BUTTERWORTHS COMPANY LAW HANDBOOK

BUTTERWORTHS COMPANY LAW HANDBOOK

Twenty-first edition

Consultant Editor

KEITH WALMSLEY, LLB, FCIS, Barrister

LexisNexis® Butterworths

Members of the LexisNexis Group worldwide

United Kingdom	LexisNexis Butterworths, a Division of Reed Elsevier (UK) Ltd, Halsbury House, 35 Chancery Lane, London, WC2A 1EL, and London House, 20–22 East London Street, Edinburgh EH7 4BQ
Argentina	LexisNexis Argentina, BUENOS AIRES
Australia	LexisNexis Butterworths, CHATSWOOD, New South Wales
Austria	LexisNexis Verlag ARD Orac GmbH & Co KG, VIENNA
Benelux	LexisNexis Benelux, AMSTERDAM
Canada	LexisNexis Canada, MARKHAM, Ontario
Chile	LexisNexis Chile Ltda, SANTIAGO
China	LexisNexis China, BEIJING and SHANGHAI
France	LexisNexis SA, PARIS
Germany	LexisNexis Deutschland GmbH MUNSTER
Hong Kong	LexisNexis Hong Kong, HONG KONG
India	LexisNexis India, NEW DELHI
Italy	Giuffrè Editore, MILAN
Japan	LexisNexis Japan, TOKYO
Malaysia	Malayan Law Journal Sdn Bhd, KUALA LUMPUR
Mexico	LexisNexis Mexico, MEXICO
New Zealand	LexisNexis NZ ltd, WELLINGTON
Poland	Wydawnictwo Prawnicze LexisNexis Sp, WARSAW
Singapore	LexisNexis Singapore, SINGAPORE
South Africa	LexisNexis Butterworths, DURBAN
USA	LexisNexis, DAYTON, Ohio

Published by LexisNexis Butterworths

A CIP Catalogue record for this book is available from the British Library.

ISBN 13: 978 1 4057 2538 5

Typeset by Columns Design Ltd, Reading, England
Printed in the United Kingdom by Polestar Wheatons Ltd

Visit LexisNexis Butterworths at www.lexisnexis.co.uk

INTRODUCTION

The aim of this Handbook is to make available in a convenient and up-to-date form the full text of the most important company law statutes, statutory instruments and European legislation. The Handbook is published annually.

How to use this book

The book is divided into six parts—

Part I—Companies Legislation
— A. Pre-2006 Companies Legislation
— B. The Companies Act 2006
— C. Table of Origins for the Companies Act 2006
— D. Tables of Destinations (Companies Acts 1985 and 1989)

Part II—Financial Services and Markets Act 2000

Part III—Other Legislation

Part IV—Statutory Instruments
— A. FSMA 2000: Statutory Instruments
— B. Other Statutory Instruments

Part V—European Community Legislation

Appendices

Within each Part, the contents are printed in chronological order. All the legislation is reproduced as amended. A list of all the amending provisions is provided at the beginning of each statute and statutory instrument. An amending or repealing provision is not normally reproduced. Where that provision is in force, effect is given to it in the text of the provision amended or repealed; where the amendment or repeal is not yet in force, it is noted below the amended provision.

The publication of this, the twenty-first edition of this work, occurs at a time of transition for those involved in the field of company law. The 'old' regime under the 1985 and 1989 Acts is, to a large extent, still extant as only a limited number of provisions of the 2006 Act have been brought into force. As people attempt to come to terms with the new regime introduced by the 2006 Act, the publishers of this work are faced with a more mundane problem: how to fit all the relevant material into one volume.

Regular users of this work will notice that this year's edition is nearly one thousand pages larger than last year's and is at the very limit of what can be bound in a one volume work. But, despite this, a few changes have had to be made simply in order to fit in all the relevant material. Some items of legislation, of lesser relevance to users of this particular Handbook, have been removed (and replaced with a note) in order to create space for the new Companies Act 2006 material. However, material omitted from this edition to save space continues to be reproduced in full in the CD and online versions of this work. In addition, the standard practice in the *Handbooks* series of putting commencement notes at provision level for any provision brought into force within the last five years has been abandoned in this edition. Commencement information is now not given at provision level if a section, article, etc came into force *for all purposes* before 1 July 2005.

Companies legislation and other legislation (Parts I and III)

The full text of the Companies Act 2006 is now included together with tables of origins and destinations relative to that Act and its predecessor Acts. The Explanatory Notes to the 2006 Act, which were included in the Supplement to the twentieth edition, have not been reproduced in this edition, again for reasons of space, and users are referred to that Supplement or the CD and online versions of this work for those Notes.

All the texts of the statutes have been updated including the amendments made by the Companies Act 2006 and all commencements, etc, made by the first and second commencement orders, as well as the draft third commencement order (as to which see below).

This edition also includes the Fraud Act 2006 and those provisions of the Bankruptcy and Diligence etc (Scotland) Act 2007 that are concerned with floating charges.

Financial Services and Markets Act 2000 (Part II)

The Financial Services and Markets Act 2000 (FSMA 2000) provides for a single legal framework with the Financial Services Authority (FSA) acting as a single regulatory body in respect of the provision of financial services in the UK. The full text of the Act is reproduced in Part II, printed with all amendments to 1 July 2007.

Rules, Regulations and Guidance made by the FSA are not reproduced. They can be accessed at *www.fsa.gov.uk/Pages/handbook/*

Statutory Instruments (Part IV)

A. FSMA Statutory Instruments

This section includes the texts of those statutory instruments made under FSMA 2000 that are most relevant to corporate lawyers. New to this edition are the

Financial Services and Markets Act 2000 (Regulated Activities) (Amendment) (No 2) Order 2006 and the Financial Services and Markets Act 2000 (Regulated Activities) (Amendment No 3) Order 2006.

B. Other Statutory Instruments

New statutory instruments reproduced include the Capital Requirements Regulations 2006, the Companies (Registrar, Languages and Trading Disclosures) Regulations 2006, the Companies Acts (Unregistered Companies) Regulations 2007, and the Financial Services and Markets Act 2000 (Markets in Financial Instruments) Regulations 2007 (made under the European Communities Act 1972).

The Companies Act 2006 (Commencement No 1, Transitional Provisions and Savings) Order 2006 and the Companies Act 2006 (Commencement No 2, Consequential Amendments, Transitional Provisions and Savings) Order 2007 are also reproduced in full and the sections of the Companies Act 2006 (and earlier legislation) commenced or otherwise affected by those Orders are duly annotated.

At the time this Handbook went to press, the Companies Act 2006 (Commencement No 3, Consequential Amendments, Transitional Provisions and Savings) Order 2007, which brings into force various provisions of the 2006 Act on 1 October 2007, was still in draft. The draft Order is reproduced in Appendix 12 and, for the convenience of users, the sections of the Companies Act 2006 (and earlier

legislation) commenced or affected by the Order are appropriately annotated (showing the effect of the Order, on the assumption that it has been made).
[Note: the commencement order was made on 26 July 2007 (SI 2007/2194) but, as of 30 July 2007, had not been published. As this work was in the final stages of going to press at that date, there was no time to change references to it in this Handbook. Accordingly, it is referred to as the draft third commencement order throughout this work.]

Statutory instruments that are outside the scope of this Handbook are reproduced in companion Butterworths Handbook volumes, namely *Butterworths Banking Law Handbook*, *Butterworths Financial Services Law Handbook* and *Butterworths Insurance Law Handbook*. Materials on corporate governance may be found in *Butterworths Corporate Governance Handbook.*

European Community Legislation (Part V)

New to this edition are: Commission Regulation 1287/2006/EC implementing Directive 2004/39/EC of the European Parliament and of the Council as regards record-keeping obligations for investment firms, transaction reporting, market transparency, admission of financial instruments to trading, and defined terms for the purposes of that Directive; European Parliament and Council Directive 2006/68/EC amending Council Directive 77/91/EEC as regards the formation of public limited liability companies and the maintenance and alteration of their capital; Commission Directive 2006/73/EC implementing Directive 2004/39/EC of the European Parliament and of the Council as regards organisational requirements and operating conditions for investment firms and defined terms for the purposes of that Directive; and Commission Directive 2007/14/EC laying down detailed rules for the implementation of certain provisions of Directive 2004/109/EC on the harmonisation of transparency requirements in relation to information about issuers whose securities are admitted to trading on a regulated market.

Appendices

Throughout the text of the legislation, there are cross-references to the fees instruments and forms tables contained in Appendices 3 and 4 at the end of this book. The text of the Companies Act 1948 Table A is reproduced because this version of Table A continues to apply to many companies incorporated prior to 1 July 1985 (Appendix 1). For convenience, the Companies Act 1985 Table A is also set out in Appendix 2, following the 1948 Table A. Users should be aware that, for companies incorporated on or after 1 October 2007, amendments to the 1985 Table A were, when this edition went to press, under consideration by the government but, at that time, the text of such amendments was not available.

A complete list of all statutory instruments made under FSMA 2000, including a brief summary of their effect or, as appropriate, a cross-reference to where they are reproduced in the Handbook is set out in Appendix 5. Also included is a table listing the domestic implementation measures of all the European Directives reproduced in Part V (Appendix 6).

New to this edition are: Appendix 7 (Companies Act 2006 – Duties of Company Directors) and Appendix 8 (Table of commencements for the Companies Act 2006). Appendices 9–12 set out the draft Companies (Fees for Inspection and Copying of Company Records) Regulations 2007, the draft Limited Liability Partnerships (Amendment) Regulations 2007, the draft Companies (Political Expenditure Exemption) Order 2007, and the draft third Commencement Order respectively.

Standard Scale; Statutory Maximum

There are numerous references to the standard scale, and to the statutory maximum, throughout the legislation contained in this Handbook. For reasons of space, notes have not been made at every place where the references appear, but users should refer back to this note.

The standard scale is the scale set out in the Criminal Justice Act 1982, s 37(2), but different amounts may be substituted by order under the Magistrates' Courts Act 1980, s 143. The scale (as substituted by the Criminal Justice Act 1991, s 17(1), as from 1 October 1992) is—

level 1: £200;

level 2: £500;

level 3: £1,000;

level 4: £2,500; and

level 5: £5,000.

The statutory maximum is the prescribed sum within the meaning of the Magistrates' Courts Act 1980, s 32. Section 32(9) of the 1980 Act (as amended by the Criminal Justice Act 1991, s 17(2)(c), as from 1 October 1992), provides that the prescribed sum is £5,000, but a different sum may be substituted by order under s 143 of the 1980 Act.

The contents are reproduced as amended to include materials published at 1 July 2007, though later amendments have been noted where possible.

LexisNexis Butterworths
July 2007

CONTENTS

B. Other Statutory Instruments

PART V EUROPEAN COMMUNITY LEGISLATION

APPENDICES

PART I
COMPANIES LEGISLATION

A. Pre-2006 Companies Legislation

COMPANIES ACT 1985

(1985 c 6)

NOTES

This Act is reproduced as amended by the following Acts:

1985	Insolvency Act 1985.
1986	Building Societies Act 1986; Company Directors Disqualification Act 1986; FSA 1986; Insolvency Act 1986.
1987	Banking Act 1987.
1988	Copyright, Designs and Patents Act 1988; FA 1988.
1989	CA 1989.
1990	FA 1990; Law Reform (Miscellaneous Provisions) (Scotland) Act 1990.
1991	Age of Legal Capacity (Scotland) Act 1991.
1992	Charities Act 1992; Friendly Societies Act 1992.
1993	Charities Act 1993; Criminal Justice Act 1993; Pension Schemes Act 1993; Statute Law (Repeals) Act 1993; Welsh Language Act 1993.
1994	Deregulation and Contracting Out Act 1994; Law of Property (Miscellaneous Provisions) Act 1994; Trade Marks Act 1994.
1995	Criminal Procedure (Consequential Provisions) (Scotland) Act 1995; Disability Discrimination Act 1995; Insurance Companies (Reserves) Act 1995; Pensions Act 1995; Requirements of Writing (Scotland) Act 1995.
1998	Bank of England Act 1998.
1999	Youth Justice and Criminal Evidence Act 1999.
2000	Abolition of Feudal Tenure etc (Scotland) Act 2000; Political Parties, Elections and Referendums Act 2000.
2001	Criminal Justice and Police Act 2001.
2002	Enterprise Act 2002.
2004	Statute Law (Repeals) Act 2004; Companies (Audit, Investigations and Community Enterprise) Act 2004; Civil Partnership Act 2004; Pensions Act 2004.
2005	Constitutional Reform Act 2005; Charities and Trustee Investment (Scotland) Act 2005.
2006	Charities Act 2006; Fraud Act 2006; Companies Act 2006.
2007	Bankruptcy and Diligence etc (Scotland) Act 2007.

This Act is reproduced as amended by the following SIs:

1987	Companies (Mergers and Divisions) Regulations 1987, SI 1987/1991.
1990	Companies Act 1989 (Commencement No 4 and Transitional and Saving Provisions) Order 1990, SI 1990/355; Companies Act 1989 (Commencement No 6 and Transitional and Saving Provisions) Order 1990, SI 1990/1392; Companies (Fair Dealing by Directors) (Increase in Financial Limits) Order 1990, SI 1990/1393; Companies Act 1989 (Commencement No 7 and Transitional and Savings Provisions) Order 1990, SI 1990/1707.
1991	Companies (Disclosure of Interests in Shares) (Orders imposing restrictions on shares) Regulations 1991, SI 1991/1646; Companies Act 1989 (Eligibility for Appointment as Company Auditor) (Consequential Amendments) Regulations 1991, SI 1991/1997; Companies Act 1985 (Bank Accounts) Regulations 1991, SI 1991/2705.

1992	Companies Act 1985 (Welsh Language Accounts) Regulations 1992, SI 1992/1083; Transfer of Functions (Financial Services) Order 1992, SI 1992/1315; Companies (Single Member Private Limited Companies) Regulations 1992, SI 1992/1699; Companies Act 1985 (Accounts of Small and Medium-Sized Enterprises and Publication of Accounts in ECUs) Regulations 1992, SI 1992/2452; Companies Act 1985 (Amendment of Sections 250 and 251) Regulations 1992, SI 1992/3003; Companies Act 1985 (Disclosure of Branches and Bank Accounts) Regulations 1992, SI 1992/3178; Oversea Companies and Credit and Financial Institutions (Branch Disclosure) Regulations 1992, SI 1992/3179.
1993	Disclosure of Interests in Shares (Amendment) Regulations 1993, SI 1993/1819; Partnerships and Unlimited Companies (Accounts) Regulations 1993, SI 1993/1820; Companies Act 1985 (Insurance Companies Accounts) Regulations 1993, SI 1993/3246.
1994	Companies Act 1985 (Bank Accounts) Regulations 1994, SI 1994/233; Companies Act 1985 (Audit Exemption) Regulations 1994, SI 1994/1935.
1995	Companies Act 1985 (Audit Exemption) (Amendment) Regulations 1995, SI 1995/589; Uncertificated Securities Regulations 1995, SI 1995/3272.
1996	Companies Act 1985 (Miscellaneous Accounting Amendments) Regulations 1996, SI 1996/189; Deregulation (Resolutions of Private Companies) Order 1996, SI 1996/1471; Disclosure of Interests in Shares (Amendment) Regulations 1996, SI 1996/1560; Open-Ended Investment Companies (Investment Companies with Variable Capital) Regulations 1996, SI 1996/2827; Companies Act 1985 (Audit Exemption) (Amendment) Regulations 1996, SI 1996/3080.
1997	Companies Act 1985 (Accounts of Small and Medium-sized Companies and Minor Accounting Amendments) Regulations 1997, SI 1997/220; Company Accounts (Disclosure of Directors' Emoluments) Regulations 1997, SI 1997/570; Companies Act 1985 (Directors' Report) (Statement of Payment Practice) Regulations 1997, SI 1997/571; Companies Act 1985 (Audit Exemption) (Amendment) Regulations 1997, SI 1997/936; Companies Overseas Branch Registers (Hong Kong) Order 1997, SI 1997/1313; Companies (Membership of Holding Company) (Dealers in Securities) Regulations 1997, SI 1997/2306; Companies Act 1985 (Insurance Companies Accounts) (Minor Amendments) Regulations 1997, SI 1997/2704.
1999	Scotland Act 1998 (Consequential Modifications) (No 2) Order 1999, SI 1999/1820; Companies (Contents of Annual Return) Regulations 1999, SI 1999/2322; Companies (Investment Companies) (Distribution of Profits) Regulations 1999, SI 1999/2770.
2000	Companies Act 1985 (Audit Exemption) (Amendment) Regulations 2000, SI 2000/1430; Banking Consolidation Directive (Consequential Amendments) Regulations 2000, SI 2000/2952; Companies Act 1985 (Electronic Communications) Order 2000, SI 2000/3373.
2001	Limited Liability Partnerships Regulations 2001, SI 2001/1090; Open-Ended Investment Companies Regulations 2001, SI 2001/1228; Financial Services and Markets Act 2000 (Dissolution of Insurance Brokers Registration Council) (Consequential Provisions) Order 2001, SI 2001/1283; Financial Services and Markets Act 2000 (Consequential Amendments and Repeals) Order 2001, SI 2001/3649; Uncertificated Securities Regulations 2001, SI 2001/3755.
2002	Electronic Money (Miscellaneous Amendments) Regulations 2002, SI 2002/765; Companies (Particulars of Usual Residential Address) (Confidentiality Orders) Regulations 2002, SI 2002/912; Financial Services and Markets Act 2000 (Consequential Amendments) Order 2002, SI 2002/1555; Directors' Remuneration Report Regulations 2002, SI 2002/1986; Regulatory Reform (Removal of 20 Member Limit in Partnerships etc) Order 2002, SI 2002/3203.
2003	Companies (Acquisition of Own Shares) (Treasury Shares) Regulations 2003, SI 2003/1116; Collective Investment Schemes (Miscellaneous Amendments) Regulations 2003, SI 2003/2066; Stamp Duty and Stamp Duty Land Tax (Consequential Amendment of Enactments) Regulations 2003, SI 2003/2868; Companies (Acquisition of Own Shares) (Treasury Shares) No 2 Regulations 2003, SI 2003/3031.
2004	Companies Act 1985 (Accounts of Small and Medium-Sized Enterprises and Audit Exemption) (Amendment) Regulations 2004, SI 2004/16; Financial Services and Markets Act 2000 (Consequential Amendments) Order 2004, SI 2004/355; Companies Act 1985 (International Accounting Standards and Other Accounting Amendments) Regulations 2004, SI 2004/2947; Life Assurance Consolidation Directive (Consequential Amendments) Regulations 2004, SI 2004/3379.

2005	Regulatory Reform (Trading Stamps) Order 2005, SI 2005/781; Companies Act 1985 (Operating and Financial Review and Directors' Report etc) Regulations 2005, SI 2005/1011; Regulatory Reform (Execution of Deeds and Documents) Order 2005, SI 2005/1906; Companies Act 1985 (Investment Companies and Accounting and Audit Amendments) Regulations 2005, SI 2005/2280; Companies Act 1985 (Operating and Financial Review) (Repeal) Regulations 2005, SI 2005/3442; Civil Partnership Act 2004 (International Immunities and Privileges, Companies and Adoption) Order 2005, SI 2005/3542.
2006	Charities and Trustee Investment (Scotland) Act 2005 (Consequential Provisions and Modifications) Order 2006, SI 2006/242; Companies (Disclosure of Information) (Designated Authorities) Order 2006, SI 2006/1644; Financial Services and Markets Act 2000 (Regulated Activities) (Amendment) (No 2) Order 2006, SI 2006/2383; Companies Act 1985 (Small Companies' Accounts and Audit) Regulations 2006, SI 2006/2782; Capital Requirements Regulations 2006, SI 2006/3221; Companies (Registrar, Languages and Trading Disclosures) Regulations 2006, SI 2006/3429.
2007	Financial Services and Markets Act 2000 (Markets in Financial Instruments) Regulations 2007, SI 2007/126; Companies (EEA State) Regulations 2007, SI 2007/732; Companies Act 2006 (Commencement No 2, Consequential Amendments, Transitional Provisions and Savings) Order 2007, SI 2007/1093; Government of Wales Act 2006 (Consequential Modifications and Transitional Provisions) Order 2007, SI 2007/1388; the draft Companies Act 2006 (Commencement No 3, Consequential Amendments, Transitional Provisions and Savings) Order 2007.

ARRANGEMENT OF SECTIONS

PART I
FORMATION AND REGISTRATION OF COMPANIES; JURIDICAL STATUS AND MEMBERSHIP

CHAPTER I
COMPANY FORMATION

Memorandum of association

Articles of association

Registration and its consequences

A company's membership

CHAPTER II
COMPANY NAMES

CHAPTER III
A COMPANY'S CAPACITY; FORMALITIES OF CARRYING ON BUSINESS

PART II
RE-REGISTRATION AS A MEANS OF ALTERING A COMPANY'S STATUS

Private company becoming public

Limited company becoming unlimited

Unlimited company becoming limited

Public company becoming private

PART III
CAPITAL ISSUES

CHAPTER I
ISSUES BY COMPANIES REGISTERED, OR TO BE REGISTERED, IN GREAT BRITAIN

The prospectus

PART IV
ALLOTMENT OF SHARES AND DEBENTURES

General provisions as to allotment

Pre-emption rights

Commissions and discounts

Amount to be paid for shares; the means of payment

Valuation provisions

Other matters arising out of allotment, &c

PART V
SHARE CAPITAL, ITS INCREASE, MAINTENANCE AND REDUCTION

CHAPTER I
GENERAL PROVISIONS ABOUT SHARE CAPITAL

Registration and investigation of share acquisitions and disposals

Supplementary

PART VII
ACCOUNTS AND AUDIT

CHAPTER I
PROVISIONS APPLYING TO COMPANIES GENERALLY

Accounting records

A company's financial year and accounting reference periods

Annual accounts

Approval and signing of accounts

Directors' report

Auditors' report

CHAPTER III
SUPPLEMENTARY PROVISIONS

Accounting standards

Power to alter accounting requirements

Parents and subsidiary undertakings

Other interpretation provisions

PART VIII
DISTRIBUTION OF PROFITS AND ASSETS

Limits of company's power of distribution

Relevant accounts

Supplementary

PART IX
A COMPANY'S MANAGEMENT; DIRECTORS AND SECRETARIES; THEIR QUALIFICATIONS, DUTIES AND RESPONSIBILITIES

Officers and registered office

Provisions governing appointment of directors

Removal of directors

Other provisions about directors and officers

PART X
ENFORCEMENT OF FAIR DEALING BY DIRECTORS

Restrictions on directors taking financial advantage

Restrictions on a company's power to make loans, etc, to directors and persons connected with them

Supplementary

PART XA
CONTROL OF POLITICAL DONATIONS

PART XI
COMPANY ADMINISTRATION AND PROCEDURE

CHAPTER I
COMPANY IDENTIFICATION

CHAPTER II
REGISTER OF MEMBERS

CHAPTER III
ANNUAL RETURN

CHAPTER IV
MEETINGS AND RESOLUTIONS

Meetings

Resolutions

Written resolutions of private companies

Records of proceedings

CHAPTER V
AUDITORS

Appointment of auditors

Rights of auditors

Remuneration of auditors

Removal, resignation, &c of auditors

PART XII
REGISTRATION OF CHARGES

CHAPTER I
REGISTRATION OF CHARGES (ENGLAND AND WALES)

CHAPTER II
REGISTRATION OF CHARGES (SCOTLAND)

PART XIII
ARRANGEMENTS AND RECONSTRUCTIONS

PART XIIIA
TAKEOVER OFFERS

PART XIV
INVESTIGATION OF COMPANIES AND THEIR AFFAIRS; REQUISITION OF DOCUMENTS

Appointment and functions of inspectors

Other powers of investigation available to the Secretary of State

Powers of Secretary of State to give directions to inspectors

Resignation, removal and replacement of inspectors

Power to obtain information from former inspectors etc

Requisition and seizure of books and papers

PART XXII
BODIES CORPORATE SUBJECT, OR BECOMING SUBJECT, TO THIS ACT (OTHERWISE THAN BY ORIGINAL FORMATION UNDER PART I)

CHAPTER I
COMPANIES FORMED OR REGISTERED UNDER FORMER COMPANIES ACTS

CHAPTER II
COMPANIES NOT FORMED UNDER COMPANIES LEGISLATION, BUT AUTHORISED TO REGISTER

PART XXIII
OVERSEA COMPANIES

CHAPTER I
REGISTRATION, ETC

CHAPTER II
DELIVERY OF ACCOUNTS AND REPORTS

CHAPTER III
REGISTRATION OF CHARGES

CHAPTER IV
WINDING UP ETC

PART XXIV
THE REGISTRAR OF COMPANIES, HIS FUNCTIONS AND OFFICES

PART XXV
MISCELLANEOUS AND SUPPLEMENTARY PROVISIONS

An Act to consolidate the greater part of the Companies Acts

[11 March 1985]

NOTES

Commencement:

Unless otherwise indicated, this Act came into force on 1 July 1985; see s 746 at **[632]**. Where any provision in this work (including any inserted or substituted provision) came into force for all purposes on or before 1 July 2005, commencement information is not noted at provision level.

Repeal and amendment of this Act by the Companies Act 2006:

The vast majority of this Act is repealed by the Companies Act 2006, as from a day to be appointed (see s 1295 of, and Sch 16 to, the 2006 Act at **[S1295]**, **[S1331]** which repeal ss 1–430F, 438, 446, 458–461, 651–746 of, and Schs 1–15B, 20–25 to, this Act). The only provisions not repealed by the 2006 Act are: (a) Part XIV (Investigation of Companies and their Affairs; Requisition of Documents) (including Schs 15C, 15D but not including ss 438, 446 which are repealed); (b) Part XV (Orders

Imposing Restrictions on Shares); (c) Part XVIII (Floating Charges and Receivers (Scotland)); and (d) section 747 (citation). For provision relating to the continuity of law, see s 1297 of the 2006 Act at **[S1297]**. The 2006 Act also makes a number of amendments to this Act (including amendments to provisions which it also repeals). See, in particular: (a) s 992 of, and Sch 15, Pt 1 to, the 2006 Act (amendments to Part VII of this Act); and (b) Part 32 of, and Sch 3 to, the 2006 Act (amendments to Part XIV of this Act). Details of all repeals and amendments are noted to the provisions affected.

Note also that Part XVIII (Floating Charges and Receivers (Scotland)) is repealed by the Bankruptcy and Diligence etc (Scotland) Act 2007, s 46(1), as from a day to be appointed. For savings see the introductory note to that Part (preceding **[496]**).

Application of this Act to other companies, etc:

This Act, or particular parts of it, is applied to various other types of companies and bodies, as follows:

Limited liability partnerships: the provisions of this Act relating to companies are applied with modifications to limited liability partnerships; see the Limited Liability Partnerships (Scotland) Regulations 2001, SSI 2001/128 at **[6974]**, and the Limited Liability Partnerships Regulations 2001, SI 2001/1090 at **[6982]**. Further provisions of this Act are applied to limited liability partnerships, subject to modifications, by the Limited Liability Partnership (No 2) Regulations 2002, SI 2002/913 at **[7076]**. See also the Limited Liability Partnerships Act 2000 at **[3500]** et seq. Cross-references are provided throughout this Act on the provisions affected by the Regulations noted above. See also the Companies Act 2006 (Commencement No 1, Transitional Provisions and Savings) Order 2006, SI 2006/3428, art 8(2), the Companies Act 2006 (Commencement No 2, Consequential Amendments, Transitional Provisions and Savings) Order 2007, SI 2007/1093, art 11(1), and the draft Companies Act 2006 (Commencement No 3, Consequential Amendments, Transitional Provisions and Savings) Order 2007, art 12(2). Those articles provide that nothing in those Orders (which either amend this Act or commence amendments and repeals made by CA 2006) affect the application of any provision of this Act (as applied by the Limited Liability Partnerships Regulations 2001) to LLPs. Art 11(2) of SI 2007/1093 further provides that the repeal of s 723C(1)(a) by s 1295 of, and Sch 16 to CA 2006 (brought into force by art 7(a) of the first commencement order) does not apply to the application of the said s 723C(1)(a) to LLPs by the Limited Liability Partnerships (No 2) Regulations 2002.

Community interest companies: as to the application of this Act (subject to certain modifications) to community interest companies, see the Companies (Audit, Investigations and Community Enterprise) Act 2004 at **[894]** et seq. See, in particular, Part 2 of that Act at **[900]** et seq.

European Economic Interest Groupings: certain provisions of this Act are applied with modifications to European Economic Interest Groupings and their establishments registered, or in the process of being registered, under the European Economic Interest Grouping Regulations 1989, SI 1989/638; see reg 18 of, and Sch 4 to, the 1989 Regulations at **[6619]** and **[6624]**.

Unregistered companies: as to the application of this Act (subject to certain modifications) to unregistered companies incorporated in, and having a principal place of business in, Great Britain; see s 718 at **[590]**, Sch 22 at **[687]** and the Companies (Unregistered Companies) Regulations 1985, SI 1985/680 at **[6022]**.

Societas Europaea: as to the application of certain provisions of this Act to SEs, see the European Public Limited-Liability Company Regulations 2004, SI 2004/2326 at **[7249]**. See in particular, Sch 2 (provisions of the 1985 Act applying to the registration of SEs) at **[7334]**, and Sch 4 (modifications of the 1985 Act and the Insolvency Act 1986) at **[7338]**.

Open-ended investment companies: see the Open-Ended Investment Companies Regulations 2001, SI 2001/1228, reg 70, Sch 6.

European Grouping of Territorial Cooperation: see the European Grouping of Territorial Cooperation Regulations 2007, SI 2007/1949.

Statutory water companies: see the Statutory Water Companies Act 1991, the Water Consolidation (Consequential Provisions) Act 1991, s 2(1), Sch 1, para 40(1), s 9(1), (3), and the Companies Act 1985 (Modifications for Statutory Water Companies) Regulations 1989, SI 1989/1461.

Miscellaneous:

Private companies: references in any enactment or instrument to the period for laying and delivering accounts, and reports including those in s 244 *post* (which defines that period), shall be read in relation to a private company as references to the period for delivering accounts and reports; see the draft Companies Act 2006 (Commencement No 3, Consequential Amendments, Transitional Provisions and Savings) Order 2007, art 10(1), Sch 4, Pt 1, para 3(4), (8) (at **[A12]**).

Offences under this Act: see further the Companies Act 2006, ss 1131 at **[S1131]**.

Amendment by Companies Act 1989: extensive transitional provisions and savings were made in connection with the commencement of the 1989 Act by the Orders noted to s 215 of that Act at **[865]**. These provided for the continuity of law between the old (ie, 1985 Act regime) and the changes effected to this Act by the amendments made by the 1989 Act. To a large extent these are now effectively spent and they have been omitted from this Edition in order to save space. The complete table of commencements for the 1989 Act and the transitional provisions and savings are, however, still included at paragraph **[876]** of the electronic versions of this work.

Civil Procedure Rules: the Civil Procedure Rules 1998, SI 1998/3132, rule 49, states that, as from 26 April 1999, those Rules apply to proceedings under this Act subject to the provisions of the relevant practice direction which applies to those proceedings.

Registrar of companies (England and Wales): the Contracting Out (Functions in relation to the Registration of Companies) Order 1995, SI 1995/1013 provides for the contracting out of the following functions of the registrar in England and Wales: (i) any function of receiving any return, account or other document required to be filed with, delivered or sent, or notice of any matter required to be given, to the registrar which is conferred by or under any enactment; (ii) any functions relating to the incorporation of companies and the change of name of companies by or under Chapters I and II of Part I of the Act; (iii) any functions relating to the re-registration and change of status of companies by or under Part II and ss 138, 139 and 147; (iv) subject to certain exceptions, functions conferred by, or under, ss 705, 705A, 706, 707, 709, 710, 710A; see art 3 of, and Sch 1 to, the 1995 Order at **[6838]** and **[6841]**.

Registrar of companies (Scotland): the Contracting Out (Functions in relation to the Registration of Companies) Order 1995, SI 1995/1013 provides for the contracting out of certain functions of the registrar in Scotland conferred by, or under, ss 242, 705, 705A, 706, 707, 707A, 708(5), 709, 710A, 713; see art 4 of, and Sch 2 to, the 1995 Order at **[6839]** and **[6842]**.

Official Receiver: as to the contracting out of functions of the Official Receiver conferred by or under this Act, see the Contracting Out (Functions of the Official Receiver) Order 1995, SI 1995/1386 at **[6844]**.

Forms: for the relevant forms see the Companies (Forms) Regulations 1985, SI 1985/854 (as amended) in Appendix 4 at **[A4]**. Cross-references are included throughout this Act to that Appendix where a particular form, etc, is prescribed for the purposes of any section.

PART I
FORMATION AND REGISTRATION OF COMPANIES; JURIDICAL STATUS AND MEMBERSHIP

CHAPTER I
COMPANY FORMATION

Memorandum of association

1 Mode of forming incorporated company

(1) Any two or more persons associated for a lawful purpose may, by subscribing their names to a memorandum of association and otherwise complying with the requirements of this Act in respect of registration, form an incorporated company, with or without limited liability.

(2) A company so formed may be either—

(a) a company having the liability of its members limited by the memorandum to the amount, if any, unpaid on the shares respectively held by them ("a company limited by shares");

(b) a company having the liability of its members limited by the memorandum to such amount as the members may respectively thereby undertake to contribute to the assets of the company in the event of its being wound up ("a company limited by guarantee"); or

(c) a company not having any limit on the liability of its members ("an unlimited company").

(3) A "public company" is a company limited by shares or limited by guarantee and having a share capital, being a company—

(a) the memorandum of which states that it is to be a public company, and

(b) in relation to which the provisions of this Act or the former Companies Acts as to the registration or re-registration of a company as a public company have been complied with on or after 22nd December 1980;

and a "private company" is a company that is not a public company.

[(3A) Notwithstanding subsection (1), one person may, for a lawful purpose, by subscribing his name to a memorandum of association and otherwise complying with the requirements of this Act in respect of registration, form an incorporated company being a private company limited by shares or by guarantee.]

(4) With effect from 22nd December 1980, a company cannot be formed as, or become, a company limited by guarantee with a share capital.

[1]

NOTES

Repealed by the Companies Act 2006, s 1295, Sch 16, as from a day to be appointed.

Sub-s (3A): inserted by the Companies (Single Member Private Limited Companies) Regulations 1992, SI 1992/1699, reg 2(1)(b), Schedule, para 1, as from 15 July 1992.

Public company: until the enactment of the Companies Act 1980 (repealed) the term "public company" had not been defined in the companies legislation and it was used therein hardly at all. So far as it was used, it was generally understood to mean any company which was not a "private company" as defined (before 1980) by the Companies Act 1948, s 28 (repealed). The 1980 Act in effect reversed the position by defining the term "public company" (in s 1) and by describing a "private company" as a company which was not a public company. References in this Act (other than in the provisions derived from the Companies Act 1980, ss 1–13 (repealed)) and other than in s 33 to a public company or a company other than a private company include (unless the context otherwise requires) references to an "old public company" (as defined in the Companies Consolidation (Consequential Provisions) Act 1985, s 1(1) at **[702]**) and references to a private company in this Act are to be read accordingly; see s 1(2) of the 1985 Act. See generally as to old public companies, the Companies Consolidation (Consequential Provisions) Act 1985, ss 1–9 at **[702]–[709]**.

Private company limited by shares or by guarantee: by the Companies (Single Member Private Limited Companies) Regulations 1992, SI 1992/1699, reg 2(1) at **[6743]**, notwithstanding any enactment or rule of law to the contrary, a private company limited by shares or by guarantee within the meaning of this section may be formed by one person and may have one member; and accordingly, any enactment or rule of law which applies in relation to a private company limited by shares or by guarantee is to apply, in the absence of any express provision to the contrary, with such modifications as may be necessary in relation to such a company which is formed by one person or which has only one person as a member as it does in relation to such a company which is formed by two or more persons as members. The 1992 Regulations (which were made under the European Communities Act 1972) implement the Twelfth Council Company Law Directive 89/667/EEC on single-member private limited-liability companies.

Community interest companies: as to the incorporation of community interest companies, see the Companies (Audit, Investigations and Community Enterprise) Act 2004, s 26 at **[900]**.

2 Requirements with respect to memorandum

(*1*) *The memorandum of every company must state—*

(*a*) *the name of the company;*

(*b*) *whether the registered office of the company is to be situated in England and Wales, or in Scotland;*

(*c*) *the objects of the company.*

(*2*) *Alternatively to subsection* (*1*)(*b*), *the memorandum may contain a statement that the company's registered office is to be situated in Wales; and a company whose registered office is situated in Wales may by special resolution alter its memorandum so as to provide that its registered office is to be so situated.*

(*3*) *The memorandum of a company limited by shares or by guarantee must also state that the liability of its members is limited.*

(*4*) *The memorandum of a company limited by guarantee must also state that each member undertakes to contribute to the assets of the company if it should be wound up while he is a member, or within one year after he ceases to be a member, for payment of the debts and liabilities of the company contracted before he ceases to be a member, and of the costs, charges and expenses of winding up, and for adjustment of the rights of the contributories among themselves, such amount as may be required, not exceeding a specified amount.*

(*5*) *In the case of a company having a share capital—*

(*a*) *the memorandum must also* (*unless it is an unlimited company*) *state the amount of the share capital with which the company proposes to be registered and the division of the share capital into shares of a fixed amount;*

(*b*) *no subscriber of the memorandum may take less than one share; and*

(*c*) *there must be shown in the memorandum against the name of each subscriber the number of shares he takes.*

(*6*) *[Subject to subsection* (*6A*), *the memorandum] must be signed by each subscriber in the presence of at least one witness, who must attest the signature; and that attestation is sufficient in Scotland as well as in England and Wales.*

[(*6A*) *Where the memorandum is delivered to the registrar otherwise than in legible form and is authenticated by each subscriber in such manner as is directed by the registrar, the requirements in subsection* (*6*) *for signature in the presence of at least one witness and for attestation of the signature do not apply.]*

(*7*) *A company may not alter the conditions contained in its memorandum except in the cases, in the mode and to the extent, for which express provision is made by this Act.*

[2]

NOTES

Repealed by the Companies Act 2006, s 1295, Sch 16, as from a day to be appointed.

Sub-s (6): words in square brackets substituted by the Companies Act 1985 (Electronic Communications) Order 2000, SI 2000/3373, art 2(1), (2), as from 22 December 2000; words "; and that attestation is sufficient in Scotland as well as in England and Wales" repealed in relation to Scotland by the Requirements of Writing (Scotland) Act 1995, s 14(2), Sch 5, as from 1 August 1995.

Sub-s (6A): inserted by SI 2000/3373, art 2(1), (3), as from 22 December 2000.

3 Forms of memorandum

(1) Subject to the provisions of sections 1 and 2, the form of the memorandum of association of—

- *(a) a public company, being a company limited by shares,*
- *(b) a public company, being a company limited by guarantee and having a share capital,*
- *(c) a private company limited by shares,*
- *(d) a private company limited by guarantee and not having a share capital,*
- *(e) a private company limited by guarantee and having a share capital, and*
- *(f) an unlimited company having a share capital,*

shall be as specified respectively for such companies by regulations made by the Secretary of State, or as near to that form as circumstances admit.

(2) Regulations under this section shall be made by statutory instrument subject to annulment in pursuance of a resolution of either House of Parliament.

[3]

NOTES

Repealed by the Companies Act 2006, s 1295, Sch 16, as from a day to be appointed.

Regulations: the Companies (Tables A to F) Regulations 1985, SI 1985/805 at **[6037]**. See also Appendix 2 at **[A2]** (Table A 1985) and Appendix 1 at **[A1]** (Table A 1948).

[3A Statement of company's objects: general commercial company

Where the company's memorandum states that the object of the company is to carry on business as a general commercial company—

- *(a) the object of the company is to carry on any trade or business whatsoever, and*
- *(b) the company has power to do all such things as are incidental or conducive to the carrying on of any trade or business by it.]*

[4]

NOTES

Inserted by CA 1989, s 110(1), as from 4 February 1991.

Repealed by the Companies Act 2006, s 1295, Sch 16, as from a day to be appointed.

[4 Resolution to alter objects

(1) A company may by special resolution alter its memorandum with respect to the statement of the company's objects.

(2) If an application is made under the following section, an alteration does not have effect except in so far as it is confirmed by the court.]

[5]

NOTES

Substituted by CA 1989, s 110(2), as from 4 February 1991.

Repealed by the Companies Act 2006, s 1295, Sch 16, as from a day to be appointed.

Community interest companies: regulations may restrict a community interest company's ability under this section to amend its objects as stated in its memorandum. An existing company must not submit its application to become a community interest company, and a community interest company must not submit its application to become a charitable company, if the members of the company apply to the court under s 5 of this Act, until either the changes to its memorandum under this section or s 17 of this Act have been confirmed by the court or the deadline for objecting has passed; see the Companies (Audit, Investigations and Community Enterprise) Act 2004, ss 26, 32(6), 37, 54 at **[900]**, **[906]**, **[911]**, **[928]**.

5 Procedure for objecting to alteration

(1) Where a company's memorandum has been altered by special resolution under section 4, application may be made to the court for the alteration to be cancelled.

(2) Such an application may be made—

- *(a) by the holders of not less in the aggregate than 15 per cent in nominal value of the company's issued share capital or any class of it or, if the company is not limited by shares, not less than 15 per cent of the company's members; or* (*b*) *by the holders of not less than 15 per cent of the company's debentures entitling the holders to object to an alteration of its objects;*

but an application shall not be made by any person who has consented to or voted in favour of the alteration.

(*3*) *The application must be made within 21 days after the date on which the resolution altering the company's objects was passed, and may be made on behalf of the persons entitled to make the application by such one or more of their number as they may appoint in writing for the purpose.*

(*4*) *The court may on such an application make an order confirming the alteration either wholly or in part and on such terms and conditions as it thinks fit, and may—*

(*a*) *if it thinks fit, adjourn the proceedings in order that an arrangement may be made to its satisfaction for the purchase of the interests of dissentient members, and*

(*b*) *give such directions and make such orders as it thinks expedient for facilitating or carrying into effect any such arrangement.*

(*5*) *The court's order may (if the court thinks fit) provide for the purchase by the company of the shares of any members of the company, and for the reduction accordingly of its capital, and may make such alterations in the company's memorandum and articles as may be required in consequence of that provision.*

(*6*) *If the court's order requires the company not to make any, or any specified, alteration in its memorandum or articles, the company does not then have power without the leave of the court to make any such alteration in breach of that requirement.*

(*7*) *An alteration in the memorandum or articles of a company made by virtue of an order under this section, other than one made by resolution of the company, is of the same effect as if duly made by resolution; and this Act applies accordingly to the memorandum or articles as so altered.*

[(7A) For the purposes of subsection (2)(a), any of the company's issued share capital held as treasury shares must be disregarded.]

(*8*) *The debentures entitling the holders to object to an alteration of a company's objects are any debentures secured by a floating charge which were issued or first issued before 1st December 1947 or form part of the same series as any debentures so issued; and a special resolution altering a company's objects requires the same notice to the holders of any such debentures as to members of the company.*

In the absence of provisions regulating the giving of notice to any such debenture holders, the provisions of the company's articles regulating the giving of notice to members apply.

[6]

NOTES

Repealed by the Companies Act 2006, s 1295, Sch 16, as from a day to be appointed.

Sub-s (7A): inserted by the Companies (Acquisition of Own Shares) (Treasury Shares) Regulations 2003, SI 2003/1116, reg 4, Schedule, para 1, as from 1 December 2003.

Community interest companies: see the note to s 4 at **[5]**.

6 Provisions supplementing ss 4, 5

(*1*) *Where a company passes a resolution altering its objects, then—*

(*a*) *if with respect to the resolution no application is made under section 5, the company shall within 15 days from the end of the period for making such an application deliver to the registrar of companies a printed copy of its memorandum as altered; and*

(*b*) *if such an application is made, the company shall—*

(*i*) *forthwith give notice (in the prescribed form) of that fact to the registrar, and*

(*ii*) *within 15 days from the date of any order cancelling or confirming the alteration, deliver to the registrar an office copy of the order and, in the case of an order confirming the alteration, a printed copy of the memorandum as altered.*

(*2*) *The court may by order at any time extend the time for the delivery of documents to the registrar under subsection (1)(b) for such period as the court may think proper.*

(3) If a company makes default in giving notice or delivering any document to the registrar of companies as required by subsection (1), the company and every officer of it who is in default is liable to a fine and, for continued contravention, to a daily default fine.

(4) The validity of an alteration of a company's memorandum with respect to the objects of the company shall not be questioned on the ground that it was not authorised by section 4, except in proceedings taken for the purpose (whether under section 5 or otherwise) before the expiration of 21 days after the date of the resolution in that behalf.

(5) Where such proceedings are taken otherwise than under section 5, subsections (1) to (3) above apply in relation to the proceedings as if they had been taken under that section, and as if an order declaring the alteration invalid were an order cancelling it, and as if an order dismissing the proceedings were an order confirming the alteration.

[7]

NOTES

Repealed by the Companies Act 2006, s 1295, Sch 16, as from a day to be appointed.
Prescribed form: see Appendix 4 (Forms table) at **[A4]**.

Articles of association

7 Articles prescribing regulations for companies

(1) There may in the case of a company limited by shares, and there shall in the case of a company limited by guarantee or unlimited, be registered with the memorandum articles of association signed by the subscribers to the memorandum and prescribing regulations for the company.

(2) In the case of an unlimited company having a share capital, the articles must state the amount of share capital with which the company proposes to be registered.

(3) Articles must—

(a) be printed,

(b) be divided into paragraphs numbered consecutively, and

(c) [subject to subsection (3A),] be signed by each subscriber of the memorandum in the presence of at least one witness who must attest the signature (which attestation is sufficient in Scotland as well as in England and Wales).

[(3A) Where the articles are delivered to the registrar otherwise than in legible form and are authenticated by each subscriber to the memorandum in such manner as is directed by the registrar, the requirements in subsection (3)(c) for signature in the presence of at least one witness and for attestation of the signature do not apply.]

[8]

NOTES

Repealed by the Companies Act 2006, s 1295, Sch 16, as from a day to be appointed.
Sub-s (3): words in square brackets in para (c) inserted by the Companies Act 1985 (Electronic Communications) Order 2000, SI 2000/3373, art 3(1), (2), as from 22 December 2000; words "(which attestation is sufficient in Scotland as well as in England and Wales)" in para (c) repealed in relation to Scotland by the Requirements of Writing (Scotland) Act 1995, s 14(2), Sch 5, as from 1 August 1995.
Sub-s (3A): added by SI 2000/3373, art 3(1), (3), as from 22 December 2000.
Community interest companies: sub-s (1) of this section applies to a community interest company limited by shares as if it were a company limited by guarantee (so that articles must be registered); see the Companies (Audit, Investigations and Community Enterprise) Act 2004, ss 26, 32(2) at **[900]**, **[906]**.

8 Tables A, C, D and E

(1) Table A is as prescribed by regulations made by the Secretary of State; and a company may for its articles adopt the whole or any part of that Table.

(2) In the case of a company limited by shares, if articles are not registered or, if articles are registered, in so far as they do not exclude or modify Table A, that Table (so far as applicable, and as in force at the date of the company's registration) constitutes the company's articles, in the same manner and to the same extent as if articles in the form of that Table had been duly registered.

(3) If in consequence of regulations under this section Table A is altered, the alteration does not affect a company registered before the alteration takes effect, or repeal as respects that company any portion of the Table.

(4) The form of the articles of association of—

(a) a company limited by guarantee and not having a share capital,

(b) a company limited by guarantee and having a share capital, and

(c) an unlimited company having a share capital,

shall be respectively in accordance with Table C, D or E prescribed by regulations made by the Secretary of State, or as near to that form as circumstances admit.

(5) Regulations under this section shall be made by statutory instrument subject to annulment in pursuance of a resolution of either House of Parliament.

[9]

NOTES

Repealed by the Companies Act 2006, s 1295, Sch 16, as from a day to be appointed.

Regulations: the Companies (Tables A to F) Regulations 1985, SI 1985/805 at **[6037]**. See also Appendix 2 at **[A2]** (Table A 1985) and Appendix 1 at **[A1]** (Table A 1948).

[8A Table G

(1) The Secretary of State may by regulations prescribe a Table G containing articles of association appropriate for a partnership company, that is, a company limited by shares whose shares are intended to be held to a substantial extent by or on behalf of its employees.

(2) A company limited by shares may for its articles adopt the whole or any part of that Table.

(3) If in consequence of regulations under this section Table G is altered, the alteration does not affect a company registered before the alteration takes effect, or repeal as respects that company any portion of the Table.

(4) Regulations under this section shall be made by statutory instrument which shall be subject to annulment in pursuance of a resolution of either House of Parliament.]

[10]

NOTES

Commencement: to be appointed.

Inserted by CA 1989, s 128, as from a day to be appointed.

Repealed by the Companies Act 2006, s 1295, Sch 16, as from a day to be appointed.

9 Alteration of articles by special resolution

(1) Subject to the provisions of this Act and to the conditions contained in its memorandum, a company may by special resolution alter its articles.

(2) Alterations so made in the articles are (subject to this Act) as valid as if originally contained in them, and are subject in like manner to alteration by special resolution.

[11]

NOTES

Repealed by the Companies Act 2006, s 1295, Sch 16, as from a day to be appointed.

Registration and its consequences

10 Documents to be sent to registrar

(1) The company's memorandum and articles (if any) shall be delivered—

(a) to the registrar of companies for England and Wales, if the memorandum states that the registered office of the company is to be situated in England and Wales, or that it is to be situated in Wales; and

(b) to the registrar of companies for Scotland, if the memorandum states that the registered office of the company is to be situated in Scotland.

(2) With the memorandum there shall be delivered a statement in the prescribed form containing the names and requisite particulars of—

(*a*) *the person who is, or the persons who are, to be the first director or directors of the company; and*

(*b*) *the person who is, or the persons who are, to be the first secretary or joint secretaries of the company;*

and the requisite particulars in each case are those set out in Schedule 1.

[(2A) Where any statement delivered under subsection (2) includes an address specified in reliance on paragraph 5 of Schedule 1 there shall be delivered with the statement, a statement in the prescribed form containing particulars of the usual residential address of the director or secretary whose address is so specified.]

(3) The statement [under subsection (2)] shall be signed by or on behalf of the subscribers of the memorandum and shall contain a consent signed by each of the persons named in it as a director, as secretary or as one of joint secretaries, to act in the relevant capacity.

(4) Where a memorandum is delivered by a person as agent for the subscribers, the statement shall specify that fact and the person's name and address.

(5) An appointment by any articles delivered with the memorandum of a person as director or secretary of the company is void unless he is named as a director or secretary in the statement.

(6) There shall in the statement be specified the intended situation of the company's registered office on incorporation.

[12]

NOTES

Repealed by the Companies Act 2006, s 1295, Sch 16, as from a day to be appointed.

Sub-s (2A): inserted by the Companies (Particulars of Usual Residential Address) (Confidentiality Orders) Regulations 2002, SI 2002/912, reg 16, Sch 2, para 1(1), (2), as from 2 April 2002.

Sub-s (3): words in square brackets inserted by SI 2002/912, reg 16, Sch 2, para 1(1), (3), as from 2 April 2002.

Community interest companies: if a company is to be formed as a community interest company, both the normal documents required for formation as a company and additional documents, "the prescribed formation documents", must be delivered to the registrar of companies under this section; see the Companies (Audit, Investigations and Community Enterprise) Act 2004, ss 26, 36 at **[900]**, **[910]**.

Fees: see Appendix 3 (Fees Instruments) at **[A3]**.

Statement in the prescribed form: see Appendix 4 (Forms table) at **[A4]**.

11 Minimum authorised capital (public companies)

When a memorandum delivered to the registrar of companies under section 10 states that the association to be registered is to be a public company, the amount of the share capital stated in the memorandum to be that with which the company proposes to be registered must not be less than the authorised minimum (defined in section 118).

[13]

NOTES

Repealed by the Companies Act 2006, s 1295, Sch 16, as from a day to be appointed.

12 Duty of registrar

(1) The registrar of companies shall not register a company's memorandum delivered under section 10 unless he is satisfied that all the requirements of this Act in respect of registration and of matters precedent and incidental to it have been complied with.

(2) Subject to this, the registrar shall retain and register the memorandum and articles (if any) delivered to him under that section.

(3) [Subject to subsection (3A), a statutory declaration] in the prescribed form by—

(*a*) *a solicitor engaged in the formation of a company, or*

(*b*) *a person named as a director or secretary of the company in the statement delivered under section 10(2),*

that those requirements have been complied with shall be delivered to the registrar of companies, and the registrar may accept such a declaration as sufficient evidence of compliance.

[(3A) In place of the statutory declaration referred to in subsection (3), there may be delivered to the registrar of companies using electronic communications a statement made by a person mentioned in paragraph (a) or (b) of subsection (3) that the requirements mentioned in subsection (1) have been complied with; and the registrar may accept such a statement as sufficient evidence of compliance.

(3B) Any person who makes a false statement under subsection (3A) which he knows to be false or does not believe to be true is liable to imprisonment or a fine, or both.]

[14]

NOTES

Repealed by the Companies Act 2006, s 1295, Sch 16, as from a day to be appointed.

Sub-s (3): words in square brackets substituted by the Companies Act 1985 (Electronic Communications) Order 2000, SI 2000/3373, art 4(1), (2), as from 22 December 2000.

Sub-ss (3A), (3B): added by SI 2000/3373, art 4(1), (3), as from 22 December 2000.

Community interest companies: this section applies if a company is eligible to be formed as a community interest company; see the Companies (Audit, Investigations and Community Enterprise) Act 2004, ss 26, 36(7) at **[900]**, **[910]**.

Statutory declaration in the prescribed form: see Appendix 4 (Forms table) at **[A4]**.

Insolvency Act: ie, the Insolvency Act 1986.

13 Effect of registration

(1) On the registration of a company's memorandum, the registrar of companies shall give a certificate that the company is incorporated and, in the case of a limited company, that it is limited.

(2) The certificate may be signed by the registrar, or authenticated by his official seal.

(3) From the date of incorporation mentioned in the certificate, the subscribers of the memorandum, together with such other persons as may from time to time become members of the company, shall be a body corporate by the name contained in the memorandum.

(4) That body corporate is then capable forthwith of exercising all the functions of an incorporated company, but with such liability on the part of its members to contribute to its assets in the event of its being wound up as is provided by this Act [and the Insolvency Act].

This is subject, in the case of a public company, to section 117 (additional certificate as to amount of allotted share capital).

(5) The persons named in the statement under section 10 as directors, secretary or joint secretaries are, on the company's incorporation, deemed to have been respectively appointed as its first directors, secretary or joint secretaries.

(6) Where the registrar registers an association's memorandum which states that the association is to be a public company, the certificate of incorporation shall contain a statement that the company is a public company.

(7) A certificate of incorporation given in respect of an association is conclusive evidence—

- *(a) that the requirements of this Act in respect of registration and of matters precedent and incidental to it have been complied with, and that the association is a company authorised to be registered, and is duly registered, under this Act, and*
- *(b) if the certificate contains a statement that the company is a public company, that the company is such a company.*

[15]

NOTES

Repealed by the Companies Act 2006, s 1295, Sch 16, as from a day to be appointed.

Sub-s (4): words in square brackets inserted by the Insolvency Act 1986, s 439(1), Sch 13, Pt I, as from 29 December 1986.

Community interest companies: if a company is formed as a community interest company, the certificate of incorporation under this section is to contain a statement that the company is a community interest company; see the Companies (Audit, Investigations and Community Enterprise) Act 2004, ss 26, 36(8), (9) at **[900]**, **[910]**.

Registration under earlier legislation: nothing in this Act, nor in the Companies Consolidation (Consequential Provisions) Act 1985, the Company Securities (Insider Dealing) Act 1985 (repealed and replaced by the Criminal Justice Act 1993, Pt V), nor the Business Names Act 1985, affects the registration of any company under the Companies Acts 1948 to 1983 or the continued existence of any company by virtue of such registration; see the Companies Consolidation (Consequential Provisions) Act 1985, s 31(1), (8) at **[728]**.

Insolvency Act: ie, the Insolvency Act 1986.

14 Effect of memorandum and articles

(*1*) *Subject to the provisions of this Act, the memorandum and articles, when registered, bind the company and its members to the same extent as if they respectively had been signed and sealed by each member, and contained covenants on the part of each member to observe all the provisions of the memorandum and of the articles.*

(*2*) *Money payable by a member to the company under the memorandum or articles is a debt due from him to the company, and in England and Wales is of the nature of a specialty debt.*

[16]

NOTES

Repealed by the Companies Act 2006, s 1295, Sch 16, as from a day to be appointed.

Contractual rights of third parties: the Contracts (Rights of Third Parties) Act 1999, s 1, confers no rights on a third party in the case of any contract binding on a company and its members under this section; see s 6(2) of the 1999 Act.

15 Memorandum and articles of company limited by guarantee

(*1*) *In the case of a company limited by guarantee and not having a share capital, every provision in the memorandum or articles, or in any resolution of the company purporting to give any person a right to participate in the divisible profits of the company otherwise than as a member, is void.*

(*2*) *For purposes of provisions of this Act relating to the memorandum of a company limited by guarantee, and for those of section 1(4) and this section, every provision in the memorandum or articles, or in any resolution, of a company so limited purporting to divide the company's undertaking into shares or interests is to be treated as a provision for a share capital, notwithstanding that the nominal amount or number of the shares or interests is not specified by the provision.*

[17]

NOTES

Repealed by the Companies Act 2006, s 1295, Sch 16, as from a day to be appointed.

Companies registered before 1 January 1901: this section does not apply to companies registered before 1 January 1901 (the date on which the Companies Act 1900 came into force); see the Companies Consolidation (Consequential Provisions) Act 1985, s 10 at **[710]**.

16 Effect of alteration on company's members

(*1*) *A member of a company is not bound by an alteration made in the memorandum or articles after the date on which he became a member, if and so far as the alteration—*

- (*a*) *requires him to take or subscribe for more shares than the number held by him at the date on which the alteration is made; or*
- (*b*) *in any way increases his liability as at that date to contribute to the company's share capital or otherwise to pay money to the company.*

(*2*) *Subsection* (*1*) *operates notwithstanding anything in the memorandum or articles; but it does not apply in a case where the member agrees in writing, either before or after the alteration is made, to be bound by the alteration.*

[18]

NOTES

Repealed by the Companies Act 2006, s 1295, Sch 16, as from a day to be appointed.

17 Conditions in memorandum which could have been in articles

(*1*) *A condition contained in a company's memorandum which could lawfully have been contained in articles of association instead of in the memorandum may be altered by the company by special resolution; but if an application is made to the court for the alteration to be cancelled, the alteration does not have effect except in so far as it is confirmed by the court.*

(2) This section—

(*a*) *is subject to section 16, and also to Part XVII (court order protecting minority), and*

(*b*) *does not apply where the memorandum itself provides for or prohibits the alteration of all or any of the conditions above referred to, and does not authorise any variation or abrogation of the special rights of any class of members.*

(3) Section 5 (except subsections (2)(b) and (8)) and section 6(1) to (3) apply in relation to any alteration and to any application made under this section as they apply in relation to alterations and applications under sections 4 to 6.

[19]

NOTES

Repealed by the Companies Act 2006, s 1295, Sch 16, as from a day to be appointed.
Community interest companies: see the note to s 4 at **[5]**.

18 Amendments of memorandum or articles to be registered

(1) Where an alteration is made in a company's memorandum or articles by any statutory provision, whether contained in an Act of Parliament or in an instrument made under an Act, a printed copy of the Act or instrument shall, not later than 15 days after that provision comes into force, be forwarded to the registrar of companies and recorded by him.

(2) Where a company is required (by this section or otherwise) to send to the registrar any document making or evidencing an alteration in the company's memorandum or articles (other than a special resolution under section 4), the company shall send with it a printed copy of the memorandum or articles as altered.

(3) If a company fails to comply with this section, the company and any officer of it who is in default is liable to a fine and, for continued contravention, to a daily default fine.

[20]

NOTES

Repealed by the Companies Act 2006, s 1295, Sch 16, as from a day to be appointed.

19 Copies of memorandum and articles to be given to members

(1) A company shall, on being so required by any member, send to him a copy of the memorandum and of the articles (if any), and a copy of any Act of Parliament which alters the memorandum, subject to payment—

(*a*) *in the case of a copy of the memorandum and of the articles, of 5 pence or such less sum as the company may prescribe, and*

(*b*) *in the case of a copy of an Act, of such sum not exceeding its published price as the company may require.*

(2) If a company makes default in complying with this section, the company and every officer of it who is in default is liable for each offence to a fine.

[21]

NOTES

Repealed by the Companies Act 2006, s 1295, Sch 16, as from a day to be appointed.

20 Issued copy of memorandum to embody alterations

(1) Where an alteration is made in a company's memorandum, every copy of the memorandum issued after the date of the alteration shall be in accordance with the alteration.

(2) If, where any such alteration has been made, the company at any time after the date of the alteration issues any copies of the memorandum which are not in accordance with the alteration, it is liable to a fine, and so too is every officer of the company who is in default.

[22]

NOTES

Repealed by the Companies Act 2006, s 1295, Sch 16, as from a day to be appointed.

21 *(Repealed by the Welsh Language Act 1993, ss 30(1), (2), 35(1), Sch 2, as from 1 February 1994.)*

A company's membership

22 Definition of "member"

(1) The subscribers of a company's memorandum are deemed to have agreed to become members of the company, and on its registration shall be entered as such in its register of members.

(2) Every other person who agrees to become a member of a company, and whose name is entered in its register of members, is a member of the company.

[23]

NOTES

Repealed by the Companies Act 2006, s 1295, Sch 16, as from a day to be appointed.

[23 Membership of holding company

(1) Except as mentioned in this section, a body corporate cannot be a member of a company which is its holding company and any allotment or transfer of shares in a company to its subsidiary is void.

(2) The prohibition does not apply where the subsidiary is concerned only as personal representative or trustee unless, in the latter case, the holding company or a subsidiary of it is beneficially interested under the trust.

For the purpose of ascertaining whether the holding company or a subsidiary is so interested, there shall be disregarded—

- *(a) any interest held only by way of security for the purposes of a transaction entered into by the holding company or subsidiary in the ordinary course of a business which includes the lending of money;*
- *(b) any such interest as is mentioned in Part I of Schedule 2.*

[(3) The prohibition does not apply where shares in the holding company are held by the subsidiary in the ordinary course of its business as an intermediary.

For this purpose a person is an intermediary if that person—

- *(a) carries on a bona fide business of dealing in securities;*
- *(b) is a member of an EEA exchange (and satisfies any requirements for recognition as a dealer in securities laid down by that exchange) or is otherwise approved or supervised as a dealer in securities under the laws of an EEA State; and*
- *(c) does not carry on an excluded business.*

(3A) The excluded businesses are the following—

- *(a) any business which consists wholly or mainly in the making or managing of investments;*
- *(b) any business which consists wholly or mainly in, or is carried on wholly or mainly for the purpose of, providing services to persons who are connected with the person carrying on the business;*
- *(c) any business which consists in insurance business;*
- *(d) any business which consists in managing or acting as trustee in relation to a pension scheme or which is carried on by the manager or trustee of such a scheme in connection with or for the purposes of the scheme;*
- *(e) any business which consists in operating or acting as trustee in relation to a collective investment scheme or is carried on by the operator or trustee of such a scheme in connection with or for the purposes of the scheme.*

(3B) For the purposes of subsections (3) and (3A)—

- *(a) the question whether a person is connected with another shall be determined in accordance with the provisions of section 839 of the Income and Corporation Taxes Act 1988;*
- *(b) "collective investment scheme" has the meaning given in [section 236 of the Financial Services and Markets Act 2000];*

(c) *"EEA exchange" means a market which appears on the list drawn up by an EEA State pursuant to Article 16 of Council Directive 93/22/EEC on investment services in the securities field;*

[(d) *"insurance business" means business which consists of the effecting or carrying out of contracts of insurance;*

(e) *"securities" includes—*

(i) *options,*

(ii) *futures, and*

(iii) *contracts for differences,*

and rights or interests in those investments;]

(f) *"trustee" and "the operator" shall, in relation to a collective investment scheme, be construed in accordance with [section 237(2) of the Financial Services and Markets Act 2000].*

[(3BA) *Subsection (3B) must be read with—*

(a) *section 22 of the Financial Services and Markets Act 2000;*

(b) *any relevant order under that section; and*

(c) *Schedule 2 to that Act.]*

(3C) *Where—*

(a) *a subsidiary which is a dealer in securities has purportedly acquired shares in its holding company in contravention of the prohibition in subsection (1); and*

(b) *a person acting in good faith has agreed, for value and without notice of that contravention, to acquire shares in the holding company from the subsidiary or from someone who has purportedly acquired the shares after their disposal by the subsidiary,*

any transfer to that person of the shares mentioned in paragraph (a) shall have the same effect as it would have had if their original acquisition by the subsidiary had not been in contravention of the prohibition.]

(4) *Where a body corporate became a holder of shares in a company—*

(a) *before 1st July 1948, or*

(b) *on or after that date and before [20th October 1997], in circumstances in which this section as it then had effect did not apply,*

but at any time [on or after [20th October 1997]] falls within the prohibition in subsection (1) above in respect of those shares, it may continue to be a member of that company; but for so long as that prohibition would apply, apart from this subsection, it has no right to vote in respect of those shares at meetings of the company or of any class of its members.

(5) *Where a body corporate becomes a holder of shares in a company [on or after [20th October 1997]] in circumstances in which the prohibition in subsection (1) does not apply, but subsequently falls within that prohibition in respect of those shares, it may continue to be a member of that company; but for so long as that prohibition would apply, apart from this subsection, it has no right to vote in respect of those shares at meetings of the company or of any class of its members.*

(6) *Where a body corporate is permitted to continue as a member of a company by virtue of subsection (4) or (5), an allotment to it of fully paid shares in the company may be validly made by way of capitalisation of reserves of the company; but for so long as the prohibition in subsection (1) would apply, apart from subsection (4) or (5), it has no right to vote in respect of those shares at meetings of the company or of any class of its members.*

(7) *The provisions of this section apply to a nominee acting on behalf of a subsidiary as to the subsidiary itself.*

(8) *In relation to a company other than a company limited by shares, the references in this section to shares shall be construed as references to the interest of its members as such, whatever the form of that interest.]*

[24]

NOTES

Substituted by CA 1989, s 129(1), as from 1 November 1990, subject to transitional provisions; see CA 1989, s 144(4), Sch 18, para 32 at **[823]** and **[874]**.

Repealed by the Companies Act 2006, s 1295, Sch 16, as from a day to be appointed.

Sub-ss (3), (3A), (3C): substituted, together with sub-s (3B) for original sub-s (3), by the Companies (Membership of Holding Company) (Dealers in Securities) Regulations 1997, SI 1997/2306, reg 2, as from 20 October 1997.

Sub-s (3B): substituted as noted above; words in square brackets in paras (b), (f), and the whole of paras (d), (e), substituted by the Financial Services and Markets Act 2000 (Consequential Amendments and Repeals) Order 2001, SI 2001/3649, art 4(1)–(4), as from 1 December 2001; for the words "Article 16 of Council Directive 93/22/EEC on investment services in the securities field" in para (c) there are substituted the words "Article 47 of Directive 2004/39/EC of the European Parliament and of the Council of 21 April 2004 on markets in financial instruments" by the Financial Services and Markets Act 2000 (Markets in Financial Instruments) Regulations 2007, SI 2007/126, reg 3(6), Sch 6, Pt 1, para 7(1), (2), as from 1 November 2007 (for the full commencement details of SI 2007/126, see reg 1 of those Regulations at **[7596]**).

Sub-s (3BA): inserted by SI 2001/3649, art 4(1), (5), as from 1 December 2001.

Sub-s (4): words in first pair and third (inner) pair of square brackets substituted by SI 1997/2306, reg 3, as from 20 October 1997; words in second (outer) pair of square brackets substituted by the Companies Act 1989 (Commencement No 6 and Transitional and Saving Provisions) Order 1990, SI 1990/1392, art 8 (as amended by SI 1990/1707, art 8) as from 9 July 1990.

Sub-s (5): words in first (outer) pair of square brackets substituted by SI 1990/1392, art 8, as from 9 July 1990 (as amended by SI 1990/1707, art 8); words in second (inner) pair of square brackets substituted by SI 1997/2306, reg 3, as from 20 October 1997.

Transitional provisions, etc: as to the effect of this section prior to 1 November 1990, see CA 1989, Sch 18, para 32 at **[874]**.

24 Minimum membership for carrying on business

[(1)] If a company[, other than a private company limited by shares or by guarantee,] carries on business without having at least two members and does so for more than 6 months, a person who, for the whole or any part of the period that it so carries on business after those 6 months—

(*a*) *is a member of the company, and*

(*b*) *knows that it is carrying on business with only one member,*

is liable (jointly and severally with the company) for the payment of the company's debts contracted during the period or, as the case may be, that part of it.

[(2) For the purposes of this section references to a member of a company do not include the company itself where it is such a member only by virtue of its holding shares as treasury shares.]

[25]

NOTES

Repealed by the Companies Act 2006, s 1295, Sch 16, as from a day to be appointed.

Sub-s (1): numbered as such by the Companies (Acquisition of Own Shares) (Treasury Shares) Regulations 2003, SI 2003/1116, reg 4, Schedule, para 2, as from 1 December 2003; words in square brackets inserted by the Companies (Single Member Private Limited Companies) Regulations 1992, SI 1992/1699, reg 2(1)(b), Schedule, para 2, as from 15 July 1992 (for transitional provisions see reg 3 thereof at **[6744]**).

Sub-s (2): added by SI 2003/1116, reg 4, Schedule, para 2, as from 1 December 2003.

Application to limited liability partnerships: see the Limited Liability Partnerships Regulations 2001, SI 2001/1090, reg 4(1), Sch 2, Pt 1 at **[6985]**, **[6993]**.

CHAPTER II
COMPANY NAMES

25 Name as stated in memorandum

(1) The name of a public company must end with the words "public limited company" or, if the memorandum states that the company's registered office is to be situated in Wales, those words or their equivalent in Welsh ("cwmni cyfyngedig cyhoeddus"); and those words or that equivalent may not be preceded by the word "limited" or its equivalent in Welsh ("cyfyngedig").

(2) In the case of a company limited by shares or by guarantee (not being a public company), the name must have "limited" as its last word, except that—

(*a*) *this is subject to section 30 (exempting, in certain circumstances, a company from the requirement to have "limited" as part of the name), and*

(*b*) *if the company is to be registered with a memorandum stating that its registered office is to be situated in Wales, the name may have "cyfyngedig" as its last word.*

[26]

NOTES

Repealed by the Companies Act 2006, s 1295, Sch 16, as from a day to be appointed.

Community interest companies: this section does not apply to community interest companies; see the Companies (Audit, Investigations and Community Enterprise) Act 2004, ss 26, 33(5) at **[900]**, **[907]**.

26 Prohibition on registration of certain names

(*1*) *A company shall not be registered under this Act by a name—*

(*a*) *which includes, otherwise than at the end of the name, any of the following words or expressions, that is to say, "limited", "unlimited"[, "public limited company", "community interest company" or "community interest public limited company"] or their Welsh equivalents ("cyfyngedig", "anghyfyngedig"[, "cwmni cyfyngedig cyhoeddus", "cwmni buddiant cymunedol" and "cwmni buddiant cymunedol cyhoeddus cyfyngedig"] respectively);*

(*b*) *which includes, otherwise than at the end of the name, an abbreviation of any of those words or expressions;*

[(*bb*) *which includes, at any place in the name, the expressions "investment company with variable capital" or "open-ended investment company" or their Welsh equivalents ("cwmni buddsoddi â chyfalaf newidiol" and "cwmni buddsoddiant penagored" respectively);]*

[(*bbb*) *which includes, at any place in the name, the expression "limited liability partnership" or its Welsh equivalent ("partneriaeth atebolrwydd cyfyngedig");]*

(*c*) *which is the same as a name appearing in the registrar's index of company names;*

(*d*) *the use of which by the company would in the opinion of the Secretary of State constitute a criminal offence; or*

(*e*) *which in the opinion of the Secretary of State is offensive.*

(*2*) *Except with the approval of the Secretary of State, a company shall not be registered under this Act by a name which—*

(*a*) *in the opinion of the Secretary of State would be likely to give the impression that the company is connected in any way with Her Majesty's Government[, with the Welsh Assembly Government] or with any local authority; or*

(*b*) *includes any word or expression for the time being specified in regulations under section 29.*

"Local authority" means any local authority within the meaning of the Local Government Act 1972 or the Local Government (Scotland) Act 1973, the Common Council of the City of London or the Council of the Isles of Scilly.

(*3*) *In determining for purposes of subsection (1)(c) whether one name is the same as another, there are to be disregarded—*

(*a*) *the definite article, where it is the first word of the name;*

(*b*) *the following words and expressions where they appear at the end of the name, that is to say—*

"company" or its Welsh equivalent ("cwmni"),

"and company" or its Welsh equivalent ("a'r cwmni"),

"company limited" or its Welsh equivalent ("cwmni cyfyngedig"),

"and company limited" or its Welsh equivalent ("a'r cwmni cyfyngedig"),

"limited" or its Welsh equivalent ("cyfyngedig"),

"unlimited" or its Welsh equivalent ("anghyfyngedig"), …

"public limited company" or its Welsh equivalent ("cwmni cyfyngedig cyhoeddus"); […

["community interest company" or its Welsh equivalent ("cwmni buddiant cymunedol");

"community interest public limited company" or its Welsh equivalent ("cwmni buddiant cymunedol cyhoeddus cyfyngedig");]

"investment company with variable capital" or its Welsh equivalent ("cwmni buddsoddi â chyfalaf newidiol");] [and

"open-ended investment company" or its Welsh equivalent ("cwmni buddsoddiant penagored");]

(*c*) *abbreviations of any of those words or expressions where they appear at the end of the name; and*

(*d*) *type and case of letters, accents, spaces between letters and punctuation marks;*

and "and" and "&" are to be taken as the same.

[27]

NOTES

Repealed by the Companies Act 2006, s 1295, Sch 16, as from a day to be appointed.

Sub-s (1): words in square brackets in para (a) substituted by the Companies (Audit, Investigations and Community Enterprise) Act 2004, s 33, Sch 6, paras 1, 2(1), (2), as from 1 July 2005; para (bb) inserted by the Open-Ended Investment Companies (Investment Companies with Variable Capital) Regulations 1996, SI 1996/2827, reg 75, Sch 8, Pt I, para 4(a), as from 6 January 1997, and substituted by the Open-Ended Investment Companies Regulations 2001, SI 2001/1228, reg 84, Sch 7, para 3(1), (2), as from 1 December 2001; para (bbb) inserted by the Limited Liability Partnerships Regulations 2001, SI 2001/1090, reg 9, Sch 5, para 9, as from 6 April 2001.

Sub-s (2): words in square brackets in para (a) inserted by the Government of Wales Act 2006 (Consequential Modifications and Transitional Provisions) Order 2007, SI 2007/1388, art 3, Sch 1, para 19, as from 2 May 2007.

Sub-s (3) is amended as follows—

Word omitted from the end of the entry beginning "unlimited" repealed, and entry beginning "investment company with variable capital" (and the word "and" which originally preceded it) inserted by SI 1996/2827, reg 75, Sch 8, Pt I, para 4(b), as from 6 January 1997.

Entries beginning "community interest company" and "community interest public limited company" inserted by the Companies (Audit, Investigations and Community Enterprise) Act 2004, s 33, Sch 6, paras 1, 2(1), (3), as from 1 July 2005.

Word omitted from the end of the entry beginning "public limited company" repealed, and entry beginning "open-ended investment company" inserted, by SI 2001/1228, reg 84, Sch 7, para 3(1), (3), as from 1 December 2001.

Secretary of State: by the Contracting Out (Functions in relation to the Registration of Companies) Order 1995, SI 1995/1013, art 5, Sch 3, para 1 at **[6840]** and **[6843]**, the functions of the Secretary of State conferred by or under sub-s (2) above and ss 244(5), 702(5), may be exercised by, or by employees of, such person (if any) as may be authorised in that behalf by the Secretary of State.

27 Alternatives of statutory designations

(1) A company which by any provision of this Act is either required or entitled to include in its name, as its last part, any of the words specified in subsection (4) below may, instead of those words, include as the last part of the name the abbreviations there specified as alternatives in relation to those words.

(2) A reference in this Act to the name of a company or to the inclusion of any of those words in a company's name includes a reference to the name including (in place of any of the words so specified) the appropriate alternative, or to the inclusion of the appropriate alternative, as the case may be.

(3) A provision of this Act requiring a company not to include any of those words in its name also requires it not to include the abbreviated alternative specified in subsection (4).

(4) For the purposes of this section—

(a) the alternative of "limited" is "ltd.";

(b) the alternative of "public limited company" is "p.l.c.";

(c) the alternative of "cyfyngedig" is "cyf."; ...

(d) the alternative of "cwmni cyfyngedig cyhoeddus" is "c.c.c."

[(e) the alternative of "community interest company" is "cic";

(f) the alternative of "cwmni buddiant cymunedol" is "cbc";

(g) the alternative of "community interest public limited company" is "community interest plc"; and

(h) the alternative of "cwmni buddiant cymunedol cyhoeddus cyfyngedig" is "cwmni buddiant cymunedol ccc."].

[28]

NOTES

Repealed by the Companies Act 2006, s 1295, Sch 16, as from a day to be appointed.

Sub-s (4): word omitted from para (c) repealed, and paras (e)–(h) added, by the Companies (Audit, Investigations and Community Enterprise) Act 2004, ss 33, 64, Sch 6, paras 1, 3, Sch 8, as from 1 July 2005.

28 Change of name

(1) A company may by special resolution change its name (but subject to section 31 in the case of a company which has received a direction under subsection (2) of that section from the Secretary of State).

(2) Where a company has been registered by a name which—

(a) is the same as or, in the opinion of the Secretary of State, too like a name appearing at the time of the registration in the registrar's index of company names, or

(*b*) *is the same as or, in the opinion of the Secretary of State, too like a name which should have appeared in that index at that time,*

the Secretary of State may within 12 months of that time, in writing, direct the company to change its name within such period as he may specify.

Section 26(3) applies in determining under this subsection whether a name is the same as or too like another.

(*3*) *If it appears to the Secretary of State that misleading information has been given for the purpose of a company's registration with a particular name, or that undertakings or assurances have been given for that purpose and have not been fulfilled, he may within 5 years of the date of its registration with that name in writing direct the company to change its name within such period as he may specify.*

(*4*) *Where a direction has been given under subsection* (*2*) *or* (*3*), *the Secretary of State may by a further direction in writing extend the period within which the company is to change its name, at any time before the end of that period.*

(*5*) *A company which fails to comply with a direction under this section, and any officer of it who is in default, is liable to a fine and, for continued contravention, to a daily default fine.*

(*6*) *Where a company changes its name under this section, the registrar of companies shall* (*subject to section 26*) *enter the new name on the register in place of the former name, and shall issue a certificate of incorporation altered to meet the circumstances of the case; and the change of name has effect from the date on which the altered certificate is issued.*

(*7*) *A change of name by a company under this section does not affect any rights or obligations of the company or render defective any legal proceedings by or against it; and any legal proceedings that might have been continued or commenced against it by its former name may be continued or commenced against it by its new name.*

[29]

NOTES

Repealed by the Companies Act 2006, s 1295, Sch 16, as from a day to be appointed.

Community interest companies: this section applies where an existing company is eligible to be formed as a community interest company ("CIC") and where a CIC is eligible to cease being a CIC. Where a charitable company converts to CIC status without consent, the altered certificate of incorporation issued on the change of name under sub-s (6) of this section may be quashed by order of the High Court or Court of Session; see the Companies (Audit, Investigations and Community Enterprise) Act 2004, ss 26, 38(6), (8), 39(2), 40(2), (5), 55(6) at **[900]**, **[912]**, **[913]**, **[914]**, **[929]**.

Fees: see Appendix 3 (Fees Instruments) at **[A3]**.

29 Regulations about names

(*1*) *The Secretary of State may by regulations—*

(*a*) *specify words or expressions for the registration of which as or as part of a company's corporate name his approval is required under section 26*(*2*)(*b*), *and*

(*b*) *in relation to any such word or expression, specify a Government department or other body as the relevant body for purposes of the following subsection.*

(*2*) *Where a company proposes to have as, or as part of, its corporate name any such word or expression and a Government department or other body is specified under subsection* (*1*)(*b*) *in relation to that word or expression, a request shall be made* (*in writing*) *to the relevant body to indicate whether* (*and if so why*) *it has any objections to the proposal; and the person to make the request is—*

(*a*) *in the case of a company seeking to be registered under this Part, the person making the statutory declaration [under section 12*(*3*) *or statement under section 12*(*3A*) (*as the case may be*)*],*

(*b*) *in the case of a company seeking to be registered under section 680, the persons making the statutory declaration [under section 686*(*2*) *or statement under section 686*(*2A*) (*as the case may be*)*], and*

(*c*) *in any other case, a director or secretary of the company concerned.*

(*3*) *The person who has made that request to the relevant body shall submit to the registrar of companies a statement that it has been made and a copy of any response received from that body, together with—*

(*a*) *the requisite statutory declaration [or statement], or*

(*b*) *a copy of the special resolution changing the company's name, according as the case is one or other of those mentioned in subsection* (2).

(4) ...

(5) *Regulations under this section may contain such transitional provisions and savings as the Secretary of State thinks appropriate and may make different provision for different cases or classes of case.*

(6) *The regulations shall be made by statutory instrument, to be laid before Parliament after it is made; and the regulations shall cease to have effect at the end of 28 days beginning with the day on which the regulations were made (but without prejudice to anything previously done by virtue of them or to the making of new regulations), unless during that period they are approved by resolution of each House. In reckoning that period, no account is to be taken of any time during which Parliament is dissolved or prorogued or during which both Houses are adjourned for more than 4 days.*

[30]

NOTES

Repealed by the Companies Act 2006, s 1295, Sch 16, as from 1 January 2007 (in so far as relating to sub-s (4)), and as from a day to be appointed (otherwise).

Sub-s (2): words in square brackets substituted by the Companies Act 1985 (Electronic Communications) Order 2000, SI 2000/3373, art 31(1)(a), (b), as from 22 December 2000.

Sub-s (3): words in square brackets inserted by SI 2000/3373, art 31(1)(c), as from 22 December 2000.

Sub-s (4): repealed as noted above.

Chamber of commerce: by the Company and Business Names (Chamber of Commerce, etc) Act 1999, s 1, the Secretary of State is required to include the title "chamber of commerce" (and its Welsh equivalent) in the list of controlled titles maintained in accordance with regulations made under this section.

Regulations: no regulations have been made under this section, but by virtue of the Companies Consolidation (Consequential Provisions) Act 1985, s 31(2), (11) and the Interpretation Act 1978, s 17(2)(b), the Company and Business Names Regulations 1981, SI 1981/1685 at **[6001]** have effect as if made under this section.

30 Exemption from requirement of "limited" as part of the name

(*1*) *Certain companies are exempt from requirements of this Act relating to the use of "limited" as part of the company name.*

(*2*) *A private company limited by guarantee is exempt from those requirements, and so too is a company which on 25th February 1982 was a private company limited by shares with a name which, by virtue of a licence under section 19 of the Companies Act 1948, did not include "limited"; but in either case the company must, to have the exemption, comply with the requirements of the following subsection.*

(*3*) *Those requirements are that—*

(*a*) *the objects of the company are* (*or, in the case of a company about to be registered, are to be*) *the promotion of commerce, art, science, education, religion, charity or any profession, and anything incidental or conducive to any of those objects; and*

(*b*) *the company's memorandum or articles—*

(*i*) *require its profits* (*if any*) *or other income to be applied in promoting its objects,*

(*ii*) *prohibit the payment of dividends to its members, and*

(*iii*) *require all the assets which would otherwise be available to its members generally to be transferred on its winding up either to another body with objects similar to its own or to another body the objects of which are the promotion of charity and anything incidental or conducive thereto* (*whether or not the body is a member of the company*).

(*4*) *[Subject to subsection* (*5A*), *a statutory declaration] that a company complies with the requirements of subsection* (*3*) *may be delivered to the registrar of companies, who may accept the declaration as sufficient evidence of the matters stated in it ...*

(*5*) *The statutory declaration must be in the prescribed form and be made—*

(*a*) *in the case of a company to be formed, by a solicitor engaged in its formation or by a person named as director or secretary in the statement delivered under section 10*(*2*);

(*b*) *in the case of a company to be registered in pursuance of section 680, by two or more directors or other principal officers of the company; and*

(c) *in the case of a company proposing to change its name so that it ceases to have the word "limited" as part of its name, by a director or secretary of the company.*

[(5A) In place of the statutory declaration referred to in subsection (4), there may be delivered to the registrar of companies using electronic communications a statement made by a person falling within the applicable paragraph of subsection (5) stating that the company complies with the requirements of subsection (3); and the registrar may accept such a statement as sufficient evidence of the matters stated in it.

(5B) The registrar may refuse to register a company by a name which does not include the word "limited" unless a statutory declaration under subsection (4) or statement under subsection (5A) has been delivered to him.

(5C) Any person who makes a false statement under subsection (5A) which he knows to be false or does not believe to be true is liable to imprisonment or a fine, or both.]

(6) References in this section to the word "limited" include (in an appropriate case) its Welsh equivalent ("cyfyngedig"), and the appropriate alternative ("ltd." or "cyf.", as the case may be).

(7) A company which [under this section] is exempt from requirements relating to the use of "limited" and does not include that word as part of its name, is also exempt from the requirements of this Act relating to the publication of its name and the sending of lists of members to the registrar of companies.

[31]

NOTES

Repealed by the Companies Act 2006, s 1295, Sch 16, as from a day to be appointed.

Sub-s (4): words in square brackets substituted, and words omitted repealed, by the Companies Act 1985 (Electronic Communications) Order 2000, SI 2000/3373, art 5(1), (2), as from 22 December 2000.

Sub-ss (5A)–(5C): inserted by SI 2000/3373, art 5(1), (3), as from 22 December 2000.

Sub-s (7): words in square brackets inserted by the Companies (Audit, Investigations and Community Enterprise) Act 2004, s 33, Sch 6, paras 1, 4, as from 1 July 2005.

Companies Act 1948, s 19: repealed by the Companies Act 1981, s 119, Sch 4.

Prescribed form: see Appendix 4 (Forms table) at **[A4]**.

31 Provisions applying to company exempt under s 30

(1) A company which is exempt under section 30 and whose name does not include "limited" shall not alter its memorandum or articles of association so that it ceases to comply with the requirements of subsection (3) of that section.

(2) If it appears to the Secretary of State that such a company—

(a) *has carried on any business other than the promotion of any of the objects mentioned in that subsection, or*

(b) *has applied any of its profits or other income otherwise than in promoting such objects, or*

(c) *has paid a dividend to any of its members,*

he may, in writing, direct the company to change its name by resolution of the directors within such period as may be specified in the direction, so that its name ends with "limited".

A resolution passed by the directors in compliance with a direction under this subsection is subject to section 380 of this Act (copy to be forwarded to the registrar of companies within 15 days).

[(2A) Where such a resolution is passed by the directors, the company must give notice to the registrar of companies of the change.

(2B) Where a company changes its name under this section, the registrar of companies shall (subject to section 26) enter the new name on the register in place of the former name, and shall issue a certificate of incorporation altered to meet the circumstances of the case; and the change of name has effect from the date on which the altered certificate is issued.

(2C) A change of name by a company under this section does not affect any right or obligations of the company or render defective any legal proceedings by or against it; and any legal proceedings that might have been continued or commenced against it by its former name may be continued or commenced against it by its new name.]

(3) A company which has received a direction under subsection (2) shall not thereafter be registered by a name which does not include "limited", without the approval of the Secretary of State.

(4) References in this section to the word "limited" include (in an appropriate case) its Welsh equivalent ("cyfyngedig"), and the appropriate alternative ("ltd." or "cyf.", as the case may be).

(5) A company which contravenes subsection (1), and any officer of it who is in default, is liable to a fine and, for continued contravention, to a daily default fine.

(6) A company which fails to comply with a direction by the Secretary of State under subsection (2), and any officer of the company who is in default, is liable to a fine and, for continued contravention, to a daily default fine.

[32]

NOTES

Repealed by the Companies Act 2006, s 1295, Sch 16, as from a day to be appointed.

Sub-s (2): second sentence repealed by the draft Companies Act 2006 (Commencement No 3, Consequential Amendments, Transitional Provisions and Savings) Order 2007, art 10(1), Sch 4, Pt 1, para 1(1), as from 1 October 2007 (see **[A12]**).

Sub-ss (2A)–(2C): inserted by the draft Companies Act 2006 (Commencement No 3, Consequential Amendments, Transitional Provisions and Savings) Order 2007, art 10(1), Sch 4, Pt 1, para 1(1), as from 1 October 2007 (see **[A12]**).

32 Power to require company to abandon misleading name

(1) If in the Secretary of State's opinion the name by which a company is registered gives so misleading an indication of the nature of its activities as to be likely to cause harm to the public, he may direct it to change its name.

(2) The direction must, if not duly made the subject of an application to the court under the following subsection, be complied with within a period of 6 weeks from the date of the direction or such longer period as the Secretary of State may think fit to allow.

(3) The company may, within a period of 3 weeks from the date of the direction, apply to the court to set it aside; and the court may set the direction aside or confirm it and, if it confirms the direction, shall specify a period within which it must be complied with.

(4) If a company makes default in complying with a direction under this section, it is liable to a fine and, for continued contravention, to a daily default fine.

(5) Where a company changes its name under this section, the registrar shall (subject to section 26) enter the new name on the register in place of the former name, and shall issue a certificate of incorporation altered to meet the circumstances of the case; and the change of name has effect from the date on which the altered certificate is issued.

(6) A change of name by a company under this section does not affect any of the rights or obligations of the company, or render defective any legal proceedings by or against it; and any legal proceedings that might have been continued or commenced against it by its former name may be continued or commenced against it by its new name.

[33]

NOTES

Repealed by the Companies Act 2006, s 1295, Sch 16, as from a day to be appointed.

33 Prohibition on trading under misleading name

(1) A person who is not a public company is guilty of an offence if he carries on any trade, profession or business under a name which includes, as its last part, the words "public limited company" or their equivalent in Welsh ("cwmni cyfyngedig cyhoeddus")[; and a community interest company which is not a public company is guilty of an offence if it does so under a name which includes, as its last part, the words "cwmni buddiant cymunedol cyhoeddus cyfyngedig].

(2) A public company is guilty of an offence if, in circumstances in which the fact that it is a public company is likely to be material to any person, it uses a name which may reasonably be expected to give the impression that it is a private company.

(3) A person guilty of an offence under subsection (1) or (2) and, if that person is a company, any officer of the company who is in default, is liable to a fine and, for continued contravention, to a daily default fine.

[34]

NOTES

Repealed by the Companies Act 2006, s 1295, Sch 16, as from a day to be appointed.

Sub-s (1): words in square brackets inserted by the Companies (Audit, Investigations and Community Enterprise) Act 2004, s 33, Sch 6, paras 1, 5, as from 1 July 2005.

34 Penalty for improper use of "limited" or "cyfyngedig"

If any person trades or carries on business under a name or title of which "limited" or "cyfyngedig", or any contraction or imitation of either of those words, is the last word, that person, unless duly incorporated with limited liability, is liable to a fine and, for continued contravention, to a daily default fine.

[35]

NOTES

Repealed by the Companies Act 2006, s 1295, Sch 16, as from a day to be appointed.

[34A Penalty for improper use of "community interest company" etc

(1) A company which is not a community interest company is guilty of an offence if it carries on any trade, profession or business under a name which includes any of the expressions specified in subsection (3).

(2) A person other than a company is guilty of an offence if it carries on any trade, profession or business under a name which includes any of those expressions (or any contraction of them) as its last part.

(3) The expressions are—

(a) "community interest company" or its Welsh equivalent ("cwmni buddiant cymunedol"), and

(b) "community interest public limited company" or its Welsh equivalent ("cwmni buddiant cymunedol cyhoeddus cyfyngedig").

(4) Subsections (1) and (2) do not apply—

(a) to a person who was carrying on a trade, profession or business under the name in question at any time during the period beginning with 1st September 2003 and ending with 4th December 2003, or

(b) if the name in question was on 4th December 2003 a registered trade mark or Community trade mark (within the meaning of the Trade Marks Act 1994 (c 26)), to a person who was on that date a proprietor or licensee of that trade mark.

(5) A person guilty of an offence under subsection (1) or (2) and, if that person is a company, any officer of the company who is in default, is liable to a fine and, for continued contravention, to a daily default fine.]

[35A]

NOTES

Inserted by the Companies (Audit, Investigations and Community Enterprise) Act 2004, s 33, Sch 6, paras 1, 6, as from 1 July 2005.

Repealed by the Companies Act 2006, s 1295, Sch 16, as from a day to be appointed.

CHAPTER III
A COMPANY'S CAPACITY; FORMALITIES OF CARRYING ON BUSINESS

[35 A company's capacity not limited by its memorandum

(1) The validity of an act done by a company shall not be called into question on the ground of lack of capacity by reason of anything in the company's memorandum.

(2) A member of a company may bring proceedings to restrain the doing of an act which but for subsection (1) would be beyond the company's capacity; but no such proceedings shall lie in respect of an act to be done in fulfilment of a legal obligation arising from a previous act of the company.

(3) *It remains the duty of the directors to observe any limitations on their powers flowing from the company's memorandum; and action by the directors which but for subsection (1) would be beyond the company's capacity may only be ratified by the company by special resolution.*

A resolution ratifying such action shall not affect any liability incurred by the directors or any other person; relief from any such liability must be agreed to separately by special resolution.

(4) *The operation of this section is restricted by [section 65(1) of the Charities Act 1993] and section 112(3) of the Companies Act 1989 in relation to companies which are charities; and section 322A below (invalidity of certain transactions to which directors or their associates are parties) has effect notwithstanding this section.]*

[36]

NOTES

Substituted, together with ss 35A, 35B for original s 35, by CA 1989, s 108(1), as from 4 February 1991.

Repealed by the Companies Act 2006, s 1295, Sch 16, as from a day to be appointed.

Sub-s (4): words in square brackets substituted by the Charities Act 1993, s 98(1), Sch 6, para 20(1), (2), as from 1 August 1993.

[35A Power of directors to bind the company

(1) *In favour of a person dealing with a company in good faith, the power of the board of directors to bind the company, or authorise others to do so, shall be deemed to be free of any limitation under the company's constitution.*

(2) *For this purpose—*

(a) *a person "deals with" a company if he is a party to any transaction or other act to which the company is a party;*

(b) *a person shall not be regarded as acting in bad faith by reason only of his knowing that an act is beyond the powers of the directors under the company's constitution; and*

(c) *a person shall be presumed to have acted in good faith unless the contrary is proved.*

(3) *The references above to limitations on the directors' power under the company's constitution include limitations deriving—*

(a) *from a resolution of the company in general meeting or a meeting of any class of shareholders, or*

(b) *from any agreement between the members of the company or of any class of shareholders.*

(4) *Subsection (1) does not affect any right of a member of the company to bring proceedings to restrain the doing of an act which is beyond the powers of the directors; but no such proceedings shall lie in respect of an act to be done in fulfilment of a legal obligation arising from a previous act of the company.*

(5) *Nor does that subsection affect any liability incurred by the directors, or any other person, by reason of the directors' exceeding their powers.*

(6) *The operation of this section is restricted by [section 65(1) of the Charities Act 1993] and section 112(3) of the Companies Act 1989 in relation to companies which are charities; and section 322A below (invalidity of certain transactions to which directors or their associates are parties) has effect notwithstanding this section.]*

[37]

NOTES

Substituted as noted to s 35 at **[36]**.

Repealed by the Companies Act 2006, s 1295, Sch 16, as from a day to be appointed.

Sub-s (6): words in square brackets substituted by the Charities Act 1993, s 98(1), Sch 6, para 20(1), (2), as from 1 August 1993.

[35B No duty to enquire as to capacity of company or authority of directors

A party to a transaction with a company is not bound to enquire as to whether it is permitted by the company's memorandum or as to any limitation on the powers of the board of directors to bind the company or authorise others to do so.]

[38]

NOTES

Substituted as noted to s 35 at **[36]**.
Repealed by the Companies Act 2006, s 1295, Sch 16, as from a day to be appointed.

[36 Company contracts: England and Wales

Under the law of England and Wales a contract may be made—

(*a*) *by a company, by writing under its common seal, or*

(*b*) *on behalf of a company, by any person acting under its authority, express or implied;*

and any formalities required by law in the case of a contract made by an individual also apply, unless a contrary intention appears, to a contract made by or on behalf of a company.]

[39]

NOTES

Substituted by CA 1989, s 130(1), as from 31 July 1990.
Repealed by the Companies Act 2006, s 1295, Sch 16, as from a day to be appointed.
Application to limited liability partnerships: see the Limited Liability Partnerships Regulations 2001, SI 2001/1090, reg 4(1), Sch 2, Pt 1 at **[6985]**, **[6993]**.
Companies incorporated outside Great Britain: this section is applied, with modifications, in relation to companies incorporated outside Great Britain, by the Foreign Companies (Execution of Documents) Regulations 1994, SI 1994/950, regs 2–4 at **[6788]**–**[6790]**.

[36A Execution of documents: England and Wales

(*1*) *Under the law of England and Wales the following provisions have effect with respect to the execution of documents by a company.*

(*2*) *A document is executed by a company by the affixing of its common seal.*

(*3*) *A company need not have a common seal, however, and the following subsections apply whether it does or not.*

(*4*) *A document signed by a director and the secretary of a company, or by two directors of a company, and expressed (in whatever form of words) to be executed by the company has the same effect as if executed under the common seal of the company.*

[(4A) Where a document is to be signed by a person as a director or the secretary of more than one company, it shall not be taken to be duly signed by that person for the purposes of subsection (4) unless the person signs it separately in each capacity.]

(*5*) …

(*6*) *In favour of a purchaser a document shall be deemed to have been duly executed by a company if it purports to be signed by a director and the secretary of the company, or by two directors of the company, …*

A "purchaser" means a purchaser in good faith for valuable consideration and includes a lessee, mortgagee or other person who for valuable consideration acquires an interest in property.]

[(7) This section applies in the case of a document which is (or purports to be) executed by a company in the name or on behalf of another person whether or not that person is also a company.]

[(8) For the purposes of this section, a document is (or purports to be) signed, in the case of a director or the secretary of a company which is not an individual, if it is (or purports to be) signed by an individual authorised by the director or secretary to sign on its behalf.]

[40]

NOTES

Inserted by CA 1989, s 130(2), as from 31 July 1990.
Repealed by the Companies Act 2006, s 1295, Sch 16, as from a day to be appointed.

Sub-ss (4A), (7), (8): inserted and added respectively by the Regulatory Reform (Execution of Deeds and Documents) Order 2005, SI 2005/1906, arts 7(2), 10(1), Sch 1, paras 9–11, as from 15 September 2005, except in relation to any instrument executed before that date.
Sub-s (5): repealed by SI 2005/1906, art 10(2), Sch 2, as from 15 September 2005, except in relation to any instrument executed before that date.
Sub-s (6): words omitted repealed by SI 2005/1906, arts 5, 10(2), Sch 2, as from 15 September 2005, except in relation to any instrument executed before that date.
Application to limited liability partnerships: see the Limited Liability Partnerships Regulations 2001, SI 2001/1090, reg 4(1), Sch 2, Pt 1 at **[6985]**, **[6993]**.
Companies incorporated outside Great Britain: this section is applied, with modifications, in relation to companies incorporated outside Great Britain, by the Foreign Companies (Execution of Documents) Regulations 1994, SI 1994/950, regs 2, 3, 5 at **[6788]**, **[6789]**, **[6791]**.

[36AA Execution of deeds: England and Wales

(1) A document is validly executed by a company as a deed for the purposes of section 1(2)(b) of the Law of Property (Miscellaneous Provisions) Act 1989, if and only if—

(a) it is duly executed by the company, and

(b) it is delivered as a deed.

(2) A document shall be presumed to be delivered for the purposes of subsection (1)(b) upon its being executed, unless a contrary intention is proved.]

[40A]

NOTES

Commencement: 15 September 2005.
Inserted by the Regulatory Reform (Execution of Deeds and Documents) Order 2005, SI 2005/1906, art 6, as from 15 September 2005, except in relation to any instrument executed before that date.
Repealed by the Companies Act 2006, s 1295, Sch 16, as from a day to be appointed.

[36B Execution of documents by companies

(1) Notwithstanding the provisions of any enactment, a company need not have a company seal.

(2) For the purposes of any enactment—

(a) providing for a document to be executed by a company by affixing its common seal; or

(b) referring (in whatever terms) to a document so executed,

a document signed or subscribed by or on behalf of the company in accordance with the provisions of the Requirements of Writing (Scotland) Act 1995 shall have effect as if so executed.

(3) In this section "enactment" includes an enactment contained in a statutory instrument.]

[41]

NOTES

Inserted by CA 1989, s 130(3), as from 31 July 1990; substituted by the Requirements of Writing (Scotland) Act 1995, s 14(1), Sch 4, para 51, as from 1 August 1995.
Repealed by the Companies Act 2006, s 1295, Sch 16, as from a day to be appointed.
Application to limited liability partnerships: see the Limited Liability Partnerships (Scotland) Regulations 2001, SSI 2001/128, Sch 1 at **[6980]**.
Companies incorporated outside Great Britain: this section and s 36C are applied, with modifications, in relation to companies incorporated outside Great Britain, by the Foreign Companies (Execution of Documents) Regulations 1994, SI 1994/950, regs 2, 3 at **[6788]**, **[6789]**.

[36C Pre-incorporation contracts, deeds and obligations

(1) A contract which purports to be made by or on behalf of a company at a time when the company has not been formed has effect, subject to any agreement to the contrary, as one made with the person purporting to act for the company or as agent for it, and he is personally liable on the contract accordingly.

(2) Subsection (1) applies—

(a) to the making of a deed under the law of England and Wales, and

(*b*) *to the undertaking of an obligation under the law of Scotland,*
as it applies to the making of a contract.]

[42]

NOTES

Inserted by CA 1989, s 130(4), as from 31 July 1990.
Repealed by the Companies Act 2006, s 1295, Sch 16, as from a day to be appointed.
Application to limited liability partnerships: see the Limited Liability Partnerships Regulations 2001, SI 2001/1090, reg 4(1), Sch 2, Pt 1 at **[6985]**, **[6993]**.
Companies incorporated outside Great Britain: see the note to s 36B at **[41]**.

37 Bills of exchange and promissory notes

A bill of exchange or promissory note is deemed to have been made, accepted or endorsed on behalf of a company if made, accepted or endorsed in the name of, or by or on behalf or on account of, the company by a person acting under its authority.

[43]

NOTES

Repealed by the Companies Act 2006, s 1295, Sch 16, as from a day to be appointed.
Application to limited liability partnerships: see the Limited Liability Partnerships Regulations 2001, SI 2001/1090, reg 4(1), Sch 2, Pt 1 at **[6985]**, **[6993]**.

38 Execution of deeds abroad

(*1*) *A company may […], by writing under its common seal, empower any person, either generally or in respect of any specified matters, as its attorney, to execute deeds on its behalf in any place elsewhere than in the United Kingdom.*

[(2) A deed executed by such an attorney on behalf of the company has the same effect as if it were executed under the company's common seal.]

[(3) This section does not extend to Scotland.]

[44]

NOTES

Repealed by the Companies Act 2006, s 1295, Sch 16, as from a day to be appointed.
Sub-s (1): words omitted (as originally inserted by CA 1989, s 130(7), Sch 17, para 1) repealed by the Law Reform (Miscellaneous Provisions) (Scotland) Act 1990, s 74(1), (2), Sch 8, para 33(2), Sch 9, as from 1 December 1990.
Sub-s (2): substituted by CA 1989, s 130(7), Sch 17, para 1, as from 31 July 1990.
Sub-s (3): added by the Requirements of Writing (Scotland) Act 1995, s 14(1), Sch 4, para 52, as from 1 August 1995.
Application to limited liability partnerships: see the Limited Liability Partnerships Regulations 2001, SI 2001/1090, reg 4(1), Sch 2, Pt 1 at **[6985]**, **[6993]**.

39 Power of company to have official seal for use abroad

(*1*) *A company [which has a common seal] whose objects require or comprise the transaction of business in foreign countries may, if authorised by its articles, have for use in any territory, district, or place elsewhere than in the United Kingdom, an official seal, which shall be a facsimile of [its common seal], with the addition on its face of the name of every territory, district or place where it is to be used.*

[(2) The official seal when duly affixed to a document has the same effect as the company's common seal.]

[(2A) Subsection (2) does not extend to Scotland.]

(*3*) *A company having an official seal for use in any such territory, district or place may, by writing under its common seal [or as respects Scotland by writing subscribed in accordance with the Requirements of Writing (Scotland) Act 1995] […] authorise any person appointed for the purpose in that territory, district or place to affix the official seal to any deed or other document to which the company is party in that territory, district or place.*

(*4*) *As between the company and a person dealing with such an agent, the agent's authority continues during the period (if any) mentioned in the instrument conferring the authority, or if no period is there mentioned, then until notice of the revocation or determination of the agent's authority has been given to the person dealing with him.*

(5) The person affixing the official seal shall certify in writing on the deed or other instrument to which the seal is affixed the date on which and the place at which it is affixed.
[45]

NOTES

Repealed by the Companies Act 2006, s 1295, Sch 16, as from a day to be appointed.

Sub-s (1): words in first pair of square brackets inserted, and words in second pair of square brackets substituted, by CA 1989, s 130(7), Sch 17, para 2, as from 31 July 1990.

Sub-s (2): substituted by CA 1989, s 130(7), Sch 17, para 2, as from 31 July 1990.

Sub-s (2A): inserted by the Requirements of Writing (Scotland) Act 1995, s 14(1), Sch 4, para 53(a), as from 1 August 1995.

Sub-s (3): words in square brackets inserted the Requirements of Writing (Scotland) Act 1995, s 14(1), Sch 4, para 53(b), as from 1 August 1995; words omitted (as originally inserted by CA 1989, s 130(7), Sch 17, para 2) repealed by the Law Reform (Miscellaneous Provisions) (Scotland) Act 1990, s 74(1), (2), Sch 8, para 33(3), Sch 9, as from 1 December 1990.

Application to limited liability partnerships: see the Limited Liability Partnerships Regulations 2001, SI 2001/1090, reg 4(1), Sch 2, Pt 1 at **[6985]**, **[6993]**.

40 Official seal for share certificates, etc

[(1)] A company [which has a common seal] may have, for use for sealing securities issued by the company and for sealing documents creating or evidencing securities so issued, an official seal which is a facsimile of [its common seal] with the addition on its face of the word "Securities".

[The official seal when duly affixed to a document has the same effect as the company's common seal.]

[(2) Nothing in this section shall affect the right of a company registered in Scotland to subscribe such securities and documents in accordance with the Requirements of Writing (Scotland) Act 1995.]
[46]

NOTES

Repealed by the Companies Act 2006, s 1295, Sch 16, as from a day to be appointed.

Sub-s (1): numbered as such by the Requirements of Writing (Scotland) Act 1995, s 14(1), Sch 4, para 54, as from 1 August 1995; words in first pair of square brackets inserted, words in second pair of square brackets substituted, and words in third pair of square brackets added, by CA 1989, s 130(7), Sch 17, para 3, as from 31 July 1990.

Sub-s (2): added by the Requirements of Writing (Scotland) Act 1995, s 14(1), Sch 4, para 54, as from 1 August 1995.

Companies incorporated before 12 February 1979: companies which were incorporated before 12 February 1979 (the date on which the Stock Exchange (Completion of Bargains) Act 1976, s 2(2) came into force) and which have an official seal which accords with the provisions of this section, may use the seal for sealing securities and documents, notwithstanding antecedent requirements to the contrary or as to signature; see the Companies Consolidation (Consequential Provisions) Act 1985, s 11 at **[711]**.

41 Authentication of documents

A document or proceeding requiring authentication by a company [is sufficiently authenticated for the purposes of the law of England and Wales by the signature of a director, secretary or other authorised officer of the company].
[47]

NOTES

Repealed by the Companies Act 2006, s 1295, Sch 16, as from 6 April 2007. This section is reproduced only because of its continued application to limited liability partnerships (see the note below).

Words in square brackets substituted by CA 1989, s 130(7), Sch 17, para 4, as from 31 July 1990.

Application to limited liability partnerships: see the Limited Liability Partnerships Regulations 2001, SI 2001/1090, reg 4(1), Sch 2, Pt 1 at **[6985]**, **[6993]**. Note also that nothing in the Companies Act 2006 (Commencement No 1, Transitional Provisions and Savings) Order 2006, SI 2006/3428 affects any provision of this Act as applied by the 2001 Regulations to LLPs (see art 8(2) at **[7581]** and the introductory notes to this Act).

42 Events affecting a company's status

(1) A company is not entitled to rely against other persons on the happening of any of the following events—

(*a*) *the making of a winding-up order in respect of the company, or the appointment of a liquidator in a voluntary winding up of the company, or*

(*b*) *any alteration of the company's memorandum or articles, or*

(*c*) *any change among the company's directors, or*

(*d*) (*as regards service of any document on the company*) *any change in the situation of the company's registered office,*

if the event had not been officially notified at the material time and is not shown by the company to have been known at that time to the person concerned, or if the material time fell on or before the 15th day after the date of official notification (*or, where the 15th day was a non-business day, on or before the next day that was not*) *and it is shown that the person concerned was unavoidably prevented from knowing of the event at that time.*

(2) *In subsection* (*1*)*—*

(*a*) *"official notification" and "officially notified" have the meanings given by section 711*(2) (*registrar of companies to give public notice of the issue or receipt by him of certain documents*), *and*

(*b*) *"non-business day" means a Saturday or Sunday, Christmas Day, Good Friday and any other day which is a bank holiday in the part of Great Britain where the company is registered.*

[48]

NOTES

Repealed by the Companies Act 2006, s 1295, Sch 16, as from 1 January 2007. This section is reproduced only because of its continued application to limited liability partnerships (see the note below).

Application to limited liability partnerships: see the Limited Liability Partnerships Regulations 2001, SI 2001/1090, reg 4(1), Sch 2, Pt 1 at **[6985]**, **[6993]**. Note also that nothing in the Companies Act 2006 (Commencement No 1, Transitional Provisions and Savings) Order 2006, SI 2006/3428 affects any provision of this Act as applied by the 2001 Regulations to LLPs (see art 8(2) at **[7581]** and the introductory notes to this Act).

PART II
RE-REGISTRATION AS A MEANS OF ALTERING A COMPANY'S STATUS

Private company becoming public

43 Re-registration of private company as public

(*1*) *Subject to this and the following five sections, a private company* (*other than a company not having a share capital*) *may be re-registered as a public company if—*

(*a*) *a special resolution that it should be so re-registered is passed; and*

(*b*) *an application for re-registration is delivered to the registrar of companies, together with the necessary documents.*

A company cannot be re-registered under this section if it has previously been re-registered as unlimited.

(*2*) *The special resolution must—*

(*a*) *alter the company's memorandum so that it states that the company is to be a public company; and*

(*b*) *make such other alterations in the memorandum as are necessary to bring it* (*in substance and in form*) *into conformity with the requirements of this Act with respect to the memorandum of a public company* (*the alterations to include compliance with section 25*(*1*)[*, or section 33 of the Companies* (*Audit, Investigations and Community Enterprise*) *Act 2004,*] *as regards the company's name*)*; and*

(*c*) *make such alterations in the company's articles as are requisite in the circumstances.*

(*3*) *The application must be in the prescribed form and be signed by a director or secretary of the company; and the documents to be delivered with it are the following—*

(*a*) *a printed copy of the memorandum and articles as altered in pursuance of the resolution;*

(*b*) *a copy of a written statement by the company's auditors that in their opinion the relevant balance sheet shows that at the balance sheet date the amount of the company's net assets (within the meaning given to that expression by section 264(2)) was not less than the aggregate of its called-up share capital and undistributable reserves;*

(*c*) *a copy of the relevant balance sheet, together with a copy of an unqualified report (defined in section 46) by the company's auditors in relation to that balance sheet;*

(*d*) *if section 44 applies, a copy of the valuation report under subsection* (2)(*b*) *of that section; and*

(*e*) *[subject to subsection (3A),] a statutory declaration in the prescribed form by a director or secretary of the company—*

(*i*) *that the special resolution required by this section has been passed and that the conditions of the following two sections (so far as applicable) have been satisfied, and*

(*ii*) *that, between the balance sheet date and the application for re-registration, there has been no change in the company's financial position that has resulted in the amount of its net assets becoming less than the aggregate of its called-up share capital and undistributable reserves.*

[(3A) In place of the statutory declaration referred to in paragraph (e) of subsection (3), there may be delivered to the registrar of companies using electronic communications a statement made by a director or secretary of the company as to the matters set out in sub-paragraphs (i) and (ii) of that paragraph.

(3B) Any person who makes a false statement under subsection (3A) which he knows to be false or does not believe to be true is liable to imprisonment or a fine, or both.]

(4) "Relevant balance sheet" means a balance sheet prepared as at a date not more than 7 months before the company's application under this section.

(5) A resolution that a company be re-registered as a public company may change the company name by deleting the word "company" or the words "and company", or its or their equivalent in Welsh ("cwmni", "a'r cwmni"), including any abbreviation of them.

[49]

NOTES

Repealed by the Companies Act 2006, s 1295, Sch 16, as from a day to be appointed.

Sub-s (2): words in square brackets in para (b) inserted by the Companies (Audit, Investigations and Community Enterprise) Act 2004, s 33, Sch 6, paras 1, 7, as from 1 July 2005.

Sub-s (3): words in square brackets inserted by the Companies Act 1985 (Electronic Communications) Order 2000, SI 2000/3373, art 6(1), (2), as from 22 December 2000.

Sub-ss (3A), (3B): inserted by SI 2000/3373, art 6(1), (3), as from 22 December 2000.

Re-registration under earlier legislation: nothing in this Act, nor in the Companies Consolidation (Consequential Provisions) Act 1985, the Company Securities (Insider Dealing) Act 1985 (repealed and replaced by the Criminal Justice Act 1993, Pt V), nor the Business Names Act 1985, affects the re-registration of any company under the Companies Acts 1948 to 1983 or the continued existence of any company by virtue of such registration; see the Companies Consolidation (Consequential Provisions) Act 1985, s 31(1), (8) at **[728]**.

Community interest companies: if a community interest company which is not a public company re-registers as a public company under this section, the certificate of incorporation issued under s 47(1)(b) of this Act is to contain a statement that the company is a community interest company; see the Companies (Audit, Investigations and Community Enterprise) Act 2004, ss 26, 52(2), (3) at **[900]**, **[926]**.

Fees: see Appendix 3 (Fees Instruments) at **[A3]**.

Application … in the prescribed form; statutory declaration in the prescribed form: see Appendix 4 (Forms table) at **[A4]**.

44 Consideration for shares recently allotted to be valued

(1) The following applies if shares have been allotted by the company between the date as at which the relevant balance sheet was prepared and the passing of the special resolution under section 43, and those shares were allotted as fully or partly paid up as to their nominal value or any premium on them otherwise than in cash.

(2) Subject to the following provisions, the registrar of companies shall not entertain an application by the company under section 43 unless beforehand—

(*a*) *the consideration for the allotment has been valued in accordance with section 108, and*

(*b*) *a report with respect to the value of the consideration has been made to the company (in accordance with that section) during the 6 months immediately preceding the allotment of the shares.*

(3) Where an amount standing to the credit of any of the company's reserve accounts, or of its profit and loss account, has been applied in paying up (to any extent) any of the shares allotted or any premium on those shares, the amount applied does not count as consideration for the allotment, and accordingly subsection (2) does not apply to it.

(4) Subsection (2) does not apply if the allotment is in connection with an arrangement providing for it to be on terms that the whole or part of the consideration for the shares allotted is to be provided by the transfer to the company or the cancellation of all or some of the shares, or of all or some of the shares of a particular class, in another company (with or without the issue to the company applying under section 43 of shares, or of shares of any particular class, in that other company).

(5) But subsection (4) does not exclude the application of subsection (2), unless under the arrangement it is open to all the holders of the shares of the other company in question (or, where the arrangement applies only to shares of a particular class, all the holders of the other company's shares of that class) to take part in the arrangement.

In determining whether that is the case, shares held by or by a nominee of the company allotting shares in connection with the arrangement, or by or by a nominee of a company which is that company's holding company or subsidiary or a company which is a subsidiary of its holding company, are to be disregarded.

(6) Subsection (2) does not apply to preclude an application under section 43, if the allotment of the company's shares is in connection with its proposed merger with another company; that is, where one of the companies concerned proposes to acquire all the assets and liabilities of the other in exchange for the issue of shares or other securities of that one to shareholders of the other, with or without any cash payment to shareholders.

(7) In this section—

(a) "arrangement" means any agreement, scheme or arrangement, including an arrangement sanctioned in accordance with section 425 (company compromise with creditors and members) or [section 110 of the Insolvency Act] (liquidator in winding up accepting shares as consideration for sale of company's property), and

(b) "another company" includes any body corporate ...

[50]

NOTES

Repealed by the Companies Act 2006, s 1295, Sch 16, as from a day to be appointed.

Sub-s (7): words in square brackets in para (a) substituted by the Insolvency Act 1986, s 439(1), Sch 13, Pt I, as from 29 December 1986, for transitional provisions see s 437 of, and Sch 11, Pt I to, that Act at **[3456]** and **[3481]**; words omitted from para (b) repealed by the Statute Law (Repeals) Act 2004, as from 22 July 2004.

Insolvency Act, s 110: ie, the Insolvency Act 1986, s 110.

Chartered Companies Act 1837: repealed by the Statute Law (Repeals) Act 1993.

45 Additional requirements relating to share capital

(1) For a private company to be re-registered under section 43 as a public company, the following conditions with respect to its share capital must be satisfied at the time the special resolution under that section is passed.

(2) Subject to subsections (5) to (7) below—

(a) the nominal value of the company's allotted share capital must be not less than the authorised minimum, and

(b) each of the company's allotted shares must be paid up at least as to one-quarter of the nominal value of that share and the whole of any premium on it.

(3) Subject to subsection (5), if any shares in the company or any premium on them have been fully or partly paid up by an undertaking given by any person that he or another should do work or perform services (whether for the company or any other person), the undertaking must have been performed or otherwise discharged.

(4) Subject to subsection (5), if shares have been allotted as fully or partly paid up as to their nominal value or any premium on them otherwise than in cash, and the consideration for the allotment consists of or includes an undertaking to the company (other than one to which subsection (3) applies), then either—

(a) the undertaking must have been performed or otherwise discharged, or

(*b*) *there must be a contract between the company and some person pursuant to which the undertaking is to be performed within 5 years from the time the resolution under section 43 is passed.*

(*5*) *For the purpose of determining whether subsections* (*2*)(*b*), (*3*) *and* (*4*) *are complied with, certain shares in the company may be disregarded; and these are—*

(*a*) *subject to the next subsection, any share which was allotted before 22nd June 1982, and*

(*b*) *any share which was allotted in pursuance of an employees' share scheme and by reason of which the company would, but for this subsection, be precluded under subsection* (*2*)(*b*) (*but not otherwise*) *from being re-registered as a public company.*

(*6*) *A share is not to be disregarded under subsection* (*5*)(*a*) *if the aggregate in nominal value of that share and other shares proposed to be so disregarded is more than one-tenth of the nominal value of the company's allotted share capital; but for this purpose the allotted share capital is treated as not including any shares disregarded under subsection* (*5*)(*b*).

(*7*) *Any shares disregarded under subsection* (*5*) *are treated as not forming part of the allotted share capital for the purposes of subsection* (*2*)(*a*).

[51]

NOTES

Repealed by the Companies Act 2006, s 1295, Sch 16, as from a day to be appointed.

46 Meaning of "unqualified report" in s 43(3)

(*1*) *The following subsections explain the reference in section 43*(*3*)(*c*) *to an unqualified report of the company's auditors on the relevant balance sheet.*

[(*2*) *If the balance sheet was prepared for a financial year of the company, the reference is to an auditors' report stating without material qualification the auditors' opinion that the balance sheet has been properly prepared in accordance with this Act.*

(*3*) *If the balance sheet was not prepared for a financial year of the company, the reference is to an auditors' report stating without material qualification the auditors' opinion that the balance sheet has been properly prepared in accordance with the provisions of this Act which would have applied if it had been so prepared.*

For the purposes of an auditors' report under this subsection the provisions of this Act shall be deemed to apply with such modifications as are necessary by reason of the fact that the balance sheet is not prepared for a financial year of the company.

(*4*) *A qualification shall be regarded as material unless the auditors state in their report that the matter giving rise to the qualification is not material for the purpose of determining* (*by reference to the company's balance sheet*) *whether at the balance sheet date the amount of the company's net assets was not less than the aggregate of its called up share capital and undistributable reserves.*

In this subsection "net assets" and "undistributable reserves" have the meaning given by section 264(*2*) *and* (*3*).*]*

[52]

NOTES

Repealed by the Companies Act 2006, s 1295, Sch 16, as from a day to be appointed.

Sub-ss (2)–(4): substituted, for original sub-ss (2)–(6), by CA 1989, s 23, Sch 10, para 1, as from 1 April 1990.

47 Certificate of re-registration under s 43

(*1*) *If the registrar of companies is satisfied, on an application under section 43, that a company may be re-registered under that section as a public company, he shall—*

(*a*) *retain the application and other documents delivered to him under the section; and*

(*b*) *issue the company with a certificate of incorporation stating that the company is a public company.*

(*2*) *The registrar may accept a declaration under section 43*(*3*)(*e*) *[or a statement under section 43*(*3A*)*] as sufficient evidence that the special resolution required by that section has been passed and the other conditions of re-registration satisfied.*

(3) The registrar shall not issue the certificate if it appears to him that the court has made an order confirming a reduction of the company's capital which has the effect of bringing the nominal value of the company's allotted share capital below the authorised minimum.

(4) Upon the issue to a company of a certificate of incorporation under this section—

(a) the company by virtue of the issue of that certificate becomes a public company; and

(b) any alterations in the memorandum and articles set out in the resolution take effect accordingly.

(5) The certificate is conclusive evidence—

(a) that the requirements of this Act in respect of re-registration and of matters precedent and incidental thereto have been complied with; and

(b) that the company is a public company.

[53]

NOTES

Repealed by the Companies Act 2006, s 1295, Sch 16, as from a day to be appointed.

Sub-s (2): words in square brackets inserted by the Companies Act 1985 (Electronic Communications) Order 2000, SI 2000/3373, art 7, as from 22 December 2000.

Re-registration under earlier legislation: see the note to s 43 at **[49]**.

Community interest companies: see the note to s 43 at **[49]**.

48 Modification for unlimited company re-registering

(1) In their application to unlimited companies, sections 43 to 47 are modified as follows.

(2) The special resolution required by section 43(1) must, in addition to the matters mentioned in subsection (2) of that section—

(a) state that the liability of the members is to be limited by shares, and what the company's share capital is to be; and

(b) make such alterations in the company's memorandum as are necessary to bring it in substance and in form into conformity with the requirements of this Act with respect to the memorandum of a company limited by shares.

(3) The certificate of incorporation issued under section 47(1) shall, in addition to containing the statement required by paragraph (b) of that subsection, state that the company has been incorporated as a company limited by shares; and—

(a) the company by virtue of the issue of the certificate becomes a public company so limited; and

(b) the certificate is conclusive evidence of the fact that it is such a company.

[54]

NOTES

Repealed by the Companies Act 2006, s 1295, Sch 16, as from a day to be appointed.

Limited company becoming unlimited

49 Re-registration of limited company as unlimited

(1) Subject as follows, a company which is registered as limited may be re-registered as unlimited in pursuance of an application in that behalf complying with the requirements of this section.

(2) A company is excluded from re-registering under this section if it is limited by virtue of re-registration under section 44 of the Companies Act 1967 or section 51 of this Act.

(3) A public company cannot be re-registered under this section; nor can a company which has previously been re-registered as unlimited.

(4) An application under this section must be in the prescribed form and be signed by a director or the secretary of the company, and be lodged with the registrar of companies, together with the documents specified in subsection (8) below.

(5) The application must set out such alterations in the company's memorandum as—

(*a*) *if it is to have a share capital, are requisite to bring it (in substance and in form) into conformity with the requirements of this Act with respect to the memorandum of a company to be formed as an unlimited company having a share capital; or*

(*b*) *if it is not to have a share capital, are requisite in the circumstances.*

(6) If articles have been registered, the application must set out such alterations in them as—

(*a*) *if the company is to have a share capital, are requisite to bring the articles (in substance and in form) into conformity with the requirements of this Act with respect to the articles of a company to be formed as an unlimited company having a share capital; or*

(*b*) *if the company is not to have a share capital, are requisite in the circumstances.*

(7) If articles have not been registered, the application must have annexed to it, and request the registration of, printed articles; and these must, if the company is to have a share capital, comply with the requirements mentioned in subsection (6)(a) and, if not, be articles appropriate to the circumstances.

(8) The documents to be lodged with the registrar are—

(*a*) *the prescribed form of assent to the company's being registered as unlimited, subscribed by or on behalf of all the members of the company;*

(*b*) *[subject to subsection (8A),] a statutory declaration made by the directors of the company—*

(i) that the persons by whom or on whose behalf the form of assent is subscribed constitute the whole membership of the company, and

(ii) if any of the members have not subscribed that form themselves, that the directors have taken all reasonable steps to satisfy themselves that each person who subscribed it on behalf of a member was lawfully empowered to do so;

(*c*) *a printed copy of the memorandum incorporating the alterations in it set out in the application; and*

(*d*) *if articles have been registered, a printed copy of them incorporating the alterations set out in the application.*

[(8A) In place of the lodging of a statutory declaration under paragraph (b) of subsection (8), there may be delivered to the registrar of companies using electronic communications a statement made by the directors of the company as to the matters set out in sub-paragraphs (i) and (ii) of that paragraph.

(8B) Any person who makes a false statement under subsection (8A) which he knows to be false or does not believe to be true is liable to imprisonment or a fine, or both.]

(9) For purposes of this section—

(*a*) *subscription to a form of assent by the legal personal representative of a deceased member of a company is deemed subscription by him; and*

(*b*) *a trustee in bankruptcy of a member of a company is, to the exclusion of the latter, deemed a member of the company.*

[55]

NOTES

Repealed by the Companies Act 2006, s 1295, Sch 16, as from a day to be appointed.

Sub-s (8): words in square brackets inserted by the Companies Act 1985 (Electronic Communications) Order 2000, SI 2000/3373, art 8(1), (2), as from 22 December 2000.

Sub-ss (8A), (8B): inserted by SI 2000/3373, art 8(1), (3), as from 22 December 2000.

Re-registration under earlier legislation: see the note to s 43 at **[49]**.

Community interest companies: a community interest company is excluded from re-registering under this section; see the Companies (Audit, Investigations and Community Enterprise) Act 2004, ss 26, 52(1) at **[900]**, **[926]**.

Companies Act 1967, s 44: repealed by the Companies Consolidation (Consequential Provisions) Act 1985, s 29, Sch 1, and partly replaced by ss 51 and 52 of this Act.

Fees: see Appendix 3 (Fees Instruments) at **[A3]**.

Application … in the prescribed form; prescribed form of assent: see Appendix 4 (Forms table) at **[A4]**.

50 Certificate of re-registration under s 49

(1) The registrar of companies shall retain the application and other documents lodged with him under section 49 and shall—

(*a*) *if articles are annexed to the application, register them; and* (*b*) *issue to the company a certificate of incorporation appropriate to the status to be assumed by it by virtue of that section.*

(2) *On the issue of the certificate—*

(*a*) *the status of the company, by virtue of the issue, is changed from limited to unlimited; and*

(*b*) *the alterations in the memorandum set out in the application and (if articles have been previously registered) any alterations to the articles so set out take effect as if duly made by resolution of the company; and*

(*c*) *the provisions of this Act apply accordingly to the memorandum and articles as altered.*

(3) *The certificate is conclusive evidence that the requirements of section 49 in respect of re-registration and of matters precedent and incidental to it have been complied with, and that the company was authorised to be re-registered under this Act in pursuance of that section and was duly so re-registered.*

[56]

NOTES

Repealed by the Companies Act 2006, s 1295, Sch 16, as from a day to be appointed.

Unlimited company becoming limited

51 Re-registration of unlimited company as limited

(*1*) *Subject as follows, a company which is registered as unlimited may be re-registered as limited if a special resolution that it should be so re-registered is passed, and the requirements of this section are complied with in respect of the resolution and otherwise.*

(2) *A company cannot under this section be re-registered as a public company; and a company is excluded from re-registering under it if it is unlimited by virtue of re-registration under section 43 of the Companies Act 1967 or section 49 of this Act.*

(3) *The special resolution must state whether the company is to be limited by shares or by guarantee and—*

(*a*) *if it is to be limited by shares, must state what the share capital is to be and provide for the making of such alterations in the memorandum as are necessary to bring it (in substance and in form) into conformity with the requirements of this Act with respect to the memorandum of a company so limited, and such alterations in the articles as are requisite in the circumstances;*

(*b*) *if it is to be limited by guarantee, must provide for the making of such alterations in its memorandum and articles as are necessary to bring them (in substance and in form) into conformity with the requirements of this Act with respect to the memorandum and articles of a company so limited.*

(*4*) *The special resolution is subject to section 380 of this Act (copy to be forwarded to registrar within 15 days); and an application for the company to be re-registered as limited, framed in the prescribed form and signed by a director or by the secretary of the company, must be lodged with the registrar of companies, together with the necessary documents, not earlier than the day on which the copy of the resolution forwarded under section 380 is received by him.*

(*5*) *The documents to be lodged with the registrar are—*

(*a*) *a printed copy of the memorandum as altered in pursuance of the resolution; and*

(*b*) *a printed copy of the articles as so altered.*

(*6*) *This section does not apply in relation to the re-registration of an unlimited company as a public company under section 43.*

[57]

NOTES

Repealed by the Companies Act 2006, s 1295, Sch 16, as from a day to be appointed.

Sub-s (4): the words from "The special resolution" to "15 days); and" are repealed, and for the words "under section 380" there are substituted the words "under section 30 of the Companies Act 2006", by the draft Companies Act 2006 (Commencement No 3, Consequential Amendments, Transitional Provisions and Savings) Order 2007, art 10(1), Sch 4, Pt 1, para 1(2), as from 1 October 2007 (see **[A12]**).

Re-registration under earlier legislation: see the note to s 43 at **[49]**.

Companies Act 1967, s 43: repealed by the Companies Consolidation (Consequential Provisions) Act 1985, s 29, Sch 1, and partly replaced by ss 49 and 50 of this Act.
Fees: see Appendix 3 (Fees Instruments) at **[A3]**.
Application … in the prescribed form: see Appendix 4 (Forms table) at **[A4]**.

52 Certificate of re-registration under s 51

(1) The registrar shall retain the application and other documents lodged with him under section 51, and shall issue to the company a certificate of incorporation appropriate to the status to be assumed by the company by virtue of that section.

(2) On the issue of the certificate—

(a) the status of the company is, by virtue of the issue, changed from unlimited to limited; and

(b) the alterations in the memorandum specified in the resolution and the alterations in, and additions to, the articles so specified take effect.

(3) The certificate is conclusive evidence that the requirements of section 51 in respect of re-registration and of matters precedent and incidental to it have been complied with, and that the company was authorised to be re-registered in pursuance of that section and was duly so re-registered.

[58]

NOTES

Repealed by the Companies Act 2006, s 1295, Sch 16, as from a day to be appointed.

Public company becoming private

53 Re-registration of public company as private

(1) A public company may be re-registered as a private company if—

(a) a special resolution complying with subsection (2) below that it should be so re-registered is passed and has not been cancelled by the court under the following section;

(b) an application for the purpose in the prescribed form and signed by a director or the secretary of the company is delivered to the registrar of companies, together with a printed copy of the memorandum and articles of the company as altered by the resolution; and

(c) the period during which an application for the cancellation of the resolution under the following section may be made has expired without any such application having been made; or

(d) where such an application has been made, the application has been withdrawn or an order has been made under section 54(5) confirming the resolution and a copy of that order has been delivered to the registrar.

(2) The special resolution must alter the company's memorandum so that it no longer states that the company is to be a public company and must make such other alterations in the company's memorandum and articles as are requisite in the circumstances.

(3) A company cannot under this section be re-registered otherwise than as a company limited by shares or by guarantee.

[59]

NOTES

Repealed by the Companies Act 2006, s 1295, Sch 16, as from a day to be appointed.
Re-registration under earlier legislation: see the note to s 43 at **[49]**.
Community interest companies: if a community interest company which is a public company re-registers as a private company under this section, the certificate of incorporation issued under s 55(1)(b) of this Act is to contain a statement that the company is a community interest company; see the Companies (Audit, Investigations and Community Enterprise) Act 2004, ss 26, 52(2), (3) at **[900]**, **[926]**.
Fees: see Appendix 3 (Fees Instruments) at **[A3]**.
Application … in the prescribed form: see Appendix 4 (Forms table) at **[A4]**.

54 Litigated objection to resolution under s 53

(*1*) *Where a special resolution by a public company to be re-registered under section 53 as a private company has been passed, an application may be made to the court for the cancellation of that resolution.*

(*2*) *The application may be made—*

(*a*) *by the holders of not less in the aggregate than 5 per cent in nominal value of the company's issued share capital or any class thereof;*

(*b*) *if the company is not limited by shares, by not less than 5 per cent of its members; or*

(*c*) *by not less than 50 of the company's members;*

but not by a person who has consented to or voted in favour of the resolution.

[(2A) For the purposes of subsection (2)(a), any of the company's issued share capital held as treasury shares must be disregarded.]

(*3*) *The application must be made within 28 days after the passing of the resolution and may be made on behalf of the persons entitled to make the application by such one or more of their number as they may appoint in writing for the purpose.*

(*4*) *If such an application is made, the company shall forthwith give notice in the prescribed form of that fact to the registrar of companies.*

(*5*) *On the hearing of the application, the court shall make an order either cancelling or confirming the resolution and—*

(*a*) *may make that order on such terms and conditions as it thinks fit, and may (if it thinks fit) adjourn the proceedings in order that an arrangement may be made to the satisfaction of the court for the purchase of the interests of dissentient members; and*

(*b*) *may give such directions and make such orders as it thinks expedient for facilitating or carrying into effect any such arrangement.*

(*6*) *The court's order may, if the court thinks fit, provide for the purchase by the company of the shares of any of its members and for the reduction accordingly of the company's capital, and may make such alterations in the company's memorandum and articles as may be required in consequence of that provision.*

(*7*) *The company shall, within 15 days from the making of the court's order, or within such longer period as the court may at any time by order direct, deliver to the registrar of companies [a copy] of the order.*

(*8*) *If the court's order requires the company not to make any, or any specified, alteration in its memorandum or articles, the company has not then power without the leave of the court to make any such alteration in breach of the requirement.*

(*9*) *An alteration in the memorandum or articles made by virtue of an order under this section, if not made by resolution of the company, is of the same effect as if duly made by resolution; and this Act applies accordingly to the memorandum or articles as so altered.*

(*10*) *A company which fails to comply with subsection (4) or subsection (7), and any officer of it who is in default, is liable to a fine and, for continued contravention, to a daily default fine.*

[60]

NOTES

Repealed by the Companies Act 2006, s 1295, Sch 16, as from a day to be appointed.

Sub-s (2A): inserted by the Companies (Acquisition of Own Shares) (Treasury Shares) Regulations 2003, SI 2003/1116, reg 4, Schedule, para 3, as from 1 December 2003.

Sub-s (7): words in square brackets substituted by the Companies (Registrar, Languages and Trading Disclosures) Regulations 2006, SI 2006/3429, reg 3(1)(a), as from 1 January 2007.

Notice in the prescribed form: see Appendix 4 (Forms table) at **[A4]**.

55 Certificate of re-registration under s 53

(*1*) *If the registrar of companies is satisfied that a company may be re-registered under section 53, he shall—*

(*a*) *retain the application and other documents delivered to him under that section; and* (*b*) *issue the company with a certificate of incorporation appropriate to a private company.*

(2) *On the issue of the certificate—*

(*a*) *the company by virtue of the issue becomes a private company; and*

(*b*) *the alterations in the memorandum and articles set out in the resolution under section 53 take effect accordingly.*

(3) *The certificate is conclusive evidence—*

(*a*) *that the requirements of section 53 in respect of re-registration and of matters precedent and incidental to it have been complied with; and*

(*b*) *that the company is a private company.*

[61]

NOTES

Repealed by the Companies Act 2006, s 1295, Sch 16, as from a day to be appointed.

Re-registration under earlier legislation: see the note to s 43 at **[49]**.

Community interest companies: see the note to s 53 at **[59]**.

PART III
CAPITAL ISSUES

NOTES

This Part (together with the other provisions mentioned in (i) and (ii) below) has been repealed (subject to limited savings) in accordance with the notes set out below following the coming into force of the Public Offers of Securities Regulations 1995, SI 1995/1537 (now revoked). It is also repealed by the Companies Act 2006, s 1295, Sch 16, as from a day to be appointed.

Certain sections in Part III (ss 58, 59, 60 and 62) and Sch 3, para 2 were preserved by the Financial Services Act 1986 (Commencement) (No 13) Order 1995, SI 1995/1538 for the sole purpose of interpreting other provisions of the Companies Act 1985 (i e ss 81, 83, 246, 248 and 744); see further head (v) below and see also the notes to the individual sections in this Part for any subsequent repeal for all remaining purposes.

Sections 56–79, 693 (in part) and Sch 3 are repealed by FSA 1986, s 212(3), Sch 17, Pt I as follows—

(i) to the extent to which they would apply in relation to any investment which is listed or the subject of an application for listing in accordance with FSA 1986, Pt IV—

(a) *as from 12 January 1987* for the purposes specified in art 5(a) of the Financial Services Act 1986 (Commencement) (No 3) Order 1986, SI 1986/2246, i e for all purposes relating to the admission of securities offered by or on behalf of a Minister of the Crown or a body corporate controlled by a Minister of the Crown or a subsidiary of such a body corporate to the Official List in respect of which an application is made after that date;

(b) *as from 16 February 1987* for the purposes specified in art 5(b) of SI 1986/2246, i e purposes relating to the admission of securities in respect of which an application is made after that date other than those referred to in art 5(a) of that Order (see (a) above) and otherwise for all purposes;

These repeals also affected ss 81–87, 97, 693, 709. Note, FSA 1986 was repealed by SI 2001/3649, art 3(1)(c), as from 1 December 2001.

(ii) *as from 29 April 1988* insofar as is necessary to have the effect that they cease to apply to a prospectus offering for subscription, or to any form of application for, units in a body corporate which is an open-ended investment company which is a recognised scheme (Financial Services Act 1986 (Commencement) (No 8) Order 1988, SI 1988/740, art 2, Schedule);

This repeal also affected ss 81–87, 97, 449(1)(d), 693, 707, 744.

(iii) subject to NOTES below—

(a) *as from 31 December 1988* insofar as is necessary to have the effect that, to the extent that they do apply, they cease to apply to a prospectus offering for subscription, or to any application form for, units in an open-ended investment company which *does not* fulfil the conditions described in art 3(a)(i) or (a)(ii) of the Financial Services Act 1986 (Commencement) (No 10) Order 1988, SI 1988/1960.

These conditions are—

(1) it is managed in and authorised under the law of a country or territory in respect of which an order under section 87 of the 1986 Act is in force on 31 December 1988 and which is of a class specified in that Order; or

(2) it is constituted in a member state in respect of which an order under para 10 of Sch 15 to the 1986 Act is in force on 31 December 1988 and which meets the requirements specified in that Order.

(b) *as from 1 March 1989* insofar as is necessary to have the effect that, to the extent that they do apply, they cease to apply to a prospectus offering for subscription, or to any application form for, units in an open-ended investment company which *does* fulfil the conditions described in art 3(a)(i) or (a)(ii) of SI 1988/1960 (set out above).

The dates above were appointed by SI 1988/1960, art 4, as amended by SI 1988/2285, art 6.

NOTES: art 4, cited above, does not have effect in relation to a prospectus offering for subscription, or to any application form for, units in an open-ended investment company which fulfils the conditions described in art 2(a) of the Financial Services Act 1986 (Commencement) (No 11) Order 1988, SI 1988/2285, i e it is an open-ended investment company managed in and authorised under the law of Bermuda, units in which are, on 31 December 1988, included in the Official List of the International Stock Exchange of the United Kingdom and the Republic of Ireland Limited (SI 1988/2285, art 3).

The above repeals also affected s 693.

(iv)(a) *as from 1 May 1989* insofar as is necessary to have the effect that, to the extent that they do apply, they cease to apply to a prospectus offering for subscription, or to any application form for, units in an open-ended investment company falling within art 4(a) of SI 1988/2285, i e an open-ended investment company which fulfils the conditions described in art 2(a) of SI 1988/2285 (which are set out in NOTES to (iii) above), and which is a scheme of a class specified in the Schedule to the Financial Services (Designated Countries and Territories) (Overseas Collective Investment Schemes) (Bermuda) Order 1988, SI 1988/2284;

(b) *as from 28 February 1989* insofar as is necessary to have the effect that, to the extent that they do apply, they cease to apply to a prospectus offering for subscription, or to any application form for, units in an open-ended investment company falling within art 2(a) of SI 1988/2285 (which is set out in NOTES to (iii) above), but not within art 4(a) (which is set out in (iv)(a) above);

These dates were appointed by SI 1988/2285, art 5.

(v) *as from 19 June 1995* for all remaining purposes except for repeals of ss 58, 59, 60 (so far as necessary for the purposes of ss 81, 83, 246, 248, 744), Sch 3, para 2 (so far as necessary for the purposes of s 83(1)(a)) and s 62 (so far as necessary for the purposes of s 744) (SI 1995/1538, art 2(a)).

(vi) *as from 10 May 1999* so far as relates to repeals of or in (i) ss 82, 83, and the corresponding provisions of the Companies (Northern Ireland) Order 1986, SI 1986/1032, for all remaining purposes except for the purposes of prospectuses to which SI 1995/1537, reg 8 applies; and (ii) ss 86, 87, and the corresponding provisions of SI 1986/1032, for all remaining purposes (SI 1999/727).

Transfer of functions: by the Transfer of Functions (Financial Services) Order 1992, SI 1992/1315, art 2(3) at **[6730]**, any functions retained by the Secretary of State under this Part (ss 56–79) are transferred to the Treasury, with the exception of the functions under ss 65(3)(b), 77(5)(a) which are retained by the Secretary of State (see SI 1992/1315, art 3, Sch 1, para 2 at **[6731]**, **[6739]**).

CHAPTER I
ISSUES BY COMPANIES REGISTERED, OR TO BE REGISTERED, IN GREAT BRITAIN

The prospectus

56, 57 (*Repealed; see Note at the beginning of this Part.*)

58 Document offering shares etc for sale deemed a prospectus

(1) If a company allots or agrees to allot its shares or debentures with a view to all or any of them being offered for sale to the public, any document by which the offer for sale to the public is made is deemed for all purposes a prospectus issued by the company.

(2) All enactments and rules of law as to the contents of prospectuses, and to liability in respect of statements in and omissions from prospectuses, or otherwise relating to prospectuses, apply and have effect accordingly, as if the shares or debentures had been offered to the public for subscription and as if persons accepting the offer in respect of any shares or debentures were subscribers for those shares or debentures.

This is without prejudice to the liability (if any) of the persons by whom the offer is made, in respect of mis-statements in the document or otherwise in respect of it.

(3) For purposes of this Act it is evidence (unless the contrary is proved) that an allotment of, or an agreement to allot, shares or debentures was made with a view to their being offered for sale to the public if it is shown—

(a) that an offer of the shares or debentures (or of any of them) for sale to the public was made within 6 months after the allotment or agreement to allot, or

(b) that at the date when the offer was made the whole consideration to be received by the company in respect of the shares or debentures had not been so received.

(*4*) *Section 56 as applied by this section has effect as if it required a prospectus to state, in addition to the matters required by that section—*

(*a*) *the net amount of the consideration received or to be received by the company in respect of the shares or debentures to which the offer relates, and*

(*b*) *the place and time at which the contract under which those shares or debentures have been or are to be allotted may be inspected.*

[62]

NOTES

Repealed as noted at the beginning of this Part.

Repealed by the Companies Act 2006, s 1295, Sch 16, as from a day to be appointed.

59–61 (*In so far as ss 59, 60 continued to have effect* (*see Note at the beginning of this Part*)*, they were repealed by the Financial Services and Markets Act 2000* (*Consequential Amendments and Repeals*) *Order 2001, SI 2001/3649, art 5, as from 1 December 2001; s 61 repealed, see Note at the beginning of this Part.*)

62 Meaning of "expert"

The expression "expert", in both Chapters of this Part, includes engineer, valuer, accountant and any other person whose profession gives authority to a statement made by him.

[63]

NOTES

Repealed as noted at the beginning of this Part.

Repealed by the Companies Act 2006, s 1295, Sch 16, as from a day to be appointed.

63–79 (*Repealed; see Note at the beginning of this Part.*)

PART IV
ALLOTMENT OF SHARES AND DEBENTURES

General provisions as to allotment

80 Authority of company required for certain allotments

(*1*) *The directors of a company shall not exercise any power of the company to allot relevant securities, unless they are, in accordance with this section [or section 80A], authorised to do so by—*

(*a*) *the company in general meeting; or*

(*b*) *the company's articles.*

(*2*) *In this section "relevant securities" means—*

(*a*) *shares in the company other than shares shown in the memorandum to have been taken by the subscribers to it or shares allotted in pursuance of an employees' share scheme, and*

(*b*) *any right to subscribe for, or to convert any security into, shares in the company* (*other than shares so allotted*)*;*

and a reference to the allotment of relevant securities includes the grant of such a right but (*subject to subsection* (*6*) *below*)*, not the allotment of shares pursuant to such a right.*

(*3*) *Authority under this section may be given for a particular exercise of the power or for its exercise generally, and may be unconditional or subject to conditions.*

(*4*) *The authority must state the maximum amount of relevant securities that may be allotted under it and the date on which it will expire, which must be not more than 5 years from whichever is relevant of the following dates—*

(*a*) *in the case of an authority contained in the company's articles at the time of its original incorporation, the date of that incorporation; and*

(*b*) *in any other case, the date on which the resolution is passed by virtue of which the authority is given;*

but such an authority (*including an authority contained in the articles*) *may be previously revoked or varied by the company in general meeting.*

(5) The authority may be renewed or further renewed by the company in general meeting for a further period not exceeding 5 years; but the resolution must state (or restate) the amount of relevant securities which may be allotted under the authority or, as the case may be, the amount remaining to be allotted under it, and must specify the date on which the renewed authority will expire.

(6) In relation to authority under this section for the grant of such rights as are mentioned in subsection (2)(b), the reference in subsection (4) (as also the corresponding reference in subsection (5)) to the maximum amount of relevant securities that may be allotted under the authority is to the maximum amount of shares which may be allotted pursuant to the rights.

(7) The directors may allot relevant securities, notwithstanding that authority under this section has expired, if they are allotted in pursuance of an offer or agreement made by the company before the authority expired and the authority allowed it to make an offer or agreement which would or might require relevant securities to be allotted after the authority expired.

(8) A resolution of a company to give, vary, revoke or renew such an authority may, notwithstanding that it alters the company's articles, be an ordinary resolution; but it is in any case subject to section 380 of this Act (copy to be forwarded to registrar within 15 days).

(9) A director who knowingly and wilfully contravenes, or permits or authorises a contravention of, this section is liable to a fine.

(10) Nothing in this section affects the validity of any allotment.

(11) This section does not apply to any allotment of relevant securities by a company, other than a public company registered as such on its original incorporation, if it is made in pursuance of an offer or agreement made before the earlier of the following two dates—

- *(a) the date of the holding of the first general meeting of the company after its registration or re-registration as a public company, and*
- *(b) 22nd June 1982;*

but any resolution to give, vary or revoke an authority for the purposes of section 14 of the Companies Act 1980 or this section has effect for those purposes if passed at any time after the end of April 1980.

[64]

NOTES

Repealed by the Companies Act 2006, s 1295, Sch 16, as from a day to be appointed.

Sub-s (1): words in square brackets inserted by CA 1989, s 115(1), as from 1 April 1990.

Sub-s (8): for the words "but it is in any case subject to section 380" to the end there are substituted the words "but in any case Chapter 3 of Part 3 of the Companies Act 2006 (resolutions affecting a company's constitution) applies to it" by the draft Companies Act 2006 (Commencement No 3, Consequential Amendments, Transitional Provisions and Savings) Order 2007, art 10(1), Sch 4, Pt 1, para 1(3), as from 1 October 2007 (see **[A12]**).

Companies Act 1980, s 14: repealed by the Companies Consolidation (Consequential Provisions) Act 1985, s 29, Sch 1, and replaced by this section.

[80A Election by private company as to duration of authority

(1) A private company may elect (by elective resolution in accordance with section 379A) that the provisions of this section shall apply, instead of the provisions of section 80(4) and (5), in relation to the giving or renewal, after the election, of an authority under that section.

(2) The authority must state the maximum amount of relevant securities that may be allotted under it and may be given—

- *(a) for an indefinite period, or*
- *(b) for a fixed period, in which case it must state the date on which it will expire.*

(3) In either case an authority (including an authority contained in the articles) may be revoked or varied by the company in general meeting.

(4) An authority given for a fixed period may be renewed or further renewed by the company in general meeting.

(5) A resolution renewing an authority—

(*a*) *must state, or re-state, the amount of relevant securities which may be allotted under the authority or, as the case may be, the amount remaining to be allotted under it, and*

(*b*) *must state whether the authority is renewed for an indefinite period or for a fixed period, in which case it must state the date on which the renewed authority will expire.*

(6) The references in this section to the maximum amount of relevant securities that may be allotted shall be construed in accordance with section 80(6).

(7) If an election under this section ceases to have effect, an authority then in force which was given for an indefinite period or for a fixed period of more than five years—

(*a*) *if given five years or more before the election ceases to have effect, shall expire forthwith, and*

(*b*) *otherwise, shall have effect as if it had been given for a fixed period of five years.]*

[65]

NOTES

Inserted by CA 1989, s 115(1), as from 1 April 1990.

Repealed by the Companies Act 2006, s 1295, Sch 16, as from a day to be appointed.

81 Restriction on public offers by private company

(1) A private limited company (other than a company limited by guarantee and not having a share capital) commits an offence if it—

(*a*) *offers to the public (whether for cash or otherwise) any shares in or debentures of the company; or*

(*b*) *allots or agrees to allot (whether for cash or otherwise) any shares in or debentures of the company with a view to all or any of those shares or debentures being offered for sale to the public (within the meaning given to that expression by [sections 58 and 742A]).*

(2) A company guilty of an offence under this section, and any officer of it who is in default, is liable to a fine.

(3) Nothing in this section affects the validity of any allotment or sale of shares or debentures, or of any agreement to allot or sell shares or debentures.

[66]

NOTES

Repealed for limited purposes, together with ss 82, 83, certain words in ss 84(1), 85(1), ss 86, 87, 97(2)(b), (3), (4), 709(2), (3), and certain entries in Schs 22, 24, by FSA 1986, s 212(3), Sch 17, Pt I, to the extent, and as from the dates, specified in the note at the beginning of Part III.

Repealed by the Companies Act 2006, s 1295, Sch 16, as from a day to be appointed.

Sub-s (1): words in square brackets in para (b) substituted by the Financial Services and Markets Act 2000 (Consequential Amendments) Order 2004, SI 2004/355, art 2(1), (2), as from 4 March 2004.

82 Application for, and allotment of, shares and debentures

(1) No allotment shall be made of a company's shares or debentures in pursuance of a prospectus issued generally, and no proceedings shall be taken on applications made in pursuance of a prospectus so issued, until the beginning of the third day after that on which the prospectus is first so issued or such later time (if any) as may be specified in the prospectus.

(2) The beginning of that third day, or that later time, is "the time of the opening of the subscription lists".

(3) In subsection (1), the reference to the day on which the prospectus is first issued generally is to the day when it is first so issued as a newspaper advertisement; and if it is not so issued as a newspaper advertisement before the third day after that on which it is first so issued in any other manner, the reference is to the day on which it is first so issued in any manner.

(4) In reckoning for this purpose the third day after another day—

(*a*) *any intervening day which is a Saturday or Sunday, or is a bank holiday in any part of Great Britain, is to be disregarded; and* (*b*) *if the third day (as so reckoned) is itself a Saturday or Sunday, or a bank holiday, there is to be substituted the first day after that which is none of them.*

(*5*) *The validity of an allotment is not affected by any contravention of subsections (1) to (4); but in the event of contravention, the company and every officer of it who is in default is liable to a fine.*

(*6*) *As applying to a prospectus offering shares or debentures for sale, the above provisions are modified as follows—*

(*a*) *for references to allotment, substitute references to sale; and*

(*b*) *for the reference to the company and every officer of it who is in default, substitute a reference to any person by or through whom the offer is made and who knowingly and wilfully authorises or permits the contravention.*

(*7*) *An application for shares in or debentures of a company which is made in pursuance of a prospectus issued generally is not revocable until after the expiration of the third day after the time of the opening of the subscription lists, or the giving before the expiration of that day of the appropriate public notice; and that notice is one given by some person responsible under sections 67 to 69 for the prospectus and having the effect under those sections of excluding or limiting the responsibility of the giver.*

[67]

NOTES

Repealed for limited purposes as noted to s 81 at **[66]**.
Repealed by the Companies Act 2006, s 1295, Sch 16, as from a day to be appointed.

83 No allotment unless minimum subscription received

(*1*) *No allotment shall be made of any share capital of a company offered to the public for subscription unless—*

(*a*) *there has been subscribed the amount stated in the prospectus as the minimum amount which, in the opinion of the directors, must be raised by the issue of share capital in order to provide for the matters specified in paragraph 2 of Schedule 3 (preliminary expenses, purchase of property, working capital, etc); and*

(*b*) *the sum payable on application for the amount so stated has been paid to and received by the company.*

(*2*) *For purposes of subsection (1)(b), a sum is deemed paid to the company, and received by it, if a cheque for that sum has been received in good faith by the company and the directors have no reason for suspecting that the cheque will not be paid.*

(*3*) *The amount so stated in the prospectus is to be reckoned exclusively of any amount payable otherwise than in cash and is known as "the minimum subscription".*

(*4*) *If the above conditions have not been complied with on the expiration of 40 days after the first issue of the prospectus, all money received from applicants for shares shall be forthwith repaid to them without interest.*

(*5*) *If any of the money is not repaid within 48 days after the issue of the prospectus, the directors of the company are jointly and severally liable to repay it with interest at the rate of 5 per cent per annum from the expiration of the 48th day; except that a director is not so liable if he proves that the default in the repayment of the money was not due to any misconduct or negligence on his part.*

(*6*) *Any condition requiring or binding an applicant for shares to waive compliance with any requirement of this section is void.*

(*7*) *This section does not apply to an allotment of shares subsequent to the first allotment of shares offered to the public for subscription.*

[68]

NOTES

Repealed for limited purposes as noted to s 81 at **[66]**.
Repealed by the Companies Act 2006, s 1295, Sch 16, as from a day to be appointed.
Sch 3, para 2: Sch 3 to this Act is repealed to the extent noted at the beginning of Pt III of this Act.

84 Allotment where issue not fully subscribed

(1) No allotment shall be made of any share capital of a public company offered for subscription unless—

(a) that capital is subscribed for in full; or

(b) the offer states that, even if the capital is not subscribed for in full, the amount of that capital subscribed for may be allotted in any event or in the event of the conditions specified in the offer being satisfied;

and, where conditions are so specified, no allotment of the capital shall be made by virtue of paragraph (b) unless those conditions are satisfied.

This is without prejudice to section 83.

(2) If shares are prohibited from being allotted by subsection (1) and 40 days have elapsed after the first issue of the prospectus, all money received from applicants for shares shall be forthwith repaid to them without interest.

(3) If any of the money is not repaid within 48 days after the issue of the prospectus, the directors of the company are jointly and severally liable to repay it with interest at the rate of 5 per cent per annum from the expiration of the 48th day; except that a director is not so liable if he proves that the default in repayment was not due to any misconduct or negligence on his part.

(4) This section applies in the case of shares offered as wholly or partly payable otherwise than in cash as it applies in the case of shares offered for subscription (the word "subscribed" in subsection (1) being construed accordingly).

(5) In subsections (2) and (3) as they apply to the case of shares offered as wholly or partly payable otherwise than in cash, references to the repayment of money received from applicants for shares include—

(a) the return of any other consideration so received (including, if the case so requires, the release of the applicant from any undertaking), or

(b) if it is not reasonably practicable to return the consideration, the payment of money equal to its value at the time it was so received,

and references to interest apply accordingly.

(6) Any condition requiring or binding an applicant for shares to waive compliance with any requirement of this section is void.

[69]

NOTES

Repealed by the Companies Act 2006, s 1295, Sch 16, as from a day to be appointed.

Sub-s (1): words "This is without prejudice to section 83" repealed for limited purposes as noted to s 81 at **[66]**.

85 Effect of irregular allotment

(1) An allotment made by a company to an applicant in contravention of section 83 or 84 is voidable at the instance of the applicant within one month after the date of the allotment, and not later, and is so voidable notwithstanding that the company is in the course of being wound up.

(2) If a director of a company knowingly contravenes, or permits or authorises the contravention of, any provision of either of those sections with respect to allotment, he is liable to compensate the company and the allottee respectively for any loss, damages or costs which the company or the allottee may have sustained or incurred by the contravention.

(3) But proceedings to recover any such loss, damages or costs shall not be commenced after the expiration of 2 years from the date of the allotment.

[70]

NOTES

Repealed by the Companies Act 2006, s 1295, Sch 16, as from a day to be appointed.

Sub-s (1): words "83 or" repealed for limited purposes as noted to s 81 at **[66]**.

86 Allotment of shares, etc to be dealt in on stock exchange

(1) The following applies where a prospectus, whether issued generally or not, states that application has been or will be made for permission for the shares or debentures offered by it to be listed on any stock exchange.

(2) An allotment made on an application in pursuance of the prospectus is, whenever made, void if the permission has not been applied for before the third day after the first issue of the prospectus or if the permission has been refused before the expiration of 3 weeks from the date of the closing of the subscription lists or such longer period (not exceeding 6 weeks) as may, within those 3 weeks, be notified to the applicant for permission by or on behalf of the stock exchange.

(3) In reckoning for this purpose the third day after another day—
- *(a) any intervening day which is a Saturday or Sunday, or is a bank holiday in any part of Great Britain, is to be disregarded; and*
- *(b) if the third day (as so reckoned) is itself a Saturday or Sunday, or a bank holiday, there is to be substituted the first day after that which is none of them.*

(4) Where permission has not been applied for as above, or has been refused as above, the company shall forthwith repay (without interest) all money received from applicants in pursuance of the prospectus.

(5) If any of the money is not repaid within 8 days after the company becomes liable to repay it, the directors of the company are jointly and severally liable to repay the money with interest at the rate of 5 per cent per annum from the expiration of the 8th day, except that a director is not liable if he proves that the default in the repayment of the money was not due to any misconduct or negligence on his part.

(6) All money received from applicants in pursuance of the prospectus shall be kept in a separate bank account so long as the company may become liable to repay it under subsection (4); and if default is made in complying with this subsection, the company and every officer of it who is in default is liable to a fine.

(7) Any condition requiring or binding an applicant for shares or debentures to waive compliance with any requirement of this section is void.

(8) For purposes of this section, permission is not deemed to be refused if it is intimated that the application for it, though not at present granted, will be given further consideration.

(9) This section has effect in relation to shares or debentures agreed to be taken by a person underwriting an offer of them by a prospectus as if he applied for them in pursuance of the prospectus.

[71]

NOTES

Repealed for limited purposes as noted to s 81 at **[66]**.
Repealed by the Companies Act 2006, s 1295, Sch 16, as from a day to be appointed.

87 Operation of s 86 where prospectus offers shares for sale

(1) The following has effect as regards the operation of section 86 in relation to a prospectus offering shares for sale.

(2) Subsections (1) and (2) of that section apply, but with the substitution for the reference in subsection (2) to allotment of a reference to sale.

(3) Subsections (4) and (5) of that section do not apply; but—
- *(a) if the permission referred to in section 86(2) has not been applied for as there mentioned, or has been refused as there mentioned, the offeror of the shares shall forthwith repay (without interest) all money received from applicants in pursuance of the prospectus, and*
- *(b) if any such money is not repaid within 8 days after the offeror becomes liable to repay it, he becomes liable to pay interest on the money due, at the rate of 5 per cent per annum from the end of the 8th day.*

(4) Subsections (6) to (9) apply, except that in subsection (6)—
- *(a) for the first reference to the company there is substituted a reference to the offeror, and*
- *(b) for the reference to the company and every officer of the company who is in*

default there is substituted a reference to any person by or through whom the offer is made and who knowingly and wilfully authorises or permits the default.

[72]

NOTES

Repealed for limited purposes as noted to s 81 at **[66]**.

Repealed by the Companies Act 2006, s 1295, Sch 16, as from a day to be appointed.

88 Return as to allotments, etc

(1) This section applies to a company limited by shares and to a company limited by guarantee and having a share capital.

(2) When such a company makes an allotment of its shares, the company shall within one month thereafter deliver to the registrar of companies for registration—

(a) a return of the allotments (in the prescribed form) stating the number and nominal amount of the shares comprised in the allotment, the names and addresses of the allottees, and the amount (if any) paid or due and payable on each share, whether on account of the nominal value of the share or by way of premium; and

(b) in the case of shares allotted as fully or partly paid up otherwise than in cash—

(i) a contract in writing constituting the title of the allottee to the allotment together with any contract of sale, or for services or other consideration in respect of which that allotment was made (such contracts being duly stamped), and

(ii) a return stating the number and nominal amount of shares so allotted, the extent to which they are to be treated as paid up, and the consideration for which they have been allotted.

(3) Where such a contract as above mentioned is not reduced to writing, the company shall within one month after the allotment deliver to the registrar of companies for registration the prescribed particulars of the contract …

(4) …

(5) If default is made in complying with this section, every officer of the company who is in default is liable to a fine and, for continued contravention, to a daily default fine, but subject as follows.

(6) In the case of default in delivering to the registrar within one month after the allotment any document required by this section to be delivered, the company, or any officer liable for the default, may apply to the court for relief; and the court, if satisfied that the omission to deliver the document was accidental or due to inadvertence, or that it is just and equitable to grant relief, may make an order extending the time for the delivery of the document for such period as the court thinks proper.

[73]

NOTES

Repealed by the Companies Act 2006, s 1295, Sch 16, as from a day to be appointed.

Sub-s (3): words omitted repealed by the Stamp Duty and Stamp Duty Land Tax (Consequential Amendment of Enactments) Regulations 2003, SI 2003/2868, reg 2(1), (2), as from 1 December 2003, in relation to contracts mentioned in sub-s (2)(b)(i) above entered into on or after that date.

Sub-s (4): repealed by SI 2003/2868, reg 2(1), (3), as from 1 December 2003, in relation to contracts mentioned in sub-s (2)(b)(i) above entered into on or after that date.

Return of the allotments (in the prescribed form); prescribed particulars of the contract: see Appendix 4 (Forms table) at **[A4]**.

See also, the Companies (Registrar, Languages and Trading Disclosures) Regulations 2006, SI 2006/3429, reg 4 at **[7594]**, which provides that s 1106 of the Companies Act 2006 (documents that may be drawn up and delivered in languages other than English) applies to contracts required to be delivered to the registrar under sub-s (2)(b)(i) above.

Pre-emption rights

89 Offers to shareholders to be on pre-emptive basis

(1) Subject to the provisions of this section and the seven sections next following, a company proposing to allot equity securities (defined in section 94)—

(a) shall not allot any of them on any terms to a person unless it has made an offer to

each person who holds relevant shares or relevant employee shares to allot to him on the same or more favourable terms a proportion of those securities which is as nearly as practicable equal to the proportion in nominal value held by him of the aggregate of relevant shares and relevant employee shares, and

(*b*) *shall not allot any of those securities to a person unless the period during which any such offer may be accepted has expired or the company has received notice of the acceptance or refusal of every offer so made.*

(2) Subsection (3) below applies to any provision of a company's memorandum or articles which requires the company, when proposing to allot equity securities consisting of relevant shares of any particular class, not to allot those securities on any terms unless it has complied with the condition that it makes such an offer as is described in subsection (1) to each person who holds relevant shares or relevant employee shares of that class.

(3) If in accordance with a provision to which this subsection applies—

(*a*) *a company makes an offer to allot securities to such a holder, and*

(*b*) *he or anyone in whose favour he has renounced his right to their allotment accepts the offer,*

subsection (1) does not apply to the allotment of those securities, and the company may allot them accordingly; but this is without prejudice to the application of subsection (1) in any other case.

(4) Subsection (1) does not apply to a particular allotment of equity securities if these are, or are to be, wholly or partly paid up otherwise than in cash; and securities which a company has offered to allot to a holder of relevant shares or relevant employee shares may be allotted to him, or anyone in whose favour he has renounced his right to their allotment, without contravening subsection (1)(b).

(5) Subsection (1) does not apply to the allotment of securities which would, apart from a renunciation or assignment of the right to their allotment, be held under an employees' share scheme.

[(6) Where a company holds relevant shares as treasury shares—

(*a*) *for the purposes of subsections (1) and (2), the company is not a "person who holds relevant shares"; and*

(*b*) *for the purposes of subsection (1), the shares held as treasury shares do not form part of "the aggregate of relevant shares and relevant employee shares".]*

[74]

NOTES

Repealed by the Companies Act 2006, s 1295, Sch 16, as from a day to be appointed.

Sub-s (6): added by the Companies (Acquisition of Own Shares) (Treasury Shares) Regulations 2003, SI 2003/1116, reg 4, Schedule, para 4, as from 1 December 2003; substituted by the Companies (Acquisition of Own Shares) (Treasury Shares) No 2 Regulations 2003, SI 2003/3031, reg 2(1), as from 18 December 2003.

Transitional provisions: the Companies (Acquisition of Own Shares) (Treasury Shares) No 2 Regulations 2003, SI 2003/3031, reg 2(2) provides that where a company holds relevant shares as treasury shares, and immediately before 18 December 2003, its memorandum or articles included a provision that met the requirements of sub-s (2) above, that provision shall have effect as if it had been modified so as to comply with the requirements of that subsection as it has effect after that date.

90 Communication of pre-emption offers to shareholders

(1) This section has effect as to the manner in which offers required by section 89(1), or by a provision to which section 89(3) applies, are to be made to holders of a company's shares.

(2) Subject to the following subsections, an offer shall be in writing and shall be made to a holder of shares either personally or by sending it by post (that is to say, prepaying and posting a letter containing the offer) to him or to his registered address or, if he has no registered address in the United Kingdom, to the address in the United Kingdom supplied by him to the company for the giving of notice to him.

If sent by post, the offer is deemed to be made at the time at which the letter would be delivered in the ordinary course of post.

(3) Where shares are held by two or more persons jointly, the offer may be made to the joint holder first named in the register of members in respect of the shares.

(4) *In the case of a holder's death or bankruptcy, the offer may be made—*

(*a*) *by sending it by post in a prepaid letter addressed to the persons claiming to be entitled to the shares in consequence of the death or bankruptcy by name, or by the title of representatives of the deceased, or trustee of the bankrupt, or by any like description, at the address in the United Kingdom supplied for the purpose by those so claiming, or*

(*b*) (*until such an address has been so supplied*) *by giving the notice in any manner in which it might have been given if the death or bankruptcy had not occurred.*

(5) *If the holder—*

(*a*) *has no registered address in the United Kingdom and has not given to the company an address in the United Kingdom for the service of notices on him, or*

(*b*) *is the holder of a share warrant,*

the offer may be made by causing it, or a notice specifying where a copy of it can be obtained or inspected, to be published in the Gazette.

(6) *The offer must state a period of not less than 21 days during which it may be accepted; and the offer shall not be withdrawn before the end of that period.*

(7) *This section does not invalidate a provision to which section 89(3) applies by reason that that provision requires or authorises an offer under it to be made in contravention of any of subsections (1) to (6) above; but, to the extent that the provision requires or authorises such an offer to be so made, it is of no effect.*

[75]

NOTES

Repealed by the Companies Act 2006, s 1295, Sch 16, as from a day to be appointed.

91 Exclusion of ss 89, 90 by private company

(1) *Section 89(1), section 90(1) to (5) or section 90(6) may, as applying to allotments by a private company of equity securities or to such allotments of a particular description, be excluded by a provision contained in the memorandum or articles of that company.*

(2) *A requirement or authority contained in the memorandum or articles of a private company, if it is inconsistent with any of those subsections, has effect as a provision excluding that subsection; but a provision to which section 89(3) applies is not to be treated as inconsistent with section 89(1).*

[76]

NOTES

Repealed by the Companies Act 2006, s 1295, Sch 16, as from a day to be appointed.

92 Consequences of contravening ss 89, 90

(1) *If there is a contravention of section 89(1), or of section 90(1) to (5) or section 90(6), or of a provision to which section 89(3) applies, the company, and every officer of it who knowingly authorised or permitted the contravention, are jointly and severally liable to compensate any person to whom an offer should have been made under the subsection or provision contravened for any loss, damage, costs or expenses which the person has sustained or incurred by reason of the contravention.*

(2) *However, no proceedings to recover any such loss, damage, costs or expenses shall be commenced after the expiration of 2 years from the delivery to the registrar of companies of the return of allotments in question or, where equity securities other than shares are granted, from the date of the grant.*

[77]

NOTES

Repealed by the Companies Act 2006, s 1295, Sch 16, as from a day to be appointed.

93 Saving for other restrictions as to offers

(1) *Sections 89 to 92 are without prejudice to any enactment by virtue of which a company is prohibited (whether generally or in specified circumstances) from offering or allotting equity securities to any person.*

(2) Where a company cannot by virtue of such an enactment offer or allot equity securities to a holder of relevant shares or relevant employee shares, those sections have effect as if the shares held by that holder were not relevant shares or relevant employee shares.

[78]

NOTES

Repealed by the Companies Act 2006, s 1295, Sch 16, as from a day to be appointed.

94 Definitions for ss 89–96

(1) The following subsections apply for the interpretation of sections 89 to 96.

(2) "Equity security", in relation to a company, means a relevant share in the company (other than a share shown in the memorandum to have been taken by a subscriber to the memorandum or a bonus share), or a right to subscribe for, or to convert securities into, relevant shares in the company.

(3) A reference to the allotment of equity securities or of equity securities consisting of relevant shares of a particular class includes the grant of a right to subscribe for, or to convert any securities into, relevant shares in the company or (as the case may be) relevant shares of a particular class; but such a reference does not include the allotment of any relevant shares pursuant to such a right.

[(3A) A reference to the allotment of equity securities or of equity securities consisting of relevant shares of a particular class also includes the sale of any relevant shares in the company or (as the case may be) relevant shares of a particular class if, immediately before the sale, the shares were held by the company as treasury shares.]

(4) "Relevant employee shares", in relation to a company, means shares of the company which would be relevant in it but for the fact that they are held by a person who acquired them in pursuance of an employees' share scheme.

(5) "Relevant shares", in relation to a company, means shares in the company other than—

- *(a) shares which as respects dividends and capital carry a right to participate only up to a specified amount in a distribution, and*
- *(b) shares which are held by a person who acquired them in pursuance of an employees' share scheme or, in the case of shares which have not been allotted, are to be allotted in pursuance of such a scheme [or, in the case of shares held by the company as treasury shares, are to be transferred in pursuance of such a scheme].*

(6) A reference to a class of shares is to shares to which the same rights are attached as to voting and as to participation, both as respects dividends and as respects capital, in a distribution.

(7) In relation to an offer to allot securities required by section 89(1) or by any provision to which section 89(3) applies, a reference in sections 89 to 94 (however expressed) to the holder of shares of any description is to whoever was at the close of business on a date, to be specified in the offer and to fall in the period of 28 days immediately before the date of the offer, the holder of shares of that description.

[79]

NOTES

Repealed by the Companies Act 2006, s 1295, Sch 16, as from a day to be appointed.

Sub-s (3A): inserted by the Companies (Acquisition of Own Shares) (Treasury Shares) Regulations 2003, SI 2003/1116, reg 4, Schedule, para 5(1), (3), as from 1 December 2003.

Sub-s (5): words in square brackets in para (b) added by SI 2003/1116, reg 4, Schedule, para 5(1), (2), as from 1 December 2003.

95 Disapplication of pre-emption rights

(1) Where the directors of a company are generally authorised for purposes of section 80, they may be given power by the articles, or by a special resolution of the company, to allot equity securities pursuant to that authority as if—

- *(a) section 89(1) did not apply to the allotment, or*

(*b*) *that subsection applied to the allotment with such modifications as the directors may determine;*

and where the directors make an allotment under this subsection, sections 89 to 94 have effect accordingly.

(*2*) *Where the directors of a company are authorised for purposes of section 80 (whether generally or otherwise), the company may by special resolution resolve either—*

(*a*) *that section 89(1) shall not apply to a specified allotment of equity securities to be made pursuant to that authority, or*

(*b*) *that that subsection shall apply to the allotment with such modifications as may be specified in the resolution;*

and where such a resolution is passed, sections 89 to 94 have effect accordingly.

[(2A) Subsections (1) and (2) apply in relation to a sale of shares which is an allotment of equity securities by virtue of section 94(3A) as if—

(*a*) *in subsection (1) for "Where the directors of a company are generally authorised for purposes of section 80, they" there were substituted "The directors of a company" and the words "pursuant to that authority" were omitted, and*

(*b*) *in subsection (2), the words from "Where" to "otherwise)," and, in paragraph (a), the words "to be made pursuant to that authority" were omitted.]*

(*3*) *The power conferred by subsection (1) or a special resolution under subsection (2) ceases to have effect when the authority to which it relates is revoked or would (if not renewed) expire; but if the authority is renewed, the power or (as the case may be) the resolution may also be renewed, for a period not longer than that for which the authority is renewed, by a special resolution of the company.*

(*4*) *Notwithstanding that any such power or resolution has expired, the directors may allot equity securities in pursuance of an offer or agreement previously made by the company, if the power or resolution enabled the company to make an offer or agreement which would or might require equity securities to be allotted after it expired.*

(*5*) *A special resolution under subsection (2), or a special resolution to renew such a resolution, shall not be proposed unless it is recommended by the directors and there has been circulated, with the notice of the meeting at which the resolution is proposed, to the members entitled to have that notice a written statement by the directors setting out—*

(*a*) *their reasons for making the recommendation,*

(*b*) *the amount to be paid to the company in respect of the equity securities to be allotted, and*

(*c*) *the directors' justification of that amount.*

(*6*) *A person who knowingly or recklessly authorises or permits the inclusion in a statement circulated under subsection (5) of any matter which is misleading, false or deceptive in a material particular is liable to imprisonment or a fine, or both.*

[80]

NOTES

Repealed by the Companies Act 2006, s 1295, Sch 16, as from a day to be appointed.

Sub-s (2A): inserted by the Companies (Acquisition of Own Shares) (Treasury Shares) Regulations 2003, SI 2003/1116, reg 4, Schedule, para 6, as from 1 December 2003.

96 Saving for company's pre-emption procedure operative before 1982

(*1*) *Where a company which is re-registered or registered as a public company is or, but for the provisions of the Companies Act 1980 and the enactments replacing it, would be subject at the time of re-registration or (as the case may be) registration to a pre-1982 pre-emption requirement, sections 89 to 95 do not apply to an allotment of the equity securities which are subject to that requirement.*

(*2*) *A "pre-1982 pre-emption requirement" is a requirement imposed (whether by the company's memorandum or articles, or otherwise) before the relevant date in 1982 by virtue of which the company must, when making an allotment of equity securities, make an offer to allot those securities or some of them in a manner which (otherwise than because involving a contravention of section 90(1) to (5) or 90(6)) is inconsistent with sections 89 to 94; and "the relevant date in 1982" is—*

(*a*) *except in a case falling within the following paragraph, 22nd June in that year, and* (*b*) *in the case of a company which was re-registered or registered as a public company on an application made before that date, the date on which the application was made.*

(*3*) *A requirement which—*

(*a*) *is imposed on a private company (having been so imposed before the relevant date in 1982) otherwise than by the company's memorandum or articles, and*

(*b*) *if contained in the company's memorandum or articles, would have effect under section 91 to the exclusion of any provisions of sections 89 to 94,*

has effect, so long as the company remains a private company, as if it were contained in the memorandum or articles.

(*4*) *If on the relevant date in 1982 a company, other than a public company registered as such on its original incorporation, was subject to such a requirement as is mentioned in section 89(2) imposed otherwise than by the memorandum or articles, the requirement is to be treated for purposes of sections 89 to 94 as if it were contained in the memorandum or articles.*

[81]

NOTES

Repealed by the Companies Act 2006, s 1295, Sch 16, as from a day to be appointed.

Companies Act 1980: repealed by the Companies Consolidation (Consequential Provisions) Act 1985, s 29, Sch 1.

Commissions and discounts

97 Power of company to pay commissions

(*1*) *It is lawful for a company to pay a commission to any person in consideration of his subscribing or agreeing to subscribe (whether absolutely or conditionally) for any shares in the company, or procuring or agreeing to procure subscriptions (whether absolute or conditional) for any shares in the company, if the following conditions are satisfied.*

(2) *The payment of the commission must be authorised by the company's articles; and—*

(*a*) *the commission paid or agreed to be paid must not exceed 10 per cent of the price at which the shares are issued or the amount or rate authorised by the articles, whichever is the less; and*

(*b*) *the amount or rate per cent of commission paid or agreed to be paid, and the number of shares which persons have agreed for a commission to subscribe absolutely, must be disclosed in the manner required by the following subsection.*

(*3*) *Those matters must, in the case of shares offered to the public for subscription, be disclosed in the prospectus; and in the case of shares not so offered—*

(*a*) *they must be disclosed in a statement in the prescribed form signed by every director of the company or by his agent authorised in writing, and delivered (before payment of the commission) to the registrar of companies for registration; and*

(*b*) *where a circular or notice (not being a prospectus) inviting subscription for the shares is issued, they must also be disclosed in that circular or notice.*

(*4*) *If default is made in complying with subsection (3)(a) as regards delivery to the registrar of the statement in prescribed form, the company and every officer of it who is in default is liable to a fine.*

[82]

NOTES

Repealed by the Companies Act 2006, s 1295, Sch 16, as from a day to be appointed.

Sub-s (1): formerly amended by FSA 1986, s 212(2), Sch 16, para 16, as from a day to be appointed, which was repealed without having been brought into force by the Public Offers of Securities Regulations 1995, SI 1995/1537, reg 17, Sch 2, Pt II, para 5(e) (revoked).

Sub-s (2): para (a) formerly amended by FSA 1986, s 212(2), Sch 16, para 16, as noted above; para (b), and the word immediately preceding it, repealed as noted to s 81 at **[66]**.

Sub-ss (3), (4): repealed as noted to s 81 at **[66]**.

Prescribed form: see Appendix 4 (Forms table) at **[A4]**.

98 Apart from s 97, commissions and discounts barred

(1) Except as permitted by section 97, no company shall apply any of its shares or capital money, either directly or indirectly in payment of any commission, discount or allowance to any person in consideration of his subscribing or agreeing to subscribe (whether absolutely or conditionally) for any shares in the company, or procuring or agreeing to procure subscriptions (whether absolute or conditional) for any shares in the company.

(2) This applies whether the shares or money be so applied by being added to the purchase money of any property acquired by the company or to the contract price of any work to be executed for the company, or the money be paid out of the nominal purchase money or contract price, or otherwise.

(3) Nothing in section 97 or this section affects the power of a company to pay such brokerage as has previously been lawful.

(4) A vendor to, or promoter of, or other person who receives payment in money or shares from, a company has, and is deemed always to have had, power to apply any part of the money or shares so received in payment of any commission, the payment of which, if made directly by the company, would have been lawful under section 97 and this section.

[83]

NOTES

Repealed by the Companies Act 2006, s 1295, Sch 16, as from a day to be appointed.

Amount to be paid for shares; the means of payment

99 General rules as to payment for shares on allotment

(1) Subject to the following provisions of this Part, shares allotted by a company, and any premium on them, may be paid up in money or money's worth (including goodwill and know-how).

(2) A public company shall not accept at any time, in payment up of its shares or any premium on them, an undertaking given by any person that he or another should do work or perform services for the company or any other person.

(3) If a public company accepts such an undertaking in payment up of its shares or any premium on them, the holder of the shares when they or the premium are treated as paid up (in whole or in part) by the undertaking is liable—

- *(a) to pay the company in respect of those shares an amount equal to their nominal value, together with the whole of any premium or, if the case so requires, such proportion of that amount as is treated as paid up by the undertaking; and*
- *(b) to pay interest at the appropriate rate on the amount payable under paragraph (a) above.*

(4) This section does not prevent a company from allotting bonus shares to its members or from paying up, with sums available for the purpose, any amounts for the time being unpaid on any of its shares (whether on account of the nominal value of the shares or by way of premium).

(5) The reference in subsection (3) to the holder of shares includes any person who has an unconditional right to be included in the company's register of members in respect of those shares or to have an instrument of transfer of them executed in his favour.

[84]

NOTES

Repealed by the Companies Act 2006, s 1295, Sch 16, as from a day to be appointed.

Application to a company whose directors have passed and not revoked a resolution to be re-registered under s 2 of this Act: see the Companies Consolidation (Consequential Provisions) Act 1985, s 9 at **[709]**.

100 Prohibition on allotment of shares at a discount

(1) A company's shares shall not be allotted at a discount.

(2) If shares are allotted in contravention of this section, the allottee is liable to pay the company an amount equal to the amount of the discount, with interest at the appropriate rate.

[85]

NOTES

Repealed by the Companies Act 2006, s 1295, Sch 16, as from a day to be appointed.

101 Shares to be allotted as at least one-quarter paid-up

(1) A public company shall not allot a share except as paid up at least as to one-quarter of its nominal value and the whole of any premium on it.

(2) Subsection (1) does not apply to shares allotted in pursuance of an employees' share scheme.

(3) If a company allots a share in contravention of subsection (1), the share is to be treated as if one-quarter of its nominal value, together with the whole of any premium on it, had been received.

(4) But the allottee is liable to pay the company the minimum amount which should have been received in respect of the share under subsection (1) (less the value of any consideration actually applied in payment up, to any extent, of the share and any premium on it), with interest at the appropriate rate.

(5) Subsections (3) and (4) do not apply to the allotment of bonus shares, unless the allottee knew or ought to have known the shares were allotted in contravention of subsection (1).

[86]

NOTES

Repealed by the Companies Act 2006, s 1295, Sch 16, as from a day to be appointed.

Application to a company whose directors have passed and not revoked a resolution to be re-registered under s 2 of this Act: see the Companies Consolidation (Consequential Provisions) Act 1985, s 9 at **[709]**.

102 Restriction on payment by long-term undertaking

(1) A public company shall not allot shares as fully or partly paid up (as to their nominal value or any premium on them) otherwise than in cash if the consideration for the allotment is or includes an undertaking which is to be, or may be, performed more than 5 years after the date of the allotment.

(2) If a company allots shares in contravention of subsection (1), the allottee is liable to pay the company an amount equal to the aggregate of their nominal value and the whole of any premium (or, if the case so requires, so much of that aggregate as is treated as paid up by the undertaking), with interest at the appropriate rate.

(3) Where a contract for the allotment of shares does not contravene subsection (1), any variation of the contract which has the effect that the contract would have contravened the subsection, if the terms of the contract as varied had been its original terms, is void.

(4) Subsection (3) applies also to the variation by a public company of the terms of a contract entered into before the company was re-registered as a public company.

(5) The following subsection applies where a public company allots shares for a consideration which consists of or includes (in accordance with subsection (1)) an undertaking which is to be performed within 5 years of the allotment, but the undertaking is not performed within the period allowed by the contract for the allotment of the shares.

(6) The allottee is then liable to pay the company, at the end of the period so allowed, an amount equal to the aggregate of the nominal value of the shares and the whole of any premium (or, if the case so requires, so much of that aggregate as is treated as paid up by the undertaking), with interest at the appropriate rate.

(7) A reference in this section to a contract for the allotment of shares includes an ancillary contract relating to payment in respect of them.

[87]

NOTES

Repealed by the Companies Act 2006, s 1295, Sch 16, as from a day to be appointed.

Application to a company whose directors have passed and not revoked a resolution to be re-registered under s 2 of this Act: see the Companies Consolidation (Consequential Provisions) Act 1985, s 9 at **[709]**.

103 Non-cash consideration to be valued before allotment

(*1*) *A public company shall not allot shares as fully or partly paid up (as to their nominal value or any premium on them) otherwise than in cash unless—*

(*a*) *the consideration for the allotment has been independently valued under section 108; and*

(*b*) *a report with respect to its value has been made to the company by a person appointed by the company (in accordance with that section) during the 6 months immediately preceding the allotment of the shares; and*

(*c*) *a copy of the report has been sent to the proposed allottee.*

(*2*) *Where an amount standing to the credit of any of a company's reserve accounts, or of its profit and loss account, is applied in paying up (to any extent) any shares allotted to members of the company or any premiums on shares so allotted, the amount applied does not count as consideration for the allotment, and accordingly subsection* (*1*) *does not apply in that case.*

(*3*) *Subsection* (*1*) *does not apply to the allotment of shares by a company in connection with an arrangement providing for the allotment of shares in that company on terms that the whole or part of the consideration for the shares allotted is to be provided by the transfer to that company (or the cancellation) of all or some of the shares, or of all or some of the shares of a particular class, in another company (with or without the issue to that company of shares, or of shares of any particular class, in that other company).*

(*4*) *But subsection* (*3*) *does not exclude the application of subsection* (*1*) *unless under the arrangement it is open to all the holders of the shares in the other company in question [("the relevant company")] (or, where the arrangement applies only to shares of a particular class, to all the holders of shares in [the relevant company], being holders of shares of that class) to take part in the arrangement.*

[In determining whether that is the case, the following shall be disregarded—

(*a*) *shares held by or by a nominee of the company proposing to allot the shares in connection with the arrangement ("the allotting company");*

(*b*) *shares held by or by a nominee of a company which is—*

(*i*) *the holding company, or a subsidiary, of the allotting company, or*

(*ii*) *a subsidiary of that holding company; and*

(*c*) *shares held as treasury shares by the relevant company.]*

(*5*) *Subsection* (*1*) *also does not apply to the allotment of shares by a company in connection with its proposed merger with another company; that is, where one of the companies proposes to acquire all the assets and liabilities of the other in exchange for the issue of shares or other securities of that one to shareholders of the other, with or without any cash payment to shareholders.*

(*6*) *If a company allots shares in contravention of subsection* (*1*) *and either—*

(*a*) *the allottee has not received the valuer's report required by that subsection to be sent to him; or*

(*b*) *there has been some other contravention of this section or section 108 which the allottee knew or ought to have known amounted to a contravention,*

the allottee is liable to pay the company an amount equal to the aggregate of the nominal value of the shares and the whole of any premium (or, if the case so requires, so much of that aggregate as is treated as paid up by the consideration), with interest at the appropriate rate.

(*7*) *In this section—*

(*a*) *"arrangement" means any agreement, scheme or arrangement (including an arrangement sanctioned in accordance with section 425 (company compromise with creditors and members) or [section 110 of the Insolvency Act] (liquidator in winding up accepting shares as consideration for sale of company property)), and*

(*b*) *any reference to a company, except where it is or is to be construed as a reference to a public company, includes any body corporate …*

[88]

NOTES

Repealed by the Companies Act 2006, s 1295, Sch 16, as from a day to be appointed.

Sub-s (4): words in first pair of square brackets inserted, and words in second and third pair of square brackets substituted, by the Companies (Acquisition of Own Shares) (Treasury Shares) Regulations 2003, SI 2003/1116, reg 4, Schedule, para 7, as from 1 December 2003.

Sub-s (7): words in square brackets in para (a) substituted by the Insolvency Act 1986, s 439(1), Sch 13, Pt I, as from 29 December 1986 (for transitional provisions see s 437 of, and Sch 11, Pt I to, that Act at **[3456]**, **[3481]**); words omitted from para (b) repealed by the Statute Law (Repeals) Act 2004, as from 22 July 2004.

Application to a company whose directors have passed and not revoked a resolution to be re-registered under s 2 of this Act: see the Companies Consolidation (Consequential Provisions) Act 1985, s 9 at **[709]**.

Insolvency Act, s 110: ie, the Insolvency Act 1986, s 110.

Chartered Companies Act 1837: repealed by the Statute Law (Repeals) Act 1993.

104 Transfer to public company of non-cash asset in initial period

(1) A public company formed as such shall not, unless the conditions of this section have been complied with, enter into an agreement with a person for the transfer by him during the initial period of one or more non-cash assets to the company or another, if—

(a) that person is a subscriber to the company's memorandum, and

(b) the consideration for the transfer to be given by the company is equal in value at the time of the agreement to one-tenth or more of the company's nominal share capital issued at that time.

(2) The "initial period" for this purpose is 2 years beginning with the date of the company being issued with a certificate under section 117 (or the previous corresponding provision) that it was entitled to do business.

(3) This section applies also to a company re-registered as a public company (except one re-registered under section 8 of the Companies Act 1980 or section 2 of the Consequential Provisions Act), or registered under section 685 (joint stock company) or the previous corresponding provision; but in that case—

(a) there is substituted a reference in subsection (1)(a) to a person who is a member of the company on the date of registration or re-registration, and

(b) the initial period is then 2 years beginning with that date.

In this subsection the reference to a company re-registered as a public company includes a private company so re-registered which was a public company before it was a private company.

(4) The conditions of this section are as follows—

(a) the consideration to be received by the company, and any consideration other than cash to be given by the company, must have been independently valued under section 109;

(b) a report with respect to the consideration to be so received and given must have been made to the company in accordance with that section during the 6 months immediately preceding the date of the agreement;

(c) the terms of the agreement must have been approved by an ordinary resolution of the company; and

(d) not later than the giving of the notice of the meeting at which the resolution is proposed, copies of the resolution and report must have been circulated to the members of the company entitled to receive the notice and, if the person with whom the agreement in question is proposed to be made is not then a member of the company so entitled, to that person.

(5) In subsection (4)(a)—

(a) the reference to the consideration to be received by the company is to the asset to be transferred to it or the advantage to the company of the asset's transfer to another person; and

(b) the specified condition is without prejudice to any requirement to value any consideration for purposes of section 103.

(6) In the case of the following agreements, this section does not apply—

(a) where it is part of the company's ordinary business to acquire, or arrange for other persons to acquire, assets of a particular description, an agreement entered into by the company in the ordinary course of its business for the transfer of an asset of that description to it or to such a person, as the case may be;

(b) an agreement entered into by the company under the supervision of the court, or of an officer authorised by the court for the purpose, for the transfer of an asset to the company or to another.

[89]

NOTES

Repealed by the Companies Act 2006, s 1295, Sch 16, as from a day to be appointed.

Companies Act 1980, s 8: repealed by the Companies Consolidation (Consequential Provisions) Act 1985, s 29, Sch 1 and replaced by ss 1–4 of that Act at **[702]–[705]**.

Consequential Provisions Act: ie, the Companies Consolidation (Consequential Provisions) Act 1985.

105 Agreements contravening s 104

(1) The following subsection applies if a public company enters into an agreement contravening section 104, the agreement being made with the person referred to in subsection (1)(a) or (as the case may be) subsection (3) of that section, and either—

(*a*) *that person has not received the valuer's report required for compliance with the conditions of the section, or*

(*b*) *there has been some other contravention of the section or of section 108(1), (2) or (5) or section 109, which he knew or ought to have known amounted to a contravention.*

(2) The company is then entitled to recover from that person any consideration given by it under the agreement, or an amount equal to the value of the consideration at the time of the agreement; and the agreement, so far as not carried out, is void.

(3) However, if the agreement is or includes an agreement for the allotment of shares in the company, then—

(*a*) *whether or not the agreement also contravenes section 103, subsection (2) does not apply to it in so far as it is for the allotment of shares; and*

(*b*) *the allottee is liable to pay the company an amount equal to the aggregate of the nominal value of the shares and the whole of any premium (or, if the case so requires, so much of that aggregate as is treated as paid up by the consideration), with interest at the appropriate rate.*

[90]

NOTES

Repealed by the Companies Act 2006, s 1295, Sch 16, as from a day to be appointed.

106 Shares issued to subscribers of memorandum

Shares taken by a subscriber to the memorandum of a public company in pursuance of an undertaking of his in the memorandum, and any premium on the shares, shall be paid up in cash.

[91]

NOTES

Repealed by the Companies Act 2006, s 1295, Sch 16, as from a day to be appointed.

Application to a company whose directors have passed and not revoked a resolution to be re-registered under s 2 of this Act: see the Companies Consolidation (Consequential Provisions) Act 1985, s 9 at **[709]**.

107 Meaning of "the appropriate rate"

In sections 99 to 105 "the appropriate rate", in relation to interest, means 5 per cent per annum or such other rate as may be specified by order made by the Secretary of State by statutory instrument subject to annulment in pursuance of a resolution of either House of Parliament.

[92]

NOTES

Repealed by the Companies Act 2006, s 1295, Sch 16, as from a day to be appointed.

Valuation provisions

108 Valuation and report (s 103)

(1) The valuation and report required by section 103 (or, where applicable, section 44) shall be made by an independent person, that is to say a person qualified at the time of the report to be appointed, or continue to be, an auditor of the company.

(2) However, where it appears to the independent person (from here on referred to as "the valuer") to be reasonable for the valuation of the consideration, or part of it, to be made (or for him to accept such a valuation) by another person who—

(a) appears to him to have the requisite knowledge and experience to value the consideration or that part of it; and

(b) is not an officer or servant of the company or any other body corporate which is that company's subsidiary or holding company or a subsidiary of that company's holding company or a partner or employee of such an officer or servant,

he may arrange for or accept such a valuation, together with a report which will enable him to make his own report under this section and provide the note required by subsection (6) below.

(3) The reference in subsection (2)(b) to an officer or servant does not include an auditor.

(4) The valuer's report shall state—

(a) the nominal value of the shares to be wholly or partly paid for by the consideration in question;

(b) the amount of any premium payable on the shares;

(c) the description of the consideration and, as respects so much of the consideration as he himself has valued, a description of that part of the consideration, the method used to value it and the date of the valuation;

(d) the extent to which the nominal value of the shares and any premium are to be treated as paid up—

(i) by the consideration;

(ii) in cash.

(5) Where the consideration or part of it is valued by a person other than the valuer himself, the latter's report shall state that fact and shall also—

(a) state the former's name and what knowledge and experience he has to carry out the valuation, and

(b) describe so much of the consideration as was valued by the other person, and the method used to value it, and specify the date of the valuation.

(6) The valuer's report shall contain or be accompanied by a note by him—

(a) in the case of a valuation made by a person other than himself, that it appeared to himself reasonable to arrange for it to be so made or to accept a valuation so made;

(b) whoever made the valuation, that the method of valuation was reasonable in all the circumstances;

(c) that it appears to the valuer that there has been no material change in the value of the consideration in question since the valuation; and

(d) that on the basis of the valuation the value of the consideration, together with any cash by which the nominal value of the shares or any premium payable on them is to be paid up, is not less than so much of the aggregate of the nominal value and the whole of any such premium as is treated as paid up by the consideration and any such cash.

(7) Where the consideration to be valued is accepted partly in payment up of the nominal value of the shares and any premium and partly for some other consideration given by the company, section 103 (and, where applicable, section 44) and the foregoing provisions of this section apply as if references to the consideration accepted by the company included the proportion of that consideration which is properly attributable to the payment up of that value and any premium; and—

(a) the valuer shall carry out, or arrange for, such other valuations as will enable him to determine that proportion; and

(b) his report shall state what valuations have been made under this subsection and also the reason for, and method and date of, any such valuation and any other matters which may be relevant to that determination.

[93]

NOTES

Repealed by the Companies Act 2006, s 1295, Sch 16, as from a day to be appointed.

Application to a company whose directors have passed and not revoked a resolution to be re-registered under s 2 of this Act: see the Companies Consolidation (Consequential Provisions) Act 1985, s 9 at **[709]**.

109 Valuation and report (s 104)

(1) Subsections (1) to (3) and (5) of section 108 apply also as respects the valuation and report for the purposes of section 104.

(2) The valuer's report for those purposes shall—

(a) state the consideration to be received by the company, describing the asset in question (specifying the amount to be received in cash) and the consideration to be given by the company (specifying the amount to be given in cash);

(b) state the method and date of valuation;

(c) contain or be accompanied by a note as to the matters mentioned in section 108(6)(a) to (c); and

(d) contain or be accompanied by a note that on the basis of the valuation the value of the consideration to be received by the company is not less than the value of the consideration to be given by it.

(3) A reference in section 104 or this section to consideration given for the transfer of an asset includes consideration given partly for its transfer; but—

(a) the value of any consideration partly so given is to be taken as the proportion of the consideration properly attributable to its transfer;

(b) the valuer shall carry out or arrange for such valuations of anything else as will enable him to determine that proportion; and

(c) his report for purposes of section 104 shall state what valuation has been made under this subsection and also the reason for and method and date of any such valuation and any other matters which may be relevant to that determination.

[94]

NOTES

Repealed by the Companies Act 2006, s 1295, Sch 16, as from a day to be appointed.

110 Entitlement of valuer to full disclosure

(1) A person carrying out a valuation or making a report under section 103 or 104, with respect to any consideration proposed to be accepted or given by a company, is entitled to require from the officers of the company such information and explanation as he thinks necessary to enable him to carry out the valuation or make the report and provide a note under section 108(6) or (as the case may be) section 109(2)(c).

(2) A person who knowingly or recklessly makes a statement which—

(a) is misleading, false or deceptive in a material particular, and

(b) is a statement to which this subsection applies,

is guilty of an offence and liable to imprisonment or a fine, or both.

(3) Subsection (2) applies to any statement made (whether orally or in writing) to a person carrying out a valuation or making a report under section 108 or 109, being a statement which conveys or purports to convey any information or explanation which that person requires, or is entitled to require, under subsection (1) of this section.

[95]

NOTES

Repealed by the Companies Act 2006, s 1295, Sch 16, as from a day to be appointed.

Application to a company whose directors have passed and not revoked a resolution to be re-registered under s 2 of this Act: see the Companies Consolidation (Consequential Provisions) Act 1985, s 9 at **[709]**.

111 Matters to be communicated to registrar

(1) A company to which a report is made under section 108 as to the value of any consideration for which, or partly for which, it proposes to allot shares shall deliver a copy of the report to the registrar of companies for registration at the same time that it files the return of the allotments of those shares under section 88.

(2) A company which has passed a resolution under section 104 with respect to the transfer of an asset shall, within 15 days of so doing, deliver to the registrar of companies a copy of the resolution together with the valuer's report required by that section.

(3) If default is made in complying with subsection (1), every officer of the company who is in default is liable to a fine and, for continued contravention, to a daily default fine; but this

is subject to the same exception as is made by section 88(6) (relief on application to the court) in the case of default in complying with that section.

(4) If a company fails to comply with subsection (2), it and every officer of it who is in default is liable to a fine and, for continued contravention, to a daily default fine.

[96]

NOTES

Repealed by the Companies Act 2006, s 1295, Sch 16, as from a day to be appointed.

Application to a company whose directors have passed and not revoked a resolution to be re-registered under s 2 of this Act: see the Companies Consolidation (Consequential Provisions) Act 1985, s 9 at **[709]**.

Other matters arising out of allotment, &c

[111A Right to damages, &c not affected

A person is not debarred from obtaining damages or other compensation from a company by reason only of his holding or having held shares in the company or any right to apply or subscribe for shares or to be included in the company's register in respect of shares.]

[97]

NOTES

Inserted by CA 1989, s 131(1), as from 1 April 1990.

Repealed by the Companies Act 2006, s 1295, Sch 16, as from a day to be appointed.

Application to a company whose directors have passed and not revoked a resolution to be re-registered under s 2 of this Act: see the Companies Consolidation (Consequential Provisions) Act 1985, s 9 at **[709]**.

112 Liability of subsequent holders of shares allotted

(1) If a person becomes a holder of shares in respect of which—

(a) there has been a contravention of section 99, 100, 101 or 103; and

(b) by virtue of that contravention, another is liable to pay any amount under the section contravened,

that person is also liable to pay that amount (jointly and severally with any other person so liable), unless he is exempted from liability by subsection (3) below.

(2) If a company enters into an agreement in contravention of section 104 and—

(a) the agreement is or includes an agreement for the allotment of shares in the company; and

(b) a person becomes a holder of shares allotted under the agreement; and

(c) by virtue of the agreement and allotment under it, another person is liable to pay any amount under section 105,

the person who becomes the holder of the shares is also liable to pay that amount (jointly and severally with any other person so liable), unless he is exempted from liability by the following subsection; and this applies whether or not the agreement also contravenes section 103.

(3) A person otherwise liable under subsection (1) or (2) is exempted from that liability if either—

(a) he is a purchaser for value and, at the time of the purchase, he did not have actual notice of the contravention concerned; or

(b) he derived title to the shares (directly or indirectly) from a person who became a holder of them after the contravention and was not liable under subsection (1) or (as the case may be) subsection (2).

(4) References in this section to a holder, in relation to shares in a company, include any person who has an unconditional right to be included in the company's register of members in respect of those shares or to have an instrument of transfer of the shares executed in his favour.

(5) As subsections (1) and (3) apply in relation to the contraventions there mentioned, they also apply—

(a) to a contravention of section 102; and

(b) to a failure to carry out a term of a contract as mentioned in subsections (5) and (6) of that section.

[98]

NOTES

Repealed by the Companies Act 2006, s 1295, Sch 16, as from a day to be appointed.

Application to a company whose directors have passed and not revoked a resolution to be re-registered under s 2 of this Act: see the Companies Consolidation (Consequential Provisions) Act 1985, s 9 at **[709]**.

113 Relief in respect of certain liabilities under ss 99 ff

(1) Where a person is liable to a company under—

(a) section 99, 102, 103 or 105;

(b) section 112(1) by reference to a contravention of section 99 or 103; or

(c) section 112(2) or (5),

in relation to payment in respect of any shares in the company, or is liable by virtue of an undertaking given to it in, or in connection with, payment for any such shares, the person so liable may make an application to the court to be exempted in whole or in part from the liability.

(2) If the liability mentioned in subsection (1) arises in relation to payment in respect of any shares, the court may, on an application under that subsection, exempt the applicant from the liability only—

(a) if and to the extent that it appears to the court just and equitable to do so having regard to the matters mentioned in the following subsection,

(b) if and to the extent that it appears to the court just and equitable to do so in respect of any interest which he is liable to pay the company under any of the relevant sections.

(3) The matters to be taken into account by the court under subsection (2)(a) are—

(a) whether the applicant has paid, or is liable to pay, any amount in respect of any other liability arising in relation to those shares under any of the relevant sections, or of any liability arising by virtue of any undertaking given in or in connection with payment for those shares;

(b) whether any person other than the applicant has paid or is likely to pay (whether in pursuance of an order of the court or otherwise) any such amount; and

(c) whether the applicant or any other person has performed in whole or in part, or is likely so to perform, any such undertaking, or has done or is likely to do any other thing in payment or part payment for the shares.

(4) Where the liability arises by virtue of an undertaking given to the company in, or in connection with, payment for shares in it, the court may, on an application under subsection (1), exempt the applicant from the liability only if and to the extent that it appears to the court just and equitable to do so having regard to—

(a) whether the applicant has paid or is liable to pay any amount in respect of liability arising in relation to the shares under any of the provisions mentioned in that subsection; and

(b) whether any person other than the applicant has paid or is likely to pay (whether in pursuance of an order of the court or otherwise) any such amount.

(5) In determining whether it should exempt the applicant in whole or in part from any liability, the court shall have regard to the following overriding principles, namely—

(a) that a company which has allotted shares should receive money or money's worth at least equal in value to the aggregate of the nominal value of those shares and the whole of any premium or, if the case so requires, so much of that aggregate as is treated as paid up; and

(b) subject to this, that where such a company would, if the court did not grant the exemption, have more than one remedy against a particular person, it should be for the company to decide which remedy it should remain entitled to pursue.

(6) If a person brings proceedings against another ("the contributor") for a contribution in respect of liability to a company arising under any of sections 99 to 105 or 112, and it appears to the court that the contributor is liable to make such a contribution, the court may exercise the powers of the following subsection.

(7) The court may, if and to the extent that it appears to it, having regard to the respective culpability (in respect of the liability to the company) of the contributor and the person bringing the proceedings, that it is just and equitable to do so—

(a) exempt the contributor in whole or in part from his liability to make such a contribution; or

(*b*) *order the contributor to make a larger contribution than, but for this subsection, he would be liable to make.*

(8) Where a person is liable to a company under section 105(2), the court may, on application, exempt him in whole or in part from that liability if and to the extent that it appears to the court just and equitable to do so having regard to any benefit accruing to the company by virtue of anything done by him towards the carrying out of the agreement mentioned in that subsection.

[99]

NOTES

Repealed by the Companies Act 2006, s 1295, Sch 16, as from a day to be appointed.

Application to a company whose directors have passed and not revoked a resolution to be re-registered under s 2 of this Act: see the Companies Consolidation (Consequential Provisions) Act 1985, s 9 at **[709]**.

114 Penalty for contravention

If a company contravenes any of the provisions of sections 99 to 104 and 106 the company and any officer of it who is in default is liable to a fine.

[100]

NOTES

Repealed by the Companies Act 2006, s 1295, Sch 16, as from a day to be appointed.

Application to a company whose directors have passed and not revoked a resolution to be re-registered under s 2 of this Act: see the Companies Consolidation (Consequential Provisions) Act 1985, s 9 at **[709]**.

115 Undertakings to do work, etc

(1) Subject to section 113, an undertaking given by any person, in or in connection with payment for shares in a company, to do work or perform services or to do any other thing, if it is enforceable by the company apart from this Act, is so enforceable notwithstanding that there has been a contravention in relation to it of section 99, 102 or 103.

(2) Where such an undertaking is given in contravention of section 104 in respect of the allotment of shares, it is so enforceable notwithstanding the contravention.

[101]

NOTES

Repealed by the Companies Act 2006, s 1295, Sch 16, as from a day to be appointed.

Application to a company whose directors have passed and not revoked a resolution to be re-registered under s 2 of this Act: see the Companies Consolidation (Consequential Provisions) Act 1985, s 9 at **[709]**.

116 Application of ss 99 ff to special cases

Except as provided by section 9 of the Consequential Provisions Act (transitional cases dealt with by section 31 of the Companies Act 1980), sections 99, 101 to 103, 106, 108 [110, 111 and 112 to 115] apply—

(*a*) *to a company which has passed and not revoked a resolution to be re-registered under section 43 as a public company, and*

(*b*) *to a joint stock company which has passed, and not revoked, a resolution that the company be a public company,*

as those sections apply to a public company.

[102]

NOTES

Repealed by the Companies Act 2006, s 1295, Sch 16, as from a day to be appointed.

Words in square brackets substituted by CA 1989, s 131(2), as from 1 April 1990.

Consequential Provisions Act: ie, the Companies Consolidation (Consequential Provisions) Act 1985.

Companies Act 1980, s 31: repealed by the Companies Consolidation (Consequential Provisions) Act 1985, s 29, Sch 1, and replaced by this section and s 9 of that Act at **[709]**.

PART V
SHARE CAPITAL, ITS INCREASE, MAINTENANCE AND REDUCTION

CHAPTER I
GENERAL PROVISIONS ABOUT SHARE CAPITAL

117 Public company share capital requirements

(1) A company registered as a public company on its original incorporation shall not do business or exercise any borrowing powers unless the registrar of companies has issued it with a certificate under this section or the company is re-registered as a private company.

(2) The registrar shall issue a company with such a certificate if, on an application made to him by the company in the prescribed form, he is satisfied that the nominal value of the company's allotted share capital is not less than the authorised minimum, and there is delivered to him a statutory declaration complying with the following subsection.

[This subsection is subject to subsection (3A).]

(3) The statutory declaration must be in the prescribed form and be signed by a director or secretary of the company; and it must—

- *(a) state that the nominal value of the company's allotted share capital is not less than the authorised minimum;*
- *(b) specify the amount paid up, at the time of the application, on the allotted share capital of the company;*
- *(c) specify the amount, or estimated amount, of the company's preliminary expenses and the persons by whom any of those expenses have been paid or are payable; and*
- *(d) specify any amount or benefit paid or given, or intended to be paid or given, to any promoter of the company, and the consideration for the payment or benefit.*

[(3A) In place of the statutory declaration referred to in subsection (2), there may be delivered to the registrar of companies using electronic communications a statement made by a director or secretary of the company complying with the requirements of subsection (3)(a) to (d).]

(4) For the purposes of subsection (2), a share allotted in pursuance of an employees' share scheme may not be taken into account in determining the nominal value of the company's allotted share capital unless it is paid up at least as to one-quarter of the nominal value of the share and the whole of any premium on the share.

(5) The registrar may accept a statutory declaration [or statement] delivered to him under this section as sufficient evidence of the matters stated in it.

(6) A certificate under this section in respect of a company is conclusive evidence that the company is entitled to do business and exercise any borrowing powers.

(7) If a company does business or exercises borrowing powers in contravention of this section, the company and any officer of it who is in default is liable to a fine.

[(7A) Any person who makes a false statement under subsection (3A) which he knows to be false or does not believe to be true is liable to imprisonment or a fine, or both.]

(8) Nothing in this section affects the validity of any transaction entered into by a company; but, if a company enters into a transaction in contravention of this section and fails to comply with its obligations in that connection within 21 days from being called upon to do so, the directors of the company are jointly and severally liable to indemnify the other party to the transaction in respect of any loss or damage suffered by him by reason of the company's failure to comply with those obligations.

[103]

NOTES

Repealed by the Companies Act 2006, s 1295, Sch 16, as from a day to be appointed.

Sub-ss (2), (5): words in square brackets inserted by the Companies Act 1985 (Electronic Communications) Order 2000, SI 2000/3373, art 9(1), (2), (4), as from 22 December 2000.

Sub-ss (3A), (7A): inserted by SI 2000/3373, art 9(1), (3), (5), as from 22 December 2000.

Application … in the prescribed form; statutory declaration … in the prescribed form: see Appendix 4 (Forms table) at **[A4]**.

118 The authorised minimum

(1) In this Act, "the authorised minimum" means £50,000, or such other sum as the Secretary of State may by order made by statutory instrument specify instead.

(2) An order under this section which increases the authorised minimum may—

(a) require any public company having an allotted share capital of which the nominal value is less than the amount specified in the order as the authorised minimum to increase that value to not less than that amount or make application to be re-registered as a private company;

(b) make, in connection with any such requirement, provision for any of the matters from which provision is made by this Act relating to a company's registration, re-registration or change of name, to payment for any share comprised in a company's capital and to offers of shares in or debentures of a company to the public, including provision as to the consequences (whether in criminal law or otherwise) of a failure to comply with any requirement of the order; and

(c) contain such supplemental and transitional provisions as the Secretary of State thinks appropriate, make different provision for different cases and, in particular, provide for any provision of the order to come into operation on different days for different purposes.

(3) An order shall not be made under this section unless a draft of it has been laid before Parliament and approved by resolution of each House.

[104]

NOTES

Repealed by the Companies Act 2006, s 1295, Sch 16, as from a day to be appointed.

119 Provision for different amounts to be paid on shares

A company, if so authorised by its articles, may do any one or more of the following things—

(a) make arrangements on the issue of shares for a difference between the shareholders in the amounts and times of payment of calls on their shares;

(b) accept from any member the whole or a part of the amount remaining unpaid on any shares held by him, although no part of that amount has been called up;

(c) pay dividend in proportion to the amount paid up on each share where a larger amount is paid up on some shares than on others.

[105]

NOTES

Repealed by the Companies Act 2006, s 1295, Sch 16, as from a day to be appointed.

120 Reserve liability of limited company

A limited company may by special resolution determine that any portion of its share capital which has not been already called up shall not be capable of being called up except in the event and for the purposes of the company being wound up; and that portion of its share capital is then not capable of being called up except in that event and for those purposes.

[106]

NOTES

Repealed by the Companies Act 2006, s 1295, Sch 16, as from a day to be appointed.

121 Alteration of share capital (limited companies)

(1) A company limited by shares or a company limited by guarantee and having a share capital, if so authorised by its articles, may alter the conditions of its memorandum in any of the following ways.

(2) The company may—

(a) increase its share capital by new shares of such amount as it thinks expedient;

(b) consolidate and divide all or any of its share capital into shares of larger amount than its existing shares;

(c) convert all or any of its paid-up shares into stock, and re-convert that stock into paid-up shares of any denomination;

(*d*) *sub-divide its shares, or any of them, into shares of smaller amount than is fixed by the memorandum (but subject to the following subsection);*

(*e*) *cancel shares which, at the date of the passing of the resolution to cancel them, have not been taken or agreed to be taken by any person, and diminish the amount of the company's share capital by the amount of the shares so cancelled.*

(3) In any sub-division under subsection (2)(d) the proportion between the amount paid and the amount, if any, unpaid on each reduced share must be the same as it was in the case of the share from which the reduced share is derived.

(4) The powers conferred by this section must be exercised by the company in general meeting.

(5) A cancellation of shares under this section does not for purposes of this Act constitute a reduction of share capital.

[107]

NOTES

Repealed by the Companies Act 2006, s 1295, Sch 16, as from a day to be appointed.

122 Notice to registrar of alteration

(1) If a company having a share capital has—

(*a*) *consolidated and divided its share capital into shares of larger amount than its existing shares; or*

(*b*) *converted any shares into stock; or*

(*c*) *re-converted stock into shares; or*

(*d*) *sub-divided its shares or any of them; or*

(*e*) *redeemed any redeemable shares; or*

(*f*) *cancelled any shares (otherwise than in connection with a reduction of share capital under section 135),*

it shall within one month after so doing give notice in the prescribed form to the registrar of companies, specifying (as the case may be) the shares consolidated, divided, converted, sub-divided, redeemed or cancelled, or the stock re-converted.

(2) If default is made in complying with this section, the company and every officer of it who is in default is liable to a fine and, for continued contravention, to a daily default fine.

[108]

NOTES

Repealed by the Companies Act 2006, s 1295, Sch 16, as from a day to be appointed.
Notice in the prescribed form: see Appendix 4 (Forms table) at **[A4]**.

123 Notice to registrar of increased share capital

(1) If a company having a share capital (whether or not its shares have been converted into stock) increases its share capital beyond the registered capital, it shall within 15 days after the passing of the resolution authorising the increase, give to the registrar of companies notice of the increase, and the registrar shall record the increase.

(2) The notice must include such particulars as may be prescribed with respect to the classes of shares affected and the conditions subject to which the new shares have been or are to be issued.

(3) There shall be forwarded to the registrar together with the notice a printed copy of the resolution authorising the increase, or a copy of the resolution in some other form approved by the registrar.

(4) If default is made in complying with this section, the company and every officer of it who is in default is liable to a fine and, for continued contravention, to a daily default fine.

[109]

NOTES

Repealed by the Companies Act 2006, s 1295, Sch 16, as from a day to be appointed.
Prescribed particulars: see Appendix 4 (Forms table) at **[A4]**.

124 Reserve capital of unlimited company

An unlimited company having a share capital may by its resolution for re-registration as a public company under section 43, or as a limited company under section 51—

- *(a)* *increase the nominal amount of its share capital by increasing the nominal amount of each of its shares (but subject to the condition that no part of the increased capital is to be capable of being called up except in the event and for the purpose of the company being wound up), and*
- *(b)* *alternatively or in addition, provide that a specified portion of its uncalled share capital is not to be capable of being called up except in that event and for that purpose.*

[110]

NOTES

Repealed by the Companies Act 2006, s 1295, Sch 16, as from a day to be appointed.

CHAPTER II
CLASS RIGHTS

125 Variation of class rights

(1) This section is concerned with the variation of the rights attached to any class of shares in a company whose share capital is divided into shares of different classes.

(2) Where the rights are attached to a class of shares otherwise than by the company's memorandum, and the company's articles do not contain provision with respect to the variation of the rights, those rights may be varied if, but only if—

- *(a)* *the holders of three-quarters in nominal value of the issued shares of that class [(excluding any shares of that class held as treasury shares)] consent in writing to the variation; or*
- *(b)* *an extraordinary resolution passed at a separate general meeting of the holders of that class sanctions the variation;*

and any requirement (howsoever imposed) in relation to the variation of those rights is complied with to the extent that it is not comprised in paragraphs (a) and (b) above.

(3) Where—

- *(a)* *the rights are attached to a class of shares by the memorandum or otherwise;*
- *(b)* *the memorandum or articles contain provision for the variation of those rights; and*
- *(c)* *the variation of those rights is connected with the giving, variation, revocation or renewal of an authority for allotment under section 80 or with a reduction of the company's share capital under section 135;*

those rights shall not be varied unless—

- *(i)* *the condition mentioned in subsection (2)(a) or (b) above is satisfied; and*
- *(ii)* *any requirement of the memorandum or articles in relation to the variation of rights of that class is complied with to the extent that it is not comprised in that condition.*

(4) If the rights are attached to a class of shares in the company by the memorandum or otherwise and—

- *(a)* *where they are so attached by the memorandum, the articles contain provision with respect to their variation which had been included in the articles at the time of the company's original incorporation; or*
- *(b)* *where they are so attached otherwise, the articles contain such provision (whenever first so included),*

and in either case the variation is not connected as mentioned in subsection (3)(c), those rights may only be varied in accordance with that provision of the articles.

(5) If the rights are attached to a class of shares by the memorandum, and the memorandum and articles do not contain provision with respect to the variation of those rights, those rights may be varied if all the members of the company [(excluding any member holding shares as treasury shares)] agree to the variation.

(6) The provisions of section 369 (length of notice for calling company meetings), section 370 (general provisions as to meetings and votes), and sections 376 and 377 (circulation of members' resolutions) and the provisions of the articles relating to general

meetings shall, so far as applicable, apply in relation to any meeting of shareholders required by this section or otherwise to take place in connection with the variation of the rights attached to a class of shares, and shall so apply with the necessary modifications and subject to the following provisions, namely—

(*a*) *the necessary quorum at any such meeting other than an adjourned meeting shall be two persons holding or representing by proxy at least one-third in nominal value of the issued shares of the class in question [(excluding any shares of that class held as treasury shares)] and at an adjourned meeting one person holding shares of the class in question or his proxy;*

(*b*) *any holder of shares of the class in question present in person or by proxy may demand a poll.*

(7) Any alteration of a provision contained in a company's articles for the variation of the rights attached to a class of shares, or the insertion of any such provision into the articles, is itself to be treated as a variation of those rights.

(8) In this section and (except where the context otherwise requires) in any provision for the variation of the rights attached to a class of shares contained in a company's memorandum or articles, references to the variation of those rights are to be read as including references to their abrogation.

[111]

NOTES

Repealed by the Companies Act 2006, s 1295, Sch 16, as from 1 October 2007 (in so far as relating to sub-s (6)), and as from a day to be appointed (otherwise). For savings see the note below.

Sub-s (2): words in square brackets inserted by the Companies (Acquisition of Own Shares) (Treasury Shares) Regulations 2003, SI 2003/1116, reg 4, Schedule, para 8, as from 1 December 2003; for the words "an extraordinary resolution" there are substituted the words "a special resolution" by the draft Companies Act 2006 (Commencement No 3, Consequential Amendments, Transitional Provisions and Savings) Order 2007, art 10(1), Sch 4, Pt 1, para 2, as from 1 October 2007 (see **[A12]**). This amendment applies (i) to written resolutions for which the circulation date (see s 290 of the Companies Act 2006) is on or after 1 October 2007; and (ii) to resolutions passed at a meeting of which notice is given on or after that date.

Sub-s (5): words in square brackets inserted by the Companies (Acquisition of Own Shares) (Treasury Shares) Regulations 2003, SI 2003/1116, reg 4, Schedule, para 8, as from 1 December 2003.

Sub-s (6): repealed as noted above; words in square brackets inserted by the Companies (Acquisition of Own Shares) (Treasury Shares) Regulations 2003, SI 2003/1116, reg 4, Schedule, para 8, as from 1 December 2003.

Savings: sub-s (6) continues to apply to meetings of which notice is given before 1 October 2007 (see the draft Companies Act 2006 (Commencement No 3, Consequential Amendments, Transitional Provisions and Savings) Order 2007, Sch 3, para 31 at **[A12]**).

126 Saving for court's powers under other provisions

Nothing in subsections (2) to (5) of section 125 derogates from the powers of the court under the following sections of this Act, namely—

sections 4 to 6 (company resolution to alter objects),
section 54 (litigated objection to public company becoming private by re-registration),
section 425 (court control of company compromising with members and creditors),
section 427 (company reconstruction or amalgamation),
sections 459 to 461 (protection of minorities).

[112]

NOTES

Repealed by the Companies Act 2006, s 1295, Sch 16, as from a day to be appointed.

For the words "sections 459 to 461 (protection of minorities)" there are substituted the words "Part 30 of the Companies Act 2006 (protection of members against unfair prejudice)" by the draft Companies Act 2006 (Commencement No 3, Consequential Amendments, Transitional Provisions and Savings) Order 2007, art 10(1), Sch 4, Pt 1, para 9, as from 1 October 2007 (see **[A12]**).

127 Shareholders' right to object to variation

(1) This section applies if, in the case of a company whose share capital is divided into different classes of shares—

(*a*) *provision is made by the memorandum or articles for authorising the variation of the rights attached to any class of shares in the company, subject to—*

(*i*) *the consent of any specified proportion of the holders of the issued shares of that class, or*

(ii) the sanction of a resolution passed at a separate meeting of the holders of those shares,

and in pursuance of that provision the rights attached to any such class of shares are at any time varied; or

(b) the rights attached to any class of shares in the company are varied under section 125(2).

(2) The holders of not less in the aggregate than 15 per cent of the issued shares of the class in question (being persons who did not consent to or vote in favour of the resolution for the variation), may apply to the court to have the variation cancelled; and if such an application is made, the variation has no effect unless and until it is confirmed by the court.

[(2A) For the purposes of subsection (2), any of the company's issued share capital held as treasury shares must be disregarded.]

(3) Application to the court must be made within 21 days after the date on which the consent was given or the resolution was passed (as the case may be), and may be made on behalf of the shareholders entitled to make the application by such one or more of their number as they may appoint in writing for the purpose.

(4) The court, after hearing the applicant and any other persons who apply to the court to be heard and appear to the court to be interested in the application, may, if satisfied having regard to all the circumstances of the case, that the variation would unfairly prejudice the shareholders of the class represented by the applicant, disallow the variation and shall, if not satisfied, confirm it.

The decision of the court on any such application is final.

(5) The company shall within 15 days after the making of an order by the court on such an application forward a copy of the order to the registrar of companies; and, if default is made in complying with this provision, the company and every officer of it who is in default is liable to a fine and, for continued contravention, to a daily default fine.

(6) "Variation", in this section, includes abrogation; and "varied" is to be construed accordingly.

[113]

NOTES

Repealed by the Companies Act 2006, s 1295, Sch 16, as from a day to be appointed.

Sub-s (2A): inserted by the Companies (Acquisition of Own Shares) (Treasury Shares) Regulations 2003, SI 2003/1116, reg 4, Schedule, para 9, as from 1 December 2003.

128 Registration of particulars of special rights

(1) If a company allots shares with rights which are not stated in its memorandum or articles, or in any resolution or agreement which is required by section 380 to be sent to the registrar of companies, the company shall deliver to the registrar of companies, within one month from allotting the shares, a statement in the prescribed form containing particulars of those rights.

(2) This does not apply if the shares are in all respects uniform with shares previously allotted; and shares are not for this purpose to be treated as different from shares previously allotted by reason only that the former do not carry the same rights to dividends as the latter during the 12 months immediately following the former's allotment.

(3) Where the rights attached to any shares of a company are varied otherwise than by an amendment of the company's memorandum or articles or by a resolution or agreement subject to section 380, the company shall within one month from the date on which the variation is made deliver to the registrar of companies a statement in the prescribed form containing particulars of the variation.

(4) Where a company (otherwise than by any such amendment, resolution or agreement as is mentioned above) assigns a name or other designation, or a new name or other designation, to any class of its shares, it shall within one month from doing so deliver to the registrar of companies a notice in the prescribed form giving particulars of the name or designation so assigned.

(5) If a company fails to comply with this section, the company and every officer of it who is in default is liable to a fine and, for continued contravention, to a daily default fine.

[114]

NOTES

Repealed by the Companies Act 2006, s 1295, Sch 16, as from a day to be appointed.

Sub-s (1): for the words "section 380" there are substituted the words "section 30 of the Companies Act 2006" by the draft Companies Act 2006 (Commencement No 3, Consequential Amendments, Transitional Provisions and Savings) Order 2007, art 10(1), Sch 4, Pt 1, para 1(4), as from 1 October 2007 (see **[A12]**).

Statement in the prescribed form; notice in the prescribed form: see Appendix 4 (Forms table) at **[A4]**.

129 Registration of newly created class rights

(1) If a company not having a share capital creates a class of members with rights which are not stated in its memorandum or articles or in a resolution or agreement to which section 380 applies, the company shall deliver to the registrar of companies within one month from the date on which the new class is created a statement in the prescribed form containing particulars of the rights attached to that class.

(2) If the rights of any class of members of the company are varied otherwise than by an amendment of the memorandum or articles or by a resolution or agreement subject to section 380, the company shall within one month from the date on which the variation is made deliver to the registrar a statement in the prescribed form containing particulars of the variation.

(3) If a company (otherwise than by such an amendment, resolution or agreement as is mentioned above) assigns a name or other designation, or a new name or other designation, to any class of its members, it shall within one month from doing so deliver to the registrar a notice in the prescribed form giving particulars of the name or designation so assigned.

(4) If a company fails to comply with this section, the company and every officer of it who is in default is liable to a fine and, for continued contravention, to a daily default fine.

[115]

NOTES

Repealed by the Companies Act 2006, s 1295, Sch 16, as from a day to be appointed.

Sub-s (1): for the words "section 380" there are substituted the words "section 30 of the Companies Act 2006" by the draft Companies Act 2006 (Commencement No 3, Consequential Amendments, Transitional Provisions and Savings) Order 2007, art 10(1), Sch 4, Pt 1, para 1(5), as from 1 October 2007 (see **[A12]**).

Statement in the prescribed form: see Appendix 4 (Forms table) at **[A4]**.

CHAPTER III
SHARE PREMIUMS

130 Application of share premiums

(1) If a company issues shares at a premium, whether for cash or otherwise, a sum equal to the aggregate amount or value of the premiums on those shares shall be transferred to an account called "the share premium account".

(2) The share premium account may be applied by the company in paying up unissued shares to be allotted to members as fully paid bonus shares, or in writing off—

- *(a) the company's preliminary expenses; or*
- *(b) the expenses of, or the commission paid or discount allowed on, any issue of shares or debentures of the company,*

or in providing for the premium payable on redemption of debentures of the company.

(3) Subject to this, the provisions of this Act relating to the reduction of a company's share capital apply as if the share premium account were part of its paid up share capital.

(4) Sections 131 and 132 below give relief from the requirements of this section, and in those sections references to the issuing company are to the company issuing shares as above mentioned.

[116]

NOTES

Repealed by the Companies Act 2006, s 1295, Sch 16, as from a day to be appointed.

131 Merger relief

(1) With the exception made by [section 132(8)] (group reconstruction) this section applies where the issuing company has secured at least a 90 per cent equity holding in another company in pursuance of an arrangement providing for the allotment of equity shares in the issuing company on terms that the consideration for the shares allotted is to be provided—

(a) by the issue or transfer to the issuing company of equity shares in the other company, or

(b) by the cancellation of any such shares not held by the issuing company.

(2) If the equity shares in the issuing company allotted in pursuance of the arrangement in consideration for the acquisition or cancellation of equity shares in the other company are issued at a premium, section 130 does not apply to the premiums on those shares.

(3) Where the arrangement also provides for the allotment of any shares in the issuing company on terms that the consideration for those shares is to be provided by the issue or transfer to the issuing company of non-equity shares in the other company or by the cancellation of any such shares in that company not held by the issuing company, relief under subsection (2) extends to any shares in the issuing company allotted on those terms in pursuance of the arrangement.

(4) Subject to the next subsection, the issuing company is to be regarded for purposes of this section as having secured at least a 90 per cent equity holding in another company in pursuance of such an arrangement as is mentioned in subsection (1) if in consequence of an acquisition or cancellation of equity shares in that company (in pursuance of that arrangement) it holds equity shares in that company (whether all or any of those shares were acquired in pursuance of that arrangement, or not) of an aggregate nominal value equal to 90 per cent or more of the nominal value of that company's equity share capital [(excluding any shares in that company held as treasury shares)].

(5) Where the equity share capital of the other company is divided into different classes of shares, this section does not apply unless the requirements of subsection (1) are satisfied in relation to each of those classes of shares taken separately.

(6) Shares held by a company which is the issuing company's holding company or subsidiary, or a subsidiary of the issuing company's holding company, or by its or their nominees, are to be regarded for purposes of this section as held by the issuing company.

(7) In relation to a company and its shares and capital, the following definitions apply for purposes of this section—

(a) "equity shares" means shares comprised in the company's equity share capital; and

(b) "non-equity shares" means shares (of any class) not so comprised;

and "arrangement" means any agreement, scheme or arrangement (including an arrangement sanctioned under section 425 (company compromise with members and creditors) or [section 110 of the Insolvency Act] (liquidator accepting shares etc as consideration for sale of company property)).

(8) The relief allowed by this section does not apply if the issue of shares took place before 4th February 1981.

[117]

NOTES

Repealed by the Companies Act 2006, s 1295, Sch 16, as from a day to be appointed.

Sub-s (1): words in square brackets substituted by CA 1989, s 145, Sch 19, para 1, which also provides that this amendment is deemed always to have had effect.

Sub-s (4): words in square brackets added by the Companies (Acquisition of Own Shares) (Treasury Shares) Regulations 2003, SI 2003/1116, reg 4, Schedule, para 10, as from 1 December 2003.

Sub-s (7): words in square brackets substituted by the Insolvency Act 1986, s 439(1), Sch 13, Pt I, as from 29 December 1986; for transitional provisions see s 437 of, and Sch 11, Pt I to, that Act at **[3456]**, **[3481]**.

Insolvency Act, s 110: ie, the Insolvency Act 1986, s 110.

132 Relief in respect of group reconstructions

(1) This section applies where the issuing company—

(a) is a wholly-owned subsidiary of another company ("the holding company"), and

(b) allots shares to the holding company or to another wholly-owned subsidiary of the

holding company in consideration for the transfer to the issuing company of assets other than cash, being assets of any company ("the transferor company") which is a member of the group of companies which comprises the holding company and all its wholly-owned subsidiaries.

(2) Where the shares in the issuing company allotted in consideration for the transfer are issued at a premium, the issuing company is not required by section 130 to transfer any amount in excess of the minimum premium value to the share premium account.

(3) In subsection (2), "the minimum premium value" means the amount (if any) by which the base value of the consideration for the shares allotted exceeds the aggregate nominal value of those shares.

(4) For the purposes of subsection (3), the base value of the consideration for the shares allotted is the amount by which the base value of the assets transferred exceeds the base value of any liabilities of the transferor company assumed by the issuing company as part of the consideration for the assets transferred.

(5) For the purposes of subsection (4)—

(a) the base value of assets transferred is to be taken as—

(i) the cost of those assets to the transferor company, or

(ii) the amount at which those assets are stated in the transferor company's accounting records immediately before the transfer,

whichever is the less; and

(b) the base value of the liabilities assumed is to be taken as the amount at which they are stated in the transferor company's accounting records immediately before the transfer.

(6) The relief allowed by this section does not apply (subject to the next subsection) if the issue of shares took place before the date of the coming into force of the Companies (Share Premium Account) Regulations 1984 (which were made on 21st December 1984).

(7) To the extent that the relief allowed by this section would have been allowed by section 38 of the Companies Act 1981 as originally enacted (the text of which section is set out in Schedule 25 to this Act), the relief applies where the issue of shares took place before the date of the coming into force of those Regulations, but not if the issue took place before 4th February 1981.

(8) Section 131 does not apply in a case falling within this section.

[118]

NOTES

Repealed by the Companies Act 2006, s 1295, Sch 16, as from a day to be appointed.

Companies (Share Premium Account) Regulations 1984, SI 1984/2007: the 1984 Regulations were made under the Companies Act 1981, s 41 which was replaced by s 134 of this Act. The effect of the Regulations is incorporated into this section.

Companies Act 1981, s 38: repealed by the Companies Consolidation (Consequential Provisions) Act 1985, s 29, Sch 1 and replaced by this section and Sch 25 at **[690]**.

133 Provisions supplementing ss 131, 132

(1) An amount corresponding to one representing the premiums or part of the premiums on shares issued by a company which by virtue of sections 131 or 132 of this Act, or section 12 of the Consequential Provisions Act, is not included in the company's share premium account may also be disregarded in determining the amount at which any shares or other consideration provided for the shares issued is to be included in the company's balance sheet.

(2) References in this Chapter (however expressed) to—

(a) the acquisition by a company of shares in another company; and

(b) the issue or allotment of shares to, or the transfer of shares to or by, a company,

include (respectively) the acquisition of any of those shares by, and the issue or allotment or (as the case may be) the transfer of any of those shares to or by, nominees of that company; and the reference in section 132 to the company transferring the shares is to be construed accordingly.

(3) References in this Chapter to the transfer of shares in a company include the transfer of a right to be included in the company's register of members in respect of those shares.

(4) In sections 131 to 133 "company", except in references to the issuing company, includes any body corporate.

[119]

NOTES

Repealed by the Companies Act 2006, s 1295, Sch 16, as from a day to be appointed.
Consequential Provisions Act: ie, the Companies Consolidation (Consequential Provisions) Act 1985.

134 Provision for extending or restricting relief from s 130

(1) The Secretary of State may by regulations in a statutory instrument make such provision as appears to him to be appropriate—

- *(a) for relieving companies from the requirements of section 130 in relation to premiums other than cash premiums, or*
- *(b) for restricting or otherwise modifying any relief from those requirements provided by this Chapter.*

(2) Regulations under this section may make different provision for different cases or classes of case and may contain such incidental and supplementary provisions as the Secretary of State thinks fit.

(3) No such regulations shall be made unless a draft of the instrument containing them has been laid before Parliament and approved by a resolution of each House.

[120]

NOTES

Repealed by the Companies Act 2006, s 1295, Sch 16, as from a day to be appointed.

CHAPTER IV
REDUCTION OF SHARE CAPITAL

135 Special resolution for reduction of share capital

(1) Subject to confirmation by the court, a company limited by shares or a company limited by guarantee and having a share capital may, if so authorised by its articles, by special resolution reduce its share capital in any way.

(2) In particular, and without prejudice to subsection (1), the company may—

- *(a) extinguish or reduce the liability on any of its shares in respect of share capital not paid up; or*
- *(b) either with or without extinguishing or reducing liability on any of its shares, cancel any paid-up share capital which is lost or unrepresented by available assets; or*
- *(c) either with or without extinguishing or reducing liability on any of its shares, pay off any paid-up share capital which is in excess of the company's wants;*

and the company may, if and so far as is necessary, alter its memorandum by reducing the amount of its share capital and of its shares accordingly.

(3) A special resolution under this section is in this Act referred to as "a resolution for reducing share capital".

[121]

NOTES

Repealed by the Companies Act 2006, s 1295, Sch 16, as from a day to be appointed.

136 Application to court for order of confirmation

(1) Where a company has passed a resolution for reducing share capital, it may apply to the court for an order confirming the reduction.

(2) If the proposed reduction of share capital involves either—

- *(a) diminution of liability in respect of unpaid share capital; or*
- *(b) the payment to a shareholder of any paid-up share capital,*

and in any other case if the court so directs, the next three subsections have effect, but subject throughout to subsection (6).

(3) Every creditor of the company who at the date fixed by the court is entitled to any debt or claim which, if that date were the commencement of the winding up of the company, would be admissible in proof against the company is entitled to object to the reduction of capital.

(4) The court shall settle a list of creditors entitled to object, and for that purpose—

(a) shall ascertain, as far as possible without requiring an application from any creditor, the names of those creditors and the nature and amount of their debts or claims; and

(b) may publish notices fixing a day or days within which creditors not entered on the list are to claim to be so entered or are to be excluded from the right of objecting to the reduction of capital.

(5) If a creditor entered on the list whose debt or claim is not discharged or has not determined does not consent to the reduction, the court may, if it thinks fit, dispense with the consent of that creditor, on the company securing payment of his debt or claim by appropriating (as the court may direct) the following amount—

(a) if the company admits the full amount of the debt or claim or, though not admitting it, is willing to provide for it, then the full amount of the debt or claim;

(b) if the company does not admit, and is not willing to provide for, the full amount of the debt or claim, or if the amount is contingent or not ascertained, then an amount fixed by the court after the like enquiry and adjudication as if the company were being wound up by the court.

(6) If a proposed reduction of share capital involves either the diminution of any liability in respect of unpaid share capital or the payment to any shareholder of any paid-up share capital, the court may, if having regard to any special circumstances of the case it thinks proper to do so, direct that subsections (3) to (5) of this section shall not apply as regards any class or any classes of creditors.

[122]

NOTES

Repealed by the Companies Act 2006, s 1295, Sch 16, as from a day to be appointed.

137 Court order confirming reduction

(1) The court, if satisfied with respect to every creditor of the company who under section 136 is entitled to object to the reduction of capital that either—

(a) his consent to the reduction has been obtained; or

(b) his debt or claim has been discharged or has determined, or has been secured,

may make an order confirming the reduction on such terms and conditions as it thinks fit.

(2) Where the court so orders, it may also—

(a) if for any special reason it thinks proper to do so, make an order directing that the company shall, during such period (commencing on or at any time after the date of the order) as is specified in the order, add to its name as its last words the words "and reduced"; and

(b) make an order requiring the company to publish (as the court directs) the reasons for reduction of capital or such other information in regard to it as the court thinks expedient with a view to giving proper information to the public and (if the court thinks fit) the causes which led to the reduction.

(3) Where a company is ordered to add to its name the words "and reduced", those words are, until the expiration of the period specified in the order, deemed to be part of the company's name.

[123]

NOTES

Repealed by the Companies Act 2006, s 1295, Sch 16, as from a day to be appointed.

138 Registration of order and minute of reduction

(1) The registrar of companies, on production to him of an order of the court confirming the reduction of a company's share capital, and the delivery to him of a copy of the order and of a minute (approved by the court) showing, with respect to the company's share capital as altered by the order—

(a) the amount of the share capital;
(b) the number of shares into which it is to be divided, and the amount of each share; and
(c) the amount (if any) at the date of the registration deemed to be paid up on each share,

shall register the order and minute (but subject to section 139).

(2) On the registration of the order and minute, and not before, the resolution for reducing share capital as confirmed by the order so registered takes effect.

(3) Notice of the registration shall be published in such manner as the court may direct.

(4) The registrar shall certify the registration of the order and minute; and the certificate—
(a) may be either signed by the registrar, or authenticated by his official seal;
(b) is conclusive evidence that all the requirements of this Act with respect to the reduction of share capital have been complied with, and that the company's share capital is as stated in the minute.

(5) The minute when registered is deemed to be substituted for the corresponding part of the company's memorandum, and is valid and alterable as if it had been originally contained therein.

(6) The substitution of such a minute for part of the company's memorandum is deemed an alteration of the memorandum for purposes of section 20.

[124]

NOTES
Repealed by the Companies Act 2006, s 1295, Sch 16, as from a day to be appointed.

139 Public company reducing capital below authorised minimum

(1) This section applies where the court makes an order confirming a reduction of a public company's capital which has the effect of bringing the nominal value of its allotted share capital below the authorised minimum.

(2) The registrar of companies shall not register the order under section 138 unless the court otherwise directs, or the company is first re-registered as a private company.

(3) The court may authorise the company to be so re-registered without its having passed the special resolution required by section 53; and where that authority is given, the court shall specify in the order the alterations in the company's memorandum and articles to be made in connection with that re-registration.

(4) The company may then be re-registered as a private company, if an application in the prescribed form and signed by a director or secretary of the company is delivered to the registrar, together with a printed copy of the memorandum and articles as altered by the court's order.

(5) On receipt of such an application, the registrar shall retain it and the other documents delivered with it and issue the company with a certificate of incorporation appropriate to a company that is not a public company; and—
(a) the company by virtue of the issue of the certificate becomes a private company, and the alterations in the memorandum and articles set out in the court's order take effect; and
(b) the certificate is conclusive evidence that the requirements of this section in respect of re-registration and of matters precedent and incidental thereto have been complied with, and that the company is a private company.

[125]

NOTES
Repealed by the Companies Act 2006, s 1295, Sch 16, as from a day to be appointed.
Application in the prescribed form: see Appendix 4 (Forms table) at **[A4]**.

140 Liability of members on reduced shares

(1) Where a company's share capital is reduced, a member of the company (past or present) is not liable in respect of any share to any call or contribution exceeding in amount

the difference (if any) between the amount of the share as fixed by the minute and the amount paid on the share or the reduced amount (if any), which is deemed to have been paid on it, as the case may be.

(2) But the following two subsections apply if—

(a) a creditor, entitled in respect of a debt or claim to object to the reduction of share capital, by reason of his ignorance of the proceedings for reduction of share capital, or of their nature and effect with respect to his claim, is not entered on the list of creditors; and

(b) after the reduction of capital, the company is unable (within the meaning of [section 123 of the Insolvency Act]) to pay the amount of his debt or claim.

(3) Every person who was a member of the company at the date of the registration of the order for reduction and minute is then liable to contribute for the payment of the debt or claim in question an amount not exceeding that which he would have been liable to contribute if the company had commenced to be wound up on the day before that date.

(4) If the company is wound up, the court, on the application of the creditor in question and proof of ignorance referred to in subsection (2)(a), may (if it thinks fit) settle accordingly a list of persons so liable to contribute, and make and enforce calls and orders on the contributories settled on the list, as if they were ordinary contributories in a winding up.

(5) Nothing in this section affects the rights of the contributories among themselves.

[126]

NOTES

Repealed by the Companies Act 2006, s 1295, Sch 16, as from a day to be appointed.

Sub-s (2): words in square brackets substituted by the Insolvency Act 1986, s 439(1), Sch 13, Pt I, as from 29 December 1986; for transitional provisions see s 437 of, and Sch 11, Pt I to, that Act at **[3456]**, **[3481]**.

Insolvency Act, s 123: ie, the Insolvency Act 1986, s 123.

141 Penalty for concealing name of creditor, etc

If an officer of the company—

(a) wilfully conceals the name of a creditor entitled to object to the reduction of capital; or

(b) wilfully misrepresents the nature or amount of the debt or claim of any creditor; or

(c) aids, abets or is privy to any such concealment or misrepresentation as is mentioned above,

he is guilty of an offence and liable to a fine.

[127]

NOTES

Repealed by the Companies Act 2006, s 1295, Sch 16, as from a day to be appointed.

CHAPTER V
MAINTENANCE OF CAPITAL

142 Duty of directors on serious loss of capital

(1) Where the net assets of a public company are half or less of its called-up share capital, the directors shall, not later than 28 days from the earliest day on which that fact is known to a director of the company, duly convene an extraordinary general meeting of the company for a date not later than 56 days from that day for the purpose of considering whether any, and if so what, steps should be taken to deal with the situation.

(2) If there is a failure to convene an extraordinary general meeting as required by subsection (1), each of the directors of the company who—

(a) knowingly and wilfully authorises or permits the failure, or

(b) after the expiry of the period during which that meeting should have been convened, knowingly and wilfully authorises or permits the failure to continue,

is liable to a fine.

(3) Nothing in this section authorises the consideration, at a meeting convened in pursuance of subsection (1), of any matter which could not have been considered at that meeting apart from this section.

[128]

NOTES

Repealed by the Companies Act 2006, s 1295, Sch 16, as from a day to be appointed.

143 General rule against company acquiring own shares

(1) Subject to the following provisions, a company limited by shares or limited by guarantee and having a share capital shall not acquire its own shares, whether by purchase, subscription or otherwise.

(2) If a company purports to act in contravention of this section, the company is liable to a fine, and every officer of the company who is in default is liable to imprisonment or a fine, or both; and[, subject to subsection (2A),] the purported acquisition is void.

[(2A) Where a company purchases qualifying shares out of distributable profits under section 162, any contravention by the company of any provision of section 162B(1) or (2) shall not render the acquisition void under subsection (2) above.]

(3) A company limited by shares may acquire any of its own fully paid shares otherwise than for valuable consideration; and subsection (1) does not apply in relation to—

- *(a) the redemption or purchase of shares in accordance with Chapter VII of this Part,*
- *(b) the acquisition of shares in a reduction of capital duly made,*
- *(c) the purchase of shares in pursuance of an order of the court under section 5 (alteration of objects), section 54 (litigated objection to resolution for company to be re-registered as private) or Part XVII (relief to members unfairly prejudiced), or*
- *(d) the forfeiture of shares, or the acceptance of shares surrendered in lieu, in pursuance of the articles, for failure to pay any sum payable in respect of the shares.*

[129]

NOTES

Repealed by the Companies Act 2006, s 1295, Sch 16, as from a day to be appointed.

Sub-s (2): words in square brackets inserted by the Companies (Acquisition of Own Shares) (Treasury Shares) Regulations 2003, SI 2003/1116, reg 4, Schedule, para 11(a), as from 1 December 2003.

Sub-s (2A): inserted by SI 2003/1116, reg 4, Schedule, para 11(b), as from 1 December 2003.

144 Acquisition of shares by company's nominee

(1) Subject to section 145, where shares are issued to a nominee of a company mentioned in section 143(1), or are acquired by a nominee of such a company from a third person as partly paid up, then, for all purposes—

- *(a) the shares are to be treated as held by the nominee on his own account; and*
- *(b) the company is to be regarded as having no beneficial interest in them.*

(2) Subject to that section, if a person is called on to pay any amount for the purpose of paying up, or paying any premium on, any shares in such a company which were issued to him, or which he otherwise acquired, as the company's nominee and he fails to pay that amount within 21 days from being called on to do so, then—

- *(a) if the shares were issued to him as subscriber to the memorandum by virtue of an undertaking of his in the memorandum, the other subscribers to the memorandum, or*
- *(b) if the shares were otherwise issued to or acquired by him, the directors of the company at the time of the issue or acquisition,*

are jointly and severally liable with him to pay that amount.

(3) If in proceedings for the recovery of any such amount from any such subscriber or director under this section it appears to the court—

- *(a) that he is or may be liable to pay that amount, but*
- *(b) that he has acted honestly and reasonably and, having regard to all the circumstances of the case, he ought fairly to be excused from liability,*

the court may relieve him, either wholly or partly, from his liability on such terms as the court thinks fit.

(4) Where any such subscriber or director has reason to apprehend that a claim will or might be made for the recovery of any such amount from him, he may apply to the court for relief; and the court has the same power to relieve him as it would have had in proceedings for the recovery of that amount.

[130]

NOTES

Repealed by the Companies Act 2006, s 1295, Sch 16, as from a day to be appointed.

145 Exceptions from s 144

(1) Section 144(1) does not apply to shares acquired otherwise than by subscription by a nominee of a public company, where a person acquires shares in the company with financial assistance given to him directly or indirectly by the company for the purpose of or in connection with the acquisition, and the company has a beneficial interest in the shares.

(2) Section 144(1) and (2) do not apply—

(a) to shares acquired by a nominee of a company when the company has no beneficial interest in those shares, or

(b) to shares issued in consequence of an application made before 22nd December 1980, or transferred in pursuance of an agreement to acquire them made before that date.

(3) Schedule 2 to this Act has effect for the interpretation of references in this section to a company having, or not having, a beneficial interest in shares.

[131]

NOTES

Repealed by the Companies Act 2006, s 1295, Sch 16, as from a day to be appointed.

146 Treatment of shares held by or for public company

(1) Except as provided by section 148, the following applies to a public company—

(a) where shares in the company are forfeited, or surrendered to the company in lieu, in pursuance of the articles, for failure to pay any sum payable in respect of the shares;

[(aa) where shares in the company are surrendered to the company in pursuance of section 102C(1)(b) of the Building Societies Act 1986;]

(b) where shares in the company are acquired by it (otherwise than by any of the methods mentioned in section 143(3)(a) to (d)) and the company has a beneficial interest in the shares;

(c) where the nominee of the company acquires shares in the company from a third person without financial assistance being given directly or indirectly by the company and the company has a beneficial interest in the shares; or

(d) where a person acquires shares in the company with financial assistance given to him directly or indirectly by the company for the purpose of or in connection with the acquisition, and the company has a beneficial interest in the shares.

Schedule 2 to this Act has effect for the interpretation of references in this subsection to the company having a beneficial interest in shares.

(2) Unless the shares or any interest of the company in them are previously disposed of, the company must, not later than the end of the relevant period from their forfeiture or surrender or, in a case within subsection (1)(b), (c) or (d), their acquisition—

(a) cancel them and diminish the amount of the share capital by the nominal value of the shares cancelled, and

(b) where the effect of cancelling the shares will be that the nominal value of the company's allotted share capital is brought below the authorised minimum, apply for re-registration as a private company, stating the effect of the cancellation.

(3) For this purpose "the relevant period" is—

(a) 3 years in the case of shares forfeited or surrendered to the company in lieu of forfeiture, or acquired as mentioned in subsection (1)(b) or (c);

(*b*) *one year in the case of shares acquired as mentioned in subsection (1)(d).*

(*4*) *The company and, in a case within subsection (1)(c) or (d), the company's nominee or (as the case may be) the other shareholder must not exercise any voting rights in respect of the shares; and any purported exercise of those rights is void.*

[132]

NOTES

Repealed by the Companies Act 2006, s 1295, Sch 16, as from a day to be appointed.

Sub-s (1): para (aa) inserted by the Building Societies Act 1986, s 102C(5) (as inserted by the Building Societies (Distributions) Act 1997, s 1(1)), as from 22 January 1997.

References to a public company in this section and ss 147–149 do not include an old public company; and references in to a private company are to be read accordingly: see the Companies Consolidation (Consequential Provisions) Act 1985, s 6 at **[707]**.

147 Matters arising out of compliance with s 146(2)

(*1*) *The directors may take such steps as are requisite to enable the company to carry out its obligations under section 146(2) without complying with sections 135 and 136 (resolution to reduce share capital; application to court for approval).*

(*2*) *The steps taken may include the passing of a resolution to alter the company's memorandum so that it no longer states that the company is to be a public company; and the resolution may make such other alterations in the memorandum as are requisite in the circumstances.*

Such a resolution is subject to section 380 (copy to be forwarded to registrar within 15 days).

(*3*) *The application for re-registration required by section 146(2)(b) must be in the prescribed form and be signed by a director or secretary of the company, and must be delivered to the registrar of companies together with a printed copy of the memorandum and articles of the company as altered by the resolution.*

(*4*) *If the registrar is satisfied that the company may be re-registered under section 146, he shall retain the application and other documents delivered with it and issue the company with a certificate of incorporation appropriate to a company that is not a public company; and—*

(*a*) *the company by virtue of the issue of the certificate becomes a private company, and the alterations in the memorandum and articles set out in the resolution take effect accordingly, and*

(*b*) *the certificate is conclusive evidence that the requirements of sections 146 to 148 in respect of re-registration and of matters precedent and incidental to it have been complied with, and that the company is a private company.*

[133]

NOTES

Repealed by the Companies Act 2006, s 1295, Sch 16, as from a day to be appointed.

Sub-s (2): for the second sentence there is substituted "Chapter 3 of Part 3 of the Companies Act 2006 (resolutions affecting a company's constitution) applies to such a resolution" by the draft Companies Act 2006 (Commencement No 3, Consequential Amendments, Transitional Provisions and Savings) Order 2007, art 10(1), Sch 4, Pt 1, para 1(6), as from 1 October 2007 (see **[A12]**).

References to a public company, etc: see the note to s 146 at **[132]**.

Application … in the prescribed form: see Appendix 4 (Forms table) at **[A4]**.

148 Further provisions supplementing ss 146, 147

(*1*) *Where, after shares in a private company—*

(*a*) *are forfeited in pursuance of the company's articles or are surrendered to the company in lieu of forfeiture, or*

(*b*) *are acquired by the company (otherwise than by such surrender or forfeiture, and otherwise than by any of the methods mentioned in section 143(3)), the company having a beneficial interest in the shares, or*

(*c*) *are acquired by the nominee of a company in the circumstances mentioned in section 146(1)(c), or*

(*d*) *are acquired by any person in the circumstances mentioned in section 146(1)(d), the company is re-registered as a public company, sections 146 and 147, and also section 149, apply to the company as if it had been a public company at the time of the forfeiture, surrender or acquisition, but with the modification required by the following subsection.*

(2) *That modification is to treat any reference to the relevant period from the forfeiture, surrender or acquisition as referring to the relevant period from the re-registration of the company as a public company.*

(3) *Schedule 2 to this Act has effect for the interpretation of the reference in subsection (1)(b) to the company having a beneficial interest in shares.*

(4) *Where a public company or a nominee of a public company acquires shares in the company or an interest in such shares, and those shares are (or that interest is) shown in a balance sheet of the company as an asset, an amount equal to the value of the shares or (as the case may be) the value to the company of its interest in them shall be transferred out of profits available for dividend to a reserve fund and are not then available for distribution.*

[134]

NOTES

Repealed by the Companies Act 2006, s 1295, Sch 16, as from a day to be appointed.
References to a public company, etc: see the note to s 146 at **[132]**.

149 Sanctions for non-compliance

(1) *If a public company required by section 146(2) to apply to be re-registered as a private company fails to do so before the end of the relevant period referred to in that subsection, section 81 (restriction on public offers) applies to it as if it were a private company such as is mentioned in that section; but, subject to this, the company continues to be treated for the purpose of this Act as a public company until it is so re-registered.*

(2) *If a company when required to do so by section 146(2) (including that subsection as applied by section 148(1)) fails to cancel any shares in accordance with paragraph (a) of that subsection or to make an application for re-registration in accordance with paragraph (b) of it, the company and every officer of it who is in default is liable to a fine and, for continued contravention, to a daily default fine.*

[135]

NOTES

Repealed by the Companies Act 2006, s 1295, Sch 16, as from a day to be appointed.
References to a public company, etc: see the note to s 146 at **[132]**.

150 Charges of public companies on own shares

(1) *A lien or other charge of a public company on its own shares (whether taken expressly or otherwise), except a charge permitted by any of the following subsections, is void.*

This is subject to section 6 of the Consequential Provisions Act (saving for charges of old public companies on their own shares).

(2) *In the case of any description of company, a charge on its own shares is permitted if the shares are not fully paid and the charge is for any amount payable in respect of the shares.*

(3) *In the case of a company whose ordinary business—*

(a) *includes the lending of money, or*

(b) *consists of the provision of credit or the bailment (in Scotland, hiring) of goods under a hire purchase agreement, or both,*

a charge of the company on its own shares is permitted (whether the shares are fully paid or not) if it arises in connection with a transaction entered into by the company in the ordinary course of its business.

(4) *In the case of a company which is re-registered or is registered under section 680 as a public company, a charge on its own shares is permitted if the charge was in existence immediately before the company's application for re-registration or (as the case may be) registration.*

This subsection does not apply in the case of such a company as is referred to in section 6(3) of the Consequential Provisions Act (old public company remaining such after 22nd March 1982, not having applied to be re-registered as public company).

[136]

NOTES

Repealed by the Companies Act 2006, s 1295, Sch 16, as from a day to be appointed.
Consequential Provisions Act: ie, the Companies Consolidation (Consequential Provisions) Act 1985.

CHAPTER VI
FINANCIAL ASSISTANCE BY A COMPANY FOR ACQUISITION OF ITS OWN SHARES

Provisions applying to both public and private companies

151 Financial assistance generally prohibited

(*1*) *Subject to the following provisions of this Chapter, where a person is acquiring or is proposing to acquire shares in a company, it is not lawful for the company or any of its subsidiaries to give financial assistance directly or indirectly for the purpose of that acquisition before or at the same time as the acquisition takes place.*

(2) *Subject to those provisions, where a person has acquired shares in a company and any liability has been incurred (by that or any other person), for the purpose of that acquisition, it is not lawful for the company or any of its subsidiaries to give financial assistance directly or indirectly for the purpose of reducing or discharging the liability so incurred.*

(3) *If a company acts in contravention of this section, it is liable to a fine, and every officer of it who is in default is liable to imprisonment or a fine, or both.*

[137]

NOTES

Repealed by the Companies Act 2006, s 1295, Sch 16, as from a day to be appointed.

152 Definitions for this Chapter

(*1*) *In this Chapter—*

(*a*) *"financial assistance" means—*

(*i*) *financial assistance given by way of gift,*

(*ii*) *financial assistance given by way of guarantee, security or indemnity, other than an indemnity in respect of the indemnifier's own neglect or default, or by way of release or waiver,*

(*iii*) *financial assistance given by way of a loan or any other agreement under which any of the obligations of the person giving the assistance are to be fulfilled at a time when in accordance with the agreement any obligation of another party to the agreement remains unfulfilled, or by way of the novation of, or the assignment of rights arising under, a loan or such other agreement, or*

(*iv*) *any other financial assistance given by a company the net assets of which are thereby reduced to a material extent or which has no net assets;*

(*b*) *"distributable profits", in relation to the giving of any financial assistance—*

(*i*) *means those profits out of which the company could lawfully make a distribution equal in value to that assistance, and*

(*ii*) *includes, in a case where the financial assistance is or includes a non-cash asset, any profit which, if the company were to make a distribution of that asset, would under section 276 (distributions in kind) be available for that purpose, and*

(*c*) *"distribution" has the meaning given by section 263(2).*

(2) *In subsection (1)(a)(iv), "net assets" means the aggregate of the company's assets, less the aggregate of its liabilities ("liabilities" to include any [provision for liabilities] within paragraph 89 of Schedule 4 [that is made in Companies Act individual accounts and any provision that is made in IAS individual accounts]).*

(*3*) *In this Chapter—*

(*a*) *a reference to a person incurring a liability includes his changing his financial position by making an agreement or arrangement (whether enforceable or unenforceable, and whether made on his own account or with any other person) or by any other means, and*

(*b*) *a reference to a company giving financial assistance for the purpose of reducing or discharging a liability incurred by a person for the purpose of the acquisition of shares includes its giving such assistance for the purpose of wholly or partly restoring his financial position to what it was before the acquisition took place.*

[138]

NOTES

Repealed by the Companies Act 2006, s 1295, Sch 16, as from a day to be appointed.

Sub-s (2): words in first pair of square brackets substituted, and words in second pair of square brackets inserted, by the Companies Act 1985 (International Accounting Standards and Other Accounting Amendments) Regulations 2004, SI 2004/2947, regs 3, 15, Sch 1, paras 1, 2, Sch 7, Pt 1, paras 1, 2, as from 12 November 2004, in relation to companies' financial years which begin on or after 1 January 2005.

153 Transactions not prohibited by s 151

(*1*) *Section 151*(*1*) *does not prohibit a company from giving financial assistance for the purpose of an acquisition of shares in it or its holding company if—*

(*a*) *the company's principal purpose in giving that assistance is not to give it for the purpose of any such acquisition, or the giving of the assistance for that purpose is but an incidental part of some larger purpose of the company, and*

(*b*) *the assistance is given in good faith in the interests of the company.*

(2) *Section 151*(2) *does not prohibit a company from giving financial assistance if—*

(*a*) *the company's principal purpose in giving the assistance is not to reduce or discharge any liability incurred by a person for the purpose of the acquisition of shares in the company or its holding company, or the reduction or discharge of any such liability is but an incidental part of some larger purpose of the company, and*

(*b*) *the assistance is given in good faith in the interests of the company.*

(*3*) *Section 151 does not prohibit—*

(*a*) *a distribution of a company's assets by way of dividend lawfully made or a distribution made in the course of the company's winding up,*

(*b*) *the allotment of bonus shares,*

(*c*) *a reduction of capital confirmed by order of the court under section 137,*

(*d*) *a redemption or purchase of shares made in accordance with Chapter VII of this Part,*

(*e*) *anything done in pursuance of an order of the court under section 425 (compromises and arrangements with creditors and members),*

(*f*) *anything done under an arrangement made in pursuance of [section 110 of the Insolvency Act] (acceptance of shares by liquidator in winding up as consideration for sale of property), or*

(*g*) *anything done under an arrangement made between a company and its creditors which is binding on the creditors by virtue of [Part I of the Insolvency Act].*

(*4*) *Section 151 does not prohibit—*

(*a*) *where the lending of money is part of the ordinary business of the company, the lending of money by the company in the ordinary course of its business,*

[(*b*) *the provision by a company, in good faith in the interests of the company, of financial assistance for the purposes of an employees' share scheme,*]

[(*bb*) *without prejudice to paragraph* (*b*), *the provision of financial assistance by a company or any of its subsidiaries for the purposes of or in connection with anything done by the company (or [a company in the same group]) for the purpose of enabling or facilitating transactions in shares in the first-mentioned company between, and involving the acquisition of beneficial ownership of those shares by, any of the following persons—*

(*i*) *the bona fide employees or former employees of that company or of another company in the same group; or*

(ii) *the [spouses, civil partners, surviving spouses, surviving civil partners], children or step-children under the age of eighteen of any such employees or former employees,]*

(c) *the making by a company of loans to persons (other than directors) employed in good faith by the company with a view to enabling those persons to acquire fully paid shares in the company or its holding company to be held by them by way of beneficial ownership.*

[(5) For the purposes of subsection (4)(bb) a company is in the same group as another company if it is a holding company or subsidiary of that company, or a subsidiary of a holding company of that company.]

[139]

NOTES

Repealed by the Companies Act 2006, s 1295, Sch 16, as from a day to be appointed.

Sub-s (3): words in square brackets in paras (f), (g) substituted by the Insolvency Act 1986, s 439(1), Sch 13, Pt I, as from 29 December 1986; for transitional provisions see s 437 of, and Sch 11, Pt I to, that Act at **[3456]**, **[3481]**.

Sub-s (4): para (b) substituted by CA 1989, s 132, as from 1 April 1990; para (bb) inserted by FSA 1986, s 196, as from 1 December 1987; words in first pair of square brackets in para (bb) substituted by CA 1989, s 144(4), Sch 18, para 33, as from 1 November 1990; words in second pair of square brackets in para (bb) substituted by the Civil Partnership Act 2004 (International Immunities and Privileges, Companies and Adoption) Order 2005, SI 2005/3542, art 3(1), as from 23 December 2005.

Sub-s (5): added by FSA 1986, s 196, as from 1 December 1987; substituted by CA 1989, s 144(4), Sch 18, para 33, as from 1 November 1990.

Insolvency Act: ie, the Insolvency Act 1986.

Step-children: this includes relationships arising through civil partnerships; see the Civil Partnership Act 2004, ss 246, 247, Sch 21.

154 Special restriction for public companies

(1) In the case of a public company, section 153(4) authorises the giving of financial assistance only if the company has net assets which are not thereby reduced or, to the extent that those assets are thereby reduced, if the assistance is provided out of distributable profits.

(2) For this purpose the following definitions apply—

(a) *"net assets" means the amount by which the aggregate of the company's assets exceeds the aggregate of its liabilities (taking the amount of both assets and liabilities to be as stated in the company's accounting records immediately before the financial assistance is given);*

(b) *"liabilities" includes any amount retained as reasonably necessary for the purpose of providing for any liability [the nature of which is clearly defined and] which is either likely to be incurred, or certain to be incurred but uncertain as to amount or as to the date on which it will arise.*

[140]

NOTES

Repealed by the Companies Act 2006, s 1295, Sch 16, as from a day to be appointed.

Sub-s (2): words in square brackets substituted by the Companies Act 1985 (International Accounting Standards and Other Accounting Amendments) Regulations 2004, SI 2004/2947, reg 15, Sch 7, Pt 1, paras 1, 3, as from 12 November 2004, in relation to companies' financial years which begin on or after 1 January 2005.

Private companies

155 Relaxation of s 151 for private companies

(1) Section 151 does not prohibit a private company from giving financial assistance in a case where the acquisition of shares in question is or was an acquisition of shares in the company or, if it is a subsidiary of another private company, in that other company if the following provisions of this section, and sections 156 to 158, are complied with as respects the giving of that assistance.

(2) The financial assistance may only be given if the company has net assets which are not thereby reduced or, to the extent that they are reduced, if the assistance is provided out of distributable profits.

Section 154(2) applies for the interpretation of this subsection.

(3) This section does not permit financial assistance to be given by a subsidiary, in a case where the acquisition of shares in question is or was an acquisition of shares in its holding company, if it is also a subsidiary of a public company which is itself a subsidiary of that holding company.

(4) Unless the company proposing to give the financial assistance is a wholly-owned subsidiary, the giving of assistance under this section must be approved by special resolution of the company in general meeting.

(5) Where the financial assistance is to be given by the company in a case where the acquisition of shares in question is or was an acquisition of shares in its holding company, that holding company and any other company which is both the company's holding company and a subsidiary of that other holding company (except, in any case, a company which is a wholly-owned subsidiary) shall also approve by special resolution in general meeting the giving of the financial assistance.

(6) [Subject to subsection (6A), the directors of the company] proposing to give the financial assistance and, where the shares acquired or to be acquired are shares in its holding company, the directors of that company and of any other company which is both the company's holding company and a subsidiary of that other holding company shall before the financial assistance is given make a statutory declaration in the prescribed form complying with the section next following.

[(6A) In place of the statutory declaration referred to in subsection (6), there may be delivered to the registrar of companies under section 156(5) a statement made by the persons mentioned in subsection (6) above complying with the section next following.]

[141]

NOTES

Repealed by the Companies Act 2006, s 1295, Sch 16, as from a day to be appointed.

Sub-s (6): words in square brackets substituted by the Companies Act 1985 (Electronic Communications) Order 2000, SI 2000/3373, art 10(1), (2), as from 22 December 2000.

Sub-s (6A): added by SI 2000/3373, art 10(1), (3), as from 22 December 2000.

Statutory declaration in the prescribed form: see Appendix 4 (Forms table) at **[A4]**.

156 Statutory declaration under s 155

(1) A statutory declaration made by a company's directors under section 155(6) shall contain such particulars of the financial assistance to be given, and of the business of the company of which they are directors, as may be prescribed, and shall identify the person to whom the assistance is to be given.

[(1A) A statement made by a company's directors under section 155(6A) shall state—

- *(a) the names and addresses of all the directors of the company,*
- *(b) whether the business of the company is that of a banking company or insurance company or some other business,*
- *(c) that the company or (as the case may be) a company (naming such company) of which it is the holding company is proposing to give financial assistance in connection with the acquisition of shares in the company or (as the case may be) its holding company (naming that holding company),*
- *(d) whether the assistance is for the purpose of that acquisition or for reducing or discharging a liability incurred for the purpose of that acquisition,*
- *(e) the name and address of the person to whom the assistance is to be given (and in the case of a company its registered office),*
- *(f) the name of the person who has acquired or will acquire the shares and the number and class of the shares acquired or to be acquired,*
- *(g) the principal terms on which the assistance will be given,*
- *(h) the form the financial assistance will take (stating the amount of cash or value of any asset to be transferred to the person assisted), and*
- *(i) the date on which the assistance is to be given.]*

(2) The declaration [under section 155(6) or (as the case may be) statement under section 155(6A)] shall state that the directors have formed the opinion, as regards the company's initial situation immediately following the date on which the assistance is proposed to be given, that there will be no ground on which it could then be found to be unable to pay its debts; and either—

(*a*) *if it is intended to commence the winding up of the company within 12 months of that date, that the company will be able to pay its debts in full within 12 months of the commencement of the winding up, or*

(*b*) *in any other case, that the company will be able to pay its debts as they fall due during the year immediately following that date.*

(*3*) *In forming their opinion for purposes of subsection* (2), *the directors shall take into account the same liabilities (including contingent and prospective liabilities) as would be relevant under [section 122 of the Insolvency Act] (winding up by the court) to the question whether the company is unable to pay its debts.*

(*4*) *The directors' statutory declaration [or statement] shall have annexed to it a report addressed to them by their company's auditors stating that—*

(*a*) *they have enquired into the state of affairs of the company, and*

(*b*) *they are not aware of anything to indicate that the opinion expressed by the directors in the declaration [or statement] as to any of the matters mentioned in subsection* (2) *of this section is unreasonable in all the circumstances.*

(*5*) *The statutory declaration [or statement] and auditors' report shall be delivered to the registrar of companies—*

(*a*) *together with a copy of any special resolution passed by the company under section 155 and delivered to the registrar in compliance with section 380, or*

(*b*) *where no such resolution is required to be passed, within 15 days after the making of the declaration [or statement].*

(*6*) *If a company fails to comply with subsection* (5), *the company and every officer of it who is in default is liable to a fine and, for continued contravention, to a daily default fine.*

(*7*) *A director of a company who makes a statutory declaration [or statement] under section 155 without having reasonable grounds for the opinion expressed in it is liable to imprisonment or a fine, or both.*

[142]

NOTES

Repealed by the Companies Act 2006, s 1295, Sch 16, as from a day to be appointed.

Sub-s (1A): inserted by the Companies Act 1985 (Electronic Communications) Order 2000, SI 2000/3373, art 11, as from 22 December 2000.

Sub-ss (2), (4), (7): words in square brackets inserted by SI 2000/3373, art 11, as from 22 December 2000.

Sub-s (3): words in square brackets substituted by the Insolvency Act 1986, s 439(1), Sch 13, Pt I, as from 29 December 1986; for transitional provisions see s 437 of, and Sch 11, Pt I to, that Act at **[3456]**, **[3481]**.

Sub-s (5): words in square brackets inserted by SI 2000/3373, art 11, as from 22 December 2000; for the words "section 380" there are substituted the words "section 30 of the Companies Act 2006" by the draft Companies Act 2006 (Commencement No 3, Consequential Amendments, Transitional Provisions and Savings) Order 2007, art 10(1), Sch 4, Pt 1, para 1(7), as from 1 October 2007 (see **[A12]**).

Insolvency Act, s 122: ie, the Insolvency Act 1986, s 122.

157 Special resolution under s 155

(*1*) *A special resolution required by section 155 to be passed by a company approving the giving of financial assistance must be passed on the date on which the directors of that company make the statutory declaration [or statement] required by that section in connection with the giving of that assistance, or within the week immediately following that date.*

(*2*) *Where such a resolution has been passed, an application may be made to the court for the cancellation of the resolution—*

(*a*) *by the holders of not less in the aggregate than 10 per cent in nominal value of the company's issued share capital or any class of it, or*

(*b*) *if the company is not limited by shares, by not less than 10 per cent of the company's members;*

but the application shall not be made by a person who has consented to or voted in favour of the resolution.

(*3*) *Subsections* (3) *to* (10) *of section 54 (litigation to cancel resolution under section 53) apply to applications under this section as to applications under section 54.*

(*4*) *A special resolution passed by a company is not effective for purposes of section 155—*

(*a*) *unless the declaration [or statement] made in compliance with subsection (6) of that section by the directors of the company, together with the auditors' report annexed to it, is available for inspection by members of the company at the meeting at which the resolution is passed,*

(*b*) *if it is cancelled by the court on an application under this section.*

[143]

NOTES

Repealed by the Companies Act 2006, s 1295, Sch 16, as from a day to be appointed.

Sub-ss (1), (4): words in square brackets inserted by the Companies Act 1985 (Electronic Communications) Order 2000, SI 2000/3373, art 31(2), as from 22 December 2000. Note, art 31(2) purports to amend s 157(2), (4), (5) and (7) but it is believed that the amendment should be as noted above.

Prescribed form: see Appendix 4 (Forms table) at **[A4]**.

158 Time for giving financial assistance under s 155

(*1*) *This section applies as to the time before and after which financial assistance may not be given by a company in pursuance of section 155.*

(*2*) *Where a special resolution is required by that section to be passed approving the giving of the assistance, the assistance shall not be given before the expiry of the period of 4 weeks beginning with—*

(*a*) *the date on which the special resolution is passed, or*

(*b*) *where more than one such resolution is passed, the date on which the last of them is passed,*

unless, as respects that resolution (or, if more than one, each of them), every member of the company which passed the resolution who is entitled to vote at general meetings of the company voted in favour of the resolution.

(*3*) *If application for the cancellation of any such resolution is made under section 157, the financial assistance shall not be given before the final determination of the application unless the court otherwise orders.*

(*4*) *The assistance shall not be given after the expiry of the period of 8 weeks beginning with—*

(*a*) *the date on which the directors of the company proposing to give the assistance made their statutory declaration [or statement] under section 155, or*

(*b*) *where that company is a subsidiary and both its directors and the directors of any of its holding companies made such a declaration [or statement], the date on which the earliest of the declarations [or statements] is made,*

unless the court, on an application under section 157, otherwise orders.

[144]

NOTES

Repealed by the Companies Act 2006, s 1295, Sch 16, as from a day to be appointed.

Sub-s (4): words in square brackets inserted by the Companies Act 1985 (Electronic Communications) Order 2000, SI 2000/3373, art 31(2), as from 22 December 2000.

CHAPTER VII
REDEEMABLE SHARES; PURCHASE BY A COMPANY OF ITS OWN SHARES

Redemption and purchase generally

159 Power to issue redeemable shares

(*1*) *Subject to the provisions of this Chapter, a company limited by shares or limited by guarantee and having a share capital may, if authorised to do so by its articles, issue shares which are to be redeemed or are liable to be redeemed at the option of the company or the shareholder.*

(*2*) *No redeemable shares may be issued at a time when there are no issued shares of the company which are not redeemable.*

(*3*) *Redeemable shares may not be redeemed unless they are fully paid; and the terms of redemption must provide for payment on redemption.*

[145]

PART I COMPANIES LEGISLATION

NOTES

Repealed by the Companies Act 2006, s 1295, Sch 16, as from a day to be appointed.

[159A Terms and manner of redemption

(1) Redeemable shares may not be issued unless the following conditions are satisfied as regards the terms and manner of redemption.

(2) The date on or by which, or dates between which, the shares are to be or may be redeemed must be specified in the company's articles or, if the articles so provide, fixed by the directors, and in the latter case the date or dates must be fixed before the shares are issued.

(3) Any other circumstances in which the shares are to be or may be redeemed must be specified in the company's articles.

(4) The amount payable on redemption must be specified in, or determined in accordance with, the company's articles, and in the latter case the articles must not provide for the amount to be determined by reference to any person's discretion or opinion.

(5) Any other terms and conditions of redemption shall be specified in the company's articles.

(6) Nothing in this section shall be construed as requiring a company to provide in its articles for any matter for which provision is made by this Act.]

[146]

NOTES

Commencement: to be appointed.
Inserted by CA 1989, s 133(1), (2), as from a day to be appointed.
Repealed by the Companies Act 2006, s 1295, Sch 16, as from a day to be appointed.

160 Financing etc of redemption

(1) Subject to the next subsection and to sections 171 (private companies redeeming or purchasing own shares out of capital) and 178(4) (terms of redemption or purchase enforceable in a winding up)—

- *(a) redeemable shares may only be redeemed out of distributable profits of the company or out of the proceeds of a fresh issue of shares made for the purposes of the redemption; and*
- *(b) any premium payable on redemption must be paid out of distributable profits of the company.*

(2) If the redeemable shares were issued at a premium, any premium payable on their redemption may be paid out of the proceeds of a fresh issue of shares made for the purposes of the redemption, up to an amount equal to—

- *(a) the aggregate of the premiums received by the company on the issue of the shares redeemed, or*
- *(b) the current amount of the company's share premium account (including any sum transferred to that account in respect of premiums on the new shares),*

whichever is the less; and in that case the amount of the company's share premium account shall be reduced by a sum corresponding (or by sums in the aggregate corresponding) to the amount of any payment made by virtue of this subsection out of the proceeds of the issue of the new shares.

(3) Subject to the following provisions of this Chapter, redemption of shares may be effected on such terms and in such manner as may be provided by the company's articles.

(4) Shares redeemed under this section shall be treated as cancelled on redemption, and the amount of the company's issued share capital shall be diminished by the nominal value of those shares accordingly; but the redemption of shares by a company is not to be taken as reducing the amount of the company's authorised share capital.

(5) Without prejudice to subsection (4), where a company is about to redeem shares, it has power to issue shares up to the nominal value of the shares to be redeemed as if those shares had never been issued.

[147]

NOTES

Repealed by the Companies Act 2006, s 1295, Sch 16, as from a day to be appointed.

Sub-s (3): repealed by CA 1989, ss 133(1), (3)(a), 212, Sch 24, as from a day to be appointed.

Sub-s (4): for the words "redeemed under this section" there are substituted the words "redeemed under this Chapter" by CA 1989, s 133(3)(1), (b), as from a day to be appointed.

161 (*Repealed by FA 1988, s 148, Sch 14, Pt XI, with effect from 22 March 1988.*)

162 Power of company to purchase own shares

(1) Subject to the following provisions of this Chapter, a company limited by shares or limited by guarantee and having a share capital may, if authorised to do so by its articles, purchase its own shares (including any redeemable shares).

[(2) Sections 159 and 160 apply to the purchase by a company under this section of its own shares as they apply to the redemption of redeemable shares.

This is subject to subsections (2A) and (2B).

(2A) The terms and manner of a purchase under this section need not be determined by the articles as required by section 160(3).

(2B) Where a company makes a purchase of qualifying shares out of distributable profits under this section, section 162A applies to the shares purchased; and accordingly section 160(4) does not apply to those shares.]

(3) A company may not under this section purchase its shares if as a result of the purchase there would no longer be any member of the company holding shares other than redeemable shares [or shares held as treasury shares].

[(4) For the purposes of this Chapter "qualifying shares" are shares which—

(a) are included in the official list in accordance with the provisions of Part 6 of the Financial Services and Markets Act 2000,

(b) are traded on the market known as the Alternative Investment Market established under the rules of London Stock Exchange plc,

(c) are officially listed in an EEA State, or

(d) are traded on a market established in an EEA State which is a regulated market for the purposes of Article 16 of Council Directive 93/22/EEC on investment services in the securities field

and in paragraph (a) "the official list" has the meaning given in section 103(1) of the Financial Services and Markets Act 2000.]

[148]

NOTES

Repealed by the Companies Act 2006, s 1295, Sch 16, as from a day to be appointed.

Sub-ss (2), (2A), (2B): substituted, for original sub-s (2), by the Companies (Acquisition of Own Shares) (Treasury Shares) Regulations 2003, SI 2003/1116, reg 2(1), (2), as from 1 December 2003.

Sub-s (3): words in square brackets added by SI 2003/1116, reg 2(1), (3), as from 1 December 2003.

Sub-s (4): added by SI 2003/1116, reg 2(1), (4), as from 1 December 2003; for the words "for the purposes of Article 16 of Council Directive 93/22/EEC on investment services in the securities field" in para (d) there are substituted the words "which appears on the list drawn up by that State pursuant to Article 47 of Directive 2004/39/EC of the European Parliament and of the Council of 21 April 2004 on markets in financial instruments," by the Financial Services and Markets Act 2000 (Markets in Financial Instruments) Regulations 2007, SI 2007/126, reg 3(6), Sch 6, Pt 1, para 7(1), (3), as from 1 November 2007 (for the full commencement details of SI 2007/126, see reg 1 of those Regulations at **[7596]**).

[162A Treasury shares

(1) Where qualifying shares are purchased by a company out of distributable profits in accordance with section 162, the company may—

(a) hold the shares (or any of them), or

(b) deal with any of them, at any time, in accordance with section 162D.

(2) Where shares are held under subsection (1)(a) then, for the purposes of section 352, the company must be entered in the register as the member holding those shares.

(3) In this Act, references to a company holding shares as treasury shares are references to the company holding shares which—

(*a*) *were (or are treated as having been) purchased by it in circumstances in which this section applies, and*
(*b*) *have been held by the company continuously since they were so purchased.]*

[148A]

NOTES

Inserted, together with ss 162B–162G, by the Companies (Acquisition of Own Shares) (Treasury Shares) Regulations 2003, SI 2003/1116, reg 3, as from 1 December 2003.

Repealed by the Companies Act 2006, s 1295, Sch 16, as from a day to be appointed.

[162B Treasury shares: maximum holdings

(1) Where a company has shares of only one class, the aggregate nominal value of shares held as treasury shares must not at any time exceed 10 per cent of the nominal value of the issued share capital of the company at that time.

(2) Where the share capital of a company is divided into shares of different classes, the aggregate nominal value of the shares of any class held as treasury shares must not at any time exceed 10 per cent of the nominal value of the issued share capital of the shares in that class at that time.

(3) Where subsection (1) or (2) is contravened by a company, the company must dispose of or cancel the excess shares, in accordance with section 162D, before the end of the period of 12 months beginning with the day on which that contravention occurs.

For this purpose "the excess shares" means such number of the shares, held by the company as treasury shares at the time in question, as resulted in the limit being exceeded.]

[148B]

NOTES

Inserted as noted to s 162A at **[148A]**.

Repealed by the Companies Act 2006, s 1295, Sch 16, as from a day to be appointed.

[162C Treasury shares: voting and other rights

(1) This section applies to shares which are held by a company as treasury shares ("the treasury shares").

(2) The company must not exercise any right in respect of the treasury shares, and any purported exercise of such a right is void.

(3) The rights to which subsection (2) applies include any right to attend or vote at meetings (including meetings under section 425).

(4) No dividend may be paid, and no other distribution (whether in cash or otherwise) of the company's assets (including any distribution of assets to members on a winding up) may be made, to the company in respect of the treasury shares.

(5) Nothing in this section is to be taken as preventing—
(*a*) *an allotment of shares as fully paid bonus shares in respect of the treasury shares, or*
(*b*) *the payment of any amount payable on the redemption of the treasury shares (if they are redeemable shares).*

(6) Any shares allotted as fully paid bonus shares in respect of the treasury shares shall be treated for the purposes of this Act as if they were purchased by the company at the time they were allotted, in circumstances in which section 162A(1) applied.]

[148C]

NOTES

Inserted as noted to s 162A at **[148A]**.

Repealed by the Companies Act 2006, s 1295, Sch 16, as from a day to be appointed.

[162D Treasury shares: disposal and cancellation

(1) Where shares are held as treasury shares, a company may at any time—
(*a*) *sell the shares (or any of them) for cash,*

(*b*) *transfer the shares* (*or any of them*) *for the purposes of or pursuant to an employees' share scheme, or*

(*c*) *cancel the shares* (*or any of them*).

(*2*) *For the purposes of subsection* (*1*)(*a*), *"cash", in relation to a sale of shares by a company, means—*

(*a*) *cash* (*including foreign currency*) *received by the company, or*

(*b*) *a cheque received by the company in good faith which the directors have no reason for suspecting will not be paid, or*

(*c*) *a release of a liability of the company for a liquidated sum, or*

(*d*) *an undertaking to pay cash to the company on or before a date not more than 90 days after the date on which the company agrees to sell the shares.*

(*3*) *But if the company receives a notice under [section 979 of the Companies Act 2006]* (*right of offeror to buy out minority shareholders*) *that a person desires to acquire any of the shares, the company must not, under subsection* (*1*), *sell or transfer the shares to which the notice relates except to that person.*

(*4*) *If under subsection* (*1*) *the company cancels shares held as treasury shares, the company must diminish the amount of the issued share capital by the nominal value of the shares cancelled; but the cancellation is not to be taken as reducing the amount of the company's authorised share capital.*

(*5*) *The directors may take such steps as are requisite to enable the company to cancel its shares under subsection* (*1*) *without complying with sections 135 and 136* (*resolution to reduce issued share capital; application to court for approval*).*]*

[148D]

NOTES

Inserted as noted to s 162A at **[148A]**.

Repealed by the Companies Act 2006, s 1295, Sch 16, as from a day to be appointed.

Sub-s (3): words in square brackets substituted by the Companies Act 2006 (Commencement No 2, Consequential Amendments, Transitional Provisions and Savings) Order 2007, SI 2007/1093, art 6(1), Sch 3, para 1, as from 6 April 2007.

[162E Treasury shares: mandatory cancellation

(*1*) *If shares held as treasury shares cease to be qualifying shares, the company must forthwith cancel the shares in accordance with section 162D.*

(*2*) *For the purposes of subsection* (*1*), *shares are not to be regarded as ceasing to be qualifying shares by virtue only of—*

(*a*) *the suspension of their listing in accordance with the applicable rules in the EEA State in which the shares are officially listed, or*

(*b*) *the suspension of their trading in accordance with—*

(*i*) *in the case of shares traded on the market known as the Alternative Investment Market, the rules of London Stock Exchange plc, and*

(*ii*) *in any other case, the rules of the regulated market on which they are traded.*

(*3*) *For the purposes of this section "regulated market" means a market which is a regulated market for the purposes of Article 16 of Council Directive 93/22/EEC on investment services in the securities field.]*

[148E]

NOTES

Inserted as noted to s 162A at **[148A]**.

Repealed by the Companies Act 2006, s 1295, Sch 16, as from a day to be appointed.

Sub-s (3): for the words "is a regulated market for the purposes of Article 16 of Council Directive 93/22/EEC on investment services in the securities field" there are substituted the words "appears on the list drawn up by an EEA State pursuant to Article 47 of Directive 2004/39/EC of the European Parliament and of the Council of 21 April 2004 on markets in financial instruments" by the Financial Services and Markets Act 2000 (Markets in Financial Instruments) Regulations 2007, SI 2007/126, reg 3(6), Sch 6, Pt 1, para 7(1), (4), as from 1 November 2007 (for the full commencement details of SI 2007/126, see reg 1 of those Regulations at **[7596]**).

[162F Treasury shares: proceeds of sale

(*1*) *Where shares held as treasury shares are sold, the proceeds of sale shall be dealt with in accordance with this section.*

(*2*) *Where the proceeds of sale are equal to or less than the purchase price paid by the company for the shares, the proceeds shall be treated for the purposes of Part 8 as a realised profit of the company.*

(*3*) *Where the proceeds of sale exceed the purchase price paid by the company for the shares—*

- (*a*) *that part of the proceeds of sale that is equal to the purchase price paid shall be treated for the purposes of Part 8 as a realised profit of the company, and*
- (*b*) *a sum equal to the excess shall be transferred to the company's share premium account.*

(*4*) *The purchase price paid by the company for the shares shall be determined by the application of a weighted average price method.*

(*5*) *Where the shares were allotted to the company as fully paid bonus shares, the purchase price paid for them shall, for the purposes of subsection (4), be treated as being nil.]*

[148F]

NOTES

Inserted as noted to s 162A at **[148A]**.

Repealed by the Companies Act 2006, s 1295, Sch 16, as from a day to be appointed.

[162G Treasury shares: penalty for contravention

If a company contravenes any provision of sections 162A to 162F every officer of it who is in default is liable to a fine.]

[148G]

NOTES

Inserted as noted to s 162A at **[148A]**.

Repealed by the Companies Act 2006, s 1295, Sch 16, as from a day to be appointed.

163 Definitions of "off-market" and "market" purchase

(*1*) *A purchase by a company of its own shares is "off-market" if the shares either—*

- (*a*) *are purchased otherwise than on [a recognised investment exchange], or*
- (*b*) *are purchased on [a recognised investment exchange] but are not subject to a marketing arrangement on [that investment exchange].*

(*2*) *For this purpose, a company's shares are subject to a marketing arrangement on [a recognised investment exchange] if either—*

- (*a*) *they are listed [under [Part 6 of the Financial Services and Markets Act 2000]]; or*
- (*b*) *the company has been afforded facilities for dealings in those shares to take place on [that investment exchange] without prior permission for individual transactions from the authority governing [that investment exchange] and without limit as to the time during which those facilities are to be available.*

(*3*) *A purchase by a company of its own shares is a "market purchase" if it is a purchase made on [a recognised investment exchange], other than a purchase which is an off-market purchase by virtue of subsection (1)(b).*

[(4) "Recognised investment exchange" means a recognised investment exchange other than an overseas investment exchange.

(*5*) *Expressions used in the definition contained in subsection (4) have the same meaning as in Part 18 of the Financial Services and Markets Act 2000.]*

[149]

NOTES

Repealed by the Companies Act 2006, s 1295, Sch 16, as from a day to be appointed.

Sub-ss (1), (3): words in square brackets substituted by FSA 1986, s 212(2), Sch 16, para 17, as from 29 April 1988.

Sub-s (2): words in first, fourth and fifth pairs of square brackets substituted by FSA 1986, s 212(2), Sch 16, para 17, as from 29 April 1988; words in second (outer) pair of square brackets substituted by FSA 1986, s 212(2), Sch 16, para 17, as from 12 January 1987; words in third (inner) pair of square brackets substituted by the Financial Services and Markets Act 2000 (Consequential Amendments and Repeals) Order 2001, SI 2001/3649, art 6(1), (2), as from 1 December 2001.

Sub-ss (4), (5): substituted (for sub-s (4) as added by FSA 1986, s 212(2), Sch 16, para 17) by SI 2001/3649, art 6(1), (3), as from 1 December 2001.

164 Authority for off-market purchase

(1) A company may only make an off-market purchase of its own shares in pursuance of a contract approved in advance in accordance with this section or under section 165 below.

(2) The terms of the proposed contract must be authorised by a special resolution of the company before the contract is entered into; and the following subsections apply with respect to that authority and to resolutions conferring it.

(3) Subject to the next subsection, the authority may be varied, revoked or from time to time renewed by special resolution of the company.

(4) In the case of a public company, the authority conferred by the resolution must specify a date on which the authority is to expire; and in a resolution conferring or renewing authority that date must not be later than 18 months after that on which the resolution is passed.

(5) A special resolution to confer, vary, revoke or renew authority is not effective if any member of the company holding shares to which the resolution relates exercises the voting rights carried by any of those shares in voting on the resolution and the resolution would not have been passed if he had not done so.

For this purpose—

- *(a) a member who holds shares to which the resolution relates is regarded as exercising the voting rights carried by those shares not only if he votes in respect of them on a poll on the question whether the resolution shall be passed, but also if he votes on the resolution otherwise than on a poll;*
- *(b) notwithstanding anything in the company's articles, any member of the company may demand a poll on that question; and*
- *(c) a vote and a demand for a poll by a person as proxy for a member are the same respectively as a vote and a demand by the member.*

(6) Such a resolution is not effective for the purposes of this section unless (if the proposed contract is in writing) a copy of the contract or (if not) a written memorandum of its terms is available for inspection by members of the company both—

- *(a) at the company's registered office for not less than 15 days ending with the date of the meeting at which the resolution is passed, and*
- *(b) at the meeting itself.*

A memorandum of contract terms so made available must include the names of any members holding shares to which the contract relates; and a copy of the contract so made available must have annexed to it a written memorandum specifying any such names which do not appear in the contract itself.

(7) A company may agree to a variation of an existing contract so approved, but only if the variation is authorised by a special resolution of the company before it is agreed to; and subsections (3) to (6) above apply to the authority for a proposed variation as they apply to the authority for a proposed contract, save that a copy of the original contract or (as the case may require) a memorandum of its terms, together with any variations previously made, must also be available for inspection in accordance with subsection (6).

[150]

NOTES

Repealed by the Companies Act 2006, s 1295, Sch 16, as from a day to be appointed.

165 Authority for contingent purchase contract

(1) A contingent purchase contract is a contract entered into by a company and relating to any of its shares—

- *(a) which does not amount to a contract to purchase those shares, but* (*b*) *under which the company may (subject to any conditions) become entitled or obliged to purchase those shares.*

(2) *A company may only make a purchase of its own shares in pursuance of a contingent purchase contract if the contract is approved in advance by a special resolution of the company before the contract is entered into; and subsections (3) to (7) of section 164 apply to the contract and its terms.*

[151]

NOTES

Repealed by the Companies Act 2006, s 1295, Sch 16, as from a day to be appointed.

166 Authority for market purchase

(*1*) *A company shall not make a market purchase of its own shares unless the purchase has first been authorised by the company in general meeting.*

(2) *That authority—*

(*a*) *may be general for that purpose, or limited to the purchase of shares of any particular class or description, and*
(*b*) *may be unconditional or subject to conditions.*

(*3*) *The authority must—*

(*a*) *specify the maximum number of shares authorised to be acquired,*
(*b*) *determine both the maximum and the minimum prices which may be paid for the shares, and*
(*c*) *specify a date on which it is to expire.*

(*4*) *The authority may be varied, revoked or from time to time renewed by the company in general meeting, but this is subject to subsection (3) above; and in a resolution to confer or renew authority, the date on which the authority is to expire must not be later than 18 months after that on which the resolution is passed.*

(*5*) *A company may under this section make a purchase of its own shares after the expiry of the time limit imposed to comply with subsection (3)(c), if the contract of purchase was concluded before the authority expired and the terms of the authority permitted the company to make a contract of purchase which would or might be executed wholly or partly after its expiration.*

(*6*) *A resolution to confer or vary authority under this section may determine either or both the maximum and minimum prices for purchase by—*

(*a*) *specifying a particular sum, or*
(*b*) *providing a basis or formula for calculating the amount of the price in question without reference to any person's discretion or opinion.*

(*7*) *A resolution of a company conferring, varying, revoking or renewing authority under this section is subject to section 380 (resolution to be sent to registrar of companies within 15 days).*

[152]

NOTES

Repealed by the Companies Act 2006, s 1295, Sch 16, as from a day to be appointed.
Sub-s (7): substituted by the draft Companies Act 2006 (Commencement No 3, Consequential Amendments, Transitional Provisions and Savings) Order 2007, art 10(1), Sch 4, Pt 1, para 1(8), as from 1 October 2007 (see **[A12]**), as follows—

"(7) Chapter 3 of Part 3 of the Companies Act 2006 (resolutions affecting a company's constitution) applies to a resolution of a company conferring, varying, revoking or renewing authority under this section.".

167 Assignment or release of company's right to purchase own shares

(*1*) *The rights of a company under a contract approved under section 164 or 165, or under a contract for a purchase authorised under section 166, are not capable of being assigned.*

(*2*) *An agreement by a company to release its rights under a contract approved under section 164 or 165 is void unless the terms of the release agreement are approved in advance by a special resolution of the company before the agreement is entered into; and subsections (3) to (7) of section 164 apply to approval for a proposed release agreement as to authority for a proposed variation of an existing contract.*

[153]

NOTES

Repealed by the Companies Act 2006, s 1295, Sch 16, as from a day to be appointed.

168 Payments apart from purchase price to be made out of distributable profits

(*1*) *A payment made by a company in consideration of—*

(*a*) *acquiring any right with respect to the purchase of its own shares in pursuance of a contract approved under section 165, or*

(*b*) *the variation of a contract approved under section 164 or 165, or*

(*c*) *the release of any of the company's obligations with respect to the purchase of any of its own shares under a contract approved under section 164 or 165 or under a contract for a purchase authorised under section 166,*

must be made out of the company's distributable profits.

(2) *If the requirements of subsection (1) are not satisfied in relation to a contract—*

(*a*) *in a case within paragraph (a) of the subsection, no purchase by the company of its own shares in pursuance of that contract is lawful under this Chapter,*

(*b*) *in a case within paragraph (b), no such purchase following the variation is lawful under this Chapter, and*

(*c*) *in a case within paragraph (c), the purported release is void.*

[154]

NOTES

Repealed by the Companies Act 2006, s 1295, Sch 16, as from a day to be appointed.

169 Disclosure by company of purchase of own shares

(*1*) *Within the period of 28 days beginning with the date on which any shares purchased by a company under this Chapter are delivered to it, the company shall deliver to the registrar of companies for registration a return in the prescribed form stating with respect to shares of each class purchased the number and nominal value of those shares and the date on which they were delivered to the company.*

[(1A) But in the case of a company which has purchased its own shares in circumstances in which section 162A applies, the requirement to deliver a return under subsection (1) shall apply only where some or all of the shares have been cancelled forthwith after the date of their delivery in accordance with section 162D(1) and in those circumstances the particulars required by that subsection to be stated with respect to the shares purchased shall apply only to such of the shares as have been so cancelled.

(1B) Where a company has purchased its own shares in circumstances in which section 162A applies, the company shall within the period of 28 days beginning with the date on which such shares are delivered to it (except where all of the shares have been cancelled forthwith after the date of their delivery in the circumstances referred to in subsection (1A)) deliver to the registrar of companies for registration a return in the prescribed form stating with respect to shares of each class purchased (other than any shares which have been cancelled in the circumstances referred to in subsection (1A)) the number and nominal value of each of those shares which are held as treasury shares and the date on which they were delivered to the company.]

(2) *In the case of a public company, [any return under subsection (1) or (1B)] shall also state—*

(*a*) *the aggregate amount paid by the company for the shares; and*

(*b*) *the maximum and minimum prices paid in respect of shares of each class purchased.*

(*3*) *Particulars of shares delivered to the company on different dates and under different contracts may be included in a single return [under either subsection (1) or (1B)] to the registrar; and in such a case the amount required to be stated under subsection (2)(a) is the aggregate amount paid by the company for all the shares to which the return relates.*

(4) Where a company enters into a contract approved under section 164 or 165, or a contract for a purchase authorised under section 166, the company shall keep at its registered office—

(a) if the contract is in writing, a copy of it; and

(b) if not, a memorandum of its terms,

from the conclusion of the contract until the end of the period of 10 years beginning with the date on which the purchase of all the shares in pursuance of the contract is completed or (as the case may be) the date on which the contract otherwise determines.

(5) Every copy and memorandum so required to be kept shall ... be open to inspection without charge—

(a) by any member of the company, and

(b) if it is a public company, by any other person.

(6) If default is made in delivering to the registrar any return required by this section, every officer of the company who is in default is liable to a fine and, for continued contravention, to a daily default fine.

(7) If default is made in complying with subsection (4), or if an inspection required under subsection (5) is refused, the company and every officer of it who is in default is liable to a fine and, for continued contravention, to a daily default fine.

(8) In the case of a refusal of an inspection required under subsection (5) of a copy or memorandum, the court may by order compel an immediate inspection of it.

(9) The obligation of a company under subsection (4) to keep a copy of any contract or (as the case may be) a memorandum of its terms applies to any variation of the contract so long as it applies to the contract.

[155]

NOTES

Repealed by the Companies Act 2006, s 1295, Sch 16, as from a day to be appointed.

Sub-ss (1A), (1B): inserted by the Companies (Acquisition of Own Shares) (Treasury Shares) Regulations 2003, SI 2003/1116, reg 4, Schedule, para 12(1), (2), as from 1 December 2003.

Sub-s (2): words in square brackets substituted by SI 2003/1116, reg 4, Schedule, para 12(1), (3), as from 1 December 2003.

Sub-s (3): words in square brackets inserted by the Companies (Acquisition of Own Shares) (Treasury Shares) No 2 Regulations 2003, SI 2003/3031, reg 3, as from 18 December 2003.

Sub-s (5): words omitted repealed by CA 1989, ss 143(2), 212, Sch 24, as from 1 November 1991.

Inspection: for provisions relating to the inspection of documents, registers and fees under this section, see the Companies (Inspection and Copying of Registers, Indices and Documents) Regulations 1991, SI 1991/1998 at **[6716]** et seq.

Return in the prescribed form: see Appendix 4 (Forms table) at **[A4]**.

[169A Disclosure by company of cancellation or disposal of treasury shares

(1) Subsection (2) applies in relation to any shares held by a company as treasury shares if—

(a) the company is or was required to make a return under section 169(1B) in relation to the shares, and

(b) the shares have—

(i) been cancelled in accordance with section 162D(1), or

(ii) been sold or transferred for the purposes of or pursuant to an employees' share scheme under section 162D(1).

(2) Within the period of 28 days beginning with the date on which such shares are cancelled or disposed of, the company shall deliver to the registrar of companies for registration a return in the prescribed form stating with respect to shares of each class cancelled or disposed of—

(a) the number and nominal value of those shares, and

(b) the date on which they were cancelled or disposed of.

(3) Particulars of shares cancelled or disposed of on different dates may be included in a single return to the registrar.

(4) If default is made in delivering to the registrar any return required by this section, every officer of the company who is in default is liable to a fine and, for continued contravention, to a daily default fine.]

[155A]

NOTES

Inserted by the Companies (Acquisition of Own Shares) (Treasury Shares) Regulations 2003, SI 2003/1116, reg 4, Schedule, para 13, as from 1 December 2003.

Repealed by the Companies Act 2006, s 1295, Sch 16, as from a day to be appointed.

Return in the prescribed form: see Appendix 4 (Forms table) at **[A4]**.

170 The capital redemption reserve

(1) Where under this Chapter shares of a company are redeemed or purchased wholly out of the company's profits, the amount by which the company's issued share capital is diminished in accordance with section 160(4) on cancellation of the shares redeemed or purchased[, or in accordance with section 162D(4) on cancellation of shares held as treasury shares,] shall be transferred to a reserve, called "the capital redemption reserve".

(2) If the shares are redeemed or purchased wholly or partly out of the proceeds of a fresh issue and the aggregate amount of those proceeds is less than the aggregate nominal value of the shares redeemed or purchased, the amount of the difference shall be transferred to the capital redemption reserve.

(3) But subsection (2) does not apply if the proceeds of the fresh issue are applied by the company in making a redemption or purchase of its own shares in addition to a payment out of capital under section 171.

(4) The provisions of this Act relating to the reduction of a company's share capital apply as if the capital redemption reserve were paid-up share capital of the company, except that the reserve may be applied by the company in paying up its unissued shares to be allotted to members of the company as fully paid bonus shares.

[156]

NOTES

Repealed by the Companies Act 2006, s 1295, Sch 16, as from a day to be appointed.

Sub-s (1): words in square brackets inserted by the Companies (Acquisition of Own Shares) (Treasury Shares) Regulations 2003, SI 2003/1116, reg 4, Schedule, para 14, as from 1 December 2003.

Redemption or purchase of own shares out of capital (private companies only)

171 Power of private companies to redeem or purchase own shares out of capital

(1) Subject to the following provisions of this Chapter, a private company limited by shares or limited by guarantee and having a share capital may, if so authorised by its articles, make a payment in respect of the redemption or purchase under section 160 or (as the case may be) section 162, of its own shares otherwise than out of its distributable profits or the proceeds of a fresh issue of shares.

(2) References below in this Chapter to payment out of capital are (subject to subsection (6)) to any payment so made, whether or not it would be regarded apart from this section as a payment out of capital.

(3) The payment which may (if authorised in accordance with the following provisions of this Chapter) be made by a company out of capital in respect of the redemption or purchase of its own shares is such an amount as, taken together with—

- *(a) any available profits of the company, and*
- *(b) the proceeds of any fresh issue of shares made for the purposes of the redemption or purchase,*

is equal to the price of redemption or purchase; and the payment permissible under this subsection is referred to below in this Chapter as the permissible capital payment for the shares.

(4) Subject to subsection (6), if the permissible capital payment for shares redeemed or purchased is less than their nominal amount, the amount of the difference shall be transferred to the company's capital redemption reserve.

(5) Subject to subsection (6), if the permissible capital payment is greater than the nominal amount of the shares redeemed or purchased—

- *(a) the amount of any capital redemption reserve, share premium account or fully paid share capital of the company, and* (*b*) *any amount representing unrealised profits of the company for the time being standing to the credit of any reserve maintained by the company in accordance with paragraph 34 of Schedule 4 [or paragraph 34 of Schedule 8]* (*revaluation reserve*),

may be reduced by a sum not exceeding (*or by sums not in the aggregate exceeding*) *the amount by which the permissible capital payment exceeds the nominal amount of the shares.*

(*6*) *Where the proceeds of a fresh issue are applied by a company in making any redemption or purchase of its own shares in addition to a payment out of capital under this section, the references in subsections* (*4*) *and* (*5*) *to the permissible capital payment are to be read as referring to the aggregate of that payment and those proceeds.*

[157]

NOTES

Repealed by the Companies Act 2006, s 1295, Sch 16, as from a day to be appointed.

Sub-s (5): words in square brackets inserted by the Companies Act 1985 (Accounts of Small and Medium-sized Companies and Minor Accounting Amendments) Regulations 1997, SI 1997/220, reg 7(1), in relation to annual accounts approved by the board of directors on or after 1 March 1997, and to directors' and auditors' reports on such accounts (subject to transitional provisions in relation to a financial year of a company ending on or before 24 March 1997).

172 Availability of profits for purposes of s 171

(*1*) *The reference in section 171*(*3*)(*a*) *to available profits of the company is to the company's profits which are available for distribution* (*within the meaning of Part VIII*); *but the question whether a company has any profits so available and the amount of any such profits are to be determined for purposes of that section in accordance with the following subsections, instead of sections 270 to 275 in that Part.*

(*2*) *Subject to the next subsection, that question is to be determined by reference to [the following items as stated in the relevant accounts for determining the permissible capital payments for shares]—*

(*a*) *profits, losses, assets and liabilities,*

(*b*) *[the following provisions—*

(*i*) *in the case of Companies Act individual accounts,] provisions of any of the kinds mentioned in paragraphs 88 and 89 of Schedule 4* (*depreciation, diminution in value of assets, retentions to meet liabilities, etc*)*[, and*

(*ii*) *in the case of IAS individual accounts, provisions of any kind], and*

(*c*) *share capital and reserves* (*including undistributable reserves*),

…

(*3*) *The relevant accounts for this purpose are such accounts, prepared as at any date within the period for determining the amount of the permissible capital payment, as are necessary to enable a reasonable judgment to be made as to the amounts of any of the items mentioned in subsection* (2)(*a*) *to* (*c*) *above.*

(*4*) *For purposes of determining the amount of the permissible capital payment for shares, the amount of the company's available profits* (*if any*) *determined in accordance with subsections* (*2*) *and* (*3*) *is treated as reduced by the amount of any distributions lawfully made by the company after the date of the relevant accounts and before the end of the period for determining the amount of that payment.*

(*5*) *The reference in subsection* (*4*) *to distributions lawfully made by the company includes—*

(*a*) *financial assistance lawfully given out of distributable profits in a case falling within section 154 or 155,*

(*b*) *any payment lawfully made by the company in respect of the purchase by it of any shares in the company* (*except a payment lawfully made otherwise than out of distributable profits*), *and*

(*c*) *a payment of any description specified in section 168*(*1*) *lawfully made by the company.*

(*6*) *References in this section to the period for determining the amount of the permissible capital payment for shares are to the period of 3 months ending with the date on which the statutory declaration of the directors purporting to specify the amount of that payment is made in accordance with subsection* (*3*) *of the section next following.*

[158]

NOTES

Repealed by the Companies Act 2006, s 1295, Sch 16, as from a day to be appointed.

Sub-s (2): words in square brackets inserted, and words omitted repealed, by the Companies Act 1985 (International Accounting Standards and Other Accounting Amendments) Regulations 2004, SI 2004/2947, reg 3, Sch 1, paras 1, 3, as from 12 November 2004, in relation to companies' financial years which begin on or after 1 January 2005.

173 Conditions for payment out of capital

(1) Subject to any order of the court under section 177, a payment out of capital by a private company for the redemption or purchase of its own shares is not lawful unless the requirements of this and the next two sections are satisfied.

(2) The payment out of capital must be approved by a special resolution of the company.

(3) The company's directors must make a statutory declaration specifying the amount of the permissible capital payment for the shares in question and stating that, having made full inquiry into the affairs and prospects of the company, they have formed the opinion—

(a) as regards its initial situation immediately following the date on which the payment out of capital is proposed to be made, that there will be no grounds on which the company could then be found unable to pay its debts, and

(b) as regards its prospects for the year immediately following that date, that, having regard to their intentions with respect to the management of the company's business during that year and to the amount and character of the financial resources which will in their view be available to the company during that year, the company will be able to continue to carry on business as a going concern (and will accordingly be able to pay its debts as they fall due) throughout that year.

(4) In forming their opinion for purposes of subsection (3)(a), the directors shall take into account the same liabilities (including prospective and contingent liabilities) as would be relevant under [section 122 of the Insolvency Act] (winding up by the court) to the question whether a company is unable to pay its debts.

(5) The directors' statutory declaration must be in the prescribed form and contain such information with respect to the nature of the company's business as may be prescribed, and must in addition have annexed to it a report addressed to the directors by the company's auditors stating that—

(a) they have inquired into the company's state of affairs; and

(b) the amount specified in the declaration as the permissible capital payment for the shares in question is in their view properly determined in accordance with sections 171 and 172; and

(c) they are not aware of anything to indicate that the opinion expressed by the directors in the declaration as to any of the matters mentioned in subsection (3) is unreasonable in all the circumstances.

(6) A director who makes a declaration under this section without having reasonable grounds for the opinion expressed in the declaration is liable to imprisonment or a fine, or both.

[159]

NOTES

Repealed by the Companies Act 2006, s 1295, Sch 16, as from a day to be appointed.

Sub-s (4): words in square brackets substituted by the Insolvency Act 1986, s 439(1), Sch 13, Pt I, as from 29 December 1986; for transitional provisions see s 437 of, and Sch 11, Pt I to, that Act at **[3456]**, **[3481]**.

Insolvency Act, s 122: ie, the Insolvency Act 1986, s 122.

Prescribed form: see Appendix 4 (Forms table) at **[A4]**.

174 Procedure for special resolution under s 173

(1) The resolution required by section 173 must be passed on, or within the week immediately following, the date on which the directors make the statutory declaration required by that section; and the payment out of capital must be made no earlier than 5 nor more than 7 weeks after the date of the resolution.

(2) The resolution is ineffective if any member of the company holding shares to which the resolution relates exercises the voting rights carried by any of those shares in voting on the resolution and the resolution would not have been passed if he had not done so.

(3) For purposes of subsection (2), a member who holds such shares is to be regarded as exercising the voting rights carried by them in voting on the resolution not only if he votes in respect of them on a poll on the question whether the resolution shall be passed, but also if he votes on the resolution otherwise than on a poll; and, notwithstanding anything in a company's articles, any member of the company may demand a poll on that question.

(4) The resolution is ineffective unless the statutory declaration and auditors' report required by the section are available for inspection by members of the company at the meeting at which the resolution is passed.

(5) For purposes of this section a vote and a demand for a poll by a person as proxy for a member are the same (respectively) as a vote and demand by the member.

[160]

NOTES

Repealed by the Companies Act 2006, s 1295, Sch 16, as from a day to be appointed.

175 Publicity for proposed payment out of capital

(1) Within the week immediately following the date of the resolution for payment out of capital the company must cause to be published in the Gazette a notice—

- *(a) stating that the company has approved a payment out of capital for the purpose of acquiring its own shares by redemption or purchase or both (as the case may be);*
- *(b) specifying the amount of the permissible capital payment for the shares in question and the date of the resolution under section 173;*
- *(c) stating that the statutory declaration of the directors and the auditors' report required by that section are available for inspection at the company's registered office; and*
- *(d) stating that any creditor of the company may at any time within the 5 weeks immediately following the date of the resolution for payment out of capital apply to the court under section 176 for an order prohibiting the payment.*

(2) Within the week immediately following the date of the resolution the company must also either cause a notice to the same effect as that required by subsection (1) to be published in an appropriate national newspaper or give notice in writing to that effect to each of its creditors.

(3) "An appropriate national newspaper" means a newspaper circulating throughout England and Wales (in the case of a company registered in England and Wales), and a newspaper circulating throughout Scotland (in the case of a company registered in Scotland).

(4) References below in this section to the first notice date are to the day on which the company first publishes the notice required by subsection (1) or first publishes or gives the notice required by subsection (2) (whichever is the earlier).

(5) Not later than the first notice date the company must deliver to the registrar of companies a copy of the statutory declaration of the directors and of the auditors' report required by section 173.

(6) The statutory declaration and auditors' report—

- *(a) shall be kept at the company's registered office throughout the period beginning with the first notice date and ending 5 weeks after the date of the resolution for payment out of capital, and*
- *(b) shall … be open to the inspection of any member or creditor of the company without charge.*

(7) If an inspection required under subsection (6) is refused, the company and every officer of it who is in default is liable to a fine and, for continued contravention, to a daily default fine.

(8) In the case of refusal of an inspection required under subsection (6) of a declaration or report, the court may by order compel an immediate inspection of that declaration or report.

[161]

NOTES

Repealed by the Companies Act 2006, s 1295, Sch 16, as from a day to be appointed.
Sub-s (6): words omitted repealed by CA 1989, ss 143(3), 212, Sch 24, as from 1 November 1991.

Inspection: for provisions relating to the inspection of documents, registers and fees under this section, see the Companies (Inspection and Copying of Registers, Indices and Documents) Regulations 1991, SI 1991/1998 at **[6716]** et seq.

176 Objections by company's members or creditors

(1) Where a private company passes a special resolution approving for purposes of this Chapter any payment out of capital for the redemption or purchase of any of its shares—

(a) any member of the company other than one who consented to or voted in favour of the resolution; and

(b) any creditor of the company,

may within 5 weeks of the date on which the resolution was passed apply to the court for cancellation of the resolution.

(2) The application may be made on behalf of the persons entitled to make it by such one or more of their number as they may appoint in writing for the purpose.

(3) If an application is made, the company shall—

(a) forthwith give notice in the prescribed form of that fact to the registrar of companies; and

(b) within 15 days from the making of any order of the court on the hearing of the application, or such longer period as the court may by order direct, deliver an office copy of the order to the registrar.

(4) A company which fails to comply with subsection (3), and any officer of it who is in default, is liable to a fine and for continued contravention, to a daily default fine.

[162]

NOTES

Repealed by the Companies Act 2006, s 1295, Sch 16, as from a day to be appointed.
Notice in the prescribed form: see Appendix 4 (Forms table) at **[A4]**.

177 Powers of court on application under s 176

(1) On the hearing of an application under section 176 the court may, if it thinks fit, adjourn the proceedings in order that an arrangement may be made to the court's satisfaction for the purchase of the interests of dissentient members or for the protection of dissentient creditors (as the case may be); and the court may give such directions and make such orders as it thinks expedient for facilitating or carrying into effect any such arrangement.

(2) Without prejudice to its powers under subsection (1), the court shall make an order on such terms and conditions as it thinks fit either confirming or cancelling the resolution; and, if the court confirms the resolution, it may in particular by order alter or extend any date or period of time specified in the resolution or in any provision in this Chapter which applies to the redemption or purchase of shares to which the resolution refers.

(3) The court's order may, if the court thinks fit, provide for the purchase by the company of the shares of any of its members and for the reduction accordingly of the company's capital, and may make such alterations in the company's memorandum and articles as may be required in consequence of that provision.

(4) If the court's order requires the company not to make any, or any specified, alteration in its memorandum or articles, the company has not then power without leave of the court to make any such alteration in breach of the requirement.

(5) An alteration in the memorandum or articles made by virtue of an order under this section, if not made by resolution of the company, is of the same effect as if duly made by resolution; and this Act applies accordingly to the memorandum or articles as so altered.

[163]

NOTES

Repealed by the Companies Act 2006, s 1295, Sch 16, as from a day to be appointed.

Supplementary

178 Effect of company's failure to redeem or purchase

(*1*) *This section has effect where a company has, on or after 15th June 1982,—*

(*a*) *issued shares on terms that they are or are liable to be redeemed, or*

(*b*) *agreed to purchase any of its own shares.*

(*2*) *The company is not liable in damages in respect of any failure on its part to redeem or purchase any of the shares.*

(*3*) *Subsection* (*2*) *is without prejudice to any right of the holder of the shares other than his right to sue the company for damages in respect of its failure; but the court shall not grant an order for specific performance of the terms of redemption or purchase if the company shows that it is unable to meet the costs of redeeming or purchasing the shares in question out of distributable profits.*

(*4*) *If the company is wound up and at the commencement of the winding up any of the shares have not been redeemed or purchased, the terms of redemption or purchase may be enforced against the company; and when shares are redeemed or purchased under this subsection, they are treated as cancelled.*

(*5*) *However, subsection* (*4*) *does not apply if—*

(*a*) *the terms provided for the redemption or purchase to take place at a date later than that of the commencement of the winding up, or*

(*b*) *during the period beginning with the date on which the redemption or purchase was to have taken place and ending with the commencement of the winding up the company could not at any time have lawfully made a distribution equal in value to the price at which the shares were to have been redeemed or purchased.*

(*6*) *There shall be paid in priority to any amount which the company is liable under subsection* (*4*) *to pay in respect of any shares—*

(*a*) *all other debts and liabilities of the company* (*other than any due to members in their character as such*),

(*b*) *if other shares carry rights* (*whether as to capital or as to income*) *which are preferred to the rights as to capital attaching to the first-mentioned shares, any amount due in satisfaction of those preferred rights;*

but, subject to that, any such amount shall be paid in priority to any amounts due to members in satisfaction of their rights (*whether as to capital or income*) *as members.*

(*7*) ...

[164]

NOTES

Repealed by the Companies Act 2006, s 1295, Sch 16, as from a day to be appointed.
Sub-s (7): repealed by the Insolvency Act 1985, s 235(3), Sch 10, Pt II, as from 29 December 1986.

179 Power for Secretary of State to modify this Chapter

(*1*) *The Secretary of State may by regulations made by statutory instrument modify the provisions of this Chapter with respect to any of the following matters—*

(*a*) *the authority required for a purchase by a company of its own shares,*

(*b*) *the authority required for the release by a company of its rights under a contract for the purchase of its own shares or a contract under which the company may* (*subject to any conditions*) *become entitled or obliged to purchase its own shares,*

(*c*) *the information to be included in a return delivered by a company to the registrar of companies in accordance with section 169*(*1*),

(*d*) *the matters to be dealt with in the statutory declaration of the directors under section 173 with a view to indicating their opinion of their company's ability to make a proposed payment out of capital with due regard to its financial situation and prospects, and*

(*e*) *the contents of the auditors' report required by that section to be annexed to that declaration.*

(*2*) *The Secretary of State may also by regulations so made make such provision* (*including modification of the provisions of this Chapter*) *as appears to him to be appropriate—*

(*a*) *for wholly or partly relieving companies from the requirement of section 171*(*3*)(*a*) *that any available profits must be taken into account in determining the amount of the permissible capital payment for shares under that section, or*

(*b*) *for permitting a company's share premium account to be applied, to any extent appearing to the Secretary of State to be appropriate, in providing for the premiums payable on redemption or purchase by the company of any of its own shares.*

(*3*) *Regulations under this section—*

(*a*) *may make such further modification of any provisions of this Chapter as appears to the Secretary of State to be reasonably necessary in consequence of any provision made under such regulations by virtue of subsection* (*1*) *or* (*2*),

(*b*) *may make different provision for different cases or classes of case, and*

(*c*) *may contain such further consequential provisions, and such incidental and supplementary provisions, as the Secretary of State thinks fit.*

(*4*) *No regulations shall be made under this section unless a draft of the instrument containing them has been laid before Parliament and approved by resolution of each House.*

[165]

NOTES

Repealed by the Companies Act 2006, s 1295, Sch 16, as from a day to be appointed.

The power to make regulations under this section has been extended by the Insolvency Act 1986, ss 76(6), 79(3), 124(3) at **[3232]**, **[3235]**, **[3280]**.

180 Transitional cases arising under this Chapter; and savings

(*1*) *Any preference shares issued by a company before 15th June 1982 which could but for the repeal by the Companies Act 1981 of section 58 of the Companies Act 1948* (*power to issue redeemable preference shares*) *have been redeemed under that section are subject to redemption in accordance with the provisions of this Chapter.*

(*2*) *In a case to which sections 159 and 160 apply by virtue of this section, any premium payable on redemption may, notwithstanding the repeal by the 1981 Act of any provision of the 1948 Act, be paid out of the share premium account instead of out of profits, or partly out of that account and partly out of profits* (*but subject to the provisions of this Chapter so far as payment is out of profits*).

(*3*) *Any capital redemption reserve fund established before 15th June 1982 by a company for the purposes of section 58 of the Act of 1948 is to be known as the company's capital redemption reserve and be treated as if it had been established for the purposes of section 170 of this Act; and accordingly, a reference in any enactment or in the articles of any company, or in any other instrument, to a company's capital redemption reserve fund is to be construed as a reference to the company's capital redemption reserve.*

[166]

NOTES

Repealed by the Companies Act 2006, s 1295, Sch 16, as from a day to be appointed.

Companies Act 1981: repealed by the Companies Consolidation (Consequential Provisions) Act 1985, s 29, Sch 1.

Companies Act 1948, s 58: repealed by the Companies Act 1981, ss 62(2), 119, Sch 4.

181 Definitions for Chapter VII

In this Chapter—

(*a*) *"distributable profits", in relation to the making of any payment by a company, means those profits out of which it could lawfully make a distribution* (*within the meaning given by section 263*(*2*)) *equal in value to the payment, and*

(*b*) *"permissible capital payment" means the payment permitted by section 171;*

and references to payment out of capital are to be construed in accordance with section 171.

[167]

NOTES

Repealed by the Companies Act 2006, s 1295, Sch 16, as from a day to be appointed.

CHAPTER VIII
MISCELLANEOUS PROVISIONS ABOUT SHARES AND DEBENTURES

Share and debenture certificates, transfers and warrants

182 Nature, transfer and numbering of shares

(1) The shares or other interest of any member in a company—

(a) are personal estate or, in Scotland, moveable property and are not in the nature of real estate or heritage,

(b) are transferable in manner provided by the company's articles, but subject to the Stock Transfer Act 1963 (which enables securities of certain descriptions to be transferred by a simplified process) [and to regulations made under section 207 of the Companies Act 1989 (which enable title to securities to be evidenced and transferred without a written instrument)].

(2) Each share in a company having a share capital shall be distinguished by its appropriate number; except that, if at any time all the issued shares in a company, or all the issued shares in it of a particular class, are fully paid up and rank pari passu for all purposes, none of those shares need thereafter have a distinguishing number so long as it remains fully paid up and ranks pari passu for all purposes with all shares of the same class for the time being issued and fully paid up.

[168]

NOTES

Repealed by the Companies Act 2006, s 1295, Sch 16, as from a day to be appointed.

Sub-s (1): the words in square brackets were originally added by the Uncertificated Securities Regulations 1995, SI 1995/3272, reg 40(1), as from 19 December 1995; the 1995 Regulations were revoked by the Uncertificated Securities Regulations 2001, SI 2001/3755, reg 52, as from 26 November 2001, and reg 51 of, and Sch 7, Pt 1, para 7 to, the 2001 Regulations added the same words as from that date.

Regulations made under section 207 of the Companies Act 1989: see the Uncertificated Securities Regulations 2001, SI 2001/3755 at **[7001]**. The 2001 Regulations (as amended) make provision for the transfer without a written instrument, and the evidencing otherwise than by a certificate, of title to a unit of a security, in accordance with a computer-based system. They modify this Chapter (and related provisions of this Act) in relation to such transfers. Note that s 207 of the 1989 Act is repealed by the Companies Act 2006, s 1295, Sch 16, as from a day to be appointed.

183 Transfer and registration

(1) It is not lawful for a company to register a transfer of shares in or debentures of the company unless a proper instrument of transfer has been delivered to it, or the transfer is an exempt transfer within the Stock Transfer Act 1982 [or is in accordance with regulations made under section 207 of the Companies Act 1989].

This applies notwithstanding anything in the company's articles.

(2) Subsection (1) does not prejudice any power of the company to register as shareholder or debenture holder a person to whom the right to any shares in or debentures of the company has been transmitted by operation of law.

(3) A transfer of the share or other interest of a deceased member of a company made by his personal representative, although the personal representative is not himself a member of the company, is as valid as if he had been such a member at the time of the execution of the instrument of transfer.

(4) On the application of the transferor of any share or interest in a company, the company shall enter in its register of members the name of the transferee in the same manner and subject to the same conditions as if the application for the entry were made by the transferee.

(5) If a company refuses to register a transfer of shares or debentures, the company shall, within 2 months after the date on which the transfer was lodged with it, send to the transferee notice of the refusal.

(6) If default is made in complying with subsection (5), the company and every officer of it who is in default is liable to a fine and, for continued contravention, to a daily default fine.

[169]

NOTES

Repealed by the Companies Act 2006, s 1295, Sch 16, as from a day to be appointed.

Sub-s (1): the words in square brackets were originally inserted by the Uncertificated Securities Regulations 1995, SI 1995/3272, reg 40(1), as from 19 December 1995; the 1995 Regulations were revoked by the Uncertificated Securities Regulations 2001, SI 2001/3755, reg 52, as from 26 November 2001, and reg 51 of, and Sch 7, Pt 1, para 8 to, the 2001 Regulations inserted the same words as from that date.

Application to limited liability partnerships: see the Limited Liability Partnerships Regulations 2001, SI 2001/1090, reg 4(1), Sch 2, Pt 1 at **[6985]**, **[6993]**.

Exempt transfer within the Stock Transfer Act 1982: "exempt transfer" is defined by s 1(2) of that Act. By virtue of s 2(1), the Act applies to "specified securities" and these are listed in Sch 1 to the 1982 Act.

Regulations made under section 207 of the Companies Act 1989: see the note to s 182 at **[168]**.

184 Certification of transfers

(1) The certification by a company of any instrument of transfer of any shares in, or debentures of, the company is to be taken as a representation by the company to any person acting on the faith of the certification that there have been produced to the company such documents as on their face show a prima facie title to the shares or debentures in the transferor named in the instrument.

However, the certification is not to be taken as a representation that the transferor has any title to the shares or debentures.

(2) Where a person acts on the faith of a false certification by a company made negligently, the company is under the same liability to him as if the certification had been made fraudulently.

(3) For purposes of this section—

(a) an instrument of transfer is deemed certificated if it bears the words "certificate lodged" (or words to the like effect);

(b) the certification of an instrument of transfer is deemed made by a company if—

(i) the person issuing the instrument is a person authorised to issue certificated instruments of transfer on the company's behalf, and

(ii) the certification is signed by a person authorised to certificate transfers on the company's behalf or by an officer or servant either of the company or of a body corporate so authorised;

(c) a certification is deemed signed by a person if—

(i) it purports to be authenticated by his signature or initials (whether handwritten or not), and

(ii) it is not shown that the signature or initials was or were placed there neither by himself nor by a person authorised to use the signature or initials for the purpose of certificating transfers on the company's behalf.

[170]

NOTES

Repealed by the Companies Act 2006, s 1295, Sch 16, as from a day to be appointed.

Application to limited liability partnerships: see the Limited Liability Partnerships Regulations 2001, SI 2001/1090, reg 4(1), Sch 2, Pt 1 at **[6985]**, **[6993]**.

185 Duty of company as to issue of certificates

(1) Subject to the following provisions, every company shall—

(a) within 2 months after the allotment of any of its shares, debentures or debenture stock, and

(b) within 2 months after the date on which a transfer of any such shares, debentures or debenture stock is lodged with the company,

complete and have ready for delivery the certificates of all shares, the debentures and the certificates of all debenture stock allotted or transferred (unless the conditions of issue of the shares, debentures or debenture stock otherwise provide).

(2) For this purpose, "transfer" means a transfer duly stamped and otherwise valid, or an exempt transfer within the Stock Transfer Act 1982, and does not include such a transfer as the company is for any reason entitled to refuse to register and does not register.

(3) Subsection (1) does not apply in the case of a transfer to any person where, by virtue of regulations under section 3 of the Stock Transfer Act 1982, he is not entitled to a certificate or other document of or evidencing title in respect of the securities transferred; but if in such a case the transferee—

(a) subsequently becomes entitled to such a certificate or other document by virtue of any provision of those regulations, and

(b) gives notice in writing of that fact to the company,

this section has effect as if the reference in subsection (1)(b) to the date of the lodging of the transfer were a reference to the date of the notice.

[(4) Subsection (4A) applies in relation to a company—

(a) of which shares or debentures are allotted to a financial institution,

(b) of which debenture stock is allotted to a financial institution, or

(c) with which a transfer for transferring shares, debentures or debenture stock to a financial institution is lodged.

(4A) The company is not required, in consequence of that allotment or transfer, to comply with subsection (1).

(4B) "Financial institution" means—

(a) a recognised clearing house acting in relation to a recognised investment exchange; or

(b) a nominee of—

(i) a recognised clearing house acting in that way; or

(ii) a recognised investment exchange.

(4C) No person may be a nominee for the purposes of this section unless he is a person designated for those purposes in the rules of the recognised investment exchange in question.

(4D) Expressions used in subsections (4B) and (4C) have the same meaning as in Part 18 of the Financial Services and Markets Act 2000.]

(5) If default is made in complying with subsection (1), the company and every officer of it who is in default is liable to a fine and, for continued contravention, to a daily default fine.

(6) If a company on which a notice has been served requiring it to make good any default in complying with subsection (1) fails to make good the default within 10 days after service of the notice, the court may, on the application of the person entitled to have the certificates or the debentures delivered to him, exercise the power of the following subsection.

(7) The court may make an order directing the company and any officer of it to make good the default within such time as may be specified in the order; and the order may provide that all costs of and incidental to the application shall be borne by the company or by an officer of it responsible for the default.

[171]

NOTES

Repealed by the Companies Act 2006, s 1295, Sch 16, as from a day to be appointed.

Sub-ss (4), (4A)–(4D): substituted, for original sub-s (4), by the Financial Services and Markets Act 2000 (Consequential Amendments and Repeals) Order 2001, SI 2001/3649, art 7, as from 1 December 2001.

Application to limited liability partnerships: see the Limited Liability Partnerships Regulations 2001, SI 2001/1090, reg 4(1), Sch 2, Pt 1 at **[6985]**, **[6993]**.

[186 Certificate to be evidence of title

[(1)] A certificate under the common seal of the company … specifying any shares held by a member is—

(a) in England and Wales, prima facie evidence, and

(b) in Scotland, sufficient evidence unless the contrary is shown,

of his title to the shares.]

[(2) Without prejudice to subsection (1), as respects Scotland a certificate specifying any shares held by a member and subscribed by the company in accordance with the Requirements of Writing (Scotland) Act 1995 is, unless the contrary is shown, sufficient evidence of his title to the shares.]

[172]

NOTES

Substituted by CA 1989, s 130(7), Sch 17, para 5, as from 31 July 1990.

Repealed by the Companies Act 2006, s 1295, Sch 16, as from a day to be appointed.

Sub-s (1): numbered as such by the Requirements of Writing (Scotland) Act 1995, s 14(1), Sch 4, para 55, as from 1 August 1995; words omitted repealed by the Law Reform (Miscellaneous Provisions) (Scotland) Act 1990, s 74(1), (2), Sch 8, para 33(4), Sch 9, as from 1 December 1990.

Sub-s (2): added by the Requirements of Writing (Scotland) Act 1995, s 14(1), Sch 4, para 55, as from 1 August 1995.

187 Evidence of grant of probate or confirmation as executor

The production to a company of any document which is by law sufficient evidence of probate of the will, or letters of administration of the estate, or confirmation as executor, of a deceased person having been granted to some person shall be accepted by the company as sufficient evidence of the grant.

This has effect notwithstanding anything in the company's articles.

[173]

NOTES

Repealed by the Companies Act 2006, s 1295, Sch 16, as from a day to be appointed.

[188 Issue and effect of share warrant to bearer

(*1*) *A company limited by shares may, if so authorised by its articles, issue with respect to any fully paid shares a warrant (a "share warrant") stating that the bearer of the warrant is entitled to the shares specified in it.*

(2) *A share warrant issued under the company's common seal [(or, in the case of a company registered in Scotland, subscribed in accordance with the Requirements of Writing (Scotland) Act 1995)] … entitles the bearer to the shares specified in it; and the shares may be transferred by delivery of the warrant.*

(*3*) *A company which issues a share warrant may, if so authorised by its articles, provide (by coupons or otherwise) for the payment of the future dividends on the shares included in the warrant.]*

[174]

NOTES

Substituted by CA 1989, s 130(7), Sch 17, para 6, as from 31 July 1990.

Repealed by the Companies Act 2006, s 1295, Sch 16, as from a day to be appointed.

Sub-s (2): words in square brackets inserted by the Requirements of Writing (Scotland) Act 1995, s 14(1), Sch 4, para 56, as from 1 August 1995; words omitted repealed by the Law Reform (Miscellaneous Provisions) (Scotland) Act 1990, s 74(1), (2), Sch 8, para 33(5), Sch 9, as from 1 December 1990.

189 Offences in connection with share warrants (Scotland)

(*1*) *If in Scotland a person—*

(*a*) *with intent to defraud, forges or alters, or offers, utters, disposes of, or puts off, knowing the same to be forged or altered, any share warrant or coupon, or any document purporting to be a share warrant or coupon, issued in pursuance of this Act; or*

(*b*) *by means of any such forged or altered share warrant, coupon, or document, purporting as aforesaid, demands or endeavours to obtain or receive any share or interest in any company under this Act, or to receive any dividend or money payable in respect thereof, knowing the warrant, coupon, or document to be forged or altered;*

he is on conviction thereof liable to imprisonment or a fine, or both.

(2) *If in Scotland a person without lawful authority or excuse (proof whereof lies on him)—*

(*a*) *engraves or makes on any plate, wood, stone, or other material, any share warrant or coupon purporting to be—*

(*i*) *a share warrant or coupon issued or made by any particular company in pursuance of this Act; or*

(ii) *a blank share warrant or coupon so issued or made; or*
(iii) *a part of such a share warrant or coupon; or*

(*b*) *uses any such plate, wood, stone, or other material, for the making or printing of any such share warrant or coupon, or of any such blank share warrant or coupon, or any part thereof respectively; or*

(*c*) *knowingly has in his custody or possession any such plate, wood, stone, or other material;*

he is on conviction thereof liable to imprisonment or a fine, or both.

[175]

NOTES

Repealed by the Companies Act 2006, s 1295, Sch 16, as from a day to be appointed.

Debentures

190 Register of debenture holders

(*1*) *A company registered in England and Wales shall not keep in Scotland any register of holders of debentures of the company or any duplicate of any such register or part of any such register which is kept outside Great Britain.*

(*2*) *A company registered in Scotland shall not keep in England and Wales any such register or duplicate as above-mentioned.*

(*3*) *Neither a register of holders of debentures of a company nor a duplicate of any such register or part of any such register which is kept outside Great Britain shall be kept in England and Wales* (*in the case of a company registered in England and Wales*) *or in Scotland* (*in the case of a company registered in Scotland*) *elsewhere than—*

(*a*) *at the company's registered office; or*

(*b*) *at any office of the company at which the work of making it up is done; or*

(*c*) *if the company arranges with some other person for the making up of the register or duplicate to be undertaken on its behalf by that other person, at the office of that other person at which the work is done.*

(*4*) *Where a company keeps* (*in England and Wales or in Scotland, as the case may be*) *both such a register and such a duplicate, it shall keep them at the same place.*

(*5*) *Every company which keeps any such register or duplicate in England and Wales or Scotland shall send to the registrar of companies notice* (*in the prescribed form*) *of the place where the register or duplicate is kept and of any change in that place.*

(*6*) *But a company is not bound to send notice under subsection* (*5*) *where the register or duplicate has, at all times since it came into existence, been kept at the company's registered office.*

[176]

NOTES

Repealed by the Companies Act 2006, s 1295, Sch 16, as from a day to be appointed.

Application to limited liability partnerships: see the Limited Liability Partnerships Regulations 2001, SI 2001/1090, reg 4(1), Sch 2, Pt 1 at **[6985]**, **[6993]**.

Inspection, etc: for provisions relating to the inspection, etc, of a register of debenture holders maintained under this section, see the Companies (Inspection and Copying of Registers, Indices and Documents) Regulations 1991, SI 1991/1998, reg 4 at **[6719]**.

Notice (in the prescribed form): see Appendix 4 (Forms table) at **[A4]**.

191 Right to inspect register

(*1*) *Every register of holders of debentures of a company shall, except when duly closed ... , be open to the inspection—*

(*a*) *of the registered holder of any such debentures or any holder of shares in the company without fee; and*

(*b*) *of any other person on payment of [such fee as may be prescribed].*

(*2*) *Any such registered holder of debentures or holder of shares, or any other person, may require a copy of the register of the holders of debentures of the company or any part of it, on payment of [such fee as may be prescribed].*

(*3*) *A copy of any trust deed for securing an issue of debentures shall be forwarded to every holder of any such debentures at his request on payment [of such fee as may be prescribed] …*

(*4*) *If inspection is refused, or a copy is refused or not forwarded, the company and every officer of it who is in default is liable to a fine and, for continued contravention, to a daily default fine.*

(*5*) *Where a company is in default as above-mentioned, the court may by order compel an immediate inspection of the register or direct that the copies required be sent to the person requiring them.*

(*6*) *For purposes of this section, a register is deemed to be duly closed if closed in accordance with provisions contained in the articles or in the debentures or, in the case of debenture stock, in the stock certificates, or in the trust deed or other document securing the debentures or debenture stock, during such period or periods not exceeding in the whole 30 days in any year, as may be therein specified.*

(*7*) *Liability incurred by a company from the making or deletion of an entry in its register of debenture holders, or from a failure to make or delete any such entry, is not enforceable more than 20 years after the date on which the entry was made or deleted or, in the case of any such failure, the failure first occurred.*

This is without prejudice to any lesser period of limitation.

[177]

NOTES

Repealed by the Companies Act 2006, s 1295, Sch 16, as from a day to be appointed.

Sub-s (1): words omitted repealed, and words in square brackets substituted, by CA 1989, ss 143(4)(a), 212, Sch 24, as from 1 November 1991.

Sub-s (2): words in square brackets substituted by CA 1989, s 143(4)(b), as from 1 November 1991.

Sub-s (3): words omitted repealed, and words in square brackets inserted, by CA 1989, ss 143(4)(c), 212, Sch 24, as from 1 November 1991.

Application to limited liability partnerships: see the Limited Liability Partnerships Regulations 2001, SI 2001/1090, reg 4(1), Sch 2, Pt 1 at **[6985]**, **[6993]**.

Inspection: for provisions relating to the inspection of documents, registers and fees under this section, see the Companies (Inspection and Copying of Registers, Indices and Documents) Regulations 1991, SI 1991/1998 at **[6716]** et seq (partly made under this section).

192 Liability of trustees of debentures

(*1*) *Subject to this section, any provision contained—*

(*a*) *in a trust deed for securing an issue of debentures, or*

(*b*) *in any contract with the holders of debentures secured by a trust deed,*

is void in so far as it would have the effect of exempting a trustee of the deed from, or indemnifying him against, liability for breach of trust where he fails to show the degree of care and diligence required of him as trustee, having regard to the provisions of the trust deed conferring on him any powers, authorities or discretions.

(2) *Subsection* (*1*) *does not invalidate—*

(*a*) *a release otherwise validly given in respect of anything done or omitted to be done by a trustee before the giving of the release; or*

(*b*) *any provision enabling such a release to be given—*

(*i*) *on the agreement thereto of a majority of not less than three-fourths in value of the debenture holders present and voting in person or, where proxies are permitted, by proxy at a meeting summoned for the purpose, and*

(*ii*) *either with respect to specific acts or omissions or on the trustee dying or ceasing to act.*

(*3*) *Subsection* (*1*) *does not operate—*

(*a*) *to invalidate any provision in force on 1st July 1948 so long as any person then entitled to the benefit of that provision or afterwards given the benefit of that provision under the following subsection remains a trustee of the deed in question; or*

(*b*) *to deprive any person of any exemption or right to be indemnified in respect of anything done or omitted to be done by him while any such provision was in force.*

(4) While any trustee of a trust deed remains entitled to the benefit of a provision saved by subsection (3), the benefit of that provision may be given either—

(a) to all trustees of the deed, present and future; or

(b) to any named trustees or proposed trustees of it,

by a resolution passed by a majority of not less than three-fourths in value of the debenture holders present in person or, where proxies are permitted, by proxy at a meeting summoned for the purpose in accordance with the provisions of the deed or, if the deed makes no provision for summoning meetings, a meeting summoned for the purpose in any manner approved by the court.

[178]

NOTES

Repealed by the Companies Act 2006, s 1295, Sch 16, as from a day to be appointed.

Application to limited liability partnerships: see the Limited Liability Partnerships Regulations 2001, SI 2001/1090, reg 4(1), Sch 2, Pt 1 at **[6985]**, **[6993]**.

193 Perpetual debentures

A condition contained in debentures, or in a deed for securing debentures, is not invalid by reason only that the debentures are thereby made irredeemable or redeemable only on the happening of a contingency (however remote), or on the expiration of a period (however long), any rule of equity to the contrary notwithstanding.

This applies to debentures whenever issued, and to deeds whenever executed.

[179]

NOTES

Repealed by the Companies Act 2006, s 1295, Sch 16, as from a day to be appointed.

Application to limited liability partnerships: see the Limited Liability Partnerships Regulations 2001, SI 2001/1090, reg 4(1), Sch 2, Pt 1 at **[6985]**, **[6993]**.

194 Power to re-issue redeemed debentures

(1) Where (at any time) a company has redeemed debentures previously issued, then—

(a) unless provision to the contrary, whether express or implied, is contained in the articles or in any contract entered into by the company; or

(b) unless the company has, by passing a resolution to that effect or by some other act, manifested its intention that the debentures shall be cancelled,

the company has, and is deemed always to have had, power to re-issue the debentures, either by re-issuing the same debentures or by issuing other debentures in their place.

(2) On a re-issue of redeemed debentures, the person entitled to the debentures has, and is deemed always to have had, the same priorities as if the debentures had never been redeemed.

(3) Where a company has (at any time) deposited any of its debentures to secure advances from time to time on current account or otherwise, the debentures are not deemed to have been redeemed by reason only of the company's account having ceased to be in debit while the debentures remained so deposited.

(4) The re-issue of a debenture or the issue of another debenture in its place under the power which by this section is given to or deemed to be possessed by a company is to be treated as the issue of a new debenture for purposes of stamp duty; but it is not to be so treated for the purposes of any provision limiting the amount or number of debentures to be issued.

This applies whenever the issue or re-issue was made.

(5) A person lending money on the security of a debenture re-issued under this section which appears to be duly stamped may give the debenture in evidence in any proceedings for enforcing his security without payment of the stamp duty or any penalty in respect of it, unless he had notice (or, but for his negligence, might have discovered) that the debenture was not duly stamped; but in that case the company is liable to pay the proper stamp duty and penalty.

[180]

NOTES

Repealed by the Companies Act 2006, s 1295, Sch 16, as from a day to be appointed.

Application to limited liability partnerships: see the Limited Liability Partnerships Regulations 2001, SI 2001/1090, reg 4(1), Sch 2, Pt 1 at **[6985]**, **[6993]**.

Saving: for a saving, in the case of certain re-issued debentures, for the rights of certain mortgagees, see the Companies Consolidation (Consequential Provisions) Act 1985, s 13 at **[713]**.

195 Contract to subscribe for debentures

A contract with a company to take up and pay for debentures of the company may be enforced by an order for specific performance.

[181]

NOTES

Repealed by the Companies Act 2006, s 1295, Sch 16, as from a day to be appointed.

Application to limited liability partnerships: see the Limited Liability Partnerships Regulations 2001, SI 2001/1090, reg 4(1), Sch 2, Pt 1 at **[6985]**, **[6993]**.

196 Payment of debts out of assets subject to floating charge (England and Wales)

[(1) The following applies in the case of a company registered in England and Wales, where debentures of the company are secured by a charge which, as created, was a floating charge.

(2) If possession is taken, by or on behalf of the holders of any of the debentures, of any property comprised in or subject to the charge, and the company is not at that time in course of being wound up, the company's preferential debts shall be paid out of assets coming to the hands of the person taking possession in priority to any claims for principal or interest in respect of the debentures.

(3) "Preferential debts" means the categories of debts listed in Schedule 6 to the Insolvency Act; and for the purposes of that Schedule "the relevant date" is the date of possession being taken as above mentioned.

(4) Payments made under this section shall be recouped, as far as may be, out of the assets of the company available for payment of general creditors.]

[182]

NOTES

Substituted by the Insolvency Act 1986, s 439(1), Sch 13, Pt I, as from 29 December 1986; for transitional provisions see s 437 of, and Sch 11, Pt I to, that Act at **[3456]**, **[3481]**. Note that the original section heading has been retained.

Repealed by the Companies Act 2006, s 1295, Sch 16, as from a day to be appointed.

Application to limited liability partnerships: see the Limited Liability Partnerships Regulations 2001, SI 2001/1090, reg 4(1), Sch 2, Pt 1 at **[6985]**, **[6993]**.

Insolvency Act: ie, the Insolvency Act 1986.

197 Debentures to bearer (Scotland)

Notwithstanding anything in the statute of the Scots Parliament of 1696, chapter 25, debentures to bearer issued in Scotland are valid and binding according to their terms.

[183]

NOTES

Repealed by the Companies Act 2006, s 1295, Sch 16, as from a day to be appointed.

PART VI
DISCLOSURE OF INTERESTS IN SHARES

Individual and group acquisitions

198 Obligation of disclosure: the cases in which it may arise and "the relevant time"

(1) Where a person either—

(a) to his knowledge acquires an interest in shares comprised in a public company's relevant share capital, or ceases to be interested in shares so comprised (whether or not retaining an interest in other shares so comprised), or

(*b*) *becomes aware that he has acquired an interest in shares so comprised or that he has ceased to be interested in shares so comprised in which he was previously interested,*

then in certain circumstances he comes under an obligation ("the obligation of disclosure") to make notification to the company [with respect to his interests (if any)], in its shares.

(2) *In relation to a public company, "relevant share capital" means the company's issued share capital of a class carrying rights to vote in all circumstances at general meetings of the company [(excluding any shares in the company held as treasury shares)]; and it is hereby declared for the avoidance of doubt that—*

(*a*) *where a company's share capital is divided into different classes of shares, references in this Part to a percentage of the nominal value of its relevant share capital are to a percentage of the nominal value of the issued shares comprised in each of the classes taken separately [(excluding any shares of each class held as treasury shares)], and*

(*b*) *the temporary suspension of voting rights in respect of shares comprised in issued share capital of a company of any such class does not affect the application of this Part in relation to interests in those or any other shares comprised in that class.*

(3) *Where, otherwise than in circumstances within subsection (1), a person—*

(*a*) *is aware at the time when it occurs of any change of circumstances affecting facts relevant to the application of the next following section to an existing interest of his in shares comprised in a company's share capital of any description, or*

(*b*) *otherwise becomes aware of any such facts (whether or not arising from any such change of circumstances),*

then in certain circumstances he comes under the obligation of disclosure.

(4) *The existence of the obligation in a particular case depends (in part) on circumstances obtaining before and after whatever is in that case the relevant time; and that is—*

(*a*) *in a case within subsection (1)(a) or (3)(a), the time of the event or change of circumstances there mentioned, and*

(*b*) *in a case within subsection (1)(b) or (3)(b), the time at which the person became aware of the facts in question.*

[184]

NOTES

Repealed by the Companies Act 2006, s 1295, Sch 16, as from 20 January 2007 (for transitional provisions and savings see the note below).

Sub-s (1): words in square brackets substituted by the Disclosure of Interests in Shares (Amendment) Regulations 1993, SI 1993/1819, regs 2, 3, as from 18 September 1993 (subject to transitional provisions in relation to interests which become notifiable as a result of the coming into force of the 1993 Regulations).

Sub-s (2): words in square brackets inserted by the Companies (Acquisition of Own Shares) (Treasury Shares) Regulations 2003, SI 2003/1116, reg 4, Schedule, para 15, as from 1 December 2003.

Transitional provisions and savings: the Companies Act 2006 (Commencement No 1, Transitional Provisions and Savings) Order 2006, SI 2006/3428, Sch 5, para 2 provides as follows—

2 Information about interests in a company's shares

(1) The repeal of sections 198 to 210 and 220 of the 1985 Act or Articles 206 to 218 and 228 of the 1986 Order (obligation to disclose acquisitions and disposals of interests in shares) does not affect any obligation to which a person became subject under section 198 of that Act or Article 206 of that Order before 20th January 2007.

(2) The repeal of sections 212 to 220 of the 1985 Act or Articles 220 to 228 of the 1986 Order (power of public company to require disclosure of interests in shares) does not affect the operation of those provisions in relation to a notice issued by a company under section 212 of the 1985 Act or Article 220 of the 1986 Order before 20th January 2007.

(3) On and after 20th January 2007 any separate part of a register kept by a company under section 213 of the 1985 Act or Article 221 of the 1986 Order (register of interests disclosed in response to requirement by company) shall continue to be kept by the company and shall be treated as a register kept under and for the purposes of section 808 of the Companies Act 2006.

(4) Until regulations under section 1136 of the Companies Act 2006 (regulations about where certain company records are to be kept available for inspection) are made specifying a place for the purposes of section 809(1)(b) of that Act—

(a) the register kept under section 808 of that Act (register of interests disclosed) may be kept by a company at any place where its register of members is kept; and

(b) no notice need be given to the registrar of companies under section 809(2) of that Act.

199 Interests to be disclosed

(1) For the purposes of the obligation of disclosure, the interests to be taken into account are those in relevant share capital of the company concerned.

[(2) Where a person is interested in shares comprised in relevant share capital, then—

(a) if in some or all of those shares he has interests which are material interests, he has a notifiable interest at any time when the aggregate nominal value of the shares in which those material interests subsist is equal to or more than 3 per cent of the nominal value of that share capital; and

(b) he has a notifiable interest at any time when, not having such an interest by virtue of paragraph (a), the aggregate nominal value of the shares in which he has interests (whether or not including material interests) is equal to or more than 10 per cent of the nominal value of the relevant share capital.

(2A) For the purposes of this Part, a material interest is any interest other than—

(a) an interest which a person [who may lawfully] manage investments belonging to another has by virtue of having the management of such investments under an agreement in or evidenced in writing;

(b) an interest which a person has by virtue of being the operator of—

(i) an authorised unit trust scheme;

(ii) a recognised scheme; or

(iii) a UCITS (as defined in subsection (8));

[(bb) an interest belonging to an [open-ended investment company];]

(c) an interest in shares in a listed company which, if that company were not listed, would fall to be disregarded by virtue of section 209(10); or

(d) an interest of another which a person is taken to have by virtue of the application of section 203 or 205, where the interest of that other person falls within paragraph [(a), (b), (bb), (c)].]

(3) All facts relevant to determining whether a person has a notifiable interest at any time (or the percentage level of his interest) are taken to be what he knows the facts to be at that time.

(4) The obligation of disclosure arises under section 198(1) or (3) where the person has a notifiable interest immediately after the relevant time, but did not have such an interest immediately before that time.

(5) The obligation also arises under section 198(1) [or (3)] where—

(a) the person had a notifiable interest immediately before the relevant time, but does not have such an interest immediately after it, or

(b) he had a notifiable interest immediately before that time, and has such an interest immediately after it, but the percentage levels of his interest immediately before and immediately after that time are not the same.

[[(6) For the purposes of subsection (2A), a person ("A") may lawfully manage investments belonging to another if—

(a) A can manage those investments in accordance with a permission which A has under Part 4 of the Financial Services and Markets Act 2000;

(b) A is an EEA firm of the kind mentioned in sub-paragraph (a) or (b) of paragraph 5 of Schedule 3 to that Act, and can manage those investments in accordance with its EEA authorisation;

(c) A can, in accordance with section 327 of that Act, manage those investments without contravening the prohibition contained in section 19 of that Act; or

(d) A can lawfully manage those investments in another Member State and would, if he were to manage those investments in the United Kingdom, require permission under Part 4 of that Act.

(7) References in this section to the management of investments must be read with—

(a) section 22 of the Financial Services and Markets Act 2000;

(b) any relevant order under that section; and

(c) Schedule 2 to that Act.]

(8) In this Part "UCITS" means a collective investment scheme which—

(*a*) *is constituted in a member State other than the United Kingdom, and*
(*b*) *[is certified by the competent authority in that member State as complying with the conditions imposed] by [Council Directive 85/611/EEC on the co-ordination of laws, regulations and administrative provisions relating to undertakings for collective investment in transferable securities, as last amended by European Parliament and Council Directive 2001/108/EC]*

and [subsection (5) of section 264 of the Financial Services and Markets Act 2000] (meaning of "constituted in a member State") applies for the purposes of paragraph (a) of this subsection as it applies for the purposes of that section.]

[185]

NOTES

Repealed by the Companies Act 2006, s 1295, Sch 16, as from 20 January 2007 (for transitional provisions and savings see the note to s 198 at **[184]**).

Sub-s (2): substituted, together with sub-s (2A), for original sub-s (2), by the Disclosure of Interests in Shares (Amendment) Regulations 1993, SI 1993/1819, regs 2, 4(1), as from 18 September 1993 (subject to transitional provisions in relation to interests which become notifiable as a result of the coming into force of the 1993 Regulations).

Sub-s (2A): substituted as noted above; words in square brackets in para (a) substituted by the Financial Services and Markets Act 2000 (Consequential Amendments and Repeals) Order 2001, SI 2001/3649, art 8(1), (2), as from 1 December 2001; para (bb) inserted by the Open-Ended Investment Companies (Investment Companies with Variable Capital) Regulations 1996, SI 1996/2827, reg 75, Sch 8, Pt I, para 5, as from 6 January 1997, and words in square brackets therein substituted by the Open-Ended Investment Companies Regulations 2001, SI 2001/1228, reg 84, Sch 7, para 4(1), (2), as from 1 December 2001; words in square brackets in para (d) substituted by SI 2001/1228, reg 84, Sch 7, para 4(1), (3), as from 1 December 2001.

Sub-s (5): words in square brackets inserted by SI 1993/1819, regs 2, 4(2), as from 18 September 1993 (subject to transitional provisions as noted above).

Sub-ss (6), (7): added, together with sub-s (8), by SI 1993/1819, regs 2, 4(3), as from 18 September 1993 (subject to transitional provisions as noted above); substituted by SI 2001/3649, art 8(1), (3), as from 1 December 2001.

Sub-s (8): added as noted above; words in first and third pairs of square brackets substituted by SI 2001/3649, art 8(1), (4), as from 1 December 2001; words in second pair of square brackets substituted by the Collective Investment Schemes (Miscellaneous Amendments) Regulations 2003, SI 2003/2066, reg 13(1), as from 13 February 2004.

[200 "Percentage level" in relation to notifiable interests

(1) Subject to the qualifications mentioned below, "percentage level", in section 199(5)(b), means the percentage figure found by expressing the aggregate nominal value of all the shares comprised in the share capital concerned in which the person has material interests immediately before or (as the case may be) immediately after the relevant time as a percentage of the nominal value of that share capital and rounding that figure down, if it is not a whole number, to the next whole number.

(2) In relation to a notifiable interest which a person has when the aggregate nominal value of the shares in which he is interested is equal to or more than 10 per cent of the nominal value of that relevant share capital, subsection (1) shall have effect as if for the words "has material interests" there were substituted "is interested".

(3) Where the nominal value of the share capital is greater immediately after the relevant time than it was immediately before, the percentage level of the person's interest immediately before (as well as immediately after) that time is determined by reference to the larger amount.]

[186]

NOTES

Substituted by the Disclosure of Interests in Shares (Amendment) Regulations 1993, SI 1993/1819, regs 2, 5, as from 18 September 1993 (subject to transitional provisions in relation to interests which become notifiable as a result of the coming into force of the 1993 Regulations).

Repealed by the Companies Act 2006, s 1295, Sch 16, as from 20 January 2007 (for transitional provisions and savings see the note to s 198 at **[184]**).

201 *(Repealed by CA 1989, s 212, Sch 24, as from 31 May 1990.)*

202 Particulars to be contained in notification

(1) Where notification is required by section 198 with respect to a person's interest (if any) in shares comprised in relevant share capital of a public company, the obligation to

make the notification must … be performed within the period of [2 days] next following the day on which that obligation arises; and the notification must be in writing to the company.

(2) *The notification must specify the share capital to which it relates, and must also—*

[(a) subject to subsections (2A) and (2B), state the number of shares comprised in that share capital in which the person making the notification knows he had material interests immediately after the time when the obligation arose, or]

(b) in a case where the person no longer has a notifiable interest in shares comprised in that share capital, state that he no longer has that interest.

[(2A) Where, immediately after the relevant time, the aggregate nominal value of the shares in which the person making the notification is interested is equal to or more than 10 per cent of the nominal value of that relevant share capital, subsection (2)(a) shall have effect as if for the words "had material interests" there were substituted "was interested".

(2B) Nothing in subsection (2) or (2A) requires a notification to state, in relation to any shares, whether the interest of the person making the notification is (or is not) a material interest.]

[(3) A notification (other than one stating that a person no longer has a notifiable interest) shall include the following particulars, so far as known to the person making the notification at the date when it is made—

(a) the identity of each registered holder of shares to which the notification relates and the number of such shares held by each of them, and

(b) the number of such shares in which the interest of the person giving the notification is such an interest as is mentioned in section 208(5).]

(4) A person who has an interest in shares comprised in a company's relevant share capital, that interest being notifiable, is under obligation to notify the company in writing—

(a) of any particulars in relation to those shares which are specified in subsection (3), and

(b) of any change in those particulars,

of which in either case he becomes aware at any time after any interest notification date and before the first occasion following that date on which he comes under any further obligation of disclosure with respect to his interest in shares comprised in that share capital.

An obligation arising under this section must be performed within the period of [2 days] next following the day on which it arises.

(5) The reference in subsection (4) to an interest notification date, in relation to a person's interest in shares comprised in a public company's relevant share capital, is to either of the following—

(a) the date of any notification made by him with respect to his interest under this Part, and

(b) where he has failed to make a notification, the date on which the period allowed for making it came to an end.

(6) A person who at any time has an interest in shares which is notifiable is to be regarded under subsection (4) as continuing to have a notifiable interest in them unless and until he comes under obligation to make a notification stating that he no longer has such an interest in those shares.

[187]

NOTES

Repealed by the Companies Act 2006, s 1295, Sch 16, as from 20 January 2007 (for transitional provisions and savings see the note to s 198 at **[184]**).

Sub-s (1): words omitted repealed, and words in square brackets substituted, by CA 1989, ss 134(1), (3), 212, Sch 24, as from 31 May 1990.

Sub-s (2): para (a) substituted by the Disclosure of Interests in Shares (Amendment) Regulations 1993, SI 1993/1819, regs 2, 6(1), as from 18 September 1993 (subject to transitional provisions in relation to interests which become notifiable as a result of the coming into force of the 1993 Regulations).

Sub-ss (2A), (2B): inserted by SI 1993/1819, regs 2, 6(2), as from 18 September 1993 (subject to transitional provisions as noted above).

Sub-s (3): substituted by CA 1989, s 134(1), (4), as from 1 November 1991.

Sub-s (4): words in square brackets substituted by CA 1989, s 134(3), as from 31 May 1990.

203 Notification of family and corporate interests

(1) For purposes of sections 198 to 202, a person is taken to be interested in any shares in which his spouse [or civil partner] or any infant child or step-child of his is interested; and "infant" means, in relation to Scotland, [person under the age of 18 years].

(2) For those purposes, a person is taken to be interested in shares if a body corporate is interested in them and—

(a) that body or its directors are accustomed to act in accordance with his directions or instructions, or

(b) he is entitled to exercise or control the exercise of one-third or more of the voting power at general meetings of that body corporate.

(3) Where a person is entitled to exercise or control the exercise of one-third or more of the voting power at general meetings of a body corporate and that body corporate is entitled to exercise or control the exercise of any of the voting power at general meetings of another body corporate ("the effective voting power") then, for purposes of subsection (2)(b), the effective voting power is taken as exercisable by that person.

(4) For purposes of subsections (2) and (3), a person is entitled to exercise or control the exercise of voting power if—

(a) he has a right (whether subject to conditions or not) the exercise of which would make him so entitled, or

(b) he is under an obligation (whether or not so subject) the fulfilment of which would make him so entitled.

[188]

NOTES

Repealed by the Companies Act 2006, s 1295, Sch 16, as from 20 January 2007 (for transitional provisions and savings see the note to s 198 at **[184]**).

Sub-s (1): words in first pair of square brackets inserted by the Civil Partnership Act 2004, s 261(1), Sch 27, para 99, as from 5 December 2005; words in second pair of square brackets substituted by the Age of Legal Capacity (Scotland) Act 1991, s 10(1), Sch 1, para 39, as from 25 September 1991.

Step-child: this includes relationships arising through civil partnerships; see the Civil Partnership Act 2004, ss 246, 247, Sch 21.

204 Agreement to acquire interests in a particular company

(1) In certain circumstances the obligation of disclosure may arise from an agreement between two or more persons which includes provision for the acquisition by any one or more of them of interests in shares of a particular public company ("the target company"), being shares comprised in the relevant share capital of that company.

(2) This section applies to such an agreement if—

(a) the agreement also includes provisions imposing obligations or restrictions on any one or more of the parties to it with respect to their use, retention or disposal of their interests in that company's shares acquired in pursuance of the agreement (whether or not together with any other interests of theirs in the company's shares to which the agreement relates), and

(b) any interest in the company's shares is in fact acquired by any of the parties in pursuance of the agreement;

and in relation to such an agreement references below in this section, and in sections 205 and 206, to the target company are to the company which is the target company for that agreement in accordance with this and the previous subsection.

(3) The reference in subsection (2)(a) to the use of interests in shares in the target company is to the exercise of any rights or of any control or influence arising from those interests (including the right to enter into any agreement for the exercise, or for control of the exercise, of any of those rights by another person).

(4) Once any interest in shares in the target company has been acquired in pursuance of such an agreement as is mentioned above, this section continues to apply to that agreement irrespective of—

(a) whether or not any further acquisitions of interests in the company's shares take place in pursuance of the agreement, and

(b) any change in the persons who are for the time being parties to it, and

(c) any variation of the agreement,

so long as the agreement continues to include provisions of any description mentioned in subsection (2)(a).

References in this subsection to the agreement include any agreement having effect (whether directly or indirectly) in substitution for the original agreement.

(5) In this section, and also in references elsewhere in this Part to an agreement to which this section applies, "agreement" includes any agreement or arrangement; and references in this section to provisions of an agreement—

(*a*) *accordingly include undertakings, expectations or understandings operative under any arrangement, and*

(*b*) *(without prejudice to the above) also include any provisions, whether express or implied and whether absolute or not.*

(6) However, this section does not apply to an agreement which is not legally binding unless it involves mutuality in the undertakings, expectations or understandings of the parties to it; nor does the section apply to an agreement to underwrite or sub-underwrite any offer of shares in a company, provided the agreement is confined to that purpose and any matters incidental to it.

[189]

NOTES

Repealed by the Companies Act 2006, s 1295, Sch 16, as from 20 January 2007 (for transitional provisions and savings see the note to s 198 at **[184]**).

205 Obligation of disclosure arising under s 204

(1) In the case of an agreement to which section 204 applies, each party to the agreement is taken (for purposes of the obligation of disclosure) to be interested in all shares in the target company in which any other party to it is interested apart from the agreement (whether or not the interest of the other party in question was acquired, or includes any interest which was acquired, in pursuance of the agreement).

(2) For those purposes, and also for those of the next section, an interest of a party to such an agreement in shares in the target company is an interest apart from the agreement if he is interested in those shares otherwise than by virtue of the application of section 204 and this section in relation to the agreement.

(3) Accordingly, any such interest of the person (apart from the agreement) includes for those purposes any interest treated as his under section 203 or by the application of section 204 and this section in relation to any other agreement with respect to shares in the target company to which he is a party.

(4) A notification with respect to his interest in shares in the target company made to that company under this Part by a person who is for the time being a party to an agreement to which section 204 applies shall—

(*a*) *state that the person making the notification is a party to such an agreement,*

(*b*) *include the names and (so far as known to him) the addresses of the other parties to the agreement, identifying them as such, and*

(*c*) *state whether or not any of the shares to which the notification relates are shares in which he is interested by virtue of section 204 and this section and, if so, the number of those shares.*

(5) Where a person makes a notification to a company under this Part in consequence of ceasing to be interested in any shares of that company by virtue of the fact that he or any other person has ceased to be a party to an agreement to which section 204 applies, the notification shall include a statement that he or that other person has ceased to be a party to the agreement (as the case may require) and also (in the latter case) the name and (if known to him) the address of that other.

[190]

NOTES

Repealed by the Companies Act 2006, s 1295, Sch 16, as from 20 January 2007 (for transitional provisions and savings see the note to s 198 at **[184]**).

206 Obligation of persons acting together to keep each other informed

(*1*) *A person who is a party to an agreement to which section 204 applies is subject to the requirements of this section at any time when—*

(*a*) *the target company is a public company, and he knows it to be so, and*

(*b*) *the shares in that company to which the agreement relates consist of or include shares comprised in relevant share capital of the company, and he knows that to be the case; and*

(*c*) *he knows the facts which make the agreement one to which section 204 applies.*

(2) *Such a person is under obligation to notify every other party to the agreement, in writing, of the relevant particulars of his interest (if any) apart from the agreement in shares comprised in relevant share capital of the target company—*

(*a*) *on his first becoming subject to the requirements of this section, and*

(*b*) *on each occurrence after that time while he is still subject to those requirements of any event or circumstances within section 198(1) (as it applies to his case otherwise than by reference to interests treated as his under section 205 as applying to that agreement).*

(3) *The relevant particulars to be notified under subsection (2) are—*

(*a*) *the number of shares (if any) comprised in the target company's relevant share capital in which the person giving the notice would be required to state his interest [if he were under the wide obligation of disclosure with respect to that interest] (apart from the agreement) immediately after the time when the obligation to give notice under subsection (2) arose, and*

(*b*) *the relevant particulars with respect to the registered ownership of those shares, so far as known to him at the date of the notice [and*

(*c*) *except in the circumstances mentioned in subsection (3A), the number of shares (if any) out of the number given under paragraph (a) in which he knows that, immediately after the time when the obligation to give the notice arose, he had interests (apart from the agreement) which were not material interests.]*

[(3A) The circumstance referred to in subsection (3)(c) is that the aggregate nominal value of the shares comprised in relevant share capital in which the person is interested (apart from the agreement) is equal to or more than 10 per cent of the nominal value of the relevant share capital.

(3B) For the purposes of subsection (3)(a) "the wide obligation of disclosure" means the obligation to disclose the number of shares in which the person concerned has any interest (material or otherwise).]

(4) *A person who is for the time being subject to the requirements of this section is also under obligation to notify every other party to the agreement, in writing—*

(*a*) *of any relevant particulars with respect to the registered ownership of any shares comprised in relevant share capital of the target company in which he is interested apart from the agreement, and*

(*b*) *of any change in those particulars,*

of which in either case he becomes aware at any time after any interest notification date and before the first occasion following that date on which he becomes subject to any further obligation to give notice under subsection (2) with respect to his interest in shares comprised in that share capital.

(5) *The reference in subsection (4) to an interest notification date, in relation to a person's interest in shares comprised in the target company's relevant share capital, is to either of the following—*

(*a*) *the date of any notice given by him with respect to his interest under subsection (2), and*

(*b*) *where he has failed to give that notice, the date on which the period allowed by this section for giving the notice came to an end.*

(6) *A person who is a party to an agreement to which section 204 applies is under an obligation to notify each other party to the agreement, in writing, of his current address—*

(*a*) *on his first becoming subject to the requirements of this section, and*

(*b*) *on any change in his address occurring after that time and while he is still subject to those requirements.*

(7) *A reference to the relevant particulars with respect to the registered ownership of shares is to such particulars in relation to those shares as are mentioned in section 202(3)(a) or (b).*

(*8*) *A person's obligation to give any notice required by this section to any other person must be performed within the period of [2 days] next following the day on which that obligation arose.*

[191]

NOTES

Repealed by the Companies Act 2006, s 1295, Sch 16, as from 20 January 2007 (for transitional provisions and savings see the note to s 198 at **[184]**).

Sub-s (3): words in square brackets in para (a) substituted, and para (c) and the word immediately preceding it added, by the Disclosure of Interests in Shares (Amendment) Regulations 1993, SI 1993/1819, regs 2, 7(1), as from 18 September 1993 (subject to transitional provisions in relation to interests which become notifiable as a result of the coming into force of the 1993 Regulations).

Sub-ss (3A), (3B): inserted by SI 1993/1819, regs 2, 7(2), as from 18 September 1993 (subject to transitional provisions as noted above).

Sub-s (8): words in square brackets substituted by CA 1989, s 134(1), (3), as from 31 May 1990.

207 Interests in shares by attribution

(*1*) *Where section 198 or 199 refers to a person acquiring an interest in shares or ceasing to be interested in shares, that reference in certain cases includes his becoming or ceasing to be interested in those shares by virtue of another person's interest.*

(*2*) *Such is the case where he becomes or ceases to be interested by virtue of section 203 or (as the case may be) section 205 whether—*

(*a*) *by virtue of the fact that the person who is interested in the shares becomes or ceases to be a person whose interests (if any) fall by virtue of either section to be treated as his, or*

(*b*) *in consequence of the fact that such a person has become or ceased to be interested in the shares, or*

(*c*) *in consequence of the fact that he himself becomes or ceases to be a party to an agreement to which section 204 applies to which the person interested in the shares is for the time being a party, or*

(*d*) *in consequence of the fact that an agreement to which both he and that person are parties becomes or ceases to be one to which that section applies.*

(*3*) *The person is then to be treated as knowing he has acquired an interest in the shares or (as the case may be) that he has ceased to be interested in them, if and when he knows both—*

(*a*) *the relevant facts with respect to the other person's interest in the shares, and*

(*b*) *the relevant facts by virtue of which he himself has become or ceased to be interested in them in accordance with section 203 or 205.*

(*4*) *He has the knowledge referred to in subsection (3)(a) if he knows (whether contemporaneously or not) either of the subsistence of the other person's interest at any material time or of the fact that the other has become or ceased to be interested in the shares at any such time; and "material time" is any time at which the other's interests (if any) fall or fell to be treated as his under section 203 or 205.*

(*5*) *A person is to be regarded as knowing of the subsistence of another's interest in shares or (as the case may be) that another has become or ceased to be interested in shares if he has been notified under section 206 of facts with respect to the other's interest which indicate that he is or has become or ceased to be interested in the shares (whether on his own account or by virtue of a third party's interest in them).*

[192]

NOTES

Repealed by the Companies Act 2006, s 1295, Sch 16, as from 20 January 2007 (for transitional provisions and savings see the note to s 198 at **[184]**).

208 Interests in shares which are to be notified

(*1*) *This section applies, subject to the section next following, in determining for purposes of sections 198 to 202 whether a person has a notifiable interest in shares.*

(*2*) *A reference to an interest in shares is to be read as including an interest of any kind whatsoever in the shares; and accordingly there are to be disregarded any restraints or restrictions to which the exercise of any right attached to the interest is or may be subject.*

(*3*) *Where property is held on trust and an interest in shares is comprised in the property, a beneficiary of the trust who apart from this subsection does not have an interest in the shares is to be taken as having such an interest.*

(*4*) *A person is taken to have an interest in shares if—*

(*a*) *he enters into a contract for their purchase by him (whether for cash or other consideration), or*

(*b*) *not being the registered holder, he is entitled to exercise any right conferred by the holding of the shares or is entitled to control the exercise of any such right.*

(*5*) *A person is taken to have an interest in shares if, otherwise than by virtue of having an interest under a trust—*

(*a*) *he has a right to call for delivery of the shares to himself or to his order, or*

(*b*) *he has a right to acquire an interest in shares or is under an obligation to take an interest in shares,*

whether in any case the right or obligation is conditional or absolute.

(*6*) *For purposes of subsection (4)(b), a person is entitled to exercise or control the exercise of any right conferred by the holding of shares if he—*

(*a*) *has a right (whether subject to conditions or not) the exercise of which would make him so entitled, or*

(*b*) *is under an obligation (whether so subject or not) the fulfilment of which would make him so entitled.*

(*7*) *Persons having a joint interest are taken each of them to have that interest.*

(*8*) *It is immaterial that shares in which a person has an interest are unidentifiable.*

[193]

NOTES

Repealed by the Companies Act 2006, s 1295, Sch 16, as from 20 January 2007 (for transitional provisions and savings see the note to s 198 at **[184]**).

[209 Interests to be disregarded

(*1*) *Subject to subsections (5) and (6), the following interests in shares are disregarded for the purposes of sections 198 to 202—*

(*a*) *where property is held on trust and an interest in shares is comprised in that property, an interest of a person, being a discretionary interest or an interest in reversion or remainder or an interest of a bare trustee;*

(*b*) *an interest which a person has by virtue of holding units in—*

(*i*) *an authorised unit trust scheme;*

(*ii*) *a recognised scheme; or*

(*iii*) *a UCITS;*

(*c*) *an interest of a person which is an exempt security interest within the meaning of subsection (2);*

(*d*) *an interest which a person has by virtue of his being a beneficiary under a retirement benefits scheme as defined in section 611 of the Income and Corporation Taxes Act 1988;*

(*e*) *an interest which a person has in shares as a result of the acceptance of a takeover offer made by him (either alone or jointly with one or more other persons) for shares where—*

(*i*) *the offer is subject to a threshold acceptance condition; and*

(*ii*) *the threshold acceptance condition is not fulfilled;*

(*f*) *an interest of a person which is an exempt custodian interest within the meaning of subsection (4);*

(*g*) *an interest which a person has by virtue of his being a personal representative of any estate;*

(*h*) *an interest which a person has—*

(*i*) *by virtue of his being a trustee of an authorised unit trust scheme, ...*

(*ii*) *in relation to a recognised scheme or a UCITS, by virtue of his being entrusted with the custody of the property in question (whether or not under a trust) [or*

[(iii) by virtue of his being a depositary, within the meaning of the Open-Ended Investment Companies Regulations 2001, of an open-ended investment company]].

[(2) An interest in shares is an exempt security interest for the purposes of subsection (1)(c) if the condition mentioned in subsection (2A) is satisfied and it is held by—

(a) a person who has permission under Part 4 of the Financial Services and Markets Act 2000 to accept deposits;

(b) an EEA firm of the kind mentioned in paragraph 5(b) of Schedule 3 to that Act [which falls within [Article 4(1)(a)] of the banking consolidation directive (within the meaning of that Schedule)];

(c) a person authorised under the law of a member State other than the United Kingdom to accept deposits who—

(i) would not qualify for authorisation under paragraph 12 of Schedule 3 to that Act; and

(ii) would require permission under another provision of that Act to accept such deposits in the United Kingdom;

(d) an authorised insurance undertaking;

(e) a person authorised under the law of a member State to deal in securities or derivatives, who deals in securities or derivatives on a relevant stock exchange or a relevant investment exchange, whether as a member or otherwise;

(f) a relevant stock exchange;

(g) a relevant investment exchange;

(h) a recognised clearing house;

(i) the Bank of England; or

(j) the central bank of a member State other than the United Kingdom.

(2A) The condition is that the interest in the shares must be held by way of security only for the purposes of a transaction entered into in the ordinary course of his or its business as a person or other body falling within any of paragraphs (a) to (j) of subsection (2).

(2B) Paragraphs (a) to (c) of subsection (2) must be read with—

(a) section 22 of the Financial Services and Markets Act 2000;

(b) any relevant order under that section; and

(c) Schedule 2 to that Act.

(2C) But paragraph (a) of subsection (2) does not include—

(a) a building society incorporated, or deemed to be incorporated, under the Building Societies Act 1986; or

(b) a credit union, within the meaning of the Credit Unions Act 1979 or the Credit Unions (Northern Ireland) Order 1985.]

(3) For the purposes of subsection (1)(e)—

(a) "takeover offer" has the same meaning as in Part XIIIA; and

(b) "a threshold acceptance condition" means a condition that acceptances are received in respect of such proportion of the shares for which the takeover offer is made as is specified in or determined in accordance with the terms of the takeover offer.

(4) For the purposes of subsection (1)(f) an interest of a person is an exempt custodian interest if it is held by him—

(a) as a custodian (whether under a trust or by a contract); or

(b) under an arrangement pursuant to which he has issued, or is to issue, depository receipts in respect of the shares concerned.

(5) An interest referred to in any paragraph of subsection (1) (except for paragraph (c)) is disregarded only if the person referred to in the relevant paragraph or in subsection (4) is not entitled to exercise or control the exercise of voting rights in respect of the shares concerned; and for this purpose he is not so entitled if he is bound (whether by contract or otherwise) not to exercise the voting rights, or not to exercise them otherwise than in accordance with the instructions of another.

(6) In the case of an interest referred to in paragraph (c) of subsection (1), an interest of a person referred to in subsection (2) is disregarded only if that person—

(a) is not entitled (within the meaning of subsection (5)) to exercise or control the exercise of voting rights in respect of the shares concerned; or

(b) is so entitled, but has not evidenced any intention to exercise them or control their exercise nor taken any step to do so.

(7) For the purposes of subsections (5) and (6), voting rights which a person is entitled to exercise or of which he is entitled to control the exercise only in certain circumstances shall be taken into account only when the circumstances have arisen and for so long as they continue to obtain.

(8) An interest in shares of a company is also disregarded for the purposes of sections 198 to 202—

- *(a) if it is held by a market maker in securities or derivatives for the purposes of his business, but*
- *(b) only in so far as it is not used by him for the purpose of intervening in the management of the company.*

(9) For the purposes of subsection (8) a person is a market maker in securities or derivatives if—

- *(a) he is authorised under the law of a member State to deal in securities or derivatives and so deals on a relevant stock exchange or on a relevant investment exchange (whether as a member or otherwise); and*
- *(b) he holds himself out at all normal times as willing to acquire and dispose of securities or derivatives at prices specified by him and in so doing is subject to the rules of that exchange;*

and he holds an interest for the purposes of his business if he holds it for the purposes of a business carried on by him as a market maker in a member State.

[(9A) Where—

- *(a) in pursuance of arrangements made with the operator of a relevant system—*
  - *(i) securities of a particular aggregate value are on any day transferred by means of that system from a person ("A") to another person ("B");*
  - *(ii) the securities are of kinds and amounts determined by the operator-system; and*
  - *(iii) the securities, or securities of the same kinds and amounts, are on the following day transferred by means of the relevant system from B to A; and*
- *(b) the securities comprise any shares of a company,*

any interest of B in those shares is also disregarded for the purposes of sections 198 to 202.

(9B) For the purposes of subsection (9A)—

- *(a) any day which, in England and Wales, is a non-business day for the purposes of the Bills of Exchange Act 1882 is disregarded; and*
- *(b) expressions which are used in the [Uncertificated Securities Regulations 2001] have the same meanings as in those Regulations.]*

(10) The following interests in shares in a public company which is not listed are also disregarded for the purposes of sections 198 to 202—

- *(a) an interest which subsists by virtue of—*
  - *(i) a scheme made under section 24 or 25 of the Charities Act 1993, section 25 of the Charities Act (Northern Ireland) 1964, section 11 of the Trustee Investments Act 1961 or section 42 of the Administration of Justice Act 1982, or*
  - *(ii) the scheme set out in the Schedule to the Church Funds Investment Measure 1958;*
- *(b) an interest of the Church of Scotland General Trustees or of the Church of Scotland Trust in shares held by them or of any other person in shares held by those Trustees or that Trust otherwise than as simple trustees;*
- *(c) an interest for the life of himself or another of a person under a settlement in the case of which the property comprised in the settlement consists of or includes shares, and the conditions mentioned in subsection (11) are satisfied;*
- *(d) …*
- *(e) an interest of the Accountant General of the Supreme Court in shares held by him;*
- *(f) an interest of the Public Trustee;*
- *(g) an interest of the Probate Judge subsisting by virtue of section 3 of the Administration of Estates Act (Northern Ireland) 1955.*

(11) The conditions referred to in subsection (10)(c) are, in relation to a settlement—

- *(a) that it is irrevocable, and*
- *(b) that the settlor (within the meaning of section 670 of the Income and Corporation Taxes Act 1988) has no interest in any income arising under, or property comprised in, the settlement.*

(12) A person is not by virtue of section 208(4)(b) taken to be interested in shares by reason only that he has been appointed a proxy to vote at a specified meeting of a company or of any class of its members and at any adjournment of that meeting, or has been appointed by a corporation to act as its representative at any meeting of a company or of any class of its members.

(13) In the application of subsection (1)(a) to property held on trust according to the law of Scotland, for the words "or remainder or an interest of a bare trustee" there shall be substituted "or in fee or an interest of a simple trustee".]

[194]

NOTES

Substituted by the Disclosure of Interests in Shares (Amendment) Regulations 1993, SI 1993/1819, regs 2, 8, as from 18 September 1993 (subject to transitional provisions in relation to interests which become notifiable as a result of the coming into force of the 1993 Regulations).

Repealed by the Companies Act 2006, s 1295, Sch 16, as from 20 January 2007 (for transitional provisions and savings see the note to s 198 at **[184]**).

Sub-s (1): in para (h), word omitted repealed, and sub-para (iii) and the word immediately preceding added, by the Open-Ended Investment Companies (Investment Companies with Variable Capital) Regulations 1996, SI 1996/2827, reg 75, Sch 8, Pt I, para 6, as from 6 January 1997, sub-para (h)(iii) substituted by the Open-Ended Investment Companies Regulations 2001, SI 2001/1228, reg 84, Sch 7, para 5, as from 1 December 2001.

Sub-s (2): substituted, together with sub-ss (2A)–(2C) for original sub-s (2), by the Financial Services and Markets Act 2000 (Consequential Amendments and Repeals) Order 2001, SI 2001/3649, art 9, as from 1 December 2001; words in first (outer) pair of square brackets in para (b) added by the Electronic Money (Miscellaneous Amendments) Regulations 2002, SI 2002/765, reg 2(1), as from 27 April 2002; words in second (inner) pair of square brackets in para (b) substituted by the Capital Requirements Regulations 2006, SI 2006/3221, reg 29(2), Sch 4, para 2(1), (2), as from 1 January 2007.

Sub-ss (2A)–(2C): substituted as noted above.

Sub-s (9A): inserted, together with sub-s (9B), by the Disclosure of Interests in Shares (Amendment) Regulations 1996, SI 1996/1560, reg 2, as from 15 July 1996.

Sub-s (9B): inserted as noted above; words in square brackets substituted by the Uncertificated Securities Regulations 2001, SI 2001/3755, reg 51, Sch 7, Pt 1, para 9, as from 26 November 2001.

Sub-s (10): para (d) repealed by the Law of Property (Miscellaneous Provisions) Act 1994, s 21(2), Sch 2, as from 1 July 1995; for the words "Supreme Court" in para (e) there are substituted the words "Senior Courts" by the Constitutional Reform Act 2005, s 59, Sch 11, Pt 2, para 4, as from a day to be appointed.

Income and Corporation Taxes Act 1988, s 670: repealed by the Finance Act 1995, s 162, Sch 29, Pt VIII(8).

210 Other provisions about notification under this Part

(1) Where a person authorises another ("the agent") to acquire or dispose of, on his behalf, interests in shares comprised in relevant share capital of a public company, he shall secure that the agent notifies him immediately of acquisitions or disposals effected by the agent which will or may give rise to any obligation of disclosure imposed on him by this Part with respect to his interest in that share capital.

(2) An obligation of disclosure imposed on a person by any provision of sections 198 to 202 is treated as not being fulfilled unless the notice by means of which it purports to be fulfilled identifies him and gives his address and, in a case where he is a director of the company, is expressed to be given in fulfilment of that obligation.

(3) A person who—

(a) fails to fulfil, within the proper period, an obligation of disclosure imposed on him by this Part, or

(b) in purported fulfilment of any such obligation makes to a company a statement which he knows to be false, or recklessly makes to a company a statement which is false, or

(c) fails to fulfil, within the proper period, an obligation to give another person a notice required by section 206, or

(d) fails without reasonable excuse to comply with subsection (1) of this section,

is guilty of an offence and liable to imprisonment or a fine, or both.

(4) It is a defence for a person charged with an offence under subsection (3)(c) to prove that it was not possible for him to give the notice to the other person required by section 206 within the proper period, and either—

(a) that it has not since become possible for him to give the notice so required, or

(b) that he gave the notice as soon after the end of that period as it became possible for him to do so.

(5) Where a person is convicted of an offence under this section (other than an offence relating to his ceasing to be interested in a company's shares), the Secretary of State may by order direct that the shares in relation to which the offence was committed shall, until further order, be subject to the restrictions of Part XV of this Act; and such an order may be made notwithstanding any power in the company's memorandum or articles enabling the company to impose similar restrictions on those shares.

[(5A) If the Secretary of State is satisfied that an order under subsection (5) may unfairly affect the rights of third parties in respect of shares then the Secretary of State, for the purpose of protecting such rights and subject to such terms as he thinks fit, may direct that such acts by such persons or descriptions of persons and for such purposes as may be set out in the order, shall not constitute a breach of the restrictions of Part XV of this Act.]

(6) Sections 732 (restriction on prosecutions) and 733(2) and (3) (liability of directors, etc) apply to offences under this section.

[195]

NOTES

Repealed by the Companies Act 2006, s 1295, Sch 16, as from 20 January 2007 (for transitional provisions and savings see the note to s 198 at **[184]**).

Sub-s (5A): inserted by the Companies (Disclosure of Interests in Shares) (Orders imposing restrictions on shares) Regulations 1991, SI 1991/1646, reg 3, as from 18 July 1991.

[210A Power to make further provision by regulations

(1) The Secretary of State may by regulations amend—

(a) the definition of "relevant share capital" (section 198(2)),

(b) the percentage giving rise to a "notifiable interest" (section 199(2)),

(c) the periods within which an obligation of disclosure must be fulfilled or a notice must be given (sections 202(1) and (4) and 206(8)),

(d) the provisions as to what is taken to be an interest in shares (section 208) and what interests are to be disregarded (section 209), and

(e) the provisions as to company investigations (section 212);

and the regulations may amend, replace or repeal the provisions referred to above and make such other consequential amendments or repeals of provisions of this Part as appear to the Secretary of State to be appropriate.

(2) The regulations may in any case make different provision for different descriptions of company; and regulations under subsection (1)(b), (c) or (d) may make different provision for different descriptions of person, interest or share capital.

(3) The regulations may contain such transitional and other supplementary and incidental provisions as appear to the Secretary of State to be appropriate, and may in particular make provision as to the obligations of a person whose interest in a company's shares becomes or ceases to be notifiable by virtue of the regulations.

(4) Regulations under this section shall be made by statutory instrument.

(5) No regulations shall be made under this section unless a draft of the regulations has been laid before and approved by a resolution of each House of Parliament.]

[196]

NOTES

Inserted by CA 1989, s 134(1), (5), as from 31 May 1990.

Repealed by the Companies Act 2006, s 1295, Sch 16, as from 20 January 2007 (for transitional provisions and savings see the note to s 198 at **[184]**).

Regulations: the Disclosure of Interests in Shares (Amendment) Regulations 1993, SI 1993/1819 at **[6745]**; the Disclosure of Interests in Shares (Amendment) Regulations 1996, SI 1996/1560. These Regulations amended certain provisions in this Part (subject to transitional provisions in the case of the 1993 Regulations) and effectively became spent on the repeal of this Part on 20 January 2007.

Registration and investigation of share acquisitions and disposals

211 Register of interests in shares

(1) Every public company shall keep a register for purposes of sections 198 to 202, and whenever the company receives information from a person in consequence of the fulfilment of

an obligation imposed on him by any of those sections, it is under obligation to inscribe in the register, against that person's name, that information and the date of the inscription.

(2) Without prejudice to subsection (1), where a company receives a notification under this Part which includes a statement that the person making the notification, or any other person, has ceased to be a party to an agreement to which section 204 applies, the company is under obligation to record that information against the name of that person in every place where his name appears in the register as a party to that agreement (including any entry relating to him made against another person's name).

(3) An obligation imposed by subsection (1) or (2) must be fulfilled within the period of 3 days next following the day on which it arises.

(4) The company is not, by virtue of anything done for the purposes of this section, affected with notice of, or put upon enquiry as to, the rights of any person in relation to any shares.

(5) The register must be so made up that the entries against the several names entered in it appear in chronological order.

(6) Unless the register is in such form as to constitute in itself an index, the company shall keep an index of the names entered in the register which shall in respect of each name contain a sufficient indication to enable the information entered against it to be readily found; and the company shall, within 10 days after the date on which a name is entered in the register, make any necessary alteration in the index.

(7) If the company ceases to be a public company it shall continue to keep the register and any associated index until the end of the period of 6 years beginning with the day next following that on which it ceases to be such a company.

(8) The register and any associated index—

- *(a) shall be kept at the place at which the register required to be kept by the company by section 325 (register of directors' interests) is kept, and*
- *(b) subject to the next subsection, shall be available for inspection in accordance with section 219 below.*

(9) Neither the register nor any associated index shall be available for inspection in accordance with that section in so far as it contains information with respect to a company for the time being entitled to avail itself of the benefit conferred by [section 231(3)] (disclosure of shareholdings not required if it would be harmful to company's business).

(10) If default is made in complying with subsection (1) or (2), or with any of subsections (5) to (7), the company and every officer of it who is in default is liable to a fine and, for continued contravention, to a daily default fine.

(11) Any register kept by a company immediately before 15th June 1982 under section 34 of the Companies Act 1967 shall continue to be kept by the company under and for the purposes of this section.

[197]

NOTES

Repealed by the Companies Act 2006, s 1295, Sch 16, as from 20 January 2007 (for transitional provisions and savings see the note to s 198 at **[184]**).

Sub-s (9): words in square brackets substituted by CA 1989, s 23, Sch 10, para 3, as from 1 April 1990.

Companies Act 1967, s 34: repealed by the Companies Act 1981, ss 83(1), 199(5), Sch 4 (repealed).

212 Company investigations

(1) A public company may by notice in writing require a person whom the company knows or has reasonable cause to believe to be or, at any time during the 3 years immediately preceding the date on which the notice is issued, to have been interested in shares comprised in the company's relevant share capital—

- *(a) to confirm that fact or (as the case may be) to indicate whether or not it is the case, and*
- *(b) where he holds or has during that time held an interest in shares so comprised, to give such further information as may be required in accordance with the following subsection.*

(2) A notice under this section may require the person to whom it is addressed—

(*a*) *to give particulars of his own past or present interest in shares comprised in relevant share capital of the company (held by him at any time during the 3-year period mentioned in subsection (1)),*

(*b*) *where the interest is a present interest and any other interest in the shares subsists or, in any case, where another interest in the shares subsisted during that 3-year period at any time when his own interest subsisted, to give (so far as lies within his knowledge) such particulars with respect to that other interest as may be required by the notice,*

(*c*) *where his interest is a past interest, to give (so far as lies within his knowledge) particulars of the identity of the person who held that interest immediately upon his ceasing to hold it.*

(3) The particulars referred to in subsection (2)(a) and (b) include particulars of the identity of persons interested in the shares in question and of whether persons interested in the same shares are or were parties to any agreement to which section 204 applies or to any agreement or arrangement relating to the exercise of any rights conferred by the holding of the shares.

(4) A notice under this section shall require any information given in response to the notice to be given in writing within such reasonable time as may be specified in the notice.

(5) Sections 203 to 205 and 208 apply for the purpose of construing references in this section to persons interested in shares and to interests in shares respectively, as they apply in relation to sections 198 to 201 (but with the omission of any reference to section 209).

(6) This section applies in relation to a person who has or previously had, or is or was entitled to acquire, a right to subscribe for shares in a public company which would on issue be comprised in relevant share capital of that company as it applies in relation to a person who is or was interested in shares so comprised; and references above in this section to an interest in shares so comprised and to shares so comprised are to be read accordingly in any such case as including respectively any such right and shares which would on issue be so comprised.

[198]

NOTES

Repealed by the Companies Act 2006, s 1295, Sch 16, as from 20 January 2007 (for transitional provisions and savings see the note to s 198 at **[184]**).

213 Registration of interests disclosed under s 212

(1) Whenever in pursuance of a requirement imposed on a person under section 212 a company receives information to which this section applies relating to shares comprised in its relevant share capital, it is under obligation to enter against the name of the registered holder of those shares, in a separate part of its register of interests in shares—

(*a*) *the fact that the requirement was imposed and the date on which it was imposed, and*

(*b*) *any information to which this section applies received in pursuance of the requirement.*

(2) This section applies to any information received in pursuance of a requirement imposed by section 212 which relates to the present interests held by any persons in shares comprised in relevant share capital of the company in question.

(3) Subsections (3) to (10) of section 211 apply in relation to any part of the register maintained in accordance with subsection (1) of this section as they apply in relation to the remainder of the register, reading references to subsection (1) of that section to include subsection (1) of this.

(4) In the case of a register kept by a company immediately before 15th June 1982 under section 34 of the Companies Act 1967, any part of the register so kept for the purposes of section 27 of the Companies Act 1976 shall continue to be kept by the company under and for the purposes of this section.

[199]

NOTES

Repealed by the Companies Act 2006, s 1295, Sch 16, as from 20 January 2007 (for transitional provisions and savings see the note to s 198 at **[184]**).

Companies Act 1967, s 34; Companies Act 1976, s 27: repealed by the Companies Act 1981, ss 83(1), 199(5), Sch 4 (repealed).

214 Company investigation on requisition by members

(1) A company may be required to exercise its powers under section 212 on the requisition of members of the company holding at the date of the deposit of the requisition not less than one-tenth of such of the paid-up capital of the company as carries at that date the right of voting at general meetings of the company [(excluding any shares in the company held as treasury shares)].

(2) The requisition must—

(a) state that the requisitionists are requiring the company to exercise its powers under section 212,

(b) specify the manner in which they require those powers to be exercised, and

(c) give reasonable grounds for requiring the company to exercise those powers in the manner specified,

and must be signed by the requisitionists and deposited at the company's registered office.

(3) The requisition may consist of several documents in like form each signed by one or more requisitionists.

(4) On the deposit of a requisition complying with this section it is the company's duty to exercise its powers under section 212 in the manner specified in the requisition.

(5) If default is made in complying with subsection (4), the company and every officer of it who is in default is liable to a fine.

[200]

NOTES

Repealed by the Companies Act 2006, s 1295, Sch 16, as from 20 January 2007 (for transitional provisions and savings see the note to s 198 at **[184]**).

Sub-s (1): words in square brackets added by the Companies (Acquisition of Own Shares) (Treasury Shares) Regulations 2003, SI 2003/1116, reg 4, Schedule, para 16, as from 1 December 2003.

215 Company report to members

(1) On the conclusion of an investigation carried out by a company in pursuance of a requisition under section 214, it is the company's duty to cause a report of the information received in pursuance of that investigation to be prepared, and the report shall be made available at the company's registered office within a reasonable period after the conclusion of that investigation.

(2) Where—

(a) a company undertakes an investigation in pursuance of a requisition under section 214, and

(b) the investigation is not concluded before the end of 3 months beginning with the date immediately following the date of the deposit of the requisition,

it is the duty of the company to cause to be prepared, in respect of that period and each successive period of 3 months ending before the conclusion of the investigation, an interim report of the information received during that period in pursuance of the investigation. Each such report shall be made available at the company's registered office within a reasonable period after the end of the period to which it relates.

(3) The period for making any report prepared under this section available as required by subsection (1) or (2) shall not exceed 15 days.

(4) Such a report shall not include any information with respect to a company entitled to avail itself of the benefit conferred by [section 231(3)] (disclosure of shareholdings not required if it would be harmful to company's business); but where any such information is omitted, that fact shall be stated in the report.

(5) The company shall, within 3 days of making any report prepared under this section available at its registered office, notify the requisitionists that the report is so available.

(6) An investigation carried out by a company in pursuance of a requisition under section 214 is regarded for purposes of this section as concluded when the company has made

all such inquiries as are necessary or expedient for the purposes of the requisition and in the case of each such inquiry, either a response has been received by the company or the time allowed for a response has elapsed.

(7) *A report prepared under this section—*
- (a) *shall be kept at the company's registered office from the day on which it is first available there in accordance with subsection (1) or (2) until the expiration of 6 years beginning with the day next following that day, and*
- (b) *shall be available for inspection in accordance with section 219 below so long as it is so kept.*

(8) *If default is made in complying with subsection (1), (2), (5) or (7)(a), the company and every officer of it who is in default is liable to a fine.*

[201]

NOTES

Repealed by the Companies Act 2006, s 1295, Sch 16, as from 20 January 2007 (for transitional provisions and savings see the note to s 198 at **[184]**).

Sub-s (4): words in square brackets substituted by CA 1989, s 23, Sch 10, para 3, as from 1 April 1990.

216 Penalty for failure to provide information

(1) *Where notice is served by a company under section 212 on a person who is or was interested in shares of the company and that person fails to give the company any information required by the notice within the time specified in it, the company may apply to the court for an order directing that the shares in question be subject to the restrictions of Part XV of this Act.*

[(1A) On an application made under subsection (1), the court may make an interim order and any such order may be made unconditionally or on such terms as the court thinks fit.

(1B) If the court is satisfied that an order under subsection (1) may unfairly affect the rights of third parties in respect of shares then the court, for the purpose of protecting such rights and subject to such terms as it thinks fit, may direct that such acts by such persons or descriptions of persons and for such purposes as may be set out in the order, shall not constitute a breach of the restrictions of Part XV of this Act.]

(2) *[An order under this section] may be made by the court notwithstanding any power contained in the applicant company's memorandum or articles enabling the company itself to impose similar restrictions on the shares in question.*

(3) *Subject to the following subsections, a person who fails to comply with a notice under section 212 or who, in purported compliance with such a notice, makes any statement which he knows to be false in a material particular or recklessly makes any statement which is false in a material particular is guilty of an offence and liable to imprisonment or a fine, or both.*

Section 733(2) and (3) of this Act (liability of individuals for corporate default) apply to offences under this subsection.

(4) *A person is not guilty of an offence by virtue of failing to comply with a notice under section 212 if he proves that the requirement to give the information was frivolous or vexatious.*

(5) *A person is not obliged to comply with a notice under section 212 if he is for the time being exempted by the Secretary of State from the operation of that section; but the Secretary of State shall not grant any such exemption unless—*
- (a) *he has consulted with the Governor of the Bank of England, and*
- (b) *he (the Secretary of State) is satisfied that, having regard to any undertaking given by the person in question with respect to any interest held or to be held by him in any shares, there are special reasons why that person should not be subject to the obligations imposed by that section.*

[202]

NOTES

Repealed by the Companies Act 2006, s 1295, Sch 16, as from 20 January 2007 (for transitional provisions and savings see the note to s 198 at **[184]**).

Sub-ss (1A), (1B): inserted by the Companies (Disclosure of Interests in Shares) (Orders imposing restrictions on shares) Regulations 1991, SI 1991/1646, reg 4(a), as from 18 July 1991.

Sub-s (2): words in square brackets substituted by SI 1991/1646, reg 4(b), as from 18 July 1991.

217 Removal of entries from register

(1) A company may remove an entry against a person's name from its register of interests in shares if more than 6 years have elapsed since the date of the entry being made, and either—

(*a*) *that entry recorded the fact that the person in question had ceased to have an interest notifiable under this Part in relevant share capital of the company, or*

(*b*) *it has been superseded by a later entry made under section 211 against the same person's name;*

and in a case within paragraph (*a*) *the company may also remove that person's name from the register.*

(2) *If a person in pursuance of an obligation imposed on him by any provision of this Part gives to a company the name and address of another person as being interested in shares in the company, the company shall, within 15 days of the date on which it was given that information, notify the other person that he has been so named and shall include in that notification—*

(*a*) *particulars of any entry relating to him made, in consequence of its being given that information, by the company in its register of interests in shares, and*

(*b*) *a statement informing him of his right to apply to have the entry removed in accordance with the following provisions of this section.*

(*3*) *A person who has been notified by a company in pursuance of subsection* (2) *that an entry relating to him has been made in the company's register of interests in shares may apply in writing to the company for the removal of that entry from the register; and the company shall remove the entry if satisfied that the information in pursuance of which the entry was made was incorrect.*

(*4*) *If a person who is identified in a company's register of interests in shares as being a party to an agreement to which section 204 applies* (*whether by an entry against his own name or by an entry relating to him made against another person's name as mentioned in subsection* (2)(*a*)) *ceases to be a party to that agreement, he may apply in writing to the company for the inclusion of that information in the register; and if the company is satisfied that he has ceased to be a party to the agreement, it shall record that information* (*if not already recorded*) *in every place where his name appears as a party to that agreement in the register.*

(*5*) *If an application under subsection* (*3*) *or* (*4*) *is refused* (*in a case within subsection* (*4*), *otherwise than on the ground that the information has already been recorded*) *the applicant may apply to the court for an order directing the company to remove the entry in question from the register or* (*as the case may be*) *to include the information in question in the register; and the court may, if it thinks fit, make such an order.*

(*6*) *Where a name is removed from a company's register of interests in shares in pursuance of subsection* (*1*) *or* (*3*) *or an order under subsection* (*5*), *the company shall within 14 days of the date of that removal make any necessary alteration in any associated index.*

(*7*) *If default is made in complying with subsection* (2) *or* (*6*), *the company and every officer of it who is in default is liable to a fine and, for continued contravention, to a daily default fine.*

[203]

NOTES

Repealed by the Companies Act 2006, s 1295, Sch 16, as from 20 January 2007 (for transitional provisions and savings see the note to s 198 at **[184]**).

218 Otherwise, entries not to be removed

(*1*) *Entries in a company's register of interests in shares shall not be deleted except in accordance with section 217.*

(2) *If an entry is deleted from a company's register of interests in shares in contravention of subsection* (*1*), *the company shall restore that entry to the register as soon as is reasonably practicable.*

(3) If default is made in complying with subsection (1) or (2), the company and every officer of it who is in default is liable to a fine and, for continued contravention of subsection (2), to a daily default fine.

[204]

NOTES

Repealed by the Companies Act 2006, s 1295, Sch 16, as from 20 January 2007 (for transitional provisions and savings see the note to s 198 at **[184]**).

219 Inspection of register and reports

(1) Any register of interests in shares and any report which is required by section 215(7) to be available for inspection in accordance with this section shall, ... be open to the inspection of any member of the company or of any other person without charge.

(2) Any such member or other person may require a copy of any such register or report, or any part of it, on payment of [such fee as may be prescribed]; and the company shall cause any copy so required by a person to be sent to him before the expiration of the period of 10 days beginning with the day next following that on which the requirement is received by the company.

(3) If an inspection required under this section is refused or a copy so required is not sent within the proper period, the company and every officer of it who is in default is liable to a fine and, for continued contravention, to a daily default fine.

(4) In the case of a refusal of an inspection required under this section of any register or report, the court may by order compel an immediate inspection of it; and in the case of failure to send a copy required under this section, the court may by order direct that the copy required shall be sent to the person requiring it.

(5) The Secretary of State may by regulations made by statutory instrument substitute a sum specified in the regulations for the sum for the time being mentioned in subsection (2).

[205]

NOTES

Repealed by the Companies Act 2006, s 1295, Sch 16, as from 20 January 2007 (for transitional provisions and savings see the note to s 198 at **[184]**).

Sub-s (1): words omitted repealed by CA 1989, ss 143(5)(a), 212, Sch 24, as from 1 November 1991.

Sub-s (2): words in square brackets substituted by CA 1989, s 143(5)(b), as from 1 November 1991.

Inspection: for provisions relating to the inspection of documents, registers and fees under this section, see the Companies (Inspection and Copying of Registers, Indices and Documents) Regulations 1991, SI 1991/1998 at **[6716]** et seq (partly made under this section).

Supplementary

220 Definitions for Part VI

[(1) In this Part of this Act—

"associated index", in relation to a register, means the index kept in relation to that register in pursuance of section 211(6);

.....

"authorised insurance undertaking" means an insurance undertaking which has been authorised in accordance with Article 6 or 23 of Council Directive 73/239/EEC or [Article 4 or 51 of Directive 2002/83/EC of the European Parliament and of the Council of 5th November 2002 concerning life assurance], or is authorised under the law of a member State to carry on insurance business restricted to re-insurance;

"authorised unit trust scheme" has the same meaning as in [Part 17 of the Financial Services and Markets Act 2000];

"depositary receipt" means a certificate or other record (whether or not in the form of a document)—

- *(a) which is issued by or on behalf of a person who holds shares or who holds evidence of the right to receive shares, or has an interest in shares, in a particular company; and*
- *(b) which evidences or acknowledges that another person is entitled to rights in relation to those shares or shares of the same kind, which shall include*

the right to receive such shares (or evidence of the right to receive such shares) from the person mentioned in paragraph (a);

["derivatives" means options and futures in relation to shares;]

.....

["EEA authorisation" has the same meaning as in paragraph 6 of Schedule 3 to the Financial Services and Markets Act 2000;]

[.....]

"listed company" means a company any of the shares in which are officially listed on a relevant stock exchange and "listed" shall be construed accordingly;

"material interest" shall be construed in accordance with section 199(2A);

["open-ended investment company" has the same meaning as in the Open-Ended Investment Companies Regulations 2001;]

"operator", in relation to a collective investment scheme, shall be construed in accordance with [section 237(2) of the Financial Services and Markets Act 2000];

["recognised clearing house" has the same meaning as in the Financial Services and Markets Act 2000;

"recognised scheme" has the same meaning as in Part 17 of the Financial Services and Markets Act 2000;]

"register of interest in shares" means the register kept in pursuance of section 211 including, except where the context otherwise requires, that part of the register kept in pursuance of section 213;

"relevant investment exchange" means an exchange situated or operating in a member State on which derivatives are traded;

"relevant share capital" has the meaning given by section 198(2);

"relevant stock exchange" means a stock exchange situated or operating in a member State;

"UCITS" has the meaning given by section 199(8);

"units" has the same meaning as in [section 237(2) of the Financial Services and Markets Act 2000].]

[(1A) References in subsection (1) to contracts of insurance (of any description), options and futures must be read with—

(a) section 22 of the Financial Services and Markets Act 2000;

(b) any relevant order under that section; and

(c) Schedule 2 to that Act.]

(2) Where the period allowed by any provision of this Part for fulfilling an obligation is expressed as a number of days, any day that is a Saturday or Sunday or a bank holiday in any part of Great Britain is to be disregarded in reckoning that period.

[206]

NOTES

Repealed by the Companies Act 2006, s 1295, Sch 16, as from 20 January 2007 (for transitional provisions and savings see the note to s 198 at **[184]**).

Sub-s (1): substituted by the Disclosure of Interest in Shares (Amendment) Regulations 1993, SI 1993/1819, regs 2, 9, as from 18 September 1993 (subject to transitional provisions in relation to interests which become notifiable as a result of the coming into force of the 1993 Regulations); and further amended as follows—

Definitions "authorised credit institution" and "designated agency" repealed, words in square brackets in definitions "authorised unit trust scheme", "operator" and "units" substituted, definition "derivatives" substituted, definitions "recognised clearing house" and "recognised scheme" substituted (for original definitions "recognised clearing house", "recognised professional body", "recognised scheme", and "recognised self-regulating organisation"), and definition "EEA authorisation" inserted, by the Financial Services and Markets Act 2000 (Consequential Amendments and Repeals) Order 2001, SI 2001/3649, art 10(1)–(8), as from 1 December 2001.

In definition "authorised insurance undertaking" words in square brackets substituted by the Life Assurance Consolidation Directive (Consequential Amendments) Regulations 2004, SI 2004/3379, reg 2(1), (2), as from 11 January 2005.

Definition "investment company with variable capital" inserted by the Open-Ended Investment Companies (Investment Companies with Variable Capital) Regulations 1996, SI 1996/2827, reg 75, Sch 8, Pt I, para 7, as from 6 January 1997, and repealed by the Open-Ended Investment Companies Regulations 2001, SI 2001/1228, reg 84, Sch 7, para 6, as from 1 December 2001.

Definition "open-ended investment company" inserted by SI 2001/1228, reg 84, Sch 7, para 6, as from 1 December 2001.

Sub-s (1A): inserted by SI 2001/3649, art 10(1), (9), as from 1 December 2001.

PART VII
ACCOUNTS AND AUDIT

NOTES

Original Pt VII (ss 221–262) replaced by the insertion of new ss 221–262A by CA 1989, ss 2–22. Extensive transitional provisions and savings relating to the insertion of the new Pt VII are made by the Companies Act 1989 (Commencement No 4 and Transitional and Saving Provisions) Order 1990, SI 1990/355. Principally, these provide that the rules relating to accounts and reports of companies under Pt VII of this Act prior to its amendment by the 1989 Act can have effect for financial years of a company commencing before 23 December 1989. Savings are also made to ensure the continuity of the law between the old and new Pt VII of this Act.

Private companies: references in any enactment or instrument to the period for laying and delivering accounts, and reports including those in s 244 *post* (which defines that period), shall be read in relation to a private company as references to the period for delivering accounts and reports; see the draft Companies Act 2006 (Commencement No 3, Consequential Amendments, Transitional Provisions and Savings) Order 2007, art 10(1), Sch 4, Pt 1, para 3(4) (at **[A12]**).

Overseas companies: as to the application of Pt VII to overseas companies, and the requirements from which overseas companies are exempted, see the Oversea Companies (Accounts) (Modifications and Exemptions) Order 1990, SI 1990/440 at **[6655]** et seq.

As to the application of Pt VII, subject to modifications, to accounts prepared under the Partnerships and Unlimited Companies (Accounts) Regulations 1993, SI 1993/1820, reg 4, see reg 4(3) of, and Schedule, paras 1, 2 to, those Regulations at **[6751]**, **[6758]**.

Application to insurance undertakings: see (i) the Companies Act 1985 (Insurance Companies Accounts) Regulations 1993, SI 1993/3246 at **[6764]** (which implements Council Directive 91/674/EEC on the annual accounts and consolidated accounts of insurance undertakings in respect of bodies corporate to which this Part applies); (ii) the Insurance Accounts Directive (Miscellaneous Insurance Undertakings) Regulations 1993, SI 1993/3245 (which implement the Directive in so far as it is applicable to bodies corporate or unincorporate other than bodies corporate to which this Part applies, and friendly societies; (iii) the Insurance Accounts Directive (Lloyd's Syndicate and Aggregate Accounts) Regulations 2004, SI 2004/3219 (which implements the Directive (as amended by Directive 2003/51/EC ("the Modernisation Directive")) in relation to Lloyd's of London).

CHAPTER I
PROVISIONS APPLYING TO COMPANIES GENERALLY

[Accounting records

221 Duty to keep accounting records

(1) Every company shall keep accounting records which are sufficient to show and explain the company's transactions and are such as to—

(a) disclose with reasonable accuracy, at any time, the financial position of the company at that time, and

(b) enable the directors to ensure that [any accounts required to be prepared under this Part comply] with the requirements of this Act [(and, where applicable, of Article 4 of the IAS Regulation)].

(2) The accounting records shall in particular contain—

(a) entries from day to day of all sums of money received and expended by the company, and the matters in respect of which the receipt and expenditure takes place, and

(b) a record of the assets and liabilities of the company.

(3) If the company's business involves dealing in goods, the accounting records shall contain—

(a) statements of stock held by the company at the end of each financial year of the company,

(b) all statements of stocktakings from which any such statement of stock as is mentioned in paragraph (a) has been or is to be prepared, and

(c) except in the case of goods sold by way of ordinary retail trade, statements of all goods sold and purchased, showing the goods and the buyers and sellers in sufficient detail to enable all these to be identified.

(4) A parent company which has a subsidiary undertaking in relation to which the above requirements do not apply shall take reasonable steps to secure that the undertaking keeps such accounting records as to enable the directors of the parent company to ensure that [any accounts required to be prepared under this Part comply] with the requirements of this Act [(and, where applicable, of Article 4 of the IAS Regulation)].

(5) If a company fails to comply with any provision of this section, every officer of the company who is in default is guilty of an offence unless he shows that he acted honestly and that in the circumstances in which the company's business was carried on the default was excusable.

(6) A person guilty of an offence under this section is liable to imprisonment or a fine, or both.]

[207]

NOTES

Inserted, with the preceding heading and s 222, by CA 1989, s 2, as from 1 April 1990.

Repealed by the Companies Act 2006, s 1295, Sch 16, as from a day to be appointed.

Sub-ss (1), (4): words in first pair of square brackets substituted, and words in second pair of square brackets inserted, by the Companies Act 1985 (International Accounting Standards and Other Accounting Amendments) Regulations 2004, SI 2004/2947, reg 3, Sch 1, paras 1, 4, as from 12 November 2004, in relation to companies' financial years which begin on or after 1 January 2005.

Application to limited liability partnerships: see the Limited Liability Partnerships Regulations 2001, SI 2001/1090, reg 3, Sch 1 at **[6984]**, **[6992]**.

[222 Where and for how long records to be kept

(1) A company's accounting records shall be kept at its registered office or such other place as the directors think fit, and shall at all times be open to inspection by the company's officers.

(2) If accounting records are kept at a place outside Great Britain, accounts and returns with respect to the business dealt with in the accounting records so kept shall be sent to, and kept at, a place in Great Britain, and shall at all times be open to such inspection.

(3) The accounts and returns to be sent to Great Britain shall be such as to—

(a) disclose with reasonable accuracy the financial position of the business in question at intervals of not more than six months, and

(b) enable the directors to ensure that [the accounts required to be prepared under this Part] comply with the requirements of this Act [(and, where applicable, Article 4 of the IAS Regulation)].

(4) If a company fails to comply with any provision of subsections (1) to (3), every officer of the company who is in default is guilty of an offence, and liable to imprisonment or a fine or both, unless he shows that he acted honestly and that in the circumstances in which the company's business was carried on the default was excusable.

(5) Accounting records which a company is required by section 221 to keep shall be preserved by it—

(a) in the case of a private company, for three years from the date on which they are made, and

(b) in the case of a public company, for six years from the date on which they are made.

This is subject to any provision contained in rules made under section 411 of the Insolvency Act 1986 (company insolvency rules).

(6) An officer of a company is guilty of an offence, and liable to imprisonment or a fine or both, if he fails to take all reasonable steps for securing compliance by the company with subsection (5) or intentionally causes any default by the company under that subsection.]

[208]

NOTES

Inserted as noted to s 221 at **[207]**.

Repealed by the Companies Act 2006, s 1295, Sch 16, as from a day to be appointed.

Sub-s (3): words in first pair of square brackets in para (b) substituted, and words in second pair of square brackets inserted, by the Companies Act 1985 (International Accounting Standards and Other Accounting Amendments) Regulations 2004, SI 2004/2947, reg 3, Sch 1, paras 1, 5, as from 12 November 2004, in relation to companies' financial years which begin on or after 1 January 2005.

Application to limited liability partnerships: see the Limited Liability Partnerships Regulations 2001, SI 2001/1090, reg 3, Sch 1 at **[6984]**, **[6992]**.

[A company's financial year and accounting reference periods

223 A company's financial year

(1) A company's "financial year" is determined as follows.

(2) Its first financial year begins with the first day of its first accounting reference period and ends with the last day of that period or such other date, not more than seven days before or after the end of that period, as the directors may determine.

(3) Subsequent financial years begin with the day immediately following the end of the company's previous financial year and end with the last day of its next accounting reference period or such other date, not more than seven days before or after the end of that period, as the directors may determine.

(4) In relation to an undertaking which is not a company, references in this Act to its financial year are to any period in respect of which a profit and loss account of the undertaking is required to be made up (by its constitution or by the law under which it is established), whether that period is a year or not.

(5) The directors of a parent company shall secure that, except where in their opinion there are good reasons against it, the financial year of each of its subsidiary undertakings coincides with the company's own financial year.]

[209]

NOTES

Inserted, together with the preceding heading and ss 224, 225, by CA 1989, s 3, as from 1 April 1990.
Repealed by the Companies Act 2006, s 1295, Sch 16, as from a day to be appointed.
Application to limited liability partnerships: see the Limited Liability Partnerships Regulations 2001, SI 2001/1090, reg 3, Sch 1 at **[6984]**, **[6992]**.

[224 Accounting reference periods and accounting reference date

(1) A company's accounting reference periods are determined according to its accounting reference date.

(2) A company [incorporated before 1st April 1996] may, at any time before the end of the period of nine months beginning with the date of its incorporation, by notice in the prescribed form given to the registrar specify its accounting reference date, that is, the date on which its accounting reference period ends in each calendar year.

(3) Failing such notice, [the accounting reference date of such a company] is—
(a) in the case of a company incorporated before [1st April 1990], 31st March;
(b) in the case of a company incorporated after [1st April 1990], the last day of the month in which the anniversary of its incorporation falls.

[(3A) The accounting reference date of a company incorporated on or after 1st April 1996 is the last day of the month in which the anniversary of its incorporation falls.]

(4) A company's first accounting reference period is the period of more than six months, but not more than 18 months, beginning with the date of its incorporation and ending with its accounting reference date.

(5) Its subsequent accounting reference periods are successive periods of twelve months beginning immediately after the end of the previous accounting reference period and ending with its accounting reference date.

(6) This section has effect subject to the provisions of section 225 relating to the alteration of accounting reference dates and the consequences of such alteration.]

[210]

NOTES

Inserted as noted to s 223 at **[209]**.
Repealed by the Companies Act 2006, s 1295, Sch 16, as from a day to be appointed.
Sub-s (2): words in square brackets inserted by the Companies Act 1985 (Miscellaneous Accounting Amendments) Regulations 1996, SI 1996/189, reg 2(1), (2), as from 1 April 1996.
Sub-s (3): words in first pair of square brackets substituted by SI 1996/189, reg 2(1), (3), as from 1 April 1996; words in second and third pairs of square brackets substituted by the Companies Act 1989 (Commencement No 4 and Transitional and Saving Provisions) Order 1990, SI 1990/355, art 15, as from 26 February 1990.
Sub-s (3A): inserted by SI 1996/189, reg 2(1), (4), as from 1 April 1996.

Application to limited liability partnerships: see the Limited Liability Partnerships Regulations 2001, SI 2001/1090, reg 3, Sch 1 at **[6984]**, **[6992]**.

Prescribed form: see Appendix 4 (Forms table) at **[A4]**.

[225 Alteration of accounting reference date

(1) A company may by notice in the prescribed form given to the registrar specify a new accounting reference date [having effect in relation to—

(a) the company's current accounting reference period and subsequent periods; or

(b) the company's previous accounting reference period and subsequent periods.

A company's "previous accounting reference period" means that immediately preceding its current accounting reference period.]

(2) ...

(3) The notice shall state whether the current or previous accounting reference period—

(a) is to be shortened, so as to come to an end on the first occasion on which the new accounting reference date falls or fell after the beginning of the period, or

(b) is to be extended, so as to come to an end on the second occasion on which that date falls or fell after the beginning of the period.

(4) A notice under subsection (1) stating that the current [or previous] accounting reference period is to be extended is ineffective, except as mentioned below, if given less than five years after the end of an earlier accounting reference period of the company which was extended by virtue of this section.

This subsection does not apply—

[(a) to a notice given by a company which is a subsidiary undertaking or parent undertaking of another EEA undertaking if the new accounting reference date coincides with that of the other EEA undertaking or, where that undertaking is not a company, with the last day of its financial year, or]

(b) where [the company is in administration] under Part II of the Insolvency Act 1986,

or where the Secretary of State directs that it should not apply, which he may do with respect to a notice which has been given or which may be given.

(5) A notice under [subsection (1)] may not be given [in respect of a previous accounting reference period] if the period allowed for laying and delivering accounts and reports in relation to [that period] has already expired.

(6) [A company's accounting reference period may not in any case, unless the company is in administration] under Part II of the Insolvency Act 1986, be extended so as to exceed 18 months and a notice under this section is ineffective if the current or previous accounting reference period as extended in accordance with the notice would exceed that limit.]

[(7) In this section "EEA undertaking" means an undertaking established under the law of any part of the United Kingdom or the law of any other EEA State.]

[211]

NOTES

Inserted as noted to s 223 at **[209]**.

Repealed by the Companies Act 2006, s 1295, Sch 16, as from a day to be appointed.

Sub-s (1): words in square brackets substituted by the Companies Act 1985 (Miscellaneous Accounting Amendments) Regulations 1996, SI 1996/189, reg 3(1), (2), as from 1 April 1996.

Sub-s (2): repealed by SI 1996/189, reg 3(1), (3), as from 1 April 1996.

Sub-s (4): words in first pair of square brackets inserted, and para (a) substituted, by SI 1996/189, reg 3(1), (4), as from 1 April 1996; words in square brackets in para (b) substituted by the Enterprise Act 2002, s 248(3), Sch 17, paras 3, 4(a), as from 15 September 2003 (for savings and transitional provisions, see the note to the Insolvency Act 1986, s 8 at **[3164]**).

Sub-s (5): words in first and third pairs of square brackets substituted, and words in second pair of square brackets inserted, by SI 1996/189, reg 3(1), (5), as from 1 April 1996.

Sub-s (6): words in square brackets substituted by the Enterprise Act 2002, s 248(3), Sch 17, paras 3, 4(b), as from 15 September 2003 (for savings and transitional provisions, see the note to the Insolvency Act 1986, s 8 at **[3164]**).

Sub-s (7): added by SI 1996/189, reg 3(1), (6), as from 1 April 1996.

Application to limited liability partnerships: see the Limited Liability Partnerships Regulations 2001, SI 2001/1090, reg 3, Sch 1 at **[6984]**, **[6992]**.

Notice in the prescribed form: see Appendix 4 (Forms table) at **[A4]**.

[Annual accounts

[226 Duty to prepare individual accounts

(1) The directors of every company shall prepare accounts for the company for each of its financial years.

Those accounts are referred to in this Part as the company's "individual accounts".

(2) A company's individual accounts may be prepared—
- *(a) in accordance with section 226A ("Companies Act individual accounts"), or*
- *(b) in accordance with international accounting standards ("IAS individual accounts").*

This subsection is subject to the following provisions of this section and section 227C (consistency of accounts).

(3) The individual accounts of a company that is a charity must be Companies Act individual accounts.

(4) After the first financial year in which the directors of a company prepare IAS individual accounts ("the first IAS year"), all subsequent individual accounts of the company must be prepared in accordance with international accounting standards unless there is a relevant change of circumstance.

(5) There is a relevant change of circumstance if, at any time during or after the first IAS year—
- *(a) the company becomes a subsidiary undertaking of another undertaking that does not prepare IAS individual accounts,*
- *(b) the company ceases to be a company with securities admitted to trading on a regulated market, or*
- *(c) a parent undertaking of the company ceases to be an undertaking with securities admitted to trading on a regulated market.*

In this subsection "regulated market" has the same meaning as it has in Council Directive 93/22/EEC on investment services in the securities field.

(6) If, having changed to preparing Companies Act individual accounts following a relevant change of circumstance, the directors again prepare IAS individual accounts for the company, subsections (4) and (5) apply again as if the first financial year for which such accounts are again prepared were the first IAS year.]]

[212]

NOTES

Originally inserted, together with the preceding heading, by CA 1989, s 4(1), as from 1 April 1990.

Ss 226, 227 subsequently substituted by new ss 226, 226A, 226B, 227, 227A–227C by the Companies Act 1985 (International Accounting Standards and Other Accounting Amendments) Regulations 2004, SI 2004/2947, reg 2, as from 12 November 2004, in relation to companies' financial years which begin on or after 1 January 2005.

Repealed by the Companies Act 2006, s 1295, Sch 16, as from a day to be appointed.

Sub-s (5): for the words "Council Directive 93/22/EEC on investment services in the securities field" there are substituted the words "Directive 2004/39/EC of the European Parliament and of the Council of 21 April 2004 on markets in financial instruments" by the Financial Services and Markets Act 2000 (Markets in Financial Instruments) Regulations 2007, SI 2007/126, reg 3(6), Sch 6, Pt 1, para 7(1), (5), as from 1 November 2007 (for the full commencement details of SI 2007/126, see reg 1 of those Regulations at **[7596]**).

Application to limited liability partnerships: see the Limited Liability Partnerships Regulations 2001, SI 2001/1090, reg 3, Sch 1 at **[6984]**, **[6992]**.

[226A Companies Act individual accounts

(1) Companies Act individual accounts must comprise—
- *(a) a balance sheet as at the last day of the financial year, and*
- *(b) a profit and loss account.*

(2) The balance sheet must give a true and fair view of the state of affairs of the company as at the end of the financial year; and the profit and loss account must give a true and fair view of the profit or loss of the company for the financial year.

(3) Companies Act individual accounts must comply with the provisions of Schedule 4 as to the form and content of the balance sheet and profit and loss account and additional information to be provided by way of notes to the accounts.

(4) Where compliance with the provisions of that Schedule, and the other provisions of this Act as to the matters to be included in a company's individual accounts or in notes to those accounts, would not be sufficient to give a true and fair view, the necessary additional information must be given in the accounts or in a note to them.

(5) If in special circumstances compliance with any of those provisions is inconsistent with the requirement to give a true and fair view, the directors must depart from that provision to the extent necessary to give a true and fair view.

(6) Particulars of any such departure, the reasons for it and its effect must be given in a note to the accounts.]

[212A]

NOTES

Substituted as noted to s 226 at **[212]**.

Repealed by the Companies Act 2006, s 1295, Sch 16, as from a day to be appointed.

Application to limited liability partnerships: see the Limited Liability Partnerships Regulations 2001, SI 2001/1090, reg 3, Sch 1 at **[6984]**, **[6992]**.

[226B IAS individual accounts

Where the directors of a company prepare IAS individual accounts, they must state in the notes to those accounts that the accounts have been prepared in accordance with international accounting standards.]

[212B]

NOTES

Substituted as noted to s 226 at **[212]**.

Repealed by the Companies Act 2006, s 1295, Sch 16, as from a day to be appointed.

Application to limited liability partnerships: see the Limited Liability Partnerships Regulations 2001, SI 2001/1090, reg 3, Sch 1 at **[6984]**, **[6992]**.

[227 Duty to prepare group accounts

(1) If at the end of a financial year a company is a parent company the directors, as well as preparing individual accounts for the year, shall prepare consolidated accounts for the group for the year.

Those accounts are referred to in this Part as the company's "group accounts".

(2) The group accounts of certain parent companies are required by Article 4 of the IAS Regulation to be prepared in accordance with international accounting standards ("IAS group accounts").

(3) The group accounts of other companies may be prepared—

- *(a) in accordance with section 227A ("Companies Act group accounts"), or*
- *(b) in accordance with international accounting standards ("IAS group accounts").*

This subsection is subject to the following provisions of this section.

(4) The group accounts of a parent company that is a charity must be Companies Act group accounts.

(5) After the first financial year in which the directors of a parent company prepare IAS group accounts ("the first IAS year"), all subsequent group accounts of the company must be prepared in accordance with international accounting standards unless there is a relevant change of circumstance.

(6) There is a relevant change of circumstance if, at any time during or after the first IAS year—

- *(a) the company becomes a subsidiary undertaking of another undertaking that does not prepare IAS group accounts,*
- *(b) the company ceases to be a company with securities admitted to trading on a regulated market, or*
- *(c) a parent undertaking of the company ceases to be an undertaking with securities admitted to trading on a regulated market.*

In this subsection "regulated market" has the same meaning as it has in Council Directive 93/22/EEC on investment services in the securities field.

(7) If, having changed to preparing Companies Act group accounts following a relevant change of circumstance, the directors again prepare IAS group accounts for the company, subsections (5) and (6) apply again as if the first financial year for which such accounts are again prepared were the first IAS year.

(8) This section is subject to the exemptions provided by sections 228 (parent companies included in accounts of larger EEA group), 228A (parent companies included in non-EEA group accounts), 229(5) (all subsidiary undertakings excluded from consolidation) and 248 (small and medium-sized groups).]

[213]

NOTES

Originally inserted by CA 1989, s 5(1), as from 1 April 1990.

Substituted as noted to s 226 at **[212]**.

Repealed by the Companies Act 2006, s 1295, Sch 16, as from a day to be appointed.

Sub-s (6): for the words "Council Directive 93/22/EEC on investment services in the securities field" there are substituted the words "Directive 2004/39/EC of the European Parliament and of the Council of 21 April 2004 on markets in financial instruments" by the Financial Services and Markets Act 2000 (Markets in Financial Instruments) Regulations 2007, SI 2007/126, reg 3(6), Sch 6, Pt 1, para 7(1), (6), as from 1 November 2007 (for the full commencement details of SI 2007/126, see reg 1 of those Regulations at **[7596]**).

Application to limited liability partnerships: see the Limited Liability Partnerships Regulations 2001, SI 2001/1090, reg 3, Sch 1 at **[6984]**, **[6992]**.

[227A Companies Act group accounts

(1) Companies Act group accounts must comprise—

(a) a consolidated balance sheet dealing with the state of affairs of the parent company and its subsidiary undertakings, and

(b) a consolidated profit and loss account dealing with the profit or loss of the parent company and its subsidiary undertakings.

(2) The accounts must give a true and fair view of the state of affairs as at the end of the financial year, and the profit or loss for the financial year, of the undertakings included in the consolidation as a whole, so far as concerns members of the company.

(3) Companies Act group accounts must comply with the provisions of Schedule 4A as to the form and content of the consolidated balance sheet and consolidated profit and loss account and additional information to be provided by way of notes to the accounts.

(4) Where compliance with the provisions of that Schedule, and the other provisions of this Act as to the matters to be included in a company's group accounts or in notes to those accounts, would not be sufficient to give a true and fair view, the necessary additional information must be given in the accounts or in a note to them.

(5) If in special circumstances compliance with any of those provisions is inconsistent with the requirement to give a true and fair view, the directors must depart from that provision to the extent necessary to give a true and fair view.

(6) Particulars of any such departure, the reasons for it and its effect must be given in a note to the accounts.]

[213A]

NOTES

Substituted as noted to s 226 at **[212]**.

Repealed by the Companies Act 2006, s 1295, Sch 16, as from a day to be appointed.

Application to limited liability partnerships: see the Limited Liability Partnerships Regulations 2001, SI 2001/1090, reg 3, Sch 1 at **[6984]**, **[6992]**.

[227B IAS group accounts

Where the directors of a parent company prepare IAS group accounts, they must state in the notes to those accounts that the accounts have been prepared in accordance with international accounting standards.]

[213B]

NOTES

Substituted as noted to s 226 at **[212]**.

Repealed by the Companies Act 2006, s 1295, Sch 16, as from a day to be appointed.

Application to limited liability partnerships: see the Limited Liability Partnerships Regulations 2001, SI 2001/1090, reg 3, Sch 1 at **[6984]**, **[6992]**.

[227C Consistency of accounts

(1) The directors of a parent company must secure that the individual accounts of—
- (*a*) *the parent company, and*
- (*b*) *each of its subsidiary undertakings,*

are all prepared using the same financial reporting framework, except to the extent that in their opinion there are good reasons for not doing so.

(2) Subsection (1) does not apply if the directors do not prepare group accounts for the parent company.

(3) Subsection (1) only applies to accounts of subsidiary undertakings that are required to be prepared under this Part.

(4) Subsection (1) does not require accounts of undertakings that are charities to be prepared using the same financial reporting framework as accounts of undertakings which are not charities.

(5) Subsection (1)(a) does not apply where the directors of a parent company prepare IAS group accounts and IAS individual accounts.]

[213C]

NOTES

Substituted as noted to s 226 at **[212]**.

Repealed by the Companies Act 2006, s 1295, Sch 16, as from a day to be appointed.

Application to limited liability partnerships: see the Limited Liability Partnerships Regulations 2001, SI 2001/1090, reg 3, Sch 1 at **[6984]**, **[6992]**.

[228 Exemption for parent companies included in accounts of larger group

(1) A company is exempt from the requirement to prepare group accounts if it is itself a subsidiary undertaking and its immediate parent undertaking is established under the law of [an EEA State], in the following cases—
- (*a*) *where the company is a wholly-owned subsidiary of that parent undertaking;*
- (*b*) *where that parent undertaking holds more than 50 per cent of the shares in the company and notice requesting the preparation of group accounts has not been served on the company by shareholders holding in aggregate—*
  - *(i) more than half of the remaining shares in the company, or*
  - *(ii) 5 per cent of the total shares in the company.*

Such notice must be served not later than six months after the end of the financial year before that to which it relates.

(2) *Exemption is conditional upon compliance with all of the following conditions—*
- (*a*) *that the company is included in consolidated accounts for a larger group drawn up to the same date, or to an earlier date in the same financial year, by a parent undertaking established under the law of [an EEA State];*
- (*b*) *that those accounts are drawn up and audited, and that parent undertaking's annual report is drawn up, according to that law, in accordance with the provisions of the Seventh Directive (83/349/EEC) [(where applicable as modified by the provisions of the Bank Accounts Directive (86/635/EEC) [or the Insurance Accounts Directive (91/674/EEC)]) [or in accordance with international accounting standards]];*
- (*c*) *that the company discloses in its individual accounts that it is exempt from the obligation to prepare and deliver group accounts;*
- (*d*) *that the company states in its individual accounts the name of the parent undertaking which draws up the group accounts referred to above and—*
  - *(i) if it is incorporated outside Great Britain, the country in which it is incorporated,*
  - *(ii) … , and*
  - *(iii) if it is unincorporated, the address of its principal place of business;*
- (*e*) *that the company delivers to the registrar, within the period allowed for delivering its individual accounts, copies of those group accounts and of the parent undertaking's annual report, together with the auditors' report on them; and*

(f) *[…] that if any document comprised in accounts and reports delivered in accordance with paragraph (e) is in a language other than English, there is annexed to the copy of that document delivered a translation of it into English, certified in the prescribed manner to be a correct translation.*

(3) The exemption does not apply to a company any of whose securities are [admitted to trading on a regulated market of any EEA State within the meaning of Council Directive 93/22/EEC on investment services in the securities field].

(4) Shares held by directors of a company for the purpose of complying with any share qualification requirement shall be disregarded in determining for the purposes of subsection (1)(a) whether the company is a wholly-owned subsidiary.

(5) For the purposes of subsection (1)(b) shares held by a wholly-owned subsidiary of the parent undertaking, or held on behalf of the parent undertaking or a wholly-owned subsidiary, shall be attributed to the parent undertaking.

(6) In subsection (3) "securities" includes—

(a) shares and stock,

(b) debentures, including debenture stock, loan stock, bonds, certificates of deposit and other instruments creating or acknowledging indebtedness,

(c) warrants or other instruments entitling the holder to subscribe for securities falling within paragraph (a) or (b), and

(d) certificates or other instruments which confer—

(i) property rights in respect of a security falling within paragraph (a), (b) or (c),

(ii) any right to acquire, dispose of, underwrite or convert a security, being a right to which the holder would be entitled if he held any such security to which the certificate or other instrument relates, or

(iii) a contractual right (other than an option) to acquire any such security otherwise than by subscription.]

[214]

NOTES

Inserted, together with s 229, by CA 1989, s 5(3), as from 1 April 1990.

Repealed by the Companies Act 2006, s 1295, Sch 16, as from 1 January 2007 (in so far as relating to the words omitted from sub-s (2)(f)), and as from a day to be appointed (otherwise).

Sub-s (1): words in square brackets substituted by the Companies Act 1985 (International Accounting Standards and Other Accounting Amendments) Regulations 2004, SI 2004/2947, reg 15, Sch 7, Pt 1, para 4(1), (2), as from 12 November 2004, in relation to companies' financial years which begin on or after 1 January 2005.

Sub-s (2): words in square brackets in para (a) substituted by SI 2004/2947, reg 15, Sch 7, Pt 1, para 4(1), (2), as from 12 November 2004, in relation to companies' financial years which begin on or after 1 January 2005; words in first (outer) pair of square brackets in para (b) added by the Companies Act 1985 (Disclosure of Branches and Bank Accounts) Regulations 1992, SI 1992/3178, reg 4, as from 1 January 1993; words in second (inner) pair of square brackets in para (b) added by the Companies Act 1985 (Insurance Companies Accounts) Regulations 1993, SI 1993/3246, reg 5(1), Sch 2, para 1, as from 19 December 1993, subject to exemptions in relation to certain companies contained in reg 6 (at **[6765]**) and general transitional provisions in reg 7 (at **[6766]**); words in third (inner) pair of square brackets in para (b) inserted by the Companies Act 1985 (International Accounting Standards and Other Accounting Amendments) Regulations 2004, SI 2004/2947, reg 3, Sch 1, paras 1, 6, as from 12 November 2004, in relation to companies' financial years which begin on or after 1 January 2005; para (d)(ii) repealed, in relation to any financial year ending on or after 2 February 1996, by the Companies Act 1985 (Miscellaneous Accounting Amendments) Regulations 1996, SI 1996/189, regs 4, 16(1) (subject to transitional provisions in relation to financial years ending on or before 24 March 1996); words in square brackets in para (f) inserted by the Welsh Language Act 1993, s 30(1), (3), as from 1 February 1994, and repealed as noted above (those words previously read "(subject to section 710B(6) (delivery of certain Welsh documents without a translation))").

Sub-s (3): words in square brackets substituted by SI 2004/2947, reg 15, Sch 7, Pt 1, para 4(1), (3), as from 12 November 2004, in relation to companies' financial years which begin on or after 1 January 2005; for the words "Council Directive 93/22/EEC on investment services in the securities field" there are substituted the words "Directive 2004/39/EC of the European Parliament and of the Council of 21 April 2004 on markets in financial instruments" by the Financial Services and Markets Act 2000 (Markets in Financial Instruments) Regulations 2007, SI 2007/126, reg 3(6), Sch 6, Pt 1, para 7(1), (7), as from 1 November 2007 (for the full commencement details of SI 2007/126, see reg 1 of those Regulations at **[7596]**).

Application to limited liability partnerships: see the Limited Liability Partnerships Regulations 2001, SI 2001/1090, reg 3, Sch 1 at **[6984]**, **[6992]**. Note also that nothing in the Companies Act 2006 (Commencement No 1, Transitional Provisions and Savings) Order 2006, SI 2006/3428 affects any provision of this Act as applied by the 2001 Regulations to LLPs (see art 8(2) at **[7581]** and the introductory notes to this Act)..

Modification: the reference in sub-s (6)(b) to securities, instruments or investments creating or acknowledging indebtedness (or creating or acknowledging a present or future indebtedness) includes a reference to uncertificated units of eligible debt securities; see the Uncertificated Securities (Amendment) (Eligible Debt Securities) Regulations 2003, SI 2003/1633, reg 15, Sch 2, para 8.

Certified in the prescribed manner to be a correct translation: see the Companies (Forms) (Amendment) Regulations 1990, SI 1990/572, reg 5(1), (2) (made, inter alia, under this section) which provides as follows—

"(1) From 1st April 1990, for the purposes of the provisions set out in paragraph (2) below, a translation of a document into English shall be certified to be a correct translation:—

(a) if the translation was made in the United Kingdom, by:—

(i) a notary public in any part of the United Kingdom;

(ii) a solicitor (if the translation was made in Scotland), a solicitor of the Supreme Court of Judicature of England and Wales (if it was made in England or Wales), or a *solicitor of the Supreme Court of Judicature of Northern Ireland* (if it was made in Northern Ireland); or

(iii) a person certified by a person mentioned above to be known to him to be competent to translate the document into English; or

(b) if the translation was made outside the United Kingdom, by:—

(i) a notary public;

(ii) a person authorised in the place where the translation was made to administer an oath;

(iii) any of the British officials mentioned in section 6 of the Commissioners for Oaths Act 1889;

(iv) a person certified by a person mentioned in sub-subparagraph (i), (ii) or (iii) of this subparagraph to be known to him to be competent to translate the document into English.

(2) The provisions referred to in paragraph (1) above are sections 228(2)(f), 242(1), 243(4) and 702(1) of the 1985 Act and paragraph 6 of Part II of Schedule 9 to that Act.".

In para (1)(a)(ii) above for the words in italics there are substituted the words "solicitor of the Court of Judicature of Northern Ireland" by the Constitutional Reform Act 2005, s 59, Sch 11, Pt 2, para 5, as from a day to be appointed.

Supreme Court of England and Wales: the Supreme Court of England and Wales is renamed the Senior Courts of England and Wales; see the Constitutional Reform Act 2005, s 59(1) (as from a day to be appointed).

[228A Exemption for parent companies included in non-EEA group accounts

(1) A company is exempt from the requirement to prepare group accounts if it is itself a subsidiary undertaking and its parent undertaking is not established under the law of an EEA State, in the following cases—

(a) where the company is a wholly-owned subsidiary of that parent undertaking;

(b) where that parent undertaking holds more than 50 per cent of the shares in the company and notice requesting the preparation of group accounts has not been served on the company by shareholders holding in aggregate—

(i) more than half of the remaining shares in the company, or

(ii) 5 per cent of the total shares in the company.

Such notice must be served not later than six months after the end of the financial year before that to which it relates.

(2) Exemption is conditional upon compliance with all of the following conditions—

(a) that the company and all of its subsidiary undertakings are included in consolidated accounts for a larger group drawn up to the same date, or to an earlier date in the same financial year, by a parent undertaking;

(b) that those accounts and, where appropriate, the group's annual report, are drawn up in accordance with the provisions of the Seventh Directive (83/349/EEC) (where applicable as modified by the provisions of the Bank Accounts Directive (86/635/EEC) or the Insurance Accounts Directive (91/674/EEC)), or in a manner equivalent to consolidated accounts and consolidated annual reports so drawn up;

(c) that the consolidated accounts are audited by one or more persons authorised to audit accounts under the law under which the parent undertaking which draws them up is established;

(d) that the company discloses in its individual accounts that it is exempt from the obligation to prepare and deliver group accounts;

(e) that the company states in its individual accounts the name of the parent undertaking which draws up the group accounts referred to above and—

(i) if it is incorporated outside Great Britain, the country in which it is incorporated, and

(ii) if it is unincorporated, the address of its principal place of business;

(f) that the company delivers to the registrar, within the period allowed for delivering its individual accounts, copies of the group accounts and, where appropriate, of the consolidated annual report, together with the auditors' report on them; and

(g) ... that if any document comprised in accounts and reports delivered in accordance with paragraph (f) is in a language other than English, there is annexed to the copy of that document delivered a translation of it into English, certified in the prescribed manner to be a correct translation.

(3) The exemption does not apply to a company any of whose securities are admitted to trading on a regulated market of any EEA State within the meaning of Council Directive 93/22/EEC on investment services in the securities field.

(4) Shares held by directors of a company for the purpose of complying with any share qualification requirement are disregarded in determining for the purposes of subsection (1)(a) whether the company is a wholly-owned subsidiary.

(5) For the purposes of subsection (1)(b), shares held by a wholly-owned subsidiary of the parent undertaking, or held on behalf of the parent undertaking or a wholly-owned subsidiary, are attributed to the parent undertaking.

(6) In subsection (3) "securities" includes—

(a) shares and stock,

(b) debentures, including debenture stock, loan stock, bonds, certificates of deposit and other instruments creating or acknowledging indebtedness,

(c) warrants or other instruments entitling the holder to subscribe for securities falling within paragraph (a) or (b), and

(d) certificates or other instruments which confer—

(i) property rights in respect of a security falling within paragraph (a), (b) or (c),

(ii) any right to acquire, dispose of, underwrite or convert a security, being a right to which the holder would be entitled if he held any such security to which the certificate or other instrument relates, or

(iii) a contractual right (other than an option) to acquire any such security otherwise than by subscription.]

[214A]

NOTES

Inserted by the Companies Act 1985 (International Accounting Standards and Other Accounting Amendments) Regulations 2004, SI 2004/2947, reg 4, as from 12 November 2004, in relation to companies' financial years which begin on or after 1 January 2005.

Repealed by the Companies Act 2006, s 1295, Sch 16, as from 1 January 2007 (in so far as relating to the words omitted from sub-s (2)(g)), and as from a day to be appointed (otherwise).

Sub-s (2): words omitted repealed as noted above (those words "previously read subject to section 710B(6) (delivery of certain Welsh documents without a translation)").

Sub-s (3): for the words "Council Directive 93/22/EEC on investment services in the securities field" there are substituted the words "Directive 2004/39/EC of the European Parliament and of the Council of 21 April 2004 on markets in financial instruments" by the Financial Services and Markets Act 2000 (Markets in Financial Instruments) Regulations 2007, SI 2007/126, reg 3(6), Sch 6, Pt 1, para 7(1), (8), as from 1 November 2007 (for the full commencement details of SI 2007/126, see reg 1 of those Regulations at **[7596]**).

Application to limited liability partnerships: see the Limited Liability Partnerships Regulations 2001, SI 2001/1090, reg 3, Sch 1 at **[6984]**, **[6992]**. Note also that nothing in the Companies Act 2006 (Commencement No 1, Transitional Provisions and Savings) Order 2006, SI 2006/3428 affects any provision of this Act as applied by the 2001 Regulations to LLPs (see art 8(2) at **[7581]** and the introductory notes to this Act).

[229 Subsidiary undertakings included in the consolidation

(1) [In the case of Companies Act group accounts,] subject to the exceptions authorised ... by this section, all the subsidiary undertakings of the parent company shall be included in the consolidation.

(2) A subsidiary undertaking may be excluded from consolidation [in Companies Act group accounts] if its inclusion is not material for the purpose of giving a true and fair view; but two or more undertakings may be excluded only if they are not material taken together.

(3) In addition, a subsidiary undertaking may be excluded from consolidation [in Companies Act group accounts] where—

(*a*) *severe long-term restrictions substantially hinder the exercise of the rights of the parent company over the assets or management of that undertaking, or*

(*b*) *the information necessary for the preparation of group accounts cannot be obtained without disproportionate expense or undue delay, or*

(*c*) *the interest of the parent company is held exclusively with a view to subsequent resale ...*

The reference in paragraph (a) to the rights of the parent company and the reference in paragraph (c) to the interest of the parent company are, respectively, to rights and interests held by or attributed to the company for the purposes of section 258 (definition of "parent undertaking") in the absence of which it would not be the parent company.

(*4*) ...

[(5) A parent company is exempt from the requirement to prepare group accounts if under subsection (2) or (3) all of its subsidiary undertakings could be excluded from consolidation in Companies Act group accounts.]]

[215]

NOTES

Inserted as noted to s 228 at **[214]**.

Repealed by the Companies Act 2006, s 1295, Sch 16, as from a day to be appointed.

Sub-ss (1), (3): words in square brackets inserted, and words omitted repealed, by the Companies Act 1985 (International Accounting Standards and Other Accounting Amendments) Regulations 2004, SI 2004/2947, regs 3, 5(a), Sch 1, paras 1, 7(a), (b), as from 12 November 2004, in relation to companies' financial years which begin on or after 1 January 2005.

Sub-s (2): words in square brackets inserted by SI 2004/2947, reg 3, Sch 1, paras 1, 7(b), as from 12 November 2004, in relation to companies' financial years which begin on or after 1 January 2005.

Sub-s (4): repealed by SI 2004/2947, reg 5(b), as from 12 November 2004, in relation to companies' financial years which begin on or after 1 January 2005.

Sub-s (5): substituted by SI 2004/2947, reg 3, Sch 1, paras 1, 7(c), as from 12 November 2004, in relation to companies' financial years which begin on or after 1 January 2005.

Application to limited liability partnerships: see the Limited Liability Partnerships Regulations 2001, SI 2001/1090, reg 3, Sch 1 at **[6984]**, **[6992]**.

[230 Treatment of individual profit and loss account where group accounts prepared

(*1*) *The following provisions apply with respect to the individual profit and loss account of a parent company where—*

(*a*) *the company is required to prepare and does prepare group accounts in accordance with this Act, and*

(*b*) *the notes to the company's individual balance sheet show the company's profit or loss for the financial year determined in accordance with this Act.*

(2) *[Where the company prepares Companies Act individual accounts,] the profit and loss account need not contain the information specified in paragraphs 52 to 57 of Schedule 4 (information supplementing the profit and loss account).*

(*3*) *The profit and loss account must be approved in accordance with section 233(1) (approval by board of directors) but may be omitted from the company's annual accounts for the purposes of the other provisions below in this Chapter.*

(*4*) *The exemption conferred by this section is conditional upon its being disclosed in the company's annual accounts that the exemption applies.]*

[216]

NOTES

Inserted by CA 1989, s 5(4), as from 1 April 1990.

Repealed by the Companies Act 2006, s 1295, Sch 16, as from a day to be appointed.

Sub-s (2): words in square brackets inserted by the Companies Act 1985 (International Accounting Standards and Other Accounting Amendments) Regulations 2004, SI 2004/2947, reg 3, Sch 1, paras 1, 8, as from 12 November 2004, in relation to companies' financial years which begin on or after 1 January 2005.

Application to limited liability partnerships: see the Limited Liability Partnerships Regulations 2001, SI 2001/1090, reg 3, Sch 1 at **[6984]**, **[6992]**.

[231 Disclosure required in notes to accounts: related undertakings

(*1*) *The information specified in Schedule 5 shall be given in notes to a company's annual accounts.*

(2) Where the company is not required to prepare group accounts, the information specified in Part I of that Schedule shall be given; and where the company is required to prepare group accounts, the information specified in Part II of that Schedule shall be given.

(3) The information required by Schedule 5 need not be disclosed with respect to an undertaking which—

(a) is established under the law of a country outside the United Kingdom, or

(b) carries on business outside the United Kingdom,

if in the opinion of the directors of the company the disclosure would be seriously prejudicial to the business of that undertaking, or to the business of the company or any of its subsidiary undertakings, and the Secretary of State agrees that the information need not be disclosed.

This subsection does not apply in relation to the information required under [paragraph … 6, 9A, 20 or 28A] of that Schedule.

(4) Where advantage is taken of subsection (3), that fact shall be stated in a note to the company's annual accounts.

(5) If the directors of the company are of the opinion that the number of undertakings in respect of which the company is required to disclose information under any provision of Schedule 5 to this Act is such that compliance with that provision would result in information of excessive length being given, the information need only be given in respect of—

(a) the undertakings whose results or financial position, in the opinion of the directors, principally affected the figures shown in the company's annual accounts, and

(b) undertakings excluded from consolidation under section 229(3) …

…

(6) If advantage is taken of subsection (5)—

(a) there shall be included in the notes to the company's annual accounts a statement that the information is given only with respect to such undertakings as are mentioned in that subsection, and

(b) the full information (both that which is disclosed in the notes to the accounts and that which is not) shall be annexed to the company's next annual return.

For this purpose the "next annual return" means that next delivered to the registrar after the accounts in question have been approved under section 233.

(7) If a company fails to comply with subsection (6)(b), the company and every officer of it who is in default is liable to a fine and, for continued contravention, to a daily default fine.]

[217]

NOTES

Inserted by CA 1989, s 6(1), as from 1 April 1990.

Repealed by the Companies Act 2006, s 1295, Sch 16, as from a day to be appointed.

Sub-s (3): words in square brackets substituted by the Partnerships and Unlimited Companies (Accounts) Regulations 1993, SI 1993/1820, reg 11(1), as from 21 July 1993 (subject to transitional provisions in relation to financial years commencing before 23 December 1994); number omitted repealed in relation to any financial year ending on or after 2 February 1996, by the Companies Act 1985 (Miscellaneous Accounting Amendments) Regulations 1996, SI 1996/189, regs 15(1), 16(1) (subject to transitional provisions in relation to financial years ending on or before 24 March 1996).

Sub-s (5): first words omitted repealed by the Companies Act 1985 (International Accounting Standards and Other Accounting Amendments) Regulations 2004, SI 2004/2947, reg 15, Sch 7, Pt 1, paras 1, 5, as from 12 November 2004, in relation to companies' financial years which begin on or after 1 January 2005; second words omitted repealed in relation to any financial year ending on or after 2 February 1996, by SI 1996/189, regs 15(1), 16(1) (subject to transitional provisions as noted above).

Application to limited liability partnerships: see the Limited Liability Partnerships Regulations 2001, SI 2001/1090, reg 3, Sch 1 at **[6984]**, **[6992]**.

[231A Disclosure required in notes to annual accounts: particulars of staff

(1) The following information with respect to the employees of the company must be given in notes to the company's annual accounts—

(a) the average number of persons employed by the company in the financial year, and

(b) the average number of persons so employed within each category of persons employed by the company.

(2) The average number required by subsection (1)(a) or (b) is determined by dividing the relevant annual number by the number of months in the financial year.

(3) The relevant annual number is determined by ascertaining for each month in the financial year—

(a) for the purposes of subsection (1)(a), the number of persons employed under contracts of service by the company in that month (whether throughout the month or not);

(b) for the purposes of subsection (1)(b), the number of persons in the category in question of persons so employed;

and, in either case, adding together all the monthly numbers.

(4) In respect of all persons employed by the company during the financial year who are taken into account in determining the relevant annual number for the purposes of subsection (1)(a) there must also be stated the aggregate amounts respectively of—

(a) wages and salaries paid or payable in respect of that year to those persons;
(b) social security costs incurred by the company on their behalf; and
(c) other pension costs so incurred.

This does not apply in so far as those amounts, or any of them, are stated elsewhere in the company's accounts.

(5) For the purposes of subsection (1)(b), the categories of person employed by the company are such as the directors may select, having regard to the manner in which the company's activities are organised.

(6) This section applies in relation to group accounts as if the undertakings included in the consolidation were a single company.

(7) In this section "social security costs" and "pension costs" have the same meaning as in Schedule 4 (see paragraph 94(1) and (2) of that Schedule).]

[217A]

NOTES

Inserted by the Companies Act 1985 (International Accounting Standards and Other Accounting Amendments) Regulations 2004, SI 2004/2947, reg 3, Sch 1, paras 1, 9, as from 12 November 2004, in relation to companies' financial years which begin on or after 1 January 2005.

Repealed by the Companies Act 2006, s 1295, Sch 16, as from a day to be appointed.

Application to limited liability partnerships: see the Limited Liability Partnerships Regulations 2001, SI 2001/1090, reg 3, Sch 1 at **[6984]**, **[6992]**.

[232 Disclosure required in notes to accounts: emoluments and other benefits of directors and others

[(1) The information specified in Schedule 6 shall be given in notes to a company's annual accounts, save that the information specified in paragraphs 2–14 in Part I of Schedule 6 shall be given only in the case of a company which is not a quoted company.]

(2) In that Schedule—

Part I relates to the emoluments of directors (including emoluments waived), pensions of directors and past directors, compensation for loss of office to directors and past directors and sums paid to third parties in respect of directors' services,

Part II relates to loans, quasi-loans and other dealings in favour of directors and connected persons, and

Part III relates to transactions, arrangements and agreements made by the company or a subsidiary undertaking for officers of the company other than directors.

(3) It is the duty of any director of a company, and any person who is or has at any time in the preceding five years been an officer of the company, to give notice to the company of such matters relating to himself as may be necessary for the purposes of Part I of Schedule 6.

(4) A person who makes default in complying with subsection (3) commits an offence and is liable to a fine.]

[218]

NOTES

Inserted by CA 1989, s 6(3), as from 1 April 1990.

Repealed by the Companies Act 2006, s 1295, Sch 16, as from a day to be appointed.

Sub-s (1): substituted by the Directors' Remuneration Report Regulations 2002, SI 2002/1986, reg 2, as from 1 August 2002, with effect as respects companies' financial years ending on or after 31 December 2002.

Application to limited liability partnerships: see the Limited Liability Partnerships Regulations 2001, SI 2001/1090, reg 3, Sch 1 at **[6984]**, **[6992]**.

[Approval and signing of accounts

233 Approval and signing of accounts

(1) A company's annual accounts shall be approved by the board of directors and signed on behalf of the board by a director of the company.

(2) The signature shall be on the company's balance sheet.

(3) Every copy of the balance sheet which is laid before the company in general meeting, or which is otherwise circulated, published or issued, shall state the name of the person who signed the balance sheet on behalf of the board.

(4) The copy of the company's balance sheet which is delivered to the registrar shall be signed on behalf of the board by a director of the company.

(5) If annual accounts are approved which do not comply with the requirements of this Act [(or, where applicable, of Article 4 of the IAS Regulation)], every director of the company who is party to their approval and who knows that they do not comply or is reckless as to whether they comply is guilty of an offence and liable to a fine.

For this purpose every director of the company at the time the accounts are approved shall be taken to be a party to their approval unless he shows that he took all reasonable steps to prevent their being approved.

(6) If a copy of the balance sheet—

(a) is laid before the company, or otherwise circulated, published or issued, without the balance sheet having been signed as required by this section or without the required statement of the signatory's name being included, or

(b) is delivered to the registrar without being signed as required by this section,

the company and every officer of it who is in default is guilty of an offence and liable to a fine.]

[219]

NOTES

Inserted, together with the preceding heading, by CA 1989, s 7, partly as from 1 April 1990, partly as from 7 January 1991.

Repealed by the Companies Act 2006, s 1295, Sch 16, as from a day to be appointed.

Sub-s (5): words in square brackets inserted by the Companies Act 1985 (International Accounting Standards and Other Accounting Amendments) Regulations 2004, SI 2004/2947, reg 3, Sch 1, paras 1, 10, as from 12 November 2004, in relation to companies' financial years which begin on or after 1 January 2005.

Application to limited liability partnerships: see the Limited Liability Partnerships Regulations 2001, SI 2001/1090, reg 3, Sch 1 at **[6984]**, **[6992]**.

[Directors' report

234 Duty to prepare directors' report

(1) The directors of a company shall for each financial year prepare a report (a "directors' report") complying with the general requirements of section 234ZZA and containing—

(a) the business review specified in section 234ZZB, and

(b) if section 234ZA applies to the report, the statement as to disclosure of information to auditors required by that section.

(2) For a financial year in which—

(a) the company is a parent company, and

(b) the directors of the company prepare group accounts,

the directors' report must be a consolidated report (a "group directors' report") relating, to the extent specified in the following provisions of this Part, to the company and its subsidiary undertakings included in the consolidation.

(3) A group directors' report may, where appropriate, give greater emphasis to the matters that are significant to the company and its subsidiary undertakings included in the consolidation, taken as a whole.

(4) ...

(5) If a directors' report does not comply with the provisions of this Part relating to the preparation and contents of the report, every director of the company who—

(a) knew that it did not comply or was reckless as to whether it complied, and

(b) failed to take all reasonable steps to secure compliance with the provision in question,

is guilty of an offence and liable to a fine.]

[220]

NOTES

Section 234 was inserted (together with the preceding heading and s 234A) by CA 1989, s 8(1), as from 1 April 1990. It was subsequently substituted by new ss 234, 234ZZA, 234ZZB, by the Companies Act 1985 (Operating and Financial Review and Directors' Report etc) Regulations 2005, SI 2005/1011, reg 2, as from 22 March 2005, in relation to companies' financial years which begin on or after 1 April 2005.

Repealed by the Companies Act 2006, s 1295, Sch 16, as from 1 October 2007 (in so far as relating to sub-s (1)(a)), and as from a day to be appointed (otherwise). For savings see the note below.

Sub-s (1): para (a) repealed as noted above.

Sub-s (4): repealed by the Companies Act 1985 (Operating and Financial Review) (Repeal) Regulations 2005, SI 2005/3442, reg 2(2)(a), Sch 1, para 1, as from 12 January 2006.

Savings: sub-s (1)(a) continues to apply to directors' reports for financial years beginning before 1 October 2007 (see the draft Companies Act 2006 (Commencement No 3, Consequential Amendments, Transitional Provisions and Savings) Order 2007, Sch 3, para 43 at **[A12]**).

Application to limited liability partnerships: see the Limited Liability Partnerships Regulations 2001, SI 2001/1090, reg 3, Sch 1 at **[6984]**, **[6992]**. Note also that nothing in the draft Companies Act 2006 (Commencement No 3, Consequential Amendments, Transitional Provisions and Savings) Order 2007 affects any provision of this Act as applied by the 2001 Regulations to LLPs (see art 12(2) at **[A12]** and the introductory notes to this Act).

Community interest companies: Regulations may apply the provisions of this Act relating to directors' reports to community interest company reports (with any appropriate modifications); see the Companies (Audit, Investigations and Community Enterprise) Act 2004, ss 26, 34(1), (3)(c) at **[900]**, **[908]**.

[234ZZA Directors' report: general requirements

(1) The directors' report for a financial year must state—

(a) the names of the persons who, at any time during the financial year, were directors of the company,

(b) the principal activities of the company in the course of the year, and

(c) the amount (if any) that the directors recommend should be paid by way of dividend.

(2) In relation to a group directors' report subsection (1)(b) has effect as if the reference to the company was a reference to the company and its subsidiary undertakings included in the consolidation.

(3) The report must also comply with Schedule 7 as regards the disclosure of the matters mentioned there.

(4) In Schedule 7—

Part 1 relates to matters of a general nature, including changes in asset values, directors' shareholdings and other interests and contributions for political and charitable purposes;

Part 2 relates to the acquisition by a company of its own shares or a charge on them;

Part 3 relates to the employment, training and advancement of disabled persons;

Part 5 relates to the involvement of employees in the affairs, policy and performance of the company;

Part 6 relates to the company's policy and practice on the payment of creditors;

[Part 7 specifies information to be disclosed by certain publicly- traded companies].

[(5) A directors' report shall also contain any necessary explanatory material with regard to information that is required to be included in the report by Part 7 of Schedule 7.]]

[220ZA]

NOTES

Substituted as noted to s 234 at **[220]**.

Repealed by the Companies Act 2006, s 1295, Sch 16, as from a day to be appointed. Note that this section is also amended by the 2006 Act (see below).

Sub-s (4): words in square brackets inserted by the Companies Act 2006, s 992(1), (3), (6), as from 6 April 2007, in relation to directors' reports for financial years beginning on or after 20 May 2006.

Sub-s (5): added by the Companies Act 2006, s 992(1), (4), (6), as from 6 April 2007, in relation to directors' reports for financial years beginning on or after 20 May 2006.

Application to limited liability partnerships: see the Limited Liability Partnerships Regulations 2001, SI 2001/1090, reg 3, Sch 1 at **[6984]**, **[6992]**. Note also that nothing in the Companies Act 2006 (Commencement No 2, Consequential Amendments, Transitional Provisions and Savings) Order 2007, SI 2007/1093 affects any provision of this Act as applied by the 2001 Regulations to LLPs (see art 12(1) at **[7624]** and the introductory notes to this Act).

Note: this section is amended by s 992 (in Part 28) of the Companies Act 2006 as noted above. Part 28 is the domestic implementation of the Takeovers Directive (Directive of the European Parliament and of the Council 2004/25/EC on takeover bids) and was brought into force on 6 April 2007. The Takeovers Directive had to be implemented by 20 May 2006 and this was achieved by the Takeovers Directive (Interim Implementation) Regulations 2006, SI 2006/1183 (see regs 25, 26 of those Regulations as to the application of this section to a directors' report for a financial year beginning on or after that date (at **[7533]**, **[7534]**)). The 2006 Interim Regulations were also revoked as from 6 April 2007 (subject to savings).

[234ZZB Directors' report: business review

(*1*) *The directors' report for a financial year must contain—*

(*a*) *a fair review of the business of the company, and*

(*b*) *a description of the principal risks and uncertainties facing the company.*

(*2*) *The review required is a balanced and comprehensive analysis of—*

(*a*) *the development and performance of the business of the company during the financial year, and*

(*b*) *the position of the company at the end of that year,*

consistent with the size and complexity of the business.

(*3*) *The review must, to the extent necessary for an understanding of the development, performance or position of the business of the company, include—*

(*a*) *analysis using financial key performance indicators, and*

(*b*) *where appropriate, analysis using other key performance indicators, including information relating to environmental matters and employee matters.*

(*4*) *The review must, where appropriate, include references to, and additional explanations of, amounts included in the annual accounts of the company.*

(*5*) *In this section, "key performance indicators" means factors by reference to which the development, performance or position of the business of the company can be measured effectively.*

(*6*) *In relation to a group directors' report this section has effect as if the references to the company were references to the company and its subsidiary undertakings included in the consolidation.]*

[220ZB]

NOTES

Substituted as noted to s 234 at **[220]**.

Repealed by the Companies Act 2006, s 1295, Sch 16, as from 1 October 2007. For savings see the note below.

Savings: this section continues to apply to directors' reports for financial years beginning before 1 October 2007 (see the draft Companies Act 2006 (Commencement No 3, Consequential Amendments, Transitional Provisions and Savings) Order 2007, Sch 3, para 43 at **[A12]**).

Application to limited liability partnerships: see the Limited Liability Partnerships Regulations 2001, SI 2001/1090, reg 3, Sch 1 at **[6984]**, **[6992]**. Note also that nothing in the draft Companies Act 2006 (Commencement No 3, Consequential Amendments, Transitional Provisions and Savings) Order 2007 affects any provision of this Act as applied by the 2001 Regulations to LLPs (see art 12(2) at **[A12]** and the introductory notes to this Act).

[234ZA Statement as to disclosure of information to auditors

(*1*) *This section applies to a directors' report unless the directors have taken advantage of the exemption conferred by section 249A(1) or 249AA(1).*

(*2*) *The report must contain a statement to the effect that, in the case of each of the persons who are directors at the time when the report is approved under section 234A, the following applies—*

(*a*) *so far as the director is aware, there is no relevant audit information of which the company's auditors are unaware, and*

(*b*) *he has taken all the steps that he ought to have taken as a director in order to make himself aware of any relevant audit information and to establish that the company's auditors are aware of that information.*

(*3*) *In subsection* (2) *"relevant audit information" means information needed by the company's auditors in connection with preparing their report.*

(*4*) *For the purposes of subsection* (2) *a director has taken all the steps that he ought to have taken as a director in order to do the things mentioned in paragraph* (*b*) *of that subsection if he has—*

(*a*) *made such enquiries of his fellow directors and of the company's auditors for that purpose, and*

(*b*) *taken such other steps* (*if any*) *for that purpose,*

as were required by his duty as a director of the company to exercise due care, skill and diligence.

(*5*) *In determining for the purposes of subsection* (2) *the extent of that duty in the case of a particular director, the following considerations* (*in particular*) *are relevant—*

(*a*) *the knowledge, skill and experience that may reasonably be expected of a person carrying out the same functions as are carried out by the director in relation to the company, and*

(*b*) (*so far as they exceed what may reasonably be so expected*) *the knowledge, skill and experience that the director in fact has.*

(*6*) *Where a directors' report containing the statement required by subsection* (2) *is approved under section 234A but the statement is false, every director of the company who—*

(*a*) *knew that the statement was false, or was reckless as to whether it was false, and*

(*b*) *failed to take reasonable steps to prevent the report from being approved,*

is guilty of an offence and liable to imprisonment or a fine, or both.]

[220A]

NOTES

Inserted by the Companies (Audit, Investigations and Community Enterprise) Act 2004, s 9(1), (3), as from 6 April 2005 (except in relation to any report of the directors of a company prepared under s 234 concerning a financial year beginning before 1 April 2005 or ending before 6 April 2005; see the Companies (Audit, Investigations and Community Enterprise) Act 2004 (Commencement) and Companies Act 1989 (Commencement No 18) Order 2004, SI 2004/3322, art 4 at **[7342]**).

Repealed by the Companies Act 2006, s 1295, Sch 16, as from a day to be appointed.

Application to limited liability partnerships: see the Limited Liability Partnerships Regulations 2001, SI 2001/1090, reg 3, Sch 1 at **[6984]**, **[6992]**.

[234A Approval and signing of directors' report

(*1*) *The directors' report shall be approved by the board of directors and signed on behalf of the board by a director or the secretary of the company.*

(*2*) *Every copy of the directors' report which is laid before the company in general meeting, or which is otherwise circulated, published or issued, shall state the name of the person who signed it on behalf of the board.*

(*3*) *The copy of the directors' report which is delivered to the registrar shall be signed on behalf of the board by a director or the secretary of the company.*

(*4*) *If a copy of the directors' report—*

(*a*) *is laid before the company, or otherwise circulated, published or issued, without the report having been signed as required by this section or without the required statement of the signatory's name being included, or*

(*b*) *is delivered to the registrar without being signed as required by this section,*

the company and every officer of it who is in default is guilty of an offence and liable to a fine.]

[221]

NOTES

Inserted as noted to s 234 at **[220]**.

Repealed by the Companies Act 2006, s 1295, Sch 16, as from a day to be appointed.

Application to limited liability partnerships: see the Limited Liability Partnerships Regulations 2001, SI 2001/1090, reg 3, Sch 1 at **[6984]**, **[6992]**.

234AA, 234AB (*Inserted by the Companies Act 1985 (Operating and Financial Review and Directors' Report etc) Regulations 2005, SI 2005/1011, reg 8, as from 22 March 2005, in relation to companies' financial years which begin on or after 1 April 2005; repealed by the Companies Act 1985 (Operating and Financial Review) (Repeal) Regulations 2005, SI 2005/3442, reg 2(1), (2)(a), Sch 1, paras 2, 3, as from 12 January 2006.*)

[Quoted companies: directors' remuneration report

234B Duty to prepare directors' remuneration report

(1) The directors of a quoted company shall for each financial year prepare a directors' remuneration report which shall contain the information specified in Schedule 7A and comply with any requirement of that Schedule as to how information is to be set out in the report.

(2) In Schedule 7A—

Part 1 is introductory,

Part 2 relates to information about remuneration committees, performance related remuneration and liabilities in respect of directors' contracts,

Part 3 relates to detailed information about directors' remuneration (information included under Part 3 is required to be reported on by the auditors, see section 235), and

Part 4 contains interpretative and supplementary provisions.

(3) In the case of any failure to comply with the provisions of this Part as to the preparation of a directors' remuneration report and the contents of the report, every person who was a director of the quoted company immediately before the end of the period for laying and delivering accounts and reports for the financial year in question is guilty of an offence and liable to a fine.

(4) In proceedings against a person for an offence under subsection (3) it is a defence for him to prove that he took all reasonable steps for securing compliance with the requirements in question.

(5) It is the duty of any director of a company, and any person who has at any time in the preceding five years been a director of the company, to give notice to the company of such matters relating to himself as may be necessary for the purposes of Parts 2 and 3 of Schedule 7A.

(6) A person who makes default in complying with subsection (5) commits an offence and is liable to a fine.]

[221A]

NOTES

Inserted, together with the preceding heading and s 234C, by the Directors' Remuneration Report Regulations 2002, SI 2002/1986, reg 3, as from 1 August 2002, with effect as respects companies' financial years ending on or after 31 December 2002.

Repealed by the Companies Act 2006, s 1295, Sch 16, as from a day to be appointed.

Application to limited liability partnerships: see the Limited Liability Partnerships Regulations 2001, SI 2001/1090, reg 3, Sch 1 at **[6984]**, **[6992]**.

[234C Approval and signing of directors' remuneration report

(1) The directors' remuneration report shall be approved by the board of directors and signed on behalf of the board by a director or the secretary of the company.

(2) Every copy of the directors' remuneration report which is laid before the company in general meeting, or which is otherwise circulated, published or issued, shall state the name of the person who signed it on behalf of the board.

(3) The copy of the directors' remuneration report which is delivered to the registrar shall be signed on behalf of the board by a director or the secretary of the company.

(4) If a copy of the directors' remuneration report—

(a) is laid before the company, or otherwise circulated, published or issued, without

the report having been signed as required by this section or without the required statement of the signatory's name being included, or

(*b*) *is delivered to the registrar without being signed as required by this section,*

the company and every officer of it who is in default is guilty of an offence and liable to a fine.]

[221B]

NOTES

Inserted as noted to s 234B at **[221A]**.

Repealed by the Companies Act 2006, s 1295, Sch 16, as from a day to be appointed.

Application to limited liability partnerships: see the Limited Liability Partnerships Regulations 2001, SI 2001/1090, reg 3, Sch 1 at **[6984]**, **[6992]**.

[Auditors' report

235 Auditors' report

(*1*) *A company's auditors shall make a report to the company's members on all annual accounts of the company of which copies are to be laid before the company in general meeting during their tenure of office.*

[(1A) The auditors' report must include—

(*a*) *an introduction identifying the annual accounts that are the subject of the audit and the financial reporting framework that has been applied in their preparation;*

(*b*) *a description of the scope of the audit identifying the auditing standards in accordance with which the audit was conducted.*

(*1B*) *The report must state clearly whether in the auditors' opinion the annual accounts have been properly prepared in accordance with the requirements of this Act (and, where applicable, Article 4 of the IAS Regulation).*

(*2*) *The report must state in particular whether the annual accounts give a true and fair view, in accordance with the relevant financial reporting framework—*

(*a*) *in the case of an individual balance sheet, of the state of affairs of the company as at the end of the financial year,*

(*b*) *in the case of an individual profit and loss account, of the profit or loss of the company for the financial year,*

(*c*) *in the case of group accounts, of the state of affairs as at the end of the financial year and of the profit or loss for the financial year, of the undertakings included in the consolidation as a whole, so far as concerns members of the company.*

(2A) *The auditors' report—*

(*a*) *must be either unqualified or qualified, and*

(*b*) *must include a reference to any matters to which the auditors wish to draw attention by way of emphasis without qualifying the report.]*

[(3) The auditors must state in their report whether in their opinion the information given in the directors' report for the financial year for which the annual accounts are prepared is consistent with those accounts.]

[(3A) …]

[(4) If a directors' remuneration report is prepared for the financial year for which the annual accounts are prepared the auditors shall in their report

(*a*) *report to the company's members on the auditable part of the directors' remuneration report, and*

(*b*) *state whether in their opinion that part of the directors' remuneration report has been properly prepared in accordance with this Act.*

(*5*) *For the purposes of this Part, "the auditable part" of a directors' remuneration report is the part containing the information required by Part 3 of Schedule 7A.]]*

[222]

NOTES

Inserted, together with the preceding heading and ss 236, 237, by CA 1989, s 9, as from 1 April 1990.

Repealed by the Companies Act 2006, s 1295, Sch 16, as from a day to be appointed.

Sub-s (1): for the words from "are to be laid before the company" to the end there are substituted the following words by the draft Companies Act 2006 (Commencement No 3, Consequential Amendments, Transitional Provisions and Savings) Order 2007, art 10(1), Sch 4, Pt 1, para 3(1), (8), as from 1 October 2007 (see **[A12]** and note that this amendment has effect for financial years ending on or after 1 October 2007)—

"are, during their tenure of office—

(a) in the case of a private company, to be sent out to members under section 238(1);

(b) in the case of a public company, to be laid before the company in general meeting under section 241.".

Sub-ss (1A), (1B), (2), (2A): substituted, for original sub-s (2), by the Companies Act 1985 (International Accounting Standards and Other Accounting Amendments) Regulations 2004, SI 2004/2947, reg 6, as from 12 November 2004, in relation to companies' financial years which begin on or after 1 January 2005.

Sub-s (3): substituted by the Companies Act 1985 (Operating and Financial Review and Directors' Report etc) Regulations 2005, SI 2005/1011, reg 3, as from 22 March 2005, in relation to companies' financial years which begin on or after 1 April 2005.

Sub-s (3A): inserted by SI 2005/1011, reg 10, as from 22 March 2005, in relation to companies' financial years which begin on or after 1 April 2005; repealed by the Companies Act 1985 (Operating and Financial Review) (Repeal) Regulations 2005, SI 2005/3442, reg 2(2)(a), Sch 1, para 4, as from 12 January 2006.

Sub-ss (4), (5): added by the Directors' Remuneration Report Regulations 2002, SI 2002/1986, reg 4, as from 1 August 2002, with effect as respects companies' financial years ending on or after 31 December 2002.

Application to limited liability partnerships: see the Limited Liability Partnerships Regulations 2001, SI 2001/1090, reg 3, Sch 1 at **[6984]**, **[6992]**. Note also that nothing in the draft Companies Act 2006 (Commencement No 3, Consequential Amendments, Transitional Provisions and Savings) Order 2007 affects any provision of this Act as applied by the 2001 Regulations to LLPs (see art 12(2) at **[A12]** and the introductory notes to this Act).

[236 Signature of auditors' report

(1) The auditors' report shall state the names of the auditors and be signed [and dated] by them.

(2) Every copy of the auditors' report which is laid before the company in general meeting, or which is otherwise circulated, published or issued, shall state the names of the auditors.

(3) The copy of the auditors' report which is delivered to the registrar shall state the names of the auditors and be signed by them.

(4) If a copy of the auditors' report—

(a) is laid before the company, or otherwise circulated, published or issued, without the required statement of the auditors' names, or

(b) is delivered to the registrar without the required statement of the auditors' names or without being signed as required by this section,

the company and every officer of it who is in default is guilty of an offence and liable to a fine.

(5) References in this section to signature by the auditors are, where the office of auditor is held by a body corporate or partnership, to signature in the name of the body corporate or partnership by a person authorised to sign on its behalf.]

[223]

NOTES

Inserted as noted to s 235 at **[222]**.

Repealed by the Companies Act 2006, s 1295, Sch 16, as from a day to be appointed.

Sub-s (1): words in square brackets inserted by the Companies Act 1985 (International Accounting Standards and Other Accounting Amendments) Regulations 2004, SI 2004/2947, reg 7, as from 12 November 2004, in relation to companies' financial years which begin on or after 1 January 2005.

Application to limited liability partnerships: see the Limited Liability Partnerships Regulations 2001, SI 2001/1090, reg 3, Sch 1 at **[6984]**, **[6992]**.

[237 Duties of auditors

(1) A company's auditors shall, in preparing their report, carry out such investigations as will enable them to form an opinion as to—

(a) whether proper accounting records have been kept by the company and proper returns adequate for their audit have been received from branches not visited by them, and

(*b*) *whether the company's individual accounts are in agreement with the accounting records and returns, [and*

(*c*) *(in the case of a quoted company) whether the auditable part of the company's directors' remuneration report is in agreement with the accounting records and returns.]*

(*2*) *If the auditors are of opinion that proper accounting records have not been kept, or that proper returns adequate for their audit have not been received from branches not visited by them, or if the company's individual accounts are not in agreement with the accounting records and returns, [or if in the case of a quoted company the auditable part of its directors' remuneration report is not in agreement with the accounting records and returns,] the auditors shall state that fact in their report.*

(*3*) *If the auditors fail to obtain all the information and explanations which, to the best of their knowledge and belief, are necessary for the purposes of their audit, they shall state that fact in their report.*

[(4) If—

(*a*) *the requirements of Schedule 6 (disclosure of information: emoluments and other benefits of directors and others) are not complied with in the annual accounts, or*

(*b*) *where a directors' remuneration report is required to be prepared, the requirements of Part 3 of Schedule 7A (directors' remuneration report) are not complied with in that report,*

the auditors shall include in their report, so far as they are reasonably able to do so, a statement giving the required particulars.]

[(4A) If the directors of the company have taken advantage of the exemption conferred by section 248 (exemption for small and medium-sized groups from the need to prepare group accounts) and in the auditors' opinion they were not entitled so to do, the auditors shall state that fact in their report.]]

[224]

NOTES

Inserted as noted to s 235 at **[222]**.

Repealed by the Companies Act 2006, s 1295, Sch 16, as from a day to be appointed.

Sub-s (1): para (c) and the word immediately preceding it added by the Directors' Remuneration Report Regulations 2002, SI 2002/1986, reg 5, as from 1 August 2002, with effect as respects companies' financial years ending on or after 31 December 2002.

Sub-s (2): words in square brackets inserted by SI 2002/1986, reg 10(1), (2), as from 1 August 2002, with effect as respects companies' financial years ending on or after 31 December 2002.

Sub-s (4): substituted by SI 2002/1986, reg 6, as from 1 August 2002, with effect as respects companies' financial years ending on or after 31 December 2002.

Sub-s (4A): added by the Companies Act 1985 (Miscellaneous Accounting Amendments) Regulations 1996, SI 1996/189, regs 6, 16(5), in relation to any annual accounts of a company which are approved by the board of directors on or after 2 February 1996.

Application to limited liability partnerships: see the Limited Liability Partnerships Regulations 2001, SI 2001/1090, reg 3, Sch 1 at **[6984]**, **[6992]**.

[Publication of accounts and reports

238 Persons entitled to receive copies of accounts and reports

(*1*) *[A copy of each of the documents mentioned in subsection (1A)] shall be sent to—*

(*a*) *every member of the company,*

(*b*) *every holder of the company's debentures, and*

(*c*) *every person who is entitled to receive notice of general meetings,*

not less than 21 days before the date of the meeting at which copies of those documents are to be laid in accordance with section 241.

[(1A) Those documents are—

(*a*) *the company's annual accounts for the financial year,*

(*b*) *the directors' report for that financial year,*

[(ba) ...]

(*c*) *(in the case of a quoted company) the directors' remuneration report for that financial year, and [(d) the auditors' report on those accounts and that directors' report and (in the case of a quoted company) on ... the auditable part of that directors' remuneration report.]]*

(2) Copies need not be sent—

(a) to a person who is not entitled to receive notices of general meetings and of whose address the company is unaware, or

(b) to more than one of the joint holders of shares or debentures none of whom is entitled to receive such notices, or

(c) in the case of joint holders of shares or debentures some of whom are, and some not, entitled to receive such notices, to those who are not so entitled.

(3) In the case of a company not having a share capital, copies need not be sent to anyone who is not entitled to receive notices of general meetings of the company.

(4) If copies are sent less than 21 days before the date of the meeting, they shall, notwithstanding that fact, be deemed to have been duly sent if it is so agreed by all the members entitled to attend and vote at the meeting.

[(4A) References in this section to sending to any person [copies of the documents mentioned in subsection (1A)] include references to using electronic communications for sending copies of those documents to such address as may for the time being be notified to the company by that person for that purpose.

(4B) For the purposes of this section copies of those documents are also to be treated as sent to a person where—

(a) the company and that person have agreed to his having access to the documents on a web site (instead of their being sent to him);

(b) the documents are documents to which that agreement applies; and

(c) that person is notified, in a manner for the time being agreed for the purpose between him and the company, of—

(i) the publication of the documents on a web site;

(ii) the address of that web site; and

(iii) the place on that web site where the documents may be accessed, and how they may be accessed.

(4C) For the purposes of this section documents treated in accordance with subsection (4B) as sent to any person are to be treated as sent to him not less than 21 days before the date of a meeting if, and only if—

(a) the documents are published on the web site throughout a period beginning at least 21 days before the date of the meeting and ending with the conclusion of the meeting; and

(b) the notification given for the purposes of paragraph (c) of that subsection is given not less than 21 days before the date of the meeting.

(4D) Nothing in subsection (4C) shall invalidate the proceedings of a meeting where—

(a) any documents that are required to be published as mentioned in paragraph (a) of that subsection are published for a part, but not all, of the period mentioned in that paragraph; and

(b) the failure to publish those documents throughout that period is wholly attributable to circumstances which it would not be reasonable to have expected the company to prevent or avoid.

(4E) A company may, notwithstanding any provision to the contrary in its articles, take advantage of any of subsections (4A) to (4D).]

(5) If default is made in complying with this section [or section 238A], the company and every officer of it who is in default is guilty of an offence and liable to a fine.

(6) Where copies are sent out under this section over a period of days, references elsewhere in this Act to the day on which copies are sent out shall be construed as references to the last day of that period.]

[225]

NOTES

Inserted, together with the preceding heading and ss 239, 240, by CA 1989, s 10, as from 1 April 1990.

Repealed by the Companies Act 2006, s 1295, Sch 16, as from 20 January 2007 (in so far as relating to sub-ss (4A)–(4E)), and as from a day to be appointed (otherwise) (for transitional provisions see the note below).

Sub-s (1): words in square brackets substituted by the Directors' Remuneration Report Regulations 2002, SI 2002/1986, reg 10(1), (3), as from 1 August 2002, with effect as respects companies' financial years ending on or after 31 December 2002; the words from "not less than 21 days" to the end are repealed by the draft Companies Act 2006 (Commencement No 3, Consequential Amendments, Transitional Provisions and Savings) Order 2007, art 10(1), Sch 4, Pt 1, para 3(2)(a), (8), as from 1 October 2007, with effect for financial years ending on or after that date (see **[A12]**).

Sub-s (1A) is amended as follows:

Inserted by SI 2002/1986, reg 10(1), (4), as from 1 August 2002, with effect as respects companies' financial years ending on or after 31 December 2002.

Para (ba) inserted, and para (d) substituted, by the Companies Act 1985 (Operating and Financial Review and Directors' Report etc) Regulations 2005, SI 2005/1011, reg 19, Schedule, paras 1, 2, as from 22 March 2005, in relation to companies' financial years which begin on or after 1 April 2005.

Para (ba) repealed, and the words omitted from para (d) repealed, by the Companies Act 1985 (Operating and Financial Review) (Repeal) Regulations 2005, SI 2005/3442, reg 2(2)(a), Sch 1, para 5, as from 12 January 2006.

Sub-s (4): repealed by the draft Companies Act 2006 (Commencement No 3, Consequential Amendments, Transitional Provisions and Savings) Order 2007, art 10(1), Sch 4, Pt 1, para 3(2)(b), (8), as from 1 October 2007, with effect for financial years ending on or after that date (see **[A12]**).

Sub-s (4A): inserted, together with sub-ss (4B)–(4E), by the Companies Act 1985 (Electronic Communications) Order 2000, SI 2000/3373, art 12, as from 22 December 2000, and repealed as noted above; words in square brackets substituted by SI 2002/1986, reg 10(1), (5), as from 1 August 2002, with effect as respects companies' financial years ending on or after 31 December 2002. Note it is believed that there is an error in the Queen's Printer's copy of SI 2002/1986, reg 10(1), (5), and that this substitution should have been for the words "*copies of* a company's annual accounts, of the directors' report and of the auditors' report". The original words "copies of" have, therefore been removed from the above text.

Sub-ss (4B)–(4E): inserted and repealed as noted above.

Sub-s (5): words in square brackets inserted by the draft Companies Act 2006 (Commencement No 3, Consequential Amendments, Transitional Provisions and Savings) Order 2007, art 10(1), Sch 4, Pt 1, para 3(2)(c), (8), as from 1 October 2007, with effect for financial years ending on or after that date (see **[A12]**).

Transitional provisions: the Companies Act 2006 (Commencement No 1, Transitional Provisions and Savings) Order 2006, SI 2006/3428, Sch 5, paras 3–5 provide as follows—

3 False or misleading statements in reports

Section 463 of the Companies Act 2006 (liability for false or misleading statements in reports) does not apply to a directors' report, directors' remuneration report or summary financial statement first sent to members and others under section 238 or 251 of the 1985 Act, or Article 246 or 259 of the 1986 Order, before 20th January 2007.

4 Existing agreements to communication by electronic means

(1) This paragraph applies where an address has been notified by a person to a company for the purposes of—

(a) section 238(4A) or 239(2A) of the 1985 Act or Article 246(4A) or 247(2A) of the 1986 Order (sending or supply of accounts and reports by means of electronic communications);

(b) section 251(2A) of the 1985 Act or Article 259(2A) of the 1986 Order (sending of summary financial statement by means of electronic communications); or

(c) section 369(4A) or 379A(2B) of the 1985 Act or Article 377(5) or 387A(2B) of the 1986 Order (notice of meeting given by means of electronic communications).

(2) Any such notification that is in force immediately before 20th January 2007 shall have effect on and after that date, in relation to the matters to which it relates, as an agreement under paragraph 6(a) of Schedule 5 to the Companies Act 2006 (agreement to accept documents or information in electronic form) and as an address specified under paragraph 7(1) of Schedule 5 to that Act (address for communications in electronic form).

5.—(1) This paragraph applies where an agreement between a person and a company has been entered into for the purposes of—

(a) section 238(4B) of the 1985 Act or Article 246(4B) of the 1986 Order (sending or supply of copies of accounts and reports by means of website);

(b) section 251(2B) of the 1985 Act or Article 259(2B) of the 1986 Order (sending of summary financial statement by means of website); or

(c) section 369(4B) or 379A(2C) of the 1985 Act or Article 377(6) or 387A(2C) of the 1986 Order (notice of meeting given by means of website).

(2) Any such agreement that is in force immediately before 20th January 2007 shall have effect on and after that date, in relation to the matters to which it relates, as an agreement under paragraph 9(a) of Schedule 5 to the Companies Act 2006 (agreement to accept documents or information by means of a website).

Application to limited liability partnerships: see the Limited Liability Partnerships Regulations 2001, SI 2001/1090, reg 3, Sch 1 at **[6984]**, **[6992]**. Note that nothing in the Companies Act 2006 (Commencement No 1, Transitional Provisions and Savings) Order 2006, SI 2006/3428 affects any provision of this Act as applied by the 2001 Regulations to LLPs (see art 8(2) at **[7581]** and the introductory notes to this Act). Note also that nothing in the draft Companies Act 2006 (Commencement

No 3, Consequential Amendments, Transitional Provisions and Savings) Order 2007 affects any provision of this Act as applied by the 2001 Regulations to LLPs (see art 12(2) at **[A12]** and the introductory notes to this Act).

[238A Time allowed for sending out copies of accounts and reports

(1) The time allowed for sending out copies of the company's annual accounts and reports is as follows.

(2) A private company must comply with section 238(1) not later than—

(a) the end of the period for delivering accounts and reports (see section 244), or

(b) if earlier, the date on which it actually delivers its accounts and reports under section 242.

(3) A public company must comply with section 238(1) not less than 21 days before the date of the meeting at which copies of the documents are to be laid in accordance with section 241.

(4) If in the case of a public company copies are sent out later than is required by subsection (3), they shall, despite that, be deemed to have been duly sent if it is so agreed by all the members entitled to attend and vote at the meeting.]

[225A]

NOTES

Commencement: 1 October 2007 (for effect see below)

Inserted by the draft Companies Act 2006 (Commencement No 3, Consequential Amendments, Transitional Provisions and Savings) Order 2007, art 10(1), Sch 4, Pt 1, para 3(3), (8), as from 1 October 2007, with effect for financial years ending on or after that date (see **[A12]**).

Application to limited liability partnerships: see the Limited Liability Partnerships Regulations 2001, SI 2001/1090, reg 3, Sch 1 at **[6984]**, **[6992]**. Note also that nothing in the draft Companies Act 2006 (Commencement No 3, Consequential Amendments, Transitional Provisions and Savings) Order 2007 affects any provision of this Act as applied by the 2001 Regulations to LLPs (see art 12(2) at **[A12]** and the introductory notes to this Act).

[239 Right to demand copies of accounts and reports

(1) Any member of a company and any holder of a company's debentures is entitled to be furnished, on demand and without charge, [with a copy of—

(a) the company's last annual accounts,

(b) the last directors' report,

[(ba) …]

(c) (in the case of a quoted company) the last directors' remuneration report, and

[(d) the auditors' report on those accounts and that directors' report and (in the case of a quoted company) on … the auditable part of that directors' remuneration report.]]

(2) The entitlement under this section is to a single copy of those documents, but that is in addition to any copy to which a person may be entitled under section 238.

[(2A) Any obligation by virtue of subsection (1) to furnish a person with a document may be complied with by using electronic communications for sending that document to such address as may for the time being be notified to the company by that person for that purpose.

(2B) A company may, notwithstanding any provision to the contrary in its articles, take advantage of subsection (2A).]

(3) If a demand under this section is not complied with within seven days, the company and every officer of it who is in default is guilty of an offence and liable to a fine and, for continued contravention, to a daily default fine.

(4) If in proceedings for such an offence the issue arises whether a person had already been furnished with a copy of the relevant document under this section, it is for the defendant to prove that he had.]

[226]

NOTES

Inserted as noted to s 238 at **[225]**.

Repealed by the Companies Act 2006, s 1295, Sch 16, as from 20 January 2007 (in so far as relating to sub-ss (2A), (2B)), and as from a day to be appointed (otherwise) (for transitional provisions see the note to s 238 at **[225]**).

Sub-s (1) is amended as follows:

Words in first (outer) pair of square brackets substituted by the Directors' Remuneration Report Regulations 2002, SI 2002/1986, reg 10(1), (6), as from 1 August 2002, with effect as respects companies' financial years ending on or after 31 December 2002.

Para (ba) inserted, and para (d) substituted, by the Companies Act 1985 (Operating and Financial Review and Directors' Report etc) Regulations 2005, SI 2005/1011, reg 19, Schedule, paras 1, 3, as from 22 March 2005, in relation to companies' financial years which begin on or after 1 April 2005.

Para (ba) repealed, and the words omitted from para (d) repealed, by the Companies Act 1985 (Operating and Financial Review) (Repeal) Regulations 2005, SI 2005/3442, reg 2(2)(a), Sch 1, para 6, as from 12 January 2006.

Sub-ss (2A), (2B): inserted by the Companies Act 1985 (Electronic Communications) Order 2000, SI 2000/3373, art 13, as from 22 December 2000, and repealed as note above.

Application to limited liability partnerships: see the Limited Liability Partnerships Regulations 2001, SI 2001/1090, reg 3, Sch 1 at **[6984]**, **[6992]**. Note also that nothing in the Companies Act 2006 (Commencement No 1, Transitional Provisions and Savings) Order 2006, SI 2006/3428 affects any provision of this Act as applied by the 2001 Regulations to LLPs (see art 8(2) at **[7581]** and the introductory notes to this Act).

[240 Requirements in connection with publication of accounts

(1) If a company publishes any of its statutory accounts, they must be accompanied by the relevant auditors' report under section 235 [or, as the case may be, the relevant report made for the purposes of section 249A(2)].

(2) A company which is required to prepare group accounts for a financial year shall not publish its statutory individual accounts for that year without also publishing with them its statutory group accounts.

(3) If a company publishes non-statutory accounts, it shall publish with them a statement indicating—

(a) that they are not the company's statutory accounts,

(b) whether statutory accounts dealing with any financial year with which the non-statutory accounts purport to deal have been delivered to the registrar,

(c) whether the company's auditors have made a report under section 235 on the statutory accounts for any such financial year [and, if no such report has been made, whether the company's reporting accountant has made a report for the purposes of section 249A(2) on the statutory accounts for any financial year], … [and]

[(d) whether any such auditors' report—

(i) was qualified or unqualified, or included a reference to any matters to which the auditors drew attention by way of emphasis without qualifying the report, or

(ii) contained a statement under section 237(2) or (3) (accounting records or returns inadequate, accounts not agreeing with records and returns or failure to obtain necessary information and explanations); and

(e) whether any report made for the purposes of section 249A(2) was qualified;]

and it shall not publish with the non-statutory accounts any auditors' report under section 235 [or any report made for the purposes of section 249A(2)].

(4) For the purposes of this section a company shall be regarded as publishing a document if it publishes, issues or circulates it or otherwise makes it available for public inspection in a manner calculated to invite members of the public generally, or any class of members of the public, to read it.

(5) References in this section to a company's statutory accounts are to its individual or group accounts for a financial year as required to be delivered to the registrar under section 242; and references to the publication by a company of "non-statutory accounts" are to the publication of—

(a) any balance sheet or profit and loss account relating to, or purporting to deal with, a financial year of the company, or

(b) an account in any form purporting to be a balance sheet or profit and loss account for the group consisting of the company and its subsidiary undertakings relating to, or purporting to deal with, a financial year of the company,

otherwise than as part of the company's statutory accounts.

(6) A company which contravenes any provision of this section, and any officer of it who is in default, is guilty of an offence and liable to a fine.]

[227]

NOTES

Inserted as noted to s 238 at **[225]**.

Repealed by the Companies Act 2006, s 1295, Sch 16, as from a day to be appointed. Note that this section is also amended by the 2006 Act (see below).

Sub-s (1): words in square brackets added by the Companies Act 1985 (Audit Exemption) Regulations 1994, SI 1994/1935, reg 4, Sch 1, para 1(1), (2), as from 11 August 1994, in relation to annual accounts of a company which are approved by the board of directors on or after 11 August 1994 (and do not apply to any annual accounts the period for laying and delivering of which expired before that date), and repealed by the Companies Act 2006, s 1175, Sch 9, Pt 1, para 1(a), as from a day to be appointed.

Sub-s (3) is amended as follows:

First and final words in square brackets inserted SI 1994/1935, reg 4, Sch 1, para 1(1), (3)(a), (c), as from 11 August 1994 (for effect see the note above), and repealed by the Companies Act 2006, s 1175, Sch 9, Pt 1, para 1(b), (e), as from a day to be appointed.

Word omitted from para (c) repealed by the Companies Act 1985 (International Accounting Standards and Other Accounting Amendments) Regulations 2004, SI 2004/2947, reg 8(a), as from 12 November 2004, in relation to companies' financial years which begin on or after 1 January 2005.

Word "and" at the end of para (c) added by the Companies Act 2006, s 1175, Sch 9, Pt 1, para 1(c), as from a day to be appointed.

Paras (d), (e) substituted for original para (d) by SI 2004/2947, reg 8(b), as from 12 November 2004, in relation to companies' financial years which begin on or after 1 January 2005.

Para (e) and the word immediately preceding it repealed by the Companies Act 2006, s 1175, Sch 9, Pt 1, para 1(d), as from a day to be appointed.

Application to limited liability partnerships: see the Limited Liability Partnerships Regulations 2001, SI 2001/1090, reg 3, Sch 1 at **[6984]**, **[6992]**.

[Laying and delivering of accounts and reports

241 Accounts and reports to be laid before company in general meeting

(1) The directors of a company shall in respect of each financial year lay before the company in general meeting [copies of—

(a) the company's annual accounts,

(b) the directors' report,

[(ba) ...]

(c) (in the case of a quoted company) the directors' remuneration report, and

[(d) the auditors' report on those accounts and that directors' report and (in the case of a quoted company) on ... the auditable part of that directors' remuneration report.]]

(2) If the requirements of subsection (1) are not complied with before the end of the period allowed for laying and delivering accounts and reports, every person who immediately before the end of that period was a director of the company is guilty of an offence and liable to a fine and, for continued contravention, to a daily default fine.

(3) It is a defence for a person charged with such an offence to prove that he took all reasonable steps for securing that those requirements would be complied with before the end of that period.

(4) It is not a defence to prove that the documents in question were not in fact prepared as required by this Part.]

[228]

NOTES

Inserted, together with the preceding heading and ss 242, 243, 244, by CA 1989, s 11, as from 1 April 1990.

Repealed by the Companies Act 2006, s 1295, Sch 16, as from 1 October 2007 (in so far as relating to private companies), and as from a day to be appointed (otherwise). For savings see the note below.

Sub-s (1) is amended as follows:

Words in first (outer) pair of square brackets substituted by the Directors' Remuneration Report Regulations 2002, SI 2002/1986, reg 10(1), (7), as from 1 August 2002, with effect as respects companies' financial years ending on or after 31 December 2002.

Para (ba) inserted, and para (d) substituted, by the Companies Act 1985 (Operating and Financial Review and Directors' Report etc) Regulations 2005, SI 2005/1011, reg 19, Schedule, paras 1, 4, as from 22 March 2005, in relation to companies' financial years which begin on or after 1 April 2005.

Para (ba) repealed, and the words omitted from para (d) repealed, by the Companies Act 1985 (Operating and Financial Review) (Repeal) Regulations 2005, SI 2005/3442, reg 2(2)(a), Sch 1, para 7, as from 12 January 2006.

Savings: this section continues to have effect in relation to annual accounts or reports for financial years ending before 1 October 2007 (see the draft Companies Act 2006 (Commencement No 3, Consequential Amendments, Transitional Provisions and Savings) Order 2007, Sch 3, para 49 at **[A12]**).

Application to limited liability partnerships: see the Limited Liability Partnerships Regulations 2001, SI 2001/1090, reg 3, Sch 1 at **[6984]**, **[6992]**. Note also that nothing in the draft Companies Act 2006 (Commencement No 3, Consequential Amendments, Transitional Provisions and Savings) Order 2007 affects any provision of this Act as applied by the 2001 Regulations to LLPs (see art 12(2) at **[A12]** and the introductory notes to this Act).

[241A Members' approval of directors' remuneration report

(1) This section applies to every company that is a quoted company immediately before the end of a financial year.

(2) In this section "the meeting" means the general meeting of the company before which the company's annual accounts for the financial year are to be laid.

(3) The company must, prior to the meeting, give to the members of the company entitled to be sent notice of the meeting notice of the intention to move at the meeting, as an ordinary resolution, a resolution approving the directors' remuneration report for the financial year.

(4) Notice under subsection (3) shall be given to each such member in any manner permitted for the service on him of notice of the meeting.

(5) The business that may be dealt with at the meeting includes the resolution.

(6) The existing directors must ensure that the resolution is put to the vote of the meeting.

(7) Subsection (5) has effect notwithstanding—

(a) any default in complying with subsections (3) and (4);

(b) anything in the company's articles.

(8) No entitlement of a person to remuneration is made conditional on the resolution being passed by reason only of the provision made by this section.

(9) In the event of default in complying with the requirements of subsections (3) and (4), every officer of the company who is in default is liable to a fine.

(10) If the resolution is not put to the vote of the meeting, each existing director is guilty of an offence and liable to a fine.

(11) If an existing director is charged with an offence under subsection (10), it is a defence for him to prove that he took all reasonable steps for securing that the resolution was put to the vote of the meeting.

(12) In this section "existing director" means a person who, immediately before the meeting, is a director of the company.]

[228A]

NOTES

Inserted by the Directors' Remuneration Report Regulations 2002, SI 2002/1986, reg 7, as from 1 August 2002, with effect as respects companies' financial years ending on or after 31 December 2002.

Repealed by the Companies Act 2006, s 1295, Sch 16, as from a day to be appointed.

Application to limited liability partnerships: see the Limited Liability Partnerships Regulations 2001, SI 2001/1090, reg 3, Sch 1 at **[6984]**, **[6992]**.

[242 Accounts and reports to be delivered to the registrar

(1) The directors of a company shall in respect of each financial year deliver to the registrar [a copy of—

(a) the company's annual accounts,

(b) the directors' report,

[(ba) …]

(c) (in the case of a quoted company) the directors' remuneration report, and

[(d) the auditors' report on those accounts and that directors' report and (in the case of a quoted company) on … the auditable part of that directors' remuneration report.]]

[If any document comprised in those accounts or reports is in a language other than English … , the directors must annex to the copy of that document delivered a translation of it into English, certified in the prescribed manner to be a correct translation.]

(2) *If the requirements of subsection (1) are not complied with before the end of the period allowed for laying and delivering accounts and reports, every person who immediately before the end of that period was a director of the company is guilty of an offence and liable to a fine and, for continued contravention, to a daily default fine.*

(3) *Further, if the directors of the company fail to make good the default within 14 days after the service of a notice on them requiring compliance, the court may on the application of any member or creditor of the company or of the registrar, make an order directing the directors (or any of them) to make good the default within such time as may be specified in the order.*

The court's order may provide that all costs of and incidental to the application shall be borne by the directors.

(4) *It is a defence for a person charged with an offence under this section to prove that he took all reasonable steps for securing that the requirements of subsection (1) would be complied with before the end of the period allowed for laying and delivering accounts and reports.*

(5) *It is not a defence in any proceedings under this section to prove that the documents in question were not in fact prepared as required by this Part].*

[229]

NOTES

Inserted as noted to s 241 at **[228]**.

Repealed by the Companies Act 2006, s 1295, Sch 16, as from 1 January 2007 (in so far as relating to the final words omitted from sub-s (1)), and as from a day to be appointed (otherwise).

Sub-s (1) is amended as follows:

Words in first (outer) pair of square brackets substituted by the Directors' Remuneration Report Regulations 2002, SI 2002/1986, reg 10(1), (8), as from 1 August 2002, with effect as respects companies' financial years ending on or after 31 December 2002.

Para (ba) and the final words in square brackets inserted, and para (d) substituted, by the Companies Act 1985 (Operating and Financial Review and Directors' Report etc) Regulations 2005, SI 2005/1011, reg 19, Schedule, paras 1, 5, as from 22 March 2005, in relation to companies' financial years which begin on or after 1 April 2005.

Para (ba) repealed, and the words omitted from para (d) repealed, by the Companies Act 1985 (Operating and Financial Review) (Repeal) Regulations 2005, SI 2005/3442, reg 2(2)(a), Sch 1, para 8, as from 12 January 2006.

Final words omitted repealed as noted above (those words previously read "then, subject to section 710B(6) (delivery of certain Welsh documents without a translation)").

Certified in the prescribed manner: as to the requirements of this, see the Companies (Forms) (Amendment) Regulations 1990, SI 1990/572, reg 5, and the note relating to that regulation to s 228 at **[214]**.

Application to limited liability partnerships: see the Limited Liability Partnerships Regulations 2001, SI 2001/1090, reg 3, Sch 1 at **[6984]**, **[6992]**. Note also that nothing in the Companies Act 2006 (Commencement No 1, Transitional Provisions and Savings) Order 2006, SI 2006/3428 affects any provision of this Act as applied by the 2001 Regulations to LLPs (see art 8(2) at **[7581]** and the introductory notes to this Act).

Community interest companies: sub-s (1) of this section is to be treated as requiring the directors of a community interest company to deliver to the registrar of companies a copy of the community interest company report; see the Companies (Audit, Investigations and Community Enterprise) Act 2004, ss 26, 34(1), (2) at **[900]**, **[908]**.

[242A Civil penalty for failure to deliver accounts

(1) *Where the requirements of section 242(1) are not complied with before the end of the period allowed for laying and delivering accounts and reports, the company is liable to a civil penalty.*

This is in addition to any liability of the directors under section 242.

(2) *The amount of the penalty is determined by reference to the length of the period between the end of the period allowed for laying and delivering accounts and reports and the day on which the requirements are complied with, and whether the company is a public or private company, as follows—*

Length of period	*Public company*	*Private company*
Not more than 3 months	*£500*	*£100*
More than 3 months but not more than 6 months	*£1,000*	*£250*
More than 6 months but not more than 12 months	*£2,000*	*£500*
More than 12 months	*£5,000*	*£1,000*

(*3*) *The penalty may be recovered by the registrar and shall be paid by him into the Consolidated Fund.*

(*4*) *It is not a defence in proceedings under this section to prove that the documents in question were not in fact prepared as required by this Part.]*

[230]

NOTES

Inserted by CA 1989, s 11, as from 1 July 1992.

Repealed by the Companies Act 2006, s 1295, Sch 16, as from a day to be appointed.

Application to limited liability partnerships: see the Limited Liability Partnerships Regulations 2001, SI 2001/1090, reg 3, Sch 1 at **[6984]**, **[6992]**.

[242B Delivery and publication of accounts in ECUs

(*1*) *The amounts set out in the annual accounts of a company may also be shown in the same accounts translated into ECUs.*

(2) *When complying with section 242, the directors of a company may deliver to the registrar an additional copy of the company's annual accounts in which the amounts have been translated into ECUs.*

(3) *In both cases—*

(*a*) *the amounts must have been translated at the relevant exchange rate prevailing on the balance sheet date, and*

(*b*) *that rate must be disclosed in the notes to the accounts.*

(*4*) *For the purposes of section 240 any additional copy of the company's annual accounts delivered to the registrar under subsection* (2) *shall be treated as statutory accounts of the company and, in the case of such a copy, references in section 240 to the auditors' report under section 235 shall be read as references to the auditors' report on the annual accounts of which it is a copy.*

(*5*) *In this section—*

"ECU" means a unit with a value equal to the value of the unit known as the ecu used in the European Monetary System, and

"relevant exchange rate" means the rate of exchange used for translating the value of the ecu for the purposes of that System.]

[231]–[232]

NOTES

Inserted by the Companies Act 1985 (Accounts of Small and Medium-Sized Enterprises and Publication of Accounts in ECUs) Regulations 1992, SI 1992/2452, reg 3, in relation to annual accounts in respect of financial years ending on or after 16 November 1992, and to directors' and auditors' reports on such accounts.

Repealed by the Companies Act 2006, s 1295, Sch 16, as from a day to be appointed.

Application to limited liability partnerships: see the Limited Liability Partnerships Regulations 2001, SI 2001/1090, reg 3, Sch 1 at **[6984]**, **[6992]**.

243 (*Repealed by the Companies Act 1985* (*International Accounting Standards and Other Accounting Amendments*) *Regulations 2004, SI 2004/2947, reg 15, Sch 7, Pt 1, paras 1, 6, as from 12 November 2004, in relation to companies' financial years which begin on or after 1 January 2005.*)

[244 Period allowed for laying and delivering accounts and reports

(*1*) *The period allowed for laying and delivering accounts and reports is—*

(*a*) *for a private company, 10 months after the end of the relevant accounting reference period, and*

(*b*) *for a public company, 7 months after the end of that period.*

This is subject to the following provisions of this section.

(2) *If the relevant accounting reference period is the company's first and is a period of more than 12 months, the period allowed is—*

(*a*) *10 months or 7 months, as the case may be, from the first anniversary of the incorporation of the company, or*

(*b*) *3 months from the end of the accounting reference period,*

whichever last expires.

(3) …

(4) *If the relevant accounting period is treated as shortened by virtue of a notice given by the company under section 225 (alteration of accounting reference date), the period allowed for laying and delivering accounts is that applicable in accordance with the above provisions or 3 months from the date of the notice under that section, whichever last expires.*

(5) *If for any special reason the Secretary of State thinks fit he may, on an application made before the expiry of the period otherwise allowed, by notice in writing to a company extend that period by such further period as may be specified in the notice.*

(6) *In this section "the relevant accounting reference period" means the accounting reference period by reference to which the financial year for the accounts in question was determined.]*

[233]

NOTES

Inserted as noted to s 241 at **[228]**.

Repealed by the Companies Act 2006, s 1295, Sch 16, as from a day to be appointed.

Sub-s (3): repealed by the Companies Act 1985 (International Accounting Standards and Other Accounting Amendments) Regulations 2004, SI 2004/2947, reg 9, as from 12 November 2004, in relation to companies' financial years which begin on or after 1 January 2005.

Private companies: references in any enactment or instrument to the period for laying and delivering accounts, and reports including those in this section (which defines that period), shall be read in relation to a private company as references to the period for delivering accounts and reports; see the draft Companies Act 2006 (Commencement No 3, Consequential Amendments, Transitional Provisions and Savings) Order 2007, art 10(1), Sch 4, Pt 1, para 3(4) (at **[A12]**).

Secretary of State: as to the contracting out of the function of the Secretary of State under sub-s (5) above, see the note to s 26 at **[27]**.

Application to limited liability partnerships: see the Limited Liability Partnerships Regulations 2001, SI 2001/1090, reg 3, Sch 1 at **[6984]**, **[6992]**.

Prescribed form: see Appendix 4 (Forms table) at **[A4]**.

[Revision of defective accounts and reports

245 Voluntary revision of annual accounts or directors' report

(*1*) *If it appears to the directors of a company that any annual accounts [or summary financial statement] of the company, or any directors' report […] [or directors' remuneration report], did not comply with the requirements of this Act [(or, where applicable, of Article 4 of the IAS Regulation)], they may prepare revised accounts or a [revised statement or report].*

(2) *Where copies of the previous accounts [or report] have been laid before the company in general meeting or delivered to the registrar, the revisions shall be confined to—*

(*a*) *the correction of those respects in which the previous accounts [or report] did not comply with the requirements of this Act [(or, where applicable, of Article 4 of the IAS Regulation)], and*

(*b*) *the making of any necessary consequential alterations.*

(*3*) *The Secretary of State may make provision by regulations as to the application of the provisions of this Act in relation to revised annual accounts [or a revised summary financial statement] or a revised directors' report […] [or a revised directors' remuneration report].*

(*4*) *The regulations may, in particular—*

(*a*) *make different provision according to whether the previous accounts [statement or report] are replaced or are supplemented by a document indicating the corrections to be made;*

(*b*) *make provision with respect to the functions of the company's auditors [or reporting accountant] in relation to the revised accounts [statement or report];*

(*c*) *require the directors to take such steps as may be specified in the regulations where the previous accounts [or report] have been—*

(*i*) *sent out to members and others under section 238(1),*

(*ii*) *laid before the company in general meeting, or*

(*iii*) *delivered to the registrar,*

or where a summary financial statement [containing information [derived from the previous accounts or report]] has been sent to members under section 251;

(*d*) *apply the provisions of this Act (including those creating criminal offences) subject to such additions, exceptions and modifications as are specified in the regulations.*

(5) *Regulations under this section shall be made by statutory instrument which shall be subject to annulment in pursuance of a resolution of either House of Parliament.]*

[234]

NOTES

Inserted, together with the preceding heading, and ss 245A–245C, by CA 1989, s 12, as from 7 January 1991.

Repealed by the Companies Act 2006, s 1295, Sch 16, as from a day to be appointed. Note that this section is also amended by the 2006 Act (see below).

Sub-s (1) is amended as follows:

Words in first and fourth pairs of square brackets inserted by the Companies Act 1985 (International Accounting Standards and Other Accounting Amendments) Regulations 2004, SI 2004/2947, regs 3, 10(1), (2)(a), Sch 1, paras 1, 11, as from 12 November 2004, in relation to companies' financial years which begin on or after 1 January 2005.

Words in second pair of square brackets originally inserted by the Companies Act 1985 (Operating and Financial Review and Directors' Report etc) Regulations 2005, SI 2005/1011, reg 14(1), (2), as from 22 March 2005, with effect from 1 April 2005; repealed by the Companies Act 1985 (Operating and Financial Review) (Repeal) Regulations 2005, SI 2005/3442, reg 2(2)(a), Sch 1, para 9(1), (2)(a), as from 12 January 2006.

Words in third pair of square brackets inserted by the Directors' Remuneration Report Regulations 2002, SI 2002/1986, reg 10(1), (9)(a), as from 1 August 2002, with effect as respects companies' financial years ending on or after 31 December 2002.

Words in final pair of square brackets substituted by SI 2005/3442, reg 2(2)(a), Sch 1, para 9(1), (2)(b), as from 12 January 2006.

Sub-s (2): words in first and second pairs of square brackets substituted by SI 2005/3442, reg 2(2)(a), Sch 1, para 9(1), (3), as from 12 January 2006; words in third pair of square brackets inserted by SI 2004/2947, reg 3, Sch 1, paras 1, 11, as from 12 November 2004, in relation to companies' financial years which begin on or after 1 January 2005.

Sub-s (3): words in first pair of square brackets inserted by SI 2004/2947, reg 10(1), (3), as from 12 November 2004, in relation to companies' financial years which begin on or after 1 January 2005; words in second pair of square brackets originally inserted by SI 2005/1011, reg 14(1), (4), as from 22 March 2005, with effect from 1 April 2005, and repealed by SI 2005/3442, reg 2(2)(a), Sch 1, para 9(1), (4), as from 12 January 2006; words in third pair of square brackets added by SI 2002/1986, reg 10(1), (9)(b), as from 1 August 2002, with effect as respects companies' financial years ending on or after 31 December 2002.

Sub-s (4) is amended as follows:

Words in square brackets in para (a) and words in second pair of square brackets in para (b) substituted by SI 2005/3442, reg 2(2)(a), Sch 1, para 9(1), (5), as from 12 January 2006.

Words in first pair of square brackets in para (b) inserted by the Companies Act 1985 (Audit Exemption) Regulations 1994, SI 1994/1935, reg 4, Sch 1, Pt I, para 2, as from 11 August 1994, in relation to annual accounts of a company which are approved by the board of directors on or after 11 August 1994 (and do not apply to any annual accounts the period for laying and delivering of which expired before that date), and repealed by the Companies Act 2006, s 1175, Sch 9, Pt 1, para 2, as from a day to be appointed.

Words in first pair and third (inner) pair of square brackets in para (c) substituted by SI 2005/3442, reg 2(2)(a), Sch 1, para 9(1), (6), as from 12 January 2006.

Words in second (outer) pair of square brackets in para (c) substituted by SI 2005/1011, reg 14(1), (6), as from 22 March 2005, with effect from 1 April 2005.

Application to limited liability partnerships: see the Limited Liability Partnerships Regulations 2001, SI 2001/1090, reg 3, Sch 1 at **[6984]**, **[6992]**.

Regulations: the Companies (Revision of Defective Accounts and Report) Regulations 1990, SI 1990/2570 at **[6671]**; the Companies Act 1985 (Audit Exemption) Regulations 1994, SI 1994/1935 at **[6792]**; the Companies (Summary Financial Statement) Regulations 1995, SI 1995/2092 at **[6882]**.

[245A Secretary of State's notice in respect of annual accounts

[(1) Where—

(*a*) *copies of a company's annual accounts, [or directors' report] have been sent out under section 238, or*

(*b*) *a copy of a company's annual accounts, [or directors' report] has been laid before the company in general meeting or delivered to the registrar,*

and it appears to the Secretary of State that there is, or may be, a question whether the accounts [or report] comply with the requirements of this Act, he may give notice to the directors of the company indicating the respects in which it appears to him that such a question arises or may arise.]

(2) The notice shall specify a period of not less than one month for the directors to give him an explanation of the accounts [[or report] or prepare revised accounts or [a revised report]].

(3) If at the end of the specified period, or such longer period as he may allow, it appears to the Secretary of State that [the directors have not—

(*a*) *given a satisfactory explanation of the accounts [or report], or*

(*b*) *revised the accounts [or report] so as to comply with the requirements of this Act,*

he may if he thinks fit apply to the court].

[(4) The provisions of this section apply equally to revised annual accounts [and revised directors' reports], in which case they have effect as if the references to revised accounts [or reports] were references to further revised accounts [or reports].]]

[235]

NOTES

Inserted as noted to s 245 at **[234]**.

Repealed by the Companies Act 2006, s 1295, Sch 16, as from a day to be appointed.

Sub-s (1): substituted by the Companies Act 1985 (Operating and Financial Review and Directors' Report etc) Regulations 2005, SI 2005/1011, reg 15(1), (2), as from 22 March 2005, in relation to annual accounts, directors' reports and operating and financial reviews prepared for companies' financial years which begin on or after 1 April 2006; words in square brackets substituted by the Companies Act 1985 (Operating and Financial Review) (Repeal) Regulations 2005, SI 2005/3442, reg 2(2)(a), Sch 1, para 10(1), (2), as from 12 January 2006.

Sub-s (2): words in first (outer) pair of square brackets substituted by SI 2005/1011, reg 15(1), (3), as from 22 March 2005, in relation to annual accounts, directors' reports and operating and financial reviews prepared for companies' financial years which begin on or after 1 April 2006; words in second and third (inner) pairs of square brackets substituted by SI 2005/3442, reg 2(2)(a), Sch 1, para 10(1), (3), as from 12 January 2006.

Sub-s (3): words in first (outer) pair of square brackets substituted by SI 2005/1011, reg 15(1), (4), as from 22 March 2005, in relation to annual accounts, directors' reports and operating and financial reviews prepared for companies' financial years which begin on or after 1 April 2006; words in second and third (inner) pairs of square brackets substituted by SI 2005/3442, reg 2(2)(a), Sch 1, para 10(1), (4), as from 12 January 2006.

Sub-s (4): substituted by SI 2005/1011, reg 15(1), (5), as from 22 March 2005, in relation to annual accounts, directors' reports and operating and financial reviews prepared for companies' financial years which begin on or after 1 April 2006; words in square brackets substituted by SI 2005/3442, reg 2(2)(a), Sch 1, para 10(1), (5), as from 12 January 2006.

Application to limited liability partnerships: see the Limited Liability Partnerships Regulations 2001, SI 2001/1090, reg 3, Sch 1 at **[6984]**, **[6992]**.

[245B Application to court in respect of defective accounts

(1) An application may be made to the court—

(*a*) *by the Secretary of State, after having complied with section 245A, or*

(*b*) *by a person authorised by the Secretary of State for the purposes of this section,*

for a declaration or declarator that the annual accounts of a company do not comply[, or a directors' report … does not comply,] with the requirements of this Act [(or, where applicable, of Article 4 of the IAS Regulation)] and for an order requiring the directors of the company to prepare revised accounts [or a revised report …].

(2) Notice of the application, together with a general statement of the matters at issue in the proceedings, shall be given by the applicant to the registrar for registration.

(3) If the court orders the preparation of revised accounts, it may give directions with respect to—

(*a*) *the auditing of the accounts,*

(*b*) *the revision of any directors' report[, directors' remuneration report] or summary financial statement, and*

(*c*) *the taking of steps by the directors to bring the making of the order to the notice of persons likely to rely on the previous accounts,*

and such other matters as the court thinks fit.

[(3A) If the court orders the preparation of a revised directors' report ... it may give directions with respect to—

(*a*) *the review of the directors' report ... by the auditors,*

(*b*) *the revision of any directors' report, directors' remuneration report ... or summary financial statement,*

(*c*) *the taking of steps by the directors to bring the making of the order to the notice of persons likely to rely on the previous report ..., and*

(*d*) *such other matters as the court thinks fit.]*

(4) If the court finds that the accounts [or report] did not comply with the requirements of this Act [(or, where applicable, of Article 4 of the IAS Regulation)] it may order that all or part of—

(*a*) *the costs (or in Scotland expenses) of and incidental to the application, and*

(*b*) *any reasonable expenses incurred by the company in connection with or in consequence of the preparation of revised accounts [or a revised report ...],*

shall be borne by such of the directors as were party to the approval of the [defective accounts or report].

For this purpose every director of the company at the time [of the [approval of the accounts or report]] shall be taken to have been a party to [the approval] unless he shows that he took all reasonable steps to prevent [that approval].

(5) Where the court makes an order under subsection (4) it shall have regard to whether the directors party to the approval of the defective accounts [or report] knew or ought to have known that the accounts [or report] did not comply with the requirements of this Act [(or, where applicable, of Article 4 of the IAS Regulation)], and it may exclude one or more directors from the order or order the payment of different amounts by different directors.

(6) On the conclusion of proceedings on an application under this section, the applicant shall give to the registrar for registration an office copy of the court order or, as the case may be, notice that the application has failed or been withdrawn.

[(7) The provisions of this section apply equally to revised annual accounts [and revised directors' reports], in which case they have effect as if the references to revised accounts [or reports] were references to further revised accounts [or reports].]]

[236]

NOTES

Inserted as noted to s 245 at **[234]**.

Repealed by the Companies Act 2006, s 1295, Sch 16, as from a day to be appointed.

Sub-s (1): words in first and third pairs of square brackets inserted by the Companies Act 1985 (Operating and Financial Review and Directors' Report etc) Regulations 2005, SI 2005/1011, reg 16(1), (2), as from 22 March 2005, in relation to annual accounts, directors' reports and operating and financial reviews prepared for companies' financial years which begin on or after 1 April 2006; words omitted repealed by the Companies Act 1985 (Operating and Financial Review) (Repeal) Regulations 2005, SI 2005/3442, reg 2(2)(a), Sch 1, para 11(1), (2), as from 12 January 2006; words in second pair of square brackets inserted by the Companies Act 1985 (International Accounting Standards and Other Accounting Amendments) Regulations 2004, SI 2004/2947, reg 3, Sch 1, paras 1, 11, as from 12 November 2004, in relation to companies' financial years which begin on or after 1 January 2005.

Sub-s (3): words in square brackets inserted by the Directors' Remuneration Report Regulations 2002, SI 2002/1986, reg 10(1), (10), as from 1 August 2002, with effect as respects companies' financial years ending on or after 31 December 2002.

Sub-s (3A): inserted by SI 2005/1011, reg 16(1), (3), as from 22 March 2005, in relation to annual accounts, directors' reports and operating and financial reviews prepared for companies' financial years which begin on or after 1 April 2006; words omitted repealed by SI 2005/3442, reg 2(2)(a), Sch 1, para 11(1), (3), as from 12 January 2006.

Sub-s (4) is amended as follows:

Words in first and fourth pairs of square brackets substituted by SI 2005/3442, reg 2(2)(a), Sch 1, para 11(1), (4)(a), (c) as from 12 January 2006.

Words in second pair of square brackets inserted by SI 2004/2947, reg 3, Sch 1, paras 1, 11, as from 12 November 2004, in relation to companies' financial years which begin on or after 1 January 2005.

Words in third pair of square brackets inserted by SI 2005/1011, reg 16(1), (4)(b), as from 22 March 2005, in relation to annual accounts, directors' reports and operating and financial reviews prepared for companies' financial years which begin on or after 1 April 2006; words omitted therefrom repealed by SI 2005/3442, reg 2(2)(a), Sch 1, para 11(1), (4)(b), as from 12 January 2006.

Words in fifth (outer) pair of square brackets substituted by SI 2005/1011, reg 16(1), (4)(d), as from 22 March 2005, in relation to annual accounts, directors' reports and operating and financial reviews prepared for companies' financial years which begin on or after 1 April 2006.

Words in sixth (inner) pair of square brackets substituted by SI 2005/3442, reg 2(2)(a), Sch 1, para 11(1), (4)(d), as from 12 January 2006.

Words in seventh and final pairs of square brackets substituted by SI 2005/1011, reg 16(1), (4)(e), (f), as from 22 March 2005, in relation to annual accounts, directors' reports and operating and financial reviews prepared for companies' financial years which begin on or after 1 April 2006.

Sub-s (5): words in first and second pairs of square brackets originally inserted by SI 2005/1011, reg 16(1), (5), as from 22 March 2005, in relation to annual accounts, directors' reports and operating and financial reviews prepared for companies' financial years which begin on or after 1 April 2006, and substituted by SI 2005/3442, reg 2(2)(a), Sch 1, para 11(1), (4)(d), as from 12 January 2006; words in third pair of square brackets inserted by SI 2004/2947, reg 3, Sch 1, paras 1, 11, as from 12 November 2004, in relation to companies' financial years which begin on or after 1 January 2005.

Sub-s (7): substituted by SI 2005/1011, reg 16(1), (6), as from 22 March 2005, in relation to annual accounts, directors' reports and operating and financial reviews prepared for companies' financial years which begin on or after 1 April 2006; words in square brackets substituted by SI 2005/3442, reg 2(2)(a), Sch 1, para 11(1), (6), as from 12 January 2006.

Application to limited liability partnerships: see the Limited Liability Partnerships Regulations 2001, SI 2001/1090, reg 3, Sch 1 at **[6984]**, **[6992]**.

Person authorised by the Secretary of State: see the Companies (Defective Accounts) (Authorised Person) Order 2005, SI 2005/699 at **[7393G]**.

[245C Other persons authorised to apply to court

(1) The Secretary of State may authorise for the purposes of section 245B any person appearing to him—

(a) to have an interest in, and to have satisfactory procedures directed to securing, compliance by companies with [the requirements of this Act relating to accounts [and directors' reports]] [(or, where applicable, of Article 4 of the IAS Regulation)],

(b) to have satisfactory procedures for receiving and investigating complaints about the [companies' annual accounts [and directors' reports]], and

(c) otherwise to be a fit and proper person to be authorised.

[(1A) But where the order giving authorisation (see subsection (4)) is to contain any requirements or other provisions specified under subsection (4A), the Secretary of State may not authorise a person unless, in addition, it appears to him that the person would, if authorised, exercise his functions as an authorised person in accordance with any such requirements or provisions.]

(2) A person may be authorised generally or in respect of particular classes of case, and different persons may be authorised in respect of different classes of case.

(3) The Secretary of State may refuse to authorise a person if he considers that his authorisation is unnecessary having regard to the fact that there are one or more other persons who have been or are likely to be authorised.

(4) Authorisation shall be by order made by statutory instrument which shall be subject to annulment in pursuance of a resolution of either House of Parliament.

[(4A) An order under subsection (4) may contain such requirements or other provisions relating to the exercise of functions by the authorised person as appear to the Secretary of State to be appropriate.

(4B) If the authorised person is an unincorporated association, any relevant proceedings may be brought by or against that association in the name of any body corporate whose constitution provides for the establishment of the association.

For this purpose "relevant proceedings" means proceedings brought in, or in connection with, the exercise of any function by the association as an authorised person.]

(5) Where authorisation is revoked, the revoking order may make such provision as the Secretary of State thinks fit with respect to pending proceedings.

(6) ...]

[237]

NOTES

Inserted as noted to s 245 at **[234]**.

Repealed by the Companies Act 2006, s 1295, Sch 16, as from a day to be appointed.

Sub-s (1): words in first (outer) pair of square brackets in para (a) substituted by the Companies Act 1985 (Operating and Financial Review and Directors' Report etc) Regulations 2005, SI 2005/1011, reg 17(a), as from 22 March 2005, in relation to annual accounts, directors' reports and operating and financial reviews prepared for companies' financial years which begin on or after 1 April 2006; words in second (inner) pair of square brackets in para (a) substituted by the Companies Act 1985 (Operating and Financial Review) (Repeal) Regulations 2005, SI 2005/3442, reg 2(2)(a), Sch 1, para 12, as from 12 January 2006; words in third pair of square brackets in para (a) inserted by the Companies Act 1985 (International Accounting Standards and Other Accounting Amendments) Regulations 2004, SI 2004/2947, reg 3, Sch 1, paras 1, 11, as from 12 November 2004, in relation to companies' financial years which begin on or after 1 January 2005; words in first (outer) pair of square brackets in para (b) substituted by SI 2005/1011, reg 17(b), as from 22 March 2005, in relation to annual accounts, directors' reports and operating and financial reviews prepared for companies' financial years which begin on or after 1 April 2006; words in second (inner) pair of square brackets in para (b) substituted by SI 2005/3442, reg 2(2)(a), Sch 1, para 12, as from 12 January 2006.

Sub-ss (1A), (4A), (4B): inserted by the Companies (Audit, Investigations and Community Enterprise) Act 2004, s 10, as from 1 January 2005.

Sub-s (6): repealed by the Companies (Audit, Investigations and Community Enterprise) Act 2004, s 64, Sch 8, as from 1 January 2005.

Application to limited liability partnerships: see the Limited Liability Partnerships Regulations 2001, SI 2001/1090, reg 3, Sch 1 at **[6984]**, **[6992]**.

Orders: the Companies (Defective Accounts) (Authorised Person) Order 2005, SI 2005/699 at **[7393G]**.

[245D Disclosure of information held by Inland Revenue to persons authorised to apply to court

(1) Information which is held by or on behalf of the Commissioners of Inland Revenue may be disclosed to a person who is authorised under section 245C of this Act, or under Article 253C of the Companies (Northern Ireland) Order 1986 (SI 1986/1032 (NI 6)), if the disclosure—

(a) is made for a permitted purpose, and

(b) is made by the Commissioners or is authorised by them.

(2) Such information—

(a) may be so disclosed despite any other restriction on the disclosure of information whether imposed by any statutory provision or otherwise, but

(b) in the case of personal data (within the meaning of the Data Protection Act 1998), may not be disclosed in contravention of that Act.

(3) For the purposes of subsection (1), a disclosure is made for a permitted purpose if it is made for the purpose of facilitating—

(a) the taking of steps by the authorised person to discover whether there are grounds for an application to the court under section 245B of this Act or Article 253B of the Companies (Northern Ireland) Order 1986; or

(b) a determination by the authorised person as to whether or not to make such an application.

(4) The power of the Commissioners to authorise a disclosure under subsection (1)(b) may be delegated (either generally or for a specified purpose) to an officer of the Board of Inland Revenue.]

[237A]

NOTES

Inserted, together with s 245E, by the Companies (Audit, Investigations and Community Enterprise) Act 2004, s 11(1), as from 6 April 2005.

Repealed by the Companies Act 2006, s 1295, Sch 16, as from a day to be appointed.

Application to limited liability partnerships: see the Limited Liability Partnerships Regulations 2001, SI 2001/1090, reg 3, Sch 1 at **[6984]**, **[6992]**.

Commissioners of Inland Revenue: a reference to the Commissioners of Inland Revenue is now to be taken as a reference to the Commissioners for Her Majesty's Revenue and Customs; see the Commissioners for Revenue and Customs Act 2005, s 50(1), (7).

[245E Restrictions on use and further disclosure of information disclosed under section 245D

(1) Information that is disclosed to an authorised person under section 245D may not be used except in or in connection with—

(a) taking steps to discover whether there are grounds for an application to the court as mentioned in section 245D(3)(a);

(b) determining whether or not to make such an application; or

(c) proceedings on any such application.

(2) Information that is disclosed to an authorised person under section 245D may not be further disclosed except—

(a) to the person to whom the information relates; or

(b) in or in connection with proceedings on any such application to the court.

(3) A person who contravenes subsection (1) or (2) is guilty of an offence and liable to imprisonment or a fine, or both.

(4) It is a defence for a person charged with an offence under subsection (3) to prove—

(a) that he did not know, and had no reason to suspect, that the information had been disclosed under section 245D; or

(b) that he took all reasonable steps and exercised all due diligence to avoid the commission of the offence.

(5) Sections 732 (restriction on prosecutions), 733(2) and (3) (liability of individuals for corporate default) and 734 (criminal proceedings against unincorporated bodies) apply to offences under this section.]

[237B]

NOTES

Inserted as noted to s 245D at **[237A]**.

Repealed by the Companies Act 2006, s 1295, Sch 16, as from a day to be appointed.

Application to limited liability partnerships: see the Limited Liability Partnerships Regulations 2001, SI 2001/1090, reg 3, Sch 1 at **[6984]**, **[6992]**.

[245F Power of authorised persons to require documents, information and explanations

(1) This section applies where it appears to a person who is authorised under section 245C of this Act that there is, or may be, a question whether the [a company's annual accounts [or directors' report]] comply with the requirements of this Act [(or, where applicable, of Article 4 of the IAS Regulation)].

(2) The authorised person may require any of the persons mentioned in subsection (3) to produce any document, or to provide him with any information or explanations, that he may reasonably require for the purpose of—

(a) discovering whether there are grounds for an application to the court under section 245B; or

(b) determining whether or not to make such an application.

(3) Those persons are—

(a) the company;

(b) any officer, employee, or auditor of the company;

(c) any persons who fell within paragraph (b) at a time to which the document or information required by the authorised person relates.

(4) If a person fails to comply with a requirement under subsection (2), the authorised person may apply to the court for an order under subsection (5).

(5) If on such an application the court decides that the person has failed to comply with the requirement under subsection (2), it may order the person to take such steps as it directs for securing that the documents are produced or the information or explanations are provided.

(6) A statement made by a person in response to a requirement under subsection (2) or an order under subsection (5) may not be used in evidence against him in any criminal proceedings.

(7) *Nothing in this section compels any person to disclose documents or information in respect of which in an action in the High Court a claim to legal professional privilege, or in an action in the Court of Session a claim to confidentiality of communications, could be maintained.*

(8) *In this section "document" includes information recorded in any form.]*

[237C]

NOTES

Inserted, together with s 245G, by the Companies (Audit, Investigations and Community Enterprise) Act 2004, s 12(1), as from 6 April 2005.

Repealed by the Companies Act 2006, s 1295, Sch 16, as from a day to be appointed.

Sub-s (1): words in first (outer) pair of square brackets substituted by the Companies Act 1985 (Operating and Financial Review and Directors' Report etc) Regulations 2005, SI 2005/1011, reg 18, as from 22 March 2005, in relation to annual accounts, directors' reports and operating and financial reviews prepared for companies' financial years which begin on or after 1 April 2006; words in second (inner) pair of square brackets substituted by the Companies Act 1985 (Operating and Financial Review) (Repeal) Regulations 2005, SI 2005/3442, reg 2(2)(a), Sch 1, para 13, as from 12 January 2006; words in third pair of square brackets inserted by SI 2005/1011, reg 19, Schedule, paras 1, 6, as from 22 March 2005, in relation to companies' financial years which begin on or after 1 April 2005.

Application to limited liability partnerships: see the Limited Liability Partnerships Regulations 2001, SI 2001/1090, reg 3, Sch 1 at **[6984]**, **[6992]**.

[245G Restrictions on further disclosure of information obtained under section 245F

(1) *This section applies to information (in whatever form) which—*

(a) *has been obtained in pursuance of a requirement or order under section 245F, and*

(b) *relates to the private affairs of an individual or to any particular business.*

(2) *No such information may, during the lifetime of that individual or so long as that business continues to be carried on, be disclosed without the consent of that individual or the person for the time being carrying on that business.*

(3) *Subsection (2) does not apply to any disclosure of information which—*

(a) *is made for the purpose of facilitating the carrying out by a person authorised under section 245C of his functions under section 245B;*

(b) *is made to a person specified in Part 1 of Schedule 7B;*

(c) *is of a description specified in Part 2 of that Schedule; or*

(d) *is made in accordance with Part 3 of that Schedule.*

(4) *The Secretary of State may by order amend Schedule 7B.*

(5) *An order under subsection (4) must not—*

(a) *amend Part 1 of Schedule 7B by specifying a person unless the person exercises functions of a public nature (whether or not he exercises any other function);*

(b) *amend Part 2 of Schedule 7B by adding or modifying a description of disclosure unless the purpose for which the disclosure is permitted is likely to facilitate the exercise of a function of a public nature;*

(c) *amend Part 3 of Schedule 7B so as to have the effect of permitting disclosures to be made to a body other than one that exercises functions of a public nature in a country or territory outside the United Kingdom.*

(6) *An order under subsection (4) shall be made by statutory instrument which shall be subject to annulment in pursuance of a resolution of either House of Parliament.*

(7) *A person who discloses any information in contravention of this section—*

(a) *is guilty of an offence, and*

(b) *is liable on conviction to imprisonment or a fine, or both.*

(8) *However, it is a defence for a person charged with an offence under subsection (7) to prove—*

(a) *that he did not know, and had no reason to suspect, that the information had been disclosed under section 245F; or*

(b) *that he took all reasonable steps and exercised all due diligence to avoid the commission of the offence.*

(9) *Sections 732 (restriction on prosecutions), 733 (liability of individuals for corporate default) and 734 (criminal proceedings against unincorporated bodies) apply to offences under this section.*

(10) This section does not prohibit the disclosure of information if the information is or has been available to the public from any other source.

(11) Nothing in this section authorises the making of a disclosure in contravention of the Data Protection Act 1998.]

[237D]

NOTES

Inserted as noted to s 245F at **[237C]**.

Repealed by the Companies Act 2006, s 1295, Sch 16, as from a day to be appointed.

Application to limited liability partnerships: see the Limited Liability Partnerships Regulations 2001, SI 2001/1090, reg 3, Sch 1 at **[6984]**, **[6992]**.

[CHAPTER II
EXEMPTIONS, EXCEPTIONS AND SPECIAL PROVISIONS

Small and medium-sized companies and groups

[246 Special provisions for small companies

(1) Subject to section 247A, this section applies where a company qualifies as a small company in relation to a financial year.

(2) If the company's individual accounts for the year [are Companies Act individual accounts and]—

- *(a) comply with the provisions of Schedule 8, or*
- *(b) fail to comply with those provisions only in so far as they comply instead with one or more corresponding provisions of Schedule 4,*

they need not comply with the provisions or, as the case may be, the remaining provisions of Schedule 4; and where advantage is taken of this subsection, references in [section 226A] to compliance with the provisions of Schedule 4 shall be construed accordingly.

[(3) The company's individual accounts for the year—

- *(a) may give the total of the aggregates required by paragraphs (a), (c) and (d) of paragraph 1(1) of Schedule 6 (emoluments and other benefits etc of directors) instead of giving those aggregates individually; and*
- *(b) need not give the information required by—*
  - *[(ai) section 231A (disclosure required in notes to annual accounts: particulars of staff);]*
  - *(i) paragraph 4 of Schedule 5 (financial years of subsidiary undertakings);*
  - *(ii) paragraph 1(2)(b) of Schedule 6 (numbers of directors exercising share options and receiving shares under long term incentive schemes);*
  - *(iii) paragraph 2 of Schedule 6 (details of highest paid director's emoluments etc); or*
  - *(iv) paragraph 7 of Schedule 6 (excess retirement benefits of directors and past directors).]*

(4) The directors' report for the year need not give the information required by—

- *[(a) sections 234ZZA(1)(c) (directors' report: amount to be paid as dividend) and 234ZZB (directors' report: business review);]*
- *(b) paragraph 1(2) of Schedule 7 (statement of market value of fixed assets where substantially different from balance sheet amount);*
- *[(ba) paragraph 5A of Schedule 7 (disclosures relating to the use of financial instruments);]*
- *(c) paragraph 6 of Schedule 7 (miscellaneous disclosures); or*
- *(d) paragraph 11 of Schedule 7 (employee involvement).*

(5) Notwithstanding anything in section 242(1), the directors of the company need not deliver to the registrar any of the following, namely—

- *(a) a copy of the company's profit and loss account for the year;*
- *(b) a copy of the directors' report for the year; and*
- *(c) if [they prepare Companies Act individual accounts and] they deliver a copy of a balance sheet drawn up as at the last day of the year which complies with the requirements of Schedule 8A, a copy of the company's balance sheet drawn up as at that day.*

(6) Neither a copy of the company's accounts for the year delivered to the registrar under section 242(1), nor a copy of a balance sheet delivered to the registrar under subsection (5)(c), need give the information required by—

(*a*) *paragraph 4 of Schedule 5 (financial years of subsidiary undertakings);*
(*b*) *paragraph 6 of Schedule 5 (shares of company held by subsidiary undertakings);*
(*c*) *Part I of Schedule 6 (directors' and chairman's emoluments, pensions and compensation for loss of office); or*
(*d*) *section 390A(3) (amount of auditors' remuneration).*

(7) The provisions of section 233 as to the signing of the copy of the balance sheet delivered to the registrar apply to a copy of a balance sheet delivered under subsection (5)(c).

(8) Subject to subsection (9), each of the following, namely—

(*a*) *accounts prepared in accordance with subsection (2) or (3),*
(*b*) *a report prepared in accordance with subsection (4), and*
(*c*) *a copy of accounts delivered to the registrar in accordance with subsection (5) or (6),*

shall contain a statement in a prominent position on the balance sheet, in the report or, as the case may be, on the copy of the balance sheet, above the signature required by section 233, 234A or subsection (7), that they are prepared in accordance with the special provisions of this Part relating to small companies.

(9) Subsection (8) does not apply where [the directors of the company have taken advantage of the exemption from audit conferred by section 249AA (dormant companies].]

[238]

NOTES

This section (as inserted with the preceding heading and s 247 by CA 1989, s 13(1), as from 1 April 1990, was substituted by the Companies Act 1985 (Accounts of Small and Medium-sized Companies and Minor Accounting Amendments) Regulations 1997, SI 1997/220, reg 2(1), in relation to annual accounts approved by the board of directors on or after 1 March 1997, and to directors' and auditors' reports on such accounts (subject to transitional provisions in relation to a financial year of a company ending on or before 24 March 1997).

Repealed by the Companies Act 2006, s 1295, Sch 16, as from 1 October 2007 (in so far as relating to the words "and 234ZZB (directors' report: business review)" in sub-s (4)(a)), and as from a day to be appointed (otherwise). For savings see the note below.

Sub-s (2): words in first pair of square brackets inserted, and words in second pair of square brackets substituted, by the Companies Act 1985 (International Accounting Standards and Other Accounting Amendments) Regulations 2004, SI 2004/2947, reg 3, Sch 1, paras 1, 12(1), (2), as from 12 November 2004, in relation to companies' financial years which begin on or after 1 January 2005.

Sub-s (3): substituted by the Company Accounts (Disclosure of Directors' Emoluments) Regulations 1997, SI 1997/570, reg 6(1), as from 31 March 1997, with effect in relation to companies' financial years ending on or after that date; sub-para (b)(ai) inserted by the Companies Act 1985 (Investment Companies and Accounting and Audit Amendments) Regulations 2005, SI 2005/2280, reg 12, as from 1 October 2005, in relation to companies' financial years which begin on or after 1 January 2005 and which end on or after 1 October 2005.

Sub-s (4): para (a) substituted by the Companies Act 1985 (Operating and Financial Review and Directors' Report etc) Regulations 2005, SI 2005/1011, reg 4, as from 22 March 2005, in relation to companies' financial years which begin on or after 1 April 2005 (see also the second note *above*); para (ba) inserted by SI 2004/2947, reg 13(2), as from 12 November 2004, in relation to companies' financial years which begin on or after 1 January 2005.

Sub-s (5): words in square brackets inserted by SI 2004/2947, reg 3, Sch 1, paras 1, 12(1), (3), as from 12 November 2004, in relation to companies' financial years which begin on or after 1 January 2005.

Sub-s (9): words in square brackets substituted by the Companies Act 1985 (Audit Exemption) (Amendment) Regulations 2000, SI 2000/1430, reg 8(1), as from 26 May 2000, in relation to annual reports and reports in respect of financial years ending two months or more after that date.

Savings: the words "and 234ZZB (directors' report: business review)" in sub-s (4)(a) continue to apply to directors' reports for financial years beginning before 1 October 2007 (see the draft Companies Act 2006 (Commencement No 3, Consequential Amendments, Transitional Provisions and Savings) Order 2007, Sch 3, para 43 at **[A12]**).

Application to limited liability partnerships: see the Limited Liability Partnerships Regulations 2001, SI 2001/1090, reg 3, Sch 1 at **[6984]**, **[6992]**. Note also that nothing in the draft Companies Act 2006 (Commencement No 3, Consequential Amendments, Transitional Provisions and Savings) Order 2007 affects any provision of this Act as applied by the 2001 Regulations to LLPs (see art 12(2) at **[A12]** and the introductory notes to this Act).

[246A Special provisions for medium-sized companies

(1) Subject to section 247A, this section applies where a company qualifies as a medium-sized company in relation to a financial year [and its directors prepare Companies Act individual accounts for that year].

(2) The company's individual accounts for the year need not comply with the requirements of paragraph 36A of Schedule 4 (disclosure with respect to compliance with accounting standards).

[(2A) The directors' report for the year need not comply with the requirements of section 234ZZB(3) (business review to include analysis using key performance indicators) so far as they relate to non-financial information.]

(3) The company may deliver to the registrar a copy of the company's accounts for the year—

(a) which includes a profit and loss account in which the following items listed in the profit and loss account formats set out in Part I of Schedule 4 are combined as one item under the heading "gross profit or loss"—
Items 1, 2, 3 and 6 in Format 1;
Items 1 to 5 in Format 2;
Items A.1, B.1 and B.2 in Format 3;
Items A.1, A.2 and B.1 to B.4 in Format 4;

(b) which does not contain the information required by paragraph 55 of Schedule 4 (particulars of turnover).

(4) A copy of accounts delivered to the registrar in accordance with subsection (3) shall contain a statement in a prominent position on the copy of the balance sheet, above the signature required by section 233, that the accounts are prepared in accordance with the special provisions of this Part relating to medium-sized companies.]

[239]

NOTES

Inserted by the Companies Act 1985 (Accounts of Small and Medium-sized Companies and Minor Accounting Amendments) Regulations 1997, SI 1997/220, reg 3, in relation to annual accounts approved by the board of directors on or after 1 March 1997, and to directors' and auditors' reports on such accounts (subject to transitional provisions in relation to a financial year of a company ending on or before 24 March 1997).

Repealed by the Companies Act 2006, s 1295, Sch 16, as from 1 October 2007 (in so far as relating to sub-s (2A)), and as from a day to be appointed (otherwise). For savings see the note below.

Sub-s (1): words in square brackets added by the Companies Act 1985 (International Accounting Standards and Other Accounting Amendments) Regulations 2004, SI 2004/2947, reg 3, Sch 1, paras 1, 13, as from 12 November 2004, in relation to companies' financial years which begin on or after 1 January 2005.

Sub-s (2A): inserted by the Companies Act 1985 (Operating and Financial Review and Directors' Report etc) Regulations 2005, SI 2005/1011, reg 5, as from 22 March 2005, in relation to companies' financial years which begin on or after 1 April 2005; repealed as noted above.

Savings: sub-s (2A) continues to apply to directors' reports for financial years beginning before 1 October 2007 (see the draft Companies Act 2006 (Commencement No 3, Consequential Amendments, Transitional Provisions and Savings) Order 2007, Sch 3, para 43 at **[A12]**).

Application to limited liability partnerships: see the Limited Liability Partnerships Regulations 2001, SI 2001/1090, reg 3, Sch 1 at **[6984]**, **[6992]**. Note also that nothing in the draft Companies Act 2006 (Commencement No 3, Consequential Amendments, Transitional Provisions and Savings) Order 2007 affects any provision of this Act as applied by the 2001 Regulations to LLPs (see art 12(2) at **[A12]** and the introductory notes to this Act).

[247 Qualification of company as small or medium-sized

(1) A company qualifies as small or medium-sized in relation to a financial year if the qualifying conditions are met—

(a) in the case of the company's first financial year, in that year, and

(b) in the case of any subsequent financial year, in that year and the preceding year.

(2) A company shall be treated as qualifying as small or medium-sized in relation to a financial year—

(a) if it so qualified in relation to the previous financial year under [subsection (1) above or was treated as so qualifying under paragraph (b) below]; or

(b) if it was treated as so qualifying in relation to the previous year by virtue of paragraph (a) and the qualifying conditions are met in the year in question.

(3) The qualifying conditions are met by a company in a year in which it satisfies two or more of the following requirements—

Small company	
1. Turnover	*[Not more than £5.6 million]*
2. Balance sheet total	*[Not more than £2.8 million]*
3. Number of employees	*Not more than 50*

Medium-sized company	
1. Turnover	*[Not more than £22.8 million]*
2. Balance sheet total	*[Not more than £11.4 million]*
3. Number of employees	*Not more than 250.*

(4) For a period which is a company's financial year but not in fact a year the maximum figures for turnover shall be proportionately adjusted.

[(5) The balance sheet total means—

(a) in the case of Companies Act individual accounts—

(i) the aggregate of the amounts shown in the balance sheet under the headings corresponding to items A to D of Format 1 in Part 1 of Schedule 4 or Part 1 of Schedule 8, or

(ii) if Format 2 is adopted, the aggregate of the amounts shown under the general heading "ASSETS";

(b) in the case of IAS individual accounts, the aggregate of the amounts shown as assets in the balance sheet.]

(6) The number of employees means the average number of persons employed by the company in the year (determined on a [monthly] basis).

That number shall be determined by applying the method of calculation prescribed by paragraph 56(2) and (3) of Schedule 4 for determining the corresponding number required to be stated in a note to the company's accounts.]

[240]

NOTES

Inserted as noted to s 246 at **[238]**.

Repealed by the Companies Act 2006, s 1295, Sch 16, as from a day to be appointed.

Sub-s (2): words in square brackets substituted by the Companies Act 1985 (Accounts of Small and Medium-Sized Enterprises and Publication of Accounts in ECUs) Regulations 1992, SI 1992/2452, reg 5(1), (2), in relation to annual accounts in respect of financial years ending on or after 16 November 1992, and to directors' and auditors' reports on such accounts.

Sub-s (3): words in square brackets substituted by the Companies Act 1985 (Accounts of Small and Medium-Sized Enterprises and Audit Exemption) (Amendment) Regulations 2004, SI 2004/16, reg 2, as from 30 January 2004, in relation to financial years ending on or after that date.

Sub-s (5): substituted by the Companies Act 1985 (International Accounting Standards and Other Accounting Amendments) Regulations 2004, SI 2004/2947, reg 3, Sch 1, paras 1, 14, as from 12 November 2004, in relation to companies' financial years which begin on or after 1 January 2005.

Sub-s (6): word in square brackets substituted by the Companies Act 1985 (Miscellaneous Accounting Amendments) Regulations 1996, SI 1996/189, regs 8, 16(5), in relation to any annual accounts of a company which are approved by the board of directors on or after 2 February 1996.

Transitional provisions:

The Companies Act 1985 (Accounts of Small and Medium-Sized Enterprises and Publication of Accounts in ECUs) Regulations 1992, SI 1992/2452, reg 7(2) provides as follows (note that by virtue of reg 1 these Regulations came into force on 16 November 1992)—

"(2) In determining under section 247 or 249 of the 1985 Act whether a company or group qualifies as small or medium-sized in relation to financial years subsequent to its first financial year which end on or after the date of coming into force of these Regulations:

(a) the company or group shall be treated as having qualified as small or medium-sized (as the case may be) in each previous financial year ending on or after 9th November 1990 in which it would have so qualified under section 247(3) or 249(3) as amended by these Regulations; and

(b) the company or group shall be treated as having qualified as small or medium-sized in any such financial year if they would have been so entitled had the company or group had the qualification it is treated as having had under sub-paragraph (a) above.".

The Companies Act 1985 (Accounts of Small and Medium-Sized Enterprises and Audit Exemption) (Amendment) Regulations 2004, SI 2004/16, reg 7(2), (3) provides as follows (by virtue of reg 1(2), the "commencement date" is 30 January 2004)—

"(2) For the purposes of determining whether a company or group qualifies, or is treated as qualifying, as small or medium-sized under section 247 or 249 of the 1985 Act in relation to a financial year ending on or after the commencement date, the company or group shall be treated as having qualified as small or medium-sized (as the case may be) in any previous financial year in which it would have so qualified, or have been treated as so qualifying, under section 247 or 249 as amended by regulations 2 and 3.

(3) In paragraphs (1) and (2) references to financial years ending on or after the commencement date do not include financial years which only end on or after that date by reason of an exercise of the power conferred by section 225 of the 1985 Act (alteration of accounting reference date) by the giving of a notice to the registrar on or after the date on which these Regulations are made.".

Application to limited liability partnerships: see the Limited Liability Partnerships Regulations 2001, SI 2001/1090, reg 3, Sch 1 at **[6984]**, **[6992]**.

[247A Cases in which special provisions do not apply

[(1) If a company is, or was at any time within the financial year to which the accounts relate, an ineligible company, sections 246 and 246A do not apply.

(1A) If a company does not fall within subsection (1) but is, or was at any time within the financial year to which the accounts relate, a member of an ineligible group—

- *(a) section 246(4) and (5)(b) and section 246A(2A) (provisions relating to directors' report) apply;*
- *(b) the other provisions of sections 246 and 246A do not apply.*

[(1B) A company that qualifies as small in relation to the financial year to which the accounts relate is ineligible if—

- *(a) it is a public company,*
- *(b) it is an authorised insurance company, a banking company, an e-money issuer, an ISD investment firm or a UCITS management company, or*
- *(c) it carries on an insurance market activity.*

(1C) A company that qualifies as medium-sized in relation to the financial year to which the accounts relate is ineligible if—

- *(a) it is a public company,*
- *(b) it has permission under Part 4 of the Financial Services and Markets Act 2000 to carry on a regulated activity, or*
- *(c) it carries on an insurance market activity.]]*

(2) A group is ineligible if any of its members is—

- *(a) a public company or a body corporate which (not being a company) has power under its constitution to offer its shares or debentures to the public and may lawfully exercise that power,*
- *[(b) a person [(other than a small company)] who has permission under Part 4 of the Financial Services and Markets Act 2000 to carry on a regulated activity,*
- *[(ba) a small company that is an authorised insurance company, a banking company, an e-money issuer, an ISD investment firm or a UCITS management company, or]*
- *(c) a person who carries on an insurance market activity.]*

[(2A) A company is a small company for the purposes of subsection (2) if it qualified as small in relation to its last financial year ending on or before the end of the financial year to which the accounts relate.]

(3) A parent company shall not be treated as qualifying as a small company in relation to a financial year unless the group headed by it qualifies as a small group, and shall not be treated as qualifying as a medium-sized company in relation to a financial year unless that group qualifies as a medium-sized group (see section 249).]

[241]

NOTES

Inserted by the Companies Act 1985 (Accounts of Small and Medium-sized Companies and Minor Accounting Amendments) Regulations 1997, SI 1997/220, reg 4, in relation to annual accounts approved by the board of directors on or after 1 March 1997, and to directors' and auditors' reports on such accounts (subject to transitional provisions in relation to a financial year of a company ending on or before 24 March 1997).

Repealed by the Companies Act 2006, s 1295, Sch 16, as from a day to be appointed.

Sub-ss (1), (1A): substituted, together with sub-s (1B) for original sub-s (1), by the Companies Act 1985 (Operating and Financial Review and Directors' Report etc) Regulations 2005, SI 2005/1011, reg 6, as from 22 March 2005 (as to the effect of this amendment, see further the final note below).

Sub-s (1B): originally substituted as noted above; further substituted (by new sub-ss (1B), (1C)) by the Companies Act 1985 (Small Companies' Accounts and Audit) Regulations 2006, SI 2006/2782, reg 2(1), (2), as from 8 November 2006, in relation to annual accounts and reports in respect of financial years ending on or after 31 December 2006.

Sub-s (1C): substituted as noted above.

Sub-s (2): paras (b), (c) substituted, for original paras (b)–(d), by SI 2001/3649, art 11(1), (3), as from 1 December 2001; words in square brackets in para (b) inserted, and para (ba) substituted for the original word "or" at the end of para (b), by SI 2006/2782, reg 2(1), (3), as from 8 November 2006, in relation to annual accounts and reports in respect of financial years ending on or after 31 December 2006.

Sub-s (2A): inserted by SI 2006/2782, reg 2(1), (4), as from 8 November 2006, in relation to annual accounts and reports in respect of financial years ending on or after 31 December 2006.

Application to limited liability partnerships: see the Limited Liability Partnerships Regulations 2001, SI 2001/1090, reg 3, Sch 1 at **[6984]**, **[6992]**.

Note: the Companies Act 1985 (Operating and Financial Review and Directors' Report etc) Regulations 2005, SI 2005/1011, reg 1(3) originally provided that the amendment made by reg 6 of those Regulations to this section would have effect as respects companies' financial years which begin on or after 1 April 2005. See now, the Companies Act 1985 (Investment Companies and Accounting and Audit Amendments) Regulations 2005, SI 2005/2280, reg 14, which provides as follows—

"14 Application of SI 2005/1011, regulation 6

Regulation 6 of the Companies Act 1985 (Operating and Financial Review and Directors. Report etc) Regulations 2005 (which amends section 247A of the 1985 Act so as to enable a small company to take advantage of certain exemptions despite being a member of an ineligible group) has effect in relation to a financial year—

(a) beginning before 1st April 2005 but on or after 1st January 2005, and

(b) ending on or after 1st October 2005,

as it has effect in relation to a financial year beginning on or after 1st April 2005.".

[247B Special auditors' report

(1) This section applies where—

(a) the directors of a company propose to deliver to the registrar copies of accounts ("abbreviated accounts") prepared in accordance with section 246(5) or (6) or 246A(3) ("the relevant provision"),

(b) the directors have not taken advantage of the exemption from audit conferred by section 249A(1) or (2) [or section 249AA], …

(c) …

(2) If abbreviated accounts prepared in accordance with the relevant provision are delivered to the registrar, they shall be accompanied by a copy of a special report of the auditors stating that in their opinion—

(a) the company is entitled to deliver abbreviated accounts prepared in accordance with that provision, and

(b) the abbreviated accounts to be delivered are properly prepared in accordance with that provision.

(3) In such a case a copy of the auditors' report under section 235 need not be delivered, but—

(a) if that report was qualified, the special report shall set out that report in full together with any further material necessary to understand the qualification; and

(b) if that report contained a statement under—

(i) section 237(2) (accounts, records or returns inadequate or accounts not agreeing with records and returns), or

(ii) section 237(3) (failure to obtain necessary information and explanations),

the special report shall set out that statement in full.

(4) Section 236 (signature of auditors' report) applies to a special report under this section as it applies to a report under section 235.

(5) If abbreviated accounts prepared in accordance with the relevant provision are delivered to the registrar, references in section 240 (requirements in connection with

publication of accounts) to the auditors' report under section 235 shall be read as references to the special auditors' report under this section.]

[242]

NOTES

Inserted by the Companies Act 1985 (Accounts of Small and Medium-sized Companies and Minor Accounting Amendments) Regulations 1997, SI 1997/220, reg 5, in relation to annual accounts approved by the board of directors on or after 1 March 1997, and to directors' and auditors' reports on such accounts (subject to transitional provisions in relation to a financial year of a company ending on or before 24 March 1997).

Repealed by the Companies Act 2006, s 1295, Sch 16, as from a day to be appointed.

Sub-s (1): words in square brackets inserted, and words omitted repealed, by the Companies Act 1985 (Audit Exemption) (Amendment) Regulations 2000, SI 2000/1430, reg 8(2), as from 26 May 2000, in relation to annual reports and reports in respect of financial years ending two months or more after that date.

Application to limited liability partnerships: see the Limited Liability Partnerships Regulations 2001, SI 2001/1090, reg 3, Sch 1 at **[6984]**, **[6992]**.

[248 Exemption for small and medium-sized groups

(1) A parent company need not prepare group accounts for a financial year in relation to which the group headed by that company qualifies as a small or medium-sized group and is not an ineligible group.

(2) A group is ineligible if any of its members is—

(a) a public company or body corporate which (not being a company) has power under its constitution to offer its shares or debentures to the public and may lawfully exercise that power,

[(b) a person [(other than a small company)] who has permission under Part 4 of the Financial Services and Markets Act 2000 to carry on a regulated activity,

[(ba) a small company that is an authorised insurance company, a banking company, an e-money issuer, an ISD investment firm or a UCITS management company, or]

(c) a person who carries on an insurance market activity.]

[(2A) A company is a small company for the purposes of subsection (2) if it qualified as small in relation to its last financial year ending on or before the end of the financial year to which the group accounts relate.]

(3), (4) …]

[243]

NOTES

Inserted, together with s 249, by CA 1989, s 13(3), as from 1 April 1990.

Repealed by the Companies Act 2006, s 1295, Sch 16, as from a day to be appointed.

Sub-s (2): paras (b), (c) substituted, for original paras (b)–(d), by the Financial Services and Markets Act 2000 (Consequential Amendments and Repeals) Order 2001, SI 2001/3649, art 12, as from 1 December 2001; words in square brackets in para (b) inserted, and para (ba) substituted for the original word "or" at the end of para (b), by the Companies Act 1985 (Small Companies' Accounts and Audit) Regulations 2006, SI 2006/2782, reg 3(1), (2), as from 8 November 2006, in relation to annual accounts and reports in respect of financial years ending on or after 31 December 2006.

Sub-s (2A): inserted by SI 2006/2782, reg 3(1), (3), as from 8 November 2006, in relation to annual accounts and reports in respect of financial years ending on or after 31 December 2006.

Sub-ss (3), (4): repealed by the Companies Act 1985 (Miscellaneous Accounting Amendments) Regulations 1996, SI 1996/189, regs 9, 16(1), in relation to any financial year ending on or after 2 February 1996 (subject to transitional provisions in relation to financial years ending on or before 24 March 1996).

Application to limited liability partnerships: see the Limited Liability Partnerships Regulations 2001, SI 2001/1090, reg 3, Sch 1 at **[6984]**, **[6992]**.

[248A Group accounts prepared by small company

(1) This section applies where a small company—

(a) has prepared individual accounts for a financial year in accordance with section 246(2) or (3), and

(b) is preparing [Companies Act group accounts] in respect of the same year.

(2) If the group accounts—

(a) comply with the provisions of Schedule 8, or

(*b*) *fail to comply with those provisions only in so far as they comply instead with one or more corresponding provisions of Schedule 4,*

they need not comply with the provisions or, as the case may be, the remaining provisions of Schedule 4; and where advantage is taken of this subsection, references in Schedule 4A to compliance with the provisions of Schedule 4 shall be construed accordingly.

(*3*) *For the purposes of this section, Schedule 8 shall have effect as if, in each balance sheet format set out in that Schedule, for item B.III there were substituted the following item—*

"B.III Investments

1 Shares in group undertakings

2 Interests in associated undertakings

3 Other participating interests

4 Loans to group undertakings and undertakings in which a participating interest is held

5 Other investments other than loans

6 Others."

(*4*) *The group accounts need not give the information required by the provisions specified in section 246(3).*

(*5*) *Group accounts prepared in accordance with this section shall contain a statement in a prominent position on the balance sheet, above the signature required by section 233, that they are prepared in accordance with the special provisions of this Part relating to small companies.]*

[244]

NOTES

Inserted by the Companies Act 1985 (Accounts of Small and Medium-sized Companies and Minor Accounting Amendments) Regulations 1997, SI 1997/220, reg 6, in relation to annual accounts approved by the board of directors on or after 1 March 1997, and to directors' and auditors' reports on such accounts (subject to transitional provisions in relation to a financial year of a company ending on or before 24 March 1997).

Repealed by the Companies Act 2006, s 1295, Sch 16, as from a day to be appointed.

Sub-s (1): words in square brackets substituted by the Companies Act 1985 (International Accounting Standards and Other Accounting Amendments) Regulations 2004, SI 2004/2947, reg 3, Sch 1, paras 1, 15, as from 12 November 2004, in relation to companies' financial years which begin on or after 1 January 2005.

Application to limited liability partnerships: see the Limited Liability Partnerships Regulations 2001, SI 2001/1090, reg 3, Sch 1 at **[6984]**, **[6992]**.

[249 Qualification of group as small or medium-sized

(*1*) *A group qualifies as small or medium-sized in relation to a financial year if the qualifying conditions are met—*

(*a*) *in the case of the parent company's first financial year, in that year, and*

(*b*) *in the case of any subsequent financial year, in that year and the preceding year.*

(*2*) *A group shall be treated as qualifying as small or medium-sized in relation to a financial year—*

(*a*) *if it so qualified in relation to the previous financial year under [subsection* (*1*) *above or was treated as so qualifying under paragraph* (*b*) *below]; or*

(*b*) *if it was treated as so qualifying in relation to the previous year by virtue of paragraph* (*a*) *and the qualifying conditions are met in the year in question.*

(*3*) *The qualifying conditions are met by a group in a year in which it satisfies two or more of the following requirements—*

	Small group
1. Aggregate turnover	*[Not more than £5.6 million net* (*or £6.72 million gross*)*]*
2. Aggregate balance sheet total	*[Not more than £2.8 million net* (*or £3.36 million gross*)*]*
3. Aggregate number of employees	*Not more than 50*

Medium-sized group	
1. Aggregate turnover	*[Not more than £22.8 million net (or £27.36 million gross)]*
2. Aggregate balance sheet total	*[Not more than £11.4 million net (or £13.68 million gross)]*
3. Aggregate number of employees	*Not more than 250.*

(4) The aggregate figures shall be ascertained by aggregating the relevant figures determined in accordance with section 247 for each member of the group.

In relation to the aggregate figures for turnover and balance sheet total, "net" means with the set-offs and other adjustments required by Schedule 4A in the case of group accounts and "gross" means without those set-offs and other adjustments; and a company may satisfy the relevant requirements on the basis of either the net or the gross figure.

(5) The figures for each subsidiary undertaking shall be those included in its accounts for the relevant financial year, that is—

(a) if its financial year ends with that of the parent company, that financial year, and
(b) if not, its financial year ending last before the end of the financial year of the parent company.

(6) If those figures cannot be obtained without disproportionate expense or undue delay, the latest available figures shall be taken.]

[245]

NOTES

Inserted as noted to s 248 at **[243]**.

Repealed by the Companies Act 2006, s 1295, Sch 16, as from a day to be appointed.

Sub-s (2): words in square brackets substituted by the Companies Act 1985 (Accounts of Small and Medium-Sized Enterprises and Publication of Accounts in ECUs) Regulations 1992, SI 1992/2452, reg 6(1), (2), in relation to annual accounts in respect of financial years ending on or after 16 November 1992, and to directors' and auditors' reports on such accounts.

Sub-s (3): words in square brackets substituted by the Companies Act 1985 (Accounts of Small and Medium-Sized Enterprises and Audit Exemption) (Amendment) Regulations 2004, SI 2004/16, reg 3, as from 30 January 2004, in relation to financial years ending on or after that date.

Transitional provisions: see the note to s 247 at **[240]**.

Application to limited liability partnerships: see the Limited Liability Partnerships Regulations 2001, SI 2001/1090, reg 3, Sch 1 at **[6984]**, **[6992]**.

[Exemptions from audit for certain categories of small company

249A Exemptions from audit

(1) Subject to section 249B, a company which meets the total exemption conditions set out below in respect of a financial year is exempt from the provisions of this Part relating to the audit of accounts in respect of that year.

(2) Subject to section 249B, [a company which is a charity and] which meets the report conditions set out below in respect of a financial year is exempt from the provisions of this Part relating to the audit of accounts in respect of that year if the directors cause a report in respect of the company's individual accounts for that year to be prepared in accordance with section 249C and made to the company's members.

(3) The total exemption conditions are met by a company in respect of a financial year if—

(a) it qualifies as a small company in relation to that year for the purposes of section 246,
(b) its turnover in that year is not more than [£5.6 million], and
(c) its balance sheet total for that year is not more than [£2.8 million].

[(3A) In relation to any company which is a charity, subsection (3)(b) shall have effect with the substitution—

(a) for the reference to turnover of a reference to gross income, and

(*b*) *for the reference to [£5.6 million] of a reference to £90,000.]*

(*4*) *The report conditions are met by [a company which is a charity] in respect of a financial year if—*

(*a*) *it qualifies as a small company in relation to that year for the purposes of section 246,*

(*b*) *its [gross income] in that year is more than £90,000 but not more than [£500,000], and*

(*c*) *its balance sheet total for that year is not more than [£2.8 million].*

(*5*) …

(*6*) *For a period which is a company's financial year but not in fact a year the maximum figures for turnover or gross income shall be proportionately adjusted.*

[(6A) A company is entitled to the exemption conferred by subsection (*1*) *or* (*2*) *notwithstanding that it falls within paragraph* (*a*) *or* (*b*) *of [section 249AA(1)].]*

(*7*) *In this section—*

"balance sheet total" has the meaning given by section 247(5), and

"gross income" means the company's income from all sources, as shown in the company's income and expenditure account.]

[246]

NOTES

Inserted, together with preceding heading and ss 249B–249E, by the Companies Act 1985 (Audit Exemption) Regulations 1994, SI 1994/1935, reg 2, as from 11 August 1994, in relation to annual accounts of a company which are approved by the board of directors on or after 11 August 1994 (and does not apply to any annual accounts the period for laying and delivering of which expired before that date).

Repealed by the Companies Act 2006, s 1295, Sch 16, as from a day to be appointed. Note that this section is also amended by the 2006 Act (see below).

Sub-s (2): repealed by the Companies Act 2006, s 1175, Sch 9, Pt 1, para 3(a), as from a day to be appointed; words in square brackets substituted by the Companies Act 1985 (Audit Exemption) (Amendment) Regulations 1997, SI 1997/936, reg 2(1), (2), as from 15 April 1997, in relation to the annual accounts of any company for any financial year ending two months or more after that date.

Sub-s (3): words in square brackets substituted by the Companies Act 1985 (Accounts of Small and Medium-Sized Enterprises and Audit Exemption) (Amendment) Regulations 2004, SI 2004/16, regs 4, 7(4), as from 30 January 2004, in relation to financial years ending two months or more after that date.

Sub-s (3A): inserted by SI 1997/936, reg 2(1), (4), as from 15 April 1997, in relation to the annual accounts of any company for any financial year ending two months or more after that date, and repealed by the Companies Act 2006, s 1175, Sch 9, Pt 1, para 3(a), as from a day to be appointed; words in square brackets substituted by SI 2004/16, regs 4, 7(4), as from 30 January 2004, in relation to financial years ending two months or more after that date.

Sub-s (4): repealed by the Companies Act 2006, s 1175, Sch 9, Pt 1, para 3(a), as from a day to be appointed; words in first pair of square brackets, and words in first pair of square brackets in para (b), substituted by SI 1997/936, reg 2(1), (5), as from 15 April 1997, in relation to the annual accounts of any company for any financial year ending two months or more after that date; sums "£500,000" and "£2.8 million" in square brackets substituted by the Charities Act 2006, s 32(1), as from 27 February 2007.

Sub-s (5): repealed by SI 1997/936, reg 2(1), (6), as from 15 April 1997, in relation to the annual accounts of any company for any financial year ending two months or more after that date.

Sub-s (6): for the words "figures for turnover or gross income" there are substituted the words "figure for turnover" by the Companies Act 2006, s 1175, Sch 9, Pt 1, para 3(b), as from a day to be appointed.

Sub-s (6A): inserted by SI 1997/936, reg 2(1), (7), (8), which amendment is deemed always to have had effect; words "or (2)" repealed by the Companies Act 2006, s 1175, Sch 9, Pt 1, para 3(c), as from a day to be appointed; words in square brackets substituted by SI 2000/1430, reg 2(1), (3), as from 26 May 2000, in relation to annual reports and reports in respect of financial years ending two months or more after that date.

Sub-s (7): definition "gross income" and the word immediately preceding it repealed by the Companies Act 2006, s 1175, Sch 9, Pt 1, para 3(b), as from a day to be appointed.

Application to limited liability partnerships: see the Limited Liability Partnerships Regulations 2001, SI 2001/1090, reg 3, Sch 1 at **[6984]**, **[6992]**.

[249AA Dormant companies

(*1*) *Subject to section 249B(2) to (5), a company is exempt from the provisions of this Part relating to the audit of accounts in respect of a financial year if—*

(*a*) *it has been dormant since its formation, or*

(*b*) *it has been dormant since the end of the previous financial year and subsection* (2) *applies.*

(*2*) *This subsection applies if the company—*

(*a*) *is entitled in respect of its individual accounts for the financial year in question to prepare accounts in accordance with section 246, or would be so entitled but for the application [to it of subsection (1A), (1B)(a) or (1C)(a) of section 247A], and*

(*b*) *is not required to prepare group accounts for that year.*

(*3*) *Subsection (1) does not apply if at any time in the financial year in question the company was—*

[[(*a*) *an authorised insurance company, a banking company, an e-money issuer, an ISD investment firm or a UCITS management company;]*

(*b*) *a person who carries on insurance market activity].*

(*4*) *A company is "dormant" during any period in which it has no significant accounting transaction.*

(*5*) *"Significant accounting transaction" means a transaction which—*

(*a*) *is required by section 221 to be entered in the company's accounting records; but*

(*b*) *is not a transaction to which subsection (6) or (7) applies.*

(*6*) *This subsection applies to a transaction arising from the taking of shares in the company by a subscriber to the memorandum as a result of an undertaking of his in the memorandum.*

(*7*) *This subsection applies to a transaction consisting of the payment of—*

(*a*) *a fee to the registrar on a change of name under section 28 (change of name),*

(*b*) *a fee to the registrar on the re-registration of a company under Part II (re-registration as a means of altering a company's status),*

(*c*) *a penalty under section 242A (penalty for failure to deliver accounts), or*

(*d*) *a fee to the registrar for the registration of an annual return under Chapter III of Part XI.]*

[247]

NOTES

Inserted by the Companies Act 1985 (Audit Exemption) (Amendment) Regulations 2000, SI 2000/1430, reg 3, as from 26 May 2000, in relation to annual reports and reports in respect of financial years ending two months or more after that date.

Repealed by the Companies Act 2006, s 1295, Sch 16, as from a day to be appointed.

Sub-s (2): words in square brackets in para (a) substituted by the Companies Act 1985 (Small Companies' Accounts and Audit) Regulations 2006, SI 2006/2782, reg 4(1), (2), as from 8 November 2006, in relation to annual accounts and reports in respect of financial years ending on or after 31 December 2006.

Sub-s (3): paras (a), (b) originally substituted by the Financial Services and Markets Act 2000 (Consequential Amendments and Repeals) Order 2001, SI 2001/3649, art 13, as from 1 December 2001; para (a) further substituted by SI 2006/2782, reg 4(1), (3), as from 8 November 2006, in relation to annual accounts and reports in respect of financial years ending on or after 31 December 2006.

Application to limited liability partnerships: see the Limited Liability Partnerships Regulations 2001, SI 2001/1090, reg 3, Sch 1 at **[6984]**, **[6992]**.

[249B Cases where exemptions not available

(*1*) *[Subject to [subsections (1A) to (1C)],] a company is not entitled to the exemption conferred by subsection (1) or (2) of section 249A in respect of a financial year if at any time within that year—*

(*a*) *it was a public company,*

[(*b*) *it was an authorised insurance company, a banking company, an e-money issuer, an ISD investment firm or a UCITS management company,]*

[(*bb*) *it carried on an insurance market activity,]*

(*c*), (*d*) …

(*e*) *it was a special register body as defined in section 117(1) of the Trade Union and Labour Relations (Consolidation) Act 1992 or an employers' association as defined in section 122 of that Act, or*

(*f*) *it was a parent company or a subsidiary undertaking.*

[(1A) A company which, apart from this subsection, would fall within subsection (1)(f) by virtue of its being a subsidiary undertaking for any period within a financial year shall not be treated as so falling if it is dormant (within the meaning of [section 249AA]) throughout that period.]

[(1B) A company which, apart from this subsection, would fall within subsection (1)(f) by virtue of its being a parent company or a subsidiary undertaking for any period within a

financial year, shall not be treated as so falling if throughout that period it was a member of a group meeting the conditions set out in subsection (1C).

(1C) The conditions referred to in subsection (1B) are—

(a) that the group qualifies as a small group, in relation to the financial year within which the period falls, for the purposes of section 249 [(or if all bodies corporate in such group were companies, would so qualify)] and is not, and was not at any time within that year, an ineligible group within the meaning of section 248(2),

(b) that the group's aggregate turnover in that year (calculated in accordance with section 249) is[, where the company referred to in subsection (1B) is a charity,] not more than £350,000 net (or £420,000 gross) [or, where the company so referred to is not a charity, [not more than £5.6 million net (or £6.72 million gross)]], and

(c) that the group's aggregate balance sheet total for that year (calculated in accordance with section 249) is [not more than £2.8 million net (or £3.36 million gross)].]

(2) Any member or members holding not less in the aggregate than 10 per cent in nominal value of the company's issued share capital or any class of it or, if the company does not have a share capital, not less than 10 per cent in number of the members of the company, may, by notice in writing deposited at the registered office of the company during a financial year but not later than one month before the end of that year, require the company to obtain an audit of its accounts for that year.

(3) Where a notice has been deposited under subsection (2), the company is not entitled to the exemption conferred by subsection (1) or (2) of section 249A [or by subsection (1) of section 249AA] in respect of the financial year to which the notice relates.

(4) A company is not entitled to the exemption conferred by subsection (1) or (2) of section 249A [or by subsection (1) of section 249AA] unless its balance sheet contains a statement by the directors—

(a) [to the effect] that for the year in question the company was entitled to exemption under subsection (1) or (2)... of section 249A [or subsection (1) of section 249AA],

[(b) to the effect that members have not required the company to obtain an audit of its accounts for the year in question in accordance with subsection (2) of this section], and

(c) [to the effect] that the directors acknowledge their responsibilities for—

(i) ensuring that the company keeps accounting records which comply with section 221, and

(ii) preparing accounts which give a true and fair view of the state of affairs of the company as at the end of the financial year and of its profit or loss for the financial year in accordance with the requirements of section 226, and which otherwise comply with the requirements of this Act relating to accounts, so far as applicable to the company.

(5) The statement required by subsection (4) shall appear in the balance sheet [above the signature required by section 233].]

[248]

NOTES

Inserted as noted to s 249A at **[246]**.

Repealed by the Companies Act 2006, s 1295, Sch 16, as from a day to be appointed. Note that this section is also amended by the 2006 Act (see below).

Sub-s (1) is amended as follows:

Words in first (outer) pair of square brackets inserted by the Companies Act 1985 (Miscellaneous Accounting Amendments) Regulations 1996, SI 1996/189, regs 10(1), (2), 16(5), in relation to any annual accounts of a company which are approved by the board of directors on or after 2 February 1996.

Words in second (inner) pair of square brackets substituted by the Companies Act 1985 (Audit Exemption) (Amendment) Regulations 1997, SI 1997/936, reg 3(1), (2), as from 15 April 1997, in relation to the annual accounts of any company for any financial year ending two months or more after that date.

Words "or (2)" repealed by the Companies Act 2006, s 1175, Sch 9, Pt 1, para 4(a), as from a day to be appointed.

Para (b) originally substituted by the Financial Services and Markets Act 2000 (Consequential Amendments and Repeals) Order 2001, SI 2001/3649, art 14(1), (2), as from 1 December 2001; further substituted by the Companies Act 1985 (Small Companies' Accounts and Audit) Regulations 2006, SI 2006/2782, reg 5(1), (2), as from 8 November 2006, in relation to annual accounts and reports in respect of financial years ending on or after 31 December 2006.

Para (bb) inserted by SI 2001/3649, art 14(1), (3), as from 1 December 2001.
Para (c) repealed by the Financial Services and Markets Act 2000 (Dissolution of Insurance Brokers Registration Council) (Consequential Provisions) Order 2001, SI 2001/1283, art 3(3)(a), as from 30 April 2001.
Para (d) repealed by SI 2006/2782, reg 5(1), (3), as from 8 November 2006, in relation to annual accounts and reports in respect of financial years ending on or after 31 December 2006.
Sub-s (1A): inserted by SI 1996/189, regs 10(1), (3), 16(5), in relation to any annual accounts of a company which are approved by the board of directors on or after 2 February 1996; words in square brackets substituted by the Companies Act 1985 (Audit Exemption) (Amendment) Regulations 2000, SI 2000/1430, reg 4(1), (2), as from 26 May 2000, in relation to annual accounts and reports in respect of financial years ending two months or more after that date.
Sub-s (1B): inserted, together with sub-s (1C), by SI 1997/936, reg 3(1), (3), as from 15 April 1997, in relation to the annual accounts of any company for any financial year ending two months or more after that date.
Sub-s (1C): inserted as noted above; words in first, second and third (outer) pairs of square brackets inserted by SI 2000/1430, reg 4(1), (3), as from 26 May 2000, in relation to annual accounts and reports in respect of financial years ending two months or more after that date; words in fourth (inner) and fifth pairs of square brackets substituted by the Companies Act 1985 (Accounts of Small and Medium-Sized Enterprises and Audit Exemption) (Amendment) Regulations 2004, SI 2004/16, regs 5, 7(4), as from 30 January 2004, in relation to financial years ending two months or more after that date; for the words "£350,000 net (or £420,000 gross)" in para (b) there are substituted the words "£700,000 net (or £840,000 gross)" by the Charities Act 2006, s 32(2), as from 27 February 2007, except in relation to Scotland; words from "where the company referred to in subsection (1B)" to "is not a charity" repealed by the Companies Act 2006, s 1175, Sch 9, Pt 1, para 4(b), as from a day to be appointed.
Sub-s (3): words "or (2)" repealed by the Companies Act 2006, s 1175, Sch 9, Pt 1, para 4(c), as from a day to be appointed; words in square brackets inserted by SI 2000/1430, reg 4(1), (4), as from 26 May 2000, in relation to annual accounts and reports in respect of financial years ending two months or more after that date.
Sub-s (4): words "or (2)" (in both places they occur) repealed by the Companies Act 2006, s 1175, Sch 9, Pt 1, para 4(d), as from a day to be appointed; words in first and third pairs of square brackets inserted, words omitted repealed, and para (b) substituted, by SI 2000/1430, reg 4(1), (5), as from 26 May 2000, in relation to annual accounts and reports in respect of financial years ending two months or more after that date; words in second and fourth pairs of square brackets inserted by SI 1996/189, regs 10(1), (4), 16(1), in relation to any financial year ending on or after 2 February 1996 (subject to transitional provisions in relation to financial years ending on or before 24 March 1996).
Sub-s (5): words in square brackets substituted by SI 1996/189, regs 10(1), (5), 16(1), in relation to any financial year ending on or after 2 February 1996 (subject to transitional provisions as noted above).
Application to limited liability partnerships: see the Limited Liability Partnerships Regulations 2001, SI 2001/1090, reg 3, Sch 1 at **[6984]**, **[6992]**.

[249C The report required for the purposes of section 249A(2)

(1) The report required for the purposes of section 249A(2) shall be prepared by a person (referred to in this Part as "the reporting accountant") who is eligible under section 249D.

(2) The report shall state whether in the opinion of the reporting accountant making it—
- *(a) the accounts of the company for the financial year in question are in agreement with the accounting records kept by the company under section 221, and*
- *(b) having regard only to, and on the basis of, the information contained in those accounting records, those accounts have been drawn up in a manner consistent with the provisions of this Act specified in subsection (6), so far as applicable to the company.*

(3) The report shall also state that in the opinion of the reporting accountant, having regard only to, and on the basis of, the information contained in the accounting records kept by the company under section 221, the company satisfied the requirements of subsection (4) of section 249A … for the financial year in question, and did not fall within section 249B(1)(a) to (f) at any time within that financial year.

(4) The report shall state the name of the reporting accountant and be signed by him.

(5) Where the reporting accountant is a body corporate or partnership, any reference to signature of the report, or any copy of the report, by the reporting accountant is a reference to signature in the name of the body corporate or partnership by a person authorised to sign on its behalf.

(6) The provisions referred to in subsection (2)(b) are—
- *(a) [section 226A(3)] and Schedule 4,*
- *(b) section 231 and paragraphs 7 to 9A and 13(1), (3) and (4) of Schedule 5, and*
- *(c) section 232 and Schedule 6,*

where appropriate as modified by [section 246(2) and (3)].]

[249]

NOTES

Inserted as noted to s 249A at **[246]**.

Repealed by the Companies Act 2006, s 1175, Sch 9, Pt 1, para 5, as from a day to be appointed. Note that this section is also repealed by s 1295 of, and Sch 16 to, the 2006 Act, as from a day to be appointed.

Sub-s (3): words omitted repealed by the Companies Act 1985 (Audit Exemption) (Amendment) Regulations 2000, SI 2000/1430, reg 8(3), as from 26 May 2000, in relation to annual reports and reports in respect of financial years ending two months or more after that date.

Sub-s (6): words in first pair of square brackets substituted by the Companies Act 1985 (International Accounting Standards and Other Accounting Amendments) Regulations 2004, SI 2004/2947, reg 3, Sch 1, para 16, as from 12 November 2004, in relation to companies' financial years which begin on or after 1 January 2005; words in second pair of square brackets substituted by the Companies Act 1985 (Accounts of Small and Medium-sized Companies and Minor Accounting Amendments) Regulations 1997, SI 1997/220, reg 7(3), in relation to annual accounts approved by the board of directors on or after 1 March 1997, and to directors' and auditors' reports on such accounts (subject to transitional provisions in relation to a financial year of a company ending on or before 24 March 1997).

Application to limited liability partnerships: see the Limited Liability Partnerships Regulations 2001, SI 2001/1090, reg 3, Sch 1 at **[6984]**, **[6992]**.

[249D The reporting accountant

[(1) The reporting accountant shall be either—

(a) any member of a body listed in subsection (3) who, under the rules of the body—

(i) is entitled to engage in public practice, and

(ii) is not ineligible for appointment as a reporting accountant, or

(b) any person (whether or not a member of any such body) who—

(i) is subject to the rules of any such body in seeking appointment or acting as auditor under Chapter V of Part XI, and

(ii) under those rules, is eligible for appointment as auditor under that Chapter.

(1A) In subsection (1), references to the rules of a body listed in subsection (3) are to the rules (whether or not laid down by the body itself) which the body has power to enforce and which are relevant for the purposes of Part II of the Companies Act 1989 or this section.

This includes rules relating to the admission and expulsion of members of the body, so far as relevant for the purposes of that Part or this section.]

(2) An individual, a body corporate or a partnership may be appointed as a reporting accountant, and section 26 of the Companies Act 1989 (effect of appointment of partnership) shall apply to the appointment as reporting accountant of a partnership constituted under the law of England and Wales or Northern Ireland, or under the law of any other country or territory in which a partnership is not a legal person.

(3) The bodies referred to in [subsections (1) and (1A)] are—

(a) the Institute of Chartered Accountants in England and Wales,

(b) the Institute of Chartered Accountants of Scotland,

(c) the Institute of Chartered Accountants in Ireland,

(d) [the Association of Chartered Certified Accountants], ...

(e) the Association of Authorised Public Accountants.

(f) the Association of Accounting Technicians,

(g) the Association of International Accountants, ...

(h) the Chartered Institute of Management Accountants[, and

(i) the Institute of Chartered Secretaries and Administrators].]

(4) A person is ineligible for appointment by a company as reporting accountant if he would be ineligible for appointment as an auditor of that company under section 27 of the Companies Act 1989 (ineligibility on ground of lack of independence).]

[250]

NOTES

Inserted as noted to s 249A at **[246]**.

Repealed by the Companies Act 2006, s 1175, Sch 9, Pt 1, para 6, as from a day to be appointed. Note that this section is also repealed by s 1295 of, and Sch 16 to, the 2006 Act, as from a day to be appointed.

Sub-ss (1), (1A): substituted, for original sub-s (1), by the Companies Act 1985 (Audit Exemption) (Amendment) Regulations 1995, SI 1995/589, reg 2(1), (2), as from 30 March 1995 (for transitional provisions see the note below).

Sub-s (3): words in first pair of square brackets substituted by SI 1995/589, reg 2(1), (3), as from 30 March 1995 (for transitional provisions see the note below); words in square brackets in para (d) substituted by the Companies Act 1985 (Audit Exemption) (Amendment) Regulations 1997, SI 1997/936, reg 4, in relation to the annual accounts of any company for any financial year ending two months or more after 15 April 1997; word omitted from para (d) repealed, and paras (f)–(h) added, by the Companies Act 1985 (Audit Exemption) (Amendment) Regulations 1996, SI 1996/3080, reg 2, as from 1 January 1997; word omitted from para (g) repealed, and para (i) added, by the Companies Act 1985 (Accounts of Small and Medium-Sized Enterprises and Audit Exemption) (Amendment) Regulations 2004, SI 2004/16, regs 6, 7(5), as from 30 January 2004, in relation to financial years ending on or after that date.

Transitional provisions: the Companies Act 1985 (Audit Exemption) (Amendment) Regulations 1995, SI 1995/589, reg 3 provides as follows—

"(1) This Regulation applies to any report made for the purposes of section 249A(2) of the Companies Act 1985 ("the 1985 Act") before the commencement of these Regulations.

(2) Any report to which this Regulation applies which was prepared by a person who was not eligible under section 249D of the 1985 Act to prepare it, but who would have been so eligible if the amendments made by regulation 2 of these Regulations had been in force when the report was prepared, shall be taken for the purposes of the 1985 Act to have been prepared by a person who was eligible under that section.".

Application to limited liability partnerships: see the Limited Liability Partnerships Regulations 2001, SI 2001/1090, reg 3, Sch 1 at **[6984]**, **[6992]**.

[249E Effect of exemptions

(1) Where the directors of a company have taken advantage of the exemption conferred by section 249A(1) [or 249AA(1)]—

(a) *sections 238 and 239 (right to receive or demand copies of accounts and reports) shall have effect with the omission of references to the auditors' report;*

(b) *no copy of an auditors' report need be delivered to the registrar or laid before the company in general meeting;*

(c) *subsections (3) to (5) of section 271 (accounts by reference to which distribution to be justified) shall not apply.*

[(1A) Where the directors of a company have taken advantage of the exemption conferred by section 249AA, then for the purposes of that section the company shall be treated as a company entitled to prepare accounts in accordance with section 246 even though it is a member of an ineligible group.]

(2) *Where the directors of a company have taken advantage of the exemption conferred by section 249A(2)—*

(a) *subsections (2) to (4) of section 236 (which require copies of the auditors' report to state the names of the auditors) shall have effect with the substitution for references to the auditors and the auditors' report of references to the reporting accountant and the report made for the purposes of section 249A(2) respectively;*

(b) *sections 238 and 239 (right to receive or demand copies of accounts and reports), section 241 (accounts and reports to be laid before company in general meeting) and section 242 (accounts and reports to be delivered to the registrar) shall have effect with the substitution for references to the auditors' report of references to the report made for the purposes of section 249A(2);*

(c) *subsections (3) to (5) of section 271 (accounts by reference to which distribution to be justified) shall not apply;*

(d) *[sections 389A(1) and 389B(1) and (5)] (rights to information) shall have effect with the substitution for references to [an auditor] of references to the reporting accountant.]*

[251]

NOTES

Inserted as noted to s 249A at **[246]**.

Repealed by the Companies Act 2006, s 1295, Sch 16, as from a day to be appointed. Note that this section is also amended by the 2006 Act (see below).

Sub-s (1): words in square brackets inserted by the Companies Act 1985 (Audit Exemption) (Amendment) Regulations 2000, SI 2000/1430, reg 8(4), as from 26 May 2000, in relation to annual accounts and reports in respect of financial years ending two months or more after that date.

Sub-s (1A): inserted by SI 2000/1430, reg 8(5), as from 26 May 2000, in relation to annual accounts and reports in respect of financial years ending two months or more after that date.

Sub-s (2): repealed by the Companies Act 2006, s 1175, Sch 9, Pt 1, para 7, as from a day to be appointed; words in square brackets in para (d) substituted by the Companies (Audit, Investigations and Community Enterprise) Act 2004, s 25, Sch 2, Pt 2, paras 5, 6, as from 6 April 2005.

Application to limited liability partnerships: see the Limited Liability Partnerships Regulations 2001, SI 2001/1090, reg 3, Sch 1 at **[6984]**, **[6992]**.

250 (*Repealed by the Companies Act 1985 (Audit Exemption) (Amendment) Regulations 2000, SI 2000/1430, reg 8(6), as from 26 May 2000, in relation to annual accounts and reports in respect of financial years ending two months or more after that date.*)

[[Summary financial statement]

251 Provision of summary financial statement to shareholders

(1) [A company] need not, in such cases as may be specified by regulations made by the Secretary of State, and provided any conditions so specified are complied with, send copies of the documents referred to in [section 238(1A)] to [entitled persons], but may instead send them a summary financial statement.

[In this section—

"entitled persons", in relation to a company, means such of the persons specified in paragraphs (a) to (c) of subsection (1) of section 238 as are or would apart from this section be entitled to be sent copies of those documents relating to the company which are referred to in that subsection;

["summary financial statement" means a statement that is derived from the company's annual accounts and (in the case of a quoted company) the directors' remuneration report and prepared in accordance with this section and regulations made under it;]

[.....

.....]]

(2) Copies of the documents referred to in [section 238(1A)] shall, however, be sent to [any entitled person] who wishes to receive them; and the Secretary of State may by regulations make provision as to the manner in which it is to be ascertained [(whether before or after he becomes an entitled person)] whether [an entitled person] wishes to receive them.

[(2ZA) ...]

[(2ZB) A company that sends to an entitled person a summary financial statement instead of a copy of its directors' report shall—

- *(a) include in the statement the explanatory material required to be included in the directors' report by section 234ZZA(5), or*
- *(b) send that material to the entitled person at the same time as it sends the statement.*

For the purposes of paragraph (b), subsections (2A) to (2E) apply in relation to the material referred to in that paragraph as they apply in relation to a summary financial statement.]

[(2A) References in this section to sending a summary financial statement to an entitled person include references to using electronic communications for sending the statement to such address as may for the time being be notified to the company by that person for that purpose.

(2B) For the purposes of this section a summary financial statement is also to be treated as sent to an entitled person where—

- *(a) the company and that person have agreed to his having access to summary financial statements on a web site (instead of their being sent to him);*
- *(b) the statement is a statement to which that agreement applies; and*
- *(c) that person is notified, in a manner for the time being agreed for the purpose between him and the company, of—*
  - *(i) the publication of the statement on a web site;*
  - *(ii) the address of that web site; and*
  - *(iii) the place on that web site where the statement may be accessed, and how it may be accessed.*

(2C) For the purposes of this section a statement treated in accordance with subsection (2B) as sent to an entitled person is to be treated as sent to him if, and only if—

- *(a) the statement is published on the web site throughout a period beginning at least 21 days before the date of the meeting at which the accounts and [directors' remuneration report] from which the statement is derived are to be laid and ending with the conclusion of that meeting; and*

PART I COMPANIES LEGISLATION

(*b*) *the notification given for the purposes of paragraph* (*c*) *of that subsection is given not less than 21 days before the date of the meeting.*

(2D) Nothing in [subsection ... (2C)] shall invalidate the proceedings of a meeting where—

[(a) any ... statement that is required to be published on a web site as mentioned in those subsections is published for a part, but not all, of the period mentioned in those subsections; and]

(*b*) *the failure to publish that [...] statement throughout that period is wholly attributable to circumstances which it would not be reasonable to have expected the company to prevent or avoid.*

(2E) A company may, notwithstanding any provision to the contrary in its articles, take advantage of any of subsections (2A) to (2D).]

[(3) The summary financial statement must—

(*a*) *be in such form, and*

(*b*) *contain such information,*

as the Secretary of State may by regulations specify, including information derived from the company's directors' report ...

(3A) Nothing in this section or regulations made under it prevents a company from including in its summary financial statement additional information derived from the company's annual accounts, directors' remuneration report [or directors' report].]

[(4) Every summary financial statement shall—

(*a*) *state that it is only a summary of information in the company's annual accounts, ... and (in the case of a quoted company) the directors' remuneration report;*

[(aa) state whether it contains additional information derived from the directors' report ... and, if so, state that it does not contain the full text of that report ... ;

(*ab*) *state how an entitled person can obtain a full copy of the documents referred to in section 238(1A);*

(*ac*) *...]*

(*b*) *contain a statement by the company's auditors of their opinion as to whether the summary financial statement—*

[(i) is consistent with the company's annual accounts and directors' remuneration report and (where information derived from the directors' report ... is included in the statement) with that report ... , and

(ii)] complies with the requirements of this section and regulations made under it;

(*c*) *state whether the auditors' report on the annual accounts, or on the annual accounts and the auditable part of the directors' remuneration report, was unqualified or qualified, and if it was qualified set out the report in full together with any further material needed to understand the qualification;*

[(ca) state whether, in that report, the auditor's statement under section 235(3) (whether directors' report is consistent with accounts) was qualified or unqualified and, if qualified, set out the qualified statement in full together with any further material needed to understand the qualification;]

(*d*) *state whether that auditors' report contained a statement under—*

(*i*) *section 237(2) (accounting records or returns inadequate or accounts or directors' remuneration report not agreeing with records and returns); or*

(*ii*) *section 237(3) (failure to obtain necessary information and explanations),*

and if so, set out the statement in full.]

(5) Regulations under this section shall be made by statutory instrument which shall be subject to annulment in pursuance of a resolution of either House of Parliament.

(6) If default is made in complying with this section or regulations made under it, the company and every officer of it who is in default is guilty of an offence and liable to a fine.

(7) Section 240 (requirements in connection with publication of accounts) does not apply in relation to the provision to [entitled persons] of a summary financial statement in accordance with this section.]

[252]

NOTES

Inserted, together with preceding heading, by CA 1989, s 15, as from 1 March 1990. The heading preceding this section was subsequently substituted by the Companies Act 1985 (International Accounting Standards and Other Accounting Amendments) Regulations 2004, SI 2004/2947, reg 11(1), as from 12 November 2004, in relation to companies' financial years which begin on or after 1 January 2005.

Repealed by the Companies Act 2006, s 1295, Sch 16, as from 20 January 2007 (in so far as relating to sub-ss (2A)–(2E)), and as from a day to be appointed (otherwise) (for transitional provisions see the note to s 238 at **[225]**). Note that this section is also amended by the 2006 Act (see below).

Sub-s (1) is amended as follows:

Words in first pair of square brackets substituted by SI 2004/2947, reg 11(2)(a), as from 12 November 2004, in relation to companies' financial years which begin on or after 1 January 2005.

Words in second pair of square brackets substituted by the Companies Act 1985 (Operating and Financial Review and Directors' Report etc) Regulations 2005, SI 2005/1011, reg 12(1), (2)(a), as from 22 March 2005, in relation to companies' financial years which begin on or after 1 April 2005.

Words in third pair and fourth (outer) pair of square brackets substituted by SI 1992/3003, reg 3, as from 4 December 1992.

Definition "summary financial statement" inserted by SI 2005/1011, reg 12(1), (2)(b), as from 22 March 2005, in relation to companies' financial years which begin on or after 1 April 2005.

Definitions "listed" and "the official list" substituted, for original definition "listed" and the word immediately preceding it, by the Financial Services and Markets Act 2000 (Consequential Amendments and Repeals) Order 2001, SI 2001/3649, art 15, as from 1 December 2001, and repealed by SI 2004/2947, reg 11(2)(b), as from 12 November 2004, in relation to companies' financial years which begin on or after 1 January 2005.

Sub-s (2): words in first pair of square brackets substituted by SI 2005/1011, reg 12(1), (3), as from 22 March 2005, in relation to companies' financial years which begin on or after 1 April 2005; words in second and fourth pairs of square brackets substituted, and words in third pair of square brackets inserted, by SI 1992/3003, reg 3(1), (4), as from 4 December 1992.

Sub-s (2ZA): inserted by SI 2005/1011, reg 12(1), (4), as from 22 March 2005, in relation to companies' financial years which begin on or after 1 April 2005; repealed by the Companies Act 1985 (Operating and Financial Review) (Repeal) Regulations 2005, SI 2005/3442, reg 2(2)(a), Sch 1, para 14(1), (2), as from 12 January 2006.

Sub-s (2ZB): inserted by the Companies Act 2006, s 992(1), (5), (6), as from 6 April 2007, in relation to directors' reports for financial years beginning on or after 20 May 2006.

Sub-ss (2A), (2B), (2E): inserted, together with sub-ss (2C), (2D), by the Companies Act 1985 (Electronic Communications) Order 2000, SI 2000/3373, art 14, as from 22 December 2000, and repealed as noted above.

Sub-s (2C): inserted and repealed as noted above; words in square brackets substituted by SI 2005/1011, reg 12(1), (5), as from 22 March 2005, in relation to companies' financial years which begin on or after 1 April 2005.

Sub-s (2D): inserted and repealed as noted above; words in first pair of square brackets substituted, para (a) substituted, and words in square brackets in para (b) inserted, by SI 2005/1011, reg 12(1), (6), as from 22 March 2005, in relation to companies' financial years which begin on or after 1 April 2005; words omitted repealed by SI 2005/3442, reg 2(2)(a), Sch 1, para 14(1), (3), as from 12 January 2006.

Sub-s (3): substituted by the Directors' Remuneration Report Regulations 2002, SI 2002/1986, reg 8(1), (2), as from 1 August 2002, with effect as respects companies' financial years ending on or after 31 December 2002; further substituted by new sub-s (3), (3A) by SI 2005/1011, reg 12(1), (7), as from 22 March 2005, in relation to companies' financial years which begin on or after 1 April 2005; words omitted repealed by SI 2005/3442, reg 2(2)(a), Sch 1, para 14(1), (4), as from 12 January 2006.

Sub-s (3A): substituted as noted above; words in square brackets substituted by SI 2005/3442, reg 2(2)(a), Sch 1, para 14(1), (5), as from 12 January 2006.

Sub-s (4): substituted by SI 2002/1986, reg 8(1), (3), as from 1 August 2002, with effect as respects companies' financial years ending on or after 31 December 2002; words omitted from para (a) repealed, paras (aa)–(a), (ca) inserted, and words in square brackets in para (b) substituted, by SI 2005/1011, reg 12(1), (8), as from 22 March 2005, in relation to companies' financial years which begin on or after 1 April 2005; words omitted from paras (aa), (b)(i), and the whole of para (ac), repealed, and para (ca) substituted, by SI 2005/3442, reg 2(2)(a), Sch 1, para 14(1), (6), as from 12 January 2006.

Sub-s (7): words in square brackets substituted by SI 1992/3003, reg 3(1), (5), as from 4 December 1992.

Transitional provisions: the Companies Act 1985 (Operating and Financial Review and Directors' Report etc) Regulations 2005, SI 2005/1011, reg 13 provides as follows (note that by virtue of reg 1(2) of the 2005 Regulations, they came into force on 22 March 2005)—

"13 Transitional provision

As respects companies' financial years beginning on or after 1st April 2005, regulations made by the Secretary of State under section 251 of the 1985 Act before the date on which these Regulations come into force have effect as if—

(a) any requirement in the regulations that a summary financial statement contain information derived from the company's directors' report was omitted, and

(b) the regulations had been made (with those omissions) under section 251 as amended by these Regulations.".

Application to limited liability partnerships: see the Limited Liability Partnerships Regulations 2001, SI 2001/1090, reg 3, Sch 1 at **[6984]**, **[6992]**. Note also that nothing in the Companies Act 2006 (Commencement No 2, Consequential Amendments, Transitional Provisions and Savings) Order 2007, SI 2007/1093 affects any provision of this Act as applied by the 2001 Regulations to LLPs (see art 12(1) at **[7624]** and the introductory notes to this Act).

Note: this section is amended by s 992 (in Part 28) of the Companies Act 2006 as noted above. Part 28 is the domestic implementation of the Takeovers Directive (Directive of the European Parliament and of the Council 2004/25/EC on takeover bids) and was brought into force on 6 April 2007. The Takeovers Directive had to be implemented by 20 May 2006 and this was achieved by the Takeovers Directive (Interim Implementation) Regulations 2006, SI 2006/1183 (see reg 27 of those Regulations as to summary financial statements for a financial year beginning on or after that date (at **[7535]**)). The 2006 Interim Regulations were also revoked as from 6 April 2007 (subject to savings).

Regulations: the Companies (Summary Financial Statement) Regulations 1995, SI 1995/2092 at **[6882]**.

[Private companies

252 Election to dispense with laying of accounts and reports before general meeting

(1) A private company may elect (by elective resolution in accordance with section 379A) to dispense with the laying of accounts and reports before the company in general meeting.

(2) An election has effect in relation to the accounts and reports in respect of the financial year in which the election is made and subsequent financial years.

(3) Whilst an election is in force, the references in the following provisions of this Act to the laying of accounts before the company in general meeting shall be read as references to the sending of copies of the accounts to members and others under section 238(1)—

(a) section 235(1) (accounts on which auditors are to report),

(b) section 270(3) and (4) (accounts by reference to which distributions are justified), and

(c) section 320(2) (accounts relevant for determining company's net assets for purposes of ascertaining whether approval required for certain transactions);

and the requirement in section 271(4) that the auditors' statement under that provision be laid before the company in general meeting shall be read as a requirement that it be sent to members and others along with the copies of the accounts sent to them under section 238(1).

(4) If an election under this section ceases to have effect, section 241 applies in relation to the accounts and reports in respect of the financial year in which the election ceases to have effect and subsequent financial years.]

[253]

NOTES

Inserted, together with preceding heading and s 253, by CA 1989, s 16, as from 1 April 1990.

Repealed by the Companies Act 2006, s 1295, Sch 16, as from 1 October 2007. For savings see the note below.

Savings: this section continues to have effect in relation to annual accounts or reports for financial years ending before 1 October 2007 (see the draft Companies Act 2006 (Commencement No 3, Consequential Amendments, Transitional Provisions and Savings) Order 2007, Sch 3, para 49 at **[A12]**).

Application to limited liability partnerships: see the Limited Liability Partnerships Regulations 2001, SI 2001/1090, reg 3, Sch 1 at **[6984]**, **[6992]**. Note also that nothing in the draft Companies Act 2006 (Commencement No 3, Consequential Amendments, Transitional Provisions and Savings) Order 2007 affects any provision of this Act as applied by the 2001 Regulations to LLPs (see art 12(2) at **[A12]** and the introductory notes to this Act).

[253 Right of shareholder to require laying of accounts

(1) Where an election under section 252 is in force, the copies of the accounts and reports sent out in accordance with section 238(1)—

(a) shall be sent not less than 28 days before the end of the period allowed for laying and delivering accounts and reports, and

(b) shall be accompanied, in the case of a member of the company, by a notice informing him of his right to require the laying of the accounts and reports before a general meeting;

and section 238(5) (penalty for default) applies in relation to the above requirements as to the requirements contained in that section.

(2) Before the end of the period of 28 days beginning with the day on which the accounts and reports are sent out in accordance with section 238(1), any member or auditor of the company may by notice in writing deposited at the registered office of the company require that a general meeting be held for the purpose of laying the accounts and reports before the company.

[(2A) …]

(3) If the directors do not within 21 days from the date of[—

(a) the deposit of a notice containing a requirement under subsection (2), or

(b) the receipt of such a requirement contained in an electronic communication,

proceed] duly to convene a meeting, the person who [required the holding of the meeting] may do so himself.

(4) A meeting so convened shall not be held more than three months from that date and shall be convened in the same manner, as nearly as possible, as that in which meetings are to be convened by directors.

(5) Where the directors do not duly convene a meeting, any reasonable expenses incurred by reason of that failure by the person who [required the holding of the meeting] shall be made good to him by the company, and shall be recouped by the company out of any fees, or other remuneration in respect of their services, due or to become due to such of the directors as were in default.

(6) The directors shall be deemed not to have duly convened a meeting if they convene a meeting for a date more than 28 days after the date of the notice convening it.]

[254]

NOTES

Inserted as noted to s 252 at **[253]**.

Repealed by the Companies Act 2006, s 1295, Sch 16, as from 1 October 2007. For savings see the note below.

Sub-s (2A): inserted by the Companies Act 1985 (Electronic Communications) Order 2000, SI 2000/3373, art 15(1), (2), as from 22 December 2000, and repealed as noted above

Sub-ss (3), (5): words in square brackets substituted by SI 2000/3373, art 15(1), (3), (4), as from 22 December 2000.

Savings: this section continues to have effect in relation to annual accounts or reports for financial years ending before 1 October 2007 (see the draft Companies Act 2006 (Commencement No 3, Consequential Amendments, Transitional Provisions and Savings) Order 2007, Sch 3, para 49 at **[A12]**).

Application to limited liability partnerships: see the Limited Liability Partnerships Regulations 2001, SI 2001/1090, reg 3, Sch 1 at **[6984]**, **[6992]**. Note also that nothing in the draft Companies Act 2006 (Commencement No 3, Consequential Amendments, Transitional Provisions and Savings) Order 2007 affects any provision of this Act as applied by the 2001 Regulations to LLPs (see art 12(2) at **[A12]** and the introductory notes to this Act).

[Unlimited companies

254 Exemption from requirement to deliver accounts and reports

(1) The directors of an unlimited company are not required to deliver accounts and reports to the registrar in respect of a financial year if the following conditions are met.

(2) The conditions are that at no time during the relevant accounting reference period—

(a) has the company been, to its knowledge, a subsidiary undertaking of an undertaking which was then limited, or

(b) have there been, to its knowledge, exercisable by or on behalf of two or more undertakings which were then limited, rights which if exercisable by one of them would have made the company a subsidiary undertaking of it, or

(c) has the company been a parent company of an undertaking which was then limited.

The references above to an undertaking being limited at a particular time are to an undertaking (under whatever law established) the liability of whose members is at that time limited.

(3) The exemption conferred by this section does not apply [if—

(a) the company is a banking [or insurance] company or the parent company of a banking [or insurance] group, or

(*b*) *the company is a qualifying company within the meaning of the Partnerships and Unlimited Companies (Accounts) Regulations 1993, …*

(*c*)] …

(*4*) *Where a company is exempt by virtue of this section from the obligation to deliver accounts, section 240 (requirements in connection with publication of accounts) has effect with the following modifications—*

(*a*) *in subsection (3)(b) for the words from "whether statutory accounts" to "have been delivered to the registrar" substitute "that the company is exempt from the requirement to deliver statutory accounts", and*

(*b*) *in subsection (5) for "as required to be delivered to the registrar under section 242" substitute "as prepared in accordance with this Part and approved by the board of directors".]*

[255]

NOTES

Inserted, together with preceding heading, by CA 1989, s 17, as from 1 April 1990.

Repealed by the Companies Act 2006, s 1295, Sch 16, as from a day to be appointed.

Sub-s (3): words in first (outer) pair of square brackets substituted (for words inserted by the Companies Act 1985 (Bank Accounts) Regulations 1991, SI 1991/2705, reg 6, Sch 2, para 1, as from 2 December 1991), by the Partnerships and Unlimited Companies (Accounts) Regulations 1993, SI 1993/1820, reg 10, as from 21 July 1993; words in second and third (inner) pairs of square brackets inserted by the Companies Act 1985 (Insurance Companies Accounts) Regulations 1993, SI 1993/3246, reg 5(1), Sch 2, para 2, as from 19 December 1993, subject to exemptions in relation to certain companies contained in reg 6 (at **[6765]**) and general transitional provisions in reg 7 (at **[6766]**); para (c) and the word immediately preceding it repealed by the Regulatory Reform (Trading Stamps) Order 2005, SI 2005/781, art 6, Schedule, as from 6 April 2005.

Application to limited liability partnerships: see the Limited Liability Partnerships Regulations 2001, SI 2001/1090, reg 3, Sch 1 at **[6984]**, **[6992]**.

[Banking and insurance companies and groups

255 Special provisions for banking and insurance companies

(*1*) *A banking company shall prepare its individual accounts in accordance with Part I of Schedule 9 rather than Schedule 4.*

(*2*) *An insurance company [shall] prepare its individual accounts in accordance with Part I of Schedule 9A rather than Schedule 4.*

(*3*) *Accounts so prepared shall contain a statement that they are prepared in accordance with the special provisions of this Part relating to banking companies or insurance companies, as the case may be.*

(*4*) *In relation to the preparation of individual accounts in accordance with the special provisions of this Part, the references to Schedule 4 in section 226(4) and (5) (relationship between specific requirements and duty to give true and fair view) shall be read as references to the provisions of Part I of Schedule 9, in the case of the accounts of banking companies, or to the provisions of Part I of Schedule 9A, in the case of the accounts of insurance companies.*

[(4A) References to Companies Act individual accounts include accounts prepared in accordance with this section.

(4B) This section does not apply to banking companies and insurance companies that prepare IAS individual accounts.]

(*5*) … *]*

[256]

NOTES

Substituted, together with ss 255A, 255B, for ss 255, 255A, 255B (as inserted by CA 1989, s 18(1), as from 1 April 1990), by the Companies Act 1985 (Bank Accounts) Regulations 1991, SI 1991/2705, regs 3, 9, as from 2 December 1991 (subject to transitional provisions in relation to a financial year of a company beginning before 23 December 1992).

Repealed by the Companies Act 2006, s 1295, Sch 16, as from a day to be appointed.

Sub-s (2): word in square brackets substituted by the Companies Act 1985 (Insurance Companies Accounts) Regulations 1993, SI 1993/3246, reg 2(1), as from 19 December 1993, subject to exemptions in relation to certain companies contained in reg 6 (at **[6765]**) and general transitional provisions in reg 7 (at **[6766]**).

Sub-ss (4A), (4B): inserted by the Companies Act 1985 (International Accounting Standards and Other Accounting Amendments) Regulations 2004, SI 2004/2947, reg 3, Sch 1, paras 1, 17, as from 12 November 2004, in relation to companies' financial years which begin on or after 1 January 2005.

Sub-s (5): repealed by SI 1993/3246, reg 2(2), as from 19 December 1993 (subject to exemptions and transitional provisions as noted above).

Application to limited liability partnerships: see the Limited Liability Partnerships Regulations 2001, SI 2001/1090, reg 3, Sch 1 at **[6984]**, **[6992]**.

[255A Special provisions for banking and insurance groups

(1) The parent company of a banking group shall prepare group accounts in accordance with the provisions of this Part as modified by Part II of Schedule 9.

(2) The parent company of an insurance group [shall] prepare group accounts in accordance with the provisions of this Part as modified by Part II of Schedule 9A.

(3) Accounts so prepared shall contain a statement that they are prepared in accordance with the special provisions of this Part relating to banking groups or to insurance groups, as the case may be.

[(4) References in this Part to a banking group are to a group where the parent company is a banking company or where—

(a) the parent company's principal subsidiary undertakings are wholly or mainly credit institutions, and

(b) the parent company does not itself carry on any material business apart from the acquisition, management and disposal of interests in subsidiary undertakings.

(5) References in this Part to an insurance group are to a group where the parent company is an insurance company or where—

(a) the parent company's principal subsidiary undertakings are wholly or mainly insurance companies, and

(b) the parent company does not itself carry on any material business apart from the acquisition, management and disposal of interests in subsidiary undertakings.

(5A) For the purposes of subsections (4) and (5) above—

(a) a parent company's principal subsidiary undertakings are the subsidiary undertakings of the company whose results or financial position would principally affect the figures shown in the group accounts, and

(b) the management of interests in subsidiary undertakings includes the provision of services to such undertakings.]

(6) In relation to the preparation of group accounts in accordance with the special provisions of this Part:

(a) the references to the provisions of Schedule 4A in [section 227A(4) and (5)] (relationship between specific requirements and duty to give true and fair view) shall be read as references to those provisions as modified by Part II of Schedule 9, in the case of the group accounts of a banking group, or Part II of Schedule 9A, in the case of the group accounts of an insurance group; and

(b) the reference to paragraphs 52 to 57 of Schedule 4 in section 230(2) (relief from obligation to comply with those paragraphs where group accounts prepared) shall be read as a reference to paragraphs [75 to 77], 80 and 81 of Part I of Schedule 9, in the case of the group accounts of a banking group[, and as a reference to paragraphs 73, 74, 79 and 80 of Part I of Schedule 9A, in the case of the group accounts of an insurance group].

[(6A) References to Companies Act group accounts include accounts prepared in accordance with subsections (1) to (3).

(6B) Subsections (1) to (3) and (6) do not apply to parent companies of banking groups or insurance groups that prepare IAS group accounts.]

(7) …

[257]

NOTES

Substituted as noted to s 255 at **[256]**.

Repealed by the Companies Act 2006, s 1295, Sch 16, as from a day to be appointed.

Sub-s (2): word in square brackets substituted by the Companies Act 1985 (Insurance Companies Accounts) Regulations 1993, SI 1993/3246, reg 3(1), as from 19 December 1993, subject to exemptions in relation to certain companies contained in reg 6 (at **[6765]**) and general transitional provisions in reg 7 (at **[6766]**).

Sub-ss (4), (5), (5A): substituted, for original sub-ss (4), (5), by SI 1993/3246, reg 3(2), as from 19 December 1993 (subject to exemptions and transitional provisions as noted above).

Sub-s (6): words in first pair of square brackets substituted by the Companies Act 1985 (International Accounting Standards and Other Accounting Amendments) Regulations 2004, SI 2004/2947, reg 3, Sch 1, paras 1, 18(1), (2), as from 12 November 2004, in relation to companies' financial years which begin on or after 1 January 2005; words in second pair of square brackets substituted by the Companies Act 1985 (Miscellaneous Accounting Amendments) Regulations 1996, SI 1996/189, regs 15(2), 16(1), in relation to any financial year ending on or after 2 February 1996 (subject to transitional provisions in relation to financial years ending on or before 24 March 1996) (note, in relation to this amendment, the word "paragraphs" has not been substituted as specified, in order to preserve the sense of the text); words in third pair of square brackets added by SI 1993/3246, reg 3(3), as from 19 December 1993 (subject to exemptions and transitional provisions as noted above).

Sub-ss (6A), (6B): inserted by SI 2004/2947, reg 3, Sch 1, paras 1, 18(1), (3), as from 12 November 2004, in relation to companies' financial years which begin on or after 1 January 2005.

Sub-s (7): repealed by SI 1993/3246, reg 3(4), as from 19 December 1993 (subject to exemptions and transitional provisions as noted above).

Application to limited liability partnerships: see the Limited Liability Partnerships Regulations 2001, SI 2001/1090, reg 3, Sch 1 at **[6984]**, **[6992]**.

[255B Modification of disclosure requirements in relation to banking company or group

(1) In relation to a banking company, or the [parent company of a banking group], the provisions of Schedule 5 (Disclosure of information: related undertakings) have effect subject to Part III of Schedule 9.

(2) In relation to a banking company, or the [holding company of a credit institution], the provisions of Schedule 6 (Disclosure of information: emoluments and other benefits of directors and others) have effect subject to Part IV of Schedule 9.]

[258]

NOTES

Substituted as noted to s 255 at **[256]**.

Repealed by the Companies Act 2006, s 1295, Sch 16, as from a day to be appointed.

Sub-s (1): words in square brackets substituted by the Companies Act 1985 (Disclosure of Branches and Bank Accounts) Regulations 1992, SI 1992/3178, regs 6, 8(b), as from 1 January 1993 (subject to transitional provisions in relation to any financial year of a company beginning before 23 December 1992).

Sub-s (2): words in square brackets substituted by the Companies Act 1985 (Bank Accounts) Regulations 1994, SI 1994/233, reg 3, as from 28 February 1994.

Application to limited liability partnerships: see the Limited Liability Partnerships Regulations 2001, SI 2001/1090, reg 3, Sch 1 at **[6984]**, **[6992]**.

255C *(Inserted by CA 1989, s 18(1), as from 1 April 1990, and repealed by the Companies Act 1985 (Insurance Companies Accounts) Regulations 1993, SI 1993/3246, reg 5(1), Sch 2, para 3, as from 19 December 1993, subject to exemptions in relation to certain companies contained in reg 6 (at* **[6765]***) and general transitional provisions in reg 7 (at* **[6766]***). Also Repealed by the Companies Act 2006, s 1295, Sch 16, as from a day to be appointed.)*

[255D Power to apply provisions to banking partnerships

(1) The Secretary of State may by regulations apply to banking partnerships, subject to such exceptions, adaptations and modifications as he considers appropriate, the provisions of this Part applying to banking companies.

[(2) A "banking partnership" means a partnership which has permission under Part 4 of the Financial Services and Markets Act 2000.

(2A) But a partnership is not a banking partnership if it has permission to accept deposits only for the purpose of carrying on another regulated activity in accordance with that permission.]

(3) Regulations under this section shall be made by statutory instrument.

(4) No regulations under this section shall be made unless a draft of the instrument containing the regulations has been laid before Parliament and approved by a resolution of each House.

[(5) Subsections (2) and (2A) must be read with—
(*a*) *section 22 of the Financial Services and Markets Act 2000;*
(*b*) *any relevant order under that section; and*
(*c*) *Schedule 2 to that Act.]]*

[259]

NOTES

Inserted by CA 1989, s 18(2), as from 1 April 1990.

Repealed by the Companies Act 2006, s 1295, Sch 16, as from a day to be appointed.

Sub-ss (2), (2A): substituted, for original sub-s (2), by the Financial Services and Markets Act 2000 (Consequential Amendments and Repeals) Order 2001, SI 2001/3649, art 16(1), as from 1 December 2001.

Sub-s (5): added by SI 2001/3649, art 16(2), as from 1 December 2001.

Application to limited liability partnerships: see the Limited Liability Partnerships Regulations 2001, SI 2001/1090, reg 3, Sch 1 at **[6984]**, **[6992]**.

255E (*Inserted by the Companies Act 1985 (Welsh Language Accounts) Regulations 1992, SI 1992/1083, reg 2(1), (4), as from 1 June 1992, and repealed by the Welsh Language Act 1993, ss 30(1), (5), 35(1), Sch 2, as from 1 February 1994.*)

[CHAPTER III
SUPPLEMENTARY PROVISIONS

Accounting standards

256 Accounting standards

(*1*) *In this Part "accounting standards" means statements of standard accounting practice issued by such body or bodies as may be prescribed by regulations.*

(*2*) *References in this Part to accounting standards applicable to a company's annual accounts are to such standards as are, in accordance with their terms, relevant to the company's circumstances and to the accounts.*

(*3*) …

(*4*) *Regulations under this section may contain such transitional and other supplementary and incidental provisions as appear to the Secretary of State to be appropriate.]*

[260]

NOTES

Inserted, together with preceding headings, by CA 1989, s 19, as from 1 April 1990.

Repealed by the Companies Act 2006, s 1295, Sch 16, as from a day to be appointed.

Sub-s (3): repealed by the Companies (Audit, Investigations and Community Enterprise) Act 2004, ss 16(7), 64, Sch 8, as from 1 January 2005.

Application to limited liability partnerships: see the Limited Liability Partnerships Regulations 2001, SI 2001/1090, reg 3, Sch 1 at **[6984]**, **[6992]**.

Regulations: the Accounting Standards (Prescribed Body) Regulations 2005, SI 2005/697 at **[7393C]**.

256A (*Inserted by the Companies Act 1985 (Operating and Financial Review and Directors' Report etc) Regulations 2005, SI 2005/1011, reg 11, as from 22 March 2005, in relation to companies' financial years which begin on or after 1 April 2005; repealed by the Companies Act 1985 (Operating and Financial Review) (Repeal) Regulations 2005, SI 2005/3442, reg 2(2)(a), Sch 1, para 15, as from 12 January 2006.*)

[Power to alter accounting requirements

257 Power of Secretary of State to alter accounting requirements

(*1*) *The Secretary of State may by regulations made by statutory instrument modify the provisions of this Part.*

(*2*) *Regulations which—*
(*a*) *add to the classes of documents required to be prepared, laid before the company in general meeting or delivered to the registrar,*

(*b*) *restrict the classes of company which have the benefit of any exemption, exception or special provision,*

(*c*) *require additional matter to be included in a document of any class, or*

(*d*) *otherwise render the requirements of this Part more onerous,*

shall not be made unless a draft of the instrument containing the regulations has been laid before Parliament and approved by a resolution of each House.

(*3*) *Otherwise, a statutory instrument containing regulations under this section shall be subject to annulment in pursuance of a resolution of either House of Parliament.*

(*4*) *Regulations under this section may—*

(*a*) *make different provision for different cases or classes of case,*

(*b*) *repeal and re-enact provisions with modifications of form or arrangement, whether or not they are modified in substance,*

(*c*) *make consequential amendments or repeals in other provisions of this Act, or in other enactments, and*

(*d*) *contain such transitional and other incidental and supplementary provisions as the Secretary of State thinks fit.*

[(*4A*) *Regulations under this section may also make provision—*

(*a*) *for the issuing, by such body or bodies as may be specified, of standards in relation to matters to be contained in reports which are required by this Part to be prepared by the directors of a company;*

(*b*) *for directors of a company who have complied with any such standard, or any of its provisions, in relation to any such report, to be presumed (unless the contrary is proved) to have complied with any requirements of this Part relating to the contents of the report to which the standard or provision relates.*

(*4B*) *In subsection (4A) "specified" means specified in an order made by the Secretary of State; and such an order—*

(*a*) *shall be made by statutory instrument which shall be subject to annulment in pursuance of a resolution of either House of Parliament;*

(*b*) *may contain such transitional provisions as the Secretary of State thinks fit.]*

(*5*) *Any modification by regulations under this section of section 258 or Schedule 10A (parent and subsidiary undertakings) does not apply for the purposes of enactments outside the Companies Acts unless the regulations so provide.]*

[261]

NOTES

Inserted, together with preceding heading, by CA 1989, s 20, as from 1 April 1990.

Repealed by the Companies Act 2006, s 1295, Sch 16, as from a day to be appointed.

Sub-ss (4A), (4B): inserted by the Companies (Audit, Investigations and Community Enterprise) Act 2004, s 13, as from 1 January 2005.

Application to limited liability partnerships: see the Limited Liability Partnerships Regulations 2001, SI 2001/1090, reg 3, Sch 1 at **[6984]**, **[6992]**.

Regulations: the Companies Act 1985 (Bank Accounts) Regulations 1991, SI 1991/2705; the Companies Act 1985 (Accounts of Small and Medium-sized Enterprises and Publication of Accounts in ECUs) Regulations 1992, SI 1992/2452; the Companies Act 1985 (Amendment of Sections 250 and 251) Regulations 1992, SI 1992/3003; the Companies Act 1985 (Disclosure of Branches and Bank Accounts) Regulations 1992, SI 1992/3178; the Partnerships and Unlimited (Accounts) Regulations 1993, SI 1993/1820 at **[6747]**; the Companies Act 1985 (Insurance Companies Accounts) Regulations 1993, SI 1993/3246 at **[6764]**; the Companies Act 1985 (Bank Accounts) Regulations 1994, SI 1994/233 at **[6783]**; the Companies Act 1985 (Audit Exemption) Regulations 1994, SI 1994/1935 at **[6792]**; Companies Act 1985 (Audit Exemption) (Amendment) Regulations 1994, SI 1994/2879; the Companies Act 1985 (Audit Exemption) (Amendment) Regulations 1995, SI 1995/589; the Companies Act 1985 (Miscellaneous Accounting Amendments) Regulations 1996, SI 1996/189 at **[6899]**; the Companies Act 1985 (Audit Exemption) (Amendment) Regulations 1996, SI 1996/3080; the Companies Act 1985 (Accounts of Small and Medium-sized Companies and Minor Accounting Amendments) Regulations 1997, SI 1997/220 at **[6929]**; the Company Accounts (Disclosure of Directors' Emoluments) Regulations 1997, SI 1997/570; the Companies Act 1985 (Directors' Report) (Statement of Payment Practice) Regulations 1997, SI 1997/571; the Companies Act 1985 (Audit Exemption) (Amendment) Regulations 1997, SI 1997/936; the Companies Act 1985 (Insurance Companies Accounts) (Minor Amendments) Regulations 1997, SI 1997/2704; the Companies Act 1985 (Audit Exemption) (Amendment) Regulations 2000, SI 2000/1430; the Directors' Remuneration Report Regulations 2002, SI 2002/1986; the Companies Act 1985 (Accounts of Small and Medium-Sized Enterprises and Audit Exemption) (Amendment) Regulations 2004, SI 2004/16; the Companies Act 1985 (International Accounting Standards and Other Accounting Amendments) Regulations 2004, SI 2004/2947; the Companies Act 1985 (Operating and Financial Review and Directors' Report etc) Regulations 2005, SI 2005/1011; the Companies Act 1985 (Investment Companies and Accounting and Audit Amendments)

Regulations 2005, SI 2005/2280; the Companies Act 1985 (Operating and Financial Review) (Repeal) Regulations 2005, SI 2005/3442; the Companies Act 1985 (Small Companies' Accounts and Audit) Regulations 2006, SI 2006/2782.

Orders: the Reporting Standards (Specified Body) Order 2005, SI 2005/692 at **[7393A]**.

[Parent and subsidiary undertakings

258 Parent and subsidiary undertakings

(1) The expressions "parent undertaking" and "subsidiary undertaking" in this Part shall be construed as follows; and a "parent company" means a parent undertaking which is a company.

(2) An undertaking is a parent undertaking in relation to another undertaking, a subsidiary undertaking, if—

(a) it holds a majority of the voting rights in the undertaking, or

(b) it is a member of the undertaking and has the right to appoint or remove a majority of its board of directors, or

(c) it has the right to exercise a dominant influence over the undertaking—

(i) by virtue of provisions contained in the undertaking's memorandum or articles, or

(ii) by virtue of a control contract, or

(d) it is a member of the undertaking and controls alone, pursuant to an agreement with other shareholders or members, a majority of the voting rights in the undertaking.

(3) For the purposes of subsection (2) an undertaking shall be treated as a member of another undertaking—

(a) if any of its subsidiary undertakings is a member of that undertaking, or

(b) if any shares in that other undertaking are held by a person acting on behalf of the undertaking or any of its subsidiary undertakings.

(4) An undertaking is also a parent undertaking in relation to another undertaking, a subsidiary undertaking, if ...—

[(a) it has the power to exercise, or actually exercises, dominant influence or control over it, or]

(b) it and the subsidiary undertaking are managed on a unified basis.

(5) A parent undertaking shall be treated as the parent undertaking of undertakings in relation to which any of its subsidiary undertakings are, or are to be treated as, parent undertakings; and references to its subsidiary undertakings shall be construed accordingly.

(6) Schedule 10A contains provisions explaining expressions used in this section and otherwise supplementing this section.]

[262]

NOTES

Inserted, together with preceding heading, by CA 1989, s 21(1), as from 1 April 1990.

Repealed by the Companies Act 2006, s 1295, Sch 16, as from a day to be appointed.

Sub-s (4): words omitted repealed, and para (a) substituted, by the Companies Act 1985 (International Accounting Standards and Other Accounting Amendments) Regulations 2004, SI 2004/2947, reg 12(1), as from 12 November 2004, in relation to companies' financial years which begin on or after 1 January 2005.

Note that SI 2004/2947, reg 12(2) also provides that the amendments noted above also apply for the purposes of he Building Societies Act 1986, and the Financial Services and Markets Act 2000.

Application to limited liability partnerships: see the Limited Liability Partnerships Regulations 2001, SI 2001/1090, reg 3, Sch 1 at **[6984]**, **[6992]**.

[Other interpretation provisions

259 Meaning of "undertaking" and related expressions

(1) In this Part "undertaking" means—

(a) a body corporate or partnership, or

(b) an unincorporated association carrying on a trade or business, with or without a view to profit.

(2) *In this Part references to shares—*

(*a*) *in relation to an undertaking with a share capital, are to allotted shares;*

(*b*) *in relation to an undertaking with capital but no share capital, are to rights to share in the capital of the undertaking; and*

(*c*) *in relation to an undertaking without capital, are to interests—*

(*i*) *conferring any right to share in the profits or liability to contribute to the losses of the undertaking, or*

(*ii*) *giving rise to an obligation to contribute to the debts or expenses of the undertaking in the event of a winding up.*

(3) *Other expressions appropriate to companies shall be construed, in relation to an undertaking which is not a company, as references to the corresponding persons, officers, documents or organs, as the case may be, appropriate to undertakings of that description.*

This is subject to provision in any specific context providing for the translation of such expressions.

(4) *References in this Part to "fellow subsidiary undertakings" are to undertakings which are subsidiary undertakings of the same parent undertaking but are not parent undertakings or subsidiary undertakings of each other.*

(5) *In this Part "group undertaking", in relation to an undertaking, means an undertaking which is—*

(*a*) *a parent undertaking or subsidiary undertaking of that undertaking, or*

(*b*) *a subsidiary undertaking of any parent undertaking of that undertaking.]*

[263]

NOTES

Inserted, together with preceding heading and ss 260, 261, 262, 262A, by CA 1989, s 22, as from 1 April 1990.

Repealed by the Companies Act 2006, s 1295, Sch 16, as from a day to be appointed.

Application to limited liability partnerships: see the Limited Liability Partnerships Regulations 2001, SI 2001/1090, reg 3, Sch 1 at **[6984]**, **[6992]**.

[260 Participating interests

(*1*) *In this Part a "participating interest" means an interest held by an undertaking in the shares of another undertaking which it holds on a long-term basis for the purpose of securing a contribution to its activities by the exercise of control or influence arising from or related to that interest.*

(2) *A holding of 20 per cent or more of the shares of an undertaking shall be presumed to be a participating interest unless the contrary is shown.*

(3) *The reference in subsection (1) to an interest in shares includes—*

(*a*) *an interest which is convertible into an interest in shares, and*

(*b*) *an option to acquire shares or any such interest;*

and an interest or option falls within paragraph (a) or (b) notwithstanding that the shares to which it relates are, until the conversion or the exercise of the option, unissued.

(4) *For the purposes of this section an interest held on behalf of an undertaking shall be treated as held by it.*

(5) …

(6) *In the balance sheet and profit and loss formats set out in Part I of Schedule 4[, [Part I of Schedule 8, Schedule 8A,] Chapter I of Part I of Schedule 9 and Chapter I of Part I of Schedule 9A], "participating interest" does not include an interest in a group undertaking.*

(7) *For the purposes of this section as it applies in relation to the expression "participating interest"—*

(*a*) *in those formats as they apply in relation to group accounts, and*

(*b*) *in paragraph 20 of Schedule 4A (group accounts: undertakings to be accounted for as associated undertakings),*

the references in subsections (1) to (4) to the interest held by, and the purposes and activities of, the undertaking concerned shall be construed as references to the interest held by, and the purposes and activities of, the group (within the meaning of paragraph 1 of that Schedule).]

[264]

NOTES

Inserted as noted to s 259 at **[263]**.

Repealed by the Companies Act 2006, s 1295, Sch 16, as from a day to be appointed.

Sub-s (5): repealed by the Companies Act 1985 (International Accounting Standards and Other Accounting Amendments) Regulations 2004, SI 2004/2947, reg 15, Sch 7, Pt 1, paras 1, 7, as from 12 November 2004, in relation to companies' financial years which begin on or after 1 January 2005.

Sub-s (6): words in first (outer) pair of square brackets (as originally inserted by the Companies Act 1985 (Bank Accounts) Regulations 1991, SI 1991/2705, reg 6, Sch 2, para 2, as from 2 December 1991) substituted by the Companies Act 1985 (Insurance Companies Accounts) Regulations 1993, SI 1993/3246, reg 5(1), Sch 2, para 4, as from 19 December 1993, subject to exemptions in relation to certain companies contained in reg 6 (at **[6765]**) and general transitional provisions in reg 7 (at **[6766]**); words in second (inner) pair of square brackets inserted by the Companies Act 1985 (Accounts of Small and Medium-sized Companies and Minor Accounting Amendments) Regulations 1997, SI 1997/220, reg 7(5), in relation to annual accounts approved by the board of directors on or after 1 March 1997, and to directors' and auditors' reports on such accounts (subject to transitional provisions in relation to a financial year of a company ending on or before 24 March 1997).

Application to limited liability partnerships: see the Limited Liability Partnerships Regulations 2001, SI 2001/1090, reg 3, Sch 1 at **[6984]**, **[6992]**.

[261 Notes to the accounts

(1) Information required by this Part to be given in notes to a company's annual accounts may be contained in the accounts or in a separate document annexed to the accounts.

(2) References in this Part to a company's annual accounts, or to a balance sheet or profit and loss account, include notes to the accounts giving information which is required by any provision of this Act [or international accounting standards], and required or allowed by any such provision to be given in a note to company accounts.]

[265]

NOTES

Inserted as noted to s 259 at **[263]**.

Repealed by the Companies Act 2006, s 1295, Sch 16, as from a day to be appointed.

Sub-s (2): words in square brackets inserted by the Companies Act 1985 (International Accounting Standards and Other Accounting Amendments) Regulations 2004, SI 2004/2947, reg 3, Sch 1, paras 1, 19, as from 12 November 2004, in relation to companies' financial years which begin on or after 1 January 2005.

Application to limited liability partnerships: see the Limited Liability Partnerships Regulations 2001, SI 2001/1090, reg 3, Sch 1 at **[6984]**, **[6992]**.

[262 Minor definitions

(1) In this Part—

[.....]

"annual accounts" means—

(a) the individual accounts required by section 226, and

(b) any group accounts required by section 227,

(but see also section 230 (treatment of individual profit and loss account where group accounts prepared));

"annual report", in relation to a company, means the directors' report required by section 234;

"balance sheet date" means the date as at which the balance sheet was made up;

"capitalisation", in relation to work or costs, means treating that work or those costs as a fixed asset;

["Companies Act accounts" means Companies Act individual accounts or Companies Act group accounts;]

["credit institution" means a credit institution as defined in [Article 4(1)(a) of Directive 2006/48/EC of the European Parliament and of the Council of 14 June 2006] relating to the taking up and pursuit of the business of credit institutions, that is to say an undertaking whose business is to receive deposits or other repayable funds from the public and to grant credits for its own account;]

[.....]

["e-money issuer" means a person who has permission under Part 4 of the Financial Services and Markets Act 2000 to carry on the activity of issuing electronic money within the meaning of article 9B of the Financial Services and Markets Act 2000 (Regulated Activities) Order 2001;]

"fixed assets" means assets of a company which are intended for use on a continuing basis in the company's activities, and "current assets" means assets not intended for such use;

"group" means a parent undertaking and its subsidiary undertakings;

["IAS accounts" means IAS individual accounts or IAS group accounts;]

["IAS Regulation" means EC Regulation No 1606/2002 of the European Parliament and of the Council of 19th July 2002 on the application of international accounting standards;]

"included in the consolidation", in relation to group accounts, or "included in consolidated group accounts", means that the undertaking is included in the accounts by the method of full (and not proportional) consolidation, and references to an undertaking excluded from consolidation shall be construed accordingly;

["international accounting standards" means the international accounting standards, within the meaning of the IAS Regulation, adopted from time to time by the European Commission in accordance with that Regulation;]

["ISD investment firm" has the same meaning as in the General Provisions and Glossary Instrument 2001 made by the Financial Services Authority under the Financial Services and Markets Act 2000;]

["profit and loss account", in relation to a company that prepares IAS accounts, includes an income statement or other equivalent financial statement required to be prepared by international accounting standards;]

"purchase price", in relation to an asset of a company or any raw materials or consumables used in the production of such an asset, includes any consideration (whether in cash or otherwise) given by the company in respect of that asset or those materials or consumables, as the case may be;

"qualified", in relation to an auditors' report, means that the report does not state the auditors' unqualified opinion that the accounts have been properly prepared in accordance with this Act or, in the case of an undertaking not required to prepare accounts in accordance with this Act, under any corresponding legislation under which it is required to prepare accounts;

["quoted company" means a company whose equity share capital—

- *(a) has been included in the official list in accordance with the provisions of Part VI of the Financial Services and Markets Act 2000; or*
- *(b) is officially listed in an EEA State; or*
- *(c) is admitted to dealing on either the New York Stock Exchange or the exchange known as Nasdaq;*

and in paragraph (a) "the official list" shall have the meaning given it by section 103(1) of the Financial Services and Markets Act 2000;]

["regulated activity" has the meaning given by section 744, except that it does not include activities of the kind specified in any of the following provisions of the Financial Services and Markets Act 2000 (Regulated Activities) Order 2001—

- *(a) article 25A (arranging regulated mortgage contracts),*
- *[(aa) article 25B (arranging regulated home reversion plans),*
- *(ab) article 25C (arranging regulated home purchase plans),]*
- *(b) article 39A (assisting administration and performance of a contract of insurance),*
- *(c) article 53A (advising on regulated mortgage contracts), …*
- *[(ca) article 53B (advising on regulated home reversion plans),*
- *(cb) article 53C (advising on regulated home purchase plans), …]*
- *(d) article 21 (dealing as agent), article 25 (arranging deals in investments) or article 53 (advising on investments) where the activity concerns relevant investments that are not contractually based investments (within the meaning of article 3 of that Order)[, or*
- *(e) article 64 (agreeing to carry on a regulated activity of the kind mentioned in paragraphs (a) to (d) above);]]*

.....

"turnover", in relation to a company, means the amounts derived from the provision of goods and services falling within the company's ordinary activities, after deduction of—

- *(i) trade discounts,*
- *(ii) value added tax, and*
- *(iii) any other taxes based on the amounts so derived;*

["UCITS management company" has the same meaning as in the Collective Investment Schemes (UCITS Amending Directive) Instrument 2003 made by the Financial Services Authority under the Financial Services and Markets Act 2000].

(2) *In the case of an undertaking not trading for profit, any reference in this Part to a profit and loss account is to an income and expenditure account; and references to profit and loss and, in relation to group accounts, to a consolidated profit and loss account shall be construed accordingly.*

[(2A) References in this Part to accounts giving a "true and fair view" are references—
- (*a*) *in the case of Companies Act individual accounts, to the requirement under section 226A that such accounts give a true and fair view;*
- (*b*) *in the case of Companies Act group accounts, to the requirement under section 227A that such accounts give a true and fair view; and*
- (*c*) *in the case of IAS accounts, to the requirement under international accounting standards that such accounts achieve a fair presentation.]*

(*3*) *References in this Part to "realised profits" and "realised losses", in relation to a company's accounts, are to such profits or losses of the company as fall to be treated as realised in accordance with principles generally accepted, at the time when the accounts are prepared, with respect to the determination for accounting purposes of realised profits or losses.*

This is without prejudice to—
- (*a*) *the construction of any other expression (where appropriate) by reference to accepted accounting principles or practice, or*
- (*b*) *any specific provision for the treatment of profits or losses of any description as realised.]*

[266]

NOTES

Inserted as noted to s 259 at **[263]**.

Repealed by the Companies Act 2006, s 1295, Sch 16, as from 20 January 2007 (in so far as relating to the definition "address" in sub-s (1)), and as from a day to be appointed (otherwise).

Sub-s (1) is amended as follows:

Definition "address" inserted by the Companies Act 1985 (Electronic Communications) Order 2000, SI 2000/3373, art 16(1), as from 22 December 2000, and repealed as noted above. The definition previously read as follows—

> *""address", except in section 228, in relation to electronic communications, includes any number or address used for the purposes of such communications;".*

Definitions "Companies Act accounts", "IAS accounts", "IAS Regulation", "international accounting standards", and "profit and loss account" inserted, and definition "true and fair view" repealed, by the Companies Act 1985 (International Accounting Standards and Other Accounting Amendments) Regulations 2004, SI 2004/2947, reg 3, Sch 1, paras 1, 20(1), (2), as from 12 November 2004, in relation to companies' financial years which begin on or after 1 January 2005.

Definition "credit institution" substituted by the Banking Consolidation Directive (Consequential Amendments) Regulations 2000, SI 2000/2952, reg 2(1), (3), as from 22 November 2000; words in square brackets substituted by the Capital Requirements Regulations 2006, SI 2006/3221, reg 29(2), Sch 4, para 2(1), (3), as from 1 January 2007.

Definition "EEA State" originally inserted by the Companies Act 1985 (Miscellaneous Accounting Amendments) Regulations 1996, SI 1996/189, regs 12(1), 16(1), in relation to any financial year ending on or after 2 February 1996; repealed by the Companies (Membership of Holding Company) (Dealers in Securities) Regulations 1997, SI 1997/2306, reg 4(2), as from 20 October 1997.

Definitions "e-money issuer", "ISD investment firm", and "UCITS management company" inserted by the Companies Act 1985 (Small Companies' Accounts and Audit) Regulations 2006, SI 2006/2782, reg 6(1), (2), as from 8 November 2006, in relation to annual accounts and reports in respect of financial years ending on or after 31 December 2006.

Definition "quoted company" inserted by the Directors' Remuneration Report Regulations 2002, SI 2002/1986, reg 10(1), (11), as from 1 August 2002, with effect as respects companies' financial years ending on or after 31 December 2002.

Definition "regulated activity" inserted by the Companies Act 1985 (Investment Companies and Accounting and Audit Amendments) Regulations 2005, SI 2005/2280, reg 17(1), as from 5 September 2005, in relation to accounts copies of which are delivered to the registrar of companies on or after that date; paras (aa), (ab), (ca), (cb) inserted, and the word omitted from para (c) repealed, by the Financial Services and Markets Act 2000 (Regulated Activities) (Amendment) (No 2) Order 2006, SI 2006/2383, art 26, as from 6 April 2007 (for the full commencement details of SI 2006/2383, see art 1 of that Order at **[4820]**); word omitted from para (cb) repealed, and para (e) inserted, by SI 2006/2782, reg 6(1), (3), as from 8 November 2006, in relation to annual accounts and reports in respect of financial years ending on or after 31 December 2006.

Sub-s (2A): inserted by SI 2004/2947, reg 3, Sch 1, paras 1, 20(1), (3), as from 12 November 2004, in relation to companies' financial years which begin on or after 1 January 2005.

Application to limited liability partnerships: see the Limited Liability Partnerships Regulations 2001, SI 2001/1090, reg 3, Sch 1 at **[6984]**, **[6992]**. Note also that nothing in the Companies Act 2006

(Commencement No 1, Transitional Provisions and Savings) Order 2006, SI 2006/3428 affects any provision of this Act as applied by the 2001 Regulations to LLPs (see art 8(2) at **[7581]** and the introductory notes to this Act).

[262A Index of defined expressions

The following Table shows the provisions of this Part defining or otherwise explaining expressions used in this Part (other than expressions used only in the same section or paragraph)—

[the 1982 Act (in Schedule 9A)	*paragraph 81 of Part I of that Schedule]*
accounting reference date and accounting reference period	*section 224*
accounting standards and applicable accounting standards	*section 256*
[.....]	
annual accounts	
(generally)	*section 262(1)*
(includes notes to the accounts)	*section 261(2)*
annual report	*section 262(1)*
associated undertaking (in Schedule 4A)	*paragraph 20 of that Schedule*
[auditable part (of a directors' remuneration report)	*section 235(5)]*
balance sheet (includes notes)	*section 261(2)*
balance sheet date	*section 262(1)*
[.....]	
banking group	*[section 255A(4)]*
[.....]	
capitalisation (in relation to work or costs)	*section 262(1)*
[Companies Act accounts	*Section 262(1)]*
[Companies Act group accounts	*Sections 227(2) and 255A(6A)]*
[Companies Act individual accounts	*Sections 226(2) and 255(4A)]*
credit institution	*section 262(1)*
current assets	*section 262(1)*
[directors' report	*section 23]*
[.....]	
[e-money issuer	*section 262]*
fellow subsidiary undertaking	*section 259(4)*
[financial fixed assets (in Schedule 9)	*paragraph 82 of Part I of that Schedule]*
financial year	*section 223*
fixed assets	*section 262(1)*
[general business (in Schedule 9A)	*paragraph 81 of Part I of that Schedule]*
group	*section 262(1)*
[group accounts	*Section 227(1)]*
[group directors' report	*section 234]*
[.....]	
group undertaking	*section 259(5)*

[historical cost accounting rules	
—in Schedule 4	*paragraph 29 of that Schedule*
[—in Schedule 8	*paragraph 29 of that Schedule]*
—in Schedule 9	*paragraph 39 of Part I of that Schedule*
[—in Schedule 9A	*paragraph 20(1) of Part I of that Schedule]]*
[IAS accounts	*Section 262(1)]*
[IAS group accounts	*Section 227(2) and (3)]*
[IAS individual accounts	*Section 226(2)]*
[IAS Regulation	*Section 262(1)]*
included in the consolidation and related expressions	*section 262(1)*
individual accounts	*section 226(1)*
insurance group	*[section 255A(5)]*
[international accounting standards	*Section 262(1)]*
[ISD investment firm	*section 262]*
land of freehold tenure and land of leasehold tenure (in relation to Scotland)	
—in Schedule 4	*paragraph 93 of that Schedule*
[—in Schedule 9	*paragraph 86 of Part I of that Schedule]*
[—in Schedule 9A	*paragraph 85 of Part I of that Schedule]*
lease, long lease and short lease	
—in Schedule 4	*paragraph 83 of that Schedule*
[—in Schedule 9	*paragraph 82 of Part I of that Schedule]*
[—in Schedule 9A	*paragraph 81 of Part I of that Schedule]*
listed investment	
—in Schedule 4	*paragraph 84 of that Schedule*
[—in Schedule 8	*paragraph 54 of that Schedule]*
[—in Schedule 9A	*paragraph 81 of Part I of that Schedule]*
[listed security (in Schedule 9)	*paragraph 82 of Part I of that Schedule]*
[long term business (in Schedule 9A)	*paragraph 81 of Part I of that Schedule*
long term fund (in Schedule 9A)	*paragraph 81 of Part I of that Schedule]*
notes to the accounts	*section 261(1)*
[.....]	
parent undertaking (and parent company)	*section 258 and Schedule 10A*
participating interest	*section 260*
[pension costs	
—in Schedule 4	*paragraph 94(2) of that Schedule*
—in Schedule 8	*paragraph 59(2) of that Schedule*
—in Schedule 9	*paragraph 87(b) of Part I of that Schedule*
—in Schedule 9A	*paragraph 86(b) of Part I of that Schedule]*
period allowed for laying and delivering accounts and reports	*section 244*
[policy holder (in Schedule 9A)	*paragraph 81 of Part I of that Schedule]*
profit and loss account	

(includes notes)	*section 261(2)*
[(in relation to IAS accounts)	*Section 262(1)]*
(in relation to a company not trading for profit)	*section 262(2)*
provision	
—in Schedule 4	*paragraphs 88 and 89 of that Schedule*
[—in Schedule 8	*paragraphs 57 and 58 of that Schedule]*
[—in Schedule 9	*paragraph 85 of Part I of that Schedule]*
[—in Schedule 9A	*paragraph 84 of Part I of that Schedule]*
[provision for unexpired risks (in Schedule 9A)	*paragraph 81 of Part I of that Schedule]*
purchase price	*section 262(1)*
qualified	*section 262(1)*
[quoted company	*section 262(1)]*
realised losses and realised profits	*section 262(3)*
[regulated activity	*sections 262 and 744]*
[repayable on demand (in Schedule 9)	*paragraph 82 of Part I of that Schedule]*
[reporting accountant	*section 249C(1)]*
[.....]	
reserve (in [Schedule 9A])	*paragraph 32 of that Schedule*
[sale and repurchase transaction (in Schedule 9)	*paragraph 82 of Part I of that Schedule*
sale and option to resell transaction (in Schedule 9)	*paragraph 82 of Part I of that Schedule]*
shares	*section 259(2)*
[social security costs	
—in Schedule 4	*paragraph 94(1) and (3) of that Schedule*
[—in Schedule 8	*paragraph 59(1) and (3) of that Schedule]*
—in Schedule 9	*paragraph 87(a) and (c) of Part I of that Schedule*
[—in Schedule 9A	*paragraph 86(a) and (c) of Part I of that Schedule]]*
special provisions for banking and insurance companies and groups	*sections 255 and 255A*
subsidiary undertaking	*section 258 and Schedule 10A*
[true and fair view	*section 262(2A)]*
turnover	*section 262(1)*
[UCITS management company	*section 262]*
undertaking and related expressions	*section 259(1) to (3).]*

[267]

NOTES

Inserted as noted to s 259 at **[263]**.

Repealed by the Companies Act 2006, s 1295, Sch 16, as from 20 January 2007 (in so far as relating to the entry "address"), and as from a day to be appointed (otherwise). Note that this section is also amended by the 2006 Act (see below).

Entries relating to "the 1982 Act (in Schedule 9A)", "general business (in Schedule 9A)", "long term business (in Schedule 9A)", "long term fund (in Schedule 9A)", "policy holder (in Schedule 9A)", "provision for unexpired risks (in Schedule 9A)" inserted by the Companies Act 1985 (Insurance Companies Accounts) Regulations 1993, SI 1993/3246, regs 5(1), Sch 2, para 5(a), as from

19 December 1993, subject to exemptions in relation to certain companies contained in reg 6 (at **[6765]**) and general transitional provisions in reg 7 (at **[6766]**).

Entries relating to "auditable part (of a directors' remuneration report)" and "quoted company" inserted by the Directors' Remuneration Report Regulations 2002, SI 2002/1986, reg 10(1), (12), as from 1 August 2002, with effect as respects companies' financial years ending on or after 31 December 2002 (it was previously defined in s 262(1)).

Entry relating to "address" inserted by the Companies Act 1985 (Electronic Communications) Order 2000, SI 2000/3373, art 16(2), as from 22 December 2000, and repealed as noted above.

Entries relating to "banking activities" and "banking transactions" (originally inserted by the Companies Act 1985 (Bank Accounts) Regulations 1991, SI 1991/2705, reg 6, Sch 2, para 3, as from 2 December 1991) repealed by the Companies Act 1985 (Bank Accounts) Regulations 1994, SI 1994/233, reg 4(2), as from 11 February 1994 (subject to transitional provisions in relation to financial years beginning before 23 December 1992).

Entries "Companies Act accounts", "Companies Act group accounts", "Companies Act individual accounts", "group accounts", "IAS accounts", "IAS group accounts", "IAS individual accounts", "IAS Regulation", "international accounting standards", and "(in relation to IAS accounts)" inserted, and entry "true and fair view" substituted, by the Companies Act 1985 (International Accounting Standards and Other Accounting Amendments) Regulations 2004, SI 2004/2947, reg 3, Sch 1, paras 1, 21, as from 12 November 2004, in relation to companies' financial years which begin on or after 1 January 2005.

Entries "directors' report", "group directors' report", "group operating and financial review", "operating and financial review", and "reporting standards and relevant reporting standards" inserted by the Companies Act 1985 (Operating and Financial Review and Directors' Report etc) Regulations 2005, SI 2005/1011, reg 19, Schedule, paras 1, 7, as from 22 March 2005, in relation to companies' financial years which begin on or after 1 April 2005.

Entry relating to "EEA State" (originally inserted by the Companies Act 1985 (Miscellaneous Accounting Amendments) Regulations 1996, SI 1996/189, regs 12(2), 16(1), in relation to any financial year ending on or after 2 February 1996); repealed by the Companies (Membership of Holding Company) (Dealers in Securities) Regulations 1997, SI 1997/2306, reg 4(4), as from 20 October 1997.

Entries "e-money issuer", "ISD investment firm", and "UCITS management company" inserted by the Companies Act 1985 (Small Companies' Accounts and Audit) Regulations 2006, SI 2006/2782, reg 6(1), (4), as from 8 November 2006, in relation to annual accounts and reports in respect of financial years ending on or after 31 December 2006.

Entries relating to "financial fixed assets", "listed security", "repayable on demand", "sale and repurchase transaction", "sale and option to resell transaction" inserted, and words in square brackets in entries relating to "banking group" and "insurance group" substituted, by SI 1991/2705, reg 6, Sch 2, para 3, as from 2 December 1991 (subject to transitional provisions in relation to a financial year of a company beginning before 23 December 1992).

Entries "group operating and financial review", "operating and financial review", and "reporting standards and relevant reporting standards" repealed by the Companies Act 1985 (Operating and Financial Review) (Repeal) Regulations 2005, SI 2005/3442, reg 2(2)(a), Sch 1, para 16, as from 12 January 2006.

Entry relating to "historical cost accounting rules" substituted by SI 1991/2705, reg 6, Sch 2, para 3, as from 2 December 1991 (subject to transitional provisions in relation to a financial year of a company beginning before 23 December 1992); words in first pair of square brackets in that entry inserted by the Companies Act 1985 (Accounts of Small and Medium-sized Companies and Minor Accounting Amendments) Regulations 1997, SI 1997/220, reg 7(6)(a), in relation to annual accounts approved by the board of directors on or after 1 March 1997, and to directors' and auditors' reports on such accounts (subject to transitional provisions in relation to a financial year of a company ending on or before 24 March 1997); words in second pair of square brackets in that entry inserted by SI 1993/3246, reg 5(1), Sch 2, para 5(b), as from 19 December 1993, subject to exemptions in relation to certain companies contained in reg 6 (at **[6765]**) and general transitional provisions in reg 7 (at **[6766]**).

In entries relating to "land of freehold tenure and land of leasehold tenure (in relation to Scotland)" and "lease, long lease and short lease" words in first pair of square brackets inserted by SI 1991/2705, reg 6, Sch 2, para 3, as from 2 December 1991 (subject to transitional provisions in relation to a financial year of a company beginning before 23 December 1992); words in second pair of square brackets in those entries substituted by SI 1993/3246, reg 5(1), Sch 2, para 5(c), (d), (g), as from 19 December 1993, subject to exemptions in relation to certain companies contained in reg 6 (at **[6765]**) and general transitional provisions in reg 7 (at **[6766]**).

In entry relating to "listed investment" words in first pair of square brackets inserted by SI 1997/220, reg 7(6)(b), in relation to annual accounts approved by the board of directors on or after 1 March 1997, and to directors' and auditors' reports on such accounts (subject to transitional provisions in relation to a financial year of a company ending on or before 24 March 1997); words in second pair of square brackets in that entry substituted by SI 1993/3246, reg 5(1), Sch 2, para 5(e), as from 19 December 1993, subject to exemptions in relation to certain companies contained in reg 6 (at **[6765]**) and general transitional provisions in reg 7 (at **[6766]**).

Entry relating to "pension costs" substituted by SI 1997/220, reg 7(6)(c), in relation to annual accounts approved by the board of directors on or after 1 March 1997, and to directors' and auditors' reports on such accounts (subject to transitional provisions in relation to a financial year of a company ending on or before 24 March 1997).

In entry relating to "provision" words in first pair of square brackets inserted by SI 1997/220, reg 7(6)(d), in relation to annual accounts approved by the board of directors on or after 1 March 1997, and to directors' and auditors' reports on such accounts (subject to transitional provisions in relation to a financial year of a company ending on or before 24 March 1997); words in second pair of square brackets in that entry inserted by SI 1991/2705, reg 6, Sch 2, para 3, as from 2 December 1991 (subject to transitional provisions in relation to a financial year of a company beginning before 23 December 1992);

words in third pair of square brackets substituted by SI 1993/3246, reg 5(1), Sch 2, para 5(c), (d), (g), as from 19 December 1993, subject to exemptions in relation to certain companies contained in reg 6 (at **[6765]**) and general transitional provisions in reg 7 (at **[6766]**).

Entry relating to "regulated activity" inserted by the Companies Act 1985 (Investment Companies and Accounting and Audit Amendments) Regulations 2005, SI 2005/2280, reg 17(2), as from 5 September 2005, in relation to accounts copies of which are delivered to the registrar of companies on or after that date.

Entry relating to "reporting accountant" inserted by the Companies Act 1985 (Audit Exemption) Regulations 1994, SI 1994/1935, reg 4, Sch 1, para 3, as from 11 August 1994, in relation to annual accounts of a company which are approved by the board of directors on or after 11 August 1994 (and does not apply to any annual accounts the period for laying and delivering of which expired before that date); repealed by the Companies Act 2006, s 1175, Sch 9, Pt 1, para 8, as from a day to be appointed.

Entry relating to "social security costs" substituted by SI 1991/2705, reg 6, Sch 2, para 3, as from 2 December 1991 (subject to transitional provisions in relation to a financial year of a company beginning before 23 December 1992); words in first pair of square brackets in that entry inserted by SI 1997/220, reg 7(6)(e), in relation to annual accounts approved by the board of directors on or after 1 March 1997, and to directors' and auditors' reports on such accounts (subject to transitional provisions in relation to a financial year of a company ending on or before 24 March 1997); words in second pair of square brackets inserted by SI 1993/3246, reg 5(1), Sch 2, para 5(h), as from 19 December 1993, subject to exemptions in relation to certain companies contained in reg 6 (at **[6765]**) and general transitional provisions in reg 7 (at **[6766]**).

Application to limited liability partnerships: see the Limited Liability Partnerships Regulations 2001, SI 2001/1090, reg 3, Sch 1 at **[6984]**, **[6992]**. Note also that nothing in the Companies Act 2006 (Commencement No 1, Transitional Provisions and Savings) Order 2006, SI 2006/3428 affects any provision of this Act as applied by the 2001 Regulations to LLPs (see art 8(2) at **[7581]** and the introductory notes to this Act).

PART VIII
DISTRIBUTION OF PROFITS AND ASSETS

Limits of company's power of distribution

263 Certain distributions prohibited

(1) A company shall not make a distribution except out of profits available for the purpose.

(2) In this Part, "distribution" means every description of distribution of a company's assets to its members, whether in cash or otherwise, except distribution by way of—

- *(a) an issue of shares as fully or partly paid bonus shares,*
- *(b) the redemption or purchase of any of the company's own shares out of capital (including the proceeds of any fresh issue of shares) or out of unrealised profits in accordance with Chapter VII of Part V,*
- *(c) the reduction of share capital by extinguishing or reducing the liability of any of the members on any of the company's shares in respect of share capital not paid up, or by paying off paid up share capital, and*
- *(d) a distribution of assets to members of the company on its winding up.*

(3) For purposes of this Part, a company's profits available for distribution are its accumulated, realised profits, so far as not previously utilised by distribution or capitalisation, less its accumulated, realised losses, so far as not previously written off in a reduction or reorganisation of capital duly made.

This is subject to the provision made by sections 265 and 266 for investment and other companies.

(4) A company shall not apply an unrealised profit in paying up debentures, or any amounts unpaid on its issued shares.

(5) Where the directors of a company are, after making all reasonable enquiries, unable to determine whether a particular profit made before 22nd December 1980 is realised or unrealised, they may treat the profit as realised; and where after making such enquiries they are unable to determine whether a particular loss so made is realised or unrealised, they may treat the loss as unrealised.

[268]

NOTES

Repealed by the Companies Act 2006, s 1295, Sch 16, as from a day to be appointed.

264 Restriction on distribution of assets

(1) A public company may only make a distribution at any time—

(a) if at that time the amount of its net assets is not less than the aggregate of its called-up share capital and undistributable reserves, and

(b) if, and to the extent that, the distribution does not reduce the amount of those assets to less than that aggregate.

This is subject to the provision made by sections 265 and 266 for investment and other companies.

(2) In subsection (1), "net assets" means the aggregate of the company's assets less the aggregate of its liabilities ("liabilities" to include any [provision for liabilities] within paragraph 89 of Schedule 4 [that is made in Companies Act accounts and any provision that is made in IAS accounts]).

(3) A company's undistributable reserves are—

(a) the share premium account,

(b) the capital redemption reserve,

(c) the amount by which the company's accumulated, unrealised profits, so far as not previously utilised by capitalisation of a description to which this paragraph applies, exceed its accumulated, unrealised losses (so far as not previously written off in a reduction or reorganisation of capital duly made), and

(d) any other reserve which the company is prohibited from distributing by any enactment (other than one contained in this Part) or by its memorandum or articles;

and paragraph (c) applies to every description of capitalisation except a transfer of profits of the company to its capital redemption reserve on or after 22nd December 1980.

(4) A public company shall not include any uncalled share capital as an asset in any accounts relevant for purposes of this section.

[269]

NOTES

Repealed by the Companies Act 2006, s 1295, Sch 16, as from a day to be appointed.

Sub-s (2): words in first pair of square brackets substituted, and words in second pair of square brackets inserted, by the Companies Act 1985 (International Accounting Standards and Other Accounting Amendments) Regulations 2004, SI 2004/2947, regs 3, 15, Sch 1, paras 1, 22, Sch 7, Pt 1, paras 1, 8, as from 12 November 2004, in relation to companies' financial years which begin on or after 1 January 2005.

265 Other distributions by investment companies

(1) Subject to the following provisions of this section, an investment company (defined in section 266) may also make a distribution at any time out of its accumulated, realised revenue profits, so far as not previously utilised by a distribution or capitalisation, less its accumulated revenue losses (whether realised or unrealised), so far as not previously written off in a reduction or reorganisation of capital duly made—

(a) if at that time the amount of its assets is at least equal to one and a half times the aggregate of its liabilities [to creditors], and

(b) if, and to the extent that, the distribution does not reduce that amount to less than one and a half times that aggregate.

(2) In subsection (1)(a), "liabilities" [to creditors] includes any [provision for liabilities] [to creditors] (within the meaning of paragraph 89 of Schedule 4) [that is made in Companies Act accounts and any provision [for liabilities to creditors] that is made in IAS accounts].

(3) The company shall not include any uncalled share capital as an asset in any accounts relevant for purposes of this section.

(4) An investment company may not make a distribution by virtue of subsection (1) unless—

(a) its shares are listed on a [recognised investment exchange other than an overseas investment …], and

(b) during the relevant period it has not—

(i) distributed any of its capital profits [otherwise than by way of the

redemption or purchase of any of the company's own shares in accordance with section 160 or 162 in Chapter VII of Part V], or

(*ii*) *applied any unrealised profits or any capital profits (realised or unrealised) in paying up debentures or amounts unpaid on its issued shares.*

[(4A) In subsection (4)(a) "recognised investment exchange" and "overseas investment exchange" have the same meaning as in Part 18 of the Financial Services and Markets Act 2000.]

(5) The "relevant period" under subsection (4) is the period beginning with—

(*a*) *the first day of the accounting reference period immediately preceding that in which the proposed distribution is to be made, or*

(*b*) *where the distribution is to be made in the company's first accounting reference period, the first day of that period,*

and ending with the date of the distribution.

(6) An investment company may not make a distribution by virtue of subsection (1) unless the company gave to the registrar of companies the requisite notice (that is, notice under section 266(1)) of the company's intention to carry on business as an investment company—

(*a*) *before the beginning of the relevant period under subsection (4), or*

(*b*) *in the case of a company incorporated on or after 22nd December 1980, as soon as may have been reasonably practicable after the date of its incorporation.*

[270]

NOTES

Repealed by the Companies Act 2006, s 1295, Sch 16, as from a day to be appointed.

Sub-s (1): words in square brackets inserted by the Companies Act 1985 (Investment Companies and Accounting and Audit Amendments) Regulations 2005, SI 2005/2280, reg 2(1), (2), as from 1 October 2005.

Sub-s (2): words in first pair, third pair and fifth (inner) pair of square brackets inserted by SI 2005/2280, reg 2(1), (3), as from 1 October 2005; words in second pair of square brackets substituted, and words in fourth (outer) pair of square brackets inserted, by the Companies Act 1985 (International Accounting Standards and Other Accounting Amendments) Regulations 2004, SI 2004/2947, regs 3, 15, Sch 1, paras 1, 23, Sch 7, Pt 1, paras 1, 9, as from 12 November 2004, in relation to companies' financial years which begin on or after 1 January 2005.

Sub-s (4): words in square brackets in para (a) substituted by FSA 1986, s 212(2), Sch 16, para 19, as from 29 April 1988, and words omitted therefrom repealed by the Financial Services and Markets Act 2000 (Consequential Amendments and Repeals) Order 2001, SI 2001/3649, art 17(1), (2), as from 1 December 2001; words in square brackets in para (b) inserted by the Companies (Investment Companies) (Distribution of Profits) Regulations 1999, SI 1999/2770, regs 2, 4, as from 8 November 1999, except in relation to any part of a relevant period (as defined in s 265(5)) which falls before the date.

Sub-s (4A): inserted by SI 2001/3649, art 17(1), (3), as from 1 December 2001.

266 Meaning of "investment company"

(1) In section 265 "investment company" means a public company which has given notice in the prescribed form (which has not been revoked) to the registrar of companies of its intention to carry on business as an investment company, and has since the date of that notice complied with the requirements specified below.

(2) Those requirements are—

(*a*) *that the business of the company consists of investing its funds mainly in securities, with the aim of spreading investment risk and giving members of the company the benefit of the results of the management of its funds,*

(*b*) *that none of the company's holdings in companies (other than those which are for the time being in investment companies) represents more than 15 per cent by value of the investing company's investments,*

(*c*) *that [subject to subsection (2A),] distribution of the company's capital profits is prohibited by its memorandum or articles of association,*

(*d*) *that the company has not retained, otherwise than in compliance with this Part, in respect of any accounting reference period more than 15 per cent of the income it derives from securities.*

[(2A) An investment company need not be prohibited by its memorandum or articles from redeeming or purchasing its own shares in accordance with section 160 or 162 in Chapter VII of Part V out of its capital profits.]

(3) Notice to the registrar of companies under subsection (1) may be revoked at any time by the company on giving notice in the prescribed form to the registrar that it no longer wishes to be an investment company within the meaning of this section; and, on giving such notice, the company ceases to be such a company.

[(4) Subsections (1A) to (3) of section 842 of the Income and Corporation Taxes Act 1988 apply for the purposes of subsection (2)(b) above as for those of subsection (1)(b) of that section.]

[271]

NOTES

Repealed by the Companies Act 2006, s 1295, Sch 16, as from a day to be appointed.

Sub-s (2): words in square brackets inserted by the Companies (Investment Companies) (Distribution of Profits) Regulations 1999, SI 1999/2770, reg 3(a), as from 8 November 1999.

Sub-s (2A): inserted by SI 1999/2770, reg 3(b), as from 8 November 1999.

Sub-s (4): substituted by FA 1988, s 117(3), with respect to companies' accounting periods ending after 5 April 1988.

Prescribed forms: see Appendix 4 (Forms table) at **[A4]**.

267 Extension of ss 265, 266 to other companies

(1) The Secretary of State may by regulations in a statutory instrument extend the provisions of sections 265 and 266 (with or without modifications) to companies whose principal business consists of investing their funds in securities, land or other assets with the aim of spreading investment risk and giving their members the benefit of the results of the management of the assets.

(2) Regulations under this section—

(a) may make different provision for different classes of companies and may contain such transitional and supplemental provisions as the Secretary of State considers necessary, and

(b) shall not be made unless a draft of the statutory instrument containing them has been laid before Parliament and approved by a resolution of each House.

[272]

NOTES

Repealed by the Companies Act 2006, s 1295, Sch 16, as from a day to be appointed.

268 Realised profits of insurance company with long term business

(1) Where [an authorised insurance company] carries on long term business—

[(a) any amount included in the relevant part of the balance sheet of the company which represents a surplus in the fund or funds maintained by it in respect of that business and which has not been allocated to policy holders [or, as the case may be, carried forward unappropriated, in accordance with asset identification rules made under section 142(2) of the Financial Services and Markets Act 2000], and]

(b) any deficit in that fund or those funds,

are to be (respectively) treated, for purposes of this Part, as a realised profit and a realised loss; and, subject to this, any profit or loss arising in that business is to be left out of account for those purposes.

(2) In subsection (1)—

[(aa) the reference to the relevant part of the balance sheet is—

[(i) in the case of Companies Act individual accounts,] to that part of the balance sheet which represents Liabilities item A.V (profit and loss account) in the balance sheet format set out in section B of Chapter I of Part I of Schedule 9A, [and

(ii) in the case of IAS individual accounts, to that part of the balance sheet which represents accumulated profit or loss,]]

(a) the reference to a surplus in any fund or funds of an insurance company is to an excess of the assets representing that fund or those funds over the liabilities of the company attributable to its long term business, as shown by an actuarial investigation, and

(b) the reference to a deficit in any such fund or funds is to the excess of those liabilities over those assets, as so shown.

(3) In this section—

[(a) "actuarial investigation" means—

(i) an investigation made into the financial condition of an authorised insurance company in respect of its long term business, carried out once in every period of twelve months in accordance with rules made under Part 10 of the Financial Services and Markets Act 2000 by an actuary appointed as actuary to that company; or

(ii) an investigation made into the financial condition of an authorised insurance company in respect of its long term business carried out in accordance with a requirement imposed under section 166 of that Act by an actuary appointed as actuary to that company;]

[(b) "long term business" means business which consists of effecting or carrying out contracts of long term insurance.]

[(4) The definition of "long term business" in subsection (3) must be read with—

(a) section 22 of the Financial Services and Markets Act 2000;

(b) any relevant order under that section; and

(c) Schedule 2 to that Act.]

[273]

NOTES

Repealed by the Companies Act 2006, s 1295, Sch 16, as from a day to be appointed.

Sub-s (1): words in first pair of square brackets and words in square brackets in para (a) substituted by the Financial Services and Markets Act 2000 (Consequential Amendments and Repeals) Order 2001, SI 2001/3649, art 18(1), (2), as from 1 December 2001; para (a) substituted by the Companies Act 1985 (Miscellaneous Accounting Amendments) Regulations 1996, SI 1996/189, regs 13(1), (2), 16(6), in respect of any distribution made on or after 2 February 1996.

Sub-s (2): para (aa) inserted by SI 1996/189, regs 13(1), (3), 16(6), in respect of any distribution made on or after 2 February 1996; words in square brackets in para (aa) inserted by the Companies Act 1985 (International Accounting Standards and Other Accounting Amendments) Regulations 2004, SI 2004/2947, reg 3, Sch 1, paras 1, 24, as from 12 November 2004, in relation to companies' financial years which begin on or after 1 January 2005.

Sub-s (3): paras (a), (b) substituted by SI 2001/3649, art 18(1), (3), as from 1 December 2001.

Sub-s (4): added by SI 2001/3649, art 18(1), (4), as from 1 December 2001.

269 Treatment of development costs

(1) Subject as follows, where development costs are shown as an asset in a company's accounts, any amount shown in respect of those costs is to be treated—

(a) under section 263, as a realised loss, and

(b) under section 265, as a realised revenue loss.

(2) This does not apply to any part of that amount representing an unrealised profit made on revaluation of those costs; nor does it apply if—

(a) there are special circumstances in the company's case justifying the directors in deciding that the amount there mentioned is not to be treated as required by subsection (1), …

(b) [it is stated—

(i) in the case of Companies Act individual accounts, in] the note to the accounts required by paragraph 20 of Schedule 4 [paragraph 20 of Schedule 8] (reasons for showing development costs as an asset) [, or

(ii) in the case of IAS individual accounts, in any note to the accounts,] that the amount is not to be so treated [, and

(c) the note explains] the circumstances relied upon to justify the decision of the directors to that effect.

[274]

NOTES

Repealed by the Companies Act 2006, s 1295, Sch 16, as from a day to be appointed.

Sub-s (2): word omitted from para (a) repealed, words in first pair of square brackets inserted, and words in third and fourth pairs of square brackets substituted, by the Companies Act 1985 (International Accounting Standards and Other Accounting Amendments) Regulations 2004, SI 2004/2947, reg 3, Sch 1, paras 1, 25, as from 12 November 2004, in relation to companies' financial years which begin on or after 1 January 2005; words in second pair of square brackets inserted by the Companies Act 1985 (Accounts of Small and Medium-sized Companies and Minor Accounting Amendments) Regulations 1997, SI 1997/220, reg 7(7), in relation to annual accounts approved by the board of directors on or after 1 March 1997, and to directors' and auditors' reports on such accounts (subject to transitional provisions in relation to a financial year of a company ending on or before 24 March 1997).

Relevant accounts

270 Distribution to be justified by reference to company's accounts

(1) This section and sections 271 to 276 below are for determining the question whether a distribution may be made by a company without contravening sections 263, 264 or 265.

(2) The amount of a distribution which may be made is determined by reference to the following items as stated in the company's accounts—

(a) *profits, losses, assets and liabilities,*

(b) *[the following provisions—*

(i) *in the case of Companies Act individual accounts,] provisions of any of the kinds mentioned in paragraphs 88 and 89 of Schedule 4 (depreciation, diminution in value of assets, retentions to meet liabilities, etc)[, and*

(ii) *in the case of IAS individual accounts, provisions of any kind], and*

(c) *share capital and reserves (including undistributable reserves).*

(3) Except in a case falling within the next subsection, the company's accounts which are relevant for this purpose are its last annual accounts, that is to say those prepared under Part VII which were laid in respect of the last preceding accounting reference period in respect of which accounts so prepared were laid; and for this purpose accounts are laid if section 241(1) has been complied with in relation to them.

(4) In the following two cases—

(a) *where the distribution would be found to contravene the relevant section if reference were made only to the company's last annual accounts, or*

(b) *where the distribution is proposed to be declared during the company's first accounting reference period, or before any accounts are laid in respect of that period,*

the accounts relevant under this section (called "interim accounts" in the first case, and "initial accounts" in the second) are those necessary to enable a reasonable judgment to be made as to the amounts of the items mentioned in subsection (2) above.

(5) The relevant section is treated as contravened in the case of a distribution unless the statutory requirements about the relevant accounts (that is, the requirements of this and the following three sections, as and where applicable) are complied with in relation to that distribution.

[275]

NOTES

Repealed by the Companies Act 2006, s 1295, Sch 16, as from a day to be appointed.

Sub-s (2): words in square brackets inserted by the Companies Act 1985 (International Accounting Standards and Other Accounting Amendments) Regulations 2004, SI 2004/2947, reg 3, Sch 1, paras 1, 26, as from 12 November 2004, in relation to companies' financial years which begin on or after 1 January 2005.

Sub-s (3): for the words from "that is to say" to the end there are substituted the following words by the draft Companies Act 2006 (Commencement No 3, Consequential Amendments, Transitional Provisions and Savings) Order 2007, art 10(1), Sch 4, Pt 1, para 3(6), (8), as from 1 October 2007, with effect for financial years ending on or after that date (see **[A12]**)—

"that is to say—

(a) in the case of a private company, those prepared under Part 7 that were last sent to members in accordance with section 238(1);

(b) in the case of a public company, those prepared under Part 7 which were laid in respect of the last preceding accounting reference period in respect of which accounts so prepared were laid (and for this purpose accounts are laid if section 241(1) has been complied with in relation to them).".

271 Requirements for last annual accounts

(1) If the company's last annual accounts constitute the only accounts relevant under section 270, the statutory requirements in respect of them are as follows.

(2) The accounts must have been properly prepared in accordance with this Act, or have been so prepared subject only to matters which are not material for determining, by reference to items mentioned in section 270(2), whether the distribution would contravene the relevant section; and, without prejudice to the foregoing—

(a) *so much of the accounts as consists of a balance sheet must give a true and fair view of the state of the company's affairs as at the balance sheet date, and* (*b*) *so much of the accounts as consists of a profit and loss account must give a true and fair view of the company's profit or loss for the period in respect of which the accounts were prepared.*

(3) The auditors must have made their report on the accounts under [section 235]; and the following subsection applies if the report is a qualified report, that is to say, it is not a report without qualification to the effect that in the auditors' opinion the accounts have been properly prepared in accordance with this Act.

(4) The auditors must in that case also have stated in writing (either at the time of their report or subsequently) whether, in their opinion, the matter in respect of which their report is qualified is material for determining, by reference to items mentioned in section 270(2), whether the distribution would contravene the relevant section; and a copy of the statement must have been laid before the company in general meeting.

[(4A) A copy of the auditors' statement under subsection (4) must—

(*a*) *in the case of a private company, have been circulated to members along with the copies of the accounts sent to them under section 238(1);*

(*b*) *in the case of a public company, have been laid before the company in general meeting.]*

(5) A statement under subsection (4) suffices for purposes of a particular distribution not only if it relates to a distribution which has been proposed but also if it relates to distributions of any description which includes that particular distribution, notwithstanding that at the time of the statement it has not been proposed.

[276]

NOTES

Repealed by the Companies Act 2006, s 1295, Sch 16, as from a day to be appointed.

Sub-s (3): words in square brackets substituted by CA 1989, s 23, Sch 10, para 4, as from 1 April 1990.

Sub-s (4): words from "and a copy" to the end repealed by the draft Companies Act 2006 (Commencement No 3, Consequential Amendments, Transitional Provisions and Savings) Order 2007, art 10(1), Sch 4, Pt 1, para 3(7)(a), (8), as from 1 October 2007, with effect for financial years ending on or after that date (see **[A12]**).

Sub-s (4A): inserted by the draft Companies Act 2006 (Commencement No 3, Consequential Amendments, Transitional Provisions and Savings) Order 2007, art 10(1), Sch 4, Pt 1, para 3(7)(b), (8), as from 1 October 2007, with effect for financial years ending on or after that date (see **[A12]**).

272 Requirements for interim accounts

(1) The following are the statutory requirements in respect of interim accounts prepared for a proposed distribution by a public company.

(2) The accounts must have been properly prepared, or have been so prepared subject only to matters which are not material for determining, by reference to items mentioned in section 270(2), whether the proposed distribution would contravene the relevant section.

(3) "Properly prepared" means that the accounts must comply with [section 226] (applying that section [and sections 226A and 226B] and Schedule 4 with such modifications as are necessary because the accounts are prepared otherwise than in respect of an accounting reference period) and any balance sheet comprised in the accounts must have been signed in accordance with [section 233]; and, without prejudice to the foregoing—

(*a*) *so much of the accounts as consists of a balance sheet must give a true and fair view of the state of the company's affairs as at the balance sheet date, and*

(*b*) *so much of the accounts as consists of a profit and loss account must give a true and fair view of the company's profit or loss for the period in respect of which the accounts were prepared.*

(4) A copy of the accounts must have been delivered to the registrar of companies.

(5) If the accounts are in a language other than English and [the second sentence of section 242(1)] (translation) does not apply, […] a translation into English of the accounts, certified in the prescribed manner to be a correct translation, must also have been delivered to the registrar.

[277]

NOTES

Repealed by the Companies Act 2006, s 1295, Sch 16, as from 1 January 2007 (in so far as relating to the words omitted from sub-s (5)), and as from a day to be appointed (otherwise).

Sub-s (3): words in first and third pairs of square brackets substituted by CA 1989, s 23, Sch 10, para 5, as from 1 April 1990; words in second pair of square brackets inserted by the Companies Act 1985 (International Accounting Standards and Other Accounting Amendments) Regulations 2004, SI 2004/2947, reg 3, Sch 1, paras 1, 27, as from 12 November 2004, in relation to companies' financial years which begin on or after 1 January 2005.

Sub-s (5): words in first pair of square brackets substituted by CA 1989, s 23, Sch 10, para 6, as from 1 April 1990; words in second pair of square brackets inserted by the Welsh Language Act 1993, s 30(1), (4), as from 1 February 1994, and repealed as noted above.

Certified in the prescribed manner to be a correct translation: as to the requirements of this, see the Companies (Forms) Regulations 1985, SI 1985/854, reg 6 (partly made under this section), which (as amended by SI 1990/572) provides as follows—

"For the purposes of sections 21, 65(3), 72(2)(c), 77(5)(a), … 272(5), 273(7), 691(1)(a), 698 … of the Act, a translation of a document into English shall be certified to be a correct translation:—

(a) if the translation was made in the United Kingdom, by
- (i) a notary public in any part of the United Kingdom;
- (ii) a solicitor (if the translation was made in Scotland), a solicitor of the Supreme Court of Judicature of England and Wales (if it was made in England or Wales), or a *solicitor of the Supreme Court of Judicature of Northern Ireland* (if it was made in Northern Ireland); or
- (iii) a person certified by a person mentioned above to be known to him to be competent to translate the document into English; or

(b) if the translation was made outside the United Kingdom, by
- (i) a notary public;
- (ii) a person authorised in the place where the translation was made to administer an oath;
- (iii) any of the British officials mentioned in section 6 of the Commissioners for Oaths Act 1889;
- (iv) a person certified by a person mentioned in sub-paragraph (i), (ii) or (iii) of this paragraph to be known to him to be competent to translate the document into English.".

In para (1)(a)(ii) above, for the words in italics there are substituted the words "solicitor of the Court of Judicature of Northern Ireland" by the Constitutional Reform Act 2005, s 59, Sch 11, Pt 2, para 5, as from a day to be appointed.

Supreme Court of England and Wales: the Supreme Court of England and Wales is renamed the Senior Courts of England and Wales; see the Constitutional Reform Act 2005, s 59(1) (as from a day to be appointed).

---

273 Requirements for initial accounts

(1) The following are the statutory requirements in respect of initial accounts prepared for a proposed distribution by a public company.

(2) The accounts must have been properly prepared, or they must have been so prepared subject only to matters which are not material for determining, by reference to items mentioned in section 270(2), whether the proposed distribution would contravene the relevant section.

(3) Section 272(3) applies as respects the meaning of "properly prepared".

(4) The company's auditors must have made a report stating whether, in their opinion, the accounts have been properly prepared; and the following subsection applies if their report is a qualified report, that is to say it is not a report without qualification to the effect that in the auditors' opinion the accounts have been so prepared.

(5) The auditors must in that case also have stated in writing whether, in their opinion, the matter in respect of which their report is qualified is material for determining, by reference to items mentioned in section 270(2), whether the distribution would contravene the relevant section.

(6) A copy of the accounts, of the auditors' report under subsection (4) and of the auditors' statement (if any) under subsection (5) must have been delivered to the registrar of companies.

(7) If the accounts are, or the auditors' report under subsection (4) or their statement (if any) under subsection (5) is, in a language other than English and [the second sentence of section 242(1)] (translation) does not apply, […] a translation into English of the accounts, the report or the statement (as the case may be), certified in the prescribed manner to be a correct translation, must also have been delivered to the registrar.

[278]

NOTES

Repealed by the Companies Act 2006, s 1295, Sch 16, as from 1 January 2007 (in so far as relating to the words omitted from sub-s (7)), and as from a day to be appointed (otherwise).

Sub-s (7): words in first pair of square brackets substituted by CA 1989, s 23, Sch 10, para 6, as from 1 April 1990; words in second pair of square brackets inserted by the Welsh Language Act 1993, s 30(1), (4), as from 1 February 1994, and repealed as noted above.

Certified in the prescribed manner to be a correct translation: see the note to s 272 at **[277]**.

274 Method of applying s 270 to successive distributions

(1) For the purpose of determining by reference to particular accounts whether a proposed distribution may be made by a company, section 270 has effect, in a case where one or more distributions have already been made in pursuance of determinations made by reference to those same accounts, as if the amount of the proposed distribution was increased by the amount of the distributions so made.

(2) Subsection (1) of this section applies (if it would not otherwise do so) to—

- *(a) financial assistance lawfully given by a public company out of its distributable profits in a case where the assistance is required to be so given by section 154,*
- *(b) financial assistance lawfully given by a private company out of its distributable profits in a case where the assistance is required to be so given by section 155(2),*
- *(c) financial assistance given by a company in contravention of section 151, in a case where the giving of that assistance reduces the company's net assets or increases its net liabilities,*
- *(d) a payment made by a company in respect of the purchase by it of shares in the company (except a payment lawfully made otherwise than out of distributable profits), and*
- *(e) a payment of any description specified in section 168 (company's purchase of right to acquire its own shares, etc),*

being financial assistance given or payment made since the relevant accounts were prepared, as if any such financial assistance or payment were a distribution already made in pursuance of a determination made by reference to those accounts.

(3) In this section the following definitions apply—

"financial assistance" means the same as in Chapter VI of Part V;

"net assets" has the meaning given by section 154(2)(a); and

"net liabilities", in relation to the giving of financial assistance by a company, means the amount by which the aggregate amount of the company's liabilities (within the meaning of section 154(2)(b)) exceeds the aggregate amount of its assets, taking the amount of the assets and liabilities to be as stated in the company's accounting records immediately before the financial assistance is given.

(4) Subsections (2) and (3) of this section are deemed to be included in Chapter VII of Part V for purposes of the Secretary of State's power to make regulations under section 179.

[279]

NOTES

Repealed by the Companies Act 2006, s 1295, Sch 16, as from a day to be appointed.

275 Treatment of assets in the relevant accounts

[(1) For purposes of sections 263 and 264, the following are treated as realised losses—

- *(a) in the case of Companies Act individual accounts, provisions of any kind mentioned in paragraphs 88 and 89 of Schedule 4 (other than revaluation provisions), and*
- *(b) in the case of IAS individual accounts, provisions of any kind (other than revaluation provisions).*

(1A) In subsection (1), a revaluation provision means a provision in respect of a diminution in value of a fixed asset appearing on a revaluation of all the fixed assets of the company, or of all of its fixed assets other than goodwill.]

(2) If, on the revaluation of a fixed asset, an unrealised profit is shown to have been made and, on or after the revaluation, a sum is written off or retained for depreciation of that asset over a period, then an amount equal to the amount by which that sum exceeds the sum which

would have been so written off or retained for the depreciation of that asset over that period, if that profit had not been made, is treated for purposes of sections 263 and 264 as a realised profit made over that period.

(3) Where there is no record of the original cost of an asset, or a record cannot be obtained without unreasonable expense or delay, then for the purpose of determining whether the company has made a profit or loss in respect of that asset, its cost is taken to be the value ascribed to it in the earliest available record of its value made on or after its acquisition by the company.

(4) Subject to subsection (6), any consideration by the directors of the value at a particular time of a fixed asset is treated as a revaluation of the asset for the purposes of determining whether any such revaluation of the company's fixed assets as is required for purposes of the exception from subsection (1) has taken place at that time.

(5) But where any such assets which have not actually been revalued are treated as revalued for those purposes under subsection (4), that exception applies only if the directors are satisfied that their aggregate value at the time in question is not less than the aggregate amount at which they are for the time being stated in the company's accounts.

(6) Where section 271(2), 272(2) or 273(2) applies to the relevant accounts, subsections (4) and (5) above do not apply for the purpose of determining whether a revaluation of the company's fixed assets affecting the amount of the relevant items (that is, the items mentioned in section 270(2)) as stated in those accounts has taken place, unless it is stated in a note to the accounts—

- *(a) that the directors have considered the value at any time of any fixed assets of the company, without actually revaluing those assets,*
- *(b) that they are satisfied that the aggregate value of those assets at the time in question is or was not less than the aggregate amount at which they are or were for the time being stated in the company's accounts, and*
- *(c) that the relevant items in question are accordingly stated in the relevant accounts on the basis that a revaluation of the company's fixed assets which by virtue of subsections (4) and (5) included the assets in question took place at that time.*

[280]

NOTES

Repealed by the Companies Act 2006, s 1295, Sch 16, as from a day to be appointed.

Sub-ss (1), (1A): substituted, for original sub-s (1), by the Companies Act 1985 (International Accounting Standards and Other Accounting Amendments) Regulations 2004, SI 2004/2947, reg 3, Sch 1, 28, as from 12 November 2004, in relation to companies' financial years which begin on or after 1 January 2005.

276 Distributions in kind

Where a company makes a distribution of or including a non-cash asset, and any part of the amount at which that asset is stated in the accounts relevant for the purposes of the distribution in accordance with sections 270 to 275 represents an unrealised profit, that profit is to be treated as a realised profit—

- *(a) for the purpose of determining the lawfulness of the distribution in accordance with this Part (whether before or after the distribution takes place), and*
- *(b) for the purpose of the application of paragraphs 12(a) and [34(3)(a)] of Schedule 4 [or paragraphs 12(a) and 34(3)(a) of Schedule 8] (only realised profits to be included in or transferred to the profit and loss account) in relation to anything done with a view to or in connection with the making of that distribution.*

[281]

NOTES

Repealed by the Companies Act 2006, s 1295, Sch 16, as from a day to be appointed.

Figures in first pair of square brackets in para (b) substituted by CA 1989, s 23, Sch 10, para 7, as from 1 April 1990; words in second pair of square brackets in para (b) inserted by the Companies Act 1985 (Accounts of Small and Medium-sized Companies and Minor Accounting Amendments) Regulations 1997, SI 1997/220, reg 7(8), in relation to annual accounts approved by the board of directors on or after 1 March 1997, and to directors' and auditors' reports on such accounts (subject to transitional provisions in relation to a financial year of a company ending on or before 24 March 1997).

Supplementary

277 Consequences of unlawful distribution

(*1*) *Where a distribution, or part of one, made by a company to one of its members is made in contravention of this Part and, at the time of the distribution, he knows or has reasonable grounds for believing that it is so made, he is liable to repay it* (*or that part of it, as the case may be*) *to the company or* (*in the case of a distribution made otherwise than in cash*) *to pay the company a sum equal to the value of the distribution* (*or part*) *at that time.*

(*2*) *The above is without prejudice to any obligation imposed apart from this section on a member of a company to repay a distribution unlawfully made to him; but this section does not apply in relation to—*

(*a*) *financial assistance given by a company in contravention of section 151, or*

(*b*) *any payment made by a company in respect of the redemption or purchase by the company of shares in itself.*

(*3*) *Subsection* (*2*) *of this section is deemed included in Chapter VII of Part V for purposes of the Secretary of State's power to make regulations under section 179.*

[282]

NOTES

Repealed by the Companies Act 2006, s 1295, Sch 16, as from a day to be appointed.

278 Saving for provision in articles operative before Act of 1980

Where immediately before 22nd December 1980 a company was authorised by a provision of its articles to apply its unrealised profits in paying up in full or in part unissued shares to be allotted to members of the company as fully or partly paid bonus shares, that provision continues (*subject to any alteration of the articles*) *as authority for those profits to be so applied after that date.*

[283]

NOTES

Repealed by the Companies Act 2006, s 1295, Sch 16, as from a day to be appointed.

[279 Distributions by banking or insurance companies

Where a company's accounts relevant for the purposes of this Part are prepared in accordance with the special provisions of Part VII relating to banking or insurance companies, sections 264 to 275 apply with the modifications shown in Schedule 11.]

[284]

NOTES

Substituted by CA 1989, s 23, Sch 10, para 8, as from 1 April 1990.
Repealed by the Companies Act 2006, s 1295, Sch 16, as from a day to be appointed.

280 Definitions for Part VIII

(*1*) *The following has effect for the interpretation of this Part.*

(*2*) *"Capitalisation", in relation to a company's profits, means any of the following operations* (*whenever carried out*)*—*

(*a*) *applying the profits in wholly or partly paying up unissued shares in the company to be allotted to members of the company as fully or partly paid bonus shares, or*

(*b*) *transferring the profits to capital redemption reserve.*

(*3*) *References to profits and losses of any description are* (*respectively*) *to profits and losses of that description made at any time and, except where the context otherwise requires, are* (*respectively*) *to revenue and capital profits and revenue and capital losses.*

[285]

NOTES

Repealed by the Companies Act 2006, s 1295, Sch 16, as from a day to be appointed.

281 Saving for other restraints on distribution

The provisions of this Part are without prejudice to any enactment or rule of law, or any provision of a company's memorandum or articles, restricting the sums out of which, or the cases in which, a distribution may be made.

[286]

NOTES

Repealed by the Companies Act 2006, s 1295, Sch 16, as from a day to be appointed.

PART IX
A COMPANY'S MANAGEMENT; DIRECTORS AND SECRETARIES; THEIR QUALIFICATIONS, DUTIES AND RESPONSIBILITIES

Officers and registered office

282 Directors

(*1*) *Every company registered on or after 1st November 1929* (*other than a private company*) *shall have at least two directors.*

(*2*) *Every company registered before that date* (*other than a private company*) *shall have at least one director.*

(*3*) *Every private company shall have at least one director.*

[287]

NOTES

Repealed by the Companies Act 2006, s 1295, Sch 16, as from 1 October 2007.

283 Secretary

(*1*) *Every company shall have a secretary.*

(*2*) *A sole director shall not also be secretary.*

(*3*) *Anything required or authorised to be done by or to the secretary may, if the office is vacant or there is for any other reason no secretary capable of acting, be done by or to any assistant or deputy secretary or, if there is no assistant or deputy secretary capable of acting, by or to any officer of the company authorised generally or specially in that behalf by the directors.*

(*4*) *No company shall—*

(*a*) *have as secretary to the company a corporation the sole director of which is a sole director of the company;*

(*b*) *have as sole director of the company a corporation the sole director of which is secretary to the company.*

[288]

NOTES

Repealed by the Companies Act 2006, s 1295, Sch 16, as from a day to be appointed.

284 Acts done by person in dual capacity

A provision requiring or authorising a thing to be done by or to a director and the secretary is not satisfied by its being done by or to the same person acting both as director and as, or in place of, the secretary.

[289]

NOTES

Repealed by the Companies Act 2006, s 1295, Sch 16, as from a day to be appointed.

285 Validity of acts of directors

The acts of a director or manager are valid notwithstanding any defect that may afterwards be discovered in his appointment or qualification; and this provision is not excluded by section 292(2) (void resolution to appoint).

[290]

NOTES

Repealed by the Companies Act 2006, s 1295, Sch 16, as from 1 October 2007. For savings see the note below.

Savings: this section continues to apply to acts done before 1 October 2007 (see the draft Companies Act 2006 (Commencement No 3, Consequential Amendments, Transitional Provisions and Savings) Order 2007, Sch 3, para 4 at **[A12]**).

286 Qualifications of company secretaries

(*1*) *It is the duty of the directors of a public company to take all reasonable steps to secure that the secretary (or each joint secretary) of the company is a person who appears to them to have the requisite knowledge and experience to discharge the functions of secretary of the company and who—*

(*a*) *on 22nd December 1980 held the office of secretary or assistant or deputy secretary of the company; or*

(*b*) *for at least 3 of the 5 years immediately preceding his appointment as secretary held the office of secretary of a company other than a private company; or*

(*c*) *is a member of any of the bodies specified in the following subsection; or*

(*d*) *is a barrister, advocate or solicitor called or admitted in any part of the United Kingdom; or*

(*e*) *is a person who, by virtue of his holding or having held any other position or his being a member of any other body, appears to the directors to be capable of discharging those functions.*

(2) *The bodies referred to in subsection (1)(c) are—*

(*a*) *the Institute of Chartered Accountants in England and Wales;*

(*b*) *the Institute of Chartered Accountants of Scotland;*

(*c*) *the Chartered Association of Certified Accountants;*

(*d*) *the Institute of Chartered Accountants in Ireland;*

(*e*) *the Institute of Chartered Secretaries and Administrators;*

(*f*) *the Institute of Cost and Management Accountants;*

(*g*) *the Chartered Institute of Public Finance and Accountancy.*

[291]

NOTES

Repealed by the Companies Act 2006, s 1295, Sch 16, as from a day to be appointed.

[287 Registered office

(*1*) *A company shall at all times have a registered office to which all communications and notices may be addressed.*

(2) *On incorporation the situation of the company's registered office is that specified in the statement sent to the registrar under section 10.*

(3) *The company may change the situation of its registered office from time to time by giving notice in the prescribed form to the registrar.*

(4) *The change takes effect upon the notice being registered by the registrar, but until the end of the period of 14 days beginning with the date on which it is registered a person may validly serve any document on the company at its previous registered office.*

(5) *For the purposes of any duty of a company—*

(*a*) *to keep at its registered office, or make available for public inspection there, any register, index or other document, or*

(*b*) *to mention the address of its registered office in any document,*

a company which has given notice to the registrar of a change in the situation of its registered office may act on the change as from such date, not more than 14 days after the notice is given, as it may determine.

(6) Where a company unavoidably ceases to perform at its registered office any such duty as is mentioned in subsection (5)(a) in circumstances in which it was not practicable to give prior notice to the registrar of a change in the situation of its registered office, but—

(a) resumes performance of that duty at other premises as soon as practicable, and

(b) gives notice accordingly to the registrar of a change in the situation of its registered office within 14 days of doing so,

it shall not be treated as having failed to comply with that duty.

(7) In proceedings for an offence of failing to comply with any such duty as is mentioned in subsection (5), it is for the person charged to show that by reason of the matters referred to in that subsection or subsection (6) no offence was committed.]

[292]

NOTES

Substituted by CA 1989, s 136, as from 1 April 1990.

Repealed by the Companies Act 2006, s 1295, Sch 16, as from a day to be appointed.

Application to limited liability partnerships: see the Limited Liability Partnerships Regulations 2001, SI 2001/1090, reg 4(1), Sch 2, Pt 1 at **[6985]**, **[6993]**.

Notice in the prescribed form: see Appendix 4 (Forms table) at **[A4]**.

288 Register of directors and secretaries

(1) Every company shall keep at its registered office a register of its directors and secretaries; and the register shall, with respect to the particulars to be contained in it of those persons, comply with sections 289 and 290 below.

(2) The company shall, within the period of 14 days from the occurrence of—

(a) any change among its directors or in its secretary, or

(b) any change in the particulars contained in the register,

send to the registrar of companies a notification in the prescribed form of the change and of the date on which it occurred; and a notification of a person having become a director or secretary, or one of joint secretaries, of the company shall contain a consent, signed by that person, to act in the relevant capacity.

(3) The register shall … be open to the inspection of any member of the company without charge and of any other person on payment of [such fee as may be prescribed].

(4) If an inspection required under this section is refused, or if default is made in complying with subsection (1) or (2), the company and every officer of it who is in default is liable to a fine and, for continued contravention, to a daily default fine.

(5) In the case of a refusal of inspection of the register, the court may by order compel an immediate inspection of it.

[(5A) Where a confidentiality order made under section 723B is in force in respect of a director or secretary of a company, subsections (3) and (5) shall not apply in relation to that part of the register of the company as contains particulars of the usual residential address of that individual.]

(6) For purposes of this and the next section, a shadow director of a company is deemed a director and officer of it.

[(7) …]

[293]

NOTES

Repealed by the Companies Act 2006, s 1295, Sch 16, as from a day to be appointed.

Sub-s (3): words omitted repealed, and words in square brackets substituted, by CA 1989, ss 143(6), 212, Sch 24, as from 1 November 1991.

Sub-s (5A): inserted by the Companies (Particulars of Usual Residential Address) (Confidentiality Orders) Regulations 2002, SI 2002/912, reg 16, Sch 2, para 2(1), (2), as from 2 April 2002.

Sub-s (7): added by the Criminal Justice and Police Act 2001, s 45(1), (3), as from 19 June 2001 (for the purpose of making regulations or orders), and as from 2 April 2002 (otherwise); repealed by SI 2002/912, reg 16, Sch 2, para 2(1), (3), as from 2 April 2002.

Application to limited liability partnerships: see the Limited Liability Partnerships Regulations 2001, SI 2001/1090, reg 4(1), Sch 2, Pt 1 at **[6985]**, **[6993]**.

Inspection: for provisions relating to the inspection of documents, registers and fees under this section, see the Companies (Inspection and Copying of Registers, Indices and Documents) Regulations 1991, SI 1991/1998 at **[6716]** et seq (partly made under this section).

Community interest companies: where a change of directors arises from the use of the power of the Regulator of Community Interest Companies to appoint a person to be a director of a community interest company, the Regulator, rather than the company, is required to notify the change to the registrar of companies under sub-s (2) of this section. However, if the person appointed subsequently ceases to be a director, the community interest company is required to notify the Regulator rather than the registrar of companies of the change in its directors; see the Companies (Audit, Investigations and Community Enterprise) Act 2004, ss 26, 45(8), (9), 46(12) at **[900]**, **[919]**, **[920]**.

Notification in the prescribed form: see Appendix 4 (Forms table) at **[A4]**.

[288A If an individual in respect of whom a confidentiality order under section 723B as applied to limited liability partnerships becomes a member of a limited liability partnership—

(a) the notice to be delivered to the registrar under section 9(1) of the Limited Liability Partnerships Act 2000 shall contain the address for the time being notified by the member to the limited liability partnership under the Limited Liability Partnerships (Particulars of Usual Residential Address) (Confidentiality Orders) Regulations 2002 but shall not contain his usual residential address; and

(b) with that notice the limited liability partnership shall deliver to the registrar a notice in the prescribed form containing the usual residential address of that member.]

[294]

NOTES

Inserted by the Limited Liability Partnerships (Particulars of Usual Residential Address) (Confidentiality Orders) Regulations 2002, SI 2002/915, reg 16, Sch 2, para 2, as from 2 April 2002.

Repealed by the Companies Act 2006, s 1295, Sch 16, as from a day to be appointed.

Notice in the prescribed form: see Appendix 4 (Forms table) at **[A4]**.

289 Particulars of directors to be registered under s 288

(1) Subject to the provisions of this section, the register kept by a company under section 288 shall contain the following particulars with respect to each director—

(a) in the case of an individual—

(i) his present [name],

(ii) any former [name],

(iii) his usual residential address,

(iv) his nationality,

(v) his business occupation (if any),

(vi) particulars of any other directorships held by him or which have been held by him, and

[(vii) the date of his birth;]

(b) in the case of a corporation [or Scottish firm], its corporate [or firm] name and registered or principal office.

[(1A) Where a confidentiality order made under section 723B is in force in respect of a director, the register shall contain, in addition to the particulars specified in subsection (1)(a), such address as is for the time being notified by the director to the company under regulations made under sections 723B to 723F.]

[(2) In subsection (1)(a)—

(a) "name" means a person's Christian name (or other forename) and surname, except that in the case of a peer, or an individual usually known by a title, the title may be stated instead of his Christian name (or other forename) and surname, or in addition to either or both of them; and

(b) the reference to a former name does not include—

(i) in the case of a peer, or an individual normally known by a British title, the name by which he was known previous to the adoption of or succession to the title, or

(ii) in the case of any person, a former name which was changed or disused before he attained the age of 18 years or which has been changed or disused for 20 years or more, or

(iii) in the case of a married woman, the name by which she was known previous to the marriage.]

(3) It is not necessary for the register to contain on any day particulars of a directorship—

(a) which has not been held by a director at any time during the 5 years preceding that day,

(*b*) *which is held by a director in a company which—*
  (*i*) *is dormant or grouped with the company keeping the register, and*
  (*ii*) *if he also held that directorship for any period during those 5 years, was for the whole of that period either dormant or so grouped,*
(*c*) *which was held by a director for any period during those 5 years in a company which for the whole of that period was either dormant or grouped with the company keeping the register.*

(*4*) *For purposes of subsection* (*3*), *"company" includes any body corporate incorporated in Great Britain; and—*
(*a*) *[section 249AA(3)] applies as regards whether and when a company is or has been dormant, and*
(*b*) *a company is to be regarded as being, or having been, grouped with another at any time if at that time it is or was a company of which the other is or was a wholly-owned subsidiary, or if it is or was a wholly-owned subsidiary of the other or of another company of which that other is or was a wholly-owned subsidiary.*

[295]

NOTES

Repealed by the Companies Act 2006, s 1295, Sch 16, as from a day to be appointed.

Sub-s (1): words in square brackets in para (a) substituted, and words in square brackets in para (b) inserted, by CA 1989, s 145, Sch 19, para 2, as from 1 October 1990.

Sub-s (1A): inserted by the Companies (Particulars of Usual Residential Address) (Confidentiality Orders) Regulations 2002, SI 2002/912, reg 16, Sch 2, para 3, as from 2 April 2002.

Sub-s (2): substituted by CA 1989, s 145, Sch 19, para 2, as from 1 October 1990.

Sub-s (4): words in square brackets substituted by the Companies Act 1985 (Audit Exemption) (Amendment) Regulations 2000, SI 2000/1430, reg 8(7), as from 26 May 2000, in relation to annual reports and reports in respect of financial years ending two months or more after that date.

290 Particulars of secretaries to be registered under s 288

(*1*) *The register to be kept by a company under section 288 shall contain the following particulars with respect to the secretary or, where there are joint secretaries, with respect to each of them—*
(*a*) *in the case of an individual, his present [name], any former [name] and his usual residential address, and*
(*b*) *in the case of a corporation or a Scottish firm, its corporate or firm name and registered or principal office.*

[(1A) Where a confidentiality order made under section 723B is in force in respect of a secretary the register shall contain, in addition to the particulars specified in subsection (1)(a), such address as is for the time being notified by the secretary to the company under regulations made under sections 723B to 723F.]

(*2*) *Where all the partners in a firm are joint secretaries, the name and principal office of the firm may be stated instead of the particulars specified above.*

[(3) Section 289(2)(a) and (b) apply for the purposes of the obligation under subsection (1)(a) of this section to state the name or former name of an individual.]

[296]

NOTES

Repealed by the Companies Act 2006, s 1295, Sch 16, as from a day to be appointed.

Sub-s (1): words in square brackets in para (a) substituted by CA 1989, s 145, Sch 19, para 3, as from 1 October 1990.

Sub-s (1A): inserted by the Companies (Particulars of Usual Residential Address) (Confidentiality Orders) Regulations 2002, SI 2002/912, reg 16, Sch 2, para 4, as from 2 April 2002.

Sub-s (3): substituted by CA 1989, s 145, Sch 19, para 3, as from 1 October 1990.

Provisions governing appointment of directors

291 Share qualification of directors

(*1*) *It is the duty of every director who is by the company's articles required to hold a specified share qualification, and who is not already qualified, to obtain his qualification within 2 months after his appointment, or such shorter time as may be fixed by the articles.*

(2) For the purpose of any provision of the articles requiring a director or manager to hold any specified share qualification, the bearer of a share warrant is not deemed the holder of the shares specified in the warrant.

(3) The office of director of a company is vacated if the director does not within 2 months from the date of his appointment (or within such shorter time as may be fixed by the articles) obtain his qualification, or if after the expiration of that period or shorter time he ceases at any time to hold his qualification.

(4) A person vacating office under this section is incapable of being reappointed to be a director of the company until he has obtained his qualification.

(5) If after the expiration of that period or shorter time any unqualified person acts as a director of the company, he is liable to a fine and, for continued contravention, to a daily default fine.

[297]

NOTES

Repealed by the Companies Act 2006, s 1295, Sch 16, as from a day to be appointed.

292 Appointment of directors to be voted on individually

(1) At a general meeting of a public company, a motion for the appointment of two or more persons as directors of the company by a single resolution shall not be made, unless a resolution that it shall be so made has first been agreed to by the meeting without any vote being given against it.

(2) A resolution moved in contravention of this section is void, whether or not its being so moved was objected to at the time; but where a resolution so moved is passed, no provision for the automatic reappointment of retiring directors in default of another appointment applies.

(3) For purposes of this section, a motion for approving a person's appointment, or for nominating a person for appointment, is to be treated as a motion for his appointment.

(4) Nothing in this section applies to a resolution altering the company's articles.

[298]–[300]

NOTES

Repealed by the Companies Act 2006, s 1295, Sch 16, as from 1 October 2007.

293–302 *(S 293 (Age limit for directors) repealed by the Companies Act 2006, s 1295, Sch 16, as from 6 April 2007 (note that the Companies Act 2006 (Commencement No 1, Transitional Provisions and Savings) Order 2006, SI 2006/3428, Sch 5, para 7 provides that the repeal of sub-s (3) of that section does not affect the validity of acts done by a person acting as director to whom that section applied. Sub-s (3) previously read as follows: "A director of such a company shall vacate his office at the conclusion of the annual general meeting commencing next after he attains the age of 70; but acts done by a person as director are valid notwithstanding that it is afterwards discovered that his appointment had terminated under this subsection"; s 294 repealed by the Companies Act 2006, s 1295, Sch 16, as from 6 April 2007; ss 295–299, 301, 302 repealed with savings by the Company Directors Disqualification Act 1986, s 23(2), Schs 3, 4; s 300 repealed by the Insolvency Act 1985, s 235(3), Sch 10, Pt II. These sections are also repealed by the Companies Act 2006, s 1295, Sch 16, as from a day to be appointed.)*

Removal of directors

303 Resolution to remove director

(1) A company may by ordinary resolution remove a director before the expiration of his period of office, notwithstanding anything in its articles or in any agreement between it and him.

(2) Special notice is required of a resolution to remove a director under this section or to appoint somebody instead of a director so removed at the meeting at which he is removed.

(3) A vacancy created by the removal of a director under this section, if not filled at the meeting at which he is removed, may be filled as a casual vacancy.

(4) A person appointed director in place of a person removed under this section is treated, for the purpose of determining the time at which he or any other director is to retire, as if he had become director on the day on which the person in whose place he is appointed was last appointed a director.

(5) This section is not to be taken as depriving a person removed under it of compensation or damages payable to him in respect of the termination of his appointment as director or of any appointment terminating with that as director, or as derogating from any power to remove a director which may exist apart from this section.

[301]

NOTES

Repealed by the Companies Act 2006, s 1295, Sch 16, as from 1 October 2007.

Sub-s (1) above does not, in the case of a private company, authorise the removal of a director holding office for life on 18 July 1945; see the Companies Consolidation (Consequential Provisions) Act 1985, s 14 at **[714]**.

304 Director's right to protest removal

(1) On receipt of notice of an intended resolution to remove a director under section 303, the company shall forthwith send a copy of the notice to the director concerned; and he (whether or not a member of the company) is entitled to be heard on the resolution at the meeting.

(2) Where notice is given of an intended resolution to remove a director under that section, and the director concerned makes with respect to it representations in writing to the company (not exceeding a reasonable length) and requests their notification to members of the company, the company shall, unless the representations are received by it too late for it to do so—

- *(a) in any notice of the resolution given to members of the company state the fact of the representations having been made; and*
- *(b) send a copy of the representations to every member of the company to whom notice of the meeting is sent (whether before or after receipt of the representations by the company).*

(3) If a copy of the representations is not sent as required by subsection (2) because received too late or because of the company's default, the director may (without prejudice to his right to be heard orally) require that the representations shall be read out at the meeting.

(4) But copies of the representations need not be sent out and the representations need not be read out at the meeting if, on the application either of the company or of any other person who claims to be aggrieved, the court is satisfied that the rights conferred by this section are being abused to secure needless publicity for defamatory matter.

(5) The court may order the company's costs on an application under this section to be paid in whole or in part by the director, notwithstanding that he is not a party to the application.

[302]

NOTES

Repealed by the Companies Act 2006, s 1295, Sch 16, as from 1 October 2007. For savings see the note below.

Savings: sub-s (4) continues to apply where the representations are received by the company before 1 October 2007 (see the draft Companies Act 2006 (Commencement No 3, Consequential Amendments, Transitional Provisions and Savings) Order 2007, Sch 3, para 5 at **[A12]**).

Other provisions about directors and officers

305 Directors' names on company correspondence, etc

(1) A company to which this section applies shall not state, in any form, the name of any of its directors (otherwise than in the text or as a signatory) on any business letter on which the company's name appears unless it states on the letter in legible characters [the name of every director of the company].

(2) *This section applies to—*

(*a*) *every company registered under this Act or under the former Companies Acts (except a company registered before 23rd November 1916); and*

(*b*) *every company incorporated outside Great Britain which has an established place of business within Great Britain, unless it had established such a place of business before that date.*

(*3*) *If a company makes default in complying with this section, every officer of the company who is in default is liable for each offence to a fine; and for this purpose, where a corporation is an officer of the company, any officer of the corporation is deemed an officer of the company.*

[(4) For the purposes of the obligation under subsection (*1*) *to state the name of every director of the company, a person's "name" means—*

(*a*) *in the case of an individual, his Christian name* (*or other forename*) *and surname; and*

(*b*) *in the case of a corporation or Scottish firm, its corporate or firm name.*

(*5*) *The initial or a recognised abbreviation of a person's Christian name or other forename may be stated instead of the full Christian name or other forename.*

(*6*) *In the case of a peer, or an individual usually known by a title, the title may be stated instead of his Christian name* (*or other forename*) *and surname or in addition to either or both of them.*

(*7*) *In this section "director" includes a shadow director and the reference in subsection* (*3*) *to an "officer" shall be construed accordingly.]*

[303]

NOTES

Repealed by the Companies Act 2006, s 1295, Sch 16, as from a day to be appointed.

Sub-s (1): words in square brackets substituted by CA 1989, s 145, Sch 19, para 4, as from 1 October 1990.

Sub-ss (4)–(7): substituted, for original sub-s (4), by CA 1989, s 145, Sch 19, para 4, as from 1 October 1990.

306 Limited company may have directors with unlimited liability

(*1*) *In the case of a limited company the liability of the directors or managers, or of the managing director, may, if so provided by the memorandum, be unlimited.*

(*2*) *In the case of a limited company in which the liability of a director or manager is unlimited, the directors and any managers of the company and the member who proposes any person for election or appointment to the office of director or manager, shall add to that proposal a statement that the liability of the person holding that office will be unlimited.*

(*3*) *Before the person accepts the office or acts in it, notice in writing that his liability will be unlimited shall be given to him by the following or one of the following persons, namely—*

(*a*) *the promoters of the company,*

(*b*) *the directors of the company,*

(*c*) *any managers of the company,*

(*d*) *the company secretary.*

(*4*) *If a director, manager or proposer makes default in adding such a statement, or if a promoter, director, manager or secretary makes default in giving the notice required by subsection* (*3*), *then—*

(*a*) *he is liable to a fine, and*

(*b*) *he is also liable for any damage which the person so elected or appointed may sustain from the default;*

but the liability of the person elected or appointed is not affected by the default.

[304]

NOTES

Repealed by the Companies Act 2006, s 1295, Sch 16, as from a day to be appointed.

307 Special resolution making liability of directors unlimited

(*1*) *A limited company, if so authorised by its articles, may by special resolution alter its memorandum so as to render unlimited the liability of its directors or managers, or of any managing director.*

(*2*) *When such a special resolution is passed, its provisions are as valid as if they had been originally contained in the memorandum.*

[305]

NOTES

Repealed by the Companies Act 2006, s 1295, Sch 16, as from a day to be appointed.

308 Assignment of office by directors

If provision is made by a company's articles, or by any agreement entered into between any person and the company, for empowering a director or manager of the company to assign his office as such to another person, any assignment of office made in pursuance of that provision is (notwithstanding anything to the contrary contained in the provision) of no effect unless and until it is approved by a special resolution of the company.

[306]

NOTES

Repealed by the Companies Act 2006, s 1295, Sch 16, as from a day to be appointed.

309 Directors to have regard to interests of employees

(*1*) *The matters to which the directors of a company are to have regard in the performance of their functions include the interests of the company's employees in general, as well as the interests of its members.*

(*2*) *Accordingly, the duty imposed by this section on the directors is owed by them to the company (and the company alone) and is enforceable in the same way as any other fiduciary duty owed to a company by its directors.*

(*3*) *This section applies to shadow directors as it does to directors.*

[307]

NOTES

Repealed by the Companies Act 2006, s 1295, Sch 16, as from 1 October 2007. For savings, etc, see the note below.

Savings, etc: the draft Companies Act 2006 (Commencement No 3, Consequential Amendments, Transitional Provisions and Savings) Order 2007, Sch 3, paras 15–17 (at **[A12]**) provide as follows—

"15 Directors' liabilities (ss 232 to 239)

(1) Sections 232 to 236 of the Companies Act 2006 (restrictions on provision protecting directors from liability) apply to any provision made on or after 1st October 2007.

(2) Sections 309A, 309B and 309C(1) to (3) and (6) of the 1985 Act or Article 318 of the 1986 Order (so far as it relates to directors) continue to apply in relation to any provision to which they applied immediately before that date.

16.—(1) Sections 237 and 238 of the Companies Act 2006 (copies of qualifying indemnity provision to be available for inspection etc) apply to—

(a) qualifying indemnity provision within the meaning of section 237 made on or after 1st October 2007, and

(b) qualifying third party indemnity provision within the meaning of section 309B(1) of the 1985 Act to which section 309C(4) and (5) of that Act applied immediately before that date.

(2) Until regulations under section 1136 of the Companies Act 2006 are made specifying a place for the purposes of section 237(3)(b), the copies and memoranda referred to in section 237 may be kept by a company—

(a) at any place where its register of members is kept, or

(b) at its principal place of business,

provided that place is situated in the part of the United Kingdom in which the company is registered.

(3) Until section 1068(1) of the Companies Act 2006 comes into force the notice referred to in section 237(5) must be given on the form prescribed for the purposes of section 318(4) of the 1985 Act or Article 326(4) of the 1986 Order.

(4) The provisions of section 318 of the 1985 Act, as applied by section 309C(4) and (5), continue to apply in relation to—

(a) any default before 1st October 2007 in complying with section 318(1) or (5), as so applied;
(b) any request for inspection under section 318(7), as so applied, made before that date;
(c) any duty to give notice under section 318(4), as so applied, arising before that date.

17.—(1) Section 239 of the Companies Act 2006 (ratification of acts of directors giving rise to liability) applies to conduct by a director on or after 1st October 2007.

(2) Conduct by a director before that date is subject to the law relating to ratification that applied immediately before that date.".

[309A Provisions protecting directors from liability

(1) This section applies in relation to any liability attaching to a director of a company in connection with any negligence, default, breach of duty or breach of trust by him in relation to the company.

(2) Any provision which purports to exempt (to any extent) a director of a company from any liability within subsection (1) is void.

(3) Any provision by which a company directly or indirectly provides (to any extent) an indemnity for a director of—

(a) the company, or
(b) an associated company,

against any liability within subsection (1) is void

This is subject to subsections (4) and (5).

(4) Subsection (3) does not apply to a qualifying third party indemnity provision (see section 309B(1)).

(5) Subsection (3) does not prevent a company from purchasing and maintaining for a director of—

(a) the company, or
(b) an associated company,

insurance against any liability within subsection (1).

(6) In this section—

"associated company", in relation to a company ("C"), means a company which is C's subsidiary, or C's holding company or a subsidiary of C's holding company;

"provision" means a provision of any nature, whether or not it is contained in a company's articles or in any contract with a company.]

[307A]

NOTES

Inserted, together with ss 309B, 309C, by the Companies (Audit, Investigations and Community Enterprise) Act 2004, s 19(1), as from 6 April 2005, except in relation to provisions made before 29 October 2004 which are not void under old s 310; see the Companies (Audit, Investigations and Community Enterprise) Act 2004 (Commencement) and Companies Act 1989 (Commencement No 18) Order 2004, SI 2004/3322, art 5 at **[7343]**.

Repealed by the Companies Act 2006, s 1295, Sch 16, as from 1 October 2007. For savings, etc, see the note to s 390 at **[307]**.

[309B Qualifying third party indemnity provisions

(1) For the purposes of section 309A(4) a provision is a qualifying third party indemnity provision if it is a provision such as is mentioned in section 309A(3) in relation to which conditions A to C below are satisfied.

(2) Condition A is that the provision does not provide any indemnity against any liability incurred by the director—

(a) to the company, or
(b) to any associated company.

(3) Condition B is that the provision does not provide any indemnity against any liability incurred by the director to pay—

(a) a fine imposed in criminal proceedings, or
(b) a sum payable to a regulatory authority by way of a penalty in respect of non-compliance with any requirement of a regulatory nature (however arising).

(4) Condition C is that the provision does not provide any indemnity against any liability incurred by the director—

(a) in defending any criminal proceedings in which he is convicted, or

(b) in defending any civil proceedings brought by the company, or an associated company, in which judgment is given against him, or

(c) in connection with any application under any of the following provisions in which the court refuses to grant him relief, namely—

(i) section 144(3) or (4) (acquisition of shares by innocent nominee), or

(ii) section 727 (general power to grant relief in case of honest and reasonable conduct).

(5) In paragraph (a), (b) or (c) of subsection (4) the reference to any such conviction, judgment or refusal of relief is a reference to one that has become final.

(6) For the purposes of subsection (5) a conviction, judgment or refusal of relief becomes final—

(a) if not appealed against, at the end of the period for bringing an appeal, or

(b) if appealed against, at the time when the appeal (or any further appeal) is disposed of.

(7) An appeal is disposed of—

(a) if it is determined and the period for bringing any further appeal has ended, or

(b) if it is abandoned or otherwise ceases to have effect.

(8) In this section "associated company" and "provision" have the same meaning as in section 309A.]

[307B]

NOTES

Inserted as noted to s 309A at **[307A]**.

Repealed by the Companies Act 2006, s 1295, Sch 16, as from 1 October 2007. For savings, etc, see the note to s 390 at **[307]**.

[309C Disclosure of qualifying third party indemnity provisions

(1) Subsections (2) and (3) impose disclosure requirements in relation to a directors' report under section 234 in respect of a financial year.

(2) If—

(a) at the time when the report is approved under section 234A, any qualifying third party indemnity provision (whether made by the company or otherwise) is in force for the benefit of one or more directors of the company, or

(b) at any time during the financial year, any such provision was in force for the benefit of one or more persons who were then directors of the company,

the report must state that any such provision is or (as the case may be) was so in force.

(3) If the company has made a qualifying third party indemnity provision and—

(a) at the time when the report is approved under section 234A, any qualifying third party indemnity provision made by the company is in force for the benefit of one or more directors of an associated company, or

(b) at any time during the financial year, any such provision was in force for the benefit of one or more persons who were then directors of an associated company,

the report must state that any such provision is or (as the case may be) was so in force.

(4) Subsection (5) applies where a company has made a qualifying third party indemnity provision for the benefit of a director of the company or of an associated company.

(5) Section 318 shall apply to—

(a) the company, and

(b) if the director is a director of an associated company, the associated company,

as if a copy of the provision, or (if it is not in writing) a memorandum setting out its terms, were included in the list of documents in section 318(1).

(6) In this section—

"associated company" and "provision" have the same meaning as in section 309A; and

"qualifying third party indemnity provision" has the meaning given by section 309B(1).]

[307C]

NOTES

Inserted as noted to s 309A at **[307A]**.

Repealed by the Companies Act 2006, s 1295, Sch 16, as from 1 October 2007. For savings, etc, see the note to s 390 at **[307]**.

310 Provisions [protecting] auditors from liability

(1) This section applies to any provision, whether contained in a company's articles or in any contract with the company or otherwise, for exempting … any person (whether an officer or not) employed by the company as auditor from, or indemnifying him against, any liability which by virtue of any rule of law would otherwise attach to him in respect of any negligence, default, breach of duty or breach of trust of which he may be guilty in relation to the company.

(2) Except as provided by the following subsection, any such provision is void.

[(3) This section does not prevent a company—

(a) from purchasing and maintaining for any such … auditor insurance against any such liability, or

(b) from indemnifying any such … auditor against any liability incurred by him—

(i) in defending any proceedings (whether civil or criminal) in which judgment is given in his favour or he is acquitted, or

(ii) in connection with any application under … section 727 (general power to grant relief in case of honest and reasonable conduct) in which relief is granted to him by the court.]

[308]–[309]

NOTES

Repealed by the Companies Act 2006, s 1295, Sch 16, as from a day to be appointed.

Section heading: word in square brackets substituted by the Companies (Audit, Investigations and Community Enterprise) Act 2004, s 19(2), as from 6 April 2005 (for transitional provisions see the note to s 309A at **[307A]**).

Sub-s (1): words omitted repealed by the Companies (Audit, Investigations and Community Enterprise) Act 2004, ss 19(2)(a), 64, Sch 8, as from 6 April 2005 (for transitional provisions see the note to s 309A at **[307A]**).

Sub-s (3): substituted by CA 1989, s 137(1), as from 1 April 1990; words omitted repealed by the Companies (Audit, Investigations and Community Enterprise) Act 2004, ss 19(2)(b), 64, Sch 8, as from 6 April 2005 (for transitional provisions see the note to s 309A at **[307A]**).

PART X
ENFORCEMENT OF FAIR DEALING BY DIRECTORS

Restrictions on directors taking financial advantage

311 *(Repealed by the Companies Act 2006, ss 1177, 1295, Sch 16, as from 6 April 2007.)*

312 Payment to director for loss of office, etc

It is not lawful for a company to make to a director of the company any payment by way of compensation for loss of office, or as consideration for or in connection with his retirement from office, without particulars of the proposed payment (including its amount) being disclosed to members of the company and the proposal being approved by the company.

[310]

NOTES

Repealed by the Companies Act 2006, s 1295, Sch 16, as from 1 October 2007. For savings see the note below.

Savings: this section and ss 313–316 continue to apply in relation to loss of office or retirement occurring before 1 October 2007; see the draft Companies Act 2006 (Commencement No 3, Consequential Amendments, Transitional Provisions and Savings) Order 2007, Sch 3, para 12(3), (4) (at **[A12]**).

313 Company approval for property transfer

(1) It is not lawful, in connection with the transfer of the whole or any part of the undertaking or property of a company, for any payment to be made to a director of the

company by way of compensation for loss of office, or as consideration for or in connection with his retirement from office, unless particulars of the proposed payment (including its amount) have been disclosed to members of the company and the proposal approved by the company.

(2) *Where a payment unlawful under this section is made to a director, the amount received is deemed to be received by him in trust for the company.*

[311]

NOTES

Repealed by the Companies Act 2006, s 1295, Sch 16, as from 1 October 2007. For savings see the note to s 312 at **[310]**.

314 Director's duty of disclosure on takeover, etc

(*1*) *This section applies where, in connection with the transfer to any persons of all or any of the shares in a company, being a transfer resulting from—*

- (*a*) *an offer made to the general body of shareholders; or*
- (*b*) *an offer made by or on behalf of some other body corporate with a view to the company becoming its subsidiary or a subsidiary of its holding company; or*
- (*c*) *an offer made by or on behalf of an individual with a view to his obtaining the right to exercise or control the exercise of not less than one-third of the voting power at any general meeting of the company; or*
- (*d*) *any other offer which is conditional on acceptance to a given extent,*

a payment is to be made to a director of the company by way of compensation for loss of office, or as consideration for or in connection with his retirement from office.

(2) *It is in those circumstances the director's duty to take all reasonable steps to secure that particulars of the proposed payment (including its amount) are included in or sent with any notice of the offer made for their shares which is given to any shareholders.*

(*3*) *If—*

- (*a*) *the director fails to take those steps, or*
- (*b*) *any person who has been properly required by the director to include those particulars in or send them with the notice required by subsection (2) fails to do so,*

he is liable to a fine.

[312]

NOTES

Repealed by the Companies Act 2006, s 1295, Sch 16, as from 1 October 2007. For savings see the note to s 312 at **[310]**.

315 Consequences of non-compliance with s 314

(*1*) *If in the case of any such payment to a director as is mentioned in section 314(1)—*

- (*a*) *his duty under that section is not complied with, or*
- (*b*) *the making of the proposed payment is not, before the transfer of any shares in pursuance of the offer, approved by a meeting (summoned for the purpose) of the holders of the shares to which the offer relates and of other holders of shares of the same class as any of those shares,*

any sum received by the director on account of the payment is deemed to have been received by him in trust for persons who have sold their shares as a result of the offer made; and the expenses incurred by him in distributing that sum amongst those persons shall be borne by him and not retained out of that sum.

(2) *Where—*

- (*a*) *the shareholders referred to in subsection (1)(b) are not all the members of the company, and*
- (*b*) *no provision is made by the articles for summoning or regulating the meeting referred to in that paragraph,*

the provisions of this Act and of the company's articles relating to general meetings of the company apply (for that purpose) to the meeting either without modification or with such modifications as the Secretary of State on the application of any person concerned may direct for the purpose of adapting them to the circumstances of the meeting.

(3) If at a meeting summoned for the purpose of approving any payment as required by subsection (1)(b) a quorum is not present and, after the meeting has been adjourned to a later date, a quorum is again not present, the payment is deemed for the purposes of that subsection to have been approved.

[313]

NOTES

Repealed by the Companies Act 2006, s 1295, Sch 16, as from 1 October 2007. For savings see the note to s 312 at **[310]**.

316 Provisions supplementing ss 312 to 315

(1) Where in proceedings for the recovery of any payment as having, by virtue of section 313(2) or 315(1) been received by any person in trust, it is shown that—

- *(a) the payment was made in pursuance of any arrangement entered into as part of the agreement for the transfer in question, or within one year before or two years after that agreement or the offer leading to it; and*
- *(b) the company or any person to whom the transfer was made was privy to that arrangement,*

the payment is deemed, except in so far as the contrary is shown, to be one to which the provisions mentioned above in this subsection apply.

(2) If in connection with any such transfer as is mentioned in any of sections 313 to 315—

- *(a) the price to be paid to a director of the company whose office is to be abolished or who is to retire from office for any shares in the company held by him is in excess of the price which could at the time have been obtained by other holders of the like shares; or*
- *(b) any valuable consideration is given to any such director,*

the excess or the money value of the consideration (as the case may be) is deemed for the purposes of that section to have been a payment made to him by way of compensation for loss of office or as consideration for or in connection with his retirement from office.

(3) References in sections 312 to 315 to payments made to a director by way of compensation for loss of office or as consideration for or in connection with his retirement from office, do not include any bona fide payment by way of damages for breach of contract or by way of pension in respect of past services.

"Pension" here includes any superannuation allowance, superannuation gratuity or similar payment.

(4) Nothing in sections 313 to 315 prejudices the operation of any rule of law requiring disclosure to be made with respect to such payments as are there mentioned, or with respect to any other like payments made or to be made to a company's directors.

[314]

NOTES

Repealed by the Companies Act 2006, s 1295, Sch 16, as from 1 October 2007. For savings see the note to s 312 at **[310]**.

317 Directors to disclose interest in contracts

(1) It is the duty of a director of a company who is in any way, whether directly or indirectly, interested in a contract or proposed contract with the company to declare the nature of his interest at a meeting of the directors of the company.

(2) In the case of a proposed contract, the declaration shall be made—

- *(a) at the meeting of the directors at which the question of entering into the contract is first taken into consideration; or*
- *(b) if the director was not at the date of that meeting interested in the proposed contract, at the next meeting of the directors held after he became so interested;*

and, in a case where the director becomes interested in a contract after it is made, the declaration shall be made at the first meeting of the directors held after he becomes so interested.

(3) For purposes of this section, a general notice given to the directors of a company by a director to the effect that—

(*a*) *he is a member of a specified company or firm and is to be regarded as interested in any contract which may, after the date of the notice, be made with that company or firm; or*

(*b*) *he is to be regarded as interested in any contract which may after the date of the notice be made with a specified person who is connected with him (within the meaning of section 346 below),*

is deemed a sufficient declaration of interest in relation to any such contract.

(*4*) *However, no such notice is of effect unless either it is given at a meeting of the directors or the director takes reasonable steps to secure that it is brought up and read at the next meeting of the directors after it is given.*

(*5*) *A reference in this section to a contract includes any transaction or arrangement (whether or not constituting a contract) made or entered into on or after 22nd December 1980.*

(*6*) *For purposes of this section, a transaction or arrangement of a kind described in section 330 (prohibition of loans, quasi-loans etc to directors) made by a company for a director of the company or a person connected with such a director is treated (if it would not otherwise be so treated, and whether or not it is prohibited by that section) as a transaction or arrangement in which that director is interested.*

(*7*) *A director who fails to comply with this section is liable to a fine.*

(*8*) *This section applies to a shadow director as it applies to a director, except that a shadow director shall declare his interest, not at a meeting of the directors, but by a notice in writing to the directors which is either—*

(*a*) *a specific notice given before the date of the meeting at which, if he had been a director, the declaration would be required by subsection (2) to be made; or*

(*b*) *a notice which under subsection (3) falls to be treated as a sufficient declaration of that interest (or would fall to be so treated apart from subsection (4)).*

(*9*) *Nothing in this section prejudices the operation of any rule of law restricting directors of a company from having an interest in contracts with the company.*

[315]

NOTES

Repealed by the Companies Act 2006, s 1295, Sch 16, as from a day to be appointed.

Sub-s (6): for the words "section 330" there are substituted the words "section 197, 198, 200, 201 or 203 of the Companies Act 2006" by the draft Companies Act 2006 (Commencement No 3, Consequential Amendments, Transitional Provisions and Savings) Order 2007, art 10(1), Sch 4, Pt 1, para 5, as from 1 October 2007 (see **[A12]**).

Note that the repeal of s 346 of this Act does not affect sub-s (3)(b) above; see the draft Companies Act 2006 (Commencement No 3, Consequential Amendments, Transitional Provisions and Savings) Order 2007, Sch 3 para 50(a) (at **[A12]**).

318 Directors' service contracts to be open to inspection

(*1*) *Subject to the following provisions, every company shall keep at an appropriate place—*

(*a*) *in the case of each director whose contract of service with the company is in writing, a copy of that contract;*

(*b*) *in the case of each director whose contract of service with the company is not in writing, a written memorandum setting out its terms; and*

(*c*) *in the case of each director who is employed under a contract of service with a subsidiary of the company, a copy of that contract or, if it is not in writing, a written memorandum setting out its terms.*

(*2*) *All copies and memoranda kept by a company in pursuance of subsection (1) shall be kept at the same place.*

(*3*) *The following are appropriate places for the purposes of subsection (1)—*

(*a*) *the company's registered office;*

(*b*) *the place where its register of members is kept (if other than its registered office);*

(*c*) *its principal place of business, provided that is situated in that part of Great Britain in which the company is registered.*

(4) Every company shall send notice in the prescribed form to the registrar of companies of the place where copies and memoranda are kept in compliance with subsection (1), and of any change in that place, save in a case in which they have at all times been kept at the company's registered office.

(5) Subsection (1) does not apply to a director's contract of service with the company or with a subsidiary of it if that contract required him to work wholly or mainly outside the United Kingdom; but the company shall keep a memorandum—

(a) in the case of a contract of service with the company, giving the director's name and setting out the provisions of the contract relating to its duration;

(b) in the case of a contract of service with a subsidiary, giving the director's name and the name and place of incorporation of the subsidiary, and setting out the provisions of the contract relating to its duration,

at the same place as copies and memoranda are kept by the company in pursuance of subsection (1).

(6) A shadow director is treated for purposes of this section as a director.

(7) Every copy and memorandum required by subsection (1) or (5) to be kept shall, . . . , be open to inspection of any member of the company without charge.

(8) If—

(a) default is made in complying with subsection (1) or (5), or

(b) an inspection required under subsection (7) is refused, or

(c) default is made for 14 days in complying with subsection (4),

the company and every officer of it who is in default is liable to a fine and, for continued contravention, to a daily default fine.

(9) In the case of a refusal of an inspection required under subsection (7) of a copy or memorandum, the court may by order compel an immediate inspection of it.

(10) Subsections (1) and (5) apply to a variation of a director's contract of service as they apply to the contract.

(11) This section does not require that there be kept a copy of, or memorandum setting out the terms of, a contract (or its variation) at a time when the unexpired portion of the term for which the contract is to be in force is less than 12 months, or at a time at which the contract can, within the next ensuing 12 months, be terminated by the company without payment of compensation.

[316]

NOTES

Repealed by the Companies Act 2006, s 1295, Sch 16, as from 1 October 2007. For savings see the note below.

Sub-s (7): words omitted repealed by CA 1989, ss 143(7), 212, Sch 24, as from 1 November 1991.

Savings: see the draft Companies Act 2006 (Commencement No 3, Consequential Amendments, Transitional Provisions and Savings) Order 2007, Sch 3, para 13(4) at **[A12]** which provides as follows—

"(4) The provisions of section 318 of the 1985 Act or Article 326 of the 1986 Order continue to apply in relation to—

(a) any default before 1st October 2007 in complying with section 318(1) or (5) or Article 326(1) or (5);

(b) any request for inspection under section 318(7) or Article 326(7) made before that date;

(c) any duty to give notice under section 318(4) or Article 326(4) arising before that date.".

See also para 16(4) of that Schedule for savings in relation to this section as applied by s 309C(4), (5).

Inspection: for provisions relating to the inspection of documents, registers and fees under this section, see the Companies (Inspection and Copying of Registers, Indices and Documents) Regulations 1991, SI 1991/1998 at **[6716]** et seq.

Notice in the prescribed form: see Appendix 4 (Forms table) at **[A4]**.

319 Director's contract of employment for more than 5 years

(1) This section applies in respect of any term of an agreement whereby a director's employment with the company of which he is a director or, where he is the director of a holding company, his employment within the group is to continue, or may be continued, otherwise than at the instance of the company (whether under the original agreement or under a new agreement entered into in pursuance of it), for a period of more than 5 years during which the employment—

(a) cannot be terminated by the company by notice; or

(*b*) *can be so terminated only in specified circumstances.*

(*2*) *In any case where—*

(*a*) *a person is or is to be employed with a company under an agreement which cannot be terminated by the company by notice or can be so terminated only in specified circumstances; and*

(*b*) *more than 6 months before the expiration of the period for which he is or is to be so employed, the company enters into a further agreement (otherwise than in pursuance of a right conferred by or under the original agreement on the other party to it) under which he is to be employed with the company or, where he is a director of a holding company, within the group,*

this section applies as if to the period for which he is to be employed under that further agreement there were added a further period equal to the unexpired period of the original agreement.

(*3*) *A company shall not incorporate in an agreement such a term as is mentioned in subsection (1), unless the term is first approved by a resolution of the company in general meeting and, in the case of a director of a holding company, by a resolution of that company in general meeting.*

(*4*) *No approval is required to be given under this section by any body corporate unless it is a company within the meaning of this Act, or is registered under section 680, or if it is a wholly-owned subsidiary of any body corporate, wherever incorporated.*

(*5*) *A resolution of a company approving such a term as is mentioned in subsection (1) shall not be passed at a general meeting of the company unless a written memorandum setting out the proposed agreement incorporating the term is available for inspection by members of the company both—*

(*a*) *at the company's registered office for not less than 15 days ending with the date of the meeting; and*

(*b*) *at the meeting itself.*

(*6*) *A term incorporated in an agreement in contravention of this section is, to the extent that it contravenes the section, void; and that agreement and, in a case where subsection (2) applies, the original agreement are deemed to contain a term entitling the company to terminate it at any time by the giving of reasonable notice.*

(*7*) *In this section—*

(*a*) *"employment" includes employment under a contract for services; and*

(*b*) *"group", in relation to a director of a holding company, means the group which consists of that company and its subsidiaries;*

and for purposes of this section a shadow director is treated as a director.

[317]

NOTES

Repealed by the Companies Act 2006, s 1295, Sch 16, as from 1 October 2007. For savings see the note below.

Savings: this section continues to apply to agreements made before 1 October 2007 (see the draft Companies Act 2006 (Commencement No 3, Consequential Amendments, Transitional Provisions and Savings) Order 2007, Sch 3, para 6 at **[A12]**).

320 Substantial property transactions involving directors, etc

(*1*) *With the exceptions provided by the section next following, a company shall not enter into an arrangement—*

(*a*) *whereby a director of the company or its holding company, or a person connected with such a director, acquires or is to acquire one or more non-cash assets of the requisite value from the company; or*

(*b*) *whereby the company acquires or is to acquire one or more non-cash assets of the requisite value from such a director or a person so connected,*

unless the arrangement is first approved by a resolution of the company in general meeting and, if the director or connected person is a director of its holding company or a person connected with such a director, by a resolution in general meeting of the holding company.

(*2*) *For this purpose a non-cash asset is of the requisite value if at the time the arrangement in question is entered into its value is not less than [£2,000] but (subject to that) exceeds [£100,000] or 10 per cent of the company's asset value, that is—*

(*a*) *except in a case falling within paragraph* (*b*) *below, the value of the company's net assets determined by reference to the accounts prepared and laid under Part VII in respect of the last preceding financial year in respect of which such accounts were so laid; and*

(*b*) *where no accounts have been so prepared and laid before that time, the amount of the company's called-up share capital.*

(*3*) *For purposes of this section and sections 321 and 322, a shadow director is treated as a director.*

[318]

NOTES

Repealed by the Companies Act 2006, s 1295, Sch 16, as from 1 October 2007. For savings see the note below.

Sub-s (2): sums in square brackets substituted by the Companies (Fair Dealing by Directors) (Increase in Financial Limits) Order 1990, SI 1990/1393, as from 31 July 1990.

Savings: this section and ss 321, 322 continue to apply in relation to arrangements or transactions entered into before 1 October 2007 (see the draft Companies Act 2006 (Commencement No 3, Consequential Amendments, Transitional Provisions and Savings) Order 2007, Sch 3, para 7 at **[A12]**).

321 Exceptions from s 320

(*1*) *No approval is required to be given under section 320 by any body corporate unless it is a company within the meaning of this Act or registered under section 680 or, if it is a wholly-owned subsidiary of any body corporate, wherever incorporated.*

(2) *Section 320(1) does not apply to an arrangement for the acquisition of a non-cash asset—*

(*a*) *if the asset is to be acquired by a holding company from any of its wholly-owned subsidiaries or from a holding company by any of its wholly-owned subsidiaries, or by one wholly-owned subsidiary of a holding company from another wholly-owned subsidiary of that same holding company, or*

(*b*) *if the arrangement is entered into by a company which is being wound up, unless the winding up is a members' voluntary winding up.*

(*3*) *Section 320(1)(a) does not apply to an arrangement whereby a person is to acquire an asset from a company of which he is a member, if the arrangement is made with that person in his character as a member.*

[(4) Section 320(1) does not apply to a transaction on a recognised investment exchange which is effected by a director, or a person connected with him, through the agency of a person who in relation to the transaction acts as an independent broker.

For this purpose an "independent broker" means—

(*a*) *in relation to a transaction on behalf of a director, a person who independently of the director selects the person with whom the transaction is to be effected, and*

(*b*) *in relation to a transaction on behalf of a person connected with a director, a person who independently of that person or the director selects the person with whom the transaction is to be effected;*

and "recognised", in relation to an investment exchange, means recognised under the [Financial Services and Markets Act 2000].]

[319]

NOTES

Repealed by the Companies Act 2006, s 1295, Sch 16, as from 1 October 2007. For savings see the note to s 320 at **[318]**.

Sub-s (4): added by CA 1989, s 145, Sch 19, para 8, as from 1 March 1990; words in square brackets substituted by the Financial Services and Markets Act 2000 (Consequential Amendments and Repeals) Order 2001, SI 2001/3649, art 19, as from 1 December 2001.

322 Liabilities arising from contravention of s 320

(*1*) *An arrangement entered into by a company in contravention of section 320, and any transaction entered into in pursuance of the arrangement (whether by the company or any other person) is voidable at the instance of the company unless one or more of the conditions specified in the next subsection is satisfied.*

(2) *Those conditions are that—*

(*a*) *restitution of any money or other asset which is the subject-matter of the arrangement or transaction is no longer possible or the company has been indemnified in pursuance of this section by any other person for the loss or damage suffered by it; or*

(*b*) *any rights acquired bona fide for value and without actual notice of the contravention by any person who is not a party to the arrangement or transaction would be affected by its avoidance; or*

(*c*) *the arrangement is, within a reasonable period, affirmed by the company in general meeting and, if it is an arrangement for the transfer of an asset to or by a director of its holding company or a person who is connected with such a director, is so affirmed with the approval of the holding company given by a resolution in general meeting.*

(*3*) *If an arrangement is entered into with a company by a director of the company or its holding company or a person connected with him in contravention of section 320, that director and the person so connected, and any other director of the company who authorised the arrangement or any transaction entered into in pursuance of such an arrangement, is liable—*

(*a*) *to account to the company for any gain which he has made directly or indirectly by the arrangement or transaction, and*

(*b*) *(jointly and severally with any other person liable under this subsection) to indemnify the company for any loss or damage resulting from the arrangement or transaction.*

(*4*) *Subsection* (*3*) *is without prejudice to any liability imposed otherwise than by that subsection, and is subject to the following two subsections; and the liability under subsection* (*3*) *arises whether or not the arrangement or transaction entered into has been avoided in pursuance of subsection* (*1*).

(*5*) *If an arrangement is entered into by a company and a person connected with a director of the company or its holding company in contravention of section 320, that director is not liable under subsection* (*3*) *if he shows that he took all reasonable steps to secure the company's compliance with that section.*

(*6*) *In any case, a person so connected and any such other director as is mentioned in subsection* (*3*) *is not so liable if he shows that, at the time the arrangement was entered into, he did not know the relevant circumstances constituting the contravention.*

[320]

NOTES

Repealed by the Companies Act 2006, s 1295, Sch 16, as from 1 October 2007. For savings see the note to s 320 at **[318]**.

[322A Invalidity of certain transactions involving directors, etc

(*1*) *This section applies where a company enters into a transaction to which the parties include—*

(*a*) *a director of the company or of its holding company, or*

(*b*) *a person connected with such a director or a company with whom such a director is associated,*

and the board of directors, in connection with the transaction, exceed any limitation on their powers under the company's constitution.

(*2*) *The transaction is voidable at the instance of the company.*

(*3*) *Whether or not it is avoided, any such party to the transaction as is mentioned in subsection* (*1*)(*a*) *or* (*b*), *and any director of the company who authorised the transaction, is liable—*

(*a*) *to account to the company for any gain which he has made directly or indirectly by the transaction, and*

(*b*) *to indemnify the company for any loss or damage resulting from the transaction.*

(*4*) *Nothing in the above provisions shall be construed as excluding the operation of any other enactment or rule of law by virtue of which the transaction may be called in question or any liability to the company may arise.*

(*5*) *The transaction ceases to be voidable if—*

PART I
COMPANIES LEGISLATION

(*a*) *restitution of any money or other asset which was the subject-matter of the transaction is no longer possible, or*

(*b*) *the company is indemnified for any loss or damage resulting from the transaction, or*

(*c*) *rights acquired bona fide for value and without actual notice of the directors' exceeding their powers by a person who is not party to the transaction would be affected by the avoidance, or*

(*d*) *the transaction is ratified by the company in general meeting, by ordinary or special resolution or otherwise as the case may require.*

(*6*) *A person other than a director of the company is not liable under subsection* (*3*) *if he shows that at the time the transaction was entered into he did not know that the directors were exceeding their powers.*

(*7*) *This section does not affect the operation of section 35A in relation to any party to the transaction not within subsection* (*1*)(*a*) *or* (*b*).

But where a transaction is voidable by virtue of this section and valid by virtue of that section in favour of such a person, the court may, on the application of that person or of the company, make such order affirming, severing or setting aside the transaction, on such terms, as appear to the court to be just.

(*8*) *In this section "transaction" includes any act; and the reference in subsection* (*1*) *to limitations under the company's constitution includes limitations deriving—*

(*a*) *from a resolution of the company in general meeting or a meeting of any class of shareholders, or*

(*b*) *from any agreement between the members of the company or of any class of shareholders.]*

[321]

NOTES

Inserted by CA 1989, s 109(1), as from 4 February 1991.

Repealed by the Companies Act 2006, s 1295, Sch 16, as from a day to be appointed.

[322B Contracts with sole members who are directors

(*1*) *Subject to subsection* (*2*), *where a private company limited by shares or by guarantee having only one member enters into a contract with the sole member of the company and the sole member is also a director of the company, the company shall, unless the contract is in writing, ensure that the terms of the contract are either set out in a written memorandum or are recorded in the minutes of the first meeting of the directors of the company following the making of the contract.*

(*2*) *Subsection* (*1*) *shall not apply to contracts entered into in the ordinary course of the company's business.*

(*3*) *For the purposes of this section a sole member who is a shadow director is treated as a director.*

(*4*) *If a company fails to comply with subsection* (*1*), *the company and every officer of it who is in default is liable to a fine.*

(*5*) *Subject to subsection* (*6*), *nothing in this section shall be construed as excluding the operation of any other enactment or rule of law applying to contracts between a company and a director of that company.*

(*6*) *Failure to comply with subsection* (*1*) *with respect to a contract shall not affect the validity of that contract.]*

[322]–[329]

NOTES

Inserted by the Companies (Single Member Private Limited Companies) Regulations 1992, SI 1992/1699, reg 2, Schedule, para 3(1), as from 15 July 1992.

Repealed by the Companies Act 2006, s 1295, Sch 16, as from 1 October 2007. For savings see the note below.

Savings: this section continues to apply to contracts entered into before 1 October 2007 (see the draft Companies Act 2006 (Commencement No 3, Consequential Amendments, Transitional Provisions and Savings) Order 2007, Sch 3, para 14 at **[A12]**).

323–329 *(Repealed by the Companies Act 2006, ss 1177, 1295, Sch 16, as from 6 April 2007.)*

Restrictions on a company's power to make loans, etc, to directors and persons connected with them

330 General restriction on loans etc to directors and persons connected with them

(1) The prohibitions listed below in this section are subject to the exceptions in sections 332 to 338.

(2) A company shall not—

(a) make a loan to a director of the company or of its holding company;

(b) enter into any guarantee or provide any security in connection with a loan made by any person to such a director.

(3) A relevant company shall not—

(a) make a quasi-loan to a director of the company or of its holding company;

(b) make a loan or a quasi-loan to a person connected with such a director;

(c) enter into a guarantee or provide any security in connection with a loan or quasi-loan made by any other person for such a director or a person so connected.

(4) A relevant company shall not—

(a) enter into a credit transaction as creditor for such a director or a person so connected;

(b) enter into any guarantee or provide any security in connection with a credit transaction made by any other person for such a director or a person so connected.

(5) For purposes of sections 330 to 346, a shadow director is treated as a director.

(6) A company shall not arrange for the assignment to it, or the assumption by it, of any rights, obligations or liabilities under a transaction which, if it had been entered into by the company, would have contravened subsection (2), (3) or (4); but for the purposes of sections 330 to 347 the transaction is to be treated as having been entered into on the date of the arrangement.

(7) A company shall not take part in any arrangement whereby—

(a) another person enters into a transaction which, if it had been entered into by the company, would have contravened any of subsections (2), (3), (4) or (6); and

(b) that other person, in pursuance of the arrangement, has obtained or is to obtain any benefit from the company or its holding company or a subsidiary of the company or its holding company.

[330]

NOTES

Repealed by the Companies Act 2006, s 1295, Sch 16, as from 1 October 2007. For savings, etc, see the note below.

Savings, etc: see the draft Companies Act 2006 (Commencement No 3, Consequential Amendments, Transitional Provisions and Savings) Order 2007, Sch 3, paras 8–11 (at **[A12]**) which provide as follows—

"8 Transactions requiring members' approval: loans, quasi-loans and credit transactions (ss 197 to 214)

(1) Sections 197 to 214 of the Companies Act 2006 (loans, quasi-loans and credit transactions: requirement of members' approval) apply to transactions or arrangements entered into on or after 1st October 2007.

(2) A resolution passed before that date approving a transaction or arrangement is effective for the purposes of those sections if it complies with the requirements of those sections.

(3) Sections 330 to 342 of the 1985 Act or Articles 338 to 350 of the 1986 Order continue to apply in relation to a contravention occurring before that date.

9. Approval is not required under section 197, 198, 200 or 201 of the Companies Act 2006 (requirement of members' approval for loans etc) for anything done by a company in pursuance of an agreement entered into before 1st October 2007 that, by virtue of section 337A of the 1985 Act or Article 345A of the 1986 Order (funding of director's expenditure on defending proceedings), would not have required approval if done before that date.

10.—(1) This paragraph applies where before 1st October 2007 a company has done anything—

(a) pursuant to section 337(1) or (2) of the 1985 Act or Article 345(1) or (2) of the 1986 Order (funding of director's expenditure on duty to company), and

(b) on the condition mentioned in section 337(3)(b) of that Act or Article 345(3)(b) of that Order (condition requiring repayment of loan etc if approval of company in general meeting not given within six months).

(2) If that condition has not been satisfied before that date, it continues to apply notwithstanding the repeal of that section or that Article, but subject as follows.

(3) In the case of a private company that by reason of the repeal of section 366 of the 1985 Act or Article 374 of the 1986 Order with effect from that date ceases to be required to hold an annual general meeting, the condition shall be read as if it provided—

(a) that the approval of the company is required on or before the last date on which the company would have been required to hold an annual general meeting but for the repeal, and

(b) that the loan is to be repaid within six months from that date if such approval is not forthcoming.

11.—(1) This paragraph applies where before 1st October 2007 a company has done anything—

(a) pursuant to section 337A(1) or (3) of the 1985 Act or Article 345A(1) or (3) of the 1986 Order (funding of director's expenditure on defending proceedings), and

(b) on the terms mentioned in section 337A(4) of that Act or Article 345A(4) of that Order (terms requiring repayment of loan etc if defendant convicted, has judgment given against him or refused relief).

(2) If immediately before that date—

(a) it is not yet known whether repayment will be required, or

(b) repayment is required but had not been made,

those terms continue to apply notwithstanding the repeal of that section or that Article.".

331 Definitions for ss 330 ff

(1) The following subsections apply for the interpretation of sections 330 to 346.

(2) "Guarantee" includes indemnity, and cognate expressions are to be construed accordingly.

(3) A quasi-loan is a transaction under which one party ("the creditor") agrees to pay, or pays otherwise than in pursuance of an agreement, a sum for another ("the borrower") or agrees to reimburse, or reimburses otherwise than in pursuance of an agreement, expenditure incurred by another party for another ("the borrower")—

(a) on terms that the borrower (or a person on his behalf) will reimburse the creditor; or

(b) in circumstances giving rise to a liability on the borrower to reimburse the creditor.

(4) Any reference to the person to whom a quasi-loan is made is a reference to the borrower; and the liabilities of a borrower under a quasi-loan include the liabilities of any person who has agreed to reimburse the creditor on behalf of the borrower.

(5) …

(6) "Relevant company" means a company which—

(a) is a public company, or

(b) is a subsidiary of a public company, or

(c) is a subsidiary of a company which has as another subsidiary a public company, or

(d) has a subsidiary which is a public company.

(7) A credit transaction is a transaction under which one party ("the creditor")—

(a) supplies any goods or sells any land under a hire-purchase agreement or a conditional sale agreement;

(b) leases or hires any land or goods in return for periodical payments;

(c) otherwise disposes of land or supplies goods or services on the understanding that payment (whether in a lump sum or instalments or by way of periodical payments or otherwise) is to be deferred.

(8) "Services" means anything other than goods or land.

(*9*) *A transaction or arrangement is made "for" a person if—*

(*a*) *in the case of a loan or quasi-loan, it is made to him;*

(*b*) *in the case of a credit transaction, he is the person to whom goods or services are supplied, or land is sold or otherwise disposed of, under the transaction;*

(*c*) *in the case of a guarantee or security, it is entered into or provided in connection with a loan or quasi-loan made to him or a credit transaction made for him;*

(*d*) *in the case of an arrangement within subsection* (*6*) *or* (*7*) *of section 330, the transaction to which the arrangement relates was made for him; and*

(*e*) *in the case of any other transaction or arrangement for the supply or transfer of, or of any interest in, goods, land or services, he is the person to whom the goods, land or services* (*or the interest*) *are supplied or transferred.*

(*10*) *"Conditional sale agreement" means the same as in the Consumer Credit Act 1974.*

[331]

NOTES

Repealed by the Companies Act 2006, s 1295, Sch 16, as from 1 October 2007. For savings, etc, see the note to s 330 at **[330]**.

Sub-s (5): repealed by the Banking Act 1987, s 108(2), Sch 7, Pt I, as from 1 October 1987.

332 Short-term quasi-loans

(*1*) *Subsection* (*3*) *of section 330 does not prohibit a company ("the creditor") from making a quasi-loan to one of its directors or to a director of its holding company if—*

(*a*) *the quasi-loan contains a term requiring the director or a person on his behalf to reimburse the creditor his expenditure within 2 months of its being incurred; and*

(*b*) *the aggregate of the amount of that quasi-loan and of the amount outstanding under each relevant quasi-loan does not exceed [£5,000].*

(*2*) *A quasi-loan is relevant for this purpose if it was made to the director by virtue of this section by the creditor or its subsidiary or, where the director is a director of the creditor's holding company, any other subsidiary of that company; and "the amount outstanding" is the amount of the outstanding liabilities of the person to whom the quasi-loan was made.*

[332]

NOTES

Repealed by the Companies Act 2006, s 1295, Sch 16, as from 1 October 2007. For savings, etc, see the note to s 330 at **[330]**.

Sub-s (1): sum in square brackets substituted by CA 1989, s 138(a), as from 31 July 1990.

333 Inter-company loans in same group

In the case of a relevant company which is a member of a group of companies (meaning a holding company and its subsidiaries), paragraphs (*b*) *and* (*c*) *of section 330*(*3*) *do not prohibit the company from—*

(*a*) *making a loan or quasi-loan to another member of that group; or*

(*b*) *entering into a guarantee or providing any security in connection with a loan or quasi-loan made by any person to another member of the group,*

by reason only that a director of one member of the group is associated with another.

[333]

NOTES

Repealed by the Companies Act 2006, s 1295, Sch 16, as from 1 October 2007. For savings, etc, see the note to s 330 at **[330]**.

334 Loans of small amounts

Without prejudice to any other provision of sections 332 to 338, paragraph (*a*) *of section 330*(*2*) *does not prohibit a company from making a loan to a director of the company or of its holding company if the aggregate of the relevant amounts does not exceed [£5,000].*

[334]

NOTES

Repealed by the Companies Act 2006, s 1295, Sch 16, as from 1 October 2007. For savings, etc, see the note to s 330 at **[330]**.

Sum in square brackets substituted by CA 1989, s 138(b), as from 31 July 1990.

335 Minor and business transactions

(1) Section 330(4) does not prohibit a company from entering into a transaction for a person if the aggregate of the relevant amounts does not exceed [£10,000].

(2) Section 330(4) does not prohibit a company from entering into a transaction for a person if—

- *(a) the transaction is entered into by the company in the ordinary course of its business; and*
- *(b) the value of the transaction is not greater, and the terms on which it is entered into are no more favourable, in respect of the person for whom the transaction is made, than that or those which it is reasonable to expect the company to have offered to or in respect of a person of the same financial standing but unconnected with the company.*

[335]

NOTES

Repealed by the Companies Act 2006, s 1295, Sch 16, as from 1 October 2007. For savings, etc, see the note to s 330 at **[330]**.

Sub-s (1): sum in square brackets substituted by the Companies (Fair Dealing by Directors) (Increase in Financial Limits) Order 1990, SI 1990/1393, as from 31 July 1990.

336 Transactions at behest of holding company

The following transactions are excepted from the prohibitions of section 330—

- *(a) a loan or quasi-loan by a company to its holding company, or a company entering into a guarantee or providing any security in connection with a loan or quasi-loan made by any person to its holding company;*
- *(b) a company entering into a credit transaction as creditor for its holding company, or entering into a guarantee or providing any security in connection with a credit transaction made by any other person for its holding company.*

[336]

NOTES

Repealed by the Companies Act 2006, s 1295, Sch 16, as from 1 October 2007. For savings, etc, see the note to s 330 at **[330]**.

337 Funding of director's expenditure on duty to company

(1) A company is not prohibited by section 330 from doing anything to provide a director with funds to meet expenditure incurred or to be incurred by him for the purposes of the company or for the purpose of enabling him properly to perform his duties as an officer of the company.

(2) Nor does the section prohibit a company from doing any thing to enable a director to avoid incurring such expenditure.

(3) Subsections (1) and (2) apply only if one of the following conditions is satisfied—

- *(a) the thing in question is done with prior approval of the company given at a general meeting at which there are disclosed all the matters mentioned in the next subsection;*
- *(b) that thing is done on condition that, if the approval of the company is not so given at or before the next annual general meeting, the loan is to be repaid, or any other liability arising under any such transaction discharged, within 6 months from the conclusion of that meeting;*

but those subsections do not authorise a relevant company to enter into any transaction if the aggregate of the relevant amounts exceeds [£20,000].

(4) The matters to be disclosed under subsection (3)(a) are—

(*a*) *the purpose of the expenditure incurred or to be incurred, or which would otherwise be incurred, by the director,*
(*b*) *the amount of the funds to be provided by the company, and*
(*c*) *the extent of the company's liability under any transaction which is or is connected with the thing in question.*

[337]

NOTES

Repealed by the Companies Act 2006, s 1295, Sch 16, as from 1 October 2007. For savings, etc, see the note to s 330 at **[330]**.

Sub-s (3): sum in square brackets substituted by the Companies (Fair Dealing by Directors) (Increase in Financial Limits) Order 1990, SI 1990/1393, as from 31 July 1990.

[337A Funding of director's expenditure on defending proceedings

(1) A company is not prohibited by section 330 from doing anything to provide a director with funds to meet expenditure incurred or to be incurred by him—
(*a*) *in defending any criminal or civil proceedings, or*
(*b*) *in connection with any application under any of the provisions mentioned in subsection (2).*

(2) The provisions are—
section 144(3) and (4) (acquisition of shares by innocent nominee), and
section 727 (general power to grant relief in case of honest and reasonable conduct).

(3) Nor does section 330 prohibit a company from doing anything to enable a director to avoid incurring such expenditure.

(4) Subsections (1) and (3) only apply to a loan or other thing done as mentioned in those subsections if the terms on which it is made or done will result in the loan falling to be repaid, or any liability of the company under any transaction connected with the thing in question falling to be discharged, not later than—
(*a*) *in the event of the director being convicted in the proceedings, the date when the conviction becomes final,*
(*b*) *in the event of judgment being given against him in the proceedings, the date when the judgment becomes final, or*
(*c*) *in the event of the court refusing to grant him relief on the application, the date when the refusal of relief becomes final.*

(5) For the purposes of subsection (4) a conviction, judgment or refusal of relief becomes final—
(*a*) *if not appealed against, at the end of the period for bringing an appeal, or*
(*b*) *if appealed against, at the time when the appeal (or any further appeal) is disposed of.*

(6) An appeal is disposed of—
(*a*) *if it is determined and the period for bringing any further appeal has ended, or*
(*b*) *if it is abandoned or otherwise ceases to have effect.]*

[337A]

NOTES

Inserted by the Companies (Audit, Investigations and Community Enterprise) Act 2004, s 20, as from 6 April 2005.

Repealed by the Companies Act 2006, s 1295, Sch 16, as from 1 October 2007. For savings, etc, see the note to s 330 at **[330]**.

338 Loan or quasi-loan by money-lending company

(1) There is excepted from the prohibitions in section 330—
(*a*) *a loan or quasi-loan made by a money-lending company to any person; or*
(*b*) *a money-lending company entering into a guarantee in connection with any other loan or quasi-loan.*

(2) "Money-lending company" means a company whose ordinary business includes the making of loans or quasi-loans, or the giving of guarantees in connection with loans or quasi-loans.

(3) Subsection (1) applies only if both the following conditions are satisfied—

(*a*) *the loan or quasi-loan in question is made by the company, or it enters into the guarantee, in the ordinary course of the company's business; and*

(*b*) *the amount of the loan or quasi-loan, or the amount guaranteed, is not greater, and the terms of the loan, quasi-loan or guarantee are not more favourable, in the case of the person to whom the loan or quasi-loan is made or in respect of whom the guarantee is entered into, than that or those which it is reasonable to expect that company to have offered to or in respect of a person of the same financial standing but unconnected with the company.*

(4) But subsection (1) does not authorise a relevant company (unless it is [a banking company]) to enter into any transaction if the aggregate of the relevant amounts exceeds [£100,000].

(5) In determining that aggregate, a company which a director does not control is deemed not to be connected with him.

(6) The condition specified in subsection (3)(b) does not of itself prevent a company from making a loan to one of its directors or a director of its holding company—

(*a*) *for the purpose of facilitating the purchase, for use as that director's only or main residence, of the whole or part of any dwelling-house together with any land to be occupied and enjoyed with it;*

(*b*) *for the purpose of improving a dwelling-house or part of a dwelling-house so used or any land occupied and enjoyed with it;*

(*c*) *in substitution for any loan made by any person and falling within paragraph (a) or (b) of this subsection,*

if loans of that description are ordinarily made by the company to its employees and on terms no less favourable than those on which the transaction in question is made, and the aggregate of the relevant amounts does not exceed [£100,000].

[338]

NOTES

Repealed by the Companies Act 2006, s 1295, Sch 16, as from 1 October 2007. For savings, etc, see the note to s 330 at **[330]**.

Sub-s (4): words in first pair of square brackets substituted by CA 1989, s 23, Sch 10, para 10, as from 1 April 1990; sum in second pair of square brackets substituted by CA 1989, s 138(c), as from 31 July 1990.

Sub-s (6): sum in square brackets substituted by CA 1989, s 138(c), as from 31 July 1990.

339 "Relevant amounts" for purposes of ss 334 ff

(1) This section has effect for defining the "relevant amounts" to be aggregated under sections 334, 335(1), 337(3) and 338(4); and in relation to any proposed transaction or arrangement and the question whether it falls within one or other of the exceptions provided by those sections, "the relevant exception" is that exception; but where the relevant exception is the one provided by section 334 (loan of small amount), references in this section to a person connected with a director are to be disregarded.

(2) Subject as follows, the relevant amounts in relation to a proposed transaction or arrangement are—

(*a*) *the value of the proposed transaction or arrangement,*

(*b*) *the value of any existing arrangement which—*

 (*i*) *falls within subsection (6) or (7) of section 330, and*

 (*ii*) *also falls within subsection (3) of this section, and*

 (*iii*) *was entered into by virtue of the relevant exception by the company or by a subsidiary of the company or, where the proposed transaction or arrangement is to be made for a director of its holding company or a person connected with such a director, by that holding company or any of its subsidiaries;*

(*c*) *the amount outstanding under any other transaction—*

 (*i*) *falling within subsection (3) below, and*

 (*ii*) *made by virtue of the relevant exception, and*

 (*iii*) *made by the company or by a subsidiary of the company or, where the proposed transaction or arrangement is to be made for a director of its holding company or a person connected with such a director, by that holding company or any of its subsidiaries.*

(3) A transaction falls within this subsection if it was made—

(*a*) *for the director for whom the proposed transaction or arrangement is to be made, or for any person connected with that director; or*

(*b*) *where the proposed transaction or arrangement is to be made for a person connected with a director of a company, for that director or any person connected with him;*

and an arrangement also falls within this subsection if it relates to a transaction which does so.

(*4*) *But where the proposed transaction falls within section 338 and is one which [a banking company] proposes to enter into under subsection* (*6*) *of that section* (*housing loans, etc*), *any other transaction or arrangement which apart from this subsection would fall within subsection* (*3*) *of this section does not do so unless it was entered into in pursuance of section 338*(*6*).

(*5*) *A transaction entered into by a company which is* (*at the time of that transaction being entered into*) *a subsidiary of the company which is to make the proposed transaction, or is a subsidiary of that company's holding company, does not fall within subsection* (*3*) *if at the time when the question arises* (*that is to say, the question whether the proposed transaction or arrangement falls within any relevant exception*), *it no longer is such a subsidiary.*

(*6*) *Values for purposes of subsection* (*2*) *of this section are to be determined in accordance with the section next following; and "the amount outstanding" for purposes of subsection* (*2*)(*c*) *above is the value of the transaction less any amount by which that value has been reduced.*

[339]

NOTES

Repealed by the Companies Act 2006, s 1295, Sch 16, as from 1 October 2007. For savings, etc, see the note to s 330 at **[330]**.

Sub-s (4): words in square brackets substituted by CA 1989, s 23, Sch 10, para 10, as from 1 April 1990.

340 "Value" of transactions and arrangements

(*1*) *This section has effect for determining the value of a transaction or arrangement for purposes of sections 330 to 339.*

(*2*) *The value of a loan is the amount of its principal.*

(*3*) *The value of a quasi-loan is the amount, or maximum amount, which the person to whom the quasi-loan is made is liable to reimburse the creditor.*

(*4*) *The value of a guarantee or security is the amount guaranteed or secured.*

(*5*) *The value of an arrangement to which section 330*(*6*) *or* (*7*) *applies is the value of the transaction to which the arrangement relates less any amount by which the liabilities under the arrangement or transaction of the person for whom the transaction was made have been reduced.*

(*6*) *The value of a transaction or arrangement not falling within subsections* (*2*) *to* (*5*) *above is the price which it is reasonable to expect could be obtained for the goods, land or services to which the transaction or arrangement relates if they had been supplied* (*at the time the transaction or arrangement is entered into*) *in the ordinary course of business and on the same terms* (*apart from price*) *as they have been supplied, or are to be supplied, under the transaction or arrangement in question.*

(*7*) *For purposes of this section, the value of a transaction or arrangement which is not capable of being expressed as a specific sum of money* (*because the amount of any liability arising under the transaction or arrangement is unascertainable, or for any other reason*), *whether or not any liability under the transaction or arrangement has been reduced, is deemed to exceed [£100,000].*

[340]

NOTES

Repealed by the Companies Act 2006, s 1295, Sch 16, as from 1 October 2007. For savings, etc, see the note to s 330 at **[330]**.

Sub-s (7): sum in square brackets substituted by the Companies (Fair Dealing by Directors) (Increase in Financial Limits) Order 1990, SI 1990/1393, as from 31 July 1990.

341 Civil remedies for breach of s 330

(*1*) *If a company enters into a transaction or arrangement in contravention of section 330, the transaction or arrangement is voidable at the instance of the company unless—*

(*a*) *restitution of any money or any other asset which is the subject matter of the arrangement or transaction is no longer possible, or the company has been indemnified in pursuance of subsection (2)(b) below for the loss or damage suffered by it, or*

(*b*) *any rights acquired bona fide for value and without actual notice of the contravention by a person other than the person for whom the transaction or arrangement was made would be affected by its avoidance.*

(*2*) *Where an arrangement or transaction is made by a company for a director of the company or its holding company or a person connected with such a director in contravention of section 330, that director and the person so connected and any other director of the company who authorised the transaction or arrangement (whether or not it has been avoided in pursuance of subsection (1)) is liable—*

(*a*) *to account to the company for any gain which he has made directly or indirectly by the arrangement or transaction; and*

(*b*) *(jointly and severally with any other person liable under this subsection) to indemnify the company for any loss or damage resulting from the arrangement or transaction.*

(*3*) *Subsection (2) is without prejudice to any liability imposed otherwise than by that subsection, but is subject to the next two subsections.*

(*4*) *Where an arrangement or transaction is entered into by a company and a person connected with a director of the company or its holding company in contravention of section 330, that director is not liable under subsection (2) of this section if he shows that he took all reasonable steps to secure the company's compliance with that section.*

(*5*) *In any case, a person so connected and any such other director as is mentioned in subsection (2) is not so liable if he shows that, at the time the arrangement or transaction was entered into, he did not know the relevant circumstances constituting the contravention.*

[341]

NOTES

Repealed by the Companies Act 2006, s 1295, Sch 16, as from 1 October 2007. For savings, etc, see the note to s 330 at **[330]**.

342 Criminal penalties for breach of s 330

(*1*) *A director of a relevant company who authorises or permits the company to enter into a transaction or arrangement knowing or having reasonable cause to believe that the company was thereby contravening section 330 is guilty of an offence.*

(*2*) *A relevant company which enters into a transaction or arrangement for one of its directors or for a director of its holding company in contravention of section 330 is guilty of an offence.*

(*3*) *A person who procures a relevant company to enter into a transaction or arrangement knowing or having reasonable cause to believe that the company was thereby contravening section 330 is guilty of an offence.*

(*4*) *A person guilty of an offence under this section is liable to imprisonment or a fine, or both.*

(*5*) *A relevant company is not guilty of an offence under subsection (2) if it shows that, at the time the transaction or arrangement was entered into, it did not know the relevant circumstances.*

[342]–[344]

NOTES

Repealed by the Companies Act 2006, s 1295, Sch 16, as from 1 October 2007. For savings, etc, see the note to s 330 at **[330]**.

343, 344 *(Repealed by the Companies Act 2006, ss 1177, 1295, Sch 16, as from 6 April 2007.)*

Supplementary

345 Power to increase financial limits

(1) The Secretary of State may by order in a statutory instrument substitute for any sum of money specified in this Part a larger sum specified in the order.

(2) An order under this section is subject to annulment in pursuance of a resolution of either House of Parliament.

(3) Such an order does not have effect in relation to anything done or not done before its coming into force; and accordingly, proceedings in respect of any liability (whether civil or criminal) incurred before that time may be continued or instituted as if the order had not been made.

[345]

NOTES

Repealed by the Companies Act 2006, s 1295, Sch 16, as from 1 October 2007.

Orders: the Companies (Fair Dealing by Directors) (Increase in Financial Limits) Order 1990, SI 1990/1393.

346 "Connected persons", etc

(1) This section has effect with respect to references in this Part to a person being "connected" with a director of a company, and to a director being "associated with" or "controlling" a body corporate.

(2) A person is connected with a director of a company if, but only if, he (not being himself a director of it) is—

(a) that director's spouse, [civil partner,] child or step-child; or

(b) except where the context otherwise requires, a body corporate with which the director is associated; or

(c) a person acting in his capacity as trustee of any trust the beneficiaries of which include—

(i) the director, his spouse [or civil partner] or any children or step-children of his, or

(ii) a body corporate with which he is associated,

or of a trust whose terms confer a power on the trustees that may be exercised for the benefit of the director, his spouse [or civil partner], or any children or step-children of his, or any such body corporate; or

(d) a person acting in his capacity as partner of that director or of any person who, by virtue of paragraph (a), (b) or (c) of this subsection, is connected with that director; or

(e) a Scottish firm in which—

(i) that director is a partner,

(ii) a partner is a person who, by virtue of paragraph (a), (b) or (c) above, is connected with that director, or

(iii) a partner is a Scottish firm in which that director is a partner or in which there is a partner who, by virtue of paragraph (a), (b) or (c) above, is connected with that director.

(3) In subsection (2)—

(a) a reference to the child or step-child of any person includes an illegitimate child of his, but does not include any person who has attained the age of 18; and

(b) paragraph (c) does not apply to a person acting in his capacity as trustee under an employees' share scheme or a pension scheme.

(4) A director of a company is associated with a body corporate if, but only if, he and the persons connected with him, together—

(a) are interested in shares comprised in the equity share capital of that body corporate of a nominal value equal to at least one-fifth of that share capital [(excluding any shares in the company held as treasury shares)]; or

(b) are entitled to exercise or control the exercise of more than one-fifth of the voting

power at any general meeting of that body [(excluding any voting rights attached to any shares in the company held as treasury shares)].

(5) A director of a company is deemed to control a body corporate if, but only if—

(a) he or any person connected with him is interested in any part of the equity share capital of that body or is entitled to exercise or control the exercise of any part of the voting power at any general meeting of that body; and

(b) that director, the persons connected with him and the other directors of that company, together, are interested in more than one-half of that share capital [(excluding any shares in the company held as treasury shares)] or are entitled to exercise or control the exercise of more than one-half of that voting power [(excluding any voting rights attached to any shares in the company held as treasury shares)].

(6) For purposes of subsections (4) and (5)—

(a) a body corporate with which a director is associated is not to be treated as connected with that director unless it is also connected with him by virtue of subsection (2)(c) or (d); and

(b) a trustee of a trust the beneficiaries of which include (or may include) a body corporate with which a director is associated is not to be treated as connected with a director by reason only of that fact.

(7) The rules set out in Part I of Schedule 13 apply for the purposes of subsections (4) and (5).

(8) References in those subsections to voting power the exercise of which is controlled by a director include voting power whose exercise is controlled by a body corporate controlled by him; but this is without prejudice to other provisions of subsections (4) and (5).

[346]

NOTES

Repealed by the Companies Act 2006, s 1295, Sch 16, as from 1 October 2007. For savings see the note below.

Sub-s (2): words in square brackets inserted by the Civil Partnership Act 2004, s 261(1), Sch 27, para 102, as from 5 December 2005.

Sub-ss (4), (5): words in square brackets inserted by the Companies (Acquisition of Own Shares) (Treasury Shares) Regulations 2003, SI 2003/1116, reg 4, Schedule, para 17, as from 1 December 2003.

Savings: see the draft Companies Act 2006 (Commencement No 3, Consequential Amendments, Transitional Provisions and Savings) Order 2007, Sch 3, para 50 (at **[A12]**) which provides as follows—

"50 Repeal of definition of "connected person"

The repeal of section 346 of and Schedule 13 to the 1985 Act or Article 354 of and Schedule 13 to the 1986 Order (meaning of "connected person") does not affect—

(a) section 317(3)(b) of the 1985 Act or Article 325(3)(b) of the 1986 Order (directors to disclose interest in contracts);

(b) section 7E and 7F(3) of the Industrial and Provident Societies Act 1965 or section 7D and 7E(3) of the Industrial and Provident Societies Act (Northern Ireland) 1969 (transactions with committee members: whether person "connected with" committee member or "associated with" society);

(c) section 96B(2)(a) of the Financial Services and Markets Act 2000 (disclosure rules: responsibility for compliance: meaning of person connected with person having managerial responsibilities within an issuer).".

Step-child: this includes relationships arising through civil partnership; see the Civil Partnership Act 2004, ss 246, 247, Sch 21.

347 Transactions under foreign law

For purposes of sections 319 to 322 and 330 to 343, it is immaterial whether the law which (apart from this Act) governs any arrangement or transaction is the law of the United Kingdom, or of a part of it, or not.

[347]

NOTES

Repealed by the Companies Act 2006, s 1295, Sch 16, as from 1 October 2007.

[PART XA
CONTROL OF POLITICAL DONATIONS

347A Introductory provisions

(1) This Part has effect for controlling—
- *(a) contributions and other donations made by companies to registered parties and other EU political organisations; and*
- *(b) EU political expenditure incurred by companies.*

(2) The following provisions have effect for the purposes of this Part, but subsections (4) and (7) have effect subject to section 347B.

(3) "Director" includes shadow director.

(4) "Donation", in relation to an organisation, means anything that would constitute a donation for the purposes of Part IV of the Political Parties, Elections and Referendums Act 2000 in accordance with sections 50 to 52 of that Act (references in those sections to a registered party being read as applying equally to an organisation which is not such a party); and—
- *(a) subsections (3) to (8) of section 50 of that Act shall apply, with any necessary modifications, for the purpose of determining whether something is a donation to an organisation for the purposes of this Part as they apply for the purpose of determining whether something is a donation to a registered party for the purposes of Part IV of that Act; and*
- *(b) section 53 of that Act shall similarly apply for the purpose of determining, for the purposes of this Part, the value of any donation.*

(5) "EU political expenditure", in relation to a company, means any expenditure incurred by the company—
- *(a) in respect of the preparation, publication or dissemination of any advertising or any other promotional or publicity material—*
  - *(i) of whatever nature, and*
  - *(ii) however published or otherwise disseminated,*

  which, at the time of publication or dissemination, is capable of being reasonably regarded as intended to affect public support for any EU political organisation, or
- *(b) in respect of any activities on the part of the company such as are mentioned in subsection (7)(b) or (c).*

(6) "EU political organisation" means—
- *(a) a registered party; or*
- *(b) any other organisation to which subsection (7) applies.*

(7) This subsection applies to an organisation if—
- *(a) it is a political party which carries on, or proposes to carry on, activities for the purpose of or in connection with the participation of the party in any election or elections to public office held in a member State other than the United Kingdom;*
- *(b) it carries on, or proposes to carry on, activities which are capable of being reasonably regarded as intended to affect public support for—*
  - *(i) any registered party,*
  - *(ii) any other political party within paragraph (a), or*
  - *(iii) independent candidates at any election or elections of the kind mentioned in that paragraph; or*
- *(c) it carries on, or proposes to carry on, activities which are capable of being reasonably regarded as intended to influence voters in relation to any national or regional referendum held under the law of any member State.*

(8) "Organisation" includes any body corporate and any combination of persons or other unincorporated association.

(9) "Registered party" means a party registered under Part II of the Political Parties, Elections and Referendums Act 2000.

(10) "The relevant time", in relation to any donation or expenditure made or incurred by a company or subsidiary undertaking, means—
- *(a) the time when the donation or expenditure is made or incurred; or*
- *(b) if earlier, the time when any contract is entered into by the company or undertaking in pursuance of which the donation or expenditure is made or incurred.*

(11) "Subsidiary undertaking" has the same meaning as in Part VII.]

[348]

NOTES

Inserted, together with preceding heading and ss 347B–347K (Pt XA) by the Political Parties, Elections and Referendums Act 2000, s 139(1), Sch 19, as from 30 November 2000 (in so far as confers power to make Orders or Regulations), and as from 16 February 2001 (otherwise). By virtue of s 163(7) of, and Sch 23, Pt II, para 12 to, the 2000 Act, Pt XA shall not apply to a company in relation to any time falling before the relevant date for the company; namely the date (if held within the first year after s 139(1) comes into force) of the annual general meeting of the company, or otherwise the date immediately following the end of that year.

Repealed by the Companies Act 2006, s 1295, Sch 16, as from 1 October 2007. For savings, etc, see the note below.

Savings, etc: see the draft Companies Act 2006 (Commencement No 3, Consequential Amendments, Transitional Provisions and Savings) Order 2007, Sch 3, paras 41, 42 (at **[A12]**) which provides as follows—

"41 Political donations and expenditure (ss 362 to 379)

(1) Sections 362 to 379 of the Companies Act 2006 (political donations and expenditure) apply to donations made or expenditure incurred on or after 1st October 2007.

Section 379(2) of that Act applies as to the time when a donation is regarded as made or expenditure as incurred, including where it is made or incurred in pursuance of a contract entered into before that date.

(2) Part 10A of the 1985 Act continues to apply to donations or expenditure in relation to which the relevant time, as defined in section 347A(10) of that Act, is before that date.

(3) The repeal of that Part does not affect paragraph 3(4) of Schedule 7 to the 1985 Act (matters to be dealt with in directors' report: expressions to have same meaning as in Part 10A).

42. An approval resolution passed in accordance with section 347C of the 1985 Act before 1st October 2007 is treated as complying with the requirements of section 367 of the Companies Act 2006 (form of authorising resolution) although it does not comply with the requirements of that section as to the heads under which donations and expenditure are to be stated.".

[347B Exemptions

(1) Section 347A(4) does not extend to a subscription paid to an EU trade association for membership of the association, and accordingly such a payment is not a donation to the association for the purposes of this Part.

(2) In subsection (1)—

"EU trade association" means any organisation formed for the purpose of furthering the trade interests—

(a) of its members, or

(b) of persons represented by its members,

which carries on its activities wholly or mainly in one or more of the member States;

"subscription", in relation to a trade association, does not include any payment to the association to the extent that it is made for the purpose of financing any particular activity of the association.

(3) Section 347A(7) does not apply to any all-party parliamentary group composed of members of one or both of the Houses of Parliament (or of such members and other persons), and accordingly any such group is not an EU political organisation for the purposes of this Part.

(4) For the purposes of this Part—

(a) a company does not need to be authorised as mentioned in section 347C(1) or section 347D(2) or (3), and

(b) a subsidiary undertaking does not need to be authorised as mentioned in section 347E(2),

in connection with any donation or donations to any EU political organisation or organisations made in a particular qualifying period, except to the extent (if any) that the amount or aggregate amount of any such donation or donations made in that period exceeds £5,000.

(5) The restrictions imposed by sections 347C(1), 347D(2) and (3) and 347E(2) accordingly have effect subject to subsection (4); and, where a resolution is passed for the purposes of any of those provisions, any amount of donations in relation to which, by virtue of subsection (4), no authorisation is needed shall accordingly not count towards the sum specified in the resolution.

(6) In subsection (4) "qualifying period" means—

(a) the period of 12 months beginning with the relevant date for the company or (in the case of a subsidiary undertaking) the parent company; and

(b) each succeeding period of twelve months.

(7) For the purposes of subsection (6) the relevant date for a company is—

(a) if an annual general meeting of the company is held within the period of 12 months beginning with the date of the coming into force of this section, the date of that meeting; and

(b) otherwise, the date immediately following the end of that period.

(8) For the purposes of this Part—

(a) a company does not need to be authorised as mentioned in section 347C(1) or section 347D(2) or (3), and

(b) a subsidiary undertaking does not need to be authorised as mentioned in section 347E(2),

in connection with any EU political expenditure in relation to which an exemption is conferred on the company or (as the case may be) subsidiary undertaking by virtue of an order made by the Secretary of State by statutory instrument.

(9) The restrictions imposed by sections 347C(1), 347D(2) and (3) and 347E(2) accordingly have effect subject to subsection (8); and, where a resolution is passed for the purposes of any of those provisions, any amount of EU political expenditure in relation to which, by virtue of subsection (8), no authorisation is needed shall accordingly not count towards the sum specified in the resolution.

(10) An order under subsection (8) may confer an exemption for the purposes of that subsection in relation to—

(a) companies or subsidiary undertakings of any description or category specified in the order, or

(b) expenditure of any description or category so specified (whether framed by reference to goods, services or other matters in respect of which such expenditure is incurred or otherwise),

or both.

(11) An order shall not be made under subsection (8) unless a draft of the statutory instrument containing the order has been laid before and approved by each House of Parliament.]

[349]

NOTES

Inserted as noted to s 347A at **[348]**.

Repealed by the Companies Act 2006, s 1295, Sch 16, as from 1 October 2007. For savings, etc, see the note to s 347A at **[348]**.

Orders: the Companies (EU Political Expenditure) Exemption Order 2001, SI 2001/445.

[347C Prohibition on donations and political expenditure by companies

(1) A company must not—

(a) make any donation to any registered party or to any other EU political organisation, or

(b) incur any EU political expenditure,

unless the donation or expenditure is authorised by virtue of an approval resolution passed by the company in general meeting before the relevant time.

This subsection has effect subject to section 347D(3).

(2) For the purposes of this section an approval resolution is a qualifying resolution which authorises the company to do either (or both) of the following, namely—

(a) make donations to EU political organisations not exceeding in total a sum specified in the resolution, or

(b) incur EU political expenditure not exceeding in total a sum so specified,

during the requisite period beginning with the date of the resolution.

(3) In subsection (2)—

(a) "qualifying resolution" means an ordinary resolution or, if the directors so determine or the articles so require—

(i) *a special resolution, or*

(ii) *a resolution passed by any percentage of the members greater than that required for an ordinary resolution;*

(*b*) *"the requisite period" means four years or such shorter period as the directors may determine or the articles may require;*

and the directors may make a determination for the purposes of paragraph (*a*) *or* (*b*) *above except where any provision of the articles operates to prevent them from doing so.*

(*4*) *The resolution must be expressed in general terms conforming with subsection* (*2*), *and accordingly may not purport to authorise particular donations or expenditure.*

(*5*) *Where a company makes any donation or incurs any expenditure in contravention of subsection* (*1*), *no ratification or other approval made or given by the company or its members after the relevant time is capable of operating to nullify that contravention.*

(*6*) *Nothing in this section enables a company to be authorised to do anything that it could not lawfully do apart from this section.]*

[350]

NOTES

Inserted as noted to s 347A at **[348]**.

Repealed by the Companies Act 2006, s 1295, Sch 16, as from 1 October 2007. For savings, etc, see the note to s 347A at **[348]**.

[347D Special rules for subsidiaries

(*1*) *This section applies where a company is a subsidiary of another company ("the holding company").*

(2) *Where the subsidiary is not a wholly-owned subsidiary of the holding company—*

(*a*) *it must not make any donation or incur any expenditure to which subsection* (*1*) *of section 347C applies unless the donation or expenditure is authorised by virtue of a subsidiary approval resolution passed by the holding company in general meeting before the relevant time; and*

(*b*) *this requirement applies in addition to that imposed by that subsection.*

(*3*) *Where the subsidiary is a wholly-owned subsidiary of the holding company—*

(*a*) *it must not make any donation or incur any expenditure to which subsection* (*1*) *of section 347C applies unless the donation or expenditure is authorised by virtue of a subsidiary approval resolution passed by the holding company in general meeting before the relevant time; and*

(*b*) *this requirement applies in place of that imposed by that subsection.*

(*4*) *For the purposes of this section a subsidiary approval resolution is a qualifying resolution of the holding company which authorises the subsidiary to do either* (*or both*) *of the following, namely—*

(*a*) *make donations to EU political organisations not exceeding in total a sum specified in the resolution, or*

(*b*) *incur EU political expenditure not exceeding in total a sum so specified,*

during the requisite period beginning with the date of the resolution.

(*5*) *Subsection* (*3*) *of section 347C shall apply for the purposes of subsection* (*4*) *above as it applies for the purposes of subsection* (*2*) *of that section.*

(*6*) *The resolution must be expressed in general terms conforming with subsection* (*4*), *and accordingly may not purport to authorise particular donations or expenditure.*

(*7*) *The resolution may not relate to donations or expenditure by more than one subsidiary.*

(*8*) *Where a subsidiary makes any donation or incurs any expenditure in contravention of subsection* (*2*) *or* (*3*), *no ratification or other approval made or given by the holding company or its members after the relevant time is capable of operating to nullify that contravention.*

(*9*) *Nothing in this section enables a company to be authorised to do anything that it could not lawfully do apart from this section.]*

[351]

NOTES

Inserted as noted to s 347A at **[348]**.

Repealed by the Companies Act 2006, s 1295, Sch 16, as from 1 October 2007. For savings, etc, see the note to s 347A at **[348]**.

[347E Special rule for parent company of non-GB subsidiary undertaking

(1) This section applies where a company ("the parent company") has a subsidiary undertaking which is incorporated or otherwise established outside Great Britain.

(2) The parent company shall take all such steps as are reasonably open to it to secure that the subsidiary undertaking does not make any donation or incur any expenditure to which subsection (1) of section 347C applies except to the extent that the donation or expenditure is authorised by virtue of a subsidiary approval resolution passed by the parent company in general meeting before the relevant time.

(3) For the purposes of this section a subsidiary approval resolution is a qualifying resolution of the parent company which authorises the subsidiary undertaking to do either (or both) of the following, namely—

- *(a) make donations to EU political organisations not exceeding in total a sum specified in the resolution, or*
- *(b) incur EU political expenditure not exceeding in total a sum so specified,*

during the requisite period beginning with the date of the resolution.

(4) Subsection (3) of section 347C shall apply for the purposes of subsection (3) above as it applies for the purposes of subsection (2) of that section.

(5) The resolution must be expressed in general terms conforming with subsection (3), and accordingly may not purport to authorise particular donations or expenditure.

(6) The resolution may not relate to donations or expenditure by more than one subsidiary undertaking.

(7) Where a subsidiary undertaking makes any donation or incurs any expenditure which (to any extent) is not authorised as mentioned in subsection (2), no ratification or other approval made or given by the parent company or its members after the relevant time is capable of operating to authorise that donation or expenditure.]

[352]

NOTES

Inserted as noted to s 347A at **[348]**.

Repealed by the Companies Act 2006, s 1295, Sch 16, as from 1 October 2007. For savings, etc, see the note to s 347A at **[348]**.

[347F Remedies for breach of prohibitions on company donations etc

(1) This section applies where a company has made any donation or incurred any expenditure in contravention of any of the provisions of sections 347C and 347D.

(2) Every person who was a director of the company at the relevant time is liable to pay the company—

- *(a) the amount of the donation or expenditure made or incurred in contravention of the provisions in question; and*
- *(b) damages in respect of any loss or damage sustained by the company as a result of the donation or expenditure having been made or incurred in contravention of those provisions.*

(3) Every such person is also liable to pay the company interest on the amount mentioned in subsection (2)(a) in respect of the period—

- *(a) beginning with the date when the donation or expenditure was made or incurred, and*
- *(b) ending with the date when that amount is paid to the company by any such person;*

and such interest shall be payable at such rate as the Secretary of State may prescribe by regulations.

(4) Where two or more persons are subject to a particular liability arising by virtue of any provision of this section, each of those persons is jointly and severally liable.

(5) Where only part of any donation or expenditure was made or incurred in contravention of any of the provisions of sections 347C and 347D, this section applies only to so much of it as was so made or incurred.

(6) Where—

(a) this section applies as mentioned in subsection (1), and

(b) the company in question is a subsidiary of another company ("the holding company"),

then (subject to subsection (7)) subsections (2) to (5) shall, in connection with the donation or expenditure made or incurred by the subsidiary, apply in relation to the holding company as they apply in relation to the subsidiary.

(7) Those subsections do not apply in relation to the holding company if—

(a) the subsidiary is not a wholly-owned subsidiary of the holding company; and

(b) the donation or expenditure was authorised by such a resolution of the holding company as is mentioned in section 347D(2)(a).

(8) Nothing in section 727 shall apply in relation to any liability of any person arising under this section.]

[353]

NOTES

Inserted as noted to s 347A at **[348]**.

Repealed by the Companies Act 2006, s 1295, Sch 16, as from 1 October 2007. For savings, etc, see the note to s 347A at **[348]**.

[347G Remedy for unauthorised donation or expenditure by non-GB subsidiary

(1) This section applies where—

(a) a company ("the parent company") has a subsidiary undertaking falling within subsection (1) of section 347E;

(b) the subsidiary undertaking has made any donation or incurred any expenditure to which subsection (1) of section 347C applies; and

(c) the parent company has, in relation to that donation or expenditure, failed to discharge its duty under subsection (2) of section 347E to take all such steps as are mentioned in that subsection.

(2) Subsections (2) to (4) of section 347F shall, in connection with the donation or expenditure made or incurred by the subsidiary undertaking, apply in relation to the holding company as if—

(a) it were a company falling within subsection (1) of that section, and

(b) the donation or expenditure had been made or incurred by it in contravention of section 347C or 347D.

(3) Where only part of the donation or expenditure was not authorised as mentioned in section 347E(2), those subsections shall so apply only to that part of it.

(4) Section 347F(8) applies to any liability of any person arising under section 347F by virtue of this section.]

[354]

NOTES

Inserted as noted to s 347A at **[348]**.

Repealed by the Companies Act 2006, s 1295, Sch 16, as from 1 October 2007. For savings, etc, see the note to s 347A at **[348]**.

[347H Exemption of directors from liability in respect of unauthorised donation or expenditure

(1) Where proceedings are brought against a director or former director of a company in respect of any liability arising under section 347F(2)(a) in connection with a donation or expenditure made or incurred by the company, it shall be a defence for that person to show that—

(a) the unauthorised amount has been repaid to the company, together with any interest on that amount due under section 347F(3);

(b) that repayment has been approved by the company in general meeting; and

(c) *in the notice of the relevant resolution submitted to that meeting full disclosure was made—*

(i) *of the circumstances in which the donation or expenditure was made or incurred in contravention of section 347C or 347D, and*

(ii) *of the circumstances in which, and the person or persons by whom, the repayment was made.*

(2) *Where proceedings are brought against a director or former director of a holding company in respect of any liability arising under section 347F(2)(a) in connection with a donation or expenditure made or incurred by a subsidiary of the company, it shall be a defence for that person to show that—*

(a) *the unauthorised amount has been repaid either to the subsidiary or to the holding company, together with any interest on that amount due under section 347F(3);*

(b) *that repayment has been approved—*

(i) *(if made to the subsidiary) by both the subsidiary and the holding company in general meeting, or*

(ii) *(if made to the holding company) by the holding company in general meeting; and*

(c) *in the notice of the relevant resolution submitted to each of those meetings or (as the case may be) to that meeting, full disclosure was made—*

(i) *of the circumstances in which the donation or expenditure was made in contravention of section 347D, and*

(ii) *of the circumstances in which, and the person or persons by whom, the repayment was made.*

(3) *If the subsidiary is a wholly-owned subsidiary of the holding company, it is not necessary for the purposes of subsection (2) to show (where the repayment was made to the subsidiary) that the repayment has been approved by the subsidiary, and paragraphs (b) and (c) of that subsection shall apply accordingly.*

(4) *Where proceedings are brought against a director or former director of a holding company in respect of any liability arising under section 347F(2)(a) in connection with a donation or expenditure made or incurred by a subsidiary of the company which is not a wholly-owned subsidiary, then (subject to subsection (5)) it shall be a defence for that person to show that—*

(a) *proceedings have been instituted by the subsidiary against all or any of its directors in respect of the unauthorised amount; and*

(b) *those proceedings are being pursued with due diligence by the subsidiary.*

(5) *A person may not avail himself of the defence provided by subsection (4) except with the leave of the court; and on an application for leave under this subsection the court may make such order as it thinks fit, including an order adjourning, or sanctioning the continuation of, the proceedings against the applicant on such terms and conditions as it thinks fit.*

(6) *Where proceedings are brought against a director or former director of a company in respect of any liability arising under section 347F(2)(a) (as applied by virtue of section 347G) in connection with a donation or expenditure made or incurred by a subsidiary undertaking of the company, it shall be a defence for that person to show that—*

(a) *the unauthorised amount has been repaid to the subsidiary undertaking, together with any interest on that amount due under section 347F(3) (as so applied);*

(b) *that repayment has been approved by the company in general meeting; and*

(c) *in the notice of the relevant resolution submitted to that meeting full disclosure was made—*

(i) *of the circumstances in which the donation or expenditure was made without having been authorised as mentioned in section 347E(2), and*

(ii) *of the circumstances in which, and the person or persons by whom, the repayment was made.*

(7) *In this section "the unauthorised amount", in relation to any donation or expenditure, means the amount of the donation or expenditure—*

(a) *which was made or incurred in contravention of section 347C or 347D, or*

(b) *which was not authorised as mentioned in section 347E(2),*

as the case may be.]

[355]

NOTES

Inserted as noted to s 347A at **[348]**.

Repealed by the Companies Act 2006, s 1295, Sch 16, as from 1 October 2007. For savings, etc, see the note to s 347A at **[348]**.

[347I Enforcement of directors' liabilities by shareholder action

(1) Any liability of any person under section 347F or 347G as a director or former director of a company is (in addition to being enforceable by proceedings brought by the company) enforceable by proceedings brought under this section in the name of the company by an authorised group of members of the company.

(2) For the purposes of this section "authorised group", in relation to the members of a company, means any such combination of members as is specified in section 54(2)(a), (b) or (c).

(3) An authorised group of members of a company may not bring proceedings under this section unless—

(a) the group has given written notice to the company stating—

(i) the cause of action and a summary of the facts on which the proceedings are to be based,

(ii) the names and addresses of the members of the company comprising the group, and

(iii) the grounds on which it is alleged that those members constitute an authorised group; and

(b) not less than 28 days have elapsed between the date of the giving of the notice to the company and the institution of the proceedings.

(4) Where such a notice is given to a company, any director may apply to the court within the period of 28 days beginning with the date of the giving of the notice for an order directing that the proposed proceedings are not to be instituted.

(5) An application under subsection (4) may be made on one or more of the following grounds—

(a) that the unauthorised amount within the meaning of section 347H has been repaid to the company or subsidiary undertaking as mentioned in subsection (1), (2), (4) or (6) of that section (as the case may be) and the other conditions mentioned in that subsection were satisfied with respect to that repayment;

(b) that proceedings to enforce the liability have been instituted by the company and are being pursued with due diligence by the company;

(c) that the members proposing to institute proceedings under this section do not constitute an authorised group.

(6) Where such an application is made on the ground mentioned in subsection (5)(b), the court may make such order as it thinks fit; and such an order may, as an alternative to directing that the proposed proceedings under this section are not to be instituted, direct—

(a) that those proceedings may be instituted on such terms and conditions as the court thinks fit;

(b) that the proceedings instituted by the company are to be discontinued;

(c) that the proceedings instituted by the company may be continued on such terms and conditions as the court thinks fit.

(7) If proceedings are brought under this section by an authorised group of members of a company, the group shall owe the same duties to the company in relation to the bringing of those proceedings on behalf of the company as would be owed by the directors of the company if the proceedings were being brought by the company itself; but no proceedings to enforce any duty owed by virtue of this subsection shall be brought by the company except with the leave of the court.

(8) Proceedings brought under this section may not be discontinued or settled by the group except with the leave of the court; and the court may grant leave under this subsection on such terms as it thinks fit.]

[356]

NOTES

Inserted as noted to s 347A at **[348]**.

Repealed by the Companies Act 2006, s 1295, Sch 16, as from 1 October 2007. For savings, etc, see the note to s 347A at **[348]**.

[347J Costs of shareholder action

(1) This section applies in relation to proceedings brought under section 347I by an authorised group of members of a company ("the group").

(2) The group may apply to the court for an order directing the company to indemnify the group in respect of costs incurred or to be incurred by the group in connection with the proceedings; and on such an application the court may make such an order on such terms as it thinks fit.

(3) The group shall not be entitled to be paid any such costs out of the assets of the company except by virtue of such an order.

(4) If—

(a) the company is awarded costs in connection with the proceedings or it is agreed that costs incurred by the company in connection with the proceedings should be paid by any defendant, and

(b) no order has been made with respect to the proceedings under subsection (2),

the costs shall be paid to the group.

(5) If—

(a) any defendant is awarded costs in connection with the proceedings or it is agreed that any defendant should be paid costs incurred by him in connection with the proceedings, and

(b) no order has been made with respect to the proceedings under subsection (2),

the costs shall be paid by the group.

(6) In the application of this section to Scotland references to costs are to expenses and references to any defendant are to any defender.]

[357]

NOTES

Inserted as noted to s 347A at **[348]**.

Repealed by the Companies Act 2006, s 1295, Sch 16, as from 1 October 2007. For savings, etc, see the note to s 347A at **[348]**.

[347K Information for purposes of shareholder action

(1) Where any proceedings have been instituted under section 347I by an authorised group within the meaning of that section, the group is entitled to require the company to provide the group with all information relating to the subject matter of the proceedings which is in the company's possession or under its control or which is reasonably obtainable by it.

(2) If the company, having been required by the group to provide the information referred to in subsection (1), refuses to provide the group with all or any of the information, the court may, on an application made by the group, make an order directing—

(a) the company, and

(b) any of its officers or employees specified in the application,

to provide the group with the information in question in such form and by such means as the court may direct.]

[358]

NOTES

Inserted as noted to s 347A at **[348]**.

Repealed by the Companies Act 2006, s 1295, Sch 16, as from 1 October 2007. For savings, etc, see the note to s 347A at **[348]**.

PART XI
COMPANY ADMINISTRATION AND PROCEDURE

CHAPTER I
COMPANY IDENTIFICATION

348 Company name to appear outside place of business

(1) Every company shall paint or affix, and keep painted or affixed, its name on the outside of every office or place in which its business is carried on, in a conspicuous position and in letters easily legible.

(2) If a company does not paint or affix its name as required above, the company and every officer of it who is in default is liable to a fine; and if a company does not keep its name painted or affixed as so required, the company and every officer of it who is in default is liable to a fine and, for continued contravention, to a daily default fine.

[359]

NOTES

Repealed by the Companies Act 2006, s 1295, Sch 16, as from a day to be appointed.

Application to limited liability partnerships: see the Limited Liability Partnerships Regulations 2001, SI 2001/1090, reg 4(1), Sch 2, Pt 1 at **[6985]**, **[6993]**.

349 Company's name to appear in its correspondence, etc

(1) Every company shall have its name mentioned in legible characters—

(a) in all business letters [and order forms] of the company,

(b) in all its notices and other official publications,

[(ba) on all its websites,]

(c) in all bills of exchange, promissory notes, endorsements, cheques and orders for money or goods purporting to be signed by or on behalf of the company, and

(d) in all its bills of parcels, invoices, receipts and letters of credit.

(2) If a company fails to comply with subsection (1) it is liable to a fine.

(3) If an officer of a company or a person on its behalf—

(a) issues or authorises the issue of any business letter [or order form] of the company, or any notice or other official publication of the company, in which the company's name is not mentioned as required by subsection (1), …

[(aa) causes or authorises the appearance of a website of the company on which the company's name is not so mentioned, or]

(b) issues or authorises the issue of any bill of parcels, invoice, receipt or letter of credit of the company in which its name is not so mentioned,

he is liable to a fine.

(4) If an officer of a company or a person on its behalf signs or authorises to be signed on behalf of the company any bill of exchange, promissory note, endorsement, cheque or order for money or goods in which the company's name is not mentioned as required by subsection (1), he is liable to a fine; and he is further personally liable to the holder of the bill of exchange, promissory note, cheque or order for money or goods for the amount of it (unless it is duly paid by the company).

[(5) References in this section to a document of any type are to a document of that type in hard copy, electronic or any other form.]

[360]

NOTES

Repealed by the Companies Act 2006, s 1295, Sch 16, as from a day to be appointed.

Sub-s (1): words in square brackets in para (a) and the whole of para (ba) inserted by the Companies (Registrar, Languages and Trading Disclosures) Regulations 2006, SI 2006/3429, reg 6, Sch 1, para 1(1), (2), as from 1 January 2007.

Sub-s (3): words in square brackets in para (a) and the whole of para (aa) inserted, and word omitted from para (a) repealed, by SI 2006/3429, reg 6, Sch 1, para 1(1), (3), as from 1 January 2007.

Sub-s (5): added by the Companies (Registrar, Languages and Trading Disclosures) Regulations 2006, SI 2006/3429, reg 6, Sch 1, para 1(1), (4), as from 1 January 2007.

Application to limited liability partnerships: see the Limited Liability Partnerships Regulations 2001, SI 2001/1090, reg 4(1), Sch 2, Pt 1 at **[6985]**, **[6993]**.

350 Company seal

[(1) A company which has a common seal shall have its name engraved in legible characters on the seal; and if it fails to comply with this subsection it is liable to a fine.]

(2) If an officer of a company or a person on its behalf uses or authorises the use of any seal purporting to be a seal of the company on which its name is not engraved as required by subsection (1), he is liable to a fine.

[361]

NOTES

Repealed by the Companies Act 2006, s 1295, Sch 16, as from a day to be appointed.

Sub-s (1): substituted by CA 1989, s 130(7), Sch 17, para 7, as from 31 July 1990.

Application to limited liability partnerships: see the Limited Liability Partnerships Regulations 2001, SI 2001/1090, reg 4(1), Sch 2, Pt 1 at **[6985]**, **[6993]**.

351 Particulars in correspondence etc

(1) Every company shall have the following particulars mentioned in legible characters in all business letters and order forms of the company[, and on all the company's websites], that is to say—

- *(a) the company's place of registration and the number with which it is registered,*
- *(b) the address of its registered office,*
- *(c) in the case of an investment company (as defined in section 266), the fact that it is such a company, and*
- *(d) in the case of a limited company exempt from the obligation to use the word "limited" as part of its name [under section 30 or a community interest company which is not a public company], the fact that it is a limited company.*

[(2) If in the case of a company having a share capital there is a reference to the amount of share capital—

- *(a) on the stationery used for any such letters,*
- *(b) on the company's order forms, or*
- *(c) on any of the company's websites,*

the reference must be to paid-up share capital.]

(3), (4) …

(5) As to contraventions of this section, the following applies—

- *(a) if a company fails to comply with subsection (1) or (2), it is liable to a fine,*
- *(b) if an officer of a company or a person on its behalf issues or authorises the issue of any business letter or order form not complying with those subsections, he is liable to a fine, …*
- *[(ba) if an officer of a company or a person on its behalf causes or authorises the appearance of a website not complying with those subsections, he is liable to a fine].*
- *(c) …*

[(6) References in this section to a document of any type are to a document of that type in hard copy, electronic or any other form.]

[362]

NOTES

Repealed by the Companies Act 2006, s 1295, Sch 16, as from a day to be appointed.

Sub-s (1): words in first pair of square brackets inserted by the Companies (Registrar, Languages and Trading Disclosures) Regulations 2006, SI 2006/3429, reg 6, Sch 1, para 2(1), (2), as from 1 January 2007; words in square brackets in para (d) inserted by the Companies (Audit, Investigations and Community Enterprise) Act 2004, s 33, Sch 6, paras 1, 8, as from 1 July 2005.

Sub-s (2): substituted by SI 2006/3429, reg 6, Sch 1, para 2(1), (3), as from 1 January 2007.

Sub-ss (3), (4): repealed by the Welsh Language Act 1993, ss 31, 35(1), Sch 2, as from 1 February 1994.

Sub-s (5): para (ba) inserted by SI 2006/3429, reg 6, Sch 1, para 2(1), (4), as from 1 January 2007; para (c) and the word immediately preceding it repealed by the Welsh Language Act 1993, s 35(1), Sch 2, as from 1 February 1994.

Sub-s (6): added by SI 2006/3429, reg 6, Sch 1, para 2(1), (5), as from 1 January 2007.

Application to limited liability partnerships: see the Limited Liability Partnerships Regulations 2001, SI 2001/1090, reg 4(1), Sch 2, Pt 1 at **[6985]**, **[6993]**.

CHAPTER II
REGISTER OF MEMBERS

352 Obligation to keep and enter up register

(1) Every company shall keep a register of its members and enter in it the particulars required by this section.

(2) There shall be entered in the register—

(a) the names and addresses of the members;

(b) the date on which each person was registered as a member; and

(c) the date at which any person ceased to be a member.

(3) The following applies in the case of a company having a share capital—

(a) with the names and addresses of the members there shall be entered a statement—

(i) of the shares held by each member, distinguishing each share by its number (so long as the share has a number) and, where the company has more than one class of issued shares, by its class, and

(ii) of the amount paid or agreed to be considered as paid on the shares of each member;

(b) where the company has converted any of its shares into stock and given notice of the conversion to the registrar of companies, the register shall show the amount and class of stock held by each member, instead of the amount of shares and the particulars relating to shares specified in paragraph (a).

[(3A) Where a company purchases one or more of its own shares in circumstances in which section 162A applies—

(a) the requirements of subsection (2) and (3) must be complied with unless the company cancels all of the shares forthwith after the purchase in accordance with section 162D(1), but

(b) any share which is so cancelled must be disregarded for the purposes of subsection (3).]

(4) In the case of a company which does not have a share capital but has more than one class of members, there shall be entered in the register, with the names and addresses of the members, the class to which each member belongs.

(5) If a company makes default in complying with this section, the company and every officer of it who is in default is liable to a fine and, for continued contravention, to a daily default fine.

(6) An entry relating to a former member of the company may be removed from the register after the expiration of 20 years from the date on which he ceased to be a member.

(7) Liability incurred by a company from the making or deletion of an entry in its register of members, or from a failure to make or delete any such entry, is not enforceable more than 20 years after the date on which the entry was made or deleted or, in the case of any such failure, the failure first occurred.

This is without prejudice to any lesser period of limitation.

[363]

NOTES

Repealed by the Companies Act 2006, s 1295, Sch 16, as from a day to be appointed.

Sub-s (3A): inserted by the Companies (Acquisition of Own Shares) (Treasury Shares) Regulations 2003, SI 2003/1116, reg 4, Schedule, para 18, as from 1 December 2003.

Inspection, etc: for provisions relating to the inspection, etc, of a register of debenture holders maintained under this section, see the Companies (Inspection and Copying of Registers, Indices and Documents) Regulations 1991, SI 1991/1998, reg 4 at **[6719]**.

[352A Statement that company has only one member

(1) If the number of members of a private company limited by shares or by guarantee falls to one there shall upon the occurrence of that event be entered in the company's register of members with the name and address of the sole member—

(i) a statement that the company has only one member, and

(ii) the date on which the company became a company having only one member.

(2) If the membership of a private company limited by shares or by guarantee increases from one to two or more members there shall upon the occurrence of that event be entered in the company's register of members, with the name and address of the person who was formerly the sole member, a statement that the company has ceased to have only one member together with the date on which that event occurred.

(3) If a company makes default in complying with this section, the company and every officer of it who is in default is liable to a fine and, for continued contravention, to a daily default fine.]

[364]

NOTES

Inserted by the Companies (Single Member Private Limited Companies) Regulations 1992, SI 1992/1699, reg 2, Schedule, para 4, as from 15 July 1992.

Repealed by the Companies Act 2006, s 1295, Sch 16, as from a day to be appointed.

353 Location of register

(1) A company's register of members shall be kept at its registered office, except that—

(a) if the work of making it up is done at another office of the company, it may be kept there; and

(b) if the company arranges with some other person for the making up of the register to be undertaken on its behalf by that other, it may be kept at the office of the other at which the work is done;

but it must not be kept, in the case of a company registered in England and Wales, at any place elsewhere than in England and Wales or, in the case of a company registered in Scotland, at any place elsewhere than in Scotland.

(2) Subject as follows, every company shall send notice in the prescribed form to the registrar of companies of the place where its register of members is kept, and of any change in that place.

(3) The notice need not be sent if the register has, at all times since it came into existence (or, in the case of a register in existence on 1st July 1948, at all times since then) been kept at the company's registered office.

(4) If a company makes default for 14 days in complying with subsection (2), the company and every officer of it who is in default is liable to a fine and, for continued contravention, to a daily default fine.

[365]

NOTES

Repealed by the Companies Act 2006, s 1295, Sch 16, as from a day to be appointed.

Notice in the prescribed form: see Appendix 4 (Forms table) at **[A4]**.

354 Index of members

(1) Every company having more than 50 members shall, unless the register of members is in such a form as to constitute in itself an index, keep an index of the names of the members of the company and shall, within 14 days after the date on which any alteration is made in the register of members, make any necessary alteration in the index.

(2) The index shall in respect of each member contain a sufficient indication to enable the account of that member in the register to be readily found.

(3) The index shall be at all times kept at the same place as the register of members.

(4) If default is made in complying with this section, the company and every officer of it who is in default is liable to a fine and, for continued contravention, to a daily default fine.

[366]

NOTES

Repealed by the Companies Act 2006, s 1295, Sch 16, as from a day to be appointed.

Inspection, etc: for provisions relating to the inspection, etc, of a register of debenture holders maintained under this section, see the Companies (Inspection and Copying of Registers, Indices and Documents) Regulations 1991, SI 1991/1998, reg 4 at **[6719]**.

355 Entries in register in relation to share warrants

(*1*) *On the issue of a share warrant the company shall strike out of its register of members the name of the member then entered in it as holding the shares specified in the warrant as if he had ceased to be a member, and shall enter in the register the following particulars, namely—*

(*a*) *the fact of the issue of the warrant;*

(*b*) *a statement of the shares included in the warrant, distinguishing each share by its number so long as the share has a number; and*

(*c*) *the date of the issue of the warrant.*

(*2*) *Subject to the company's articles, the bearer of a share warrant is entitled, on surrendering it for cancellation, to have his name entered as a member in the register of members.*

(*3*) *The company is responsible for any loss incurred by any person by reason of the company entering in the register the name of a bearer of a share warrant in respect of the shares specified in it without the warrant being surrendered and cancelled.*

(*4*) *Until the warrant is surrendered, the particulars specified in subsection* (*1*) *are deemed to be those required by this Act to be entered in the register of members; and, on the surrender, the date of the surrender must be entered.*

(*5*) *Except as provided by section 291*(*2*) (*director's share qualification*), *the bearer of a share warrant may, if the articles of the company so provide, be deemed a member of the company within the meaning of this Act, either to the full extent or for any purposes defined in the articles.*

[367]

NOTES

Repealed by the Companies Act 2006, s 1295, Sch 16, as from a day to be appointed.

356 Inspection of register and index

(*1*) *Except when the register of members is closed under the provisions of this Act, the register and the index of members' names shall ... be open to the inspection of any member of the company without charge, and of any other person on payment of [such fee as may be prescribed].*

(*2*) ...

(*3*) *Any member of the company or other person may require a copy of the register, or of any part of it, on payment of [such fee as may be prescribed]; and the company shall cause any copy so required by a person to be sent to him within 10 days beginning with the day next following that on which the requirement is received by the company.*

(*4*) ...

(*5*) *If an inspection required under this section is refused, or if a copy so required is not sent within the proper period, the company and every officer of it who is in default is liable in respect of each offence to a fine.*

(*6*) *In the case of such refusal or default, the court may by order compel an immediate inspection of the register and index, or direct that the copies required be sent to the persons requiring them.*

[368]

NOTES

Repealed by the Companies Act 2006, s 1295, Sch 16, as from 1 October 2007. For savings see the note below.

Sub-s (1): words omitted repealed, and words in square brackets substituted, by CA 1989, ss 143(8), 212, Sch 24, as from 1 November 1991.

Sub-ss (2), (4): repealed by CA 1989, ss 143(8), 212, Sch 24, as from 1 November 1991.

Sub-s (3): words in square brackets substituted by CA 1989, s 143(8), as from 1 November 1991.

Savings: this section and s 357 continue to apply to requests made before 1 October 2007 (see the draft Companies Act 2006 (Commencement No 3, Consequential Amendments, Transitional Provisions and Savings) Order 2007, Sch 3, para 2 at [**A12**]).

Inspection: for provisions relating to the inspection of documents, registers and fees under this section, see the Companies (Inspection and Copying of Registers, Indices and Documents) Regulations 1991, SI 1991/1998 at **[6716]** et seq (partly made under this section).

357 Non-compliance with ss 353, 354, 356; agent's default

Where under section 353(1)(b), the register of members is kept at the office of some person other than the company, and by reason of any default of his the company fails to comply with—

section 353(2) (notice to registrar),
section 354(3) (index to be kept with register), or
section 356 (inspection),

or with any requirement of this Act as to the production of the register, that other person is liable to the same penalties as if he were an officer of the company who was in default, and the power of the court under section 356(6) extends to the making of orders against that other and his officers and servants.

[369]

NOTES

Repealed by the Companies Act 2006, s 1295, Sch 16 (in so far as relating to the words "section 356 (inspection)" and "and the power of the court under section 356(6) extends to the making of orders against that other and his officers and servants"), and as from a day to be appointed (otherwise). For savings see the note to s 356 at **[368]**.

358 Power to close register

A company may, on giving notice by advertisement in a newspaper circulating in the district in which the company's registered office is situated, close the register of members for any time or times not exceeding in the whole 30 days in each year.

[370]

NOTES

Repealed by the Companies Act 2006, s 1295, Sch 16, as from a day to be appointed.

359 Power of court to rectify register

(1) If—

(a) the name of any person is, without sufficient cause, entered in or omitted from a company's register of members, or

(b) default is made or unnecessary delay takes place in entering on the register the fact of any person having ceased to be a member,

the person aggrieved, or any member of the company, or the company, may apply to the court for rectification of the register.

(2) The court may either refuse the application or may order rectification of the register and payment by the company of any damages sustained by any party aggrieved.

(3) On such an application the court may decide any question relating to the title of a person who is a party to the application to have his name entered in or omitted from the register, whether the question arises between members or alleged members, or between members or alleged members on the one hand and the company on the other hand, and generally may decide any question necessary or expedient to be decided for rectification of the register.

(4) In the case of a company required by this Act to send a list of its members to the registrar of companies, the court, when making an order for rectification of the register, shall by its order direct notice of the rectification to be given to the registrar.

[371]

NOTES

Repealed by the Companies Act 2006, s 1295, Sch 16, as from a day to be appointed.

360 Trusts not to be entered on register in England and Wales

No notice of any trust, expressed, implied or constructive, shall be entered on the register, or be receivable by the registrar, in the case of companies registered in England and Wales.

[372]

NOTES

Repealed by the Companies Act 2006, s 1295, Sch 16, as from a day to be appointed.

361 Register to be evidence

The register of members is prima facie evidence of any matters which are by this Act directed or authorised to be inserted in it.

[373]

NOTES

Repealed by the Companies Act 2006, s 1295, Sch 16, as from a day to be appointed.

362 Overseas branch registers

(1) A company having a share capital whose objects comprise the transaction of business in any of the countries or territories specified in Part I of Schedule 14 to this Act may cause to be kept in any such country or territory in which it transacts business a branch register of members resident in that country or territory.

(2) Such a branch register is to be known as an "overseas branch register"; and—

(a) any dominion register kept by a company under section 119 of the Companies Act 1948 is to become known as an overseas branch register of the company;

(b) where any Act or instrument (including in particular a company's articles) refers to a company's dominion register, that reference is to be read (unless the context otherwise requires) as being to an overseas branch register kept under this section; and

(c) references to a colonial register occurring in articles registered before 1st November 1929 are to be read as referring to an overseas branch register.

(3) Part II of Schedule 14 has effect with respect to overseas branch registers kept under this section; and Part III of the Schedule enables corresponding facilities in Great Britain to be accorded to companies incorporated in other parts of the world.

(4) The Foreign Jurisdiction Act 1890 has effect as if subsection (1) of this section, and Part II of Schedule 14, were included among the enactments which by virtue of section 5 of that Act may be applied by Order in Council to foreign countries in which for the time being Her Majesty has jurisdiction.

(5) Her Majesty may by Order in Council direct that subsection (1) above and Part II of Schedule 14 shall extend, with such exceptions, modifications or adaptations (if any) as may be specified in the Order, to any territories under Her Majesty's protection to which those provisions cannot be extended under the Foreign Jurisdiction Act 1890.

[374]

NOTES

Repealed by the Companies Act 2006, s 1295, Sch 16, as from a day to be appointed.

Companies Act 1948, s 119: repealed by the Companies Consolidation (Consequential Provisions) Act 1985, s 29, Sch 1, and replaced by this section and Sch 14.

Orders: no Order in Council had been made under sub-s (5) above or by virtue of sub-s (4) above and it is thought that no Order in Council has effect under either subsection by virtue of the Companies Consolidation (Consequential Provisions) Act 1985, s 31(2), (11) and the Interpretation Act 1978, s 17(2)(b), since the effect of the Orders in Council made under the provisions replaced by those subsections appears to have been reproduced in sub-s (1) above and Sch 14, Pt I.

Prescribed form: see Appendix 4 (Forms table) at **[A4]**.

[CHAPTER III
ANNUAL RETURN

363 Duty to deliver annual returns

(1) Every company shall deliver to the registrar successive annual returns each of which is made up to a date not later than the date which is from time to time the company's "return date", that is—

(a) the anniversary of the company's incorporation, or

(b) if the company's last return delivered in accordance with this Chapter was made up to a different date, the anniversary of that date.

(2) Each return shall—

(a) be in the prescribed form,

(*b*) *contain the information required by or under the following provisions of this Chapter, and*

(*c*) *be signed by a director or the secretary of the company;*

and it shall be delivered to the registrar within 28 days after the date to which it is made up.

(*3*) *If a company fails to deliver an annual return in accordance with this Chapter before the end of the period of 28 days after a return date, the company is guilty of an offence and liable to a fine and, in the case of continued contravention, to a daily default fine.*

The contravention continues until such time as an annual return made up to that return date and complying with the requirements of subsection (2) (*except as to date of delivery*) *is delivered by the company to the registrar.*

(*4*) *Where a company is guilty of an offence under subsection* (*3*), *every director or secretary of the company is similarly liable unless he shows that he took all reasonable steps to avoid the commission or continuation of the offence.*

(*5*) *The references in this section to a return being delivered "in accordance with this Chapter" are—*

(*a*) *in relation to a return made [on or after 1st October 1990], to a return with respect to which all the requirements of subsection* (2) *are complied with;*

(*b*) *in relation to a return made before [1st October 1990], to a return with respect to which the formal and substantive requirements of this Chapter as it then had effect were complied with, whether or not the return was delivered in time.]*

[375]

NOTES

This Chapter (i e Chapter III (ss 363, 364, 364A, 365)) was substituted, for the original Chapter III, by CA 1989, s 139(1), as from 1 October 1990.

Repealed by the Companies Act 2006, s 1295, Sch 16, as from a day to be appointed.

Sub-s (5): words in square brackets substituted by the Companies Act 1989 (Commencement No 7 and Transitional and Savings Provisions) Order 1990, SI 1990/1707, art 7, as from 1 October 1990.

Application to limited liability partnerships: see the Limited Liability Partnerships Regulations 2001, SI 2001/1090, reg 4(1), Sch 2, Pt 1 at **[6985]**, **[6993]**.

Fees: see Appendix 3 (Fees Instruments) at **[A3]**.

Prescribed form: see Appendix 4 (Forms table) at **[A4]**.

[364 Contents of annual return: general

(*1*) *Every annual return shall state the date to which it is made up and shall contain the following information—*

(*a*) *the address of the company's registered office;*

(*b*) *the type of company it is and its principal business activities;*

(*c*) *the name and address of the company secretary;*

(*d*) *the name and address of every director of the company;*

(*e*) *in the case of each individual director—*

(*i*) *his nationality, date of birth and business occupation, …*

(*ii*) …

(*f*) …

(*g*) *if the register of members is not kept at the company's registered office, the address of the place where it is kept;*

(*h*) *if any register of debenture holders* (*or a duplicate of any such register or a part of it*) *is not kept at the company's registered office, the address of the place where it is kept;*

(*i*) …

(*2*) *The information as to the company's type shall be given by reference to the classification scheme prescribed for the purposes of this section.*

(*3*) *The information as to the company's principal business activities may be given by reference to one or more categories of any prescribed system of classifying business activities.*

(*4*) *A person's "name" and "address" mean, respectively—*

(*a*) *in the case of an individual, his Christian name* (*or other forename*) *and surname and his usual residential address;*

(*b*) *in the case of a corporation or Scottish firm, its corporate or firm name and its registered or principal office.*

(5) *In the case of a peer, or an individual usually known by a title, the title may be stated instead of his Christian name (or other forename) and surname or in addition to either or both of them.*

(6) *Where all the partners in a firm are joint secretaries, the name and principal office of the firm may be stated instead of the names and addresses of the partners.]*

[376]

NOTES

Substituted as noted to s 363 at **[375]**.

Repealed by the Companies Act 2006, s 1295, Sch 16, as from a day to be appointed.

Sub-s (1): para (e)(ii) and the word immediately preceding it, and paras (f), (i) repealed by the Companies (Contents of Annual Return) Regulations 1999, SI 1999/2322, as from 13 September 1999.

Application to limited liability partnerships: see the Limited Liability Partnerships Regulations 2001, SI 2001/1090, reg 4(1), Sch 2, Pt 1 at **[6985]**, **[6993]**.

Prescribed scheme: the Companies (Forms Amendment No 2 and Company's Type and Principal Business Activities) Regulations 1990, SI 1990/1766, reg 5, Sch 3, Pt I, prescribe the following classification scheme—

T1 Public Limited Company
T2 Private Company Limited by Shares
T3 Private Company Limited by Guarantee without Share Capital
T4 Private Company Limited by Shares Exempt under CA 1985, s 30
T5 Private Company Limited by Guarantee Exempt under CA 1985, s 30
T6 Private Unlimited Company with Share Capital
T7 Private Unlimited Company without Share Capital.

A company required to deliver an annual return under CA 1985, s 699 or 718 shall give the type of company it is by reference to the category which is, in the opinion of its directors, the most appropriate to its circumstances.

Prescribed system: Sch 3, Pt II to the 1990 Regulations, as substituted by SI 2002/3081, reg 2(1), (4), prescribe for the purpose of sub-s (2), the UK Standard Industrial Classification of Economic Activities 2003 with the addition of the following code: 9800 residents' property management company.

[364A Contents of annual return: particulars of share capital and shareholders

(1) *The annual return of a company having a share capital shall contain the following information with respect to its share capital and members.*

(2) *The return shall state the total number of issued shares of the company at the date to which the return is made up and the aggregate nominal value of those shares.*

(3) *The return shall state with respect to each class of shares in the company—*
- (*a*) *the nature of the class, and*
- (*b*) *the total number and aggregate nominal value of issued shares of that class at the date to which the return is made up.*

(4) *The return shall contain a list of the names and addresses of every person who—*
- (*a*) *is a member of the company on the date to which the return is made up, or*
- (*b*) *has ceased to be a member of the company since the date to which the last return was made up (or, in the case of the first return, since the incorporation of the company);*

and if the names are not arranged in alphabetical order the return shall have annexed to it an index sufficient to enable the name of any person in the list to be easily found.

(5) *The return shall also state—*
- (*a*) *the number of shares of each class held by each member of the company at the date to which the return is made up, and*
- (*b*) *the number of shares of each class transferred since the date to which the last return was made up (or, in the case of the first return, since the incorporation of the company) by each member or person who has ceased to be a member, and the dates of registration of the transfers.*

(6) *The return may, if either of the two immediately preceding returns has given the full particulars required by subsections (4) and (5), give only such particulars as relate to persons ceasing to be or becoming members since the date of the last return and to shares transferred since that date.*

(7) *Subsections (4) and (5) do not require the inclusion of particulars entered in an overseas branch register if copies of those entries have not been received at the company's registered office by the date to which the return is made up.*

Those particulars shall be included in the company's next annual return after they are received.

(8) Where the company has converted any of its shares into stock, the return shall give the corresponding information in relation to that stock, stating the amount of stock instead of the number or nominal value of shares.]

[377]

NOTES

Substituted as noted to s 363 at **[375]**.
Repealed by the Companies Act 2006, s 1295, Sch 16, as from a day to be appointed.

[365 Supplementary provisions: regulations and interpretation

(1) The Secretary of State may by regulations make further provision as to the information to be given in a company's annual return, which may amend or repeal the provisions of sections 364 and 364A.

(2) Regulations under this section shall be made by statutory instrument which shall be subject to annulment in pursuance of a resolution of either House of Parliament.

(3) For the purposes of this Chapter, except section 363(2)(c) (signature of annual return), a shadow director shall be deemed to be a director.]

[378]

NOTES

Substituted as noted to s 363 at **[375]**.
Repealed by the Companies Act 2006, s 1295, Sch 16, as from a day to be appointed.
Regulations: the Companies (Contents of Annual Return) Regulations 1999, SI 1999/2322.

CHAPTER IV
MEETINGS AND RESOLUTIONS

Meetings

366 Annual general meeting

(1) Every company shall in each year hold a general meeting as its annual general meeting in addition to any other meetings in that year, and shall specify the meeting as such in the notices calling it.

(2) However, so long as a company holds its first annual general meeting within 18 months of its incorporation, it need not hold it in the year of its incorporation or in the following year.

(3) Not more than 15 months shall elapse between the date of one annual general meeting of a company and that of the next.

(4) If default is made in holding a meeting in accordance with this section, the company and every officer of it who is in default is liable to a fine.

[379]

NOTES

Repealed by the Companies Act 2006, s 1295, Sch 16, as from 1 October 2007. For savings, etc, see the note below.
Savings, etc: the draft Companies Act 2006 (Commencement No 3, Consequential Amendments, Transitional Provisions and Savings) Order 2007, Sch 3, paras 22–40 make a variety of savings and transitional provisions in relation to the repeal of this Chapter and the commencement of Part 13 of the Companies Act 2006 (Resolutions and Meetings). See that draft Order in Appendix 12 at **[A12]**. In relation to this section, see also the savings note on s 337 of this Act at **[337]**.

[366A Election by private company to dispense with annual general meetings

(1) A private company may elect (by elective resolution in accordance with section 379A) to dispense with the holding of annual general meetings.

(2) An election has effect for the year in which it is made and subsequent years, but does not affect any liability already incurred by reason of default in holding an annual general meeting.

(3) In any year in which an annual general meeting would be required to be held but for the election, and in which no such meeting has been held, any member of the company may, by notice to the company not later than three months before the end of the year, require the holding of an annual general meeting in that year.

[(3A) ...]

(4) If such a notice is given [or electronic communication is transmitted], the provisions of section 366(1) and (4) apply with respect to the calling of the meeting and the consequences of default.

(5) If the election ceases to have effect, the company is not obliged under section 366 to hold an annual general meeting in that year if, when the election ceases to have effect, less than three months of the year remains.

This does not affect any obligation of the company to hold an annual general meeting in that year in pursuance of a notice given [or electronic communication transmitted] under subsection (3).

[(5A) ...]]

[380]

NOTES

Inserted by CA 1989, s 115(2), as from 1 April 1990.

Repealed by the Companies Act 2006, s 1295, Sch 16, as from 20 January 2007 (in so far as relating to sub-ss (3A), (5A)), and as from 1 October 2007 (otherwise). For savings, etc, see the note below.

Sub-s (3A): inserted by the Companies Act 1985 (Electronic Communications) Order 2000, SI 2000/3373, art 17(1), (2), as from 22 December 2000, and repealed as noted above.

Sub-ss (4), (5): words in square brackets inserted by SI 2000/3373, art 17(1), (3), (4), as from 22 December 2000.

Sub-s (5A): added by SI 2000/3373, art 17(1), (5), as from 22 December 2000, and repealed as noted above.

Savings, etc: the draft Companies Act 2006 (Commencement No 3, Consequential Amendments, Transitional Provisions and Savings) Order 2007, Sch 3, paras 22–40 make a variety of savings and transitional provisions in relation to the repeal of this Chapter and the commencement of Part 13 of the Companies Act 2006 (Resolutions and Meetings). See that draft Order in Appendix 12 at **[A12]**.

367 Secretary of State's power to call meeting in default

(1) If default is made in holding a meeting in accordance with section 366, the Secretary of State may, on the application of any member of the company, call, or direct the calling of, a general meeting of the company and give such ancillary or consequential directions as he thinks expedient, including directions modifying or supplementing, in relation to the calling, holding and conduct of the meeting, the operation of the company's articles.

(2) The directions that may be given under subsection (1) include a direction that one member of the company present in person or by proxy shall be deemed to constitute a meeting.

(3) If default is made in complying with directions of the Secretary of State under subsection (1), the company and every officer of it who is in default is liable to a fine.

(4) A general meeting held under this section shall, subject to any directions of the Secretary of State, be deemed to be an annual general meeting of the company; but, where a meeting so held is not held in the year in which the default in holding the company's annual general meeting occurred, the meeting so held shall not be treated as the annual general meeting for the year in which it is held unless at that meeting the company resolves that it be so treated.

(5) Where a company so resolves, a copy of the resolution shall, within 15 days after its passing, be forwarded to the registrar of companies and recorded by him; and if default is made in complying with this subsection, the company and every officer of it who is in default is liable to a fine and, for continued contravention, to a daily default fine.

[381]

NOTES

Repealed by the Companies Act 2006, s 1295, Sch 16, as from 1 October 2007. For savings see the note below.

Savings, etc: the draft Companies Act 2006 (Commencement No 3, Consequential Amendments, Transitional Provisions and Savings) Order 2007, Sch 3, paras 22–40 make a variety of savings and transitional provisions in relation to the repeal of this Chapter and the commencement of Part 13 of the Companies Act 2006 (Resolutions and Meetings). See that draft Order in Appendix 12 at **[A12]**.

368 Extraordinary general meeting on members' requisition

(1) The directors of a company shall, on a members' requisition, forthwith proceed duly to convene an extraordinary general meeting of the company.

This applies notwithstanding anything in the company's articles.

(2) A members' requisition is a requisition of—

(a) members of the company holding at the date of the deposit of the requisition not less than one-tenth of such of the paid-up capital of the company as at that date carries the right of voting at general meetings of the company; or

(b) in the case of a company not having a share capital, members of it representing not less than one-tenth of the total voting rights of all the members having at the date of deposit of the requisition a right to vote at general meetings.

[(2A) For the purposes of subsection (2)(a) any of the company's paid up capital held as treasury shares must be disregarded.]

(3) The requisition must state the objects of the meeting, and must be signed by the requisitionists and deposited at the registered office of the company, and may consist of several documents in like form each signed by one or more requisitionists.

(4) If the directors do not within 21 days from the date of the deposit of the requisition proceed duly to convene a meeting, the requisitionists, or any of them representing more than one half of the total voting rights of all of them, may themselves convene a meeting, but any meeting so convened shall not be held after the expiration of 3 months from that date.

(5) A meeting convened under this section by requisitionists shall be convened in the same manner, as nearly as possible, as that in which meetings are to be convened by directors.

(6) Any reasonable expenses incurred by the requisitionists by reason of the failure of the directors duly to convene a meeting shall be repaid to the requisitionists by the company, and any sum so repaid shall be retained by the company out of any sums due or to become due from the company by way of fees or other remuneration in respect of their services to such of the directors as were in default.

(7) In the case of a meeting at which a resolution is to be proposed as a special resolution, the directors are deemed not to have duly convened the meeting if they do not give the notice required for special resolutions by section 378(2).

[(8) The directors are deemed not to have duly convened a meeting if they convene a meeting for a date more than 28 days after the date of the notice convening the meeting.]

[382]

NOTES

Repealed by the Companies Act 2006, s 1295, Sch 16, as from 1 October 2007. For savings, etc, see the note below.

Sub-s (2A): inserted by the Companies (Acquisition of Own Shares) (Treasury Shares) Regulations 2003, SI 2003/1116, reg 4, Schedule, para 19, as from 1 December 2003.

Sub-s (8): added by CA 1989, s 145, Sch 19, para 9, as from 1 March 1990.

Savings, etc: the draft Companies Act 2006 (Commencement No 3, Consequential Amendments, Transitional Provisions and Savings) Order 2007, Sch 3, paras 22–40 make a variety of savings and transitional provisions in relation to the repeal of this Chapter and the commencement of Part 13 of the Companies Act 2006 (Resolutions and Meetings). See that draft Order in Appendix 12 at **[A12]**.

Section 972 (in Part 28) of the Companies Act 2006 (at **[S972]**) provides for transitory modifications of this section where a takeover bid is made for an opted-in company before this repeal comes into force. Part 28 is the domestic implementation of the Takeovers Directive (Directive of the European Parliament and of the Council 2004/25/EC on takeover bids) and was brought into force on 6 April 2007. The Takeovers Directive had to be implemented by 20 May 2006 and this was achieved by the Takeovers Directive (Interim Implementation) Regulations 2006, SI 2006/1183 (see reg 23 of those Regulations as to the application of this section where a takeover bid is made for an opted-in company from 20 May 2006 (at **[7531]**)). The 2006 Interim Regulations were also revoked from 6 April 2007.

369 Length of notice for calling meetings

(1) A provision of a company's articles is void in so far as it provides for the calling of a meeting of the company (other than an adjourned meeting) by a shorter notice than—

(*a*) *in the case of the annual general meeting, 21 days' notice in writing; and*
(*b*) *in the case of a meeting other than an annual general meeting or a meeting for the passing of a special resolution—*
  (*i*) *7 days' notice in writing in the case of an unlimited company, and*
  (*ii*) *otherwise, 14 days' notice in writing.*

(2) *Save in so far as the articles of a company make other provision in that behalf (not being a provision avoided by subsection (1)), a meeting of the company (other than an adjourned meeting) may be called—*
(*a*) *in the case of the annual general meeting, by 21 days' notice in writing; and*
(*b*) *in the case of a meeting other than an annual general meeting or a meeting for the passing of a special resolution—*
  (*i*) *by 7 days' notice in writing in the case of an unlimited company, and*
  (*ii*) *otherwise, 14 days' notice in writing.*

(3) *Notwithstanding that a meeting is called by shorter notice than that specified in subsection (2) or in the company's articles (as the case may be), it is deemed to have been duly called if it is so agreed—*
(*a*) *in the case of a meeting called as the annual general meeting, by all the members entitled to attend and vote at it; and*
(*b*) *otherwise, by the requisite majority.*

(4) *The requisite majority for this purpose is a majority in number of the members having a right to attend and vote at the meeting, being a majority—*
(*a*) *together holding not less than 95 per cent in nominal value of the shares giving a right to attend and vote at the meeting [(excluding any shares in the company held as treasury shares)]; or*
(*b*) *in the case of a company not having a share capital, together representing not less than 95 per cent of the total voting rights at that meeting of all the members.*

[A private company may elect (by elective resolution in accordance with section 379A) that the above provisions shall have effect in relation to the company as if for the references to 95 per cent there were substituted references to such lesser percentage, but not less than 90 per cent, as may be specified in the resolution or subsequently determined by the company in general meeting.]

[(4A) For the purposes of this section the cases in which notice in writing of a meeting is to be taken as given to a person include any case in which notice of the meeting is sent using electronic communications to such address as may for the time being be notified by that person to the company for that purpose.

(4B) For the purposes of this section a notice in writing of a meeting is also to be treated as given to a person where—
(*a*) *the company and that person have agreed that notices of meetings required to be given to that person may instead be accessed by him on a web site;*
(*b*) *the meeting is a meeting to which that agreement applies;*
(*c*) *that person is notified, in a manner for the time being agreed between him and the company for the purpose, of—*
  (*i*) *the publication of the notice on a web site;*
  (*ii*) *the address of that web site; and*
  (*iii*) *the place on that web site where the notice may be accessed, and how it may be accessed;*

and
(*d*) *the notice continues to be published on that web site throughout the period beginning with the giving of that notification and ending with the conclusion of the meeting;*

and for the purposes of this section a notice treated in accordance with this subsection as given to any person is to be treated as so given at the time of the notification mentioned in paragraph (c).

(4C) A notification given for the purposes of subsection (4B)(c) must—
(*a*) *state that it concerns a notice of a company meeting served in accordance with this Act,*
(*b*) *specify the place, date and time of the meeting, and*
(*c*) *state whether the meeting is to be an annual or extraordinary general meeting.*

(4D) Nothing in subsection (4B) shall invalidate the proceedings of a meeting where—

(*a*) *any notice that is required to be published as mentioned in paragraph* (*d*) *of that subsection is published for a part, but not all, of the period mentioned in that paragraph; and*

(*b*) *the failure to publish that notice throughout that period is wholly attributable to circumstances which it would not be reasonable to have expected the company to prevent or avoid.*

(*4E*) *A company may, notwithstanding any provision to the contrary in a company's articles, take advantage of any of subsections* (*4A*) *to* (*4D*).

(*4F*) *In so far as the articles of the company do not provide for notices and notifications to be served using electronic communications, the provisions of Table A* (*as for the time being in force*) *as to such service shall apply.*

(*4G*) *In this section, "address" includes any number or address used for the purposes of electronic communications.]*

[383]

NOTES

Repealed by the Companies Act 2006, s 1295, Sch 16, as from 20 January 2007 (in so far as relating to sub-ss (4A)–(4G)), and as from 1 October 2007 (otherwise). For transitional provisions see the note to s 238 at **[225]** and for savings, etc, see the note below.

Sub-s (4): words in square brackets in para (a) inserted by the Companies (Acquisition of Own Shares) (Treasury Shares) Regulations 2003, SI 2003/1116, reg 4, Schedule, para 20, as from 1 December 2003; words in second pair of square brackets added by CA 1989, s 115(3), as from 1 April 1990.

Sub-ss (4A)–(4G): added by the Companies Act 1985 (Electronic Communications) Order 2000, SI 2000/3373, art 18, as from 22 December 2000, and repealed as noted above.

Repealed by the Companies Act 2006, s 1295, Sch 16, as from 1 October 2007. For savings, etc, see the note below.

Savings, etc: the draft Companies Act 2006 (Commencement No 3, Consequential Amendments, Transitional Provisions and Savings) Order 2007, Sch 3, paras 22–40 make a variety of savings and transitional provisions in relation to the repeal of this Chapter and the commencement of Part 13 of the Companies Act 2006 (Resolutions and Meetings). See that draft Order in Appendix 12 at **[A12]**.

370 General provisions as to meetings and votes

(*1*) *The following provisions have effect in so far as the articles of the company do not make other provision in that behalf.*

(*2*) *Notice of the meeting of a company shall be served on every member of it in the manner in which notices are required to be served by Table A* (*as for the time being in force*).

(*3*) *Two or more members holding not less than one-tenth of the issued share capital [(excluding any shares in the company held as treasury shares)] or, if the company does not have a share capital, not less than 5 per cent in number of the members of the company may call a meeting.*

(*4*) *Two members personally present are a quorum.*

(*5*) *Any member elected by the members present at a meeting may be chairman of it.*

(*6*) *In the case of a company originally having a share capital, every member has one vote in respect of each share or each £10 of stock held by him; and in any other case every member has one vote.*

[384]

NOTES

Repealed by the Companies Act 2006, s 1295, Sch 16, as from 1 October 2007. For savings, etc, see the note below.

Sub-s (3): words in square brackets inserted by the Companies (Acquisition of Own Shares) (Treasury Shares) Regulations 2003, SI 2003/1116, reg 4, Schedule, para 21, as from 1 December 2003.

Savings, etc: the draft Companies Act 2006 (Commencement No 3, Consequential Amendments, Transitional Provisions and Savings) Order 2007, Sch 3, paras 22–40 make a variety of savings and transitional provisions in relation to the repeal of this Chapter and the commencement of Part 13 of the Companies Act 2006 (Resolutions and Meetings). See that draft Order in Appendix 12 at **[A12]**.

[370A Quorum at meetings of the sole member

Notwithstanding any provision to the contrary in the articles of a private company limited by shares or by guarantee having only one member, one member present in person or by proxy shall be a quorum.]

[385]

NOTES

Inserted by the Companies (Single Member Private Limited Companies) Regulations 1992, SI 1992/1699, reg 2, Schedule, para 5, as from 15 July 1992.

Repealed by the Companies Act 2006, s 1295, Sch 16, as from 1 October 2007. For savings, etc, see the note below.

Savings, etc: the draft Companies Act 2006 (Commencement No 3, Consequential Amendments, Transitional Provisions and Savings) Order 2007, Sch 3, paras 22–40 make a variety of savings and transitional provisions in relation to the repeal of this Chapter and the commencement of Part 13 of the Companies Act 2006 (Resolutions and Meetings). See that draft Order in Appendix 12 at **[A12]**.

371 Power of court to order meeting

(1) If for any reason it is impracticable to call a meeting of a company in any manner in which meetings of that company may be called, or to conduct the meeting in manner prescribed by the articles or this Act, the court may, either of its own motion or on the application—

(a) of any director of the company, or

(b) of any member of the company who would be entitled to vote at the meeting,

order a meeting to be called, held and conducted in any manner the court thinks fit.

(2) Where such an order is made, the court may give such ancillary or consequential directions as it thinks expedient; and these may include a direction that one member of the company present in person or by proxy be deemed to constitute a meeting.

(3) A meeting called, held and conducted in accordance with an order under subsection (1) is deemed for all purposes a meeting of the company duly called, held and conducted.

[386]

NOTES

Repealed by the Companies Act 2006, s 1295, Sch 16, as from 1 October 2007. For savings, etc, see the note below.

Savings, etc: the draft Companies Act 2006 (Commencement No 3, Consequential Amendments, Transitional Provisions and Savings) Order 2007, Sch 3, paras 22–40 make a variety of savings and transitional provisions in relation to the repeal of this Chapter and the commencement of Part 13 of the Companies Act 2006 (Resolutions and Meetings). See that draft Order in Appendix 12 at **[A12]**.

372 Proxies

(1) Any member of a company entitled to attend and vote at a meeting of it is entitled to appoint another person (whether a member or not) as his proxy to attend and vote instead of him; and in the case of a private company a proxy appointed to attend and vote instead of a member has also the same right as the member to speak at the meeting.

(2) But, unless the articles otherwise provide—

(a) subsection (1) does not apply in the case of a company not having a share capital; and

(b) a member of a private company is not entitled to appoint more than one proxy to attend on the same occasion; and

(c) a proxy is not entitled to vote except on a poll.

[(2A), (2B) …]

(3) In the case of a company having a share capital, in every notice calling a meeting of the company there shall appear with reasonable prominence a statement that a member entitled to attend and vote is entitled to appoint a proxy or, where that is allowed, one or more proxies to attend and vote instead of him, and that a proxy need not also be a member.

(4) If default is made in complying with subsection (3) as respects any meeting, every officer of the company who is in default is liable to a fine.

(5) A provision contained in a company's articles is void in so far as it would have the effect of requiring [the appointment of a proxy or any] document necessary to show the

validity of, or otherwise relating to, the appointment of a proxy, to be received by the company or any other person more than 48 hours before a meeting or adjourned meeting in order that the appointment may be effective.

(6) If for the purpose of any meeting of a company invitations to appoint as proxy a person or one of a number of persons specified in the invitations are issued at the company's expense to some only of the members entitled to be sent a notice of the meeting and to vote at it by proxy, then every officer of the company who knowingly and wilfully authorises or permits their issue in that manner is liable to a fine.

However, an officer is not so liable by reason only of the issue to a member at his request ... of a form of appointment naming the proxy, or of a list of persons willing to act as proxy, if the form or list is available on request ... to every member entitled to vote at the meeting by proxy.

[(6A) ...]

(7) This section applies to meetings of any class of members of a company as it applies to general meetings of the company.

[387]

NOTES

Repealed by the Companies Act 2006, s 1295, Sch 16, as from 20 January 2007 (in so far as relating to sub-ss (2A), (2B), (6A)), and as from 1 October 2007 (otherwise). For savings, etc, see the note below.

Sub-ss (2A), (2B), (6A): inserted by the Companies Act 1985 (Electronic Communications) Order 2000, SI 2000/3373, art 19(1), (2), (5), as from 22 December 2000, and repealed as noted above.

Sub-s (5): words in square brackets substituted by SI 2000/3373, art 19(1), (3), as from 22 December 2000.

Sub-s (6): words omitted repealed by SI 2000/3373, art 19(1), (4), as from 22 December 2000.

Savings, etc: the draft Companies Act 2006 (Commencement No 3, Consequential Amendments, Transitional Provisions and Savings) Order 2007, Sch 3, paras 22–40 make a variety of savings and transitional provisions in relation to the repeal of this Chapter and the commencement of Part 13 of the Companies Act 2006 (Resolutions and Meetings). See that draft Order in Appendix 12 at **[A12]**.

373 Right to demand a poll

(1) A provision contained in a company's articles is void in so far as it would have the effect either—

- *(a) of excluding the right to demand a poll at a general meeting on any question other than the election of the chairman of the meeting or the adjournment of the meeting; or*
- *(b) of making ineffective a demand for a poll on any such question which is made either—*
  - *(i) by not less than 5 members having the right to vote at the meeting; or*
  - *(ii) by a member or members representing not less than one-tenth of the total voting rights of all the members having the right to vote at the meeting [(excluding any voting rights attached to any shares in the company held as treasury shares)]; or*
  - *(iii) by a member or members holding shares in the company conferring a right to vote at the meeting, being shares on which an aggregate sum has been paid up equal to not less than one-tenth of the total sum paid up on all the shares conferring that right [(excluding any shares in the company conferring a right to vote at the meeting which are held as treasury shares)].*

(2) [The appointment of] a proxy to vote at a meeting of a company is deemed also to confer authority to demand or join in demanding a poll; and for the purposes of subsection (1) a demand by a person as proxy for a member is the same as a demand by the member.

[388]

NOTES

Repealed by the Companies Act 2006, s 1295, Sch 16, as from 1 October 2007. For savings, etc, see the note below.

Sub-s (1): words in square brackets inserted by the Companies (Acquisition of Own Shares) (Treasury Shares) Regulations 2003, SI 2003/1116, reg 4, Schedule, para 22, as from 1 December 2003.

Sub-s (2): words in square brackets substituted by the Companies Act 1985 (Electronic Communications) Order 2000, SI 2000/3373, art 20, as from 22 December 2000.

Savings, etc: the draft Companies Act 2006 (Commencement No 3, Consequential Amendments, Transitional Provisions and Savings) Order 2007, Sch 3, paras 22–40 make a variety of savings and transitional provisions in relation to the repeal of this Chapter and the commencement of Part 13 of the Companies Act 2006 (Resolutions and Meetings). See that draft Order in Appendix 12 at **[A12]**.

374 Voting on a poll

On a poll taken at a meeting of a company or a meeting of any class of members of a company, a member entitled to more than one vote need not, if he votes, use all his votes or cast all the votes he uses in the same way.

[389]

NOTES

Repealed by the Companies Act 2006, s 1295, Sch 16, as from 1 October 2007. For savings, etc, see the note below.

Savings, etc: the draft Companies Act 2006 (Commencement No 3, Consequential Amendments, Transitional Provisions and Savings) Order 2007, Sch 3, paras 22–40 make a variety of savings and transitional provisions in relation to the repeal of this Chapter and the commencement of Part 13 of the Companies Act 2006 (Resolutions and Meetings). See that draft Order in Appendix 12 at **[A12]**.

375 Representation of corporations at meetings

(*1*) *A corporation, whether or not a company within the meaning of this Act, may—*

(*a*) *if it is a member of another corporation, being such a company, by resolution of its directors or other governing body authorise such person as it thinks fit to act as its representative at any meeting of the company or at any meeting of any class of members of the company;*

(*b*) *if it is a creditor (including a holder of debentures) of another corporation, being such a company, by resolution of its directors or other governing body authorise such person as it thinks fit to act as its representative at any meeting of creditors of the company held in pursuance of this Act or of rules made under it, or in pursuance of the provisions contained in any debenture or trust deed, as the case may be.*

(*2*) *A person so authorised is entitled to exercise the same powers on behalf of the corporation which he represents as that corporation could exercise if it were an individual shareholder, creditor or debenture-holder of the other company.*

[390]

NOTES

Repealed by the Companies Act 2006, s 1295, Sch 16, as from 1 October 2007. For savings, etc, see the note below.

Savings, etc: the draft Companies Act 2006 (Commencement No 3, Consequential Amendments, Transitional Provisions and Savings) Order 2007, Sch 3, paras 22–40 make a variety of savings and transitional provisions in relation to the repeal of this Chapter and the commencement of Part 13 of the Companies Act 2006 (Resolutions and Meetings). See that draft Order in Appendix 12 at **[A12]**.

Resolutions

376 Circulation of members' resolutions

(*1*) *Subject to the section next following, it is the duty of a company, on the requisition in writing of such number of members as is specified below and (unless the company otherwise resolves) at the expense of the requisitionists—*

(*a*) *to give to members of the company entitled to receive notice of the next annual general meeting notice of any resolution which may properly be moved and is intended to be moved at that meeting;*

(*b*) *to circulate to members entitled to have notice of any general meeting sent to them any statement of not more than 1,000 words with respect to the matter referred to in any proposed resolution or the business to be dealt with at that meeting.*

(*2*) *The number of members necessary for a requisition under subsection (1) is—*

(*a*) *any number representing not less than one-twentieth of the total voting rights of all the members having at the date of the requisition a right to vote at the meeting to which the requisition relates [(excluding any voting rights attached to any shares in the company held as treasury shares)]; or*

(*b*) *not less than 100 members holding shares in the company on which there has been paid up an average sum, per member, of not less than £100.*

(*3*) *Notice of any such resolution shall be given, and any such statement shall be circulated, to members of the company entitled to have notice of the meeting sent to them, by serving a copy of the resolution or statement on each such member in any manner permitted for service of notice of the meeting.*

(*4*) *Notice of any such resolution shall be given to any other member of the company by giving notice of the general effect of the resolution in any manner permitted for giving him notice of meetings of the company.*

(*5*) *For compliance with subsections (3) and (4), the copy must be served, or notice of the effect of the resolution be given (as the case may be) in the same manner and (so far as practicable) at the same time as notice of the meeting; and, where it is not practicable for it to be served or given at the same time, it must be served or given as soon as practicable thereafter.*

(*6*) *The business which may be dealt with at an annual general meeting includes any resolution of which notice is given in accordance with this section; and for purposes of this subsection notice is deemed to have been so given notwithstanding the accidental omission, in giving it, of one or more members. This has effect notwithstanding anything in the company's articles.*

(*7*) *In the event of default in complying with this section, every officer of the company who is in default is liable to a fine.*

[391]

NOTES

Repealed by the Companies Act 2006, s 1295, Sch 16, as from 1 October 2007. For savings, etc, see the note below.

Sub-s (2): words in square brackets in para (a) inserted by the Companies (Acquisition of Own Shares) (Treasury Shares) Regulations 2003, SI 2003/1116, reg 4, Schedule, para 23, as from 1 December 2003.

Savings, etc: the draft Companies Act 2006 (Commencement No 3, Consequential Amendments, Transitional Provisions and Savings) Order 2007, Sch 3, paras 22–40 make a variety of savings and transitional provisions in relation to the repeal of this Chapter and the commencement of Part 13 of the Companies Act 2006 (Resolutions and Meetings). See that draft Order in Appendix 12 at **[A12]**.

377 In certain cases, compliance with s 376 not required

(*1*) *A company is not bound under section 376 to give notice of a resolution or to circulate a statement unless—*

(*a*) *a copy of the requisition signed by the requisitionists (or two or more copies which between them contain the signatures of all the requisitionists) is deposited at the registered office of the company—*

(*i*) *in the case of a requisition requiring notice of a resolution, not less than 6 weeks before the meeting, and*

(*ii*) *otherwise, not less than one week before the meeting; and*

(*b*) *there is deposited or tendered with the requisition a sum reasonably sufficient to meet the company's expenses in giving effect to it.*

(*2*) *But if, after a copy of a requisition requiring notice of a resolution has been deposited at the company's registered office, an annual general meeting is called for a date 6 weeks or less after the copy has been deposited, the copy (though not deposited within the time required by subsection (1)) is deemed properly deposited for the purposes of that subsection.*

(*3*) *The company is also not bound under section 376 to circulate a statement if, on the application either of the company or of any other person who claims to be aggrieved, the court is satisfied that the rights conferred by that section are being abused to secure needless publicity for defamatory matter; and the court may order the company's costs on such an application to be paid in whole or in part by the requisitionists, notwithstanding that they are not parties to the application.*

[392]

NOTES

Repealed by the Companies Act 2006, s 1295, Sch 16, as from 1 October 2007. For savings, etc, see the note below.

Savings, etc: the draft Companies Act 2006 (Commencement No 3, Consequential Amendments, Transitional Provisions and Savings) Order 2007, Sch 3, paras 22–40 make a variety of savings and transitional provisions in relation to the repeal of this Chapter and the commencement of Part 13 of the Companies Act 2006 (Resolutions and Meetings). See that draft Order in Appendix 12 at **[A12]**.

378 Extraordinary and special resolutions

(1) A resolution is an extraordinary resolution when it has been passed by a majority of not less than three-fourths of such members as (being entitled to do so) vote in person or, where proxies are allowed, by proxy, at a general meeting of which notice specifying the intention to propose the resolution as an extraordinary resolution has been duly given.

(2) A resolution is a special resolution when it has been passed by such a majority as is required for the passing of an extraordinary resolution and at a general meeting of which not less than 21 days' notice, specifying the intention to propose the resolution as a special resolution, has been duly given.

(3) If it is so agreed by a majority in number of the members having the right to attend and vote at such a meeting, being a majority—

- *(a) together holding not less than 95 per cent in nominal value of the shares giving that right [(excluding any shares in the company held as treasury shares)]; or*
- *(b) in the case of a company not having a share capital, together representing not less than 95 per cent of the total voting rights at that meeting of all the members,*

a resolution may be proposed and passed as a special resolution at a meeting of which less than 21 days' notice has been given.

[A private company may elect (by elective resolution in accordance with section 379A) that the above provisions shall have effect in relation to the company as if for the references to 95 per cent there were substituted references to such lesser percentage, but not less than 90 per cent, as may be specified in the resolution or subsequently determined by the company in general meeting.]

(4) At any meeting at which an extraordinary resolution or a special resolution is submitted to be passed, a declaration by the chairman that the resolution is carried is, unless a poll is demanded, conclusive evidence of the fact without proof of the number or proportion of the votes recorded in favour of or against the resolution.

(5) In computing the majority on a poll demanded on the question that an extraordinary resolution or a special resolution be passed, reference is to be had to the number of votes cast for and against the resolution.

(6) For purposes of this section, notice of a meeting is deemed duly given, and the meeting duly held, when the notice is given and the meeting held in the manner provided by this Act or the company's articles.

[393]

NOTES

Repealed by the Companies Act 2006, s 1295, Sch 16, as from 1 October 2007. For savings, etc, see the note below.

Sub-s (3): words in square brackets in para (a) inserted by the Companies (Acquisition of Own Shares) (Treasury Shares) Regulations 2003, SI 2003/1116, reg 4, Schedule, para 24, as from 1 December 2003; words in second pair of square brackets added by CA 1989, s 115(3), as from 1 April 1990.

Savings, etc: the draft Companies Act 2006 (Commencement No 3, Consequential Amendments, Transitional Provisions and Savings) Order 2007, Sch 3, paras 22–40 make a variety of savings and transitional provisions in relation to the repeal of this Chapter and the commencement of Part 13 of the Companies Act 2006 (Resolutions and Meetings). See that draft Order in Appendix 12 at **[A12]**.

Section 972 (in Part 28) of the Companies Act 2006 (at **[S972]**) provides for transitory modifications of this section where a takeover bid is made for an opted-in company before this repeal comes into force. Part 28 is the domestic implementation of the Takeovers Directive (Directive of the European Parliament and of the Council 2004/25/EC on takeover bids) and was brought into force on 6 April 2007. The Takeovers Directive had to be implemented by 20 May 2006 and this was achieved by the Takeovers Directive (Interim Implementation) Regulations 2006, SI 2006/1183 (see reg 23 of those Regulations as to the application of this section where a takeover bid is made for an opted-in company from 20 May 2006 (at **[7531]**)). The 2006 Interim Regulations were also revoked from 6 April 2007.

379 Resolution requiring special notice

(1) Where by any provision of this Act special notice is required of a resolution, the resolution is not effective unless notice of the intention to move it has been given to the company at least 28 days before the meeting at which it is moved.

(2) The company shall give its members notice of any such resolution at the same time and in the same manner as it gives notice of the meeting or, if that is not practicable, shall give them notice either by advertisement in a newspaper having an appropriate circulation or in any other mode allowed by the company's articles, at least 21 days before the meeting.

(3) If, after notice of the intention to move such a resolution has been given to the company, a meeting is called for a date 28 days or less after the notice has been given, the notice is deemed properly given, though not given within the time required.

[394]

NOTES

Repealed by the Companies Act 2006, s 1295, Sch 16, as from 1 October 2007. For savings, etc, see the note below.

Savings, etc: the draft Companies Act 2006 (Commencement No 3, Consequential Amendments, Transitional Provisions and Savings) Order 2007, Sch 3, paras 22–40 make a variety of savings and transitional provisions in relation to the repeal of this Chapter and the commencement of Part 13 of the Companies Act 2006 (Resolutions and Meetings). See that draft Order in Appendix 12 at **[A12]**.

[379A Elective resolution of private company

(1) An election by a private company for the purposes of—

(a) section 80A (election as to duration of authority to allot shares),

(b) section 252 (election to dispense with laying of accounts and reports before general meeting),

(c) section 366A (election to dispense with holding of annual general meeting),

(d) section 369(4) or 378(3) (election as to majority required to authorise short notice of meeting), or

(e) section 386 (election to dispense with appointment of auditors annually),

shall be made by resolution of the company in general meeting in accordance with this section.

Such a resolution is referred to in this Act as an "elective resolution".

(2) An elective resolution is not effective unless—

(a) at least 21 days' notice in writing is given of the meeting, stating that an elective resolution is to be proposed and stating the terms of the resolution, and

(b) the resolution is agreed to at the meeting, in person or by proxy, by all the members entitled to attend and vote at the meeting.

[(2A) An elective resolution is effective notwithstanding the fact that less than 21 days' notice in writing of the meeting is given if all the members entitled to attend and vote at the meeting so agree.]

[(2B) For the purposes of this section, notice in writing of the meeting is to be taken as given to a person where notice of the meeting is sent using electronic communications to such address as may for the time being be notified by that person to the company for that purpose.

(2C) For the purposes of this section a notice in writing of the meeting is also to be treated as given to a person where—

(a) the company and that person have agreed that notices of meetings required to be given to that person may instead be accessed by him on a web site;

(b) the meeting is a meeting to which that agreement applies;

(c) that person is notified, in a manner for the time being agreed between him and the company for the purpose, of—

(i) the publication of the notice on a web site;

(ii) the address of that web site; and

(iii) the place on that web site where the notice may be accessed, and how it may be accessed; and

(d) the notice continues to be published on that web site throughout the period beginning with the giving of that notification and ending with the conclusion of the meeting;

and for the purposes of this section a notice treated in accordance with this subsection as given to any person is to be treated as so given at the time of the notification mentioned in paragraph (c).

(2D) A notification given for the purposes of subsection (2C)(c) must—

(a) state that it concerns a notice of a company meeting at which an elective resolution is to be proposed, and

(b) specify the place, date and time of the meeting.

(2E) Nothing in subsection (2C) shall invalidate the proceedings of a meeting where—

(a) any notice that is required to be published as mentioned in paragraph (d) of that subsection is published for a part, but not all, of the period mentioned in that paragraph; and

(b) the failure to publish that notice throughout that period is wholly attributable to circumstances which it would not be reasonable to have expected the company to prevent or avoid.

(2F) In so far as the articles of the company do not provide for notices and notifications to be served using electronic communications, the provisions of Table A (as for the time being in force) as to such service shall apply.]

(3) The company may revoke an elective resolution by passing an ordinary resolution to that effect.

(4) An elective resolution shall cease to have effect if the company is re-registered as a public company.

(5) An elective resolution may be passed or revoked in accordance with this section, and the provisions referred to in [subsections (1) and (2B) to (2E)] have effect, notwithstanding any contrary provision in the company's articles of association.

[(5A) In this section, "address" includes any number or address used for the purposes of electronic communications.]]

[395]

NOTES

Inserted by CA 1989, s 116(1), (2), as from 1 April 1990.

Repealed by the Companies Act 2006, s 1295, Sch 16, as from 20 January 2007 (in so far as relating to sub-ss (2B)–(2F), (5A)), as from 1 October 2007 (in so far as relating to sub-s (1)(b)–(e)), and as from a day to be appointed (otherwise). For transitional provisions see the note to s 238 at **[225]**, and for savings, etc, see the note below.

Sub-s (1): paras (b), (e) repealed as noted above.

Sub-s (2A): inserted by the Deregulation (Resolutions of Private Companies) Order 1996, SI 1996/1471, art 2, as from 19 June 1996.

Sub-ss (2B)–(2F): inserted by the Companies Act 1985 (Electronic Communications) Order 2000, SI 2000/3373, art 21(1), (2), as from 22 December 2000, and repealed as noted above.

Sub-s (5): words in square brackets substituted by SI 2000/3373, art 21(1), (3), as from 22 December 2000.

Sub-s (5A): added by SI 2000/3373, art 21(1), (4), as from 22 December 2000, and repealed as noted above.

Savings, etc: the draft Companies Act 2006 (Commencement No 3, Consequential Amendments, Transitional Provisions and Savings) Order 2007, Sch 3, paras 22–40 make a variety of savings and transitional provisions in relation to the repeal of this Chapter and the commencement of Part 13 of the Companies Act 2006 (Resolutions and Meetings). See that draft Order in Appendix 12 at **[A12]**.

380 Registration, etc of resolutions and agreements

(1) A copy of every resolution or agreement to which this section applies shall, within 15 days after it is passed or made, be forwarded to the registrar of companies and recorded by him; and it must be either a printed copy or else a copy in some other form approved by the registrar.

(2) Where articles have been registered, a copy of every such resolution or agreement for the time being in force shall be embodied in or annexed to every copy of the articles issued after the passing of the resolution or the making of the agreement.

(3) Where articles have not been registered, a printed copy of every such resolution or agreement shall be forwarded to any member at his request on payment of 5 pence or such less sum as the company may direct.

(4) [Except as mentioned in subsection (4ZB),] this section applies to—

(*a*) *special resolutions;*
(*b*) *extraordinary resolutions;*
[(bb) an elective resolution or a resolution revoking such a resolution;]
(*c*) *resolutions or agreements which have been agreed to by all the members of a company but which, if not so agreed to, would not have been effective for their purpose unless (as the case may be) they had been passed as special resolutions or as extraordinary resolutions;*
(*d*) *resolutions or agreements which have been agreed to by all the members of some class of shareholders but which, if not so agreed to, would not have been effective for their purpose unless they had been passed by some particular majority or otherwise in some particular manner, and all resolutions or agreements which effectively bind all the members of any class of shareholders though not agreed to by all those members;*
(*e*) *a resolution passed by the directors of a company in compliance with a direction under section 31(2) (change of name on Secretary of State's direction);*
(*f*) *a resolution of a company to give, vary, revoke or renew an authority to the directors for the purposes of section 80 (allotment of relevant securities);*
(*g*) *a resolution of the directors passed under section 147(2) (alteration of memorandum on company ceasing to be a public company, following acquisition of its own shares);*
(*h*) *a resolution conferring, varying, revoking or renewing authority under section 166 (market purchase of company's own shares);*
(*j*) *a resolution for voluntary winding up, passed under [section 84(1)(a) of the Insolvency Act];*
(*k*) *a resolution passed by the directors of an old public company, under section 2(1) of the Consequential Provisions Act, that the company should be re-registered as a public company;*
[(l) a resolution of the directors passed by virtue of regulation 16(2) of the Uncertificated Securities Regulations 2001 (which allows title to a company's shares to be evidenced and transferred without written instrument); and
(*m*) *a resolution of a company passed by virtue of regulation 16(6) of the Uncertificated Securities Regulations 2001 (which prevents or reverses a resolution of the directors under regulation 16(2) of those Regulations)].*

[(4ZA) This section does not, despite paragraphs (a) to (c) of subsection (4), apply to any resolution of a company which is—
(*a*) *registered as a company in Scotland, and*
(*b*) *entered in the Scottish Charity Register,*
where that resolution is of either of the types mentioned in section 56(5) of the Charities and Trustee Investment (Scotland) Act 2005 (asp 10).]

[(4ZB) Paragraphs (a) and (c) of subsection (4) do not apply to the resolutions of a charitable company mentioned in paragraphs (a) and (b) respectively of section 69G(6) of the Charities Act 1993.]

[(4A) For the purposes of this section, references to a member of a company do not include the company itself where it is such a member by virtue only of its holding shares as treasury shares, and accordingly, in such circumstances, the company is not, for those purposes, to be treated as a member of any class of the company's shareholders.]

(5) If a company fails to comply with subsection (1), the company and every officer of it who is in default is liable to a fine and, for continued contravention, to a daily default fine.

(6) If a company fails to comply with subsection (2) or (3), the company and every officer of it who is in default is liable to a fine.

(7) For purposes of subsections (5) and (6), a liquidator of a company is deemed an officer of it.

[396]

NOTES

Repealed by the Companies Act 2006, s 1295, Sch 16, as from 1 October 2007 (in so far as relating to sub-ss (1), (4)–(5)), and as from a day to be appointed (otherwise). For savings see the note below.

Sub-s (1): repealed as noted above.

Sub-s (2): for the words "every such resolution or agreement" there are substituted the words "every resolution or agreement to which Chapter 3 of Part 3 of the Companies Act 2006 applies (resolutions and agreements affecting a company's constitution) and which is" by the draft Companies Act 2006

(Commencement No 3, Consequential Amendments, Transitional Provisions and Savings) Order 2007, art 10(1), Sch 4, Pt 1, para 1(9), as from 1 October 2007 (see **[A12]**).

Sub-s (4): repealed as noted above; words in first pair of square brackets inserted by the Charities Act 2006, s 75, Sch 8, paras 74, 75(1), (2), as from a day to be appointed; para (bb) inserted by CA 1989, s 116(3), as from 1 April 1990; words in square brackets in para (j) substituted by the Insolvency Act 1986, s 439(1), Sch 13, Pt I, as from 29 December 1986 (for transitional provisions see s 437 of, and Sch 11, Pt I to, that Act at **[3456]**, **[3481]**); paras (l), (m) were originally added by the Uncertificated Securities Regulations 1995, SI 1995/3272, reg 40(3), as from 19 December 1995; the 1995 Regulations were revoked by the Uncertificated Securities Regulations 2001, SI 2001/3755, reg 52, as from 26 November 2001, and reg 51 of, and Sch 7, Pt 1, para 10 to, the 2001 Regulations added new paras (l), (m) as from that date.

Sub-s (4ZA): inserted by the Charities and Trustee Investment (Scotland) Act 2005, s 104, Sch 4, Pt 1, para 6, as from 1 April 2006.

Sub-s (4ZB): inserted by the Charities Act 2006, s 75, Sch 8, paras 74, 75(1), (3), as from a day to be appointed.

Sub-s (4A): inserted by the Companies (Acquisition of Own Shares) (Treasury Shares) Regulations 2003, SI 2003/1116, reg 4, Schedule, para 25, as from 1 December 2003.

Sub-s (5): repealed as noted above.

Savings, etc: the draft Companies Act 2006 (Commencement No 3, Consequential Amendments, Transitional Provisions and Savings) Order 2007, Sch 3, paras 22–40 make a variety of savings and transitional provisions in relation to the repeal of this Chapter and the commencement of Part 13 of the Companies Act 2006 (Resolutions and Meetings). See that draft Order in Appendix 12 at **[A12]**. See also Sch 3, para 1 to that Order which provides that sub-ss (1), (5) continue to apply in relation to resolutions passed and agreements made, but not forwarded to the registrar, before 1 October 2007.

Community interest companies: copies of the special resolutions making an organisation, already incorporated as a company, a community interest company, or making a community interest company a charitable company, must be forwarded to the registrar of companies, together with the memorandum and articles in the form that they will take once altered by the special resolutions; see the Companies (Audit, Investigations and Community Enterprise) Act 2004, ss 26, 37, 54 at **[900]**, **[911]**, **[928]**. If a copy of a special resolution under s 4(1) is delivered to the registrar pursuant to this section, the company must also deliver (a) a community interest statement, and (b) a statement, in a form approved by the Regulator, of the steps that have been taken to bring the proposed alteration to the notice of persons affected by the company's activities; see the Community Interest Company Regulations 2005, SI 2005/1788, reg 14 at **[7412]**.

Insolvency Act, s 84(1)(a): ie, the Insolvency Act 1986, s 84(1)(a).

Consequential Provisions Act: ie, the Companies Consolidation (Consequential Provisions) Act 1985.

381 Resolution passed at adjourned meeting

Where a resolution is passed at an adjourned meeting of—

(*a*) *a company;*

(*b*) *the holders of any class of shares in a company;*

(*c*) *the directors of a company;*

the resolution is for all purposes to be treated as having been passed on the date on which it was in fact passed, and is not to be deemed passed on any earlier date.

[397]

NOTES

Repealed by the Companies Act 2006, s 1295, Sch 16, as from 1 October 2007. For savings, etc, see the note below.

Savings, etc: the draft Companies Act 2006 (Commencement No 3, Consequential Amendments, Transitional Provisions and Savings) Order 2007, Sch 3, paras 22–40 make a variety of savings and transitional provisions in relation to the repeal of this Chapter and the commencement of Part 13 of the Companies Act 2006 (Resolutions and Meetings). See that draft Order in Appendix 12 at **[A12]**.

[Written resolutions of private companies

381A Written resolutions of private companies

(*1*) *Anything which in the case of a private company may be done—*

(*a*) *by resolution of the company in general meeting, or*

(*b*) *by resolution of a meeting of any class of members of the company,*

may be done, without a meeting and without any previous notice being required, by resolution in writing signed by or on behalf of all the members of the company who at the date of the resolution would be entitled to attend and vote at such meeting.

(2) *The signatures need not be on a single document provided each is on a document which accurately states the terms of the resolution.*

(3) The date of the resolution means when the resolution is signed by or on behalf of the last member to sign.

(4) A resolution agreed to in accordance with this section has effect as if passed—

(a) by the company in general meeting, or

(b) by a meeting of the relevant class of members of the company,

as the case may be; and any reference in any enactment to a meeting at which a resolution is passed or to members voting in favour of a resolution shall be construed accordingly.

(5) Any reference in any enactment to the date of passing of a resolution is, in relation to a resolution agreed to in accordance with this section, a reference to the date of the resolution, …

(6) A resolution may be agreed to in accordance with this section which would otherwise be required to be passed as a special, extraordinary or elective resolution; and any reference in any enactment to a special, extraordinary or elective resolution includes such a resolution.

(7) This section has effect subject to the exceptions specified in Part I of Schedule 15A; and in relation to certain descriptions of resolution under this section the procedural requirements of this Act have effect with the adaptations specified in Part II of that Schedule.]

[398]

NOTES

Inserted, together with preceding heading and ss 381B, 381C, by CA 1989, s 113(1), (2), as from 1 April 1990.

Repealed by the Companies Act 2006, s 1295, Sch 16, as from 1 October 2007. For savings, etc, see the note below.

Sub-s (5): words omitted repealed by the Deregulation (Resolutions of Private Companies) Order 1996, SI 1996/1471, art 3(2)(a), (3), with effect in relation to written resolutions first proposed on or after 19 June 1996.

Savings, etc: the draft Companies Act 2006 (Commencement No 3, Consequential Amendments, Transitional Provisions and Savings) Order 2007, Sch 3, paras 22–40 make a variety of savings and transitional provisions in relation to the repeal of this Chapter and the commencement of Part 13 of the Companies Act 2006 (Resolutions and Meetings). See that draft Order in Appendix 12 at **[A12]**.

[381B Duty to notify auditors of proposed written resolution

(1) If a director or secretary of a company—

(a) knows that it is proposed to seek agreement to a resolution in accordance with section 381A, and

(b) knows the terms of the resolution,

he shall, if the company has auditors, secure that a copy of the resolution is sent to them, or that they are otherwise notified of its contents, at or before the time the resolution is supplied to a member for signature.

(2) A person who fails to comply with subsection (1) is liable to a fine.

(3) In any proceedings for an offence under this section it is a defence for the accused to prove—

(a) that the circumstances were such that it was not practicable for him to comply with subsection (1), or

(b) that he believed on reasonable grounds that a copy of the resolution had been sent to the company's auditors or that they had otherwise been informed of its contents.

(4) Nothing in this section affects the validity of any resolution.]

[399]

NOTES

Inserted as noted to s 381A at **[398]**. Subsequently substituted by the Deregulation (Resolutions of Private Companies) Order 1996, SI 1996/1471, art 3(1), (3), with effect in relation to written resolutions first proposed on or after 19 June 1996.

Repealed by the Companies Act 2006, s 1295, Sch 16, as from 1 October 2007. For savings, etc, see the note below.

Savings, etc: the draft Companies Act 2006 (Commencement No 3, Consequential Amendments, Transitional Provisions and Savings) Order 2007, Sch 3, paras 22–40 make a variety of savings and transitional provisions in relation to the repeal of this Chapter and the commencement of Part 13 of the Companies Act 2006 (Resolutions and Meetings). See that draft Order in Appendix 12 at **[A12]**.

[381C Written resolutions: supplementary provisions

(*1*) *Sections 381A and 381B have effect notwithstanding any provision of the company's memorandum or article[, but do not prejudice any power conferred by any such provision].*

(*2*) *Nothing in those sections affects any enactment or rule of law as to—*
(*a*) *things done otherwise than by passing a resolution, or*
(*b*) *cases in which a resolution is treated as having been passed, or a person is precluded from alleging that a resolution has not been duly passed.]*

[400]

NOTES

Inserted as noted to s 381A at **[398]**.

Repealed by the Companies Act 2006, s 1295, Sch 16, as from 1 October 2007. For savings, etc, see the note below.

Sub-s (1): words in square brackets added by the Deregulation (Resolutions of Private Companies) Order 1996, SI 1996/1471, art 4, as from 19 June 1996.

Savings, etc: the draft Companies Act 2006 (Commencement No 3, Consequential Amendments, Transitional Provisions and Savings) Order 2007, Sch 3, paras 22–40 make a variety of savings and transitional provisions in relation to the repeal of this Chapter and the commencement of Part 13 of the Companies Act 2006 (Resolutions and Meetings). See that draft Order in Appendix 12 at **[A12]**.

Records of proceedings

382 Minutes of meetings

(*1*) *Every company shall cause minutes of all proceedings of general meetings, all proceedings at meetings of its directors and, where there are managers, all proceedings at meetings of its managers to be entered in books kept for that purpose.*

(*2*) *Any such minute, if purporting to be signed by the chairman of the meeting at which the proceedings were had, or by the chairman of the next succeeding meeting, is evidence of the proceedings.*

(*3*) *Where a shadow director by means of a notice required by section 317(8) declares an interest in a contract or proposed contract, this section applies—*
(*a*) *if it is a specific notice under paragraph (a) of that subsection, as if the declaration had been made at the meeting there referred to, and*
(*b*) *otherwise, as if it had been made at the meeting of the directors next following the giving of the notice;*

and the making of the declaration is in either case deemed to form part of the proceedings at the meeting.

(*4*) *Where minutes have been made in accordance with this section of the proceedings at any general meeting of the company or meeting of directors or managers, then, until the contrary is proved, the meeting is deemed duly held and convened, and all proceedings had at the meeting to have been duly had; and all appointments of directors, managers or liquidators are deemed valid.*

(*5*) *If a company fails to comply with subsection (1), the company and every officer of it who is in default is liable to a fine and, for continued contravention, to a daily default fine.*

[401]

NOTES

Repealed by the Companies Act 2006, s 1295, Sch 16, as from 1 October 2007. For savings, etc, see the note below.

Savings, etc: the draft Companies Act 2006 (Commencement No 3, Consequential Amendments, Transitional Provisions and Savings) Order 2007, Sch 3, paras 22–40 make a variety of savings and transitional provisions in relation to the repeal of this Chapter and the commencement of Part 13 of the Companies Act 2006 (Resolutions and Meetings). See that draft Order in Appendix 12 at **[A12]**.

[382A Recording of written resolutions

(*1*) *Where a written resolution is agreed to in accordance with section 381A which has effect as if agreed by the company in general meeting, the company shall cause a record of the resolution (and of the signatures) to be entered in a book in the same way as minutes of proceedings of a general meeting of the company.*

(2) Any such record, if purporting to be signed by a director of the company or by the company secretary, is evidence of the proceedings in agreeing to the resolution; and where a record is made in accordance with this section, then, until the contrary is proved, the requirements of this Act with respect to those proceedings shall be deemed to be complied with.

(3) Section 382(5) (penalties) applies in relation to a failure to comply with subsection (1) above as it applies in relation to a failure to comply with subsection (1) of that section; and section 383 (inspection of minute books) applies in relation to a record made in accordance with this section as it applies in relation to the minutes of a general meeting.]

[402]

NOTES

Inserted by CA 1989, s 113(1), (3), as from 1 April 1990.

Repealed by the Companies Act 2006, s 1295, Sch 16, as from 1 October 2007. For savings, etc, see the note below.

Savings, etc: the draft Companies Act 2006 (Commencement No 3, Consequential Amendments, Transitional Provisions and Savings) Order 2007, Sch 3, paras 22–40 make a variety of savings and transitional provisions in relation to the repeal of this Chapter and the commencement of Part 13 of the Companies Act 2006 (Resolutions and Meetings). See that draft Order in Appendix 12 at **[A12]**.

[382B Recording of decisions by the sole member

(1) Where a private company limited by shares or by guarantee has only one member and he takes any decision which may be taken by the company in general meeting and which has effect as if agreed by the company in general meeting, he shall (unless that decision is taken by way of a written resolution) provide the company with a written record of that decision.

(2) If the sole member fails to comply with subsection (1) he shall be liable to a fine.

(3) Failure by the sole member to comply with subsection (1) shall not affect the validity of any decision referred to in that subsection.]

[403]

NOTES

Inserted by the Companies (Single Member Private Limited Companies) Regulations 1992, SI 1992/1699, reg 2, Schedule, para 6(1), as from 15 July 1992.

Repealed by the Companies Act 2006, s 1295, Sch 16, as from 1 October 2007. For savings, etc, see the note below.

Savings, etc: the draft Companies Act 2006 (Commencement No 3, Consequential Amendments, Transitional Provisions and Savings) Order 2007, Sch 3, paras 22–40 make a variety of savings and transitional provisions in relation to the repeal of this Chapter and the commencement of Part 13 of the Companies Act 2006 (Resolutions and Meetings). See that draft Order in Appendix 12 at **[A12]**.

383 Inspection of minute books

(1) The books containing the minutes of proceedings of any general meeting of a company held on or after 1st November 1929 shall be kept at the company's registered office, and shall … be open to the inspection of any member without charge.

(2) …

(3) Any member shall be entitled [on payment of such fee as may be prescribed] to be furnished, within 7 days after he has made a request in that behalf to the company, with a copy of any such minutes as are referred to above, …

(4) If an inspection required under this section is refused or if a copy required under this section is not sent within the proper time, the company and every officer of it who is in default is liable in respect of each offence to a fine.

(5) In the case of any such refusal or default, the court may by order compel an immediate inspection of the books in respect of all proceedings of general meetings, or direct that the copies required be sent to the persons requiring them.

[404]

NOTES

Repealed by the Companies Act 2006, s 1295, Sch 16, as from 1 October 2007. For savings, etc, see the note below.

Sub-s (1): words omitted repealed by CA 1989, ss 143(9), 212, Sch 24, as from 1 November 1991.
Sub-s (2): repealed by CA 1989, ss 143(9), 212, Sch 24, as from 1 November 1991.
Sub-s (3): words in square brackets inserted, and words omitted repealed, by CA 1989, ss 143(9), 212, Sch 24, as from 1 November 1991.
Savings, etc: the draft Companies Act 2006 (Commencement No 3, Consequential Amendments, Transitional Provisions and Savings) Order 2007, Sch 3, paras 22–40 make a variety of savings and transitional provisions in relation to the repeal of this Chapter and the commencement of Part 13 of the Companies Act 2006 (Resolutions and Meetings). See that draft Order in Appendix 12 at **[A12]**.
Inspection: for provisions relating to the inspection of documents, registers and fees under this section, see the Companies (Inspection and Copying of Registers, Indices and Documents) Regulations 1991, SI 1991/1998 at **[6716]** et seq (partly made under this section).

CHAPTER V
AUDITORS

[Appointment of auditors

384 Duty to appoint auditors

(1) Every company shall appoint an auditor or auditors in accordance with this Chapter.

This is subject to section 388A ([certain companies] exempt from obligation to appoint auditors).

(2) Auditors shall be appointed in accordance with section 385 (appointment at general meeting at which accounts are laid), except in the case of a private company which has elected to dispense with the laying of accounts in which case the appointment shall be made in accordance with section 385A.

(3) References in this Chapter to the end of the time for appointing auditors are to the end of the time within which an appointment must be made under section 385(2) or 385A(2), according to whichever of those sections applies.

(4) Sections 385 and 385A have effect subject to section 386 under which a private company may elect to dispense with the obligation to appoint auditors annually.]

[405]

NOTES

Substituted, together with preceding heading and ss 385, 385A, 386–388, 388A, by CA 1989, ss 118, 119(1), as from 1 April 1990.
Repealed by the Companies Act 2006, s 1295, Sch 16, as from 1 October 2007 (in so far as relating to private companies), and as from a day to be appointed (otherwise). For savings, etc, see the note below.
Sub-s (1): for the words "Every company" there are substituted the words "Every public company" by the draft Companies Act 2006 (Commencement No 3, Consequential Amendments, Transitional Provisions and Savings) Order 2007, art 10(1), Sch 4, Pt 1, para 6(1)(a), (6), as from 1 October 2007, with effect in relation to appointments for financial years beginning on or after that date (see **[A12]**); words in square brackets substituted by the Companies Act 1985 (Audit Exemption) Regulations 1994, SI 1994/1935, reg 4, Sch 1, Pt I, para 4, as from 11 August 1994, in relation to annual accounts of a company which are approved by the board of directors on or after 11 August 1994 (and do not apply to any annual accounts the period for laying and delivering of which expired before that date).
Sub-s (2): words from "except in the case of a private company" to the end repealed by the draft Companies Act 2006 (Commencement No 3, Consequential Amendments, Transitional Provisions and Savings) Order 2007, art 10(1), Sch 4, Pt 1, para 6(1)(b), (6), as from 1 October 2007, with effect in relation to appointments for financial years beginning on or after that date (see **[A12]**).
Sub-s (3): words from "or 385A(2)" to the end repealed by the draft Companies Act 2006 (Commencement No 3, Consequential Amendments, Transitional Provisions and Savings) Order 2007, art 10(1), Sch 4, Pt 1, para 6(1)(c), (6), as from 1 October 2007, with effect in relation to appointments for financial years beginning on or after that date (see **[A12]**).
Sub-s (4): repealed by the draft Companies Act 2006 (Commencement No 3, Consequential Amendments, Transitional Provisions and Savings) Order 2007, art 10(1), Sch 4, Pt 1, para 6(1)(d), (6), as from 1 October 2007, with effect in relation to appointments for financial years beginning on or after that date (see **[A12]**).
Savings, etc: see the draft Companies Act 2006 (Commencement No 3, Consequential Amendments, Transitional Provisions and Savings) Order 2007, Sch 3, paras 44, 45 (at **[A12]**) which provide as follows—

"44 Appointment of auditors of private companies (ss 485 to 488)

(1) Sections 485 to 488 of the Companies Act 2006 (appointment of auditors of private companies) apply in relation to appointments for financial years beginning on or after 1st October 2007.

(2) Sections 384 to 388A of the 1985 Act or Articles 392 to 396A of the 1986 Order continue to apply in relation to appointments for financial years beginning before that date.

(3) Where—

(a) a private company has elected under section 386 of the 1985 Act or Article 394 of the 1986 Order to dispense with the annual appointment of auditors, and

(b) the election is in force immediately before 1st October 2007,

section 487(2)(a) of the Companies Act 2006 (no deemed reappointment of auditors appointed by directors) does not prevent the deemed reappointment under that subsection of auditors first appointed before 1st October 2007.

45.—(1) This paragraph applies where immediately before 1st October 2007 a resolution of a private company under section 390A of the 1985 Act or Article 398A of the 1986 Order (remuneration of auditors) was in force and was expressed (in whatever terms) to continue to have effect so long as a resolution under section 386 of that Act or Article 394 of that Order (election to dispense with annual appointment of auditors) continued in force.

(2) The repeal of section 386 of the 1985 Act or Article 394 of the 1986 Order does not affect the continued operation of the resolution, which shall continue to have effect until—

(a) it is revoked or superseded by a further resolution,

(b) the auditors to which it applies cease to hold office, or

(c) it otherwise ceases to have effect in accordance with its terms.".

Application to limited liability partnerships: see the Limited Liability Partnerships Regulations 2001, SI 2001/1090, reg 4(1), Sch 2, Pt 1 at **[6985]**, **[6993]**. Note also that nothing in the draft Companies Act 2006 (Commencement No 3, Consequential Amendments, Transitional Provisions and Savings) Order 2007 affects any provision of this Act as applied by the 2001 Regulations to LLPs (see art 12(2) at **[A12]** and the introductory notes to this Act).

[385 Appointment at general meeting at which accounts laid

(1) This section applies to every public company and to a private company which has not elected to dispense with the laying of accounts.

(2) The company shall, at each general meeting at which accounts are laid, appoint an auditor or auditors to hold office from the conclusion of that meeting until the conclusion of the next general meeting at which accounts are laid.

(3) The first auditors of the company may be appointed by the directors at any time before the first general meeting of the company at which accounts are laid; and auditors so appointed shall hold office until the conclusion of that meeting.

(4) If the directors fail to exercise their powers under subsection (3), the powers may be exercised by the company in general meeting.]

[406]

NOTES

Substituted as noted to s 384 at **[405]**.

Repealed by the Companies Act 2006, s 1295, Sch 16, as from 1 October 2007 (in so far as relating to private companies), and as from a day to be appointed (otherwise). For savings, etc, see the note to s 384 at **[405]**.

Sub-s (1): words from "and to a private company" to the end repealed by the draft Companies Act 2006 (Commencement No 3, Consequential Amendments, Transitional Provisions and Savings) Order 2007, art 10(1), Sch 4, Pt 1, para 6(2), (6), as from 1 October 2007, with effect in relation to appointments for financial years beginning on or after that date (see **[A12]**).

Application to limited liability partnerships: see the Limited Liability Partnerships Regulations 2001, SI 2001/1090, reg 4(1), Sch 2, Pt 1 at **[6985]**, **[6993]**. Note also that nothing in the draft Companies Act 2006 (Commencement No 3, Consequential Amendments, Transitional Provisions and Savings) Order 2007 affects any provision of this Act as applied by the 2001 Regulations to LLPs (see art 12(2) at **[A12]** and the introductory notes to this Act).

[385A Appointment by private company which is not obliged to lay accounts

(1) This section applies to a private company which has elected in accordance with section 252 to dispense with the laying of accounts before the company in general meeting.

(2) Auditors shall be appointed by the company in general meeting before the end of the period of 28 days beginning with the day on which copies of the company's annual accounts for the previous financial year are sent to members under section 238 or, if notice is given under section 253(2) requiring the laying of the accounts before the company in general meeting, the conclusion of that meeting.

Auditors so appointed shall hold office from the end of that period or, as the case may be, the conclusion of that meeting until the end of the time for appointing auditors for the next financial year.

(3) The first auditors of the company may be appointed by the directors at any time before—

- *(a) the end of the period of 28 days beginning with the day on which copies of the company's first annual accounts are sent to members under section 238, or*
- *(b) if notice is given under section 253(2) requiring the laying of the accounts before the company in general meeting, the beginning of that meeting;*

and auditors so appointed shall hold office until the end of that period or, as the case may be, the conclusion of that meeting.

(4) If the directors fail to exercise their powers under subsection (3), the powers may be exercised by the company in general meeting.

(5) Auditors holding office when the election is made shall, unless the company in general meeting determines otherwise, continue to hold office until the end of the time for appointing auditors for the next financial year; and auditors holding office when an election ceases to have effect shall continue to hold office until the conclusion of the next general meeting of the company at which accounts are laid.]

[407]

NOTES

Substituted as noted to s 384 at **[405]**.

Repealed by the Companies Act 2006, s 1295, Sch 16, as from 1 October 2007. For savings, etc, see the note to s 384 at **[405]**.

[386 Election by private company to dispense with annual appointment

(1) A private company may elect (by elective resolution in accordance with section 379A) to dispense with the obligation to appoint auditors annually.

(2) When such an election is in force the company's auditors shall be deemed to be re-appointed for each succeeding financial year on the expiry of the time for appointing auditors for that year, unless—

- *[(a) the directors of the company have taken advantage of the exemption conferred by section 249A or 249AA, or]*
- *(b) a resolution has been passed under section 393 to the effect that their appointment should be brought to an end.*

(3) If the election ceases to be in force, the auditors then holding office shall continue to hold office—

- *(a) where section 385 then applies, until the conclusion of the next general meeting of the company at which accounts are laid;*
- *(b) where section 385A then applies, until the end of the time for appointing auditors for the next financial year under that section.*

(4) No account shall be taken of any loss of the opportunity of further deemed re-appointment under this section in ascertaining the amount of any compensation or damages payable to an auditor on his ceasing to hold office for any reason.]

[408]

NOTES

Substituted as noted to s 384 at **[405]**.

Repealed by the Companies Act 2006, s 1295, Sch 16, as from 1 October 2007. For savings, etc, see the note to s 384 at **[405]**.

Sub-s (2): para (a) substituted by the Companies Act 1985 (Audit Exemption) (Amendment) Regulations 2000, SI 2000/1430, reg 8(8), as from 26 May 2000, in relation to annual reports and reports in respect of financial years ending two months or more after that date.

Prescribed notice: see Appendix 4 (Forms table) at **[A4]**.

[387 Appointment by Secretary of State in default of appointment by company

(1) If in any case no auditors are appointed, re-appointed or deemed to be re-appointed before the end of the time for appointing auditors, the Secretary of State may appoint a person to fill the vacancy.

(2) In such a case the company shall within one week of the end of the time for appointing auditors give notice to the Secretary of State of his power having become exercisable.

If a company fails to give the notice required by this subsection, the company and every officer of it who is in default is guilty of an offence and liable to a fine and, for continued contravention, to a daily default fine.]

[409]

NOTES

Substituted as noted to s 384 at **[405]**.

Repealed by the Companies Act 2006, s 1295, Sch 16, as from 1 October 2007 (in so far as relating to private companies), and as from a day to be appointed (otherwise). For savings, etc, see the note to s 384 at **[405]**.

Sub-s (1): for the words "If in any case" there are substituted the words "If in the case of a public company" by the draft Companies Act 2006 (Commencement No 3, Consequential Amendments, Transitional Provisions and Savings) Order 2007, art 10(1), Sch 4, Pt 1, para 6(3), (6), as from 1 October 2007, with effect in relation to appointments for financial years beginning on or after that date (see **[A12]**).

Application to limited liability partnerships: see the Limited Liability Partnerships Regulations 2001, SI 2001/1090, reg 4(1), Sch 2, Pt 1 at **[6985]**, **[6993]**. Note also that nothing in the draft Companies Act 2006 (Commencement No 3, Consequential Amendments, Transitional Provisions and Savings) Order 2007 affects any provision of this Act as applied by the 2001 Regulations to LLPs (see art 12(2) at **[A12]** and the introductory notes to this Act).

[388 Filling of casual vacancies

(1) The directors [of a public company], or the company in general meeting, may fill a casual vacancy in the office of auditor.

(2) While such a vacancy continues, any surviving or continuing auditor or auditors may continue to act.

(3) Special notice is required for a resolution at a general meeting of a company—

(a) filling a casual vacancy in the office of auditor, or

(b) re-appointing as auditor a retiring auditor who was appointed by the directors to fill a casual vacancy.

(4) On receipt of notice of such an intended resolution the company shall forthwith send a copy of it—

(a) to the person proposed to be appointed, and

(b) if the casual vacancy was caused by the resignation of an auditor, to the auditor who resigned.]

[410]

NOTES

Substituted as noted to s 384 at **[405]**.

Repealed by the Companies Act 2006, s 1295, Sch 16, as from 1 October 2007 (in so far as relating to private companies), and as from a day to be appointed (otherwise). For savings, etc, see the note to s 384 at **[405]**.

Sub-s (1): words in square brackets inserted by the draft Companies Act 2006 (Commencement No 3, Consequential Amendments, Transitional Provisions and Savings) Order 2007, art 10(1), Sch 4, Pt 1, para 6(4)(a), (6), as from 1 October 2007, with effect in relation to appointments for financial years beginning on or after that date (see **[A12]**).

Sub-s (3): for the words "a company" there are substituted the words "a public company" by the draft Companies Act 2006 (Commencement No 3, Consequential Amendments, Transitional Provisions and Savings) Order 2007, art 10(1), Sch 4, Pt 1, para 6(4)(b), (6), as from 1 October 2007, with effect in relation to appointments for financial years beginning on or after that date (see **[A12]**).

Application to limited liability partnerships: see the Limited Liability Partnerships Regulations 2001, SI 2001/1090, reg 4(1), Sch 2, Pt 1 at **[6985]**, **[6993]**. Note also that nothing in the draft Companies Act 2006 (Commencement No 3, Consequential Amendments, Transitional Provisions and Savings) Order 2007 affects any provision of this Act as applied by the 2001 Regulations to LLPs (see art 12(2) at **[A12]** and the introductory notes to this Act).

[388A Certain companies exempt from obligation to appoint auditors

(1) A company which by virtue of section 249A (certain categories of small company) or [section 249AA] (dormant companies) is exempt from the provisions of Part VII relating to the audit of accounts is also exempt from the obligation to appoint auditors.

(2) The following provisions apply if a company which has been exempt from those provisions ceases to be so exempt.

(3) Where section 385 applies (appointment at general meeting at which accounts are laid), the directors may appoint auditors at any time before the next meeting of the company at which accounts are to be laid; and auditors so appointed shall hold office until the conclusion of that meeting.

(4) Where section 385A applies (appointment by private company not obliged to lay accounts), the directors may appoint auditors at any time before—

- *(a) the end of the period of 28 days beginning with the day on which copies of the company's annual accounts are next sent to members under section 238, or*
- *(b) if notice is given under section 253(2) requiring the laying of the accounts before the company in general meeting, the beginning of that meeting;*

and auditors so appointed shall hold office until the end of that period or, as the case may be, the conclusion of that meeting.

(5) If the directors fail to exercise their powers under subsection (3) or (4), the powers may be exercised by the company in general meeting.]

[411]

NOTES

Substituted as noted to s 384 at **[405]**, and further substituted by the Companies Act 1985 (Audit Exemption) Regulations 1994, SI 1994/1935, reg 3, as from 11 August 1994, in relation to annual accounts of a company which are approved by the board of directors on or after 11 August 1994 (and does not apply to any annual accounts the period for laying and delivering of which expired before that date).

Repealed by the Companies Act 2006, s 1295, Sch 16, as from 1 October 2007 (in so far as relating to private companies), and as from a day to be appointed (otherwise). For savings, etc, see the note to s 384 at **[405]**.

Sub-s (1): for the words "A company" there are substituted the words "A public company" by the draft Companies Act 2006 (Commencement No 3, Consequential Amendments, Transitional Provisions and Savings) Order 2007, art 10(1), Sch 4, Pt 1, para 6(5)(a), (6), as from 1 October 2007, with effect in relation to appointments for financial years beginning on or after that date (see **[A12]**); words in square brackets substituted by the Companies Act 1985 (Audit Exemption) (Amendment) Regulations 2000, SI 2000/1430, reg 8(9), as from 26 May 2000, in relation to annual reports and reports in respect of financial years ending two months or more after that date.

Sub-s (2): for the words "a company" there are substituted the words "a public company" by the draft Companies Act 2006 (Commencement No 3, Consequential Amendments, Transitional Provisions and Savings) Order 2007, art 10(1), Sch 4, Pt 1, para 6(5)(b), (6), as from 1 October 2007, with effect in relation to appointments for financial years beginning on or after that date (see **[A12]**).

Sub-s (4): repealed by the draft Companies Act 2006 (Commencement No 3, Consequential Amendments, Transitional Provisions and Savings) Order 2007, art 10(1), Sch 4, Pt 1, para 6(5)(c), (6), as from 1 October 2007, with effect in relation to appointments for financial years beginning on or after that date (see **[A12]**).

Sub-s (5): words "or (4)" repealed by the draft Companies Act 2006 (Commencement No 3, Consequential Amendments, Transitional Provisions and Savings) Order 2007, art 10(1), Sch 4, Pt 1, para 6(5)(d), (6), as from 1 October 2007, with effect in relation to appointments for financial years beginning on or after that date (see **[A12]**).

Application to limited liability partnerships: see the Limited Liability Partnerships Regulations 2001, SI 2001/1090, reg 4(1), Sch 2, Pt 1 at **[6985]**, **[6993]**. Note also that nothing in the draft Companies Act 2006 (Commencement No 3, Consequential Amendments, Transitional Provisions and Savings) Order 2007 affects any provision of this Act as applied by the 2001 Regulations to LLPs (see art 12(2) at **[A12]** and the introductory notes to this Act).

389 *(Repealed by CA 1989, s 212, Sch 24, as from 1 October 1991.)*

[Rights of auditors

[389A Rights to information

(1) An auditor of a company—

- *(a) has a right of access at all times to the company's books, accounts and vouchers (in whatever form they are held), and*
- *(b) may require any of the persons mentioned in subsection (2) to provide him with such information or explanations as he thinks necessary for the performance of his duties as auditor.*

(2) Those persons are—

- *(a) any officer or employee of the company;*

(*b*) *any person holding or accountable for any of the company's books, accounts or vouchers;*

(*c*) *any subsidiary undertaking of the company which is a body corporate incorporated in Great Britain;*

(*d*) *any officer, employee or auditor of any such subsidiary undertaking or any person holding or accountable for any books, accounts or vouchers of any such subsidiary undertaking;*

(*e*) *any person who fell within any of paragraphs (a) to (d) at a time to which the information or explanations required by the auditor relates or relate.*

(*3*) *Where a parent company has a subsidiary undertaking which is not a body corporate incorporated in Great Britain, the auditor of the parent company may require it to obtain from any of the persons mentioned in subsection (4) such information or explanations as he may reasonably require for the purposes of his duties as auditor.*

(*4*) *Those persons are—*

(*a*) *the undertaking;*

(*b*) *any officer, employee or auditor of the undertaking;*

(*c*) *any person holding or accountable for any of the undertaking's books, accounts or vouchers;*

(*d*) *any person who fell within paragraph (b) or (c) at a time to which the information or explanations relates or relate.*

(*5*) *If so required, the parent company must take all such steps as are reasonably open to it to obtain the information or explanations from the person within subsection (4) from whom the auditor has required the company to obtain the information or explanations.*

(*6*) *A statement made by a person in response to a requirement under subsection (1)(b) or (3) may not be used in evidence against him in any criminal proceedings except proceedings for an offence under section 389B.*

(*7*) *Nothing in this section or section 389B compels any person to disclose information in respect of which in an action in the High Court a claim to legal professional privilege, or in an action in the Court of Session a claim to confidentiality of communications, could be maintained.]]*

[412]

NOTES

Inserted, together with preceding heading and s 390, by CA 1989, ss 118, 120(1), as from 1 April 1990.

Substituted, together with s 389B, by the Companies (Audit, Investigations and Community Enterprise) Act 2004, s 8, as from 6 April 2005.

Repealed by the Companies Act 2006, s 1295, Sch 16, as from a day to be appointed.

Application to limited liability partnerships: see the Limited Liability Partnerships Regulations 2001, SI 2001/1090, reg 4(1), Sch 2, Pt 1 at **[6985]**, **[6993]**.

[389B Offences relating to the provision of information to auditors

(*1*) *If a person knowingly or recklessly makes to an auditor of a company a statement (oral or written) that—*

(*a*) *conveys or purports to convey any information or explanations which the auditor requires, or is entitled to require, under section 389A(1)(b), and*

(*b*) *is misleading, false or deceptive in a material particular,*

the person is guilty of an offence and liable to imprisonment or a fine, or both.

(*2*) *A person who fails to comply with a requirement under section 389A(1)(b) without delay is guilty of an offence and is liable to a fine.*

(*3*) *However, it is a defence for a person charged with an offence under subsection (2) to prove that it was not reasonably practicable for him to provide the required information or explanations.*

(*4*) *If a company fails to comply with section 389A(5), the company and every officer of it who is in default is guilty of an offence and liable to a fine.*

(*5*) *Nothing in this section affects any right of an auditor to apply for an injunction to enforce any of his rights under section 389A.]*

[412A]

NOTES

Substituted as noted to s 389A at **[412]**.

Repealed by the Companies Act 2006, s 1295, Sch 16, as from a day to be appointed.

[390 Right to attend company meetings, &c

(1) A company's auditors are entitled—

(a) to receive all notices of, and other communications relating to, any general meeting which a member of the company is entitled to receive;

(b) to attend any general meeting of the company; and

(c) to be heard at any general meeting which they attend on any part of the business of the meeting which concerns them as auditors.

[(1A) Subsections (4A) to (4G) of section 369 (electronic communication of notices of meetings) apply for the purpose of determining whether notice of a meeting is received by the company's auditors as they apply in determining whether such a notice is given to any person.]

(2) In relation to a written resolution proposed to be agreed to by a private company in accordance with section 381A, the company's auditors are entitled—

(a) to receive all such communications relating to the resolution as, by virtue of any provision of Schedule 15A, are required to be supplied to a member of the company,

(b)–(d) …

(3) The right to attend or be heard at a meeting is exercisable in the case of a body corporate or partnership by an individual authorised by it in writing to act as its representative at the meeting.]

[413]

NOTES

Inserted as noted to s 389A at **[412]**.

Repealed by the Companies Act 2006, s 1295, Sch 16, as from a day to be appointed.

Sub-s (1A): inserted by the Companies Act 1985 (Electronic Communications) Order 2000, SI 2000/3373, art 31(3), as from 22 December 2000; repealed by the draft Companies Act 2006 (Commencement No 3, Consequential Amendments, Transitional Provisions and Savings) Order 2007, art 10(1), Sch 4, Pt 1, para 4(1), (2), as from 1 October 2007 (see **[A12]**).

Sub-s (2): words "in accordance with section 381A" repealed, and for the words "Schedule 15A" there are substituted the words "Chapter 2 of Part 13 of the Companies Act 2006", by the draft Companies Act 2006 (Commencement No 3, Consequential Amendments, Transitional Provisions and Savings) Order 2007, art 10(1), Sch 4, Pt 1, para 4(1), (3), as from 1 October 2007 (see **[A12]**); paras (b)–(d) repealed by the Deregulation (Resolutions of Private Companies) Order 1996, SI 1996/1471, art 3(2)(b), (3), with effect in relation to written resolutions first proposed on or after 19 June 1996.

Application to limited liability partnerships: see the Limited Liability Partnerships Regulations 2001, SI 2001/1090, reg 4(1), Sch 2, Pt 1 at **[6985]**, **[6993]**. Note also that nothing in the draft Companies Act 2006 (Commencement No 3, Consequential Amendments, Transitional Provisions and Savings) Order 2007 affects any provision of this Act as applied by the 2001 Regulations to LLPs (see art 12(2) at **[A12]** and the introductory notes to this Act).

[Remuneration of auditors

390A Remuneration of auditors

(1) The remuneration of auditors appointed by the company in general meeting shall be fixed by the company in general meeting or in such manner as the company in general meeting may determine.

(2) The remuneration of auditors appointed by the directors or the Secretary of State shall be fixed by the directors or the Secretary of State, as the case may be.

(3) …

(4) For the purposes of this section "remuneration" includes sums paid in respect of expenses.

(5) This section applies in relation to benefits in kind as to [payments of money].]

[414]

NOTES

Inserted, together with preceding heading and s 390B, by CA 1989, ss 118, 121, as from 1 April 1990.
Repealed by the Companies Act 2006, s 1295, Sch 16, as from a day to be appointed.

Sub-s (3): repealed by the Companies (Audit, Investigations and Community Enterprise) Act 2004, ss 7(2)(a), 64, Sch 8, as from 1 October 2005, except in relation to the accounts of a company for a financial year beginning before 1 October 2005; see the Companies (Audit, Investigations and Community Enterprise) Act 2004 (Commencement) and Companies Act 1989 (Commencement No 18) Order 2004, SI 2004/3322, art 3 at **[7341]**.

Sub-s (5): words in square brackets substituted by the Companies (Audit, Investigations and Community Enterprise) Act 2004, s 7(2)(b), as from 1 October 2005.

Application to limited liability partnerships: see the Limited Liability Partnerships Regulations 2001, SI 2001/1090, reg 4(1), Sch 2, Pt 1 at **[6985]**, **[6993]**.

[390B Disclosure of services provided by auditors or associates and related remuneration

(*1*) *The Secretary of State may make provision by regulations for securing the disclosure of—*

(*a*) *the nature of any services provided for a company by the company's auditors (whether in their capacity as such or otherwise) or by their associates;*

(*b*) *the amount of any remuneration received or receivable by a company's auditors, or their associates, in respect of any services within paragraph* (*a*).

(*2*) *The regulations may provide—*

(*a*) *for disclosure of the nature of any services provided to be made by reference to any class or description of services specified in the regulations (or any combination of services, however described);*

(*b*) *for the disclosure of amounts of remuneration received or receivable in respect of services of any class or description specified in the regulations (or any combination of services, however described);*

(*c*) *for the disclosure of separate amounts so received or receivable by the company's auditors or any of their associates, or of aggregate amounts so received or receivable by all or any of those persons.*

(*3*) *The regulations may—*

(*a*) *provide that "remuneration" includes sums paid in respect of expenses;*

(*b*) *apply to benefits in kind as well as to payments of money, and require the disclosure of the nature of any such benefits and their estimated money value;*

(*c*) *apply to services provided for associates of a company as well as to those provided for a company;*

(*d*) *define "associate" in relation to an auditor and a company respectively.*

(*4*) *The regulations may provide that any disclosure required by the regulations is to be made—*

(*a*) *in a note to the company's annual accounts (in the case of its individual accounts) or in such manner as is specified in the regulations (in the case of group accounts),*

(*b*) *in the directors' report required by section 234, or*

(*c*) *in the auditors' report under section 235.*

(*5*) *If the regulations provide that any such disclosure is to be made as mentioned in subsection* (4)(*a*) *or* (*b*), *the regulations may—*

(*a*) *require the auditors to supply the directors of the company with any information necessary to enable the disclosure to be made;*

(*b*) *provide for any provision within subsection* (6) *to apply in relation to a failure to make the disclosure as it applies in relation to a failure to comply with a requirement of this Act or (as the case may be) a provision of Part 7.*

(*6*) *The provisions are—*

(*a*) *sections 233(5) and 234(5); and*

(*b*) *any provision of sections 245 to 245C*

(*7*) *The regulations may make different provision for different cases.*

(*8*) *Nothing in subsections* (2) *to* (7) *affects the generality of subsection* (*1*).

(9) Regulations under this section shall be made by statutory instrument which shall be subject to annulment in pursuance of a resolution of either House of Parliament.]

[415]

NOTES

Inserted as noted to s 390A at **[414]**.

Substituted by the Companies (Audit, Investigations and Community Enterprise) Act 2004, s 7(1), as from 1 October 2005, except in relation to the accounts of a company for a financial year beginning before 1 October 2005 (see the Companies (Audit, Investigations and Community Enterprise) Act 2004 (Commencement) and Companies Act 1989 (Commencement No 18) Order 2004, SI 2004/3322, art 3 at **[7341]**).

Repealed by the Companies Act 2006, s 1295, Sch 16, as from a day to be appointed.

Application to limited liability partnerships: see the Limited Liability Partnerships Regulations 2001, SI 2001/1090, reg 4(1), Sch 2, Pt 1 at **[6985]**, **[6993]**.

Extension: the power of the Secretary of State to make regulations under this section is extended by the Open-Ended Investment Companies Regulations 2001, SI 2001/1228, reg 69, Sch 5, para 11.

Regulations: the Companies Act 1985 (Disclosure of Remuneration for Non-Audit Work) Regulations 1991, SI 1991/2128 at **[6722]** (which are disapplied in relation to the accounts of a company for any financial year beginning on or after 1 October 2005 by SI 2005/2417); the Companies (Disclosure of Auditor Remuneration) Regulations 2005, SI 2005/2417 at **[7444]**.

[Removal, resignation, &c of auditors

391 Removal of auditors

(1) A company may by ordinary resolution at any time remove an auditor from office, notwithstanding anything in any agreement between it and him.

(2) Where a resolution removing an auditor is passed at a general meeting of a company, the company shall within 14 days give notice of that fact in the prescribed form to the registrar.

If a company fails to give the notice required by this subsection, the company and every officer of it who is in default is guilty of an offence and liable to a fine and, for continued contravention, to a daily default fine.

(3) Nothing in this section shall be taken as depriving a person removed under it of compensation or damages payable to him in respect of the termination of his appointment as auditor or of any appointment terminating with that as auditor.

(4) An auditor of a company who has been removed has, notwithstanding his removal, the rights conferred by section 390 in relation to any general meeting of the company—

(a) at which his term of office would otherwise have expired, or

(b) at which it is proposed to fill the vacancy caused by his removal.

In such a case the references in that section to matters concerning the auditors as auditors shall be construed as references to matters concerning him as a former auditor.]

[416]

NOTES

Inserted, together with preceding heading and ss 391A, 392, 392A, 393, by CA 1989, ss 118, 122(1), as from 1 April 1990.

Repealed by the Companies Act 2006, s 1295, Sch 16, as from a day to be appointed.

Application to limited liability partnerships: see the Limited Liability Partnerships Regulations 2001, SI 2001/1090, reg 4(1), Sch 2, Pt 1 at **[6985]**, **[6993]**.

Prescribed form: see Appendix 4 (Forms table) at **[A4]**.

[391A Rights of auditors who are removed or not re-appointed

(1) Special notice is required for a resolution at a general meeting of a company—

(a) removing an auditor before the expiration of his term of office, or

(b) appointing as auditor a person other than a retiring auditor.

(2) On receipt of notice of such an intended resolution the company shall forthwith send a copy of it to the person proposed to be removed or, as the case may be, to the person proposed to be appointed and to the retiring auditor.

(3) The auditor proposed to be removed or (as the case may be) the retiring auditor may make with respect to the intended resolution representations in writing to the company (not exceeding a reasonable length) and request their notification to members of the company.

(4) The company shall (unless the representations are received by it too late for it to do so)—

(a) in any notice of the resolution given to members of the company, state the fact of the representations having been made, and

(b) send a copy of the representations to every member of the company to whom notice of the meeting is or has been sent.

(5) If a copy of any such representations is not sent out as required because received too late or because of the company's default, the auditor may (without prejudice to his right to be heard orally) require that the representations be read out at the meeting.

(6) Copies of the representations need not be sent out and the representations need not be read at the meeting if, on the application either of the company or of any other person claiming to be aggrieved, the court is satisfied that the rights conferred by this section are being abused to secure needless publicity for defamatory matter; and the court may order the company's costs on the application to be paid in whole or in part by the auditor, notwithstanding that he is not a party to the application.]

[417]

NOTES

Inserted as noted to s 391 at **[416]**.

Repealed by the Companies Act 2006, s 1295, Sch 16, as from a day to be appointed.

Application to limited liability partnerships: see the Limited Liability Partnerships Regulations 2001, SI 2001/1090, reg 4(1), Sch 2, Pt 1 at **[6985]**, **[6993]**.

[392 Resignation of auditors

(1) An auditor of a company may resign his office by depositing a notice in writing to that effect at the company's registered office.

The notice is not effective unless it is accompanied by the statement required by section 394.

(2) An effective notice of resignation operates to bring the auditor's term of office to an end as of the date on which the notice is deposited or on such later date as may be specified in it.

(3) The company shall within 14 days of the deposit of a notice of resignation send a copy of the notice to the registrar of companies.

If default is made in complying with this subsection, the company and every officer of it who is in default is guilty of an offence and liable to a fine and, for continued contravention, a daily default fine.]

[418]

NOTES

Inserted as noted to s 391 at **[416]**.

Repealed by the Companies Act 2006, s 1295, Sch 16, as from a day to be appointed.

Application to limited liability partnerships: see the Limited Liability Partnerships Regulations 2001, SI 2001/1090, reg 4(1), Sch 2, Pt 1 at **[6985]**, **[6993]**.

[392A Rights of resigning auditors

(1) This section applies where an auditor's notice of resignation is accompanied by a statement of circumstances which he considers should be brought to the attention of members or creditors of the company.

(2) He may deposit with the notice a signed requisition calling on the directors of the company forthwith duly to convene an extraordinary general meeting of the company for the purpose of receiving and considering such explanation of the circumstances connected with his resignation as he may wish to place before the meeting.

(3) He may request the company to circulate to its members—

(a) before the meeting convened on his requisition, or

(b) before any general meeting at which his term of office would otherwise have expired or at which it is proposed to fill the vacancy caused by his resignation,

a statement in writing (not exceeding a reasonable length) of the circumstances connected with his resignation.

(4) The company shall (unless the statement is received too late for it to comply)—

(a) in any notice of the meeting given to members of the company, state the fact of the statement having been made, and

(b) send a copy of the statement to every member of the company to whom notice of the meeting is or has been sent.

(5) If the directors do not within 21 days from the date of the deposit of a requisition under this section proceed duly to convene a meeting for a day not more than 28 days after the date on which the notice convening the meeting is given, every director who failed to take all reasonable steps to secure that a meeting was convened as mentioned above is guilty of an offence and liable to a fine.

(6) If a copy of the statement mentioned above is not sent out as required because received too late or because of the company's default, the auditor may (without prejudice to his right to be heard orally) require that the statement be read out at the meeting.

(7) Copies of a statement need not be sent out and the statement need not be read out at the meeting if, on the application either of the company or of any other person who claims to be aggrieved, the court is satisfied that the rights conferred by this section are being abused to secure needless publicity for defamatory matter; and the court may order the company's costs on such an application to be paid in whole or in part by the auditor, notwithstanding that he is not a party to the application.

(8) An auditor who has resigned has, notwithstanding his resignation, the rights conferred by section 390 in relation to any such general meeting of the company as is mentioned in subsection (3)(a) or (b).

In such a case the references in that section to matters concerning the auditors as auditors shall be construed as references to matters concerning him as a former auditor.]

[419]

NOTES

Inserted as noted to s 391 at **[416]**.

Repealed by the Companies Act 2006, s 1295, Sch 16, as from a day to be appointed.

Application to limited liability partnerships: see the Limited Liability Partnerships Regulations 2001, SI 2001/1090, reg 4(1), Sch 2, Pt 1 at **[6985]**, **[6993]**.

[393 Termination of appointment of auditors not appointed annually

(1) When an election is in force under section 386 (election by private company to dispense with annual appointment), any member of the company may deposit notice in writing at the company's registered office proposing that the appointment of the company's auditors be brought to an end.

No member may deposit more than one such notice in any financial year of the company.

(2) If such a notice is deposited it is the duty of the directors—

(a) to convene a general meeting of the company for a date not more than 28 days after the date on which the notice was given, and

(b) to propose at the meeting a resolution in a form enabling the company to decide whether the appointment of the company's auditors should be brought to an end.

(3) If the decision of the company at the meeting is that the appointment of the auditors should be brought to an end, the auditors shall not be deemed to be re appointed when next they would be and, if the notice was deposited within the period immediately following the distribution of accounts, any deemed re appointment for the financial year following that to which those accounts relate which has already occurred shall cease to have effect.

The period immediately following the distribution of accounts means the period beginning with the day on which copies of the company's annual accounts are sent to members of the company under section 238 and ending 14 days after that day.

(4) If the directors do not within 14 days from the date of the deposit of the notice proceed duly to convene a meeting, the member who deposited the notice (or, if there was more than one, any of them) may himself convene the meeting; but any meeting so convened shall not be held after the expiration of three months from that date.

(5) A meeting convened under this section by a member shall be convened in the same manner, as nearly as possible, as that in which meetings are to be convened by directors.

(6) Any reasonable expenses incurred by a member by reason of the failure of the directors duly to convene a meeting shall be made good to him by the company; and any such sums shall be recouped by the company from such of the directors as were in default out of any sums payable, or to become payable, by the company by way of fees or other remuneration in respect of their services.

(7) This section has effect notwithstanding anything in any agreement between the company and its auditors; and no compensation or damages shall be payable by reason of the auditors' appointment being terminated under this section.]

[420]

NOTES

Inserted as noted to s 391 at **[416]**.
Repealed by the Companies Act 2006, s 1295, Sch 16, as from 1 October 2007.

[394 Statement by person ceasing to hold office as auditor

(1) Where an auditor ceases for any reason to hold office, he shall deposit at the company's registered office a statement of any circumstances connected with his ceasing to hold office which he considers should be brought to the attention of the members or creditors of the company or, if he considers that there are no such circumstances, a statement that there are none.

(2) In the case of resignation, the statement shall be deposited along with the notice of resignation; in the case of failure to seek re-appointment, the statement shall be deposited not less than 14 days before the end of the time allowed for next appointing auditors; in any other case, the statement shall be deposited not later than the end of the period of 14 days beginning with the date on which he ceases to hold office.

(3) If the statement is of circumstances which the auditor considers should be brought to the attention of the members or creditors of the company, the company shall within 14 days of the deposit of the statement either—

- *(a) send a copy of it to every person who under section 238 is entitled to be sent copies of the accounts, or*
- *(b) apply to the court.*

(4) The company shall if it applies to the court notify the auditor of the application.

(5) Unless the auditor receives notice of such an application before the end of the period of 21 days beginning with the day on which he deposited the statement, he shall within a further seven days send a copy of the statement to the registrar.

(6) If the court is satisfied that the auditor is using the statement to secure needless publicity for defamatory matter—

- *(a) it shall direct that copies of the statement need not be sent out, and*
- *(b) it may further order the company's costs on the application to be paid in whole or in part by the auditor, notwithstanding that he is not a party to the application;*

and the company shall within 14 days of the court's decision send to the persons mentioned in subsection (3)(a) a statement setting out the effect of the order.

(7) If the court is not so satisfied, the company shall within 14 days of the court's decision—

- *(a) send copies of the statement to the persons mentioned in subsection (3)(a), and*
- *(b) notify the auditor of the court's decision;*

and the auditor shall within seven days of receiving such notice send a copy of the statement to the registrar.]

[421]

NOTES

Inserted, together with s 394A, by CA 1989, ss 118, 123(1), as from 1 April 1990.
Repealed by the Companies Act 2006, s 1295, Sch 16, as from a day to be appointed.
Application to limited liability partnerships: see the Limited Liability Partnerships Regulations 2001, SI 2001/1090, reg 4(1), Sch 2, Pt 1 at **[6985]**, **[6993]**.

[394A Offences of failing to comply with s 394

(1) If a person ceasing to hold office as auditor fails to comply with section 394 he is guilty of an offence and liable to a fine.

(2) In proceedings for an offence under subsection (1) it is a defence for the person charged to show that he took all reasonable steps and exercised all due diligence to avoid the commission of the offence.

(3) Sections 733 (liability of individuals for corporate default) and 734 (criminal proceedings against unincorporated bodies) apply to an offence under subsection (1).

(4) If a company makes default in complying with section 394, the company and every officer of it who is in default is guilty of an offence and liable to a fine and, for continued contravention, to a daily default fine.]

[422]

NOTES

Inserted as noted to s 394 at **[421]**.

Repealed by the Companies Act 2006, s 1295, Sch 16, as from a day to be appointed.

Application to limited liability partnerships: see the Limited Liability Partnerships Regulations 2001, SI 2001/1090, reg 4(1), Sch 2, Pt 1 at **[6985]**, **[6993]**.

PART XII
REGISTRATION OF CHARGES

NOTES

Prospective amendment.

(**a**) New ss 395–420 (provisions relating to the registration of charges with respect to companies registered in Great Britain) which apply throughout Great Britain are prospectively inserted into this Part by CA 1989, ss 92–104, in place of the current ss 395–408 (applying to England and Wales), and ss 410–423 (applying to Scotland), as from a day to be appointed. For some time it has been understood that these substitutions are unlikely to be brought into force in their present form. Note also that CA 1989, ss 92–104 are repealed by the Companies Act 2006, ss 1180, 1295, Sch 16, as from a day to be appointed. For reasons of space, and because the new provisions are unlikely to ever come into force, the new ss 395–420 have been omitted from this edition of the Company Law Handbook. The provisions were printed in the twentieth edition of this work and have not changed since 1 July 2006. The provisions are also reproduced in the CD version of this work (which may be ordered from the LexisNexis Butterworths Customer Services Department) and can be accessed online at www.lexisnexis.com/uk/legal.

(**b**) Ss 409, 424 (relating to registration of charges with respect to oversea companies) are prospectively replaced by the insertion of a new Chapter III of Part XXIII (ss 703A–703N) by CA 1989, ss 92(b), 105, Sch 15, as from a day to be appointed; see **[554]**–**[567]**. Note that those provisions of the 1989 Act are repealed by the Companies Act 2006, ss 1180, 1295, Sch 16, as from a day to be appointed.

CHAPTER I
REGISTRATION OF CHARGES (ENGLAND AND WALES)

395 Certain charges void if not registered

(1) Subject to the provisions of this Chapter, a charge created by a company registered in England and Wales and being a charge to which this section applies is, so far as any security on the company's property or undertaking is conferred by the charge, void against the liquidator [or administrator] and any creditor of the company, unless the prescribed particulars of the charge together with the instrument (if any) by which the charge is created or evidenced, are delivered to or received by the registrar of companies for registration in the manner required by this Chapter within 21 days after the date of the charge's creation.

(2) Subsection (1) is without prejudice to any contract or obligation for repayment of the money secured by the charge; and when a charge becomes void under this section, the money secured by it immediately becomes payable.

[423]

NOTES

Repealed by the Companies Act 2006, s 1295, Sch 16, as from a day to be appointed.

Prospective replacement: see note (a) preceding this section.

Sub-s (1): words in square brackets inserted by the Insolvency Act 1985, s 109(1), Sch 6, para 10.

Application to limited liability partnerships: see the Limited Liability Partnerships Regulations 2001, SI 2001/1090, reg 4(1), Sch 2, Pt 1 at **[6985]**, **[6993]**.

Prescribed particulars: see Appendix 4 (Forms table) at **[A4]**.

396 Charges which have to be registered

(1) Section 395 applies to the following charges—

(a) a charge for the purpose of securing any issue of debentures,

(b) a charge on uncalled share capital of the company,

(c) a charge created or evidenced by an instrument which, if executed by an individual, would require registration as a bill of sale,

(d) a charge on land (wherever situated) or any interest in it, but not including a charge for any rent or other periodical sum issuing out of the land,

(e) a charge on book debts of the company,

(f) a floating charge on the company's undertaking or property,

(g) a charge on calls made but not paid,

(h) a charge on a ship or aircraft, or any share in a ship,

(j) a charge on goodwill, [or on any intellectual property].

(2) Where a negotiable instrument has been given to secure the payment of any book debts of a company, the deposit of the instrument for the purpose of securing an advance to the company is not, for purposes of section 395, to be treated as a charge on those book debts.

(3) The holding of debentures entitling the holder to a charge on land is not for purposes of this section deemed to be an interest in land.

[(3A) The following are "intellectual property" for the purposes of this section—

(a) any patent, trade mark, ... registered design, copyright or design right;

(b) any licence under or in respect of any such right.]

(4) In this Chapter, "charge" includes mortgage.

[424]

NOTES

Repealed by the Companies Act 2006, s 1295, Sch 16, as from a day to be appointed.

Prospective replacement: see note (a) preceding s 395.

Sub-s (1): words in square brackets substituted by the Copyright, Designs and Patents Act 1988, s 303(1), Sch 7, para 31(1), (2), as from 1 August 1989.

Sub-s (3A): inserted by the Copyright, Designs and Patents Act 1988, s 303(1), Sch 7, para 31(1), (2), as from 1 August 1989; words omitted repealed by the Trade Marks Act 1994, s 106(2), Sch 5, as from 31 October 1994.

Application to limited liability partnerships: see the Limited Liability Partnerships Regulations 2001, SI 2001/1090, reg 4(1), Sch 2, Pt 1 at **[6985]**, **[6993]**.

Trade mark: by the Trade Marks Act 1994, s 106(1), Sch 4, para 1, the reference in sub-s (3A)(a) above to a trade mark is to be construed as a reference to a trade mark within the meaning of the 1994 Act.

397 Formalities of registration (debentures)

(1) Where a series of debentures containing, or giving by reference to another instrument, any charge to the benefit of which the debenture holders of that series are entitled pari passu is created by a company, it is for purposes of section 395 sufficient if there are delivered to or received by the registrar, within 21 days after the execution of the deed containing the charge (or, if there is no such deed, after the execution of any debentures of the series), the following particulars in the prescribed form—

(a) the total amount secured by the whole series, and

(b) the dates of the resolutions authorising the issue of the series and the date of the covering deed (if any) by which the security is created or defined, and

(c) a general description of the property charged, and

(d) the names of the trustees (if any) for the debenture holders,

together with the deed containing the charge or, if there is no such deed, one of the debentures of the series:

Provided that there shall be sent to the registrar of companies, for entry in the register, particulars in the prescribed form of the date and amount of each issue of debentures of the series, but any omission to do this does not affect the validity of any of those debentures.

(2) Where any commission, allowance or discount has been paid or made either directly or indirectly by a company to a person in consideration of his—

(a) subscribing or agreeing to subscribe, whether absolutely or conditionally, for debentures of the company, or

(b) procuring or agreeing to procure subscriptions, whether absolute or conditional, for such debentures,

the particulars required to be sent for registration under section 395 shall include particulars as to the amount or rate per cent of the commission, discount or allowance so paid or made, but omission to do this does not affect the validity of the debentures issued.

(3) The deposit of debentures as security for a debt of the company is not, for the purposes of subsection (2), treated as the issue of the debentures at a discount.

[425]

NOTES

Repealed by the Companies Act 2006, s 1295, Sch 16, as from a day to be appointed.

Prospective replacement: see note (a) preceding s 395.

Application to limited liability partnerships: see the Limited Liability Partnerships Regulations 2001, SI 2001/1090, reg 4(1), Sch 2, Pt 1 at **[6985]**, **[6993]**.

Particulars in the prescribed form: see Appendix 4 (Forms table) at **[A4]**.

398 Verification of charge on property outside United Kingdom

(1) In the case of a charge created out of the United Kingdom comprising property situated outside the United Kingdom, the delivery to and the receipt by the registrar of companies of a copy (verified in the prescribed manner) of the instrument by which the charge is created or evidenced has the same effect for purposes of sections 395 to 398 as the delivery and receipt of the instrument itself.

(2) In that case, 21 days after the date on which the instrument or copy could, in due course of post (and if despatched with due diligence), have been received in the United Kingdom are substituted for the 21 days mentioned in section 395(1) (or as the case may be, section 397(1)) as the time within which the particulars and instrument or copy are to be delivered to the registrar.

(3) Where a charge is created in the United Kingdom but comprises property outside the United Kingdom, the instrument creating or purporting to create the charge may be sent for registration under section 395 notwithstanding that further proceedings may be necessary to make the charge valid or effectual according to the law of the country in which the property is situated.

(4) Where a charge comprises property situated in Scotland or Northern Ireland and registration in the country where the property is situated is necessary to make the charge valid or effectual according to the law of that country, the delivery to and receipt by the registrar of a copy (verified in the prescribed manner) of the instrument by which the charge is created or evidenced, together with a certificate in the prescribed form stating that the charge was presented for registration in Scotland or Northern Ireland (as the case may be) on the date on which it was so presented has, for purposes of sections 395 to 398, the same effect as the delivery and receipt of the instrument itself.

[426]

NOTES

Repealed by the Companies Act 2006, s 1295, Sch 16, as from a day to be appointed.

Prospective replacement: see note (a) preceding s 395.

Application to limited liability partnerships: see the Limited Liability Partnerships Regulations 2001, SI 2001/1090, reg 4(1), Sch 2, Pt 1 at **[6985]**, **[6993]**.

Copy (verified in the prescribed manner); certificate in the prescribed form: see Appendix 4 (Forms table) at **[A4]**.

399 Company's duty to register charges it creates

(1) It is a company's duty to send to the registrar of companies for registration the particulars of every charge created by the company and of the issues of debentures of a series requiring registration under sections 395 to 398; but registration of any such charge may be effected on the application of any person interested in it.

(2) Where registration is effected on the application of some person other than the company, that person is entitled to recover from the company the amount of any fees properly paid by him to the registrar on the registration.

(3) If a company fails to comply with subsection (1), then, unless the registration has been effected on the application of some other person, the company and every officer of it who is in default is liable to a fine and, for continued contravention, to a daily default fine.

[427]

NOTES

Repealed by the Companies Act 2006, s 1295, Sch 16, as from a day to be appointed.
Prospective replacement: see note (a) preceding s 395.
Application to limited liability partnerships: see the Limited Liability Partnerships Regulations 2001, SI 2001/1090, reg 4(1), Sch 2, Pt 1 at **[6985]**, **[6993]**.

400 Charges existing on property acquired

(1) This section applies where a company registered in England and Wales acquires property which is subject to a charge of any such kind as would, if it had been created by the company after the acquisition of the property, have been required to be registered under this Chapter.

(2) The company shall cause the prescribed particulars of the charge, together with a copy (certified in the prescribed manner to be a correct copy) of the instrument (if any) by which the charge was created or is evidenced, to be delivered to the registrar of companies for registration in manner required by this Chapter within 21 days after the date on which the acquisition is completed.

(3) However, if the property is situated and the charge was created outside Great Britain, 21 days after the date on which the copy of the instrument could in due course of post, and if despatched with due diligence, have been received in the United Kingdom is substituted for the 21 days above-mentioned as the time within which the particulars and copy of the instrument are to be delivered to the registrar.

(4) If default is made in complying with this section, the company and every officer of it who is in default is liable to a fine and, for continued contravention, to a daily default fine.

[428]

NOTES

Repealed by the Companies Act 2006, s 1295, Sch 16, as from a day to be appointed.
Prospective replacement: see note (a) preceding s 395.
Application to limited liability partnerships: see the Limited Liability Partnerships Regulations 2001, SI 2001/1090, reg 4(1), Sch 2, Pt 1 at **[6985]**, **[6993]**.
Prescribed particulars; copy (certified in the prescribed manner): see Appendix 4 (Forms table) at **[A4]**.

401 Register of charges to be kept by registrar of companies

(1) The registrar of companies shall keep, with respect to each company, a register in the prescribed form of all the charges requiring registration under this Chapter; and he shall enter in the register with respect to such charges the following particulars—

- *(a) in the case of a charge to the benefit of which the holders of a series of debentures are entitled, the particulars specified in section 397(1),*
- *(b) in the case of any other charge—*
  - *(i) if it is a charge created by the company, the date of its creation, and if it is a charge which was existing on property acquired by the company, the date of the acquisition of the property, and*
  - *(ii) the amount secured by the charge, and*
  - *(iii) short particulars of the property charged, and*
  - *(iv) the persons entitled to the charge.*

(2) The registrar shall give a certificate of the registration of any charge registered in pursuance of this Chapter, stating the amount secured by the charge.

The certificate—

- *(a) shall be either signed by the registrar, or authenticated by his official seal, and*
- *(b) is conclusive evidence that the requirements of this Chapter as to registration have been satisfied.*

(3) The register kept in pursuance of this section shall be open to inspection by any person.

[429]

NOTES

Repealed by the Companies Act 2006, s 1295, Sch 16, as from a day to be appointed.
Prospective replacement: see note (a) preceding s 395.

Application to limited liability partnerships: see the Limited Liability Partnerships Regulations 2001, SI 2001/1090, reg 4(1), Sch 2, Pt 1 at **[6985]**, **[6993]**.

Register: the Companies Act 1948, s 459(12), saved any register kept under former enactments relating to companies and deemed them part of the register to be kept under the corresponding provisions of the 1948 Act. The saving made by that section remains in force notwithstanding the repeal of the whole of the 1948 Act; see the Companies Consolidation (Consequential Provisions) Act 1985, s 31(9) at **[728]**.

Prescribed form: see Appendix 4 (Forms table) at **[A4]**.

402 Endorsement of certificate on debentures

(1) The company shall cause a copy of every certificate of registration given under section 401 to be endorsed on every debenture or certificate of debenture stock which is issued by the company, and the payment of which is secured by the charge so registered.

(2) But this does not require a company to cause a certificate of registration of any charge so given to be endorsed on any debenture or certificate of debenture stock issued by the company before the charge was created.

(3) If a person knowingly and wilfully authorises or permits the delivery of a debenture or certificate of debenture stock which under this section is required to have endorsed on it a copy of a certificate of registration, without the copy being so endorsed upon it, he is liable (without prejudice to any other liability) to a fine.

[430]

NOTES

Repealed by the Companies Act 2006, s 1295, Sch 16, as from a day to be appointed.

Prospective replacement: see note (a) preceding s 395.

Application to limited liability partnerships: see the Limited Liability Partnerships Regulations 2001, SI 2001/1090, reg 4(1), Sch 2, Pt 1 at **[6985]**, **[6993]**.

403 Entries of satisfaction and release

(1) [Subject to subsection (1A), the registrar] of companies, on receipt of a statutory declaration in the prescribed form verifying, with respect to a registered charge,—

(a) that the debt for which the charge was given has been paid or satisfied in whole or in part, or

(b) that part of the property or undertaking charged has been released from the charge or has ceased to form part of the company's property or undertaking,

may enter on the register a memorandum of satisfaction in whole or in part, or of the fact that part of the property or undertaking has been released from the charge or has ceased to form part of the company's property or undertaking (as the case may be).

[(1A) The registrar of companies may make any such entry as is mentioned in subsection (1) where, instead of receiving such a statutory declaration as is mentioned in that subsection, he receives a statement by a director, secretary, administrator or administrative receiver of the company which is contained in an electronic communication and that statement—

(a) verifies the matters set out in paragraph (a) or (b) of that subsection,

(b) contains a description of the charge,

(c) states the date of creation of the charge and the date of its registration under this Chapter,

(d) states the name and address of the chargee or, in the case of a debenture, trustee, and

(e) where paragraph (b) of subsection (1) applies, contains short particulars of the property or undertaking which has been released from the charge, or which has ceased to form part of the company's property or undertaking (as the case may be).]

(2) Where the registrar enters a memorandum of satisfaction in whole, he shall if required furnish the company with a copy of it.

[(2A) Any person who makes a false statement under subsection (1A) which he knows to be false or does not believe to be true is liable to imprisonment or a fine, or both.]

[431]

NOTES

Repealed by the Companies Act 2006, s 1295, Sch 16, as from a day to be appointed.

Prospective replacement: see note (a) preceding s 395.

Sub-s (1): words in square brackets substituted by the Companies Act 1985 (Electronic Communications) Order 2000, SI 2000/3373, art 22(1), (2), as from 22 December 2000.
Sub-ss (1A), (2A): inserted by SI 2000/3373, art 22(1), (3), (4), as from 22 December 2000.
Application to limited liability partnerships: see the Limited Liability Partnerships Regulations 2001, SI 2001/1090, reg 4(1), Sch 2, Pt 1 at **[6985]**, **[6993]**.
Prescribed form: see Appendix 4 (Forms table) at **[A4]**.

404 Rectification of register of charges

(*1*) *The following applies if the court is satisfied that the omission to register a charge within the time required by this Chapter or that the omission or mis-statement of any particular with respect to any such charge or in a memorandum of satisfaction was accidental, or due to inadvertence or to some other sufficient cause, or is not of a nature to prejudice the position of creditors or shareholders of the company, or that on other grounds it is just and equitable to grant relief.*

(2) *The court may, on the application of the company or a person interested, and on such terms and conditions as seem to the court just and expedient, order that the time for registration shall be extended or, as the case may be, that the omission or mis-statement shall be rectified.*

[432]

NOTES

Repealed by the Companies Act 2006, s 1295, Sch 16, as from a day to be appointed.
Prospective replacement: see note (a) preceding s 395.
Application to limited liability partnerships: see the Limited Liability Partnerships Regulations 2001, SI 2001/1090, reg 4(1), Sch 2, Pt 1 at **[6985]**, **[6993]**.

405 Registration of enforcement of security

(*1*) *If a person obtains an order for the appointment of a receiver or manager of a company's property, or appoints such a receiver or manager under powers contained in an instrument, he shall within 7 days of the order or of the appointment under those powers, give notice of the fact to the registrar of companies; and the registrar shall enter the fact in the register of charges.*

(2) *Where a person appointed receiver or manager of a company's property under powers contained in an instrument ceases to act as such receiver or manager, he shall, on so ceasing, give the registrar notice to that effect, and the registrar shall enter the fact in the register of charges.*

(3) *A notice under this section shall be in the prescribed form.*

(4) *If a person makes default in complying with the requirements of this section, he is liable to a fine and, for continued contravention, to a daily default fine.*

[433]

NOTES

Repealed by the Companies Act 2006, s 1295, Sch 16, as from a day to be appointed.
Prospective replacement: see note (a) preceding s 395.
Application to limited liability partnerships: see the Limited Liability Partnerships Regulations 2001, SI 2001/1090, reg 4(1), Sch 2, Pt 1 at **[6985]**, **[6993]**.
Notice … in the prescribed form: see Appendix 4 (Forms table) at **[A4]**.

406 Companies to keep copies of instruments creating charges

(*1*) *Every company shall cause a copy of every instrument creating a charge requiring registration under this Chapter to be kept at its registered office.*

(2) *In the case of a series of uniform debentures, a copy of one debenture of the series is sufficient.*

[434]

NOTES

Repealed by the Companies Act 2006, s 1295, Sch 16, as from a day to be appointed.
Prospective replacement: see note (a) preceding s 395.
Application to limited liability partnerships: see the Limited Liability Partnerships Regulations 2001, SI 2001/1090, reg 4(1), Sch 2, Pt 1 at **[6985]**, **[6993]**.

407 Company's register of charges

(1) Every limited company shall keep at its registered office a register of charges and enter in it all charges specifically affecting property of the company and all floating charges on the company's undertaking or any of its property.

(2) The entry shall in each case give a short description of the property charged, the amount of the charge and, except in the case of securities to bearer, the names of the persons entitled to it.

(3) If an officer of the company knowingly and wilfully authorises or permits the omission of an entry required to be made in pursuance of this section, he is liable to a fine.

[435]

NOTES

Repealed by the Companies Act 2006, s 1295, Sch 16, as from a day to be appointed.

Prospective replacement: see note (a) preceding s 395.

Application to limited liability partnerships: see the Limited Liability Partnerships Regulations 2001, SI 2001/1090, reg 4(1), Sch 2, Pt 1 at **[6985]**, **[6993]**.

408 Right to inspect instruments which create charges, etc

(1) The copies of instruments creating any charge requiring registration under this Chapter with the registrar of companies, and the register of charges kept in pursuance of section 407, shall be open during business hours (but subject to such reasonable restrictions as the company in general meeting may impose, so that not less than 2 hours in each day be allowed for inspection) to the inspection of any creditor or member of the company without fee.

(2) The register of charges shall also be open to the inspection of any other person on payment of such fee, not exceeding 5 pence, for each inspection, as the company may prescribe.

(3) If inspection of the copies referred to, or of the register, is refused, every officer of the company who is in default is liable to a fine and, for continued contravention, to a daily default fine.

(4) If such a refusal occurs in relation to a company registered in England and Wales, the court may by order compel an immediate inspection of the copies or register.

[436]

NOTES

Repealed by the Companies Act 2006, s 1295, Sch 16, as from a day to be appointed.

Prospective replacement: see note (a) preceding s 395.

Application to limited liability partnerships: see the Limited Liability Partnerships Regulations 2001, SI 2001/1090, reg 4(1), Sch 2, Pt 1 at **[6985]**, **[6993]**.

409 Charges on property in England and Wales created by overseas company

(1) This Chapter extends to charges on property in England and Wales which are created, and to charges on property in England and Wales which is acquired, by a company (whether a company within the meaning of this Act or not) incorporated outside Great Britain which has an established place of business in England and Wales.

(2) In relation to such a company, sections 406 and 407 apply with the substitution, for the reference to the company's registered office, of a reference to its principal place of business in England and Wales.

[437]

NOTES

Repealed by the Companies Act 2006, s 1295, Sch 16, as from a day to be appointed.

Prospective replacement: see note (b) preceding s 395.

CHAPTER II
REGISTRATION OF CHARGES (SCOTLAND)

410 Charges void unless registered

(1) The following provisions of this Chapter have effect for the purpose of securing the registration in Scotland of charges created by companies.

(2) Every charge created by a company, being a charge to which this section applies, is, so far as any security on the company's property or any part of it is conferred by the charge, void against the liquidator [or administrator] and any creditor of the company unless the prescribed particulars of the charge, together with a copy (certified in the prescribed manner to be a correct copy) of the instrument (if any) by which the charge is created or evidenced, are delivered to or received by the registrar of companies for registration in the manner required by this Chapter within 21 days after the date of the creation of the charge.

(3) Subsection (2) is without prejudice to any contract or obligation for repayment of the money secured by the charge; and when a charge becomes void under this section the money secured by it immediately becomes payable.

(4) This section applies to the following charges—
- *(a) a charge on land wherever situated, or any interest in such land (not including a charge for any rent … or other periodical sum payable in respect of the land, but including a charge created by a heritable security within the meaning of section 9(8) of the Conveyancing and Feudal Reform (Scotland) Act 1970),*
- *(b) a security over the uncalled share capital of the company,*
- *(c) a security over incorporeal moveable property of any of the following categories—*
  - *(i) the book debts of the company,*
  - *(ii) calls made but not paid,*
  - *(iii) goodwill,*
  - *(iv) a patent or a licence under a patent,*
  - *(v) a trademark,*
  - *(vi) a copyright or a licence under a copyright,*
  - *[(vii) a registered design or a licence in respect of such a design,*
  - *(viii) a design right or a licence under a design right,]*
- *(d) a security over a ship or aircraft or any share in a ship, and*
- *(e) a floating charge.*

(5) In this Chapter "company" (except in section 424) means an incorporated company registered in Scotland; "registrar of companies" means the registrar or other officer performing under this Act the duty of registration of companies in Scotland; and references to the date of creation of a charge are—
- *(a) in the case of a floating charge, the date on which the instrument creating the floating charge was executed by the company creating the charge, and*
- *(b) in any other case, the date on which the right of the person entitled to the benefit of the charge was constituted as a real right.*

[438]

NOTES

Repealed by the Companies Act 2006, s 1295, Sch 16, as from a day to be appointed.

Prospective replacement: see note (a) preceding s 395.

Sub-s (2): words in square brackets inserted by the Insolvency Act 1985, s 109(1), Sch 6, para 10, as from 29 December 1986.

Sub-s (4): words omitted from para (a) repealed by the Abolition of Feudal Tenure etc (Scotland) Act 2000, s 76(1), (2), Sch 12, Pt I, para 46(1)–(4), Sch 13, Pt I, as from 28 November 2004; paras (c)(vii), (viii) added by the Copyright, Designs and Patents Act 1988, s 303(1), Sch 7, para 31(3), as from 1 August 1989.

Application to limited liability partnerships: see the Limited Liability Partnerships Regulations 2001, SI 2001/1090, reg 4(1), Sch 2, Pt 1 at **[6985]**, **[6993]**.

Trade mark: by the Trade Marks Act 1994, s 106(1), Sch 4, para 1, the reference to a trade mark in sub-s (4)(c)(v) above is to be construed as a reference to a trade mark within the meaning of the 1994 Act.

Prescribed particulars of the charge; copy (certified in the prescribed manner …): see Appendix 4 (Forms table) at **[A4]**.

411 Charges on property outside United Kingdom

(1) In the case of a charge created out of the United Kingdom comprising property situated outside the United Kingdom, the period of 21 days after the date on which the copy of

the instrument creating it could (in due course of post, and if despatched with due diligence) have been received in the United Kingdom is substituted for the period of 21 days after the date of the creation of the charge as the time within which, under section 410(2), the particulars and copy are to be delivered to the registrar.

(2) *Where a charge is created in the United Kingdom but comprises property outside the United Kingdom, the copy of the instrument creating or purporting to create the charge may be sent for registration under section 410 notwithstanding that further proceedings may be necessary to make the charge valid or effectual according to the law of the country in which the property is situated.*

[439]

NOTES

Repealed by the Companies Act 2006, s 1295, Sch 16, as from a day to be appointed.

Prospective replacement: see note (a) preceding s 395.

Application to limited liability partnerships: see the Limited Liability Partnerships Regulations 2001, SI 2001/1090, reg 4(1), Sch 2, Pt 1 at **[6985]**, **[6993]**.

412 Negotiable instrument to secure book debts

Where a negotiable instrument has been given to secure the payment of any book debts of a company, the deposit of the instrument for the purpose of securing an advance to the company is not, for purposes of section 410, to be treated as a charge on those book debts.

[440]

NOTES

Repealed by the Companies Act 2006, s 1295, Sch 16, as from a day to be appointed.

Prospective replacement: see note (a) preceding s 395.

Application to limited liability partnerships: see the Limited Liability Partnerships Regulations 2001, SI 2001/1090, reg 4(1), Sch 2, Pt 1 at **[6985]**, **[6993]**.

413 Charges associated with debentures

(*1*) *The holding of debentures entitling the holder to a charge on land is not, for the purposes of section 410, deemed to be an interest in land.*

(2) *Where a series of debentures containing, or giving by reference to any other instrument, any charge to the benefit of which the debenture-holders of that series are entitled pari passu, is created by a company, it is sufficient for purposes of section 410 if there are delivered to or received by the registrar of companies within 21 days after the execution of the deed containing the charge or if there is no such deed, after the execution of any debentures of the series, the following particulars in the prescribed form—*

(*a*) *the total amount secured by the whole series,*

(*b*) *the dates of the resolutions authorising the issue of the series and the date of the covering deed (if any) by which the security is created or defined,*

(*c*) *a general description of the property charged,*

(*d*) *the names of the trustees (if any) for the debenture holders, and*

(*e*) *in the case of a floating charge, a statement of any provisions of the charge and of any instrument relating to it which prohibit or restrict or regulate the power of the company to grant further securities ranking in priority to, or pari passu with, the floating charge, or which vary or otherwise regulate the order of ranking of the floating charge in relation to subsisting securities,*

together with a copy of the deed containing the charge or, if there is no such deed, of one of the debentures of the series:

Provided that where more than one issue is made of debentures in the series, there shall be sent to the registrar of companies for entry in the register particulars (in the prescribed form) of the date and amount of each issue of debentures of the series, but any omission to do this does not affect the validity of any of those debentures.

(*3*) *Where any commission, allowance or discount has been paid or made, either directly or indirectly, by a company to any person in consideration of his subscribing or agreeing to subscribe, whether absolutely or conditionally, for any debentures of the company, or procuring or agreeing to procure subscriptions (whether absolute or conditional) for any such debentures, the particulars required to be sent for registration under section 410 include particulars as to the amount or rate per cent of the commission, discount or allowance so paid or made; but any omission to do this does not affect the validity of the debentures issued.*

The deposit of any debentures as security for any debt of the company is not, for purposes of this subsection, treated as the issue of the debentures at a discount.

[441]

NOTES

Repealed by the Companies Act 2006, s 1295, Sch 16, as from a day to be appointed.

Prospective replacement: see note (a) preceding s 395.

Application to limited liability partnerships: see the Limited Liability Partnerships Regulations 2001, SI 2001/1090, reg 4(1), Sch 2, Pt 1 at **[6985]**, **[6993]**.

Particulars in the prescribed form: see Appendix 4 (Forms table) at **[A4]**.

414 Charge by way of ex facie absolute disposition, etc

(*1*) *For the avoidance of doubt, it is hereby declared that, in the case of a charge created by way of an ex facie absolute disposition or assignation qualified by a back letter or other agreement, or by a standard security qualified by an agreement, compliance with section 410(2) does not of itself render the charge unavailable as security for indebtedness incurred after the date of compliance.*

(*2*) *Where the amount secured by a charge so created is purported to be increased by a further back letter or agreement, a further charge is held to have been created by the ex facie absolute disposition or assignation or (as the case may be) by the standard security, as qualified by the further back letter or agreement; and the provisions of this Chapter apply to the further charge as if—*

(*a*) *references in this Chapter (other than in this section) to the charge were references to the further charge, and*

(*b*) *references to the date of the creation of the charge were references to the date on which the further back letter or agreement was executed.*

[442]

NOTES

Repealed by the Companies Act 2006, s 1295, Sch 16, as from a day to be appointed.

Prospective replacement: see note (a) preceding s 395.

Application to limited liability partnerships: see the Limited Liability Partnerships Regulations 2001, SI 2001/1090, reg 4(1), Sch 2, Pt 1 at **[6985]**, **[6993]**.

415 Company's duty to register charges created by it

(*1*) *It is a company's duty to send to the registrar of companies for registration the particulars of every charge created by the company and of the issues of debentures of a series requiring registration under sections 410 to 414; but registration of any such charge may be effected on the application of any person interested in it.*

(*2*) *Where registration is effected on the application of some person other than the company, that person is entitled to recover from the company the amount of any fees properly paid by him to the registrar on the registration.*

(*3*) *If a company makes default in sending to the registrar for registration the particulars of any charge created by the company or of the issues of debentures of a series requiring registration as above mentioned, then, unless the registration has been effected on the application of some other person, the company and every officer of it who is in default is liable to a fine and, for continued contravention, to a daily default fine.*

[443]

NOTES

Repealed by the Companies Act 2006, s 1295, Sch 16, as from a day to be appointed.

Prospective replacement: see note (a) preceding s 395.

Application to limited liability partnerships: see the Limited Liability Partnerships Regulations 2001, SI 2001/1090, reg 4(1), Sch 2, Pt 1 at **[6985]**, **[6993]**.

416 Duty to register charges existing on property acquired

(*1*) *Where a company acquires any property which is subject to a charge of any kind as would, if it had been created by the company after the acquisition of the property, have been required to be registered under this Chapter, the company shall cause the prescribed particulars of the charge, together with a copy (certified in the prescribed manner to be a correct copy) of the instrument (if any) by which the charge was created or is evidenced, to be delivered to the registrar of companies for registration in the manner required by this Chapter within 21 days after the date on which the transaction was settled.*

(2) If, however, the property is situated and the charge was created outside Great Britain, 21 days after the date on which the copy of the instrument could (in due course of post, and if despatched with due diligence) have been received in the United Kingdom are substituted for 21 days after the settlement of the transaction as the time within which the particulars and the copy of the instrument are to be delivered to the registrar.

(3) If default is made in complying with this section, the company and every officer of it who is in default is liable to a fine and, for continued contravention, to a daily default fine.

[444]

NOTES

Repealed by the Companies Act 2006, s 1295, Sch 16, as from a day to be appointed.

Prospective replacement: see note (a) preceding s 395.

Application to limited liability partnerships: see the Limited Liability Partnerships Regulations 2001, SI 2001/1090, reg 4(1), Sch 2, Pt 1 at **[6985]**, **[6993]**.

Prescribed particulars; prescribed manner: see Appendix 4 (Forms table) at **[A4]**.

417 Register of charges to be kept by registrar of companies

(1) The registrar of companies shall keep, with respect to each company, a register in the prescribed form of all the charges requiring registration under this Chapter, and shall enter in the register with respect to such charges the particulars specified below.

(2) In the case of a charge to the benefit of which the holders of a series of debentures are entitled, there shall be entered in the register the particulars specified in section 413(2).

(3) In the case of any other charge there shall be entered—

- *(a) if it is a charge created by the company, the date of its creation, and if it was a charge existing on property acquired by the company, the date of the acquisition of the property,*
- *(b) the amount secured by the charge,*
- *(c) short particulars of the property charged,*
- *(d) the persons entitled to the charge, and*
- *(e) in the case of a floating charge, a statement of any of the provisions of the charge and of any instrument relating to it which prohibit or restrict or regulate the company's power to grant further securities ranking in priority to, or pari passu with, the floating charge, or which vary or otherwise regulate the order of ranking of the floating charge in relation to subsisting securities.*

(4) The register kept in pursuance of this section shall be open to inspection by any person.

[445]

NOTES

Repealed by the Companies Act 2006, s 1295, Sch 16, as from a day to be appointed.

Prospective replacement: see note (a) preceding s 395.

Application to limited liability partnerships: see the Limited Liability Partnerships Regulations 2001, SI 2001/1090, reg 4(1), Sch 2, Pt 1 at **[6985]**, **[6993]**.

Register: see the note to s 401 at **[429]**.

Prescribed form: see Appendix 4 (Forms table) at **[A4]**.

418 Certificate of registration to be issued

(1) The registrar of companies shall give a certificate of the registration of any charge registered in pursuance of this Chapter.

(2) The certificate—

- *(a) shall be either signed by the registrar, or authenticated by his official seal,*
- *(b) shall state the name of the company and the person first-named in the charge among those entitled to the benefit of the charge (or, in the case of a series of debentures, the name of the holder of the first such debenture to be issued) and the amount secured by the charge, and*

(*c*) *is conclusive evidence that the requirements of this Chapter as to registration have been complied with.*

[446]

NOTES

Repealed by the Companies Act 2006, s 1295, Sch 16, as from a day to be appointed.
Prospective replacement: see note (a) preceding s 395.
Application to limited liability partnerships: see the Limited Liability Partnerships Regulations 2001, SI 2001/1090, reg 4(1), Sch 2, Pt 1 at **[6985]**, **[6993]**.

419 Entries of satisfaction and relief

(1) [Subject to subsections (1A) and (1B), the registrar] of companies, on application being made to him in the prescribed form, and on receipt of a statutory declaration in the prescribed form verifying, with respect to any registered charge,—

(*a*) *that the debt for which the charge was given has been paid or satisfied in whole or in part, or*

(*b*) *that part of the property charged has been released from the charge or has ceased to form part of the company's property,*

may enter on the register a memorandum of satisfaction (in whole or in part) regarding that fact.

[(1A) On an application being made to him in the prescribed form, the registrar of companies may make any such entry as is mentioned in subsection (1) where, instead of receiving such a statutory declaration as is mentioned in that subsection, he receives a statement by a director, secretary, liquidator, receiver or administrator of the company which is contained in an electronic communication and that statement—

(*a*) *verifies the matters set out in paragraph (a) or (b) of that subsection,*

(*b*) *contains a description of the charge,*

(*c*) *states the date of creation of the charge and the date of its registration under this Chapter,*

(*d*) *states the name and address of the chargee or, in the case of a debenture, trustee, and*

(*e*) *where paragraph (b) of subsection (1) applies, contains short particulars of the property which has been released from the charge, or which has ceased to form part of the company's property (as the case may be).*

(1B) Where the statement under subsection (1A) concerns the satisfaction of a floating charge, then there shall be delivered to the registrar a further statement which—

(*a*) *is made by the creditor entitled to the benefit of the floating charge or a person authorised to act on his behalf;*

(*b*) *is incorporated into, or logically associated with, the electronic communication containing the statement; and*

(*c*) *certifies that the particulars contained in the statement are correct.]*

(2) Where the registrar enters a memorandum of satisfaction in whole, he shall, if required, furnish the company with a copy of the memorandum.

(3) Without prejudice to the registrar's duty under this section to require to be satisfied as above mentioned, he shall not be so satisfied unless—

(*a*) *the creditor entitled to the benefit of the floating charge, or a person authorised to do so on his behalf, certifies as correct the particulars submitted to the registrar with respect to the entry on the register of a memorandum under this section, or*

(*b*) *the court, on being satisfied that such certification cannot readily be obtained, directs him accordingly.*

(4) Nothing in this section requires the company to submit particulars with respect to the entry in the register of a memorandum of satisfaction where the company, having created a floating charge over all or any part of its property, disposes of part of the property subject to the floating charge.

(5) A memorandum or certification required for the purposes of this section shall be in such form as may be prescribed.

[(5A) Any person who makes a false statement under subsection (1A) or (1B) which he knows to be false or does not believe to be true is liable to imprisonment or a fine, or both.]

[447]

NOTES

Repealed by the Companies Act 2006, s 1295, Sch 16, as from a day to be appointed.

Prospective replacement: see note (a) preceding s 395.

Sub-s (1): words in square brackets substituted by the Companies Act 1985 (Electronic Communications) Order 2000, SI 2000/3373, art 23(1), (2), as from 22 December 2000.

Sub-ss (1A), (1B), (5A): inserted and added respectively by SI 2000/3373, art 23(1), (3), (4), as from 22 December 2000.

Application to limited liability partnerships: see the Limited Liability Partnerships Regulations 2001, SI 2001/1090, reg 4(1), Sch 2, Pt 1 at **[6985]**, **[6993]**.

Application … in the prescribed form; statutory declaration in the prescribed form; such form as may be prescribed: see Appendix 4 (Forms table) at **[A4]**.

420 Rectification of register

The court, on being satisfied that the omission to register a charge within the time required by this Act or that the omission or mis-statement of any particular with respect to any such charge or in a memorandum of satisfaction was accidental, or due to inadvertence or to some other sufficient cause, or is not of a nature to prejudice the position of creditors or shareholders of the company, or that it is on other grounds just and equitable to grant relief, may, on the application of the company or any person interested, and on such terms and conditions as seem to the court just and expedient, order that the time for registration shall be extended or (as the case may be) that the omission or mis-statement shall be rectified.

[448]

NOTES

Repealed by the Companies Act 2006, s 1295, Sch 16, as from a day to be appointed.

Prospective replacement: see note (a) preceding s 395.

Application to limited liability partnerships: see the Limited Liability Partnerships Regulations 2001, SI 2001/1090, reg 4(1), Sch 2, Pt 1 at **[6985]**, **[6993]**.

421 Copies of instruments creating charges to be kept by company

(*1*) *Every company shall cause a copy of every instrument creating a charge requiring registration under this Chapter to be kept at the company's registered office.*

(*2*) *In the case of a series of uniform debentures, a copy of one debenture of the series is sufficient.*

[449]

NOTES

Repealed by the Companies Act 2006, s 1295, Sch 16, as from a day to be appointed.

Prospective replacement: see note (a) preceding s 395.

Application to limited liability partnerships: see the Limited Liability Partnerships Regulations 2001, SI 2001/1090, reg 4(1), Sch 2, Pt 1 at **[6985]**, **[6993]**.

422 Company's register of charges

(*1*) *Every company shall keep at its registered office a register of charges and enter in it all charges specifically affecting property of the company, and all floating charges on any property of the company.*

(*2*) *There shall be given in each case a short description of the property charged, the amount of the charge and, except in the case of securities to bearer, the names of the persons entitled to it.*

(*3*) *If an officer of the company knowingly and wilfully authorises or permits the omission of an entry required to be made in pursuance of this section, he is liable to a fine.*

[450]

NOTES

Repealed by the Companies Act 2006, s 1295, Sch 16, as from a day to be appointed.

Prospective replacement: see note (a) preceding s 395.

Application to limited liability partnerships: see the Limited Liability Partnerships Regulations 2001, SI 2001/1090, reg 4(1), Sch 2, Pt 1 at **[6985]**, **[6993]**.

423 Right to inspect copies of instruments, and company's register

(*1*) *The copies of instruments creating charges requiring registration under this Chapter with the registrar of companies, and the register of charges kept in pursuance of section 422, shall be open during business hours (but subject to such reasonable restrictions as the company in general meeting may impose, so that not less than 2 hours in each day be allowed for inspection) to the inspection of any creditor or member of the company without fee.*

(*2*) *The register of charges shall be open to the inspection of any other person on payment of such fee, not exceeding 5 pence for each inspection, as the company may prescribe.*

(*3*) *If inspection of the copies or register is refused, every officer of the company who is in default is liable to a fine and, for continued contravention, to a daily default fine.*

(*4*) *If such a refusal occurs in relation to a company, the court may by order compel an immediate inspection of the copies or register.*

[451]

NOTES

Repealed by the Companies Act 2006, s 1295, Sch 16, as from a day to be appointed.

Prospective replacement: see note (a) preceding s 395.

Application to limited liability partnerships: see the Limited Liability Partnerships Regulations 2001, SI 2001/1090, reg 4(1), Sch 2, Pt 1 at **[6985]**, **[6993]**.

424 Extension of Chapter II

(*1*) *This Chapter extends to charges on property in Scotland which are created, and to charges on property in Scotland which is acquired, by a company incorporated outside Great Britain which has a place of business in Scotland.*

(*2*) *In relation to such a company, sections 421 and 422 apply with the substitution, for the reference to the company's registered office, of a reference to its principal place of business in Scotland.*

[452]

NOTES

Repealed by the Companies Act 2006, s 1295, Sch 16, as from a day to be appointed.

Prospective replacement: see note (b) preceding s 395.

PART XIII
ARRANGEMENTS AND RECONSTRUCTIONS

425 Power of company to compromise with creditors and members

(*1*) *Where a compromise or arrangement is proposed between a company and its creditors, or any class of them, or between the company and its members, or any class of them, the court may on the application of the company or any creditor or member of it or, in the case of a company being wound up, [or [in administration], of the liquidator or administrator], order a meeting of the creditors or class of creditors, or of the members of the company or class of members (as the case may be), to be summoned in such manner as the court directs.*

(*2*) *If a majority in number representing three-fourths in value of the creditors or class of creditors or members or class of members (as the case may be), present and voting either in person or by proxy at the meeting, agree to any compromise or arrangement, the compromise or arrangement, if sanctioned by the court, is binding on all creditors or the class of creditors or on the members or class of members (as the case may be), and also on the company or, in the case of a company in the course of being wound up, on the liquidator and contributories of the company.*

(*3*) *The court's order under subsection (2) has no effect until [a copy] of it has been delivered to the registrar of companies for registration; and a copy of every such order shall be annexed to every copy of the company's memorandum issued after the order has been made or, in the case of a company not having a memorandum, of every copy so issued of the instrument constituting the company or defining its constitution.*

(4) If a company makes default in complying with subsection (3), the company and every officer of it who is in default is liable to a fine.

(5) An order under subsection (1) pronounced in Scotland by the judge acting as vacation judge in pursuance of section 4 of the Administration of Justice (Scotland) Act 1933 is not subject to review, reduction, suspension or stay of execution.

(6) In this section and the next—

(a) "company" means any company liable to be wound up under this Act, and

(b) "arrangement" includes a reorganisation of the company's share capital by the consolidation of shares of different classes or by the division of shares into shares of different classes, or by both of those methods.

[453]

NOTES

Repealed by the Companies Act 2006, s 1295, Sch 16, as from a day to be appointed.

Sub-s (1): words in first (outer) pair of square brackets substituted by the Insolvency Act 1985, s 109(1), Sch 6, para 11, as from 29 December 1986; words in second (inner) pair of square brackets substituted by the Enterprise Act 2002, s 248(3), Sch 17, paras 3, 5, as from 15 September 2003 (for savings and transitional provisions, see the note to the Insolvency Act 1986, s 8 at **[3164]**).

Sub-s (3): words in square brackets substituted by the Companies (Registrar, Languages and Trading Disclosures) Regulations 2006, SI 2006/3429, reg 3(1)(b), as from 1 January 2007.

Application to limited liability partnerships: see the Limited Liability Partnerships Regulations 2001, SI 2001/1090, reg 4(1), Sch 2, Pt 1 at **[6985]**, **[6993]**. Note also that in so far as this section applies to LLPs by virtue of the Limited Liability Partnerships Regulations 2001, SI 2001/1090, the substitution of the words "a copy" for the original words "an office copy" in sub-s (3) has no effect; see the Companies (Registrar, Languages and Trading Disclosures) Regulations 2006, SI 2006/3429, reg 3(3).

Compromise or arrangement: if an administrator concludes that a company in administration can be rescued as a going concern, he may include proposals for a compromise or arrangement to be sanctioned under this section. Any creditor or member of the company may apply to the court challenging the administrator's conduct of the company; see the Insolvency Act 1986, s 8, Sch B1, para 49, 73, 74 at **[3164]**, **[3469A]**.

426 Information as to compromise to be circulated

(1) The following applies where a meeting of creditors or any class of creditors, or of members or any class of members, is summoned under section 425.

(2) With every notice summoning the meeting which is sent to a creditor or member there shall be sent also a statement explaining the effect of the compromise or arrangement and in particular stating any material interests of the directors of the company (whether as directors or as members or as creditors of the company or otherwise) and the effect on those interests of the compromise or arrangement, in so far as it is different from the effect on the like interests of other persons.

(3) In every notice summoning the meeting which is given by advertisement there shall be included either such a statement as above-mentioned or a notification of the place at which, and the manner in which, creditors or members entitled to attend the meeting may obtain copies of the statement.

(4) Where the compromise or arrangement affects the rights of debenture holders of the company, the statement shall give the like explanation as respects the trustees of any deed for securing the issue of the debentures as it is required to give as respects the company's directors.

(5) Where a notice given by advertisement includes a notification that copies of a statement explaining the effect of the compromise or arrangement proposed can be obtained by creditors or members entitled to attend the meeting, every such creditor or member shall, on making application in the manner indicated by the notice, be furnished by the company free of charge with a copy of the statement.

(6) If a company makes default in complying with any requirement of this section, the company and every officer of it who is in default is liable to a fine; and for this purpose a liquidator [or administrator] of the company and a trustee of a deed for securing the issue of debentures of the company is deemed an officer of it.

However, a person is not liable under this subsection if he shows that the default was due to the refusal of another person, being a director or trustee for debenture holders, to supply the necessary particulars of his interests.

(7) It is the duty of any director of the company, and of any trustee for its debenture holders, to give notice to the company of such matters relating to himself as may be necessary for purposes of this section; and any person who makes default in complying with this subsection is liable to a fine.

[454]

NOTES

Repealed by the Companies Act 2006, s 1295, Sch 16, as from a day to be appointed.

Sub-s (6): words in square brackets inserted by the Insolvency Act 1985, s 109(1), Sch 6, para 12, as from 29 December 1986.

Application to limited liability partnerships: see the Limited Liability Partnerships Regulations 2001, SI 2001/1090, reg 4(1), Sch 2, Pt 1 at **[6985]**, **[6993]**.

427 Provisions for facilitating company reconstruction or amalgamation

(1) The following applies where application is made to the court under section 425 for the sanctioning of a compromise or arrangement proposed between a company and any such persons as are mentioned in that section.

(2) If it is shown—

- *(a) that the compromise or arrangement has been proposed for the purposes of, or in connection with, a scheme for the reconstruction of any company or companies, or the amalgamation of any two or more companies, and*
- *(b) that under the scheme the whole or any part of the undertaking or the property of any company concerned in the scheme ("a transferor company") is to be transferred to another company ("the transferee company"),*

the court may, either by the order sanctioning the compromise or arrangement or by any subsequent order, make provision for all or any of the following matters.

(3) The matters for which the court's order may make provision are—

- *(a) the transfer to the transferee company of the whole or any part of the undertaking and of the property or liabilities of any transferor company,*
- *(b) the allotting or appropriation by the transferee company of any shares, debentures, policies or other like interests in that company which under the compromise or arrangement are to be allotted or appropriated by that company to or for any person,*
- *(c) the continuation by or against the transferee company of any legal proceedings pending by or against any transferor company,*
- *(d) the dissolution, without winding up, of any transferor company,*
- *(e) the provision to be made for any persons who, within such time and in such manner as the court directs, dissent from the compromise or arrangement,*
- *(f) such incidental, consequential and supplemental matters as are necessary to secure that the reconstruction or amalgamation is fully and effectively carried out.*

(4) If an order under this section provides for the transfer of property or liabilities, then—

- *(a) that property is by virtue of the order transferred to, and vests in, the transferee company, and*
- *(b) those liabilities are, by virtue of the order, transferred to and become liabilities of that company;*

and property (if the order so directs) vests freed from any charge which is by virtue of the compromise or arrangement to cease to have effect.

(5) Where an order is made under this section, every company in relation to which the order is made shall cause [a copy] of the order to be delivered to the registrar of companies for registration within 7 days after its making; and if default is made in complying with this subsection, the company and every officer of it who is in default is liable to a fine and, for continued contravention, to a daily default fine.

(6) In this section the expression "property" includes property, rights and powers of every description; the expression "liabilities" includes duties and "company" includes only a company as defined in section 735(1).

[455]

NOTES

Repealed by the Companies Act 2006, s 1295, Sch 16, as from a day to be appointed.

Sub-s (5): words in square brackets substituted by the Companies (Registrar, Languages and Trading Disclosures) Regulations 2006, SI 2006/3429, reg 3(1)(c), as from 1 January 2007.

Application to limited liability partnerships: see the Limited Liability Partnerships Regulations 2001, SI 2001/1090, reg 4(1), Sch 2, Pt 1 at **[6985]**, **[6993]**. Note also that in so far as this section applies to LLPs by virtue of the Limited Liability Partnerships Regulations 2001, SI 2001/1090, the substitution of the words "a copy" for the original words "an office copy" in sub-s (5) has no effect; see the Companies (Registrar, Languages and Trading Disclosures) Regulations 2006, SI 2006/3429, reg 3(3).

[427A Application of ss 425–427 to mergers and divisions of public companies

(1) Where—

(a) a compromise or arrangement is proposed between a public company and any such persons as are mentioned in section 425(1) for the purposes of, or in connection with, a scheme for the reconstruction of any company or companies or the amalgamation of any two or more companies,

(b) the circumstances are as specified in any of the Cases described in subsection (2), and

(c) the consideration for the transfer or each of the transfers envisaged in the Case in question is to be shares in the transferee company or any of the transferee companies receivable by members of the transferor company or transferor companies, with or without any cash payment to members,

sections 425 to 427 shall, as regards that compromise or arrangement, have effect subject to the provisions of this section and Schedule [15B].

(2) The Cases referred to in subsection (1) are as follows—

Case 1

Where under the scheme the undertaking, property and liabilities of the company in respect of which the compromise or arrangement in question is proposed are to be transferred to another public company, other than one formed for the purpose of, or in connection with, the scheme.

Case 2

Where under the scheme the undertaking, property and liabilities of each of two or more public companies concerned in the scheme, including the company in respect of which the compromise or arrangement in question is proposed, are to be transferred to a company (whether or not a public company) formed for the purpose of, or in connection with, the scheme.

Case 3

Where under the scheme the undertaking, property and liabilities of the company in respect of which the compromise or arrangement in question is proposed are to be divided among and transferred to two or more companies each of which is either—

(a) a public company, or

(b) a company (whether or not a public company) formed for the purposes of, or in connection with, the scheme.

(3) Before sanctioning any compromise or arrangement under section 425(2) the court may, on the application of any pre-existing transferee company or any member or creditor of it or, [where the company is in administration], the administrator, order a meeting of the members of the company or any class of them or of the creditors of the company or any class of them to be summoned in such manner as the court directs.

(4) This section does not apply where the company in respect of which the compromise or arrangement is proposed is being wound up.

(5) This section does not apply to compromise or arrangements in respect of which an application has been made to the court for an order under section 425(1) before 1st January 1988.

(6) Where section 427 would apply in the case of a scheme but for the fact that the transferee company or any of the transferee companies is a company within the meaning of

Article 3 of the Companies (Northern Ireland) Order 1986 (and thus not within the definition of "company" in subsection (6) of section 427), section 427 shall apply notwithstanding that fact.

(7) *In the case of a scheme mentioned in subsection (1), for a company within the meaning of Article 3 of the Companies (Northern Ireland) Order 1986, the reference in section 427(5) to the registrar of companies shall have effect as a reference to the registrar as defined in Article 2 of that Order.*

(8) *In this section and Schedule [15B]—*

"transferor company" means a company whose undertaking, property and liabilities are to be transferred by means of a transfer envisaged in any of the Cases specified in subsection (2);

"transferee company" means a company to which a transfer envisaged in any of those Cases is to be made;

"pre-existing transferee company" means a transferee company other than one formed for the purpose of, or in connection with, the scheme;

"compromise or arrangement" means a compromise or arrangement to which subsection (1) applies;

"the scheme" means the scheme mentioned in subsection (1)(a);

"company" includes only a company as defined in section 735(1) except that, in the case of a transferee company, it also includes a company as defined in Article 3 of the Companies (Northern Ireland) Order 1986 (referred to in these definitions as a "Northern Ireland company");

"public company" means, in relation to a transferee company which is a Northern Ireland company, a public company within the meaning of Article 12 of the Companies (Northern Ireland) Order 1986;

"the registrar of companies" means, in relation to a transferee company which is a Northern Ireland company, the registrar as defined in Article 2 of the Companies (Northern Ireland) Order 1986;

"the Gazette" means, in relation to a transferee company which is a Northern Ireland company, the Belfast Gazette;

"Case 1 Scheme", "Case 2 Scheme" and "Case 3 Scheme" mean a scheme of the kind described in Cases 1, 2 and 3 of subsection (2) respectively;

"property" and "liabilities" have the same meaning as in section 427.]

[456]

NOTES

Inserted by the Companies (Mergers and Divisions) Regulations 1987, SI 1987/1991, reg 2(a), Schedule, Pt I, as from 1 January 1988.

Repealed by the Companies Act 2006, s 1295, Sch 16, as from a day to be appointed.

Sub-ss (1), (8): figures in square brackets substituted by CA 1989, s 114(2), as from 1 April 1990.

Sub-s (3): words in square brackets substituted by the Enterprise Act 2002, s 248(3), Sch 17, paras 3, 6, as from 15 September 2003 (for savings and transitional provisions, see the note to the Insolvency Act 1986, s 8 at **[3164]**).

[PART XIIIA
TAKEOVER OFFERS

NOTES

Transitional provisions, etc: with regard to takeover offers made before 1 November 1990, see CA 1989, Sch 18, para 35 at **[874]**.

This Part is repealed, as from 6 April 2007, by the Companies Act 2006, s 1295, Sch 16 (for savings regarding the operation of this Part in relation to a takeover offer where the date of the offer is before 6 April 2007, see the Companies Act 2006 (Commencement No 2, Consequential Amendments, Transitional Provisions and Savings) Order 2007, SI 2007/1093, Sch 6, para 1 at **[7629]**). As to takeovers generally, see now the Companies Act 2006, Part 28 (at **[S942]** et seq) and see also the note below.

This Part is disapplied where a takeover offer (where the date of the offer is on or after 20 May 2006) is made for a company that has securities carrying voting rights admitted to trading on a regulated market; see the Takeovers Directive (Interim Implementation) Regulations 2006, SI 2006/1183, regs 29, 30 at **[7537]**, **[7536]**. In such circumstances, Sch 2 to those Regulations (at **[7544]**) applies. As to the meaning of "date of the offer", see Sch 2, para 11. Note that the 2006 Regulations were revoked, as from 6 April 2007, by the Companies Act 2006 (Commencement No 2, Consequential Amendments, Transitional Provisions and Savings) Order 2007, SI 2007/1093, art 7, Sch 5, subject to certain savings in relation to (i) takeover offers (where the date of offer is before 6 April 2007) and (ii) offences committed before that date (see Sch 6, paras 2, 3 to the 2007 Order at **[7629]**).

428 Takeover offers

(1) In this Part of this Act "takeover offer" means an offer to acquire all the shares, or all the shares of any class or classes, in a company (other than shares which at the date of the offer are already held by the offeror), being an offer on terms which are the same in relation to all the shares to which the offer relates or, where those shares include shares of different classes, in relation to all the shares of each class.

[(2) In subsection (1) "shares" means shares (other than relevant treasury shares) which have been allotted on the date of the offer, but a takeover offer may include among the shares to which it relates—

- *(a) all or any shares that are allotted after the date of the offer but before a specified date;*
- *(b) all or any relevant treasury shares that cease to be held as treasury shares before a specified date;*
- *(c) all or any other relevant treasury shares.*

(2A) In this section—

"relevant treasury shares" means shares which—

- *(a) are held by the company as treasury shares on the date of the offer; or*
- *(b) become shares held by the company as treasury shares after that date but before a specified date;*

"specified date" means a date specified in or determined in accordance with the terms of the offer.]

(3) The terms offered in relation to any shares shall for the purposes of this section be treated as being the same in relation to all the shares or, as the case may be, all the shares of a class to which the offer relates notwithstanding any variation permitted by subsection (4).

(4) A variation is permitted by this subsection where—

- *(a) the law of a country or territory outside the United Kingdom precludes an offer of consideration in the form or any of the forms specified in the terms in question or precludes it except after compliance by the offeror with conditions with which he is unable to comply or which he regards as unduly onerous; and*
- *(b) the variation is such that the persons to whom an offer of consideration in that form is precluded are able to receive consideration otherwise than in that form but of substantially equivalent value.*

(5) The reference in subsection (1) to shares already held by the offeror includes a reference to shares which he has contracted to acquire but that shall not be construed as including shares which are the subject of a contract binding the holder to accept the offer when it is made, being a contract entered into by the holder either for no consideration and under seal or for no consideration other than a promise by the offeror to make the offer.

(6) In the application of subsection (5) to Scotland the words "and under seal" shall be omitted.

(7) Where the terms of an offer make provision for their revision and for acceptances on the previous terms to be treated as acceptances on the revised terms, the revision shall not be regarded for the purposes of this Part of this Act as the making of a fresh offer and references in this Part of this Act to the date of the offer shall accordingly be construed as references to the date on which the original offer was made.

(8) In this Part of this Act "the offeror" means, subject to section 430D, the person making a takeover offer and "the company" means the company whose shares are the subject of the offer.]

[457]

NOTES

Substituted, together with preceding headings and ss 429–430F, for original ss 428–430, by FSA 1986, s 172(1), Sch 12, as from 30 April 1987, save in any case in which the offer in respect of the scheme or contract mentioned in sub-s (1) above was made before that date.

Repealed by the Companies Act 2006, s 1295, Sch 16, as from 6 April 2007, except in relation to a takeover offer where the date of the offer is before that date (see the Companies Act 2006 (Commencement No 2, Consequential Amendments, Transitional Provisions and Savings) Order 2007, SI 2007/1093, Sch 6, para 1 at **[7629]**).

Sub-ss (2), (2A): substituted, for original sub-s (2), by the Companies (Acquisition of Own Shares) (Treasury Shares) No 2 Regulations 2003, SI 2003/3031, reg 5, as from 18 December 2003.

Repeal of this Part; disapplication of this Part; savings: see the note preceding this section.

[429 Right of offeror to buy out minority shareholders

(*1*) *If, in a case in which a takeover offer does not relate to shares of different classes, the offeror has by virtue of acceptances of the offer acquired or contracted to acquire not less than nine-tenths in value of the shares to which the offer relates […] he may give notice to the holder of any shares to which the offer relates which the offeror has not acquired or contracted to acquire that he desires to acquire those shares.*

(*2*) *If, in a case in which a takeover offer relates to shares of different classes, the offeror has by virtue of acceptances of the offer acquired or contracted to acquire not less than nine-tenths in value of the shares of any class to which the offer relates […], he may give notice to the holder of any shares of that class which the offeror has not acquired or contracted to acquire that he desires to acquire those shares.*

(*3*) *No notice shall be given under subsection* (*1*) *or* (*2*) *unless the offeror has acquired or contracted to acquire the shares necessary to satisfy the minimum specified in that subsection before the end of the period of four months beginning with the date of the offer; and no such notice shall be given after the end of the period of two months beginning with the date on which he has acquired or contracted to acquire shares which satisfy that minimum.*

(*4*) *Any notice under this section shall be given in the prescribed manner; and when the offeror gives the first notice in relation to an offer he shall send a copy of it to the company together with a statutory declaration by him in the prescribed form stating that the conditions for the giving of the notice are satisfied.*

(*5*) *Where the offeror is a company* (*whether or not a company within the meaning of this Act*) *the statutory declaration shall be signed by a director.*

(*6*) *Any person who fails to send a copy of a notice or a statutory declaration as required by subsection* (*4*) *or makes such a declaration for the purposes of that subsection knowing it to be false or without having reasonable grounds for believing it to be true shall be liable to imprisonment or a fine, or both, and for continued failure to send the copy or declaration, to a daily default fine.*

(*7*) *If any person is charged with an offence for failing to send a copy of a notice as required by subsection* (*4*) *it is a defence for him to prove that he took reasonable steps for securing compliance with that subsection.*

(*8*) *Where during the period within which a takeover offer can be accepted the offeror acquires or contracts to acquire any of the shares to which the offer relates but otherwise than by virtue of acceptances of the offer, then, if—*

- (*a*) *the value of the consideration for which they are acquired or contracted to be acquired* (*"the acquisition consideration"*) *does not at that time exceed the value of the consideration specified in the terms of the offer; or*
- (*b*) *those terms are subsequently revised so that when the revision is announced the value of the acquisition consideration, at the time mentioned in paragraph* (*a*) *above, no longer exceeds the value of the consideration specified in those terms,*

the offeror shall be treated for the purposes of this section as having acquired or contracted to acquire those shares by virtue of acceptances of the offer; but in any other case those shares shall be treated as excluded from those to which the offer relates.]

[458]

NOTES

Substituted as noted to s 428 at **[457]**.

Repealed with savings (as from 6 April 2007) as noted to s 428 at **[457]**.

Sub-ss (1), (2): words omitted originally inserted by the Companies (Acquisition of Own Shares) (Treasury Shares) Regulations 2003, SI 2003/1116, reg 4, Schedule, para 26, as from 1 December 2003, and repealed by the Companies (Acquisition of Own Shares) (Treasury Shares) No 2 Regulations 2003, SI 2003/3031, reg 6, as from 18 December 2003.

Repeal of this Part; disapplication of this Part; savings: see the note preceding s 428 at **[457]**.

Prescribed manner; prescribed form: see Appendix 4 (Forms table) at **[A4]** and the Companies (Forms) (Amendment) Regulations 1987, SI 1987/752 at **[6581]**.

[430 Effect of notice under s 429

(*1*) *The following provisions shall, subject to section 430C, have effect where a notice is given in respect of any shares under section 429.*

(*2*) *The offeror shall be entitled and bound to acquire those shares on the terms of the offer.*

(3) Where the terms of an offer are such as to give the holder of any shares a choice of consideration the notice shall give particulars of the choice and state—

(a) that the holder of the shares may within six weeks from the date of the notice indicate his choice by a written communication sent to the offeror at an address specified in the notice; and

(b) which consideration specified in the offer is to be taken as applying in default of his indicating a choice as aforesaid;

and the terms of the offer mentioned in subsection (2) shall be determined accordingly.

(4) Subsection (3) applies whether or not any time-limit or other conditions applicable to the choice under the terms of the offer can still be complied with; and if the consideration chosen by the holder of the shares—

(a) is not cash and the offeror is no longer able to provide it; or

(b) was to have been provided by a third party who is no longer bound or able to provide it,

the consideration shall be taken to consist of an amount of cash payable by the offeror which at the date of the notice is equivalent to the chosen consideration.

(5) At the end of six weeks from the date of the notice the offeror shall forthwith—

(a) send a copy of the notice to the company; and

(b) pay or transfer to the company the consideration for the shares to which the notice relates.

(6) If the shares to which the notice relates are registered the copy of the notice sent to the company under subsection (5)(a) shall be accompanied by an instrument of transfer executed on behalf of the shareholder by a person appointed by the offeror; and on receipt of that instrument the company shall register the offeror as the holder of those shares.

(7) If the shares to which the notice relates are transferable by the delivery of warrants or other instruments the copy of the notice sent to the company under subsection (5)(a) shall be accompanied by a statement to that effect; and the company shall on receipt of the statement issue the offeror with warrants or other instruments in respect of the shares and those already in issue in respect of the shares shall become void.

(8) Where the consideration referred to in paragraph (b) of subsection (5) consists of shares or securities to be allotted by the offeror the reference in that paragraph to the transfer of the consideration shall be construed as a reference to the allotment of the shares or securities to the company.

(9) Any sum received by a company under paragraph (b) of subsection (5) and any other consideration received under that paragraph shall be held by the company on trust for the person entitled to the shares in respect of which the sum or other consideration was received.

(10) Any sum received by a company under paragraph (b) of subsection (5), and any dividend or other sum accruing from any other consideration received by a company under that paragraph, shall be paid into a separate bank account, being an account the balance on which bears interest at an appropriate rate and can be withdrawn by such notice (if any) as is appropriate.

(11) Where after reasonable enquiry made at such intervals as are reasonable the person entitled to any consideration held on trust by virtue of subsection (9) cannot be found and twelve years have elapsed since the consideration was received or the company is wound up the consideration (together with any interest, dividend or other benefit that has accrued from it) shall be paid into court.

(12) In relation to a company registered in Scotland, subsections (13) and (14) shall apply in place of subsection (11).

(13) Where after reasonable enquiry made at such intervals as are reasonable the person entitled to any consideration held on trust by virtue of subsection (9) cannot be found and twelve years have elapsed since the consideration was received or the company is wound up—

(a) the trust shall terminate;

(b) the company or, as the case may be, the liquidator shall sell any consideration other than cash and any benefit other than cash that has accrued from the consideration; and

(c) a sum representing—

(i) the consideration so far as it is cash;

(ii) the proceeds of any sale under paragraph (b) above; and

(iii) *any interest, dividend or other benefit that has accrued from the consideration,*

shall be deposited in the name of the Accountant of Court in a bank account such as is referred to in subsection (10) and the receipt for the deposit shall be transmitted to the Accountant of Court.

(14) Section 58 of the Bankruptcy (Scotland) Act 1985 (so far as consistent with this Act) shall apply with any necessary modifications to sums deposited under subsection (13) as that section applies to sums deposited under section 57(1)(a) of that Act.

(15) The expenses of any such enquiry as is mentioned in subsection (11) or (13) may be defrayed out of the money or other property held on trust for the person or persons to whom the enquiry relates.]

[459]

NOTES

Substituted as noted to s 428 at **[457]**.
Repealed with savings (as from 6 April 2007) as noted to s 428 at **[457]**.
Repeal of this Part; disapplication of this Part; savings: see the note preceding s 428 at **[457]**.

[430A Right of minority shareholder to be bought out by offeror

(1) If a takeover offer relates to all the shares in a company and at any time before the end of the period within which the offer can be accepted—

- *(a)* *the offeror has by virtue of acceptances of the offer acquired or contracted to acquire some (but not all) of the shares to which the offer relates; and*
- *(b)* *those shares, with or without any other shares in the company which he has acquired or contracted to acquire, amount to not less than nine-tenths in value of all the shares in the company […],*

the holder of any shares to which the offer relates who has not accepted the offer may by a written communication addressed to the offeror require him to acquire those shares.

[(1A) For the purposes of subsection (1), a takeover offer relates to all the shares in a company if it is an offer to acquire all the shares in the company within the meaning of section 428.]

(2) If a takeover offer relates to shares of any class or classes and at any time before the end of the period within which the offer can be accepted—

- *(a)* *the offeror has by virtue of acceptances of the offer acquired or contracted to acquire some (but not all) of the shares of any class to which the offer relates; and*
- *(b)* *those shares, with or without any other shares of that class which he has acquired or contracted to acquire, amount to not less than nine-tenths in value of all the shares of that class […],*

the holder of any shares of that class who has not accepted the offer may by a written communication addressed to the offeror require him to acquire those shares.

[(2A) For the purposes of subsections (1) and (2), in calculating nine-tenths of the value of all the shares in the company, or all the shares of any class or classes of shares of the company, any shares held by the company as treasury shares shall be treated as having been acquired by the offeror.]

(3) Within one month of the time specified in subsection (1) or, as the case may be, subsection (2) the offeror shall give any shareholder who has not accepted the offer notice in the prescribed manner of the rights that are exercisable by him under that subsection; and if the notice is given before the end of the period mentioned in that subsection it shall state that the offer is still open for acceptance.

(4) A notice under subsection (3) may specify a period for the exercise of the rights conferred by this section and in that event the rights shall not be exercisable after the end of that period; but no such period shall end less than three months after the end of the period within which the offer can be accepted.

(5) Subsection (3) does not apply if the offeror has given the shareholder a notice in respect of the shares in question under section 429.

(6) If the offeror fails to comply with subsection (3) he and, if the offeror is a company, every officer of the company who is in default or to whose neglect the failure is attributable, shall be liable to a fine and for continued contravention, to a daily default fine.

(7) If an offeror other than a company is charged with an offence for failing to comply with subsection (3) it is a defence for him to prove that he took all reasonable steps for securing compliance with that subsection.]

[460]

NOTES

Substituted as noted to s 428 at **[457]**.

Repealed with savings (as from 6 April 2007) as noted to s 428 at **[457]**.

Sub-ss (1), (2): words omitted originally inserted by the Companies (Acquisition of Own Shares) (Treasury Shares) Regulations 2003, SI 2003/1116, reg 4, Schedule, para 27, as from 1 December 2003, and repealed by the Companies (Acquisition of Own Shares) (Treasury Shares) No 2 Regulations 2003, SI 2003/3031, reg 7(1), as from 18 December 2003.

Sub-ss (1A), (2A): inserted by SI 2003/3031, reg 7(2), (3), as from 18 December 2003.

Repeal of this Part; disapplication of this Part; savings: see the note preceding s 428 at **[457]**.

Notice in the prescribed manner: see Appendix 4 (Forms table) at **[A4]** and the Companies (Forms) (Amendment) Regulations 1987, SI 1987/752 at **[6581]**.

[430B Effect of requirement under s 430A

(1) The following provisions shall, subject to section 430C, have effect where a shareholder exercises his rights in respect of any shares under section 430A.

(2) The offeror shall be entitled and bound to acquire those shares on the terms of the offer or on such other terms as may be agreed.

(3) Where the terms of an offer are such as to give the holder of shares a choice of consideration the holder of the shares may indicate his choice when requiring the offeror to acquire them and the notice given to the holder under section 430A(3)—

(a) shall give particulars of the choice and of the rights conferred by this subsection; and

(b) may state which consideration specified in the offer is to be taken as applying in default of his indicating a choice;

and the terms of the offer mentioned in subsection (2) shall be determined accordingly.

(4) Subsection (3) applies whether or not any time-limit or other conditions applicable to the choice under the terms of the offer can still be complied with; and if the consideration chosen by the holder of the shares—

(a) is not cash and the offeror is no longer able to provide it; or

(b) was to have been provided by a third party who is no longer bound or able to provide it,

the consideration shall be taken to consist of an amount of cash payable by the offeror which at the date when the holder of the shares requires the offeror to acquire them is equivalent to the chosen consideration.]

[461]

NOTES

Substituted as noted to s 428 at **[457]**.

Repealed with savings (as from 6 April 2007) as noted to s 428 at **[457]**.

Repeal of this Part; disapplication of this Part; savings: see the note preceding s 428 at **[457]**.

[430C Applications to the court

(1) Where a notice is given under section 429 to the holder of any shares the court may, on an application made by him within six weeks from the date on which the notice was given—

(a) order that the offeror shall not be entitled and bound to acquire the shares; or

(b) specify terms of acquisition different from those of the offer.

(2) If an application to the court under subsection (1) is pending at the end of the period mentioned in subsection (5) of section 430 that subsection shall not have effect until the application has been disposed of.

(3) Where the holder of any shares exercises his rights under section 430A the court may, on an application made by him or the offeror, order that the terms on which the offeror is entitled and bound to acquire the shares shall be such as the court thinks fit.

(4) No order for costs or expenses shall be made against a shareholder making an application under subsection (1) or (3) unless the court considers—

(*a*) *that the application was unnecessary, improper or vexatious; or*

(*b*) *that there has been unreasonable delay in making the application or unreasonable conduct on his part in conducting the proceedings on the application.*

(5) Where a takeover offer has not been accepted to the extent necessary for entitling the offeror to give notices under subsection (1) or (2) of section 429 the court may, on the application of the offeror, make an order authorising him to give notices under that subsection if satisfied—

(*a*) *that the offeror has after reasonable enquiry been unable to trace one or more of the persons holding shares to which the offer relates;*

(*b*) *that the shares which the offeror has acquired or contracted to acquire by virtue of acceptances of the offer, together with the shares held by the person or persons mentioned in paragraph (a), amount to not less than the minimum specified in that subsection; and*

(*c*) *that the consideration offered is fair and reasonable;*

but the court shall not make an order under this subsection unless it considers that it is just and equitable to do so having regard, in particular, to the number of shareholders who have been traced but who have not accepted the offer.]

[462]

NOTES

Substituted as noted to s 428 at **[457]**.

Repealed with savings (as from 6 April 2007) as noted to s 428 at **[457]**.

Repeal of this Part; disapplication of this Part; savings: see the note preceding s 428 at **[457]**.

[430D Joint offers

(1) A takeover offer may be made by two or more persons jointly and in that event this Part of this Act has effect with the following modifications.

(2) The conditions for the exercise of the rights conferred by sections 429 and 430A shall be satisfied by the joint offerors acquiring or contracting to acquire the necessary shares jointly (as respects acquisitions by virtue of acceptances of the offer) and either jointly or separately (in other cases); and, subject to the following provisions, the rights and obligations of the offeror under those sections and sections 430 and 430B shall be respectively joint rights and joint and several obligations of the joint offerors.

(3) It shall be a sufficient compliance with any provision of those sections requiring or authorising a notice or other document to be given or sent by or to the joint offerors that it is given or sent by or to any of them; but the statutory declaration required by section 429(4) shall be made by all of them and, in the case of a joint offeror being a company, signed by a director of that company.

(4) In sections 428, 430(8) and 430E references to the offeror shall be construed as references to the joint offerors or any of them.

(5) In section 430(6) and (7) references to the offeror shall be construed as references to the joint offerors or such of them as they may determine.

(6) In sections 430(4)(a) and 430B(4)(a) references to the offeror being no longer able to provide the relevant consideration shall be construed as references to none of the joint offerors being able to do so.

(7) In section 430C references to the offeror shall be construed as references to the joint offerors except that any application under subsection (3) or (5) may be made by any of them and the reference in subsection (5)(a) to the offeror having been unable to trace one or more of the persons holding shares shall be construed as a reference to none of the offerors having been able to do so.]

[463]

NOTES

Substituted as noted to s 428 at **[457]**.

Repealed with savings (as from 6 April 2007) as noted to s 428 at **[457]**.

Repeal of this Part; disapplication of this Part; savings: see the note preceding s 428 at **[457]**.

[430E Associates

(1) The requirement in section 428(1) that a takeover offer must extend to all the shares, or all the shares of any class or classes, in a company shall be regarded as satisfied notwithstanding that the offer does not extend to shares which associates of the offeror hold or have contracted to acquire; but, subject to subsection (2), shares which any such associate holds or has contracted to acquire, whether at the time when the offer is made or subsequently, shall be disregarded for the purposes of any reference in this Part of this Act to the shares to which a takeover offer relates.

(2) Where during the period within which a takeover offer can be accepted any associate of the offeror acquires or contracts to acquire any of the shares to which the offer relates, then, if the condition specified in subsection (8)(a) or (b) of section 429 is satisfied as respects those shares they shall be treated for the purposes of that section as shares to which the offer relates.

(3) In section 430A(1)(b) and (2)(b) the reference to shares which the offeror has acquired or contracted to acquire shall include a reference to shares which any associate of his has acquired or contracted to acquire.

(4) In this section "associate", in relation to an offeror means—

- *(a) a nominee of the offeror;*
- *(b) a holding company, subsidiary or fellow subsidiary of the offeror or a nominee of such a holding company, subsidiary or fellow subsidiary;*
- *(c) a body corporate in which the offeror is substantially interested; or*
- *(d) any person who is, or is a nominee of, a party to an agreement with the offeror for the acquisition of, or of an interest in, the shares which are the subject of the takeover offer, being an agreement which includes provisions imposing obligations or restrictions such as are mentioned in section 204(2)(a).*

(5) For the purposes of subsection (4)(b) a company is a fellow subsidiary of another body corporate if both are subsidiaries of the same body corporate but neither is a subsidiary of the other.

(6) For the purposes of subsection (4)(c) an offeror has a substantial interest in a body corporate if—

- *(a) that body or its directors are accustomed to act in accordance with his directions or instructions; or*
- *(b) he is entitled to exercise or control the exercise of one-third or more of the voting power at general meetings of that body.*

(7) Subsections (5) and (6) of section 204 shall apply to subsection (4)(d) above as they apply to that section and subsections (3) and (4) of section 203 shall apply for the purposes of subsection (6) above as they apply for the purposes of subsection (2)(b) of that section.

(8) Where the offeror is an individual his associates shall also include his spouse [or civil partner] and any minor child or step-child of his.]

[464]

NOTES

Substituted as noted to s 428 at **[457]**.

Repealed with savings (as from 6 April 2007) as noted to s 428 at **[457]**.

Sub-s (8): words in square brackets inserted by the Civil Partnership Act 2004, s 261(1), Sch 27, para 103, as from 5 December 2005.

Repeal of this Part; disapplication of this Part; savings: see the note preceding s 428 at **[457]**.

Step-child: this includes relationships arising through civil partnership; see the Civil Partnership Act 2004, ss 246, 247, Sch 21.

[430F Convertible securities

(1) For the purposes of this Part of this Act securities of a company shall be treated as shares in the company if they are convertible into or entitle the holder to subscribe for such shares; and references to the holder of shares or a shareholder shall be construed accordingly.

(2) Subsection (1) shall not be construed as requiring any securities to be treated—

- *(a) as shares of the same class as those into which they are convertible or for which the holder is entitled to subscribe; or* (*b*) *as shares of the same class as other securities by reason only that the shares into which they are convertible or for which the holder is entitled to subscribe are of the same class.]*

[465]

NOTES

Substituted as noted to s 428 at **[457]**.

Repealed with savings (as from 6 April 2007) as noted to s 428 at **[457]**.

Repeal of this Part; disapplication of this Part; savings: see the note preceding s 428 at **[457]**.

PART XIV
INVESTIGATION OF COMPANIES AND THEIR AFFAIRS; REQUISITION OF DOCUMENTS

NOTES

Note: this Part is not repealed by the Companies Act 2006.

Appointment and functions of inspectors

431 Investigation of a company on its own application or that of its members

(1) The Secretary of State may appoint one or more competent inspectors to investigate the affairs of a company and to *report on them in such manner as he may direct*.

(2) The appointment may be made—

(a) in the case of a company having a share capital, on the application either of not less than 200 members or of members holding not less than one-tenth of the shares issued [(excluding any shares held as treasury shares)],

(b) in the case of a company not having a share capital, on the application of not less than one-fifth in number of the persons on the company's register of members, and

(c) in any case, on application of the company.

(3) The application shall be supported by such evidence as the Secretary of State may require for the purpose of showing that the applicant or applicants have good reason for requiring the investigation.

(4) The Secretary of State may, before appointing inspectors, require the applicant or applicants to give security, to an amount not exceeding £5,000, or such other sum as he may by order specify, for payment of the costs of the investigation.

An order under this subsection shall be made by statutory instrument subject to annulment in pursuance of a resolution of either House of Parliament.

[466]

NOTES

Sub-s (1): for the words in italics there are substituted the words "report the result of their investigations to him" by the Companies Act 2006, s 1035(2), as from 1 October 2007, with effect where an inspector is appointed under a provision of Pt 14 of this Act on or after that date.

Sub-s (2): words in square brackets in para (a) inserted by the Companies (Acquisition of Own Shares) (Treasury Shares) Regulations 2003, SI 2003/1116, reg 4, Schedule, para 28, as from 1 December 2003.

Application to limited liability partnerships: see the Limited Liability Partnerships Regulations 2001, SI 2001/1090, reg 4(1), Sch 2, Pt 1 at **[6985]**, **[6993]**. Note also that nothing in the draft Companies Act 2006 (Commencement No 3, Consequential Amendments, Transitional Provisions and Savings) Order 2007 affects any provision of this Act as applied by the 2001 Regulations to LLPs (see art 12(2) at **[A12]** and the introductory notes to this Act).

432 Other company investigations

(1) The Secretary of State shall appoint one or more competent inspectors to investigate the affairs of a company and *report on them in such manner as he directs*, if the court by order declares that its affairs ought to be so investigated.

(2) The Secretary of State may make such an appointment if it appears to him that there are circumstances suggesting—

(a) that the company's affairs are being or have been conducted with intent to defraud its creditors or the creditors of any other person, or otherwise for a fraudulent or unlawful purpose, or in a manner which is unfairly prejudicial to some part of its members, or

(b) that any actual or proposed act or omission of the company (including an act or omission on its behalf) is or would be so prejudicial, or that the company was formed for any fraudulent or unlawful purpose, or

(c) that persons concerned with the company's formation or the management of its affairs have in connection therewith been guilty of fraud, misfeasance or other misconduct towards it or towards its members, or

(d) that the company's members have not been given all the information with respect to its affairs which they might reasonably expect.

[(2A) Inspectors may be appointed under subsection (2) on terms that any report they may make is not for publication; and in such a case, the provisions of section 437(3) (availability and publication of inspectors' reports) do not apply.]

(3) Subsections (1) and (2) are without prejudice to the powers of the Secretary of State under section 431; and the power conferred by subsection (2) is exercisable with respect to a body corporate notwithstanding that it is in course of being voluntarily wound up.

(4) The reference in subsection (2)(a) to a company's members includes any person who is not a member but to whom shares in the company have been transferred or transmitted by operation of law.

[467]

NOTES

Sub-s (1): for the words in italics there are substituted the words "report the result of their investigations to him" by the Companies Act 2006, s 1035(3), as from 1 October 2007, with effect where an inspector is appointed under a provision of Pt 14 of this Act on or after that date.

Sub-s (2A): inserted by CA 1989, s 55, as from 21 February 1990.

Application to limited liability partnerships: see the Limited Liability Partnerships Regulations 2001, SI 2001/1090, reg 4(1), Sch 2, Pt 1 at **[6985]**, **[6993]**. Note also that nothing in the draft Companies Act 2006 (Commencement No 3, Consequential Amendments, Transitional Provisions and Savings) Order 2007 affects any provision of this Act as applied by the 2001 Regulations to LLPs (see art 12(2) at **[A12]** and the introductory notes to this Act).

433 Inspectors' powers during investigation

(1) If inspectors appointed under section 431 or 432 to investigate the affairs of a company think it necessary for the purposes of their investigation to investigate also the affairs of another body corporate which is or at any relevant time has been the company's subsidiary or holding company, or a subsidiary of its holding company or a holding company of its subsidiary, they have power to do so; and they shall report on the affairs of the other body corporate so far as they think that the results of their investigation of its affairs are relevant to the investigation of the affairs of the company first mentioned above.

(2) ...

[468]

NOTES

Sub-s (2): repealed by FSA 1986, ss 182, 212(3), Sch 13, para 7, Sch 17, Pt I, as from 27 November 1986.

Application to limited liability partnerships: see the Limited Liability Partnerships Regulations 2001, SI 2001/1090, reg 4(1), Sch 2, Pt 1 at **[6985]**, **[6993]**.

434 Production of documents and evidence to inspectors

(1) When inspectors are appointed under section 431 or 432, it is the duty of all officers and agents of the company, and of all officers and agents of any other body corporate whose affairs are investigated under section 433(1)—

(a) to produce to the inspectors all [documents] of or relating to the company or, as the case may be, the other body corporate which are in their custody or power,

(b) to attend before the inspectors when required to do so, and

(c) otherwise to give the inspectors all assistance in connection with the investigation which they are reasonably able to give.

[(2) If the inspectors consider that an officer or agent of the company or other body corporate, or any other person, is or may be in possession of information relating to a matter which they believe to be relevant to the investigation, they may require him—

(a) to produce to them any documents in his custody or power relating to that matter,

(b) to attend before them, and

(c) otherwise to give them all assistance in connection with the investigation which he is reasonably able to give;

and it is that person's duty to comply with the requirement.

(3) An inspector may for the purposes of the investigation examine any person on oath, and may administer an oath accordingly.]

(4) In this section a reference to officers or to agents includes past, as well as present, officers or agents (as the case may be); and "agents", in relation to a company or other body corporate, includes its bankers and solicitors and persons employed by it as auditors, whether these persons are or are not officers of the company or other body corporate.

(5) An answer given by a person to a question put to him in exercise of powers conferred by this section (whether as it has effect in relation to an investigation under any of sections 431 to 433, or as applied by any other section in this Part) may be used in evidence against him.

[(5A) However, in criminal proceedings in which that person is charged with an offence to which this subsection applies—

(a) no evidence relating to the answer may be adduced, and

(b) no question relating to it may be asked,

by or on behalf of the prosecution, unless evidence relating to it is adduced, or a question relating to it is asked, in the proceedings by or on behalf of that person.

(5B) Subsection (5A) applies to any offence other than—

(a) an offence under section 2 or 5 of the Perjury Act 1911 (false statements made on oath otherwise than in judicial proceedings or made otherwise than on oath); or

(b) an offence under section 44(1) or (2) of the Criminal Law (Consolidation) (Scotland) Act 1995 (false statements made on oath or otherwise than on oath).]

[(6) In this section "documents" includes information recorded in any form; and, in relation to information recorded otherwise than in legible form, the power to require its production includes power to require the production of a copy of the information in legible form[, or in a form from which it can readily be produced in visible and legible form].]

[469]

NOTES

Sub-s (1): word in square brackets substituted by CA 1989, s 56(1), (2), as from 21 February 1990.

Sub-ss (2), (3): substituted by CA 1989, s 56(1), (3), (4), as from 21 February 1990.

Sub-ss (5A), (5B): inserted by the Youth Justice and Criminal Evidence Act 1999, s 59, Sch 3, paras 4, 5, as from 14 April 2000 (in relation to England and Wales), and 1 January 2001 (in relation to Scotland).

Sub-s (6): added by CA 1989, s 56(1), (5), as from 21 February 1990; words in square brackets added by the Criminal Justice and Police Act 2001, s 70, Sch 2, Pt 2, para 17, as from 1 April 2003; whole subsection substituted by the Companies Act 2006, s 1038(1), as from 1 October 2007, with effect where an inspector is appointed under a provision of Pt 14 of this Act on or after that date, as follows—

"(6) In this section "document" includes information recorded in any form.

(7) The power under this section to require production of a document includes power, in the case of a document not in hard copy form, to require the production of a copy of the document—

(a) in hard copy form, or

(b) in a form from which a hard copy can be readily obtained.

(8) An inspector may take copies of or extracts from a document produced in pursuance of this section.".

Application to limited liability partnerships: see the Limited Liability Partnerships Regulations 2001, SI 2001/1090, reg 4(1), Sch 2, Pt 1 at **[6985]**, **[6993]**. Note also that nothing in the draft Companies Act 2006 (Commencement No 3, Consequential Amendments, Transitional Provisions and Savings) Order 2007 affects any provision of this Act as applied by the 2001 Regulations to LLPs (see art 12(2) at **[A12]** and the introductory notes to this Act).

Solicitors: the reference to a solicitor in sub-s (4) includes a reference to a recognised body within the meaning of the Administration of Justice Act 1985, s 9; see the Solicitors' Incorporated Practices Order 1991, SI 1991/2684, arts 2–5, Sch 1.

435 (*Repealed by CA 1989, s 212, Sch 24, as from 21 February 1990.*)

436 Obstruction of inspectors treated as contempt of court

[(1) If any person—

(a) fails to comply with section 434(1)(a) or (c),

(b) refuses to comply with a requirement under section 434(1)(b) or (2), or

(c) refuses to answer any question put to him by the inspectors for the purposes of the investigation,

the inspectors may certify that fact in writing to the court.]

(3) The court may thereupon enquire into the case; and, after hearing any witnesses who may be produced against or on behalf of the alleged offender and after hearing any statement which may be offered in defence, the court may punish the offender in like manner as if he had been guilty of contempt of the court.

[470]

NOTES

Sub-s (1): substituted, for original sub-ss (1), (2), by CA 1989, s 56(6), as from 21 February 1990.

Application to limited liability partnerships: see the Limited Liability Partnerships Regulations 2001, SI 2001/1090, reg 4(1), Sch 2, Pt 1 at **[6985]**, **[6993]**.

437 Inspectors' reports

(1) The inspectors may, and if so directed by the Secretary of State shall, make interim reports to the Secretary of State, and on the conclusion of their investigation shall make a final report to him.

Any such report shall be written or printed, as the Secretary of State directs.

[(1A) Any persons who have been appointed under section 431 or 432 may at any time and, if the Secretary of State directs them to do so, shall inform him of any matters coming to their knowledge as a result of their investigations.]

[(1B) If it appears to the Secretary of State that matters have come to light in the course of the inspectors' investigation which suggest that a criminal offence has been committed, and those matters have been referred to the appropriate prosecuting authority, he may direct the inspectors to take no further steps in the investigation or to take only such further steps as are specified in the direction.

(1C) Where an investigation is the subject of a direction under subsection (1B), the inspectors shall make a final report to the Secretary of State only where—

(a) they were appointed under section 432(1) (appointment in pursuance of an order of the court), or

(b) the Secretary of State directs them to do so.]

(2) If the inspectors were appointed under section 432 in pursuance of an order of the court, the Secretary of State shall furnish a copy of any report of theirs to the court.

(3) In any case the Secretary of State may, if he thinks fit—

(a) forward a copy of any report made by the inspectors to the company's registered office,

(b) furnish a copy on request and on payment of the prescribed fee to—

(i) any member of the company or other body corporate which is the subject of the report,

(ii) any person whose conduct is referred to in the report,

(iii) the auditors of that company or body corporate,

(iv) the applicants for the investigation,

(v) any other person whose financial interests appear to the Secretary of State to be affected by the matters dealt with in the report, whether as a creditor of the company or body corporate, or otherwise, and

(c) cause any such report to be printed and published.

[471]

NOTES

Sub-s (1): words in italics repealed by the Companies Act 2006, ss 1035(4)(a) 1295, Sch 16, as from 1 October 2007, with effect where an inspector is appointed under a provision of Pt 14 of this Act on or after that date.

Sub-s (1A): inserted by FSA 1986, s 182, Sch 13, para 7, as from 15 November 1986 (for the purposes of anything done or which may be done under, or by virtue of, any provision brought into force by the Financial Services Act 1986 (Commencement No 1) Order 1986, SI 1986/1940), and as from 27 November 1986 (otherwise).

Sub-ss (1B), (1C): inserted by CA 1989, s 57, as from 21 February 1990; repealed by the Companies Act 2006, ss 1035(4)(b) 1295, Sch 16, as from 1 October 2007, with effect where an inspector is appointed under a provision of Pt 14 of this Act on or after that date.

Application to limited liability partnerships: see the Limited Liability Partnerships Regulations 2001, SI 2001/1090, reg 4(1), Sch 2, Pt 1 at **[6985]**, **[6993]**. Note also that nothing in the draft Companies Act 2006 (Commencement No 3, Consequential Amendments, Transitional Provisions and Savings) Order 2007 affects any provision of this Act as applied by the 2001 Regulations to LLPs (see art 12(2) at **[A12]** and the introductory notes to this Act).

Fees: see Appendix 3 (Fees Instruments) at **[A3]**.

438 Power to bring civil proceedings on company's behalf

(1) [If from any report made or information obtained under this Part it appears to the Secretary of State] that any civil proceedings ought in the public interest to be brought by any body corporate, he may himself bring such proceedings in the name and on behalf of the body corporate.

(2) The Secretary of State shall indemnify the body corporate against any costs or expenses incurred by it in or in connection with proceedings brought under this section.

[472]

NOTES

Repealed by the Companies Act 2006, ss 1176(1), (4), 1295, Sch 16, as from 6 April 2007, except in relation to proceedings brought under this section before that date. See also the final note below.

Sub-s (1): words in square brackets substituted by CA 1989, s 58, as from 21 February 1990.

Application to limited liability partnerships: see the Limited Liability Partnerships Regulations 2001, SI 2001/1090, reg 4(1), Sch 2, Pt 1 at **[6985]**, **[6993]**. Note also that nothing in the Companies Act 2006 (Commencement No 1, Transitional Provisions and Savings) Order 2006, SI 2006/3428 affects any provision of this Act as applied by the 2001 Regulations to LLPs (see art 8(2) at **[7581]** and the introductory notes to this Act).

439 Expenses of investigating a company's affairs

[(1) The expenses of an investigation under any of the powers conferred by this Part shall be defrayed in the first instance by the Secretary of State, but he may recover those expenses from the persons liable in accordance with this section.

There shall be treated as expenses of the investigation, in particular, such reasonable sums as the Secretary of State may determine in respect of general staff costs and overheads.]

(2) A person who is convicted on a prosecution instituted as a result of the investigation, *or is ordered to pay the whole or any part of the costs of proceedings brought under section 438,* may in the same proceedings be ordered to pay those expenses to such extent as may be specified in the order.

(3) A body corporate in whose name proceedings are brought under that section is liable to the amount or value of any sums or property recovered by it as a result of those proceedings; and any amount for which a body corporate is liable under this subsection is a first charge on the sums or property recovered.

(4) A body corporate dealt with by [an inspectors' report], where the inspectors were appointed otherwise than of the Secretary of State's own motion, is liable except where it was the applicant for the investigation, and except so far as the Secretary of State otherwise directs.

[(5) Where inspectors were appointed—

(a) under section 431, or

(b) on an application under section 442(3),

the applicant or applicants for the investigation is or are liable to such extent (if any) as the Secretary of State may direct.]

(6) The report of inspectors appointed otherwise than of the Secretary of State's own motion may, if they think fit, and shall if the Secretary of State so directs, include a recommendation as to the directions (if any) which they think appropriate, in the light of their investigation, to be given under subsection (4) or (5) of this section.

(7) For purposes of this section, any costs or expenses incurred by the Secretary of State in or in connection with proceedings brought under section 438 (including expenses incurred under subsection (2) of it) are to be treated as expenses of the investigation giving rise to the proceedings.

(8) Any liability to repay the Secretary of State imposed by [subsection (2)] above is (subject to satisfaction of his right to repayment) a liability also to indemnify all persons against liability under subsections (4) and (5)*; and any such liability imposed by subsection (2) is (subject as mentioned above) a liability also to indemnify all persons against liability under subsection (3)*.

(9) A person liable under any one of those subsections is entitled to contribution from any other person liable under the same subsection, according to the amount of their respective liabilities under it.

(10) Expenses to be defrayed by the Secretary of State under this section shall, so far as not recovered under it, be paid out of money provided by Parliament.

[473]

NOTES

Sub-ss (1), (5): substituted by CA 1989, s 59(1), (2), (4), as from 21 February 1990.

Sub-s (2): words in italics repealed by the Companies Act 2006, ss 1176(2)(a), (4), 1295, Sch 16, as from 6 April 2007, except in relation to proceedings brought under s 438 before that date.

Sub-ss (3), (7): repealed by the Companies Act 2006, ss 1176(2)(b), (4), 1295, Sch 16, as from 6 April 2007, except in relation to proceedings brought under s 438 before that date.

Sub-s (4): words in square brackets substituted by CA 1989, s 59(1), (3), as from 21 February 1990.

Sub-s (8): words in square brackets substituted (for the original words "subsections (2) and (3)"), and words in italics repealed, by the Companies Act 2006, ss 1176(2)(c), (4), 1295, Sch 16, as from 6 April 2007, except in relation to proceedings brought under s 438 before that date.

Application to limited liability partnerships: see the Limited Liability Partnerships Regulations 2001, SI 2001/1090, reg 4(1), Sch 2, Pt 1 at **[6985]**, **[6993]**. Note also that nothing in the Companies Act 2006 (Commencement No 1, Transitional Provisions and Savings) Order 2006, SI 2006/3428 affects any provision of this Act as applied by the 2001 Regulations to LLPs (see art 8(2) at **[7581]** and the introductory notes to this Act).

440 (*Repealed by CA 1989, ss 60(1), 212, Sch 24, as from 21 February 1990.*)

441 Inspectors' report to be evidence

(1) A copy of any report of inspectors appointed under [this Part], certified by the Secretary of State to be a true copy, is admissible in any legal proceedings as evidence of the opinion of the inspectors in relation to any matter contained in the report [and, in proceedings on an application under [section 8 of the Company Directors Disqualification Act 1986], as evidence of any fact stated therein].

(2) A document purporting to be such a certificate as is mentioned above shall be received in evidence and be deemed to be such a certificate, unless the contrary is proved.

[474]

NOTES

Sub-s (1): words in first pair of square brackets substituted by CA 1989, s 61, as from 21 February 1990; words in second (outer) pair of square brackets added by the Insolvency Act 1985, s 109, Sch 6, para 3, as from 29 December 1986; words in third (inner) pair of square brackets substituted by the Insolvency Act 1986, s 439(1), Sch 13, Pt I, as from 29 December 1986.

Application to limited liability partnerships: see the Limited Liability Partnerships Regulations 2001, SI 2001/1090, reg 4(1), Sch 2, Pt 1 at **[6985]**, **[6993]**.

Other powers of investigation available to the Secretary of State

442 Power to investigate company ownership

(1) Where it appears to the Secretary of State that there is good reason to do so, he may appoint one or more competent inspectors to investigate and report on the membership of any company, and otherwise with respect to the company, for the purpose of determining the true persons who are or have been financially interested in the success or failure (real or apparent) of the company or able to control or materially to influence its policy.

(2) *The appointment of inspectors under this section may define the scope of their investigation (whether as respects the matter or the period to which it is to extend or otherwise) and in particular may limit the investigation to matters connected with particular shares or debentures.*

[(3) If an application for investigation under this section with respect to particular shares or debentures of a company is made to the Secretary of State by members of the company, and the number of applicants or the amount of shares held by them is not less than that required for an application for the appointment of inspectors under section 431(2)(a) or (b), then, subject to the following provisions, the Secretary of State shall appoint inspectors to conduct the investigation applied for.

(3A) The Secretary of State shall not appoint inspectors if he is satisfied that the application is vexatious; and where inspectors are appointed their terms of appointment shall exclude any matter in so far as the Secretary of State is satisfied that it is unreasonable for it to be investigated.

(3B) The Secretary of State may, before appointing inspectors, require the applicant or applicants to give security, to an amount not exceeding £5,000, or such other sum as he may by order specify, for payment of the costs of the investigation.

An order under this subsection shall be made by statutory instrument which shall be subject to annulment in pursuance of a resolution of either House of Parliament.

(3C) If on an application under subsection (3) it appears to the Secretary of State that the powers conferred by section 444 are sufficient for the purposes of investigating the matters which inspectors would be appointed to investigate, he may instead conduct the investigation under that section.]

(4) Subject to the terms of their appointment, the inspectors' powers extend to the investigation of any circumstances suggesting the existence of an arrangement or understanding which, though not legally binding, is or was observed or likely to be observed in practice and which is relevant to the purposes of the investigation.

[475]

NOTES

Sub-s (2): repealed by the Companies Act 2006, ss 1035(5), 1295, Sch 16, as from 1 October 2007, with effect where an inspector is appointed under a provision of Pt 14 of this Act on or after that date.

Sub-ss (3), (3A)–(3C): substituted, for original sub-s (3), by CA 1989, s 62, as from 21 February 1990.

443 Provisions applicable on investigation under s 442

(1) For purposes of an investigation under section 442, sections 433(1), 434, 436 and 437 apply with the necessary modifications of references to the affairs of the company or to those of any other body corporate, subject however to the following subsections.

(2) Those sections apply to—

(a) all persons who are or have been, or whom the inspector has reasonable cause to believe to be or have been, financially interested in the success or failure or the apparent success or failure of the company or any other body corporate whose membership is investigated with that of the company, or able to control or materially influence its policy (including persons concerned only on behalf of others), and

(b) any other person whom the inspector has reasonable cause to believe possesses information relevant to the investigation,

as they apply in relation to officers and agents of the company or the other body corporate (as the case may be).

(3) If the Secretary of State is of opinion that there is good reason for not divulging any part of a report made by virtue of section 442 and this section, he may under section 437 disclose the report with the omission of that part; and he may cause to be kept by the registrar of companies a copy of the report with that part omitted or, in the case of any other such report, a copy of the whole report.

(4) …

[476]

NOTES

Sub-s (4): repealed by CA 1989, s 212, Sch 24, as from 21 February 1990.

444 Power to obtain information as to those interested in shares, etc

(1) If it appears to the Secretary of State that there is good reason to investigate the ownership of any shares in or debentures of a company and that it is unnecessary to appoint inspectors for the purpose, he may require any person whom he has reasonable cause to believe to have or to be able to obtain any information as to the present and past interests in those shares or debentures and the names and addresses of the persons interested and of any persons who act or have acted on their behalf in relation to the shares or debentures to give any such information to the Secretary of State.

(2) For this purpose a person is deemed to have an interest in shares or debentures if he has any right to acquire or dispose of them or of any interest in them, or to vote in respect of them, or if his consent is necessary for the exercise of any of the rights of other persons interested in them, or if other persons interested in them can be required, or are accustomed, to exercise their rights in accordance with his instructions.

(3) A person who fails to give information required of him under this section, or who in giving such information makes any statement which he knows to be false in a material particular, or recklessly makes any statement which is false in a material particular, *is liable to imprisonment or a fine, or both.*

[(4) A person guilty of an offence under this section is liable—

(a) on conviction on indictment, to imprisonment for a term not exceeding two years or a fine (or both);

(b) on summary conviction—

(i) in England and Wales, to imprisonment for a term not exceeding twelve months or to a fine not exceeding the statutory maximum (or both) and, for continued contravention, a daily default fine not exceeding one- fiftieth of the statutory maximum;

(ii) in Scotland or Northern Ireland, to imprisonment for a term not exceeding six months, or to a fine not exceeding the statutory maximum (or both) and, for continued contravention, a daily default fine not exceeding one-fiftieth of the statutory maximum.]

[477]

NOTES

Sub-s (3): for the words in italics there are substituted the words "commits an offence" by the Companies Act 2006, s 1124, Sch 3, para 1(1), as from 1 October 2007.

Sub-s (4): added by the Companies Act 2006, s 1124, Sch 3, para 1(2), as from 1 October 2007 (see further the note below).

Transitional adaptations: art 6 of the draft Companies Act 2006 (Commencement No 3, Consequential Amendments, Transitional Provisions and Savings) Order 2007 provides that the provisions brought into force by that Order shall have effect subject to any transitional adaptations specified in Sch 1 to that Order. Schedule 1, para 20 to the Order (at **[A12]**) provides that in the sub-s (4) added to this section the words "or Northern Ireland" should be omitted from sub-para (b)(ii).

445 Power to impose restrictions on shares and debentures

(1) If in connection with an investigation under either section 442 or 444 it appears to the Secretary of State that there is difficulty in finding out the relevant facts about any shares (whether issued or to be issued), he may by order direct that the shares shall until further order be subject to the restrictions of Part XV of this Act.

[(1A) If the Secretary of State is satisfied that an order under subsection (1) may unfairly affect the rights of third parties in respect of shares then the Secretary of State, for the purpose of protecting such rights and subject to such terms as he thinks fit, may direct that such acts by such persons or descriptions of persons and for such purposes as may be set out in the order, shall not constitute a breach of the restrictions of Part XV of this Act.]

(2) This section, and Part XV in its application to orders under it, apply in relation to debentures as in relation to shares [save that subsection (1A) shall not so apply].

[478]

NOTES

Sub-s (1A): inserted by the Companies (Disclosure of Interests in Shares) (Orders imposing restrictions on shares) Regulations 1991, SI 1991/1646, reg 5(a), as from 18 July 1991.

Sub-s (2): words in square brackets added by SI 1991/1646, reg 5(b), as from 18 July 1991.

446 Investigation of share dealings

(1) If it appears to the Secretary of State that there are circumstances suggesting that contraventions may have occurred, in relation to a company's shares or debentures, of section 323 or 324 (taken with Schedule 13), or of subsections (3) to (5) of section 328 (restrictions on share dealings by directors and their families; obligation of director to disclose shareholding in his own company), he may appoint one or more competent inspectors to carry out such investigations as are requisite to establish whether or not such contraventions have occurred and to report the result of their investigations to him.

(2) The appointment of inspectors under this section may limit the period to which their investigation is to extend or confine it to shares or debentures of a particular class, or both.

(3) For purposes of an investigation under this section, sections 434 [to 437] apply—

(a) with the substitution, for references to any other body corporate whose affairs are investigated under section 433(1), of a reference to any other body corporate which is, or has at any relevant time been, the company's subsidiary or holding company, or a subsidiary of its holding company, …

(b) …

[(4) Sections 434 to 436 apply for the purposes of an investigation under this section to the following persons as they apply to officers of the company or of the other body corporate—

(a) an authorised person;

(b) a relevant professional;

(c) a person not falling within paragraph (a) or (b) who may carry on a regulated activity without contravening the prohibition imposed by section 19 of the Financial Services and Markets Act 2000; and

(d) in relation to an authorised person, to a relevant professional or to a person falling within paragraph (c)—

(i) if it is a body corporate, any person who is or has been an officer of it;

(ii) if it is a partnership, any person who is or has been a partner in it;

(iii) if it is an unincorporated association, any person who is or has been a member of its governing body or an officer of it.

(4A) In subsection (4)—

"authorised person" has the meaning given in section 31(2) of the Financial Services and Markets Act 2000;

"relevant professional" means a member of a profession in relation to which a body has been designated under section 326(1) of that Act, and, in relation to such a profession, "member" has the meaning given in section 325(2) of that Act.]

(5)–(7) …

[479]

NOTES

Repealed by the Companies Act 2006, s 1295, Sch 16, as from 1 October 2007.

Sub-s (3): words in square brackets substituted by FSA 1986, s 182, Sch 13, para 8, as from 27 November 1986; para (b) repealed by CA 1989, s 212, Sch 24, as from 21 February 1990.

Sub-ss (4), (4A): substituted, for original sub-s (4), by the Financial Services and Markets Act 2000 (Consequential Amendments and Repeals) Order 2001, SI 2001/3649, art 21, as from 1 December 2001.

Sub-ss (5), (6): repealed by FSA 1986, ss 182, 212(3), Sch 13, para 8, Sch 17, Pt I, as from 27 November 1986.

Sub-s (7): repealed by CA 1989, s 212, Sch 24, as from 21 February 1990.

[Powers of Secretary of State to give directions to inspectors

446A General powers to give directions

(1) In exercising his functions an inspector shall comply with any direction given to him by the Secretary of State under this section.

(2) The Secretary of State may give an inspector appointed under section 431, 432(2) or 442(1) a direction—

(a) as to the subject matter of his investigation (whether by reference to a specified area of a company's operation, a specified transaction, a period of time or otherwise), or

(b) which requires the inspector to take or not to take a specified step in his investigation.

(3) The Secretary of State may give an inspector appointed under any provision of this Part a direction requiring him to secure that a specified report under section 437—

(a) includes the inspector's views on a specified matter,
(b) does not include any reference to a specified matter,
(c) is made in a specified form or manner, or
(d) is made by a specified date.

(4) A direction under this section—

(a) may be given on an inspector's appointment,
(b) may vary or revoke a direction previously given, and
(c) may be given at the request of an inspector.

(5) In this section—

(a) a reference to an inspector's investigation includes any investigation he undertakes, or could undertake, under section 433(1) (power to investigate affairs of holding company or subsidiary);
(b) "specified" means specified in a direction under this section.]

[479A]

NOTES

Commencement: 1 October 2007 (for effect see below).

Inserted, together with the preceding heading and s 446B, by the Companies Act 2006, s 1035(1), as from 1 October 2007, with effect where an inspector is appointed under a provision of Pt 14 of this Act on or after that date.

[446B Direction to terminate investigation

(1) The Secretary of State may direct an inspector to take no further steps in his investigation.

(2) The Secretary of State may give a direction under this section to an inspector appointed under section 432(1) or 442(3) only on the grounds that it appears to him that—

(a) matters have come to light in the course of the inspector's investigation which suggest that a criminal offence has been committed, and

(b) those matters have been referred to the appropriate prosecuting authority.

(3) Where the Secretary of State gives a direction under this section, any direction already given to the inspector under section 437(1) to produce an interim report, and any direction given to him under section 446A(3) in relation to such a report, shall cease to have effect.

(4) Where the Secretary of State gives a direction under this section, the inspector shall not make a final report to the Secretary of State unless—

(a) the direction was made on the grounds mentioned in subsection (2) and the Secretary of State directs the inspector to make a final report to him, or

(b) the inspector was appointed under section 432(1) (appointment in pursuance of order of the court).

(5) An inspector shall comply with any direction given to him under this section.

(6) In this section, a reference to an inspector's investigation includes any investigation he undertakes, or could undertake, under section 433(1) (power to investigate affairs of holding company or subsidiary).]

[479B]

NOTES

Commencement: 1 October 2007 (for effect see s 446A at **[479A]**).

Inserted as noted to s 446A at **[479A]**.

[Resignation, removal and replacement of inspectors

446C Resignation and revocation of appointment

(1) An inspector may resign by notice in writing to the Secretary of State.

(2) The Secretary of State may revoke the appointment of an inspector by notice in writing to the inspector.]

[479C]

NOTES

Commencement: 1 October 2007 (for effect see below).

Inserted, together with the preceding heading and s 446D, by the Companies Act 2006, s 1036, as from 1 October 2007, with effect where an inspector is appointed under a provision of Pt 14 of this Act on or after that date.

[446D Appointment of replacement inspectors

(1) Where—

(a) an inspector resigns,

(b) an inspector's appointment is revoked, or

(c) an inspector dies,

the Secretary of State may appoint one or more competent inspectors to continue the investigation.

(2) An appointment under subsection (1) shall be treated for the purposes of this Part (apart from this section) as an appointment under the provision of this Part under which the former inspector was appointed.

(3) The Secretary of State must exercise his power under subsection (1) so as to secure that at least one inspector continues the investigation.

(4) Subsection (3) does not apply if—

(a) the Secretary of State could give any replacement inspector a direction under section 446B (termination of investigation), and

(b) such a direction would (under subsection (4) of that section) result in a final report not being made.

(5) In this section, references to an investigation include any investigation the former inspector conducted under section 433(1) (power to investigate affairs of holding company or subsidiary).]

[479D]

NOTES

Commencement: 1 October 2007 (for effect see s 446C at **[479C]**).

Inserted as noted to s 446C at **[479C]**.

[Power to obtain information from former inspectors etc

446E Obtaining information from former inspectors etc

(1) This section applies to a person who was appointed as an inspector under this Part—

(a) who has resigned, or

(b) whose appointment has been revoked.

(2) This section also applies to an inspector to whom the Secretary of State has given a direction under section 446B (termination of investigation).

(3) The Secretary of State may direct a person to whom this section applies to produce documents obtained or generated by that person during the course of his investigation to—

(a) the Secretary of State, or

(b) an inspector appointed under this Part.

(4) The power under subsection (3) to require production of a document includes power, in the case of a document not in hard copy form, to require the production of a copy of the document—

(a) in hard copy form, or

(b) in a form from which a hard copy can be readily obtained.

(5) The Secretary of State may take copies of or extracts from a document produced in pursuance of this section.

(6) The Secretary of State may direct a person to whom this section applies to inform him of any matters that came to that person's knowledge as a result of his investigation.

(7) A person shall comply with any direction given to him under this section.

(8) In this section—

(a) references to the investigation of a former inspector or inspector include any investigation he conducted under section 433(1) (power to investigate affairs of holding company or subsidiary), and

(b) "document" includes information recorded in any form.]

[479E]

NOTES

Commencement: 1 October 2007 (for effect see below).

Inserted, together with the preceding heading, by the Companies Act 2006, s 1037(1), as from 1 October 2007, with effect where an inspector is appointed under a provision of Pt 14 of this Act on or after that date.

Requisition and seizure of books and papers

[447 Power to require documents and information

(1) The Secretary of State may act under subsections (2) and (3) in relation to a company.

(2) The Secretary of State may give directions to the company requiring it—

(a) to produce such documents (or documents of such description) as may be specified in the directions;

(b) to provide such information (or information of such description) as may be so specified.

(3) The Secretary of State may authorise a person (an investigator) to require the company or any other person—

(a) to produce such documents (or documents of such description) as the investigator may specify;

(b) to provide such information (or information of such description) as the investigator may specify.

(4) A person on whom a requirement under subsection (3) is imposed may require the investigator to produce evidence of his authority.

(5) A requirement under subsection (2) or (3) must be complied with at such time and place as may be specified in the directions or by the investigator (as the case may be).

(6) The production of a document in pursuance of this section does not affect any lien which a person has on the document.

(7) The Secretary of State or the investigator (as the case may be) may take copies of or extracts from a document produced in pursuance of this section.

(8) A "document" includes information recorded in any form.

(9) In relation to information recorded otherwise than in legible form, the power to require production of it includes power to require the production of a copy of it in legible form or in a form from which it can readily be produced in visible and legible form.]

[480]

NOTES

Substituted by the Companies (Audit, Investigations and Community Enterprise) Act 2004, s 21, as from 6 April 2005 (for transitional provisions see the Companies (Audit, Investigations and Community Enterprise) Act 2004 (Commencement) and Companies Act 1989 (Commencement No 18) Order 2004, SI 2004/3322, arts 6–13 at **[7344]–[7351]**).

Sub-s (9): substituted by the Companies Act 2006, s 1038(2), as from 1 October 2007, with effect where an inspector is appointed under a provision of Pt 14 of this Act on or after that date, as follows—

"(9) The power under this section to require production of a document includes power, in the case of a document not in hard copy form, to require the production of a copy of the document—

(a) in hard copy form, or
(b) in a form from which a hard copy can be readily obtained.".

Application to limited liability partnerships: see the Limited Liability Partnerships Regulations 2001, SI 2001/1090, reg 4(1), Sch 2, Pt 1 at **[6985]**, **[6993]**. Note also that nothing in the draft Companies Act 2006 (Commencement No 3, Consequential Amendments, Transitional Provisions and Savings) Order 2007 affects any provision of this Act as applied by the 2001 Regulations to LLPs (see art 12(2) at **[A12]** and the introductory notes to this Act).

[447A Information provided: evidence

(1) A statement made by a person in compliance with a requirement under section 447 may be used in evidence against him.

(2) But in criminal proceedings in which the person is charged with a relevant offence—
(a) no evidence relating to the statement may be adduced by or on behalf of the prosecution, and
(b) no question relating to it may be asked by or on behalf of the prosecution,

unless evidence relating to it is adduced or a question relating to it is asked in the proceedings by or on behalf of that person.

(3) A relevant offence is any offence other than the following—
(a) an offence under section 451,
(b) an offence under section 5 of the Perjury Act 1911 (false statement made otherwise than on oath), or
(c) an offence under section 44(2) of the Criminal Law (Consolidation) (Scotland) Act 1995 (false statement made otherwise than on oath).]

[480A]

NOTES

Inserted by the Companies (Audit, Investigations and Community Enterprise) Act 2004, s 25, Sch 2, Pt 3, paras 16, 17, as from 6 April 2005 (for transitional provisions see the Companies (Audit, Investigations and Community Enterprise) Act 2004 (Commencement) and Companies Act 1989 (Commencement No 18) Order 2004, SI 2004/3322, art 9 at **[7347]**).

Application to limited liability partnerships: see the draft Limited Liability Partnerships (Amendment) Regulations 2007 in Appendix 10 at **[A10]**. Those draft Regulations amend the Limited Liability Partnerships Regulations 2001, SI 2001/1090, Sch 2, Pt 1 at **[6993]** by adding an entry for this section into that Schedule.

[448 Entry and search of premises

(1) A justice of the peace may issue a warrant under this section if satisfied on information on oath given by or on behalf of the Secretary of State, or by a person appointed or authorised to exercise powers under this Part, that there are reasonable grounds for believing that there are on any premises documents whose production has been required under this Part and which have not been produced in compliance with the requirement.

(2) A justice of the peace may also issue a warrant under this section if satisfied on information on oath given by or on behalf of the Secretary of State, or by a person appointed or authorised to exercise powers under this Part—
(a) that there are reasonable grounds for believing that an offence has been committed for which the penalty on conviction on indictment is imprisonment for a term of not less than two years and that there are on any premises documents relating to whether the offence has been committed,
(b) that the Secretary of State, or the person so appointed or authorised, has power to require the production of the documents under this Part, and
(c) that there are reasonable grounds for believing that if production was so required the documents would not be produced but would be removed from the premises, hidden, tampered with or destroyed.

(3) A warrant under this section shall authorise a constable, together with any other person named in it and any other constables—
(a) to enter the premises specified in the information, using such force as is reasonably necessary for the purpose;
(b) to search the premises and take possession of any documents appearing to be such documents as are mentioned in subsection (1) or (2), as the case may be, or to take, in relation to any such documents, any other steps which may appear to be necessary for preserving them or preventing interference with them;

(c) to take copies of any such documents; and

(d) to require any person named in the warrant to provide an explanation of them or to state where they may be found.

(4) If in the case of a warrant under subsection (2) the justice of the peace is satisfied on information on oath that there are reasonable grounds for believing that there are also on the premises other documents relevant to the investigation, the warrant shall also authorise the actions mentioned in subsection (3) to be taken in relation to such documents.

(5) A warrant under this section shall continue in force until the end of the period of one month beginning with the day on which it is issued.

(6) Any documents of which possession is taken under this section may be retained—

(a) for a period of three months; or

(b) if within that period proceedings to which the documents are relevant are commenced against any person for any criminal offence, until the conclusion of those proceedings.

(7) Any person who intentionally obstructs the exercise of any rights conferred by a warrant issued under this section or fails without reasonable excuse to comply with any requirement imposed in accordance with subsection (3)(d) is guilty of an offence *and liable to a fine*.

Sections 732 (restriction on prosecutions), 733 (liability of individuals for corporate default) and 734 (criminal proceedings against unincorporated bodies) apply to this offence.

[(7A) A person guilty of an offence under this section is liable—

(a) on conviction on indictment, to a fine;

(b) on summary conviction, to a fine not exceeding the statutory maximum.]

(8) For the purposes of sections 449 and 451A (provision for security of information) documents obtained under this section shall be treated as if they had been obtained under the provision of this Part under which their production was or, as the case may be, could have been required.

(9) In the application of this section to Scotland for the references to a justice of the peace substitute references to a justice of the peace or a sheriff, and for the references to information on oath substitute references to evidence on oath.

(10) In this section "document" includes information recorded in any form.]

[481]

NOTES

Substituted by CA 1989, s 64(1), as from 21 February 1990.

Sub-s (7): words in italics repealed by the Companies Act 2006, ss 1124, 1295, Sch 3, para 2(1), Sch 16, as from 1 October 2007.

Sub-s (7A): inserted by the Companies Act 2006, s 1124, Sch 3, para 2(2), as from 1 October 2007.

Application to limited liability partnerships: see the Limited Liability Partnerships Regulations 2001, SI 2001/1090, reg 4(1), Sch 2, Pt 1 at **[6985]**, **[6993]**. Note also that nothing in the draft Companies Act 2006 (Commencement No 3, Consequential Amendments, Transitional Provisions and Savings) Order 2007 affects any provision of this Act as applied by the 2001 Regulations to LLPs (see art 12(2) at **[A12]** and the introductory notes to this Act).

Take possession of, etc: the power of seizure conferred by sub-s (3) is a power to which Criminal Justice and Police Act 2001, s 50 applies (additional powers of seizure from premises); see s 50 of, and Sch 1, Pt 1, para 35 to, that Act.

[448A Protection in relation to certain disclosures: information provided to Secretary of State

(1) A person who makes a relevant disclosure is not liable by reason only of that disclosure in any proceedings relating to a breach of an obligation of confidence.

(2) A relevant disclosure is a disclosure which satisfies each of the following conditions—

(a) it is made to the Secretary of State otherwise than in compliance with a requirement under this Part;

(b) it is of a kind that the person making the disclosure could be required to make in pursuance of this Part;

(c) the person who makes the disclosure does so in good faith and in the reasonable belief that the disclosure is capable of assisting the Secretary of State for the purposes of the exercise of his functions under this Part;

(d) the information disclosed is not more than is reasonably necessary for the purpose of assisting the Secretary of State for the purposes of the exercise of those functions;

(e) the disclosure is not one falling within subsection (3) or (4).

(3) A disclosure falls within this subsection if the disclosure is prohibited by virtue of any enactment.

(4) A disclosure falls within this subsection if—

(a) it is made by a person carrying on the business of banking or by a lawyer, and

(b) it involves the disclosure of information in respect of which he owes an obligation of confidence in that capacity.

(5) An enactment includes an enactment—

(a) comprised in, or in an instrument made under, an Act of the Scottish Parliament;

(b) comprised in subordinate legislation (within the meaning of the Interpretation Act 1978);

(c) whenever passed or made.]

[481A]

NOTES

Inserted by the Companies (Audit, Investigations and Community Enterprise) Act 2004, s 22, as from 6 April 2005.

Application to limited liability partnerships: see the draft Limited Liability Partnerships (Amendment) Regulations 2007 in Appendix 10 at **[A10]**. Those draft Regulations amend the Limited Liability Partnerships Regulations 2001, SI 2001/1090, Sch 2, Pt 1 at **[6993]** by adding an entry for this section into that Schedule.

[449 Provision for security of information obtained

(1) This section applies to information (in whatever form) obtained—

(a) in pursuance of a requirement imposed under section 447;

(b) by means of a relevant disclosure within the meaning of section 448A(2);

(c) by an investigator in consequence of the exercise of his powers under section 453A.

(2) Such information must not be disclosed unless the disclosure—

(a) is made to a person specified in Schedule 15C, or

(b) is of a description specified in Schedule 15D.

(3) The Secretary of State may by order amend Schedules 15C and 15D.

(4) An order under subsection (3) must not—

(a) amend Schedule 15C by specifying a person unless the person exercises functions of a public nature (whether or not he exercises any other function);

(b) amend Schedule 15D by adding or modifying a description of disclosure unless the purpose for which the disclosure is permitted is likely to facilitate the exercise of a function of a public nature.

(5) An order under subsection (3) must be made by statutory instrument subject to annulment in pursuance of a resolution of either House of Parliament.

(6) A person who discloses any information in contravention of this section—

(a) is guilty of an offence, and

(b) is liable on conviction to imprisonment or a fine or to both.

[(6A) A person guilty of an offence under this section is liable—

(a) on conviction on indictment, to imprisonment for a term not exceeding two years or a fine (or both);

(b) on summary conviction—

(i) in England and Wales, to imprisonment for a term not exceeding twelve months or to a fine not exceeding the statutory maximum (or both);

(ii) in Scotland or Northern Ireland, to imprisonment for a term not exceeding six months, or to a fine not exceeding the statutory maximum (or both).]

(7) Sections 732 (restriction on prosecutions), 733 (liability of individuals for corporate default) and 734 (criminal proceedings against unincorporated bodies) apply to the offence under subsection (6).

(8) Any information which may by virtue of this section be disclosed to a person specified in Schedule 15C may be disclosed to any officer or employee of the person.

(9) This section does not prohibit the disclosure of information if the information is or has been available to the public from any other source.

(10) For the purposes of this section, information obtained by an investigator in consequence of the exercise of his powers under section 453A includes information obtained by a person accompanying the investigator in pursuance of subsection (4) of that section in consequence of that person's accompanying the investigator.

(11) Nothing in this section authorises the making of a disclosure in contravention of the Data Protection Act 1998.]

[482]

NOTES

Substituted by the Companies (Audit, Investigations and Community Enterprise) Act 2004, s 25, Sch 2, Pt 3, paras 16, 18, as from 6 April 2005 (for transitional provisions, see the Companies (Audit, Investigations and Community Enterprise) Act 2004 (Commencement) and Companies Act 1989 (Commencement No 18) Order 2004, SI 2004/3322, art 10 at **[7348]**).

Sub-s (6): for the words in italics there are substituted the words "is guilty of an offence" by the Companies Act 2006, s 1124, Sch 3, para 3(1), (2), as from 1 October 2007.

Sub-s (6A): inserted by the Companies Act 2006, s 1124, Sch 3, para 3(1), (3), as from 1 October 2007 (see further the transitional adaptations note below).

Sub-s (7): repealed by the Companies Act 2006, ss 1124, 1295, Sch 3, para 3(1), (4), Sch 16, as from 1 October 2007.

Transitional adaptations: art 6 of the draft Companies Act 2006 (Commencement No 3, Consequential Amendments, Transitional Provisions and Savings) Order 2007 provides that the provisions brought into force by that Order shall have effect subject to any transitional adaptations specified in Sch 1 to that Order. Schedule 1, para 20 to the Order (at **[A12]**) provides that in the sub-s (6A) added to this section the words "or Northern Ireland" should be omitted from sub-para (b)(ii).

Application to limited liability partnerships: see the Limited Liability Partnerships Regulations 2001, SI 2001/1090, reg 4(1), Sch 2, Pt 1 at **[6985]**, **[6993]**. Note also that nothing in the draft Companies Act 2006 (Commencement No 3, Consequential Amendments, Transitional Provisions and Savings) Order 2007 affects any provision of this Act as applied by the 2001 Regulations to LLPs (see art 12(2) at **[A12]** and the introductory notes to this Act).

Orders: the Companies (Disclosure of Information) (Designated Authorities) Order 2006, SI 2006/1644.

450 Punishment for destroying, mutilating etc company documents

(1) [An officer of a company …] … who—

(a) destroys, mutilates or falsifies, or is privy to the destruction, mutilation or falsification of a document affecting or relating to the [company's] property or affairs, or

(b) makes, or is privy to the making of, a false entry in such a document,

is guilty of an offence, unless he proves that he had no intention to conceal the state of affairs of [the company] or to defeat the law.

[(1A) Subsection (1) applies to an officer of an authorised insurance company which is not a body corporate as it applies to an officer of a company.]

(2) Such a person as above mentioned who fraudulently either parts with, alters or makes an omission in any such document or is privy to fraudulent parting with, fraudulent altering or fraudulent making of an omission in, any such document, is guilty of an offence.

(3) A person guilty of an offence under this section is liable to imprisonment or a fine, or both.

[(4) Sections 732 (restriction on prosecutions), 733 (liability of individuals for corporate default) and 734 (criminal proceedings against unincorporated bodies) apply to an offence under this section.]

[(5) In this section "document" includes information recorded in any form.]

[483]

NOTES

Sub-s (1): words in square brackets substituted by CA 1989, s 66(1), (2), as from 21 February 1990; words omitted repealed by the Financial Services and Markets Act 2000 (Consequential Amendments and Repeals) Order 2001, SI 2001/3649, art 23(1), (2), as from 1 December 2001.

Sub-s (1A): inserted by SI 2001/3649, art 22(1), (3), as from 1 December 2001.

Sub-s (3): substituted by the Companies Act 2006, s 1124, Sch 3, para 4(1), as from 1 October 2007, as follows (see also the transitional adaptations note below)—

"(3) A person guilty of an offence under this section is liable—
(a) on conviction on indictment, to imprisonment for a term not exceeding seven years or a fine (or both);
(b) on summary conviction—
(i) in England and Wales, to imprisonment for a term not exceeding twelve months or to a fine not exceeding the statutory maximum (or both);
(ii) in Scotland or Northern Ireland, to imprisonment for a term not exceeding six months, or to a fine not exceeding the statutory maximum (or both).".

Sub-s (4): substituted by CA 1989, s 66(1), (3), as from 21 February 1990; repealed by the Companies Act 2006, ss 1124, 1295, Sch 3, para 4(2), Sch 16, as from 1 October 2007.

Sub-s (5): added by CA 1989, s 66(1), (4), as from 21 February 1990.

Transitional adaptations: art 6 of the draft Companies Act 2006 (Commencement No 3, Consequential Amendments, Transitional Provisions and Savings) Order 2007 provides that the provisions brought into force by that Order shall have effect subject to any transitional adaptations specified in Sch 1 to that Order. Schedule 1, para 20 to the Order (at **[A12]**) provides that in sub-s (3) the words "or Northern Ireland" should be omitted from sub-para (b)(ii).

Application to limited liability partnerships: see the Limited Liability Partnerships Regulations 2001, SI 2001/1090, reg 4(1), Sch 2, Pt 1 at **[6985]**, **[6993]**. Note also that nothing in the draft Companies Act 2006 (Commencement No 3, Consequential Amendments, Transitional Provisions and Savings) Order 2007 affects any provision of this Act as applied by the 2001 Regulations to LLPs (see art 12(2) at **[A12]** and the introductory notes to this Act).

[451 Punishment for furnishing false information

(1) A person commits an offence if in purported compliance with a requirement under section 447 to provide information—

(a) he provides information which he knows to be false in a material particular;

(b) he recklessly provides information which is false in a material particular.

(2) A person guilty of an offence under this section is liable on conviction to imprisonment or a fine or to both.

(3) Sections 732 (restriction on prosecutions), 733 (liability of individuals for corporate default) and 734 (criminal proceedings against unincorporated bodies) apply to an offence under this section.]

[484]

NOTES

Substituted by the Companies (Audit, Investigations and Community Enterprise) Act 2004, s 25, Sch 2, Pt 3, paras 16, 19, as from 6 April 2005 (for transitional provisions, see the Companies (Audit, Investigations and Community Enterprise) Act 2004 (Commencement) and Companies Act 1989 (Commencement No 18) Order 2004, SI 2004/3322, arts 7–9 at **[7345]**–**[7347]**).

Sub-s (2): substituted by the Companies Act 2006, s 1124, Sch 3, para 5(1), as from 1 October 2007, as follows (see also the transitional adaptations note below)—

"(2) A person guilty of an offence under this section is liable—
(a) on conviction on indictment, to imprisonment for a term not exceeding two years or a fine (or both);
(b) on summary conviction—
(i) in England and Wales, to imprisonment for a term not exceeding twelve months or to a fine not exceeding the statutory maximum (or both);
(ii) in Scotland or Northern Ireland, to imprisonment for a term not exceeding six months, or to a fine not exceeding the statutory maximum (or both).".

Sub-s (3): repealed by the Companies Act 2006, ss 1124, 1295, Sch 3, para 5(2), Sch 16, as from 1 October 2007.

Transitional adaptations: art 6 of the draft Companies Act 2006 (Commencement No 3, Consequential Amendments, Transitional Provisions and Savings) Order 2007 provides that the provisions brought into force by that Order shall have effect subject to any transitional adaptations specified in Sch 1 to that Order. Schedule 1, para 20 to the Order (at **[A12]**) provides that in sub-s (2) the words "or Northern Ireland" should be omitted from sub-para (b)(ii).

Application to limited liability partnerships: see the Limited Liability Partnerships Regulations 2001, SI 2001/1090, reg 4(1), Sch 2, Pt 1 at **[6985]**, **[6993]**. Note also that nothing in the draft Companies

Act 2006 (Commencement No 3, Consequential Amendments, Transitional Provisions and Savings) Order 2007 affects any provision of this Act as applied by the 2001 Regulations to LLPs (see art 12(2) at **[A12]** and the introductory notes to this Act).

[451A Disclosure of information by Secretary of State or inspector

[(1) This section applies to information obtained—

(a) under sections 434 to *446*;

(b) by an inspector in consequence of the exercise of his powers under section 453A.]

(2) The Secretary of State may, if he thinks fit—

(a) disclose any information to which this section applies to any person to whom, or for any purpose for which, disclosure is permitted under section 449, or

(b) authorise or require an inspector appointed under this Part to disclose such information to any such person or for any such purpose.

[(3) Information to which this section applies may also be disclosed by an inspector appointed under this Part to—

(a) another inspector appointed under this Part;

(b) a person appointed under—

(i) section 167 of the Financial Services and Markets Act 2000 (general investigations),

(ii) section 168 of that Act (investigations in particular cases),

(iii) section 169(1)(b) of that Act (investigation in support of overseas regulator),

(iv) section 284 of that Act (investigations into affairs of certain collective investment schemes), or

(v) regulations made as a result of section 262(2)(k) of that Act (investigations into open-ended investment companies),

to conduct an investigation; or

(c) a person authorised to exercise powers under—

(i) section 447 of this Act; or

(ii) section 84 of the Companies Act 1989 (exercise of powers to assist overseas regulatory authority).]

(4) Any information which may by virtue of subsection (3) be disclosed to any person may be disclosed to any officer or servant of that person.

(5) The Secretary of State may, if he thinks fit, disclose any information obtained under section 444 to—

(a) the company whose ownership was the subject of the investigation,

(b) any member of the company,

(c) any person whose conduct was investigated in the course of the investigation,

(d) the auditors of the company, or

(e) any person whose financial interests appear to the Secretary of State to be affected by matters covered by the investigation.]

[(6) For the purposes of this section, information obtained by an inspector in consequence of the exercise of his powers under section 453A includes information obtained by a person accompanying the inspector in pursuance of subsection (4) of that section in consequence of that person's accompanying the inspector.

(7) The reference to an inspector in subsection (2)(b) above includes a reference to a person accompanying an inspector in pursuance of section 453A(4).]

[485]

NOTES

Inserted by FSA 1986, s 182, Sch 13, para 10; substituted by CA 1989, s 68, as from 21 February 1990.

Sub-s (1): substituted by the Companies (Audit, Investigations and Community Enterprise) Act 2004, s 25, Sch 2, Pt 3, paras 16, 20(1), (2), as from 6 April 2005; for the figure in italics in para (a) there is substituted the figure "446E" by the Companies Act 2006, s 1037(2), as from 1 October 2007, with effect where an inspector is appointed under a provision of Pt 14 of this Act on or after that date.

Sub-s (3): substituted by the Financial Services and Markets Act 2000 (Consequential Amendments and Repeals) Order 2001, SI 2001/3649, art 24, as from 1 December 2001.

Sub-ss (6), (7): added by the Companies (Audit, Investigations and Community Enterprise) Act 2004, s 25, Sch 2, Pt 3, paras 16, 20(1), (3), as from 6 April 2005.

Application to limited liability partnerships: see the Limited Liability Partnerships Regulations 2001, SI 2001/1090, reg 4(1), Sch 2, Pt 1 at **[6985]**, **[6993]**. Note also that nothing in the draft Companies

Act 2006 (Commencement No 3, Consequential Amendments, Transitional Provisions and Savings) Order 2007 affects any provision of this Act as applied by the 2001 Regulations to LLPs (see art 12(2) at **[A12]** and the introductory notes to this Act).

Supplementary

452 Privileged information

[(1) Nothing in sections 431 to *446* compels the disclosure by any person to the Secretary of State or to an inspector appointed by him of information in respect of which in an action in the High Court a claim to legal professional privilege, or in an action in the Court of Session a claim to confidentiality of communications, could be maintained.]

[(1A) Nothing in sections 434, 443 or 446 requires a person (except as mentioned in subsection (1B) below) to disclose information or produce documents in respect of which he owes an obligation of confidence by virtue of carrying on the business of banking unless—

(a) the person to whom the obligation of confidence is owed is the company or other body corporate under investigation,

(b) the person to whom the obligation of confidence is owed consents to the disclosure or production, or

(c) the making of the requirement is authorised by the Secretary of State.

(1B) Subsection (1A) does not apply where the person owing the obligation of confidence is the company or other body corporate under investigation under section 431, 432 or 433.]

[(2) Nothing in sections 447 to 451—

(a) compels the production by any person of a document or the disclosure by any person of information in respect of which in an action in the High Court a claim to legal professional privilege, or in an action in the Court of Session a claim to confidentiality of communications, could be maintained;

(b) authorises the taking of possession of any such document which is in the person's possession.

(3) The Secretary of State must not under section 447 require, or authorise a person to require—

(a) the production by a person carrying on the business of banking of a document relating to the affairs of a customer of his, or

(b) the disclosure by him of information relating to those affairs,

unless one of the conditions in subsection (4) is met.

(4) The conditions are—

(a) the Secretary of State thinks it is necessary to do so for the purpose of investigating the affairs of the person carrying on the business of banking;

(b) the customer is a person on whom a requirement has been imposed under section 447;

(c) the customer is a person on whom a requirement to produce information or documents has been imposed by an investigator appointed by the Secretary of State in pursuance of section 171 or 173 of the Financial Services and Markets Act 2000 (powers of persons appointed under section 167 or as a result of section 168(2) to conduct an investigation).

(5) Despite subsections (1) and (2) a person who is a lawyer may be compelled to disclose the name and address of his client.]

[486]

NOTES

Sub-s (1): substituted by the Companies (Audit, Investigations and Community Enterprise) Act 2004, s 25, Sch 2, Pt 3, paras 16, 21(a), as from 6 April 2005; for the figure in italics there is substituted the figure "446E" by the Companies Act 2006, s 1037(3), as from 1 October 2007, with effect where an inspector is appointed under a provision of Pt 14 of this Act on or after that date.

Sub-ss (1A), (1B): inserted by CA 1989, s 69(3), as from 21 February 1990.

Sub-ss (2)–(5): substituted, for original sub-ss (2), (3), by the Companies (Audit, Investigations and Community Enterprise) Act 2004, s 25, Sch 2, Pt 3, paras 16, 21(b), as from 6 April 2005.

Application to limited liability partnerships: see the Limited Liability Partnerships Regulations 2001, SI 2001/1090, reg 4(1), Sch 2, Pt 1 at **[6985]**, **[6993]**. Note also that nothing in the draft Companies

Act 2006 (Commencement No 3, Consequential Amendments, Transitional Provisions and Savings) Order 2007 affects any provision of this Act as applied by the 2001 Regulations to LLPs (see art 12(2) at **[A12]** and the introductory notes to this Act).

453 Investigation of oversea companies

[(1) The provisions of this Part apply to bodies corporate incorporated outside Great Britain which are carrying on business in Great Britain, or have at any time carried on business there, as they apply to companies under this Act; but subject to the following exceptions, adaptations and modifications.

(1A) The following provisions do not apply to such bodies—

(a) section 431 (investigation on application of company or its members),

(b) section 438 (power to bring civil proceedings on the company's behalf),

(c) sections 442 to 445 (investigation of company ownership and power to obtain information as to those interested in shares, &c), *and*

(d) section 446 (investigation of share dealings).

(1B) The other provisions of this Part apply to such bodies subject to such adaptations and modifications as may be specified by regulations made by the Secretary of State.]

(2) Regulations under this section shall be made by statutory instrument subject to annulment in pursuance of a resolution of either House of Parliament.

[487]

NOTES

Sub-ss (1), (1B): substituted (together with sub-s (1A)), for original sub-s (1), by CA 1989, s 70, as from 21 February 1990.

Sub-s (1A): substituted as noted above; para (b) repealed by the Companies Act 2006, ss 1176(3), (4), 1295, Sch 16, as from 6 April 2007, except in relation to proceedings brought under s 438 before that date; para (d) (and the word immediately preceding it) repealed by s 1295 of, and Sch 16 to, the 2006 Act, as from 1 October 2007.

[453A Power to enter and remain on premises

(1) An inspector or investigator may act under subsection (2) in relation to a company if—

(a) he is authorised to do so by the Secretary of State, and

(b) he thinks that to do so will materially assist him in the exercise of his functions under this Part in relation to the company.

(2) An inspector or investigator may at all reasonable times—

(a) require entry to relevant premises, and

(b) remain there for such period as he thinks necessary for the purpose mentioned in subsection (1)(b).

(3) Relevant premises are premises which the inspector or investigator believes are used (wholly or partly) for the purposes of the company's business.

(4) In exercising his powers under subsection (2), an inspector or investigator may be accompanied by such other persons as he thinks appropriate.

(5) A person who intentionally obstructs a person lawfully acting under subsection (2) or (4)—

(a) is guilty of an offence, and

(b) is liable on conviction to a fine.

[(5A) A person guilty of an offence under this section is liable—

(a) on conviction on indictment, to a fine;

(b) on summary conviction, to a fine not exceeding the statutory maximum.]

(6) Sections 732 (restriction on prosecutions), 733 (liability of individuals for corporate default) and 734 (criminal proceedings against unincorporated bodies) apply to the offence under subsection (5).

(7) An inspector is a person appointed under section 431, 432 or 442.

(8) An investigator is a person authorised for the purposes of section 447.]

[487A]

NOTES

Inserted, together with s 453B, by the Companies (Audit, Investigations and Community Enterprise) Act 2004, s 23, as from 6 April 2005 (for transitional provisions, see the Companies (Audit, Investigations and Community Enterprise) Act 2004 (Commencement) and Companies Act 1989 (Commencement No 18) Order 2004, SI 2004/3322, art 11 at **[7349]**).

Sub-s (5): for the words in italics there are substituted the words "is guilty of an offence" by the Companies Act 2006, s 1124, Sch 3, para 6(1), (2), as from 1 October 2007.

Sub-s (5A): inserted by the Companies Act 2006, s 1124, Sch 3, para 6(1), (3), as from 1 October 2007.

Sub-s (6): repealed by the Companies Act 2006, ss 1124, 1295, Sch 3, para 6(1), (4), Sch 16, as from 1 October 2007.

Application to limited liability partnerships: see the draft Limited Liability Partnerships (Amendment) Regulations 2007 in Appendix 10 at **[A10]**. Those draft Regulations amend the Limited Liability Partnerships Regulations 2001, SI 2001/1090, Sch 2, Pt 1 at **[6993]** by adding an entry for this section into that Schedule.

[453B Power to enter and remain on premises: procedural

(1) This section applies for the purposes of section 453A.

(2) The requirements of subsection (3) must be complied with at the time an inspector or investigator seeks to enter relevant premises under section 453A(2)(a).

(3) The requirements are—

(a) the inspector or investigator must produce evidence of his identity and evidence of his appointment or authorisation (as the case may be);

(b) any person accompanying the inspector or investigator must produce evidence of his identity.

(4) The inspector or investigator must, as soon as practicable after obtaining entry, give to an appropriate recipient a written statement containing such information as to—

(a) the powers of the investigator or inspector (as the case may be) under section 453A;

(b) the rights and obligations of the company, occupier and the persons present on the premises,

as may be prescribed by regulations.

(5) If during the time the inspector or investigator is on the premises there is no person present who appears to him to be an appropriate recipient for the purposes of subsection (8), the inspector or investigator must as soon as reasonably practicable send to the company—

(a) a notice of the fact and time that the visit took place, and

(b) the statement mentioned in subsection (4).

(6) As soon as reasonably practicable after exercising his powers under section 453A(2), the inspector or investigator must prepare a written record of the visit and—

(a) if requested to do so by the company he must give it a copy of the record;

(b) in a case where the company is not the sole occupier of the premises, if requested to do so by an occupier he must give the occupier a copy of the record.

(7) The written record must contain such information as may be prescribed by regulations.

(8) If the inspector or investigator thinks that the company is the sole occupier of the premises an appropriate recipient is a person who is present on the premises and who appears to the inspector or investigator to be—

(a) an officer of the company, or

(b) a person otherwise engaged in the business of the company if the inspector or investigator thinks that no officer of the company is present on the premises.

(9) If the inspector or investigator thinks that the company is not the occupier or sole occupier of the premises an appropriate recipient is—

(a) a person who is an appropriate recipient for the purposes of subsection (8), and (if different)

(b) a person who is present on the premises and who appears to the inspector or investigator to be an occupier of the premises or otherwise in charge of them.

(10) A statutory instrument containing regulations made under this section is subject to annulment in pursuance of a resolution of either House of Parliament.]

[487B]

NOTES

Inserted as noted to s 453A at **[487A]**.

Application to limited liability partnerships: see the draft Limited Liability Partnerships (Amendment) Regulations 2007 in Appendix 10 at **[A10]**. Those draft Regulations amend the Limited Liability Partnerships Regulations 2001, SI 2001/1090, Sch 2, Pt 1 at **[6993]** by adding an entry for this section into that Schedule.

Regulations: the Companies Act 1985 (Power to Enter and Remain on Premises: Procedural) Regulations 2005, SI 2005/684 at **[7391]**.

[453C Failure to comply with certain requirements

(1) This section applies if a person fails to comply with a requirement imposed by an inspector, the Secretary of State or an investigator in pursuance of either of the following provisions—

(a) section 447;
(b) section 453A.

(2) The inspector, Secretary of State or investigator (as the case may be) may certify the fact in writing to the court.

(3) If, after hearing—

(a) any witnesses who may be produced against or on behalf of the alleged offender;
(b) any statement which may be offered in defence,

the court is satisfied that the offender failed without reasonable excuse to comply with the requirement, it may deal with him as if he had been guilty of contempt of the court.]

[487C]

NOTES

Inserted by the Companies (Audit, Investigations and Community Enterprise) Act 2004, s 24, as from 6 April 2005 (for transitional provisions, see the Companies (Audit, Investigations and Community Enterprise) Act 2004 (Commencement) and Companies Act 1989 (Commencement No 18) Order 2004, SI 2004/3322, arts 7–11 at **[7345]–[7349]**).

Application to limited liability partnerships: see the draft Limited Liability Partnerships (Amendment) Regulations 2007 in Appendix 10 at **[A10]**. Those draft Regulations amend the Limited Liability Partnerships Regulations 2001, SI 2001/1090, Sch 2, Pt 1 at **[6993]** by adding an entry for this section into that Schedule.

PART XV
ORDERS IMPOSING RESTRICTIONS ON SHARES
(*SECTIONS 210, 216, 445*)

NOTES

Note: this Part is not repealed by the Companies Act 2006.

For the words in italics there are substituted the words "SECTION 445" by the draft Companies Act 2006 (Commencement No 3, Consequential Amendments, Transitional Provisions and Savings) Order 2007, art 10(1), Sch 4, Pt 1, para 11(1), (2), as from 1 October 2007 (see **[A12]**).

454 Consequence of order imposing restrictions

(1) So long as any shares are directed to be subject to the restrictions of this Part [then, subject to any directions made in relation to an order *pursuant to sections 210(5A), 216(1B), 445(1A) or 456(1A) or subject in the case of an interim order pursuant to section 216(1A) to the terms of that order*]—

(a) any transfer of those shares or, in the case of unissued shares, any transfer of the right to be issued with them, and any issue of them, is void;
(b) no voting rights are exercisable in respect of the shares;
(c) no further shares shall be issued in right of them or in pursuance of any offer made to their holder; and
(d) except in a liquidation, no payment shall be made of any sums due from the company on the shares, whether in respect of capital or otherwise.

(2) Where shares are subject to the restrictions of subsection (1)(a), any agreement to transfer the shares or, in the case of unissued shares, the right to be issued with them is void (except [such agreement or right as may be made or exercised under the terms of directions

made by the Secretary of State or the court under *sections 210(5A), 216(1B), 445(1A), 456(1A) or of an interim order made under section 216(1A)* or] an agreement to [transfer] the shares on the making of an order under section 456(3)(b) below).

(3) Where shares are subject to the restrictions of subsection (1)(c) or (d), an agreement to transfer any right to be issued with other shares in right of those shares, or to receive any payment on them (otherwise than in a liquidation) is void (except [such agreement or right as may be made or exercised under the terms of directions made by the Secretary of State or the court under *sections 210(5A), 216(1B), 445(1A), 456(1A) or of an interim order made under section 216(1A)* or] an agreement to transfer any such right on the [transfer] of the shares on the making of an order under section 456(3)(b) below).

[488]

NOTES

Sub-s (1): words in square brackets inserted by the Companies (Disclosure of Interests in Shares) (Orders imposing restrictions on shares) Regulations 1991, SI 1991/1646, reg 6(a), as from 18 July 1991; for the words in italics there are substituted the words "pursuant to section 445(1A) or 456(1A)" by the draft Companies Act 2006 (Commencement No 3, Consequential Amendments, Transitional Provisions and Savings) Order 2007, art 10(1), Sch 4, Pt 1, para 11(1), (3), as from 1 October 2007 (see **[A12]**).

Sub-ss (2), (3): words in first pair of square brackets inserted by SI 1991/1646, reg 6(b), (c) as from 18 July 1991; word in second pair of square brackets substituted by CA 1989, s 145, Sch 19, para 10(2), as from 7 January 1991; for the words in italics there are substituted the words "section 445(1A) or 456(1A)" by the draft Companies Act 2006 (Commencement No 3, Consequential Amendments, Transitional Provisions and Savings) Order 2007, art 10(1), Sch 4, Pt 1, para 11(1), (4), (5), as from 1 October 2007 (see **[A12]**).

455 Punishment for attempted evasion of restrictions

(1) [Subject to the terms of any directions made under *sections 210(5A), 216(1B), 445(1A) or 456 or of an interim order made under section 216(1A)*] a person *is liable to a fine if he*—

- (a) exercises or purports to exercise any right to dispose of any shares which, to his knowledge, are for the time being subject to the restrictions of this Part or of any right to be issued with any such shares, or
- (b) votes in respect of any such shares (whether as holder or proxy), or appoints a proxy to vote in respect of them, or
- (c) being the holder of any such shares, fails to notify of their being subject to those restrictions any person whom he does not know to be aware of that fact but does know to be entitled (apart from the restrictions) to vote in respect of those shares whether as holder or as proxy, or
- (d) being the holder of any such shares, or being entitled to any right to be issued with other shares in right of them, or to receive any payment on them (otherwise than in a liquidation), enters into any agreement which is void under section 454(2) or (3).

(2) [Subject to the terms of any directions made under *sections 210(5A), 216(1B), 445(1A) or 456 or of an interim order made under section 216(1A)*] if shares in a company are issued in contravention of the restrictions, *the company and every officer of it who is in default is liable to a fine.*

[(2A) A person guilty of an offence under this section is liable—

- (a) on conviction on indictment, to a fine;
- (b) on summary conviction, to a fine not exceeding the statutory maximum.]

(3) Section 732 (restriction on prosecutions) applies to an offence under this section.

[489]

NOTES

Sub-s (1): words in square brackets inserted by the Companies (Disclosure of Interests in Shares) (Orders imposing restrictions on shares) Regulations 1991, SI 1991/1646, reg 7, as from 18 July 1991; for the first words in italics there are substituted the words "section 445(1A) or 456" by the draft Companies Act 2006 (Commencement No 3, Consequential Amendments, Transitional Provisions and Savings) Order 2007, art 10(1), Sch 4, Pt 1, para 11(1), (6), as from 1 October 2007 (see **[A12]**); for the second words in italics there are substituted the words "commits an offence if he" by the Companies Act 2006, s 1124, Sch 3, para 7(1), as from 1 October 2007.

Sub-s (2): words in square brackets inserted by SI 1991/1646, reg 7, as from 18 July 1991; for the first words in italics there are substituted the words "section 445(1A) or 456" by the draft Companies Act 2006 (Commencement No 3, Consequential Amendments, Transitional Provisions and Savings)

Order 2007, art 10(1), Sch 4, Pt 1, para 11(1), (7), as from 1 October 2007 (see **[A12]**); for the second words in italics there are substituted the following words by the Companies Act 2006, s 1124, Sch 3, para 7(2), as from 1 October 2007—

"an offence is committed by—

(a) the company, and

(b) every officer of the company who is in default".

Sub-s (2A): inserted by the Companies Act 2006, s 1124, Sch 3, para 7(3), as from 1 October 2007.

Sub-s (3): repealed by the draft Companies Act 2006 (Commencement No 3, Consequential Amendments, Transitional Provisions and Savings) Order 2007, art 10(3), Sch 5, as from 1 October 2007 (see **[A12]**).

456 Relaxation and removal of restrictions

(1) Where shares in a company are by order made subject to the restrictions of this Part, application may be made to the court for an order directing that the shares be no longer so subject.

[(1A) Where the court is satisfied that an order subjecting the shares to the restrictions of this Part unfairly affects the rights of third parties in respect of shares then the court, for the purpose of protecting such rights and subject to such terms as it thinks fit and in addition to any order it may make under subsection (1), may direct on an application made under that subsection that such acts by such persons or descriptions of persons and for such purposes, as may be set out in the order, shall not constitute a breach of the restrictions of Part XV of this Act.

Subsection (3) does not apply to an order made under this subsection.]

(2) If the order applying the restrictions was made by the Secretary of State, or he has refused to make an order disapplying them, the application may be made by any person aggrieved; *and if the order was made by the court under section 216 (non-disclosure of share holding), it may be made by any such person or by the company.*

(3) Subject as follows, an order of the court or the Secretary of State directing that shares shall cease to be subject to the restrictions may be made only if—

(a) the court or (as the case may be) the Secretary of State is satisfied that the relevant facts about the shares have been disclosed to the company and no unfair advantage has accrued to any person as a result of the earlier failure to make that disclosure, or

(b) the shares are to be [transferred for valuable consideration] and the court (in any case) or the Secretary of State (if the order was made under section *210 or* 445) approves the [transfer].

(4) [Without prejudice to the power of the court to give directions under subsection (1A),] where shares in a company are subject to the restrictions, the court may on application order the shares to be sold, subject to the court's approval as to the sale, and may also direct that the shares shall cease to be subject to the restrictions.

An application to the court under this subsection may be made by the Secretary of State (*unless the restrictions were imposed by court order under section 216*), or by the company.

(5) Where an order has been made under subsection (4), the court may on application make such further order relating to the sale or transfer of the shares as it thinks fit.

An application to the court under this subsection may be made—

(a) by the Secretary of State (*unless the restrictions on the shares were imposed by court order under section 216*), or

(b) by the company, or

(c) by the person appointed by or in pursuance of the order to effect the sale, or

(d) by any person interested in the shares.

(6) An order (whether of the Secretary of State or the court) directing that shares shall cease to be subject to the restrictions of this Part, if it is—

(a) expressed to be made with a view to permitting a transfer of the shares, or

(b) made under subsection (4) of this section,

may continue the restrictions mentioned in paragraphs (c) and (d) of section 454(1), either in whole or in part, so far as they relate to any right acquired or offer made before the transfer.

(7) Subsection (3) does not apply to an order directing that shares shall cease to be subject to any restrictions which have been continued in force in relation to those shares under subsection (6).

[490]

NOTES

Sub-s (1A): inserted by the Companies (Disclosure of Interests in Shares) (Orders imposing restrictions on shares) Regulations 1991, SI 1991/1646, reg 8(a), as from 18 July 1991.

Sub-ss (2), (5): words in italics repealed by the draft Companies Act 2006 (Commencement No 3, Consequential Amendments, Transitional Provisions and Savings) Order 2007, art 10(1), (3), Sch 4, Pt 1, para 11(1), (8), (11), Sch 5, as from 1 October 2007 (see **[A12]**).

Sub-s (3): words in square brackets in para (b) substituted by CA 1989, s 145, Sch 19, para 10(1), as from 7 January 1991; words in italics repealed by the draft Companies Act 2006 (Commencement No 3, Consequential Amendments, Transitional Provisions and Savings) Order 2007, art 10(1), (3), Sch 4, Pt 1, para 11(1), (9), Sch 5, as from 1 October 2007 (see **[A12]**).

Sub-s (4): words in square brackets inserted by SI 1991/1646, reg 8(b), as from 18 July 1991; words in italics repealed by the draft Companies Act 2006 (Commencement No 3, Consequential Amendments, Transitional Provisions and Savings) Order 2007, art 10(1), (3), Sch 4, Pt 1, para 11(1), (10), Sch 5, as from 1 October 2007 (see **[A12]**).

Court … may direct: by virtue of SI 1991/1646, reg 9, the power of the court to give a direction under sub-s (1A) above is exercisable in respect of any order made under s 210(5), 216(1) or 445(1), including such orders as may be in force on 18 July 1991 (commencement of SI 1991/1646).

457 Further provisions on sale by court order of restricted shares

(1) Where shares are sold in pursuance of an order of the court under section 456(4) the proceeds of sale, less the costs of the sale, shall be paid into court for the benefit of the persons who are beneficially interested in the shares; and any such person may apply to the court for the whole or part of those proceeds to be paid to him.

(2) On application under subsection (1) the court shall (subject as provided below) order the payment to the applicant of the whole of the proceeds of sale together with any interest thereon or, if any other person had a beneficial interest in the shares at the time of their sale, such proportion of those proceeds and interest as is equal to the proportion which the value of the applicant's interest in the shares bears to the total value of the shares.

(3) On granting an application for an order under section 456(4) or (5) the court may order that the applicant's costs be paid out of the proceeds of sale; and if that order is made, the applicant is entitled to payment of his costs out of those proceeds before any person interested in the shares in question receives any part of those proceeds.

[491]

PART XVI
FRAUDULENT TRADING BY A COMPANY

458 Punishment for fraudulent trading

If any business of a company is carried on with intent to defraud creditors of the company or creditors of any other person, or for any fraudulent purpose, every person who was knowingly a party to the carrying on of the business in that manner is liable to imprisonment or a fine, or both.

This applies whether or not the company has been, or is in the course of being, wound up.

[492]

NOTES

Repealed by the Companies Act 2006, s 1295, Sch 16, as from 1 October 2007. For savings see the note below.

Savings: see the draft Companies Act 2006 (Commencement No 3, Consequential Amendments, Transitional Provisions and Savings) Order 2007, Sch 3, para 46 (at **[A12]**) which provides as follows—

"46 Fraudulent trading (s 993)

(1) Section 458 of the 1985 Act or Article 451 of the 1986 Order (offences of fraudulent trading) continues to apply to offences completed before 1st October 2007.

(2) Where, in the case of an offence—

(a) a relevant event occurs before 1st October 2007, and

(b) another relevant event occurs on or after 1st October 2007, the offence must be charged under section 993 of the Companies Act 2006 (and not under section 458 of the 1985 Act or Article 451 of the 1986 Order).

(3) If in the case of any such offence a relevant event occurred before 15th January 2007 section 993(3)(a) applies with the substitution of "seven years" for "ten years".

(4) "Relevant event" means an act, omission or other event (including any result of one or more acts or omissions) proof of which is required for conviction of the offence."

Application to limited liability partnerships: see the Limited Liability Partnerships Regulations 2001, SI 2001/1090, reg 4(1), Sch 2, Pt 1 at **[6985]**, **[6993]**. Note also that nothing in the draft Companies Act 2006 (Commencement No 3, Consequential Amendments, Transitional Provisions and Savings) Order 2007 affects any provision of this Act as applied by the 2001 Regulations to LLPs (see art 12(2) at **[A12]** and the introductory notes to this Act).

Business of a company: as to sole traders, etc, see the Fraud Act 2006, s 9 at **[3642]**.

PART XVII
PROTECTION OF COMPANY'S MEMBERS AGAINST UNFAIR PREJUDICE

459 Order on application of company member

(1) A member of a company may apply to the court by petition for an order under this Part on the ground that the company's affairs are being or have been conducted in a manner which is [unfairly prejudicial to the interests of its members generally or of some part of its members] (including at least himself) or that any actual or proposed act or omission of the company (including an act or omission on its behalf) is or would be so prejudicial.

(2) The provisions of this Part apply to a person who is not a member of a company but to whom shares in the company have been transferred or transmitted by operation of law, as those provisions apply to a member of the company; and references to a member or members are to be construed accordingly.

[(3) In this section (and so far as applicable for the purposes of this section, in section 461(2)) "company" means any company within the meaning of this Act or any company which is not such a company but is a statutory water company within the meaning of [the Statutory Water Companies Act 1991].]

[493]

NOTES

Repealed by the Companies Act 2006, s 1295, Sch 16, as from a day to be appointed.

Sub-s (1): words in square brackets substituted by CA 1989, s 145, Sch 19, para 11, as from 4 February 1991.

Sub-s (3): added by the Water Act 1989, s 190(1), Sch 25, para 71(3), as from 1 September 1989; words in square brackets substituted by the Water Consolidation (Consequential Provisions) Act 1991, s 2(1), Sch 1, para 40(2), as from 1 December 1991.

Application to limited liability partnerships: see the Limited Liability Partnerships Regulations 2001, SI 2001/1090, reg 4(1), Sch 2, Pt 1 at **[6985]**, **[6993]**.

Apply to the court by petition: see the Companies (Unfair Prejudice Applications) Proceedings Rules 1986, SI 1986/2000 at **[6574]**.

460 Order on application of Secretary of State

[(1) If it appears to the Secretary of State that—

(a) the affairs of a company to which this subsection applies are being or have been conducted in a manner which is unfairly prejudicial to the interests of its members generally or of some part of its members, or

(b) any actual or proposed act or omission of a company to which this subsection applies, including an act or omission on its behalf, is or would be so prejudicial,

he may himself (in addition to or instead of presenting a petition for the winding up of the company) apply to the court by petition for an order under this Part.

(1A) Subsection (1) applies to a company in respect of which—

(a) the Secretary of State has received a report under section 437 of this Act;

(b) the Secretary of State has exercised his powers under section 447 or 448 of this Act;

(c) the Secretary of State or the Financial Services Authority has exercised his or its powers under Part 11 of the Financial Services and Markets Act 2000; or

(*d*) *the Secretary of State has received a report from an investigator appointed by him or the Financial Services Authority under that Part.]*

(*2*) *In this section (and, so far as applicable for its purposes, in the section next following) "company" means any body corporate which is liable to be wound up under this Act.*

[494]

NOTES

Repealed by the Companies Act 2006, s 1295, Sch 16, as from a day to be appointed.

Sub-ss (1), (1A): substituted, for original sub-s (1), by the Financial Services and Markets Act 2000 (Consequential Amendments and Repeals) Order 2001, SI 2001/3649, art 26, as from 1 December 2001.

Application to limited liability partnerships: see the Limited Liability Partnerships Regulations 2001, SI 2001/1090, reg 4(1), Sch 2, Pt 1 at **[6985]**, **[6993]**.

Apply to the court by petition: see the Companies (Unfair Prejudice Applications) Proceedings Rules 1986, SI 1986/2000 at **[6574]**.

461 Provisions as to petitions and orders under this Part

(*1*) *If the court is satisfied that a petition under this Part is well founded, it may make such order as it thinks fit for giving relief in respect of the matters complained of.*

(*2*) *Without prejudice to the generality of subsection (1), the court's order may—*

(*a*) *regulate the conduct of the company's affairs in the future,*

(*b*) *require the company to refrain from doing or continuing an act complained of by the petitioner or to do an act which the petitioner has complained it has omitted to do,*

(*c*) *authorise civil proceedings to be brought in the name and on behalf of the company by such person or persons and on such terms as the court may direct,*

(*d*) *provide for the purchase of the shares of any members of the company by other members or by the company itself and, in the case of a purchase by the company itself, the reduction of the company's capital accordingly.*

(*3*) *If an order under this Part requires the company not to make any, or any specified, alteration in the memorandum or articles, the company does not then have power without leave of the court to make any such alteration in breach of that requirement.*

(*4*) *Any alteration in the company's memorandum or articles made by virtue of an order under this Part is of the same effect as if duly made by resolution of the company, and the provisions of this Act apply to the memorandum or articles as so altered accordingly.*

(*5*) *An office copy of an order under this Part altering, or giving leave to alter, a company's memorandum or articles shall, within 14 days from the making of the order or such longer period as the court may allow, be delivered by the company to the registrar of companies for registration; and if a company makes default in complying with this subsection, the company and every officer of it who is in default is liable to a fine and, for continued contravention, to a daily default fine.*

[(6) The power under [section 411 of the Insolvency Act] to make rules shall, so far as it relates to a winding-up petition, apply for the purposes of a petition under this Part.]

[495]

NOTES

Repealed by the Companies Act 2006, s 1295, Sch 16, as from a day to be appointed.

Sub-s (6): substituted by the Insolvency Act 1985, s 109, Sch 6, para 24, as from 1 March 1986; words in square brackets substituted by the Insolvency Act 1986, s 439(1), Sch 13, Pt I, as from 29 December 1986.

Application to limited liability partnerships: see the Limited Liability Partnerships Regulations 2001, SI 2001/1090, reg 4(1), Sch 2, Pt 1 at **[6985]**, **[6993]**.

Insolvency Act: ie, the Insolvency Act 1986.

PART XVIII
FLOATING CHARGES AND RECEIVERS (SCOTLAND)

NOTES

This Part is repealed by the Bankruptcy and Diligence etc (Scotland) Act 2007, s 46(1), as from a day to be appointed (subject to savings). Note that it was not repealed by the Companies Act 2006.

Section 46(2), (3) of the 2007 Act provide that nothing in Part 2 of the 2007 Act (except ss 40, 41 of that Act in so far as they concern the ranking of floating charges subsisting immediately before the coming into force of s 46) affects the validity or operation of floating charges subsisting before the coming into force of s 46 and, therefore, despite the repeal of Chapters I and III of Part XVIII of this Act, those provisions continue to have effect for the purposes of such floating charges. The relevant provisions of the 2007 Act are at **[3649]** et seq.

CHAPTER I
FLOATING CHARGES

462 Power of incorporated company to create floating charge

(1) It is competent under the law of Scotland for an incorporated company (whether a company within the meaning of this Act or not), for the purpose of securing any debt or other obligation (including a cautionary obligation) incurred or to be incurred by, or binding upon, the company or any other person, to create in favour of the creditor in the debt or obligation a charge, in this Part referred to as a floating charge, over all or any part of the property (including uncalled capital) which may from time to time be comprised in its property and undertaking.

(2), (3) …

(4) References in this Part to the instrument by which a floating charge was created are, in the case of a floating charge created by words in a bond or other written acknowledgment, references to the bond or, as the case may be, the other written acknowledgment.

(5) Subject to this Act, a floating charge has effect in accordance with this Part [and Part III of the Insolvency Act 1986] in relation to any heritable property in Scotland to which it relates, notwithstanding that the instrument creating it is not recorded in the Register of Sasines or, as appropriate, registered in accordance with the Land Registration (Scotland) Act 1979.

[496]

NOTES

Repealed by the Bankruptcy and Diligence etc (Scotland) Act 2007, s 46(1), as from a day to be appointed (for savings see the introductory note to this Part).

Sub-s (2): substituted, for original sub-ss (2), (3), by CA 1989, s 130(7), Sch 17, para 8; repealed by the Law Reform (Miscellaneous Provisions) (Scotland) Act 1990, s 74(1), (2), Sch 8, para 33(6), Sch 9, as from 1 December 1990.

Sub-s (3): substituted as noted above and repealed again by the Requirements of Writing (Scotland) Act 1995, s 14(2), Sch 5, as from 1 August 1995.

Sub-s (5): words in square brackets inserted by the Insolvency Act 1986, s 439(1), Sch 13, Pt I, as from 29 December 1986.

Application to limited liability partnerships: see the Limited Liability Partnerships (Scotland) Regulations 2001, SSI 2001/128, Sch 1 at **[6980]**.

463 Effect of floating charge on winding up

(1) [Where a company goes into liquidation within the meaning of section 247(2) of the Insolvency Act 1986], a floating charge created by the company attaches to the property then comprised in the company's property and undertaking or, as the case may be, in part of that property and undertaking, but does so subject to the rights of any person who—

(a) has effectually executed diligence on the property or any part of it; or

(b) holds a fixed security over the property or any part of it ranking in priority to the floating charge; or

(c) holds over the property or any part of it another floating charge so ranking.

(2) The provisions of [Part IV of the Insolvency Act (except section 185)] have effect in relation to a floating charge, subject to subsection (1), as if the charge were a fixed security over the property to which it has attached in respect of the principal of the debt or obligation to which it relates and any interest due or to become due thereon.

[(3) Nothing in this section derogates from the provisions of sections 53(7) and 54(6) of the Insolvency Act (attachment of floating charge on appointment of receiver), or prejudices the operation of sections 175 and 176 of that Act (payment of preferential debts in winding up).]

(4) ... interest accrues, in respect of a floating charge which after 16th November 1972 attaches to the property of the company, until payment of the sum due under the charge is made.

[497]

NOTES

Repealed by the Bankruptcy and Diligence etc (Scotland) Act 2007, s 46(1), as from a day to be appointed (for savings see the introductory note to this Part).

Sub-s (1): words in square brackets substituted by CA 1989, s 140(1), as from 3 July 1995.

Sub-s (2): words in square brackets substituted by the Insolvency Act 1986, s 439(1), Sch 13, Pt I, as from 29 December 1986.

Sub-s (3): substituted by the Insolvency Act 1986, s 439(1), Sch 13, Pt I, as from 29 December 1986.

Sub-s (4): words omitted repealed by the Insolvency Act 1986, s 438, Sch 12, as from 29 December 1986.

Application to limited liability partnerships: see the Limited Liability Partnerships (Scotland) Regulations 2001, SSI 2001/128, Sch 1 at **[6980]**.

464 Ranking of floating charges

(1) Subject to subsection (2), the instrument creating a floating charge over all or any part of the company's property under section 462 may contain—

- *(a) provisions prohibiting or restricting the creation of any fixed security or any other floating charge having priority over, or ranking pari passu with, the floating charge; or*
- *(b) [with the consent of the holder of any subsisting floating charge or fixed security which would be adversely affected] provisions regulating the order in which the floating charge shall rank with any other subsisting or future floating charges or fixed securities over that property or any part of it.*

[(1A) Where an instrument creating a floating charge contains any such provision as is mentioned in subsection (1)(a), that provision shall be effective to confer priority on the floating charge over any fixed security or floating charge created after the date of the instrument.]

(2) Where all or any part of the property of a company is subject both to a floating charge and to a fixed security arising by operation of law, the fixed security has priority over the floating charge.

[(3) The order of ranking of the floating charges with any other subsisting or future floating charges or fixed securities over all or any part of the company's property is determined in accordance with the provisions of subsections (4) and (5) except where it is determined in accordance with any provision such as is mentioned in paragraph (a) or (b) of subsection (1).]

(4) Subject to the provisions of this section—

- *(a) a fixed security, the right to which has been constituted as a real right before a floating charge has attached to all or any part of the property of the company, has priority of ranking over the floating charge;*
- *(b) floating charges rank with one another according to the time of registration in accordance with Chapter II of Part XII;*
- *(c) floating charges which have been received by the registrar for registration by the same postal delivery rank with one another equally.*

(5) Where the holder of a floating charge over all or any part of the company's property which has been registered in accordance with Chapter II of Part XII has received intimation in writing of the subsequent registration in accordance with that Chapter of another floating charge over the same property or any part thereof, the preference in ranking of the first-mentioned floating charge is restricted to security for—

- *(a) the holder's present advances;*
- *(b) future advances which he may be required to make under the instrument creating the floating charge or under any ancillary document;*
- *(c) interest due or to become due on all such advances; ...*
- *(d) any expenses or outlays which may reasonably be incurred by the holder[; and*
- *(e) (in the case of a floating charge to secure a contingent liability other than a liability arising under any further advances made from time to time) the maximum sum to which that contingent liability is capable of amounting whether or not it is contractually limited.]*

(6) This section is subject to [Part XII and to] [sections 175 and 176 of the Insolvency Act] (preferential debts in winding up).

[498]

NOTES

Repealed by the Bankruptcy and Diligence etc (Scotland) Act 2007, s 46(1), as from a day to be appointed (for savings see the introductory note to this Part).

Sub-s (1): words in square brackets in para (b) inserted by CA 1989, s 140(2), (3), as from 3 July 1995.

Sub-s (1A): inserted by CA 1989, s 140(2), (4), as from 3 July 1995.

Sub-s (3): substituted by CA 1989, s 140(2), (5), as from 3 July 1995.

Sub-s (5): word omitted from para (c) repealed, and para (e) and the word immediately preceding it added, by CA 1989, ss 140(2), (6), 212, Sch 24, as from 3 July 1995.

Sub-s (6): words in first pair of square brackets inserted by CA 1989, s 140(2), (7), as from a day to be appointed; words in second pair of square brackets substituted by the Insolvency Act 1986, s 439(1), Sch 13, Pt I, as from 29 December 1986.

Application to limited liability partnerships: see the Limited Liability Partnerships Regulations 2001, SI 2001/1090, reg 4(1), Sch 2, Pt 1 at **[6985]**, **[6993]**.

465 Continued effect of certain charges validated by Act of 1972

(1) Any floating charge which—

(a) purported to subsist as a floating charge on 17th November 1972, and

(b) if it had been created on or after that date, would have been validly created by virtue of the Companies (Floating Charges and Receivers) (Scotland) Act 1972,

is deemed to have subsisted as a valid floating charge as from the date of its creation.

(2) Any provision which—

(a) is contained in an instrument creating a floating charge or in any ancillary document executed prior to, and still subsisting at, the commencement of that Act,

(b) relates to the ranking of charges, and

(c) if it had been made after the commencement of that Act, would have been a valid provision,

is deemed to have been a valid provision as from the date of its making.

[499]

NOTES

Repealed by the Bankruptcy and Diligence etc (Scotland) Act 2007, s 46(1), as from a day to be appointed (for savings see the introductory note to this Part).

466 Alteration of floating charges

(1) The instrument creating a floating charge under section 462 or any ancillary document may be altered by the execution of an instrument of alteration by the company, the holder of the charge and the holder of any other charge (including a fixed security) which would be adversely affected by the alteration.

(2) [Without prejudice to any enactment or rule of law regarding the execution of documents,] such an instrument of alteration is validly executed if it is executed—

(a) …

(b) where trustees for debenture-holders are acting under and in accordance with a trust deed, by those trustees[; or]

(c) where, in the case of a series of secured debentures, no such trustees are acting, by or on behalf of—

(i) a majority in nominal value of those present or represented by proxy and voting at a meeting of debenture-holders at which the holders of at least one-third in nominal value of the outstanding debentures of the series are present or so represented; or

(ii) where no such meeting is held, the holders of at least one-half in nominal value of the outstanding debentures of the series; …

(d) …

(3) Section 464 applies to an instrument of alteration under this section as it applies to an instrument creating a floating charge.

(4) Subject to the next subsection, section 410(2) and (3) and section 420 apply to an instrument of alteration under this section which—

(*a*) *prohibits or restricts the creation of any fixed security or any other floating charge having priority over, or ranking pari passu with, the floating charge; or*

(*b*) *varies, or otherwise regulates the order of, the ranking of the floating charge in relation to fixed securities or to other floating charges; or*

(*c*) *releases property from the floating charge; or*

(*d*) *increases the amount secured by the floating charge.*

(*5*) *Section 410(2) and (3) and section 420 apply to an instrument of alteration falling under subsection (4) of this section as if references in the said sections to a charge were references to an alteration to a floating charge, and as if in section 410(2) and (3)—*

(*a*) *references to the creation of a charge were references to the execution of such alteration; and*

(*b*) *for the words from the beginning of subsection (2) to the word "applies" there were substituted the words "Every alteration to a floating charge created by a company".*

(*6*) *Any reference (however expressed) in any enactment, including this Act, to a floating charge is, for the purposes of this section and unless the context otherwise requires, to be construed as including a reference to the floating charge as altered by an instrument of alteration falling under subsection (4) of this section.*

[500]

NOTES

Repealed by the Bankruptcy and Diligence etc (Scotland) Act 2007, s 46(1), as from a day to be appointed (for savings see the introductory note to this Part).

Sub-s (2): words in square brackets inserted, and words omitted repealed, by CA 1989, ss 130(7), 212, Sch 17, para 9, Sch 24, as from 31 July 1990.

Sub-ss (4), (5): repealed by CA 1989, ss 140(8), 212, Sch 24, as from a day to be appointed.

Sub-s (6): words "falling under subsection (4) of this section" repealed by CA 1989, ss 140(8), 212, Sch 24, as from a day to be appointed.

Application to limited liability partnerships: see the Limited Liability Partnerships Regulations 2001, SI 2001/1090, reg 4(1), Sch 2, Pt 1 at **[6985]**, **[6993]**, and the Limited Liability Partnerships (Scotland) Regulations 2001, SSI 2001/128, Sch 1 at **[6980]**.

Particulars of an instrument of alteration to a floating charge: see Appendix 4 (Forms table) at **[A4]**.

467–485 *((Chapter II) repealed, with savings, by the Insolvency Act 1986, ss 437, 438, Schs 11, 12, as from 29 December 1986.)*

CHAPTER III
GENERAL

486 Interpretation for Part XVIII generally

(*1*) *In this Part, unless the context otherwise requires, the following expressions have the following meanings respectively assigned to them, that is to say—*

"ancillary document" means—

(*a*) *a document which relates to the floating charge and which was executed by the debtor or creditor in the charge before the registration of the charge in accordance with Chapter II of Part XII; or*

(*b*) *an instrument of alteration such as is mentioned in section 466 in this Part;*

"company", ... means an incorporated company (whether a company within the meaning of this Act or not);

"fixed security", in relation to any property of a company, means any security, other than a floating charge or a charge having the nature of a floating charge, which on the winding up of the company in Scotland would be treated as an effective security over that property, and (without prejudice to that generality) includes a security over that property, being a heritable security within the meaning of section 9(8) of the Conveyancing and Feudal Reform (Scotland) Act 1970;

.....

"Register of Sasines" means the appropriate division of the General Register of Sasines.

[501]

NOTES

Repealed by the Bankruptcy and Diligence etc (Scotland) Act 2007, s 46(1), as from a day to be appointed (for savings see the introductory note to this Part).

Words omitted repealed by the Insolvency Act 1986, s 438, Sch 12, as from 29 December 1986.

Application to limited liability partnerships: see the Limited Liability Partnerships Regulations 2001, SI 2001/1090, reg 4(1), Sch 2, Pt 1 at **[6985]**, **[6993]**, and the Limited Liability Partnerships (Scotland) Regulations 2001, SSI 2001/128, Sch 1 at **[6980]**.

487 Extent of Part XVIII

This Part extends to Scotland only.

[502]

NOTES

Repealed by the Bankruptcy and Diligence etc (Scotland) Act 2007, s 46(1), as from a day to be appointed (for savings see the introductory note to this Part).

Application to limited liability partnerships: see the Limited Liability Partnerships Regulations 2001, SI 2001/1090, reg 4(1), Sch 2, Pt 1 at **[6985]**, **[6993]**, and the Limited Liability Partnerships (Scotland) Regulations 2001, SSI 2001/128, Sch 1 at **[6980]**.

488–500 *((Pt XIX) repealed, with savings, by the Insolvency Act 1986, ss 437, 438, Schs 11, 12, as from 29 December 1986.)*

PART XX
WINDING UP OF COMPANIES REGISTERED UNDER THIS ACT OR THE FORMER COMPANIES ACTS

NOTES

For savings in relation to certain old liquidations, see the Companies Consolidation (Consequential Provisions) Act 1985, s 22 at **[721]**.

501–650 *((Chapters I–V) repealed, with savings, by the Insolvency Act 1986, ss 437, 438, Schs 11, 12, as from 29 December 1986.)*

CHAPTER VI
MATTERS ARISING SUBSEQUENT TO WINDING UP

651 Power of court to declare dissolution of company void

(1) Where a company has been dissolved, the court may … , on an application made for the purpose by the liquidator of the company or by any other person appearing to the court to be interested, make an order, on such terms as the court thinks fit, declaring the dissolution to have been void.

(2) Thereupon such proceedings may be taken as might have been taken if the company had not been dissolved.

(3) It is the duty of the person on whose application the order was made, within 7 days after its making (or such further time as the court may allow), to deliver to the registrar of companies for registration an office copy of the order.

If the person fails to do so, he is liable to a fine and, for continued contravention, to a daily default fine.

[(4) Subject to the following provisions, an application under this section may not be made after the end of the period of two years from the date of the dissolution of the company.

(5) An application for the purpose of bringing proceedings against the company—

- *(a) for damages in respect of personal injuries (including any sum claimed by virtue of section 1(2)(c) of the Law Reform (Miscellaneous Provisions) Act 1934 (funeral expenses)), or*
- *(b) for damages under the Fatal Accidents Act 1976 or the Damages (Scotland) Act 1976,*

may be made at any time; but no order shall be made on such an application if it appears to the court that the proceedings would fail by virtue of any enactment as to the time within which proceedings must be brought.

(6) Nothing in subsection (5) affects the power of the court on making an order under this section to direct that the period between the dissolution of the company and the making of the order shall not count for the purposes of any such enactment.

(7) In subsection (5)(a) "personal injuries" includes any disease and any impairment of a person's physical or mental condition.]

[503]

NOTES

Repealed by the Companies Act 2006, s 1295, Sch 16, as from a day to be appointed.

Sub-s (1): words omitted repealed by CA 1989, ss 141(2), 212, Sch 24, as from 16 November 1989, subject to transitional provisions in relation to a company dissolved before that date (see s 141(4), (5) of that Act at **[822]**).

Sub-ss (4)–(7): added by CA 1989, s 141(3), as from 16 November 1989 (subject to transitional provisions as noted above).

Application to limited liability partnerships: see the Limited Liability Partnerships Regulations 2001, SI 2001/1090, reg 4(1), Sch 2, Pt 1 at **[6985]**, **[6993]**.

Community interest companies: if a community interest company has been dissolved, the Regulator of Community Interest Companies may apply under this section for an order declaring the dissolution to have been void; see the Companies (Audit, Investigations and Community Enterprise) Act 2004, ss 26, 27(1), 51(1) at **[900]**, **[901]**, **[925]**.

652 Registrar may strike defunct company off register

(1) If the registrar of companies has reasonable cause to believe that a company is not carrying on business or in operation, he may send to the company by post a letter inquiring whether the company is carrying on business or in operation.

(2) If the registrar does not within one month of sending the letter receive any answer to it, he shall within 14 days after the expiration of that month send to the company by post a registered letter referring to the first letter, and stating that no answer to it has been received, and that if an answer is not received to the second letter within one month from its date, a notice will be published in the Gazette with a view to striking the company's name off the register.

(3) If the registrar either receives an answer to the effect that the company is not carrying on business or in operation, or does not within one month after sending the second letter receive any answer, he may publish in the Gazette, and send to the company by post, a notice that at the expiration of 3 months from the date of that notice the name of the company mentioned in it will, unless cause is shown to the contrary, be struck off the register and the company will be dissolved.

(4) If, in a case where a company is being wound up, the registrar has reasonable cause to believe either that no liquidator is acting, or that the affairs of the company are fully wound up, and the returns required to be made by the liquidator have not been made for a period of 6 consecutive months, the registrar shall publish in the Gazette and send to the company or the liquidator (if any) a like notice as is provided in subsection (3).

(5) At the expiration of the time mentioned in the notice the registrar may, unless cause to the contrary is previously shown by the company, strike its name off the register, and shall publish notice of this in the Gazette; and on the publication of that notice in the Gazette the company is dissolved.

(6) However—

- *(a) the liability (if any) of every director, managing officer and member of the company continues and may be enforced as if the company had not been dissolved, and*
- *(b) nothing in subsection (5) affects the power of the court to wind up a company the name of which has been struck off the register.*

(7) A notice to be sent to a liquidator under this section may be addressed to him at his last known place of business; and a letter or notice to be sent under this section to a company may be addressed to the company at its registered office or, if no office has been registered, to the care of some officer of the company.

If there is no officer of the company whose name and address are known to the registrar of companies, the letter or notice may be sent to each of the persons who subscribed the memorandum, addressed to him at the address mentioned in the memorandum.

[504]

NOTES

Repealed by the Companies Act 2006, s 1295, Sch 16, as from a day to be appointed.

Application to limited liability partnerships: see the Limited Liability Partnerships Regulations 2001, SI 2001/1090, reg 4(1), Sch 2, Pt 1 at **[6985]**, **[6993]**.

Community interest companies: if a community interest company has been struck off the register under this section, the Regulator of Community Interest Companies may apply under s 653(2) of this Act for an order that the company's name be restored; see the Companies (Audit, Investigations and Community Enterprise) Act 2004, ss 26, 27(1), 51(2) at **[900]**, **[901]**, **[925]**.

[652A Registrar may strike private company off register on application

(1) On application by a private company, the registrar of companies may strike the company's name off the register.

(2) An application by a company under this section shall—
- *(a) be made on its behalf by its directors or by a majority of them,*
- *(b) be in the prescribed form, and*
- *(c) contain the prescribed information.*

(3) The registrar shall not strike a company off under this section until after the expiration of 3 months from the publication by him in the Gazette of a notice—
- *(a) stating that he may exercise his power under this section in relation to the company, and*
- *(b) inviting any person to show cause why he should not do so.*

(4) Where the registrar strikes a company off under this section, he shall publish notice of that fact in the Gazette.

(5) On the publication in the Gazette of a notice under subsection (4), the company to which the notice relates is dissolved.

(6) However, the liability (if any) of every director, managing officer and member of the company continues and may be enforced as if the company had not been dissolved.

(7) Nothing in this section affects the power of the court to wind up a company the name of which has been struck off the register.]

[505]

NOTES

Inserted, together with ss 652B–652F, by the Deregulation and Contracting Out Act 1994, s 13(1), Sch 5, paras 1, 2, as from 1 July 1995.

Repealed by the Companies Act 2006, s 1295, Sch 16, as from a day to be appointed.

Application to limited liability partnerships: see the Limited Liability Partnerships Regulations 2001, SI 2001/1090, reg 4(1), Sch 2, Pt 1 at **[6985]**, **[6993]**.

Community interest companies: if an application under this section is made on behalf of a community interest company, s 652B(6) of this Act (persons to be notified of application) is to be treated as also requiring a copy of the application to be given to the Regulator of Community Interest Companies; see the Companies (Audit, Investigations and Community Enterprise) Act 2004, ss 26, 27(1), 51(3) at **[900]**, **[901]**, **[925]**.

Fees: see Appendix 3 (Fees Instruments) at **[A3]**.

Prescribed form; prescribed information: see Appendix 4 (Forms table) at **[A4]**.

[652B Duties in connection with making application under section 652A

(1) A person shall not make an application under section 652A on behalf of a company if, at any time in the previous 3 months, the company has—
- *(a) changed its name,*
- *(b) traded or otherwise carried on business,*
- *(c) made a disposal for value of property or rights which, immediately before ceasing to trade or otherwise carry on business, it held for the purpose of disposal for gain in the normal course of trading or otherwise carrying on business, or*
- *(d) engaged in any other activity, except one which is—*
  - *(i) necessary or expedient for the purpose of making an application under section 652A, or deciding whether to do so,*
  - *(ii) necessary or expedient for the purpose of concluding the affairs of the company,*
  - *(iii) necessary or expedient for the purpose of complying with any statutory requirement, or*
  - *(iv) specified by the Secretary of State by order for the purposes of this sub-paragraph.*

(2) For the purposes of subsection (1), a company shall not be treated as trading or otherwise carrying on business by virtue only of the fact that it makes a payment in respect of a liability incurred in the course of trading or otherwise carrying on business.

(3) A person shall not make an application under section 652A on behalf of a company at a time when any of the following is the case—

(a) an application has been made to the court under section 425 on behalf of the company for the sanctioning of a compromise or arrangement and the matter has not been finally concluded;

(b) a voluntary arrangement in relation to the company has been proposed under Part I of the Insolvency Act 1986 and the matter has not been finally concluded;

[(c) the company is in administration under Part II of that Act;

(ca) an application to the court for an administration order in respect of the company has been made and not finally dealt with or withdrawn;

(cb) a copy of notice of intention to appoint an administrator of the company under paragraph 14 of Schedule B1 to that Act has been filed with the court and neither of the events mentioned in paragraph 44(2)(a) and (b) of that Schedule has occurred;

(cc) a copy of notice of intention to appoint an administrator of the company under paragraph 22 of that Schedule has been filed with the court and neither of the events mentioned in paragraph 44(4)(a) and (b) of that Schedule has occurred;]

(d) the company is being wound up under Part IV of that Act, whether voluntarily or by the court, or a petition under that Part for the winding up of the company by the court has been presented and not finally dealt with or withdrawn;

(e) there is a receiver or manager of the company's property;

(f) the company's estate is being administered by a judicial factor.

(4) For the purposes of subsection (3)(a), the matter is finally concluded if—

(a) the application has been withdrawn,

(b) the application has been finally dealt with without a compromise or arrangement being sanctioned by the court, or

(c) a compromise or arrangement has been sanctioned by the court and has, together with anything required to be done under any provision made in relation to the matter by order of the court, been fully carried out.

(5) For the purposes of subsection (3)(b), the matter is finally concluded if—

(a) no meetings are to be summoned under section 3 of the Insolvency Act 1986,

(b) meetings summoned under that section fail to approve the arrangement with no, or the same, modifications,

(c) an arrangement approved by meetings summoned under that section, or in consequence of a direction under section 6(4)(b) of that Act, has been fully implemented, or

(d) the court makes an order under subsection (5) of section 6 of that Act revoking approval given at previous meetings and, if the court gives any directions under subsection (6) of that section, the company has done whatever it is required to do under those directions.

(6) A person who makes an application under section 652A on behalf of a company shall secure that a copy of the application is given, within 7 days from the day on which the application is made, to every person who, at any time on that day, is—

(a) a member of the company,

(b) an employee of the company,

(c) a creditor of the company,

(d) a director of the company,

(e) a manager or trustee of any pension fund established for the benefit of employees of the company, or

(f) a person of a description specified for the purposes of this paragraph by regulations made by the Secretary of State.

(7) Subsection (6) shall not require a copy of the application to be given to a director who is a party to the application.

(8) The duty imposed by subsection (6) shall cease to apply if the application is withdrawn before the end of the period for giving the copy application.

(9) The Secretary of State may by order amend subsection (1) for the purpose of altering the period in relation to which the doing of the things mentioned in paragraphs (a) to (d) of that subsection is relevant.]

[506]

NOTES

Inserted as noted to s 652A at **[505]**.

Repealed by the Companies Act 2006, s 1295, Sch 16, as from a day to be appointed.

Sub-s (3): paras (c)–(cc) substituted, for original para (c), by the Enterprise Act 2002, s 248(3), Sch 17, paras 3, 7, as from 15 September 2003 (for savings and transitional provisions, see the note to the Insolvency Act 1986, s 8 at **[3164]**).

Application to limited liability partnerships: see the Limited Liability Partnerships Regulations 2001, SI 2001/1090, reg 4(1), Sch 2, Pt 1 at **[6985]**, **[6993]**.

Community interest companies: see the note to s 652A at **[505]**.

[652C Directors' duties following application under section 652A

(1) Subsection (2) applies in relation to any time after the day on which a company makes an application under section 652A and before the day on which the application is finally dealt with or withdrawn.

(2) A person who is a director of the company at the end of a day on which a person other than himself becomes—

(a) a member of the company,
(b) an employee of the company,
(c) a creditor of the company,
(d) a director of the company,
(e) a manager or trustee of any pension fund established for the benefit of employees of the company, or
(f) a person of a description specified for the purposes of this paragraph by regulations made by the Secretary of State,

shall secure that a copy of the application is given to that person within 7 days from that day.

(3) The duty imposed by subsection (2) shall cease to apply if the application is finally dealt with or withdrawn before the end of the period for giving the copy application.

(4) Subsection (5) applies where, at any time on or after the day on which a company makes an application under section 652A and before the day on which the application is finally dealt with or withdrawn—

(a) the company—
(i) changes its name,
(ii) trades or otherwise carries on business,
(iii) makes a disposal for value of any property or rights other than those which it was necessary or expedient for it to hold for the purpose of making, or proceeding with, an application under section 652A, or
(iv) engages in any other activity, except one to which subsection (6) applies;
(b) an application is made to the court under section 425 on behalf of the company for the sanctioning of a compromise or arrangement;
(c) a voluntary arrangement in relation to the company is proposed under Part I of the Insolvency Act 1986;
[(d) an application to the court for an administration order in respect of the company is made under paragraph 12 of Schedule B1 to that Act;
(da) an administrator is appointed in respect of the company under paragraph 14 or 22 of that Schedule;
(db) a copy of notice of intention to appoint an administrator of the company under paragraph 14 or 22 of that Schedule is filed with the court;]
(e) there arise any of the circumstances in which, under section 84(1) of that Act, the company may be voluntarily wound up;
(f) a petition is presented for the winding up of the company by the court under Part IV of that Act;
(g) a receiver or manager of the company's property is appointed; or
(h) a judicial factor is appointed to administer the company's estate.

(5) A person who, at the end of a day on which an event mentioned in any of paragraphs (a) to (h) of subsection (4) occurs, is a director of the company shall secure that the company's application is withdrawn forthwith.

(6) This subsection applies to any activity which is—

(a) necessary or expedient for the purpose of making, or proceeding with, an application under section 652A,
(b) necessary or expedient for the purpose of concluding affairs of the company which

are outstanding because of what has been necessary or expedient for the purpose of making, or proceeding with, such an application,

(*c*) *necessary or expedient for the purpose of complying with any statutory requirement, or*

(*d*) *specified by the Secretary of State by order for the purposes of this subsection.*

(*7*) *For the purposes of subsection* (*4*)(*a*), *a company shall not be treated as trading or otherwise carrying on business by virtue only of the fact that it makes a payment in respect of a liability incurred in the course of trading or otherwise carrying on business.]*

[507]

NOTES

Inserted as noted to s 652A at **[505]**.

Repealed by the Companies Act 2006, s 1295, Sch 16, as from a day to be appointed.

Sub-s (4): paras (d)–(db) substituted, for original para (d), by the Enterprise Act 2002, s 248(3), Sch 17, paras 3, 8, as from 15 September 2003 (for savings and transitional provisions, see the note to the Insolvency Act 1986, s 8 at **[3164]**).

Application to limited liability partnerships: see the Limited Liability Partnerships Regulations 2001, SI 2001/1090, reg 4(1), Sch 2, Pt 1 at **[6985]**, **[6993]**.

[652D Sections 652B and 652C: supplementary provisions

(*1*) *For the purposes of sections 652B(6) and 652C(2), a document shall be treated as given to a person if it is delivered to him or left at his proper address or sent by post to him at that address.*

(*2*) *For the purposes of subsection* (*1*) *and section 7 of the Interpretation Act 1978* (*which relates to the service of documents by post*) *in its application to that subsection, the proper address of any person shall be his last known address, except that—*

(*a*) *in the case of a body corporate, other than one to which subsection* (*3*) *applies, it shall be the address of its registered or principal office,*

(*b*) *in the case of a partnership, other than one to which subsection* (*3*) *applies, it shall be the address of its principal office, and*

(*c*) *in the case of a body corporate or partnership to which subsection* (*3*) *applies, it shall be the address of its principal office in the United Kingdom.*

(*3*) *This subsection applies to a body corporate or partnership which—*

(*a*) *is incorporated or formed under the law of a country or territory outside the United Kingdom, and*

(*b*) *has a place of business in the United Kingdom.*

(*4*) *Where a creditor of the company has more than one place of business, subsection* (*1*) *shall have effect, so far as concerns the giving of a document to him, as if for the words from "delivered" to the end there were substituted "left, or sent by post to him, at each place of business of his with which the company has had dealings in relation to a matter by virtue of which he is a creditor of the company."*

(*5*) *Any power to make an order or regulations under section 652B or 652C shall—*

(*a*) *include power to make different provision for different cases or classes of case,*

(*b*) *include power to make such transitional provisions as the Secretary of State considers appropriate, and*

(*c*) *be exercisable by statutory instrument subject to annulment in pursuance of a resolution of either House of Parliament.*

(*6*) *For the purposes of sections 652B and 652C, an application under section 652A is withdrawn if notice of withdrawal in the prescribed form is given to the registrar of companies.*

(*7*) *In sections 652B and 652C, "disposal" includes part disposal.*

(*8*) *In sections 652B and 652C and this section, "creditor" includes a contingent or prospective creditor.]*

[508]

NOTES

Inserted as noted to s 652A at **[505]**.

Repealed by the Companies Act 2006, s 1295, Sch 16, as from a day to be appointed.

Application to limited liability partnerships: see the Limited Liability Partnerships Regulations 2001, SI 2001/1090, reg 4(1), Sch 2, Pt 1 at **[6985]**, **[6993]**.
Prescribed form: see Appendix 4 (Forms table) at **[A4]**.

[652E Sections 652B and 652C: enforcement

(1) A person who breaches or fails to perform a duty imposed on him by section 652B or 652C is guilty of an offence and liable to a fine.

(2) A person who fails to perform a duty imposed on him by section 652B(6) or 652C(2) with the intention of concealing the making of the application in question from the person concerned is guilty of an offence and liable to imprisonment or a fine, or both.

(3) In any proceedings for an offence under subsection (1) consisting of breach of a duty imposed by section 652B(1) or (3), it shall be a defence for the accused to prove that he did not know, and could not reasonably have known, of the existence of the facts which led to the breach.

(4) In any proceedings for an offence under subsection (1) consisting of failure to perform the duty imposed by section 652B(6), it shall be a defence for the accused to prove that he took all reasonable steps to perform the duty.

(5) In any proceedings for an offence under subsection (1) consisting of failure to perform a duty imposed by section 652C(2) or (5), it shall be a defence for the accused to prove—

(a) that at the time of the failure he was not aware of the fact that the company had made an application under section 652A, or

(b) that he took all reasonable steps to perform the duty.]

[509]

NOTES

Inserted as noted to s 652A at **[505]**.
Repealed by the Companies Act 2006, s 1295, Sch 16, as from a day to be appointed.
Application to limited liability partnerships: see the Limited Liability Partnerships Regulations 2001, SI 2001/1090, reg 4(1), Sch 2, Pt 1 at **[6985]**, **[6993]**.

[652F Other offences connected with section 652A

(1) Where a company makes an application under section 652A, any person who, in connection with the application, knowingly or recklessly furnishes any information to the registrar of companies which is false or misleading in a material particular is guilty of an offence and liable to a fine.

(2) Any person who knowingly or recklessly makes an application to the registrar of companies which purports to be an application under section 652A, but which is not, is guilty of an offence and liable to a fine.]

[510]

NOTES

Inserted as noted to s 652A at **[505]**.
Repealed by the Companies Act 2006, s 1295, Sch 16, as from a day to be appointed.
Application to limited liability partnerships: see the Limited Liability Partnerships Regulations 2001, SI 2001/1090, reg 4(1), Sch 2, Pt 1 at **[6985]**, **[6993]**.

653 Objection to striking off by person aggrieved

(1) [Subsection (2)] applies if a company or any member or creditor of it feels aggrieved by the company having been struck off the register [under section 652].

(2) The court, on an application by the company or the member or creditor made before the expiration of 20 years from publication in the Gazette of notice under section 652, may, if satisfied that the company was at the time of the striking off carrying on business or in operation, or otherwise that it is just that the company be restored to the register, order the company's name to be restored.

[(2A) Subsections (2B) and (2D) apply if a company has been struck off the register under section 652A.

(2B) The court, on an application by a notifiable person made before the expiration of 20 years from publication in the Gazette of notice under section 652A(4), may, if satisfied—

(a) that any duty under section 652B or 652C with respect to the giving to that person of a copy of the company's application under section 652A was not performed,

(b) that the making of the company's application under section 652A involved a breach of duty under section 652B(1) or (3), or

(c) that it is for some other reason just to do so,

order the company's name to be restored to the register.

(2C) In subsection (2B), "notifiable person" means a person to whom a copy of the company's application under section 652A was required to be given under section 652B or 652C.

(2D) The court, on an application by the Secretary of State made before the expiration of 20 years from publication in the Gazette of notice under section 652A(4), may, if satisfied that it is in the public interest to do so, order the company's name to be restored.]

(3) On an office copy of [an order under subsection (2), (2B) or (2D)] being delivered to the registrar of companies for registration the company [to which the order relates] is deemed to have continued in existence as if its name had not been struck off; and the court may by the order give such directions and make such provisions as seem just for placing the company and all other persons in the same position (as nearly as may be) as if the company's name had not been struck off.

[511]

NOTES

Repealed by the Companies Act 2006, s 1295, Sch 16, as from a day to be appointed.

Sub-ss (1), (3): words in first pair of square brackets substituted, and words in second pair of square brackets inserted, by the Deregulation and Contracting Out Act 1994, s 13(1), Sch 5, paras 1, 3(1), (2), (4), as from 1 July 1995.

Sub-ss (2A)–(2D) inserted by the Deregulation and Contracting Out Act 1994, s 13(1), Sch 5, paras 1, 3(1), (3), as from 1 July 1995.

Application to limited liability partnerships: see the Limited Liability Partnerships Regulations 2001, SI 2001/1090, reg 4(1), Sch 2, Pt 1 at **[6985]**, **[6993]**.

Community interest companies: see the note to s 652 at **[504]**.

654 Property of dissolved company to be bona vacantia

(1) When a company is dissolved, all property and rights whatsoever vested in or held on trust for the company immediately before its dissolution (including leasehold property, but not including property held by the company on trust for any other person) are deemed to be bona vacantia and—

(a) accordingly belong to the Crown, or to the Duchy of Lancaster or to the Duke of Cornwall for the time being (as the case may be), and

(b) vest and may be dealt with in the same manner as other bona vacantia accruing to the Crown, to the Duchy of Lancaster or to the Duke of Cornwall.

(2) Except as provided by the section next following, the above has effect subject and without prejudice to any order made by the court under section 651 or 653.

[512]

NOTES

Repealed by the Companies Act 2006, s 1295, Sch 16, as from a day to be appointed.

Application to limited liability partnerships: see the Limited Liability Partnerships Regulations 2001, SI 2001/1090, reg 4(1), Sch 2, Pt 1 at **[6985]**, **[6993]**.

655 Effect on s 654 of company's revival after dissolution

(1) The person in whom any property or right is vested by section 654 may dispose of, or of an interest in, that property or right notwithstanding that an order may be made under section 651 or 653.

(2) Where such an order is made—

(a) it does not affect the disposition (but without prejudice to the order so far as it relates to any other property or right previously vested in or held on trust for the company), and

(b) the Crown or, as the case may be, the Duke of Cornwall shall pay to the company an amount equal to—

(i) *the amount of any consideration received for the property or right, or interest therein, or*
(ii) *the value of any such consideration at the time of the disposition,*

or, if no consideration was received, an amount equal to the value of the property, right or interest disposed of, as at the date of the disposition.

(3) *Where a liability accrues under subsection (2) in respect of any property or right which, before the order under section 651 or 653 was made, had accrued as bona vacantia to the Duchy of Lancaster, the Attorney General of the Duchy shall represent Her Majesty in any proceedings arising in connection with that liability.*

(4) *Where a liability accrues under subsection (2) in respect of any property or right which, before the order under section 651 or 653 was made, had accrued as bona vacantia to the Duchy of Cornwall, such persons as the Duke of Cornwall (or other possessor for the time being of the Duchy) may appoint shall represent the Duke (or other possessor) in any proceedings arising out of that liability.*

(5) *This section applies in relation to the disposition of any property, right or interest on or after 22nd December 1981, whether the company concerned was dissolved before, on or after that day.*

[513]

NOTES

Repealed by the Companies Act 2006, s 1295, Sch 16, as from a day to be appointed.
Application to limited liability partnerships: see the Limited Liability Partnerships Regulations 2001, SI 2001/1090, reg 4(1), Sch 2, Pt 1 at **[6985]**, **[6993]**.

656 Crown disclaimer of property vesting as bona vacantia

(1) *Where property vests in the Crown under section 654, the Crown's title to it under that section may be disclaimed by a notice signed by the Crown representative, that is to say the Treasury Solicitor, or, in relation to property in Scotland, the Queen's and Lord Treasurer's Remembrancer.*

(2) *The right to execute a notice of disclaimer under this section may be waived by or on behalf of the Crown either expressly or by taking possession or other act evincing that intention.*

(3) *A notice of disclaimer under this section is of no effect unless it is executed—*
(a) *within 12 months of the date on which the vesting of the property under section 654 came to the notice of the Crown representative, or*
(b) *if an application in writing is made to the Crown representative by any person interested in the property requiring him to decide whether he will or will not disclaim, within a period of 3 months after the receipt of the application or such further period as may be allowed by the court which would have had jurisdiction to wind up the company if it had not been dissolved.*

(4) *A statement in a notice of disclaimer of any property under this section that the vesting of it came to the notice of the Crown representative on a specified date, or that no such application as above mentioned was received by him with respect to the property before a specified date, is sufficient evidence of the fact stated, until the contrary is proved.*

(5) *A notice of disclaimer under this section shall be delivered to the registrar of companies and retained and registered by him; and copies of it shall be published in the Gazette and sent to any persons who have given the Crown representative notice that they claim to be interested in the property.*

(6) *This section applies to property vested in the Duchy of Lancaster or the Duke of Cornwall under section 654 as if for references to the Crown and the Crown representative there were respectively substituted references to the Duchy of Lancaster and to the Solicitor to that Duchy, or to the Duke of Cornwall and to the Solicitor to the Duchy of Cornwall, as the case may be.*

[514]

NOTES

Repealed by the Companies Act 2006, s 1295, Sch 16, as from a day to be appointed.
Application to limited liability partnerships: see the Limited Liability Partnerships Regulations 2001, SI 2001/1090, reg 4(1), Sch 2, Pt 1 at **[6985]**, **[6993]**.

657 Effect of Crown disclaimer under s 656

(*1*) *Where notice of disclaimer is executed under section 656 as respects any property, that property is deemed not to have vested in the Crown under section 654.*

[(2) As regards property in England and Wales, [section 178(4) and sections 179 to 182 of the Insolvency Act] shall apply as if the property had been disclaimed by the liquidator under the said section 91 immediately before the dissolution of the company.]

(*3*) *As regards property in Scotland, the following 4 subsections apply.*

(*4*) *The Crown's disclaimer operates to determine, as from the date of the disclaimer, the rights, interests and liabilities of the company, and the property of the company, in or in respect of the property disclaimed; but it does not (except so far as is necessary for the purpose of releasing the company and its property from liability) affect the rights or liabilities of any other person.*

(*5*) *The court may, on application by a person who either claims an interest in disclaimed property or is under a liability not discharged by this Act in respect of disclaimed property, and on hearing such persons as it thinks fit, make an order for the vesting of the property in or its delivery to any persons entitled to it, or to whom it may seem just that the property should be delivered by way of compensation for such liability, or a trustee for him, and on such terms as the court thinks just.*

(*6*) *On such a vesting order being made, the property comprised in it vests accordingly in the person named in that behalf in the order, without conveyance or assignation for that purpose.*

(*7*) *Part II of Schedule 20 has effect for the protection of third parties where the property disclaimed is held under a lease.*

[515]

NOTES

Repealed by the Companies Act 2006, s 1295, Sch 16, as from a day to be appointed.

Sub-s (2): substituted by the Insolvency Act 1985, s 109(1), Sch 6, para 46, as from 29 December 1986; words in square brackets substituted, subject to transitional provisions, by the Insolvency Act 1986, ss 437, 439(1), Sch 11, Pt I, Sch 13, Pt I, as from 29 December 1986.

Application to limited liability partnerships: see the Limited Liability Partnerships Regulations 2001, SI 2001/1090, reg 4(1), Sch 2, Pt 1 at **[6985]**, **[6993]**.

Said section 91: the section referred to is the Insolvency Act 1985, s 91 (repealed). It is thought that this reference should also have been altered by the Insolvency Act 1986 to a reference to ss 178–180 of that Act.

Insolvency Act, ss 178(4), 179–182: ie, the Insolvency Act 1986, ss 178(4), 179–182.

658 Liability for rentcharge on company's land after dissolution

[(1) [Section 180 of the Insolvency Act] shall apply to land in England and Wales which by operation of law vests subject to a rentcharge in the Crown or any other person on the dissolution of a company as it applies to land so vesting on a disclaimer under that section.]

(2) *In this section "company" includes any body corporate.*

[516]

NOTES

Repealed by the Companies Act 2006, s 1295, Sch 16, as from a day to be appointed.

Sub-s (1): substituted by the Insolvency Act 1985, s 109(1), Sch 6, para 47, as from 29 December 1986; words in square brackets substituted, subject to transitional provisions, by the Insolvency Act 1986, ss 437, 439(1), Sch 11, Pt I, Sch 13, Pt I, as from 29 December 1986.

Application to limited liability partnerships: see the Limited Liability Partnerships Regulations 2001, SI 2001/1090, reg 4(1), Sch 2, Pt 1 at **[6985]**, **[6993]**.

Insolvency Act, s 180: ie, the Insolvency Act 1986, s 180.

659–674 ((*Pt XX, Chapter VII, Pt XXI*) *repealed, with savings, by the Insolvency Act 1986, ss 437, 438, Schs 11, 12, as from 29 December 1986. Also Repealed by the Companies Act 2006, s 1295, Sch 16, as from a day to be appointed.*)

PART XXII
BODIES CORPORATE SUBJECT, OR BECOMING SUBJECT, TO THIS ACT (OTHERWISE THAN BY ORIGINAL FORMATION UNDER PART I)

CHAPTER I
COMPANIES FORMED OR REGISTERED UNDER FORMER COMPANIES ACTS

675 Companies formed and registered under former Companies Acts

(1) In its application to existing companies, this Act applies in the same manner—

(a) in the case of a limited company (other than a company limited by guarantee) as if the company had been formed and registered under Part I of this Act as a company limited by shares,

(b) in the case of a company limited by guarantee, as if the company had been formed and registered under that Part as a company limited by guarantee, and

(c) in the case of a company other than a limited company, as if the company had been formed and registered under that Part as an unlimited company.

(2) But reference, express or implied, to the date of registration is to be read as the date at which the company was registered under the Joint Stock Companies Acts, the Companies Act 1862, the Companies (Consolidation) Act 1908, the Companies Act 1929, or the Companies Act 1948.

[517]

NOTES

Repealed by the Companies Act 2006, s 1295, Sch 16, as from a day to be appointed.
Companies Act 1862: repealed by the Companies (Consolidation) Act 1908, s 286, Sch 6, Pt I.
Companies (Consolidation) Act 1908: repealed by the Companies Act 1929, s 381, Sch 12, Pt I.
Companies Act 1929: repealed by the Companies Act 1948, s 459(1), Sch 17.
Companies Act 1948: repealed by the Companies Consolidation (Consequential Provisions) Act 1985, s 29, Sch 1.

676 Companies registered but not formed under former Companies Acts

(1) This Act applies to every company registered but not formed under the Joint Stock Companies Acts, the Companies Act 1862, the Companies (Consolidation) Act 1908, the Companies Act 1929, or the Companies Act 1948, in the same manner as it is in Chapter II of this Part declared to apply to companies registered but not formed under this Act.

(2) But reference, express or implied, to the date of registration is to be read as referring to the date at which the company was registered under the Joint Stock Companies Acts, the Companies Act 1862, the Companies (Consolidation) Act 1908, the Companies Act 1929, or the Companies Act 1948.

[518]

NOTES

Repealed by the Companies Act 2006, s 1295, Sch 16, as from a day to be appointed.
Companies Act 1862; Companies (Consolidation) Act 1908; Companies Act 1929; Companies Act 1948: repealed (see the notes to s 675 at **[517]**);

677 Companies re-registered with altered status under former Companies Acts

(1) This Act applies to every unlimited company registered or re-registered as limited in pursuance of the Companies Act 1879, section 57 of the Companies (Consolidation) Act 1908, section 16 of the Companies Act 1929, section 16 of the Companies Act 1948 or section 44 of the Companies Act 1967 as it (this Act) applies to an unlimited company re-registered as limited in pursuance of Part II of this Act.

(2) But reference, express or implied, to the date of registration or re-registration is to be read as referring to the date at which the company was registered or re-registered as a limited company under the relevant enactment.

[519]

NOTES

Repealed by the Companies Act 2006, s 1295, Sch 16, as from a day to be appointed.
Companies Act 1879: repealed by the Companies (Consolidation) Act 1908, s 286, Sch 6, Pt I.

Companies (Consolidation) Act 1908; Companies Act 1929; Companies Act 1948: repealed (see the notes to s 675 at **[517]**);

Companies Act 1967, s 44: repealed by the Companies Consolidation (Consequential Provisions) Act 1985, s 29, Sch 1.

678 Companies registered under Joint Stock Companies Acts

(1) A company registered under the Joint Stock Companies Acts may cause its shares to be transferred in manner hitherto in use, or in such other manner as the company may direct.

(2) The power of altering articles under section 9 of this Act extends, in the case of an unlimited company formed and registered under the Joint Stock Companies Acts, to altering any regulations relating to the amount of capital or to its distribution into shares, notwithstanding that those regulations are contained in the memorandum.

[520]

NOTES

Repealed by the Companies Act 2006, s 1295, Sch 16, as from a day to be appointed.

Joint Stock Companies Acts: the Joint Stock Companies Act 1856, the Joint Stock Companies Acts 1856, 1857, the Joint Stock Banking Companies Act 1857 and the Act to enable Joint Stock Banking Companies to be formed on the principle of limited liability, or any one or more of those Acts (as the case may require), but does not include the Joint Stock Companies Act 1844.

679 Northern Ireland and Irish companies

Nothing in sections 675 to 678 applies to companies registered in Northern Ireland or the Republic of Ireland.

[521]

NOTES

Repealed by the Companies Act 2006, s 1295, Sch 16, as from a day to be appointed.

CHAPTER II
COMPANIES NOT FORMED UNDER COMPANIES LEGISLATION, BUT AUTHORISED TO REGISTER

680 Companies capable of being registered under this Chapter

(1) With the exceptions and subject to the provisions contained in this section and the next—

- (*a*) *any company consisting of two or more members, which was in existence on 2nd November 1862, including any company registered under the Joint Stock Companies Acts, and*
- (*b*) *any company formed after that date (whether before or after the commencement of this Act), in pursuance of any Act of Parliament (other than this Act), or of letters patent, or being otherwise duly constituted according to law, and consisting of two or more members,*

may at any time, on making application in the prescribed form, register under this Act as an unlimited company, or as a company limited by shares, or as a company limited by guarantee; and the registration is not invalid by reason that it has taken place with a view to the company's being wound up.

[(1A) A company shall not be prevented from registering under this Act as a private company limited by shares or guarantee solely because it has only one member.]

(2) A company registered in any part of the United Kingdom under the Companies Act 1862, the Companies (Consolidation) Act 1908, the Companies Act 1929 or the Companies Act 1948 shall not register under this section.

(3) A company having the liability of its members limited by Act of Parliament or letters patent, and not being a joint stock company, shall not register under this section.

(4) A company having the liability of its members limited by Act of Parliament or letters patent shall not register in pursuance of this section as an unlimited company or as a company limited by guarantee.

(5) A company that is not a joint stock company shall not register under this section as a company limited by shares.

[522]

NOTES

Repealed by the Companies Act 2006, s 1295, Sch 16, as from a day to be appointed.

Sub-s (1A): inserted by the Companies (Single Member Private Limited Companies) Regulations 1992, SI 1992/1699, reg 2, Schedule, para 7, as from 15 July 1992.

Joint Stock Companies Acts: the Joint Stock Companies Act 1856, the Joint Stock Companies Acts 1856, 1857, the Joint Stock Banking Companies Act 1857 and the Act to enable Joint Stock Banking Companies to be formed on the principle of limited liability, or any one or more of those Acts (as the case may require), but does not include the Joint Stock Companies Act 1844.

Companies Act 1862; Companies (Consolidation) Act 1908; Companies Act 1929; Companies Act 1948: repealed (see the notes to s 675 at **[517]**);

Fees: see Appendix 3 (Fees Instruments) at **[A3]**.

Prescribed form: see Appendix 4 (Forms table) at **[A4]**.

681 Procedural requirements for registration

(1) A company shall not register under section 680 without the assent of a majority of such of its members as are present in person or by proxy (in cases where proxies are allowed) at a general meeting summoned for the purpose.

(2) Where a company not having the liability of its members limited by Act of Parliament or letters patent is about to register as a limited company, the majority required to assent as required by subsection (1) shall consist of not less than three-fourths of the members present in person or by proxy at the meeting.

(3) In computing any majority under this section when a poll is demanded, regard is to be had to the number of votes to which each member is entitled according to the company's regulations.

(4) Where a company is about to register (under section 680) as a company limited by guarantee, the assent to its being so registered shall be accompanied by a resolution declaring that each member undertakes to contribute to the company's assets, in the event of its being wound up while he is a member, or within one year after he ceases to be a member, for payment of the company's debts and liabilities contracted before he ceased to be a member, and of the costs and expenses of winding up and for the adjustment of the rights of the contributories among themselves, such amount as may be required, not exceeding a specified amount.

(5) Before a company is registered under section 680, it shall deliver to the registrar of companies—

- *(a) a statement that the registered office of the company is to be situated in England and Wales, or in Wales, or in Scotland (as the case may be),*
- *(b) a statement specifying the intended situation of the company's registered office after registration, and*
- *(c) in an appropriate case, if the company wishes to be registered with the Welsh equivalent of "public limited company" or, as the case may be, "limited" as the last words or word of its name, a statement to that effect.*

(6) Any statement delivered to the registrar under subsection (5) shall be made in the prescribed form.

[523]

NOTES

Repealed by the Companies Act 2006, s 1295, Sch 16, as from a day to be appointed.

Prescribed form: see Appendix 4 (Forms table) at **[A4]**.

682 Change of name on registration

(1) Where the name of a company seeking registration under section 680 is a name by which it is precluded from registration by section 26 of this Act, either because it falls within subsection (1) of that section or, if it falls within subsection (2), because the Secretary of State would not approve the company's being registered with that name, the company may change its name with effect from the date on which it is registered under this Chapter.

(2) *A change of name under this section requires the like assent of the company's members as is required by section 681 for registration.*

[524]

NOTES

Repealed by the Companies Act 2006, s 1295, Sch 16, as from a day to be appointed.

683 Definition of "joint stock company"

(*1*) *For purposes of this Chapter, as far as relates to registration of companies as companies limited by shares, "joint stock company" means a company—*

(*a*) *having a permanent paid-up or nominal share capital of fixed amount divided into shares, also of fixed amount, or held and transferable as stock, or divided and held partly in one way and partly in the other, and*

(*b*) *formed on the principle of having for its members the holders of those shares or that stock, and no other persons.*

(2) *Such a company when registered with limited liability under this Act is deemed a company limited by shares.*

[525]

NOTES

Repealed by the Companies Act 2006, s 1295, Sch 16, as from a day to be appointed.

684 Requirements for registration by joint stock companies

(*1*) *Before the registration under section 680 of a joint stock company, there shall be delivered to the registrar of companies the following documents—*

(*a*) *a statement in the prescribed form specifying the name with which the company is proposed to be registered,*

(*b*) *a list in the prescribed form showing the names and addresses of all persons who on a day named in the list [(not more than 28 clear days before the day of registration)] were members of the company, with the addition of the shares or stock held by them respectively (distinguishing, in cases where the shares are numbered, each share by its number), and*

(*c*) *a copy of any Act of Parliament, royal charter, letters patent, deed of settlement, contract of copartnery or other instrument constituting or regulating the company.*

(2) *If the company is intended to be registered as a limited company, there shall also be delivered to the registrar of companies a statement in the prescribed form specifying the following particulars—*

(*a*) *the nominal share capital of the company and the number of shares into which it is divided, or the amount of stock of which it consists, and*

(*b*) *the number of shares taken and the amount paid on each share.*

[526]

NOTES

Repealed by the Companies Act 2006, s 1295, Sch 16, as from a day to be appointed.

Sub-s (1): words in square brackets in para (b) substituted by CA 1989, s 145, Sch 19, para 12, as from 1 March 1990.

Prescribed form: see Appendix 4 (Forms table) at **[A4]**.

685 Registration of joint stock company as public company

(*1*) *A joint stock company applying to be registered under section 680 as a company limited by shares may, subject to—*

(*a*) *satisfying the conditions set out in section 44(2)(a) and (b) (where applicable) and section 45(2) to (4) as applied by this section, and*

(*b*) *complying with subsection (4) below,*

apply to be so registered as a public company.

(2) *Sections 44 and 45 apply for this purpose as in the case of a private company applying to be re-registered under section 43, but as if a reference to the special resolution required by section 43 were to the joint stock company's resolution that it be a public company.*

(3) The resolution may change the company's name by deleting the word "company" or the words "and company", or its or their equivalent in Welsh ("cwmni", "a'r cwmni"), including any abbreviation of them.

(4) The joint stock company's application shall be made in the form prescribed for the purpose, and shall be delivered to the registrar of companies together with the following documents (as well as those required by section 684), namely—

- *(a) a copy of the resolution that the company be a public company,*
- *(b) a copy of a written statement by an accountant with the appropriate qualifications that in his opinion a relevant balance sheet shows that at the balance sheet date the amount of the company's net assets was not less than the aggregate of its called up share capital and undistributable reserves,*
- *(c) a copy of the relevant balance sheet, together with a copy of an unqualified report (by an accountant with such qualifications) in relation to that balance sheet,*
- *(d) a copy of any valuation report prepared under section 44(2)(b) as applied by this section, and*
- *(e) [subject to subsection (4A),] a statutory declaration in the prescribed form by a director or secretary of the company—*
  - *(i) that the conditions set out in section 44(2)(a) and (b) (where applicable) and section 45(2) to (4) have been satisfied, and*
  - *(ii) that, between the balance sheet date referred to in paragraph (b) of this subsection and the joint stock company's application, there has been no change in the company's financial position that has resulted in the amount of its net assets becoming less than the aggregate of its called up share capital and undistributable reserves.*

[(4A) In place of the statutory declaration referred to in paragraph (e) of subsection (4), there may be delivered to the registrar of companies using electronic communications a statement made by a director or secretary of the company as to the matters set out in sub-paragraphs (i) and (ii) of that paragraph.]

(5) The registrar may accept a declaration under subsection (4)(e) [or statement under subsection (4A)] as sufficient evidence that the conditions referred to in that paragraph have been satisfied.

(6) In this section—

"accountant with the appropriate qualifications" means [a person who would be eligible] for appointment as the company's auditor, if it were a company registered under this Act,

"relevant balance sheet" means a balance sheet prepared as at a date not more than 7 months before the joint stock company's application to be registered as a public company limited by shares, and

"undistributable reserves" has the meaning given by section 264(3);

and section 46 applies (with necessary modifications) for the interpretation of the reference in subsection (4)(c) above to an unqualified report by the accountant.

[(6A) Any person who makes a false statement under subsection (4A) which he knows to be false or does not believe to be true is liable to imprisonment or a fine, or both.]

[527]

NOTES

Repealed by the Companies Act 2006, s 1295, Sch 16, as from a day to be appointed.

Sub-ss (4), (5): words in square brackets inserted by the Companies Act 1985 (Electronic Communications) Order 2000, SI 2000/3373, art 24(1), (2), (4), as from 22 December 2000.

Sub-s (4A): inserted by SI 2000/3373, art 24(1), (3), as from 22 December 2000.

Sub-s (6): words in square brackets substituted by the Companies Act 1989 (Eligibility for Appointment as Company Auditor) (Consequential Amendments) Regulations 1991, SI 1991/1997, reg 2, Schedule, para 53(1), (2), as from 1 October 1991 (for transitional provisions see reg 4 of those Regulations at **[6715]**).

Sub-s (6A): added by SI 2000/3373, art 24(1), (5), as from 22 December 2000.

Form prescribed; prescribed form: see Appendix 4 (Forms table) at **[A4]**.

686 Other requirements for registration

(1) Before the registration in pursuance of this Chapter of any company (not being a joint stock company), there shall be delivered to the registrar of companies—

- *(a) a statement in the prescribed form specifying the name with which the company is proposed to be registered, [(b) a list showing with respect to each director or manager of the company—*

(i) in the case of an individual, his name, address, occupation and date of birth,

(ii) in the case of a corporation or Scottish firm, its corporate or firm name and registered or principal office,]

(c) a copy of any Act of Parliament, letters patent, deed of settlement, contract of copartnery or other instrument constituting or regulating the company, and

(d) in the case of a company intended to be registered as a company limited by guarantee, a copy of the resolution declaring the amount of the guarantee.

[(1A) For the purposes of subsection (1)(b)(i) a person's "name" means his Christian name (or other forename) and surname, except that in the case of a peer, or an individual usually known by a title, the title may be stated instead of his Christian name (or other forename) and surname or in addition to either or both of them.]

(2) [Subject to subsection (2A), the lists] of members and directors and any other particulars relating to the company which are required by this Chapter to be delivered to the registrar shall be verified by a statutory declaration in the prescribed form made by any two or more directors or other principal officers of the company.

[(2A) In place of the statutory declaration referred to in subsection (2), there may be delivered to the registrar of companies using electronic communications a statement made by any two or more directors or other principal officers of the company verifying the matters set out in that subsection.]

(3) The registrar may require such evidence as he thinks necessary for the purpose of satisfying himself whether a company proposing to be registered is or is not a joint stock company as defined by section 683.

[(3A) Any person who makes a false statement under subsection (2A) which he knows to be false or does not believe to be true is liable to imprisonment or a fine, or both.]

[528]

NOTES

Repealed by the Companies Act 2006, s 1295, Sch 16, as from a day to be appointed.

Sub-s (1): para (b) substituted by CA 1989, s 145, Sch 19, para 5(1), (2), as from 1 October 1990.

Sub-s (1A): inserted by CA 1989, s 145, Sch 19, para 5(1), (3), as from 1 October 1990.

Sub-s (2): words in square brackets substituted by the Companies Act 1985 (Electronic Communications) Order 2000, SI 2000/3373, art 25(1), (2), as from 22 December 2000.

Sub-ss (2A), (3A): inserted and added respectively by SI 2000/3373, art 25(1), (3), (4), as from 22 December 2000.

Prescribed form: see Appendix 4 (Forms table) at **[A4]**.

687 Name of company registering

(1) The following applies with respect to the name of a company registering under this Chapter (whether a joint stock company or not).

(2) If the company is to be registered as a public company, its name must end with the words "public limited company" or, if it is stated that the company's registered office is to be situated in Wales, with those words or their equivalent in Welsh ("cwmni cyfyngedig chyoeddus"); and those words or that equivalent may not be preceded by the word "limited" or its equivalent in Welsh ("cyfyngedig").

(3) In the case of a company limited by shares or by guarantee (not being a public company), the name must have "limited" as its last word (or, if the company's registered office is to be situated in Wales, "cyfyngedig"); but this is subject to section 30 (exempting a company, in certain circumstances, from having "limited" as part of the name).

(4) If the company is registered with limited liability, then any additions to the company's name set out in the statements delivered under section 684(1)(a) or 686(1)(a) shall form and be registered as the last part of the company's name.

[529]

NOTES

Repealed by the Companies Act 2006, s 1295, Sch 16, as from a day to be appointed.

688 Certificate of registration under this Chapter

(1) On compliance with the requirements of this Chapter with respect to registration, the registrar of companies shall give a certificate (which may be signed by him, or authenticated by his official seal) that the company applying for registration is incorporated as a company under this Act and, in the case of a limited company, that it is limited.

(2) On the issue of the certificate, the company shall be so incorporated; and a banking company in Scotland so incorporated is deemed a bank incorporated, constituted or established by or under Act of Parliament.

(3) The certificate is conclusive evidence that the requirements of this Chapter in respect of registration, and of matters precedent and incidental to it, have been complied with.

(4) Where on an application by a joint stock company to register as a public company limited by shares the registrar of companies is satisfied that the company may be registered as a public company so limited, the certificate of incorporation given under this section shall state that the company is a public company; and that statement is conclusive evidence that the requirements of section 685 have been complied with and that the company is a public company so limited.

[530]

NOTES

Repealed by the Companies Act 2006, s 1295, Sch 16, as from a day to be appointed.

689 Effect of registration

Schedule 21 to this Act has effect with respect to the consequences of registration under this Chapter, the vesting of property, savings for existing liabilities, continuation of existing actions, status of the company following registration, and other connected matters.

[531]

NOTES

Repealed by the Companies Act 2006, s 1295, Sch 16, as from a day to be appointed.

690 Power to substitute memorandum and articles for deed of settlement

(1) Subject as follows, a company registered in pursuance of this Chapter may by special resolution alter the form of its constitution by substituting a memorandum and articles for a deed of settlement.

(2) The provisions of sections 4 to 6 of this Act with respect to applications to the court for cancellation of alterations of the objects of a company and matters consequential on the passing of resolutions for such alterations (so far as applicable) apply, but with the following modifications—

- *(a) there is substituted for the printed copy of the altered memorandum required to be delivered to the registrar of companies a printed copy of the substituted memorandum and articles, and*
- *(b) on the delivery to the registrar of the substituted memorandum and articles or the date when the alteration is no longer liable to be cancelled by order of the court (whichever is the later)—*
  - *(i) the substituted memorandum and articles apply to the company in the same manner as if it were a company registered under Part I with that memorandum and those articles, and*
  - *(ii) the company's deed of settlement ceases to apply to the company.*

(3) An alteration under this section may be made either with or without alteration of the company's objects.

(4) In this section "deed of settlement" includes any contract of copartnery or other instrument constituting or regulating the company, not being an Act of Parliament, a royal charter or letters patent.

[532]

NOTES

Repealed by the Companies Act 2006, s 1295, Sch 16, as from a day to be appointed.

PART XXIII
OVERSEA COMPANIES

CHAPTER I
REGISTRATION, ETC

[690A Branch registration under the Eleventh Company Law Directive (89/66/EEC)

(*1*) *This section applies to any limited company which—*

(*a*) *is incorporated outside the United Kingdom and Gibraltar, and*

(*b*) *has a branch in Great Britain.*

(*2*) *Schedule 21A to this Act* (*Branch registration under the Eleventh Company Law Directive* (*89/666/EEC*)) *shall have effect in relation to any company to which this section applies.]*

[533]

NOTES

Inserted, together with s 690B, by the Oversea Companies and Credit and Financial Institutions (Branch Disclosure) Regulations 1992, SI 1992/3179, reg 3, Sch 2, Pt I, paras 1, 2, as from 1 January 1993; for transitional provisions see Sch 4 to those Regulations at **[6744B]**.

Repealed by the Companies Act 2006, s 1295, Sch 16, as from a day to be appointed.

[690B Scope of sections 691 and 692

Sections 691 and 692 shall not apply to any limited company which—

(*a*) *is incorporated outside the United Kingdom and Gibraltar, and*

(*b*) *has a branch in the United Kingdom.]*

[534]

NOTES

Inserted as noted to s 690A at **[533]**.

Repealed by the Companies Act 2006, s 1295, Sch 16, as from a day to be appointed.

691 Documents to be delivered to registrar

(*1*) *When a company incorporated outside Great Britain establishes a place of business in Great Britain, it shall within one month of doing so deliver to the registrar of companies for registration—*

(*a*) *a certified copy of the charter, statutes or memorandum and articles of the company or other instrument constituting or defining the company's constitution, and, if the instrument is not written in the English language, a certified translation of it; and*

(*b*) *a return in the prescribed form containing—*

(*i*) *a list of the company's directors and secretary, containing [(subject to subsection* (*5*))*] the particulars specified in the next subsection,*

(*ii*) *a list of the names and addresses of some one or more persons resident in Great Britain authorised to accept on the company's behalf service of process and any notices required to be served on it,*

(*iii*) *a list of the documents delivered in compliance with paragraph* (*a*) *of this subsection, and*

(*iv*) *[subject to subsection* (*3A*)*,] a statutory declaration* (*made by a director or secretary of the company or by any person whose name and address are given in the list required by sub-paragraph* (*ii*)), *stating the date on which the company's place of business in Great Britain was established.*

[(*2*) *The list referred to in subsection* (*1*)(*b*)(*i*) *shall contain the following particulars with respect to each director—*

(*a*) *in the case of an individual—*

(*i*) *his name,*

(*ii*) *any former name,*

(*iii*) *his usual residential address,*

(*iv*) *his nationality,*

(*v*) *his business occupation* (*if any*),

(vi) *if he has no business occupation but holds other directorships, particulars of them, and*

(vii) *his date of birth;*

(*b*) *in the case of a corporation or Scottish firm, its corporate or firm name and registered or principal office.*

(3) *The list referred to in subsection (1)(b)(i) shall contain the following particulars with respect to the secretary (or, where there are joint secretaries, with respect to each of them)—*

(*a*) *in the case of an individual, his name, any former name and his usual residential address;*

(*b*) *in the case of a corporation or Scottish firm, its corporate or firm name and registered or principal office.*

Where all the partners in a firm are joint secretaries of the company, the name and principal office of the firm may be stated instead of the particulars required by paragraph (a).

[(3A) In place of the statutory declaration referred to in sub-paragraph (iv) of paragraph (b) of subsection (1), there may be delivered to the registrar of companies using electronic communications a statement made by any person by whom the declaration could have been made stating the date on which the company's place of business in Great Britain was established.]

(4) *In subsections (2)(a) and (3)(a) above—*

(*a*) *"name" means a person's Christian name (or other forename) and surname, except that in the case of a peer, or an individual usually known by a title, the title may be stated instead of his Christian name (or other forename) and surname, or in addition to either or both of them; and*

(*b*) *the reference to a former name does not include—*

(i) *in the case of a peer, or an individual normally known by a British title, the name by which he was known previous to the adoption of or succession to the title, or*

(ii) *in the case of any person, a former name which was changed or disused before he attained the age of 18 years or which has been changed or disused for 20 years or more, or*

(iii) *in the case of a married woman, the name by which she was known previous to the marriage.]*

[(4A) Any person who makes a false statement under subsection (3A) which he knows to be false or does not believe to be true is liable to imprisonment or a fine, or both.]

[(5) Where a confidentiality order made under section 723B is in force in respect of a director or secretary required to be specified in the list under subsection (1)(b)(i)—

(*a*) *if the order is in respect of a director, subsection (2) has effect in respect of that director as if the reference in subsection (2)(a)(iii) to his usual residential address were a reference to the address for the time being notified by him to the company under regulations made under sections 723B to 723F;*

(*b*) *if the order is in respect of a secretary, subsection (3) has effect in respect of that secretary as if the reference in subsection (3)(a) to his usual residential address were a reference to the address for the time being notified by him to the company under such regulations; and*

(*c*) *in either case the company shall deliver to the registrar, in addition to the return required by subsection (1), a return in the prescribed form containing the usual residential address of the director or secretary to whom the confidentiality order relates, and any such return shall be delivered to the registrar within one month of the company establishing a place of business in Great Britain.]*

[535]

NOTES

Repealed by the Companies Act 2006, s 1295, Sch 16, as from a day to be appointed.

Sub-s (1): words in first pair of square brackets in para (b) inserted by the Companies (Particulars of Usual Residential Address) (Confidentiality Orders) Regulations 2002, SI 2002/912, reg 16, Sch 2, para 5(1), (2), as from 2 April 2002; words in second pair of square brackets in para (b) inserted by the Companies Act 1985 (Electronic Communications) Order 2000, SI 2000/3373, art 26(1), (2), as from 22 December 2000.

Sub-ss (2), (3), (4): substituted, for original sub-s (2), by CA 1989, s 145, Sch 19, para 6, as from 1 October 1990.

Sub-ss (3A), (4A): inserted and added respectively by SI 2000/3373, art 26(1), (3), (4), as from 22 December 2000.

Sub-s (5): added by SI 2002/912, reg 16, Sch 2, para 5(1), (3), as from 2 April 2002.

PART I COMPANIES LEGISLATION

Certified translation: see s 698 at **[545]**, the Companies (Forms) Regulations 1985, SI 1985/854, reg 6 and the note relating to that regulation to s 272 at **[277]**.
Fees: see Appendix 3 (Fees Instruments) at **[A3]**.
Prescribed form: see Appendix 4 (Forms table) at **[A4]**.

692 Registration of altered particulars

(1) If any alteration is made in—

(a) the charter, statutes, or memorandum and articles of an oversea company or any such instrument as is mentioned above, or

(b) the directors or secretary of an oversea company or the particulars contained in the list of the directors and secretary, or

(c) the names or addresses of the persons authorised to accept service on behalf of an oversea company,

the company shall, within the time specified below, deliver to the registrar of companies for registration a return containing the prescribed particulars of the alteration.

[(1A) If an individual in respect of whom a confidentiality order under section 723B is in force becomes a director or secretary of an oversea company—

(a) the return required to be delivered to the registrar under subsection (1) shall contain the address for the time being notified by the director or secretary to the company under regulations made under sections 723B to 723F, but shall not contain his usual residential address; and

(b) with that return the company shall deliver to the registrar a return in the prescribed form containing the usual residential address of that director or secretary.

(1B) If a confidentiality order under section 723B is made in respect of an existing director or secretary of an oversea company, the company shall within the time specified below deliver to the registrar of companies for registration a return in the prescribed form containing the address for the time being notified to it by the director or secretary under regulations made under sections 723B to 723F.

(1C) If while a confidentiality order made under section 723B is in force in respect of a director or secretary of an oversea company there is an alteration in his usual residential address, the company shall within the time specified below deliver to the registrar of companies for registration a return in the prescribed form containing the new address.]

(2) If any change is made in the corporate name of an oversea company, the company shall, within the time specified below, deliver to the registrar of companies for registration a return containing the prescribed particulars of the change.

(3) The time for delivery of the returns required by subsections (1)[, (1B), (1C)] and (2) is—

(a) in the case of an alteration to which subsection (1)(c) applies, 21 days after the making of the alteration, and

(b) otherwise, 21 days after the date on which notice of the alteration or change in question could have been received in Great Britain in due course of post (if despatched with due diligence).

[536]

NOTES

Repealed by the Companies Act 2006, s 1295, Sch 16, as from a day to be appointed.
Sub-ss (1A)–(1C): inserted by the Companies (Particulars of Usual Residential Address) (Confidentiality Orders) Regulations 2002, SI 2002/912, reg 16, Sch 2, para 6(1), (2), as from 2 April 2002.
Sub-s (3): words in square brackets inserted by SI 2002/912, reg 16, Sch 2, para 6(1), (3), as from 2 April 2002.
Prescribed particulars of the alteration; prescribed particulars of the change: see Appendix 4 (Forms table) at **[A4]**.

[692A Change in registration regime

(1) Where a company ceases to be a company to which section 690A applies and, immediately after ceasing to be such a company—

(a) continues to have in Great Britain a place of business which it had immediately before ceasing to be such a company, and

(*b*) *does not have a branch in Northern Ireland,*

it shall be treated for the purposes of section 691 as having established the place of business on the date when it ceased to be a company to which section 690A applies.

(2) *Where a limited company incorporated outside the United Kingdom and Gibraltar—*

(*a*) *ceases to have a branch in Northern Ireland, and*

(*b*) *both immediately before and immediately after ceasing to do so, has a place of business, but not a branch, in Great Britain,*

it shall be treated for the purposes of section 691 as having established the place of business on the date when it ceased to have a branch in Northern Ireland.

(3) *Where a company—*

(*a*) *becomes a company to which section 690A applies,*

(*b*) *immediately after becoming such a company, has in a part of Great Britain an established place of business but no branch, and*

(*c*) *immediately before becoming such a company, had an established place of business in that part,*

sections 691 and 692 shall, in relation to that part, continue to apply to the company (*notwithstanding section 690B*) *until such time as it gives notice to the registrar for that part that it is a company to which that section applies.*

(4) *Schedule 21B to this Act* (*transitional provisions in relation to change in registration regime*) *shall have effect.]*

[537]

NOTES

Inserted by the Oversea Companies and Credit and Financial Institutions (Branch Disclosure) Regulations 1992, SI 1992/3179, reg 3(1), Sch 2, Pt I, paras 1, 4, as from 1 January 1993; for transitional provisions see Sch 4 to those Regulations at **[6744B]**.

Repealed by the Companies Act 2006, s 1295, Sch 16, as from a day to be appointed.

693 Obligation to state name and other particulars

[(1)] Every oversea company shall—

(*a*) *in every prospectus inviting subscriptions for its shares or debentures in Great Britain, state the country in which the company is incorporated,*

(*b*) *conspicuously exhibit on every place where it carries on business in Great Britain the company's name and the country in which it is incorporated,*

(*c*) *cause the company's name and the country in which it is incorporated to be stated in legible characters in all bill-heads and letter paper, and in all notices and other official publications of the company, and*

(*d*) *if the liability of the members of the company is limited, cause notice of that fact to be stated in legible characters in every such prospectus as above mentioned and in all bill-heads, letter paper, notices and other official publications of the company in Great Britain, and to be affixed on every place where it carries on its business.*

[(2) Every company to which section 690A applies shall, in the case of each branch of the company registered under paragraph 1 of Schedule 21A, cause the following particulars to be stated in legible characters in all letter paper and order forms used in carrying on the business of the branch—

(*a*) *the place of registration of the branch, and*

(*b*) *the registered number of the branch.*

(3) *Every company to which section 690A applies, which is not incorporated in a Member State and which is required by the law of the country in which it is incorporated to be registered shall, in the case of each branch of the company registered under paragraph 1 of Schedule 21A, cause the following particulars to be stated in legible characters in all letter paper and order forms used in carrying on the business of the branch—*

(*a*) *the identity of the registry in which the company is registered in its country of incorporation, and*

(*b*) *the number with which it is registered.*

(4) *Every company to which section 690A applies and which is not incorporated in a Member State shall, in the case of each branch of the company registered under paragraph 1 of Schedule 21A, cause the following particulars to be stated in legible characters in all letter paper and order forms used in carrying on the business of the branch—*

(*a*) *the legal form of the company,*

(*b*) *the location of its head office, and*

(*c*) *if applicable, the fact that it is being wound up.]*

[538]

NOTES

Repealed by the Companies Act 2006, s 1295, Sch 16, as from a day to be appointed.

Sub-s (1): numbered as such by the Oversea Companies and Credit and Financial Institutions (Branch Disclosure) Regulations 1992, SI 1992/3179, reg 3(1), Sch 2, Pt I, paras 1, 6, as from 1 January 1993, for transitional provisions see Sch 4 to those Regulations at **[6744B]**; para (a) and the words "in every such prospectus as above mentioned and" in para (d) repealed by FSA 1986, s 212(3), Sch 17, Pt I, to the extent specified in heads (i)–(iv) of the note at the beginning of Pt III.

Sub-ss (2)–(4): added by SI 1992/3179, reg 3(1), Sch 2, Pt I, paras 1, 6, as from 1 January 1993; for transitional provisions see Sch 4 to those Regulations at **[6744B]**.

Application to limited liability partnerships: see the Limited Liability Partnerships Regulations 2001, SI 2001/1090, reg 4(1), Sch 2, Pt 1 at **[6985]**, **[6993]**.

694 Regulation of oversea companies in respect of their names

(1) If it appears to the Secretary of State that the corporate name of an oversea company is a name by which the company, had it been formed under this Act, would on the relevant date [(determined in accordance with subsections (3A) and (3B))] have been precluded from being registered by section 26 either—

(*a*) *because it falls within subsection (1) of that section, or*

(*b*) *if it falls within subsection (2) of that section, because the Secretary of State would not approve the company's being registered with that name,*

the Secretary of State may serve a notice on the company, stating why the name would not have been registered.

(2) If the corporate name of an oversea company is in the Secretary of State's opinion too like a name appearing on the relevant date in the index of names kept by the registrar of companies under section 714 or which should have appeared in that index on that date, or is the same as a name which should have so appeared, the Secretary of State may serve a notice on the company specifying the name in the index which the company's name is too like or which is the same as the company's name.

(3) No notice shall be served on a company under subsection (1) or (2) later than 12 months after the relevant date, …

[(3A) For the purposes of subsections (1) to (3), the relevant date, in relation to a company, is the date on which it has complied with paragraph 1 of Schedule 21A or section 691(1) or, if there is more than one such date, the first date on which it has complied with that paragraph or that subsection since becoming an oversea company.

(3B) But where the company's corporate name has changed since the date ascertained in accordance with subsection (3A), the relevant date is the date on which the company has, in respect of the change or, if more than one, the latest change, complied with paragraph 7(1) of Schedule 21A or section 692(2), as the case may be.]

(4) An oversea company on which a notice is served under subsection (1) or (2)—

(*a*) *may deliver to the registrar of companies for registration a statement in the prescribed form specifying a name approved by the Secretary of State other than its corporate name under which it proposes to carry on business in Great Britain, and*

(*b*) *may, after that name has been registered, at any time deliver to the registrar for registration a statement in the prescribed form specifying a name approved by the Secretary of State (other than its corporate name) in substitution for the name previously registered.*

(5) The name by which an oversea company is for the time being registered under subsection (4) is, for all purposes of the law applying in Great Britain (including this Act and the Business Names Act 1985), deemed to be the company's corporate name; but—

(*a*) *this does not affect references to the corporate name in this section, or any rights or obligations of the company, or render defective any legal proceedings by or against the company, and*

(*b*) *any legal proceedings that might have been continued or commenced against the company by its corporate name or its name previously registered under this section may be continued or commenced against it by its name for the time being so registered.*

(*6*) *An oversea company on which a notice is served under subsection* (*1*) *or* (*2*) *shall not at any time after the expiration of 2 months from the service of that notice* (*or such longer period as may be specified in that notice*) *carry on business in Great Britain under its corporate name.*

Nothing in this subsection, or in section 697(*2*) (*which imposes penalties for its contravention*) *invalidates any transaction entered into by the company.*

(*7*) *The Secretary of State may withdraw a notice served under subsection* (*1*) *or* (*2*) *at any time before the end of the period mentioned in subsection* (*6*)*; and that subsection does not apply to a company served with a notice which has been withdrawn.*

[539]

NOTES

Repealed by the Companies Act 2006, s 1295, Sch 16, as from a day to be appointed.

Sub-s (1): words in square brackets substituted by the Oversea Companies and Credit and Financial Institutions (Branch Disclosure) Regulations 1992, SI 1992/3179, reg 3(1), Sch 2, Pt I, paras 1, 7(1), (2), as from 1 January 1993; for transitional provisions see Sch 4 to those Regulations at **[6744B]**.

Sub-s (3): words omitted repealed by SI 1992/3179, reg 3(1), Sch 2, Pt I, paras 1, 7(1), (3), as from 1 January 1993; for transitional provisions see Sch 4 to those Regulations at **[6744B]**.

Sub-ss (3A), (3B): inserted by SI 1992/3179, reg 3(1), Sch 2, Pt I, paras 1, 7(1), (4), as from 1 January 1993; for transitional provisions see Sch 4 to those Regulations at **[6744B]**.

Fees: see Appendix 3 (Fees Instruments) at **[A3]**.

Statement in the prescribed form: see Appendix 4 (Forms table) at **[A4]**.

[694A Service of documents: companies to which section 690A applies

(*1*) *This section applies to any company to which section 690A applies.*

(*2*) *Any process or notice required to be served on a company to which this section applies in respect of the carrying on of the business of a branch registered by it under paragraph 1 of Schedule 21A is sufficiently served if—*

(*a*) *addressed to any person whose name has, in respect of the branch, been delivered to the registrar as a person falling within paragraph 3*(*e*) *of that Schedule, and*

(*b*) *left at or sent by post to the address for that person which has been so delivered.*

(*3*) *Where—*

(*a*) *a company to which this section applies makes default, in respect of a branch, in delivering to the registrar the particulars mentioned in paragraph 3*(*e*) *of Schedule 21A, or*

(*b*) *all the persons whose names have, in respect of a branch, been delivered to the registrar as persons falling within paragraph 3*(*e*) *of that Schedule are dead or have ceased to reside in Great Britain, or refuse to accept service on the company's behalf, or for any reason cannot be served,*

a document may be served on the company in respect of the carrying on of the business of the branch by leaving it at, or sending it by post to, any place of business established by the company in Great Britain.

(*4*) *Where a company to which this section applies has more than one branch in Great Britain, any notice or process required to be served on the company which is not required to be served in respect of the carrying on of the business of one branch rather than another shall be treated for the purposes of this section as required to be served in respect of the carrying on of the business of each of its branches.*]

[540]

NOTES

Inserted by the Oversea Companies and Credit and Financial Institutions (Branch Disclosure) Regulations 1992, SI 1992/3179, reg 3(1), Sch 2, Pt I, paras 1, 8, as from 1 January 1993; for transitional provisions see Sch 4 to those Regulations at **[6744B]**.

Repealed by the Companies Act 2006, s 1295, Sch 16, as from a day to be appointed.

695 Service of documents on oversea company

(1) Any process or notice required to be served on an oversea company [to which section 691 applies] is sufficiently served if addressed to any person whose name has been delivered to the registrar under preceding sections in this Part and left at or sent by post to the address which has been so delivered.

(2) However—

(a) where such a company makes default in delivering to the registrar the name and address of a person resident in Great Britain who is authorised to accept on behalf of the company service of process or notices, or

(b) if at any time all the persons whose names and addresses have been so delivered are dead or have ceased so to reside, or refuse to accept service on the company's behalf, or for any reason cannot be served,

a document may be served on the company by leaving it at, or sending it by post to, any place of business established by the company in Great Britain.

[541]

NOTES

Repealed by the Companies Act 2006, s 1295, Sch 16, as from a day to be appointed.

Sub-s (1): words in square brackets inserted by the Oversea Companies and Credit and Financial Institutions (Branch Disclosure) Regulations 1992, SI 1992/3179, reg 3(1), Sch 2, Pt I, paras 1, 9, as from 1 January 1993; for transitional provisions see Sch 4 to those Regulations at **[6744B]**.

[695A Registrar to whom documents to be delivered: companies to which section 690A applies

(1) References to the registrar, in relation to a company to which section 690A applies, (except references in Schedule 21C [or Chapter III of this Part]) shall be construed in accordance with the following provisions.

(2) The documents which a company is required to deliver to the registrar shall be delivered—

(a) to the registrar for England and Wales, if required to be delivered in respect of a branch in England and Wales; and

(b) to the registrar for Scotland, if required to be delivered in respect of a branch in Scotland.

(3) If a company closes a branch in a part of Great Britain, it shall forthwith give notice of that fact to the registrar for that part; and from the date on which notice is so given it is no longer obliged to deliver documents to that registrar in respect of that branch.

(4) In subsection (3) above, the reference to closing a branch in either part of Great Britain includes a reference to a branch ceasing to be situated in that part on becoming situated elsewhere.]

[542]

NOTES

Inserted by the Oversea Companies and Credit and Financial Institutions (Branch Disclosure) Regulations 1992, SI 1992/3179, reg 3(1), Sch 2, Pt I, paras 1, 10, as from 1 January 1993; for transitional provisions see Sch 4 to those Regulations at **[6744B]**.

Repealed by the Companies Act 2006, s 1295, Sch 16, as from a day to be appointed.

Sub-s (1): words in square brackets inserted by CA 1989, s 107, Sch 16, para 1A (as inserted by SI 1992/3179, reg 4, Sch 3, para 16), as from a day to be appointed.

696 Office where documents to be filed

(1) Any document which an oversea company [to which section 691 applies] is required to deliver to the registrar of companies shall be delivered to the registrar at the registration office in England and Wales or Scotland, according to where the company has established a place of business.

(2) If the company has established a place of business both in England and Wales and in Scotland, the document shall be delivered at the registration office both in England and Wales and in Scotland.

(3) References in this Part [(except references in Schedule 21C)] to the registrar of companies[, in relation to a company to which section 691 applies,] are to be construed in accordance with the above subsections.

(4) If an oversea company [to which section 691 applies] ceases to have a place of business in either part of Great Britain, it shall forthwith give notice of that fact to the registrar of companies for that part; and as from the date on which notice is so given the obligation of the company to deliver any document to the registrar ceases.

[543]

NOTES

Repealed by the Companies Act 2006, s 1295, Sch 16, as from a day to be appointed.

Substituted by CA 1989, s 145, Sch 19, para 13 (as amended by SI 1992/3179, reg 4, Sch 3, para 17), as from a day to be appointed, as follows (note that Sch 19, para 13 is also repealed by the 2006 Act)—

"696 Registrar to whom documents to be delivered

(1) References to the registrar in relation to an oversea company [to which section 691 applies] (except references [in Schedule 21C or Chapter III of this Part)], shall be construed in accordance with the following provisions.

(2) The documents which an oversea company is required to deliver to the registrar shall be delivered—

(a) to the registrar for England and Wales if the company has established a place of business in England and Wales, and

(b) to the registrar for Scotland if the company has established a place of business in Scotland;

and if the company has an established place of business in both parts of Great Britain, the documents shall be delivered to both registrars.

(3) If a company ceases to have a place of business in either part of Great Britain, it shall forthwith give notice of that fact to the registrar for that part; and from the date on which notice is so given it is no longer obliged to deliver documents to that registrar.".

Sub-ss (1), (3), (4): words in square brackets inserted by SI 1992/3179, regs 3(1), 4, Sch 2, Pt I, paras 1, 11, Sch 3, paras 3, 4, as from 1 January 1993; for transitional provisions see Sch 4 to those Regulations at **[6744B]**.

697 Penalties for non-compliance

(1) If an oversea company fails to comply with any of sections 691 to 693 and 696, the company, and every officer or agent of the company who knowingly and wilfully authorises or permits the default, is liable to a fine and, in the case of a continuing offence, to a daily default fine for continued contravention.

(2) If an oversea company contravenes section 694(6), the company and every officer or agent of it who knowingly and wilfully authorises or permits the contravention is guilty of an offence and liable to a fine and, for continued contravention, to a daily default fine.

[(3) If an oversea company fails to comply with section 695A or Schedule 21A, the company, and every officer or agent of the company who knowingly and wilfully authorises or permits the default, is liable to a fine and, in the case of a continuing offence, to a daily default fine for continued contravention.]

[544]

NOTES

Repealed by the Companies Act 2006, s 1295, Sch 16, as from a day to be appointed.

Sub-s (3): added by the Oversea Companies and Credit and Financial Institutions (Branch Disclosure) Regulations 1992, SI 1992/3179, reg 3(1), Sch 2, Pt I, paras 1, 12, as from 1 January 1993; for transitional provisions see Sch 4 to those Regulations at **[6744B]**.

698 Definitions ...

[(1)] For purposes of this Chapter—

"certified" means certified in the prescribed manner to be a true copy or a correct translation;

"director", in relation to an oversea company, includes shadow director; and

"secretary" includes any person occupying the position of secretary by whatever name called.

[(2) For the purposes of this Part (except section 699A and Schedule 21C)—

(a) where a branch comprises places of business in more than one part of the United Kingdom the branch shall be treated as being situated in that part of the United Kingdom where its principal place of business is situated; and

(*b*) *"branch" means a branch within the meaning of the Council Directive concerning disclosure requirements in respect of branches opened in a Member State by certain types of company governed by the law of another State (the Eleventh Company Law Directive, 89/666/EEC).]*

[545]

NOTES

Repealed by the Companies Act 2006, s 1295, Sch 16, as from a day to be appointed.

Words omitted from the section heading repealed by the Oversea Companies and Credit and Financial Institutions (Branch Disclosure) Regulations 1992, SI 1992/3179, reg 3(1), Sch 2, Pt I, paras 1, 13(1), (2), as from 1 January 1993; for transitional provisions see Sch 4 to those Regulations at **[6744B]**.

Sub-s (1) numbered as such, and sub-s (2) added, by SI 1992/3179, reg 3(1), Sch 2, Pt I, paras 1, 13, as from 1 January 1993; for transitional provisions see Sch 4 to those Regulations at **[6744B]**.

Prescribed manner to be a true copy or a correct translation: as to the requirements of this, see the Companies (Forms) Regulations 1985, SI 1985/854, reg 6 and the note relating to that regulation to s 272 at **[277]**.

699 Channel Islands and Isle of Man companies

(1) With the exceptions specified in subsection (3) below, the provisions of this Act [and the Companies Act 2006] requiring documents to be forwarded or delivered to or filed with the registrar of companies and applying to companies formed and registered under Part I apply also (if they would not otherwise) to an oversea company [to which section 691 applies] incorporated in the Channel Islands or the Isle of Man.

(2) Those provisions apply to such a company—

(*a*) *if it has established a place of business in England and Wales, as if it were registered in England and Wales,*

(*b*) *if it has established a place of business in Scotland, as if it were registered in Scotland, and*

(*c*) *if it has established a place of business both in England and Wales and in Scotland, as if it were registered in both England and Wales and Scotland,*

with such modifications as may be necessary and, in particular, apply in a similar way to documents relating to things done outside Great Britain as if they had been done in Great Britain.

(3) The exceptions are—

section 6(1) (resolution altering company's objects),

section 18 (alteration of memorandum or articles by statute or statutory instrument),

[section 242(1)] (directors' duty to file accounts),

section 288(2) (notice to registrar of change of directors or secretary), and

section 380 (copies of certain resolutions and agreements to be sent to registrar within 15 days), so far as applicable to a resolution altering a company's memorandum or articles.

[546]

NOTES

Repealed by the Companies Act 2006, s 1295, Sch 16, as from a day to be appointed.

Sub-s (1): words in first pair of square brackets inserted by the draft Companies Act 2006 (Commencement No 3, Consequential Amendments, Transitional Provisions and Savings) Order 2007, art 10(1), Sch 4, Pt 1, para 1(10)(a), as from 1 October 2007 (see **[A12]**); words in second pair of square brackets inserted by the Oversea Companies and Credit and Financial Institutions (Branch Disclosure) Regulations 1992, SI 1992/3179, reg 3(1), Sch 2, Pt I, paras 1, 14, as from 1 January 1993 (for transitional provisions see Sch 4 to those Regulations at **[6744B]**).

Sub-s (3): words in square brackets substituted by CA 1989, s 23, Sch 10, para 12, as from 1 April 1990; for the words from "section 380" to "15 days)" there are substituted the words "Chapter 3 of Part 3 of the Companies Act 2006 (resolutions and agreements affecting a company's constitution)" by the draft Companies Act 2006 (Commencement No 3, Consequential Amendments, Transitional Provisions and Savings) Order 2007, art 10(1), Sch 4, Pt 1, para 1(10)(b), as from 1 October 2007 (see **[A12]**).

[CHAPTER II
DELIVERY OF ACCOUNTS AND REPORTS]

[699A Credit and financial institutions to which the Bank Branches Directive (89/117/EEC) applies

(1) This section applies to any credit or financial institution—

(*a*) *which is incorporated or otherwise formed outside the United Kingdom and Gibraltar,*

(*b*) *whose head office is outside the United Kingdom and Gibraltar, and*

(*c*) *which has a branch in Great Britain.*

(*2*) *Schedule 21C (delivery of accounts and reports) shall have effect in relation to any institution to which this section applies.*

(*3*) *In this section—*

"branch", in relation to a credit or financial institution, means a place of business which forms a legally dependent part of the institution and which conducts directly all or some of the operations inherent in its business;

["credit institution" means a credit institution as defined in [Article 4(1)(a) of Directive 2006/48/EC of the European Parliament and of the Council of 14 June 2006] relating to the taking up and pursuit of the business of credit institutions, that is to say an undertaking whose business is to receive deposits or other repayable funds from the public and to grant credits for its own account;]

"financial institution" means a financial institution within the meaning of Article 1 of the Council Directive on the obligations of branches established in a Member State of credit and financial institutions having their head offices outside that Member State regarding the publication of annual accounting documents (the Bank Branches Directive, 89/117/EEC); and

"undertaking" has the same meaning as in Part VII.]

[547]

NOTES

Inserted, together with ss 699AA, 699B, by the Oversea Companies and Credit and Financial Institutions (Branch Disclosure) Regulations 1992, SI 1992/3179, regs 2(1), 3(1), Sch 2, Pt II, paras 15, 16, as from 1 January 1993; for transitional provisions see Sch 4 to those Regulations at **[6744B]**.

Repealed by the Companies Act 2006, s 1295, Sch 16, as from a day to be appointed.

Sub-s (3): definition "credit institution" substituted by the Banking Consolidation Directive (Consequential Amendments) Regulations 2000, SI 2000/2952, reg 2(1), (3), as from 20 November 2000; words in square brackets substituted by the Capital Requirements Regulations 2006, SI 2006/3221, reg 29(2), Sch 4, para 2(1), (3), as from 1 January 2007.

[699AA Companies to which the Eleventh Company Law Directive applies

(*1*) *This section applies to any limited company which—*

(*a*) *is incorporated outside the United Kingdom and Gibraltar,*

(*b*) *has a branch in Great Britain, and*

(*c*) *is not an institution to which section 699A applies.*

(*2*) *Schedule 21D to this Act (delivery of accounts and reports) shall have effect in relation to any company to which this section applies.]*

[548]

NOTES

Inserted as noted to s 699A at **[547]**.

Repealed by the Companies Act 2006, s 1295, Sch 16, as from a day to be appointed.

[699B Scope of sections 700 to 703

Sections 700 to 703 shall not apply to any institution to which section 699A applies [or to any limited company which is incorporated outside the United Kingdom and Gibraltar and has a branch in the United Kingdom].]

[549]

NOTES

Inserted as noted to s 699A at **[547]**. (Note that SI 1992/3179 actually numbered this section as "s 669B" but this is assumed to be an error.)

Repealed by the Companies Act 2006, s 1295, Sch 16, as from a day to be appointed.

Words in square brackets added by the Oversea Companies and Credit and Financial Institutions (Branch Disclosure) Regulations 1992, SI 1992/3179, reg 3(1), Sch 2, Pt II, paras 15, 17, as from 1 January 1993; for transitional provisions see Sch 4 to those Regulations at **[6744B]**.

[700 Preparation of accounts and reports by oversea companies

(1) Every oversea company shall in respect of each financial year of the company prepare the like accounts and directors' report, and cause to be prepared such an auditors' report, as would be required if the company were formed and registered under this Act.

(2) The Secretary of State may by order—

(a) modify the requirements referred to in subsection (1) for the purpose of their application to oversea companies;

(b) exempt an oversea company from those requirements or from such of them as may be specified in the order.

(3) An order may make different provision for different cases or classes of case and may contain such incidental and supplementary provisions as the Secretary of State thinks fit.

(4) An order under this section shall be made by statutory instrument which shall be subject to annulment in pursuance of a resolution of either House of Parliament.]

[550]

NOTES

This section, the headings preceding s 699A, and ss 701–703, substituted by CA 1989, s 23, Sch 10, para 13, as from 1 April 1990.

Repealed by the Companies Act 2006, s 1295, Sch 16, as from a day to be appointed.

Orders: the Oversea Companies (Accounts) (Modifications and Exemptions) Order 1990, SI 1990/440 at **[6655]**.

Fees: see Appendix 3 (Fees Instruments) at **[A3]**.

[701 Oversea company's financial year and accounting reference periods

(1) Sections 223 to 225 (financial year and accounting reference periods) apply to an oversea company, subject to the following modifications.

(2) For the references to the incorporation of the company substitute references to the company establishing a place of business in Great Britain.

(3) Omit section 225(4) (restriction on frequency with which current accounting reference period may be extended).]

[551]

NOTES

Substituted as noted to s 700 at **[550]**.

Repealed by the Companies Act 2006, s 1295, Sch 16, as from a day to be appointed.

[702 Delivery to registrar of accounts and reports of oversea company

(1) An oversea company shall in respect of each financial year of the company deliver to the registrar copies of the accounts and reports prepared in accordance with section 700.

If any document comprised in those accounts or reports is in a language other than English, the directors shall annex to the copy delivered a translation of it into English, certified in the prescribed manner to be a correct translation.

(2) In relation to an oversea company the period allowed for delivering accounts and reports is 13 months after the end of the relevant accounting reference period.

This is subject to the following provisions of this section.

(3) If the relevant accounting reference period is the company's first and is a period of more than 12 months, the period allowed is 13 months from the first anniversary of the company's establishing a place of business in Great Britain.

(4) If the relevant accounting period is treated as shortened by virtue of a notice given by the company under section 225 (alteration of accounting reference date), the period allowed is that applicable in accordance with the above provisions or three months from the date of the notice under that section, whichever last expires.

(5) If for any special reason the Secretary of State thinks fit he may, on an application made before the expiry of the period otherwise allowed, by notice in writing to an oversea company extend that period by such further period as may be specified in the notice.

(6) In this section "the relevant accounting reference period" means the accounting reference period by reference to which the financial year for the accounts in question was determined.]

[552]

NOTES

Substituted as noted to s 700 at **[550]**.

Repealed by the Companies Act 2006, s 1295, Sch 16, as from a day to be appointed.

Secretary of State: as to the contracting out of the function of the Secretary of State under sub-s (5) above, see the note to s 26 at **[27]**.

Certified in the prescribed manner: as to the requirements of this, see the Companies (Forms) (Amendment) Regulations 1990, SI 1990/572, reg 5 and the note relating to that regulation to s 228 at **[214]**.

[703 Penalty for non-compliance

(1) If the requirements of section 702(1) are not complied with before the end of the period allowed for delivering accounts and reports, or if the accounts and reports delivered do not comply with the requirements of this Act, the company and every person who immediately before the end of that period was a director of the company is guilty of an offence and liable to a fine and, for continued contravention, to a daily default fine.

(2) It is a defence for a person charged with such an offence to prove that he took all reasonable steps for securing that the requirements in question would be complied with.

(3) It is not a defence in relation to a failure to deliver copies to the registrar to prove that the documents in question were not in fact prepared as required by this Act.]

[553]

NOTES

Substituted as noted to s 700 at **[550]**.

Repealed by the Companies Act 2006, s 1295, Sch 16, as from a day to be appointed.

[CHAPTER III
REGISTRATION OF CHARGES

703A Introductory provisions

(1) The provisions of this Chapter have effect for securing the registration in Great Britain of charges on the property of a registered oversea company.

(2) Section 395(2) and (3) (meaning of "charge" and "property") have effect for the purposes of this Chapter.

(3) A "registered oversea company", in relation to England and Wales or Scotland, means an oversea company which—

- *[(a) has duly delivered documents under paragraph 1 of Schedule 21A to the registrar for that part of Great Britain and has not subsequently given notice to him under section 695A(3) that it has closed the branch in respect of which the documents were registered, or*
- *(b)] has duly delivered documents to the registrar for that part of Great Britain under section 691 and has not subsequently given notice to him under section 696(4) that it has ceased to have an established place of business in that part.*

(4) References in this Chapter to the registrar shall be construed in accordance with section 703E below and references to registration, in relation to a charge, are to registration in the register kept by him under this Chapter.]

[554]

NOTES

Commencement: to be appointed.

This Chapter (this section and ss 703B–703N) inserted by CA 1989, s 105, Sch 15, as from a day to be appointed. It should be noted that references in this Chapter to provisions of Pt XII of this Act are references to those provisions as substituted as from a day to be appointed. Note also that those provisions of the 1989 Act are also repealed by the Companies Act 2006, s 1295, Sch 16, as from a day to be appointed.

Repealed by the Companies Act 2006, s 1295, Sch 16, as from a day to be appointed.

Sub-s (3): words in square brackets inserted by the Oversea Companies and Credit and Financial Institutions (Branch Disclosure) Regulations 1992, S1 1992/3179, reg 4, Sch 3, paras 11, 12, as from 1 January 1993; for transitional provisions see Sch 4 to those Regulations at **[6744B]**.

[703B Charges requiring registration

(1) The charges requiring registration under this Chapter are those which if created by a company registered in Great Britain would require registration under Part XII of this Act.

(2) Whether a charge is one requiring registration under this Chapter shall be determined—

[(a) in the case of a charge over property of a company at the date when it becomes a registered oversea company, as at that date,]

(b) in the case of a charge created by a registered oversea company, as at the date the charge is created, and

(c) in the case of a charge over property acquired by a registered oversea company, as at the date of the acquisition.

(3) In the following provisions of this Chapter references to a charge are, unless the context otherwise requires, to a charge requiring registration under this Chapter.

Where a charge not otherwise requiring registration relates to property by virtue of which it requires to be registered and to other property, the references are to the charge so far as it relates to property of the former description.]

[555]

NOTES

Commencement: to be appointed.

Inserted as noted to s 703A at **[554]**.

Repealed by the Companies Act 2006, s 1295, Sch 16, as from a day to be appointed.

Sub-s (2): para (a) substituted by the Oversea Companies and Credit and Financial Institutions (Branch Disclosure) Regulations 1992, SI 1992/3179, reg 4, Sch 3, paras 11, 13, as from 1 January 1993; for transitional provisions see Sch 4 to those Regulations at **[6744B]**.

[703C The register

(1) The registrar shall keep for each registered oversea company a register, in such form as he thinks fit, of charges on property of the company.

(2) The register shall consist of a file containing with respect to each such charge the particulars and other information delivered to the registrar under or by virtue of the following provisions of this Chapter.

(3) Section 397(3) to (5) (registrar's certificate as to the date of delivery of particulars) applies in relation to the delivery of any particulars or other information under this Chapter.]

[556]

NOTES

Commencement: to be appointed.

Inserted as noted to s 703A at **[554]**.

Repealed by the Companies Act 2006, s 1295, Sch 16, as from a day to be appointed.

[703D Company's duty to deliver particulars of charges for registration

(1) If when an oversea company

[(a) delivers documents for registration under paragraph 1 of Schedule 21A—

(i) in respect of a branch in England and Wales, or

(ii) in respect of a branch in Scotland,

for the first time since becoming a company to which section 690A applies, or

(b) delivers documents for registration under section 691,]

any of its property is situated in Great Britain and subject to a charge, it is the company's duty at the same time to deliver the prescribed particulars of the charge, in the prescribed form, to the registrar for registration.

[(1A) Subsection (1) above does not apply in relation to a charge if—

(a) the particulars of it required to be delivered under that subsection have already been so delivered to the registrar to whom the documents mentioned in subsection (1) above are delivered, and

(*b*) *the company has at all times since they were so delivered to him been a registered oversea company in relation to the part of Great Britain for which he is registrar.]*

(2) *Where a registered oversea company—*

(*a*) *creates a charge on property situated in Great Britain, or*

(*b*) *acquires property which is situated in Great Britain and subject to a charge,*

it is the company's duty to deliver the prescribed particulars of the charge in the prescribed form, to the registrar for registration within 21 days after the date of the charge's creation or, as the case may be, the date of the acquisition.

This subsection does not apply if the property subject to the charge is at the end of that period no longer situated in Great Britain.

(*3*) *Where the preceding subsections do not apply and property of a registered oversea company is for a continuous period of four months situated in Great Britain and subject to a charge, it is the company's duty before the end of that period to deliver the prescribed particulars of the charge, in the prescribed form, to the registrar for registration.*

(*4*) *Particulars of a charge required to be delivered under subsection* (*1*), (2) *or* (*3*) *may be delivered for registration by any person interested in the charge.*

(*5*) *If a company fails to comply with subsection* (*1*), (2) *or* (*3*), *then, unless particulars of the charge have been delivered for registration by another person, the company and every officer of it who is in default is liable to a fine.*

(*6*) *Section 398*(2), (*4*) *and* (*5*) (*recovery of fees paid in connection with registration, filing of particulars in register and sending of copy of particulars filed and note as to date*) *apply in relation to particulars delivered under this Chapter.]*

[557]

NOTES

Commencement: to be appointed.

Inserted as noted to s 703A at **[554]**.

Repealed by the Companies Act 2006, s 1295, Sch 16, as from a day to be appointed.

Sub-s (1): words in square brackets substituted by the Oversea Companies and Credit and Financial Institutions (Branch Disclosure) Regulations 1992, SI 1992/3179, reg 4, Sch 3, paras 11, 14(1), (2), as from 1 January 1993; for transitional provisions see Sch 4 to those Regulations at **[6744B]**.

Sub-s (1A): inserted by SI 1992/3179, reg 4, Sch 3, paras 11, 14(1), (3), as from 1 January 1993; for transitional provisions see Sch 4 to those Regulations at **[6744B]**.

[703E Registrar to whom particulars, &c to be delivered

(*1*) *The particulars required to be delivered by section 703D*(*1*) (*charges over property of oversea company becoming registered in a part of Great Britain*) *shall be delivered to the registrar to whom the documents are delivered under [paragraph 1 of Schedule 21A or, as the case may be,] section 691.*

(2) *The particulars required to be delivered by section 703D*(2) *or* (*3*) (*charges over property of registered oversea company*) *shall be delivered—*

[(*a*) *where the company is a company to which section 690A applies—*

(*i*) *if it has registered a branch in one part of Great Britain but has not registered a branch in the other, to the registrar for the part in which it has registered a branch,*

(*ii*) *if it has registered a branch in both parts of Great Britain but the property subject to the charge is situated in one part of Great Britain only, to the registrar for that part, and*

(*iii*) *in any other case, to the registrars for both parts of Great Britain; and*

(*b*) *where the company is a company to which section 691 applies—*

(*i*) *if it is registered in one part of Great Britain and not in the other, to the registrar for the part in which it is registered,*

(*ii*) *if it is registered in both parts of Great Britain but the property subject to the charge is situated in one part of Great Britain only, to the registrar for that part, and*

(*iii*) *in any other case, to the registrar for both parts of Great Britain.]*

(*3*) *Other documents required or authorised by virtue of this Chapter to be delivered to the registrar shall be delivered to the registrar or registrars to whom particulars of the charge to which they relate have been, or ought to have been, delivered.*

(4) [If a company ceases to be a registered oversea company in relation to either part of Great Britain, charges over property of the company shall cease to be subject to the provisions of this Chapter, as regards registration in that part of Great Britain, as from the date on which the notice under section 695A(3) or, as the case may be, 696(3) is given.]

This is without prejudice to rights arising by reason of events occurring before that date.]

[558]

NOTES

Commencement: to be appointed.
Inserted as noted to s 703A at **[554]**.
Repealed by the Companies Act 2006, s 1295, Sch 16, as from a day to be appointed.
Sub-s (1): words in square brackets inserted by the Oversea Companies and Credit and Financial Institutions (Branch Disclosure) Regulations 1992, SI 1992/3179, reg 4, Sch 3, paras 11, 15(1), (2), as from 1 January 1993; for transitional provisions see Sch 4 to those Regulations at **[6744B]**.
Sub-ss (2), (4): words in square brackets substituted by SI 1992/3179, reg 4, Sch 3, paras 11, 15(1), (3), (4), as from 1 January 1993; for transitional provisions see Sch 4 to those Regulations at **[6744B]**.

[703F Effect of failure to deliver particulars, late delivery and effect of errors and omissions

(1) The following provisions of Part XII—

- *(a) section 399 (effect of failure to deliver particulars),*
- *(b) section 400 (late delivery of particulars), and*
- *(c) section 402 (effect of errors and omissions in particulars delivered),*

apply, with the following modifications, in relation to a charge created by a registered oversea company of which particulars are required to be delivered under this Chapter.

(2) Those provisions do not apply to a charge of which particulars are required to be delivered under section 703D(1) (charges existing when company delivers documents under section 691).

(3) In relation to a charge of which particulars are required to be delivered under section 703D(3) (charges registrable by virtue of property being within Great Britain for requisite period), the references to the period of 21 days after the charge's creation shall be construed as references to the period of four months referred to in that subsection.]

[559]

NOTES

Commencement: to be appointed.
Inserted as noted to s 703A at **[554]**.
Repealed by the Companies Act 2006, s 1295, Sch 16, as from a day to be appointed.

[703G Delivery of further particulars or memorandum

Sections 401 and 403 (delivery of further particulars and memorandum of charge ceasing to affect company's property) apply in relation to a charge of which particulars have been delivered under this Chapter.]

[560]

NOTES

Commencement: to be appointed.
Inserted as noted to s 703A at **[554]**.
Repealed by the Companies Act 2006, s 1295, Sch 16, as from a day to be appointed.

[703H Further provisions with respect to voidness of charges

(1) The following provisions of Part XII apply in relation to the voidness of a charge by virtue of this Chapter—

- *(a) section 404 (exclusion of voidness as against unregistered charges),*
- *(b) section 405 (restrictions on cases in which charge is void),*
- *(c) section 406 (effect of exercise of power of sale), and*
- *(d) section 407 (effect of voidness on obligation secured).*

(2) In relation to a charge of which particulars are required to be delivered under section 703D(3) (charges registrable by virtue of property being within Great Britain for

requisite period), the reference in section 404 to the period of 21 days after the charge's creation shall be construed as a reference to the period of four months referred to in that subsection.]

[561]

NOTES

Commencement: to be appointed.
Inserted as noted to s 703A at **[554]**.
Repealed by the Companies Act 2006, s 1295, Sch 16, as from a day to be appointed.

[703I Additional information to be registered

(1) Section 408 (particulars of taking up of issue of debentures) applies in relation to a charge of which particulars have been delivered under this Chapter.

(2) Section 409 (notice of appointment of receiver or manager) applies in relation to the appointment of a receiver or manager of property of a registered oversea company.

(3) Regulations under section 410 (notice of crystallisation of floating charge, &c) may apply in relation to a charge of which particulars have been delivered under this Chapter; but subject to such exceptions, adaptations and modifications as may be specified in the regulations.]

[562]

NOTES

Commencement: to be appointed.
Inserted as noted to s 703A at **[554]**.
Repealed by the Companies Act 2006, s 1295, Sch 16, as from a day to be appointed.

[703J Copies of instruments and register to be kept by company

(1) Sections 411 and 412 (copies of instruments and register to be kept by company) apply in relation to a registered oversea company and any charge over property of the company situated in Great Britain.

(2) They apply to any charge, whether or not particulars are required to be delivered to the registrar.

(3) In relation to such a company the references to the company's registered office shall be construed as references to its principal place of business in Great Britain.]

[563]

NOTES

Commencement: to be appointed.
Inserted as noted to s 703A at **[554]**.
Repealed by the Companies Act 2006, s 1295, Sch 16, as from a day to be appointed.

[703K Power to make further provision by regulations

(1) The Secretary of State may by regulations make further provision as to the application of the provisions of this Chapter, or the provisions of Part XII applied by this Chapter, in relation to charges of any description specified in the regulations.

(2) The regulations may apply any provisions of regulations made under section 413 (power to make further provision with respect to application of Part XII) or make any provision which may be made under that section with respect to the application of provisions of Part XII.]

[564]

NOTES

Commencement: to be appointed.
Inserted as noted to s 703A at **[554]**.
Repealed by the Companies Act 2006, s 1295, Sch 16, as from a day to be appointed.

[703L Provisions as to situation of property

(1) The following provisions apply for determining for the purposes of this Chapter whether a vehicle which is the property of an oversea company is situated in Great Britain—

(*a*) *a ship, aircraft or hovercraft shall be regarded as situated in Great Britain if, and only if, it is registered in Great Britain;*

(*b*) *any further description of vehicle shall be regarded as situated in Great Britain on a day if, and only if, at any time on that day the management of the vehicle is directed from a place of business of the company in Great Britain;*

and for the purposes of this Chapter a vehicle shall not be regarded as situated in one part of Great Britain only.

(2) *For the purposes of this Chapter as it applies to a charge on future property, the subject-matter of the charge shall be treated as situated in Great Britain unless it relates exclusively to property of a kind which cannot, after being acquired or coming into existence, be situated in Great Britain; and references to property situated in a part of Great Britain shall be similarly construed.]*

[565]

NOTES

Commencement: to be appointed.
Inserted as noted to s 703A at **[554]**.
Repealed by the Companies Act 2006, s 1295, Sch 16, as from a day to be appointed.

[703M Other supplementary provisions

The following provisions of Part XII apply for the purposes of this Chapter—

(*a*) *section 414* (*construction of references to date of creation of charge*),
(*b*) *section 415* (*prescribed particulars and related expressions*),
(*c*) *section 416* (*notice of matters disclosed in the register*),
(*d*) *section 417* (*power of court to dispense with signature*),
(*e*) *section 418* (*regulations*) *and*
(*f*) *section 419* (*minor definitions*).*]*

[566]

NOTES

Commencement: to be appointed.
Inserted as noted to s 703A at **[554]**.
Repealed by the Companies Act 2006, s 1295, Sch 16, as from a day to be appointed.

[703N Index of defined expressions

The following Table shows the provisions of this Chapter and Part XII defining or otherwise explaining expressions used in this Chapter (*other than expressions used only in the same section*)*—*

charge	*sections 703A*(*2*), *703B*(*3*) *and 395*(*2*)
charge requiring registration	*sections 703B*(*1*) *and 396*
creation of charge	*sections 703M*(*f*) *and 419*(*2*)
date of acquisition (*of property by a company*)	*sections 703M*(*f*) *and 419*(*3*)
date of creation of charge	*sections 703M*(*a*) *and 414*
property	*sections 703A*(*2*) *and 395*(*2*)
registered oversea company	*section 703A*(*3*)
registrar and registration in relation to a charge	*sections 703A*(*4*) *and 703E*
situated in Great Britain	
—in relation to vehicles	*section 703L*(*1*)
—in relation to future property	*section 703L*(*2*).*]*

[567]

NOTES

Commencement: to be appointed.
Inserted as noted to s 703A at **[554]**.
Repealed by the Companies Act 2006, s 1295, Sch 16, as from a day to be appointed.

[CHAPTER IV
WINDING UP ETC

703O Scope of Chapter

This Chapter applies to any company to which section 690A applies.]

[568]

NOTES

This Chapter (ss 703O–703R) inserted by the Oversea Companies and Credit and Financial Institutions (Branch Disclosure) Regulations 1992, SI 1992/3179, reg 3(1), Sch 2, Pt III, para 19, as from 1 January 1993; for transitional provisions see Sch 4 to those Regulations at **[6744B]**.

Repealed by the Companies Act 2006, s 1295, Sch 16, as from a day to be appointed.

[703P Particulars to be delivered: winding up

(*1*) *Subject to subsection* (*8*), *where a company to which this Chapter applies is being wound up, it shall deliver to the registrar for registration a return in the prescribed form containing the following particulars—*

(*a*) *the name of the company;*

(*b*) *whether the company is being wound up by an order of a court and, if so, the name and address of the court and the date of the order;*

(*c*) *if the company is not being so wound up, as a result of what action the winding up has commenced;*

(*d*) *whether the winding up has been instigated by—*

(*i*) *the company's members;*
(*ii*) *the company's creditors; or*
(*iii*) *some other person or persons,*

and, in the case of (*iii*) *the identity of that person or those persons shall be given; and*

(*e*) *the date on which the winding up became or will become effective.*

(*2*) *The period allowed for delivery of a return under subsection* (*1*) *above is 14 days from the date on which the winding up begins.*

(*3*) *Subject to subsection* (*8*), *a person appointed to be the liquidator of a company to which this Chapter applies shall deliver to the registrar for registration a return in the prescribed form containing the following particulars—*

(*a*) *his name and address,*

(*b*) *the date of his appointment, and*

(*c*) *a description of such of his powers, if any, as are derived otherwise than from the general law or the company's constitution.*

(*4*) *The period allowed for delivery of a return under subsection* (*3*) *above is 14 days from the date of the liquidator's appointment.*

(*5*) *Subject to subsection* (*8*), *the liquidator of a company to which this Chapter applies shall deliver to the registrar for registration a return in the prescribed form upon the occurrence of the following events—*

(*a*) *the termination of the winding up of the company, and*

(*b*) *the company ceasing to be registered, in circumstances where ceasing to be registered is an event of legal significance.*

The following particulars shall be given—

(*i*) *in the case of* (*a*), *the name of the company and the date on which the winding up terminated; and*
(*ii*) *in the case of* (*b*), *the name of the company and the date on which the company ceased to be registered.*

(*6*) *The period allowed for delivery of a return under subsection* (*5*) *is 14 days from the date of the event concerned.*

(*7*) *The obligation to deliver a return under subsection* (*1*), (*3*) *or* (*5*) *above shall apply in respect of each branch which the company has in Great Britain (though where the company has more than one branch in a part of Great Britain a return which gives the branch numbers of two or more such branches is to be regarded as a return in respect of each branch whose number is given).*

(*8*) *No return is required under subsection* (*1*), (*3*) *or* (*5*) *above in respect of a winding up under Part V of the Insolvency Act 1986.]*

[569]

NOTES

Inserted as noted to s 703O at **[568]**.
Repealed by the Companies Act 2006, s 1295, Sch 16, as from a day to be appointed.
Prescribed form: see Appendix 4 (Forms table) at **[A4]**.

[703Q Particulars to be delivered to the registrar: insolvency proceedings etc

(*1*) *Where a company to which this Chapter applies becomes subject to any of the following proceedings* (*other than proceedings for the winding up of the company*), *that is to say, insolvency proceedings or an arrangement or composition or any analogous proceedings, it shall deliver to the registrar for registration a return in the prescribed form containing the following particulars—*

- (*a*) *the name of the company;*
- (*b*) *whether the proceedings are by order of a court and, if so, the name and address of the court and the date of the order;*
- (*c*) *if the proceedings are not by order of a court, as a result of what action the proceedings have been commenced;*
- (*d*) *whether the proceedings have been instigated by—*
  - (*i*) *the company's members;*
  - (*ii*) *the company's creditors; or*
  - (*iii*) *some other person or persons,*

and, in the case of (*iii*) *the identity of that person or those persons shall be given; and*

- (*e*) *the date on which the proceedings became or will become effective.*

(*2*) *Where a company to which this Chapter applies ceases to be subject to any of the proceedings mentioned in subsection* (*1*) *it shall deliver to the registrar for registration a return in the prescribed form containing the following particulars—*

- (*a*) *the name of the company; and*
- (*b*) *the date on which it ceased to be subject to the proceedings.*

(*3*) *The period allowed for delivery of a return under subsection* (*1*) *or* (*2*) *is 14 days from the date on which the company becomes subject, or* (*as the case may be*) *ceases to be subject to the proceedings concerned.*

(*4*) *The obligation to deliver a return under subsection* (*1*) *or* (*2*) *shall apply in respect of each branch which the company has in Great Britain* (*though where the company has more than one branch in a part of Great Britain a return which gives the branch numbers of two or more such branches is to be regarded as a return in respect of each branch whose number is given*)*.]*

[570]

NOTES

Inserted as noted to s 703O at **[568]**.
Repealed by the Companies Act 2006, s 1295, Sch 16, as from a day to be appointed.
Prescribed form: see Appendix 4 (Forms table) at **[A4].**

[703R Penalty for non-compliance

(*1*) *If a company fails to comply with section 703P*(*1*) *or 703Q*(*1*) *or* (*2*) *within the period allowed for compliance, it, and every person who immediately before the end of that period was a director of it, is guilty of an offence and liable to a fine and, for continued contravention, to a daily default fine.*

(*2*) *If a liquidator fails to comply with section 703P*(*3*) *or* (*5*) *within the period allowed for compliance, he is guilty of an offence and liable to a fine and, for continued contravention, to a daily default fine.*

(*3*) *It is a defence for a person charged with an offence under this section to prove that he took all reasonable steps for securing compliance with the requirements concerned.]*

[571]

NOTES

Inserted as noted to s 703O at **[568]**.
Repealed by the Companies Act 2006, s 1295, Sch 16, as from a day to be appointed.

PART XXIV
THE REGISTRAR OF COMPANIES, HIS FUNCTIONS AND OFFICES

NOTES

Community interest companies: Regulations under the Companies (Audit, Investigations and Community Enterprise) Act 2004, s 58 (at **[932]**) may make amendments or modifications of any provision contained in this Part (ss 704–715A) in consequence of any provision contained in, or made under, Pt 2 (ss 26–63 and Schs 3–7) of the 2004 Act (see the Community Interest Company Regulations 2005, SI 2005/1788 at **[7399]**).

704 Registration offices

(1) For the purposes of the registration of companies under the Companies Acts, there shall continue to be offices in England and Wales and in Scotland, at such places as the Secretary of State thinks fit.

(2) The Secretary of State may appoint such registrars, assistant registrars, clerks and servants as he thinks necessary for that purpose, and may make regulations with respect to their duties, and may remove any persons so appointed.

(3) The salaries of the persons so appointed continue to be fixed by the Secretary of State, with the concurrence of the Treasury, and shall be paid out of money provided by Parliament.

(4) The Secretary of State may direct a seal or seals to be prepared for the authentication of documents required for or in connection with the registration of companies; and any seal so prepared is referred to in this Act as the registrar's official seal.

(5) Wherever any act is by the Companies Acts directed to be done to or by the registrar of companies, it shall (until the Secretary of State otherwise directs) be done to or by the existing registrar of companies in England and Wales or in Scotland (as the case may be), or to or by such person as the Secretary of State may for the time being authorise.

(6) In the event of the Secretary of State altering the constitution of the existing registration offices or any of them, any such act shall be done to or by such officer and at such place with reference to the local situation of the registered offices of the companies to be registered as the Secretary of State may appoint.

[(7) Subsection (8) below applies where by virtue of an order made under section 69 of the Deregulation and Contracting Out Act 1994 a person is authorised by the registrar of companies to accept delivery of any class of documents which are under any provision of the Companies Acts to be delivered to the registrar.

(8) If—

- *(a) the registrar directs that documents of that class shall be delivered to a specified address of the authorised person; and*
- *(b) the direction is printed and made available to the public (with or without payment),*

any document of that class which is delivered to an address other than the specified address shall be treated for the purposes of those Acts as not having been delivered.]

[572]

NOTES

Repealed by the Companies Act 2006, s 1295, Sch 16, as from a day to be appointed.
Sub-ss (7), (8): added by the Deregulation and Contracting Out Act 1994, s 76, Sch 16, para 8, as from 3 January 1995.
Application to limited liability partnerships: see the Limited Liability Partnerships Regulations 2001, SI 2001/1090, reg 4(1), Sch 2, Pt 1 at **[6985]**, **[6993]**.

[705 Companies' registered numbers

(1) The registrar shall allocate to every company a number, which shall be known as the company's registered number.

(2) Companies' registered numbers shall be in such form, consisting of one or more sequences of figures or letters, as the registrar may from time to time determine.

(3) The registrar may upon adopting a new form of registered number make such changes of existing registered numbers as appear to him necessary.

(4) A change of a company's registered number has effect from the date on which the company is notified by the registrar of the change; but for a period of three years beginning with the date on which that notification is sent by the registrar the requirement of section 351(1)(a) as to the use of the company's registered number on [business letters, order forms and websites] is satisfied by the use of either the old number or the new.

(5) In this section "company" includes—

[(za) any oversea company which has complied with paragraph 1 of Schedule 21A other than a company which appears to the registrar not to have a branch in Great Britain;]

(a) any oversea company which has complied with section 691 (delivery of statutes to registrar, &c), other than a company which appears to the registrar not to have a place of business in Great Britain; and

(b) any body to which any provision of this Act applies by virtue of section 718 (unregistered companies).]

[573]

NOTES

Substituted by CA 1989, s 145, Sch 19, para 14, as from 1 October 1990.

Repealed by the Companies Act 2006, s 1295, Sch 16, as from a day to be appointed.

Sub-s (4): words in square brackets substituted by the Companies (Registrar, Languages and Trading Disclosures) Regulations 2006, SI 2006/3429, reg 6, Sch 1, para 3, as from 1 January 2007.

Sub-s (5): para (za) inserted by the Oversea Companies and Credit and Financial Institutions (Branch Disclosure) Regulations 1992, SI 1992/3179, reg 4, Sch 3, paras 3, 5, as from 1 January 1993; for transitional provisions see Sch 4 to those Regulations at **[6744B]**.

Application to limited liability partnerships: see the Limited Liability Partnerships Regulations 2001, SI 2001/1090, reg 4(1), Sch 2, Pt 1 at **[6985]**, **[6993]**.

[705A Registration of branches of oversea companies

(1) For each company to which section 690A applies the registrar, shall keep, in such form as he thinks fit, a register of the branches registered by the company under paragraph 1 of Schedule 21A.

(2) The registrar shall allocate to every branch registered by him under this section a number, which shall be known as the branch's registered number.

(3) Branches' registered numbers shall be in such form, consisting of one or more sequences of figures or letters, as the registrar may from time to time determine.

(4) The registrar may upon adopting a new form of registered number make such changes of existing registered numbers as appear to him necessary.

(5) A change of a branch's registered number has effect from the date on which the company is notified by the registrar of the change; but for a period of three years beginning with the date on which that notification is sent by the registrar the requirement of section 693(2) as to the use of the branch's registered number on business letters and order forms is satisfied by the use of either the old number or the new.

(6) Where an oversea company to which section 690A applies files particulars, in any circumstances permitted by this Act, by—

(i) adopting particulars already filed in respect of another branch; or

(ii) including in one document particulars which are to relate to two or more branches,

the registrar shall ensure that the particulars concerned become part of the registered particulars of each branch concerned.]

[574]

NOTES

Inserted by the Oversea Companies and Credit and Financial Institutions (Branch Disclosure) Regulations 1992, SI 1992/3179, reg 3(2), as from 1 January 1993; for transitional provisions see Sch 4 to those Regulations at **[6744B]**.

Repealed by the Companies Act 2006, s 1295, Sch 16, as from a day to be appointed.

[706 Delivery to the registrar of documents in legible form

(1) This section applies to the delivery to the registrar under any provision of the Companies Acts of documents in legible form.

(2) The document must—

- (*a*) *state in a prominent position the registered number of the company to which it relates [and, if the document is delivered under sections 695A(3), 703P or 703Q or Schedules 21A or 21D the registered number of the branch to which it relates,]*
- (*b*) *satisfy any requirements prescribed by regulations for the purposes of this section, and*
- (*c*) *conform to such requirements as the registrar may specify for the purpose of enabling him to copy the document.*

(3) If a document is delivered to the registrar which does not comply with the requirements of this section, he may serve on the person by whom the document was delivered (or, if there are two or more such persons, on any of them) a notice indicating the respect in which the document does not comply.

(4) Where the registrar serves such a notice, then, unless a replacement document—

- (*a*) *is delivered to him within 14 days after the service of the notice, and*
- (*b*) *complies with the requirements of this section (or section [707B]) or is not rejected by him for failure to comply with those requirements,*

the original document shall be deemed not to have been delivered to him.

But for the purposes of any enactment imposing a penalty for failure to deliver, so far as it imposes a penalty for continued contravention, no account shall be taken of the period between the delivery of the original document and the end of the period of 14 days after service of the registrar's notice.

(5) Regulations made for the purposes of this section may make different provision with respect to different descriptions of document.]

[575]

NOTES

Substituted by CA 1989, s 125(1), as from 7 January 1991.

Repealed by the Companies Act 2006, s 1295, Sch 16, as from a day to be appointed.

Sub-s (2): words in square brackets in para (a) inserted by the Oversea Companies and Credit and Financial Institutions (Branch Disclosure) Regulations 1992, SI 1992/3179, reg 4, Sch 3, paras 3, 6, as from 1 January 1993; for transitional provisions see Sch 4 to those Regulations at **[6744B]**.

Sub-s (4): figure in square brackets substituted by the Companies Act 1985 (Electronic Communications) Order 2000, SI 2000/3373, art 31(4)(a), as from 22 December 2000.

Application to limited liability partnerships: see the Limited Liability Partnerships Regulations 2001, SI 2001/1090, reg 4(1), Sch 2, Pt 1 at **[6985]**, **[6993]**.

707 (*Repealed by the Companies Act 1985 (Electronic Communications) Order 2000, SI 2000/3373, art 31(4), as from 22 December 2000.*)

[707A The keeping of company records by the registrar

(1) ...

(2) The originals of documents delivered to the registrar in legible form shall be kept by him for ten years, after which they may be destroyed.

(3) Where a company has been dissolved, the registrar may, at any time after the expiration of two years from the date of the dissolution, direct that any records in his custody relating to the company may be removed to the Public Record Office; and records in respect of which such a direction is given shall be disposed of in accordance with the enactments relating to that Office and the rules made under them.

This subsection does not extend to Scotland.

(4) In subsection (3) "company" includes a company provisionally or completely registered under the Joint Stock Companies Act 1844.]

[576]

NOTES

Inserted by CA 1989, s 126(1), as from 1 July 1991.

Repealed by the Companies Act 2006, s 1295, Sch 16, as from 1 January 2007 (in so far as relating to sub-s (1)), and as from a day to be appointed (otherwise).

Sub-s (1): repealed as noted above. It previously read as follows—

"(1) The information contained in a document delivered to the registrar under the Companies Acts may be recorded and kept by him in any form he thinks fit, provided it is possible to inspect the information and to produce a copy of it in legible form.

This is sufficient compliance with any duty of his to keep, file or register the document.".

Application to limited liability partnerships: see the Limited Liability Partnerships Regulations 2001, SI 2001/1090, reg 4(1), Sch 2, Pt 1 at **[6985]**, **[6993]**. Note also that nothing in the Companies Act 2006 (Commencement No 1, Transitional Provisions and Savings) Order 2006, SI 2006/3428 affects any provision of this Act as applied by the 2001 Regulations to LLPs (see art 8(2) at **[7581]** and the introductory notes to this Act).

Joint Stock Companies Act 1844: repealed by the Companies Act 1862, s 205, Sch 3.

[707B Delivery to the registrar using electronic communications

(1) Electronic communications may be used for the delivery of any document to the registrar under any provision of the Companies Acts (including delivery of a document in the prescribed form), provided that such delivery is in such form and manner as is directed by the registrar.

(2) Where the document is required under any provision of the Companies Acts to be signed or sealed, it shall instead be authenticated in such manner as is directed by the registrar.

(3) The document must contain in a prominent position—

(a) the name and registered number of the company to which it relates, or

(b) if the document is delivered under Part XXIII, the registered number of the branch or place of business of the company to which it relates.

(4) If a document is delivered to the registrar which does not comply with the requirements imposed by or under this section, he may serve on the person by whom the document was delivered (or, if there are two or more such persons, on any of them) a notice indicating the respect in which the document does not comply.

(5) Where the registrar serves such a notice, then unless a replacement document—

(a) is delivered to him within 14 days after the service of the notice, and

(b) complies with the requirements of this section (or section 706) or is not rejected by him for failure to comply with those requirements,

the original document shall be deemed not to have been delivered to him.

But for the purposes of any enactment imposing a penalty for failure to deliver, so far as it imposes a penalty for continued contravention, no account shall be taken of the period between the delivery of the original document and the end of the period of 14 days after service of the registrar's notice.

(6) In this section references to the delivery of a document include references to the forwarding, lodging, registering, sending or submission of a document and to the giving of a notice, and cognate expressions are to be construed accordingly.]

[577]

NOTES

Inserted by the Companies Act 1985 (Electronic Communications) Order 2000, SI 2000/3373, art 27.

Repealed by the Companies Act 2006, s 1295, Sch 16, as from a day to be appointed.

Application to limited liability partnerships: see the Limited Liability Partnerships Regulations 2001, SI 2001/1090, reg 4(1), Sch 2, Pt 1 at **[6985]**, **[6993]**.

708 Fees payable to registrar

(1) The Secretary of State may by regulations made by statutory instrument require the payment to the registrar of companies of such fees as may be specified in the regulations in respect of—

(*a*) *the performance by the registrar of such functions under the Companies Acts as may be so specified, including the receipt by him of [any document which under those Acts is required to be delivered to him],*

(*b*) *the inspection of documents ... kept by him under those Acts.*

(2) A statutory instrument containing regulations under this section requiring the payment of a fee in respect of a matter for which no fee was previously payable, or increasing a fee, shall be laid before Parliament after being made and shall cease to have effect at the end of the period of 28 days beginning with the day on which the regulations were made (but without prejudice to anything previously done under the regulations or to the making of further regulations) unless in that period the regulations are approved by resolution of each House of Parliament.

In reckoning that period of 28 days no account is to be taken of any time during which Parliament is dissolved or prorogued or during which both Houses are adjourned for more than 4 days.

(3) A statutory instrument containing regulations under this section, where subsection (2) does not apply, is subject to annulment in pursuance of a resolution of either House of Parliament.

(4) Fees paid to the registrar under the Companies Acts shall be paid into the Consolidated Fund.

(5) ...

[578]

NOTES

Repealed by the Companies Act 2006, s 1295, Sch 16, as from 6 April 2007 (in so far as relating to sub-s (5)), and as from a day to be appointed (otherwise) (for transitional provisions see the note below).

Sub-s (1): words in square brackets substituted, and words omitted repealed, by CA 1989, ss 127(2), 212, Sch 24, as from 7 January 1991.

Sub-s (5): repealed as noted above. It previously read as follows—

"(5) It is hereby declared that the registrar may charge a fee for any services provided by him otherwise than in pursuance of an obligation imposed on him by law.".

Application to limited liability partnerships: see the Limited Liability Partnerships Regulations 2001, SI 2001/1090, reg 4(1), Sch 2, Pt 1 at **[6985]**, **[6993]**. Note also that nothing in the Companies Act 2006 (Commencement No 1, Transitional Provisions and Savings) Order 2006, SI 2006/3428 affects any provision of this Act as applied by the 2001 Regulations to LLPs (see art 8(2) at **[7581]** and the introductory notes to this Act).

Transitional provisions: the Companies Act 2006 (Commencement No 1, Transitional Provisions and Savings) Order 2006, SI 2006/3428, Sch 5, para 6(3) provides as follows—

"(3) The repeal of section 708(5) of the 1985 Act shall not prevent the registrar from continuing to charge fees thereunder of which notice had before the repeal been given to those to whom the services in question have been, are being or are to be provided (including notice by publication of a list of fees in respect of services provided to any person who seeks their provision).".

Regulations: the Open-Ended Investment Companies (Investment Companies with Variable Capital) (Fees) Regulations 1998, SI 1998/3087; the Companies (Competent Authority) (Fees) Regulations 2002, SI 2002/502; the Limited Liability Partnerships (Competent Authority) (Fees) Regulations 2002, SI 2002/503; the Limited Liability Partnerships (Fees) Regulations 2004, SI 2004/2620; the Companies (Fees) Regulations 2004, SI 2004/2621 (see Appendix 3 (Fees Instruments) at **[A3]**).

[709 Inspection, &c of records kept by the registrar

(1) [Subject to section 723B,] any person may inspect any records kept by the registrar for the purposes of the Companies Acts and may require—

(*a*) *a copy, in such form as the registrar considers appropriate, of any information contained in those records, or*

(*b*) *a certified copy of, or extract from, any such record.*

(2) The right of inspection extends to the originals of documents delivered to the registrar in legible form only where the record kept by the registrar of the contents of the document is illegible or unavailable.

(3) A copy of or extract from a record kept at any of the offices for the registration of companies in England and Wales or Scotland, certified in writing by the registrar (whose official position it is unnecessary to prove) to be an accurate record of the contents of any document delivered to him under the Companies Acts, is in all legal proceedings admissible in

evidence as of equal validity with the original document and as evidence of any fact stated therein of which direct oral evidence would be admissible.

…

(*4*) *Copies of or extracts from records furnished by the registrar may, instead of being certified by him in writing to be an accurate record, be sealed with his official seal.*

(*5*) *No process for compelling the production of a record kept by the registrar shall issue from any court except with the leave of the court; and any such process shall bear on it a statement that it is issued with the leave of the court.]*

[579]

NOTES

Substituted, together with ss 710, 710A, for original ss 709, 710, by CA 1989, s 126(2), as from 1 July 1991.

Repealed by the Companies Act 2006, s 1295, Sch 16, as from 1 January 2007. This section is reproduced only because of its continued application to limited liability partnerships (see the note below).

Sub-s (1): words in square brackets inserted by the Criminal Justice and Police Act 2001, s 45(1), (4), as from 19 June 2001 (for the purpose of making regulations or orders), and as from 2 April 2002 (otherwise).

Sub-s (3): words omitted repealed by the Youth Justice and Criminal Evidence Act 1999, s 67, Sch 6, as from 14 April 2000.

Application to limited liability partnerships: see the Limited Liability Partnerships Regulations 2001, SI 2001/1090, reg 4(1), Sch 2, Pt 1 at **[6985]**, **[6993]**. Note also that nothing in the Companies Act 2006 (Commencement No 1, Transitional Provisions and Savings) Order 2006, SI 2006/3428 affects any provision of this Act as applied by the 2001 Regulations to LLPs (see art 8(2) at **[7581]** and the introductory notes to this Act).

Fees: see Appendix 3 (Fees Instruments) at **[A3]**.

[710 Certificate of incorporation

Any person may require a certificate of the incorporation of a company, signed by the registrar or authenticated by his official seal.]

[580]

NOTES

Substituted as noted to s 709 at **[579]**.

Repealed by the Companies Act 2006, s 1295, Sch 16, as from a day to be appointed.

Application to limited liability partnerships: see the Limited Liability Partnerships Regulations 2001, SI 2001/1090, reg 4(1), Sch 2, Pt 1 at **[6985]**, **[6993]**.

[710A Provision and authentication by registrar of documents in non-legible form

(*1*) *Any requirement of the Companies Acts as to the supply by the registrar of a document may, if the registrar thinks fit, be satisfied by the communication by the registrar of the requisite information in any non-legible form prescribed for the purposes of this section by regulations or approved by him.*

(*2*) *Where the document is required to be signed by him or sealed with his official seal, it shall instead be authenticated in such manner as may be prescribed by regulations or approved by the registrar.]*

[581]

NOTES

Substituted as noted to s 709 at **[579]**.

Repealed by the Companies Act 2006, s 1295, Sch 16, as from a day to be appointed.

Application to limited liability partnerships: see the Limited Liability Partnerships Regulations 2001, SI 2001/1090, reg 4(1), Sch 2, Pt 1 at **[6985]**, **[6993]**.

[710B Documents relating to Welsh companies

(*1*) *This section applies to any document which—*

(*a*) *is delivered to the registrar under this Act[, the Insolvency Act 1986 or Part 2 of the Companies (Audit, Investigations and Community Enterprise) Act 2004], and*

(*b*) *relates to a company (whether already registered or to be registered) whose memorandum states that its registered office is to be situated in Wales.*

(2) A document to which this section applies may be in Welsh but, subject to subsection (3), shall on delivery to the registrar be accompanied by a certified translation into English.

(3) The requirement for a translation imposed by subsection (2) shall not apply—
- *(a) to documents of such descriptions as may be prescribed for the purposes of this paragraph, or*
- *(b) to documents in a form prescribed in Welsh (or partly in Welsh and partly in English) by virtue of section 26 of the Welsh Language Act 1993.*

(4) Where by virtue of subsection (3) the registrar receives a document in Welsh without a certified translation into English, he shall, if that document is to be available for inspection, himself obtain such a translation; and that translation shall be treated as delivered to him in accordance with the same provision as the original.

(5) A company whose memorandum states that its registered office is to be situated in Wales may deliver to the registrar a certified translation into Welsh of any document in English which relates to the company and which is or has been delivered to the registrar.

(6) The provisions within subsection (7) (which require certified translations into English of certain documents delivered to the registrar) shall not apply where a translation is required by subsection (2) or would be required but for subsection (3).

(7) The provisions within this subsection are section 228(2)(f), the second sentence of section 242(1), sections 243(4), 272(5) and 273(7) and paragraph 7(3) of Part II of Schedule 9.

(8) In this section "certified translation" means a translation certified in the prescribed manner to be a correct translation.]

[582]

NOTES

Inserted by the Welsh Language Act 1993, s 30(1), (6), as from 25 January 1994 (in so far as enables prescription of description of documents for the purposes of sub-s (3)(a) and in so far as enables prescription of manner in which a translation is to be certified for the purpose of sub-s (8)), and as from 1 February 1994 (otherwise).

Repealed by the Companies Act 2006, s 1295, Sch 16, as from 1 January 2007. This section is reproduced only because of its continued application to limited liability partnerships (see the note below).

Sub-s (1): words in square brackets in para (a) substituted by the Community Interest Company Regulations 2005, SI 2005/1788, reg 34(3), as from 1 July 2005.

Application to limited liability partnerships: see the Limited Liability Partnerships Regulations 2001, SI 2001/1090, reg 4(1), Sch 2, Pt 1 at **[6985]**, **[6993]**. Note also that nothing in the Companies Act 2006 (Commencement No 1, Transitional Provisions and Savings) Order 2006, SI 2006/3428 affects any provision of this Act as applied by the 2001 Regulations to LLPs (see art 8(2) at **[7581]** and the introductory notes to this Act).

Prescribed; prescribed manner: see Appendix 4 (Forms table) at **[A4]**.

Transitional provisions: the Companies Act 2006 (Commencement No 1, Transitional Provisions and Savings) Order 2006, SI 2006/3428, Sch 5, para 1 (at **[7589]**) provides that regs 4 and 5 of the Companies (Welsh Language Forms and Documents) Regulations 1994 (SI 1994/117) continue to have effect notwithstanding the repeal of this section subject to certain adaptations.

Regulations: the Companies (Welsh Language Forms and Documents) Regulations 1994, SI 1994/117 (see also the transitional provisions note above).

711 Public notice by registrar of receipt and issue of certain documents

(1) The registrar of companies shall cause to be published in the Gazette notice of the issue or receipt by him of documents of any of the following descriptions (stating in the notice the name of the company, the description of document and the date of issue or receipt)—
- *(a) any certificate of incorporation of a company,*
- *(b) any document making or evidencing an alteration in a company's memorandum or articles,*
- *(c) any notification of a change among the directors of a company,*
- *(d) any copy of a resolution of a public company which gives, varies, revokes or renews an authority for the purposes of section 80 (allotment of relevant securities),*
- *(e) any copy of a special resolution of a public company passed under section 95(1), (2) or (3) (disapplication of pre-emption rights),*
- *(f) any report under section 103 or 104 as to the value of a non-cash asset,*
- *(g) any statutory declaration [or statement] delivered under section 117 (public company share capital requirements),*

(*h*) *any notification (given under section 122) of the redemption of shares,*
(*j*) *any statement or notice delivered by a public company under section 128 (registration of particulars of special rights),*
(*k*) *any documents delivered by a company under [section 242(1) (accounts and reports)],*
(*l*) *a copy of any resolution or agreement to which section 380 applies and which—*
  (*i*) *states the rights attached to any shares in a public company, other than shares which are in all respects uniform (for purposes of section 128) with shares previously allotted, or*
  (*ii*) *varies rights attached to any shares in a public company, or*
  (*iii*) *assigns a name or other designation, or a new name or designation, to any class of shares in a public company,*
(*m*) *any return of allotments of a public company,*
(*n*) *any notice of a change in the situation of a company's registered office,*
(*p*) *any copy of a winding-up order in respect of a company,*
(*q*) *any order for the dissolution of a company on a winding up,*
(*r*) *any return by a liquidator of the final meeting of a company on a winding up,*
[(*s*) *any copy of a draft of the terms of a scheme delivered to the registrar of companies under paragraph 2(1) of Schedule 15A,*
(*t*) *any copy of an order under section 425(2) or section 427 in respect of a compromise or arrangement to which section 427A(1) applies],*
[(*u*) *any return delivered under paragraph 1, 7 or 8 of Schedule 21A (branch registration),*
(*v*) *any document delivered under paragraph 1 or 8 of that Schedule,*
(*w*) *any notice under section 695A(3) of the closure of a branch,*
(*x*) *any document delivered under Schedule 21C (accounts and reports of foreign credit and financial institutions),*
(*y*) *any document delivered under Schedule 21D (accounts and reports of oversea companies subject to branch registration, other than credit and financial institutions),*
(*z*) *any return delivered under section 703P (particulars of winding up of oversea companies subject to branch registration).]*

(2) *In section 42 "official notification" means—*
(*a*) *in relation to anything stated in a document of any of the above descriptions, the notification of that document in the Gazette under this section, and*
(*b*) *in relation to the appointment of a liquidator in a voluntary winding up, the notification of it in the Gazette under [section 109 of the Insolvency Act];*

and "officially notified" is to be construed accordingly.

[583]

NOTES

Repealed by the Companies Act 2006, s 1295, Sch 16, as from 1 January 2007. This section is reproduced only because of its continued application to limited liability partnerships (see the note below).

Sub-s (1): words in square brackets in para (g) inserted by the Companies Act 1985 (Electronic Communications) Order 2000, SI 2000/3373, art 31(5), as from 22 December 2000; words in square brackets in para (k) substituted by CA 1989, s 23, Sch 10, para 14, as from 1 April 1990; paras (s), (t) added by the Companies (Mergers and Divisions) Regulations 1987, SI 1987/1991, reg 2(b), as from 1 January 1988; paras (u)–(z) added by the Oversea Companies and Credit and Financial Institutions (Branch Disclosure) Regulations 1992, SI 1992/3179, reg 4, Sch 3, paras 3, 7, as from 1 January 1993, for transitional provisions see Sch 4 to those Regulations at **[6744B]**.

Sub-s (2): words in square brackets substituted, subject to transitional provisions, by the Insolvency Act 1986, ss 437, 439(1), Sch 11, Pt I, Sch 13, Pt I, as from 29 December 1986.

Application to limited liability partnerships: see the Limited Liability Partnerships Regulations 2001, SI 2001/1090, reg 4(1), Sch 2, Pt 1 at **[6985]**, **[6993]**. Note also that nothing in the Companies Act 2006 (Commencement No 1, Transitional Provisions and Savings) Order 2006, SI 2006/3428 affects any provision of this Act as applied by the 2001 Regulations to LLPs (see art 8(2) at **[7581]** and the introductory notes to this Act).

Note: the reference in sub-s (1)(s) to "Schedule 15A" should now refer to "Schedule 15B" as a result of the renumbering of Schedule 15A as 15B: see **[678]**.

[711A Exclusion of deemed notice

(*1*) *A person shall not be taken to have notice of any matter merely because of its being disclosed in any document kept by the registrar of companies (and thus available for inspection) or made available by the company for inspection.*

(2) This does not affect the question whether a person is affected by notice of any matter by reason of a failure to make such inquiries as ought reasonably to be made.

(3) In this section "document" includes any material which contains information.

(4) Nothing in this section affects the operation of—

(a) section 416 of this Act (under which a person taking a charge over a company's property is deemed to have notice of matters disclosed on the companies charges register), or

(b) section 198 of the Law of Property Act 1925 as it applies by virtue of section 3(7) of the Land Charges Act 1972 (under which the registration of certain land charges under Part XII, or Chapter III of Part XXIII, of this Act is deemed to constitute actual notice for all purposes connected with the land affected).]

[584]

NOTES

Commencement: to be appointed.
Inserted by CA 1989, s 142(1), as from a day to be appointed.
Repealed by the Companies Act 2006, s 1295, Sch 16, as from a day to be appointed.

712 (*Repealed by CA 1989, ss 127(3), 212, Sch 24, as from 1 July 1991.*)

713 Enforcement of company's duty to make returns

(1) If a company, having made default in complying with any provision of the Companies Acts which requires it to [deliver a document to the registrar of companies], or to give notice to him of any matter, fails to make good the default within 14 days after the service of a notice on the company requiring it to do so, the court may, on an application made to it by any member or creditor of the company or by the registrar of companies, make an order directing the company and any officer of it to make good the default within such time as may be specified in the order.

(2) The court's order may provide that all costs of and incidental to the application shall be borne by the company or by any officers of it responsible for the default.

(3) Nothing in this section prejudices the operation of any enactment imposing penalties on a company or its officers in respect of any such default as is mentioned above.

[585]

NOTES

Repealed by the Companies Act 2006, s 1295, Sch 16, as from a day to be appointed.
Sub-s (1): words in square brackets substituted by CA 1989, s 127(4), as from 7 January 1991.
Application to limited liability partnerships: see the Limited Liability Partnerships Regulations 2001, SI 2001/1090, reg 4(1), Sch 2, Pt 1 at **[6985]**, **[6993]**.

714 Registrar's index of company and corporate names

(1) The registrar of companies shall keep an index of the names of the following bodies—

(a) companies as defined by this Act,

[(aa) companies incorporated outside the United Kingdom and Gibraltar which have complied with paragraph 1 of Schedule 21A and which do not appear to the registrar of companies not to have a branch in Great Britain,]

(b) companies incorporated outside Great Britain which have complied with section 691 and which do not appear to the registrar of companies not to have a place of business in Great Britain,

(c) incorporated and unincorporated bodies to which any provision of this Act applies by virtue of section 718 (unregistered companies),

(d) limited partnerships registered under the Limited Partnerships Act 1907,

[(da) limited liability partnerships incorporated under the Limited Liability Partnerships Act 2000,]

(e) companies within the meaning of the Companies Act (Northern Ireland) 1960,

(f) companies incorporated outside Northern Ireland which have complied with section 356 of that Act (which corresponds with section 691 of this Act), and which do not appear to the registrar not to have a place of business in Northern Ireland, and

(*g*) *societies registered under the Industrial and Provident Societies Act 1965 or the Industrial and Provident Societies Act* (*Northern Ireland*) *1969.*

(*2*) *The Secretary of State may by order in a statutory instrument vary subsection* (*1*) *by the addition or deletion of any class of body, except any within paragraph* (*a*) *or* (*b*) *of the subsection, whether incorporated or unincorporated; and any such statutory instrument is subject to annulment in pursuance of a resolution of either House of Parliament.*

[586]

NOTES

Repealed by the Companies Act 2006, s 1295, Sch 16, as from a day to be appointed.

Sub-s (1): para (aa) inserted by the Oversea Companies and Credit and Financial Institutions (Branch Disclosure) Regulations 1992, SI 1992/3179, reg 4, Sch 3, paras 3, 8, as from 1 January 1993, for transitional provisions see Sch 4 to those Regulations at **[6744B]**; para (da) inserted by the Limited Liability Partnerships Act 2000, s 1(6), Schedule, Pt I, para 1, as from 6 April 2001.

Application to limited liability partnerships: see the Limited Liability Partnerships Regulations 2001, SI 2001/1090, reg 4(1), Sch 2, Pt 1 at **[6985]**, **[6993]**.

715 (*Repealed by CA 1989, ss 127(3), 212, Sch 24, as from 1 July 1991.*)

[715A Interpretation

(*1*) *In this Part—*

"document" includes information recorded in any form; and

"legible", in the context of documents in legible or non-legible form, means capable of being read with the naked eye.

(*2*) *References in this Part to delivering a document include sending, forwarding, producing or* (*in the case of a notice*) *giving it.*

[(*3*) *References in this Part to the Companies Acts include Part 2 of the Companies* (*Audit, Investigations and Community Enterprise*) *Act 2004.]]*

[587]–[589]

NOTES

Inserted by CA 1989, s 127(1), as from 7 January 1991.

Repealed by the Companies Act 2006, s 1295, Sch 16, as from a day to be appointed.

Sub-s (3): added by the Community Interest Company Regulations 2005, SI 2005/1788, reg 34(2), as from 1 July 2005.

Application to limited liability partnerships: see the Limited Liability Partnerships Regulations 2001, SI 2001/1090, reg 4(1), Sch 2, Pt 1 at **[6985]**, **[6993]**.

PART XXV
MISCELLANEOUS AND SUPPLEMENTARY PROVISIONS

NOTES

Community interest companies: Regulations under the Companies (Audit, Investigations and Community Enterprise) Act 2004, s 58 (at **[932]**) may make amendments or modifications of any provision contained in this Part (ss 718–734) in consequence of any provision contained in, or made under, Pt 2 (ss 26–63 and Schs 3–7) of the 2004 Act. See the Community Interest Company Regulations 2005, SI 2005/1788.

716, 717 (*Repealed by the Regulatory Reform* (*Removal of 20 Member Limit in Partnerships etc*) *Order 2002, SI 2002/3203, reg 2, as from 21 December 2002.*)

718 Unregistered companies

(*1*) *The provisions of this Act specified in the first column of Schedule 22* (*relating respectively to the matters specified in the second column of the Schedule*) *apply to all bodies corporate incorporated in and having a principal place of business in Great Britain, other than those mentioned in subsection* (*2*) *below, as if they were companies registered under this Act, but subject to any limitations mentioned in relation to those provisions respectively in the third column and to such adaptations and modifications* (*if any*) *as may be specified by regulations made by the Secretary of State.*

(2) Those provisions of this Act do not apply by virtue of this section to any of the following—

(a) any body incorporated by or registered under any public general Act of Parliament,

(b) any body not formed for the purpose of carrying on a business which has for its object the acquisition of gain by the body or its individual members,

(c) any body for the time being exempted by direction of the Secretary of State (or before him by the Board of Trade),

[(d) any open-ended investment company within the meaning of the Open-Ended Investment Companies Regulations 2001.]

(3) Where against any provision of this Act specified in the first column of Schedule 22 there appears in the third column the entry "Subject to section 718(3)", it means that the provision is to apply by virtue of this section so far only as may be specified by regulations made by the Secretary of State and to such bodies corporate as may be so specified.

(4) …

(5) This section does not repeal or revoke in whole or in part any enactment, royal charter or other instrument constituting or regulating any body in relation to which those provisions are applied by virtue of this section, or restrict the power of Her Majesty to grant a charter in lieu or supplementary to any such charter as above mentioned; but, in relation to any such body, the operation of any such enactment, charter or instrument is suspended in so far as it is inconsistent with any of those provisions as they apply for the time being to that body.

(6) The power to make regulations conferred by this section (whether regulations under subsection (1) or subsection (3)) is exercisable by statutory instrument subject to annulment in pursuance of a resolution of either House of Parliament.

[590]

NOTES

Repealed by the Companies Act 2006, s 1295, Sch 16, as from a day to be appointed.

Sub-s (2): para (d) added by the Open-Ended Investment Companies (Investment Companies with Variable Capital) Regulations 1996, SI 1996/2827, reg 75, Sch 8, Pt I, para 9, as from 6 January 1997, and substituted by the Open-Ended Investment Companies Regulations 2001, SI 2001/1228, reg 84, Sch 7, para 8, as from 1 December 2001.

Sub-s (4): repealed by the Statute Law (Repeals) Act 2004, as from 22 July 2004.

Regulations: the Companies (Unregistered Companies) Regulations 1985, SI 1985/680 at **[6022]**.

719 Power of company to provide for employees on cessation or transfer of business

(1) The powers of a company include (if they would not otherwise do so apart from this section) power to make the following provision for the benefit of persons employed or formerly employed by the company or any of its subsidiaries, that is to say, provision in connection with the cessation or the transfer to any person of the whole or part of the undertaking of the company or that subsidiary.

(2) The power conferred by subsection (1) is exercisable notwithstanding that its exercise is not in the best interests of the company.

(3) The power which a company may exercise by virtue only of subsection (1) shall only be exercised by the company if sanctioned—

(a) in a case not falling within paragraph (b) or (c) below, by an ordinary resolution of the company, or

(b) if so authorised by the memorandum or articles, a resolution of the directors, or

(c) if the memorandum or articles require the exercise of the power to be sanctioned by a resolution of the company of some other description for which more than a simple majority of the members voting is necessary, with the sanction of a resolution of that description;

and in any case after compliance with any other requirements of the memorandum or articles applicable to its exercise.

(4) Any payment which may be made by a company under this section may, if made before the commencement of any winding up of the company, be made out of profits of the company which are available for dividend.

[591]–[592]

NOTES

Repealed by the Companies Act 2006, s 1295, Sch 16, as from 1 October 2007. For savings see the note below.

Transitional provision: for transitional provisions in relation to this section, see CA 1989, Sch 18, para 36 at **[874]**.

Savings: this section continues to apply (a) to provision made before 1 October 2007, and (b) to anything sanctioned in accordance with sub-s (3) before that date (see the draft Companies Act 2006 (Commencement No 3, Consequential Amendments, Transitional Provisions and Savings) Order 2007, Sch 3, para 18 at **[A12]**).

On the winding up of a company the liquidator may make any payment which the company has, before the commencement of the winding up, decided to make under this section, and the powers which a company may exercise by virtue only of this section may be exercised, in certain circumstances, by the liquidator himself; see the Insolvency Act 1986, s 187 at **[3344]**.

720 (*Repealed by the Companies Act 2006, ss 1178, 1295, Sch 16, as from 6 April 2007.*)

721 Production and inspection of books where offence suspected

(1) The following applies if on an application made—

(a) in England and Wales, to a judge of the High Court by the Director of Public Prosecutions, the Secretary of State or a chief officer of police, or

(b) in Scotland, to one of the Lords Commissioners of Justiciary by the Lord Advocate,

there is shown to be reasonable cause to believe that any person has, while an officer of a company, committed an offence in connection with the management of the company's affairs and that evidence of the commission of the offence is to be found in any books or papers of or under the control of the company.

(2) An order may be made—

(a) authorising any person named in it to inspect the books or papers in question, or any of them, for the purpose of investigating and obtaining evidence of the offence, or

(b) requiring the secretary of the company or such other officer of it as may be named in the order to produce the books or papers (or any of them) to a person named in the order at a place so named.

(3) The above applies also in relation to any books or papers of a person carrying on the business of banking so far as they relate to the company's affairs, as it applies to any books or papers of or under the control of the company, except that no such order as is referred to in subsection (2)(b) shall be made by virtue of this subsection.

(4) The decision of a judge of the High Court or of any of the Lords Commissioners of Justiciary on an application under this section is not appealable.

[593]

NOTES

Repealed by the Companies Act 2006, s 1295, Sch 16, as from a day to be appointed.

Application to limited liability partnerships: see the Limited Liability Partnerships Regulations 2001, SI 2001/1090, reg 4(1), Sch 2, Pt 1 at **[6985]**, **[6993]**.

722 Form of company registers, etc

(1) Any register, index, minute book or accounting records required by the Companies Acts to be kept by a company may be kept either by making entries in bound books or by recording the matters in question in any other manner.

(2) Where any such register, index, minute book or accounting record is not kept by making entries in a bound book, but by some other means, adequate precautions shall be taken for guarding against falsification and facilitating its discovery.

(3) If default is made in complying with subsection (2), the company and every officer of it who is in default is liable to a fine and, for continued contravention, to a daily default fine.

[594]

NOTES

Repealed by the Companies Act 2006, s 1295, Sch 16, as from a day to be appointed.

Application to limited liability partnerships: see the Limited Liability Partnerships Regulations 2001, SI 2001/1090, reg 4(1), Sch 2, Pt 1 at **[6985]**, **[6993]**.

723 Use of computers for company records

(1) The power conferred on a company by section 722(1) to keep a register or other record by recording the matters in question otherwise than by making entries in bound books includes power to keep the register or other record by recording those matters otherwise than in a legible form, so long as the recording is capable of being reproduced in a legible form.

(2) Any provision of an instrument made by a company before 12th February 1979 which requires a register of holders of the company's debentures to be kept in a legible form is to be read as requiring the register to be kept in a legible or non-legible form.

(3) If any such register or other record of a company as is mentioned in section 722(1), or a register of holders of a company's debentures, is kept by the company by recording the matters in question otherwise than in a legible form, any duty imposed on the company by this Act to allow inspection of, or to furnish a copy of, the register or other record or any part of it is to be treated as a duty to allow inspection of, or to furnish, a reproduction of the recording or of the relevant part of it in a legible form.

(4) The Secretary of State may by regulations in a statutory instrument make such provision in addition to subsection (3) as he considers appropriate in connection with such registers or other records as are mentioned in that subsection, and are kept as so mentioned; and the regulations may make modifications of provisions of this Act relating to such registers or other records.

(5) A statutory instrument under subsection (4) is subject to annulment in pursuance of a resolution of either House of Parliament.

[595]

NOTES

Repealed by the Companies Act 2006, s 1295, Sch 16, as from a day to be appointed.

Application to limited liability partnerships: see the Limited Liability Partnerships Regulations 2001, SI 2001/1090, reg 4(1), Sch 2, Pt 1 at **[6985]**, **[6993]**.

Regulations: the Companies (Registers and other Records) Regulations 1985, SI 1985/724 at **[6028]**.

[723A Obligations of company as to inspections of registers, &c

(1) The Secretary of State may make provision by regulations as to the obligations of a company which is required by any provision of this Act—

(a) to make available for inspection any register, index or document, or

(b) to provide copies of any such register, index or document, or part of it;

and a company which fails to comply with the regulations shall be deemed to have refused inspection or, as the case may be, to have failed to provide a copy.

(2) The regulations may make provision as to the time, duration and manner of inspection, including the circumstances in which and extent to which the copying of information is permitted in the course of inspection.

(3) The regulations may define what may be required of the company as regards the nature, extent and manner of extracting or presenting any information for the purposes of inspection or the provision of copies.

(4) Where there is a power to charge a fee, the regulations may make provision as to the amount of the fee and the basis of its calculation.

(5) Regulations under this section may make different provision for different classes of case.

(6) Nothing in any provision of this Act or in the regulations shall be construed as preventing a company from affording more extensive facilities than are required by the regulations or, where a fee may be charged, from charging a lesser fee than that prescribed or no fee at all.

(7) Regulations under this section shall be made by statutory instrument which shall be subject to annulment in pursuance of a resolution of either House of Parliament.]

[596]

NOTES

Inserted by CA 1989, s 143(1), as from 1 November 1991.

Repealed by the Companies Act 2006, s 1295, Sch 16, as from a day to be appointed.

Application to limited liability partnerships: see the Limited Liability Partnerships Regulations 2001, SI 2001/1090, reg 4(1), Sch 2, Pt 1 at **[6985]**, **[6993]**.

Regulations: the Companies (Inspection and Copying of Registers, Indices and Documents) Regulations 1991, SI 1991/1998 at **[6716]**.

[723B Confidentiality orders

(1) Subject to the provisions of this section, an individual may make an application under this section to the Secretary of State where the condition in subsection (2) is satisfied.

(2) That condition is that the individual—

- *(a) is or proposes to become a director, secretary or permanent representative of a relevant company; and*
- *(b) considers that the availability for inspection by members of the public of particulars of his usual residential address creates, or (if an order is not made under this section) is likely to create, a serious risk that he or a person who lives with him will be subjected to violence or intimidation.*

(3) Where, on an application made by an individual under this section, the Secretary of State is satisfied that the availability for inspection by members of the public of particulars of the individual's usual residential address creates, or (if an order is not made under this section) is likely to create, a serious risk that the individual, or a person who lives with him, will be subjected to violence or intimidation, he shall make an order under this section ("a confidentiality order") in relation to him.

(4) Otherwise, he shall dismiss the application.

(5) An application under this section shall specify, in relation to each company of which the individual is a director, secretary or permanent representative, an address satisfying such conditions as may be prescribed.

(6) The Secretary of State shall give the applicant notice of his decision under subsection (3) or (4); and a notice under this subsection shall be given within the prescribed period after the making of the decision and contain such information as may be prescribed.

(7) Regulations may make provision about applications for confidentiality orders; and the regulations may in particular—

- *(a) require the payment, on the making of an application, of such fees as may be specified in the regulations;*
- *(b) make provision about the form and manner in which applications are to be made;*
- *(c) provide that applications shall contain such information, and be accompanied by such evidence, as the Secretary of State may from time to time direct.*

(8) Regulations may make provision—

- *(a) about the manner in which determinations are to be made under subsection (3) or (4);*
- *(b) for questions to be referred to such persons as the Secretary of State thinks fit for the purposes of such determinations;*
- *(c) about the review of such determinations;*
- *(d) about the period for which confidentiality orders shall remain in force and the renewal of confidentiality orders.*

(9) The Secretary of State may at any time revoke a confidentiality order if he is satisfied that such conditions as may be prescribed are satisfied.

(10) Regulations may make provision about the manner in which a determination under subsection (9) is to be made and notified to the individual concerned.]

[597]

NOTES

Inserted by the Criminal Justice and Police Act 2001, s 45(1), (2), as from 19 June 2001 (for the purpose of making regulations or orders), and as from 2 April 2002 (otherwise).

Repealed by the Companies Act 2006, s 1295, Sch 16, as from a day to be appointed.

Application to limited liability partnerships: see the Limited Liability Partnership (No 2) Regulations 2002, SI 2002/913, Schedule at **[7079]**.

Regulations: the Companies (Particulars of Usual Residential Address) (Confidentiality Orders) Regulations 2002, SI 2002/912 at **[7058]**; the Limited Liability Partnerships (Particulars of Usual Residential Address) (Confidentiality Orders) Regulations 2002, SI 2002/915 at **[7080]**.

[723C Effect of confidentiality orders

(1) At any time when a confidentiality order is in force in relation to an individual—

(*a*) ...

(*b*) *section 364 shall have effect in relation to each affected company of which the individual is a director or secretary as if the reference in subsection (4)(a) of that section to the individual's usual residential address were a reference to the address for the time being specified by the individual in relation to that company under section 723B(5) or subsection (7) below.*

(2) Regulations may make provision about the inspection and copying of confidential records, and such provision may include—

(*a*) *provision as to the persons by whom, and the circumstances in which, confidential records may be inspected or copies taken of such records;*

(*b*) *provision under which the registrar may be required to provide certified copies of, or of extracts from, such records.*

(3) Provision under subsection (2) may include provision—

(*a*) *for persons of a prescribed description to be entitled to apply to the court for authority to inspect or take copies of confidential records;*

(*b*) *as to the criteria to be used by the court in determining whether an authorisation should be given.*

(4) Regulations may make provision for restricting the persons to whom, and the purposes for which, relevant information may be disclosed.

(5) In subsection (4) "relevant information" means information, relating to the usual residential address of an individual in relation to whom a confidentiality order is in force, which has been obtained in prescribed circumstances.

(6) Regulations may—

(*a*) *provide that, where a confidentiality order is in force in relation to an individual who is a director or secretary of a company, subsections (3) and (5) of section 288 shall not apply in relation to so much of the register kept by the company under that section as contains particulars of the usual residential address of that individual ("the protected part of the register"); and*

(*b*) *make provision as to the persons by whom the protected part of the register may be inspected and the conditions (which may include conditions as to the payment of a fee) on which they may inspect it.*

(7) Regulations may make provision—

(*a*) *requiring any individual in relation to whom a confidentiality order is in force to specify in the prescribed manner, in relation to each company of which he becomes a director, secretary or permanent representative at a time when the order is in force, an address satisfying such conditions as may be prescribed;*

(*b*) *as to the manner in which the address specified in relation to a company under section 723B(5) or this subsection may be changed.*

(8) A company is an affected company for the purposes of subsection (1) if—

(*a*) *it is required to deliver annual returns in accordance with section 363; and*

(*b*) *the individual has specified an address in relation to it under section 723B(5) or subsection (7) above.]*

[598]

NOTES

Inserted as noted to s 723B at **[597]**.

Repealed by the Companies Act 2006, s 1295, Sch 16, as from 1 January 2007 (in so far as relating to sub-s (1)(a)), and as from a day to be appointed (otherwise).

Sub-s (1): para (a) repealed as noted above. It previously read as follows—

"(a) section 709(1) shall not apply to so much of any record kept by the registrar as contains information which is recorded as particulars of the individual's usual residential address that were contained in a document delivered to the registrar after the order came into force;".

Application to limited liability partnerships: see the Limited Liability Partnership (No 2) Regulations 2002, SI 2002/913, Schedule at **[7079]**. Note also that nothing in the Companies Act 2006

(Commencement No 2, Consequential Amendments, Transitional Provisions and Savings) Order 2007, SI 2007/1093 affects any provision of this Act as applied by the 2001 Regulations to LLPs (see art 12(1) at **[7624]** and the introductory notes to this Act).

Regulations: the Companies (Particulars of Usual Residential Address) (Confidentiality Orders) Regulations 2002, SI 2002/912 at **[7058]**; the Limited Liability Partnerships (Particulars of Usual Residential Address) (Confidentiality Orders) Regulations 2002, SI 2002/915 at **[7080]**.

[723D Construction of sections 723B and 723C

(1) In section 723B "relevant company" means—

(a) a company formed and registered under this Act or an existing company; or

(b) an overseas company.

(2) For the purposes of sections 723B and 723C, an individual is a permanent representative of a company if—

(a) the company is a company to which section 690A applies; and

(b) he is authorised to represent the company as a permanent representative of the company for the business of one or more of its branches in Great Britain.

(3) In section 723C "confidential records" means so much of any records kept by the registrar for the purposes of the Companies Acts as contains information—

(a) which relates to an individual in relation to whom a confidentiality order is in force; and

(b) is recorded as particulars of the individual's usual residential address that were contained in a document delivered to the registrar after the order came into force.

(4) In sections 723B and 723C—

"confidentiality order" means an order under section 723B;

"the court" means such court as may be specified in regulations;

"director" and "secretary", in relation to an overseas company, have the same meanings as in Chapter 1 of Part 23 of this Act;

"document" has the same meaning as in Part 24 of this Act;

"prescribed" means prescribed by regulations.

(5) Section 715A(2) applies in relation to sections 723B and 723C as it applies in relation to Part 24 of this Act.

(6) Regulations may provide that in determining for the purposes of sections 723B and 723C whether a document has been delivered after the coming into force of a confidentiality order, any document delivered to the registrar after the latest time permitted for the delivery of that document shall be deemed to have been delivered at that time.

(7) For the purposes of section 723B(2)(a) and subsection (2) above it is immaterial whether or not the company in question has already been incorporated or become a relevant company or a company to which section 690A applies at the time of the application under section 723B.

(8) For the purposes of section 723C(1) and subsection (3) above, it is immaterial whether the record in question consists in the original document concerned.]

[599]

NOTES

Inserted as noted to s 723B at **[597]**.

Repealed by the Companies Act 2006, s 1295, Sch 16, as from a day to be appointed.

Application to limited liability partnerships: see the Limited Liability Partnership (No 2) Regulations 2002, SI 2002/913, Schedule at **[7079]**.

Regulations: the Companies (Particulars of Usual Residential Address) (Confidentiality Orders) Regulations 2002, SI 2002/912 at **[7058]**; the Limited Liability Partnerships (Particulars of Usual Residential Address) (Confidentiality Orders) Regulations 2002, SI 2002/915 at **[7080]**.

[723E Sections 723B and 723C: offences

(1) Regulations may provide—

(a) that any person who in an application under section 723B makes a statement which he knows to be false in a material particular, or recklessly makes a statement which is false in a material particular, shall be guilty of an offence;

(b) that any person who discloses information in contravention of regulations under section 723C(4) shall be guilty of an offence.

(2) *Regulations may provide that a person guilty of an offence under subsection (1) shall be liable—*

(*a*) *on conviction on indictment, to imprisonment for a term not exceeding two years, or to a fine, or to both; and*

(*b*) *on summary conviction, to imprisonment for a term not exceeding six months, or to a fine not exceeding the statutory maximum, or to both.]*

[600]

NOTES

Inserted as noted to s 723B at **[597]**.

Repealed by the Companies Act 2006, s 1295, Sch 16, as from a day to be appointed.

Application to limited liability partnerships: see the Limited Liability Partnership (No 2) Regulations 2002, SI 2002/913, Schedule at **[7079]**.

Regulations: the Companies (Particulars of Usual Residential Address) (Confidentiality Orders) Regulations 2002, SI 2002/912 at **[7058]**; the Limited Liability Partnerships (Particulars of Usual Residential Address) (Confidentiality Orders) Regulations 2002, SI 2002/915 at **[7080]**.

[723F Regulations under sections 723B to 723E

(1) *In sections 723B to 723E "regulations" means regulations made by the Secretary of State.*

(2) *Any power of the Secretary of State to make regulations under any of those sections shall be exercisable by statutory instrument.*

(3) *Regulations under sections 723B to 723E—*

(*a*) *may make different provision for different cases;*

(*b*) *may contain such incidental, supplemental, consequential and transitional provision, as the Secretary of State thinks fit.*

(4) *The provision that may be made by virtue of subsection (3)(b) includes provision repealing or modifying any enactment.*

(5) *No regulations shall be made under any of sections 723B to 723E unless a draft of the instrument containing them has been laid before Parliament and approved by a resolution of each House.]*

[601]

NOTES

Inserted as noted to s 723B at **[597]**.

Repealed by the Companies Act 2006, s 1295, Sch 16, as from a day to be appointed.

Application to limited liability partnerships: see the Limited Liability Partnership (No 2) Regulations 2002, SI 2002/913, Schedule at **[7079]**.

Regulations: the Limited Liability Partnerships (Particulars of Usual Residential Address) (Confidentiality Orders) Regulations 2002, SI 2002/915 at **[7080]**.

724 (*Repealed, with savings, by the Insolvency Act 1986, ss 437, 438, Schs 11, 12, as from 29 December 1986. Also Repealed by the Companies Act 2006, s 1295, Sch 16, as from a day to be appointed.*)

725 Service of documents

(1) *A document may be served on a company by leaving it at, or sending it by post to, the company's registered office.*

(2) *Where a company registered in Scotland carries on business in England and Wales, the process of any court in England and Wales may be served on the company by leaving it at, or sending it by post to, the company's principal place of business in England and Wales, addressed to the manager or other head officer in England and Wales of the company.*

(3) *Where process is served on a company under subsection (2), the person issuing out the process shall send a copy of it by post to the company's registered office.*

[602]

NOTES

Repealed by the Companies Act 2006, s 1295, Sch 16, as from a day to be appointed.

Application to limited liability partnerships: see the Limited Liability Partnerships Regulations 2001, SI 2001/1090, reg 4(1), Sch 2, Pt 1 at **[6985]**, **[6993]**.

726 Costs and expenses in actions by certain limited companies

(1) Where in England and Wales a limited company is plaintiff in an action or other legal proceeding, the court having jurisdiction in the matter may, if it appears by credible testimony that there is reason to believe that the company will be unable to pay the defendant's costs if successful in his defence, require sufficient security to be given for those costs, and may stay all proceedings until the security is given.

(2) Where in Scotland a limited company is pursuer in an action or other legal proceeding, the court having jurisdiction in the matter may, if it appears by credible testimony that there is reason to believe that the company will be unable to pay the defender's expenses if successful in his defence, order the company to find caution and sist the proceedings until caution is found.

[603]

NOTES

Repealed by the Companies Act 2006, s 1295, Sch 16, as from a day to be appointed.

Application to limited liability partnerships: see the Limited Liability Partnerships Regulations 2001, SI 2001/1090, reg 4(1), Sch 2, Pt 1 at **[6985]**, **[6993]**.

727 Power of court to grant relief in certain cases

(1) If in any proceedings for negligence, default, breach of duty or breach of trust against an officer of a company or a person employed by a company as auditor (whether he is or is not an officer of the company) it appears to the court hearing the case that that officer or person is or may be liable in respect of the negligence, default, breach of duty or breach of trust, but that he has acted honestly and reasonably, and that having regard to all the circumstances of the case (including those connected with his appointment) he ought fairly to be excused for the negligence, default, breach of duty or breach of trust, that court may relieve him, either wholly or partly, from his liability on such terms as it thinks fit.

(2) If any such officer or person as above-mentioned has reason to apprehend that any claim will or might be made against him in respect of any negligence, default, breach of duty or breach of trust, he may apply to the court for relief; and the court on the application has the same power to relieve him as under this section it would have had if it had been a court before which proceedings against that person for negligence, default, breach of duty or breach of trust had been brought.

(3) Where a case to which subsection (1) applies is being tried by a judge with a jury, the judge, after hearing the evidence, may, if he is satisfied that the defendant or defender ought in pursuance of that subsection to be relieved either in whole or in part from the liability sought to be enforced against him, withdraw the case in whole or in part from the jury and forthwith direct judgment to be entered for the defendant or defender on such terms as to costs or otherwise as the judge may think proper.

[604]

NOTES

Repealed by the Companies Act 2006, s 1295, Sch 16, as from a day to be appointed.

Application to limited liability partnerships: see the Limited Liability Partnerships Regulations 2001, SI 2001/1090, reg 4(1), Sch 2, Pt 1 at **[6985]**, **[6993]**.

728 Enforcement of High Court orders

Orders made by the High Court under this Act may be enforced in the same manner as orders made in an action pending in that court.

[605]

NOTES

Repealed by the Companies Act 2006, s 1295, Sch 16, as from a day to be appointed.

Application to limited liability partnerships: see the Limited Liability Partnerships Regulations 2001, SI 2001/1090, reg 4(1), Sch 2, Pt 1 at **[6985]**, **[6993]**.

729 Annual report by Secretary of State

The Secretary of State shall cause a general annual report of matters within the Companies Acts to be prepared and laid before both Houses of Parliament.

[606]

NOTES

Repealed by the Companies Act 2006, ss 1179, 1295, Sch 16, as from 6 April 2007. This section is reproduced only because of its continued application to limited liability partnerships (see the note below).

Application to limited liability partnerships: see the Limited Liability Partnerships Regulations 2001, SI 2001/1090, reg 4(1), Sch 2, Pt 1 at **[6985]**, **[6993]**. Note also that nothing in the Companies Act 2006 (Commencement No 1, Transitional Provisions and Savings) Order 2006, SI 2006/3428 affects any provision of this Act as applied by the 2001 Regulations to LLPs (see art 8(2) at **[7581]** and the introductory notes to this Act).

730 Punishment of offences

(1) Schedule 24 to this Act has effect with respect to the way in which offences under this Act [(other than an offence under Part 14 or 15)] are punishable on conviction.

(2) In relation to an offence under a provision of this Act specified in the first column of the Schedule (the general nature of the offence being described in the second column), the third column shows whether the offence is punishable on conviction on indictment, or on summary conviction, or either in the one way or the other.

(3) The fourth column of the Schedule shows, in relation to an offence, the maximum punishment by way of fine or imprisonment under this Act which may be imposed on a person convicted of the offence in the way specified in relation to it in the third column (that is to say, on indictment or summarily), a reference to a period of years or months being to a term of imprisonment of that duration.

(4) The fifth column shows (in relation to an offence for which there is an entry in that column) that a person convicted of the offence after continued contravention is liable to a daily default fine; that is to say, he is liable on a second or subsequent summary conviction of the offence to the fine specified in that column for each day on which the contravention is continued (instead of the penalty specified for the offence in the fourth column of the Schedule).

(5) For the purpose of any enactment in the Companies Acts which provides that an officer of a company [or other body] who is in default is liable to a fine or penalty, the expression "officer who is in default" means any officer of the company [or other body] who knowingly and wilfully authorises or permits the default, refusal or contravention mentioned in the enactment.

[607]

NOTES

Repealed by the Companies Act 2006, s 1295, Sch 16, as from a day to be appointed.

Sub-s (1): words in square brackets inserted by the draft Companies Act 2006 (Commencement No 3, Consequential Amendments, Transitional Provisions and Savings) Order 2007, art 10(1), Sch 4, Pt 1, para 12, as from 1 October 2007 (see **[A12]**).

Sub-s (5): words in square brackets inserted by CA 1989, s 145, Sch 19, para 17, as from 1 April 1990; repealed by the draft Companies Act 2006 (Commencement No 3, Consequential Amendments, Transitional Provisions and Savings) Order 2007, art 10(1), Sch 4, Pt 1, para 13, as from 1 October 2007 (see **[A12]**).

Application to limited liability partnerships: see the Limited Liability Partnerships Regulations 2001, SI 2001/1090, reg 4(1), Sch 2, Pt 1 at **[6985]**, **[6993]**. Note also that nothing in the draft Companies Act 2006 (Commencement No 3, Consequential Amendments, Transitional Provisions and Savings) Order 2007 affects any provision of this Act as applied by the 2001 Regulations to LLPs (see art 12(2) at **[A12]** and the introductory notes to this Act).

[730A Meaning of "officer in default"

(1) This section applies to—

(a) offences under this Act (other than an offence under Part 14 or 15),

(b) offences under the insider dealing legislation, and

(c) offences under the Companies Consolidation (Consequential Provisions) Act 1985.

(2) For the purposes of an offence to which this section applies "officer who is in default" means any officer who knowingly and wilfully authorises or permits the default, refusal or contravention in question.]

[607]

NOTES

Commencement: 1 October 2007.

Inserted by the draft Companies Act 2006 (Commencement No 3, Consequential Amendments, Transitional Provisions and Savings) Order 2007, art 10(1), Sch 4, Pt 1, para 13, as from 1 October 2007 (see **[A12]**).

731 Summary proceedings

[(A1) This section applies to—

(*a*) *offences under this Act (other than an offence under Part 14 or 15),*

(*b*) *offences under the insider dealing legislation, and*

(*c*) *offences under the Companies Consolidation (Consequential Provisions) Act 1985.]*

(*1*) *Summary proceedings for any offence under the Companies Acts may (without prejudice to any jurisdiction exercisable apart from this subsection) be taken against a body corporate at any place at which the body has a place of business, and against any other person at any place at which he is for the time being.*

(*2*) *Notwithstanding anything in section 127(1) of the Magistrates' Courts Act 1980, an information relating to an offence under the Companies Acts which is triable by a magistrates' court in England and Wales may be so tried if it is laid at any time within 3 years after the commission of the offence and within 12 months after the date on which evidence sufficient in the opinion of the Director of Public Prosecutions or the Secretary of State (as the case may be) to justify the proceedings comes to his knowledge.*

(*3*) *Summary proceedings in Scotland for an offence under the Companies Acts shall not be commenced after the expiration of 3 years from the commission of the offence.*

Subject to this (and notwithstanding anything in [section 136 of the Criminal Procedure (Scotland) Act 1995]), such proceedings may (in Scotland) be commenced at any time within 12 months after the date on which evidence sufficient in the Lord Advocate's opinion to justify the proceedings came to his knowledge or, where such evidence was reported to him by the Secretary of State, within 12 months after the date on which it came to the knowledge of the latter; and subsection (3) of that section applies for the purpose of this subsection as it applies for the purpose of that section.

(*4*) *For purposes of this section, a certificate of the Director of Public Prosecutions, the Lord Advocate or the Secretary of State (as the case may be) as to the date on which such evidence as is referred to above came to his knowledge is conclusive evidence.*

[608]

NOTES

Repealed by the Companies Act 2006, s 1295, Sch 16, as from a day to be appointed.

Sub-s (A1): inserted by the draft Companies Act 2006 (Commencement No 3, Consequential Amendments, Transitional Provisions and Savings) Order 2007, art 10(1), Sch 4, Pt 1, para 14(1), (2), as from 1 October 2007 (see **[A12]**).

Sub-s (1): for the words "any offence under the Companies Acts" there are substituted the words "an offence to which this section applies" by the draft Companies Act 2006 (Commencement No 3, Consequential Amendments, Transitional Provisions and Savings) Order 2007, art 10(1), Sch 4, Pt 1, para 14(1), (3), as from 1 October 2007 (see **[A12]**).

Sub-s (2): for the words "an offence under the Companies Acts" there are substituted the words "an offence to which this section applies" by the draft Companies Act 2006 (Commencement No 3, Consequential Amendments, Transitional Provisions and Savings) Order 2007, art 10(1), Sch 4, Pt 1, para 14(1), (4), as from 1 October 2007 (see **[A12]**).

Sub-s (3): for the words "an offence under the Companies Acts" there are substituted the words "an offence to which this section applies" by the draft Companies Act 2006 (Commencement No 3, Consequential Amendments, Transitional Provisions and Savings) Order 2007, art 10(1), Sch 4, Pt 1, para 14(1), (4), as from 1 October 2007 (see **[A12]**); words in square brackets substituted by the Criminal Procedure (Consequential Provisions) (Scotland) Act 1995, s 5, Sch 4, para 56(3), as from 1 April 1996.

Application to limited liability partnerships: see the Limited Liability Partnerships Regulations 2001, SI 2001/1090, reg 4(1), Sch 2, Pt 1 at **[6985]**, **[6993]**. Note also that nothing in the draft Companies Act 2006 (Commencement No 3, Consequential Amendments, Transitional Provisions and Savings) Order 2007 affects any provision of this Act as applied by the 2001 Regulations to LLPs (see art 12(2) at **[A12]** and the introductory notes to this Act).

732 Prosecution by public authorities

(1) In respect of an offence under any of sections 210, [245E, 245G,] 324, 329, [448, 449 to 451, 453A] and 455, proceedings shall not, in England and Wales, be instituted except by or with the consent of the appropriate authority.

(2) That authority is—

- *(a) for an offence under any of sections 210, [245E, 245G,] 324 and 329, the Secretary of State or the Director of Public Prosecutions,*
- *(b) for an offence under any of sections [448, 449 to 451 and 453A], either one of those two persons or the Industrial Assurance Commissioner, and*
- *(c) for an offence under section 455, the Secretary of State.*

(3) Where proceedings are instituted under the Companies Acts against any person by the Director of Public Prosecutions or by or on behalf of the Secretary of State or the Lord Advocate, nothing in those Acts is to be taken to require any person to disclose any information which he is entitled to refuse to disclose on grounds of legal professional privilege [or, in Scotland, confidentiality of communications].

[609]

NOTES

Repealed by the Companies Act 2006, s 1295, Sch 16, as from a day to be appointed.

Sub-ss (1), (2): figures in first pair of square brackets inserted, and words in second pair of square brackets substituted, by the Companies (Audit, Investigations and Community Enterprise) Act 2004, s 25, Sch 2, Pts 2, 3, paras 5, 7, 16, 22(a), (b), as from 6 April 2005 (for transitional provisions, see the Companies (Audit, Investigations and Community Enterprise) Act 2004 (Commencement) and Companies Act 1989 (Commencement No 18) Order 2004, SI 2004/3322, art 7 at **[7345]**). Sub-ss (1), (2) are also substituted by the draft Companies Act 2006 (Commencement No 3, Consequential Amendments, Transitional Provisions and Savings) Order 2007, art 10(1), Sch 4, Pt 1, para 15, as from 1 October 2007 (see **[A12]**), as follows—

"(1) Proceedings in England and Wales for an offence under section 245E or 245G may only be brought by or with the consent of the Secretary of State or the Director of Public Prosecutions.".

Sub-s (3): words in square brackets inserted by the Companies (Audit, Investigations and Community Enterprise) Act 2004, s 25, Sch 2, Pt 3, paras 16, 22(c), as from 6 April 2005.

Application to limited liability partnerships: see the Limited Liability Partnerships Regulations 2001, SI 2001/1090, reg 4(1), Sch 2, Pt 1 at **[6985]**, **[6993]**. Note also that nothing in the draft Companies Act 2006 (Commencement No 3, Consequential Amendments, Transitional Provisions and Savings) Order 2007 affects any provision of this Act as applied by the 2001 Regulations to LLPs (see art 12(2) at **[A12]** and the introductory notes to this Act).

Industrial Assurance Commissioner: by the Friendly Societies Act 1992 (Transitional and Consequential Provisions) Regulations 1995, SI 1995/710, reg 5 (revoked), any reference to the Industrial Assurance Commissioner was to be construed as a reference to the Friendly Societies Commission. The functions of the Friendly Societies Commission were in due course transferred to the Financial Services Authority (see the Friendly Societies Act 1992, s 1 (as substituted by the Financial Services and Markets Act 2000 (Mutual Societies) Order 2001, SI 2001/2617, art 13(1), Sch 3, Pt I, paras 53, 54).

733 Offences by bodies corporate

(1) The following applies to offences under any of sections 210, 216(3)[, 245E(3), 245G(7)] […] [, 394A(1)][, 448, 449 to 451 and 453A].

(2) Where a body corporate is guilty of such an offence and it is proved that the offence occurred with the consent or connivance of, or was attributable to any neglect on the part of any director, manager, secretary or other similar officer of the body, or any person who was purporting to act in any such capacity, he as well as the body corporate is guilty of that offence and is liable to be proceeded against and punished accordingly.

(3) Where the affairs of a body corporate are managed by its members, … subsection (2) above applies in relation to the acts and defaults of a member in connection with his functions of management as if he were a director of the body corporate.

(4) In this section "director", in relation to an offence under any of sections [448, 449 to 451 and 453A], includes a shadow director.

[610]

NOTES

Repealed by the Companies Act 2006, s 1295, Sch 16, as from a day to be appointed.

Sub-s (1): figure in first pair of square brackets inserted, and words in final pair of square brackets substituted, by the Companies (Audit, Investigations and Community Enterprise) Act 2004, s 25, Sch 2,

Pts 2, 3, paras 5, 8, 16, 23(a), as from 6 April 2005 (for transitional provisions, see the Companies (Audit, Investigations and Community Enterprise) Act 2004 (Commencement) and Companies Act 1989 (Commencement No 18) Order 2004, SI 2004/3322, art 7 at **[7345]**); figure omitted (as inserted by the Insolvency Act 1985, s 109, Sch 6, para 7(2)) repealed by the Insolvency Act 1986, s 439(1), Sch 13, Pt I, as from 29 December 1986; figure in penultimate pair of square brackets inserted by CA 1989, s 123(3), as from 1 April 1990; for the words from "any of sections 210" to "453A" there are substituted the words "section 245E(3), 245G(7) or 394A(1)" by the draft Companies Act 2006 (Commencement No 3, Consequential Amendments, Transitional Provisions and Savings) Order 2007, art 10(1), Sch 4, Pt 1, para 16(1)(a), as from 1 October 2007 (see **[A12]**).

Sub-s (3): words omitted repealed by CA 1989, s 212, Sch 24, as from 1 October 1990.

Sub-s (4): repealed by the draft Companies Act 2006 (Commencement No 3, Consequential Amendments, Transitional Provisions and Savings) Order 2007, art 10(1), Sch 4, Pt 1, para 16(1)(b), as from 1 October 2007 (see **[A12]**); words in square brackets substituted by the Companies (Audit, Investigations and Community Enterprise) Act 2004, s 25, Sch 2, Pt 3, paras 16, 23(b), as from 6 April 2005 (for transitional provisions, see SI 2004/3322, art 7 at **[7345]**).

Application to limited liability partnerships: see the Limited Liability Partnerships Regulations 2001, SI 2001/1090, reg 4(1), Sch 2, Pt 1 at **[6985]**, **[6993]**. Note also that nothing in the draft Companies Act 2006 (Commencement No 3, Consequential Amendments, Transitional Provisions and Savings) Order 2007 affects any provision of this Act as applied by the 2001 Regulations to LLPs (see art 12(2) at **[A12]** and the introductory notes to this Act).

734 Criminal proceedings against unincorporated bodies

(1) Proceedings for an offence alleged to have been committed under [section 245E(3), section 245G(7),] [...] [section 394A(1) or] any of sections [448, 449 to 451 or section 453A] by an unincorporated body shall be brought in the name of that body (and not in that of any of its members), and for the purposes of any such proceedings, any rules of court relating to the service of documents apply as if that body were a corporation.

(2) A fine imposed on an unincorporated body on its conviction of such an offence shall be paid out of the funds of that body.

(3) In a case in which an unincorporated body is charged in England and Wales with such an offence, section 33 of the Criminal Justice Act 1925 and Schedule 3 to the Magistrates' Courts Act 1980 (procedure on charge of an offence against a corporation) have effect in like manner as in the case of a corporation so charged.

(4) In relation to proceedings on indictment in Scotland for such an offence alleged to have been committed by an unincorporated body, [section 70 of the Criminal Procedure (Scotland) Act 1995] (proceedings on indictment against bodies corporate) has effect as if that body were a body corporate.

[(5) Where such an offence committed by a partnership is proved to have been committed with the consent or connivance of, or to be attributable to any neglect on the part of, a partner, he as well as the partnership is guilty of the offence and liable to be proceeded against and punished accordingly.

(6) Where such an offence committed by an unincorporated body (other than a partnership) is proved to have been committed with the consent or connivance of, or to be attributable to any neglect on the part of, any officer of the body or any member of its governing body, he as well as the body is guilty of the offence and liable to be proceeded against and punished accordingly.]

[611]

NOTES

Repealed by the Companies Act 2006, s 1295, Sch 16, as from 1 October 2007 (in so far as relating to sub-s (1)), and as from a day to be appointed (otherwise).

Sub-s (1): repealed as noted above; words in first pair of square brackets inserted, and words in final pair of square brackets substituted, by the Companies (Audit, Investigations and Community Enterprise) Act 2004, s 25, Sch 2, Pt 2, paras 5, 9(a), as from 6 April 2005 (for transitional provisions, see the Companies (Audit, Investigations and Community Enterprise) Act 2004 (Commencement) and Companies Act 1989 (Commencement No 18) Order 2004, SI 2004/3322, art 7 at **[7345]**); words omitted originally inserted by CA 1989, s 120(2), as from 1 April 1990, and repealed by the Companies (Audit, Investigations and Community Enterprise) Act 2004, ss 25, 64, Sch 2, Pt 2, paras 5, 8(b), Sch 8, as from 6 April 2005; words in third pair of square brackets inserted by CA 1989, s 123(4), as from 1 April 1990; for the words from "section 245E(3)" to "453A" there are substituted the words "section 245E(3), 245G(7) or 394A(1)" by the draft Companies Act 2006 (Commencement No 3, Consequential Amendments, Transitional Provisions and Savings) Order 2007, art 10(1), Sch 4, Pt 1, para 16(2), as from 1 October 2007 (see **[A12]**).

Sub-s (4): words in square brackets substituted by the Criminal Procedure (Consequential Provisions) (Scotland) Act 1995, s 5, Sch 4, para 56(4), as from 1 April 1996.

Sub-ss (5), (6): added by CA 1989, s 145, Sch 19, para 18, as from 1 April 1990.

Application to limited liability partnerships: see the Limited Liability Partnerships Regulations 2001, SI 2001/1090, reg 4(1), Sch 2, Pt 1 at **[6985]**, **[6993]**. Note also that nothing in the draft Companies Act 2006 (Commencement No 3, Consequential Amendments, Transitional Provisions and Savings) Order 2007 affects any provision of this Act as applied by the 2001 Regulations to LLPs (see art 12(2) at **[A12]** and the introductory notes to this Act).

PART XXVI
INTERPRETATION

735 "Company", etc

(*1*) *In this Act—*

(*a*) *"company" means a company formed and registered under this Act, or an existing company;*

(*b*) *"existing company" means a company formed and registered under the former Companies Acts, but does not include a company registered under the Joint Stock Companies Acts, the Companies Act 1862 or the Companies (Consolidation) Act 1908 in what was then Ireland;*

(*c*) *"the former Companies Acts" means the Joint Stock Companies Acts, the Companies Act 1862, the Companies (Consolidation) Act 1908, the Companies Act 1929 and the Companies Acts 1948 to 1983.*

(*2*) *"Public company" and "private company" have the meanings given by section 1(3).*

(*3*) *"The Joint Stock Companies Acts" means the Joint Stock Companies Act 1856, the Joint Stock Companies Acts 1856, 1857, the Joint Stock Banking Companies Act 1857 and the Act to enable Joint Stock Banking Companies to be formed on the principle of limited liability, or any one or more of those Acts (as the case may require), but does not include the Joint Stock Companies Act 1844.*

(*4*) *The definitions in this section apply unless the contrary intention appears.*

[612]

NOTES

Repealed by the Companies Act 2006, s 1295, Sch 16, as from a day to be appointed.

Companies Act 1862: repealed by the Companies (Consolidation) Act 1908, s 286, Sch 6, Pt I.

Companies (Consolidation) Act 1908: repealed by the Companies Act 1929, s 381, Sch 12, Pt I.

Companies Act 1929: repealed by the Companies Act 1948, s 459(1), Sch 17.

Companies Act 1948: repealed by the Companies Consolidation (Consequential Provisions) Act 1985, s 29, Sch 1.

Companies Acts 1948 to 1983: by virtue of the Companies Act 1981, s 119(2), as read with the Companies Act 1983, s 7(2), the following Acts could be cited by this collective title: the Companies Act 1948; the Companies Act 1967, Pts I, III; the Companies (Floating Charges and Receivers) (Scotland) Act 1972; the European Communities Act 1972, s 9; the Stock Exchange (Completion of Bargains) Act 1976, ss 1–4; the Insolvency Act 1976, s 9; the Companies Act 1976; the Companies Act 1980; the Companies Act 1981, except ss 28, 29; and the Companies (Beneficial Interests) Act 1983. Those provisions are all repealed by the Companies Consolidation (Consequential Provisions) Act 1985, s 29, Sch 1.

Joint Stock Companies Acts: the Joint Stock Companies Act 1856, the Joint Stock Companies Acts 1856, 1857 (i e the Joint Stock Companies Act 1856 and the Joint Stock Companies Act 1857), the Joint Stock Banking Companies Act 1857 and the Act to enable Joint Stock Banking Companies to be formed on the principle of limited liability (21 & 22 Vict c 91) (1858) were repealed by the Companies Act 1862, s 205, Sch 3 (repealed). The Joint Stock Companies Act 1844 was also repealed by the Companies Act 1862, s 205, Sch 3.

[735A Relationship of this Act to Insolvency Act

(*1*) *In this Act "the Insolvency Act" means the Insolvency Act 1986; and in the following provisions of this Act, namely, sections 375(1)(b), 425(6)(a), … 460(2), 675, 676, 677, 699(1), 728 and Schedule 21, paragraph 6(1), the words "this Act" are to be read as including Parts I to VII of that Act, sections 411, 413, 414, 416 and 417 in Part XV of that Act, and also the Company Directors Disqualification Act 1986.*

(*2*) *In [sections 704(5), (7) and (8)], 706(1), [707B(1)], [707A(1),] 708(1)(a) and (4), [709(1) and (3),] [710A], 713(1), 729 and 732(3) references to the Companies Acts include Parts I to VII of the Insolvency Act, sections 411, 413, 414, 416 and 417 in Part XV of that Act, and also the Company Directors Disqualification Act 1986.*

(3) Subsections (1) and (2) apply unless the contrary intention appears.]

[613]

NOTES

Inserted by the Insolvency Act 1986, s 439(1), Sch 13, Pt II, as from 29 December 1986.

Repealed by the Companies Act 2006, s 1295, Sch 16, as from a day to be appointed.

Sub-s (1): words omitted repealed by CA 1989, s 212, Sch 24, as from 21 February 1990.

Sub-s (2): words in first pair of square brackets substituted by the Deregulation and Contracting Out Act 1994, s 76, Sch 16, para 9, as from 3 January 1995; figure in second pair of square brackets substituted by the Companies Act 1985 (Electronic Communications) Order 2000, SI 2000/3373, art 31(4)(b), as from 22 December 2000; figure in third pair of square brackets and words in fourth pair of square brackets inserted, and figure in fifth pair of square brackets substituted, by CA 1989, s 127(5), as from 1 July 1991.

Application to limited liability partnerships: see the Limited Liability Partnerships Regulations 2001, SI 2001/1090, reg 4(1), Sch 2, Pt 1 at **[6985]**, **[6993]**.

[735B Relationship of this Act to [Part 6 of the Financial Services and Markets Act 2000]

In [sections 704(5), (7) and (8)], 706(1), 707(1), 707A(1), 708(1)(a) and (4), 709(1) and (3), 710A and 713(1) references to the Companies Acts include [Part 6 of the Financial Services and Markets Act 2000].]

[614]

NOTES

Inserted by CA 1989, s 127(6), as from 1 July 1991.

Repealed by the Companies Act 2006, s 1295, Sch 16, as from a day to be appointed.

Words in square brackets in the section heading and words in final pair of square brackets substituted by the Financial Services and Markets Act 2000 (Consequential Amendments and Repeals) Order 2001, SI 2001/3649, art 28, as from 1 December 2001; other words in square brackets substituted by the Deregulation and Contracting Out Act 1994, s 76, Sch 16, para 10, as from 3 January 1995.

[736 "Subsidiary", "holding company" and "wholly-owned subsidiary"

(1) A company is a "subsidiary" of another company, its "holding company", if that other company—

(a) holds a majority of the voting rights in it, or

(b) is a member of it and has the right to appoint or remove a majority of its board of directors, or

(c) is a member of it and controls alone, pursuant to an agreement with other shareholders or members, a majority of the voting rights in it,

or if it is a subsidiary of a company which is itself a subsidiary of that other company.

(2) A company is a "wholly-owned subsidiary" of another company if it has no members except that other and that other's wholly-owned subsidiaries or persons acting on behalf of that other or its wholly-owned subsidiaries.

(3) In this section "company" includes any body corporate.]

[615]

NOTES

Substituted, together with s 736A, for original s 736, by CA 1989, s 144(1), as from 1 November 1990.

Repealed by the Companies Act 2006, s 1295, Sch 16, as from a day to be appointed.

The original s 736 is reproduced here because of its continuing application for limited purposes (as to which see the Companies Act 1989, Sch 18, the Companies Act 1989 (Commencement No 4 and Transitional and Saving Provisions) Order 1990, SI 1990/355, arts 7, 10, Schs 2, 4, and the Companies Act 1989 (Commencement No 6 and Transitional and Saving Provisions) Order 1990, SI 1990/1392, art 6)—

"736 "Holding company", "subsidiary" and "wholly-owned subsidiary"

(1) For the purposes of this Act, a company is deemed to be a subsidiary of another if (but only if)—

(a) that other either—

(i) is a member of it and controls the composition of its board of directors, or

(ii) holds more than half in nominal value of its equity share capital, or

(b) the first-mentioned company is a subsidiary of any company which is that other's subsidiary.

The above is subject to subsection (4) below in this section.

(2) For purposes of subsection (1), the composition of a company's board of directors is deemed to be controlled by another company if (but only if) that other company by the exercise of some power exercisable by it without the consent or concurrence of any other person can appoint or remove the holders of all or a majority of the directorships.

(3) For purposes of this last provision, the other company is deemed to have power to appoint to a directorship with respect to which any of the following conditions is satisfied—

(a) that a person cannot be appointed to it without the exercise in his favour by the other company of such a power as is mentioned above, or

(b) that a person's appointment to the directorship follows necessarily from his appointment as director of the other company, or

(c) that the directorship is held by the other company itself or by a subsidiary of it.

(4) In determining whether one company is a subsidiary of another—

(a) any shares held or power exercisable by the other in a fiduciary capacity are to be treated as not held or exercisable by it,

(b) subject to the two following paragraphs, any shares held or power exercisable—

(i) by any person as nominee for the other (except where the other is concerned only in a fiduciary capacity), or

(ii) by, or by a nominee for, a subsidiary of the other (not being a subsidiary which is concerned only in a fiduciary capacity),

are to be treated as held or exercisable by the other,

(c) any shares held or power exercisable by any person by virtue of the provisions of any debentures of the first-mentioned company or of a trust deed for securing any issue of such debentures are to be disregarded,

(d) any shares held or power exercisable by, or by a nominee for, the other or its subsidiary (not being held or exercisable as mentioned in paragraph (c)) are to be treated as not held or exercisable by the other if the ordinary business of the other or its subsidiary (as the case may be) includes the lending of money and the shares are held or the power is exercisable as above mentioned by way of security only for the purposes of a transaction entered into in the ordinary course of that business.

(5) For purposes of this Act—

(a) a company is deemed to be another's holding company if (but only if) the other is its subsidiary, and

(b) a body corporate is deemed the wholly-owned subsidiary of another if it has no members except that other and that other's wholly-owned subsidiaries and its or their nominees.

(6) In this section "company" includes any body corporate.".

Application to limited liability partnerships: see the Limited Liability Partnerships Regulations 2001, SI 2001/1090, reg 4(1), Sch 2, Pt 1 at **[6985]**, **[6993]**.

[736A Provisions supplementing s 736

(1) The provisions of this section explain expressions used in section 736 and otherwise supplement that section.

(2) In section 736(1)(a) and (c) the references to the voting rights in a company are to the rights conferred on shareholders in respect of their shares or, in the case of a company not having a share capital, on members, to vote at general meetings of the company on all, or substantially all, matters.

(3) In section 736(1)(b) the reference to the right to appoint or remove a majority of the board of directors is to the right to appoint or remove directors holding a majority of the voting rights at meetings of the board on all, or substantially all, matters; and for the purposes of that provision—

(a) a company shall be treated as having the right to appoint to a directorship if—

(i) a person's appointment to it follows necessarily from his appointment as director of the company, or

(ii) the directorship is held by the company itself; and

(b) a right to appoint or remove which is exercisable only with the consent or concurrence of another person shall be left out of account unless no other person has a right to appoint or, as the case may be, remove in relation to that directorship.

(4) Rights which are exercisable only in certain circumstances shall be taken into account only—

(a) when the circumstances have arisen, and for so long as they continue to obtain, or

(b) when the circumstances are within the control of the person having the rights;

and rights which are normally exercisable but are temporarily incapable of exercise shall continue to be taken into account.

(5) *Rights held by a person in a fiduciary capacity shall be treated as not held by him.*

(6) *Rights held by a person as nominee for another shall be treated as held by the other; and rights shall be regarded as held as nominee for another if they are exercisable only on his instructions or with his consent or concurrence.*

(7) *Rights attached to shares held by way of security shall be treated as held by the person providing the security—*

(*a*) *where apart from the right to exercise them for the purpose of preserving the value of the security, or of realising it, the rights are exercisable only in accordance with his instructions;*

(*b*) *where the shares are held in connection with the granting of loans as part of normal business activities and apart from the right to exercise them for the purpose of preserving the value of the security, or of realising it, the rights are exercisable only in his interests.*

(8) *Rights shall be treated as held by a company if they are held by any of its subsidiaries; and nothing in subsection* (6) *or* (7) *shall be construed as requiring rights held by a company to be treated as held by any of its subsidiaries.*

(9) *For the purposes of subsection* (7) *rights shall be treated as being exercisable in accordance with the instructions or in the interests of a company if they are exercisable in accordance with the instructions of or, as the case may be, in the interests of—*

(*a*) *any subsidiary or holding company of that company, or*

(*b*) *any subsidiary of a holding company of that company.*

(10) *The voting rights in a company shall be reduced by any rights held by the company itself.*

(11) *References in any provision of subsections* (5) *to* (10) *to rights held by a person include rights falling to be treated as held by him by virtue of any other provision of those subsections but not rights which by virtue of any such provision are to be treated as not held by him.*

(12) *In this section "company" includes any body corporate.]*

[616]

NOTES

Substituted as noted to s 736 at **[615]**.

Repealed by the Companies Act 2006, s 1295, Sch 16, as from a day to be appointed.

Application to limited liability partnerships: see the Limited Liability Partnerships Regulations 2001, SI 2001/1090, reg 4(1), Sch 2, Pt 1 at **[6985]**, **[6993]**.

[736B Power to amend ss 736 and 736A

(1) *The Secretary of State may by regulations amend sections 736 and 736A so as to alter the meaning of the expressions "holding company", "subsidiary" or "wholly-owned subsidiary".*

(2) *The regulations may make different provision for different cases or classes of case and may contain such incidental and supplementary provisions as the Secretary of State thinks fit.*

(3) *Regulations under this section shall be made by statutory instrument which shall be subject to annulment in pursuance of a resolution of either House of Parliament.*

(4) *Any amendment made by regulations under this section does not apply for the purposes of enactments outside the Companies Acts unless the regulations so provide.*

(5) *So much of section 23*(3) *of the Interpretation Act 1978 as applies section 17*(2)(*a*) *of that Act* (*effect of repeal and re-enactment*) *to deeds, instruments and documents other than enactments shall not apply in relation to any repeal and re-enactment effected by regulations made under this section.]*

[617]

NOTES

Inserted by CA 1989, s 144(3), as from 1 November 1990.

Repealed by the Companies Act 2006, s 1295, Sch 16, as from a day to be appointed.

737 "Called-up share capital"

(1) In this Act, "called-up share capital", in relation to a company, means so much of its share capital as equals the aggregate amount of the calls made on its shares (whether or not those calls have been paid), together with any share capital paid up without being called and any share capital to be paid on a specified future date under the articles, the terms of allotment of the relevant shares or any other arrangements for payment of those shares.

(2) "Uncalled share capital" is to be construed accordingly.

(3) The definitions in this section apply unless the contrary intention appears.

[618]

NOTES

Repealed by the Companies Act 2006, s 1295, Sch 16, as from a day to be appointed.

738 "Allotment" and "paid up"

(1) In relation to an allotment of shares in a company, the shares are to be taken for the purposes of this Act to be allotted when a person acquires the unconditional right to be included in the company's register of members in respect of those shares.

(2) For purposes of this Act, a share in a company is deemed paid up (as to its nominal value or any premium on it) in cash, or allotted for cash, if the consideration for the allotment or payment up is cash received by the company, or is a cheque received by it in good faith which the directors have no reason for suspecting will not be paid, or is a release of a liability of the company for a liquidated sum, or is an undertaking to pay cash to the company at a future date.

(3) In relation to the allotment or payment up of any shares in a company, references in this Act (except sections 89 to 94) to consideration other than cash and to the payment up of shares and premiums on shares otherwise than in cash include the payment of, or any undertaking to pay, cash to any person other than the company.

(4) For the purpose of determining whether a share is or is to be allotted for cash, or paid up in cash, "cash" includes foreign currency.

[619]

NOTES

Repealed by the Companies Act 2006, s 1295, Sch 16, as from a day to be appointed.

739 "Non-cash asset"

(1) In this Act "non-cash asset" means any property or interest in property other than cash; and for this purpose "cash" includes foreign currency.

(2) A reference to the transfer or acquisition of a non-cash asset includes the creation or extinction of an estate or interest in, or a right over, any property and also the discharge of any person's liability, other than a liability for a liquidated sum.

[620]

NOTES

Repealed by the Companies Act 2006, s 1295, Sch 16, as from a day to be appointed.

Application to limited liability partnerships: see the Limited Liability Partnerships Regulations 2001, SI 2001/1090, reg 4(1), Sch 2, Pt 1 at **[6985]**, **[6993]**.

740 "Body corporate" and "corporation"

References in this Act to a body corporate or to a corporation do not include a corporation sole, but include a company incorporated elsewhere than in Great Britain.

Such references to a body corporate do not include a Scottish firm.

[621]

NOTES

Repealed by the Companies Act 2006, s 1295, Sch 16, as from a day to be appointed.

Application to limited liability partnerships: see the Limited Liability Partnerships Regulations 2001, SI 2001/1090, reg 4(1), Sch 2, Pt 1 at **[6985]**, **[6993]**.

741 "Director" and "shadow director"

(*1*) *In this Act, "director" includes any person occupying the position of director, by whatever name called.*

(*2*) *In relation to a company, "shadow director" means a person in accordance with whose directions or instructions the directors of the company are accustomed to act.*

However, a person is not deemed a shadow director by reason only that the directors act on advice given by him in a professional capacity.

(*3*) *For the purposes of the following provisions of this Act, namely—*
section 309 (directors' duty to have regard to interests of employees),
section 319 (directors' long-term contracts of employment),
sections 320 to 322 (substantial property transactions involving directors), ...
[section 322B (contracts with sole members who are directors), and]
sections 330 to 346 (general restrictions on power of companies to make loans, etc, to directors and others connected with them),
(being provisions under which shadow directors are treated as directors), a body corporate is not to be treated as a shadow director of any of its subsidiary companies by reason only that the directors of the subsidiary are accustomed to act in accordance with its directions or instructions.

[622]

NOTES

Repealed by the Companies Act 2006, s 1295, Sch 16, as from 1 October 2007.

Sub-s (3): word omitted repealed, and words in square brackets inserted, by the Companies (Single Member Private Limited Companies) Regulations 1992, SI 1992/1699, reg 2, Schedule, para 3(2), as from 15 July 1992.

Application to limited liability partnerships: see the Limited Liability Partnerships Regulations 2001, SI 2001/1090, reg 4(1), Sch 2, Pt 1 at **[6985]**, **[6993]**. Note also that nothing in the draft Companies Act 2006 (Commencement No 3, Consequential Amendments, Transitional Provisions and Savings) Order 2007 affects any provision of this Act as applied by the 2001 Regulations to LLPs (see art 12(2) at **[A12]** and the introductory notes to this Act).

[742 Expressions used in connection with accounts

(*1*) *In this Act, unless a contrary intention appears, the following expressions have the same meaning as in Part VII (accounts)—*
"annual accounts",
"accounting reference date" and "accounting reference period",
"balance sheet" and "balance sheet date",
["Companies Act accounts"]
["Companies Act individual accounts"]
"current assets",
"financial year", in relation to a company,
"fixed assets",
["IAS accounts"]
["IAS individual accounts"]
"parent company" and "parent undertaking",
"profit and loss account", and
"subsidiary undertaking".

(*2*) *References in this Act to "realised profits" and "realised losses", in relation to a company's accounts, shall be construed in accordance with section 262(3).]*

[(2A) References in this Act to sending or sending out copies of any of the documents referred to in section 238(1) include sending or sending out such copies in accordance with section 238(4A) or (4B).]

[623]

NOTES

Substituted by CA 1989, s 23, Sch 10, para 15, as from 1 April 1990.

Repealed by the Companies Act 2006, s 1295, Sch 16, as from a day to be appointed.

Sub-s (1): entries in square brackets inserted the Companies Act 1985 (International Accounting Standards and Other Accounting Amendments) Regulations 2004, SI 2004/2947, reg 3, Sch 1, paras 1, 29, as from 12 November 2004, in relation to companies' financial years which begin on or after 1 January 2005.

Sub-s (2A): added by the Companies Act 1985 (Electronic Communications) Order 2000, SI 2000/3373, art 28, as from 22 December 2000.

Application to limited liability partnerships: see the Limited Liability Partnerships Regulations 2001, SI 2001/1090, reg 4(1), Sch 2, Pt 1 at **[6985]**, **[6993]**.

[742A Meaning of "offer to the public"

(1) Any reference in Part IV (allotment of shares and debentures) or [Part 7 (accounts) or section 744 (general interpretation)] to offering shares or debentures to the public is to be read as including a reference to offering them to any section of the public, however selected.

(2) This section does not require an offer to be treated as made to the public if it can properly be regarded, in all the circumstances—

(a) as not being calculated to result, directly or indirectly, in the shares or debentures becoming available for subscription or purchase by persons other than those receiving the offer; or

(b) as being a domestic concern of the persons receiving and making it.

(3) An offer of shares in or debentures of a private company (other than an offer to which subsection (5) applies) is to be regarded (unless the contrary is proved) as being a domestic concern of the persons making and receiving it if—

(a) it is made to—

(i) an existing member of the company making the offer,

(ii) an existing employee of that company,

(iii) the widow or widower [or surviving civil partner] of a person who was a member or employee of that company,

(iv) a member of the family of a person who is or was a member or employee of that company, or

(v) an existing debenture holder; or

(b) it is an offer to subscribe for shares or debentures to be held under an employee's share scheme.

(4) Subsection (5) applies to an offer—

(a) which falls within paragraph (a) or (b) of subsection (3); but

(b) which is made on terms which permit the person to whom it is made to renounce his right to the allotment of shares or issue of debentures.

(5) The offer is to be regarded (unless the contrary is proved) as being a domestic concern of the persons making and receiving it if the terms are such that the right may be renounced only in favour—

(a) of any person mentioned in subsection (3)(a), or

(b) in the case of an employee's share scheme, of a person entitled to hold shares or debentures under the scheme.

(6) For the purposes of subsection (3)(a)(iv), the members of a person's family are—

(a) the person's spouse [or civil partner] and children (including step-children) and their descendants, and

(b) any trustee (acting in his capacity as such) of a trust the principal beneficiary of which is the person him or herself or of any of those relatives.

(7) Where an application has been made to the competent authority in any EEA State for the admission of any securities to official listing, then an offer of those securities for subscription or sale to a person whose ordinary business it is to buy or sell shares or debentures (whether as principal or agent) is not to be regarded as an offer to the public for the purposes of this Part.

(8) For the purposes of subsection (7)—

(a) "competent authority" means a competent authority appointed for the purposes of the Council Directive of 28 May 2001 on the admission of securities to official stock exchange listing and on information to be published on those securities; and

(b) "official listing" means official listing pursuant to that directive.]

[624]

NOTES

Inserted, together with ss 742B, 742C, by the Financial Services and Markets Act 2000 (Consequential Amendments and Repeals) Order 2001, SI 2001/3649, art 29, as from 1 December 2001.

Repealed by the Companies Act 2006, s 1295, Sch 16, as from a day to be appointed.

Sub-s (1): words in square brackets substituted by the Financial Services and Markets Act 2000 (Consequential Amendments) Order 2004, SI 2004/355, art 2(1), (3), as from 4 March 2004.

Sub-ss (3), (6): words in square brackets inserted by the Civil Partnership Act 2004, s 261(1), Sch 27, para 104, as from 5 December 2005.

Step-children: this includes relationships arising through civil partnership; see the Civil Partnership Act 2004, ss 246, 247, Sch 21.

[742B Meaning of "banking company"

(1) Subject to subsection (2), "banking company" means a person who has permission under Part 4 of the Financial Services and Markets Act 2000 to accept deposits.

(2) A banking company does not include—

(a) a person who is not a company, and

(b) a person who has permission to accept deposits only for the purpose of carrying on another regulated activity in accordance with that permission.

(3) This section must be read with—

(a) section 22 of the Financial Services and Markets Act 2000;

(b) any relevant order under that section; and

(c) Schedule 2 to that Act.]

[625]

NOTES

Inserted as noted to s 742A at **[624]**.

Repealed by the Companies Act 2006, s 1295, Sch 16, as from a day to be appointed.

[742C Meaning of "insurance company" and "authorised insurance company"

(1) For the purposes of this Act, "insurance company" has the meaning given in subsection (2) and "authorised insurance company" has the meaning given in subsection (4).

(2) Subject to subsection (3), "insurance company" means a person (whether incorporated or not)—

(a) who has permission under Part 4 of the Financial Services and Markets Act 2000 to effect or carry out contracts of insurance; or

(b) who carries on insurance market activity; or

(c) who may effect or carry out contracts of insurance under which the benefits provided by that person are exclusively or primarily benefits in kind in the event of accident to or breakdown of a vehicle, and does not fall within paragraph (a).

(3) An insurance company does not include a friendly society, within the meaning of section 116 of the Friendly Societies Act 1992.

(4) An "authorised insurance company" means a person falling within paragraph (a) of subsection (2).

(5) References in this section to contracts of insurance and the effecting or carrying out of such contracts must be read with—

(a) section 22 of the Financial Services and Markets Act 2000;

(b) any relevant order under that section; and

(c) Schedule 2 to that Act.]

[626]

NOTES

Inserted as noted to s 742A at **[624]**.

Repealed by the Companies Act 2006, s 1295, Sch 16, as from a day to be appointed.

743 "Employees' share scheme"

For purposes of this Act, an employees' share scheme is a scheme for encouraging or facilitating the holding of shares or debentures in a company by or for the benefit of—

(a) the bona fide employees or former employees of the company, the company's subsidiary or holding company or a subsidiary of the company's holding company, or

(*b*) *the [spouses, civil partners, surviving spouses, surviving civil partners] or children or step-children under the age of 18 of such employees or former employees.*

[627]

NOTES

Repealed by the Companies Act 2006, s 1295, Sch 16, as from a day to be appointed.

Words in square brackets substituted by the Civil Partnership Act 2004 (International Immunities and Privileges, Companies and Adoption) Order 2005, SI 2005/3542, art 3(2), as from 23 December 2005.

Transitional provisions, etc: for the purposes of this section a company which immediately before 1 November 1990 was a subsidiary of another company is not to be treated as ceasing to be such a subsidiary by reason of the substitution of s 736 of this Act; see the CA 1989, Sch 18, para 37 at **[874]**.

[743A Meaning of "office copy" in Scotland

References in this Act to an office copy of a court order shall be construed, as respects Scotland, as references to a certified copy interlocutor.]

[628]

NOTES

Inserted by CA 1989, s 145, Sch 19, para 19, as from 1 March 1990.

Repealed by the Companies Act 2006, s 1295, Sch 16, as from a day to be appointed.

Application to limited liability partnerships: see the Limited Liability Partnerships Regulations 2001, SI 2001/1090, reg 4(1), Sch 2, Pt 1 at **[6985]**, **[6993]**.

744 Expressions used generally in this Act

In this Act, unless the contrary intention appears, the following definitions apply—

"agent" does not include a person's counsel acting as such;

.....

"articles" means, in relation to a company, its articles of association, as originally framed or as altered by resolution, including (so far as applicable to the company) regulations contained in or annexed to any enactment relating to companies passed before this Act, as altered by or under any such enactment;

[.....]

"authorised minimum" has the meaning given by section 118;

"bank holiday" means a holiday under the Banking and Financial Dealings Act 1971;

[.....]

"books and papers" and "books or papers" include accounts, deeds, writings and documents;

["communication" means the same as in the Electronic Communications Act 2000;]

"the Companies Acts" means this Act, the [insider dealing legislation] and the Consequential Provisions Act;

"the Consequential Provisions Act" means the Companies Consolidation (Consequential Provisions) Act 1985;

"the court", in relation to a company, means the court having jurisdiction to wind up the company;

"debenture" includes debenture stock, bonds and any other securities of a company, whether constituting a charge on the assets of the company or not;

"document" includes summons, notice, order, and other legal process, and registers;

[.....]

["electronic communication" means the same as in the Electronic Communications Act 2000;]

"equity share capital" means, in relation to a company, its issued share capital excluding any part of that capital which, neither as respects dividends nor as respects capital, carries any right to participate beyond a specified amount in a distribution;

"expert" has the meaning given by section 62;

"floating charge" includes a floating charge within the meaning given by section 462;

"the Gazette" means, as respects companies registered in England and Wales, the London Gazette and, as respects companies registered in Scotland, the Edinburgh Gazette;

.....

"hire-purchase agreement" has the same meaning as in the Consumer Credit Act 1974;

["the insider dealing legislation" means Part V of the Criminal Justice Act 1993 (insider dealing).]

.....

["insurance market activity" has the meaning given in section 316(3) of the Financial Services and Markets Act 2000;]

"joint stock company" has the meaning given by section 683;

"memorandum", in relation to a company, means its memorandum of association, as originally framed or as altered in pursuance of any enactment;

"number", in relation to shares, includes amount, where the context admits of the reference to shares being construed to include stock;

"officer", in relation to a body corporate, includes a director, manager or secretary;

"official seal", in relation to the registrar of companies, means a seal prepared under section 704(4) for the authentication of documents required for or in connection with the registration of companies;

"oversea company" means—

(*a*) *a company incorporated elsewhere than in Great Britain which, after the commencement of this Act, establishes a place of business in Great Britain, and*

(*b*) *a company so incorporated which has, before that commencement, established a place of business and continues to have an established place of business in Great Britain at that commencement;*

"place of business" includes a share transfer or share registration office;

"prescribed" means—

(*a*) *as respects provisions of this Act relating to winding up, prescribed by general rules ... , and*

(*b*) *otherwise, prescribed by statutory instrument made by the Secretary of State;*

"prospectus" means any prospectus, notice, circular, advertisement, or other invitation, offering to the public for subscription or purchase any shares in or debentures of a company;

"prospectus issued generally" means a prospectus issued to persons who are not existing members of the company or holders of its debentures;

.....

["regulated activity" has the meaning given in section 22 of the Financial Services and Markets Act 2000;]

"the registrar of companies" and "the registrar" mean the registrar or other officer performing under this Act the duty of registration of companies in England and Wales or in Scotland, as the case may require;

"share" means share in the share capital of a company, and includes stock (except where a distinction between shares and stock is express or implied); and

"undistributable reserves" has the meaning given by section 264(3).

[629]

NOTES

Repealed by the Companies Act 2006, s 1295, Sch 16, as from 6 April 2007 (in so far as relating to the definition "EEA State"), and as from a day to be appointed (otherwise).

Definition "annual return" repealed by CA 1989, s 212, Sch 24, as from 3 July 1995.

Definitions "authorised minimum", "expert", "floating charge", "joint stock company" and "undistributable reserves" repealed by CA 1989, s 212, Sch 24, as from a day to be appointed.

Definition "authorised institution" (as inserted by the Banking Act 1987, s 108(1), Sch 6, para 18(8)) repealed by CA 1989, ss 23, 212, Sch 10, Pt I, para 16, Sch 24, as from 1 April 1990.

Definition "banking company" inserted by CA 1989, s 23, Sch 10, Pt I, para 16, as from 1 April 1990; repealed by the Financial Services and Markets Act 2000 (Consequential Amendments and Repeals) Order 2001, SI 2001/3649, art 30(a), as from 1 December 2001.

Definitions "communication" and "electronic communication" inserted by the Companies Act 1985 (Electronic Communications) Order 2000, SI 2000/3373, art 29, as from 22 December 2000.

Words in square brackets in definition "the Companies Acts" and the whole of the definition "the insider dealing legislation" substituted by the Criminal Justice Act 1993, s 79(13), Sch 5, Pt I, para 4, as from 1 March 1994.

Definition "EEA State" inserted by the Companies (Membership of Holding Company) (Dealers in Securities) Regulations 1997, SI 1997/2306, reg 4(1), as from 20 October 1997; substituted by the Companies (EEA State) Regulations 2007, SI 2007/732, reg 2, as from 9 March 2007; repealed as noted above. It previously read as follows—

""EEA State" has the meaning given by Schedule 1 to the Interpretation Act 1978;".

Definition "general rules", and words omitted from definition "prescribed", repealed by the Insolvency Act 1985, s 235(3), Sch 10, Pt II, as from 1 March 1986.

Definition "insurance company" repealed by SI 2001/3649, art 30(a), as from 1 December 2001.

Definition "insurance market activity" inserted by SI 2001/3649, art 30(b), as from 1 December 2001.

Definition "prospectus issued generally" and "recognised stock exchange" repealed by FSA 1986, s 212(3), Sch 17, Pt I, to the extent noted in at the beginning of Pt III of this Act in the case of the definition "prospectus issued generally".

Definition "recognised bank" repealed by the Banking Act 1987, s 108, Sch 6, para 18(8), Sch 7, Pt I, as from 1 October 1987.

Definition "regulated activity" inserted by SI 2001/3649, art 30(c), as from 1 December 2001.

Application to limited liability partnerships: see the Limited Liability Partnerships Regulations 2001, SI 2001/1090, reg 4(1), Sch 2, Pt 1 at **[6985]**, **[6993]**. Note also that nothing in the Companies Act 2006 (Commencement No 2, Consequential Amendments, Transitional Provisions and Savings) Order 2007, SI 2007/1093 affects any provision of this Act as applied by the 2001 Regulations to LLPs (see art 12(1) at **[7624]** and the introductory notes to this Act).

Prescribed: by virtue of the Transfer of Functions (Financial Services) Order 1992, SI 1992/1315, art 10(1), Sch 4, para 2, this section has effect, in relation to any provision of this Act conferring a function transferred to the Treasury by that Order (as to which, see **[6729]** et seq), as if "prescribed" means prescribed by statutory instrument made by the Treasury.

[744A Index of defined expressions

The following Table shows provisions defining or otherwise explaining expressions for the purposes of this Act generally—

accounting reference date, accounting reference period	*sections 224 and 742(1)*
acquisition (in relation to a non-cash asset)	*section 739(2)*
agent	*section 744*
allotment (and related expressions)	*section 738*
annual accounts	*sections 261(2), 262(1) and 742(1)*
annual general meeting	*section 366*
annual return	*section 363*
articles	*section 744*
[authorised insurance company	*section 742C]*
authorised minimum	*section 118*
balance sheet and balance sheet date	*sections 261(2), 262(1) and 742(1)*
bank holiday	*section 744*
banking company	*[section 742B]*
body corporate	*section 740*
books and papers, books or papers	*section 744*
called-up share capital	*section 737(1)*
capital redemption reserve	*section 170(1)*
[communication	*section 744]*
the Companies Acts	*section 744*
[Companies Act accounts	*Sections 262(1) and 742(1)]*
[Companies Act individual accounts	*Sections 226(2), 255(4A) and 742(1)]*
companies charges register	*section 397*
company	*section 735(1)*
the Consequential Provisions Act	*section 744*
corporation	*section 740*
the court (in relation to a company)	*section 744*
current assets	*sections 262(1) and 742(1)*
debenture	*section 744*
director	*section 741(1)*
document	*section 744*

[EEA State	*section 744]*
elective resolution	*section 379A*
[electronic communication	*section 744]*
employees' share scheme	*section 743*
equity share capital	*section 744*
existing company	*section 735(1)*
extraordinary general meeting	*section 368*
extraordinary resolution	*section 378(1)*
financial year (of a company)	*sections 223 and 742(1)*
fixed assets	*sections 262(1) and 742(1)*
floating charge (in Scotland)	*section 462*
the former Companies Acts	*section 735(1)*
the Gazette	*section 744*
hire-purchase agreement	*section 744*
holding company	*section 736*
[IAS accounts	*Sections 262(1) and 742(1)]*
[IAS individual accounts	*Sections 226(2) and 742(1)]*
the [insider dealing legislation]	*section 744*
the Insolvency Act	*section 735A(1)*
insurance company	*[section 742C]*
[insurance market activity	*section 744]*
the Joint Stock Companies Acts	*section 735(3)*
limited company	*section 1(2)*
member (of a company)	*section 22*
memorandum (in relation to a company)	*section 744*
non-cash asset	*section 739(1)*
number (in relation to shares)	*section 744*
office copy (in relation to a court order in Scotland)	*section 743A*
officer (in relation to a body corporate)	*section 744*
official seal (in relation to the register of companies)	*section 744*
oversea company	*section 744*
overseas branch register	*section 362*
paid up (and related expressions)	*section 738*
parent company and parent undertaking	*sections 258 and 742(1)*
place of business	*section 744*
prescribed	*section 744*
private company	*section 1(3)*
profit and loss account	*sections 261(2), [262(1) and (2)] and 742(1)*
prospectus	*section 744*
public company	*section 1(3)*
realised profits or losses	*sections 262(3) and 742(2)*
registered number (of a company)	*section 705(1)*

registered office (of a company)	*section 287*
registrar and registrar of companies	*section 744*
[regulated activity	*section 744]*
resolution for reducing share capital	*section 135(3)*
shadow director	*section 741(2) and (3)*
share	*section 744*
share premium account	*section 130(1)*
share warrant	*section 188*
special notice (in relation to a resolution)	*section 379*
special resolution	*section 378(2)*
subsidiary	*section 736*
subsidiary undertaking	*sections 258 and 742(1)*
transfer (in relation to a non-cash asset)	*section 739(2)*
[treasury shares	*section 162A(3)]*
uncalled share capital	*section 737(2)*
undistributable reserves	*section 264(3)*
unlimited company	*section 1(2)*
unregistered company	*section 718*
wholly-owned subsidiary	*section 736(2).]*

[630]

NOTES

Inserted by CA 1989, s 145, Sch 19, para 20, as from 3 July 1995.

Repealed by the Companies Act 2006, s 1295, Sch 16, as from a day to be appointed.

Entry "authorised insurance company" inserted by the Financial Services and Markets Act 2000 (Consequential Amendments and Repeals) Order 2001, SI 2001/3649, art 31(a), as from 1 December 2001.

In entry relating to "banking company" words in square brackets substituted by SI 2001/3649, art 31(b), as from 1 December 2001.

Entry "communication" inserted by the Companies Act 1985 (Electronic Communications) Order 2000, SI 2000/3373, art 30, as from 22 December 2000.

Entry "Companies Act accounts" inserted by the Companies Act 1985 (International Accounting Standards and Other Accounting Amendments) Regulations 2004, SI 2004/2947, reg 3, Sch 1, paras 1, 30(1), (2), as from 12 November 2004, in relation to companies' financial years which begin on or after 1 January 2005.

Entry "Companies Act individual accounts" inserted by SI 2004/2947, reg 3, Sch 1, paras 1, 30(1), (2), as from 12 November 2004, in relation to companies' financial years which begin on or after 1 January 2005.

Entry "EEA State" inserted by the Companies (Membership of Holding Company) (Dealers in Securities) Regulations 1997, SI 1997/2306, reg 4(1), (3), as from 20 October 1997.

Entry "electronic communication" inserted by the Companies Act 1985 (Electronic Communications) Order 2000, SI 2000/3373, art 30, as from 22 December 2000.

Entry "IAS accounts" inserted by SI 2004/2947, reg 3, Sch 1, paras 1, 30(1), (2), as from 12 November 2004, in relation to companies' financial years which begin on or after 1 January 2005.

Entry "IAS individual accounts" inserted by SI 2004/2947, reg 3, Sch 1, paras 1, 30(1), (2), as from 12 November 2004, in relation to companies' financial years which begin on or after 1 January 2005.

In entry relating to "insider dealing legislation" words in square brackets substituted by the Criminal Justice Act 1993, s 79(13), Sch 5, Pt I, para 4(2), as from 1 March 1994.

In entry relating to "insurance company" words in square brackets substituted by SI 2001/3649, art 31(c), as from 1 December 2001.

Entry "insurance market activity" inserted by SI 2001/3649, art 31(d), as from 1 December 2001.

In entry "profit and loss account" words in square brackets substituted by SI 2004/2947, reg 3, Sch 1, paras 1, 30(1), (3), as from 12 November 2004, in relation to companies' financial years which begin on or after 1 January 2005.

Entry "regulated activity" inserted by SI 2001/3649, art 31(e), as from 1 December 2001.

Entry "treasury shares" inserted by the Companies (Acquisition of Own Shares) (Treasury Shares) Regulations 2003, SI 2003/1116, reg 4, Schedule, para 29, as from 1 December 2003.

Application to limited liability partnerships: see the Limited Liability Partnerships Regulations 2001, SI 2001/1090, reg 4(1), Sch 2, Pt 1 at **[6985]**, **[6993]**.

PART XXVII
FINAL PROVISIONS

745 Northern Ireland

(1) Except where otherwise expressly provided, nothing in this Act (except provisions relating expressly to companies registered or incorporated in Northern Ireland or outside Great Britain) applies to or in relation to companies so registered or incorporated.

(2) Subject to any such provision, and to any express provision as to extent, this Act does not extend to Northern Ireland.

[631]

NOTES

Repealed by the Companies Act 2006, s 1295, Sch 16, as from a day to be appointed.

Section heading: the heading to this section does not cover its subject-matter fully as sub-s (1) is concerned with companies registered or incorporated anywhere outside Great Britain as well as companies registered or incorporated in Northern Ireland.

As to the application of this Act to Northern Ireland, see now the Companies Act 2006, s 1284(1) (at **[S1284]**) which provides that this Act, in so far as it remains in force, extends to Northern Ireland.

746 Commencement

... this Act comes into force on 1st July 1985.

[632]

NOTES

Repealed by the Companies Act 2006, s 1295, Sch 16, as from a day to be appointed.

Words omitted repealed by CA 1989, s 212, Sch 24, as from 1 April 1990.

747 Citation

This Act may be cited as the Companies Act 1985.

[633]

SCHEDULES

SCHEDULE 1
PARTICULARS OF DIRECTORS ETC TO BE CONTAINED IN STATEMENT UNDER SECTION 10

Section 10

Directors

1. Subject as provided below, the statement under section 10(2) shall contain the following particulars with respect to each person named as director—

(*a*) *in the case of an individual, his present [name], any former [name], his usual residential address, his nationality, his business occupation (if any), particulars of any other directorships held by him, or which have been held by him [and his date of birth];*

(*b*) *in the case of a corporation [or Scottish firm], its corporate [or firm] name and registered or principal office.*

2.—(1) It is not necessary for the statement to contain particulars of a directorship—

(*a*) *which has not been held by a director at any time during the 5 years preceding the date on which the statement is delivered to the registrar,*

(*b*) *which is held by a director in a company which—*

(*i*) *is dormant or grouped with the company delivering the statement, and*

(*ii*) *if he also held that directorship for any period during those 5 years, was for the whole of that period either dormant or so grouped,*

(*c*) *which was held by a director for any period during those 5 years in a company which for the whole of that period was either dormant or grouped with the company delivering the statement.*

(2) For these purposes, "company" includes any body corporate incorporated in Great Britain; and—

(a) *[section 249AA(3)] applies as regards whether and when a company is or has been "dormant", and*

(b) *a company is treated as being or having been at any time grouped with another company if at that time it is or was a company of which that other is or was a wholly-owned subsidiary, or if it is or was a wholly-owned subsidiary of the other or of another company of which that other is or was a wholly-owned subsidiary.*

Secretaries

3.—(1) The statement shall contain the following particulars with respect to the person named as secretary or, where there are to be joint secretaries, with respect to each person named as one of them—

(a) *in the case of an individual, his present [name], any former [name] and his usual residential address,*

(b) *in the case of a corporation or a Scottish firm, its corporate or firm name and registered or principal office.*

(2) *However, if all the partners in a firm are joint secretaries, the name and principal office of the firm may be stated instead of the particulars otherwise required by this paragraph.*

Interpretation

4. In paragraphs 1(a) and 3(1)(a) above—

(a) *"name" means a person's Christian name (or other forename) and surname, except that in the case of a peer, or an individual usually known by a title, the title may be stated instead of his Christian name (or other forename) and surname or in addition to either or both of them; and*

(b) *the reference to a former name does not include—*

(i) *in the case of a peer, or an individual normally known by a British title, the name by which he was known previous to the adoption of or succession to the title, or*

(ii) *in the case of any person, a former name which was changed or disused before he attained the age of 18 years or which has been changed or disused for 20 years or more, or*

(iii) *in the case of a married woman, the name by which she was known previous to the marriage.]*

[5. Where a confidentiality order made under section 723B is in force in respect of any individual named as a director or secretary, paragraphs 1(a) and 3(1)(a) have effect as if the references to the usual residential address of the individual were references to the address for the time being notified by him under regulations made under sections 723B to 723F to any companies or oversea companies of which he is a director, secretary or permanent representative, or, if he is not such a director, secretary or permanent representative either the address specified in his application for a confidentiality order under regulations made under section 723B or the address last notified by him under regulations made under sections 723B to 723F as the case may be.]

[634]

NOTES

Repealed by the Companies Act 2006, s 1295, Sch 16, as from a day to be appointed.

Para 1: words in square brackets in sub-para (a) substituted, and words in square brackets in sub-para (b) inserted, by CA 1989, s 145, Sch 19, para 7(1)–(3), as from 1 October 1990.

Para 2: words in square brackets in sub-para (2)(a) substituted by the Companies Act 1985 (Audit Exemption) (Amendment) Regulations 2000, SI 2000/1430, reg 8(10), as from 26 May 2000, in relation to annual reports and reports in respect of financial years ending two months or more after that date.

Para 3: words in square brackets in sub-para (1)(a) substituted by CA 1989, s 145, Sch 19, para 7(1), (4), as from 1 October 1990.

Para 4: substituted by CA 1989, s 145, Sch 19, para 7(1), (5), as from 1 October 1990.

Para 5: added by the Companies (Particulars of Usual Residential Address) (Confidentiality Orders) Regulations 2002, SI 2002/912, reg 16, Sch 2, para 7, as from 2 April 2002.

SCHEDULE 2
INTERPRETATION OF REFERENCES TO "BENEFICIAL INTEREST"

Sections 23, 145, 146, 148

[PART I
REFERENCES IN SECTIONS 23, 145, 146 AND 148]

Residual interests under pension and employees' share schemes

1.—(1) Where shares in a company are held on trust for the purposes of a pension scheme or an employees' share scheme, there is to be disregarded any residual interest which has not vested in possession, being an interest of the company or, [as this paragraph applies for the purposes of section 23(2)] … of any subsidiary of the company.

(2) In this paragraph, "a residual interest" means a right of the company or subsidiary in question ("the residual beneficiary") to receive any of the trust property in the event of—

- *(a) all the liabilities arising under the scheme having been satisfied or provided for, or*
- *(b) the residual beneficiary ceasing to participate in the scheme, or*
- *(c) the trust property at any time exceeding what is necessary for satisfying the liabilities arising or expected to arise under the scheme.*

(3) In sub-paragraph (2), references to a right include a right dependent on the exercise of a discretion vested by the scheme in the trustee or any other person; and references to liabilities arising under a scheme include liabilities that have resulted or may result from the exercise of any such discretion.

(4) For purposes of this paragraph, a residual interest vests in possession—

- *(a) in a case within (a) of sub-paragraph (2), on the occurrence of the event there mentioned, whether or not the amount of the property receivable pursuant to the right mentioned in that sub-paragraph is then ascertained, and*
- *(b) in a case within (b) or (c) of that sub-paragraph, when the residual beneficiary becomes entitled to require the trustee to transfer to that beneficiary any of the property receivable pursuant to that right.*

(5) …

2.—(1) The following has effect as regards the operation of sections … 144, 145 and 146 to 149 in cases where a residual interest vests in possession.

(2) …

(3) Where by virtue of paragraph 1 of this Schedule any shares are exempt from section 144 or 145 at the time when they are issued or acquired but the residual interest in question vests in possession before they are disposed of or fully paid up, those sections apply to the shares as if they had been issued or acquired on the date on which that interest vests in possession.

(4) Where by virtue of paragraph 1 any shares are exempt from sections 146 to 149 at the time when they are acquired but the residual interest in question vests in possession before they are disposed of, those sections apply to the shares as if they had been acquired on the date on which that interest vests in possession.

(5) The above sub-paragraphs apply irrespective of the date on which the residual interest vests or vested in possession; but where the date on which it vested was before 26th July 1983 (the passing of the Companies (Beneficial Interests) Act 1983), they have effect as if the vesting had occurred on that date.

Employer's charges and other rights of recovery

3.—(1) Where shares in a company are held on trust, there are to be disregarded—

- *(a) if the trust is for the purposes of a pension scheme, any such rights as are mentioned in the following sub-paragraph, and*
- *(b) if the trust is for the purposes of an employees' share scheme, any such rights as are mentioned in (a) of the sub-paragraph,*

being rights of the company or, [as this paragraph applies for the purposes of section 23(2)] … of any subsidiary of the company.

(2) The rights referred to are—

(a) any charge or lien on, or set-off against, any benefit or other right or interest under the scheme for the purpose of enabling the employer or former employer of a member of the scheme to obtain the discharge of a monetary obligation due to him from the member, and

(b) any right to receive from the trustee of the scheme, or as trustee of the scheme to retain, an amount that can be recovered or retained under [section 61 of the Pension Schemes Act 1993 (deduction of contributions equivalent premium from refund of scheme contributions)] or otherwise as reimbursement or partial reimbursement for any [contributions equivalent premium] paid in connection with the scheme under Part III of that Act.

(3) …

Trustee's right to expenses, remuneration, indemnity, etc

4.—(1) Where a company is a trustee … , there are to be disregarded any rights which the company has in its capacity as trustee including, in particular, any right to recover its expenses or be remunerated out of the trust property and any right to be indemnified out of that property for any liability incurred by reason of any act or omission of the company in the performance of its duties as trustee.

(2) [As this paragraph applies for the purposes of section 23(2)] … , sub-paragraph (1) has effect as if references to a company included any body corporate which is a subsidiary of a company.

[(3) As respects sections 145, 146 and 148, sub-paragraph (1) above applies where a company is a personal representative as it applies where a company is a trustee.]

Supplementary

5.—(1) The following applies for the interpretation of [this Part of this Schedule].

(2) "Pension scheme" means any scheme for the provision of benefits consisting of or including relevant benefits for or in respect of employees or former employees; and "relevant benefits" means any pension, lump sum, gratuity or other like benefit given or to be given on retirement or on death or in anticipation of retirement or, in connection with past service, after retirement or death.

(3) In sub-paragraph (2) of this paragraph, and in paragraph 3(2)(a), "employer" and "employee" are to be read as if a director of a company were employed by it.

[635]

NOTES

Repealed by the Companies Act 2006, s 1295, Sch 16, as from a day to be appointed.

Original Sch 2 renumbered as Sch 2, Pt I and Part heading added by CA 1989, s 23, Sch 10, Pt I, para 18(1), (2), as from 1 April 1990.

Para 1: words omitted from sub-para (1) and the whole of sub-para (5) repealed by CA 1989, ss 23, 212, Sch 10, para 18(1), (3), Sch 24, as from 1 April 1990; words in square brackets in sub-para (1) substituted by CA 1989, s 129(2), as from 1 November 1990.

Para 2: word omitted from sub-para (1) and the whole of sub-para (2) repealed by CA 1989, s 212, Sch 24, as from 1 April 1990.

Para 3: words omitted from sub-para (1) and the whole of sub-para (3) repealed by CA 1989, ss 23, 212, Sch 10, para 18(1), (4), Sch 24, as from 1 April 1990; words in square brackets in sub-para (1) substituted by CA 1989, s 129(2), as from 1 November 1990; words in first pair of square brackets in sub-para (2)(b) substituted by the Pension Schemes Act 1993, s 190, Sch 8, para 16(a), as from 7 February 1994; words in second pair of square brackets in sub-para (2)(b) substituted by the Pensions Act 1995, s 151, Sch 5, para 11, as from 6 April 1997.

Para 4: words omitted from sub-paras (1), (2) repealed, and sub-para (3) added, by CA 1989, ss 23, 212, Sch 10, para 18(1), (5), Sch 24, as from 1 April 1990; words in square brackets in sub-para (2) substituted by CA 1989, s 129(2), as from 1 November 1990.

Para 5: words in square brackets in sub-para (1) substituted by CA 1989, s 23, Sch 10, para 18(1), (6), as from 1 April 1990.

Companies (Beneficial Interests) Act 1983: repealed by the Companies Consolidation (Consequential Provisions) Act 1985, s 29, Sch 1.

[PART II
REFERENCES IN SCHEDULE 5

Residual interests under pension and employees' share schemes

6.—(1) Where shares in an undertaking are held on trust for the purposes of a pension scheme or an employees' share scheme, there shall be disregarded any residual interest which has not vested in possession, being an interest of the undertaking or any of its subsidiary undertakings.

(2) In this paragraph a "residual interest" means a right of the undertaking in question (the "residual beneficiary") to receive any of the trust property in the event of—

- *(a) all the liabilities arising under the scheme having been satisfied or provided for, or*
- *(b) the residual beneficiary ceasing to participate in the scheme, or*
- *(c) the trust property at any time exceeding what is necessary for satisfying the liabilities arising or expected to arise under the scheme.*

(3) In sub-paragraph (2) references to a right include a right dependent on the exercise of a discretion vested by the scheme in the trustee or any other person; and references to liabilities arising under a scheme include liabilities that have resulted or may result from the exercise of any such discretion.

(4) For the purposes of this paragraph a residual interest vests in possession—

- *(a) in a case within sub-paragraph (2)(a), on the occurrence of the event there mentioned, whether or not the amount of the property receivable pursuant to the right mentioned in that sub-paragraph is then ascertained;*
- *(b) in a case within sub-paragraph (2)(b) or (c), when the residual beneficiary becomes entitled to require the trustee to transfer to that beneficiary any of the property receivable pursuant to that right.*

Employer's charges and other rights of recovery

7.—(1) Where shares in an undertaking are held on trust, there shall be disregarded—

- *(a) if the trust is for the purposes of a pension scheme, any such rights as are mentioned in sub-paragraph (2) below;*
- *(b) if the trust is for the purposes of an employees' share scheme, any such rights as are mentioned in paragraph (a) of that sub-paragraph,*

being rights of the undertaking or any of its subsidiary undertakings.

(2) The rights referred to are—

- *(a) any charge or lien on, or set-off against, any benefit or other right or interest under the scheme for the purpose of enabling the employer or former employer of a member of the scheme to obtain the discharge of a monetary obligation due to him from the member, and*
- *(b) any right to receive from the trustee of the scheme, or as trustee of the scheme to retain, an amount that can be recovered or retained under [section 61 of the Pension Schemes Act 1993 (deduction of contributions equivalent premium from refund of scheme contributions)] or otherwise as reimbursement or partial reimbursement for any [contributions equivalent premium] paid in connection with the scheme under [Chapter III of Part III] of that Act.*

Trustee's right to expenses, remuneration, indemnity, &c

8. Where an undertaking is a trustee, there shall be disregarded any rights which the undertaking has in its capacity as trustee including, in particular, any right to recover its expenses or be remunerated out of the trust property and any right to be indemnified out of that property for any liability incurred by reason of any act or omission of the undertaking in the performance of its duties as trustee.

Supplementary

9.—(1) The following applies for the interpretation of this Part of this Schedule.

(2) "Undertaking" and "shares", in relation to an undertaking, have the same meaning as in Part VII.

(3) This Part of this Schedule applies in relation to debentures as it applies in relation to shares.

(4) "Pension scheme" means any scheme for the provision of benefits consisting of or including relevant benefits for or in respect of employees or former employees; and "relevant benefits" means any pension, lump sum, gratuity or other like benefit given or to be given on retirement or on death or in anticipation of retirement or, in connection with past service, after retirement or death.

(5) In sub-paragraph (4) of this paragraph and in paragraph 7(2) "employee" and "employer" shall be read as if a director of an undertaking were employed by it.]

[636]

NOTES

This Part (paras 6–9) of this Schedule added by CA 1989, s 23, Sch 10, para 18(1), (7), as from 1 April 1990.

Repealed by the Companies Act 2006, s 1295, Sch 16, as from a day to be appointed.

Para 7: words in first and third pairs of square brackets in sub-para (2)(b) substituted by the Pensions Schemes Act 1993, s 190, Sch 8, para 16(b), as from 7 February 1994; words in second pair of square brackets in sub-para (2)(b) substituted by the Pensions Act 1995, s 151, Sch 5, para 11, as from 6 April 1997.

(Sch 3 repealed by FSA 1986, s 212(3), Sch 17, Pt I to the extent noted at the beginning of Pt III of this Act.)

SCHEDULE 4
FORM AND CONTENT OF COMPANY ACCOUNTS

Sections 228, 230

PART I
GENERAL RULES AND FORMATS

SECTION A
GENERAL RULES

1.—(1) Subject to the following provisions of this Schedule—

(a) every balance sheet of a company shall show the items listed in either of the balance sheet formats set out below in section B of this Part; and

(b) every profit and loss account of a company shall show the items listed in any one of the profit and loss account formats so set out;

in either case in the order and under the headings and sub-headings given in the format adopted.

(2) Sub-paragraph (1) above is not to be read as requiring the heading or sub-heading for any item to be distinguished by any letter or number assigned to that item in the format adopted.

2.—(1) Where in accordance with paragraph 1 a company's balance sheet or profit and loss account for any financial year has been prepared by reference to one of the formats set out in section B below, the directors of the company shall adopt the same format in preparing the accounts for subsequent financial years of the company unless in their opinion there are special reasons for a change.

(2) Particulars of any change in the format adopted in preparing a company's balance sheet or profit and loss account in accordance with paragraph 1 shall be disclosed, and the reasons for the change shall be explained, in a note to the accounts in which the new format is first adopted.

3.—(1) Any item required in accordance with paragraph 1 to be shown in a company's balance sheet or profit and loss account may be shown in greater detail than required by the format adopted.

(2) A company's balance sheet or profit and loss account may include an item representing or covering the amount of any asset or liability, income or expenditure not otherwise covered by any of the items listed in the format adopted, but the following shall not be treated as assets in any company's balance sheet—

(a) preliminary expenses;

(b) expenses of and commission on any issue of shares or debentures; and

(c) costs of research.

(3) In preparing a company's balance sheet or profit and loss account the directors of the company shall adapt the arrangement and headings and sub-headings otherwise required by paragraph 1 in respect of items to which an Arabic number is assigned in the format adopted, in any case where the special nature of the company's business requires such adaptation.

(4) Items to which Arabic numbers are assigned in any of the formats set out in section B below may be combined in a company's accounts for any financial year if either—

(a) their individual amounts are not material to assessing the state of affairs or profit or loss of the company for that year; or

(b) the combination facilitates that assessment;

but in a case within paragraph (b) the individual amounts of any items so combined shall be disclosed in a note to the accounts.

(5) Subject to paragraph 4(3) below, a heading or sub-heading corresponding to an item listed in the format adopted in preparing a company's balance sheet or profit and loss account shall not be included if there is no amount to be shown for that item in respect of the financial year to which the balance sheet or profit and loss account relates.

(6) Every profit and loss account of a company shall show the amount of the company's profit or loss on ordinary activities before taxation.

(7) …

4.—(1) In respect of every item shown in a company's balance sheet or profit and loss account the corresponding amount for the financial year immediately preceding that to which the balance sheet or profit and loss account relates shall also be shown.

(2) Where that corresponding amount is not comparable with the amount to be shown for the item in question in respect of the financial year to which the balance sheet or profit and loss account relates, the former amount [may be adjusted] and [particulars of the non-comparability and of any adjustment] shall be disclosed in a note to the accounts.

(3) Paragraph 3(5) does not apply in any case where an amount can be shown for the item in question in respect of the financial year immediately preceding that to which the balance sheet or profit and loss account relates, and that amount shall be shown under the heading or sub-heading required by paragraph 1 for that item.

5. Amounts in respect of items representing assets or income may not be set off against amounts in respect of items representing liabilities or expenditure (as the case may be), or vice versa.

[5A. The directors of a company must, in determining how amounts are presented within items in the profit and loss account and balance sheet, have regard to the substance of the reported transaction or arrangement, in accordance with generally accepted accounting principles or practice.]

SECTION B
THE REQUIRED FORMATS FOR ACCOUNTS

Preliminary

6. References in this Part of this Schedule to the items listed in any of the formats set out below are to those items read together with any of the notes following the formats which apply to any of those items, and the requirement imposed by paragraph 1 to show the items listed in any such format in the order adopted in the format is subject to any provision in those notes for alternative positions for any particular items.

7. A number in brackets following any item in any of the formats set out below is a reference to the note of that number in the notes following the formats.

8. In the notes following the formats—

(a) the heading of each note gives the required heading or sub-heading for the item to which it applies and a reference to any letters and numbers assigned to that item in the formats set out below (taking a reference in the case of Format 2 of the balance sheet formats to the item listed under "Assets" or under "Liabilities" as the case may require); and

(b) references to a numbered format are to the balance sheet format or (as the case may require) to the profit and loss account format of that number set out below.

Balance Sheet Formats

Format 1

A. Called up share capital not paid (1)

B. Fixed assets

I Intangible assets
- *1. Development costs*
- *2. Concessions, patents, licences, trade marks and similar rights and assets (2)*
- *3. Goodwill (3)*
- *4. Payments on account*

II Tangible assets
- *1. Land and buildings*
- *2. Plant and machinery*
- *3. Fixtures, fittings, tools and equipment*
- *4. Payments on account and assets in course of construction*

III Investments
- *1. Shares in [group undertakings]*
- *2. Loans to [group undertakings]*
- *3. [Participating interests]*
- *4. Loans to [undertakings in which the company has a participating interest]*
- *5. Other investments other than loans*
- *6. Other loans*
- *7. Own shares (4)*

C. Current assets

I Stocks
- *1. Raw materials and consumables*
- *2. Work in progress*
- *3. Finished goods and goods for resale*
- *4. Payments on account*

II Debtors (5)
- *1. Trade debtors*
- *2. Amounts owed by [group undertakings]*
- *3. Amounts owed by [undertakings in which the company has a participating interest]*
- *4. Other debtors*
- *5. Called up share capital not paid (1)*
- *6. Prepayments and accrued income (6)*

III Investments
- *1. Shares in [group undertakings]*
- *2. Own shares (4)*
- *3. Other investments*

IV Cash at bank and in hand

D. Prepayments and accrued income (6)

E. Creditors: amounts falling due within one year
- *1. Debenture loans (7)*
- *2. Bank loans and overdrafts*
- *3. Payments received on account (8)*
- *4. Trade creditors*
- *5. Bills of exchange payable*
- *6. Amounts owed to [group undertakings]*

7. Amounts owed to [undertakings in which the company has a participating interest]
8. Other creditors including taxation and social security (*9*)
9. Accruals and deferred income (*10*)

F. Net current assets (*liabilities*) (*11*)

G. Total assets less current liabilities

H. Creditors: amounts falling due after more than one year
1. Debenture loans (*7*)
2. Bank loans and overdrafts
3. Payments received on account (*8*)
4. Trade creditors
5. Bills of exchange payable
6. Amounts owed to [group undertakings]
7. Amounts owed to [undertakings in which the company has a participating interest]
8. Other creditors including taxation and social security (*9*)
9. Accruals and deferred income (*10*)

I. [Provisions for liabilities]
1. Pensions and similar obligations
2. Taxation, including deferred taxation
3. Other provisions

J. Accruals and deferred income (*10*)

K. Capital and reserves
I Called up share capital (*12*)
II Share premium account
III Revaluation reserve
IV Other reserves
1. Capital redemption reserve
2. Reserve for own shares
3. Reserves provided for by the articles of association
4. Other reserves
V Profit and loss account

Balance Sheet Formats

Format 2

ASSETS

A. Called up share capital not paid (*1*)

B. Fixed assets
I Intangible assets
1. Development costs
2. Concessions, patents, licences, trade marks and similar rights and assets (*2*)
3. Goodwill (*3*)
4. Payments on account
II Tangible assets
1. Land and buildings
2. Plant and machinery
3. Fixtures, fittings, tools and equipment
4. Payments on account and assets in course of construction
III Investments
1. Shares in [group undertakings]
2. Loans to [group undertakings]
3. [Participating interests]
4. Loans to [undertakings in which the company has a participating interest]
5. Other investments other than loans
6. Other loans
7. Own shares (*4*)

C. Current assets
I Stocks
1. Raw materials and consumables

2. *Work in progress*
3. *Finished goods and goods for resale*
4. *Payments on account*

II *Debtors* (5)
1. *Trade debtors*
2. *Amounts owed by [group undertakings]*
3. *Amounts owed by [undertakings in which the company has a participating interest]*
4. *Other debtors*
5. *Called up share capital not paid* (1)
6. *Prepayments and accrued income* (6)

III *Investments*
1. *Shares in [group undertakings]*
2. *Own shares* (4)
3. *Other investments*

IV *Cash at bank and in hand*

D. *Prepayments and accrued income* (6)

LIABILITIES

A. *Capital and reserves*

I *Called up share capital* (12)

II *Share premium account*

III *Revaluation reserve*

IV *Other reserves*
1. *Capital redemption reserve*
2. *Reserve for own shares*
3. *Reserves provided for by the articles of association*
4. *Other reserves*

V *Profit and loss account*

B. *[Provisions for liabilities]*
1. *Pensions and similar obligations*
2. *Taxation including deferred taxation*
3. *Other provisions*

C. *Creditors* (13)
1. *Debenture loans* (7)
2. *Bank loans and overdrafts*
3. *Payments received on account* (8)
4. *Trade creditors*
5. *Bills of exchange payable*
6. *Amounts owed to [group undertakings]*
7. *Amounts owed to [undertakings in which the company has a participating interest]*
8. *Other creditors including taxation and social security* (9)
9. *Accruals and deferred income* (10)

D. *Accruals and deferred income* (10)

Notes on the balance sheet formats

(1) *Called up share capital not paid*

(*Formats 1 and 2, items A and C.II.5.*)

This item may be shown in either of the two positions given in Formats 1 and 2.

(2) *Concessions, patents, licences, trade marks and similar rights and assets*

(*Formats 1 and 2, item B.I.2.*)

Amounts in respect of assets shall only be included in a company's balance sheet under this item if either—

(*a*) *the assets were acquired for valuable consideration and are not required to be shown under goodwill; or*

(*b*) *the assets in question were created by the company itself.*

(3) *Goodwill*

(*Formats 1 and 2, item B.I.3.*)

Amounts representing goodwill shall only be included to the extent that the goodwill was acquired for valuable consideration.

(4) Own shares

(Formats 1 and 2, items B.III.7 and C.III.2.)

The nominal value of the shares held shall be shown separately.

(5) Debtors

(Formats 1 and 2, items C.II.1 to 6.)

The amount falling due after more than one year shall be shown separately for each item included under debtors.

(6) Prepayments and accrued income

(Formats 1 and 2, items C.II.6 and D.)

This item may be shown in either of the two positions given in Formats 1 and 2.

(7) Debenture loans

(Format 1, items E.1 and H.1 and Format 2, item C.1.)

The amount of any convertible loans shall be shown separately.

(8) Payments received on account

(Format 1, items E.3 and H.3 and Format 2, item C.3.)

Payments received on account of orders shall be shown for each of these items in so far as they are not shown as deductions from stocks.

(9) Other creditors including taxation and social security

(Format 1, items E.8 and H.8 and Format 2, item C.8.)

The amount for creditors in respect of taxation and social security shall be shown separately from the amount for other creditors.

(10) Accruals and deferred income

(Format 1, items E.9, H.9 and J and Format 2, items C.9 and D.)

The two positions given for this item in Format 1 at E.9 and H.9 are an alternative to the position at J, but if the item is not shown in a position corresponding to that at J it may be shown in either or both of the other two positions (as the case may require).

The two positions given for this item in Format 2 are alternatives.

(11) Net current assets (liabilities)

(Format 1, item F.)

In determining the amount to be shown for this item any amounts shown under "prepayments and accrued income" shall be taken into account wherever shown.

(12) Called up share capital

(Format 1, item K.I and Format 2, item A.I.)

The amount of allotted share capital and the amount of called up share capital which has been paid up shall be shown separately.

(13) Creditors

(Format 2, items C.1 to 9.)

Amounts falling due within one year and after one year shall be shown separately for each of these items [and for the aggregate of all of these items].

Profit and loss account formats

Format 1
(see note (17) below)

1. Turnover

2. Cost of sales (14)

3. *Gross profit or loss*
4. *Distribution costs* (*14*)
5. *Administrative expenses* (*14*)
6. *Other operating income*
7. *Income from shares in [group undertakings]*
8. *Income from [participating interests]*
9. *Income from other fixed asset investments* (*15*)
10. *Other interest receivable and similar income* (*15*)
11. *Amounts written off investments*
12. *Interest payable and similar charges* (*16*)
13. *Tax on profit or loss on ordinary activities*
14. *Profit or loss on ordinary activities after taxation*
15. *Extraordinary income*
16. *Extraordinary charges*
17. *Extraordinary profit or loss*
18. *Tax on extraordinary profit or loss*
19. *Other taxes not shown under the above items*
20. *Profit or loss for the financial year*

Profit and loss account formats

Format 2

1. *Turnover*
2. *Change in stocks of finished goods and in work in progress*
3. *Own work capitalised*
4. *Other operating income*
5.
   (*a*) *Raw materials and consumables*
   (*b*) *Other external charges*
6. *Staff costs—*
   (*a*) *wages and salaries*
   (*b*) *social security costs*
   (*c*) *other pension costs*
7.
   (*a*) *Depreciation and other amounts written off tangible and intangible fixed assets*
   (*b*) *Exceptional amounts written off current assets*
8. *Other operating charges*
9. *Income from shares in [group undertakings]*
10. *Income from [participating interests]*
11. *Income from other fixed asset investments* (*15*)
12. *Other interest receivable and similar income* (*15*)
13. *Amounts written off investments*
14. *Interest payable and similar charges* (*16*)
15. *Tax on profit or loss on ordinary activities*
16. *Profit or loss on ordinary activities after taxation*
17. *Extraordinary income*

18. Extraordinary charges

19. Extraordinary profit or loss

20. Tax on extraordinary profit or loss

21. Other taxes not shown under the above items

22. Profit or loss for the financial year

Profit and loss account formats

Format 3
(*see note* (*17*) *below*)

A. Charges
- *1. Cost of sales* (*14*)
- *2. Distribution costs* (*14*)
- *3. Administrative expenses* (*14*)
- *4. Amounts written off investments*
- *5. Interest payable and similar charges* (*16*)
- *6. Tax on profit or loss on ordinary activities*
- *7. Profit or loss on ordinary activities after taxation*
- *8. Extraordinary charges*
- *9. Tax on extraordinary profit or loss*
- *10. Other taxes not shown under the above items*
- *11. Profit or loss for the financial year*

B. Income
- *1. Turnover*
- *2. Other operating income*
- *3. Income from shares in [group undertakings]*
- *4. Income from [participating interests]*
- *5. Income from other fixed asset investments* (*15*)
- *6. Other interest receivable and similar income* (*15*)
- *7. Profit or loss on ordinary activities after taxation*
- *8. Extraordinary income*
- *9. Profit or loss for the financial year*

Profit and loss account formats

Format 4

A. Charges
- *1. Reduction in stocks of finished goods and in work in progress*
- *2.*
  - (*a*) *Raw materials and consumables*
  - (*b*) *Other external charges*
- *3. Staff costs—*
  - (*a*) *wages and salaries*
  - (*b*) *social security costs*
  - (*c*) *other pension costs*
- *4.*
  - (*a*) *Depreciation and other amounts written off tangible and intangible fixed assets*
  - (*b*) *Exceptional amounts written off current assets*
- *5. Other operating charges*
- *6. Amounts written off investments*
- *7. Interest payable and similar charges* (*16*)
- *8. Tax on profit or loss on ordinary activities*
- *9. Profit or loss on ordinary activities after taxation*
- *10. Extraordinary charges*
- *11. Tax on extraordinary profit or loss*
- *12. Other taxes not shown under the above items*
- *13. Profit or loss for the financial year*

B. Income
- *1. Turnover*
- *2. Increase in stocks of finished goods and in work in progress*
- *3. Own work capitalised*

4. *Other operating income*
5. *Income from shares in [group undertakings]*
6. *Income from [participating interests]*
7. *Income from other fixed asset investments (15)*
8. *Other interest receivable and similar income (15)*
9. *Profit or loss on ordinary activities after taxation*
10. *Extraordinary income*
11. *Profit or loss for the financial year*

Notes on the profit and loss account formats

(14) Cost of sales: distribution costs: administrative expenses

(Format 1, items 2, 4 and 5 and Format 3, items A.1, 2 and 3.)

These items shall be stated after taking into account any necessary provisions for depreciation or diminution in value of assets.

(15) Income from other fixed asset investments: other interest receivable and similar income

(Format 1, items 9 and 10: Format 2, items 11 and 12: Format 3, items B.5 and 6: Format 4, items B.7 and 8.)

Income and interest derived from [group undertakings] shall be shown separately from income and interest derived from other sources.

(16) Interest payable and similar charges

(Format 1, item 12: Format 2, item 14: Format 3, item A.5: Format 4, item A.7.)

The amount payable to [group undertakings] shall be shown separately.

(17) Formats 1 and 3

The amount of any provisions for depreciation and diminution in value of tangible and intangible fixed assets falling to be shown under items 7(a) and A.4(a) respectively in Formats 2 and 4 shall be disclosed in a note to the accounts in any case where the profit and loss account is prepared by reference to Format 1 or Format 3.

[637]

NOTES

Repealed by the Companies Act 2006, s 1295, Sch 16, as from a day to be appointed.

Para 3: sub-para (7) repealed by the Companies Act 1985 (International Accounting Standards and Other Accounting Amendments) Regulations 2004, SI 2004/2947, reg 14(1), Sch 2, paras 1, 2, as from 12 November 2004, in relation to companies' financial years which begin on or after 1 January 2005.

Para 4: words in square brackets substituted by the Companies Act 1985 (Investment Companies and Accounting and Audit Amendments) Regulations 2005, SI 2005/2280, reg 3, as from 1 October 2005, in relation to companies' financial years which begin on or after 1 January 2005 and which end on or after 1 October 2005.

Para 5A: inserted by SI 2004/2947, reg 14(1), Sch 2, paras 1, 3, as from 12 November 2004, in relation to companies' financial years which begin on or after 1 January 2005.

Words "provisions for liabilities" in square brackets in balance sheet format 1 and balance sheet format 2 substituted by SI 2004/2947, reg 14(1), Sch 2, paras 1, 4, as from 12 November 2004, in relation to companies' financial years which begin on or after 1 January 2005.

Words in square brackets in note (13) of the notes on the balance sheet formats substituted by the Companies Act 1985 (Miscellaneous Accounting Amendments) Regulations 1996, SI 1996/189, regs 14(1), 16(1), Sch 1, paras 1, 3, in relation to any financial year ending on or after 2 February 1996 (subject to transitional provisions in relation to financial years ending on or before 24 March 1996).

Other words in square brackets substituted by CA 1989, s 4(2), Sch 1, paras 1–4, as from 1 April 1990.

Application to limited liability partnerships: see the Limited Liability Partnerships Regulations 2001, SI 2001/1090, reg 3, Sch 1 at **[6984]**, **[6992]**.

Trade marks: by the Trade Marks Act 1994, s 106(1), Sch 4, para 1, references in Balance Sheet Formats 1 and 2 and Note (2) to trade marks are to be construed as references to trade marks within the meaning of the 1994 Act.

PART II
ACCOUNTING PRINCIPLES AND RULES

SECTION A
ACCOUNTING PRINCIPLES

Preliminary

9. Subject to paragraph 15 below, the amounts to be included in respect of all items shown in a company's accounts shall be determined in accordance with the principles set out in paragraphs 10 to 14.

Accounting principles

10. The company shall be presumed to be carrying on business as a going concern.

[11. Accounting policies shall be applied consistently within the same accounts as from one financial year to the next.]

12. The amount of any item shall be determined on a prudent basis, and in particular—

(a) only profits realised at the balance sheet date shall be included in the profit and loss account; and

(b) all liabilities … which have arisen … in respect of the financial year to which the accounts relate or a previous financial year shall be taken into account, including those which only become apparent between the balance sheet date and the date on which it is signed on behalf of the board of directors in pursuance of [section 233] of this Act.

13. All income and charges relating to the financial year to which the accounts relate shall be taken into account, without regard to the date of receipt or payment.

14. In determining the aggregate amount of any item the amount of each individual asset or liability that falls to be taken into account shall be determined separately.

Departure from the accounting principles

15. If it appears to the directors of a company that there are special reasons for departing from any of the principles stated above in preparing the company's accounts in respect of any financial year they may do so, but particulars of the departure, the reasons for it and its effect shall be given in a note to the accounts.

SECTION B
HISTORICAL COST ACCOUNTING RULES

Preliminary

16. [Subject to sections C and D] of this Part of this Schedule, the amounts to be included in respect of all items shown in a company's accounts shall be determined in accordance with the rules set out in paragraphs 17 to 28.

Fixed assets

General rules

17. Subject to any provision for depreciation or diminution in value made in accordance with paragraph 18 or 19 the amount to be included in respect of any fixed asset shall be its purchase price or production cost.

18. In the case of any fixed asset which has a limited useful economic life, the amount of—

(a) its purchase price or production cost; or

(b) where it is estimated that any such asset will have a residual value at the end of the period of its useful economic life, its purchase price or production cost less that estimated residual value;

shall be reduced by provisions for depreciation calculated to write off that amount systematically over the period of the asset's useful economic life.

19.—(1) Where a fixed asset investment of a description falling to be included under item B.III of either of the balance sheet formats set out in Part I of this Schedule has diminished in value provisions for diminution in value may be made in respect of it and the amount to be included in respect of it may be reduced accordingly; and any such provisions which are not shown in the profit and loss account shall be disclosed (either separately or in aggregate) in a note to the accounts.

(2) Provisions for diminution in value shall be made in respect of any fixed asset which has diminished in value if the reduction in its value is expected to be permanent (whether its useful economic life is limited or not), and the amount to be included in respect of it shall be reduced accordingly; and any such provisions which are not shown in the profit and loss account shall be disclosed (either separately or in aggregate) in a note to the accounts.

(3) Where the reasons for which any provision was made in accordance with sub-paragraph (1) or (2) have ceased to apply to any extent, that provision shall be written back to the extent that it is no longer necessary; and any amounts written back in accordance with this sub-paragraph which are not shown in the profit and loss account shall be disclosed (either separately or in aggregate) in a note to the accounts.

Rules for determining particular fixed asset items

20.—(1) Notwithstanding that an item in respect of "development costs" is included under "fixed assets" in the balance sheet formats set out in Part I of this Schedule, an amount may only be included in a company's balance sheet in respect of development costs in special circumstances.

(2) If any amount is included in a company's balance sheet in respect of development costs the following information shall be given in a note to the accounts—

- *(a) the period over which the amount of those costs originally capitalised is being or is to be written off; and*
- *(b) the reasons for capitalising the development costs in question.*

21.—(1) The application of paragraphs 17 to 19 in relation to goodwill (in any case where goodwill is treated as an asset) is subject to the following provisions of this paragraph.

(2) Subject to sub-paragraph (3) below, the amount of the consideration for any goodwill acquired by a company shall be reduced by provisions for depreciation calculated to write off that amount systematically over a period chosen by the directors of the company.

(3) The period chosen shall not exceed the useful economic life of the goodwill in question.

(4) In any case where any goodwill acquired by a company is shown or included as an asset in the company's balance sheet the period chosen for writing off the consideration for that goodwill and the reasons for choosing that period shall be disclosed in a note to the accounts.

Current assets

22. Subject to paragraph 23, the amount to be included in respect of any current asset shall be its purchase price or production cost.

23.—(1) If the net realisable value of any current asset is lower than its purchase price or production cost the amount to be included in respect of that asset shall be the net realisable value.

(2) Where the reasons for which any provision for diminution in value was made in accordance with sub-paragraph (1) have ceased to apply to any extent, that provision shall be written back to the extent that it is no longer necessary.

Miscellaneous and supplementary provisions

Excess of money owed over value received as an asset item

24.—(1) Where the amount repayable on any debt owed by a company is greater than the value of the consideration received in the transaction giving rise to the debt, the amount of the difference may be treated as an asset.

(2) Where any such amount is so treated—

(a) it shall be written off by reasonable amounts each year and must be completely written off before repayment of the debt; and

(b) if the current amount is not shown as a separate item in the company's balance sheet it must be disclosed in a note to the accounts.

Assets included at a fixed amount

25.—(1) Subject to the following sub-paragraph, assets which fall to be included—

(a) amongst the fixed assets of a company under the item "tangible assets"; or

(b) amongst the current assets of a company under the item "raw materials and consumables";

may be included at a fixed quantity and value.

(2) Sub-paragraph (1) applies to assets of a kind which are constantly being replaced, where—

(a) their overall value is not material to assessing the company's state of affairs; and

(b) their quantity, value and composition are not subject to material variation.

Determination of purchase price or production cost

26.—(1) The purchase price of an asset shall be determined by adding to the actual price paid any expenses incidental to its acquisition.

(2) The production cost of an asset shall be determined by adding to the purchase price of the raw materials and consumables used the amount of the costs incurred by the company which are directly attributable to the production of that asset.

(3) In addition, there may be included in the production cost of an asset—

(a) a reasonable proportion of the costs incurred by the company which are only indirectly attributable to the production of that asset, but only to the extent that they relate to the period of production; and

(b) interest on capital borrowed to finance the production of that asset, to the extent that it accrues in respect of the period of production;

provided, however, in a case within paragraph (b) above, that the inclusion of the interest in determining the cost of that asset and the amount of the interest so included is disclosed in a note to the accounts.

(4) In the case of current assets distribution costs may not be included in production costs.

27.—(1) Subject to the qualification mentioned below, the purchase price or production cost of—

(a) any assets which fall to be included under any item shown in a company's balance sheet under the general item "stocks"; and

(b) any assets which are fungible assets (including investments);

may be determined by the application of any of the methods mentioned in sub-paragraph (2) below in relation to any such assets of the same class.

The method chosen must be one which appears to the directors to be appropriate in the circumstances of the company.

(2) Those methods are—

(a) the method known as "first in, first out" (FIFO);

(b) the method known as "last in, first out" (LIFO);

(c) a weighted average price; and

(d) any other method similar to any of the methods mentioned above.

(3) Where in the case of any company—

(a) the purchase price or production cost of assets falling to be included under any item shown in the company's balance sheet has been determined by the application of any method permitted by this paragraph; and

(b) the amount shown in respect of that item differs materially from the relevant alternative amount given below in this paragraph;

the amount of that difference shall be disclosed in a note to the accounts.

(4) Subject to sub-paragraph (5) below, for the purposes of sub-paragraph (3)(b) above, the relevant alternative amount, in relation to any item shown in a company's balance sheet, is the amount which would have been shown in respect of that item if assets of any class included under that item at an amount determined by any method permitted by this paragraph had instead been included at their replacement cost as at the balance sheet date.

(5) The relevant alternative amount may be determined by reference to the most recent actual purchase price or production cost before the balance sheet date of assets of any class included under the item in question instead of by reference to their replacement cost as at that date, but only if the former appears to the directors of the company to constitute the more appropriate standard of comparison in the case of assets of that class.

(6) For the purposes of this paragraph, assets of any description shall be regarded as fungible if assets of that description are substantially indistinguishable one from another.

Substitution of original stated amount where price or cost unknown

28. Where there is no record of the purchase price or production cost of any asset of a company or of any price, expenses or costs relevant for determining its purchase price or production cost in accordance with paragraph 26, or any such record cannot be obtained without unreasonable expense or delay, its purchase price or production cost shall be taken for the purposes of paragraphs 17 to 23 to be the value ascribed to it in the earliest available record of its value made on or after its acquisition or production by the company.

SECTION C
ALTERNATIVE ACCOUNTING RULES

Preliminary

29.—(1) The rules set out in section B are referred to below in this Schedule as the historical cost accounting rules.

(2) Those rules, with the omission of paragraphs 16, 21 and 25 to 28, are referred to below in this Part of this Schedule as the depreciation rules; and references below in this Schedule to the historical cost accounting rules do not include the depreciation rules as they apply by virtue of paragraph 32.

30. Subject to paragraphs 32 to 34, the amounts to be included in respect of assets of any description mentioned in paragraph 31 may be determined on any basis so mentioned.

Alternative accounting rules

31.—(1) Intangible fixed assets, other than goodwill, may be included at their current cost.

(2) Tangible fixed assets may be included at a market value determined as at the date of their last valuation or at their current cost.

(3) Investments of any description falling to be included under item B.III of either of the balance sheet formats set out in Part I of this Schedule may be included either—

(a) at a market value determined as at the date of their last valuation; or

(b) at a value determined on any basis which appears to the directors to be appropriate in the circumstances of the company;

but in the latter case particulars of the method of valuation adopted and of the reasons for adopting it shall be disclosed in a note to the accounts.

(4) Investments of any description falling to be included under item C.III of either of the balance sheet formats set out in Part I of this Schedule may be included at their current cost.

(5) Stocks may be included at their current cost.

Application of the depreciation rules

32.—(1) Where the value of any asset of a company is determined on any basis mentioned in paragraph 31, that value shall be, or (as the case may require) be the starting point for determining, the amount to be included in respect of that asset in the company's accounts, instead of its purchase price or production cost or any value previously so determined for that asset; and the depreciation rules shall apply accordingly in relation to any such asset with the substitution for any reference to its purchase price or production cost of a reference to the value most recently determined for that asset on any basis mentioned in paragraph 31.

(2) *The amount of any provision for depreciation required in the case of any fixed asset by paragraph 18 or 19 as it applies by virtue of sub-paragraph (1) is referred to below in this paragraph as the adjusted amount, and the amount of any provision which would be required by that paragraph in the case of that asset according to the historical cost accounting rules is referred to as the historical cost amount.*

(3) *Where sub-paragraph (1) applies in the case of any fixed asset the amount of any provision for depreciation in respect of that asset—*

(a) *included in any item shown in the profit and loss account in respect of amounts written off assets of the description in question; or*

(b) *taken into account in stating any item so shown which is required by note (14) of the notes on the profit and loss account formats set out in Part I of this Schedule to be stated after taking into account any necessary provisions for depreciation or diminution in value of assets included under it;*

may be the historical cost amount instead of the adjusted amount, provided that the amount of any difference between the two is shown separately in the profit and loss account or in a note to the accounts.

Additional information to be provided in case of departure from historical cost accounting rules

33.—(1) This paragraph applies where the amounts to be included in respect of assets covered by any items shown in a company's accounts have been determined on any basis mentioned in paragraph 31.

(2) *The items affected and the basis of valuation adopted in determining the amounts of the assets in question in the case of each such item shall be disclosed in a note to the accounts.*

(3) *In the case of each balance sheet item affected (except stocks) either—*

(a) *the comparable amounts determined according to the historical cost accounting rules; or*

(b) *the differences between those amounts and the corresponding amounts actually shown in the balance sheet in respect of that item;*

shall be shown separately in the balance sheet or in a note to the accounts.

(4) *In sub-paragraph (3) above, references in relation to any item to the comparable amounts determined as there mentioned are references to—*

(a) *the aggregate amount which would be required to be shown in respect of that item if the amounts to be included in respect of all the assets covered by that item were determined according to the historical cost accounting rules; and*

(b) *the aggregate amount of the cumulative provisions for depreciation or diminution in value which would be permitted or required in determining those amounts according to those rules.*

Revaluation reserve

34.—(1) With respect to any determination of the value of an asset of a company on any basis mentioned in paragraph 31, the amount of any profit or loss arising from that determination (after allowing, where appropriate, for any provisions for depreciation or diminution in value made otherwise than by reference to the value so determined and any adjustments of any such provisions made in the light of that determination) shall be credited or (as the case may be) debited to a separate reserve ("the revaluation reserve").

(2) *The amount of the revaluation reserve shall be shown in the company's balance sheet under a separate sub-heading in the position given for the item "revaluation reserve" in Format 1 or 2 of the balance sheet formats set out in Part I of this Schedule, but need not be shown under that name.*

[(3) *An amount may be transferred—*

[(a) *from the revaluation reserve—*

(i) *to the profit and loss account, if the amount was previously charged to that account or represents realised profit, or*

(ii) *on capitalisation,*

(*b*) *to or from the revaluation reserve in respect of the taxation relating to any profit or loss credited or debited to the reserve;]*

and the revaluation reserve shall be reduced to the extent that the amounts transferred to it are no longer necessary for the purposes of the valuation method used.

(3A) In [sub-paragraph (3)(a)(ii)] "capitalisation", in relation to an amount standing to the credit of the revaluation reserve, means applying it in wholly or partly paying up unissued shares in the company to be allotted to members of the company as fully or partly paid shares.

(3B) The revaluation reserve shall not be reduced except as mentioned in this paragraph.]

(4) The treatment for taxation purposes of amounts credited or debited to the revaluation reserve shall be disclosed in a note to the accounts.

[SECTION D
FAIR VALUE ACCOUNTING

Inclusion of financial instruments at fair value

34A.—(1) Subject to sub-paragraphs (2) to (4), financial instruments (including derivatives) may be included at fair value.

(2) Sub-paragraph (1) does not apply to financial instruments which constitute liabilities unless—

(a) they are held as part of a trading portfolio, or
(b) they are derivatives.

(3) Sub-paragraph (1) does not apply to—

(a) financial instruments (other than derivatives) held to maturity;
(b) loans and receivables originated by the company and not held for trading purposes;
(c) interests in subsidiary undertakings, associated undertakings and joint ventures;
(d) equity instruments issued by the company;
(e) contracts for contingent consideration in a business combination;
(f) other financial instruments with such special characteristics that the instruments, according to generally accepted accounting principles or practice, should be accounted for differently from other financial instruments.

(4) If the fair value of a financial instrument cannot be determined reliably in accordance with paragraph 34B, sub-paragraph (1) does not apply to that financial instrument.

(5) In this paragraph—

"associated undertaking" has the meaning given by paragraph 20 of Schedule 4A; and "joint venture" has the meaning given by paragraph 19 of that Schedule.

Determination of fair value

34B.—(1) The fair value of a financial instrument is determined in accordance with this paragraph.

(2) If a reliable market can readily be identified for the financial instrument, its fair value is determined by reference to its market value.

(3) If a reliable market cannot readily be identified for the financial instrument but can be identified for its components or for a similar instrument, its fair value is determined by reference to the market value of its components or of the similar instrument.

(4) If neither sub-paragraph (2) nor (3) applies, the fair value of the financial instrument is a value resulting from generally accepted valuation models and techniques.

(5) Any valuation models and techniques used for the purposes of sub-paragraph (4) must ensure a reasonable approximation of the market value.

Inclusion of hedged items at fair value

34C. A company may include any assets and liabilities that qualify as hedged items under a fair value hedge accounting system, or identified portions of such assets or liabilities, at the amount required under that system.

Other assets that may be included at fair value

34D.—(1) This paragraph applies to—

(a) investment property, and

(b) living animals and plants,

that, under international accounting standards, may be included in accounts at fair value.

(2) Such investment property and such living animals and plants may be included at fair value, provided that all such investment property or, as the case may be, all such living animals and plants are so included where their fair value can reliably be determined.

(3) In this paragraph, "fair value" means fair value determined in accordance with relevant international accounting standards.

Accounting for changes in value

34E.—(1) This paragraph applies where a financial instrument is valued in accordance with paragraph 34A or 34C or an asset is valued in accordance with paragraph 34D.

(2) Notwithstanding paragraph 12 of this Schedule, and subject to sub-paragraphs (3) and (4) below, a change in the value of the financial instrument or of the investment property or living animal or plant must be included in the profit and loss account.

(3) Where—

(a) the financial instrument accounted for is a hedging instrument under a hedge accounting system that allows some or all of the change in value not to be shown in the profit and loss account, or

(b) the change in value relates to an exchange difference arising on a monetary item that forms part of a company's net investment in a foreign entity,

the amount of the change in value must be credited to or (as the case may be) debited from a separate reserve ("the fair value reserve").

(4) Where the instrument accounted for—

(a) is an available for sale financial asset, and

(b) is not a derivative,

the change in value may be credited to or (as the case may be) debited from the fair value reserve.

The fair value reserve

34F.—(1) The fair value reserve must be adjusted to the extent that the amounts shown in it are no longer necessary for the purposes of paragraph 34E(3) or (4).

(2) The treatment for taxation purposes of amounts credited or debited to the fair value reserve must be disclosed in a note to the accounts.]

[638]

NOTES

Repealed by the Companies Act 2006, s 1295, Sch 16, as from a day to be appointed.

Para 11: substituted by CA 1989, s 4(2), Sch 1, para 5, as from 1 April 1990.

Para 12: words omitted repealed by the Companies Act 1985 (International Accounting Standards and Other Accounting Amendments) Regulations 2004, SI 2004/2947, reg 14(1), Sch 2, paras 1, 5, as from 12 November 2004, in relation to companies' financial years which begin on or after 1 January 2005; words in square brackets in sub-para (b) substituted by CA 1989, s 23, Sch 10, para 20, as from 1 April 1990.

Para 16: words in square brackets substituted by SI 2004/2947, reg 14(1), Sch 2, paras 1, 6(1), (2), as from 12 November 2004, in relation to companies' financial years which begin on or after 1 January 2005.

Para 34: sub-paras (3), (3A), (3B) substituted, for original sub-para (3), by CA 1989, s 4(2), Sch 1, para 6, as from 1 April 1990; words in square brackets in sub-paras (3), (3A) substituted by the Companies Act 1985 (Miscellaneous Accounting Amendments) Regulations 1996, SI 1996/189, regs 14(1), 16(1), Sch 1, paras 1, 4, in relation to any financial year ending on or after 2 February 1996 (subject to transitional provisions in relation to financial years ending on or before 24 March 1996).

Paras 34A–34F: added by SI 2004/2947, reg 14(1), Sch 2, paras 1, 6(1), (3), as from 12 November 2004, in relation to companies' financial years which begin on or after 1 January 2005.

Application to limited liability partnerships: see the Limited Liability Partnerships Regulations 2001, SI 2001/1090, reg 3, Sch 1 at **[6984]**, **[6992]**.

PART III
NOTES TO THE ACCOUNTS

Preliminary

35. Any information required in the case of any company by the following provisions of this Part of this Schedule shall (if not given in the company's accounts) be given by way of a note to those accounts.

[Reserves and dividends

35A. There must be stated—

(a) any amount set aside or proposed to be set aside to, or withdrawn or proposed to be withdrawn from, reserves,

(b) the aggregate amount of dividends paid in the financial year (other than those for which a liability existed at the immediately preceding balance sheet date),

(c) the aggregate amount of dividends that the company is liable to pay at the balance sheet date, and

(d) the aggregate amount of dividends that are proposed before the date of approval of the accounts, and not otherwise disclosed under paragraph (b) or (c).]

Disclosure of accounting policies

36. The accounting policies adopted by the company in determining the amounts to be included in respect of items shown in the balance sheet and in determining the profit or loss of the company shall be stated (including such policies with respect to the depreciation and diminution in value of assets).

[36A. It shall be stated whether the accounts have been prepared in accordance with applicable accounting standards and particulars of any material departure from those standards and the reasons for it shall be given.]

Information supplementing the balance sheet

37. Paragraphs 38 to 51 require information which either supplements the information given with respect to any particular items shown in the balance sheet or is otherwise relevant to assessing the company's state of affairs in the light of the information so given.

Share capital and debentures

38.—(1) The following information shall be given with respect to the company's share capital—

(a) the authorised share capital; …

(b) where shares of more than one class have been allotted, the number and aggregate nominal value of shares of each class allotted[; and

(c) where shares are held as treasury shares, the number and aggregate nominal value of the treasury shares and, where shares of more than one class have been allotted, the number and aggregate nominal value of the shares of each class held as treasury shares.]

(2) In the case of any part of the allotted share capital that consists of redeemable shares, the following information shall be given—

(a) the earliest and latest dates on which the company has power to redeem those shares;

(b) whether those shares must be redeemed in any event or are liable to be redeemed at the option of the company or of the shareholder; and

(c) whether any (and, if so, what) premium is payable on redemption.

39. If the company has allotted any shares during the financial year, the following information shall be given—

(a) …

(b) the classes of shares allotted; and

(c) as respects each class of shares, the number allotted, their aggregate nominal value, and the consideration received by the company for the allotment.

40.—(1) With respect to any contingent right to the allotment of shares in the company the following particulars shall be given—

(*a*) *the number, description and amount of the shares in relation to which the right is exercisable;*
(*b*) *the period during which it is exercisable; and*
(*c*) *the price to be paid for the shares allotted.*

(2) In sub-paragraph (1) above "contingent right to the allotment of shares" means any option to subscribe for shares and any other right to require the allotment of shares to any person whether arising on the conversion into shares of securities of any other description or otherwise.

41.—(1) If the company has issued any debentures during the financial year to which the accounts relate, the following information shall be given—

(*a*) …
(*b*) *the classes of debentures issued; and*
(*c*) *as respects each class of debentures, the amount issued and the consideration received by the company for the issue.*

(2) …

(3) Where any of the company's debentures are held by a nominee of or trustee for the company, the nominal amount of the debentures and the amount at which they are stated in the accounting records kept by the company in accordance with section 221 of this Act shall be stated.

Fixed assets

42.—(1) In respect of each item which is or would but for paragraph 3(4)(b) be shown under the general item "fixed assets" in the company's balance sheet the following information shall be given—

(*a*) *the appropriate amounts in respect of that item as at the date of the beginning of the financial year and as at the balance sheet date respectively;*
(*b*) *the effect on any amount shown in the balance sheet in respect of that item of—*
  (*i*) *any revision of the amount in respect of any assets included under that item made during that year on any basis mentioned in paragraph 31;*
  (*ii*) *acquisitions during that year of any assets;*
  (*iii*) *disposals during that year of any assets; and*
  (*iv*) *any transfers of assets of the company to and from that item during that year.*

(2) The reference in sub-paragraph (1)(a) to the appropriate amounts in respect of any item as at any date there mentioned is a reference to amounts representing the aggregate amounts determined, as at that date, in respect of assets falling to be included under that item on either of the following bases, that is to say—

(*a*) *on the basis of purchase price or production cost (determined in accordance with paragraphs 26 and 27); or*
(*b*) *on any basis mentioned in paragraph 31,*

(leaving out of account in either case any provisions for depreciation or diminution in value).

(3) In respect of each item within sub-paragraph (1)—

(*a*) *the cumulative amount of provisions for depreciation or diminution in value of assets included under that item as at each date mentioned in sub-paragraph (1)(a);*
(*b*) *the amount of any such provisions made in respect of the financial year;*
(*c*) *the amount of any adjustments made in respect of any such provisions during that year in consequence of the disposal of any assets; and*
(*d*) *the amount of any other adjustments made in respect of any such provisions during that year;*

shall also be stated.

43. Where any fixed assets of the company (other than listed investments) are included under any item shown in the company's balance sheet at an amount determined on any basis mentioned in paragraph 31, the following information shall be given—

(*a*) *the years (so far as they are known to the directors) in which the assets were severally valued and the several values; and* (*b*) *in the case of assets that have been valued during the financial year, the names of the persons who valued them or particulars of their qualifications for doing so and (whichever is stated) the bases of valuation used by them.*

44. In relation to any amount which is or would but for paragraph 3(4)(b) be shown in respect of the item "land and buildings" in the company's balance sheet there shall be stated—

(*a*) *how much of that amount is ascribable to land of freehold tenure and how much to land of leasehold tenure; and*

(*b*) *how much of the amount ascribable to land of leasehold tenure is ascribable to land held on long lease and how much to land held on short lease.*

Investments

45.—(1) In respect of the amount of each item which is or would but for paragraph 3(4)(b) be shown in the company's balance sheet under the general item "investments" (whether as fixed assets or as current assets) there shall be stated—

(*a*) *how much of that amount is ascribable to listed investments; …*

(*b*) …

(2) *Where the amount of any listed investments is stated for any item in accordance with sub-paragraph (1)(a), the following amounts shall also be stated—*

(*a*) *the aggregate market value of those investments where it differs from the amount so stated; and*

(*b*) *both the market value and the stock exchange value of any investments of which the former value is, for the purposes of the accounts, taken as being higher than the latter.*

[Information about fair value of assets and liabilities

45A.—(1) This paragraph applies where financial instruments have been valued in accordance with paragraph 34A or 34C

(2) *There must be stated—*

(*a*) *where the fair value of the instruments has been determined in accordance with paragraph 34B(4), the significant assumptions underlying the valuation models and techniques used,*

(*b*) *for each category of financial instrument, the fair value of the instruments in that category and the changes in value—*

(*i*) *included in the profit and loss account, or*

(*ii*) *credited to or (as the case may be) debited from the fair value reserve,*

in respect of those instruments, and

(*c*) *for each class of derivatives, the extent and nature of the instruments, including significant terms and conditions that may affect the amount, timing and certainty of future cash flows.*

(3) *Where any amount is transferred to or from the fair value reserve during the financial year, there must be stated in tabular form—*

(*a*) *the amount of the reserve as at the date of the beginning of the financial year and as at the balance sheet date respectively;*

(*b*) *the amount transferred to or from the reserve during that year; and*

(*c*) *the source and application respectively of the amounts so transferred.*

45B. Where the company has derivatives that it has not included at fair value, there must be stated for each class of such derivatives—

(*a*) *the fair value of the derivatives in that class, if such a value can be determined in accordance with paragraph 34B, and*

(*b*) *the extent and nature of the derivatives.*

45C.—(1) Sub-paragraph (2) applies if—

(*a*) *the company has financial fixed assets that could be included at fair value by virtue of paragraph 34A,*

(*b*) *the amount at which those assets are included under any item in the company's accounts is in excess of their fair value, and* (*c*) *the company has not made provision for diminution in value of those assets in accordance with paragraph 19(1) of this Schedule.*

(2) *There must be stated—*

(*a*) *the amount at which either the individual assets or appropriate groupings of those individual assets are included in the company's accounts,*

(*b*) *the fair value of those assets or groupings, and*

(*c*) *the reasons for not making a provision for diminution in value of those assets, including the nature of the evidence that provides the basis for the belief that the amount at which they are stated in the accounts will be recovered.*

Information where investment property and living animals and plants included at fair value

45D.—(1) This paragraph applies where the amounts to be included in a company's accounts in respect of investment property or living animals and plants have been determined in accordance with paragraph 34D.

(2) *The balance sheet items affected and the basis of valuation adopted in determining the amounts of the assets in question in the case of each such item must be disclosed in a note to the accounts.*

(3) *In the case of investment property, for each balance sheet item affected there must be shown, either separately in the balance sheet or in a note to the accounts—*

(*a*) *the comparable amounts determined according to the historical cost accounting rules; or*

(*b*) *the differences between those amounts and the corresponding amounts actually shown in the balance sheet in respect of that item.*

(4) *In sub-paragraph (3) above, references in relation to any item to the comparable amounts determined in accordance with that sub-paragraph are references to—*

(*a*) *the aggregate amount which would be required to be shown in respect of that item if the amounts to be included in respect of all the assets covered by that item were determined according to the historical cost accounting rules; and*

(*b*) *the aggregate amount of the cumulative provisions for depreciation or diminution in value which would be permitted or required in determining those amounts according to those rules.]*

Reserves and provisions

46.—(1) Where any amount is transferred—

(*a*) *to or from any reserves; or*

(*b*) *to any [provisions for liabilities]; or*

(*c*) *from any [provision for liabilities] otherwise than for the purpose for which the provision was established;*

and the reserves or provisions are or would but for paragraph 3(4)(b) be shown as separate items in the company's balance sheet, the information mentioned in the following sub-paragraph shall be given in respect of the aggregate of reserves or provisions included in the same item.

(2) *That information is—*

(*a*) *the amount of the reserves or provisions as at the date of the beginning of the financial year and as at the balance sheet date respectively;*

(*b*) *any amounts transferred to or from the reserves or provisions during that year; and*

(*c*) *the source and application respectively of any amounts so transferred.*

(3) *Particulars shall be given of each provision included in the item "other provisions" in the company's balance sheet in any case where the amount of that provision is material.*

Provision for taxation

[47. The amount of any provision for deferred taxation shall be stated separately from the amount of any provision for other taxation.]

Details of indebtedness

48.—[(1) In respect of each item shown under "creditors" in the company's balance sheet there shall be stated the aggregate of the following amounts, that is to say—

- *(a) the amount of any debts included under that item which are payable or repayable otherwise than by instalments and fall due for payment or repayment after the end of the period of five years beginning with the day next following the end of the financial year; and*
- *[(b) in the case of any debts so included which are payable or repayable by instalments, the amount of any instalments which fall due for payment after the end of that period.]]*

(2) Subject to sub-paragraph (3), in relation to each debt falling to be taken into account under sub-paragraph (1), the terms of payment or repayment and the rate of any interest payable on the debt shall be stated.

(3) If the number of debts is such that, in the opinion of the directors, compliance with sub-paragraph (2) would result in a statement of excessive length, it shall be sufficient to give a general indication of the terms of payment or repayment and the rates of any interest payable on the debts.

(4) In respect of each item shown under "creditors" in the company's balance sheet there shall be stated—

- *(a) the aggregate amount of any debts included under that item in respect of which any security has been given by the company; and*
- *(b) an indication of the nature of the securities so given.*

(5) References above in this paragraph to an item shown under "creditors" in the company's balance sheet include references, where amounts falling due to creditors within one year and after more than one year are distinguished in the balance sheet—

- *(a) in a case within sub-paragraph (1), to an item shown under the latter of those categories; and*
- *(b) in a case within sub-paragraph (4), to an item shown under either of those categories;*

and references to items shown under "creditors" include references to items which would but for paragraph 3(4)(b) be shown under that heading.

49. If any fixed cumulative dividends on the company's shares are in arrear, there shall be stated—

- *(a) the amount of the arrears; and*
- *(b) the period for which the dividends or, if there is more than one class, each class of them are in arrear.*

Guarantees and other financial commitments

50.—(1) Particulars shall be given of any charge on the assets of the company to secure the liabilities of any other person, including, where practicable, the amount secured.

(2) The following information shall be given with respect to any other contingent liability not provided for—

- *(a) the amount or estimated amount of that liability;*
- *(b) its legal nature; and*
- *(c) whether any valuable security has been provided by the company in connection with that liability and if so, what.*

(3) There shall be stated, where practicable—

- *(a) the aggregate amount or estimated amount of contracts for capital expenditure, so far as not provided for; ...*
- *(b) ...*

(4) Particulars shall be given of—

- *(a) any pension commitments included under any provision shown in the company's balance sheet; and*
- *(b) any such commitments for which no provision has been made;*

and where any such commitment relates wholly or partly to pensions payable to past directors of the company separate particulars shall be given of that commitment so far as it relates to such pensions.

(5) Particulars shall also be given of any other financial commitments which—

(a) have not been provided for; and

(b) are relevant to assessing the company's state of affairs.

(6) …

Miscellaneous matters

51.—(1) Particulars shall be given of any case where the purchase price or production cost of any asset is for the first time determined under paragraph 28.

(2) Where any outstanding loans made under the authority of section 153(4)(b)[, (bb)] or (c) or section 155 of this Act (various cases of financial assistance by a company for purchase of its own shares) are included under any item shown in the company's balance sheet, the aggregate amount of those loans shall be disclosed for each item in question.

(3) …

Information supplementing the profit and loss account

52. Paragraphs 53 to 57 require information which either supplements the information given with respect to any particular items shown in the profit and loss account or otherwise provides particulars of income or expenditure of the company or of circumstances affecting the items shown in the profit and loss account.

Separate statement of certain items of income and expenditure

53.—(1) Subject to the following provisions of this paragraph, each of the amounts mentioned below shall be stated.

(2) The amount of the interest on or any similar charges in respect of—

(a) bank loans and overdrafts, … ; and

(b) loans of any other kind made to the company.

This sub-paragraph does not apply to interest or charges on loans to the company from [group undertakings], but, with that exception, it applies to interest or charges on all loans, whether made on the security of debentures or not.

(3)–(7) …

Particulars of tax

54.—(1) …

(2) Particulars shall be given of any special circumstances which affect liability in respect of taxation of profits, income or capital gains for the financial year or liability in respect of taxation of profits, income or capital gains for succeeding financial years.

(3) The following amounts shall be stated—

(a) the amount of the charge for United Kingdom corporation tax;

(b) if that amount would have been greater but for relief from double taxation, the amount which it would have been but for such relief;

(c) the amount of the charge for United Kingdom income tax; and

(d) the amount of the charge for taxation imposed outside the United Kingdom of profits, income and (so far as charged to revenue) capital gains.

These amounts shall be stated separately in respect of each of the amounts which is or would but for paragraph 3(4)(b) be shown under the following items in the profit and loss account, that is to say "tax on profit or loss on ordinary activities" and "tax on extraordinary profit or loss".

Particulars of turnover

55.—(1) If in the course of the financial year the company has carried on business of two or more classes that, in the opinion of the directors, differ substantially from each other, there shall be stated in respect of each class (describing it)—

(*a*) *the amount of the turnover attributable to that class; …*

(*b*) …

(2) *If in the course of the financial year the company has supplied markets that, in the opinion of the directors, differ substantially from each other, the amount of the turnover attributable to each such market shall also be stated.*

In this paragraph "market" means a market delimited by geographical bounds.

(3) *In analysing for the purposes of this paragraph the source (in terms of business or in terms of market) of turnover … , the directors of the company shall have regard to the manner in which the company's activities are organised.*

(4) *For the purposes of this paragraph—*

(*a*) *classes of business which, in the opinion of the directors, do not differ substantially from each other shall be treated as one class; and*

(*b*) *markets which, in the opinion of the directors, do not differ substantially from each other shall be treated as one market;*

and any amounts properly attributable to one class of business or (as the case may be) to one market which are not material may be included in the amount stated in respect of another.

(5) *Where in the opinion of the directors the disclosure of any information required by this paragraph would be seriously prejudicial to the interests of the company, that information need not be disclosed, but the fact that any such information has not been disclosed must be stated.*

56. …

Miscellaneous matters

57.—(1) Where any amount relating to any preceding financial year is included in any item in the profit and loss account, the effect shall be stated.

(2) *Particulars shall be given of any extraordinary income or charges arising in the financial year.*

(3) *The effect shall be stated of any transactions that are exceptional by virtue of size or incidence though they fall within the ordinary activities of the company.*

General

58.—(1) Where sums originally denominated in foreign currencies have been brought into account under any items shown in the balance sheet or profit and loss account, the basis on which those sums have been translated into sterling shall be stated.

(2), (3) …

[Dormant Companies Acting as Agents

58A. Where the directors of a company take advantage of the exemption conferred by section 249AA, and the company has during the financial year in question acted as an agent for any person, the fact that it has so acted must be stated.]

[639]

NOTES

Repealed by the Companies Act 2006, s 1295, Sch 16, as from a day to be appointed.

Para 35A: inserted by the Companies Act 1985 (International Accounting Standards and Other Accounting Amendments) Regulations 2004, SI 2004/2947, reg 14(1), Sch 2, paras 1, 7(1), (2), as from 12 November 2004, in relation to companies' financial years which begin on or after 1 January 2005.

Para 36A: inserted by CA 1989, s 4(2), Sch 1, para 7, as from 1 April 1990.

Para 38: word omitted repealed, and sub-para (1)(c) and the word immediately preceding it added, by the Companies (Acquisition of Own Shares) (Treasury Shares) Regulations 2003, SI 2003/1116, reg 4, Schedule, para 30, as from 1 December 2003.

Para 39: sub-para (a) repealed by the Companies Act 1985 (Miscellaneous Accounting Amendments) Regulations 1996, SI 1996/189, regs 14(1), 16(1), Sch 1, paras 1, 5, in relation to any financial year ending on or after 2 February 1996 (subject to transitional provisions in relation to financial years ending on or before 24 March 1996).

Para 41: sub-paras (1)(a), (2) repealed by SI 1996/189, regs 14(1), 16(1), Sch 1, paras 1, 6, in relation to any financial year ending on or after 2 February 1996 (subject to transitional provisions as noted above).

Para 45: sub-para (1)(b) and the word immediately preceding it repealed by SI 1996/189, regs 14(1), 16(1), Sch 1, paras 1, 7, in relation to any financial year ending on or after 2 February 1996 (subject to transitional provisions as noted above).

Paras 45A–45D: inserted by SI 2004/2947, reg 14(1), Sch 2, paras 1, 7(1), (3), as from 12 November 2004, in relation to companies' financial years which begin on or after 1 January 2005.

Para 46: words in square brackets in sub-para (1)(b), (c) substituted by SI 2004/2947, reg 14(1), Sch 2, paras 1, 8, as from 12 November 2004, in relation to companies' financial years which begin on or after 1 January 2005.

Para 47: substituted by CA 1989, s 4(2), Sch 1, para 8, as from 1 April 1990.

Para 48: sub-para (1) substituted by SI 1996/189, regs 14(1), 16(1), Sch 1, paras 1, 8, in relation to any financial year ending on or after 2 February 1996 (subject to transitional provisions as noted above); sub-para (1)(b) further substituted, in relation to annual accounts approved by the board of directors on or after 1 March 1997, and to directors' and auditors' reports on such accounts, by the Companies Act 1985 (Accounts of Small and Medium-sized Companies and Minor Accounting Amendments) Regulations 1997, SI 1997/220, reg 7(9) (subject to transitional provisions in relation to a financial year of a company ending on or before 24 March 1997).

Para 50: sub-para (3)(b) and the word immediately preceding it repealed by SI 1996/189, regs 14(1), 16(1), Sch 1, paras 1, 9, in relation to any financial year ending on or after 2 February 1996 (subject to transitional provisions as noted above); sub-para (6) repealed by CA 1989, s 212, Sch 24, as from 1 April 1990.

Para 51: words in square brackets in sub-para (2) inserted by CA 1989, s 4(2), Sch 1, para 9, as from 1 April 1990; sub-para (3) repealed by SI 1996/189, regs 14(1), 16(1), Sch 1, paras 1, 10, in relation to any financial year ending on or after 2 February 1996 (subject to transitional provisions as noted above).

Para 53: words omitted from sub-para (2), and the whole of sub-paras (3)–(6), repealed by SI 1996/189, regs 14(1), 16(1), Sch 1, paras 1, 11, in relation to any financial year ending on or after 2 February 1996 (subject to transitional provisions as noted above); words in square brackets in sub-para (2) substituted, and sub-para (7) repealed, by CA 1989, ss 4(2), 212, Sch 1, para 2, Sch 24, as from 1 April 1990.

Para 54: sub-para (1) repealed by SI 1996/189, regs 14(1), 16(1), Sch 1, paras 1, 12, in relation to any financial year ending on or after 2 February 1996 (subject to transitional provisions as noted above).

Para 55: sub-para (1)(b), the word immediately preceding it, and the words omitted from sub-para (3), repealed by SI 1996/189, regs 14(1), 16(1), Sch 1, paras 1, 13, in relation to any financial year ending on or after 2 February 1996 (subject to transitional provisions as noted above).

Para 56: repealed by SI 2004/2947, reg 3, Sch 1, paras 1, 31(1), (2), as from 12 November 2004, in relation to companies' financial years which begin on or after 1 January 2005.

Para 58: sub-paras (2), (3) repealed by the Companies Act 1985 (Investment Companies and Accounting and Audit Amendments) Regulations 2005, SI 2005/2280, reg 4, as from 1 October 2005, in relation to companies' financial years which begin on or after 1 January 2005 and which end on or after 1 October 2005.

Para 58A: added by the Companies Act 1985 (Audit Exemption) (Amendment) Regulations 2000, SI 2000/1430, reg 5, as from 26 May 2000, in relation to annual reports and reports in respect of financial years ending two months or more after that date.

Application to limited liability partnerships: see the Limited Liability Partnerships Regulations 2001, SI 2001/1090, reg 3, Sch 1 at **[6984]**, **[6992]**.

[PART IV
SPECIAL PROVISIONS WHERE COMPANY IS A PARENT COMPANY OR SUBSIDIARY UNDERTAKING]

Company's own accounts

59. …

[Guarantees and other financial commitments in favour of group undertakings

59A. Commitments within any of sub-paragraphs (1) to (5) of paragraph 50 (guarantees and other financial commitments) which are undertaken on behalf of or for the benefit of—

(a) any parent undertaking or fellow subsidiary undertaking, or

(b) any subsidiary undertaking of the company,

shall be stated separately from the other commitments within that sub-paragraph, and commitments within paragraph (a) shall also be stated separately from those within paragraph (b).]

60.–70. …

[640]

NOTES

Repealed by the Companies Act 2006, s 1295, Sch 16, as from a day to be appointed.

Para 59: substituted as noted below and subsequently repealed by the Companies Act 1985 (Miscellaneous Accounting Amendments) Regulations 1996, SI 1996/189, regs 14(1), 16(1), Sch 1, paras 1, 15, in relation to any financial year ending on or after 2 February 1996 (subject to transitional provisions in relation to financial years ending on or before 24 March 1996).

Para 59A: substituted (together with para 59, the preceding heading and the heading to this Part of the Schedule) by CA 1989, s 4(2), Sch 1, para 11, as from 1 April 1990.

Paras 60–70: repealed by CA 1989, s 212, Sch 24, as from 1 April 1990.

Application to limited liability partnerships: see the Limited Liability Partnerships Regulations 2001, SI 2001/1090, reg 3, Sch 1 at **[6984]**, **[6992]**.

PART V
SPECIAL PROVISIONS WHERE THE COMPANY IS AN INVESTMENT COMPANY

71.—(1) Paragraph 34 does not apply to the amount of any profit or loss arising from a determination of the value of any investments of an investment company on any basis mentioned in paragraph 31(3).

(2) Any provisions made by virtue of paragraph 19(1) or (2) in the case of an investment company in respect of any fixed asset investments need not be charged to the company's profit and loss account provided they are either—

- *(a) charged against any reserve account to which any amount excluded by sub-paragraph (1) from the requirements of paragraph 34 has been credited; or*
- *(b) shown as a separate item in the company's balance sheet under the sub-heading "other reserves".*

(3) For the purposes of this paragraph, as it applies in relation to any company, "fixed asset investment" means any asset falling to be included under any item shown in the company's balance sheet under the subdivision "investments" under the general item "fixed assets".

72.—(1) Any distribution made by an investment company which reduces the amount of its net assets to less than the aggregate of its called-up share capital and undistributable reserves shall be disclosed in a note to the company's accounts.

(2) For purposes of this paragraph, a company's net assets are the aggregate of its assets less the aggregate of its liabilities (including any [provision for liabilities] within paragraph 89 [that is made in Companies Act accounts and any provision that is made in IAS accounts]); and "undistributable reserves" has the meaning given by section 264(3) of this Act.

73. A company shall be treated as an investment company for the purposes of this Part of this Schedule in relation to any financial year of the company if—

- *(a) during the whole of that year it was an investment company as defined by section 266 of this Act, and*
- *(b) it was not at any time during that year prohibited under section 265(4) of this Act (no distribution where capital profits have been distributed, etc) from making a distribution by virtue of that section.*

74. ...

[641]

NOTES

Repealed by the Companies Act 2006, s 1295, Sch 16, as from a day to be appointed.

Para 72: words in first pair of square brackets in sub-para (2) substituted, and words in second pair of square brackets in sub-para (2) inserted, by the Companies Act 1985 (International Accounting Standards and Other Accounting Amendments) Regulations 2004, SI 2004/2947, regs 3, 14(1), Sch 1, paras 1, 31(1), (3), Sch 2, paras 1, 9, as from 12 November 2004, in relation to companies' financial years which begin on or after 1 January 2005.

Para 74: repealed by CA 1989, s 212, Sch 24, as from 1 April 1990.

Application to limited liability partnerships: see the Limited Liability Partnerships Regulations 2001, SI 2001/1090, reg 3, Sch 1 at **[6984]**, **[6992]**.

(Pt VI (para 75) repealed by CA 1989, s 212, Sch 24, as from 1 April 1990.)

PART VII
INTERPRETATION OF SCHEDULE

76. The following paragraphs apply for the purposes of this Schedule and its interpretation.

[Financial instruments

76A. References to "derivatives" include commodity-based contracts that give either contracting party the right to settle in cash or in some other financial instrument, except when such contracts—

- *(a) were entered into for the purpose of, and continue to meet, the company's expected purchase, sale or usage requirements,*
- *(b) were designated for such purpose at their inception, and*
- *(c) are expected to be settled by delivery of the commodity.*

76B.—(1) The expressions listed in sub-paragraph (2) have the same meaning as they have in Council Directive 78/660/EEC on the annual accounts of certain types of companies, as amended.

(2) Those expressions are "available for sale financial asset", "business combination", "commodity-based contracts", "derivative", "equity instrument", "exchange difference", "fair value hedge accounting system", "financial fixed asset", "financial instrument", "foreign entity", "hedge accounting", "hedge accounting system", "hedged items", "hedging instrument", "held for trading purposes", "held to maturity", "monetary item", "receivables", "reliable market" and "trading portfolio".]

Historical cost accounting rules

77.–81. …

82. References to the historical cost accounting rules shall be read in accordance with paragraph 29.

[Investment property

82A "Investment property" means land held to earn rent or for capital appreciation.]

Leases

83.—(1) "Long lease" means a lease in the case of which the portion of the term for which it was granted remaining unexpired at the end of the financial year is not less than 50 years.

(2) "Short lease" means a lease which is not a long lease.

(3) "Lease" includes an agreement for a lease.

Listed investments

[84. "Listed investment" means an investment as respects which there has been granted a listing [on a recognised investment exchange other than an overseas investment exchange within the meaning of the Financial Services Act 1986 or on any stock exchange of repute outside Great Britain].

Loans

85. A loan is treated as falling due for repayment, and an instalment of a loan is treated as falling due for payment, on the earliest date on which the lender could require repayment or (as the case may be) payment, if he exercised all options and rights available to him.

Materiality

86. Amounts which in the particular context of any provision of this Schedule are not material may be disregarded for the purposes of that provision.

87. ...

Provisions

88.—(1) References to provisions for depreciation or diminution in value of assets are to any amount written off by way of providing for depreciation or diminution in value of assets.

(2) Any reference in the profit and loss account formats set out in Part I of this Schedule to the depreciation of, or amounts written off, assets of any description is to any provision for depreciation or diminution in value of assets of that description.

89. References to [provisions for liabilities] are to any amount retained as reasonably necessary for the purpose of providing for any liability [the nature of which is clearly defined and] which is either likely to be incurred, or certain to be incurred but uncertain as to amount or as to the date on which it will arise.

90.–92. ...

Scots land tenure

93. In the application of this Schedule to Scotland, "land of freehold tenure" means land in respect of which the company ... is the owner; "land of leasehold tenure" means land of which the company is the tenant under a lease ...

Staff costs

94.—(1) "Social security costs" means any contributions by the company to any state social security or pension scheme, fund or arrangement.

[(2) "Pension costs" includes any costs incurred by the company in respect of any pension scheme established for the purpose of providing pensions for persons currently or formerly employed by the company, any sums set aside for the future payment of pensions directly by the company to current or former employees and any pensions paid directly to such persons without having first been set aside.]

(3) Any amount stated in respect of [the item "social security costs"] or in respect of the item "wages and salaries" in the company's profit and loss account shall be determined by reference to payments made or costs incurred in respect of all persons employed by the company during the financial year who are taken into account in determining the relevant annual number for the purposes of [section 231A(1)(a)].

95. ...

[642]

NOTES

Repealed by the Companies Act 2006, s 1295, Sch 16, as from a day to be appointed.

Paras 76A, 76B, 82A: inserted by the Companies Act 1985 (International Accounting Standards and Other Accounting Amendments) Regulations 2004, SI 2004/2947, reg 14(1), Sch 2, paras 1, 10, 11, as from 12 November 2004, in relation to companies' financial years which begin on or after 1 January 2005.

Paras 77–81, 87, 90–92, 95: repealed by CA 1989, s 212, Sch 24, as from 1 April 1990.

Para 84: substituted by the Financial Services and Markets Act 2000 (Consequential Amendments and Repeals) Order 2001, SI 2001/3649, art 32, as from 1 December 2001.

Para 89: words in square brackets substituted by SI 2004/2947, reg 14(1), Sch 2, paras 1, 12, as from 12 November 2004, in relation to companies' financial years which begin on or after 1 January 2005.

Para 93: words omitted repealed by the Abolition of Feudal Tenure etc (Scotland) Act 2000, s 76(1), (2), Sch 12, Pt I, para 46(1), (5), Sch 13, Pt I, as from 28 November 2004.

Para 94: sub-para (2) and words in first pair of square brackets in sub-para (3) substituted by the Companies Act 1985 (Miscellaneous Accounting Amendments) Regulations 1996, SI 1996/189, regs 14(1), 16(1), Sch 1, paras 1, 16, in relation to any financial year ending on or after 2 February 1996 (subject to transitional provisions in relation to financial years ending on or before 24 March 1996); words in second pair of square brackets in sub-para (3) substituted by SI 2004/2947, reg 3, Sch 1, paras 1, 31(1), (4), as from 12 November 2004, in relation to companies' financial years which begin on or after 1 January 2005.

Application to limited liability partnerships: see the Limited Liability Partnerships Regulations 2001, SI 2001/1090, reg 3, Sch 1 at **[6984]**, **[6992]**.

[SCHEDULE 4A
FORM AND CONTENT OF GROUP ACCOUNTS

Section 227

General rules

1.—(1) Group accounts shall comply so far as practicable with the [provisions of … Schedule 4 (form and content of company accounts)] as if the undertakings included in the consolidation ("the group") were a single company.

(2) …

(3) Where the parent company is treated as an investment company for the purposes of Part V of that Schedule (special provisions for investment companies) the group shall be similarly treated.

2.—(1) The consolidated balance sheet and profit and loss account shall incorporate in full the information contained in the individual accounts of the undertakings included in the consolidation, subject to the adjustments authorised or required by the following provisions of this Schedule and to such other adjustments (if any) as may be appropriate in accordance with generally accepted accounting principles or practice.

(2) If the financial year of a subsidiary undertaking included in the consolidation [does not end with that of the parent company], the group accounts shall be made up—

- (*a*) *from the accounts of the subsidiary undertaking for its financial year last ending before the end of the parent company's financial year, provided that year ended no more than three months before that of the parent company, or*
- (*b*) *from interim accounts prepared by the subsidiary undertaking as at the end of the parent company's financial year.*

3.—(1) Where assets and liabilities to be included in the group accounts have been valued or otherwise determined by undertakings according to accounting rules differing from those used for the group accounts, the values or amounts shall be adjusted so as to accord with the rules used for the group accounts.

(2) If it appears to the directors of the parent company that there are special reasons for departing from sub-paragraph (1) they may do so, but particulars of any such departure, the reasons for it and its effect shall be given in a note to the accounts.

(3) The adjustments referred to in this paragraph need not be made if they are not material for the purpose of giving a true and fair view.

4. Any differences of accounting rules as between a parent company's individual accounts for a financial year and its group accounts shall be disclosed in a note to the latter accounts and the reasons for the difference given.

5. Amounts which in the particular context of any provision of this Schedule are not material may be disregarded for the purposes of that provision.

Elimination of group transactions

6.—(1) Debts and claims between undertakings included in the consolidation, and income and expenditure relating to transactions between such undertakings, shall be eliminated in preparing the group accounts.

(2) Where profits and losses resulting from transactions between undertakings included in the consolidation are included in the book value of assets, they shall be eliminated in preparing the group accounts.

(3) The elimination required by sub-paragraph (2) may be effected in proportion to the group's interest in the shares of the undertakings.

(4) Sub-paragraphs (1) and (2) need not be complied with if the amounts concerned are not material for the purpose of giving a true and fair view.

Acquisition and merger accounting

7.—(1) The following provisions apply where an undertaking becomes a subsidiary undertaking of the parent company.

(2) That event is referred to in those provisions as an "acquisition", and references to the "undertaking acquired" shall be construed accordingly.

8. An acquisition shall be accounted for by the acquisition method of accounting unless the conditions for accounting for it as a merger are met and the merger method of accounting is adopted.

9.—(1) The acquisition method of accounting is as follows.

(2) The identifiable assets and liabilities of the undertaking acquired shall be included in the consolidated balance sheet at their fair values as at the date of acquisition.

In this paragraph the "identifiable" assets or liabilities of the undertaking acquired means the assets or liabilities which are capable of being disposed of or discharged separately, without disposing of a business of the undertaking.

(3) The income and expenditure of the undertaking acquired shall be brought into the group accounts only as from the date of the acquisition.

(4) There shall be set off against the acquisition cost of the interest in the shares of the undertaking held by the parent company and its subsidiary undertakings the interest of the parent company and its subsidiary undertakings in the adjusted capital and reserves of the undertaking acquired.

For this purpose—

"the acquisition cost" means the amount of any cash consideration and the fair value of any other consideration, together with such amount (if any) in respect of fees and other expenses of the acquisition as the company may determine, and

"the adjusted capital and reserves" of the undertaking acquired means its capital and reserves at the date of the acquisition after adjusting the identifiable assets and liabilities of the undertaking to fair values as at that date.

(5) The resulting amount if positive shall be treated as goodwill, and if negative as a negative consolidation difference.

10.—(1) The conditions for accounting for an acquisition as a merger are—

- *(a) that at least 90 per cent of the nominal value of the relevant shares in the undertaking acquired [(excluding any shares in the undertaking held as treasury shares)] is held by or on behalf of the parent company and its subsidiary undertakings,*
- *(b) that the proportion referred to in paragraph (a) was attained pursuant to an arrangement providing for the issue of equity shares by the parent company or one or more of its subsidiary undertakings,*
- *(c) that the fair value of any consideration other than the issue of equity shares given pursuant to the arrangement by the parent company and its subsidiary undertakings did not exceed 10 per cent of the nominal value of the equity shares issued, and*
- *(d) that adoption of the merger method of accounting accords with generally accepted accounting principles or practice.*

(2) The reference in sub-paragraph (1)(a) to the "relevant shares" in an undertaking acquired is to those carrying unrestricted rights to participate both in distributions and in the assets of the undertaking upon liquidation.

11.—(1) The merger method of accounting is as follows.

(2) The assets and liabilities of the undertaking acquired shall be brought into the group accounts at the figures at which they stand in the undertaking's accounts, subject to any adjustment authorised or required by this Schedule.

(3) The income and expenditure of the undertaking acquired shall be included in the group accounts for the entire financial year, including the period before the acquisition.

(4) The group accounts shall show corresponding amounts relating to the previous financial year as if the undertaking acquired had been included in the consolidation throughout that year.

(5) There shall be set off against the aggregate of—

- *(a) the appropriate amount in respect of qualifying shares issued by the parent company or its subsidiary undertakings in consideration for the acquisition of shares in the undertaking acquired, and*
- *(b) the fair value of any other consideration for the acquisition of shares in the undertaking acquired, determined as at the date when those shares were acquired,*

the nominal value of the issued share capital of the undertaking acquired held by the parent company and its subsidiary undertakings.

(6) The resulting amount shall be shown as an adjustment to the consolidated reserves.

(7) In sub-paragraph (5)(a) "qualifying shares" means—

- *(a) shares in relation to which section 131 (merger relief) applies, in respect of which the appropriate amount is the nominal value; or*
- *(b) shares in relation to which section 132 (relief in respect of group reconstructions) applies, in respect of which the appropriate amount is the nominal value together with any minimum premium value within the meaning of that section.*

12.—(1) Where a group is acquired, paragraphs 9 to 11 apply with the following adaptations.

(2) References to shares of the undertaking acquired shall be construed as references to shares of the parent undertaking of the group.

(3) Other references to the undertaking acquired shall be construed as references to the group; and references to the assets and liabilities, income and expenditure and capital and reserves of the undertaking acquired shall be construed as references to the assets and liabilities, income and expenditure and capital and reserves of the group after making the set-offs and other adjustments required by this Schedule in the case of group accounts.

13.—(1) The following information with respect to acquisitions taking place in the financial year shall be given in a note to the accounts.

(2) There shall be stated—

- *(a) the name of the undertaking acquired or, where a group was acquired, the name of the parent undertaking of that group, and*
- *(b) whether the acquisition has been accounted for by the acquisition or the merger method of accounting;*

and in relation to an acquisition which significantly affects the figures shown in the group accounts, the following further information shall be given.

(3) The composition and fair value of the consideration for the acquisition given by the parent company and its subsidiary undertakings shall be stated.

(4) …

(5) Where the acquisition method of accounting has been adopted, the book values immediately prior to the acquisition, and the fair values at the date of acquisition, of each class of assets and liabilities of the undertaking or group acquired shall be stated in tabular form, including a statement of the amount of any goodwill or negative consolidation difference arising on the acquisition, together with an explanation of any significant adjustments made.

(6) Where the merger method of accounting has been adopted, an explanation shall be given of any significant adjustments made in relation to the amounts of the assets and liabilities of the undertaking or group acquired, together with a statement of any resulting adjustment to the consolidated reserves (including the re-statement of opening consolidated reserves).

(7) In ascertaining for the purposes of sub-paragraph … , (5) or (6) the profit or loss of a group, the book values and fair values of assets and liabilities of a group or the amount of the assets and liabilities of a group, the set-offs and other adjustments required by this Schedule in the case of group accounts shall be made.

14.—(1) There shall also be stated in a note to the accounts the cumulative amount of goodwill resulting from acquisitions in that and earlier financial years which has been written off [otherwise than in the consolidated profit and loss account for that or any earlier financial year].

(2) That figure shall be shown net of any goodwill attributable to subsidiary undertakings or businesses disposed of prior to the balance sheet date.

15. Where during the financial year there has been a disposal of an undertaking or group which significantly affects the figures shown in the group accounts, there shall be stated in a note to the accounts—

- *(a) the name of that undertaking or, as the case may be, of the parent undertaking of that group, and*
- *(b) the extent to which the profit or loss shown in the group accounts is attributable to profit or loss of that undertaking or group.*

16. The information required by paragraph 13, 14 or 15 above need not be disclosed with respect to an undertaking which—

- *(a) is established under the law of a country outside the United Kingdom, or*
- *(b) carries on business outside the United Kingdom,*

if in the opinion of the directors of the parent company the disclosure would be seriously prejudicial to the business of that undertaking or to the business of the parent company or any of its subsidiary undertakings and the Secretary of State agrees that the information should not be disclosed.

Minority interests

17.—(1) The formats set out in Schedule 4 have effect in relation to group accounts with the following additions.

(2) In the Balance Sheet Formats a further item headed "Minority interests" shall be added—

- *(a) in Format 1, either after item J or at the end (after item K), and*
- *(b) in Format 2, under the general heading "LIABILITIES", between items A and B;*

and under that item shall be shown the amount of capital and reserves attributable to shares in subsidiary undertakings included in the consolidation held by or on behalf of persons other than the parent company and its subsidiary undertakings.

(3) In the Profit and Loss Account Formats a further item headed "Minority interests" shall be added—

- *(a) in Format 1, between items 14 and 15,*
- *(b) in Format 2, between items 16 and 17,*
- *(c) in Format 3, between items 7 and 8 in both sections A and B, and*
- *(d) in Format 4, between items 9 and 10 in both sections A and B;*

and under that item shall be shown the amount of any profit or loss on ordinary activities attributable to shares in subsidiary undertakings included in the consolidation held by or on behalf of persons other than the parent company and its subsidiary undertakings.

(4) In the Profit and Loss Account Formats a further item headed "Minority interests" shall be added—

- *(a) in Format 1, between items 18 and 19,*
- *(b) in Format 2, between items 20 and 21,*
- *(c) in Format 3, between items 9 and 10 in section A and between items 8 and 9 in section B, and*
- *(d) in Format 4, between items 11 and 12 in section A and between items 10 and 11 in section B;*

and under that item shall be shown the amount of any profit or loss on extraordinary activities attributable to shares in subsidiary undertakings included in the consolidation held by or on behalf of persons other than the parent company and its subsidiary undertakings.

(5) *For the purposes of paragraph 3(3) and (4) of Schedule 4 (power to adapt or combine items)—*

(*a*) *the additional item required by sub-paragraph (2) above shall be treated as one to which a letter is assigned, and*

(*b*) *the additional items required by sub-paragraphs (3) and (4) above shall be treated as ones to which an Arabic number is assigned.*

18. ...

Joint ventures

19.—(1) Where an undertaking included in the consolidation manages another undertaking jointly with one or more undertakings not included in the consolidation, that other undertaking ("the joint venture") may, if it is not—

(*a*) *a body corporate, or*

(*b*) *a subsidiary undertaking of the parent company,*

be dealt with in the group accounts by the method of proportional consolidation.

(2) *The provisions of [this Schedule] relating to the preparation of consolidated accounts apply, with any necessary modifications, to proportional consolidation under this paragraph.*

Associated undertakings

20.—(1) An "associated undertaking" means an undertaking in which an undertaking included in the consolidation has a participating interest and over whose operating and financial policy it exercises a significant influence, and which is not—

(*a*) *a subsidiary undertaking of the parent company, or*

(*b*) *a joint venture dealt with in accordance with paragraph 19.*

(2) *Where an undertaking holds 20 per cent or more of the voting rights in another undertaking, it shall be presumed to exercise such an influence over it unless the contrary is shown.*

(3) *The voting rights in an undertaking means the rights conferred on shareholders in respect of their shares or, in the case of an undertaking not having a share capital, on members, to vote at general meetings of the undertaking on all, or substantially all, matters.*

(4) *The provisions of paragraphs 5 to 11 of Schedule 10A (rights to be taken into account and attribution of rights) apply in determining for the purposes of this paragraph whether an undertaking holds 20 per cent or more of the voting rights in another undertaking.*

21.—(1) The formats set out in Schedule 4 have effect in relation to group accounts with the following modifications.

(2) *In the Balance Sheet Formats the items headed "Participating interests", that is—*

(*a*) *in Format 1, item B.III.3, and*

(*b*) *in Format 2, item B.III.3 under the heading "ASSETS",*

shall be replaced by two items, "Interests in associated undertakings" and "Other participating interests".

(3) *In the Profit and Loss Account Formats, the items headed "Income from participating interests", that is—*

(*a*) *in Format 1, item 8,*

(*b*) *in Format 2, item 10,*

(*c*) *in Format 3, item B.4, and*

(*d*) *in Format 4, item B.6,*

shall be replaced by two items, "Income from interests in associated undertakings" and "Income from other participating interests".

22.—(1) The interest of an undertaking in an associated undertaking, and the amount of profit or loss attributable to such an interest, shall be shown by the equity method of accounting (including dealing with any goodwill arising in accordance with paragraphs 17 to 19 and 21 of Schedule 4).

(2) Where the associated undertaking is itself a parent undertaking, the net assets and profits or losses to be taken into account are those of the parent and its subsidiary undertakings (after making any consolidation adjustments).

(3) The equity method of accounting need not be applied if the amounts in question are not material for the purpose of giving a true and fair view.]

[643]

NOTES

Inserted by CA 1989, s 5(2), Sch 2, as from 1 April 1990.

Repealed by the Companies Act 2006, s 1295, Sch 16, as from a day to be appointed.

Para 1: words in square brackets in sub-para (1) substituted by the Companies Act 1985 (Miscellaneous Accounting Amendments) Regulations 1996, SI 1996/189, regs 14(2), 16(1), Sch 2, paras 1, 2, in relation to any financial year ending on or after 2 February 1996 (subject to transitional provisions in relation to financial years ending on or before 24 March 1996); words omitted from sub-para (1) repealed by the Companies (Audit, Investigations and Community Enterprise) Act 2004, ss 7(3), 64, Sch 8, as from 1 October 2005 (except in relation to the accounts of a company for a financial year beginning before that date, see the Companies (Audit, Investigations and Community Enterprise) Act 2004 (Commencement) and Companies Act 1989 (Commencement No 18) Order 2004, SI 2004/3322, art 3 at **[7341]**); sub-para (2) repealed by the Companies Act 1985 (Accounts of Small and Medium-sized Companies and Minor Accounting Amendments) Regulations 1997, SI 1997/220, reg 7(10)(a), in relation to annual accounts approved by the board of directors on or after 1 March 1997, and to directors' and auditors' reports on such accounts (subject to transitional provisions in relation to a financial year of a company ending on or before 24 March 1997).

Para 2: words in square brackets in sub-para (2) substituted by SI 1996/189, regs 14(2), 16(1), Sch 2, paras 1, 3, in relation to any financial year ending on or after 2 February 1996 (subject to transitional provisions as noted above).

Para 10: words in square brackets inserted by the Companies (Acquisition of Own Shares) (Treasury Shares) Regulations 2003, SI 2003/1116, reg 4, Schedule, para 31, as from 31 December 2003.

Para 13: sub-para (4) and the figure omitted from sub-para (7) repealed by SI 1996/189, regs 14(2), 16(1), Sch 2, paras 1, 4, in relation to any financial year ending on or after 2 February 1996 (subject to transitional provisions as noted above).

Para 14: words in square brackets in sub-para (1) added by SI 1996/189, regs 14(2), 16(1), Sch 2, paras 1, 5, in relation to any financial year ending on or after 2 February 1996 (subject to transitional provisions as noted above).

Para 18: repealed by the Companies Act 1985 (International Accounting Standards and Other Accounting Amendments) Regulations 2004, SI 2004/2947, reg 15, Sch 7, Pt 1, paras 1, 10, as from 12 November 2004, in relation to companies' financial years which begin on or after 1 January 2005.

Para 19: words in square brackets in sub-para (2) substituted by SI 1997/220, reg 7(10)(b), in relation to annual accounts approved by the board of directors on or after 1 March 1997, and to directors' and auditors' reports on such accounts (subject to transitional provisions in relation to a financial year of a company ending on or before 24 March 1997).

Application to limited liability partnerships: see the Limited Liability Partnerships Regulations 2001, SI 2001/1090, reg 3, Sch 1 at **[6984]**, **[6992]**.

[SCHEDULE 5
DISCLOSURE OF INFORMATION: RELATED UNDERTAKINGS

Section 231

PART I
COMPANIES NOT REQUIRED TO PREPARE GROUP ACCOUNTS

Subsidiary undertakings

1.—(1) The following information shall be given where at the end of the financial year the company has subsidiary undertakings.

(2) The name of each subsidiary undertaking shall be stated.

(3) There shall be stated with respect to each subsidiary undertaking—

(a) if it is incorporated outside Great Britain, the country in which it is incorporated;

(b) …

(c) if it is unincorporated, the address of its principal place of business.

(4) The reason why the company is not required to prepare group accounts shall be stated.

(5) *If the reason is that all the subsidiary undertakings of the company fall within the exclusions provided for in section 229, it shall be stated with respect to each subsidiary undertaking which of those exclusions applies.*

Holdings in subsidiary undertakings

2.—(1) There shall be stated in relation to shares of each class held by the company in a subsidiary undertaking—

- (*a*) *the identity of the class, and*
- (*b*) *the proportion of the nominal value of the shares of that class represented by those shares.*

(2) *The shares held by or on behalf of the company itself shall be distinguished from those attributed to the company which are held by or on behalf of a subsidiary undertaking.*

Financial information about subsidiary undertakings

3.—(1) There shall be disclosed with respect to each subsidiary undertaking—

- (*a*) *the aggregate amount of its capital and reserves as at the end of its relevant financial year, and*
- (*b*) *its profit or loss for that year.*

(2) *That information need not be given if the company is exempt by virtue of section 228 from the requirement to prepare group accounts (parent company included in accounts of larger group).*

[(2A) That information need not be given if the company's investment in the subsidiary undertaking is included in the company's accounts by way of the equity method of valuation.]

(3) *That information need not be given if—*

- (*a*) *the subsidiary undertaking is not required by any provision of this Act to deliver a copy of its balance sheet for its relevant financial year and does not otherwise publish that balance sheet in Great Britain or elsewhere, and*
- (*b*) *the company's holding is less than 50 per cent of the nominal value of the shares in the undertaking.*

(4) *Information otherwise required by this paragraph need not be given if it is not material.*

(5) *For the purposes of this paragraph the "relevant financial year" of a subsidiary undertaking is—*

- (*a*) *if its financial year ends with that of the company, that year, and*
- (*b*) *if not, its financial year ending last before the end of the company's financial year.*

Financial years of subsidiary undertakings

[4. Where—

- (*a*) *disclosure is made under paragraph 3(1) with respect to a subsidiary undertaking, and*
- (*b*) *that undertaking's financial year does not end with that of the company,*

there shall be stated in relation to that undertaking the date on which its last financial year ended (last before the end of the company's financial year).]

Further information about subsidiary undertakings

5. …

Shares and debentures of company held by subsidiary undertakings

6.—(1) The number, description and amount of the shares in … the company held by or on behalf of its subsidiary undertakings shall be disclosed.

(2) *Sub-paragraph (1) does not apply in relation to shares … in the case of which the subsidiary undertaking is concerned as personal representative or, subject as follows, as trustee.*

(3) *The exception for shares … in relation to which the subsidiary undertaking is concerned as trustee does not apply if the company, or any subsidiary undertaking of the company, is beneficially interested under the trust, otherwise than by way of security only for the purposes of a transaction entered into by it in the ordinary course of a business which includes the lending of money.*

(4) *Schedule 2 to this Act has effect for the interpretation of the reference in sub-paragraph (3) to a beneficial interest under a trust.*

Significant holdings in undertakings other than subsidiary undertakings

7.—(1) *The information required by paragraphs 8 and 9 shall be given where at the end of the financial year the company has a significant holding in an undertaking which is not a subsidiary undertaking of the company.*

(2) *A holding is significant for this purpose if—*
(a) *it amounts to [20 per cent] or more of the nominal value of any class of shares in the undertaking, or*
(b) *the amount of the holding (as stated or included in the company's accounts) exceeds [one-fifth] of the amount (as so stated) of the company's assets.*

8.—(1) *The name of the undertaking shall be stated.*

(2) *There shall be stated—*
(a) *if the undertaking is incorporated outside Great Britain, the country in which it is incorporated;*
(b) …
(c) *if it is unincorporated, the address of its principal place of business.*

(3) *There shall also be stated—*
(a) *the identity of each class of shares in the undertaking held by the company, and*
(b) *the proportion of the nominal value of the shares of that class represented by those shares.*

9.—(1) … *there shall also be stated—*
(a) *the aggregate amount of the capital and reserves of the undertaking as at the end of its relevant financial year, and*
(b) *its profit or loss for that year.*

(2) *That information need not be given if—*
(a) *the company is exempt by virtue of section 228 from the requirement to prepare group accounts (parent company included in accounts of larger group), and*
(b) *the investment of the company in all undertakings in which it has such a holding as is mentioned in sub-paragraph (1) is shown, in aggregate, in the notes to the accounts by way of the equity method of valuation.*

(3) *That information need not be given in respect of an undertaking if—*
(a) *the undertaking is not required by any provision of this Act to deliver a copy of its balance sheet for its relevant financial year and does not otherwise publish that balance sheet in Great Britain or elsewhere, and*
(b) *the company's holding is less than 50 per cent of the nominal value of the shares in the undertaking.*

(4) *Information otherwise required by this paragraph need not be given if it is not material.*

(5) *For the purposes of this paragraph the "relevant financial year" of an undertaking is—*
(a) *if its financial year ends with that of the company, that year, and*
(b) *if not, its financial year ending last before the end of the company's financial year.*

[Membership of certain undertakings

9A.—(1) The information required by this paragraph shall be given where at the end of the financial year the company is a member of a qualifying undertaking.

(2) There shall be stated—
(a) the name and legal form of the undertaking, and
(b) the address of the undertaking's registered office (whether in or outside Great Britain) or, if it does not have such an office, its head office (whether in or outside Great Britain).

(3) Where the undertaking is a qualifying partnership there shall also be stated either—
(a) that a copy of the latest accounts of the undertaking has been or is to be appended to the copy of the company's accounts sent to the registrar under section 242 of this Act, or
(b) the name of at least one body corporate (which may be the company) in whose group accounts the undertaking has been or is to be dealt with on a consolidated basis.

(4) Information otherwise required by sub-paragraph (2) above need not be given if it is not material.

(5) Information otherwise required by sub-paragraph (3)(b) above need not be given if the notes to the company's accounts disclose that advantage has been taken of the exemption conferred by regulation 7 of the Partnerships and Unlimited Companies (Accounts) Regulations 1993.

(6) In this paragraph—
"dealt with on a consolidated basis", "member", "qualifying company" and "qualifying partnership" have the same meanings as in the Partnerships and Unlimited Companies (Accounts) Regulations 1993;
"qualifying undertaking" means a qualifying partnership or a qualifying company.]

10. …

Parent undertaking drawing up accounts for larger group

11.—(1) Where the company is a subsidiary undertaking, the following information shall be given with respect to the parent undertaking of—
(a) the largest group of undertakings for which group accounts are drawn up and of which the company is a member, and
(b) the smallest such group of undertakings.

(2) The name of the parent undertaking shall be stated.

(3) There shall be stated—
(a) if the undertaking is incorporated outside Great Britain, the country in which it is incorporated;
(b) …
(c) if it is unincorporated, the address of its principal place of business.

(4) If copies of the group accounts referred to in sub-paragraph (1) are available to the public, there shall also be stated the addresses from which copies of the accounts can be obtained.

Identification of ultimate parent company

12.—(1) Where the company is a subsidiary undertaking, the following information shall be given with respect to the company (if any) regarded by the directors as being the company's ultimate parent company.

(2) The name of that company shall be stated.

(3) If known to the directors, there shall be stated—
(a) if that company is incorporated outside Great Britain, the country in which it is incorporated;

(*b*) ...

(4) *In this paragraph "company" includes any body corporate.*

Constructions of references to shares held by company

13.—(1) References in this Part of this Schedule to shares held by a company shall be construed as follows.

(2) *For the purposes of [paragraphs 2 to 4] (information about subsidiary undertakings)—*

(*a*) *there shall be attributed to the company any shares held by a subsidiary undertaking, or by a person acting on behalf of the company or a subsidiary undertaking; but*

(*b*) *there shall be treated as not held by the company any shares held on behalf of a person other than the company or a subsidiary undertaking.*

(3) *For the purposes of paragraphs 7 to 9 (information about undertakings other than subsidiary undertakings)—*

(*a*) *there shall be attributed to the company shares held on its behalf by any person; but*

(*b*) *there shall be treated as not held by a company shares held on behalf of a person other than the company.*

(4) *For the purposes of any of those provisions, shares held by way of security shall be treated as held by the person providing the security—*

(*a*) *where apart from the right to exercise them for the purpose of preserving the value of the security, or of realising it, the rights attached to the shares are exercisable only in accordance with his instructions, and*

(*b*) *where the shares are held in connection with the granting of loans as part of normal business activities and apart from the right to exercise them for the purpose of preserving the value of the security, or of realising it, the rights attached to the shares are exercisable only in his interests.]*

[644]

NOTES

Substituted by CA 1989, s 6(2), Sch 3, as from 1 April 1990.

Repealed by the Companies Act 2006, s 1295, Sch 16, as from a day to be appointed.

Paras 1, 11, 12: sub-para (3)(b) repealed by the Companies Act 1985 (Miscellaneous Accounting Amendments) Regulations 1996, SI 1996/189, regs 14(3), 16(1), Sch 3, paras 1, 2, 11, 12, in relation to any financial year ending on or after 2 February 1996 (subject to transitional provisions in relation to financial years ending on or before 24 March 1996).

Para 3: sub-para (2A) inserted by SI 1996/189, regs 14(3), 16(1), Sch 3, paras 1, 3, in relation to any financial year ending on or after 2 February 1996 (subject to transitional provisions as noted above).

Para 4: substituted by SI 1996/189, regs 14(3), 16(1), Sch 3, paras 1, 4, in relation to any financial year ending on or after 2 February 1996 (subject to transitional provisions as noted above).

Paras 5, 10: repealed by SI 1996/189, regs 14(3), 16(1), Sch 3, paras 1, 5, 10, in relation to any financial year ending on or after 2 February 1996 (subject to transitional provisions as noted above).

Paras 6, 8, 9: words omitted repealed by SI 1996/189, regs 14(3), 16(1), Sch 3, paras 1, 6, 8, 9, in relation to any financial year ending on or after 2 February 1996 (subject to transitional provisions as noted above).

Paras 7, 13: words in square brackets in sub-para (2) substituted by SI 1996/189, regs 14(3), 16(1), Sch 3, paras 1, 7, 13, in relation to any financial year ending on or after 2 February 1996 (subject to transitional provisions as noted above).

Para 9A: inserted by the Partnerships and Unlimited Companies (Accounts) Regulations 1993, SI 1993/1820, reg 11(2), as from 21 July 1993 (subject to transitional provisions in relation to financial years commencing before 23 December 1994).

Application to limited liability partnerships: see the Limited Liability Partnerships Regulations 2001, SI 2001/1090, reg 3, Sch 1 at **[6984]**, **[6992]**.

[PART II
COMPANIES REQUIRED TO PREPARE GROUP ACCOUNTS

Introductory

14. In this Part of this Schedule "the group" means the group consisting of the parent company and its subsidiary undertakings.

Subsidiary undertakings

15.—(1) The following information shall be given with respect to the undertakings which are subsidiary undertakings of the parent company at the end of the financial year.

(2) The name of each undertaking shall be stated.

(3) There shall be stated—

- *(a) if the undertaking is incorporated outside Great Britain, the country in which it is incorporated;*
- *(b) …*
- *(c) if it is unincorporated, the address of its principal place of business.*

(4) It shall also be stated whether the subsidiary undertaking is included in the consolidation and, if it is not, the reasons for excluding it from consolidation shall be given.

(5) It shall be stated with respect to each subsidiary undertaking by virtue of which of the conditions specified in section 258(2) or (4) it is a subsidiary undertaking of its immediate parent undertaking.

That information need not be given if the relevant condition is that specified in subsection (2)(a) of that section (holding of a majority of the voting rights) and the immediate parent undertaking holds the same proportion of the shares in the undertaking as it holds voting rights.

Holdings in subsidiary undertakings

16.—(1) The following information shall be given with respect to the shares of a subsidiary undertaking held—

- *(a) by the parent company, and*
- *(b) by the group;*

and the information under paragraphs (a) and (b) shall (if different) be shown separately.

(2) There shall be stated—

- *(a) the identity of each class of shares held, and*
- *(b) the proportion of the nominal value of the shares of that class represented by those shares.*

Financial information about subsidiary undertakings not included in the consolidation

17.—(1) There shall be shown with respect to each subsidiary undertaking not included in the consolidation—

- *(a) the aggregate amount of its capital and reserves as at the end of its relevant financial year, and*
- *(b) its profit or loss for that year.*

(2) That information need not be given if the group's investment in the undertaking is included in the accounts by way of the equity method of valuation or if—

- *(a) the undertaking is not required by any provision of this Act to deliver a copy of its balance sheet for its relevant financial year and does not otherwise publish that balance sheet in Great Britain or elsewhere, and*
- *(b) the holding of the group is less than 50 per cent of the nominal value of the shares in the undertaking.*

(3) Information otherwise required by this paragraph need not be given if it is not material.

(4) For the purposes of this paragraph the "relevant financial year" of a subsidiary undertaking is—

- *(a) if its financial year ends with that of the company, that year, and*
- *(b) if not, its financial year ending last before the end of the company's financial year.*

18, 19. …

Shares and debentures of company held by subsidiary undertakings

20.—(1) The number, description and amount of the shares in … the company held by or on behalf of its subsidiary undertakings shall be disclosed.

(2) Sub-paragraph (1) does not apply in relation to shares … in the case of which the subsidiary undertaking is concerned as personal representative or, subject as follows, as trustee.

(3) The exception for shares … in relation to which the subsidiary undertaking is concerned as trustee does not apply if the company or any of its subsidiary undertakings is beneficially interested under the trust, otherwise than by way of security only for the purposes of a transaction entered into by it in the ordinary course of a business which includes the lending of money.

(4) Schedule 2 to this Act has effect for the interpretation of the reference in sub-paragraph (3) to a beneficial interest under a trust.

Joint ventures

21.—(1) The following information shall be given where an undertaking is dealt with in the consolidated accounts by the method of proportional consolidation in accordance with paragraph 19 of Schedule 4A (joint ventures)—

- *(a) the name of the undertaking;*
- *(b) the address of the principal place of business of the undertaking;*
- *(c) the factors on which joint management of the undertaking is based; and*
- *(d) the proportion of the capital of the undertaking held by undertakings included in the consolidation.*

(2) Where the financial year of the undertaking did not end with that of the company, there shall be stated the date on which a financial year of the undertaking last ended before that date.

Associated undertakings

22.—(1) The following information shall be given where an undertaking included in the consolidation has an interest in an associated undertaking.

(2) The name of the associated undertaking shall be stated.

(3) There shall be stated—

- *(a) if the undertaking is incorporated outside Great Britain, the country in which it is incorporated;*
- *(b) …*
- *(c) if it is unincorporated, the address of its principal place of business.*

(4) The following information shall be given with respect to the shares of the undertaking held—

- *(a) by the parent company, and*
- *(b) by the group;*

and the information under paragraphs (a) and (b) shall be shown separately.

(5) There shall be stated—

- *(a) the identity of each class of shares held, and*
- *(b) the proportion of the nominal value of the shares of that class represented by those shares.*

(6) In this paragraph "associated undertaking" has the meaning given by paragraph 20 of Schedule 4A; and the information required by this paragraph shall be given notwithstanding that paragraph 22(3) of that Schedule (materiality) applies in relation to the accounts themselves.

Other significant holdings of parent company or group

23.—(1) The information required by paragraphs 24 and 25 shall be given where at the end of the financial year the parent company has a significant holding in an undertaking which is not one of its subsidiary undertakings and does not fall within paragraph 21 (joint ventures) or paragraph 22 (associated undertakings).

(2) A holding is significant for this purpose if—

(a) it amounts to [20 per cent] or more of the nominal value of any class of shares in the undertaking, or

(b) the amount of the holding (as stated or included in the company's individual accounts) exceeds [one-fifth] of the amount of its assets (as so stated).

24.—(1) The name of the undertaking shall be stated.

(2) There shall be stated—

(a) if the undertaking is incorporated outside Great Britain, the country in which it is incorporated;

(b) …

(c) if it is unincorporated, the address of its principal place of business.

(3) The following information shall be given with respect to the shares of the undertaking held by the parent company.

(4) There shall be stated—

(a) the identity of each class of shares held, and

(b) the proportion of the nominal value of the shares of that class represented by those shares.

25.—(1) … there shall also be stated—

(a) the aggregate amount of the capital and reserves of the undertaking as at the end of its relevant financial year, and

(b) its profit or loss for that year.

(2) That information need not be given in respect of an undertaking if—

(a) the undertaking is not required by any provision of this Act to deliver a copy of its balance sheet for its relevant financial year and does not otherwise publish that balance sheet in Great Britain or elsewhere, and

(b) the company's holding is less than 50 per cent of the nominal value of the shares in the undertaking.

(3) Information otherwise required by this paragraph need not be given if it is not material.

(4) For the purposes of this paragraph the "relevant financial year" of an undertaking is—

(a) if its financial year ends with that of the company, that year, and

(b) if not, its financial year ending last before the end of the company's financial year.

26.—(1) The information required by paragraphs 27 and 28 shall be given where at the end of the financial year the group has a significant holding in an undertaking which is not a subsidiary undertaking of the parent company and does not fall within paragraph 21 (joint ventures) or paragraph 22 (associated undertakings).

(2) A holding is significant for this purpose if—

(a) it amounts to [20 per cent] or more of the nominal value of any class of shares in the undertaking, or

(b) the amount of the holding (as stated or included in the group accounts) exceeds [one-fifth] of the amount of the group's assets (as so stated).

27.—(1) The name of the undertaking shall be stated.

(2) There shall be stated—

(a) if the undertaking is incorporated outside Great Britain, the country in which it is incorporated;

(b) …

(c) if it is unincorporated, the address of its principal place of business.

(3) The following information shall be given with respect to the shares of the undertaking held by the group.

(4) There shall be stated—

(a) the identity of each class of shares held, and

(b) the proportion of the nominal value of the shares of that class represented by those shares.

28.—(1) ... there shall also be stated—

(a) the aggregate amount of the capital and reserves of the undertaking as at the end of its relevant financial year, and

(b) its profit or loss for that year.

(2) That information need not be given if—

(a) the undertaking is not required by any provision of this Act to deliver a copy of its balance sheet for its relevant financial year and does not otherwise publish that balance sheet in Great Britain or elsewhere, and

(b) the holding of the group is less than 50 per cent of the nominal value of the shares in the undertaking.

(3) Information otherwise required by this paragraph need not be given if it is not material.

(4) For the purposes of this paragraph the "relevant financial year" of an outside undertaking is—

(a) if its financial year ends with that of the parent company, that year, and

(b) if not, its financial year ending last before the end of the parent company's financial year.

[Parent company's or group's membership of certain undertakings

28A.—(1) The information required by this paragraph shall be given where at the end of the financial year the parent company or group is a member of a qualifying undertaking.

(2) There shall be stated—

(a) the name and legal form of the undertaking, and

(b) the address of the undertaking's registered office (whether in or outside Great Britain) or, if it does not have such an office, its head office (whether in or outside Great Britain).

(3) Where the undertaking is a qualifying partnership there shall also be stated either—

(a) that a copy of the latest accounts of the undertaking has been or is to be appended to the copy of the company's accounts sent to the registrar under section 242 of this Act, or

(b) the name of at least one body corporate (which may be the company) in whose group accounts the undertaking has been or is to be dealt with on a consolidated basis.

(4) Information otherwise required by sub-paragraph (2) above need not be given if it is not material.

(5) Information otherwise required by sub-paragraph (3)(b) above need not be given if the notes to the company's accounts disclose that advantage has been taken of the exemption conferred by regulation 7 of the Partnerships and Unlimited Companies (Accounts) Regulations 1993.

(6) In this paragraph—

"dealt with on a consolidated basis", "member", "qualifying company" and "qualifying partnership" have the same meanings as in the Partnerships and Unlimited Companies (Accounts) Regulations 1993;

"qualifying undertaking" means a qualifying partnership or a qualifying company.]

29. ...

Parent undertaking drawing up accounts for larger group

30.—(1) Where the parent company is itself a subsidiary undertaking, the following information shall be given with respect to that parent undertaking of the company which heads—

(*a*) *the largest group of undertakings for which group accounts are drawn up and of which that company is a member, and*
(*b*) *the smallest such group of undertakings.*

(2) *The name of the parent undertaking shall be stated.*

(3) *There shall be stated—*
(*a*) *if the undertaking is incorporated outside Great Britain, the country in which it is incorporated;*
(*b*) …
(*c*) *if it is unincorporated, the address of its principal place of business.*

(4) *If copies of the group accounts referred to in sub-paragraph (1) are available to the public, there shall also be stated the addresses from which copies of the accounts can be obtained.*

Identification of ultimate parent company

31.—(1) Where the parent company is itself a subsidiary undertaking, the following information shall be given with respect to the company (if any) regarded by the directors as being that company's ultimate parent company.

(2) *The name of that company shall be stated.*

(3) *If known to the directors, there shall be stated—*
(*a*) *if that company is incorporated outside Great Britain, the country in which it is incorporated;*
(*b*) …

(4) *In this paragraph "company" includes any body corporate.*

Construction of references to shares held by parent company or group

32.—(1) References in this Part of this Schedule to shares held by the parent company or the group shall be construed as follows.

(2) *For the purposes of paragraphs 16, 22(4) and (5) and 23 to 25 (information about holdings in subsidiary and other undertakings)—*
(*a*) *there shall be attributed to the parent company shares held on its behalf by any person; but*
(*b*) *there shall be treated as not held by the parent company shares held on behalf of a person other than the company.*

(3) *References to shares held by the group are to any shares held by or on behalf of the parent company or any of its subsidiary undertakings; but there shall be treated as not held by the group any shares held on behalf of a person other than the parent company or any of its subsidiary undertakings.*

(4) *Shares held by way of security shall be treated as held by the person providing the security—*
(*a*) *where apart from the right to exercise them for the purpose of preserving the value of the security, or of realising it, the rights attached to the shares are exercisable only in accordance with his instructions, and*
(*b*) *where the shares are held in connection with the granting of loans as part of normal business activities and apart from the right to exercise them for the purpose of preserving the value of the security, or of realising it, the rights attached to the shares are exercisable only in his interests.]*

[645]

NOTES

Substituted as noted to Pt I of this Schedule at **[644]**.

Repealed by the Companies Act 2006, s 1295, Sch 16, as from a day to be appointed.

Paras 15, 20, 22, 24, 25, 27, 28, 30, 31: words omitted repealed by the Companies Act 1985 (Miscellaneous Accounting Amendments) Regulations 1996, SI 1996/189, regs 14(3), 16(1), Sch 3, paras 1, 14, 17, 18, 20–22, 24, 25, in relation to any financial year ending on or after 2 February 1996 (subject to transitional provisions in relation to financial years ending on or before 24 March 1996).

Paras 18, 19, 29: repealed by SI 1996/189, regs 14(3), 16(1), Sch 3, paras 1, 15, 16, 23, in relation to any financial year ending on or after 2 February 1996 (subject to transitional provisions as noted above).

Paras 23, 26: words in square brackets in sub-para (2) substituted by SI 1996/189, regs 14(3), 16(1), Sch 3, paras 1, 19, in relation to any financial year ending on or after 2 February 1996 (subject to transitional provisions as noted above).

Para 28A: inserted by the Partnerships and Unlimited Companies (Accounts) Regulations 1993, SI 1993/1820, reg 11(3), as from 21 July 1993 (subject to transitional provisions in relation to financial years commencing before 23 December 1994).

Application to limited liability partnerships: see the Limited Liability Partnerships Regulations 2001, SI 2001/1090, reg 3, Sch 1 at **[6984]**, **[6992]**.

SCHEDULE 6
[DISCLOSURE OF INFORMATION:
EMOLUMENTS AND OTHER BENEFITS OF DIRECTORS AND OTHERS]

Section 232

[PART I
CHAIRMAN'S AND DIRECTORS' EMOLUMENTS, PENSIONS AND COMPENSATION FOR LOSS OF OFFICE

[CHAPTER 1
PROVISIONS APPLYING TO QUOTED AND UNQUOTED COMPANIES]

[Aggregate amount of directors' emoluments etc

1.—(1) Subject to sub-paragraph (2), the following shall be shown, namely—

(a) the aggregate amount of emoluments paid to or receivable by directors in respect of qualifying services;

(b) the aggregate of the amount of gains made by directors on the exercise of share options;

(c) the aggregate of the following, namely—

(i) the amount of money paid to or receivable by directors under long term incentive schemes in respect of qualifying services; and

(ii) the net value of assets (other than money and share options) received or receivable by directors under such schemes in respect of such services;

(d) the aggregate value of any company contributions paid, or treated as paid, to a pension scheme in respect of directors' qualifying services, being contributions by reference to which the rate or amount of any money purchase benefits that may become payable will be calculated; and

(e) in the case of each of the following, namely—

(i) money purchase schemes; and

(ii) defined benefit schemes,

the number of directors (if any) to whom retirement benefits are accruing under such schemes in respect of qualifying services.

(2) [In the case of a company which is not a quoted company and whose equity share capital is not listed on the market known as AIM]—

(a) sub-paragraph (1) shall have effect as if paragraph (b) were omitted and, in paragraph (c)(ii), "assets" did not include shares; and

(b) the number of each of the following (if any) shall be shown, namely—

(i) the directors who exercised share options; and

(ii) the directors in respect of whose qualifying services shares were received or receivable under long term incentive schemes.

(3) In this paragraph "emoluments" of a director—

(a) includes salary, fees and bonuses, sums paid by way of expenses allowance (so far as they are chargeable to United Kingdom income tax) and, subject to paragraph (b), the estimated money value of any other benefits received by him otherwise than in cash; but

(b) does not include any of the following, namely—

(i) the value of any share options granted to him or the amount of any gains made on the exercise of any such options;

(ii) any company contributions paid, or treated as paid, in respect of him under any pension scheme or any benefits to which he is entitled under any such scheme; or

(iii) any money or other assets paid to or received or receivable by him under any long term incentive scheme.

(4) In this paragraph "long term incentive scheme" means any agreement or arrangement under which money or other assets may become receivable by a director and which includes one or more qualifying conditions with respect to service or performance which cannot be fulfilled within a single financial year; and for this purpose the following shall be disregarded, namely—

- *(a) bonuses the amount of which falls to be determined by reference to service or performance within a single financial year;*
- *(b) compensation for loss of office, payments for breach of contract and other termination payments; and*
- *(c) retirement benefits.*

(5) In this paragraph—

"amount", in relation to a gain made on the exercise of a share option, means the difference between—

- *(a) the market price of the shares on the day on which the option was exercised; and*
- *(b) the price actually paid for the shares;*

"company contributions", in relation to a pension scheme and a director, means any payments (including insurance premiums) made, or treated as made, to the scheme in respect of the director by a person other than the director;

"defined benefits" means retirement benefits payable under a pension scheme which are not money purchase benefits;

"defined benefit scheme", in relation to a director, means a pension scheme which is not a money purchase scheme;

.....

"money purchase benefits", in relation to a director, means retirement benefits payable under a pension scheme the rate or amount of which is calculated by reference to payments made, or treated as made, by the director or by any other person in respect of the director and which are not average salary benefits;

"money purchase scheme", in relation to a director, means a pension scheme under which all of the benefits that may become payable to or in respect of the director are money purchase benefits;

"net value", in relation to any assets received or receivable by a director, means value after deducting any money paid or other value given by the director in respect of those assets;

["the official list" has the meaning given in section 103(1) of the Financial Services and Markets Act 2000;]

"qualifying services", in relation to any person, means his services as a director of the company, and his services while director of the company—

- *(a) as director of any of its subsidiary undertakings; or*
- *(b) otherwise in connection with the management of the affairs of the company or any of its subsidiary undertakings;*

["recognised investment exchange" has the same meaning as in the Financial Services and Markets Act 2000;]

"shares" means shares (whether allotted or not) in the company, or any undertaking which is a group undertaking in relation to the company, and includes a share warrant as defined by section 188(1);

"share option" means a right to acquire shares;

"value", in relation to shares received or receivable by a director on any day, means the market price of the shares on that day.

(6) For the purposes of this paragraph—

- *(a) any information, other than the aggregate amount of gains made by directors on the exercise of share options, shall be treated as shown if it is capable of being readily ascertained from other information which is shown; and*
- *(b) emoluments paid or receivable or share options granted in respect of a person's accepting office as a director shall be treated as emoluments paid or receivable or share options granted in respect of his services as a director.*

(7) Where a pension scheme provides for any benefits that may become payable to or in respect of any director to be whichever are the greater of—

- *(a) money purchase benefits as determined by or under the scheme; and*
- *(b) defined benefits as so determined,*

the company may assume for the purposes of this paragraph that those benefits will be money purchase benefits, or defined benefits, according to whichever appears more likely at the end of the financial year.

(8) For the purpose of determining whether a pension scheme is a money purchase or defined benefit scheme, any death in service benefits provided for by the scheme shall be disregarded.]

[CHAPTER 2
PROVISIONS APPLYING ONLY TO UNQUOTED COMPANIES]

[Details of highest paid director's emoluments etc

2.—(1) Where the aggregates shown under paragraph 1(1)(a), (b) and (c) total £200,000 or more, the following shall be shown, namely—
- *(a) so much of the total of those aggregates as is attributable to the highest paid director; and*
- *(b) so much of the aggregate mentioned in paragraph 1(1)(d) as is so attributable.*

(2) Where sub-paragraph (1) applies and the highest paid director has performed qualifying services during the financial year by reference to which the rate or amount of any defined benefits that may become payable will be calculated, there shall also be shown—
- *(a) the amount at the end of the year of his accrued pension; and*
- *(b) where applicable, the amount at the end of the year of his accrued lump sum.*

(3) Subject to sub-paragraph (4), where sub-paragraph (1) applies in the case of a company which is not a listed company, there shall also be shown—
- *(a) whether the highest paid director exercised any share options; and*
- *(b) whether any shares were received or receivable by that director in respect of qualifying services under a long term incentive scheme.*

(4) Where the highest paid director has not been involved in any of the transactions specified in sub-paragraph (3), that fact need not be stated.

(5) In this paragraph—

"accrued pension" and "accrued lump sum", in relation to any pension scheme and any director, mean respectively the amount of the annual pension, and the amount of the lump sum, which would be payable under the scheme on his attaining normal pension age if—
- *(a) he had left the company's service at the end of the financial year;*
- *(b) there were no increase in the general level of prices in Great Britain during the period beginning with the end of that year and ending with his attaining that age;*
- *(c) no question arose of any commutation of the pension or inverse commutation of the lump sum; and*
- *(d) any amounts attributable to voluntary contributions paid by the director to the scheme, and any money purchase benefits which would be payable under the scheme, were disregarded;*

"the highest paid director" means the director to whom is attributable the greatest part of the total of the aggregates shown under paragraph 1(1)(a), (b) and (c);

"normal pension age", in relation to any pension scheme and any director, means the age at which the director will first become entitled to receive a full pension on retirement of an amount determined without reduction to take account of its payment before a later age (but disregarding any entitlement to pension upon retirement in the event of illness, incapacity or redundancy).

(6) Sub-paragraphs (4) to (8) of paragraph 1 apply for the purposes of this paragraph as they apply for the purposes of that paragraph.]

[Excess retirement benefits of directors and past directors

7.—(1) Subject to sub-paragraph (2), there shall be shown the aggregate amount of—
- *(a) so much of retirement benefits paid to or receivable by directors under pension schemes; and*
- *(b) so much of retirement benefits paid to or receivable by past directors under such schemes,*

as (in each case) is in excess of the retirement benefits to which they were respectively entitled on the date on which the benefits first became payable or 31st March 1997, whichever is the later.

(2) Amounts paid or receivable under a pension scheme need not be included in the aggregate amount if—

(*a*) *the funding of the scheme was such that the amounts were or, as the case may be, could have been paid without recourse to additional contributions; and*

(*b*) *amounts were paid to or receivable by all pensioner members of the scheme on the same basis;*

and in this sub-paragraph "pensioner member", in relation to a pension scheme, means any person who is entitled to the present payment of retirement benefits under the scheme.

(3) In this paragraph—

(*a*) *references to retirement benefits include benefits otherwise than in cash; and*

(*b*) *in relation to so much of retirement benefits as consists of a benefit otherwise than in cash, references to their amount are to the estimated money value of the benefit;*

and the nature of any such benefit shall also be disclosed.]

Compensation to directors for loss of office

8.—(1) There shall be shown the aggregate amount of any compensation to directors or past directors in respect of loss of office.

(2) This amount includes compensation received or receivable by a director or past director for—

(*a*) *loss of office as director of the company, or*

(*b*) *loss, while director of the company or on or in connection with his ceasing to be a director of it, of—*

(i) any other office in connection with the management of the company's affairs, or

(ii) any office as director or otherwise in connection with the management of the affairs of any subsidiary undertaking of the company;

…

(3) References to compensation include benefits otherwise than in cash; and in relation to such compensation references to its amount are to the estimated money value of the benefit.

The nature of any such compensation shall be disclosed

[(4) In this paragraph, references to compensation for loss of office include the following, namely—

(*a*) *compensation in consideration for, or in connection with, a person's retirement from office; and*

(*b*) *where such a retirement is occasioned by a breach of the person's contract with the company or with a subsidiary undertaking of the company—*

(i) payments made by way of damages for the breach; or

(ii) payments made by way of settlement or compromise of any claim in respect of the breach.

(5) Sub-paragraph (6)(a) of paragraph 1 applies for the purposes of this paragraph as it applies for the purposes of that paragraph.]

Sums paid to third parties in respect of directors' services

9.—(1) There shall be shown the aggregate amount of any consideration paid to or receivable by third parties for making available the services of any person—

(*a*) *as a director of the company, or*

(*b*) *while director of the company—*

(i) as director of any of its subsidiary undertakings, or

(ii) otherwise in connection with the management of the affairs of the company or any of its subsidiary undertakings.

(2) The reference to consideration includes benefits otherwise than in cash; and in relation to such consideration the reference to its amount is to the estimated money value of the benefit.

The nature of any such consideration shall be disclosed.

(3) The reference to third parties is to persons other than—

(*a*) *the director himself or a person connected with him or body corporate controlled by him, and*
(*b*) *the company or any of its subsidiary undertakings.*

Supplementary

10.—(1) The following applies with respect to the amounts to be shown under [this Part of this Schedule].

(2) The amount in each case includes all relevant sums paid by or receivable from—
(*a*) *the company; and*
(*b*) *the company's subsidiary undertakings; and*
(*c*) *any other person,*

except sums to be accounted for to the company or any of its subsidiary undertakings or, by virtue of sections 314 and 315 of this Act (duty of directors to make disclosure on company takeover; consequence of non-compliance), to past or present members of the company or any of its subsidiaries or any class of those members.

(3) …

(4) References to amounts paid to or receivable by a person include amounts paid to or receivable by a person connected with him or a body corporate controlled by him (but not so as to require an amount to be counted twice).

11.—(1) The amounts to be shown for any financial year under [this Part of this Schedule] are the sums receivable in respect of that year (whenever paid) or, in the case of sums not receivable in respect of a period, the sums paid during that year.

(2) But where—
(*a*) *any sums are not shown in a note to the accounts for the relevant financial year on the ground that the person receiving them is liable to account for them as mentioned in paragraph 10(2), but the liability is thereafter wholly or partly released or is not enforced within a period of 2 years; or*
(*b*) *any sums paid by way of expenses allowance are charged to United Kingdom income tax after the end of the relevant financial year,*

those sums shall, to the extent to which the liability is released or not enforced or they are charged as mentioned above (as the case may be), be shown in a note to the first accounts in which it is practicable to show them and shall be distinguished from the amounts to be shown apart from this provision.

12. Where it is necessary to do so for the purpose of making any distinction required by the preceding paragraphs in an amount to be shown in compliance with this Part of this Schedule, the directors may apportion any payments between the matters in respect of which these have been paid or are receivable in such manner as they think appropriate.

Interpretation

13.—(1) The following applies for the interpretation of this Part of this Schedule.

(2) A reference to a subsidiary undertaking of the company—
(*a*) *in relation to a person who is or was, while a director of the company, a director also, by virtue of the company's nomination (direct or indirect) of any other undertaking, includes (subject to the following sub-paragraph) that undertaking, whether or not it is or was in fact a subsidiary undertaking of the company, and*
(*b*) *for the purposes of paragraphs 1 to 7 … is to an undertaking which is a subsidiary undertaking at the time the services were rendered, and for the purposes of paragraph 8 to a subsidiary undertaking immediately before the loss of office as director.*

[(3) The following definitions apply—
(*a*) *"pension scheme" has the meaning assigned to "retirement benefits scheme" by section 611 of the Income and Corporation Taxes Act 1988;*
(*b*) *"retirement benefits" has the meaning assigned to relevant benefits by section 612(1) of that Act.]*

(4) References in this Part of this Schedule to a person being "connected" with a director, and to a director "controlling" a body corporate, shall be construed in accordance with section 346.

Supplementary

14. This Part of this Schedule requires information to be given only so far as it is contained in the company's books and papers or the company has the right to obtain it from the persons concerned.]

[646]

NOTES

This Part of this Schedule inserted, and heading to this Schedule substituted, by CA 1989, s 6(4), Sch 4, paras 1–3, as from 1 April 1990.

Repealed by the Companies Act 2006, s 1295, Sch 16, as from a day to be appointed.

Chapter 1 heading inserted by the Directors' Remuneration Report Regulations 2002, SI 2002/1986, reg 10(1), (13)(a), as from 1 August 2002, with effect as respects companies' financial years ending on or after 31 December 2002.

Para 1: substituted, together with the heading preceding it, by the Company Accounts (Disclosure of Directors' Emoluments) Regulations 1997, SI 1997/570, reg 2, as from 31 March 1997, with effect in relation to companies' financial years ending on or after that date; words in square brackets in sub-para (2) substituted by SI 2002/1986, reg 10(1), (13)(b), as from 1 August 2002, with effect as respects companies' financial years ending on or after 31 December 2002; definitions "the official list" and "recognised investment exchange" in sub-para (5) inserted by the Financial Services and Markets Act 2000 (Consequential Amendments and Repeals) Order 2001, SI 2001/3649, art 33(1), (3), (4), as from 1 December 2001; definition "listed company" in sub-para (5) repealed by SI 2002/1986, reg 10(1), (13)(c), as from 1 August 2002, with effect as respects companies' financial years ending on or after 31 December 2002.

Chapter 2 heading inserted by SI 2002/1986, reg 10(1), (13)(d), as from 1 August 2002, with effect as respects companies' financial years ending on or after 31 December 2002.

Para 2: substituted, together with the heading preceding it for original paras 2–6, by SI 1997/570, reg 3(1), as from 31 March 1997, with effect in relation to companies' financial years ending on or after that date.

Para 7: substituted, together with the heading preceding it, by SI 1997/570, reg 4, as from 31 March 1997, with effect in relation to companies' financial years ending on or after that date.

Para 8: words omitted from sub-para (2)(b) repealed, and sub-paras (4), (5) substituted for original sub-para (4), by SI 1997/570, reg 5, as from 31 March 1997, with effect in relation to companies' financial years ending on or after that date.

Para 10: words in square brackets in sub-para (1) substituted, and sub-para (3) repealed, by SI 1997/570, reg 6(2), as from 31 March 1997, with effect in relation to companies' financial years ending on or after that date.

Para 11: words in square brackets in sub-para (1) substituted by SI 1997/570, reg 6(3), as from 31 March 1997, with effect in relation to companies' financial years ending on or after that date.

Para 13: words omitted from sub-para (2) repealed, and sub-para (3) substituted, by SI 1997/570, reg 6(4), (5), as from 31 March 1997, with effect in relation to companies' financial years ending on or after that date.

Application to limited liability partnerships: see the Limited Liability Partnerships Regulations 2001, SI 2001/1090, reg 3, Sch 1 at **[6984]**, **[6992]**.

[PART II
LOANS, QUASI-LOANS AND OTHER DEALINGS IN FAVOUR OF DIRECTORS]

[15]. [The group accounts of a holding company, or if it is not required to prepare group accounts its individual accounts,] shall contain the particulars required by this Schedule of—

- *(a) any transaction or arrangement of a kind described in section 330 entered into by the company or by a subsidiary of the company for a person who at any time during the financial year was a director of the company or its holding company, or was connected with such a director;*
- *(b) an agreement by the company or by a subsidiary of the company to enter into any such transaction or arrangement for a person who was at any time during the financial year a director of the company or its holding company, or was connected with such a director; and*
- *(c) any other transaction or arrangement with the company or a subsidiary of it in which a person who at any time during the financial year was a director of the company or its holding company had, directly or indirectly, a material interest.*

[16]. The accounts prepared by a company other than a holding company shall contain the particulars required by this Schedule of—

(*a*) *any transaction or arrangement of a kind described in section 330 entered into by the company for a person who at any time during the financial year was a director of it or of its holding company or was connected with such a director;*

(*b*) *an agreement by the company to enter into any such transaction or arrangement for a person who at any time during the financial year was a director of the company or its holding company or was connected with such a director; and*

(*c*) *any other transaction or arrangement with the company in which a person who at any time during the financial year was a director of the company or of its holding company had, directly or indirectly, a material interest.*

[17].—(1) For purposes of paragraphs [15](c) and [16](c), a transaction or arrangement between a company and a director of it or of its holding company, or a person connected with such a director, is to be treated (if it would not otherwise be so) as a transaction, arrangement or agreement in which that director is interested.

(2) An interest in such a transaction or arrangement is not "material" for purposes of those sub-paragraphs if in the board's opinion it is not so; but this is without prejudice to the question whether or not such an interest is material in a case where the board have not considered the matter.

"The board" here means the directors of the company preparing the accounts, or a majority of those directors, but excluding in either case the director whose interest it is.

.....

[18]. Paragraphs [15] and [16] do not apply in relation to the following transactions, arrangements and agreements—

(*a*) *a transaction, arrangement or agreement between one company and another in which a director of the former or of its subsidiary or holding company is interested only by virtue of his being a director of the latter;*

(*b*) *a contract of service between a company and one of its directors or a director of its holding company, or between a director of a company and any of that company's subsidiaries;*

(*c*) *a transaction, arrangement or agreement which was not entered into during the financial year and which did not subsist at any time during that year.*

[19]. Paragraphs [15] and [16] apply whether or not—

(*a*) *the transaction or arrangement was prohibited by section 330;*

(*b*) *the person for whom it was made was a director of the company or was connected with a director of it at the time it was made;*

(*c*) *in the case of a transaction or arrangement made by a company which at any time during a financial year is a subsidiary of another company, it was a subsidiary of that other company at the time the transaction or arrangement was made.*

[20]. Neither paragraph [15](c) nor paragraph [16](c) applies in relation to any transaction or arrangement if—

(*a*) *each party to the transaction or arrangement which is a member of the same group of companies (meaning a holding company and its subsidiaries) as the company entered into the transaction or arrangement in the ordinary course of business, and*

(*b*) *the terms of the transaction or arrangement are not less favourable to any such party than it would be reasonable to expect if the interest mentioned in that sub-paragraph had not been an interest of a person who was a director of the company or of its holding company.*

[21]. Neither paragraph [15](c) nor paragraph [16](c) applies in relation to any transaction or arrangement if—

(*a*) *the company is a member of a group of companies (meaning a holding company and its subsidiaries), and*

(*b*) *either the company is a wholly-owned subsidiary or no body corporate (other than the company or a subsidiary of the company) which is a member of the group of companies which includes the company's ultimate holding company was a party to the transaction or arrangement, and*

(*c*) *the director in question was at some time during the relevant period associated with the company, and* (*d*) *the material interest of the director in question in the transaction or arrangement would not have arisen if he had not been associated with the company at any time during the relevant period.*

The particulars required by this Part

[22].—(1) Subject to the next paragraph, the particulars required by this Part are those of the principal terms of the transaction, arrangement or agreement.

(2) Without prejudice to the generality of sub-paragraph (1), the following particulars are required—

- *(a) a statement of the fact either that the transaction, arrangement or agreement was made or subsisted (as the case may be) during the financial year;*
- *(b) the name of the person for whom it was made and, where that person is or was connected with a director of the company or of its holding company, the name of that director;*
- *(c) in a case where paragraph [15](c) or [16](c) applies, the name of the director with the material interest and the nature of that interest;*
- *(d) in the case of a loan or an agreement for a loan or an arrangement within section 330(6) or (7) of this Act relating to a loan—*
  - *(i) the amount of the liability of the person to whom the loan was or was agreed to be made, in respect of principal and interest, at the beginning and at the end of the financial year;*
  - *(ii) the maximum amount of that liability during that year;*
  - *(iii) the amount of any interest which, having fallen due, has not been paid; and*
  - *(iv) the amount of any provision (within the meaning of Schedule 4 to this Act) made in respect of any failure or anticipated failure by the borrower to repay the whole or part of the loan or to pay the whole or part of any interest on it;*
- *(e) in the case of a guarantee or security or an arrangement within section 330(6) relating to a guarantee or security—*
  - *(i) the amount for which the company (or its subsidiary) was liable under the guarantee or in respect of the security both at the beginning and at the end of the financial year;*
  - *(ii) the maximum amount for which the company (or its subsidiary) may become so liable; and*
  - *(iii) any amount paid and any liability incurred by the company (or its subsidiary) for the purpose of fulfilling the guarantee or discharging the security (including any loss incurred by reason of the enforcement of the guarantee or security); and*
- *(f) in the case of any transaction, arrangement or agreement other than those mentioned in sub-paragraphs (d) and (e), the value of the transaction or arrangement or (as the case may be) the value of the transaction or arrangement to which the agreement relates.*

[23]. In paragraph [22](2) above, sub-paragraphs (c) to (f) do not apply in the case of a loan or quasi-loan made or agreed to be made by a company to or for a body corporate which is either—

- *(a) a body corporate of which that company is a wholly-owned subsidiary, or*
- *(b) a wholly-owned subsidiary of a body corporate of which that company is a wholly-owned subsidiary, or*
- *(c) a wholly-owned subsidiary of that company,*

if particulars of that loan, quasi-loan or agreement for it would not have been required to be included in that company's annual accounts if the first-mentioned body corporate had not been associated with a director of that company at any time during the relevant period.

[Excluded transactions]

[24].—(1) In relation to a company's accounts for a financial year, compliance with this Part is not required in the case of transactions of a kind mentioned in the following sub-paragraph which are made by the company or a subsidiary of it for a person who at any time during that financial year was a director of the company or of its holding company, or was connected with such a director, if the aggregate of the values of each transaction, arrangement or agreement so made for that director or any person connected with him, less

the amount (if any) by which the liabilities of the person for whom the transaction or arrangement was made has been reduced, did not at any time during the financial year exceed £5,000.

(2) *The transactions in question are—*
- (*a*) *credit transactions,*
- (*b*) *guarantees provided or securities entered into in connection with credit transactions,*
- (*c*) *arrangements within subsection (6) or (7) of section 330 relating to credit transactions,*
- (*d*) *agreements to enter into credit transactions.*

[25]. In relation to a company's accounts for a financial year, compliance with this Part is not required by virtue of paragraph [15](c) or [16](c) in the case of any transaction or arrangement with a company or any of its subsidiaries in which a director of the company or its holding company had, directly or indirectly, a material interest if—
- (*a*) *the value of each transaction or arrangement within paragraph [15](c) or [16](c) (as the case may be) in which that director had (directly or indirectly) a material interest and which was made after the commencement of the financial year with the company or any of its subsidiaries, and*
- (*b*) *the value of each such transaction or arrangement which was made before the commencement of the financial year less the amount (if any) by which the liabilities of the person for whom the transaction or arrangement was made have been reduced,*

did not at any time during the financial year exceed in the aggregate £1,000 or, if more, did not exceed £5,000 or 1 per cent of the value of the net assets of the company preparing the accounts in question as at the end of the financial year, whichever is the less.

For this purpose a company's net assets are the aggregate of its assets, less the aggregate of its liabilities ("liabilities" to include any [provisions for liabilities] within paragraph 89 of Schedule 4 [that is made in Companies Act accounts and any provision that is made in IAS accounts]).

[26]. Section 345 of this Act (power of Secretary of State to alter sums by statutory instrument subject to negative resolution in Parliament) applies as if the money sums specified in paragraph [24] or [25] above were specified in Part X.

Interpretation

[27].—[(1)] The following provisions of this Act apply for purposes of this Part of this Schedule—
- (*a*) *section 331(2), … and (7), as regards the meaning of "guarantee", … and "credit transaction";*
- (*b*) *section 331(9), as to the interpretation of references to a transaction or arrangement being made "for" a person;*
- (*c*) *section 340, in assigning values to transactions and arrangements, and*
- (*d*) *section 346, as to the interpretation of references to a person being "connected with" a director of a company.*

[(2) In this Part of this Schedule "director" includes a shadow director.]

[647]

NOTES

Repealed by the Companies Act 2006, s 1295, Sch 16, as from a day to be appointed.

Heading to this Part of this Schedule substituted, paragraphs of this Part renumbered 15–27 and internal cross-references accordingly renumbered, para 4 (as originally numbered) repealed, words in square brackets in para 15 (as renumbered) and heading preceding para 24 (as renumbered) substituted, and the original para 27 (as renumbered) renumbered para 27(1), and para 27(2) inserted, by CA 1989, s 6(4), Sch 4, paras 1, 4, 5, as from 1 April 1990.

Paras 15, 16: for the words "section 330" in sub-para (a) there are substituted the words "section 197, 198, 200, 201 or 203 of the Companies Act 2006" by the draft Companies Act 2006 (Commencement No 3, Consequential Amendments, Transitional Provisions and Savings) Order 2007, art 10(1), Sch 4, Pt 1, para 6(1), (2), (11), as from 1 October 2007, in relation to arrangements and transactions entered into on or after that date (see **[A12]**).

Para 19: for the words "was prohibited by section 330" in sub-para (a) there are substituted the words "was one in respect of which approval was required under section 197, 198, 200, 201 or 203 of the Companies Act 2006" by the draft Companies Act 2006 (Commencement No 3, Consequential

Amendments, Transitional Provisions and Savings) Order 2007, art 10(1), Sch 4, Pt 1, para 6(1), (3), (11), as from 1 October 2007, in relation to arrangements and transactions entered into on or after that date (see **[A12]**).

Para 22: for the words "section 330(6) or (7) of this Act" in sub-para (2)(d) there are substituted the words "section 203 of the Companies Act 2006", and for the words "section 330(6)" in sub-para (2)(e) there are substituted the words "section 203(1)(b) of the Companies Act 2006", by the draft Companies Act 2006 (Commencement No 3, Consequential Amendments, Transitional Provisions and Savings) Order 2007, art 10(1), Sch 4, Pt 1, para 6(1), (4), (11), as from 1 October 2007, in relation to arrangements and transactions entered into on or after that date (see **[A12]**).

Para 24: for the words "subsection (6) or (7) of section 330" in sub-para (2)(c) there are substituted the words "section 203 of the Companies Act 2006" by the draft Companies Act 2006 (Commencement No 3, Consequential Amendments, Transitional Provisions and Savings) Order 2007, art 10(1), Sch 4, Pt 1, para 6(1), (5), (11), as from 1 October 2007, in relation to arrangements and transactions entered into on or after that date (see **[A12]**).

Para 25: words in first pair of square brackets substituted, and words in second pair of square brackets inserted, by the Companies Act 1985 (International Accounting Standards and Other Accounting Amendments) Regulations 2004, SI 2004/2947, regs 3, 15, Sch 1, paras 1, 32, Sch 7, Pt 1, paras 1, 11, as from 12 November 2004, in relation to companies' financial years which begin on or after 1 January 2005.

Para 26: for the words "Section 345 of this Act" there are substituted the words "Section 258 of the Companies Act 2006", and for the words "Part 10" there are substituted the words "Part 10 of that Act", by the draft Companies Act 2006 (Commencement No 3, Consequential Amendments, Transitional Provisions and Savings) Order 2007, art 10(1), Sch 4, Pt 1, para 6(1), (6), (11), as from 1 October 2007, in relation to arrangements and transactions entered into on or after that date (see **[A12]**).

Para 27: words omitted from sub-para (1) (as renumbered) repealed by the Banking Act 1987, s 108(2), Sch 7, Pt I, as from 1 October 1987; sub-para (1) substituted by the draft Companies Act 2006 (Commencement No 3, Consequential Amendments, Transitional Provisions and Savings) Order 2007, art 10(1), Sch 4, Pt 1, para 6(1), (7), (11), as from 1 October 2007, in relation to arrangements and transactions entered into on or after that date (see **[A12]**) as follows—

"(1) The following provisions of the Companies Act 2006 apply for the purposes of this Part of this Schedule—

(a) section 202 (meaning of "credit transaction");
(b) section 211 (value of transactions and arrangements);
(c) section 212 (person for whom a transaction or arrangement is entered into);
(d) sections 252 to 255 and Schedule 1 (persons connected with a director).".

Application to limited liability partnerships: see the Limited Liability Partnerships Regulations 2001, SI 2001/1090, reg 3, Sch 1 at **[6984]**, **[6992]**. Note also that nothing in the draft Companies Act 2006 (Commencement No 3, Consequential Amendments, Transitional Provisions and Savings) Order 2007 affects any provision of this Act as applied by the 2001 Regulations to LLPs (see art 12(2) at **[A12]** and the introductory notes to this Act).

[PART III
OTHER TRANSACTIONS, ARRANGEMENTS AND AGREEMENTS]

[28]. This Part of this Schedule applies in relation to the following classes of transactions, arrangements and agreements—

(a) loans, guarantees and securities relating to loans, arrangements of a kind described in subsection (6) or (7) of section 330 of this Act relating to loans and agreements to enter into any of the foregoing transactions and arrangements;

(b) quasi-loans, guarantees and securities relating to quasi-loans, arrangements of a kind described in either of those subsections relating to quasi-loans and agreements to enter into any of the foregoing transactions and arrangements;

(c) credit transactions, guarantees and securities relating to credit transactions, arrangements of a kind described in either of those subsections relating to credit transactions and agreements to enter into any of the foregoing transactions and arrangements.

[29].—(1) To comply with this Part of this Schedule, the accounts must contain a statement, in relation to transactions, arrangements and agreements [made by the company or a subsidiary of it for persons who at any time during the financial year were officers of the company (but not directors or shadow directors)], of—

(a) the aggregate amounts outstanding at the end of the financial year under transactions, arrangements and agreements within sub-paragraphs (a), (b) and (c) respectively of paragraph [28] above, and

(b) the numbers of officers for whom the transactions, arrangements and agreements falling within each of those sub-paragraphs were made.

(2) *This paragraph does not apply to transactions, arrangements and agreements made by the company or any of its subsidiaries for an officer of the company if the aggregate amount outstanding at the end of the financial year under the transactions, arrangements and agreements so made for that officer does not exceed £2,500.*

(3) *Section 345 of this Act (power of Secretary of State to alter money sums by statutory instrument subject to negative resolution in Parliament) applies as if the money sum specified above in this paragraph were specified in Part X.*

[30]. The following provisions of this Act apply for purposes of this Part—

(*a*) *section 331(2), (3), … and (7), as regards the meaning of "guarantee", "quasi-loan", … and "credit transaction", and*

(*b*) *section 331(9), as to the interpretation of references to a transaction or arrangement being made "for" a person;*

and "amount outstanding" means the amount of the outstanding liabilities of the person for whom the transaction, arrangement or agreement was made or, in the case of a guarantee or security, the amount guaranteed or secured.

[648]

NOTES

Repealed by the Companies Act 2006, s 1295, Sch 16, as from a day to be appointed.

Heading to this Part of this Schedule substituted, paragraphs of this Part renumbered 28–30 and internal cross-references accordingly renumbered, words in square brackets in para 29 (as renumbered) substituted, and original Pt III of this Schedule repealed, by CA 1989, s 6(4), Sch 4, paras 1, 6, 7, as from 1 April 1990.

Para 28: for the words "subsection (6) or (7) of section 330 of this Act" in sub-para (a) there are substituted the words "section 203 of the Companies Act 2006", and for the words "either of those subsections" in sub-paras (b), (c) there are substituted the words "that section", by the draft Companies Act 2006 (Commencement No 3, Consequential Amendments, Transitional Provisions and Savings) Order 2007, art 10(1), Sch 4, Pt 1, para 6(1), (8), (11), as from 1 October 2007, in relation to arrangements and transactions entered into on or after that date (see **[A12]**).

Para 29: for the words "Section 345 of this Act" in sub-para (3) there are substituted the words "Section 258 of the Companies Act 2006", and for the words "Part 10" there are substituted the words "Part 10 of that Act", by the draft Companies Act 2006 (Commencement No 3, Consequential Amendments, Transitional Provisions and Savings) Order 2007, art 10(1), Sch 4, Pt 1, para 6(1), (9), (11), as from 1 October 2007, in relation to arrangements and transactions entered into on or after that date (see **[A12]**).

Para 30: words omitted from sub-para (a) (as renumbered) repealed by the Banking Act 1987, s 108(2), Sch 7, Pt I, as from 1 October 1987; for the words from "of this Act" to the end of para (b) there are substituted the following words by the draft Companies Act 2006 (Commencement No 3, Consequential Amendments, Transitional Provisions and Savings) Order 2007, art 10(1), Sch 4, Pt 1, para 6(1), (10), (11), as from 1 October 2007, in relation to arrangements and transactions entered into on or after that date (see **[A12]**)—

"of the Companies Act 2006 apply for the purposes of this Part of this Schedule—

(a) section 199 (meaning of "quasi-loan"),

(b) section 202 (meaning of "credit transaction"), and

(c) section 212 (person for whom a transaction or arrangement is entered into);".

Application to limited liability partnerships: see the Limited Liability Partnerships Regulations 2001, SI 2001/1090, reg 3, Sch 1 at **[6984]**, **[6992]**. Note also that nothing in the draft Companies Act 2006 (Commencement No 3, Consequential Amendments, Transitional Provisions and Savings) Order 2007 affects any provision of this Act as applied by the 2001 Regulations to LLPs (see art 12(2) at **[A12]** and the introductory notes to this Act).

SCHEDULE 7
MATTERS TO BE DEALT WITH IN DIRECTORS' REPORT

Section 234

PART I
MATTERS OF A GENERAL NATURE

Asset values

1.—(1) …

(2) *If, in the case of [such of the fixed assets of the company …] as consist in interests in land, their market value (as at the end of the financial year) differs substantially from the*

amount at which they are included in the balance sheet, and the difference is, in the directors' opinion, of such significance as to require that the attention of members of the company or of holders of its debentures should be drawn to it, the report shall indicate the difference with such degree of precision as is practicable.

[(3) In relation to a group directors' report sub-paragraph (2) has effect as if the reference to the fixed assets of the company was a reference to the fixed assets of the company and of its subsidiary undertakings included in the consolidation.]

Directors' interests

[2.—(1) The information required by paragraphs 2A and 2B shall be given in the directors' report, or by way of notes to the company's annual accounts, with respect to each person who at the end of the financial year was a director of the company.

(2) In those paragraphs—

- *(a) "the register" means the register of directors' interests kept by the company under section 325; and*
- *(b) references to a body corporate being in the same group as the company are to its being a subsidiary or holding company, or another subsidiary of a holding company, of the company.*

2A.—(1) It shall be stated with respect to each director whether, according to the register, he was at the end of the financial year interested in shares in or debentures of the company or any other body corporate in the same group.

(2) If he was so interested, there shall be stated the number of shares in and amount of debentures of each body (specifying it) in which, according to the register, he was then interested.

(3) If a director was interested at the end of the financial year in shares in or debentures of the company or any other body corporate in the same group—

- *(a) it shall also be stated whether, according to the register, he was at the beginning of the financial year (or, if he was not then a director, when he became one) interested in shares in or debentures of the company or any other body corporate in the same group, and*
- *(b) if he was so interested, there shall be stated the number of shares in and amount of debentures of each body (specifying it) in which, according to the register, he was then interested.*

(4) In this paragraph references to an interest in shares or debentures have the same meaning as in section 324; and references to the interest of a director include any interest falling to be treated as his for the purposes of that section.

(5) The reference above to the time when a person became a director is, in the case of a person who became a director on more than one occasion, to the time when he first became a director.

2B.—(1) It shall be stated with respect to each director whether, according to the register, any right to subscribe for shares in or debentures of the company or another body corporate in the same group was during the financial year granted to, or exercised by, the director or a member of his immediate family.

(2) If any such right was granted to, or exercised by, any such person during the financial year, there shall be stated the number of shares in and amount of debentures of each body (specifying it) in respect of which, according to the register, the right was granted or exercised.

(3) A director's "immediate family" means his or her spouse [or civil partner] and infant children; and for this purpose "children" includes step-children, and "infant", in relation to Scotland, means pupil or minor.

(4) The reference above to a member of the director's immediate family does not include a person who is himself or herself a director of the company.]

[Political donations and expenditure

3.—(1) If—

(a) the company (not being the wholly-owned subsidiary of a company incorporated in Great Britain) has in the financial year—

(i) made any donation to any registered party or to any other EU political organisation, or

(ii) incurred any EU political expenditure, and

(b) the amount of the donation or expenditure, or (as the case may be) the aggregate amount of all donations and expenditure falling within paragraph (a), exceeded £200,

the directors' report for the year shall contain the particulars specified in sub-paragraph (2).

(2) Those particulars are—

(a) as respects donations falling within sub-paragraph (1)(a)(i)—

(i) the name of each registered party or other organisation to whom any such donation has been made, and

(ii) the total amount given to that party or organisation by way of such donations in the financial year; and

(b) as respects expenditure falling within sub-paragraph (1)(a)(ii), the total amount incurred by way of such expenditure in the financial year.

(3) If—

(a) at the end of the financial year the company has subsidiaries which have, in that year, made any donations or incurred any such expenditure as is mentioned in sub-paragraph (1)(a), and

(b) it is not itself the wholly-owned subsidiary of a company incorporated in Great Britain,

the directors' report for the year is not, by virtue of sub-paragraph (1), required to contain the particulars specified in sub-paragraph (2); but, if the total amount of any such donations or expenditure (or both) made or incurred in that year by the company and the subsidiaries between them exceeds £200, the directors' report for the year shall contain those particulars in relation to each body by whom any such donation or expenditure has been made or incurred.

(4) Any expression used in this paragraph which is also used in Part XA of this Act has the same meaning as in that Part.

4.—(1) If the company (not being the wholly-owned subsidiary of a company incorporated in Great Britain) has in the financial year made any contribution to a non-EU political party, the directors' report for the year shall contain—

(a) a statement of the amount of the contribution, or

(b) (if it has made two or more such contributions in the year) a statement of the total amount of the contributions.

(2) If—

(a) at the end of the financial year the company has subsidiaries which have, in that year, made any such contributions as are mentioned in sub-paragraph (1), and

(b) it is not itself the wholly-owned subsidiary of a company incorporated in Great Britain,

the directors' report for the year is not, by virtue of sub-paragraph (1), required to contain any such statement as is there mentioned, but it shall instead contain a statement of the total amount of the contributions made in the year by the company and the subsidiaries between them.

(3) In this paragraph "contribution", in relation to an organisation, means—

(a) any gift of money to the organisation (whether made directly or indirectly);

(b) any subscription or other fee paid for affiliation to, or membership of, the organisation; or

(c) any money spent (otherwise than by the organisation or a person acting on its behalf) in paying any expenses incurred directly or indirectly by the organisation.

(4) In this paragraph "non-EU political party" means any political party which carries on, or proposes to carry on, its activities wholly outside the member States.

Charitable donations

5.—(1) If—

(a) the company (not being the wholly-owned subsidiary of a company incorporated in Great Britain) has in the financial year given money for charitable purposes, and

(b) the money given exceeded £200 in amount,

the directors' report for the year shall contain, in the case of each of the purposes for which money has been given, a statement of the amount of money given for that purpose.

(2) If—

(a) at the end of the financial year the company has subsidiaries which have, in that year, given money for charitable purposes, and

(b) it is not itself the wholly-owned subsidiary of a company incorporated in Great Britain,

sub-paragraph (1) does not apply to the company; but, if the amount given in that year for charitable purposes by the company and the subsidiaries between them exceeds £200, the directors' report for the year shall contain, in the case of each of the purposes for which money has been given by the company and the subsidiaries between them, a statement of the amount of money given for that purpose.

(3) Money given for charitable purposes to a person who, when it was given, was ordinarily resident outside the United Kingdom is to be left out of account for the purposes of this paragraph.

(4) For the purposes of this paragraph "charitable purposes" means purposes which are exclusively charitable, and as respects Scotland [a purpose is charitable if it is listed in section 7(2) of the Charities and Trustee Investment (Scotland) Act 2005].]

[Financial instruments

5A.—(1) In relation to the use of financial instruments by a company ... the directors' report must contain an indication of—

(a) the financial risk management objectives and policies of the company ... , including the policy for hedging each major type of forecasted transaction for which hedge accounting is used, and

(b) the exposure of the company ... to price risk, credit risk, liquidity risk and cash flow risk,

unless such information is not material for the assessment of the assets, liabilities, financial position and profit or loss of the company ...

[(1A) In relation to a group directors' report sub-paragraph (1) has effect as if the references to the company were references to the company and its subsidiary undertakings included in the consolidation.]

(2) In sub-paragraph (1) the expressions "hedge accounting", "price risk", "credit risk", "liquidity risk" and "cash flow risk" have the same meaning as they have in Council Directive 78/660/EEC on the annual accounts of certain types of companies, and in Council Directive 83/349/EEC on consolidated accounts, as amended.]

Miscellaneous

6.—[(1)] The directors' report shall contain—

(a) particulars of any important events affecting the company ... which have occurred since the end of the financial year,

(b) an indication of likely future developments in the business of the company ...

(c) an indication of the activities (if any) of the company ... in the field of research and development[, and

(d) (unless the company is an unlimited company) an indication of the existence of branches (as defined in section 698(2)) of the company outside the United Kingdom].

[(2) In relation to a group directors' report paragraphs (a), (b) and (c) of sub-paragraph (1) have effect as if the references to the company were references to the company and its subsidiary undertakings included in the consolidation.]

[649]

NOTES

Repealed by the Companies Act 2006, s 1295, Sch 16, as from 6 April 2007 (in so far as relating to paras 2. 2A, 2B), and as from a day to be appointed (otherwise). Note that the repeal of paras 2, 2A and 2B does not affect the operation of those provisions in relation to any directors' report referred to in s 234 of this Act that is approved before 6 April 2007 (see the Companies Act 2006 (Commencement No 2, Consequential Amendments, Transitional Provisions and Savings) Order 2007, SI 2007/1093, Sch 6, para 5 at **[7629]**).

Para 1: sub-para (1) repealed, and words in square brackets in sub-para (2) substituted, by the Companies Act 1985 (Miscellaneous Accounting Amendments) Regulations 1996, SI 1996/189, regs 14(4)(a), 15(3), 16(1), in relation to any financial year ending on or after 2 February 1996 (subject to transitional provisions in relation to financial years ending on or before 24 March 1996); words omitted from sub-para (2) repealed, and sub-para (3) added, by the Companies Act 1985 (Operating and Financial Review and Directors' Report etc) Regulations 2005, SI 2005/1011, reg 7(1), (2), as from 22 March 2005, in relation to companies' financial years which begin on or after 1 April 2005.

Paras 2, 2A: substituted, together with para 2B for original para 2, by CA 1989, s 8(2), Sch 5, as from 1 April 1990; repealed as noted above.

Para 2B: substituted as noted above; words in square brackets in sub-para (3) inserted by the Civil Partnership Act 2004, s 261(1), Sch 27, para 105, as from 5 December 2005; repealed as noted above.

Paras 3, 4: substituted, together with para 5, by the Political Parties, Elections and Referendums Act 2000, s 140, as from 16 February 2001. By virtue of s 163(7), Sch 23, Pt II, para 13 to the 2000 Act, this substitution applies only in relation to directors' reports for financial years beginning on or after the first anniversary of the date which is the relevant date for the purposes of Sch 23, Pt II, para 12 to that Act; namely the date (if held within the first year after s 139(1) comes into force) of the annual general meeting of the company, or otherwise the date immediately following the end of that year.

Para 5: substituted as noted above; words in square brackets in sub-para (4) substituted by the Charities and Trustee Investment (Scotland) Act 2005 (Consequential Provisions and Modifications) Order 2006, SI 2006/242, art 5, Schedule, Pt 1, para 3, as from 1 April 2006.

Para 5A: inserted by the Companies Act 1985 (International Accounting Standards and Other Accounting Amendments) Regulations 2004, SI 2004/2947, reg 13(1), as from 12 November 2004, in relation to companies' financial years which begin on or after 1 January 2005 (note that previously a para 5A had been inserted by CA 1989, s 137(2), partly as from 1 April 1990 and partly as from a day to be appointed, and repealed by SI 1996/189, regs 14(4)(b), 16(1), in relation to any financial year ending on or after 2 February 1996 (subject to transitional provisions as noted above); words omitted from sub-para (1) repealed, and sub-para (1A) inserted, by the Companies Act 1985 (Operating and Financial Review and Directors' Report etc) Regulations 2005, SI 2005/1011, reg 7(1), (3), as from 22 March 2005, in relation to companies' financial years which begin on or after 1 April 2005.

Para 6: sub-para (1) numbered as such, words omitted from that sub-paragraph repealed, and sub-para (2) added, by the Companies Act 1985 (Operating and Financial Review and Directors' Report etc) Regulations 2005, SI 2005/1011, reg 7(1), (4), as from 22 March 2005, in relation to companies' financial years which begin on or after 1 April 2005; sub-para (1)(d) and the word immediately preceding it added, by the Companies Act 1985 (Disclosure of Branches and Bank Accounts) Regulations 1992, SI 1992/3178, regs 3, 8(a), as from 1 January 1993 (subject to transitional provisions in relation to the preparation of a directors' report under s 234 of this Act for a financial year of the company beginning before 1 January 1993).

Application to limited liability partnerships: see the Limited Liability Partnerships Regulations 2001, SI 2001/1090, reg 3, Sch 1 at **[6984]**, **[6992]**. Note also that nothing in the Companies Act 2006 (Commencement No 2, Consequential Amendments, Transitional Provisions and Savings) Order 2007, SI 2007/1093 affects any provision of this Act as applied by the 2001 Regulations to LLPs (see art 12(1) at **[7624]** and the introductory notes to this Act).

PART II
DISCLOSURE REQUIRED BY COMPANY ACQUIRING ITS OWN SHARES, ETC

7. This Part of this Schedule applies where shares in a company—

- *(a) are purchased by the company or are acquired by it by forfeiture or surrender in lieu of forfeiture, or in pursuance of section 143(3) of this Act (acquisition of own shares by company limited by shares), or*
- *(b) are acquired by another person in circumstances where paragraph (c) or (d) of section 146(1) applies (acquisition by company's nominee, or by another with company financial assistance, the company having a beneficial interest), or*
- *(c) are made subject to a lien or other charge taken (whether expressly or otherwise) by the company and permitted by section 150(2) or (4), or section 6(3) of the Consequential Provisions Act (exceptions from general rule against a company having a lien or charge on its own shares).*

8. The directors' report with respect to a financial year shall state—

(*a*) *the number and nominal value of the shares so purchased, the aggregate amount of the consideration paid by the company for such shares and the reasons for their purchase;*

(*b*) *the number and nominal value of the shares so acquired by the company, acquired by another person in such circumstances and so charged respectively during the financial year;*

(*c*) *the maximum number and nominal value of shares which, having been so acquired by the company, acquired by another person in such circumstances or so charged (whether or not during that year) are held at any time by the company or that other person during that year;*

(*d*) *the number and nominal value of the shares so acquired by the company, acquired by another person in such circumstances or so charged (whether or not during that year) which are disposed of by the company or that other person or cancelled by the company during that year;*

(*e*) *where the number and nominal value of the shares of any particular description are stated in pursuance of any of the preceding sub-paragraphs, the percentage of the called-up share capital which shares of that description represent;*

(*f*) *where any of the shares have been so charged the amount of the charge in each case; and*

(*g*) *where any of the shares have been disposed of by the company or the person who acquired them in such circumstances for money or money's worth the amount or value of the consideration in each case.*

[650]

NOTES

Repealed by the Companies Act 2006, s 1295, Sch 16, as from a day to be appointed.

Application to limited liability partnerships: see the Limited Liability Partnerships Regulations 2001, SI 2001/1090, reg 3, Sch 1 at **[6984]**, **[6992]**.

Consequential Provisions Act: ie, the Companies Consolidation (Consequential Provisions) Act 1985.

PART III
DISCLOSURE CONCERNING EMPLOYMENT, ETC, OF DISABLED PERSONS

9.—(1) This Part of this Schedule applies to the directors' report where the average number of persons employed by the company in each week during the financial year exceeded 250.

(2) That average number is the quotient derived by dividing, by the number of weeks in the financial year, the number derived by ascertaining, in relation to each of those weeks, the number of persons who, under contracts of service, were employed in the week (whether throughout it or not) by the company, and adding up the numbers ascertained.

(3) The directors' report shall in that case contain a statement describing such policy as the company has applied during the financial year—

(*a*) *for giving full and fair consideration to applications for employment by the company made by disabled persons, having regard to their particular aptitudes and abilities,*

(*b*) *for continuing the employment of, and for arranging appropriate training for, employees of the company who have become disabled persons during the period when they were employed by the company, and*

(*c*) *otherwise for the training, career development and promotion of disabled persons employed by the company.*

(4) In this Part—

(*a*) *"employment" means employment other than employment to work wholly or mainly outside the United Kingdom, and "employed" and "employee" shall be construed accordingly; and*

(*b*) *"disabled person" means the same as in the [Disability Discrimination Act 1995].*

[651]

NOTES

Repealed by the Companies Act 2006, s 1295, Sch 16, as from a day to be appointed.

Para 9: words in square brackets substituted by the Disability Discrimination Act 1995, s 70(4), Sch 6, para 4, as from 2 December 1996.

Application to limited liability partnerships: see the Limited Liability Partnerships Regulations 2001, SI 2001/1090, reg 3, Sch 1 at **[6984]**, **[6992]**.

(Pt IV (para 10) repealed, in relation to any financial year ending on or after 2 February 1996, by the Companies Act 1985 (Miscellaneous Accounting Amendments) Regulations 1996, SI 1996/189, regs 14(4)(c), 16(1) (subject to transitional provisions in relation to financial years ending on or before 24 March 1996).)

PART V
EMPLOYEE INVOLVEMENT

11.—(1) This Part of this Schedule applies to the directors' report where the average number of persons employed by the company in each week during the financial year exceeded 250.

(2) That average number is the quotient derived by dividing by the number of weeks in the financial year the number derived by ascertaining, in relation to each of those weeks, the number of persons who, under contracts of service, were employed in the week (whether throughout it or not) by the company, and adding up the numbers ascertained.

(3) The directors' report shall in that case contain a statement describing the action that has been taken during the financial year to introduce, maintain or develop arrangements aimed at—

- *(a) providing employees systematically with information on matters of concern to them as employees,*
- *(b) consulting employees or their representatives on a regular basis so that the views of employees can be taken into account in making decisions which are likely to affect their interests,*
- *(c) encouraging the involvement of employees in the company's performance through an employees' share scheme or by some other means,*
- *(d) achieving a common awareness on the part of all employees of the financial and economic factors affecting the performance of the company.*

(4) In sub-paragraph (3) "employee" does not include a person employed to work wholly or mainly outside the United Kingdom; and for the purposes of sub-paragraph (2) no regard is to be had to such a person.

[652]

NOTES

Repealed by the Companies Act 2006, s 1295, Sch 16, as from a day to be appointed.

Application to limited liability partnerships: see the Limited Liability Partnerships Regulations 2001, SI 2001/1090, reg 3, Sch 1 at **[6984]**, **[6992]**.

[PART VI
POLICY AND PRACTICE ON PAYMENT OF CREDITORS

12.—(1) This Part of this Schedule applies to the directors' report for a financial year if—

- *(a) the company was at any time within the year a public company, or*
- *(b) the company did not qualify as small or medium-sized in relation to the year by virtue of section 247 and was at any time within the year a member of a group of which the parent company was a public company.*

(2) The report shall state, with respect to the next following financial year—

- *(a) whether in respect of some or all of its suppliers it is the company's policy to follow any code or standard on payment practice and, if so, the name of the code or standard and the place where information about, and copies of, the code or standard can be obtained,*
- *(b) whether in respect of some or all of its suppliers it is the company's policy—*
  - *(i) to settle the terms of payment with those suppliers when agreeing the terms of each transaction,*
  - *(ii) to ensure that those suppliers are made aware of the terms of payment, and*
  - *(iii) to abide by the terms of payment,*

(*c*) *where the company's policy is not as mentioned in paragraph* (*a*) *or* (*b*) *in respect of some or all of its suppliers, what its policy is with respect to the payment of those suppliers;*

and if the company's policy is different for different suppliers or classes of suppliers, the report shall identify the suppliers to which the different policies apply.

In this sub-paragraph references to the company's suppliers are references to persons who are or may become its suppliers.

(*3*) *The report shall also state the number of days which bears to the number of days in the financial year the same proportion as X bears to Y where—*

X = the aggregate of the amounts which were owed to trade creditors at the end of the year; and

Y = the aggregate of the amounts in which the company was invoiced by suppliers during the year.

(*4*) *For the purposes of sub-paragraphs* (*2*) *and* (*3*) *a person is a supplier of the company at any time if—*

(*a*) *at that time, he is owed an amount in respect of goods or services supplied, and*

(*b*) *that amount would be included under the heading corresponding to item E.4* (*trade creditors*) *in Format 1 if—*

(*i*) *the company's accounts fell to be prepared as at that time,*

(*ii*) *those accounts were prepared in accordance with Schedule 4, and*

(*iii*) *that Format were adopted.*

(*5*) *For the purpose of sub-paragraph* (*3*), *the aggregate of the amounts which at the end of the financial year were owed to trade creditors shall be taken to be—*

(*a*) *where in the company's accounts Format 1 of the balance sheet formats set out in Part I of Schedule 4 is adopted, the amount shown under the heading corresponding to item E.4* (*trade creditors*) *in that Format,*

(*b*) *where Format 2 is adopted, the amount which, under the heading corresponding to item C.4* (*trade creditors*) *in that Format, is shown as falling due within one year, and*

(*c*) *where the company's accounts are prepared in accordance with Schedule 9 or 9A [or the company's accounts are IAS accounts], the amount which would be shown under the heading corresponding to item E.4* (*trade creditors*) *in Format 1 if the company's accounts were prepared in accordance with Schedule 4 and that Format were adopted.]*

[653]

NOTES

Inserted by the Companies Act 1985 (Miscellaneous Accounting Amendments) Regulations 1996, SI 1996/189, regs 14(5), 16(1), in relation to any financial year ending on or after 2 February 1996 (subject to transitional provisions in relation to financial years ending on or before 24 March 1996); substituted by the Companies Act 1985 (Directors' Report) (Statement of Payment Practice) Regulations 1997, SI 1997/571, reg 2(2), as from 4 March 1997 (for transitional provisions relating to financial years ending on or before 24 March 1997, see reg 3 of those Regulations).

Repealed by the Companies Act 2006, s 1295, Sch 16, as from a day to be appointed.

Para 12: words in square brackets in sub-para (5)(c) inserted by the Companies Act 1985 (International Accounting Standards and Other Accounting Amendments) Regulations 2004, SI 2004/2947, reg 3, Sch 1, paras 1, 33, as from 12 November 2004, in relation to companies' financial years which begin on or after 1 January 2005.

Application to limited liability partnerships: see the Limited Liability Partnerships Regulations 2001, SI 2001/1090, reg 3, Sch 1 at **[6984]**, **[6992]**.

[PART VII
DISCLOSURE REQUIRED BY CERTAIN PUBLICLY-TRADED COMPANIES

13.—(*1*) *This Part of this Schedule applies to the directors' report for a financial year if the company had securities carrying voting rights admitted to trading on a regulated market at the end of that year.*

(*2*) *The report shall contain detailed information, by reference to the end of that year, on the following matters—*

(*a*) *the structure of the company's capital, including in particular—*

(*i*) *the rights and obligations attaching to the shares or, as the case may be, to each class of shares in the company, and*

(ii) *where there are two or more such classes, the percentage of the total share capital represented by each class;*

(b) *any restrictions on the transfer of securities in the company, including in particular—*

(i) *limitations on the holding of securities, and*

(ii) *requirements to obtain the approval of the company, or of other holders of securities in the company, for a transfer of securities;*

(c) *in the case of each person with a significant direct or indirect holding of securities in the company, such details as are known to the company of—*

(i) *the identity of the person,*

(ii) *the size of the holding, and*

(iii) *the nature of the holding;*

(d) *in the case of each person who holds securities carrying special rights with regard to control of the company—*

(i) *the identity of the person, and*

(ii) *the nature of the rights;*

(e) *where—*

(i) *the company has an employees' share scheme, and*

(ii) *shares to which the scheme relates have rights with regard to control of the company that are not exercisable directly by the employees,*

how those rights are exercisable;

(f) *any restrictions on voting rights, including in particular—*

(i) *limitations on voting rights of holders of a given percentage or number of votes,*

(ii) *deadlines for exercising voting rights, and*

(iii) *arrangements by which, with the company's co- operation, financial rights carried by securities are held by a person other than the holder of the securities;*

(g) *any agreements between holders of securities that are known to the company and may result in restrictions on the transfer of securities or on voting rights;*

(h) *any rules that the company has about—*

(i) *appointment and replacement of directors, or*

(ii) *amendment of the company's articles of association;*

(i) *the powers of the company's directors, including in particular any powers in relation to the issuing or buying back by the company of its shares;*

(j) *any significant agreements to which the company is a party that take effect, alter or terminate upon a change of control of the company following a takeover bid, and the effects of any such agreements;*

(k) *any agreements between the company and its directors or employees providing for compensation for loss of office or employment (whether through resignation, purported redundancy or otherwise) that occurs because of a takeover bid.*

(3) *For the purposes of sub-paragraph (2)(a) a company's capital includes any securities in the company that are not admitted to trading on a regulated market.*

(4) *For the purposes of sub-paragraph (2)(c) a person has an indirect holding of securities if—*

(a) *they are held on his behalf, or*

(b) *he is able to secure that rights carried by the securities are exercised in accordance with his wishes.*

(5) *Sub-paragraph (2)(j) does not apply to an agreement if—*

(a) *disclosure of the agreement would be seriously prejudicial to the company, and*

(b) *the company is not under any other obligation to disclose it.*

(6) *In this paragraph—*

"securities" means shares or debentures;

"takeover bid" has the same meaning as in the Takeovers Directive;

"the Takeovers Directive" means Directive 2004/25/EC of the European Parliament and of the Council;

"voting rights" means rights to vote at general meetings of the company in question, including rights that arise only in certain circumstances.]

[653AA]

NOTES

Commencement: 6 April 2007.

Inserted by the Companies Act 2006, s 992(1), (2), (6), as from 6 April 2007, in relation to directors' reports for financial years beginning on or after 20 May 2006.

Repealed by the Companies Act 2006, s 1295, Sch 16, as from a day to be appointed.

Application to limited liability partnerships: nothing in the Companies Act 2006 (Commencement No 2, Consequential Amendments, Transitional Provisions and Savings) Order 2007, SI 2007/1093 affects any provision of this Act as applied by the 2001 Regulations to LLPs (see art 12(1) at **[7624]** and the introductory notes to this Act).

(Sch 7ZA inserted by the Companies Act 1985 (Operating and Financial Review and Directors' Report etc) Regulations 2005, SI 2005/1011, reg 9, as from 22 March 2005, in relation to companies' financial years which begin on or after 1 April 2005; repealed by the Companies Act 1985 (Operating and Financial Review) (Repeal) Regulations 2005, SI 2005/3442, reg 2(2)(a), Sch 1, para 17, as from 12 January 2006.)

[SCHEDULE 7A
DIRECTORS' REMUNERATION REPORT

Section 234B

PART 1
INTRODUCTORY

1.—(1) In the directors' remuneration report for a financial year ("the relevant financial year") there shall be shown the information specified in Parts 2 and 3 below.

(2) Information required to be shown in the report for or in respect of a particular person shall be shown in the report in a manner that links the information to that person identified by name.]

[653A]

NOTES

Inserted by the Directors' Remuneration Report Regulations 2002, SI 2002/1986, reg 9, Schedule, as from 1 August 2002, with effect as respects companies' financial years ending on or after 31 December 2002.

Repealed by the Companies Act 2006, s 1295, Sch 16, as from a day to be appointed.

Application to limited liability partnerships: see the Limited Liability Partnerships Regulations 2001, SI 2001/1090, reg 3, Sch 1 at **[6984]**, **[6992]**.

[PART 2
INFORMATION NOT SUBJECT TO AUDIT

Consideration by the directors of matters relating to directors' remuneration

2.—(1) If a committee of the company's directors has considered matters relating to the directors' remuneration for the relevant financial year, the directors' remuneration report shall—

(a) name each director who was a member of the committee at any time when the committee was considering any such matter;

(b) name any person who provided to the committee advice, or services, that materially assisted the committee in their consideration of any such matter;

(c) in the case of any person named under paragraph (b), who is not a director of the company, state—

(i) the nature of any other services that that person has provided to the company during the relevant financial year; and

(ii) whether that person was appointed by the committee.

(2) In sub-paragraph (1)(b) "person" includes (in particular) any director of the company who does not fall within sub-paragraph (1)(a).

Statement of company's policy on directors' remuneration

3.—(1) The directors' remuneration report shall contain a statement of the company's policy on directors' remuneration for the following financial year and for financial years subsequent to that.

(2) The policy statement shall include—

(a) for each director, a detailed summary of any performance conditions to which any entitlement of the director—
(i) to share options, or
(ii) under a long-term incentive scheme,

is subject;
(b) an explanation as to why any such performance conditions were chosen;
(c) a summary of the methods to be used in assessing whether any such performance conditions are met and an explanation as to why those methods were chosen;
(d) if any such performance condition involves any comparison with factors external to the company—
(i) a summary of the factors to be used in making each such comparison, and
(ii) if any of the factors relates to the performance of another company, of two or more other companies or of an index on which the securities of a company or companies are listed, the identity of that company, of each of those companies or of the index;
(e) a description of, and an explanation for, any significant amendment proposed to be made to the terms and conditions of any entitlement of a director to share options or under a long term incentive scheme; and
(f) if any entitlement of a director to share options, or under a long-term incentive scheme, is not subject to performance conditions, an explanation as to why that is the case.

(3) The policy statement shall, in respect of each director's terms and conditions relating to remuneration, explain the relative importance of those elements which are, and those which are not, related to performance.

(4) The policy statement shall summarise, and explain, the company's policy on—
(a) the duration of contracts with directors, and
(b) notice periods, and termination payments, under such contracts.

(5) In sub-paragraphs (2) and (3), references to a director are to any person who serves as a director of the company at any time in the period beginning with the end of the relevant financial year and ending with date on which the directors' remuneration report is laid before the company in general meeting.

Performance Graph

4.—(1) The directors' remuneration report shall—
(a) contain a line graph that shows for each of—
(i) a holding of shares of that class of the company's equity share capital whose listing, or admission to dealing, has resulted in the company falling within the definition of "quoted company", and
(ii) a hypothetical holding of shares made up of shares of the same kinds and number as those by reference to which a broad equity market index is calculated,

a line drawn by joining up points plotted to represent, for each of the financial years in the relevant period, the total shareholder return on that holding; and
(b) state the name of the index selected for the purposes of the graph and set out the reasons for selecting that index.

(2) For the purposes of sub-paragraphs (1) and (4), "relevant period" means the five financial years of which the last is the relevant financial year.

(3) Where the relevant financial year
(a) is the company's second, third or fourth financial year, sub-paragraph (2) has effect with the substitution of "two", "three" or "four" (as the case may be) for "five"; and
(b) is the company's first financial year, "relevant period", for the purposes of sub-paragraphs (1) and (4), means the relevant financial year.

(4) For the purposes of sub-paragraph (1), the "total shareholder return" for a relevant period on a holding of shares must be calculated using a fair method that—
(a) takes as its starting point the percentage change over the period in the market price of the holding;
(b) involves making—
(i) the assumptions specified in sub-paragraph (5) as to reinvestment of income, and

(ii) *the assumption specified in sub-paragraph (7) as to the funding of liabilities; and*

(*c*) *makes provision for any replacement of shares in the holding by shares of a different description;*

and the same method must be used for each of the holdings mentioned in sub-paragraph (1).

(5) *The assumptions as to reinvestment of income are—*

(*a*) *that any benefit in the form of shares of the same kind as those in the holding is added to the holding at the time the benefit becomes receivable; and*

(*b*) *that any benefit in cash, and an amount equal to the value of any benefit not in cash and not falling within paragraph (a), is applied at the time the benefit becomes receivable in the purchase at their market price of shares of the same kind as those in the holding and that the shares purchased are added to the holding at that time.*

(6) *In sub-paragraph (5) "benefit" means any benefit (including, in particular, any dividend) receivable in respect of any shares in the holding by the holder from the company of whose share capital the shares form part.*

(7) *The assumption as to the funding of liabilities is that, where the holder has a liability to the company of whose capital the shares in the holding form part, shares are sold from the holding—*

(*a*) *immediately before the time by which the liability is due to be satisfied, and*

(*b*) *in such numbers that, at the time of the sale, the market price of the shares sold equals the amount of the liability in respect of the shares in the holding that are not being sold.*

(8) *In sub-paragraph (7) "liability" means a liability arising in respect of any shares in the holding or from the exercise of a right attached to any of those shares.*

Service contracts

5.—(1) *The directors' remuneration report shall contain, in respect of the contract of service or contract for services of each person who has served as a director of the company at any time during the relevant financial year, the following information:*

(*a*) *the date of the contract, the unexpired term and the details of any notice periods;*

(*b*) *any provision for compensation payable upon early termination of the contract; and*

(*c*) *such details of other provisions in the contract as are necessary to enable members of the company to estimate the liability of the company in the event of early termination of the contract.*

(2) *The directors' remuneration report shall contain an explanation for any significant award made to a person in the circumstances described in paragraph 14.]*

[653B]

NOTES

Inserted as noted to Pt 1 at **[653A]**.

Repealed by the Companies Act 2006, s 1295, Sch 16, as from a day to be appointed.

Application to limited liability partnerships: see the Limited Liability Partnerships Regulations 2001, SI 2001/1090, reg 3, Sch 1 at **[6984]**, **[6992]**.

[PART 3
INFORMATION SUBJECT TO AUDIT

Amount of each director's emoluments and compensation in the relevant financial year

6.—(1) *The directors' remuneration report shall for the relevant financial year show, for each person who has served as a director of the company at any time during that year, each of the following—*

(*a*) *the total amount of salary and fees paid to or receivable by the person in respect of qualifying services;*

(*b*) *the total amount of bonuses so paid or receivable;*

(*c*) *the total amount of sums paid by way of expenses allowance that are—*

(i) *chargeable to United Kingdom income tax (or would be if the person were an individual); and*
(ii) *paid to or receivable by the person in respect of qualifying services;*
(d) *the total amount of—*
(i) *any compensation for loss of office paid to or receivable by the person, and*
(ii) *any other payments paid to or receivable by the person in connection with the termination of qualifying services;*
(e) *the total estimated value of any benefits received by the person otherwise than in cash that—*
(i) *do not fall within any of sub-paragraphs (a)–(d) or paragraphs 7–11 below,*
(ii) *are emoluments of the person, and*
(iii) *are received by the person in respect of qualifying services; and*
(f) *the amount that is the total of the sums mentioned in paragraphs (a) to (e).*

(2) *The directors' remuneration report shall show, for each person who has served as a director of the company at any time during the relevant financial year, the amount that for the financial year preceding the relevant financial year is the total of the sums mentioned in paragraphs (a) to (e) of sub-paragraph (1).*

(3) *The directors' remuneration report shall also state the nature of any element of a remuneration package which is not cash.*

(4) *The information required by sub-paragraphs (1) and (2) shall be presented in tabular form.*

Share options

7.—(1) *The directors' remuneration report shall contain, in respect of each person who has served as a director of the company at any time in the relevant financial year, the information specified in paragraph 8.*

(2) *Sub-paragraph (1) is subject to paragraph 9 (aggregation of information to avoid excessively lengthy reports).*

(3) *The information specified in paragraphs (a) to (c) of paragraph 8 shall be presented in tabular form in the report.*

(4) *In paragraph 8 "share option", in relation to a person, means a share option granted in respect of qualifying services of the person.*

8. *The information required by sub-paragraph (1) of paragraph 7 in respect of such a person as is mentioned in that sub-paragraph is—*
(a) *the number of shares that are subject to a share option—*
(i) *at the beginning of the relevant financial year or, if later, on the date of the appointment of the person as a director of the company, and*
(ii) *at the end of the relevant financial year or, if earlier, on the cessation of the person's appointment as a director of the company,*

in each case differentiating between share options having different terms and conditions;
(b) *information identifying those share options that have been awarded in the relevant financial year, those that have been exercised in that year, those that in that year have expired unexercised and those whose terms and conditions have been varied in that year;*
(c) *for each share option that is unexpired at any time in the relevant financial year—*
(i) *the price paid, if any, for its award,*
(ii) *the exercise price,*
(iii) *the date from which the option may be exercised, and*
(iv) *the date on which the option expires;*
(d) *a description of any variation made in the relevant financial year in the terms and conditions of a share option;*
(e) *a summary of any performance criteria upon which the award or exercise of a share option is conditional, including a description of any variation made in such performance criteria during the relevant financial year;*
(f) *for each share option that has been exercised during the relevant financial year, the market price of the shares, in relation to which it is exercised, at the time of exercise; and*
(g) *for each share option that is unexpired at the end of the relevant financial year—*
(i) *the market price at the end of that year, and*

(ii) the highest and lowest market prices during that year,
of each share that is subject to the option.

9.—(1) If, in the opinion of the directors of the company, disclosure in accordance with paragraphs 7 and 8 would result in a disclosure of excessive length then, (subject to sub-paragraphs (2) and (3))—

(a) information disclosed for a person under paragraph 8(a) need not differentiate between share options having different terms and conditions;

(b) for the purposes of disclosure in respect of a person under paragraph 8(c)(i) and (ii) and (g), share options may be aggregated and (instead of disclosing prices for each share option) disclosure may be made of weighted average prices of aggregations of share options;

(c) for the purposes of disclosure in respect of a person under paragraph 8(c)(iii) and (iv), share options may be aggregated and (instead of disclosing dates for each share option) disclosure may be made of ranges of dates for aggregation of share options.

(2) Sub-paragraph (1)(b) and (c) does not permit the aggregation of—

(a) share options in respect of shares whose market price at the end of the relevant financial year is below the option exercise price, with

(b) share options in respect of shares whose market price at the end of the relevant financial year is equal to, or exceeds, the option exercise price.

(3) Sub-paragraph (1) does not apply (and accordingly, full disclosure must be made in accordance with paragraphs 7 and 8) in respect of share options that during the relevant financial year have been awarded or exercised or had their terms and conditions varied.

Long term incentive schemes

10.—(1) The directors' remuneration report shall contain, in respect of each person who has served as a director of the company at any time in the relevant financial year, the information specified in paragraph 11.

(2) Sub-paragraph (1) does not require the report to contain share option details that are contained in the report in compliance with paragraphs 7 to 9.

(3) The information specified in paragraph 11 shall be presented in tabular form in the report.

(4) For the purposes of paragraph 11—

(a) "scheme interest", in relation to a person, means an interest under a long term incentive scheme that is an interest in respect of which assets may become receivable under the scheme in respect of qualifying services of the person; and

(b) such an interest "vests" at the earliest time when—

(i) it has been ascertained that the qualifying conditions have been fulfilled, and

(ii) the nature and quantity of the assets receivable under the scheme in respect of the interest have been ascertained.

(5) In this Schedule "long term incentive scheme" means any agreement or arrangement under which money or other assets may become receivable by a person and which includes one or more qualifying conditions with respect to service or performance that cannot be fulfilled within a single financial year, and for this purpose the following shall be disregarded, namely—

(a) any bonus the amount of which falls to be determined by reference to service or performance within a single financial year;

(b) compensation in respect of loss of office, payments for breach of contract and other termination payments; and

(c) retirement benefits.

11.—(1) The information required by sub-paragraph (1) of paragraph 10 in respect of such a person as is mentioned in that sub-paragraph is—

(a) details of the scheme interests that the person has at the beginning of the relevant financial year or if later on the date of the appointment of the person as a director of the company;

(b) details of the scheme interests awarded to the person during the relevant financial year;

(c) details of the scheme interests that the person has at the end of the relevant financial year or if earlier on the cessation of the person's appointment as a director of the company;

(d) for each scheme interest within paragraphs (a) to (c)—

(i) the end of the period over which the qualifying conditions for that interest have to be fulfilled (or if there are different periods for different conditions, the end of whichever of those periods ends last); and

(ii) a description of any variation made in the terms and conditions of the scheme interests during the relevant financial year; and

(e) for each scheme interest that has vested in the relevant financial year—

(i) the relevant details (see sub-paragraph (3)) of any shares,

(ii) the amount of any money, and

(iii) the value of any other assets,

that have become receivable in respect of the interest.

(2) The details that sub-paragraph (1)(b) requires of a scheme interest awarded during the relevant financial year include, if shares may become receivable in respect of the interest, the following—

(a) the number of those shares;

(b) the market price of each of those shares when the scheme interest was awarded; and

(c) details of qualifying conditions that are conditions with respect to performance.

(3) In sub-paragraph (1)(e)(i) "the relevant details", in relation to any shares that have become receivable in respect of a scheme interest, means—

(a) the number of those shares;

(b) the date on which the scheme interest was awarded;

(c) the market price of each of those shares when the scheme interest was awarded;

(d) the market price of each of those shares when the scheme interest vested; and

(e) details of qualifying conditions that were conditions with respect to performance.

Pensions

12.—(1) The directors' remuneration report shall, for each person who has served as a director of the company at any time during the relevant financial year, contain the information in respect of pensions that is specified in sub-paragraphs (2) and (3).

(2) Where the person has rights under a pension scheme that is a defined benefit scheme in relation to the person and any of those rights are rights to which he has become entitled in respect of qualifying services of his—

(a) details

(i) of any changes during the relevant financial year in the person's accrued benefits under the scheme, and

(ii) of the person's accrued benefits under the scheme as at the end of that year;

(b) the transfer value, calculated in a manner consistent with "Retirement Benefit Schemes—Transfer Values (GN 11)" published by the Institute of Actuaries and the Faculty of Actuaries and dated 6th April 2001, of the person's accrued benefits under the scheme at the end of the relevant financial year;

(c) the transfer value of the person's accrued benefits under the scheme that in compliance with paragraph (b) was contained in the director's remuneration report for the previous financial year or, if there was no such report or no such value was contained in that report, the transfer value, calculated in such a manner as is mentioned in paragraph (b), of the person's accrued benefits under the scheme at the beginning of the relevant financial year;

(d) the amount obtained by subtracting—

(i) the transfer value of the person's accrued benefits under the scheme that is required to be contained in the report by paragraph (c), from

(ii) the transfer value of those benefits that is required to be contained in the report by paragraph (b),

and then subtracting from the result of that calculation the amount of any contributions made to the scheme by the person in the relevant financial year.

(3) Where—

(a) the person has rights under a pension scheme that is a money purchase scheme in relation to the person, and

(*b*) *any of those rights are rights to which he has become entitled in respect of qualifying services of his,*

details of any contribution to the scheme in respect of the person that is paid or payable by the company for the relevant financial year or paid by the company in that year for another financial year.

Excess retirement benefits of directors and past directors

13.—(1) Subject to sub-paragraph (3), the directors' remuneration report shall show in respect of each person who has served as a director of the company—

(*a*) *at any time during the relevant financial year, or*

(*b*) *at any time before the beginning of that year,*

the amount of so much of retirement benefits paid to or receivable by the person under pension schemes as is in excess of the retirement benefits to which he was entitled on the date on which the benefits first became payable or 31st March 1997, whichever is the later.

(2) In subsection (1) "retirement benefits" means retirement benefits to which the person became entitled in respect of qualifying services of his.

(3) Amounts paid or receivable under a pension scheme need not be included in an amount required to be shown under sub-paragraph (1) if—

(*a*) *the funding of the scheme was such that the amounts were or, as the case may be, could have been paid without recourse to additional contributions; and*

(*b*) *amounts were paid to or receivable by all pensioner members of the scheme on the same basis;*

and in this sub-paragraph "pensioner member", in relation to a pension scheme, means any person who is entitled to the present payment of retirement benefits under the scheme.

(4) In this paragraph—

(*a*) *references to retirement benefits include benefits otherwise than in cash; and*

(*b*) *in relation to so much of retirement benefits as consists of a benefit otherwise than in cash, references to their amount are to the estimated money value of the benefit;*

and the nature of any such benefit shall also be shown in the report.

Compensation for past directors

14. The directors' remuneration report shall contain details of any significant award made in the relevant financial year to any person who was not a director of the company at the time the award was made but had previously been a director of the company, including (in particular) compensation in respect of loss of office and pensions but excluding any sums which have already been shown in the report under paragraph 6(1)(d).

Sums paid to third parties in respect of a director's services

15.—(1) The directors' remuneration report shall show, in respect of each person who served as a director of the company at any time during the relevant financial year, the aggregate amount of any consideration paid to or receivable by third parties for making available the services of the person—

(*a*) *as a director of the company, or*

(*b*) *while director of the company—*

  (*i*) *as director of any of its subsidiary undertakings, or*

  (*ii*) *as director of any other undertaking of which he was (while director of the company) a director by virtue of the company's nomination (direct or indirect), or*

  (*iii*) *otherwise in connection with the management of the affairs of the company or any such other undertaking.*

(2) The reference to consideration includes benefits otherwise than in cash; and in relation to such consideration the reference to its amount is to the estimated money value of the benefit.

The nature of any such consideration shall be shown in the report.

(3) The reference to third parties is to persons other than—

(*a*) *the person himself or a person connected with him or a body corporate controlled by him, and*

(*b*) *the company or any such other undertaking as is mentioned in sub-paragraph (1)(b)(ii).]*

[653C]

NOTES

Inserted as noted to Pt 1 at **[653A]**.

Repealed by the Companies Act 2006, s 1295, Sch 16, as from a day to be appointed.

Application to limited liability partnerships: see the Limited Liability Partnerships Regulations 2001, SI 2001/1090, reg 3, Sch 1 at **[6984]**, **[6992]**.

[PART 4
INTERPRETATION AND SUPPLEMENTARY

16.—(1) In this Schedule—

"amount", in relation to a gain made on the exercise of a share option, means the difference between—

(*a*) *the market price of the shares on the day on which the option was exercised; and*

(*b*) *the price actually paid for the shares;*

"company contributions", in relation to a pension scheme and a person, means any payments (including insurance premiums) made, or treated as made, to the scheme in respect of the person by anyone other than the person;

"defined benefit scheme", in relation to a person, means a pension scheme which is not a money purchase scheme in relation to the person;

"emoluments" of a person—

(*a*) *includes salary, fees and bonuses, sums paid by way of expenses allowance (so far as they are chargeable to United Kingdom income tax or would be if the person were an individual) but,*

(*b*) *does not include any of the following, namely—*

(*i*) *the value of any share options granted to him or the amount of any gains made on the exercise of any such options;*

(*ii*) *any company contributions paid, or treated as paid, in respect of him under any pension scheme or any benefits to which he is entitled under any such scheme; or*

(*iii*) *any money or other assets paid to or received or receivable by him under any long term incentive scheme;*

"long term incentive scheme" has the meaning given by paragraph 10(5);

"money purchase benefits", in relation to a person, means retirement benefits the rate or amount of which is calculated by reference to payments made, or treated as made, by the person or by any other person in respect of that person and which are not average salary benefits;

"money purchase scheme", in relation to a person, means a pension scheme under which all of the benefits that may become payable to or in respect of the person are money purchase benefits in relation to the person;

"pension scheme" means a retirement benefits scheme within the meaning given by section 611 of the Income and Corporation Taxes Act 1988;

"qualifying services", in relation to any person, means his services as a director of the company, and his services at any time while he is a director of the company—

(*a*) *as a director of an undertaking that is a subsidiary undertaking of the company at that time;*

(*b*) *as a director of any other undertaking of which he is a director by virtue of the company's nomination (direct or indirect); or*

(*c*) *otherwise in connection with the management of the affairs of the company or any such subsidiary undertaking or any such other undertaking;*

"retirement benefits" means relevant benefits within the meaning given by section 612(1) of the Income and Corporation Taxes Act 1988;

"shares" means shares (whether allotted or not) in the company, or any undertaking which is a group undertaking in relation to the company, and includes a share warrant as defined by section 188(1);

"share option" means a right to acquire shares;

"value", in relation to shares received or receivable on any day by a person who is or has been a director of the company, means the market price of the shares on that day.

(2) In this Schedule "compensation in respect of loss of office" includes compensation received or receivable by a person for—

(a) loss of office as director of the company, or

(b) loss, while director of the company or on or in connection with his ceasing to be a director of it, of—

(i) any other office in connection with the management of the company's affairs, or

(ii) any office as director or otherwise in connection with the management of the affairs of any undertaking that, immediately before the loss, is a subsidiary undertaking of the company or an undertaking of which he is a director by virtue of the company's nomination (direct or indirect);

(c) compensation in consideration for, or in connection with, a person's retirement from office; and

(d) where such a retirement is occasioned by a breach of the person's contract with the company or with an undertaking that, immediately before the breach, is a subsidiary undertaking of the company or an undertaking of which he is a director by virtue of the company' s nomination (direct or indirect)—

(i) payments made by way of damages for the breach; or

(ii) payments made by way of settlement or compromise of any claim in respect of the breach.

(3) References in this Schedule to compensation include benefits otherwise than in cash; and in relation to such compensation references in this Schedule to its amount are to the estimated money value of the benefit.

(4) References in this Schedule to a person being "connected" with a director, and to a director "controlling" a body corporate, shall be construed in accordance with section 346.

17.—(1) For the purposes of this Schedule emoluments paid or receivable or share options granted in respect of a person's accepting office as a director shall be treated as emoluments paid or receivable or share options granted in respect of his services as a director.

(2) Where a pension scheme provides for any benefits that may become payable to or in respect of a person to be whichever are the greater of—

(a) such benefits determined by or under the scheme as are money purchase benefits in relation to the person; and

(b) such retirement benefits determined by or under the scheme to be payable to or in respect of the person as are not money purchase benefits in relation to the person,

the company may assume for the purposes of this Schedule that those benefits will be money purchase benefits in relation to the person, or not, according to whichever appears more likely at the end of the relevant financial year.

(3) In determining for the purposes of this Schedule whether a pension scheme is a money purchase scheme in relation to a person or a defined benefit scheme in relation to a person, any death in service benefits provided for by the scheme shall be disregarded.

18.—(1) The following applies with respect to the amounts to be shown under this Schedule.

(2) The amount in each case includes all relevant sums paid by or receivable from—

(a) the company; and

(b) the company's subsidiary undertakings; and

(c) any other person,

except sums to be accounted for to the company or any of its subsidiary undertakings or any other undertaking of which any person has been a director while director of the company, by virtue of sections 314 and 315 of this Act (duty of directors to make disclosure on company takeover; consequence of non-compliance), to past or present members of the company or any of its subsidiaries or any class of those members.

(3) References to amounts paid to or receivable by a person include amounts paid to or receivable by a person connected with him or a body corporate controlled by him (but not so as to require an amount to be counted twice).

19.—(1) The amounts to be shown for any financial year under Part 3 of this Schedule are the sums receivable in respect of that year (whenever paid) or, in the case of sums not receivable in respect of a period, the sums paid during that year.

(2) But where—

(a) any sums are not shown in the directors' remuneration report for the relevant

financial year on the ground that the person receiving them is liable to account for them as mentioned in paragraph 18(2), but the liability is thereafter wholly or partly released or is not enforced within a period of 2 years; or

(*b*) *any sums paid by way of expenses allowance are charged to United Kingdom income tax after the end of the relevant financial year or, in the case of any such sums paid otherwise than to an individual, it does not become clear until the end of the relevant financial year that those sums would be charged to such tax were the person an individual,*

those sums shall, to the extent to which the liability is released or not enforced or they are charged as mentioned above (as the case may be), be shown in the first directors' remuneration report in which it is practicable to show them and shall be distinguished from the amounts to be shown apart from this provision.

20. Where it is necessary to do so for the purpose of making any distinction required by the preceding paragraphs in an amount to be shown in compliance with this Part of this Schedule, the directors may apportion any payments between the matters in respect of which these have been paid or are receivable in such manner as they think appropriate.

21. This Schedule requires information to be given only so far as it is contained in the company's books and papers, available to members of the public or the company has the right to obtain it."]

[653D]

NOTES

Inserted as noted to Pt 1 at **[653A]**.

Repealed by the Companies Act 2006, s 1295, Sch 16, as from a day to be appointed.

Application to limited liability partnerships: see the Limited Liability Partnerships Regulations 2001, SI 2001/1090, reg 3, Sch 1 at **[6984]**, **[6992]**.

[SCHEDULE 7B
SPECIFIED PERSONS, DESCRIPTIONS OF DISCLOSURES ETC FOR THE PURPOSES OF SECTION 245G

Section 245G(3)

PART 1
SPECIFIED PERSONS

1. The Secretary of State.

2. The Department of Enterprise, Trade and Investment for Northern Ireland.

3. The Treasury.

4. The Bank of England.

5. The Financial Services Authority.

6. The Commissioners of Inland Revenue.]

[653E]

NOTES

Inserted by the Companies (Audit, Investigations and Community Enterprise) Act 2004, s 12, Sch 1, as from 6 April 2005.

Repealed by the Companies Act 2006, s 1295, Sch 16, as from a day to be appointed.

Application to limited liability partnerships: see the Limited Liability Partnerships Regulations 2001, SI 2001/1090, reg 3, Sch 1 at **[6984]**, **[6992]**.

Commissioners of Inland Revenue: a reference to the Commissioners of Inland Revenue is now to be taken as a reference to the Commissioners for Her Majesty's Revenue and Customs; see the Commissioners for Revenue and Customs Act 2005, s 50(1), (7).

[PART 2
SPECIFIED DESCRIPTIONS OF DISCLOSURES

7. A disclosure for the purpose of assisting a body designated by an order under section 46 of the Companies Act 1989 (delegation of functions of Secretary of State) to exercise its functions under Part 2 of that Act.

8. A disclosure with a view to the institution of, or otherwise for the purposes of, disciplinary proceedings relating to the performance by an accountant or auditor of his professional duties.

9. A disclosure for the purpose of enabling or assisting the Secretary of State or the Treasury to exercise any of their functions under any of the following—
- (*a*) *this Act;*
- (*b*) *the insider dealing legislation;*
- (*c*) *the Insolvency Act 1986;*
- (*d*) *the Company Directors Disqualification Act 1986;*
- (*e*) *the Financial Services and Markets Act 2000.*

10. A disclosure for the purpose of enabling or assisting the Department of Enterprise, Trade and Investment for Northern Ireland to exercise any powers conferred on it by the enactments relating to companies or insolvency.

11. A disclosure for the purpose of enabling or assisting the Bank of England to exercise its functions.

12. A disclosure for the purpose of enabling or assisting the Commissioners of Inland Revenue to exercise their functions.

13. A disclosure for the purpose of enabling or assisting the Financial Services Authority to exercise its functions under any of the following—
- (*a*) *the legislation relating to friendly societies or to industrial and provident societies;*
- (*b*) *the Building Societies Act 1986;*
- (*c*) *Part 7 of the Companies Act 1989;*
- (*d*) *the Financial Services and Markets Act 2000.*

14. A disclosure in pursuance of any Community obligation.]

[653F]

NOTES

Inserted as noted to Pt 1 at **[653E]**.

Repealed by the Companies Act 2006, s 1295, Sch 16, as from a day to be appointed.

Application to limited liability partnerships: see the Limited Liability Partnerships Regulations 2001, SI 2001/1090, reg 3, Sch 1 at **[6984]**, **[6992]**.

Commissioners of Inland Revenue: a reference to the Commissioners of Inland Revenue is now to be taken as a reference to the Commissioners for Her Majesty's Revenue and Customs; see the Commissioners for Revenue and Customs Act 2005, s 50(1), (7).

[PART 3
OVERSEAS REGULATORY BODIES

15. A disclosure is made in accordance with this Part of this Schedule if—
- (*a*) *it is made to a body within paragraph 16, and*
- (*b*) *it is made for the purpose of enabling or assisting that body to exercise the functions mentioned in that paragraph.*

16. A body is within this paragraph if it exercises functions of a public nature under legislation in any country or territory outside the United Kingdom which appear to the authorised person to be similar to his functions under section 245B of this Act.

17. In determining whether to disclose information to a body in accordance with this Part of this Schedule, the authorised person must have regard to the following considerations—

(*a*) *whether the use which the body is likely to make of the information is sufficiently important to justify making the disclosure; and*

(*b*) *whether the body has adequate arrangements to prevent the information from being used or further disclosed other than for the purposes of carrying out the functions mentioned in paragraph 16 or any other purposes substantially similar to those for which information disclosed to the authorised person could be used or further disclosed.]*

[653G]

NOTES

Inserted as noted to Pt 1 at **[653E]**.

Repealed by the Companies Act 2006, s 1295, Sch 16, as from a day to be appointed.

Application to limited liability partnerships: see the Limited Liability Partnerships Regulations 2001, SI 2001/1090, reg 3, Sch 1 at **[6984]**, **[6992]**.

[SCHEDULE 8
FORM AND CONTENT OF ACCOUNTS PREPARED BY SMALL COMPANIES

Sections 246, 248A

PART I
GENERAL RULES AND FORMATS

SECTION A
GENERAL RULES

1.—(1) Subject to the following provisions of this Schedule—

(*a*) *every balance sheet of a small company shall show the items listed in either of the balance sheet formats set out below in section B of this Part; and*

(*b*) *every profit and loss account of a small company shall show the items listed in any one of the profit and loss account formats so set out;*

in either case in the order and under the headings and sub-headings given in the format adopted.

(2) *Sub-paragraph (1) above is not to be read as requiring the heading or sub-heading for any item to be distinguished by any letter or number assigned to that item in the format adopted.*

2.—(1) Where in accordance with paragraph 1 a small company's balance sheet or profit and loss account for any financial year has been prepared by reference to one of the formats set out in section B below, the directors of the company shall adopt the same format in preparing the accounts for subsequent financial years of the company unless in their opinion there are special reasons for a change.

(2) *Particulars of any change in the format adopted in preparing a small company's balance sheet or profit and loss account in accordance with paragraph 1 shall be disclosed, and the reasons for the change shall be explained, in a note to the accounts in which the new format is first adopted.*

3.—(1) Any item required in accordance with paragraph 1 to be shown in a small company's balance sheet or profit and loss account may be shown in greater detail than required by the format adopted.

(2) *A small company's balance sheet or profit and loss account may include an item representing or covering the amount of any asset or liability, income or expenditure not otherwise covered by any of the items listed in the format adopted, but the following shall not be treated as assets in any small company's balance sheet—*

(*a*) *preliminary expenses;*

(*b*) *expenses of and commission on any issue of shares or debentures; and*

(*c*) *costs of research.*

(3) *In preparing a small company's balance sheet or profit and loss account the directors of the company shall adapt the arrangement and headings and sub-headings otherwise required by paragraph 1 in respect of items to which an Arabic number is assigned in the format adopted, in any case where the special nature of the company's business requires such adaptation.*

(4) Items to which Arabic numbers are assigned in any of the formats set out in section B below may be combined in a small company's accounts for any financial year if either—

(a) their individual amounts are not material to assessing the state of affairs or profit or loss of the company for that year; or

(b) the combination facilitates that assessment;

but in a case within paragraph (b) the individual amounts of any items so combined shall be disclosed in a note to the accounts.

(5) Subject to paragraph 4(3) below, a heading or sub-heading corresponding to an item listed in the format adopted in preparing a small company's balance sheet or profit and loss account shall not be included if there is no amount to be shown for that item in respect of the financial year to which the balance sheet or profit and loss account relates.

(6) Every profit and loss account of a small company shall show the amount of the company's profit or loss on ordinary activities before taxation.

(7) ...

4.—(1) In respect of every item shown in a small company's balance sheet or profit and loss account the corresponding amount for the financial year immediately preceding that to which the balance sheet or profit and loss account relates shall also be shown.

(2) Where that corresponding amount is not comparable with the amount to be shown for the item in question in respect of the financial year to which the balance sheet or profit and loss account relates, the former amount [may be adjusted] and [particulars of the non-comparability and of any adjustment] shall be disclosed in a note to the accounts.

(3) Paragraph 3(5) does not apply in any case where an amount can be shown for the item in question in respect of the financial year immediately preceding that to which the balance sheet or profit and loss account relates, and that amount shall be shown under the heading or sub-heading required by paragraph 1 for that item.

5. Amounts in respect of items representing assets or income may not be set off against amounts in respect of items representing liabilities or expenditure (as the case may be), or vice versa.

[5A. The directors of a company must, in determining how amounts are presented within items in the profit and loss account and balance sheet, have regard to the substance of the reported transaction or arrangement, in accordance with generally accepted accounting principles or practice.]

SECTION B
THE REQUIRED FORMATS FOR ACCOUNTS

Preliminary

6. References in this Part of this Schedule to the items listed in any of the formats set out below are to those items read together with any of the notes following the formats which apply to any of those items, and the requirement imposed by paragraph 1 to show the items listed in any such format in the order adopted in the format is subject to any provision in those notes for alternative positions for any particular items.

7. A number in brackets following any item in any of the formats set out below is a reference to the note of that number in the notes following the formats.

8. In the notes following the formats—

(a) the heading of each note gives the required heading or sub-heading for the item to which it applies and a reference to any letters and numbers assigned to that item in the formats set out below (taking a reference in the case of Format 2 of the balance sheet formats to the item listed under "Assets" or under "Liabilities" as the case may require); and

(b) references to a numbered format are to the balance sheet format or (as the case may require) to the profit and loss account format of that number set out below.

Balance Sheet Formats

Format 1

A. *Called up share capital not paid (1)*

B. *Fixed assets*
- I *Intangible assets*
  - 1. *Goodwill (2)*
  - 2. *Other intangible assets (3)*
- II *Tangible assets*
  - 1. *Land and buildings*
  - 2. *Plant and machinery etc*
- III *Investments*
  - 1. *Shares in group undertakings and participating interests*
  - 2. *Loans to group undertakings and undertakings in which the company has a participating interest*
  - 3. *Other investments other than loans*
  - 4. *Other investments (4)*

C. *Current assets*
- I *Stocks*
  - 1. *Stocks*
  - 2. *Payments on account*
- II *Debtors (5)*
  - 1. *Trade debtors*
  - 2. *Amounts owed by group undertakings and undertakings in which the company has a participating interest*
  - 3. *Other debtors*
- III *Investments*
  - 1. *Shares in group undertakings*
  - 2. *Other investments*
- IV *Cash at bank and in hand*

D. *Prepayments and accrued income (6)*

E. *Creditors: amounts falling due within one year*
- 1. *Bank loans and overdrafts*
- 2. *Trade creditors*
- 3. *Amounts owed to group undertakings and undertakings in which the company has a participating interest*
- 4. *Other creditors (7)*

F. *Net current assets (liabilities) (8)*

G. *Total assets less current liabilities*

H. *Creditors: amounts falling due after more than one year*
- 1. *Bank loans and overdrafts*
- 2. *Trade creditors*
- 3. *Amounts owed to group undertakings and undertakings in which the company has a participating interest*
- 4. *Other creditors (7)*

I. *[Provisions for liabilities]*

J. *Accruals and deferred income (7)*

K. *Capital and reserves*
- I *Called up share capital (9)*
- II *Share premium account*
- III *Revaluation reserve*
- IV *Other reserves*
- V *Profit and loss account*

Balance Sheet Formats

Format 2

ASSETS

A. *Called up share capital not paid (1)*

B. Fixed assets

I Intangible assets

1. Goodwill (2)

2. Other intangible assets (3)

II Tangible assets

1. Land and buildings

2. Plant and machinery etc

III Investments

1. Shares in group undertakings and participating interests

2. Loans to group undertakings and undertakings in which the company has a participating interest

3. Other investments other than loans

4. Other investments (4)

C. Current assets

I Stocks

1. Stocks

2. Payments on account

II Debtors (5)

1. Trade debtors

2. Amounts owed by group undertakings and undertakings in which the company has a participating interest

3. Other debtors

III Investments

1. Shares in group undertakings

2. Other investments

IV Cash at bank and in hand

D. Prepayments and accrued income (6)

LIABILITIES

A. Capital and reserves

I Called up share capital (9)

II Share premium account

III Revaluation reserve

IV Other reserves

V Profit and loss account

B. [Provisions for liabilities]

C. Creditors (10)

1. Bank loans and overdrafts

2. Trade creditors

3. Amounts owed to group undertakings and undertakings in which the company has a participating interest

4. Other creditors (7)

D. Accruals and deferred income (7)

Notes on the balance sheet formats

(1) Called up share capital not paid

(Formats 1 and 2, items A and C.II.3.)

This item may either be shown at item A or included under item C.II.3 in Format 1 or 2.

(2) Goodwill

(Formats 1 and 2, item B.I.1.)

Amounts representing goodwill shall only be included to the extent that the goodwill was acquired for valuable consideration.

(3) Other intangible assets

(Formats 1 and 2, item B.I.2.)

Amounts in respect of concessions, patents, licences, trade marks and similar rights and assets shall only be included in a company's balance sheet under this item if either—

(a) the assets were acquired for valuable consideration and are not required to be shown under goodwill; or

(*b*) *the assets in question were created by the company itself.*

(*4*) *Others: Other investments*

(*Formats 1 and 2, items B.III.4 and C.III.2.*)

Where amounts in respect of own shares held are included under either of these items, the nominal value of such shares shall be shown separately.

(*5*) *Debtors*

(*Formats 1 and 2, items C.II.1 to 3.*)

The amount falling due after more than one year shall be shown separately for each item included under debtors unless the aggregate amount of debtors falling due after more than one year is disclosed in the notes to the accounts.

(*6*) *Prepayments and accrued income*

(*Formats 1 and 2, item D.*)

This item may alternatively be included under item C.II.3 in Format 1 or 2.

(*7*) *Other creditors*

(*Format 1, items E.4, H.4 and J and Format 2, items C.4 and D.*)

There shall be shown separately—
(*a*) *the amount of any convertible loans, and*
(*b*) *the amount for creditors in respect of taxation and social security.*

Payments received on account of orders shall be included in so far as they are not shown as deductions from stocks.

In Format 1, accruals and deferred income may be shown under item J or included under item E.4 or H.4, or both (as the case may require). In Format 2, accruals and deferred income may be shown under item D or within item C.4 under Liabilities.

(*8*) *Net current assets (liabilities)*

(*Format 1, item F.*)

In determining the amount to be shown under this item any prepayments and accrued income shall be taken into account wherever shown.

(*9*) *Called up share capital*

(*Format 1, item K.I and Format 2, item A.I.*)

The amount of allotted share capital and the amount of called up share capital which has been paid up shall be shown separately.

(*10*) *Creditors*

(*Format 2, items C.I to 4.*)

Amounts falling due within one year and after one year shall be shown separately for each of these items and for the aggregate of all of these items unless the aggregate amount of creditors falling due within one year and the aggregate amount of creditors falling due after more than one year is disclosed in the notes to the accounts.

Profit and loss account formats

Format 1
(*see note (14) below*)

1. *Turnover*
2. *Cost of sales (11)*
3. *Gross profit or loss*
4. *Distribution costs (11)*
5. *Administrative expenses (11)*
6. *Other operating income*
7. *Income from shares in group undertakings*

8. *Income from participating interests*

8. *Income from other fixed asset investments* (*12*)

10. *Other interest receivable and similar income* (*12*)

11. *Amounts written off investments*

12. *Interest payable and similar charges* (*13*)

13. *Tax on profit or loss on ordinary activities*

14. *Profit or loss on ordinary activities after taxation*

15. *Extraordinary income*

16. *Extraordinary charges*

17. *Extraordinary profit or loss*

18. *Tax on extraordinary profit or loss*

19. *Other taxes not shown under the above items*

20. *Profit or loss for the financial year*

Profit and loss account formats

Format 2

1. *Turnover*

2. *Change in stocks of finished goods and in work in progress*

3. *Own work capitalised*

4. *Other operating income*

5.
    (*a*) *Raw materials and consumables*
    (*b*) *Other external charges*

6. *Staff costs:*
    (*a*) *wages and salaries*
    (*b*) *social security costs*
    (*c*) *other pension costs*

7.
    (*a*) *Depreciation and other amounts written off tangible and intangible fixed assets*
    (*b*) *Exceptional amounts written off current assets*

8. *Other operating charges*

9. *Income from shares in group undertakings*

10. *Income from participating interests*

11. *Income from other fixed asset investments* (*12*)

12. *Other interest receivable and similar income* (*12*)

13. *Amounts written off investments*

14. *Interest payable and similar charges* (*13*)

15. *Tax on profit or loss on ordinary activities*

16. *Profit or loss on ordinary activities after taxation*

17. *Extraordinary income*

18. *Extraordinary charges*

19. *Extraordinary profit or loss*

20. *Tax on extraordinary profit or loss*

21. *Other taxes not shown under the above items*

22. *Profit or loss for the financial year*

Profit and loss account formats

Format 3
(see note (14) below)

A. *Charges*
  1. *Cost of sales (11)*
  2. *Distribution costs (11)*
  3. *Administrative expenses (11)*
  4. *Amounts written off investments*
  5. *Interest payable and similar charges (13)*
  6. *Tax on profit or loss on ordinary activities*
  7. *Profit or loss on ordinary activities after taxation*
  8. *Extraordinary charges*
  9. *Tax on extraordinary profit or loss*
  10. *Other taxes not shown under the above items*
  11. *Profit or loss for the financial year*

B. *Income*
  1. *Turnover*
  2. *Other operating income*
  3. *Income from shares in group undertakings*
  4. *Income from participating interests*
  5. *Income from other fixed asset investments (12)*
  6. *Other interest receivable and similar income (12)*
  7. *Profit or loss on ordinary activities after taxation*
  8. *Extraordinary income*
  9. *Profit or loss for the financial year*

Profit and loss account formats

Format 4

A. *Charges*
  1. *Reduction in stocks of finished goods and in work in progress*
  2.
    (*a*) *Raw materials and consumables*
    (*b*) *Other external charges*
  3. *Staff costs:*
    (*a*) *wages and salaries*
    (*b*) *social security costs*
    (*c*) *other pension costs*
  4.
    (*a*) *Depreciation and other amounts written off tangible and intangible fixed assets*
    (*b*) *Exceptional amounts written off current assets*
  5. *Other operating charges*
  6. *Amounts written off investments*
  7. *Interest payable and similar charges (13)*
  8. *Tax on profit or loss on ordinary activities*
  9. *Profit or loss on ordinary activities after taxation*
  10. *Extraordinary charges*
  11. *Tax on extraordinary profit or loss*
  12. *Other taxes not shown under the above items*
  13. *Profit or loss for the financial year*

B. *Income*
  1. *Turnover*
  2. *Increase in stocks of finished goods and in work in progress*
  3. *Own work capitalised*
  4. *Other operating income*
  5. *Income from shares in group undertakings*
  6. *Income from participating interests*
  7. *Income from other fixed asset investments (12)*
  8. *Other interest receivable and similar income (12)*
  9. *Profit or loss on ordinary activities after taxation*
  10. *Extraordinary income*
  11. *Profit or loss for the financial year*

Notes on the profit and loss account formats

(11) Cost of sales: distribution costs: administrative expenses

(Format 1, items 2, 4 and 5 and Format 3, items A.1, 2 and 3.)

These items shall be stated after taking into account any necessary provisions for depreciation or diminution in value of assets.

(12) Income from other fixed asset investments: other interest receivable and similar income

(Format 1, items 9 and 10: Format 2, items 11 and 12: Format 3, items B.5 and 6: Format 4, items B.7 and 8.)

Income and interest derived from group undertakings shall be shown separately from income and interest derived from other sources.

(13) Interest payable and similar charges

(Format 1, item 12: Format 2, item 14: Format 3, item A.5: Format 4, item A.7.)

The amount payable to group undertakings shall be shown separately.

(14) Formats 1 and 3

The amount of any provisions for depreciation and diminution in value of tangible and intangible fixed assets falling to be shown under items 7(a) and A.4(a) respectively in Formats 2 and 4 shall be disclosed in a note to the accounts in any case where the profit and loss account is prepared by reference to Format 1 or Format 3.]

[654]

NOTES

Whole Schedule substituted by the Companies Act 1985 (Accounts of Small and Medium-sized Companies and Minor Accounting Amendments) Regulations 1997, SI 1997/220, reg 2(2), Sch 1, in relation to annual accounts approved by the board of directors on or after 1 March 1997, and to directors' and auditors' reports on such accounts (subject to transitional provisions in relation to a financial year of a company ending on or before 24 March 1997).

Repealed by the Companies Act 2006, s 1295, Sch 16, as from a day to be appointed.

Para 3: sub-para (7) repealed by the Companies Act 1985 (International Accounting Standards and Other Accounting Amendments) Regulations 2004, SI 2004/2947, reg 14(2), Sch 3, paras 1, 2, as from 12 November 2004, in relation to companies' financial years which begin on or after 1 January 2005.

Para 4: words in square brackets in sub-para (2) substituted by the Companies Act 1985 (Investment Companies and Accounting and Audit Amendments) Regulations 2005, SI 2005/2280, reg 5, as from 1 October 2005, in relation to companies' financial years which begin on or after 1 January 2005 and which end on or after 1 October 2005.

Para 5A: inserted by SI 2004/2947, reg 14(2), Sch 3, paras 1, 3, as from 12 November 2004, in relation to companies' financial years which begin on or after 1 January 2005.

Words in square brackets in balance sheet format 1 and balance sheet format 2 substituted by SI 2004/2947, reg 14(2), Sch 3, paras 1, 4, as from 12 November 2004, in relation to companies' financial years which begin on or after 1 January 2005.

Application to limited liability partnerships: see the Limited Liability Partnerships Regulations 2001, SI 2001/1090, reg 3, Sch 1 at **[6984]**, **[6992]**.

[PART II
ACCOUNTING PRINCIPLES AND RULES

SECTION A
ACCOUNTING PRINCIPLES

Preliminary

9. Subject to paragraph 15 below, the amounts to be included in respect of all items shown in a small company's accounts shall be determined in accordance with the principles set out in paragraphs 10 to 14.

Accounting principles

10. The company shall be presumed to be carrying on business as a going concern.

11. Accounting policies shall be applied consistently within the same accounts and from one financial year to the next.

12. The amount of any item shall be determined on a prudent basis, and in particular—
(a) only profits realised at the balance sheet date shall be included in the profit and loss account; and
(b) all liabilities ... which have arisen ... in respect of the financial year to which the accounts relate or a previous financial year shall be taken into account, including those which only become apparent between the balance sheet date and the date on which it is signed on behalf of the board of directors in pursuance of section 233 of this Act.

13. All income and charges relating to the financial year to which the accounts relate shall be taken into account, without regard to the date of receipt or payment.

14. In determining the aggregate amount of any item the amount of each individual asset or liability that falls to be taken into account shall be determined separately.

Departure from the accounting principles

15. If it appears to the directors of a small company that there are special reasons for departing from any of the principles stated above in preparing the company's accounts in respect of any financial year they may do so, but particulars of the departure, the reasons for it and its effect shall be given in a note to the accounts.

SECTION B
HISTORICAL COST ACCOUNTING RULES

Preliminary

16. [Subject to sections C and D] of this Part of this Schedule, the amounts to be included in respect of all items shown in a small company's accounts shall be determined in accordance with the rules set out in paragraphs 17 to 28.

Fixed assets

General rules

17. Subject to any provision for depreciation or diminution in value made in accordance with paragraph 18 or 19 the amount to be included in respect of any fixed asset shall be its purchase price or production cost.

18. In the case of any fixed asset which has a limited useful economic life, the amount of—
(a) its purchase price or production cost; or
(b) where it is estimated that any such asset will have a residual value at the end of the period of its useful economic life, its purchase price or production cost less that estimated residual value;

shall be reduced by provisions for depreciation calculated to write off that amount systematically over the period of the asset's useful economic life.

19.—(1) Where a fixed asset investment of a description falling to be included under item B.III of either of the balance sheet formats set out in Part I of this Schedule has diminished in value provisions for diminution in value may be made in respect of it and the amount to be included in respect of it may be reduced accordingly; and any such provisions which are not shown in the profit and loss account shall be disclosed (either separately or in aggregate) in a note to the accounts.

(2) Provisions for diminution in value shall be made in respect of any fixed asset which has diminished in value if the reduction in its value is expected to be permanent (whether its useful economic life is limited or not), and the amount to be included in respect of it shall be reduced accordingly; and any such provisions which are not shown in the profit and loss account shall be disclosed (either separately or in aggregate) in a note to the accounts.

(3) Where the reasons for which any provision was made in accordance with sub-paragraph (1) or (2) have ceased to apply to any extent, that provision shall be written back to the extent that it is no longer necessary; and any amounts written back in accordance with this sub-paragraph which are not shown in the profit and loss account shall be disclosed (either separately or in aggregate) in a note to the accounts.

Rules for determining particular fixed asset items

20.—(1) Notwithstanding that an item in respect of "development costs" is included under "fixed assets" in the balance sheet formats set out in Part I of this Schedule, an amount may only be included in a small company's balance sheet in respect of development costs in special circumstances.

(2) If any amount is included in a small company's balance sheet in respect of development costs the following information shall be given in a note to the accounts—

- *(a) the period over which the amount of those costs originally capitalised is being or is to be written off; and*
- *(b) the reasons for capitalising the development costs in question.*

21.—(1) The application of paragraphs 17 to 19 in relation to goodwill (in any case where goodwill is treated as an asset) is subject to the following provisions of this paragraph.

(2) Subject to sub-paragraph (3) below, the amount of the consideration for any goodwill acquired by a small company shall be reduced by provisions for depreciation calculated to write off that amount systematically over a period chosen by the directors of the company.

(3) The period chosen shall not exceed the useful economic life of the goodwill in question.

(4) In any case where any goodwill acquired by a small company is shown or included as an asset in the company's balance sheet the period chosen for writing off the consideration for that goodwill and the reasons for choosing that period shall be disclosed in a note to the accounts.

Current assets

22. Subject to paragraph 23, the amount to be included in respect of any current asset shall be its purchase price or production cost.

23.—(1) If the net realisable value of any current asset is lower than its purchase price or production cost the amount to be included in respect of that asset shall be the net realisable value.

(2) Where the reasons for which any provision for diminution in value was made in accordance with sub-paragraph (1) have ceased to apply to any extent, that provision shall be written back to the extent that it is no longer necessary.

Miscellaneous and supplementary provisions

Excess of money owed over value received as an asset item

24.—(1) Where the amount repayable on any debt owed by a small company is greater than the value of the consideration received in the transaction giving rise to the debt, the amount of the difference may be treated as an asset.

(2) Where any such amount is so treated—

- *(a) it shall be written off by reasonable amounts each year and must be completely written off before repayment of the debt; and*
- *(b) if the current amount is not shown as a separate item in the company's balance sheet it must be disclosed in a note to the accounts.*

Assets included at a fixed amount

25.—(1) Subject to the following sub-paragraph, assets which fall to be included—

- *(a) amongst the fixed assets of a small company under the item "tangible assets"; or* (*b*) *amongst the current assets of a small company under the item "raw materials and consumables";*

may be included at a fixed quantity and value.

(2) *Sub-paragraph (1) applies to assets of a kind which are constantly being replaced, where—*

(*a*) *their overall value is not material to assessing the company's state of affairs; and*
(*b*) *their quantity, value and composition are not subject to material variation.*

Determination of purchase price or production cost

26.—(1) The purchase price of an asset shall be determined by adding to the actual price paid any expenses incidental to its acquisition.

(2) *The production cost of an asset shall be determined by adding to the purchase price of the raw materials and consumables used the amount of the costs incurred by the company which are directly attributable to the production of that asset.*

(3) *In addition, there may be included in the production cost of an asset—*

(*a*) *a reasonable proportion of the costs incurred by the company which are only indirectly attributable to the production of that asset, but only to the extent that they relate to the period of production; and*
(*b*) *interest on capital borrowed to finance the production of that asset, to the extent that it accrues in respect of the period of production;*

provided, however, in a case within paragraph (b) above, that the inclusion of the interest in determining the cost of that asset and the amount of the interest so included is disclosed in a note to the accounts.

(4) *In the case of current assets distribution costs may not be included in production costs.*

27.—(1) Subject to the qualification mentioned below, the purchase price or production cost of—

(*a*) *any assets which fall to be included under any item shown in a small company's balance sheet under the general item "stocks"; and*
(*b*) *any assets which are fungible assets (including investments);*

may be determined by the application of any of the methods mentioned in sub-paragraph (2) below in relation to any such assets of the same class.

The method chosen must be one which appears to the directors to be appropriate in the circumstances of the company.

(2) *Those methods are—*

(*a*) *the method known as "first in, first out" (FIFO);*
(*b*) *the method known as "last in, first out" (LIFO);*
(*c*) *a weighted average price; and*
(*d*) *any other method similar to any of the methods mentioned above.*

(3) *For the purposes of this paragraph, assets of any description shall be regarded as fungible if assets of that description are substantially indistinguishable one from another.*

Substitution of original stated amount where price or cost unknown

28. Where there is no record of the purchase price or production cost of any asset of a small company or of any price, expenses or costs relevant for determining its purchase price or production cost in accordance with paragraph 26, or any such record cannot be obtained without unreasonable expense or delay, its purchase price or production cost shall be taken for the purposes of paragraphs 17 to 23 to be the value ascribed to it in the earliest available record of its value made on or after its acquisition or production by the company.

SECTION C
ALTERNATIVE ACCOUNTING RULES

Preliminary

29.—(1) The rules set out in section B are referred to below in this Schedule as the historical cost accounting rules.

(2) Those rules, with the omission of paragraphs 16, 21 and 25 to 28, are referred to below in this Part of this Schedule as the depreciation rules; and references below in this Schedule to the historical cost accounting rules do not include the depreciation rules as they apply by virtue of paragraph 32.

30. Subject to paragraphs 32 to 34, the amounts to be included in respect of assets of any description mentioned in paragraph 31 may be determined on any basis so mentioned.

Alternative accounting rules

31.—(1) Intangible fixed assets, other than goodwill, may be included at their current cost.

(2) Tangible fixed assets may be included at a market value determined as at the date of their last valuation or at their current cost.

(3) Investments of any description falling to be included under item B III of either of the balance sheet formats set out in Part I of this Schedule may be included either—

- *(a) at a market value determined as at the date of their last valuation; or*
- *(b) at a value determined on any basis which appears to the directors to be appropriate in the circumstances of the company;*

but in the latter case particulars of the method of valuation adopted and of the reasons for adopting it shall be disclosed in a note to the accounts.

(4) Investments of any description falling to be included under item C III of either of the balance sheet formats set out in Part I of this Schedule may be included at their current cost.

(5) Stocks may be included at their current cost.

Application of the depreciation rules

32.—(1) Where the value of any asset of a small company is determined on any basis mentioned in paragraph 31, that value shall be, or (as the case may require) be the starting point for determining, the amount to be included in respect of that asset in the company's accounts, instead of its purchase price or production cost or any value previously so determined for that asset; and the depreciation rules shall apply accordingly in relation to any such asset with the substitution for any reference to its purchase price or production cost of a reference to the value most recently determined for that asset on any basis mentioned in paragraph 31.

(2) The amount of any provision for depreciation required in the case of any fixed asset by paragraph 18 or 19 as it applies by virtue of sub-paragraph (1) is referred to below in this paragraph as the adjusted amount, and the amount of any provision which would be required by that paragraph in the case of that asset according to the historical cost accounting rules is referred to as the historical cost amount.

(3) Where sub-paragraph (1) applies in the case of any fixed asset the amount of any provision for depreciation in respect of that asset—

- *(a) included in any item shown in the profit and loss account in respect of amounts written off assets of the description in question; or*
- *(b) taken into account in stating any item so shown which is required by note (11) of the notes on the profit and loss account formats set out in Part I of this Schedule to be stated after taking into account any necessary provision for depreciation or diminution in value of assets included under it;*

may be the historical cost amount instead of the adjusted amount, provided that the amount of any difference between the two is shown separately in the profit and loss account or in a note to the accounts.

Additional information to be provided in case of departure from historical cost accounting rules

33.—(1) This paragraph applies where the amounts to be included in respect of assets covered by any items shown in a small company's accounts have been determined on any basis mentioned in paragraph 31.

(2) The items affected and the basis of valuation adopted in determining the amounts of the assets in question in the case of each such item shall be disclosed in a note to the accounts.

(3) In the case of each balance sheet item affected (except stocks) either—

(a) the comparable amounts determined according to the historical cost accounting rules; or

(b) the differences between those amounts and the corresponding amounts actually shown in the balance sheet in respect of that item;

shall be shown separately in the balance sheet or in a note to the accounts.

(4) In sub-paragraph (3) above, references in relation to any item to the comparable amounts determined as there mentioned are references to—

(a) the aggregate amount which would be required to be shown in respect of that item if the amounts to be included in respect of all the assets covered by that item were determined according to the historical cost accounting rules; and

(b) the aggregate amount of the cumulative provisions for depreciation or diminution in value which would be permitted or required in determining those amounts according to those rules.

Revaluation reserve

34.—(1) With respect to any determination of the value of an asset of a small company on any basis mentioned in paragraph 31, the amount of any profit or loss arising from that determination (after allowing, where appropriate, for any provisions for depreciation or diminution in value made otherwise than by reference to the value so determined and any adjustments of any such provisions made in the light of that determination) shall be credited or (as the case may be) debited to a separate reserve ("the revaluation reserve").

(2) The amount of the revaluation reserve shall be shown in the company's balance sheet under a separate sub-heading in the position given for the item "revaluation reserve" in Format 1 or 2 of the balance sheet formats set out in Part I of this Schedule, but need not be shown under that name.

(3) An amount may be transferred—

(a) from the revaluation reserve—

(i) to the profit and loss account, if the amount was previously charged to that account or represents realised profit, or

(ii) on capitalisation,

(b) to or from the revaluation reserve in respect of the taxation relating to any profit or loss credited or debited to the reserve;

and the revaluation reserve shall be reduced to the extent that the amounts transferred to it are no longer necessary for the purposes of the valuation method used.

(4) In sub-paragraph (3)(a)(ii) "capitalisation", in relation to an amount standing to the credit of the revaluation reserve, means applying it in wholly or partly paying up unissued shares in the company to be allotted to members of the company as fully or partly paid shares.

(5) The revaluation reserve shall not be reduced except as mentioned in this paragraph.

(6) The treatment for taxation purposes of amounts credited or debited to the revaluation reserve shall be disclosed in a note to the accounts.]

[SECTION D
FAIR VALUE ACCOUNTING

Inclusion of financial instruments at fair value

34A.—(1) Subject to sub-paragraphs (2) to (4), financial instruments (including derivatives) may be included at fair value.

(2) Sub-paragraph (1) does not apply to financial instruments which constitute liabilities unless—
- *(a) they are held as part of a trading portfolio, or*
- *(b) they are derivatives.*

(3) Sub-paragraph (1) does not apply to—
- *(a) financial instruments (other than derivatives) held to maturity;*
- *(b) loans and receivables originated by the company and not held for trading purposes;*
- *(c) interests in subsidiary undertakings, associated undertakings and joint ventures;*
- *(d) equity instruments issued by the company;*
- *(e) contracts for contingent consideration in a business combination;*
- *(f) other financial instruments with such special characteristics that the instruments, according to generally accepted accounting principles or practice, should be accounted for differently from other financial instruments.*

(4) If the fair value of a financial instrument cannot be determined reliably in accordance with paragraph 34B, sub-paragraph (1) does not apply to that financial instrument.

(5) In this paragraph—
"associated undertaking" has the meaning given by paragraph 20 of Schedule 4A; and
"joint venture" has the meaning given by paragraph 19 of that Schedule.

Determination of fair value

34B.—(1) The fair value of a financial instrument is determined in accordance with this paragraph.

(2) If a reliable market can readily be identified for the financial instrument, its fair value is determined by reference to its market value.

(3) If a reliable market cannot readily be identified for the financial instrument but can be identified for its components or for a similar instrument, its fair value is determined by reference to the market value of its components or of the similar instrument.

(4) If neither sub-paragraph (2) nor (3) applies, the fair value of the financial instrument is a value resulting from generally accepted valuation models and techniques.

(5) Any valuation models and techniques used for the purposes of sub-paragraph (4) must ensure a reasonable approximation of the market value.

Inclusion of hedged items at fair value

34C. A company may include any assets and liabilities that qualify as hedged items under a fair value hedge accounting system, or identified portions of such assets or liabilities, at the amount required under that system.

Other assets that may be included at fair value

34D.—(1) This paragraph applies to—
- *(a) investment property, and*
- *(b) living animals and plants,*

that, under international accounting standards, may be included in accounts at fair value.

(2) Such investment property and such living animals and plants may be included at fair value, provided that all such investment property or, as the case may be, all such living animals and plants are so included where their fair value can reliably be determined.

(3) In this paragraph, "fair value" means fair value determined in accordance with relevant international accounting standards.

Accounting for changes in value

34E.—(1) This paragraph applies where a financial instrument is valued in accordance with paragraph 34A or 34C or an asset is valued in accordance with paragraph 34D.

(2) Notwithstanding paragraph 12 of this Schedule, and subject to sub-paragraphs (3) and (4) below, a change in the value of the financial instrument or of the investment property or living animal or plant must be included in the profit and loss account.

(3) Where—

(a) the financial instrument accounted for is a hedging instrument under a hedge accounting system that allows some or all of the change in value not to be shown in the profit and loss account, or

(b) the change in value relates to an exchange difference arising on a monetary item that forms part of a company's net investment in a foreign entity,

the amount of the change in value must be credited to or (as the case may be) debited from a separate reserve ("the fair value reserve").

(4) Where the instrument accounted for—

(a) is an available for sale financial asset, and

(b) is not a derivative,

the change in value may be credited to or (as the case may be) debited from the fair value reserve.

The fair value reserve

34F.—(1) The fair value reserve must be adjusted to the extent that the amounts shown in it are no longer necessary for the purposes of paragraph 34E(3) or (4).

(2) The treatment for taxation purposes of amounts credited or debited to the fair value reserve must be disclosed in a note to the accounts.]

[655]

NOTES

Substituted as noted to Pt I at **[654]**.

Repealed by the Companies Act 2006, s 1295, Sch 16, as from a day to be appointed.

Para 12: words omitted repealed by the Companies Act 1985 (International Accounting Standards and Other Accounting Amendments) Regulations 2004, SI 2004/2947, reg 14(2), Sch 3, paras 1, 5, as from 12 November 2004, in relation to companies' financial years which begin on or after 1 January 2005.

Para 16: words in square brackets substituted by SI 2004/2947, reg 14(2), Sch 3, paras 1, 6(1), (2), as from 12 November 2004, in relation to companies' financial years which begin on or after 1 January 2005.

Paras 34A–34F: added by SI 2004/2947, reg 14(2), Sch 3, paras 1, 6(1), (3), as from 12 November 2004, in relation to companies' financial years which begin on or after 1 January 2005.

Application to limited liability partnerships: see the Limited Liability Partnerships Regulations 2001, SI 2001/1090, reg 3, Sch 1 at **[6984]**, **[6992]**.

[PART III
NOTES TO THE ACCOUNTS

Preliminary

35. Any information required in the case of any small company by the following provisions of this Part of this Schedule shall (if not given in the company's accounts) be given by way of a note to those accounts.

[Reserves and dividends

35A. There must be stated—

(a) any amount set aside or proposed to be set aside to, or withdrawn or proposed to be withdrawn from, reserves,

(b) the aggregate amount of dividends paid in the financial year (other than those for which a liability existed at the immediately preceding balance sheet date),

(c) the aggregate amount of dividends that the company is liable to pay at the balance sheet date, and

(d) the aggregate amount of dividends that are proposed before the date of approval of the accounts, and not otherwise disclosed under paragraph (b) or (c).]

Disclosure of accounting policies

36. The accounting policies adopted by the company in determining the amounts to be included in respect of items shown in the balance sheet and in determining the profit or loss of the company shall be stated (including such policies with respect to the depreciation and diminution in value of assets).

Information supplementing the balance sheet

37. Paragraphs 38 to 47 require information which either supplements the information given with respect to any particular items shown in the balance sheet or is otherwise relevant to assessing the company's state of affairs in the light of the information so given.

Share capital and debentures

38.—(1) The following information shall be given with respect to the company's share capital—

(a) the authorised share capital; and

(b) where shares of more than one class have been allotted, the number and aggregate nominal value of shares of each class allotted.

(2) In the case of any part of the allotted share capital that consists of redeemable shares, the following information shall be given—

(a) the earliest and latest dates on which the company has power to redeem those shares;

(b) whether those shares must be redeemed in any event or are liable to be redeemed at the option of the company or of the shareholder; and

(c) whether any (and, if so, what) premium is payable on redemption.

39. If the company has allotted any shares during the financial year, the following information shall be given—

(a) the classes of shares allotted; and

(b) as respects each class of shares, the number allotted, their aggregate nominal value, and the consideration received by the company for the allotment.

Fixed assets

40.—(1) In respect of each item which is or would but for paragraph 3(4)(b) be shown under the general item "fixed assets" in the company's balance sheet the following information shall be given—

(a) the appropriate amounts in respect of that item as at the date of the beginning of the financial year and as at the balance sheet date respectively;

(b) the effect on any amount shown in the balance sheet in respect of that item of—

(i) any revision of the amount in respect of any assets included under that item made during that year on any basis mentioned in paragraph 31;

(ii) acquisitions during that year of any assets;

(iii) disposals during that year of any assets; and

(iv) any transfers of assets of the company to and from that item during that year.

(2) The reference in sub-paragraph (1)(a) to the appropriate amounts in respect of any item as at any date there mentioned is a reference to amounts representing the aggregate amounts determined, as at that date, in respect of assets falling to be included under that item on either of the following bases, that is to say—

(a) on the basis of purchase price or production cost (determined in accordance with paragraphs 26 and 27); or

(b) on any basis mentioned in paragraph 31,

(leaving out of account in either case any provisions for depreciation or diminution in value).

(3) In respect of each item within sub-paragraph (1)—

(a) the cumulative amount of provisions for depreciation or diminution in value of assets included under that item as at each date mentioned in sub-paragraph (1)(a);

(b) the amount of any such provisions made in respect of the financial year;

(c) the amount of any adjustments made in respect of any such provisions during that year in consequence of the disposal of any assets; and

(d) the amount of any other adjustments made in respect of any such provisions during that year;

shall also be stated.

41. Where any fixed assets of the company (other than listed investments) are included under any item shown in the company's balance sheet at an amount determined on any basis mentioned in paragraph 31, the following information shall be given—

(a) the years (so far as they are known to the directors) in which the assets were severally valued and the several values; and

(b) in the case of assets that have been valued during the financial year, the names of the persons who valued them or particulars of their qualifications for doing so and (whichever is stated) the bases of valuation used by them.

Investments

42.—(1) In respect of the amount of each item which is or would but for paragraph 3(4)(b) be shown in the company's balance sheet under the general item "investments" (whether as fixed assets or as current assets) there shall be stated how much of that amount is ascribable to listed investments.

(2) Where the amount of any listed investments is stated for any item in accordance with sub-paragraph (1), the following amounts shall also be stated—

(a) the aggregate market value of those investments where it differs from the amount so stated; and

(b) both the market value and the stock exchange value of any investments of which the former value is, for the purposes of the accounts, taken as being higher than the latter.

[Information about fair value of assets and liabilities

42A.—(1) This paragraph applies where financial instruments have been valued in accordance with paragraph 34A or 34C

(2) There must be stated—

(a) where the fair value of the instruments has been determined in accordance with paragraph 34B(4), the significant assumptions underlying the valuation models and techniques used,

(b) for each category of financial instrument, the fair value of the instruments in that category and the changes in value—

(i) included in the profit and loss account, and

(ii) credited to or (as the case may be) debited from the fair value reserve,

in respect of those instruments, and

(c) for each class of derivatives, the extent and nature of the instruments, including significant terms and conditions that may affect the amount, timing and certainty of future cash flows.

(3) Where any amount is transferred to or from the fair value reserve during the financial year, there must be stated in tabular form—

(a) the amount of the reserve as at the date of the beginning of the financial year and as at the balance sheet date respectively;

(b) the amount transferred to or from the reserve during that year; and

(c) the source and application respectively of the amounts so transferred.

42B.—(1) Sub-paragraph (2) applies if—

(a) the company has financial fixed assets that could be included at fair value by virtue of paragraph 34A,

(b) the amount at which those assets are included under any item in the company's accounts is in excess of their fair value, and

(c) the company has not made provision for diminution in value of those assets in accordance with paragraph 19(1) of this Schedule.

(2) There must be stated—

(*a*) *the amount at which either the individual assets or appropriate groupings of those individual assets are included in the company's accounts,*
(*b*) *the fair value of those assets or groupings, and*
(*c*) *the reasons for not making a provision for diminution in value of those assets, including the nature of the evidence that provides the basis for the belief that the amount at which they are stated in the accounts will be recovered.*

Information where investment property and living animals and plants included at fair value

42C.—(1) This paragraph applies where the amounts to be included in a company's accounts in respect of investment property or living animals and plants have been determined in accordance with paragraph 34D.

(2) The balance sheet items affected and the basis of valuation adopted in determining the amounts of the assets in question in the case of each such item must be disclosed in a note to the accounts.

(3) In the case of investment property, for each balance sheet item affected there must be shown, either separately in the balance sheet or in a note to the accounts—
(*a*) *the comparable amounts determined according to the historical cost accounting rules; or*
(*b*) *the differences between those amounts and the corresponding amounts actually shown in the balance sheet in respect of that item.*

(4) In sub-paragraph (3) above, references in relation to any item to the comparable amounts determined in accordance with that sub-paragraph are references to—
(*a*) *the aggregate amount which would be required to be shown in respect of that item if the amounts to be included in respect of all the assets covered by that item were determined according to the historical cost accounting rules; and*
(*b*) *the aggregate amount of the cumulative provisions for depreciation or diminution in value which would be permitted or required in determining those amounts according to those rules.]*

Reserves and provisions

43.—(1) Where any amount is transferred—
(*a*) *to or from any reserves; or*
(*b*) *to any [provisions for liabilities]; or*
(*c*) *from any [provision for liabilities] otherwise than for the purpose for which the provision was established;*

and the reserves or provisions are or would but for paragraph 3(4)(b) be shown as separate items in the company's balance sheet, the information mentioned in the following sub-paragraph shall be given in respect of the aggregate of reserves or provisions included in the same item.

(2) That information is—
(*a*) *the amount of the reserves or provisions as at the date of the beginning of the financial year and as at the balance sheet date respectively;*
(*b*) *any amounts transferred to or from the reserves or provisions during that year; and*
(*c*) *the source and application respectively of any amounts so transferred.*

(3) Particulars shall be given of each provision included in the item "other provisions" in the company's balance sheet in any case where the amount of that provision is material.

Details of indebtedness

44.—(1) For the aggregate of all items shown under "creditors" in the company's balance sheet there shall be stated the aggregate of the following amounts, that is to say—
(*a*) *the amount of any debts included under "creditors" which are payable or repayable otherwise than by instalments and fall due for payment or repayment after the end of the period of five years beginning with the day next following the end of the financial year; and*

(*b*) *in the case of any debts so included which are payable or repayable by instalments, the amount of any instalments which fall due for payment after the end of that period.*

(2) *In respect of each item shown under "creditors" in the company's balance sheet there shall be stated the aggregate amount of any debts included under that item in respect of which any security has been given by the company.*

(3) *References above in this paragraph to an item shown under "creditors" in the company's balance sheet include references, where amounts falling due to creditors within one year and after more than one year are distinguished in the balance sheet—*

(*a*) *in a case within sub-paragraph* (*1*), *to an item shown under the latter of those categories; and*

(*b*) *in a case within sub-paragraph* (2), *to an item shown under either of those categories;*

and references to items shown under "creditors" include references to items which would but for paragraph 3(4)(b) be shown under that heading.

45. *If any fixed cumulative dividends on the company's shares are in arrear, there shall be stated—*

(*a*) *the amount of the arrears; and*

(*b*) *the period for which the dividends or, if there is more than one class, each class of them are in arrear.*

Guarantees and other financial commitments

46.—(*1*) *Particulars shall be given of any charge on the assets of the company to secure the liabilities of any other person, including, where practicable, the amount secured.*

(2) *The following information shall be given with respect to any other contingent liability not provided for—*

(*a*) *the amount or estimated amount of that liability;*

(*b*) *its legal nature; and*

(*c*) *whether any valuable security has been provided by the company in connection with that liability and if so, what.*

(*3*) *There shall be stated, where practicable, the aggregate amount or estimated amount of contracts for capital expenditure, so far as not provided for.*

(4) *Particulars shall be given of—*

(*a*) *any pension commitments included under any provision shown in the company's balance sheet; and*

(*b*) *any such commitments for which no provision has been made;*

and where any such commitment relates wholly or partly to pensions payable to past directors of the company separate particulars shall be given of that commitment so far as it relates to such pensions.

(5) *Particulars shall also be given of any other financial commitments which—*

(*a*) *have not been provided for; and*

(*b*) *are relevant to assessing the company's state of affairs.*

(6) *Commitments within any of sub-paragraphs* (*1*) *to* (5) *which are undertaken on behalf of or for the benefit of—*

(*a*) *any parent undertaking or fellow subsidiary undertaking, or*

(*b*) *any subsidiary undertaking of the company,*

shall be stated separately from the other commitments within that sub-paragraph, and commitments within paragraph (*a*) *shall also be stated separately from those within paragraph* (*b*).

Miscellaneous matters

47. *Particulars shall be given of any case where the purchase price or production cost of any asset is for the first time determined under paragraph 28.*

Information supplementing the profit and loss account

48. Paragraphs 49 and 50 require information which either supplements the information given with respect to any particular items shown in the profit and loss account or otherwise provides particulars of income or expenditure of the company or of circumstances affecting the items shown in the profit and loss account.

Particulars of turnover

49.—(1) If the company has supplied geographical markets outside the United Kingdom during the financial year in question, there shall be stated the percentage of its turnover that, in the opinion of the directors, is attributable to those markets.

(2) In analysing for the purposes of this paragraph the source of turnover, the directors of the company shall have regard to the manner in which the company's activities are organised.

Miscellaneous matters

50.—(1) Where any amount relating to any preceding financial year is included in any item in the profit and loss account, the effect shall be stated.

(2) Particulars shall be given of any extraordinary income or charges arising in the financial year.

(3) The effect shall be stated of any transactions that are exceptional by virtue of size or incidence though they fall within the ordinary activities of the company.

General

51.—(1) Where sums originally denominated in foreign currencies have been brought into account under any items shown in the balance sheet or profit and loss account, the basis on which those sums have been translated into sterling shall be stated.

(*2*), (*3*) …

[Dormant Companies Acting as Agents

51A. Where the directors of a company take advantage of the exemption conferred by section 249AA, and the company has during the financial year in question acted as an agent for any person, the fact that it has so acted must be stated.]

[656]

NOTES

Substituted as noted to Pt I at **[654]**.

Repealed by the Companies Act 2006, s 1295, Sch 16, as from a day to be appointed.

Paras 35A, 42A–42C: inserted by the Companies Act 1985 (International Accounting Standards and Other Accounting Amendments) Regulations 2004, SI 2004/2947, reg 14(2), Sch 3, paras 1, 7, as from 12 November 2004, in relation to companies' financial years which begin on or after 1 January 2005.

Para 43: words in square brackets in sub-para (1) substituted by SI 2004/2947, reg 14(2), Sch 3, paras 1, 8, as from 12 November 2004, in relation to companies' financial years which begin on or after 1 January 2005.

Para 51: sub-paras (2), (3) repealed by the Companies Act 1985 (Investment Companies and Accounting and Audit Amendments) Regulations 2005, SI 2005/2280, reg 6, as from 1 October 2005, in relation to companies' financial years which begin on or after 1 January 2005 and which end on or after 1 October 2005.

Para 51A: added by the Companies Act 1985 (Audit Exemption) (Amendment) Regulations 2000, SI 2000/1430, reg 6, as from 26 May 2000, in relation to annual reports and reports in respect of financial years ending two months or more after that date.

Application to limited liability partnerships: see the Limited Liability Partnerships Regulations 2001, SI 2001/1090, reg 3, Sch 1 at **[6984]**, **[6992]**.

[PART IV
INTERPRETATION OF SCHEDULE

52. The following paragraphs apply for the purposes of this Schedule and its interpretation.

[Financial instruments

52A. References to "derivatives" include commodity-based contracts that give either contracting party the right to settle in cash or in some other financial instrument, except when such contracts—

(*a*) *were entered into for the purpose of, and continue to meet, the company's expected purchase, sale or usage requirements,*

(*b*) *were designated for such purpose at their inception, and*

(*c*) *are expected to be settled by delivery of the commodity.*

52B.—(1) The expressions listed in sub-paragraph (2) have the same meaning as they have in Council Directive 78/660/EEC on the annual accounts of certain types of companies, as amended.

(2) Those expressions are "available for sale financial asset", "business combination", "commodity-based contracts", "derivative", "equity instrument", "exchange difference", "fair value hedge accounting system", "financial fixed asset", "financial instrument", "foreign entity", "hedge accounting", "hedge accounting system", "hedged items", "hedging instrument", "held for trading purposes", "held to maturity", "monetary item", "receivables", "reliable market" and "trading portfolio".]

Historical cost accounting rules

53. References to the historical cost accounting rules shall be read in accordance with paragraph 29.

[Investment property

53A. "Investment property" means land held to earn rent or for capital appreciation.]

Listed investments

[54.—(1) "Listed investment" means an investment as respects which there has been granted a listing on—

(*a*) *a recognised investment exchange other than an overseas investment exchange; or*

(*b*) *a stock exchange of repute outside Great Britain.*

(2) "Recognised investment exchange" and "overseas investment exchange" have the meaning given in Part 18 of the Financial Services and Markets Act 2000.]

Loans

55. A loan is treated as falling due for repayment, and an instalment of a loan is treated as falling due for payment, on the earliest date on which the lender could require repayment or (as the case may be) payment, if he exercised all options and rights available to him.

Materiality

56. Amounts which in the particular context of any provision of this Schedule are not material may be disregarded for the purposes of that provision.

Provisions

57.—(1) References to provisions for depreciation or diminution in value of assets are to any amount written off by way of providing for depreciation or diminution in value of assets.

(2) Any reference in the profit and loss account formats set out in Part I of this Schedule to the depreciation of, or amounts written off, assets of any description is to any provision for depreciation or diminution in value of assets of that description.

58. References to [provisions for liabilities] are to any amount retained as reasonably necessary for the purpose of providing for any liability [the nature of which is clearly defined and] which is either likely to be incurred, or certain to be incurred but uncertain as to amount or as to the date on which it will arise.

Staff costs

59.—(1) "Social security costs" means any contributions by the company to any state social security or pension scheme, fund or arrangement.

(2) "Pension costs" includes any costs incurred by the company in respect of any pension scheme established for the purpose of providing pensions for persons currently or formerly employed by the company, any sums set aside for the future payment of pensions directly by the company to current or former employees and any pensions paid directly to such persons without having first been set aside.

(3) Any amount stated in respect of the item "social security costs" or in respect of the item "wages and salaries" in the company's profit and loss account shall be determined by reference to payments made or costs incurred in respect of all persons employed by the company during the financial year under contracts of service.]

[657]

NOTES

Substituted as noted to Pt I at **[654]**.

Repealed by the Companies Act 2006, s 1295, Sch 16, as from a day to be appointed.

Paras 52A, 52B, 53A: inserted by the Companies Act 1985 (International Accounting Standards and Other Accounting Amendments) Regulations 2004, SI 2004/2947, reg 14(2), Sch 3, paras 1, 9, 10, as from 12 November 2004, in relation to companies' financial years which begin on or after 1 January 2005.

Para 54: substituted by the Financial Services and Markets Act 2000 (Consequential Amendments and Repeals) Order 2001, SI 2001/3649, art 34, as from 1 December 2001.

Para 58: words in square brackets substituted by SI 2004/2947, reg 14(2), Sch 3, paras 1, 11, as from 12 November 2004, in relation to companies' financial years which begin on or after 1 January 2005.

Application to limited liability partnerships: see the Limited Liability Partnerships Regulations 2001, SI 2001/1090, reg 3, Sch 1 at **[6984]**, **[6992]**.

[SCHEDULE 8A
FORM AND CONTENT OF ABBREVIATED ACCOUNTS OF SMALL COMPANIES DELIVERED TO REGISTRAR

Section 246

PART I
BALANCE SHEET FORMATS

1. A small company may deliver to the registrar a copy of the balance sheet showing the items listed in either of the balance sheet formats set out in paragraph 2 below in the order and under the headings and sub-headings given in the format adopted, but in other respects corresponding to the full balance sheet.

2. The formats referred to in paragraph 1 are as follows—

Balance Sheet Formats

Format 1

A. Called up share capital not paid

B. Fixed assets
I Intangible assets
II Tangible assets
III Investments

C. Current assets
I Stocks
II Debtors (1)

III *Investments*
IV *Cash at bank and in hand*

D. *Prepayments and accrued income*

E. *Creditors: amounts falling due within one year*

F. *Net current assets (liabilities)*

G. *Total assets less current liabilities*

H. *Creditors: amounts falling due after more than one year*

I. *[Provisions for liabilities]*

J. *Accruals and deferred income*

K. *Capital and reserves*
I *Called up share capital*
II *Share premium account*
III *Revaluation reserve*
IV *Other reserves*
V *Profit and loss account*

Balance Sheet Formats

Format 2

ASSETS

A. *Called up share capital not paid*

B. *Fixed assets*
I *Intangible assets*
II *Tangible assets*
III *Investments*

C. *Current assets*
I *Stocks*
II *Debtors (1)*
III *Investments*
IV *Cash at bank and in hand*

D. *Prepayments and accrued income*

LIABILITIES

A. *Capital and reserves*
I *Called up share capital*
II *Share premium account*
III *Revaluation reserve*
IV *Other reserves*
V *Profit and loss account*

B. *[Provisions for liabilities]*

C. *Creditors* (2)

D. *Accruals and deferred income*

Notes on the balance sheet formats

(*1*) *Debtors*

(*Formats 1 and 2, item C.II.*)

The aggregate amount of debtors falling due after more than one year shall be shown separately, unless it is disclosed in the notes to the accounts.

(2) *Creditors*

(*Format 2, Liabilities item C.*)

The aggregate amount of creditors falling due within one year and of creditors falling due after more than one year shall be shown separately, unless it is disclosed in the notes to the accounts.

[658]

NOTES

Inserted by the Companies Act 1985 (Accounts of Small and Medium-sized Companies and Minor Accounting Amendments) Regulations 1997, SI 1997/220, reg 2(3), Sch 2, in relation to annual accounts approved by the board of directors on or after 1 March 1997, and to directors' and auditors' reports on such accounts (subject to transitional provisions in relation to a financial year of a company ending on or before 24 March 1997).

Repealed by the Companies Act 2006, s 1295, Sch 16, as from a day to be appointed.

Words in square brackets in balance sheet format 1 and balance sheet format 2 substituted by the Companies Act 1985 (International Accounting Standards and Other Accounting Amendments) Regulations 2004, SI 2004/2947, reg 14(3), Sch 4, paras 1, 2, as from 12 November 2004, in relation to companies' financial years which begin on or after 1 January 2005.

Application to limited liability partnerships: see the Limited Liability Partnerships Regulations 2001, SI 2001/1090, reg 3, Sch 1 at **[6984]**, **[6992]**.

PART II
NOTES TO THE ACCOUNTS

Preliminary

3. Any information required in the case of any small company by the following provisions of this Part of this Schedule shall (if not given in the company's accounts) be given by way of a note to those accounts.

Disclosure of accounting policies

4. The accounting policies adopted by the company in determining the amounts to be included in respect of items shown in the balance sheet and in determining the profit or loss of the company shall be stated (including such policies with respect to the depreciation and diminution in value of assets).

Information supplementing the balance sheet

Share capital and debentures

5.—(1) The following information shall be given with respect to the company's share capital—

(a) the authorised share capital; and

(b) where shares of more than one class have been allotted, the number and aggregate nominal value of shares of each class allotted.

(2) In the case of any part of the allotted share capital that consists of redeemable shares, the following information shall be given—

(a) the earliest and latest dates on which the company has power to redeem those shares;

(b) whether those shares must be redeemed in any event or are liable to be redeemed at the option of the company or of the shareholder; and

(c) whether any (and, if so, what) premium is payable on redemption.

6. If the company has allotted any shares during the financial year, the following information shall be given—

(a) the classes of shares allotted; and

(b) as respects each class of shares, the number allotted, their aggregate nominal value, and the consideration received by the company for the allotment.

Fixed assets

7.—(1) In respect of each item to which a letter or Roman number is assigned under the general item "fixed assets" in the company's balance sheet the following information shall be given—

(a) the appropriate amounts in respect of that item as at the date of the beginning of the financial year and as at the balance sheet date respectively;

(b) the effect on any amount shown in the balance sheet in respect of that item of—

(i) any revision of the amount in respect of any assets included under that item made during that year on any basis mentioned in paragraph 31 of Schedule 8;
(ii) acquisitions during that year of any assets;
(iii) disposals during that year of any assets; and
(iv) any transfers of assets of the company to and from that item during that year.

(2) The reference in sub-paragraph (1)(a) to the appropriate amounts in respect of any item as at any date there mentioned is a reference to amounts representing the aggregate amounts determined, as at that date, in respect of assets falling to be included under that item on either of the following bases, that is to say—
(a) on the basis of purchase price or production cost (determined in accordance with paragraphs 26 and 27 of Schedule 8); or
(b) on any basis mentioned in paragraph 31 of that Schedule,

(leaving out of account in either case any provisions for depreciation or diminution in value).

(3) In respect of each item within sub-paragraph (1)—
(a) the cumulative amount of provisions for depreciation or diminution in value of assets included under that item as at each date mentioned in sub-paragraph (1)(a);
(b) the amount of any such provisions made in respect of the financial year;
(c) the amount of any adjustments made in respect of any such provisions during that year in consequence of the disposal of any assets; and
(d) the amount of any other adjustments made in respect of any such provisions during that year;

shall also be stated.

[Financial fixed assets

7A.—(1) Sub-paragraph (2) applies if—
(a) the company has financial fixed assets that could be included at fair value by virtue of paragraph 34A of Schedule 8,
(b) the amount at which those assets are included under any item in the company's accounts is in excess of their fair value, and
(c) the company has not made provision for diminution in value of those assets in accordance with paragraph 19(1) of that Schedule.

(2) There must be stated—
(a) the amount at which either the individual assets or appropriate groupings of those individual assets are included in the company's accounts,
(b) the fair value of those assets or groupings, and
(c) the reasons for not making a provision for diminution in value of those assets, including the nature of the evidence that provides the basis for the belief that the amount at which they are stated in the accounts will be recovered.]

Details of indebtedness

8.—(1) For the aggregate of all items shown under "creditors" in the company's balance sheet there shall be stated the aggregate of the following amounts, that is to say—
(a) the amount of any debts included under "creditors" which are payable or repayable otherwise than by instalments and fall due for payment or repayment after the end of the period of five years beginning with the day next following the end of the financial year; and
(b) in the case of any debts so included which are payable or repayable by instalments, the amount of any instalments which fall due for payment after the end of that period.

(2) In respect of each item shown under "creditors" in the company's balance sheet there shall be stated the aggregate amount of any debts included under that item, in respect of which any security has been given by the company.

General

9.—(1) Where sums originally denominated in foreign currencies have been brought into account under any items shown in the balance sheet or profit and loss account, the basis on which those sums have been translated into sterling shall be stated.

(2), (3) …

[Dormant Companies Acting as Agents

9A. Where the directors of a company take advantage of the exemption conferred by section 249AA, and the company has during the financial year in question acted as an agent for any person, the fact that it has so acted must be stated.]]

[659]

NOTES

Inserted as noted to Pt I at **[658]**.

Repealed by the Companies Act 2006, s 1295, Sch 16, as from a day to be appointed.

Para 7A: inserted by the Companies Act 1985 (International Accounting Standards and Other Accounting Amendments) Regulations 2004, SI 2004/2947, reg 14(3), Sch 4, paras 1, 3, as from 12 November 2004, in relation to companies' financial years which begin on or after 1 January 2005.

Para 9: sub-paras (2), (3) repealed by the Companies Act 1985 (Investment Companies and Accounting and Audit Amendments) Regulations 2005, SI 2005/2280, reg 7, as from 1 October 2005, in relation to companies' financial years which begin on or after 1 January 2005 and which end on or after 1 October 2005.

Para 9A: added by the Companies Act 1985 (Audit Exemption) (Amendment) Regulations 2000, SI 2000/1430, reg 7, as from 26 May 2000, in relation to annual reports and reports in respect of financial years ending two months or more after that date.

Application to limited liability partnerships: see the Limited Liability Partnerships Regulations 2001, SI 2001/1090, reg 3, Sch 1 at **[6984]**, **[6992]**.

SCHEDULE 9
[SPECIAL PROVISIONS FOR BANKING COMPANIES AND GROUPS]

Sections 255, 255A, 255B

[PART I
INDIVIDUAL ACCOUNTS

CHAPTER 1
GENERAL RULES AND FORMATS

SECTION A
GENERAL RULES

1.—(1) Subject to the following provisions of this Part of this Schedule—

- *(a) every balance sheet of a company shall show the items listed in the balance sheet format set out below in section B of this Chapter of this Schedule; and*
- *(b) every profit and loss account of a company shall show the items listed in either of the profit and loss account formats so set out;*

in either case in the order and under the headings and sub-headings given in the format adopted.

(2) Sub-paragraph (1) above is not to be read as requiring the heading or sub-heading for any item to be distinguished by any number or letter assigned to that item in the format adopted.

(3) Where the heading of an item in the format adopted contains any wording in square brackets, that wording may be omitted if not applicable to the company.

2.—(1) Where in accordance with paragraph 1 a company's profit and loss account for any financial year has been prepared by reference to one of the formats set out in section B below, the directors of the company shall adopt the same format in preparing the profit and loss account for subsequent financial years of the company unless in their opinion there are special reasons for a change.

(2) Particulars of any change in the format adopted in preparing a company's profit and loss account in accordance with paragraph 1 shall be disclosed, and the reasons for the change shall be explained, in a note to the accounts in which the new format is first adopted.

3.—(1) Any item required in accordance with paragraph 1 to be shown in a company's balance sheet or profit and loss account may be shown in greater detail than so required.

(2) A company's balance sheet or profit and loss account may include an item representing or covering the amount of any asset or liability, income or expenditure not specifically covered by any of the items listed in the balance sheet format provided or the profit and loss account format adopted, but the following shall not be treated as assets in any company's balance sheet:

(i) preliminary expenses;
(ii) expenses of and commission on any issue of shares or debentures; and
(iii) costs of research.

(3) Items to which lower case letters are assigned in any of the formats set out in section B below may be combined in a company's accounts for any financial year if either:

(a) their individual amounts are not material for the purpose of giving a true and fair view; or
(b) the combination facilitates the assessment of the state of affairs or profit or loss of the company for that year;

but in a case within paragraph (b) the individual amounts of any items so combined shall be disclosed in a note to the accounts and any notes required by this Schedule to the items so combined shall, notwithstanding the combination, be given.

(4) Subject to paragraph 4(3) below, a heading or sub-heading corresponding to an item listed in the balance sheet format or the profit and loss account format adopted in preparing a company's balance sheet or profit and loss account shall not be included if there is no amount to be shown for that item in respect of the financial year to which the balance sheet or profit and loss account relates.

4.—(1) In respect of every item shown in the balance sheet or profit and loss account, there shall be shown or stated the corresponding amount for the financial year immediately preceding that to which the accounts relate.

(2) Where the corresponding amount is not comparable with the amount to be shown for the item in question in respect of the financial year to which the balance sheet or profit and loss account relates, the former amount [may be adjusted] and [particulars of the non-comparability and of any adjustment] shall be given in a note to the accounts.

(3) Paragraph 3(4) does not apply in any case where an amount can be shown for the item in question in respect of the financial year immediately preceding that to which the balance sheet or profit and loss account relates, and that amount shall be shown under the heading or sub-heading required by paragraph 1 for that item.

5.—(1) Subject to the following provisions of this paragraph and without prejudice to note (6) to the balance sheet format, amounts in respect of items representing assets or income may not be set off against amounts in respect of items representing liabilities or expenditure (as the case may be), or vice versa.

(2) Charges required to be included in profit and loss account format 1, items 11(a) and 11(b) or format 2, items A7(a) and A7(b) may however be set off against income required to be included in format 1, items 12(a) and 12(b) or format 2, items B5(a) and B5(b) and the resulting figure shown as a single item (in format 2 at position A7 if negative and at position B5 if positive).

(3) Charges required to be included in profit and loss account format 1, item 13 or format 2, item A8 may also be set off against income required to be included in format 1, item 14 or format 2, item B6 and the resulting figure shown as a single item (in format 2 at position A8 if negative and at position B6 if positive).

6.—(1) Assets shall be shown under the relevant balance sheet headings even where the company has pledged them as security for its own liabilities or for those of third parties or has otherwise assigned them as security to third parties.

(2) A company shall not include in its balance sheet assets pledged or otherwise assigned to it as security unless such assets are in the form of cash in the hands of the company.

7. Assets acquired in the name of and on behalf of third parties shall not be shown in the balance sheet.

8. …

[8A. The directors of a company must, in determining how amounts are presented within items in the profit and loss account and balance sheet, have regard to the substance of the reported transaction or arrangement, in accordance with generally accepted accounting principles or practice.]

SECTION B
THE REQUIRED FORMATS FOR ACCOUNTS

Preliminary

9.—(1) References in this Part of this Schedule to the balance sheet format or to profit and loss account formats are to the balance sheet format or profit and loss account formats set out below and references to the items listed in any of the formats are to those items read together with any of the notes following the formats which apply to any of those items.

(2) The requirement imposed by paragraph 1 of this Part of this Schedule to show the items listed in any such format in the order adopted in the format is subject to any provision in the notes following the formats for alternative positions for any particular items.

10. A number in brackets following any item in any of the formats set out below is a reference to the note of that number in the notes following the formats.

Balance Sheet Format

ASSETS

1. Cash and balances at central (or post office) banks (1)

2. Treasury bills and other eligible bills (20)
(a) Treasury bills and similar securities (2)
(b) Other eligible bills (3)

3. Loans and advances to banks (4), (20)
(a) Repayable on demand
(b) Other loans and advances

4. Loans and advances to customers (5), (20)

5. Debt securities (and other fixed income securities) (6), (20)
(a) Issued by public bodies
(b) Issued by other issuers

6. Equity shares (and other variable-yield securities)

7. Participating interests

8. Shares in group undertakings

9. Intangible fixed assets (7)

10. Tangible fixed assets (8)

11. Called up capital not paid (9)

12. Own shares (10)

13. Other assets

14. Called up capital not paid (9)

15. Prepayments and accrued income

Total assets

LIABILITIES

1. *Deposits by banks* (*11*), (*20*)
   (*a*) *Repayable on demand*
   (*b*) *With agreed maturity dates or periods of notice*
2. *Customer accounts* (*12*), (*20*)
   (*a*) *Repayable on demand*
   (*b*) *With agreed maturity dates or periods of notice*
3. *Debt securities in issue* (*13*), (*20*)
   (*a*) *Bonds and medium term notes*
   (*b*) *Others*
4. *Other liabilities*
5. *Accruals and deferred income*
6. *[Provisions for liabilities]*
   (*a*) *Provisions for pensions and similar obligations*
   (*b*) *Provisions for tax*
   (*c*) *Other provisions*
7. *Subordinated liabilities* (*14*), (*20*)
8. *Called up share capital* (*15*)
9. *Share premium account*
10. *Reserves*
   (*a*) *Capital redemption reserve*
   (*b*) *Reserve for own shares*
   (*c*) *Reserves provided for by the articles of association*
   (*d*) *Other reserves*
11. *Revaluation reserve*
12. *Profit and loss account*

Total liabilities

MEMORANDUM ITEMS

1. *Contingent liabilities* (*16*)
   (*1*) *Acceptances and endorsements*
   (*2*) *Guarantees and assets pledged as collateral security* (*17*)
   (*3*) *Other contingent liabilities*
2. *Commitments* (*18*)
   (*1*) *Commitments arising out of sale and option to resell transactions* (*19*)
   (*2*) *Other commitments*

Notes on the balance sheet format and memorandum items

(*1*) *Cash and balances at central* (*or post office*) *banks*

(*Assets item 1*)

Cash shall comprise all currency including foreign notes and coins.

Only those balances which may be withdrawn without notice and which are deposited with central or post office banks of the country or countries in which the company is established shall be included in this item. All other claims on central or post office banks must be shown under Assets items 3 or 4.

(*2*) *Treasury bills and other eligible bills: Treasury bills and similar securities*

(*Assets item 2*(*a*))

Treasury bills and similar securities shall comprise treasury bills and similar debt instruments issued by public bodies which are eligible for refinancing with central banks of the country or countries in which the company is established. Any treasury bills or similar debt instruments not so eligible shall be included under Assets item 5, sub-item (*a*).

(*3*) *Treasury bills and other eligible bills: Other eligible bills*

(*Assets item 2*(*b*))

Other eligible bills shall comprise all bills purchased to the extent that they are eligible, under national law, for refinancing with the central banks of the country or countries in which the company is established.

(4) Loans and advances to banks

(Assets item 3)

Loans and advances to banks shall comprise all loans and advances to domestic or foreign credit institutions made by the company arising out of banking transactions. However loans and advances to credit institutions represented by debt securities or other fixed income securities shall be included under Assets item 5 and not this item.

(5) Loans and advances to customers

(Assets item 4)

Loans and advances to customers shall comprise all types of assets in the form of claims on domestic and foreign customers other than credit institutions. However loans and advances represented by debt securities or other fixed income securities shall be included under Assets item 5 and not this item.

(6) Debt securities (and other fixed income securities)

(Assets item 5)

This item shall comprise transferable debt securities and any other transferable fixed income securities issued by credit institutions, other undertakings or public bodies. Debt securities and other fixed income securities issued by public bodies shall however only be included in this item if they may not be shown under Assets item 2.

Where a company holds its own debt securities these shall not be included under this item but shall be deducted from Liabilities item 3(a) or (b), as appropriate.

Securities bearing interest rates that vary in accordance with specific factors, for example the interest rate on the inter-bank market or on the Euromarket, shall also be regarded as fixed income securities to be included under this item.

(7) Intangible fixed assets

(Assets item 9)

This item shall comprise:
- *(a) development costs;*
- *(b) concessions, patents, licences, trade marks and similar rights and assets;*
- *(c) goodwill; and*
- *(d) payments on account.*

Amounts shall, however, be included in respect of (b) only if the assets were acquired for valuable consideration or the assets in question were created by the company itself.

Amounts representing goodwill shall only be included to the extent that the goodwill was acquired for valuable consideration.

There shall be disclosed, in a note to the accounts, the amount of any goodwill included in this item.

(8) Tangible fixed assets

(Assets item 10)

This item shall comprise:
- *land and buildings;*
- *plant and machinery;*
- *fixtures and fittings, tools and equipment; and*
- *payments on account and assets in the course of construction.*

There shall be disclosed in a note to the accounts the amount included in this item with respect to land and buildings occupied by the company for its own activities.

(9) Called up capital not paid

(Assets items 11 and 14)

The two positions shown for this item are alternatives.

(10) Own shares

(Assets item 12)

The nominal value of the shares held shall be shown separately under this item.

(11) Deposits by banks

(Liabilities item 1)

Deposits by banks shall comprise all amounts arising out of banking transactions owed to other domestic or foreign credit institutions by the company. However liabilities in the form of debt securities and any liabilities for which transferable certificates have been issued shall be included under Liabilities item 3 and not this item.

(12) Customer accounts

(Liabilities item 2)

This item shall comprise all amounts owed to creditors that are not credit institutions. However liabilities in the form of debt securities and any liabilities for which transferable certificates have been issued shall be shown under Liabilities item 3 and not this item.

(13) Debt securities in issue

(Liabilities item 3)

This item shall include both debt securities and debts for which transferable certificates have been issued, including liabilities arising out of own acceptances and promissory notes. (Only acceptances which a company has issued for its own refinancing and in respect of which it is the first party liable shall be treated as own acceptances.)

(14) Subordinated liabilities

(Liabilities item 7)

This item shall comprise all liabilities in respect of which there is a contractual obligation that, in the event of winding up or bankruptcy, they are to be repaid only after the claims of other creditors have been met.

This item shall include all subordinated liabilities, whether or not a ranking has been agreed between the subordinated creditors concerned.

(15) Called up share capital

(Liabilities item 8)

The amount of allotted share capital and the amount of called up share capital which has been paid up shall be shown separately.

(16) Contingent liabilities

(Memorandum item 1)

This item shall include all transactions whereby the company has underwritten the obligations of a third party.

Liabilities arising out of the endorsement of rediscounted bills shall be included in this item.

Acceptances other than own acceptances shall also be included.

(17) Contingent liabilities: Guarantees and assets pledged as collateral security

(Memorandum item 1(2))

This item shall include all guarantee obligations incurred and assets pledged as collateral security on behalf of third parties, particularly in respect of sureties and irrevocable letters of credit.

(18) Commitments

(Memorandum item 2)

This item shall include every irrevocable commitment which could give rise to a credit risk.

(19) Commitments: Commitments arising out of sale and option to resell transactions

(Memorandum item 2(1))

This sub-item shall comprise commitments entered into by the company in the context of sale and option to resell transactions.

(20) Claims on, and liabilities to, undertakings in which a participating interest is held or group undertakings

(Assets items 2 to 5, Liabilities items 1 to 3 and 7)

The following information must be given either by way of subdivision of the relevant items or by way of notes to the accounts.

The amount of the following must be shown for each of Assets items 2 to 5:
- (*a*) *claims on group undertakings included therein; and*
- (*b*) *claims on undertakings in which the company has a participating interest included therein.*

The amount of the following must be shown for each of Liabilities items 1, 2, 3 and 7:
- *(i) liabilities to group undertakings included therein; and*
- *(ii) liabilities to undertakings in which the company has a participating interest included therein.*

Special rules

Subordinated assets

11.—(1) The amount of any assets that are subordinated must be shown either as a subdivision of any relevant asset item or in the notes to the accounts; in the latter case disclosure shall be by reference to the relevant asset item or items in which the assets are included.

(2) In the case of Assets items 2 to 5 in the balance sheet format, the amounts required to be shown by note (20) to the format as sub-items of those items shall be further subdivided so as to show the amount of any claims included therein that are subordinated.

(3) For this purpose, assets are subordinated if there is a contractual obligation to the effect that, in the event of winding up or bankruptcy, they are to be repaid only after the claims of other creditors have been met, whether or not a ranking has been agreed between the subordinated creditors concerned.

Syndicated loans

12.—(1) Where a company is a party to a syndicated loan transaction the company shall include only that part of the total loan which it itself has funded.

(2) Where a company is a party to a syndicated loan transaction and has agreed to reimburse (in whole or in part) any other party to the syndicate any funds advanced by that party or any interest thereon upon the occurrence of any event, including the default of the borrower, any additional liability by reason of such a guarantee shall be included as a contingent liability in Memorandum item 1, sub-item (2).

Sale and repurchase transactions

13.—(1) The following rules apply where a company is a party to a sale and repurchase transaction.

(2) Where the company is the transferor of the assets under the transaction:
- (*a*) *the assets transferred shall, notwithstanding the transfer, be included in its balance sheet;*
- (*b*) *the purchase price received by it shall be included in its balance sheet as an amount owed to the transferee; and*
- (*c*) *the value of the assets transferred shall be disclosed in a note to its accounts.*

(3) Where the company is the transferee of the assets under the transaction it shall not include the assets transferred in its balance sheet but the purchase price paid by it to the transferor shall be so included as an amount owed by the transferor.

Sale and option to resell transactions

14.—(1) The following rules apply where a company is a party to a sale and option to resell transaction.

(2) Where the company is the transferor of the assets under the transaction it shall not include in its balance sheet the assets transferred but it shall enter under Memorandum item 2 an amount equal to the price agreed in the event of repurchase.

(3) Where the company is the transferee of the assets under the transaction it shall include those assets in its balance sheet.

Managed funds

15.—(1) For the purposes of this paragraph "managed funds" are funds which the company administers in its own name but on behalf of others and to which it has legal title.

(2) The company shall, in any case where claims and obligations arising in respect of managed funds fall to be treated as claims and obligations of the company, adopt the following accounting treatment: claims and obligations representing managed funds are to be included in the company's balance sheet, with the notes to the accounts disclosing the total amount included with respect to such assets and liabilities in the balance sheet and showing the amount included under each relevant balance sheet item in respect of such assets or (as the case may be) liabilities.

Profit and Loss Account Formats

Format 1
Vertical layout

1. *Interest receivable (1)*
   (1) *Interest receivable and similar income arising from debt securities (and other fixed income securities)*
   (2) *Other interest receivable and similar income*
2. *Interest payable (2)*
3. *Dividend income*
   (a) *Income from equity shares (and other variable-yield securities)*
   (b) *Income from participating interests*
   (c) *Income from shares in group undertakings*
4. *Fees and commissions receivable (3)*
5. *Fees and commissions payable (4)*
6. *Dealing (profits) (losses) (5)*
7. *Other operating income*
8. *Administrative expenses*
   (a) *Staff costs*
      (i) *Wages and salaries*
      (ii) *Social security costs*
      (iii) *Other pension costs*
   (b) *Other administrative expenses*
9. *Depreciation and amortisation (6)*
10. *Other operating charges*
11. *Provisions*
    (a) *Provisions for bad and doubtful debts (7)*
    (b) *Provisions for contingent liabilities and commitments (8)*
12. *Adjustments to provisions*
    (a) *Adjustments to provisions for bad and doubtful debts (9)*
    (b) *Adjustments to provisions for contingent liabilities and commitments (10)*
13. *Amounts written off fixed asset investments (11)*
14. *Adjustments to amounts written off fixed asset investments (12)*

15. *(Profit) (loss) on ordinary activities before tax*
16. *Tax on (profit) (loss) on ordinary activities*
17. *(Profit) (loss) on ordinary activities after tax*
18. *Extraordinary income*
19. *Extraordinary charges*
20. *Extraordinary (profit) (loss)*
21. *Tax on extraordinary (profit) (loss)*
22. *Extraordinary (profit) (loss) after tax*
23. *Other taxes not shown under the preceding items*
24. *(Profit) (loss) for the financial year*

Format 2
Horizontal layout

A. Charges
- *1. Interest payable (2)*
- *2. Fees and commissions payable (4)*
- *3. Dealing losses (5)*
- *4. Administrative expenses*
  - *(a) Staff costs*
    - *(i) Wages and salaries*
    - *(ii) Social security costs*
    - *(iii) Other pension costs*
  - *(b) Other administrative expenses*
- *5. Depreciation and amortisation (6)*
- *6. Other operating charges*
- *7. Provisions*
  - *(a) Provisions for bad and doubtful debts (7)*
  - *(b) Provisions for contingent liabilities and commitments (8)*
- *8. Amounts written off fixed asset investments (11)*
- *9. Profit on ordinary activities before tax*
- *10. Tax on (profit) (loss) on ordinary activities*
- *11. Profit on ordinary activities after tax*
- *12. Extraordinary charges*
- *13. Tax on extraordinary (profit) (loss)*
- *14. Extraordinary loss after tax*
- *15. Other taxes not shown under the preceding items*
- *16. Profit for the financial year*

B. Income
- *1. Interest receivable (1)*
  - *(1) Interest receivable and similar income arising from debt securities (and other fixed income securities)*
  - *(2) Other interest receivable and similar income*
- *2. Dividend income*
  - *(a) Income from equity shares (and other variable-yield securities)*
  - *(b) Income from participating interests*
  - *(c) Income from shares in group undertakings*
- *3. Fees and commissions receivable (3)*
- *4. Dealing profits (5)*
- *5. Adjustments to provisions*
  - *(a) Adjustments to provisions for bad and doubtful debts (9)*
  - *(b) Adjustments to provisions for contingent liabilities and commitments (10)*
- *6. Adjustments to amounts written off fixed asset investments (12)*
- *7. Other operating income*
- *8. Loss on ordinary activities before tax*
- *9. Loss on ordinary activities after tax*
- *10. Extraordinary income*
- *11. Extraordinary profit after tax*
- *12. Loss for the financial year*

Notes on the profit and loss account formats

(*1*) *Interest receivable*

(*Format 1, item 1; Format 2, item B.1*)

This item shall include all income arising out of banking activities, including:
- (*a*) *income from assets included in Assets items 1 to 5 in the balance sheet format, however calculated;*
- (*b*) *income resulting from covered forward contracts spread over the actual duration of the contract and similar in nature to interest; and*
- (*c*) *fees and commissions receivable similar in nature to interest and calculated on a time basis or by reference to the amount of the claim* (*but not other fees and commissions receivable*).

(*2*) *Interest payable*

(*Format 1, item 2; Format 2, item A.1*)

This item shall include all expenditure arising out of banking activities, including:
- (*a*) *charges arising out of liabilities included in Liabilities items 1, 2, 3 and 7 in the balance sheet format, however calculated;*
- (*b*) *charges resulting from covered forward contracts, spread over the actual duration of the contract and similar in nature to interest; and*
- (*c*) *fees and commissions payable similar in nature to interest and calculated on a time basis or by reference to the amount of the liability* (*but not other fees and commissions payable*).

(*3*) *Fees and commissions receivable*

(*Format 1, item 4; Format 2, item B.3*)

Fees and commissions receivable shall comprise income in respect of all services supplied by the company to third parties, but not fees or commissions required to be included under interest receivable (*Format 1, item 1; Format 2, item B.1*).

In particular the following fees and commissions receivable must be included (*unless required to be included under interest receivable*):
- — *fees and commissions for guarantees, loan administration on behalf of other lenders and securities transactions;*
- — *fees, commissions and other income in respect of payment transactions, account administration charges and commissions for the safe custody and administration of securities;*
- — *fees and commissions for foreign currency transactions and for the sale and purchase of coin and precious metals; and*
- — *fees and commissions charged for brokerage services in connection with savings and insurance contracts and loans.*

(*4*) *Fees and commissions payable*

(*Format 1, item 5; Format 2, item A.2*)

Fees and commissions payable shall comprise charges for all services rendered to the company by third parties but not fees or commissions required to be included under interest payable (*Format 1, item 2; Format 2, item A.1*).

In particular the following fees and commissions payable must be included (*unless required to be included under interest payable*):
- — *fees and commissions for guarantees, loan administration and securities transactions;*
- — *fees, commissions and other charges in respect of payment transactions, account administration charges and commissions for the safe custody and administration of securities;*
- — *fees and commissions for foreign currency transactions and for the sale and purchase of coin and precious metals; and*
- — *fees and commissions for brokerage services in connection with savings and insurance contracts and loans.*

(*5*) *Dealing* (*profits*) (*losses*)

(*Format 1, item 6; Format 2, items B.4 and A.3*)

This item shall comprise:
- (*a*) *the net profit or net loss on transactions in securities which are not held as*

financial fixed assets together with amounts written off or written back with respect to such securities, including amounts written off or written back as a result of the application of paragraph 34(1) below;

(*b*) *the net profit or loss on exchange activities, save in so far as the profit or loss is included in interest receivable or interest payable (Format 1, items 1 or 2; Format 2, items B.1 or A.1); and*

(*c*) *the net profits and losses on other dealing operations involving financial instruments, including precious metals.*

(*6*) *Depreciation and amortisation*

(*Format 1, item 9; Format 2, item A.5*)

This item shall comprise depreciation and other amounts written off in respect of balance sheet Assets items 9 and 10.

(*7*) *Provisions: Provisions for bad and doubtful debts*

(*Format 1, item 11(a); Format 2, item A.7(a)*)

Provisions for bad and doubtful debts shall comprise charges for amounts written off and for provisions made in respect of loans and advances shown under balance sheet Assets items 3 and 4.

(*8*) *Provisions: Provisions for contingent liabilities and commitments*

(*Format 1, item 11(b); Format 2, item A.7(b)*)

This item shall comprise charges for provisions for contingent liabilities and commitments of a type which would, if not provided for, be shown under Memorandum items 1 and 2.

(*9*) *Adjustments to provisions: Adjustments to provisions for bad and doubtful debts*

(*Format 1, item 12(a); Format 2, item B.5(a)*)

This item shall include credits from the recovery of loans that have been written off, from other advances written back following earlier write offs and from the reduction of provisions previously made with respect to loans and advances.

(*10*) *Adjustments to provisions: Adjustments to provisions for contingent liabilities and commitments*

(*Format 1, item 12(b); Format 2, item B.5(b)*)

This item comprises credits from the reduction of provisions previously made with respect to contingent liabilities and commitments.

(*11*) *Amounts written off fixed asset investments*

(*Format 1, item 13; Format 2, item A.8*)

Amounts written off fixed asset investments shall comprise amounts written off in respect of assets which are transferable securities held as financial fixed assets, participating interests and shares in group undertakings and which are included in Assets items 5 to 8 in the balance sheet format.

(*12*) *Adjustments to amounts written off fixed asset investments*

(*Format 1, item 14; Format 2, item B.6*)

Adjustments to amounts written off fixed asset investments shall include amounts written back following earlier write offs and provisions in respect of assets which are transferable securities held as financial fixed assets, participating interests and group undertakings and which are included in Assets items 5 to 8 in the balance sheet format.

CHAPTER II
ACCOUNTING PRINCIPLES AND RULES

SECTION A
ACCOUNTING PRINCIPLES

16. Subject to paragraph 22 below, the amounts to be included in respect of all items shown in a company's accounts shall be determined in accordance with the principles set out in paragraphs 17 to 21.

Accounting principles

17. The company shall be presumed to be carrying on business as a going concern.

18. Accounting policies shall be applied consistently within the same accounts and from one financial year to the next.

19. The amount of any item shall be determined on a prudent basis, and in particular:
- (*a*) *only profits realised at the balance sheet date shall be included in the profit and loss account; and*
- (*b*) *all liabilities … which have arisen … in respect of the financial year to which the accounts relate or a previous financial year shall be taken into account, including those which only become apparent between the balance sheet date and the date on which it is signed on behalf of the board of directors in pursuance of section 233 of this Act.*

20. All income and charges relating to the financial year to which the accounts relate shall be taken into account, without regard to the date of receipt or payment.

21. In determining the aggregate amount of any item the amount of each individual asset or liability that falls to be taken into account shall be determined separately.

Departure from the accounting principles

22. If it appears to the directors of a company that there are special reasons for departing from any of the principles stated above in preparing the company's accounts in respect of any financial year they may do so, but particulars of the departure, the reasons for it and its effect shall be given in a note to the accounts.

SECTION B
VALUATION RULES

HISTORICAL COST ACCOUNTING RULES

Preliminary

23. Subject to [paragraphs 39 to 44F] of this Part of this Schedule, the amounts to be included in respect of all items shown in a company's accounts shall be determined in accordance with the rules set out in paragraphs 24 to 38 of this Part of this Schedule.

Fixed assets

General rules

24. Subject to any provision for depreciation or diminution in value made in accordance with paragraph 25 or 26 the amount to be included in respect of any fixed asset shall be its cost.

25. In the case of any fixed asset which has a limited useful economic life, the amount of:
- (*a*) *its cost; or*
- (*b*) *where it is estimated that any such asset will have a residual value at the end of the period of its useful economic life, its cost less that estimated residual value;*

shall be reduced by provisions for depreciation calculated to write off that amount systematically over the period of the asset's useful economic life.

26.—(1) Where a fixed asset investment of a description falling to be included under Assets items 7 (Participating interests) or 8 (Shares in group undertakings) in the balance sheet format, or any other holding of securities held as a financial fixed asset, has diminished in value, provisions for diminution in value may be made in respect of it and the amount to be included in respect of it may be reduced accordingly; and any such provisions which are not shown in the profit and loss account shall be disclosed (either separately or in aggregate) in a note to the accounts.

(2) Provisions for diminution in value shall be made in respect of any fixed asset which has diminished in value if the reduction in its value is expected to be permanent (whether its useful economic life is limited or not), and the amount to be included in respect of it shall be reduced accordingly; and any such provisions which are not shown in the profit and loss account shall be disclosed (either separately or in aggregate) in a note to the accounts.

(3) Where the reasons for which any provision was made in accordance with sub-paragraph (1) or (2) have ceased to apply to any extent, that provision shall be written back to the extent that it is no longer necessary; and any amounts written back in accordance with this sub-paragraph which are not shown in the profit and loss account shall be disclosed (either separately or in aggregate) in a note to the accounts.

Development costs

27.—(1) Notwithstanding that amounts representing "development costs" may be included under Assets item 9 in the balance sheet format, an amount may only be included in a company's balance sheet in respect of development costs in special circumstances.

(2) If any amount is included in a company's balance sheet in respect of development costs the following information shall be given in a note to the accounts:

- *(a) the period over which the amount of those costs originally capitalised is being or is to be written off; and*
- *(b) the reasons for capitalising the development costs in question.*

Goodwill

28.—(1) The application of paragraphs 24 to 26 in relation to goodwill (in any case where goodwill is treated as an asset) is subject to the following provisions of this paragraph.

(2) Subject to sub-paragraph (3) below the amount of the consideration for any goodwill acquired by a company shall be reduced by provisions for depreciation calculated to write off that amount systematically over a period chosen by the directors of the company.

(3) The period chosen shall not exceed the useful economic life of the goodwill in question.

(4) In any case where any goodwill acquired by a company is included as an asset in the company's balance sheet the period chosen for writing off the consideration for that goodwill and the reasons for choosing that period shall be disclosed in a note to the accounts.

Intangible and tangible fixed assets

29. Assets included in Assets items 9 (Intangible fixed assets) and 10 (Tangible fixed assets) in the balance sheet format shall be valued as fixed assets.

Other fixed assets

30. Other assets falling to be included in the balance sheet shall be valued as fixed assets where they are intended for use on a continuing basis in the company's activities.

Financial fixed assets

31.—(1) Debt securities, including fixed income securities, held as financial fixed assets shall be included in the balance sheet at an amount equal to their maturity value plus any premium, or less any discount, on their purchase, subject to the following provisions of this paragraph.

(2) The amount included in the balance sheet with respect to such securities purchased at a premium shall be reduced each financial year on a systematic basis so as to write the premium off over the period to the maturity date of the security and the amounts so written off shall be charged to the profit and loss account for the relevant financial years.

(3) The amount included in the balance sheet with respect to such securities purchased at a discount shall be increased each financial year on a systematic basis so as to extinguish the discount over the period to the maturity date of the security and the amounts by which the amount is increased shall be credited to the profit and loss account for the relevant years.

(4) The notes to the accounts shall disclose the amount of any unamortised premium or discount not extinguished which is included in the balance sheet by virtue of sub-paragraph (1).

(5) For the purposes of this paragraph "premium" means any excess of the amount paid for a security over its maturity value and "discount" means any deficit of the amount paid for a security over its maturity value.

Current assets

32. The amount to be included in respect of loans and advances, debt or other fixed income securities and equity shares or other variable yield securities not held as financial fixed assets shall be their cost, subject to paragraphs 33 and 34 below.

33.—(1) If the net realisable value of any asset referred to in paragraph 32 is lower than its cost the amount to be included in respect of that asset shall be the net realisable value.

(2) Where the reasons for which any provision for diminution in value was made in accordance with sub-paragraph (1) have ceased to apply to any extent, that provision shall be written back to the extent that it is no longer necessary.

34.—(1) Subject to paragraph 33 above, the amount to be included in the balance sheet in respect of transferable securities not held as financial fixed assets may be the higher of their cost or their market value at the balance sheet date.

(2) The difference between the cost of any securities included in the balance sheet at a valuation under sub-paragraph (1) and their market value shall be shown (in aggregate) in the notes to the accounts.

Miscellaneous and supplementary provisions

Excess of money owed over value received as an asset item

35.—(1) Where the amount repayable on any debt owed by a company is greater than the value of the consideration received in the transaction giving rise to the debt, the amount of the difference may be treated as an asset.

(2) Where any such amount is so treated:
- *(a) it shall be written off by reasonable amounts each year and must be completely written off before repayment of the debt; and*
- *(b) if the current amount is not shown as a separate item in the company's balance sheet it must be disclosed in a note to the accounts.*

Determination of cost

36.—(1) The cost of an asset that has been acquired by the company shall be determined by adding to the actual price paid any expenses incidental to its acquisition.

(2) The cost of an asset constructed by the company shall be determined by adding to the purchase price of the raw materials and consumables used the amount of the costs incurred by the company which are directly attributable to the construction of that asset.

(3) In addition, there may be included in the cost of an asset constructed by the company:
- *(a) a reasonable proportion of the costs incurred by the company which are only indirectly attributable to the construction of that asset, but only to the extent that they relate to the period of construction; and*
- *(b) interest on capital borrowed to finance the construction of that asset, to the extent that it accrues in respect of the period of construction;*

provided, however, in a case within sub-paragraph (b) above, that the inclusion of the interest in determining the cost of that asset and the amount of the interest so included is disclosed in a note to the accounts.

37.—(1) Subject to the qualification mentioned below, the cost of any assets which are fungible assets (including investments) may be determined by the application of any of the methods mentioned in sub-paragraph (2) below in relation to any such assets of the same class.

The method chosen must be one which appears to the directors to be appropriate in the circumstances of the company.

(2) Those methods are:

(a) the method known as "first in, first out" (FIFO);
(b) the method known as "last in, first out" (LIFO);
(c) a weighted average price; and
(d) any other method similar to any of the methods mentioned above.

(3) Where in the case of any company:

(a) the cost of assets falling to be included under any item shown in the company's balance sheet has been determined by the application of any method permitted by this paragraph; and
(b) the amount shown in respect of that item differs materially from the relevant alternative amount given below in this paragraph;

the amount of that difference shall be disclosed in a note to the accounts.

(4) Subject to sub-paragraph (5) below, for the purposes of sub-paragraph (3)(b) above, the relevant alternative amount, in relation to any item shown in a company's balance sheet, is the amount which would have been shown in respect of that item if assets of any class included under that item at an amount determined by any method permitted by this paragraph had instead been included at their replacement cost as at the balance sheet date.

(5) The relevant alternative amount may be determined by reference to the most recent actual purchase price before the balance sheet date of assets of any class included under the item in question instead of by reference to their replacement cost as at that date, but only if the former appears to the directors of the company to constitute the more appropriate standard of comparison in the case of assets of that class.

Substitution of original amount where price or cost unknown

38. Where there is no record of the purchase price of any asset acquired by a company or of any price, expenses or costs relevant for determining its cost in accordance with paragraph 36, or any such record cannot be obtained without unreasonable expense or delay, its cost shall be taken for the purposes of paragraphs 24 to 34 to be the value ascribed to it in the earliest available record of its value made on or after its acquisition by the company.

ALTERNATIVE ACCOUNTING RULES

Preliminary

39.—(1) The rules set out in paragraphs 24 to 38 are referred to below in this Schedule as the historical cost accounting rules.

(2) Paragraphs 24 to 27 and 31 to 35 are referred to below in this section of this Part of this Schedule as the depreciation rules; and references below in this Schedule to the historical cost accounting rules do not include the depreciation rules as they apply by virtue of paragraph 42.

40. Subject to paragraphs 42 to 44, the amounts to be included in respect of assets of any description mentioned in paragraph 41 may be determined on any basis so mentioned.

Alternative accounting rules

41.—(1) Intangible fixed assets, other than goodwill, may be included at their current cost.

(2) Tangible fixed assets may be included at a market value determined as at the date of their last valuation or at their current cost.

(3) Investments of any description falling to be included under Assets items 7 (Participating interests) or 8 (Shares in group undertakings) of the balance sheet format and any other securities held as financial fixed assets may be included either:

(*a*) *at a market value determined as at the date of their last valuation; or*
(*b*) *at a value determined on any basis which appears to the directors to be appropriate in the circumstances of the company;*

but in the latter case particulars of the method of valuation adopted and of the reasons for adopting it shall be disclosed in a note to the accounts.

(*4*) *Securities of any description not held as financial fixed assets (if not valued in accordance with paragraph 34 above) may be included at their current cost.*

Application of the depreciation rules

42.—(1) Where the value of any asset of a company is determined in accordance with paragraph 41, that value shall be, or (as the case may require) be the starting point for determining, the amount to be included in respect of that asset in the company's accounts, instead of its cost or any value previously so determined for that asset; and the depreciation rules shall apply accordingly in relation to any such asset with the substitution for any reference to its cost of a reference to the value most recently determined for that asset in accordance with paragraph 41.

(*2*) *The amount of any provision for depreciation required in the case of any fixed asset by paragraph 25 or 26 as it applies by virtue of sub-paragraph (1) is referred to below in this paragraph as the "adjusted amount", and the amount of any provision which would be required by that paragraph in the case of that asset according to the historical cost accounting rules is referred to as the "historical cost amount".*

(*3*) *Where sub-paragraph (1) applies in the case of any fixed asset the amount of any provision for depreciation in respect of that asset included in any item shown in the profit and loss account in respect of amounts written off assets of the description in question may be the historical cost amount instead of the adjusted amount, provided that the amount of any difference between the two is shown separately in the profit and loss account or in a note to the accounts.*

Additional information to be provided in case of departure from historical cost accounting rules

43.—(1) This paragraph applies where the amounts to be included in respect of assets covered by any items shown in a company's accounts have been determined in accordance with paragraph 41.

(*2*) *The items affected and the basis of valuation adopted in determining the amounts of the assets in question in the case of each such item shall be disclosed in a note to the accounts.*

(*3*) *In the case of each balance sheet item affected either:*
(*a*) *the comparable amounts determined according to the historical cost accounting rules; or*
(*b*) *the differences between those amounts and the corresponding amounts actually shown in the balance sheet in respect of that item;*

shall be shown separately in the balance sheet or in a note to the accounts.

(*4*) *In sub-paragraph (3) above, references in relation to any item to the comparable amounts determined as there mentioned are references to:*
(*a*) *the aggregate amount which would be required to be shown in respect of that item if the amounts to be included in respect of all the assets covered by that item were determined according to the historical cost accounting rules; and*
(*b*) *the aggregate amount of the cumulative provisions for depreciation or diminution in value which would be permitted or required in determining those amounts according to those rules.*

Revaluation reserve

44.—(1) With respect to any determination of the value of an asset of a company in accordance with paragraph 41, the amount of any profit or loss arising from that determination (after allowing, where appropriate, for any provisions for depreciation or diminution in value made otherwise than by reference to the value so determined and any adjustments of any such provisions made in the light of that determination) shall be credited or (as the case may be) debited to a separate reserve ("the revaluation reserve").

(2) The amount of the revaluation reserve shall be shown in the company's balance sheet under Liabilities item 11 in the balance sheet format, but need not be shown under that name.

(3) An amount may be transferred

[(a) from the revaluation reserve—

(i) to the profit and loss account, if the amount was previously charged to that account or represents realised profit, or

(ii) on capitalisation,

(b) to or from the revaluation reserve in respect of the taxation relating to any profit or loss credited or debited to the reserve;]

and the revaluation reserve shall be reduced to the extent that the amounts transferred to it are no longer necessary for the purposes of the valuation method used.

(4) In [sub-paragraph (3)(a)(ii)] "capitalisation", in relation to an amount standing to the credit of the revaluation reserve, means applying it in wholly or partly paying up unissued shares in the company to be allotted to members of the company as fully or partly paid shares.

(5) The revaluation reserve shall not be reduced except as mentioned in this paragraph.

(6) The treatment for taxation purposes of amounts credited or debited to the revaluation reserve shall be disclosed in a note to the accounts.

[FAIR VALUE ACCOUNTING

Inclusion of financial instruments at fair value

44A.—(1) Subject to sub-paragraphs (2) to (4), financial instruments (including derivatives) may be included at fair value.

(2) Sub-paragraph (1) does not apply to financial instruments which constitute liabilities unless—

(a) they are held as part of a trading portfolio, or

(b) they are derivatives.

(3) Sub-paragraph (1) does not apply to—

(a) financial instruments (other than derivatives) held to maturity;

(b) loans and receivables originated by the company and not held for trading purposes;

(c) interests in subsidiary undertakings, associated undertakings and joint ventures;

(d) equity instruments issued by the company;

(e) contracts for contingent consideration in a business combination;

(f) other financial instruments with such special characteristics that the instruments, according to generally accepted accounting principles or practice, should be accounted for differently from other financial instruments.

(4) If the fair value of a financial instrument cannot be determined reliably in accordance with paragraph 44B, sub-paragraph (1) does not apply to that financial instrument.

(5) In this paragraph—

"associated undertaking" has the meaning given by paragraph 20 of Schedule 4A; and

"joint venture" has the meaning given by paragraph 19 of that Schedule.

Determination of fair value

44B.—(1) The fair value of a financial instrument is determined in accordance with this paragraph.

(2) If a reliable market can readily be identified for the financial instrument, its fair value is determined by reference to its market value.

(3) If a reliable market cannot readily be identified for the financial instrument but can be identified for its components or for a similar instrument, its fair value is determined by reference to the market value of its components or of the similar instrument.

(4) If neither sub-paragraph (2) nor (3) applies, the fair value of the financial instrument is a value resulting from generally accepted valuation models and techniques.

(5) Any valuation models and techniques used for the purposes of sub-paragraph (4) must ensure a reasonable approximation of the market value.

Inclusion of hedged items at fair value

44C. A company may include any assets and liabilities that qualify as hedged items under a fair value hedge accounting system, or identified portions of such assets or liabilities, at the amount required under that system.

Other assets that may be included at fair value

44D.—(1) This paragraph applies to—

(a) investment property, and

(b) living animals and plants,

that, under international accounting standards, may be included in accounts at fair value.

(2) Such investment property and such living animals and plants may be included at fair value, provided that all such investment property or, as the case may be, all such living animals and plants are so included where their fair value can reliably be determined.

(3) In this paragraph, "fair value" means fair value determined in accordance with relevant international accounting standards.

Accounting for changes in value

44E.—(1) This paragraph applies where a financial instrument is valued in accordance with paragraph 44A or 44C or an asset is valued in accordance with paragraph 44D.

(2) Notwithstanding paragraph 19 of this Schedule, and subject to sub-paragraphs (3) and (4) below, a change in the value of the financial instrument or of the investment property or living animal or plant must be included in the profit and loss account.

(3) Where—

(a) the financial instrument accounted for is a hedging instrument under a hedge accounting system that allows some or all of the change in value not to be shown in the profit and loss account, or

(b) the change in value relates to an exchange difference arising on a monetary item that forms part of a company's net investment in a foreign entity,

the amount of the change in value must be credited to or (as the case may be) debited from a separate reserve ("the fair value reserve").

(4) Where the instrument accounted for—

(a) is an available for sale financial asset, and

(b) is not a derivative,

the change in value may be credited to or (as the case may be) debited from the fair value reserve.

The fair value reserve

44F.—(1) The fair value reserve must be adjusted to the extent that the amounts shown in it are no longer necessary for the purposes of paragraph 44E(3) or (4).

(2) The treatment for taxation purposes of amounts credited or debited to the fair value reserve shall be disclosed in a note to the accounts.]

ASSETS AND LIABILITIES DENOMINATED IN FOREIGN CURRENCIES

45.—(1) Subject to the following sub-paragraphs, amounts to be included in respect of assets and liabilities denominated in foreign currencies shall be in sterling (or the currency in which the accounts are drawn up) after translation at an appropriate spot rate of exchange prevailing at the balance sheet date.

(2) An appropriate rate of exchange prevailing on the date of purchase may however be used for assets held as financial fixed assets and assets to be included under Assets items 9 (Intangible fixed assets) and 10 (Tangible fixed assets) in the balance sheet format, if they are not covered or not specifically covered in either the spot or forward currency markets.

(3) An appropriate spot rate of exchange prevailing at the balance sheet date shall be used for translating uncompleted spot exchange transactions.

(4) An appropriate forward rate of exchange prevailing at the balance sheet date shall be used for translating uncompleted forward exchange transactions.

(5) This paragraph does not apply to any assets or liabilities held, or any transactions entered into, for hedging purposes or to any assets or liabilities which are themselves hedged.

46.—(1) Subject to sub-paragraph (2), any difference between the amount to be included in respect of an asset or liability under paragraph 45 and the book value, after translation into sterling (or the currency in which the accounts are drawn up) at an appropriate rate, of that asset or liability shall be credited or, as the case may be, debited to the profit and loss account.

(2) In the case, however, of assets held as financial fixed assets, of assets to be included under Assets items 9 (Intangible fixed assets) and 10 (Tangible fixed assets) in the balance sheet format and of transactions undertaken to cover such assets, any such difference may be deducted from or credited to any non-distributable reserve available for the purpose.

CHAPTER III
NOTES TO THE ACCOUNTS

Preliminary

47.—(1) Any information required in the case of a company by the following provisions of this Part of this Schedule shall [(if not given in the company's accounts)] be given by way of a note to the accounts ...

(2), (3) ...

General

Disclosure of accounting policies

48. The accounting policies adopted by the company in determining the amounts to be included in respect of items shown in the balance sheet and in determining the profit or loss of the company shall be stated (including such policies with respect to the depreciation and diminution in value of assets).

49. It shall be stated whether the accounts have been prepared in accordance with applicable accounting standards and particulars of any material departure from those standards and the reasons for it shall be given.

Sums denominated in foreign currencies

50. Where any sums originally denominated in foreign currencies have been brought into account under any items shown in the balance sheet format or the profit and loss account formats, the basis on which those sums have been translated into sterling (or the currency in which the accounts are drawn up) shall be stated.

[Reserves and dividends

50A. There must be stated—

- (*a*) *any amount set aside or proposed to be set aside to, or withdrawn or proposed to be withdrawn from, reserves,*
- (*b*) *the aggregate amount of dividends paid in the financial year (other than those for which a liability existed at the immediately preceding balance sheet date),*
- (*c*) *the aggregate amount of dividends that the company is liable to pay at the balance sheet date, and*
- (*d*) *the aggregate amount of dividends that are proposed before the date of approval of the accounts, and not otherwise disclosed under paragraph (b) or (c).]*

Information supplementing the balance sheet

Share capital and debentures

51.—(1) The following information shall be given with respect to the company's share capital:

(a) the authorised share capital; and

(b) where shares of more than one class have been allotted, the number and aggregate nominal value of shares of each class allotted.

(2) In the case of any part of the allotted share capital that consists of redeemable shares, the following information shall be given:

(a) the earliest and latest dates on which the company has power to redeem those shares;

(b) whether those shares must be redeemed in any event or are liable to be redeemed at the option of the company or of the shareholder; and

(c) whether any (and, if so, what) premium is payable on redemption.

52. If the company has allotted any shares during the financial year, the following information shall be given:

(a) …

(b) the classes of shares allotted; and

(c) as respects each class of shares, the number allotted, their aggregate nominal value and the consideration received by the company for the allotment.

53.—(1) With respect to any contingent right to the allotment of shares in the company the following particulars shall be given:

(a) the number, description and amount of the shares in relation to which the right is exercisable;

(b) the period during which it is exercisable; and

(c) the price to be paid for the shares allotted.

(2) In sub-paragraph (1) above "contingent right to the allotment of shares" means any option to subscribe for shares and any other right to require the allotment of shares to any person whether arising on the conversion into shares of securities of any other description or otherwise.

54.—(1) If the company has issued any debentures during the financial year to which the accounts relate, the following information shall be given:

(a) …

(b) the classes of debentures issued; and

(c) as respects each class of debentures, the amount issued and the consideration received by the company for the issue.

(2) …

(3) Where any of the company's debentures are held by a nominee of or trustee for the company, the nominal amount of the debentures and the amount at which they are stated in the accounting records kept by the company in accordance with section 221 of this Act shall be stated.

Fixed assets

55.—(1) In respect of any fixed assets of the company included in any assets item in the company's balance sheet the following information shall be given by reference to each such item:

(a) the appropriate amounts in respect of those assets included in the item as at the date of the beginning of the financial year and as at the balance sheet date respectively;

(b) the effect on any amount included in the item in respect of those assets of:

(i) any determination during that year of the value to be ascribed to any of those assets in accordance with paragraph 41 above;

(ii) acquisitions during that year of any fixed assets;

(iii) disposals during that year of any fixed assets; and

(iv) any transfers of fixed assets of the company to and from the item during that year.

(2) The reference in sub-paragraph (1)(a) to the appropriate amounts in respect of any fixed assets (included in an assets item) as at any date there mentioned is a reference to amounts representing the aggregate amounts determined, as at that date, in respect of fixed assets falling to be included under the item on either of the following bases, that is to say:

- *(a) on the basis of cost (determined in accordance with paragraphs 36 and 37); or*
- *(b) on any basis permitted by paragraph 41;*

(leaving out of account in either case any provisions for depreciation or diminution in value).

(3) In addition, in respect of any fixed assets of the company included in any assets item in the company's balance sheet, there shall be stated (by reference to each such item):

- *(a) the cumulative amount of provisions for depreciation or diminution in value of those assets included under the item as at each date mentioned in sub-paragraph (1)(a);*
- *(b) the amount of any such provisions made in respect of the financial year;*
- *(c) the amount of any adjustments made in respect of any such provisions during that year in consequence of the disposal of any of those assets; and*
- *(d) the amount of any other adjustments made in respect of any such provisions during that year.*

(4) The requirements of this paragraph need not be complied with to the extent that a company takes advantage of the option of setting off charges and income afforded by paragraph 5(3) of this Part of this Schedule.

56. Where any fixed assets of the company (other than listed investments) are included under any item shown in the company's balance sheet at an amount determined in accordance with paragraph 41, the following information shall be given:

- *(a) the years (so far as they are known to the directors) in which the assets were severally valued and the several values; and*
- *(b) in the case of assets that have been valued during the financial year, the names of the persons who valued them or particulars of their qualifications for doing so and (whichever is stated) the bases of valuation used by them.*

57. In relation to any amount which is included under Assets item 10 in the balance sheet format (Tangible fixed assets) with respect to land and buildings there shall be stated:

- *(a) how much of that amount is ascribable to land of freehold tenure and how much to land of leasehold tenure; and*
- *(b) how much of the amount ascribable to land of leasehold tenure is ascribable to land held on long lease and how much to land held on short lease.*

58. There shall be disclosed separately the amount of:

- *(a) any participating interests; and*
- *(b) any shares in group undertakings that are held in credit institutions.*

[Information about fair value of assets and liabilities

58A.—(1) This paragraph applies where financial instruments have been valued in accordance with paragraph 44A or 44C

(2) There must be stated—

- *(a) where the fair value of the instruments has been determined in accordance with paragraph 44B(4), the significant assumptions underlying the valuation models and techniques used,*
- *(b) for each category of financial instrument, the fair value of the instruments in that category and the changes in value—*
  - *(i) included in the profit and loss account, and*
  - *(ii) credited to or (as the case may be) debited from the fair value reserve,*

in respect of those instruments, and

- *(c) for each class of derivatives, the extent and nature of the instruments, including significant terms and conditions that may affect the amount, timing and certainty of future cash flows.*

(3) Where any amount is transferred to or from the fair value reserve during the financial year, there must be stated in tabular form—

- *(a) the amount of the reserve as at the date of the beginning of the financial year and as at the balance sheet date respectively;*
- *(b) the amount transferred to or from the reserve during that year; and*

(c) the source and application respectively of the amounts so transferred.

58B. Where the company has derivatives that it has not included at fair value, there must be stated for each class of such derivatives—

(a) the fair value of the derivatives in that class, if such a value can be determined in accordance with paragraph 44B, and

(b) the extent and nature of the derivatives.

58C.—(1) Sub-paragraph (2) applies if—

(a) the company has financial fixed assets that could be included at fair value by virtue of paragraph 44A,

(b) the amount at which those assets are included under any item in the company's accounts is in excess of their fair value, and

(c) the company has not made provision for diminution in value of those assets in accordance with paragraph 26(1) of this Part of this Schedule.

(2) There must be stated—

(a) the amount at which either the individual assets or appropriate groupings of those individual assets are included in the company's accounts,

(b) the fair value of those assets or groupings, and

(c) the reasons for not making a provision for diminution in value of those assets, including the nature of the evidence that provides the basis for the belief that the amount at which they are stated in the accounts will be recovered.

Information where investment property and living animals and plants included at fair value

58D.—(1) This paragraph applies where the amounts to be included in a company's accounts in respect of investment property or living animals and plants have been determined in accordance with paragraph 44D.

(2) The balance sheet items affected and the basis of valuation adopted in determining the amounts of the assets in question in the case of each such item must be disclosed in a note to the accounts.

(3) In the case of investment property, for each balance sheet item affected there must be shown, either separately in the balance sheet or in a note to the accounts—

(a) the comparable amounts determined according to the historical cost accounting rules; or

(b) the differences between those amounts and the corresponding amounts actually shown in the balance sheet in respect of that item.

(4) In sub-paragraph (3) above, references in relation to any item to the comparable amounts determined in accordance with that sub-paragraph are references to—

(a) the aggregate amount which would be required to be shown in respect of that item if the amounts to be included in respect of all the assets covered by that item were determined according to the historical cost accounting rules; and

(b) the aggregate amount of the cumulative provisions for depreciation or diminution in value which would be permitted or required in determining those amounts according to those rules.]

Reserves and provisions

59.—(1) Where any amount is transferred:

(a) to or from any reserves;

(b) to any [provisions for liabilities]; or

(c) from any [provision for liabilities] otherwise than for the purpose for which the provision was established;

and the reserves or provisions are or would but for paragraph 3(3) of this Part of this Schedule be shown as separate items in the company's balance sheet, the information mentioned in the following sub-paragraph shall be given in respect of the aggregate of reserves or provisions included in the same item.

(2) That information is:

(a) the amount of the reserves or provisions as at the date of the beginning of the financial year and as at the balance sheet date respectively;

(b) any amounts transferred to or from the reserve or provisions during that year; and (*c*) *the source and application respectively of any amounts so transferred.*

(3) Particulars shall be given of each provision included in Liabilities item 6(c) (Other provisions) in the company's balance sheet in any case where the amount of that provision is material.

Provision for taxation

60. The amount of any provision for deferred taxation shall be stated separately from the amount of any provision for other taxation.

Maturity analysis

61.—(1) A company shall disclose separately for each of Assets items 3(b) and 4 and Liabilities items 1(b), 2(b) and 3(b) the aggregate amount of the loans and advances and liabilities included in those items broken down into the following categories:

(*a*) *those repayable in not more than three months*
(*b*) *those repayable in more than three months but not more than one year*
(*c*) *those repayable in more than one year but not more than five years*
(*d*) *those repayable in more than five years*

from the balance sheet date.

(2) A company shall also disclose the aggregate amounts of all loans and advances falling within Assets item 4 (Loans and advances to customers) which are:

(*a*) *repayable on demand; or*
(*b*) *are for an indeterminate period, being repayable upon short notice.*

(3) For the purposes of sub-paragraph (1), where a loan or advance or liability is repayable by instalments, each such instalment is to be treated as a separate loan or advance or liability.

Debt and other fixed income securities

62. A company shall disclose the amount of debt and fixed income securities included in Assets item 5 (Debt securities [and other fixed income securities]) and the amount of such securities included in Liabilities item 3(a) (Bonds and medium term notes) that (in each case) will become due within one year of the balance sheet date.

Subordinated liabilities

63.—(1) The following information must be disclosed in relation to any borrowing included in Liabilities item 7 (Subordinated liabilities) that exceeds 10 per cent of the total for that item:

(*a*) *its amount;*
(*b*) *the currency in which it is denominated;*
(*c*) *the rate of interest and the maturity date (or the fact that it is perpetual);*
(*d*) *the circumstances in which early repayment may be demanded;*
(*e*) *the terms of the subordination; and*
(*f*) *the existence of any provisions whereby it may be converted into capital or some other form of liability and the terms of any such provisions.*

(2) The general terms of any other borrowings included in Liabilities item 7 shall also be stated.

Fixed cumulative dividends

64. If any fixed cumulative dividends on the company's shares are in arrear, there shall be stated:

(*a*) *the amount of the arrears; and*
(*b*) *the period for which the dividends or, if there is more than one class, each class of them are in arrear.*

Details of assets charged

65.—(1) There shall be disclosed, in relation to each liabilities and memorandum item of the balance sheet format, the aggregate amount of any assets of the company which have been charged to secure any liability or potential liability included thereunder, the aggregate amount of the liabilities or potential liabilities so secured and an indication of the nature of the security given.

(2) Particulars shall also be given of any other charge on the assets of the company to secure the liabilities of any other person, including, where practicable, the amount secured.

Guarantees and other financial commitments

66.—(1) There shall be stated, where practicable:
- *(a) the aggregate amount or estimated amount of contracts for capital expenditure, so far as not provided for; …*
- *(b) …*

(2) Particulars shall be given of:
- *(a) any pension commitments included under any provision shown in the company's balance sheet; and*
- *(b) any such commitments for which no provision has been made;*

and where any such commitment relates wholly or partly to pensions payable to past directors of the company separate particulars shall be given of that commitment so far as it relates to such pensions.

(3) Particulars shall also be given of any other financial commitments, including any contingent liabilities, which:
- *(a) have not been provided for;*
- *(b) have not been included in the memorandum items in the balance sheet format; and*
- *(c) are relevant to assessing the company's state of affairs.*

(4) Commitments within any of the preceding sub-paragraphs undertaken on behalf of or for the benefit of:
- *(a) any parent company or fellow subsidiary undertaking of the company; or*
- *(b) any subsidiary undertaking of the company;*

shall be stated separately from the other commitments within that sub-paragraph (and commitments within paragraph (a) shall be stated separately from those within paragraph (b)).

(5) There shall be disclosed the nature and amount of any contingent liabilities and commitments included in Memorandum items 1 and 2 which are material in relation to the company's activities.

Memorandum items: Group undertakings

67.—(1) With respect to contingent liabilities required to be included under Memorandum item 1 in the balance sheet format, there shall be stated in a note to the accounts the amount of such contingent liabilities incurred on behalf of or for the benefit of:
- *(a) any parent undertaking or fellow subsidiary undertaking; or*
- *(b) any subsidiary undertaking*

of the company; in addition the amount incurred in respect of the undertakings referred to in paragraph (a) shall be stated separately from the amount incurred in respect of the undertakings referred to in paragraph (b).

(2) With respect to commitments required to be included under Memorandum item 2 in the balance sheet format, there shall be stated in a note to the accounts the amount of such commitments undertaken on behalf of or for the benefit of:
- *(a) any parent undertaking or fellow subsidiary undertaking; or*
- *(b) any subsidiary undertaking*

of the company; in addition the amount incurred in respect of the undertakings referred to in paragraph (a) shall be stated separately from the amount incurred in respect of the undertakings referred to in paragraph (b).

Transferable securities

68.—(1) There shall be disclosed for each of Assets items 5 to 8 in the balance sheet format the amount of transferable securities included under those items:
- *(a) that are listed and the amount of those that are unlisted; …*
- *(b) …*

(2) In the case of each amount shown in respect of listed securities under sub-paragraph (1)(a) above, there shall also be disclosed the aggregate market value of those securities, if different from the amount shown.

(3) There shall also be disclosed for each of Assets items 5 and 6 the amount of transferable securities included under those items that are held as financial fixed assets and the amount of those that are not so held, together with the criterion used by the directors to distinguish those held as financial fixed assets.

Leasing transactions

69. The aggregate amount of all property (other than land) leased by the company to other persons shall be disclosed, broken down so as to show the aggregate amount included in each relevant balance sheet item.

Assets and liabilities denominated in a currency other than sterling (or the currency in which the accounts are drawn up)

70.—(1) The aggregate amount, in sterling (or the currency in which the accounts are drawn up), of all assets denominated in a currency other than sterling (or the currency used), together with the aggregate amount, in sterling (or the currency used), of all liabilities so denominated, is to be disclosed.

(2) For the purposes of this paragraph an appropriate rate of exchange prevailing at the balance sheet date shall be used to determine the amounts concerned.

Sundry assets and liabilities

71. Where any amount shown under either of the following items is material, particulars shall be given of each type of asset or liability included therein, including an explanation of the nature of the asset or liability and the amount included with respect to assets or liabilities of that type:
- *(a) Assets item 13 (Other assets)*
- *(b) Liabilities item 4 (Other liabilities).*

Unmatured forward transactions

72.—(1) The following shall be disclosed with respect to unmatured forward transactions outstanding at the balance sheet date:
- *(a) the categories of such transactions, by reference to an appropriate system of classification;*
- *(b) whether, in the case of each such category, they have been made, to any material extent, for the purpose of hedging the effects of fluctuations in interest rates, exchange rates and market prices or whether they have been made, to any material extent, for dealing purposes.*

(2) Transactions falling within sub-paragraph (1) shall include all those in relation to which income or expenditure is to be included in:
- *(a) format 1, item 6 or format 2, items B4 or A3 (Dealing [profits] [losses]),*
- *(b) format 1, items 1 or 2, or format 2, items B1 or A1, by virtue of notes (1)(b) and (2)(b) to the profit and loss account formats (forward contracts, spread over the actual duration of the contract and similar in nature to interest).*

Miscellaneous matters

73.—(1) Particulars shall be given of any case where the cost of any asset is for the first time determined under paragraph 38 of this Part of this Schedule.

(2) Where any outstanding loans made under the authority of section 153(4)(b), (bb) or (c) or section 155 of this Act (various cases of financial assistance by a company for purchase of its own shares) are included under any item shown in the company's balance sheet, the aggregate amount of those loans shall be disclosed for each item in question.

(3) ...

Information supplementing the profit and loss account

74. ...

Particulars of tax

75.—(1) ...

(2) Particulars shall be given of any special circumstances which affect liability in respect of taxation of profits, income or capital gains for the financial year or liability in respect of taxation of profits, income or capital gains for succeeding financial years.

(3) The following amounts shall be stated:
- *(a) the amount of the charge for United Kingdom corporation tax;*
- *(b) if that amount would have been greater but for relief from double taxation, the amount which it would have been but for such relief;*
- *(c) the amount of the charge for United Kingdom income tax; and*
- *(d) the amount of the charge for taxation imposed outside the United Kingdom of profits, income and (so far as charged to revenue) capital gains.*

These amounts shall be stated separately in respect of each of the amounts which is shown under the following items in the profit and loss account, that is to say format 1 item 16, format 2 item A10 (Tax on [profit] [loss] on ordinary activities) and format 1 item 21, format 2 item A13 (Tax on extraordinary [profit] [loss]).

Particulars of income

76.—(1) A company shall disclose, with respect to income included in the following items in the profit and loss account formats, the amount of that income attributable to each of the geographical markets in which the company has operated during the financial year:
- *(a) format 1 item 1, format 2 item B1 (Interest receivable);*
- *(b) format 1 item 3, format 2 item B2 (Dividend income);*
- *(c) format 1 item 4, format 2 item B3 (Fees and commissions receivable);*
- *(d) format 1 item 6, format 2 item B4 (Dealing profits); and*
- *(e) format 1 item 7, format 2 item B7 (Other operating income).*

(2) In analysing for the purposes of this paragraph the source of any income, the directors shall have regard to the manner in which the company's activities are organised.

(3) For the purposes of this paragraph, markets which do not differ substantially from each other shall be treated as one market.

(4) Where in the opinion of the directors the disclosure of any information required by this paragraph would be seriously prejudicial to the interests of the company, that information need not be disclosed, but the fact that any such information has not been disclosed must be stated.

77. ...

Management and agency services

78. A company providing any management and agency services to customers shall disclose that fact, if the scale of such services provided is material in the context of its business as a whole.

Subordinated liabilities

79. Any amounts charged to the profit and loss account representing charges incurred during the year with respect to subordinated liabilities shall be disclosed.

Sundry income and charges

80. Where any amount to be included in any of the following items is material, particulars shall be given of each individual component of the figure, including an explanation of their nature and amount:

(*a*) *In format 1:*
  (*i*) *Items 7 and 10* (*Other operating income and charges*)
  (*ii*) *Items 18 and 19* (*Extraordinary income and charges*)*;*

(*b*) *In format 2:*
  (*i*) *Items A6 and B7* (*Other operating charges and income*)
  (*ii*) *Items A12 and B10* (*Extraordinary charges and income*).

Miscellaneous matters

81.—(1) Where any amount relating to any preceding financial year is included in any item in the profit and loss account, the effect shall be stated.

(2) *The effect shall be stated of any transactions that are exceptional by virtue of size or incidence though they fall within the ordinary activities of the company.*

CHAPTER IV
INTERPRETATION OF PART I

General

82. The following definitions apply for the purposes of this Part of this Schedule and its interpretation:

.....

"Financial fixed assets" means loans and advances and securities held as fixed assets; participating interests and shareholdings in group undertakings shall be regarded as financial fixed assets;

"Fungible assets" means assets of any description which are substantially indistinguishable one from another;

["Investment property" means land held to earn rent or for capital appreciation;]

"Lease" includes an agreement for a lease;

"Listed security" means a security listed on a recognised stock exchange, or on any stock exchange of repute outside Great Britain and the expression "unlisted security" shall be construed accordingly;

"Long lease" means a lease in the case of which the portion of the term for which it was granted remaining unexpired at the end of the financial year is not less than 50 years;

"Repayable on demand", in connection with deposits, loans or advances, means those amounts which can at any time be withdrawn or demanded without notice or for which a maturity or period of notice of not more than 24 hours or one working day has been agreed;

"Sale and repurchase transaction" means a transaction which involves the transfer by a credit institution or customer ("the transferor") to another credit institution or customer ("the transferee") of assets subject to an agreement that the same assets, or (in the case of fungible assets) equivalent assets, will subsequently be transferred back to the transferor at a specified price on a date specified or to be specified by the transferor; but the following shall not be regarded as sale and repurchase transactions: forward exchange transactions, options, transactions involving the issue of debt securities with a commitment to repurchase all or part of the issue before maturity or any similar transactions;

"Sale and option to resell transaction" means a transaction which involves the transfer by a credit institution or customer ("the transferor") to another credit institution or customer ("the transferee") of assets subject to an agreement that the transferee is entitled to require the subsequent transfer of the same assets, or (in the case of

fungible assets) equivalent assets, back to the transferor at the purchase price or another price agreed in advance on a date specified or to be specified; and

"Short lease" means a lease which is not a long lease.

[Financial instruments

82A. For the purposes of this Part of this Schedule, references to "derivatives" include commodity-based contracts that give either contracting party the right to settle in cash or in some other financial instrument, except when such contracts—

(a) were entered into for the purpose of, and continue to meet, the company's expected purchase, sale or usage requirements,

(b) were designated for such purpose at their inception, and

(c) are expected to be settled by delivery of the commodity.

82B.—(1) The expressions listed in sub-paragraph (2) have the same meaning in paragraphs 44A to 44F, 58A to 58C and 82A of this Part of this Schedule as they have in Council Directives 78/660/EEC on the annual accounts of certain types of companies and 86/635/EEC on the annual accounts and consolidated accounts of banks and other financial institutions, as amended.

(2) Those expressions are "available for sale financial asset", "business combination", "commodity-based contracts", "derivative", "equity instrument", "exchange difference", "fair value hedge accounting system", "financial fixed asset", "financial instrument", "foreign entity", "hedge accounting", "hedge accounting system", "hedged items", "hedging instrument", "held for trading purposes", "held to maturity", "monetary item", "receivables", "reliable market" and "trading portfolio".]

Loans

83. For the purposes of this Part of this Schedule a loan or advance (including a liability comprising a loan or advance) is treated as falling due for repayment, and an instalment of a loan or advance is treated as falling due for payment, on the earliest date on which the lender could require repayment or (as the case may be) payment, if he exercised all options and rights available to him.

Materiality

84. For the purposes of this Part of this Schedule amounts which in the particular context of any provision of this Part are not material may be disregarded for the purposes of that provision.

Provisions

85. For the purposes of this Part of this Schedule and its interpretation:

(a) references in this Part to provisions for depreciation or diminution in value of assets are to any amount written off by way of providing for depreciation or diminution in value of assets;

(b) any reference in the profit and loss account formats or the notes thereto set out in Section B of this Part to the depreciation of, or amounts written off, assets of any description is to any provision for depreciation or diminution in value of assets of that description; and

(c) references in this Part to [provisions for liabilities] are to any amount retained as reasonably necessary for the purpose of providing for any liability [the nature of which is clearly defined and] which is either likely to be incurred, or certain to be incurred but uncertain as to amount or as to the date on which it will arise.

Scots land tenure

86. In the application of this Part of this Schedule to Scotland, "land of freehold tenure" means land in respect of which the company ... is the owner; "land of leasehold tenure" means land of which the company is the tenant under a lease ...

Staff costs

87. For the purposes of this Part of this Schedule and its interpretation:

(a) "Social security costs" means any contributions by the company to any state social security or pension scheme, fund or arrangement;

[(b) "Pension costs" includes any costs incurred by the company in respect of any pension scheme established for the purpose of providing pensions for persons currently or formerly employed by the company, any sums set aside for the future payment of pensions directly by the company to current or former employees and any pensions paid directly to such persons without having first been set aside; and]

(c) any amount stated in respect of [social security costs] or in respect of the item "wages and salaries" in the company's profit and loss account shall be determined by reference to payments made or costs incurred in respect of all persons employed by the company during the financial year who are taken into account in determining the relevant annual number for the purposes of [section 231A(1)(a)].]

[660]

NOTES

The original Pts I–V of this Schedule were renumbered Pt I of this Schedule, and the provisions of Pts II, III, IV of CA 1989, Sch 7, had effect as Pts II, III, IV of this Schedule, by virtue of CA 1989, s 18(3), (4), Sch 7, preliminary paragraph. Pts I, II of this Schedule (as recast) formed a new Sch 9A to this Act (since substituted), Pt III of this Schedule (as recast) was repealed, the heading to this Schedule was substituted, and Sch 1, Pts I–III to the Companies Act 1985 (Bank Accounts) Regulations 1991, SI 1991/2705, were inserted as Pts I–III of this Schedule, by virtue of reg 5 of, Sch 1 to, those Regulations (subject to transitional provisions in relation to a financial year of a company beginning before 23 December 1992).

Repealed by the Companies Act 2006, s 1295, Sch 16, as from a day to be appointed.

Para 4: words in square brackets in sub-para (2) substituted by the Companies Act 1985 (Investment Companies and Accounting and Audit Amendments) Regulations 2005, SI 2005/2280, reg 8, as from 1 October 2005, in relation to companies' financial years which begin on or after 1 January 2005 and which end on or after 1 October 2005.

Para 8: repealed by the Companies Act 1985 (International Accounting Standards and Other Accounting Amendments) Regulations 2004, SI 2004/2947, reg 14(4), Sch 5, paras 1, 2, as from 12 November 2004, in relation to companies' financial years which begin on or after 1 January 2005.

Paras 8A, 44A–44F, 50A, 58A–58D, 82A, 82B: inserted by SI 2004/2947, reg 14(4), Sch 5, paras 1, 3, 7, 8, 11, as from 12 November 2004, in relation to companies' financial years which begin on or after 1 January 2005.

Words in square brackets in the balance sheet format following para 10 substituted by SI 2004/2947, reg 14(4), Sch 5, paras 1, 4, as from 12 November 2004, in relation to companies' financial years which begin on or after 1 January 2005.

Para 19: words omitted repealed by SI 2004/2947, reg 14(4), Sch 5, paras 1, 5, as from 12 November 2004, in relation to companies' financial years which begin on or after 1 January 2005.

Paras 23, 59, 85: words in square brackets substituted by SI 2004/2947, reg 14(4), Sch 5, paras 1, 6, 9, 12, as from 12 November 2004, in relation to companies' financial years which begin on or after 1 January 2005.

Para 44: words in square brackets in sub-paras (3), (4) substituted by SI 1996/189, regs 14(6), 16(1), Sch 4, paras 1, 3, in relation to any financial year ending on or after 2 February 1996 (subject to transitional provisions in relation to financial years ending on or before 24 March 1996).

Para 47: words in square brackets in sub-para (1) inserted, and words omitted repealed, by SI 1996/189, regs 14(6), 16(1), Sch 4, paras 1, 4, in relation to any financial year ending on or after 2 February 1996 (subject to transitional provisions as noted above); sub-paras (2), (3) repealed by SI 2005/2280, reg 9, as from 1 October 2005, in relation to companies' financial years which begin on or after 1 January 2005 and which end on or after 1 October 2005.

Paras 52, 54, 66, 68, 73, 75: words omitted repealed by SI 1996/189, regs 14(6), 16(1), Sch 4, paras 1, 5, 6, 7, 8, 9, 11, in relation to any financial year ending on or after 2 February 1996 (subject to transitional provisions as noted above).

Para 74: repealed by SI 1996/189, regs 14(6), 16(1), Sch 4, paras 1, 10, in relation to any financial year ending on or after 2 February 1996 (subject to transitional provisions as noted above).

Para 77: repealed by SI 2004/2947, reg 3, Sch 1, paras 1, 34(a), as from 12 November 2004, in relation to companies' financial years which begin on or after 1 January 2005.

Para 82: definitions "Banking activities" and "Banking transactions" repealed by the Companies Act 1985 (Bank Accounts) Regulations 1994, SI 1994/233, reg 4(1), as from 11 February 1994 (subject to transitional provisions in relation to financial years beginning before 23 December 1992); definition "Investment property" inserted by SI 2004/2947, reg 14(4), Sch 5, paras 1, 10, as from 12 November 2004, in relation to companies' financial years which begin on or after 1 January 2005.

Para 86: words omitted repealed by the Abolition of Feudal Tenure etc (Scotland) Act 2000, s 76(1), (2), Sch 12, Pt I, para 46(1), (6), Sch 13, Pt I, as from 28 November 2004.

Para 87: sub-para (b) and words in first pair of square brackets in sub-para (c) substituted by SI 1996/189, regs 14(6), 16(1), Sch 4, paras 1, 13, in relation to any financial year ending on or after 2 February 1996 (subject to transitional provisions as noted above); words in second pair of square brackets in sub-para (c) substituted by SI 2004/2947, reg 3, Sch 1, paras 1, 34(b), as from 12 November 2004, in relation to companies' financial years which begin on or after 1 January 2005.

Application to limited liability partnerships: see the Limited Liability Partnerships Regulations 2001, SI 2001/1090, reg 3, Sch 1 at **[6984]**, **[6992]**.

Treasury bills: a reference to a Treasury bill in this Part includes a reference to uncertificated units of eligible Treasury bills; see the Uncertificated Securities (Amendment) (Eligible Debt Securities) Regulations 2003, SI 2003/1633, reg 15, Sch 2, para 2(e).

Trade marks: by the Trade Marks Act 1994, s 106(1), Sch 4, para 1, the reference in Note 7(b) in Pt I, Chapter I, Section B above to a trade mark are to be construed as a reference to a trade mark within the meaning of the 1994 Act.

[PART II
CONSOLIDATED ACCOUNTS

1. …

General application of provisions applicable to individual accounts

2.—(1) In paragraph 1 of Schedule 4A (application to group accounts of provisions applicable to individual accounts), the reference in sub-paragraph (1) to the provisions of Schedule 4 shall be construed as a reference to the provisions of Part I of this Schedule; and accordingly:

(a) …

(b) sub-paragraph (3) shall be omitted.

(2) The general application of the provisions of Part I of this Schedule in place of those of Schedule 4 is subject to the following provisions.

Minority interests and associated undertakings

3.—(1) The provisions of this paragraph shall have effect so as to adapt paragraphs 17 and 21 of Schedule 4A (which require items in respect of "Minority interests" and associated undertakings to be added to the formats set out in Schedule 4) to the formats prescribed by Part I of this Schedule.

(2) The item required to be added to the balance sheet format by paragraph 17(2) shall be added either between Liabilities items 7 and 8 or after Liabilities item 12.

(3) The item required to be added to the profit and loss account format by paragraph 17(3) shall be added:

(a) in the case of format 1, between items 17 and 18; or

(b) in the case of format 2, between items A11 and A12 or between items B9 and B10.

(4) The item required to be added to the profit and loss account format by paragraph 17(4) shall be added:

(a) in the case of format 1, between items 22 and 23; or

(b) in the case of format 2, between items A14 and A15 or between items B11 and B12.

(5) Paragraph 17(5) shall not apply but for the purposes of paragraph 3(3) of Part I of this Schedule (power to combine items) the additional items required by the foregoing provisions of this paragraph shall be treated as items to which a letter is assigned.

(6) Paragraph 21(2) shall apply with respect to a balance sheet prepared under this Schedule as if it required Assets item 7 (Participating interests) in the balance sheet format to be replaced by the two replacement items referred to in that paragraph.

(7) Paragraph 21(3) shall not apply, but the following items in the profit and loss account formats, namely:

(*a*) *format 1 item 3(b) (Income from participating interests)*
(*b*) *format 2 item B2(b) (Income from participating interests),*

shall be replaced by the following two replacement items:

(*i*) *"Income from participating interests other than associated undertakings", which shall be shown at position 3(b) in format 1 and position B2(b) in format 2; and*
(*ii*) *"Income from associated undertakings", which shall be shown at an appropriate position.*

4. Paragraphs 18 and 22(1) of Schedule 4A shall apply as if, in substitution for the references therein to paragraphs 17 to 19 and 21 of Schedule 4, they referred to paragraphs 24 to 26 and 28 of Part I of this Schedule.

Foreign currency translation

5. Any difference between:

(*a*) *the amount included in the consolidated accounts for the previous financial year with respect to any undertaking included in the consolidation or the group's interest in any associated undertaking, together with the amount of any transactions undertaken to cover any such interest; and*
(*b*) *the opening amount for the financial year in respect of those undertakings and in respect of any such transactions*

arising as a result of the application of paragraph 45 of Part I of this Schedule may be credited to (where (a) is less than (b)), or deducted from (where (a) is greater than (b)), (as the case may be) consolidated reserves.

6. Any income and expenditure of undertakings included in the consolidation and associated undertakings in a foreign currency may be translated for the purposes of the consolidated accounts at the average rates of exchange prevailing during the financial year.

Information as to undertaking in which shares held as a result of financial assistance operation

7.—(1) The following provisions apply where the parent company of a banking group has a subsidiary undertaking which:

(*a*) *is a credit institution of which shares are held as a result of a financial assistance operation with a view to its reorganisation or rescue; and*
(*b*) *is excluded from consolidation under section 229(3)(c) (interest held with a view to resale).*

(2) Information as to the nature and terms of the operations shall be given in a note to the group accounts and there shall be appended to the copy of the group accounts delivered to the registrar in accordance with section 242 a copy of the undertaking's latest individual accounts and, if it is a parent undertaking, its latest group accounts.

If the accounts appended are required by law to be audited, a copy of the auditors' report shall also be appended.

(3) […] if any document required to be appended is in a language other than English […], the directors shall annex a translation of it into English certified in the prescribed manner to be a correct translation.

(4) The above requirements are subject to the following qualifications:

(*a*) *an undertaking is not required to prepare for the purposes of this paragraph accounts which would not otherwise be prepared, and if no accounts satisfying the above requirements are prepared none need be appended;*
(*b*) *the accounts of an undertaking need not be appended if they would not otherwise be required to be published, or made available for public inspection, anywhere in the world, but in that case the reason for not appending the accounts shall be stated in a note to the consolidated accounts.*

(5) Where a copy of an undertaking's accounts is required to be appended to the copy of the group accounts delivered to the registrar, that fact shall be stated in a note to the group accounts.

(6) Sub-sections (2) to (4) of section 242 (penalties, &c in case of default) apply in relation to the requirements of this paragraph as regards the delivery of documents to the registrar as they apply in relation to the requirements of sub-section (1) of that section.]

[661]

NOTES

Inserted as noted to Pt I at **[660]**.

Repealed by the Companies Act 2006, s 1295, Sch 16, as from 1 January 2007 (in so far as relating to the second words omitted from para 7(3)), and as from a day to be appointed (otherwise).

Para 1: repealed by the Companies Act 1985 (International Accounting Standards and Other Accounting Amendments) Regulations 2004, SI 2004/2947, reg 15, Sch 7, Pt 1, paras 1, 12, as from 12 November 2004, in relation to companies' financial years which begin on or after 1 January 2005.

Para 2: sub-para (1)(a) repealed by the Companies Act 1985 (Accounts of Small and Medium-sized Companies and Minor Accounting Amendments) Regulations 1997, SI 1997/220, reg 7(11), in relation to annual accounts approved by the board of directors on or after 1 March 1997, and to directors' and auditors' reports on such accounts (subject to transitional provisions in relation to a financial year of a company ending on or before 24 March 1997).

Para 7: first words omitted from sub-para (3) (as inserted by the Companies Act 1985 (Welsh Language Accounts) Regulations 1992, SI 1992/1083, reg 2(1), (5), as from 1 June 1992) repealed, and words in second pair of square brackets in that sub-paragraph inserted, by the Welsh Language Act 1993, ss 30(1), (4), 35(1), Sch 2, as from 1 February 1994; second words omitted (as inserted by the Welsh Language Act 1993 as noted ante) repealed as noted above (those words were "then, subject to section 710B(6) (delivery of certain Welsh documents without a translation),").

Application to limited liability partnerships: see the Limited Liability Partnerships Regulations 2001, SI 2001/1090, reg 3, Sch 1 at **[6984]**, **[6992]**. Note also that nothing in the Companies Act 2006 (Commencement No 1, Transitional Provisions and Savings) Order 2006, SI 2006/3428 affects any provision of this Act as applied by the 2001 Regulations to LLPs (see art 8(2) at **[7581]** and the introductory notes to this Act).

Prescribed manner: for the relevant Regulations, see, by virtue of the Interpretation Act 1978, s 17(2)(b), the Companies (Forms) (Amendment) Regulations 1990, SI 1990/572, reg 5 and the note relating to that regulation to s 228 at **[214]**.

[PART III
ADDITIONAL DISCLOSURE: RELATED UNDERTAKINGS

1.—(1) Where accounts are prepared in accordance with the special provisions of this Schedule relating to banking companies or groups:

- (*a*) *the information required by paragraphs 8 and 24 of Schedule 5 (information about significant holdings of the company in undertakings other than subsidiary undertakings) need only be given in respect of undertakings (otherwise falling within the class of undertakings in respect of which disclosure is required) in which the company has a significant holding amounting to 20 per cent or more of the nominal value of the shares in the undertaking; and*
- (*b*) *the information required by paragraph 27 of Schedule 5 (information about significant holdings of the group in undertakings other than subsidiary undertakings) need only be given in respect of undertakings (otherwise falling within the class of undertakings in respect of which disclosure is required) in which the group has a significant holding amounting to 20 per cent or more of the nominal value of the shares in the undertaking.*

In addition any information required by those paragraphs may be omitted if it is not material.

(2) Paragraph 13(3) and (4) of Schedule 5 shall apply mutatis mutandis for the purposes of sub-paragraph (1)(a) above and paragraph 32(3) and (4) of that Schedule shall apply mutatis mutandis for the purposes of sub-paragraph (1)(b) above.]

[662]

NOTES

Inserted as noted to Pt I at **[660]**.

Repealed by the Companies Act 2006, s 1295, Sch 16, as from a day to be appointed.

Application to limited liability partnerships: see the Limited Liability Partnerships Regulations 2001, SI 2001/1090, reg 3, Sch 1 at **[6984]**, **[6992]**.

[PART IV
ADDITIONAL DISCLOSURE: EMOLUMENTS AND OTHER BENEFITS OF DIRECTORS AND OTHERS

1. The provisions of this Part of this Schedule have effect with respect to the application of Schedule 6 (additional disclosure: emoluments and other benefits of directors and others) to a banking company or [the holding company of a credit institution].

Loans, quasi-loans and other dealings

[2. Where a banking company, or a company which is the holding company of a credit institution, prepares annual accounts for a financial year, it need not comply with the provisions of Part II of Schedule 6 (loans, quasi-loans and other dealings) in relation to a transaction or arrangement of a kind mentioned in section 330, or an agreement to enter into such a transaction or arrangement, to which that banking company or (as the case may be) credit institution is a party.]

Other transactions, arrangements and agreements

3.—(1) [Where a banking company, or a company which is the holding company of a credit institution, takes advantage of the provisions of paragraph 2 of this Part of this Schedule for the purposes of its annual; accounts for a financial year, then, in preparing those accounts, it shall comply with the provisions of Part III of Schedule 6 (other transactions, arrangements and agreements) only in relation to a transaction, arrangement or agreement made by that banking company or (as the case may be) credit institution for—]

(a) a person who was a director of the company preparing the accounts or who was connected with such a director, or

(b) a person who was a chief executive or manager ([...]) of that company or its holding company.

(2) References in that Part to officers of the company shall be construed accordingly as including references to such persons.

[(3) In this paragraph—

(a) "director" includes a shadow director;

(b) "chief executive" has the meaning given in section 417 of the Financial Services and Markets Act 2000; and

(c) "manager" has the meaning given in section 423(3) of that Act.]

(4) For the purposes of that Part as it applies by virtue of this paragraph, a [body corporate] which a person does not control shall not be treated as connected with him.

(5) Section 346 of this Act applies for the purposes of this paragraph as regards the interpretation of references to a person being connected with a director or controlling a [body corporate].]

[663]

NOTES

Inserted by CA 1989, s 18(3), (4), Sch 7, Pt IV, as from 1 April 1990.

Repealed by the Companies Act 2006, s 1295, Sch 16, as from a day to be appointed.

Para 1: words in square brackets substituted by the Companies Act 1985 (Bank Accounts) Regulations 1994, SI 1994/233, reg 5(1), (2), as from 28 February 1994.

Para 2: substituted by SI 1994/233, reg 5(1), (3), as from 28 February 1994; for the words "section 330" there are substituted the words "section 197, 198, 200, 201 or 203 of the Companies Act 2006" by the draft Companies Act 2006 (Commencement No 3, Consequential Amendments, Transitional Provisions and Savings) Order 2007, art 10(1), Sch 4, Pt 1, para 7(1)(a), (2), as from 1 October 2007, in relation to arrangements and transactions entered into on or after that date (see **[A12]**).

Para 3: words in first pair of square brackets in sub-para (1), and words in square brackets in sub-para (4), substituted by SI 1994/233, reg 5(1), (4), (5), as from 28 February 1994; words omitted from second pair of square brackets in sub-para (1) (as substituted by the Financial Services and Markets Act 2000 (Consequential Amendments and Repeals) Order 2001, SI 2001/3649, art 35(1), (3), as from 1 December 2001) repealed by the Financial Services and Markets Act 2000 (Consequential Amendments) Order 2002, SI 2002/1555, art 12(1), (2), as from 3 July 2002; sub-para (3) substituted by SI 2002/555, art 12(1), (3), as from 3 July 2002; for the words "Section 346 of this Act applies" in sub-para (5) there are substituted the words "Sections 252 to 255 of, and Schedule 1 to, the Companies Act 2006 apply" by the draft Companies Act 2006 (Commencement No 3, Consequential Amendments, Transitional Provisions and Savings) Order 2007, art 10(1), Sch 4, Pt 1, para 7(1)(b), (2), as from 1 October 2007, in relation to arrangements and transactions entered into on or after that date (see **[A12]**).

Application to limited liability partnerships: see the Limited Liability Partnerships Regulations 2001, SI 2001/1090, reg 3, Sch 1 at **[6984]**, **[6992]**. Note also that nothing in the draft Companies Act 2006 (Commencement No 3, Consequential Amendments, Transitional Provisions and Savings) Order 2007 affects any provision of this Act as applied by the 2001 Regulations to LLPs (see art 12(2) at **[A12]** and the introductory notes to this Act).

[SCHEDULE 9A
FORM AND CONTENT OF ACCOUNTS OF INSURANCE COMPANIES AND GROUPS

Sections 255, 255A, 255B

PART I
INDIVIDUAL ACCOUNTS

CHAPTER I
GENERAL RULES AND FORMATS

SECTION A
GENERAL RULES

1.—(1) Subject to the following provisions of this Part of this Schedule—

(a) every balance sheet of a company shall show the items listed in the balance sheet format set out below in section B of this Chapter; and

(b) every profit and loss account of a company shall show the items listed in the profit and loss account format so set out,

in either case in the order and under the headings and sub-headings given in the format.

(2) Sub-paragraph (1) above is not to be read as requiring the heading or sub-heading for any item to be distinguished by any letter or number assigned to that item in the format.

2.—(1) Any item required in accordance with paragraph 1 above to be shown in a company's balance sheet or profit and loss account may be shown in greater detail than so required.

(2) A company's balance sheet or profit and loss account may include an item representing or covering the amount of any asset or liability, income or expenditure not specifically covered by any of the items listed in the balance sheet or profit and loss account format set out in section B below, but the following shall not be treated as assets in any company's balance sheet—

(a) preliminary expenses;

(b) expenses of and commission on any issue of shares or debentures; and

(c) costs of research.

(3) Items to which Arabic numbers are assigned in the balance sheet format set out in section B below (except for items concerning technical provisions and the reinsurers' share of technical provisions), and items to which lower case letters in parentheses are assigned in the profit and loss account format so set out (except for items within items I.1 and 4 and II.1, 5 and 6) may be combined in a company's accounts for any financial year if either—

(a) their individual amounts are not material for the purpose of giving a true and fair view; or

(b) the combination facilitates the assessment of the state of affairs or profit or loss of the company for that year;

but in a case within paragraph (b) above the individual amounts of any items so combined shall be disclosed in a note to the accounts and any notes required by this Schedule to the items so combined under that paragraph shall, notwithstanding the combination, be given.

(4) Subject to paragraph 3(3) below, a heading or sub-heading corresponding to an item listed in the format adopted in preparing a company's balance sheet or profit and loss account shall not be included if there is no amount to be shown for that item in respect of the financial year to which the balance sheet or profit and loss account relates.

3.—(1) In respect of every item shown in the balance sheet or profit and loss account, there shall be shown or stated the corresponding amount for the financial year immediately preceding that to which the accounts relate.

(2) *Where the corresponding amount is not comparable with the amount to be shown for the item in question in respect of the financial year to which the balance sheet or profit and loss account relates, the former amount [may be adjusted] and [particulars of the non-comparability and of any adjustment] shall be given in a note to the accounts.*

(3) *Paragraph 2(4) above does not apply in any case where an amount can be shown for the item in question in respect of the financial year immediately preceding that to which the balance sheet or profit and loss account relates, and that amount shall be shown under the heading or sub-heading required by paragraph 1 above for that item.*

4. *Subject to the provisions of this Schedule, amounts in respect of items representing assets or income may not be set off against amounts in respect of items representing liabilities or expenditure (as the case may be), or vice versa.*

5. ...

6.—[(1)] *The provisions of this Schedule which relate to long term business shall apply, with necessary modifications, [to business which consists of effecting or carrying out relevant contracts of general insurance] which—*

(a) *is transacted exclusively or principally according to the technical principles of long term business, and*

(b) *is a significant amount of the business of the company.*

[(2) *For the purposes of paragraph (1), a contract of general insurance is a relevant contract if the risk insured against relates to—*

(a) *accident; or*

(b) *sickness.*

(3) *Sub-paragraph (2) must be read with—*

(a) *section 22 of the Financial Services and Markets Act 2000;*

(b) *any relevant order under that section; and*

(c) *Schedule 2 to that Act.]*

[6A. *The directors of a company must, in determining how amounts are presented within items in the profit and loss account and balance sheet, have regard to the substance of the reported transaction or arrangement, in accordance with generally accepted accounting principles or practice.]*

SECTION B
THE REQUIRED FORMATS FOR ACCOUNTS

Preliminary

7.—(1) *References in this Part of this Schedule to the balance sheet format or profit and loss account format are to the balance sheet format or profit and loss account format set out below, and references to the items listed in either of the formats are to those items read together with any of the notes following the formats which apply to any of those items.*

(2) *The requirement imposed by paragraph 1 to show the items listed in either format in the order adopted in the format is subject to any provision in the notes following the format for alternative positions for any particular items.*

(3) *Where in respect of any item to which an Arabic number is assigned in either format, the gross amount and reinsurance amount or reinsurers' share are required to be shown, a sub-total of those amounts shall also be given.*

(4) *Where in respect of any item to which an Arabic number is assigned in the profit and loss account format, separate items are required to be shown, then a separate sub-total of those items shall also be given in addition to any sub-total required by sub-paragraph (3) above.*

8. *A number in brackets following any item in either of the formats set out below is a reference to the note of that number in the notes following the format.*

9.—[(1)] *In the profit and loss account format set out below—*

(a) *the heading "Technical account—General business" is for [business which consists of effecting or carrying out contracts of general insurance]; and* (*b*) *the heading "Technical account—Long term business" is for [business which consists of effecting or carrying out contracts of long term insurance].*

[(2) In sub-paragraph (1), references to—

(*a*) *contracts of general or long term insurance; and*

(*b*) *the effecting or carrying out of such contracts,*

must be read with section 22 of the Financial Services and Markets Act 2000, any relevant order under that section, and Schedule 2 to that Act.]

Balance Sheet Format

ASSETS

A. *Called up share capital not paid (1)*

B. *Intangible assets*
- 1. *Development costs*
- 2. *Concessions, patents, licences, trade marks and similar rights and assets (2)*
- 3. *Goodwill (3)*
- 4. *Payments on account*

C. *Investments*
- I *Land and buildings (4)*
- II *Investments in group undertakings and participating interests*
  - 1. *Shares in group undertakings*
  - 2. *Debt securities issued by, and loans to, group undertakings*
  - 3. *Participating interests*
  - 4. *Debt securities issued by, and loans to, undertakings in which the company has a participating interest*
- III *Other financial investments*
  - 1. *Shares and other variable-yield securities and units in unit trusts*
  - 2. *Debt securities and other fixed income securities (5)*
  - 3. *Participation in investment pools (6)*
  - 4. *Loans secured by mortgages (7)*
  - 5. *Other loans (7)*
  - 6. *Deposits with credit institutions (8)*
  - 7. *Other (9)*
- IV *Deposits with ceding undertakings (10)*

D. *Assets held to cover linked liabilities (11)*

Da. *Reinsurers' share of technical provisions (12)*
- 1. *Provision for unearned premiums*
- 2. *Long term business provision*
- 3. *Claims outstanding*
- 4. *Provisions for bonuses and rebates*
- 5. *Other technical provisions*
- 6. *Technical provisions for unit-linked liabilities*

E. *Debtors (13)*
- I *Debtors arising out of direct insurance operations*
  - 1. *Policy holders*
  - 2. *Intermediaries*
- II *Debtors arising out of reinsurance operations*
- III *Other debtors*
- IV *Called up share capital not paid (1)*

F. *Other assets*
- I *Tangible assets*
  - 1. *Plant and machinery*
  - 2. *Fixtures, fittings, tools and equipment*
  - 3. *Payments on account (other than deposits paid on land and buildings) and assets (other than buildings) in course of construction*
- II *Stocks*
  - 1. *Raw materials and consumables*
  - 2. *Work in progress*
  - 3. *Finished goods and goods for resale*
  - 4. *Payments on account*
- III *Cash at bank and in hand*

IV Own shares (14)
V Other (15)

G. Prepayments and accrued income
I Accrued interest and rent (16)
II Deferred acquisition costs (17)
III Other prepayments and accrued income

LIABILITIES

A. Capital and reserves
I Called up share capital or equivalent funds
II Share premium account
III Revaluation reserve
IV Reserves
1. Capital redemption reserve
2. Reserve for own shares
3. Reserves provided for by the articles of association
4. Other reserves
V Profit and loss account

B. Subordinated liabilities (18)

Ba. Fund for future appropriations (19)

C. Technical provisions
1. Provision for unearned premiums (20)
(a) gross amount
(b) reinsurance amount (12)
2. Long term business provision (20) (21) (26)
(a) gross amount
(b) reinsurance amount (12)
3. Claims outstanding (22)
(a) gross amount
(b) reinsurance amount (12)
4. Provision for bonuses and rebates (23)
(a) gross amount
(b) reinsurance amount (12)
5. Equalisation provision (24)
6. Other technical provisions (25)
(a) gross amount
(b) reinsurance amount (12)

D. Technical provisions for linked liabilities (26)
(a) gross amount
(b) reinsurance amount (12)

E. [Provisions for other risks]
1. Provisions for pensions and similar obligations
2. Provisions for taxation
3. Other provisions

F. Deposits received from reinsurers (27)

G. Creditors (28)
I Creditors arising out of direct insurance operations
II Creditors arising out of reinsurance operations
III Debenture loans (29)
IV Amounts owed to credit institutions
V Other creditors including taxation and social security

H. Accruals and deferred income

Notes on the balance sheet format

(1) Called up share capital not paid

(Assets items A and E.IV)

This item may be shown in either of the positions given in the format.

(2) Concessions, patents, licences, trade marks and similar rights and assets

(Assets item B.2)

Amounts in respect of assets shall only be included in a company's balance sheet under this item if either—

(*a*) *the assets were acquired for valuable consideration and are not required to be shown under goodwill; or*

(*b*) *the assets in question were created by the company itself.*

(*3*) *Goodwill*

(Assets item B.3)

Amounts representing goodwill shall only be included to the extent that the goodwill was acquired for valuable consideration.

(*4*) *Land and buildings*

(Assets item C.I.)

The amount of any land and buildings occupied by the company for its own activities shall be shown separately in the notes to the accounts.

(*5*) *Debt securities and other fixed income securities*

(Assets item C.III.2)

This item shall comprise transferable debt securities and any other transferable fixed income securities issued by credit institutions, other undertakings or public bodies, in so far as they are not covered by Assets item C.II.2 or C.II.4.

Securities bearing interest rates that vary in accordance with specific factors, for example the interest rate on the inter-bank market or on the Euromarket, shall also be regarded as debt securities and other fixed income securities and so be included under this item.

(*6*) *Participation in investment pools*

(Assets item C.III.3)

This item shall comprise shares held by the company in joint investments constituted by several undertakings or pension funds, the management of which has been entrusted to one of those undertakings or to one of those pension funds.

(*7*) *Loans secured by mortgages and other loans*

(Assets items C.III.4 and C.III.5)

Loans to policy holders for which the policy is the main security shall be included under "Other loans" and their amount shall be disclosed in the notes to the accounts. Loans secured by mortgage shall be shown as such even where they are also secured by insurance policies. Where the amount of "Other loans" not secured by policies is material, an appropriate breakdown shall be given in the notes to the accounts.

(*8*) *Deposits with credit institutions*

(Assets item C.III.6)

This item shall comprise sums the withdrawal of which is subject to a time restriction. Sums deposited with no such restriction shall be shown under Assets item F.III even if they bear interest.

(*9*) *Other*

(Assets item C.III.7)

This item shall comprise those investments which are not covered by Assets items C.III.1 to 6. Where the amount of such investments is significant, they must be disclosed in the notes to the accounts.

(*10*) *Deposits with ceding undertakings*

(Assets item C.IV)

Where the company accepts reinsurance this item shall comprise amounts, owed by the ceding undertakings and corresponding to guarantees, which are deposited with those ceding undertakings or with third parties or which are retained by those undertakings.

These amounts may not be combined with other amounts owed by the ceding insurer to the reinsurer or set off against amounts owed by the reinsurer to the ceding insurer.

Securities deposited with ceding undertakings or third parties which remain the property of the company shall be entered in the company's accounts as an investment, under the appropriate item.

(11) Assets held to cover linked liabilities

(Assets item D)

In respect of long term business, this item shall comprise investments made pursuant to long term policies under which the benefits payable to the policy holder are wholly or partly to be determined by reference to the value of, or the income from, property of any description (whether or not specified in the contract) or by reference to fluctuations in, or in an index of, the value of property of any description (whether or not so specified).

This item shall also comprise investments which are held on behalf of the members of a tontine and are intended for distribution among them.

(12) Reinsurance amounts

(Assets item Da: Liabilities items C.1(b), 2(b), 3(b), 4(b) and 6(b) and D(b))

The reinsurance amounts may be shown either under Assets item Da or under Liabilities items C.1(b), 2(b), 3(b), 4(b) and 6(b) and D(b).

The reinsurance amounts shall comprise the actual or estimated amounts which, under contractual reinsurance arrangements, are deducted from the gross amounts of technical provisions.

As regards the provision for unearned premiums, the reinsurance amounts shall be calculated according to the methods referred to in paragraph 44 above or in accordance with the terms of the reinsurance policy.

(13) Debtors

(Assets item E)

Amounts owed by group undertakings and undertakings in which the company has a participating interest shall be shown separately as sub-items of Assets items E.I, II and III.

(14) Own shares

(Assets item F.IV)

The nominal value of the shares shall be shown separately under this item.

(15) Other

(Assets item F.V)

This item shall comprise those assets which are not covered by Assets items F.I to IV. Where such assets are material they must be disclosed in the notes to the accounts.

(16) Accrued interest and rent

(Assets item G.I)

This item shall comprise those items that represent interest and rent that have been earned up to the balance-sheet date but have not yet become receivable.

(17) Deferred acquisition costs

(Assets item G.II)

This item shall comprise the costs of acquiring insurance policies which are incurred during a financial year but relate to a subsequent financial year ("deferred acquisition costs"), except in so far as—

- *(a) allowance has been made in the computation of the long term business provision made under paragraph 46 below and shown under Liabilities item C2 or D in the balance sheet, for—*
  - *(i) the explicit recognition of such costs, or*
  - *(ii) the implicit recognition of such costs by virtue of the anticipation of future income from which such costs may prudently be expected to be recovered, or*
- *(b) allowance has been made for such costs in respect of general business policies by a deduction from the provision for unearned premiums made under paragraph 44 below and shown under Liabilities item C.I in the balance sheet.*

Deferred acquisition costs arising in general business shall be distinguished from those arising in long term business.

In the case of general business, the amount of any deferred acquisition costs shall be established on a basis compatible with that used for unearned premiums.

There shall be disclosed in the notes to the accounts—

(*a*) *how the deferral of acquisition costs has been treated* (*unless otherwise expressly stated in the accounts*), *and*

(*b*) *where such costs are included as a deduction from the provisions at Liabilities item C.1, the amount of such deduction, or*

(*c*) *where the actuarial method used in the calculation of the provisions at Liabilities item C.2 or D has made allowance for the explicit recognition of such costs, the amount of the costs so recognised.*

(*18*) *Subordinated liabilities*

(*Liabilities item B*)

This item shall comprise all liabilities in respect of which there is a contractual obligation that, in the event of winding up or of bankruptcy, they are to be repaid only after the claims of all other creditors have been met (*whether or not they are represented by certificates*).

(*19*) *Fund for future appropriations*

(*Liabilities item Ba*)

This item shall comprise all funds the allocation of which either to policy holders or to shareholders has not been determined by the end of the financial year.

Transfers to and from this item shall be shown in item II.12a in the profit and loss account.

(*20*) *Provision for unearned premiums*

(*Liabilities item C.1*)

In the case of long term business the provision for unearned premiums may be included in Liabilities item C.2 rather than in this item.

The provision for unearned premiums shall comprise the amount representing that part of gross premiums written which is estimated to be earned in the following financial year or to subsequent financial years.

(*21*) *Long term business provision*

(*Liabilities item C.2*)

This item shall comprise the actuarially estimated value of the company's liabilities (*excluding technical provisions included in Liabilities item D*), *including bonuses already declared and after deducting the actuarial value of future premiums.*

This item shall also comprise claims incurred but not reported, plus the estimated costs of settling such claims.

(*22*) *Claims outstanding*

(*Liabilities item C.3*)

This item shall comprise the total estimated ultimate cost to the company of settling all claims arising from events which have occurred up to the end of the financial year (*including, in the case of general business, claims incurred but not reported*) *less amounts already paid in respect of such claims.*

(*23*) *Provision for bonuses and rebates*

(*Liabilities item C.4*)

This item shall comprise amounts intended for policy holders or contract beneficiaries by way of bonuses and rebates as defined in Note (*5*) *on the profit and loss account format to the extent that such amounts have not been credited to policy holders or contract beneficiaries or included in Liabilities item Ba or in Liabilities item C.2.*

(24) Equalisation provision

(Liabilities item C.5)

[This item shall comprise [the amount of any equalisation reserve maintained in respect of general business by the company, in accordance with rules made by the Financial Services Authority under Part X of the Financial Services and Markets Act 2000].]

This item shall [also] comprise any amounts which, in accordance with Council Directive 87/343/EEC, are required to be set aside by a company to equalise fluctuations in loss ratios in future years or to provide for special risks.

A company which otherwise constitutes reserves to equalise fluctuations in loss ratios in future years or to provide for special risks shall disclose that fact in the notes to the accounts.

(25) Other technical provisions

(Liabilities item C.6)

This item shall comprise, inter alia, the provision for unexpired risks as defined in paragraph 81 below. Where the amount of the provision for unexpired risks is significant, it shall be disclosed separately either in the balance sheet or in the notes to the accounts.

(26) Technical provisions for linked liabilities

(Liabilities item D)

This item shall comprise technical provisions constituted to cover liabilities relating to investment in the context of long term policies under which the benefits payable to policy holders are wholly or partly to be determined by reference to the value of, or the income from, property of any description (whether or not specified in the contract) or by reference to fluctuations in, or in an index of, the value of property of any description (whether or not so specified).

Any additional technical provisions constituted to cover death risks, operating expenses or other risks (such as benefits payable at the maturity date or guaranteed surrender values) shall be included under Liabilities item C.2.

This item shall also comprise technical provisions representing the obligations of a tontine's organiser in relation to its members.

(27) Deposits received from reinsurers

(Liabilities item F)

Where the company cedes reinsurance, this item shall comprise amounts deposited by or withheld from other insurance undertakings under reinsurance contracts. These amounts may not be merged with other amounts owed to or by those other undertakings.

Where the company cedes reinsurance and has received as a deposit securities which have been transferred to its ownership, this item shall comprise the amount owed by the company by virtue of the deposit.

(28) Creditors

(Liabilities item G)

Amounts owed to group undertakings and undertakings in which the company has a participating interest shall be shown separately as sub-items.

(29) Debenture loans

(Liabilities item G.III)

The amount of any convertible loans shall be shown separately.

Special rules for balance sheet format

Additional items

10.—(1) Every balance sheet of a company which carries on long term business shall show separately as an additional item the aggregate of any amounts included in Liabilities item A (capital and reserves) which are required not to be treated as realised profits under section 268 of this Act.

(2) A company which carries on long term business shall show separately, in the balance sheet or in the notes to the accounts, the total amount of assets representing the long term fund valued in accordance with the provisions of this Schedule.

Managed funds

11.—(1) For the purposes of this paragraph "managed funds" are funds of a group pension fund—

[(a) the management of which constitutes long term insurance business, and]
(b) which the company administers in its own name but on behalf of others, and
(c) to which it has legal title.

(2) The company shall, in any case where assets and liabilities arising in respect of managed funds fall to be treated as assets and liabilities of the company, adopt the following accounting treatment: assets and liabilities representing managed funds are to be included in the company's balance sheet, with the notes to the accounts disclosing the total amount included with respect to such assets and liabilities in the balance sheet and showing the amount included under each relevant balance sheet item in respect of such assets or (as the case may be) liabilities.

Deferred acquisition costs

12. The costs of acquiring insurance policies which are incurred during a financial year but which relate to a subsequent financial year shall be deferred in a manner specified in Note (17) on the balance sheet format.

Profit and loss account format

I Technical account—General business

1. Earned premiums, net of reinsurance
  (a) gross premiums written (1)
  (b) outward reinsurance premiums (2)
  (c) change in the gross provision for unearned premiums
  (d) change in the provision for unearned premiums, reinsurers' share

2. Allocated investment return transferred from the non-technical account (item III.6) (10)

2a. Investment income (8) (10)
  (a) income from participating interests, with a separate indication of that derived from group undertakings
  (b) income from other investments, with a separate indication of that derived from group undertakings
    (aa) income from land and buildings
    (bb) income from other investments
  (c) value re-adjustments on investments
  (d) gains on the realisation of investments

3. Other technical income, net of reinsurance

4. Claims incurred, net of reinsurance (4)
  (a) claims paid
    (aa) gross amount
    (bb) reinsurers' share
  (b) change in the provision for claims
    (aa) gross amount
    (bb) reinsurers' share

5. Changes in other technical provisions, net of reinsurance, not shown under other headings

6. Bonuses and rebates, net of reinsurance (5)

7. Net operating expenses
  (a) acquisition costs (6)
  (b) change in deferred acquisition costs
  (c) administrative expenses (7)
  (d) reinsurance commissions and profit participation

8. Other technical charges, net of reinsurance

8a. Investment expenses and charges (8)
  (a) investment management expenses, including interest

(*b*) *value adjustments on investments*
(*c*) *losses on the realisation of investments*

9. *Change in the equalisation provision*
10. *Sub-total* (*balance on the technical account for general business*) (*item III.1*)

II Technical account—Long term business

1. *Earned premiums, net of reinsurance*
   (*a*) *gross premiums written* (*1*)
   (*b*) *outward reinsurance premiums* (2)
   (*c*) *change in the provision for unearned premiums, net of reinsurance* (*3*)
2. *Investment income* (*8*) (*10*)
   (*a*) *income from participating interests, with a separate indication of that derived from group undertakings*
   (*b*) *income from other investments, with a separate indication of that derived from group undertakings*
      (*aa*) *income from land and buildings*
      (*bb*) *income from other investments*
   (*c*) *value re-adjustments on investments*
   (*d*) *gains on the realisation of investments*
3. *Unrealised gains on investments* (*9*)
4. *Other technical income, net of reinsurance*
5. *Claims incurred, net of reinsurance* (*4*)
   (*a*) *claims paid*
      (*aa*) *gross amount*
      (*bb*) *reinsurers' share*
   (*b*) *change in the provision for claims*
      (*aa*) *gross amount*
      (*bb*) *reinsurers' share*
6. *Change in other technical provisions, net of reinsurance, not shown under other headings*
   (*a*) *long term business provision, net of reinsurance* (*3*)
      (*aa*) *gross amount*
      (*bb*) *reinsurers' share*
   (*b*) *other technical provisions, net of reinsurance*
7. *Bonuses and rebates, net of reinsurance* (*5*)
8. *Net operating expenses*
   (*a*) *acquisition costs* (*6*)
   (*b*) *change in deferred acquisition costs*
   (*c*) *administrative expenses* (*7*)
   (*d*) *reinsurance commissions and profit participation*
9. *Investment expenses and charges* (*8*)
   (*a*) *investment management expenses, including interest*
   (*b*) *value adjustments on investments*
   (*c*) *losses on the realisation of investments*
10. *Unrealised losses on investments* (*9*)
11. *Other technical charges, net of reinsurance*

11a. *Tax attributable to the long term business*

12. *Allocated investment return transferred to the non-technical account* (*item III.4*)

12a. *Transfers to or from the fund for future appropriations*

13. *Sub-total* (*balance on the technical account—long term business*) (*item III.2*)

III Non-technical account

1. *Balance on the general business technical account—*(*item I.10*)
2. *Balance on the long term business technical account—*(*item II.13*)

[2a. *Tax credit attributable to balance on the long term business technical account*]

3. *Investment income* (*8*)
   (*a*) *income from participating interests, with a separate indication of that derived from group undertakings*
   (*b*) *income from other investments, with a separate indication of that derived from group undertakings*
      (*aa*) *income from land and buildings*
      (*bb*) *income from other investments*
   (*c*) *value re-adjustments on investments*
   (*d*) *gains on the realisation of investments*

3a. *Unrealised gains on investments* (*9*)

4. *Allocated investment return transferred from the long term business technical account* (*item II.12*) (*10*)

5. *Investment expenses and charges* (*8*)
   (*a*) *investment management expenses, including interest*
   (*b*) *value adjustments on investments*
   (*c*) *losses on the realisation of investments*
5a. *Unrealised losses on investments* (*9*)
6. *Allocated investment return transferred to the general business technical account* (*item I.2*) (*10*)
7. *Other income*
8. *Other charges, including value adjustments*
8a. *Profit or loss on ordinary activities before tax*
9. *Tax on profit or loss on ordinary activities*
10. *Profit or loss on ordinary activities after tax*
11. *Extraordinary income*
12. *Extraordinary charges*
13. *Extraordinary profit or loss*
14. *Tax on extraordinary profit or loss*
15. *Other taxes not shown under the preceding items*
16. *Profit or loss for the financial year*

Notes on the profit and loss account format

(*1*) *Gross premiums written*

(*General business technical account: item I.1.*(*a*)

Long term business technical account: item II.1.(*a*))

This item shall comprise all amounts due during the financial year in respect of insurance contracts entered into regardless of the fact that such amounts may relate in whole or in part to a later financial year, and shall include inter alia—

(*i*) *premiums yet to be determined, where the premium calculation can be done only at the end of the year;*
(*ii*) *single premiums, including annuity premiums, and, in long term business, single premiums resulting from bonus and rebate provisions in so far as they must be considered as premiums under the terms of the contract;*
(*iii*) *additional premiums in the case of half-yearly, quarterly or monthly payments and additional payments from policy holders for expenses borne by the company;*
(*iv*) *in the case of co-insurance, the company's portion of total premiums;*
(*v*) *reinsurance premiums due from ceding and retroceding insurance undertakings, including portfolio entries,*

after deduction of cancellations and portfolio withdrawals credited to ceding and retroceding insurance undertakings.

The above amounts shall not include the amounts of taxes or duties levied with premiums.

(*2*) *Outward reinsurance premiums*

(*General business technical account: item I.1.*(*b*)

Long term business technical account: item II.l.(*b*))

This item shall comprise all premiums paid or payable in respect of outward reinsurance contracts entered into by the company. Portfolio entries payable on the conclusion or amendment of outward reinsurance contracts shall be added; portfolio withdrawals receivable must be deducted.

(*3*) *Change in the provision for unearned premiums, net of reinsurance*

(*Long term business technical account: items II.1.*(*c*) *and II.6.*(*a*))

In the case of long term business, the change in unearned premiums may be included either in item II.1.(*c*) *or in item II.6.*(*a*) *of the long term business technical account.*

(*4*) *Claims incurred, net of reinsurance*

(*General business technical account: item I.4*

Long term business technical account: item II.5)

This item shall comprise all payments made in respect of the financial year with the addition of the provision for claims (but after deducting the provision for claims for the preceding financial year).

These amounts shall include annuities, surrenders, entries and withdrawals of loss provisions to and from ceding insurance undertakings and reinsurers and external and internal claims management costs and charges for claims incurred but not reported such as are referred to in paragraphs 47(2) and 49 below.

Sums recoverable on the basis of subrogation and salvage (within the meaning of paragraph 47 below) shall be deducted.

Where the difference between—

(a) the loss provision made at the beginning of the year for outstanding claims incurred in previous years, and

(b) the payments made during the year on account of claims incurred in previous years and the loss provision shown at the end of the year for such outstanding claims,

is material, it shall be shown in the notes to the accounts, broken down by category and amount.

(5) Bonuses and rebates, net of reinsurance

(General business technical account: item I.6

Long term business technical account: item II.7)

Bonuses shall comprise all amounts chargeable for the financial year which are paid or payable to policy holders and other insured parties or provided for their benefit, including amounts used to increase technical provisions or applied to the reduction of future premiums, to the extent that such amounts represent an allocation of surplus or profit arising on business as a whole or a section of business, after deduction of amounts provided in previous years which are no longer required.

Rebates shall comprise such amounts to the extent that they represent a partial refund of premiums resulting from the experience of individual contracts.

Where material, the amount charged for bonuses and that charged for rebates shall be disclosed separately in the notes to the accounts.

(6) Acquisition costs

(General business technical account: item I.7.(a)

Long term business technical account: item II.8.(a))

This item shall comprise the costs arising from the conclusion of insurance contracts. They shall cover both direct costs, such as acquisition commissions or the cost of drawing up the insurance document or including the insurance contract in the portfolio, and indirect costs, such as advertising costs or the administrative expenses connected with the processing of proposals and the issuing of policies.

In the case of long term business, policy renewal commissions shall be included under item II.8.(c) in the long term business technical account.

(7) Administrative expenses

(General business technical account: item I.7.(c)

Long term business technical account: item II.8.(c))

This item shall include the costs arising from premium collection, portfolio administration, handling of bonuses and rebates, and inward and outward reinsurance. They shall in particular include staff costs and depreciation provisions in respect of office furniture and equipment in so far as these need not be shown under acquisition costs, claims incurred or investment charges.

Item II.8.(c) shall also include policy renewal commissions.

(8) Investment income, expenses and charges

(General business technical account: items I.2a and 8a

Long term business technical account: items II.2 and 9

Non-technical account: items III.3 and 5)

Investment income, expenses and charges shall, to the extent that they arise in the long term fund, be disclosed in the long term business technical account. Other investment income, expenses and charges shall either be disclosed in the non-technical account or attributed between the appropriate technical and non-technical accounts. Where the company makes such an attribution it shall disclose the basis for it in the notes to the accounts.

(9) Unrealised gains and losses on investments

(Long term business technical account: items II.3 and 10

Non-technical account: items III.3a and 5a)

In the case of investments attributed to the long term fund, the difference between the valuation of the investments and their purchase price or, if they have previously been valued, their valuation as at the last balance sheet date, may be disclosed (in whole or in part) in item II.3 or II.10 (as the case may be) of the long term business technical account, and in the case of investments shown as assets under Assets item D (assets held to cover linked liabilities) shall be so disclosed.

In the case of other investments, the difference between the valuation of the investments and their purchase price or, if they have previously been valued, their valuation as at the last balance sheet date, may be disclosed (in whole or in part) in item III.3a or III.5a (as the case may require) of the non-technical account.

(10) Allocated investment return

(General business technical account: [item I.2]

Long term business technical account: [item II.12]

Non-technical account: items III.4 and 6)

The allocated return may be transferred from one part of the profit and loss account to another.

Where part of the investment return is transferred to the general business technical account, the transfer from the non-technical account shall be deducted from item III.6 and added to item I.2.

Where part of the investment return disclosed in the long term business technical account is transferred to the non-technical account, the transfer to the non-technical account shall be deducted from item II.12 and added to item III.4.

The reasons for such transfers (which may consist of a reference to any relevant statutory requirement) and the bases on which they are made shall be disclosed in the notes to the accounts.

CHAPTER II
ACCOUNTING PRINCIPLES AND RULES

SECTION A
ACCOUNTING PRINCIPLES

Preliminary

13. Subject to paragraph 19 below, the amounts to be included in respect of all items shown in a company's accounts shall be determined in accordance with the principles set out in paragraphs 14 to 18 below.

Accounting principles

14. The company shall be presumed to be carrying on business as a going concern.

15. Accounting policies shall be applied consistently within the same accounts and from one financial year to the next.

16. The amount of any item shall be determined on a prudent basis, and in particular—

(a) subject to note (9) on the profit and loss account format, only profits realised at the balance sheet date shall be included in the profit and loss account; and

(b) all liabilities ... which have arisen ... in respect of the financial year to which the accounts relate or a previous financial year shall be taken into account, including those which only become apparent between the balance sheet date and the date on which it is signed on behalf of the board of directors in pursuance of section 233 of this Act.

17. All income and charges relating to the financial year to which the accounts relate shall be taken into account, without regard to the date of receipt or payment.

18. In determining the aggregate amount of any item the amount of each individual asset or liability that falls to be taken into account shall be determined separately.

Departure from accounting principles

19. If it appears to the directors of a company that there are special reasons for departing from any of the principles stated above in preparing the company's accounts in respect of any financial year they may do so, but particulars of the departure, the reasons for it and its effect shall be given in a note to the accounts.

[Valuation

19A.—(1) The amounts to be included in respect of assets of any description mentioned in paragraph 22 (valuation of assets: general) are determined either—

(a) in accordance with that paragraph and paragraph 24 (but subject to paragraphs 27 to 29); or

(b) so far as applicable to an asset of that description, in accordance with section BA (valuation at fair value).

(2) The amounts to be included in respect of assets of any description mentioned in paragraph 23 (alternative valuation of fixed-income securities) may be determined—

(a) in accordance with that paragraph (but subject to paragraphs 27 to 29); or

(b) so far as applicable to an asset of that description, in accordance with section BA.

(3) The amounts to be included in respect of assets which—

(a) are not assets of a description mentioned in paragraph 22 or 23, but

(b) are assets of a description to which section BA is applicable,

may be determined in accordance with that section.

(4) Subject to sub-paragraphs (1) to (3), the amounts to be included in respect of all items shown in a company's accounts are determined in accordance with section C.]

SECTION B
CURRENT VALUE ACCOUNTING RULES

20, 21. ...

Valuation of assets: general

22.—(1) Subject to paragraph 24 below, investments falling to be included under Assets item C (investments) shall be included at their current value calculated in accordance with paragraphs 25 and 26 below.

(2) Investments falling to be included under Assets item D (assets held to cover linked liabilities) shall be shown at their current value calculated in accordance with paragraphs 25 and 26 below.

23.—(1) Intangible assets other than goodwill may be shown at their current cost.

(2) Assets falling to be included under Assets items F.I (tangible assets) and F.IV (own shares) in the balance sheet format may be shown at their current value calculated in accordance with paragraphs 25 and 26 below or at their current cost.

(3) Assets falling to be included under Assets item F.II (stocks) may be shown at current cost.

Alternative valuation of fixed-income securities

24.—(1) This paragraph applies to debt securities and other fixed-income securities shown as assets under Assets items C.II (investments in group undertakings and participating interests) and C.III (other financial investments).

(2) Securities to which this paragraph applies may either be valued in accordance with paragraph 22 above or their amortised value may be shown in the balance sheet, in which case the provisions of this paragraph apply.

(3) Subject to sub-paragraph (4) below, where the purchase price of securities to which this paragraph applies exceeds the amount repayable at maturity, the amount of the difference—

(a) shall be charged to the profit and loss account, and

(b) shall be shown separately in the balance sheet or in the notes to the accounts.

(4) The amount of the difference referred to in sub-paragraph (3) above may be written off in instalments so that it is completely written off when the securities are repaid, in which case there shall be shown separately in the balance sheet or in the notes to the accounts the difference between the purchase price (less the aggregate amount written off) and the amount repayable at maturity.

(5) Where the purchase price of securities to which this paragraph applies is less than the amount repayable at maturity, the amount of the difference shall be released to income in instalments over the period remaining until repayment, in which case there shall be shown separately in the balance sheet or in the notes to the accounts the difference between the purchase price (plus the aggregate amount released to income) and the amount repayable at maturity.

(6) Both the purchase price and the current value of securities valued in accordance with this paragraph shall be disclosed in the notes to the accounts.

(7) Where securities to which this paragraph applies which are not valued in accordance with paragraph 22 above are sold before maturity, and the proceeds are used to purchase other securities to which this paragraph applies, the difference between the proceeds of sale and their book value may be spread uniformly over the period remaining until the maturity of the original investment.

Meaning of "current value"

25.—(1) Subject to sub-paragraph (5) below, in the case of investments other than land and buildings, current value shall mean market value determined in accordance with this paragraph.

(2) In the case of listed investments, market value shall mean the value on the balance sheet date or, when the balance sheet date is not a stock exchange trading day, on the last stock exchange trading day before that date.

(3) Where a market exists for unlisted investments, market value shall mean the average price at which such investments were traded on the balance sheet date or, when the balance sheet date is not a trading day, on the last trading day before that date.

(4) Where, on the date on which the accounts are drawn up, listed or unlisted investments have been sold or are to be sold within the short term, the market value shall be reduced by the actual or estimated realisation costs.

(5) Except where the equity method of accounting is applied, all investments other than those referred to in sub-paragraphs (2) and (3) above shall be valued on a basis which has prudent regard to the likely realisable value.

26.—(1) In the case of land and buildings, current value shall mean the market value on the date of valuation, where relevant reduced as provided in sub-paragraphs (4) and (5) below.

(2) Market value shall mean the price at which land and buildings could be sold under private contract between a willing seller and an arm's length buyer on the date of valuation, it being assumed that the property is publicly exposed to the market, that market conditions permit orderly disposal and that a normal period, having regard to the nature of the property, is available for the negotiation of the sale.

(3) The market value shall be determined through the separate valuation of each land and buildings item, carried out at least every five years in accordance with generally recognised methods of valuation.

(4) Where the value of any land and buildings item has diminished since the preceding valuation under sub-paragraph (3), an appropriate value adjustment shall be made.

(5) The lower value arrived at under sub-paragraph (4) shall not be increased in subsequent balance sheets unless such increase results from a new determination of market value arrived at in accordance with sub-paragraphs (2) and (3).

(6) Where, on the date on which the accounts are drawn up, land and buildings have been sold or are to be sold within the short term, the value arrived at in accordance with sub-paragraphs (2) and (4) shall be reduced by the actual or estimated realisation costs.

(7) Where it is impossible to determine the market value of a land and buildings item, the value arrived at on the basis of the principle of purchase price or production cost shall be deemed to be its current value.

Application of the depreciation rules

27.—(1) Where—

(a) the value of any asset of a company is determined in accordance with paragraph 22 or 23 above, and

(b) in the case of a determination under paragraph 22 above, the asset falls to be included under Assets item C.I,

that value shall be, or (as the case may require) be the starting point for determining, the amount to be included in respect of that asset in the company's accounts, instead of its cost or any value previously so determined for that asset; and paragraphs 31 to 35 and 37 below shall apply accordingly in relation to any such asset with the substitution for any reference to its cost of a reference to the value most recently determined for that asset in accordance with paragraph 22 or 23 above (as the case may be).

(2) The amount of any provision for depreciation required in the case of any asset by paragraph 32 or 33 below as it applies by virtue of sub-paragraph (1) is referred to below in this paragraph as the "adjusted amount", and the amount of any provision which would be required by that paragraph in the case of that asset according to the historical cost accounting rules is referred to as the "historical cost amount".

(3) Where sub-paragraph (1) applies in the case of any asset the amount of any provision for depreciation in respect of that asset included in any item shown in the profit and loss account in respect of amounts written off assets of the description in question may be the historical cost amount instead of the adjusted amount, provided that the amount of any difference between the two is shown separately in the profit and loss account or in a note to the accounts.

Additional information to be provided

28.—(1) This paragraph applies where the amounts to be included in respect of assets covered by any items shown in a company's accounts have been determined in accordance with paragraph 22 or 23 above.

(2) The items affected and the basis of valuation adopted in determining the amounts of the assets in question in the case of each such item shall be disclosed in a note to the accounts.

(3) The purchase price of investments valued in accordance with paragraph 22 above shall be disclosed in the notes to the accounts.

(4) In the case of each balance sheet item valued in accordance with paragraph 23 above either—

(a) the comparable amounts determined according to the historical cost accounting rules (without any provision for depreciation or diminution in value); or

(b) the differences between those amounts and the corresponding amounts actually shown in the balance sheet in respect of that item,

shall be shown separately in the balance sheet or in a note to the accounts.

(5) In sub-paragraph (4) above, references in relation to any item to the comparable amounts determined as there mentioned are references to—

(a) the aggregate amount which would be required to be shown in respect of that item if the amounts to be included in respect of all the assets covered by that item were determined according to the historical cost accounting rules; and

(b) the aggregate amount of the cumulative provisions for depreciation or diminution in value which would be permitted or required in determining those amounts according to those rules.

Revaluation reserve

29.—(1) *Subject to sub-paragraph (7) below, with respect to any determination of the value of an asset of a company in accordance with paragraph 22 or 23 above, the amount of any profit or loss arising from that determination (after allowing, where appropriate, for any provisions for depreciation or diminution in value made otherwise than by reference to the value so determined and any adjustments of any such provisions made in the light of that determination) shall be credited or (as the case may be) debited to a separate reserve ("the revaluation reserve").*

(2) *The amount of the revaluation reserve shall be shown in the company's balance sheet under Liabilities item A.III, but need not be shown under the name "revaluation reserve".*

(3) *An amount may be transferred*

[(a) *from the revaluation reserve—*

(i) *to the profit and loss account, if the amount was previously charged to that account or represents realised profit, or*

(ii) *on capitalisation,*

(b) *to or from the revaluation reserve in respect of the taxation relating to any profit or loss credited or debited to the reserve;]*

and the revaluation reserve shall be reduced to the extent that the amounts transferred to it are no longer necessary for the purposes of the valuation method used.

(4) *In [sub-paragraph (3)(a)(ii)] "capitalisation", in relation to an amount standing to the credit of the revaluation reserve, means applying it in wholly or partly paying up unissued shares in the company to be allotted to members of the company as fully or partly paid shares.*

(5) *The revaluation reserve shall not be reduced except as mentioned in this paragraph.*

(6) *The treatment for taxation purposes of amounts credited or debited to the revaluation reserve shall be disclosed in a note to the accounts.*

(7) *This paragraph does not apply to the difference between the valuation of investments and their purchase price or previous valuation shown in the long term business technical account or the non-technical account in accordance with note (9) on the profit and loss account format.*

[SECTION BA
VALUATION AT FAIR VALUE

Inclusion of financial instruments at fair value

29A.—(1) *Subject to sub-paragraphs (2) to (4), financial instruments (including derivatives) may be included at fair value.*

(2) *Sub-paragraph (1) does not apply to financial instruments which constitute liabilities unless—*

(a) *they are held as part of a trading portfolio, or*

(b) *they are derivatives.*

(3) *Except where they fall to be included under Assets item D (assets held to cover linked liabilities), sub-paragraph (1) does not apply to—*

(a) *financial instruments (other than derivatives) held to maturity;*

(b) *loans and receivables originated by the company and not held for trading purposes;*

(c) *interests in subsidiary undertakings, associated undertakings and joint ventures;*

(d) *equity instruments issued by the company;*

(e) *contracts for contingent consideration in a business combination;*

(f) *other financial instruments with such special characteristics that the instruments, according to generally accepted accounting principles or practice, should be accounted for differently from other financial instruments.*

(4) *If the fair value of a financial instrument cannot be determined reliably in accordance with paragraph 29B, sub-paragraph (1) does not apply to that financial instrument.*

(5) *In this paragraph—*

"associated undertaking" has the meaning given by paragraph 20 of Schedule 4A; and "joint venture" has the meaning given by paragraph 19 of that Schedule.

Determination of fair value

29B.—(1) The fair value of a financial instrument is determined in accordance with this paragraph.

(2) If a reliable market can readily be identified for the financial instrument, its fair value is determined by reference to its market value.

(3) If a reliable market cannot readily be identified for the financial instrument but can be identified for its components or for a similar instrument, its fair value is determined by reference to the market value of its components or of the similar instrument.

(4) If neither sub-paragraph (2) nor (3) applies, the fair value of the financial instrument is a value resulting from generally accepted valuation models and techniques.

(5) Any valuation models and techniques used for the purposes of sub-paragraph (4) must ensure a reasonable approximation of the market value.

Inclusion of hedged items at fair value

29C. A company may include any assets and liabilities that qualify as hedged items under a fair value hedge accounting system, or identified portions of such assets or liabilities, at the amount required under that system.

Other assets that may be included at fair value

29D.—(1) This paragraph applies to—
- *(a) investment property, and*
- *(b) living animals and plants,*

that, under international accounting standards, may be included in accounts at fair value.

(2) Such investment property and such living animals and plants may be included at fair value, provided that all such investment property or, as the case may be, all such living animals and plants are so included where their fair value can reliably be determined.

(3) In this paragraph, "fair value" means fair value determined in accordance with relevant international accounting standards.

Accounting for changes in value

29E.—(1) This paragraph applies where a financial instrument is valued in accordance with paragraph 29A or 29C or an asset is valued in accordance with paragraph 29D.

(2) Notwithstanding paragraph 16 in this Part of this Schedule, and subject to sub-paragraphs (3) and (4) below, a change in the value of the financial instrument or of the investment property or living animal or plant must be included in the profit and loss account.

(3) Where—
- *(a) the financial instrument accounted for is a hedging instrument under a hedge accounting system that allows some or all of the change in value not to be shown in the profit and loss account, or*
- *(b) the change in value relates to an exchange difference arising on a monetary item that forms part of a company's net investment in a foreign entity,*

the amount of the change in value must be credited to or (as the case may be) debited from a separate reserve ("the fair value reserve").

(4) Where the instrument accounted for—
- *(a) is an available for sale financial asset, and*
- *(b) is not a derivative,*

the change in value may be credited to or (as the case may be) debited from the fair value reserve.

The fair value reserve

29F.—(1) The fair value reserve must be adjusted to the extent that the amounts shown in it are no longer necessary for the purposes of paragraph 29E(3) or (4).

(2) The treatment for taxation purposes of amounts credited or debited to the fair value reserve shall be disclosed in a note to the accounts.]

SECTION C
HISTORICAL COST ACCOUNTING RULES

Preliminary

30. ...

Valuation of assets

General rules

31. Subject to any provision for depreciation or diminution in value made in accordance with paragraph 32 or 33 below, the amount to be included in respect of any asset in the balance sheet format shall be its cost.

32. In the case of any asset included under Assets item B (intangible assets), C.I (land and buildings), F.I. (tangible assets) or F.II (stocks) which has a limited useful economic life, the amount of—

(a) its cost; or

(b) where it is estimated that any such asset will have a residual value at the end of the period of its useful economic life, its cost less that estimated residual value,

shall be reduced by provisions for depreciation calculated to write off that amount systematically over the period of the asset's useful economic life.

33.—(1) This paragraph applies to any asset included under Assets item B (tangible assets), C (investments), F.I (tangible assets) or F.IV (own shares).

(2) Where an asset to which this paragraph applies has diminished in value, provisions for diminution in value may be made in respect of it and the amount to be included in respect of it may be reduced accordingly; and any such provisions which are not shown in the profit and loss account shall be disclosed (either separately or in aggregate) in a note to the accounts.

(3) Provisions for diminution in value shall be made in respect of any asset to which this paragraph applies if the reduction in its value is expected to be permanent (whether its useful economic life is limited or not), and the amount to be included in respect of it shall be reduced accordingly; and any such provisions which are not shown in the profit and loss account shall be disclosed (either separately or in aggregate) in a note to the accounts.

(4) Where the reasons for which any provision was made in accordance with sub-paragraph (1) or (2) have ceased to apply to any extent, that provision shall be written back to the extent that it is no longer necessary; and any amounts written back in accordance with this sub-paragraph which are not shown in the profit and loss account shall be disclosed (either separately or in aggregate) in a note to the accounts.

34.—(1) This paragraph applies to assets included under Assets items E.I, II and III (debtors) and F.III (cash at bank and in hand) in the balance sheet.

(2) If the net realisable value of an asset to which this paragraph applies is lower than its cost the amount to be included in respect of that asset shall be the net realisable value.

(3) Where the reasons for which any provision for diminution in value was made in accordance with sub-paragraph (2) have ceased to apply to any extent, that provision shall be written back to the extent that it is no longer necessary.

Development costs

35.—(1) Notwithstanding that amounts representing "development costs" may be included under Assets item B (intangible assets) in the balance sheet format, an amount may only be included in a company's balance sheet in respect of development costs in special circumstances.

(2) If any amount is included in a company's balance sheet in respect of development costs the following information shall be given in a note to the accounts—

(a) the period over which the amount of those costs originally capitalised is being or is to be written off; and

(b) the reasons for capitalising the development costs in question.

Goodwill

36.—(1) The application of paragraphs 31 to 33 above in relation to goodwill (in any case where goodwill is treated as an asset) is subject to the following provisions of this paragraph.

(2) Subject to sub-paragraph (3) below, the amount of the consideration for any goodwill acquired by a company shall be reduced by provisions for depreciation calculated to write off that amount systematically over a period chosen by the directors of the company.

(3) The period chosen shall not exceed the useful economic life of the goodwill in question.

(4) In any case where any goodwill acquired by a company is included as an asset in the company's balance sheet the period chosen for writing off the consideration for that goodwill and the reasons for choosing that period shall be disclosed in a note to the accounts.

Miscellaneous and supplemental

Excess of money owed over value received as an asset item

37.—(1) Where the amount repayable on any debt owed by a company is greater than the value of the consideration received in the transaction giving rise to the debt, the amount of the difference may be treated as an asset.

(2) Where any such amount is so treated—

(a) it shall be written off by reasonable amounts each year and must be completely written off before repayment of the debt; and

(b) if the current amount is not shown as a separate item in the company's balance sheet it must be disclosed in a note to the accounts.

Assets included at a fixed amount

38.—(1) Subject to the following sub-paragraph, assets which fall to be included under Assets item F.I (tangible assets) in the balance sheet format may be included at a fixed quantity and value.

(2) Sub-paragraph (1) applies to assets of a kind which are constantly being replaced, where—

(a) their overall value is not material to assessing the company's state of affairs; and

(b) their quantity, value and composition are not subject to material variation.

Determination of cost

39.—(1) The cost of an asset that has been acquired by the company shall be determined by adding to the actual price paid any expenses incidental to its acquisition.

(2) The cost of an asset constructed by the company shall be determined by adding to the purchase price of the raw materials and consumables used the amount of the costs incurred by the company which are directly attributable to the construction of that asset.

(3) In addition, there may be included in the cost of an asset constructed by the company—

(a) a reasonable proportion of the costs incurred by the company which are only indirectly attributable to the construction of that asset, but only to the extent that they relate to the period of construction; and

(b) interest on capital borrowed to finance the construction of that asset, to the extent that it accrues in respect of the period of construction;

provided, however, in a case within sub-paragraph (b) above, that the inclusion of the interest in determining the cost of that asset and the amount of the interest so included is disclosed in a note to the accounts.

40.—(1) Subject to the qualification mentioned below, the cost of any assets which are fungible assets may be determined by the application of any of the methods mentioned in sub-paragraph (2) below in relation to any such assets of the same class.

The method chosen must be one which appears to the directors to be appropriate in the circumstances of the company.

(2) Those methods are—
- *(a) the method known as "first in, first out" (FIFO);*
- *(b) the method known as "last in, first out" (LIFO);*
- *(c) a weighted average price; and*
- *(d) any other method similar to any of the methods mentioned above.*

(3) Where in the case of any company—
- *(a) the cost of assets falling to be included under any item shown in the company's balance sheet has been determined by the application of any method permitted by this paragraph; and*
- *(b) the amount shown in respect of that item differs materially from the relevant alternative amount given below in this paragraph;*

the amount of that difference shall be disclosed in a note to the accounts.

(4) Subject to sub-paragraph (5) below, for the purposes of sub-paragraph (3)(b) above, the relevant alternative amount, in relation to any item shown in a company's balance sheet, is the amount which would have been shown in respect of that item if assets of any class included under that item at an amount determined by any method permitted by this paragraph had instead been included at their replacement cost as at the balance sheet date.

(5) The relevant alternative amount may be determined by reference to the most recent actual purchase price before the balance sheet date of assets of any class included under the item in question instead of by reference to their replacement cost as at that date, but only if the former appears to the directors of the company to constitute the more appropriate standard of comparison in the case of assets of that class.

Substitution of original amount where price or cost unknown

41. Where there is no record of the purchase price of any asset acquired by a company or of any price, expenses or costs relevant for determining its cost in accordance with paragraph 39 above, or any such record cannot be obtained without unreasonable expense or delay, its cost shall be taken for the purposes of paragraphs 31 to 36 above to be the value ascribed to it in the earliest available record of its value made on or after its acquisition by the company.

SECTION D
RULES FOR DETERMINING PROVISIONS

Preliminary

42. Provisions which are to be shown in a company's accounts shall be determined in accordance with paragraphs 43 to 53 below.

Technical provisions

43. The amount of technical provisions must at all times be sufficient to cover any liabilities arising out of insurance contracts as far as can reasonably be foreseen.

Provision for unearned premiums

44.—(1) The provision for unearned premiums shall in principle be computed separately for each insurance contract, save that statistical methods (and in particular proportional and flat rate methods) may be used where they may be expected to give approximately the same results as individual calculations.

(2) Where the pattern of risk varies over the life of a contract, this shall be taken into account in the calculation methods.

Provision for unexpired risks

45. The provision for unexpired risks (as defined in paragraph 81 below) shall be computed on the basis of claims and administrative expenses likely to arise after the end of the financial year from contracts concluded before that date, in so far as their estimated value exceeds the provision for unearned premiums and any premiums receivable under those contracts.

Long term business provision

46.—(1) The long term business provision shall in principle be computed separately for each long term contract, save that statistical or mathematical methods may be used where they may be expected to give approximately the same results as individual calculations.

(2) A summary of the principal assumptions in making the provision under sub-paragraph (1) shall be given in the notes to the accounts.

(3) The computation shall be made annually by a Fellow of the Institute or Faculty of Actuaries on the basis of recognised actuarial methods, with due regard to the actuarial principles laid down in [Directive 2002/83/EC of the European Parliament and of the Council of 5th November 2002 concerning life assurance].

Provisions for claims outstanding

General business

47.—(1) A provision shall in principle be computed separately for each claim on the basis of the costs still expected to arise, save that statistical methods may be used if they result in an adequate provision having regard to the nature of the risks.

(2) This provision shall also allow for claims incurred but not reported by the balance sheet date, the amount of the allowance being determined having regard to past experience as to the number and magnitude of claims reported after previous balance sheet dates.

(3) All claims settlement costs (whether direct or indirect) shall be included in the calculation of the provision.

(4) Recoverable amounts arising out of subrogation or salvage shall be estimated on a prudent basis and either deducted from the provision for claims outstanding (in which case if the amounts are material they shall be shown in the notes to the accounts) or shown as assets.

(5) In sub-paragraph (4) above, "subrogation" means the acquisition of the rights of policy holders with respect to third parties, and "salvage" means the acquisition of the legal ownership of insured property.

(6) Where benefits resulting from a claim must be paid in the form of annuity, the amounts to be set aside for that purpose shall be calculated by recognised actuarial methods, and paragraph 48 below shall not apply to such calculations.

(7) Implicit discounting or deductions, whether resulting from the placing of a current value on a provision for an outstanding claim which is expected to be settled later at a higher figure or otherwise effected, is prohibited.

48.—(1) Explicit discounting or deductions to take account of investment income is permitted, subject to the following conditions:
- *(a) the expected average interval between the date for the settlement of claims being discounted and the accounting date shall be at least four years;*
- *(b) the discounting or deductions shall be effected on a recognised prudential basis;*

(c) when calculating the total cost of settling claims, the company shall take account of all factors that could cause increases in that cost;
(d) the company shall have adequate data at its disposal to construct a reliable model of the rate of claims settlements;
(e) the rate of interest used for the calculation of present values shall not exceed a rate prudently estimated to be earned by assets of the company which are appropriate in magnitude and nature to cover the provisions for claims being discounted during the period necessary for the payment of such claims, and shall not exceed either—
 (i) a rate justified by the performance of such assets over the preceding five years, or
 (ii) a rate justified by the performance of such assets during the year preceding the balance sheet date.

(2) When discounting or effecting deductions, the company shall, in the notes to the accounts, disclose—
(a) the total amount of provisions before discounting or deductions,
(b) the categories of claims which are discounted or from which deductions have been made,
(c) for each category of claims, the methods used, in particular the rates used for the estimates referred to in sub-paragraph (1)(d) and (e), and the criteria adopted for estimating the period that will elapse before the claims are settled.

Long term business

49. The amount of the provision for claims shall be equal to the sums due to beneficiaries, plus the costs of settling claims.

[Equalisation reserves

50. The amount of any equalisation reserve maintained in respect of general business, in accordance with rules made by the Financial Services Authority under Part X of the Financial Services and Markets Act 2000, shall be determined in accordance with such rules.]

Accounting on a non-annual basis

51.—(1) Either of the methods described in paragraphs 52 and 53 below may be applied where, because of the nature of the class or type of insurance in question, information about premiums receivable or claims payable (or both) for the underwriting years is insufficient when the accounts are drawn up for reliable estimates to be made.

(2) The use of either of the methods referred to in sub-paragraph (1) shall be disclosed in the notes to the accounts together with the reasons for adopting it.

(3) Where one of the methods referred to in sub-paragraph (1) above is adopted, it shall be applied systematically in successive years unless circumstances justify a change.

(4) In the event of a change in the method applied, the effect on the assets, liabilities, financial position and profit or loss shall be stated in the notes to the accounts.

(5) For the purposes of this paragraph and paragraph 52 below, "underwriting year" means the financial year in which the insurance contracts in the class or type of insurance in question commenced.

52.—(1) The excess of the premiums written over the claims and expenses paid in respect of contracts commencing in the underwriting year shall form a technical provision included in the technical provision for claims outstanding shown in the balance sheet under Liabilities item C.3.

(2) The provision may also be computed on the basis of a given percentage of the premiums written where such a method is appropriate for the type of risk insured.

(3) If necessary, the amount of this technical provision shall be increased to make it sufficient to meet present and future obligations.

(4) The technical provision constituted under this paragraph shall be replaced by a provision for claims outstanding estimated in accordance with paragraph 47 above as soon as sufficient information has been gathered and not later than the end of the third year following the underwriting year.

(5) The length of time that elapses before a provision for claims outstanding is constituted in accordance with sub-paragraph (4) above shall be disclosed in the notes to the accounts.

53.—(1) The figures shown in the technical account or in certain items within it shall relate to a year which wholly or partly precedes the financial year (but by no more than 12 months).

(2) The amounts of the technical provisions shown in the accounts shall if necessary be increased to make them sufficient to meet present and future obligations.

(3) The length of time by which the earlier year to which the figures relate precedes the financial year and the magnitude of the transactions concerned shall be disclosed in the notes to the accounts.

CHAPTER III
NOTES TO THE ACCOUNTS

Preliminary

[54.—(1) Any information required in the case of any company by the following provisions of this Part of this Schedule shall (if not given in the company's accounts) be given by way of a note to those accounts.

(2), (3) …]

General

Disclosure of accounting policies

55. The accounting policies adopted by the company in determining the amounts to be included in respect of items shown in the balance sheet and in determining the profit or loss of the company shall be stated (including such accounting policies with respect to the depreciation and diminution in value of assets).

56. It shall be stated whether the accounts have been prepared in accordance with applicable accounting standards and particulars of any material departure from those standards and the reasons for it shall be given.

Sums denominated in foreign currencies

57. Where any sums originally denominated in foreign currencies have been brought into account under any items shown in the balance sheet or profit and loss account format, the basis on which those sums have been translated into sterling (or the currency in which the accounts are drawn up) shall be stated.

[Reserves and dividends

57A. There must be stated—

- *(a) any amount set aside or proposed to be set aside to, or withdrawn or proposed to be withdrawn from, reserves,*
- *(b) the aggregate amount of dividends paid in the financial year (other than those for which a liability existed at the immediately preceding balance sheet date),*
- *(c) the aggregate amount of dividends that the company is liable to pay at the balance sheet date, and*
- *(d) the aggregate amount of dividends that are proposed before the date of approval of the accounts, and not otherwise disclosed under paragraph (b) or (c).]*

Information supplementing the balance sheet

Share capital and debentures

58.—(1) The following information shall be given with respect to the company's share capital—
- *(a) the authorised share capital; and*
- *(b) where shares of more than one class have been allotted, the number and aggregate nominal value of shares of each class allotted.*

(2) In the case of any part of the allotted share capital that consists of redeemable shares, the following information shall be given—
- *(a) the earliest and latest dates on which the company has power to redeem those shares;*
- *(b) whether those shares must be redeemed in any event or are liable to be redeemed at the option of the company or of the shareholder; and*
- *(c) whether any (and, if so, what) premium is payable on redemption.*

59. If the company has allotted any shares during the financial year, the following information shall be given—
- *(a) …*
- *(b) the classes of shares allotted; and*
- *(c) as respects each class of shares, the number allotted, their aggregate nominal value and the consideration received by the company for the allotment.*

60.—(1) With respect to any contingent right to the allotment of shares in the company the following particulars shall be given—
- *(a) the number, description and amount of the shares in relation to which the right is exercisable;*
- *(b) the period during which it is exercisable; and*
- *(c) the price to be paid for the shares allotted.*

(2) In sub-paragraph (1) above "contingent right to the allotment of shares" means any option to subscribe for shares and any other right to require the allotment of shares to any person whether arising on the conversion into shares of securities of any other description or otherwise.

61.—(1) If the company has issued any debentures during the financial year to which the accounts relate, the following information shall be given—
- *(a) …*
- *(b) the classes of debentures issued; and*
- *(c) as respects each class of debentures, the amount issued and the consideration received by the company for the issue.*

(2) …

(3) Where any of the company's debentures are held by a nominee of or trustee for the company, the nominal amount of the debentures and the amount at which they are stated in the accounting records kept by the company in accordance with section 221 of this Act shall be stated.

Assets

62.—(1) In respect of any assets of the company included in Assets items B (intangible assets), C.I (land and buildings) and C.II (investments in group undertakings and participating interests) in the company's balance sheet the following information shall be given by reference to each such item—
- *(a) the appropriate amounts in respect of those assets included in the item as at the date of the beginning of the financial year and as at the balance sheet date respectively;*
- *(b) the effect on any amount included in Assets item B in respect of those assets of—*
  - *(i) any determination during that year of the value to be ascribed to any of those assets in accordance with paragraph 23 above;*
  - *(ii) acquisitions during that year of any assets;*
  - *(iii) disposals during that year of any assets; and*

(iv) any transfers of assets of the company to and from the item during that year.

(2) The reference in sub-paragraph (1)(a) to the appropriate amounts in respect of any assets (included in an assets item) as at any date there mentioned is a reference to amounts representing the aggregate amounts determined, as at that date, in respect of assets falling to be included under the item on either of the following bases, that is to say—

(a) on the basis of cost (determined in accordance with paragraphs 39 and 40 above); or

(b) on any basis permitted by paragraph 22 or 23 above,

(leaving out of account in either case any provisions for depreciation or diminution in value).

(3) In addition, in respect of any assets of the company included in any assets item in the company's balance sheet, there shall be stated (by reference to each such item)—

(a) the cumulative amount of provisions for depreciation or diminution in value of those assets included under the item as at each date mentioned in sub-paragraph (1)(a);

(b) the amount of any such provisions made in respect of the financial year;

(c) the amount of any adjustments made in respect of any such provisions during that year in consequence of the disposal of any of those assets; and

(d) the amount of any other adjustments made in respect of any such provisions during that year.

63. Where any assets of the company (other than listed investments) are included under any item shown in the company's balance sheet at an amount determined on any basis mentioned in paragraph 22 or 23 above, the following information shall be given—

(a) the years (so far as they are known to the directors) in which the assets were severally valued and the several values; and

(b) in the case of assets that have been valued during the financial year, the names of the persons who valued them or particulars of their qualifications for doing so and (whichever is stated) the bases of valuation used by them.

64. In relation to any amount which is included under Assets item C.I (land and buildings) there shall be stated—

(a) how much of that amount is ascribable to land of freehold tenure and how much to land of leasehold tenure; and

(b) how much of the amount ascribable to land of leasehold tenure is ascribable to land held on long lease and how much to land held on short lease.

Investments

65. In respect of the amount of each item which is shown in the company's balance sheet under Assets item C (investments) there shall be stated—

(a) how much of that amount is ascribable to listed investments; …

(b) …

[Information about fair value of assets and liabilities

65A.—(1) This paragraph applies where financial instruments have been valued in accordance with paragraph 29A or 29C.

(2) The items affected and the basis of valuation adopted in determining the amounts of the financial instruments must be disclosed.

(3) The purchase price of the financial instruments must be disclosed.

(4) There must be stated—

(a) where the fair value of the instruments has been determined in accordance with paragraph 29B(4), the significant assumptions underlying the valuation models and techniques used,

(b) for each category of financial instrument, the fair value of the instruments in that category and the changes in value—

(i) included in the profit and loss account, or

(ii) credited to or (as the case may be) debited from the fair value reserve,

in respect of those instruments, and

(c) *for each class of derivatives, the extent and nature of the instruments, including significant terms and conditions that may affect the amount, timing and certainty of future cash flows.*

(5) Where any amount is transferred to or from the fair value reserve during the financial year, there must be stated in tabular form—

(a) *the amount of the reserve as at the date of the beginning of the financial year and as at the balance sheet date respectively;*

(b) *the amount transferred to or from the reserve during that year; and*

(c) *the source and application respectively of the amounts so transferred.*

65B. Where the company has derivatives that it has not included at fair value, there must be stated for each class of such derivatives—

(a) *the fair value of the derivatives in that class, if such a value can be determined in accordance with paragraph 29B, and*

(b) *the extent and nature of the derivatives.*

65C.—(1) Sub-paragraph (2) applies if—

(a) *the company has financial fixed assets that could be included at fair value by virtue of paragraph 29A,*

(b) *the amount at which those assets are included under any item in the company's accounts is in excess of their fair value, and*

(c) *the company has not made provision for diminution in value of those assets in accordance with paragraph 33(2) of this Part of this Schedule.*

(2) There must be stated—

(a) *the amount at which either the individual assets or appropriate groupings of those individual assets are included in the company's accounts,*

(b) *the fair value of those assets or groupings, and*

(c) *the reasons for not making a provision for diminution in value of those assets, including the nature of the evidence that provides the basis for the belief that the amount at which they are stated in the accounts will be recovered.*

Information where investment property and living animals and plants included at fair value

65D.—(1) This paragraph applies where the amounts to be included in a company's accounts in respect of investment property or living animals and plants have been determined in accordance with paragraph 29D.

(2) The balance sheet items affected and the basis of valuation adopted in determining the amounts of the assets in question in the case of each such item must be disclosed in a note to the accounts.

(3) In the case of investment property, for each balance sheet item affected there must be shown, either separately in the balance sheet or in a note to the accounts—

(a) *the comparable amounts determined according to the historical cost accounting rules; or*

(b) *the differences between those amounts and the corresponding amounts actually shown in the balance sheet in respect of that item.*

(4) In sub-paragraph (3) above, references in relation to any item to the comparable amounts determined in accordance with that sub-paragraph are references to—

(a) *the aggregate amount which would be required to be shown in respect of that item if the amounts to be included in respect of all the assets covered by that item were determined according to the historical cost accounting rules; and*

(b) *the aggregate amount of the cumulative provisions for depreciation or diminution in value which would be permitted or required in determining those amounts according to those rules.]*

Reserves and provisions

66.—(1) Where any amount is transferred—

(a) *to or from any reserves;*

(b) *to any [provisions for other risks]; or*

(c) *from any [provisions for other risks] otherwise than for the purpose for which the provision was established;*

and the reserves or provisions are or would but for paragraph 2(3) above be shown as separate items in the company's balance sheet, the information mentioned in the following sub-paragraph shall be given in respect of the aggregate of reserves or provisions included in the same item.

(2) *That information is—*

(*a*) *the amount of the reserves or provisions as at the date of the beginning of the financial year and as at the balance sheet date respectively;*

(*b*) *any amounts transferred to or from the reserves or provisions during that year; and*

(*c*) *the source and application respectively of any amounts so transferred.*

(3) *Particulars shall be given of each provision included in Liabilities item E.3 (other provisions) in the company's balance sheet in any case where the amount of that provision is material.*

Provision for taxation

67. *The amount of any provision for deferred taxation shall be stated separately from the amount of any provision for other taxation.*

Details of indebtedness

68.—[(*1*) *In respect of each item shown under "creditors" in the company's balance sheet there shall be stated the aggregate of the following amounts, that is to say—*

(*a*) *the amount of any debts included under that item which are payable or repayable otherwise than by instalments and fall due for payment or repayment after the end of the period of five years beginning with the day next following the end of the financial year; and*

[(*b*) *in the case of any debts so included which are payable or repayable by instalments, the amount of any instalments which fall due for payment after the end of that period.*]]

(2) *Subject to sub-paragraph* (*3*), *in relation to each debt falling to be taken into account under sub-paragraph* (*1*), *the terms of payment or repayment and the rate of any interest payable on the debt shall be stated.*

(3) *If the number of debts is such that, in the opinion of the directors, compliance with sub-paragraph* (2) *would result in a statement of excessive length, it shall be sufficient to give a general indication of the terms of payment or repayment and the rates of any interest payable on the debts.*

(4) *In respect of each item shown under "creditors" in the company's balance sheet there shall be stated—*

(*a*) *the aggregate amount of any debts included under that item in respect of which any security has been given by the company; and*

(*b*) *an indication of the nature of the securities so given.*

(5) *References above in this paragraph to an item shown under "creditors" in the company's balance sheet include references, where amounts falling due to creditors within one year and after more than one year are distinguished in the balance sheet—*

(*a*) *in a case within sub-paragraph* (*1*), *to an item shown under the latter of those categories; and*

(*b*) *in a case within sub-paragraph* (4), *to an item shown under either of those categories;*

and references to items shown under "creditors" include references to items which would but for paragraph 2(3)(b) above be shown under that heading.

69. *If any fixed cumulative dividends on the company's shares are in arrear, there shall be stated—*

(*a*) *the amount of the arrears; and*

(*b*) *the period for which the dividends or, if there is more than one class, each class of them are in arrear.*

Guarantees and other financial commitments

70.—(1) Particulars shall be given of any charge on the assets of the company to secure the liabilities of any other person, including, where practicable, the amount secured.

(2) The following information shall be given with respect to any other contingent liability not provided for (other than a contingent liability arising out of an insurance contract)—

(a) the amount or estimated amount of that liability;
(b) its legal nature;
(c) whether any valuable security has been provided by the company in connection with that liability and if so, what.

(3) There shall be stated, where practicable—

(a) the aggregate amount or estimated amount of contracts for capital expenditure, so far as not provided for; …
(b) …

(4) Particulars shall be given of—

(a) any pension commitments included under any provision shown in the company's balance sheet; and
(b) any such commitments for which no provision has been made;

and where any such commitment relates wholly or partly to pensions payable to past directors of the company separate particulars shall be given of that commitment so far as it relates to such pensions.

(5) Particulars shall also be given of any other financial commitments, other than commitments arising out of insurance contracts, which—

(a) have not been provided for; and
(b) are relevant to assessing the company's state of affairs.

(6) Commitments within any of the preceding sub-paragraphs undertaken on behalf of or for the benefit of—

(a) any parent undertaking or fellow subsidiary undertaking, or
(b) any subsidiary undertaking of the company,

shall be stated separately from the other commitments within that sub-paragraph, and commitments within paragraph (a) shall also be stated separately from those within paragraph (b).

71. …

Miscellaneous matters

72.—(1) Particulars shall be given of any case where the cost of any asset is for the first time determined under paragraph 41 above.

(2) Where any outstanding loans made under the authority of section 153(4)(b), (bb) or (c) or section 155 of this Act (various cases of financial assistance by a company for purchase of its own shares) are included under any item shown in the company's balance sheet, the aggregate amount of those loans shall be disclosed for each item in question.

(3) …

Information supplementing the profit and loss account

Separate statement of certain items of income and expenditure

73.—(1) Subject to the following provisions of this paragraph, each of the amounts mentioned below shall be stated.

(2) The amount of the interest on or any similar charges in respect of—

(a) bank loans and overdrafts, … and
(b) loans of any other kind made to the company.

This sub-paragraph does not apply to interest or charges on loans to the company from group undertakings, but, with that exception, it applies to interest or charges on all loans, whether made on the security of debentures or not.

(3)–(5) …

Particulars of tax

74.—(1) ...

(2) Particulars shall be given of any special circumstances which affect liability in respect of taxation of profits, income or capital gains for the financial year or liability in respect of taxation of profits, income or capital gains for succeeding financial years.

(3) The following amounts shall be stated—

(a) the amount of the charge for United Kingdom corporation tax;
(b) if that amount would have been greater but for relief from double taxation, the amount which it would have been but for such relief;
(c) the amount of the charge for United Kingdom income tax; and
(d) the amount of the charge for taxation imposed outside the United Kingdom of profits, income and (so far as charged to revenue) capital gains.

Those amounts shall be stated separately in respect of each of the amounts which is shown under the following items in the profit and loss account, that is to say item III.9 (tax on profit or loss on ordinary activities) and item III.14 (tax on extraordinary profit or loss).

Particulars of business

75.—(1) As regards general business a company shall disclose—

(a) gross premiums written,
(b) gross premiums earned,
(c) gross claims incurred,
(d) gross operating expenses, and
(e) the reinsurance balance.

(2) The amounts required to be disclosed by sub-paragraph (1) shall be broken down between direct insurance and reinsurance acceptances, if reinsurance acceptances amount to 10 per cent or more of gross premiums written.

(3) Subject to sub-paragraph (4) below, the amounts required to be disclosed by sub-paragraphs (1) and (2) above with respect to direct insurance shall be further broken down into the following groups of classes—

(a) accident and health,
(b) motor (third party liability),
(c) motor (other classes),
(d) marine, aviation and transport,
(e) fire and other damage to property,
(f) third-party liability,
(g) credit and suretyship,
(h) legal expenses,
(i) assistance, and
(j) miscellaneous,

where the amount of the gross premiums written in direct insurance for each such group exceeds 10 million ECUs.

(4) The company shall in any event disclose the amounts relating to the three largest groups of classes in its business.

76.—(1) As regards long term business, the company shall disclose—

(a) gross premiums written, and
(b) the reinsurance balance.

(2) Subject to sub-paragraph (3) below—

(a) gross premiums written shall be broken down between those written by way of direct insurance and those written by way of reinsurance; and
(b) gross premiums written by way of direct insurance shall be broken down—
    (i) between individual premiums and premiums under group contracts;
    (ii) between periodic premiums and single premiums; and
    (iii) between premiums from non-participating contracts, premiums from participating contracts and premiums from contracts where the investment risk is borne by policy holders.

(3) Disclosure of any amount referred to in sub-paragraph (2)(a) or (2)(b)(i), (ii) or (iii) above shall not be required if it does not exceed 10 per cent of the gross premiums written or (as the case may be) of the gross premiums written by way of direct insurance.

77.—(1) Subject to sub-paragraph (2) below, there shall be disclosed as regards both general and long term business the total gross direct insurance premiums resulting from contracts concluded by the company—

- *(a) in the member State of its head office,*
- *(b) in the other member States, and*
- *(c) in other countries.*

(2) Disclosure of any amount referred to in sub-paragraph (1) above shall not be required if it does not exceed 5 per cent of total gross premiums.

Commissions

78. There shall be disclosed the total amount of commissions for direct insurance business accounted for in the financial year, including acquisition, renewal, collection and portfolio management commissions.

79. …

Miscellaneous matters

80.—(1) Where any amount relating to any preceding financial year is included in any item in the profit and loss account, the effect shall be stated.

(2) Particulars shall be given of any extraordinary income or charges arising in the financial year.

(3) The effect shall be stated of any transactions that are exceptional by virtue of size or incidence though they fall within the ordinary activities of the company.

CHAPTER IV
INTERPRETATIONS OF PART I

General

81.—(1) The following definitions apply for the purposes of this Part of this Schedule and its interpretation—

.....

"fungible assets" means assets of any description which are substantially indistinguishable one from another;

["general business" means business which consists of effecting or carrying out contracts of general insurance;]

["investment property" means land held to earn rent or for capital appreciation.]

"lease" includes an agreement for a lease;

"listed investment" means an investment listed on a recognised stock exchange, or on any stock exchange of repute outside Great Britain and the expression "unlisted investment" shall be construed accordingly;

"long lease" means a lease in the case of which the portion of the term for which it was granted remaining unexpired at the end of the financial year is not less than 50 years;

["long term business" means business which consists of effecting or carrying out contracts of long term insurance;]

"long term fund" means the fund or funds maintained by a company in respect of its long term business [in accordance with rules made by the Financial Services Authority under Part X of the Financial Services and Markets Act 2000];

["policy holder" has the meaning given in any relevant order under section 424(2) of the Financial Services and Markets Act 2000;]

"provision for unexpired risks" means the amount set aside in addition to unearned premiums in respect of risks to be borne by the company after the end of the financial

year, in order to provide for all claims and expenses in connection with insurance contracts in force in excess of the related unearned premiums and any premiums receivable on those contracts;

"short lease" means a lease which is not a long lease.

(2) In this Part of this Schedule the "ECU" means the unit of account of that name defined in Council Regulation (EEC) No 3180/78 as amended.

The exchange rates as between the ECU and the currencies of the member States to be applied for each financial year shall be the rates applicable on the last day of the preceding October for which rates for the currencies of all the member States were published in the Official Journal of the Communities.

[Financial instruments

81A. For the purposes of this Part of this Schedule, references to "derivatives" include commodity-based contracts that give either contracting party the right to settle in cash or some other financial instrument, except when such contracts—

(a) were entered into for the purpose of, and continue to meet, the company's expected purchase, sale or usage requirements,

(b) were designated for such purpose at their inception, and

(c) are expected to be settled by delivery of the commodity.

81B.—(1) The expressions listed in sub-paragraph (2) have the same meaning in Section BA of Chapter 2 and paragraphs 65A to 65C and 81A of this Part of this Schedule as they have in Council Directives 78/660/EEC on the annual accounts of certain types of companies and 91/674/EEC on the annual accounts and consolidated accounts of insurance undertakings, as amended.

(2) Those expressions are "available for sale financial asset", "business combination", "commodity-based contracts", "derivative", "equity instrument", "exchange difference", "fair value hedge accounting system", "financial fixed asset", "financial instrument", "foreign entity", "hedge accounting", "hedge accounting system", "hedged items", "hedging instrument", "held for trading purposes", "held to maturity", "monetary item", "receivables", "reliable market" and "trading portfolio".]

Loans

82. For the purposes of this Part of this Schedule a loan or advance (including a liability comprising a loan or advance) is treated as falling due for repayment, and an instalment of a loan or advance is treated as falling due for payment, on the earliest date on which the lender could require repayment or (as the case may be) payment, if he exercised all options and rights available to him.

Materiality

83. For the purposes of this Part of this Schedule amounts which in the particular context of any provision of this Part are not material may be disregarded for the purposes of that provision.

Provisions

84. For the purposes of this Part of this Schedule and its interpretation—

(a) references in this Part to provisions for depreciation or diminution in value of assets are to any amount written off by way of providing for depreciation or diminution in value of assets;

(b) any reference in the profit and loss account format or the notes thereto set out in Section B of this Part to the depreciation of, or amounts written off, assets of any description is to any provision for depreciation or diminution in value of assets of that description; and

(c) references in this Part to [provisions for other risks] ... are to any amount retained as reasonably necessary for the purpose of providing for any liability [the nature

of which is clearly defined and] which is either likely to be incurred, or certain to be incurred but uncertain as to amount or as to the date on which it will arise.

Scots land tenure

85. In the application of this Part of this Schedule to Scotland—
"land of freehold tenure" means land in respect of which the company is the proprietor of the dominium utile or, in the case of land not held on feudal tenure, is the owner;
"land of leasehold tenure" means land of which the company is the tenant under a lease;
and the reference to ground-rents, rates and other outgoings includes feu-duty and ground annual.

Staff costs

86. For the purposes of this Part of this Schedule and its interpretation—
(a) "Social security costs" means any contributions by the company to any state social security or pension scheme, fund or arrangement;
[(b) "Pension costs" includes any costs incurred by the company in respect of any pension scheme established for the purpose of providing pensions for persons currently or formerly employed by the company, any sums set aside for the future payment of pensions directly by the company to current or former employees and any pensions paid directly to such persons without having first been set aside; and]
(c) any amount stated in respect of [the item "social security costs"] or in respect of the item "wages and salaries" in the company's profit and loss account shall be determined by reference to payments made or costs incurred in respect of all persons employed by the company during the financial year who are taken into account in determining the relevant annual number for the purposes of [section 231A(1)(a)].

[664]

NOTES

This Schedule, formed by the original Sch 9, Pts I, II (now substituted as noted to Sch 9, Pt I at **[660]** by the Companies Act 1985 (Bank Accounts) Regulations 1991, SI 1991/2705, reg 5(1), (3)), substituted by the Companies Act 1985 (Insurance Companies Accounts) Regulations 1993, SI 1993/3246, reg 4, Sch 1, as from 19 December 1993, subject to exemptions in relation to certain companies contained in reg 6 (at **[6765]**) and general transitional provisions in reg 7 (at **[6766]**).

Repealed by the Companies Act 2006, s 1295, Sch 16, as from a day to be appointed.

Para 3: words in square brackets substituted by the Companies Act 1985 (Investment Companies and Accounting and Audit Amendments) Regulations 2005, SI 2005/2280, reg 10, as from 1 October 2005, in relation to companies' financial years which begin on or after 1 January 2005 and which end on or after 1 October 2005.

Para 5: repealed by the Companies Act 1985 (International Accounting Standards and Other Accounting Amendments) Regulations 2004, SI 2004/2947, reg 14(5), Sch 6, paras 1, 2, as from 12 November 2004, in relation to companies' financial years which begin on or after 1 January 2005.

Para 6: sub-para (1) numbered as such and words in square brackets therein substituted, and sub-paras (2), (3) added, by the Financial Services and Markets Act 2000 (Consequential Amendments and Repeals) Order 2001, SI 2001/3649, art 36(1), (2), as from 1 December 2001.

Paras 6A, 19A, 29A–29F, 57A, 65A–65D, 81A, 81B: inserted by SI 2004/2947, reg 14(5), Sch 6, paras 1, 3, 6(1), 7(1), 8, 9, 12, as from 12 November 2004, in relation to companies' financial years which begin on or after 1 January 2005.

Para 9: sub-para (1) numbered as such and words in square brackets therein substituted, and sub-para (2) added, by SI 2001/3649, art 36(1), (3), as from 1 December 2001.

Words in square brackets in the balance sheet format following para 9 substituted by SI 2004/2947, reg 14(5), Sch 6, paras 1, 4, as from 12 November 2004, in relation to companies' financial years which begin on or after 1 January 2005.

In Note (24) to the notes on the balance sheet format words in first (outer) pair and third pair of square brackets inserted by the Insurance Companies (Reserves) Act 1995, s 3(1), (2), as from 30 April 1996; words in second (inner) pair of square brackets substituted by SI 2001/3649, art 36(1), (4), as from 1 December 2001.

Para 11: sub-para (a) substituted by SI 2001/3649, art 36(1), (5), as from 1 December 2001.

Para 12: item 2a under head III in the profit and loss account format inserted by SI 1996/189, regs 14(7), 16(5), Sch 5, paras 1, 3, in relation to any annual accounts of a company which are approved by the board of directors on or after 2 February 1996; words in square brackets in note (10) substituted by the Companies Act 1985 (Insurance Companies Accounts) (Minor Amendments) Regulations 1997, SI 1997/2704, reg 2, as from 31 December 1997.

Para 16: words omitted repealed by SI 2004/2947, reg 14(5), Sch 6, paras 1, 5, as from 12 November 2004, in relation to companies' financial years which begin on or after 1 January 2005.

Paras 20, 30: repealed by SI 2004/2947, reg 14(5), Sch 6, paras 1, 6(2), 7(2), as from 12 November 2004, in relation to companies' financial years which begin on or after 1 January 2005.

Paras 21: repealed by SI 1996/189, regs 14(7), 16(5), Sch 5, paras 1, 4, in relation to any annual accounts of a company which are approved by the board of directors on or after 2 February 1996.

Para 29: words in square brackets in sub-paras (3), (4) substituted by SI 1996/189, regs 14(7), 16(1), Sch 5, paras 1, 5, in relation to any financial year ending on or after 2 February 1996 (subject to transitional provisions in relation to financial years ending on or before 24 March 1996).

Para 46: words in square brackets in sub-para (3) substituted by the Life Assurance Consolidation Directive (Consequential Amendments) Regulations 2004, SI 2004/3379, reg 2(1), (2), as from 11 January 2005.

Para 50: substituted by SI 2001/3649, art 36(1), (6), as from 1 December 2001.

Para 54: substituted by SI 1996/189, regs 14(7), 16(5), Sch 5, paras 1, 6, in relation to any annual accounts of a company which are approved by the board of directors on or after 2 February 1996; sub-paras (2), (3) repealed by SI 2005/2280, reg 11, as from 1 October 2005, in relation to companies' financial years which begin on or after 1 January 2005 and which end on or after 1 October 2005.

Paras 59, 61, 65, 70, 72–74: words omitted repealed by SI 1996/189, regs 14(7), 16(1), Sch 5, paras 1, 7–9, 12, 14–16, in relation to any financial year ending on or after 2 February 1996 (subject to transitional provisions as noted above).

Para 66: words in square brackets in sub-para (1) substituted by SI 2004/2947, reg 14(5), Sch 6, paras 1, 10, as from 12 November 2004, in relation to companies' financial years which begin on or after 1 January 2005.

Para 68: sub-para (1) substituted by SI 1996/189, regs 14(7), 16(1), Sch 5, paras 1, 11, in relation to any financial year ending on or after 2 February 1996 (subject to transitional provisions as noted above); sub-para (1)(b) further substituted by the Companies Act 1985 (Accounts of Small and Medium-sized Companies and Minor Accounting Amendments) Regulations 1997, SI 1997/220, reg 7(9), in relation to annual accounts approved by the board of directors on or after 1 March 1997, and to directors' and auditors' reports on such accounts (subject to transitional provisions in relation to a financial year of a company ending on or before 24 March 1997).

Para 71: repealed by SI 1996/189, regs 14(7), 16(1), Sch 5, paras 1, 13, in relation to any financial year ending on or after 2 February 1996 (subject to transitional provisions as noted above).

Para 79: repealed by SI 2004/2947, reg 3, Sch 1, paras 1, 35(a), as from 12 November 2004, in relation to companies' financial years which begin on or after 1 January 2005.

Para 81: definition "the 1982 Act" repealed, definitions "general business", "long term business" and "policy holder" substituted, and words in square brackets in definition "long term fund" substituted, by SI 2001/3649, art 36(1), (7), as from 1 December 2001; definition "investment property" inserted by SI 2004/2947, reg 14(5), Sch 6, paras 1, 11, as from 12 November 2004, in relation to companies' financial years which begin on or after 1 January 2005.

Para 84: words in square brackets in sub-para (c) substituted by SI 2004/2947, reg 14(5), Sch 6, paras 1, 13, as from 12 November 2004, in relation to companies' financial years which begin on or after 1 January 2005; words omitted from sub-para (c) repealed by SI 1996/189, regs 14(7), 16(5), Sch 5, paras 1, 18, in relation to any annual accounts of a company which are approved by the board of directors on or after 2 February 1996.

Para 86: sub-para (b) and words in first pair of square brackets in sub-para (c) substituted by SI 1996/189, regs 14(7), 16(1), Sch 5, paras 1, 19, in relation to any financial year ending on or after 2 February 1996 (subject to transitional provisions as noted above); words in second pair of square brackets in sub-para (c) substituted by SI 2004/2947, reg 3, Sch 1, paras 1, 35(b), as from 12 November 2004, in relation to companies' financial years which begin on or after 1 January 2005.

Application to limited liability partnerships: see the Limited Liability Partnerships Regulations 2001, SI 2001/1090, reg 3, Sch 1 at **[6984]**, **[6992]**.

Trade marks: by the Trade Marks Act 1994, s 106(1), Sch 4, para 1, the references in Pt I, Chapter I, Section B above to a trade mark are to be construed as references to a trade mark within the meaning of the 1994 Act.

PART II
CONSOLIDATED ACCOUNTS

Schedule 4A to apply Part I of this Schedule with modifications

1.—(1) In its application to insurance groups, Schedule 4A shall have effect with the following modifications.

(2) *In paragraph 1—*

(*a*) *for the reference in sub-paragraph (1) to the provisions of Schedule 4 there shall be substituted a reference to the provisions of Part I of this Schedule modified as mentioned in paragraph 2 below;*

(*b*) …

(*c*) *sub-paragraph (3) shall be omitted.*

(3) In paragraph 2(2)(a), for the words "three months" there shall be substituted the words "six months".

(4) In paragraph 3, after sub-paragraph (1) there shall be inserted the following sub-paragraphs—

"(1A) Sub-paragraph (1) shall not apply to those liabilities items the valuation of which by the undertakings included in a consolidation is based on the application of provisions applying only to insurance undertakings, nor to those assets items changes in the values of which also affect or establish policy holders' rights.

(1B) Where sub-paragraph (1A) applies, that fact shall be disclosed in the notes on the consolidated accounts."

(5) For sub-paragraph (4) of paragraph 6 there shall be substituted the following sub-paragraphs—

"(4) Sub-paragraphs (1) and (2) need not be complied with—

(a) where a transaction has been concluded according to normal market conditions and a policy holder has rights in respect of that transaction, or

(b) if the amounts concerned are not material for the purpose of giving a true and fair view.

(5) Where advantage is taken of sub-paragraph (4)(a) above that fact shall be disclosed in the notes to the accounts, and where the transaction in question has a material effect on the assets, liabilities, financial position and profit or loss of all the undertakings included in the consolidation that fact shall also be so disclosed."

(6) In paragraph 17—

(a) in sub-paragraph (1), for the reference to Schedule 4 there shall be substituted a reference to Part I of this Schedule;

(b) in sub-paragraph (2), paragraph (a) and, in paragraph (b), the words "in Format 2" shall be omitted;

(c) in sub-paragraph (3), for paragraphs (a) to (d) there shall be substituted the words "between items 10 and 11 in section III";

(d) in sub-paragraph (4), for paragraphs (a) to (d) there shall be substituted the words "between items 14 and 15 in section III"; and

(e) for sub-paragraph (5) there shall be substituted the following sub-paragraph—

"(5) Paragraph 2(3) of Part I of Schedule 9A (power to combine items) shall not apply in relation to the additional items required by the foregoing provisions of this paragraph."

(7) In paragraph 18, for the reference to paragraphs 17 to 19 and 21 of Schedule 4 there shall be substituted a reference to paragraphs 31 to 33 and 36 of Part I of this Schedule.

(8) In paragraph 21—

(a) in sub-paragraph (1), for the reference to Schedule 4 there shall be substituted a reference to Part I of this Schedule; and

(b) for sub-paragraphs (2) and (3) there shall be substituted the following sub-paragraphs—

"(2) In the Balance Sheet Format, Asset item C.II.3 (participating interests) shall be replaced by two items, "Interests in associated undertakings" and "Other participating interests".

(3) In the Profit and Loss Account Format, items II.2(a) and III.3(a) (income from participating interests, with a separate indication of that derived from group undertakings) shall each be replaced by the following items—

(a) "Income from participating interests other than associated undertakings, with a separate indication of that derived from group undertakings", which shall be shown as items II.2(a) and III.3(a), and

(b) "Income from associated undertakings", which shall be shown as items II.2(aa) and III.3(aa)."

(9) In paragraph 22(1), for the reference to paragraphs 17 to 19 and 21 of Schedule 4 there shall be substituted a reference to paragraphs 31 to 33 and 36 of Part I of this Schedule.

Modifications of Part I of this Schedule for purposes of paragraph 1

2.—(1) For the purposes of paragraph 1 above, Part I of this Schedule shall be modified as follows.

(2) The information required by paragraph 10 need not be given.

(3) In the case of general business, investment income, expenses and charges may be disclosed in the non-technical account rather than in the technical account.

(4) In the case of subsidiary undertakings which are not authorised to carry on long term business in Great Britain, notes (8) and (9) to the profit and loss account format shall have effect as if references to investment income, expenses and charges arising in the long term fund or to investments attributed to the long term fund were references to investment income, expenses and charges or (as the case may be) investments relating to long term business.

(5) In the case of subsidiary undertakings which do not have a head office in Great Britain, the computation required by paragraph 46 shall be made annually by an actuary or other specialist in the field on the basis of recognised actuarial methods.

(6) The information required by paragraphs 75 to 78 need not be shown.]

[665]

NOTES

Substituted as noted to Pt I at **[664]**.

Repealed by the Companies Act 2006, s 1295, Sch 16, as from a day to be appointed.

Para 1: sub-para (2)(b) repealed by the Companies Act 1985 (Accounts of Small and Medium-sized Companies and Minor Accounting Amendments) Regulations 1997, SI 1997/220, reg 7(12), in relation to annual accounts approved by the board of directors on or after 1 March 1997, and to directors' and auditors' reports on such accounts (subject to transitional provisions in relation to a financial year of a company ending on or before 24 March 1997).

Application to limited liability partnerships: see the Limited Liability Partnerships Regulations 2001, SI 2001/1090, reg 3, Sch 1 at **[6984]**, **[6992]**.

(Sch 10 repealed by the Companies Act 1985 (Insurance Companies Accounts) Regulations 1993, SI 1993/3246, reg 5(1), Sch 2, para 7, as from 19 December 1993, subject to exemptions in relation to certain companies contained in reg 6 (at **[6765]***) and general transitional provisions in reg 7 (at* **[6766]***). Also repealed by the Companies Act 2006, s 1295, Sch 16, as from a day to be appointed.)*

[SCHEDULE 10A
PARENT AND SUBSIDIARY UNDERTAKINGS: SUPPLEMENTARY PROVISIONS

Section 258

Introduction

1. The provisions of this Schedule explain expressions used in section 258 (parent and subsidiary undertakings) and otherwise supplement that section.

Voting rights in an undertaking

2.—(1) In section 258(2)(a) and (d) the references to the voting rights in an undertaking are to the rights conferred on shareholders in respect of their shares or, in the case of an undertaking not having a share capital, on members, to vote at general meetings of the undertaking on all, or substantially all, matters.

(2) In relation to an undertaking which does not have general meetings at which matters are decided by the exercise of voting rights, the references to holding a majority of the voting rights in the undertaking shall be construed as references to having the right under the constitution of the undertaking to direct the overall policy of the undertaking or to alter the terms of its constitution.

Right to appoint or remove a majority of the directors

3.—(1) In section 258(2)(b) the reference to the right to appoint or remove a majority of the board of directors is to the right to appoint or remove directors holding a majority of the voting rights at meetings of the board on all, or substantially all, matters.

(2) *An undertaking shall be treated as having the right to appoint to a directorship if—*

(*a*) *a person's appointment to it follows necessarily from his appointment as director of the undertaking, or*

(*b*) *the directorship is held by the undertaking itself.*

(3) A right to appoint or remove which is exercisable only with the consent or concurrence of another person shall be left out of account unless no other person has a right to appoint or, as the case may be, remove in relation to that directorship.

Right to exercise dominant influence

4.—(1) For the purposes of section 258(2)(c) an undertaking shall not be regarded as having the right to exercise a dominant influence over another undertaking unless it has a right to give directions with respect to the operating and financial policies of that other undertaking which its directors are obliged to comply with whether or not they are for the benefit of that other undertaking.

(2) *A "control contract" means a contract in writing conferring such a right which—*

(*a*) *is of a kind authorised by the memorandum or articles of the undertaking in relation to which the right is exercisable, and*

(*b*) *is permitted by the law under which that undertaking is established.*

(3) This paragraph shall not be read as affecting the construction of the expression "actually exercises a dominant influence" in section 258(4)(a).

Rights exercisable only in certain circumstances or temporarily incapable of exercise

5.—(1) Rights which are exercisable only in certain circumstances shall be taken into account only—

(*a*) *when the circumstances have arisen, and for so long as they continue to obtain, or*

(*b*) *when the circumstances are within the control of the person having the rights.*

(2) *Rights which are normally exercisable but are temporarily incapable of exercise shall continue to be taken into account.*

Rights held by one person on behalf of another

6. Rights held by a person in a fiduciary capacity shall be treated as not held by him.

7.—(1) Rights held by a person as nominee for another shall be treated as held by the other.

(2) *Rights shall be regarded as held as nominee for another if they are exercisable only on his instructions or with his consent or concurrence.*

Rights attached to shares held by way of security

8. Rights attached to shares held by way of security shall be treated as held by the person providing the security—

(*a*) *where apart from the right to exercise them for the purpose of preserving the value of the security, or of realising it, the rights are exercisable only in accordance with his instructions, and*

(*b*) *where the shares are held in connection with the granting of loans as part of normal business activities and apart from the right to exercise them for the purpose of preserving the value of the security, or of realising it, the rights are exercisable only in his interests.*

Rights attributed to parent undertaking

9.—(1) Rights shall be treated as held by a parent undertaking if they are held by any of its subsidiary undertakings.

(2) Nothing in paragraph 7 or 8 shall be construed as requiring rights held by a parent undertaking to be treated as held by any of its subsidiary undertakings.

(3) For the purposes of paragraph 8 rights shall be treated as being exercisable in accordance with the instructions or in the interests of an undertaking if they are exercisable in accordance with the instructions of or, as the case may be, in the interests of any group undertaking.

Disregard of certain rights

10. The voting rights in an undertaking shall be reduced by any rights held by the undertaking itself.

Supplementary

11. References in any provision of paragraphs 6 to 10 to rights held by a person include rights falling to be treated as held by him by virtue of any other provision of those paragraphs but not rights which by virtue of any such provision are to be treated as not held by him.]

[666]

NOTES

Inserted by CA 1989, s 21(2), Sch 9, as from 1 April 1990.
Repealed by the Companies Act 2006, s 1295, Sch 16, as from a day to be appointed.

SCHEDULE 11
[MODIFICATIONS OF PART VIII WHERE COMPANY'S ACCOUNTS PREPARED IN ACCORDANCE WITH SPECIAL PROVISIONS FOR BANKING OR INSURANCE COMPANIES]

Section 279

[1. Paragraphs 2 to 6 below apply where a company has prepared accounts in accordance with the special provisions of Part VII relating to banking companies and paragraphs 7 to 13 below apply where a company has prepared accounts in accordance with the special provisions of Part VII relating to insurance companies.

Modifications where accounts prepared in accordance with special provisions for banking companies

2. Section 264(2) shall apply as if the reference to paragraph 89 of Schedule 4 therein was a reference to paragraph 85(c) of Part I of Schedule 9.

3. Section 269 shall apply as if:

(a) there were substituted for the words "are shown as an asset" in sub-section (1) the words "are included as an asset"; and

(b) the reference to paragraph 20 of Schedule 4 in sub-section (2)(b) was to paragraph 27 of Part I of Schedule 9.

4. Sections 270(2) and 275 shall apply as if the references therein to paragraphs 88 and 89 of Schedule 4 were to paragraph 85 of Part I of Schedule 9.

5. Sections 272 and 273 shall apply as if in section 272(3) there were substituted for the references to [sections 226, 226A and 226B] and Schedule 4, references to section 255 and Part I of Schedule 9.

6. Section 276 shall apply as if the references to paragraphs 12(a) and 34(3)(a) of Schedule 4 were to paragraphs 19(a) and 44(3)(a) of Schedule 9.]

[Modifications where accounts prepared in accordance with special provisions for insurance companies

[7. Section 264(2) shall apply as if for the words in parentheses there were substituted "("liabilities" to include any provision for other risks and charges within paragraph 84(c) of Part I of Schedule 9A and any amount included under Liabilities items Ba (fund for future appropriations), C (technical provisions) and D (technical provisions for linked liabilities) in a balance sheet drawn up in accordance with the balance sheet format set out in section B of Part I of Schedule 9A)".]

8. Section 269 shall apply as if the reference to paragraph 20 of Schedule 4 in subsection (2)(b) were a reference to paragraph 35 of Part I of Schedule 9A.

[9. [In the case of Companies Act accounts,] sections 270(2) and 275 shall apply as if the reference to provisions of any of the kinds mentioned in paragraphs 88 and 89 of Schedule 4 were a reference to provisions of any of the kinds mentioned in paragraph 84 of Part I of Schedule 9A and to any amount included under Liabilities items Ba (fund for future appropriations), C (technical provisions) and D (technical provisions for linked liabilities) in a balance sheet drawn up in accordance with the balance sheet format set out in section B of Part I of Schedule 9A.]

10. Sections 272 and 273 shall apply as if the references in section 272(3) to [sections 226, 226A and 226B] and Schedule 4 were references to section 255 and Part I of Schedule 9A.

11. Section 276 shall apply as if the references to paragraphs 12(a) and 34(3)(a) of Schedule 4(d) were references to paragraphs 16(a) and 29(3)(a) of Part I of Schedule 9A.]
[667]

NOTES

Repealed by the Companies Act 2006, s 1295, Sch 16, as from a day to be appointed.

Schedule heading substituted by the Companies Act 1989, s 23, Sch 10, para 21, as from 1 April 1990.

Paras 1–6: inserted before original para 1, and original paras 1–7 renumbered paras 7–13, and the heading preceding those paragraphs inserted, by the Companies Act 1985 (Bank Accounts) Regulations 1991, SI 1991/2705, reg 7, Sch 3, as from 19 December 1991 (subject to transitional provisions in relation to a financial year of a company beginning before 23 December 1992).

Paras 5, 10: words in square brackets substituted by the Companies Act 1985 (International Accounting Standards and Other Accounting Amendments) Regulations 2004, SI 2004/2947, reg 3, Sch 1, paras 1, 36(1), (2), (4), as from 12 November 2004, in relation to companies' financial years which begin on or after 1 January 2005.

Paras 7–11: substituted for the renumbered paras 7–13 by the Companies Act 1985 (Insurance Companies Accounts) Regulations 1993, SI 1993/3246, reg 5(1), Sch 2, para 8, as from 19 December 1993, subject to exemptions in relation to certain companies contained in reg 6 (at **[6765]**) and general transitional provisions in reg 7 (at **[6766]**).

Paras 7, 9: further substituted by the Companies Act 1985 (Miscellaneous Accounting Amendments) Regulations 1996, SI 1996/189, regs 14(8), 16(6), Sch 6, in relation to any distribution made on or after 2 February 1996; words in square brackets in para 9 inserted by SI 2004/2947, reg 3, Sch 1, paras 1, 36(1), (3), as from 12 November 2004, in relation to companies' financial years which begin on or after 1 January 2005.

(Sch 12 repealed by the Company Directors Disqualification Act 1986, s 23(1), (2), Schs 3, 4, as from 29 December 1986, subject to transitional provisions and savings. Also repealed by the Companies Act 2006, s 1295, Sch 16, as from a day to be appointed.)

SCHEDULE 13
PROVISIONS SUPPLEMENTING AND INTERPRETING SECTIONS 324 TO 328

Sections 324, 325, 326, 328 and 346

PART I
RULES FOR INTERPRETATION OF THE SECTIONS AND ALSO SECTION 346(4) AND (5)

1.—(1) A reference to an interest in shares or debentures is to be read as including any interest of any kind whatsoever in shares or debentures.

(2) Accordingly, there are to be disregarded any restraints or restrictions to which the exercise of any right attached to the interest is or may be subject.

2. Where property is held on trust and any interest in shares or debentures is comprised in the property, any beneficiary of the trust who (apart from this paragraph) does not have an interest in the shares or debentures is to be taken as having such an interest; but this paragraph is without prejudice to the following provisions of this Part of this Schedule.

3.—(1) A person is taken to have an interest in shares or debentures if—

(a) he enters into a contract for their purchase by him (whether for cash or other consideration), or

(b) not being the registered holder, he is entitled to exercise any right conferred by the holding of the shares or debentures, or is entitled to control the exercise of any such right.

(2) For purposes of sub-paragraph (1)(b), a person is taken to be entitled to exercise or control the exercise of a right conferred by the holding of shares or debentures if he—

(a) has a right (whether subject to conditions or not) the exercise of which would make him so entitled, or

(b) is under an obligation (whether or not so subject) the fulfilment of which would make him so entitled.

(3) A person is not by virtue of sub-paragraph (1)(b) taken to be interested in shares or debentures by reason only that he—

(a) has been appointed a proxy to vote at a specified meeting of a company or of any class of its members and at any adjournment of that meeting, or

(b) has been appointed by a corporation to act as its representative at any meeting of a company or of any class of its members.

4. A person is taken to be interested in shares or debentures if a body corporate is interested in them and—

(a) that body corporate or its directors are accustomed to act in accordance with his directions or instructions, or

(b) he is entitled to exercise or control the exercise of one-third or more of the voting power at general meetings of that body corporate.

As this paragraph applies for the purposes of section 346(4) and (5), "more than one-half" is substituted for "one-third or more".

5. Where a person is entitled to exercise or control the exercise of one-third or more of the voting power at general meetings of a body corporate, and that body corporate is entitled to exercise or control the exercise of any of the voting power at general meetings of another body corporate ("the effective voting power"), then, for purposes of paragraph 4(b), the effective voting power is taken to be exercisable by that person.

As this paragraph applies for the purposes of section 346(4) and (5), "more than one-half" is substituted for "one-third or more".

6.—(1) A person is taken to have an interest in shares or debentures if, otherwise than by virtue of having an interest under a trust—

(a) he has a right to call for delivery of the shares or debentures to himself or to his order, or

(b) he has a right to acquire an interest in shares or debentures or is under an obligation to take an interest in shares or debentures;

whether in any case the right or obligation is conditional or absolute.

(2) Rights or obligations to subscribe for shares or debentures are not to be taken, for purposes of sub-paragraph (1), to be rights to acquire, or obligations to take, an interest in shares or debentures.

This is without prejudice to paragraph 1.

7. Persons having a joint interest are deemed each of them to have that interest.

8. It is immaterial that shares or debentures in which a person has an interest are unidentifiable.

9. So long as a person is entitled to receive, during the lifetime of himself or another, income from trust property comprising shares or debentures, an interest in the shares or debentures in reversion or remainder or (as regards Scotland) in fee, are to be disregarded.

10. A person is to be treated as uninterested in shares or debentures if, and so long as, he holds them under the law in force in England and Wales as a bare trustee or as a custodian trustee, or under the law in force in Scotland, as a simple trustee.

11.—[(1)] There is to be disregarded an interest of a person subsisting by virtue of—

[(a) any unit trust scheme which is an authorised unit trust scheme ...];

(b) a scheme made under section 22 [or 22A] of the Charities Act 1960 [or section 24 or 25 of the Charities Act 1993], section 11 of the Trustee Investments Act 1961 or section 1 of the Administration of Justice Act 1965; or

(c) the scheme set out in the Schedule to the Church Funds Investment Measure 1958.

[(2) "Unit trust scheme" and "authorised unit trust scheme" have the meaning given in section 237 of the Financial Services and Markets Act 2000.]

12. There is to be disregarded any interest—

(a) of the Church of Scotland General Trustees or of the Church of Scotland Trust in shares or debentures held by them;

(b) of any other person in shares or debentures held by those Trustees or that Trust otherwise than as simple trustees.

"The Church of Scotland General Trustees" are the body incorporated by the order confirmed by the Church of Scotland (General Trustees) Order Confirmation Act 1921; and "the Church of Scotland Trust" is the body incorporated by the order confirmed by the Church of Scotland Trust Order Confirmation Act 1932.

13. Delivery to a person's order of shares or debentures in fulfilment of a contract for the purchase of them by him or in satisfaction of a right of his to call for their delivery, or failure to deliver shares or debentures in accordance with the terms of such a contract or on which such a right falls to be satisfied, is deemed to constitute an event in consequence of the occurrence of which he ceases to be interested in them, and so is the lapse of a person's right to call for delivery of shares or debentures.

[668]–[671]

NOTES

Repealed by the Companies Act 2006, s 1295, Sch 16, as from 1 October 2007. For savings see the note to s 346 at **[346]**.

Para 11: sub-para (1) numbered as such, and sub-para (2) added, by the Financial Services and Markets Act 2000 (Consequential Amendments and Repeals) Order 2001, SI 2001/3649, art 37(1), (2), (4), as from 1 December 2001; sub-para (1)(a) substituted by FSA 1986, s 212(2), Sch 16, para 25, as from 29 April 1988, and words omitted repealed by SI 2001/3649, art 37(1), (3), as from 1 December 2001; in sub-para (b), words in first pair of square brackets inserted by the Charities Act 1992, s 78(1), Sch 6, para 11(b), as from 1 September 1992, and words in second pair of square brackets inserted by the Charities Act 1993, s 98(1), Sch 6, para 20(1), (3), as from 1 August 1993.

Charities Act 1960, ss 22, 22A: repealed by the Charities Act 1993, s 98(2), Sch 7, and replaced by ss 24, 25 of the 1993 Act.

Administration of Justice Act 1965, s 1: repealed by the Administration of Justice Act 1982, s 75, Sch 9, Pt I, and replaced by s 42 of the 1982 Act.

(Sch 13, Pts II–IV repealed by the Companies Act 2006, ss 1177, 1295, Sch 16, as from 6 April 2007.)

SCHEDULE 14
OVERSEAS BRANCH REGISTERS

Section 362

PART I
COUNTRIES AND TERRITORIES IN WHICH OVERSEAS BRANCH REGISTER MAY BE KEPT

Northern Ireland

Any part of Her Majesty's dominions outside the United Kingdom, the Channel Islands or the Isle of Man

Bangladesh

Cyprus

Dominica

The Gambia

Ghana

Guyana

[The Hong Kong Special Administrative Region of the People's Republic of China]

India

Kenya

Kiribati

Lesotho

Malawi

Malaysia

Malta

Nigeria

Pakistan

Republic of Ireland

Seychelles

Sierra Leone

Singapore

South Africa

Sri Lanka

Swaziland

Trinidad and Tobago

Uganda

Zimbabwe

[672]

NOTES

Repealed by the Companies Act 2006, s 1295, Sch 16, as from a day to be appointed.

Entry in square brackets inserted by the Companies Overseas Branch Registers (Hong Kong) Order 1997, SI 1997/1313, art 2, as from 1 July 1997.

PART II
GENERAL PROVISIONS WITH RESPECT TO OVERSEAS BRANCH REGISTERS

1.—(1) A company keeping an overseas branch register shall give to the registrar of companies notice in the prescribed form of the situation of the office where any overseas branch register is kept and of any change in its situation, and, if it is discontinued, of its discontinuance.

(2) Any such notice shall be given within 14 days of the opening of the office or of the change or discontinuance, as the case may be.

(3) If default is made in complying with this paragraph, the company and every officer of it who is in default is liable to a fine and, for continued contravention, to a daily default fine.

2.—(1) An overseas branch register is deemed to be part of the company's register of members ("the principal register").

(2) It shall be kept in the same manner in which the principal register is by this Act required to be kept, except that the advertisement before closing the register shall be inserted in a newspaper circulating in the district where the overseas branch register is kept.

3.—(1) A competent court in a country or territory where an overseas branch register is kept may exercise the same jurisdiction of rectifying the register as is under this Act exercisable by the court in Great Britain; and the offences of refusing inspection or copies of the register, and of authorising or permitting the refusal, may be prosecuted summarily before any tribunal having summary criminal jurisdiction.

(2) This paragraph extends only to those countries and territories where, immediately before the coming into force of this Act, provision to the same effect made by section 120(2) of the Companies Act 1948 had effect as part of the local law.

4.—(1) The company shall—

(a) transmit to its registered office a copy of every entry in its overseas branch register as soon as may be after the entry is made, and

(*b*) *cause to be kept at the place where the company's principal register is kept a duplicate of its overseas branch register duly entered up from time to time.*

Every such duplicate is deemed for all purposes of this Act to be part of the principal register.

(2) If default is made in complying with sub-paragraph (1), the company and every officer of it who is in default is liable to a fine and, for continued contravention, to a daily default fine.

(3) Where, by virtue of section 353(1)(b), the principal register is kept at the office of some person other than the company, and by reason of any default of his the company fails to comply with sub-paragraph (1)(b) above he is liable to the same penalty as if he were an officer of the company who was in default.

5. Subject to the above provisions with respect to the duplicate register, the shares registered in an overseas branch register shall be distinguished from those registered in the principal register; and no transaction with respect to any shares registered in an overseas branch register shall, during the continuance of that registration, be registered in any other register.

6. A company may discontinue to keep an overseas branch register, and thereupon all entries in that register shall be transferred to some other overseas branch register kept by the company in the same country or territory, or to the principal register.

7. Subject to the provisions of this Act, any company may, by its articles, make such provisions as it thinks fit respecting the keeping of overseas branch registers.

8. An instrument of transfer of a share registered in an overseas branch register (other than such a register kept in Northern Ireland) is deemed a transfer of property situated outside the United Kingdom and, unless executed in a part of the United Kingdom, is exempt from stamp duty chargeable in Great Britain.

[673]

NOTES

Repealed by the Companies Act 2006, s 1295, Sch 16, as from a day to be appointed.

Para 8: words "and, unless executed in a part of the United Kingdom, is exempt from stamp duty chargeable in Great Britain" repealed by FA 1990, s 132, Sch 19, Pt VI; for the effect of this repeal see the notes to Sch 19, Pt VI to the 1990 Act.

Companies Act 1948, s 120(2): repealed by the Companies Consolidation (Consequential Provisions) Act 1985, s 29, Sch 1.

Notice in the prescribed form: see Appendix 4 (Forms table) at **[A4]**.

PART III
PROVISIONS FOR BRANCH REGISTERS OF OVERSEA COMPANIES TO BE KEPT IN GREAT BRITAIN

9.—(1) If by virtue of the law in force in any country or territory to which this paragraph applies companies incorporated under that law have power to keep in Great Britain branch registers of their members resident in Great Britain, Her Majesty may by Order in Council direct that—

(*a*) *so much of section 353 as requires a company's register of members to be kept at its registered office,*

(*b*) *section 356 (register to be open to inspection by members), and*

(*c*) *section 359 (power of court to rectify),*

shall, subject to any modifications and adaptations specified in the Order, apply to and in relation to any such branch registers kept in Great Britain as they apply to and in relation to the registers of companies subject to those sections.

(2) The countries and territories to which this paragraph applies are—

(*a*) *all those specified in Part I of this Schedule, plus the Channel Islands and the Isle of Man,*

(*b*) *Botswana, Zambia and Tonga, and*

(*c*) *any territory for the time being under Her Majesty's protection or administered by the Government of the United Kingdom under the Trusteeship System of the United Nations.*

[674]

NOTES

Repealed by the Companies Act 2006, s 1295, Sch 16, as from a day to be appointed.

SCHEDULE 15
CONTENTS OF ANNUAL RETURN OF A COMPANY HAVING A SHARE CAPITAL

Section 363

1. The address of the registered office of the company.

2.—(1) If the register of members is, under the provisions of this Act, kept elsewhere than at the registered office of the company, the address of the place where it is kept.

(2) If any register of holders of debentures of the company or any duplicate of any such register or part of any such register is, under the provisions of this Act, kept, in England and Wales in the case of a company registered in England and Wales or in Scotland in the case of a company registered in Scotland, elsewhere than at the registered office of the company, the address of the place where it is kept.

3. A summary, distinguishing between shares issued for cash and shares issued as fully or partly paid up otherwise than in cash, specifying the following particulars—

(*a*) *the amount of the share capital of the company and the number of shares into which it is divided;*
(*b*) *the number of shares taken from the commencement of the company up to the date of the return;*
(*c*) *the amount called up on each share;*
(*d*) *the total amount of calls received;*
(*e*) *the total amount of calls unpaid;*
(*f*) *the total amount of the sums (if any) paid by way of commission in respect of any shares or debentures;*
(*g*) *the discount allowed on the issue of any shares issued at a discount or so much of that discount as has not been written off at the date on which the return is made;*
(*h*) *the total amount of the sums (if any) allowed by way of discount in respect of any debentures since the date of the last return;*
(*i*) *the total number of shares forfeited;*
(*j*) *the total number of shares for which share warrants are outstanding at the date of the return and of share warrants issued and surrendered respectively since the date of the last return, and the number of shares comprised in each warrant.*

4. Particulars of the total amount of the company's indebtedness in respect of all mortgages and charges (whenever created) of any description specified in section 396(1) or, in the case of a company registered in Scotland, section 410(4).

5. A list—

(*a*) *containing the names and addresses of all persons who, on the fourteenth day after the company's annual general meeting for the year, are members of the company, and of persons who have ceased to be members since the date of the last return or, in the case of the first return, since the incorporation of the company;*
(*b*) *stating the number of shares held by each of the existing members at the date of the return, specifying shares transferred since the date of the last return (or, in the case of the first return, since the incorporation of the company) by persons who are still members and have ceased to be members respectively and the dates of registration of the transfers;*
(*c*) *if the names are not arranged in alphabetical order, having annexed to it an index sufficient to enable the name of any person in the list to be easily found.*

6. All such particulars with respect to the persons who at the date of the return are the directors of the company and any person who at that date is the secretary of the company as are by this Act required to be contained with respect to directors and the secretary respectively in the register of the directors and secretaries of a company.

[675]

NOTES

Repealed by CA 1989, s 212, Sch 24 as from 7 January 1991; this Schedule still has limited effect in view of the transitional provisions and savings contained in the Companies Act 1989 (Commencement No 7 and Transitional and Saving Provisions) Order 1990, SI 1990/1707.

Repealed by the Companies Act 2006, s 1295, Sch 16, as from a day to be appointed.

[SCHEDULE 15A
WRITTEN RESOLUTIONS OF PRIVATE COMPANIES

Section 381A(7)

PART I
EXCEPTIONS

1. Section 381A does not apply to—

- (*a*) *a resolution under section 303 removing a director before the expiration of his period of office, or*
- (*b*) *a resolution under section 391 removing an auditor before the expiration of his term of office.*

[676]

NOTES

Inserted by CA 1989, s 114(1), as from 1 April 1990.

Repealed by the Companies Act 2006, s 1295, Sch 16, as from 1 October 2007. For savings see the note below.

Savings: this Schedule continues to apply to resolutions sent or circulated to any relevant member before 1 October 2007 (see the draft Companies Act 2006 (Commencement No 3, Consequential Amendments, Transitional Provisions and Savings) Order 2007, Sch 3, para 24 at **[A12]**).

PART II
ADAPTATION OF PROCEDURAL REQUIREMENTS

Introductory

2.—(1) In this Part of this Schedule (which adapts certain requirements of this Act in relation to proceedings under section 381A)—

- (*a*) *a "written resolution" means a resolution agreed to, or proposed to be agreed to, in accordance with that section, and*
- (*b*) *a "relevant member" means a member by whom, or on whose behalf, the resolution is required to be signed in accordance with that section.*

(2) A written resolution is not effective if any of the requirements of this Part of this Schedule is not complied with.

Section 95 (disapplication of pre-emption rights)

3.—(1) The following adaptations have effect in relation to a written resolution under section 95(2) (disapplication of pre-emption rights), or renewing a resolution under that provision.

(2) So much of section 95(5) as requires the circulation of a written statement by the directors with a notice of meeting does not apply, but such a statement must be supplied to each relevant member at or before the time at which the resolution is supplied to him for signature.

(3) Section 95(6) (offences) applies in relation to the inclusion in any such statement of matter which is misleading, false or deceptive in a material particular.

Section 155 (financial assistance for purchase of company's own shares or those of holding company)

4. In relation to a written resolution giving approval under section 155(4) or (5) (financial assistance for purchase of company's own shares or those of holding company), section 157(4)(a) (documents to be available at meeting) does not apply, but the documents referred to in that provision must be supplied to each relevant member at or before the time at which the resolution is supplied to him for signature.

Sections 164, 165 and 167 (authority for off-market purchase or contingent purchase contract of company's own shares)

5.—(1) The following adaptations have effect in relation to a written resolution—

(a) conferring authority to make an off-market purchase of the company's own shares under section 164(2),

(b) conferring authority to vary a contract for an off-market purchase of the company's own shares under section 164(7), or

(c) varying, revoking or renewing any such authority under section 164(3).

(2) Section 164(5) (resolution ineffective if passed by exercise of voting rights by member holding shares to which the resolution relates) does not apply; but for the purposes of section 381A(1) a member holding shares to which the resolution relates shall not be regarded as a member who would be entitled to attend and vote.

(3) Section 164(6) (documents to be available at company's registered office and at meeting) does not apply, but the documents referred to in that provision and, where that provision applies by virtue of section 164(7), the further documents referred to in that provision must be supplied to each relevant member at or before the time at which the resolution is supplied to him for signature.

(4) The above adaptations also have effect in relation to a written resolution in relation to which the provisions of section 164(3) to (7) apply by virtue of—

(a) section 165(2) (authority for contingent purchase contract), or

(b) section 167(2) (approval of release of rights under contract approved under section 164 or 165).

Section 173 (approval for payment out of capital)

6.—(1) The following adaptations have effect in relation to a written resolution giving approval under section 173(2) (redemption or purchase of company's own shares out of capital).

(2) Section 174(2) (resolution ineffective if passed by exercise of voting rights by member holding shares to which the resolution relates) does not apply; but for the purposes of section 381A(1) a member holding shares to which the resolution relates shall not be regarded as a member who would be entitled to attend and vote.

(3) Section 174(4) (documents to be available at meeting) does not apply, but the documents referred to in that provision must be supplied to each relevant member at or before the time at which the resolution is supplied to him for signature.

Section 319 (approval of director's service contract)

7. In relation to a written resolution approving any such term as is mentioned in section 319(1) (director's contract of employment for more than five years), section 319(5) (documents to be available at company's registered office and at meeting) does not apply, but the documents referred to in that provision must be supplied to each relevant member at or before the time at which the resolution is supplied to him for signature.

Section 337 (funding of director's expenditure in performing his duties)

8. In relation to a written resolution giving approval under section 337(3)(a) (funding a director's expenditure in performing his duties), the requirement of that provision that certain matters be disclosed at the meeting at which the resolution is passed does not apply, but those matters must be disclosed to each relevant member at or before the time at which the resolution is supplied to him for signature.]

[677]

NOTES

Inserted as noted to Pt I at **[676]**.

Repealed by the Companies Act 2006, s 1295, Sch 16, as from 1 October 2007. For savings see the note to Pt I of this Schedule at **[376]**.

[SCHEDULE [15B]
PROVISIONS SUBJECT TO WHICH SS 425–427 HAVE EFFECT IN THEIR APPLICATION TO MERGERS AND DIVISIONS OF PUBLIC COMPANIES

Section 427A

Meetings of transferee company

1. Subject to paragraphs 10(1), 12(4) and 14(2), the court shall not sanction a compromise or arrangement under section 425(2) unless a majority in number representing three-fourths in value of each class of members of every pre-existing transferee company concerned in the scheme, present and voting either in person or by proxy at a meeting, agree to the scheme.

Draft terms of merger

2.—(1) The court shall not sanction the compromise or arrangement under section 425(2) unless—

- *(a) a draft of the proposed terms of the scheme (from here on referred to as the "draft terms") has been drawn up and adopted by the directors of all the transferor and pre-existing transferee companies concerned in the scheme,*
- *(b) subject to paragraph 11(3), in the case of each of those companies the directors have delivered a copy of the draft terms to the registrar of companies and the registrar has published in the Gazette notice of receipt by him of a copy of the draft terms from that company, and*
- *(c) subject to paragraphs 10 to 14, that notice was so published at least one month before the date of any meeting of that company summoned under section 425(1) or for purposes of paragraph 1.*

(2) Subject to paragraph 12(2), the draft terms shall give particulars of at least the following matters—

- *(a) in respect of each transferor company and transferee company concerned in the scheme, its name, the address of its registered office and whether it is a company limited by shares or a company limited by guarantee and having a share capital;*
- *(b) the number of shares in any transferee company to be allotted to members of any transferor company for a given number of their shares (from here on referred to as the "share exchange ratio") and the amount of any cash payment;*
- *(c) the terms relating to the allotment of shares in any transferee company;*
- *(d) the date from which the holding of shares in a transferee company will entitle the holders to participate in profits, and any special conditions affecting that entitlement;*
- *(e) the date from which the transactions of any transferor company are to be treated for accounting purposes as being those of any transferee company;*
- *(f) any rights or restrictions attaching to shares or other securities in any transferee company to be allotted under the scheme to the holders of shares to which any special rights or restrictions attach, or of other securities, in any transferor company, or the measures proposed concerning them;*
- *(g) any amount of benefit paid or given or intended to be paid or given to any of the experts referred to in paragraph 5 or to any director of a transferor company or pre-existing transferee company, and the consideration for the payment of benefit.*

(3) Where the scheme is a Case 3 Scheme the draft terms shall also—

- *(a) give particulars of the property and liabilities to be transferred (to the extent these are known to the transferor company) and their allocation among the transferee companies;*

(*b*) *make provision for the allocation among and transfer to the transferee companies of any other property and liabilities which the transferor company has or may subsequently acquire; and*

(*c*) *specify the allocation to members of the transferor company of shares in the transferee companies and the criteria upon which that allocation is based.*

Documents and information to be made available

3. Subject to paragraphs 10 to 14, the court shall not sanction the compromise or arrangement under section 425(2) unless—

(*a*) *in the case of each transferor company and each pre-existing transferee company the directors have drawn up and adopted a report complying with paragraph 4 (from here on referred to as a "directors' report");*

(*b*) *where the scheme is a Case 3 Scheme, the directors of the transferor company have reported to every meeting of the members or any class of members of that company summoned under section 425(1), and to the directors of each transferee company, any material changes in the property and liabilities of the transferor company between the date when the draft terms were adopted and the date of the meeting in question;*

(*c*) *where the directors of a transferor company have reported to the directors of a transferee company such a change as is mentioned in sub-paragraph (b) above, the latter have reported that change to every meeting of the members or any class of members of that transferee company summoned for the purposes of paragraph 1, or have sent a report of that change to every member who would have been entitled to receive a notice of such a meeting;*

(*d*) *a report complying with paragraph 5 has been drawn up on behalf of each transferor company and pre-existing transferee company (from here on referred to as an "expert's report");*

(*e*) *the members of any transferor company or transferee company were able to inspect at the registered office of that company copies of the documents listed in paragraph 6(1) in relation to every transferor company and pre-existing transferee company concerned in the scheme during a period beginning one month before, and ending on, the date of the first meeting of the members or any class of members of the first-mentioned transferor or transferee company summoned either under section 425(1) or for the purposes of paragraph 1 and those members were able to obtain copies of those documents or any part of them on request during that period free of charge; and*

(*f*) *the memorandum and articles of association of any transferee company which is not a pre-existing transferee company, or a draft thereof, has been approved by ordinary resolution of every transferor company concerned in the scheme.*

Directors' report

4.—(1) The directors' report shall consist of—

(*a*) *the statement required by section 426, and*

(*b*) *insofar as that statement does not contain the following matters, a further statement—*

(*i*) *setting out the legal and economic grounds for the draft terms, and in particular for the share exchange ratio, and, where the scheme is a Case 3 Scheme, for the criteria upon which the allocation to the members of the transferor company of shares in the transferee companies was based, and*

(*ii*) *specifying any special valuation difficulties.*

(2) Where the scheme is a Case 3 Scheme the directors' report shall also state whether a report has been made to the transferee company under section 103 (non-cash consideration to be valued before allotment) and, if so, whether that report has been delivered to the registrar of companies.

Expert's report

5.—(1) Except where a joint expert is appointed under sub-paragraph (2) below, an expert's report shall consist of a separate written report on the draft terms to the members of one transferor company or pre-existing transferee company concerned in the scheme drawn up by a separate expert appointed on behalf of that company.

(2) *The court may, on the joint application of all the transferor companies and pre-existing transferee companies concerned in the scheme, approve the appointment of a joint expert to draw up a single report on behalf of all those companies.*

(3) *An expert shall be independent of any of the companies concerned in the scheme, that is to say a person qualified at the time of the report to be appointed, or to continue to be, an auditor of those companies.*

(4) *However, where it appears to an expert that a valuation is reasonably necessary to enable him to draw up the report, and it appears to him to be reasonable for that valuation, or part of it, to be made (or for him to accept such a valuation) by another person who—*

- (*a*) *appears to him to have the requisite knowledge and experience to make the valuation or that part of it; and*
- (*b*) *is not an officer or servant of any of the companies concerned in the scheme or any other body corporate which is one of those companies' subsidiary or holding company or a subsidiary of one of those companies' holding company or a partner or employee of such an officer or servant,*

he may arrange for or accept such a valuation, together with a report which will enable him to make his own report under this paragraph.

(5) *The reference in sub-paragraph* (4) *above to an officer or servant does not include an auditor.*

(6) *Where any valuation is made by a person other than the expert himself, the latter's report shall state that fact and shall also—*

- (*a*) *state the former's name and what knowledge and experience he has to carry out the valuation, and*
- (*b*) *describe so much of the undertaking, property and liabilities as were valued by the other person, and the method used to value them, and specify the date of the valuation.*

(7) *An expert's report shall—*

- (*a*) *indicate the method or methods used to arrive at the share exchange ratio proposed;*
- (*b*) *give an opinion as to whether the method or methods used are reasonable in all the circumstances of the case, indicate the values arrived at using each such method and* (*if there is more than one method*) *give an opinion on the relative importance attributed to such methods in arriving at the value decided on;*
- (*c*) *describe any special valuation difficulties which have arisen;*
- (*d*) *state whether in the expert's opinion the share exchange ratio is reasonable; and*
- (*e*) *in the case of a valuation made by a person other than himself, state that it appeared to himself reasonable to arrange for it to be so made or to accept a valuation so made.*

(8) *Each expert has the right of access to all such documents of all the transferor companies and pre-existing transferee companies concerned in the scheme, and the right to require from the companies' officers all such information, as he thinks necessary for the purpose of making his report.*

Inspection of documents

6.—(*1*) *The documents referred to in paragraph 3*(*e*) *are, in relation to any company—*

- (*a*) *the draft terms;*
- (*b*) *the directors' report [referred to in paragraph 4 above];*
- (*c*) *the expert's report;*
- [(*d*) *the company's annual accounts, together with the relevant directors' report and auditors' report, for the last three financial years ending on or before the relevant date; and*
- (*e*) *if the last of those financial years ended more than six months before the relevant date, an accounting statement in the form described in the following provisions.]*

[In paragraphs (*d*) *and* (*e*) *"the relevant date" means one month before the first meeting of the company summoned under section 425*(*1*) *or for the purposes of paragraph 1.]*

[(2) *The accounting statement shall consist of—*

(*a*) *a balance sheet dealing with the state of the affairs of the company as at a date not more than three months before the draft terms were adopted by the directors, and*

(*b*) *where the company would be required to prepare group accounts if that date were the last day of a financial year, a consolidated balance sheet dealing with the state of affairs of the company and its subsidiary undertakings as at that date.*

(*3*) *The requirements of this Act as to balance sheets forming part of a company's annual accounts, and the matters to be included in notes thereto, apply to any balance sheet required for the accounting statement, with such modifications as are necessary by reason of its being prepared otherwise than as at the last day of a financial year.*

(*4*) *Any balance sheet required for the accounting statement shall be approved by the board of directors and signed on behalf of the board by a director of the company.*

(*5*) *In relation to a company within the meaning of Article 3 of the Companies (Northern Ireland) Order 1986, the references in this paragraph to the requirements of this Act shall be construed as reference to the corresponding requirements of that Order.]*

Transferor company holding its own shares

7. The court shall not sanction under section 425(2) a compromise or arrangement under which any shares in a transferee company are to be allotted to a transferor company or its nominee in respect of shares in that transferor company held by it or its nominee.

8.—(1) Where any security of a transferor company to which special rights are attached is held by a person other than as a member or creditor of the company, the court shall not sanction a compromise or arrangement under section 425(2) unless under the scheme that person is to receive rights in a transferee company of equivalent value.

(2) *Sub-paragraph (1) above shall not apply in the case of any such security where—*

(*a*) *the holder has agreed otherwise; or*

(*b*) *the holder is, or under the scheme is to be, entitled to have the security purchased by a transferee company involved in the scheme on terms which the court considers reasonable.*

Date and consequences of the compromise or arrangement

9.—(1) The following provisions of this paragraph shall apply where the court sanctions a compromise or arrangement.

(*2*) *The court shall in the order sanctioning the compromise or arrangement or in a subsequent order under section 427 fix a date on which the transfer or transfers to the transferee company or transferee companies of the undertaking, property and liabilities of the transferor company shall take place; and any such order which provides for the dissolution of the transferor company shall fix the same date for the dissolution.*

(*3*) *If it is necessary for the transferor company to take any steps to ensure that the undertaking, property and liabilities are fully transferred, the court shall fix a date, not later than six months after the date fixed under sub-paragraph (2) above, by which such steps must be taken and for that purpose may postpone the dissolution of the transferor company until that date.*

(*4*) *The court may postpone or further postpone the date fixed under sub-paragraph (3) above if it is satisfied that the steps there mentioned cannot be completed by the date (or latest date) fixed under that sub-paragraph.*

Exceptions

10.—(1) The court may sanction a compromise or arrangement under section 425(2) notwithstanding that—

(*a*) *any meeting otherwise required by paragraph 1 has not been summoned by a pre-existing transferee company ("the relevant company"), and*

(*b*) *paragraphs 2(1)(c) and 3(e) have not been complied with in respect of that company, if the court is satisfied that the conditions specified in sub-paragraph* (2) *below have been complied with.*

(2) *Subject to paragraph 11*(3) *and 12*(3), *the conditions mentioned in sub-paragraph* (*1*) *above are—*

(*a*) *that the publication of notice of receipt of the draft terms by the registrar of companies referred to in paragraph 2*(*1*)(*b*) *took place in respect of the relevant company at least one month before the date of any meeting of members of any transferor company concerned in the scheme summoned under section 425*(*1*);

(*b*) *that the members of the relevant company were able to inspect at the registered office of that company the documents listed in paragraph 6*(*1*) *in relation to every transferor company and transferee company concerned in the scheme during a period* ("*the relevant period*") *beginning one month before, and ending on, the date of any such meeting, and that they were able to obtain copies of those documents or any part of them on request during that period free of charge; and*

(*c*) *that one or more members of the relevant company, who together held not less than five per cent of the paid-up capital of that company which carried the right to vote at general meetings of the company [(excluding any shares in the company held as treasury shares)], would have been able during the relevant period to require that a meeting of each class of members be called for the purpose of deciding whether or not to agree to the scheme but that no such requisition had been made.*

11.—(*1*) *The following sub-paragraphs apply where the scheme is a Case 3 Scheme.*

(2) *Sub-paragraphs* (*a*) *to* (*d*) *of paragraph 3 shall not apply and sub-paragraph* (*e*) *of that paragraph shall not apply as regards the documents listed in paragraph 6*(*1*)(*b*), (*c*) *and* (*e*), *if all members holding shares in, and all persons holding other securities of, any of the transferor companies and pre-existing transferee companies concerned in the scheme on the date of the application to the court under section 425*(*1*), *being shares or securities which as at that date carry the right to vote in general meetings of the company, so agree.*

(3) *The court may by order direct in respect of any transferor company or pre-existing transferee company that the requirements relating to—*

(*a*) *delivering copies of the draft terms and publication of notice of receipt of the draft terms under paragraph 2*(*1*)(*b*) *and* (*c*), *or*

(*b*) *inspection under paragraph 3*(*e*),

shall not apply, and may by order direct that paragraph 10 shall apply to any pre-existing transferee company with the omission of sub-paragraph (2)(*a*) *and* (*b*) *of that paragraph.*

(4) *The court shall not make any order under paragraph* (3) *above unless it is satisfied that the following conditions will be fulfilled—*

(*a*) *that the members of the company will have received or will have been able to obtain free of charge copies of the documents listed in paragraph 6*(*1*) *in time to examine them before the date of the first meeting of the members or any class of members of the company summoned under section 425*(*1*) *or for the purposes of paragraph 1;*

(*b*) *in the case of a pre-existing transferee company, where in the circumstances described in paragraph 10 no meeting is held, that the members of that company will have received or will have been able to obtain free of charge copies of those documents in time to require a meeting under paragraph 10*(*2*)(*c*);

(*c*) *that the creditors of the company will have received or will have been able to obtain free of charge copies of the draft terms in time to examine them before the date of the meeting of the members or any class of members of the company, or, in the circumstances referred to in paragraph* (*b*) *above, at the same time as the members of the company; and*

(*d*) *that no prejudice would be caused to the members or creditors of any transferor company or transferee company concerned in the scheme by making the order in question.*

Transferee company or companies holding shares in the transferor company

12.—(*1*) *Where the scheme is a Case 1 Scheme and in the case of every transferor company concerned—*

(*a*) *the shares in that company, and*

(*b*) *such securities of that company* (*other than shares*) *as carry the right to vote at general meetings of that company,*

are all held by or on behalf of the transferee company, section 427A and this Schedule shall apply subject to the following sub-paragraphs.

(2) *The draft terms need not give particulars of the matters mentioned in paragraph 2*(2)(*b*), (*c*) *or* (*d*).

(3) *Section 426 and sub-paragraphs* (*a*) *and* (*d*) *of paragraph 3 shall not apply, and sub-paragraph* (*e*) *of that paragraph shall not apply as regards the documents listed in paragraph 6*(*1*)(*b*) *and* (*c*).

(4) *The court may sanction the compromise or arrangement under section 425*(2) *notwithstanding that—*

(*a*) *any meeting otherwise required by section 425 or paragraph 1 has not been summoned by any company concerned in the scheme, and*
(*b*) *paragraphs 2*(*1*)(*c*) *and 3*(*e*) *have not been complied with in respect of that company,*

if it is satisfied that the conditions specified in the following sub-paragraphs have been complied with.

(5) *The conditions mentioned in the previous sub-paragraph are—*

(*a*) *that the publication of notice of receipt of the draft items by the registrar of companies referred to in paragraph 2*(*1*)(*b*) *took place in respect of every transferor company and transferee company concerned in the scheme at least one month before the date of the order under section 425*(2) (*"the relevant date"*);
(*b*) *that the members of the transferee company were able to inspect at the registered office of that company copies of the documents listed in paragraphs 6*(*1*)(*a*), (*d*) *and* (*e*) *in relation to every transferor company or transferee company concerned in the scheme during a period* (*"the relevant period"*) *beginning one month before, and ending on, the relevant date and that they were able to obtain copies of those documents or any part of them on request during that period free of charge; and*
(*c*) *that one or more members of the transferee company who together held not less than five per cent of the paid-up capital of the company which carried the right to vote at general meetings of the company [*(*excluding any shares in the company held as treasury shares*)*] would have been able during the relevant period to require that a meeting of each class of members be called for the purpose of deciding whether or not to agree to the scheme but that no such requisition has been made.*

13.—(*1*) *Where the scheme is a Case 3 Scheme and—*

(*a*) *the shares in the transferor company, and*
(*b*) *such securities of that company* (*other than shares*) *as carry the right to vote at general meetings of that company,*

are all held by or on behalf of one or more transferee companies, section 427A and this Schedule shall apply subject to the following sub-paragraphs.

(2) *The court may sanction a compromise or arrangement under section 425*(2) *notwithstanding that—*

(*a*) *any meeting otherwise required by section 425 has not been summoned by the transferor company, and*
(*b*) *paragraphs 2*(*1*)(*c*) *and 3*(*b*) *and* (*e*) *have not been complied with in respect of that company,*

if it is satisfied that the conditions specified in the following sub-paragraph have been complied with.

(3) *The conditions referred to in the previous sub-paragraph are—*

(*a*) *the conditions set out in paragraph 12*(*5*)(*a*) *and* (*c*);
(*b*) *that the members of the transferor company and every transferee company concerned in the scheme were able to inspect at the registered office of the company of which they were members copies of the documents listed in paragraph 6*(*1*) *in relation to every such company during a period beginning one month before, and ending on, the date of the order under section 425*(2) (*"the relevant date"*), *and that they were able to obtain copies of those documents or any part of them on request during that period free of charge; and*
(*c*) *that the directors of the transferor company have sent to every member who would have been entitled to receive a notice of the meeting* (*had it been called*), *and to*

the directors of each transferee company, a report of any material changes in the property and liabilities of the transferor company between the date when the draft terms were adopted and a date one month before the relevant date.

14.—(1) When the scheme is a Case 1 Scheme and in the case of every transferor company concerned ninety per cent or more (but not all) of—

(*a*) *the shares in that company, and*

(*b*) *such securities of that company (other than shares) as carry the right to vote at general meetings of that company,*

are held by or on behalf of the transferee company, section 427A and this Schedule shall apply subject to the following sub-paragraphs.

(2) The court may sanction a compromise or arrangement under section 425(2) notwithstanding that—

(*a*) *any meeting otherwise required by paragraph 1 has not been summoned by the transferee company, and*

(*b*) *paragraph 2(1)(c) and 3(e) have not been complied with in respect of that company,*

if the court is satisfied that the conditions specified in the following sub-paragraph have been complied with.

(3) The conditions referred to in the previous sub-paragraph are the same conditions as those specified in paragraph 10(2), save that for this purpose the condition contained in paragraph 10(2)(b) shall be treated as referring only to the documents listed in paragraph 6(1)(a), (d) and (e).

Liability of transferee companies for the default of another

15.—(1) Where the scheme is a Case 3 Scheme, each transferee company shall be jointly and severally liable, subject to sub-paragraph (2) below, for any liability transferred to any other transferee company under the scheme to the extent that that other company has made default in satisfying that liability, but so that no transferee company shall be so liable for an amount greater than the amount arrived at by calculating the value at the time of the transfer of the property transferred to it under the scheme less the amount at that date of the liabilities so transferred.

(2) If a majority in number representing three-fourths in value of the creditors or any class of creditors of the transferor company present and voting either in person or by proxy at a meeting summoned under section 425(1) so agree, sub-paragraph (1) above shall not apply in respect of the liabilities of the creditors or that class of creditors.]

[678]

NOTES

Inserted (as Sch 15A) by the Companies (Mergers and Divisions) Regulations 1987, SI 1987/1991, reg 2(c), Schedule, Pt II, as from 1 January 1988, and renumbered by CA 1989, s 114(2), as from 1 April 1990.

Repealed by the Companies Act 2006, s 1295, Sch 16, as from a day to be appointed.

Para 6: words in square brackets in sub-para (1)(b) inserted, sub-paras (1)(d), (e), (2)–(5) substituted, and words in square brackets at end of sub-para (1) added, by CA 1989, s 23, Sch 10, Pt I, para 22, as from 1 April 1990.

Paras 10, 12: words in square brackets inserted by the Companies (Acquisition of Own Shares) (Treasury Shares) Regulations 2003, SI 2003/1116, reg 4, Schedule, para 32, as from 1 December 2003.

[SCHEDULE 15C
SPECIFIED PERSONS

Section 449

1. The Secretary of State.

2. The Department of Enterprise, Trade and Investment for Northern Ireland.

3. The Treasury.

4. The Lord Advocate.

5. The Director of Public Prosecutions.

6. The Director of Public Prosecutions for Northern Ireland.

7. The Financial Services Authority.

8. A constable.

9. A procurator fiscal.

10. The Scottish Ministers.]

[678A]

NOTES

Inserted, together with Sch 15D, by the Companies (Audit, Investigations and Community Enterprise) Act 2004, s 25, Sch 2, Pt 3, paras 16, 25, as from 6 April 2005 (for transitional provisions, see the Companies (Audit, Investigations and Community Enterprise) Act 2004 (Commencement) and Companies Act 1989 (Commencement No 18) Order 2004, SI 2004/3322, art 10 at **[7348]**).

Application to limited liability partnerships: see the draft Limited Liability Partnerships (Amendment) Regulations 2007 in Appendix 10 at **[A10]**. Those draft Regulations amend the Limited Liability Partnerships Regulations 2001, SI 2001/1090, Sch 2, Pt 1 at **[6993]** by adding an entry for this Schedule into that Schedule.

[SCHEDULE 15D
DISCLOSURES

Section 449

1. A disclosure for the purpose of enabling or assisting a person authorised under section 245C to exercise his functions.

2. A disclosure for the purpose of enabling or assisting an inspector appointed under Part 14 to exercise his functions.

3. A disclosure for the purpose of enabling or assisting a person authorised under section 447 of this Act or section 84 of the Companies Act 1989 to exercise his functions.

4. A disclosure for the purpose of enabling or assisting a person appointed under section 167 of the Financial Services and Markets Act 2000 (general investigations) to conduct an investigation to exercise his functions.

5. A disclosure for the purpose of enabling or assisting a person appointed under section 168 of the Financial Services and Markets Act 2000 (investigations in particular cases) to conduct an investigation to exercise his functions.

6. A disclosure for the purpose of enabling or assisting a person appointed under section 169(1)(b) of the Financial Services and Markets Act 2000 (investigation in support of overseas regulator) to conduct an investigation to exercise his functions.

7. A disclosure for the purpose of enabling or assisting a person appointed under section 284 of the Financial Services and Markets Act 2000 (investigations into affairs of certain collective investment schemes) to conduct an investigation to exercise his functions.

8. A disclosure for the purpose of enabling or assisting a person appointed under regulations made under sections 262(1) and (2)(k) of the Financial Services and Markets Act 2000 (investigations into open-ended investment companies) to conduct an investigation to exercise his functions.

9. A disclosure for the purpose of enabling or assisting the Secretary of State or the Treasury to exercise any of their functions under any of the following—

(a) this Act;
(b) the insider dealing legislation;
(c) the Insolvency Act 1986;
(d) the Company Directors Disqualification Act 1986;
(e) Part 2, 3 or 7 of the Companies Act 1989;

(f) the Financial Services and Markets Act 2000.

10. A disclosure for the purpose of enabling or assisting the Scottish Ministers to exercise their functions under the enactments relating to insolvency.

11. A disclosure for the purpose of enabling or assisting the Department of Enterprise, Trade and Investment for Northern Ireland to exercise any powers conferred on it by the enactments relating to companies or insolvency.

12. A disclosure for the purpose of enabling or assisting a person appointed or authorised by the Department of Enterprise, Trade and Investment for Northern Ireland under the enactments relating to companies or insolvency to exercise his functions.

[13. A disclosure for the purpose of enabling or assisting the Pensions Regulator to exercise the functions conferred on it by or by virtue of any of the following—

(a) the Pension Schemes Act 1993;
(b) the Pensions Act 1995;
(c) the Welfare Reform and Pensions Act 1999;
(d) the Pensions Act 2004;
(e) any enactment in force in Northern Ireland corresponding to any of those enactments.]

[13A. A disclosure for the purpose of enabling or assisting the Board of the Pension Protection Fund to exercise the functions conferred on it by or by virtue of Part 2 of the Pensions Act 2004 or any enactment in force in Northern Ireland corresponding to that Part.]

14. A disclosure for the purpose of enabling or assisting the Bank of England to exercise its functions.

15. A disclosure for the purpose of enabling or assisting the body known as the Panel on Takeovers and Mergers to exercise its functions.

16. A disclosure for the purpose of enabling or assisting organs of the Society of Lloyd's (being organs constituted by or under the Lloyd's Act 1982) to exercise their functions under or by virtue of the Lloyd's Acts 1871 to 1982.

17. A disclosure for the purpose of enabling or assisting the Office of Fair Trading to exercise its functions under any of the following—

(a) the Fair Trading Act 1973;
(b) the Consumer Credit Act 1974;
(c) the Estate Agents Act 1979;
(d) the Competition Act 1980;
(e) the Competition Act 1998;
(f) the Financial Services and Markets Act 2000;
(g) the Enterprise Act 2002;
(h) the Control of Misleading Advertisements Regulations 1988 (SI 1988/915);
(i) the Unfair Terms in Consumer Contracts Regulations 1999 (SI 1999/2083).

18. A disclosure for the purpose of enabling or assisting the Competition Commission to exercise its functions under any of the following—

(a) the Fair Trading Act 1973;
(b) the Competition Act 1980;
(c) the Competition Act 1998;
(d) the Enterprise Act 2002.

19. A disclosure with a view to the institution of, or otherwise for the purposes of, proceedings before the Competition Appeal Tribunal.

20. A disclosure for the purpose of enabling or assisting an enforcer under Part 8 of the Enterprise Act 2002 to exercise its functions under that Part.

21. A disclosure for the purpose of enabling or assisting the [Charity Commission to exercise its] functions.

22. A disclosure for the purpose of enabling or assisting the Attorney General to exercise his functions in connection with charities.

23. A disclosure for the purpose of enabling or assisting the National Lottery Commission to exercise its functions under sections 5 to 10 and 15 of the National Lottery etc Act 1993.

24. A disclosure by the National Lottery Commission to the National Audit Office for the purpose of enabling or assisting the Comptroller and Auditor General to carry out an examination under Part 2 of the National Audit Act 1983 into the economy, effectiveness and efficiency with which the National Lottery Commission has used its resources in discharging its functions under sections 5 to 10 of the National Lottery etc Act 1993.

25. A disclosure for the purpose of enabling or assisting a qualifying body under the Unfair Terms in Consumer Contracts Regulations 1999 (SI 1999/2083) to exercise its functions under those Regulations.

26. A disclosure for the purpose of enabling or assisting an enforcement authority under the Consumer Protection (Distance Selling) Regulations 2000 (SI 2000/2334) to exercise its functions under those Regulations.

27. A disclosure for the purpose of enabling or assisting a local weights and measures authority in England and Wales to exercise its functions under section 230(2) of the Enterprise Act 2002.

28. A disclosure for the purpose of enabling or assisting the Financial Services Authority to exercise its functions under any of the following—

(a) the legislation relating to friendly societies or to industrial and provident societies;
(b) the Building Societies Act 1986;
(c) Part 7 of the Companies Act 1989;
(d) the Financial Services and Markets Act 2000.

29. A disclosure for the purpose of enabling or assisting the competent authority for the purposes of Part 6 of the Financial Services and Markets Act 2000 to exercise its functions under that Part.

30. A disclosure for the purpose of enabling or assisting a body corporate established in accordance with section 212(1) of the Financial Services and Markets Act 2000 (compensation scheme manager) to exercise its functions.

31.—(1) A disclosure for the purpose of enabling or assisting a recognised investment exchange or a recognised clearing house to exercise its functions as such.

(2) Recognised investment exchange and recognised clearing house have the same meaning as in section 285 of the Financial Services and Markets Act 2000.

32. A disclosure for the purpose of enabling or assisting a body designated under section 326(1) of the Financial Services and Markets Act 2000 (designated professional bodies) to exercise its functions in its capacity as a body designated under that section.

33. A disclosure with a view to the institution of, or otherwise for the purposes of, civil proceedings arising under or by virtue of the Financial Services and Markets Act 2000.

34. A disclosure for the purpose of enabling or assisting a body designated by order under section 46 of the Companies Act 1989 (delegation of functions of Secretary of State) to exercise its functions under Part 2 of that Act.

35. A disclosure for the purpose of enabling or assisting a recognised supervisory or qualifying body (within the meaning of Part 2 of the Companies Act 1989) to exercise its functions as such.

36. A disclosure for the purpose of enabling or assisting an official receiver (including the Accountant in Bankruptcy in Scotland and the Official Assignee in Northern Ireland) to exercise his functions under the enactments relating to insolvency.

37. A disclosure for the purpose of enabling or assisting the Insolvency Practitioners Tribunal to exercise its functions under the Insolvency Act 1986.

38. A disclosure for the purpose of enabling or assisting a body which is for the time being a recognised professional body for the purposes of section 391 of the Insolvency Act 1986 (recognised professional bodies) to exercise its functions as such.

39.—(1) A disclosure for the purpose of enabling or assisting an overseas regulatory authority to exercise its regulatory functions.

(2) Overseas regulatory authority and regulatory functions have the same meaning as in section 82 of the Companies Act 1989.

40. A disclosure for the purpose of enabling or assisting the Regulator of Community Interest Companies to exercise functions under the Companies (Audit, Investigations and Community Enterprise) Act 2004.

41. A disclosure with a view to the institution of, or otherwise for the purposes of, criminal proceedings.

42. A disclosure with a view to the institution of, or otherwise for the purposes of, proceedings on an application under section 6, 7 or 8 of the Company Directors Disqualification Act 1986.

43. A disclosure with a view to the institution of, or otherwise for the purposes of, proceedings before the Financial Services and Markets Tribunal.

44. A disclosure for the purposes of proceedings before the Financial Services Tribunal by virtue of the Financial Services and Markets Act 2000 (Transitional Provisions) (Partly Completed Procedures) Order 2001 (SI 2001/3592).

[44A. A disclosure for the purposes of proceedings before the Pensions Regulator Tribunal.]

45. A disclosure for the purpose of enabling or assisting a body appointed under section 14 of the Companies (Audit, Investigations and Community Enterprise) Act 2004 (supervision of periodic accounts and reports of issuers of listed securities) to exercise functions mentioned in subsection (2) of that section.

46. A disclosure with a view to the institution of, or otherwise for the purposes of, disciplinary proceedings relating to the performance by a solicitor, barrister, auditor, accountant, valuer or actuary of his professional duties.

47.—(1) A disclosure with a view to the institution of, or otherwise for the purposes of, disciplinary proceedings relating to the performance by a public servant of his duties.

(2) Public servant means an officer or employee of the Crown or of any public or other authority for the time being designated for the purposes of this paragraph by the Secretary of State by order.

(3) An order under sub-paragraph (2) must be made by statutory instrument subject to annulment in pursuance of a resolution of either House of Parliament.

48. A disclosure for the purpose of the provision of a summary or collection of information framed in such a way as not to enable the identity of any person to whom the information relates to be ascertained.

49. A disclosure in pursuance of any Community obligation.

[50. A disclosure for the purpose of enabling or assisting the Gambling Commission to exercise its functions under the Gambling Act 2005.]]

[678B]

NOTES

Inserted as noted to Sch 15C at **[678A]**.

Para 13: substituted by the Pensions Act 2004, s 319, Sch 12, para 5(1), (3)(a), as from 6 April 2005.

Paras 13A, 44A: inserted by the Pensions Act 2004, ss 102, 319, Sch 4, Pt 4, para 19, Sch 12, para 5(1), (3)(b), as from 6 April 2005.

Para 21: words in square brackets substituted by the Charities Act 2006, s 75, Sch 8, paras 74, 76, as from 27 February 2007.

Para 50: added by the Companies (Disclosure of Information) (Designated Authorities) Order 2006, SI 2006/1644, art 2, as from 1 October 2006.

Application to limited liability partnerships: see the draft Limited Liability Partnerships (Amendment) Regulations 2007 in Appendix 10 at **[A10]**. Those draft Regulations amend the Limited Liability Partnerships Regulations 2001, SI 2001/1090, Sch 2, Pt 1 at **[6993]** by adding an entry for this Schedule into that Schedule.

Charity Commissioners: as to the abolition of the office of Charity Commissioner for England and Wales, the establishment of the Charity Commission for England and Wales, and the transfer of the functions, rights, liabilities, etc from the Charity Commissioners for England and Wales to the Charity Commission, see the Charities Act 2006, s 6.

(Sch 16 repealed by the Insolvency Act 1986, s 438, Sch 12, as from 29 December 1986; Schs 17–19 repealed by the Insolvency Act 1985, s 235(3), Sch 10, Pt II, as from 29 December 1986.)

SCHEDULE 20
VESTING OF DISCLAIMED PROPERTY; PROTECTION OF THIRD PARTIES

Section 619

(Pt I repealed by the Insolvency Act 1985, s 235(3), Sch 10, Pt II.)

PART II
CROWN DISCLAIMER UNDER SECTION 656 (SCOTLAND ONLY)

5. The court shall not under section 657 make a vesting order, where the property disclaimed is held under a lease, in favour of a person claiming under the company (whether as sub-lessee or as creditor in a duly registered or, as appropriate, recorded heritable security over a lease), except on the following terms.

6. The person must by the order be made subject—

- *(a) to the same liabilities and obligations as those to which the company was subject under the lease in respect of the property at the commencement of the winding up, or*
- *(b) (if the court thinks fit) only to the same liabilities and obligations as if the lease had been assigned to him at that date;*

and in either event (if the case so requires) the liabilities and obligations must be as if the lease had comprised only the property comprised in the vesting order.

7. A creditor or sub-lessee declining to accept a vesting order on such terms is excluded from all interest in and security over the property.

8. If there is no person claiming under the company who is willing to accept an order on such terms, the court has power to vest the company's estate and interest in the property in any person liable (either personally or in a representative character, and either alone or jointly with the company) to perform the lessee's obligations under the lease, freed and discharged from all interests, rights and obligations created by the company in the lease or in relation to the lease.

9. For the purposes of paragraph 5 above, a heritable security is duly recorded if it is recorded in the Register of Sasines and is duly registered if registered in accordance with the Land Registration (Scotland) Act 1979.

[679]

NOTES

Repealed by the Companies Act 2006, s 1295, Sch 16, as from a day to be appointed.

SCHEDULE 21
EFFECT OF REGISTRATION UNDER SECTION 680

Section 689

Interpretation

1. In this Schedule—

"registration" means registration in pursuance of section 680 in Chapter II of Part XXII of this Act, and "registered" has the corresponding meaning, and

"instrument" includes deed of settlement, contract of copartnery and letters patent.

Vesting of property

2. All property belonging to or vested in the company at the date of its registration passes to and vests in the company on registration for all the estate and interest of the company in the property.

Existing liabilities

3. Registration does not affect the company's rights or liabilities in respect of any debt or obligation incurred, or contract entered into, by, to, with or on behalf of the company before registration.

Pending actions at law

4.—(1) All actions and other legal proceedings which at the time of the company's registration are pending by or against the company, or the public officer or any member of it, may be continued in the same manner as if the registration had not taken place.

(2) However, execution shall not issue against the effects of any individual member of the company on any judgment, decree or order obtained in such an action or proceeding; but in the event of the company's property and effects being insufficient to satisfy the judgment, decree or order, an order may be obtained for winding up the company.

The company's constitution

5.—(1) All provisions contained in any Act of Parliament or other instrument constituting or regulating the company are deemed to be conditions and regulations of the company, in the same manner and with the same incidents as if so much of them as would, if the company had been formed under this Act, have been required to be inserted in the memorandum, were contained in a registered memorandum, and the residue were contained in registered articles.

(2) The provisions brought in under this paragraph include, in the case of a company registered as a company limited by guarantee, those of the resolution declaring the amount of the guarantee; and they include also the statement under section 681(5)(a), and any statement under section 684(2).

6.—(1) All the provisions of this Act apply to the company, and to its members, contributories and creditors, in the same manner in all respects as if it had been formed under this Act, subject as follows.

(2) Table A does not apply unless adopted by special resolution.

(3) Provisions relating to the numbering of shares do not apply to any joint stock company whose shares are not numbered.

(4) Subject to the provisions of this Schedule, the company does not have power—

(a) to alter any provision contained in an Act of Parliament relating to the company,

(b) without the sanction of the Secretary of State, to alter any provision contained in letters patent relating to the company.

(5) The company does not have power to alter any provision contained in a royal charter or letters patent with respect to the company's objects.

[(6) When by virtue of sub-paragraph (4) or (5) a company does not have power to alter a provision, it does not have power to ratify acts of the directors in contravention of the provision.]

Capital structure

7. Provisions of this Act with respect to—

- *(a) the registration of an unlimited company as limited,*
- *(b) the powers of an unlimited company on registration as a limited company to increase the nominal amount of its share capital and to provide that a portion of its share capital shall not be capable of being called up except in the event of winding up, and*
- *(c) the power of a limited company to determine that a portion of its share capital shall not be capable of being called up except in that event,*

apply, notwithstanding any provisions contained in an Act of Parliament, royal charter or other instrument constituting or regulating the company.

Supplementary

8. Nothing in paragraphs 5 to 7 authorises a company to alter any such provisions contained in an instrument constituting or regulating the company as would, if the company had originally been formed under this Act, have been required to be contained in the memorandum and are not authorised to be altered by this Act.

9. None of the provisions of this Act (except section 461(3)) derogate from any power of altering the company's constitution or regulations which may, by virtue of any Act of Parliament or other instrument constituting or regulating it, be vested in the company.

[680]

NOTES

Repealed by the Companies Act 2006, s 1295, Sch 16, as from a day to be appointed.

Para 6: sub-para (6) added by CA 1989, s 108(2), as from 4 February 1991.

Para 9: for the words "None of the provisions of this Act (except section 461(3)" there are substituted the words "None of the provisions of this Act, and none of the provisions of the Companies Act 2006 (except section 996(2)),", by the draft Companies Act 2006 (Commencement No 3, Consequential Amendments, Transitional Provisions and Savings) Order 2007, art 10(1), Sch 4, Pt 1, para 10, as from 1 October 2007 (see **[A12]**).

[SCHEDULE 21A
BRANCH REGISTRATION UNDER THE ELEVENTH COMPANY LAW DIRECTIVE (89/666/EEC)

Section 690A

Duty to register

1.—(1) A company shall, within one month of having opened a branch in a part of Great Britain, deliver to the registrar for registration a return in the prescribed form containing—

- *(a) such particulars about the company as are specified in paragraph 2,*
- *(b) such particulars about the branch as are specified in paragraph 3, and*
- *(c) if the company is one to which section 699AA applies, such particulars in relation to the registration of documents under Schedule 21D as are specified in paragraph 4.*

(2) The return shall, except where sub-paragraph (3) below applies, be accompanied by the documents specified in paragraph 5 and, if the company is one to which Part I of Schedule 21D applies, the documents specified in paragraph 6.

(3) This sub-paragraph applies where—

- *(a) at the time the return is delivered, the company has another branch in the United Kingdom,*
- *(b) the return contains a statement to the effect that the documents specified in*

paragraph 5, and, if the company is one to which Part I of Schedule 21D applies, paragraph 6, are included in the material registered in respect of the other branch, and

(*c*) *the return states where the other branch is registered and what is its registered number.*

(*4*) *In sub-paragraph (1) above, the reference to having opened a branch in a part of Great Britain includes a reference to a branch having become situated there on ceasing to be situated elsewhere.*

(*5*) *If at the date on which the company opens the branch in Great Britain the company is subject to any proceedings referred to in section 703P(1) (winding up) or 703Q(1) (insolvency proceedings etc), the company shall deliver a return under section 703P(1) or (as the case may be) 703Q(1) within one month of that date.*

If on or before that date a person has been appointed to be liquidator of the company and continues in that office at that date, section 703P(3) and (4) (liquidator to make return within 14 days of appointment) shall have effect as if it required a return to be made under that section within one month of the date of the branch being opened.

Particulars required

2.—(1) The particulars referred to in paragraph 1(1)(a) are —

(*a*) *the corporate name of the company,*

(*b*) *its legal form,*

(*c*) *if it is registered in the country of its incorporation, the identity of the register in which it is registered and the number with which it is so registered,*

(*d*) *a list of its directors and secretary, containing [(subject to paragraph 4A)]—*

  (*i*) *with respect to each director, the particulars specified in sub-paragraph (3) below, and*

  (*ii*) *with respect to the secretary (or where there are joint secretaries, with respect to each of them) the particulars specified in sub-paragraph (4) below,*

(*e*) *the extent of the powers of the directors to represent the company in dealings with third parties and in legal proceedings, together with a statement as to whether they may act alone or must act jointly and, if jointly, the name of any other person concerned, and*

(*f*) *whether the company is an institution to which section 699A (or the equivalent provision in Northern Ireland) applies.*

(*2*) *In the case of a company which is not incorporated in a Member State, those particulars also include—*

(*a*) *the law under which the company is incorporated,*

(*b*) *(in the case of a company to which either paragraphs 2 and 3 of Part I of Schedule 21C or Schedule 21D applies) the period for which the company is required by the law under which it is incorporated to prepare accounts, together with the period allowed for the preparation and public disclosure of accounts for such a period, and*

(*c*) *unless disclosed by the documents specified in paragraph 5—*

  (*i*) *the address of its principal place of business in its country of incorporation,*

  (*ii*) *its objects, and*

  (*iii*) *the amount of its issued share capital.*

(*3*) *The particulars referred to in sub-paragraph (1)(d)(i) above are—*

(*a*) *in the case of an individual—*

  (*i*) *his name,*

  (*ii*) *any former name,*

  (*iii*) *his usual residential address,*

  (*iv*) *his nationality,*

  (*v*) *his business occupation (if any),*

  (*vi*) *particulars of any other directorships held by him, and*

  (*vii*) *his date of birth;*

(*b*) *in the case of a corporation or Scottish firm, its corporate or firm name and registered or principal office.*

(*4*) *The particulars referred to in sub-paragraph (1)(d)(ii) above are—*

(*a*) *in the case of an individual, his name, any former name and his usual residential address;*

(*b*) *in the case of a corporation or Scottish firm, its corporate or firm name and registered or principal office.*

Where all the partners in a firm are joint secretaries of the company, the name and principal office of the firm may be stated instead of the particulars required by paragraph (a) above.

(5) In sub-paragraphs (3)(a) and (4)(a) above—

(*a*) *"name" means a person's forename and surname, except that in the case of a peer, or an individual usually known by a title, the title may be stated instead of his forename and surname, or in addition to either or both of them; and*

(*b*) *the reference to a former name does not include—*

(i) in the case of a peer, or an individual normally known by a title, the name by which he was known previous to the adoption of or succession to the title;

(ii) in the case of any person, a former name which was changed or disused before he attained the age of 18 years or which has been changed or disused for 20 years or more;

(iii) in the case of a married woman, the name by which she was known previous to the marriage.

(6) Where—

(*a*) *at the time a return is delivered under paragraph 1(1) the company has another branch in the same part of Great Britain as the branch covered by the return; and*

(*b*) *the company has delivered the particulars required by sub-paragraphs (1)(b) to (f) and (2) to (5) to the registrar with respect to that branch (or to the extent it is required to do so by virtue of Schedule 21B to this Act) and has no outstanding obligation to make a return to the registrar in respect of that branch under paragraph 7 in relation to any alteration to those particulars,*

the company may adopt the particulars so delivered as particulars which the registrar is to treat as having been filed by the return by referring in the return to the fact that the particulars have been filed in respect of that other branch and giving the number with which the other branch is registered.

3. The particulars referred to in paragraph 1(1)(b) are—

(*a*) *the address of the branch,*

(*b*) *the date on which it was opened,*

(*c*) *the business carried on at it,*

(*d*) *if different from the name of the company, the name in which that business is carried on,*

(*e*) *a list of the names and addresses of all persons resident in Great Britain authorised to accept on the company's behalf service of process in respect of the business of the branch and of any notices required to be served on the company in respect of the business of the branch,*

(*f*) *a list of the names and [(subject to paragraph 4A)] usual residential addresses of all persons authorised to represent the company as permanent representatives of the company for the business of the branch,*

(*g*) *the extent of the authority of any person falling within paragraph (f) above, including whether that person is authorised to act alone or jointly, and*

(*h*) *if a person falling within paragraph (f) above is not authorised to act alone, the name of any person with whom he is authorised to act.*

4. The particulars referred to in paragraph 1(1)(c) are—

(*a*) *whether it is intended to register documents under paragraph 2(2) or, as the case may be, 10(1) of Schedule 21D in respect of the branch or in respect of some other branch in the United Kingdom, and*

(*b*) *if it is, where that other branch is registered and what is its registered number.*

[4A. Where a confidentiality order made under section 723B is in force in respect of a director or secretary required to be specified in the list under paragraph 2(1)(d) or a permanent representative required to be specified in the list under paragraph 3(f)—

(*a*) *if the order is in respect of a director, paragraph 2(1)(d) has effect in respect of that director as if the reference in paragraph 2(3)(a)(iii) to his usual residential address were a reference to the address for the time being notified by him to the company under regulations made under sections 723B to 723F;*

(*b*) *if the order is in respect of a secretary, paragraph 2(1)(d) has effect in respect of that secretary as if the reference in paragraph 2(4)(a) to his usual residential address were a reference to the address for the time being notified by him to the company under such regulations;*

(c) *if the order is in respect of a permanent representative, paragraph 3(f) has effect in respect of that representative as if the reference to his usual residential address were a reference to the address for the time being notified by him to the company under such regulations; and*

(d) *in any case the company shall deliver to the registrar, in addition to the return required by paragraph 1(1) a return in the prescribed form containing particulars of the usual residential address of the director, secretary or permanent representative to whom the confidentiality order relates, and any such return shall be delivered to the registrar within one month of having opened a branch in a part of Great Britain.]*

Documents required

5. *The first documents referred to in paragraph 1(2) are—*

(a) *a certified copy of the charter, statutes or memorandum and articles of the company (or other instrument constituting or defining the company's constitution), and*

(b) *if any of the documents mentioned in paragraph (a) above is not written in the English language, a translation of it into English certified in the prescribed manner to be a correct translation.*

6.—(1) *The second documents referred to in paragraph 1(2) are—*

(a) *copies of the latest accounting documents prepared in relation to a financial period of the company to have been publicly disclosed in accordance with the law of the country in which it is incorporated before the end of the period allowed for compliance with paragraph 1 in respect of the branch or, if earlier, the date on which the company complies with paragraph 1 in respect of the branch, and*

(b) *if any of the documents mentioned in paragraph (a) above is not written in the English language, a translation of it into English certified in the prescribed manner to be a correct translation.*

(2) *In sub-paragraph (1)(a) above, "financial period" and "accounting documents" shall be construed in accordance with paragraph 6 of Schedule 21D.*

Alterations

7.—(1) *If, after a company has delivered a return under paragraph 1(1) above, any alteration is made in—*

(a) *its charter, statutes or memorandum and articles (or other instrument constituting or defining its constitution), or*

(b) *any of the particulars referred to in paragraph 1(1),*

the company shall, within the time specified below, deliver to the registrar for registration a return in the prescribed form containing the prescribed particulars of the alteration.

In the case of an alteration in any of the documents referred to in paragraph (a), the return shall be accompanied by a certified copy of the document as altered, together with, if the document is not written in the English language, a translation of it into English certified in the prescribed manner to be a correct translation.

(2) *The time for the delivery of the return required by sub-paragraph (1) above is—*

(a) *in the case of an alteration in any of the particulars specified in paragraph 3, 21 days after the alteration is made; or*

(b) *in the case of any other alteration, 21 days after the date on which notice of the alteration in question could have been received in Great Britain in due course of post (if despatched with due diligence).*

(3) *Where—*

(a) *a company has more than one branch in Great Britain, and*

(b) *an alteration relates to more than one of those branches,*

sub-paragraph (1) above shall have effect to require the company to deliver a return in respect of each of the branches to which the alteration relates.

(4) *For the purposes of sub-paragraph (3) above—*

(a) an alteration in any of the particulars specified in paragraph 2 shall be treated as relating to every branch of the company (though where the company has more than one branch in a part of Great Britain a return in respect of an alteration in any of those particulars which gives the branch numbers of two or more such branches shall be treated as a return in respect of each branch whose number is given), but

(b) an alteration in the company's charter, statutes or memorandum and articles (or other instrument constituting or defining its constitution) shall only be treated as relating to a branch if the document altered is included in the material registered in respect of it.

8.—(1) Sub-paragraph (2) below applies where—

(a) a company's return under paragraph 1(1) includes a statement to the effect mentioned in paragraph 1(3)(b), and

(b) the statement ceases to be true so far as concerns the documents specified in paragraph 5.

(2) The company shall, within the time specified below, deliver to the registrar of companies for registration in respect of the branch to which the return relates—

(a) the documents specified in paragraph 5, or

(b) a return in the prescribed form—

(i) containing a statement to the effect that those documents are included in the material which is registered in respect of another branch of the company in the United Kingdom, and

(ii) stating where the other branch is registered and what is its registered number.

(3) The time for complying with sub-paragraph (2) above is 21 days after the date on which notice of the fact that the statement in the earlier return has ceased to be true could have been received in Great Britain in due course of post (if despatched with due diligence).

(4) Sub-paragraph (2) above shall also apply where, after a company has made a return under sub-paragraph (2)(b) above, the statement to the effect mentioned in sub-paragraph (2)(b)(i) ceases to be true.

(5) For the purposes of sub-paragraph (2)(b), where the company has more than one branch in a part of Great Britain a return which gives the branch numbers of two or more such branches shall be treated as a return in respect of each branch whose number is given.

[9.—(1) If an individual in respect of whom a confidentiality order under section 723B is in force becomes a director, secretary or permanent representative of a company that has delivered a return under paragraph (1)—

(a) the return required to be delivered to the registrar under paragraph 7(1) shall contain the address for the time being notified to the company by the director, secretary or permanent representative under regulations made under sections 723B to 723F, but shall not contain his usual residential address; and

(b) with the return under paragraph 7(1) the company shall deliver to the registrar a return in the prescribed form containing the usual residential address of that director, secretary or permanent representative.

(2) If after a company has delivered a return under paragraph 1(1) a confidentiality order under section 723B is made in respect of an existing director, secretary or permanent representative of the company, the company shall within the time specified below deliver to the registrar of companies for registration a return in the prescribed form containing the address for the time being notified to it by the director, secretary or permanent representative under regulations made under sections 723B to 723F.

(3) Sub-paragraph (4) applies if, at any time after a company has delivered a return under paragraph 1(1), there is an alteration in the usual residential address of a director, secretary or permanent representative of the company in respect of whom a confidentiality order under section 723B is in force.

(4) The company shall within the time specified below deliver to the registrar of companies for registration a return in the prescribed form containing the new address.

(5) The time for the delivery of a return required by sub-paragraph (2) or (4) is 21 days after the date on which notice of the alteration in question could have been received in Great Britain in due course of post (if despatched with due diligence).

(6) Where a company has more than one branch in Great Britain and any provision of this paragraph requires a return to be made to the registrar, that provision requires the company to deliver a return in respect of each of the branches; but a return which gives the branch numbers of two or more such branches shall be treated as a return in respect of each branch whose number is given.]]

[681]

NOTES

Inserted by the Oversea Companies and Credit and Financial Institutions (Branch Disclosure) Regulations 1992, SI 1992/3179, reg 3(1), Sch 2, Pt I, paras 1, 3, as from 1 January 1993; subject to transitional provisions in Sch 4 to those Regulations at **[6744B]**

Repealed by the Companies Act 2006, s 1295, Sch 16, as from a day to be appointed.

Paras 2, 3: words in square brackets inserted by the Companies (Particulars of Usual Residential Address) (Confidentiality Orders) Regulations 2002, SI 2002/912, reg 16, Sch 2, para 8(1), (2), as from 2 April 2002.

Paras 4A, 9: inserted and added respectively by SI 2002/912, reg 16, Sch 2, para 8(1), (3), (4), as from 2 April 2002.

Fees: see Appendix 3 (Fees Instruments) at **[A3]**.

Prescribed forms; prescribed manner: see Appendix 4 (Forms table) at **[A4]**.

[SCHEDULE 21B
CHANGE IN THE REGISTRATION REGIME: TRANSITIONAL PROVISIONS

Section 692A

1.—(1) This paragraph applies where a company which becomes a company to which section 690A applies was, immediately before becoming such a company (referred to in this paragraph as the relevant time), a company to which section 691 applies.

(2) The company need not include the particulars specified in paragraph 2(1)(d) of Schedule 21A in the first return to be delivered under paragraph 1(1) of that Schedule to the registrar for a part of Great Britain if at the relevant time—

- *(a) it had an established place of business in that part,*
- *(b) it had complied with its obligations under section 691(1)(b)(i), and*
- *(c) it had no outstanding obligation to make a return to the registrar for that part under subsection (1) of section 692, so far as concerns any alteration of the kind mentioned in subsection (1)(b) of that section,*

and if it states in the return that the particulars have been previously filed in respect of a place of business of the company in that part, giving the company's registered number.

(3) The company shall not be required to deliver the documents mentioned in paragraph 5 of Schedule 21A with the first return to be delivered under paragraph 1(1) of that Schedule to the registrar for a part of Great Britain if at the relevant time—

- *(a) it had an established place of business in that part,*
- *(b) it had delivered the documents mentioned in section 691(1)(a) to the registrar for that part, and*
- *(c) it had no outstanding obligation to make a return to that registrar under subsection (1) of section 692, so far as concerns any alteration in any of the documents mentioned in paragraph (a) of that subsection,*

and if it states in the return that the documents have been previously filed in respect of a place of business of the company in that part, giving the company's registered number.

2.—(1) This paragraph applies where a company which becomes a company to which section 691 applies was, immediately before becoming such a company (referred to in this paragraph as the relevant time), a company to which section 690A applies.

(2) The company shall not be required to deliver the documents mentioned in section 691(1)(a) to the registrar for a part of Great Britain if at the relevant time—

- *(a) it had a branch in that part,*
- *(b) the documents mentioned in paragraph 5 of Schedule 21A were included in the material registered in respect of the branch, and*
- *(c) it had no outstanding obligation to make a return to the registrar for that part under paragraph 7 of that Schedule, so far as concerns any alteration in any of the documents mentioned in sub-paragraph (1)(a) of that paragraph,*

and if it states in the return that the documents have been previously filed in respect of a branch of the company, giving the branch's registered number.

(3) The company need not include the particulars mentioned in section 691(1)(b)(i) in the return to be delivered under section 691(1)(b) to the registrar for a part of Great Britain if at the relevant time—

(a) it had a branch in that part,

(b) it had complied with its obligations under paragraph 1(1)(a) of Schedule 21A in respect of the branch so far as the particulars required by paragraph 2(1)(d) of that Schedule are concerned, and

(c) it had no outstanding obligation to make a return to the registrar for that part under paragraph 7 of that Schedule, so far as concerns any alteration in any of the particulars required by paragraph 2(1)(d) of that Schedule,

and if it states in the return that the particulars have been previously filed in respect of a branch of the company, giving the branch's registered number.

(4) Where sub-paragraph (3) above applies, the reference in section 692(1)(b) to the list of the directors and secretary shall be construed as a reference to the list contained in the return under paragraph 1(1) of Schedule 21A with any alterations in respect of which a return under paragraph 7(1) of that Schedule has been made.]

[682]

NOTES

Inserted by the Oversea Companies and Credit and Financial Institutions (Branch Disclosure) Regulations 1992, SI 1992/3179, reg 3(1), Sch 2, Pt I, paras 1, 5, as from 1 January 1993; subject to transitional provisions in Sch 4 to those Regulations at **[6744B]**.

Repealed by the Companies Act 2006, s 1295, Sch 16, as from a day to be appointed.

[SCHEDULE 21C
DELIVERY OF REPORTS AND ACCOUNTS: CREDIT AND FINANCIAL INSTITUTIONS TO WHICH THE BANK BRANCHES DIRECTIVE (89/117/EEC) APPLIES

Section 699A

PART I
INSTITUTIONS REQUIRED TO PREPARE ACCOUNTS UNDER PARENT LAW

Scope of Part and Interpretation

1.—(1) This Part of this Schedule applies to any institution to which section 699A applies which is required by its parent law to prepare and have audited accounts for its financial periods and whose only or principal branch within the United Kingdom is in Great Britain.

(2) In this Part of this Schedule, "branch" has the meaning given by section 699A.

Duty to deliver copies in Great Britain

2.—(1) An institution to which this Part of this Schedule applies shall, within one month of becoming such an institution, deliver to the registrar for registration—

(a) copies of the latest accounting documents of the institution prepared in accordance with its parent law to have been disclosed before the end of the period allowed for compliance with this sub-paragraph or, if earlier, the date of compliance with it, and

(b) if any of the documents mentioned in paragraph (a) above is not written in the English language, a translation of it into English certified in the prescribed manner to be a correct translation.

Where an institution to which this Part of this Schedule applies had, immediately prior to becoming such an institution, a branch in Northern Ireland which was its only or principal branch within the United Kingdom it may, instead of delivering the documents mentioned in sub-paragraph (1)(a) under that paragraph, deliver thereunder a notice that it has become an institution to which this Part of this Schedule applies, provided that those documents have been delivered to the registrar for Northern Ireland pursuant to the Companies (Northern Ireland) Order 1986.

3.—(1) An institution to which this Part of this Schedule applies shall deliver to the registrar for registration—

(*a*) *copies of all the accounting documents of the institution prepared in accordance with its parent law which are disclosed on or after the end of the period allowed for compliance with paragraph 2(1) or, if earlier, the date on which it complies with that paragraph, and*

(*b*) *if any of the documents mentioned in paragraph (a) above is not written in the English language, a translation of it into English, certified in the prescribed manner to be a correct translation.*

(2) *The period allowed for delivery, in relation to a document required to be delivered under this paragraph, is 3 months from the date on which the document is first disclosed.*

4. *Where an institution's parent law permits it to discharge an obligation with respect to the disclosure of accounting documents by disclosing documents in a modified form, it may discharge its obligation under paragraph 2 or 3 by delivering copies of documents modified as permitted by that law.*

5.—(1) *Neither paragraph 2 nor paragraph 3 shall require an institution to deliver documents to the registrar if at the end of the period allowed for compliance with that paragraph—*

(*a*) *it is not required by its parent law to register them,*

(*b*) *they are made available for inspection at each branch of the institution in Great Britain, and*

(*c*) *copies of them are available on request at a cost not exceeding the cost of supplying them.*

(2) *Where by virtue of sub-paragraph (1) above an institution is not required to deliver documents under paragraph 2 or 3 and any of the conditions specified in that sub-paragraph ceases to be met, the institution shall deliver the documents to the registrar for registration within 7 days of the condition ceasing to be met.*

Registrar to whom documents to be delivered

6. *The documents which an institution is required to deliver to the registrar under this Part of this Schedule shall be delivered—*

(*a*) *to the registrar for England and Wales if the institution's only branch, or (if it has more than one) its principal branch within the United Kingdom, is in England and Wales; or*

(*b*) *to the registrar for Scotland if the institution's only branch, or (if it has more than one) its principal branch within the United Kingdom, is in Scotland.*

Penalty for non-compliance

7.—(1) *If an institution fails to comply with paragraph 2, 3 or 5(2) before the end of the period allowed for compliance, the institution and every person who immediately before the end of that period was a director of the institution, or, in the case of an institution which does not have directors, a person occupying an equivalent office, is guilty of an offence and liable to a fine and, for continued contravention, to a daily default fine.*

(2) *It is a defence for a person charged with an offence under this paragraph to prove that he took all reasonable steps for securing compliance with paragraph 2, 3 or 5(2), as the case may be.*

Interpretation

8.—(1) *In this Part of this Schedule—*

"financial period" in relation to an institution, means a period for which the institution is required or permitted by its parent law to prepare accounts;

"parent law", in relation to an institution, means the law of the country in which the institution has its head office;

and references to disclosure are to public disclosure, except where an institution is not required under its parent law, any enactment (including any subordinate legislation within the meaning of section 21 of the Interpretation Act 1978) having effect for Great Britain or its constitution to publicly disclose its accounts, in which case such references are to the disclosure of the accounts to the persons for whose information they have been prepared.

(2) *For the purposes of this Part of this Schedule, the following are accounting documents in relation to a financial period of an institution—*

(*a*) *the accounts of the institution for the period, including, if it has one or more subsidiaries, any consolidated accounts of the group,*

(*b*) *any annual report of the directors (or, in the case of an institution which does not have directors, the persons occupying equivalent offices) for the period,*

(*c*) *the report of the auditors on the accounts mentioned in paragraph* (*a*) *above, and*

(*d*) *any report of the auditors on the report mentioned in paragraph* (*b*) *above.*

[683]

NOTES

Inserted by the Oversea Companies and Credit and Financial Institutions (Branch Disclosure) Regulations 1992, SI 1992/3179, reg 2(2), Sch 1, as from 1 January 1993; subject to transitional provisions in Sch 4 to those Regulations at **[6744B]**.

Repealed by the Companies Act 2006, s 1295, Sch 16, as from a day to be appointed.

Prescribed manner: see Appendix 4 (Forms table) at **[A4]**.

PART II
INSTITUTIONS NOT REQUIRED TO PREPARE ACCOUNTS UNDER PARENT LAW

Scope of Part and Interpretation

9.—(1) This Part of this Schedule applies to any institution to which section 699A applies which—

(*a*) *is incorporated, and*

(*b*) *is not required by the law of the country in which it has its head office to prepare and have audited accounts.*

(2) *In this Part of this Schedule, "branch" has the meaning given by section 699A.*

Preparation of accounts and reports

10. An institution to which this Part of this Schedule applies shall in respect of each financial year of the institution prepare the like accounts and directors' report, and cause to be prepared such an auditor's report, as would be required if the institution were a company to which section 700 applied.

11. Sections 223 to 225 apply to an institution to which this Part of this Schedule applies subject to the following modifications—

(*a*) *for the references to the incorporation of the company there shall be substituted references to the institution becoming an institution to which this Part of this Schedule applies; and*

(*b*) *section 225(4) shall be omitted.*

Duty to deliver accounts and reports

12.—(1) An institution to which this Part of this Schedule applies shall in respect of each financial year of the institution deliver to the registrar copies of the accounts and reports prepared in accordance with paragraph 10.

(2) *If any document comprised in those accounts or reports is in a language other than English, the institution shall annex to the copy delivered a translation of it into English, certified in the prescribed manner to be a correct translation.*

Time for delivery

13.—(1) The period allowed for delivering accounts and reports under paragraph 12 above is 13 months after the end of the relevant accounting reference period, subject to the following provisions of this paragraph.

(2) If the relevant accounting reference period is the institution's first and is a period of more than 12 months, the period allowed is 13 months from the first anniversary of the institution's becoming an institution to which this Part of this Schedule applies.

(3) If the relevant accounting reference period is treated as shortened by virtue of a notice given by the institution under section 225, the period allowed is that applicable in accordance with the above provisions or 3 months from the date of the notice under that section, whichever last expires.

(4) If for any special reason the Secretary of State thinks fit he may, on an application made before the expiry of the period otherwise allowed, by notice in writing to an institution to which this Part of this Schedule applies, extend that period by such further period as may be specified in the notice.

(5) In this paragraph "the relevant accounting reference period" means the accounting reference period by reference to which the financial year for the accounts in question was determined.

Registrar to whom documents to be delivered

14. The documents which an institution is required to deliver to the registrar under this Part of the Schedule shall be delivered—

- *(a) to the registrar for England and Wales if the institution's only branch, or (if it has more than one) its principal branch within Great Britain, is in England and Wales; or*
- *(b) to the registrar for Scotland if the institution's only branch, or (if it has more than one) its principal branch within Great Britain, is in Scotland.*

Penalty for non-compliance

15.—(1) If the requirements of paragraph 12 are not complied with before the end of the period allowed for delivering accounts and reports, or if the accounts and reports delivered do not comply with the requirements of this Act, the institution and every person who immediately before the end of that period was a director of the institution, or, in the case of an institution which does not have directors, a person occupying an equivalent office, is guilty of an offence and liable to a fine and, for continued contravention, to a daily default fine.

(2) It is a defence for a person charged with such an offence to prove that he took all reasonable steps for securing that the requirements in question would be complied with.

(3) It is not a defence in relation to a failure to deliver copies to the registrar to prove that the documents in question were not in fact prepared as required by this Schedule.]

[684]

NOTES

Inserted as noted to Pt I at **[683]**.

Repealed by the Companies Act 2006, s 1295, Sch 16, as from a day to be appointed.

Prescribed manner: see Appendix 4 (Forms table) at **[A4]**.

[SCHEDULE 21D
DELIVERY OF REPORTS AND ACCOUNTS: COMPANIES TO WHICH THE ELEVENTH COMPANY LAW DIRECTIVE APPLIES

Section 699AA

PART I
COMPANIES REQUIRED TO MAKE DISCLOSURE UNDER PARENT LAW

Scope of Part

1. This Part of this Schedule applies to any company to which section 699AA applies which is required by its parent law to prepare, have audited and disclose accounts.

Duty to deliver copies in Great Britain

2.—(1) This paragraph applies in respect of each branch which a company to which this Part of this Schedule applies has in Great Britain.

(2) The company shall deliver to the registrar for registration in respect of the branch copies of all the accounting documents prepared in relation to a financial period of the company which are disclosed in accordance with its parent law on or after the end of the period allowed for compliance in respect of the branch with paragraph 1 of Schedule 21A or, if earlier, the date on which the company complies with that paragraph in respect of the branch.

(3) Where the company's parent law permits it to discharge its obligation with respect to the disclosure of accounting documents by disclosing documents in a modified form, it may discharge its obligation under sub-paragraph (2) above by delivering copies of documents modified as permitted by that law.

(4) If any document, a copy of which is delivered under sub-paragraph (2) above, is in a language other than English, the company shall annex to the copy delivered a translation of it into English, certified in the prescribed manner to be a correct translation.

3. Paragraph 2 above shall not require documents to be delivered in respect of a branch if—
(a) before the end of the period allowed for compliance with that paragraph, they are delivered in respect of another branch in the United Kingdom, and
(b) the particulars registered under Schedule 21A in respect of the branch indicate an intention that they are to be registered in respect of that other branch and include the details of that other branch mentioned in paragraph 4(b) of that Schedule.

Time for delivery

4. The period allowed for delivery, in relation to a document required to be delivered under paragraph 2, is 3 months from the date on which the document is first disclosed in accordance with the company's parent law.

Penalty for non-compliance

5.—(1) If a company fails to comply with paragraph 2 before the end of the period allowed for compliance, it, and every person who immediately before the end of that period was a director of it, is guilty of an offence and liable to a fine and, for continued contravention, to a daily default fine.

(2) It is a defence for a person charged with an offence under this paragraph to prove that he took all reasonable steps for securing compliance with paragraph 2.

Interpretation

6.—(1) In this Part of this Schedule—

"financial period", in relation to a company, means a period for which the company is required or permitted by its parent law to prepare accounts;

"parent law", in relation to a company, means the law of the country in which the company is incorporated;

and references to disclosure are to public disclosure.

(2) For the purposes of this Part of this Schedule, the following are accounting documents in relation to a financial period of a company—

- *(a) the accounts of the company for the period, including, if it has one or more subsidiaries, any consolidated accounts of the group,*
- *(b) any annual report of the directors for the period,*
- *(c) the report of the auditors on the accounts mentioned in paragraph (a) above, and*
- *(d) any report of the auditors on the report mentioned in paragraph (b) above.*

[685]

NOTES

Inserted by the Oversea Companies and Credit and Financial Institutions (Branch Disclosure) Regulations 1992, SI 1992/3179, reg 3(1), Sch 2, Pt II, paras 15, 18, as from 1 January 1993; subject to transitional provisions in Sch 4 to those Regulations at **[6744B]**.

Repealed by the Companies Act 2006, s 1295, Sch 16, as from a day to be appointed.

Prescribed manner: see Appendix 4 (Forms table) at **[A4]**.

PART II
COMPANIES NOT REQUIRED TO MAKE DISCLOSURE UNDER PARENT LAW

Scope of Part

7. This Part of this Schedule applies to any company to which section 699AA applies which is not required by the law of the country in which it is incorporated to prepare, have audited and publicly disclose accounts.

Preparation of accounts and reports

8. A company to which this Part of this Schedule applies shall in respect of each financial year of the company prepare the like accounts and directors' report, and cause to be prepared such an auditors' report, as would be required if the company were a company to which section 700 applied.

9. Sections 223 to 225 apply to a company to which this Part of this Schedule applies subject to the following modifications—

- *(a) for the references to the incorporation of the company there shall be substituted references to the company becoming a company to which this Part of this Schedule applies, and*
- *(b) section 225(4) shall be omitted.*

Duty to deliver accounts and reports

10.—(1) A company to which this Part of this Schedule applies shall in respect of each financial year of the company deliver to the registrar copies of the accounts and reports prepared in accordance with paragraph 8.

(2) If any document comprised in those accounts or reports is in a language other than English, the company shall annex to the copy delivered a translation of it into English, certified in the prescribed manner to be a correct translation.

(3) A company required to deliver documents under this paragraph is respect of a financial year shall deliver them in respect of each branch which it has in Great Britain at the end of that year.

(4) Sub-paragraph (3) above is without prejudice to section 695A(3).

11. Paragraph 10 shall not require documents to be delivered in respect of a branch if—

(*a*) *before the end of the period allowed for compliance with that paragraph, they are delivered in respect of another branch in the United Kingdom, and*

(*b*) *the particulars registered under paragraph 1 of Schedule 21A in respect of the branch indicate an intention that they are to be registered in respect of that other branch and include the details of that other branch mentioned in paragraph 4(b) of that Schedule.*

Time for delivery

12.—(1) The period allowed for delivering accounts and reports under paragraph 10 is 13 months after the end of the relevant accounting reference period, subject to the following provisions of this paragraph.

(2) If the relevant accounting reference period is the company's first and is a period of more than 12 months, the period allowed is 13 months from the first anniversary of the company's becoming a company to which this Part of this Schedule applies.

(3) If the relevant accounting reference period is treated as shortened by virtue of a notice given by the company under section 225, the period allowed is that applicable in accordance with the above provisions or 3 months from the date of the notice under that section, whichever last expires.

(4) If for any special reason the Secretary of State thinks fit he may, on application made before the expiry of the period otherwise allowed, by notice in writing to a company to which this Part of this Schedule applies extend that period by such further period as may be specified in the notice.

(5) In this paragraph "the relevant accounting reference period" means the accounting reference period by reference to which the financial year for the accounts in question was determined.

Penalty for non-compliance

13.—(1) If the requirements of paragraph 10 are not complied with before the end of the period allowed for delivering accounts and reports, or if the accounts and reports delivered do not comply with the requirements of this Act, the company and every person who immediately before the end of that period was a director of the company is guilty of an offence and liable to a fine and, for continued contravention, to a daily default fine.

(2) It is a defence for a person charged with such an offence to prove that he took all reasonable steps for securing that the requirements in question would be complied with.

(3) It is not a defence in relation to a failure to deliver copies to the registrar to prove that the documents in question were not in fact prepared as required by this Act.]

[686]

NOTES

Inserted as noted to Pt I at **[685]**.
Repealed by the Companies Act 2006, s 1295, Sch 16, as from a day to be appointed.
Para 10: it is thought that the word "is" in sub-para (3) should read "in".
Prescribed form: see Appendix 4 (Forms table) at **[A4]**.

SCHEDULE 22
PROVISIONS OF THIS ACT APPLYING TO UNREGISTERED COMPANIES

Section 718

Provisions of this Act applied	*Subject matter*	*Limitations and exceptions (if any)*
In Part I—		
section 18	*Statutory and other amendments of memorandum and articles to be registered*	*Subject to section 718(3).*
[sections 35 to 35B]	*Company's capacity; power of directors to bind it*	*Subject to section 718(3).*
[section 36	*Company contracts*	*Subject to section 718(3).*
sections 36A[, 36AA] and 36B	*Execution of documents [and deeds]*	*Subject to section 718(3).*
section 36C	*Pre-incorporation contracts, deeds and obligations*	*Subject to section 718(3).]*
	.....	
section 40	*Official seal for share certificates, etc*	*Subject to section 718(3).*
section 42	*Events affecting a company's status to be officially notified*	*Subject to section 718(3).*
	.....	
In Part IV, sections 82, 86 and 87	*Allotments*	*Subject to section 718(3).*
In Part V—		
section 185(4)	*Exemption from duty to prepare certificates where shares etc issued to [clearing house or] nominee*	*Subject to section 718(3).*
section 186	*Certificate as evidence of title*	*Subject to section 718(3).*
Part VII, with—	*Accounts and audit*	*Subject to section 718(3).*
[Schedules 4 to 9]		
[Schedule 9A] … , and		
[Schedules 10 and 10A]		

Provisions of this Act applied	Subject matter	Limitations and exceptions (if any)
In Part IX—		
section 287	*Registered office*	*Subject to section 718(3).*
sections 288 to 290	*Register of directors and secretaries*	*—*
In Part X—		
[section 322A	*Invalidity of certain transactions involving directors, etc*	*Subject to section 718(3).]*
sections 343 to 347	*Register to be kept of certain transactions not disclosed in accounts; other related matters*	*Subject to section 718(3).*
[Part XA	*Control of political donations by companies*	*Subject to section 718(3).]*
In Part XI—		
section 351(1), (2) and (5)(a)	*Particulars of company to be given in correspondence*	*Subject to section 718(3).*
sections 363 … to 365	*Annual return*	*Subject to section 718(3).*
sections 384 to [394A]	*Appointment, … , etc, of auditors*	*Subject to section 718(3).*
[Part XII	*Registration of company charges; copies of instruments and register to be kept by company*	*Subject to section 718(3).]*
[Part XIV (except section 446)	*Investigation of companies and their affairs; requisition of documents*	*—]*
Part XV	*Effect of order imposing restrictions on shares*	*To apply so far only as relates to orders under section 445.*
[Part XVI	*Fraudulent trading by a company*	*—]*
In Part XXIV—		
[sections 706 to 710A, 713 and 715A]	*Miscellaneous provisions about registration*	*—*
section 711	*Public notice by registrar of companies with respect to certain documents*	*Subject to section 718(3).*
[section 711A	*Abolition of doctrine of deemed notice*	*Subject to section 718(3).]*
In Part XXV—		

Provisions of this Act applied	*Subject matter*	*Limitations and exceptions (if any)*
section 720	*Companies to publish periodical statement*	*Subject to section 718(3).*
section 721	*Production and inspection of company's books*	*To apply so far only as these provisions have effect in relation to provisions applying by virtue of the foregoing provisions of this Schedule.*
section 722	*Form of company registers, etc*	
section 723	*Use of computers for company records*	
[section 723A	*Rights of inspection and related matters]*	
section 725	*Service of documents*	
section 730, with Schedule 24	*Punishment of offences; meaning of "officer in default"*	
section 731	*Summary proceedings*	
section 732	*Prosecution by public authorities*	
Part XXVI	*Interpretation*	*To apply so far as requisite for the interpretation of other provisions applied by section 718 and this Schedule.*

[687]–[688]

NOTES

Repealed by the Companies Act 2006, s 1295, Sch 16, as from a day to be appointed.

Entry relating to ss 35–35B substituted by CA 1989, s 108(3), as from 1 February 1991.

Entries relating to ss 36, 36A, 36B, 36C inserted by CA 1989, s 130(5), and entry relating to s 36(4) repealed by s 212 of, and Sch 24 to, the 1989 Act, both as from 31 July 1990; figure ", 36AA" in the first column and words "and deeds" in square brackets in the second column inserted by the Regulatory Reform (Execution of Deeds and Documents) Order 2005, SI 2005/1906, art 10(1), Sch 1, para 12, as from 15 September 2005, except in relation to any instrument executed before that date

Entry relating to Pt III repealed, and entry relating to Pt IV repealed for certain purposes, by FSA 1986, s 212(3), Sch 17, Pt I (see the note preceding s 56 ante).

Words in square brackets in the entry relating to s 185(4) substituted by FSA 1986, s 212(2), Sch 16, para 26, as from 29 April 1988.

Entry relating to Part XA inserted by the Political Parties, Elections and Referendums Act 2000, s 139(2), as from 16 February 2001; this insertion applies only in relation to directors' reports for financial years beginning on or after the first anniversary of the date which is the relevant date for the purposes of Sch 23, Pt II, para 12 to that Act; namely the date (if held within the first year after s 139(1) comes into force) of the annual general meeting of the company, or otherwise the date immediately following the end of that year.

Entry relating to Schs 4–9 substituted by the Companies Act 1985 (Bank Accounts) Regulations 1991, SI 1991/2705, reg 7, Sch 3, para 2, as from 2 December 1991 (subject to transitional provisions in relation to a financial year of a company beginning before 23 December 1992).

Words in square brackets in the entry relating to Sch 9A substituted by SI 1991/2705, reg 7, Sch 3, para 2, as from 2 December 1991 (subject to transitional provisions as noted above); words omitted from that entry repealed by the Companies Act 1985 (Insurance Companies Accounts) Regulations 1993, SI 1993/3246, reg 5(1), Sch 2, para 9, as from 19 December 1993, subject to exemptions in relation to certain companies contained in reg 6 (at **[6765]**) and general transitional provisions in reg 7 (at **[6766]**).

Entry relating to Schs 10, 10A substituted by CA 1989, s 23, Sch 10, para 23, as from 1 April 1990.

Entry relating to s 322A inserted by CA 1989, s 109(2), as from 4 February 1991.

In the entries relating to ss 363–365 and ss 384–394A, words in square brackets substituted, and words omitted repealed, by CA 1989, ss 123(5), 212, Sch 24, as from 1 April 1990.

Entry relating to Pt XII inserted by CA 1989, s 106, as from a day to be appointed.

Entry relating to Pt XIV substituted by CA 1989, s 71, as from 21 February 1990.

Entry relating to Pt XVI inserted by CA 1989, s 145, Sch 19, para 21, as from 1 March 1990.

Entry relating to ss 706–710A, 713, 715A substituted by CA 1989, s 127(7), partly as from 7 January 1991 (ss 706, 707, 715A) and partly as from 1 July 1991 (otherwise).

Entry relating to s 711A inserted by CA 1989, s 142(2), as from a day to be appointed.

Entry relating to s 723A inserted by CA 1989, s 143(11), as from 1 November 1991.

Regulations: the Companies (Unregistered Companies) Regulations 1985, SI 1985/680 at **[6022]**.

(Sch 23 repealed by the Companies Act 2006, ss 1177, 1295, Sch 16, as from 6 April 2007.)

SCHEDULE 24
PUNISHMENT OF OFFENCES UNDER THIS ACT

Section 730

…

Section of Act creating offence	*General nature of offence*	*Mode of prosecution*	*Punishment*	*Daily default fine (where applicable)*
6(3)	*Company failing to deliver to registrar notice or other document, following alteration of its objects*	*Summary*	*One-fifth of the statutory maximum*	*One-fiftieth of the statutory maximum.*
[12(3B)	*Person making false statement under section 12(3A) which he knows to be false or does not believe to be true*	*1. On indictment* *2. Summary*	*2 years or a fine; or both* *6 months or the statutory maximum; or both]*	
18(3)	*Company failing to register change in memorandum or articles*	*Summary*	*One-fifth of the statutory maximum*	*One-fiftieth of the statutory maximum.*
19(2)	*Company failing to send to one of its members a copy of the memorandum or articles, when so required by the member*	*Summary*	*One-fifth of the statutory maximum*	
20(2)	*Where company's memorandum altered, company issuing copy of the memorandum without the alteration*	*Summary*	*One-fifth of the statutory maximum for each occasion on which copies are so issued after the date of the alteration*	
28(5)	*Company failing to change name on direction of Secretary of State*	*Summary*	*One-fifth of the statutory maximum*	*One-fiftieth of the statutory maximum.*
[30(5C)	*Person making false statement under section 30(5A) which he knows to be false or does not believe to be true*	*1. On indictment* *2. Summary*	*2 years or a fine; or both* *6 months or the statutory maximum; or both]*	

Section of Act creating offence	General nature of offence	Mode of prosecution	Punishment	Daily default fine (where applicable)
31(5)	*Company altering its memorandum or articles, so ceasing to be exempt from having "limited" as part of its name*	*Summary*	*The statutory maximum*	*One-tenth of the statutory maximum.*
31(6)	*Company failing to change name, on Secretary of State's direction, so as to have "limited" (or Welsh equivalent) at the end*	*Summary*	*One-fifth of the statutory maximum*	*One-fiftieth of the statutory maximum.*
32(4)	*Company failing to comply with Secretary of State's direction to change its name, on grounds that the name is misleading.*	*Summary*	*One-fifth of the statutory maximum*	*One-fiftieth of the statutory maximum.*
33	*Trading under misleading name (use of "public limited company" or Welsh equivalent [etc] when not so entitled); purporting to be a private company*	*Summary*	*One-fifth of the statutory maximum*	*One-fiftieth of the statutory maximum.*
34	*Trading or carrying on business with improper use of "limited" or "cyfyngedig"*	*Summary*	*One-fifth of the statutory maximum*	*One-fiftieth of the statutory maximum.*
[34A	*Trading with improper use of "community interest company" etc*	*Summary*	*Level 3 on the standard scale*	*One-tenth of level 3 on the standard scale.]*
[43(3B)	*Person making false statement under section 43(3A) which he knows to be false or does not believe to be true*	*1. On indictment* *2. Summary*	*2 years or a fine; or both* *6 months or the statutory maximum; or both*	
49(8B)	*Person making false statement under section 49(8A) which he knows to be false or does not believe to be true*	*1. On indictment* *2. Summary*	*2 years or a fine; or both* *6 months or the statutory maximum; or both]*	
54(10)	*Public company failing to give notice, or copy of court order, to registrar, concerning application to re-register as private company*	*Summary*	*One-fifth of the statutory maximum*	*One-fiftieth of the statutory maximum.*
56(4)	…	…	…	

Section of Act creating offence	*General nature of offence*	*Mode of prosecution*	*Punishment*	*Daily default fine (where applicable)*
61	...	...	...	
64(5)	...	...	...	...
70(1)	...	...	...	
78(1)	...	...	...	
80(9)	*Directors exercising company's power of allotment without the authority required by section 80(1)*	*1. On indictment* *2. Summary*	*A fine* *The statutory maximum*	
81(2)	*Private limited company offering shares to the public, or allotting shares with a view to their being so offered*	*1. On indictment* *2. Summary*	*A fine* *The statutory maximum*	
82(5)	*Allotting shares or debentures before third day after issue of prospectus*	*1. On indictment* *2. Summary*	*A fine* *The statutory maximum*	
86(6)	*Company failing to keep money in separate bank account, where received in pursuance of prospectus stating that stock exchange listing is to be applied for*	*1. On indictment* *2. Summary*	*A fine* *The statutory maximum*	
87(4)	*Offeror of shares for sale failing to keep proceeds in separate bank account*	*1. On indictment* *2. Summary*	*A fine* *The statutory maximum*	
88(5)	*Officer of company failing to deliver return of allotments, etc, to registrar*	*1. On indictment* *2. Summary*	*A fine* *The statutory maximum*	*One-tenth of the statutory maximum.*
95(6)	*Knowingly or recklessly authorising or permitting misleading, false or deceptive material in statement by directors under section 95(5)*	*1. On indictment* *2. Summary*	*2 years or a fine; or both* *6 months or the statutory maximum; or both*	
97(4)	*Company failing to deliver to registrar the prescribed form disclosing amount or rate of share commission*	*Summary*	*One-fifth of the statutory maximum*	

Section of Act creating offence	*General nature of offence*	*Mode of prosecution*	*Punishment*	*Daily default fine (where applicable)*
110(2)	*Making misleading, false or deceptive statement in connection with valuation under section 103 or 104*	*1. On indictment* *2. Summary*	*2 years or a fine; or both* *6 months or the statutory maximum; or both*	
111(3)	*Officer of company failing to deliver copy of asset valuation report to registrar*	*1. On indictment* *2. Summary*	*A fine* *The statutory maximum*	*One-tenth of the statutory maximum.*
111(4)	*Company failing to deliver to registrar copy of resolution under section 104(4), with respect to transfer of an asset as consideration for allotment*	*Summary*	*One-fifth of the statutory maximum*	*One-fiftieth of the statutory maximum.*
114	*Contravention of any of the provisions of sections 99 to 104, 106*	*1. On indictment* *2. Summary*	*A fine* *The statutory maximum*	
117(7)	*Company doing business or exercising borrowing powers contrary to section 117*	*1. On indictment* *2. Summary*	*A fine* *The statutory maximum*	
[117(7A)	*Person making false statement under section 117(3A) which he knows to be false or does not believe to be true*	*1. On indictment* *2. Summary*	*2 years or a fine; or both* *6 months or the statutory maximum; or both]*	
122(2)	*Company failing to give notice to registrar of reorganisation of share capital*	*Summary*	*One-fifth of the statutory maximum*	*One-fiftieth of the statutory maximum.*
123(4)	*Company failing to give notice to registrar of increase of share capital*	*Summary*	*One-fifth of the statutory maximum*	*One-fiftieth of the statutory maximum.*
127(5)	*Company failing to forward to registrar copy of court order, when application made to cancel resolution varying shareholders' rights*	*Summary*	*One-fifth of the statutory maximum*	*One-fiftieth of the statutory maximum.*
128(5)	*Company failing to send to registrar statement or notice required by section 128 (particulars of shares carrying special rights)*	*Summary*	*One-fifth of the statutory maximum*	*One-fiftieth of the statutory maximum.*

Section of Act creating offence	*General nature of offence*	*Mode of prosecution*	*Punishment*	*Daily default fine (where applicable)*
129(4)	*Company failing to deliver to registrar statement or notice required by section 129 (registration of newly created class rights)*	*Summary*	*One-fifth of the statutory maximum*	*One-fiftieth of the statutory maximum.*
141	*Officer of company concealing name of creditor entitled to object to reduction of capital, or wilfully misrepresenting nature or amount of debt or claim, etc*	*1. On indictment* *2. Summary*	*A fine* *The statutory maximum*	
142(2)	*Director authorising or permitting non-compliance with section 142 (requirement to convene company meeting to consider serious loss of capital)*	*1. On indictment* *2. Summary*	*A fine* *The statutory maximum*	
143(2)	*Company acquiring its own shares in breach of section 143*	*1. On indictment*	*In the case of the company, a fine* *In the case of an officer of the company who is in default, 2 years or a fine; or both*	
		2. Summary	*In the case of the company, the statutory maximum* *In the case of an officer of the company who is in default, 6 months or the statutory maximum; or both*	
149(2)	*Company failing to cancel its own shares, acquired by itself, as required by section 146(2); or failing to apply for re-registration as private company as so required in the case there mentioned*	*Summary*	*One-fifth of the statutory maximum*	*One-fiftieth of the statutory maximum.*

Section of Act creating offence	*General nature of offence*	*Mode of prosecution*	*Punishment*	*Daily default fine (where applicable)*
151(3)	*Company giving financial assistance towards acquisition of its own shares*	*1. On indictment*	*Where the company is convicted, a fine* *Where an officer of the company is convicted, 2 years or a fine; or both*	
		2. Summary	*Where the company is convicted, the statutory maximum* *Where an officer of the company is convicted, 6 months or the statutory maximum; or both*	
156(6)	*Company failing to register statutory declaration [or statement] under section 155*	*Summary*	*The statutory maximum*	*One-fiftieth of the statutory maximum.*
156(7)	*Director making statutory declaration [or statement] under section 155, without having reasonable grounds for opinion expressed in it*	*1. On indictment* *2. Summary*	*2 years or a fine; or both* *6 months or the statutory maximum; or both*	
[162G	*Contravention of any provision of sections 162A–162F (dealings by company in treasury shares, etc)*	*1. On indictment* *2. Summary*	*A fine* *The statutory maximum]*	
169(6)	*Default by company's officer in delivering to registrar the return required by section 169 (disclosure by company of purchase of own shares)*	*1. On indictment* *2. Summary*	*A fine* *The statutory maximum*	*One-tenth of the statutory maximum.*
169(7)	*Company failing to keep copy of contract, etc, at registered office; refusal of inspection to person demanding it*	*Summary*	*One-fifth of the statutory maximum*	*One-fiftieth of the statutory maximum.*

Section of Act creating offence	*General nature of offence*	*Mode of prosecution*	*Punishment*	*Daily default fine (where applicable)*
[169A(4)	*Default by company's officer in delivering to registrar the return required by section 169A (disclosure by company of cancellation or disposal of treasury shares)*	*1. On indictment* *2. Summary*	*A fine* *The statutory maximum*	*One-tenth of the statutory maximum.]*
173(6)	*Director making statutory declaration under section 173 without having reasonable grounds for the opinion expressed in the declaration*	*1. On indictment* *2. Summary*	*2 years or a fine; or both* *6 months or the statutory maximum; or both*	
175(7)	*Refusal of inspection of statutory declaration and auditors' report under section 173, etc*	*Summary*	*One-fifth of the statutory maximum*	*One-fiftieth of the statutory maximum.*
176(4)	*Company failing to give notice to registrar of application to court under section 176, or to register court order*	*Summary*	*One-fifth of the statutory maximum*	*One-fiftieth of the statutory maximum.*
183(6)	*Company failing to send notice of refusal to register a transfer of shares or debentures*	*Summary*	*One-fifth of the statutory maximum*	*One-fiftieth of the statutory maximum.*
185(5)	*Company default in compliance with section 185(1) (certificates to be made ready following allotment or transfer of shares, etc)*	*Summary*	*One-fifth of the statutory maximum*	*One-fiftieth of the statutory maximum.*
189(1)	*Offences of fraud and forgery in connection with share warrants in Scotland*	*1. On indictment* *2. Summary*	*7 years or a fine; or both* *6 months or the statutory maximum; or both*	
189(2)	*Unauthorised making of, or using or possessing apparatus for making, share warrants in Scotland*	*1. On indictment* *2. Summary*	*7 years or a fine; or both* *6 months or the statutory maximum; or both*	
191(4)	*Refusal of inspection or copy of register of debenture-holders, etc*	*Summary*	*One-fifth of the statutory maximum*	*One-fiftieth of the statutory maximum.*

Section of Act creating offence	General nature of offence	Mode of prosecution	Punishment	Daily default fine (where applicable)
210(3)	Failure to discharge obligation of disclosure under Part VI; other forms of non-compliance with that Part	1. On indictment 2. Summary	2 years or a fine; or both 6 months or the statutory maximum; or both	
211(10)	Company failing to keep register of interests disclosed under Part VI; other contraventions of section 211	Summary	One-fifth of the statutory maximum	One-fiftieth of the statutory maximum.
214(5)	Company failing to exercise powers under section 212, when so required by the members	1. On indictment 2. Summary	A fine The statutory maximum	
215(8)	Company default in compliance with section 215 (company report of investigation of shareholdings on members' requisition)	1. On indictment 2. Summary	A fine The statutory maximum	
216(3)	Failure to comply with company notice under section 212; making false statement in response, etc	1. On indictment 2. Summary	2 years or a fine; or both 6 months or the statutory maximum; or both	
217(7)	Company failing to notify a person that he has been named as a shareholder; on removal of name from register, failing to alter associated index	Summary	One-fifth of the statutory maximum	One-fiftieth of the statutory maximum.
218(3)	Improper removal of entry from register of interests disclosed; company failing to restore entry improperly removed	Summary	One-fifth of the statutory maximum	For continued contravention of section 218(2) one-fiftieth of the statutory maximum.
219(3)	Refusal of inspection of register or report under Part VI; failure to send copy when required	Summary	One-fifth of the statutory maximum	One-fiftieth of the statutory maximum.

PART I
COMPANIES LEGISLATION

Section of Act creating offence	*General nature of offence*	*Mode of prosecution*	*Punishment*	*Daily default fine (where applicable)*
[221(5) or 222(4)]	*Company failing to keep accounting records (liability of officers)*	*1. On indictment* *2. Summary*	*2 years or a fine; or both* *6 months or the statutory maximum; or both*	
[222(6)]	*Officer of company failing to secure compliance with, or intentionally causing default under, section [222(5)] (preservation of accounting records for requisite number of years)*	*1. On indictment* *2. Summary*	*2 years or a fine; or both* *6 months or the statutory maximum; or both*	
[231(6)]	*Company failing to annex to its annual return certain particulars required by Schedule 5 and not included in annual accounts*	*Summary*	*One-fifth of the statutory maximum*	*One-fiftieth of the statutory maximum.*
[232(4)]	*Default by director or officer of a company in giving notice of matters relating to himself for purposes of [Schedule 6, Part I]*	*Summary*	*One-fifth of the statutory maximum*	
[233(5)	*Approving defective accounts*	*1. On indictment* *2. Summary*	*A fine* *The statutory maximum]*	
[233(6)]	*Laying or delivery of unsigned balance sheet; circulating copies of balance sheet without signatures*	*Summary*	*One-fifth of the statutory maximum*	
[234(5)]	*Non-compliance with [Part VII], as to directors' report and its content; directors individually liable*	*1. On indictment* *2. Summary*	*A fine* *The statutory maximum*	
[234ZA(6)	*Making a statement in a directors' report as mentioned in section 234ZA(2) which is false*	*1. On indictment* *2. Summary*	*2 years or a fine; or both* *12 months or the statutory maximum; or both]*	
[234A(4)	*Laying, circulating or delivering directors' report without required signature*	*Summary*	*One-fifth of the statutory maximum*	

Section of Act creating offence	General nature of offence	Mode of prosecution	Punishment	Daily default fine (where applicable)
[234AA(5)	…	…	…	
234AB(4)	…	…	…]	
[234B(3)	Non-compliance with requirements as to preparation and content of directors' remuneration report	Summary	One-fifth of the statutory maximum	
234B(6)	Default in complying with section 234B(5)	Summary	One-fifth of the statutory maximum]	
236(4)	Laying, circulating or delivering auditors' report without required signature	Summary	One-fifth of the statutory maximum.]	
[238(5)]	Failing to send [company's annual accounts], directors' report and auditors' report to those entitled to receive them	1. On indictment 2. Summary	A fine The statutory maximum	
[239(3)]	Company failing to supply copy of accounts [and reports] to shareholder on his demand	Summary	One-fifth of the statutory maximum	One-fiftieth of the statutory maximum.
[240(6)]	[Failure to comply with requirements in connection with publication of accounts]	Summary	One-fifth of the statutory maximum	
[241(2) or 242(2)]	Director in default as regards duty to lay and deliver [company's annual accounts, directors' report and auditors' report]	Summary	The statutory maximum	One-tenth of the statutory maximum.
[241A(9)	Default in complying with the requirements of section 241A(3) and (4)	Summary	One-fifth of the statutory maximum	
241A(10)	Failure to put resolution to vote of meeting	Summary	One-fifth of the statutory maximum]	
[245E(3)	Using or disclosing tax information in contravention of section 245E(1) or (2)	1. On indictment 2. Summary	2 years or a fine; or both 12 months or the statutory maximum; or both]	

Section of Act creating offence	*General nature of offence*	*Mode of prosecution*	*Punishment*	*Daily default fine (where applicable)*
[245G(7)	*Disclosing information in contravention of section 245G(2) and (3)*	*1. On indictment* *2. Summary*	*2 years or a fine; or both* *12 months or the statutory maximum; or both]*	
245(1)	…	…	…	
245(2)	…	…	…	
[251(6)	*Failure to comply with requirements in relation to summary financial statements*	*Summary*	*One-fifth of the statutory maximum]*	
255(5)	…	…	…	
260(3)	…	…	…	
287(3)	…	…	…	…
288(4)	*Default in complying with section 288 (keeping register of directors and secretaries, refusal of inspection)*	*Summary*	*The statutory maximum*	*One-tenth of the statutory maximum.*
291(5)	*Acting as director of a company without having the requisite share qualification*	*Summary*	*One-fifth of the statutory maximum*	*One-fiftieth of the statutory maximum.*
294(3)	*Director failing to give notice of his attaining retirement age; acting as director under appointment invalid due to his attaining it*	*Summary*	*One-fifth of the statutory maximum*	*One-fiftieth of the statutory maximum.*
295(7)	…	…	…	
302(1)	…	…	…	
305(3)	*Company default in complying with section 305 (directors' names to appear on company correspondence, etc)*	*Summary*	*One-fifth of the statutory maximum*	

Section of Act creating offence	*General nature of offence*	*Mode of prosecution*	*Punishment*	*Daily default fine (where applicable)*
306(4)	*Failure to state that liability of proposed director or manager is unlimited; failure to give notice of that fact to person accepting office*	*1. On indictment* *2. Summary*	*A fine* *The statutory maximum*	
314(3)	*Director failing to comply with section 314 (duty to disclose compensation payable on takeover, etc); a person's failure to include required particulars in a notice he has to give of such matters*	*Summary*	*One-fifth of the statutory maximum*	
317(7)	*Director failing to disclose interest in contract*	*1. On indictment* *2. Summary*	*A fine* *The statutory maximum*	
318(8)	*Company default in complying with section 318(1) or (5) (directors' service contracts to be open to inspection); 14 days' default in complying with section 318(4) (notice to registrar as to where copies of contracts and memoranda are kept); refusal of inspection required under section 318(7)*	*Summary*	*One-fifth of the statutory maximum*	*One-fiftieth of the statutory maximum.*
[322B(4)	*Terms of unwritten contract between sole member of a private company limited by shares or by guarantee and the company not set out in a written memorandum or recorded in minutes of a directors' meeting*	*Summary*	*Level 5 on the standard scale]*	
323(2)	*Director dealing in options to buy or sell company's listed shares or debentures*	*1. On indictment* *2. Summary*	*2 years or a fine; or both* *6 months or the statutory maximum; or both*	
324(7)	*Director failing to notify interest in company's shares; making false statement in purported notification*	*1. On indictment* *2. Summary*	*2 years or a fine; or both* *6 months or the statutory maximum; or both*	

Section of Act creating offence	*General nature of offence*	*Mode of prosecution*	*Punishment*	*Daily default fine (where applicable)*
326(2), (3), (4), (5)	*Various defaults in connection with company register of directors' interests*	*Summary*	*One-fifth of the statutory maximum*	*Except in the case of section 326(5), one fiftieth of the statutory maximum.*
328(6)	*Director failing to notify company that members of his family have, or have exercised, options to buy shares or debentures; making false statement in purported notification*	*1. On indictment* *2. Summary*	*2 years or a fine; or both* *6 months or the statutory maximum; or both*	
329(3)	*Company failing to notify [investment exchange] of acquisition of its securities by a director*	*Summary*	*One-fifth of the statutory maximum*	*One-fiftieth of the statutory maximum.*
342(1)	*Director of relevant company authorising or permitting company to enter into transaction or arrangement, knowing or suspecting it to contravene section 330*	*1. On indictment* *2. Summary*	*2 years or a fine; or both* *6 months or the statutory maximum; or both*	
342(2)	*Relevant company entering into transaction or arrangement for a director in contravention of section 330*	*1. On indictment* *2. Summary*	*2 years or a fine; or both* *6 months or the statutory maximum; or both*	
342(3)	*Procuring a relevant company to enter into transaction or arrangement known to be contrary to section 330*	*1. On indictment* *2. Summary*	*2 years or a fine; or both* *6 months or the statutory maximum; or both*	
343(8)	*Company failing to maintain register of transactions, etc, made with and for directors and not disclosed in company accounts; failing to make register available at registered office or at company meeting*	*1. On indictment* *2. Summary*	*A fine* *The statutory maximum*	

Section of Act creating offence	*General nature of offence*	*Mode of prosecution*	*Punishment*	*Daily default fine (where applicable)*
348(2)	*Company failing to paint or affix name; failing to keep it painted or affixed*	*Summary*	*One-fifth of the statutory maximum*	*In the case of failure to keep the name painted or affixed, one fiftieth of the statutory maximum.*
349(2)	*Company failing to have name on business correspondence, invoices, etc*	*Summary*	*One-fifth of the statutory maximum*	
349(3)	*Officer of company issuing business letter or document not bearing company's name [or causing appearance of website in which company's name not mentioned]*	*Summary*	*One-fifth of the statutory maximum*	
349(4)	*Officer of company signing cheque, bill of exchange, etc on which company's name not mentioned*	*Summary*	*One-fifth of the statutory maximum*	
350(*1*)	*Company failing to have its name engraved on company seal*	*Summary*	*One-fifth of the statutory maximum*	
350(2)	*Officer of company, etc, using company seal without name engraved on it*	*Summary*	*One-fifth of the statutory maximum*	
351(5)(*a*)	*Company failing to comply with section 351*(*1*) *or* (2) (*matters to be stated on business correspondence, etc*)	*Summary*	*One-fifth of the statutory maximum*	
351(5)(*b*)	*Officer or agent of company issuing, or authorising issue of, business document not complying with those subsections*	*Summary*	*One-fifth of the statutory maximum*	
[351(5)(ba)	Officer or agent of company causing appearance of website not complying with section 351(1) or (2)	*Summary*	*Level 3 on the standard scale]*	

PART I
COMPANIES LEGISLATION

Section of Act creating offence	General nature of offence	Mode of prosecution	Punishment	Daily default fine (where applicable)
351(5)(c)	*Contravention of section 351(3) or (4) (information in English to be stated on Welsh company's business correspondence, etc)*	*Summary*	*One-fifth of the statutory maximum*	*For contravention of section 351(3), one-fiftieth of the statutory maximum.*
352(5)	*Company default in complying with section 352 (requirement to keep register of members and their particulars)*	*Summary*	*One-fifth of the statutory maximum*	*One-fiftieth of the statutory maximum.*
[352A(3)	*Company default in complying with section 352A (statement that company has only one member)*	*Summary*	*Level 2 on the standard scale*	*One-tenth of level 2 on the standard scale.]*
353(4)	*Company failing to send notice to registrar as to place where register of members is kept*	*Summary*	*One-fifth of the statutory maximum*	*One-fiftieth of the statutory maximum.*
354(4)	*Company failing to keep index of members*	*Summary*	*One-fifth of the statutory maximum*	*One-fiftieth of the statutory maximum.*
356(5)	*Refusal of inspection of members' register; failure to send copy on requisition*	*Summary*	*One-fifth of the statutory maximum*	
[363(3)]	*Company with share capital failing to make annual return*	*Summary*	*The statutory maximum*	*One-tenth of the statutory maximum.*
364(4)	*Company without share capital failing to complete and register annual return in due time*	*Summary*	*The statutory maximum*	*One-tenth of the statutory maximum.*
365(3)	...	...	...	...
366(4)	*Company default in holding annual general meeting*	*1. On indictment* *2. Summary*	*A fine* *The statutory maximum*	
367(3)	*Company default in complying with Secretary of State's direction to hold company meeting*	*1. On indictment* *2. Summary*	*A fine* *The statutory maximum*	

Section of Act creating offence	General nature of offence	Mode of prosecution	Punishment	Daily default fine (where applicable)
367(5)	Company failing to register resolution that meeting held under section 367 is to be its annual general meeting	Summary	One-fifth of the statutory maximum	One-fiftieth of the statutory maximum.
372(4)	Failure to give notice, to member entitled to vote at company meeting, that he may do so by proxy	Summary	One-fifth of the statutory maximum	
372(6)	Officer of company authorising or permitting issue of irregular invitations to appoint proxies	Summary	One-fifth of the statutory maximum	
376(7)	Officer of company in default as to circulation of members' resolutions for company meeting	1. On indictment 2. Summary	A fine The statutory maximum	
380(5)	Company failing to comply with section 380 (copies of certain resolutions etc to be sent to registrar of companies)	Summary	One-fifth of the statutory maximum	One-fiftieth of the statutory maximum.
380(6)	Company failing to include copy of resolution to which section 380 applies in articles; failing to forward copy to member on request	Summary	One-fifth of the statutory maximum for each occasion on which copies are issued or, as the case may be, requested	
[381B(2)	Director or secretary of company failing to notify auditors of proposed written resolution	Summary	Level 3 on the standard scale]	
382(5)	Company failing to keep minutes of proceedings at company and board meetings, etc	Summary	One-fifth of the statutory maximum	One-fiftieth of the statutory maximum.
[382B(2)	Failure of sole member to provide the company with a written record of a decision	Summary	Level 2 on the standard scale]	

PART I
COMPANIES LEGISLATION

Section of Act creating offence	*General nature of offence*	*Mode of prosecution*	*Punishment*	*Daily default fine (where applicable)*
383(4)	*Refusal of inspection of minutes of general meeting; failure to send copy of minutes on member's request*	*Summary*	*One-fifth of the statutory maximum*	
384(5)	…	…	…	…
386(2)	…	…	…	…
[387(2)	*Company failing to give Secretary of State notice of non-appointment of auditors*	*Summary*	*One-fifth of the statutory maximum*	*One-fiftieth of the statutory maximum.]*
389(10)	*Person acting as company auditor knowing himself to be disqualified; failing to give notice vacating office when he becomes disqualified*	*1. On indictment* *2. Summary*	*A fine* *The statutory maximum.*	*One-tenth of the statutory maximum*
[389B(1)	*Person making false, misleading or deceptive statement to auditor*	*1. On indictment* *2. Summary*	*2 years or a fine; or both* *12 months or the statutory maximum; or both*	
389B(2)	*Failure to provide information or explanations to auditor*	*Summary*	*Level 3 on the standard scale*	
389B(4)	*Parent company failing to obtain from subsidiary undertaking information for purposes of audit*	*Summary*	*Level 3 on the standard scale]*	
390(7)	…	…	…	…
[391(2)	*Failing to give notice to registrar of removal of auditor*	*Summary*	*One-fifth of the statutory maximum*	*One-fiftieth of the statutory maximum.*
391(4)	…	…	…	…
392(2)	…	…	…	
392(3)	*Company failing to forward notice of auditor's resignation to registrar*	*1. On indictment* *2. Summary*	*A fine* *The statutory maximum*	*One-tenth of the statutory maximum.*

Section of Act creating offence	General nature of offence	Mode of prosecution	Punishment	Daily default fine (where applicable)
392A(5)	*Directors failing to convene meeting requisitioned by resigning auditor*	*1. On indictment* *2. Summary*	*A fine* *The statutory maximum]*	
393	…	…	…	
[394A(1)	*Person ceasing to hold office as auditor failing to deposit statement as to circumstances*	*1. On indictment* *2. Summary*	*A fine* *The statutory maximum*	
394A(4)	*Company failing to comply with requirements as to statement of person ceasing to hold office as auditor*	*1. On indictment* *2. Summary*	*A fine* *The statutory maximum*	*One-tenth of the statutory maximum.]*
399(3)	*Company failing to send to registrar particulars of charge created by it, or of issue of debentures which requires registration*	*1. On indictment* *2. Summary*	*A fine* *The statutory maximum*	*One-tenth of the statutory maximum.*
400(4)	*Company failing to send to registrar particulars of charge on property acquired*	*1. On indictment* *2. Summary*	*A fine* *The statutory maximum*	*One-tenth of the statutory maximum.*
402(3)	*Authorising or permitting delivery of debenture or certificate of debenture stock, without endorsement on it of certificate of registration of charge*	*Summary*	*One-fifth of the statutory maximum*	
[403(2A)	*Person making false statement under section 403(1A) which he knows to be false or does not believe to be true*	*1. On indictment* *2. Summary*	*2 years or a fine; or both* *6 months or the statutory maximum; or both]*	
405(4)	*Failure to give notice to registrar of appointment of receiver or manager, or of his ceasing to act*	*Summary*	*One-fifth of the statutory maximum*	*One-fiftieth of the statutory maximum.*
407(3)	*Authorising or permitting omission from company register of charges*	*1. On indictment* *2. Summary*	*A fine* *The statutory maximum*	

PART I
COMPANIES LEGISLATION

Section of Act creating offence	*General nature of offence*	*Mode of prosecution*	*Punishment*	*Daily default fine (where applicable)*
408(3)	*Officer of company refusing inspection of charging instrument, or of register of charges*	*Summary*	*One-fifth of the statutory maximum*	*One-fiftieth of the statutory maximum.*
415(3)	*Scottish company failing to send to registrar particulars of charge created by it, or of issue of debentures which requires registration*	*1. On indictment* *2. Summary*	*A fine* *The statutory maximum*	*One-tenth of the statutory maximum.*
416(3)	*Scottish company failing to send to registrar particulars of charge on property acquired by it*	*1. On indictment* *2. Summary*	*A fine* *The statutory maximum*	*One-tenth of the statutory maximum.*
[419(5A)	*Person making false statement under section 419(1A) or (1B) which he knows to be false or does not believe to be true*	*1. On indictment* *2. Summary*	*2 years or a fine; or both* *6 months or the statutory maximum; or both]*	
422(3)	*Scottish company authorising or permitting omission from its register of charges*	*1. On indictment* *2. Summary*	*A fine* *The statutory maximum*	
423(3)	*Officer of Scottish company refusing inspection of charging instrument, or of register of charges*	*Summary*	*One-fifth of the statutory maximum*	*One-fiftieth of the statutory maximum.*
425(4)	*Company failing to annex to memorandum court order sanctioning compromise or arrangement with creditors*	*Summary*	*One-fifth of the statutory maximum*	
426(6)	*Company failing to comply with requirements of section 426 (information to members and creditors about compromise or arrangement)*	*1. On indictment* *2. Summary*	*A fine* *The statutory maximum*	
426(7)	*Director or trustee for debenture holders failing to give notice to company of matters necessary for purposes of section 426*	*Summary*	*One-fifth of the statutory maximum*	

Section of Act creating offence	General nature of offence	Mode of prosecution	Punishment	Daily default fine (where applicable)
427(5)	Failure to deliver to registrar office copy of court order under section 427 (company reconstruction or amalgamation)	Summary	One-fifth of the statutory maximum	One-fiftieth of the statutory maximum.
[429(6)	Offeror failing to send copy of notice or making statutory declaration knowing it to be false, etc	1. On indictment 2. Summary	2 years or a fine; or both 6 months or the statutory maximum; or both	One-fiftieth of the statutory maximum.
430A(6)	Offeror failing to give notice of rights to minority shareholder	1. On indictment 2. Summary	A fine The statutory maximum	One-fiftieth of the statutory maximum.]
444(3)	Failing to give Secretary of State, when required to do so, information about interests in shares, etc; giving false information	1. On indictment 2. Summary	2 years or a fine; or both 6 months or the statutory maximum; or both	
447(6)	…	…	…	
[448(7)]	[Obstructing the exercise of any rights conferred by a warrant or failing to comply with a requirement imposed under subsection (3)(d)]	1. On indictment 2. Summary	A fine The statutory maximum	
[449(6)	Wrongful disclosure of information to which section 449 applies.	1. On indictment. 2. Summary.	2 years, or a fine; or both. 12 months, or the statutory maximum; or both.]	
450	Destroying or mutilating company documents; falsifying such documents or making false entries; parting with such documents or altering them or making omissions	1. On indictment 2. Summary	7 years or a fine; or both 6 months or the statutory maximum; or both	
[451	Providing false information in purported compliance with section 447.	1. On indictment. 2. Summary.	2 years, or a fine; or both. 12 months, or the statutory maximum; or both.]	

Section of Act creating offence	*General nature of offence*	*Mode of prosecution*	*Punishment*	*Daily default fine (where applicable)*
[453A(5)	*Intentionally obstructing a person lawfully acting under section 453A(2) or (4).*	*1. On indictment.* *2. Summary.*	*A fine.* *The statutory maximum.]*	
455(1)	*Exercising a right to dispose of, or vote in respect of, shares which are subject to restrictions under Part XV; failing to give notice in respect of shares so subject; entering into agreement void under section 454(2), (3)*	*1. On indictment* *2. Summary*	*A fine* *The statutory maximum*	
455(2)	*Issuing shares in contravention of restrictions of Part XV*	*1. On indictment* *2. Summary*	*A fine* *The statutory maximum*	
458	*Being a party to carrying on company's business with intent to defraud creditors, or for any fraudulent purpose*	*1. On indictment* *2. Summary*	*[10 years] or a fine; or both* *6 months or the statutory maximum; or both*	
461(5)	*Failure to register office copy of court order under Part XVII altering, or giving leave to alter, company's memorandum*	*Summary*	*One-fifth of the statutory maximum*	*One-fiftieth of the statutory maximum.*
467(4), 467(5)	…	…	…	
469(2), 470(3), 478(5)	…	…	…	…
480(2)	…	…	…	
481(7), 482(5)	…	…	…	…
489, 490, 493(2)	…	…	…	
495(7), 496(6), 497(7), 498(4), 528(7), 568(3), 573(2)	…	…	…	…
577(4)	…	…	…	
577(6)	…	…	…	…

Section of Act creating offence	*General nature of offence*	*Mode of prosecution*	*Punishment*	*Daily default fine (where applicable)*
583(2), 584(2)	…	…	…	
585(3), 585(6)	…	…	…	…
585(7), 588(5), 594(2)	…	…	…	
595(4), 595(7)	…	…	…	…
595(8)	…	…	…	
600(2)	…	…	…	…
624(2), 624(5), 625, 626, 627, 628, 629, 634, 635, 637(2), 640(4)	…	…	…	
641(2)	…	…	…	…
651(3)	*Person obtaining court order to declare company's dissolution void, then failing to register the order*	*Summary*	*One-fifth of the statutory maximum*	*One-fiftieth of the statutory maximum.*
[652E(1)	*Person breaching or failing to perform duty imposed by section 652B or 652C*	*1. On indictment* *2. Summary*	*A fine* *The statutory maximum*	
652E(2)	*Person failing to perform duty imposed by section 652B(6) or 652C(2) with intent to conceal the making of application under section 652A*	*1. On indictment* *2. Summary*	*7 years or a fine; or both* *6 months or the statutory maximum; or both*	
652F(1)	*Person furnishing false or misleading information in connection with application under section 652A*	*1. On indictment* *2. Summary*	*A fine* *The statutory maximum.*	
652F(2)	*Person making false application under section 652A*	*1. On indictment* *2. Summary*	*A fine* *The statutory maximum.]*	

PART I
COMPANIES LEGISLATION

Section of Act creating offence	*General nature of offence*	*Mode of prosecution*	*Punishment*	*Daily default fine (where applicable)*
[685(6A)	*Person making false statement under section 685(4A) which he knows to be false or does not believe to be true*	*1. On indictment* *2. Summary*	*2 years or a fine; or both* *6 months or the statutory maximum; or both*	
686(3A)	*Person making false statement under section 686(2A) which he knows to be false or does not believe to be true*	*1. On indictment* *2. Summary*	*2 years or a fine; or both* *6 months or the statutory maximum; or both*	
691(4A)	*Person making false statement under section 691(3A) which he knows to be false or does not believe to be true*	*1. On indictment* *2. Summary*	*2 years or a fine; or both* *6 months or the statutory maximum; or both]*	
697(1)	*Oversea company failing to comply with any of sections 691 to 693 or 696*	*Summary*	*For an offence which is not a continuing offence, one-fifth of the statutory maximum*	
			For an offence which is a continuing offence, one-fifth of the statutory maximum	*One-fiftieth of the statutory maximum.*
697(2)	*Oversea company contravening section 694(6) (carrying on business under its corporate name after Secretary of State's direction)*	*1. On indictment* *2. Summary*	*A fine* *The statutory maximum*	*One-tenth of the statutory maximum.*
[697(3)	*Oversea Company failing to comply with Section 695A or Schedule 21A*	*Summary*	*For an offence which is not a continuing offence, one fifth of level 5 of the standard scale*	*£100]*
			For an offence which is a continuing offence one fifth of level 5 of the standard scale	
703(1)	*Oversea company failing to comply with [requirements as to accounts and reports]*	*1. On indictment* *2. Summary*	*A fine* *The statutory maximum*	*One-tenth of the statutory maximum.*

Section of Act creating offence	General nature of offence	Mode of prosecution	Punishment	Daily default fine (where applicable)
703D(5)	Oversea company failing to deliver particulars of charge to registrar	1. On indictment 2. Summary	A fine The statutory maximum	
[703R(1)	Company failing to register winding up or commencement of insolvency proceedings etc	1. On indictment 2. Summary	A fine The statutory maximum	£100]
[703R(2)	Liquidator failing to register appointment, termination of winding up or striking-off of company	1. On indictment 2. Summary	A fine The statutory maximum	£100]
710(4)	…	…	…	
720(4)	Insurance company etc failing to send twice-yearly statement in form of Schedule 23	Summary	One-fifth of the statutory maximum	One-fiftieth of the statutory maximum.
722(3)	Company failing to comply with section 722(2), as regards the manner of keeping registers, minute books and accounting records	Summary	One-fifth of the statutory maximum	One-fiftieth of the statutory maximum.
Sch 14, Pt II, para 1(3)	Company failing to give notice of location of overseas branch register, etc	Summary	One-fifth of the statutory maximum	One-fiftieth of the statutory maximum.
Sch 14, Pt II, para 4(2)	Company failing to transmit to its registered office in Great Britain copies of entries in overseas branch register, or to keep a duplicate of overseas branch register	Summary	One-fifth of the statutory maximum	One-fiftieth of the statutory maximum.
[Sch 21C, Pt I, para 7	Credit or financial institution failing to deliver accounting documents	1. On indictment 2. Summary	A fine The statutory maximum	£100]
[Sch 21C, Pt II, para 15	Credit or financial institution failing to deliver accounts and reports	1. On indictment 2. Summary	A fine The statutory maximum	£100]
[Sch 21D, Pt I, para 5	Company failing to deliver accounting documents	1. On indictment 2. Summary	A fine The statutory maximum	£100]

Section of Act creating offence	*General nature of offence*	*Mode of prosecution*	*Punishment*	*Daily default fine (where applicable)*
[Sch 21D, Pt I, para 13	*Company failing to deliver accounts and reports*	*1. On indictment* *2. Summary*	*A fine* *The statutory maximum*	*£100]*

[689]

NOTES

Repealed by the Companies Act 2006, s 1295, Sch 16, as from 1 October 2007 (in so far as relating to the entries specified in the note immediately below), and as from a day to be appointed (otherwise).

Entries repealed as from 1 October 2007 and savings in relation to those entries: the following entries are repealed as from 1 October 2007: (a) ss 210(3), 211(10), 214(5), 215(8), 216(3), 217(7), 218(3) and 219(3); (b) s 241(2), as it applies to private companies; (c) ss 314(3), 318(8), 322B(4), 323(2), 324(7), 326(2), (3), (4) and (5), 328(6), 329(3), 342(1), (2) and (3), 343(8), 356(5), 366(4), 367(3) and (5), 372(4) and (6), 376(7), 380(5), 381B(2), 382(5), 382B(2) and 383(4); (d) s 387(2), as it applies to private companies; and (e) ss 429(6), 430A(6), 444(3), 448(7), 449(6), 450, 451, 453A(5), 455(1) and (2), 458, 461(5) and 720(4). Note that the draft Companies Act 2006 (Commencement No 3, Consequential Amendments, Transitional Provisions and Savings) Order 2007, Sch 3, para 51 (at **[A12]**) provides as follows—

"51 Provisions relating to trial and punishment of offences

Any saving in this Schedule for the effect of a provision of the 1985 Act or 1986 Order that creates an offence extends to the entry relating to that provision in Schedule 24 to that Act or Schedule 23 to that Order (punishment of offences).".

The Note at the beginning of this Schedule was repealed by the Statue law (Repeals) Act 1993, as from 5 November 1993.

Entries relating to ss 12(3B), 30(5C), 43(3B), 49(8B), 117(7A), 403(2A), 419(5A), 685(6A), 686(3A), 691(4A), and words in square brackets in entries relating to ss 156(6), (7) inserted by the Companies Act 1985 (Electronic Communications) Order 2000, SI 2000/3373, art 31(6), as from 22 December 2000.

In entry relating to s 33 word in square brackets in the second column, and the entry relating to s 34A, inserted by the Companies (Audit, Investigations and Community Enterprise) Act 2004, s 33, Sch 6, paras 1, 9, as from 1 July 2005.

Entries relating to ss 56(4), 61, 64(5), 70(1), 78(1) repealed by FSA 1986, s 212(3), Sch 17, Pt I, as from 19 June 1995.

Entries relating to ss 81(2), 82(5), 86(6), 87(4), 97(4) repealed for certain purposes by FSA 1986, s 212(3), Sch 17, Pt I, as noted to s 81 at **[66]**.

Entries relating to ss 162G, 169A(4) inserted by the Companies (Acquisition of Own Shares) (Treasury Shares) Regulations 2003, SI 2003/1116, reg 4, Schedule, para 33, as from 1 December 2003.

In the entries relating to ss 221–234 words in square brackets substituted by CA 1989, s 23, Sch 10, para 24(1), (2), as from 7 January 1991.

Entries relating to ss 233(5), 234A(4), 236(4), 251(6) inserted by CA 1989, s 23, Sch 10, para 24(1), (3), partly as from 1 April 1990, and partly as from 7 January 1991.

Entries relating to sections 234ZA(6), 245E(3), 245G(7) inserted by the Companies (Audit, Investigations and Community Enterprise) Act 2004, s 25, Sch 2, Pt 2, paras 5, 10(1)–(3), as from 6 April 2005 (for modifications of this amendment in relation to England and Wales (in the case of an offence committed before the Criminal Justice Act 2003, s 154(1) comes into force), and for modifications in relation to Scotland, see s 25 of the 2004 Act at **[899]**).

Entries relating to sections 234AA(5), 234AB(4) inserted by the Companies Act 1985 (Operating and Financial Review and Directors' Report etc) Regulations 2005, SI 2005/1011, reg 19, Schedule, paras 1, 8, as from 22 March 2005, in relation to companies' financial years which begin on or after 1 April 2005; repealed by the Companies Act 1985 (Operating and Financial Review) (Repeal) Regulations 2005, SI 2005/3442, reg 2(2)(a), Sch 1, para 18, as from 12 January 2006.

Entries relating to ss 234B(3), (6), 241A(9), (10) inserted by the Directors' Remuneration Report Regulations 2002, SI 2002/1986, reg 10(1), (14), as from 1 August 2002, with effect as respects companies' financial years ending on or after 31 December 2002.

In the entries relating to ss 238–242, words in square brackets substituted by CA 1989, s 23, Sch 10, para 24(1), (2), as from 7 January 1991.

Entries relating to ss 245(1), (2), 255(5), 260(3), 287(3) repealed by CA 1989, ss 23, 212, Sch 10, para 24(1), (2), Sch 24, partly as from 1 April 1990, and partly as from 7 January 1991.

Entries relating to ss 295(7), 302(1) repealed by the Company Directors Disqualification Act 1986, s 23(2), Sch 4, as from 29 December 1986.

Entry relating to s 322B(4) inserted by the Companies (Single Member Private Limited Companies) Regulations 1992, SI 1992/1699, reg 2, Schedule, para 3(3), as from 15 July 1992.

In the entry relating to s 329(3) words in square brackets substituted by FSA 1986, s 212(2), Sch 16, para 27(a), as from 29 April 1988.

In entry relating to s 349(3) words in square brackets inserted by the Companies (Registrar, Languages and Trading Disclosures) Regulations 2006, SI 2006/3429, reg 6, Sch 1, para 4(a), as from 1 January 2007.

Entry relating to s 351(5)(ba) inserted by SI 2006/3429, reg 6, Sch 1, para 4(b), as from 1 January 2007.

Entry relating to s 352A(3) inserted by SI 1992/1699, reg 2, Schedule, para 4(2), as from 15 July 1992.

In the entry relating to s 363(3) words in square brackets substituted by CA 1989, s 139(3), as from 1 October 1990.

Entry relating to s 365(3) repealed by CA 1989, s 212, Sch 24, as from 1 October 1990.

Entry relating to s 381B(2) inserted by the Deregulation (Resolutions of Private Companies) Order 1996, SI 1996/1471, art 3(2)(c), (3), in relation to written resolutions first proposed on or after 19 June 1996.

Entry relating to s 382B(2) inserted by SI 1992/1699, reg 2, Schedule, para 6(2), as from 15 July 1992.

Entries relating to ss 384(5), 386(2) repealed by CA 1989, s 212, Sch 24, as from 1 April 1990.

Entry relating to s 387(2) inserted by CA 1989, s 119(2), as from 1 April 1990.

Entry relating to s 389(10) repealed by CA 1989, s 212, Sch 24, as from a day to be appointed.

Entries relating to s 389B(1), (2), (4) substituted for original entries relating to s 389A(2)–(4) (as inserted by CA 1989, s 120(3)), by the Companies (Audit, Investigations and Community Enterprise) Act 2004, s 25, Sch 2, Pt 2, paras 5, 10(1), (4), as from 6 April 2005 (for modifications of this amendment in relation to England and Wales (in the case of an offence committed before the Criminal Justice Act 2003, s 154(1) comes into force), and for modifications in relation to Scotland, see s 25 of the 2004 Act at **[899]**).

Entries relating to ss 390(7), 391(4), 392(2), 393 repealed by CA 1989, s 212, Sch 24, as from 1 April 1990.

Entries relating to ss 391(2), 392(3), 392A(5) inserted by CA 1989, s 122(2), as from 1 April 1990.

Entries relating to s 394A(1), (4) inserted by CA 1989, s 123(2), as from 1 April 1990.

Original entries relating to ss 399(3)–423(3) substituted by CA 1989, s 107, Sch 16, para 2(1), (2), as from a day to be appointed, as follows—

"398(3)	Company failing to deliver particulars of charge to registrar	1. On indictment 2. Summary	A fine The statutory maximum.	
408(3)	Company failing to deliver particulars of taking up of issue of debentures	Summary	One-fifth of the statutory maximum.	
409(4)	Failure to give notice to registrar of appointment of receiver or manager, or of his ceasing to act	Summary	One-fifth of the statutory maximum.	
410(4)	Failure to comply with requirements of regulations under s 410	Summary	One-fifth of the statutory maximum.	
411(4)	Failure to keep copies of charging instruments or register at registered office	1. On indictment 2. Summary	A fine The statutory maximum.	

412(4)	Refusing inspection of charging instrument or register or failing to supply copies	Summary	One-fifth of the statutory maximum.”.	

Entries relating to ss 429(6), 430A(6) inserted by FSA 1986, s 212(2), Sch 16, para 27(b), as from 4 June 1987.

Entry relating to s 447(6) repealed by the Companies (Audit, Investigations and Community Enterprise) Act 2004, s 64, Sch 8, as from 6 April 2005 (for transitional provisions, see the Companies (Audit, Investigations and Community Enterprise) Act 2004 (Commencement) and Companies Act 1989 (Commencement No 18) Order 2004, SI 2004/3322, art 7 at **[7345]**).

In the entry relating to s 448(7) words in square brackets substituted by CA 1989, s 64(2), as from 21 February 1990.

Entry relating to s 449(6) substituted for original entry relating to s 449(2), and entry relating to entry 451 substituted, by the Companies (Audit, Investigations and Community Enterprise) Act 2004, s 25, Sch 2, Pt 3, paras 16, 26(1)–(3), as from 6 April 2005 (for modifications of these amendments in relation to England and Wales (in the case of an offence committed before the Criminal Justice Act 2003, s 154(1) comes into force), and for modifications in relation to Scotland, see s 25 of the 2004 Act at **[899]**).

Entry relating to s 453A(5) inserted by the Companies (Audit, Investigations and Community Enterprise) Act 2004, s 25, Sch 2, Pt 3, paras 16, 26(1), (4), as from 6 April 2005.

In the entry relating to s 458 words in square brackets substituted by the Fraud Act 2006, s 10(1), as from 15 January 2007.

Entries relating to ss 467–641(2) repealed by the Insolvency Act 1986, s 438, Sch 12, as from 29 December 1986.

Entries relating to ss 652E(1), (2), 652F(1), (2) inserted by the Deregulation and Contracting Out Act 1994, s 13(1), Sch 5, paras 1, 4, as from 1 July 1995.

Entries relating to ss 697(3), 703R(1), (2), Schs 21C, 21D inserted by the Oversea Companies and Credit and Financial Institutions (Branch Disclosure) Regulations 1992, SI 1992/3179, reg 4, Sch 3, paras 3, 9, as from 1 January 1993 (for transitional provisions, see Sch 4 to those Regulations at **[6744B]**).

In the entry relating to s 703(1) words in square brackets substituted by CA 1989, s 23, Sch 10, para 24(1), (4), as from 1 April 1990.

Entry relating to s 703D(5) inserted by CA 1989, s 107, Sch 16, para 2(1), (3), as from a day to be appointed.

Entry relating to s 710(4) repealed by the Insolvency Act 1986, s 438, Sch 12, as from 29 December 1986.

Application to limited liability partnerships: see the Limited Liability Partnerships Regulations 2001, SI 2001/1090, reg 4(1), Sch 2, Pt 1 at **[6985]**, **[6993]**. Note also that nothing in the draft Companies Act 2006 (Commencement No 3, Consequential Amendments, Transitional Provisions and Savings) Order 2007 affects any provision of this Act as applied by the 2001 Regulations to LLPs (see art 12(2) at **[A12]** and the introductory notes to this Act).

SCHEDULE 25
COMPANIES ACT 1981, SECTION 38, AS ORIGINALLY ENACTED
Section 132(7)

38 Relief from section 56 in respect of group reconstructions

(1) This section applies where the issuing company—
(a) is a wholly-owned subsidiary of another company ("the holding company"); and
(b) allots shares to the holding company or to another wholly-owned subsidiary of the holding company in consideration for the transfer to it of shares in another subsidiary (whether wholly-owned or not) of the holding company.

(2) Where the shares in the issuing company allotted in consideration for the transfer are issued at a premium, the issuing company shall not be required by section 56 of the 1948 Act to transfer any amount in excess of the minimum premium value to the share premium account.

(3) In subsection (2) above "the minimum premium value" means the amount (if any) by which the base value of the shares transferred exceeds the aggregate nominal value of the shares allotted in consideration for the transfer.

(4) For the purposes of subsection (3) above, the base value of the shares transferred shall be taken as—
(a) the cost of those shares to the company transferring them; or
(b) the amount at which those shares are stated in that company's accounting records immediately before the transfer;
whichever is the less.

(5) Section 37 of this Act shall not apply in a case to which this section applies.

[690]

NOTES

Repealed by the Companies Act 2006, s 1295, Sch 16, as from a day to be appointed.

Subsidiary: for the purposes of this Schedule, "subsidiary" has the meaning given by s 736 of this Act as originally enacted; see CA 1989, Sch 18, para 38 at **[874]**.

Companies Act 1981, s 38, as originally enacted: i e that section as it existed before its substitution by the Companies (Share Premium Account) Regulations 1984, SI 1984/2007. The whole of the 1981 Act was repealed by the Companies Consolidation (Consequential Provisions) Act 1985, s 29, Sch 1.

1948 Act: by the Companies Act 1981, s 118(1) (repealed) this meant the Companies Act 1948. The 1948 Act was repealed by the Companies Consolidation (Consequential Provisions) Act 1985, s 29, Sch 1, and s 56 is replaced by s 130.

BUSINESS NAMES ACT 1985

(1985 c 7)

NOTES

This Act is reproduced as amended by: the Statute law (Repeals) Act 1993; the Scotland Act 1998 (Consequential Modifications) (No 2) Order 1999, SI 1999/1820; the Limited Liability Partnerships Regulations 2001, SI 2001/1090; the Government of Wales Act 2006 (Consequential Modifications and Transitional Provisions) Order 2007, SI 2007/1388. See also the note below.

Repeal of this Act by the Companies Act 2006: the whole of this Act is repealed by the Companies Act 2006, as from a day to be appointed (see s 1295 of, and Sch 16 to, the 2006 Act at **[S1295]**, **[S1331]**). For provision relating to the continuity of law, see s 1297 of the 2006 Act at **[S1297]**.

Commencement: this Act came into force on 1 July 1985 (see s 10 at **[700]**). Where any provision in this work (including any inserted or substituted provision) came into force for all purposes on or before 1 July 2005, commencement information is not noted at provision level.

ARRANGEMENT OF SECTIONS

An Act to consolidate certain enactments relating to the names under which persons may carry on business in Great Britain

[11 March 1985]

NOTES

European Economic Interest Groupings: as to the application of this Act to European Economic Interest Groupings, see the European Economic Interest Grouping Regulations 1989, SI 1989/638, reg 17 at **[6618]**.

1 Persons subject to this Act

(*1*) *This Act applies to any person who has a place of business in Great Britain and who carries on business in Great Britain under a name which—*

(*a*) *in the case of a partnership, does not consist of the surnames of all partners who are individuals and the corporate names of all partners who are bodies corporate without any addition other than an addition permitted by this Act;*

(*b*) *in the case of an individual, does not consist of his surname without any addition other than one so permitted;*

(*c*) *in the case of a company, being a company which is capable of being wound up under the Companies Act 1985, does not consist of its corporate name without any addition other than one so permitted;*

[(*d*) *in the case of a limited liability partnership, does not consist of its corporate name without any addition other than one so permitted.*]

(2) *The following are permitted additions for the purposes of subsection (1)—*

(*a*) *in the case of a partnership, the forenames of individual partners or the initials of those forenames or, where two or more individual partners have the same surname, the addition of "s" at the end of that surname; or*

(*b*) *in the case of an individual, his forename or its initial;*

(*c*) *in any case, any addition merely indicating that the business is carried on in succession to a former owner of the business.*

[691]

NOTES

Repealed by the Companies Act 2006, s 1295, Sch 16, as from a day to be appointed.

Sub-s (1): para (d) added by the Limited Liability Partnerships Regulations 2001, SI 2001/1090, reg 9, Sch 5, para 10, as from 6 April 2001.

Company which is capable of being wound up under the Companies Act 1985: as to the winding up of companies, see now the Insolvency Act 1986.

2 Prohibition of use of certain business names

(*1*) *Subject to the following subsections, a person to whom this Act applies shall not, without the written approval of the Secretary of State, carry on business in Great Britain under a name which—*

(*a*) *would be likely to give the impression that the business is connected with Her Majesty's Government[, with any part of the Scottish Administration,] [with the Welsh Assembly Government,] or with any local authority; or*

(*b*) *includes any word or expression for the time being specified in regulations made under this Act.*

(2) *Subsection (1) does not apply to the carrying on of a business by a person—*

(*a*) *to whom the business has been transferred on or after 26th February 1982; and*

(*b*) *who carries on the business under the name which was its lawful business name immediately before that transfer,*

during the period of 12 months beginning with the date of that transfer.

(3) *Subsection (1) does not apply to the carrying on of a business by a person who—*

(*a*) *carried on that business immediately before 26th February 1982; and* (*b*) *continues to carry it on under the name which immediately before that date was its lawful business name.*

(*4*) *A person who contravenes subsection* (*1*) *is guilty of an offence.*

[692]

NOTES

Repealed by the Companies Act 2006, s 1295, Sch 16, as from a day to be appointed.

Sub-s (1): words in first pair of square brackets in para (a) inserted by the Scotland Act 1998 (Consequential Modifications) (No 2) Order 1999, SI 1999/1820, art 4, Sch 2, Pt I, para 79, as from 1 July 1999; words in second pair of square brackets in that paragraph inserted by the Government of Wales Act 2006 (Consequential Modifications and Transitional Provisions) Order 2007, SI 2007/1388, art 3, Sch 1, para 20, as from 25 May 2007.

Secretary of State: by the Contracting Out (Functions in relation to the Registration of Companies) Order 1995, SI 1995/1013, art 5, Sch 3, paras 2, 3 at **[6840]**, **[6843]**, the functions of the Secretary of State conferred by or under this section may be exercised by, or by employees of, such person (if any) as may be authorised in that behalf by the Secretary of State.

Application to Scotland: the function of the Secretary of State so far as relating to an individual who (a) has a place of business in Scotland, and (b) carries on business in Scotland under a name to which either sub-s (1)(a) or (b) applies, shall be treated as exercisable in or as regards Scotland and may be exercised separately; see the Scotland Act 1998 (Modification of Functions) Order 1999, SI 1999/1756.

3 Words and expressions requiring Secretary of State's approval

(*1*) *The Secretary of State may by regulations—*

(*a*) *specify words or expressions for the use of which as or as part of a business name his approval is required by section 2*(*1*)(*b*)*; and*

(*b*) *in relation to any such word or expression, specify a Government department or other body as the relevant body for purposes of the following subsection.*

(*2*) *Where a person to whom this Act applies proposes to carry on a business under a name which is or includes any such word or expression, and a Government department or other body is specified under subsection* (*1*)(*b*) *in relation to that word or expression, that person shall—*

(*a*) *request* (*in writing*) *the relevant body to indicate whether* (*and if so why*) *it has any objections to the proposal; and*

(*b*) *submit to the Secretary of State a statement that such a request has been made and a copy of any response received from the relevant body.*

[693]

NOTES

Repealed by the Companies Act 2006, s 1295, Sch 16, as from a day to be appointed.

Regulations: the Company and Business Names Regulations 1981, SI 1981/1685 at **[6001]**.

4 Disclosure required of persons using business names

(*1*) *A person to whom this Act applies shall—*

(*a*) *[subject to subsections* (*3*) *and* (*3A*)*], state in legible characters on all business letters, written orders for goods or services to be supplied to the business, invoices and receipts issued in the course of the business and written demands for payment of debts arising in the course of the business—*

(*i*) *in the case of a partnership, the name of each partner,*

(*ii*) *in the case of an individual, his name,*

(*iii*) *in the case of a company, its corporate name, …*

[(*iiia*) *in the case of a limited liability partnership, its corporate name and the name of each member, and]*

(*iv*) *in relation to each person so named, an address in Great Britain at which service of any document relating in any way to the business will be effective; and*

(*b*) *in any premises where the business is carried on and to which the customers of the business or suppliers of any goods or services to the business have access, display in a prominent position so that it may easily be read by such customers or suppliers a notice containing such names and addresses.*

(*2*) *A person to whom this Act applies shall secure that the names and addresses required by subsection* (*1*)(*a*) *to be stated on his business letters, or which would have been so required but for [subsection (3) or (3A)], are immediately given, by written notice to any person with whom anything is done or discussed in the course of the business and who asks for such names and addresses.*

(3) Subsection (1)(a) does not apply in relation to any document issued by a partnership of more than 20 persons which maintains at its principal place of business a list of the names of all the partners if—

(a) none of the names of the partners appears in the document otherwise than in the text or as a signatory; and

(b) the document states in legible characters the address of the partnership's principal place of business and that the list of the partners' names is open to inspection at that place.

[(3A) Subsection (1)(a) does not apply in relation to any document issued by a limited liability partnership with more than 20 members which maintains at its principal place of business a list of the names of all the members if—

(a) none of the names of the members appears in the document otherwise than in the text or as a signatory; and

(b) the document states in legible characters the address of the principal place of business of the limited liability partnership and that the list of the members' names is open to inspection at that place.]

(4) Where a partnership maintains a list of the partners' names for purposes of subsection (3), any person may inspect the list during office hours.

[(4A) Where a limited liability partnership maintains a list of the members' names for the purposes of subsection (3A), any person may inspect the list during office hours.]

(5) The Secretary of State may by regulations require notices under subsection (1)(b) or (2) to be displayed or given in a specified form.

(6) A person who without reasonable excuse contravenes subsection (1) or (2), or any regulations made under subsection (5), is guilty of an offence.

(7) Where an inspection required by a person in accordance with subsection (4) [or (4A)] is refused, any partner of the partnership concerned[, or any member of the limited liability partnership concerned,] who without reasonable excuse refused that inspection, or permitted it to be refused, is guilty of an offence.

[694]

NOTES

Repealed by the Companies Act 2006, s 1295, Sch 16, as from a day to be appointed.

Sub-s (1): words in first pair of square brackets in para (a) substituted, word omitted from para (a)(iii) repealed, and para (a)(iiia) inserted, by the Limited Liability Partnerships Regulations 2001, SI 2001/1090, reg 9, Sch 5, para 11(1), (2), as from 6 April 2001.

Sub-s (2): words in square brackets substituted by SI 2001/1090, reg 9, Sch 5, para 11(1), (3), as from 6 April 2001.

Sub-ss (3A), (4A): inserted by SI 2001/1090, reg 9, Sch 5, para 11(1), (4), (5), as from 6 April 2001.

Sub-s (7): words in square brackets inserted by SI 2001/1090, reg 9, Sch 5, para 11(1), (6), as from 6 April 2001.

5 Civil remedies for breach of s 4

(1) Any legal proceedings brought by a person to whom this Act applies to enforce a right arising out of a contract made in the course of a business in respect of which he was, at the time the contract was made, in breach of subsection (1) or (2) of section 4 shall be dismissed if the defendant (or, in Scotland, the defender) to the proceedings shows—

(a) that he has a claim against the plaintiff (pursuer) arising out of that contract which he has been unable to pursue by reason of the latter's breach of section 4(1) or (2), or

(b) that he has suffered some financial loss in connection with the contract by reason of the plaintiff's (pursuer's) breach of section 4(1) or (2),

unless the court before which the proceedings are brought is satisfied that it is just and equitable to permit the proceedings to continue.

(2) This section is without prejudice to the right of any person to enforce such rights as he may have against another person in any proceedings brought by that person.

[695]

NOTES

Repealed by the Companies Act 2006, s 1295, Sch 16, as from a day to be appointed.

6 Regulations

(*1*) *Regulations under this Act shall be made by statutory instrument and may contain such transitional provisions and savings as the Secretary of State thinks appropriate, and may make different provision for different cases or classes of case.*

(*2*) *In the case of regulations made under section 3, the statutory instrument containing them shall be laid before Parliament after the regulations are made and shall cease to have effect at the end of the period of 28 days beginning with the day on which they were made (but without prejudice to anything previously done by virtue of them or to the making of new regulations) unless during that period they are approved by a resolution of each House of Parliament.*

In reckoning this period of 28 days, no account is to be taken of any time during which Parliament is dissolved or prorogued, or during which both Houses are adjourned for more than 4 days.

(*3*) *In the case of regulations made under section 4, the statutory instrument containing them is subject to annulment in pursuance of a resolution of either House of Parliament.*

[696]

NOTES

Repealed by the Companies Act 2006, s 1295, Sch 16, as from a day to be appointed.

7 Offences

(*1*) *Offences under this Act are punishable on summary conviction.*

(*2*) *A person guilty of an offence under this Act is liable to a fine not exceeding one-fifth of the statutory maximum.*

(*3*) *If after a person has been convicted summarily of an offence under section 2 or 4(6) the original contravention is continued, he is liable on a second or subsequent summary conviction of the offence to a fine not exceeding one-fiftieth of the statutory maximum for each day on which the contravention is continued (instead of to the penalty which may be imposed on the first conviction of the offence).*

(*4*) *Where an offence under section 2 or 4(6) or (7) committed by a body corporate is proved to have been committed with the consent or connivance of, or to be attributable to any neglect on the part of, any director, manager, secretary or other similar officer of the body corporate, or any person who was purporting to act in any such capacity, he as well as the body corporate is guilty of the offence and liable to be proceeded against and punished accordingly.*

(*5*) *Where the affairs of a body corporate are managed by its members, subsection (4) applies in relation to the acts and defaults of a member in connection with his functions of managements as if he were a director of the body corporate.*

(*6*) *For purposes of the following provisions of the Companies Act 1985—*

(*a*) *section 731 (summary proceedings under the Companies Acts), and*

(*b*) *section 732(3) (legal professional privilege),*

this Act is to be treated as included in those Acts.

[697]

NOTES

Repealed by the Companies Act 2006, s 1295, Sch 16, as from a day to be appointed.

8 Interpretation

(*1*) *The following definitions apply for purposes of this Act—*

"business" includes a profession;

"initial" includes any recognised abbreviation of a name;

"lawful business name", in relation to a business, means a name under which the business was carried on without contravening section 2(1) of this Act or section 2 of the Registration of Business Names Act 1916;

"local authority" means any local authority within the meaning of the Local Government Act 1972 or the Local Government (Scotland) Act 1973, the Common Council of the City of London or the Council of the Isles of Scilly;

"partnership" includes a foreign partnership;

.....

and "surname", in relation to a peer or person usually known by a British title different from his surname, means the title by which he is known.

(2) *Any expression used in this Act and also in the Companies Act 1985 has the same meaning in this Act as in that.*

[698]

NOTES

Repealed by the Companies Act 2006, s 1295, Sch 16, as from a day to be appointed.

Sub-s (1): definition "statutory maximum" repealed by the Statute law (Repeals) Act 1993, as from 5 November 1993.

9 Northern Ireland

This Act does not extend to Northern Ireland.

[699]

NOTES

Repealed by the Companies Act 2006, s 1295, Sch 16, as from a day to be appointed.

10 Commencement

This Act comes into force on 1st July 1985.

[700]

NOTES

Repealed by the Companies Act 2006, s 1295, Sch 16, as from a day to be appointed.

11 Citation

This Act may be cited as the Business Names Act 1985.

[701]

NOTES

Repealed by the Companies Act 2006, s 1295, Sch 16, as from a day to be appointed.

COMPANIES CONSOLIDATION (CONSEQUENTIAL PROVISIONS) ACT 1985

(1985 c 9)

NOTES

This Act (as reproduced here) is reproduced as amended by: FSA 1986; the Banking Act 1987; the Requirements of Writing (Scotland) Act 1995; the Statute Law (Repeals) Act 2004; the Financial Services and Markets Act 2000 (Consequential Amendments and Repeals) Order 2001, SI 2001/3649. See also the prospective amendments made to this Act by the draft Companies Act 2006 (Commencement No 3, Consequential Amendments, Transitional Provisions and Savings) Order 2007 (see **[A12]**).

Note that this Act is not amended by the Companies Act 2006.

Offences under this Act: see further the Companies Act 2006, ss 1131 at **[S1131]**.

Commencement: this Act came into force on 1 July 1985 (see s 34 at **[731]**). Where any provision in this work (including any inserted or substituted provision) came into force for all purposes on or before 1 July 2005, commencement information is not noted at provision level.

ARRANGEMENT OF SECTIONS

Old public companies

Miscellaneous savings

Repeals, etc consequential on Companies Acts consolidation; continuity of law

General

SCHEDULES

An Act to make, in connection with the consolidation of the Companies Acts 1948 to 1983 and other enactments relating to companies, provision for transitional matters and savings, repeals (including the repeal, in accordance with recommendations of the Law Commission, of certain provisions of the Companies Act 1948 which are no longer of practical utility) and consequential amendments of other Acts

[11 March 1985]

Old public companies

1 Meaning of "old public company"

(1) For the purposes of the Companies Act 1985 ("the principal Act") and this Act, an "old public company" is a company limited by shares or by guarantee and having a share capital in respect of which the following conditions are satisfied—

(a) the company either existed on 22nd December 1980 or was incorporated after that date pursuant to an application made before that date,

(b) on that date or, if later, on the day of the company's incorporation the company was not or (as the case may be) would not have been a private company within section 28 of the Companies Act 1948, and

(c) the company has not since that date or the day of the company's incorporation (as the case may be) either been re-registered as a public company or become a private company.

(2) References in the principal Act (other than so much of it as is derived from Part I of the Companies Act 1980, and other than section 33 (penalty for trading under misleading name)) to a public company or a company other than a private company are to be read as including (unless the context otherwise requires) references to an old public company, and references in that Act to a private company are to be read accordingly.
[702]

2 Re-registration as public company

(1) An old public company may be re-registered as a public company if—
(a) the directors pass a resolution, complying with the following subsection, that it should be so re-registered, and
(b) an application for the purpose in the prescribed form and signed by a director or secretary of the company is delivered to the registrar of companies together with the documents mentioned in subsection (4) below, and
(c) at the time of the resolution, the conditions specified in section 3 below are satisfied.

(2) The resolution must alter the company's memorandum so that it states that the company is to be a public company and make such other alterations in it as are necessary to bring it in substance and in form into conformity with the requirements of the principal Act with respect to the memorandum of a public company.

(3) A resolution of the directors under this section is subject to section 380 of the principal Act (copy of resolution to be forwarded to registrar of companies within 15 days).

(4) The documents referred to in subsection (1)(b) are—
(a) a printed copy of the memorandum as altered in pursuance of the resolution, and
(b) a statutory declaration in the prescribed form by a director or secretary of the company that the resolution has been passed and that the conditions specified in section 3 of this Act were satisfied at the time of the resolution.

(5) The registrar may accept a declaration under subsection (4)(b) as sufficient evidence that the resolution has been passed and the necessary conditions were satisfied.

(6) Section 47(1) and (3) to (5) of the principal Act apply on an application for re-registration under this section as they apply on an application under section 43 of that Act.
[703]

NOTES

Prescribed form: see Appendix 4 (Forms table) at **[A4]**.

3 Conditions for re-registering under s 2

(1) The following are the conditions referred to in section 2(1)(c) (being conditions also relevant under section 4).

(2) At the time concerned, the nominal value of the company's allotted share capital must not be less than the authorised minimum (defined in section 118 of the principal Act).

(3) In the case of all the shares of the company, or of all those of its shares which are comprised in a portion of the share capital which satisfies the condition in subsection (2)—
(a) each share must be paid up at least as to one-quarter of the nominal value of that share and the whole of any premium on it;
(b) where any of the shares in question or any premium payable on them has been fully or partly paid up by an undertaking given by any person that he or another should do work or perform services for the company or another, the undertaking must have been performed or otherwise discharged; and
(c) where any of the shares in question has been allotted as fully or partly paid up as to its nominal value or any premium payable on it otherwise than in cash, and the consideration for the allotment consists of or includes an undertaking (other than one to which paragraph (b) applies) to the company, then either—
(i) that undertaking must have been either performed or otherwise discharged, or
(ii) there must be a contract between the company and some person pursuant to which the undertaking is to be performed within 5 years from the time of the resolution.
[704]

4 Old public company becoming private

(1) An old public company may pass a special resolution not to be re-registered under section 2 as a public company; and section 54 of the principal Act (litigated objection by shareholders) applies to the resolution as it would apply to a special resolution by a public company to be re-registered as private.

(2) If either—

(a) 28 days from the passing of the resolution elapse without an application being made under section 54 of the principal Act (as applied), or

(b) such an application is made and proceedings are concluded on the application without the court making an order for the cancellation of the resolution,

the registrar of companies shall issue the company with a certificate stating that it is a private company; and the company then becomes a private company by virtue of the issue of the certificate.

(3) For the purposes of subsection (2)(b), proceedings on the application are concluded—

(a) except in a case within the following paragraph, when the period mentioned in section 54(7) of the principal Act (as applied) for delivering an office copy of the court's order under that section to the registrar of companies has expired, or

(b) when the company has been notified that the application has been withdrawn.

(4) If an old public company delivers to the registrar of companies a statutory declaration in the prescribed form by a director or secretary of the company that the company does not at the time of the declaration satisfy the conditions specified in section 3 for the company to be re-registered as public, the registrar shall issue the company with a certificate stating that it is a private company; and the company then becomes a private company by virtue of the issue of the certificate.

(5) A certificate issued to a company under subsection (2) or (4) is conclusive evidence that the requirements of that subsection have been complied with and that the company is a private company.

[705]

NOTES

Prescribed form: see Appendix 4 (Forms table) at **[A4]**.

---

5 Failure by old public company to obtain new classification

(1) If at any time a company which is an old public company has not delivered to the registrar of companies a declaration under section 4(4), the company and any officer of it who is in default is guilty of an offence unless at that time the company—

(a) has applied to be re-registered under section 2, and the application has not been refused or withdrawn, or

(b) has passed a special resolution not to be re-registered under that section, and the resolution has not been revoked, and has not been cancelled under section 54 of the principal Act as applied by section 4 above.

(2) A person guilty of an offence under subsection (1) is liable on summary conviction to a fine not exceeding one-fifth of the statutory maximum or, on conviction after continued contravention, to a daily default fine not exceeding one-fiftieth of the statutory maximum for every day on which the subsection is contravened.

[706]

6 Shares of old public company held by itself; charges on own shares

(1) The following has effect notwithstanding section 1(2).

(2) References to a public company in sections 146 to 149 of the principal Act (treatment of a company's shares when acquired by itself) do not include an old public company; and references in those sections to a private company are to be read accordingly.

(3) In the case of a company which after 22nd March 1982 remained an old public company and did not before that date apply to be re-registered under section 8 of the Act of 1980 as a public company, any charge on its own shares which was in existence on or immediately before that date is a permitted charge for the purposes of Chapter V of Part V of the principal Act and accordingly not void under section 150 of that Act.

[707]

7 (*Repealed by FSA 1986, s 212(3), Sch 17, Pt I.*)

8 Trading under misleading name

(1) An old public company is guilty of an offence if it carries on any trade, profession or business under a name which includes, as its last part, the words "public limited company" or "cwmni cyfyngedig cyhoeddus".

(2) A company guilty of an offence under this section, and any officer of the company who is in default, is liable on summary conviction as for an offence under section 33 of the principal Act.

[708]

9 Payment for share capital

(1) Subject as follows, sections 99, 101 to 103, 106, 108 and 110 to 115 in Part IV of the principal Act apply to a company whose directors have passed and not revoked a resolution to be re-registered under section 2 of this Act, as those sections apply to a public company.

(2) Sections 99, 101 to 103, 108 and 112 of the principal Act do not apply to the allotment of shares by a company, other than a public company registered as such on its original incorporation, where the contract for the allotment was entered into—

- (a) except in a case falling within the following paragraph, on or before 22nd June 1982;
- (b) in the case of a company re-registered or registered as a public company in pursuance of—
  - (i) a resolution to be re-registered under section 43 of the principal Act,
  - (ii) a resolution to be re-registered under section 2 of this Act, or
  - (iii) a resolution by a joint stock company that the company be a public company,

being a resolution that was passed on or before 22nd June 1982, before the date on which the resolution was passed.

[709]

Miscellaneous savings

10 Pre-1901 companies limited by guarantee

Section 15 of the principal Act does not apply in the case of companies registered before 1st January 1901.

[710]

11 Company official seal

(1) A company which was incorporated before 12th February 1979 and which has such an official seal as is mentioned in section 40 of the principal Act may use the seal for sealing such securities and documents as are there mentioned, notwithstanding anything in any instrument constituting or regulating the company or in any instrument made before that date which relates to any securities issued by the company.

(2) Any provision of such an instrument which requires any such securities or documents to be signed shall not apply to the securities or documents if they are sealed with that seal.

[(3) The foregoing provisions of this section are without prejudice to the right of a company to subscribe such securities and documents in accordance with the Requirements of Writing (Scotland) Act 1995.]

[711]

NOTES

Sub-s (3): added by the Requirements of Writing (Scotland) Act 1995, s 14(1), Sch 4, para 57, as from 1 August 1995, in relation to Scotland only.

12 Share premiums: retrospective relief

(1) The relief given by this section (being a replacement of section 39 of the Companies Act 1981) applies only where a company has issued shares in circumstances to which this section applies before 4th February 1981.

(2) Subject as follows, this section applies where the issuing company (that is, the company issuing shares as mentioned in section 130 of the principal Act) has issued at a premium shares which were allotted in pursuance of any arrangement providing for the allotment of shares in the issuing company on terms that the consideration for the shares allotted was to be provided by the issue or transfer to the issuing company of shares in another company or by the cancellation of any shares in that other company not held by the issuing company.

(3) The other company in question must either have been at the time of the arrangement a subsidiary of the issuing company or of any company which was then the issuing company's holding company or have become such a subsidiary on the acquisition or cancellation of its shares in pursuance of the arrangement.

(4) Any part of the premiums on the shares so issued which was not transferred to the company's share premium account in accordance with section 56 of the Act of 1948 shall be treated as if that section had never applied to those premiums (and may accordingly be disregarded in determining the sum to be included in the company's share premium account).

(5) Section 133(2) and (3) of the principal Act apply for the interpretation of this section; and for the purposes of this section—

(a) "company" (except in references to the issuing company) includes any body corporate, and

(b) the definition of "arrangement" in section 131(7) of the principal Act applies.

(6) This section is deemed included in Chapter III of Part V of the principal Act for the purpose of the Secretary of State's power under section 134 of that Act to make regulations in respect of relief from the requirements of section 130 of that Act.

[712]

13 Saving, in case of re-issued debentures, of rights of certain mortgagees

Whereas by section 104 of the Companies (Consolidation) Act 1908 it was provided that, upon the re-issue of redeemed debentures, the person entitled to the debentures should have the same rights and priorities as if the debentures had not previously been issued:

And whereas section 45 of the Companies Act 1928 amended section 104 of the Act of 1908 so as to provide (among other things) that the said person should have the same priorities as if the debentures had never been redeemed, but saved, in the case of debentures redeemed before, but re-issued after, 1st November 1929, the rights and priorities of persons under mortgages and charges created before that date:

Now, therefore, where any debentures which were redeemed before the date last mentioned have been re-issued after that date and before the commencement of the Act of 1948 (1st July 1948), or are or have been re-issued after that commencement, the re-issue of the debentures does not prejudice, and is deemed never to have prejudiced, any right or priority which any person would have had under or by virtue of any such mortgage or charge as above referred to if section 104 of the Act of 1908, as originally enacted, had been enacted in the Act of 1948 instead of section 90 of that Act, and in the principal Act instead of section 194 of that Act.

[713]

14 Removal of directors appointed for life pre-1945

Section 303(1) of the principal Act does not, in the case of a private company, authorise the removal of a director holding office for life on 18th July 1945, whether or not subject to retirement under an age limit by virtue of the articles or otherwise.

[714]

NOTES

Repealed by the draft Companies Act 2006 (Commencement No 3, Consequential Amendments, Transitional Provisions and Savings) Order 2007, art 10(3), Sch 5, as from 1 October 2007 (see **[A12]**).

15 Tax-free payments to directors

Section 311(1) of the principal Act does not apply to remuneration under a contract which was in force on 18th July 1945 and provides expressly (and not by reference to the articles) for payment of remuneration as mentioned in that subsection; and section 311(2) does not apply to any provision contained in such a contract.

[715]

NOTES

Repealed by the draft Companies Act 2006 (Commencement No 3, Consequential Amendments, Transitional Provisions and Savings) Order 2007, art 10(3), Sch 5, as from 1 October 2007 (see **[A12]**).

16 Statutory declaration of solvency in voluntary winding up

In relation to a winding up commenced before 22nd December 1981, section 577 of the principal Act applies in the form of section 283 of the Act of 1948, without the amendment of that section made by section 105 of the Act of 1981.

[716]

17 Court's power to control proceedings

Nothing in section 603 of the principal Act affects the practice or powers of the court as existing immediately before 1st November 1929, with respect to the staying of proceedings against a company registered in England and Wales and in course of being wound up.

[717]

18 Effect of floating charge in winding up

In relation to a charge created on or before 31st December 1947, section 617(1) of the principal Act has effect with the substitution of "6 months" for "12 months".

[718]

19 Saving from s 649 of principal Act

Nothing in section 649 of the principal Act affects the practice or powers of the court as existing immediately before 1st November 1929, with respect to the costs of an application for leave to proceed with an action or proceeding against a company which is being wound up in England and Wales.

[719]–[720]

20, 21 *(S 20 repealed by the Banking Act 1987, s 108(2), Sch 7, Pt I, as from 1 October 1987; s 21 repealed by the Statute Law (Repeals) Act 2004, as from 22 July 2004.)*

22 Saving as to certain old liquidations

(1) The provisions of the principal Act with respect to winding up (other than sections 635, 658 and 620 as applied for the purposes of section 620 and subsection (2) below) shall not apply to any company of which the winding up commenced before 1st November 1929; but every such company shall be wound up in the same manner and with the same incidents as if the Companies Act 1929, the Act of 1948 and the principal Act (apart from the sections above-mentioned) had not passed; and, for the purposes of the winding up, the Act or Acts under which the winding up commenced shall be deemed to remain in full force.

(2) A copy of every order staying or sisting the proceedings in a winding up commenced as above shall forthwith be forwarded by the company, or otherwise as may be prescribed, to the registrar of companies, who shall enter the order in his records relating to the company.

[721]

23 Restrictions on shares imposed pre-1982

Where before 3rd December 1981 shares in a company were directed by order of the Secretary of State to be subject to the restrictions imposed by section 174 of the Act of 1948, and the order remains in force at the commencement date, nothing in this Act prevents the continued application of the order with such effect as it had immediately before the repeal of section 174 took effect.

[722]

24 Saving for conversion of winding up under 1981 s 107

(1) The repeal of section 107 of the 1981 Act (conversion of creditors' winding up into members' voluntary winding up, due to circumstances arising in the period April to August 1981) does not affect the enablement for such a conversion by means of a statutory declaration (complying with subsection (2) of the section) delivered to the registrar of companies after the commencement date.

(2) For the purposes of sections 577(4) and 583 of the principal Act (consequences of actual or prospective failure to pay debts in full within the period stated by the directors in the declaration of solvency), the period stated in the declaration in the case of a winding up converted under section 107 is taken to have been 12 months from the commencement of the winding up, unless the contrary is shown.

[723]–[725]

25–28 *(S 25 repealed by the Financial Services and Markets Act 2000 (Consequential Amendments and Repeals) Order 2001, SI 2001/3649, art 38(a), as from 1 December 2001; s 26 amends the Industrial and Provident Societies Act 1967 (outside the scope of this work); ss 27, 28 repealed by the Statute Law (Repeals) Act 2004, as from 22 July 2004.)*

Repeals, etc consequential on Companies Acts consolidation; continuity of law

29 Repeals

The enactments specified in the second column of Schedule 1 to this Act are repealed to the extent specified in the third column of the Schedule.

[726]

30 Amendment of post-1948 statutes

The enactments specified in the first column of Schedule 2 to this Act (being enactments passed after the Act of 1948 and containing references to that Act or others of the Companies Acts 1948 to 1983) are amended as shown in the second column of the Schedule.

[727]

31 Continuity of law

(1) In this section—

(a) "the new Acts" means the principal Act, the Company Securities (Insider Dealing) Act 1985, the Business Names Act 1985 and this Act;

(b) "the old Acts" means the Companies Acts 1948 to 1983 and any other enactment which is repealed by this Act and replaced by a corresponding provision in the new Acts; and

(c) "the commencement date" means 1st July 1985.

(2) So far as anything done or treated as done under or for the purposes of any provision of the old Acts could have been done under or for the purposes of the corresponding provision of the new Acts, it is not invalidated by the repeal of that provision but has effect as if done under or for the purposes of the corresponding provision; and any order, regulation or other instrument made or having effect under any provision of the old Acts shall, in so far as its effect is preserved by this subsection, be treated for all purposes as made and having effect under the corresponding provision.

(3) Where any period of time specified in a provision of the old Acts is current immediately before the commencement date, the new Acts have effect as if the corresponding provision had been in force when the period began to run; and (without prejudice to the foregoing) any period of time so specified and current is deemed for the purposes of the new Acts—

(a) to run from the date or event from which it was running immediately before the commencement date, and

(b) to expire (subject to any provision of the new Acts for its extension) whenever it would have expired if the new Acts had not been passed;

and any rights, priorities, liabilities, reliefs, obligations, requirements, powers, duties or exemptions dependent on the beginning, duration or end of such a period as above mentioned shall be under the new Acts as they were or would have been under the old.

(4) Where in any provision of the new Acts there is a reference to another provision of those Acts, and the first-mentioned provision operates, or is capable of operating, in relation to things done or omitted, or events occurring or not occurring, in the past (including in particular past acts of compliance with any enactment, failures of compliance, contraventions, offences and convictions of offences), the reference to that other provision is to be read as including a reference to the corresponding provision of the old Acts.

(5) A contravention of any provision of the old Acts committed before the commencement date shall not be visited with any severer punishment under or by virtue of the new Acts than would have been applicable under that provision at the time of the contravention; but—

(a) where an offence for the continuance of which a penalty was provided has been committed under any provision of the old Acts, proceedings may be taken under the new Acts in respect of the continuance of the offence after the commencement date in the like manner as if the offence had been committed under the corresponding provision of the new Acts; and

(b) the repeal of any transitory provision of the old Acts (not replaced by any corresponding provision of the new Acts) requiring a thing to be done within a certain time does not affect a person's continued liability to be prosecuted and punished in respect of the failure, or continued failure, to do that thing.

(6) A reference in any enactment, instrument or document (whether express or implied, and in whatever phraseology) to a provision (whether first in force before or after the Act of 1948 or contained in that Act) which is replaced by a corresponding provision of the new Acts is to be read, where necessary to retain for the enactment, instrument or document the same force and effect as it would have had but for the passing of the new Acts, as, or as including, a reference to that corresponding provision.

(7) The generality of subsection (6) is not affected by any specific conversion of references made by this Act, nor by the inclusion in any provision of the new Acts of a reference (whether express or implied, and in whatever phraseology) to the provision of the old Acts corresponding to that provision, or to a provision of the old Acts which is replaced by a corresponding provision of the new.

(8) Nothing in the new Acts affects—

(a) the registration or re-registration of any company under the former Companies Acts, or the continued existence of any company by virtue of such registration or re-registration; or

(b) the application of—

(i) Table B in the Joint Stock Companies Act 1856, or

(ii) Table A in the Companies Act 1862, the Companies (Consolidation) Act 1908, the Companies Act 1929 or the Companies Act 1948,

to any company existing immediately before the commencement date; or

(c) the operation of any enactment providing for any partnership, association or company being wound up, or being wound up as a company or as an unregistered company under any of the former Companies Acts.

(9) Anything saved from repeal by section 459 of the Act of 1948 and still in force immediately before the commencement date remains in force notwithstanding the repeal of the whole of that Act.

(10) Where any provision of the new Acts was, immediately before the commencement date, contained in or given effect by a statutory instrument (whether or not made under a power in any of the old Acts), then—

(a) the foregoing provisions of this section have effect as if that provision was contained in the old Acts, and

(b) insofar as the provision was, immediately before that date, subject to a power (whether or not under the old Acts) of variation or revocation, nothing in the new Acts is to be taken as prejudicing any future exercise of the power.

(11) The provisions of this section are without prejudice to the operation of sections 16 and 17 of the Interpretation Act 1978 (savings from, and effect of, repeals); and for the purposes of section 17(2) of that Act (construction of references to enactments repealed and replaced; continuity of powers preserved in repealing enactment), any provision of the old Acts which is replaced by a provision of the principal Act, the Company Securities (Insider Dealing) Act 1985 or the Business Names Act 1985 is deemed to have been repealed and re-enacted by that one of the new Acts and not by this Act.

[728]

General

32 Interpretation

In this Act—

"the Act of 1948" means the Companies Act 1948,
"the Act of 1980" means the Companies Act 1980,
"the Act of 1981" means the Companies Act 1981, and
"the principal Act" means the Companies Act 1985;

and expressions used in this Act and also in the principal Act have the same meanings in this Act as in that (the provisions of Part XXVI of that Act to apply accordingly).

[729]

NOTES

Companies Act 1948; Companies Act 1980; Companies Act 1981: repealed by s 29 of, and Sch 1 to, this Act.

33 Northern Ireland

Except in so far as it has effect for maintaining the continuity of the law, or—

(a) repeals any enactment which extends to Northern Ireland, or
(b) amends any enactment which extends to Northern Ireland (otherwise than by the insertion of provisions expressed not so to extend),

nothing in this Act extends to Northern Ireland.

[730]

NOTES

As to the application of this Act to Northern Ireland, see now the Companies Act 2006, s 1284(1) (at **[S1284]**) which provides that this Act, in so far as it remains in force, extends to Northern Ireland.

34 Commencement

This Act comes into force on 1st July 1985.

[731]

35 Citation

This Act may be cited as the Companies Consolidation (Consequential Provisions) Act 1985.

[732]

SCHEDULES

SCHEDULE 1
ENACTMENTS REPEALED

Section 29

Chapter	*Short title*	*Extent of repeal*
1948 c 38.	Companies Act 1948.	The whole Act.
1952 c 33.	Finance Act 1952.	In section 30, subsections (2) and (3); in subsection (5) the words "(2) or (3)"; and in subsection (6) the words from "and subsection (3)" to the end.
1961 c 46.	Companies (Floating Charges) (Scotland) Act 1961.	Section 7.
1966 c 18.	Finance Act 1966.	In Schedule 6, in paragraph 14, the words "section 319(1)(a)(ii) of the Companies Act 1948 and in".
1966 c 29.	Singapore Act 1966.	In the Schedule, paragraph 14.

Chapter	*Short title*	*Extent of repeal*
1967 c 81.	Companies Act 1967.	The whole Act, except so much of Part II as remains unrepealed immediately before the commencement of this Act.
1970 c 8.	Insolvency Services (Accounting and Investment) Act 1970.	In section 1(3), paragraph (c) (with the "and" immediately preceding it).
1972 c 67.	Companies (Floating Charges and Receivers) (Scotland) Act 1972.	The whole Act.
1972 c 68.	European Communities Act 1972.	Section 9.
1973 c 38.	Social Security Act 1973.	In Schedule 27, paragraph 9.
1973 c 48.	Pakistan Act 1973.	In Schedule 3, paragraph 3(1) and (4).
1973 c 51.	Finance Act 1973.	In Schedule 19, paragraph 14.
1974 c 37.	Health and Safety at Work Etc Act 1974.	Section 79.
1975 c 18.	Social Security (Consequential Provisions) Act 1975.	In Schedule 2, paragraph 7.
1975 c 45.	Finance (No 2) Act 1975.	In Part IV of Schedule 12, paragraph 6(1)(e).
1975 c 60.	Social Security Pensions Act 1975.	In Schedule 4, paragraph 3.
1976 c 47.	Stock Exchange (Completion of Bargains) Act 1976.	Sections 1 to 4. Section 7(3).
1976 c 60.	Insolvency Act 1976.	In section 1(1), the words "the winding up of companies and". Section 9. Section 14(3). In section 14(6), the word "9". In Part I of Schedule 1, the heading "The Companies Act 1948" and the entries under that heading; and in Part II of that Schedule in paragraph 1, sub-paragraph (c), in paragraph 2, sub-paragraph (c), paragraph 6, and in paragraph 7, sub-paragraph (b). In Schedule 2, paragraphs 3 and 4.
1976 c 69.	Companies Act 1976.	The whole Act.
1979 c 53.	Charging Orders Act 1979.	In section 4, the words "and in section 325 of the Companies Act 1948", and the words "in each case".
1980 c 22.	Companies Act 1980.	The whole Act.
1981 c 54.	Supreme Court Act 1981.	In Schedule 5, the entry relating to the Companies Act 1948.
1981 c 62.	Companies Act 1981.	The whole Act.

Chapter	Short title	Extent of repeal
1981 c 63.	Betting and Gaming Duties Act 1981.	In section 30(1), the word "or" at the end of paragraph (b), and paragraph (c). In section 30(2), paragraph (c).
1981 c 65.	Trustee Savings Banks Act 1981.	In Schedule 6, the entry under "COMPANIES ACT 1948".
1982 c 4.	Stock Transfer Act 1982.	In Schedule 2, paragraphs 4 and 5.
1982 c 46.	Employment Act 1982.	Section 1.
1982 c 48.	Criminal Justice Act 1982.	In section 46(4)(a) the words from "except" to "1981".
1982 c 50.	Insurance Companies Act 1982.	In Schedule 4, paragraph 14.
1983. c 50.	Companies (Beneficial Interests) Act 1983.	The whole Act.
1983 c 53.	Car Tax Act 1983.	In Schedule 1, in paragraph 4(1), the word "or" at the end of sub-paragraph (b), and sub-paragraph (c); and in that Schedule, in paragraph 4(2), sub-paragraph (c).
1983 c 55.	Value Added Tax Act 1983.	In Schedule 7, in paragraph 12(1), the word "or" at the end of sub-paragraph (b), and sub-paragraph (c); and in that Schedule, in paragraph 12(2), sub-paragraph (c).

[733]

NOTES

Supreme Court Act 1981: see the Constitutional Reform Act 2005, s 59(5), Sch 11, Pt 1, para 1(2), which provides that the "Supreme Court Act 1981" shall be renamed the "Senior Courts Act 1981" (as from a day to be appointed).

(*In so far as still in force, Sch 2 makes amendments consequential upon the consolidation of the Companies Acts and, in so far as they are relevant to this work, they have been incorporated in the appropriate place.*)

DESTINATION TABLES
CONSOLIDATION OF THE COMPANIES ACTS: 1948–1983 (NOTE)

NOTES

In order to save space and, therefore, include new substantive legislation, the destination tables have been omitted from this edition of the Company Law Handbook. The tables are, however, still included in electronic versions of this Handbook. See www.lexisnexis.co.uk.

[734]

DERIVATION TABLES CONSOLIDATION OF THE COMPANIES ACTS: 1948–1983 (NOTE)

NOTES

In order to save space and, therefore, include new substantive legislation, the derivation tables have been omitted from this edition of the Company Law Handbook. The tables are, however, still included in electronic versions of this Handbook. See www.lexisnexis.co.uk.

[735]

COMPANY DIRECTORS DISQUALIFICATION ACT 1986

(1986 c 46)

NOTES

This Act is reproduced as amended by: CA 1989; the Friendly Societies Act 1992; the Deregulation and Contracting Out Act 1994; the Youth Justice and Criminal Evidence Act 1999; the Insolvency Act 2000; the Enterprise Act 2002; the Communications Act 2003; the Water Act 2003; the Health and Social Care (Community Health and Standards) Act 2003; the Courts Act 2003; the Railways and Transport Safety Act 2003; the Companies (Audit, Investigations and Community Enterprise) Act 2004; the National Health Service (Consequential Provisions) Act 2006; the Companies Act 2006; the Open-Ended Investment Companies (Investment Companies with Variable Capital) Regulations 1996, SI 1996/2827; the Open-Ended Investment Companies Regulations 2001, SI 2001/1228; the Financial Services and Markets Act 2000 (Consequential Amendments and Repeals) Order 2001, SI 2001/3649; the Enterprise Act 2002 (Insolvency) Order 2003, SI 2003/2096; the Insolvency Act 2000 (Company Directors Disqualification Undertakings) Order 2004, SI 2004/1941. See also the prospective amendments made to this Act by the draft Companies Act 2006 (Commencement No 3, Consequential Amendments, Transitional Provisions and Savings) Order 2007 (see **[A12]**).

ARRANGEMENT OF SECTIONS

An Act to consolidate certain enactments relating to the disqualification of persons from being directors of companies, and from being otherwise concerned with a company's affairs

[25 July 1986]

NOTES

Limited liability partnerships: the Limited Liability Partnerships Regulations 2001, SI 2001/1090, reg 4(2) (at **[6985]**) provides that the provisions of this Act shall apply to limited liability partnerships, except where the context otherwise requires, with the general modifications specified in that paragraph. See also Sch 2, Pt II to the 2001 Regulations (at **[6994]**) for specific modifications of Sch 1, Pt II to this Act.

European Economic Interest Groupings: as to the application of ss 1, 2, 4–11, 12(2), 15–17, 20, 22 of, and Sch 1 to, this Act, to European Economic Interest Groupings, see the European Economic Interest Grouping Regulations 1989, SI 1989/638, reg 20 at **[6621]**.

Insolvent partnerships: as to the application, with modifications, of this Act in relation to insolvent partnerships, see the Insolvent Partnerships Order 1994, SI 1994/2421.

Official Receiver: as to the contracting out of certain functions of the Official Receiver conferred by or under this Act, see the Contracting Out (Functions of the Official Receiver) Order 1995, SI 1995/1386 at **[6844]**.

Preliminary

1 Disqualification orders: general

(1) In the circumstances specified below in this Act a court may, and under [sections 6 and 9A] shall, make against a person a disqualification order, that is to say an order that [for a period specified in the order—

(a) he shall not be a director of a company, act as receiver of a company's property or in any way, whether directly or indirectly, be concerned or take part in the promotion, formation or management of a company unless (in each case) he has the leave of the court, and

(b) he shall not act as an insolvency practitioner.]

(2) In each section of this Act which gives to a court power or, as the case may be, imposes on it the duty to make a disqualification order there is specified the maximum (and,

in section 6, the minimum) period of disqualification which may or (as the case may be) must be imposed by means of the order [and, unless the court otherwise orders, the period of disqualification so imposed shall begin at the end of the period of 21 days beginning with the date of the order].

(3) Where a disqualification order is made against a person who is already subject to such an order [or to a disqualification undertaking], the periods specified in those orders [or, as the case may be, in the order and the undertaking] shall run concurrently.

(4) A disqualification order may be made on grounds which are or include matters other than criminal convictions, notwithstanding that the person in respect of whom it is to be made may be criminally liable in respect of those matters.

[736]

NOTES

Sub-s (1): words in first pair of square brackets substituted by the Enterprise Act 2002, s 204(1), (3), as from 20 June 2003; words in second pair of square brackets substituted by the Insolvency Act 2000, s 5(1), as from 2 April 2001.

Sub-ss (2), (3): words in square brackets inserted by the Insolvency Act 2000, ss 5(2), 8, Sch 4, Pt I, paras 1, 2, as from 2 April 2001.

[1A Disqualification undertakings: general

(1) In the circumstances specified in sections 7 and 8 the Secretary of State may accept a disqualification undertaking, that is to say an undertaking by any person that, for a period specified in the undertaking, the person—

(a) will not be a director of a company, act as receiver of a company's property or in any way, whether directly or indirectly, be concerned or take part in the promotion, formation or management of a company unless (in each case) he has the leave of a court, and

(b) will not act as an insolvency practitioner.

(2) The maximum period which may be specified in a disqualification undertaking is 15 years; and the minimum period which may be specified in a disqualification undertaking under section 7 is two years.

(3) Where a disqualification undertaking by a person who is already subject to such an undertaking or to a disqualification order is accepted, the periods specified in those undertakings or (as the case may be) the undertaking and the order shall run concurrently.

(4) In determining whether to accept a disqualification undertaking by any person, the Secretary of State may take account of matters other than criminal convictions, notwithstanding that the person may be criminally liable in respect of those matters.]

[737]

NOTES

Inserted by the Insolvency Act 2000, s 6(1), (2), as from 2 April 2001.

Disqualification for general misconduct in connection with companies

2 Disqualification on conviction of indictable offence

(1) The court may make a disqualification order against a person where he is convicted of an indictable offence (whether on indictment or summarily) in connection with the promotion, formation, management[, liquidation or striking off] of a company [with the receivership of a company's property or with his being an administrative receiver of a company].

(2) "The court" for this purpose means—

(a) any court having jurisdiction to wind up the company in relation to which the offence was committed, or

(b) the court by or before which the person is convicted of the offence, or

(c) in the case of a summary conviction in England and Wales, any other magistrates' court acting [in the same local justice] area;

and for the purposes of this section the definition of "indictable offence" in Schedule 1 to the Interpretation Act 1978 applies for Scotland as it does for England and Wales.

(3) The maximum period of disqualification under this section is—

(a) where the disqualification order is made by a court of summary jurisdiction, 5 years, and

(b) in any other case, 15 years.

[738]

NOTES

Sub-s (1): words in first pair of square brackets substituted by the Deregulation and Contracting Out Act 1994, s 39, Sch 11, para 6, as from 1 July 1995; words in second pair of square brackets substituted by the Insolvency Act 2000, s 8, Sch 4, Pt I, paras 1, 3, as from 2 April 2001.

Sub-s (2): words in square brackets substituted by the Courts Act 2003, s 109(1), Sch 8, para 300, as from 1 April 2005 (for transitional provisions and savings in connection with the commencement of the Courts Act 2003 and the continuity of functions, etc, see SI 2005/911).

3 Disqualification for persistent breaches of companies legislation

(1) The court may make a disqualification order against a person where it appears to it that he has been persistently in default in relation to provisions of the companies legislation requiring any return, account or other document to be filed with, delivered or sent, or notice of any matter to be given, to the registrar of companies.

(2) On an application to the court for an order to be made under this section, the fact that a person has been persistently in default in relation to such provisions as are mentioned above may (without prejudice to its proof in any other manner) be conclusively proved by showing that in the 5 years ending with the date of the application he has been adjudged guilty (whether or not on the same occasion) of three or more defaults in relation to those provisions.

(3) A person is to be treated under subsection (2) as being adjudged guilty of a default in relation to any provision of that legislation if—

(a) he is convicted (whether on indictment or summarily) of an offence consisting in a contravention of or failure to comply with that provision (whether on his own part or on the part of any company), or

(b) a default order is made against him, that is to say an order under any of the following provisions—

(i) [section 242(4)] of the Companies Act (order requiring delivery of company accounts),

[(ia) section 245B of that Act (order requiring preparation of revised accounts),]

(ii) section 713 of that Act (enforcement of company's duty to make returns),

(iii) section 41 of the Insolvency Act (enforcement of receiver's or manager's duty to make returns), or

(iv) section 170 of that Act (corresponding provision for liquidator in winding up),

in respect of any such contravention of or failure to comply with that provision (whether on his own part or on the part of any company).

(4) In this section "the court" means any court having jurisdiction to wind up any of the companies in relation to which the offence or other default has been or is alleged to have been committed.

(5) The maximum period of disqualification under this section is 5 years.

[739]

NOTES

Sub-s (3): words in square brackets in para (b)(i) substituted by CA 1989, s 23, Sch 10, para 35(2)(a), as from 1 April 1990, and para (b)(ia) inserted by CA 1989, s 23, Sch 10, para 35(2)(b), as from 7 January 1991.

4 Disqualification for fraud, etc, in winding up

(1) The court may make a disqualification order against a person if, in the course of the winding up of a company, it appears that he—

(a) has been guilty of an offence for which he is liable (whether he has been convicted or not) under section 458 of the Companies Act (fraudulent trading), or

(b) has otherwise been guilty, while an officer or liquidator of the company [receiver of the company's property or administrative receiver of the company], of any fraud in relation to the company or of any breach of his duty as such officer, liquidator, [receiver or administrative receiver].

(2) In this section "the court" means any court having jurisdiction to wind up any of the companies in relation to which the offence or other default has been or is alleged to have been committed; and "officer" includes a shadow director.

(3) The maximum period of disqualification under this section is 15 years.

[740]

NOTES

Sub-s (1): words in square brackets substituted by the Insolvency Act 2000, s 8, Sch 4, Pt I, paras 1, 4, as from 2 April 2001.

5 Disqualification on summary conviction

(1) An offence counting for the purposes of this section is one of which a person is convicted (either on indictment or summarily) in consequence of a contravention of, or failure to comply with, any provision of the companies legislation requiring a return, account or other document to be filed with, delivered or sent, or notice of any matter to be given, to the registrar of companies (whether the contravention or failure is on the person's own part or on the part of any company).

(2) Where a person is convicted of a summary offence counting for those purposes, the court by which he is convicted (or, in England and Wales, any other magistrates' court acting [in the same local justice] area) may make a disqualification order against him if the circumstances specified in the next subsection are present.

(3) Those circumstances are that, during the 5 years ending with the date of the conviction, the person has had made against him, or has been convicted of, in total not less than 3 default orders and offences counting for the purposes of this section; and those offences may include that of which he is convicted as mentioned in subsection (2) and any other offence of which he is convicted on the same occasion.

(4) For the purposes of this section—

(a) the definition of "summary offence" in Schedule 1 to the Interpretation Act 1978 applies for Scotland as for England and Wales, and

(b) "default order" means the same as in section 3(3)(b).

(5) The maximum period of disqualification under this section is 5 years.

[741]

NOTES

Sub-s (2): words in square brackets substituted by the Courts Act 2003, s 109(1), Sch 8, para 300, as from 1 April 2005 (for transitional provisions and savings in connection with the commencement of the Courts Act 2003 and the continuity of functions, etc, see SI 2005/911).

Disqualification for unfitness

6 Duty of court to disqualify unfit directors of insolvent companies

(1) The court shall make a disqualification order against a person in any case where, on an application under this section, it is satisfied—

(a) that he is or has been a director of a company which has at any time become insolvent (whether while he was a director or subsequently), and

(b) that his conduct as a director of that company (either taken alone or taken together with his conduct as a director of any other company or companies) makes him unfit to be concerned in the management of a company.

(2) For the purposes of this section and the next, a company becomes insolvent if—

(a) the company goes into liquidation at a time when its assets are insufficient for the payment of its debts and other liabilities and the expenses of the winding up,

[(b) the company enters administration,] or

(c) an administrative receiver of the company is appointed;

and references to a person's conduct as a director of any company or companies include, where that company or any of those companies has become insolvent, that person's conduct in relation to any matter connected with or arising out of the insolvency of that company.

[(3) In this section and section 7(2), "the court" means—

(a) where the company in question is being or has been wound up by the court, that court,

(b) where the company in question is being or has been wound up voluntarily, any court which has or (as the case may be) had jurisdiction to wind it up,

[(c) where neither paragraph (a) nor (b) applies but an administrator or administrative receiver has at any time been appointed in respect of the company in question, any court which has jurisdiction to wind it up.]

(3A) Sections 117 and 120 of the Insolvency Act 1986 (jurisdiction) shall apply for the purposes of subsection (3) as if the references in the definitions of "registered office" to the presentation of the petition for winding up were references—

(a) in a case within paragraph (b) of that subsection, to the passing of the resolution for voluntary winding up,

[(b) in a case within paragraph (c) of that subsection, to the appointment of the administrator or (as the case may be) administrative receiver.]

(3B) Nothing in subsection (3) invalidates any proceedings by reason of their being taken in the wrong court; and proceedings—

(a) for or in connection with a disqualification order under this section, or

(b) in connection with a disqualification undertaking accepted under section 7,

may be retained in the court in which the proceedings were commenced, although it may not be the court in which they ought to have been commenced.

(3C) In this section and section 7, "director" includes a shadow director.]

(4) Under this section the minimum period of disqualification is 2 years, and the maximum period is 15 years.

[742]

NOTES

Sub-s (2): para (b) substituted by the Enterprise Act 2002, s 248(3), Sch 17, paras 40, 41(a), as from 15 September 2003 (for savings and transitional provisions, see the note to the Insolvency Act 1986, s 8 at **[3164]**).

Sub-s (3): substituted, together with sub-ss (3A), (3B), (3C) for original sub-s (3), by the Insolvency Act 2000, s 8, Sch 4, Pt I, paras 1, 5, as from 2 April 2001; para (c) substituted by the Enterprise Act 2002, s 248(3), Sch 17, paras 40, 41(b), as from 15 September 2003 (for savings and transitional provisions, see the note to the Insolvency Act 1986, s 8 at **[3164]**).

Sub-s (3A): substituted as noted above; para (b) substituted by the Enterprise Act 2002, s 248(3), Sch 17, paras 40, 41(c), as from 15 September 2003 (for savings and transitional provisions, see the note to the Insolvency Act 1986, s 8 at **[3164]**).

Sub-ss (3B), (3C): substituted as noted above.

7 [Disqualification order or undertaking; and reporting provisions]

(1) If it appears to the Secretary of State that it is expedient in the public interest that a disqualification order under section 6 should be made against any person, an application for the making of such an order against that person may be made—

(a) by the Secretary of State, or

(b) if the Secretary of State so directs in the case of a person who is or has been a director of a company which is being [or has been] wound up by the court in England and Wales, by the official receiver.

(2) Except with the leave of the court, an application for the making under that section of a disqualification order against any person shall not be made after the end of the period of 2 years beginning with the day on which the company of which that person is or has been a director became insolvent.

[(2A) If it appears to the Secretary of State that the conditions mentioned in section 6(1) are satisfied as respects any person who has offered to give him a disqualification undertaking, he may accept the undertaking if it appears to him that it is expedient in the public interest that he should do so (instead of applying, or proceeding with an application, for a disqualification order).]

(3) If it appears to the office-holder responsible under this section, that is to say—

(a) in the case of a company which is being wound up by the court in England and Wales, the official receiver,

(b) in the case of a company which is being wound up otherwise, the liquidator,

[(c) in the case of a company which is in administration, the administrator,] or

(d) in the case of a company of which there is an administrative receiver, that receiver,

that the conditions mentioned in section 6(1) are satisfied as respects a person who is or has been a director of that company, the officer-holder shall forthwith report the matter to the Secretary of State.

(4) The Secretary of State or the official receiver may require the liquidator, administrator or administrative receiver of a company, or the former liquidator, administrator or administrative receiver of a company—

(a) to furnish him with such information with respect to any person's conduct as a director of the company, and

(b) to produce and permit inspection of such books, papers and other records relevant to that person's conduct as such a director,

as the Secretary of State or the official receiver may reasonably require for the purpose of determining whether to exercise, or of exercising, any function of his under this section.

[743]

NOTES

Section heading: substituted by the Insolvency Act 2000, s 8, Sch 4, Pt I, paras 1, 6(b), as from 2 April 2001.

Sub-s (1): words in square brackets inserted by the Insolvency Act 2000, s 8, Sch 4, Pt I, paras 1, 6(a), as from 2 April 2001.

Sub-s (2A): inserted by the Insolvency Act 2000, s 6(1), (3), as from 2 April 2001.

Sub-s (3): para (c) substituted by the Enterprise Act 2002, s 248(3), Sch 17, paras 40, 42, as from 15 September 2003 (for savings and transitional provisions, see the note to the Insolvency Act 1986, s 8 at **[3164]**).

8 Disqualification after investigation of company

[(1) If it appears to the Secretary of State from investigative material that it is expedient in the public interest that a disqualification order should be made against a person who is, or has been, a director or shadow director of a company, he may apply to the court for such an order.

(1A) "Investigative material" means—

(a) a report made by inspectors under—

(i) section 437 of the Companies Act 1985;

(ii) section 167, 168, 169 or 284 of the Financial Services and Markets Act 2000; or

(iii) where the company is an open-ended investment company (within the meaning of that Act) regulations made as a result of section 262(2)(k) of that Act; and

(b) information or documents obtained under—

(i) section [437, 446E,] 447[, 448[, 451A] or 453A] of the Companies Act 1985;

(ii) section 2 of the Criminal Justice Act 1987;

(iii) section 28 of the Criminal Law (Consolidation) (Scotland) Act 1995;

(iv) section 83 of the Companies Act 1989; or

(v) section 165, 171, 172, 173 or 175 of the Financial Services and Markets Act 2000.]

(2) The court may make a disqualification order against a person where, on an application under this section, it is satisfied that his conduct in relation to the company makes him unfit to be concerned in the management of a company.

[(2A) Where it appears to the Secretary of State from such report, information or documents that, in the case of a person who has offered to give him a disqualification undertaking—

(a) the conduct of the person in relation to a company of which the person is or has been a director or shadow director makes him unfit to be concerned in the management of a company, and

(b) it is expedient in the public interest that he should accept the undertaking (instead of applying, or proceeding with an application, for a disqualification order),

he may accept the undertaking.]

(3) In this section "the court" means the High Court or, in Scotland, the Court of Session.

(4) The maximum period of disqualification under this section is 15 years.

[744]

NOTES

Sub-s (1): substituted, together with sub-s (1A) for original sub-s (1), by the Financial Services and Markets Act 2000 (Consequential Amendments and Repeals) Order 2001, SI 2001/3649, art 39, as from 1 December 2001.

Sub-s (1A): substituted as noted above; figures in first pair and third (inner) pair of square brackets inserted by the Companies Act 2006, s 1039, as from 1 October 2007, with effect where an inspector is appointed under a provision of CA 1985, Pt 14 on or after that date; words in second (outer) pair of square brackets substituted by the Companies (Audit, Investigations and Community Enterprise) Act 2004, s 25, Sch 2, Pt 3, para 28, as from 6 April 2005 (for transitional provisions, see the Companies (Audit, Investigations and Community Enterprise) Act 2004 (Commencement) and Companies Act 1989 (Commencement No 18) Order 2004, SI 2004/3322, art 12 at **[7350]**).

Sub-s (2A): inserted by the Insolvency Act 2000, s 6(1), (4), as from 2 April 2001.

[8A Variation etc of disqualification undertaking

(1) The court may, on the application of a person who is subject to a disqualification undertaking—

(a) reduce the period for which the undertaking is to be in force, or

(b) provide for it to cease to be in force.

(2) On the hearing of an application under subsection (1), the Secretary of State shall appear and call the attention of the court to any matters which seem to him to be relevant, and may himself give evidence or call witnesses.

[(2A) Subsection (2) does not apply to an application in the case of an undertaking given under section 9B, and in such a case on the hearing of the application whichever of the OFT or a specified regulator (within the meaning of section 9E) accepted the undertaking—

(a) must appear and call the attention of the court to any matters which appear to it or him (as the case may be) to be relevant;

(b) may give evidence or call witnesses.]

[(3) In this section "the court"—

(a) in the case of an undertaking given under section 9B means the High Court or (in Scotland) the Court of Session;

(b) in any other case has the same meaning as in section 7(2) or 8 (as the case may be).]

[745]

NOTES

Inserted by the Insolvency Act 2000, s 6(1), (5), as from 2 April 2001.

Sub-s (2A): inserted by the Enterprise Act 2002, s 204(1), (4), as from 20 June 2003.

Sub-s (3): substituted by the Enterprise Act 2002, s 204(1), (5), as from 20 June 2003.

9 Matters for determining unfitness of directors

(1) Where it falls to a court to determine whether a person's conduct as a director … of any particular company or companies makes him unfit to be concerned in the management of a company, the court shall, as respects his conduct as a director of that company or, as the case may be, each of those companies, have regard in particular—

(a) to the matters mentioned in Part I of Schedule 1 to this Act, and

(b) where the company has become insolvent, to the matters mentioned in Part II of that Schedule;

and references in that Schedule to the director and the company are to be read accordingly.

[(1A) In determining whether he may accept a disqualification undertaking from any person the Secretary of State shall, as respects the person's conduct as a director of any company concerned, have regard in particular—

(a) to the matters mentioned in Part I of Schedule 1 to this Act, and

(b) where the company has become insolvent, to the matters mentioned in Part II of that Schedule;

and references in that Schedule to the director and the company are to be read accordingly.]

(2) Section 6(2) applies for the purposes of this section and Schedule 1 as it applies for the purposes of sections 6 and 7 [and in this section and that Schedule "director" includes a shadow director].

(3) Subject to the next subsection, any reference in Schedule 1 to an enactment contained in the Companies Act or the Insolvency Act includes, in relation to any time before the coming into force of that enactment, the corresponding enactment in force at that time.

(4) The Secretary of State may by order modify any of the provisions of Schedule 1; and such an order may contain such transitional provisions as may appear to the Secretary of State necessary or expedient.

(5) The power to make orders under this section is exercisable by statutory instrument subject to annulment in pursuance of a resolution of either House of Parliament.

[746]

NOTES

Sub-s (1): words omitted repealed by the Insolvency Act 2000, ss 8, 15(1), Sch 4, Pt I, paras 1, 7(a), Sch 5, as from 2 April 2001.

Sub-s (1A): inserted by the Insolvency Act 2000, s 6(1), (6), as from 2 April 2001.

Sub-s (2): words in square brackets added by the Insolvency Act 2000, s 8, Sch 4, Pt I, paras 1, 7(b), as from 2 April 2001.

[Disqualification for competition infringements

9A Competition disqualification order

(1) The court must make a disqualification order against a person if the following two conditions are satisfied in relation to him.

(2) The first condition is that an undertaking which is a company of which he is a director commits a breach of competition law.

(3) The second condition is that the court considers that his conduct as a director makes him unfit to be concerned in the management of a company.

(4) An undertaking commits a breach of competition law if it engages in conduct which infringes any of the following—

- (a) the Chapter 1 prohibition (within the meaning of the Competition Act 1998) (prohibition on agreements, etc preventing, restricting or distorting competition);
- (b) the Chapter 2 prohibition (within the meaning of that Act) (prohibition on abuse of a dominant position);
- (c) Article 81 of the Treaty establishing the European Community (prohibition on agreements, etc preventing, restricting or distorting competition);
- (d) Article 82 of that Treaty (prohibition on abuse of a dominant position).

(5) For the purpose of deciding under subsection (3) whether a person is unfit to be concerned in the management of a company the court—

- (a) must have regard to whether subsection (6) applies to him;
- (b) may have regard to his conduct as a director of a company in connection with any other breach of competition law;
- (c) must not have regard to the matters mentioned in Schedule 1.

(6) This subsection applies to a person if as a director of the company—

- (a) his conduct contributed to the breach of competition law mentioned in subsection (2);
- (b) his conduct did not contribute to the breach but he had reasonable grounds to suspect that the conduct of the undertaking constituted the breach and he took no steps to prevent it;
- (c) he did not know but ought to have known that the conduct of the undertaking constituted the breach.

(7) For the purposes of subsection (6)(a) it is immaterial whether the person knew that the conduct of the undertaking constituted the breach.

(8) For the purposes of subsection (4)(a) or (c) references to the conduct of an undertaking are references to its conduct taken with the conduct of one or more other undertakings.

(9) The maximum period of disqualification under this section is 15 years.

(10) An application under this section for a disqualification order may be made by the OFT or by a specified regulator.

(11) Section 60 of the Competition Act 1998 (c 41) (consistent treatment of questions arising under United Kingdom and Community law) applies in relation to any question arising by virtue of subsection (4)(a) or (b) above as it applies in relation to any question arising under Part 1 of that Act.]

[746A]

NOTES

Inserted, together with preceding heading and ss 9B–9E, by the Enterprise Act 2002, s 204(1), (2), as from 20 June 2003.

[9B Competition undertakings

(1) This section applies if—

(a) the OFT or a specified regulator thinks that in relation to any person an undertaking which is a company of which he is a director has committed or is committing a breach of competition law,

(b) the OFT or the specified regulator thinks that the conduct of the person as a director makes him unfit to be concerned in the management of a company, and

(c) the person offers to give the OFT or the specified regulator (as the case may be) a disqualification undertaking.

(2) The OFT or the specified regulator (as the case may be) may accept a disqualification undertaking from the person instead of applying for or proceeding with an application for a disqualification order.

(3) A disqualification undertaking is an undertaking by a person that for the period specified in the undertaking he will not—

(a) be a director of a company;

(b) act as receiver of a company's property;

(c) in any way, whether directly or indirectly, be concerned or take part in the promotion, formation or management of a company;

(d) act as an insolvency practitioner.

(4) But a disqualification undertaking may provide that a prohibition falling within subsection (3)(a) to (c) does not apply if the person obtains the leave of the court.

(5) The maximum period which may be specified in a disqualification undertaking is 15 years.

(6) If a disqualification undertaking is accepted from a person who is already subject to a disqualification undertaking under this Act or to a disqualification order the periods specified in those undertakings or the undertaking and the order (as the case may be) run concurrently.

(7) Subsections (4) to (8) of section 9A apply for the purposes of this section as they apply for the purposes of that section but in the application of subsection (5) of that section the reference to the court must be construed as a reference to the OFT or a specified regulator (as the case may be).]

[746B]

NOTES

Inserted as noted to s 9A at **[746A]**.

[9C Competition investigations

(1) If the OFT or a specified regulator has reasonable grounds for suspecting that a breach of competition law has occurred it or he (as the case may be) may carry out an investigation for the purpose of deciding whether to make an application under section 9A for a disqualification order.

(2) For the purposes of such an investigation sections 26 to 30 of the Competition Act 1998 (c 41) apply to the OFT and the specified regulators as they apply to the OFT for the purposes of an investigation under section 25 of that Act.

(3) Subsection (4) applies if as a result of an investigation under this section the OFT or a specified regulator proposes to apply under section 9A for a disqualification order.

(4) Before making the application the OFT or regulator (as the case may be) must—

(a) give notice to the person likely to be affected by the application, and
(b) give that person an opportunity to make representations.]

[746C]

NOTES

Inserted as noted to s 9A at **[746A]**.

[9D Co-ordination

(1) The Secretary of State may make regulations for the purpose of co-ordinating the performance of functions under sections 9A to 9C (relevant functions) which are exercisable concurrently by two or more persons.

(2) Section 54(5) to (7) of the Competition Act 1998 (c 41) applies to regulations made under this section as it applies to regulations made under that section and for that purpose in that section—

(a) references to Part 1 functions must be read as references to relevant functions;
(b) references to a regulator must be read as references to a specified regulator;
(c) a competent person also includes any of the specified regulators.

(3) The power to make regulations under this section must be exercised by statutory instrument subject to annulment in pursuance of a resolution of either House of Parliament.

(4) Such a statutory instrument may—

(a) contain such incidental, supplemental, consequential and transitional provision as the Secretary of State thinks appropriate;
(b) make different provision for different cases.]

[746D]

NOTES

Inserted as noted to s 9A at **[746A]**.

[9E Interpretation

(1) This section applies for the purposes of sections 9A to 9D.

(2) Each of the following is a specified regulator for the purposes of a breach of competition law in relation to a matter in respect of which he or it has a function—

[(a) the Office of Communications;]
(b) the Gas and Electricity Markets Authority;
[(c) the Water Services Regulation Authority;]
(d) [the Office of Rail Regulation];
(e) the Civil Aviation Authority.

(3) The court is the High Court or (in Scotland) the Court of Session.

(4) Conduct includes omission.

(5) Director includes shadow director.]

[746E]

NOTES

Inserted as noted to s 9A at **[746A]**.

Sub-s (2): para (a) substituted by the Communications Act 2003, s 406, Sch 17, para 83, as from 29 December 2003; para (c) substituted by the Water Act 2003, s 101(1), Sch 7, Pt 2, para 25, as from 1 April 2006; words in square brackets in para (d) substituted by the Railways and Transport Safety Act 2003, s 16, Sch 2, Pt 2. para 19(j), as from 5 July 2004 (for transitional provisions in relation to the transfer of functions to the Office of Rail Regulation, see Sch 3 to the 2003 Act).

Other cases of disqualification

10 Participation in wrongful trading

(1) Where the court makes a declaration under section 213 or 214 of the Insolvency Act that a person is liable to make a contribution to a company's assets, then, whether or not an

application for such an order is made by any person, the court may, if it thinks fit, also make a disqualification order against the person to whom the declaration relates.

(2) The maximum period of disqualification under this section is 15 years.

[747]

11 Undischarged bankrupts

[(1) It is an offence for a person to act as director of a company or directly or indirectly to take part in or be concerned in the promotion, formation or management of a company, without the leave of the court, at a time when—

(a) he is an undischarged bankrupt, or

(b) a bankruptcy restrictions order is in force in respect of him.]

(2) "The court" for this purpose is the court by which the person was adjudged bankrupt or, in Scotland, sequestration of his estates was awarded.

(3) In England and Wales, the leave of the court shall not be given unless notice of intention to apply for it has been served on the official receiver; and it is the latter's duty, if he is of opinion that it is contrary to the public interest that the application should be granted, to attend on the hearing of the application and oppose it.

[748]

NOTES

Sub-s (1): substituted, in relation to England and Wales only, by the Enterprise Act 2002, s 257(3), Sch 21, para 5, as from 1 April 2004; the original sub-s (1) read as follows—

"(1) It is an offence for a person who is an undischarged bankrupt to act as director of, or directly or indirectly to take part in or be concerned in the promotion, formation or management of, a company, except with the leave of the court.".

12 Failure to pay under county court administration order

(1) The following has effect where a court under section 429 of the Insolvency Act revokes an administration order under Part VI of the County Courts Act 1984.

(2) A person to whom that section applies by virtue of the order under section 429(2)(b) shall not, except with the leave of the court which made the order, act as director or liquidator of, or directly or indirectly take part or be concerned in the promotion, formation or management of, a company.

[749]

[12A Northern Irish disqualification orders

A person subject to a disqualification order under Part II of the Companies (Northern Ireland) Order 1989—

(a) shall not be a director of a company, act as receiver of a company's property or in any way, whether directly or indirectly, be concerned or take part in the promotion, formation or management of a company unless (in each case) he has the leave of the High Court of Northern Ireland, and

(b) shall not act as an insolvency practitioner.]

[750]

NOTES

Inserted by the Insolvency Act 2000, s 7(1), as from 2 April 2001, except in relation to a person subject to a disqualification order under the Companies (Northern Ireland) Order 1989, SI 1989/2404, Pt II made before that date.

[12B Northern Irish disqualification undertakings

A person subject to a disqualification undertaking under the Company Directors Disqualification (Northern Ireland) Order 2002—

(a) shall not be a director of a company, act as receiver of a company's property or in any way, whether directly or indirectly, be concerned or take part in the promotion, formation or management of a company unless (in each case) he has the leave of the High Court of Northern Ireland, and

(b) shall not act as an insolvency practitioner.]

[750A]

NOTES

Inserted by the Insolvency Act 2000 (Company Directors Disqualification Undertakings) Order 2004, SI 2004/1941, art 2(1), (2), as from 1 September 2004, in relation to disqualification undertakings under the Company Directors Disqualification (Northern Ireland) Order 2002 accepted on or after that date.

Consequences of contravention

13 Criminal penalties

If a person acts in contravention of a disqualification order or [disqualification undertaking or in contravention] of section 12(2)[, 12A or 12B], or is guilty of an offence under section 11, he is liable—

(a) on conviction on indictment, to imprisonment for not more than 2 years or a fine, or both; and

(b) on summary conviction, to imprisonment for not more than 6 months or a fine not exceeding the statutory maximum, or both.

[751]

NOTES

Words in first pair of square brackets inserted by the Insolvency Act 2000, s 8, Sch 4, Pt I, paras 1, 8, as from 2 April 2001; words in second pair of square brackets substituted by the Insolvency Act 2000 (Company Directors Disqualification Undertakings) Order 2004, SI 2004/1941, art 2(1), (3), as from 1 September 2004, in relation to disqualification undertakings under the Company Directors Disqualification (Northern Ireland) Order 2002 accepted on or after that date.

14 Offences by body corporate

(1) Where a body corporate is guilty of an offence of acting in contravention of a disqualification order [or disqualification undertaking or in contravention of section 12A] [or 12B], and it is proved that the offence occurred with the consent or connivance of, or was attributable to any neglect on the part of any director, manager, secretary or other similar officer of the body corporate, or any person who was purporting to act in any such capacity he, as well as the body corporate, is guilty of the offence and liable to be proceeded against and punished accordingly.

(2) Where the affairs of a body corporate are managed by its members, subsection (1) applies in relation to the acts and defaults of a member in connection with his functions of management as if he were a director of the body corporate.

[752]

NOTES

Sub-s (1): words in first pair of square brackets inserted by the Insolvency Act 2000, s 8, Sch 4, Pt I, paras 1, 9, as from 2 April 2001; words in second pair of square brackets inserted by the Insolvency Act 2000 (Company Directors Disqualification Undertakings) Order 2004, SI 2004/1941, art 2(1), (4), as from 1 September 2004, in relation to disqualification undertakings under the Company Directors Disqualification (Northern Ireland) Order 2002 accepted on or after that date.

15 Personal liability for company's debts where person acts while disqualified

(1) A person is personally responsible for all the relevant debts of a company if at any time—

(a) in contravention of a disqualification order or [disqualification undertaking or in contravention] of section 11[, 12A or 12B] of this Act he is involved in the management of the company, or

(b) as a person who is involved in the management of the company, he acts or is willing to act on instructions given without the leave of the court by a person whom he knows at that time to be the subject of a disqualification order [or disqualification undertaking or a disqualification order under Part II of the Companies (Northern Ireland) Order 1989] [or disqualification undertaking under the Company Directors Disqualification (Northern Ireland) Order 2002] or to be an undischarged bankrupt.

(2) Where a person is personally responsible under this section for the relevant debts of a company, he is jointly and severally liable in respect of those debts with the company and any other person who, whether under this section or otherwise, is so liable.

(3) For the purposes of this section the relevant debts of a company are—

(a) in relation to a person who is personally responsible under paragraph (a) of subsection (1), such debts and other liabilities of the company as are incurred at a time when that person was involved in the management of the company, and

(b) in relation to a person who is personally responsible under paragraph (b) of that subsection, such debts and other liabilities of the company as are incurred at a time when that person was acting or was willing to act on instructions given as mentioned in that paragraph.

(4) For the purposes of this section, a person is involved in the management of a company if he is a director of the company or if he is concerned, whether directly or indirectly, or takes part, in the management of the company.

(5) For the purposes of this section a person who, as a person involved in the management of a company, has at any time acted on instructions given without the leave of the court by a person whom he knew at that time to be the subject of a disqualification order [or disqualification undertaking or a disqualification order under Part II of the Companies (Northern Ireland) Order 1989] [or disqualification undertaking under the Company Directors Disqualification (Northern Ireland) Order 2002] or to be an undischarged bankrupt is presumed, unless the contrary is shown, to have been willing at any time thereafter to act on any instructions given by that person.

[753]

NOTES

Sub-s (1): words in first and third pairs of square brackets inserted by the Insolvency Act 2000, s 8, Sch 4, Pt I, paras 1, 10, as from 2 April 2001; words in second pair of square brackets substituted, and words in final pair of square brackets inserted, by the Insolvency Act 2000 (Company Directors Disqualification Undertakings) Order 2004, SI 2004/1941, art 2(1), (5)(a), as from 1 September 2004, in relation to disqualification undertakings under the Company Directors Disqualification (Northern Ireland) Order 2002 accepted on or after that date.

Sub-s (5): words in first pair of square brackets inserted by the Insolvency Act 2000, s 8, Sch 4, Pt I, paras 1, 10, as from 2 April 2001; words in second pair of square brackets inserted by SI 2004/1941, art 2(1), (5)(b), as from 1 September 2004, in relation to disqualification undertakings under the Company Directors Disqualification (Northern Ireland) Order 2002 accepted on or after that date.

Supplementary provisions

16 Application for disqualification order

(1) A person intending to apply for the making of a disqualification order by the court having jurisdiction to wind up a company shall give not less than 10 days' notice of his intention to the person against whom the order is sought; and on the hearing of the application the last-mentioned person may appear and himself give evidence or call witnesses.

(2) An application to a court with jurisdiction to wind up companies for the making against any person of a disqualification order under any of sections 2 to [4] may be made by the Secretary of State or the official receiver, or by the liquidator or any past or present member or creditor of any company in relation to which that person has committed or is alleged to have committed an offence or other default.

(3) On the hearing of any application under this Act made by [a person falling within subsection (4)], the applicant shall appear and call the attention of the court to any matters which seem to him to be relevant, and may himself give evidence or call witnesses.

[(4) The following fall within this subsection—

(a) the Secretary of State;

(b) the official receiver;

(c) the OFT;

(d) the liquidator;

(e) a specified regulator (within the meaning of section 9E).]

[754]

NOTES

Sub-s (2): figure in square brackets substituted by the Insolvency Act 2000, s 8, Sch 4, Pt I, paras 1, 11, as from 2 April 2001.

Sub-s (3): words in square brackets substituted by the Enterprise Act 2002, s 204(1), (6), as from 20 June 2003.

Sub-s (4): added by the Enterprise Act 2002, s 204(1), (7), as from 20 June 2003.

[17 Application for leave under an order or undertaking

(1) Where a person is subject to a disqualification order made by a court having jurisdiction to wind up companies, any application for leave for the purposes of section 1(1)(a) shall be made to that court.

(2) Where—

(a) a person is subject to a disqualification order made under section 2 by a court other than a court having jurisdiction to wind up companies, or

(b) a person is subject to a disqualification order made under section 5,

any application for leave for the purposes of section 1(1)(a) shall be made to any court which, when the order was made, had jurisdiction to wind up the company (or, if there is more than one such company, any of the companies) to which the offence (or any of the offences) in question related.

(3) Where a person is subject to a disqualification undertaking accepted at any time under section 7 or 8, any application for leave for the purposes of section 1A(1)(a) shall be made to any court to which, if the Secretary of State had applied for a disqualification order under the section in question at that time, his application could have been made.

[(3A) Where a person is subject to a disqualification undertaking accepted at any time under section 9B any application for leave for the purposes of section 9B(4) must be made to the High Court or (in Scotland) the Court of Session.]

(4) But where a person is subject to two or more disqualification orders or undertakings (or to one or more disqualification orders and to one or more disqualification undertakings), any application for leave for the purposes of section 1(1)(a) [1A(1)(a) or 9B(4)] shall be made to any court to which any such application relating to the latest order to be made, or undertaking to be accepted, could be made.

(5) On the hearing of an application for leave for the purposes of section 1(1)(a) or 1A(1)(a), the Secretary of State shall appear and call the attention of the court to any matters which seem to him to be relevant, and may himself give evidence or call witnesses.

[(6) Subsection (5) does not apply to an application for leave for the purposes of section 1(1)(a) if the application for the disqualification order was made under section 9A.

(7) In such a case and in the case of an application for leave for the purposes of section 9B(4) on the hearing of the application whichever of the OFT or a specified regulator (within the meaning of section 9E) applied for the order or accepted the undertaking (as the case may be)—

(a) must appear and draw the attention of the court to any matters which appear to it or him (as the case may be) to be relevant;

(b) may give evidence or call witnesses.]]

[755]

NOTES

Substituted by the Insolvency Act 2000, s 8, Sch 4, Pt I, paras 1, 12, as from 2 April 2001, subject to transitional provisions in relation to cases where a person subject to a disqualification order, made on the application of the Secretary of State, the official receiver or the liquidator, has applied for leave of the court under this section before that date (see SI 2001/766, art 3).

Sub-ss (3A), (6), (7): inserted and added respectively by the Enterprise Act 2002, s 204(1), (8), (10), as from 20 June 2003.

Sub-s (4): words in square brackets substituted by the Enterprise Act 2002, s 204(1), (9), as from 20 June 2003.

18 [Register of disqualification orders and undertakings]

(1) The Secretary of State may make regulations requiring officers of courts to furnish him with such particulars as the regulations may specify of cases in which—

(a) a disqualification order is made, or

(b) any action is taken by a court in consequence of which such an order [or a disqualification undertaking] is varied or ceases to be in force, or

(c) leave is granted by a court for a person subject to such an order to do any thing which otherwise the order prohibits him from doing; [or

(d) leave is granted by a court for a person subject to such an undertaking to do anything which otherwise the undertaking prohibits him from doing]

and the regulations may specify the time within which, and the form and manner in which, such particulars are to be furnished.

(2) The Secretary of State shall, from the particulars so furnished, continue to maintain the register of orders, and of cases in which leave has been granted as mentioned in subsection (1)(c), which was set up by him under section 29 of the Companies Act 1976 and continued under section 301 of the Companies Act 1985.

[(2A) The Secretary of State must include in the register such particulars as he considers appropriate of—

(a) disqualification undertakings accepted by him under section 7 or 8;

(b) disqualification undertakings accepted by the OFT or a specified regulator under section 9B;

(c) cases in which leave has been granted as mentioned in subsection (1)(d).]

(3) When an order [or undertaking] of which entry is made in the register ceases to be in force, the Secretary of State shall delete the entry from the register and all particulars relating to it which have been furnished to him under this section or any previous corresponding provision [and, in the case of a disqualification undertaking, any other particulars he has included in the register].

(4) The register shall be open to inspection on payment of such fee as may be specified by the Secretary of State in regulations.

[(4A) Regulations under this section may extend the preceding provisions of this section, to such extent and with such modifications as may be specified in the regulations, to disqualification orders made under Part II of the Companies (Northern Ireland) Order 1989 [or disqualification undertakings made under the Company Directors Disqualification (Northern Ireland) Order 2002].]

(5) Regulations under this section shall be made by statutory instrument subject to annulment in pursuance of a resolution of either House of Parliament.

[756]

NOTES

Section heading: substituted by the Insolvency Act 2000, s 8, Sch 4, Pt I, paras 1, 13(1), (6), as from 2 April 2001.

Sub-ss (1), (3): words in square brackets inserted by the Insolvency Act 2000, s 8, Sch 4, Pt I, paras 1, 13(1), (2), (4), as from 2 April 2001.

Sub-s (2A): inserted by the Insolvency Act 2000, s 8, Sch 4, Pt I, paras 1, 13(1), (3), as from 2 April 2001; substituted by the Enterprise Act 2002, s 204(1), (11), as from 20 June 2003.

Sub-s (4A): inserted by the Insolvency Act 2000, s 8, Sch 4, Pt I, paras 1, 13(1), (5), as from 2 April 2001; words in square brackets added by the Insolvency Act 2000 (Company Directors Disqualification Undertakings) Order 2004, SI 2004/1941, art 2(1), (6), as from 1 September 2004, in relation to disqualification undertakings under the Company Directors Disqualification (Northern Ireland) Order 2002 accepted on or after that date.

Regulations: the Companies (Disqualification Orders) Regulations 2001, SI 2001/967 at **[6981A]**.

19 Special savings from repealed enactments

Schedule 2 to this Act has effect—

(a) in connection with certain transitional cases arising under sections 93 and 94 of the Companies Act 1981, so as to limit the power to make a disqualification order, or to restrict the duration of an order, by reference to events occurring or things done before those sections came into force,

(b) to preserve orders made under section 28 of the Companies Act 1976 (repealed by the Act of 1981), and

(c) to preclude any applications for a disqualification order under section 6 or 8, where the relevant company went into liquidation before 28th April 1986.

[757]

Miscellaneous and general

20 Admissibility in evidence of statements

[(1)] In any proceedings (whether or not under this Act), any statement made in pursuance of a requirement imposed by or under sections 6 to 10, 15 or 19(c) of, or Schedule 1 to, this Act, or by or under rules made for the purposes of this Act under the Insolvency Act, may be used in evidence against any person making or concurring in making the statement.

[(2) However, in criminal proceedings in which any such person is charged with an offence to which this subsection applies—

(a) no evidence relating to the statement may be adduced, and

(b) no question relating to it may be asked,

by or on behalf of the prosecution, unless evidence relating to it is adduced, or a question relating to it is asked, in the proceedings by or on behalf of that person.

(3) Subsection (2) applies to any offence other than—

(a) an offence which is—

(i) created by rules made for the purposes of this Act under the Insolvency Act, and

(ii) designated for the purposes of this subsection by such rules or by regulations made by the Secretary of State;

(b) an offence which is—

(i) created by regulations made under any such rules, and

(ii) designated for the purposes of this subsection by such regulations;

(c) an offence under section 5 of the Perjury Act 1911 (false statements made otherwise than on oath); or

(d) an offence under section 44(2) of the Criminal Law (Consolidation) (Scotland) Act 1995 (false statements made otherwise than on oath).

(4) Regulations under subsection (3)(a)(ii) shall be made by statutory instrument and, after being made, shall be laid before each House of Parliament.]

[758]

NOTES

Sub-s (1) numbered as such, and sub-ss (2)–(4) added, by the Youth Justice and Criminal Evidence Act 1999, s 59, Sch 3, para 8, as from 14 April 2000 (in relation to England and Wales), and 1 January 2001 (in relation to Scotland).

21 Interaction with Insolvency Act

(1) References in this Act to the official receiver, in relation to the winding up of a company or the bankruptcy of an individual, are to any person who, by virtue of section 399 of the Insolvency Act, is authorised to act as the official receiver in relation to that winding up or bankruptcy; and, in accordance with section 401(2) of that Act, references in this Act to an official receiver includes a person appointed as his deputy.

(2) Sections [1A,] 6 to 10, [13, 14,] 15, 19(c) and 20 of, and Schedule 1 to, this Act [and sections 1 and 17 of this Act as they apply for the purposes of those provisions] are deemed included in Parts I to VII of the Insolvency Act for the purposes of the following sections of that Act—

section 411 (power to make insolvency rules);

section 414 (fees orders);

section 420 (orders extending provisions about insolvent companies to insolvent partnerships);

section 422 (modification of such provisions in their application to recognised banks);

...

(3) Section 434 of that Act (Crown application) applies to sections [1A,] 6 to 10, [13, 14,] 15, 19(c) and 20 of, and Schedule 1 to, this Act [and sections 1 and 17 of this Act as they apply for the purposes of those provisions] as it does to the provisions of that Act which are there mentioned.

[(4) For the purposes of summary proceedings in Scotland, section 431 of that Act applies to summary proceedings for an offence under section 11 or 13 of this Act as it applies to summary proceedings for an offence under Parts I to VII of that Act.]

[759]

NOTES

Sub-s (2): words in square brackets inserted by the Insolvency Act 2000, s 8, Sch 4, Pt I, paras 1, 14(1), (2), as from 2 April 2001; words omitted repealed by CA 1989, s 212, Sch 24, as from 1 March 1990.

Sub-s (3): words in square brackets inserted by the Insolvency Act 2000, s 8, Sch 4, Pt I, paras 1, 14(1), (3), as from 2 April 2001.

Sub-s (4): added by CA 1989, s 208, as from 1 March 1990.

As to Rules and Orders having effect under this section, see the notes to the sections listed in sub-s (2) above.

22 Interpretation

(1) This section has effect with respect to the meaning of expressions used in this Act, and applies unless the context otherwise requires.

(2) The expression "company"—

- (a) in section 11, includes an unregistered company and a company incorporated outside Great Britain which has an established place of business in Great Britain, and
- (b) elsewhere, includes any company which may be wound up under Part V of the Insolvency Act.

(3) Section 247 in Part VII of the Insolvency Act (interpretation for the first Group of Parts of that Act) applies as regards references to a company's insolvency and to its going into liquidation; and "administrative receiver" has the meaning given by section 251 of that Act [and references to acting as an insolvency practitioner are to be read in accordance with section 388 of that Act].

(4) "Director" includes any person occupying the position of director, by whatever name called …

(5) "Shadow director", in relation to a company, means a person in accordance with whose directions or instructions the directors of the company are accustomed to act (but so that a person is not deemed a shadow director by reason only that the directors act on advice given by him in a professional capacity).

(6) Section 740 of the Companies Act applies as regards the meaning of "body corporate"; and "officer" has the meaning given by section 744 of that Act.

(7) In references to legislation other than this Act—

"the Companies Act" means the Companies Act 1985;

"the Companies Acts" has the meaning given by section 744 of that Act; and

"the Insolvency Act" means the Insolvency Act 1986;

and in section 3(1) and 5(1) of this Act "the companies legislation" means the Companies Acts (except the Insider Dealing Act), Parts I to VII of the Insolvency Act and, in Part XV of that Act, sections 411, 413, 414, 416 and 417.

(8) Any reference to provisions, or a particular provision, of the Companies Acts or the Insolvency Act includes the corresponding provisions or provision of the former Companies Acts (as defined by section 735(1)(c) of the Companies Act, but including also that Act itself) or, as the case may be, the Insolvency Act 1985.

(9) Any expression for whose interpretation provision is made by Part XXVI of the Companies Act (and not by subsections (3) to (8) above) is to be construed in accordance with that provision.

[(10) Any reference to acting as receiver—

- (a) includes acting as manager or as both receiver and manager, but
- (b) does not include acting as administrative receiver;

and "receivership" is to be read accordingly.]

[760]

NOTES

Sub-s (3): words in square brackets added by the Insolvency Act 2000, s 8, Sch 4, Pt I, paras 1, 15(1), (2), as from 2 April 2001.

Sub-s (4): words omitted repealed by the Insolvency Act 2000, ss 8, 15(1), Sch 4, Pt I, paras 1, 15(1), (3), Sch 5, as from 2 April 2001.

Sub-s (10): added by the Insolvency Act 2000, s 5(3), as from 2 April 2001.

[22A Application of Act to building societies

(1) This Act applies to building societies as it applies to companies.

(2) References in this Act to a company, or to a director or an officer of a company include, respectively, references to a building society within the meaning of the Building Societies Act 1986 or to a director or officer, within the meaning of that Act, of a building society.

(3) In relation to a building society the definition of "shadow director" in section 22(5) applies with the substitution of "building society" for "company".

(4) In the application of Schedule 1 to the directors of a building society, references to provisions of the Insolvency Act or the Companies Act include references to the corresponding provisions of the Building Societies Act 1986.]

[761]

NOTES

Inserted by CA 1989, s 211(3), as from 31 July 1990.

[22B Application of Act to incorporated friendly societies

(1) This Act applies to incorporated friendly societies as it applies to companies.

(2) References in this Act to a company, or to a director or an officer of a company include, respectively, references to an incorporated friendly society within the meaning of the Friendly Societies Act 1992 or to a member of the committee of management or officer, within the meaning of that Act, of an incorporated friendly society.

(3) In relation to an incorporated friendly society every reference to a shadow director shall be omitted.

(4) In the application of Schedule 1 to the members of the committee of management of an incorporated friendly society, references to provisions of the Insolvency Act or the Companies Act include references to the corresponding provisions of the Friendly Societies Act 1992.]

[762]

NOTES

Inserted by the Friendly Societies Act 1992, s 120(1), Sch 21, Pt I, para 8, as from 1 February 1993.

[22C Application of Act to NHS foundation trusts

(1) This Act applies to NHS foundation trusts as it applies to companies within the meaning of this Act.

(2) References in this Act to a company, or to a director or officer of a company, include, respectively, references to an NHS foundation trust or to a director or officer of the trust; but references to shadow directors are omitted.

(3) In the application of Schedule 1 to the directors of an NHS foundation trust, references to the provisions of the Insolvency Act or the Companies Act include references to the corresponding provisions of [Chapter 5 of Part 2 of the National Health Service Act 2006].]

[762A]

NOTES

Commencement: 1 April 2004 (England and Wales); to be appointed (Scotland).

Inserted by the Health and Social Care (Community Health and Standards) Act 2003, s 34, Sch 4, paras 67, 68, as from 1 April 2004 (in relation to England and Wales), and as from a day to be appointed (in relation to Scotland).

Sub-s (3): words in square brackets substituted by the National Health Service (Consequential Provisions) Act 2006, s 2, Sch 1, paras 91, 92, as from 1 March 2007.

23 Transitional provisions, savings, repeals

(1) The transitional provisions and savings in Schedule 3 to this Act have effect, and are without prejudice to anything in the Interpretation Act 1978 with regard to the effect of repeals.

(2) The enactments specified in the second column of Schedule 4 to this Act are repealed to the extent specified in the third column of that Schedule.

[763]

24 Extent

(1) This Act extends to England and Wales and to Scotland.

(2) Nothing in this Act extends to Northern Ireland.

[764]

25 Commencement

This Act comes into force simultaneously with the Insolvency Act 1986.

[765]

26 Citation

This Act may be cited as the Company Directors Disqualification Act 1986.

[766]

SCHEDULES

SCHEDULE 1
MATTERS FOR DETERMINING UNFITNESS OF DIRECTORS

Section 9

PART I
MATTERS APPLICABLE IN ALL CASES

1. Any misfeasance or breach of any fiduciary or other duty by the director in relation to the company.

2. Any misapplication or retention by the director of, or any conduct by the director giving rise to an obligation to account for, any money or other property of the company.

3. The extent of the director's responsibility for the company entering into any transaction liable to be set aside under Part XVI of the Insolvency Act (provisions against debt avoidance).

4. The extent of the director's responsibility for any failure by the company to comply with any of the following provisions of the Companies Act, namely—

(a) section 221 (companies to keep accounting records);
(b) section 222 (where and for how long records to be kept);
(c) section 288 (register of directors and secretaries);
(d) section 352 (obligation to keep and enter up register of members);
(e) section 353 (location of register of members);
[(f) section 363 (duty of company to make annual returns);] and
(*h*) *sections 399 and 415* (*company's duty to register charges it creates*).

[5. The extent of the director's responsibility for any failure by the directors of the company to comply with—

(a) section 226 or 227 of the Companies Act (duty to prepare annual accounts), or
(b) section 233 of that Act (approval and signature of accounts).]

[5A. In the application of this Part of this Schedule in relation to any person who is a director of an open-ended investment company, any reference to a provision of the Companies

Act is to be taken to be a reference to the corresponding provision of the Open-Ended Investment Companies Regulations 2001 or of any rules made under regulation 6 of those Regulations (Financial Services Authority rules).]

[767]

NOTES

Para 4: sub-para (f) substituted, for original sub-paras (f), (g), by CA 1989, s 139(4), as from 1 October 1991; sub-para (h) substituted by CA 1989, s 107, Sch 16, para 4, as from a day to be appointed, as follows—

"(h) sections 398 and 703D (duty of company to deliver particulars of charges on its property).".

Para 5: substituted by CA 1989, s 23, Sch 10, para 35(1), (3), as from 1 April 1990.

Para 5A: inserted by the Open-Ended Investment Companies (Investment Companies with Variable Capital) Regulations 1996, SI 1996/2827, reg 75, Sch 8, Pt I, para 10, as from 6 January 1997, and substituted by the Open-Ended Investment Companies Regulations 2001, SI 2001/1228, reg 84, Sch 7, para 9, as from 1 December 2001.

PART II
MATTERS APPLICABLE WHERE COMPANY HAS BECOME INSOLVENT

6. The extent of the director's responsibility for the causes of the company becoming insolvent.

7. The extent of the director's responsibility for any failure by the company to supply any goods or services which have been paid for (in whole or in part).

8. The extent of the director's responsibility for the company entering into any transaction or giving any preference, being a transaction or preference—

(a) liable to be set aside under section 127 or sections 238 to 240 of the Insolvency Act, or

(b) challengeable under section 242 or 243 of that Act or under any rule of law in Scotland.

9. The extent of the director's responsibility for any failure by the directors of the company to comply with section 98 of the Insolvency Act (duty to call creditors' meeting in creditors' voluntary winding up).

10. Any failure by the director to comply with any obligation imposed on him by or under any of the following provisions of the Insolvency Act—

(a) [paragraph 47 of Schedule B1] (company's statement of affairs in administration);
(b) section 47 (statement of affairs to administrative receiver);
(c) section 66 (statement of affairs in Scottish receivership);
(d) section 99 (directors' duty to attend meeting; statement of affairs in creditors' voluntary winding up);
(e) section 131 (statement of affairs in winding up by the court);
(f) section 234 (duty of any one with company property to deliver it up);
(g) section 235 (duty to co-operate with liquidator, etc).

[768]

NOTES

Para 10: words in square brackets in sub-para (a) substituted by the Enterprise Act 2002 (Insolvency) Order 2003, SI 2003/2096, arts 4, 6, Schedule, Pt 1, para 12, as from 15 September 2003, except in relation to any case where a petition for an administration order was presented before that date.

Limited liability partnerships: see the introductory notes to this Act.

SCHEDULE 2
SAVINGS FROM COMPANIES ACT 1981 SS 93, 94, AND INSOLVENCY ACT 1985 SCHEDULE 9

Section 19

1. Sections 2 and 4(1)(b) do not apply in relation to anything done before 15th June 1982 by a person in his capacity as liquidator of a company or as receiver or manager of a company's property.

2. Subject to paragraph 1—
   (a) section 2 applies in a case where a person is convicted on indictment of an offence which he committed (and, in the case of a continuing offence, has ceased to commit) before 15th June 1982; but in such a case a disqualification order under that section shall not be made for a period in excess of 5 years;
   (b) that section does not apply in a case where a person is convicted summarily—
      (i) in England and Wales, if he had consented so to be tried before that date, or
      (ii) in Scotland, if the summary proceedings commenced before that date.

3. Subject to paragraph 1, section 4 applies in relation to an offence committed or other thing done before 15th June 1982; but a disqualification order made on the grounds of such an offence or other thing done shall not be made for a period in excess of 5 years.

4. The powers of a court under section 5 are not exercisable in a case where a person is convicted of an offence which he committed (and, in the case of a continuing offence, had ceased to commit) before 15th June 1982.

5. For purposes of section 3(1) and section 5, no account is to be taken of any offence which was committed, or any default order which was made, before 1st June 1977.

6. An order made under section 28 of the Companies Act 1976 has effect as if made under section 3 of this Act; and an application made before 15th June 1982 for such an order is to be treated as an application for an order under the section last mentioned.

7. Where—
   (a) an application is made for a disqualification order under section 6 of this Act by virtue of paragraph (a) of subsection (2) of that section, and
   (b) the company in question went into liquidation before 28th April 1986 (the coming into force of the provision replaced by section 6),

the court shall not make an order under that section unless it could have made a disqualification order under section 300 of the Companies Act as it had effect immediately before the date specified in sub-paragraph (b) above.

8. An application shall not be made under section 8 of this Act in relation to a report made or information or documents obtained before 28th April 1986.

[769]

SCHEDULE 3
TRANSITIONAL PROVISIONS AND SAVINGS

Section 23(1)

1. In this Schedule, "the former enactments" means so much of the Companies Act, and so much of the Insolvency Act, as is repealed and replaced by this Act; and "the appointed day" means the day on which this Act comes into force.

2. So far as anything done or treated as done under or for the purposes of any provision of the former enactments could have been done under or for the purposes of the corresponding provision of this Act, it is not invalidated by the repeal of that provision but has effect as if done under or for the purposes of the corresponding provision; and any order, regulation, rule or other instrument made or having effect under any provision of the former enactments shall, insofar as its effect is preserved by this paragraph, be treated for all purposes as made and having effect under the corresponding provision.

3. Where any period of time specified in a provision of the former enactments is current immediately before the appointed day, this Act has effect as if the corresponding provision had been in force when the period began to run; and (without prejudice to the foregoing) any period of time so specified and current is deemed for the purposes of this Act—
   (a) to run from the date or event from which it was running immediately before the appointed day, and
   (b) to expire (subject to any provision of this Act for its extension) whenever it would have expired if this Act had not been passed;

and any rights, priorities, liabilities, reliefs, obligations, requirements, powers, duties or exemptions dependent on the beginning, duration or end of such a period as above mentioned shall be under this Act as they were or would have been under the former enactments.

4. Where in any provision of this Act there is a reference to another such provision, and the first-mentioned provision operates, or is capable of operating, in relation to things done or omitted, or events occurring or not occurring, in the past (including in particular past acts of compliance with any enactment, failures of compliance, contraventions, offences and convictions of offences) the reference to the other provision is to be read as including a reference to the corresponding provision of the former enactments.

5. Offences committed before the appointed day under any provision of the former enactments may, notwithstanding any repeal by this Act, be prosecuted and punished after that day as if this Act had not passed.

6. A reference in any enactment, instrument or document (whether express or implied, and in whatever phraseology) to a provision of the former enactments (including the corresponding provision of any yet earlier enactment) is to be read, where necessary to retain for the enactment, instrument or document the same force and effect as it would have had but for the passing of this Act, as, or as including, a reference to the corresponding provision by which it is replaced in this Act.

[770]–[771]

(*Sch 4 repeals CA 1985, ss 295–299, 301, 302, Sch 2* (*the entries relating to ss 295*(*7*), *302*(*1*) *only*), *Sch 12, and IA 1985, ss 12–14, 16, 18, 108*(*2*), *Sch 2, Sch 6, paras 1, 2, 7, 14, Sch 9, paras 2, 3.*)

COMPANIES ACT 1989

(1989 c 40)

NOTES

This Act is reproduced as amended by the following Acts:

1990	Law Reform (Miscellaneous Provisions) (Scotland) Act 1990.
1991	Water Consolidation (Consequential Provisions) Act 1991.
1992	Friendly Societies Act 1992; Trade Union and Labour Relations (Consolidation) Act 1992.
1993	Charities Act 1993; Criminal Justice Act 1993.
1994	Coal Industry Act 1994.
1995	Criminal Procedure (Consequential Provisions) (Scotland) Act 1995; Crown Agents Act 1995; Pensions Act 1995.
1998	Bank of England Act 1998; Competition Act 1998; National Lottery Act 1998; Northern Ireland Act 1998.
1999	Youth Justice and Criminal Evidence Act 1999.
2000	Insolvency Act 2000.
2002	Enterprise Act 2002.
2004	Finance Act 2004; Statute Law (Repeals) Act 2004; Companies (Audit, Investigations and Community Enterprise) Act 2004; Civil Partnership Act 2004; Pensions Act 2004.
2006	Companies Act 2006.
2007	Bankruptcy and Diligence etc (Scotland) Act 2007.

This Act is reproduced as amended by the following SIs:

1991	Financial Markets and Insolvency Regulations 1991, SI 1991/880.
1992	Transfer of Functions (Financial Services) Order 1992, SI 1992/1315.
1993	Financial Services (Disclosure of Information) (Designated Authorities) (No 7) Order 1993, SI 1993/1826.
1994	Financial Services (Disclosure of Information) (Designated Authorities) (No 8) Order 1994, SI 1994/340.
1995	Public Offers of Securities Regulations 1995, SI 1995/1537.

1998	Financial Markets and Insolvency Regulations 1998, SI 1998/1748.
1999	Competition Act 1998 (Competition Commission) Transitional, Consequential and Supplemental Provisions Order 1999, SI 1999/506; Scotland Act 1998 (Consequential Modifications) (No 2) Order 1999, SI 1999/1820.
2000	Competition Act 1998 (Transitional, Consequential and Supplemental Provisions) Order 2000, SI 2000/311.
2001	Financial Services and Markets Act 2000 (Dissolution of the Insurance Brokers Registration Council) (Consequential Provisions) Order 2001, SI 2001/1283; Financial Services and Markets Act 2000 (Consequential Amendments and Repeals) Order 2001, SI 2001/3649; Civil Jurisdiction and Judgments Order 2001, SI 2001/3929.
2002	Companies (Disclosure of Information) (Designated Authorities) (No 2) Order 2002, SI 2002/1889.
2003	Companies (Acquisition of Own Shares) (Treasury Shares) Regulations 2003, SI 2003/1116; Enterprise Act 2002 (Consequential and Supplemental Provisions) Order 2003, SI 2003/1398.
2004	Competition Act 1998 and other enactments (Amendment) Regulations 2004, SI 2004/1261.
2005	Regulatory Reform (Trading Stamps) Order 2005, SI 2005/781; Prospectus Regulations 2005, SI 2005/1433; Regulatory Reform (Execution of Deeds and Documents) Order 2005, SI 2005/1906.
2006	Charities and Trustee Investment (Scotland) Act 2005 (Consequential Provisions and Modifications) Order 2006, SI 2006/242; Companies (Disclosure of Information) (Designated Authorities) Order 2006, SI 2006/1644; Financial Services and Markets Act 2000 (Regulated Activities) (Amendment No 3) Order 2006, SI 2006/3384.
2007	Civil Jurisdiction and Judgments Regulations 2007, SI 2007/1655.

See also the prospective amendments made to this Act by the draft Companies Act 2006 (Commencement No 3, Consequential Amendments, Transitional Provisions and Savings) Order 2007 (see **[A12]**).

Commencement: most of this Act came into force between 16 November 1989 (Royal assent) and 3 July 1995, although a limited number of provisions were commenced after 1995, and a few are yet to be brought into force. Where any provision in this work (including any inserted or substituted provision) came into force for all purposes on or before 1 July 2005, commencement information is not noted at provision level. Extensive transitional provisions and savings were made in connection with the commencement of this Act by the Orders noted to s 215 at **[865]**. These provided for the continuity of law between the original 1985 Act regime and the changes effected to the 1985 Act by the amendments made by this Act. To a large extent these are now effectively spent and they have been omitted from this Edition in order to create space for other legislation (ie, the Companies Act 2006 and the associated destination and derivation tables). The complete table of commencements for this Act and the transitional provisions and savings are, however, still included at paragraph **[876]** of the electronic versions of this work.

Civil Procedure Rules. The Civil Procedure Rules 1998, SI 1998/3132, r 49, states that, as from 26 April 1999, those Rules apply to proceedings under this Act subject to the provisions of the relevant practice direction which applies to proceedings.

ARRANGEMENT OF SECTIONS

PART I
COMPANY ACCOUNTS

Introduction

PART II
ELIGIBILITY FOR APPOINTMENT AS AUDITOR

Introduction

Eligibility for appointment

Recognition of supervisory bodies and professional qualifications

Miscellaneous

PART VII
FINANCIAL MARKETS AND INSOLVENCY

Introduction

Recognised investment exchanges and clearing houses

Other exchanges and clearing houses

Market charges

Market property

Supplementary provisions

PART IX
TRANSFER OF SECURITIES

PART X
MISCELLANEOUS AND GENERAL PROVISIONS

General

SCHEDULES

An Act to amend the law relating to company accounts; to make new provision with respect to the persons eligible for appointment as company auditors; to amend the Companies Act 1985 and certain other enactments with respect to investigations and powers to obtain information and to confer new powers exercisable to assist overseas regulatory authorities; to make new provision with respect to the registration of company charges and otherwise to amend the law relating to companies; to amend the Fair Trading Act 1973; to enable provision to be made for the payment of fees in connection with the exercise by the Secretary of State, the Director General of Fair Trading and the Monopolies and Mergers Commission of their functions under Part V of that Act; to make provision for safeguarding the operation of certain financial markets; to amend the Financial Services Act 1986; to enable provision to be made for the recording and transfer of title to securities without a written instrument; to amend the Company Directors Disqualification Act 1986, the Company Securities (Insider Dealing) Act 1985, the Policyholders Protection Act 1975 and the law relating to building societies; and for connected purposes

[16 November 1989]

PART I
COMPANY ACCOUNTS

Introduction

1 Introduction

The provisions of this Part amend Part VII of the Companies Act 1985 (accounts and audit) by—

(*a*) *inserting new provisions in place of sections 221 to 262 of that Act, and*

(*b*) *amending or replacing Schedules 4 to 10 to that Act and inserting new Schedules.*

[772]

NOTES

Repealed by the Companies Act 2006, s 1295, Sch 16, as from a day to be appointed.

2–23 (*Ss 1–22 (which are repealed by the Companies Act 2006, s 1295, Sch 16, as from 1 October 2007 (in so far as relating to s 16), and as from a day to be appointed (otherwise)) make the following amendments: ss 2, 3, 4(1) insert CA 1985, ss 221–226 at* **[207]** *et seq; s 4(2) introduces Sch 1 to this Act; s 5 inserts ss 227, 228, 229, 230 of the 1985 Act at* **[213]** *et seq and introduces Sch 2 to this Act; s 6 inserts ss 231, 232 of the 1985 Act at* **[217]** *et seq and introduces Schs 3, 4 to this Act; s 7 inserts s 233 of the 1985 Act at* **[219]**; *s 8 inserts ss 234, 234A of the 1985 Act at* **[220]** *et seq and introduces Sch 5 to this Act; ss 9, 10 insert ss 235–240 of the 1985 Act at* **[222]** *et seq; s 11 inserts ss 241, 242, 242A, 243 (repealed), 244 of the 1985 Act at* **[228]** *et seq; s 12 inserts ss 245, 245A, 245B, 245C of the 1985 Act at* **[234]** *et seq; ss 13–18 insert Pt VII, Chapter II of the 1985 Act at* **[238]** *et seq, and introduce Schs 6–8 to this Act; ss 19–22 insert Pt VII, Chapter III of the 1985 Act at* **[260]** *et seq, and introduces Sch 9 to this Act; s 23 introduces Sch 10 to this Act.*)

PART II
ELIGIBILITY FOR APPOINTMENT AS COMPANY AUDITOR

NOTES

Transfer of functions: as to the transfer of the Secretary of State's functions under this Part to the Professional Oversight Board for Accountancy, together with transitional provisions and consequential modifications, see the Companies Act 1989 (Delegation) Order 2005, SI 2005/2337 at **[7444]**. Note also that as from 5 May 2006 the Board changed its name to the Professional Oversight Board.

Application: as to the application of this Part of this Act to auditors appointed for the purposes of the Partnerships and Unlimited Companies (Accounts) Regulations 1993, SI 1993/1820, reg 4, see reg 4(3) of, and the Schedule, para 3 to, those regulations at **[6751]**, **[6758]**; by the Insurance Accounts Directive (Miscellaneous Insurance Undertakings) Regulations 1993, SI 1993/3245, reg 3(5), this Part of this Act applies to auditors appointed for the purposes of reg 3 of those Regulations, subject to modifications where the body concerned is unincorporated.

Introduction

24 Introduction

(1) The main purposes of this Part are to secure that only persons who are properly supervised and appropriately qualified are appointed company auditors, and that audits by persons so appointed are carried out properly and with integrity and with a proper degree of independence.

(2) A "company auditor" means a person appointed as auditor under Chapter V of Part XI of the Companies Act 1985; and the expressions "company audit" and "company audit work" shall be construed accordingly.

[773]

NOTES

Repealed by the Companies Act 2006, s 1295, Sch 16, as from a day to be appointed.

Eligibility for appointment

25 Eligibility for appointment

(1) A person is eligible for appointment as a company auditor only if he—

(a) is a member of a recognised supervisory body, and

(b) is eligible for the appointment under the rules of that body.

(2) An individual or a firm may be appointed a company auditor.

(3) In the cases to which section 34 applies (individuals retaining only 1967 Act authorisation) a person's eligibility for appointment as a company auditor is restricted as mentioned in that section.

[774]

NOTES

Repealed by the Companies Act 2006, s 1295, Sch 16, as from a day to be appointed.

Community interest companies: a person eligible for appointment as a company auditor under this section is qualified to audit the annual accounts of a community interest company; see the Companies (Audit, Investigations and Community Enterprise) Act 2004, ss 26, 43(2) at **[900]**, **[917]**.

26 Effect of appointment of partnership

(1) The following provisions apply to the appointment as company auditor of a partnership constituted under the law of England and Wales or Northern Ireland, or under the law of any other country or territory in which a partnership is not a legal person.

(2) The appointment is (unless a contrary intention appears) an appointment of the partnership as such and not of the partners.

(3) Where the partnership ceases, the appointment shall be treated as extending to—

(a) any partnership which succeeds to the practice of that partnership and is eligible for the appointment, and

(*b*) *any person who succeeds to that practice having previously carried it on in partnership and is eligible for the appointment.*

(*4*) *For this purpose a partnership shall be regarded as succeeding to the practice of another partnership only if the members of the successor partnership are substantially the same as those of the former partnership; and a partnership or other person shall be regarded as succeeding to the practice of a partnership only if it or he succeeds to the whole or substantially the whole of the business of the former partnership.*

(*5*) *Where the partnership ceases and no person succeeds to the appointment under subsection (3), the appointment may with the consent of the company be treated as extending to a partnership or other person eligible for the appointment who succeeds to the business of the former partnership or to such part of it as is agreed by the company shall be treated as comprising the appointment.*

[775]

NOTES

Repealed by the Companies Act 2006, s 1295, Sch 16, as from a day to be appointed.

27 Ineligibility on ground of lack of independence

(*1*) *A person is ineligible for appointment as company auditor of a company if he is—*

(*a*) *an officer or employee of the company, or*

(*b*) *a partner or employee of such a person, or a partnership of which such a person is a partner,*

or if he is ineligible by virtue of paragraph (a) or (b) for appointment as company auditor of any associated undertaking of the company.

For this purpose an auditor of a company shall not be regarded as an officer or employee of the company.

(*2*) *A person is also ineligible for appointment as company auditor of a company if there exists between him or any associate of his and the company or any associated undertaking a connection of any such description as may be specified by regulations made by the Secretary of State.*

The regulations may make different provisions for different cases.

(*3*) *In this section "associated undertaking", in relation to a company, means—*

(*a*) *a parent undertaking or subsidiary undertaking of the company, or*

(*b*) *a subsidiary undertaking of any parent undertaking of the company.*

(*4*) *Regulations under this section shall be made by statutory instrument which shall be subject to annulment in pursuance of a resolution of either House of Parliament.*

[776]

NOTES

Repealed by the Companies Act 2006, s 1295, Sch 16, as from a day to be appointed.

Application: the power of the Secretary of State to make regulations under this section is exercisable in relation to the appointment of auditors of open-ended investment companies for like purposes and subject to the same conditions; see the Open-Ended Investment Companies Regulations 2001, SI 2001/1228, reg 69, Sch 5, para 2(3). As to the transfer of the Secretary of State's functions under this Part, see the introductory note to this Part.

28 Effect of ineligibility

(*1*) *No person shall act as a company auditor if he is ineligible for appointment to the office.*

(*2*) *If during his term of office a company auditor becomes ineligible for appointment to the office, he shall thereupon vacate office and shall forthwith give notice in writing to the company concerned that he has vacated it by reason of ineligibility.*

(*3*) *A person who acts as company auditor in contravention of subsection (1), or fails to give notice of vacating his office as required by subsection (2), is guilty of an offence and liable—*

(*a*) *on conviction on indictment, to a fine, and*

(*b*) *on summary conviction, to a fine not exceeding the statutory maximum.*

(4) In the case of continued contravention he is liable on a second or subsequent summary conviction (instead of the fine mentioned in subsection (3)(b)) to a fine not exceeding one-tenth of the statutory maximum in respect of each day on which the contravention is continued.

(5) In proceedings against a person for an offence under this section it is a defence for him to show that he did not know and had no reason to believe that he was, or had become, ineligible for appointment.

[777]

NOTES

Repealed by the Companies Act 2006, s 1295, Sch 16, as from a day to be appointed.

29 Power of Secretary of State to require second audit

(1) Where a person appointed company auditor was, for any part of the period during which the audit was conducted, ineligible for appointment to that office, the Secretary of State may direct the company concerned to retain a person eligible for appointment as auditor of the company—

(a) to audit the relevant accounts again, or

(b) to review the first audit and to report (giving his reasons) whether a second audit is needed;

and the company shall comply with such a direction within 21 days of its being given.

(2) If a second audit is recommended the company shall forthwith take such steps as are necessary to comply with the recommendation.

(3) Where a direction is given under this section, the Secretary of State shall send a copy of the direction to the registrar of companies; and the company shall within 21 days of receiving any report under subsection (1)(b) send a copy of it to the registrar of companies.

The provisions of the Companies Act 1985 relating to the delivery of documents to the registrar apply for the purposes of this subsection.

(4) Any statutory or other provisions applying in relation to the first audit shall apply, so far as practicable, in relation to a second audit under this section.

(5) If a company fails to comply with the requirements of this section, it is guilty of an offence and liable on summary conviction to a fine not exceeding the statutory maximum; and in the case of continued contravention it is liable on a second or subsequent summary conviction (instead of the fine mentioned above) to a fine not exceeding one-tenth of the statutory maximum in respect of each day on which the contravention is continued.

(6) A direction under this section is, on the application of the Secretary of State, enforceable by injunction or, in Scotland, by an order under section 45 of the Court of Session Act 1988.

(7) If a person accepts an appointment, or continues to act, as company auditor at a time when he knows he is ineligible, the company concerned may recover from him any costs incurred by it in complying with the requirements of this section.

[778]

NOTES

Repealed by the Companies Act 2006, s 1295, Sch 16, as from a day to be appointed.

Recognition of supervisory bodies and professional qualifications

30 Supervisory bodies

(1) In this Part a "supervisory body" means a body established in the United Kingdom (whether a body corporate or an unincorporated association) which maintains and enforces rules as to—

(a) the eligibility of persons to seek appointment as company auditors, and

(b) the conduct of company audit work,

which are binding on persons seeking appointment or acting as company auditors either because they are members of that body or because they are otherwise subject to its control.

(2) *In this Part references to the members of a supervisory body are to the persons who, whether or not members of the body, are subject to its rules in seeking appointment or acting as company auditors.*

(3) *In this Part references to the rules of a supervisory body are to the rules (whether or not laid down by the body itself) which the body has power to enforce and which are relevant for the purposes of this Part.*

This includes rules relating to the admission and expulsion of members of the body, so far as relevant for the purposes of this Part.

(4) *In this Part references to guidance issued by a supervisory body are to guidance issued or any recommendation made by it to all or any class of its members or persons seeking to become members which would, if it were a rule, fall within subsection (3).*

(5) *The provisions of [Parts I, II and III] of Schedule 11 have effect with respect to the recognition of supervisory bodies for the purposes of this Part.*

[779]

NOTES

Repealed by the Companies Act 2006, s 1295, Sch 16, as from a day to be appointed.

Sub-s (5): words in square brackets substituted by the Companies (Audit, Investigations and Community Enterprise) Act 2004, s 25, Sch 2, Pt 1, paras 1, 2, as from 6 April 2005.

31 Meaning of "appropriate qualification"

(1) *A person holds an appropriate qualification for the purposes of this Part if—*

(a) *he was, by virtue of membership of a body recognised for the purposes of section 389(1)(a) of the Companies Act 1985, qualified for appointment as auditor of a company under that section immediately before 1st January 1990 and immediately before the commencement of section 25 above,*

(b) *he holds a recognised professional qualification obtained in the United Kingdom, or*

(c) *he holds an approved overseas qualification and satisfies any additional educational requirements applicable in accordance with section 33(4).*

(2) *A person who immediately before 1st January 1990 and immediately before the commencement of section 25 above, was qualified for appointment as auditor of a company under section 389 of the Companies Act 1985 otherwise than by virtue of membership of a body recognised for the purposes of section 389(1)(a)—*

(a) *shall be treated as holding an appropriate qualification for twelve months from the day on which section 25 comes into force, and*

(b) *shall continue to be so treated if within that period he notifies the Secretary of State that he wishes to retain the benefit of his qualification.*

The notice shall be in writing and shall contain such information as the Secretary of State may require.

(3) *If a person fails to give such notice within the time allowed he may apply to the Secretary of State, giving such information as would have been required in connection with a notice, and the Secretary of State may, if he is satisfied—*

(a) *that there was good reason why the applicant did not give notice in time, and*

(b) *that the applicant genuinely intends to practise as an auditor in Great Britain,*

direct that he shall be treated as holding an appropriate qualification for the purposes of this Part.

(4) *A person who—*

(a) *began before 1st January 1990 a course of study or practical training leading to a professional qualification in accountancy offered by a body established in the United Kingdom, and*

(b) *obtained that qualification on or after that date and before 1st January 1996,*

shall be treated as holding an appropriate qualification if the qualification is approved by the Secretary of State for the purposes of this subsection.

(5) *Approval shall not be given unless the Secretary of State is satisfied that the body concerned has or, as the case may be, had at the relevant time adequate arrangements to ensure that the qualification is, or was, awarded only to persons educated and trained to a standard equivalent to that required in the case of a recognised professional qualification.*

(6) A person shall not be regarded as holding an appropriate qualification for the purposes of this Part except in the above cases.

[780]

NOTES

Repealed by the Companies Act 2006, s 1295, Sch 16, as from a day to be appointed.

32 Qualifying bodies and recognised professional qualifications

(1) In this Part a "qualifying body" means a body established in the United Kingdom (whether a body corporate or an unincorporated association) which offers a professional qualification in accountancy.

(2) In this Part references to the rules of a qualifying body are to the rules (whether or not laid down by the body itself) which the body has power to enforce and which are relevant for the purposes of this Part.

This includes rules relating to—

- *(a) admission to or expulsion from a course of study leading to a qualification,*
- *(b) the award or deprivation of a qualification, or*
- *(c) the approval of a person for the purposes of giving practical training or the withdrawal of such approval,*

so far as relevant for the purposes of this Part.

(3) In this Part references to guidance issued by any such body are to any guidance which the body issues, or any recommendation it makes to all or any class of persons holding or seeking to hold a qualification, or approved or seeking to be approved by the body for the purpose of giving practical training, which would, if it were a rule, fall within subsection (2).

(4) The provisions of Parts I and II of Schedule 12 have effect with respect to the recognition for the purposes of this Part of a professional qualification offered by a qualifying body.

[781]

NOTES

Repealed by the Companies Act 2006, s 1295, Sch 16, as from a day to be appointed.

33 Approval of overseas qualifications

[(1) The Secretary of State may declare that the following are to be regarded for the purposes of this Part as holding an approved overseas qualification—

- *(a) persons who are qualified to audit accounts under the law of a specified country or territory outside the United Kingdom;*
- *(b) persons who hold a specified professional qualification in accountancy obtained in a specified country or territory outside the United Kingdom.*

(1A) Approval of a qualification under subsection (1)(b) may be expressed to be subject to any specified requirement or requirements being satisfied.

(2) A qualification must not be approved under subsection (1) unless the Secretary of State is satisfied that the qualification, taken with any requirement or requirements to be specified under subsection (1A), affords an assurance of professional competence equivalent to that afforded by a recognised professional qualification.]

(3) In exercising the power conferred by subsection (1) the Secretary of State may have regard to the extent to which persons—

- *(a) eligible under this Part for appointment as a company auditor, or*
- *(b) holding a professional qualification recognised under this Part,*

are recognised by the law of the country or territory in question as qualified to audit accounts there.

(4) The Secretary of State may direct that a person holding an approved overseas qualification shall not be treated as holding an appropriate qualification for the purposes of this Part unless he holds such additional educational qualifications as the Secretary of State may specify for the purpose of ensuring that such persons have an adequate knowledge of the law and practice in the United Kingdom relevant to the audit of accounts.

(5) Different directions may be given in relation to different qualifications.

[(6) The Secretary of State may if he thinks fit, having regard to the considerations mentioned in subsections (2) and (3)—

- *(a) withdraw his approval of an overseas qualification in relation to persons becoming qualified as mentioned in subsection (1)(a), or obtaining such a qualification as is mentioned in subsection (1)(b), after such date as he may specify; or*
- *(b) vary or revoke a requirement mentioned in subsection (1A) from such date as he may specify.]*

[782]

NOTES

Repealed by the Companies Act 2006, s 1295, Sch 16, as from a day to be appointed.

Sub-ss (1), (1A), (2): substituted, for original sub-ss (1), (2), by the Companies (Audit, Investigations and Community Enterprise) Act 2004, s 6(1), (2), as from 6 April 2005.

Sub-s (6): substituted by the Companies (Audit, Investigations and Community Enterprise) Act 2004, s 6(1), (3), as from 6 April 2005.

34 Eligibility of individuals retaining only 1967 Act authorisation

(1) A person whose only appropriate qualification is that he retains an authorisation granted by the Board of Trade or the Secretary of State under section 13(1) of the Companies Act 1967 is eligible only for appointment as auditor of an unquoted company.

(2) A company is "unquoted" if, at the time of the person's appointment, no shares or debentures of the company, or of a parent undertaking of which it is a subsidiary undertaking, have been quoted on a stock exchange (in Great Britain or elsewhere) or offered (whether in Great Britain or elsewhere) to the public for subscription or purchase.

(3) ...

(4) References to a person eligible for appointment as company auditor under section 25 in enactments relating to eligibility for appointment as auditor of a body other than a company do not include a person to whom this section applies.

[783]

NOTES

Repealed by the Companies Act 2006, s 1295, Sch 16, as from a day to be appointed.

Sub-s (3): repealed by the Regulatory Reform (Trading Stamps) Order 2005, SI 2005/781, art 6, Schedule, as from 6 April 2005.

Duties of recognised bodies

35 The register of auditors

(1) The Secretary of State shall make regulations requiring the keeping of a register of—

- *(a) the individuals and firms eligible for appointment as company auditor, and*
- *(b) the individuals holding an appropriate qualification who are responsible for company audit work on behalf of such firms.*

(2) The regulations shall provide that each person's entry in the register shall give—

- *(a) his name and address, and*
- *(b) in the case of a person eligible as mentioned in subsection (1)(a), the name of the relevant supervisory body,*

together with such other information as may be specified by the regulations.

(3) The regulations may impose such obligations as the Secretary of State thinks fit—

- *(a) on recognised supervisory bodies,*
- *(b) on persons eligible for appointment as company auditor, and*
- *(c) on any person with whom arrangements are made by one or more recognised supervisory bodies with respect to the keeping of the register.*

(4) The regulations may include provision—

- *(a) requiring the register to be open to inspection at such times and places as may be specified in the regulations or determined in accordance with them,* (*b*) *enabling a person to require a certified copy of an entry in the register, and*

(*c*) *authorising the charging of fees for inspection, or the provision of copies, of such reasonable amount as may be specified in the regulations or determined in accordance with them;*

and may contain such other supplementary and incidental provisions as the Secretary of State thinks fit.

(*5*) *Regulations under this section shall be made by statutory instrument which shall be subject to annulment in pursuance of a resolution of either House of Parliament.*

(*6*) *The obligations imposed by regulations under this section on such persons as are mentioned in subsection (3)(a) or (c) are enforceable on the application of the Secretary of State by injunction or, in Scotland, by order under section 45 of the Court of Session Act 1988.*
[784]

NOTES

Repealed by the Companies Act 2006, s 1295, Sch 16, as from a day to be appointed.

Regulations: the Companies Act 1989 (Register of Auditors and Information about Audit Firms) Regulations 1991, SI 1991/1566 at **[6703]**.

36 Information about firms to be available to public

(*1*) *The Secretary of State shall make regulations requiring recognised supervisory bodies to keep and make available to the public the following information with respect to the firms eligible under their rules for appointment as a company auditor—*

(*a*) *in relation to a body corporate, the name and address of each person who is a director of the body or holds any shares in it,*

(*b*) *in relation to a partnership, the name and address of each partner,*

and such other information as may be specified in the regulations.

(*2*) *The regulations may impose such obligations as the Secretary of State thinks fit—*

(*a*) *on recognised supervisory bodies,*

(*b*) *on persons eligible for appointment as company auditor, and*

(*c*) *on any person with whom arrangements are made by one or more recognised supervisory bodies with respect to the keeping of the information.*

(*3*) *The regulations may include provision—*

(*a*) *requiring that the information be open to inspection at such times and places as may be specified in the regulations or determined in accordance with them,*

(*b*) *enabling a person to require a certified copy of the information or any part of it, and*

(*c*) *authorising the charging of fees for inspection, or the provision of copies, of such reasonable amount as may be specified in the regulations or determined in accordance with them;*

and may contain such other supplementary and incidental provisions as the Secretary of State thinks fit.

(*4*) *The regulations may make different provision in relation to different descriptions of information and may contain such other supplementary and incidental provisions as the Secretary of State thinks fit.*

(*5*) *Regulations under this section shall be made by statutory instrument which shall be subject to annulment in pursuance of a resolution of either House of Parliament.*

(*6*) *The obligations imposed by regulations under this section on such persons as are mentioned in subsection (2)(a) or (c) are enforceable on the application of the Secretary of State by injunction or, in Scotland, by an order under section 45 of the Court of Session Act 1988.*
[785]

NOTES

Repealed by the Companies Act 2006, s 1295, Sch 16, as from a day to be appointed.

Regulations: the Companies Act 1989 (Register of Auditors and Information about Audit Firms) Regulations 1991, SI 1991/1566 at **[6703]**.

37 Matters to be notified to the Secretary of State

(*1*) *The Secretary of State may require a recognised supervisory or qualifying body—*

(*a*) *to notify him forthwith of the occurrence of such events as he may specify in writing and to give him such information in respect of those events as is so specified;*

(*b*) *to give him, at such times or in respect of such periods as he may specify in writing, such information as is so specified.*

(*2*) *The notices and information required to be given shall be such as the Secretary of State may reasonably require for the exercise of his functions under this Part.*

(*3*) *The Secretary of State may require information given under this section to be given in a specified form or verified in a specified manner.*

(*4*) *Any notice or information required to be given under this section shall be given in writing unless the Secretary of State specifies or approves some other manner.*

[786]

NOTES

Repealed by the Companies Act 2006, s 1295, Sch 16, as from a day to be appointed.

38 Power to call for information

(*1*) *The Secretary of State may by notice in writing require a recognised supervisory or qualifying body to give him such information as he may reasonably require for the exercise of his functions under this Part.*

(*2*) *The Secretary of State may require that any information which he requires under this section shall be given within such reasonable time and verified in such manner as he may specify.*

[787]

NOTES

Repealed by the Companies Act 2006, s 1295, Sch 16, as from a day to be appointed.

39 Compliance orders

(*1*) *If at any time it appears to the Secretary of State—*

(*a*) *in the case of a recognised supervisory body, that any requirement of Schedule 11 is not satisfied,*

(*b*) *in the case of a recognised professional qualification, that any requirement of Schedule 12 is not satisfied, or*

(*c*) *that a recognised supervisory or qualifying body has failed to comply with an obligation to which it is subject by virtue of this Part,*

he may, instead of revoking the relevant recognition order, make an application to the court under this section.

(*2*) *If on such application the court decides that the subsection or requirement in question is not satisfied or, as the case may be, that the body has failed to comply with the obligation in question it may order the supervisory or qualifying body in question to take such steps as the court directs for securing that the subsection or requirement is satisfied or that the obligation is complied with.*

(*3*) *The jurisdiction conferred by this section is exercisable by the High Court and the Court of Session.*

[788]

NOTES

Repealed by the Companies Act 2006, s 1295, Sch 16, as from a day to be appointed.

40 Directions to comply with international obligations

(*1*) *If it appears to the Secretary of State—*

(*a*) *that any action proposed to be taken by a recognised supervisory or qualifying body, or a body [designated] by order under section 46, would be incompatible with Community obligations or any other international obligations of the United Kingdom, or* (*b*) *that any action which that body has power to take is required for the purpose of implementing any such obligations,*

he may direct the body not to take or, as the case may be, to take the action in question.

(*2*) *A direction may include such supplementary or incidental requirements as the Secretary of State thinks necessary or expedient.*

(*3*) *A direction under this section is enforceable on the application of the Secretary of State by injunction or, in Scotland, by an order under section 45 of the Court of Session Act 1988.*

[789]

NOTES

Repealed by the Companies Act 2006, s 1295, Sch 16, as from a day to be appointed.

Sub-s (1): word in square brackets substituted by the Companies (Audit, Investigations and Community Enterprise) Act 2004, s 25, Sch 2, Pt 1, paras 1, 3(a), as from 1 January 2005.

Offences

41 False and misleading statements

(*1*) *A person commits an offence if—*

(*a*) *for the purposes of or in connection with any application under this Part, or*

(*b*) *in purported compliance with any requirement imposed on him by or under this Part,*

he furnishes information which he knows to be false or misleading in a material particular or recklessly furnishes information which is false or misleading in a material particular.

(*2*) *It is an offence for a person whose name does not appear on the register of auditors kept under regulations under section 35 to describe himself as a registered auditor or so to hold himself out as to indicate, or be reasonably understood to indicate, that he is a registered auditor.*

(*3*) *It is an offence for a body which is not a recognised supervisory or qualifying body to describe itself as so recognised or so to describe itself or hold itself out as to indicate, or be reasonably understood to indicate, that it is so recognised.*

(*4*) *A person guilty of an offence under subsection (1) is liable—*

(*a*) *on conviction on indictment, to imprisonment for a term not exceeding two years or to a fine or both;*

(*b*) *on summary conviction, to imprisonment for a term not exceeding six months or to a fine not exceeding the statutory maximum or both.*

(*5*) *A person guilty of an offence under subsection (2) or (3) is liable on summary conviction to imprisonment for a term not exceeding six months or to a fine not exceeding level 5 on the standard scale or both.*

Where a contravention of subsection (2) or (3) involves a public display of the offending description, the maximum fine that may be imposed is (in place of that mentioned above) an amount equal to level 5 on the standard scale multiplied by the number of days for which the display has continued.

(*6*) *It is a defence for a person charged with an offence under subsection (2) or (3) to show that he took all reasonable precautions and exercised all due diligence to avoid the commission of the offence.*

[790]

NOTES

Repealed by the Companies Act 2006, s 1295, Sch 16, as from a day to be appointed.

42 Offences by bodies corporate, partnerships and unincorporated associations

(*1*) *Where an offence under this Part committed by a body corporate is proved to have been committed with the consent or connivance of, or to be attributable to any neglect on the part of, a director, manager, secretary or other similar officer of the body, or a person purporting to act in any such capacity, he as well as the body corporate is guilty of the offence and liable to be proceeded against and punished accordingly.*

(2) Where the affairs of a body corporate are managed by its members, subsection (1) applies in relation to the acts and defaults of a member in connection with his functions of management as to a director of a body corporate.

(3) Where an offence under this Part committed by a partnership is proved to have been committed with the consent or connivance of, or to be attributable to any neglect on the part of, a partner, he as well as the partnership is guilty of the offence and liable to be proceeded against and punished accordingly.

(4) Where an offence under this Part committed by an unincorporated association (other than a partnership) is proved to have been committed with the consent or connivance of, or to be attributable to any neglect on the part of, any officer of the association or any member of its governing body, he as well as the association is guilty of the offence and liable to be proceeded against and punished accordingly.

[791]

NOTES

Repealed by the Companies Act 2006, s 1295, Sch 16, as from a day to be appointed.

43 Time limits for prosecution of offences

(1) An information relating to an offence under this Part which is triable by a magistrates' court in England and Wales may be so tried on an information laid at any time within twelve months after the date on which evidence sufficient in the opinion of the Director of Public Prosecutions or the Secretary of State to justify the proceedings comes to his knowledge.

(2) Proceedings in Scotland for an offence under this Part may be commenced at any time within twelve months after the date on which evidence sufficient in the Lord Advocate's opinion to justify the proceedings came to his knowledge or, where such evidence was reported to him by the Secretary of State, within twelve months after the date on which it came to the knowledge of the latter.

For the purposes of this subsection proceedings shall be deemed to be commenced on the date on which a warrant to apprehend or to cite the accused is granted, if the warrant is executed without undue delay.

(3) Subsection (1) does not authorise the trial of an information laid, and subsection (2) does not authorise the commencement of proceedings, more than three years after the commission of the offence.

(4) For the purposes of this section a certificate of the Director of Public Prosecutions, the Lord Advocate or the Secretary of State as to the date on which such evidence as is referred to above came to his knowledge is conclusive evidence.

(5) Nothing in this section affects proceedings within the time limits prescribed by section 127(1) of the Magistrates' Courts Act 1980 or section 331 of the Criminal Procedure (Scotland) Act 1975 (the usual time limits for criminal proceedings).

[792]

NOTES

Repealed by the Companies Act 2006, s 1295, Sch 16, as from a day to be appointed.

44 Jurisdiction and procedure in respect of offences

(1) Summary proceedings for an offence under this Part may, without prejudice to any jurisdiction exercisable apart from this section, be taken against a body corporate or unincorporated association at any place at which it has a place of business and against an individual at any place where he is for the time being.

(2) Proceedings for an offence alleged to have been committed under this Part by an unincorporated association shall be brought in the name of the association (and not in that of any of its members), and for the purposes of any such proceedings any rules of court relating to the service of documents apply as in relation to a body corporate.

(3) Section 33 of the Criminal Justice Act 1925 and Schedule 3 to the Magistrates' Courts Act 1980 (procedure on charge of offence against a corporation) apply in a case in which an unincorporated association is charged in England and Wales with an offence under this Part as they apply in the case of a corporation.

(4) In relation to proceedings on indictment in Scotland for an offence alleged to have been committed under this Part by an unincorporated association, [section 70 of the Criminal Procedure (Scotland) Act 1995] (proceedings on indictment against bodies corporate) applies as if the association were a body corporate.

(5) A fine imposed on an unincorporated association on its conviction of such an offence shall be paid out of the funds of the association.

[793]

NOTES

Repealed by the Companies Act 2006, s 1295, Sch 16, as from a day to be appointed.

Sub-s (4): words in square brackets substituted by the Criminal Procedure (Consequential Provisions) (Scotland) Act 1995, s 5, Sch 4, para 74(2), as from 1 April 1996.

Supplementary provisions

45 Fees

(1) An applicant for a recognition order under this Part shall pay such fee in respect of his application as may be prescribed; and no application shall be regarded as duly made unless this subsection is complied with.

(2) Every recognised supervisory or qualifying body shall pay such periodical fees to the Secretary of State as may be prescribed.

(3) In this section "prescribed" means prescribed by regulations made by the Secretary of State, which may make different provision for different cases or classes of case.

(4) Regulations under this section shall be made by statutory instrument which shall be subject to annulment in pursuance of a resolution of either House of Parliament.

(5) Fees received by the Secretary of State by virtue of this Part shall be paid into the Consolidated Fund.

[794]

NOTES

Repealed by the Companies Act 2006, s 1295, Sch 16, as from a day to be appointed.

Regulations: the Company Auditors (Recognition Orders) (Application Fees) and the Companies Act 1989 (Recognised Supervisory Bodies) (Periodical Fees) (Revocation) Regulations 2005, SI 2005/2243. The 2005 Regulations revoke the Company Auditors (Recognition Orders) (Application Fees) Regulations 1990, SI 1990/1206, and the Companies Act 1989 (Recognised Supervisory Bodies) (Periodical Fees) Regulations 1993, SI 1993/1881 (see further, Appendix 3 (Fees Instruments) at **[A3]**).

46 Delegation of functions of Secretary of State

[(1) The Secretary of State may make an order under this section (a "delegation order" for the purpose of enabling functions of the Secretary of State under this Part to be exercised by a body designated by the order.

(1A) The body so designated may be either—

- *(a) a body corporate which is established by the order, or*
- *(b) subject to section 46A, a body (whether a body corporate or an unincorporated association) which is already in existence ("an existing body").]*

(2) A delegation order has the effect of transferring to the body [designated] by it, subject to such exceptions and reservations as may be specified in the order, all the functions of the Secretary of State under this Part except—

- *(a) ...*
- *(b) his functions in relation to the body itself;*

and the order may also confer on the body such other functions supplementary or incidental to those transferred as appear to the Secretary of State to be appropriate.

(3) Any transfer of the functions under the following provisions shall be subject to the reservation that they remain exercisable concurrently by the Secretary of State—

- *(a) section 38 (power to call for information), and*
- *(b) section 40 (directions to comply with international obligations);*

and any transfer of the function of refusing to approve an overseas qualification, or withdrawing such approval, on the grounds referred to in section 33(3) (lack of reciprocity) shall be subject to the reservation that the function is exercisable only with the consent of the Secretary of State.

(4) A delegation order may be amended or, if it appears to the Secretary of State that it is no longer in the public interest that the order should remain in force, revoked by a further order under this section.

(5) Where functions are transferred or resumed, the Secretary of State may by order confer or, as the case may be, take away such other functions supplementary or incidental to those transferred or resumed as appear to him to be appropriate.

[(6) Where a delegation order is made, the provisions of Schedule 13 have effect with respect to—

- *(a) the status of the body designated by the order in exercising functions of the Secretary of State under this Part;*
- *(b) the constitution and proceedings of the body where it is established by the order;*
- *(c) the exercise by the body of certain functions transferred to it; and*
- *(d) other supplementary matters.]*

(7) An order under this section shall be made by statutory instrument.

(8) An order which has the effect of transferring or resuming any functions shall not be made unless a draft of it has been laid before and approved by resolution of each House of Parliament; and any other description of order shall be subject to annulment in pursuance of a resolution of either House of Parliament.

[795]–[796]

NOTES

Repealed by the Companies Act 2006, s 1295, Sch 16, as from a day to be appointed.

Sub-ss (1), (1A): substituted, for original sub-s (1), by the Companies (Audit, Investigations and Community Enterprise) Act 2004, s 3(1), (2), as from 1 January 2005.

Sub-s (2): word in square brackets substituted by the Companies (Audit, Investigations and Community Enterprise) Act 2004, s 3(1), (3), as from 1 January 2005; para (a) repealed by the Competition Act 1998 and other enactments (Amendment) Regulations 2004, SI 2004/1261, reg 5, Sch 2, para 2(1), (2), as from 1 May 2004.

Sub-s (6): substituted by the Companies (Audit, Investigations and Community Enterprise) Act 2004, s 3(1), (4), as from 1 January 2005.

As to the disclosure of information in connection with defective accounts and company investigations for the purposes of enabling or assisting a body designated by an Order under this section to exercise its functions under Pt II of this Act, see the Companies Act 1985, ss 245F, 245G, 449, Sch 7B, Pt 2, para 7, Sch 15D, para 34 (as inserted or substituted by the Companies (Audit, Investigations and Community Enterprise) Act 2004). As to the disclosure of information obtained under the Companies Act 2006, s 459, for the purpose of assisting a body designated by an Order under this section, see s 461(4) of that Act at **[S461]**.

Orders: the Companies Act 1989 (Delegation) Order 2005, SI 2005/2337 at **[7444]**.

[46A Circumstances in which Secretary of State may delegate functions to existing body

(1) The Secretary of State's power to make a delegation order under section 46 which designates an existing body (see section 46(1A)(b)) is exercisable in accordance with this section.

(2) The Secretary of State may make such an order if it appears to the Secretary of State—

- *(a) that the body is willing and able to exercise the functions that would be transferred by the order; and*
- *(b) that the body has arrangements in place relating to the exercise of those functions which are such as to be likely to ensure that the conditions in subsection (3) are met.*

(3) The conditions are—

- *(a) that the functions in question will be exercised effectively; and*
- *(b) where the delegation order is to contain any requirements or other provisions specified under subsection (4), that those functions will be exercised in accordance with any such requirements or provisions.*

(4) The delegation order may contain such requirements or other provisions relating to the exercise of the functions by the designated body as appear to the Secretary of State to be appropriate.

(5) An existing body—

(a) may be designated by a delegation order under section 46, and

(b) may accordingly exercise functions of the Secretary of State in pursuance of the order,

despite any involvement of the body in the exercise of any functions under arrangements within any of paragraphs 17, 18, 19(1) or 20(1) of Schedule 11.]

[796A]

NOTES

Inserted by the Companies (Audit, Investigations and Community Enterprise) Act 2004, s 4, as from 1 January 2005.

Repealed by the Companies Act 2006, s 1295, Sch 16, as from a day to be appointed.

Orders: the Companies Act 1989 (Delegation) Order 2005, SI 2005/2337 at **[7444]**.

47 *(Repealed by the Competition Act 1998 and other enactments (Amendment) Regulations 2004, SI 2004/1261, reg 5, Sch 2, para 2(1), (2), as from 1 May 2004.)*

48 Exemption from liability for damages

(1) Neither a recognised supervisory body, nor any of its officers or employees or members of its governing body, shall be liable in damages for anything done or omitted in the discharge or purported discharge of functions to which this subsection applies, unless the act or omission is shown to have been in bad faith.

(2) Subsection (1) applies to the functions of the body so far as relating to, or to matters arising out of—

(a) such rules, practices, powers and arrangements of the body to which the requirements of Part II of Schedule 11 apply, or

(b) the obligations with which paragraph 16 of that Schedule requires the body to comply,

(c) any guidance issued by the body, or

(d) the obligations to which the body is subject by virtue of this Part.

(3) …

[797]

NOTES

Repealed by the Companies Act 2006, s 1295, Sch 16, as from a day to be appointed.

Sub-s (3): repealed by the Companies (Audit, Investigations and Community Enterprise) Act 2004, s 64, Sch 8, as from 1 January 2005.

49 Service of notices

(1) This section has effect in relation to any notice, direction or other document required or authorised by or under this Part to be given to or served on any person other than the Secretary of State.

(2) Any such document may be given to or served on the person in question—

(a) by delivering it to him,

(b) by leaving it at his proper address, or

(c) by sending it by post to him at that address.

(3) Any such document may—

(a) in the case of a body corporate, be given to or served on the secretary or clerk of that body;

(b) in the case of a partnership, be given to or served on any partner;

(c) in the case of an unincorporated association other than a partnership, be given to or served on any member of the governing body of the association.

(4) For the purposes of this section and section 7 of the Interpretation Act 1978 (service of documents by post) in its application to this section, the proper address of any person is his last known address (whether of his residence or of a place where he carries on business or is employed) and also—

(*a*) *in the case of a person who is eligible under the rules of a recognised supervisory body for appointment as company auditor and who does not have a place of business in the United Kingdom, the address of that body;*
(*b*) *in the case of a body corporate, its secretary or its clerk, the address of its registered or principal office in the United Kingdom;*
(*c*) *in the case of an unincorporated association (other than a partnership) or a member of its governing body, its principal office in the United Kingdom.*

[798]

NOTES

Repealed by the Companies Act 2006, s 1295, Sch 16, as from a day to be appointed.

50 Power to make consequential amendments

(*1*) *The Secretary of State may by regulations make such amendments of enactments as appear to him to be necessary or expedient in consequence of the provisions of this Part having effect in place of section 389 of the Companies Act 1985.*

(*2*) *That power extends to making such amendments as appear to the Secretary of State necessary or expedient of—*
(*a*) *enactments referring by name to the bodies of accountants recognised for the purposes of section 389(1)(a) of the Companies Act 1985, and*
(*b*) *enactments making with respect to other statutory auditors provision as to the matters dealt with in relation to company auditors by section 389 of the Companies Act 1985.*

(*3*) *The provision which may be made with respect to other statutory auditors includes provision as to—*
(*a*) *eligibility for the appointment,*
(*b*) *the effect of appointing a partnership which is not a legal person and the manner of exercise of the auditor's rights in such a case, and*
(*c*) *ineligibility on the ground of lack of independence or any other ground.*

(*4*) *The regulations may contain such supplementary, incidental and transitional provision as appears to the Secretary of State to be necessary or expedient.*

(*5*) *The Secretary of State shall not make regulations under this section with respect to any statutory auditors without the consent of—*
(*a*) *the Minister responsible for their appointment or responsible for the body or person by, or in relation to whom, they are appointed, or*
(*b*) *if there is no such Minister, the person by whom they are appointed.*

(*6*) *In this section a "statutory auditor" means a person appointed auditor in pursuance of any enactment authorising or requiring the appointment of an auditor or auditors.*

(*7*) *Regulations under this section shall be made by statutory instrument which shall be subject to annulment in pursuance of a resolution of either House of Parliament.*

[799]

NOTES

Repealed by the Companies Act 2006, s 1295, Sch 16, as from a day to be appointed.
Regulations: the Companies Act 1989 (Eligibility for Appointment as Company Auditor) (Consequential Amendments) Regulations 1991, SI 1991/1997 at **[6712]**; the Companies Act 1989 Part II (Consequential Amendments) Regulations 1995, SI 1995/1163; the Companies Act 1989 Part II (Consequential Amendment) (No 2) Regulations 1995, SI 1995/2723.

51 Power to make provision in consequence of changes affecting accountancy bodies

(*1*) *The Secretary of State may by regulations make such amendments of enactments as appear to him to be necessary or expedient in consequence of any change of name, merger or transfer of engagements affecting—*
(*a*) *a recognised supervisory or qualifying body under this Part, or*
(*b*) *a body of accountants referred to in, or approved, authorised or otherwise recognised for the purposes of, any other enactment.*

(*2*) *Regulations under this section shall be made by statutory instrument which shall be subject to annulment in pursuance of a resolution of either House of Parliament.*

[800]

NOTES

Repealed by the Companies Act 2006, s 1295, Sch 16, as from a day to be appointed.

52 Meaning of "associate"

(*1*) *In this Part "associate", in relation to a person, shall be construed as follows.*

(2) *In relation to an individual "associate" means—*

(*a*) *that individual's spouse [or civil partner] or minor child or step-child,*

(*b*) *any body corporate of which that individual is a director, and*

(*c*) *any employee or partner of that individual.*

(*3*) *In relation to a body corporate "associate" means—*

(*a*) *any body corporate of which that body is a director,*

(*b*) *any body corporate in the same group as that body, and*

(*c*) *any employee or partner of that body or of any body corporate in the same group.*

(*4*) *In relation to a Scottish firm, or a partnership constituted under the law of any other country or territory in which a partnership is a legal person, "associate" means—*

(*a*) *any body corporate of which the firm is a director,*

(*b*) *any employee of or partner in the firm, and*

(*c*) *any person who is an associate of a partner in the firm.*

(*5*) *In relation to a partnership constituted under the law of England and Wales or Northern Ireland, or the law of any other country or territory in which a partnership is not a legal person, "associate" means any person who is an associate of any of the partners.*

[801]

NOTES

Repealed by the Companies Act 2006, s 1295, Sch 16, as from a day to be appointed.

Sub-s (1): words in square brackets inserted by the Civil Partnership Act 2004, s 261(1), Sch 27, para 128, as from 5 December 2005.

Step-child: this includes relationships arising through civil partnerships; see the Civil Partnership Act 2004, ss 246, 247, Sch 21.

53 Minor definitions

(*1*) *In this Part—*

"address" means—

(*a*) *in relation to an individual, his usual residential or business address, and*

(*b*) *in relation to a firm, its registered or principal office in Great Britain;*

"company" means any company or other body to which section 384 of the Companies Act 1985 (duty to appoint auditors) applies;

"director", in relation to a body corporate, includes any person occupying in relation to it the position of a director (by whatever name called) and any person in accordance with whose directions or instructions (not being advice given in a professional capacity) the directors of the body are accustomed to act;

"enactment" includes an enactment contained in subordinate legislation within the meaning of the Interpretation Act 1978;

"firm" means a body corporate or a partnership;

"group", in relation to a body corporate, means the body corporate, any other body corporate which is its holding company or subsidiary and any other body corporate which is a subsidiary of that holding company; and

"holding company" and "subsidiary" have the meaning given by section 736 of the Companies Act 1985;

"parent undertaking" and "subsidiary undertaking" have the same meaning as in Part VII of the Companies Act 1985.

(2) *For the purposes of this Part a body shall be regarded as "established in the United Kingdom" if and only if—*

(*a*) *it is incorporated or formed under the law of the United Kingdom or a part of the United Kingdom, or*

(*b*) *its central management and control is exercised in the United Kingdom;*

and any reference to a qualification "obtained in the United Kingdom" is to a qualification obtained from such a body.

[802]

NOTES

Repealed by the Companies Act 2006, s 1295, Sch 16, as from a day to be appointed.

54 Index of defined expressions

The following Table shows provisions defining or otherwise explaining expressions used in this Part (other than provisions defining or explaining an expression used only in the same section)—

address	*section 53(1)*
appropriate qualification	*section 31*
associate	*section 52*
company	*section 53(1)*
company auditor, company audit and company audit work	*section 24(2)*
delegation order	*section 46*
director (of a body corporate)	*section 53(1)*
…	…
enactment	*section 53(1)*
established in the United Kingdom	*section 53(2)*
firm	*section 53(1)*
group (in relation to a body corporate)	*section 53(1)*
guidance	
—of a qualifying body	*section 32(3)*
—of a supervisory body	*section 30(4)*
holding company	*section 53(1)*
member (of a supervisory body)	*section 30(2)*
obtained in the United Kingdom	*section 53(2)*
parent undertaking	*section 53(1)*
purposes of this Part	*section 24(1)*
qualifying body	*section 32(1)*
recognised	
—in relation to a professional qualification	*section 32(4) and Schedule 12*
—in relation to a qualifying body	*paragraph 2(1) of Schedule 12*
—in relation to a supervisory body	*section 30(5) and Schedule 11*
rules	
—of a qualifying body	*section 32(2)*
—of a supervisory body	*section 30(3)*
subsidiary and subsidiary undertaking	*section 53(1)*
supervisory body	*section 30(1)*

[803]

NOTES

Repealed by the Companies Act 2006, s 1295, Sch 16, as from a day to be appointed.

Entry "Director (in Schedule 14)" repealed by the Competition Act 1998 and other enactments (Amendment) Regulations 2004, SI 2004/1261, reg 5, Sch 2, para 2(1), (3), as from 1 May 2004.

PART III
INVESTIGATIONS AND POWERS TO OBTAIN INFORMATION

55–81 *(S 55 inserts CA 1985, s 432(2A) at* **[467]***; s 56(1)–(5) amend s 434 of the 1985 Act at* **[469]** *(s 56(5) is repealed by the Companies Act 2006, s 1295, Sch 16, as from a day to be appointed); s 56(6) substitutes s 436(1) of the 1985 Act at* **[470]***; s 57 inserts s 437(1B), (1C) of the 1985 Act at* **[471]** *(and is repealed by the Companies Act 2006, s 1295, Sch 16, as from a day to be appointed); s 58 repealed by the Companies Act 2006, s 1295, Sch 16, as from 6 April 2007; s 59 amends s 439 of the 1985 Act at* **[473]***; s 60 repeals s 440 of the 1985 Act, amends the Insolvency Act 1986, s 124(4) at* **[3280]***, and inserts s 124A of that Act at* **[3281]***; s 61 amends CA 1985, s 441 at* **[474]***; s 62 substitutes s 442(3) of that Act at* **[475]***; s 63 repealed by the Companies (Audit, Investigations and Community Enterprise) Act 2004, s 64, Sch 8, as from 6 April 2005; s 64(1) substitutes s 448 of that Act at* **[481]***; s 64(2) amends Sch 24 to that Act at* **[689]** *(and is repealed by the Companies Act 2006, s 1295, Sch 16, as from a day to be appointed); s 65 repealed by the Companies (Audit, Investigations and Community Enterprise) Act 2004, s 64, Sch 8, as from 6 April 2005; s 66(1), (2), (4) amend s 450 of that Act at* **[483]***; s 66(3) substitutes s 450(4) of that Act (and is repealed by the Companies Act 2006, s 1295, Sch 16, as from a day to be appointed); s 67 repealed by the Companies (Audit, Investigations and Community Enterprise) Act 2004, s 64, Sch 8, as from 6 April 2005; s 68 substitutes s 451A of that Act at* **[485]***; s 69 amends s 452 of that Act at* **[486]***, and is repealed in part by the Companies (Audit, Investigations and Community Enterprise) Act 2004, s 64, Sch 8, as from 6 April 2005; s 70 substitutes s 453(1) of that Act at* **[487]***; s 71 amends Sch 22 to that Act at* **[687]** *(and is repealed by the Companies Act 2006, s 1295, Sch 16, as from a day to be appointed); ss 72–77 repealed by the Financial Services and Markets Act 2000 (Consequential Amendments and Repeals) Order 2001, SI 2001/3649, art 75(a), as from 1 December 2001; s 78 repealed by the Insolvency Act 2000, s 15(1), Sch 5, as from 2 April 2001; s 79 repealed by SI 2001/3649, art 75(b), as from 1 December 2001; s 80 spent (amended the Building Societies Act 1986, s 53 which was substituted by a new s 53A by SI 2001/2617); s 81 repealed by SI 2001/3649, art 75(c), as from 1 December 2001.)*

Powers exercisable to assist overseas regulatory authorities

82 Request for assistance by overseas regulatory authority

(1) The powers conferred by section 83 are exercisable by the Secretary of State for the purpose of assisting an overseas regulatory authority which has requested his assistance in connection with inquiries being carried out by it or on its behalf.

(2) An "overseas regulatory authority" means an authority which in a country or territory outside the United Kingdom exercises—

[(a) any function corresponding to—
  (i) any function of the Secretary of State under the Companies Act 1985;
  (ii) any function of the Financial Services Authority under the Financial Services and Markets Act 2000;
  (iii) any function exercised by the competent authority under Part VI of that Act …], or

(b) any function in connection with the investigation of, or the enforcement of rules (whether or not having the force of law) relating to, conduct of the kind prohibited by [Part V of the Criminal Justice Act 1993 (insider dealing)], or

(c) any function prescribed for the purposes of this subsection by order of the Secretary of State, being a function which in the opinion of the Secretary of State relates to companies or financial services.

An order under paragraph (c) shall be made by statutory instrument which shall be subject to annulment in pursuance of a resolution of either House of Parliament.

(3) The Secretary of State shall not exercise the powers conferred by section 83 unless [he and the Financial Services Authority are] satisfied that the assistance requested by the overseas regulatory authority is for the purposes of its regulatory functions.

An authority's "regulatory functions" means any functions falling within subsection (2) and any other functions relating to companies or financial services.

(4) In deciding whether to exercise those powers the Secretary of State may take into account, in particular—

(a) whether corresponding assistance would be given in that country or territory to an authority exercising regulatory functions in the United Kingdom;

(b) whether the inquiries relate to the possible breach of a law, or other requirement, which has no close parallel in the United Kingdom or involves the assertion of a jurisdiction not recognised by the United Kingdom;

(c) the seriousness of the matter to which the inquiries relate, the importance to the inquiries of the information sought in the United Kingdom and whether the assistance could be obtained by other means;

(d) whether it is otherwise appropriate in the public interest to give the assistance sought.

(5) Before deciding whether to exercise those powers in a case where the overseas regulatory authority is a banking supervisor, the Secretary of State shall consult the [Financial Services Authority].

A "banking supervisor" means an overseas regulatory authority with respect to which the [Financial Services Authority] has notified the Secretary of State, for the purposes of this subsection, that it exercises functions corresponding to those of the [Authority] [in relation to authorised persons with permission under the Financial Services and Markets Act 2000 to accept deposits].

[(5A) In subsection (5), "authorised person" has the meaning given in the Financial Services and Markets Act 2000 and the references to deposits and their acceptance must be read with—

(a) section 22 of that Act;

(b) any relevant order under that section; and

(c) Schedule 2 to that Act.]

(6) The Secretary of State may decline to exercise those powers unless the overseas regulatory authority undertakes to make such contribution towards the costs of their exercise as the Secretary of State considers appropriate.

(7) References in this section to financial services include, in particular, investment business, insurance and banking.

[804]

NOTES

Sub-s (2): para (a) substituted by the Financial Services and Markets Act 2000 (Consequential Amendments and Repeals) Order 2001, SI 2001/3649, art 76(1), (2), as from 1 December 2001; words omitted from para (a) repealed by the Prospectus Regulations 2005, SI 2005/1433, reg 2(3), Sch 3, para 1, as from 1 July 2005; words in square brackets in para (b) substituted by the Criminal Justice Act 1993, s 79(13), Sch 5, Pt I, para 16, as from 1 March 1994.

Sub-s (3): words in square brackets substituted by SI 2001/3649, art 76(1), (3), as from 1 December 2001.

Sub-s (5): words in first, second and third pairs of square brackets substituted by the Bank of England Act 1998, s 23(1), Sch 5, Pt IV, Ch II, para 66(1), (2)(b), as from 1 June 1998; words in fourth pair of square brackets substituted by SI 2001/3649, art 76(1), (4), as from 1 December 2001.

Sub-s (5A): inserted by SI 2001/3649, art 76(1), (5), as from 1 December 2001.

Transfer of functions: by the Transfer of Functions (Financial Services) Order 1992, SI 1992/1315, art 5, Sch 3, para 3 at **[6733]**, **[6741]**, the function of the Secretary of State under sub-s (3) above is exercisable concurrently by the Secretary of State and the Treasury.

83 Power to require information, documents or other assistance

(1) The following powers may be exercised in accordance with section 82, if the Secretary of State considers there is good reason for their exercise.

(2) The Secretary of State may require any person—

(a) to attend before him at a specified time and place and answer questions or otherwise furnish information with respect to any matter relevant to the inquiries,

(b) to produce at a specified time and place any specified documents which appear to the Secretary of State to relate to any matter relevant to the inquiries, and

(c) otherwise to give him such assistance in connection with the inquiries as he is reasonably able to give.

(3) The Secretary of State may examine a person on oath and may administer an oath accordingly.

(4) Where documents are produced the Secretary of State may take copies or extracts from them.

(5) A person shall not under this section be required to disclose information or produce a document which he would be entitled to refuse to disclose or produce on grounds of legal professional privilege in proceedings in the High Court or on grounds of confidentiality as between client and professional legal adviser in proceedings in the Court of Session, except that a lawyer may be required to furnish the name and address of his client.

(6) A statement by a person in compliance with a requirement imposed under this section may be used in evidence against him.

[(6A) However, in criminal proceedings in which that person is charged with an offence to which this subsection applies—

(a) no evidence relating to the statement may be adduced, and

(b) no question relating to it may be asked,

by or on behalf of the prosecution, unless evidence relating to it is adduced, or a question relating to it is asked, in the proceedings by or on behalf of that person.

(6B) Subsection (6A) applies to any offence other than—

(a) an offence under section 85;

(b) an offence under section 2 or 5 of the Perjury Act 1911 (false statements made on oath otherwise than in judicial proceedings or made otherwise than on oath);

(c) an offence under section 44(1) or (2) of the Criminal Law (Consolidation) (Scotland) Act 1995 (false statements made on oath or otherwise than on oath); or

(d) an offence under Article 7 or 10 of the Perjury (Northern Ireland) Order 1979 (false statements made on oath otherwise than in judicial proceedings or made otherwise than on oath).]

(7) Where a person claims a lien on a document, its production under this section is without prejudice to his lien.

(8) In this section "documents" includes information recorded in any form; and, in relation to information recorded otherwise than in legible form, the power to require its production includes power to require the production of a copy of it in legible form.

[805]

NOTES

Sub-ss (6A), (6B): inserted by the Youth Justice and Criminal Evidence Act 1999, s 59, Sch 3, para 21, as from 14 April 2000 (in relation to England and Wales), and as from 1 January 2001 (in relation to Scotland).

84 Exercise of powers by officer, &c

(1) The Secretary of State may authorise an officer of his or any other competent person to exercise on his behalf all or any of the powers conferred by section 83.

(2) No such authority shall be granted except for the purpose of investigating—

(a) the affairs, or any aspects of the affairs, of a person specified in the authority, or

(b) a subject-matter so specified,

being a person who, or subject-matter which, is the subject of the inquiries being carried out by or on behalf of the overseas regulatory authority.

(3) No person shall be bound to comply with a requirement imposed by a person exercising powers by virtue of an authority granted under this section unless he has, if required, produced evidence of his authority.

(4) A person shall not by virtue of an authority under this section be required to disclose any information or produce any documents in respect of which he owes an obligation of confidence by virtue of carrying on the business of banking unless—

(a) the imposing on him of a requirement with respect to such information or documents has been specifically authorised by the Secretary of State, or

(b) the person to whom the obligation of confidence is owed consents to the disclosure or production.

In this subsection "documents" has the same meaning as in section 83.

(5) Where the Secretary of State authorises a person other than one of his officers to exercise any powers by virtue of this section, that person shall make a report to the Secretary of State in such manner as he may require on the exercise of those powers and the results of exercising them.

[806]

85 Penalty for failure to comply with requirement, &c

(1) A person who without reasonable excuse fails to comply with a requirement imposed on him under section 83 commits an offence and is liable on summary conviction to imprisonment for a term not exceeding six months or to a fine not exceeding level 5 on the standard scale, or both.

(2) A person who in purported compliance with any such requirement furnishes information which he knows to be false or misleading in a material particular, or recklessly furnishes information which is false or misleading in a material particular, commits an offence and is liable—

- (a) on conviction on indictment, to imprisonment for a term not exceeding two years or to a fine, or both;
- (b) on summary conviction, to imprisonment for a term not exceeding six months or to a fine not exceeding the statutory maximum, or both.

[807]

86 Restrictions on disclosure of information

(1) This section applies to information relating to the business or other affairs of a person which—

- (a) is supplied by an overseas regulatory authority in connection with a request for assistance, or
- (b) is obtained by virtue of the powers conferred by section 83, whether or not any requirement to supply it is made under that section.

(2) Except as permitted by section 87 below, such information shall not be disclosed for any purpose—

- (a) by the primary recipient, or
- (b) by any person obtaining the information directly or indirectly from him,

without the consent of the person from whom the primary recipient obtained the information and, if different, the person to whom it relates.

(3) The "primary recipient" means, as the case may be—

- (a) the Secretary of State,
- (b) any person authorised under section 84 to exercise powers on his behalf, and
- (c) any officer or servant of any such person.

(4) Information shall not be treated as information to which this section applies if it has been made available to the public by virtue of being disclosed in any circumstances in which, or for any purpose for which, disclosure is not precluded by this section.

(5) A person who contravenes this section commits an offence and is liable—

- (a) on conviction on indictment, to imprisonment for a term not exceeding two years or to a fine, or both;
- (b) on summary conviction, to imprisonment for a term not exceeding three months or to a fine not exceeding the statutory maximum, or both.

[808]

87 Exceptions from restrictions on disclosure

(1) Information to which section 86 applies may be disclosed—

- (a) to any person with a view to the institution of, or otherwise for the purposes of, relevant proceedings,
- (b) for the purpose of enabling or assisting a relevant authority to discharge any relevant function (including functions in relation to proceedings),
- (c) to the Treasury, if the disclosure is made in the interests of investors or in the public interest,
- (d) if the information is or has been available to the public from other sources,
- (e) in a summary or collection of information framed in such a way as not to enable the identity of any person to whom the information relates to be ascertained, or
- (f) in pursuance of any Community obligation.

(2) The relevant proceedings referred to in subsection (1)(a) are—
(a) any criminal proceedings,
[(b) civil proceedings arising under or by virtue of the Financial Services and Markets Act 2000 and proceedings before the Financial Services and Markets Tribunal], and
(c) disciplinary proceedings relating to—
(i) the exercise by a solicitor, auditor, accountant, valuer or actuary of his professional duties, or
(ii) the discharge by a public servant of his duties;
[(d) proceedings before the Pensions Regulator Tribunal].

(3) In subsection (2)(c)(ii) "public servant" means an officer or servant of the Crown or of any public or other authority for the time being designated for the purposes of that provision by order of the Secretary of State.

(4) The relevant authorities referred to in subsection (1)(b), and the relevant functions in relation to each such authority, are as follows—

Authority	*Functions*
[The Secretary of State.	Functions under— (a) the enactments relating to companies or insolvency; (b) Part 2, this Part or Part 7 of this Act; (c) the Financial Services and Markets Act 2000.]
[The Treasury	Functions under— (a) this Part or Part 7 of this Act; (b) the Financial Services and Markets Act 2000.]
[An inspector appointed under Part 14 of the Companies Act 1985.	Functions under that Part.]
[A person authorised to exercise powers under section 447 of the Companies Act 1985 or section 84 of this Act.	Functions under that section.]
[A person appointed under— (a) section 167 of the Financial Services and Markets Act 2000 (general investigations), (b) section 168 of that Act (investigations in particular cases), (c) section 169(1)(b) of that Act (investigation in support of overseas regulator), (d) section 284 of that Act (investigations into affairs of certain collective investment schemes), or (e) regulations made as a result of section 262(2)(k) of that Act (investigations into open-ended investment companies), to conduct an investigation.	Functions in relation to the investigation.]
An overseas regulatory authority.	Its regulatory functions (within the meaning of section 82 of this Act).

Authority	*Functions*
The Department of Economic Development in Northern Ireland or a person appointed or authorised by that Department.	Functions conferred on it or him by the enactments relating to companies or insolvency.
…	…
…	…
…	…
…	…
…	…
[…	…]
The Bank of England.	[Any of its functions]
[The Financial Services Authority.	Functions under the enactments relating to friendly societies, under the Building Societies Act 1986 and under the Financial Services and Markets Act 2000.]
[A body corporate established in accordance with section 212(1) of that Act.	Functions under the Financial Services Compensation Scheme, established in accordance with section 213 of that Act.]
[A recognised investment exchange or a recognised clearing house (as defined by section 285 of that Act).	Functions in its capacity as an exchange or clearing house recognised under that Act.]
[A body designated under section 326(1) of the Financial Services and Markets Act 2000.	Functions in its capacity as a body designated under that section.]
…	…
A body [designated] by order under section 46 of this Act.	Functions under Part II of this Act.
A recognised supervisory or qualifying body within the meaning of Part II of this Act.	Functions as such a body.
…	…
…	…
The Official Receiver or, in Northern Ireland, the Official Assignee for company liquidations or for bankruptcy.	Functions under the enactments relating to insolvency.
A recognised professional body (within the meaning of section 391 of the Insolvency Act 1986).	Functions in its capacity as such a body under the Insolvency Act 1986.
…	…
[The Pensions Regulator	Functions conferred by or by virtue of— (a) the Pension Schemes Act 1993, (b) the Pensions Act 1995, (c) the Welfare Reform and Pensions Act 1999, (d) the Pensions Act 2004, or any enactment in force in Northern Ireland corresponding to an enactment mentioned in paragraphs (a) to (d) above.

Authority	*Functions*
The Board of the Pension Protection Fund	Functions conferred by or by virtue of Part 2 of the Pensions Act 2004 or any enactment in force in Northern Ireland corresponding to that Part.]
[The Office of Fair Trading.]	Functions under the [Financial Services and Markets Act 2000].
[A person authorised by the Secretary of State under section 245C of the Companies Act 1985.	Functions relating to the securing of compliance by companies with the accounting requirements of that Act.]
[The [Commission] of the National Lottery.	Functions under sections 5 to 10 inclusive and section 15 of the National Lottery etc Act 1993.]
[The Comptroller and Auditor General	Functions under Part 2 of the National Audit Act 1983.]
[The Scottish Ministers	Functions under the enactments relating to insolvency]
[The Accountant in Bankruptcy	Functions he has under the enactments relating to insolvency.]
[The Regulator of Community Interest Companies.	Functions under the Companies (Audit, Investigations and Community Enterprise) Act 2004."
[The Gambling Commission	Functions under the Gambling Act 2005.]
[The Regulator of Community Interest Companies for Northern Ireland.	Functions under the Companies (Audit, Investigations and Community Enterprise) (Northern Ireland) Order 2005.]

[*Note*: Article 3(4) of the Companies (Disclosure of Information) (Designated Authorities) (No 2) Order 2002 restricts the circumstances in which disclosure for the purpose of enabling or assisting the Comptroller and Auditor General to discharge his relevant functions is permitted.]

(5) The Secretary of State may by order amend the Table in subsection (4) so as to—

(a) add any public or other authority to the Table and specify the relevant functions of that authority,

(b) remove any authority from the Table, or

(c) add functions to, or remove functions from, those which are relevant functions in relation to an authority specified in the Table;

and the order may impose conditions subject to which, or otherwise restrict the circumstances in which, disclosure is permitted.

(6) An order under this section shall be made by statutory instrument which shall be subject to annulment in pursuance of a resolution of either House of Parliament.

[809]

NOTES

Sub-s (2): para (b) substituted by the Financial Services and Markets Act 2000 (Consequential Amendments and Repeals) Order 2001, SI 2001/3649, art 77(1), (2), as from 1 December 2001; para (d) added by the Pensions Act 2004, s 102, Sch 4, Pt 4, para 20, as from 6 April 2005.

Sub-s (4) is amended as follows:

Entry "The Secretary of State" substituted by SI 2001/3649, art 77(1), (3), (5), as from 1 December 2001.

Entry "The Treasury" inserted by the Transfer of Functions (Financial Services) Order 1992, SI 1992/1315, art 10(1), Sch 4, para 12, as from 7 June 1992; substituted by SI 2001/3649, art 77(1), (3), (6), as from 1 December 2001.

Entry beginning "An inspector appointed under Part 14" substituted by SI 2001/3649, art 77(1), (3), (7), as from 1 December 2001.

Entry beginning "A person authorised to exercise powers" and subsequent entry substituted for the original entry beginning with those words by SI 2001/3649, art 77(1), (3), (8), as from 1 December 2001.

First, second, third, fourth, fifth, seventh, eighth and tenth entries omitted repealed by SI 2001/3649, art 77(1), (3), (4), as from 1 December 2001

Sixth entry omitted originally inserted by the Friendly Societies Act 1992, s 120, Sch 21, Pt I, para 11, and repealed by SI 2001/3649, 77(1), (3), (4), as from 1 December 2001.

In entry "The Bank of England" words in square brackets substituted by the Bank of England Act 1998, s 23(1), Sch 5, para 66(1), (3), as from 1 June 1998.

Entry "The Financial Services Authority" inserted by the Bank of England Act 1998, s 23(1), Sch 5, para 66(1), (3), as from 1 June 1998; substituted by SI 2001/3649, art 77(1), (3), (9), as from 1 December 2001.

Entry "A body corporate established in accordance with section 212(1) of that Act" inserted by SI 2001/3649, art 77(1), (3), (10), as from 1 December 2001.

Entry beginning "A recognised investment exchange or a recognised clearing house" inserted by SI 2001/3649, art 77(1), (3), (10), as from 1 December 2001.

Entry "A body designated under section 326(1) of the Financial Services and Markets Act 2000" inserted by SI 2001/3649, art 77(1), (3), (10), as from 1 December 2001.

Ninth entry omitted repealed by the Financial Services and Markets Act 2000 (Dissolution of the Insurance Brokers Registration Council) (Consequential Provisions) Order 2001, SI 2001/1283, art 3(4), as from 30 April 2001.

In entry "A body designated by order under section 46 of this Act" word in square brackets substituted by the Companies (Audit, Investigations and Community Enterprise) Act 2004, s 25, Sch 2, Pt 1, paras 1, 3(b), as from 1 January 2005.

Entries "The Pensions Regulator" and "The Board of the Pension Protection Fund" substituted for the entry "The Occupational Pensions Regulatory Authority" (as inserted by the Pensions Act 1995, s 122, Sch 3, para 19, as from 6 April 1997) by the Pensions Act 2004, s 319, Sch 12, para 6, as from 6 April 2005.

In entry "The Office of Fair Trading" (formerly "The Director General of Fair Trading") words in square brackets in column 1 substituted by the Enterprise Act 2002, s 278(1), Sch 25, para 21(1), (3), as from 1 April 2003; words in square brackets in column 2 substituted by SI 2001/3649, art 77(1), (3), (11), as from 1 December 2001.

Entry beginning "A person authorised by the Secretary of State" inserted by the Financial Services (Disclosure of Information) (Designated Authorities) (No 7) Order 1993, SI 1993/1826, art 3, as from 16 August 1993.

Entry relating to "the National Lottery" inserted by the Financial Services (Disclosure of Information) (Designated Authorities) (No 8) Order 1994, SI 1994/340, art 3, as from 10 March 1994; word in square brackets substituted by the National Lottery Act 1998, s 1(5), Sch 1, para 4, as from 1 April 1999.

Entry "The Comptroller and Auditor General" inserted by the Companies (Disclosure of Information) (Designated Authorities) (No 2) Order 2002, SI 2002/1889, art 3(1), (2), as from 14 August 2002. See further the note below.

Entry "The Scottish Ministers" added by the Scotland Act 1998 (Consequential Modifications) (No 2) Order 1999, SI 1999/1820, art 4, Sch 2, Pt I, para 96, as from 1 July 1999.

Entry "The Accountant in Bankruptcy" added by the Scotland Act 1998 (Consequential Modifications) (No 2) Order 1999, SI 1999/1820, art 4, Sch 2, Pt I, para 96, as from 1 July 1999.

Entry "The Regulator of Community Interest Companies" added by the Companies (Audit, Investigations and Community Enterprise) Act 2004, s 25, Sch 2, Pt 3, para 29, as from 1 July 2005.

Entry "The Gambling Commission" inserted by the Companies (Disclosure of Information) (Designated Authorities) Order 2006, SI 2006/1644, art 3, as from 1 October 2006.

Entry "The Regulator of Community Interest Companies for Northern Ireland" added by the Companies (Audit, Investigations and Community Enterprise) (Northern Ireland) Order 2005, SI 2005/1967, art 24(1), Sch 2, Pt 2, para 22, as from a day to be appointed.

Table note: added by SI 2002/1889, art 3(1), (3), as from 14 August 2002. See further the note below.

Note: SI 2002/1889, art 3(4) provides—

"(4) Disclosure under section 87(1)(b) of the 1989 Act is permitted by virtue of the amendment made by paragraph (2) only where the disclosure is made by the National Lottery Commission to the National Audit Office for the purpose of enabling or assisting the Comptroller and Auditor General to carry out an examination into the economy, efficiency and effectiveness with which the National Lottery Commission has used its resources in discharging its functions under sections 5 to 10 of the National Lottery etc Act 1993."

Sub-s (1) above has effect in accordance with the Anti-terrorism, Crime and Security Act 2001, s 17. That section, which clarifies and extends a number of information disclosure provisions available to public authorities, permits disclosure to assist any criminal investigation or criminal proceedings being carried out in the UK or abroad or to facilitate determinations of whether or not such investigations or proceedings should begin or end.

Orders: the Financial Services (Disclosure of Information) (Designated Authorities) (No 7) Order 1993, SI 1993/1826; the Financial Services (Disclosure of Information) (Designated Authorities) (No 8) Order 1994, SI 1994/340; the Companies (Disclosure of Information) (Designated Authorities) (No 2) Order 2002, SI 2002/1889; the Companies (Disclosure of Information) (Designated Authorities) Order 2006, SI 2006/1644.

88 Exercise of powers in relation to Northern Ireland

(1) The following provisions apply where it appears to the Secretary of State that a request for assistance by an overseas regulatory authority may involve the powers conferred

by section 83 being exercised in Northern Ireland in relation to matters which are transferred matters within the meaning of the Northern Ireland Constitution Act 1973.

(2) The Secretary of State shall before deciding whether to accede to the request consult the Department of Economic Development in Northern Ireland, and if he decides to accede to the request and it appears to him—

(a) that the powers should be exercised in Northern Ireland, and
(b) that the purposes for which they should be so exercised relate wholly or primarily to transferred matters,

he shall by instrument in writing authorise the Department to exercise in Northern Ireland his powers under section 83.

(3) The following provisions have effect in relation to the exercise of powers by virtue of such an authority with the substitution for references to the Secretary of State of references to the Department of Economic Development in Northern Ireland—

(a) section 84 (exercise of powers by officer, &c),
[(b) section 449 of the Companies Act 1985 and sections 86 and 87 above (restrictions on disclosure of information),] and
(c) section 89 (authority for institution of criminal proceedings);

and references to the Secretary of State in other enactments which proceed by reference to those provisions shall be construed accordingly as being or including references to the Department.

(4) The Secretary of State may after consultation with the Department of Economic Development in Northern Ireland revoke an authority given to the Department under this section.

(5) In that case nothing in the provisions referred to in subsection (3)(b) shall apply so as to prevent the Department from giving the Secretary of State any information obtained by virtue of the authority; and (without prejudice to their application in relation to disclosure by the Department) those provisions shall apply to the disclosure of such information by the Secretary of State as if it had been obtained by him in the first place.

(6) Nothing in this section affects the exercise by the Secretary of State of any powers in Northern Ireland—

(a) in a case where at the time of acceding to the request it did not appear to him that the circumstances were such as to require him to authorise the Department of Economic Development in Northern Ireland to exercise those powers, or
(b) after the revocation by him of any such authority;

and no objection shall be taken to anything done by or in relation to the Secretary of State or the Department on the ground that it should have been done by or in relation to the other.

[810]

NOTES

Sub-s (3): para (b) substituted by the Financial Services and Markets Act 2000 (Consequential Amendments and Repeals) Order 2001, SI 2001/3649, art 78, as from 1 December 2001.

89 Prosecutions

Proceedings for an offence under section 85 or 86 shall not be instituted—

(a) in England and Wales, except by or with the consent of the Secretary of State or the Director of Public Prosecutions;
(b) in Northern Ireland, except by or with the consent of the Secretary of State or the Director of Public Prosecutions for Northern Ireland.

[811]

90 Offences by bodies corporate, partnerships and unincorporated associations

(1) Where an offence under section 85 or 86 committed by a body corporate is proved to have been committed with the consent or connivance of, or to be attributable to any neglect on the part of, a director, manager, secretary or other similar officer of the body, or a person purporting to act in any such capacity, he as well as the body corporate is guilty of the offence and liable to be proceeded against and punished accordingly.

(2) Where the affairs of a body corporate are managed by its members, subsection (1) applies in relation to the acts and defaults of a member in connection with his functions of management as to a director of a body corporate.

(3) Where an offence under section 85 or 86 committed by a partnership is proved to have been committed with the consent or connivance of, or to be attributable to any neglect on the part of, a partner, he as well as the partnership is guilty of the offence and liable to be proceeded against and punished accordingly.

(4) Where an offence under section 85 or 86 committed by an unincorporated association (other than a partnership) is proved to have been committed with the consent or connivance of, or to be attributable to any neglect on the part of, any officer of the association or any member of its governing body, he as well as the association is guilty of the offence and liable to be proceeded against and punished accordingly.

[812]

91 Jurisdiction and procedure in respect of offences

(1) Summary proceedings for an offence under section 85 may, without prejudice to any jurisdiction exercisable apart from this section, be taken against a body corporate or unincorporated association at any place at which it has a place of business and against an individual at any place where he is for the time being.

(2) Proceedings for an offence alleged to have been committed under section 85 or 86 by an unincorporated association shall be brought in the name of the association (and not in that of any of its members), and for the purposes of any such proceedings any rules of court relating to the service of documents apply as in relation to a body corporate.

(3) Section 33 of the Criminal Justice Act 1925 and Schedule 3 to the Magistrates' Courts Act 1980 (procedure on charge of offence against a corporation) apply in a case in which an unincorporated association is charged in England and Wales with an offence under section 85 or 86 as they apply in the case of a corporation.

(4) In relation to proceedings on indictment in Scotland for an offence alleged to have been committed under section 85 or 86 by an unincorporated association, section 74 of the Criminal Procedure (Scotland) Act 1975 (proceedings on indictment against bodies corporate) applies as if the association were a body corporate.

(5) Section 18 of the Criminal Justice Act (Northern Ireland) 1945 and Schedule 4 to the Magistrates' Courts (Northern Ireland) Order 1981 (procedure on charge of offence against a corporation) apply in a case in which an unincorporated association is charged in Northern Ireland with an offence under section 85 or 86 as they apply in the case of a corporation.

(6) A fine imposed on an unincorporated association on its conviction of such an offence shall be paid out of the funds of the association.

[813]

PART IV
REGISTRATION OF COMPANY CHARGES

Introduction

92 Introduction

The provisions of this Part amend the provisions of the Companies Act 1985 relating to the registration of company charges—

(*a*) *by inserting in Part XII of that Act (in place of sections 395 to 408 and 410 to 423) new provisions with respect to companies registered in Great Britain, and*

(*b*) *by inserting as Chapter III of Part XXIII of that Act (in place of sections 409 and 424) new provisions with respect to oversea companies.*

[814]

NOTES

Commencement: to be appointed.

Repealed by the Companies Act 2006, s 1180, as from a day to be appointed. Note that this section is also repealed by s 1295 of, and Sch 16 to, the 2006 Act, as from a day to be appointed.

Note: it is understood that the amendments made by this Part are now unlikely to be brought into force in their present form.

93–107 (*Ss 93–107 are repealed by the Companies Act 2006, s 1180, as from a day to be appointed (note that these sections are also repealed by s 1295 of, and Sch 16 to, the 2006*

Act, as from a day to be appointed); the sections make the following amendments: s 93 inserts CA 1985, ss 395, 396, as from a day to be appointed; s 94 inserts s 397 of the 1985 Act, as from a day to be appointed; s 95 inserts ss 398–400 of the 1985 Act, as from a day to be appointed; s 96 inserts s 401 of the 1985 Act, as from a day to be appointed; s 97 inserts s 402 of the 1985 Act, as from a day to be appointed; s 98 inserts s 403 of the 1985 Act, as from a day to be appointed; s 99 inserts ss 404–407 of the 1985 Act, as from a day to be appointed; s 100 inserts ss 408–410 of the 1985 Act, as from a day to be appointed; s 101 inserts ss 411, 412 of the 1985 Act, as from a day to be appointed; s 102 inserts s 413 of the 1985 Act, as from a day to be appointed; s 103 inserts ss 414–417 of the 1985 Act, as from a day to be appointed; s 104 inserts ss 418–420 of the 1985 Act, as from a day to be appointed (in relation to all of these insertions, see the note preceding CA 1985, s 395 at **[423]***); s 105 introduces Sch 15 to this Act; s 106 amends Sch 22 to the 1985 Act at* **[687]***, as from a day to be appointed; s 107 introduces Sch 16 to this Act.)*

PART V
OTHER AMENDMENTS OF COMPANY LAW

A company's capacity and related matters

108–111 *(S 108 substitutes CA 1985, ss 35, 35A, 35B for original s 35 and amends Schs 21, 22 to that Act at* **[36]–[38]**, **[680]**, **[687]** *(and is repealed by the Companies Act 2006, s 1295, Sch 16, as from a day to be appointed); s 109 inserts s 322A of the 1985 Act and amends Sch 22 to that Act at* **[321]**, **[687]** *(and is repealed by the Companies Act 2006, s 1295, Sch 16, as from a day to be appointed); s 110 inserts s 3A and substitutes s 4 of the 1985 Act at* **[4]**, **[5]** *(and is repealed by the Companies Act 2006, s 1295, Sch 16, as from a day to be appointed); s 111 repealed by the Charities Act 1993, s 98(2), Sch 7, as from 1 August 1993.)*

112 Charitable companies (Scotland)

(1) In the following provisions (which extend to Scotland only)—

(a) "company" means a company formed and registered under the Companies Act 1985, or to which the provisions of that Act apply as they apply to such a company; and

(b) "charity" means a body [entered in the Scottish Charity Register].

(2) Where a charity is a company or other body corporate having power to alter the instruments establishing or regulating it as a body corporate, no exercise of that power which has the effect of the body ceasing to be a charity shall be valid so as to affect the application of—

(a) any property acquired by virtue of any transfer, contract or obligation previously effected otherwise than for full consideration in money or money's worth, or any property representing property so acquired,

(b) any property representing income which has accrued before the alteration is made, or

(c) the income from any such property as aforesaid.

(3) Sections 35 and 35A of the Companies Act 1985 (capacity of company not limited by its memorandum; power of directors to bind company) do not apply to the acts of a company which is a charity except in favour of a person who—

(a) gives full consideration in money or money's worth in relation to the act in question, and

(b) does not know that the act is not permitted by the company's memorandum or, as the case may be, is beyond the powers of the directors,

or who does not know at the time the act is done that the company is a charity.

(4) However, where such a company purports to transfer or grant an interest in property, the fact that the act was not permitted by the company's memorandum or, as the case may be, that the directors in connection with the act exceeded any limitation on their powers under the company's constitution, does not affect the title of a person who subsequently acquires the property or any interest in it for full consideration without actual notice of any such circumstances affecting the validity of the company's act.

(5) In any proceedings arising out of subsection (3) the burden of proving—

(a) that a person knew that an act was not permitted by the company's memorandum or was beyond the powers of the directors, or

(b) that a person knew that the company was a charity,

lies on the person making that allegation.

(6) Where a company is a charity and its name does not include the word "charity" or the word "charitable", the fact that the company is a charity shall be stated in English in legible characters—

(a) in all business letters of the company,

(b) in all its notices and other official publications,

(c) in all bills of exchange, promissory notes, endorsements, cheques and orders for money or goods purporting to be signed by or on behalf of the company,

(d) in all conveyances purporting to be executed by the company, and

(e) in all its bills of parcels, invoices, receipts and letters of credit.

(7) In subsection (6)(d) "conveyance" means any document for the creation, transfer, variation or extinction of an interest in land.

(8) Section 349(2) to (4) of the Companies Act 1985 (offences in connection with failure to include required particulars in business letters, &c) apply in relation to a contravention of subsection (6) above.

[815]

NOTES

Sub-s (1): words in square brackets in para (b) substituted by the Charities and Trustee Investment (Scotland) Act 2005 (Consequential Provisions and Modifications) Order 2006, SI 2006/242, art 5, Schedule, Pt 1, para 4, as from 1 April 2006.

De-regulation of private companies

113–116 (*Ss 113–116 (which are repealed by the Companies Act 2006, s 1295, Sch 16, as from 1 October 2007 (in so far as relating to s 113, 114(1), 115(2), (3)), and as from a day to be appointed (otherwise)) make the following amendments: s 113(1), (2) insert CA 1985, ss 381A–381C at* **[398]**–**[400]**; *s 113(1), (3) insert s 382A of the 1985 Act at* **[402]**; *s 114(1) inserts Sch 15A to the 1985 Act at* **[676]**; *s 114(2) amends s 427A of the 1985 Act and renumbers the original Sch 15A thereto as Sch 15B at* **[456]**, **[678]**; *s 115(1) amends s 80(1) and inserts s 80A of the 1985 Act at* **[64]**, **[65]**; *s 115(2) inserts s 366A of the 1985 Act at* **[380]**; *s 115(3) amends ss 369(4), 378(3) of the 1985 Act at* **[383]**, **[393]**; *s 116 inserts ss 379A, 380(4)(bb) of the 1985 Act at* **[395]**, **[396]**.)

117 Power to make further provision by regulations

(1) The Secretary of State may by regulations make provision enabling private companies to elect, by elective resolution in accordance with section 379A of the Companies Act 1985, to dispense with compliance with such requirements of that Act as may be specified in the regulations, being requirements which appear to the Secretary of State to relate primarily to the internal administration and procedure of companies.

(2) The regulations may add to, amend or repeal provisions of that Act; and may provide for any such provision to have effect, where an election is made, subject to such adaptations and modifications as appear to the Secretary of State to be appropriate.

(3) The regulations may make different provision for different cases and may contain such supplementary, incidental and transitional provisions as appear to the Secretary of State to be appropriate.

(4) Regulations under this section shall be made by statutory instrument.

(5) No regulations under this section shall be made unless a draft of the instrument containing the regulations has been laid before Parliament and approved by a resolution of each House.

[816]

NOTES

Repealed by the Companies Act 2006, s 1295, Sch 16, as from a day to be appointed.

Appointment and removal of auditors and related matters

118 Introduction

(1) The following sections amend the provisions of the Companies Act 1985 relating to auditors by inserting new provisions in Chapter V of Part XI of that Act.

(2) The new provisions, together with the amendment made by section 124, replace the present provisions of that Chapter except section 389 (qualification for appointment as auditor) which is replaced by provisions in Part II of this Act.

[817]

NOTES

Repealed by the Companies Act 2006, s 1295, Sch 16, as from a day to be appointed.

119–127 *(Ss 119–127 (which are repealed by the Companies Act 2006, s 1295, Sch 16, as from a day to be appointed) make the following amendments: s 119 inserts CA 1985, ss 384, 385, 385A, 386–388, 388A and amends Sch 24 to that Act at* **[405]**, **[406]**, **[407]**, **[408]**–**[410]**, **[411]**, **[689]** *and the Banking Act 1987, s 46(2), and is repealed in part by the Financial Services and Markets Act 2000 (Consequential Amendments and Repeals) Order 2001, SI 2001/3649, art 75(d), as from 1 December 2001; s 120(1) inserts ss 389A, 390 of the 1985 Act at* **[412]**, **[413]**; *s 120(2), (3) repealed by the Companies (Audit, Investigations and Community Enterprise) Act 2004, s 64, Sch 8, as from 6 April 2005; s 120(4) repealed by the Statute Law (Repeals) Act 2004, as from 22 July 2004; s 121 inserts CA 1985, ss 390A, 390B at* **[414]**, **[415]**; *s 122(1) inserts ss 391, 391A, 392, 392A, 393 of the 1985 Act at* **[416]**, **[417]**, **[418]**, **[419]**, **[420]**; *s 122(2) amends Sch 24 to the 1985 Act at* **[689]**; *s 123(1) inserts ss 394, 394A of the 1985 Act at* **[421]**, **[422]**; *s 123(2) amends Sch 24 to the 1985 Act at* **[689]**; *s 123(3) amends s 733(1) of the 1985 Act at* **[610]**; *s 123(4) amends s 734(1) of the 1985 Act at* **[611]**; *s 123(5) amends Sch 22 to the 1985 Act at* **[687]**; *s 124 repealed by the Trade Union and Labour Relations (Consolidation) Act 1992, s 300(1), Sch 1; s 125 substitutes CA 1985, ss 706 at* **[575]**, *and 707 (repealed); s 126(1) inserts s 707A of the 1985 Act at* **[576]**; *s 126(2) substitutes ss 709, 710, 710A of the 1985 Act at* **[579]**, **[580]**, **[581]** *for ss 709, 710; s 127(1) inserts s 715A of the 1985 Act at* **[587]**; *s 127(2)–(5), (7) amend ss 708, 713, 735A of, and Sch 22 to, the 1985 Act at* **[578]**, **[585]**, **[613]**, **[687]**, *and repeal ss 712, 715 of the 1985 Act, and are repealed in part by the Statute Law (Repeals) Act 2004, as from 22 July 2004; s 127(6) inserts s 735B of the 1985 Act at* **[614]**.)

Miscellaneous

128, 129 *(S 128 inserts CA 1985, s 8A at* **[10]**, *as from a day to be appointed (and is repealed by the Companies Act 2006, s 1295, Sch 16, as from a day to be appointed); s 129(1) substitutes s 23 of the 1985 Act at* **[24]** *(and is repealed by the Companies Act 2006, s 1295, Sch 16, as from a day to be appointed); s 129(2) amends Sch 2, Pt I to the 1985 Act at* **[635]** *(and is repealed by the Companies Act 2006, s 1295, Sch 16, as from a day to be appointed).)*

130 Company contracts and execution of documents by companies

(1)–(5) ...

(6) The Secretary of State may make provision by regulations applying sections 36 to 36C of the Companies Act 1985 (company contracts; execution of documents; [execution of deeds;] pre-incorporation contracts, deeds and obligations) to companies incorporated outside Great Britain, subject to such exceptions, adaptations or modifications as may be specified in the regulations.

Regulations under this subsection shall be made by statutory instrument which shall be subject to annulment in pursuance of a resolution of either House of Parliament.

(7) Schedule 17 contains further minor and consequential amendments relating to company contracts, the execution of documents by companies and related matters.

[818]–[819]

NOTES

Repealed by the Companies Act 2006, s 1295, Sch 16, as from a day to be appointed.

Sub-s (1) substitutes CA 1985, s 36 at **[39]**; sub-s (2) inserts s 36A of the 1985 Act at **[40]**; sub-s (4) inserts s 36C of the 1985 Act at **[42]**; sub-s (5) amends Sch 22 to the 1985 Act at **[687]**.

Sub-s (3): repealed by the Law Reform (Miscellaneous Provisions) (Scotland) Act 1990, s 74(2), Sch 9, as from 1 December 1990.

Sub-s (6): words in square brackets inserted by the Regulatory Reform (Execution of Deeds and Documents) Order 2005, SI 2005/1906, art 10(1), Sch 1, para 16, as from 15 September 2005, except in relation to any instrument executed before that date.

Regulations: the Foreign Companies (Execution of Documents) Regulations 1994, SI 1994/950 at **[6787]**.

131–134 *(S 131(1) inserts CA 1985, s 111A at* **[97]** *(and is repealed by the Companies Act 2006, s 1295, Sch 16, as from a day to be appointed); s 131(2) amends s 116 of the 1985 Act at* **[102]** *(and is repealed by the Companies Act 2006, s 1295, Sch 16, as from a day to be appointed); s 132 amends s 153 of the 1985 Act at* **[139]** *(and is repealed by the Companies Act 2006, s 1295, Sch 16, as from a day to be appointed); s 133 inserts s 159A and amends ss 160, 162 of the 1985 Act at* **[146]**, **[147]**, **[148]**, *as from a day to be appointed, and is partly repealed by the Companies (Acquisition of Own Shares) (Treasury Shares) Regulations 2003, SI 2003/1116, reg 4, Schedule, para 34, as from 1 December 2003 (and is completely repealed by the Companies Act 2006, s 1295, Sch 16, as from a day to be appointed); s 134 repealed by the Companies Act 2006, s 1295, Sch 16, as from 20 January 2007.)*

135 Orders imposing restrictions on shares

(1) The Secretary of State may by regulations made by statutory instrument make such amendments of the provisions of the Companies Act 1985 relating to orders imposing restrictions on shares as appear to him necessary or expedient—

- *(a) for enabling orders to be made in a form protecting the rights of third parties;*
- *(b) with respect to the circumstances in which restrictions may be relaxed or removed;*
- *(c) with respect to the making of interim orders by a court.*

(2) The provisions referred to in subsection (1) are section 210(5), section 216(1) and (2), section 445 and Part XV of the Companies Act 1985.

(3) The regulations may make different provision for different cases and may contain such transitional and other supplementary and incidental provisions as appear to the Secretary of State to be appropriate.

(4) Regulations under this section shall not be made unless a draft of the regulations has been laid before Parliament and approved by resolution of each House of Parliament.

[820]

NOTES

Repealed by the Companies Act 2006, s 1295, Sch 16, as from a day to be appointed.

Regulations: the Companies (Disclosure of Interests in Shares) (Orders imposing restrictions on shares) Regulations 1991, SI 1991/1646.

136–138 *(S 136 substitutes CA 1985, s 287 at* **[292]** *(and is repealed by the Companies Act 2006, s 1295, Sch 16, as from a day to be appointed); s 137(1) substitutes s 310(3) of the 1985 Act at* **[308]** *(and is repealed by the Companies Act 2006, s 1295, Sch 16, as from a day to be appointed); s 137(2) repealed by the Statute Law (Repeals) Act 2004, as from 22 July 2004; s 138 amends ss 332, 334, 338 of the 1985 Act at* **[332]**, **[334]**, **[338]** *(and is repealed by the Companies Act 2006, s 1295, Sch 16, as from 1 October 2007).)*

139 Annual returns

(1) …

(2) Where a company was, immediately before the commencement of this section, in default with respect to the delivery of one or more annual returns, this section does not affect its obligation to make such a return (in accordance with Chapter III of Part XI of the Companies Act 1985 as it then had effect) or any liability arising from failure to do so.

(3)–(5) …

[821]

NOTES

Sub-s (1) substitutes CA 1985, Pt XI, Chapter III (ss 363–365) at **[375]**–**[378]** and is repealed by the Companies Act 2006, s 1295, Sch 16, as from a day to be appointed.

Sub-s (2): repealed by the Companies Act 2006, s 1295, Sch 16, as from a day to be appointed.
Sub-s (3) amends Sch 24 to the 1985 Act at **[689]** and is repealed by the Companies Act 2006, s 1295, Sch 16, as from a day to be appointed.
Sub-s (4) substitutes the Company Directors Disqualification Act 1986, Sch 1, Pt I, para 4(f) for Sch 1, Pt I, para 4(f), (g) at **[767]**.
Sub-s (5): repealed by the Finance Act 2004, s 326, Sch 42, Part 2, as from 22 July 2004 in accordance with s 77 of the 2004 Act.

140 (*Repealed by the Bankruptcy and Diligence etc (Scotland) Act 2007, s 46(4), as from a day to be appointed (for savings, see the introductory note to the Companies Act 1985, Pt XVIII); sub-s (1) of s 140 amends CA 1985, s 463 at* **[497]***; sub-ss (2)–(6) amend s 464 of the 1985 Act at* **[498]***; sub-s (7) amends s 464(6) of the 1985 Act, as from a day to be appointed; sub-s (8) amends s 466 of the 1985 Act at* **[500]***, as from a day to be appointed.*)

141 Application to declare dissolution of company void

(1)–(3) …

(4) An application may be made under section 651(5) of the Companies Act 1985 as inserted by subsection (3) above (proceedings for damages for personal injury, &c) in relation to a company dissolved before the commencement of this section notwithstanding that the time within which the dissolution might formerly have been declared void under that section had expired before commencement.

But no such application shall be made in relation to a company dissolved more than twenty years before the commencement of this section.

(5) Except as provided by subsection (4), the amendments made by this section do not apply in relation to a company which was dissolved more than two years before the commencement of this section.

[822]

NOTES

Repealed by the Companies Act 2006, s 1295, Sch 16, as from a day to be appointed.
Sub-ss (1)–(3): amend CA 1985, s 651 at **[503]**.

142, 143 (*S 142(1) inserts CA 1985, s 711A at* **[584]***, as from a day to be appointed (and is repealed by the Companies Act 2006, s 1295, Sch 16, as from a day to be appointed); s 142(2) amends Sch 22 to the 1985 Act at* **[687]***, as from a day to be appointed (and is repealed by the Companies Act 2006, s 1295, Sch 16, as from a day to be appointed); s 143(1) inserts s 723A of the 1985 Act at* **[596]** *(and is repealed by the Companies Act 2006, s 1295, Sch 16, as from a day to be appointed); s 143(2)–(11) amend ss 169(5), 175(6), 191, 219, 288, 318, 356, 383 of, and Sch 13, Pt IV, Sch 22 to, the 1985 Act at* **[155]**, **[161]**, **[177]**, **[205]**, **[293]**, **[316]**, **[368]**, **[404]**, **[671]**, **[687]** *(and are repealed by the Companies Act 2006, s 1295, Sch 16, as from 20 January 2007 (in so far as relating to sub-s (5)), as from 6 April 2007 (in so far as relating to sub-s (1)), as from 1 October 2007 (in so far as relating to sub-ss (8), (9)), and as from a day to be appointed (otherwise)).*)

144 "Subsidiary", "holding company" and "wholly-owned subsidiary"

(1) …

(2) Any reference in any enactment (including any enactment contained in subordinate legislation within the meaning of the Interpretation Act 1978) to a "subsidiary" or "holding company" within the meaning of section 736 of the Companies Act 1985 shall, subject to any express amendment or saving made by or under this Act, be read as referring to a subsidiary or holding company as defined in section 736 as substituted by subsection (1) above.

This applies whether the reference is specific or general, or express or implied.

(3) …

(4) Schedule 18 contains amendments and savings consequential on the amendments made by this section; and the Secretary of State may by regulations make such further amendments or savings as appear to him to be necessary or expedient.

(5) Regulations under this section shall be made by statutory instrument which shall be subject to annulment in pursuance of a resolution of either House of Parliament.

(6) So much of section 23(3) of the Interpretation Act 1978 as applies section 17(2)(a) of that Act (presumption as to meaning of references to enactments repealed and re-enacted) to deeds or other instruments or documents does not apply in relation to the repeal and re-enactment by this section of section 736 of the Companies Act 1985.

[823]–[826]

NOTES

Sub-s (1): substitutes CA 1985, ss 736, 736A (at **[615]**, **[616]**) for original s 736, and is repealed by the Companies Act 2006, s 1295, Sch 16, as from a day to be appointed.

Sub-ss (2), (6): repealed by the Companies Act 2006, s 1295, Sch 16, as from a day to be appointed.

Sub-s (3): inserts s 736B of the 1985 Act at **[617]**, and is repealed by the Companies Act 2006, s 1295, Sch 16, as from a day to be appointed.

Regulations: the Definition of Subsidiary (Consequential Amendments) Regulations 1990, SI 1990/1395 (which amend the Electricity Act 1989, s 77).

145–153 *(S 145 introduces Sch 19 (Minor amendments of CA1985); Pt VII (ie, ss 146–153 (Mergers and related matters)) provides as follows: ss 146–150 amended the Fair Trading Act 1973 and were repealed by the Enterprise Act 2002, s 278(2), Sch 26, as from 20 June 2003 (for all purposes except in relation to the merger of water or sewerage undertakings), and from 29 December 2004 (otherwise) (for transitional provisions see Sch 24 to the 2002 Act at* **[3632]***, and SI 2003/1397 and SI 2004/3233); s 151 inserts the Fair Trading Act 1973, s 93B; s 152 repealed by the Enterprise Act 2002, s 278(2), Sch 26, as from 29 December 2004; s 153 introduces Sch 20 (Amendments about Mergers and Related Matters).)*

PART VII
FINANCIAL MARKETS AND INSOLVENCY

NOTES

Transfer of functions: by the Transfer of Functions (Financial Services) Order 1992, SI 1992/1315, art 2(1)(c) at **[6730]**, the functions of the Secretary of State under this Part of this Act are transferred to the Treasury. However, by art 4 of, and Sch 2, para 7 to, that order at **[6732]** and **[6740]**, the functions of the Secretary of State under ss 158(4), (5), 160(5), 170 (other than the function under s 170(1) of approving an overseas investment exchange) 171–174, 181, 185, and so much of his functions under s 186 as relate to any function under the aforementioned provisions, are to be exercisable jointly by the Secretary of State and the Treasury. See also the European Communities (Designation) (No 4) Order 2002, SI 2002/2840 in relation to certain open-ended collective investment schemes, and the Financial Markets and Insolvency Regulations 1996, SI 1996/1469.

Introduction

154 Introduction

This Part has effect for the purposes of safeguarding the operation of certain financial markets by provisions with respect to—

(a) the insolvency, winding up or default of a person party to transactions in the market (sections 155 to 172),

(b) the effectiveness or enforcement of certain charges given to secure obligations in connection with such transactions (sections 173 to 176), and

(c) rights and remedies in relation to certain property provided as cover for margin in relation to such transactions or subject to such a charge (sections 177 to 181).

[827]

Recognised investment exchanges and clearing houses

155 Market contracts

(1) This Part applies to the following descriptions of contract connected with a recognised investment exchange or recognised clearing house.

The contracts are referred to in this Part as "market contracts".

[(2) Except as provided in subsection (2A), in relation to a recognised investment exchange this Part applies to—

(a) contracts entered into by a member or designated non-member of the exchange [with a person other than the exchange] which are either

(i) contracts made on the exchange or an exchange to whose undertaking the exchange has succeeded whether by amalgamation, merger or otherwise; or

(ii) contracts in the making of which the member or designated non-member was subject to the rules of the exchange or of an exchange to whose undertaking the exchange has succeeded whether by amalgamation, merger or otherwise; and

[(b) contracts entered into by the exchange with its members for the purpose of enabling the rights and liabilities of that member under transactions in investments to be settled.]

A "designated non-member" means a person in respect of whom action may be taken under the default rules of the exchange but who is not a member of the exchange.

(2A) This Part does not apply to contracts falling within paragraph (a) of subsection (2) above where the exchange in question is a recognised overseas investment exchange.]

[(3) In relation to a recognised clearing house, this Part applies to contracts entered into by the clearing house with a member of the clearing house for the purpose of enabling the rights and liabilities of that member under transactions in investments to be settled.]

(4) The Secretary of State may by regulations make further provision as to the contracts to be treated as "market contracts", for the purposes of this Part, in relation to a recognised investment exchange or recognised clearing house.

(5) The regulations may add to, amend or repeal the provisions of subsections (2) and (3) above.

[828]

NOTES

Sub-s (2): substituted, together with sub-s (2A) for original sub-s (2), by the Financial Markets and Insolvency Regulations 1991, SI 1991/880, reg 3, as from 25 April 1991; words in first pair of square brackets inserted, and para (b) substituted, by the Financial Markets and Insolvency Regulations 1998, SI 1998/1748, reg 3, as from 11 August 1998.

Sub-s (2A): substituted as noted above.

Sub-s (3): substituted by SI 1998/1748, reg 4, as from 11 August 1998.

Regulations: the Financial Markets and Insolvency Regulations 1991, SI 1991/880 at **[6691]**; the Financial Markets and Insolvency Regulations 1998, SI 1998/1748.

156 (*Repealed by the Financial Services and Markets Act 2000* (*Consequential Amendments and Repeals*) *Order 2001*, *SI 2001/3649*, *art 75*(*e*), *as from 1 December 2001.*)

157 Change in default rules

(1) A recognised UK investment exchange or recognised UK clearing house shall give the [Authority] at least 14 days' notice of any proposal to amend, revoke or add to its default rules; and the [Authority] may within 14 days from receipt of the notice direct the exchange or clearing house not to proceed with the proposal, in whole or in part.

(2) A direction under this section may be varied or revoked.

(3) Any amendment or revocation of, or addition to, the default rules of an exchange or clearing house in breach of a direction under this section is ineffective.

[829]

NOTES

Sub-s (1): words in square brackets substituted by the Financial Services and Markets Act 2000 (Consequential Amendments and Repeals) Order 2001, SI 2001/3649, art 79, as from 1 December 2001.

158 Modifications of the law of insolvency

(1) The general law of insolvency has effect in relation to market contracts, and action taken under the rules of a recognised investment exchange or recognised clearing house with respect to such contracts, subject to the provisions of sections 159 to 165.

(2) So far as those provisions relate to insolvency proceedings in respect of a person other than a defaulter, they apply in relation to—

(a) proceedings in respect of a member or designated non-member of a recognised investment exchange or a member of a recognised clearing house, and

(b) proceedings in respect of a party to a market contract begun after a recognised investment exchange or recognised clearing house has taken action under its default rules in relation to a person party to the contract as principal,

but not in relation to any other insolvency proceedings, notwithstanding that rights or liabilities arising from market contracts fall to be dealt with in the proceedings.

(3) The reference in subsection (2)(b) to the beginning of insolvency proceedings is to—

(a) the presentation of a bankruptcy petition or a petition for sequestration of a person's estate, or

[(b) the application for an administration order or the presentation of a winding-up petition or the passing of a resolution for voluntary winding up,] or

(c) the appointment of an administrative receiver.

[(3A) In subsection (3)(b) the reference to an application for an administration order shall be taken to include a reference to—

(a) in a case where an administrator is appointed under paragraph 14 or 22 of Schedule B1 to the Insolvency Act 1986 (appointment by floating charge holder, company or directors) following filing with the court of a copy of a notice of intention to appoint under that paragraph, the filing of the copy of the notice, and

(b) in a case where an administrator is appointed under either of those paragraphs without a copy of a notice of intention to appoint having been filed with the court, the appointment of the administrator.]

(4) The Secretary of State may make further provision by regulations modifying the law of insolvency in relation to the matters mentioned in subsection (1).

(5) The regulations may add to, amend or repeal the provisions mentioned in subsection (1), and any other provision of this Part as it applies for the purposes of those provisions, or provide that those provisions have effect subject to such additions, exceptions or adaptations as are specified in the regulations.

[830]

NOTES

Sub-s (3): para (b) substituted by the Enterprise Act 2002, s 248(3), Sch 17, paras 43, 44(a), as from 15 September 2003 (for savings and transitional provisions, see the note to the Insolvency Act 1986, s 8 at **[3164]**).

Sub-s (3A): inserted by the Enterprise Act 2002, s 248(3), Sch 17, paras 43, 44(b), as from 15 September 2003 (for savings and transitional provisions, see the note to the Insolvency Act 1986, s 8 at **[3164]**).

Regulations: the Financial Markets and Insolvency Regulations 1991, SI 1991/880 at **[6691]**.

159 Proceedings of exchange or clearing house take precedence over insolvency procedures

(1) None of the following shall be regarded as to any extent invalid at law on the ground of inconsistency with the law relating to the distribution of the assets of a person on bankruptcy, winding up or sequestration, or in the administration of an insolvent estate—

(a) a market contract,

(b) the default rules of a recognised investment exchange or recognised clearing house,

(c) the rules of a recognised investment exchange or recognised clearing house as to the settlement of market contracts not dealt with under its default rules.

(2) The powers of a relevant office-holder in his capacity as such, and the powers of the court under the Insolvency Act 1986 or the Bankruptcy (Scotland) Act 1985 shall not be exercised in such a way as to prevent or interfere with—

(a) the settlement in accordance with the rules of a recognised investment exchange or recognised clearing house of a market contract not dealt with under its default rules, or

(b) any action taken under the default rules of such an exchange or clearing house.

This does not prevent a relevant office-holder from afterwards seeking to recover any amount under section 163(4) or 164(4) or prevent the court from afterwards making any such order or decree as is mentioned in section 165(1) or (2) (but subject to subsections (3) and (4) of that section).

(3) Nothing in the following provisions of this Part shall be construed as affecting the generality of the above provisions.

(4) A debt or other liability arising out of a market contract which is the subject of default proceedings may not be proved in a winding up or bankruptcy, or in Scotland claimed in a winding up or sequestration, until the completion of the default proceedings.

A debt or other liability which by virtue of this subsection may not be proved or claimed shall not be taken into account for the purposes of any set-off until the completion of the default proceedings.

[(4A) However, prior to the completion of default proceedings—

(a) where it appears to the chairman of the meeting of creditors that a sum will be certified under section 162(1) to be payable, subsection (4) shall not prevent any proof or claim including or consisting of an estimate of that sum which has been lodged or, in Scotland, submitted, from being admitted or, in Scotland, accepted, for the purpose only of determining the entitlement of a creditor to vote at a meeting of creditors; and

(b) a creditor whose claim or proof has been lodged and admitted or, in Scotland, submitted and accepted, for the purpose of determining the entitlement of a creditor to vote at a meeting of creditors and which has not been subsequently wholly withdrawn, disallowed or rejected, is eligible as a creditor to be a member of a liquidation committee or, in bankruptcy proceedings in England and Wales, a creditors' committee.]

(5) For the purposes of [subsections (4) and (4A)] the default proceedings shall be taken to be completed in relation to a person when a report is made under section 162 stating the sum (if any) certified to be due to or from him.

[831]

NOTES

Sub-s (4A): inserted by the Financial Markets and Insolvency Regulations 1991, SI 1991/880, reg 4(1), (2), as from 25 April 1991.

Sub-s (5): words in square brackets substituted by SI 1991/880, reg 4(1), (3), as from 25 April 1991.

160 Duty to give assistance for purposes of default proceedings

(1) It is the duty of—

(a) any person who has or had control of any assets of a defaulter, and

(b) any person who has or had control of any documents of or relating to a defaulter,

to give a recognised investment exchange or recognised clearing house such assistance as it may reasonably require for the purposes of its default proceedings.

This applies notwithstanding any duty of that person under the enactments relating to insolvency.

(2) A person shall not under this section be required to provide any information or produce any document which he would be entitled to refuse to provide or produce on grounds of legal professional privilege in proceedings in the High Court or on grounds of confidentiality as between client and professional legal adviser in proceedings in the Court of Session.

(3) Where original documents are supplied in pursuance of this section, the exchange or clearing house shall return them forthwith after the completion of the relevant default proceedings, and shall in the meantime allow reasonable access to them to the person by whom they were supplied and to any person who would be entitled to have access to them if they were still in the control of the person by whom they were supplied.

(4) The expenses of a relevant office-holder in giving assistance under this section are recoverable as part of the expenses incurred by him in the discharge of his duties; and he shall not be required under this section to take any action which involves expenses which cannot be so recovered, unless the exchange or clearing house undertakes to meet them.

There shall be treated as expenses of his such reasonable sums as he may determine in respect of time spent in giving the assistance [and for the purpose of determining the priority in which his expenses are payable out of the assets, sums in respect of time spent shall be treated as his remuneration and other sums shall be treated as his disbursements or, in Scotland, outlays].

(5) The Secretary of State may by regulations make further provision as to the duties of persons to give assistance to a recognised investment exchange or recognised clearing house for the purposes of its default proceedings, and the duties of the exchange or clearing house with respect to information supplied to it.

The regulations may add to, amend or repeal the provisions of subsections (1) to (4) above.

(6) In this section "document" includes information recorded in any form.

[832]

NOTES

Sub-s (4): words in square brackets inserted by the Financial Markets and Insolvency Regulations 1991, SI 1991/880, reg 5, as from 25 April 1991.

Regulations: the Financial Markets and Insolvency Regulations 1991, SI 1991/880 at **[6691]**.

161 Supplementary provisions as to default proceedings

(1) If the court is satisfied on an application by a relevant office-holder that a party to a market contract with a defaulter intends to dissipate or apply his assets so as to prevent the officer-holder recovering such sums as may become due upon the completion of the default proceedings, the court may grant such interlocutory relief (in Scotland, such interim order) as it thinks fit.

(2) A liquidator or trustee of a defaulter or, in Scotland, a permanent trustee on the sequestrated estate of the defaulter shall not—

(a) declare or pay any dividend to the creditors, or

(b) return any capital to contributories,

unless he has retained what he reasonably considers to be an adequate reserve in respect of any claims arising as a result of the default proceedings of the exchange or clearing house concerned.

(3) The court may on an application by a relevant office-holder make such order as it thinks fit altering or dispensing from compliance with such of the duties of his office as are affected by the fact that default proceedings are pending or could be taken, or have been or could have been taken.

(4) Nothing in [section 126, 128, 130, 185 or 285 of, or paragraph 42 or 43 (including paragraph 43(6) as applied by paragraph 44) of Schedule B1 to, the Insolvency Act 1986] (which restrict the taking of certain legal proceedings and other steps), and nothing in any rule of law in Scotland to the like effect as the said section 285, in the Bankruptcy (Scotland) Act 1985 or in the Debtors (Scotland) Act 1987 as to the effect of sequestration, shall affect any action taken by an exchange or clearing house for the purpose of its default proceedings.

[833]

NOTES

Sub-s (4): words in square brackets substituted by the Enterprise Act 2002, s 248(3), Sch 17, paras 43, 45, as from 15 September 2003 (for savings and transitional provisions, see the note to the Insolvency Act 1986, s 8 at **[3164]**).

162 Duty to report on completion of default proceedings

(1) [Subject to subsection (1A),] a recognised investment exchange or recognised clearing house shall, on the completion of proceedings under its default rules, report to the [Authority] on its proceedings stating in respect of each creditor or debtor the sum certified by them to be payable from or to the defaulter or, as the case may be, the fact that no sum is payable.

[(1A) A recognised overseas investment exchange or recognised overseas clearing house shall not be subject to the obligation under subsection (1) unless it has been notified by the [Authority] that a report is required for the purpose of insolvency proceedings in any part of the United Kingdom.]

(2) The exchange or clearing house may make a single report or may make reports from time to time as proceedings are completed with respect to the transactions affecting particular persons.

(3) The exchange or clearing house shall supply a copy of every report under this section to the defaulter and to any relevant office-holder acting in relation to him or his estate.

(4) When a report under this section is received by the [Authority, it] shall publish notice of that fact in such manner as [it] thinks appropriate for bringing [the report] to the attention of creditors and debtors of the defaulter.

(5) An exchange or clearing house shall make available for inspection by a creditor or debtor of the defaulter so much of any report by it under this section as relates to the sum (if any) certified to be due to or from him or to the method by which that sum was determined.

(6) Any such person may require the exchange or clearing house, on payment of such reasonable fee as the exchange or clearing house may determine, to provide him with a copy of any part of a report which he is entitled to inspect.

[834]

NOTES

Sub-s (1): words in first pair of square brackets inserted by the Financial Markets and Insolvency Regulations 1991, SI 1991/880, reg 6(1), (2), as from 25 April 1991; word in second pair of square brackets substituted by the Financial Services and Markets Act 2000 (Consequential Amendments and Repeals) Order 2001, SI 2001/3649, art 80(1), (2), as from 1 December 2001.

Sub-s (1A): inserted by SI 1991/880, reg 6(1), (3), as from 25 April 1991; word in square brackets substituted by SI 2001/3649, art 80(1), (3), as from 1 December 2001.

Sub-s (4): words in square brackets substituted by SI 2001/3649, art 80(1), (4), as from 1 December 2001.

163 Net sum payable on completion of default proceedings

(1) The following provisions apply with respect to the net sum certified by a recognised investment exchange or recognised clearing house, upon proceedings under its default rules being duly completed in accordance with this Part, to be payable by or to a defaulter.

(2) If, in England and Wales, a bankruptcy or winding-up order has been made, or a resolution for voluntary winding up has been passed, the debt—

(a) is provable in the bankruptcy or winding up or, as the case may be, is payable to the relevant officer-holder, and

(b) shall be taken into account, where appropriate, under section 323 of the Insolvency Act 1986 (mutual dealings and set-off) or the corresponding provision applicable in the case of winding up,

in the same way as a debt due before the commencement of the bankruptcy, the date on which the body corporate goes into liquidation (within the meaning of section 247 of the Insolvency Act 1986) or, in the case of a partnership, the date of the winding-up order.

(3) If, in Scotland, an award of sequestration or a winding-up order has been made, or a resolution for voluntary winding up has been passed, the debt—

(a) may be claimed in the sequestration or winding up or, as the case may be, is payable to the relevant officer-holder, and

(b) shall be taken into account for the purposes of any rule of law relating to set-off applicable in sequestration or winding up,

in the same way as a debt due before the date of sequestration (within the meaning of section 73(1) of the Bankruptcy (Scotland) Act 1985) or the commencement of the winding up (within the meaning of section 129 of the Insolvency Act 1986).

(4) However, where (or to the extent that) a sum is taken into account by virtue of subsection (2)(b) or (3)(b) which arises from a contract entered into at a time when the creditor had notice—

(a) that a bankruptcy petition or, in Scotland, a petition for sequestration was pending, or

(b) that a meeting of creditors had been summoned under section 98 of the Insolvency Act 1986 or that a winding-up petition was pending,

the value of any profit to him arising from the sum being so taken into account (or being so taken into account to that extent) is recoverable from him by the relevant office-holder unless the court directs otherwise.

(5) Subsection (4) does not apply in relation to a sum arising from a contract effected under the default rules of a recognised investment exchange or recognised clearing house.

(6) Any sum recoverable by virtue of subsection (4) ranks for priority, in the event of the insolvency of the person from whom it is due, immediately before preferential or, in Scotland, preferred debts.

[835]

164 Disclaimer of property, rescission of contracts, &c

(1) Sections 178, 186, 315 and 345 of the Insolvency Act 1986 (power to disclaim onerous property and court's power to order rescission of contracts, &c) do not apply in relation to—

(a) a market contract, or

(b) a contract effected by the exchange or clearing house for the purpose of realising property provided as margin in relation to market contracts.

In the application of this subsection in Scotland, the reference to sections 178, 315 and 345 shall be construed as a reference to any rule of law having the like effect as those sections.

(2) In Scotland, a permanent trustee on the sequestrated estate of a defaulter or a liquidator is bound by any market contract to which that defaulter is a party and by any contract as is mentioned in subsection (1)(b) above notwithstanding section 42 of the Bankruptcy (Scotland) Act 1985 or any rule of law to the like effect applying in liquidations.

(3) Sections 127 and 284 of the Insolvency Act 1986 (avoidance of property dispositions effected after commencement of winding up or presentation of bankruptcy petition), and section 32(8) of the Bankruptcy (Scotland) Act 1985 (effect of dealing with debtor relating to estate vested in permanent trustee) do not apply to—

(a) a market contract, or any disposition of property in pursuance of such a contract,

(b) the provision of margin in relation to market contracts,

(c) a contract effected by the exchange or clearing house for the purpose of realising property provided as margin in relation to a market contract, or any disposition of property in pursuance of such a contract, or

(d) any disposition of property in accordance with the rules of the exchange or clearing house as to the application of property provided as margin.

(4) However, where—

(a) a market contract is entered into by a person who has notice that a petition has been presented for the winding up or bankruptcy or sequestration of the estate of the other party to the contract, or

(b) margin in relation to a market contract is accepted by a person who has notice that such a petition has been presented in relation to the person by whom or on whose behalf the margin is provided,

the value of any profit to him arising from the contract or, as the case may be, the amount or value of the margin is recoverable from him by the relevant office-holder unless the court directs otherwise.

(5) Subsection (4)(a) does not apply where the person entering into the contract is a recognised investment exchange or recognised clearing house acting in accordance with its rules, or where the contract is effected under the default rules of such an exchange or clearing house; but subsection (4)(b) applies in relation to the provision of margin in relation to such a contract.

(6) Any sum recoverable by virtue of subsection (4) ranks for priority, in the event of the insolvency of the person from whom it is due, immediately before preferential or, in Scotland, preferred debts.

[836]

165 Adjustment of prior transactions

(1) No order shall be made in relation to a transaction to which this section applies under—

(a) section 238 or 339 of the Insolvency Act 1986 (transactions at an undervalue),

(b) section 239 or 340 of that Act (preferences), or

(c) section 423 of that Act (transactions defrauding creditors).

(2) As respects Scotland, no decree shall be granted in relation to any such transaction—

(a) under section 34 or 36 of the Bankruptcy (Scotland) Act 1985 or section 242 or 243 of the Insolvency Act 1986 (gratuitous alienations and unfair preferences), or

(b) at common law on grounds of gratuitous alienations or fraudulent preferences.

(3) This section applies to—

(a) a market contract to which a recognised investment exchange or recognised clearing house is a party or which is entered into under its default rules, and

(b) a disposition of property in pursuance of such a market contract.

(4) Where margin is provided in relation to a market contract and (by virtue of subsection (3)(a) or otherwise) no such order or decree as is mentioned in subsection (1) or (2) has been, or could be, made in relation to that contract, this section applies to—

(a) the provision of the margin,

(b) any contract effected by the exchange or clearing house in question for the purpose of realising the property provided as margin, and

(c) any disposition of property in accordance with the rules of the exchange or clearing house as to the application of property provided as margin.

[837]

166 Powers of Secretary of State to give directions

(1) The powers conferred by this section are exercisable in relation to a recognised UK investment exchange or recognised UK clearing house.

(2) Where in any case an exchange or clearing house has not taken action under its default rules—

(a) if it appears to the [Authority] that it could take action, [the Authority] may direct it to do so, and

(b) if it appears to the [Authority] that it is proposing to take or may take action, [the Authority] may direct it not to do so.

(3) Before giving such a direction the [Authority] shall consult the exchange or clearing house in question; and [it] shall not give a direction unless [it] is satisfied, in the light of that consultation—

(a) in the case of a direction to take action, that failure to take action would involve undue risk to investors or other participants in the market, or

(b) in the case of a direction not to take action, that the taking of action would be premature or otherwise undesirable in the interests of investors or other participants in the market.

(4) A direction shall specify the grounds on which it is given.

(5) A direction not to take action may be expressed to have effect until the giving of a further direction (which may be a direction to take action or simply revoking the earlier direction).

(6) No direction shall be given not to take action if, in relation to the person in question—

(a) a bankruptcy order or an award of sequestration of his estate has been made, or an interim receiver or interim trustee has been appointed, or

(b) a winding up order has been made, a resolution for voluntary winding up has been passed or an administrator, administrative receiver or provisional liquidator has been appointed;

and any previous direction not to take action shall cease to have effect on the making or passing of any such order, award or appointment.

(7) Where an exchange or clearing house has taken or been directed to take action under its default rules, the [Authority] may direct it to do or not to do such things (being things which it has power to do under its default rules) as are specified in the direction.

The [Authority] shall not give such a direction unless [it is satisfied that the direction] will not impede or frustrate the proper and efficient conduct of the default proceedings.

(8) A direction under this section is enforceable, on the application of the [Authority], by injunction or, in Scotland, by an order under section 45 of the Court of Session Act 1988; and where an exchange or clearing house has not complied with a direction, the court may make such order as it thinks fit for restoring the position to what it would have been if the direction had been complied with.

[838]

NOTES

Sub-ss (2), (3), (7), (8): words in square brackets substituted by the Financial Services and Markets Act 2000 (Consequential Amendments and Repeals) Order 2001, SI 2001/3649, art 81, as from 1 December 2001.

In consequence of these amendments it is thought that the heading to this section should refer to the powers of the Authority.

167 Application to determine whether default proceedings to be taken

(1) Where there has been made or passed in relation to a member or designated non-member of a recognised investment exchange or a member of a recognised clearing house—

(a) a bankruptcy order or an award of sequestration of his estate, or an order appointing an interim receiver of his property, or

(b) an administration or winding up order, a resolution for voluntary winding up or an order appointing a provisional liquidator,

and the exchange or clearing house has not taken action under its default rules in consequence of the order, award or resolution or the matters giving rise to it, a relevant office-holder appointed by, or in consequence of or in connection with, the order, award or resolution may apply to the [Authority].

[(1A) In subsection (1) a reference to an administration order shall be taken to include a reference to the appointment of an administrator under—

(a) paragraph 14 of Schedule B1 to the Insolvency Act 1986 (c 45) (appointment by holder of qualifying floating charge), or

(b) paragraph 22 of that Schedule (appointment by company or directors).]

(2) The application shall specify the exchange or clearing house concerned and the grounds on which it is made.

(3) On receipt of the application the [Authority] shall notify the exchange or clearing house, and unless within three business days after the day on which the notice is received the exchange or clearing house—

(a) takes action under its default rules, or

(b) notifies the [Authority] that it proposes to do so forthwith,

then, subject as follows, the provisions of sections 158 to 165 above do not apply in relation to market contracts to which the member or designated non-member in question is a party or to anything done by the exchange or clearing house for the purposes of, or in connection with, the settlement of any such contract.

For this purpose a "business day" means any day which is not a Saturday or Sunday, Christmas Day, Good Friday or a bank holiday in any part of the United Kingdom under the Banking and Financial Dealings Act 1971.

(4) The provisions of sections 158 to 165 are not disapplied if before the end of the period mentioned in subsection (3) the [Authority] gives the exchange or clearing house a direction under section 166(2)(a) (direction to take action under default rules).

No such direction may be given after the end of that period.

(5) If the exchange or clearing house notifies the [Authority] that it proposes to take action under its default rules forthwith, it shall do so; and that duty is enforceable, on the application of the [Authority], by injunction or, in Scotland, by an order under section 45 of the Court of Session Act 1988.

[839]

NOTES

Sub-ss (1), (3)–(5): words in square brackets substituted by the Financial Services and Markets Act 2000 (Consequential Amendments and Repeals) Order 2001, SI 2001/3649, art 82, as from 1 December 2001.

Sub-s (1A): inserted by the Enterprise Act 2002, s 248(3), Sch 17, paras 43, 46, as from 15 September 2003 (for savings and transitional provisions, see the note to the Insolvency Act 1986, s 8 at **[3164]**).

---

168 (*Repealed by the Financial Services and Markets Act 2000 (Consequential Amendments and Repeals) Order 2001, SI 2001/3649, art 75(f), as from 1 December 2001.*)

169 Supplementary provisions

(1) …

(2) [Sections 296 and 297 of the Financial Services and Markets Act 2000 apply] in relation to a failure by a recognised investment exchange or recognised clearing house to comply with an obligation under this Part as to a failure to comply with an obligation under that Act.

(3) Where the recognition of an investment exchange or clearing house is revoked under the [Financial Services and Markets Act 2000, the appropriate authority] may, before or after

the revocation order, give such directions as [it] thinks fit with respect to the continued application of the provisions of this Part, with such exceptions, additions and adaptations as may be specified in the direction, in relation to cases where a relevant event of any description specified in the directions occurred before the revocation order takes effect.

[(3A) "The appropriate authority" means—

(a) in the case of an overseas investment exchange or clearing house, the Treasury; and

(b) in the case of a UK investment exchange or clearing house, the Authority.]

(4) …

(5) [Regulations under section 414 of the Financial Services and Markets Act 2000 (service of notices) may make provision] in relation to a notice, direction or other document required or authorised by or under this Part to be given to or served on any person other than the [Treasury or the Authority].

[840]

NOTES

Sub-s (1): repealed by the Financial Services and Markets Act 2000 (Consequential Amendments and Repeals) Order 2001, SI 2001/3649, art 75(g), as from 1 December 2001.

Sub-ss (2), (3), (5): words in square brackets substituted by SI 2001/3649, art 83(1)–(3), (5), as from 1 December 2001.

Sub-s (3A): inserted by SI 2001/3649, art 83(1), (4), as from 1 December 2001.

Sub-s (4): repealed (without having been brought into force) by SI 2001/3649, art 75(g), as from 1 December 2001.

Other exchanges and clearing houses

170 Certain overseas exchanges and clearing houses

(1) The Secretary of State [and the Treasury] may by regulations provide that this Part applies in relation to contracts connected with an overseas investment exchange or clearing house which is approved by [the Treasury] in accordance with such procedures as may be specified in the regulations, as satisfying such requirements as may be so specified, as it applies in relation to contracts connected with a recognised investment exchange or clearing house.

(2) The [Treasury] shall not approve an overseas investment exchange or clearing house unless [they are] satisfied—

(a) that the rules and practices of the body, together with the law of the country in which the body's head office is situated, provide adequate procedures for dealing with the default of persons party to contracts connected with the body, and

(b) that it is otherwise appropriate to approve the body.

(3) The reference in subsection (2)(a) to default is to a person being unable to meet his obligations.

(4) The regulations may apply in relation to the approval of a body under this section such of the provisions of the [Financial Services and Markets Act 2000] as the Secretary of State considers appropriate.

(5) The Secretary of State may make regulations which, in relation to a body which is so approved—

(a) apply such of the provisions of the [Financial Services and Markets Act 2000] as the Secretary of State considers appropriate, and

(b) provide that the provisions of this Part apply with such exceptions, additions and adaptations as appear to the Secretary of State to be necessary or expedient;

and different provision may be made with respect to different bodies or descriptions of body.

(6) Where the regulations apply any provisions of the [Financial Services and Markets Act 2000], they may provide that those provisions apply with such exceptions, additions and adaptations as appear to the Secretary of State to be necessary or expedient.

[841]

NOTES

Commencement: 25 March 1991 (certain purposes); not in force (otherwise); see the final note below.

Sub-s (1): words in first pair of square brackets inserted, and words in second pair of square brackets substituted, by the Financial Services and Markets Act 2000 (Consequential Amendments and Repeals) Order 2001, SI 2001/3649, art 84(1), (2), as from 1 December 2001.

Sub-ss (2), (4)–(6): words in square brackets substituted by SI 2001/3649, art 84(1), (3), (4), as from 1 December 2001.

Note: the Companies Act 1989 (Commencement No 9 and Saving and Transitional Provisions) Order 1991, SI 1991/488 provided that this Part (ie, ss 154–191, Schs 21, 22) comes into force on 25 March 1991 in so far as necessary to enable Regulations to be made under ss 155(4), (5), 158(4), (5), 160(5), 173(4), (5), 174(2)–(4), 185, 186, 187(3), Sch 21, para 2(3). As of 1 July 2007 this section (and ss 172, 178) had not been commenced for other purposes.

171 *(Repealed by the Financial Services and Markets Act 2000 (Consequential Amendments and Repeals) Order 2001, SI 2001/3649, art 75(h), as from 1 December 2001.)*

172 Settlement arrangements provided by the Bank of England

(1) The Secretary of State may by regulations provide that this Part applies to contracts of any specified description in relation to which settlement arrangements are provided by the Bank of England, as it applies to contracts connected with a recognised investment exchange or recognised clearing house.

(2) Regulations under this section may provide that the provisions of this Part apply with such exceptions, additions and adaptations as appear to the Secretary of State to be necessary or expedient.

(3) Before making any regulations under this section, the Secretary of State [and the Treasury shall consult] the Bank of England.

[842]

NOTES

Commencement: 25 March 1991 (certain purposes); not in force (otherwise).

Sub-s (3): words in square brackets substituted by the Transfer of Functions (Financial Services) Order 1992, SI 1992/1315, art 10(1), Sch 4, para 13, as from 7 June 1992.

As to the commencement of this section, see the note to s 170 at **[841]**.

Market charges

173 Market charges

(1) In this Part "market charge" means a charge whether fixed or floating, granted—

(a) in favour of a recognised investment exchange, for the purpose of securing debts or liabilities arising in connection with the settlement of market contracts,

[(aa) in favour of The Stock Exchange, for the purpose of securing debts or liabilities arising in connection with short term certificates;]

(b) in favour of a recognised clearing house, for the purpose of securing debts or liabilities arising in connection with their ensuring the performance of market contracts, or

(c) in favour of a person who agrees to make payments as a result of the transfer [or allotment] of specified securities made through the medium of a computer-based system established by the Bank of England and The Stock Exchange, for the purpose of securing debts or liabilities of the transferee [or allottee] arising in connection therewith.

(2) Where a charge is granted partly for purposes specified in subsection (1)(a), [(aa),] (b) or (c) and partly for other purposes, it is a "market charge" so far as it has effect for the specified purposes.

(3) [In subsection (1)—

"short term certificate" means an instrument issued by The Stock Exchange undertaking to procure the transfer of property of a value and description specified in the instrument to or to the order of the person to whom the instrument is issued or his endorsee or to a person acting on behalf of either of them and also undertaking to make appropriate payments in cash, in the event that the obligation to procure the transfer of property cannot be discharged in whole or in part;]

"specified securities" means securities for the time being specified in the list in Schedule 1 to the Stock Transfer Act 1982, and includes any right to such securities; and "transfer", in relation to any such securities or right, means a transfer of the beneficial interest.

(4) The Secretary of State may by regulations make further provision as to the charges granted in favour of any such person as is mentioned in subsection (1)(a), (b) or (c) which are to be treated as "market charges" for the purposes of this Part; and the regulations may add to, amend or repeal the provisions of subsections (1) to (3) above.

(5) The regulations may provide that a charge shall or shall not be treated as a market charge if or to the extent that it secures obligations of a specified description, is a charge over property of a specified description or contains provisions of a specified description.

(6) Before making regulations under this section in relation to charges granted in favour of a person within subsection (1)(c), the Secretary of State [and the Treasury shall consult] the Bank of England.

[843]

NOTES

Sub-s (1): para (aa), and words in square brackets in para (c), inserted by the Financial Markets and Insolvency Regulations 1991, SI 1991/880, reg 9(a), (b), as from 25 April 1991.

Sub-s (2): words in square brackets inserted by SI 1991/880, reg 9(c), as from 25 April 1991.

Sub-s (3): words in square brackets substituted by SI 1991/880, reg 9(d), as from 25 April 1991.

Sub-s (6): words in square brackets substituted by the Transfer of Functions (Financial Services) Order 1992, SI 1992/1315, art 10(1), Sch 4, para 13, as from 7 June 1992.

Regulations: the Financial Markets and Insolvency Regulations 1991, SI 1991/880 at **[6691]**; the Financial Markets and Insolvency (CGO Service) Regulations 1999, SI 1999/1209.

174 Modifications of the law of insolvency

(1) The general law of insolvency has effect in relation to market charges and action taken in enforcing them subject to the provisions of section 175.

(2) The Secretary of State may by regulations make further provision modifying the law of insolvency in relation to the matters mentioned in subsection (1).

(3) The regulations may add to, amend or repeal the provisions mentioned in subsection (1), and any other provision of this Part as it applies for the purposes of those provisions, or provide that those provisions have effect with such exceptions, additions or adaptations as are specified in the regulations.

(4) The regulations may make different provision for cases defined by reference to the nature of the charge, the nature of the property subject to it, the circumstances, nature or extent of the obligations secured by it or any other relevant factor.

(5) Before making regulations under this section in relation to charges granted in favour of a person within section 173(1)(c), the Secretary of State [and the Treasury shall consult] the Bank of England.

[844]

NOTES

Sub-s (5): words in square brackets substituted by the Transfer of Functions (Financial Services) Order 1992, SI 1992/1315, art 10(1), Sch 4, para 13, as from 7 June 1992.

Regulations: the Financial Markets and Insolvency Regulations 1991, SI 1991/880 at **[6691]**; the Financial Markets and Insolvency (CGO Service) Regulations 1999, SI 1999/1209.

175 Administration orders, &c

[(1) The following provisions of Schedule B1 to the Insolvency Act 1986 (administration) do not apply in relation to a market charge—

(a) paragraph 43(2) and (3) (restriction on enforcement of security or repossession of goods) (including that provision as applied by paragraph 44 (interim moratorium)), and

(b) paragraphs 70, 71 and 72 (power of administrator to deal with charged or hire-purchase property).

(1A) Paragraph 41(2) of that Schedule (receiver to vacate office at request of administrator) does not apply to a receiver appointed under a market charge.]

(2) However, where a market charge falls to be enforced after [the occurrence of an event to which subsection (2A) applies], and there exists another charge over some or all of the

same property ranking in priority to or *pari passu* with the market charge [on the application of any person interested], the court may order that there shall be taken after enforcement of the market charge such steps as the court may direct for the purpose of ensuring that the chargee under the other charge is not prejudiced by the enforcement of the market charge.

[(2A) This subsection applies to—

(a) making an administration application under paragraph 12 of Schedule B1 to the Insolvency Act 1986,

(b) appointing an administrator under paragraph 14 or 22 of that Schedule (appointment by floating charge holder, company or directors),

(c) filing with the court a copy of notice of intention to appoint an administrator under either of those paragraphs.]

(3) The following provisions of the Insolvency Act 1986 (which relate to the powers of receivers) do not apply in relation to a market charge—

(a) section 43 (power of administrative receiver to dispose of charged property), and

(b) section 61 (power of receiver in Scotland to dispose of an interest in property).

(4) Sections 127 and 284 of the Insolvency Act 1986 (avoidance of property dispositions effected after commencement of winding up or presentation of bankruptcy petition), and section 32(8) of the Bankruptcy (Scotland) Act 1985 (effect of dealing with debtor relating to estate vested in permanent trustee), do not apply to a disposition of property as a result of which the property becomes subject to a market charge or any transaction pursuant to which that disposition is made.

(5) However, if a person (other than the chargee under the market charge) who is party to a disposition mentioned in subsection (4) has notice at the time of the disposition that a petition has been presented for the winding up or bankruptcy or sequestration of the estate of the party making the disposition, the value of any profit to him arising from the disposition is recoverable from him by the relevant office-holder unless the court directs otherwise.

(6) Any sum recoverable by virtue of subsection (5) ranks for priority, in the event of the insolvency of the person from whom it is due, immediately before preferential or, in Scotland, preferred debts.

(7) In a case falling within both subsection (4) above (as a disposition of property as a result of which the property becomes subject to a market charge) and section 164(3) (as the provision of margin in relation to a market contract), section 164(4) applies with respect to the recovery of the amount or value of the margin and subsection (5) above does not apply.

[845]

NOTES

Sub-ss (1), (1A): substituted, for original sub-s (1), by the Enterprise Act 2002, s 248(3), Sch 17, paras 43, 47(1), (2), as from 15 September 2003 (for savings and transitional provisions, see the note to the Insolvency Act 1986, s 8 at **[3164]**).

Sub-s (2): words in first pair of square brackets substituted by the Enterprise Act 2002, s 248(3), Sch 17, paras 43, 47(1), (3), as from 15 September 2003 (for savings and transitional provisions, see the note to the Insolvency Act 1986, s 8 at **[3164]**); words in second pair of square brackets inserted by the Financial Markets and Insolvency Regulations 1991, SI 1991/880, reg 18, as from 25 April 1991.

Sub-s (2A): inserted by the Enterprise Act 2002, s 248(3), Sch 17, paras 43, 47(1), (4), as from 15 September 2003 (for savings and transitional provisions, see the note to the Insolvency Act 1986, s 8 at **[3164]**).

176 Power to make provision about certain other charges

(1) The Secretary of State may by regulations provide that the general law of insolvency has effect in relation to charges of such descriptions as may be specified in the regulations, and action taken in enforcing them, subject to such provisions as may be specified in the regulations.

(2) The regulations may specify any description of charge granted in favour of—

(a) a body approved under section 170 (certain overseas exchanges and clearing houses),

(b) a person included in the list maintained by the [... Authority] for the purposes of [section 301 of the Financial Services and Markets Act 2000] (certain money market institutions),

(c) the Bank of England,

[(d) a person who has permission under Part 4 of the Financial Services and Markets Act 2000 to carry on a relevant regulated activity, or

(e) an international securities self-regulating organisation approved for the purposes of an order made under section 22 of the Financial Services and Markets Act 2000,]

for the purpose of securing debts or liabilities arising in connection with or as a result of the settlement of contracts or the transfer of assets, rights or interests on a financial market.

(3) The regulations may specify any description of charge granted for that purpose in favour of any other person in connection with exchange facilities or clearing services provided by a recognised investment exchange or recognised clearing house or by any such body, person, authority or organisation as is mentioned in subsection (2).

(4) Where a charge is granted partly for the purpose specified in subsection (2) and partly for other purposes, the power conferred by this section is exercisable in relation to the charge so far as it has effect for that purpose.

(5) The regulations may—

(a) make the same or similar provision in relation to the charges to which they apply as is made by or under sections 174 and 175 in relation to market charges, or

(b) apply any of those provisions with such exceptions, additions or adaptations as are specified in the regulations.

[(6) Before making regulations under this section relating to a description of charges defined by reference to their being granted in favour of a person included in the list maintained by the … Authority for the purposes of [section 301 of the Financial Services and Markets Act 2000], or in connection with exchange facilities or clearing services provided by a person included in that list, the Secretary of State and the Treasury shall consult the Authority and the Bank of England.

(6A) Before making regulations under this section relating to a description of charges defined by reference to their being granted in favour of the Bank of England, or in connection with settlement arrangements provided by the Bank, the Secretary of State and the Treasury shall consult the Bank.]

(7) Regulations under this section may provide that they apply or do not apply to a charge if or to the extent that it secures obligations of a specified description, is a charge over property of a specified description or contains provisions of a specified description.

[(8) For the purposes of subsection (2)(d), "relevant regulated activity" means—

(a) dealing in investments as principal or as agent;

(b) arranging deals in investments;

[(ba) operating a multilateral trading facility;]

(c) managing investments;

(d) safeguarding and administering investments;

(e) sending dematerialised instructions; or

(f) establishing etc a collective investment scheme.

(9) Subsection (8) must be read with—

(a) section 22 of the Financial Services and Markets Act 2000;

(b) any relevant order under that section; and

(c) Schedule 2 to that Act.]

[846]

NOTES

Sub-s (2): words in first pair of square brackets in para (b) substituted by the Bank of England Act 1998, s 23(1), Sch 5, Pt III, paras 46, 48(1), (2), as from 1 June 1998; words omitted therefrom repealed, and words in second pair of square brackets substituted, by the Financial Services and Markets Act 2000 (Consequential Amendments and Repeals) Order 2001, SI 2001/3649, art 85(1), (2), as from 1 December 2001. Note that the sidenote to the Financial Services and Markets Act 2000, s 301 is "supervision of certain contracts" and not "certain money market institutions" as stated in sub-s (2)(b) above, therefore it is thought that the words "certain money market institutions" should be deleted from the text of this subsection. Paras (d), (e) substituted by SI 2001/3649, art 85(1), (3), as from 1 December 2001.

Sub-s (6): substituted, together with sub-s (6A) for original sub-s (6), by the Bank of England Act 1998, s 23(1), Sch 5, Pt III, paras 46, 48(1), (3), as from 1 June 1998; words omitted repealed, and words in square brackets substituted, by SI 2001/3649, art 85(1), (4), as from 1 December 2001.

Sub-s (6A): substituted as noted above.

Sub-s (8): added, together with sub-s (9), by SI 2001/3649, art 85(1), (5), as from 1 December 2001; para (ba) inserted by the Financial Services and Markets Act 2000 (Regulated Activities) (Amendment No 3) Order 2006, SI 2006/3384, art 32, as from 1 November 2007 (for the full commencement details of SI 2006/3384, see the Note for that Order at **[4826A]**).
Sub-s (9): added as noted above.

Market property

177 Application of margin not affected by certain other interests

(1) The following provisions have effect with respect to the application by a recognised investment exchange or recognised clearing house of property (other than land) held by the exchange or clearing house as margin in relation to a market contract.

(2) So far as necessary to enable the property to be applied in accordance with the rules of the exchange or clearing house, it may be so applied notwithstanding any prior equitable interest or right, or any right or remedy arising from a breach of fiduciary duty, unless the exchange or clearing house had notice of the interest, right or breach of duty at the time the property was provided as margin.

(3) No right or remedy arising subsequently to the property being provided as margin may be enforced so as to prevent or interfere with the application of the property by the exchange or clearing house in accordance with its rules.

(4) Where an exchange or clearing house has power by virtue of the above provisions to apply property notwithstanding an interest, right or remedy, a person to whom the exchange or clearing house disposes of the property in accordance with its rules takes free from that interest, right or remedy.

[847]

178 Priority of floating market charge over subsequent charges

(1) The Secretary of State may by regulations provide that a market charge which is a floating charge has priority over a charge subsequently created or arising, including a fixed charge.

(2) The regulations may make different provision for cases defined, as regards the market charge or the subsequent charge, by reference to the description of charge, its terms, the circumstances in which it is created or arises, the nature of the charge, the person in favour of whom it is granted or arises or any other relevant factor.

[848]

NOTES

Commencement: 25 March 1991 (certain purposes); not in force (otherwise).
As to the commencement of this section, see the note to s 170 at **[841]**.

179 Priority of market charge over unpaid vendor's lien

Where property subject to an unpaid vendor's lien becomes subject to a market charge, the charge has priority over the lien unless the chargee had actual notice of the lien at the time the property became subject to the charge.

[849]

180 Proceedings against market property by unsecured creditors

(1) Where property (other than land) is held by a recognised investment exchange or recognised clearing house as margin in relation to market contracts or is subject to a market charge, no execution or other legal process for the enforcement of a judgment or order may be commenced or continued, and no distress may be levied, against the property by a person not seeking to enforce any interest in or security over the property, except with the consent of—

(a) in the case of property provided as cover for margin, the investment exchange or clearing house in question, or

(b) in the case of property subject to a market charge, the person in whose favour the charge was granted.

(2) Where consent is given the proceedings may be commenced or continued notwithstanding any provision of the Insolvency Act 1986 or the Bankruptcy (Scotland) Act 1985.

(3) Where by virtue of this section a person would not be entitled to enforce a judgment or order against any property, any injunction or other remedy granted with a view to facilitating the enforcement of any such judgment or order shall not extend to that property.

(4) In the application of this section to Scotland, the reference to execution being commenced or continued includes a reference to diligence being carried out or continued, and the reference to distress being levied shall be omitted.

[850]

181 Power to apply provisions to other cases

(1) [A power to which this subsection applies includes the] power to apply sections 177 to 180 to any description of property provided as cover for margin in relation to contracts in relation to which the power is exercised or, as the case may be, property subject to charges in relation to which the power is exercised.

(2) The regulations may provide that those sections apply with such exceptions, additions and adaptations as may be specified in the regulations.

[(3) Subsection (1) applies to the powers of the Secretary of State and the Treasury to act jointly under—

(a) sections 170, 172 and 176 of this Act; and

(b) section 301 of the Financial Services and Markets Act 2000 (supervision of certain contracts).]

[851]

NOTES

Sub-s (1): words in square brackets substituted by the Financial Services and Markets Act 2000 (Consequential Amendments and Repeals) Order 2001, SI 2001/3649, art 86(1), (2), as from 1 December 2001.

Sub-s (3): added by SI 2001/3649, art 86(1), (3), as from 1 December 2001.

Supplementary provisions

182 Powers of court in relation to certain proceedings begun before commencement

(1) The powers conferred by this section are exercisable by the court where insolvency proceedings in respect of—

(a) a member of a recognised investment exchange or a recognised clearing house, or

(b) a person by whom a market charge has been granted,

are begun on or after 22nd December 1988 and before the commencement of this section.

That person is referred to in this section as "the relevant person".

(2) For the purposes of this section "insolvency proceedings" means proceedings under Part II, IV, V or IX of the Insolvency Act 1986 (administration, winding up and bankruptcy) or under the Bankruptcy (Scotland) Act 1985; and references in this section to the beginning of such proceedings are to—

(a) the presentation of a petition on which an administration order, winding-up order, bankruptcy order or award of sequestration is made, or

(b) the passing of a resolution for voluntary winding up.

(3) This section applies in relation to—

(a) in England and Wales, the administration of the insolvent estate of a deceased person, and

(b) in Scotland, the administration by a judicial factor appointed under section 11A of the Judicial Factors (Scotland) Act 1889 of the insolvent estate of a deceased person,

as it applies in relation to insolvency proceedings.

In such a case references to the beginning of the proceedings shall be construed as references to the death of the relevant person.

(4) The court may on an application made, within three months after the commencement of this section, by—

(a) a recognised investment exchange or recognised clearing house, or

(b) a person in whose favour a market charge has been granted, make such order as it thinks fit for achieving, except so far as assets of the relevant person have been distributed before the making of the application, the same result as if the provisions of Schedule 22 had come into force on 22nd December 1988.

(5) The provisions of that Schedule ("the relevant provisions") reproduce the effect of certain provisions of this Part as they appeared in the Bill for this Act as introduced into the House of Lords and published on that date.

(6) The court may in particular—

(a) require the relevant person or a relevant office-holder—

(i) to return property provided as cover for margin or which was subject to a market charge, or to pay to the applicant or any other person the proceeds of realisation of such property, or

(ii) to pay to the applicant or any other person such amount as the court estimates would have been payable to that person if the relevant provisions had come into force on 22nd December 1988 and market contracts had been settled in accordance with the rules of the recognised investment exchange or recognised clearing house, or a proportion of that amount if the property of the relevant person or relevant office-holder is not sufficient to meet the amount in full;

(b) provide that contracts, rules and dispositions shall be treated as not having been void;

(c) modify the functions of a relevant office-holder, or the duties of the applicant or any other person, in relation to the insolvency proceedings, or indemnify any such person in respect of acts or omissions which would have been proper if the relevant provisions had been in force;

(d) provide that conduct which constituted an offence be treated as not having done so;

(e) dismiss proceedings which could not have been brought if the relevant provisions had come into force on 22nd December 1988, and reverse the effect of any order of a court which could not, or would not, have been made if those provisions had come into force on that date.

(7) An order under this section shall not be made against a relevant office-holder if the effect would be that his remuneration, costs and expenses could not be met.

[852]

183 Insolvency proceedings in other jurisdictions

(1) The references to insolvency law in section 426 of the Insolvency Act 1986 (co-operation with courts exercising insolvency jurisdiction in other jurisdictions) include, in relation to a part of the United Kingdom, the provisions made by or under this Part and, in relation to a relevant country or territory within the meaning of that section, so much of the law of that country or territory as corresponds to any provisions made by or under this Part.

(2) A court shall not, in pursuance of that section or any other enactment or rule of law, recognise or give effect to—

(a) any order of a court exercising jurisdiction in relation to insolvency law in a country or territory outside the United Kingdom, or

(b) any act of a person appointed in such a country or territory to discharge any functions under insolvency law,

in so far as the making of the order or the doing of the act would be prohibited in the case of a court in the United Kingdom or a relevant office-holder by provisions made by or under this Part.

(3) Subsection (2) does not affect the recognition or enforcement of a judgment required to be recognised or enforced under or by virtue of the Civil Jurisdiction and Judgments Act 1982 [or Council Regulation (EC) No 44/2001 of 22nd December 2000 on jurisdiction and the recognition and enforcement of judgments in civil and commercial matters][, as amended from time to time and as applied by the Agreement made on 19th October 2005 between the European Community and the Kingdom of Denmark on jurisdiction and the recognition and enforcement of judgments in civil and commercial matters (OJ No L299 16.11.2005 at p 62)].

[853]

NOTES

Sub-s (3): words in first pair of square brackets added by the Civil Jurisdiction and Judgments Order 2001, SI 2001/3929, art 5, Sch 3, para 21, as from 1 March 2002; words in second pair of square brackets added by the Civil Jurisdiction and Judgments Regulations 2007, SI 2007/1655, reg 5, Schedule, Pt 1, para 15, as from 1 July 2007.

184 Indemnity for certain acts, &c

(1) Where a relevant office-holder takes any action in relation to property of a defaulter which is liable to be dealt with in accordance with the default rules of a recognised investment exchange or recognised clearing house, and believes and has reasonable grounds for believing that he is entitled to take that action, he is not liable to any person in respect of any loss or damage resulting from his action except in so far as the loss or damage is caused by the office-holder's own negligence.

(2) Any failure by a recognised investment exchange or recognised clearing house to comply with its own rules in respect of any matter shall not prevent that matter being treated for the purposes of this Part as done in accordance with those rules so long as the failure does not substantially affect the rights of any person entitled to require compliance with the rules.

(3) No recognised investment exchange or recognised clearing house, nor any officer or servant or member of the governing body of a recognised investment exchange or recognised clearing house, shall be liable in damages for anything done or omitted in the discharge or purported discharge of any functions to which this subsection applies unless the act or omission is shown to have been in bad faith.

(4) The functions to which subsection (3) applies are the functions of the exchange or clearing house so far as relating to, or to matters arising out of—

(a) its default rules, or

(b) any obligations to which it is subject by virtue of this Part.

(5) No person [to whom the exercise of any function of a recognised investment exchange or recognised clearing house is delegated under its default rules], nor any officer or servant of such a person, shall be liable in damages for anything done or omitted in the discharge or purported discharge of those functions unless the act or omission is shown to have been in bad faith.

[854]

NOTES

Sub-s (5): words in square brackets substituted by the Financial Services and Markets Act 2000 (Consequential Amendments and Repeals) Order 2001, SI 2001/3649, art 87, as from 1 December 2001.

185 Power to make further provision by regulations

(1) The Secretary of State may by regulations make such further provision as appears to him necessary or expedient for the purposes of this Part.

(2) Provision may, in particular, be made—

(a) for integrating the provisions of this Part with the general law of insolvency, and

(b) for adapting the provisions of this Part in their application to overseas investment exchanges and clearing houses.

(3) Regulations under this section may add to, amend or repeal any of the provisions of this Part or provide that those provisions have effect subject to such additions, exceptions or adaptations as are specified in the regulations.

[(4) References in this section to the provisions of this Part include any provision made under section 301 of the Financial Services and Markets Act 2000.]

[855]

NOTES

Sub-s (4): added by the Financial Services and Markets Act 2000 (Consequential Amendments and Repeals) Order 2001, SI 2001/3649, art 88, as from 1 December 2001.

Regulations: the Financial Markets and Insolvency Regulations 1991, SI 1991/880 at **[6691]**; the Financial Markets and Insolvency Regulations 1996, SI 1996/1469, at **[6908]**; the Financial Markets and Insolvency Regulations 1998, SI 1998/1748; the Financial Markets and Insolvency (CGO Service) Regulations 1999, SI 1999/1209.

186 Supplementary provisions as to regulations

(1) Regulations under this Part may make different provision for different cases and may contain such incidental, transitional and other supplementary provisions as appear to the Secretary of State to be necessary or expedient.

(2) Regulations under this Part shall be made by statutory instrument which shall be subject to annulment in pursuance of a resolution of either House of Parliament.

[856]

NOTES

Regulations: the Financial Markets and Insolvency Regulations 1996, SI 1996/1469, at **[6908]**; the Financial Markets and Insolvency Regulations 1998, SI 1998/1748; the Financial Markets and Insolvency (CGO Service) Regulations 1999, SI 1999/1209.

187 Construction of references to parties to market contracts

(1) Where a person enters into market contracts in more than one capacity, the provisions of this Part apply (subject as follows) as if the contracts entered into in each different capacity were entered into by different persons.

(2) References in this Part to a market contract to which a person is a party include (subject as follows, and unless the context otherwise requires) contracts to which he is party as agent.

(3) The Secretary of State may by regulations—

(a) modify or exclude the operation of subsections (1) and (2), and

(b) make provision as to the circumstances in which a person is to be regarded for the purposes of those provisions as acting in different capacities.

[857]

NOTES

Regulations: the Financial Markets and Insolvency Regulations 1991, SI 1991/880 at **[6691]**.

188 Meaning of "default rules" and related expressions

(1) In this Part "default rules" means rules of a recognised investment exchange or recognised clearing house which provide for the taking of action in the event of a person appearing to be unable, or likely to become unable, to meet his obligations in respect of one or more market contracts connected with the exchange or clearing house.

(2) References in this Part to a "defaulter" are to a person in respect of whom action has been taken by a recognised investment exchange or recognised clearing house under its default rules, whether by declaring him to be a defaulter or otherwise; and references in this Part to "default" shall be construed accordingly.

(3) In this Part "default proceedings" means proceedings taken by a recognised investment exchange or recognised clearing house under its default rules.

(4) If an exchange or clearing house takes action under its default rules in respect of a person, all subsequent proceedings under its rules for the purposes of or in connection with the settlement of market contracts to which the defaulter is a party shall be treated as done under its default rules.

[858]

189 Meaning of "relevant office-holder"

(1) The following are relevant office-holders for the purposes of this Part—

(a) the official receiver,

(b) any person acting in relation to a company as its liquidator, provisional liquidator, administrator or administrative receiver,

(c) any person acting in relation to an individual (or, in Scotland, any debtor within the meaning of the Bankruptcy (Scotland) Act 1985) as his trustee in bankruptcy or interim receiver of his property or as permanent or interim trustee in the sequestration of his estate,

(d) any person acting as administrator of an insolvent estate of a deceased person.

(2) In subsection (1)(b) "company" means any company, society, association, partnership or other body which may be wound up under the Insolvency Act 1986.

[859]

190 Minor definitions

(1) In this Part—

"administrative receiver" has the meaning given by section 251 of the Insolvency Act 1986;

["the Authority" means the Financial Services Authority;]

"charge" means any form of security, including a mortgage and, in Scotland, a heritable security;

.....

"interim trustee" and "permanent trustee" have the same meaning as in the Bankruptcy (Scotland) Act 1985;

.....

"overseas", in relation to an investment exchange or clearing house, means having its head office outside the United Kingdom;

.....

["recognised clearing house" and "recognised investment exchange" have the same meaning as in the Financial Services and Markets Act 2000;]

"set-off", in relation to Scotland, includes compensation;

["The Stock Exchange" means the London Stock Exchange Limited;]

"UK", in relation to an investment exchange or clearing house, means having its head office in the United Kingdom.

(2) References in this Part to settlement in relation to a market contract are to the discharge of the rights and liabilities of the parties to the contract, whether by performance, compromise or otherwise.

(3) In this Part the expressions "margin" and "cover for margin" have the same meaning.

(4) …

(5) For the purposes of this Part a person shall be taken to have notice of a matter if he deliberately failed to make enquiries as to that matter in circumstances in which a reasonable and honest person would have done so.

This does not apply for the purposes of a provision requiring "actual notice".

(6) References in this Part to the law of insolvency include references to every provision made by or under the Insolvency Act 1986 or the Bankruptcy (Scotland) Act 1985; and in relation to a building society references to insolvency law or to any provision of the Insolvency Act 1986 are to that law or provision as modified by the Building Societies Act 1986.

(7) In relation to Scotland, references in this Part—

(a) to sequestration include references to the administration by a judicial factor of the insolvent estate of a deceased person, and

(b) to an interim or permanent trustee include references to a judicial factor on the insolvent estate of a deceased person,

unless the context otherwise requires.

[860]

NOTES

Sub-s (1): definitions "the Authority", "recognised clearing house" and "recognised investment exchange" inserted, definitions "clearing house", "investment", "investment exchange" and "recognised" repealed, and definition "The Stock Exchange" substituted, by the Financial Services and Markets Act 2000 (Consequential Amendments and Repeals) Order 2001, SI 2001/3649, art 89(1)–(5), as from 1 December 2001.

Sub-s (4): repealed by SI 2001/3649, art 89(1), (6), as from 1 December 2001.

191 Index of defined expressions

The following Table shows provisions defining or otherwise explaining expressions used in this Part (other than provisions defining or explaining an expression used only in the same section or paragraph)—

administrative receiver	section 190(1)
[the Authority	section 190(1)]
charge	section 190(1)
…	…
cover for margin	section 190(3)
default rules (and related expressions)	section 188
designated non-member	section 155(2)
…	…
insolvency law (and similar expressions)	section 190(6)
interim trustee	section 190(1) and (7)(b)
…	…
…	…
margin	section 190(3)
market charge	section 173
market contract	section 155
notice	section 190(5)
overseas (in relation to an investment exchange or clearing house)	section 190(1)
party (in relation to a market contract)	section 187
permanent trustee	section 190(1) and (7)(b)
…	…
[recognised clearing house and recognised investment exchange	section 190(1)]
relevant office-holder	section 189
sequestration	section 190(7)(a)
set off (in relation to Scotland)	section 190(1)
settlement and related expressions (in relation to a market contract)	section 190(2)
The Stock Exchange	section 190(1)
trustee, interim or permanent (in relation to Scotland)	section 190(7)(b)
UK (in relation to an investment exchange or clearing house)	section 190(1).

[861]

NOTES

Entries relating to "clearing house", "ensuring the performance of a transaction", "investment," "investment exchange" and "recognised" repealed, and entries relating to "the Authority" and "recognised clearing house and recognised investment exchange" inserted, by the Financial Services and Markets Act 2000 (Consequential Amendments and Repeals) Order 2001, SI 2001/3649, art 89(7), as from 1 December 2001.

192–206 (*Ss 192–206 (Pt VIII: Amendments of FSA 1986): ss 192–197 repealed by the Financial Services and Markets Act 2000 (Consequential Amendments and Repeals) Order 2001, SI 2001/3649, art 75(i), as from 1 December 2001; ss 198, 199 repealed by the Public Offers of Securities Regulations 1995, SI 1995/1537, reg 17, Sch 2, Pt II, para 10, as from 19 June 1995; s 200 repealed in part by SI 2001/3649, art 75(j), as from 1 December 2001 and the reminder of the section is effectively spent (it amended the Civil Jurisdiction and Judgments Act 1982 by inserting a reference to FSA 1986, s 188 into Sch 5 to the 1982 Act – that reference has now been superseded by a reference to FSMA 2000, s 415); ss 201–206 repealed by SI 2001/3649, art 75(k), as from 1 December 2001.*)

PART IX
TRANSFER OF SECURITIES

207 Transfer of securities

(1) The Secretary of State may make provision by regulations for enabling title to securities to be evidenced and transferred without a written instrument.

In this section—

(*a*) *"securities" means shares, stock, debentures, debenture stock, loan stock, bonds, units of a collective investment scheme within the meaning of the [Financial Services and Markets Act 2000] and other securities of any description;*

(*b*) *references to title to securities include any legal or equitable interest in securities; and*

(*c*) *references to a transfer of title include a transfer by way of security.*

(2) The regulations may make provision—

(*a*) *for procedures for recording and transferring title to securities, and*

(*b*) *for the regulation of those procedures and the persons responsible for or involved in their operation.*

(3) The regulations shall contain such safeguards as appear to the Secretary of State appropriate for the protection of investors and for ensuring that competition is not restricted, distorted or prevented.

(4) The regulations may for the purpose of enabling or facilitating the operation of the new procedures make provision with respect to the rights and obligations of persons in relation to securities dealt with under the procedures.

But the regulations shall be framed so as to secure that the rights and obligations in relation to securities dealt with under the new procedures correspond, so far as practicable, with those which would arise apart from any regulations under this section.

(5) The regulations may include such supplementary, incidental and transitional provisions as appear to the Secretary of State to be necessary or expedient.

In particular, provision may be made for the purpose of giving effect to—

(*a*) *the transmission of title to securities by operation of law;*

(*b*) *any restriction on the transfer of title to securities arising by virtue of the provisions of any enactment or instrument, court order or agreement;*

(*c*) *any power conferred by any such provision on a person to deal with securities on behalf of the person entitled.*

(6) The regulations may make provision with respect to the persons responsible for the operation of the new procedures—

(*a*) *as to the consequences of their insolvency or incapacity, or*

(*b*) *as to the transfer from them to other persons of their functions in relation to the new procedures.*

(7) The regulations may for the purposes mentioned above—

(*a*) *modify or exclude any provision of any enactment or instrument, or any rule of law;*

(*b*) *apply, with such modifications as may be appropriate, the provisions of any enactment or instrument (including provisions creating criminal offences);*

(*c*) *require the payment of fees, or enable persons to require the payment of fees, of such amounts as may be specified in the regulations or determined in accordance with them;*

(*d*) *empower the Secretary of State to delegate to any person willing and able to discharge them any functions of his under the regulations.*

(8) The regulations may make different provision for different cases.

(9) Regulations under this section shall be made by statutory instrument; and no such regulations shall be made unless a draft of the instrument has been laid before and approved by resolution of each House of Parliament.

[(10) In subsection (1), the reference to transfer without a written instrument includes, in relation to bearer securities, transfer without delivery.]

[862]–[863]

NOTES

Repealed by the Companies Act 2006, s 1295, Sch 16, as from a day to be appointed.

Sub-s (1): words in square brackets substituted by the Financial Services and Markets Act 2000 (Consequential Amendments and Repeals) Order 2001, SI 2001/3649, art 90, as from 1 December 2001.

Sub-s (10): added by the Bank of England Act 1998, s 35, as from 1 June 1998.

Transfer of functions: by the Transfer of Functions (Financial Services) Order 1992, SI 1992/1315, art 2(1)(c) at **[6730]**, the functions of the Secretary of State under this Part of this Act are transferred to the Treasury.

Regulations: the Uncertificated Securities Regulations 2001, SI 2001/3755 at **[7001]**; the Uncertificated Securities (Amendment) (Eligible Debt Securities) Regulations 2003, SI 2003/1633.

PART X
MISCELLANEOUS AND GENERAL PROVISIONS

208–212 *(S 208 adds the Company Directors Disqualification Act 1986, s 21(4) at* **[759]***; s 209 repealed by the Criminal Justice Act 1993, s 79(14), Sch 6, Pt I, as from 1 March 1994; s 210 spent (amended the Policyholders Protection Act 1975, Sch 3 (repealed)); s 211 amends the Building Societies Act 1986, s 104, Sch 15 and inserts the Company Directors Disqualification Act 1986, s 22A at* **[761]***; s 212 introduces Sch 24 (Repeals).)*

General

213 Provisions extending to Northern Ireland

(1) The provisions of this Act extend to Northern Ireland so far as they amend, or provide for the amendment of, an enactment which so extends.

(2) So far as any provision of this Act amends the Companies Act 1985 or the Insolvency Act 1986, its application to companies registered or incorporated in Northern Ireland is subject to section 745(1) of the Companies Act 1985 or section 441(2) of the Insolvency Act 1986, as the case may be.

(3) In Part III (investigations and powers to obtain information), sections 82 to 91, (powers exercisable to assist overseas regulatory authorities) extend to Northern Ireland.

(4) Part VI (mergers and related matters) extends to Northern Ireland.

(5) In Part VII (financial markets and insolvency) the following provisions extend to Northern Ireland—

(a) sections 154 and 155 (introductory provisions and definition of "market contract"),

(b) …

(c) sections 157, 160, 162, and 166 to 169 (provisions relating to recognised investment exchanges and clearing houses),

(d) sections 170 to 172 (power to extend provisions to other financial markets),

(e) section 184 (indemnity for certain acts), and

(f) sections 185 to 191 (supplementary provisions).

(6) …

(7) Part IX (transfer of securities) extends to Northern Ireland.

…

(8) In Part X (miscellaneous and general provisions), this section and sections 214 to 216 (general provisions) extend to Northern Ireland.

(9) Except as mentioned above, the provisions of this Act do not extend to Northern Ireland.

[864]

NOTES

Sub-s (5): para (b) repealed by the Financial Services and Markets Act 2000 (Consequential Amendments and Repeals) Order 2001, SI 2001/3649, art 75(l), as from 1 December 2001.

Sub-s (6): repealed by SI 2001/3649, art 75(l), as from 1 December 2001.

Sub-s (7): words omitted repealed by the Northern Ireland Act 1998, s 100(2), Sch 15, as from 2 December 1999.

214 (*Repealed by the Financial Services and Markets Act 2000 (Consequential Amendments and Repeals) Order 2001, SI 2001/3649, art 75(m), as from 1 December 2001.*)

215 Commencement and transitional provisions

(1) The following provisions of this Act come into force on Royal Assent—

(a) in Part V (amendments of company law), section 141 (application to declare dissolution of company void);

(b) in Part VI (mergers)—

(i) sections 147 to 150, and

(ii) paragraphs 2 to 12, 14 to 16, 18 to 20, 22 to 25 of Schedule 20, and section 153 so far as relating to those paragraphs;

(c) in Part VIII (amendments of the Financial Services Act 1986), section 202 (offers of short-dated debentures);

(d) in Part X (miscellaneous and general provisions), the repeals made by Schedule 24 in sections 71, 74, 88 and 89 of, and Schedule 9 to, the Fair Trading Act 1973, and section 212 so far as relating to those repeals.

(2) The other provisions of this Act come into force on such day as the Secretary of State may appoint by order made by statutory instrument; and different days may be appointed for different provisions and different purposes.

(3) An order bringing into force any provision may contain such transitional provisions and savings as appear to the Secretary of State to be necessary or expedient.

(4) The Secretary of State may also by order under this section amend any enactment which refers to the commencement of a provision brought into force by the order so as to substitute a reference to the actual date on which it comes into force.

[865]

NOTES

Transfer of functions: as to the exercise of functions under this section, see the Transfer of Functions (Financial Services) Order 1992, SI 1992/1315, art 2(2)(c) at **[6730]**.

Financial Services Act 1986: repealed by the Financial Services and Markets Act 2000 (Consequential Amendments and Repeals) Order 2001, SI 2001/3649, art 3(1)(c), as from 1 December 2001.

Orders: the Companies Act 1989 (Commencement No 1) Order 1990, SI 1990/98; the Companies Act 1989 (Commencement No 2) Order 1990, SI 1990/142 (as amended by SI 1990/355); the Companies Act 1989 (Commencement No 3, Transitional Provisions and Transfer of Functions under the Financial Services Act 1986) Order 1990, SI 1990/354; the Companies Act 1989 (Commencement No 4, Transitional and Saving Provisions) Order 1990, SI 1990/355 (as amended by SI 1990/1707, SI 1990/2569, SI 1993/3246); the Companies Act 1989 (Commencement No 5 and Transitional and Saving Provisions) Order 1990, SI 1990/713; the Companies Act 1989 (Commencement No 6 and Transitional and Savings Provisions) Order 1990, SI 1990/1392 (as amended by SI 1990/1707); the Companies Act 1989 (Commencement No 7, Transitional and Saving Provisions) Order 1990, SI 1990/1707; the Companies Act 1989 (Commencement No 8 and Transitional and Saving Provisions) Order 1990, SI 1990/2569; the Companies Act 1989 (Commencement No 9 and Saving and Transitional Provisions) Order 1991, SI 1991/488; the Companies Act 1989 (Commencement No 10 and Saving Provisions) Order 1991, SI 1991/878; the Companies Act 1989 (Commencement No 11) Order 1991, SI 1991/1452; the Companies Act 1989 (Commencement No 12 and Transitional Provision) Order 1991, SI 1991/1996; the Companies Act 1989 (Commencement No 13) Order 1991, SI 1991/2173; the Companies Act 1989 (Commencement No 14 and Transitional Provision) Order 1991, SI 1991/2945; the Companies Act 1989 (Commencement No 15 and Transitional and Savings Provisions) Order 1995, SI 1995/1352; the Companies Act 1989 (Commencement No 16) Order 1995, SI 1995/1591; the Companies Act 1989 (Commencement No 17) Order 1998, SI 1998/1747; the Companies (Audit, Investigations and Community Enterprise) Act 2004 (Commencement) and Companies Act 1989 (Commencement No 18) Order 2004, SI 2004/3322 (at **[7339]**).

216 Short title

This Act may be cited as the Companies Act 1989.

[866]

SCHEDULES

(*Sch 1 amends CA 1985, Sch 4 at* **[637]** *et seq (and is repealed by the Companies Act 2006, s 1295, Sch 16, as from a day to be appointed); Sch 2 inserts Sch 4A to the 1985 Act at* **[643]** *(and is repealed by CA 2006, s 1295, Sch 16, as from a day to be appointed); Sch 3 substitutes Sch 5 to the 1985 Act at* **[644]** *et seq (and is repealed by CA 2006, s 1295, Sch 16, as from a day to be appointed); Sch 4 amends Sch 6 to the 1985 Act at* **[646]** *et seq and is repealed in* *part by the Statute Law (Repeals) Act 2004, as from 22 July 2004 (and is completely repealed by CA 2006, s 1295, Sch 16, as from a day to be appointed); Sch 5 amends Sch 7 to the 1985 Act at* **[649]** *et seq and is repealed in part by the Statute Law (Repeals) Act 2004, as from 22 July 2004 (and is completely repealed by CA 2006, s 1295, Sch 16, as from a day to be appointed); Sch 6 substitutes Sch 8 to the 1985 Act at* **[654]** *et seq (and is repealed by CA 2006, s 1295, Sch 16, as from a day to be appointed); Sch 7 substitutes the heading to Sch 9 to the 1985 Act, repeals the introductory paragraph preceding Pt I together with its heading, renames the original Pts I–V thereof as Pt I and amends that Part, and inserts new Pts II–IV thereof at* **[660]** *et seq (and is repealed by CA 2006, s 1295, Sch 16, as from a day to be appointed); Sch 8 (which is repealed by CA 2006, s 1295, Sch 16, as from a day to be appointed) substituted Sch 10 to the 1985 Act (repealed by the Companies Act 1985 (Insurance Companies Accounts) Regulations 1993, SI 1993/3246, reg 5(1), Sch 2, para 7, as from 19 December 1993, subject to a transitional provision in reg 7 thereof at* **[6766]**; *Sch 9 inserts Sch 10A to the 1985 Act at* **[666]** *(and is repealed by CA 2006, s 1295, Sch 16, as from a day to be appointed); Sch 10 (Amendments consequential on Part I) contains various amendments to CA 1985 and other legislation which, in so far as relevant to this work, and still in force, are incorporated at the appropriate place (note that this Schedule is repealed by CA 2006, s 1295, Sch 16, as from 20 January 2007 (in part), as from 1 October 2007 (in part) and as from a day to be appointed (otherwise).)*

SCHEDULE 11
RECOGNITION OF SUPERVISORY BODY

Section 30(5)

PART I
GRANT AND REVOCATION OF RECOGNITION

Application for recognition of supervisory body

1.—(1) A supervisory body may apply to the Secretary of State for an order declaring it to be a recognised supervisory body for the purposes of this Part of this Act.

(2) *Any such application—*

(*a*) *shall be made in such manner as the Secretary of State may direct, and*

(*b*) *shall be accompanied by such information as the Secretary of State may reasonably require for the purpose of determining the application.*

(3) At any time after receiving an application and before determining it the Secretary of State may require the applicant to furnish additional information.

(4) The directions and requirements given or imposed under sub-paragraphs (2) and (3) may differ as between different applications.

(5) Any information to be furnished to the Secretary of State under this paragraph shall, if he so requires, be in such form or verified in such manner as he may specify.

(6) Every application shall be accompanied by a copy of the applicant's rules and of any guidance issued by the applicant which is intended to have continuing effect and is issued in writing or other legible form.

Grant and refusal of recognition

2.—(1) The Secretary of State may, on an application duly made in accordance with paragraph 1 and after being furnished with all such information as he may require under that paragraph, make or refuse to make an order (a "recognition order") declaring the applicant to be a recognised supervisory body for the purposes of this Part of this Act.

(2) The Secretary of State shall not make a recognition order unless it appears to him, from the information furnished by the body and having regard to any other information in his possession, that the requirements of Part II of this Schedule are satisfied as respects that body.

(3) The Secretary of State may refuse to make a recognition order in respect of a body if he considers that its recognition is unnecessary having regard to the existence of one or more other bodies which maintain and enforce rules as to the appointment and conduct of company auditors and which have been or are likely to be recognised.

(4) Where the Secretary of State refuses an application for a recognition order he shall give the applicant a written notice to that effect specifying which requirements in the opinion of the Secretary of State are not satisfied or stating that the application is refused on the ground mentioned in sub-paragraph (3).

(5) A recognition order shall state the date on which it takes effect.

Revocation of recognition

3.—(1) A recognition order may be revoked by a further order made by the Secretary of State if at any time it appears to him—

- *(a) that any requirement of Part II of this Schedule is not satisfied in the case of the body to which the recognition order relates ("the recognised body"),*
- *(b) that the recognised body has failed to comply with any obligation to which it is subject by virtue of this Part of this Act, or*
- *(c) that the continued recognition of the body is undesirable having regard to the existence of one or more other bodies which have been or are to be recognised.*

(2) An order revoking a recognition order shall state the date on which it takes effect and that date shall not be earlier than three months after the day on which the revocation order is made.

(3) Before revoking a recognition order the Secretary of State shall give written notice of his intention to do so to the recognised body, take such steps as he considers reasonably practicable for bringing the notice to the attention of members of the body and publish it in such manner as he thinks appropriate for bringing it to the attention of any other persons who are in his opinion likely to be affected.

(4) A notice under sub-paragraph (3) shall state the reasons for which the Secretary of State proposes to act and give particulars of the rights conferred by sub-paragraph (5).

(5) A body on which a notice is served under sub-paragraph (3), any member of the body and any other person who appears to the Secretary of State to be affected may within three months after the date of service or publication, or within such longer time as the Secretary of State may allow, make written representations to the Secretary of State and, if desired, oral representations to a person appointed for that purpose by the Secretary of State; and the Secretary of State shall have regard to any representations made in accordance with this sub-paragraph in determining whether to revoke the recognition order.

(6) If in any case the Secretary of State considers it essential to do so in the public interest he may revoke a recognition order without regard to the restriction imposed by sub-paragraph (2) and notwithstanding that no notice has been given or published under sub-paragraph (3) or that the time for making representations in pursuance of such a notice has not expired.

(7) An order revoking a recognition order may contain such transitional provisions as the Secretary of State thinks necessary or expedient.

(8) A recognition order may be revoked at the request or with the consent of the recognised body and any such revocation shall not be subject to the restrictions imposed by sub-paragraphs (1) and (2) or the requirements of sub-paragraphs (3) to (5).

(9) On making an order revoking a recognition order the Secretary of State shall give the body written notice of the making of the order, take such steps as he considers reasonably practicable for bringing the making of the order to the attention of members of the body and publish a notice of the making of the order in such manner as he thinks appropriate for bringing it to the attention of any other persons who are in his opinion likely to be affected.
[867]

NOTES

Repealed by the Companies Act 2006, s 1295, Sch 16, as from a day to be appointed.

PART II
REQUIREMENTS FOR RECOGNITION

Holding of appropriate qualification

4.—(1) The body must have rules to the effect that a person is not eligible for appointment as a company auditor unless—

(*a*) *in the case of an individual, he holds an appropriate qualification;*

(*b*) *in the case of a firm—*

(*i*) *the individuals responsible for company audit work on behalf of the firm hold an appropriate qualification, and*

(*ii*) *the firm is controlled by qualified persons (see paragraph 5 below).*

(2) This does not prevent the body from imposing more stringent requirements.

(3) A firm which has ceased to comply with the conditions mentioned in sub-paragraph (1)(b) may be permitted to remain eligible for appointment as a company auditor for a period of not more than three months.

5.—(1) The following provisions explain what is meant in paragraph 4(1)(b)(ii) by a firm being "controlled by qualified persons".

(2) For this purpose references to a person being qualified are, in relation to an individual, to his holding an appropriate qualification, and in relation to a firm, to its being eligible for appointment as a company auditor.

(3) A firm shall be treated as controlled by qualified persons if, and only if—

(*a*) *a majority of the members of the firm are qualified persons, and*

(*b*) *where the firm's affairs are managed by a board of directors, committee or other management body, a majority of the members of that body are qualified persons or, if the body consists of two persons only, that at least one of them is a qualified person.*

(4) A majority of the members of a firm means—

(*a*) *where under the firm's constitution matters are decided upon by the exercise of voting rights, members holding a majority of the rights to vote on all, or substantially all, matters;*

(*b*) *in any other case, members having such rights under the constitution of the firm as enable them to direct its overall policy or alter its constitution.*

(5) A majority of the members of the management body of a firm means—

(*a*) *where matters are decided at meetings of the management body by the exercise of voting rights, members holding a majority of the rights to vote on all, or substantially all, matters at such meetings;*

(*b*) *in any other case, members having such rights under the constitution of the firm as enable them to direct its overall policy or alter its constitution.*

(6) The provisions of paragraphs 5 to 11 of Schedule 10A to the Companies Act 1985 (rights to be taken into account and attribution of rights) apply for the purposes of this paragraph.

Auditors to be fit and proper persons

6.—(1) The body must have adequate rules and practices designed to ensure that the persons eligible under its rules for appointment as a company auditor are fit and proper persons to be so appointed.

(2) The matters which the body may take into account for this purpose in relation to a person must include—

(*a*) *any matter relating to any person who is or will be employed by or associated with him for the purposes of or in connection with company audit work; and*

(*b*) *in the case of a body corporate, any matter relating to any director or controller of the body, to any other body corporate in the same group or to any director or controller of any such other body; and*

(*c*) *in the case of a partnership, any matter relating to any of the partners, any director or controller of any of the partners, any body corporate in the same group as any of the partners and any director or controller of any such other body.*

(3) In sub-paragraph (2)(b) and (c) "controller", in relation to a body corporate, means a person who either alone or with any associate or associates is entitled to exercise or control the exercise of 15 per cent or more of the rights to vote on all, or substantially all, matters at general meetings of the body or another body corporate of which it is a subsidiary.

Professional integrity and independence

7.—(1) The body must have adequate rules and practices designed to ensure—

- *(a) that company audit work is conducted properly and with integrity, and*
- *(b) that persons are not appointed company auditor in circumstances in which they have any interest likely to conflict with the proper conduct of the audit.*

[(1A) The body must participate in arrangements within paragraph 17, and the rules and practices mentioned in sub-paragraph (1) above must include provision requiring compliance with any standards for the time being determined under such arrangements.]

(2) The body must also have adequate rules and practices designed to ensure that no firm is eligible under its rules for appointment as a company auditor unless the firm has arrangements to prevent—

- *(a) individuals who do not hold an appropriate qualification, and*
- *(b) persons who are not members of the firm,*

from being able to exert any influence over the way in which an audit is conducted in circumstances in which that influence would be likely to affect the independence or integrity of the audit.

Technical standards

8.—[(1)] The body must have rules and practices as to the technical standards to be applied in company audit work and as to the manner in which those standards are to be applied in practice.

[(2) The body must participate in arrangements within paragraph 18, and the rules and practices mentioned in sub-paragraph (1) above must include provision requiring compliance with any standards for the time being determined under such arrangements.]

Procedures for maintaining competence

9. The body must have rules and practices designed to ensure that persons eligible under its rules for appointment as a company auditor continue to maintain an appropriate level of competence in the conduct of company audits.

Monitoring and enforcement

10.—(1) The body must have adequate arrangements and resources for the effective monitoring and enforcement of compliance with its rules.

(2) The arrangements for monitoring may make provision for that function to be performed on behalf of the body (and without affecting its responsibility) by any other body or person who is able and willing to perform it.

[Independent monitoring of audits of listed and other major companies

10A.—(1) The body must—

- *(a) participate in arrangements within paragraph 19(1), and*
- *(b) have rules designed to ensure that members of the body who perform any company audit functions in respect of major audits take such steps as may be reasonably required of them to enable their performance of any such functions to be monitored by means of inspections carried out under the arrangements.*

(2) Any monitoring of such persons under the arrangements is to be regarded (so far as their performance of company audit functions in respect of major audits is concerned) as monitoring of compliance with the body's rules for the purposes of paragraph 10(1).

(3) In this paragraph "company audit function" and "major audit" have the same meaning as in paragraph 19.]

Membership, eligibility and discipline

11. The rules and practices of the body relating to—

(a) the admission and expulsion of members,

(b) the grant and withdrawal of eligibility for appointment as a company auditor, and

(c) the discipline it exercises over its members,

must be fair and reasonable and include adequate provision for appeals.

Investigation of complaints

12.—(1) The body must have effective arrangements for the investigation of complaints—

(a) against persons who are eligible under its rules to be appointed company auditor, or

(b) against the body in respect of matters arising out of its functions as a supervisory body.

(2) The arrangements may make provision for the whole or part of that function to be performed by and to be the responsibility of a body or person independent of the body itself.

[Independent investigation for disciplinary purposes of public interest cases

12A.—(1) The body must—

(a) participate in arrangements within paragraph 20(1), and

(b) have rules and practices designed to ensure that, where the designated persons have decided that any particular disciplinary action should be taken against a member of the body following the conclusion of an investigation under such arrangements, that decision is to be treated as if it were a decision made by the body in disciplinary proceedings against the member.

(2) In sub-paragraph (1) "the designated persons" means the persons who, under the arrangements, have the function of deciding whether (and, if so, what) disciplinary action should be taken against a member of the body in the light of an investigation carried out under the arrangements.]

Meeting of claims arising out of audit work

13.—(1) The body must have adequate rules or arrangements designed to ensure that persons eligible under its rules for appointment as a company auditor take such steps as may reasonably be expected of them to secure that they are able to meet claims against them arising out of company audit work.

(2) This may be achieved by professional indemnity insurance or other appropriate arrangements.

Register of auditors and other information to be made available

14. The body must have rules requiring persons eligible under its rules for appointment as a company auditor to comply with any obligations imposed on them by regulations under section 35 or 36.

Taking account of costs of compliance

15. The body must have satisfactory arrangements for taking account, in framing its rules, of the cost to those to whom the rules would apply of complying with those rules and any other controls to which they are subject.

Promotion and maintenance of standards

16. The body must be able and willing to promote and maintain high standards of integrity in the conduct of company audit work and to co-operate, by the sharing of information and otherwise, with the Secretary of State and any other authority, body or person having responsibility in the United Kingdom for the qualification, supervision or regulation of auditors.

[868]

NOTES

Repealed by the Companies Act 2006, s 1295, Sch 16, as from a day to be appointed.

Para 7: sub-para (1A) inserted by the Companies (Audit, Investigations and Community Enterprise) Act 2004, s 1(1), (2), as from 6 April 2005.

Para 8: sub-para (1) numbered as such, and sub-para (2) added, by the Companies (Audit, Investigations and Community Enterprise) Act 2004, s 1(1), (3), as from 6 April 2005.

Paras 10A, 12A: inserted by the Companies (Audit, Investigations and Community Enterprise) Act 2004, s 1(1), (4), (5), as from 6 April 2005.

[PART 3
ARRANGEMENTS IN WHICH SUPERVISORY BODIES ARE REQUIRED TO PARTICIPATE

Arrangements for setting standards relating to professional integrity and independence

17. The arrangements referred to in paragraph 7(1A) are appropriate funded arrangements—

- (*a*) *for the determining of standards for the purposes of the rules and practices mentioned in paragraph 7(1), and*
- (*b*) *for ensuring that the determination of those standards is done independently of the body.*

Arrangements for setting technical standards

18. The arrangements referred to in paragraph 8(2) are appropriate funded arrangements—

- (*a*) *for the determining of standards for the purposes of the rules and practices mentioned in paragraph 8(1), and*
- (*b*) *for ensuring that the determination of those standards is done independently of the body.*

Arrangements for independent monitoring of audits of listed and other major companies

19.—(1) The arrangements referred to in paragraph 10A(1) are appropriate funded arrangements—

- (*a*) *for enabling the performance by members of the body of company audit functions in respect of major audits to be monitored by means of inspections carried out under the arrangements, and*
- (*b*) *for ensuring that the carrying out of such monitoring and inspections is done independently of the body.*

(2) *In this paragraph—*

"company audit function" means any function performed as a company auditor;

"major audit" means an audit conducted in respect of—

- (*a*) *a company any of whose securities have been admitted to the official list (within the meaning of Part 6 of the Financial Services and Markets Act 2000), or*
- (*b*) *any other company in whose financial condition there is a major public interest.*

Arrangements for independent investigation for disciplinary purposes of public interest cases

20.—(1) The arrangements referred to in paragraph 12A(1) are appropriate funded arrangements—

(*a*) *for the carrying out of investigations into public interest cases arising in connection with the performance of company audit functions by members of the body,*

(*b*) *for the holding of disciplinary hearings relating to members of the body which appear to be desirable following the conclusion of such investigations,*

(*c*) *for requiring such hearings to be held in public except where the interests of justice otherwise require,*

(*d*) *for the persons before whom such hearings have taken place to decide whether (and, if so, what) disciplinary action should be taken against the members to whom the hearings related, and*

(*e*) *for ensuring that the carrying out of those investigations, the holding of those hearings, and the taking of those decisions are done independently of the body.*

(2) In this paragraph—

"company audit function" means any function performed as a company auditor;

"public interest cases" means matters which raise or appear to raise important issues affecting the public interest.

Supplementary: arrangements to operate independently of body

21.—(1) This paragraph applies for the purposes of—

paragraph 17(b),

paragraph 18(b),

paragraph 19(1)(b), or

paragraph 20(1)(e).

(2) Arrangements cannot be regarded as appropriate for the purpose of ensuring that the thing or things mentioned in that provision is or are done independently of the body unless they are designed to ensure that the body—

(*a*) *will have no involvement in the appointment or selection of any of the persons who are to be responsible for doing the thing or things in question, and*

(*b*) *will not otherwise be involved in the doing of that thing or those things.*

(3) Sub-paragraph (2) imposes a minimum requirement and does not preclude the possibility that additional criteria may need to be satisfied in order for the arrangements to be regarded as appropriate for the purpose in question.

Supplementary: "funded" arrangements etc

22.—(1) For the purposes of any of paragraphs 17, 18, 19 and 20, arrangements are "funded" arrangements if, in the event of their providing for the payment of costs of maintaining the arrangements, such costs are to be paid by the body in accordance with the arrangements.

(2) Arrangements can qualify as arrangements within any of paragraphs 17, 18, 19(1) and 20(1) even though the matters for which they provide are more extensive in any respect than those mentioned in that provision."

[868A]

NOTES

Inserted by the Companies (Audit, Investigations and Community Enterprise) Act 2004, s 2, as from 6 April 2005.

Repealed by the Companies Act 2006, s 1295, Sch 16, as from a day to be appointed.

SCHEDULE 12
RECOGNITION OF PROFESSIONAL QUALIFICATION

Section 32(4)

PART I
GRANT AND REVOCATION OF RECOGNITION

Application for recognition of professional qualification

1.—(1) A qualifying body may apply to the Secretary of State for an order declaring a qualification offered by it to be a recognised professional qualification for the purposes of this Part of this Act.

(2) Any such application—

(a) shall be made in such manner as the Secretary of State may direct, and

(b) shall be accompanied by such information as the Secretary of State may reasonably require for the purpose of determining the application.

(3) At any time after receiving an application and before determining it the Secretary of State may require the applicant to furnish additional information.

(4) The directions and requirements given or imposed under sub-paragraphs (2) and (3) may differ as between different applications.

(5) Any information to be furnished to the Secretary of State under this section shall, if he so requires, be in such form or verified in such manner as he may specify.

In the case of examination standards, the verification required may include independent moderation of the examinations over such period as the Secretary of State considers necessary.

(6) Every application shall be accompanied by a copy of the applicant's rules and of any guidance issued by it which is intended to have continuing effect and is issued in writing or other legible form.

Grant and refusal of recognition

2.—(1) The Secretary of State may, on an application duly made in accordance with paragraph 1 and after being furnished with all such information as he may require under that paragraph, make or refuse to make an order (a "recognition order") declaring the qualification in respect of which the application was made to be a recognised professional qualification for the purposes of this Part of this Act.

In this Part of this Act a "recognised qualifying body" means a qualifying body offering a recognised professional qualification.

(2) The Secretary of State shall not make a recognition order unless it appears to him, from the information furnished by the applicant and having regard to any other information in his possession, that the requirements of Part II of this Schedule are satisfied as respects the qualification.

(3) Where the Secretary of State refuses an application for a recognition order he shall give the applicant a written notice to that effect specifying which requirements, in his opinion, are not satisfied.

(4) A recognition order shall state the date on which it takes effect.

Revocation of recognition

3.—(1) A recognition order may be revoked by a further order made by the Secretary of State if at any time it appears to him—

(a) that any requirement of Part II of this Schedule is not satisfied in relation to the qualification to which the recognition order relates, or

(b) that the qualifying body has failed to comply with any obligation to which it is subject by virtue of this Part of this Act.

(2) An order revoking a recognition order shall state the date on which it takes effect and that date shall not be earlier than three months after the day on which the revocation order is made.

(3) Before revoking a recognition order the Secretary of State shall give written notice of his intention to do so to the qualifying body, take such steps as he considers reasonably practicable for bringing the notice to the attention of persons holding the qualification or in the course of studying for it and publish it in such manner as he thinks appropriate for bringing it to the attention of any other persons who are in his opinion likely to be affected.

(4) A notice under sub-paragraph (3) shall state the reasons for which the Secretary of State proposes to act and give particulars of the rights conferred by sub-paragraph (5).

(5) A body on which a notice is served under sub-paragraph (3), any person holding the qualification or in the course of studying for it and any other person who appears to the Secretary of State to be affected may within three months after the date of service or publication, or within such longer time as the Secretary of State may allow, make written representations to the Secretary of State and, if desired, oral representations to a person appointed for that purpose by the Secretary of State; and the Secretary of State shall have regard to any representations made in accordance with this subsection in determining whether to revoke the recognition order.

(6) If in any case the Secretary of State considers it essential to do so in the public interest he may revoke a recognition order without regard to the restriction imposed by sub-paragraph (2) and notwithstanding that no notice has been given or published under sub-paragraph (3) or that the time for making representations in pursuance of such a notice has not expired.

(7) An order revoking a recognition order may contain such transitional provisions as the Secretary of State thinks necessary or expedient.

(8) A recognition order may be revoked at the request or with the consent of the qualifying body and any such revocation shall not be subject to the restrictions imposed by sub-paragraphs (1) and (2) or the requirements of sub-paragraphs (3) to (5).

(9) On making an order revoking a recognition order the Secretary of State shall give the qualifying body written notice of the making of the order, take such steps as he considers reasonably practicable for bringing the making of the order to the attention of persons holding the qualification or in the course of studying for it and publish a notice of the making of the order in such manner as he thinks appropriate for bringing it to the attention of any other persons who are in his opinion likely to be affected.

[869]

NOTES

Repealed by the Companies Act 2006, s 1295, Sch 16, as from a day to be appointed.

PART II
REQUIREMENTS FOR RECOGNITION

Entry requirements

4.—(1) The qualification must only be open to persons who have attained university entrance level or have a sufficient period of professional experience.

(2) In relation to a person who has not been admitted to a university or other similar establishment in the United Kingdom, attaining university entrance level means—

- *(a) being educated to such a standard as would entitle him to be considered for such admission on the basis of—*
  - *(i) academic or professional qualifications obtained in the United Kingdom and recognised by the Secretary of State to be of an appropriate standard, or*
  - *(ii) academic or professional qualifications obtained outside the United Kingdom which the Secretary of State considers to be of an equivalent standard; or*
- *(b) being assessed on the basis of written tests of a kind appearing to the Secretary of State to be adequate for the purpose, with or without oral examination, as of such a standard of ability as would entitle him to be considered for such admission.*

(3) The assessment, tests and oral examination referred to in sub-paragraph (2)(b) may be conducted by the qualifying body or by some other body approved by the Secretary of State.

Course of theoretical instruction

5. The qualification must be restricted to persons who have completed a course of theoretical instruction in the subjects prescribed for the purposes of paragraph 7 or have a sufficient period of professional experience.

Sufficient period of professional experience

6.—(1) The references in paragraphs 4 and 5 to a sufficient period of professional experience are to not less than seven years' experience in a professional capacity in the fields of finance, law and accountancy.

(2) Periods of theoretical instruction in the fields of finance, law and accountancy may be deducted from the required period of professional experience, provided the instruction—

- *(a) lasted at least one year, and*
- *(b) is attested by an examination recognised by the Secretary of State for the purposes of this paragraph;*

but the period of professional experience may not be so reduced by more than four years.

(3) The period of professional experience together with the practical training required in the case of persons satisfying the requirement in paragraph 5 by virtue of having a sufficient period of professional experience must not be shorter than the course of theoretical instruction referred to in that paragraph and the practical training required in the case of persons satisfying the requirement of that paragraph by virtue of having completed such a course.

Examination

7.—(1) The qualification must be restricted to persons who have passed an examination (at least part of which is in writing) testing—

- *(a) theoretical knowledge of the subjects prescribed for the purposes of this paragraph by regulations made by the Secretary of State, and*
- *(b) ability to apply that knowledge in practice,*

and requiring a standard of attainment at least equivalent to that required to obtain a degree from a university or similar establishment in the United Kingdom.

(2) The qualification may be awarded to a person without his theoretical knowledge of a subject being tested by examination if he has passed a university or other examination of equivalent standard in that subject or holds a university degree or equivalent qualification in it.

(3) The qualification may be awarded to a person without his ability to apply his theoretical knowledge of a subject in practice being tested by examination if he has received practical training in that subject which is attested by an examination or diploma recognised by the Secretary of State for the purposes of this paragraph.

(4) Regulations under this paragraph shall be made by statutory instrument which shall be subject to annulment in pursuance of a resolution of either House of Parliament.

Practical training

8.—(1) The qualification must be restricted to persons who have completed at least three years' practical training of which—

- *(a) part was spent being trained in company audit work, and*
- *(b) a substantial part was spent being trained in company audit work or other audit work of a description approved by the Secretary of State as being similar to company audit work.*

For this purpose "company audit work" includes the work of a person appointed as auditor under the Companies (Northern Ireland) Order 1986 or under the law of a country or territory outside the United Kingdom where it appears to the Secretary of State that the law and practice with respect to the audit of company accounts is similar to that in the United Kingdom.

(2) The training must be given by persons approved by the body offering the qualification as persons as to whom the body is satisfied, in the light of undertakings given by them and the supervision to which they are subject (whether by the body itself or some other body or organisation), that they will provide adequate training.

(3) At least two-thirds of the training must be given by a fully-qualified auditor, that is, a person—

(a) eligible in accordance with this Part of this Act to be appointed as a company auditor, or

(b) satisfying the corresponding requirements of the law of Northern Ireland or another member State of the European Economic Community.

The body offering the qualification

9.—(1) The body offering the qualification must have—

(a) rules and arrangements adequate to ensure compliance with the requirements of paragraphs 4 to 8, and

(b) adequate arrangements for the effective monitoring of its continued compliance with those requirements.

(2) The arrangements must include arrangements for monitoring the standard of its examinations and the adequacy of the practical training given by the persons approved by it for that purpose.

[870]

NOTES

Repealed by the Companies Act 2006, s 1295, Sch 16, as from a day to be appointed.

Regulations: the Company Auditors (Examinations) Regulations 1990, SI 1990/1146, prescribing (as from 20 June 1990) the following subjects for the purposes of para 7 above—

Auditing; analysis and critical assessment of annual accounts; general accounting; cost and management accounting; consolidated accounts; internal control; standards relating to the preparation of annual and consolidated accounts and to methods of valuing balance sheet items and of computing profits and losses; legal and professional standards and professional guidance relating to the statutory auditing of accounting documents and to those carrying out such audits; and those aspects of the following which are relevant to auditing: company law, law of insolvency and similar procedures, tax law, civil and commercial law, social security law and law of employment, information and computer systems, business, general and financial economics, mathematics and statistics, and basic principles of financial management of undertakings.

SCHEDULE 13
SUPPLEMENTARY PROVISIONS WITH RESPECT TO DELEGATION ORDER

Section 46(6)

[Operation of this Schedule

1.—(1) This Schedule has effect in relation to a body designated by an order under section 46 as follows—

(a) paragraphs 2 to 12 have effect in relation to the body where it is established by the order;

(b) paragraphs 2 and 6 to 11 have effect in relation to the body where it is an existing body (see section 46(1A)(b)); and

(c) paragraph 13 has effect in relation to the body where it is an existing body that is an unincorporated association.

(2) In their operation in accordance with sub-paragraph (1)(b), paragraphs 2 and 6 apply only in relation to—

(a) things done by or in relation to the body in or in connection with the exercise of functions transferred to it by the order, and

(b) functions of the body which are functions so transferred.

(3) Any power conferred by this Schedule to make provision by order is a power to make provision by an order under section 46.]

Status

2. *The body shall not be regarded as acting on behalf of the Crown and its members, officers and employees shall not be regarded as Crown servants.*

Name, members and chairman

3.—(1) *The body shall be known by such name as may be specified in the delegation order.*

(2) *The body shall consist of such persons (not being less than eight) as the Secretary of State may appoint after such consultation as he thinks appropriate; and the chairman of the body shall be such person as the Secretary of State may appoint from amongst its members.*

(3) *The Secretary of State may make provision by order as to the terms on which the members of the body are to hold and vacate office and as to the terms on which a person appointed as chairman is to hold and vacate the office of chairman.*

Financial provisions

4.—(1) *The body shall pay to its chairman and members such remuneration, and such allowances in respect of expenses properly incurred by them in the performance of their duties, as the Secretary of State may determine.*

(2) *As regards any chairman or member in whose case the Secretary of State so determines, the body shall pay or make provision for the payment of—*

(a) *such pension, allowance or gratuity to or in respect of that person on his retirement or death, or*

(b) *such contributions or other payment towards the provision of such a pension, allowance or gratuity,*

as the Secretary of State may determine.

(3) *Where a person ceases to be a member of the body otherwise than on the expiry of his term of office and it appears to the Secretary of State that there are special circumstances which make it right for him to receive compensation, the body shall make a payment to him by way of compensation of such amount as the Secretary of State may determine.*

Proceedings

5.—(1) *The delegation order may contain such provision as the Secretary of State considers appropriate with respect to the proceedings of the body.*

(2) *The order may, in particular—*

(a) *authorise the body to discharge any functions by means of committees consisting wholly or partly of members of the body;*

(b) *provide that the validity of proceedings of the body, or of any such committee, is not affected by any vacancy among the members or any defect in the appointment of any member.*

Fees

6.—(1) *The body may retain fees payable to it.*

(2) *The fees shall be applied for meeting the expenses of the body in discharging its functions and for any purposes incidental to those functions.*

(3) *Those expenses include any expenses incurred by the body on such staff, accommodation, services and other facilities as appear to it to be necessary or expedient for the proper performance of its functions.*

(4) *In prescribing the amount of fees in the exercise of the functions transferred to it the body shall prescribe such fees as appear to it sufficient to defray those expenses, taking one year with another.*

(5) *Any exercise by the body of the power to prescribe fees requires the approval of the Secretary of State; and the Secretary of State may, after consultation with the body, by order vary or revoke any regulations made by it prescribing fees.*

Legislative functions

7.—(1) Regulations made by the body in the exercise of the functions transferred to it shall be made by instrument in writing, but not by statutory instrument.

(2) The instrument shall specify the provision of this Part of this Act under which it is made.

(3) The Secretary of State may by order impose such requirements as he thinks necessary or expedient as to the circumstances and manner in which the body must consult on any regulations it proposes to make.

8.—(1) Immediately after an instrument is made it shall be printed and made available to the public with or without payment.

(2) A person shall not be taken to have contravened any regulation if he shows that at the time of the alleged contravention the instrument containing the regulation had not been made available as required by this paragraph.

9.—(1) The production of a printed copy of an instrument purporting to be made by the body on which is endorsed a certificate signed by an officer of the body authorised by it for the purpose and stating—

- *(a) that the instrument was made by the body,*
- *(b) that the copy is a true copy of the instrument, and*
- *(c) that on a specified date the instrument was made available to the public as required by paragraph 8,*

is prima facie evidence or, in Scotland, sufficient evidence of the facts stated in the certificate.

(2) A certificate purporting to be signed as mentioned in sub-paragraph (1) shall be deemed to have been duly signed unless the contrary is shown.

(3) Any person wishing in any legal proceedings to cite an instrument made by the body may require the body to cause a copy of it to be endorsed with such a certificate as is mentioned in this paragraph.

Report and accounts

10.—(1) The body shall at least once in each year for which the delegation order is in force make a report to the Secretary of State on the discharge of the functions transferred to it and on such other matters as the Secretary of State may by order require.

(2) The Secretary of State shall lay before Parliament copies of each report received by him under this paragraph.

[(2A) The following provisions of this paragraph apply as follows—

- *(a) sub-paragraphs (3) and (4) apply only where the body is established by the order, and*
- *(b) sub-paragraphs (5) and (6) apply only where the body is an existing body.]*

(3) The Secretary of State may, with the consent of the Treasury, give directions to the body with respect to its accounts and the audit of its accounts and it is the duty of the body to comply with the directions.

(4) A person shall not be appointed auditor of the body unless he is eligible for appointment as a company auditor under section 25.

[(5) Unless the body is a company to which section 226 of the Companies Act 1985 (duty to prepare individual company accounts) applies—

- *(a) the Secretary of State may, with the consent of the Treasury, give directions to the body with respect to its accounts and the audit of its accounts, and*
- *(b) it is the duty of the body to comply with the directions.*

(6) Whether or not the body is a company to which section 226 of the Companies Act 1985 applies—

- *(a) the Secretary of State may give directions to the body providing that any provisions of that Act specified in the directions are to apply to the body, with or without any modifications so specified, and*
- *(b) it is the duty of the body to comply with the directions.]*

Other supplementary provisions

11.—(1) The transfer of a function to a body established by a delegation order does not affect anything previously done in the exercise of the function transferred; and the resumption of a function so transferred does not affect anything previously done in exercise of the function resumed.

(2) The Secretary of State may by order make such transitional and other supplementary provision as he thinks necessary or expedient in relation to the transfer or resumption of a function.

(3) The provision that may be made in connection with the transfer of a function includes, in particular, provision—

- *(a) for modifying or excluding any provision of this Part of this Act in its application to the function transferred;*
- *(b) for applying to the body established by the delegation order, in connection with the function transferred, any provision applying to the Secretary of State which is contained in or made under any other enactment;*
- *(c) for the transfer of any property, rights or liabilities from the Secretary of State to that body;*
- *(d) for the carrying on and completion by that body of anything in process of being done by the Secretary of State when the order takes effect;*
- *(e) for the substitution of that body for the Secretary of State in any instrument, contract or legal proceedings.*

(4) The provision that may be made in connection with the resumption of a function includes, in particular, provision—

- *(a) for the transfer of any property, rights or liabilities from that body to the Secretary of State;*
- *(b) for the carrying on and completion by the Secretary of State of anything in process of being done by that body when the order takes effect;*
- *(c) for the substitution of the Secretary of State for that body in any instrument, contract or legal proceedings.*

12. Where a delegation order is revoked, the Secretary of State may by order make provision—

- *(a) for the payment of compensation to persons ceasing to be employed by the body established by the delegation order; and*
- *(b) as to the winding up and dissolution of the body.*

[13.—(1) This paragraph applies where the body is an unincorporated association.

(2) Any relevant proceedings may be brought by or against the body in the name of any body corporate whose constitution provides for the establishment of the body.

(3) In sub-paragraph (2) "relevant proceedings" means proceedings brought in or in connection with the exercise of any transferred function.

(4) In relation to proceedings brought as mentioned in sub-paragraph (2), any reference in paragraph 11(3)(e) or (4)(c) to the body replacing or being replaced by the Secretary of State in any legal proceedings is to be read with the appropriate modifications.]

[871]–[873]

NOTES

Repealed by the Companies Act 2006, s 1295, Sch 16, as from a day to be appointed.

Para 1: substituted by the Companies (Audit, Investigations and Community Enterprise) Act 2004, s 5(1), (2), as from 1 January 2005.

Para 10: sub-paras (2A), (5), (6) inserted by the Companies (Audit, Investigations and Community Enterprise) Act 2004, s 5(1), (3), as from 1 January 2005.

Para 11: word in square brackets substituted by the Companies (Audit, Investigations and Community Enterprise) Act 2004, s 5(1), (4), as from 1 January 2005.

Para 13: added by the Companies (Audit, Investigations and Community Enterprise) Act 2004, s 5(1), (5), as from 1 January 2005.

Orders: the Companies Act 1989 (Delegation) Order 2005, SI 2005/2337 at **[7444]**.

(Sch 14 repealed by the Competition Act 1998 and other enactments (Amendment) Regulations 2004, SI 2004/1261, reg 5, Sch 2, para 2(1), (2), as from 1 May 2004; Sch 15 inserts CA 1985, Pt XXIII, Chapter III (ss 703A–703N) at **[554]** *et seq, as from a day to be*

appointed (and is repealed by the Companies Act 2006, ss 1180, 1295, Sch 16, as from a day to be appointed); Sch 16 (which is repealed by CA 2006, ss 1180, 1295, Sch 16, as from a day to be appointed) makes the following amendments: para 1 amends legislation outside the scope of this work; para 1A (as inserted by the Oversea Companies and Credit and Financial Institutions (Branch Disclosure) Regulations 1992, SI 1992/3179, reg 4, Sch 3, para 16) amends CA 1985, s 695A(1) at **[542]**, *as from a day to be appointed; para 2 amends CA 1985, Sch 24 at* **[689]**, *as from a day to be appointed; para 3 amends the Insolvency Act 1986, ss 45, 53, 54, 62 at* **[3201]**, **[3209]**, **[3210]**, **[3218]**, *as from a day to be appointed; para 4 amends the Company Directors Disqualification Act 1986, Sch 1, Pt I at* **[767]**, *as from a day to be appointed; Sch 17 (which is repealed by CA 2006, s 1295, Sch 16, as from 6 April 2007 (certain purposes), and as from a day to be appointed (otherwise)) makes the following amendments: paras 1–7 amend CA 1985, ss 38–41 at* **[44]**–**[47]** *and substitute ss 186, 188, 350(1) of the 1985 Act, at* **[172]**, **[174]**, **[361]**; *paras 8–10 amend CA 1985, ss 462, 466 at* **[496]**, **[500]** *and the Insolvency Act 1986, s 3 at* **[3155]**.)

SCHEDULE 18
"SUBSIDIARY" AND RELATED EXPRESSIONS: CONSEQUENTIAL AMENDMENTS AND SAVINGS

Section 144(4)

1.–31. (*Contain minor amendments to provisions that are outside the scope of this work.*)

Companies Act 1985 (c 6)

32.—(1) The following provisions have effect with respect to the operation of section 23 of the Companies Act 1985 (prohibition on subsidiary being a member of its holding company).

(2) In relation to times, circumstances and purposes before the commencement of section 144(1) of this Act, the references in section 23 to a subsidiary or holding company shall be construed in accordance with section 736 of the Companies Act 1985 as originally enacted.

(3) Where a body corporate becomes or ceases to be a subsidiary of a holding company by reason of section 144(1) coming into force, the prohibition in section 23 of the Companies Act 1985 shall apply (in the absence of exempting circumstances), or cease to apply, accordingly.

33. (amends CA 1985, s 153 at **[139]**.)

34. Section 293 of the Companies Act 1985 (age limit for directors) does not apply in relation to a director of a company if—

(*a*) *he had attained the age of 70 before the commencement of section 144(1) of this Act, and*

(*b*) *the company became a subsidiary of a public company by reason only of the commencement of that subsection.*

35. Nothing in section 144(1) affects the operation of Part XIIIA of the Companies Act 1985 (takeover offers) in relation to a takeover offer made before the commencement of that subsection.

36. For the purposes of section 719 of the Companies Act 1985 (power to provide for employees on transfer or cessation of business), a company which immediately before the commencement of section 144(1) was a subsidiary of another company shall not be treated as ceasing to be such a subsidiary by reason of that subsection coming into force.

37. For the purposes of section 743 of the Companies Act 1985 (meaning of "employees' share scheme"), a company which immediately before the commencement of section 144(1) was a subsidiary of another company shall not be treated as ceasing to be such a subsidiary by reason of that subsection coming into force.

38. In Schedule 25 to the Companies Act 1985 "subsidiary" has the meaning given by section 736 of that Act as originally enacted.

39.–47. (*Contain minor amendments to provisions that are outside the scope of this work.*)
[874]–[875]

NOTES

Paras 32–38: repealed by the Companies Act 2006, s 1295, Sch 16, as from 1 October 2007 (in so far as relating to paras 34–36), and as from a day to be appointed (otherwise).

(Sch 19 (Minor Amendments of the Companies Act 1985) makes various amendments to CA 1985 which have been incorporated at the appropriate place (note that most of this Schedule is repealed by the Companies Act 2006, s 1295, Sch 16, as from 1 October 2007 (in part), and as from a day to be appointed (otherwise), though a small number of paragraphs remain in force for limited purposes); Sch 20 (Amendments about Mergers and Related Matters) this Schedule has been repealed, or is spent, except in so far as it relates to a minor amendment to the Fair Trading Act 1973, s 132; Schs 21–23 repealed by SI 2001/3649, art 75(p)–(r), as from 1 December 2001; Sch 24 contains various repeals to the Harbours Act 1964, the Fair Trading Act 1973, CA 1985, IA 1985, IA 1986, the Building Societies Act 1986, the Company Directors Disqualification Act 1986, FSA 1986, the Banking Act 1987, the Criminal Justice (Scotland) Act 1987, ICTA 1988, the Criminal Justice Act 1988, and the Copyright, Designs and Patents Act 1988 and, in so far as relevant to this work, are incorporated at the appropriate place.)

APPENDIX
COMMENCEMENT DATES OF COMPANIES ACT 1989 (NOTE)

NOTES

The Appendix of commencement dates for the Companies Act 1989 has been omitted from this edition in order to create space for other legislation (ie, the Companies Act 2006 and the associated destination and derivation tables). The Appendix has not changed since 1 July 2006 and is reproduced in the CD version of this work (which may be ordered from the LexisNexis Butterworths Customer Services Department) and can be accessed online at www.lexisnexis.com/uk/legal.

[876]

CRIMINAL JUSTICE ACT 1993

(1993 c 36)

NOTES

This Act is reproduced as amended by: the Drug Trafficking Act 1994; the Financial Services and Markets Act 2000 (Consequential Amendments and Repeals) Order 2001, SI 2001/3649; the Financial Services and Markets Act 2000 (Market Abuse) Regulations 2005, SI 2005/381.

ARRANGEMENT OF SECTIONS

PART V
INSIDER DEALING

The offence of insider dealing

Interpretation

Miscellaneous

PART VII
SUPPLEMENTARY

SCHEDULES

An Act to make provision about the jurisdiction of courts in England and Wales in relation to certain offences of dishonesty and blackmail; to amend the law about drug trafficking offences and to implement provisions of the Community Council Directive No 91/308/EEC; to amend Part VI of the Criminal Justice Act 1988; to make provision with respect to the financing of terrorism, the proceeds of terrorist-related activities and the investigation of terrorist activities; to amend Part I of the Criminal Justice Act 1991; to implement provisions of the Community Council Directive No 89/592/EEC and to amend and restate the law about insider dealing in securities; to provide for certain offences created by the Banking Coordination (Second Council Directive) Regulations 1992 to be punishable in the same way as offences under sections 39, 40 and 41 of the Banking Act 1987 and to enable regulations implementing Article 15 of the Community Council Directive No 89/646/EEC and Articles 3, 6 and 7 of the Community Council Directive No 92/30/EEC to create offences punishable in that way; to make provision with respect to the penalty for causing death by dangerous driving or causing death by careless driving while under the influence of drink or drugs; to make it an offence to assist in or induce certain conduct which for the purposes of, or in connection with, the provisions of Community law is unlawful in another member State; to provide for the introduction of safeguards in connection with the return of persons under backing of warrants arrangements; to amend the Criminal Procedure (Scotland) Act 1975 and Part I of the Prisoners and Criminal Proceedings (Scotland) Act 1993; and for connected purposes

[27 July 1993]

NOTES

Only those provisions of this Act relating to company law are reproduced. Provisions not reproduced are not annotated.

PART V
INSIDER DEALING

The offence of insider dealing

52 The offence

(1) An individual who has information as an insider is guilty of insider dealing if, in the circumstances mentioned in subsection (3), he deals in securities that are price-affected securities in relation to the information.

(2) An individual who has information as an insider is also guilty of insider dealing if—

(a) he encourages another person to deal in securities that are (whether or not that other knows it) price-affected securities in relation to the information, knowing or having reasonable cause to believe that the dealing would take place in the circumstances mentioned in subsection (3); or

(b) he discloses the information, otherwise than in the proper performance of the functions of his employment, office or profession, to another person.

(3) The circumstances referred to above are that the acquisition or disposal in question occurs on a regulated market, or that the person dealing relies on a professional intermediary or is himself acting as a professional intermediary.

(4) This section has effect subject to section 53.

[877]

53 Defences

(1) An individual is not guilty of insider dealing by virtue of dealing in securities if he shows—

(a) that he did not at the time expect the dealing to result in a profit attributable to the fact that the information in question was price-sensitive information in relation to the securities, or
(b) that at the time he believed on reasonable grounds that the information had been disclosed widely enough to ensure that none of those taking part in the dealing would be prejudiced by not having the information, or
(c) that he would have done what he did even if he had not had the information.

(2) An individual is not guilty of insider dealing by virtue of encouraging another person to deal in securities if he shows—
(a) that he did not at the time expect the dealing to result in a profit attributable to the fact that the information in question was price-sensitive information in relation to the securities, or
(b) that at the time he believed on reasonable grounds that the information had been or would be disclosed widely enough to ensure that none of those taking part in the dealing would be prejudiced by not having the information, or
(c) that he would have done what he did even if he had not had the information.

(3) An individual is not guilty of insider dealing by virtue of a disclosure of information if he shows—
(a) that he did not at the time expect any person, because of the disclosure, to deal in securities in the circumstances mentioned in subsection (3) of section 52; or
(b) that, although he had such an expectation at the time, he did not expect the dealing to result in a profit attributable to the fact that the information was price-sensitive information in relation to the securities.

(4) Schedule 1 (special defences) shall have effect.

(5) The Treasury may by order amend Schedule 1.

(6) In this section references to a profit include references to the avoidance of a loss.
[878]

Interpretation

54 Securities to which Part V applies

(1) This Part applies to any security which—
(a) falls within any paragraph of Schedule 2; and
(b) satisfies any conditions applying to it under an order made by the Treasury for the purposes of this subsection;

and in the provisions of this Part (other than that Schedule) any reference to a security is a reference to a security to which this Part applies.

(2) The Treasury may by order amend Schedule 2.
[879]

NOTES

Orders: the Insider Dealing (Securities and Regulated Markets) Order 1994, SI 1994/187 at **[6767]**.

---

55 "Dealing" in securities

(1) For the purposes of this Part, a person deals in securities if—
(a) he acquires or disposes of the securities (whether as principal or agent); or
(b) he procures, directly or indirectly, an acquisition or disposal of the securities by any other person.

(2) For the purposes of this Part, "acquire", in relation to a security, includes—
(a) agreeing to acquire the security; and
(b) entering into a contract which creates the security.

(3) For the purposes of this Part, "dispose", in relation to a security, includes—
(a) agreeing to dispose of the security; and
(b) bringing to an end a contract which created the security.

(4) For the purposes of subsection (1), a person procures an acquisition or disposal of a security if the security is acquired or disposed of by a person who is—

(a) his agent,
(b) his nominee, or
(c) a person who is acting at his direction,

in relation to the acquisition or disposal.

(5) Subsection (4) is not exhaustive as to the circumstances in which one person may be regarded as procuring an acquisition or disposal of securities by another.

[880]

56 "Inside information", etc

(1) For the purposes of this section and section 57, "inside information" means information which—

(a) relates to particular securities or to a particular issuer of securities or to particular issuers of securities and not to securities generally or to issuers of securities generally;
(b) is specific or precise;
(c) has not been made public; and
(d) if it were made public would be likely to have a significant effect on the price of any securities.

(2) For the purposes of this Part, securities are "price-affected securities" in relation to inside information, and inside information is "price-sensitive information" in relation to securities, if and only if the information would, if made public, be likely to have a significant effect on the price of the securities.

(3) For the purposes of this section "price" includes value.

[881]

57 "Insiders"

(1) For the purposes of this Part, a person has information as an insider if and only if—

(a) it is, and he knows that it is, inside information, and
(b) he has it, and knows that he has it, from an inside source.

(2) For the purposes of subsection (1), a person has information from an inside source if and only if—

(a) he has it through—
  (i) being a director, employee or shareholder of an issuer of securities; or
  (ii) having access to the information by virtue of his employment, office or profession; or
(b) the direct or indirect source of his information is a person within paragraph (a).

[882]

58 Information "made public"

(1) For the purposes of section 56, "made public", in relation to information, shall be construed in accordance with the following provisions of this section; but those provisions are not exhaustive as to the meaning of that expression.

(2) Information is made public if—

(a) it is published in accordance with the rules of a regulated market for the purpose of informing investors and their professional advisers;
(b) it is contained in records which by virtue of any enactment are open to inspection by the public;
(c) it can be readily acquired by those likely to deal in any securities—
  (i) to which the information relates, or
  (ii) of an issuer to which the information relates; or
(d) it is derived from information which has been made public.

(3) Information may be treated as made public even though—

(a) it can be acquired only by persons exercising diligence or expertise;
(b) it is communicated to a section of the public and not to the public at large;
(c) it can be acquired only by observation;
(d) it is communicated only on payment of a fee; or
(e) it is published only outside the United Kingdom.

[883]

59 "Professional intermediary"

(1) For the purposes of this Part, a "professional intermediary" is a person—

(a) who carries on a business consisting of an activity mentioned in subsection (2) and who holds himself out to the public or any section of the public (including a section of the public constituted by persons such as himself) as willing to engage in any such business; or

(b) who is employed by a person falling within paragraph (a) to carry out any such activity.

(2) The activities referred to in subsection (1) are—

(a) acquiring or disposing of securities (whether as principal or agent); or

(b) acting as an intermediary between persons taking part in any dealing in securities.

(3) A person is not to be treated as carrying on a business consisting of an activity mentioned in subsection (2)—

(a) if the activity in question is merely incidental to some other activity not falling within subsection (2); or

(b) merely because he occasionally conducts one of those activities.

(4) For the purposes of section 52, a person dealing in securities relies on a professional intermediary if and only if a person who is acting as a professional intermediary carries out an activity mentioned in subsection (2) in relation to that dealing.

[884]

60 Other interpretation provisions

(1) For the purposes of this Part, "regulated market" means any market, however operated, which, by an order made by the Treasury, is identified (whether by name or by reference to criteria prescribed by the order) as a regulated market for the purposes of this Part.

(2) For the purposes of this Part an "issuer", in relation to any securities, means any company, public sector body or individual by which or by whom the securities have been or are to be issued.

(3) For the purposes of this Part—

(a) "company" means any body (whether or not incorporated and wherever incorporated or constituted) which is not a public sector body; and

(b) "public sector body" means—

(i) the government of the United Kingdom, of Northern Ireland or of any country or territory outside the United Kingdom;

(ii) a local authority in the United Kingdom or elsewhere;

(iii) any international organisation the members of which include the United Kingdom or another member state;

(iv) the Bank of England; or

(v) the central bank of any sovereign State.

(4) For the purposes of this Part, information shall be treated as relating to an issuer of securities which is a company not only where it is about the company but also where it may affect the company's business prospects.

[885]

NOTES

Orders: the Insider Dealing (Securities and Regulated Markets) Order 1994, SI 1994/187 at **[6767]**.

Miscellaneous

61 Penalties and prosecution

(1) An individual guilty of insider dealing shall be liable—

(a) on summary conviction, to a fine not exceeding the statutory maximum or imprisonment for a term not exceeding six months or to both; or

(b) on conviction on indictment, to a fine or imprisonment for a term not exceeding seven years or to both.

(2) Proceedings for offences under this Part shall not be instituted in England and Wales except by or with the consent of—

(a) the Secretary of State; or

(b) the Director of Public Prosecutions.

(3) In relation to proceedings in Northern Ireland for offences under this Part, subsection (2) shall have effect as if the reference to the Director of Public Prosecutions were a reference to the Director of Public Prosecutions for Northern Ireland.

[886]

62 Territorial scope of offence of insider dealing

(1) An individual is not guilty of an offence falling within subsection (1) of section 52 unless—

(a) he was within the United Kingdom at the time when he is alleged to have done any act constituting or forming part of the alleged dealing;

(b) the regulated market on which the dealing is alleged to have occurred is one which, by an order made by the Treasury, is identified (whether by name or by reference to criteria prescribed by the order) as being, for the purposes of this Part, regulated in the United Kingdom; or

(c) the professional intermediary was within the United Kingdom at the time when he is alleged to have done anything by means of which the offence is alleged to have been committed.

(2) An individual is not guilty of an offence falling within subsection (2) of section 52 unless—

(a) he was within the United Kingdom at the time when he is alleged to have disclosed the information or encouraged the dealing; or

(b) the alleged recipient of the information or encouragement was within the United Kingdom at the time when he is alleged to have received the information or encouragement.

[887]

NOTES

Orders: the Insider Dealing (Securities and Regulated Markets) Order 1994, SI 1994/187 at **[6767]**.

63 Limits on section 52

(1) Section 52 does not apply to anything done by an individual acting on behalf of a public sector body in pursuit of monetary policies or policies with respect to exchange rates or the management of public debt or foreign exchange reserves.

(2) No contract shall be void or unenforceable by reason only of section 52.

[888]

64 Orders

(1) Any power under this Part to make an order shall be exercisable by statutory instrument.

(2) No order shall be made under this Part unless a draft of it has been laid before and approved by a resolution of each House of Parliament.

(3) An order under this Part—

(a) may make different provision for different cases; and

(b) may contain such incidental, supplemental and transitional provisions as the Treasury consider expedient.

[889]

PART VII
SUPPLEMENTARY

78 Commencement etc

(1) Sections 70 and 71 shall come into force at the end of the period of two months beginning with the day on which this Act is passed.

(2) Sections 68, 69, 75, 76 and 79(1) to (12), paragraph 2 of Schedule 5 and, in so far as relating to the Criminal Procedure (Scotland) Act 1975, and the Prisoners and Criminal Proceedings (Scotland) Act 1993, Schedule 6, shall come into force on the passing of this Act.

(3) The other provisions of this Act shall come into force on such day as may be appointed by the Secretary of State by an order made by statutory instrument.

(4) Different days may be appointed under subsection (3) for different provisions and different purposes.

(5)–(9) (*Outside the scope of this work.*)

(10) An order under subsection (3) may contain such transitional provisions and savings as the Secretary of State considers appropriate.

(11), (12) (*Outside the scope of this work.*)

[890]

NOTES

Orders: the relevant commencement order is the Criminal Justice Act 1993 (Commencement No 5) Order 1994, SI 1994/242 which brought Pt V (including Schs 1, 2) into force on 1 March 1994.

79 Short title, extent etc

(1) This Act may be cited as the Criminal Justice Act 1993.

(2) The following provisions of this Act extend to the United Kingdom—

Part V;

sections 21(1) and (3)(h), 23, … 45 to 51, 70 to 72, 77, 78 and this section;

Schedules 1 and 2; and

paragraphs 4 … and 6 of Schedule 4.

(3)–(14) (*Outside the scope of this work.*)

[891]

NOTES

Sub-s (2): words omitted repealed by the Drug Trafficking Act 1994, ss 65(1), 67(1), Sch 1, para 30(1)–(3), Sch 3, as from 3 February 1995.

SCHEDULES

SCHEDULE 1
SPECIAL DEFENCES

Section 53(4)

Market makers

1.—(1) An individual is not guilty of insider dealing by virtue of dealing in securities or encouraging another person to deal if he shows that he acted in good faith in the course of—

(a) his business as a market maker, or

(b) his employment in the business of a market maker.

(2) A market maker is a person who—

(a) holds himself out at all normal times in compliance with the rules of a regulated market or an approved organisation as willing to acquire or dispose of securities; and

(b) is recognised as doing so under those rules.

(3) In this paragraph "approved organisation" means an international securities self-regulating organisation approved [by the Treasury under any relevant order under section 22 of the Financial Services and Markets Act 2000].

Market information

2.—(1) An individual is not guilty of insider dealing by virtue of dealing in securities or encouraging another person to deal if he shows that—

(a) the information which he had as an insider was market information; and

(b) it was reasonable for an individual in his position to have acted as he did despite having that information as an insider at the time.

(2) In determining whether it is reasonable for an individual to do any act despite having market information at the time, there shall, in particular, be taken into account—

(a) the content of the information;

(b) the circumstances in which he first had the information and in what capacity; and

(c) the capacity in which he now acts.

3. An individual is not guilty of insider dealing by virtue of dealing in securities or encouraging another person to deal if he shows—

(a) that he acted—

(i) in connection with an acquisition or disposal which was under consideration or the subject of negotiation, or in the course of a series of such acquisitions or disposals; and

(ii) with a view to facilitating the accomplishment of the acquisition or disposal or the series of acquisitions or disposals; and

(b) that the information which he had as an insider was market information arising directly out of his involvement in the acquisition or disposal or series of acquisitions or disposals.

4. For the purposes of paragraphs 2 and 3 market information is information consisting of one or more of the following facts—

(a) that securities of a particular kind have been or are to be acquired or disposed of, or that their acquisition or disposal is under consideration or the subject of negotiation;

(b) that securities of a particular kind have not been or are not to be acquired or disposed of;

(c) the number of securities acquired or disposed of or to be acquired or disposed of or whose acquisition or disposal is under consideration or the subject of negotiation;

(d) the price (or range of prices) at which securities have been or are to be acquired or disposed of or the price (or range of prices) at which the securities whose acquisition or disposal is under consideration or the subject of negotiation may be acquired or disposed of;

(e) the identity of the persons involved or likely to be involved in any capacity in an acquisition or disposal.

Price stabilisation

5.—(1) An individual is not guilty of insider dealing by virtue of dealing in securities or encouraging another person to deal if he shows that he acted in conformity with the price stabilisation rules [or with the relevant provisions of Commission Regulation (EC) No 2273/2003 of 22 December 2003 implementing Directive 2003/6/EC of the European Parliament and of the Council as regards exemptions for buy-back programmes and stabilisation of financial instruments].

[(2) "Price stabilisation rules" means rules made under section 144(1) of the Financial Services and Markets Act 2000.]

[892]

NOTES

Para 1: words in square brackets in sub-para (3) substituted by the Financial Services and Markets Act 2000 (Consequential Amendments and Repeals) Order 2001, SI 2001/3649, art 341(1), (2), as from 1 December 2001.

Para 5: words in square brackets in sub-para (1) added by the Financial Services and Markets Act 2000 (Market Abuse) Regulations 2005, SI 2005/381, reg 3, as from 17 March 2005; sub-para (2) substituted by SI 2001/3649, art 341(1), (3), as from 1 December 2001.

SCHEDULE 2
SECURITIES

Section 54

Shares

1. Shares and stock in the share capital of a company ("shares").

Debt securities

2. Any instrument creating or acknowledging indebtedness which is issued by a company or public sector body, including, in particular, debentures, debenture stock, loan stock, bonds and certificates of deposit ("debt securities").

Warrants

3. Any right (whether conferred by warrant or otherwise) to subscribe for shares or debt securities ("warrants").

Depositary receipts

4.—(1) The rights under any depositary receipt.

(2) For the purposes of sub-paragraph (1) a "depositary receipt" means a certificate or other record (whether or not in the form of a document)—
- (a) which is issued by or on behalf of a person who holds any relevant securities of a particular issuer; and
- (b) which acknowledges that another person is entitled to rights in relation to the relevant securities or relevant securities of the same kind.

(3) In sub-paragraph (2) "relevant securities" means shares, debt securities and warrants.

Options

5. Any option to acquire or dispose of any security falling within any other paragraph of this Schedule.

Futures

6.—(1) Rights under a contract for the acquisition or disposal of relevant securities under which delivery is to be made at a future date and at a price agreed when the contract is made.

(2) In sub-paragraph (1)—
- (a) the references to a future date and to a price agreed when the contract is made include references to a date and a price determined in accordance with terms of the contract; and
- (b) "relevant securities" means any security falling within any other paragraph of this Schedule.

Contracts for differences

7.—(1) Rights under a contract which does not provide for the delivery of securities but whose purpose or pretended purpose is to secure a profit or avoid a loss by reference to fluctuations in—
- (a) a share index or other similar factor connected with relevant securities;
- (b) the price of particular relevant securities; or
- (c) the interest rate offered on money placed on deposit.

(2) In sub-paragraph (1) "relevant securities" means any security falling within any other paragraph of this Schedule.

[893]

NOTES

Modification: the reference in para 2 to securities, instruments or investments creating or acknowledging indebtedness (or creating or acknowledging a present or future indebtedness) includes a reference to uncertificated units of eligible debt securities; see the Uncertificated Securities (Amendment) (Eligible Debt Securities) Regulations 2003, SI 2003/1633, reg 15, Sch 2, para 8.

COMPANIES (AUDIT, INVESTIGATIONS AND COMMUNITY ENTERPRISE) ACT 2004

(2004 c 27)

NOTES

This Act is reproduced as amended by: the Charities Act 2006; the Companies Act 2006; the Prospectus Regulations 2005, SI 2005/1433; the Companies (Audit, Investigations and Community Enterprise) (Northern Ireland) Order 2005, SI 2005/1967; the Charities and Trustee Investment (Scotland) Act 2005 (Consequential Provisions and Modifications) Order 2006, SI 2006/242; the Companies Act 2006 (Commencement No 2, Consequential Amendments, Transitional Provisions and Savings) Order 2007, SI 2007/1093. See also the prospective amendments made to this Act by the draft Companies Act 2006 (Commencement No 3, Consequential Amendments, Transitional Provisions and Savings) Order 2007 (see **[A12]**).

Commencement: see s 65 at **[938]** and the Orders noted thereto. Where any provision in this work (including any inserted or substituted provision) came into force for all purposes on or before 1 July 2005, commencement information is not noted at provision level.

Offences under this Act: see further the Companies Act 2006, ss 1131 at **[S1131]**.

ARRANGEMENT OF SECTIONS

An Act to amend the law relating to company auditors and accounts, to the provision that may be made in respect of certain liabilities incurred by a company's officers, and to company investigations; to make provision for community interest companies; and for connected purposes

[28 October 2004]

PART 1
AUDITORS, ACCOUNTS, DIRECTORS' LIABILITIES AND INVESTIGATIONS

1–7 (*Ss 1–7* (*Chap 1*) *which are repealed by the Companies Act 2006, s 1295, Sch 16, as from a day to be appointed make the following amendments: s 1 amends CA 1989, Sch 11, Pt 2 at* **[868]**; *s 3 adds CA 1989, Sch 11, Pt 3 at* **[868A]**; *s 3 amends CA 1989, s 46 at* **[795]**; *s 4 inserts CA 1989, s 46A at* **[796A]**; *s 5 amends CA 1989, Sch 13 at* **[871]**; *s 6 amends CA 1989, s 33 at* **[782]**; *s 7 substitutes CA 1985, s 390B at* **[415]**, *and amends s 390A and Sch 4A at* **[414]**, **[643]**.)

CHAPTER 2
ACCOUNTS AND REPORTS

8–13 *(Ss 8–13 which are repealed by the Companies Act 2006, s 1295, Sch 16, as from a day to be appointed make the following amendments: s 8 substitutes CA 1985, s 389A at* **[412]***; s 9 amends CA 1985, s 234 at* **[220]***, and inserts s 234ZA at* **[220A]***; s 10 amends CA 1985, s 245C at* **[237]***; s 11 inserts CA 1985, ss 245D, 245E at* **[237A]**, **[237B]***, and amends the Companies (Northern Ireland) Order 1986, SI 1986/1032 (NI 6); s 12 inserts CA 1985, ss 245F, 245G at* **[237C]**, **[237D]***, and introduces Sch 1 to this Act (which inserts CA 1985, Sch 7B); s 13 amends CA 1985, s 257 at* **[261]**.)

Supervision of accounts and reports

14 Supervision of periodic accounts and reports of issuers of listed securities

(1) The Secretary of State may make an order appointing a body ("the prescribed body") to exercise the functions mentioned in subsection (2).

(2) The functions are—
- (a) keeping under review periodic accounts and reports that are produced by issuers of [transferable] securities and are required to comply with any accounting requirements imposed by [Part 6] rules; and
- (b) if the prescribed body thinks fit, informing the Financial Services Authority of any conclusions reached by the body in relation to any such accounts or report.

(3) A body may be appointed under this section if it is a body corporate or an unincorporated association which appears to the Secretary of State—
- (a) to have an interest in, and to have satisfactory procedures directed to, monitoring compliance by issuers of [transferable] securities with accounting requirements imposed by [Part 6] rules in relation to periodic accounts and reports produced by such issuers; and
- (b) otherwise to be a fit and proper body to be appointed.

(4) But where the order is to contain any requirements or other provisions specified under subsection (8), the Secretary of State may not appoint a body unless, in addition, it appears to him that the body would, if appointed, exercise its functions as a prescribed body in accordance with any such requirements or provisions.

(5) A body may be appointed either generally or in respect of any of the following, namely—
- (a) any particular class or classes of issuers,
- (b) any particular class or classes of periodic accounts or reports,

and different bodies may be appointed in respect of different classes within either or both of paragraphs (a) and (b).

(6) In relation to the appointment of a body in respect of any such class or classes, subsections (2) and (3) are to be read as referring to issuers, or (as the case may be) to periodic accounts or reports, of the class or classes concerned.

(7) Where—
- (a) a body is so appointed, but
- (b) the Financial Services Authority requests the body to exercise its functions under subsection (2) in relation to any particular issuer of [transferable] securities in relation to whom those functions would not otherwise be exercisable,

the body is to exercise those functions in relation to that issuer as well.

(8) An order under this section may contain such requirements or other provisions relating to the exercise of functions by the prescribed body as appear to the Secretary of State to be appropriate.

(9) If the prescribed body is an unincorporated association, any relevant proceedings may be brought by or against that body in the name of any body corporate whose constitution provides for the establishment of the body.

For this purpose "relevant proceedings" means proceedings brought in or in connection with the exercise of any function by the body as a prescribed body.

(10) Where an appointment is revoked, the revoking order may make such provision as the Secretary of State thinks fit with respect to pending proceedings.

(11) The power to make an order under this section is exercisable by statutory instrument subject to annulment in pursuance of a resolution of either House of Parliament.

(12) In this section—

[["Part 6 Rules" has] have the meaning given by section 103(1) of the Financial Services and Markets Act 2000 (c 8) (interpretation of Part 6);

["issuer" has the meaning given by section 102A(6) of that Act;]]

"periodic" accounts and reports means accounts and reports which are required by [Part 6] rules to be produced periodically;

["transferable securities" has the meaning given by section 102A(3) of that Act]. **[894]**

NOTES

Sub-ss (2), (3), (7): words in square brackets substituted by the Companies Act 2006, s 1272, Sch 15, Pt 2, paras 13, 14(1)–(4), as from 8 November 2006.

Sub-s (12): words in first (outer) pair of square brackets substituted by the Prospectus Regulations 2005, SI 2005/1433, reg 2(3), Sch 3, para 5, as from 1 July 2005; other words in square brackets substituted, and definition "transferable securities" inserted, by the Companies Act 2006, s 1272, Sch 15, Pt 2, paras 13, 14(1), (5), as from 8 November 2006.

Orders: the Supervision of Accounts and Reports (Prescribed Body) Order 2005, SI 2005/715 at **[7394]**.

15 Application of provisions inserted by sections 11 and 12 to bodies appointed under section 14

(1) The following provisions apply, in accordance with this section, in relation to prescribed bodies and their functions under section 14 of this Act—

(a) sections 245D and 245E of the Companies Act 1985 (c 6) (as inserted by section 11(1) of this Act),

(b) Articles 253D and 253E of the Companies (Northern Ireland) Order 1986 (SI 1986/1032 (NI 6)) (as inserted by section 11(2) of this Act), and

(c) sections 245F and 245G of and Schedule 7B to the Companies Act 1985 (as inserted by section 12(1) of this Act)[, and

(d) Articles 253F and 253G of and Schedule 7B to the 1986 Order].

(2) Sections 245D and 245E apply in relation to prescribed bodies and their functions as they apply in relation to persons authorised under section 245C of that Act and persons authorised under Article 253C of the Companies (Northern Ireland) Order 1986 and the functions of such persons mentioned in sections 245D(3) and 245E(1).

But section 245E so applies as if subsection (2)(b) of that section were omitted.

(3) Articles 253D and 253E apply in relation to prescribed bodies and their functions as they apply in relation to persons authorised under Article 253C of that Order and persons authorised under section 245C of the Companies Act 1985 and the functions of such persons mentioned in Articles 253D(3) and 253E(1).

But Article 253E so applies as if paragraph (2)(b) of that Article were omitted.

(4) Sections 245F and 245G and Schedule 7B apply in relation to prescribed bodies and their functions as they apply in relation to persons authorised under section 245C of that Act and the functions of such persons mentioned in section 245F(2), section 245G(3)(a) and paragraph 16 of Schedule 7B.

(5) But section 245F so applies as if—

(a) subsection (1) of that section provided that the section applies where it appears to a prescribed body that there is, or may be, a question whether any relevant accounts or reports produced by an issuer of [transferable] securities comply with any accounting requirements imposed by [Part 6] rules;

(b) the references in section 245F(3)(a) and (b) to "the company" were references to that issuer; and

(c) the references in section 245F(4) and (5) to "the court" were to the High Court or, in Scotland, the Court of Session.

[(5A) Articles 253F and 253G of and Schedule 7B to the 1986 Order apply in relation to prescribed bodies and their functions as they apply in relation to persons authorised under Article 253C of that Order and the functions of such persons mentioned in Article 253F(2), Article 253G(3)(a) of and paragraph 16 of Schedule 7B to that Order.

(5B) But Article 253F so applies as if—

(a) paragraph (1) of that Article provided that the Article applies where it appears to a prescribed body that there is, or may be, a question whether any relevant accounts or reports produced by an issuer of [transferable] securities comply with any accounting requirements imposed by [Part 6] rules; and

(b) the references in Article 253F(3)(a) and (b) to "the company" were references to that issuer.]

(6) In subsection (5) [and subsection (5B)]—

(a) "relevant accounts or reports" means accounts or reports in relation to which the prescribed body has functions under section 14; and

(b) "issuer", ["Part 6 rules" and "transferable securities"] have the same meanings as in section 14.

(7) In this section "prescribed body" has the same meaning as in section 14.

[895]

NOTES

Sub-s (1): para (d) and the word immediately preceding it inserted by the Companies (Audit, Investigations and Community Enterprise) (Northern Ireland) Order 2005, SI 2005/1967, art 15(1), (2), as from a day to be appointed.

Sub-s (5): words in square brackets substituted by the Companies Act 2006, s 1272, Sch 15, Pt 2, paras 13, 15(1), (2), as from 8 November 2006.

Sub-s (5A): inserted, together with sub-s (5B), by SI 2005/1967, art 15(1), (3), as from a day to be appointed.

Sub-s (5B): inserted as noted above; words in square brackets substituted by the Companies Act 2006, s 1272, Sch 15, Pt 2, paras 13, 15(1), (3), as from 8 November 2006.

Sub-s (6): words in first pair of square brackets inserted by SI 2005/1967, art 15(1), (4), as from a day to be appointed; words in second pair of square brackets substituted by the Companies Act 2006, s 1272, Sch 15, Pt 2, paras 13, 15(1), (4), as from 8 November 2006.

Bodies concerned with accounting standards etc

16 Grants to bodies concerned with accounting standards etc

(1) The Secretary of State may make grants to any body carrying on activities concerned with any of the matters set out in subsection (2).

(2) The matters are—

(a) issuing accounting standards;

(b) issuing standards in respect of matters to be contained in reports required to be produced by auditors or company directors;

(c) investigating departures from standards within paragraph (a) or (b) or from the accounting requirements of the Companies Act 1985 (c 6) [or the 1986 Order] or any requirements of directly applicable Community legislation relating to company accounts;

(d) taking steps to secure compliance with such standards or requirements;

(e) keeping under review periodic accounts and reports that are produced by issuers of listed securities and are required to comply with any accounting requirements imposed by listing rules;

(f) establishing, maintaining or carrying out arrangements within *paragraph 17, 18, 19(1) or 20(1) of Schedule 11 to the Companies Act 1989* (*c 40*);

(g) exercising functions of the Secretary of State under *Part 2 of that Act*;

(h) carrying out investigations into public interest cases arising in connection with the performance of accountancy functions by members of professional accountancy bodies;

(i) holding disciplinary hearings relating to members of such bodies following the conclusion of such investigations;

(j) deciding whether (and, if so, what) disciplinary action should be taken against members of such bodies to whom such hearings related;

(k) supervising the exercise by such bodies of regulatory functions in relation to their members;

[(ka) exercising functions of the Independent Supervisor appointed under Chapter 3 of Part 42 of the Companies Act 2006;]

[(kb) establishing, maintaining or carrying out arrangements within paragraph 1 or 2 of Schedule 12 to the Companies Act 2006;]

[(l) issuing standards to be applied in actuarial work;
(m) issuing standards in respect of matters to be contained in reports or other communications required to be produced or made by actuaries or in accordance with standards within paragraph (l);
(n) investigating departures from standards within paragraph (l) or (m);
(o) taking steps to secure compliance with standards within paragraph (l) or (m);
(p) carrying out investigations into public interest cases arising in connection with the performance of actuarial functions by members of professional actuarial bodies;
(q) holding disciplinary hearings relating to members of professional actuarial bodies following the conclusion of investigations within paragraph (p);
(r) deciding whether (and, if so, what) disciplinary action should be taken against members of professional actuarial bodies to whom hearings within paragraph (q) related;
(s) supervising the exercise by professional actuarial bodies of regulatory functions in relation to their members;
(t) overseeing or directing any of the matters mentioned above.]

(3) A grant may be made to a body within subsection (1) in respect of any of its activities.

(4) For the purposes of this section—
(a) a body is to be regarded as carrying on any subsidiary activities of the body; and
(b) a body's "subsidiary activities" are activities carried on by any of its subsidiaries or by any body established under its constitution or under the constitution of such a subsidiary.

(5) In this section—

"accountancy functions" means functions performed as an accountant, whether in the capacity of auditor or otherwise;

"company" means a company within the meaning of the Companies Act 1985 (c 6) [or the 1986 Order];

["listed securities" and "listing rules" have the meaning given by section 103(1) of the Financial Services and Markets Act 2000 (c 8) (interpretation of Part 6);

"issuer", in relation to listed securities, has the meaning given by section 102A(6)(b) of the Financial Services and Markets Act 2000 (meaning of "securities" etc,);]

"professional accountancy body" means—
(a) a supervisory body which is recognised for the purposes of *Part 2 of the Companies Act 1989 (c 40)*, or
(b) a qualifying body, as defined by *section 32* of that Act, which enforces rules as to the performance of accountancy functions by its members,

and references to the members of professional accountancy bodies include persons who, although not members of such bodies, are subject to their rules in performing accountancy functions;

["professional actuarial body" means—
(a) the Institute of Actuaries, or
(b) the Faculty of Actuaries in Scotland,

and the "members" of a professional actuarial body include persons who, although not members of the body, are subject to its rules in performing actuarial functions;]

"public interest cases" means matters which raise or appear to raise important issues affecting the public interest;

"regulatory functions", in relation to professional accountancy bodies, means any of the following functions—
(a) investigatory or disciplinary functions exercised by such bodies in relation to the performance by their members of accountancy functions,
(b) the setting by such bodies of standards in relation to the performance by their members of accountancy functions, and
(c) the determining by such bodies of requirements in relation to the education and training of their members;

["regulatory functions", in relation to professional actuarial bodies, means any of the following—
(a) investigatory or disciplinary functions exercised by such bodies in relation to the performance by their members of actuarial functions,
(b) the setting by such bodies of standards in relation to the performance by their members of actuarial functions, and
(c) the determining by such bodies of requirements in relation to the education and training of their members;]

"subsidiary" has the meaning given by section 736 of the Companies Act 1985 [or Article 4 of the 1986 Order];

["the 1986 Order" means the Companies (Northern Ireland) Order 1986 (SI 1986/1032 (NI 6)).]

[(6) In their application to Scotland, subsection (2)(a) to (t) are to be read as referring only to matters provision relating to which would be outside the legislative competence of the Scottish Parliament.]

(7) …

[896]

NOTES

Sub-s (2) is amended as follows:

Words in square brackets in para (c) inserted by the Companies Act 2006, s 1276(1), (3), as from 8 November 2006.

For the words in italics in paras (f), (g) there are substituted the words "paragraph 21, 22, 23(1) or 24(1) of Schedule 10 to the Companies Act 2006" and "Part 42 of that Act" respectively, by the Companies Act 2006, s 1264, Sch 14, paras 1(1), (2), as from a day to be appointed.

Paras (ka), (kb) inserted by the Companies Act 2006, s 1238, 1247, as from a day to be appointed.

Paras (l)–(t) substituted, for original para (l), by the Companies Act 2006, s 1274(1), (2), as from 8 November 2006.

Sub-s (5) is amended as follows:

Words in square brackets in definitions "company" and "subsidiary" inserted by the Companies Act 2006, s 1276(1), (4)(a), (b), as from 8 November 2006.

Definitions "listed securities", "listing rules" and "issuer" substituted for the original definitions "issuer", "listing rules" and "security" by the Prospectus Regulations 2005, SI 2005/1433, reg 2(3), Sch 3, para 6, as from 1 July 2005.

For the words in italics in the definition "professional accountancy body" there are substituted the words "Part 42 of the Companies Act 2006" and "section 1220" respectively, by the Companies Act 2006, s 1264, Sch 14, paras 1(1), (2), as from a day to be appointed.

Definitions "professional actuarial body" and "regulatory functions" (in relation to professional actuarial bodies) inserted by the Companies Act 2006, s 1274(1), (3), as from 8 November 2006.

Definition "the 1986 Order" inserted by the Companies Act 2006, s 1276(1), (4)(c), as from 8 November 2006.

Sub-s (6): substituted by the Companies Act 2006, s 1276(1), (2), as from 8 November 2006.

Sub-s (7): repeals the Companies Act 1985, s 256(3).

17 Levy to pay expenses of bodies concerned with accounting standards etc

(1) For the purpose of meeting any part of the expenses of a grant-aided body, the Secretary of State may by regulations provide for a levy to be payable to that body ("the specified recipient") by bodies or persons which are specified, or are of a description specified, in the regulations.

(2) For the purposes of this section—

(a) "grant-aided body" means a body to whom the Secretary of State has paid, or is proposing to pay, grant under section 16; and

(b) any expenses of any body carrying on subsidiary activities of the grant-aided body (within the meaning of that section) are to be regarded as expenses of the grant-aided body.

(3) The power to specify (or to specify descriptions of) bodies or persons must be exercised in such a way that the levy is only payable by—

(a) bodies corporate to which[, or persons within subsection (3A) to whom,] the Secretary of State considers that any of the activities of the specified recipient, or any of its subsidiary activities, are relevant to a significant extent, or

(b) bodies or persons who the Secretary of State considers have a major interest in any of those activities being carried on.

[(3A) The following persons are within this subsection—

(a) the administrators of a public service pension scheme (within the meaning of section 1 of the Pension Schemes Act 1993);

(b) the trustees or managers of an occupational or personal pension scheme (within the meaning of that section).]

(4) Regulations under this section may in particular—

(a) specify the rate of the levy and the period in respect of which it is payable at that rate;

(b) make provision as to the times when, and the manner in which, payments are to be made in respect of the levy;

[(c) make different provision for different cases].

(5) In determining the rate of the levy payable in respect of a particular period, the Secretary of State—

(a) must take into account the amount of any grant which is to be or has been made to the specified recipient in respect of that period under section 16;

(b) may take into account estimated as well as actual expenses of that body in respect of that period.

(6) Any amount of levy payable by any body or person is a debt due from the body or person to the specified recipient, and is recoverable accordingly.

(7) The specified recipient must—

(a) keep proper accounts in respect of amounts of levy received, and

(b) prepare in relation to each levy period a statement of account relating to such amounts in such form and manner as is specified in the regulations.

(8) Those accounts must be audited, and the statement certified, by persons appointed by the Secretary of State.

(9) The power to make regulations under this section is exercisable by statutory instrument.

(10) Regulations to which this subsection applies may not be made unless a draft of the regulations has been laid before, and approved by a resolution of, each House of Parliament.

(11) Subsection (10) applies to—

(a) the first regulations under this section, and

(b) any other regulations under this section that would result in any change in the bodies or persons by whom the levy is payable.

(12) Otherwise, any statutory instrument containing regulations under this section is subject to annulment in pursuance of a resolution of either House of Parliament.

[(13) If a draft of any regulations to which subsection (10) applies would, apart from this subsection, be treated for the purposes of the standing orders of either House of Parliament as a hybrid instrument, it is to proceed in that House as if it were not such an instrument.]

[897]

NOTES

Sub-s (3): words in square brackets inserted by the Companies Act 2006, s 1275(1), (2), (6), as from a day to be appointed, subject to transitional provisions as noted below.

Sub-ss (3A), (13): inserted and added respectively by the Companies Act 2006, s 1275(1), (3), (5), (6), as from a day to be appointed, subject to transitional provisions as noted below.

Sub-s (4): para (c) inserted by the Companies Act 2006, s 1275(1), (4), (6), as from a day to be appointed, subject to transitional provisions as noted below.

Transitional provisions: the Companies Act 2006, s 1275(6) provides that the amendments made to this section by s 1275(1)–(5) of the 2006 Act have effect in relation to any exercise of the power to make Regulations under this section after s 1275 into force, regardless of when the expenses to be met by the levy in respect of which the Regulations are made were incurred.

18 Exemption from liability

(1) Where a grant has been paid by the Secretary of State to a body under section 16, this section prevents any liability in damages arising in respect of certain acts or omissions occurring during the period of 12 months beginning with the date on which the grant was paid.

(2) In this section—

"the exemption period" means the period of 12 months mentioned in subsection (1);

"a relevant body" means the body mentioned in that subsection or a body carrying on any subsidiary activities of that body (within the meaning of section 16);

"section 16(2) activities" means activities concerned with any of the matters set out in section 16(2).

(3) Neither a relevant body, nor any person who is (or is acting as) a member, officer or member of staff of a relevant body, is to be liable in damages for anything done, or omitted to be done, during the exemption period for the purposes of or in connection with—

(a) the carrying on of any section 16(2) activities of the body, or

(b) the purported carrying on of any such activities.

(4) Subsection (3) does not apply—

(a) if the act or omission is shown to have been in bad faith; or

(b) so as to prevent an award of damages in respect of the act or omission on the grounds that it was unlawful as a result of section 6(1) of the Human Rights Act 1998 (c 42) (acts of public authorities incompatible with Convention rights).

[898]

19–24 *((Chaps 3, 4): s 19 inserts CA 1985, ss 309A–309C at* **[307A]–[307C]** *and amends s 310 at* **[308]** *(and is repealed by the Companies Act 2006, s 1295, Sch 16, as from 1 October 2007 (in so far as elating to sub-s (1)), and as from a day to be appointed (otherwise)); s 20 inserts CA 1985, s 337A at* **[337A]** *(and is repealed by CA 2006, s 1295, Sch 16, as from 1 October 2007); s 21 substitutes CA 1985, s 447 at* **[480]***; s 22 inserts CA 1985, s 448A at* **[481A]***; s 23 inserts CA 1985, ss 453A, 453B at* **[487A]**, **[487B]***; s 24 inserts CA 1985, s 453C at* **[487C]**.)

CHAPTER 5
SUPPLEMENTARY

25 Minor and consequential amendments

(1) Schedule 2 (minor and consequential amendments relating to Part 1) has effect.

(2) That Schedule has effect subject to the modifications set out in subsection (3)—

(a) in relation to England and Wales, in the case of an offence committed before section 154(1) of the Criminal Justice Act 2003 (c 44) comes into force, and

(b) in relation to Scotland.

(3) The modifications are—

(a) the amendment in paragraph 10(2) has effect as if for "12 months" there were substituted "6 months";

(b) the amendment in paragraph 10(3) has effect as if for "12 months", in both places where it occurs, there were substituted "3 months";

(c) the amendment in paragraph 10(4) has effect as if for "12 months" there were substituted "6 months";

(d) the amendment in paragraph 26(2) has effect as if for "12 months" there were substituted "6 months"; and

(e) the amendment in paragraph 26(3) has effect as if for "12 months" there were substituted "6 months".

[899]

PART 2
COMMUNITY INTEREST COMPANIES

Introductory

26 Community interest companies

(1) There is to be a new type of company to be known as the community interest company.

(2) In accordance with this Part—

(a) a company limited by shares or a company limited by guarantee and not having a share capital may be formed as or become a community interest company, and

(b) a company limited by guarantee and having a share capital may become a community interest company.

(3) A community interest company established for charitable purposes is to be treated as not being so established and accordingly—

(a) is not [an English charity or a Northern Ireland charity], and

(b) must not be [entered in the Scottish Charity Register].

[900]

NOTES

Sub-s (3): words in square brackets in para (a) substituted by the Companies Act 2006 (Commencement No 2, Consequential Amendments, Transitional Provisions and Savings) Order 2007, SI 2007/1093, art 6(2), Sch 4, Pt 1, para 1, as from 6 April 2007; words in square brackets in para (b) substituted by the Charities and Trustee Investment (Scotland) Act 2005 (Consequential Provisions and Modifications) Order 2006, SI 2006/242, art 5, Schedule, Pt 1, para 8(1), (2), as from 1 April 2006.

27 Regulator

(1) There is to be an officer known as the Regulator of Community Interest Companies (referred to in this Part as "the Regulator").

(2) The Secretary of State must appoint a person to be the Regulator.

(3) The Regulator has such functions relating to community interest companies as are conferred or imposed by or by virtue of this Act or any other enactment.

(4) The Regulator must adopt an approach to the discharge of those functions which is based on good regulatory practice, that is an approach adopted having regard to—

- (a) the likely impact on those who may be affected by the discharge of those functions,
- (b) the outcome of consultations with, and with organisations representing, community interest companies and others with relevant experience, and
- (c) the desirability of using the Regulator's resources in the most efficient and economic way.

(5) The Regulator may issue guidance, or otherwise provide assistance, about any matter relating to community interest companies.

(6) The Secretary of State may require the Regulator to issue guidance or otherwise provide assistance about any matter relating to community interest companies which is specified by the Secretary of State.

(7) Any guidance issued under this section must be such that it is readily accessible to, and capable of being easily understood by, those at whom it is aimed; and any other assistance provided under this section must be provided in the manner which the Regulator considers is most likely to be helpful to those to whom it is provided.

(8) Schedule 3 (further provisions about the Regulator) has effect.

[901]

28 Appeal Officer

(1) There is to be an officer known as the Appeal Officer for Community Interest Companies (referred to in this Part as "the Appeal Officer").

(2) The Secretary of State must appoint a person to be the Appeal Officer.

(3) The Appeal Officer has the function of determining appeals against decisions and orders of the Regulator which under or by virtue of this Act or any other enactment lie to the Appeal Officer.

(4) An appeal to the Appeal Officer against a decision or order of the Regulator may be brought on the ground that the Regulator made a material error of law or fact.

(5) On such an appeal the Appeal Officer must—

- (a) dismiss the appeal,
- (b) allow the appeal, or
- (c) remit the case to the Regulator.

(6) Where a case is remitted the Regulator must reconsider it in accordance with any rulings of law and findings of fact made by the Appeal Officer.

(7) Schedule 4 (further provisions about the Appeal Officer) has effect.

[902]

29 Official Property Holder

(1) There is to be an officer known as the Official Property Holder for Community Interest Companies (referred to in this Part as "the Official Property Holder").

(2) The Regulator must appoint a member of the Regulator's staff to be the Official Property Holder.

(3) The Official Property Holder has such functions relating to property of community interest companies as are conferred or imposed by or by virtue of this Act or any other enactment.

(4) Schedule 5 (further provisions about the Official Property Holder) has effect.

[903]

Requirements

30 Cap on distributions and interest

(1) Community interest companies must not distribute assets to their members unless regulations make provision authorising them to do so.

(2) If regulations authorise community interest companies to distribute assets to their members, the regulations may impose limits on the extent to which they may do so.

(3) Regulations may impose limits on the payment of interest on debentures issued by, or debts of, community interest companies.

(4) Regulations under this section may make provision for limits to be set by the Regulator.

(5) The Regulator—

(a) may set a limit by reference to a rate determined by any other person (as it has effect from time to time), and

(b) may set different limits for different descriptions of community interest companies.

(6) The Regulator must (in accordance with section 27)—

(a) undertake appropriate consultation before setting a limit, and

(b) in setting a limit, have regard to its likely impact on community interest companies.

(7) Regulations under this section may include power for the Secretary of State to require the Regulator to review a limit or limits.

(8) Where the Regulator sets a limit he must publish notice of it in the Gazette.

[904]

NOTES

Regulations: the Community Interest Company Regulations 2005, SI 2005/1788 at **[7399]**.

31 Distribution of assets on winding up

(1) Regulations may make provision for and in connection with the distribution, on the winding up of a community interest company, of any assets of the company which remain after satisfaction of the company's liabilities.

(2) The regulations may, in particular, amend or modify the operation of any enactment or instrument.

[905]

NOTES

Regulations: the Community Interest Company Regulations 2005, SI 2005/1788 at **[7399]**.

32 Memorandum and articles

(1) The memorandum of a community interest company must state that the company is to be a community interest company.

(2) [Section 7(1) of the 1985 Act or Article 18(1) of the 1986 Order] (articles) applies in relation to a community interest company limited by shares as if it were a company limited by guarantee (so that articles must be registered).

(3) The memorandum and articles of a community interest company of any description—

(a) must at all times include such provisions as regulations require to be included in the memorandum and articles of every community interest company or a community interest company of that description, and

(b) must not include such provisions as regulations require not to be so included.

(4) The provisions required by regulations under subsection (3)(a) to be included in the memorandum or articles of a community interest company may (in particular) include—

(a) provisions about the transfer and distribution of the company's assets (including their distribution on a winding up),

(b) provisions about the payment of interest on debentures issued by the company or debts of the company,

(c) provisions about membership of the company,

(d) provisions about the voting rights of members of the company,

(e) provisions about the appointment and removal of directors of the company, and

(f) provisions about voting at meetings of directors of the company.

(5) The memorandum and articles of a community interest company are of no effect to the extent that they—

(a) are inconsistent with provisions required to be included in the memorandum or articles of the company by regulations under subsection (3)(a), or

(b) include provisions required not to be included by regulations under subsection (3)(b).

(6) Regulations may make provision for and in connection with restricting the ability of a community interest company under [section 4 of the 1985 Act or Article 15 of the 1986 Order] to alter its memorandum with respect to the statement of its objects.

[906]

NOTES

Sub-ss (2), (6): words in square brackets substituted by the Companies Act 2006 (Commencement No 2, Consequential Amendments, Transitional Provisions and Savings) Order 2007, SI 2007/1093, art 6(2), Sch 4, Pt 1, para 2, as from 6 April 2007.

Regulations: the Community Interest Company Regulations 2005, SI 2005/1788 at **[7399]**.

33 Names

(1) The name of a community interest company which is not a public company must end with—

(a) "community interest company", or

(b) "cic".

(2) But the name of such a company may (instead) end with—

(a) "cwmni buddiant cymunedol", or

(b) "cbc",

if the memorandum of the company states that the company's registered office is to be situated in Wales.

(3) The name of a community interest company which is a public company must end with—

(a) "community interest public limited company", or

(b) "community interest plc".

(4) But the name of such a company may (instead) end with—

(a) "cwmni buddiant cymunedol cyhoeddus cyfyngedig", or

(b) "cwmni buddiant cymunedol ccc",

if the memorandum of the company states that the company's registered office is to be situated in Wales.

(5) [Section 25 of the 1985 Act or Article 35 of the 1986 Order] (company name to end with "public limited company" or "limited" or equivalent) does not apply to community interest companies.

(6) Schedule 6 (further provisions about names) has effect.

[907]

NOTES

Sub-s (5): words in square brackets substituted by the Companies Act 2006 (Commencement No 2, Consequential Amendments, Transitional Provisions and Savings) Order 2007, SI 2007/1093, art 6(2), Sch 4, Pt 1, para 3, as from 6 April 2007.

34 Community interest company reports

(1) The directors of a community interest company must prepare in respect of each financial year a report about the company's activities during the financial year (a "community interest company report").

(2) [Section 242(1) of the 1985 Act or Article 250(1) of the 1986 Order] is to be treated as requiring the directors of a community interest company to deliver to the registrar of companies a copy of the community interest company report.

(3) Regulations—

(a) must make provision requiring community interest company reports to include information about the remuneration of directors,

(b) may make provision as to the form of, and other information to be included in, community interest company reports, and

(c) may apply provisions of [the 1985 Act or the 1986 Order] relating to directors' reports to community interest company reports (with any appropriate modifications).

(4) The registrar of companies must forward to the Regulator a copy of each community interest company report delivered to the registrar by virtue of this section.

[908]

NOTES

Sub-ss (2), (3): words in square brackets substituted by the Companies Act 2006 (Commencement No 2, Consequential Amendments, Transitional Provisions and Savings) Order 2007, SI 2007/1093, art 6(2), Sch 4, Pt 1, para 4, as from 6 April 2007.

Regulations: the Community Interest Company Regulations 2005, SI 2005/1788 at **[7399]**.

35 Community interest test and excluded companies

(1) This section has effect for the purposes of this Part.

(2) A company satisfies the community interest test if a reasonable person might consider that its activities are being carried on for the benefit of the community.

(3) An object stated in the memorandum of a company is a community interest object of the company if a reasonable person might consider that the carrying on of activities by the company in furtherance of the object is for the benefit of the community.

(4) Regulations may provide that activities of a description prescribed by the regulations are to be treated as being, or as not being, activities which a reasonable person might consider are activities carried on for the benefit of the community.

(5) "Community" includes a section of the community (whether in [the United Kingdom] or anywhere else); and regulations may make provision about what does, does not or may constitute a section of the community.

(6) A company is an excluded company if it is a company of a description prescribed by regulations.

[909]

NOTES

Sub-s (5): words in square brackets substituted by the Companies Act 2006 (Commencement No 2, Consequential Amendments, Transitional Provisions and Savings) Order 2007, SI 2007/1093, art 6(2), Sch 4, Pt 1, para 5, as from 6 April 2007.

Regulations: the Community Interest Company Regulations 2005, SI 2005/1788 at **[7399]**.

Becoming a community interest company

36 New companies

(1) If a company is to be formed as a community interest company, the documents delivered to the registrar of companies under [section 10 of the 1985 Act or Article 21 of the 1986 Order] (memorandum, articles and statement of names and particulars of directors and secretary) must be accompanied by the prescribed formation documents.

(2) "The prescribed formation documents" means such statutory declarations or other declarations or statements as are required by regulations to accompany the documents delivered under that section, in such form as may be approved in accordance with the regulations.

(3) On receiving the documents delivered under that section and the prescribed formation documents the registrar of companies must (instead of registering the memorandum and articles)—

(a) forward a copy of each of the documents to the Regulator, and
(b) retain the documents pending the Regulator's decision.

(4) The Regulator must decide whether the company is eligible to be formed as a community interest company.

(5) A company is eligible to be formed as a community interest company if—

(a) the memorandum and articles comply with the requirements imposed by and by virtue of section 32 and the company's name complies with section 33, and
(b) the Regulator, having regard to the documents delivered under [section 10 of the 1985 Act or Article 21 of the 1986 Order], the prescribed formation documents and any other relevant considerations, considers that the company will satisfy the community interest test and is not an excluded company.

(6) The Regulator must give notice of the decision to the registrar of companies (but the registrar is not required to record it).

(7) If the Regulator gives notice of a decision that the company is eligible to be formed as a community interest company, [section 12 of the 1985 Act or Article 23 of the 1986 Order] (registration of memorandum and articles) applies; and if the registrar registers the memorandum and articles he must also retain and record the prescribed formation documents.

(8) The certificate of incorporation under [section 13 of the 1985 Act or Article 24 of the 1986 Order] (effect of registration) is to contain a statement that the company is a community interest company.

(9) The fact that the certificate of incorporation contains such a statement is conclusive evidence that the company is a community interest company.

(10) If the Regulator decides that the company is not eligible to be formed as a community interest company, any subscriber to the memorandum may appeal to the Appeal Officer against the decision.

[910]

NOTES

Sub-ss (1), (5), (7), (8): words in square brackets substituted by the Companies Act 2006 (Commencement No 2, Consequential Amendments, Transitional Provisions and Savings) Order 2007, SI 2007/1093, art 6(2), Sch 4, Pt 1, para 6, as from 6 April 2007.

Regulations: the Community Interest Company Regulations 2005, SI 2005/1788 at **[7399]**.

37 Existing companies: requirements

(1) If a company is to become a community interest company, the company must—

(a) by special resolution alter its memorandum to state that it is to be a community interest company,
(b) by special resolutions under [the 1985 Act or the 1986 Order] make such alterations of its memorandum and articles as it considers necessary to comply with requirements imposed by and by virtue of section 32 or otherwise appropriate in connection with becoming a community interest company, and
(c) by special resolution change its name to comply with section 33.

(2) [Section 380(1) of the 1985 Act or Article 388(1) of the 1986 Order] (forwarding of copies of special resolutions to registrar of companies) must be complied with in relation to each of the special resolutions at the same time.

(3) If the special resolutions include one under [section 4 or 17 of the 1985 Act or Article 15 or 28 of the 1986 Order] (alterations of memorandum)—

(a) copies of the special resolutions must not be forwarded to the registrar of companies before the relevant date, and

(b) [section 380(1) of the 1985 Act or Article 388(1) of the 1986 Order] has effect in relation to them as if it referred to 15 days after the relevant date.

(4) If an application is made under [section 5 of the 1985 Act or Article 16 of the 1986 Order] (objection to alteration of memorandum …), the relevant date is—

(a) the date on which the court determines the application (or, if there is more than one application, the date on which the last to be determined by the court is determined), or

(b) such later date as the court may order.

(5) If there is no application under [section 5 of the 1985 Act or Article 16 of the 1986 Order], the relevant date is the end of the period for making such an application.

(6) The copies of the special resolutions forwarded to the registrar of companies must be accompanied by—

(a) a copy of the memorandum and articles of the company as altered by the special resolutions, and

(b) the prescribed conversion documents.

(7) "The prescribed conversion documents" means such statutory declarations or other declarations or statements as are required by regulations to accompany the copies of the special resolutions, in such form as may be approved in accordance with the regulations.

[911]

NOTES

Sub-ss (1)–(3), (5): words in square brackets substituted by the Companies Act 2006 (Commencement No 2, Consequential Amendments, Transitional Provisions and Savings) Order 2007, SI 2007/1093, art 6(2), Sch 4, Pt 1, para 7(a)–(d), (f), as from 6 April 2007.

Sub-s (4): words in square brackets substituted, and words omitted repealed, by SI 2007/1093, art 6(2), Sch 4, Pt 1, para 7(e), as from 6 April 2007.

Regulations: the Community Interest Company Regulations 2005, SI 2005/1788 at **[7399]**.

38 Existing companies: decisions etc

(1) On receiving under section 37 the copies of the special resolutions, the memorandum and articles as altered by the special resolutions and the prescribed conversion documents, the registrar of companies must (instead of recording the special resolutions and entering a new name on the register)—

(a) forward a copy of each of the documents to the Regulator, and

(b) retain the documents pending the Regulator's decision.

(2) The alterations of the memorandum and articles made by the special resolutions are to take effect only as provided by this section.

(3) The Regulator must decide whether the company is eligible to become a community interest company.

(4) A company is eligible to become a community interest company if—

(a) the memorandum and articles as altered by the special resolutions comply with the requirements imposed by and by virtue of section 32 and the company's name as so altered complies with section 33, and

(b) the Regulator, having regard to the special resolutions, the memorandum and articles as altered, the prescribed conversion documents and any other relevant considerations, considers that the company will satisfy the community interest test and is not an excluded company.

(5) The Regulator must give notice of the decision to the registrar of companies (but the registrar is not required to record it).

(6) If the Regulator gives notice of a decision that the company is eligible to become a community interest company, [section 28(6) of the 1985 Act or Article 38(6) of the 1986 Order] (registration of new name) applies; and if the registrar of companies enters the new name of the company on the register the registrar must also retain and record the special resolutions and the prescribed conversion documents.

(7) On the special resolutions being recorded, the alterations to the company's articles and memorandum made by the special resolutions take effect.

(8) The certificate of incorporation under [section 28(6) of the 1985 Act or Article 38(6) of the 1986 Order] is to contain a statement that the company is a community interest company.

(9) The fact that the certificate of incorporation contains such a statement is conclusive evidence that the company is a community interest company.

(10) If the Regulator decides that the company is not eligible to become a community interest company, the company may appeal to the Appeal Officer against the decision.

[912]

NOTES

Sub-ss (6), (8): words in square brackets substituted by the Companies Act 2006 (Commencement No 2, Consequential Amendments, Transitional Provisions and Savings) Order 2007, SI 2007/1093, art 6(2), Sch 4, Pt 1, para 8, as from 6 April 2007.

39 Existing companies: [English] charities

(1) A [company that is an English charity] may not by special resolution change its name to comply with section 33 without the prior written consent of the [Charity Commission].

(2) If a [company that is an English charity] contravenes subsection (1), the [Charity Commission] may apply to the High Court for an order quashing any altered certificate of incorporation issued under section 28(6) of [the 1985 Act].

(3) If a [company that is an English charity] becomes a community interest company, that does not affect the application of—

- (a) any property acquired under any disposition or agreement previously made otherwise than for full consideration in money or money's worth, or any property representing property so acquired,
- (b) any property representing income which has previously accrued, or
- (c) the income from any such property.

(4) …

[913]

NOTES

Words "Charity Commission" in square brackets in sub-ss (1), (2) substituted by the Charities Act 2006, s 75, Sch 8, paras 200, 201, as from 27 February 2007; all other words in square brackets (including in the section heading) substituted, and sub-s (4) repealed, by the Companies Act 2006 (Commencement No 2, Consequential Amendments, Transitional Provisions and Savings) Order 2007, SI 2007/1093, art 6(2), Sch 4, Pt 1, para 9, as from 6 April 2007.

40 Existing companies: Scottish charities

(1) A [company that is a Scottish charity] may not become a community interest company.

(2) If a [company that is a Scottish charity] purports by special resolution to change its name to comply with section 33, the Commissioners of Inland Revenue may apply to the Court of Session for an order quashing any altered certificate of incorporation issued under section 28(6) of [the 1985 Act].

(3) Regulations may repeal subsections (1) and (2); and subsections (4) to (7) have effect on and after the day on which regulations under this subsection come into force.

(4) A [company that is a Scottish charity] may not by special resolution change its name to comply with section 33 without the prior written consent—

- (a) if the company's registered office is situated in Scotland, of the Scottish Charity Regulator, or
- (b) if the company's registered office is situated in England and Wales (or Wales), of both the Scottish Charity Regulator and the [Charity Commission].

(5) If a [company that is a Scottish charity] contravenes subsection (4)(a), the Scottish Charity Regulator may apply to the Court of Session for an order quashing any altered certificate of incorporation issued under section 28(6) of the [the 1985 Act].

(6) If a [company that is a Scottish charity] contravenes subsection (4)(b), the Scottish Charity Regulator or the [Charity Commission] may apply to the High Court for such an order.

(7) If a [company that is a Scottish charity] becomes a community interest company, [it shall continue to be under a duty to apply—

(a) any property previously acquired, or any property representing property previously acquired,

(b) any property representing income which has previously accrued, and

(c) the income from any such property,

in accordance with its purposes as set out in its entry in the Scottish Charity Register immediately before it became a community interest company.]

(8), (9) …

[914]

NOTES

Sub-ss (1), (2), (5): words in square brackets substituted by the Companies Act 2006 (Commencement No 2, Consequential Amendments, Transitional Provisions and Savings) Order 2007, SI 2007/1093, art 6(2), Sch 4, Pt 1, para 10(a), (b), as from 6 April 2007.

Sub-ss (4), (6): words in first pair of square brackets substituted by SI 2007/1093, art 6(2), Sch 4, Pt 1, para 10(a), as from 6 April 2007; words in second pair of square brackets substituted by the Charities Act 2006, s 75, Sch 8, paras 200, 202, as from 27 February 2007.

Sub-s (7): words in first pair of square brackets substituted by SI 2007/1093, art 6(2), Sch 4, Pt 1, para 10(a), as from 6 April 2007; words in second pair of square brackets substituted by the Charities and Trustee Investment (Scotland) Act 2005 (Consequential Provisions and Modifications) Order 2006, SI 2006/242, art 5, Schedule, Pt 1, para 8(1), (3)(a), as from 1 April 2006.

Sub-s (8): repealed by SI 2007/1093, art 6(2), Sch 4, Pt 1, para 10(c), as from 6 April 2007.

Sub-s (9): repealed by SI 2006/242, art 5, Schedule, Pt 1, para 8(1), (3)(c), as from 1 April 2006.

Commissioners of Inland Revenue: a reference to the Commissioners of Inland Revenue is now to be taken as a reference to the Commissioners for Her Majesty's Revenue and Customs; see the Commissioners for Revenue and Customs Act 2005, s 50(1), (7).

[40A Existing companies: Northern Ireland charities

(1) A company that is a Northern Ireland charity may not become a community interest company.

(2) If a company that is a Northern Ireland charity purports by special resolution to change its name to comply with section 33, the Commissioners of Her Majesty's Revenue and Customs may apply to the High Court for an order quashing any altered certificate of incorporation under Article 38(6) of the 1986 Order.]

[914A]

NOTES

Commencement: 1 April 2007.

Inserted by the Companies Act 2006 (Commencement No 2, Consequential Amendments, Transitional Provisions and Savings) Order 2007, SI 2007/1093, art 6(2), Sch 4, Pt 1, para 11, as from 6 April 2007.

Supervision by Regulator

41 Conditions for exercise of supervisory powers

(1) In deciding whether and how to exercise the powers conferred by sections 42 to 51 the Regulator must adopt an approach which is based on the principle that those powers should be exercised only to the extent necessary to maintain confidence in community interest companies.

(2) No power conferred on the Regulator by—

(a) section 45 (appointment of director),

(b) section 46 (removal of director),

(c) section 47 (appointment of manager), or

(d) section 48 (property),

is exercisable in relation to a community interest company unless the company default condition is satisfied in relation to the power and the company.

(3) The company default condition is satisfied in relation to a power and a company if it appears to the Regulator necessary to exercise the power in relation to the company because—

(a) there has been misconduct or mismanagement in the administration of the company,
(b) there is a need to protect the company's property or to secure the proper application of that property,
(c) the company is not satisfying the community interest test, or
(d) if the company has community interest objects, the company is not carrying on any activities in pursuit of those objects.

(4) The power conferred on the Regulator by section 49 (transfer of shares etc) is not exercisable in relation to a community interest company unless it appears to the Regulator that the company is an excluded company.

[915]

42 Investigation

(1) The Regulator may—
(a) investigate the affairs of a community interest company, or
(b) appoint any person (other than a member of the Regulator's staff) to investigate the affairs of a community interest company on behalf of the Regulator.

(2) Subsection (1)(b) is in addition to paragraph 5 of Schedule 3 (powers of Regulator exercisable by authorised members of staff) and does not affect the application of that paragraph to the Regulator's power under subsection (1)(a).

(3) Schedule 7 (further provision about investigations under this section) has effect.

[916]

43 Audit

(1) The Regulator may by order require a community interest company to allow the annual accounts of the company to be audited by a qualified auditor appointed by the Regulator.

(2) A person is a qualified auditor if he is eligible for appointment as a company auditor under section 25 of the Companies Act 1989 (c 40) [or Article 28 of the Companies (Northern Ireland) Order 1990] (eligibility for appointment as auditor).

(3) [Sections 389A and 389B of the 1985 Act or Articles 397A and 397B of the 1986 Order] (auditor's rights to information) apply in relation to an auditor appointed under this section *as in relation to an auditor appointed under [Chapter 5 of Part 11 of the 1985 Act or Chapter 5 of Part 12 of the 1986 Order]*.

(4) On completion of the audit the auditor must make a report to the Regulator on such matters and in such form as the Regulator specifies.

(5) The expenses of the audit, including the remuneration of the auditor, are to be paid by the Regulator.

(6) An audit under this section is in addition to, and does not affect, any audit required by or by virtue of any other enactment.

[917]

NOTES

Sub-s (2): words in square brackets inserted by the Companies Act 2006 (Commencement No 2, Consequential Amendments, Transitional Provisions and Savings) Order 2007, SI 2007/1093, art 6(2), Sch 4, Pt 1, para 12(a), as from 6 April 2007.

Sub-s (3): words in square brackets substituted by SI 2007/1093, art 6(2), Sch 4, Pt 1, para 12(b), as from 6 April 2007; words in italics repealed by the draft Companies Act 2006 (Commencement No 3, Consequential Amendments, Transitional Provisions and Savings) Order 2007, art 10(3), Sch 5, as from 1 October 2007 (see **[A12]**).

44 Civil proceedings

(1) The Regulator may bring civil proceedings in the name and on behalf of a community interest company.

(2) Before instituting proceedings under this section the Regulator must give written notice to the company stating—
(a) the cause of action,
(b) the remedy sought, and

(c) a summary of the facts on which the proceedings are to be based.

(3) Any director of the company may apply to the court for an order—
(a) that proposed proceedings are not to be instituted under this section, or
(b) that proceedings instituted under this section are to be discontinued.

(4) On an application under subsection (3) the court may make such order as it thinks fit.

(5) In particular the court may (as an alternative to ordering that proposed proceedings are not to be instituted under this section or that proceedings instituted under this section are to be discontinued) order—
(a) that the proposed proceedings may be instituted under this section, or the proceedings instituted under this section may be continued, on such terms and conditions as the court thinks fit,
(b) that any proceedings instituted by the company are to be discontinued, or
(c) that any proceedings instituted by the company may be continued on such terms and conditions as the court thinks fit.

(6) The Regulator must indemnify the company against any costs (or expenses) incurred by it in connection with proceedings brought under this section.

(7) Any costs (or expenses)—
(a) awarded to the company in connection with proceedings brought under this section, or
(b) incurred by the company in connection with the proceedings and which it is agreed should be paid by a defendant (or defender),
are to be paid to the Regulator.

[918]

45 Appointment of director

(1) The Regulator may by order appoint a director of a community interest company.

(2) The person appointed may be anyone whom the Regulator thinks appropriate, other than a member of the Regulator's staff.

(3) A person may be appointed as a director of a company under this section—
(a) whether or not the person is a member of the company, and
(b) irrespective of any provision made by the memorandum or articles of the company or a resolution of the company in general meeting.

(4) An order appointing a person to be a director of a company under this section must specify the terms on which the director is to hold office; and those terms have effect as if contained in a contract between the director and the company.

(5) The terms specified must include the period for which the director is to hold office, and may include terms as to the remuneration of the director by the company.

(6) A director appointed under this section has all the powers of the directors appointed by the company (including powers exercisable only by a particular director or class of directors).

(7) A director appointed under this section may not be removed by the company, but may be removed by the Regulator at any time.

(8) Where—
(a) a person is appointed to be a director of the company under this section, or
(b) a person so appointed ceases to be a director of the company,
the obligation which would otherwise be imposed on the company under [section 288(2) of the 1985 Act or Article 296(2) of the 1986 Order] (requirement that company notify change among directors to registrar) is instead an obligation of the Regulator.

(9) But if subsection (10) applies, section 288(2) [or Article 296(2)] applies as if the period within which the Regulator must send a notification to the registrar of companies is 14 days from the date on which the Regulator receives notification under that subsection.

(10) Where a person appointed to be a director of the company under this section ceases to be a director of the company (otherwise than by removal under subsection (7)), the company must give notification of that fact to the Regulator in a form approved by the Regulator before the end of the period of 14 days beginning with the date on which the person ceases to be a director.

(11) If the company fails to comply with subsection (10) it commits an offence.

(12) A person guilty of an offence under subsection (11) is liable on summary conviction to a fine not exceeding level 5 on the standard scale.

(13) The company may appeal to the Appeal Officer against an order under this section.
[919]

NOTES

Sub-s (8): words in square brackets substituted by the Companies Act 2006 (Commencement No 2, Consequential Amendments, Transitional Provisions and Savings) Order 2007, SI 2007/1093, art 6(2), Sch 4, Pt 1, para 13(a), as from 6 April 2007.

Sub-s (9): words in square brackets inserted by SI 2007/1093, art 6(2), Sch 4, Pt 1, para 13(b), as from 6 April 2007.

---

46 Removal of director

(1) The Regulator may by order remove a director of a community interest company.

(2) If a person has been removed under subsection (1)—

(a) the company may not subsequently appoint him a director of the company, and

(b) any assignment to the person of the office of director of the company is of no effect (even if approved by special resolution of the company).

(3) The Regulator may by order suspend a director of the company pending a decision whether to remove him.

(4) The maximum period for which a director may be suspended under subsection (3) is one year.

(5) If the Regulator suspends a director under subsection (3) the Regulator may give directions in relation to the performance of the director's functions.

(6) The Regulator may discharge an order made under subsection (1).

(7) The discharge of an order made under subsection (1) does not reinstate the person removed by the order as a director of the company, but on the discharge of the order subsection (2) ceases to apply to the person.

(8) The Regulator must from time to time review any order made under subsection (3) and, if it is appropriate to do so, discharge the order.

(9) Before making an order under subsection (1) or (3) in relation to a director, the Regulator must give at least 14 days' notice to—

(a) the director, and

(b) the company.

(10) Where an order is made in relation to a director under subsection (1) or (3) the director may appeal against the order—

(a) in England and Wales [or Northern Ireland], to the High Court, or

(b) in Scotland, to the Court of Session.

(11) The Regulator must, before the end of the period of 14 days beginning with the date on which—

(a) an order under subsection (1) is made or discharged,

(b) an order under subsection (3) is made or discharged or expires, or

(c) an order under subsection (1) or (3) is quashed on appeal,

give notification of that event to the registrar of companies in a form approved by the registrar of companies.

(12) Where subsection (11) imposes an obligation to notify the registrar of companies of an event, [section 288(2) of the 1985 Act or Article 296(2) of the 1986 Order] (requirement that company notify change among directors to registrar) does not apply in respect of the event.
[920]

NOTES

Sub-s (10): words in square brackets inserted by the Companies Act 2006 (Commencement No 2, Consequential Amendments, Transitional Provisions and Savings) Order 2007, SI 2007/1093, art 6(2), Sch 4, Pt 1, para 14(a), as from 6 April 2007.

Sub-s (12): words in square brackets substituted by SI 2007/1093, art 6(2), Sch 4, Pt 1, para 14(b), as from 6 April 2007.

47 Appointment of manager

(1) The Regulator may by order appoint a manager in respect of the property and affairs of a community interest company.

(2) The person appointed may be anyone whom the Regulator thinks appropriate, other than a member of the Regulator's staff.

(3) An order under subsection (1) may make provision as to the functions to be exercised by, and the powers of, the manager.

(4) The order may in particular provide—

(a) for the manager to have such of the functions of the company's directors as are specified in the order, and

(b) for the company's directors to be prevented from exercising any of those functions.

(5) In carrying out his functions the manager acts as the company's agent; and a person dealing with the manager in good faith and for value need not inquire whether the manager is acting within his powers.

(6) The appointment of the manager does not affect—

(a) any right of any person to appoint a receiver or manager of the company's property (including any right under section 51 of the Insolvency Act 1986 (c 45) [(power to appoint receiver under law of Scotland)]), or

(b) the rights of a receiver or manager appointed by a person other than the Regulator.

(7) The manager's functions are to be discharged by him under the supervision of the Regulator; and the Regulator must from time to time review the order by which the manager is appointed and, if it is appropriate to do so, discharge it in whole or in part.

(8) In particular, the Regulator must discharge the order on the appointment of a person to act as administrative receiver, administrator, provisional liquidator or liquidator of the company.

(9) The Regulator may apply to the court for directions in relation to any matter arising in connection with the manager's functions or powers.

(10) On an application under subsection (9) the court may give such directions or make such orders as it thinks fit.

(11) The costs of any application under subsection (9) are to be paid by the company.

(12) Regulations may authorise the Regulator—

(a) to require a manager to make reports,

(b) to require a manager to give security (or, in Scotland, to find caution) for the due exercise of the manager's functions, and

(c) to remove a manager in circumstances prescribed by the regulations.

(13) Regulations may—

(a) provide for a manager's remuneration to be payable from the property of the company, and

(b) authorise the Regulator to determine the amount of a manager's remuneration and to disallow any amount of remuneration in circumstances prescribed by the regulations.

(14) The company may appeal to the Appeal Officer against an order under this section. **[921]**

NOTES

Sub-s (6): words in square brackets inserted by the Companies Act 2006 (Commencement No 2, Consequential Amendments, Transitional Provisions and Savings) Order 2007, SI 2007/1093, art 6(2), Sch 4, Pt 1, para 15, as from 6 April 2007.

Regulations: the Community Interest Company Regulations 2005, SI 2005/1788 at **[7399]**.

48 Property

(1) The Regulator may by order—

(a) vest in the Official Property Holder any property held by or in trust for a community interest company, or
(b) require persons in whom such property is vested to transfer it to the Official Property Holder.

(2) The Regulator—
(a) may order a person who holds property on behalf of a community interest company, or on behalf of a trustee of a community interest company, not to part with the property without the Regulator's consent, and
(b) may order any debtor of a community interest company not to make any payment in respect of the debtor's liability to the company without the Regulator's consent.

(3) The Regulator may by order restrict—
(a) the transactions which may be entered into by a community interest company, or
(b) the nature or amount of the payments that a community interest company may make,

and the order may in particular provide that transactions may not be entered into or payments made without the Regulator's consent.

(4) The vesting or transfer of property under subsection (1) does not constitute a breach of a covenant or condition against alienation, and no right listed in subsection (5) operates or becomes exercisable as a result of the vesting or transfer.

(5) The rights are—
(a) a right of reverter (or, in Scotland, the right of the fiar on the termination of a liferent),
(b) a right of pre-emption,
(c) a right of forfeiture,
(d) a right of re-entry,
(e) a right of irritancy,
(f) an option, and
(g) any right similar to those listed in paragraphs (a) to (f).

(6) The Regulator must from time to time review any order under this section and, if it is appropriate to do so, discharge the order in whole or in part.

(7) On discharging an order under subsection (1) the Regulator may make any order as to the vesting or transfer of the property, and give any directions, which he considers appropriate.

(8) If a person fails to comply with an order under subsection (1)(b), the Regulator may certify that fact in writing to the court.

(9) If, after hearing—
(a) any witnesses who may be produced against or on behalf of the alleged offender, and
(b) any statement which may be offered in defence,

the court is satisfied that the offender failed without reasonable excuse to comply with the order, it may deal with him as if he had been guilty of contempt of the court.

(10) A person who contravenes an order under subsection (2) or (3) commits an offence, but a prosecution may be instituted[—
(a) in England and Wales, only with the consent of the Regulator or the Director of Public Prosecutions;
(b) in Northern Ireland, only with the consent of the Regulator or the Director of Public Prosecutions for Northern Ireland].

(11) A person guilty of an offence under subsection (10) is liable on summary conviction to a fine not exceeding level 5 on the standard scale.

(12) Subsections (8) to (10) do not prevent the bringing of civil proceedings in respect of a contravention of an order under subsection (1)(b), (2) or (3).

(13) The company and any person to whom the order is directed may appeal to the Appeal Officer against an order under subsection (1) or (2).

(14) The company may appeal to the Appeal Officer against an order under subsection (3).

[922]

NOTES

Sub-s (10): words in square brackets substituted by the Companies Act 2006 (Commencement No 2, Consequential Amendments, Transitional Provisions and Savings) Order 2007, SI 2007/1093, art 6(2), Sch 4, Pt 1, para 16, as from 6 April 2007.

49 Transfer of shares etc

(1) If a community interest company has a share capital, the Regulator may by order transfer specified shares in the company to specified persons.

(2) If a community interest company is a company limited by guarantee, the Regulator may by order—

(a) extinguish the interests in the company of specified members of the company (otherwise than as shareholders), and

(b) appoint a new member in place of each member whose interest has been extinguished.

(3) An order under subsection (1) may not transfer any shares in respect of which—

(a) a dividend may be paid, or

(b) a distribution of the company's assets may be made if the company is wound up.

(4) An order under this section in relation to a company—

(a) may only transfer shares to, and appoint as new members, persons who have consented to the transfer or appointment, and

(b) may be made irrespective of any provision made by the memorandum or articles of the company or a resolution of the company in general meeting.

(5) The company and any person from whom shares are transferred by the order may appeal to the Appeal Officer against an order under subsection (1).

(6) The company and any person whose interest is extinguished by the order may appeal to the Appeal Officer against an order under subsection (2).

(7) "Specified", in relation to an order, means specified in the order.

[923]

50 Petition for winding up

(1) The Regulator may present a petition for a community interest company to be wound up if the court is of the opinion that it is just and equitable that the company should be wound up.

(2) Subsection (1) does not apply if the company is already being wound up by the court.

(3) …

[924]

NOTES

Sub-s (3): inserts the Insolvency Act 1986, s 124(4A) at **[3280]**.

51 Dissolution and striking off

(1) If a community interest company has been dissolved, the Regulator may apply under [section 651 of the 1985 Act or Article 602 of the 1986 Order] for an order declaring the dissolution to have been void.

(2) If a community interest company has been struck off the register under [section 652 of the 1985 Act or Article 603 of the 1986 Order] (defunct companies), the Regulator may apply under [section 653(2) of the 1985 Act or Article 604(2) of the 1986 Order] for an order that the company's name be restored.

(3) If an application under [section 652A of the 1985 Act or Article 603A of the 1986 Order] (application to strike name of private company off register) is made on behalf of a community interest company, [section 652B(6) of the 1985 Act or Article 603B(6) of the 1986 Order] (persons to be notified of application) is to be treated as also requiring a copy of the application to be given to the Regulator.

[925]

NOTES

Words in square brackets substituted by the Companies Act 2006 (Commencement No 2, Consequential Amendments, Transitional Provisions and Savings) Order 2007, SI 2007/1093, art 6(2), Sch 4, Pt 1, para 17, as from 6 April 2007.

Change of status

52 Re-registration

(1) A community interest company is excluded from re-registering under [section 49 of the 1985 Act or Article 59 of the 1986 Order] (re-registration of limited company as unlimited).

(2) If a community interest company which is not a public company re-registers as a public company under [section 43 of the 1985 Act or Article 53 of the 1986 Order], or a community interest company which is a public company re-registers as a private company under [section 53 of the 1985 Act or Article 63 of the 1986 Order], the certificate of incorporation issued under [section 47(1)(b) or 55(1)(b) of the 1985 Act or Article 57(1)(b) or 65(1)(b) of the 1986 Order] is to contain a statement that the company is a community interest company.

(3) The fact that the certificate of incorporation contains such a statement is conclusive evidence that the company is a community interest company.

[926]

NOTES

Sub-ss (1), (2):words in square brackets substituted by the Companies Act 2006 (Commencement No 2, Consequential Amendments, Transitional Provisions and Savings) Order 2007, SI 2007/1093, art 6(2), Sch 4, Pt 1, para 18, as from 6 April 2007.

53 Ceasing to be a community interest company

A community interest company may not cease to be a community interest company except by dissolution or as provided—

(a) by sections 54 and 55 (becoming a charity or a Scottish charity), or

(b) if regulations are made under section 56 (becoming an industrial and provident society), by the regulations.

[927]

54 Becoming a charity … : requirements

(1) If a community interest company is to cease being a community interest company and become a charity … , the company must—

(a) by special resolution alter its memorandum so that it does not state that it is to be a community interest company,

(b) by special resolutions under [the 1985 Act or the 1986 Order] make such alterations of its memorandum and articles as it considers appropriate, and

(c) by special resolution change its name so that it does not comply with section 33.

(2) [Section 380(1) of the 1985 Act or Article 388(1) of the 1986 Order] (forwarding of copies of special resolutions to registrar of companies) must be complied with in relation to each of the special resolutions at the same time.

(3) If the special resolutions include one under [section 4 or 17 of the 1985 Act or Article 15 or 28 of the 1986 Order] (alterations of memorandum)—

(a) copies of the special resolutions must not be forwarded to the registrar of companies before the relevant date, and

(b) [section 380(1) of the 1985 Act or Article 388(1) of the 1986 Order] has effect in relation to them as if it referred to 15 days after the relevant date.

(4) If an application is made under [section 5 of the 1985 Act or Article 16 of the 1986 Order] (objection to alteration of memorandum …), the relevant date is—

(a) the date on which the court determines the application (or, if there is more than one application, the date on which the last to be determined by the court is determined), or

(b) such later date as the court may order.

(5) If there is no application under [section 5 of the 1985 Act or Article 16 of the 1986 Order], the relevant date is the end of the period for making such an application.

(6) The copies of the special resolutions forwarded to the registrar of companies must be accompanied by—

(a) a copy of the memorandum and articles of the company as altered by the special resolutions, and

[(b) the statement required by subsection (7), (8) or (8A)].

[(7) The statement required where the company is to become an English charity is a statement by the Charity Commissioners that, in their opinion, if the special resolutions take effect and the company ceases to be a community interest company, the company will be an English charity and will not be an exempt charity.

"Exempt charity" here has the same meaning as in the Charities Act 1993 (see section 96 of that Act).

(8) The statement required where the company is to become a Scottish charity is a statement by the Scottish Charity Regulator that, if the special resolutions take effect and the company ceases to be a community interest company, the company will be entered in the Scottish Charity Register.]

[(8A) The statement required where the company is to become a Northern Ireland charity is a statement by the Commissioners of Her Majesty's Revenue and Customs that the company has claimed exemption under section 505(1) of the Income and Corporation Taxes Act 1988.]

(9) …

[928]

NOTES

Section heading: words omitted repealed by the Companies Act 2006 (Commencement No 2, Consequential Amendments, Transitional Provisions and Savings) Order 2007, SI 2007/1093, art 6(2), Sch 4, Pt 1, para 19(1), (2), as from 6 April 2007.

Sub-ss (1), (4): words omitted repealed, and words in square brackets substituted, by SI 2007/1093, art 6(2), Sch 4, Pt 1, para 19(1)–(3), (6), as from 6 April 2007.

Sub-ss (2), (3), (5), (6): words in square brackets substituted by SI 2007/1093, art 6(2), Sch 4, Pt 1, para 19(1), (4), (5), (7), (8), as from 6 April 2007.

Sub-ss (7), (8): substituted by SI 2007/1093, art 6(2), Sch 4, Pt 1, para 19(1), (9), as from 6 April 2007.

Sub-s (8A): inserted by SI 2007/1093, art 6(2), Sch 4, Pt 1, para 19(1), (10), as from 6 April 2007.

Sub-s (9): repealed by SI 2007/1093, art 6(2), Sch 4, Pt 1, para 19(1), (11), as from 6 April 2007.

55 Becoming a charity … : decisions etc

(1) On receiving under section 54 the copies of the special resolutions, the memorandum and articles as altered by the special resolutions and the statement, the registrar must (instead of recording the special resolutions and entering a new name on the register)—

(a) forward a copy of each of the documents to the Regulator, and

(b) retain them pending the Regulator's decision.

(2) The alterations of the memorandum and articles made by the special resolutions are to take effect only as provided by this section.

(3) The Regulator must decide whether the company is eligible to cease being a community interest company.

(4) The company is eligible to cease being a community interest company if it has complied with section 54 and none of the following applies—

(a) the Regulator has under section 43 appointed an auditor to audit the company's annual accounts and the audit has not been completed,

(b) civil proceedings instituted by the Regulator in the name of the company under section 44 have not been determined or discontinued,

(c) a director of the company holds office by virtue of an order under section 45,

(d) a director of the company is suspended under section 46(3),

(e) there is a manager in respect of the property and affairs of the company appointed under section 47,

(f) the Official Property Holder holds property as trustee for the company,

(g) an order under section 48(2) or (3) is in force in relation to the company,

(h) a petition has been presented for the company to be wound up.

(5) The Regulator must give notice of the decision to the registrar of companies (but the registrar is not required to record it).

(6) If the Regulator gives notice of a decision that the company is eligible to cease being a community interest company, [section 28(6) of the 1985 Act or Article 38(6) of the 1986 Order] (registration of new name) applies; and if the registrar of companies enters the new name of the company on the register he must also retain and record the special resolutions and the statement.

(7) On the date on which the certificate of incorporation is issued the alterations to the company's articles and memorandum made by the special resolutions take effect and the company ceases to be a community interest company.

(8) If the Regulator decides that the company is not eligible to cease being a community interest company, the company may appeal to the Appeal Officer against the decision.

[929]

NOTES

Section heading: words omitted repealed by the Companies Act 2006 (Commencement No 2, Consequential Amendments, Transitional Provisions and Savings) Order 2007, SI 2007/1093, art 6(2), Sch 4, Pt 1, para 20(a), as from 6 April 2007.

Sub-s (6): words in square brackets substituted by SI 2007/1093, art 6(2), Sch 4, Pt 1, para 20(b), as from 6 April 2007.

56 Becoming an industrial and provident society

(1) Unless regulations make provision to the contrary, a community interest company may not convert itself into a registered society under section 53 of the Industrial and Provident Societies Act 1965 (c 12) [or section 62 of the Industrial and Provident Societies Act (Northern Ireland) 1969].

(2) If regulations make provision allowing the conversion of community interest companies under that section they may include provision modifying that section in its application by virtue of the regulations.

[930]

NOTES

Sub-s (1): words in square brackets inserted by the Companies Act 2006 (Commencement No 2, Consequential Amendments, Transitional Provisions and Savings) Order 2007, SI 2007/1093, art 6(2), Sch 4, Pt 1, para 21, as from 6 April 2007.

Supplementary

57 Fees

(1) Regulations may require the payment of such fees in connection with the Regulator's functions as may be specified in the regulations.

(2) The regulations may provide for fees to be paid to the registrar of companies (rather than to the Regulator).

(3) The Regulator may charge a fee for any service which is provided otherwise than in pursuance of an obligation imposed by law, other than the provision of guidance which the Regulator considers to be of general interest.

(4) Fees paid by virtue of this section are to be paid into the Consolidated Fund.

[931]

NOTES

Regulations: the Community Interest Company Regulations 2005, SI 2005/1788 at **[7399]**. For the current fees, see Appendix 3 (Fees table)at **[A3]**.

58 Extension of provisions about registrar etc

Regulations may make amendments or modifications of any provision contained in—

(a) [Part 24 of the 1985 Act or Part 24 of the 1986 Order] (registrar), or
(b) [Part 25 of the 1985 Act or Part 25 of the 1986 Order] (miscellaneous and supplementary),

in consequence of any provision contained in, or made under, this Part (in particular, so as to provide that references to the Companies Acts are to include provisions contained in, or made under, this Part).

[932]

NOTES

Words in square brackets substituted by the Companies Act 2006 (Commencement No 2, Consequential Amendments, Transitional Provisions and Savings) Order 2007, SI 2007/1093, art 6(2), Sch 4, Pt 1, para 22, as from 6 April 2007.

Regulations: the Community Interest Company Regulations 2005, SI 2005/1788 at **[7399]**.

59 Information

(1) Regulations may require the registrar of companies—
(a) to notify the Regulator of matters specified in the regulations, and
(b) to provide the Regulator with copies of documents specified in the regulations.

(2), (3) …

(4) A public authority may disclose to the Regulator, for any purpose connected with the exercise of the Regulator's functions, information received by the authority in connection with its functions.

(5) The Regulator may disclose to a public authority any information received by the Regulator in connection with the functions of the Regulator—
(a) for a purpose connected with the exercise of those functions, or
(b) for a purpose connected with the exercise by the authority of its functions.

(6) In deciding whether to disclose information to a public authority in a country or territory outside the United Kingdom the Regulator must have regard to the considerations listed in section 243(6) of the Enterprise Act 2002 (c 40) (overseas disclosures), but as if the reference to information of a kind to which section 237 of that Act applies were to information of the kind the Regulator is considering disclosing.

(7) The powers to disclose information in subsections (4) and (5) are subject to—
(a) any restriction on disclosure imposed by or by virtue of an enactment, and
(b) any express restriction on disclosure subject to which information was supplied.

(8) Information may be disclosed under subsection (4) or (5) subject to a restriction on its further disclosure.

(9) A person who discloses information in contravention of a restriction imposed under subsection (8) is guilty of an offence, but a prosecution may be instituted[—
(a) in England and Wales, only with the consent of the Regulator or the Director of Public Prosecutions;
(b) in Northern Ireland, only with the consent of the Regulator or the Director of Public Prosecutions for Northern Ireland].

(10) A person guilty of an offence under subsection (9) is liable on summary conviction to a fine not exceeding level 3 on the standard scale.

(11) "Public authority" means a person or body having functions of a public nature.

[933]

NOTES

Sub-ss (2), (3): insert the Bankruptcy (Scotland) Act 1985, s 71A, and amend the Data Protection Act 1998, s 31(2).

Sub-s (9): words in square brackets substituted by the Companies Act 2006 (Commencement No 2, Consequential Amendments, Transitional Provisions and Savings) Order 2007, SI 2007/1093, art 6(2), Sch 4, Pt 1, para 23, as from 6 April 2007.

Regulations: the Community Interest Company Regulations 2005, SI 2005/1788 at **[7399]**.

60 Offences

(1) If an offence under this Part committed by a body corporate is proved—
(a) to have been committed with the consent or connivance of an officer, or

(b) to be attributable to any neglect on the part of an officer,

the officer as well as the body corporate is guilty of the offence and liable to be proceeded against and punished accordingly.

(2) "Officer" means a director, manager, secretary or other similar officer of the body corporate, or a person purporting to act in any such capacity.

(3) "Director"—

(a) includes a shadow director, and

(b) if the affairs of a body corporate are managed by its members, means a member of the body.

[934]

61 Orders made by Regulator

(1) An order made by the Regulator under this Part must be given to the community interest company in relation to which it is made and—

(a) if the order is under section 46(1) or (3), to the director removed or suspended,

(b) if the order is under section 48(1)(b) or (2), to the person to whom the order is directed,

(c) if the order is under section 49(1), to the persons from and to whom shares are transferred,

(d) if the order is under section 49(2), to the person whose interest is extinguished and any person appointed in his place.

(2) Orders made by the Regulator under or by virtue of this Part may contain any incidental or supplementary provisions the Regulator considers expedient.

(3) When discharging an order made under or by virtue of this Part, the Regulator may make savings and transitional provisions.

(4) A document certified by the Regulator to be a true copy of an order made by the Regulator is evidence of the order without further proof; and a document purporting to be so certified shall, unless the contrary is proved, be taken to be so certified.

(5) Where the Regulator makes an order or decision against which an appeal lies under or by virtue of this Part, the Regulator must give reasons for the order or decision to the persons entitled to appeal against it.

[935]

62 Regulations

(1) Any power to make regulations under this Part is exercisable by the Secretary of State by statutory instrument.

(2) Regulations under this Part may make different provision for different cases.

(3) Regulations under this Part may confer or impose functions on the Regulator or any other person specified in the regulations (and, unless made under paragraph 4 of Schedule 4, may provide for appeals to the Appeal Officer from a person on whom functions are conferred by the regulations).

(4) No regulations to which this subsection applies are to be made unless a draft of the statutory instrument containing the regulations (whether or not together with other provisions) has been laid before, and approved by a resolution of, each House of Parliament.

(5) Subsection (4) applies to regulations under—

(a) section 30,

(b) section 31,

(c) section 32,

(d) section 34,

(e) section 35,

(f) section 36,

(g) section 37,

(h) section 47, and

(i) section 56.

(6) A statutory instrument containing regulations under this Part is (unless a draft of it has been approved by each House of Parliament under subsection (4)) subject to annulment in pursuance of a resolution of either House of Parliament.

[936]

63 Interpretation

(1) In this Part—

["the 1985 Act" means the Companies Act 1985;]

["the 1986 Order" means the Companies (Northern Ireland) Order 1986;]

"administrative receiver" has the meaning given[—

(a) in England and Wales or Scotland, by section 251 of the Insolvency Act 1986, and

(b) in Northern Ireland, by Article 5 of the Insolvency (Northern Ireland) Order 1989;]

"the Appeal Officer" has the meaning given by section 28(1),

["charity" means an English charity, a Scottish charity or a Northern Ireland charity, as defined below;]

"community interest object" is to be construed in accordance with section 35(3),

"the community interest test" is to be construed in accordance with section 35(2),

"enactment" includes an Act of the Scottish Parliament,

["English charity" means a charity within the meaning of the Charities Act 1993 (see section 96 of that Act);]

"excluded company" is to be construed in accordance with section 35(6),

["the Gazette" has the meaning given by section 1173 of the Companies Act 2006;]

["Northern Ireland charity" means a charity within the meaning of the Charities Act (Northern Ireland) 1964 (see section 35 of that Act);]

"the Official Property Holder" has the meaning given by section 29(1),

"the Regulator" has the meaning given by section 27(1), and

["Scottish charity" means a body entered in the Scottish Charity Register].

[(2) In England and Wales or Scotland, any expression used in this Part and in the 1985 Act has the same meaning in this Part as in that Act.

(3) In Northern Ireland, any expression used in this Part and in the 1986 Order has the same meaning in this Part as in that Order.]

[937]

NOTES

Sub-s (1): words in square brackets in definition "administrative receiver" substituted, definition "charity" substituted, and definitions "the 1985 Act", "the 1986 Order", "English charity", "the Gazette", and "Northern Ireland charity" inserted, by the Companies Act 2006 (Commencement No 2, Consequential Amendments, Transitional Provisions and Savings) Order 2007, SI 2007/1093, art 6(2), Sch 4, Pt 1, para 24(1)–(4), as from 6 April 2007; definition "Scottish charity" substituted by the Charities and Trustee Investment (Scotland) Act 2005 (Consequential Provisions and Modifications) Order 2006, SI 2006/242, art 5, Schedule, Pt 1, para 8(1), (5), as from 1 April 2006..

Sub-ss (2), (3): substituted, for original sub-s (2), by SI 2007/1093, art 6(2), Sch 4, Pt 1, para 24(1), (5), as from 6 April 2007.

PART 3
SUPPLEMENTARY

64 (*Introduces Schedule 8 to this Act* (*repeals and revocations*).)

65 Commencement etc

(1) This Act (apart from this section and sections 66 and 67) does not come into force until such day as the Secretary of State may by order made by statutory instrument appoint; and different days may be appointed for different provisions or otherwise for different purposes.

(2) The Secretary of State may by order made by statutory instrument make any transitional provisions or savings which appear appropriate in connection with the commencement of any provision of this Act.

[938]

NOTES

Orders: the Companies (Audit, Investigations and Community Enterprise) Act 2004 (Commencement) and Companies Act 1989 (Commencement No 18) Order 2004, SI 2004/3322 at **[7339]**.

66 Extent

(1) Any amendment made by this Act has the same extent as the provision to which it relates.

(2) Sections 14, 15(1)(b), (3) and (7) and [16 to 18] [and Part 2] extend to Northern Ireland.

(3) Subject to that, this Act (apart from section 65, this section and section 67) does not extend to Northern Ireland.

[939]

NOTES

Sub-s (2): words in first pair of square brackets substituted by the Companies Act 2006, s 1276(5), as from 8 November 2006; words in second pair of square brackets inserted by the Companies Act 2006 (Commencement No 2, Consequential Amendments, Transitional Provisions and Savings) Order 2007, SI 2007/1093, art 6(2), Sch 4, Pt 1, para 25, as from 6 April 2007.

As to the application of this Act to Northern Ireland, see also the Companies Act 2006, s 1284(1) at **[S1284]**.

67 Short title

This Act may be cited as the Companies (Audit, Investigations and Community Enterprise) Act 2004.

[940]

SCHEDULES

(*Sch 1 inserts CA 1985, Sch 7B at* **[653E]** *et seq* (*and is repealed by the Companies Act 2006, s 1295, Sch 16, as from a day to be appointed*)*; Sch 2, Pt 1* (*which is repealed by CA 2006, s 1295, Sch 16, as from a day to be appointed*) *amends CA 1989, ss 30, 40, 87 at* **[779]**, **[789]**, **[809]**, *amends CA 1989, s 47* (*which was repealed, subject to savings, by the Competition Act 1998 and other enactments* (*Amendment*) *Regulations 2004, SI 2004/1261, reg 5, Sch 2, para 2*(*1*), (*2*), *as from 1 May 2004*), *and amends the Companies* (*Northern Ireland*) *Order 1990, SI 1990/593* (*NI 5*)*; Sch 2, Pt 2* (*which is repealed by CA 2006, s 1295, Sch 16, as from 1 October 2007* (*in part*), *and as from a day to be appointed* (*otherwise*)) *amends CA 1985, ss 249E, 732–734, Sch 24 at* **[251]**, **[609]**–**[611]**, **[689]**, *and the Companies* (*Northern Ireland*) *Order 1986, SI 1986/1032* (*NI 6*)*; Sch 2, Pt 3, paras 16–21, 25 insert CA 1985, s 447, Schs 15C, 15D at* **[480A]**, **[678A]**, **[678B]**, *substitute ss 449, 451 at* **[482]**, **[484]**, *and amend ss 451A, 452 at* **[485]**, **[486]***; paras 22–24 amend ss 732–734, Sch 24 of the 1985 Act at* **[609]**–**[611]**, **[689]** (*and are repealed by Sch 16, as from 1 October 2007* (*in part*), *and as from a day to be appointed* (*otherwise*))*; para 27 amends the Insolvency Act 1986, s 124A at* **[3281]***; para 28 amends the Company Directors Disqualification Act 1986, s 8 at* **[744]***; para 29 amends CA 1989, s 87 at* **[809]***; paras 30, 31 amend the Criminal Justice and Police Act 2001, Sch 2, and the Anti-terrorism, Crime and Security Act 2001, Sch 4.*)

SCHEDULE 3
REGULATOR OF COMMUNITY INTEREST COMPANIES

Section 27

Regulator's terms of appointment

1.—(1) The period for which a person is appointed as Regulator must not exceed five years.

(2) A person who has held office as Regulator may be re-appointed, once only, for a further period not exceeding five years.

(3) The Regulator may at any time resign the office by giving notice in writing to the Secretary of State.

(4) The Secretary of State may at any time remove the Regulator on the ground of incapacity or misbehaviour.

(5) Subject to that, the Regulator holds and vacates office on the terms determined by the Secretary of State.

Remuneration and pensions

2.—(1) The Secretary of State may pay remuneration and travelling and other allowances to the Regulator.

(2) The Secretary of State may—

(a) pay a pension, allowance or gratuity to or in respect of a person who is or has been the Regulator, or

(b) make contributions or payments towards provision for a pension, allowance or gratuity for or in respect of such a person.

Staff

3.—(1) The Regulator may, after consulting the Minister for the Civil Service as to numbers and terms and conditions of service, appoint such staff as the Regulator may determine.

(2) The members of staff must include a deputy to the Regulator who is to act as Regulator—

(a) during any vacancy in that office, or

(b) if the Regulator is absent, subject to suspension or unable to act.

(3) Where a participant in a scheme under section 1 of the Superannuation Act 1972 (c 11) is appointed as the Regulator, the Minister for the Civil Service may determine that the person's term of office as the Regulator is to be treated for the purposes of the scheme as service in the employment by reference to which he was a participant (whether or not any benefits are payable by virtue of paragraph 2(2)).

4. The [chairman of the Charity Commission] may make available to the Regulator, to assist in the exercise of the Regulator's functions, [any other member of the Commission appointed under paragraph 1(2) of Schedule 1A to the Charities Act 1993 or any member of staff of the Commission appointed under paragraph 5(1) of that Schedule].

Delegation of functions

5. Anything which the Regulator is authorised or required to do may be done by a member of the Regulator's staff if authorised by the Regulator (generally or specifically) for that purpose.

Finance

6. The Secretary of State may make payments to the Regulator.

Reports and other information

7.—(1) The Regulator must, in respect of each financial year, prepare a report on the exercise of the Regulator's functions during the financial year.

(2) The Regulator must prepare accounts in respect of a financial year if the Secretary of State so directs.

(3) The Regulator must send a copy of the accounts to the Comptroller and Auditor General.

(4) The Comptroller and Auditor General must examine, certify and report on the accounts and send a copy of the report to the Regulator.

(5) The Regulator must include the accounts and the Comptroller and Auditor General's report on them in the report prepared by the Regulator in respect of the financial year to which the accounts relate.

(6) The Regulator must prepare that report as soon as possible after the end of the financial year to which it relates.

(7) The Regulator must send to the Secretary of State a copy of—

(a) each report prepared by the Regulator under sub-paragraph (1), and

(b) each report prepared by the Official Property Holder under paragraph 6 of Schedule 5.

(8) The Secretary of State must lay before each House of Parliament a copy of each of those reports.

(9) The Regulator must supply the Secretary of State with such other reports and information relating to the exercise of the Regulator's functions as the Secretary of State may require.

(10) "Financial year" means—

(a) the period beginning with the date on which a person is first appointed as the Regulator and ending with the next 31st March, and

(b) each successive period of 12 months beginning with 1st April.

Amendments

8, 9. …

[941]

NOTES

Para 4: words in square brackets substituted by the Charities Act 2006, s 75, Sch 8, paras 200, 204, as from 27 February 2007.

Para 8: amended the Parliamentary Commissioner Act 1967, Sch 2 (and is superseded by the Parliamentary Commissioner Order 2005, SI 2005/249, art 2, Sch 1).

Para 9: amends the House of Commons Disqualification Act 1975, Sch 1, Pt III.

SCHEDULE 4
APPEAL OFFICER FOR COMMUNITY INTEREST COMPANIES

Section 28

Appeal Officer's terms of appointment

1.—(1) The Appeal Officer holds office for the period determined by the Secretary of State on appointment (or re-appointment).

(2) But—

(a) the Appeal Officer may at any time resign the office by giving notice in writing to the Secretary of State, and

(b) the Secretary of State may at any time remove the Appeal Officer on the ground of incapacity or misbehaviour.

(3) Subject to that, the Appeal Officer holds and vacates office on the terms determined by the Secretary of State.

Remuneration and pensions

2.—(1) The Secretary of State may pay remuneration and travelling and other allowances to the Appeal Officer.

(2) The Secretary of State may—

(a) pay a pension, allowance or gratuity to or in respect of a person who is or has been the Appeal Officer, or

(b) make contributions or payments towards provision for a pension, allowance or gratuity for or in respect of such a person.

Finance

3. The Secretary of State may make payments to the Appeal Officer.

Procedure

4.—(1) Regulations may make provision about the practice and procedure to be followed by the Appeal Officer.

(2) Regulations under this paragraph may in particular impose time limits for bringing appeals.

PART I COMPANIES LEGISLATION

Amendments

5. …

[942]

NOTES

Paras 5, 6: amend the Parliamentary Commissioner Act 1967, Sch 2, and the House of Commons Disqualification Act 1975, Sch 1, Pt III.

Regulations: the Community Interest Company Regulations 2005, SI 2005/1788 at **[7399]**.

SCHEDULE 5
OFFICIAL PROPERTY HOLDER FOR COMMUNITY INTEREST COMPANIES

Section 29

Status

1.—(1) The Official Property Holder is a corporation sole.

(2) A document purporting to be—

(a) duly executed under the seal of the Official Property Holder, or

(b) signed on behalf of the Official Property Holder,

shall be received in evidence and shall, unless the contrary is proved, be taken to be so executed or signed.

Relationship with Regulator

2. The Regulator must make available to the Official Property Holder such members of the Regulator's staff as the Official Property Holder may require in order to exercise the functions of the office.

Effect of vacancy

3. The Regulator must appoint a member of the Regulator's staff who is to act as Official Property Holder—

(a) during any vacancy in the office, or

(b) if the Official Property Holder is absent, subject to suspension or unable to act.

Property

4.—(1) The Official Property Holder holds property vested in or transferred to him as a trustee.

(2) The Official Property Holder may release or deal with the property—

(a) to give effect to any interest in or right over the property of any person (other than the community interest company by which, or in trust for which, the property was held before it was vested or transferred), or

(b) at the request of a person appointed to act as administrative receiver, administrator, provisional liquidator or liquidator of the company.

(3) Subject to sub-paragraph (2), the Official Property Holder may not release or deal with the property except in accordance with directions given by the Regulator.

Finance

5.—(1) The Official Property Holder may recover his expenses in respect of property held by him from the property or from the community interest company by which, or in trust for which, the property was held before it was vested in or transferred to the Official Property Holder.

(2) Any expenses of the Official Property Holder not recovered under sub-paragraph (1) are to be met by the Regulator.

Reports

6.—(1) As soon as possible after the end of each financial year, the Official Property Holder must prepare a report on the exercise of the Official Property Holder's functions during the financial year.

(2) The Official Property Holder must send a copy of the report to the Regulator.

(3) "Financial year" means—

(a) the period beginning with the date on which a person is first appointed as the Official Property Holder and ending with the next 31st March, and

(b) each successive period of 12 months beginning with 1st April.

[943]

(*Sch 6: paras 1–9 amend CA 1985, ss 26, 27, 30, 33, 43, 351, Sch 24 at* **[27]**, **[28]**, **[31]**, **[34]**, **[49]**, **[362]**, **[689]**, *and insert s 34A at* **[35A]** (*and are repealed by the Companies Act 2006, s 1295, Sch 16, as from a day to be appointed*); *para 10 amends the Limited Liability Partnerships Act 2000, Schedule, para 8 at* **[3516]**.)

SCHEDULE 7
COMMUNITY INTEREST COMPANIES: INVESTIGATIONS

Section 42

Power to require documents and information

1.—(1) The investigator of a community interest company may require the company or any other person—

(a) to produce such documents (or documents of such description) as the investigator may specify;

(b) to provide such information (or information of such description) as the investigator may specify.

(2) A person on whom a requirement is imposed under sub-paragraph (1) may require the investigator to produce evidence of his authority.

(3) A requirement under sub-paragraph (1) must be complied with at such time and place as may be specified by the investigator.

(4) The production of a document in pursuance of this paragraph does not affect any lien which a person has on the document.

(5) The investigator may take copies of or extracts from a document produced in pursuance of this paragraph.

(6) In relation to information recorded otherwise than in legible form, the power to require production of it includes power to require the production of a copy of it in legible form or in a form from which it can readily be produced in visible and legible form.

(7) In this Schedule—

(a) "the investigator of a community interest company" means a person investigating the company's affairs under section 42, and

(b) "document" includes information recorded in any form.

Privileged information

2.—(1) Nothing in paragraph 1 requires a person to produce a document or provide information in respect of which a claim could be maintained—

(a) in an action in the High Court, to legal professional privilege, or

(b) in an action in the Court of Session, to confidentiality of communications,

but a person who is a lawyer may be required to provide the name and address of his client.

(2) Nothing in paragraph 1 requires a person carrying on the business of banking to produce a document, or provide information, relating to the affairs of a customer unless a requirement to produce the document, or provide the information, has been imposed on the customer under that paragraph.

Use of information as evidence

3.—(1) A statement made by a person in compliance with a requirement imposed under paragraph 1 may be used in evidence against the person.

(2) But in criminal proceedings—

(a) no evidence relating to the statement may be adduced by or on behalf of the prosecution, and

(b) no question relating to it may be asked by or on behalf of the prosecution,

unless evidence relating to it is adduced or a question relating to it is asked in the proceedings by or on behalf of that person.

(3) However, sub-paragraph (2) does not apply to proceedings in which a person is charged with—

[(a) an offence under paragraph 5 below (false information), or

(b) an offence under section 5 of the Perjury Act 1911, section 44(2) of the Criminal Law (Consolidation) (Scotland) Act 1995 or Article 10 of the Perjury (Northern Ireland) Order 1979 (false statement made otherwise than on oath).]

Failure to comply with requirement

4.—(1) This paragraph applies if a person fails to comply with a requirement imposed under paragraph 1.

(2) The investigator may certify that fact in writing to the court.

(3) If, after hearing—

(a) any witnesses who may be produced against or on behalf of the alleged offender, and

(b) any statement which may be offered in defence,

the court is satisfied that the offender failed without reasonable excuse to comply with the requirement, it may deal with him as if he had been guilty of contempt of the court.

False information

5.—(1) A person commits an offence if in purported compliance with a requirement under paragraph 1 to provide information, the person—

(a) provides information which the person knows to be false in a material particular, or

(b) recklessly provides information which is false in a material particular,

...

[(1A) A prosecution for an offence under sub-paragraph (1) may be instituted—

(a) in England and Wales, only with the consent of the Director of Public Prosecutions;

(b) in Northern Ireland, only with the consent of the Director of Public Prosecutions for Northern Ireland.]

(2) A person guilty of an offence under sub-paragraph (1) is liable—

(a) on conviction on indictment to imprisonment for a term not exceeding two years or a fine or to both,

(b) on summary conviction in England and Wales, to imprisonment for a term not exceeding twelve months or a fine of an amount not exceeding the statutory maximum or to both, and

(c) on summary conviction in Scotland [or Northern Ireland], to imprisonment for a term not exceeding six months or a fine of an amount not exceeding the statutory maximum or to both.

(3) In relation to an offence committed before section 154(1) of the Criminal Justice Act 2003 (c 44) comes into force, sub-paragraph (2)(b) has effect as if for "twelve" there were substituted "six".

[944]

NOTES

Para 3: words in square brackets in sub-para (3) substituted by the Companies Act 2006 (Commencement No 2, Consequential Amendments, Transitional Provisions and Savings) Order 2007, SI 2007/1093, art 6(2), Sch 4, Pt 1, para 26(1), (2), as from 6 April 2007.

Para 5: words omitted from sub-para (1) repealed, sub-para (1A) inserted, and words in square brackets in sub-para (2) inserted, by SI 2007/1093, art 6(2), Sch 4, Pt 1, para 26(1), (3), as from 6 April 2007.

(*Sch 8 contains repeals of or in CA 1985, ss 27, 245C, 256, 310, 390A, 734, Schs 4A, 24, IA 1986, Sch 13, and CA 1989, s 48, 63, 65, 67, 69, 120 as noted to the provisions affected. Other repeals in this Schedule are outside the scope of this work.*)

B. The Companies Act 2006

COMPANIES ACT 2006

(2006 c 46)

NOTES

Commencement: the commencement of this Act is provided for by s 1300 at **[S1300]**. See also the Orders made under that section, i e the Companies Act 2006 (Commencement No 1, Transitional Provisions and Savings) Order 2006, SI 2006/3428 at **[7574]**, and the Companies Act 2006 (Commencement No 2, Consequential Amendments, Transitional Provisions and Savings) Order 2007, SI 2007/1093 at **[7614]**. See also the note below.

Draft Companies Act 2006 (Commencement No 3, Consequential Amendments, Transitional Provisions and Savings) Order 2007: this is set out in full in Appendix 12 at **[A12]**. Commencements made by the draft Order are noted to the appropriate provisions *post*.

Interpretation of provisions in this Act: the Companies Act 2006 (Commencement No 1, Transitional Provisions and Savings) Order 2006, SI 2006/3428, art 6 (at **[7579]**) provides as set out below. Note that identical provision is also made by the Companies Act 2006 (Commencement No 2, Consequential Amendments, Transitional Provisions and Savings) Order 2007, SI 2007/1093, art 4 (at **[7617]**) and the draft Companies Act 2006 (Commencement No 3, Consequential Amendments, Transitional Provisions and Savings) Order 2007, art 7 (see **[A12]**):

"4 Interpretation of provisions brought into force

Where an expression in a provision brought into force by this Order (or in an adaptation made by this Order of such a provision)—

(a) is defined in the 1985 Act or the 1986 Order ("the old definition"); and

(b) is defined in the Companies Act 2006 by another provision that is not yet in force for the purposes of the provision brought into force ("the new definition"),

the expression has, for the purposes of the provision brought into force (or the adaptation), the meaning given by the old definition until the new definition is brought into force for the purposes of that provision.".

Application to unregistered companies: as to the application of certain parts of this Act to unregistered companies, see the Companies Acts (Unregistered Companies) Regulations 2007, SI 2007/318 at **[7607]** (made under s 1043 of this Act).

This Act is reproduced as amended by: the Companies (EEA State) Regulations 2007, SI 2007/732; the Government of Wales Act 2006 (Consequential Modifications and Transitional Provisions) Order 2007, SI 2007/1388.

ARRANGEMENT OF SECTIONS

PART 1
GENERAL INTRODUCTORY PROVISIONS

Companies and Companies Acts

Types of company

PART 2
COMPANY FORMATION

General

Requirements for registration

Registration and its effect

PART 3
A COMPANY'S CONSTITUTION

CHAPTER 1
INTRODUCTORY

CHAPTER 2
ARTICLES OF ASSOCIATION

General

Alteration of articles

Supplementary

CHAPTER 3
RESOLUTIONS AND AGREEMENTS AFFECTING A COMPANY'S CONSTITUTION

CHAPTER 4
MISCELLANEOUS AND SUPPLEMENTARY PROVISIONS

Statement of company's objects

Other provisions with respect to a company's constitution

Supplementary provisions

PART 4
A COMPANY'S CAPACITY AND RELATED MATTERS

Capacity of company and power of directors to bind it

PART I
COMPANIES LEGISLATION

Formalities of doing business under the law of England and Wales or Northern Ireland

Formalities of doing business under the law of Scotland

Other matters

PART 5
A COMPANY'S NAME

CHAPTER 1
GENERAL REQUIREMENTS

Prohibited names

Sensitive words and expressions

Permitted characters etc

CHAPTER 2
INDICATIONS OF COMPANY TYPE OR LEGAL FORM

Required indications for limited companies

Inappropriate use of indications of company type or legal form

CHAPTER 3
SIMILARITY TO OTHER NAMES

Similarity to other name on registrar's index

Similarity to other name in which person has goodwill

PART 8
A COMPANY'S MEMBERS

CHAPTER 1
THE MEMBERS OF A COMPANY

CHAPTER 2
REGISTER OF MEMBERS

General

Special cases

Supplementary

CHAPTER 3
OVERSEAS BRANCH REGISTERS

CHAPTER 4
PROHIBITION ON SUBSIDIARY BEING MEMBER OF ITS HOLDING COMPANY

General prohibition

Subsidiary acting as personal representative or trustee

Subsidiary acting as dealer in securities

Supplementary

PART 9
EXERCISE OF MEMBERS' RIGHTS

Effect of provisions in company's articles

Information rights

Exercise of rights where shares held on behalf of others

PART 10
A COMPANY'S DIRECTORS

CHAPTER 1
APPOINTMENT AND REMOVAL OF DIRECTORS

Requirement to have directors

Appointment

Register of directors, etc

Removal

CHAPTER 2
GENERAL DUTIES OF DIRECTORS

Introductory

The general duties

Supplementary provisions

CHAPTER 3
DECLARATION OF INTEREST IN EXISTING TRANSACTION OR ARRANGEMENT

CHAPTER 4
TRANSACTIONS WITH DIRECTORS REQUIRING APPROVAL OF MEMBERS

Service contracts

Substantial property transactions

Loans, quasi-loans and credit transactions

Payments for loss of office

Supplementary

CHAPTER 5
DIRECTORS' SERVICE CONTRACTS

CHAPTER 6
CONTRACTS WITH SOLE MEMBERS WHO ARE DIRECTORS

CHAPTER 7
DIRECTORS' LIABILITIES

Provision protecting directors from liability

Ratification of acts giving rise to liability

CHAPTER 8
DIRECTORS' RESIDENTIAL ADDRESSES: PROTECTION FROM DISCLOSURE

CHAPTER 9
SUPPLEMENTARY PROVISIONS

Provision for employees on cessation or transfer of business

Records of meetings of directors

Meaning of "director" and "shadow director"

Other definitions

General

PART 11
DERIVATIVE CLAIMS AND PROCEEDINGS BY MEMBERS

CHAPTER 1
DERIVATIVE CLAIMS IN ENGLAND AND WALES OR NORTHERN IRELAND

CHAPTER 2
DERIVATIVE PROCEEDINGS IN SCOTLAND

PART 12
COMPANY SECRETARIES

Private companies

Public companies

Provisions applying to private companies with a secretary and to public companies

PART 13
RESOLUTIONS AND MEETINGS

CHAPTER 1
GENERAL PROVISIONS ABOUT RESOLUTIONS

CHAPTER 2
WRITTEN RESOLUTIONS

General provisions about written resolutions

Circulation of written resolutions

Agreeing to written resolutions

Supplementary

CHAPTER 3
RESOLUTIONS AT MEETINGS

General provisions about resolutions at meetings

Calling meetings

Notice of meetings

Members' statements

Procedure at meetings

Proxies

Adjourned meetings

Electronic communications

Application to class meetings

Group accounts: general

Information to be given in notes to the accounts

Approval and signing of accounts

CHAPTER 5
DIRECTORS' REPORT

Directors' report

CHAPTER 6
QUOTED COMPANIES: DIRECTORS' REMUNERATION REPORT

CHAPTER 7
PUBLICATION OF ACCOUNTS AND REPORTS

Duty to circulate copies of accounts and reports

Option to provide summary financial statement

Quoted companies: requirements as to website publication

Right of member or debenture holder to demand copies of accounts and reports

Requirements in connection with publication of accounts and reports

CHAPTER 8
PUBLIC COMPANIES: LAYING OF ACCOUNTS AND REPORTS BEFORE GENERAL MEETING

CHAPTER 9
QUOTED COMPANIES: MEMBERS' APPROVAL OF DIRECTORS' REMUNERATION REPORT

CHAPTER 10
FILING OF ACCOUNTS AND REPORTS

Duty to file accounts and reports

Filing obligations of different descriptions of company

Requirements where abbreviated accounts delivered

Failure to file accounts and reports

CHAPTER 11
REVISION OF DEFECTIVE ACCOUNTS AND REPORTS

Voluntary revision

Secretary of State's notice

Application to court

Power of authorised person to require documents etc

CHAPTER 12
SUPPLEMENTARY PROVISIONS

Liability for false or misleading statements in reports

Accounting and reporting standards

Companies qualifying as medium-sized

General power to make further provision about accounts and reports

Other supplementary provisions

PART 16
AUDIT

CHAPTER 1
REQUIREMENT FOR AUDITED ACCOUNTS

Requirement for audited accounts

Exemption from audit: small companies

Exemption from audit: dormant companies

Companies subject to public sector audit

General power of amendment by regulations

CHAPTER 2
APPOINTMENT OF AUDITORS

Private companies

Public companies

General provisions

CHAPTER 3
FUNCTIONS OF AUDITOR

Auditor's report

Duties and rights of auditors

Supplementary provisions

CHAPTER 2
EVIDENCING AND TRANSFER OF TITLE TO SECURITIES WITHOUT WRITTEN INSTRUMENT

Introductory

Powers exercisable

Supplementary

PART 22
INFORMATION ABOUT INTERESTS IN A COMPANY'S SHARES

Introductory

Notice requiring information about interests in shares

Orders imposing restrictions on shares

Power of members to require company to act

Register of interests disclosed

PART I COMPANIES LEGISLATION

Meaning of interest in shares

Other supplementary provisions

PART 23
DISTRIBUTIONS

CHAPTER 1
RESTRICTIONS ON WHEN DISTRIBUTIONS MAY BE MADE

Introductory

General rules

Distributions by investment companies

CHAPTER 2
JUSTIFICATION OF DISTRIBUTION BY REFERENCE TO ACCOUNTS

Justification of distribution by reference to accounts

Requirements applicable in relation to relevant accounts

Application of provisions to successive distributions etc

CHAPTER 3
SUPPLEMENTARY PROVISIONS

Accounting matters

Distributions in kind

Consequences of unlawful distribution

Other matters

PART 24
A COMPANY'S ANNUAL RETURN

PART 25
COMPANY CHARGES

CHAPTER 1
COMPANIES REGISTERED IN ENGLAND AND WALES OR IN NORTHERN IRELAND

Requirement to register company charges

Special rules about debentures

Charges in other jurisdictions

Orders charging land: Northern Ireland

The register of charges

Avoidance of certain charges

Companies' records and registers

CHAPTER 2
COMPANIES REGISTERED IN SCOTLAND

Charges requiring registration

PART 28
TAKEOVERS ETC

CHAPTER 1
THE TAKEOVER PANEL

The Panel and its rules

Information

Co-operation

Hearings and appeals

Contravention of rules etc

Funding

Miscellaneous and supplementary

CHAPTER 2
IMPEDIMENTS TO TAKEOVERS

Opting in and opting out

Consequences of opting in

Supplementary

CHAPTER 3
"SQUEEZE-OUT" AND "SELL-OUT"

Takeover offers

PART I
COMPANIES LEGISLATION

CHAPTER 2
UNREGISTERED COMPANIES

PART 34
OVERSEAS COMPANIES

Introductory

Registration of particulars

Other requirements

Supplementary

PART 35
THE REGISTRAR OF COMPANIES

The registrar

Certificates of incorporation

Registered numbers

Delivery of documents to the registrar

Requirements for proper delivery

Public notice of receipt of certain documents

Meaning of "subsidiary" and related expressions

Meaning of "undertaking" and related expressions

Other definitions

General

PART 39
COMPANIES: MINOR AMENDMENTS

PART 40
COMPANY DIRECTORS: FOREIGN DISQUALIFICATION ETC

Introductory

Power to disqualify

Power to make persons liable for company's debts

Power to require statements to be sent to the registrar of companies

PART 41
BUSINESS NAMES

CHAPTER 1
RESTRICTED OR PROHIBITED NAMES

Introductory

Sensitive words or expressions

CHAPTER 6
SUPPLEMENTARY AND GENERAL

Power to require second company audit

False and misleading statements

Fees

Delegation of Secretary of State's functions

International obligations

General provision relating to offences

Notices etc

Interpretation

Miscellaneous and general

PART 43
TRANSPARENCY OBLIGATIONS AND RELATED MATTERS

Introductory

Transparency obligations

Other matters

PART 44
MISCELLANEOUS PROVISIONS

Regulation of actuaries etc

PART I
COMPANIES LEGISLATION

An Act to reform company law and restate the greater part of the enactments relating to companies; to make other provision relating to companies and other forms of business organisation; to make provision about directors' disqualification, business names, auditors and actuaries; to amend Part 9 of the Enterprise Act 2002; and for connected purposes

[8 November 2006]

PART 1
GENERAL INTRODUCTORY PROVISIONS

Companies and Companies Acts

1 Companies

(1) In the Companies Acts, unless the context otherwise requires—
"company" means a company formed and registered under this Act, that is—
(a) a company so formed and registered after the commencement of this Part, or
(b) a company that immediately before the commencement of this Part—
(i) was formed and registered under the Companies Act 1985 (c 6) or the Companies (Northern Ireland) Order 1986 (SI 1986/1032 (NI 6)), or
(ii) was an existing company for the purposes of that Act or that Order,
(which is to be treated on commencement as if formed and registered under this Act).

(2) Certain provisions of the Companies Acts apply to—
(a) companies registered, but not formed, under this Act (see Chapter 1 of Part 33), and
(b) bodies incorporated in the United Kingdom but not registered under this Act (see Chapter 2 of that Part).

(3) For provisions applying to companies incorporated outside the United Kingdom, see Part 34 (overseas companies).

[S1]

NOTES

Commencement: to be appointed.

2 The Companies Acts

(1) In this Act "the Companies Acts" means—
(a) the company law provisions of this Act,
(b) Part 2 of the Companies (Audit, Investigations and Community Enterprise) Act 2004 (c 27) (community interest companies), and
(c) the provisions of the Companies Act 1985 (c 6) and the Companies Consolidation (Consequential Provisions) Act 1985 (c 9) that remain in force.

(2) The company law provisions of this Act are—
(a) the provisions of Parts 1 to 39 of this Act, and
(b) the provisions of Parts 45 to 47 of this Act so far as they apply for the purposes of those Parts.

[S2]

NOTES

Commencement: 1 January 2007 (certain purposes); 20 January 2007 (certain purposes); 6 April 2007 (otherwise) (for transitional adaptations see the notes below).

Note: the Companies Act 2006 (Commencement No 1, Transitional Provisions and Savings) Order 2006, SI 2006/3428, arts 2(2), 3(2) provide that this section shall come into force on 1 January 2007 and 20 January 2007 respectively so far as is necessary for the purposes of the provisions of this Act brought into force on those dates by arts 2(1), 3(1) of that Order (see **[7575]**, **[7576]**).

Transitional adaptations: art 5 of the Companies Act 2006 (Commencement No 1, Transitional Provisions and Savings) Order 2006, SI 2006/3428 provides that the provisions brought into force by arts 2–4 of 2006 Order shall have effect subject to any transitional adaptations specified in Sch 1 to that Order. Schedule 1, para 1 to the Order (at **[7582]**) provides as follows—

"**1.**—(1) Section 2 (the Companies Acts) has effect with the following adaptation.

(2) For subsection (1)(c) substitute—

"(c) the provisions of the Companies Acts as defined in section 744 of the Companies Act 1985, and the Companies Orders as defined in Article 2(3) of the Companies (Northern Ireland) Order 1986, that remain in force.".".

Transitional adaptations: art 3 of the Companies Act 2006 (Commencement No 2, Consequential Amendments, Transitional Provisions and Savings) Order 2007, SI 2007/1093 provides that the provisions brought into force by art 2 of 2007 Order shall have effect subject to any transitional adaptations specified in Sch 1 to that Order. Schedule 1, para 1 to the Order (at **[7625]**) provides as follows—

"**1.**—(1) Section 2 (the Companies Acts) has effect with the following adaptation.

(2) For subsection (1)(c) substitute—

"(c) the provisions of the Companies Acts as defined in section 744 of the Companies Act 1985, and the Companies Orders as defined in Article 2(3) of the Companies (Northern Ireland) Order 1986, that remain in force"".

Types of company

3 Limited and unlimited companies

(1) A company is a "limited company" if the liability of its members is limited by its constitution.

It may be limited by shares or limited by guarantee.

(2) If their liability is limited to the amount, if any, unpaid on the shares held by them, the company is "limited by shares".

(3) If their liability is limited to such amount as the members undertake to contribute to the assets of the company in the event of its being wound up, the company is "limited by guarantee".

(4) If there is no limit on the liability of its members, the company is an "unlimited company".

[S3]

NOTES

Commencement: to be appointed.

4 Private and public companies

(1) A "private company" is any company that is not a public company.

(2) A "public company" is a company limited by shares or limited by guarantee and having a share capital—

(a) whose certificate of incorporation states that it is a public company, and
(b) in relation to which the requirements of this Act, or the former Companies Acts, as to registration or re-registration as a public company have been complied with on or after the relevant date.

(3) For the purposes of subsection (2)(b) the relevant date is—

(a) in relation to registration or re-registration in Great Britain, 22nd December 1980;
(b) in relation to registration or re-registration in Northern Ireland, 1st July 1983.

(4) For the two major differences between private and public companies, see Part 20.

[S4]

NOTES

Commencement: to be appointed.

5 Companies limited by guarantee and having share capital

(1) A company cannot be formed as, or become, a company limited by guarantee with a share capital.

(2) Provision to this effect has been in force—

(a) in Great Britain since 22nd December 1980, and
(b) in Northern Ireland since 1st July 1983.

(3) Any provision in the constitution of a company limited by guarantee that purports to divide the company's undertaking into shares or interests is a provision for a share capital.

This applies whether or not the nominal value or number of the shares or interests is specified by the provision.

[S5]

NOTES

Commencement: to be appointed.

6 Community interest companies

(1) In accordance with Part 2 of the Companies (Audit, Investigations and Community Enterprise) Act 2004 (c 27)—

(a) a company limited by shares or a company limited by guarantee and not having a share capital may be formed as or become a community interest company, and
(b) a company limited by guarantee and having a share capital may become a community interest company.

(2) The other provisions of the Companies Acts have effect subject to that Part.

[S6]

NOTES

Commencement: to be appointed.

PART 2
COMPANY FORMATION

General

7 Method of forming company

(1) A company is formed under this Act by one or more persons—

(a) subscribing their names to a memorandum of association (see section 8), and
(b) complying with the requirements of this Act as to registration (see sections 9 to 13).

(2) A company may not be so formed for an unlawful purpose.

[S7]

NOTES

Commencement: to be appointed.

8 Memorandum of association

(1) A memorandum of association is a memorandum stating that the subscribers—

(a) wish to form a company under this Act, and

(b) agree to become members of the company and, in the case of a company that is to have a share capital, to take at least one share each.

(2) The memorandum must be in the prescribed form and must be authenticated by each subscriber.

[S8]

NOTES

Commencement: 20 January 2007 (for the purpose of enabling the exercise of powers to make Orders or Regulations by statutory instrument); to be appointed (otherwise).

Requirements for registration

9 Registration documents

(1) The memorandum of association must be delivered to the registrar together with an application for registration of the company, the documents required by this section and a statement of compliance.

(2) The application for registration must state—

(a) the company's proposed name,

(b) whether the company's registered office is to be situated in England and Wales (or in Wales), in Scotland or in Northern Ireland,

(c) whether the liability of the members of the company is to be limited, and if so whether it is to be limited by shares or by guarantee, and

(d) whether the company is to be a private or a public company.

(3) If the application is delivered by a person as agent for the subscribers to the memorandum of association, it must state his name and address.

(4) The application must contain—

(a) in the case of a company that is to have a share capital, a statement of capital and initial shareholdings (see section 10);

(b) in the case of a company that is to be limited by guarantee, a statement of guarantee (see section 11);

(c) a statement of the company's proposed officers (see section 12).

(5) The application must also contain—

(a) a statement of the intended address of the company's registered office; and

(b) a copy of any proposed articles of association (to the extent that these are not supplied by the default application of model articles: see section 20).

(6) The application must be delivered—

(a) to the registrar of companies for England and Wales, if the registered office of the company is to be situated in England and Wales (or in Wales);

(b) to the registrar of companies for Scotland, if the registered office of the company is to be situated in Scotland;

(c) to the registrar of companies for Northern Ireland, if the registered office of the company is to be situated in Northern Ireland.

[S9]

NOTES

Commencement: to be appointed.

10 Statement of capital and initial shareholdings

(1) The statement of capital and initial shareholdings required to be delivered in the case of a company that is to have a share capital must comply with this section.

(2) It must state—
- (a) the total number of shares of the company to be taken on formation by the subscribers to the memorandum of association,
- (b) the aggregate nominal value of those shares,
- (c) for each class of shares—
  - (i) prescribed particulars of the rights attached to the shares,
  - (ii) the total number of shares of that class, and
  - (iii) the aggregate nominal value of shares of that class, and
- (d) the amount to be paid up and the amount (if any) to be unpaid on each share (whether on account of the nominal value of the share or by way of premium).

(3) It must contain such information as may be prescribed for the purpose of identifying the subscribers to the memorandum of association.

(4) It must state, with respect to each subscriber to the memorandum—
- (a) the number, nominal value (of each share) and class of shares to be taken by him on formation, and
- (b) the amount to be paid up and the amount (if any) to be unpaid on each share (whether on account of the nominal value of the share or by way of premium).

(5) Where a subscriber to the memorandum is to take shares of more than one class, the information required under subsection (4)(a) is required for each class.

[S10]

NOTES

Commencement: 20 January 2007 (for the purpose of enabling the exercise of powers to make Orders or Regulations by statutory instrument); to be appointed (otherwise).

11 Statement of guarantee

(1) The statement of guarantee required to be delivered in the case of a company that is to be limited by guarantee must comply with this section.

(2) It must contain such information as may be prescribed for the purpose of identifying the subscribers to the memorandum of association.

(3) It must state that each member undertakes that, if the company is wound up while he is a member, or within one year after he ceases to be a member, he will contribute to the assets of the company such amount as may be required for—
- (a) payment of the debts and liabilities of the company contracted before he ceases to be a member,
- (b) payment of the costs, charges and expenses of winding up, and
- (c) adjustment of the rights of the contributories among themselves,

not exceeding a specified amount.

[S11]

NOTES

Commencement: 20 January 2007 (for the purpose of enabling the exercise of powers to make Orders or Regulations by statutory instrument); to be appointed (otherwise).

12 Statement of proposed officers

(1) The statement of the company's proposed officers required to be delivered to the registrar must contain the required particulars of—
- (a) the person who is, or persons who are, to be the first director or directors of the company;
- (b) in the case of a company that is to be a private company, any person who is (or any persons who are) to be the first secretary (or joint secretaries) of the company;
- (c) in the case of a company that is to be a public company, the person who is (or the persons who are) to be the first secretary (or joint secretaries) of the company.

(2) The required particulars are the particulars that will be required to be stated—

(a) in the case of a director, in the company's register of directors and register of directors' residential addresses (see sections 162 to 166);
(b) in the case of a secretary, in the company's register of secretaries (see sections 277 to 279).

(3) The statement must also contain a consent by each of the persons named as a director, as secretary or as one of joint secretaries, to act in the relevant capacity.

If all the partners in a firm are to be joint secretaries, consent may be given by one partner on behalf of all of them.

[S12]

NOTES

Commencement: to be appointed.

13 Statement of compliance

(1) The statement of compliance required to be delivered to the registrar is a statement that the requirements of this Act as to registration have been complied with.

(2) The registrar may accept the statement of compliance as sufficient evidence of compliance.

[S13]

NOTES

Commencement: to be appointed.

Registration and its effect

14 Registration

If the registrar is satisfied that the requirements of this Act as to registration are complied with, he shall register the documents delivered to him.

[S14]

NOTES

Commencement: to be appointed.

15 Issue of certificate of incorporation

(1) On the registration of a company, the registrar of companies shall give a certificate that the company is incorporated.

(2) The certificate must state—
(a) the name and registered number of the company,
(b) the date of its incorporation,
(c) whether it is a limited or unlimited company, and if it is limited whether it is limited by shares or limited by guarantee,
(d) whether it is a private or a public company, and
(e) whether the company's registered office is situated in England and Wales (or in Wales), in Scotland or in Northern Ireland.

(3) The certificate must be signed by the registrar or authenticated by the registrar's official seal.

(4) The certificate is conclusive evidence that the requirements of this Act as to registration have been complied with and that the company is duly registered under this Act.

[S15]

NOTES

Commencement: to be appointed.

16 Effect of registration

(1) The registration of a company has the following effects as from the date of incorporation.

(2) The subscribers to the memorandum, together with such other persons as may from time to time become members of the company, are a body corporate by the name stated in the certificate of incorporation.

(3) That body corporate is capable of exercising all the functions of an incorporated company.

(4) The status and registered office of the company are as stated in, or in connection with, the application for registration.

(5) In the case of a company having a share capital, the subscribers to the memorandum become holders of the shares specified in the statement of capital and initial shareholdings.

(6) The persons named in the statement of proposed officers—

(a) as director, or

(b) as secretary or joint secretary of the company,

are deemed to have been appointed to that office.

[S16]

NOTES

Commencement: to be appointed.

PART 3
A COMPANY'S CONSTITUTION

CHAPTER 1
INTRODUCTORY

17 A company's constitution

Unless the context otherwise requires, references in the Companies Acts to a company's constitution include—

(a) the company's articles, and

(b) any resolutions and agreements to which Chapter 3 applies (see section 29).

[S17]

NOTES

Commencement: 1 October 2007 (certain purposes); to be appointed (otherwise) (for transitional adaptations see the notes below).

Note: the draft Companies Act 2006 (Commencement No 3, Consequential Amendments, Transitional Provisions and Savings) Order 2007, art 2(3) provides that this section shall come into force on 1 October 2007 so far as is necessary for the purposes of the provisions of this Act brought into force on that date by art 2(1), (2) of that Order (see **[A12]**).

Transitional adaptations: art 6 of the draft Companies Act 2006 (Commencement No 3, Consequential Amendments, Transitional Provisions and Savings) Order 2007 provides that the provisions brought into force by that Order shall have effect subject to any transitional adaptations specified in Sch 1 to that Order. Schedule 1, para 1 to the Order (at **[A12]**) provides as follows—

"**1 A company's constitution** (s 17)

(1) Section 17 (a company's constitution) has effect with the following adaptation.

(2) Make the existing provision subsection (1).

(3) After that subsection insert—

"(2) Unless the context otherwise requires, references in this Act to a company's articles (including the reference in subsection (1) above) include the company's memorandum.".".

CHAPTER 2
ARTICLES OF ASSOCIATION

General

18 Articles of association

(1) A company must have articles of association prescribing regulations for the company.

(2) Unless it is a company to which model articles apply by virtue of section 20 (default application of model articles in case of limited company), it must register articles of association.

(3) Articles of association registered by a company must—
(a) be contained in a single document, and
(b) be divided into paragraphs numbered consecutively.

(4) References in the Companies Acts to a company's "articles" are to its articles of association.

[S18]

NOTES
Commencement: to be appointed.

19 Power of Secretary of State to prescribe model articles

(1) The Secretary of State may by regulations prescribe model articles of association for companies.

(2) Different model articles may be prescribed for different descriptions of company.

(3) A company may adopt all or any of the provisions of model articles.

(4) Any amendment of model articles by regulations under this section does not affect a company registered before the amendment takes effect.

"Amendment" here includes addition, alteration or repeal.

(5) Regulations under this section are subject to negative resolution procedure.

[S19]

NOTES
Commencement: 20 January 2007 (for the purpose of enabling the exercise of powers to make Orders or Regulations by statutory instrument); to be appointed (otherwise).

20 Default application of model articles

(1) On the formation of a limited company—
(a) if articles are not registered, or
(b) if articles are registered, in so far as they do not exclude or modify the relevant model articles,
the relevant model articles (so far as applicable) form part of the company's articles in the same manner and to the same extent as if articles in the form of those articles had been duly registered.

(2) The "relevant model articles" means the model articles prescribed for a company of that description as in force at the date on which the company is registered.

[S20]

NOTES
Commencement: to be appointed.

Alteration of articles

21 Amendment of articles

(1) A company may amend its articles by special resolution.

(2) In the case of a company that is a charity, this is subject to—
(a) in England and Wales, section 64 of the Charities Act 1993 (c 10);
(b) in Northern Ireland, Article 9 of the Charities (Northern Ireland) Order 1987 (SI 1987/2048 (NI 19)).

(3) In the case of a company that is registered in the Scottish Charity Register, this is subject to—
(a) section 112 of the Companies Act 1989 (c 40), and

(b) section 16 of the Charities and Trustee Investment (Scotland) Act 2005 (asp 10).

[S21]

NOTES

Commencement: to be appointed.

22 Entrenched provisions of the articles

(1) A company's articles may contain provision ("provision for entrenchment") to the effect that specified provisions of the articles may be amended or repealed only if conditions are met, or procedures are complied with, that are more restrictive than those applicable in the case of a special resolution.

(2) Provision for entrenchment may only be made—

(a) in the company's articles on formation, or

(b) by an amendment of the company's articles agreed to by all the members of the company.

(3) Provision for entrenchment does not prevent amendment of the company's articles—

(a) by agreement of all the members of the company, or

(b) by order of a court or other authority having power to alter the company's articles.

(4) Nothing in this section affects any power of a court or other authority to alter a company's articles.

[S22]

NOTES

Commencement: to be appointed.

23 Notice to registrar of existence of restriction on amendment of articles

(1) Where a company's articles—

(a) on formation contain provision for entrenchment,

(b) are amended so as to include such provision, or

(c) are altered by order of a court or other authority so as to restrict or exclude the power of the company to amend its articles,

the company must give notice of that fact to the registrar.

(2) Where a company's articles—

(a) are amended so as to remove provision for entrenchment, or

(b) are altered by order of a court or other authority—

(i) so as to remove such provision, or

(ii) so as to remove any other restriction on, or any exclusion of, the power of the company to amend its articles,

the company must give notice of that fact to the registrar.

[S23]

NOTES

Commencement: to be appointed.

24 Statement of compliance where amendment of articles restricted

(1) This section applies where a company's articles are subject—

(a) to provision for entrenchment, or

(b) to an order of a court or other authority restricting or excluding the company's power to amend the articles.

(2) If the company—

(a) amends its articles, and

(b) is required to send to the registrar a document making or evidencing the amendment,

the company must deliver with that document a statement of compliance.

(3) The statement of compliance required is a statement certifying that the amendment has been made in accordance with the company's articles and, where relevant, any applicable order of a court or other authority.

(4) The registrar may rely on the statement of compliance as sufficient evidence of the matters stated in it.

[S24]

NOTES

Commencement: to be appointed.

25 Effect of alteration of articles on company's members

(1) A member of a company is not bound by an alteration to its articles after the date on which he became a member, if and so far as the alteration—

(a) requires him to take or subscribe for more shares than the number held by him at the date on which the alteration is made, or

(b) in any way increases his liability as at that date to contribute to the company's share capital or otherwise to pay money to the company.

(2) Subsection (1) does not apply in a case where the member agrees in writing, either before or after the alteration is made, to be bound by the alteration.

[S25]

NOTES

Commencement: to be appointed.

26 Registrar to be sent copy of amended articles

(1) Where a company amends its articles it must send to the registrar a copy of the articles as amended not later than 15 days after the amendment takes effect.

(2) This section does not require a company to set out in its articles any provisions of model articles that—

(a) are applied by the articles, or

(b) apply by virtue of section 20 (default application of model articles).

(3) If a company fails to comply with this section an offence is committed by—

(a) the company, and

(b) every officer of the company who is in default.

(4) A person guilty of an offence under this section is liable on summary conviction to a fine not exceeding level 3 on the standard scale and, for continued contravention, a daily default fine not exceeding one-tenth of level 3 on the standard scale.

[S26]

NOTES

Commencement: to be appointed.

27 Registrar's notice to comply in case of failure with respect to amended articles

(1) If it appears to the registrar that a company has failed to comply with any enactment requiring it—

(a) to send to the registrar a document making or evidencing an alteration in the company's articles, or

(b) to send to the registrar a copy of the company's articles as amended,

the registrar may give notice to the company requiring it to comply.

(2) The notice must—

(a) state the date on which it is issued, and

(b) require the company to comply within 28 days from that date.

(3) If the company complies with the notice within the specified time, no criminal proceedings may be brought in respect of the failure to comply with the enactment mentioned in subsection (1).

(4) If the company does not comply with the notice within the specified time, it is liable to a civil penalty of £200.

This is in addition to any liability to criminal proceedings in respect of the failure mentioned in subsection (1).

(5) The penalty may be recovered by the registrar and is to be paid into the Consolidated Fund.

[S27]

NOTES

Commencement: to be appointed.

Supplementary

28 Existing companies: provisions of memorandum treated as provisions of articles

(1) Provisions that immediately before the commencement of this Part were contained in a company's memorandum but are not provisions of the kind mentioned in section 8 (provisions of new-style memorandum) are to be treated after the commencement of this Part as provisions of the company's articles.

(2) This applies not only to substantive provisions but also to provision for entrenchment (as defined in section 22).

(3) The provisions of this Part about provision for entrenchment apply to such provision as they apply to provision made on the company's formation, except that the duty under section 23(1)(a) to give notice to the registrar does not apply.

[S28]

NOTES

Commencement: to be appointed.

CHAPTER 3
RESOLUTIONS AND AGREEMENTS AFFECTING A COMPANY'S CONSTITUTION

29 Resolutions and agreements affecting a company's constitution

(1) This Chapter applies to—

(a) any special resolution;

(b) any resolution or agreement agreed to by all the members of a company that, if not so agreed to, would not have been effective for its purpose unless passed as a special resolution;

(c) any resolution or agreement agreed to by all the members of a class of shareholders that, if not so agreed to, would not have been effective for its purpose unless passed by some particular majority or otherwise in some particular manner;

(d) any resolution or agreement that effectively binds all members of a class of shareholders though not agreed to by all those members;

(e) any other resolution or agreement to which this Chapter applies by virtue of any enactment.

(2) References in subsection (1) to a member of a company, or of a class of members of a company, do not include the company itself where it is such a member by virtue only of its holding shares as treasury shares.

[S29]

NOTES

Commencement: 1 October 2007 (for transitional provisions see the note below).

Transitional provisions: Sch 3, para 1 to the draft Companies Act 2006 (Commencement No 3, Consequential Amendments, Transitional Provisions and Savings) Order 2007 (at **[A12]**) provides as follows—

"**1 Resolutions and agreements affecting a company's constitution** (ss 29 and 30)

(1) Sections 29 and 30 of the Companies Act 2006 (resolutions and agreements affecting a company's constitution) apply to resolutions passed and agreements made on or after 1st October 2007.

(2) The provisions of section 380(1) and (5) of the 1985 Act or Article 388(1) and (5) of the 1986 Order continue to apply in relation to resolutions passed and agreements made, but not forwarded to the registrar, before that date.

This does not affect the operation of section 1297 of the Companies Act 2006 (continuity of the law) in relation to things done under those provisions.".

30 Copies of resolutions or agreements to be forwarded to registrar

(1) A copy of every resolution or agreement to which this Chapter applies, or (in the case of a resolution or agreement that is not in writing) a written memorandum setting out its terms, must be forwarded to the registrar within 15 days after it is passed or made.

(2) If a company fails to comply with this section, an offence is committed by—
- (a) the company, and
- (b) every officer of it who is in default.

(3) A person guilty of an offence under this section is liable on summary conviction to a fine not exceeding level 3 on the standard scale and, for continued contravention, a daily default fine not exceeding one-tenth of level 3 on the standard scale.

(4) For the purposes of this section, a liquidator of the company is treated as an officer of it.

[S30]

NOTES

Commencement: 1 October 2007 (for transitional provisions see the note to s 29).

CHAPTER 4
MISCELLANEOUS AND SUPPLEMENTARY PROVISIONS

Statement of company's objects

31 Statement of company's objects

(1) Unless a company's articles specifically restrict the objects of the company, its objects are unrestricted.

(2) Where a company amends its articles so as to add, remove or alter a statement of the company's objects—
- (a) it must give notice to the registrar,
- (b) on receipt of the notice, the registrar shall register it, and
- (c) the amendment is not effective until entry of that notice on the register.

(3) Any such amendment does not affect any rights or obligations of the company or render defective any legal proceedings by or against it.

(4) In the case of a company that is a charity, the provisions of this section have effect subject to—
- (a) in England and Wales, section 64 of the Charities Act 1993 (c 10);
- (b) in Northern Ireland, Article 9 of the Charities (Northern Ireland) Order 1987 (SI 1987/2048 (NI 19)).

(5) In the case of a company that is entered in the Scottish Charity Register, the provisions of this section have effect subject to the provisions of the Charities and Trustee Investment (Scotland) Act 2005 (asp 10).

[S31]

NOTES

Commencement: to be appointed.

Other provisions with respect to a company's constitution

32 Constitutional documents to be provided to members

(1) A company must, on request by any member, send to him the following documents—

(a) an up-to-date copy of the company's articles;
(b) a copy of any resolution or agreement relating to the company to which Chapter 3 applies (resolutions and agreements affecting a company's constitution) and that is for the time being in force;
(c) a copy of any document required to be sent to the registrar under—
  (i) section 34(2) (notice where company's constitution altered by enactment), or
  (ii) section 35(2)(a) (notice where order of court or other authority alters company's constitution);
(d) a copy of any court order under section 899 (order sanctioning compromise or arrangement) or section 900 (order facilitating reconstruction or amalgamation);
(e) a copy of any court order under section 996 (protection of members against unfair prejudice: powers of the court) that alters the company's constitution;
(f) a copy of the company's current certificate of incorporation, and of any past certificates of incorporation;
(g) in the case of a company with a share capital, a current statement of capital;
(h) in the case of a company limited by guarantee, a copy of the statement of guarantee.

(2) The statement of capital required by subsection (1)(g) is a statement of—
(a) the total number of shares of the company,
(b) the aggregate nominal value of those shares,
(c) for each class of shares—
  (i) prescribed particulars of the rights attached to the shares,
  (ii) the total number of shares of that class, and
  (iii) the aggregate nominal value of shares of that class, and
(d) the amount paid up and the amount (if any) unpaid on each share (whether on account of the nominal value of the share or by way of premium).

(3) If a company makes default in complying with this section, an offence is committed by every officer of the company who is in default.

(4) A person guilty of an offence under this section is liable on summary conviction to a fine not exceeding level 3 on the standard scale.

[S32]

NOTES

Commencement: 20 January 2007 (for the purpose of enabling the exercise of powers to make Orders or Regulations by statutory instrument); to be appointed (otherwise).

33 Effect of company's constitution

(1) The provisions of a company's constitution bind the company and its members to the same extent as if there were covenants on the part of the company and of each member to observe those provisions.

(2) Money payable by a member to the company under its constitution is a debt due from him to the company.

In England and Wales and Northern Ireland it is of the nature of an ordinary contract debt.

[S33]

NOTES

Commencement: to be appointed.

34 Notice to registrar where company's constitution altered by enactment

(1) This section applies where a company's constitution is altered by an enactment, other than an enactment amending the general law.

(2) The company must give notice of the alteration to the registrar, specifying the enactment, not later than 15 days after the enactment comes into force.

In the case of a special enactment the notice must be accompanied by a copy of the enactment.

(3) If the enactment amends—

(a) the company's articles, or
(b) a resolution or agreement to which Chapter 3 applies (resolutions and agreements affecting a company's constitution),

the notice must be accompanied by a copy of the company's articles, or the resolution or agreement in question, as amended.

(4) A "special enactment" means an enactment that is not a public general enactment, and includes—

(a) an Act for confirming a provisional order,
(b) any provision of a public general Act in relation to the passing of which any of the standing orders of the House of Lords or the House of Commons relating to Private Business applied, or
(c) any enactment to the extent that it is incorporated in or applied for the purposes of a special enactment.

(5) If a company fails to comply with this section an offence is committed by—

(a) the company, and
(b) every officer of the company who is in default.

(6) A person guilty of an offence under this section is liable on summary conviction to a fine not exceeding level 3 on the standard scale and, for continued contravention, a daily default fine not exceeding one-tenth of level 3 on the standard scale.

[S34]

NOTES

Commencement: to be appointed.

35 Notice to registrar where company's constitution altered by order

(1) Where a company's constitution is altered by an order of a court or other authority, the company must give notice to the registrar of the alteration not later than 15 days after the alteration takes effect.

(2) The notice must be accompanied by—

(a) a copy of the order, and
(b) if the order amends—
    (i) the company's articles, or
    (ii) a resolution or agreement to which Chapter 3 applies (resolutions and agreements affecting the company's constitution),

a copy of the company's articles, or the resolution or agreement in question, as amended.

(3) If a company fails to comply with this section an offence is committed by—

(a) the company, and
(b) every officer of the company who is in default.

(4) A person guilty of an offence under this section is liable on summary conviction to a fine not exceeding level 3 on the standard scale and, for continued contravention, a daily default fine not exceeding one-tenth of level 3 on the standard scale.

(5) This section does not apply where provision is made by another enactment for the delivery to the registrar of a copy of the order in question.

[S35]

NOTES

Commencement: to be appointed.

36 Documents to be incorporated in or accompany copies of articles issued by company

(1) Every copy of a company's articles issued by the company must be accompanied by—

(a) a copy of any resolution or agreement relating to the company to which Chapter 3 applies (resolutions and agreements affecting a company's constitution),
(b) where the company has been required to give notice to the registrar under

section 34(2) (notice where company's constitution altered by enactment), a statement that the enactment in question alters the effect of the company's constitution,

(c) where the company's constitution is altered by a special enactment (see section 34(4)), a copy of the enactment, and

(d) a copy of any order required to be sent to the registrar under section 35(2)(a) (order of court or other authority altering company's constitution).

(2) This does not require the articles to be accompanied by a copy of a document or by a statement if—

(a) the effect of the resolution, agreement, enactment or order (as the case may be) on the company's constitution has been incorporated into the articles by amendment, or

(b) the resolution, agreement, enactment or order (as the case may be) is not for the time being in force.

(3) If the company fails to comply with this section, an offence is committed by every officer of the company who is in default.

(4) A person guilty of an offence under this section is liable on summary conviction to a fine not exceeding level 3 on the standard scale for each occasion on which copies are issued, or, as the case may be, requested.

(5) For the purposes of this section, a liquidator of the company is treated as an officer of it.

[S36]

NOTES

Commencement: to be appointed.

Supplementary provisions

37 Right to participate in profits otherwise than as member void

In the case of a company limited by guarantee and not having a share capital any provision in the company's articles, or in any resolution of the company, purporting to give a person a right to participate in the divisible profits of the company otherwise than as a member is void.

[S37]

NOTES

Commencement: to be appointed.

38 Application to single member companies of enactments and rules of law

Any enactment or rule of law applicable to companies formed by two or more persons or having two or more members applies with any necessary modification in relation to a company formed by one person or having only one person as a member.

[S38]

NOTES

Commencement: to be appointed.

PART 4
A COMPANY'S CAPACITY AND RELATED MATTERS

Capacity of company and power of directors to bind it

39 A company's capacity

(1) The validity of an act done by a company shall not be called into question on the ground of lack of capacity by reason of anything in the company's constitution.

(2) This section has effect subject to section 42 (companies that are charities).

[S39]

NOTES

Commencement: to be appointed.

40 Power of directors to bind the company

(1) In favour of a person dealing with a company in good faith, the power of the directors to bind the company, or authorise others to do so, is deemed to be free of any limitation under the company's constitution.

(2) For this purpose—

(a) a person "deals with" a company if he is a party to any transaction or other act to which the company is a party,

(b) a person dealing with a company—

(i) is not bound to enquire as to any limitation on the powers of the directors to bind the company or authorise others to do so,

(ii) is presumed to have acted in good faith unless the contrary is proved, and

(iii) is not to be regarded as acting in bad faith by reason only of his knowing that an act is beyond the powers of the directors under the company's constitution.

(3) The references above to limitations on the directors' powers under the company's constitution include limitations deriving—

(a) from a resolution of the company or of any class of shareholders, or

(b) from any agreement between the members of the company or of any class of shareholders.

(4) This section does not affect any right of a member of the company to bring proceedings to restrain the doing of an action that is beyond the powers of the directors.

But no such proceedings lie in respect of an act to be done in fulfilment of a legal obligation arising from a previous act of the company.

(5) This section does not affect any liability incurred by the directors, or any other person, by reason of the directors' exceeding their powers.

(6) This section has effect subject to—

section 41 (transactions with directors or their associates), and

section 42 (companies that are charities).

[S40]

NOTES

Commencement: to be appointed.

41 Constitutional limitations: transactions involving directors or their associates

(1) This section applies to a transaction if or to the extent that its validity depends on section 40 (power of directors deemed to be free of limitations under company's constitution in favour of person dealing with company in good faith).

Nothing in this section shall be read as excluding the operation of any other enactment or rule of law by virtue of which the transaction may be called in question or any liability to the company may arise.

(2) Where—

(a) a company enters into such a transaction, and

(b) the parties to the transaction include—

(i) a director of the company or of its holding company, or

(ii) a person connected with any such director,

the transaction is voidable at the instance of the company.

(3) Whether or not it is avoided, any such party to the transaction as is mentioned in subsection (2)(b)(i) or (ii), and any director of the company who authorised the transaction, is liable—

(a) to account to the company for any gain he has made directly or indirectly by the transaction, and

(b) to indemnify the company for any loss or damage resulting from the transaction.

(4) The transaction ceases to be voidable if—

(a) restitution of any money or other asset which was the subject matter of the transaction is no longer possible, or

(b) the company is indemnified for any loss or damage resulting from the transaction, or

(c) rights acquired bona fide for value and without actual notice of the directors' exceeding their powers by a person who is not party to the transaction would be affected by the avoidance, or

(d) the transaction is affirmed by the company.

(5) A person other than a director of the company is not liable under subsection (3) if he shows that at the time the transaction was entered into he did not know that the directors were exceeding their powers.

(6) Nothing in the preceding provisions of this section affects the rights of any party to the transaction not within subsection (2)(b)(i) or (ii).

But the court may, on the application of the company or any such party, make an order affirming, severing or setting aside the transaction on such terms as appear to the court to be just.

(7) In this section—

(a) "transaction" includes any act; and

(b) the reference to a person connected with a director has the same meaning as in Part 10 (company directors).

[S41]

NOTES

Commencement: to be appointed.

42 Constitutional limitations: companies that are charities

(1) Sections 39 and 40 (company's capacity and power of directors to bind company) do not apply to the acts of a company that is a charity except in favour of a person who—

(a) does not know at the time the act is done that the company is a charity, or

(b) gives full consideration in money or money's worth in relation to the act in question and does not know (as the case may be)—

(i) that the act is not permitted by the company's constitution, or

(ii) that the act is beyond the powers of the directors.

(2) Where a company that is a charity purports to transfer or grant an interest in property, the fact that (as the case may be)—

(a) the act was not permitted by the company's constitution, or

(b) the directors in connection with the act exceeded any limitation on their powers under the company's constitution,

does not affect the title of a person who subsequently acquires the property or any interest in it for full consideration without actual notice of any such circumstances affecting the validity of the company's act.

(3) In any proceedings arising out of subsection (1) or (2) the burden of proving—

(a) that a person knew that the company was a charity, or

(b) that a person knew that an act was not permitted by the company's constitution or was beyond the powers of the directors,

lies on the person asserting that fact.

(4) In the case of a company that is a charity the affirmation of a transaction to which section 41 applies (transactions with directors or their associates) is ineffective without the prior written consent of—

(a) in England and Wales, the Charity Commission;

(b) in Northern Ireland, the Department for Social Development.

(5) This section does not extend to Scotland (but see section 112 of the Companies Act 1989 (c 40)).

[S42]

NOTES

Commencement: to be appointed.

Formalities of doing business under the law of England and Wales or Northern Ireland

43 Company contracts

(1) Under the law of England and Wales or Northern Ireland a contract may be made—

(a) by a company, by writing under its common seal, or

(b) on behalf of a company, by a person acting under its authority, express or implied.

(2) Any formalities required by law in the case of a contract made by an individual also apply, unless a contrary intention appears, to a contract made by or on behalf of a company.

[S43]

NOTES

Commencement: to be appointed.

44 Execution of documents

(1) Under the law of England and Wales or Northern Ireland a document is executed by a company—

(a) by the affixing of its common seal, or

(b) by signature in accordance with the following provisions.

(2) A document is validly executed by a company if it is signed on behalf of the company—

(a) by two authorised signatories, or

(b) by a director of the company in the presence of a witness who attests the signature.

(3) The following are "authorised signatories" for the purposes of subsection (2)—

(a) every director of the company, and

(b) in the case of a private company with a secretary or a public company, the secretary (or any joint secretary) of the company.

(4) A document signed in accordance with subsection (2) and expressed, in whatever words, to be executed by the company has the same effect as if executed under the common seal of the company.

(5) In favour of a purchaser a document is deemed to have been duly executed by a company if it purports to be signed in accordance with subsection (2).

A "purchaser" means a purchaser in good faith for valuable consideration and includes a lessee, mortgagee or other person who for valuable consideration acquires an interest in property.

(6) Where a document is to be signed by a person on behalf of more than one company, it is not duly signed by that person for the purposes of this section unless he signs it separately in each capacity.

(7) References in this section to a document being (or purporting to be) signed by a director or secretary are to be read, in a case where that office is held by a firm, as references to its being (or purporting to be) signed by an individual authorised by the firm to sign on its behalf.

(8) This section applies to a document that is (or purports to be) executed by a company in the name of or on behalf of another person whether or not that person is also a company.

[S44]

NOTES

Commencement: to be appointed.

45 Common seal

(1) A company may have a common seal, but need not have one.

(2) A company which has a common seal shall have its name engraved in legible characters on the seal.

(3) If a company fails to comply with subsection (2) an offence is committed by—

(a) the company, and

(b) every officer of the company who is in default.

(4) An officer of a company, or a person acting on behalf of a company, commits an offence if he uses, or authorises the use of, a seal purporting to be a seal of the company on which its name is not engraved as required by subsection (2).

(5) A person guilty of an offence under this section is liable on summary conviction to a fine not exceeding level 3 on the standard scale.

(6) This section does not form part of the law of Scotland.

[S45]

NOTES

Commencement: to be appointed.

46 Execution of deeds

(1) A document is validly executed by a company as a deed for the purposes of section 1(2)(b) of the Law of Property (Miscellaneous Provisions) Act 1989 (c 34) and for the purposes of the law of Northern Ireland if, and only if—

(a) it is duly executed by the company, and

(b) it is delivered as a deed.

(2) For the purposes of subsection (1)(b) a document is presumed to be delivered upon its being executed, unless a contrary intention is proved.

[S46]

NOTES

Commencement: to be appointed.

47 Execution of deeds or other documents by attorney

(1) Under the law of England and Wales or Northern Ireland a company may, by instrument executed as a deed, empower a person, either generally or in respect of specified matters, as its attorney to execute deeds or other documents on its behalf.

(2) A deed or other document so executed, whether in the United Kingdom or elsewhere, has effect as if executed by the company.

[S47]

NOTES

Commencement: to be appointed.

Formalities of doing business under the law of Scotland

48 Execution of documents by companies

(1) The following provisions form part of the law of Scotland only.

(2) Notwithstanding the provisions of any enactment, a company need not have a company seal.

(3) For the purposes of any enactment—

(a) providing for a document to be executed by a company by affixing its common seal, or

(b) referring (in whatever terms) to a document so executed,

a document signed or subscribed by or on behalf of the company in accordance with the provisions of the Requirements of Writing (Scotland) Act 1995 (c 7) has effect as if so executed.

[S48]

NOTES

Commencement: to be appointed.

Other matters

49 Official seal for use abroad

(1) A company that has a common seal may have an official seal for use outside the United Kingdom.

(2) The official seal must be a facsimile of the company's common seal, with the addition on its face of the place or places where it is to be used.

(3) The official seal when duly affixed to a document has the same effect as the company's common seal.

This subsection does not extend to Scotland.

(4) A company having an official seal for use outside the United Kingdom may—
- (a) by writing under its common seal, or
- (b) as respects Scotland, by writing subscribed in accordance with the Requirements of Writing (Scotland) Act 1995,

authorise any person appointed for the purpose to affix the official seal to any deed or other document to which the company is party.

(5) As between the company and a person dealing with such an agent, the agent's authority continues—
- (a) during the period mentioned in the instrument conferring the authority, or
- (b) if no period is mentioned, until notice of the revocation or termination of the agent's authority has been given to the person dealing with him.

(6) The person affixing the official seal must certify in writing on the deed or other document to which the seal is affixed the date on which, and place at which, it is affixed.

[S49]

NOTES

Commencement: to be appointed.

50 Official seal for share certificates etc

(1) A company that has a common seal may have an official seal for use—
- (a) for sealing securities issued by the company, or
- (b) for sealing documents creating or evidencing securities so issued.

(2) The official seal—
- (a) must be a facsimile of the company's common seal, with the addition on its face of the word "Securities", and
- (b) when duly affixed to the document has the same effect as the company's common seal.

[S50]

NOTES

Commencement: to be appointed.

51 Pre-incorporation contracts, deeds and obligations

(1) A contract that purports to be made by or on behalf of a company at a time when the company has not been formed has effect, subject to any agreement to the contrary, as one made with the person purporting to act for the company or as agent for it, and he is personally liable on the contract accordingly.

(2) Subsection (1) applies—
- (a) to the making of a deed under the law of England and Wales or Northern Ireland, and
- (b) to the undertaking of an obligation under the law of Scotland,

as it applies to the making of a contract.

[S51]

NOTES

Commencement: to be appointed.

52 Bills of exchange and promissory notes

A bill of exchange or promissory note is deemed to have been made, accepted or endorsed on behalf of a company if made, accepted or endorsed in the name of, or by or on behalf or on account of, the company by a person acting under its authority.

[S52]

NOTES

Commencement: to be appointed.

PART 5
A COMPANY'S NAME

CHAPTER 1
GENERAL REQUIREMENTS

Prohibited names

53 Prohibited names

A company must not be registered under this Act by a name if, in the opinion of the Secretary of State—

(a) its use by the company would constitute an offence, or
(b) it is offensive.

[S53]

NOTES

Commencement: to be appointed.

Sensitive words and expressions

54 Names suggesting connection with government or public authority

(1) The approval of the Secretary of State is required for a company to be registered under this Act by a name that would be likely to give the impression that the company is connected with—

(a) Her Majesty's Government, any part of the Scottish administration or Her Majesty's Government in Northern Ireland,
(b) a local authority, or
(c) any public authority specified for the purposes of this section by regulations made by the Secretary of State.

(2) For the purposes of this section—

"local authority" means—

(a) a local authority within the meaning of the Local Government Act 1972 (c 70), the Common Council of the City of London or the Council of the Isles of Scilly,
(b) a council constituted under section 2 of the Local Government etc (Scotland) Act 1994 (c 39), or
(c) a district council in Northern Ireland;

"public authority" includes any person or body having functions of a public nature.

(3) Regulations under this section are subject to affirmative resolution procedure.

[S54]

NOTES

Commencement: 20 January 2007 (for the purpose of enabling the exercise of powers to make Orders or Regulations by statutory instrument); to be appointed (otherwise).

55 Other sensitive words or expressions

(1) The approval of the Secretary of State is required for a company to be registered under this Act by a name that includes a word or expression for the time being specified in regulations made by the Secretary of State under this section.

(2) Regulations under this section are subject to approval after being made.

[S55]

NOTES

Commencement: 20 January 2007 (for the purpose of enabling the exercise of powers to make Orders or Regulations by statutory instrument); to be appointed (otherwise).

56 Duty to seek comments of government department or other specified body

(1) The Secretary of State may by regulations under—

(a) section 54 (name suggesting connection with government or public authority), or

(b) section 55 (other sensitive words or expressions),

require that, in connection with an application for the approval of the Secretary of State under that section, the applicant must seek the view of a specified Government department or other body.

(2) Where such a requirement applies, the applicant must request the specified department or other body (in writing) to indicate whether (and if so why) it has any objections to the proposed name.

(3) Where a request under this section is made in connection with an application for the registration of a company under this Act, the application must—

(a) include a statement that a request under this section has been made, and

(b) be accompanied by a copy of any response received.

(4) Where a request under this section is made in connection with a change in a company's name, the notice of the change sent to the registrar must be accompanied by—

(a) a statement by a director or secretary of the company that a request under this section has been made, and

(b) a copy of any response received.

(5) In this section "specified" means specified in the regulations.

[S56]

NOTES

Commencement: 20 January 2007 (for the purpose of enabling the exercise of powers to make Orders or Regulations by statutory instrument); to be appointed (otherwise).

Permitted characters etc

57 Permitted characters etc

(1) The Secretary of State may make provision by regulations—

(a) as to the letters or other characters, signs or symbols (including accents and other diacritical marks) and punctuation that may be used in the name of a company registered under this Act; and

(b) specifying a standard style or format for the name of a company for the purposes of registration.

(2) The regulations may prohibit the use of specified characters, signs or symbols when appearing in a specified position (in particular, at the beginning of a name).

(3) A company may not be registered under this Act by a name that consists of or includes anything that is not permitted in accordance with regulations under this section.

(4) Regulations under this section are subject to negative resolution procedure.

(5) In this section "specified" means specified in the regulations.

[S57]

NOTES

Commencement: 20 January 2007 (for the purpose of enabling the exercise of powers to make Orders or Regulations by statutory instrument); to be appointed (otherwise).

CHAPTER 2
INDICATIONS OF COMPANY TYPE OR LEGAL FORM

Required indications for limited companies

58 Public limited companies

(1) The name of a limited company that is a public company must end with "public limited company" or "p.l.c.".

(2) In the case of a Welsh company, its name may instead end with "cwmni cyfyngedig cyhoeddus" or "c.c.c.".

(3) This section does not apply to community interest companies (but see section 33(3) and (4) of the Companies (Audit, Investigations and Community Enterprise) Act 2004 (c 27)).

[S58]

NOTES

Commencement: to be appointed.

59 Private limited companies

(1) The name of a limited company that is a private company must end with "limited" or "ltd.".

(2) In the case of a Welsh company, its name may instead end with "cyfyngedig" or "cyf.".

(3) Certain companies are exempt from this requirement (see section 60).

(4) This section does not apply to community interest companies (but see section 33(1) and (2) of the Companies (Audit, Investigations and Community Enterprise) Act 2004).

[S59]

NOTES

Commencement: to be appointed.

60 Exemption from requirement as to use of "limited"

(1) A private company is exempt from section 59 (requirement to have name ending with "limited" or permitted alternative) if—

(a) it is a charity,

(b) it is exempted from the requirement of that section by regulations made by the Secretary of State, or

(c) it meets the conditions specified in—
section 61 (continuation of existing exemption: companies limited by shares), or
section 62 (continuation of existing exemption: companies limited by guarantee).

(2) The registrar may refuse to register a private limited company by a name that does not include the word "limited" (or a permitted alternative) unless a statement has been delivered to him that the company meets the conditions for exemption.

(3) The registrar may accept the statement as sufficient evidence of the matters stated in it.

(4) Regulations under this section are subject to negative resolution procedure.

[S60]

NOTES

Commencement: 20 January 2007 (for the purpose of enabling the exercise of powers to make Orders or Regulations by statutory instrument); to be appointed (otherwise).

61 Continuation of existing exemption: companies limited by shares

(1) This section applies to a private company limited by shares—

(a) that on 25th February 1982—

(i) was registered in Great Britain, and
(ii) had a name that, by virtue of a licence under section 19 of the Companies Act 1948 (c 38) (or corresponding earlier legislation), did not include the word "limited" or any of the permitted alternatives, or

(b) that on 30th June 1983—
(i) was registered in Northern Ireland, and
(ii) had a name that, by virtue of a licence under section 19 of the Companies Act (Northern Ireland) 1960 (c 22 (NI)) (or corresponding earlier legislation), did not include the word "limited" or any of the permitted alternatives.

(2) A company to which this section applies is exempt from section 59 (requirement to have name ending with "limited" or permitted alternative) so long as—
(a) it continues to meet the following two conditions, and
(b) it does not change its name.

(3) The first condition is that the objects of the company are the promotion of commerce, art, science, education, religion, charity or any profession, and anything incidental or conducive to any of those objects.

(4) The second condition is that the company's articles—
(a) require its income to be applied in promoting its objects,
(b) prohibit the payment of dividends, or any return of capital, to its members, and
(c) require all the assets that would otherwise be available to its members generally to be transferred on its winding up either—
(i) to another body with objects similar to its own, or
(ii) to another body the objects of which are the promotion of charity and anything incidental or conducive thereto,
(whether or not the body is a member of the company).

[S61]

NOTES
Commencement: to be appointed.

62 Continuation of existing exemption: companies limited by guarantee

(1) A private company limited by guarantee that immediately before the commencement of this Part—
(a) was exempt by virtue of section 30 of the Companies Act 1985 (c 6) or Article 40 of the Companies (Northern Ireland) Order 1986 (SI 1986/ 1032 (NI 6)) from the requirement to have a name including the word "limited" or a permitted alternative, and
(b) had a name that did not include the word "limited" or any of the permitted alternatives,
is exempt from section 59 (requirement to have name ending with "limited" or permitted alternative) so long as it continues to meet the following two conditions and does not change its name.

(2) The first condition is that the objects of the company are the promotion of commerce, art, science, education, religion, charity or any profession, and anything incidental or conducive to any of those objects.

(3) The second condition is that the company's articles—
(a) require its income to be applied in promoting its objects,
(b) prohibit the payment of dividends to its members, and
(c) require all the assets that would otherwise be available to its members generally to be transferred on its winding up either—
(i) to another body with objects similar to its own, or
(ii) to another body the objects of which are the promotion of charity and anything incidental or conducive thereto,
(whether or not the body is a member of the company).

[S62]

NOTES
Commencement: to be appointed.

63 Exempt company: restriction on amendment of articles

(1) A private company—

(a) that is exempt under section 61 or 62 from the requirement to use "limited" (or a permitted alternative) as part of its name, and

(b) whose name does not include "limited" or any of the permitted alternatives,

must not amend its articles so that it ceases to comply with the conditions for exemption under that section.

(2) If subsection (1) above is contravened an offence is committed by—

(a) the company, and

(b) every officer of the company who is in default.

For this purpose a shadow director is treated as an officer of the company.

(3) A person guilty of an offence under this section is liable on summary conviction to a fine not exceeding level 5 on the standard scale and, for continued contravention, a daily default fine not exceeding one-tenth of level 5 on the standard scale.

(4) Where immediately before the commencement of this section—

(a) a company was exempt by virtue of section 30 of the Companies Act 1985 (c 6) or Article 40 of the Companies (Northern Ireland) Order 1986 (SI 1986/1032 (NI 6)) from the requirement to have a name including the word "limited" (or a permitted alternative), and

(b) the company's memorandum or articles contained provision preventing an alteration of them without the approval of—

(i) the Board of Trade or a Northern Ireland department (or any other department or Minister), or

(ii) the Charity Commission,

that provision, and any condition of any such licence as is mentioned in section 61(1)(a)(ii) or (b)(ii) requiring such provision, shall cease to have effect.

This does not apply if, or to the extent that, the provision is required by or under any other enactment.

(5) It is hereby declared that any such provision as is mentioned in subsection (4)(b) formerly contained in a company's memorandum was at all material times capable, with the appropriate approval, of being altered or removed under section 17 of the Companies Act 1985 or Article 28 of the Companies (Northern Ireland) Order 1986 (SI 1986/1032 (NI 6)) (or corresponding earlier enactments).

[S63]

NOTES

Commencement: to be appointed.

64 Power to direct change of name in case of company ceasing to be entitled to exemption

(1) If it appears to the Secretary of State that a company whose name does not include "limited" or any of the permitted alternatives—

(a) has ceased to be entitled to exemption under section 60(1)(a) or (b), or

(b) in the case of a company within section 61 or 62 (which impose conditions as to the objects and articles of the company)—

(i) has carried on any business other than the promotion of any of the objects mentioned in subsection (3) of section 61 or, as the case may be, subsection (2) of section 62, or

(ii) has acted inconsistently with the provision required by subsection (4)(a) or (b) of section 61 or, as the case may be, subsection (3)(a) or (b) of section 62,

the Secretary of State may direct the company to change its name so that it ends with "limited" or one of the permitted alternatives.

(2) The direction must be in writing and must specify the period within which the company is to change its name.

(3) A change of name in order to comply with a direction under this section may be made by resolution of the directors.

This is without prejudice to any other method of changing the company's name.

(4) Where a resolution of the directors is passed in accordance with subsection (3), the company must give notice to the registrar of the change.

Sections 80 and 81 apply as regards the registration and effect of the change.

(5) If the company fails to comply with a direction under this section an offence is committed by—

(a) the company, and
(b) every officer of the company who is in default.

(6) A person guilty of an offence under this section is liable on summary conviction to a fine not exceeding level 5 on the standard scale and, for continued contravention, a daily default fine not exceeding one-tenth of level 5 on the standard scale.

(7) A company that has been directed to change its name under this section may not, without the approval of the Secretary of State, subsequently change its name so that it does not include "limited" or one of the permitted alternatives. This does not apply to a change of name on re-registration or on conversion to a community interest company.

[S64]

NOTES

Commencement: to be appointed.

Inappropriate use of indications of company type or legal form

65 Inappropriate use of indications of company type or legal form

(1) The Secretary of State may make provision by regulations prohibiting the use in a company name of specified words, expressions or other indications—

(a) that are associated with a particular type of company or form of organisation, or
(b) that are similar to words, expressions or other indications associated with a particular type of company or form of organisation.

(2) The regulations may prohibit the use of words, expressions or other indications—

(a) in a specified part, or otherwise than in a specified part, of a company's name;
(b) in conjunction with, or otherwise than in conjunction with, such other words, expressions or indications as may be specified.

(3) A company must not be registered under this Act by a name that consists of or includes anything prohibited by regulations under this section.

(4) In this section "specified" means specified in the regulations.

(5) Regulations under this section are subject to negative resolution procedure.

[S65]

NOTES

Commencement: 20 January 2007 (for the purpose of enabling the exercise of powers to make Orders or Regulations by statutory instrument); to be appointed (otherwise).

CHAPTER 3
SIMILARITY TO OTHER NAMES

Similarity to other name on registrar's index

66 Name not to be the same as another in the index

(1) A company must not be registered under this Act by a name that is the same as another name appearing in the registrar's index of company names.

(2) The Secretary of State may make provision by regulations supplementing this section.

(3) The regulations may make provision—

(a) as to matters that are to be disregarded, and

(b) as to words, expressions, signs or symbols that are, or are not, to be regarded as the same,

for the purposes of this section.

(4) The regulations may provide—

(a) that registration by a name that would otherwise be prohibited under this section is permitted—

(i) in specified circumstances, or

(ii) with specified consent, and

(b) that if those circumstances obtain or that consent is given at the time a company is registered by a name, a subsequent change of circumstances or withdrawal of consent does not affect the registration.

(5) Regulations under this section are subject to negative resolution procedure.

(6) In this section "specified" means specified in the regulations.

[S66]

NOTES

Commencement: 20 January 2007 (for the purpose of enabling the exercise of powers to make Orders or Regulations by statutory instrument); to be appointed (otherwise).

67 Power to direct change of name in case of similarity to existing name

(1) The Secretary of State may direct a company to change its name if it has been registered in a name that is the same as or, in the opinion of the Secretary of State, too like—

(a) a name appearing at the time of the registration in the registrar's index of company names, or

(b) a name that should have appeared in that index at that time.

(2) The Secretary of State may make provision by regulations supplementing this section.

(3) The regulations may make provision—

(a) as to matters that are to be disregarded, and

(b) as to words, expressions, signs or symbols that are, or are not, to be regarded as the same,

for the purposes of this section.

(4) The regulations may provide—

(a) that no direction is to be given under this section in respect of a name—

(i) in specified circumstances, or

(ii) if specified consent is given, and

(b) that a subsequent change of circumstances or withdrawal of consent does not give rise to grounds for a direction under this section.

(5) Regulations under this section are subject to negative resolution procedure.

(6) In this section "specified" means specified in the regulations.

[S67]

NOTES

Commencement: 20 January 2007 (for the purpose of enabling the exercise of powers to make Orders or Regulations by statutory instrument); to be appointed (otherwise).

68 Direction to change name: supplementary provisions

(1) The following provisions have effect in relation to a direction under section 67 (power to direct change of name in case of similarity to existing name).

(2) Any such direction—

(a) must be given within twelve months of the company's registration by the name in question, and

(b) must specify the period within which the company is to change its name.

(3) The Secretary of State may by a further direction extend that period.

Any such direction must be given before the end of the period for the time being specified.

(4) A direction under section 67 or this section must be in writing.

(5) If a company fails to comply with the direction, an offence is committed by—
(a) the company, and
(b) every officer of the company who is in default.

For this purpose a shadow director is treated as an officer of the company.

(6) A person guilty of an offence under this section is liable on summary conviction to a fine not exceeding level 3 on the standard scale and, for continued contravention, a daily default fine not exceeding one-tenth of level 3 on the standard scale.

[S68]

NOTES

Commencement: to be appointed.

Similarity to other name in which person has goodwill

69 Objection to company's registered name

(1) A person ("the applicant") may object to a company's registered name on the ground—
(a) that it is the same as a name associated with the applicant in which he has goodwill, or
(b) that it is sufficiently similar to such a name that its use in the United Kingdom would be likely to mislead by suggesting a connection between the company and the applicant.

(2) The objection must be made by application to a company names adjudicator (see section 70).

(3) The company concerned shall be the primary respondent to the application. Any of its members or directors may be joined as respondents.

(4) If the ground specified in subsection (1)(a) or (b) is established, it is for the respondents to show—
(a) that the name was registered before the commencement of the activities on which the applicant relies to show goodwill; or
(b) that the company—
(i) is operating under the name, or
(ii) is proposing to do so and has incurred substantial start-up costs in preparation, or
(iii) was formerly operating under the name and is now dormant;
or
(c) that the name was registered in the ordinary course of a company formation business and the company is available for sale to the applicant on the standard terms of that business; or
(d) that the name was adopted in good faith; or
(e) that the interests of the applicant are not adversely affected to any significant extent.

If none of those is shown, the objection shall be upheld.

(5) If the facts mentioned in subsection (4)(a), (b) or (c) are established, the objection shall nevertheless be upheld if the applicant shows that the main purpose of the respondents (or any of them) in registering the name was to obtain money (or other consideration) from the applicant or prevent him from registering the name.

(6) If the objection is not upheld under subsection (4) or (5), it shall be dismissed.

(7) In this section "goodwill" includes reputation of any description.

[S69]

NOTES

Commencement: to be appointed.

70 Company names adjudicators

(1) The Secretary of State shall appoint persons to be company names adjudicators.

(2) The persons appointed must have such legal or other experience as, in the Secretary of State's opinion, makes them suitable for appointment.

(3) An adjudicator—

(a) holds office in accordance with the terms of his appointment,

(b) is eligible for re-appointment when his term of office ends,

(c) may resign at any time by notice in writing given to the Secretary of State, and

(d) may be dismissed by the Secretary of State on the ground of incapacity or misconduct.

(4) One of the adjudicators shall be appointed Chief Adjudicator.

He shall perform such functions as the Secretary of State may assign to him.

(5) The other adjudicators shall undertake such duties as the Chief Adjudicator may determine.

(6) The Secretary of State may—

(a) appoint staff for the adjudicators;

(b) pay remuneration and expenses to the adjudicators and their staff;

(c) defray other costs arising in relation to the performance by the adjudicators of their functions;

(d) compensate persons for ceasing to be adjudicators.

[S70]

NOTES

Commencement: to be appointed.

71 Procedural rules

(1) The Secretary of State may make rules about proceedings before a company names adjudicator.

(2) The rules may, in particular, make provision—

(a) as to how an application is to be made and the form and content of an application or other documents;

(b) for fees to be charged;

(c) about the service of documents and the consequences of failure to serve them;

(d) as to the form and manner in which evidence is to be given;

(e) for circumstances in which hearings are required and those in which they are not;

(f) for cases to be heard by more than one adjudicator;

(g) setting time limits for anything required to be done in connection with the proceedings (and allowing for such limits to be extended, even if they have expired);

(h) enabling the adjudicator to strike out an application, or any defence, in whole or in part—

(i) on the ground that it is vexatious, has no reasonable prospect of success or is otherwise misconceived, or

(ii) for failure to comply with the requirements of the rules;

(i) conferring power to order security for costs (in Scotland, caution for expenses);

(j) as to how far proceedings are to be held in public;

(k) requiring one party to bear the costs (in Scotland, expenses) of another and as to the taxing (or settling) the amount of such costs (or expenses).

(3) The rules may confer on the Chief Adjudicator power to determine any matter that could be the subject of provision in the rules.

(4) Rules under this section shall be made by statutory instrument which shall be subject to annulment in pursuance of a resolution of either House of Parliament.

[S71]

NOTES

Commencement: to be appointed.

72 Decision of adjudicator to be made available to public

(1) A company names adjudicator must, within 90 days of determining an application under section 69, make his decision and his reasons for it available to the public.

(2) He may do so by means of a website or by such other means as appear to him to be appropriate.

[S72]

NOTES

Commencement: to be appointed.

73 Order requiring name to be changed

(1) If an application under section 69 is upheld, the adjudicator shall make an order—

(a) requiring the respondent company to change its name to one that is not an offending name, and

(b) requiring all the respondents—

(i) to take all such steps as are within their power to make, or facilitate the making, of that change, and

(ii) not to cause or permit any steps to be taken calculated to result in another company being registered with a name that is an offending name.

(2) An "offending name" means a name that, by reason of its similarity to the name associated with the applicant in which he claims goodwill, would be likely—

(a) to be the subject of a direction under section 67 (power of Secretary of State to direct change of name), or

(b) to give rise to a further application under section 69.

(3) The order must specify a date by which the respondent company's name is to be changed and may be enforced—

(a) in England and Wales or Northern Ireland, in the same way as an order of the High Court;

(b) in Scotland, in the same way as a decree of the Court of Session.

(4) If the respondent company's name is not changed in accordance with the order by the specified date, the adjudicator may determine a new name for the company.

(5) If the adjudicator determines a new name for the respondent company he must give notice of his determination—

(a) to the applicant,

(b) to the respondents, and

(c) to the registrar.

(6) For the purposes of this section a company's name is changed when the change takes effect in accordance with section 81(1) (on the issue of the new certification of incorporation).

[S73]

NOTES

Commencement: to be appointed.

74 Appeal from adjudicator's decision

(1) An appeal lies to the court from any decision of a company names adjudicator to uphold or dismiss an application under section 69.

(2) Notice of appeal against a decision upholding an application must be given before the date specified in the adjudicator's order by which the respondent company's name is to be changed.

(3) If notice of appeal is given against a decision upholding an application, the effect of the adjudicator's order is suspended.

(4) If on appeal the court—

(a) affirms the decision of the adjudicator to uphold the application, or

(b) reverses the decision of the adjudicator to dismiss the application,

the court may (as the case may require) specify the date by which the adjudicator's order is to be complied with, remit the matter to the adjudicator or make any order or determination that the adjudicator might have made.

(5) If the court determines a new name for the company it must give notice of the determination—

(a) to the parties to the appeal, and
(b) to the registrar.

[S74]

NOTES
Commencement: to be appointed.

CHAPTER 4
OTHER POWERS OF THE SECRETARY OF STATE

75 Provision of misleading information etc

(1) If it appears to the Secretary of State—
(a) that misleading information has been given for the purposes of a company's registration by a particular name, or
(b) that an undertaking or assurance has been given for that purpose and has not been fulfilled,

the Secretary of State may direct the company to change its name.

(2) Any such direction—
(a) must be given within five years of the company's registration by that name, and
(b) must specify the period within which the company is to change its name.

(3) The Secretary of State may by a further direction extend the period within which the company is to change its name.

Any such direction must be given before the end of the period for the time being specified.

(4) A direction under this section must be in writing.

(5) If a company fails to comply with a direction under this section, an offence is committed by—
(a) the company, and
(b) every officer of the company who is in default.

For this purpose a shadow director is treated as an officer of the company.

(6) A person guilty of an offence under this section is liable on summary conviction to a fine not exceeding level 3 on the standard scale and, for continued contravention, a daily default fine not exceeding one-tenth of level 3 on the standard scale.

[S75]

NOTES
Commencement: to be appointed.

76 Misleading indication of activities

(1) If in the opinion of the Secretary of State the name by which a company is registered gives so misleading an indication of the nature of its activities as to be likely to cause harm to the public, the Secretary of State may direct the company to change its name.

(2) The direction must be in writing.

(3) The direction must be complied with within a period of six weeks from the date of the direction or such longer period as the Secretary of State may think fit to allow.

This does not apply if an application is duly made to the court under the following provisions.

(4) The company may apply to the court to set the direction aside.

The application must be made within the period of three weeks from the date of the direction.

(5) The court may set the direction aside or confirm it.

If the direction is confirmed, the court shall specify the period within which the direction is to be complied with.

(6) If a company fails to comply with a direction under this section, an offence is committed by—
- (a) the company, and
- (b) every officer of the company who is in default.

For this purpose a shadow director is treated as an officer of the company.

(7) A person guilty of an offence under this section is liable on summary conviction to a fine not exceeding level 3 on the standard scale and, for continued contravention, a daily default fine not exceeding one-tenth of level 3 on the standard scale.

[S76]

NOTES

Commencement: to be appointed.

CHAPTER 5
CHANGE OF NAME

77 Change of name

(1) A company may change its name—
- (a) by special resolution (see section 78), or
- (b) by other means provided for by the company's articles (see section 79).

(2) The name of a company may also be changed—
- (a) by resolution of the directors acting under section 64 (change of name to comply with direction of Secretary of State under that section);
- (b) on the determination of a new name by a company names adjudicator under section 73 (powers of adjudicator on upholding objection to company name);
- (c) on the determination of a new name by the court under section 74 (appeal against decision of company names adjudicator);
- (d) under section 1033 (company's name on restoration to the register).

[S77]

NOTES

Commencement: to be appointed.

78 Change of name by special resolution

(1) Where a change of name has been agreed to by a company by special resolution, the company must give notice to the registrar.

This is in addition to the obligation to forward a copy of the resolution to the registrar.

(2) Where a change of name by special resolution is conditional on the occurrence of an event, the notice given to the registrar of the change must—
- (a) specify that the change is conditional, and
- (b) state whether the event has occurred.

(3) If the notice states that the event has not occurred—
- (a) the registrar is not required to act under section 80 (registration and issue of new certificate of incorporation) until further notice,
- (b) when the event occurs, the company must give notice to the registrar stating that it has occurred, and
- (c) the registrar may rely on the statement as sufficient evidence of the matters stated in it.

[S78]

NOTES

Commencement: to be appointed.

79 Change of name by means provided for in company's articles

(1) Where a change of a company's name has been made by other means provided for by its articles—
- (a) the company must give notice to the registrar, and

(b) the notice must be accompanied by a statement that the change of name has been made by means provided for by the company's articles.

(2) The registrar may rely on the statement as sufficient evidence of the matters stated in it.

[S79]

NOTES

Commencement: to be appointed.

80 Change of name: registration and issue of new certificate of incorporation

(1) This section applies where the registrar receives notice of a change of a company's name.

(2) If the registrar is satisfied—

(a) that the new name complies with the requirements of this Part, and

(b) that the requirements of the Companies Acts, and any relevant requirements of the company's articles, with respect to a change of name are complied with,

the registrar must enter the new name on the register in place of the former name.

(3) On the registration of the new name, the registrar must issue a certificate of incorporation altered to meet the circumstances of the case.

[S80]

NOTES

Commencement: to be appointed.

81 Change of name: effect

(1) A change of a company's name has effect from the date on which the new certificate of incorporation is issued.

(2) The change does not affect any rights or obligations of the company or render defective any legal proceedings by or against it.

(3) Any legal proceedings that might have been continued or commenced against it by its former name may be continued or commenced against it by its new name.

[S81]

NOTES

Commencement: to be appointed.

CHAPTER 6
TRADING DISCLOSURES

82 Requirement to disclose company name etc

(1) The Secretary of State may by regulations make provision requiring companies—

(a) to display specified information in specified locations,

(b) to state specified information in specified descriptions of document or communication, and

(c) to provide specified information on request to those they deal with in the course of their business.

(2) The regulations—

(a) must in every case require disclosure of the name of the company, and

(b) may make provision as to the manner in which any specified information is to be displayed, stated or provided.

(3) The regulations may provide that, for the purposes of any requirement to disclose a company's name, any variation between a word or words required to be part of the name and a permitted abbreviation of that word or those words (or vice versa) shall be disregarded.

(4) In this section "specified" means specified in the regulations.

(5) Regulations under this section are subject to affirmative resolution procedure.

[S82]

NOTES

Commencement: 20 January 2007 (for the purpose of enabling the exercise of powers to make Orders or Regulations by statutory instrument); to be appointed (otherwise).

83 Civil consequences of failure to make required disclosure

(1) This section applies to any legal proceedings brought by a company to which section 82 applies (requirement to disclose company name etc) to enforce a right arising out of a contract made in the course of a business in respect of which the company was, at the time the contract was made, in breach of regulations under that section.

(2) The proceedings shall be dismissed if the defendant (in Scotland, the defender) to the proceedings shows—

(a) that he has a claim against the claimant (pursuer) arising out of the contract that he has been unable to pursue by reason of the latter's breach of the regulations, or

(b) that he has suffered some financial loss in connection with the contract by reason of the claimant's (pursuer's) breach of the regulations,

unless the court before which the proceedings are brought is satisfied that it is just and equitable to permit the proceedings to continue.

(3) This section does not affect the right of any person to enforce such rights as he may have against another person in any proceedings brought by that person.

[S83]

NOTES

Commencement: to be appointed.

84 Criminal consequences of failure to make required disclosures

(1) Regulations under section 82 may provide—

(a) that where a company fails, without reasonable excuse, to comply with any specified requirement of regulations under that section an offence is committed by—

(i) the company, and

(ii) every officer of the company who is in default;

(b) that a person guilty of such an offence is liable on summary conviction to a fine not exceeding level 3 on the standard scale and, for continued contravention, a daily default fine not exceeding one-tenth of level 3 on the standard scale.

(2) The regulations may provide that, for the purposes of any provision made under subsection (1), a shadow director of the company is to be treated as an officer of the company.

(3) In subsection (1)(a) "specified" means specified in the regulations.

[S84]

NOTES

Commencement: 20 January 2007 (for the purpose of enabling the exercise of powers to make Orders or Regulations by statutory instrument); to be appointed (otherwise).

85 Minor variations in form of name to be left out of account

(1) For the purposes of this Chapter, in considering a company's name no account is to be taken of—

(a) whether upper or lower case characters (or a combination of the two) are used,

(b) whether diacritical marks or punctuation are present or absent,

(c) whether the name is in the same format or style as is specified under section 57(1)(b) for the purposes of registration,

provided there is no real likelihood of names differing only in those respects being taken to be different names.

(2) This does not affect the operation of regulations under section 57(1)(a) permitting only specified characters, diacritical marks or punctuation.

[S85]

NOTES

Commencement: to be appointed.

PART 6

A COMPANY'S REGISTERED OFFICE

General

86 A company's registered office

A company must at all times have a registered office to which all communications and notices may be addressed.

[S86]

NOTES

Commencement: to be appointed.

87 Change of address of registered office

(1) A company may change the address of its registered office by giving notice to the registrar.

(2) The change takes effect upon the notice being registered by the registrar, but until the end of the period of 14 days beginning with the date on which it is registered a person may validly serve any document on the company at the address previously registered.

(3) For the purposes of any duty of a company—

(a) to keep available for inspection at its registered office any register, index or other document, or

(b) to mention the address of its registered office in any document,

a company that has given notice to the registrar of a change in the address of its registered office may act on the change as from such date, not more than 14 days after the notice is given, as it may determine.

(4) Where a company unavoidably ceases to perform at its registered office any such duty as is mentioned in subsection (3)(a) in circumstances in which it was not practicable to give prior notice to the registrar of a change in the address of its registered office, but—

(a) resumes performance of that duty at other premises as soon as practicable, and

(b) gives notice accordingly to the registrar of a change in the situation of its registered office within 14 days of doing so,

it is not to be treated as having failed to comply with that duty.

[S87]

NOTES

Commencement: to be appointed.

Welsh companies

88 Welsh companies

(1) In the Companies Acts a "Welsh company" means a company as to which it is stated in the register that its registered office is to be situated in Wales.

(2) A company—

(a) whose registered office is in Wales, and

(b) as to which it is stated in the register that its registered office is to be situated in England and Wales, may by special resolution require the register to be amended so that it states that the company's registered office is to be situated in Wales.

(3) A company—

(a) whose registered office is in Wales, and

(b) as to which it is stated in the register that its registered office is to be situated in Wales,

may by special resolution require the register to be amended so that it states that the company's registered office is to be situated in England and Wales.

(4) Where a company passes a resolution under this section it must give notice to the registrar, who shall—

(a) amend the register accordingly, and

(b) issue a new certificate of incorporation altered to meet the circumstances of the case.

[S88]

NOTES

Commencement: to be appointed.

PART 7
RE-REGISTRATION AS A MEANS OF ALTERING A COMPANY'S STATUS

Introductory

89 Alteration of status by re-registration

A company may by re-registration under this Part alter its status—

(a) from a private company to a public company (see sections 90 to 96);

(b) from a public company to a private company (see sections 97 to 101);

(c) from a private limited company to an unlimited company (see sections 102 to 104);

(d) from an unlimited private company to a limited company (see sections 105 to 108);

(e) from a public company to an unlimited private company (see sections 109 to 111).

[S89]

NOTES

Commencement: to be appointed.

Private company becoming public

90 Re-registration of private company as public

(1) A private company (whether limited or unlimited) may be re-registered as a public company limited by shares if—

(a) a special resolution that it should be so re-registered is passed,

(b) the conditions specified below are met, and

(c) an application for re-registration is delivered to the registrar in accordance with section 94, together with—

(i) the other documents required by that section, and

(ii) a statement of compliance.

(2) The conditions are—

(a) that the company has a share capital;

(b) that the requirements of section 91 are met as regards its share capital;

(c) that the requirements of section 92 are met as regards its net assets;

(d) if section 93 applies (recent allotment of shares for non-cash consideration), that the requirements of that section are met; and

(e) that the company has not previously been re-registered as unlimited.

(3) The company must make such changes—

(a) in its name, and

(b) in its articles,

as are necessary in connection with its becoming a public company.

(4) If the company is unlimited it must also make such changes in its articles as are necessary in connection with its becoming a company limited by shares.

[S90]

NOTES

Commencement: to be appointed.

91 Requirements as to share capital

(1) The following requirements must be met at the time the special resolution is passed that the company should be re-registered as a public company—

(a) the nominal value of the company's allotted share capital must be not less than the authorised minimum;

(b) each of the company's allotted shares must be paid up at least as to one-quarter of the nominal value of that share and the whole of any premium on it;

(c) if any shares in the company or any premium on them have been fully or partly paid up by an undertaking given by any person that he or another should do work or perform services (whether for the company or any other person), the undertaking must have been performed or otherwise discharged;

(d) if shares have been allotted as fully or partly paid up as to their nominal value or any premium on them otherwise than in cash, and the consideration for the allotment consists of or includes an undertaking to the company (other than one to which paragraph (c) applies), then either—

(i) the undertaking must have been performed or otherwise discharged, or

(ii) there must be a contract between the company and some person pursuant to which the undertaking is to be performed within five years from the time the special resolution is passed.

(2) For the purpose of determining whether the requirements in subsection (1)(b), (c) and (d) are met, the following may be disregarded—

(a) shares allotted—

(i) before 22nd June 1982 in the case of a company then registered in Great Britain, or

(ii) before 31st December 1984 in the case of a company then registered in Northern Ireland;

(b) shares allotted in pursuance of an employees' share scheme by reason of which the company would, but for this subsection, be precluded under subsection (1)(b) (but not otherwise) from being re-registered as a public company.

(3) No more than one-tenth of the nominal value of the company's allotted share capital is to be disregarded under subsection (2)(a).

For this purpose the allotted share capital is treated as not including shares disregarded under subsection (2)(b).

(4) Shares disregarded under subsection (2) are treated as not forming part of the allotted share capital for the purposes of subsection (1)(a).

(5) A company must not be re-registered as a public company if it appears to the registrar that—

(a) the company has resolved to reduce its share capital,

(b) the reduction—

(i) is made under section 626 (reduction in connection with redenomination of share capital),

(ii) is supported by a solvency statement in accordance with section 643, or

(iii) has been confirmed by an order of the court under section 648, and

(c) the effect of the reduction is, or will be, that the nominal value of the company's allotted share capital is below the authorised minimum.

[S91]

NOTES

Commencement: to be appointed.

92 Requirements as to net assets

(1) A company applying to re-register as a public company must obtain—

(a) a balance sheet prepared as at a date not more than seven months before the date on which the application is delivered to the registrar,

(b) an unqualified report by the company's auditor on that balance sheet, and

(c) a written statement by the company's auditor that in his opinion at the balance sheet date the amount of the company's net assets was not less than the aggregate of its called-up share capital and undistributable reserves.

(2) Between the balance sheet date and the date on which the application for re-registration is delivered to the registrar, there must be no change in the company's financial position that results in the amount of its net assets becoming less than the aggregate of its called-up share capital and undistributable reserves.

(3) In subsection (1)(b) an "unqualified report" means—

(a) if the balance sheet was prepared for a financial year of the company, a report stating without material qualification the auditor's opinion that the balance sheet has been properly prepared in accordance with the requirements of this Act;

(b) if the balance sheet was not prepared for a financial year of the company, a report stating without material qualification the auditor's opinion that the balance sheet has been properly prepared in accordance with the provisions of this Act which would have applied if it had been prepared for a financial year of the company.

(4) For the purposes of an auditor's report on a balance sheet that was not prepared for a financial year of the company, the provisions of this Act apply with such modifications as are necessary by reason of that fact.

(5) For the purposes of subsection (3) a qualification is material unless the auditor states in his report that the matter giving rise to the qualification is not material for the purpose of determining (by reference to the company's balance sheet) whether at the balance sheet date the amount of the company's net assets was not less than the aggregate of its called-up share capital and undistributable reserves.

(6) In this Part "net assets" and "undistributable reserves" have the same meaning as in section 831 (net asset restriction on distributions by public companies).

[S92]

NOTES

Commencement: to be appointed.

93 Recent allotment of shares for non-cash consideration

(1) This section applies where—

(a) shares are allotted by the company in the period between the date as at which the balance sheet required by section 92 is prepared and the passing of the resolution that the company should re-register as a public company, and

(b) the shares are allotted as fully or partly paid up as to their nominal value or any premium on them otherwise than in cash.

(2) The registrar shall not entertain an application by the company for re-registration as a public company unless—

(a) the requirements of section 593(1)(a) and (b) have been complied with (independent valuation of non-cash consideration; valuer's report to company not more than six months before allotment), or

(b) the allotment is in connection with—

(i) a share exchange (see subsections (3) to (5) below), or

(ii) a proposed merger with another company (see subsection (6) below).

(3) An allotment is in connection with a share exchange if—

(a) the shares are allotted in connection with an arrangement under which the whole or part of the consideration for the shares allotted is provided by—

(i) the transfer to the company allotting the shares of shares (or shares of a particular class) in another company, or

(ii) the cancellation of shares (or shares of a particular class) in another company; and

(b) the allotment is open to all the holders of the shares of the other company in question (or, where the arrangement applies only to shares of a particular class, to all the holders of the company's shares of that class) to take part in the arrangement in connection with which the shares are allotted.

(4) In determining whether a person is a holder of shares for the purposes of subsection (3), there shall be disregarded—

(a) shares held by, or by a nominee of, the company allotting the shares;

(b) shares held by, or by a nominee of—

(i) the holding company of the company allotting the shares,

(ii) a subsidiary of the company allotting the shares, or

(iii) a subsidiary of the holding company of the company allotting the shares.

(5) It is immaterial, for the purposes of deciding whether an allotment is in connection with a share exchange, whether or not the arrangement in connection with which the shares are allotted involves the issue to the company allotting the shares of shares (or shares of a particular class) in the other company.

(6) There is a proposed merger with another company if one of the companies concerned proposes to acquire all the assets and liabilities of the other in exchange for the issue of its shares or other securities to shareholders of the other (whether or not accompanied by a cash payment).

"Another company" includes any body corporate.

(7) For the purposes of this section—

(a) the consideration for an allotment does not include any amount standing to the credit of any of the company's reserve accounts, or of its profit and loss account, that has been applied in paying up (to any extent) any of the shares allotted or any premium on those shares; and

(b) "arrangement" means any agreement, scheme or arrangement, (including an arrangement sanctioned in accordance with—

(i) Part 26 of this Act (arrangements and reconstructions), or

(ii) section 110 of the Insolvency Act 1986 (c 45) or Article 96 of the Insolvency (Northern Ireland) Order 1989 (SI 1989/2405 (NI 19)) (liquidator in winding up accepting shares as consideration for sale of company's property)).

[S93]

NOTES

Commencement: to be appointed.

94 Application and accompanying documents

(1) An application for re-registration as a public company must contain—

(a) a statement of the company's proposed name on re-registration; and

(b) in the case of a company without a secretary, a statement of the company's proposed secretary (see section 95).

(2) The application must be accompanied by—

(a) a copy of the special resolution that the company should re-register as a public company (unless a copy has already been forwarded to the registrar under Chapter 3 of Part 3);

(b) a copy of the company's articles as proposed to be amended;

(c) a copy of the balance sheet and other documents referred to in section 92(1); and

(d) if section 93 applies (recent allotment of shares for non-cash consideration), a copy of the valuation report (if any) under subsection (2)(a) of that section.

(3) The statement of compliance required to be delivered together with the application is a statement that the requirements of this Part as to re-registration as a public company have been complied with.

(4) The registrar may accept the statement of compliance as sufficient evidence that the company is entitled to be re-registered as a public company.

[S94]

NOTES

Commencement: to be appointed.

95 Statement of proposed secretary

(1) The statement of the company's proposed secretary must contain the required particulars of the person who is or the persons who are to be the secretary or joint secretaries of the company.

(2) The required particulars are the particulars that will be required to be stated in the company's register of secretaries (see sections 277 to 279).

(3) The statement must also contain a consent by the person named as secretary, or each of the persons named as joint secretaries, to act in the relevant capacity. If all the partners in a firm are to be joint secretaries, consent may be given by one partner on behalf of all of them.

[S95]

NOTES

Commencement: to be appointed.

96 Issue of certificate of incorporation on re-registration

(1) If on an application for re-registration as a public company the registrar is satisfied that the company is entitled to be so re-registered, the company shall be re-registered accordingly.

(2) The registrar must issue a certificate of incorporation altered to meet the circumstances of the case.

(3) The certificate must state that it is issued on re-registration and the date on which it is issued.

(4) On the issue of the certificate—
- (a) the company by virtue of the issue of the certificate becomes a public company,
- (b) the changes in the company's name and articles take effect, and
- (c) where the application contained a statement under section 95 (statement of proposed secretary), the person or persons named in the statement as secretary or joint secretary of the company are deemed to have been appointed to that office.

(5) The certificate is conclusive evidence that the requirements of this Act as to re-registration have been complied with.

[S96]

NOTES

Commencement: to be appointed.

Public company becoming private

97 Re-registration of public company as private limited company

(1) A public company may be re-registered as a private limited company if—
- (a) a special resolution that it should be so re-registered is passed,
- (b) the conditions specified below are met, and
- (c) an application for re-registration is delivered to the registrar in accordance with section 100, together with—
  - (i) the other documents required by that section, and
  - (ii) a statement of compliance.

(2) The conditions are that—
- (a) where no application under section 98 for cancellation of the resolution has been made—
  - (i) having regard to the number of members who consented to or voted in favour of the resolution, no such application may be made, or
  - (ii) the period within which such an application could be made has expired, or
- (b) where such an application has been made—
  - (i) the application has been withdrawn, or
  - (ii) an order has been made confirming the resolution and a copy of that order has been delivered to the registrar.

(3) The company must make such changes—

(a) in its name, and
(b) in its articles,

as are necessary in connection with its becoming a private company limited by shares or, as the case may be, by guarantee.

[S97]

NOTES

Commencement: to be appointed.

98 Application to court to cancel resolution

(1) Where a special resolution by a public company to be re-registered as a private limited company has been passed, an application to the court for the cancellation of the resolution may be made—

(a) by the holders of not less in the aggregate than 5% in nominal value of the company's issued share capital or any class of the company's issued share capital (disregarding any shares held by the company as treasury shares);
(b) if the company is not limited by shares, by not less than 5% of its members; or
(c) by not less than 50 of the company's members;

but not by a person who has consented to or voted in favour of the resolution.

(2) The application must be made within 28 days after the passing of the resolution and may be made on behalf of the persons entitled to make it by such one or more of their number as they may appoint for the purpose.

(3) On the hearing of the application the court shall make an order either cancelling or confirming the resolution.

(4) The court may—

(a) make that order on such terms and conditions as it thinks fit,
(b) if it thinks fit adjourn the proceedings in order that an arrangement may be made to the satisfaction of the court for the purchase of the interests of dissentient members, and
(c) give such directions, and make such orders, as it thinks expedient for facilitating or carrying into effect any such arrangement.

(5) The court's order may, if the court thinks fit—

(a) provide for the purchase by the company of the shares of any of its members and for the reduction accordingly of the company's capital; and
(b) make such alteration in the company's articles as may be required in consequence of that provision.

(6) The court's order may, if the court thinks fit, require the company not to make any, or any specified, amendments to its articles without the leave of the court.

[S98]

NOTES

Commencement: to be appointed.

99 Notice to registrar of court application or order

(1) On making an application under section 98 (application to court to cancel resolution) the applicants, or the person making the application on their behalf, must immediately give notice to the registrar.

This is without prejudice to any provision of rules of court as to service of notice of the application.

(2) On being served with notice of any such application, the company must immediately give notice to the registrar.

(3) Within 15 days of the making of the court's order on the application, or such longer period as the court may at any time direct, the company must deliver to the registrar a copy of the order.

(4) If a company fails to comply with subsection (2) or (3) an offence is committed by—

(a) the company, and

(b) every officer of the company who is in default.

(5) A person guilty of an offence under this section is liable on summary conviction to a fine not exceeding level 3 on the standard scale and, for continued contravention, a daily default fine not exceeding one-tenth of level 3 on the standard scale.

[S99]

NOTES

Commencement: to be appointed.

100 Application and accompanying documents

(1) An application for re-registration as a private limited company must contain a statement of the company's proposed name on re-registration.

(2) The application must be accompanied by—

(a) a copy of the resolution that the company should re-register as a private limited company (unless a copy has already been forwarded to the registrar under Chapter 3 of Part 3); and

(b) a copy of the company's articles as proposed to be amended.

(3) The statement of compliance required to be delivered together with the application is a statement that the requirements of this Part as to re-registration as a private limited company have been complied with.

(4) The registrar may accept the statement of compliance as sufficient evidence that the company is entitled to be re-registered as a private limited company.

[S100]

NOTES

Commencement: to be appointed.

101 Issue of certificate of incorporation on re-registration

(1) If on an application for re-registration as a private limited company the registrar is satisfied that the company is entitled to be so re-registered, the company shall be re-registered accordingly.

(2) The registrar must issue a certificate of incorporation altered to meet the circumstances of the case.

(3) The certificate must state that it is issued on re-registration and the date on which it is issued.

(4) On the issue of the certificate—

(a) the company by virtue of the issue of the certificate becomes a private limited company, and

(b) the changes in the company's name and articles take effect.

(5) The certificate is conclusive evidence that the requirements of this Act as to re-registration have been complied with.

[S101]

NOTES

Commencement: to be appointed.

Private limited company becoming unlimited

102 Re-registration of private limited company as unlimited

(1) A private limited company may be re-registered as an unlimited company if—

(a) all the members of the company have assented to its being so re-registered,

(b) the condition specified below is met, and

(c) an application for re-registration is delivered to the registrar in accordance with section 103, together with—

(i) the other documents required by that section, and

(ii) a statement of compliance.

(2) The condition is that the company has not previously been re-registered as limited.

(3) The company must make such changes in its name and its articles—
(a) as are necessary in connection with its becoming an unlimited company; and
(b) if it is to have a share capital, as are necessary in connection with its becoming an unlimited company having a share capital.

(4) For the purposes of this section—
(a) a trustee in bankruptcy of a member of the company is entitled, to the exclusion of the member, to assent to the company's becoming unlimited; and
(b) the personal representative of a deceased member of the company may assent on behalf of the deceased.

(5) In subsection (4)(a), "a trustee in bankruptcy of a member of the company" includes—
(a) a permanent trustee or an interim trustee (within the meaning of the Bankruptcy (Scotland) Act 1985 (c 66)) on the sequestrated estate of a member of the company;
(b) a trustee under a protected trustee deed (within the meaning of the Bankruptcy (Scotland) Act 1985) granted by a member of the company.

[S102]

NOTES

Commencement: to be appointed.

103 Application and accompanying documents

(1) An application for re-registration as an unlimited company must contain a statement of the company's proposed name on re-registration.

(2) The application must be accompanied by—
(a) the prescribed form of assent to the company's being registered as an unlimited company, authenticated by or on behalf of all the members of the company;
(b) a copy of the company's articles as proposed to be amended.

(3) The statement of compliance required to be delivered together with the application is a statement that the requirements of this Part as to re-registration as an unlimited company have been complied with.

(4) The statement must contain a statement by the directors of the company—
(a) that the persons by whom or on whose behalf the form of assent is authenticated constitute the whole membership of the company, and
(b) if any of the members have not authenticated that form themselves, that the directors have taken all reasonable steps to satisfy themselves that each person who authenticated it on behalf of a member was lawfully empowered to do so.

(5) The registrar may accept the statement of compliance as sufficient evidence that the company is entitled to be re-registered as an unlimited company.

[S103]

NOTES

Commencement: 20 January 2007 (for the purpose of enabling the exercise of powers to make Orders or Regulations by statutory instrument); to be appointed (otherwise).

104 Issue of certificate of incorporation on re-registration

(1) If on an application for re-registration of a private limited company as an unlimited company the registrar is satisfied that the company is entitled to be so re-registered, the company shall be re-registered accordingly.

(2) The registrar must issue a certificate of incorporation altered to meet the circumstances of the case.

(3) The certificate must state that it is issued on re-registration and the date on which it is issued.

(4) On the issue of the certificate—

(a) the company by virtue of the issue of the certificate becomes an unlimited company, and
(b) the changes in the company's name and articles take effect.

(5) The certificate is conclusive evidence that the requirements of this Act as to re-registration have been complied with.

[S104]

NOTES

Commencement: to be appointed.

Unlimited private company becoming limited

105 Re-registration of unlimited company as limited

(1) An unlimited company may be re-registered as a private limited company if—
(a) a special resolution that it should be so re-registered is passed,
(b) the condition specified below is met, and
(c) an application for re-registration is delivered to the registrar in accordance with section 106, together with—
(i) the other documents required by that section, and
(ii) a statement of compliance.

(2) The condition is that the company has not previously been re-registered as unlimited.

(3) The special resolution must state whether the company is to be limited by shares or by guarantee.

(4) The company must make such changes—
(a) in its name, and
(b) in its articles,

as are necessary in connection with its becoming a company limited by shares or, as the case may be, by guarantee.

[S105]

NOTES

Commencement: to be appointed.

106 Application and accompanying documents

(1) An application for re-registration as a limited company must contain a statement of the company's proposed name on re-registration.

(2) The application must be accompanied by—
(a) a copy of the resolution that the company should re-register as a private limited company (unless a copy has already been forwarded to the registrar under Chapter 3 of Part 3);
(b) if the company is to be limited by guarantee, a statement of guarantee;
(c) a copy of the company's articles as proposed to be amended.

(3) The statement of guarantee required to be delivered in the case of a company that is to be limited by guarantee must state that each member undertakes that, if the company is wound up while he is a member, or within one year after he ceases to be a member, he will contribute to the assets of the company such amount as may be required for—
(a) payment of the debts and liabilities of the company contracted before he ceases to be a member,
(b) payment of the costs, charges and expenses of winding up, and
(c) adjustment of the rights of the contributories among themselves,

not exceeding a specified amount.

(4) The statement of compliance required to be delivered together with the application is a statement that the requirements of this Part as to re-registration as a limited company have been complied with.

(5) The registrar may accept the statement of compliance as sufficient evidence that the company is entitled to be re-registered as a limited company.

[S106]

NOTES

Commencement: to be appointed.

107 Issue of certificate of incorporation on re-registration

(1) If on an application for re-registration of an unlimited company as a limited company the registrar is satisfied that the company is entitled to be so re-registered, the company shall be re-registered accordingly.

(2) The registrar must issue a certificate of incorporation altered to meet the circumstances of the case.

(3) The certificate must state that it is issued on re-registration and the date on which it is so issued.

(4) On the issue of the certificate—

(a) the company by virtue of the issue of the certificate becomes a limited company, and

(b) the changes in the company's name and articles take effect.

(5) The certificate is conclusive evidence that the requirements of this Act as to re-registration have been complied with.

[S107]

NOTES

Commencement: to be appointed.

108 Statement of capital required where company already has share capital

(1) A company which on re-registration under section 107 already has allotted share capital must within 15 days after the re-registration deliver a statement of capital to the registrar.

(2) This does not apply if the information which would be included in the statement has already been sent to the registrar in—

(a) a statement of capital and initial shareholdings (see section 10), or

(b) a statement of capital contained in an annual return (see section 856(2)).

(3) The statement of capital must state with respect to the company's share capital on re-registration—

(a) the total number of shares of the company,

(b) the aggregate nominal value of those shares,

(c) for each class of shares—

(i) prescribed particulars of the rights attached to the shares,

(ii) the total number of shares of that class, and

(iii) the aggregate nominal value of shares of that class, and

(d) the amount paid up and the amount (if any) unpaid on each share (whether on account of the nominal value of the share or by way of premium).

(4) If default is made in complying with this section, an offence is committed by—

(a) the company, and

(b) every officer of the company who is in default.

(5) A person guilty of an offence under this section is liable on summary conviction to a fine not exceeding level 3 on the standard scale and, for continued contravention, a daily default fine not exceeding one-tenth of level 3 on the standard scale.

[S108]

NOTES

Commencement: 20 January 2007 (for the purpose of enabling the exercise of powers to make Orders or Regulations by statutory instrument); to be appointed (otherwise).

Public company becoming private and unlimited

109 Re-registration of public company as private and unlimited

(1) A public company limited by shares may be re-registered as an unlimited private company with a share capital if—
- (a) all the members of the company have assented to its being so re-registered,
- (b) the condition specified below is met, and
- (c) an application for re-registration is delivered to the registrar in accordance with section 110, together with—
  - (i) the other documents required by that section, and
  - (ii) a statement of compliance.

(2) The condition is that the company has not previously been re-registered—
- (a) as limited, or
- (b) as unlimited.

(3) The company must make such changes—
- (a) in its name, and
- (b) in its articles,

as are necessary in connection with its becoming an unlimited private company.

(4) For the purposes of this section—
- (a) a trustee in bankruptcy of a member of the company is entitled, to the exclusion of the member, to assent to the company's re-registration; and
- (b) the personal representative of a deceased member of the company may assent on behalf of the deceased.

(5) In subsection (4)(a), "a trustee in bankruptcy of a member of the company" includes—
- (a) a permanent trustee or an interim trustee (within the meaning of the Bankruptcy (Scotland) Act 1985 (c 66)) on the sequestrated estate of a member of the company;
- (b) a trustee under a protected trustee deed (within the meaning of the Bankruptcy (Scotland) Act 1985) granted by a member of the company.

[S109]

NOTES

Commencement: to be appointed.

110 Application and accompanying documents

(1) An application for re-registration of a public company as an unlimited private company must contain a statement of the company's proposed name on re-registration.

(2) The application must be accompanied by—
- (a) the prescribed form of assent to the company's being registered as an unlimited company, authenticated by or on behalf of all the members of the company, and
- (b) a copy of the company's articles as proposed to be amended.

(3) The statement of compliance required to be delivered together with the application is a statement that the requirements of this Part as to re-registration as an unlimited private company have been complied with.

(4) The statement must contain a statement by the directors of the company—
- (a) that the persons by whom or on whose behalf the form of assent is authenticated constitute the whole membership of the company, and
- (b) if any of the members have not authenticated that form themselves, that the directors have taken all reasonable steps to satisfy themselves that each person who authenticated it on behalf of a member was lawfully empowered to do so.

(5) The registrar may accept the statement of compliance as sufficient evidence that the company is entitled to be re-registered as an unlimited private company.

[S110]

NOTES

Commencement: 20 January 2007 (for the purpose of enabling the exercise of powers to make Orders or Regulations by statutory instrument); to be appointed (otherwise).

111 Issue of certificate of incorporation on re-registration

(1) If on an application for re-registration of a public company as an unlimited private company the registrar is satisfied that the company is entitled to be so re-registered, the company shall be re-registered accordingly.

(2) The registrar must issue a certificate of incorporation altered to meet the circumstances of the case.

(3) The certificate must state that it is issued on re-registration and the date on which it is so issued.

(4) On the issue of the certificate—

(a) the company by virtue of the issue of the certificate becomes an unlimited private company, and

(b) the changes in the company's name and articles take effect.

(5) The certificate is conclusive evidence that the requirements of this Act as to re-registration have been complied with.

[S111]

NOTES

Commencement: to be appointed.

PART 8
A COMPANY'S MEMBERS

CHAPTER 1
THE MEMBERS OF A COMPANY

112 The members of a company

(1) The subscribers of a company's memorandum are deemed to have agreed to become members of the company, and on its registration become members and must be entered as such in its register of members.

(2) Every other person who agrees to become a member of a company, and whose name is entered in its register of members, is a member of the company.

[S112]

NOTES

Commencement: to be appointed.

CHAPTER 2
REGISTER OF MEMBERS

General

113 Register of members

(1) Every company must keep a register of its members.

(2) There must be entered in the register—

(a) the names and addresses of the members,

(b) the date on which each person was registered as a member, and

(c) the date at which any person ceased to be a member.

(3) In the case of a company having a share capital, there must be entered in the register, with the names and addresses of the members, a statement of—

(a) the shares held by each member, distinguishing each share—

(i) by its number (so long as the share has a number), and

(ii) where the company has more than one class of issued shares, by its class, and

(b) the amount paid or agreed to be considered as paid on the shares of each member.

(4) If the company has converted any of its shares into stock, and given notice of the conversion to the registrar, the register of members must show the amount and class of stock held by each member instead of the amount of shares and the particulars relating to shares specified above.

(5) In the case of joint holders of shares or stock in a company, the company's register of members must state the names of each joint holder.

In other respects joint holders are regarded for the purposes of this Chapter as a single member (so that the register must show a single address).

(6) In the case of a company that does not have a share capital but has more than one class of members, there must be entered in the register, with the names and addresses of the members, a statement of the class to which each member belongs.

(7) If a company makes default in complying with this section an offence is committed by—
- (a) the company, and
- (b) every officer of the company who is in default.

(8) A person guilty of an offence under this section is liable on summary conviction to a fine not exceeding level 3 on the standard scale and, for continued contravention, a daily default fine not exceeding one-tenth of level 3 on the standard scale.

[S113]

NOTES

Commencement: to be appointed.

114 Register to be kept available for inspection

(1) A company's register of members must be kept available for inspection—
- (a) at its registered office, or
- (b) at a place specified in regulations under section 1136.

(2) A company must give notice to the registrar of the place where its register of members is kept available for inspection and of any change in that place.

(3) No such notice is required if the register has, at all times since it came into existence (or, in the case of a register in existence on the relevant date, at all times since then) been kept available for inspection at the company's registered office.

(4) The relevant date for the purposes of subsection (3) is—
- (a) 1st July 1948 in the case of a company registered in Great Britain, and
- (b) 1st April 1961 in the case of a company registered in Northern Ireland.

(5) If a company makes default for 14 days in complying with subsection (2), an offence is committed by—
- (a) the company, and
- (b) every officer of the company who is in default.

(6) A person guilty of an offence under this section is liable on summary conviction to a fine not exceeding level 3 on the standard scale and, for continued contravention, a daily default fine not exceeding one-tenth of level 3 on the standard scale.

[S114]

NOTES

Commencement: to be appointed.

115 Index of members

(1) Every company having more than 50 members must keep an index of the names of the members of the company, unless the register of members is in such a form as to constitute in itself an index.

(2) The company must make any necessary alteration in the index within 14 days after the date on which any alteration is made in the register of members.

(3) The index must contain, in respect of each member, a sufficient indication to enable the account of that member in the register to be readily found.

(4) The index must be at all times kept available for inspection at the same place as the register of members.

(5) If default is made in complying with this section, an offence is committed by—

(a) the company, and

(b) every officer of the company who is in default.

(6) A person guilty of an offence under this section is liable on summary conviction to a fine not exceeding level 3 on the standard scale and, for continued contravention, a daily default fine not exceeding one-tenth of level 3 on the standard scale.

[S115]

NOTES

Commencement: to be appointed.

116 Rights to inspect and require copies

(1) The register and the index of members' names must be open to the inspection—

(a) of any member of the company without charge, and

(b) of any other person on payment of such fee as may be prescribed.

(2) Any person may require a copy of a company's register of members, or of any part of it, on payment of such fee as may be prescribed.

(3) A person seeking to exercise either of the rights conferred by this section must make a request to the company to that effect.

(4) The request must contain the following information—

(a) in the case of an individual, his name and address;

(b) in the case of an organisation, the name and address of an individual responsible for making the request on behalf of the organisation;

(c) the purpose for which the information is to be used; and

(d) whether the information will be disclosed to any other person, and if so—

(i) where that person is an individual, his name and address,

(ii) where that person is an organisation, the name and address of an individual responsible for receiving the information on its behalf, and

(iii) the purpose for which the information is to be used by that person.

[S116]

NOTES

Commencement: 20 January 2007 (for the purpose of enabling the exercise of powers to make Orders or Regulations by statutory instrument); 1 October 2007 (otherwise) (for transitional provisions etc see the note below).

Transitional provisions, etc: Sch 3, para 2 to the draft Companies Act 2006 (Commencement No 3, Consequential Amendments, Transitional Provisions and Savings) Order 2007 (at **[A12]**) provides as follows—

"2 Inspection of register of members (**ss 116 to 119**)

(1) Sections 116 to 119 of the Companies Act 2006 (inspection of register of members) apply where—

(a) the request is made on or after 1st October 2007, and

(b) the company is not obliged to deliver an annual return under section 363 of the 1985 Act or Article 371 of the 1986 Order made up to a date before 1st October 2008.

(2) Sections 356 and 357 of the 1985 Act or Articles 364 and 365 of the 1986 Order continue to apply to requests made before 1st October 2007 or after that date to a company that is so obliged.".

Transitional adaptations: art 6 of the draft Companies Act 2006 (Commencement No 3, Consequential Amendments, Transitional Provisions and Savings) Order 2007 provides that the provisions brought into force by that Order shall have effect subject to any transitional adaptations specified in Sch 1 to that Order. Schedule 1, para 2 to the Order (at **[A12]**) provides as follows—

"2 Inspection of register of members (**s 116**)

(1) Section 116 (rights to inspect and require copies of register and index of members' names) has effect with the following adaptation.

(2) After subsection (1) (right of inspection) insert—

"(1A) The right conferred by subsection (1) is not exercisable when the register is closed under section 358 of the Companies Act 1985 or Article 366 of the Companies (Northern Ireland) Order 1986."".

117 Register of members: response to request for inspection or copy

(1) Where a company receives a request under section 116 (register of members: right to inspect and require copy), it must within five working days either—
- (a) comply with the request, or
- (b) apply to the court.

(2) If it applies to the court it must notify the person making the request.

(3) If on an application under this section the court is satisfied that the inspection or copy is not sought for a proper purpose—
- (a) it shall direct the company not to comply with the request, and
- (b) it may further order that the company's costs (in Scotland, expenses) on the application be paid in whole or in part by the person who made the request, even if he is not a party to the application.

(4) If the court makes such a direction and it appears to the court that the company is or may be subject to other requests made for a similar purpose (whether made by the same person or different persons), it may direct that the company is not to comply with any such request.

The order must contain such provision as appears to the court appropriate to identify the requests to which it applies.

(5) If on an application under this section the court does not direct the company not to comply with the request, the company must comply with the request immediately upon the court giving its decision or, as the case may be, the proceedings being discontinued.

[S117]

NOTES

Commencement: 1 October 2007 (for transitional provisions see the note to s 116).

118 Register of members: refusal of inspection or default in providing copy

(1) If an inspection required under section 116 (register of members: right to inspect and require copy) is refused or default is made in providing a copy required under that section, otherwise than in accordance with an order of the court, an offence is committed by—
- (a) the company, and
- (b) every officer of the company who is in default.

(2) A person guilty of an offence under this section is liable on summary conviction to a fine not exceeding level 3 on the standard scale and, for continued contravention, a daily default fine not exceeding one-tenth of level 3 on the standard scale.

(3) In the case of any such refusal or default the court may by order compel an immediate inspection or, as the case may be, direct that the copy required be sent to the person requesting it.

[S118]

NOTES

Commencement: 1 October 2007 (for transitional provisions see the note to s 116).

119 Register of members: offences in connection with request for or disclosure of information

(1) It is an offence for a person knowingly or recklessly to make in a request under section 116 (register of members: right to inspect or require copy) a statement that is misleading, false or deceptive in a material particular.

(2) It is an offence for a person in possession of information obtained by exercise of either of the rights conferred by that section—
- (a) to do anything that results in the information being disclosed to another person, or
- (b) to fail to do anything with the result that the information is disclosed to another person,

knowing, or having reason to suspect, that person may use the information for a purpose that is not a proper purpose.

(3) A person guilty of an offence under this section is liable—

(a) on conviction on indictment, to imprisonment for a term not exceeding two years or a fine (or both);

(b) on summary conviction—

(i) in England and Wales, to imprisonment for a term not exceeding twelve months or to a fine not exceeding the statutory maximum (or both);

(ii) in Scotland or Northern Ireland, to imprisonment for a term not exceeding six months, or to a fine not exceeding the statutory maximum (or both).

[S119]

NOTES

Commencement: 1 October 2007 (for transitional provisions see the note to s 116).

120 Information as to state of register and index

(1) When a person inspects the register, or the company provides him with a copy of the register or any part of it, the company must inform him of the most recent date (if any) on which alterations were made to the register and there were no further alterations to be made.

(2) When a person inspects the index of members' names, the company must inform him whether there is any alteration to the register that is not reflected in the index.

(3) If a company fails to provide the information required under subsection (1) or (2), an offence is committed by—

(a) the company, and

(b) every officer of the company who is in default.

(4) A person guilty of an offence under this section is liable on summary conviction to a fine not exceeding level 3 on the standard scale.

[S120]

NOTES

Commencement: to be appointed.

121 Removal of entries relating to former members

An entry relating to a former member of the company may be removed from the register after the expiration of ten years from the date on which he ceased to be a member.

[S121]

NOTES

Commencement: to be appointed.

Special cases

122 Share warrants

(1) On the issue of a share warrant the company must—

(a) enter in the register of members—

(i) the fact of the issue of the warrant,

(ii) a statement of the shares included in the warrant, distinguishing each share by its number so long as the share has a number, and

(iii) the date of the issue of the warrant,

and

(b) amend the register, if necessary, so that no person is named on the register as the holder of the shares specified in the warrant.

(2) Until the warrant is surrendered, the particulars specified in subsection (1)(a) are deemed to be those required by this Act to be entered in the register of members.

(3) The bearer of a share warrant may, if the articles of the company so provide, be deemed a member of the company within the meaning of this Act, either to the full extent or for any purposes defined in the articles.

(4) Subject to the company's articles, the bearer of a share warrant is entitled, on surrendering it for cancellation, to have his name entered as a member in the register of members.

(5) The company is responsible for any loss incurred by any person by reason of the company entering in the register the name of a bearer of a share warrant in respect of the shares specified in it without the warrant being surrendered and cancelled.

(6) On the surrender of a share warrant, the date of the surrender must be entered in the register.

[S122]

NOTES

Commencement: to be appointed.

123 Single member companies

(1) If a limited company is formed under this Act with only one member there shall be entered in the company's register of members, with the name and address of the sole member, a statement that the company has only one member.

(2) If the number of members of a limited company falls to one, or if an unlimited company with only one member becomes a limited company on re-registration, there shall upon the occurrence of that event be entered in the company's register of members, with the name and address of the sole member—

(a) a statement that the company has only one member, and

(b) the date on which the company became a company having only one member.

(3) If the membership of a limited company increases from one to two or more members, there shall upon the occurrence of that event be entered in the company's register of members, with the name and address of the person who was formerly the sole member—

(a) a statement that the company has ceased to have only one member, and

(b) the date on which that event occurred.

(4) If a company makes default in complying with this section, an offence is committed by—

(a) the company, and

(b) every officer of the company who is in default.

(5) A person guilty of an offence under this section is liable on summary conviction to a fine not exceeding level 3 on the standard scale and, for continued contravention, a daily default fine not exceeding one-tenth of level 3 on the standard scale.

[S123]

NOTES

Commencement: to be appointed.

124 Company holding its own shares as treasury shares

(1) Where a company purchases its own shares in circumstances in which section 724 (treasury shares) applies—

(a) the requirements of section 113 (register of members) need not be complied with if the company cancels all of the shares forthwith after the purchase, and

(b) if the company does not cancel all of the shares forthwith after the purchase, any share that is so cancelled shall be disregarded for the purposes of that section.

(2) Subject to subsection (1), where a company holds shares as treasury shares the company must be entered in the register as the member holding those shares.

[S124]

NOTES

Commencement: to be appointed.

Supplementary

125 Power of court to rectify register

(1) If—

(a) the name of any person is, without sufficient cause, entered in or omitted from a company's register of members, or

(b) default is made or unnecessary delay takes place in entering on the register the fact of any person having ceased to be a member,

the person aggrieved, or any member of the company, or the company, may apply to the court for rectification of the register.

(2) The court may either refuse the application or may order rectification of the register and payment by the company of any damages sustained by any party aggrieved.

(3) On such an application the court may decide any question relating to the title of a person who is a party to the application to have his name entered in or omitted from the register, whether the question arises between members or alleged members, or between members or alleged members on the one hand and the company on the other hand, and generally may decide any question necessary or expedient to be decided for rectification of the register.

(4) In the case of a company required by this Act to send a list of its members to the registrar of companies, the court, when making an order for rectification of the register, shall by its order direct notice of the rectification to be given to the registrar.

[S125]

NOTES

Commencement: to be appointed.

126 Trusts not to be entered on register

No notice of any trust, expressed, implied or constructive, shall be entered on the register of members of a company registered in England and Wales or Northern Ireland, or be receivable by the registrar.

[S126]

NOTES

Commencement: to be appointed.

127 Register to be evidence

The register of members is prima facie evidence of any matters which are by this Act directed or authorised to be inserted in it.

[S127]

NOTES

Commencement: to be appointed.

128 Time limit for claims arising from entry in register

(1) Liability incurred by a company—

(a) from the making or deletion of an entry in the register of members, or

(b) from a failure to make or delete any such entry,

is not enforceable more than ten years after the date on which the entry was made or deleted or, as the case may be, the failure first occurred.

(2) This is without prejudice to any lesser period of limitation (and, in Scotland, to any rule that the obligation giving rise to the liability prescribes before the expiry of that period).

[S128]

NOTES

Commencement: to be appointed.

CHAPTER 3
OVERSEAS BRANCH REGISTERS

129 Overseas branch registers

(1) A company having a share capital may, if it transacts business in a country or territory to which this Chapter applies, cause to be kept there a branch register of members resident there (an "overseas branch register").

(2) This Chapter applies to—

(a) any part of Her Majesty's dominions outside the United Kingdom, the Channel Islands and the Isle of Man, and

(b) the countries or territories listed below.

Bangladesh

Cyprus

Dominica

The Gambia

Ghana

Guyana

The Hong Kong Special Administrative Region of the People's Republic of China

India

Ireland

Kenya

Kiribati

Lesotho

Malawi

Malaysia

Malta

Nigeria

Pakistan

Seychelles

Sierra Leone

Singapore

South Africa

Sri Lanka

Swaziland

Trinidad and Tobago

Uganda

Zimbabwe

(3) The Secretary of State may make provision by regulations as to the circumstances in which a company is to be regarded as keeping a register in a particular country or territory.

(4) Regulations under this section are subject to negative resolution procedure.

(5) References—

(a) in any Act or instrument (including, in particular, a company's articles) to a dominion register, or

(b) in articles registered before 1st November 1929 to a colonial register,

are to be read (unless the context otherwise requires) as a reference to an overseas branch register kept under this section.

[S129]

NOTES

Commencement: 20 January 2007 (for the purpose of enabling the exercise of powers to make Orders or Regulations by statutory instrument); to be appointed (otherwise).

---

130 Notice of opening of overseas branch register

(1) A company that begins to keep an overseas branch register must give notice to the registrar within 14 days of doing so, stating the country or territory in which the register is kept.

(2) If default is made in complying with subsection (1), an offence is committed by—

(a) the company, and

(b) every officer of the company who is in default.

(3) A person guilty of an offence under subsection (2) is liable on summary conviction to a fine not exceeding level 3 on the standard scale and, for continued contravention, a daily default fine not exceeding one-tenth of level 3 on the standard scale.

[S130]

NOTES

Commencement: to be appointed.

131 Keeping of overseas branch register

(1) An overseas branch register is regarded as part of the company's register of members ("the main register").

(2) The Secretary of State may make provision by regulations modifying any provision of Chapter 2 (register of members) as it applies in relation to an overseas branch register.

(3) Regulations under this section are subject to negative resolution procedure.

(4) Subject to the provisions of this Act, a company may by its articles make such provision as it thinks fit as to the keeping of overseas branch registers.

[S131]

NOTES

Commencement: 20 January 2007 (for the purpose of enabling the exercise of powers to make Orders or Regulations by statutory instrument); to be appointed (otherwise).

132 Register or duplicate to be kept available for inspection in UK

(1) A company that keeps an overseas branch register must keep available for inspection—

(a) the register, or

(b) a duplicate of the register duly entered up from time to time,

at the place in the United Kingdom where the company's main register is kept available for inspection.

(2) Any such duplicate is treated for all purposes of this Act as part of the main register.

(3) If default is made in complying with subsection (1), an offence is committed by—

(a) the company, and

(b) every officer of the company who is in default.

(4) A person guilty of an offence under subsection (3) is liable on summary conviction to a fine not exceeding level 3 on the standard scale and, for continued contravention, a daily default fine not exceeding one-tenth of level 3 on the standard scale.

[S132]

NOTES

Commencement: to be appointed.

133 Transactions in shares registered in overseas branch register

(1) Shares registered in an overseas branch register must be distinguished from those registered in the main register.

(2) No transaction with respect to shares registered in an overseas branch register may be registered in any other register.

(3) An instrument of transfer of a share registered in an overseas branch register—

(a) is regarded as a transfer of property situated outside the United Kingdom, and

(b) unless executed in a part of the United Kingdom, is exempt from stamp duty.

[S133]

NOTES

Commencement: to be appointed.

134 Jurisdiction of local courts

(1) A competent court in a country or territory where an overseas branch register is kept may exercise the same jurisdiction as is exercisable by a court in the United Kingdom—

(a) to rectify the register (see section 125), or

(b) in relation to a request for inspection or a copy of the register (see section 117).

(2) The offences—

(a) of refusing inspection or failing to provide a copy of the register (see section 118), and

(b) of making a false, misleading or deceptive statement in a request for inspection or a copy (see section 119),

may be prosecuted summarily before any tribunal having summary criminal jurisdiction in the country or territory where the register is kept.

(3) This section extends only to those countries and territories to which paragraph 3 of Schedule 14 to the Companies Act 1985 (c 6) (which made similar provision) extended immediately before the coming into force of this Chapter.

[S134]

NOTES

Commencement: to be appointed.

135 Discontinuance of overseas branch register

(1) A company may discontinue an overseas branch register.

(2) If it does so all the entries in that register must be transferred—

(a) to some other overseas branch register kept in the same country or territory, or

(b) to the main register.

(3) The company must give notice to the registrar within 14 days of the discontinuance.

(4) If default is made in complying with subsection (3), an offence is committed by—

(a) the company, and

(b) every officer of the company who is in default.

(5) A person guilty of an offence under subsection (4) is liable on summary conviction to a fine not exceeding level 3 on the standard scale and, for continued contravention, a daily default fine not exceeding one-tenth of level 3 on the standard scale.

[S135]

NOTES

Commencement: to be appointed.

CHAPTER 4
PROHIBITION ON SUBSIDIARY BEING MEMBER OF ITS HOLDING COMPANY

General prohibition

136 Prohibition on subsidiary being a member of its holding company

(1) Except as provided by this Chapter—

(a) a body corporate cannot be a member of a company that is its holding company, and

(b) any allotment or transfer of shares in a company to its subsidiary is void.

(2) The exceptions are provided for in—

section 138 (subsidiary acting as personal representative or trustee), and

section 141 (subsidiary acting as authorised dealer in securities).

[S136]

NOTES

Commencement: to be appointed.

137 Shares acquired before prohibition became applicable

(1) Where a body corporate became a holder of shares in a company—

(a) before the relevant date, or

(b) on or after that date and before the commencement of this Chapter in circumstances in which the prohibition in section 23(1) of the Companies Act 1985 or Article 33(1) of the Companies (Northern Ireland) Order 1986 (SI 1986/1032 (NI 6)) (or any corresponding earlier enactment), as it then had effect, did not apply, or

(c) on or after the commencement of this Chapter in circumstances in which the prohibition in section 136 did not apply,

it may continue to be a member of the company.

(2) The relevant date for the purposes of subsection (1)(a) is—

(a) 1st July 1948 in the case of a company registered in Great Britain, and

(b) 1st April 1961 in the case of a company registered in Northern Ireland.

(3) So long as it is permitted to continue as a member of a company by virtue of this section, an allotment to it of fully paid shares in the company may be validly made by way of capitalisation of reserves of the company.

(4) But, so long as the prohibition in section 136 would (apart from this section) apply, it has no right to vote in respect of the shares mentioned in subsection (1) above, or any shares allotted as mentioned in subsection (3) above, on a written resolution or at meetings of the company or of any class of its members.

[S137]

NOTES

Commencement: to be appointed.

Subsidiary acting as personal representative or trustee

138 Subsidiary acting as personal representative or trustee

(1) The prohibition in section 136 (prohibition on subsidiary being a member of its holding company) does not apply where the subsidiary is concerned only—

(a) as personal representative, or

(b) as trustee,

unless, in the latter case, the holding company or a subsidiary of it is beneficially interested under the trust.

(2) For the purpose of ascertaining whether the holding company or a subsidiary is so interested, there shall be disregarded—

(a) any interest held only by way of security for the purposes of a transaction entered into by the holding company or subsidiary in the ordinary course of a business that includes the lending of money;

(b) any interest within—

section 139 (interests to be disregarded: residual interest under pension scheme or employees' share scheme), or

section 140 (interests to be disregarded: employer's rights of recovery under pension scheme or employees' share scheme);

(c) any rights that the company or subsidiary has in its capacity as trustee, including in particular—

(i) any right to recover its expenses or be remunerated out of the trust property, and

(ii) any right to be indemnified out of the trust property for any liability incurred by reason of any act or omission in the performance of its duties as trustee.

[S138]

NOTES

Commencement: to be appointed.

139 Interests to be disregarded: residual interest under pension scheme or employees' share scheme

(1) Where shares in a company are held on trust for the purposes of a pension scheme or employees' share scheme, there shall be disregarded for the purposes of section 138 any residual interest that has not vested in possession.

(2) A "residual interest" means a right of the company or subsidiary ("the residual beneficiary") to receive any of the trust property in the event of—

(a) all the liabilities arising under the scheme having been satisfied or provided for, or
(b) the residual beneficiary ceasing to participate in the scheme, or
(c) the trust property at any time exceeding what is necessary for satisfying the liabilities arising or expected to arise under the scheme.

(3) In subsection (2)—

(a) the reference to a right includes a right dependent on the exercise of a discretion vested by the scheme in the trustee or another person, and
(b) the reference to liabilities arising under a scheme includes liabilities that have resulted, or may result, from the exercise of any such discretion.

(4) For the purposes of this section a residual interest vests in possession—

(a) in a case within subsection (2)(a), on the occurrence of the event mentioned there (whether or not the amount of the property receivable pursuant to the right is ascertained);
(b) in a case within subsection (2)(b) or (c), when the residual beneficiary becomes entitled to require the trustee to transfer to him any of the property receivable pursuant to the right.

(5) In this section "pension scheme" means a scheme for the provision of benefits consisting of or including relevant benefits for or in respect of employees or former employees.

(6) In subsection (5)—

(a) "relevant benefits" means any pension, lump sum, gratuity or other like benefit given or to be given on retirement or on death or in anticipation of retirement or, in connection with past service, after retirement or death; and
(b) "employee" shall be read as if a director of a company were employed by it.

[S139]

NOTES

Commencement: to be appointed.

140 Interests to be disregarded: employer's rights of recovery under pension scheme or employees' share scheme

(1) Where shares in a company are held on trust for the purposes of a pension scheme or employees' share scheme, there shall be disregarded for the purposes of section 138 any charge or lien on, or set-off against, any benefit or other right or interest under the scheme for the purpose of enabling the employer or former employer of a member of the scheme to obtain the discharge of a monetary obligation due to him from the member.

(2) In the case of a trust for the purposes of a pension scheme there shall also be disregarded any right to receive from the trustee of the scheme, or as trustee of the scheme to retain, an amount that can be recovered or retained, under section 61 of the Pension Schemes Act 1993 (c 48) or section 57 of the Pension Schemes (Northern Ireland) Act 1993 (c 49) (deduction of contributions equivalent premium from refund of scheme contributions) or otherwise, as reimbursement or partial reimbursement for any contributions equivalent premium paid in connection with the scheme under Part 3 of that Act.

(3) In this section "pension scheme" means a scheme for the provision of benefits consisting of or including relevant benefits for or in respect of employees or former employees.

"Relevant benefits" here means any pension, lump sum, gratuity or other like benefit given or to be given on retirement or on death or in anticipation of retirement or, in connection with past service, after retirement or death.

(4) In this section "employer" and "employee" shall be read as if a director of a company were employed by it.

[S140]

NOTES

Commencement: to be appointed.

Subsidiary acting as dealer in securities

141 Subsidiary acting as authorised dealer in securities

(1) The prohibition in section 136 (prohibition on subsidiary being a member of its holding company) does not apply where the shares are held by the subsidiary in the ordinary course of its business as an intermediary.

(2) For this purpose a person is an intermediary if he—

(a) carries on a bona fide business of dealing in securities,

(b) is a member of or has access to a regulated market, and

(c) does not carry on an excluded business.

(3) The following are excluded businesses—

(a) a business that consists wholly or mainly in the making or managing of investments;

(b) a business that consists wholly or mainly in, or is carried on wholly or mainly for the purposes of, providing services to persons who are connected with the person carrying on the business;

(c) a business that consists in insurance business;

(d) a business that consists in managing or acting as trustee in relation to a pension scheme, or that is carried on by the manager or trustee of such a scheme in connection with or for the purposes of the scheme;

(e) a business that consists in operating or acting as trustee in relation to a collective investment scheme, or that is carried on by the operator or trustee of such a scheme in connection with and for the purposes of the scheme.

(4) For the purposes of this section—

(a) the question whether a person is connected with another shall be determined in accordance with section 839 of the Income and Corporation Taxes Act 1988 (c 1);

(b) "collective investment scheme" has the meaning given in section 235 of the Financial Services and Markets Act 2000 (c 8);

(c) "insurance business" means business that consists in the effecting or carrying out of contracts of insurance;

(d) "securities" includes—

(i) options,

(ii) futures, and

(iii) contracts for differences,

and rights or interests in those investments;

(e) "trustee" and "the operator" in relation to a collective investment scheme shall be construed in accordance with section 237(2) of the Financial Services and Markets Act 2000 (c 8).

(5) Expressions used in this section that are also used in the provisions regulating activities under the Financial Services and Markets Act 2000 have the same meaning here as they do in those provisions.

See section 22 of that Act, orders made under that section and Schedule 2 to that Act.

[S141]

NOTES

Commencement: to be appointed.

142 Protection of third parties in other cases where subsidiary acting as dealer in securities

(1) This section applies where—

(a) a subsidiary that is a dealer in securities has purportedly acquired shares in its holding company in contravention of the prohibition in section 136, and

(b) a person acting in good faith has agreed, for value and without notice of the contravention, to acquire shares in the holding company—

(i) from the subsidiary, or

(ii) from someone who has purportedly acquired the shares after their disposal by the subsidiary.

(2) A transfer to that person of the shares mentioned in subsection (1)(a) has the same effect as it would have had if their original acquisition by the subsidiary had not been in contravention of the prohibition.

[S142]

NOTES

Commencement: to be appointed.

Supplementary

143 Application of provisions to companies not limited by shares

In relation to a company other than a company limited by shares, the references in this Chapter to shares shall be read as references to the interest of its members as such, whatever the form of that interest.

[S143]

NOTES

Commencement: to be appointed.

144 Application of provisions to nominees

The provisions of this Chapter apply to a nominee acting on behalf of a subsidiary as to the subsidiary itself.

[S144]

NOTES

Commencement: to be appointed.

PART 9
EXERCISE OF MEMBERS' RIGHTS

Effect of provisions in company's articles

145 Effect of provisions of articles as to enjoyment or exercise of members' rights

(1) This section applies where provision is made by a company's articles enabling a member to nominate another person or persons as entitled to enjoy or exercise all or any specified rights of the member in relation to the company.

(2) So far as is necessary to give effect to that provision, anything required or authorised by any provision of the Companies Acts to be done by or in relation to the member shall instead be done, or (as the case may be) may instead be done, by or in relation to the nominated person (or each of them) as if he were a member of the company.

(3) This applies, in particular, to the rights conferred by—

(a) sections 291 and 293 (right to be sent proposed written resolution);
(b) section 292 (right to require circulation of written resolution);
(c) section 303 (right to require directors to call general meeting);
(d) section 310 (right to notice of general meetings);
(e) section 314 (right to require circulation of a statement);
(f) section 324 (right to appoint proxy to act at meeting);
(g) section 338 (right to require circulation of resolution for AGM of public company); and
(h) section 423 (right to be sent a copy of annual accounts and reports).

(4) This section and any such provision as is mentioned in subsection (1)—

(a) do not confer rights enforceable against the company by anyone other than the member, and
(b) do not affect the requirements for an effective transfer or other disposition of the whole or part of a member's interest in the company.

[S145]

NOTES

Commencement: 1 October 2007 (for transitional provisions etc see the note below).

Transitional provisions, etc: Sch 3, para 3 to the draft Companies Act 2006 (Commencement No 3, Consequential Amendments, Transitional Provisions and Savings) Order 2007 (at **[A12]**) provides as follows—

"**3 Exercise of members' rights** (**ss 145 to 153**)

(1) Section 145 of the Companies Act 2006 (effect of provisions of articles as to enjoyment or exercise of members' rights) applies in relation to things required or authorised to be done as mentioned in subsection (2) of that section on or after 1st October 2007.

(2) Nominations under section 146 of that Act (traded companies: nomination of persons to enjoy information rights) may be made at any time on or after 1st October 2007.

A company is not required to act on a nomination before 1st January 2008; but if it does so, sections 147 to 150 apply.

(3) Section 152 of that Act (exercise of rights where shares held on behalf of others: exercise in different ways) applies in relation to the exercise of rights on or after 1st October 2007.

(4) A request may be made under section 153 of that Act (exercise of rights where shares held on behalf of others: members' requests) at any time on or after 1st October 2007.".

Transitional adaptations: art 6 of the draft Companies Act 2006 (Commencement No 3, Consequential Amendments, Transitional Provisions and Savings) Order 2007 provides that the provisions brought into force by that Order shall have effect subject to any transitional adaptations specified in Sch 1 to that Order. Schedule 1, paras 3–5 to the Order (at **[A12]**) provide as follows—

"**3 Exercise of members' rights** (**ss 145 to 153**)

(1) Section 145 (effect of provision of articles as to enjoyment or exercise of members' rights) has effect with the following adaptation.

(2) In subsection (3)(h), for "section 423 (right to be sent a copy of annual accounts and reports)" substitute "section 238 of the Companies Act 1985 or Article 246 of the Companies (Northern Ireland) Order 1986 (persons entitled to receive copies of accounts and reports).".

4.—(1) Section 146 (traded companies: nomination of persons to enjoy information rights) has effect with the following adaptations.

(2) In subsection (3)(b)(i), for "section 431 or 432 (right to require copies of accounts and reports)," substitute "section 239 of the Companies Act 1985 or Article 247 of the Companies (Northern Ireland) Order 1986 (right to demand copies of accounts and annual reports),".

(3) For the second sentence of subsection (4) substitute "Section 251 of the Companies Act 1985 or Article 259 of the Companies (Northern Ireland) Order 1986 (summary financial statements) applies to copies of accounts and reports required to be sent out by virtue of this section to a person nominated to enjoy information rights as it applies to copies of accounts and reports required to be sent out to a member of the company in accordance with section 238 of that Act or Article 246 of that Order.".

5.—(1) Section 153(1) (exercise of rights held on behalf of others: members' requests) has effect with the following adaptation.

(2) Omit paragraph (d).".

Information rights

146 Traded companies: nomination of persons to enjoy information rights

(1) This section applies to a company whose shares are admitted to trading on a regulated market.

(2) A member of such a company who holds shares on behalf of another person may nominate that person to enjoy information rights.

(3) "Information rights" means—

(a) the right to receive a copy of all communications that the company sends to its members generally or to any class of its members that includes the person making the nomination, and

(b) the rights conferred by—

(i) section 431 or 432 (right to require copies of accounts and reports), and

(ii) section 1145 (right to require hard copy version of document or information provided in another form).

(4) The reference in subsection (3)(a) to communications that a company sends to its members generally includes the company's annual accounts and reports. For the application of section 426 (option to provide summary financial statement) in relation to a person nominated to enjoy information rights, see subsection (5) of that section.

(5) A company need not act on a nomination purporting to relate to certain information rights only.

[S146]

NOTES

Commencement: 1 October 2007 (for transitional provisions etc see the note to s 145).

147 Information rights: form in which copies to be provided

(1) This section applies as regards the form in which copies are to be provided to a person nominated under section 146 (nomination of person to enjoy information rights).

(2) If the person to be nominated wishes to receive hard copy communications, he must—

(a) request the person making the nomination to notify the company of that fact, and

(b) provide an address to which such copies may be sent.

This must be done before the nomination is made.

(3) If having received such a request the person making the nomination—

(a) notifies the company that the nominated person wishes to receive hard copy communications, and

(b) provides the company with that address,

the right of the nominated person is to receive hard copy communications accordingly.

(4) This is subject to the provisions of Parts 3 and 4 of Schedule 5 (communications by company) under which the company may take steps to enable it to communicate in electronic form or by means of a website.

(5) If no such notification is given (or no address is provided), the nominated person is taken to have agreed that documents or information may be sent or supplied to him by the company by means of a website.

(6) That agreement—

(a) may be revoked by the nominated person, and

(b) does not affect his right under section 1145 to require a hard copy version of a document or information provided in any other form.

[S147]

NOTES

Commencement: 1 October 2007 (for transitional provisions etc see the note to s 145).

148 Termination or suspension of nomination

(1) The following provisions have effect in relation to a nomination under section 146 (nomination of person to enjoy information rights).

(2) The nomination may be terminated at the request of the member or of the nominated person.

(3) The nomination ceases to have effect on the occurrence in relation to the member or the nominated person of any of the following—

(a) in the case of an individual, death or bankruptcy;

(b) in the case of a body corporate, dissolution or the making of an order for the winding up of the body otherwise than for the purposes of reconstruction.

(4) In subsection (3)—

(a) the reference to bankruptcy includes—

(i) the sequestration of a person's estate, and

(ii) a person's estate being the subject of a protected trust deed (within the meaning of the Bankruptcy (Scotland) Act 1985 (c 66)); and

(b) the reference to the making of an order for winding up is to—

(i) the making of such an order under the Insolvency Act 1986 (c 45) or the Insolvency (Northern Ireland) Order 1989 (SI 1989/2405 (NI 19)), or

(ii) any corresponding proceeding under the law of a country or territory outside the United Kingdom.

(5) The effect of any nominations made by a member is suspended at any time when there are more nominated persons than the member has shares in the company.

(6) Where—

(a) the member holds different classes of shares with different information rights, and

(b) there are more nominated persons than he has shares conferring a particular right,

the effect of any nominations made by him is suspended to the extent that they confer that right.

(7) Where the company—

(a) enquires of a nominated person whether he wishes to retain information rights, and

(b) does not receive a response within the period of 28 days beginning with the date on which the company's enquiry was sent,

the nomination ceases to have effect at the end of that period.

Such an enquiry is not to be made of a person more than once in any twelve-month period.

(8) The termination or suspension of a nomination means that the company is not required to act on it.

It does not prevent the company from continuing to do so, to such extent or for such period as it thinks fit.

[S148]

NOTES

Commencement: 1 October 2007 (for transitional provisions etc see the note to s 145).

149 Information as to possible rights in relation to voting

(1) This section applies where a company sends a copy of a notice of a meeting to a person nominated under section 146 (nomination of person to enjoy information rights)

(2) The copy of the notice must be accompanied by a statement that—

(a) he may have a right under an agreement between him and the member by whom he was nominated to be appointed, or to have someone else appointed, as a proxy for the meeting, and

(b) if he has no such right or does not wish to exercise it, he may have a right under such an agreement to give instructions to the member as to the exercise of voting rights.

(3) Section 325 (notice of meeting to contain statement of member's rights in relation to appointment of proxy) does not apply to the copy, and the company must either—

(a) omit the notice required by that section, or

(b) include it but state that it does not apply to the nominated person.

[S149]

NOTES

Commencement: 1 October 2007 (for transitional provisions etc see the note to s 145).

150 Information rights: status of rights

(1) This section has effect as regards the rights conferred by a nomination under section 146 (nomination of person to enjoy information rights).

(2) Enjoyment by the nominated person of the rights conferred by the nomination is enforceable against the company by the member as if they were rights conferred by the company's articles.

(3) Any enactment, and any provision of the company's articles, having effect in relation to communications with members has a corresponding effect (subject to any necessary adaptations) in relation to communications with the nominated person.

(4) In particular—
  (a) where under any enactment, or any provision of the company's articles, the members of a company entitled to receive a document or information are determined as at a date or time before it is sent or supplied, the company need not send or supply it to a nominated person—
    (i) whose nomination was received by the company after that date or time, or
    (ii) if that date or time falls in a period of suspension of his nomination; and
  (b) where under any enactment, or any provision of the company's articles, the right of a member to receive a document or information depends on the company having a current address for him, the same applies to any person nominated by him.

(5) The rights conferred by the nomination—
  (a) are in addition to the rights of the member himself, and
  (b) do not affect any rights exercisable by virtue of any such provision as is mentioned in section 145 (provisions of company's articles as to enjoyment or exercise of members' rights).

(6) A failure to give effect to the rights conferred by the nomination does not affect the validity of anything done by or on behalf of the company.

(7) References in this section to the rights conferred by the nomination are to—
  (a) the rights referred to in section 146(3) (information rights), and
  (b) where applicable, the rights conferred by section 147(3) (right to hard copy communications) and section 149 (information as to possible voting rights).

[S150]

NOTES

Commencement: 1 October 2007 (for transitional provisions etc see the note to s 145).

151 Information rights: power to amend

(1) The Secretary of State may by regulations amend the provisions of sections 146 to 150 (information rights) so as to—
  (a) extend or restrict the classes of companies to which section 146 applies,
  (b) make other provision as to the circumstances in which a nomination may be made under that section, or
  (c) extend or restrict the rights conferred by such a nomination.

(2) The regulations may make such consequential modifications of any other provisions of this Part, or of any other enactment, as appear to the Secretary of State to be necessary.

(3) Regulations under this section are subject to affirmative resolution procedure.

[S151]

NOTES

Commencement: 20 January 2007 (for the purpose of enabling the exercise of powers to make Orders or Regulations by statutory instrument); 1 October 2007 (otherwise) (for transitional provisions etc see the note to s 145).

Exercise of rights where shares held on behalf of others

152 Exercise of rights where shares held on behalf of others: exercise in different ways

(1) Where a member holds shares in a company on behalf of more than one person—
  (a) rights attached to the shares, and
  (b) rights under any enactment exercisable by virtue of holding the shares,

need not all be exercised, and if exercised, need not all be exercised in the same way.

(2) A member who exercises such rights but does not exercise all his rights, must inform the company to what extent he is exercising the rights.

(3) A member who exercises such rights in different ways must inform the company of the ways in which he is exercising them and to what extent they are exercised in each way.

(4) If a member exercises such rights without informing the company—

(a) that he is not exercising all his rights, or

(b) that he is exercising his rights in different ways,

the company is entitled to assume that he is exercising all his rights and is exercising them in the same way.

[S152]

NOTES

Commencement: 1 October 2007 (for transitional provisions etc see the note to s 145).

153 Exercise of rights where shares held on behalf of others: members' requests

(1) This section applies for the purposes of—

(a) section 314 (power to require circulation of statement),

(b) section 338 (public companies: power to require circulation of resolution for AGM),

(c) section 342 (power to require independent report on poll), and

(d) section 527 (power to require website publication of audit concerns).

(2) A company is required to act under any of those sections if it receives a request in relation to which the following conditions are met—

(a) it is made by at least 100 persons;

(b) it is authenticated by all the persons making it;

(c) in the case of any of those persons who is not a member of the company, it is accompanied by a statement—

(i) of the full name and address of a person ("the member") who is a member of the company and holds shares on behalf of that person,

(ii) that the member is holding those shares on behalf of that person in the course of a business,

(iii) of the number of shares in the company that the member holds on behalf of that person,

(iv) of the total amount paid up on those shares,

(v) that those shares are not held on behalf of anyone else or, if they are, that the other person or persons are not among the other persons making the request,

(vi) that some or all of those shares confer voting rights that are relevant for the purposes of making a request under the section in question, and

(vii) that the person has the right to instruct the member how to exercise those rights;

(d) in the case of any of those persons who is a member of the company, it is accompanied by a statement—

(i) that he holds shares otherwise than on behalf of another person, or

(ii) that he holds shares on behalf of one or more other persons but those persons are not among the other persons making the request;

(e) it is accompanied by such evidence as the company may reasonably require of the matters mentioned in paragraph (c) and (d);

(f) the total amount of the sums paid up on—

(i) shares held as mentioned in paragraph (c), and

(ii) shares held as mentioned in paragraph (d),

divided by the number of persons making the request, is not less than £100;

(g) the request complies with any other requirements of the section in question as to contents, timing and otherwise.

[S153]

NOTES

Commencement: 1 October 2007 (for transitional provisions etc see the note to s 145).

PART 10
A COMPANY'S DIRECTORS

CHAPTER 1
APPOINTMENT AND REMOVAL OF DIRECTORS

Requirement to have directors

154 Companies required to have directors

(1) A private company must have at least one director.

(2) A public company must have at least two directors.

[S154]

NOTES

Commencement: 1 October 2007.

155 Companies required to have at least one director who is a natural person

(1) A company must have at least one director who is a natural person.

(2) This requirement is met if the office of director is held by a natural person as a corporation sole or otherwise by virtue of an office.

[S155]

NOTES

Commencement: to be appointed.

156 Direction requiring company to make appointment

(1) If it appears to the Secretary of State that a company is in breach of—

section 154 (requirements as to number of directors), or

section 155 (requirement to have at least one director who is a natural person),

the Secretary of State may give the company a direction under this section.

(2) The direction must specify—

(a) the statutory requirement the company appears to be in breach of,

(b) what the company must do in order to comply with the direction, and

(c) the period within which it must do so.

That period must be not less than one month or more than three months after the date on which the direction is given.

(3) The direction must also inform the company of the consequences of failing to comply.

(4) Where the company is in breach of section 154 or 155 it must comply with the direction by—

(a) making the necessary appointment or appointments, and

(b) giving notice of them under section 167,

before the end of the period specified in the direction.

(5) If the company has already made the necessary appointment or appointments (or so far as it has done so), it must comply with the direction by giving notice of them under section 167 before the end of the period specified in the direction.

(6) If a company fails to comply with a direction under this section, an offence is committed by—

(a) the company, and

(b) every officer of the company who is in default.

For this purpose a shadow director is treated as an officer of the company.

(7) A person guilty of an offence under this section is liable on summary conviction to a fine not exceeding level 5 on the standard scale and, for continued contravention, a daily default fine not exceeding one-tenth of level 5 on the standard scale.

[S156]

NOTES

Commencement: to be appointed.

Appointment

157 Minimum age for appointment as director

(1) A person may not be appointed a director of a company unless he has attained the age of 16 years.

(2) This does not affect the validity of an appointment that is not to take effect until the person appointed attains that age.

(3) Where the office of director of a company is held by a corporation sole, or otherwise by virtue of another office, the appointment to that other office of a person who has not attained the age of 16 years is not effective also to make him a director of the company until he attains the age of 16 years.

(4) An appointment made in contravention of this section is void.

(5) Nothing in this section affects any liability of a person under any provision of the Companies Acts if he—

(a) purports to act as director, or

(b) acts as a shadow director,

although he could not, by virtue of this section, be validly appointed as a director.

(6) This section has effect subject to section 158 (power to provide for exceptions from minimum age requirement).

[S157]

NOTES

Commencement: to be appointed.

158 Power to provide for exceptions from minimum age requirement

(1) The Secretary of State may make provision by regulations for cases in which a person who has not attained the age of 16 years may be appointed a director of a company.

(2) The regulations must specify the circumstances in which, and any conditions subject to which, the appointment may be made.

(3) If the specified circumstances cease to obtain, or any specified conditions cease to be met, a person who was appointed by virtue of the regulations and who has not since attained the age of 16 years ceases to hold office.

(4) The regulations may make different provision for different parts of the United Kingdom.

This is without prejudice to the general power to make different provision for different cases.

(5) Regulations under this section are subject to negative resolution procedure.

[S158]

NOTES

Commencement: 20 January 2007 (for the purpose of enabling the exercise of powers to make Orders or Regulations by statutory instrument); to be appointed (otherwise).

159 Existing under-age directors

(1) This section applies where—

(a) a person appointed a director of a company before section 157 (minimum age for appointment as director) comes into force has not attained the age of 16 when that section comes into force, or

(b) the office of director of a company is held by a corporation sole, or otherwise by virtue of another office, and the person appointed to that other office has not attained the age of 16 years when that section comes into force,

and the case is not one excepted from that section by regulations under section 158.

(2) That person ceases to be a director on section 157 coming into force.

(3) The company must make the necessary consequential alteration in its register of directors but need not give notice to the registrar of the change.

(4) If it appears to the registrar (from other information) that a person has ceased by virtue of this section to be a director of a company, the registrar shall note that fact on the register.

[S159]

NOTES

Commencement: to be appointed.

160 Appointment of directors of public company to be voted on individually

(1) At a general meeting of a public company a motion for the appointment of two or more persons as directors of the company by a single resolution must not be made unless a resolution that it should be so made has first been agreed to by the meeting without any vote being given against it.

(2) A resolution moved in contravention of this section is void, whether or not its being so moved was objected to at the time.

But where a resolution so moved is passed, no provision for the automatic reappointment of retiring directors in default of another appointment applies.

(3) For the purposes of this section a motion for approving a person's appointment, or for nominating a person for appointment, is treated as a motion for his appointment.

(4) Nothing in this section applies to a resolution amending the company's articles.

[S160]

NOTES

Commencement: 1 October 2007.

161 Validity of acts of directors

(1) The acts of a person acting as a director are valid notwithstanding that it is afterwards discovered—

(a) that there was a defect in his appointment;

(b) that he was disqualified from holding office;

(c) that he had ceased to hold office;

(d) that he was not entitled to vote on the matter in question.

(2) This applies even if the resolution for his appointment is void under section 160 (appointment of directors of public company to be voted on individually).

[S161]

NOTES

Commencement: 1 October 2007 (for transitional provisions see the note below).

Transitional provisions, etc: Sch 3, para 4 to the draft Companies Act 2006 (Commencement No 3, Consequential Amendments, Transitional Provisions and Savings) Order 2007 (at **[A12]**) provides as follows—

"**4 Validity of acts of directors** (**s 161**)

(1) Section 161 of the Companies Act 2006 (validity of acts of directors) applies to acts done on or after 1st October 2007.

(2) Section 285 of the 1985 Act (validity of acts of director or manager) or Article 293 of the 1986 Order (validity of acts of director) continues to apply to acts done before that date.".

Register of directors, etc

162 Register of directors

(1) Every company must keep a register of its directors.

(2) The register must contain the required particulars (see sections 163, 164 and 166) of each person who is a director of the company.

(3) The register must be kept available for inspection—
- (a) at the company's registered office, or
- (b) at a place specified in regulations under section 1136.

(4) The company must give notice to the registrar—
- (a) of the place at which the register is kept available for inspection, and
- (b) of any change in that place,

unless it has at all times been kept at the company's registered office.

(5) The register must be open to the inspection—
- (a) of any member of the company without charge, and
- (b) of any other person on payment of such fee as may be prescribed.

(6) If default is made in complying with subsection (1), (2) or (3) or if default is made for 14 days in complying with subsection (4), or if an inspection required under subsection (5) is refused, an offence is committed by—
- (a) the company, and
- (b) every officer of the company who is in default.

For this purpose a shadow director is treated as an officer of the company.

(7) A person guilty of an offence under this section is liable on summary conviction to a fine not exceeding level 5 on the standard scale and, for continued contravention, a daily default fine not exceeding one-tenth of level 5 on the standard scale.

(8) In the case of a refusal of inspection of the register, the court may by order compel an immediate inspection of it.

[S162]

NOTES

Commencement: 20 January 2007 (for the purpose of enabling the exercise of powers to make Orders or Regulations by statutory instrument); to be appointed (otherwise).

163 Particulars of directors to be registered: individuals

(1) A company's register of directors must contain the following particulars in the case of an individual—
- (a) name and any former name;
- (b) a service address;
- (c) the country or state (or part of the United Kingdom) in which he is usually resident;
- (d) nationality;
- (e) business occupation (if any);
- (f) date of birth.

(2) For the purposes of this section "name" means a person's Christian name (or other forename) and surname, except that in the case of—
- (a) a peer, or
- (b) an individual usually known by a title,

the title may be stated instead of his Christian name (or other forename) and surname or in addition to either or both of them.

(3) For the purposes of this section a "former name" means a name by which the individual was formerly known for business purposes.

Where a person is or was formerly known by more than one such name, each of them must be stated.

(4) It is not necessary for the register to contain particulars of a former name in the following cases—

(a) in the case of a peer or an individual normally known by a British title, where the name is one by which the person was known previous to the adoption of or succession to the title;
(b) in the case of any person, where the former name—
  (i) was changed or disused before the person attained the age of 16 years, or
  (ii) has been changed or disused for 20 years or more.

(5) A person's service address may be stated to be "The company's registered office".

[S163]

NOTES

Commencement: to be appointed.

164 Particulars of directors to be registered: corporate directors and firms

A company's register of directors must contain the following particulars in the case of a body corporate, or a firm that is a legal person under the law by which it is governed—
(a) corporate or firm name;
(b) registered or principal office;
(c) in the case of an EEA company to which the First Company Law Directive (68/151/EEC) applies, particulars of—
  (i) the register in which the company file mentioned in Article 3 of that Directive is kept (including details of the relevant state), and
  (ii) the registration number in that register;
(d) in any other case, particulars of—
  (i) the legal form of the company or firm and the law by which it is governed, and
  (ii) if applicable, the register in which it is entered (including details of the state) and its registration number in that register.

[S164]

NOTES

Commencement: to be appointed.

165 Register of directors' residential addresses

(1) Every company must keep a register of directors' residential addresses.

(2) The register must state the usual residential address of each of the company's directors.

(3) If a director's usual residential address is the same as his service address (as stated in the company's register of directors), the register of directors' residential addresses need only contain an entry to that effect.

This does not apply if his service address is stated to be "The company's registered office".

(4) If default is made in complying with this section, an offence is committed by—
(a) the company, and
(b) every officer of the company who is in default.

For this purpose a shadow director is treated as an officer of the company.

(5) A person guilty of an offence under this section is liable on summary conviction to a fine not exceeding level 5 on the standard scale and, for continued contravention, a daily default fine not exceeding one-tenth of level 5 on the standard scale.

(6) This section applies only to directors who are individuals, not where the director is a body corporate or a firm that is a legal person under the law by which it is governed.

[S165]

NOTES

Commencement: to be appointed.

166 Particulars of directors to be registered: power to make regulations

(1) The Secretary of State may make provision by regulations amending—
section 163 (particulars of directors to be registered: individuals),

section 164 (particulars of directors to be registered: corporate directors and firms), or
section 165 (register of directors' residential addresses),

so as to add to or remove items from the particulars required to be contained in a company's register of directors or register of directors' residential addresses.

(2) Regulations under this section are subject to affirmative resolution procedure.

[S166]

NOTES

Commencement: 20 January 2007 (for the purpose of enabling the exercise of powers to make Orders or Regulations by statutory instrument); to be appointed (otherwise).

167 Duty to notify registrar of changes

(1) A company must, within the period of 14 days from—

(a) a person becoming or ceasing to be a director, or

(b) the occurrence of any change in the particulars contained in its register of directors or its register of directors' residential addresses,

give notice to the registrar of the change and of the date on which it occurred.

(2) Notice of a person having become a director of the company must—

(a) contain a statement of the particulars of the new director that are required to be included in the company's register of directors and its register of directors' residential addresses, and

(b) be accompanied by a consent, by that person, to act in that capacity.

(3) Where—

(a) a company gives notice of a change of a director's service address as stated in the company's register of directors, and

(b) the notice is not accompanied by notice of any resulting change in the particulars contained in the company's register of directors' residential addresses,

the notice must be accompanied by a statement that no such change is required.

(4) If default is made in complying with this section, an offence is committed by—

(a) the company, and

(b) every officer of the company who is in default.

For this purpose a shadow director is treated as an officer of the company.

(5) A person guilty of an offence under this section is liable on summary conviction to a fine not exceeding level 5 on the standard scale and, for continued contravention, a daily default fine not exceeding one-tenth of level 5 on the standard scale.

[S167]

NOTES

Commencement: to be appointed.

Removal

168 Resolution to remove director

(1) A company may by ordinary resolution at a meeting remove a director before the expiration of his period of office, notwithstanding anything in any agreement between it and him.

(2) Special notice is required of a resolution to remove a director under this section or to appoint somebody instead of a director so removed at the meeting at which he is removed.

(3) A vacancy created by the removal of a director under this section, if not filled at the meeting at which he is removed, may be filled as a casual vacancy.

(4) A person appointed director in place of a person removed under this section is treated, for the purpose of determining the time at which he or any other director is to retire, as if he had become director on the day on which the person in whose place he is appointed was last appointed a director.

(5) This section is not to be taken—

(a) as depriving a person removed under it of compensation or damages payable to him in respect of the termination of his appointment as director or of any appointment terminating with that as director, or

(b) as derogating from any power to remove a director that may exist apart from this section.

[S168]

NOTES

Commencement: 1 October 2007 (for transitional provisions see the note to s 169).

169 Director's right to protest against removal

(1) On receipt of notice of an intended resolution to remove a director under section 168, the company must forthwith send a copy of the notice to the director concerned.

(2) The director (whether or not a member of the company) is entitled to be heard on the resolution at the meeting.

(3) Where notice is given of an intended resolution to remove a director under that section, and the director concerned makes with respect to it representations in writing to the company (not exceeding a reasonable length) and requests their notification to members of the company, the company shall, unless the representations are received by it too late for it to do so—

(a) in any notice of the resolution given to members of the company state the fact of the representations having been made; and

(b) send a copy of the representations to every member of the company to whom notice of the meeting is sent (whether before or after receipt of the representations by the company).

(4) If a copy of the representations is not sent as required by subsection (3) because received too late or because of the company's default, the director may (without prejudice to his right to be heard orally) require that the representations shall be read out at the meeting.

(5) Copies of the representations need not be sent out and the representations need not be read out at the meeting if, on the application either of the company or of any other person who claims to be aggrieved, the court is satisfied that the rights conferred by this section are being abused.

(6) The court may order the company's costs (in Scotland, expenses) on an application under subsection (5) to be paid in whole or in part by the director, notwithstanding that he is not a party to the application.

[S169]

NOTES

Commencement: 1 October 2007 (for transitional provisions see the note below).

Transitional provisions, etc: Sch 3, para 5 to the draft Companies Act 2006 (Commencement No 3, Consequential Amendments, Transitional Provisions and Savings) Order 2007 (at **[A12]**) provides as follows—

"5 Removal of directors (ss 168 and 169)

(1) Section 169(5) of the Companies Act 2006 (circumstances in which representations need not be sent out or read out at the meeting) applies where the representations are received by the company on or after 1st October 2007.

(2) Section 304(4) of the 1985 Act or Article 312(4) of the 1986 Order continues to apply where the representations are received by the company before that date.".

CHAPTER 2
GENERAL DUTIES OF DIRECTORS

Introductory

170 Scope and nature of general duties

(1) The general duties specified in sections 171 to 177 are owed by a director of a company to the company.

(2) A person who ceases to be a director continues to be subject—
  (a) to the duty in section 175 (duty to avoid conflicts of interest) as regards the exploitation of any property, information or opportunity of which he became aware at a time when he was a director, and
  (b) to the duty in section 176 (duty not to accept benefits from third parties) as regards things done or omitted by him before he ceased to be a director.

To that extent those duties apply to a former director as to a director, subject to any necessary adaptations.

(3) The general duties are based on certain common law rules and equitable principles as they apply in relation to directors and have effect in place of those rules and principles as regards the duties owed to a company by a director.

(4) The general duties shall be interpreted and applied in the same way as common law rules or equitable principles, and regard shall be had to the corresponding common law rules and equitable principles in interpreting and applying the general duties.

(5) The general duties apply to shadow directors where, and to the extent that, the corresponding common law rules or equitable principles so apply.

[S170]

NOTES

Commencement: 1 October 2007 (for transitional adaptations see the note below).

Transitional adaptations: art 6 of the draft Companies Act 2006 (Commencement No 3, Consequential Amendments, Transitional Provisions and Savings) Order 2007 provides that the provisions brought into force by that Order shall have effect subject to any transitional adaptations specified in Sch 1 to that Order. Schedule 1, paras 6–9 to the Order (at **[A12]**) provides as follows—

"**6 General duties of directors** (**ss 170 to 181**)

(1) Section 170 (scope and nature of general duties) has effect with the following adaptations.

(2) In subsection (1), for "177" substitute "174".

(3) Omit subsection (2).

(4) In subsection (3) after "The general duties" insert "in sections 171 to 174".

7.—(1) Section 178 (civil consequences of breach of general duties) has effect with the following adaptation.

(2) In subsection (1), for "177" substitute "174".

8.—(1) Section 180 (consent, approval or authorisation by members) has effect with the following adaptations.

(2) Omit subsection (1).

(3) In subsection (2), omit the words from ", except that" to the end.

(4) In subsection (4), omit paragraph (b).

9.—(1) Section 181 (modification of provisions in relation to charitable companies) has effect with the following modifications.

(2) Omit subsections (2) and (3).".

The general duties

171 Duty to act within powers

A director of a company must—
  (a) act in accordance with the company's constitution, and
  (b) only exercise powers for the purposes for which they are conferred.

[S171]

NOTES

Commencement: 1 October 2007.

172 Duty to promote the success of the company

(1) A director of a company must act in the way he considers, in good faith, would be most likely to promote the success of the company for the benefit of its members as a whole, and in doing so have regard (amongst other matters) to—

(a) the likely consequences of any decision in the long term,
(b) the interests of the company's employees,
(c) the need to foster the company's business relationships with suppliers, customers and others,
(d) the impact of the company's operations on the community and the environment,
(e) the desirability of the company maintaining a reputation for high standards of business conduct, and
(f) the need to act fairly as between members of the company.

(2) Where or to the extent that the purposes of the company consist of or include purposes other than the benefit of its members, subsection (1) has effect as if the reference to promoting the success of the company for the benefit of its members were to achieving those purposes.

(3) The duty imposed by this section has effect subject to any enactment or rule of law requiring directors, in certain circumstances, to consider or act in the interests of creditors of the company.

[S172]

NOTES

Commencement: 1 October 2007.

173 Duty to exercise independent judgment

(1) A director of a company must exercise independent judgment.

(2) This duty is not infringed by his acting—

(a) in accordance with an agreement duly entered into by the company that restricts the future exercise of discretion by its directors, or
(b) in a way authorised by the company's constitution.

[S173]

NOTES

Commencement: 1 October 2007.

174 Duty to exercise reasonable care, skill and diligence

(1) A director of a company must exercise reasonable care, skill and diligence.

(2) This means the care, skill and diligence that would be exercised by a reasonably diligent person with—

(a) the general knowledge, skill and experience that may reasonably be expected of a person carrying out the functions carried out by the director in relation to the company, and
(b) the general knowledge, skill and experience that the director has.

[S174]

NOTES

Commencement: 1 October 2007.

175 Duty to avoid conflicts of interest

(1) A director of a company must avoid a situation in which he has, or can have, a direct or indirect interest that conflicts, or possibly may conflict, with the interests of the company.

(2) This applies in particular to the exploitation of any property, information or opportunity (and it is immaterial whether the company could take advantage of the property, information or opportunity).

(3) This duty does not apply to a conflict of interest arising in relation to a transaction or arrangement with the company.

(4) This duty is not infringed—
(a) if the situation cannot reasonably be regarded as likely to give rise to a conflict of interest; or
(b) if the matter has been authorised by the directors.

(5) Authorisation may be given by the directors—
(a) where the company is a private company and nothing in the company's constitution invalidates such authorisation, by the matter being proposed to and authorised by the directors; or
(b) where the company is a public company and its constitution includes provision enabling the directors to authorise the matter, by the matter being proposed to and authorised by them in accordance with the constitution.

(6) The authorisation is effective only if—
(a) any requirement as to the quorum at the meeting at which the matter is considered is met without counting the director in question or any other interested director, and
(b) the matter was agreed to without their voting or would have been agreed to if their votes had not been counted.

(7) Any reference in this section to a conflict of interest includes a conflict of interest and duty and a conflict of duties.

[S175]

NOTES

Commencement: to be appointed.

176 Duty not to accept benefits from third parties

(1) A director of a company must not accept a benefit from a third party conferred by reason of—
(a) his being a director, or
(b) his doing (or not doing) anything as director.

(2) A "third party" means a person other than the company, an associated body corporate or a person acting on behalf of the company or an associated body corporate.

(3) Benefits received by a director from a person by whom his services (as a director or otherwise) are provided to the company are not regarded as conferred by a third party.

(4) This duty is not infringed if the acceptance of the benefit cannot reasonably be regarded as likely to give rise to a conflict of interest.

(5) Any reference in this section to a conflict of interest includes a conflict of interest and duty and a conflict of duties.

[S176]

NOTES

Commencement: to be appointed.

177 Duty to declare interest in proposed transaction or arrangement

(1) If a director of a company is in any way, directly or indirectly, interested in a proposed transaction or arrangement with the company, he must declare the nature and extent of that interest to the other directors.

(2) The declaration may (but need not) be made—
(a) at a meeting of the directors, or
(b) by notice to the directors in accordance with—
(i) section 184 (notice in writing), or
(ii) section 185 (general notice).

(3) If a declaration of interest under this section proves to be, or becomes, inaccurate or incomplete, a further declaration must be made.

(4) Any declaration required by this section must be made before the company enters into the transaction or arrangement.

(5) This section does not require a declaration of an interest of which the director is not aware or where the director is not aware of the transaction or arrangement in question.

For this purpose a director is treated as being aware of matters of which he ought reasonably to be aware.

(6) A director need not declare an interest—

(a) if it cannot reasonably be regarded as likely to give rise to a conflict of interest;

(b) if, or to the extent that, the other directors are already aware of it (and for this purpose the other directors are treated as aware of anything of which they ought reasonably to be aware); or

(c) if, or to the extent that, it concerns terms of his service contract that have been or are to be considered—

(i) by a meeting of the directors, or

(ii) by a committee of the directors appointed for the purpose under the company's constitution.

[S177]

NOTES

Commencement: to be appointed.

Supplementary provisions

178 Civil consequences of breach of general duties

(1) The consequences of breach (or threatened breach) of sections 171 to 177 are the same as would apply if the corresponding common law rule or equitable principle applied.

(2) The duties in those sections (with the exception of section 174 (duty to exercise reasonable care, skill and diligence)) are, accordingly, enforceable in the same way as any other fiduciary duty owed to a company by its directors.

[S178]

NOTES

Commencement: 1 October 2007 (for transitional adaptations see the note to s 170).

179 Cases within more than one of the general duties

Except as otherwise provided, more than one of the general duties may apply in any given case.

[S179]

NOTES

Commencement: 1 October 2007.

180 Consent, approval or authorisation by members

(1) In a case where—

(a) section 175 (duty to avoid conflicts of interest) is complied with by authorisation by the directors, or

(b) section 177 (duty to declare interest in proposed transaction or arrangement) is complied with,

the transaction or arrangement is not liable to be set aside by virtue of any common law rule or equitable principle requiring the consent or approval of the members of the company.

This is without prejudice to any enactment, or provision of the company's constitution, requiring such consent or approval.

(2) The application of the general duties is not affected by the fact that the case also falls within Chapter 4 (transactions requiring approval of members), except that where that Chapter applies and— (a) approval is given under that Chapter, or (b) the matter is one as to which it is provided that approval is not needed, it is not necessary also to comply with section 175 (duty to avoid conflicts of interest) or section 176 (duty not to accept benefits from third parties).

(3) Compliance with the general duties does not remove the need for approval under any applicable provision of Chapter 4 (transactions requiring approval of members).

(4) The general duties—

(a) have effect subject to any rule of law enabling the company to give authority, specifically or generally, for anything to be done (or omitted) by the directors, or any of them, that would otherwise be a breach of duty, and

(b) where the company's articles contain provisions for dealing with conflicts of interest, are not infringed by anything done (or omitted) by the directors, or any of them, in accordance with those provisions.

(5) Otherwise, the general duties have effect (except as otherwise provided or the context otherwise requires) notwithstanding any enactment or rule of law.

[S180]

NOTES

Commencement: 1 October 2007 (for transitional adaptations see the note to s 170).

181 Modification of provisions in relation to charitable companies

(1) In their application to a company that is a charity, the provisions of this Chapter have effect subject to this section.

(2) Section 175 (duty to avoid conflicts of interest) has effect as if—

(a) for subsection (3) (which disapplies the duty to avoid conflicts of interest in the case of a transaction or arrangement with the company) there were substituted—

"(3) This duty does not apply to a conflict of interest arising in relation to a transaction or arrangement with the company if or to the extent that the company's articles allow that duty to be so disapplied, which they may do only in relation to descriptions of transaction or arrangement specified in the company's articles.";

(b) for subsection (5) (which specifies how directors of a company may give authority under that section for a transaction or arrangement) there were substituted—

"(5) Authorisation may be given by the directors where the company's constitution includes provision enabling them to authorise the matter, by the matter being proposed to and authorised by them in accordance with the constitution.".

(3) Section 180(2)(b) (which disapplies certain duties under this Chapter in relation to cases excepted from requirement to obtain approval by members under Chapter 4) applies only if or to the extent that the company's articles allow those duties to be so disapplied, which they may do only in relation to descriptions of transaction or arrangement specified in the company's articles.

(4) (*Inserts the Charities Act 1993, s 26(5A)* (*outside the scope of this work*).)

(5) This section does not extend to Scotland.

[S181]

NOTES

Commencement: 1 October 2007 (for transitional adaptations see the note to s 170).

CHAPTER 3
DECLARATION OF INTEREST IN EXISTING TRANSACTION OR ARRANGEMENT

182 Declaration of interest in existing transaction or arrangement

(1) Where a director of a company is in any way, directly or indirectly, interested in a transaction or arrangement that has been entered into by the company, he must declare the nature and extent of the interest to the other directors in accordance with this section.

This section does not apply if or to the extent that the interest has been declared under section 177 (duty to declare interest in proposed transaction or arrangement).

(2) The declaration must be made—

(a) at a meeting of the directors, or

(b) by notice in writing (see section 184), or

(c) by general notice (see section 185).

(3) If a declaration of interest under this section proves to be, or becomes, inaccurate or incomplete, a further declaration must be made.

(4) Any declaration required by this section must be made as soon as is reasonably practicable.

Failure to comply with this requirement does not affect the underlying duty to make the declaration.

(5) This section does not require a declaration of an interest of which the director is not aware or where the director is not aware of the transaction or arrangement in question.

For this purpose a director is treated as being aware of matters of which he ought reasonably to be aware.

(6) A director need not declare an interest under this section—

(a) if it cannot reasonably be regarded as likely to give rise to a conflict of interest;

(b) if, or to the extent that, the other directors are already aware of it (and for this purpose the other directors are treated as aware of anything of which they ought reasonably to be aware); or

(c) if, or to the extent that, it concerns terms of his service contract that have been or are to be considered—

(i) by a meeting of the directors, or

(ii) by a committee of the directors appointed for the purpose under the company's constitution.

[S182]

NOTES

Commencement: to be appointed.

183 Offence of failure to declare interest

(1) A director who fails to comply with the requirements of section 182 (declaration of interest in existing transaction or arrangement) commits an offence.

(2) A person guilty of an offence under this section is liable—

(a) on conviction on indictment, to a fine;

(b) on summary conviction, to a fine not exceeding the statutory maximum.

[S183]

NOTES

Commencement: to be appointed.

184 Declaration made by notice in writing

(1) This section applies to a declaration of interest made by notice in writing.

(2) The director must send the notice to the other directors.

(3) The notice may be sent in hard copy form or, if the recipient has agreed to receive it in electronic form, in an agreed electronic form.

(4) The notice may be sent—

(a) by hand or by post, or

(b) if the recipient has agreed to receive it by electronic means, by agreed electronic means.

(5) Where a director declares an interest by notice in writing in accordance with this section—

(a) the making of the declaration is deemed to form part of the proceedings at the next meeting of the directors after the notice is given, and

(b) the provisions of section 248 (minutes of meetings of directors) apply as if the declaration had been made at that meeting.

[S184]

NOTES

Commencement: to be appointed.

185 General notice treated as sufficient declaration

(1) General notice in accordance with this section is a sufficient declaration of interest in relation to the matters to which it relates.

(2) General notice is notice given to the directors of a company to the effect that the director—

(a) has an interest (as member, officer, employee or otherwise) in a specified body corporate or firm and is to be regarded as interested in any transaction or arrangement that may, after the date of the notice, be made with that body corporate or firm, or

(b) is connected with a specified person (other than a body corporate or firm) and is to be regarded as interested in any transaction or arrangement that may, after the date of the notice, be made with that person.

(3) The notice must state the nature and extent of the director's interest in the body corporate or firm or, as the case may be, the nature of his connection with the person.

(4) General notice is not effective unless—

(a) it is given at a meeting of the directors, or

(b) the director takes reasonable steps to secure that it is brought up and read at the next meeting of the directors after it is given.

[S185]

NOTES

Commencement: to be appointed.

186 Declaration of interest in case of company with sole director

(1) Where a declaration of interest under section 182 (duty to declare interest in existing transaction or arrangement) is required of a sole director of a company that is required to have more than one director—

(a) the declaration must be recorded in writing,

(b) the making of the declaration is deemed to form part of the proceedings at the next meeting of the directors after the notice is given, and

(c) the provisions of section 248 (minutes of meetings of directors) apply as if the declaration had been made at that meeting.

(2) Nothing in this section affects the operation of section 231 (contract with sole member who is also a director: terms to be set out in writing or recorded in minutes).

[S186]

NOTES

Commencement: to be appointed.

187 Declaration of interest in existing transaction by shadow director

(1) The provisions of this Chapter relating to the duty under section 182 (duty to declare interest in existing transaction or arrangement) apply to a shadow director as to a director, but with the following adaptations.

(2) Subsection (2)(a) of that section (declaration at meeting of directors) does not apply.

(3) In section 185 (general notice treated as sufficient declaration), subsection (4) (notice to be given at or brought up and read at meeting of directors) does not apply.

(4) General notice by a shadow director is not effective unless given by notice in writing in accordance with section 184.

[S187]

NOTES

Commencement: to be appointed.

CHAPTER 4
TRANSACTIONS WITH DIRECTORS REQUIRING APPROVAL OF MEMBERS

Service contracts

188 Directors' long-term service contracts: requirement of members' approval

(1) This section applies to provision under which the guaranteed term of a director's employment—

(a) with the company of which he is a director, or
(b) where he is the director of a holding company, within the group consisting of that company and its subsidiaries,

is, or may be, longer than two years.

(2) A company may not agree to such provision unless it has been approved—
(a) by resolution of the members of the company, and
(b) in the case of a director of a holding company, by resolution of the members of that company.

(3) The guaranteed term of a director's employment is—
(a) the period (if any) during which the director's employment—
(i) is to continue, or may be continued otherwise than at the instance of the company (whether under the original agreement or under a new agreement entered into in pursuance of it), and
(ii) cannot be terminated by the company by notice, or can be so terminated only in specified circumstances, or
(b) in the case of employment terminable by the company by notice, the period of notice required to be given,

or, in the case of employment having a period within paragraph (a) and a period within paragraph (b), the aggregate of those periods.

(4) If more than six months before the end of the guaranteed term of a director's employment the company enters into a further service contract (otherwise than in pursuance of a right conferred, by or under the original contract, on the other party to it), this section applies as if there were added to the guaranteed term of the new contract the unexpired period of the guaranteed term of the original contract.

(5) A resolution approving provision to which this section applies must not be passed unless a memorandum setting out the proposed contract incorporating the provision is made available to members—
(a) in the case of a written resolution, by being sent or submitted to every eligible member at or before the time at which the proposed resolution is sent or submitted to him;
(b) in the case of a resolution at a meeting, by being made available for inspection by members of the company both—
(i) at the company's registered office for not less than 15 days ending with the date of the meeting, and
(ii) at the meeting itself.

(6) No approval is required under this section on the part of the members of a body corporate that—
(a) is not a UK-registered company, or
(b) is a wholly-owned subsidiary of another body corporate.

(7) In this section "employment" means any employment under a director's service contract.

[S188]

NOTES

Commencement: 1 October 2007 (for transitional provisions see the note below).

Transitional provisions, etc: Sch 3, para 6 to the draft Companies Act 2006 (Commencement No 3, Consequential Amendments, Transitional Provisions and Savings) Order 2007 (at **[A12]**) provides as follows—

"6 Transactions requiring members' approval: directors' long-term service contracts (**ss 188 and 189**)

(1) Sections 188 and 189 of the Companies Act 2006 (directors' long-term service contracts: requirement of members' approval) apply to agreements made on or after 1st October 2007.

(2) A resolution passed before that date approving the provision made by such an agreement is effective for the purposes of those sections if it complies with the requirements of those sections.

(3) Section 188(4) (addition of unexpired period of earlier contract in determining guaranteed period under new contract) applies whether the original contract (within the meaning of that provision) was entered into before or after that date.

(4) Section 319 of the 1985 Act or Article 327 of the 1986 Order continues to apply to agreements made before that date.".

189 Directors' long-term service contracts: civil consequences of contravention

If a company agrees to provision in contravention of section 188 (directors' long-term service contracts: requirement of members' approval)—

(a) the provision is void, to the extent of the contravention, and

(b) the contract is deemed to contain a term entitling the company to terminate it at any time by the giving of reasonable notice.

[S189]

NOTES

Commencement: 1 October 2007 (for transitional provisions see the note to s 188).

Substantial property transactions

190 Substantial property transactions: requirement of members' approval

(1) A company may not enter into an arrangement under which—

(a) a director of the company or of its holding company, or a person connected with such a director, acquires or is to acquire from the company (directly or indirectly) a substantial non-cash asset, or

(b) the company acquires or is to acquire a substantial non-cash asset (directly or indirectly) from such a director or a person so connected,

unless the arrangement has been approved by a resolution of the members of the company or is conditional on such approval being obtained.

For the meaning of "substantial non-cash asset" see section 191.

(2) If the director or connected person is a director of the company's holding company or a person connected with such a director, the arrangement must also have been approved by a resolution of the members of the holding company or be conditional on such approval being obtained.

(3) A company shall not be subject to any liability by reason of a failure to obtain approval required by this section.

(4) No approval is required under this section on the part of the members of a body corporate that—

(a) is not a UK-registered company, or

(b) is a wholly-owned subsidiary of another body corporate.

(5) For the purposes of this section—

(a) an arrangement involving more than one non-cash asset, or

(b) an arrangement that is one of a series involving non-cash assets,

shall be treated as if they involved a non-cash asset of a value equal to the aggregate value of all the non-cash assets involved in the arrangement or, as the case may be, the series.

(6) This section does not apply to a transaction so far as it relates—

(a) to anything to which a director of a company is entitled under his service contract, or

(b) to payment for loss of office as defined in section 215 (payments requiring members' approval).

[S190]

NOTES

Commencement: 1 October 2007 (for transitional provisions see the note below).

Transitional provisions, etc: Sch 3, para 7 to the draft Companies Act 2006 (Commencement No 3, Consequential Amendments, Transitional Provisions and Savings) Order 2007 (at **[A12]**) provides as follows—

"**7 Transactions requiring members' approval: substantial property transactions** (ss 190 to 196)

(1) Sections 190 to 196 of the Companies Act 2006 (substantial property transactions: requirement of members' approval) apply to arrangements or transactions entered into on or after 1st October 2007.

(2) A resolution passed before that date approving an arrangement or transaction is effective for the purposes of those sections if it complies with the requirements of those sections.

(3) Sections 320 to 322 of the 1985 Act or Articles 328 to 330 of the 1986 Order continue to apply in relation to arrangements or transactions entered into before that date.".

191 Meaning of "substantial"

(1) This section explains what is meant in section 190 (requirement of approval for substantial property transactions) by a "substantial" non-cash asset.

(2) An asset is a substantial asset in relation to a company if its value—
(a) exceeds 10% of the company's asset value and is more than £5,000, or
(b) exceeds £100,000.

(3) For this purpose a company's "asset value" at any time is—
(a) the value of the company's net assets determined by reference to its most recent statutory accounts, or
(b) if no statutory accounts have been prepared, the amount of the company's called-up share capital.

(4) A company's "statutory accounts" means its annual accounts prepared in accordance with Part 15, and its "most recent" statutory accounts means those in relation to which the time for sending them out to members (see section 424) is most recent.

(5) Whether an asset is a substantial asset shall be determined as at the time the arrangement is entered into.

[S191]

NOTES

Commencement: 1 October 2007 (for transitional provisions etc see the note to s 190 and the note below).

Transitional adaptations: art 6 of the draft Companies Act 2006 (Commencement No 3, Consequential Amendments, Transitional Provisions and Savings) Order 2007 provides that the provisions brought into force by that Order shall have effect subject to any transitional adaptations specified in Sch 1 to that Order. Schedule 1, para 10 to the Order (at **[A12]**) provides as follows—

"10 Transactions with directors requiring approval of members (ss 188 to 226)

(1) Section 191 (meaning of "substantial" non-cash asset) has effect with the following adaptations.

(2) In subsection (4)—
(a) for "Part 15" substitute "Part 7 of the Companies Act 1985 or Part 8 of the Companies (Northern Ireland) Order 1986", and
(b) for "section 424" substitute "section 238A of that Act or Article 246A of that Order".".

192 Exception for transactions with members or other group companies

Approval is not required under section 190 (requirement of members' approval for substantial property transactions)—
(a) for a transaction between a company and a person in his character as a member of that company, or
(b) for a transaction between—
(i) a holding company and its wholly-owned subsidiary, or
(ii) two wholly-owned subsidiaries of the same holding company.

[S192]

NOTES

Commencement: 1 October 2007 (for transitional provisions see the note to s 190).

193 Exception in case of company in winding up or administration

(1) This section applies to a company—
(a) that is being wound up (unless the winding up is a members' voluntary winding up), or
(b) that is in administration within the meaning of Schedule B1 to the Insolvency Act 1986 (c 45) or the Insolvency (Northern Ireland) Order 1989 (SI 1989/2405 (NI 19)).

(2) Approval is not required under section 190 (requirement of members' approval for substantial property transactions)—

(a) on the part of the members of a company to which this section applies, or
(b) for an arrangement entered into by a company to which this section applies.

[S193]

NOTES

Commencement: 1 October 2007 (for transitional provisions see the note to s 190).

194 Exception for transactions on recognised investment exchange

(1) Approval is not required under section 190 (requirement of members' approval for substantial property transactions) for a transaction on a recognised investment exchange effected by a director, or a person connected with him, through the agency of a person who in relation to the transaction acts as an independent broker.

(2) For this purpose—

(a) "independent broker" means a person who, independently of the director or any person connected with him, selects the person with whom the transaction is to be effected; and
(b) "recognised investment exchange" has the same meaning as in Part 18 of the Financial Services and Markets Act 2000 (c 8).

[S194]

NOTES

Commencement: 1 October 2007 (for transitional provisions see the note to s 190).

195 Property transactions: civil consequences of contravention

(1) This section applies where a company enters into an arrangement in contravention of section 190 (requirement of members' approval for substantial property transactions).

(2) The arrangement, and any transaction entered into in pursuance of the arrangement (whether by the company or any other person), is voidable at the instance of the company, unless—

(a) restitution of any money or other asset that was the subject matter of the arrangement or transaction is no longer possible,
(b) the company has been indemnified in pursuance of this section by any other persons for the loss or damage suffered by it, or
(c) rights acquired in good faith, for value and without actual notice of the contravention by a person who is not a party to the arrangement or transaction would be affected by the avoidance.

(3) Whether or not the arrangement or any such transaction has been avoided, each of the persons specified in subsection (4) is liable—

(a) to account to the company for any gain that he has made directly or indirectly by the arrangement or transaction, and
(b) (jointly and severally with any other person so liable under this section) to indemnify the company for any loss or damage resulting from the arrangement or transaction.

(4) The persons so liable are—

(a) any director of the company or of its holding company with whom the company entered into the arrangement in contravention of section 190,
(b) any person with whom the company entered into the arrangement in contravention of that section who is connected with a director of the company or of its holding company,
(c) the director of the company or of its holding company with whom any such person is connected, and
(d) any other director of the company who authorised the arrangement or any transaction entered into in pursuance of such an arrangement.

(5) Subsections (3) and (4) are subject to the following two subsections.

(6) In the case of an arrangement entered into by a company in contravention of section 190 with a person connected with a director of the company or of its holding company, that director is not liable by virtue of subsection (4)(c) if he shows that he took all reasonable steps to secure the company's compliance with that section.

(7) In any case—

(a) a person so connected is not liable by virtue of subsection (4)(b), and

(b) a director is not liable by virtue of subsection (4)(d),

if he shows that, at the time the arrangement was entered into, he did not know the relevant circumstances constituting the contravention.

(8) Nothing in this section shall be read as excluding the operation of any other enactment or rule of law by virtue of which the arrangement or transaction may be called in question or any liability to the company may arise.

[S195]

NOTES

Commencement: 1 October 2007 (for transitional provisions see the note to s 190).

196 Property transactions: effect of subsequent affirmation

Where a transaction or arrangement is entered into by a company in contravention of section 190 (requirement of members' approval) but, within a reasonable period, it is affirmed—

(a) in the case of a contravention of subsection (1) of that section, by resolution of the members of the company, and

(b) in the case of a contravention of subsection (2) of that section, by resolution of the members of the holding company,

the transaction or arrangement may no longer be avoided under section 195.

[S196]

NOTES

Commencement: 1 October 2007 (for transitional provisions see the note to s 190).

Loans, quasi-loans and credit transactions

197 Loans to directors: requirement of members' approval

(1) A company may not—

(a) make a loan to a director of the company or of its holding company, or

(b) give a guarantee or provide security in connection with a loan made by any person to such a director,

unless the transaction has been approved by a resolution of the members of the company.

(2) If the director is a director of the company's holding company, the transaction must also have been approved by a resolution of the members of the holding company.

(3) A resolution approving a transaction to which this section applies must not be passed unless a memorandum setting out the matters mentioned in subsection (4) is made available to members—

(a) in the case of a written resolution, by being sent or submitted to every eligible member at or before the time at which the proposed resolution is sent or submitted to him;

(b) in the case of a resolution at a meeting, by being made available for inspection by members of the company both—

(i) at the company's registered office for not less than 15 days ending with the date of the meeting, and

(ii) at the meeting itself.

(4) The matters to be disclosed are—

(a) the nature of the transaction,

(b) the amount of the loan and the purpose for which it is required, and

(c) the extent of the company's liability under any transaction connected with the loan.

(5) No approval is required under this section on the part of the members of a body corporate that—

(a) is not a UK-registered company, or

(b) is a wholly-owned subsidiary of another body corporate.

[S197]

NOTES

Commencement: 1 October 2007 (for transitional provisions see the note below).

Transitional provisions, etc: Sch 3, paras 8–11 to the draft Companies Act 2006 (Commencement No 3, Consequential Amendments, Transitional Provisions and Savings) Order 2007 (at **[A12]**) provides as follows—

"8 Transactions requiring members' approval: loans, quasi-loans and credit transactions (ss 197 to 214)

(1) Sections 197 to 214 of the Companies Act 2006 (loans, quasi-loans and credit transactions: requirement of members' approval) apply to transactions or arrangements entered into on or after 1st October 2007.

(2) A resolution passed before that date approving a transaction or arrangement is effective for the purposes of those sections if it complies with the requirements of those sections.

(3) Sections 330 to 342 of the 1985 Act or Articles 338 to 350 of the 1986 Order continue to apply in relation to a contravention occurring before that date.

9. Approval is not required under section 197, 198, 200 or 201 of the Companies Act 2006 (requirement of members' approval for loans etc) for anything done by a company in pursuance of an agreement entered into before 1st October 2007 that, by virtue of section 337A of the 1985 Act or Article 345A of the 1986 Order (funding of director's expenditure on defending proceedings), would not have required approval if done before that date.

10.—(1) This paragraph applies where before 1st October 2007 a company has done anything—

(a) pursuant to section 337(1) or (2) of the 1985 Act or Article 345(1) or (2) of the 1986 Order (funding of director's expenditure on duty to company), and

(b) on the condition mentioned in section 337(3)(b) of that Act or Article 345(3)(b) of that Order (condition requiring repayment of loan etc if approval of company in general meeting not given within six months).

(2) If that condition has not been satisfied before that date, it continues to apply notwithstanding the repeal of that section or that Article, but subject as follows.

(3) In the case of a private company that by reason of the repeal of section 366 of the 1985 Act or Article 374 of the 1986 Order with effect from that date ceases to be required to hold an annual general meeting, the condition shall be read as if it provided—

(a) that the approval of the company is required on or before the last date on which the company would have been required to hold an annual general meeting but for the repeal, and

(b) that the loan is to be repaid within six months from that date if such approval is not forthcoming.

11.—(1) This paragraph applies where before 1st October 2007 a company has done anything—

(a) pursuant to section 337A(1) or (3) of the 1985 Act or Article 345A(1) or (3) of the 1986 Order (funding of director's expenditure on defending proceedings), and

(b) on the terms mentioned in section 337A(4) of that Act or Article 345A(4) of that Order (terms requiring repayment of loan etc if defendant convicted, has judgment given against him or refused relief).

(2) If immediately before that date—

(a) it is not yet known whether repayment will be required, or

(b) repayment is required but had not been made,

those terms continue to apply notwithstanding the repeal of that section or that Article.".

198 Quasi-loans to directors: requirement of members' approval

(1) This section applies to a company if it is—

(a) a public company, or

(b) a company associated with a public company.

(2) A company to which this section applies may not—

(a) make a quasi-loan to a director of the company or of its holding company, or

(b) give a guarantee or provide security in connection with a quasi-loan made by any person to such a director,

unless the transaction has been approved by a resolution of the members of the company.

(3) If the director is a director of the company's holding company, the transaction must also have been approved by a resolution of the members of the holding company.

(4) A resolution approving a transaction to which this section applies must not be passed unless a memorandum setting out the matters mentioned in subsection (5) is made available to members—

(a) in the case of a written resolution, by being sent or submitted to every eligible member at or before the time at which the proposed resolution is sent or submitted to him;

(b) in the case of a resolution at a meeting, by being made available for inspection by members of the company both—

(i) at the company's registered office for not less than 15 days ending with the date of the meeting, and

(ii) at the meeting itself.

(5) The matters to be disclosed are—

(a) the nature of the transaction,

(b) the amount of the quasi-loan and the purpose for which it is required, and

(c) the extent of the company's liability under any transaction connected with the quasi-loan.

(6) No approval is required under this section on the part of the members of a body corporate that—

(a) is not a UK-registered company, or

(b) is a wholly-owned subsidiary of another body corporate.

[S198]

NOTES

Commencement: 1 October 2007 (for transitional provisions see the note to s 197).

199 Meaning of "quasi-loan" and related expressions

(1) A "quasi-loan" is a transaction under which one party ("the creditor") agrees to pay, or pays otherwise than in pursuance of an agreement, a sum for another ("the borrower") or agrees to reimburse, or reimburses otherwise than in pursuance of an agreement, expenditure incurred by another party for another ("the borrower")—

(a) on terms that the borrower (or a person on his behalf) will reimburse the creditor; or

(b) in circumstances giving rise to a liability on the borrower to reimburse the creditor.

(2) Any reference to the person to whom a quasi-loan is made is a reference to the borrower.

(3) The liabilities of the borrower under a quasi-loan include the liabilities of any person who has agreed to reimburse the creditor on behalf of the borrower.

[S199]

NOTES

Commencement: 1 October 2007 (for transitional provisions see the note to s 197).

200 Loans or quasi-loans to persons connected with directors: requirement of members' approval

(1) This section applies to a company if it is—

(a) a public company, or

(b) a company associated with a public company.

(2) A company to which this section applies may not—

(a) make a loan or quasi-loan to a person connected with a director of the company or of its holding company, or

(b) give a guarantee or provide security in connection with a loan or quasi-loan made by any person to a person connected with such a director,

unless the transaction has been approved by a resolution of the members of the company.

(3) If the connected person is a person connected with a director of the company's holding company, the transaction must also have been approved by a resolution of the members of the holding company.

(4) A resolution approving a transaction to which this section applies must not be passed unless a memorandum setting out the matters mentioned in subsection (5) is made available to members—

(a) in the case of a written resolution, by being sent or submitted to every eligible member at or before the time at which the proposed resolution is sent or submitted to him;

(b) in the case of a resolution at a meeting, by being made available for inspection by members of the company both—

(i) at the company's registered office for not less than 15 days ending with the date of the meeting, and

(ii) at the meeting itself.

(5) The matters to be disclosed are—

(a) the nature of the transaction,

(b) the amount of the loan or quasi-loan and the purpose for which it is required, and

(c) the extent of the company's liability under any transaction connected with the loan or quasi-loan.

(6) No approval is required under this section on the part of the members of a body corporate that—

(a) is not a UK-registered company, or

(b) is a wholly-owned subsidiary of another body corporate.

[S200]

NOTES

Commencement: 1 October 2007 (for transitional provisions see the note to s 197).

201 Credit transactions: requirement of members' approval

(1) This section applies to a company if it is—

(a) a public company, or

(b) a company associated with a public company.

(2) A company to which this section applies may not—

(a) enter into a credit transaction as creditor for the benefit of a director of the company or of its holding company, or a person connected with such a director, or

(b) give a guarantee or provide security in connection with a credit transaction entered into by any person for the benefit of such a director, or a person connected with such a director,

unless the transaction (that is, the credit transaction, the giving of the guarantee or the provision of security, as the case may be) has been approved by a resolution of the members of the company.

(3) If the director or connected person is a director of its holding company or a person connected with such a director, the transaction must also have been approved by a resolution of the members of the holding company.

(4) A resolution approving a transaction to which this section applies must not be passed unless a memorandum setting out the matters mentioned in subsection (5) is made available to members—

(a) in the case of a written resolution, by being sent or submitted to every eligible member at or before the time at which the proposed resolution is sent or submitted to him;

(b) in the case of a resolution at a meeting, by being made available for inspection by members of the company both—

(i) at the company's registered office for not less than 15 days ending with the date of the meeting, and

(ii) at the meeting itself.

(5) The matters to be disclosed are—

(a) the nature of the transaction,

(b) the value of the credit transaction and the purpose for which the land, goods or services sold or otherwise disposed of, leased, hired or supplied under the credit transaction are required, and

(c) the extent of the company's liability under any transaction connected with the credit transaction.

(6) No approval is required under this section on the part of the members of a body corporate that—

(a) is not a UK-registered company, or

(b) is a wholly-owned subsidiary of another body corporate.

[S201]

NOTES

Commencement: 1 October 2007 (for transitional provisions see the note to s 197).

202 Meaning of "credit transaction"

(1) A "credit transaction" is a transaction under which one party ("the creditor")—

(a) supplies any goods or sells any land under a hire-purchase agreement or a conditional sale agreement,

(b) leases or hires any land or goods in return for periodical payments, or

(c) otherwise disposes of land or supplies goods or services on the understanding that payment (whether in a lump sum or instalments or by way of periodical payments or otherwise) is to be deferred.

(2) Any reference to the person for whose benefit a credit transaction is entered into is to the person to whom goods, land or services are supplied, sold, leased, hired or otherwise disposed of under the transaction.

(3) In this section—

"conditional sale agreement" has the same meaning as in the Consumer Credit Act 1974 (c 39); and

"services" means anything other than goods or land.

[S202]

NOTES

Commencement: 1 October 2007 (for transitional provisions see the note to s 197).

203 Related arrangements: requirement of members' approval

(1) A company may not—

(a) take part in an arrangement under which—

(i) another person enters into a transaction that, if it had been entered into by the company, would have required approval under section 197, 198, 200 or 201, and

(ii) that person, in pursuance of the arrangement, obtains a benefit from the company or a body corporate associated with it, or

(b) arrange for the assignment to it, or assumption by it, of any rights, obligations or liabilities under a transaction that, if it had been entered into by the company, would have required such approval,

unless the arrangement in question has been approved by a resolution of the members of the company.

(2) If the director or connected person for whom the transaction is entered into is a director of its holding company or a person connected with such a director, the arrangement must also have been approved by a resolution of the members of the holding company.

(3) A resolution approving an arrangement to which this section applies must not be passed unless a memorandum setting out the matters mentioned in subsection (4) is made available to members—

(a) in the case of a written resolution, by being sent or submitted to every eligible member at or before the time at which the proposed resolution is sent or submitted to him;

(b) in the case of a resolution at a meeting, by being made available for inspection by members of the company both—

(i) at the company's registered office for not less than 15 days ending with the date of the meeting, and

(ii) at the meeting itself.

(4) The matters to be disclosed are—

(a) the matters that would have to be disclosed if the company were seeking approval of the transaction to which the arrangement relates,

(b) the nature of the arrangement, and
(c) the extent of the company's liability under the arrangement or any transaction connected with it.

(5) No approval is required under this section on the part of the members of a body corporate that—
(a) is not a UK-registered company, or
(b) is a wholly-owned subsidiary of another body corporate.

(6) In determining for the purposes of this section whether a transaction is one that would have required approval under section 197, 198, 200 or 201 if it had been entered into by the company, the transaction shall be treated as having been entered into on the date of the arrangement.

[S203]

NOTES

Commencement: 1 October 2007 (for transitional provisions see the note to s 197).

204 Exception for expenditure on company business

(1) Approval is not required under section 197, 198, 200 or 201 (requirement of members' approval for loans etc) for anything done by a company—
(a) to provide a director of the company or of its holding company, or a person connected with any such director, with funds to meet expenditure incurred or to be incurred by him—
(i) for the purposes of the company, or
(ii) for the purpose of enabling him properly to perform his duties as an officer of the company, or
(b) to enable any such person to avoid incurring such expenditure.

(2) This section does not authorise a company to enter into a transaction if the aggregate of—
(a) the value of the transaction in question, and
(b) the value of any other relevant transactions or arrangements,
exceeds £50,000.

[S204]

NOTES

Commencement: 1 October 2007 (for transitional provisions see the note to s 197).

205 Exception for expenditure on defending proceedings etc

(1) Approval is not required under section 197, 198, 200 or 201 (requirement of members' approval for loans etc) for anything done by a company—
(a) to provide a director of the company or of its holding company with funds to meet expenditure incurred or to be incurred by him—
(i) in defending any criminal or civil proceedings in connection with any alleged negligence, default, breach of duty or breach of trust by him in relation to the company or an associated company, or
(ii) in connection with an application for relief (see subsection (5)), or
(b) to enable any such director to avoid incurring such expenditure,
if it is done on the following terms.

(2) The terms are—
(a) that the loan is to be repaid, or (as the case may be) any liability of the company incurred under any transaction connected with the thing done is to be discharged, in the event of—
(i) the director being convicted in the proceedings,
(ii) judgment being given against him in the proceedings, or
(iii) the court refusing to grant him relief on the application; and
(b) that it is to be so repaid or discharged not later than—
(i) the date when the conviction becomes final,
(ii) the date when the judgment becomes final, or
(iii) the date when the refusal of relief becomes final.

PART I COMPANIES LEGISLATION

(3) For this purpose a conviction, judgment or refusal of relief becomes final—
(a) if not appealed against, at the end of the period for bringing an appeal;
(b) if appealed against, when the appeal (or any further appeal) is disposed of.

(4) An appeal is disposed of—
(a) if it is determined and the period for bringing any further appeal has ended, or
(b) if it is abandoned or otherwise ceases to have effect.

(5) The reference in subsection (1)(a)(ii) to an application for relief is to an application for relief under—
section 661(3) or (4) (power of court to grant relief in case of acquisition of shares by innocent nominee), or
section 1157 (general power of court to grant relief in case of honest and reasonable conduct).

[S205]

NOTES

Commencement: 1 October 2007 (for transitional provisions etc see the note to s 197 and the note below).

Transitional adaptations: art 6 of the draft Companies Act 2006 (Commencement No 3, Consequential Amendments, Transitional Provisions and Savings) Order 2007 provides that the provisions brought into force by that Order shall have effect subject to any transitional adaptations specified in Sch 1 to that Order. Schedule 1, para 11 to the Order (at **[A12]**) provides as follows—

"11.—(1) Section 205 (exception for expenditure on defending proceedings etc) has effect with the following adaptation.

(2) In subsection (5), for the words from "section 661(3)" to the end substitute—

"section 144(3) or (4) of the Companies Act 1985 or Article 154(3) or (4) of the Companies (Northern Ireland) Order 1986 (acquisition of shares by innocent nominee), or

section 727 of the Companies Act 1985 or Article 675 of the Companies (Northern Ireland) Order 1986 (general power to grant relief in case of honest and reasonable conduct).".".

206 Exception for expenditure in connection with regulatory action or investigation

Approval is not required under section 197, 198, 200 or 201 (requirement of members' approval for loans etc) for anything done by a company—
(a) to provide a director of the company or of its holding company with funds to meet expenditure incurred or to be incurred by him in defending himself—
(i) in an investigation by a regulatory authority, or
(ii) against action proposed to be taken by a regulatory authority,
in connection with any alleged negligence, default, breach of duty or breach of trust by him in relation to the company or an associated company, or
(b) to enable any such director to avoid incurring such expenditure.

[S206]

NOTES

Commencement: 1 October 2007 (for transitional provisions see the note to s 197).

207 Exceptions for minor and business transactions

(1) Approval is not required under section 197, 198 or 200 for a company to make a loan or quasi-loan, or to give a guarantee or provide security in connection with a loan or quasi-loan, if the aggregate of—
(a) the value of the transaction, and
(b) the value of any other relevant transactions or arrangements,
does not exceed £10,000.

(2) Approval is not required under section 201 for a company to enter into a credit transaction, or to give a guarantee or provide security in connection with a credit transaction, if the aggregate of—
(a) the value of the transaction (that is, of the credit transaction, guarantee or security), and
(b) the value of any other relevant transactions or arrangements,
does not exceed £15,000.

(3) Approval is not required under section 201 for a company to enter into a credit transaction, or to give a guarantee or provide security in connection with a credit transaction, if—

(a) the transaction is entered into by the company in the ordinary course of the company's business, and

(b) the value of the transaction is not greater, and the terms on which it is entered into are not more favourable, than it is reasonable to expect the company would have offered to, or in respect of, a person of the same financial standing but unconnected with the company.

[S207]

NOTES

Commencement: 1 October 2007 (for transitional provisions see the note to s 197).

208 Exceptions for intra-group transactions

(1) Approval is not required under section 197, 198 or 200 for—

(a) the making of a loan or quasi-loan to an associated body corporate, or

(b) the giving of a guarantee or provision of security in connection with a loan or quasi-loan made to an associated body corporate.

(2) Approval is not required under section 201—

(a) to enter into a credit transaction as creditor for the benefit of an associated body corporate, or

(b) to give a guarantee or provide security in connection with a credit transaction entered into by any person for the benefit of an associated body corporate.

[S208]

NOTES

Commencement: 1 October 2007 (for transitional provisions see the note to s 197).

209 Exceptions for money-lending companies

(1) Approval is not required under section 197, 198 or 200 for the making of a loan or quasi-loan, or the giving of a guarantee or provision of security in connection with a loan or quasi-loan, by a money-lending company if—

(a) the transaction (that is, the loan, quasi-loan, guarantee or security) is entered into by the company in the ordinary course of the company's business, and

(b) the value of the transaction is not greater, and its terms are not more favourable, than it is reasonable to expect the company would have offered to a person of the same financial standing but unconnected with the company.

(2) A "money-lending company" means a company whose ordinary business includes the making of loans or quasi-loans, or the giving of guarantees or provision of security in connection with loans or quasi-loans.

(3) The condition specified in subsection (1)(b) does not of itself prevent a company from making a home loan—

(a) to a director of the company or of its holding company, or

(b) to an employee of the company,

if loans of that description are ordinarily made by the company to its employees and the terms of the loan in question are no more favourable than those on which such loans are ordinarily made.

(4) For the purposes of subsection (3) a "home loan" means a loan—

(a) for the purpose of facilitating the purchase, for use as the only or main residence of the person to whom the loan is made, of the whole or part of any dwelling-house together with any land to be occupied and enjoyed with it,

(b) for the purpose of improving a dwelling-house or part of a dwelling-house so used or any land occupied and enjoyed with it, or

(c) in substitution for any loan made by any person and falling within paragraph (a) or (b).

[S209]

NOTES

Commencement: 1 October 2007 (for transitional provisions see the note to s 197).

210 Other relevant transactions or arrangements

(1) This section has effect for determining what are "other relevant transactions or arrangements" for the purposes of any exception to section 197, 198, 200 or 201. In the following provisions "the relevant exception" means the exception for the purposes of which that falls to be determined.

(2) Other relevant transactions or arrangements are those previously entered into, or entered into at the same time as the transaction or arrangement in question in relation to which the following conditions are met.

(3) Where the transaction or arrangement in question is entered into—

(a) for a director of the company entering into it, or

(b) for a person connected with such a director,

the conditions are that the transaction or arrangement was (or is) entered into for that director, or a person connected with him, by virtue of the relevant exception by that company or by any of its subsidiaries.

(4) Where the transaction or arrangement in question is entered into—

(a) for a director of the holding company of the company entering into it, or

(b) for a person connected with such a director,

the conditions are that the transaction or arrangement was (or is) entered into for that director, or a person connected with him, by virtue of the relevant exception by the holding company or by any of its subsidiaries.

(5) A transaction or arrangement entered into by a company that at the time it was entered into—

(a) was a subsidiary of the company entering into the transaction or arrangement in question, or

(b) was a subsidiary of that company's holding company,

is not a relevant transaction or arrangement if, at the time the question arises whether the transaction or arrangement in question falls within a relevant exception, it is no longer such a subsidiary.

[S210]

NOTES

Commencement: 1 October 2007 (for transitional provisions see the note to s 197).

211 The value of transactions and arrangements

(1) For the purposes of sections 197 to 214 (loans etc)—

(a) the value of a transaction or arrangement is determined as follows, and

(b) the value of any other relevant transaction or arrangement is taken to be the value so determined reduced by any amount by which the liabilities of the person for whom the transaction or arrangement was made have been reduced.

(2) The value of a loan is the amount of its principal.

(3) The value of a quasi-loan is the amount, or maximum amount, that the person to whom the quasi-loan is made is liable to reimburse the creditor.

(4) The value of a credit transaction is the price that it is reasonable to expect could be obtained for the goods, services or land to which the transaction relates if they had been supplied (at the time the transaction is entered into) in the ordinary course of business and on the same terms (apart from price) as they have been supplied, or are to be supplied, under the transaction in question.

(5) The value of a guarantee or security is the amount guaranteed or secured.

(6) The value of an arrangement to which section 203 (related arrangements) applies is the value of the transaction to which the arrangement relates.

(7) If the value of a transaction or arrangement is not capable of being expressed as a specific sum of money—

(a) whether because the amount of any liability arising under the transaction or arrangement is unascertainable, or for any other reason, and

(b) whether or not any liability under the transaction or arrangement has been reduced,

its value is deemed to exceed £50,000.

[S211]

NOTES

Commencement: 1 October 2007 (for transitional provisions see the note to s 197).

212 The person for whom a transaction or arrangement is entered into

For the purposes of sections 197 to 214 (loans etc) the person for whom a transaction or arrangement is entered into is—

(a) in the case of a loan or quasi-loan, the person to whom it is made;

(b) in the case of a credit transaction, the person to whom goods, land or services are supplied, sold, hired, leased or otherwise disposed of under the transaction;

(c) in the case of a guarantee or security, the person for whom the transaction is made in connection with which the guarantee or security is entered into;

(d) in the case of an arrangement within section 203 (related arrangements), the person for whom the transaction is made to which the arrangement relates.

[S212]

NOTES

Commencement: 1 October 2007 (for transitional provisions see the note to s 197).

213 Loans etc: civil consequences of contravention

(1) This section applies where a company enters into a transaction or arrangement in contravention of section 197, 198, 200, 201 or 203 (requirement of members' approval for loans etc).

(2) The transaction or arrangement is voidable at the instance of the company, unless—

(a) restitution of any money or other asset that was the subject matter of the transaction or arrangement is no longer possible,

(b) the company has been indemnified for any loss or damage resulting from the transaction or arrangement, or

(c) rights acquired in good faith, for value and without actual notice of the contravention by a person who is not a party to the transaction or arrangement would be affected by the avoidance.

(3) Whether or not the transaction or arrangement has been avoided, each of the persons specified in subsection (4) is liable—

(a) to account to the company for any gain that he has made directly or indirectly by the transaction or arrangement, and

(b) (jointly and severally with any other person so liable under this section) to indemnify the company for any loss or damage resulting from the transaction or arrangement.

(4) The persons so liable are—

(a) any director of the company or of its holding company with whom the company entered into the transaction or arrangement in contravention of section 197, 198, 201 or 203,

(b) any person with whom the company entered into the transaction or arrangement in contravention of any of those sections who is connected with a director of the company or of its holding company,

(c) the director of the company or of its holding company with whom any such person is connected, and

(d) any other director of the company who authorised the transaction or arrangement.

(5) Subsections (3) and (4) are subject to the following two subsections.

(6) In the case of a transaction or arrangement entered into by a company in contravention of section 200, 201 or 203 with a person connected with a director of the

company or of its holding company, that director is not liable by virtue of subsection (4)(c) if he shows that he took all reasonable steps to secure the company's compliance with the section concerned.

(7) In any case—

(a) a person so connected is not liable by virtue of subsection (4)(b), and

(b) a director is not liable by virtue of subsection (4)(d),

if he shows that, at the time the transaction or arrangement was entered into, he did not know the relevant circumstances constituting the contravention.

(8) Nothing in this section shall be read as excluding the operation of any other enactment or rule of law by virtue of which the transaction or arrangement may be called in question or any liability to the company may arise.

[S213]

NOTES

Commencement: 1 October 2007 (for transitional provisions see the note to s 197).

214 Loans etc: effect of subsequent affirmation

Where a transaction or arrangement is entered into by a company in contravention of section 197, 198, 200, 201 or 203 (requirement of members' approval for loans etc) but, within a reasonable period, it is affirmed—

(a) in the case of a contravention of the requirement for a resolution of the members of the company, by a resolution of the members of the company, and

(b) in the case of a contravention of the requirement for a resolution of the members of the company's holding company, by a resolution of the members of the holding company,

the transaction or arrangement may no longer be avoided under section 213.

[S214]

NOTES

Commencement: 1 October 2007 (for transitional provisions see the note to s 197).

Payments for loss of office

215 Payments for loss of office

(1) In this Chapter a "payment for loss of office" means a payment made to a director or past director of a company—

(a) by way of compensation for loss of office as director of the company,

(b) by way of compensation for loss, while director of the company or in connection with his ceasing to be a director of it, of—

(i) any other office or employment in connection with the management of the affairs of the company, or

(ii) any office (as director or otherwise) or employment in connection with the management of the affairs of any subsidiary undertaking of the company,

(c) as consideration for or in connection with his retirement from his office as director of the company, or

(d) as consideration for or in connection with his retirement, while director of the company or in connection with his ceasing to be a director of it, from—

(i) any other office or employment in connection with the management of the affairs of the company, or

(ii) any office (as director or otherwise) or employment in connection with the management of the affairs of any subsidiary undertaking of the company.

(2) The references to compensation and consideration include benefits otherwise than in cash and references in this Chapter to payment have a corresponding meaning.

(3) For the purposes of sections 217 to 221 (payments requiring members' approval)—

(a) payment to a person connected with a director, or

(b) payment to any person at the direction of, or for the benefit of, a director or a person connected with him, is treated as payment to the director.

(4) References in those sections to payment by a person include payment by another person at the direction of, or on behalf of, the person referred to.

[S215]

NOTES

Commencement: 1 October 2007 (for transitional provisions see the note below).

Transitional provisions, etc: Sch 3, para 12 to the draft Companies Act 2006 (Commencement No 3, Consequential Amendments, Transitional Provisions and Savings) Order 2007 (at **[A12]**) provides as follows—

"12 Transactions requiring members' approval: payments for loss of office (ss 215 to 222)

(1) Sections 215 to 222 of the Companies Act 2006 (payments for loss of office: requirement of members' approval) apply in relation to any such loss of office or employment as is mentioned in section 215(1)(a) or (b), or any such retirement as is mentioned in section 215(1)(c) or (d), occurring on or after 1st October 2007.

(2) A resolution passed before that date approving a payment is effective for the purposes of those sections if it complies with the requirements of those sections.

(3) Sections 312 to 316 of the 1985 Act or Articles 320 to 324 of the 1986 Order continue to apply in relation to loss of office or retirement within the meaning of those provisions occurring before that date.

(4) For the purposes of this paragraph loss of office or retirement is regarded as occurring—

(a) in the case of a directorship, when the person ceases to be a director;

(b) in the case of any other office, when the person ceases to hold that office;

(c) in the case of employment, when the employment comes to an end.".

216 Amounts taken to be payments for loss of office

(1) This section applies where in connection with any such transfer as is mentioned in section 218 or 219 (payment in connection with transfer of undertaking, property or shares) a director of the company—

(a) is to cease to hold office, or

(b) is to cease to be the holder of—

(i) any other office or employment in connection with the management of the affairs of the company, or

(ii) any office (as director or otherwise) or employment in connection with the management of the affairs of any subsidiary undertaking of the company.

(2) If in connection with any such transfer—

(a) the price to be paid to the director for any shares in the company held by him is in excess of the price which could at the time have been obtained by other holders of like shares, or

(b) any valuable consideration is given to the director by a person other than the company,

the excess or, as the case may be, the money value of the consideration is taken for the purposes of those sections to have been a payment for loss of office.

[S216]

NOTES

Commencement: 1 October 2007 (for transitional provisions see the note to s 215).

217 Payment by company: requirement of members' approval

(1) A company may not make a payment for loss of office to a director of the company unless the payment has been approved by a resolution of the members of the company.

(2) A company may not make a payment for loss of office to a director of its holding company unless the payment has been approved by a resolution of the members of each of those companies.

(3) A resolution approving a payment to which this section applies must not be passed unless a memorandum setting out particulars of the proposed payment (including its amount) is made available to the members of the company whose approval is sought—

(a) in the case of a written resolution, by being sent or submitted to every eligible member at or before the time at which the proposed resolution is sent or submitted to him;

(b) in the case of a resolution at a meeting, by being made available for inspection by the members both—

(i) at the company's registered office for not less than 15 days ending with the date of the meeting, and

(ii) at the meeting itself.

(4) No approval is required under this section on the part of the members of a body corporate that—

(a) is not a UK-registered company, or

(b) is a wholly-owned subsidiary of another body corporate.

[S217]

NOTES

Commencement: 1 October 2007 (for transitional provisions see the note to s 215).

218 Payment in connection with transfer of undertaking etc: requirement of members' approval

(1) No payment for loss of office may be made by any person to a director of a company in connection with the transfer of the whole or any part of the undertaking or property of the company unless the payment has been approved by a resolution of the members of the company.

(2) No payment for loss of office may be made by any person to a director of a company in connection with the transfer of the whole or any part of the undertaking or property of a subsidiary of the company unless the payment has been approved by a resolution of the members of each of the companies.

(3) A resolution approving a payment to which this section applies must not be passed unless a memorandum setting out particulars of the proposed payment (including its amount) is made available to the members of the company whose approval is sought—

(a) in the case of a written resolution, by being sent or submitted to every eligible member at or before the time at which the proposed resolution is sent or submitted to him;

(b) in the case of a resolution at a meeting, by being made available for inspection by the members both—

(i) at the company's registered office for not less than 15 days ending with the date of the meeting, and

(ii) at the meeting itself.

(4) No approval is required under this section on the part of the members of a body corporate that—

(a) is not a UK-registered company, or

(b) is a wholly-owned subsidiary of another body corporate.

(5) A payment made in pursuance of an arrangement—

(a) entered into as part of the agreement for the transfer in question, or within one year before or two years after that agreement, and

(b) to which the company whose undertaking or property is transferred, or any person to whom the transfer is made, is privy,

is presumed, except in so far as the contrary is shown, to be a payment to which this section applies.

[S218]

NOTES

Commencement: 1 October 2007 (for transitional provisions see the note to s 215).

219 Payment in connection with share transfer: requirement of members' approval

(1) No payment for loss of office may be made by any person to a director of a company in connection with a transfer of shares in the company, or in a subsidiary of the company, resulting from a takeover bid unless the payment has been approved by a resolution of the relevant shareholders.

(2) The relevant shareholders are the holders of the shares to which the bid relates and any holders of shares of the same class as any of those shares.

(3) A resolution approving a payment to which this section applies must not be passed unless a memorandum setting out particulars of the proposed payment (including its amount) is made available to the members of the company whose approval is sought—

- (a) in the case of a written resolution, by being sent or submitted to every eligible member at or before the time at which the proposed resolution is sent or submitted to him;
- (b) in the case of a resolution at a meeting, by being made available for inspection by the members both—
  - (i) at the company's registered office for not less than 15 days ending with the date of the meeting, and
  - (ii) at the meeting itself.

(4) Neither the person making the offer, nor any associate of his (as defined in section 988), is entitled to vote on the resolution, but—

- (a) where the resolution is proposed as a written resolution, they are entitled (if they would otherwise be so entitled) to be sent a copy of it, and
- (b) at any meeting to consider the resolution they are entitled (if they would otherwise be so entitled) to be given notice of the meeting, to attend and speak and if present (in person or by proxy) to count towards the quorum.

(5) If at a meeting to consider the resolution a quorum is not present, and after the meeting has been adjourned to a later date a quorum is again not present, the payment is (for the purposes of this section) deemed to have been approved.

(6) No approval is required under this section on the part of shareholders in a body corporate that—

- (a) is not a UK-registered company, or
- (b) is a wholly-owned subsidiary of another body corporate.

(7) A payment made in pursuance of an arrangement—

- (a) entered into as part of the agreement for the transfer in question, or within one year before or two years after that agreement, and
- (b) to which the company whose shares are the subject of the bid, or any person to whom the transfer is made, is privy,

is presumed, except in so far as the contrary is shown, to be a payment to which this section applies.

[S219]

NOTES

Commencement: 1 October 2007 (for transitional provisions see the note to s 215).

220 Exception for payments in discharge of legal obligations etc

(1) Approval is not required under section 217, 218 or 219 (payments requiring members' approval) for a payment made in good faith—

- (a) in discharge of an existing legal obligation (as defined below),
- (b) by way of damages for breach of such an obligation,
- (c) by way of settlement or compromise of any claim arising in connection with the termination of a person's office or employment, or
- (d) by way of pension in respect of past services.

(2) In relation to a payment within section 217 (payment by company) an existing legal obligation means an obligation of the company, or any body corporate associated with it, that was not entered into in connection with, or in consequence of, the event giving rise to the payment for loss of office.

(3) In relation to a payment within section 218 or 219 (payment in connection with transfer of undertaking, property or shares) an existing legal obligation means an obligation of the person making the payment that was not entered into for the purposes of, in connection with or in consequence of, the transfer in question.

(4) In the case of a payment within both section 217 and section 218, or within both section 217 and section 219, subsection (2) above applies and not subsection (3).

(5) A payment part of which falls within subsection (1) above and part of which does not is treated as if the parts were separate payments.

[S220]

NOTES

Commencement: 1 October 2007 (for transitional provisions see the note to s 215).

221 Exception for small payments

(1) Approval is not required under section 217, 218 or 219 (payments requiring members' approval) if—

(a) the payment in question is made by the company or any of its subsidiaries, and

(b) the amount or value of the payment, together with the amount or value of any other relevant payments, does not exceed £200.

(2) For this purpose "other relevant payments" are payments for loss of office in relation to which the following conditions are met.

(3) Where the payment in question is one to which section 217 (payment by company) applies, the conditions are that the other payment was or is paid—

(a) by the company making the payment in question or any of its subsidiaries,

(b) to the director to whom that payment is made, and

(c) in connection with the same event.

(4) Where the payment in question is one to which section 218 or 219 applies (payment in connection with transfer of undertaking, property or shares), the conditions are that the other payment was (or is) paid in connection with the same transfer—

(a) to the director to whom the payment in question was made, and

(b) by the company making the payment or any of its subsidiaries.

[S221]

NOTES

Commencement: 1 October 2007 (for transitional provisions see the note to s 215).

222 Payments made without approval: civil consequences

(1) If a payment is made in contravention of section 217 (payment by company)—

(a) it is held by the recipient on trust for the company making the payment, and

(b) any director who authorised the payment is jointly and severally liable to indemnify the company that made the payment for any loss resulting from it.

(2) If a payment is made in contravention of section 218 (payment in connection with transfer of undertaking etc), it is held by the recipient on trust for the company whose undertaking or property is or is proposed to be transferred.

(3) If a payment is made in contravention of section 219 (payment in connection with share transfer)—

(a) it is held by the recipient on trust for persons who have sold their shares as a result of the offer made, and

(b) the expenses incurred by the recipient in distributing that sum amongst those persons shall be borne by him and not retained out of that sum.

(4) If a payment is in contravention of section 217 and section 218, subsection (2) of this section applies rather than subsection (1).

(5) If a payment is in contravention of section 217 and section 219, subsection (3) of this section applies rather than subsection (1), unless the court directs otherwise.

[S222]

NOTES

Commencement: 1 October 2007 (for transitional provisions see the note to s 215).

Supplementary

223 Transactions requiring members' approval: application of provisions to shadow directors

(1) For the purposes of—

(a) sections 188 and 189 (directors' service contracts),

(b) sections 190 to 196 (property transactions),

(c) sections 197 to 214 (loans etc), and

(d) sections 215 to 222 (payments for loss of office),

a shadow director is treated as a director.

(2) Any reference in those provisions to loss of office as a director does not apply in relation to loss of a person's status as a shadow director.

[S223]

NOTES

Commencement: 1 October 2007.

224 Approval by written resolution: accidental failure to send memorandum

(1) Where—

(a) approval under this Chapter is sought by written resolution, and

(b) a memorandum is required under this Chapter to be sent or submitted to every eligible member before the resolution is passed,

any accidental failure to send or submit the memorandum to one or more members shall be disregarded for the purpose of determining whether the requirement has been met.

(2) Subsection (1) has effect subject to any provision of the company's articles.

[S224]

NOTES

Commencement: 1 October 2007.

225 Cases where approval is required under more than one provision

(1) Approval may be required under more than one provision of this Chapter.

(2) If so, the requirements of each applicable provision must be met.

(3) This does not require a separate resolution for the purposes of each provision.

[S225]

NOTES

Commencement: 1 October 2007.

226 Requirement of consent of Charity Commission: companies that are charities

(*Substitutes the Charities Act 1993, ss 66, 66A for original s 66* (*outside the scope of this work.*)

[S226]

NOTES

Commencement: 1 October 2007.

CHAPTER 5
DIRECTORS' SERVICE CONTRACTS

227 Directors' service contracts

(1) For the purposes of this Part a director's "service contract", in relation to a company, means a contract under which—

(a) a director of the company undertakes personally to perform services (as director or otherwise) for the company, or for a subsidiary of the company, or

(b) services (as director or otherwise) that a director of the company undertakes personally to perform are made available by a third party to the company, or to a subsidiary of the company.

(2) The provisions of this Part relating to directors' service contracts apply to the terms of a person's appointment as a director of a company.

They are not restricted to contracts for the performance of services outside the scope of the ordinary duties of a director.

[S227]

NOTES

Commencement: 1 October 2007 (for transitional provisions see the note below).

Transitional provisions, etc: Sch 3, para 13 to the draft Companies Act 2006 (Commencement No 3, Consequential Amendments, Transitional Provisions and Savings) Order 2007 (at **[A12]**) provides as follows—

"13 Directors' service contracts (ss 227 to 230)

(1) Sections 228 to 230 of the Companies Act 2006 (directors' service contracts) apply to—
(a) contracts within section 227(1) of that Act entered into on or after 1st October 2007,
(b) appointments within section 227(2) of that Act made on or after that date, and
(c) contracts to which section 318(1) of the 1985 Act or Article 326(1) of the 1986 Order applied immediately before that date.

(2) Until regulations under section 1136 of the Companies Act 2006 are made specifying a place for the purposes of section 228(2)(b), the copies and memoranda referred to in section 228 may be kept by a company—
(a) at any place where its register of members is kept, or
(b) at its principal place of business,
provided that place is situated in the part of the United Kingdom in which the company is registered.

(3) Until section 1068(1) of the Companies Act 2006 comes into force the notice referred to in section 228(4) must be given on the form prescribed for the purposes of section 318(4) of the 1985 Act or Article 326(4) of the 1986 Order.

(4) The provisions of section 318 of the 1985 Act or Article 326 of the 1986 Order continue to apply in relation to—
(a) any default before 1st October 2007 in complying with section 318(1) or (5) or Article 326(1) or (5);
(b) any request for inspection under section 318(7) or Article 326(7) made before that date;
(c) any duty to give notice under section 318(4) or Article 326(4) arising before that date.".

228 Copy of contract or memorandum of terms to be available for inspection

(1) A company must keep available for inspection—
(a) a copy of every director's service contract with the company or with a subsidiary of the company, or
(b) if the contract is not in writing, a written memorandum setting out the terms of the contract.

(2) All the copies and memoranda must be kept available for inspection at—
(a) the company's registered office, or
(b) a place specified in regulations under section 1136.

(3) The copies and memoranda must be retained by the company for at least one year from the date of termination or expiry of the contract and must be kept available for inspection during that time.

(4) The company must give notice to the registrar—
(a) of the place at which the copies and memoranda are kept available for inspection, and
(b) of any change in that place,
unless they have at all times been kept at the company's registered office.

(5) If default is made in complying with subsection (1), (2) or (3), or default is made for 14 days in complying with subsection (4), an offence is committed by every officer of the company who is in default.

(6) A person guilty of an offence under this section is liable on summary conviction to a fine not exceeding level 3 on the standard scale and, for continued contravention, a daily default fine not exceeding one-tenth of level 3 on the standard scale.

(7) The provisions of this section apply to a variation of a director's service contract as they apply to the original contract.

[S228]

NOTES

Commencement: 1 October 2007 (for transitional provisions see the note to s 227).

229 Right of member to inspect and request copy

(1) Every copy or memorandum required to be kept under section 228 must be open to inspection by any member of the company without charge.

(2) Any member of the company is entitled, on request and on payment of such fee as may be prescribed, to be provided with a copy of any such copy or memorandum.

The copy must be provided within seven days after the request is received by the company.

(3) If an inspection required under subsection (1) is refused, or default is made in complying with subsection (2), an offence is committed by every officer of the company who is in default.

(4) A person guilty of an offence under this section is liable on summary conviction to a fine not exceeding level 3 on the standard scale and, for continued contravention, a daily default fine not exceeding one-tenth of level 3 on the standard scale.

(5) In the case of any such refusal or default the court may by order compel an immediate inspection or, as the case may be, direct that the copy required be sent to the person requiring it.

[S229]

NOTES

Commencement: 20 January 2007 (for the purpose of enabling the exercise of powers to make Orders or Regulations by statutory instrument); 1 October 2007 (otherwise) (for transitional provisions see the note to s 227).

230 Directors' service contracts: application of provisions to shadow directors

A shadow director is treated as a director for the purposes of the provisions of this Chapter.

[S230]

NOTES

Commencement: 1 October 2007 (for transitional provisions see the note to s 227).

CHAPTER 6
CONTRACTS WITH SOLE MEMBERS WHO ARE DIRECTORS

231 Contract with sole member who is also a director

(1) This section applies where—

(a) a limited company having only one member enters into a contract with the sole member,

(b) the sole member is also a director of the company, and

(c) the contract is not entered into in the ordinary course of the company's business.

(2) The company must, unless the contract is in writing, ensure that the terms of the contract are either—

(a) set out in a written memorandum, or

(b) recorded in the minutes of the first meeting of the directors of the company following the making of the contract.

(3) If a company fails to comply with this section an offence is committed by every officer of the company who is in default.

(4) A person guilty of an offence under this section is liable on summary conviction to a fine not exceeding level 5 on the standard scale.

(5) For the purposes of this section a shadow director is treated as a director.

(6) Failure to comply with this section in relation to a contract does not affect the validity of the contract.

(7) Nothing in this section shall be read as excluding the operation of any other enactment or rule of law applying to contracts between a company and a director of the company.

[S231]

NOTES

Commencement: 1 October 2007 (for transitional provisions see the note below).

Transitional provisions, etc: Sch 3, para 14 to the draft Companies Act 2006 (Commencement No 3, Consequential Amendments, Transitional Provisions and Savings) Order 2007 (at **[A12]**) provides as follows—

"**14 Contracts with sole member who is a director** (s 231)

(1) Section 231 of the Companies Act 2006 (contracts with sole member who is a director) applies to contracts entered into on or after 1st October 2007.

(2) Section 322B of the 1985 Act or Article 330B of the 1986 Order continues to apply to contracts entered into before that date.".

CHAPTER 7
DIRECTORS' LIABILITIES

Provision protecting directors from liability

232 Provisions protecting directors from liability

(1) Any provision that purports to exempt a director of a company (to any extent) from any liability that would otherwise attach to him in connection with any negligence, default, breach of duty or breach of trust in relation to the company is void.

(2) Any provision by which a company directly or indirectly provides an indemnity (to any extent) for a director of the company, or of an associated company, against any liability attaching to him in connection with any negligence, default, breach of duty or breach of trust in relation to the company of which he is a director is void, except as permitted by—

(a) section 233 (provision of insurance),
(b) section 234 (qualifying third party indemnity provision), or
(c) section 235 (qualifying pension scheme indemnity provision).

(3) This section applies to any provision, whether contained in a company's articles or in any contract with the company or otherwise.

(4) Nothing in this section prevents a company's articles from making such provision as has previously been lawful for dealing with conflicts of interest.

[S232]

NOTES

Commencement: 1 October 2007 (for transitional provisions see the note below).

Transitional provisions, etc: Sch 3, para 15 to the draft Companies Act 2006 (Commencement No 3, Consequential Amendments, Transitional Provisions and Savings) Order 2007 (at **[A12]**) provides as follows—

"**15 Directors' liabilities** (ss 232 to 239)

(1) Sections 232 to 236 of the Companies Act 2006 (restrictions on provision protecting directors from liability) apply to any provision made on or after 1st October 2007.

(2) Sections 309A, 309B and 309C(1) to (3) and (6) of the 1985 Act or Article 318 of the 1986 Order (so far as it relates to directors) continue to apply in relation to any provision to which they applied immediately before that date.".

233 Provision of insurance

Section 232(2) (voidness of provisions for indemnifying directors) does not prevent a company from purchasing and maintaining for a director of the company, or of an associated company, insurance against any such liability as is mentioned in that subsection.

[S233]

NOTES

Commencement: 1 October 2007 (for transitional provisions see the note to s 232).

234 Qualifying third party indemnity provision

(1) Section 232(2) (voidness of provisions for indemnifying directors) does not apply to qualifying third party indemnity provision.

(2) Third party indemnity provision means provision for indemnity against liability incurred by the director to a person other than the company or an associated company.

Such provision is qualifying third party indemnity provision if the following requirements are met.

(3) The provision must not provide any indemnity against—

(a) any liability of the director to pay—

(i) a fine imposed in criminal proceedings, or

(ii) a sum payable to a regulatory authority by way of a penalty in respect of non-compliance with any requirement of a regulatory nature (however arising); or

(b) any liability incurred by the director—

(i) in defending criminal proceedings in which he is convicted, or

(ii) in defending civil proceedings brought by the company, or an associated company, in which judgment is given against him, or

(iii) in connection with an application for relief (see subsection (6)) in which the court refuses to grant him relief.

(4) The references in subsection (3)(b) to a conviction, judgment or refusal of relief are to the final decision in the proceedings.

(5) For this purpose—

(a) a conviction, judgment or refusal of relief becomes final—

(i) if not appealed against, at the end of the period for bringing an appeal, or

(ii) if appealed against, at the time when the appeal (or any further appeal) is disposed of; and

(b) an appeal is disposed of—

(i) if it is determined and the period for bringing any further appeal has ended, or

(ii) if it is abandoned or otherwise ceases to have effect.

(6) The reference in subsection (3)(b)(iii) to an application for relief is to an application for relief under—

section 661(3) or (4) (power of court to grant relief in case of acquisition of shares by innocent nominee), or

section 1157 (general power of court to grant relief in case of honest and reasonable conduct).

[S234]

NOTES

Commencement: 1 October 2007 (for transitional provisions etc see the note to s 232 and the note below).

Transitional adaptations: art 6 of the draft Companies Act 2006 (Commencement No 3, Consequential Amendments, Transitional Provisions and Savings) Order 2007 provides that the provisions brought into force by that Order shall have effect subject to any transitional adaptations specified in Sch 1 to that Order. Schedule 1, para 12 to the Order (at **[A12]**) provides as follows—

"12 Directors' liabilities (ss 232 to 239)

(1) Section 234 (qualifying third party indemnity provision) has effect with the following adaptation.

(2) In subsection (6), for the words from "section 661(3)" to the end substitute—

"section 144(3) or (4) of the Companies Act 1985 or Article 154(3) or (4) of the Companies (Northern Ireland) Order 1986 (acquisition of shares by innocent nominee), or

section 727 of the Companies Act 1985 or Article 675 of the Companies (Northern Ireland) Order 1986 (general power to grant relief in case of honest and reasonable conduct).".".

235 Qualifying pension scheme indemnity provision

(1) Section 232(2) (voidness of provisions for indemnifying directors) does not apply to qualifying pension scheme indemnity provision.

(2) Pension scheme indemnity provision means provision indemnifying a director of a company that is a trustee of an occupational pension scheme against liability incurred in connection with the company's activities as trustee of the scheme.

Such provision is qualifying pension scheme indemnity provision if the following requirements are met.

(3) The provision must not provide any indemnity against—
- (a) any liability of the director to pay—
  - (i) a fine imposed in criminal proceedings, or
  - (ii) a sum payable to a regulatory authority by way of a penalty in respect of non-compliance with any requirement of a regulatory nature (however arising); or
- (b) any liability incurred by the director in defending criminal proceedings in which he is convicted.

(4) The reference in subsection (3)(b) to a conviction is to the final decision in the proceedings.

(5) For this purpose—
- (a) a conviction becomes final—
  - (i) if not appealed against, at the end of the period for bringing an appeal, or
  - (ii) if appealed against, at the time when the appeal (or any further appeal) is disposed of; and
- (b) an appeal is disposed of—
  - (i) if it is determined and the period for bringing any further appeal has ended, or
  - (ii) if it is abandoned or otherwise ceases to have effect.

(6) In this section "occupational pension scheme" means an occupational pension scheme as defined in section 150(5) of the Finance Act 2004 (c 12) that is established under a trust.

[S235]

NOTES

Commencement: 1 October 2007 (for transitional provisions see the note to s 232).

236 Qualifying indemnity provision to be disclosed in directors' report

(1) This section requires disclosure in the directors' report of—
- (a) qualifying third party indemnity provision, and
- (b) qualifying pension scheme indemnity provision.

Such provision is referred to in this section as "qualifying indemnity provision".

(2) If when a directors' report is approved any qualifying indemnity provision (whether made by the company or otherwise) is in force for the benefit of one or more directors of the company, the report must state that such provision is in force.

(3) If at any time during the financial year to which a directors' report relates any such provision was in force for the benefit of one or more persons who were then directors of the company, the report must state that such provision was in force.

(4) If when a directors' report is approved qualifying indemnity provision made by the company is in force for the benefit of one or more directors of an associated company, the report must state that such provision is in force.

(5) If at any time during the financial year to which a directors' report relates any such provision was in force for the benefit of one or more persons who were then directors of an associated company, the report must state that such provision was in force.

[S236]

NOTES

Commencement: 1 October 2007 (for transitional provisions see the note to s 232).

237 Copy of qualifying indemnity provision to be available for inspection

(1) This section has effect where qualifying indemnity provision is made for a director of a company, and applies—

(a) to the company of which he is a director (whether the provision is made by that company or an associated company), and

(b) where the provision is made by an associated company, to that company.

(2) That company or, as the case may be, each of them must keep available for inspection—

(a) a copy of the qualifying indemnity provision, or

(b) if the provision is not in writing, a written memorandum setting out its terms.

(3) The copy or memorandum must be kept available for inspection at—

(a) the company's registered office, or

(b) a place specified in regulations under section 1136.

(4) The copy or memorandum must be retained by the company for at least one year from the date of termination or expiry of the provision and must be kept available for inspection during that time.

(5) The company must give notice to the registrar—

(a) of the place at which the copy or memorandum is kept available for inspection, and

(b) of any change in that place,

unless it has at all times been kept at the company's registered office.

(6) If default is made in complying with subsection (2), (3) or (4), or default is made for 14 days in complying with subsection (5), an offence is committed by every officer of the company who is in default.

(7) A person guilty of an offence under this section is liable on summary conviction to a fine not exceeding level 3 on the standard scale and, for continued contravention, a daily default fine not exceeding one-tenth of level 3 on the standard scale.

(8) The provisions of this section apply to a variation of a qualifying indemnity provision as they apply to the original provision.

(9) In this section "qualifying indemnity provision" means—

(a) qualifying third party indemnity provision, and

(b) qualifying pension scheme indemnity provision.

[S237]

NOTES

Commencement: 1 October 2007 (for transitional provisions see the note below).

Transitional provisions, etc: Sch 3, para 16 to the draft Companies Act 2006 (Commencement No 3, Consequential Amendments, Transitional Provisions and Savings) Order 2007 (at **[A12]**) provides as follows—

"**16.**—(1) Sections 237 and 238 of the Companies Act 2006 (copies of qualifying indemnity provision to be available for inspection etc) apply to—

(a) qualifying indemnity provision within the meaning of section 237 made on or after 1st October 2007, and

(b) qualifying third party indemnity provision within the meaning of section 309B(1) of the 1985 Act to which section 309C(4) and (5) of that Act applied immediately before that date.

(2) Until regulations under section 1136 of the Companies Act 2006 are made specifying a place for the purposes of section 237(3)(b), the copies and memoranda referred to in section 237 may be kept by a company—

(a) at any place where its register of members is kept, or

(b) at its principal place of business,

provided that place is situated in the part of the United Kingdom in which the company is registered.

(3) Until section 1068(1) of the Companies Act 2006 comes into force the notice referred to in section 237(5) must be given on the form prescribed for the purposes of section 318(4) of the 1985 Act or Article 326(4) of the 1986 Order.

(4) The provisions of section 318 of the 1985 Act, as applied by section 309C(4) and (5), continue to apply in relation to—

(a) any default before 1st October 2007 in complying with section 318(1) or (5), as so applied;

(b) any request for inspection under section 318(7), as so applied, made before that date;

(c) any duty to give notice under section 318(4), as so applied, arising before that date.".

238 Right of member to inspect and request copy

(1) Every copy or memorandum required to be kept by a company under section 237 must be open to inspection by any member of the company without charge.

(2) Any member of the company is entitled, on request and on payment of such fee as may be prescribed, to be provided with a copy of any such copy or memorandum.

The copy must be provided within seven days after the request is received by the company.

(3) If an inspection required under subsection (1) is refused, or default is made in complying with subsection (2), an offence is committed by every officer of the company who is in default.

(4) A person guilty of an offence under this section is liable on summary conviction to a fine not exceeding level 3 on the standard scale and, for continued contravention, a daily default fine not exceeding one-tenth of level 3 on the standard scale.

(5) In the case of any such refusal or default the court may by order compel an immediate inspection or, as the case may be, direct that the copy required be sent to the person requiring it.

[S238]

NOTES

Commencement: 20 January 2007 (for the purpose of enabling the exercise of powers to make Orders or Regulations by statutory instrument); 1 October 2007 (otherwise) (for transitional provisions see the note to s 237).

Ratification of acts giving rise to liability

239 Ratification of acts of directors

(1) This section applies to the ratification by a company of conduct by a director amounting to negligence, default, breach of duty or breach of trust in relation to the company.

(2) The decision of the company to ratify such conduct must be made by resolution of the members of the company.

(3) Where the resolution is proposed as a written resolution neither the director (if a member of the company) nor any member connected with him is an eligible member.

(4) Where the resolution is proposed at a meeting, it is passed only if the necessary majority is obtained disregarding votes in favour of the resolution by the director (if a member of the company) and any member connected with him. This does not prevent the director or any such member from attending, being counted towards the quorum and taking part in the proceedings at any meeting at which the decision is considered.

(5) For the purposes of this section—

- (a) "conduct" includes acts and omissions;
- (b) "director" includes a former director;
- (c) a shadow director is treated as a director; and
- (d) in section 252 (meaning of "connected person"), subsection (3) does not apply (exclusion of person who is himself a director).

(6) Nothing in this section affects—

- (a) the validity of a decision taken by unanimous consent of the members of the company, or
- (b) any power of the directors to agree not to sue, or to settle or release a claim made by them on behalf of the company.

(7) This section does not affect any other enactment or rule of law imposing additional requirements for valid ratification or any rule of law as to acts that are incapable of being ratified by the company.

[S239]

NOTES

Commencement: 1 October 2007 (for transitional provisions see the note below).

Transitional provisions, etc: Sch 3, para 17 to the draft Companies Act 2006 (Commencement No 3, Consequential Amendments, Transitional Provisions and Savings) Order 2007 (at **[A12]**) provides as follows—

"17.—(1) Section 239 of the Companies Act 2006 (ratification of acts of directors giving rise to liability) applies to conduct by a director on or after 1st October 2007.

(2) Conduct by a director before that date is subject to the law relating to ratification that applied immediately before that date.".

CHAPTER 8
DIRECTORS' RESIDENTIAL ADDRESSES: PROTECTION FROM DISCLOSURE

240 Protected information

(1) This Chapter makes provision for protecting, in the case of a company director who is an individual—

(a) information as to his usual residential address;

(b) the information that his service address is his usual residential address.

(2) That information is referred to in this Chapter as "protected information".

(3) Information does not cease to be protected information on the individual ceasing to be a director of the company.

References in this Chapter to a director include, to that extent, a former director.

[S240]

NOTES

Commencement: to be appointed.

241 Protected information: restriction on use or disclosure by company

(1) A company must not use or disclose protected information about any of its directors, except—

(a) for communicating with the director concerned,

(b) in order to comply with any requirement of the Companies Acts as to particulars to be sent to the registrar, or

(c) in accordance with section 244 (disclosure under court order).

(2) Subsection (1) does not prohibit any use or disclosure of protected information with the consent of the director concerned.

[S241]

NOTES

Commencement: to be appointed.

242 Protected information: restriction on use or disclosure by registrar

(1) The registrar must omit protected information from the material on the register that is available for inspection where—

(a) it is contained in a document delivered to him in which such information is required to be stated, and

(b) in the case of a document having more than one part, it is contained in a part of the document in which such information is required to be stated.

(2) The registrar is not obliged—

(a) to check other documents or (as the case may be) other parts of the document to ensure the absence of protected information, or

(b) to omit from the material that is available for public inspection anything registered before this Chapter comes into force.

(3) The registrar must not use or disclose protected information except—

(a) as permitted by section 243 (permitted use or disclosure by registrar), or

(b) in accordance with section 244 (disclosure under court order).

[S242]

NOTES

Commencement: to be appointed.

243 Permitted use or disclosure by the registrar

(1) The registrar may use protected information for communicating with the director in question.

(2) The registrar may disclose protected information—

(a) to a public authority specified for the purposes of this section by regulations made by the Secretary of State, or

(b) to a credit reference agency.

(3) The Secretary of State may make provision by regulations—

(a) specifying conditions for the disclosure of protected information in accordance with this section, and

(b) providing for the charging of fees.

(4) The Secretary of State may make provision by regulations requiring the registrar, on application, to refrain from disclosing protected information relating to a director to a credit reference agency.

(5) Regulations under subsection (4) may make provision as to—

(a) who may make an application,

(b) the grounds on which an application may be made,

(c) the information to be included in and documents to accompany an application, and

(d) how an application is to be determined.

(6) Provision under subsection (5)(d) may in particular—

(a) confer a discretion on the registrar;

(b) provide for a question to be referred to a person other than the registrar for the purposes of determining the application.

(7) In this section—

"credit reference agency" means a person carrying on a business comprising the furnishing of information relevant to the financial standing of individuals, being information collected by the agency for that purpose; and

"public authority" includes any person or body having functions of a public nature.

(8) Regulations under this section are subject to negative resolution procedure.

[S243]

NOTES

Commencement: 20 January 2007 (for the purpose of enabling the exercise of powers to make Orders or Regulations by statutory instrument); to be appointed (otherwise).

244 Disclosure under court order

(1) The court may make an order for the disclosure of protected information by the company or by the registrar if—

(a) there is evidence that service of documents at a service address other than the director's usual residential address is not effective to bring them to the notice of the director, or

(b) it is necessary or expedient for the information to be provided in connection with the enforcement of an order or decree of the court,

and the court is otherwise satisfied that it is appropriate to make the order.

(2) An order for disclosure by the registrar is to be made only if the company—

(a) does not have the director's usual residential address, or

(b) has been dissolved.

(3) The order may be made on the application of a liquidator, creditor or member of the company, or any other person appearing to the court to have a sufficient interest.

(4) The order must specify the persons to whom, and purposes for which, disclosure is authorised.

[S244]

NOTES

Commencement: to be appointed.

245 Circumstances in which registrar may put address on the public record

(1) The registrar may put a director's usual residential address on the public record if—

(a) communications sent by the registrar to the director and requiring a response within a specified period remain unanswered, or

(b) there is evidence that service of documents at a service address provided in place of the director's usual residential address is not effective to bring them to the notice of the director.

(2) The registrar must give notice of the proposal—

(a) to the director, and

(b) to every company of which the registrar has been notified that the individual is a director.

(3) The notice must—

(a) state the grounds on which it is proposed to put the director's usual residential address on the public record, and

(b) specify a period within which representations may be made before that is done.

(4) It must be sent to the director at his usual residential address, unless it appears to the registrar that service at that address may be ineffective to bring it to the individual's notice, in which case it may be sent to any service address provided in place of that address.

(5) The registrar must take account of any representations received within the specified period.

(6) What is meant by putting the address on the public record is explained in section 246.

[S245]

NOTES

Commencement: to be appointed.

246 Putting the address on the public record

(1) The registrar, on deciding in accordance with section 245 that a director's usual residential address is to be put on the public record, shall proceed as if notice of a change of registered particulars had been given—

(a) stating that address as the director's service address, and

(b) stating that the director's usual residential address is the same as his service address.

(2) The registrar must give notice of having done so—

(a) to the director, and

(b) to the company.

(3) On receipt of the notice the company must—

(a) enter the director's usual residential address in its register of directors as his service address, and

(b) state in its register of directors' residential addresses that his usual residential address is the same as his service address.

(4) If the company has been notified by the director in question of a more recent address as his usual residential address, it must—

(a) enter that address in its register of directors as the director's service address, and

(b) give notice to the registrar as on a change of registered particulars.

(5) If a company fails to comply with subsection (3) or (4), an offence is committed by—

(a) the company, and

(b) every officer of the company who is in default.

(6) A person guilty of an offence under subsection (5) is liable on summary conviction to a fine not exceeding level 5 on the standard scale and, for continued contravention, a daily default fine not exceeding one-tenth of level 5 on the standard scale.

(7) A director whose usual residential address has been put on the public record by the registrar under this section may not register a service address other than his usual residential address for a period of five years from the date of the registrar's decision.

[S246]

NOTES

Commencement: to be appointed.

CHAPTER 9
SUPPLEMENTARY PROVISIONS

Provision for employees on cessation or transfer of business

247 Power to make provision for employees on cessation or transfer of business

(1) The powers of the directors of a company include (if they would not otherwise do so) power to make provision for the benefit of persons employed or formerly employed by the company, or any of its subsidiaries, in connection with the cessation or the transfer to any person of the whole or part of the undertaking of the company or that subsidiary.

(2) This power is exercisable notwithstanding the general duty imposed by section 172 (duty to promote the success of the company).

(3) In the case of a company that is a charity it is exercisable notwithstanding any restrictions on the directors' powers (or the company's capacity) flowing from the objects of the company.

(4) The power may only be exercised if sanctioned—
- (a) by a resolution of the company, or
- (b) by a resolution of the directors,

in accordance with the following provisions.

(5) A resolution of the directors—
- (a) must be authorised by the company's articles, and
- (b) is not sufficient sanction for payments to or for the benefit of directors, former directors or shadow directors.

(6) Any other requirements of the company's articles as to the exercise of the power conferred by this section must be complied with.

(7) Any payment under this section must be made—
- (a) before the commencement of any winding up of the company, and
- (b) out of profits of the company that are available for dividend.

[S247]

NOTES

Commencement: 1 October 2007 (for transitional provisions see the note below).

Transitional provisions, etc: Sch 3, para 18 to the draft Companies Act 2006 (Commencement No 3, Consequential Amendments, Transitional Provisions and Savings) Order 2007 (at **[A12]**) provides as follows—

"18 Power to make provision for employees on cessation or transfer of business (s 247)

(1) Section 247 of the Companies Act 2006 (power to make provision for employees on cessation or transfer of business) applies to provision made on or after 1st October 2007 (subject to sub-paragraph (2)(b)).

(2) Section 719 of the 1985 Act or Article 668 of the 1986 Order continues to apply—
- (a) to provision made before that date, and
- (b) to anything sanctioned in accordance with subsection (3) of that section or paragraph (3) of that Article before that date.".

Records of meetings of directors

248 Minutes of directors' meetings

(1) Every company must cause minutes of all proceedings at meetings of its directors to be recorded.

(2) The records must be kept for at least ten years from the date of the meeting.

(3) If a company fails to comply with this section, an offence is committed by every officer of the company who is in default.

(4) A person guilty of an offence under this section is liable on summary conviction to a fine not exceeding level 3 on the standard scale and, for continued contravention, a daily default fine not exceeding one-tenth of level 3 on the standard scale.

[S248]

NOTES

Commencement: 1 October 2007 (for transitional provisions see the note below).

Transitional provisions, etc: Sch 3, para 19 to the draft Companies Act 2006 (Commencement No 3, Consequential Amendments, Transitional Provisions and Savings) Order 2007 (at **[A12]**) provides as follows—

"19 Records of meetings of directors (ss 248 and 249)

(1) Sections 248 and 249 of the Companies Act 2006 (records of meetings of directors) apply to meetings held on or after 1st October 2007.

(2) Section 382 of the 1985 Act or Article 390 of the 1986 Order continues to apply to meetings of directors held before that date.".

249 Minutes as evidence

(1) Minutes recorded in accordance with section 248, if purporting to be authenticated by the chairman of the meeting or by the chairman of the next directors' meeting, are evidence (in Scotland, sufficient evidence) of the proceedings at the meeting.

(2) Where minutes have been made in accordance with that section of the proceedings of a meeting of directors, then, until the contrary is proved—

(a) the meeting is deemed duly held and convened,
(b) all proceedings at the meeting are deemed to have duly taken place, and
(c) all appointments at the meeting are deemed valid.

[S249]

NOTES

Commencement: 1 October 2007 (for transitional provisions see the note to s 248).

Meaning of "director" and "shadow director"

250 "Director"

In the Companies Acts "director" includes any person occupying the position of director, by whatever name called.

[S250]

NOTES

Commencement: 1 October 2007.

251 "Shadow director"

(1) In the Companies Acts "shadow director", in relation to a company, means a person in accordance with whose directions or instructions the directors of the company are accustomed to act.

(2) A person is not to be regarded as a shadow director by reason only that the directors act on advice given by him in a professional capacity.

(3) A body corporate is not to be regarded as a shadow director of any of its subsidiary companies for the purposes of—

Chapter 2 (general duties of directors),
Chapter 4 (transactions requiring members' approval), or
Chapter 6 (contract with sole member who is also a director),

by reason only that the directors of the subsidiary are accustomed to act in accordance with its directions or instructions.

[S251]

NOTES

Commencement: 1 October 2007.

Other definitions

252 Persons connected with a director

(1) This section defines what is meant by references in this Part to a person being "connected" with a director of a company (or a director being "connected" with a person).

(2) The following persons (and only those persons) are connected with a director of a company—

(a) members of the director's family (see section 253);

(b) a body corporate with which the director is connected (as defined in section 254);

(c) a person acting in his capacity as trustee of a trust—

(i) the beneficiaries of which include the director or a person who by virtue of paragraph (a) or (b) is connected with him, or

(ii) the terms of which confer a power on the trustees that may be exercised for the benefit of the director or any such person,

other than a trust for the purposes of an employees' share scheme or a pension scheme;

(d) a person acting in his capacity as partner—

(i) of the director, or

(ii) of a person who, by virtue of paragraph (a), (b) or (c), is connected with that director;

(e) a firm that is a legal person under the law by which it is governed and in which—

(i) the director is a partner,

(ii) a partner is a person who, by virtue of paragraph (a), (b) or (c) is connected with the director, or

(iii) a partner is a firm in which the director is a partner or in which there is a partner who, by virtue of paragraph (a), (b) or (c), is connected with the director.

(3) References in this Part to a person connected with a director of a company do not include a person who is himself a director of the company.

[S252]

NOTES

Commencement: 1 October 2007.

253 Members of a director's family

(1) This section defines what is meant by references in this Part to members of a director's family.

(2) For the purposes of this Part the members of a director's family are—

(a) the director's spouse or civil partner;

(b) any other person (whether of a different sex or the same sex) with whom the director lives as partner in an enduring family relationship;

(c) the director's children or step-children;

(d) any children or step-children of a person within paragraph (b) (and who are not children or step-children of the director) who live with the director and have not attained the age of 18;

(e) the director's parents.

(3) Subsection (2)(b) does not apply if the other person is the director's grandparent or grandchild, sister, brother, aunt or uncle, or nephew or niece.

[S253]

NOTES

Commencement: 1 October 2007.

254 Director "connected with" a body corporate

(1) This section defines what is meant by references in this Part to a director being "connected with" a body corporate.

(2) A director is connected with a body corporate if, but only if, he and the persons connected with him together—

(a) are interested in shares comprised in the equity share capital of that body corporate of a nominal value equal to at least 20% of that share capital, or

(b) are entitled to exercise or control the exercise of more than 20% of the voting power at any general meeting of that body.

(3) The rules set out in Schedule 1 (references to interest in shares or debentures) apply for the purposes of this section.

(4) References in this section to voting power the exercise of which is controlled by a director include voting power whose exercise is controlled by a body corporate controlled by him.

(5) Shares in a company held as treasury shares, and any voting rights attached to such shares, are disregarded for the purposes of this section.

(6) For the avoidance of circularity in the application of section 252 (meaning of "connected person") —

(a) a body corporate with which a director is connected is not treated for the purposes of this section as connected with him unless it is also connected with him by virtue of subsection (2)(c) or (d) of that section (connection as trustee or partner); and

(b) a trustee of a trust the beneficiaries of which include (or may include) a body corporate with which a director is connected is not treated for the purposes of this section as connected with a director by reason only of that fact.

[S254]

NOTES

Commencement: 1 October 2007.

255 Director "controlling" a body corporate

(1) This section defines what is meant by references in this Part to a director "controlling" a body corporate.

(2) A director of a company is taken to control a body corporate if, but only if—

(a) he or any person connected with him—

  (i) is interested in any part of the equity share capital of that body, or

  (ii) is entitled to exercise or control the exercise of any part of the voting power at any general meeting of that body, and

(b) he, the persons connected with him and the other directors of that company, together—

  (i) are interested in more than 50% of that share capital, or

  (ii) are entitled to exercise or control the exercise of more than 50% of that voting power.

(3) The rules set out in Schedule 1 (references to interest in shares or debentures) apply for the purposes of this section.

(4) References in this section to voting power the exercise of which is controlled by a director include voting power whose exercise is controlled by a body corporate controlled by him.

(5) Shares in a company held as treasury shares, and any voting rights attached to such shares, are disregarded for the purposes of this section.

(6) For the avoidance of circularity in the application of section 252 (meaning of "connected person")—

(a) a body corporate with which a director is connected is not treated for the purposes of this section as connected with him unless it is also connected with him by virtue of subsection (2)(c) or (d) of that section (connection as trustee or partner); and

(b) a trustee of a trust the beneficiaries of which include (or may include) a body corporate with which a director is connected is not treated for the purposes of this section as connected with a director by reason only of that fact.

[S255]

NOTES

Commencement: 1 October 2007.

256 Associated bodies corporate

For the purposes of this Part—

(a) bodies corporate are associated if one is a subsidiary of the other or both are subsidiaries of the same body corporate, and

(b) companies are associated if one is a subsidiary of the other or both are subsidiaries of the same body corporate.

[S256]

NOTES

Commencement: 1 October 2007.

257 References to company's constitution

(1) References in this Part to a company's constitution include—

(a) any resolution or other decision come to in accordance with the constitution, and

(b) any decision by the members of the company, or a class of members, that is treated by virtue of any enactment or rule of law as equivalent to a decision by the company.

(2) This is in addition to the matters mentioned in section 17 (general provision as to matters contained in company's constitution).

[S257]

NOTES

Commencement: 1 October 2007.

General

258 Power to increase financial limits

(1) The Secretary of State may by order substitute for any sum of money specified in this Part a larger sum specified in the order.

(2) An order under this section is subject to negative resolution procedure.

(3) An order does not have effect in relation to anything done or not done before it comes into force.

Accordingly, proceedings in respect of any liability incurred before that time may be continued or instituted as if the order had not been made.

[S258]

NOTES

Commencement: 20 January 2007 (for the purpose of enabling the exercise of powers to make Orders or Regulations by statutory instrument); 1 October 2007 (otherwise).

259 Transactions under foreign law

For the purposes of this Part it is immaterial whether the law that (apart from this Act) governs an arrangement or transaction is the law of the United Kingdom, or a part of it, or not.

[S259]

NOTES

Commencement: 1 October 2007.

PART 11
DERIVATIVE CLAIMS AND PROCEEDINGS BY MEMBERS

CHAPTER 1
DERIVATIVE CLAIMS IN ENGLAND AND WALES OR NORTHERN IRELAND

260 Derivative claims

(1) This Chapter applies to proceedings in England and Wales or Northern Ireland by a member of a company—

(a) in respect of a cause of action vested in the company, and

(b) seeking relief on behalf of the company.

This is referred to in this Chapter as a "derivative claim".

(2) A derivative claim may only be brought—

(a) under this Chapter, or

(b) in pursuance of an order of the court in proceedings under section 994 (proceedings for protection of members against unfair prejudice).

(3) A derivative claim under this Chapter may be brought only in respect of a cause of action arising from an actual or proposed act or omission involving negligence, default, breach of duty or breach of trust by a director of the company.

The cause of action may be against the director or another person (or both).

(4) It is immaterial whether the cause of action arose before or after the person seeking to bring or continue the derivative claim became a member of the company.

(5) For the purposes of this Chapter—

(a) "director" includes a former director;

(b) a shadow director is treated as a director; and

(c) references to a member of a company include a person who is not a member but to whom shares in the company have been transferred or transmitted by operation of law.

[S260]

NOTES

Commencement: 1 October 2007 (for transitional provisions see the note below).

Transitional provisions, etc: Sch 3, paras 20, 21 to the draft Companies Act 2006 (Commencement No 3, Consequential Amendments, Transitional Provisions and Savings) Order 2007 (at **[A12]**) provides as follows—

"20 Derivative claims and proceedings by members (ss 260 to 269)

(1) On and after 1st October 2007 sections 260 to 264 of the Companies Act 2006 (derivative claims in England and Wales or Northern Ireland) apply to all derivative claims, subject to the following provisions.

(2) Those sections do not apply, and the law in force immediately before 1st October 2007 continues to apply, where the claimant (in Northern Ireland, the plaintiff) has applied for permission (in Northern Ireland, leave) to continue the claim before that date.

(3) If, or to the extent that, the claim arises from acts or omissions that occurred before 1st October 2007, the court must exercise its powers under those sections so as to secure that the claim is allowed to proceed as a derivative claim only if, or to the extent that, it would have been allowed to proceed as a derivative claim under the law in force immediately before that date.

21.—(1) This paragraph applies where an application is made under section 266 or 267 (derivative proceedings in Scotland).

(2) If the cause of action arises, wholly or to any extent, from an act or omission that occurred before 1st October 2007, the court shall exercise its powers under those sections so as to secure that the proceedings in respect of that act or omission are allowed to proceed as derivative proceedings only to the extent that they could have been pursued by the applicant under the law in force immediately before that date.".

261 Application for permission to continue derivative claim

(1) A member of a company who brings a derivative claim under this Chapter must apply to the court for permission (in Northern Ireland, leave) to continue it.

(2) If it appears to the court that the application and the evidence filed by the applicant in support of it do not disclose a prima facie case for giving permission (or leave), the court—

(a) must dismiss the application, and
(b) may make any consequential order it considers appropriate.

(3) If the application is not dismissed under subsection (2), the court—

(a) may give directions as to the evidence to be provided by the company, and
(b) may adjourn the proceedings to enable the evidence to be obtained.

(4) On hearing the application, the court may—

(a) give permission (or leave) to continue the claim on such terms as it thinks fit,
(b) refuse permission (or leave) and dismiss the claim, or
(c) adjourn the proceedings on the application and give such directions as it thinks fit.

[S261]

NOTES

Commencement: 1 October 2007 (for transitional provisions see the note to s 260).

262 Application for permission to continue claim as a derivative claim

(1) This section applies where—

(a) a company has brought a claim, and
(b) the cause of action on which the claim is based could be pursued as a derivative claim under this Chapter.

(2) A member of the company may apply to the court for permission (in Northern Ireland, leave) to continue the claim as a derivative claim on the ground that—

(a) the manner in which the company commenced or continued the claim amounts to an abuse of the process of the court,
(b) the company has failed to prosecute the claim diligently, and
(c) it is appropriate for the member to continue the claim as a derivative claim.

(3) If it appears to the court that the application and the evidence filed by the applicant in support of it do not disclose a prima facie case for giving permission (or leave), the court—

(a) must dismiss the application, and
(b) may make any consequential order it considers appropriate.

(4) If the application is not dismissed under subsection (3), the court—

(a) may give directions as to the evidence to be provided by the company, and
(b) may adjourn the proceedings to enable the evidence to be obtained.

(5) On hearing the application, the court may—

(a) give permission (or leave) to continue the claim as a derivative claim on such terms as it thinks fit,
(b) refuse permission (or leave) and dismiss the application, or
(c) adjourn the proceedings on the application and give such directions as it thinks fit.

[S262]

NOTES

Commencement: 1 October 2007 (for transitional provisions see the note to s 260).

263 Whether permission to be given

(1) The following provisions have effect where a member of a company applies for permission (in Northern Ireland, leave) under section 261 or 262.

(2) Permission (or leave) must be refused if the court is satisfied—

(a) that a person acting in accordance with section 172 (duty to promote the success of the company) would not seek to continue the claim, or
(b) where the cause of action arises from an act or omission that is yet to occur, that the act or omission has been authorised by the company, or
(c) where the cause of action arises from an act or omission that has already occurred, that the act or omission—
  (i) was authorised by the company before it occurred, or
  (ii) has been ratified by the company since it occurred.

(3) In considering whether to give permission (or leave) the court must take into account, in particular—

(a) whether the member is acting in good faith in seeking to continue the claim;

(b) the importance that a person acting in accordance with section 172 (duty to promote the success of the company) would attach to continuing it;

(c) where the cause of action results from an act or omission that is yet to occur, whether the act or omission could be, and in the circumstances would be likely to be—

(i) authorised by the company before it occurs, or

(ii) ratified by the company after it occurs;

(d) where the cause of action arises from an act or omission that has already occurred, whether the act or omission could be, and in the circumstances would be likely to be, ratified by the company;

(e) whether the company has decided not to pursue the claim;

(f) whether the act or omission in respect of which the claim is brought gives rise to a cause of action that the member could pursue in his own right rather than on behalf of the company.

(4) In considering whether to give permission (or leave) the court shall have particular regard to any evidence before it as to the views of members of the company who have no personal interest, direct or indirect, in the matter.

(5) The Secretary of State may by regulations—

(a) amend subsection (2) so as to alter or add to the circumstances in which permission (or leave) is to be refused;

(b) amend subsection (3) so as to alter or add to the matters that the court is required to take into account in considering whether to give permission (or leave).

(6) Before making any such regulations the Secretary of State shall consult such persons as he considers appropriate.

(7) Regulations under this section are subject to affirmative resolution procedure.

[S263]

NOTES

Commencement: 20 January 2007 (for the purpose of enabling the exercise of powers to make Orders or Regulations by statutory instrument); 1 October 2007 (otherwise) (for transitional provisions see the note to s 260).

264 Application for permission to continue derivative claim brought by another member

(1) This section applies where a member of a company ("the claimant")—

(a) has brought a derivative claim,

(b) has continued as a derivative claim a claim brought by the company, or

(c) has continued a derivative claim under this section.

(2) Another member of the company ("the applicant") may apply to the court for permission (in Northern Ireland, leave) to continue the claim on the ground that—

(a) the manner in which the proceedings have been commenced or continued by the claimant amounts to an abuse of the process of the court,

(b) the claimant has failed to prosecute the claim diligently, and

(c) it is appropriate for the applicant to continue the claim as a derivative claim.

(3) If it appears to the court that the application and the evidence filed by the applicant in support of it do not disclose a prima facie case for giving permission (or leave), the court—

(a) must dismiss the application, and

(b) may make any consequential order it considers appropriate.

(4) If the application is not dismissed under subsection (3), the court—

(a) may give directions as to the evidence to be provided by the company, and

(b) may adjourn the proceedings to enable the evidence to be obtained.

(5) On hearing the application, the court may—

(a) give permission (or leave) to continue the claim on such terms as it thinks fit,

(b) refuse permission (or leave) and dismiss the application, or

(c) adjourn the proceedings on the application and give such directions as it thinks fit.

[S264]

NOTES

Commencement: 1 October 2007 (for transitional provisions see the note to s 260).

CHAPTER 2
DERIVATIVE PROCEEDINGS IN SCOTLAND

265 Derivative proceedings

(1) In Scotland, a member of a company may raise proceedings in respect of an act or omission specified in subsection (3) in order to protect the interests of the company and obtain a remedy on its behalf.

(2) A member of a company may raise such proceedings only under subsection (1).

(3) The act or omission referred to in subsection (1) is any actual or proposed act or omission involving negligence, default, breach of duty or breach of trust by a director of the company.

(4) Proceedings may be raised under subsection (1) against (either or both)—

(a) the director referred to in subsection (3), or

(b) another person.

(5) It is immaterial whether the act or omission in respect of which the proceedings are to be raised or, in the case of continuing proceedings under section 267 or 269, are raised, arose before or after the person seeking to raise or continue them became a member of the company.

(6) This section does not affect—

(a) any right of a member of a company to raise proceedings in respect of an act or omission specified in subsection (3) in order to protect his own interests and obtain a remedy on his own behalf, or

(b) the court's power to make an order under section 996(2)(c) or anything done under such an order.

(7) In this Chapter—

(a) proceedings raised under subsection (1) are referred to as "derivative proceedings",

(b) the act or omission in respect of which they are raised is referred to as the "cause of action",

(c) "director" includes a former director,

(d) references to a director include a shadow director, and

(e) references to a member of a company include a person who is not a member but to whom shares in the company have been transferred or transmitted by operation of law.

[S265]

NOTES

Commencement: 1 October 2007 (for transitional provisions see the note to s 260).

266 Requirement for leave and notice

(1) Derivative proceedings may be raised by a member of a company only with the leave of the court.

(2) An application for leave must—

(a) specify the cause of action, and

(b) summarise the facts on which the derivative proceedings are to be based.

(3) If it appears to the court that the application and the evidence produced by the applicant in support of it do not disclose a prima facie case for granting it, the court—

(a) must refuse the application, and

(b) may make any consequential order it considers appropriate.

(4) If the application is not refused under subsection (3)—

(a) the applicant must serve the application on the company,

(b) the court—

(i) may make an order requiring evidence to be produced by the company, and

(ii) may adjourn the proceedings on the application to enable the evidence to be obtained, and

(c) the company is entitled to take part in the further proceedings on the application.

(5) On hearing the application, the court may—

(a) grant the application on such terms as it thinks fit,

(b) refuse the application, or

(c) adjourn the proceedings on the application and make such order as to further procedure as it thinks fit.

[S266]

NOTES

Commencement: 1 October 2007 (for transitional provisions see the note to s 260).

267 Application to continue proceedings as derivative proceedings

(1) This section applies where—

(a) a company has raised proceedings, and

(b) the proceedings are in respect of an act or omission which could be the basis for derivative proceedings.

(2) A member of the company may apply to the court to be substituted for the company in the proceedings, and for the proceedings to continue in consequence as derivative proceedings, on the ground that—

(a) the manner in which the company commenced or continued the proceedings amounts to an abuse of the process of the court,

(b) the company has failed to prosecute the proceedings diligently, and

(c) it is appropriate for the member to be substituted for the company in the proceedings.

(3) If it appears to the court that the application and the evidence produced by the applicant in support of it do not disclose a prima facie case for granting it, the court—

(a) must refuse the application, and

(b) may make any consequential order it considers appropriate.

(4) If the application is not refused under subsection (3)—

(a) the applicant must serve the application on the company,

(b) the court—

(i) may make an order requiring evidence to be produced by the company, and

(ii) may adjourn the proceedings on the application to enable the evidence to be obtained, and

(c) the company is entitled to take part in the further proceedings on the application.

(5) On hearing the application, the court may—

(a) grant the application on such terms as it thinks fit,

(b) refuse the application, or

(c) adjourn the proceedings on the application and make such order as to further procedure as it thinks fit.

[S267]

NOTES

Commencement: 1 October 2007 (for transitional provisions see the note to s 260).

268 Granting of leave

(1) The court must refuse leave to raise derivative proceedings or an application under section 267 if satisfied—

(a) that a person acting in accordance with section 172 (duty to promote the success of the company) would not seek to raise or continue the proceedings (as the case may be), or

(b) where the cause of action is an act or omission that is yet to occur, that the act or omission has been authorised by the company, or

(c) where the cause of action is an act or omission that has already occurred, that the act or omission—

(i) was authorised by the company before it occurred, or

(ii) has been ratified by the company since it occurred.

(2) In considering whether to grant leave to raise derivative proceedings or an application under section 267, the court must take into account, in particular—

(a) whether the member is acting in good faith in seeking to raise or continue the proceedings (as the case may be),

(b) the importance that a person acting in accordance with section 172 (duty to promote the success of the company) would attach to raising or continuing them (as the case may be),

(c) where the cause of action is an act or omission that is yet to occur, whether the act or omission could be, and in the circumstances would be likely to be—

(i) authorised by the company before it occurs, or

(ii) ratified by the company after it occurs,

(d) where the cause of action is an act or omission that has already occurred, whether the act or omission could be, and in the circumstances would be likely to be, ratified by the company,

(e) whether the company has decided not to raise proceedings in respect of the same cause of action or to persist in the proceedings (as the case may be),

(f) whether the cause of action is one which the member could pursue in his own right rather than on behalf of the company.

(3) In considering whether to grant leave to raise derivative proceedings or an application under section 267, the court shall have particular regard to any evidence before it as to the views of members of the company who have no personal interest, direct or indirect, in the matter.

(4) The Secretary of State may by regulations—

(a) amend subsection (1) so as to alter or add to the circumstances in which leave or an application is to be refused,

(b) amend subsection (2) so as to alter or add to the matters that the court is required to take into account in considering whether to grant leave or an application.

(5) Before making any such regulations the Secretary of State shall consult such persons as he considers appropriate.

(6) Regulations under this section are subject to affirmative resolution procedure.

[S268]

NOTES

Commencement: 20 January 2007 (for the purpose of enabling the exercise of powers to make Orders or Regulations by statutory instrument); 1 October 2007 (otherwise) (for transitional provisions see the note to s 260).

269 Application by member to be substituted for member pursuing derivative proceedings

(1) This section applies where a member of a company ("the claimant")—

(a) has raised derivative proceedings,

(b) has continued as derivative proceedings raised by the company, or

(c) has continued derivative proceedings under this section.

(2) Another member of the company ("the applicant") may apply to the court to be substituted for the claimant in the action on the ground that—

(a) the manner in which the proceedings have been commenced or continued by the claimant amounts to an abuse of the process of the court,

(b) the claimant has failed to prosecute the proceedings diligently, and

(c) it is appropriate for the applicant to be substituted for the claimant in the proceedings.

(3) If it appears to the court that the application and the evidence produced by the applicant in support of it do not disclose a prima facie case for granting it, the court—

(a) must refuse the application, and

(b) may make any consequential order it considers appropriate.

(4) If the application is not refused under subsection (3)—

(a) the applicant must serve the application on the company,

(b) the court—

(i) may make an order requiring evidence to be produced by the company, and

(ii) may adjourn the proceedings on the application to enable the evidence to be obtained, and

(c) the company is entitled to take part in the further proceedings on the application.

(5) On hearing the application, the court may—

(a) grant the application on such terms as it thinks fit,

(b) refuse the application, or

(c) adjourn the proceedings on the application and make such order as to further procedure as it thinks fit.

[S269]

NOTES

Commencement: 1 October 2007 (for transitional provisions see the note to s 260).

PART 12
COMPANY SECRETARIES

Private companies

270 Private company not required to have secretary

(1) A private company is not required to have a secretary.

(2) References in the Companies Acts to a private company "without a secretary" are to a private company that for the time being is taking advantage of the exemption in subsection (1); and references to a private company "with a secretary" shall be construed accordingly.

(3) In the case of a private company without a secretary—

(a) anything authorised or required to be given or sent to, or served on, the company by being sent to its secretary—

(i) may be given or sent to, or served on, the company itself, and

(ii) if addressed to the secretary shall be treated as addressed to the company; and

(b) anything else required or authorised to be done by or to the secretary of the company may be done by or to—

(i) a director, or

(ii) a person authorised generally or specifically in that behalf by the directors.

[S270]

NOTES

Commencement: to be appointed.

Public companies

271 Public company required to have secretary

A public company must have a secretary.

[S271]

NOTES

Commencement: to be appointed.

272 Direction requiring public company to appoint secretary

(1) If it appears to the Secretary of State that a public company is in breach of section 271 (requirement to have secretary), the Secretary of State may give the company a direction under this section.

(2) The direction must state that the company appears to be in breach of that section and specify—

(a) what the company must do in order to comply with the direction, and

(b) the period within which it must do so.

That period must be not less than one month or more than three months after the date on which the direction is given.

(3) The direction must also inform the company of the consequences of failing to comply.

(4) Where the company is in breach of section 271 it must comply with the direction by—

(a) making the necessary appointment, and

(b) giving notice of it under section 276,

before the end of the period specified in the direction.

(5) If the company has already made the necessary appointment, it must comply with the direction by giving notice of it under section 276 before the end of the period specified in the direction.

(6) If a company fails to comply with a direction under this section, an offence is committed by—

(a) the company, and

(b) every officer of the company who is in default.

For this purpose a shadow director is treated as an officer of the company.

(7) A person guilty of an offence under this section is liable on summary conviction to a fine not exceeding level 5 on the standard scale and, for continued contravention, a daily default fine not exceeding one-tenth of level 5 on the standard scale.

[S272]

NOTES

Commencement: to be appointed.

273 Qualifications of secretaries of public companies

(1) It is the duty of the directors of a public company to take all reasonable steps to secure that the secretary (or each joint secretary) of the company—

(a) is a person who appears to them to have the requisite knowledge and experience to discharge the functions of secretary of the company, and

(b) has one or more of the following qualifications.

(2) The qualifications are—

(a) that he has held the office of secretary of a public company for at least three of the five years immediately preceding his appointment as secretary;

(b) that he is a member of any of the bodies specified in subsection (3);

(c) that he is a barrister, advocate or solicitor called or admitted in any part of the United Kingdom;

(d) that he is a person who, by virtue of his holding or having held any other position or his being a member of any other body, appears to the directors to be capable of discharging the functions of secretary of the company.

(3) The bodies referred to in subsection (2)(b) are—

(a) the Institute of Chartered Accountants in England and Wales;

(b) the Institute of Chartered Accountants of Scotland;

(c) the Association of Chartered Certified Accountants;

(d) the Institute of Chartered Accountants in Ireland;

(e) the Institute of Chartered Secretaries and Administrators;

(f) the Chartered Institute of Management Accountants;

(g) the Chartered Institute of Public Finance and Accountancy.

[S273]

NOTES

Commencement: to be appointed.

Provisions applying to private companies with a secretary and to public companies

274 Discharge of functions where office vacant or secretary unable to act

Where in the case of any company the office of secretary is vacant, or there is for any other reason no secretary capable of acting, anything required or authorised to be done by or to the secretary may be done—

(a) by or to an assistant or deputy secretary (if any), or

(b) if there is no assistant or deputy secretary or none capable of acting, by or to any person authorised generally or specifically in that behalf by the directors.

[S274]

NOTES

Commencement: to be appointed.

275 Duty to keep register of secretaries

(1) A company must keep a register of its secretaries.

(2) The register must contain the required particulars (see sections 277 to 279) of the person who is, or persons who are, the secretary or joint secretaries of the company.

(3) The register must be kept available for inspection—

(a) at the company's registered office, or

(b) at a place specified in regulations under section 1136.

(4) The company must give notice to the registrar—

(a) of the place at which the register is kept available for inspection, and

(b) of any change in that place,

unless it has at all times been kept at the company's registered office.

(5) The register must be open to the inspection—

(a) of any member of the company without charge, and

(b) of any other person on payment of such fee as may be prescribed.

(6) If default is made in complying with subsection (1), (2) or (3), or if default is made for 14 days in complying with subsection (4), or if an inspection required under subsection (5) is refused, an offence is committed by—

(a) the company, and

(b) every officer of the company who is in default.

For this purpose a shadow director is treated as an officer of the company.

(7) A person guilty of an offence under this section is liable on summary conviction to a fine not exceeding level 5 on the standard scale and, for continued contravention, a daily default fine not exceeding one-tenth of level 5 on the standard scale.

(8) In the case of a refusal of inspection of the register, the court may by order compel an immediate inspection of it.

[S275]

NOTES

Commencement: 20 January 2007 (for the purpose of enabling the exercise of powers to make Orders or Regulations by statutory instrument); to be appointed (otherwise).

276 Duty to notify registrar of changes

(1) A company must, within the period of 14 days from—

(a) a person becoming or ceasing to be its secretary or one of its joint secretaries, or

(b) the occurrence of any change in the particulars contained in its register of secretaries,

give notice to the registrar of the change and of the date on which it occurred.

(2) Notice of a person having become secretary, or one of joint secretaries, of the company must be accompanied by a consent by that person to act in the relevant capacity.

(3) If default is made in complying with this section, an offence is committed by every officer of the company who is in default.

For this purpose a shadow director is treated as an officer of the company.

(4) A person guilty of an offence under this section is liable on summary conviction to a fine not exceeding level 5 on the standard scale and, for continued contravention, a daily default fine not exceeding one-tenth of level 5 on the standard scale.

[S276]

NOTES

Commencement: to be appointed.

277 Particulars of secretaries to be registered: individuals

(1) A company's register of secretaries must contain the following particulars in the case of an individual—

(a) name and any former name;
(b) address.

(2) For the purposes of this section "name" means a person's Christian name (or other forename) and surname, except that in the case of—

(a) a peer, or
(b) an individual usually known by a title,

the title may be stated instead of his Christian name (or other forename) and surname or in addition to either or both of them.

(3) For the purposes of this section a "former name" means a name by which the individual was formerly known for business purposes.

Where a person is or was formerly known by more than one such name, each of them must be stated.

(4) It is not necessary for the register to contain particulars of a former name in the following cases—

(a) in the case of a peer or an individual normally known by a British title, where the name is one by which the person was known previous to the adoption of or succession to the title;
(b) in the case of any person, where the former name—
  (i) was changed or disused before the person attained the age of 16 years, or
  (ii) has been changed or disused for 20 years or more.

(5) The address required to be stated in the register is a service address. This may be stated to be "The company's registered office".

[S277]

NOTES

Commencement: to be appointed.

278 Particulars of secretaries to be registered: corporate secretaries and firms

(1) A company's register of secretaries must contain the following particulars in the case of a body corporate, or a firm that is a legal person under the law by which it is governed—

(a) corporate or firm name;
(b) registered or principal office;
(c) in the case of an EEA company to which the First Company Law Directive (68/151/EEC) applies, particulars of—
  (i) the register in which the company file mentioned in Article 3 of that Directive is kept (including details of the relevant state), and
  (ii) the registration number in that register;
(d) in any other case, particulars of—
  (i) the legal form of the company or firm and the law by which it is governed, and
  (ii) if applicable, the register in which it is entered (including details of the state) and its registration number in that register.

(2) If all the partners in a firm are joint secretaries it is sufficient to state the particulars that would be required if the firm were a legal person and the firm had been appointed secretary.

[S278]

NOTES

Commencement: to be appointed.

279 Particulars of secretaries to be registered: power to make regulations

(1) The Secretary of State may make provision by regulations amending—
section 277 (particulars of secretaries to be registered: individuals), or
section 278 (particulars of secretaries to be registered: corporate secretaries and firms),
so as to add to or remove items from the particulars required to be contained in a company's register of secretaries.

(2) Regulations under this section are subject to affirmative resolution procedure.

[S279]

NOTES

Commencement: 20 January 2007 (for the purpose of enabling the exercise of powers to make Orders or Regulations by statutory instrument); to be appointed (otherwise).

280 Acts done by person in dual capacity

A provision requiring or authorising a thing to be done by or to a director and the secretary of a company is not satisfied by its being done by or to the same person acting both as director and as, or in place of, the secretary.

[S280]

NOTES

Commencement: to be appointed.

PART 13
RESOLUTIONS AND MEETINGS

CHAPTER 1
GENERAL PROVISIONS ABOUT RESOLUTIONS

281 Resolutions

(1) A resolution of the members (or of a class of members) of a private company must be passed—

(a) as a written resolution in accordance with Chapter 2, or

(b) at a meeting of the members (to which the provisions of Chapter 3 apply).

(2) A resolution of the members (or of a class of members) of a public company must be passed at a meeting of the members (to which the provisions of Chapter 3 and, where relevant, Chapter 4 apply).

(3) Where a provision of the Companies Acts—

(a) requires a resolution of a company, or of the members (or a class of members) of a company, and

(b) does not specify what kind of resolution is required,

what is required is an ordinary resolution unless the company's articles require a higher majority (or unanimity).

(4) Nothing in this Part affects any enactment or rule of law as to—

(a) things done otherwise than by passing a resolution,

(b) circumstances in which a resolution is or is not treated as having been passed, or

(c) cases in which a person is precluded from alleging that a resolution has not been duly passed.

[S281]

NOTES

Commencement: 1 October 2007 (for transitional provisions see the note below).

Transitional provisions, etc: Sch 3, paras 22, 23 to the draft Companies Act 2006 (Commencement No 3, Consequential Amendments, Transitional Provisions and Savings) Order 2007 (at **[A12]**) provides as follows—

"22 General provisions about resolutions (ss 281 to 287)

(1) Sections 281 to 287 of the Companies Act 2006 (general provisions about resolutions), apply—

(a) to written resolutions to which sections 288 to 300 of that Act apply (see paragraph 24);

(b) to resolutions (other than written resolutions)—

(i) of which notice is given on or after 1st October 2007, or

(ii) that are proposed at a meeting of which notice is given on or after 1st October 2007, other than a meeting convened in pursuance of a requisition made under section 368 or 376 of the 1985 Act or Article 376 or 384 of the 1986 Order made before that date.

(2) The provisions of the 1985 Act or 1986 Order continue to apply to resolutions (other than written resolutions)—

(a) of which notice is given before 1st October 2007, or

(b) that are proposed at a meeting—

(i) of which notice was given before 1st October 2007, or

(ii) that is convened in pursuance of a requisition under section 368 or 376 of the 1985 Act or Article 376 or 384 of the 1986 Order made before that date.

(3) The provisions referred to in sub-paragraph (2) include—

section 370(6) of the 1985 Act or Article 378(6) of the 1986 Order (voting entitlement of members); and

section 378 of the 1985 Act or Article 386 of the 1986 Order (extraordinary and special resolutions).

(4) Where notice of a meeting is given over more than one day, it is treated for the purposes of this paragraph as given on the first of those days.

(5) Where copies of a requisition are deposited on more than one day, the references in this paragraph to the day on which the requisition is made shall be read as references to the first day on which the copies deposited are sufficient to require the company to act.

23. Any reference to an extraordinary resolution in a provision—

(a) of a company's memorandum or articles, or

(b) of a contract,

continues to have effect and shall continue to be construed in accordance with section 378 of the 1985 Act or Article 386 of the 1986 Order as if that section or Article had not been repealed.".

282 Ordinary resolutions

(1) An ordinary resolution of the members (or of a class of members) of a company means a resolution that is passed by a simple majority.

(2) A written resolution is passed by a simple majority if it is passed by members representing a simple majority of the total voting rights of eligible members (see Chapter 2).

(3) A resolution passed at a meeting on a show of hands is passed by a simple majority if it is passed by a simple majority of—

(a) the members who, being entitled to do so, vote in person on the resolution, and

(b) the persons who vote on the resolution as duly appointed proxies of members entitled to vote on it.

(4) A resolution passed on a poll taken at a meeting is passed by a simple majority if it is passed by members representing a simple majority of the total voting rights of members who (being entitled to do so) vote in person or by proxy on the resolution.

(5) Anything that may be done by ordinary resolution may also be done by special resolution.

[S282]

NOTES

Commencement: 1 October 2007 (for transitional provisions see the note to s 281).

283 Special resolutions

(1) A special resolution of the members (or of a class of members) of a company means a resolution passed by a majority of not less than 75%.

(2) A written resolution is passed by a majority of not less than 75% if it is passed by members representing not less than 75% of the total voting rights of eligible members (see Chapter 2).

(3) Where a resolution of a private company is passed as a written resolution—
- (a) the resolution is not a special resolution unless it stated that it was proposed as a special resolution, and
- (b) if the resolution so stated, it may only be passed as a special resolution.

(4) A resolution passed at a meeting on a show of hands is passed by a majority of not less than 75% if it is passed by not less than 75% of—
- (a) the members who, being entitled to do so, vote in person on the resolution, and
- (b) the persons who vote on the resolution as duly appointed proxies of members entitled to vote on it.

(5) A resolution passed on a poll taken at a meeting is passed by a majority of not less than 75% if it is passed by members representing not less than 75% of the total voting rights of the members who (being entitled to do so) vote in person or by proxy on the resolution.

(6) Where a resolution is passed at a meeting—
- (a) the resolution is not a special resolution unless the notice of the meeting included the text of the resolution and specified the intention to propose the resolution as a special resolution, and
- (b) if the notice of the meeting so specified, the resolution may only be passed as a special resolution.

[S283]

NOTES

Commencement: 1 October 2007 (for transitional provisions see the note to s 281).

284 Votes: general rules

(1) On a vote on a written resolution—
- (a) in the case of a company having a share capital, every member has one vote in respect of each share or each £10 of stock held by him, and
- (b) in any other case, every member has one vote.

(2) On a vote on a resolution on a show of hands at a meeting—
- (a) every member present in person has one vote, and
- (b) every proxy present who has been duly appointed by a member entitled to vote on the resolution has one vote.

(3) On a vote on a resolution on a poll taken at a meeting—
- (a) in the case of a company having a share capital, every member has one vote in respect of each share or each £10 of stock held by him, and
- (b) in any other case, every member has one vote.

(4) The provisions of this section have effect subject to any provision of the company's articles.

[S284]

NOTES

Commencement: 1 October 2007 (for transitional provisions see the note to s 281).

285 Votes: specific requirements

(1) Where a member entitled to vote on a resolution has appointed one proxy only, and the company's articles provide that the proxy has fewer votes in a vote on a resolution on a show of hands taken at a meeting than the member would have if he were present in person—
- (a) the provision about how many votes the proxy has on a show of hands is void, and
- (b) the proxy has the same number of votes on a show of hands as the member who appointed him would have if he were present at the meeting.

(2) Where a member entitled to vote on a resolution has appointed more than one proxy, subsection (1) applies as if the references to the proxy were references to the proxies taken together.

(3) In relation to a resolution required or authorised by an enactment, if a private company's articles provide that a member has a different number of votes in relation to a resolution when it is passed as a written resolution and when it is passed on a poll taken at a meeting—

(a) the provision about how many votes a member has in relation to the resolution passed on a poll is void, and

(b) a member has the same number of votes in relation to the resolution when it is passed on a poll as he has when it is passed as a written resolution.

[S285]

NOTES

Commencement: 1 October 2007 (for transitional provisions see the note to s 281).

286 Votes of joint holders of shares

(1) In the case of joint holders of shares of a company, only the vote of the senior holder who votes (and any proxies duly authorised by him) may be counted by the company.

(2) For the purposes of this section, the senior holder of a share is determined by the order in which the names of the joint holders appear in the register of members.

(3) Subsections (1) and (2) have effect subject to any provision of the company's articles.

[S286]

NOTES

Commencement: 1 October 2007 (for transitional provisions see the note to s 281).

287 Saving for provisions of articles as to determination of entitlement to vote

Nothing in this Chapter affects—

(a) any provision of a company's articles—

(i) requiring an objection to a person's entitlement to vote on a resolution to be made in accordance with the articles, and

(ii) for the determination of any such objection to be final and conclusive, or

(b) the grounds on which such a determination may be questioned in legal proceedings.

[S287]

NOTES

Commencement: 1 October 2007 (for transitional provisions see the note to s 281).

CHAPTER 2
WRITTEN RESOLUTIONS

General provisions about written resolutions

288 Written resolutions of private companies

(1) In the Companies Acts a "written resolution" means a resolution of a private company proposed and passed in accordance with this Chapter.

(2) The following may not be passed as a written resolution—

(a) a resolution under section 168 removing a director before the expiration of his period of office;

(b) a resolution under section 510 removing an auditor before the expiration of his term of office.

(3) A resolution may be proposed as a written resolution—

(a) by the directors of a private company (see section 291), or

(b) by the members of a private company (see sections 292 to 295).

(4) References in enactments passed or made before this Chapter comes into force to—

(a) a resolution of a company in general meeting, or

(b) a resolution of a meeting of a class of members of the company, have effect as if they included references to a written resolution of the members, or of a class of members, of a private company (as appropriate).

(5) A written resolution of a private company has effect as if passed (as the case may be)—

(a) by the company in general meeting, or

(b) by a meeting of a class of members of the company,

and references in enactments passed or made before this section comes into force to a meeting at which a resolution is passed or to members voting in favour of a resolution shall be construed accordingly.

[S288]

NOTES

Commencement: 1 October 2007 (for transitional provisions etc see the note below).

Transitional provisions, etc: Sch 3, para 24 to the draft Companies Act 2006 (Commencement No 3, Consequential Amendments, Transitional Provisions and Savings) Order 2007 (at **[A12]**) provides as follows—

"**24 Written resolutions** (**ss 288 to 300**)

(1) Sections 288 to 300 of the Companies Act 2006 (written resolutions) apply to resolutions for which the circulation date (see section 290) is on or after 1st October 2007.

(2) Section 381A to 381C of, and Schedule 15A to, the 1985 Act or Article 389A to 389C of, and Schedule 15A to, the 1986 Order continue to apply to resolutions sent or circulated to any relevant member before that date.

A "relevant member" means one whose signature is required by section 381A(1) or Article 389A(1).".

Transitional adaptations: art 6 of the draft Companies Act 2006 (Commencement No 3, Consequential Amendments, Transitional Provisions and Savings) Order 2007 provides that the provisions brought into force by that Order shall have effect subject to any transitional adaptations specified in Sch 1 to that Order. Schedule 1, para 13(1)–(3) to the Order (at **[A12]**) provide as follows—

"**13 Written resolutions** (**ss 288 to 300**)

(1) Section 288 (written resolutions of private companies) has effect with the following adaptations.

(2) In subsection (2) (resolutions that may not be passed as a written resolution)—

(a) in paragraph (b), for "a resolution under section 510" substitute "a resolution under section 391 of the Companies Act 1985 or Article 399 of the Companies (Northern Ireland) Order 1986";

(b) after that paragraph add—

"(c) a resolution under section 80A of the Companies Act 1985 or Article 90A of the Companies (Northern Ireland) Order 1986 revoking, varying or renewing the authority of the directors to allot securities.".

(3) After subsection (5) add—

"(6) A written resolution under any of the provisions of the Companies Act 1985 or the Companies (Northern Ireland) Order 1986 mentioned in sections 300A to 300D is not effective unless the procedural requirements specified in those sections are complied with."".

289 Eligible members

(1) In relation to a resolution proposed as a written resolution of a private company, the eligible members are the members who would have been entitled to vote on the resolution on the circulation date of the resolution (see section 290).

(2) If the persons entitled to vote on a written resolution change during the course of the day that is the circulation date of the resolution, the eligible members are the persons entitled to vote on the resolution at the time that the first copy of the resolution is sent or submitted to a member for his agreement.

[S289]

NOTES

Commencement: 1 October 2007 (for transitional provisions see the note to s 288).

Circulation of written resolutions

290 Circulation date

References in this Part to the circulation date of a written resolution are to the date on which copies of it are sent or submitted to members in accordance with this Chapter (or if copies are sent or submitted to members on different days, to the first of those days).

[S290]

NOTES

Commencement: 1 October 2007 (for transitional provisions see the note to s 288).

291 Circulation of written resolutions proposed by directors

(1) This section applies to a resolution proposed as a written resolution by the directors of the company.

(2) The company must send or submit a copy of the resolution to every eligible member.

(3) The company must do so—

(a) by sending copies at the same time (so far as reasonably practicable) to all eligible members in hard copy form, in electronic form or by means of a website, or

(b) if it is possible to do so without undue delay, by submitting the same copy to each eligible member in turn (or different copies to each of a number of eligible members in turn),

or by sending copies to some members in accordance with paragraph (a) and submitting a copy or copies to other members in accordance with paragraph (b).

(4) The copy of the resolution must be accompanied by a statement informing the member—

(a) how to signify agreement to the resolution (see section 296), and

(b) as to the date by which the resolution must be passed if it is not to lapse (see section 297).

(5) In the event of default in complying with this section, an offence is committed by every officer of the company who is in default.

(6) A person guilty of an offence under this section is liable—

(a) on conviction on indictment, to a fine;

(b) on summary conviction, to a fine not exceeding the statutory maximum.

(7) The validity of the resolution, if passed, is not affected by a failure to comply with this section.

[S291]

NOTES

Commencement: 1 October 2007 (for transitional provisions see the note to s 288).

292 Members' power to require circulation of written resolution

(1) The members of a private company may require the company to circulate a resolution that may properly be moved and is proposed to be moved as a written resolution.

(2) Any resolution may properly be moved as a written resolution unless—

(a) it would, if passed, be ineffective (whether by reason of inconsistency with any enactment or the company's constitution or otherwise),

(b) it is defamatory of any person, or

(c) it is frivolous or vexatious.

(3) Where the members require a company to circulate a resolution they may require the company to circulate with it a statement of not more than 1,000 words on the subject matter of the resolution.

(4) A company is required to circulate the resolution and any accompanying statement once it has received requests that it do so from members representing not less than the requisite percentage of the total voting rights of all members entitled to vote on the resolution.

(5) The "requisite percentage" is 5% or such lower percentage as is specified for this purpose in the company's articles.

(6) A request—

(a) may be in hard copy form or in electronic form,

(b) must identify the resolution and any accompanying statement, and

(c) must be authenticated by the person or persons making it.

[S292]

NOTES

Commencement: 1 October 2007 (for transitional provisions see the note to s 288).

293 Circulation of written resolution proposed by members

(1) A company that is required under section 292 to circulate a resolution must send or submit to every eligible member—

(a) a copy of the resolution, and

(b) a copy of any accompanying statement.

This is subject to section 294(2) (deposit or tender of sum in respect of expenses of circulation) and section 295 (application not to circulate members' statement).

(2) The company must do so—

(a) by sending copies at the same time (so far as reasonably practicable) to all eligible members in hard copy form, in electronic form or by means of a website, or

(b) if it is possible to do so without undue delay, by submitting the same copy to each eligible member in turn (or different copies to each of a number of eligible members in turn),

or by sending copies to some members in accordance with paragraph (a) and submitting a copy or copies to other members in accordance with paragraph (b).

(3) The company must send or submit the copies (or, if copies are sent or submitted to members on different days, the first of those copies) not more than 21 days after it becomes subject to the requirement under section 292 to circulate the resolution.

(4) The copy of the resolution must be accompanied by guidance as to—

(a) how to signify agreement to the resolution (see section 296), and

(b) the date by which the resolution must be passed if it is not to lapse (see section 297).

(5) In the event of default in complying with this section, an offence is committed by every officer of the company who is in default.

(6) A person guilty of an offence under this section is liable—

(a) on conviction on indictment, to a fine;

(b) on summary conviction, to a fine not exceeding the statutory maximum.

(7) The validity of the resolution, if passed, is not affected by a failure to comply with this section.

[S293]

NOTES

Commencement: 1 October 2007 (for transitional provisions see the note to s 288).

294 Expenses of circulation

(1) The expenses of the company in complying with section 293 must be paid by the members who requested the circulation of the resolution unless the company resolves otherwise.

(2) Unless the company has previously so resolved, it is not bound to comply with that section unless there is deposited with or tendered to it a sum reasonably sufficient to meet its expenses in doing so.

[S294]

NOTES

Commencement: 1 October 2007 (for transitional provisions see the note to s 288).

295 Application not to circulate members' statement

(1) A company is not required to circulate a members' statement under section 293 if, on an application by the company or another person who claims to be aggrieved, the court is satisfied that the rights conferred by section 292 and that section are being abused.

(2) The court may order the members who requested the circulation of the statement to pay the whole or part of the company's costs (in Scotland, expenses) on such an application, even if they are not parties to the application.

[S295]

NOTES

Commencement: 1 October 2007 (for transitional provisions see the note to s 288).

Agreeing to written resolutions

296 Procedure for signifying agreement to written resolution

(1) A member signifies his agreement to a proposed written resolution when the company receives from him (or from someone acting on his behalf) an authenticated document—

(a) identifying the resolution to which it relates, and

(b) indicating his agreement to the resolution.

(2) The document must be sent to the company in hard copy form or in electronic form.

(3) A member's agreement to a written resolution, once signified, may not be revoked.

(4) A written resolution is passed when the required majority of eligible members have signified their agreement to it.

[S296]

NOTES

Commencement: 1 October 2007 (for transitional provisions see the note to s 288).

297 Period for agreeing to written resolution

(1) A proposed written resolution lapses if it is not passed before the end of—

(a) the period specified for this purpose in the company's articles, or

(b) if none is specified, the period of 28 days beginning with the circulation date.

(2) The agreement of a member to a written resolution is ineffective if signified after the expiry of that period.

[S297]

NOTES

Commencement: 1 October 2007 (for transitional provisions see the note to s 288).

Supplementary

298 Sending documents relating to written resolutions by electronic means

(1) Where a company has given an electronic address in any document containing or accompanying a proposed written resolution, it is deemed to have agreed that any document or information relating to that resolution may be sent by electronic means to that address (subject to any conditions or limitations specified in the document).

(2) In this section "electronic address" means any address or number used for the purposes of sending or receiving documents or information by electronic means.

[S298]

NOTES

Commencement: 1 October 2007 (for transitional provisions see the note to s 288).

299 Publication of written resolution on website

(1) This section applies where a company sends—

(a) a written resolution, or

(b) a statement relating to a written resolution,

to a person by means of a website.

(2) The resolution or statement is not validly sent for the purposes of this Chapter unless the resolution is available on the website throughout the period beginning with the circulation date and ending on the date on which the resolution lapses under section 297.

[S299]

NOTES

Commencement: 1 October 2007 (for transitional provisions see the note to s 288).

300 Relationship between this Chapter and provisions of company's articles

A provision of the articles of a private company is void in so far as it would have the effect that a resolution that is required by or otherwise provided for in an enactment could not be proposed and passed as a written resolution.

[S300]

NOTES

Commencement: 1 October 2007 (for transitional provisions etc see the note to s 288 and the note below).

Transitional adaptations: art 6 of the draft Companies Act 2006 (Commencement No 3, Consequential Amendments, Transitional Provisions and Savings) Order 2007 provides that the provisions brought into force by that Order shall have effect subject to any transitional adaptations specified in Sch 1 to that Order. Schedule 1, para 13(4) to the Order (at **[A12]**) provides as follows—

"(4) After section 300 insert—

"Transitional application of procedural requirements

300A Disapplication of pre-emption rights

(1) This section applies to a written resolution—

(a) under section 95(2) of the Companies Act 1985 or Article 105(2) of the Companies (Northern Ireland) Order 1986 (disapplication of pre-emption rights), or

(b) renewing a resolution under that provision.

(2) The statement required by section 95(5) of that Act or Article 105(5) of that Order (statement by directors to be circulated with notice of meeting) must be sent or submitted to every eligible member at or before the time at which the resolution is sent or submitted to him.

(3) Section 95(6) of that Act or Article 105(6) of that Order (offences) applies in relation to the inclusion in any such statement of matter that is misleading, false or deceptive in a material particular.

300B Financial assistance for purchase of company's own shares or those of holding company

(1) This section applies to a written resolution under section 155(4) or (5) of the Companies Act 1985 or Article 165(4) or (5) of the Companies (Northern Ireland) Order 1986 (financial assistance for purchase of company's own shares or those of holding company).

(2) The documents referred to in section 157(4)(a) of that Act or Article 167(4)(a) of that Order (documents to be available at meeting) must be sent or submitted to every eligible member at or before the time at which the resolution is sent or submitted to him.

300C Authority for off-market purchase or contingent purchase contract of company's own shares

(1) This section applies to a written resolution—

(a) conferring authority to make an off-market purchase of the company's own shares under section 164(2) of the Companies Act 1985 or Article 174(2) of the Companies (Northern Ireland) Order 1986,

(b) conferring authority to vary a contract for an off-market purchase of the company's own shares under section 164(7) of that Act or Article 174(7) of that Order, or

(c) varying, revoking or renewing any such authority under section 164(3) of that Act or Article 174(3) of that Order.

(2) Section 164(5) of that Act or Article 174(5) of that Order (resolution ineffective if passed by exercise of voting rights by member holding shares to which the resolution relates) does not apply.

But for the purposes of section 289 of this Act (eligible members) a member holding shares to which the resolution relates shall not be regarded as a member who would be entitled to vote on the resolution.

(3) The documents referred to in section 164(6) of that Act or Article 174(6) of that Order (documents to be available at company's registered office and at meeting), and, where that provision applies by virtue of section 164(7) of that Act or Article 174(7) of that Order, the further documents referred to in that provision, must be sent or submitted to every eligible member at or before the time at which the resolution is sent or submitted to him.

(4) Subsections (2) and (3) above also have effect in relation to a written resolution in relation to which the provisions of section 164(3) to (7) of the Companies Act 1985 or Article 174(3) to (7) of the Companies (Northern Ireland) Order 1986 apply by virtue of—

(a) section 165(2) of that Act or Article 175(2) of that Order (authority for contingent purchase contract), or

(b) section 167(2) of that Act or Article 177(2) of that Order (approval for release of rights under contracts approved under section 164 or 165 or Article 174 or 175).

300D Approval for payment out of capital

(1) This section applies to a written resolution giving approval under section 173(2) of the Companies Act 1985 or Article 183(2) of the Companies (Northern Ireland) Order 1986 (redemption or purchase of company's own shares out of capital).

(2) Section 174(2) of that Act or Article 184(2) of that Order (resolution ineffective if passed by exercise of voting rights by member holding shares to which the resolution relates) does not apply.

But for the purposes of section 289 of this Act (eligible members) a member holding shares to which the resolution relates shall not be regarded as a member who would be entitled to vote on the resolution.

(3) The documents referred to in section 174(4) of that Act or Article 184(4) of that Order (documents to be available at meeting) must be sent or submitted to every eligible member at or before the time at which the resolution is sent or submitted to him.".".

CHAPTER 3
RESOLUTIONS AT MEETINGS

General provisions about resolutions at meetings

301 Resolutions at general meetings

A resolution of the members of a company is validly passed at a general meeting if—

(a) notice of the meeting and of the resolution is given, and

(b) the meeting is held and conducted,

in accordance with the provisions of this Chapter (and, where relevant, Chapter 4) and the company's articles.

[S301]

NOTES

Commencement: 1 October 2007.

Calling meetings

302 Directors' power to call general meetings

The directors of a company may call a general meeting of the company.

[S302]

NOTES

Commencement: 1 October 2007.

303 Members' power to require directors to call general meeting

(1) The members of a company may require the directors to call a general meeting of the company.

(2) The directors are required to call a general meeting once the company has received requests to do so from—

(a) members representing at least the required percentage of such of the paid-up capital of the company as carries the right of voting at general meetings of the company (excluding any paid-up capital held as treasury shares); or

(b) in the case of a company not having a share capital, members who represent at least the required percentage of the total voting rights of all the members having a right to vote at general meetings.

(3) The required percentage is 10% unless, in the case of a private company, more than twelve months has elapsed since the end of the last general meeting—

(a) called in pursuance of a requirement under this section, or

(b) in relation to which any members of the company had (by virtue of an enactment, the company's articles or otherwise) rights with respect to the circulation of a resolution no less extensive than they would have had if the meeting had been so called at their request,

in which case the required percentage is 5%.

(4) A request—

(a) must state the general nature of the business to be dealt with at the meeting, and

(b) may include the text of a resolution that may properly be moved and is intended to be moved at the meeting.

(5) A resolution may properly be moved at a meeting unless—

(a) it would, if passed, be ineffective (whether by reason of inconsistency with any enactment or the company's constitution or otherwise),

(b) it is defamatory of any person, or

(c) it is frivolous or vexatious.

(6) A request—

(a) may be in hard copy form or in electronic form, and

(b) must be authenticated by the person or persons making it.

[S303]

NOTES

Commencement: 1 October 2007 (for transitional provisions see the note below).

Transitional provisions, etc: Sch 3, para 25 to the draft Companies Act 2006 (Commencement No 3, Consequential Amendments, Transitional Provisions and Savings) Order 2007 (at **[A12]**) provides as follows—

"25 Members' power to require directors to call meeting (ss 303 to 305)

(1) Sections 303 to 305 of the Companies Act 2006 (meetings required by members) apply to requests made on or after 1st October 2007.

(2) Section 368 of the 1985 Act or Article 376 of the 1986 Order continues to apply to requisitions made before that date.

(3) Where requests are made or copies of a requisition are deposited on more than one day, the references in this paragraph to the day on which the request or requisition is made shall be read as references to the first day on which the requests made or copies deposited are sufficient to require the company to act.".

304 Directors' duty to call meetings required by members

(1) Directors required under section 303 to call a general meeting of the company must call a meeting—

(a) within 21 days from the date on which they become subject to the requirement, and

(b) to be held on a date not more than 28 days after the date of the notice convening the meeting.

(2) If the requests received by the company identify a resolution intended to be moved at the meeting, the notice of the meeting must include notice of the resolution.

(3) The business that may be dealt with at the meeting includes a resolution of which notice is given in accordance with this section.

(4) If the resolution is to be proposed as a special resolution, the directors are treated as not having duly called the meeting if they do not give the required notice of the resolution in accordance with section 283.

[S304]

NOTES

Commencement: 1 October 2007 (for transitional provisions see the note to s 303).

305 Power of members to call meeting at company's expense

(1) If the directors—

(a) are required under section 303 to call a meeting, and

(b) do not do so in accordance with section 304,

the members who requested the meeting, or any of them representing more than one half of the total voting rights of all of them, may themselves call a general meeting.

(2) Where the requests received by the company included the text of a resolution intended to be moved at the meeting, the notice of the meeting must include notice of the resolution.

(3) The meeting must be called for a date not more than three months after the date on which the directors become subject to the requirement to call a meeting.

(4) The meeting must be called in the same manner, as nearly as possible, as that in which meetings are required to be called by directors of the company.

(5) The business which may be dealt with at the meeting includes a resolution of which notice is given in accordance with this section.

(6) Any reasonable expenses incurred by the members requesting the meeting by reason of the failure of the directors duly to call a meeting must be reimbursed by the company.

(7) Any sum so reimbursed shall be retained by the company out of any sums due or to become due from the company by way of fees or other remuneration in respect of the services of such of the directors as were in default.

[S305]

NOTES

Commencement: 1 October 2007 (for transitional provisions see the note to s 303).

306 Power of court to order meeting

(1) This section applies if for any reason it is impracticable—

(a) to call a meeting of a company in any manner in which meetings of that company may be called, or

(b) to conduct the meeting in the manner prescribed by the company's articles or this Act.

(2) The court may, either of its own motion or on the application—

(a) of a director of the company, or

(b) of a member of the company who would be entitled to vote at the meeting,

order a meeting to be called, held and conducted in any manner the court thinks fit.

(3) Where such an order is made, the court may give such ancillary or consequential directions as it thinks expedient.

(4) Such directions may include a direction that one member of the company present at the meeting be deemed to constitute a quorum.

(5) A meeting called, held and conducted in accordance with an order under this section is deemed for all purposes to be a meeting of the company duly called, held and conducted.

[S306]

NOTES

Commencement: 1 October 2007 (for transitional adaptations see the notes below).

Transitional adaptations: art 6 of the draft Companies Act 2006 (Commencement No 3, Consequential Amendments, Transitional Provisions and Savings) Order 2007 provides that the provisions brought into force by that Order shall have effect subject to any transitional adaptations specified in Sch 1 to that Order. Schedule 1, para 14 to the Order (at **[A12]**) provides as follows—

"**14 Resolutions at meetings (ss 301 to 335)**

(1) Section 306 (power of court to order meeting) has effect with the following adaptation.

(2) In subsection (1)(b) for "or this Act" substitute "this Act, the Companies Act 1985 or the Companies (Northern Ireland) Order 1986".".

Notice of meetings

307 Notice required of general meeting

(1) A general meeting of a private company (other than an adjourned meeting) must be called by notice of at least 14 days.

(2) A general meeting of a public company (other than an adjourned meeting) must be called by notice of—

(a) in the case of an annual general meeting, at least 21 days, and

(b) in any other case, at least 14 days.

(3) The company's articles may require a longer period of notice than that specified in subsection (1) or (2).

(4) A general meeting may be called by shorter notice than that otherwise required if shorter notice is agreed by the members.

(5) The shorter notice must be agreed to by a majority in number of the members having a right to attend and vote at the meeting, being a majority who—

(a) together hold not less than the requisite percentage in nominal value of the shares giving a right to attend and vote at the meeting (excluding any shares in the company held as treasury shares), or

(b) in the case of a company not having a share capital, together represent not less than the requisite percentage of the total voting rights at that meeting of all the members.

(6) The requisite percentage is—

(a) in the case of a private company, 90% or such higher percentage (not exceeding 95%) as may be specified in the company's articles;

(b) in the case of a public company, 95%.

(7) Subsections (5) and (6) do not apply to an annual general meeting of a public company (see instead section 337(2)).

[S307]

NOTES

Commencement: 1 October 2007 (for transitional provisions see the note below).

Transitional provisions, etc: Sch 3, para 26 to the draft Companies Act 2006 (Commencement No 3, Consequential Amendments, Transitional Provisions and Savings) Order 2007 (at **[A12]**) provides as follows—

"**26 Notice of meetings (ss 307, 310 and 311)**

(1) Sections 307, 310 and 311 of the Companies Act 2006 (notice of meetings) apply in relation to meetings of which notice is given on or after 1st October 2007.

(2) The provisions of the 1985 Act or the 1986 Order continue to apply in relation to a meeting of which notice was given before that date.

(3) The provisions referred to in sub-paragraph (2) include sections 369 and 370(2) of the 1985 Act or Articles 377 and 378(2) of the 1986 Order.

(4) Where notice of a meeting is given over more than one day, it is treated for the purposes of this paragraph as given on the first of those days.".

308 Manner in which notice to be given

Notice of a general meeting of a company must be given—

(a) in hard copy form,

(b) in electronic form, or
(c) by means of a website (see section 309),

or partly by one such means and partly by another.

[S308]

NOTES

Commencement: 20 January 2007.

309 Publication of notice of meeting on website

(1) Notice of a meeting is not validly given by a company by means of a website unless it is given in accordance with this section.

(2) When the company notifies a member of the presence of the notice on the website the notification must—

(a) state that it concerns a notice of a company meeting,
(b) specify the place, date and time of the meeting, and
(c) in the case of a public company, state whether the meeting will be an annual general meeting.

(3) The notice must be available on the website throughout the period beginning with the date of that notification and ending with the conclusion of the meeting.

[S309]

NOTES

Commencement: 20 January 2007.

310 Persons entitled to receive notice of meetings

(1) Notice of a general meeting of a company must be sent to—

(a) every member of the company, and
(b) every director.

(2) In subsection (1), the reference to members includes any person who is entitled to a share in consequence of the death or bankruptcy of a member, if the company has been notified of their entitlement.

(3) In subsection (2), the reference to the bankruptcy of a member includes—

(a) the sequestration of the estate of a member;
(b) a member's estate being the subject of a protected trust deed (within the meaning of the Bankruptcy (Scotland) Act 1985 (c 66)).

(4) This section has effect subject to—

(a) any enactment, and
(b) any provision of the company's articles.

[S310]

NOTES

Commencement: 1 October 2007 (for transitional provisions see the note to s 307).

311 Contents of notices of meetings

(1) Notice of a general meeting of a company must state—

(a) the time and date of the meeting, and
(b) the place of the meeting.

(2) Notice of a general meeting of a company must state the general nature of the business to be dealt with at the meeting.

This subsection has effect subject to any provision of the company's articles.

[S311]

NOTES

Commencement: 1 October 2007 (for transitional provisions see the note to s 307).

312 Resolution requiring special notice

(1) Where by any provision of the Companies Acts special notice is required of a resolution, the resolution is not effective unless notice of the intention to move it has been given to the company at least 28 days before the meeting at which it is moved.

(2) The company must, where practicable, give its members notice of any such resolution in the same manner and at the same time as it gives notice of the meeting.

(3) Where that is not practicable, the company must give its members notice at least 14 days before the meeting—

(a) by advertisement in a newspaper having an appropriate circulation, or

(b) in any other manner allowed by the company's articles.

(4) If, after notice of the intention to move such a resolution has been given to the company, a meeting is called for a date 28 days or less after the notice has been given, the notice is deemed to have been properly given, though not given within the time required.

[S312]

NOTES

Commencement: 1 October 2007 (for transitional provisions see the note below).

Transitional provisions, etc: Sch 3, para 27 to the draft Companies Act 2006 (Commencement No 3, Consequential Amendments, Transitional Provisions and Savings) Order 2007 (at **[A12]**) provides as follows—

"**27 Special notice** (s 312)

(1) Section 312 of the Companies Act 2006 (special notice) applies in relation to resolutions for which special notice is required where notice of the intention to move the resolution is given to the company on or after 1st October 2007.

(2) Section 379 of the 1985 Act or Article 387 of the 1986 Order continues to apply to resolutions for which special notice is required where notice of the intention to move the resolution is given to the company before that date.".

313 Accidental failure to give notice of resolution or meeting

(1) Where a company gives notice of—

(a) a general meeting, or

(b) a resolution intended to be moved at a general meeting,

any accidental failure to give notice to one or more persons shall be disregarded for the purpose of determining whether notice of the meeting or resolution (as the case may be) is duly given.

(2) Except in relation to notice given under—

(a) section 304 (notice of meetings required by members),

(b) section 305 (notice of meetings called by members), or

(c) section 339 (notice of resolutions at AGMs proposed by members),

subsection (1) has effect subject to any provision of the company's articles.

[S313]

NOTES

Commencement: 1 October 2007 (for transitional provisions see the note below).

Transitional provisions, etc: Sch 3, para 28 to the draft Companies Act 2006 (Commencement No 3, Consequential Amendments, Transitional Provisions and Savings) Order 2007 (at **[A12]**) provides as follows—

"**28 Accidental failure to give notice of resolution or meeting** (s 313)

(1) Section 313 of the Companies Act 2006 (accidental failure to give notice of resolution or meeting) applies to resolutions or meetings of which notice is given on or after 1st October 2007.

(2) The reference in sub-paragraph (1) to cases in which notice is given on or after 1st October 2007 includes cases in which notice would be regarded as so given if section 313 applied.".

Members' statements

314 Members' power to require circulation of statements

(1) The members of a company may require the company to circulate, to members of the company entitled to receive notice of a general meeting, a statement of not more than 1,000 words with respect to—

(a) a matter referred to in a proposed resolution to be dealt with at that meeting, or
(b) other business to be dealt with at that meeting.

(2) A company is required to circulate a statement once it has received requests to do so from—

(a) members representing at least 5% of the total voting rights of all the members who have a relevant right to vote (excluding any voting rights attached to any shares in the company held as treasury shares), or
(b) at least 100 members who have a relevant right to vote and hold shares in the company on which there has been paid up an average sum, per member, of at least £100.

See also section 153 (exercise of rights where shares held on behalf of others).

(3) In subsection (2), a "relevant right to vote" means—

(a) in relation to a statement with respect to a matter referred to in a proposed resolution, a right to vote on that resolution at the meeting to which the requests relate, and
(b) in relation to any other statement, a right to vote at the meeting to which the requests relate.

(4) A request—

(a) may be in hard copy form or in electronic form,
(b) must identify the statement to be circulated,
(c) must be authenticated by the person or persons making it, and
(d) must be received by the company at least one week before the meeting to which it relates.

[S314]

NOTES

Commencement: 1 October 2007 (for transitional provisions see the note below).

Transitional provisions, etc: Sch 3, para 29 to the draft Companies Act 2006 (Commencement No 3, Consequential Amendments, Transitional Provisions and Savings) Order 2007 (at **[A12]**) provides as follows—

"29 Circulation of members' statements (ss 314 to 317)

(1) Sections 314 to 317 of the Companies Act 2006 (circulation of members' statements) apply to requests made on or after 1st October 2007.

(2) Sections 376 and 377 of the 1985 Act or Articles 384 and 385 of the 1986 Order continue to apply in relation to requisitions made before that date.

(3) So long as such a requisition made to a private company under section 376(1)(b) or Article 384(1)(b) is not complied with, section 366 of the 1985 Act or Article 374 of the 1986 Order (duty to hold annual general meeting) continues to apply in relation to the company.

This does not apply if the company is not required to comply with the requisition (see section 377 of the 1985 Act or Article 385 of the 1986 Order).

(4) Where requests are made or copies of a requisition are deposited on more than one day, the references in this paragraph to the day on which the request or requisition is made shall be read as references to the first day on which the requests made or copies deposited are sufficient to require the company to act.".

315 Company's duty to circulate members' statement

(1) A company that is required under section 314, to circulate a statement must send a copy of it to each member of the company entitled to receive notice of the meeting—

(a) in the same manner as the notice of the meeting, and
(b) at the same time as, or as soon as reasonably practicable after, it gives notice of the meeting.

(2) Subsection (1) has effect subject to section 316(2) (deposit or tender of sum in respect of expenses of circulation) and section 317 (application not to circulate members' statement).

(3) In the event of default in complying with this section, an offence is committed by every officer of the company who is in default.

(4) A person guilty of an offence under this section is liable—
- (a) on conviction on indictment, to a fine;
- (b) on summary conviction, to a fine not exceeding the statutory maximum.

[S315]

NOTES

Commencement: 1 October 2007 (for transitional provisions see the note to s 314).

316 Expenses of circulating members' statement

(1) The expenses of the company in complying with section 315 need not be paid by the members who requested the circulation of the statement if—
- (a) the meeting to which the requests relate is an annual general meeting of a public company, and
- (b) requests sufficient to require the company to circulate the statement are received before the end of the financial year preceding the meeting.

(2) Otherwise—
- (a) the expenses of the company in complying with that section must be paid by the members who requested the circulation of the statement unless the company resolves otherwise, and
- (b) unless the company has previously so resolved, it is not bound to comply with that section unless there is deposited with or tendered to it, not later than one week before the meeting, a sum reasonably sufficient to meet its expenses in doing so.

[S316]

NOTES

Commencement: 1 October 2007 (for transitional provisions see the note to s 314).

317 Application not to circulate members' statement

(1) A company is not required to circulate a members' statement under section 315 if, on an application by the company or another person who claims to be aggrieved, the court is satisfied that the rights conferred by section 314 and that section are being abused.

(2) The court may order the members who requested the circulation of the statement to pay the whole or part of the company's costs (in Scotland, expenses) on such an application, even if they are not parties to the application.

[S317]

NOTES

Commencement: 1 October 2007 (for transitional provisions see the note to s 314).

Procedure at meetings

318 Quorum at meetings

(1) In the case of a company limited by shares or guarantee and having only one member, one qualifying person present at a meeting is a quorum.

(2) In any other case, subject to the provisions of the company's articles, two qualifying persons present at a meeting are a quorum, unless—
- (a) each is a qualifying person only because he is authorised under section 323 to act as the representative of a corporation in relation to the meeting, and they are representatives of the same corporation; or
- (b) each is a qualifying person only because he is appointed as proxy of a member in relation to the meeting, and they are proxies of the same member.

(3) For the purposes of this section a "qualifying person" means—
(a) an individual who is a member of the company,
(b) a person authorised under section 323 (representation of corporations at meetings) to act as the representative of a corporation in relation to the meeting, or
(c) a person appointed as proxy of a member in relation to the meeting.

[S318]

NOTES

Commencement: 1 October 2007 (for transitional provisions see the note below).

Transitional provisions, etc: Sch 3, para 30 to the draft Companies Act 2006 (Commencement No 3, Consequential Amendments, Transitional Provisions and Savings) Order 2007 (at **[A12]**) provides as follows—

"**30 Procedure at meetings and proxies (ss 318 to 331)**

(1) Sections 318 to 323 of the Companies Act 2006 (procedure at meetings) and sections 324 to 331 (proxies) apply to meetings of which notice is given on or after 1st October 2007.

(2) The provisions of the 1985 Act or the 1986 Order continue to apply to meetings of which notice was given before that date.

(3) The provisions referred to in sub-paragraph (2) include sections 370, 370A, 372 to 375 and 378(4) of the 1985 Act or Articles 378, 378A, 380 to 383 and 386(4) of the 1986 Order.

(4) Where notice of a meeting is given over more than one day, it is treated for the purposes of this paragraph as given on the first of those days.".

319 Chairman of meeting

(1) A member may be elected to be the chairman of a general meeting by a resolution of the company passed at the meeting.

(2) Subsection (1) is subject to any provision of the company's articles that states who may or may not be chairman.

[S319]

NOTES

Commencement: 1 October 2007 (for transitional provisions see the note to s 318).

320 Declaration by chairman on a show of hands

(1) On a vote on a resolution at a meeting on a show of hands, a declaration by the chairman that the resolution—
(a) has or has not been passed, or
(b) passed with a particular majority,
is conclusive evidence of that fact without proof of the number or proportion of the votes recorded in favour of or against the resolution.

(2) An entry in respect of such a declaration in minutes of the meeting recorded in accordance with section 355 is also conclusive evidence of that fact without such proof.

(3) This section does not have effect if a poll is demanded in respect of the resolution (and the demand is not subsequently withdrawn).

[S320]

NOTES

Commencement: 1 October 2007 (for transitional provisions see the note to s 318).

321 Right to demand a poll

(1) A provision of a company's articles is void in so far as it would have the effect of excluding the right to demand a poll at a general meeting on any question other than—
(a) the election of the chairman of the meeting, or
(b) the adjournment of the meeting.

(2) A provision of a company's articles is void in so far as it would have the effect of making ineffective a demand for a poll on any such question which is made—
(a) by not less than 5 members having the right to vote on the resolution; or

(b) by a member or members representing not less than 10% of the total voting rights of all the members having the right to vote on the resolution (excluding any voting rights attached to any shares in the company held as treasury shares); or

(c) by a member or members holding shares in the company conferring a right to vote on the resolution, being shares on which an aggregate sum has been paid up equal to not less than 10% of the total sum paid up on all the shares conferring that right (excluding shares in the company conferring a right to vote on the resolution which are held as treasury shares).

[S321]

NOTES

Commencement: 1 October 2007 (for transitional provisions see the note to s 318).

322 Voting on a poll

On a poll taken at a general meeting of a company, a member entitled to more than one vote need not, if he votes, use all his votes or cast all the votes he uses in the same way.

[S322]

NOTES

Commencement: 1 October 2007 (for transitional provisions see the note to s 318).

323 Representation of corporations at meetings

(1) If a corporation (whether or not a company within the meaning of this Act) is a member of a company, it may by resolution of its directors or other governing body authorise a person or persons to act as its representative or representatives at any meeting of the company.

(2) Where the corporation authorises only one person, he is entitled to exercise the same powers on behalf of the corporation as the corporation could exercise if it were an individual member of the company.

(3) Where the corporation authorises more than one person, any one of them is entitled to exercise the same powers on behalf of the corporation as the corporation could exercise if it were an individual member of the company.

(4) Where the corporation authorises more than one person and more than one of them purport to exercise a power under subsection (3)—

(a) if they purport to exercise the power in the same way, the power is treated as exercised in that way,

(b) if they do not purport to exercise the power in the same way, the power is treated as not exercised.

[S323]

NOTES

Commencement: 1 October 2007 (for transitional provisions see the note to s 318).

Proxies

324 Rights to appoint proxies

(1) A member of a company is entitled to appoint another person as his proxy to exercise all or any of his rights to attend and to speak and vote at a meeting of the company.

(2) In the case of a company having a share capital, a member may appoint more than one proxy in relation to a meeting, provided that each proxy is appointed to exercise the rights attached to a different share or shares held by him, or (as the case may be) to a different £10, or multiple of £10, of stock held by him.

[S324]

NOTES

Commencement: 1 October 2007 (for transitional provisions see the note to s 318).

325 Notice of meeting to contain statement of rights

(1) In every notice calling a meeting of a company there must appear, with reasonable prominence, a statement informing the member of—

(a) his rights under section 324, and

(b) any more extensive rights conferred by the company's articles to appoint more than one proxy.

(2) Failure to comply with this section does not affect the validity of the meeting or of anything done at the meeting.

(3) If this section is not complied with as respects any meeting, an offence is committed by every officer of the company who is in default.

(4) A person guilty of an offence under this section is liable on summary conviction to a fine not exceeding level 3 on the standard scale.

[S325]

NOTES

Commencement: 1 October 2007 (for transitional provisions see the note to s 318).

326 Company-sponsored invitations to appoint proxies

(1) If for the purposes of a meeting there are issued at the company's expense invitations to members to appoint as proxy a specified person or a number of specified persons, the invitations must be issued to all members entitled to vote at the meeting.

(2) Subsection (1) is not contravened if—

(a) there is issued to a member at his request a form of appointment naming the proxy or a list of persons willing to act as proxy, and

(b) the form or list is available on request to all members entitled to vote at the meeting.

(3) If subsection (1) is contravened as respects a meeting, an offence is committed by every officer of the company who is in default.

(4) A person guilty of an offence under this section is liable on summary conviction to a fine not exceeding level 3 on the standard scale.

[S326]

NOTES

Commencement: 1 October 2007 (for transitional provisions see the note to s 318).

327 Notice required of appointment of proxy etc

(1) This section applies to—

(a) the appointment of a proxy, and

(b) any document necessary to show the validity of, or otherwise relating to, the appointment of a proxy.

(2) Any provision of the company's articles is void in so far as it would have the effect of requiring any such appointment or document to be received by the company or another person earlier than the following time—

(a) in the case of a meeting or adjourned meeting, 48 hours before the time for holding the meeting or adjourned meeting;

(b) in the case of a poll taken more than 48 hours after it was demanded, 24 hours before the time appointed for the taking of the poll;

(c) in the case of a poll taken not more than 48 hours after it was demanded, the time at which it was demanded.

(3) In calculating the periods mentioned in subsection (2) no account shall be taken of any part of a day that is not a working day.

[S327]

NOTES

Commencement: 1 October 2007 (except sub-s (2)(c)); to be appointed (otherwise) (for transitional provisions see the note to s 318).

328 Chairing meetings

(1) A proxy may be elected to be the chairman of a general meeting by a resolution of the company passed at the meeting.

(2) Subsection (1) is subject to any provision of the company's articles that states who may or who may not be chairman.

[S328]

NOTES

Commencement: 1 October 2007 (for transitional provisions see the note to s 318).

329 Right of proxy to demand a poll

(1) The appointment of a proxy to vote on a matter at a meeting of a company authorises the proxy to demand, or join in demanding, a poll on that matter.

(2) In applying the provisions of section 321(2) (requirements for effective demand), a demand by a proxy counts—

(a) for the purposes of paragraph (a), as a demand by the member;
(b) for the purposes of paragraph (b), as a demand by a member representing the voting rights that the proxy is authorised to exercise;
(c) for the purposes of paragraph (c), as a demand by a member holding the shares to which those rights are attached.

[S329]

NOTES

Commencement: 1 October 2007 (for transitional provisions see the note to s 318).

330 Notice required of termination of proxy's authority

(1) This section applies to notice that the authority of a person to act as proxy is terminated ("notice of termination").

(2) The termination of the authority of a person to act as proxy does not affect—

(a) whether he counts in deciding whether there is a quorum at a meeting,
(b) the validity of anything he does as chairman of a meeting, or
(c) the validity of a poll demanded by him at a meeting,

unless the company receives notice of the termination before the commencement of the meeting.

(3) The termination of the authority of a person to act as proxy does not affect the validity of a vote given by that person unless the company receives notice of the termination—

(a) before the commencement of the meeting or adjourned meeting at which the vote is given, or
(b) in the case of a poll taken more than 48 hours after it is demanded, before the time appointed for taking the poll.

(4) If the company's articles require or permit members to give notice of termination to a person other than the company, the references above to the company receiving notice have effect as if they were or (as the case may be) included a reference to that person.

(5) Subsections (2) and (3) have effect subject to any provision of the company's articles which has the effect of requiring notice of termination to be received by the company or another person at a time earlier than that specified in those subsections.

This is subject to subsection (6).

(6) Any provision of the company's articles is void in so far as it would have the effect of requiring notice of termination to be received by the company or another person earlier than the following time—

(a) in the case of a meeting or adjourned meeting, 48 hours before the time for holding the meeting or adjourned meeting;
(b) in the case of a poll taken more than 48 hours after it was demanded, 24 hours before the time appointed for the taking of the poll;
(c) in the case of a poll taken not more than 48 hours after it was demanded, the time at which it was demanded.

(7) In calculating the periods mentioned in subsections (3)(b) and (6) no account shall be taken of any part of a day that is not a working day.

[S330]

NOTES

Commencement: 1 October 2007 (except sub-s (6)(c)); to be appointed (otherwise) (for transitional provisions see the note to s 318).

331 Saving for more extensive rights conferred by articles

Nothing in sections 324 to 330 (proxies) prevents a company's articles from conferring more extensive rights on members or proxies than are conferred by those sections.

[S331]

NOTES

Commencement: 1 October 2007 (for transitional provisions see the note to s 318).

Adjourned meetings

332 Resolution passed at adjourned meeting

Where a resolution is passed at an adjourned meeting of a company, the resolution is for all purposes to be treated as having been passed on the date on which it was in fact passed, and is not to be deemed passed on any earlier date.

[S332]

NOTES

Commencement: 1 October 2007.

Electronic communications

333 Sending documents relating to meetings etc in electronic form

(1) Where a company has given an electronic address in a notice calling a meeting, it is deemed to have agreed that any document or information relating to proceedings at the meeting may be sent by electronic means to that address (subject to any conditions or limitations specified in the notice).

(2) Where a company has given an electronic address—

(a) in an instrument of proxy sent out by the company in relation to the meeting, or

(b) in an invitation to appoint a proxy issued by the company in relation to the meeting,

it is deemed to have agreed that any document or information relating to proxies for that meeting may be sent by electronic means to that address (subject to any conditions or limitations specified in the notice).

(3) In subsection (2), documents relating to proxies include—

(a) the appointment of a proxy in relation to a meeting,

(b) any document necessary to show the validity of, or otherwise relating to, the appointment of a proxy, and

(c) notice of the termination of the authority of a proxy.

(4) In this section "electronic address" means any address or number used for the purposes of sending or receiving documents or information by electronic means.

[S333]

NOTES

Commencement: 20 January 2007.

Application to class meetings

334 Application to class meetings

(1) The provisions of this Chapter apply (with necessary modifications) in relation to a meeting of holders of a class of shares as they apply in relation to a general meeting.

This is subject to subsections (2) and (3).

(2) The following provisions of this Chapter do not apply in relation to a meeting of holders of a class of shares—

(a) sections 303 to 305 (members' power to require directors to call general meeting), and

(b) section 306 (power of court to order meeting).

(3) The following provisions (in addition to those mentioned in subsection (2)) do not apply in relation to a meeting in connection with the variation of rights attached to a class of shares (a "variation of class rights meeting")—

(a) section 318 (quorum), and

(b) section 321 (right to demand a poll).

(4) The quorum for a variation of class rights meeting is—

(a) for a meeting other than an adjourned meeting, two persons present holding at least one-third in nominal value of the issued shares of the class in question (excluding any shares of that class held as treasury shares);

(b) for an adjourned meeting, one person present holding shares of the class in question.

(5) For the purposes of subsection (4), where a person is present by proxy or proxies, he is treated as holding only the shares in respect of which those proxies are authorised to exercise voting rights.

(6) At a variation of class rights meeting, any holder of shares of the class in question present may demand a poll.

(7) For the purposes of this section—

(a) any amendment of a provision contained in a company's articles for the variation of the rights attached to a class of shares, or the insertion of any such provision into the articles, is itself to be treated as a variation of those rights, and

(b) references to the variation of rights attached to a class of shares include references to their abrogation.

[S334]

NOTES

Commencement: 1 October 2007 (for transitional provisions see the note below).

Transitional provisions, etc: Sch 3, para 31 to the draft Companies Act 2006 (Commencement No 3, Consequential Amendments, Transitional Provisions and Savings) Order 2007 (at **[A12]**) provides as follows—

"**31 Application of provisions to class meetings (ss 334 and 335)**

(1) Sections 334 and 335 of the Companies Act 2006 (application of provisions of Chapter 3 to class meetings) apply to requests and meetings in relation to which the provisions applied by those sections have effect.

(2) Section 125(6) of the 1985 Act or Article 135(6) of the 1986 Order continues to apply to meetings of which notice is given before 1st October 2007.

(3) Where notice of a meeting is given over more than one day, it is treated for the purposes of sub-paragraph (2) as given on the first of those days.".

335 Application to class meetings: companies without a share capital

(1) The provisions of this Chapter apply (with necessary modifications) in relation to a meeting of a class of members of a company without a share capital as they apply in relation to a general meeting.

This is subject to subsections (2) and (3).

(2) The following provisions of this Chapter do not apply in relation to a meeting of a class of members—

(a) sections 303 to 305 (members' power to require directors to call general meeting), and
(b) section 306 (power of court to order meeting).

(3) The following provisions (in addition to those mentioned in subsection (2)) do not apply in relation to a meeting in connection with the variation of the rights of a class of members (a "variation of class rights meeting")—
(a) section 318 (quorum), and
(b) section 321 (right to demand a poll).

(4) The quorum for a variation of class rights meeting is—
(a) for a meeting other than an adjourned meeting, two members of the class present (in person or by proxy) who together represent at least one-third of the voting rights of the class;
(b) for an adjourned meeting, one member of the class present (in person or by proxy).

(5) At a variation of class rights meeting, any member present (in person or by proxy) may demand a poll.

(6) For the purposes of this section—
(a) any amendment of a provision contained in a company's articles for the variation of the rights of a class of members, or the insertion of any such provision into the articles, is itself to be treated as a variation of those rights, and
(b) references to the variation of rights of a class of members include references to their abrogation.

[S335]

NOTES

Commencement: 1 October 2007 (for transitional provisions see the note to s 334).

CHAPTER 4
PUBLIC COMPANIES: ADDITIONAL REQUIREMENTS FOR AGMS

336 Public companies: annual general meeting

(1) Every public company must hold a general meeting as its annual general meeting in each period of 6 months beginning with the day following its accounting reference date (in addition to any other meetings held during that period).

(2) A company that fails to comply with subsection (1) as a result of giving notice under section 392 (alteration of accounting reference date)—
(a) specifying a new accounting reference date, and
(b) stating that the current accounting reference period or the previous accounting reference period is to be shortened,

shall be treated as if it had complied with subsection (1) if it holds a general meeting as its annual general meeting within 3 months of giving that notice.

(3) If a company fails to comply with subsection (1), an offence is committed by every officer of the company who is in default.

(4) A person guilty of an offence under this section is liable—
(a) on conviction on indictment, to a fine;
(b) on summary conviction, to a fine not exceeding the statutory maximum.

[S336]

NOTES

Commencement: 1 October 2007 (for transitional provisions etc see the note below).

Transitional provisions, etc: Sch 3, paras 32–38 to the draft Companies Act 2006 (Commencement No 3, Consequential Amendments, Transitional Provisions and Savings) Order 2007 (at **[A12]**) provides as follows—

"**32 Annual general meetings** (**ss 336 to 340**)

(1) The repeal of section 366 of the 1985 Act or Article 374 of the 1986 Order (duty to hold annual general meeting) does not affect any provision of a private company's memorandum or articles that expressly requires the company to hold an annual general meeting.

(2) Any such provision continues to have such effect as it had immediately before 1st October 2007.

(3) Provision specifying that one or more directors are to retire at an annual general meeting of the company is not provision expressly requiring the company to hold an annual general meeting.

33. The repeal of section 367 of the 1985 Act (default power of Secretary of State to call AGM) has effect in relation to a private company as from 1st October 2007, even if an application under that section has been made, or the Secretary of State has called or directed the calling of a meeting under that section, before that date.

34.—(1) The repeal of sections 376 and 377 of the 1985 Act or Articles 384 and 385 of the 1986 Order does not affect their application in relation to a requisition under section 376(1)(a) or Article 384(1)(a) made to a private company before 1st October 2007.

(2) So long as such a requisition has not been complied with, section 366 of the 1985 Act or Article 374 of the 1986 Order (duty to hold annual general meeting) continues to apply in relation to the company.

This does not apply if the company is not required to comply with the requisition (see section 377 of the 1985 Act or Article 385 of the 1986 Order).

(3) Where copies of the requisition are deposited on more than one day, the reference in sub-paragraph (1) to the day on which the request or requisition is made shall be read as a reference to the first day on which the copies deposited are sufficient to require the company to act.

35.—(1) In the case of an existing public company—
- (a) section 366 of the 1985 Act or section 374 of the 1986 Order (duty to hold annual general meeting) continues to apply to determine the date by which the company must hold its first annual general meeting after 30th September 2007, and
- (b) section 336 of the Companies Act 2006 (public companies: annual general meeting) applies in relation to subsequent annual general meetings.

(2) An "existing public company" means a company formed and registered before 1st October 2007 that is a public company immediately before that date.

36. The repeal of section 367 of the 1985 Act (default power of Secretary of State to call AGM) does not affect the operation of that section in relation to a public company where an application under that section was made before 1st October 2007.

37.—(1) Section 337 of the Companies Act 2006 (public companies: notice of AGM) applies to meetings of which notice is given on or after 1st October 2007.

(2) Section 369 of the 1985 Act or Article 377 of the 1986 Order continues to apply in relation to meetings of which notice is given before that date.

(3) Where notice of a meeting is given over more than one day, it is treated for the purposes of this paragraph as given on the first of those days.

38.—(1) Sections 338 to 340 of the Companies Act 2006 (public companies: members' power to require circulation of resolutions for AGMs) apply to requests made on or after 1st October 2007.

(2) Sections 376 and 377 of the 1985 Act or Articles 384 and 385 of the 1986 Order continue to apply to requisitions made to a public company before that date.

(3) Where requests are made or copies of a requisition are deposited on more than one day, the references in this paragraph to the day on which the request or requisition is made shall be read as references to the first day on which the requests made or copies deposited are sufficient to require the company to act.".

Transitional adaptations: art 6 of the draft Companies Act 2006 (Commencement No 3, Consequential Amendments, Transitional Provisions and Savings) Order 2007 provides that the provisions brought into force by that Order shall have effect subject to any transitional adaptations specified in Sch 1 to that Order. Schedule 1, para 15 to the Order (at **[A12]**) provides as follows—

"15 Public companies: additional requirements for AGMs (**ss 336 to 340**)

(1) Section 336 (public companies: annual general meeting) has effect with the following adaptations.

(2) In subsection (1), for "6 months" substitute "7 months".

(3) In subsection (2), for "notice under section 392 (alteration of accounting reference date)" substitute "notice under section 225 of the Companies Act 1985 or Article 233 of the Companies (Northern Ireland) Order 1986 (alteration of accounting reference date)".".

337 Public companies: notice of AGM

(1) A notice calling an annual general meeting of a public company must state that the meeting is an annual general meeting.

(2) An annual general meeting may be called by shorter notice than that required by section 307(2) or by the company's articles (as the case may be), if all the members entitled to attend and vote at the meeting agree to the shorter notice.

[S337]

NOTES

Commencement: 1 October 2007 (for transitional provisions see the note to s 336).

338 Public companies: members' power to require circulation of resolutions for AGMs

(1) The members of a public company may require the company to give, to members of the company entitled to receive notice of the next annual general meeting, notice of a resolution which may properly be moved and is intended to be moved at that meeting.

(2) A resolution may properly be moved at an annual general meeting unless—

- (a) it would, if passed, be ineffective (whether by reason of inconsistency with any enactment or the company's constitution or otherwise),
- (b) it is defamatory of any person, or
- (c) it is frivolous or vexatious.

(3) A company is required to give notice of a resolution once it has received requests that it do so from—

- (a) members representing at least 5% of the total voting rights of all the members who have a right to vote on the resolution at the annual general meeting to which the requests relate (excluding any voting rights attached to any shares in the company held as treasury shares), or
- (b) at least 100 members who have a right to vote on the resolution at the annual general meeting to which the requests relate and hold shares in the company on which there has been paid up an average sum, per member, of at least £100.

See also section 153 (exercise of rights where shares held on behalf of others).

(4) A request—

- (a) may be in hard copy form or in electronic form,
- (b) must identify the resolution of which notice is to be given,
- (c) must be authenticated by the person or persons making it, and
- (d) must be received by the company not later than—
  - (i) 6 weeks before the annual general meeting to which the requests relate, or
  - (ii) if later, the time at which notice is given of that meeting.

[S338]

NOTES

Commencement: 1 October 2007 (for transitional provisions see the note to s 336).

339 Public companies: company's duty to circulate members' resolutions for AGMs

(1) A company that is required under section 338 to give notice of a resolution must send a copy of it to each member of the company entitled to receive notice of the annual general meeting—

- (a) in the same manner as notice of the meeting, and
- (b) at the same time as, or as soon as reasonably practicable after, it gives notice of the meeting.

(2) Subsection (1) has effect subject to section 340(2) (deposit or tender of sum in respect of expenses of circulation).

(3) The business which may be dealt with at an annual general meeting includes a resolution of which notice is given in accordance with this section.

(4) In the event of default in complying with this section, an offence is committed by every officer of the company who is in default.

(5) A person guilty of an offence under this section is liable—

(a) on conviction on indictment, to a fine;
(b) on summary conviction, to a fine not exceeding the statutory maximum.

[S339]

NOTES

Commencement: 1 October 2007 (for transitional provisions see the note to s 336).

340 Public companies: expenses of circulating members' resolutions for AGM

(1) The expenses of the company in complying with section 339 need not be paid by the members who requested the circulation of the resolution if requests sufficient to require the company to circulate it are received before the end of the financial year preceding the meeting.

(2) Otherwise—

(a) the expenses of the company in complying with that section must be paid by the members who requested the circulation of the resolution unless the company resolves otherwise, and
(b) unless the company has previously so resolved, it is not bound to comply with that section unless there is deposited with or tendered to it, not later than—
  (i) six weeks before the annual general meeting to which the requests relate, or
  (ii) if later, the time at which notice is given of that meeting,

a sum reasonably sufficient to meet its expenses in complying with that section.

[S340]

NOTES

Commencement: 1 October 2007 (for transitional provisions see the note to s 336).

CHAPTER 5
ADDITIONAL REQUIREMENTS FOR QUOTED COMPANIES

Website publication of poll results

341 Results of poll to be made available on website

(1) Where a poll is taken at a general meeting of a quoted company, the company must ensure that the following information is made available on a website—

(a) the date of the meeting,
(b) the text of the resolution or, as the case may be, a description of the subject matter of the poll,
(c) the number of votes cast in favour, and
(d) the number of votes cast against.

(2) The provisions of section 353 (requirements as to website availability) apply.

(3) In the event of default in complying with this section (or with the requirements of section 353 as it applies for the purposes of this section), an offence is committed by every officer of the company who is in default.

(4) A person guilty of an offence under subsection (3) is liable on summary conviction to a fine not exceeding level 3 on the standard scale.

(5) Failure to comply with this section (or the requirements of section 353) does not affect the validity of—

(a) the poll, or
(b) the resolution or other business (if passed or agreed to) to which the poll relates.

(6) This section only applies to polls taken after this section comes into force.

[S341]

NOTES

Commencement: 1 October 2007.

Independent report on poll

342 Members' power to require independent report on poll

(1) The members of a quoted company may require the directors to obtain an independent report on any poll taken, or to be taken, at a general meeting of the company.

(2) The directors are required to obtain an independent report if they receive requests to do so from—

(a) members representing not less than 5% of the total voting rights of all the members who have a right to vote on the matter to which the poll relates (excluding any voting rights attached to any shares in the company held as treasury shares), or

(b) not less than 100 members who have a right to vote on the matter to which the poll relates and hold shares in the company on which there has been paid up an average sum, per member, of not less than £100.

See also section 153 (exercise of rights where shares held on behalf of others).

(3) Where the requests relate to more than one poll, subsection (2) must be satisfied in relation to each of them.

(4) A request—

(a) may be in hard copy form or in electronic form,

(b) must identify the poll or polls to which it relates,

(c) must be authenticated by the person or persons making it, and

(d) must be received by the company not later than one week after the date on which the poll is taken.

[S342]

NOTES

Commencement: 1 October 2007 (for transitional provisions see the note below).

Transitional provisions, etc: Sch 3, para 39 to the draft Companies Act 2006 (Commencement No 3, Consequential Amendments, Transitional Provisions and Savings) Order 2007 (at **[A12]**) provides as follows—

"39 Additional requirements for quoted companies (ss 342 to 354)

(1) Sections 342 to 354 of the Companies Act 2006 apply to polls taken at meetings of which notice was given on or after 1st October 2007.

(2) Where notice of a meeting is given over more than one day, it is treated for the purposes of this paragraph as given on the first of those days.".

---

343 Appointment of independent assessor

(1) Directors who are required under section 342 to obtain an independent report on a poll or polls must appoint a person they consider to be appropriate (an "independent assessor") to prepare a report for the company on it or them.

(2) The appointment must be made within one week after the company being required to obtain the report.

(3) The directors must not appoint a person who—

(a) does not meet the independence requirement in section 344, or

(b) has another role in relation to any poll on which he is to report (including, in particular, a role in connection with collecting or counting votes or with the appointment of proxies).

(4) In the event of default in complying with this section, an offence is committed by every officer of the company who is in default.

(5) A person guilty of an offence under this section is liable on summary conviction to a fine not exceeding level 5 on the standard scale.

(6) If at the meeting no poll on which a report is required is taken—

(a) the directors are not required to obtain a report from the independent assessor, and

(b) his appointment ceases (but without prejudice to any right to be paid for work done before the appointment ceased).

[S343]

NOTES

Commencement: 1 October 2007 (for transitional provisions see the note to s 342).

344 Independence requirement

(1) A person may not be appointed as an independent assessor—

(a) if he is—

(i) an officer or employee of the company, or

(ii) a partner or employee of such a person, or a partnership of which such a person is a partner;

(b) if he is—

(i) an officer or employee of an associated undertaking of the company, or

(ii) a partner or employee of such a person, or a partnership of which such a person is a partner;

(c) if there exists between— (i) the person or an associate of his, and (ii) the company or an associated undertaking of the company, a connection of any such description as may be specified by regulations made by the Secretary of State.

(2) An auditor of the company is not regarded as an officer or employee of the company for this purpose.

(3) In this section—

"associated undertaking" means—

(a) a parent undertaking or subsidiary undertaking of the company, or

(b) a subsidiary undertaking of a parent undertaking of the company; and

"associate" has the meaning given by section 345.

(4) Regulations under this section are subject to negative resolution procedure.

[S344]

NOTES

Commencement: 20 January 2007 (for the purpose of enabling the exercise of powers to make Orders or Regulations by statutory instrument); 1 October 2007 (otherwise) (for transitional provisions see the note to s 342).

345 Meaning of "associate"

(1) This section defines "associate" for the purposes of section 344 (independence requirement).

(2) In relation to an individual, "associate" means—

(a) that individual's spouse or civil partner or minor child or step-child,

(b) any body corporate of which that individual is a director, and

(c) any employee or partner of that individual.

(3) In relation to a body corporate, "associate" means—

(a) any body corporate of which that body is a director,

(b) any body corporate in the same group as that body, and

(c) any employee or partner of that body or of any body corporate in the same group.

(4) In relation to a partnership that is a legal person under the law by which it is governed, "associate" means—

(a) any body corporate of which that partnership is a director,

(b) any employee of or partner in that partnership, and

(c) any person who is an associate of a partner in that partnership.

(5) In relation to a partnership that is not a legal person under the law by which it is governed, "associate" means any person who is an associate of any of the partners.

(6) In this section, in relation to a limited liability partnership, for "director" read "member".

[S345]

NOTES

Commencement: 1 October 2007 (for transitional provisions see the note to s 342).

346 Effect of appointment of a partnership

(1) This section applies where a partnership that is not a legal person under the law by which it is governed is appointed as an independent assessor.

(2) Unless a contrary intention appears, the appointment is of the partnership as such and not of the partners.

(3) Where the partnership ceases, the appointment is to be treated as extending to—

(a) any partnership that succeeds to the practice of that partnership, or

(b) any other person who succeeds to that practice having previously carried it on in partnership.

(4) For the purposes of subsection (3)—

(a) a partnership is regarded as succeeding to the practice of another partnership only if the members of the successor partnership are substantially the same as those of the former partnership, and

(b) a partnership or other person is regarded as succeeding to the practice of a partnership only if it or he succeeds to the whole or substantially the whole of the business of the former partnership.

(5) Where the partnership ceases and the appointment is not treated under subsection (3) as extending to any partnership or other person, the appointment may with the consent of the company be treated as extending to a partnership, or other person, who succeeds to—

(a) the business of the former partnership, or

(b) such part of it as is agreed by the company is to be treated as comprising the appointment.

[S346]

NOTES

Commencement: 1 October 2007 (for transitional provisions see the note to s 342).

---

347 The independent assessor's report

(1) The report of the independent assessor must state his opinion whether—

(a) the procedures adopted in connection with the poll or polls were adequate;

(b) the votes cast (including proxy votes) were fairly and accurately recorded and counted;

(c) the validity of members' appointments of proxies was fairly assessed;

(d) the notice of the meeting complied with section 325 (notice of meeting to contain statement of rights to appoint proxy);

(e) section 326 (company-sponsored invitations to appoint proxies) was complied with in relation to the meeting.

(2) The report must give his reasons for the opinions stated.

(3) If he is unable to form an opinion on any of those matters, the report must record that fact and state the reasons for it.

(4) The report must state the name of the independent assessor.

[S347]

NOTES

Commencement: 1 October 2007 (for transitional provisions see the note to s 342).

---

348 Rights of independent assessor: right to attend meeting etc

(1) Where an independent assessor has been appointed to report on a poll, he is entitled to attend—

(a) the meeting at which the poll may be taken, and

(b) any subsequent proceedings in connection with the poll.

(2) He is also entitled to be provided by the company with a copy of—

(a) the notice of the meeting, and

(b) any other communication provided by the company in connection with the meeting to persons who have a right to vote on the matter to which the poll relates.

(3) The rights conferred by this section are only to be exercised to the extent that the independent assessor considers necessary for the preparation of his report.

(4) If the independent assessor is a firm, the right under subsection (1) to attend the meeting and any subsequent proceedings in connection with the poll is exercisable by an individual authorised by the firm in writing to act as its representative for that purpose.

[S348]

NOTES

Commencement: 1 October 2007 (for transitional provisions see the note to s 342).

349 Rights of independent assessor: right to information

(1) The independent assessor is entitled to access to the company's records relating to—

(a) any poll on which he is to report;

(b) the meeting at which the poll or polls may be, or were, taken.

(2) The independent assessor may require anyone who at any material time was—

(a) a director or secretary of the company,

(b) an employee of the company,

(c) a person holding or accountable for any of the company's records,

(d) a member of the company, or

(e) an agent of the company,

to provide him with information or explanations for the purpose of preparing his report.

(3) For this purpose "agent" includes the company's bankers, solicitors and auditor.

(4) A statement made by a person in response to a requirement under this section may not be used in evidence against him in criminal proceedings except proceedings for an offence under section 350 (offences relating to provision of information).

(5) A person is not required by this section to disclose information in respect of which a claim to legal professional privilege (in Scotland, to confidentiality of communications) could be maintained in legal proceedings.

[S349]

NOTES

Commencement: 1 October 2007 (for transitional provisions see the note to s 342).

350 Offences relating to provision of information

(1) A person who fails to comply with a requirement under section 349 without delay commits an offence unless it was not reasonably practicable for him to provide the required information or explanation.

(2) A person guilty of an offence under subsection (1) is liable on summary conviction to a fine not exceeding level 3 on the standard scale.

(3) A person commits an offence who knowingly or recklessly makes to an independent assessor a statement (oral or written) that—

(a) conveys or purports to convey any information or explanations which the independent assessor requires, or is entitled to require, under section 349, and

(b) is misleading, false or deceptive in a material particular.

(4) A person guilty of an offence under subsection (3) is liable—

(a) on conviction on indictment, to imprisonment for a term not exceeding two years or a fine (or both);

(b) on summary conviction—

(i) in England and Wales, to imprisonment for a term not exceeding twelve months or to a fine not exceeding the statutory maximum (or both);

(ii) in Scotland or Northern Ireland, to imprisonment for a term not exceeding six months, or to a fine not exceeding the statutory maximum (or both).

(5) Nothing in this section affects any right of an independent assessor to apply for an injunction (in Scotland, an interdict or an order for specific performance) to enforce any of his rights under section 348 or 349.

[S350]

NOTES

Commencement: 1 October 2007 (for transitional provisions see the note to s 342).

351 Information to be made available on website

(1) Where an independent assessor has been appointed to report on a poll, the company must ensure that the following information is made available on a website—

(a) the fact of his appointment,

(b) his identity,

(c) the text of the resolution or, as the case may be, a description of the subject matter of the poll to which his appointment relates, and

(d) a copy of a report by him which complies with section 347.

(2) The provisions of section 353 (requirements as to website availability) apply.

(3) In the event of default in complying with this section (or with the requirements of section 353 as it applies for the purposes of this section), an offence is committed by every officer of the company who is in default.

(4) A person guilty of an offence under subsection (3) is liable on summary conviction to a fine not exceeding level 3 on the standard scale.

(5) Failure to comply with this section (or the requirements of section 353) does not affect the validity of—

(a) the poll, or

(b) the resolution or other business (if passed or agreed to) to which the poll relates.

[S351]

NOTES

Commencement: 1 October 2007 (for transitional provisions see the note to s 342).

Supplementary

352 Application of provisions to class meetings

(1) The provisions of—

section 341 (results of poll to be made available on website), and
sections 342 to 351 (independent report on poll),

apply (with any necessary modifications) in relation to a meeting of holders of a class of shares of a quoted company in connection with the variation of the rights attached to such shares as they apply in relation to a general meeting of the company.

(2) For the purposes of this section—

(a) any amendment of a provision contained in a company's articles for the variation of the rights attached to a class of shares, or the insertion of any such provision into the articles, is itself to be treated as a variation of those rights, and

(b) references to the variation of rights attached to a class of shares include references to their abrogation.

[S352]

NOTES

Commencement: 1 October 2007 (for transitional provisions see the note to s 342).

353 Requirements as to website availability

(1) The following provisions apply for the purposes of—

section 341 (results of poll to be made available on website), and
section 351 (report of independent observer to be made available on website).

(2) The information must be made available on a website that—

(a) is maintained by or on behalf of the company, and

(b) identifies the company in question.

(3) Access to the information on the website, and the ability to obtain a hard copy of the information from the website, must not be conditional on the payment of a fee or otherwise restricted.

(4) The information—
(a) must be made available as soon as reasonably practicable, and
(b) must be kept available throughout the period of two years beginning with the date on which it is first made available on a website in accordance with this section.

(5) A failure to make information available on a website throughout the period specified in subsection (4)(b) is disregarded if—
(a) the information is made available on the website for part of that period, and
(b) the failure is wholly attributable to circumstances that it would not be reasonable to have expected the company to prevent or avoid.

[S353]

NOTES

Commencement: 1 October 2007 (for transitional provisions see the note to s 342).

354 Power to limit or extend the types of company to which provisions of this Chapter apply

(1) The Secretary of State may by regulations—
(a) limit the types of company to which some or all of the provisions of this Chapter apply, or
(b) extend some or all of the provisions of this Chapter to additional types of company.

(2) Regulations under this section extending the application of any provision of this Chapter are subject to affirmative resolution procedure.

(3) Any other regulations under this section are subject to negative resolution procedure.

(4) Regulations under this section may—
(a) amend the provisions of this Chapter (apart from this section);
(b) repeal and re-enact provisions of this Chapter with modifications of form or arrangement, whether or not they are modified in substance;
(c) contain such consequential, incidental and supplementary provisions (including provisions amending, repealing or revoking enactments) as the Secretary of State thinks fit.

[S354]

NOTES

Commencement: 20 January 2007 (for the purpose of enabling the exercise of powers to make Orders or Regulations by statutory instrument); 1 October 2007 (otherwise) (for transitional provisions see the note to s 342).

CHAPTER 6
RECORDS OF RESOLUTIONS AND MEETINGS

355 Records of resolutions and meetings etc

(1) Every company must keep records comprising—
(a) copies of all resolutions of members passed otherwise than at general meetings,
(b) minutes of all proceedings of general meetings, and
(c) details provided to the company in accordance with section 357 (decisions of sole member).

(2) The records must be kept for at least ten years from the date of the resolution, meeting or decision (as appropriate).

(3) If a company fails to comply with this section, an offence is committed by every officer of the company who is in default.

(4) A person guilty of an offence under this section is liable on summary conviction to a fine not exceeding level 3 on the standard scale and, for continued contravention, a daily default fine not exceeding one-tenth of level 3 on the standard scale.

[S355]

NOTES

Commencement: 1 October 2007 (for transitional provisions see the note below).

Transitional provisions, etc: Sch 3, para 40 to the draft Companies Act 2006 (Commencement No 3, Consequential Amendments, Transitional Provisions and Savings) Order 2007 (at **[A12]**) provides as follows—

"40 Records of resolutions and meetings (ss 355 to 359)

(1) Sections 355 to 359 of the Companies Act 2006 (records of resolutions and meetings) apply to resolutions passed, meetings held or decisions taken on or after 1st October 2007.

(2) Sections 382, 382A, 382B and 383 of the 1985 Act or Articles 390, 390A, 390B and 391 of the 1986 Order continue to apply to resolutions passed, meetings held or decisions taken before that date.".

356 Records as evidence of resolutions etc

(1) This section applies to the records kept in accordance with section 355.

(2) The record of a resolution passed otherwise than at a general meeting, if purporting to be signed by a director of the company or by the company secretary, is evidence (in Scotland, sufficient evidence) of the passing of the resolution.

(3) Where there is a record of a written resolution of a private company, the requirements of this Act with respect to the passing of the resolution are deemed to be complied with unless the contrary is proved.

(4) The minutes of proceedings of a general meeting, if purporting to be signed by the chairman of that meeting or by the chairman of the next general meeting, are evidence (in Scotland, sufficient evidence) of the proceedings at the meeting.

(5) Where there is a record of proceedings of a general meeting of a company, then, until the contrary is proved—

(a) the meeting is deemed duly held and convened,

(b) all proceedings at the meeting are deemed to have duly taken place, and

(c) all appointments at the meeting are deemed valid.

[S356]

NOTES

Commencement: 1 October 2007 (for transitional provisions see the note to s 355).

357 Records of decisions by sole member

(1) This section applies to a company limited by shares or by guarantee that has only one member.

(2) Where the member takes any decision that—

(a) may be taken by the company in general meeting, and

(b) has effect as if agreed by the company in general meeting,

he must (unless that decision is taken by way of a written resolution) provide the company with details of that decision.

(3) If a person fails to comply with this section he commits an offence.

(4) A person guilty of an offence under this section is liable on summary conviction to a fine not exceeding level 2 on the standard scale.

(5) Failure to comply with this section does not affect the validity of any decision referred to in subsection (2).

[S357]

NOTES

Commencement: 1 October 2007 (for transitional provisions see the note to s 355).

358 Inspection of records of resolutions and meetings

(1) The records referred to in section 355 (records of resolutions etc) relating to the previous ten years must be kept available for inspection—

(a) at the company's registered office, or
(b) at a place specified in regulations under section 1136.

(2) The company must give notice to the registrar—
(a) of the place at which the records are kept available for inspection, and
(b) of any change in that place,
unless they have at all times been kept at the company's registered office.

(3) The records must be open to the inspection of any member of the company without charge.

(4) Any member may require a copy of any of the records on payment of such fee as may be prescribed.

(5) If default is made for 14 days in complying with subsection (2) or an inspection required under subsection (3) is refused, or a copy requested under subsection (4) is not sent, an offence is committed by every officer of the company who is in default.

(6) A person guilty of an offence under this section is liable on summary conviction to a fine not exceeding level 3 on the standard scale and, for continued contravention, a daily default fine not exceeding one-tenth of level 3 on the standard scale.

(7) In a case in which an inspection required under subsection (3) is refused or a copy requested under subsection (4) is not sent, the court may by order compel an immediate inspection of the records or direct that the copies required be sent to the persons who requested them.

[S358]

NOTES

Commencement: 20 January 2007 (for the purpose of enabling the exercise of powers to make Orders or Regulations by statutory instrument); 1 October 2007 (otherwise) (for transitional provisions see the note to s 355).

359 Records of resolutions and meetings of class of members

The provisions of this Chapter apply (with necessary modifications) in relation to resolutions and meetings of—
(a) holders of a class of shares, and
(b) in the case of a company without a share capital, a class of members,
as they apply in relation to resolutions of members generally and to general meetings.

[S359]

NOTES

Commencement: 1 October 2007 (for transitional provisions see the note to s 355).

CHAPTER 7
SUPPLEMENTARY PROVISIONS

360 Computation of periods of notice etc: clear day rule

(1) This section applies for the purposes of the following provisions of this Part—
section 307(1) and (2) (notice required of general meeting),
section 312(1) and (3) (resolution requiring special notice),
section 314(4)(d) (request to circulate members' statement),
section 316(2)(b) (expenses of circulating statement to be deposited or tendered before meeting),
section 338(4)(d)(i) (request to circulate member's resolution at AGM of public company), and
section 340(2)(b)(i) (expenses of circulating statement to be deposited or tendered before meeting).

(2) Any reference in those provisions to a period of notice, or to a period before a meeting by which a request must be received or sum deposited or tendered, is to a period of the specified length excluding—
(a) the day of the meeting, and

(b) the day on which the notice is given, the request received or the sum deposited or tendered.

[S360]

NOTES

Commencement: 1 October 2007.

361 Meaning of "quoted company"

In this Part "quoted company" has the same meaning as in Part 15 of this Act.

[S361]

NOTES

Commencement: 1 October 2007.

PART 14
CONTROL OF POLITICAL DONATIONS AND EXPENDITURE

Introductory

362 Introductory

This Part has effect for controlling—

(a) political donations made by companies to political parties, to other political organisations and to independent election candidates, and

(b) political expenditure incurred by companies.

[S362]

NOTES

Commencement: 1 October 2007 (in relation to Great Britain (subject to the exception noted below)); 1 November 2007 (in relation to Northern Ireland (subject to the exception noted below)); 1 October 2008 (otherwise).

Note: the draft Companies Act 2006 (Commencement No 3, Consequential Amendments, Transitional Provisions and Savings) Order 2007, arts 2(2), 3(1) provide that this section shall come into force on 1 October 2007 (in Great Britain) and 1 November 2007 (in Northern Ireland) with the exception of the provisions specified in art 5 of that Order (which relate to independent election candidates and which shall come into force on 1 October 2008). Article 5 provides that in this section, the words "and to independent election candidates" in para (a) shall come into force on 1 October 2008 (see the draft Order at **[A12]**).

Transitional provisions: the draft Companies Act 2006 (Commencement No 3, Consequential Amendments, Transitional Provisions and Savings) Order 2007, Sch 3, paras 41, 42 provide as follows—

"41 Political donations and expenditure (ss 362 to 379)

(1) Sections 362 to 379 of the Companies Act 2006 (political donations and expenditure) apply to donations made or expenditure incurred on or after 1st October 2007.

Section 379(2) of that Act applies as to the time when a donation is regarded as made or expenditure as incurred, including where it is made or incurred in pursuance of a contract entered into before that date.

(2) Part 10A of the 1985 Act continues to apply to donations or expenditure in relation to which the relevant time, as defined in section 347A(10) of that Act, is before that date.

(3) The repeal of that Part does not affect paragraph 3(4) of Schedule 7 to the 1985 Act (matters to be dealt with in directors' report: expressions to have same meaning as in Part 10A).

42. An approval resolution passed in accordance with section 347C of the 1985 Act before 1st October 2007 is treated as complying with the requirements of section 367 of the Companies Act 2006 (form of authorising resolution) although it does not comply with the requirements of that section as to the heads under which donations and expenditure are to be stated.".

Donations and expenditure to which this Part applies

363 Political parties, organisations etc to which this Part applies

(1) This Part applies to a political party if—

(a) it is registered under Part 2 of the Political Parties, Elections and Referendums Act 2000 (c 41), or

(b) it carries on, or proposes to carry on, activities for the purposes of or in connection with the participation of the party in any election or elections to public office held in a member State other than the United Kingdom.

(2) This Part applies to an organisation (a "political organisation") if it carries on, or proposes to carry on, activities that are capable of being reasonably regarded as intended—

(a) to affect public support for a political party to which, or an independent election candidate to whom, this Part applies, or

(b) to influence voters in relation to any national or regional referendum held under the law of the United Kingdom or another member State.

(3) This Part applies to an independent election candidate at any election to public office held in the United Kingdom or another member State.

(4) Any reference in the following provisions of this Part to a political party, political organisation or independent election candidate, or to political expenditure, is to a party, organisation, independent candidate or expenditure to which this Part applies.

[S363]

NOTES

Commencement: 1 October 2007 (in relation to Great Britain (subject to the exception noted below)); 1 November 2007 (in relation to Northern Ireland (subject to the exception noted below)); 1 October 2008 (otherwise).

Note: the draft Companies Act 2006 (Commencement No 3, Consequential Amendments, Transitional Provisions and Savings) Order 2007, arts 2(2), 3(1) provide that this section shall come into force on 1 October 2007 (in Great Britain) and 1 November 2007 (in Northern Ireland) with the exception of the provisions specified in art 5 of that Order (which relate to independent election candidates and which shall come into force on 1 October 2008). Article 5 provides that in this section, (i) the words "or an independent election candidate to whom" in sub-s (2)(a); (ii) all of sub-s (3); and (iii) the words "or independent election candidate" and "independent candidate" in sub-s (4) shall come into force on 1 October 2008 (see the draft Order at **[A12]**).

Transitional provisions: see the note to s 362.

364 Meaning of "political donation"

(1) The following provisions have effect for the purposes of this Part as regards the meaning of "political donation".

(2) In relation to a political party or other political organisation—

(a) "political donation" means anything that in accordance with sections 50 to 52 of the Political Parties, Elections and Referendums Act 2000—

(i) constitutes a donation for the purposes of Chapter 1 of Part 4 of that Act (control of donations to registered parties), or

(ii) would constitute such a donation reading references in those sections to a registered party as references to any political party or other political organisation,

and

(b) section 53 of that Act applies, in the same way, for the purpose of determining the value of a donation.

(3) In relation to an independent election candidate—

(a) "political donation" means anything that, in accordance with sections 50 to 52 of that Act, would constitute a donation for the purposes of Chapter 1 of Part 4 of that Act (control of donations to registered parties) reading references in those sections to a registered party as references to the independent election candidate, and

(b) section 53 of that Act applies, in the same way, for the purpose of determining the value of a donation.

(4) For the purposes of this section, sections 50 and 53 of the Political Parties, Elections and Referendums Act 2000 (c 41) (definition of "donation" and value of donations) shall be treated as if the amendments to those sections made by the Electoral Administration Act 2006 (which remove from the definition of "donation" loans made otherwise than on commercial terms) had not been made.

[S364]

NOTES

Commencement: 1 October 2007 (in relation to Great Britain (subject to the exception noted below)); 1 November 2007 (in relation to Northern Ireland (subject to the exception noted below)); 1 October 2008 (otherwise).

Note: the draft Companies Act 2006 (Commencement No 3, Consequential Amendments, Transitional Provisions and Savings) Order 2007, arts 2(2), 3(1) provide that this section shall come into force on 1 October 2007 (in Great Britain) and 1 November 2007 (in Northern Ireland) with the exception of the provisions specified in art 5 of that Order (which relate to independent election candidates and which shall come into force on 1 October 2008). Article 5 provides that in this section, sub-s (3) shall come into force on 1 October 2008 (see the draft Order at **[A12]**).

Transitional provisions: see the note to s 362.

365 Meaning of "political expenditure"

(1) In this Part "political expenditure", in relation to a company, means expenditure incurred by the company on—

(a) the preparation, publication or dissemination of advertising or other promotional or publicity material—

(i) of whatever nature, and

(ii) however published or otherwise disseminated,

that, at the time of publication or dissemination, is capable of being reasonably regarded as intended to affect public support for a political party or other political organisation, or an independent election candidate, or

(b) activities on the part of the company that are capable of being reasonably regarded as intended—

(i) to affect public support for a political party or other political organisation, or an independent election candidate, or

(ii) to influence voters in relation to any national or regional referendum held under the law of a member State.

(2) For the purposes of this Part a political donation does not count as political expenditure.

[S365]

NOTES

Commencement: 1 October 2007 (in relation to Great Britain (subject to the exception noted below)); 1 November 2007 (in relation to Northern Ireland (subject to the exception noted below)); 1 October 2008 (otherwise).

Note: the draft Companies Act 2006 (Commencement No 3, Consequential Amendments, Transitional Provisions and Savings) Order 2007, arts 2(2), 3(1) provide that this section shall come into force on 1 October 2007 (in Great Britain) and 1 November 2007 (in Northern Ireland) with the exception of the provisions specified in art 5 of that Order (which relate to independent election candidates and which shall come into force on 1 October 2008). Article 5 provides that in this section, the words "or an independent election candidate" in sub-s (1)(a), (b)(i) shall come into force on 1 October 2008 (see the draft Order at **[A12]**).

Transitional provisions: see the note to s 362.

Authorisation required for donations or expenditure

366 Authorisation required for donations or expenditure

(1) A company must not—

(a) make a political donation to a political party or other political organisation, or to an independent election candidate, or

(b) incur any political expenditure,

unless the donation or expenditure is authorised in accordance with the following provisions.

(2) The donation or expenditure must be authorised—

(a) in the case of a company that is not a subsidiary of another company, by a resolution of the members of the company;

(b) in the case of a company that is a subsidiary of another company by—

(i) a resolution of the members of the company, and

(ii) a resolution of the members of any relevant holding company.

(3) No resolution is required on the part of a company that is a wholly-owned subsidiary of a UK-registered company.

(4) For the purposes of subsection (2)(b)(ii) a "relevant holding company" means a company that, at the time the donation was made or the expenditure was incurred—

(a) was a holding company of the company by which the donation was made or the expenditure was incurred,

(b) was a UK-registered company, and

(c) was not a subsidiary of another UK-registered company.

(5) The resolution or resolutions required by this section—

(a) must comply with section 367 (form of authorising resolution), and

(b) must be passed before the donation is made or the expenditure incurred.

(6) Nothing in this section enables a company to be authorised to do anything that it could not lawfully do apart from this section.

[S366]

NOTES

Commencement: 1 October 2007 (in relation to Great Britain (subject to the exception noted below)); 1 November 2007 (in relation to Northern Ireland (subject to the exception noted below)); 1 October 2008 (otherwise).

Note: the draft Companies Act 2006 (Commencement No 3, Consequential Amendments, Transitional Provisions and Savings) Order 2007, arts 2(2), 3(1) provide that this section shall come into force on 1 October 2007 (in Great Britain) and 1 November 2007 (in Northern Ireland) with the exception of the provisions specified in art 5 of that Order (which relate to independent election candidates and which shall come into force on 1 October 2008). Article 5 provides that in this section, the words "or to an independent election candidate" in sub-s (1)(a) shall come into force on 1 October 2008 (see the draft Order at **[A12]**).

Transitional provisions: see the note to s 362.

367 Form of authorising resolution

(1) A resolution conferring authorisation for the purposes of this Part may relate to—

(a) the company passing the resolution,

(b) one or more subsidiaries of that company, or

(c) the company passing the resolution and one or more subsidiaries of that company.

(2) A resolution may be expressed to relate to all companies that are subsidiaries of the company passing the resolution—

(a) at the time the resolution is passed, or

(b) at any time during the period for which the resolution has effect,

without identifying them individually.

(3) The resolution may authorise donations or expenditure under one or more of the following heads—

(a) donations to political parties or independent election candidates;

(b) donations to political organisations other than political parties;

(c) political expenditure.

(4) The resolution must specify a head or heads—

(a) in the case of a resolution under subsection (2), for all of the companies to which it relates taken together;

(b) in the case of any other resolution, for each company to which it relates.

(5) The resolution must be expressed in general terms conforming with subsection (2) and must not purport to authorise particular donations or expenditure.

(6) For each of the specified heads the resolution must authorise donations or, as the case may be, expenditure up to a specified amount in the period for which the resolution has effect (see section 368).

(7) The resolution must specify such amounts—

(a) in the case of a resolution under subsection (2), for all of the companies to which it relates taken together;

(b) in the case of any other resolution, for each company to which it relates.

[S367]

NOTES

Commencement: 1 October 2007 (in relation to Great Britain (subject to the exception noted below)); 1 November 2007 (in relation to Northern Ireland (subject to the exception noted below)); 1 October 2008 (otherwise).

Note: the draft Companies Act 2006 (Commencement No 3, Consequential Amendments, Transitional Provisions and Savings) Order 2007, arts 2(2), 3(1) provide that this section shall come into force on 1 October 2007 (in Great Britain) and 1 November 2007 (in Northern Ireland) with the exception of the provisions specified in art 5 of that Order (which relate to independent election candidates and which shall come into force on 1 October 2008). Article 5 provides that in this section, the words "or independent election candidates" in sub-s (3)(a) shall come into force on 1 October 2008 (see the draft Order at **[A12]**).

Transitional provisions: see the note to s 362.

368 Period for which resolution has effect

(1) A resolution conferring authorisation for the purposes of this Part has effect for a period of four years beginning with the date on which it is passed unless the directors determine, or the articles require, that it is to have effect for a shorter period beginning with that date.

(2) The power of the directors to make a determination under this section is subject to any provision of the articles that operates to prevent them from doing so.

[S368]

NOTES

Commencement: 1 October 2007 (in relation to Great Britain); 1 November 2007 (in relation to Northern Ireland).

Transitional provisions: see the note to s 362.

Remedies in case of unauthorised donations or expenditure

369 Liability of directors in case of unauthorised donation or expenditure

(1) This section applies where a company has made a political donation or incurred political expenditure without the authorisation required by this Part.

(2) The directors in default are jointly and severally liable—

(a) to make good to the company the amount of the unauthorised donation or expenditure, with interest, and

(b) to compensate the company for any loss or damage sustained by it as a result of the unauthorised donation or expenditure having been made.

(3) The directors in default are—

(a) those who, at the time the unauthorised donation was made or the unauthorised expenditure was incurred, were directors of the company by which the donation was made or the expenditure was incurred, and

(b) where—

(i) that company was a subsidiary of a relevant holding company, and

(ii) the directors of the relevant holding company failed to take all reasonable steps to prevent the donation being made or the expenditure being incurred,

the directors of the relevant holding company.

(4) For the purposes of subsection (3)(b) a "relevant holding company" means a company that, at the time the donation was made or the expenditure was incurred—

(a) was a holding company of the company by which the donation was made or the expenditure was incurred,

(b) was a UK-registered company, and

(c) was not a subsidiary of another UK-registered company.

(5) The interest referred to in subsection (2)(a) is interest on the amount of the unauthorised donation or expenditure, so far as not made good to the company—

(a) in respect of the period beginning with the date when the donation was made or the expenditure was incurred, and

(b) at such rate as the Secretary of State may prescribe by regulations.

Section 379(2) (construction of references to date when donation made or expenditure incurred) does not apply for the purposes of this subsection.

(6) Where only part of a donation or expenditure was unauthorised, this section applies only to so much of it as was unauthorised.

[S369]

NOTES

Commencement: 20 January 2007 (for the purpose of enabling the exercise of powers to make Orders or Regulations by statutory instrument); 1 October 2007 (otherwise, in relation to Great Britain); 1 November 2007 (otherwise, in relation to Northern Ireland).

Transitional provisions: see the note to s 362.

370 Enforcement of directors' liabilities by shareholder action

(1) Any liability of a director under section 369 is enforceable—

- (a) in the case of a liability of a director of a company to that company, by proceedings brought under this section in the name of the company by an authorised group of its members;
- (b) in the case of a liability of a director of a holding company to a subsidiary, by proceedings brought under this section in the name of the subsidiary by—
  - (i) an authorised group of members of the subsidiary, or
  - (ii) an authorised group of members of the holding company.

(2) This is in addition to the right of the company to which the liability is owed to bring proceedings itself to enforce the liability.

(3) An "authorised group" of members of a company means—

- (a) the holders of not less than 5% in nominal value of the company's issued share capital,
- (b) if the company is not limited by shares, not less than 5% of its members, or
- (c) not less than 50 of the company's members.

(4) The right to bring proceedings under this section is subject to the provisions of section 371.

(5) Nothing in this section affects any right of a member of a company to bring or continue proceedings under Part 11 (derivative claims or proceedings).

[S370]

NOTES

Commencement: 1 October 2007 (in relation to Great Britain); 1 November 2007 (in relation to Northern Ireland).

Transitional provisions: see the note to s 362.

371 Enforcement of directors' liabilities by shareholder action: supplementary

(1) A group of members may not bring proceedings under section 370 in the name of a company unless—

- (a) the group has given written notice to the company stating—
  - (i) the cause of action and a summary of the facts on which the proceedings are to be based,
  - (ii) the names and addresses of the members comprising the group, and
  - (iii) the grounds on which it is alleged that those members constitute an authorised group; and
- (b) not less than 28 days have elapsed between the date of the giving of the notice to the company and the bringing of the proceedings.

(2) Where such a notice is given to a company, any director of the company may apply to the court within the period of 28 days beginning with the date of the giving of the notice for an order directing that the proposed proceedings shall not be brought, on one or more of the following grounds—

- (a) that the unauthorised amount has been made good to the company;
- (b) that proceedings to enforce the liability have been brought, and are being pursued with due diligence, by the company;
- (c) that the members proposing to bring proceedings under this section do not constitute an authorised group.

(3) Where an application is made on the ground mentioned in subsection (2)(b), the court may as an alternative to directing that the proposed proceedings under section 370 are not to be brought, direct—

- (a) that such proceedings may be brought on such terms and conditions as the court thinks fit, and

(b) that the proceedings brought by the company—
  (i) shall be discontinued, or
  (ii) may be continued on such terms and conditions as the court thinks fit.

(4) The members by whom proceedings are brought under section 370 owe to the company in whose name they are brought the same duties in relation to the proceedings as would be owed by the company's directors if the proceedings were being brought by the company.

But proceedings to enforce any such duty may be brought by the company only with the permission of the court.

(5) Proceedings brought under section 370 may not be discontinued or settled by the group except with the permission of the court, which may be given on such terms as the court thinks fit.

[S371]

NOTES

Commencement: 1 October 2007 (in relation to Great Britain); 1 November 2007 (in relation to Northern Ireland).

Transitional provisions: see the note to s 362.

372 Costs of shareholder action

(1) This section applies in relation to proceedings brought under section 370 in the name of a company ("the company") by an authorised group ("the group").

(2) The group may apply to the court for an order directing the company to indemnify the group in respect of costs incurred or to be incurred by the group in connection with the proceedings.

The court may make such an order on such terms as it thinks fit.

(3) The group is not entitled to be paid any such costs out of the assets of the company except by virtue of such an order.

(4) If no such order has been made with respect to the proceedings, then—
(a) if the company is awarded costs in connection with the proceedings, or it is agreed that costs incurred by the company in connection with the proceedings should be paid by any defendant, the costs shall be paid to the group; and
(b) if any defendant is awarded costs in connection with the proceedings, or it is agreed that any defendant should be paid costs incurred by him in connection with the proceedings, the costs shall be paid by the group.

(5) In the application of this section to Scotland for "costs" read "expenses" and for "defendant" read "defender".

[S372]

NOTES

Commencement: 1 October 2007 (in relation to Great Britain); 1 November 2007 (in relation to Northern Ireland).

Transitional provisions: see the note to s 362.

373 Information for purposes of shareholder action

(1) Where proceedings have been brought under section 370 in the name of a company by an authorised group, the group is entitled to require the company to provide it with all information relating to the subject matter of the proceedings that is in the company's possession or under its control or which is reasonably obtainable by it.

(2) If the company, having been required by the group to do so, refuses to provide the group with all or any of that information, the court may, on an application made by the group, make an order directing—
(a) the company, and
(b) any of its officers or employees specified in the application,

to provide the group with the information in question in such form and by such means as the court may direct.

[S373]

NOTES

Commencement: 1 October 2007 (in relation to Great Britain); 1 November 2007 (in relation to Northern Ireland).

Transitional provisions: see the note to s 362.

Exemptions

374 Trade unions

(1) A donation to a trade union, other than a contribution to the union's political fund, is not a political donation for the purposes of this Part.

(2) A trade union is not a political organisation for the purposes of section 365 (meaning of "political expenditure").

(3) In this section—

"trade union" has the meaning given by section 1 of Trade Union and Labour Relations (Consolidation) Act 1992 (c 52) or Article 3 of the Industrial Relations (Northern Ireland) Order 1992 (SI 1992/807 (NI 5));

"political fund" means the fund from which payments by a trade union in the furtherance of political objects are required to be made by virtue of section 82(1)(a) of that Act or Article 57(2)(a) of that Order.

[S374]

NOTES

Commencement: 1 October 2007 (in relation to Great Britain); 1 November 2007 (in relation to Northern Ireland).

Transitional provisions: see the note to s 362.

375 Subscription for membership of trade association

(1) A subscription paid to a trade association for membership of the association is not a political donation for the purposes of this Part.

(2) For this purpose—

"trade association" means an organisation formed for the purpose of furthering the trade interests of its members, or of persons represented by its members, and

"subscription" does not include a payment to the association to the extent that it is made for the purpose of financing any particular activity of the association.

[S375]

NOTES

Commencement: 1 October 2007 (in relation to Great Britain); 1 November 2007 (in relation to Northern Ireland).

Transitional provisions: see the note to s 362.

376 All-party parliamentary groups

(1) An all-party parliamentary group is not a political organisation for the purposes of this Part.

(2) An "all-party parliamentary group" means an all-party group composed of members of one or both of the Houses of Parliament (or of such members and other persons).

[S376]

NOTES

Commencement: 1 October 2007 (in relation to Great Britain); 1 November 2007 (in relation to Northern Ireland).

Transitional provisions: see the note to s 362.

377 Political expenditure exempted by order

(1) Authorisation under this Part is not needed for political expenditure that is exempt by virtue of an order of the Secretary of State under this section.

(2) An order may confer an exemption in relation to—
(a) companies of any description or category specified in the order, or
(b) expenditure of any description or category so specified (whether framed by reference to goods, services or other matters in respect of which such expenditure is incurred or otherwise),

or both.

(3) If or to the extent that expenditure is exempt from the requirement of authorisation under this Part by virtue of an order under this section, it shall be disregarded in determining what donations are authorised by any resolution of the company passed for the purposes of this Part.

(4) An order under this section is subject to affirmative resolution procedure.

[S377]

NOTES

Commencement: 20 January 2007 (for the purpose of enabling the exercise of powers to make Orders or Regulations by statutory instrument); 1 October 2007 (otherwise, in relation to Great Britain); 1 November 2007 (otherwise, in relation to Northern Ireland).

Transitional provisions: see the note to s 362.

378 Donations not amounting to more than £5,000 in any twelve month period

(1) Authorisation under this Part is not needed for a donation except to the extent that the total amount of—
(a) that donation, and
(b) other relevant donations made in the period of 12 months ending with the date on which that donation is made,

exceeds £5,000.

(2) In this section—
"donation" means a donation to a political party or other political organisation or to an independent election candidate; and
"other relevant donations" means—
(a) in relation to a donation made by a company that is not a subsidiary, any other donations made by that company or by any of its subsidiaries;
(b) in relation to a donation made by a company that is a subsidiary, any other donations made by that company, by any holding company of that company or by any other subsidiary of any such holding company.

(3) If or to the extent that a donation is exempt by virtue of this section from the requirement of authorisation under this Part, it shall be disregarded in determining what donations are authorised by any resolution passed for the purposes of this Part.

[S378]

NOTES

Commencement: 1 October 2007 (in relation to Great Britain (subject to the exception noted below)); 1 November 2007 (in relation to Northern Ireland (subject to the exception noted below)); 1 October 2008 (otherwise).

Note: the draft Companies Act 2006 (Commencement No 3, Consequential Amendments, Transitional Provisions and Savings) Order 2007, arts 2(2), 3(1) provide that this section shall come into force on 1 October 2007 (in Great Britain) and 1 November 2007 (in Northern Ireland) with the exception of the provisions specified in art 5 of that Order (which relate to independent election candidates and which shall come into force on 1 October 2008). Article 5 provides that in this section, the words "or to an independent election candidate" in sub-s (2) shall come into force on 1 October 2008 (see the draft Order at **[A12]**).

Transitional provisions: see the note to s 362.

Supplementary provisions

379 Minor definitions

(1) In this Part—
"director" includes shadow director; and
"organisation" includes any body corporate or unincorporated association and any combination of persons.

(2) Except as otherwise provided, any reference in this Part to the time at which a donation is made or expenditure is incurred is, in a case where the donation is made or expenditure incurred in pursuance of a contract, any earlier time at which that contract is entered into by the company.

[S379]

NOTES

Commencement: 1 October 2007 (in relation to Great Britain); 1 November 2007 (in relation to Northern Ireland).

Transitional provisions: see the note to s 362.

PART 15
ACCOUNTS AND REPORTS

CHAPTER 1
INTRODUCTION

General

380 Scheme of this Part

(1) The requirements of this Part as to accounts and reports apply in relation to each financial year of a company.

(2) In certain respects different provisions apply to different kinds of company.

(3) The main distinctions for this purpose are—
- (a) between companies subject to the small companies regime (see section 381) and companies that are not subject to that regime; and
- (b) between quoted companies (see section 385) and companies that are not quoted.

(4) In this Part, where provisions do not apply to all kinds of company—
- (a) provisions applying to companies subject to the small companies regime appear before the provisions applying to other companies,
- (b) provisions applying to private companies appear before the provisions applying to public companies, and
- (c) provisions applying to quoted companies appear after the provisions applying to other companies.

[S380]

NOTES

Commencement: to be appointed.

Companies subject to the small companies regime

381 Companies subject to the small companies regime

The small companies regime for accounts and reports applies to a company for a financial year in relation to which the company—
- (a) qualifies as small (see sections 382 and 383), and
- (b) is not excluded from the regime (see section 384).

[S381]

NOTES

Commencement: to be appointed.

382 Companies qualifying as small: general

(1) A company qualifies as small in relation to its first financial year if the qualifying conditions are met in that year.

(2) A company qualifies as small in relation to a subsequent financial year—
- (a) if the qualifying conditions are met in that year and the preceding financial year;

(b) if the qualifying conditions are met in that year and the company qualified as small in relation to the preceding financial year;
(c) if the qualifying conditions were met in the preceding financial year and the company qualified as small in relation to that year.

(3) The qualifying conditions are met by a company in a year in which it satisfies two or more of the following requirements—

1 Turnover	Not more than £5.6 million
2 Balance sheet total	Not more than £2.8 million
3 Number of employees	Not more than 50

(4) For a period that is a company's financial year but not in fact a year the maximum figures for turnover must be proportionately adjusted.

(5) The balance sheet total means the aggregate of the amounts shown as assets in the company's balance sheet.

(6) The number of employees means the average number of persons employed by the company in the year, determined as follows—
(a) find for each month in the financial year the number of persons employed under contracts of service by the company in that month (whether throughout the month or not),
(b) add together the monthly totals, and
(c) divide by the number of months in the financial year.

(7) This section is subject to section 383 (companies qualifying as small: parent companies).

[S382]

NOTES
Commencement: to be appointed.

383 Companies qualifying as small: parent companies

(1) A parent company qualifies as a small company in relation to a financial year only if the group headed by it qualifies as a small group.

(2) A group qualifies as small in relation to the parent company's first financial year if the qualifying conditions are met in that year.

(3) A group qualifies as small in relation to a subsequent financial year of the parent company—
(a) if the qualifying conditions are met in that year and the preceding financial year;
(b) if the qualifying conditions are met in that year and the group qualified as small in relation to the preceding financial year;
(c) if the qualifying conditions were met in the preceding financial year and the group qualified as small in relation to that year.

(4) The qualifying conditions are met by a group in a year in which it satisfies two or more of the following requirements—

1. Aggregate turnover	Not more than £5.6 million net (or £6.72 million gross)
2. Aggregate balance sheet total	Not more than £2.8 million net (or £3.36 million gross)
3. Aggregate number of employees	Not more than 50

(5) The aggregate figures are ascertained by aggregating the relevant figures determined in accordance with section 382 for each member of the group.

(6) In relation to the aggregate figures for turnover and balance sheet total—
"net" means after any set-offs and other adjustments made to eliminate group transactions—
(a) in the case of Companies Act accounts, in accordance with regulations under section 404,
(b) in the case of IAS accounts, in accordance with international accounting standards; and
"gross" means without those set-offs and other adjustments.

A company may satisfy any relevant requirement on the basis of either the net or the gross figure.

(7) The figures for each subsidiary undertaking shall be those included in its individual accounts for the relevant financial year, that is—
(a) if its financial year ends with that of the parent company, that financial year, and
(b) if not, its financial year ending last before the end of the financial year of the parent company.

If those figures cannot be obtained without disproportionate expense or undue delay, the latest available figures shall be taken.

[S383]

NOTES

Commencement: to be appointed.

384 Companies excluded from the small companies regime

(1) The small companies regime does not apply to a company that is, or was at any time within the financial year to which the accounts relate—
(a) a public company,
(b) a company that—
(i) is an authorised insurance company, a banking company, an e-money issuer, an ISD investment firm or a UCITS management company, or
(ii) carries on insurance market activity, or
(c) a member of an ineligible group.

(2) A group is ineligible if any of its members is—
(a) a public company,
(b) a body corporate (other than a company) whose shares are admitted to trading on a regulated market in an EEA State,
(c) a person (other than a small company) who has permission under Part 4 of the Financial Services and Markets Act 2000 (c 8) to carry on a regulated activity,
(d) a small company that is an authorised insurance company, a banking company, an e-money issuer, an ISD investment firm or a UCITS management company, or
(e) a person who carries on insurance market activity.

(3) A company is a small company for the purposes of subsection (2) if it qualified as small in relation to its last financial year ending on or before the end of the financial year to which the accounts relate.

[S384]

NOTES

Commencement: to be appointed.

Quoted and unquoted companies

385 Quoted and unquoted companies

(1) For the purposes of this Part a company is a quoted company in relation to a financial year if it is a quoted company immediately before the end of the accounting reference period by reference to which that financial year was determined.

(2) A "quoted company" means a company whose equity share capital—
(a) has been included in the official list in accordance with the provisions of Part 6 of the Financial Services and Markets Act 2000 (c 8), or

(b) is officially listed in an EEA State, or
(c) is admitted to dealing on either the New York Stock Exchange or the exchange known as Nasdaq.

In paragraph (a) "the official list" has the meaning given by section 103(1) of the Financial Services and Markets Act 2000.

(3) An "unquoted company" means a company that is not a quoted company.

(4) The Secretary of State may by regulations amend or replace the provisions of subsections (1) to (2) so as to limit or extend the application of some or all of the provisions of this Part that are expressed to apply to quoted companies.

(5) Regulations under this section extending the application of any such provision of this Part are subject to affirmative resolution procedure.

(6) Any other regulations under this section are subject to negative resolution procedure.

[S385]

NOTES

Commencement: 20 January 2007 (for the purpose of enabling the exercise of powers to make Orders or Regulations by statutory instrument); 1 October 2007 (certain purposes); to be appointed (otherwise) (see the note below).

Note: the draft Companies Act 2006 (Commencement No 3, Consequential Amendments, Transitional Provisions and Savings) Order 2007, art 2(3) provides that this section shall come into force on 1 October 2007 so far as is necessary for the purposes of the provisions of this Act brought into force on that date by art 2(1), (2) of that Order (see **[A12]**).

CHAPTER 2
ACCOUNTING RECORDS

386 Duty to keep accounting records

(1) Every company must keep adequate accounting records.

(2) Adequate accounting records means records that are sufficient—
(a) to show and explain the company's transactions,
(b) to disclose with reasonable accuracy, at any time, the financial position of the company at that time, and
(c) to enable the directors to ensure that any accounts required to be prepared comply with the requirements of this Act (and, where applicable, of Article 4 of the IAS Regulation).

(3) Accounting records must, in particular, contain—
(a) entries from day to day of all sums of money received and expended by the company and the matters in respect of which the receipt and expenditure takes place, and
(b) a record of the assets and liabilities of the company.

(4) If the company's business involves dealing in goods, the accounting records must contain—
(a) statements of stock held by the company at the end of each financial year of the company,
(b) all statements of stocktakings from which any statement of stock as is mentioned in paragraph (a) has been or is to be prepared, and
(c) except in the case of goods sold by way of ordinary retail trade, statements of all goods sold and purchased, showing the goods and the buyers and sellers in sufficient detail to enable all these to be identified.

(5) A parent company that has a subsidiary undertaking in relation to which the above requirements do not apply must take reasonable steps to secure that the undertaking keeps such accounting records as to enable the directors of the parent company to ensure that any accounts required to be prepared under this Part comply with the requirements of this Act (and, where applicable, of Article 4 of the IAS Regulation).

[S386]

NOTES

Commencement: to be appointed.

387 Duty to keep accounting records: offence

(1) If a company fails to comply with any provision of section 386 (duty to keep accounting records), an offence is committed by every officer of the company who is in default.

(2) It is a defence for a person charged with such an offence to show that he acted honestly and that in the circumstances in which the company's business was carried on the default was excusable.

(3) A person guilty of an offence under this section is liable—
- (a) on conviction on indictment, to imprisonment for a term not exceeding two years or a fine (or both);
- (b) on summary conviction—
  - (i) in England and Wales, to imprisonment for a term not exceeding twelve months or to a fine not exceeding the statutory maximum (or both);
  - (ii) in Scotland or Northern Ireland, to imprisonment for a term not exceeding six months, or to a fine not exceeding the statutory maximum (or both).

[S387]

NOTES

Commencement: to be appointed.

388 Where and for how long records to be kept

(1) A company's accounting records—
- (a) must be kept at its registered office or such other place as the directors think fit, and
- (b) must at all times be open to inspection by the company's officers.

(2) If accounting records are kept at a place outside the United Kingdom, accounts and returns with respect to the business dealt with in the accounting records so kept must be sent to, and kept at, a place in the United Kingdom, and must at all times be open to such inspection.

(3) The accounts and returns to be sent to the United Kingdom must be such as to—
- (a) disclose with reasonable accuracy the financial position of the business in question at intervals of not more than six months, and
- (b) enable the directors to ensure that the accounts required to be prepared under this Part comply with the requirements of this Act (and, where applicable, of Article 4 of the IAS Regulation).

(4) Accounting records that a company is required by section 386 to keep must be preserved by it—
- (a) in the case of a private company, for three years from the date on which they are made;
- (b) in the case of a public company, for six years from the date on which they are made.

(5) Subsection (4) is subject to any provision contained in rules made under section 411 of the Insolvency Act 1986 (c 45) (company insolvency rules) or Article 359 of the Insolvency (Northern Ireland) Order 1989 (SI 1989/2405 (NI 19)).

[S388]

NOTES

Commencement: to be appointed.

389 Where and for how long records to be kept: offences

(1) If a company fails to comply with any provision of subsections (1) to (3) of section 388 (requirements as to keeping of accounting records), an offence is committed by every officer of the company who is in default.

(2) It is a defence for a person charged with such an offence to show that he acted honestly and that in the circumstances in which the company's business was carried on the default was excusable.

(3) An officer of a company commits an offence if he—

(a) fails to take all reasonable steps for securing compliance by the company with subsection (4) of that section (period for which records to be preserved), or
(b) intentionally causes any default by the company under that subsection.

(4) A person guilty of an offence under this section is liable—
(a) on conviction on indictment, to imprisonment for a term not exceeding two years or a fine (or both);
(b) on summary conviction—
(i) in England and Wales, to imprisonment for a term not exceeding twelve months or to a fine not exceeding the statutory maximum (or both);
(ii) in Scotland or Northern Ireland, to imprisonment for a term not exceeding six months, or to a fine not exceeding the statutory maximum (or both).

[S389]

NOTES

Commencement: to be appointed.

CHAPTER 3
A COMPANY'S FINANCIAL YEAR

390 A company's financial year

(1) A company's financial year is determined as follows.

(2) Its first financial year—
(a) begins with the first day of its first accounting reference period, and
(b) ends with the last day of that period or such other date, not more than seven days before or after the end of that period, as the directors may determine.

(3) Subsequent financial years—
(a) begin with the day immediately following the end of the company's previous financial year, and
(b) end with the last day of its next accounting reference period or such other date, not more than seven days before or after the end of that period, as the directors may determine.

(4) In relation to an undertaking that is not a company, references in this Act to its financial year are to any period in respect of which a profit and loss account of the undertaking is required to be made up (by its constitution or by the law under which it is established), whether that period is a year or not.

(5) The directors of a parent company must secure that, except where in their opinion there are good reasons against it, the financial year of each of its subsidiary undertakings coincides with the company's own financial year.

[S390]

NOTES

Commencement: to be appointed.

391 Accounting reference periods and accounting reference date

(1) A company's accounting reference periods are determined according to its accounting reference date in each calendar year.

(2) The accounting reference date of a company incorporated in Great Britain before 1st April 1996 is—
(a) the date specified by notice to the registrar in accordance with section 224(2) of the Companies Act 1985 (c 6) (notice specifying accounting reference date given within nine months of incorporation), or
(b) failing such notice—
(i) in the case of a company incorporated before 1st April 1990, 31st March, and
(ii) in the case of a company incorporated on or after 1st April 1990, the last day of the month in which the anniversary of its incorporation falls.

(3) The accounting reference date of a company incorporated in Northern Ireland before 22nd August 1997 is—

(a) the date specified by notice to the registrar in accordance with article 232(2) of the Companies (Northern Ireland) Order 1986 (SI 1986/1032 (NI 6)) (notice specifying accounting reference date given within nine months of incorporation), or

(b) failing such notice—

(i) in the case of a company incorporated before the coming into operation of Article 5 of the Companies (Northern Ireland) Order 1990 (SI 1990/593 (NI 5)), 31st March, and

(ii) in the case of a company incorporated after the coming into operation of that Article, the last day of the month in which the anniversary of its incorporation falls.

(4) The accounting reference date of a company incorporated—

(a) in Great Britain on or after 1st April 1996 and before the commencement of this Act,

(b) in Northern Ireland on or after 22nd August 1997 and before the commencement of this Act, or

(c) after the commencement of this Act,

is the last day of the month in which the anniversary of its incorporation falls.

(5) A company's first accounting reference period is the period of more than six months, but not more than 18 months, beginning with the date of its incorporation and ending with its accounting reference date.

(6) Its subsequent accounting reference periods are successive periods of twelve months beginning immediately after the end of the previous accounting reference period and ending with its accounting reference date.

(7) This section has effect subject to the provisions of section 392 (alteration of accounting reference date).

[S391]

NOTES

Commencement: to be appointed.

392 Alteration of accounting reference date

(1) A company may by notice given to the registrar specify a new accounting reference date having effect in relation to—

(a) the company's current accounting reference period and subsequent periods, or

(b) the company's previous accounting reference period and subsequent periods.

A company's "previous accounting reference period" means the one immediately preceding its current accounting reference period.

(2) The notice must state whether the current or previous accounting reference period—

(a) is to be shortened, so as to come to an end on the first occasion on which the new accounting reference date falls or fell after the beginning of the period, or

(b) is to be extended, so as to come to an end on the second occasion on which that date falls or fell after the beginning of the period.

(3) A notice extending a company's current or previous accounting reference period is not effective if given less than five years after the end of an earlier accounting reference period of the company that was extended under this section.

This does not apply—

(a) to a notice given by a company that is a subsidiary undertaking or parent undertaking of another EEA undertaking if the new accounting reference date coincides with that of the other EEA undertaking or, where that undertaking is not a company, with the last day of its financial year, or

(b) where the company is in administration under Part 2 of the Insolvency Act 1986 (c 45) or Part 3 of the Insolvency (Northern Ireland) Order 1989 (SI 1989/2405 (NI 19)), or

(c) where the Secretary of State directs that it should not apply, which he may do with respect to a notice that has been given or that may be given.

(4) A notice under this section may not be given in respect of a previous accounting reference period if the period for filing accounts and reports for the financial year determined by reference to that accounting reference period has already expired.

(5) An accounting reference period may not be extended so as to exceed 18 months and a notice under this section is ineffective if the current or previous accounting reference period as extended in accordance with the notice would exceed that limit.

This does not apply where the company is in administration under Part 2 of the Insolvency Act 1986 (c 45) or Part 3 of the Insolvency (Northern Ireland) Order 1989 (SI 1989/2405 (NI 19)).

(6) In this section "EEA undertaking" means an undertaking established under the law of any part of the United Kingdom or the law of any other EEA State.

[S392]

NOTES

Commencement: to be appointed.

CHAPTER 4
ANNUAL ACCOUNTS

General

393 Accounts to give true and fair view

(1) The directors of a company must not approve accounts for the purposes of this Chapter unless they are satisfied that they give a true and fair view of the assets, liabilities, financial position and profit or loss—

(a) in the case of the company's individual accounts, of the company;

(b) in the case of the company's group accounts, of the undertakings included in the consolidation as a whole, so far as concerns members of the company.

(2) The auditor of a company in carrying out his functions under this Act in relation to the company's annual accounts must have regard to the directors' duty under subsection (1).

[S393]

NOTES

Commencement: to be appointed.

Individual accounts

394 Duty to prepare individual accounts

The directors of every company must prepare accounts for the company for each of its financial years.

Those accounts are referred to as the company's "individual accounts".

[S394]

NOTES

Commencement: to be appointed.

395 Individual accounts: applicable accounting framework

(1) A company's individual accounts may be prepared—

(a) in accordance with section 396 ("Companies Act individual accounts"), or

(b) in accordance with international accounting standards ("IAS individual accounts").

This is subject to the following provisions of this section and to section 407 (consistency of financial reporting within group).

(2) The individual accounts of a company that is a charity must be Companies Act individual accounts.

(3) After the first financial year in which the directors of a company prepare IAS individual accounts ("the first IAS year"), all subsequent individual accounts of the company must be prepared in accordance with international accounting standards unless there is a relevant change of circumstance.

(4) There is a relevant change of circumstance if, at any time during or after the first IAS year—

(a) the company becomes a subsidiary undertaking of another undertaking that does not prepare IAS individual accounts,

(b) the company ceases to be a company with securities admitted to trading on a regulated market in an EEA State, or

(c) a parent undertaking of the company ceases to be an undertaking with securities admitted to trading on a regulated market in an EEA State.

(5) If, having changed to preparing Companies Act individual accounts following a relevant change of circumstance, the directors again prepare IAS individual accounts for the company, subsections (3) and (4) apply again as if the first financial year for which such accounts are again prepared were the first IAS year.

[S395]

NOTES

Commencement: to be appointed.

396 Companies Act individual accounts

(1) Companies Act individual accounts must comprise—

(a) a balance sheet as at the last day of the financial year, and

(b) a profit and loss account.

(2) The accounts must—

(a) in the case of the balance sheet, give a true and fair view of the state of affairs of the company as at the end of the financial year, and

(b) in the case of the profit and loss account, give a true and fair view of the profit or loss of the company for the financial year.

(3) The accounts must comply with provision made by the Secretary of State by regulations as to—

(a) the form and content of the balance sheet and profit and loss account, and

(b) additional information to be provided by way of notes to the accounts.

(4) If compliance with the regulations, and any other provision made by or under this Act as to the matters to be included in a company's individual accounts or in notes to those accounts, would not be sufficient to give a true and fair view, the necessary additional information must be given in the accounts or in a note to them.

(5) If in special circumstances compliance with any of those provisions is inconsistent with the requirement to give a true and fair view, the directors must depart from that provision to the extent necessary to give a true and fair view.

Particulars of any such departure, the reasons for it and its effect must be given in a note to the accounts.

[S396]

NOTES

Commencement: 20 January 2007 (for the purpose of enabling the exercise of powers to make Orders or Regulations by statutory instrument); to be appointed (otherwise).

397 IAS individual accounts

Where the directors of a company prepare IAS individual accounts, they must state in the notes to the accounts that the accounts have been prepared in accordance with international accounting standards.

[S397]

NOTES

Commencement: to be appointed.

Group accounts: small companies

398 Option to prepare group accounts

If at the end of a financial year a company subject to the small companies regime is a parent company the directors, as well as preparing individual accounts for the year, may prepare group accounts for the year.

[S398]

NOTES

Commencement: to be appointed.

Group accounts: other companies

399 Duty to prepare group accounts

(1) This section applies to companies that are not subject to the small companies regime.

(2) If at the end of a financial year the company is a parent company the directors, as well as preparing individual accounts for the year, must prepare group accounts for the year unless the company is exempt from that requirement.

(3) There are exemptions under-

section 400 (company included in EEA accounts of larger group),

section 401 (company included in non-EEA accounts of larger group), and

section 402 (company none of whose subsidiary undertakings need be included in the consolidation).

(4) A company to which this section applies but which is exempt from the requirement to prepare group accounts, may do so.

[S399]

NOTES

Commencement: to be appointed.

400 Exemption for company included in EEA group accounts of larger group

(1) A company is exempt from the requirement to prepare group accounts if it is itself a subsidiary undertaking and its immediate parent undertaking is established under the law of an EEA State, in the following cases—

(a) where the company is a wholly-owned subsidiary of that parent undertaking;

(b) where that parent undertaking holds more than 50% of the allotted shares in the company and notice requesting the preparation of group accounts has not been served on the company by shareholders holding in aggregate—

(i) more than half of the remaining allotted shares in the company, or

(ii) 5% of the total allotted shares in the company.

Such notice must be served not later than six months after the end of the financial year before that to which it relates.

(2) Exemption is conditional upon compliance with all of the following conditions—

(a) the company must be included in consolidated accounts for a larger group drawn up to the same date, or to an earlier date in the same financial year, by a parent undertaking established under the law of an EEA State;

(b) those accounts must be drawn up and audited, and that parent undertaking's annual report must be drawn up, according to that law—

(i) in accordance with the provisions of the Seventh Directive (83/ 349/EEC) (as modified, where relevant, by the provisions of the Bank Accounts Directive (86/635/EEC) or the Insurance Accounts Directive (91/674/EEC)), or

(ii) in accordance with international accounting standards;

(c) the company must disclose in its individual accounts that it is exempt from the obligation to prepare and deliver group accounts;

(d) the company must state in its individual accounts the name of the parent undertaking that draws up the group accounts referred to above and—

(i) if it is incorporated outside the United Kingdom, the country in which it is incorporated, or

(ii) if it is unincorporated, the address of its principal place of business;

(e) the company must deliver to the registrar, within the period for filing its accounts and reports for the financial year in question, copies of—

(i) those group accounts, and

(ii) the parent undertaking's annual report,

together with the auditor's report on them;

(f) any requirement of Part 35 of this Act as to the delivery to the registrar of a certified translation into English must be met in relation to any document comprised in the accounts and reports delivered in accordance with paragraph (e).

(3) For the purposes of subsection (1)(b) shares held by a wholly-owned subsidiary of the parent undertaking, or held on behalf of the parent undertaking or a wholly-owned subsidiary, shall be attributed to the parent undertaking.

(4) The exemption does not apply to a company any of whose securities are admitted to trading on a regulated market in an EEA State.

(5) Shares held by directors of a company for the purpose of complying with any share qualification requirement shall be disregarded in determining for the purposes of this section whether the company is a wholly-owned subsidiary.

(6) In subsection (4) "securities" includes—

(a) shares and stock,

(b) debentures, including debenture stock, loan stock, bonds, certificates of deposit and other instruments creating or acknowledging indebtedness,

(c) warrants or other instruments entitling the holder to subscribe for securities falling within paragraph (a) or (b), and

(d) certificates or other instruments that confer—

(i) property rights in respect of a security falling within paragraph (a), (b) or (c),

(ii) any right to acquire, dispose of, underwrite or convert a security, being a right to which the holder would be entitled if he held any such security to which the certificate or other instrument relates, or

(iii) a contractual right (other than an option) to acquire any such security otherwise than by subscription.

[S400]

NOTES

Commencement: to be appointed.

401 Exemption for company included in non-EEA group accounts of larger group

(1) A company is exempt from the requirement to prepare group accounts if it is itself a subsidiary undertaking and its parent undertaking is not established under the law of an EEA State, in the following cases—

(a) where the company is a wholly-owned subsidiary of that parent undertaking;

(b) where that parent undertaking holds more than 50% of the allotted shares in the company and notice requesting the preparation of group accounts has not been served on the company by shareholders holding in aggregate—

(i) more than half of the remaining allotted shares in the company, or

(ii) 5% of the total allotted shares in the company.

Such notice must be served not later than six months after the end of the financial year before that to which it relates.

(2) Exemption is conditional upon compliance with all of the following conditions—

(a) the company and all of its subsidiary undertakings must be included in consolidated accounts for a larger group drawn up to the same date, or to an earlier date in the same financial year, by a parent undertaking;

(b) those accounts and, where appropriate, the group's annual report, must be drawn up—

(i) in accordance with the provisions of the Seventh Directive (83/ 349/EEC) (as modified, where relevant, by the provisions of the Bank Accounts Directive (86/635/EEC) or the Insurance Accounts Directive (91/674/EEC)), or

(ii) in a manner equivalent to consolidated accounts and consolidated annual reports so drawn up;

(c) the group accounts must be audited by one or more persons authorised to audit accounts under the law under which the parent undertaking which draws them up is established;

(d) the company must disclose in its individual accounts that it is exempt from the obligation to prepare and deliver group accounts;

(e) the company must state in its individual accounts the name of the parent undertaking which draws up the group accounts referred to above and—

(i) if it is incorporated outside the United Kingdom, the country in which it is incorporated, or

(ii) if it is unincorporated, the address of its principal place of business;

(f) the company must deliver to the registrar, within the period for filing its accounts and reports for the financial year in question, copies of—

(i) the group accounts, and

(ii) where appropriate, the consolidated annual report,

together with the auditor's report on them;

(g) any requirement of Part 35 of this Act as to the delivery to the registrar of a certified translation into English must be met in relation to any document comprised in the accounts and reports delivered in accordance with paragraph (f).

(3) For the purposes of subsection (1)(b), shares held by a wholly-owned subsidiary of the parent undertaking, or held on behalf of the parent undertaking or a wholly-owned subsidiary, are attributed to the parent undertaking.

(4) The exemption does not apply to a company any of whose securities are admitted to trading on a regulated market in an EEA State.

(5) Shares held by directors of a company for the purpose of complying with any share qualification requirement shall be disregarded in determining for the purposes of this section whether the company is a wholly-owned subsidiary.

(6) In subsection (4) "securities" includes—

(a) shares and stock,

(b) debentures, including debenture stock, loan stock, bonds, certificates of deposit and other instruments creating or acknowledging indebtedness,

(c) warrants or other instruments entitling the holder to subscribe for securities falling within paragraph (a) or (b), and

(d) certificates or other instruments that confer—

(i) property rights in respect of a security falling within paragraph (a), (b) or (c),

(ii) any right to acquire, dispose of, underwrite or convert a security, being a right to which the holder would be entitled if he held any such security to which the certificate or other instrument relates, or

(iii) a contractual right (other than an option) to acquire any such security otherwise than by subscription.

[S401]

NOTES

Commencement: to be appointed.

402 Exemption if no subsidiary undertakings need be included in the consolidation

A parent company is exempt from the requirement to prepare group accounts if under section 405 all of its subsidiary undertakings could be excluded from consolidation in Companies Act group accounts.

[S402]

NOTES

Commencement: to be appointed.

Group accounts: general

403 Group accounts: applicable accounting framework

(1) The group accounts of certain parent companies are required by Article 4 of the IAS Regulation to be prepared in accordance with international accounting standards ("IAS group accounts").

(2) The group accounts of other companies may be prepared—
- (a) in accordance with section 404 ("Companies Act group accounts"), or
- (b) in accordance with international accounting standards ("IAS group accounts").

This is subject to the following provisions of this section.

(3) The group accounts of a parent company that is a charity must be Companies Act group accounts.

(4) After the first financial year in which the directors of a parent company prepare IAS group accounts ("the first IAS year"), all subsequent group accounts of the company must be prepared in accordance with international accounting standards unless there is a relevant change of circumstance.

(5) There is a relevant change of circumstance if, at any time during or after the first IAS year—
- (a) the company becomes a subsidiary undertaking of another undertaking that does not prepare IAS group accounts,
- (b) the company ceases to be a company with securities admitted to trading on a regulated market in an EEA State, or
- (c) a parent undertaking of the company ceases to be an undertaking with securities admitted to trading on a regulated market in an EEA State.

(6) If, having changed to preparing Companies Act group accounts following a relevant change of circumstance, the directors again prepare IAS group accounts for the company, subsections (4) and (5) apply again as if the first financial year for which such accounts are again prepared were the first IAS year.

[S403]

NOTES
Commencement: to be appointed.

404 Companies Act group accounts

(1) Companies Act group accounts must comprise—
- (a) a consolidated balance sheet dealing with the state of affairs of the parent company and its subsidiary undertakings, and
- (b) a consolidated profit and loss account dealing with the profit or loss of the parent company and its subsidiary undertakings.

(2) The accounts must give a true and fair view of the state of affairs as at the end of the financial year, and the profit or loss for the financial year, of the undertakings included in the consolidation as a whole, so far as concerns members of the company.

(3) The accounts must comply with provision made by the Secretary of State by regulations as to—
- (a) the form and content of the consolidated balance sheet and consolidated profit and loss account, and
- (b) additional information to be provided by way of notes to the accounts.

(4) If compliance with the regulations, and any other provision made by or under this Act as to the matters to be included in a company's group accounts or in notes to those accounts, would not be sufficient to give a true and fair view, the necessary additional information must be given in the accounts or in a note to them.

(5) If in special circumstances compliance with any of those provisions is inconsistent with the requirement to give a true and fair view, the directors must depart from that provision to the extent necessary to give a true and fair view.

Particulars of any such departure, the reasons for it and its effect must be given in a note to the accounts.

[S404]

NOTES

Commencement: 20 January 2007 (for the purpose of enabling the exercise of powers to make Orders or Regulations by statutory instrument); to be appointed (otherwise).

405 Companies Act group accounts: subsidiary undertakings included in the consolidation

(1) Where a parent company prepares Companies Act group accounts, all the subsidiary undertakings of the company must be included in the consolidation, subject to the following exceptions.

(2) A subsidiary undertaking may be excluded from consolidation if its inclusion is not material for the purpose of giving a true and fair view (but two or more undertakings may be excluded only if they are not material taken together).

(3) A subsidiary undertaking may be excluded from consolidation where—

(a) severe long-term restrictions substantially hinder the exercise of the rights of the parent company over the assets or management of that undertaking, or

(b) the information necessary for the preparation of group accounts cannot be obtained without disproportionate expense or undue delay, or

(c) the interest of the parent company is held exclusively with a view to subsequent resale.

(4) The reference in subsection (3)(a) to the rights of the parent company and the reference in subsection (3)(c) to the interest of the parent company are, respectively, to rights and interests held by or attributed to the company for the purposes of the definition of "parent undertaking" (see section 1162) in the absence of which it would not be the parent company.

[S405]

NOTES

Commencement: to be appointed.

406 IAS group accounts

Where the directors of a company prepare IAS group accounts, they must state in the notes to those accounts that the accounts have been prepared in accordance with international accounting standards.

[S406]

NOTES

Commencement: to be appointed.

407 Consistency of financial reporting within group

(1) The directors of a parent company must secure that the individual accounts of—

(a) the parent company, and

(b) each of its subsidiary undertakings,

are all prepared using the same financial reporting framework, except to the extent that in their opinion there are good reasons for not doing so.

(2) Subsection (1) does not apply if the directors do not prepare group accounts for the parent company.

(3) Subsection (1) only applies to accounts of subsidiary undertakings that are required to be prepared under this Part.

(4) Subsection (1) does not require accounts of undertakings that are charities to be prepared using the same financial reporting framework as accounts of undertakings which are not charities.

(5) Subsection (1)(a) does not apply where the directors of a parent company prepare IAS group accounts and IAS individual accounts.

[S407]

NOTES

Commencement: to be appointed.

408 Individual profit and loss account where group accounts prepared

(1) This section applies where—

(a) a company prepares group accounts in accordance with this Act, and

(b) the notes to the company's individual balance sheet show the company's profit or loss for the financial year determined in accordance with this Act.

(2) The profit and loss account need not contain the information specified in section 411 (information about employee numbers and costs).

(3) The company's individual profit and loss account must be approved in accordance with section 414(1) (approval by directors) but may be omitted from the company's annual accounts for the purposes of the other provisions of the Companies Acts.

(4) The exemption conferred by this section is conditional upon its being disclosed in the company's annual accounts that the exemption applies.

[S408]

NOTES

Commencement: to be appointed.

Information to be given in notes to the accounts

409 Information about related undertakings

(1) The Secretary of State may make provision by regulations requiring information about related undertakings to be given in notes to a company's annual accounts.

(2) The regulations—

(a) may make different provision according to whether or not the company prepares group accounts, and

(b) may specify the descriptions of undertaking in relation to which they apply, and make different provision in relation to different descriptions of related undertaking.

(3) The regulations may provide that information need not be disclosed with respect to an undertaking that—

(a) is established under the law of a country outside the United Kingdom, or

(b) carries on business outside the United Kingdom,

if the following conditions are met.

(4) The conditions are—

(a) that in the opinion of the directors of the company the disclosure would be seriously prejudicial to the business of—

(i) that undertaking,

(ii) the company,

(iii) any of the company's subsidiary undertakings, or

(iv) any other undertaking which is included in the consolidation;

(b) that the Secretary of State agrees that the information need not be disclosed.

(5) Where advantage is taken of any such exemption, that fact must be stated in a note to the company's annual accounts.

[S409]

NOTES

Commencement: 20 January 2007 (for the purpose of enabling the exercise of powers to make Orders or Regulations by statutory instrument); to be appointed (otherwise).

410 Information about related undertakings: alternative compliance

(1) This section applies where the directors of a company are of the opinion that the number of undertakings in respect of which the company is required to disclose information under any provision of regulations under section 409 (related undertakings) is such that compliance with that provision would result in information of excessive length being given in notes to the company's annual accounts.

(2) The information need only be given in respect of—

(a) the undertakings whose results or financial position, in the opinion of the directors, principally affected the figures shown in the company's annual accounts, and
(b) where the company prepares group accounts, undertakings excluded from consolidation under section 405(3) (undertakings excluded on grounds other than materiality).

(3) If advantage is taken of subsection (2)—
(a) there must be included in the notes to the company's annual accounts a statement that the information is given only with respect to such undertakings as are mentioned in that subsection, and
(b) the full information (both that which is disclosed in the notes to the accounts and that which is not) must be annexed to the company's next annual return.

For this purpose the "next annual return" means that next delivered to the registrar after the accounts in question have been approved under section 414.

(4) If a company fails to comply with subsection (3)(b), an offence is committed by—
(a) the company, and
(b) every officer of the company who is in default.

(5) A person guilty of an offence under subsection (4) is liable on summary conviction to a fine not exceeding level 3 on the standard scale and, for continued contravention, a daily default fine not exceeding one-tenth of level 3 on the standard scale.

[S410]

NOTES
Commencement: to be appointed.

411 Information about employee numbers and costs

(1) In the case of a company not subject to the small companies regime, the following information with respect to the employees of the company must be given in notes to the company's annual accounts—
(a) the average number of persons employed by the company in the financial year, and
(b) the average number of persons so employed within each category of persons employed by the company.

(2) The categories by reference to which the number required to be disclosed by subsection (1)(b) is to be determined must be such as the directors may select having regard to the manner in which the company's activities are organised.

(3) The average number required by subsection (1)(a) or (b) is determined by dividing the relevant annual number by the number of months in the financial year.

(4) The relevant annual number is determined by ascertaining for each month in the financial year—
(a) for the purposes of subsection (1)(a), the number of persons employed under contracts of service by the company in that month (whether throughout the month or not);
(b) for the purposes of subsection (1)(b), the number of persons in the category in question of persons so employed;

and adding together all the monthly numbers.

(5) In respect of all persons employed by the company during the financial year who are taken into account in determining the relevant annual number for the purposes of subsection (1)(a) there must also be stated the aggregate amounts respectively of—
(a) wages and salaries paid or payable in respect of that year to those persons;
(b) social security costs incurred by the company on their behalf; and
(c) other pension costs so incurred.

This does not apply in so far as those amounts, or any of them, are stated elsewhere in the company's accounts.

(6) In subsection (5)—
"pension costs" includes any costs incurred by the company in respect of—
(a) any pension scheme established for the purpose of providing pensions for persons currently or formerly employed by the company,

(b) any sums set aside for the future payment of pensions directly by the company to current or former employees, and

(c) any pensions paid directly to such persons without having first been set aside;

"social security costs" means any contributions by the company to any state social security or pension scheme, fund or arrangement.

(7) Where the company prepares group accounts, this section applies as if the undertakings included in the consolidation were a single company.

[S411]

NOTES

Commencement: to be appointed.

412 Information about directors' benefits: remuneration

(1) The Secretary of State may make provision by regulations requiring information to be given in notes to a company's annual accounts about directors' remuneration.

(2) The matters about which information may be required include—

(a) gains made by directors on the exercise of share options;

(b) benefits received or receivable by directors under long-term incentive schemes;

(c) payments for loss of office (as defined in section 215);

(d) benefits receivable, and contributions for the purpose of providing benefits, in respect of past services of a person as director or in any other capacity while director;

(e) consideration paid to or receivable by third parties for making available the services of a person as director or in any other capacity while director.

(3) Without prejudice to the generality of subsection (1), regulations under this section may make any such provision as was made immediately before the commencement of this Part by Part 1 of Schedule 6 to the Companies Act 1985 (c 6).

(4) For the purposes of this section, and regulations made under it, amounts paid to or receivable by—

(a) a person connected with a director, or

(b) a body corporate controlled by a director,

are treated as paid to or receivable by the director.

The expressions "connected with" and "controlled by" in this subsection have the same meaning as in Part 10 (company directors).

(5) It is the duty of—

(a) any director of a company, and

(b) any person who is or has at any time in the preceding five years been a director of the company,

to give notice to the company of such matters relating to himself as may be necessary for the purposes of regulations under this section.

(6) A person who makes default in complying with subsection (5) commits an offence and is liable on summary conviction to a fine not exceeding level 3 on the standard scale.

[S412]

NOTES

Commencement: 20 January 2007 (for the purpose of enabling the exercise of powers to make Orders or Regulations by statutory instrument); to be appointed (otherwise).

413 Information about directors' benefits: advances, credit and guarantees

(1) In the case of a company that does not prepare group accounts, details of—

(a) advances and credits granted by the company to its directors, and

(b) guarantees of any kind entered into by the company on behalf of its directors,

must be shown in the notes to its individual accounts.

(2) In the case of a parent company that prepares group accounts, details of—

(a) advances and credits granted to the directors of the parent company, by that company or by any of its subsidiary undertakings, and

(b) guarantees of any kind entered into on behalf of the directors of the parent company, by that company or by any of its subsidiary undertakings,

must be shown in the notes to the group accounts.

(3) The details required of an advance or credit are—

(a) its amount,
(b) an indication of the interest rate,
(c) its main conditions, and
(d) any amounts repaid.

(4) The details required of a guarantee are—

(a) its main terms,
(b) the amount of the maximum liability that may be incurred by the company (or its subsidiary), and
(c) any amount paid and any liability incurred by the company (or its subsidiary) for the purpose of fulfilling the guarantee (including any loss incurred by reason of enforcement of the guarantee).

(5) There must also be stated in the notes to the accounts the totals—

(a) of amounts stated under subsection (3)(a),
(b) of amounts stated under subsection (3)(d),
(c) of amounts stated under subsection (4)(b), and
(d) of amounts stated under subsection (4)(c).

(6) References in this section to the directors of a company are to the persons who were a director at any time in the financial year to which the accounts relate.

(7) The requirements of this section apply in relation to every advance, credit or guarantee subsisting at any time in the financial year to which the accounts relate—

(a) whenever it was entered into,
(b) whether or not the person concerned was a director of the company in question at the time it was entered into, and
(c) in the case of an advance, credit or guarantee involving a subsidiary undertaking of that company, whether or not that undertaking was such a subsidiary undertaking at the time it was entered into.

(8) Banking companies and the holding companies of credit institutions need only state the details required by subsections (3)(a) and (4)(b).

[S413]

NOTES

Commencement: to be appointed.

Approval and signing of accounts

414 Approval and signing of accounts

(1) A company's annual accounts must be approved by the board of directors and signed on behalf of the board by a director of the company.

(2) The signature must be on the company's balance sheet.

(3) If the accounts are prepared in accordance with the provisions applicable to companies subject to the small companies regime, the balance sheet must contain a statement to that effect in a prominent position above the signature.

(4) If annual accounts are approved that do not comply with the requirements of this Act (and, where applicable, of Article 4 of the IAS Regulation), every director of the company who—

(a) knew that they did not comply, or was reckless as to whether they complied, and
(b) failed to take reasonable steps to secure compliance with those requirements or, as the case may be, to prevent the accounts from being approved,

commits an offence.

(5) A person guilty of an offence under this section is liable—

(a) on conviction on indictment, to a fine;

(b) on summary conviction, to a fine not exceeding the statutory maximum.

[S414]

NOTES

Commencement: to be appointed.

CHAPTER 5
DIRECTORS' REPORT

Directors' report

415 Duty to prepare directors' report

(1) The directors of a company must prepare a directors' report for each financial year of the company.

(2) For a financial year in which—

(a) the company is a parent company, and

(b) the directors of the company prepare group accounts,

the directors' report must be a consolidated report (a "group directors' report") relating to the undertakings included in the consolidation.

(3) A group directors' report may, where appropriate, give greater emphasis to the matters that are significant to the undertakings included in the consolidation, taken as a whole.

(4) In the case of failure to comply with the requirement to prepare a directors' report, an offence is committed by every person who—

(a) was a director of the company immediately before the end of the period for filing accounts and reports for the financial year in question, and

(b) failed to take all reasonable steps for securing compliance with that requirement.

(5) A person guilty of an offence under this section is liable—

(a) on conviction on indictment, to a fine;

(b) on summary conviction, to a fine not exceeding the statutory maximum.

[S415]

NOTES

Commencement: to be appointed.

416 Contents of directors' report: general

(1) The directors' report for a financial year must state—

(a) the names of the persons who, at any time during the financial year, were directors of the company, and

(b) the principal activities of the company in the course of the year.

(2) In relation to a group directors' report subsection (1)(b) has effect as if the reference to the company was to the undertakings included in the consolidation.

(3) Except in the case of a company subject to the small companies regime, the report must state the amount (if any) that the directors recommend should be paid by way of dividend.

(4) The Secretary of State may make provision by regulations as to other matters that must be disclosed in a directors' report.

Without prejudice to the generality of this power, the regulations may make any such provision as was formerly made by Schedule 7 to the Companies Act 1985.

[S416]

NOTES

Commencement: 20 January 2007 (for the purpose of enabling the exercise of powers to make Orders or Regulations by statutory instrument); to be appointed (otherwise).

417 Contents of directors' report: business review

(1) Unless the company is subject to the small companies' regime, the directors' report must contain a business review.

(2) The purpose of the business review is to inform members of the company and help them assess how the directors have performed their duty under section 172 (duty to promote the success of the company).

(3) The business review must contain—
(a) a fair review of the company's business, and
(b) a description of the principal risks and uncertainties facing the company.

(4) The review required is a balanced and comprehensive analysis of—
(a) the development and performance of the company's business during the financial year, and
(b) the position of the company's business at the end of that year,

consistent with the size and complexity of the business.

(5) In the case of a quoted company the business review must, to the extent necessary for an understanding of the development, performance or position of the company's business, include—
(a) the main trends and factors likely to affect the future development, performance and position of the company's business; and
(b) information about—
(i) environmental matters (including the impact of the company's business on the environment),
(ii) the company's employees, and
(iii) social and community issues,

including information about any policies of the company in relation to those matters and the effectiveness of those policies; and
(c) subject to subsection (11), information about persons with whom the company has contractual or other arrangements which are essential to the business of the company.

If the review does not contain information of each kind mentioned in paragraphs (b)(i), (ii) and (iii) and (c), it must state which of those kinds of information it does not contain.

(6) The review must, to the extent necessary for an understanding of the development, performance or position of the company's business, include—
(a) analysis using financial key performance indicators, and
(b) where appropriate, analysis using other key performance indicators, including information relating to environmental matters and employee matters.

"Key performance indicators" means factors by reference to which the development, performance or position of the company's business can be measured effectively.

(7) Where a company qualifies as medium-sized in relation to a financial year (see sections 465 to 467), the directors' report for the year need not comply with the requirements of subsection (6) so far as they relate to non-financial information.

(8) The review must, where appropriate, include references to, and additional explanations of, amounts included in the company's annual accounts.

(9) In relation to a group directors' report this section has effect as if the references to the company were references to the undertakings included in the consolidation.

(10) Nothing in this section requires the disclosure of information about impending developments or matters in the course of negotiation if the disclosure would, in the opinion of the directors, be seriously prejudicial to the interests of the company.

(11) Nothing in subsection (5)(c) requires the disclosure of information about a person if the disclosure would, in the opinion of the directors, be seriously prejudicial to that person and contrary to the public interest.

[S417]

NOTES

Commencement: 1 October 2007 (for transitional provisions etc see the note below).

Transitional provisions, etc: Sch 3, para 43 to the draft Companies Act 2006 (Commencement No 3, Consequential Amendments, Transitional Provisions and Savings) Order 2007 (at **[A12]**) provides as follows—

"43 Contents of directors' report: business review (s 417)

(1) Section 417 of the Companies Act 2006 (contents of directors' report: business review) applies to directors' reports for financial years beginning on or after 1st October 2007.

(2) Sections 234(1)(a), 234ZZB, 246(4)(a) and 246A(2A) of the 1985 Act or Articles 242(1), 242ZZB, 254(4)(a) and 254A(2A) of the 1986 Order continue to apply to directors' reports for financial years beginning before that date.".

Transitional adaptations: art 6 of the draft Companies Act 2006 (Commencement No 3, Consequential Amendments, Transitional Provisions and Savings) Order 2007 provides that the provisions brought into force by that Order shall have effect subject to any transitional adaptations specified in Sch 1 to that Order. Schedule 1, para 16 to the Order (at **[A12]**) provides as follows—

"16 Contents of directors' report: business review (s 417)

(1) Section 417 (contents of directors' report: business review) has effect with the following adaptations.

(2) For subsection (1) substitute—

"(1) Unless the company is entitled to small companies exemption in relation to the directors' report, the report must contain a business review.

(1A) A company is entitled to small companies exemption in relation to the directors' report for a financial year if it—

(a) qualifies as small in relation to that year under Part 7 of the Companies Act 1985 or Part 8 of the Companies (Northern Ireland) Order 1986, and

(b) is not, and was not at any time within that year, an ineligible company as defined in section 247A(1B) of that Act or Article 255A(1B) of that Order.".

(3) For subsection (7) substitute—

"(7) Where a company—

(a) qualifies as medium-sized in relation to a financial year under Part 7 of the Companies Act 1985 or Part 8 of the Companies (Northern Ireland) Order 1986, and

(b) is not, and was not at any time within that year, an ineligible company as defined in section 247A(1B) of that Act or Article 255A(1B) of that Order,

the directors' report for the year need not comply with the requirements of subsection (6) so far as they relate to non-financial information.".".

---

418 Contents of directors' report: statement as to disclosure to auditors

(1) This section applies to a company unless—

(a) it is exempt for the financial year in question from the requirements of Part 16 as to audit of accounts, and

(b) the directors take advantage of that exemption.

(2) The directors' report must contain a statement to the effect that, in the case of each of the persons who are directors at the time the report is approved—

(a) so far as the director is aware, there is no relevant audit information of which the company's auditor is unaware, and

(b) he has taken all the steps that he ought to have taken as a director in order to make himself aware of any relevant audit information and to establish that the company's auditor is aware of that information.

(3) "Relevant audit information" means information needed by the company's auditor in connection with preparing his report.

(4) A director is regarded as having taken all the steps that he ought to have taken as a director in order to do the things mentioned in subsection (2)(b) if he has—

(a) made such enquiries of his fellow directors and of the company's auditors for that purpose, and

(b) taken such other steps (if any) for that purpose,

as are required by his duty as a director of the company to exercise reasonable care, skill and diligence.

(5) Where a directors' report containing the statement required by this section is approved but the statement is false, every director of the company who—

(a) knew that the statement was false, or was reckless as to whether it was false, and

(b) failed to take reasonable steps to prevent the report from being approved,

commits an offence.

(6) A person guilty of an offence under subsection (5) is liable—

(a) on conviction on indictment, to imprisonment for a term not exceeding two years or a fine (or both);

(b) on summary conviction—

(i) in England and Wales, to imprisonment for a term not exceeding twelve months or to a fine not exceeding the statutory maximum (or both);

(ii) in Scotland or Northern Ireland, to imprisonment for a term not exceeding six months, or to a fine not exceeding the statutory maximum (or both).

[S418]

NOTES

Commencement: to be appointed.

419 Approval and signing of directors' report

(1) The directors' report must be approved by the board of directors and signed on behalf of the board by a director or the secretary of the company.

(2) If the report is prepared in accordance with the small companies regime, it must contain a statement to that effect in a prominent position above the signature.

(3) If a directors' report is approved that does not comply with the requirements of this Act, every director of the company who—

(a) knew that it did not comply, or was reckless as to whether it complied, and

(b) failed to take reasonable steps to secure compliance with those requirements or, as the case may be, to prevent the report from being approved,

commits an offence.

(4) A person guilty of an offence under this section is liable—

(a) on conviction on indictment, to a fine;

(b) on summary conviction, to a fine not exceeding the statutory maximum.

[S419]

NOTES

Commencement: to be appointed.

CHAPTER 6
QUOTED COMPANIES: DIRECTORS' REMUNERATION REPORT

420 Duty to prepare directors' remuneration report

(1) The directors of a quoted company must prepare a directors' remuneration report for each financial year of the company.

(2) In the case of failure to comply with the requirement to prepare a directors' remuneration report, every person who—

(a) was a director of the company immediately before the end of the period for filing accounts and reports for the financial year in question, and

(b) failed to take all reasonable steps for securing compliance with that requirement,

commits an offence.

(3) A person guilty of an offence under this section is liable—

(a) on conviction on indictment, to a fine;

(b) on summary conviction, to a fine not exceeding the statutory maximum.

[S420]

NOTES

Commencement: to be appointed.

421 Contents of directors' remuneration report

(1) The Secretary of State may make provision by regulations as to—

(a) the information that must be contained in a directors' remuneration report,

(b) how information is to be set out in the report, and

(c) what is to be the auditable part of the report.

(2) Without prejudice to the generality of this power, the regulations may make any such provision as was made, immediately before the commencement of this Part, by Schedule 7A to the Companies Act 1985 (c 6).

(3) It is the duty of—

(a) any director of a company, and

(b) any person who is or has at any time in the preceding five years been a director of the company,

to give notice to the company of such matters relating to himself as may be necessary for the purposes of regulations under this section.

(4) A person who makes default in complying with subsection (3) commits an offence and is liable on summary conviction to a fine not exceeding level 3 on the standard scale.

[S421]

NOTES

Commencement: 20 January 2007 (for the purpose of enabling the exercise of powers to make Orders or Regulations by statutory instrument); to be appointed (otherwise).

422 Approval and signing of directors' remuneration report

(1) The directors' remuneration report must be approved by the board of directors and signed on behalf of the board by a director or the secretary of the company.

(2) If a directors' remuneration report is approved that does not comply with the requirements of this Act, every director of the company who—

(a) knew that it did not comply, or was reckless as to whether it complied, and

(b) failed to take reasonable steps to secure compliance with those requirements or, as the case may be, to prevent the report from being approved,

commits an offence.

(3) A person guilty of an offence under this section is liable—

(a) on conviction on indictment, to a fine;

(b) on summary conviction, to a fine not exceeding the statutory maximum.

[S422]

NOTES

Commencement: to be appointed.

CHAPTER 7
PUBLICATION OF ACCOUNTS AND REPORTS

Duty to circulate copies of accounts and reports

423 Duty to circulate copies of annual accounts and reports

(1) Every company must send a copy of its annual accounts and reports for each financial year to—

(a) every member of the company,

(b) every holder of the company's debentures, and

(c) every person who is entitled to receive notice of general meetings.

(2) Copies need not be sent to a person for whom the company does not have a current address.

(3) A company has a "current address" for a person if—

(a) an address has been notified to the company by the person as one at which documents may be sent to him, and

(b) the company has no reason to believe that documents sent to him at that address will not reach him.

(4) In the case of a company not having a share capital, copies need not be sent to anyone who is not entitled to receive notices of general meetings of the company.

(5) Where copies are sent out over a period of days, references in the Companies Acts to the day on which copies are sent out shall be read as references to the last day of that period.

(6) This section has effect subject to section 426 (option to provide summary financial statement).

[S423]

NOTES

Commencement: to be appointed.

424 Time allowed for sending out copies of accounts and reports

(1) The time allowed for sending out copies of the company's annual accounts and reports is as follows.

(2) A private company must comply with section 423 not later than—

(a) the end of the period for filing accounts and reports, or

(b) if earlier, the date on which it actually delivers its accounts and reports to the registrar.

(3) A public company must comply with section 423 at least 21 days before the date of the relevant accounts meeting.

(4) If in the case of a public company copies are sent out later than is required by subsection (3), they shall, despite that, be deemed to have been duly sent if it is so agreed by all the members entitled to attend and vote at the relevant accounts meeting.

(5) Whether the time allowed is that for a private company or a public company is determined by reference to the company's status immediately before the end of the accounting reference period by reference to which the financial year for the accounts in question was determined.

(6) In this section the "relevant accounts meeting" means the accounts meeting of the company at which the accounts and reports in question are to be laid.

[S424]

NOTES

Commencement: to be appointed.

425 Default in sending out copies of accounts and reports: offences

(1) If default is made in complying with section 423 or 424, an offence is committed by—

(a) the company, and

(b) every officer of the company who is in default.

(2) A person guilty of an offence under this section is liable—

(a) on conviction on indictment, to a fine;

(b) on summary conviction, to a fine not exceeding the statutory maximum.

[S425]

NOTES

Commencement: to be appointed.

Option to provide summary financial statement

426 Option to provide summary financial statement

(1) A company may—

(a) in such cases as may be specified by regulations made by the Secretary of State, and

(b) provided any conditions so specified are complied with,

provide a summary financial statement instead of copies of the accounts and reports required to be sent out in accordance with section 423.

(2) Copies of those accounts and reports must, however, be sent to any person entitled to be sent them in accordance with that section and who wishes to receive them.

(3) The Secretary of State may make provision by regulations as to the manner in which it is to be ascertained, whether before or after a person becomes entitled to be sent a copy of those accounts and reports, whether he wishes to receive them.

(4) A summary financial statement must comply with the requirements of—
section 427 (form and contents of summary financial statement: unquoted companies), or
section 428 (form and contents of summary financial statement: quoted companies).

(5) This section applies to copies of accounts and reports required to be sent out by virtue of section 146 to a person nominated to enjoy information rights as it applies to copies of accounts and reports required to be sent out in accordance with section 423 to a member of the company.

(6) Regulations under this section are subject to negative resolution procedure.

[S426]

NOTES

Commencement: 20 January 2007 (for the purpose of enabling the exercise of powers to make Orders or Regulations by statutory instrument); to be appointed (otherwise).

427 Form and contents of summary financial statement: unquoted companies

(1) A summary financial statement by a company that is not a quoted company must—
(a) be derived from the company's annual accounts, and
(b) be prepared in accordance with this section and regulations made under it.

(2) The summary financial statement must be in such form, and contain such information, as the Secretary of State may specify by regulations.

The regulations may require the statement to include information derived from the directors' report.

(3) Nothing in this section or regulations made under it prevents a company from including in a summary financial statement additional information derived from the company's annual accounts or the directors' report.

(4) The summary financial statement must—
(a) state that it is only a summary of information derived from the company's annual accounts;
(b) state whether it contains additional information derived from the directors' report and, if so, that it does not contain the full text of that report;
(c) state how a person entitled to them can obtain a full copy of the company's annual accounts and the directors' report;
(d) contain a statement by the company's auditor of his opinion as to whether the summary financial statement—
(i) is consistent with the company's annual accounts and, where information derived from the directors' report is included in the statement, with that report, and
(ii) complies with the requirements of this section and regulations made under it;
(e) state whether the auditor's report on the annual accounts was unqualified or qualified and, if it was qualified, set out the report in full together with any further material needed to understand the qualification;
(f) state whether, in that report, the auditor's statement under section 496 (whether directors' report consistent with accounts) was qualified or unqualified and, if it was qualified, set out the qualified statement in full together with any further material needed to understand the qualification;
(g) state whether that auditor's report contained a statement under—
(i) section 498(2)(a) or (b) (accounting records or returns inadequate or accounts not agreeing with records and returns), or
(ii) section 498(3) (failure to obtain necessary information and explanations),
and if so, set out the statement in full.

(5) Regulations under this section may provide that any specified material may, instead of being included in the summary financial statement, be sent separately at the same time as the statement.

(6) Regulations under this section are subject to negative resolution procedure.

[S427]

NOTES

Commencement: 20 January 2007 (for the purpose of enabling the exercise of powers to make Orders or Regulations by statutory instrument); to be appointed (otherwise).

428 Form and contents of summary financial statement: quoted companies

(1) A summary financial statement by a quoted company must—

(a) be derived from the company's annual accounts and the directors' remuneration report, and

(b) be prepared in accordance with this section and regulations made under it.

(2) The summary financial statement must be in such form, and contain such information, as the Secretary of State may specify by regulations.

The regulations may require the statement to include information derived from the directors' report.

(3) Nothing in this section or regulations made under it prevents a company from including in a summary financial statement additional information derived from the company's annual accounts, the directors' remuneration report or the directors' report.

(4) The summary financial statement must—

(a) state that it is only a summary of information derived from the company's annual accounts and the directors' remuneration report;

(b) state whether it contains additional information derived from the directors' report and, if so, that it does not contain the full text of that report;

(c) state how a person entitled to them can obtain a full copy of the company's annual accounts, the directors' remuneration report or the directors' report;

(d) contain a statement by the company's auditor of his opinion as to whether the summary financial statement—

(i) is consistent with the company's annual accounts and the directors' remuneration report and, where information derived from the directors' report is included in the statement, with that report, and

(ii) complies with the requirements of this section and regulations made under it;

(e) state whether the auditor's report on the annual accounts and the auditable part of the directors' remuneration report was unqualified or qualified and, if it was qualified, set out the report in full together with any further material needed to understand the qualification;

(f) state whether that auditor's report contained a statement under—

(i) section 498(2) (accounting records or returns inadequate or accounts or directors' remuneration report not agreeing with records and returns), or

(ii) section 498(3) (failure to obtain necessary information and explanations),

and if so, set out the statement in full;

(g) state whether, in that report, the auditor's statement under section 496 (whether directors' report consistent with accounts) was qualified or unqualified and, if it was qualified, set out the qualified statement in full together with any further material needed to understand the qualification.

(5) Regulations under this section may provide that any specified material may, instead of being included in the summary financial statement, be sent separately at the same time as the statement.

(6) Regulations under this section are subject to negative resolution procedure.

[S428]

NOTES

Commencement: 20 January 2007 (for the purpose of enabling the exercise of powers to make Orders or Regulations by statutory instrument); to be appointed (otherwise).

429 Summary financial statements: offences

(1) If default is made in complying with any provision of section 426, 427 or 428, or of regulations under any of those sections, an offence is committed by—

(a) the company, and
(b) every officer of the company who is in default.

(2) A person guilty of an offence under this section is liable on summary conviction to a fine not exceeding level 3 on the standard scale.

[S429]

NOTES

Commencement: to be appointed.

Quoted companies: requirements as to website publication

430 Quoted companies: annual accounts and reports to be made available on website

(1) A quoted company must ensure that its annual accounts and reports—
(a) are made available on a website, and
(b) remain so available until the annual accounts and reports for the company's next financial year are made available in accordance with this section.

(2) The annual accounts and reports must be made available on a website that—
(a) is maintained by or on behalf of the company, and
(b) identifies the company in question.

(3) Access to the annual accounts and reports on the website, and the ability to obtain a hard copy of the annual accounts and reports from the website, must not be—
(a) conditional on the payment of a fee, or
(b) otherwise restricted, except so far as necessary to comply with any enactment or regulatory requirement (in the United Kingdom or elsewhere).

(4) The annual accounts and reports—
(a) must be made available as soon as reasonably practicable, and
(b) must be kept available throughout the period specified in subsection (1)(b).

(5) A failure to make the annual accounts and reports available on a website throughout that period is disregarded if—
(a) the annual accounts and reports are made available on the website for part of that period, and
(b) the failure is wholly attributable to circumstances that it would not be reasonable to have expected the company to prevent or avoid.

(6) In the event of default in complying with this section, an offence is committed by every officer of the company who is in default.

(7) A person guilty of an offence under subsection (6) is liable on summary conviction to a fine not exceeding level 3 on the standard scale.

[S430]

NOTES

Commencement: to be appointed.

Right of member or debenture holder to demand copies of accounts and reports

431 Right of member or debenture holder to copies of accounts and reports: unquoted companies

(1) A member of, or holder of debentures of, an unquoted company is entitled to be provided, on demand and without charge, with a copy of—
(a) the company's last annual accounts,
(b) the last directors' report, and
(c) the auditor's report on those accounts (including the statement on that report).

(2) The entitlement under this section is to a single copy of those documents, but that is in addition to any copy to which a person may be entitled under section 423.

(3) If a demand made under this section is not complied with within seven days of receipt by the company, an offence is committed by—

(a) the company, and
(b) every officer of the company who is in default.

(4) A person guilty of an offence under this section is liable on summary conviction to a fine not exceeding level 3 on the standard scale and, for continued contravention, a daily default fine not exceeding one-tenth of level 3 on the standard scale.

[S431]

NOTES
Commencement: to be appointed.

432 Right of member or debenture holder to copies of accounts and reports: quoted companies

(1) A member of, or holder of debentures of, a quoted company is entitled to be provided, on demand and without charge, with a copy of—
(a) the company's last annual accounts,
(b) the last directors' remuneration report,
(c) the last directors' report, and
(d) the auditor's report on those accounts (including the report on the directors' remuneration report and on the directors' report).

(2) The entitlement under this section is to a single copy of those documents, but that is in addition to any copy to which a person may be entitled under section 423.

(3) If a demand made under this section is not complied with within seven days of receipt by the company, an offence is committed by—
(a) the company, and
(b) every officer of the company who is in default.

(4) A person guilty of an offence under this section is liable on summary conviction to a fine not exceeding level 3 on the standard scale and, for continued contravention, a daily default fine not exceeding one-tenth of level 3 on the standard scale.

[S432]

NOTES
Commencement: to be appointed.

Requirements in connection with publication of accounts and reports

433 Name of signatory to be stated in published copies of accounts and reports

(1) Every copy of a document to which this section applies that is published by or on behalf of the company must state the name of the person who signed it on behalf of the board.

(2) In the case of an unquoted company, this section applies to copies of—
(a) the company's balance sheet, and
(b) the directors' report.

(3) In the case of a quoted company, this section applies to copies of—
(a) the company's balance sheet,
(b) the directors' remuneration report, and
(c) the directors' report.

(4) If a copy is published without the required statement of the signatory's name, an offence is committed by—
(a) the company, and
(b) every officer of the company who is in default.

(5) A person guilty of an offence under this section is liable on summary conviction to a fine not exceeding level 3 on the standard scale.

[S433]

NOTES
Commencement: to be appointed.

434 Requirements in connection with publication of statutory accounts

(1) If a company publishes any of its statutory accounts, they must be accompanied by the auditor's report on those accounts (unless the company is exempt from audit and the directors have taken advantage of that exemption).

(2) A company that prepares statutory group accounts for a financial year must not publish its statutory individual accounts for that year without also publishing with them its statutory group accounts.

(3) A company's "statutory accounts" are its accounts for a financial year as required to be delivered to the registrar under section 441.

(4) If a company contravenes any provision of this section, an offence is committed by—
- (a) the company, and
- (b) every officer of the company who is in default.

(5) A person guilty of an offence under this section is liable on summary conviction to a fine not exceeding level 3 on the standard scale.

(6) This section does not apply in relation to the provision by a company of a summary financial statement (see section 426).

[S434]

NOTES

Commencement: to be appointed.

435 Requirements in connection with publication of non-statutory accounts

(1) If a company publishes non-statutory accounts, it must publish with them a statement indicating—
- (a) that they are not the company's statutory accounts,
- (b) whether statutory accounts dealing with any financial year with which the non-statutory accounts purport to deal have been delivered to the registrar, and
- (c) whether an auditor's report has been made on the company's statutory accounts for any such financial year, and if so whether the report—
  - (i) was qualified or unqualified, or included a reference to any matters to which the auditor drew attention by way of emphasis without qualifying the report, or
  - (ii) contained a statement under section 498(2) (accounting records or returns inadequate or accounts or directors' remuneration report not agreeing with records and returns), or section 498(3) (failure to obtain necessary information and explanations).

(2) The company must not publish with non-statutory accounts the auditor's report on the company's statutory accounts.

(3) References in this section to the publication by a company of "non-statutory accounts" are to the publication of—
- (a) any balance sheet or profit and loss account relating to, or purporting to deal with, a financial year of the company, or
- (b) an account in any form purporting to be a balance sheet or profit and loss account for a group headed by the company relating to, or purporting to deal with, a financial year of the company,

otherwise than as part of the company's statutory accounts.

(4) In subsection (3)(b) "a group headed by the company" means a group consisting of the company and any other undertaking (regardless of whether it is a subsidiary undertaking of the company) other than a parent undertaking of the company.

(5) If a company contravenes any provision of this section, an offence is committed by—
- (a) the company, and
- (b) every officer of the company who is in default.

(6) A person guilty of an offence under this section is liable on summary conviction to a fine not exceeding level 3 on the standard scale.

(7) This section does not apply in relation to the provision by a company of a summary financial statement (see section 426).

[S435]

NOTES

Commencement: to be appointed.

436 Meaning of "publication" in relation to accounts and reports

(1) This section has effect for the purposes of—

section 433 (name of signatory to be stated in published copies of accounts and reports),

section 434 (requirements in connection with publication of statutory accounts), and

section 435 (requirements in connection with publication of non-statutory accounts).

(2) For the purposes of those sections a company is regarded as publishing a document if it publishes, issues or circulates it or otherwise makes it available for public inspection in a manner calculated to invite members of the public generally, or any class of members of the public, to read it.

[S436]

NOTES

Commencement: to be appointed.

CHAPTER 8
PUBLIC COMPANIES: LAYING OF ACCOUNTS AND REPORTS BEFORE GENERAL MEETING

437 Public companies: laying of accounts and reports before general meeting

(1) The directors of a public company must lay before the company in general meeting copies of its annual accounts and reports.

(2) This section must be complied with not later than the end of the period for filing the accounts and reports in question.

(3) In the Companies Acts "accounts meeting", in relation to a public company, means a general meeting of the company at which the company's annual accounts and reports are (or are to be) laid in accordance with this section.

[S437]

NOTES

Commencement: to be appointed.

438 Public companies: offence of failure to lay accounts and reports

(1) If the requirements of section 437 (public companies: laying of accounts and reports before general meeting) are not complied with before the end of the period allowed, every person who immediately before the end of that period was a director of the company commits an offence.

(2) It is a defence for a person charged with such an offence to prove that he took all reasonable steps for securing that those requirements would be complied with before the end of that period.

(3) It is not a defence to prove that the documents in question were not in fact prepared as required by this Part.

(4) A person guilty of an offence under this section is liable on summary conviction to a fine not exceeding level 5 on the standard scale and, for continued contravention, a daily default fine not exceeding one-tenth of level 5 on the standard scale.

[S438]

NOTES

Commencement: to be appointed.

CHAPTER 9
QUOTED COMPANIES: MEMBERS' APPROVAL OF DIRECTORS' REMUNERATION REPORT

439 Quoted companies: members' approval of directors' remuneration report

(1) A quoted company must, prior to the accounts meeting, give to the members of the company entitled to be sent notice of the meeting notice of the intention to move at the meeting, as an ordinary resolution, a resolution approving the directors' remuneration report for the financial year.

(2) The notice may be given in any manner permitted for the service on the member of notice of the meeting.

(3) The business that may be dealt with at the accounts meeting includes the resolution.

This is so notwithstanding any default in complying with subsection (1) or (2).

(4) The existing directors must ensure that the resolution is put to the vote of the meeting.

(5) No entitlement of a person to remuneration is made conditional on the resolution being passed by reason only of the provision made by this section.

(6) In this section—

"the accounts meeting" means the general meeting of the company before which the company's annual accounts for the financial year are to be laid; and

"existing director" means a person who is a director of the company immediately before that meeting.

[S439]

NOTES

Commencement: to be appointed.

440 Quoted companies: offences in connection with procedure for approval

(1) In the event of default in complying with section 439(1) (notice to be given of resolution for approval of directors' remuneration report), an offence is committed by every officer of the company who is in default.

(2) If the resolution is not put to the vote of the accounts meeting, an offence is committed by each existing director.

(3) It is a defence for a person charged with an offence under subsection (2) to prove that he took all reasonable steps for securing that the resolution was put to the vote of the meeting.

(4) A person guilty of an offence under this section is liable on summary conviction to a fine not exceeding level 3 on the standard scale.

(5) In this section—

"the accounts meeting" means the general meeting of the company before which the company's annual accounts for the financial year are to be laid; and

"existing director" means a person who is a director of the company immediately before that meeting.

[S440]

NOTES

Commencement: to be appointed.

CHAPTER 10
FILING OF ACCOUNTS AND REPORTS

Duty to file accounts and reports

441 Duty to file accounts and reports with the registrar

(1) The directors of a company must deliver to the registrar for each financial year the accounts and reports required by—

section 444 (filing obligations of companies subject to small companies regime),
section 445 (filing obligations of medium-sized companies),
section 446 (filing obligations of unquoted companies), or
section 447 (filing obligations of quoted companies).

(2) This is subject to section 448 (unlimited companies exempt from filing obligations).
[S441]

NOTES

Commencement: to be appointed.

442 Period allowed for filing accounts

(1) This section specifies the period allowed for the directors of a company to comply with their obligation under section 441 to deliver accounts and reports for a financial year to the registrar.

This is referred to in the Companies Acts as the "period for filing" those accounts and reports.

(2) The period is—

(a) for a private company, nine months after the end of the relevant accounting reference period, and

(b) for a public company, six months after the end of that period.

This is subject to the following provisions of this section.

(3) If the relevant accounting reference period is the company's first and is a period of more than twelve months, the period is—

(a) nine months or six months, as the case may be, from the first anniversary of the incorporation of the company, or

(b) three months after the end of the accounting reference period,

whichever last expires.

(4) If the relevant accounting reference period is treated as shortened by virtue of a notice given by the company under section 392 (alteration of accounting reference date), the period is—

(a) that applicable in accordance with the above provisions, or

(b) three months from the date of the notice under that section,

whichever last expires.

(5) If for any special reason the Secretary of State thinks fit he may, on an application made before the expiry of the period otherwise allowed, by notice in writing to a company extend that period by such further period as may be specified in the notice.

(6) Whether the period allowed is that for a private company or a public company is determined by reference to the company's status immediately before the end of the relevant accounting reference period.

(7) In this section "the relevant accounting reference period" means the accounting reference period by reference to which the financial year for the accounts in question was determined.

[S442]

NOTES

Commencement: to be appointed.

443 Calculation of period allowed

(1) This section applies for the purposes of calculating the period for filing a company's accounts and reports which is expressed as a specified number of months from a specified date or after the end of a specified previous period.

(2) Subject to the following provisions, the period ends with the date in the appropriate month corresponding to the specified date or the last day of the specified previous period.

(3) If the specified date, or the last day of the specified previous period, is the last day of a month, the period ends with the last day of the appropriate month (whether or not that is the corresponding date).

(4) If—

(a) the specified date, or the last day of the specified previous period, is not the last day of a month but is the 29th or 30th, and

(b) the appropriate month is February,

the period ends with the last day of February.

(5) "The appropriate month" means the month that is the specified number of months after the month in which the specified date, or the end of the specified previous period, falls.

[S443]

NOTES

Commencement: to be appointed.

Filing obligations of different descriptions of company

444 Filing obligations of companies subject to small companies regime

(1) The directors of a company subject to the small companies regime—

(a) must deliver to the registrar for each financial year a copy of a balance sheet drawn up as at the last day of that year, and

(b) may also deliver to the registrar—

(i) a copy of the company's profit and loss account for that year, and

(ii) a copy of the directors' report for that year.

(2) The directors must also deliver to the registrar a copy of the auditor's report on those accounts (and on the directors' report).

This does not apply if the company is exempt from audit and the directors have taken advantage of that exemption.

(3) The copies of accounts and reports delivered to the registrar must be copies of the company's annual accounts and reports, except that where the company prepares Companies Act accounts—

(a) the directors may deliver to the registrar a copy of a balance sheet drawn up in accordance with regulations made by the Secretary of State, and

(b) there may be omitted from the copy profit and loss account delivered to the registrar such items as may be specified by the regulations.

These are referred to in this Part as "abbreviated accounts".

(4) If abbreviated accounts are delivered to the registrar the obligation to deliver a copy of the auditor's report on the accounts is to deliver a copy of the special auditor's report required by section 449.

(5) Where the directors of a company subject to the small companies regime deliver to the registrar IAS accounts, or Companies Act accounts that are not abbreviated accounts, and in accordance with this section—

(a) do not deliver to the registrar a copy of the company's profit and loss account, or

(b) do not deliver to the registrar a copy of the directors' report,

the copy of the balance sheet delivered to the registrar must contain in a prominent position a statement that the company's annual accounts and reports have been delivered in accordance with the provisions applicable to companies subject to the small companies regime.

(6) The copies of the balance sheet and any directors' report delivered to the registrar under this section must state the name of the person who signed it on behalf of the board.

(7) The copy of the auditor's report delivered to the registrar under this section must—

(a) state the name of the auditor and (where the auditor is a firm) the name of the person who signed it as senior statutory auditor, or

(b) if the conditions in section 506 (circumstances in which names may be omitted) are met, state that a resolution has been passed and notified to the Secretary of State in accordance with that section.

[S444]

NOTES

Commencement: 20 January 2007 (for the purpose of enabling the exercise of powers to make Orders or Regulations by statutory instrument); to be appointed (otherwise).

445 Filing obligations of medium-sized companies

(1) The directors of a company that qualifies as a medium-sized company in relation to a financial year (see sections 465 to 467) must deliver to the registrar a copy of—
- (a) the company's annual accounts, and
- (b) the directors' report.

(2) They must also deliver to the registrar a copy of the auditor's report on those accounts (and on the directors' report).

This does not apply if the company is exempt from audit and the directors have taken advantage of that exemption.

(3) Where the company prepares Companies Act accounts, the directors may deliver to the registrar a copy of the company's annual accounts for the financial year—
- (a) that includes a profit and loss account in which items are combined in accordance with regulations made by the Secretary of State, and
- (b) that does not contain items whose omission is authorised by the regulations.

These are referred to in this Part as "abbreviated accounts".

(4) If abbreviated accounts are delivered to the registrar the obligation to deliver a copy of the auditor's report on the accounts is to deliver a copy of the special auditor's report required by section 449.

(5) The copies of the balance sheet and directors' report delivered to the registrar under this section must state the name of the person who signed it on behalf of the board.

(6) The copy of the auditor's report delivered to the registrar under this section must—
- (a) state the name of the auditor and (where the auditor is a firm) the name of the person who signed it as senior statutory auditor, or
- (b) if the conditions in section 506 (circumstances in which names may be omitted) are met, state that a resolution has been passed and notified to the Secretary of State in accordance with that section.

(7) This section does not apply to companies within section 444 (filing obligations of companies subject to the small companies regime).

[S445]

NOTES

Commencement: 20 January 2007 (for the purpose of enabling the exercise of powers to make Orders or Regulations by statutory instrument); to be appointed (otherwise).

446 Filing obligations of unquoted companies

(1) The directors of an unquoted company must deliver to the registrar for each financial year of the company a copy of—
- (a) the company's annual accounts, and
- (b) the directors' report.

(2) The directors must also deliver to the registrar a copy of the auditor's report on those accounts (and the directors' report).

This does not apply if the company is exempt from audit and the directors have taken advantage of that exemption.

(3) The copies of the balance sheet and directors' report delivered to the registrar under this section must state the name of the person who signed it on behalf of the board.

(4) The copy of the auditor's report delivered to the registrar under this section must—
- (a) state the name of the auditor and (where the auditor is a firm) the name of the person who signed it as senior statutory auditor, or
- (b) if the conditions in section 506 (circumstances in which names may be omitted) are met, state that a resolution has been passed and notified to the Secretary of State in accordance with that section.

(5) This section does not apply to companies within—
- (a) section 444 (filing obligations of companies subject to the small companies regime), or
- (b) section 445 (filing obligations of medium-sized companies).

[S446]

NOTES

Commencement: to be appointed.

447 Filing obligations of quoted companies

(1) The directors of a quoted company must deliver to the registrar for each financial year of the company a copy of—

(a) the company's annual accounts,

(b) the directors' remuneration report, and

(c) the directors' report.

(2) They must also deliver a copy of the auditor's report on those accounts (and on the directors' remuneration report and the directors' report).

(3) The copies of the balance sheet, the directors' remuneration report and the directors' report delivered to the registrar under this section must state the name of the person who signed it on behalf of the board.

(4) The copy of the auditor's report delivered to the registrar under this section must—

(a) state the name of the auditor and (where the auditor is a firm) the name of the person who signed it as senior statutory auditor, or

(b) if the conditions in section 506 (circumstances in which names may be omitted) are met, state that a resolution has been passed and notified to the Secretary of State in accordance with that section.

[S447]

NOTES

Commencement: to be appointed.

448 Unlimited companies exempt from obligation to file accounts

(1) The directors of an unlimited company are not required to deliver accounts and reports to the registrar in respect of a financial year if the following conditions are met.

(2) The conditions are that at no time during the relevant accounting reference period—

(a) has the company been, to its knowledge, a subsidiary undertaking of an undertaking which was then limited, or

(b) have there been, to its knowledge, exercisable by or on behalf of two or more undertakings which were then limited, rights which if exercisable by one of them would have made the company a subsidiary undertaking of it, or

(c) has the company been a parent company of an undertaking which was then limited.

The references above to an undertaking being limited at a particular time are to an undertaking (under whatever law established) the liability of whose members is at that time limited.

(3) The exemption conferred by this section does not apply if—

(a) the company is a banking or insurance company or the parent company of a banking or insurance group, or

(b) the company is a qualifying company within the meaning of the Partnerships and Unlimited Companies (Accounts) Regulations 1993 (SI 1993/1820).

(4) Where a company is exempt by virtue of this section from the obligation to deliver accounts—

(a) section 434(3) (requirements in connection with publication of statutory accounts: meaning of "statutory accounts") has effect with the substitution for the words "as required to be delivered to the registrar under section 441" of the words "as prepared in accordance with this Part and approved by the board of directors"; and

(b) section 435(1)(b) (requirements in connection with publication of non-statutory accounts: statement whether statutory accounts delivered) has effect with the substitution for the words from "whether statutory accounts" to "have been delivered to the registrar" of the words "that the company is exempt from the requirement to deliver statutory accounts".

(5) In this section the "relevant accounting reference period", in relation to a financial year, means the accounting reference period by reference to which that financial year was determined.

[S448]

NOTES

Commencement: to be appointed.

Requirements where abbreviated accounts delivered

449 Special auditor's report where abbreviated accounts delivered

(1) This section applies where—

(a) the directors of a company deliver abbreviated accounts to the registrar, and

(b) the company is not exempt from audit (or the directors have not taken advantage of any such exemption).

(2) The directors must also deliver to the registrar a copy of a special report of the company's auditor stating that in his opinion—

(a) the company is entitled to deliver abbreviated accounts in accordance with the section in question, and

(b) the abbreviated accounts to be delivered are properly prepared in accordance with regulations under that section.

(3) The auditor's report on the company's annual accounts need not be delivered, but—

(a) if that report was qualified, the special report must set out that report in full together with any further material necessary to understand the qualification, and

(b) if that report contained a statement under—

(i) section 498(2)(a) or (b) (accounts, records or returns inadequate or accounts not agreeing with records and returns), or

(ii) section 498(3) (failure to obtain necessary information and explanations),

the special report must set out that statement in full.

(4) The provisions of—

sections 503 to 506 (signature of auditor's report), and

sections 507 to 509 (offences in connection with auditor's report),

apply to a special report under this section as they apply to an auditor's report on the company's annual accounts prepared under Part 16.

(5) If abbreviated accounts are delivered to the registrar, the references in section 434 or 435 (requirements in connection with publication of accounts) to the auditor's report on the company's annual accounts shall be read as references to the special auditor's report required by this section.

[S449]

NOTES

Commencement: to be appointed.

450 Approval and signing of abbreviated accounts

(1) Abbreviated accounts must be approved by the board of directors and signed on behalf of the board by a director of the company.

(2) The signature must be on the balance sheet.

(3) The balance sheet must contain in a prominent position above the signature a statement to the effect that it is prepared in accordance with the special provisions of this Act relating (as the case may be) to companies subject to the small companies regime or to medium-sized companies.

(4) If abbreviated accounts are approved that do not comply with the requirements of regulations under the relevant section, every director of the company who—

(a) knew that they did not comply, or was reckless as to whether they complied, and

(b) failed to take reasonable steps to prevent them from being approved,

commits an offence.

(5) A person guilty of an offence under subsection (4) is liable—

(a) on conviction on indictment, to a fine;

(b) on summary conviction, to a fine not exceeding the statutory maximum.

[S450]

NOTES

Commencement: to be appointed.

Failure to file accounts and reports

451 Default in filing accounts and reports: offences

(1) If the requirements of section 441 (duty to file accounts and reports) are not complied with in relation to a company's accounts and reports for a financial year before the end of the period for filing those accounts and reports, every person who immediately before the end of that period was a director of the company commits an offence.

(2) It is a defence for a person charged with such an offence to prove that he took all reasonable steps for securing that those requirements would be complied with before the end of that period.

(3) It is not a defence to prove that the documents in question were not in fact prepared as required by this Part.

(4) A person guilty of an offence under this section is liable on summary conviction to a fine not exceeding level 5 on the standard scale and, for continued contravention, a daily default fine not exceeding one-tenth of level 5 on the standard scale.

[S451]

NOTES

Commencement: to be appointed.

452 Default in filing accounts and reports: court order

(1) If—

(a) the requirements of section 441 (duty to file accounts and reports) are not complied with in relation to a company's accounts and reports for a financial year before the end of the period for filing those accounts and reports, and

(b) the directors of the company fail to make good the default within 14 days after the service of a notice on them requiring compliance,

the court may, on the application of any member or creditor of the company or of the registrar, make an order directing the directors (or any of them) to make good the default within such time as may be specified in the order.

(2) The court's order may provide that all costs (in Scotland, expenses) of and incidental to the application are to be borne by the directors.

[S452]

NOTES

Commencement: to be appointed.

453 Civil penalty for failure to file accounts and reports

(1) Where the requirements of section 441 are not complied with in relation to a company's accounts and reports for a financial year before the end of the period for filing those accounts and reports, the company is liable to a civil penalty.

This is in addition to any liability of the directors under section 451.

(2) The amount of the penalty shall be determined in accordance with regulations made by the Secretary of State by reference to—

(a) the length of the period between the end of the period for filing the accounts and reports in question and the day on which the requirements are complied with, and

(b) whether the company is a private or public company.

(3) The penalty may be recovered by the registrar and is to be paid into the Consolidated Fund.

(4) It is not a defence in proceedings under this section to prove that the documents in question were not in fact prepared as required by this Part.

(5) Regulations under this section having the effect of increasing the penalty payable in any case are subject to affirmative resolution procedure. Otherwise, the regulations are subject to negative resolution procedure.

[S453]

NOTES

Commencement: 20 January 2007 (for the purpose of enabling the exercise of powers to make Orders or Regulations by statutory instrument); to be appointed (otherwise).

CHAPTER 11
REVISION OF DEFECTIVE ACCOUNTS AND REPORTS

Voluntary revision

454 Voluntary revision of accounts etc

(1) If it appears to the directors of a company that—

(a) the company's annual accounts,

(b) the directors' remuneration report or the directors' report, or

(c) a summary financial statement of the company,

did not comply with the requirements of this Act (or, where applicable, of Article 4 of the IAS Regulation), they may prepare revised accounts or a revised report or statement.

(2) Where copies of the previous accounts or report have been sent out to members, delivered to the registrar or (in the case of a public company) laid before the company in general meeting, the revisions must be confined to—

(a) the correction of those respects in which the previous accounts or report did not comply with the requirements of this Act (or, where applicable, of Article 4 of the IAS Regulation), and

(b) the making of any necessary consequential alterations.

(3) The Secretary of State may make provision by regulations as to the application of the provisions of this Act in relation to—

(a) revised annual accounts,

(b) a revised directors' remuneration report or directors' report, or

(c) a revised summary financial statement.

(4) The regulations may, in particular—

(a) make different provision according to whether the previous accounts, report or statement are replaced or are supplemented by a document indicating the corrections to be made;

(b) make provision with respect to the functions of the company's auditor in relation to the revised accounts, report or statement;

(c) require the directors to take such steps as may be specified in the regulations where the previous accounts or report have been—

(i) sent out to members and others under section 423,

(ii) laid before the company in general meeting, or

(iii) delivered to the registrar,

or where a summary financial statement containing information derived from the previous accounts or report has been sent to members under section 426;

(d) apply the provisions of this Act (including those creating criminal offences) subject to such additions, exceptions and modifications as are specified in the regulations.

(5) Regulations under this section are subject to negative resolution procedure.

[S454]

NOTES

Commencement: 20 January 2007 (for the purpose of enabling the exercise of powers to make Orders or Regulations by statutory instrument); to be appointed (otherwise).

Secretary of State's notice

455 Secretary of State's notice in respect of accounts or reports

(1) This section applies where—

(a) copies of a company's annual accounts or directors' report have been sent out under section 423, or

(b) a copy of a company's annual accounts or directors' report has been delivered to the registrar or (in the case of a public company) laid before the company in general meeting,

and it appears to the Secretary of State that there is, or may be, a question whether the accounts or report comply with the requirements of this Act (or, where applicable, of Article 4 of the IAS Regulation).

(2) The Secretary of State may give notice to the directors of the company indicating the respects in which it appears that such a question arises or may arise.

(3) The notice must specify a period of not less than one month for the directors to give an explanation of the accounts or report or prepare revised accounts or a revised report.

(4) If at the end of the specified period, or such longer period as the Secretary of State may allow, it appears to the Secretary of State that the directors have not—

(a) given a satisfactory explanation of the accounts or report, or

(b) revised the accounts or report so as to comply with the requirements of this Act (or, where applicable, of Article 4 of the IAS Regulation),

the Secretary of State may apply to the court.

(5) The provisions of this section apply equally to revised annual accounts and revised directors' reports, in which case they have effect as if the references to revised accounts or reports were references to further revised accounts or reports.

[S455]

NOTES

Commencement: to be appointed.

Application to court

456 Application to court in respect of defective accounts or reports

(1) An application may be made to the court—

(a) by the Secretary of State, after having complied with section 455, or

(b) by a person authorised by the Secretary of State for the purposes of this section,

for a declaration (in Scotland, a declarator) that the annual accounts of a company do not comply, or a directors' report does not comply, with the requirements of this Act (or, where applicable, of Article 4 of the IAS Regulation) and for an order requiring the directors of the company to prepare revised accounts or a revised report.

(2) Notice of the application, together with a general statement of the matters at issue in the proceedings, shall be given by the applicant to the registrar for registration.

(3) If the court orders the preparation of revised accounts, it may give directions as to—

(a) the auditing of the accounts,

(b) the revision of any directors' remuneration report, directors' report or summary financial statement, and

(c) the taking of steps by the directors to bring the making of the order to the notice of persons likely to rely on the previous accounts,

and such other matters as the court thinks fit.

(4) If the court orders the preparation of a revised directors' report it may give directions as to—

(a) the review of the report by the auditors,
(b) the revision of any summary financial statement,
(c) the taking of steps by the directors to bring the making of the order to the notice of persons likely to rely on the previous report, and
(d) such other matters as the court thinks fit.

(5) If the court finds that the accounts or report did not comply with the requirements of this Act (or, where applicable, of Article 4 of the IAS Regulation) it may order that all or part of—

(a) the costs (in Scotland, expenses) of and incidental to the application, and
(b) any reasonable expenses incurred by the company in connection with or in consequence of the preparation of revised accounts or a revised report,

are to be borne by such of the directors as were party to the approval of the defective accounts or report.

For this purpose every director of the company at the time of the approval of the accounts or report shall be taken to have been a party to the approval unless he shows that he took all reasonable steps to prevent that approval.

(6) Where the court makes an order under subsection (5) it shall have regard to whether the directors party to the approval of the defective accounts or report knew or ought to have known that the accounts or report did not comply with the requirements of this Act (or, where applicable, of Article 4 of the IAS Regulation), and it may exclude one or more directors from the order or order the payment of different amounts by different directors.

(7) On the conclusion of proceedings on an application under this section, the applicant must send to the registrar for registration a copy of the court order or, as the case may be, give notice to the registrar that the application has failed or been withdrawn.

(8) The provisions of this section apply equally to revised annual accounts and revised directors' reports, in which case they have effect as if the references to revised accounts or reports were references to further revised accounts or reports.

[S456]

NOTES

Commencement: to be appointed.

457 Other persons authorised to apply to the court

(1) The Secretary of State may by order (an "authorisation order") authorise for the purposes of section 456 any person appearing to him—

(a) to have an interest in, and to have satisfactory procedures directed to securing, compliance by companies with the requirements of this Act (or, where applicable, of Article 4 of the IAS Regulation) relating to accounts and directors' reports,
(b) to have satisfactory procedures for receiving and investigating complaints about companies' annual accounts and directors' reports, and
(c) otherwise to be a fit and proper person to be authorised.

(2) A person may be authorised generally or in respect of particular classes of case, and different persons may be authorised in respect of different classes of case.

(3) The Secretary of State may refuse to authorise a person if he considers that his authorisation is unnecessary having regard to the fact that there are one or more other persons who have been or are likely to be authorised.

(4) If the authorised person is an unincorporated association, proceedings brought in, or in connection with, the exercise of any function by the association as an authorised person may be brought by or against the association in the name of a body corporate whose constitution provides for the establishment of the association.

(5) An authorisation order may contain such requirements or other provisions relating to the exercise of functions by the authorised person as appear to the Secretary of State to be appropriate.

No such order is to be made unless it appears to the Secretary of State that the person would, if authorised, exercise his functions as an authorised person in accordance with the provisions proposed.

(6) Where authorisation is revoked, the revoking order may make such provision as the Secretary of State thinks fit with respect to pending proceedings.

(7) An order under this section is subject to negative resolution procedure.

[S457]

NOTES

Commencement: 20 January 2007 (for the purpose of enabling the exercise of powers to make Orders or Regulations by statutory instrument); to be appointed (otherwise).

458 Disclosure of information by tax authorities

(1) The Commissioners for Her Majesty's Revenue and Customs may disclose information to a person authorised under section 457 for the purpose of facilitating—

(a) the taking of steps by that person to discover whether there are grounds for an application to the court under section 456 (application in respect of defective accounts etc), or

(b) a decision by the authorised person whether to make such an application.

(2) This section applies despite any statutory or other restriction on the disclosure of information.

Provided that, in the case of personal data within the meaning of the Data Protection Act 1998 (c 29), information is not to be disclosed in contravention of that Act.

(3) Information disclosed to an authorised person under this section—

(a) may not be used except in or in connection with—

(i) taking steps to discover whether there are grounds for an application to the court under section 456, or

(ii) deciding whether or not to make such an application,

or in, or in connection with, proceedings on such an application; and

(b) must not be further disclosed except—

(i) to the person to whom the information relates, or

(ii) in, or in connection with, proceedings on any such application to the court.

(4) A person who contravenes subsection (3) commits an offence unless—

(a) he did not know, and had no reason to suspect, that the information had been disclosed under this section, or

(b) he took all reasonable steps and exercised all due diligence to avoid the commission of the offence.

(5) A person guilty of an offence under subsection (4) is liable—

(a) on conviction on indictment, to imprisonment for a term not exceeding two years or a fine (or both);

(b) on summary conviction—

(i) in England and Wales, to imprisonment for a term not exceeding twelve months or to a fine not exceeding the statutory maximum (or both);

(ii) in Scotland or Northern Ireland, to imprisonment for a term not exceeding six months, or to a fine not exceeding the statutory maximum (or both).

[S458]

NOTES

Commencement: to be appointed.

Power of authorised person to require documents etc

459 Power of authorised person to require documents, information and explanations

(1) This section applies where it appears to a person who is authorised under section 457 that there is, or may be, a question whether a company's annual accounts or directors' report comply with the requirements of this Act (or, where applicable, of Article 4 of the IAS Regulation).

(2) The authorised person may require any of the persons mentioned in subsection (3) to produce any document, or to provide him with any information or explanations, that he may reasonably require for the purpose of—

(a) discovering whether there are grounds for an application to the court under section 456, or

(b) deciding whether to make such an application.

(3) Those persons are—

(a) the company;

(b) any officer, employee, or auditor of the company;

(c) any persons who fell within paragraph (b) at a time to which the document or information required by the authorised person relates.

(4) If a person fails to comply with such a requirement, the authorised person may apply to the court.

(5) If it appears to the court that the person has failed to comply with a requirement under subsection (2), it may order the person to take such steps as it directs for securing that the documents are produced or the information or explanations are provided.

(6) A statement made by a person in response to a requirement under subsection (2) or an order under subsection (5) may not be used in evidence against him in any criminal proceedings.

(7) Nothing in this section compels any person to disclose documents or information in respect of which a claim to legal professional privilege (in Scotland, to confidentiality of communications) could be maintained in legal proceedings.

(8) In this section "document" includes information recorded in any form.

[S459]

NOTES

Commencement: to be appointed.

460 Restrictions on disclosure of information obtained under compulsory powers

(1) This section applies to information (in whatever form) obtained in pursuance of a requirement or order under section 459 (power of authorised person to require documents etc) that relates to the private affairs of an individual or to any particular business.

(2) No such information may, during the lifetime of that individual or so long as that business continues to be carried on, be disclosed without the consent of that individual or the person for the time being carrying on that business.

(3) This does not apply—

(a) to disclosure permitted by section 461 (permitted disclosure of information obtained under compulsory powers), or

(b) to the disclosure of information that is or has been available to the public from another source.

(4) A person who discloses information in contravention of this section commits an offence, unless—

(a) he did not know, and had no reason to suspect, that the information had been disclosed under section 459, or

(b) he took all reasonable steps and exercised all due diligence to avoid the commission of the offence.

(5) A person guilty of an offence under this section is liable—

(a) on conviction on indictment, to imprisonment for a term not exceeding two years or a fine (or both);

(b) on summary conviction—

(i) in England and Wales, to imprisonment for a term not exceeding twelve months or to a fine not exceeding the statutory maximum (or both);

(ii) in Scotland or Northern Ireland, to imprisonment for a term not exceeding six months, or to a fine not exceeding the statutory maximum (or both).

[S460]

NOTES

Commencement: to be appointed.

461 Permitted disclosure of information obtained under compulsory powers

(1) The prohibition in section 460 of the disclosure of information obtained in pursuance of a requirement or order under section 459 (power of authorised person to require documents etc) that relates to the private affairs of an individual or to any particular business has effect subject to the following exceptions.

(2) It does not apply to the disclosure of information for the purpose of facilitating the carrying out by the authorised person of his functions under section 456.

(3) It does not apply to disclosure to—

(a) the Secretary of State,

(b) the Department of Enterprise, Trade and Investment for Northern Ireland,

(c) the Treasury,

(d) the Bank of England,

(e) the Financial Services Authority, or

(f) the Commissioners for Her Majesty's Revenue and Customs.

(4) It does not apply to disclosure—

(a) for the purpose of assisting a body designated by an order under section 46 of the Companies Act 1989 (c 40) (delegation of functions of the Secretary of State) to exercise its functions under Part 2 of that Act;

(b) with a view to the institution of, or otherwise for the purposes of, disciplinary proceedings relating to the performance by an accountant or auditor of his professional duties;

(c) for the purpose of enabling or assisting the Secretary of State or the Treasury to exercise any of their functions under any of the following—

(i) the Companies Acts,

(ii) Part 5 of the Criminal Justice Act 1993 (c 36) (insider dealing),

(iii) the Insolvency Act 1986 (c 45) or the Insolvency (Northern Ireland) Order 1989 (SI 1989/2405 (NI 19)),

(iv) the Company Directors Disqualification Act 1986 (c 46) or the Company Directors Disqualification (Northern Ireland) Order 2002 (SI 2002/3150 (NI 4)),

(v) the Financial Services and Markets Act 2000 (c 8);

(d) for the purpose of enabling or assisting the Department of Enterprise, Trade and Investment for Northern Ireland to exercise any powers conferred on it by the enactments relating to companies, directors' disqualification or insolvency;

(e) for the purpose of enabling or assisting the Bank of England to exercise its functions;

(f) for the purpose of enabling or assisting the Commissioners for Her Majesty's Revenue and Customs to exercise their functions;

(g) for the purpose of enabling or assisting the Financial Services Authority to exercise its functions under any of the following—

(i) the legislation relating to friendly societies or to industrial and provident societies,

(ii) the Building Societies Act 1986 (c 53),

(iii) Part 7 of the Companies Act 1989 (c 40),

(iv) the Financial Services and Markets Act 2000; or

(h) in pursuance of any Community obligation.

(5) It does not apply to disclosure to a body exercising functions of a public nature under legislation in any country or territory outside the United Kingdom that appear to the authorised person to be similar to his functions under section 456 for the purpose of enabling or assisting that body to exercise those functions.

(6) In determining whether to disclose information to a body in accordance with subsection (5), the authorised person must have regard to the following considerations—

(a) whether the use which the body is likely to make of the information is sufficiently important to justify making the disclosure;

(b) whether the body has adequate arrangements to prevent the information from being used or further disclosed other than—

(i) for the purposes of carrying out the functions mentioned in that subsection, or

(ii) for other purposes substantially similar to those for which information disclosed to the authorised person could be used or further disclosed.

(7) Nothing in this section authorises the making of a disclosure in contravention of the Data Protection Act 1998 (c 29).

[S461]

NOTES

Commencement: to be appointed.

462 Power to amend categories of permitted disclosure

(1) The Secretary of State may by order amend section 461(3), (4) and (5).

(2) An order under this section must not—
- (a) amend subsection (3) of that section (UK public authorities) by specifying a person unless the person exercises functions of a public nature (whether or not he exercises any other function);
- (b) amend subsection (4) of that section (purposes for which disclosure permitted) by adding or modifying a description of disclosure unless the purpose for which the disclosure is permitted is likely to facilitate the exercise of a function of a public nature;
- (c) amend subsection (5) of that section (overseas regulatory authorities) so as to have the effect of permitting disclosures to be made to a body other than one that exercises functions of a public nature in a country or territory outside the United Kingdom.

(3) An order under this section is subject to negative resolution procedure.

[S462]

NOTES

Commencement: 20 January 2007 (for the purpose of enabling the exercise of powers to make Orders or Regulations by statutory instrument); to be appointed (otherwise).

CHAPTER 12
SUPPLEMENTARY PROVISIONS

Liability for false or misleading statements in reports

463 Liability for false or misleading statements in reports

(1) The reports to which this section applies are—
- (a) the directors' report,
- (b) the directors' remuneration report, and
- (c) a summary financial statement so far as it is derived from either of those reports.

(2) A director of a company is liable to compensate the company for any loss suffered by it as a result of—
- (a) any untrue or misleading statement in a report to which this section applies, or
- (b) the omission from a report to which this section applies of anything required to be included in it.

(3) He is so liable only if—
- (a) he knew the statement to be untrue or misleading or was reckless as to whether it was untrue or misleading, or
- (b) he knew the omission to be dishonest concealment of a material fact.

(4) No person shall be subject to any liability to a person other than the company resulting from reliance, by that person or another, on information in a report to which this section applies.

(5) The reference in subsection (4) to a person being subject to a liability includes a reference to another person being entitled as against him to be granted any civil remedy or to rescind or repudiate an agreement.

(6) This section does not affect—
- (a) liability for a civil penalty, or
- (b) liability for a criminal offence.

[S463]

NOTES

Commencement: 20 January 2007 (for transitional provisions see the note below).

Transitional provisions: the Companies Act 2006 (Commencement No 1, Transitional Provisions and Savings) Order 2006, SI 2006/3428, Sch 5, para 3 (at **[7590]**) provides as follows—

"3 False or misleading statements in reports

Section 463 of the Companies Act 2006 (liability for false or misleading statements in reports) does not apply to a directors' report, directors' remuneration report or summary financial statement first sent to members and others under section 238 or 251 of the 1985 Act, or Article 246 or 259 of the 1986 Order, before 20th January 2007.".

Accounting and reporting standards

464 Accounting standards

(1) In this Part "accounting standards" means statements of standard accounting practice issued by such body or bodies as may be prescribed by regulations.

(2) References in this Part to accounting standards applicable to a company's annual accounts are to such standards as are, in accordance with their terms, relevant to the company's circumstances and to the accounts.

(3) Regulations under this section may contain such transitional and other supplementary and incidental provisions as appear to the Secretary of State to be appropriate.

[S464]

NOTES

Commencement: 20 January 2007 (for the purpose of enabling the exercise of powers to make Orders or Regulations by statutory instrument); to be appointed (otherwise).

Companies qualifying as medium-sized

465 Companies qualifying as medium-sized: general

(1) A company qualifies as medium-sized in relation to its first financial year if the qualifying conditions are met in that year.

(2) A company qualifies as medium-sized in relation to a subsequent financial year—

(a) if the qualifying conditions are met in that year and the preceding financial year;

(b) if the qualifying conditions are met in that year and the company qualified as medium-sized in relation to the preceding financial year;

(c) if the qualifying conditions were met in the preceding financial year and the company qualified as medium-sized in relation to that year.

(3) The qualifying conditions are met by a company in a year in which it satisfies two or more of the following requirements—

1 Turnover	Not more than £22.8 million
2 Balance sheet total	Not more than £11.4 million
3 Number of employees	Not more than 250

(4) For a period that is a company's financial year but not in fact a year the maximum figures for turnover must be proportionately adjusted.

(5) The balance sheet total means the aggregate of the amounts shown as assets in the company's balance sheet.

(6) The number of employees means the average number of persons employed by the company in the year, determined as follows—

(a) find for each month in the financial year the number of persons employed under contracts of service by the company in that month (whether throughout the month or not),

(b) add together the monthly totals, and

(c) divide by the number of months in the financial year.

(7) This section is subject to section 466 (companies qualifying as medium-sized: parent companies).

[S465]

NOTES

Commencement: to be appointed.

466 Companies qualifying as medium-sized: parent companies

(1) A parent company qualifies as a medium-sized company in relation to a financial year only if the group headed by it qualifies as a medium-sized group.

(2) A group qualifies as medium-sized in relation to the parent company's first financial year if the qualifying conditions are met in that year.

(3) A group qualifies as medium-sized in relation to a subsequent financial year of the parent company—

(a) if the qualifying conditions are met in that year and the preceding financial year;

(b) if the qualifying conditions are met in that year and the group qualified as medium-sized in relation to the preceding financial year;

(c) if the qualifying conditions were met in the preceding financial year and the group qualified as medium-sized in relation to that year.

(4) The qualifying conditions are met by a group in a year in which it satisfies two or more of the following requirements—

1 Aggregate turnover	Not more than £22.8 million net (or £27.36 million gross)
2 Aggregate balance sheet total	Not more than £11.4 million net (or £13.68 million gross)
3 Aggregate number of employees	Not more than 250

(5) The aggregate figures are ascertained by aggregating the relevant figures determined in accordance with section 465 for each member of the group.

(6) In relation to the aggregate figures for turnover and balance sheet total—

"net" means after any set-offs and other adjustments made to eliminate group transactions—

(a) in the case of Companies Act accounts, in accordance with regulations under section 404,

(b) in the case of IAS accounts, in accordance with international accounting standards; and

"gross" means without those set-offs and other adjustments.

A company may satisfy any relevant requirement on the basis of either the net or the gross figure.

(7) The figures for each subsidiary undertaking shall be those included in its individual accounts for the relevant financial year, that is—

(a) if its financial year ends with that of the parent company, that financial year, and

(b) if not, its financial year ending last before the end of the financial year of the parent company.

If those figures cannot be obtained without disproportionate expense or undue delay, the latest available figures shall be taken.

[S466]

NOTES

Commencement: to be appointed.

467 Companies excluded from being treated as medium-sized

(1) A company is not entitled to take advantage of any of the provisions of this Part relating to companies qualifying as medium-sized if it was at any time within the financial year in question—

(a) a public company,

(b) a company that—

(i) has permission under Part 4 of the Financial Services and Markets Act 2000 (c 8) to carry on a regulated activity, or

(ii) carries on insurance market activity, or

(c) a member of an ineligible group.

(2) A group is ineligible if any of its members is—

(a) a public company,

(b) a body corporate (other than a company) whose shares are admitted to trading on a regulated market,

(c) a person (other than a small company) who has permission under Part 4 of the Financial Services and Markets Act 2000 to carry on a regulated activity,

(d) a small company that is an authorised insurance company, a banking company, an e-money issuer, an ISD investment firm or a UCITS management company, or

(e) a person who carries on insurance market activity.

(3) A company is a small company for the purposes of subsection (2) if it qualified as small in relation to its last financial year ending on or before the end of the financial year in question.

[S467]

NOTES

Commencement: to be appointed.

General power to make further provision about accounts and reports

468 General power to make further provision about accounts and reports

(1) The Secretary of State may make provision by regulations about—

(a) the accounts and reports that companies are required to prepare;

(b) the categories of companies required to prepare accounts and reports of any description;

(c) the form and content of the accounts and reports that companies are required to prepare;

(d) the obligations of companies and others as regards—

(i) the approval of accounts and reports,

(ii) the sending of accounts and reports to members and others,

(iii) the laying of accounts and reports before the company in general meeting,

(iv) the delivery of copies of accounts and reports to the registrar, and

(v) the publication of accounts and reports.

(2) The regulations may amend this Part by adding, altering or repealing provisions.

(3) But they must not amend (other than consequentially)—

(a) section 393 (accounts to give true and fair view), or

(b) the provisions of Chapter 11 (revision of defective accounts and reports).

(4) The regulations may create criminal offences in cases corresponding to those in which an offence is created by an existing provision of this Part.

The maximum penalty for any such offence may not be greater than is provided in relation to an offence under the existing provision.

(5) The regulations may provide for civil penalties in circumstances corresponding to those within section 453(1) (civil penalty for failure to file accounts and reports).

The provisions of section 453(2) to (5) apply in relation to any such penalty.

[S468]

NOTES

Commencement: 20 January 2007 (for the purpose of enabling the exercise of powers to make Orders or Regulations by statutory instrument); to be appointed (otherwise).

Other supplementary provisions

469 Preparation and filing of accounts in euros

(1) The amounts set out in the annual accounts of a company may also be shown in the same accounts translated into euros.

(2) When complying with section 441 (duty to file accounts and reports), the directors of a company may deliver to the registrar an additional copy of the company's annual accounts in which the amounts have been translated into euros.

(3) In both cases—

(a) the amounts must have been translated at the exchange rate prevailing on the date to which the balance sheet is made up, and

(b) that rate must be disclosed in the notes to the accounts.

(4) For the purposes of sections 434 and 435 (requirements in connection with published accounts) any additional copy of the company's annual accounts delivered to the registrar under subsection (2) above shall be treated as statutory accounts of the company.

In the case of such a copy, references in those sections to the auditor's report on the company's annual accounts shall be read as references to the auditor's report on the annual accounts of which it is a copy.

[S469]

NOTES

Commencement: to be appointed.

470 Power to apply provisions to banking partnerships

(1) The Secretary of State may by regulations apply to banking partnerships, subject to such exceptions, adaptations and modifications as he considers appropriate, the provisions of this Part (and of regulations made under this Part) applying to banking companies.

(2) A "banking partnership" means a partnership which has permission under Part 4 of the Financial Services and Markets Act 2000 (c 8).

But a partnership is not a banking partnership if it has permission to accept deposits only for the purpose of carrying on another regulated activity in accordance with that permission.

(3) Expressions used in this section that are also used in the provisions regulating activities under the Financial Services and Markets Act 2000 have the same meaning here as they do in those provisions.

See section 22 of that Act, orders made under that section and Schedule 2 to that Act.

(4) Regulations under this section are subject to affirmative resolution procedure.

[S470]

NOTES

Commencement: 20 January 2007 (for the purpose of enabling the exercise of powers to make Orders or Regulations by statutory instrument); to be appointed (otherwise).

471 Meaning of "annual accounts" and related expressions

(1) In this Part a company's "annual accounts", in relation to a financial year, means—

(a) the company's individual accounts for that year (see section 394), and

(b) any group accounts prepared by the company for that year (see sections 398 and 399).

This is subject to section 408 (option to omit individual profit and loss account from annual accounts where information given in group accounts).

(2) In the case of an unquoted company, its "annual accounts and reports" for a financial year are—

(a) its annual accounts,

(b) the directors' report, and

(c) the auditor's report on those accounts and the directors' report (unless the company is exempt from audit).

(3) In the case of a quoted company, its "annual accounts and reports" for a financial year are—

(a) its annual accounts,
(b) the directors' remuneration report,
(c) the directors' report, and
(d) the auditor's report on those accounts, on the auditable part of the directors' remuneration report and on the directors' report.

[S471]

NOTES

Commencement: to be appointed.

472 Notes to the accounts

(1) Information required by this Part to be given in notes to a company's annual accounts may be contained in the accounts or in a separate document annexed to the accounts.

(2) References in this Part to a company's annual accounts, or to a balance sheet or profit and loss account, include notes to the accounts giving information which is required by any provision of this Act or international accounting standards, and required or allowed by any such provision to be given in a note to company accounts.

[S472]

NOTES

Commencement: to be appointed.

473 Parliamentary procedure for certain regulations under this Part

(1) This section applies to regulations under the following provisions of this Part—

section 396 (Companies Act individual accounts),
section 404 (Companies Act group accounts),
section 409 (information about related undertakings),
section 412 (information about directors' benefits: remuneration, pensions and compensation for loss of office),
section 416 (contents of directors' report: general),
section 421 (contents of directors' remuneration report),
section 444 (filing obligations of companies subject to small companies regime),
section 445 (filing obligations of medium-sized companies),
section 468 (general power to make further provision about accounts and reports).

(2) Any such regulations may make consequential amendments or repeals in other provisions of this Act, or in other enactments.

(3) Regulations that—

(a) restrict the classes of company which have the benefit of any exemption, exception or special provision,
(b) require additional matter to be included in a document of any class, or
(c) otherwise render the requirements of this Part more onerous,

are subject to affirmative resolution procedure.

(4) Otherwise, the regulations are subject to negative resolution procedure.

[S473]

NOTES

Commencement: 20 January 2007 (for the purpose of enabling the exercise of powers to make Orders or Regulations by statutory instrument); to be appointed (otherwise).

474 Minor definitions

(1) In this Part—

"e-money issuer" means a person who has permission under Part 4 of the Financial Services and Markets Act 2000 (c 8) to carry on the activity of issuing electronic money within the meaning of article 9B of the Financial Services and Markets Act 2000 (Regulated Activities) Order 2001 (SI 2001/544);

"group" means a parent undertaking and its subsidiary undertakings;

"IAS Regulation" means EC Regulation No 1606/2002 of the European Parliament and of the Council of 19 July 2002 on the application of international accounting standards;

"included in the consolidation", in relation to group accounts, or "included in consolidated group accounts", means that the undertaking is included in the accounts by the method of full (and not proportional) consolidation, and references to an undertaking excluded from consolidation shall be construed accordingly;

"international accounting standards" means the international accounting standards, within the meaning of the IAS Regulation, adopted from time to time by the European Commission in accordance with that Regulation;

"ISD investment firm" has the meaning given by the Glossary forming part of the Handbook made by the Financial Services Authority under the Financial Services and Markets Act 2000;

"profit and loss account", in relation to a company that prepares IAS accounts, includes an income statement or other equivalent financial statement required to be prepared by international accounting standards;

"regulated activity" has the meaning given in section 22 of the Financial Services and Markets Act 2000, except that it does not include activities of the kind specified in any of the following provisions of the Financial Services and Markets Act 2000 (Regulated Activities) Order 2001 (SI 2001/544)—

- (a) article 25A (arranging regulated mortgage contracts),
- (b) article 25B (arranging regulated home reversion plans),
- (c) article 25C (arranging regulated home purchase plans),
- (d) article 39A (assisting administration and performance of a contract of insurance),
- (e) article 53A (advising on regulated mortgage contracts),
- (f) article 53B (advising on regulated home reversion plans),
- (g) article 53C (advising on regulated home purchase plans),
- (h) article 21 (dealing as agent), article 25 (arranging deals in investments) or article 53 (advising on investments) where the activity concerns relevant investments that are not contractually based investments (within the meaning of article 3 of that Order), or
- (i) article 64 (agreeing to carry on a regulated activity of the kind mentioned in paragraphs (a) to (h));

"turnover", in relation to a company, means the amounts derived from the provision of goods and services falling within the company's ordinary activities, after deduction of—

- (a) trade discounts,
- (b) value added tax, and
- (c) any other taxes based on the amounts so derived;

"UCITS management company" has the meaning given by the Glossary forming part of the Handbook made by the Financial Services Authority under the Financial Services and Markets Act 2000 (c 8).

(2) In the case of an undertaking not trading for profit, any reference in this Part to a profit and loss account is to an income and expenditure account. References to profit and loss and, in relation to group accounts, to a consolidated profit and loss account shall be construed accordingly.

[S474]

NOTES

Commencement: to be appointed.

PART 16
AUDIT

CHAPTER 1
REQUIREMENT FOR AUDITED ACCOUNTS

Requirement for audited accounts

475 Requirement for audited accounts

(1) A company's annual accounts for a financial year must be audited in accordance with this Part unless the company—

(a) is exempt from audit under—
section 477 (small companies), or
section 480 (dormant companies);

or

(b) is exempt from the requirements of this Part under section 482 (non-profit-making companies subject to public sector audit).

(2) A company is not entitled to any such exemption unless its balance sheet contains a statement by the directors to that effect.

(3) A company is not entitled to exemption under any of the provisions mentioned in subsection (1)(a) unless its balance sheet contains a statement by the directors to the effect that—

(a) the members have not required the company to obtain an audit of its accounts for the year in question in accordance with section 476, and
(b) the directors acknowledge their responsibilities for complying with the requirements of this Act with respect to accounting records and the preparation of accounts.

(4) The statement required by subsection (2) or (3) must appear on the balance sheet above the signature required by section 414.

[S475]

NOTES

Commencement: to be appointed.

476 Right of members to require audit

(1) The members of a company that would otherwise be entitled to exemption from audit under any of the provisions mentioned in section 475(1)(a) may by notice under this section require it to obtain an audit of its accounts for a financial year.

(2) The notice must be given by—

(a) members representing not less in total than 10% in nominal value of the company's issued share capital, or any class of it, or
(b) if the company does not have a share capital, not less than 10% in number of the members of the company.

(3) The notice may not be given before the financial year to which it relates and must be given not later than one month before the end of that year.

[S476]

NOTES

Commencement: to be appointed.

Exemption from audit: small companies

477 Small companies: conditions for exemption from audit

(1) A company that meets the following conditions in respect of a financial year is exempt from the requirements of this Act relating to the audit of accounts for that year.

(2) The conditions are—

(a) that the company qualifies as a small company in relation to that year,
(b) that its turnover in that year is not more than £5.6 million, and
(c) that its balance sheet total for that year is not more than £2.8 million.

(3) For a period which is a company's financial year but not in fact a year the maximum figure for turnover shall be proportionately adjusted.

(4) For the purposes of this section—
(a) whether a company qualifies as a small company shall be determined in accordance with section 382(1) to (6), and
(b) "balance sheet total" has the same meaning as in that section.

(5) This section has effect subject to—
section 475(2) and (3) (requirements as to statements to be contained in balance sheet),
section 476 (right of members to require audit),
section 478 (companies excluded from small companies exemption), and
section 479 (availability of small companies exemption in case of group company).

[S477]

NOTES

Commencement: to be appointed.

478 Companies excluded from small companies exemption

A company is not entitled to the exemption conferred by section 477 (small companies) if it was at any time within the financial year in question—
(a) a public company,
(b) a company that—
(i) is an authorised insurance company, a banking company, an e-money issuer, an ISD investment firm or a UCITS management company, or
(ii) carries on insurance market activity, or
(c) a special register body as defined in section 117(1) of the Trade Union and Labour Relations (Consolidation) Act 1992 (c 52) or an employers' association as defined in section 122 of that Act or Article 4 of the Industrial Relations (Northern Ireland) Order 1992 (SI 1992/807 (NI 5)).

[S478]

NOTES

Commencement: to be appointed.

479 Availability of small companies exemption in case of group company

(1) A company is not entitled to the exemption conferred by section 477 (small companies) in respect of a financial year during any part of which it was a group company unless—
(a) the conditions specified in subsection (2) below are met, or
(b) subsection (3) applies.

(2) The conditions are—
(a) that the group—
(i) qualifies as a small group in relation to that financial year, and
(ii) was not at any time in that year an ineligible group;
(b) that the group's aggregate turnover in that year is not more than £5.6 million net (or £6.72 million gross);
(c) that the group's aggregate balance sheet total for that year is not more than £2.8 million net (or £3.36 million gross).

(3) A company is not excluded by subsection (1) if, throughout the whole of the period or periods during the financial year when it was a group company, it was both a subsidiary undertaking and dormant.

(4) In this section—
(a) "group company" means a company that is a parent company or a subsidiary undertaking, and
(b) "the group", in relation to a group company, means that company together with all its associated undertakings.

For this purpose undertakings are associated if one is a subsidiary undertaking of the other or both are subsidiary undertakings of a third undertaking.

(5) For the purposes of this section—

(a) whether a group qualifies as small shall be determined in accordance with section 383 (companies qualifying as small: parent companies);

(b) "ineligible group" has the meaning given by section 384(2) and (3);

(c) a group's aggregate turnover and aggregate balance sheet total shall be determined as for the purposes of section 383;

(d) "net" and "gross" have the same meaning as in that section;

(e) a company may meet any relevant requirement on the basis of either the gross or the net figure.

(6) The provisions mentioned in subsection (5) apply for the purposes of this section as if all the bodies corporate in the group were companies.

[S479]

NOTES

Commencement: to be appointed.

Exemption from audit: dormant companies

480 Dormant companies: conditions for exemption from audit

(1) A company is exempt from the requirements of this Act relating to the audit of accounts in respect of a financial year if—

(a) it has been dormant since its formation, or

(b) it has been dormant since the end of the previous financial year and the following conditions are met.

(2) The conditions are that the company—

(a) as regards its individual accounts for the financial year in question—

(i) is entitled to prepare accounts in accordance with the small companies regime (see sections 381 to 384), or

(ii) would be so entitled but for having been a public company or a member of an ineligible group, and

(b) is not required to prepare group accounts for that year.

(3) This section has effect subject to—

section 475(2) and (3) (requirements as to statements to be contained in balance sheet),

section 476 (right of members to require audit), and

section 481 (companies excluded from dormant companies exemption).

[S480]

NOTES

Commencement: to be appointed.

481 Companies excluded from dormant companies exemption

A company is not entitled to the exemption conferred by section 480 (dormant companies) if it was at any time within the financial year in question a company that—

(a) is an authorised insurance company, a banking company, an e-money issuer, an ISD investment firm or a UCITS management company, or

(b) carries on insurance market activity.

[S481]

NOTES

Commencement: to be appointed.

Companies subject to public sector audit

482 Non-profit-making companies subject to public sector audit

(1) The requirements of this Part as to audit of accounts do not apply to a company for a financial year if it is non-profit-making and its accounts—

(a) are subject to audit—
  (i) by the Comptroller and Auditor General by virtue of an order under section 25(6) of the Government Resources and Accounts Act 2000 (c 20), or
  (ii) by the Auditor General for Wales by virtue of section 96, or an order under section 144, of the Government of Wales Act 1998 (c 38);

(b) are accounts—
  (i) in relation to which section 21 of the Public Finance and Accountability (Scotland) Act 2000 (asp 1) (audit of accounts: Auditor General for Scotland) applies, or
  (ii) that are subject to audit by the Auditor General for Scotland by virtue of an order under section 483 (Scottish public sector companies: audit by Auditor General for Scotland); or

(c) are subject to audit by the Comptroller and Auditor General for Northern Ireland by virtue of an order under Article 5(3) of the Audit and Accountability (Northern Ireland) Order 2003 (SI 2003/418 (NI 5)).

(2) In the case of a company that is a parent company or a subsidiary undertaking, subsection (1) applies only if every group undertaking is non-profit-making.

(3) In this section "non-profit-making" has the same meaning as in Article 48 of the Treaty establishing the European Community.

(4) This section has effect subject to section 475(2) (balance sheet to contain statement that company entitled to exemption under this section).

[S482]

NOTES

Commencement: to be appointed.

483 Scottish public sector companies: audit by Auditor General for Scotland

(1) The Scottish Ministers may by order provide for the accounts of a company having its registered office in Scotland to be audited by the Auditor General for Scotland.

(2) An order under subsection (1) may be made in relation to a company only if it appears to the Scottish Ministers that the company—

(a) exercises in or as regards Scotland functions of a public nature none of which relate to reserved matters (within the meaning of the Scotland Act 1998 (c 46)), or

(b) is entirely or substantially funded from a body having accounts falling within paragraph (a) or (b) of subsection (3).

(3) Those accounts are—

(a) accounts in relation to which section 21 of the Public Finance and Accountability (Scotland) Act 2000 (asp 1) (audit of accounts: Auditor General for Scotland) applies,

(b) accounts which are subject to audit by the Auditor General for Scotland by virtue of an order under this section.

(4) An order under subsection (1) may make such supplementary or consequential provision (including provision amending an enactment) as the Scottish Ministers think expedient.

(5) An order under subsection (1) shall not be made unless a draft of the statutory instrument containing it has been laid before, and approved by resolution of, the Scottish Parliament.

[S483]

NOTES

Commencement: 20 January 2007 (for the purpose of enabling the exercise of powers to make Orders or Regulations by statutory instrument); to be appointed (otherwise).

General power of amendment by regulations

484 General power of amendment by regulations

(1) The Secretary of State may by regulations amend this Chapter or section 539 (minor definitions) so far as applying to this Chapter by adding, altering or repealing provisions.

(2) The regulations may make consequential amendments or repeals in other provisions of this Act, or in other enactments.

(3) Regulations under this section imposing new requirements, or rendering existing requirements more onerous, are subject to affirmative resolution procedure.

(4) Other regulations under this section are subject to negative resolution procedure.

[S484]

NOTES

Commencement: 20 January 2007 (for the purpose of enabling the exercise of powers to make Orders or Regulations by statutory instrument); to be appointed (otherwise).

CHAPTER 2
APPOINTMENT OF AUDITORS

Private companies

485 Appointment of auditors of private company: general

(1) An auditor or auditors of a private company must be appointed for each financial year of the company, unless the directors reasonably resolve otherwise on the ground that audited accounts are unlikely to be required.

(2) For each financial year for which an auditor or auditors is or are to be appointed (other than the company's first financial year), the appointment must be made before the end of the period of 28 days beginning with—

(a) the end of the time allowed for sending out copies of the company's annual accounts and reports for the previous financial year (see section 424), or

(b) if earlier, the day on which copies of the company's annual accounts and reports for the previous financial year are sent out under section 423.

This is the "period for appointing auditors".

(3) The directors may appoint an auditor or auditors of the company—

(a) at any time before the company's first period for appointing auditors,

(b) following a period during which the company (being exempt from audit) did not have any auditor, at any time before the company's next period for appointing auditors, or

(c) to fill a casual vacancy in the office of auditor.

(4) The members may appoint an auditor or auditors by ordinary resolution—

(a) during a period for appointing auditors,

(b) if the company should have appointed an auditor or auditors during a period for appointing auditors but failed to do so, or

(c) where the directors had power to appoint under subsection (3) but have failed to make an appointment.

(5) An auditor or auditors of a private company may only be appointed—

(a) in accordance with this section, or

(b) in accordance with section 486 (default power of Secretary of State).

This is without prejudice to any deemed re-appointment under section 487.

[S485]

NOTES

Commencement: 1 October 2007 (for transitional provisions see the note below).

Transitional provisions, etc: Sch 3, paras 44, 45 to the draft Companies Act 2006 (Commencement No 3, Consequential Amendments, Transitional Provisions and Savings) Order 2007 (at **[A12]**) provide as follows—

"44 Appointment of auditors of private companies (ss 485 to 488)

(1) Sections 485 to 488 of the Companies Act 2006 (appointment of auditors of private companies) apply in relation to appointments for financial years beginning on or after 1st October 2007.

(2) Sections 384 to 388A of the 1985 Act or Articles 392 to 396A of the 1986 Order continue to apply in relation to appointments for financial years beginning before that date.

(3) Where—

(a) a private company has elected under section 386 of the 1985 Act or Article 394 of the 1986 Order to dispense with the annual appointment of auditors, and

(b) the election is in force immediately before 1st October 2007,

section 487(2)(a) of the Companies Act 2006 (no deemed reappointment of auditors appointed by directors) does not prevent the deemed reappointment under that subsection of auditors first appointed before 1st October 2007.

45.—(1) This paragraph applies where immediately before 1st October 2007 a resolution of a private company under section 390A of the 1985 Act or Article 398A of the 1986 Order (remuneration of auditors) was in force and was expressed (in whatever terms) to continue to have effect so long as a resolution under section 386 of that Act or Article 394 of that Order (election to dispense with annual appointment of auditors) continued in force.

(2) The repeal of section 386 of the 1985 Act or Article 394 of the 1986 Order does not affect the continued operation of the resolution, which shall continue to have effect until—

(a) it is revoked or superseded by a further resolution,

(b) the auditors to which it applies cease to hold office, or

(c) it otherwise ceases to have effect in accordance with its terms.".

Transitional adaptations: art 6 of the draft Companies Act 2006 (Commencement No 3, Consequential Amendments, Transitional Provisions and Savings) Order 2007 provides that the provisions brought into force by that Order shall have effect subject to any transitional adaptations specified in Sch 1 to that Order. Schedule 1, para 17 to the Order (at **[A12]**) provides as follows—

"17 Appointment of auditors of private company (ss 485 to 488)

(1) Section 485 (appointment of auditors of private companies: general) has effect with the following adaptations.

(2) For paragraph (a) of subsection (2) substitute—

"(a) the end of the period allowed for delivering accounts and reports under section 244 of the Companies Act 1985 or Article 252 of the Companies (Northern Ireland) Order 1986, or".

(3) In paragraph (b) of subsection (2), for "section 423" substitute "section 238 of the Companies Act 1985 or Article 246 of the Companies (Northern Ireland) Order 1986".".

486 Appointment of auditors of private company: default power of Secretary of State

(1) If a private company fails to appoint an auditor or auditors in accordance with section 485, the Secretary of State may appoint one or more persons to fill the vacancy.

(2) Where subsection (2) of that section applies and the company fails to make the necessary appointment before the end of the period for appointing auditors, the company must within one week of the end of that period give notice to the Secretary of State of his power having become exercisable.

(3) If a company fails to give the notice required by this section, an offence is committed by—

(a) the company, and

(b) every officer of the company who is in default.

(4) A person guilty of an offence under this section is liable on summary conviction to a fine not exceeding level 3 on the standard scale and, for continued contravention, a daily default fine not exceeding one-tenth of level 3 on the standard scale.

[S486]

NOTES

Commencement: 1 October 2007 (for transitional provisions see the note to s 485).

487 Term of office of auditors of private company

(1) An auditor or auditors of a private company hold office in accordance with the terms of their appointment, subject to the requirements that—

(a) they do not take office until any previous auditor or auditors cease to hold office, and

(b) they cease to hold office at the end of the next period for appointing auditors unless re-appointed.

(2) Where no auditor has been appointed by the end of the next period for appointing auditors, any auditor in office immediately before that time is deemed to be re-appointed at that time, unless—

(a) he was appointed by the directors, or

(b) the company's articles require actual re-appointment, or

(c) the deemed re-appointment is prevented by the members under section 488, or

(d) the members have resolved that he should not be re-appointed, or

(e) the directors have resolved that no auditor or auditors should be appointed for the financial year in question.

(3) This is without prejudice to the provisions of this Part as to removal and resignation of auditors.

(4) No account shall be taken of any loss of the opportunity of deemed re-appointment under this section in ascertaining the amount of any compensation or damages payable to an auditor on his ceasing to hold office for any reason.

[S487]

NOTES

Commencement: 1 October 2007 (for transitional provisions etc see the note to s 485 and the note below).

Transitional adaptations: art 6 of the draft Companies Act 2006 (Commencement No 3, Consequential Amendments, Transitional Provisions and Savings) Order 2007 provides that the provisions brought into force by that Order shall have effect subject to any transitional adaptations specified in Sch 1 to that Order. Schedule 1, para 18 to the Order (at **[A12]**) provides as follows—

"**18.**—(1) Section 487 (term of office of auditors of private company) has effect with the following adaptation.

(2) In subsection (3) for "the provisions of this Part" substitute "the provisions of Chapter 5 of Part 11 of the Companies Act 1985 or Chapter 5 of Part 12 of the Companies (Northern Ireland) Order 1986".".

488 Prevention by members of deemed re-appointment of auditor

(1) An auditor of a private company is not deemed to be re-appointed under section 487(2) if the company has received notices under this section from members representing at least the requisite percentage of the total voting rights of all members who would be entitled to vote on a resolution that the auditor should not be re-appointed.

(2) The "requisite percentage" is 5%, or such lower percentage as is specified for this purpose in the company's articles.

(3) A notice under this section—

(a) may be in hard copy or electronic form,

(b) must be authenticated by the person or persons giving it, and

(c) must be received by the company before the end of the accounting reference period immediately preceding the time when the deemed re-appointment would have effect.

[S488]

NOTES

Commencement: 1 October 2007 (for transitional provisions see the note to s 485).

Public companies

489 Appointment of auditors of public company: general

(1) An auditor or auditors of a public company must be appointed for each financial year of the company, unless the directors reasonably resolve otherwise on the ground that audited accounts are unlikely to be required.

(2) For each financial year for which an auditor or auditors is or are to be appointed (other than the company's first financial year), the appointment must be made before the end of the accounts meeting of the company at which the company's annual accounts and reports for the previous financial year are laid.

(3) The directors may appoint an auditor or auditors of the company—
(a) at any time before the company's first accounts meeting;
(b) following a period during which the company (being exempt from audit) did not have any auditor, at any time before the company's next accounts meeting;
(c) to fill a casual vacancy in the office of auditor.

(4) The members may appoint an auditor or auditors by ordinary resolution—
(a) at an accounts meeting;
(b) if the company should have appointed an auditor or auditors at an accounts meeting but failed to do so;
(c) where the directors had power to appoint under subsection (3) but have failed to make an appointment.

(5) An auditor or auditors of a public company may only be appointed—
(a) in accordance with this section, or
(b) in accordance with section 490 (default power of Secretary of State).

[S489]

NOTES
Commencement: to be appointed.

490 Appointment of auditors of public company: default power of Secretary of State

(1) If a public company fails to appoint an auditor or auditors in accordance with section 489, the Secretary of State may appoint one or more persons to fill the vacancy.

(2) Where subsection (2) of that section applies and the company fails to make the necessary appointment before the end of the accounts meeting, the company must within one week of the end of that meeting give notice to the Secretary of State of his power having become exercisable.

(3) If a company fails to give the notice required by this section, an offence is committed by—
(a) the company, and
(b) every officer of the company who is in default.

(4) A person guilty of an offence under this section is liable on summary conviction to a fine not exceeding level 3 on the standard scale and, for continued contravention, a daily default fine not exceeding one-tenth of level 3 on the standard scale.

[S490]

NOTES
Commencement: to be appointed.

491 Term of office of auditors of public company

(1) The auditor or auditors of a public company hold office in accordance with the terms of their appointment, subject to the requirements that—
(a) they do not take office until the previous auditor or auditors have ceased to hold office, and
(b) they cease to hold office at the conclusion of the accounts meeting next following their appointment, unless re-appointed.

(2) This is without prejudice to the provisions of this Part as to removal and resignation of auditors.

[S491]

NOTES
Commencement: to be appointed.

General provisions

492 Fixing of auditor's remuneration

(1) The remuneration of an auditor appointed by the members of a company must be fixed by the members by ordinary resolution or in such manner as the members may by ordinary resolution determine.

(2) The remuneration of an auditor appointed by the directors of a company must be fixed by the directors.

(3) The remuneration of an auditor appointed by the Secretary of State must be fixed by the Secretary of State.

(4) For the purposes of this section "remuneration" includes sums paid in respect of expenses.

(5) This section applies in relation to benefits in kind as to payments of money.

[S492]

NOTES

Commencement: to be appointed.

493 Disclosure of terms of audit appointment

(1) The Secretary of State may make provision by regulations for securing the disclosure of the terms on which a company's auditor is appointed, remunerated or performs his duties.

Nothing in the following provisions of this section affects the generality of this power.

(2) The regulations may—
- (a) require disclosure of—
  - (i) a copy of any terms that are in writing, and
  - (ii) a written memorandum setting out any terms that are not in writing;
- (b) require disclosure to be at such times, in such places and by such means as are specified in the regulations;
- (c) require the place and means of disclosure to be stated—
  - (i) in a note to the company's annual accounts (in the case of its individual accounts) or in such manner as is specified in the regulations (in the case of group accounts),
  - (ii) in the directors' report, or
  - (iii) in the auditor's report on the company's annual accounts.

(3) The provisions of this section apply to a variation of the terms mentioned in subsection (1) as they apply to the original terms.

(4) Regulations under this section are subject to affirmative resolution procedure.

[S493]

NOTES

Commencement: 20 January 2007 (for the purpose of enabling the exercise of powers to make Orders or Regulations by statutory instrument); to be appointed (otherwise).

494 Disclosure of services provided by auditor or associates and related remuneration

(1) The Secretary of State may make provision by regulations for securing the disclosure of—
- (a) the nature of any services provided for a company by the company's auditor (whether in his capacity as auditor or otherwise) or by his associates;
- (b) the amount of any remuneration received or receivable by a company's auditor, or his associates, in respect of any such services.

Nothing in the following provisions of this section affects the generality of this power.

(2) The regulations may provide—
- (a) for disclosure of the nature of any services provided to be made by reference to any class or description of services specified in the regulations (or any combination of services, however described);
- (b) for the disclosure of amounts of remuneration received or receivable in respect of

services of any class or description specified in the regulations (or any combination of services, however described);

(c) for the disclosure of separate amounts so received or receivable by the company's auditor or any of his associates, or of aggregate amounts so received or receivable by all or any of those persons.

(3) The regulations may—

(a) provide that "remuneration" includes sums paid in respect of expenses;

(b) apply to benefits in kind as well as to payments of money, and require the disclosure of the nature of any such benefits and their estimated money value;

(c) apply to services provided for associates of a company as well as to those provided for a company;

(d) define "associate" in relation to an auditor and a company respectively.

(4) The regulations may provide that any disclosure required by the regulations is to be made—

(a) in a note to the company's annual accounts (in the case of its individual accounts) or in such manner as is specified in the regulations (in the case of group accounts),

(b) in the directors' report, or

(c) in the auditor's report on the company's annual accounts.

(5) If the regulations provide that any such disclosure is to be made as mentioned in subsection (4)(a) or (b), the regulations may require the auditor to supply the directors of the company with any information necessary to enable the disclosure to be made.

(6) Regulations under this section are subject to negative resolution procedure.

[S494]

NOTES

Commencement: 20 January 2007 (for the purpose of enabling the exercise of powers to make Orders or Regulations by statutory instrument); to be appointed (otherwise).

CHAPTER 3
FUNCTIONS OF AUDITOR

Auditor's report

495 Auditor's report on company's annual accounts

(1) A company's auditor must make a report to the company's members on all annual accounts of the company of which copies are, during his tenure of office—

(a) in the case of a private company, to be sent out to members under section 423;

(b) in the case of a public company, to be laid before the company in general meeting under section 437.

(2) The auditor's report must include—

(a) an introduction identifying the annual accounts that are the subject of the audit and the financial reporting framework that has been applied in their preparation, and

(b) a description of the scope of the audit identifying the auditing standards in accordance with which the audit was conducted.

(3) The report must state clearly whether, in the auditor's opinion, the annual accounts—

(a) give a true and fair view—

(i) in the case of an individual balance sheet, of the state of affairs of the company as at the end of the financial year,

(ii) in the case of an individual profit and loss account, of the profit or loss of the company for the financial year,

(iii) in the case of group accounts, of the state of affairs as at the end of the financial year and of the profit or loss for the financial year of the undertakings included in the consolidation as a whole, so far as concerns members of the company;

(b) have been properly prepared in accordance with the relevant financial reporting framework; and

(c) have been prepared in accordance with the requirements of this Act (and, where applicable, Article 4 of the IAS Regulation).

Expressions used in this subsection that are defined for the purposes of Part 15 (see section 474) have the same meaning as in that Part.

(4) The auditor's report—

(a) must be either unqualified or qualified, and

(b) must include a reference to any matters to which the auditor wishes to draw attention by way of emphasis without qualifying the report.

[S495]

NOTES

Commencement: to be appointed.

496 Auditor's report on directors' report

The auditor must state in his report on the company's annual accounts whether in his opinion the information given in the directors' report for the financial year for which the accounts are prepared is consistent with those accounts.

[S496]

NOTES

Commencement: to be appointed.

497 Auditor's report on auditable part of directors' remuneration report

(1) If the company is a quoted company, the auditor, in his report on the company's annual accounts for the financial year, must—

(a) report to the company's members on the auditable part of the directors' remuneration report, and

(b) state whether in his opinion that part of the directors' remuneration report has been properly prepared in accordance with this Act.

(2) For the purposes of this Part, "the auditable part" of a directors' remuneration report is the part identified as such by regulations under section 421.

[S497]

NOTES

Commencement: to be appointed.

Duties and rights of auditors

498 Duties of auditor

(1) A company's auditor, in preparing his report, must carry out such investigations as will enable him to form an opinion as to—

(a) whether adequate accounting records have been kept by the company and returns adequate for their audit have been received from branches not visited by him, and

(b) whether the company's individual accounts are in agreement with the accounting records and returns, and

(c) in the case of a quoted company, whether the auditable part of the company's directors' remuneration report is in agreement with the accounting records and returns.

(2) If the auditor is of the opinion—

(a) that adequate accounting records have not been kept, or that returns adequate for their audit have not been received from branches not visited by him, or

(b) that the company's individual accounts are not in agreement with the accounting records and returns, or

(c) in the case of a quoted company, that the auditable part of its directors' remuneration report is not in agreement with the accounting records and returns,

the auditor shall state that fact in his report.

(3) If the auditor fails to obtain all the information and explanations which, to the best of his knowledge and belief, are necessary for the purposes of his audit, he shall state that fact in his report.

(4) If—

(a) the requirements of regulations under section 412 (disclosure of directors' benefits: remuneration, pensions and compensation for loss of office) are not complied with in the annual accounts, or

(b) in the case of a quoted company, the requirements of regulations under section 421 as to information forming the auditable part of the directors' remuneration report are not complied with in that report,

the auditor must include in his report, so far as he is reasonably able to do so, a statement giving the required particulars.

(5) If the directors of the company have prepared accounts and reports in accordance with the small companies regime and in the auditor's opinion they were not entitled so to do, the auditor shall state that fact in his report.

[S498]

NOTES

Commencement: to be appointed.

499 Auditor's general right to information

(1) An auditor of a company—

(a) has a right of access at all times to the company's books, accounts and vouchers (in whatever form they are held), and

(b) may require any of the following persons to provide him with such information or explanations as he thinks necessary for the performance of his duties as auditor.

(2) Those persons are—

(a) any officer or employee of the company;

(b) any person holding or accountable for any of the company's books, accounts or vouchers;

(c) any subsidiary undertaking of the company which is a body corporate incorporated in the United Kingdom;

(d) any officer, employee or auditor of any such subsidiary undertaking or any person holding or accountable for any books, accounts or vouchers of any such subsidiary undertaking;

(e) any person who fell within any of paragraphs (a) to (d) at a time to which the information or explanations required by the auditor relates or relate.

(3) A statement made by a person in response to a requirement under this section may not be used in evidence against him in criminal proceedings except proceedings for an offence under section 501.

(4) Nothing in this section compels a person to disclose information in respect of which a claim to legal professional privilege (in Scotland, to confidentiality of communications) could be maintained in legal proceedings.

[S499]

NOTES

Commencement: to be appointed.

500 Auditor's right to information from overseas subsidiaries

(1) Where a parent company has a subsidiary undertaking that is not a body corporate incorporated in the United Kingdom, the auditor of the parent company may require it to obtain from any of the following persons such information or explanations as he may reasonably require for the purposes of his duties as auditor.

(2) Those persons are—

(a) the undertaking;

(b) any officer, employee or auditor of the undertaking;

(c) any person holding or accountable for any of the undertaking's books, accounts or vouchers;

(d) any person who fell within paragraph (b) or (c) at a time to which the information or explanations relates or relate.

(3) If so required, the parent company must take all such steps as are reasonably open to it to obtain the information or explanations from the person concerned.

(4) A statement made by a person in response to a requirement under this section may not be used in evidence against him in criminal proceedings except proceedings for an offence under section 501.

(5) Nothing in this section compels a person to disclose information in respect of which a claim to legal professional privilege (in Scotland, to confidentiality of communications) could be maintained in legal proceedings.

[S500]

NOTES

Commencement: to be appointed.

501 Auditor's rights to information: offences

(1) A person commits an offence who knowingly or recklessly makes to an auditor of a company a statement (oral or written) that—

(a) conveys or purports to convey any information or explanations which the auditor requires, or is entitled to require, under section 499, and

(b) is misleading, false or deceptive in a material particular.

(2) A person guilty of an offence under subsection (1) is liable—

(a) on conviction on indictment, to imprisonment for a term not exceeding two years or a fine (or both);

(b) on summary conviction—

(i) in England and Wales, to imprisonment for a term not exceeding twelve months or to a fine not exceeding the statutory maximum (or both);

(ii) in Scotland or Northern Ireland, to imprisonment for a term not exceeding six months or to a fine not exceeding the statutory maximum (or both).

(3) A person who fails to comply with a requirement under section 499 without delay commits an offence unless it was not reasonably practicable for him to provide the required information or explanations.

(4) If a parent company fails to comply with section 500, an offence is committed by—

(a) the company, and

(b) every officer of the company who is in default.

(5) A person guilty of an offence under subsection (3) or (4) is liable on summary conviction to a fine not exceeding level 3 on the standard scale.

(6) Nothing in this section affects any right of an auditor to apply for an injunction (in Scotland, an interdict or an order for specific performance) to enforce any of his rights under section 499 or 500.

[S501]

NOTES

Commencement: to be appointed.

502 Auditor's rights in relation to resolutions and meetings

(1) In relation to a written resolution proposed to be agreed to by a private company, the company's auditor is entitled to receive all such communications relating to the resolution as, by virtue of any provision of Chapter 2 of Part 13 of this Act, are required to be supplied to a member of the company.

(2) A company's auditor is entitled—

(a) to receive all notices of, and other communications relating to, any general meeting which a member of the company is entitled to receive,

(b) to attend any general meeting of the company, and

(c) to be heard at any general meeting which he attends on any part of the business of the meeting which concerns him as auditor.

(3) Where the auditor is a firm, the right to attend or be heard at a meeting is exercisable by an individual authorised by the firm in writing to act as its representative at the meeting.

[S502]

NOTES

Commencement: to be appointed.

Signature of auditor's report

503 Signature of auditor's report

(1) The auditor's report must state the name of the auditor and be signed and dated.

(2) Where the auditor is an individual, the report must be signed by him.

(3) Where the auditor is a firm, the report must be signed by the senior statutory auditor in his own name, for and on behalf of the auditor.

[S503]

NOTES

Commencement: to be appointed.

504 Senior statutory auditor

(1) The senior statutory auditor means the individual identified by the firm as senior statutory auditor in relation to the audit in accordance with—

- (a) standards issued by the European Commission, or
- (b) if there is no applicable standard so issued, any relevant guidance issued by—
  - (i) the Secretary of State, or
  - (ii) a body appointed by order of the Secretary of State.

(2) The person identified as senior statutory auditor must be eligible for appointment as auditor of the company in question (see Chapter 2 of Part 42 of this Act).

(3) The senior statutory auditor is not, by reason of being named or identified as senior statutory auditor or by reason of his having signed the auditor's report, subject to any civil liability to which he would not otherwise be subject.

(4) An order appointing a body for the purpose of subsection (1)(b)(ii) is subject to negative resolution procedure.

[S504]

NOTES

Commencement: 20 January 2007 (for the purpose of enabling the exercise of powers to make Orders or Regulations by statutory instrument); to be appointed (otherwise).

505 Names to be stated in published copies of auditor's report

(1) Every copy of the auditor's report that is published by or on behalf of the company must—

- (a) state the name of the auditor and (where the auditor is a firm) the name of the person who signed it as senior statutory auditor, or
- (b) if the conditions in section 506 (circumstances in which names may be omitted) are met, state that a resolution has been passed and notified to the Secretary of State in accordance with that section.

(2) For the purposes of this section a company is regarded as publishing the report if it publishes, issues or circulates it or otherwise makes it available for public inspection in a manner calculated to invite members of the public generally, or any class of members of the public, to read it.

(3) If a copy of the auditor's report is published without the statement required by this section, an offence is committed by—

- (a) the company, and
- (b) every officer of the company who is in default.

(4) A person guilty of an offence under this section is liable on summary conviction to a fine not exceeding level 3 on the standard scale.

[S505]

NOTES

Commencement: to be appointed.

506 Circumstances in which names may be omitted

(1) The auditor's name and, where the auditor is a firm, the name of the person who signed the report as senior statutory auditor, may be omitted from—

(a) published copies of the report, and

(b) the copy of the report delivered to the registrar under Chapter 10 of Part 15 (filing of accounts and reports),

if the following conditions are met.

(2) The conditions are that the company—

(a) considering on reasonable grounds that statement of the name would create or be likely to create a serious risk that the auditor or senior statutory auditor, or any other person, would be subject to violence or intimidation, has resolved that the name should not be stated, and

(b) has given notice of the resolution to the Secretary of State, stating—

(i) the name and registered number of the company,

(ii) the financial year of the company to which the report relates, and

(iii) the name of the auditor and (where the auditor is a firm) the name of the person who signed the report as senior statutory auditor.

[S506]

NOTES

Commencement: to be appointed.

Offences in connection with auditor's report

507 Offences in connection with auditor's report

(1) A person to whom this section applies commits an offence if he knowingly or recklessly causes a report under section 495 (auditor's report on company's annual accounts) to include any matter that is misleading, false or deceptive in a material particular.

(2) A person to whom this section applies commits an offence if he knowingly or recklessly causes such a report to omit a statement required by—

(a) section 498(2)(b) (statement that company's accounts do not agree with accounting records and returns),

(b) section 498(3) (statement that necessary information and explanations not obtained), or

(c) section 498(5) (statement that directors wrongly took advantage of exemption from obligation to prepare group accounts).

(3) This section applies to—

(a) where the auditor is an individual, that individual and any employee or agent of his who is eligible for appointment as auditor of the company;

(b) where the auditor is a firm, any director, member, employee or agent of the firm who is eligible for appointment as auditor of the company.

(4) A person guilty of an offence under this section is liable—

(a) on conviction on indictment, to a fine;

(b) on summary conviction, to a fine not exceeding the statutory maximum.

[S507]

NOTES

Commencement: to be appointed.

508 Guidance for regulatory and prosecuting authorities: England, Wales and Northern Ireland

(1) The Secretary of State may issue guidance for the purpose of helping relevant regulatory and prosecuting authorities to determine how they should carry out their functions in cases where behaviour occurs that—

(a) appears to involve the commission of an offence under section 507 (offences in connection with auditor's report), and
(b) has been, is being or may be investigated pursuant to arrangements—
  (i) under paragraph 15 of Schedule 10 (investigation of complaints against auditors and supervisory bodies), or
  (ii) of a kind mentioned in paragraph 24 of that Schedule (independent investigation for disciplinary purposes of public interest cases).

(2) The Secretary of State must obtain the consent of the Attorney General before issuing any such guidance.

(3) In this section "relevant regulatory and prosecuting authorities" means—
(a) supervisory bodies within the meaning of Part 42 of this Act,
(b) bodies to which the Secretary of State may make grants under section 16(1) of the Companies (Audit, Investigations and Community Enterprise) Act 2004 (c 27) (bodies concerned with accounting standards etc),
(c) the Director of the Serious Fraud Office,
(d) the Director of Public Prosecutions or the Director of Public Prosecutions for Northern Ireland, and
(e) the Secretary of State.

(4) This section does not apply to Scotland.

[S508]

NOTES

Commencement: to be appointed.

509 Guidance for regulatory authorities: Scotland

(1) The Lord Advocate may issue guidance for the purpose of helping relevant regulatory authorities to determine how they should carry out their functions in cases where behaviour occurs that—
(a) appears to involve the commission of an offence under section 507 (offences in connection with auditor's report), and
(b) has been, is being or may be investigated pursuant to arrangements—
  (i) under paragraph 15 of Schedule 10 (investigation of complaints against auditors and supervisory bodies), or
  (ii) of a kind mentioned in paragraph 24 of that Schedule (independent investigation for disciplinary purposes of public interest cases).

(2) The Lord Advocate must consult the Secretary of State before issuing any such guidance.

(3) In this section "relevant regulatory authorities" means—
(a) supervisory bodies within the meaning of Part 42 of this Act,
(b) bodies to which the Secretary of State may make grants under section 16(1) of the Companies (Audit, Investigations and Community Enterprise) Act 2004 (c 27) (bodies concerned with accounting standards etc), and
(c) the Secretary of State.

(4) This section applies only to Scotland.

[S509]

NOTES

Commencement: to be appointed.

CHAPTER 4
REMOVAL, RESIGNATION, ETC OF AUDITORS

Removal of auditor

510 Resolution removing auditor from office

(1) The members of a company may remove an auditor from office at any time.

(2) This power is exercisable only—

(a) by ordinary resolution at a meeting, and
(b) in accordance with section 511 (special notice of resolution to remove auditor).

(3) Nothing in this section is to be taken as depriving the person removed of compensation or damages payable to him in respect of the termination—
(a) of his appointment as auditor, or
(b) of any appointment terminating with that as auditor.

(4) An auditor may not be removed from office before the expiration of his term of office except by resolution under this section.

[S510]

NOTES
Commencement: to be appointed.

511 Special notice required for resolution removing auditor from office

(1) Special notice is required for a resolution at a general meeting of a company removing an auditor from office.

(2) On receipt of notice of such an intended resolution the company must immediately send a copy of it to the auditor proposed to be removed.

(3) The auditor proposed to be removed may make with respect to the intended resolution representations in writing to the company (not exceeding a reasonable length) and request their notification to members of the company.

(4) The company must (unless the representations are received by it too late for it to do so)—
(a) in any notice of the resolution given to members of the company, state the fact of the representations having been made, and
(b) send a copy of the representations to every member of the company to whom notice of the meeting is or has been sent.

(5) If a copy of any such representations is not sent out as required because received too late or because of the company's default, the auditor may (without prejudice to his right to be heard orally) require that the representations be read out at the meeting.

(6) Copies of the representations need not be sent out and the representations need not be read at the meeting if, on the application either of the company or of any other person claiming to be aggrieved, the court is satisfied that the auditor is using the provisions of this section to secure needless publicity for defamatory matter.

The court may order the company's costs (in Scotland, expenses) on the application to be paid in whole or in part by the auditor, notwithstanding that he is not a party to the application.

[S511]

NOTES
Commencement: to be appointed.

512 Notice to registrar of resolution removing auditor from office

(1) Where a resolution is passed under section 510 (resolution removing auditor from office), the company must give notice of that fact to the registrar within 14 days.

(2) If a company fails to give the notice required by this section, an offence is committed by—
(a) the company, and
(b) every officer of it who is in default.

(3) A person guilty of an offence under this section is liable on summary conviction to a fine not exceeding level 3 on the standard scale and, for continued contravention, a daily default fine not exceeding one-tenth of level 3 on the standard scale.

[S512]

NOTES
Commencement: to be appointed.

513 Rights of auditor who has been removed from office

(1) An auditor who has been removed by resolution under section 510 has, notwithstanding his removal, the rights conferred by section 502(2) in relation to any general meeting of the company—

(a) at which his term of office would otherwise have expired, or

(b) at which it is proposed to fill the vacancy caused by his removal.

(2) In such a case the references in that section to matters concerning the auditor as auditor shall be construed as references to matters concerning him as a former auditor.

[S513]

NOTES

Commencement: to be appointed.

Failure to re-appoint auditor

514 Failure to re-appoint auditor: special procedure required for written resolution

(1) This section applies where a resolution is proposed as a written resolution of a private company whose effect would be to appoint a person as auditor in place of a person (the "outgoing auditor") whose term of office has expired, or is to expire, at the end of the period for appointing auditors.

(2) The following provisions apply if—

(a) no period for appointing auditors has ended since the outgoing auditor ceased to hold office, or

(b) such a period has ended and an auditor or auditors should have been appointed but were not.

(3) The company must send a copy of the proposed resolution to the person proposed to be appointed and to the outgoing auditor.

(4) The outgoing auditor may, within 14 days after receiving the notice, make with respect to the proposed resolution representations in writing to the company (not exceeding a reasonable length) and request their circulation to members of the company.

(5) The company must circulate the representations together with the copy or copies of the resolution circulated in accordance with section 291 (resolution proposed by directors) or section 293 (resolution proposed by members).

(6) Where subsection (5) applies—

(a) the period allowed under section 293(3) for service of copies of the proposed resolution is 28 days instead of 21 days, and

(b) the provisions of section 293(5) and (6) (offences) apply in relation to a failure to comply with that subsection as in relation to a default in complying with that section.

(7) Copies of the representations need not be circulated if, on the application either of the company or of any other person claiming to be aggrieved, the court is satisfied that the auditor is using the provisions of this section to secure needless publicity for defamatory matter.

The court may order the company's costs (in Scotland, expenses) on the application to be paid in whole or in part by the auditor, notwithstanding that he is not a party to the application.

(8) If any requirement of this section is not complied with, the resolution is ineffective.

[S514]

NOTES

Commencement: to be appointed.

515 Failure to re-appoint auditor: special notice required for resolution at general meeting

(1) This section applies to a resolution at a general meeting of a company whose effect would be to appoint a person as auditor in place of a person (the "outgoing auditor") whose term of office has ended, or is to end—

(a) in the case of a private company, at the end of the period for appointing auditors;
(b) in the case of a public company, at the end of the next accounts meeting.

(2) Special notice is required of such a resolution if—
(a) in the case of a private company—
(i) no period for appointing auditors has ended since the outgoing auditor ceased to hold office, or
(ii) such a period has ended and an auditor or auditors should have been appointed but were not;
(b) in the case of a public company—
(i) there has been no accounts meeting of the company since the outgoing auditor ceased to hold office, or
(ii) there has been an accounts meeting at which an auditor or auditors should have been appointed but were not.

(3) On receipt of notice of such an intended resolution the company shall forthwith send a copy of it to the person proposed to be appointed and to the outgoing auditor.

(4) The outgoing auditor may make with respect to the intended resolution representations in writing to the company (not exceeding a reasonable length) and request their notification to members of the company.

(5) The company must (unless the representations are received by it too late for it to do so)—
(a) in any notice of the resolution given to members of the company, state the fact of the representations having been made, and
(b) send a copy of the representations to every member of the company to whom notice of the meeting is or has been sent.

(6) If a copy of any such representations is not sent out as required because received too late or because of the company's default, the outgoing auditor may (without prejudice to his right to be heard orally) require that the representations be read out at the meeting.

(7) Copies of the representations need not be sent out and the representations need not be read at the meeting if, on the application either of the company or of any other person claiming to be aggrieved, the court is satisfied that the auditor is using the provisions of this section to secure needless publicity for defamatory matter.

The court may order the company's costs (in Scotland, expenses) on the application to be paid in whole or in part by the outgoing auditor, notwithstanding that he is not a party to the application.

[S515]

NOTES
Commencement: to be appointed.

Resignation of auditor

516 Resignation of auditor

(1) An auditor of a company may resign his office by depositing a notice in writing to that effect at the company's registered office.

(2) The notice is not effective unless it is accompanied by the statement required by section 519.

(3) An effective notice of resignation operates to bring the auditor's term of office to an end as of the date on which the notice is deposited or on such later date as may be specified in it.

[S516]

NOTES
Commencement: to be appointed.

517 Notice to registrar of resignation of auditor

(1) Where an auditor resigns the company must within 14 days of the deposit of a notice of resignation send a copy of the notice to the registrar of companies.

(2) If default is made in complying with this section, an offence is committed by—
(a) the company, and
(b) every officer of the company who is in default.

(3) A person guilty of an offence under this section is liable—
(a) on conviction on indictment, to a fine;
(b) on summary conviction, to a fine not exceeding the statutory maximum and, for continued contravention, a daily default fine not exceeding one-tenth of the statutory maximum.

[S517]

NOTES
Commencement: to be appointed.

518 Rights of resigning auditor

(1) This section applies where an auditor's notice of resignation is accompanied by a statement of the circumstances connected with his resignation (see section 519).

(2) He may deposit with the notice a signed requisition calling on the directors of the company forthwith duly to convene a general meeting of the company for the purpose of receiving and considering such explanation of the circumstances connected with his resignation as he may wish to place before the meeting.

(3) He may request the company to circulate to its members—
(a) before the meeting convened on his requisition, or
(b) before any general meeting at which his term of office would otherwise have expired or at which it is proposed to fill the vacancy caused by his resignation,

a statement in writing (not exceeding a reasonable length) of the circumstances connected with his resignation.

(4) The company must (unless the statement is received too late for it to comply)—
(a) in any notice of the meeting given to members of the company, state the fact of the statement having been made, and
(b) send a copy of the statement to every member of the company to whom notice of the meeting is or has been sent.

(5) The directors must within 21 days from the date of the deposit of a requisition under this section proceed duly to convene a meeting for a day not more than 28 days after the date on which the notice convening the meeting is given.

(6) If default is made in complying with subsection (5), every director who failed to take all reasonable steps to secure that a meeting was convened commits an offence.

(7) A person guilty of an offence under this section is liable—
(a) on conviction on indictment, to a fine;
(b) on summary conviction to a fine not exceeding the statutory maximum.

(8) If a copy of the statement mentioned above is not sent out as required because received too late or because of the company's default, the auditor may (without prejudice to his right to be heard orally) require that the statement be read out at the meeting.

(9) Copies of a statement need not be sent out and the statement need not be read out at the meeting if, on the application either of the company or of any other person who claims to be aggrieved, the court is satisfied that the auditor is using the provisions of this section to secure needless publicity for defamatory matter.

The court may order the company's costs (in Scotland, expenses) on such an application to be paid in whole or in part by the auditor, notwithstanding that he is not a party to the application.

(10) An auditor who has resigned has, notwithstanding his resignation, the rights conferred by section 502(2) in relation to any such general meeting of the company as is mentioned in subsection (3)(a) or (b) above.

In such a case the references in that section to matters concerning the auditor as auditor shall be construed as references to matters concerning him as a former auditor.

[S518]

NOTES

Commencement: to be appointed.

Statement by auditor on ceasing to hold office

519 Statement by auditor to be deposited with company

(1) Where an auditor of an unquoted company ceases for any reason to hold office, he must deposit at the company's registered office a statement of the circumstances connected with his ceasing to hold office, unless he considers that there are no circumstances in connection with his ceasing to hold office that need to be brought to the attention of members or creditors of the company.

(2) If he considers that there are no circumstances in connection with his ceasing to hold office that need to be brought to the attention of members or creditors of the company, he must deposit at the company's registered office a statement to that effect.

(3) Where an auditor of a quoted company ceases for any reason to hold office, he must deposit at the company's registered office a statement of the circumstances connected with his ceasing to hold office.

(4) The statement required by this section must be deposited—

(a) in the case of resignation, along with the notice of resignation;

(b) in the case of failure to seek re-appointment, not less than 14 days before the end of the time allowed for next appointing an auditor;

(c) in any other case, not later than the end of the period of 14 days beginning with the date on which he ceases to hold office.

(5) A person ceasing to hold office as auditor who fails to comply with this section commits an offence.

(6) In proceedings for such an offence it is a defence for the person charged to show that he took all reasonable steps and exercised all due diligence to avoid the commission of the offence.

(7) A person guilty of an offence under this section is liable—

(a) on conviction on indictment, to a fine;

(b) on summary conviction, to a fine not exceeding the statutory maximum.

[S519]

NOTES

Commencement: to be appointed.

520 Company's duties in relation to statement

(1) This section applies where the statement deposited under section 519 states the circumstances connected with the auditor's ceasing to hold office.

(2) The company must within 14 days of the deposit of the statement either—

(a) send a copy of it to every person who under section 423 is entitled to be sent copies of the accounts, or

(b) apply to the court.

(3) If it applies to the court, the company must notify the auditor of the application.

(4) If the court is satisfied that the auditor is using the provisions of section 519 to secure needless publicity for defamatory matter—

(a) it shall direct that copies of the statement need not be sent out, and

(b) it may further order the company's costs (in Scotland, expenses) on the application to be paid in whole or in part by the auditor, even if he is not a party to the application.

The company must within 14 days of the court's decision send to the persons mentioned in subsection (2)(a) a statement setting out the effect of the order.

(5) If no such direction is made the company must send copies of the statement to the persons mentioned in subsection (2)(a) within 14 days of the court's decision or, as the case may be, of the discontinuance of the proceedings.

(6) In the event of default in complying with this section an offence is committed by every officer of the company who is in default.

(7) In proceedings for such an offence it is a defence for the person charged to show that he took all reasonable steps and exercised all due diligence to avoid the commission of the offence.

(8) A person guilty of an offence under this section is liable—

(a) on conviction on indictment, to a fine;

(b) on summary conviction, to a fine not exceeding the statutory maximum.

[S520]

NOTES

Commencement: to be appointed.

521 Copy of statement to be sent to registrar

(1) Unless within 21 days beginning with the day on which he deposited the statement under section 519 the auditor receives notice of an application to the court under section 520, he must within a further seven days send a copy of the statement to the registrar.

(2) If an application to the court is made under section 520 and the auditor subsequently receives notice under subsection (5) of that section, he must within seven days of receiving the notice send a copy of the statement to the registrar.

(3) An auditor who fails to comply with subsection (1) or (2) commits an offence.

(4) In proceedings for such an offence it is a defence for the person charged to show that he took all reasonable steps and exercised all due diligence to avoid the commission of the offence.

(5) A person guilty of an offence under this section is liable—

(a) on conviction on indictment, to a fine;

(b) on summary conviction, to a fine not exceeding the statutory maximum.

[S521]

NOTES

Commencement: to be appointed.

522 Duty of auditor to notify appropriate audit authority

(1) Where—

(a) in the case of a major audit, an auditor ceases for any reason to hold office, or

(b) in the case of an audit that is not a major audit, an auditor ceases to hold office before the end of his term of office,

the auditor ceasing to hold office must notify the appropriate audit authority.

(2) The notice must—

(a) inform the appropriate audit authority that he has ceased to hold office, and

(b) be accompanied by a copy of the statement deposited by him at the company's registered office in accordance with section 519.

(3) If the statement so deposited is to the effect that he considers that there are no circumstances in connection with his ceasing to hold office that need to be brought to the attention of members or creditors of the company, the notice must also be accompanied by a statement of the reasons for his ceasing to hold office.

(4) The auditor must comply with this section—

(a) in the case of a major audit, at the same time as he deposits a statement at the company's registered office in accordance with section 519;

(b) in the case of an audit that is not a major audit, at such time (not being earlier than the time mentioned in paragraph (a)) as the appropriate audit authority may require.

(5) A person ceasing to hold office as auditor who fails to comply with this section commits an offence.

(6) If that person is a firm an offence is committed by—

(a) the firm, and
(b) every officer of the firm who is in default.

(7) In proceedings for an offence under this section it is a defence for the person charged to show that he took all reasonable steps and exercised all due diligence to avoid the commission of the offence.

(8) A person guilty of an offence under this section is liable—
(a) on conviction on indictment, to a fine;
(b) on summary conviction, to a fine not exceeding the statutory maximum.

[S522]

NOTES

Commencement: to be appointed.

523 Duty of company to notify appropriate audit authority

(1) Where an auditor ceases to hold office before the end of his term of office, the company must notify the appropriate audit authority.

(2) The notice must—
(a) inform the appropriate audit authority that the auditor has ceased to hold office, and
(b) be accompanied by—
(i) a statement by the company of the reasons for his ceasing to hold office, or
(ii) if the copy of the statement deposited by the auditor at the company's registered office in accordance with section 519 contains a statement of circumstances in connection with his ceasing to hold office that need to be brought to the attention of members or creditors of the company, a copy of that statement.

(3) The company must give notice under this section not later than 14 days after the date on which the auditor's statement is deposited at the company's registered office in accordance with section 519.

(4) If a company fails to comply with this section, an offence is committed by—
(a) the company, and
(b) every officer of the company who is in default.

(5) In proceedings for such an offence it is a defence for the person charged to show that he took all reasonable steps and exercised all due diligence to avoid the commission of the offence.

(6) A person guilty of an offence under this section is liable—
(a) on conviction on indictment, to a fine;
(b) on summary conviction, to a fine not exceeding the statutory maximum.

[S523]

NOTES

Commencement: to be appointed.

524 Information to be given to accounting authorities

(1) The appropriate audit authority on receiving notice under section 522 or 523 of an auditor's ceasing to hold office—
(a) must inform the accounting authorities, and
(b) may if it thinks fit forward to those authorities a copy of the statement or statements accompanying the notice.

(2) The accounting authorities are—
(a) the Secretary of State, and
(b) any person authorised by the Secretary of State for the purposes of section 456 (revision of defective accounts: persons authorised to apply to court).

(3) If either of the accounting authorities is also the appropriate audit authority it is only necessary to comply with this section as regards any other accounting authority.

(4) If the court has made an order under section 520(4) directing that copies of the statement need not be sent out by the company, sections 460 and 461 (restriction on further disclosure) apply in relation to the copies sent to the accounting authorities as they apply to information obtained under section 459 (power to require documents etc).

[S524]

NOTES

Commencement: to be appointed.

525 Meaning of "appropriate audit authority" and "major audit"

(1) In sections 522, 523 and 524 "appropriate audit authority" means—

(a) in the case of a major audit—

(i) the Secretary of State, or

(ii) if the Secretary of State has delegated functions under section 1252 to a body whose functions include receiving the notice in question, that body;

(b) in the case of an audit that is not a major audit, the relevant supervisory body.

"Supervisory body" has the same meaning as in Part 42 (statutory auditors) (see section 1217).

(2) In sections 522 and this section "major audit" means a statutory audit conducted in respect of—

(a) a company any of whose securities have been admitted to the official list (within the meaning of Part 6 of the Financial Services and Markets Act 2000 (c 8)), or

(b) any other person in whose financial condition there is a major public interest.

(3) In determining whether an audit is a major audit within subsection (2)(b), regard shall be had to any guidance issued by any of the authorities mentioned in subsection (1).

[S525]

NOTES

Commencement: to be appointed.

Supplementary

526 Effect of casual vacancies

If an auditor ceases to hold office for any reason, any surviving or continuing auditor or auditors may continue to act.

[S526]

NOTES

Commencement: to be appointed.

CHAPTER 5
QUOTED COMPANIES: RIGHT OF MEMBERS TO RAISE AUDIT CONCERNS AT ACCOUNTS MEETING

527 Members' power to require website publication of audit concerns

(1) The members of a quoted company may require the company to publish on a website a statement setting out any matter relating to—

(a) the audit of the company's accounts (including the auditor's report and the conduct of the audit) that are to be laid before the next accounts meeting, or

(b) any circumstances connected with an auditor of the company ceasing to hold office since the previous accounts meeting,

that the members propose to raise at the next accounts meeting of the company.

(2) A company is required to do so once it has received requests to that effect from—

(a) members representing at least 5% of the total voting rights of all the members who have a relevant right to vote (excluding any voting rights attached to any shares in the company held as treasury shares), or

(b) at least 100 members who have a relevant right to vote and hold shares in the company on which there has been paid up an average sum, per member, of at least £100.

See also section 153 (exercise of rights where shares held on behalf of others).

(3) In subsection (2) a "relevant right to vote" means a right to vote at the accounts meeting.

(4) A request—

(a) may be sent to the company in hard copy or electronic form,

(b) must identify the statement to which it relates,

(c) must be authenticated by the person or persons making it, and

(d) must be received by the company at least one week before the meeting to which it relates.

(5) A quoted company is not required to place on a website a statement under this section if, on an application by the company or another person who claims to be aggrieved, the court is satisfied that the rights conferred by this section are being abused.

(6) The court may order the members requesting website publication to pay the whole or part of the company's costs (in Scotland, expenses) on such an application, even if they are not parties to the application.

[S527]

NOTES

Commencement: to be appointed.

528 Requirements as to website availability

(1) The following provisions apply for the purposes of section 527 (website publication of members' statement of audit concerns).

(2) The information must be made available on a website that—

(a) is maintained by or on behalf of the company, and

(b) identifies the company in question.

(3) Access to the information on the website, and the ability to obtain a hard copy of the information from the website, must not be conditional on the payment of a fee or otherwise restricted.

(4) The statement—

(a) must be made available within three working days of the company being required to publish it on a website, and

(b) must be kept available until after the meeting to which it relates.

(5) A failure to make information available on a website throughout the period specified in subsection (4)(b) is disregarded if—

(a) the information is made available on the website for part of that period, and

(b) the failure is wholly attributable to circumstances that it would not be reasonable to have expected the company to prevent or avoid.

[S528]

NOTES

Commencement: to be appointed.

529 Website publication: company's supplementary duties

(1) A quoted company must in the notice it gives of the accounts meeting draw attention to—

(a) the possibility of a statement being placed on a website in pursuance of members' requests under section 527, and

(b) the effect of the following provisions of this section.

(2) A company may not require the members requesting website publication to pay its expenses in complying with that section or section 528 (requirements in connection with website publication).

(3) Where a company is required to place a statement on a website under section 527 it must forward the statement to the company's auditor not later than the time when it makes the statement available on the website.

(4) The business which may be dealt with at the accounts meeting includes any statement that the company has been required under section 527 to publish on a website.

[S529]

NOTES

Commencement: to be appointed.

530 Website publication: offences

(1) In the event of default in complying with
- (a) section 528 (requirements as to website publication), or
- (b) section 529 (companies' supplementary duties in relation to request for website publication),

an offence is committed by every officer of the company who is in default.

(2) A person guilty of an offence under this section is liable—
- (a) on conviction on indictment, to a fine;
- (b) on summary conviction, to a fine not exceeding the statutory maximum.

[S530]

NOTES

Commencement: to be appointed.

531 Meaning of "quoted company"

(1) For the purposes of this Chapter a company is a quoted company if it is a quoted company in accordance with section 385 (quoted and unquoted companies for the purposes of Part 15) in relation to the financial year to which the accounts to be laid at the next accounts meeting relate.

(2) The provisions of subsections (4) to (6) of that section (power to amend definition by regulations) apply in relation to the provisions of this Chapter as in relation to the provisions of that Part.

[S531]

NOTES

Commencement: to be appointed.

CHAPTER 6
AUDITORS' LIABILITY

Voidness of provisions protecting auditors from liability

532 Voidness of provisions protecting auditors from liability

(1) This section applies to any provision—
- (a) for exempting an auditor of a company (to any extent) from any liability that would otherwise attach to him in connection with any negligence, default, breach of duty or breach of trust in relation to the company occurring in the course of the audit of accounts, or
- (b) by which a company directly or indirectly provides an indemnity (to any extent) for an auditor of the company, or of an associated company, against any liability attaching to him in connection with any negligence, default, breach of duty or breach of trust in relation to the company of which he is auditor occurring in the course of the audit of accounts.

(2) Any such provision is void, except as permitted by—
- (a) section 533 (indemnity for costs of successfully defending proceedings), or
- (b) sections 534 to 536 (liability limitation agreements).

(3) This section applies to any provision, whether contained in a company's articles or in any contract with the company or otherwise.

(4) For the purposes of this section companies are associated if one is a subsidiary of the other or both are subsidiaries of the same body corporate.

[S532]

NOTES

Commencement: to be appointed.

Indemnity for costs of defending proceedings

533 Indemnity for costs of successfully defending proceedings

Section 532 (general voidness of provisions protecting auditors from liability) does not prevent a company from indemnifying an auditor against any liability incurred by him—

(a) in defending proceedings (whether civil or criminal) in which judgment is given in his favour or he is acquitted, or

(b) in connection with an application under section 1157 (power of court to grant relief in case of honest and reasonable conduct) in which relief is granted to him by the court.

[S533]

NOTES

Commencement: to be appointed.

Liability limitation agreements

534 Liability limitation agreements

(1) A "liability limitation agreement" is an agreement that purports to limit the amount of a liability owed to a company by its auditor in respect of any negligence, default, breach of duty or breach of trust, occurring in the course of the audit of accounts, of which the auditor may be guilty in relation to the company.

(2) Section 532 (general voidness of provisions protecting auditors from liability) does not affect the validity of a liability limitation agreement that—

(a) complies with section 535 (terms of liability limitation agreement) and of any regulations under that section, and

(b) is authorised by the members of the company (see section 536).

(3) Such an agreement—

(a) is effective to the extent provided by section 537, and

(b) is not subject—

(i) in England and Wales or Northern Ireland, to section 2(2) or 3(2)(a) of the Unfair Contract Terms Act 1977 (c 50);

(ii) in Scotland, to section 16(1)(b) or 17(1)(a) of that Act.

[S534]

NOTES

Commencement: to be appointed.

535 Terms of liability limitation agreement

(1) A liability limitation agreement—

(a) must not apply in respect of acts or omissions occurring in the course of the audit of accounts for more than one financial year, and

(b) must specify the financial year in relation to which it applies.

(2) The Secretary of State may by regulations—

(a) require liability limitation agreements to contain specified provisions or provisions of a specified description;

(b) prohibit liability limitation agreements from containing specified provisions or provisions of a specified description.

"Specified" here means specified in the regulations.

(3) Without prejudice to the generality of the power conferred by subsection (2), that power may be exercised with a view to preventing adverse effects on competition.

(4) Subject to the preceding provisions of this section, it is immaterial how a liability limitation agreement is framed.

In particular, the limit on the amount of the auditor's liability need not be a sum of money, or a formula, specified in the agreement.

(5) Regulations under this section are subject to negative resolution procedure.

[S535]

NOTES

Commencement: 20 January 2007 (for the purpose of enabling the exercise of powers to make Orders or Regulations by statutory instrument); to be appointed (otherwise).

536 Authorisation of agreement by members of the company

(1) A liability limitation agreement is authorised by the members of the company if it has been authorised under this section and that authorisation has not been withdrawn.

(2) A liability limitation agreement between a private company and its auditor may be authorised—

(a) by the company passing a resolution, before it enters into the agreement, waiving the need for approval,

(b) by the company passing a resolution, before it enters into the agreement, approving the agreement's principal terms, or

(c) by the company passing a resolution, after it enters into the agreement, approving the agreement.

(3) A liability limitation agreement between a public company and its auditor may be authorised—

(a) by the company passing a resolution in general meeting, before it enters into the agreement, approving the agreement's principal terms, or

(b) by the company passing a resolution in general meeting, after it enters into the agreement, approving the agreement.

(4) The "principal terms" of an agreement are terms specifying, or relevant to the determination of—

(a) the kind (or kinds) of acts or omissions covered,

(b) the financial year to which the agreement relates, or

(c) the limit to which the auditor's liability is subject.

(5) Authorisation under this section may be withdrawn by the company passing an ordinary resolution to that effect—

(a) at any time before the company enters into the agreement, or

(b) if the company has already entered into the agreement, before the beginning of the financial year to which the agreement relates.

Paragraph (b) has effect notwithstanding anything in the agreement.

[S536]

NOTES

Commencement: to be appointed.

537 Effect of liability limitation agreement

(1) A liability limitation agreement is not effective to limit the auditor's liability to less than such amount as is fair and reasonable in all the circumstances of the case having regard (in particular) to—

(a) the auditor's responsibilities under this Part,

(b) the nature and purpose of the auditor's contractual obligations to the company, and

(c) the professional standards expected of him.

(2) A liability limitation agreement that purports to limit the auditor's liability to less than the amount mentioned in subsection (1) shall have effect as if it limited his liability to that amount.

(3) In determining what is fair and reasonable in all the circumstances of the case no account is to be taken of—

(a) matters arising after the loss or damage in question has been incurred, or

(b) matters (whenever arising) affecting the possibility of recovering compensation from other persons liable in respect of the same loss or damage.

[S537]

NOTES

Commencement: to be appointed.

538 Disclosure of agreement by company

(1) A company which has entered into a liability limitation agreement must make such disclosure in connection with the agreement as the Secretary of State may require by regulations.

(2) The regulations may provide, in particular, that any disclosure required by the regulations shall be made—

(a) in a note to the company's annual accounts (in the case of its individual accounts) or in such manner as is specified in the regulations (in the case of group accounts), or

(b) in the directors' report.

(3) Regulations under this section are subject to negative resolution procedure.

[S538]

NOTES

Commencement: 20 January 2007 (for the purpose of enabling the exercise of powers to make Orders or Regulations by statutory instrument); to be appointed (otherwise).

CHAPTER 7
SUPPLEMENTARY PROVISIONS

539 Minor definitions

In this Part—

"e-money issuer" means a person who has permission under Part 4 of the Financial Services and Markets Act 2000 (c 8) to carry on the activity of issuing electronic money within the meaning of article 9B of the Financial Services and Markets Act 2000 (Regulated Activities) Order 2001 (SI 2001/544);

"ISD investment firm" has the meaning given by the Glossary forming part of the Handbook made by the Financial Services Authority under the Financial Services and Markets Act 2000;

"qualified", in relation to an auditor's report (or a statement contained in an auditor's report), means that the report or statement does not state the auditor's unqualified opinion that the accounts have been properly prepared in accordance with this Act or, in the case of an undertaking not required to prepare accounts in accordance with this Act, under any corresponding legislation under which it is required to prepare accounts;

"turnover", in relation to a company, means the amounts derived from the provision of goods and services falling within the company's ordinary activities, after deduction of—

(a) trade discounts,

(b) value added tax, and

(c) any other taxes based on the amounts so derived;

"UCITS management company" has the meaning given by the Glossary forming part of the Handbook made by the Financial Services Authority under the Financial Services and Markets Act 2000.

[S539]

NOTES

Commencement: to be appointed.

PART 17
A COMPANY'S SHARE CAPITAL

CHAPTER 1
SHARES AND SHARE CAPITAL OF A COMPANY

Shares

540 Shares

(1) In the Companies Acts "share", in relation to a company, means share in the company's share capital.

(2) A company's shares may no longer be converted into stock.

(3) Stock created before the commencement of this Part may be reconverted into shares in accordance with section 620.

(4) In the Companies Acts—

(a) references to shares include stock except where a distinction between share and stock is express or implied, and

(b) references to a number of shares include an amount of stock where the context admits of the reference to shares being read as including stock.

[S540]

NOTES

Commencement: 1 October 2007 (sub-ss (1), (4) certain purposes); to be appointed (otherwise) (see the note below).

Note: the draft Companies Act 2006 (Commencement No 3, Consequential Amendments, Transitional Provisions and Savings) Order 2007, art 2(3) provides that sub-ss (1), (4) shall come into force on 1 October 2007 so far as is necessary for the purposes of the provisions of this Act brought into force on that date by art 2(1), (2) of that Order (see **[A12]**).

541 Nature of shares

The shares or other interest of a member in a company are personal property (or, in Scotland, moveable property) and are not in the nature of real estate (or heritage).

[S541]

NOTES

Commencement: to be appointed.

542 Nominal value of shares

(1) Shares in a limited company having a share capital must each have a fixed nominal value.

(2) An allotment of a share that does not have a fixed nominal value is void.

(3) Shares in a limited company having a share capital may be denominated in any currency, and different classes of shares may be denominated in different currencies.

But see section 765 (initial authorised minimum share capital requirement for public company to be met by reference to share capital denominated in sterling or euros).

(4) If a company purports to allot shares in contravention of this section, an offence is committed by every officer of the company who is in default.

(5) A person guilty of an offence under this section is liable—

(a) on conviction on indictment, to a fine;

(b) on summary conviction, to a fine not exceeding the statutory maximum.

[S542]

NOTES

Commencement: to be appointed.

543 Numbering of shares

(1) Each share in a company having a share capital must be distinguished by its appropriate number, except in the following circumstances.

(2) If at any time—

(a) all the issued shares in a company are fully paid up and rank *pari passu* for all purposes, or

(b) all the issued shares of a particular class in a company are fully paid up and rank *pari passu* for all purposes,

none of those shares need thereafter have a distinguishing number so long as it remains fully paid up and ranks *pari passu* for all purposes with all shares of the same class for the time being issued and fully paid up.

[S543]

NOTES

Commencement: to be appointed.

544 Transferability of shares

(1) The shares or other interest of any member in a company are transferable in accordance with the company's articles.

(2) This is subject to—

(a) the Stock Transfer Act 1963 (c 18) or the Stock Transfer Act (Northern Ireland) 1963 (c 24 (NI)) (which enables securities of certain descriptions to be transferred by a simplified process), and

(b) regulations under Chapter 2 of Part 21 of this Act (which enable title to securities to be evidenced and transferred without a written instrument).

(3) See Part 21 of this Act generally as regards share transfers.

[S544]

NOTES

Commencement: to be appointed.

545 Companies having a share capital

References in the Companies Acts to a company having a share capital are to a company that has power under its constitution to issue shares.

[S545]

NOTES

Commencement: 1 October 2007 (certain purposes); to be appointed (otherwise) (see the note below).

Note: the draft Companies Act 2006 (Commencement No 3, Consequential Amendments, Transitional Provisions and Savings) Order 2007, art 2(3) provides that this section shall come into force on 1 October 2007 so far as is necessary for the purposes of the provisions of this Act brought into force on that date by art 2(1), (2) of that Order (see **[A12]**).

546 Issued and allotted share capital

(1) References in the Companies Acts—

(a) to "issued share capital" are to shares of a company that have been issued;

(b) to "allotted share capital" are to shares of a company that have been allotted.

(2) References in the Companies Acts to issued or allotted shares, or to issued or allotted share capital, include shares taken on the formation of the company by the subscribers to the company's memorandum.

[S546]

NOTES

Commencement: 6 April 2007 (certain purposes); 1 October 2007 (certain purposes); 1 November 2007 (certain purposes); to be appointed (otherwise) (see the notes below).

Note: the Companies Act 2006 (Commencement No 2, Consequential Amendments, Transitional Provisions and Savings) Order 2007, SI 2007/1093, art 2(2) provides that this section shall come into force on 6 April 2007 so far as is necessary for the purposes of the provisions of this Act brought into force on that date by art 2(1) of that Order (see **[7615]**).

Note: the draft Companies Act 2006 (Commencement No 3, Consequential Amendments, Transitional Provisions and Savings) Order 2007, arts 2(3) and 3(2) provide that this section shall come into force on 1 October 2007 and 1 November 2007 so far as is necessary for the purposes of the provisions of this Act brought into force on those dates by art 2(1), (2) and art 3(1) of that Order respectively (see **[A12]**).

Application to unregistered companies: see the Companies Acts (Unregistered Companies) Regulations 2007, SI 2007/318 at **[7606]**.

Share capital

547 Called-up share capital

In the Companies Acts—

"called-up share capital", in relation to a company, means so much of its share capital as equals the aggregate amount of the calls made on its shares (whether or not those calls have been paid), together with—

(a) any share capital paid up without being called, and

(b) any share capital to be paid on a specified future date under the articles, the terms of allotment of the relevant shares or any other arrangements for payment of those shares; and

"uncalled share capital" is to be construed accordingly.

[S547]

NOTES

Commencement: to be appointed.

548 Equity share capital

In the Companies Acts "equity share capital", in relation to a company, means its issued share capital excluding any part of that capital that, neither as respects dividends nor as respects capital, carries any right to participate beyond a specified amount in a distribution.

[S548]

NOTES

Commencement: 1 October 2007 (certain purposes); to be appointed (otherwise) (see the note below).

Note: the draft Companies Act 2006 (Commencement No 3, Consequential Amendments, Transitional Provisions and Savings) Order 2007, art 2(3) provides that this section shall come into force on 1 October 2007 so far as is necessary for the purposes of the provisions of this Act brought into force on that date by art 2(1), (2) of that Order (see **[A12]**).

CHAPTER 2
ALLOTMENT OF SHARES: GENERAL PROVISIONS

Power of directors to allot shares

549 Exercise by directors of power to allot shares etc

(1) The directors of a company must not exercise any power of the company—

(a) to allot shares in the company, or

(b) to grant rights to subscribe for, or to convert any security into, shares in the company,

except in accordance with section 550 (private company with single class of shares) or section 551 (authorisation by company).

(2) Subsection (1) does not apply—

(a) to the allotment of shares in pursuance of an employees' share scheme, or

(b) to the grant of a right to subscribe for, or to convert any security into, shares so allotted.

(3) If this section applies in relation to the grant of a right to subscribe for, or to convert any security into, shares, it does not apply in relation to the allotment of shares pursuant to that right.

(4) A director who knowingly contravenes, or permits or authorises a contravention of, this section commits an offence.

(5) A person guilty of an offence under this section is liable—

(a) on conviction on indictment, to a fine;

(b) on summary conviction, to a fine not exceeding the statutory maximum.

(6) Nothing in this section affects the validity of an allotment or other transaction.

[S549]

NOTES

Commencement: to be appointed.

550 Power of directors to allot shares etc: private company with only one class of shares

Where a private company has only one class of shares, the directors may exercise any power of the company—

(a) to allot shares of that class, or

(b) to grant rights to subscribe for or to convert any security into such shares,

except to the extent that they are prohibited from doing so by the company's articles.

[S550]

NOTES

Commencement: to be appointed.

551 Power of directors to allot shares etc: authorisation by company

(1) The directors of a company may exercise a power of the company—

(a) to allot shares in the company, or

(b) to grant rights to subscribe for or to convert any security into shares in the company,

if they are authorised to do so by the company's articles or by resolution of the company.

(2) Authorisation may be given for a particular exercise of the power or for its exercise generally, and may be unconditional or subject to conditions.

(3) Authorisation must—

(a) state the maximum amount of shares that may be allotted under it, and

(b) specify the date on which it will expire, which must be not more than five years from—

(i) in the case of authorisation contained in the company's articles at the time of its original incorporation, the date of that incorporation;

(ii) in any other case, the date on which the resolution is passed by virtue of which the authorisation is given.

(4) Authorisation may—

(a) be renewed or further renewed by resolution of the company for a further period not exceeding five years, and

(b) be revoked or varied at any time by resolution of the company.

(5) A resolution renewing authorisation must—

(a) state (or restate) the maximum amount of shares that may be allotted under the authorisation or, as the case may be, the amount remaining to be allotted under it, and

(b) specify the date on which the renewed authorisation will expire.

(6) In relation to rights to subscribe for or to convert any security into shares in the company, references in this section to the maximum amount of shares that may be allotted under the authorisation are to the maximum amount of shares that may be allotted pursuant to the rights.

(7) The directors may allot shares, or grant rights to subscribe for or to convert any security into shares, after authorisation has expired if—

(a) the shares are allotted, or the rights are granted, in pursuance of an offer or agreement made by the company before the authorisation expired, and

(b) the authorisation allowed the company to make an offer or agreement which would or might require shares to be allotted, or rights to be granted, after the authorisation had expired.

(8) A resolution of a company to give, vary, revoke or renew authorisation under this section may be an ordinary resolution, even though it amends the company's articles.

(9) Chapter 3 of Part 3 (resolutions affecting a company's constitution) applies to a resolution under this section.

[S551]

NOTES

Commencement: to be appointed.

Prohibition of commissions, discounts and allowances

552 General prohibition of commissions, discounts and allowances

(1) Except as permitted by section 553 (permitted commission), a company must not apply any of its shares or capital money, either directly or indirectly, in payment of any commission, discount or allowance to any person in consideration of his—

(a) subscribing or agreeing to subscribe (whether absolutely or conditionally) for shares in the company, or

(b) procuring or agreeing to procure subscriptions (whether absolute or conditional) for shares in the company.

(2) It is immaterial how the shares or money are so applied, whether by being added to the purchase money of property acquired by the company or to the contract price of work to be executed for the company, or being paid out of the nominal purchase money or contract price, or otherwise.

(3) Nothing in this section affects the payment of such brokerage as has previously been lawful.

[S552]

NOTES

Commencement: to be appointed.

553 Permitted commission

(1) A company may, if the following conditions are satisfied, pay a commission to a person in consideration of his subscribing or agreeing to subscribe (whether absolutely or conditionally) for shares in the company, or procuring or agreeing to procure subscriptions (whether absolute or conditional) for shares in the company.

(2) The conditions are that—

(a) the payment of the commission is authorised by the company's articles; and

(b) the commission paid or agreed to be paid does not exceed—

(i) 10% of the price at which the shares are issued, or

(ii) the amount or rate authorised by the articles,

whichever is the less.

(3) A vendor to, or promoter of, or other person who receives payment in money or shares from, a company may apply any part of the money or shares so received in payment of any commission the payment of which directly by the company would be permitted by this section.

[S553]

NOTES

Commencement: to be appointed.

Registration of allotment

554 Registration of allotment

(1) A company must register an allotment of shares as soon as practicable and in any event within two months after the date of the allotment.

(2) This does not apply if the company has issued a share warrant in respect of the shares (see section 779).

(3) If a company fails to comply with this section, an offence is committed by—
- (a) the company, and
- (b) every officer of the company who is in default.

(4) A person guilty of an offence under this section is liable on summary conviction to a fine not exceeding level 3 on the standard scale and, for continued contravention, a daily default fine not exceeding one-tenth of level 3 on the standard scale.

(5) For the company's duties as to the issue of share certificates etc, see Part 21 (certification and transfer of securities).

[S554]

NOTES

Commencement: to be appointed.

Return of allotment

555 Return of allotment by limited company

(1) This section applies to a company limited by shares and to a company limited by guarantee and having a share capital.

(2) The company must, within one month of making an allotment of shares, deliver to the registrar for registration a return of the allotment.

(3) The return must—
- (a) contain the prescribed information, and
- (b) be accompanied by a statement of capital.

(4) The statement of capital must state with respect to the company's share capital at the date to which the return is made up—
- (a) the total number of shares of the company,
- (b) the aggregate nominal value of those shares,
- (c) for each class of shares—
  - (i) prescribed particulars of the rights attached to the shares,
  - (ii) the total number of shares of that class, and
  - (iii) the aggregate nominal value of shares of that class, and
- (d) the amount paid up and the amount (if any) unpaid on each share (whether on account of the nominal value of the share or by way of premium).

[S555]

NOTES

Commencement: 20 January 2007 (for the purpose of enabling the exercise of powers to make Orders or Regulations by statutory instrument); to be appointed (otherwise).

556 Return of allotment by unlimited company allotting new class of shares

(1) This section applies to an unlimited company that allots shares of a class with rights that are not in all respects uniform with shares previously allotted.

(2) The company must, within one month of making such an allotment, deliver to the registrar for registration a return of the allotment.

(3) The return must contain the prescribed particulars of the rights attached to the shares.

(4) For the purposes of this section shares are not to be treated as different from shares previously allotted by reason only that the former do not carry the same rights to dividends as the latter during the twelve months immediately following the former's allotment.

[S556]

NOTES

Commencement: 20 January 2007 (for the purpose of enabling the exercise of powers to make Orders or Regulations by statutory instrument); to be appointed (otherwise).

557 Offence of failure to make return

(1) If a company makes default in complying with—

section 555 (return of allotment of shares by limited company), or

section 556 (return of allotment of new class of shares by unlimited company),

an offence is committed by every officer of the company who is in default.

(2) A person guilty of an offence under this section is liable—

(a) on conviction on indictment, to a fine;

(b) on summary conviction, to a fine not exceeding the statutory maximum and, for continued contravention, a daily default fine not exceeding one-tenth of the statutory maximum.

(3) In the case of default in delivering to the registrar within one month after the allotment the return required by section 555 or 556—

(a) any person liable for the default may apply to the court for relief, and

(b) the court, if satisfied—

(i) that the omission to deliver the document was accidental or due to inadvertence, or

(ii) that it is just and equitable to grant relief,

may make an order extending the time for delivery of the document for such period as the court thinks proper.

[S557]

NOTES

Commencement: to be appointed.

Supplementary provisions

558 When shares are allotted

For the purposes of the Companies Acts shares in a company are taken to be allotted when a person acquires the unconditional right to be included in the company's register of members in respect of the shares.

[S558]

NOTES

Commencement: 6 April 2007 (certain purposes); to be appointed (otherwise) (see the note below).

Note: the Companies Act 2006 (Commencement No 2, Consequential Amendments, Transitional Provisions and Savings) Order 2007, SI 2007/1093, art 2(2) provides that this section shall come into force on 6 April 2007 so far as is necessary for the purposes of the provisions of this Act brought into force on that date by art 2(1) of that Order (see **[7615]**).

Application to unregistered companies: see the Companies Acts (Unregistered Companies) Regulations 2007, SI 2007/318 at **[7606]**.

559 Provisions about allotment not applicable to shares taken on formation

The provisions of this Chapter have no application in relation to the taking of shares by the subscribers to the memorandum on the formation of the company.

[S559]

NOTES

Commencement: to be appointed.

CHAPTER 3
ALLOTMENT OF EQUITY SECURITIES: EXISTING SHAREHOLDERS' RIGHT OF PRE-EMPTION

Introductory

560 Meaning of "equity securities" and related expressions

(1) In this Chapter—

"equity securities" means—

(a) ordinary shares in the company, or

(b) rights to subscribe for, or to convert securities into, ordinary shares in the company;

"ordinary shares" means shares other than shares that as respects dividends and capital carry a right to participate only up to a specified amount in a distribution.

(2) References in this Chapter to the allotment of equity securities include—

(a) the grant of a right to subscribe for, or to convert any securities into, ordinary shares in the company, and

(b) the sale of ordinary shares in the company that immediately before the sale are held by the company as treasury shares.

[S560]

NOTES

Commencement: to be appointed.

Existing shareholders' right of pre-emption

561 Existing shareholders' right of pre-emption

(1) A company must not allot equity securities to a person on any terms unless—

(a) it has made an offer to each person who holds ordinary shares in the company to allot to him on the same or more favourable terms a proportion of those securities that is as nearly as practicable equal to the proportion in nominal value held by him of the ordinary share capital of the company, and

(b) the period during which any such offer may be accepted has expired or the company has received notice of the acceptance or refusal of every offer so made.

(2) Securities that a company has offered to allot to a holder of ordinary shares may be allotted to him, or anyone in whose favour he has renounced his right to their allotment, without contravening subsection (1)(b).

(3) If subsection (1) applies in relation to the grant of such a right, it does not apply in relation to the allotment of shares in pursuance of that right.

(4) Shares held by the company as treasury shares are disregarded for the purposes of this section, so that—

(a) the company is not treated as a person who holds ordinary shares, and

(b) the shares are not treated as forming part of the ordinary share capital of the company.

(5) This section is subject to—

(a) sections 564 to 566 (exceptions to pre-emption right),

(b) sections 567 and 568 (exclusion of rights of pre-emption),

(c) sections 569 to 573 (disapplication of pre-emption rights), and

(d) section 576 (saving for certain older pre-emption procedures).

[S561]

NOTES

Commencement: to be appointed.

562 Communication of pre-emption offers to shareholders

(1) This section has effect as to the manner in which offers required by section 561 are to be made to holders of a company's shares.

(2) The offer may be made in hard copy or electronic form.

(3) If the holder—

(a) has no registered address in an EEA State and has not given to the company an address in an EEA State for the service of notices on him, or

(b) is the holder of a share warrant,

the offer may be made by causing it, or a notice specifying where a copy of it can be obtained or inspected, to be published in the Gazette.

(4) The offer must state a period during which it may be accepted and the offer shall not be withdrawn before the end of that period.

(5) The period must be a period of at least 21 days beginning—

(a) in the case of an offer made in hard copy form, with the date on which the offer is sent or supplied;

(b) in the case of an offer made in electronic form, with the date on which the offer is sent;

(c) in the case of an offer made by publication in the Gazette, with the date of publication.

(6) The Secretary of State may by regulations made by statutory instrument—

(a) reduce the period specified in subsection (5) (but not to less than 14 days), or

(b) increase that period.

(7) A statutory instrument containing regulations made under subsection (6) is subject to affirmative resolution procedure.

[S562]

NOTES

Commencement: 20 January 2007 (for the purpose of enabling the exercise of powers to make Orders or Regulations by statutory instrument); to be appointed (otherwise).

563 Liability of company and officers in case of contravention

(1) This section applies where there is a contravention of—

section 561 (existing shareholders' right of pre-emption), or

section 562 (communication of pre-emption offers to shareholders).

(2) The company and every officer of it who knowingly authorised or permitted the contravention are jointly and severally liable to compensate any person to whom an offer should have been made in accordance with those provisions for any loss, damage, costs or expenses which the person has sustained or incurred by reason of the contravention.

(3) No proceedings to recover any such loss, damage, costs or expenses shall be commenced after the expiration of two years—

(a) from the delivery to the registrar of companies of the return of allotment, or

(b) where equity securities other than shares are granted, from the date of the grant.

[S563]

NOTES

Commencement: to be appointed.

Exceptions to right of pre-emption

564 Exception to pre-emption right: bonus shares

Section 561(1) (existing shareholders' right of pre-emption) does not apply in relation to the allotment of bonus shares.

[S564]

NOTES

Commencement: to be appointed.

565 Exception to pre-emption right: issue for non-cash consideration

Section 561(1) (existing shareholders' right of pre-emption) does not apply to a particular allotment of equity securities if these are, or are to be, wholly or partly paid up otherwise than in cash.

[S565]

NOTES

Commencement: to be appointed.

566 Exception to pre-emption right: securities held under employees' share scheme

Section 561 (existing shareholders' right of pre-emption) does not apply to the allotment of securities that would, apart from any renunciation or assignment of the right to their allotment, be held under an employees' share scheme.

[S566]

NOTES

Commencement: to be appointed.

Exclusion of right of pre-emption

567 Exclusion of requirements by private companies

(1) All or any of the requirements of—

(a) section 561 (existing shareholders' right of pre-emption), or

(b) section 562 (communication of pre-emption offers to shareholders)

may be excluded by provision contained in the articles of a private company.

(2) They may be excluded—

(a) generally in relation to the allotment by the company of equity securities, or

(b) in relation to allotments of a particular description.

(3) Any requirement or authorisation contained in the articles of a private company that is inconsistent with either of those sections is treated for the purposes of this section as a provision excluding that section.

(4) A provision to which section 568 applies (exclusion of pre-emption right: corresponding right conferred by articles) is not to be treated as inconsistent with section 561.

[S567]

NOTES

Commencement: to be appointed.

568 Exclusion of pre-emption right: articles conferring corresponding right

(1) The provisions of this section apply where, in a case in which section 561 (existing shareholders' right of pre-emption) would otherwise apply—

(a) a company's articles contain provision ("pre-emption provision") prohibiting the company from allotting ordinary shares of a particular class unless it has complied with the condition that it makes such an offer as is described in section 561(1) to each person who holds ordinary shares of that class, and

(b) in accordance with that provision—

(i) the company makes an offer to allot shares to such a holder, and

(ii) he or anyone in whose favour he has renounced his right to their allotment accepts the offer.

(2) In that case, section 561 does not apply to the allotment of those shares and the company may allot them accordingly.

(3) The provisions of section 562 (communication of pre-emption offers to shareholders) apply in relation to offers made in pursuance of the pre-emption provision of the company's articles.

This is subject to section 567 (exclusion of requirements by private companies).

(4) If there is a contravention of the pre-emption provision of the company's articles, the company, and every officer of it who knowingly authorised or permitted the contravention, are jointly and severally liable to compensate any person to whom an offer should have been made under the provision for any loss, damage, costs or expenses which the person has sustained or incurred by reason of the contravention.

(5) No proceedings to recover any such loss, damage, costs or expenses may be commenced after the expiration of two years—

(a) from the delivery to the registrar of companies of the return of allotment, or

(b) where equity securities other than shares are granted, from the date of the grant.

[S568]

NOTES

Commencement: to be appointed.

Disapplication of pre-emption rights

569 Disapplication of pre-emption rights: private company with only one class of shares

(1) The directors of a private company that has only one class of shares may be given power by the articles, or by a special resolution of the company, to allot equity securities of that class as if section 561 (existing shareholders' right of pre-emption)—

(a) did not apply to the allotment, or

(b) applied to the allotment with such modifications as the directors may determine.

(2) Where the directors make an allotment under this section, the provisions of this Chapter have effect accordingly.

[S569]

NOTES

Commencement: to be appointed.

570 Disapplication of pre-emption rights: directors acting under general authorisation

(1) Where the directors of a company are generally authorised for the purposes of section 551 (power of directors to allot shares etc: authorisation by company), they may be given power by the articles, or by a special resolution of the company, to allot equity securities pursuant to that authorisation as if section 561 (existing shareholders' right of pre-emption)—

(a) did not apply to the allotment, or

(b) applied to the allotment with such modifications as the directors may determine.

(2) Where the directors make an allotment under this section, the provisions of this Chapter have effect accordingly.

(3) The power conferred by this section ceases to have effect when the authorisation to which it relates—

(a) is revoked, or

(b) would (if not renewed) expire.

But if the authorisation is renewed the power may also be renewed, for a period not longer than that for which the authorisation is renewed, by a special resolution of the company.

(4) Notwithstanding that the power conferred by this section has expired, the directors may allot equity securities in pursuance of an offer or agreement previously made by the company if the power enabled the company to make an offer or agreement that would or might require equity securities to be allotted after it expired.

[S570]

NOTES

Commencement: to be appointed.

571 Disapplication of pre-emption rights by special resolution

(1) Where the directors of a company are authorised for the purposes of section 551 (power of directors to allot shares etc: authorisation by company), whether generally or otherwise, the company may by special resolution resolve that section 561 (existing shareholders' right of pre-emption)—

(a) does not apply to a specified allotment of equity securities to be made pursuant to that authorisation, or

(b) applies to such an allotment with such modifications as may be specified in the resolution.

(2) Where such a resolution is passed the provisions of this Chapter have effect accordingly.

(3) A special resolution under this section ceases to have effect when the authorisation to which it relates—

(a) is revoked, or

(b) would (if not renewed) expire.

But if the authorisation is renewed the resolution may also be renewed, for a period not longer than that for which the authorisation is renewed, by a special resolution of the company.

(4) Notwithstanding that any such resolution has expired, the directors may allot equity securities in pursuance of an offer or agreement previously made by the company if the resolution enabled the company to make an offer or agreement that would or might require equity securities to be allotted after it expired.

(5) A special resolution under this section, or a special resolution to renew such a resolution, must not be proposed unless—

(a) it is recommended by the directors, and

(b) the directors have complied with the following provisions.

(6) Before such a resolution is proposed, the directors must make a written statement setting out—

(a) their reasons for making the recommendation,

(b) the amount to be paid to the company in respect of the equity securities to be allotted, and

(c) the directors' justification of that amount.

(7) The directors' statement must—

(a) if the resolution is proposed as a written resolution, be sent or submitted to every eligible member at or before the time at which the proposed resolution is sent or submitted to him;

(b) if the resolution is proposed at a general meeting, be circulated to the members entitled to notice of the meeting with that notice.

[S571]

NOTES

Commencement: to be appointed.

572 Liability for false statement in directors' statement

(1) This section applies in relation to a directors' statement under section 571 (special resolution disapplying pre-emption rights) that is sent, submitted or circulated under subsection (7) of that section.

(2) A person who knowingly or recklessly authorises or permits the inclusion of any matter that is misleading, false or deceptive in a material particular in such a statement commits an offence.

(3) A person guilty of an offence under this section is liable—

(a) on conviction on indictment, to imprisonment for a term not exceeding two years or a fine (or both);

(b) on summary conviction—

(i) in England and Wales, to imprisonment for a term not exceeding twelve months or to a fine not exceeding the statutory maximum (or both);

(ii) in Scotland or Northern Ireland, to imprisonment for a term not exceeding six months, or to a fine not exceeding the statutory maximum (or both).

[S572]

NOTES

Commencement: to be appointed.

573 Disapplication of pre-emption rights: sale of treasury shares

(1) This section applies in relation to a sale of shares that is an allotment of equity securities by virtue of section 560(2)(b) (sale of shares held by company as treasury shares).

(2) The directors of a company may be given power by the articles, or by a special resolution of the company, to allot equity securities as if section 561 (existing shareholders' right of pre-emption)—

(a) did not apply to the allotment, or
(b) applied to the allotment with such modifications as the directors may determine.

(3) The provisions of section 570(2) and (4) apply in that case as they apply to a case within subsection (1) of that section.

(4) The company may by special resolution resolve that section 561—

(a) shall not apply to a specified allotment of securities, or
(b) shall apply to the allotment with such modifications as may be specified in the resolution.

(5) The provisions of section 571(2) and (4) to (7) apply in that case as they apply to a case within subsection (1) of that section.

[S573]

NOTES

Commencement: to be appointed.

Supplementary

574 References to holder of shares in relation to offer

(1) In this Chapter, in relation to an offer to allot securities required by—

(a) section 561 (existing shareholders' right of pre-emption), or
(b) any provision to which section 568 applies (articles conferring corresponding right),

a reference (however expressed) to the holder of shares of any description is to whoever was the holder of shares of that description at the close of business on a date to be specified in the offer.

(2) The specified date must fall within the period of 28 days immediately before the date of the offer.

[S574]

NOTES

Commencement: to be appointed.

575 Saving for other restrictions on offer or allotment

(1) The provisions of this Chapter are without prejudice to any other enactment by virtue of which a company is prohibited (whether generally or in specified circumstances) from offering or allotting equity securities to any person.

(2) Where a company cannot by virtue of such an enactment offer or allot equity securities to a holder of ordinary shares of the company, those shares are disregarded for the purposes of section 561 (existing shareholders' right of pre-emption), so that—

(a) the person is not treated as a person who holds ordinary shares, and
(b) the shares are not treated as forming part of the ordinary share capital of the company.

[S575]

NOTES

Commencement: to be appointed.

576 Saving for certain older pre-emption requirements

(1) In the case of a public company the provisions of this Chapter do not apply to an allotment of equity securities that are subject to a pre-emption requirement in relation to which section 96(1) of the Companies Act 1985 (c 6) or Article 106(1) of the Companies (Northern Ireland) Order 1986 (SI 1986/1032 (NI 6)) applied immediately before the commencement of this Chapter.

(2) In the case of a private company a pre-emption requirement to which section 96(3) of the Companies Act 1985 or Article 106(3) of the Companies (Northern Ireland) Order 1986 applied immediately before the commencement of this Chapter shall have effect, so long as the company remains a private company, as if it were contained in the company's articles.

(3) A pre-emption requirement to which section 96(4) of the Companies Act 1985 or Article 106(4) of the Companies (Northern Ireland) Order 1986 applied immediately before the commencement of this section shall be treated for the purposes of this Chapter as if it were contained in the company's articles.

[S576]

NOTES

Commencement: to be appointed.

577 Provisions about pre-emption not applicable to shares taken on formation

The provisions of this Chapter have no application in relation to the taking of shares by the subscribers to the memorandum on the formation of the company.

[S577]

NOTES

Commencement: to be appointed.

CHAPTER 4
PUBLIC COMPANIES: ALLOTMENT WHERE ISSUE NOT FULLY SUBSCRIBED

578 Public companies: allotment where issue not fully subscribed

(1) No allotment shall be made of shares of a public company offered for subscription unless—

(a) the issue is subscribed for in full, or

(b) the offer is made on terms that the shares subscribed for may be allotted—

(i) in any event, or

(ii) if specified conditions are met (and those conditions are met).

(2) If shares are prohibited from being allotted by subsection (1) and 40 days have elapsed after the first making of the offer, all money received from applicants for shares must be repaid to them forthwith, without interest.

(3) If any of the money is not repaid within 48 days after the first making of the offer, the directors of the company are jointly and severally liable to repay it, with interest at the rate for the time being specified under section 17 of the Judgments Act 1838 (c 110) from the expiration of the 48th day.

A director is not so liable if he proves that the default in the repayment of the money was not due to any misconduct or negligence on his part.

(4) This section applies in the case of shares offered as wholly or partly payable otherwise than in cash as it applies in the case of shares offered for subscription.

(5) In that case—

(a) the references in subsection (1) to subscription shall be construed accordingly;

(b) references in subsections (2) and (3) to the repayment of money received from applicants for shares include—

(i) the return of any other consideration so received (including, if the case so requires, the release of the applicant from any undertaking), or

(ii) if it is not reasonably practicable to return the consideration, the payment of money equal to its value at the time it was so received;

(c) references to interest apply accordingly.

(6) Any condition requiring or binding an applicant for shares to waive compliance with any requirement of this section is void.

[S578]

NOTES

Commencement: to be appointed.

579 Public companies: effect of irregular allotment where issue not fully subscribed

(1) An allotment made by a public company to an applicant in contravention of section 578 (public companies: allotment where issue not fully subscribed) is voidable at the instance of the applicant within one month after the date of the allotment, and not later.

(2) It is so voidable even if the company is in the course of being wound up.

(3) A director of a public company who knowingly contravenes, or permits or authorises the contravention of, any provision of section 578 with respect to allotment is liable to compensate the company and the allottee respectively for any loss, damages, costs or expenses that the company or allottee may have sustained or incurred by the contravention.

(4) Proceedings to recover any such loss, damages, costs or expenses may not be brought more than two years after the date of the allotment.

[S579]

NOTES

Commencement: to be appointed.

CHAPTER 5
PAYMENT FOR SHARES

General rules

580 Shares not to be allotted at a discount

(1) A company's shares must not be allotted at a discount.

(2) If shares are allotted in contravention of this section, the allottee is liable to pay the company an amount equal to the amount of the discount, with interest at the appropriate rate.

[S580]

NOTES

Commencement: to be appointed.

581 Provision for different amounts to be paid on shares

A company, if so authorised by its articles, may—

(a) make arrangements on the issue of shares for a difference between the shareholders in the amounts and times of payment of calls on their shares;

(b) accept from any member the whole or part of the amount remaining unpaid on any shares held by him, although no part of that amount has been called up;

(c) pay a dividend in proportion to the amount paid up on each share where a larger amount is paid up on some shares than on others.

[S581]

NOTES

Commencement: to be appointed.

582 General rule as to means of payment

(1) Shares allotted by a company, and any premium on them, may be paid up in money or money's worth (including goodwill and know-how).

(2) This section does not prevent a company—

(a) from allotting bonus shares to its members, or

(b) from paying up, with sums available for the purpose, any amounts for the time being unpaid on any of its shares (whether on account of the nominal value of the shares or by way of premium).

(3) This section has effect subject to the following provisions of this Chapter (additional rules for public companies).

[S582]

NOTES

Commencement: to be appointed.

583 Meaning of payment in cash

(1) The following provisions have effect for the purposes of the Companies Acts.

(2) A share in a company is deemed paid up (as to its nominal value or any premium on it) in cash, or allotted for cash, if the consideration received for the allotment or payment up is a cash consideration.

(3) A "cash consideration" means—

(a) cash received by the company,

(b) a cheque received by the company in good faith that the directors have no reason for suspecting will not be paid,

(c) a release of a liability of the company for a liquidated sum,

(d) an undertaking to pay cash to the company at a future date, or

(e) payment by any other means giving rise to a present or future entitlement (of the company or a person acting on the company's behalf) to a payment, or credit equivalent to payment, in cash.

(4) The Secretary of State may by order provide that particular means of payment specified in the order are to be regarded as falling within subsection (3)(e).

(5) In relation to the allotment or payment up of shares in a company—

(a) the payment of cash to a person other than the company, or

(b) an undertaking to pay cash to a person other than the company,

counts as consideration other than cash.

This does not apply for the purposes of Chapter 3 (allotment of equity securities: existing shareholders' right of pre-emption).

(6) For the purpose of determining whether a share is or is to be allotted for cash, or paid up in cash, "cash" includes foreign currency.

(7) An order under this section is subject to negative resolution procedure.

[S583]

NOTES

Commencement: 20 January 2007 (for the purpose of enabling the exercise of powers to make Orders or Regulations by statutory instrument); to be appointed (otherwise).

Additional rules for public companies

584 Public companies: shares taken by subscribers of memorandum

Shares taken by a subscriber to the memorandum of a public company in pursuance of an undertaking of his in the memorandum, and any premium on the shares, must be paid up in cash.

[S584]

NOTES

Commencement: to be appointed.

585 Public companies: must not accept undertaking to do work or perform services

(1) A public company must not accept at any time, in payment up of its shares or any premium on them, an undertaking given by any person that he or another should do work or perform services for the company or any other person.

(2) If a public company accepts such an undertaking in payment up of its shares or any premium on them, the holder of the shares when they or the premium are treated as paid up (in whole or in part) by the undertaking is liable—

(a) to pay the company in respect of those shares an amount equal to their nominal value, together with the whole of any premium or, if the case so requires, such proportion of that amount as is treated as paid up by the undertaking; and

(b) to pay interest at the appropriate rate on the amount payable under paragraph (a).

(3) The reference in subsection (2) to the holder of shares includes a person who has an unconditional right—

(a) to be included in the company's register of members in respect of those shares, or

(b) to have an instrument of transfer of them executed in his favour.

[S585]

NOTES

Commencement: to be appointed.

586 Public companies: shares must be at least one-quarter paid up

(1) A public company must not allot a share except as paid up at least as to one-quarter of its nominal value and the whole of any premium on it.

(2) This does not apply to shares allotted in pursuance of an employees' share scheme.

(3) If a company allots a share in contravention of this section—

(a) the share is to be treated as if one-quarter of its nominal value, together with the whole of any premium on it, had been received, and

(b) the allottee is liable to pay the company the minimum amount which should have been received in respect of the share under subsection (1) (less the value of any consideration actually applied in payment up, to any extent, of the share and any premium on it), with interest at the appropriate rate.

(4) Subsection (3) does not apply to the allotment of bonus shares, unless the allottee knew or ought to have known the shares were allotted in contravention of this section.

[S586]

NOTES

Commencement: to be appointed.

587 Public companies: payment by long-term undertaking

(1) A public company must not allot shares as fully or partly paid up (as to their nominal value or any premium on them) otherwise than in cash if the consideration for the allotment is or includes an undertaking which is to be, or may be, performed more than five years after the date of the allotment.

(2) If a company allots shares in contravention of subsection (1), the allottee is liable to pay the company an amount equal to the aggregate of their nominal value and the whole of any premium (or, if the case so requires, so much of that aggregate as is treated as paid up by the undertaking), with interest at the appropriate rate.

(3) Where a contract for the allotment of shares does not contravene subsection (1), any variation of the contract that has the effect that the contract would have contravened the subsection, if the terms of the contract as varied had been its original terms, is void.

This applies also to the variation by a public company of the terms of a contract entered into before the company was re-registered as a public company.

(4) Where—

(a) a public company allots shares for a consideration which consists of or includes (in accordance with subsection (1)) an undertaking that is to be performed within five years of the allotment, and

(b) the undertaking is not performed within the period allowed by the contract for the allotment of the shares,

the allottee is liable to pay the company, at the end of the period so allowed, an amount equal to the aggregate of the nominal value of the shares and the whole of any premium (or, if the case so requires, so much of that aggregate as is treated as paid up by the undertaking), with interest at the appropriate rate.

(5) References in this section to a contract for the allotment of shares include an ancillary contract relating to payment in respect of them.

[S587]

NOTES

Commencement: to be appointed.

Supplementary provisions

588 Liability of subsequent holders of shares

(1) If a person becomes a holder of shares in respect of which—

(a) there has been a contravention of any provision of this Chapter, and

(b) by virtue of that contravention another is liable to pay any amount under the provision contravened,

that person is also liable to pay that amount (jointly and severally with any other person so liable), subject as follows.

(2) A person otherwise liable under subsection (1) is exempted from that liability if either—

(a) he is a purchaser for value and, at the time of the purchase, he did not have actual notice of the contravention concerned, or

(b) he derived title to the shares (directly or indirectly) from a person who became a holder of them after the contravention and was not liable under subsection (1).

(3) References in this section to a holder, in relation to shares in a company, include any person who has an unconditional right—

(a) to be included in the company's register of members in respect of those shares, or

(b) to have an instrument of transfer of the shares executed in his favour.

(4) This section applies in relation to a failure to carry out a term of a contract as mentioned in section 587(4) (public companies: payment by long-term undertaking) as it applies in relation to a contravention of a provision of this Chapter.

[S588]

NOTES

Commencement: to be appointed.

589 Power of court to grant relief

(1) This section applies in relation to liability under—

section 585(2) (liability of allottee in case of breach by public company of prohibition on accepting undertaking to do work or perform services),

section 587(2) or (4) (liability of allottee in case of breach by public company of prohibition on payment by long-term undertaking), or

section 588 (liability of subsequent holders of shares),

as it applies in relation to a contravention of those sections.

(2) A person who—

(a) is subject to any such liability to a company in relation to payment in respect of shares in the company, or

(b) is subject to any such liability to a company by virtue of an undertaking given to it in, or in connection with, payment for shares in the company,

may apply to the court to be exempted in whole or in part from the liability.

(3) In the case of a liability within subsection (2)(a), the court may exempt the applicant from the liability only if and to the extent that it appears to the court just and equitable to do so having regard to—

(a) whether the applicant has paid, or is liable to pay, any amount in respect of—
(i) any other liability arising in relation to those shares under any provision of this Chapter or Chapter 6, or
(ii) any liability arising by virtue of any undertaking given in or in connection with payment for those shares;
(b) whether any person other than the applicant has paid or is likely to pay, whether in pursuance of any order of the court or otherwise, any such amount;
(c) whether the applicant or any other person—
(i) has performed in whole or in part, or is likely so to perform any such undertaking, or
(ii) has done or is likely to do any other thing in payment or part payment for the shares.

(4) In the case of a liability within subsection (2)(b), the court may exempt the applicant from the liability only if and to the extent that it appears to the court just and equitable to do so having regard to—
(a) whether the applicant has paid or is liable to pay any amount in respect of liability arising in relation to the shares under any provision of this Chapter or Chapter 6;
(b) whether any person other than the applicant has paid or is likely to pay, whether in pursuance of any order of the court or otherwise, any such amount.

(5) In determining whether it should exempt the applicant in whole or in part from any liability, the court must have regard to the following overriding principles—
(a) a company that has allotted shares should receive money or money's worth at least equal in value to the aggregate of the nominal value of those shares and the whole of any premium or, if the case so requires, so much of that aggregate as is treated as paid up;
(b) subject to that, where a company would, if the court did not grant the exemption, have more than one remedy against a particular person, it should be for the company to decide which remedy it should remain entitled to pursue.

(6) If a person brings proceedings against another ("the contributor") for a contribution in respect of liability to a company arising under any provision of this Chapter or Chapter 6 and it appears to the court that the contributor is liable to make such a contribution, the court may, if and to the extent that it appears to it just and equitable to do so having regard to the respective culpability (in respect of the liability to the company) of the contributor and the person bringing the proceedings—
(a) exempt the contributor in whole or in part from his liability to make such a contribution, or
(b) order the contributor to make a larger contribution than, but for this subsection, he would be liable to make.

[S589]

NOTES
Commencement: to be appointed.

590 Penalty for contravention of this Chapter

(1) If a company contravenes any of the provisions of this Chapter, an offence is committed by—
(a) the company, and
(b) every officer of the company who is in default.

(2) A person guilty of an offence under this section is liable—
(a) on conviction on indictment, to a fine;
(b) on summary conviction, to a fine not exceeding the statutory maximum.

[S590]

NOTES
Commencement: to be appointed.

591 Enforceability of undertakings to do work etc

(1) An undertaking given by any person, in or in connection with payment for shares in a company, to do work or perform services or to do any other thing, if it is enforceable by the

company apart from this Chapter, is so enforceable notwithstanding that there has been a contravention in relation to it of a provision of this Chapter or Chapter 6.

(2) This is without prejudice to section 589 (power of court to grant relief etc in respect of liabilities).

[S591]

NOTES

Commencement: to be appointed.

592 The appropriate rate of interest

(1) For the purposes of this Chapter the "appropriate rate" of interest is 5% per annum or such other rate as may be specified by order made by the Secretary of State.

(2) An order under this section is subject to negative resolution procedure.

[S592]

NOTES

Commencement: 20 January 2007 (for the purpose of enabling the exercise of powers to make Orders or Regulations by statutory instrument); to be appointed (otherwise).

CHAPTER 6
PUBLIC COMPANIES: INDEPENDENT VALUATION OF NON-CASH CONSIDERATION

Non-cash consideration for shares

593 Public company: valuation of non-cash consideration for shares

(1) A public company must not allot shares as fully or partly paid up (as to their nominal value or any premium on them) otherwise than in cash unless—

(a) the consideration for the allotment has been independently valued in accordance with the provisions of this Chapter,

(b) the valuer's report has been made to the company during the six months immediately preceding the allotment of the shares, and

(c) a copy of the report has been sent to the proposed allottee.

(2) For this purpose the application of an amount standing to the credit of—

(a) any of a company's reserve accounts, or

(b) its profit and loss account,

in paying up (to any extent) shares allotted to members of the company, or premiums on shares so allotted, does not count as consideration for the allotment.

Accordingly, subsection (1) does not apply in that case.

(3) If a company allots shares in contravention of subsection (1) and either—

(a) the allottee has not received the valuer's report required to be sent to him, or

(b) there has been some other contravention of the requirements of this section or section 596 that the allottee knew or ought to have known amounted to a contravention,

the allottee is liable to pay the company an amount equal to the aggregate of the nominal value of the shares and the whole of any premium (or, if the case so requires, so much of that aggregate as is treated as paid up by the consideration), with interest at the appropriate rate.

(4) This section has effect subject to—

section 594 (exception to valuation requirement: arrangement with another company), and

section 595 (exception to valuation requirement: merger).

[S593]

NOTES

Commencement: to be appointed.

594 Exception to valuation requirement: arrangement with another company

(1) Section 593 (valuation of non-cash consideration) does not apply to the allotment of shares by a company ("company A") in connection with an arrangement to which this section applies.

(2) This section applies to an arrangement for the allotment of shares in company A on terms that the whole or part of the consideration for the shares allotted is to be provided by—

(a) the transfer to that company, or

(b) the cancellation,

of all or some of the shares, or of all or some of the shares of a particular class, in another company ("company B").

(3) It is immaterial whether the arrangement provides for the issue to company A of shares, or shares of any particular class, in company B.

(4) This section applies to an arrangement only if under the arrangement it is open to all the holders of the shares in company B (or, where the arrangement applies only to shares of a particular class, to all the holders of shares of that class) to take part in the arrangement.

(5) In determining whether that is the case, the following shall be disregarded—

(a) shares held by or by a nominee of company A;

(b) shares held by or by a nominee of a company which is—

(i) the holding company, or a subsidiary, of company A, or

(ii) a subsidiary of such a holding company;

(c) shares held as treasury shares by company B.

(6) In this section—

(a) "arrangement" means any agreement, scheme or arrangement (including an arrangement sanctioned in accordance with—

(i) Part 26 (arrangements and reconstructions), or

(ii) section 110 of the Insolvency Act 1986 (c 45) or Article 96 of the Insolvency (Northern Ireland) Order 1989 (SI 1989/2405 (NI 19)) (liquidator in winding up accepting shares as consideration for sale of company property)), and

(b) "company", except in reference to company A, includes any body corporate.

[S594]

NOTES

Commencement: to be appointed.

595 Exception to valuation requirement: merger

(1) Section 593 (valuation of non-cash consideration) does not apply to the allotment of shares by a company in connection with a proposed merger with another company.

(2) A proposed merger is where one of the companies proposes to acquire all the assets and liabilities of the other in exchange for the issue of shares or other securities of that one to shareholders of the other, with or without any cash payment to shareholders.

(3) In this section "company", in reference to the other company, includes any body corporate.

[S595]

NOTES

Commencement: to be appointed.

596 Non-cash consideration for shares: requirements as to valuation and report

(1) The provisions of sections 1150 to 1153 (general provisions as to independent valuation and report) apply to the valuation and report required by section 593 (public company: valuation of non-cash consideration for shares).

(2) The valuer's report must state—

(a) the nominal value of the shares to be wholly or partly paid for by the consideration in question;

(b) the amount of any premium payable on the shares;

(c) the description of the consideration and, as respects so much of the consideration as he himself has valued, a description of that part of the consideration, the method used to value it and the date of the valuation;
(d) the extent to which the nominal value of the shares and any premium are to be treated as paid up—
  (i) by the consideration;
  (ii) in cash.

(3) The valuer's report must contain or be accompanied by a note by him—
(a) in the case of a valuation made by a person other than himself, that it appeared to himself reasonable to arrange for it to be so made or to accept a valuation so made,
(b) whoever made the valuation, that the method of valuation was reasonable in all the circumstances,
(c) that it appears to the valuer that there has been no material change in the value of the consideration in question since the valuation, and
(d) that, on the basis of the valuation, the value of the consideration, together with any cash by which the nominal value of the shares or any premium payable on them is to be paid up, is not less than so much of the aggregate of the nominal value and the whole of any such premium as is treated as paid up by the consideration and any such cash.

(4) Where the consideration to be valued is accepted partly in payment up of the nominal value of the shares and any premium and partly for some other consideration given by the company, section 593 and the preceding provisions of this section apply as if references to the consideration accepted by the company included the proportion of that consideration that is properly attributable to the payment up of that value and any premium.

(5) In such a case—
(a) the valuer must carry out, or arrange for, such other valuations as will enable him to determine that proportion, and
(b) his report must state what valuations have been made under this subsection and also the reason for, and method and date of, any such valuation and any other matters which may be relevant to that determination.

[S596]

NOTES
Commencement: to be appointed.

597 Copy of report to be delivered to registrar

(1) A company to which a report is made under section 593 as to the value of any consideration for which, or partly for which, it proposes to allot shares must deliver a copy of the report to the registrar for registration.

(2) The copy must be delivered at the same time that the company files the return of the allotment of those shares under section 555 (return of allotment by limited company).

(3) If default is made in complying with subsection (1) or (2), an offence is committed by every officer of the company who is in default.

(4) A person guilty of an offence under this section is liable—
(a) on conviction on indictment, to a fine;
(b) on summary conviction, to a fine not exceeding the statutory maximum and, for continued contravention, a daily default fine not exceeding one-tenth of the statutory maximum.

(5) In the case of default in delivering to the registrar any document as required by this section, any person liable for the default may apply to the court for relief.

(6) The court, if satisfied—
(a) that the omission to deliver the document was accidental or due to inadvertence, or
(b) that it is just and equitable to grant relief,

may make an order extending the time for delivery of the document for such period as the court thinks proper.

[S597]

NOTES

Commencement: to be appointed.

Transfer of non-cash asset in initial period

598 Public company: agreement for transfer of non-cash asset in initial period

(1) A public company formed as such must not enter into an agreement—

(a) with a person who is a subscriber to the company's memorandum,

(b) for the transfer by him to the company, or another, before the end of the company's initial period of one or more non-cash assets, and

(c) under which the consideration for the transfer to be given by the company is at the time of the agreement equal in value to one-tenth or more of the company's issued share capital,

unless the conditions referred to below have been complied with.

(2) The company's "initial period" means the period of two years beginning with the date of the company being issued with a certificate under section 761 (trading certificate).

(3) The conditions are those specified in—

section 599 (requirement of independent valuation), and

section 601 (requirement of approval by members).

(4) This section does not apply where—

(a) it is part of the company's ordinary business to acquire, or arrange for other persons to acquire, assets of a particular description, and

(b) the agreement is entered into by the company in the ordinary course of that business.

(5) This section does not apply to an agreement entered into by the company under the supervision of the court or of an officer authorised by the court for the purpose.

[S598]

NOTES

Commencement: to be appointed.

599 Agreement for transfer of non-cash asset: requirement of independent valuation

(1) The following conditions must have been complied with—

(a) the consideration to be received by the company, and any consideration other than cash to be given by the company, must have been independently valued in accordance with the provisions of this Chapter,

(b) the valuer's report must have been made to the company during the six months immediately preceding the date of the agreement, and

(c) a copy of the report must have been sent to the other party to the proposed agreement not later than the date on which copies have to be circulated to members under section 601(3).

(2) The reference in subsection (1)(a) to the consideration to be received by the company is to the asset to be transferred to it or, as the case may be, to the advantage to the company of the asset's transfer to another person.

(3) The reference in subsection (1)(c) to the other party to the proposed agreement is to the person referred to in section 598(1)(a).

If he has received a copy of the report under section 601 in his capacity as a member of the company, it is not necessary to send another copy under this section.

(4) This section does not affect any requirement to value any consideration for purposes of section 593 (valuation of non-cash consideration for shares).

[S599]

NOTES

Commencement: to be appointed.

600 Agreement for transfer of non-cash asset: requirements as to valuation and report

(1) The provisions of sections 1150 to 1153 (general provisions as to independent valuation and report) apply to the valuation and report required by section 599 (public company: transfer of non-cash asset).

(2) The valuer's report must state—

(a) the consideration to be received by the company, describing the asset in question (specifying the amount to be received in cash) and the consideration to be given by the company (specifying the amount to be given in cash), and

(b) the method and date of valuation.

(3) The valuer's report must contain or be accompanied by a note by him—

(a) in the case of a valuation made by a person other than himself, that it appeared to himself reasonable to arrange for it to be so made or to accept a valuation so made,

(b) whoever made the valuation, that the method of valuation was reasonable in all the circumstances,

(c) that it appears to the valuer that there has been no material change in the value of the consideration in question since the valuation, and

(d) that, on the basis of the valuation, the value of the consideration to be received by the company is not less than the value of the consideration to be given by it.

(4) Any reference in section 599 or this section to consideration given for the transfer of an asset includes consideration given partly for its transfer.

(5) In such a case—

(a) the value of any consideration partly so given is to be taken as the proportion of the consideration properly attributable to its transfer,

(b) the valuer must carry out or arrange for such valuations of anything else as will enable him to determine that proportion, and

(c) his report must state what valuations have been made for that purpose and also the reason for and method and date of any such valuation and any other matters which may be relevant to that determination.

[S600]

NOTES

Commencement: to be appointed.

601 Agreement for transfer of non-cash asset: requirement of approval by members

(1) The following conditions must have been complied with—

(a) the terms of the agreement must have been approved by an ordinary resolution of the company,

(b) the requirements of this section must have been complied with as respects the circulation to members of copies of the valuer's report under section 599, and

(c) a copy of the proposed resolution must have been sent to the other party to the proposed agreement.

(2) The reference in subsection (1)(c) to the other party to the proposed agreement is to the person referred to in section 598(1)(a).

(3) The requirements of this section as to circulation of copies of the valuer's report are as follows—

(a) if the resolution is proposed as a written resolution, copies of the valuer's report must be sent or submitted to every eligible member at or before the time at which the proposed resolution is sent or submitted to him;

(b) if the resolution is proposed at a general meeting, copies of the valuer's report must be circulated to the members entitled to notice of the meeting not later than the date on which notice of the meeting is given.

[S601]

NOTES

Commencement: to be appointed.

602 Copy of resolution to be delivered to registrar

(1) A company that has passed a resolution under section 601 with respect to the transfer of an asset must, within 15 days of doing so, deliver to the registrar a copy of the resolution together with the valuer's report required by that section.

(2) If a company fails to comply with subsection (1), an offence is committed by—

(a) the company, and

(b) every officer of the company who is in default.

(3) A person guilty of an offence under this section is liable on summary conviction to a fine not exceeding level 3 on the standard scale and, for continued contravention, to a daily default fine not exceeding one-tenth of level 3 on the standard scale.

[S602]

NOTES

Commencement: to be appointed.

603 Adaptation of provisions in relation to company re-registering as public

The provisions of sections 598 to 602 (public companies: transfer of non-cash assets) apply with the following adaptations in relation to a company re-registered as a public company—

(a) the reference in section 598(1)(a) to a person who is a subscriber to the company's memorandum shall be read as a reference to a person who is a member of the company on the date of re-registration;

(b) the reference in section 598(2) to the date of the company being issued with a certificate under section 761 (trading certificate) shall be read as a reference to the date of re-registration.

[S603]

NOTES

Commencement: to be appointed.

604 Agreement for transfer of non-cash asset: effect of contravention

(1) This section applies where a public company enters into an agreement in contravention of section 598 and either—

(a) the other party to the agreement has not received the valuer's report required to be sent to him, or

(b) there has been some other contravention of the requirements of this Chapter that the other party to the agreement knew or ought to have known amounted to a contravention.

(2) In those circumstances—

(a) the company is entitled to recover from that person any consideration given by it under the agreement, or an amount equal to the value of the consideration at the time of the agreement, and

(b) the agreement, so far as not carried out, is void.

(3) If the agreement is or includes an agreement for the allotment of shares in the company, then—

(a) whether or not the agreement also contravenes section 593 (valuation of non-cash consideration for shares), this section does not apply to it in so far as it is for the allotment of shares, and

(b) the allottee is liable to pay the company an amount equal to the aggregate of the nominal value of the shares and the whole of any premium (or, if the case so requires, so much of that aggregate as is treated as paid up by the consideration), with interest at the appropriate rate.

[S604]

NOTES

Commencement: to be appointed.

Supplementary provisions

605 Liability of subsequent holders of shares

(1) If a person becomes a holder of shares in respect of which—

(a) there has been a contravention of section 593 (public company: valuation of non-cash consideration for shares), and

(b) by virtue of that contravention another is liable to pay any amount under the provision contravened,

that person is also liable to pay that amount (jointly and severally with any other person so liable), unless he is exempted from liability under subsection (3) below.

(2) If a company enters into an agreement in contravention of section 598 (public company: agreement for transfer of non-cash asset in initial period) and—

(a) the agreement is or includes an agreement for the allotment of shares in the company,

(b) a person becomes a holder of shares allotted under the agreement, and

(c) by virtue of the agreement and allotment under it another person is liable to pay an amount under section 604,

the person who becomes the holder of the shares is also liable to pay that amount (jointly and severally with any other person so liable), unless he is exempted from liability under subsection (3) below.

This applies whether or not the agreement also contravenes section 593.

(3) A person otherwise liable under subsection (1) or (2) is exempted from that liability if either—

(a) he is a purchaser for value and, at the time of the purchase, he did not have actual notice of the contravention concerned, or

(b) he derived title to the shares (directly or indirectly) from a person who became a holder of them after the contravention and was not liable under subsection (1) or (2).

(4) References in this section to a holder, in relation to shares in a company, include any person who has an unconditional right—

(a) to be included in the company's register of members in respect of those shares, or

(b) to have an instrument of transfer of the shares executed in his favour.

[S605]

NOTES

Commencement: to be appointed.

606 Power of court to grant relief

(1) A person who—

(a) is liable to a company under any provision of this Chapter in relation to payment in respect of any shares in the company, or

(b) is liable to a company by virtue of an undertaking given to it in, or in connection with, payment for any shares in the company,

may apply to the court to be exempted in whole or in part from the liability.

(2) In the case of a liability within subsection (1)(a), the court may exempt the applicant from the liability only if and to the extent that it appears to the court just and equitable to do so having regard to—

(a) whether the applicant has paid, or is liable to pay, any amount in respect of—

(i) any other liability arising in relation to those shares under any provision of this Chapter or Chapter 5, or

(ii) any liability arising by virtue of any undertaking given in or in connection with payment for those shares;

(b) whether any person other than the applicant has paid or is likely to pay, whether in pursuance of any order of the court or otherwise, any such amount;

(c) whether the applicant or any other person—

(i) has performed in whole or in part, or is likely so to perform any such undertaking, or

(ii) has done or is likely to do any other thing in payment or part payment for the shares.

(3) In the case of a liability within subsection (1)(b), the court may exempt the applicant from the liability only if and to the extent that it appears to the court just and equitable to do so having regard to—

(a) whether the applicant has paid or is liable to pay any amount in respect of liability arising in relation to the shares under any provision of this Chapter or Chapter 5;

(b) whether any person other than the applicant has paid or is likely to pay, whether in pursuance of any order of the court or otherwise, any such amount.

(4) In determining whether it should exempt the applicant in whole or in part from any liability, the court must have regard to the following overriding principles—

(a) that a company that has allotted shares should receive money or money's worth at least equal in value to the aggregate of the nominal value of those shares and the whole of any premium or, if the case so requires, so much of that aggregate as is treated as paid up;

(b) subject to this, that where such a company would, if the court did not grant the exemption, have more than one remedy against a particular person, it should be for the company to decide which remedy it should remain entitled to pursue.

(5) If a person brings proceedings against another ("the contributor") for a contribution in respect of liability to a company arising under any provision of this Chapter or Chapter 5 and it appears to the court that the contributor is liable to make such a contribution, the court may, if and to the extent that it appears to it, just and equitable to do so having regard to the respective culpability (in respect of the liability to the company) of the contributor and the person bringing the proceedings—

(a) exempt the contributor in whole or in part from his liability to make such a contribution, or

(b) order the contributor to make a larger contribution than, but for this subsection, he would be liable to make.

(6) Where a person is liable to a company under section 604(2) (agreement for transfer of non-cash asset: effect of contravention), the court may, on application, exempt him in whole or in part from that liability if and to the extent that it appears to the court to be just and equitable to do so having regard to any benefit accruing to the company by virtue of anything done by him towards the carrying out of the agreement mentioned in that subsection.

[S606]

NOTES

Commencement: to be appointed.

607 Penalty for contravention of this Chapter

(1) This section applies where a company contravenes—

section 593 (public company allotting shares for non-cash consideration), or

section 598 (public company entering into agreement for transfer of non-cash asset).

(2) An offence is committed by—

(a) the company, and

(b) every officer of the company who is in default.

(3) A person guilty of an offence under this section is liable—

(a) on conviction on indictment, to a fine;

(b) on summary conviction, to a fine not exceeding the statutory maximum.

[S607]

NOTES

Commencement: to be appointed.

608 Enforceability of undertakings to do work etc

(1) An undertaking given by any person, in or in connection with payment for shares in a company, to do work or perform services or to do any other thing, if it is enforceable by the company apart from this Chapter, is so enforceable notwithstanding that there has been a contravention in relation to it of a provision of this Chapter or Chapter 5.

(2) This is without prejudice to section 606 (power of court to grant relief etc in respect of liabilities).

[S608]

NOTES

Commencement: to be appointed.

609 The appropriate rate of interest

(1) For the purposes of this Chapter the "appropriate rate" of interest is 5% per annum or such other rate as may be specified by order made by the Secretary of State.

(2) An order under this section is subject to negative resolution procedure.

[S609]

NOTES

Commencement: 20 January 2007 (for the purpose of enabling the exercise of powers to make Orders or Regulations by statutory instrument); to be appointed (otherwise).

CHAPTER 7
SHARE PREMIUMS

The share premium account

610 Application of share premiums

(1) If a company issues shares at a premium, whether for cash or otherwise, a sum equal to the aggregate amount or value of the premiums on those shares must be transferred to an account called "the share premium account".

(2) Where, on issuing shares, a company has transferred a sum to the share premium account, it may use that sum to write off—

(a) the expenses of the issue of those shares;

(b) any commission paid on the issue of those shares.

(3) The company may use the share premium account to pay up new shares to be allotted to members as fully paid bonus shares.

(4) Subject to subsections (2) and (3), the provisions of the Companies Acts relating to the reduction of a company's share capital apply as if the share premium account were part of its paid up share capital.

(5) This section has effect subject to—
section 611 (group reconstruction relief);
section 612 (merger relief);
section 614 (power to make further provisions by regulations).

(6) In this Chapter "the issuing company" means the company issuing shares as mentioned in subsection (1) above.

[S610]

NOTES

Commencement: to be appointed.

Relief from requirements as to share premiums

611 Group reconstruction relief

(1) This section applies where the issuing company—

(a) is a wholly-owned subsidiary of another company ("the holding company"), and

(b) allots shares—

(i) to the holding company, or

(ii) to another wholly-owned subsidiary of the holding company,

in consideration for the transfer to the issuing company of non-cash assets of a company ("the transferor company") that is a member of the group of companies that comprises the holding company and all its wholly-owned subsidiaries.

(2) Where the shares in the issuing company allotted in consideration for the transfer are issued at a premium, the issuing company is not required by section 610 to transfer any amount in excess of the minimum premium value to the share premium account.

(3) The minimum premium value means the amount (if any) by which the base value of the consideration for the shares allotted exceeds the aggregate nominal value of the shares.

(4) The base value of the consideration for the shares allotted is the amount by which the base value of the assets transferred exceeds the base value of any liabilities of the transferor company assumed by the issuing company as part of the consideration for the assets transferred.

(5) For the purposes of this section—

(a) the base value of assets transferred is taken as—

(i) the cost of those assets to the transferor company, or

(ii) if less, the amount at which those assets are stated in the transferor company's accounting records immediately before the transfer;

(b) the base value of the liabilities assumed is taken as the amount at which they are stated in the transferor company's accounting records immediately before the transfer.

[S611]

NOTES

Commencement: to be appointed.

612 Merger relief

(1) This section applies where the issuing company has secured at least a 90% equity holding in another company in pursuance of an arrangement providing for the allotment of equity shares in the issuing company on terms that the consideration for the shares allotted is to be provided—

(a) by the issue or transfer to the issuing company of equity shares in the other company, or

(b) by the cancellation of any such shares not held by the issuing company.

(2) If the equity shares in the issuing company allotted in pursuance of the arrangement in consideration for the acquisition or cancellation of equity shares in the other company are issued at a premium, section 610 does not apply to the premiums on those shares.

(3) Where the arrangement also provides for the allotment of any shares in the issuing company on terms that the consideration for those shares is to be provided—

(a) by the issue or transfer to the issuing company of non-equity shares in the other company, or

(b) by the cancellation of any such shares in that company not held by the issuing company,

relief under subsection (2) extends to any shares in the issuing company allotted on those terms in pursuance of the arrangement.

(4) This section does not apply in a case falling within section 611 (group reconstruction relief).

[S612]

NOTES

Commencement: to be appointed.

613 Merger relief: meaning of 90% equity holding

(1) The following provisions have effect to determine for the purposes of section 612 (merger relief) whether a company ("company A") has secured at least a 90% equity holding in another company ("company B") in pursuance of such an arrangement as is mentioned in subsection (1) of that section.

(2) Company A has secured at least a 90% equity holding in company B if in consequence of an acquisition or cancellation of equity shares in company B (in pursuance of that arrangement) it holds equity shares in company B of an aggregate amount equal to 90% or more of the nominal value of that company's equity share capital.

(3) For this purpose—
(a) it is immaterial whether any of those shares were acquired in pursuance of the arrangement; and
(b) shares in company B held by the company as treasury shares are excluded in determining the nominal value of company B's share capital.

(4) Where the equity share capital of company B is divided into different classes of shares, company A is not regarded as having secured at least a 90% equity holding in company B unless the requirements of subsection (2) are met in relation to each of those classes of shares taken separately.

(5) For the purposes of this section shares held by—
(a) a company that is company A's holding company or subsidiary, or
(b) a subsidiary of company A's holding company, or
(c) its or their nominees,
are treated as held by company A.

[S613]

NOTES

Commencement: to be appointed.

614 Power to make further provision by regulations

(1) The Secretary of State may by regulations make such provision as he thinks appropriate—
(a) for relieving companies from the requirements of section 610 (application of share premiums) in relation to premiums other than cash premiums;
(b) for restricting or otherwise modifying any relief from those requirements provided by this Chapter.

(2) Regulations under this section are subject to affirmative resolution procedure.

[S614]

NOTES

Commencement: 20 January 2007 (for the purpose of enabling the exercise of powers to make Orders or Regulations by statutory instrument); to be appointed (otherwise).

615 Relief may be reflected in company's balance sheet

An amount corresponding to the amount representing the premiums, or part of the premiums, on shares issued by a company that by virtue of any relief under this Chapter is not included in the company's share premium account may also be disregarded in determining the amount at which any shares or other consideration provided for the shares issued is to be included in the company's balance sheet.

[S615]

NOTES

Commencement: to be appointed.

Supplementary provisions

616 Interpretation of this Chapter

(1) In this Chapter—
"arrangement" means any agreement, scheme or arrangement (including an arrangement sanctioned in accordance with—
(a) Part 26 (arrangements and reconstructions), or
(b) section 110 of the Insolvency Act 1986 (c 45) or Article 96 of the Insolvency (Northern Ireland) Order 1989 (SI 1989/2405 (NI 19)) (liquidator in winding up accepting shares as consideration for sale of company property));
"company", except in reference to the issuing company, includes any body corporate;
"equity shares" means shares comprised in a company's equity share capital, and "non-equity shares" means shares (of any class) that are not so comprised;

"the issuing company" has the meaning given by section 610(6).

(2) References in this Chapter (however expressed) to—

(a) the acquisition by a company of shares in another company, and

(b) the issue or allotment of shares to, or the transfer of shares to or by, a company,

include (respectively) the acquisition of shares by, and the issue or allotment or transfer of shares to or by, a nominee of that company.

The reference in section 611 to the transferor company shall be read accordingly.

(3) References in this Chapter to the transfer of shares in a company include the transfer of a right to be included in the company's register of members in respect of those shares.

[S616]

NOTES

Commencement: to be appointed.

CHAPTER 8
ALTERATION OF SHARE CAPITAL

How share capital may be altered

617 Alteration of share capital of limited company

(1) A limited company having a share capital may not alter its share capital except in the following ways.

(2) The company may—

(a) increase its share capital by allotting new shares in accordance with this Part, or

(b) reduce its share capital in accordance with Chapter 10.

(3) The company may—

(a) sub-divide or consolidate all or any of its share capital in accordance with section 618, or

(b) reconvert stock into shares in accordance with section 620.

(4) The company may redenominate all or any of its shares in accordance with section 622, and may reduce its share capital in accordance with section 626 in connection with such a redenomination.

(5) Nothing in this section affects—

(a) the power of a company to purchase its own shares, or to redeem shares, in accordance with Part 18;

(b) the power of a company to purchase its own shares in pursuance of an order of the court under—

(i) section 98 (application to court to cancel resolution for re-registration as a private company),

(ii) section 721(6) (powers of court on objection to redemption or purchase of shares out of capital),

(iii) section 759 (remedial order in case of breach of prohibition of public offers by private company), or

(iv) Part 30 (protection of members against unfair prejudice);

(c) the forfeiture of shares, or the acceptance of shares surrendered in lieu, in pursuance of the company's articles, for failure to pay any sum payable in respect of the shares;

(d) the cancellation of shares under section 662 (duty to cancel shares held by or for a public company);

(e) the power of a company—

(i) to enter into a compromise or arrangement in accordance with Part 26 (arrangements and reconstructions), or

(ii) to do anything required to comply with an order of the court on an application under that Part.

[S617]

NOTES

Commencement: to be appointed.

Subdivision or consolidation of shares

618 Sub-division or consolidation of shares

(1) A limited company having a share capital may—

(a) sub-divide its shares, or any of them, into shares of a smaller nominal amount than its existing shares, or

(b) consolidate and divide all or any of its share capital into shares of a larger nominal amount than its existing shares.

(2) In any sub-division, consolidation or division of shares under this section, the proportion between the amount paid and the amount (if any) unpaid on each resulting share must be the same as it was in the case of the share from which that share is derived.

(3) A company may exercise a power conferred by this section only if its members have passed a resolution authorising it to do so.

(4) A resolution under subsection (3) may authorise a company—

(a) to exercise more than one of the powers conferred by this section;

(b) to exercise a power on more than one occasion;

(c) to exercise a power at a specified time or in specified circumstances.

(5) The company's articles may exclude or restrict the exercise of any power conferred by this section.

[S618]

NOTES

Commencement: to be appointed.

619 Notice to registrar of sub-division or consolidation

(1) If a company exercises the power conferred by section 618 (sub-division or consolidation of shares) it must within one month after doing so give notice to the registrar, specifying the shares affected.

(2) The notice must be accompanied by a statement of capital.

(3) The statement of capital must state with respect to the company's share capital immediately following the exercise of the power—

(a) the total number of shares of the company,

(b) the aggregate nominal value of those shares,

(c) for each class of shares—

(i) prescribed particulars of the rights attached to the shares,

(ii) the total number of shares of that class, and

(iii) the aggregate nominal value of shares of that class, and

(d) the amount paid up and the amount (if any) unpaid on each share (whether on account of the nominal value of the share or by way of premium).

(4) If default is made in complying with this section, an offence is committed by—

(a) the company, and

(b) every officer of the company who is in default.

(5) A person guilty of an offence under this section is liable on summary conviction to a fine not exceeding level 3 on the standard scale and, for continued contravention, a daily default fine not exceeding one-tenth of level 3 on the standard scale.

[S619]

NOTES

Commencement: 20 January 2007 (for the purpose of enabling the exercise of powers to make Orders or Regulations by statutory instrument); to be appointed (otherwise).

Reconversion of stock into shares

620 Reconversion of stock into shares

(1) A limited company that has converted paid-up shares into stock (before the repeal by this Act of the power to do so) may reconvert that stock into paid-up shares of any nominal value.

(2) A company may exercise the power conferred by this section only if its members have passed an ordinary resolution authorising it to do so.

(3) A resolution under subsection (2) may authorise a company to exercise the power conferred by this section—

(a) on more than one occasion;

(b) at a specified time or in specified circumstances.

[S620]

NOTES

Commencement: to be appointed.

621 Notice to registrar of reconversion of stock into shares

(1) If a company exercises a power conferred by section 620 (reconversion of stock into shares) it must within one month after doing so give notice to the registrar, specifying the stock affected.

(2) The notice must be accompanied by a statement of capital.

(3) The statement of capital must state with respect to the company's share capital immediately following the exercise of the power—

(a) the total number of shares of the company,

(b) the aggregate nominal value of those shares,

(c) for each class of shares—

(i) prescribed particulars of the rights attached to the shares,

(ii) the total number of shares of that class, and

(iii) the aggregate nominal value of shares of that class, and

(d) the amount paid up and the amount (if any) unpaid on each share (whether on account of the nominal value of the share or by way of premium).

(4) If default is made in complying with this section, an offence is committed by—

(a) the company, and

(b) every officer of the company who is in default.

(5) A person guilty of an offence under this section is liable on summary conviction to a fine not exceeding level 3 on the standard scale and, for continued contravention, a daily default fine not exceeding one-tenth of level 3 on the standard scale.

[S621]

NOTES

Commencement: 20 January 2007 (for the purpose of enabling the exercise of powers to make Orders or Regulations by statutory instrument); to be appointed (otherwise).

Redenomination of share capital

622 Redenomination of share capital

(1) A limited company having a share capital may by resolution redenominate its share capital or any class of its share capital.

"Redenominate" means convert shares from having a fixed nominal value in one currency to having a fixed nominal value in another currency.

(2) The conversion must be made at an appropriate spot rate of exchange specified in the resolution.

(3) The rate must be either—

(a) a rate prevailing on a day specified in the resolution, or

(b) a rate determined by taking the average of rates prevailing on each consecutive day of a period specified in the resolution.

The day or period specified for the purposes of paragraph (a) or (b) must be within the period of 28 days ending on the day before the resolution is passed.

(4) A resolution under this section may specify conditions which must be met before the redenomination takes effect.

(5) Redenomination in accordance with a resolution under this section takes effect—
(a) on the day on which the resolution is passed, or
(b) on such later day as may be determined in accordance with the resolution.

(6) A resolution under this section lapses if the redenomination for which it provides has not taken effect at the end of the period of 28 days beginning on the date on which it is passed.

(7) A company's articles may prohibit or restrict the exercise of the power conferred by this section.

(8) Chapter 3 of Part 3 (resolutions affecting a company's constitution) applies to a resolution under this section.

[S622]

NOTES

Commencement: to be appointed.

623 Calculation of new nominal values

For each class of share the new nominal value of each share is calculated as follows:

Step One

Take the aggregate of the old nominal values of all the shares of that class.

Step Two

Translate that amount into the new currency at the rate of exchange specified in the resolution.

Step Three

Divide that amount by the number of shares in the class.

[S623]

NOTES

Commencement: to be appointed.

624 Effect of redenomination

(1) The redenomination of shares does not affect any rights or obligations of members under the company's constitution, or any restrictions affecting members under the company's constitution.

In particular, it does not affect entitlement to dividends (including entitlement to dividends in a particular currency), voting rights or any liability in respect of amounts unpaid on shares.

(2) For this purpose the company's constitution includes the terms on which any shares of the company are allotted or held.

(3) Subject to subsection (1), references to the old nominal value of the shares in any agreement or statement, or in any deed, instrument or document, shall (unless the context otherwise requires) be read after the resolution takes effect as references to the new nominal value of the shares.

[S624]

NOTES

Commencement: to be appointed.

625 Notice to registrar of redenomination

(1) If a limited company having a share capital redenominates any of its share capital, it must within one month after doing so give notice to the registrar, specifying the shares redenominated.

(2) The notice must—
(a) state the date on which the resolution was passed, and
(b) be accompanied by a statement of capital.

(3) The statement of capital must state with respect to the company's share capital as redenominated by the resolution—

(a) the total number of shares of the company,
(b) the aggregate nominal value of those shares,
(c) for each class of shares—
(i) prescribed particulars of the rights attached to the shares,
(ii) the total number of shares of that class, and
(iii) the aggregate nominal value of shares of that class, and
(d) the amount paid up and the amount (if any) unpaid on each share (whether on account of the nominal value of the share or by way of premium).

(4) If default is made in complying with this section, an offence is committed by—
(a) the company, and
(b) every officer of the company who is in default.

(5) A person guilty of an offence under this section is liable on summary conviction to a fine not exceeding level 3 on the standard scale and, for continued contravention, a daily default fine not exceeding one-tenth of level 3 on the standard scale.

[S625]

NOTES

Commencement: 20 January 2007 (for the purpose of enabling the exercise of powers to make Orders or Regulations by statutory instrument); to be appointed (otherwise).

626 Reduction of capital in connection with redenomination

(1) A limited company that passes a resolution redenominating some or all of its shares may, for the purpose of adjusting the nominal values of the redenominated shares to obtain values that are, in the opinion of the company, more suitable, reduce its share capital under this section.

(2) A reduction of capital under this section requires a special resolution of the company.

(3) Any such resolution must be passed within three months of the resolution effecting the redenomination.

(4) The amount by which a company's share capital is reduced under this section must not exceed 10% of the nominal value of the company's allotted share capital immediately after the reduction.

(5) A reduction of capital under this section does not extinguish or reduce any liability in respect of share capital not paid up.

(6) Nothing in Chapter 10 applies to a reduction of capital under this section.

[S626]

NOTES

Commencement: to be appointed.

627 Notice to registrar of reduction of capital in connection with redenomination

(1) A company that passes a resolution under section 626 (reduction of capital in connection with redenomination) must within 15 days after the resolution is passed give notice to the registrar stating—
(a) the date of the resolution, and
(b) the date of the resolution under section 622 in connection with which it was passed.

This is in addition to the copies of the resolutions themselves that are required to be delivered to the registrar under Chapter 3 of Part 3.

(2) The notice must be accompanied by a statement of capital.

(3) The statement of capital must state with respect to the company's share capital as reduced by the resolution—
(a) the total number of shares of the company,
(b) the aggregate nominal value of those shares,
(c) for each class of shares—
(i) prescribed particulars of the rights attached to the shares,
(ii) the total number of shares of that class, and

(iii) the aggregate nominal value of shares of that class, and

(d) the amount paid up and the amount (if any) unpaid on each share (whether on account of the nominal value of the share or by way of premium).

(4) The registrar must register the notice and the statement on receipt.

(5) The reduction of capital is not effective until those documents are registered.

(6) The company must also deliver to the registrar, within 15 days after the resolution is passed, a statement by the directors confirming that the reduction in share capital is in accordance with section 626(4) (reduction of capital not to exceed 10% of nominal value of allotted shares immediately after reduction).

(7) If default is made in complying with this section, an offence is committed by—

(a) the company, and

(b) every officer of the company who is in default.

(8) A person guilty of an offence under this section is liable—

(a) on conviction on indictment to a fine, and

(b) on summary conviction to a fine not exceeding the statutory maximum.

[S627]

NOTES

Commencement: 20 January 2007 (for the purpose of enabling the exercise of powers to make Orders or Regulations by statutory instrument); to be appointed (otherwise).

628 Redenomination reserve

(1) The amount by which a company's share capital is reduced under section 626 (reduction of capital in connection with redenomination) must be transferred to a reserve, called "the redenomination reserve".

(2) The redenomination reserve may be applied by the company in paying up shares to be allotted to members as fully paid bonus shares.

(3) Subject to that, the provisions of the Companies Acts relating to the reduction of a company's share capital apply as if the redenomination reserve were paid-up share capital of the company.

[S628]

NOTES

Commencement: to be appointed.

CHAPTER 9
CLASSES OF SHARE AND CLASS RIGHTS

Introductory

629 Classes of shares

(1) For the purposes of the Companies Acts shares are of one class if the rights attached to them are in all respects uniform.

(2) For this purpose the rights attached to shares are not regarded as different from those attached to other shares by reason only that they do not carry the same rights to dividends in the twelve months immediately following their allotment.

[S629]

NOTES

Commencement: 1 October 2007 (certain purposes); to be appointed (otherwise) (see the note below).

Note: the draft Companies Act 2006 (Commencement No 3, Consequential Amendments, Transitional Provisions and Savings) Order 2007, art 2(3) provides that this section shall come into force on 1 October 2007 so far as is necessary for the purposes of the provisions of this Act brought into force on that date by art 2(1), (2) of that Order (see **[A12]**).

Variation of class rights

630 Variation of class rights: companies having a share capital

(1) This section is concerned with the variation of the rights attached to a class of shares in a company having a share capital.

(2) Rights attached to a class of a company's shares may only be varied—

(a) in accordance with provision in the company's articles for the variation of those rights, or

(b) where the company's articles contain no such provision, if the holders of shares of that class consent to the variation in accordance with this section.

(3) This is without prejudice to any other restrictions on the variation of the rights.

(4) The consent required for the purposes of this section on the part of the holders of a class of a company's shares is—

(a) consent in writing from the holders of at least three-quarters in nominal value of the issued shares of that class (excluding any shares held as treasury shares), or

(b) a special resolution passed at a separate general meeting of the holders of that class sanctioning the variation.

(5) Any amendment of a provision contained in a company's articles for the variation of the rights attached to a class of shares, or the insertion of any such provision into the articles, is itself to be treated as a variation of those rights.

(6) In this section, and (except where the context otherwise requires) in any provision in a company's articles for the variation of the rights attached to a class of shares, references to the variation of those rights include references to their abrogation.

[S630]

NOTES

Commencement: to be appointed.

631 Variation of class rights: companies without a share capital

(1) This section is concerned with the variation of the rights of a class of members of a company where the company does not have a share capital.

(2) Rights of a class of members may only be varied—

(a) in accordance with provision in the company's articles for the variation of those rights, or

(b) where the company's articles contain no such provision, if the members of that class consent to the variation in accordance with this section.

(3) This is without prejudice to any other restrictions on the variation of the rights.

(4) The consent required for the purposes of this section on the part of the members of a class is—

(a) consent in writing from at least three-quarters of the members of the class, or

(b) a special resolution passed at a separate general meeting of the members of that class sanctioning the variation.

(5) Any amendment of a provision contained in a company's articles for the variation of the rights of a class of members, or the insertion of any such provision into the articles, is itself to be treated as a variation of those rights.

(6) In this section, and (except where the context otherwise requires) in any provision in a company's articles for the variation of the rights of a class of members, references to the variation of those rights include references to their abrogation.

[S631]

NOTES

Commencement: to be appointed.

632 Variation of class rights: saving for court's powers under other provisions

Nothing in section 630 or 631 (variation of class rights) affects the power of the court under—

section 98 (application to cancel resolution for public company to be re-registered as private),
Part 26 (arrangements and reconstructions), or
Part 30 (protection of members against unfair prejudice).

[S632]

NOTES

Commencement: to be appointed.

633 Right to object to variation: companies having a share capital

(1) This section applies where the rights attached to any class of shares in a company are varied under section 630 (variation of class rights: companies having a share capital).

(2) The holders of not less in the aggregate than 15% of the issued shares of the class in question (being persons who did not consent to or vote in favour of the resolution for the variation) may apply to the court to have the variation cancelled.

For this purpose any of the company's share capital held as treasury shares is disregarded.

(3) If such an application is made, the variation has no effect unless and until it is confirmed by the court.

(4) Application to the court—

(a) must be made within 21 days after the date on which the consent was given or the resolution was passed (as the case may be), and

(b) may be made on behalf of the shareholders entitled to make the application by such one or more of their number as they may appoint in writing for the purpose.

(5) The court, after hearing the applicant and any other persons who apply to the court to be heard and appear to the court to be interested in the application, may, if satisfied having regard to all the circumstances of the case that the variation would unfairly prejudice the shareholders of the class represented by the applicant, disallow the variation, and shall if not so satisfied confirm it. The decision of the court on any such application is final.

(6) References in this section to the variation of the rights of holders of a class of shares include references to their abrogation.

[S633]

NOTES

Commencement: to be appointed.

634 Right to object to variation: companies without a share capital

(1) This section applies where the rights of any class of members of a company are varied under section 631 (variation of class rights: companies without a share capital).

(2) Members amounting to not less than 15% of the members of the class in question (being persons who did not consent to or vote in favour of the resolution for the variation) may apply to the court to have the variation cancelled.

(3) If such an application is made, the variation has no effect unless and until it is confirmed by the court.

(4) Application to the court must be made within 21 days after the date on which the consent was given or the resolution was passed (as the case may be) and may be made on behalf of the members entitled to make the application by such one or more of their number as they may appoint in writing for the purpose.

(5) The court, after hearing the applicant and any other persons who apply to the court to be heard and appear to the court to be interested in the application, may, if satisfied having regard to all the circumstances of the case that the variation would unfairly prejudice the members of the class represented by the applicant, disallow the variation, and shall if not so satisfied confirm it.

The decision of the court on any such application is final.

(6) References in this section to the variation of the rights of a class of members include references to their abrogation.

[S634]

NOTES

Commencement: to be appointed.

635 Copy of court order to be forwarded to the registrar

(1) The company must within 15 days after the making of an order by the court on an application under section 633 or 634 (objection to variation of class rights) forward a copy of the order to the registrar.

(2) If default is made in complying with this section an offence is committed by—
(a) the company, and
(b) every officer of the company who is in default.

(3) A person guilty of an offence under this section is liable on summary conviction to a fine not exceeding level 3 on the standard scale and, for continued contravention, a daily default fine not exceeding one-tenth of level 3 on the standard scale.

[S635]

NOTES

Commencement: to be appointed.

Matters to be notified to the registrar

636 Notice of name or other designation of class of shares

(1) Where a company assigns a name or other designation, or a new name or other designation, to any class or description of its shares, it must within one month from doing so deliver to the registrar a notice giving particulars of the name or designation so assigned.

(2) If default is made in complying with this section, an offence is committed by—
(a) the company, and
(b) every officer of the company who is in default.

(3) A person guilty of an offence under this section is liable on summary conviction to a fine not exceeding level 3 on the standard scale and, for continued contravention, a daily default fine not exceeding one-tenth of level 3 on the standard scale.

[S636]

NOTES

Commencement: to be appointed.

637 Notice of particulars of variation of rights attached to shares

(1) Where the rights attached to any shares of a company are varied, the company must within one month from the date on which the variation is made deliver to the registrar a notice giving particulars of the variation.

(2) If default is made in complying with this section, an offence is committed by—
(a) the company, and
(b) every officer of the company who is in default.

(3) A person guilty of an offence under this section is liable on summary conviction to a fine not exceeding level 3 on the standard scale and, for continued contravention, a daily default fine not exceeding one-tenth of level 3 on the standard scale.

[S637]

NOTES

Commencement: to be appointed.

638 Notice of new class of members

(1) If a company not having a share capital creates a new class of members, the company must within one month from the date on which the new class is created deliver to the registrar a notice containing particulars of the rights attached to that class.

(2) If default is made in complying with this section, an offence is committed by—

(a) the company, and

(b) every officer of the company who is in default.

(3) A person guilty of an offence under this section is liable on summary conviction to a fine not exceeding level 3 on the standard scale and, for continued contravention, a daily default fine not exceeding one-tenth of level 3 on the standard scale.

[S638]

NOTES

Commencement: to be appointed.

639 Notice of name or other designation of class of members

(1) Where a company not having a share capital assigns a name or other designation, or a new name or other designation, to any class of its members, it must within one month from doing so deliver to the registrar a notice giving particulars of the name or designation so assigned.

(2) If default is made in complying with this section, an offence is committed by—

(a) the company, and

(b) every officer of the company who is in default.

(3) A person guilty of an offence under this section is liable on summary conviction to a fine not exceeding level 3 on the standard scale and, for continued contravention, a daily default fine not exceeding one-tenth of level 3 on the standard scale.

[S639]

NOTES

Commencement: to be appointed.

640 Notice of particulars of variation of class rights

(1) If the rights of any class of members of a company not having a share capital are varied, the company must within one month from the date on which the variation is made deliver to the registrar a notice containing particulars of the variation.

(2) If default is made in complying with this section, an offence is committed by—

(a) the company, and

(b) every officer of the company who is in default.

(3) A person guilty of an offence under this section is liable on summary conviction to a fine not exceeding level 3 on the standard scale and, for continued contravention, a daily default fine not exceeding one-tenth of level 3 on the standard scale.

[S640]

NOTES

Commencement: to be appointed.

CHAPTER 10
REDUCTION OF SHARE CAPITAL

Introductory

641 Circumstances in which a company may reduce its share capital

(1) A limited company having a share capital may reduce its share capital—

(a) in the case of a private company limited by shares, by special resolution supported by a solvency statement (see sections 642 to 644);

(b) in any case, by special resolution confirmed by the court (see sections 645 to 651).

(2) A company may not reduce its capital under subsection (1)(a) if as a result of the reduction there would no longer be any member of the company holding shares other than redeemable shares.

(3) Subject to that, a company may reduce its share capital under this section in any way.

(4) In particular, a company may—

(a) extinguish or reduce the liability on any of its shares in respect of share capital not paid up, or

(b) either with or without extinguishing or reducing liability on any of its shares—

(i) cancel any paid-up share capital that is lost or unrepresented by available assets, or

(ii) repay any paid-up share capital in excess of the company's wants.

(5) A special resolution under this section may not provide for a reduction of share capital to take effect later than the date on which the resolution has effect in accordance with this Chapter.

(6) This Chapter (apart from subsection (5) above) has effect subject to any provision of the company's articles restricting or prohibiting the reduction of the company's share capital.

[S641]

NOTES

Commencement: to be appointed.

Private companies: reduction of capital supported by solvency statement

642 Reduction of capital supported by solvency statement

(1) A resolution for reducing share capital of a private company limited by shares is supported by a solvency statement if—

(a) the directors of the company make a statement of the solvency of the company in accordance with section 643 (a "solvency statement") not more than 15 days before the date on which the resolution is passed, and

(b) the resolution and solvency statement are registered in accordance with section 644.

(2) Where the resolution is proposed as a written resolution, a copy of the solvency statement must be sent or submitted to every eligible member at or before the time at which the proposed resolution is sent or submitted to him.

(3) Where the resolution is proposed at a general meeting, a copy of the solvency statement must be made available for inspection by members of the company throughout that meeting.

(4) The validity of a resolution is not affected by a failure to comply with subsection (2) or (3).

[S642]

NOTES

Commencement: to be appointed.

643 Solvency statement

(1) A solvency statement is a statement that each of the directors—

(a) has formed the opinion, as regards the company's situation at the date of the statement, that there is no ground on which the company could then be found to be unable to pay (or otherwise discharge) its debts; and

(b) has also formed the opinion—

(i) if it is intended to commence the winding up of the company within twelve months of that date, that the company will be able to pay (or otherwise discharge) its debts in full within twelve months of the commencement of the winding up; or

(ii) in any other case, that the company will be able to pay (or otherwise discharge) its debts as they fall due during the year immediately following that date.

(2) In forming those opinions, the directors must take into account all of the company's liabilities (including any contingent or prospective liabilities).

(3) The solvency statement must be in the prescribed form and must state—
- (a) the date on which it is made, and
- (b) the name of each director of the company.

(4) If the directors make a solvency statement without having reasonable grounds for the opinions expressed in it, and the statement is delivered to the registrar, an offence is committed by every director who is in default.

(5) A person guilty of an offence under subsection (4) is liable—
- (a) on conviction on indictment, to imprisonment for a term not exceeding two years or a fine (or both);
- (b) on summary conviction—
  - (i) in England and Wales, to imprisonment for a term not exceeding twelve months or to a fine not exceeding the statutory maximum (or both);
  - (ii) in Scotland or Northern Ireland, to imprisonment for a term not exceeding six months, or to a fine not exceeding the statutory maximum (or both).

[S643]

NOTES

Commencement: 20 January 2007 (for the purpose of enabling the exercise of powers to make Orders or Regulations by statutory instrument); to be appointed (otherwise).

644 Registration of resolution and supporting documents

(1) Within 15 days after the resolution for reducing share capital is passed the company must deliver to the registrar—
- (a) a copy of the solvency statement, and
- (b) a statement of capital.

This is in addition to the copy of the resolution itself that is required to be delivered to the registrar under Chapter 3 of Part 3.

(2) The statement of capital must state with respect to the company's share capital as reduced by the resolution—
- (a) the total number of shares of the company,
- (b) the aggregate nominal value of those shares,
- (c) for each class of shares—
  - (i) prescribed particulars of the rights attached to the shares,
  - (ii) the total number of shares of that class, and
  - (iii) the aggregate nominal value of shares of that class, and
- (d) the amount paid up and the amount (if any) unpaid on each share (whether on account of the nominal value of the share or by way of premium).

(3) The registrar must register the documents delivered to him under subsection (1) on receipt.

(4) The resolution does not take effect until those documents are registered.

(5) The company must also deliver to the registrar, within 15 days after the resolution is passed, a statement by the directors confirming that the solvency statement was—
- (a) made not more than 15 days before the date on which the resolution was passed, and
- (b) provided to members in accordance with section 642(2) or (3).

(6) The validity of a resolution is not affected by—
- (a) a failure to deliver the documents required to be delivered to the registrar under subsection (1) within the time specified in that subsection, or
- (b) a failure to comply with subsection (5).

(7) If the company delivers to the registrar a solvency statement that was not provided to members in accordance with section 642(2) or (3), an offence is committed by every officer of the company who is in default.

(8) If default is made in complying with this section, an offence is committed by—
- (a) the company, and
- (b) every officer of the company who is in default.

(9) A person guilty of an offence under subsection (7) or (8) is liable—

(a) on conviction on indictment, to a fine;

(b) on summary conviction, to a fine not exceeding the statutory maximum.

[S644]

NOTES

Commencement: 20 January 2007 (for the purpose of enabling the exercise of powers to make Orders or Regulations by statutory instrument); to be appointed (otherwise).

Reduction of capital confirmed by the court

645 Application to court for order of confirmation

(1) Where a company has passed a resolution for reducing share capital, it may apply to the court for an order confirming the reduction.

(2) If the proposed reduction of capital involves either—

(a) diminution of liability in respect of unpaid share capital, or

(b) the payment to a shareholder of any paid-up share capital,

section 646 (creditors entitled to object to reduction) applies unless the court directs otherwise.

(3) The court may, if having regard to any special circumstances of the case it thinks proper to do so, direct that section 646 is not to apply as regards any class or classes of creditors.

(4) The court may direct that section 646 is to apply in any other case.

[S645]

NOTES

Commencement: to be appointed.

646 Creditors entitled to object to reduction

(1) Where this section applies (see section 645(2) and (4)), every creditor of the company who at the date fixed by the court is entitled to any debt or claim that, if that date were the commencement of the winding up of the company would be admissible in proof against the company, is entitled to object to the reduction of capital.

(2) The court shall settle a list of creditors entitled to object.

(3) For that purpose the court—

(a) shall ascertain, as far as possible without requiring an application from any creditor, the names of those creditors and the nature and amount of their debts or claims, and

(b) may publish notices fixing a day or days within which creditors not entered on the list are to claim to be so entered or are to be excluded from the right of objecting to the reduction of capital.

(4) If a creditor entered on the list whose debt or claim is not discharged or has not determined does not consent to the reduction, the court may, if it thinks fit, dispense with the consent of that creditor on the company securing payment of his debt or claim.

(5) For this purpose the debt or claim must be secured by appropriating (as the court may direct) the following amount—

(a) if the company admits the full amount of the debt or claim or, though not admitting it, is willing to provide for it, the full amount of the debt or claim;

(b) if the company does not admit, and is not willing to provide for, the full amount of the debt or claim, or if the amount is contingent or not ascertained, an amount fixed by the court after the like enquiry and adjudication as if the company were being wound up by the court.

[S646]

NOTES

Commencement: to be appointed.

647 Offences in connection with list of creditors

(1) If an officer of the company—

(a) intentionally or recklessly—

(i) conceals the name of a creditor entitled to object to the reduction of capital, or

(ii) misrepresents the nature or amount of the debt or claim of a creditor, or

(b) is knowingly concerned in any such concealment or misrepresentation,

he commits an offence.

(2) A person guilty of an offence under this section is liable—

(a) on conviction on indictment, to a fine;

(b) on summary conviction, to a fine not exceeding the statutory maximum.

[S647]

NOTES

Commencement: to be appointed.

648 Court order confirming reduction

(1) The court may make an order confirming the reduction of capital on such terms and conditions as it thinks fit.

(2) The court must not confirm the reduction unless it is satisfied, with respect to every creditor of the company who is entitled to object to the reduction of capital that either—

(a) his consent to the reduction has been obtained, or

(b) his debt or claim has been discharged, or has determined or has been secured.

(3) Where the court confirms the reduction, it may order the company to publish (as the court directs) the reasons for reduction of capital, or such other information in regard to it as the court thinks expedient with a view to giving proper information to the public, and (if the court thinks fit) the causes that led to the reduction.

(4) The court may, if for any special reason it thinks proper to do so, make an order directing that the company must, during such period (commencing on or at any time after the date of the order) as is specified in the order, add to its name as its last words the words "and reduced".

If such an order is made, those words are, until the end of the period specified in the order, deemed to be part of the company's name.

[S648]

NOTES

Commencement: to be appointed.

649 Registration of order and statement of capital

(1) The registrar, on production of an order of the court confirming the reduction of a company's share capital and the delivery of a copy of the order and of a statement of capital (approved by the court), shall register the order and statement.

This is subject to section 650 (public company reducing capital below authorised minimum).

(2) The statement of capital must state with respect to the company's share capital as altered by the order—

(a) the total number of shares of the company,

(b) the aggregate nominal value of those shares,

(c) for each class of shares—

(i) prescribed particulars of the rights attached to the shares,

(ii) the total number of shares of that class, and

(iii) the aggregate nominal value of shares of that class, and

(d) the amount paid up and the amount (if any) unpaid on each share (whether on account of the nominal value of the share or by way of premium).

(3) The resolution for reducing share capital, as confirmed by the court's order, takes effect—

(a) in the case of a reduction of share capital that forms part of a compromise or arrangement sanctioned by the court under Part 26 (arrangements and reconstructions)—
   (i) on delivery of the order and statement of capital to the registrar, or
   (ii) if the court so orders, on the registration of the order and statement of capital;

(b) in any other case, on the registration of the order and statement of capital.

(4) Notice of the registration of the order and statement of capital must be published in such manner as the court may direct.

(5) The registrar must certify the registration of the order and statement of capital.

(6) The certificate—

(a) must be signed by the registrar or authenticated by the registrar's official seal, and

(b) is conclusive evidence—
   (i) that the requirements of this Act with respect to the reduction of share capital have been complied with, and
   (ii) that the company's share capital is as stated in the statement of capital.

[S649]

NOTES

Commencement: 20 January 2007 (for the purpose of enabling the exercise of powers to make Orders or Regulations by statutory instrument); to be appointed (otherwise).

Public company reducing capital below authorised minimum

650 Public company reducing capital below authorised minimum

(1) This section applies where the court makes an order confirming a reduction of a public company's capital that has the effect of bringing the nominal value of its allotted share capital below the authorised minimum.

(2) The registrar must not register the order unless either—

(a) the court so directs, or

(b) the company is first re-registered as a private company.

(3) Section 651 provides an expedited procedure for re-registration in these circumstances.

[S650]

NOTES

Commencement: to be appointed.

651 Expedited procedure for re-registration as a private company

(1) The court may authorise the company to be re-registered as a private company without its having passed the special resolution required by section 97.

(2) If it does so, the court must specify in the order the changes to the company's name and articles to be made in connection with the re-registration.

(3) The company may then be re-registered as a private company if an application to that effect is delivered to the registrar together with—

(a) a copy of the court's order, and

(b) notice of the company's name, and a copy of the company's articles, as altered by the court's order.

(4) On receipt of such an application the registrar must issue a certificate of incorporation altered to meet the circumstances of the case.

(5) The certificate must state that it is issued on re-registration and the date on which it is issued.

(6) On the issue of the certificate—

(a) the company by virtue of the issue of the certificate becomes a private company, and

(b) the changes in the company's name and articles take effect.

(7) The certificate is conclusive evidence that the requirements of this Act as to re-registration have been complied with.

[S651]

NOTES

Commencement: to be appointed.

Effect of reduction of capital

652 Liability of members following reduction of capital

(1) Where a company's share capital is reduced a member of the company (past or present) is not liable in respect of any share to any call or contribution exceeding in amount the difference (if any) between—

(a) the nominal amount of the share as notified to the registrar in the statement of capital delivered under section 644 or 649, and

(b) the amount paid on the share or the reduced amount (if any) which is deemed to have been paid on it, as the case may be.

(2) This is subject to section 653 (liability to creditor in case of omission from list).

(3) Nothing in this section affects the rights of the contributories among themselves.

[S652]

NOTES

Commencement: to be appointed.

653 Liability to creditor in case of omission from list of creditors

(1) This section applies where, in the case of a reduction of capital confirmed by the court—

(a) a creditor entitled to object to the reduction of share capital is by reason of his ignorance—

(i) of the proceedings for reduction of share capital, or

(ii) of their nature and effect with respect to his debt or claim,

not entered on the list of creditors, and

(b) after the reduction of capital the company is unable to pay the amount of his debt or claim.

(2) Every person who was a member of the company at the date on which the resolution for reducing capital took effect under section 649(3) is liable to contribute for the payment of the debt or claim an amount not exceeding that which he would have been liable to contribute if the company had commenced to be wound up on the day before that date.

(3) If the company is wound up, the court on the application of the creditor in question, and proof of ignorance as mentioned in subsection (1)(a), may if it thinks fit—

(a) settle accordingly a list of persons liable to contribute under this section, and

(b) make and enforce calls and orders on them as if they were ordinary contributories in a winding up.

(4) The reference in subsection (1)(b) to a company being unable to pay the amount of a debt or claim has the same meaning as in section 123 of the Insolvency Act 1986 (c 45) or Article 103 of the Insolvency (Northern Ireland) Order 1989 (SI 1989/2405 (NI 19)).

[S653]

NOTES

Commencement: to be appointed.

CHAPTER 11
MISCELLANEOUS AND SUPPLEMENTARY PROVISIONS

654 Treatment of reserve arising from reduction of capital

(1) A reserve arising from the reduction of a company's share capital is not distributable, subject to any provision made by order under this section.

PART I
COMPANIES LEGISLATION

(2) The Secretary of State may by order specify cases in which—
(a) the prohibition in subsection (1) does not apply, and
(b) the reserve is to be treated for the purposes of Part 23 (distributions) as a realised profit.

(3) An order under this section is subject to affirmative resolution procedure.

[S654]

NOTES

Commencement: 20 January 2007 (for the purpose of enabling the exercise of powers to make Orders or Regulations by statutory instrument); to be appointed (otherwise).

655 Shares no bar to damages against company

A person is not debarred from obtaining damages or other compensation from a company by reason only of his holding or having held shares in the company or any right to apply or subscribe for shares or to be included in the company's register of members in respect of shares.

[S655]

NOTES

Commencement: to be appointed.

656 Public companies: duty of directors to call meeting on serious loss of capital

(1) Where the net assets of a public company are half or less of its called-up share capital, the directors must call a general meeting of the company to consider whether any, and if so what, steps should be taken to deal with the situation.

(2) They must do so not later than 28 days from the earliest day on which that fact is known to a director of the company.

(3) The meeting must be convened for a date not later than 56 days from that day.

(4) If there is a failure to convene a meeting as required by this section, each of the directors of the company who—
(a) knowingly authorises or permits the failure, or
(b) after the period during which the meeting should have been convened, knowingly authorises or permits the failure to continue,
commits an offence.

(5) A person guilty of an offence under this section is liable—
(a) on conviction on indictment, to a fine;
(b) on summary conviction, to a fine not exceeding the statutory maximum.

(6) Nothing in this section authorises the consideration at a meeting convened in pursuance of subsection (1) of any matter that could not have been considered at that meeting apart from this section.

[S656]

NOTES

Commencement: to be appointed.

657 General power to make further provision by regulations

(1) The Secretary of State may by regulations modify the following provisions of this Part—

sections 552 and 553 (prohibited commissions, discounts and allowances),
Chapter 5 (payment for shares),
Chapter 6 (public companies: independent valuation of non-cash consideration),
Chapter 7 (share premiums),
sections 622 to 628 (redenomination of share capital),
Chapter 10 (reduction of capital), and
section 656 (public companies: duty of directors to call meeting on serious loss of capital).

(2) The regulations may—

(a) amend or repeal any of those provisions, or

(b) make such other provision as appears to the Secretary of State appropriate in place of any of those provisions.

(3) Regulations under this section may make consequential amendments or repeals in other provisions of this Act, or in other enactments.

(4) Regulations under this section are subject to affirmative resolution procedure.

[S657]

NOTES

Commencement: 20 January 2007 (for the purpose of enabling the exercise of powers to make Orders or Regulations by statutory instrument); to be appointed (otherwise).

PART 18
ACQUISITION BY LIMITED COMPANY OF ITS OWN SHARES

CHAPTER 1
GENERAL PROVISIONS

Introductory

658 General rule against limited company acquiring its own shares

(1) A limited company must not acquire its own shares, whether by purchase, subscription or otherwise, except in accordance with the provisions of this Part.

(2) If a company purports to act in contravention of this section—

(a) an offence is committed by—

(i) the company, and

(ii) every officer of the company who is in default, and

(b) the purported acquisition is void.

(3) A person guilty of an offence under this section is liable—

(a) on conviction on indictment, to imprisonment for a term not exceeding two years or a fine (or both);

(b) on summary conviction—

(i) in England and Wales, to imprisonment for a term not exceeding twelve months or a fine not exceeding the statutory maximum (or both);

(ii) in Scotland or Northern Ireland, to imprisonment for a term not exceeding six months or a fine not exceeding the statutory maximum (or both).

[S658]

NOTES

Commencement: to be appointed.

659 Exceptions to general rule

(1) A limited company may acquire any of its own fully paid shares otherwise than for valuable consideration.

(2) Section 658 does not prohibit—

(a) the acquisition of shares in a reduction of capital duly made;

(b) the purchase of shares in pursuance of an order of the court under—

(i) section 98 (application to court to cancel resolution for re-registration as a private company),

(ii) section 721(6) (powers of court on objection to redemption or purchase of shares out of capital),

(iii) section 759 (remedial order in case of breach of prohibition of public offers by private company), or

(iv) Part 30 (protection of members against unfair prejudice);

(c) the forfeiture of shares, or the acceptance of shares surrendered in lieu, in pursuance of the company's articles, for failure to pay any sum payable in respect of the shares.

[S659]

NOTES

Commencement: to be appointed.

Shares held by company's nominee

660 Treatment of shares held by nominee

(1) This section applies where shares in a limited company—
  (a) are taken by a subscriber to the memorandum as nominee of the company,
  (b) are issued to a nominee of the company, or
  (c) are acquired by a nominee of the company, partly paid up, from a third person.

(2) For all purposes—
  (a) the shares are to be treated as held by the nominee on his own account, and
  (b) the company is to be regarded as having no beneficial interest in them.

(3) This section does not apply—
  (a) to shares acquired otherwise than by subscription by a nominee of a public company, where—
    (i) a person acquires shares in the company with financial assistance given to him, directly or indirectly, by the company for the purpose of or in connection with the acquisition, and
    (ii) the company has a beneficial interest in the shares;
  (b) to shares acquired by a nominee of the company when the company has no beneficial interest in the shares.

[S660]

NOTES

Commencement: to be appointed.

661 Liability of others where nominee fails to make payment in respect of shares

(1) This section applies where shares in a limited company—
  (a) are taken by a subscriber to the memorandum as nominee of the company,
  (b) are issued to a nominee of the company, or
  (c) are acquired by a nominee of the company, partly paid up, from a third person.

(2) If the nominee, having been called on to pay any amount for the purposes of paying up, or paying any premium on, the shares, fails to pay that amount within 21 days from being called on to do so, then—
  (a) in the case of shares that he agreed to take as subscriber to the memorandum, the other subscribers to the memorandum, and
  (b) in any other case, the directors of the company when the shares were issued to or acquired by him,

are jointly and severally liable with him to pay that amount.

(3) If in proceedings for the recovery of an amount under subsection (2) it appears to the court that the subscriber or director—
  (a) has acted honestly and reasonably, and
  (b) having regard to all the circumstances of the case, ought fairly to be relieved from liability,

the court may relieve him, either wholly or in part, from his liability on such terms as the court thinks fit.

(4) If a subscriber to a company's memorandum or a director of a company has reason to apprehend that a claim will or might be made for the recovery of any such amount from him—
  (a) he may apply to the court for relief, and
  (b) the court has the same power to relieve him as it would have had in proceedings for recovery of that amount.

(5) This section does not apply to shares acquired by a nominee of the company when the company has no beneficial interest in the shares.

[S661]

NOTES

Commencement: to be appointed.

Shares held by or for public company

662 Duty to cancel shares in public company held by or for the company

(1) This section applies in the case of a public company—

(a) where shares in the company are forfeited, or surrendered to the company in lieu of forfeiture, in pursuance of the articles, for failure to pay any sum payable in respect of the shares;

(b) where shares in the company are surrendered to the company in pursuance of section 102C(1)(b) of the Building Societies Act 1986 (c 53);

(c) where shares in the company are acquired by it (otherwise than in accordance with this Part or Part 30 (protection of members against unfair prejudice)) and the company has a beneficial interest in the shares;

(d) where a nominee of the company acquires shares in the company from a third party without financial assistance being given directly or indirectly by the company and the company has a beneficial interest in the shares; or

(e) where a person acquires shares in the company, with financial assistance given to him, directly or indirectly, by the company for the purpose of or in connection with the acquisition, and the company has a beneficial interest in the shares.

(2) Unless the shares or any interest of the company in them are previously disposed of, the company must—

(a) cancel the shares and diminish the amount of the company's share capital by the nominal value of the shares cancelled, and

(b) where the effect is that the nominal value of the company's allotted share capital is brought below the authorised minimum, apply for re-registration as a private company, stating the effect of the cancellation.

(3) It must do so no later than—

(a) in a case within subsection (1)(a) or (b), three years from the date of the forfeiture or surrender;

(b) in a case within subsection (1)(c) or (d), three years from the date of the acquisition;

(c) in a case within subsection (1)(e), one year from the date of the acquisition.

(4) The directors of the company may take any steps necessary to enable the company to comply with this section, and may do so without complying with the provisions of Chapter 10 of Part 17 (reduction of capital).

See also section 664 (re-registration as private company in consequence of cancellation).

(5) Neither the company nor, in a case within subsection (1)(d) or (e), the nominee or other shareholder may exercise any voting rights in respect of the shares.

(6) Any purported exercise of those rights is void.

[S662]

NOTES

Commencement: to be appointed.

663 Notice of cancellation of shares

(1) Where a company cancels shares in order to comply with section 662, it must within one month after the shares are cancelled give notice to the registrar, specifying the shares cancelled.

(2) The notice must be accompanied by a statement of capital.

(3) The statement of capital must state with respect to the company's share capital immediately following the cancellation—
(a) the total number of shares of the company,
(b) the aggregate nominal value of those shares,
(c) for each class of shares—
(i) prescribed particulars of the rights attached to the shares,
(ii) the total number of shares of that class, and
(iii) the aggregate nominal value of shares of that class, and
(d) the amount paid up and the amount (if any) unpaid on each share (whether on account of the nominal value of the share or by way of premium).

(4) If default is made in complying with this section, an offence is committed by—
(a) the company, and
(b) every officer of the company who is in default.

(5) A person guilty of an offence under this section is liable on summary conviction to a fine not exceeding level 3 on the standard scale and, for continued contravention, a daily default fine not exceeding one-tenth of level 3 on the standard scale.

[S663]

NOTES

Commencement: 20 January 2007 (for the purpose of enabling the exercise of powers to make Orders or Regulations by statutory instrument); to be appointed (otherwise).

664 Re-registration as private company in consequence of cancellation

(1) Where a company is obliged to re-register as a private company to comply with section 662, the directors may resolve that the company should be so re-registered.

Chapter 3 of Part 3 (resolutions affecting a company's constitution) applies to any such resolution.

(2) The resolution may make such changes—
(a) in the company's name, and
(b) in the company's articles,
as are necessary in connection with its becoming a private company.

(3) The application for re-registration must contain a statement of the company's proposed name on re-registration.

(4) The application must be accompanied by—
(a) a copy of the resolution (unless a copy has already been forwarded under Chapter 3 of Part 3),
(b) a copy of the company's articles as amended by the resolution, and
(c) a statement of compliance.

(5) The statement of compliance required is a statement that the requirements of this section as to re-registration as a private company have been complied with.

(6) The registrar may accept the statement of compliance as sufficient evidence that the company is entitled to be re-registered as a private company.

[S664]

NOTES

Commencement: to be appointed.

665 Issue of certificate of incorporation on re-registration

(1) If on an application under section 664 the registrar is satisfied that the company is entitled to be re-registered as a private company, the company shall be re-registered accordingly.

(2) The registrar must issue a certificate of incorporation altered to meet the circumstances of the case.

(3) The certificate must state that it is issued on re-registration and the date on which it is issued.

(4) On the issue of the certificate—

(a) the company by virtue of the issue of the certificate becomes a private company, and

(b) the changes in the company's name and articles take effect.

(5) The certificate is conclusive evidence that the requirements of this Act as to re-registration have been complied with.

[S665]

NOTES

Commencement: to be appointed.

666 Effect of failure to re-register

(1) If a public company that is required by section 662 to apply to be re-registered as a private company fails to do so before the end of the period specified in subsection (3) of that section, Chapter 1 of Part 20 (prohibition of public offers by private company) applies to it as if it were a private company.

(2) Subject to that, the company continues to be treated as a public company until it is so re-registered.

[S666]

NOTES

Commencement: to be appointed.

667 Offence in case of failure to cancel shares or re-register

(1) This section applies where a company, when required to do by section 662—

(a) fails to cancel any shares, or

(b) fails to make an application for re-registration as a private company,

within the time specified in subsection (3) of that section.

(2) An offence is committed by—

(a) the company, and

(b) every officer of the company who is in default.

(3) A person guilty of an offence under this section is liable on summary conviction to a fine not exceeding level 3 on the standard scale and, for continued contravention, a daily default fine not exceeding one-tenth of level 3 on the standard scale.

[S667]

NOTES

Commencement: to be appointed.

668 Application of provisions to company re-registering as public company

(1) This section applies where, after shares in a private company—

(a) are forfeited in pursuance of the company's articles or are surrendered to the company in lieu of forfeiture,

(b) are acquired by the company (otherwise than by any of the methods permitted by this Part or Part 30 (protection of members against unfair prejudice)), the company having a beneficial interest in the shares,

(c) are acquired by a nominee of the company from a third party without financial assistance being given directly or indirectly by the company, the company having a beneficial interest in the shares, or

(d) are acquired by a person with financial assistance given to him, directly or indirectly, by the company for the purpose of or in connection with the acquisition, the company having a beneficial interest in the shares,

the company is re-registered as a public company.

(2) In that case the provisions of sections 662 to 667 apply to the company as if it had been a public company at the time of the forfeiture, surrender or acquisition, subject to the following modification.

(3) The modification is that the period specified in section 662(3)(a), (b) or (c) (period for complying with obligations under that section) runs from the date of the re-registration of the company as a public company.

[S668]

NOTES

Commencement: to be appointed.

669 Transfer to reserve on acquisition of shares by public company or nominee

(1) Where—

(a) a public company, or a nominee of a public company, acquires shares in the company, and

(b) those shares are shown in a balance sheet of the company as an asset,

an amount equal to the value of the shares must be transferred out of profits available for dividend to a reserve fund and is not then available for distribution.

(2) Subsection (1) applies to an interest in shares as it applies to shares.

As it so applies the reference to the value of the shares shall be read as a reference to the value to the company of its interest in the shares.

[S669]

NOTES

Commencement: to be appointed.

Charges of public company on own shares

670 Public companies: general rule against lien or charge on own shares

(1) A lien or other charge of a public company on its own shares (whether taken expressly or otherwise) is void, except as permitted by this section.

(2) In the case of any description of company, a charge is permitted if the shares are not fully paid up and the charge is for an amount payable in respect of the shares.

(3) In the case of a company whose ordinary business—

(a) includes the lending of money, or

(b) consists of the provision of credit or the bailment (in Scotland, hiring) of goods under a hire-purchase agreement, or both,

a charge is permitted (whether the shares are fully paid or not) if it arises in connection with a transaction entered into by the company in the ordinary course of that business.

(4) In the case of a company that has been re-registered as a public company, a charge is permitted if it was in existence immediately before the application for re-registration.

[S670]

NOTES

Commencement: to be appointed.

Supplementary provisions

671 Interests to be disregarded in determining whether company has beneficial interest

In determining for the purposes of this Chapter whether a company has a beneficial interest in shares, there shall be disregarded any such interest as is mentioned in—

section 672 (residual interest under pension scheme or employees' share scheme),
section 673 (employer's charges and other rights of recovery), or
section 674 (rights as personal representative or trustee).

[S671]

NOTES

Commencement: to be appointed.

672 Residual interest under pension scheme or employees' share scheme

(1) Where the shares are held on trust for the purposes of a pension scheme or employees' share scheme, there shall be disregarded any residual interest of the company that has not vested in possession.

(2) A "residual interest" means a right of the company to receive any of the trust property in the event of—

- (a) all the liabilities arising under the scheme having been satisfied or provided for, or
- (b) the company ceasing to participate in the scheme, or
- (c) the trust property at any time exceeding what is necessary for satisfying the liabilities arising or expected to arise under the scheme.

(3) In subsection (2)—

- (a) the reference to a right includes a right dependent on the exercise of a discretion vested by the scheme in the trustee or another person, and
- (b) the reference to liabilities arising under a scheme includes liabilities that have resulted, or may result, from the exercise of any such discretion.

(4) For the purposes of this section a residual interest vests in possession—

- (a) in a case within subsection (2)(a), on the occurrence of the event mentioned there (whether or not the amount of the property receivable pursuant to the right is ascertained);
- (b) in a case within subsection (2)(b) or (c), when the company becomes entitled to require the trustee to transfer to it any of the property receivable pursuant to that right.

(5) Where by virtue of this section shares are exempt from section 660 or 661 (shares held by company's nominee) at the time they are taken, issued or acquired but the residual interest in question vests in possession before they are disposed of or fully paid up, those sections apply to the shares as if they had been taken, issued or acquired on the date on which that interest vests in possession.

(6) Where by virtue of this section shares are exempt from sections 662 to 668 (shares held by or for public company) at the time they are acquired but the residual interest in question vests in possession before they are disposed of, those sections apply to the shares as if they had been acquired on the date on which the interest vests in possession.

[S672]

NOTES

Commencement: to be appointed.

673 Employer's charges and other rights of recovery

(1) Where the shares are held on trust for the purposes of a pension scheme there shall be disregarded—

- (a) any charge or lien on, or set-off against, any benefit or other right or interest under the scheme for the purpose of enabling the employer or former employer of a member of the scheme to obtain the discharge of a monetary obligation due to him from the member;
- (b) any right to receive from the trustee of the scheme, or as trustee of the scheme to retain, an amount that can be recovered or retained—
  - (i) under section 61 of the Pension Schemes Act 1993 (c 48), or otherwise, as reimbursement or partial reimbursement for any contributions equivalent premium paid in connection with the scheme under Part 3 of that Act, or
  - (ii) under section 57 of the Pension Schemes (Northern Ireland) Act 1993 (c 49), or otherwise, as reimbursement or partial reimbursement for any contributions equivalent premium paid in connection with the scheme under Part 3 of that Act.

(2) Where the shares are held on trust for the purposes of an employees' share scheme, there shall be disregarded any charge or lien on, or set-off against, any benefit or other right or interest under the scheme for the purpose of enabling the employer or former employer of a member of the scheme to obtain the discharge of a monetary obligation due to him from the member.

[S673]

NOTES

Commencement: to be appointed.

674 Rights as personal representative or trustee

Where the company is a personal representative or trustee, there shall be disregarded any rights that the company has in that capacity including, in particular—

(a) any right to recover its expenses or be remunerated out of the estate or trust property, and

(b) any right to be indemnified out of that property for any liability incurred by reason of any act or omission of the company in the performance of its duties as personal representative or trustee.

[S674]

NOTES

Commencement: to be appointed.

675 Meaning of "pension scheme"

(1) In this Chapter "pension scheme" means a scheme for the provision of benefits consisting of or including relevant benefits for or in respect of employees or former employees.

(2) In subsection (1) "relevant benefits" means any pension, lump sum, gratuity or other like benefit given or to be given on retirement or on death or in anticipation of retirement or, in connection with past service, after retirement or death.

[S675]

NOTES

Commencement: to be appointed.

676 Application of provisions to directors

For the purposes of this Chapter references to "employer" and "employee", in the context of a pension scheme or employees' share scheme, shall be read as if a director of a company were employed by it.

[S676]

NOTES

Commencement: to be appointed.

CHAPTER 2
FINANCIAL ASSISTANCE FOR PURCHASE OF OWN SHARES

Introductory

677 Meaning of "financial assistance"

(1) In this Chapter "financial assistance" means—

(a) financial assistance given by way of gift,

(b) financial assistance given—

(i) by way of guarantee, security or indemnity (other than an indemnity in respect of the indemnifier's own neglect or default), or

(ii) by way of release or waiver,

(c) financial assistance given—

(i) by way of a loan or any other agreement under which any of the obligations of the person giving the assistance are to be fulfilled at a time when in accordance with the agreement any obligation of another party to the agreement remains unfulfilled, or

(ii) by way of the novation of, or the assignment (in Scotland, assignation) of rights arising under, a loan or such other agreement, or

(d) any other financial assistance given by a company where—
  (i) the net assets of the company are reduced to a material extent by the giving of the assistance, or
  (ii) the company has no net assets.

(2) "Net assets" here means the aggregate amount of the company's assets less the aggregate amount of its liabilities.

(3) For this purpose a company's liabilities include—

(a) where the company draws up Companies Act individual accounts, any provision of a kind specified for the purposes of this subsection by regulations under section 396, and

(b) where the company draws up IAS individual accounts, any provision made in those accounts.

[S677]

NOTES

Commencement: to be appointed.

Circumstances in which financial assistance prohibited

678 Assistance for acquisition of shares in public company

(1) Where a person is acquiring or proposing to acquire shares in a public company, it is not lawful for that company, or a company that is a subsidiary of that company, to give financial assistance directly or indirectly for the purpose of the acquisition before or at the same time as the acquisition takes place.

(2) Subsection (1) does not prohibit a company from giving financial assistance for the acquisition of shares in it or its holding company if—

(a) the company's principal purpose in giving the assistance is not to give it for the purpose of any such acquisition, or

(b) the giving of the assistance for that purpose is only an incidental part of some larger purpose of the company,

and the assistance is given in good faith in the interests of the company.

(3) Where—

(a) a person has acquired shares in a company, and

(b) a liability has been incurred (by that or another person) for the purpose of the acquisition,

it is not lawful for that company, or a company that is a subsidiary of that company, to give financial assistance directly or indirectly for the purpose of reducing or discharging the liability if, at the time the assistance is given, the company in which the shares were acquired is a public company.

(4) Subsection (3) does not prohibit a company from giving financial assistance if—

(a) the company's principal purpose in giving the assistance is not to reduce or discharge any liability incurred by a person for the purpose of the acquisition of shares in the company or its holding company, or

(b) the reduction or discharge of any such liability is only an incidental part of some larger purpose of the company,

and the assistance is given in good faith in the interests of the company.

(5) This section has effect subject to sections 681 and 682 (unconditional and conditional exceptions to prohibition).

[S678]

NOTES

Commencement: to be appointed.

679 Assistance by public company for acquisition of shares in its private holding company

(1) Where a person is acquiring or proposing to acquire shares in a private company, it is not lawful for a public company that is a subsidiary of that company to give financial assistance directly or indirectly for the purpose of the acquisition before or at the same time as the acquisition takes place.

(2) Subsection (1) does not prohibit a company from giving financial assistance for the acquisition of shares in its holding company if—

(a) the company's principal purpose in giving the assistance is not to give it for the purpose of any such acquisition, or

(b) the giving of the assistance for that purpose is only an incidental part of some larger purpose of the company,

and the assistance is given in good faith in the interests of the company.

(3) Where—

(a) a person has acquired shares in a private company, and

(b) a liability has been incurred (by that or another person) for the purpose of the acquisition,

it is not lawful for a public company that is a subsidiary of that company to give financial assistance directly or indirectly for the purpose of reducing or discharging the liability.

(4) Subsection (3) does not prohibit a company from giving financial assistance if—

(a) the company's principal purpose in giving the assistance is not to reduce or discharge any liability incurred by a person for the purpose of the acquisition of shares in its holding company, or

(b) the reduction or discharge of any such liability is only an incidental part of some larger purpose of the company,

and the assistance is given in good faith in the interests of the company.

(5) This section has effect subject to sections 681 and 682 (unconditional and conditional exceptions to prohibition).

[S679]

NOTES

Commencement: to be appointed.

680 Prohibited financial assistance an offence

(1) If a company contravenes section 678(1) or (3) or section 679(1) or (3) (prohibited financial assistance) an offence is committed by—

(a) the company, and

(b) every officer of the company who is in default.

(2) A person guilty of an offence under this section is liable—

(a) on conviction on indictment, to imprisonment for a term not exceeding two years or a fine (or both);

(b) on summary conviction—

(i) in England and Wales, to imprisonment for a term not exceeding twelve months or to a fine not exceeding the statutory maximum (or both);

(ii) in Scotland or Northern Ireland, to imprisonment for a term not exceeding six months, or to a fine not exceeding the statutory maximum (or both).

[S680]

NOTES

Commencement: to be appointed.

Exceptions from prohibition

681 Unconditional exceptions

(1) Neither section 678 nor section 679 prohibits a transaction to which this section applies.

(2) Those transactions are—
(a) a distribution of the company's assets by way of—
(i) dividend lawfully made, or
(ii) distribution in the course of a company's winding up;
(b) an allotment of bonus shares;
(c) a reduction of capital under Chapter 10 of Part 17;
(d) a redemption of shares under Chapter 3 or a purchase of shares under Chapter 4 of this Part;
(e) anything done in pursuance of an order of the court under Part 26 (order sanctioning compromise or arrangement with members or creditors);
(f) anything done under an arrangement made in pursuance of section 110 of the Insolvency Act 1986 (c 45) or Article 96 of the Insolvency (Northern Ireland) Order 1989 (SI 1989/2405 (NI 19)) (liquidator in winding up accepting shares as consideration for sale of company's property);
(g) anything done under an arrangement made between a company and its creditors that is binding on the creditors by virtue of Part 1 of the Insolvency Act 1986 or Part 2 of the Insolvency (Northern Ireland) Order 1989 (SI 1989/2405 (NI 19)).

[S681]

NOTES

Commencement: to be appointed.

682 Conditional exceptions

(1) Neither section 678 nor section 679 prohibits a transaction to which this section applies—
(a) if the company giving the assistance is a private company, or
(b) if the company giving the assistance is a public company and—
(i) the company has net assets that are not reduced by the giving of the assistance, or
(ii) to the extent that those assets are so reduced, the assistance is provided out of distributable profits.

(2) The transactions to which this section applies are—
(a) where the lending of money is part of the ordinary business of the company, the lending of money in the ordinary course of the company's business;
(b) the provision by the company, in good faith in the interests of the company or its holding company, of financial assistance for the purposes of an employees' share scheme;
(c) the provision of financial assistance by the company for the purposes of or in connection with anything done by the company (or another company in the same group) for the purpose of enabling or facilitating transactions in shares in the first-mentioned company or its holding company between, and involving the acquisition of beneficial ownership of those shares by—
(i) bona fide employees or former employees of that company (or another company in the same group), or
(ii) spouses or civil partners, widows, widowers or surviving civil partners, or minor children or step-children of any such employees or former employees;
(d) the making by the company of loans to persons (other than directors) employed in good faith by the company with a view to enabling those persons to acquire fully paid shares in the company or its holding company to be held by them by way of beneficial ownership.

(3) The references in this section to "net assets" are to the amount by which the aggregate of the company's assets exceeds the aggregate of its liabilities.

(4) For this purpose—
(a) the amount of both assets and liabilities shall be taken to be as stated in the company's accounting records immediately before the financial assistance is given, and
(b) "liabilities" includes any amount retained as reasonably necessary for the purpose of providing for a liability the nature of which is clearly defined and that is either likely to be incurred or certain to be incurred but uncertain as to amount or as to the date on which it will arise.

(5) For the purposes of subsection (2)(c) a company is in the same group as another company if it is a holding company or subsidiary of that company or a subsidiary of a holding company of that company.

[S682]

NOTES

Commencement: to be appointed.

Supplementary

683 Definitions for this Chapter

(1) In this Chapter—

"distributable profits", in relation to the giving of any financial assistance—

(a) means those profits out of which the company could lawfully make a distribution equal in value to that assistance, and

(b) includes, in a case where the financial assistance consists of or includes, or is treated as arising in consequence of, the sale, transfer or other disposition of a non-cash asset, any profit that, if the company were to make a distribution of that character would be available for that purpose (see section 846); and

"distribution" has the same meaning as in Part 23 (distributions) (see section 829).

(2) In this Chapter—

(a) a reference to a person incurring a liability includes his changing his financial position by making an agreement or arrangement (whether enforceable or unenforceable, and whether made on his own account or with any other person) or by any other means, and

(b) a reference to a company giving financial assistance for the purposes of reducing or discharging a liability incurred by a person for the purpose of the acquisition of shares includes its giving such assistance for the purpose of wholly or partly restoring his financial position to what it was before the acquisition took place.

[S683]

NOTES

Commencement: to be appointed.

CHAPTER 3
REDEEMABLE SHARES

684 Power of limited company to issue redeemable shares

(1) A limited company having a share capital may issue shares that are to be redeemed or are liable to be redeemed at the option of the company or the shareholder ("redeemable shares"), subject to the following provisions.

(2) The articles of a private limited company may exclude or restrict the issue of redeemable shares.

(3) A public limited company may only issue redeemable shares if it is authorised to do so by its articles.

(4) No redeemable shares may be issued at a time when there are no issued shares of the company that are not redeemable.

[S684]

NOTES

Commencement: to be appointed.

685 Terms and manner of redemption

(1) The directors of a limited company may determine the terms, conditions and manner of redemption of shares if they are authorised to do so—

(a) by the company's articles, or

(b) by a resolution of the company.

(2) A resolution under subsection (1)(b) may be an ordinary resolution, even though it amends the company's articles.

(3) Where the directors are authorised under subsection (1) to determine the terms, conditions and manner of redemption of shares—

(a) they must do so before the shares are allotted, and

(b) any obligation of the company to state in a statement of capital the rights attached to the shares extends to the terms, conditions and manner of redemption.

(4) Where the directors are not so authorised, the terms, conditions and manner of redemption of any redeemable shares must be stated in the company's articles.

[S685]

NOTES

Commencement: to be appointed.

686 Payment for redeemable shares

(1) Redeemable shares in a limited company may not be redeemed unless they are fully paid.

(2) The terms of redemption of shares in a limited company may provide that the amount payable on redemption may, by agreement between the company and the holder of the shares, be paid on a date later than the redemption date.

(3) Unless redeemed in accordance with a provision authorised by subsection (2), the shares must be paid for on redemption.

[S686]

NOTES

Commencement: to be appointed.

687 Financing of redemption

(1) A private limited company may redeem redeemable shares out of capital in accordance with Chapter 5.

(2) Subject to that, redeemable shares in a limited company may only be redeemed out of—

(a) distributable profits of the company, or

(b) the proceeds of a fresh issue of shares made for the purposes of the redemption.

(3) Any premium payable on redemption of shares in a limited company must be paid out of distributable profits of the company, subject to the following provision.

(4) If the redeemable shares were issued at a premium, any premium payable on their redemption may be paid out of the proceeds of a fresh issue of shares made for the purposes of the redemption, up to an amount equal to—

(a) the aggregate of the premiums received by the company on the issue of the shares redeemed, or

(b) the current amount of the company's share premium account (including any sum transferred to that account in respect of premiums on the new shares),

whichever is the less.

(5) The amount of the company's share premium account is reduced by a sum corresponding (or by sums in the aggregate corresponding) to the amount of any payment made under subsection (4).

(6) This section is subject to section 735(4) (terms of redemption enforceable in a winding up).

[S687]

NOTES

Commencement: to be appointed.

688 Redeemed shares treated as cancelled

Where shares in a limited company are redeemed—
- (a) the shares are treated as cancelled, and
- (b) the amount of the company's issued share capital is diminished accordingly by the nominal value of the shares redeemed.

[S688]

NOTES

Commencement: to be appointed.

689 Notice to registrar of redemption

(1) If a limited company redeems any redeemable shares it must within one month after doing so give notice to the registrar, specifying the shares redeemed.

(2) The notice must be accompanied by a statement of capital.

(3) The statement of capital must state with respect to the company's share capital immediately following the redemption—
- (a) the total number of shares of the company,
- (b) the aggregate nominal value of those shares,
- (c) for each class of shares—
  - (i) prescribed particulars of the rights attached to the shares,
  - (ii) the total number of shares of that class, and
  - (iii) the aggregate nominal value of shares of that class, and
- (d) the amount paid up and the amount (if any) unpaid on each share (whether on account of the nominal value of the share or by way of premium).

(4) If default is made in complying with this section, an offence is committed by—
- (a) the company, and
- (b) every officer of the company who is in default.

(5) A person guilty of an offence under this section is liable on summary conviction to a fine not exceeding level 3 on the standard scale and, for continued contravention, a daily default fine not exceeding one-tenth of level 3 on the standard scale.

[S689]

NOTES

Commencement: 20 January 2007 (for the purpose of enabling the exercise of powers to make Orders or Regulations by statutory instrument); to be appointed (otherwise).

CHAPTER 4
PURCHASE OF OWN SHARES

General provisions

690 Power of limited company to purchase own shares

(1) A limited company having a share capital may purchase its own shares (including any redeemable shares), subject to—
- (a) the following provisions of this Chapter, and
- (b) any restriction or prohibition in the company's articles.

(2) A limited company may not purchase its own shares if as a result of the purchase there would no longer be any issued shares of the company other than redeemable shares or shares held as treasury shares.

[S690]

NOTES

Commencement: to be appointed.

691 Payment for purchase of own shares

(1) A limited company may not purchase its own shares unless they are fully paid.

(2) Where a limited company purchases its own shares, the shares must be paid for on purchase.

[S691]

NOTES
Commencement: to be appointed.

692 Financing of purchase of own shares

(1) A private limited company may purchase its own shares out of capital in accordance with Chapter 5.

(2) Subject to that—
- (a) a limited company may only purchase its own shares out of—
  - (i) distributable profits of the company, or
  - (ii) the proceeds of a fresh issue of shares made for the purpose of financing the purchase, and
- (b) any premium payable on the purchase by a limited company of its own shares must be paid out of distributable profits of the company, subject to subsection (3).

(3) If the shares to be purchased were issued at a premium, any premium payable on their purchase by the company may be paid out of the proceeds of a fresh issue of shares made for the purpose of financing the purchase, up to an amount equal to—
- (a) the aggregate of the premiums received by the company on the issue of the shares purchased, or
- (b) the current amount of the company's share premium account (including any sum transferred to that account in respect of premiums on the new shares),

whichever is the less.

(4) The amount of the company's share premium account is reduced by a sum corresponding (or by sums in the aggregate corresponding) to the amount of any payment made under subsection (3).

(5) This section has effect subject to section 735(4) (terms of purchase enforceable in a winding up).

[S692]

NOTES
Commencement: to be appointed.

Authority for purchase of own shares

693 Authority for purchase of own shares

(1) A limited company may only purchase its own shares—
- (a) by an off-market purchase, in pursuance of a contract approved in advance in accordance with section 694;
- (b) by a market purchase, authorised in accordance with section 701.

(2) A purchase is "off-market" if the shares either—
- (a) are purchased otherwise than on a recognised investment exchange, or
- (b) are purchased on a recognised investment exchange but are not subject to a marketing arrangement on the exchange.

(3) For this purpose a company's shares are subject to a marketing arrangement on a recognised investment exchange if—
- (a) they are listed under Part 6 of the Financial Services and Markets Act 2000 (c 8), or
- (b) the company has been afforded facilities for dealings in the shares to take place on the exchange—
  - (i) without prior permission for individual transactions from the authority governing that investment exchange, and
  - (ii) without limit as to the time during which those facilities are to be available.

(4) A purchase is a "market purchase" if it is made on a recognised investment exchange and is not an off-market purchase by virtue of subsection (2)(b).

(5) In this section "recognised investment exchange" means a recognised investment exchange (within the meaning of Part 18 of the Financial Services and Markets Act 2000) other than an overseas exchange (within the meaning of that Part).

[S693]

NOTES

Commencement: to be appointed.

Authority for off-market purchase

694 Authority for off-market purchase

(1) A company may only make an off-market purchase of its own shares in pursuance of a contract approved prior to the purchase in accordance with this section.

(2) Either—

(a) the terms of the contract must be authorised by a special resolution of the company before the contract is entered into, or

(b) the contract must provide that no shares may be purchased in pursuance of the contract until its terms have been authorised by a special resolution of the company.

(3) The contract may be a contract, entered into by the company and relating to shares in the company, that does not amount to a contract to purchase the shares but under which the company may (subject to any conditions) become entitled or obliged to purchase the shares.

(4) The authority conferred by a resolution under this section may be varied, revoked or from time to time renewed by a special resolution of the company.

(5) In the case of a public company a resolution conferring, varying or renewing authority must specify a date on which the authority is to expire, which must not be later than 18 months after the date on which the resolution is passed.

(6) A resolution conferring, varying, revoking or renewing authority under this section is subject to—

section 695 (exercise of voting rights), and

section 696 (disclosure of details of contract).

[S694]

NOTES

Commencement: to be appointed.

695 Resolution authorising off-market purchase: exercise of voting rights

(1) This section applies to a resolution to confer, vary, revoke or renew authority for the purposes of section 694 (authority for off-market purchase of own shares).

(2) Where the resolution is proposed as a written resolution, a member who holds shares to which the resolution relates is not an eligible member.

(3) Where the resolution is proposed at a meeting of the company, it is not effective if—

(a) any member of the company holding shares to which the resolution relates exercises the voting rights carried by any of those shares in voting on the resolution, and

(b) the resolution would not have been passed if he had not done so.

(4) For this purpose—

(a) a member who holds shares to which the resolution relates is regarded as exercising the voting rights carried by those shares not only if he votes in respect of them on a poll on the question whether the resolution shall be passed, but also if he votes on the resolution otherwise than on a poll;

(b) any member of the company may demand a poll on that question;

(c) a vote and a demand for a poll by a person as proxy for a member are the same respectively as a vote and a demand by the member.

[S695]

NOTES

Commencement: to be appointed.

696 Resolution authorising off-market purchase: disclosure of details of contract

(1) This section applies in relation to a resolution to confer, vary, revoke or renew authority for the purposes of section 694 (authority for off-market purchase of own shares).

(2) A copy of the contract (if it is in writing) or a memorandum setting out its terms (if it is not) must be made available to members—

- (a) in the case of a written resolution, by being sent or submitted to every eligible member at or before the time at which the proposed resolution is sent or submitted to him;
- (b) in the case of a resolution at a meeting, by being made available for inspection by members of the company both—
  - (i) at the company's registered office for not less than 15 days ending with the date of the meeting, and
  - (ii) at the meeting itself.

(3) A memorandum of contract terms so made available must include the names of the members holding shares to which the contract relates.

(4) A copy of the contract so made available must have annexed to it a written memorandum specifying such of those names as do not appear in the contract itself.

(5) The resolution is not validly passed if the requirements of this section are not complied with.

[S696]

NOTES

Commencement: to be appointed.

697 Variation of contract for off-market purchase

(1) A company may only agree to a variation of a contract authorised under section 694 (authority for off-market purchase) if the variation is approved in advance in accordance with this section.

(2) The terms of the variation must be authorised by a special resolution of the company before it is agreed to.

(3) That authority may be varied, revoked or from time to time renewed by a special resolution of the company.

(4) In the case of a public company a resolution conferring, varying or renewing authority must specify a date on which the authority is to expire, which must not be later than 18 months after the date on which the resolution is passed.

(5) A resolution conferring, varying, revoking or renewing authority under this section is subject to—

section 698 (exercise of voting rights), and

section 699 (disclosure of details of variation).

[S697]

NOTES

Commencement: to be appointed.

698 Resolution authorising variation: exercise of voting rights

(1) This section applies to a resolution to confer, vary, revoke or renew authority for the purposes of section 697 (variation of contract for off-market purchase of own shares).

(2) Where the resolution is proposed as a written resolution, a member who holds shares to which the resolution relates is not an eligible member.

(3) Where the resolution is proposed at a meeting of the company, it is not effective if—

(a) any member of the company holding shares to which the resolution relates exercises the voting rights carried by any of those shares in voting on the resolution, and

(b) the resolution would not have been passed if he had not done so.

(4) For this purpose—

(a) a member who holds shares to which the resolution relates is regarded as exercising the voting rights carried by those shares not only if he votes in respect of them on a poll on the question whether the resolution shall be passed, but also if he votes on the resolution otherwise than on a poll;

(b) any member of the company may demand a poll on that question;

(c) a vote and a demand for a poll by a person as proxy for a member are the same respectively as a vote and a demand by the member.

[S698]

NOTES

Commencement: to be appointed.

699 Resolution authorising variation: disclosure of details of variation

(1) This section applies in relation to a resolution under section 697 (variation of contract for off-market purchase of own shares).

(2) A copy of the proposed variation (if it is in writing) or a written memorandum giving details of the proposed variation (if it is not) must be made available to members—

(a) in the case of a written resolution, by being sent or submitted to every eligible member at or before the time at which the proposed resolution is sent or submitted to him;

(b) in the case of a resolution at a meeting, by being made available for inspection by members of the company both—

(i) at the company's registered office for not less than 15 days ending with the date of the meeting, and

(ii) at the meeting itself.

(3) There must also be made available as mentioned in subsection (2) a copy of the original contract or, as the case may be, a memorandum of its terms, together with any variations previously made.

(4) A memorandum of the proposed variation so made available must include the names of the members holding shares to which the variation relates.

(5) A copy of the proposed variation so made available must have annexed to it a written memorandum specifying such of those names as do not appear in the variation itself.

(6) The resolution is not validly passed if the requirements of this section are not complied with.

[S699]

NOTES

Commencement: to be appointed.

700 Release of company's rights under contract for off-market purchase

(1) An agreement by a company to release its rights under a contract approved under section 694 (authorisation of off-market purchase) is void unless the terms of the release agreement are approved in advance in accordance with this section.

(2) The terms of the proposed agreement must be authorised by a special resolution of the company before the agreement is entered into.

(3) That authority may be varied, revoked or from time to time renewed by a special resolution of the company.

(4) In the case of a public company a resolution conferring, varying or renewing authority must specify a date on which the authority is to expire, which must not be later than 18 months after the date on which the resolution is passed.

(5) The provisions of—

section 698 (exercise of voting rights), and
section 699 (disclosure of details of variation),

apply to a resolution authorising a proposed release agreement as they apply to a resolution authorising a proposed variation.

[S700]

NOTES

Commencement: to be appointed.

Authority for market purchase

701 Authority for market purchase

(1) A company may only make a market purchase of its own shares if the purchase has first been authorised by a resolution of the company.

(2) That authority—

(a) may be general or limited to the purchase of shares of a particular class or description, and

(b) may be unconditional or subject to conditions.

(3) The authority must—

(a) specify the maximum number of shares authorised to be acquired, and

(b) determine both the maximum and minimum prices that may be paid for the shares.

(4) The authority may be varied, revoked or from time to time renewed by a resolution of the company.

(5) A resolution conferring, varying or renewing authority must specify a date on which it is to expire, which must not be later than 18 months after the date on which the resolution is passed.

(6) A company may make a purchase of its own shares after the expiry of the time limit specified if—

(a) the contract of purchase was concluded before the authority expired, and

(b) the terms of the authority permitted the company to make a contract of purchase that would or might be executed wholly or partly after its expiration.

(7) A resolution to confer or vary authority under this section may determine either or both the maximum and minimum price for purchase by—

(a) specifying a particular sum, or

(b) providing a basis or formula for calculating the amount of the price (but without reference to any person's discretion or opinion).

(8) Chapter 3 of Part 3 (resolutions affecting a company's constitution) applies to a resolution under this section.

[S701]

NOTES

Commencement: to be appointed.

Supplementary provisions

702 Copy of contract or memorandum to be available for inspection

(1) This section applies where a company has entered into—

(a) a contract approved under section 694 (authorisation of contract for off-market purchase), or

(b) a contract for a purchase authorised under section 701 (authorisation of market purchase).

(2) The company must keep available for inspection—

(a) a copy of the contract, or

(b) if the contract is not in writing, a written memorandum setting out its terms.

(3) The copy or memorandum must be kept available for inspection from the conclusion of the contract until the end of the period of ten years beginning with—
- (a) the date on which the purchase of all the shares in pursuance of the contract is completed, or
- (b) the date on which the contract otherwise determines.

(4) The copy or memorandum must be kept available for inspection—
- (a) at the company's registered office, or
- (b) at a place specified in regulations under section 1136.

(5) The company must give notice to the registrar—
- (a) of the place at which the copy or memorandum is kept available for inspection, and
- (b) of any change in that place,

unless it has at all times been kept at the company's registered office.

(6) Every copy or memorandum required to be kept under this section must be kept open to inspection without charge—
- (a) by any member of the company, and
- (b) in the case of a public company, by any other person.

(7) The provisions of this section apply to a variation of a contract as they apply to the original contract.

[S702]

NOTES
Commencement: to be appointed.

703 Enforcement of right to inspect copy or memorandum

(1) If default is made in complying with section 702(2), (3) or (4) or default is made for 14 days in complying with section 702(5), or an inspection required under section 702(6) is refused, an offence is committed by—
- (a) the company, and
- (b) every officer of the company who is in default.

(2) A person guilty of an offence under this section is liable on summary conviction to a fine not exceeding level 3 on the standard scale and, for continued contravention, a daily default fine not exceeding one-tenth of level 3 on the standard scale.

(3) In the case of refusal of an inspection required under section 702(6) the court may by order compel an immediate inspection.

[S703]

NOTES
Commencement: to be appointed.

704 No assignment of company's right to purchase own shares

The rights of a company under a contract authorised under—
- (a) section 694 (authority for off-market purchase), or
- (b) section 701 (authority for market purchase)

are not capable of being assigned.

[S704]

NOTES
Commencement: to be appointed.

705 Payments apart from purchase price to be made out of distributable profits

(1) A payment made by a company in consideration of—
- (a) acquiring any right with respect to the purchase of its own shares in pursuance of a contingent purchase contract approved under section 694 (authorisation of off-market purchase),
- (b) the variation of any contract approved under that section, or

(c) the release of any of the company's obligations with respect to the purchase of any of its own shares under a contract—
  (i) approved under section 694, or
  (ii) authorised under section 701 (authorisation of market purchase),

must be made out of the company's distributable profits.

(2) If this requirement is not met in relation to a contract, then—
  (a) in a case within subsection (1)(a), no purchase by the company of its own shares in pursuance of that contract may be made under this Chapter;
  (b) in a case within subsection (1)(b), no such purchase following the variation may be made under this Chapter;
  (c) in a case within subsection (1)(c), the purported release is void.

[S705]

NOTES

Commencement: to be appointed.

706 Treatment of shares purchased

Where a limited company makes a purchase of its own shares in accordance with this Chapter, then—
  (a) if section 724 (treasury shares) applies, the shares may be held and dealt with in accordance with Chapter 6;
  (b) if that section does not apply—
    (i) the shares are treated as cancelled, and
    (ii) the amount of the company's issued share capital is diminished accordingly by the nominal value of the shares cancelled.

[S706]

NOTES

Commencement: to be appointed.

707 Return to registrar of purchase of own shares

(1) Where a company purchases shares under this Chapter, it must deliver a return to the registrar within the period of 28 days beginning with the date on which the shares are delivered to it.

(2) The return must distinguish—
  (a) shares in relation to which section 724 (treasury shares) applies and shares in relation to which that section does not apply, and
  (b) shares in relation to which that section applies—
    (i) that are cancelled forthwith (under section 729 (cancellation of treasury shares)), and
    (ii) that are not so cancelled.

(3) The return must state, with respect to shares of each class purchased—
  (a) the number and nominal value of the shares, and
  (b) the date on which they were delivered to the company.

(4) In the case of a public company the return must also state—
  (a) the aggregate amount paid by the company for the shares, and
  (b) the maximum and minimum prices paid in respect of shares of each class purchased.

(5) Particulars of shares delivered to the company on different dates and under different contracts may be included in a single return.

In such a case the amount required to be stated under subsection (4)(a) is the aggregate amount paid by the company for all the shares to which the return relates.

(6) If default is made in complying with this section an offence is committed by every officer of the company who is in default.

(7) A person guilty of an offence under this section is liable—
  (a) on conviction on indictment, to a fine;

(b) on summary conviction to a fine not exceeding the statutory maximum and, for continued contravention, a daily default fine not exceeding one-tenth of the statutory maximum.

[S707]

NOTES

Commencement: to be appointed.

708 Notice to registrar of cancellation of shares

(1) If on the purchase by a company of any of its own shares in accordance with this Part—

(a) section 724 (treasury shares) does not apply (so that the shares are treated as cancelled), or

(b) that section applies but the shares are cancelled forthwith (under section 729 (cancellation of treasury shares)),

the company must give notice of cancellation to the registrar, within the period of 28 days beginning with the date on which the shares are delivered to it, specifying the shares cancelled.

(2) The notice must be accompanied by a statement of capital.

(3) The statement of capital must state with respect to the company's share capital immediately following the cancellation—

(a) the total number of shares of the company,

(b) the aggregate nominal value of those shares,

(c) for each class of shares—

(i) prescribed particulars of the rights attached to the shares,

(ii) the total number of shares of that class, and

(iii) the aggregate nominal value of shares of that class, and

(d) the amount paid up and the amount (if any) unpaid on each share (whether on account of the nominal value of the share or by way of premium).

(4) If default is made in complying with this section, an offence is committed by—

(a) the company, and

(b) every officer of the company who is in default.

(5) A person guilty of an offence under this section is liable on summary conviction to a fine not exceeding level 3 on the standard scale and, for continued contravention, a daily default fine not exceeding one-tenth of level 3 on the standard scale.

[S708]

NOTES

Commencement: 20 January 2007 (for the purpose of enabling the exercise of powers to make Orders or Regulations by statutory instrument); to be appointed (otherwise).

CHAPTER 5
REDEMPTION OR PURCHASE BY PRIVATE COMPANY OUT OF CAPITAL

Introductory

709 Power of private limited company to redeem or purchase own shares out of capital

(1) A private limited company may in accordance with this Chapter, but subject to any restriction or prohibition in the company's articles, make a payment in respect of the redemption or purchase of its own shares otherwise than out of distributable profits or the proceeds of a fresh issue of shares.

(2) References below in this Chapter to payment out of capital are to any payment so made, whether or not it would be regarded apart from this section as a payment out of capital.

[S709]

NOTES

Commencement: to be appointed.

The permissible capital payment

710 The permissible capital payment

(1) The payment that may, in accordance with this Chapter, be made by a company out of capital in respect of the redemption or purchase of its own shares is such amount as, after applying for that purpose—

(a) any available profits of the company, and

(b) the proceeds of any fresh issue of shares made for the purposes of the redemption or purchase,

is required to meet the price of redemption or purchase.

(2) That is referred to below in this Chapter as "the permissible capital payment" for the shares.

[S710]

NOTES

Commencement: to be appointed.

711 Available profits

(1) For the purposes of this Chapter the available profits of the company, in relation to the redemption or purchase of any shares, are the profits of the company that are available for distribution (within the meaning of Part 23).

(2) But the question whether a company has any profits so available, and the amount of any such profits, shall be determined in accordance with section 712 instead of in accordance with sections 836 to 842 in that Part.

[S711]

NOTES

Commencement: to be appointed.

712 Determination of available profits

(1) The available profits of the company are determined as follows.

(2) First, determine the profits of the company by reference to the following items as stated in the relevant accounts—

(a) profits, losses, assets and liabilities,

(b) provisions of the following kinds—

(i) where the relevant accounts are Companies Act accounts, provisions of a kind specified for the purposes of this subsection by regulations under section 396;

(ii) where the relevant accounts are IAS accounts, provisions of any kind;

(c) share capital and reserves (including undistributable reserves).

(3) Second, reduce the amount so determined by the amount of—

(a) any distribution lawfully made by the company, and

(b) any other relevant payment lawfully made by the company out of distributable profits,

after the date of the relevant accounts and before the end of the relevant period.

(4) For this purpose "other relevant payment lawfully made" includes—

(a) financial assistance lawfully given out of distributable profits in accordance with Chapter 2,

(b) payments lawfully made out of distributable profits in respect of the purchase by the company of any shares in the company, and

(c) payments of any description specified in section 705 (payments other than purchase price to be made out of distributable profits) lawfully made by the company.

(5) The resulting figure is the amount of available profits.

(6) For the purposes of this section "the relevant accounts" are any accounts that—

(a) are prepared as at a date within the relevant period, and

(b) are such as to enable a reasonable judgment to be made as to the amounts of the items mentioned in subsection (2).

(7) In this section "the relevant period" means the period of three months ending with the date on which the directors' statement is made in accordance with section 714.

[S712]

NOTES

Commencement: to be appointed.

Requirements for payment out of capital

713 Requirements for payment out of capital

(1) A payment out of capital by a private company for the redemption or purchase of its own shares is not lawful unless the requirements of the following sections are met—

section 714 (directors' statement and auditor's report);
section 716 (approval by special resolution);
section 719 (public notice of proposed payment);
section 720 (directors' statement and auditor's report to be available for inspection).

(2) This is subject to any order of the court under section 721 (power of court to extend period for compliance on application by persons objecting to payment).

[S713]

NOTES

Commencement: to be appointed.

714 Directors' statement and auditor's report

(1) The company's directors must make a statement in accordance with this section.

(2) The statement must specify the amount of the permissible capital payment for the shares in question.

(3) It must state that, having made full inquiry into the affairs and prospects of the company, the directors have formed the opinion—

(a) as regards its initial situation immediately following the date on which the payment out of capital is proposed to be made, that there will be no grounds on which the company could then be found unable to pay its debts, and

(b) as regards its prospects for the year immediately following that date, that having regard to—

(i) their intentions with respect to the management of the company's business during that year, and

(ii) the amount and character of the financial resources that will in their view be available to the company during that year,

the company will be able to continue to carry on business as a going concern (and will accordingly be able to pay its debts as they fall due) throughout that year.

(4) In forming their opinion for the purposes of subsection (3)(a), the directors must take into account all of the company's liabilities (including any contingent or prospective liabilities).

(5) The directors' statement must be in the prescribed form and must contain such information with respect to the nature of the company's business as may be prescribed.

(6) It must in addition have annexed to it a report addressed to the directors by the company's auditor stating that—

(a) he has inquired into the company's state of affairs,

(b) the amount specified in the statement as the permissible capital payment for the shares in question is in his view properly determined in accordance with sections 710 to 712, and

(c) he is not aware of anything to indicate that the opinion expressed by the directors in their statement as to any of the matters mentioned in subsection (3) above is unreasonable in all the circumstances.

[S714]

NOTES

Commencement: 20 January 2007 (for the purpose of enabling the exercise of powers to make Orders or Regulations by statutory instrument); to be appointed (otherwise).

715 Directors' statement: offence if no reasonable grounds for opinion

(1) If the directors make a statement under section 714 without having reasonable grounds for the opinion expressed in it, an offence is committed by every director who is in default.

(2) A person guilty of an offence under this section is liable—

(a) on conviction on indictment, to imprisonment for a term not exceeding two years or a fine (or both);

(b) on summary conviction—

(i) in England and Wales, to imprisonment for a term not exceeding twelve months or a fine not exceeding the statutory maximum (or both);

(ii) in Scotland or Northern Ireland, to imprisonment for a term not exceeding six months or a fine not exceeding the statutory maximum (or both).

[S715]

NOTES

Commencement: to be appointed.

716 Payment to be approved by special resolution

(1) The payment out of capital must be approved by a special resolution of the company.

(2) The resolution must be passed on, or within the week immediately following, the date on which the directors make the statement required by section 714.

(3) A resolution under this section is subject to—

section 717 (exercise of voting rights), and

section 718 (disclosure of directors' statement and auditors' report).

[S716]

NOTES

Commencement: to be appointed.

717 Resolution authorising payment: exercise of voting rights

(1) This section applies to a resolution under section 716 (authority for payment out of capital for redemption or purchase of own shares).

(2) Where the resolution is proposed as a written resolution, a member who holds shares to which the resolution relates is not an eligible member.

(3) Where the resolution is proposed at a meeting of the company, it is not effective if—

(a) any member of the company holding shares to which the resolution relates exercises the voting rights carried by any of those shares in voting on the resolution, and

(b) the resolution would not have been passed if he had not done so.

(4) For this purpose—

(a) a member who holds shares to which the resolution relates is regarded as exercising the voting rights carried by those shares not only if he votes in respect of them on a poll on the question whether the resolution shall be passed, but also if he votes on the resolution otherwise than on a poll;

(b) any member of the company may demand a poll on that question;

(c) a vote and a demand for a poll by a person as proxy for a member are the same respectively as a vote and a demand by the member.

[S717]

NOTES

Commencement: to be appointed.

718 Resolution authorising payment: disclosure of directors' statement and auditor's report

(1) This section applies to a resolution under section 716 (resolution authorising payment out of capital for redemption or purchase of own shares).

(2) A copy of the directors' statement and auditor's report under section 714 must be made available to members—

(a) in the case of a written resolution, by being sent or submitted to every eligible member at or before the time at which the proposed resolution is sent or submitted to him;

(b) in the case of a resolution at a meeting, by being made available for inspection by members of the company at the meeting.

(3) The resolution is ineffective if this requirement is not complied with.

[S718]

NOTES

Commencement: to be appointed.

719 Public notice of proposed payment

(1) Within the week immediately following the date of the resolution under section 716 the company must cause to be published in the Gazette a notice—

(a) stating that the company has approved a payment out of capital for the purpose of acquiring its own shares by redemption or purchase or both (as the case may be),

(b) specifying—

(i) the amount of the permissible capital payment for the shares in question, and

(ii) the date of the resolution,

(c) stating where the directors' statement and auditor's report required by section 714 are available for inspection, and

(d) stating that any creditor of the company may at any time within the five weeks immediately following the date of the resolution apply to the court under section 721 for an order preventing the payment.

(2) Within the week immediately following the date of the resolution the company must also either—

(a) cause a notice to the same effect as that required by subsection (1) to be published in an appropriate national newspaper, or

(b) give notice in writing to that effect to each of its creditors.

(3) "An appropriate national newspaper" means a newspaper circulating throughout the part of the United Kingdom in which the company is registered.

(4) Not later than the day on which the company—

(a) first publishes the notice required by subsection (1), or

(b) if earlier, first publishes or gives the notice required by subsection (2),

the company must deliver to the registrar a copy of the directors' statement and auditor's report required by section 714.

[S719]

NOTES

Commencement: to be appointed.

720 Directors' statement and auditor's report to be available for inspection

(1) The directors' statement and auditor's report must be kept available for inspection throughout the period—

(a) beginning with the day on which the company—

(i) first publishes the notice required by section 719(1), or

(ii) if earlier, first publishes or gives the notice required by section 719(2), and

(b) ending five weeks after the date of the resolution for payment out of capital.

(2) They must be kept available for inspection—

(a) at the company's registered office, or

(b) at a place specified in regulations under section 1136.

(3) The company must give notice to the registrar—

(a) of the place at which the statement and report are kept available for inspection, and

(b) of any change in that place,

unless they have at all times been kept at the company's registered office.

(4) They must be open to the inspection of any member or creditor of the company without charge.

(5) If default is made for 14 days in complying with subsection (3), or an inspection under subsection (4) is refused, an offence is committed by—

(a) the company, and

(b) every officer of the company who is in default.

(6) A person guilty of an offence under this section is liable on summary conviction to a fine not exceeding level 3 on the standard scale and, for continued contravention, a daily default fine not exceeding one-tenth of level 3 on the standard scale.

(7) In the case of a refusal of an inspection required by subsection (4), the court may by order compel an immediate inspection.

[S720]

NOTES

Commencement: to be appointed.

Objection to payment by members or creditors

721 Application to court to cancel resolution

(1) Where a private company passes a special resolution approving a payment out of capital for the redemption or purchase of any of its shares—

(a) any member of the company (other than one who consented to or voted in favour of the resolution), and

(b) any creditor of the company,

may apply to the court for the cancellation of the resolution.

(2) The application—

(a) must be made within five weeks after the passing of the resolution, and

(b) may be made on behalf of the persons entitled to make it by such one or more of their number as they may appoint in writing for the purpose.

(3) On an application under this section the court may if it thinks fit—

(a) adjourn the proceedings in order that an arrangement may be made to the satisfaction of the court—

(i) for the purchase of the interests of dissentient members, or

(ii) for the protection of dissentient creditors, and

(b) give such directions and make such orders as it thinks expedient for facilitating or carrying into effect any such arrangement.

(4) Subject to that, the court must make an order either cancelling or confirming the resolution, and may do so on such terms and conditions as it thinks fit.

(5) If the court confirms the resolution, it may by order alter or extend any date or period of time specified—

(a) in the resolution, or

(b) in any provision of this Chapter applying to the redemption or purchase to which the resolution relates.

(6) The court's order may, if the court thinks fit—

(a) provide for the purchase by the company of the shares of any of its members and for the reduction accordingly of the company's capital, and

(b) make any alteration in the company's articles that may be required in consequence of that provision.

(7) The court's order may, if the court thinks fit, require the company not to make any, or any specified, amendments of its articles without the leave of the court.

[S721]

NOTES

Commencement: to be appointed.

722 Notice to registrar of court application or order

(1) On making an application under section 721 (application to court to cancel resolution) the applicants, or the person making the application on their behalf, must immediately give notice to the registrar.

This is without prejudice to any provision of rules of court as to service of notice of the application.

(2) On being served with notice of any such application, the company must immediately give notice to the registrar.

(3) Within 15 days of the making of the court's order on the application, or such longer period as the court may at any time direct, the company must deliver to the registrar a copy of the order.

(4) If a company fails to comply with subsection (2) or (3) an offence is committed by—
- (a) the company, and
- (b) every officer of the company who is in default.

(5) A person guilty of an offence under this section is liable on summary conviction to a fine not exceeding level 3 on the standard scale and, for continued contravention, a daily default fine not exceeding one-tenth of level 3 on the standard scale.

[S722]

NOTES

Commencement: to be appointed.

Supplementary provisions

723 When payment out of capital to be made

(1) The payment out of capital must be made—
- (a) no earlier than five weeks after the date on which the resolution under section 716 is passed, and
- (b) no more than seven weeks after that date.

(2) This is subject to any exercise of the court's powers under section 721(5) (power to alter or extend time where resolution confirmed after objection).

[S723]

NOTES

Commencement: to be appointed.

CHAPTER 6
TREASURY SHARES

724 Treasury shares

(1) This section applies where—
- (a) a limited company makes a purchase of its own shares in accordance with Chapter 4,
- (b) the purchase is made out of distributable profits, and
- (c) the shares are qualifying shares.

(2) For this purpose "qualifying shares" means shares that—
- (a) are included in the official list in accordance with the provisions of Part 6 of the Financial Services and Markets Act 2000 (c 8),
- (b) are traded on the market known as the Alternative Investment Market established under the rules of London Stock Exchange plc,
- (c) are officially listed in an EEA State, or

(d) are traded on a regulated market.

In paragraph (a) "the official list" has the meaning given in section 103(1) of the Financial Services and Markets Act 2000.

(3) Where this section applies the company may—

(a) hold the shares (or any of them), or

(b) deal with any of them, at any time, in accordance with section 727 or 729.

(4) Where shares are held by the company, the company must be entered in its register of members as the member holding the shares.

(5) In the Companies Acts references to a company holding shares as treasury shares are to the company holding shares that—

(a) were (or are treated as having been) purchased by it in circumstances in which this section applies, and

(b) have been held by the company continuously since they were so purchased (or treated as purchased).

[S724]

NOTES

Commencement: to be appointed.

725 Treasury shares: maximum holdings

(1) Where a company has shares of only one class, the aggregate nominal value of shares held as treasury shares must not at any time exceed 10% of the nominal value of the issued share capital of the company at that time.

(2) Where the share capital of a company is divided into shares of different classes, the aggregate nominal value of the shares of any class held as treasury shares must not at any time exceed 10% of the nominal value of the issued share capital of the shares of that class at that time.

(3) If subsection (1) or (2) is contravened by a company, the company must dispose of or cancel the excess shares, in accordance with section 727 or 729, before the end of the period of twelve months beginning with the date on which that contravention occurs.

The "excess shares" means such number of the shares held by the company as treasury shares at the time in question as resulted in the limit being exceeded.

(4) Where a company purchases qualifying shares out of distributable profits in accordance with section 724, a contravention by the company of subsection (1) or (2) above does not render the acquisition void under section 658 (general rule against limited company acquiring its own shares).

[S725]

NOTES

Commencement: to be appointed.

726 Treasury shares: exercise of rights

(1) This section applies where shares are held by a company as treasury shares.

(2) The company must not exercise any right in respect of the treasury shares, and any purported exercise of such a right is void.

This applies, in particular, to any right to attend or vote at meetings.

(3) No dividend may be paid, and no other distribution (whether in cash or otherwise) of the company's assets (including any distribution of assets to members on a winding up) may be made to the company, in respect of the treasury shares.

(4) Nothing in this section prevents—

(a) an allotment of shares as fully paid bonus shares in respect of the treasury shares, or

(b) the payment of any amount payable on the redemption of the treasury shares (if they are redeemable shares).

(5) Shares allotted as fully paid bonus shares in respect of the treasury shares are treated as if purchased by the company, at the time they were allotted, in circumstances in which section 724(1) (treasury shares) applied.

[S726]

NOTES

Commencement: to be appointed.

727 Treasury shares: disposal

(1) Where shares are held as treasury shares, the company may at any time—

(a) sell the shares (or any of them) for a cash consideration, or

(b) transfer the shares (or any of them) for the purposes of or pursuant to an employees' share scheme.

(2) In subsection (1)(a) "cash consideration" means—

(a) cash received by the company, or

(b) a cheque received by the company in good faith that the directors have no reason for suspecting will not be paid, or

(c) a release of a liability of the company for a liquidated sum, or

(d) an undertaking to pay cash to the company on or before a date not more than 90 days after the date on which the company agrees to sell the shares, or

(e) payment by any other means giving rise to a present or future entitlement (of the company or a person acting on the company's behalf) to a payment, or credit equivalent to payment, in cash.

For this purpose "cash" includes foreign currency.

(3) The Secretary of State may by order provide that particular means of payment specified in the order are to be regarded as falling within subsection (2)(e).

(4) If the company receives a notice under section 979 (takeover offers: right of offeror to buy out minority shareholders) that a person desires to acquire shares held by the company as treasury shares, the company must not sell or transfer the shares to which the notice relates except to that person.

(5) An order under this section is subject to negative resolution procedure.

[S727]

NOTES

Commencement: 20 January 2007 (for the purpose of enabling the exercise of powers to make Orders or Regulations by statutory instrument); to be appointed (otherwise).

728 Treasury shares: notice of disposal

(1) Where shares held by a company as treasury shares—

(a) are sold, or

(b) are transferred for the purposes of an employees' share scheme,

the company must deliver a return to the registrar not later than 28 days after the shares are disposed of.

(2) The return must state with respect to shares of each class disposed of—

(a) the number and nominal value of the shares, and

(b) the date on which they were disposed of.

(3) Particulars of shares disposed of on different dates may be included in a single return.

(4) If default is made in complying with this section an offence is committed by every officer of the company who is in default.

(5) A person guilty of an offence under this section is liable—

(a) on conviction on indictment, to a fine;

(b) on summary conviction, to a fine not exceeding the statutory maximum and, for continued contravention, a daily default fine not exceeding one-tenth of the statutory maximum.

[S728]

NOTES

Commencement: to be appointed.

729 Treasury shares: cancellation

(1) Where shares are held as treasury shares, the company may at any time cancel the shares (or any of them).

(2) If shares held as treasury shares cease to be qualifying shares, the company must forthwith cancel the shares.

(3) For this purpose shares are not to be regarded as ceasing to be qualifying shares by virtue only of—

(a) the suspension of their listing in accordance with the applicable rules in the EEA State in which the shares are officially listed, or

(b) the suspension of their trading in accordance with—

(i) in the case of shares traded on the market known as the Alternative Investment Market, the rules of London Stock Exchange plc, and

(ii) in any other case, the rules of the regulated market on which they are traded.

(4) If company cancels shares held as treasury shares, the amount of the company's share capital is reduced accordingly by the nominal amount of the shares cancelled.

(5) The directors may take any steps required to enable the company to cancel its shares under this section without complying with the provisions of Chapter 10 of Part 17 (reduction of share capital).

[S729]

NOTES

Commencement: to be appointed.

730 Treasury shares: notice of cancellation

(1) Where shares held by a company as treasury shares are cancelled, the company must deliver a return to the registrar not later than 28 days after the shares are cancelled.

This does not apply to shares that are cancelled forthwith on their acquisition by the company (see section 708).

(2) The return must state with respect to shares of each class cancelled—

(a) the number and nominal value of the shares, and

(b) the date on which they were cancelled.

(3) Particulars of shares cancelled on different dates may be included in a single return.

(4) The notice must be accompanied by a statement of capital.

(5) The statement of capital must state with respect to the company's share capital immediately following the cancellation—

(a) the total number of shares of the company,

(b) the aggregate nominal value of those shares,

(c) for each class of shares—

(i) prescribed particulars of the rights attached to the shares,

(ii) the total number of shares of that class, and

(iii) the aggregate nominal value of shares of that class, and

(d) the amount paid up and the amount (if any) unpaid on each share (whether on account of the nominal value of the share or by way of premium).

(6) If default is made in complying with this section, an offence is committed by—

(a) the company, and

(b) every officer of the company who is in default.

(7) A person guilty of an offence under this section is liable on summary conviction to a fine not exceeding level 3 on the standard scale and, for continued contravention, a daily default fine not exceeding one-tenth of level 3 on the standard scale.

[S730]

NOTES

Commencement: 20 January 2007 (for the purpose of enabling the exercise of powers to make Orders or Regulations by statutory instrument); to be appointed (otherwise).

731 Treasury shares: treatment of proceeds of sale

(1) Where shares held as treasury shares are sold, the proceeds of sale must be dealt with in accordance with this section.

(2) If the proceeds of sale are equal to or less than the purchase price paid by the company for the shares, the proceeds are treated for the purposes of Part 23 (distributions) as a realised profit of the company.

(3) If the proceeds of sale exceed the purchase price paid by the company—
- (a) an amount equal to the purchase price paid is treated as a realised profit of the company for the purposes of that Part, and
- (b) the excess must be transferred to the company's share premium account.

(4) For the purposes of this section—
- (a) the purchase price paid by the company must be determined by the application of a weighted average price method, and
- (b) if the shares were allotted to the company as fully paid bonus shares, the purchase price paid for them is treated as nil.

[S731]

NOTES

Commencement: to be appointed.

732 Treasury shares: offences

(1) If a company contravenes any of the provisions of this Chapter (except section 730 (notice of cancellation)), an offence is committed by—
- (a) the company, and
- (b) every officer of the company who is in default.

(2) A person guilty of an offence under this section is liable—
- (a) on conviction on indictment, to a fine;
- (b) on summary conviction to a fine not exceeding the statutory maximum.

[S732]

NOTES

Commencement: to be appointed.

CHAPTER 7
SUPPLEMENTARY PROVISIONS

733 The capital redemption reserve

(1) In the following circumstances a company must transfer amounts to a reserve, called the "capital redemption reserve".

(2) Where under this Part shares of a limited company are redeemed or purchased wholly out of the company's profits, the amount by which the company's issued share capital is diminished in accordance with—
- (a) section 688(b) (on the cancellation of shares redeemed), or
- (b) section 706(b)(ii) (on the cancellation of shares purchased),

must be transferred to the capital redemption reserve.

(3) If—
- (a) the shares are redeemed or purchased wholly or partly out of the proceeds of a fresh issue, and
- (b) the aggregate amount of the proceeds is less than the aggregate nominal value of the shares redeemed or purchased,

the amount of the difference must be transferred to the capital redemption reserve.

This does not apply in the case of a private company if, in addition to the proceeds of the fresh issue, the company applies a payment out of capital under Chapter 5 in making the redemption or purchase.

(4) The amount by which a company's share capital is diminished in accordance with section 729(4) (on the cancellation of shares held as treasury shares) must be transferred to the capital redemption reserve.

(5) The company may use the capital redemption reserve to pay up new shares to be allotted to members as fully paid bonus shares.

(6) Subject to that, the provisions of the Companies Acts relating to the reduction of a company's share capital apply as if the capital redemption reserve were part of its paid up share capital.

[S733]

NOTES

Commencement: to be appointed.

734 Accounting consequences of payment out of capital

(1) This section applies where a payment out of capital is made in accordance with Chapter 5 (redemption or purchase of own shares by private company out of capital).

(2) If the permissible capital payment is less than the nominal amount of the shares redeemed or purchased, the amount of the difference must be transferred to the company's capital redemption reserve.

(3) If the permissible capital payment is greater than the nominal amount of the shares redeemed or purchased—

(a) the amount of any capital redemption reserve, share premium account or fully paid share capital of the company, and

(b) any amount representing unrealised profits of the company for the time being standing to the credit of any revaluation reserve maintained by the company,

may be reduced by a sum not exceeding (or by sums not in total exceeding) the amount by which the permissible capital payment exceeds the nominal amount of the shares.

(4) Where the proceeds of a fresh issue are applied by the company in making a redemption or purchase of its own shares in addition to a payment out of capital under this Chapter, the references in subsections (2) and (3) to the permissible capital payment are to be read as referring to the aggregate of that payment and those proceeds.

[S734]

NOTES

Commencement: to be appointed.

735 Effect of company's failure to redeem or purchase

(1) This section applies where a company—

(a) issues shares on terms that they are or are liable to be redeemed, or

(b) agrees to purchase any of its shares.

(2) The company is not liable in damages in respect of any failure on its part to redeem or purchase any of the shares.

This is without prejudice to any right of the holder of the shares other than his right to sue the company for damages in respect of its failure.

(3) The court shall not grant an order for specific performance of the terms of redemption or purchase if the company shows that it is unable to meet the costs of redeeming or purchasing the shares in question out of distributable profits.

(4) If the company is wound up and at the commencement of the winding up any of the shares have not been redeemed or purchased, the terms of redemption or purchase may be enforced against the company.

When shares are redeemed or purchased under this subsection, they are treated as cancelled.

(5) Subsection (4) does not apply if—

(a) the terms provided for the redemption or purchase to take place at a date later than that of the commencement of the winding up, or

(b) during the period—

(i) beginning with the date on which the redemption or purchase was to have taken place, and

(ii) ending with the commencement of the winding up,

the company could not at any time have lawfully made a distribution equal in value to the price at which the shares were to have been redeemed or purchased.

(6) There shall be paid in priority to any amount that the company is liable under subsection (4) to pay in respect of any shares—

(a) all other debts and liabilities of the company (other than any due to members in their character as such), and

(b) if other shares carry rights (whether as to capital or as to income) that are preferred to the rights as to capital attaching to the first-mentioned shares, any amount due in satisfaction of those preferred rights.

Subject to that, any such amount shall be paid in priority to any amounts due to members in satisfaction of their rights (whether as to capital or income) as members.

[S735]

NOTES

Commencement: to be appointed.

736 Meaning of "distributable profits"

In this Part (except in Chapter 2 (financial assistance): see section 683) "distributable profits", in relation to the making of any payment by a company, means profits out of which the company could lawfully make a distribution (within the meaning given by section 830) equal in value to the payment.

[S736]

NOTES

Commencement: to be appointed.

737 General power to make further provision by regulations

(1) The Secretary of State may by regulations modify the provisions of this Part.

(2) The regulations may—

(a) amend or repeal any of the provisions of this Part, or

(b) make such other provision as appears to the Secretary of State appropriate in place of any of the provisions of this Part.

(3) Regulations under this section may make consequential amendments or repeals in other provisions of this Act, or in other enactments.

(4) Regulations under this section are subject to affirmative resolution procedure.

[S737]

NOTES

Commencement: 20 January 2007 (for the purpose of enabling the exercise of powers to make Orders or Regulations by statutory instrument); to be appointed (otherwise).

PART 19
DEBENTURES

General provisions

738 Meaning of "debenture"

In the Companies Acts "debenture" includes debenture stock, bonds and any other securities of a company, whether or not constituting a charge on the assets of the company.

[S738]

NOTES

Commencement: to be appointed.

739 Perpetual debentures

(1) A condition contained in debentures, or in a deed for securing debentures, is not invalid by reason only that the debentures are made—

(a) irredeemable, or

(b) redeemable only—

(i) on the happening of a contingency (however remote), or

(ii) on the expiration of a period (however long),

any rule of equity to the contrary notwithstanding.

(2) Subsection (1) applies to debentures whenever issued and to deeds whenever executed.

[S739]

NOTES

Commencement: to be appointed.

740 Enforcement of contract to subscribe for debentures

A contract with a company to take up and pay for debentures of the company may be enforced by an order for specific performance.

[S740]

NOTES

Commencement: to be appointed.

741 Registration of allotment of debentures

(1) A company must register an allotment of debentures as soon as practicable and in any event within two months after the date of the allotment.

(2) If a company fails to comply with this section, an offence is committed by—

(a) the company, and

(b) every officer of the company who is in default.

(3) A person guilty of an offence under this section is liable on summary conviction to a fine not exceeding level 3 on the standard scale and, for continued contravention, a daily default fine not exceeding one-tenth of level 3 on the standard scale.

(4) For the duties of the company as to the issue of the debentures, or certificates of debenture stock, see Part 21 (certification and transfer of securities)

[S741]

NOTES

Commencement: to be appointed.

742 Debentures to bearer (Scotland)

Notwithstanding anything in the statute of the Scots Parliament of 1696, chapter 25, debentures to bearer issued in Scotland are valid and binding according to their terms.

[S742]

NOTES

Commencement: to be appointed.

Register of debenture holders

743 Register of debenture holders

(1) Any register of debenture holders of a company that is kept by the company must be kept available for inspection—

(a) at the company's registered office, or
(b) at a place specified in regulations under section 1136.

(2) A company must give notice to the registrar of the place where any such register is kept available for inspection and of any change in that place.

(3) No such notice is required if the register has, at all times since it came into existence, been kept available for inspection at the company's registered office.

(4) If a company makes default for 14 days in complying with subsection (2), an offence is committed by—
(a) the company, and
(b) every officer of the company who is in default.

(5) A person guilty of an offence under this section is liable on summary conviction to a fine not exceeding level 3 on the standard scale and, for continued contravention, a daily default fine not exceeding one-tenth of level 3 on the standard scale.

(6) References in this section to a register of debenture holders include a duplicate—
(a) of a register of debenture holders that is kept outside the United Kingdom, or
(b) of any part of such a register.

[S743]

NOTES
Commencement: to be appointed.

744 Register of debenture holders: right to inspect and require copy

(1) Every register of debenture holders of a company must, except when duly closed, be open to the inspection—
(a) of the registered holder of any such debentures, or any holder of shares in the company, without charge, and
(b) of any other person on payment of such fee as may be prescribed.

(2) Any person may require a copy of the register, or any part of it, on payment of such fee as may be prescribed.

(3) A person seeking to exercise either of the rights conferred by this section must make a request to the company to that effect.

(4) The request must contain the following information—
(a) in the case of an individual, his name and address;
(b) in the case of an organisation, the name and address of an individual responsible for making the request on behalf of the organisation;
(c) the purpose for which the information is to be used; and
(d) whether the information will be disclosed to any other person, and if so—
(i) where that person is an individual, his name and address,
(ii) where that person is an organisation, the name and address of an individual responsible for receiving the information on its behalf, and
(iii) the purpose for which the information is to be used by that person.

(5) For the purposes of this section a register is "duly closed" if it is closed in accordance with provision contained—
(a) in the articles or in the debentures,
(b) in the case of debenture stock in the stock certificates, or
(c) in the trust deed or other document securing the debentures or debenture stock.

The total period for which a register is closed in any year must not exceed 30 days.

(6) References in this section to a register of debenture holders include a duplicate—
(a) of a register of debenture holders that is kept outside the United Kingdom, or
(b) of any part of such a register.

[S744]

NOTES
Commencement: 20 January 2007 (for the purpose of enabling the exercise of powers to make Orders or Regulations by statutory instrument); to be appointed (otherwise).

745 Register of debenture holders: response to request for inspection or copy

(1) Where a company receives a request under section 744 (register of debenture holders: right to inspect and require copy), it must within five working days either—

(a) comply with the request, or
(b) apply to the court.

(2) If it applies to the court it must notify the person making the request.

(3) If on an application under this section the court is satisfied that the inspection or copy is not sought for a proper purpose—

(a) it shall direct the company not to comply with the request, and
(b) it may further order that the company's costs (in Scotland, expenses) on the application be paid in whole or in part by the person who made the request, even if he is not a party to the application.

(4) If the court makes such a direction and it appears to the court that the company is or may be subject to other requests made for a similar purpose (whether made by the same person or different persons), it may direct that the company is not to comply with any such request.

The order must contain such provision as appears to the court appropriate to identify the requests to which it applies.

(5) If on an application under this section the court does not direct the company not to comply with the request, the company must comply with the request immediately upon the court giving its decision or, as the case may be, the proceedings being discontinued.

[S745]

NOTES
Commencement: to be appointed.

746 Register of debenture holders: refusal of inspection or default in providing copy

(1) If an inspection required under section 744 (register of debenture holders: right to inspect and require copy) is refused or default is made in providing a copy required under that section, otherwise than in accordance with an order of the court, an offence is committed by—

(a) the company, and
(b) every officer of the company who is in default.

(2) A person guilty of an offence under this section is liable on summary conviction to a fine not exceeding level 3 on the standard scale and, for continued contravention, a daily default fine not exceeding one-tenth of level 3 on the standard scale.

(3) In the case of any such refusal or default the court may by order compel an immediate inspection or, as the case may be, direct that the copy required be sent to the person requesting it.

[S746]

NOTES
Commencement: to be appointed.

747 Register of debenture holders: offences in connection with request for or disclosure of information

(1) It is an offence for a person knowingly or recklessly to make in a request under section 744 (register of debenture holders: right to inspect and require copy) a statement that is misleading, false or deceptive in a material particular.

(2) It is an offence for a person in possession of information obtained by exercise of either of the rights conferred by that section—

(a) to do anything that results in the information being disclosed to another person, or
(b) to fail to do anything with the result that the information is disclosed to another person,

knowing, or having reason to suspect, that person may use the information for a purpose that is not a proper purpose.

(3) A person guilty of an offence under this section is liable—

(a) on conviction on indictment, to imprisonment for a term not exceeding two years or a fine (or both);

(b) on summary conviction—

(i) in England and Wales, to imprisonment for a term not exceeding twelve months or to a fine not exceeding the statutory maximum (or both);

(ii) in Scotland or Northern Ireland, to imprisonment for a term not exceeding six months, or to a fine not exceeding the statutory maximum (or both).

[S747]

NOTES

Commencement: to be appointed.

748 Time limit for claims arising from entry in register

(1) Liability incurred by a company—

(a) from the making or deletion of an entry in the register of debenture holders, or

(b) from a failure to make or delete any such entry,

is not enforceable more than ten years after the date on which the entry was made or deleted or, as the case may be, the failure first occurred.

(2) This is without prejudice to any lesser period of limitation (and, in Scotland, to any rule that the obligation giving rise to the liability prescribes before the expiry of that period).

[S748]

NOTES

Commencement: to be appointed.

Supplementary provisions

749 Right of debenture holder to copy of deed

(1) Any holder of debentures of a company is entitled, on request and on payment of such fee as may be prescribed, to be provided with a copy of any trust deed for securing the debentures.

(2) If default is made in complying with this section, an offence is committed by every officer of the company who is in default.

(3) A person guilty of an offence under this section is liable on summary conviction to a fine not exceeding level 3 on the standard scale and, for continued contravention, a daily default fine not exceeding one-tenth of level 3 on the standard scale.

(4) In the case of any such default the court may direct that the copy required be sent to the person requiring it.

[S749]

NOTES

Commencement: 20 January 2007 (for the purpose of enabling the exercise of powers to make Orders or Regulations by statutory instrument); to be appointed (otherwise).

750 Liability of trustees of debentures

(1) Any provision contained in—

(a) a trust deed for securing an issue of debentures, or

(b) any contract with the holders of debentures secured by a trust deed,

is void in so far as it would have the effect of exempting a trustee of the deed from, or indemnifying him against, liability for breach of trust where he fails to show the degree of care and diligence required of him as trustee, having regard to the provisions of the trust deed conferring on him any powers, authorities or discretions.

(2) Subsection (1) does not invalidate—

(a) a release otherwise validly given in respect of anything done or omitted to be done by a trustee before the giving of the release;

(b) any provision enabling such a release to be given—
(i) on being agreed to by a majority of not less than 75% in value of the debenture holders present and voting in person or, where proxies are permitted, by proxy at a meeting summoned for the purpose, and
(ii) either with respect to specific acts or omissions or on the trustee dying or ceasing to act.

(3) This section is subject to section 751 (saving for certain older provisions).

[S750]

NOTES

Commencement: to be appointed.

751 Liability of trustees of debentures: saving for certain older provisions

(1) Section 750 (liability of trustees of debentures) does not operate—
(a) to invalidate any provision in force on the relevant date so long as any person—
(i) then entitled to the benefit of the provision, or
(ii) afterwards given the benefit of the provision under subsection (3) below,
remains a trustee of the deed in question, or
(b) to deprive any person of any exemption or right to be indemnified in respect of anything done or omitted to be done by him while any such provision was in force.

(2) The relevant date for this purpose is—
(a) 1st July 1948 in a case where section 192 of the Companies Act 1985 (c 6) applied immediately before the commencement of this section;
(b) 1st July 1961 in a case where Article 201 of the Companies (Northern Ireland) Order 1986 (SI 1986/1032 (NI 6)) then applied.

(3) While any trustee of a trust deed remains entitled to the benefit of a provision saved by subsection (1) above the benefit of that provision may be given either—
(a) to all trustees of the deed, present and future, or
(b) to any named trustees or proposed trustees of it,
by a resolution passed by a majority of not less than 75% in value of the debenture holders present in person or, where proxies are permitted, by proxy at a meeting summoned for the purpose.

(4) A meeting for that purpose must be summoned in accordance with the provisions of the deed or, if the deed makes no provision for summoning meetings, in a manner approved by the court.

[S751]

NOTES

Commencement: to be appointed.

752 Power to re-issue redeemed debentures

(1) Where a company has redeemed debentures previously issued, then unless—
(a) provision to the contrary (express or implied) is contained in the company's articles or in any contract made by the company, or
(b) the company has, by passing a resolution to that effect or by some other act, manifested its intention that the debentures shall be cancelled,
the company may re-issue the debentures, either by re-issuing the same debentures or by issuing new debentures in their place.

This subsection is deemed always to have had effect.

(2) On a re-issue of redeemed debentures the person entitled to the debentures has (and is deemed always to have had) the same priorities as if the debentures had never been redeemed.

(3) The re-issue of a debenture or the issue of another debenture in its place under this section is treated as the issue of a new debenture for the purposes of stamp duty.

It is not so treated for the purposes of any provision limiting the amount or number of debentures to be issued.

(4) A person lending money on the security of a debenture re-issued under this section which appears to be duly stamped may give the debenture in evidence in any proceedings for enforcing his security without payment of the stamp duty or any penalty in respect of it, unless he had notice (or, but for his negligence, might have discovered) that the debenture was not duly stamped. In that case the company is liable to pay the proper stamp duty and penalty.
[S752]

NOTES
Commencement: to be appointed.

753 Deposit of debentures to secure advances

Where a company has deposited any of its debentures to secure advances from time to time on current account or otherwise, the debentures are not treated as redeemed by reason only of the company's account having ceased to be in debit while the debentures remained so deposited.
[S753]

NOTES
Commencement: to be appointed.

754 Priorities where debentures secured by floating charge

(1) This section applies where debentures of a company registered in England and Wales or Northern Ireland are secured by a charge that, as created, was a floating charge.

(2) If possession is taken, by or on behalf of the holders of the debentures, of any property comprised in or subject to the charge, and the company is not at that time in the course of being wound up, the company's preferential debts shall be paid out of assets coming to the hands of the persons taking possession in priority to any claims for principal or interest in respect of the debentures.

(3) "Preferential debts" means the categories of debts listed in Schedule 6 to the Insolvency Act 1986 (c 45) or Schedule 4 to the Insolvency (Northern Ireland) Order 1989 (SI 1989/2405 (NI 19)).

For the purposes of those Schedules "the relevant date" is the date of possession being taken as mentioned in subsection (2).

(4) Payments under this section shall be recouped, as far as may be, out of the assets of the company available for payment of general creditors.
[S754]

NOTES
Commencement: to be appointed.

PART 20
PRIVATE AND PUBLIC COMPANIES

CHAPTER 1
PROHIBITION OF PUBLIC OFFERS BY PRIVATE COMPANIES

755 Prohibition of public offers by private company

(1) A private company limited by shares or limited by guarantee and having a share capital must not—

(a) offer to the public any securities of the company, or

(b) allot or agree to allot any securities of the company with a view to their being offered to the public.

(2) Unless the contrary is proved, an allotment or agreement to allot securities is presumed to be made with a view to their being offered to the public if an offer of the securities (or any of them) to the public is made—

(a) within six months after the allotment or agreement to allot, or

(b) before the receipt by the company of the whole of the consideration to be received by it in respect of the securities.

(3) A company does not contravene this section if—

(a) it acts in good faith in pursuance of arrangements under which it is to re-register as a public company before the securities are allotted, or

(b) as part of the terms of the offer it undertakes to re-register as a public company within a specified period, and that undertaking is complied with.

(4) The specified period for the purposes of subsection (3)(b) must be a period ending not later than six months after the day on which the offer is made (or, in the case of an offer made on different days, first made).

(5) In this Chapter "securities" means shares or debentures.

[S755]

NOTES

Commencement: to be appointed.

756 Meaning of "offer to the public"

(1) This section explains what is meant in this Chapter by an offer of securities to the public.

(2) An offer to the public includes an offer to any section of the public, however selected.

(3) An offer is not regarded as an offer to the public if it can properly be regarded, in all the circumstances, as—

(a) not being calculated to result, directly or indirectly, in securities of the company becoming available to persons other than those receiving the offer, or

(b) otherwise being a private concern of the person receiving it and the person making it.

(4) An offer is to be regarded (unless the contrary is proved) as being a private concern of the person receiving it and the person making it if—

(a) it is made to a person already connected with the company and, where it is made on terms allowing that person to renounce his rights, the rights may only be renounced in favour of another person already connected with the company; or

(b) it is an offer to subscribe for securities to be held under an employees' share scheme and, where it is made on terms allowing that person to renounce his rights, the rights may only be renounced in favour of—

(i) another person entitled to hold securities under the scheme, or

(ii) a person already connected with the company.

(5) For the purposes of this section "person already connected with the company" means—

(a) an existing member or employee of the company,

(b) a member of the family of a person who is or was a member or employee of the company,

(c) the widow or widower, or surviving civil partner, of a person who was a member or employee of the company,

(d) an existing debenture holder of the company, or

(e) a trustee (acting in his capacity as such) of a trust of which the principal beneficiary is a person within any of paragraphs (a) to (d).

(6) For the purposes of subsection (5)(b) the members of a person's family are the person's spouse or civil partner and children (including step-children) and their descendants.

[S756]

NOTES

Commencement: to be appointed.

757 Enforcement of prohibition: order restraining proposed contravention

(1) If it appears to the court—

(a) on an application under this section, or

(b) in proceedings under Part 30 (protection of members against unfair prejudice), that a company is proposing to act in contravention of section 755 (prohibition of public offers by private companies), the court shall make an order under this section.

(2) An order under this section is an order restraining the company from contravening that section.

(3) An application for an order under this section may be made by—

(a) a member or creditor of the company, or

(b) the Secretary of State.

[S757]

NOTES

Commencement: to be appointed.

758 Enforcement of prohibition: orders available to the court after contravention

(1) This section applies if it appears to the court—

(a) on an application under this section, or

(b) in proceedings under Part 30 (protection of members against unfair prejudice),

that a company has acted in contravention of section 755 (prohibition of public offers by private companies).

(2) The court must make an order requiring the company to re-register as a public company unless it appears to the court—

(a) that the company does not meet the requirements for re-registration as a public company, and

(b) that it is impractical or undesirable to require it to take steps to do so.

(3) If it does not make an order for re-registration, the court may make either or both of the following—

(a) a remedial order (see section 759), or

(b) an order for the compulsory winding up of the company.

(4) An application under this section may be made by—

(a) a member of the company who—

(i) was a member at the time the offer was made (or, if the offer was made over a period, at any time during that period), or

(ii) became a member as a result of the offer,

(b) a creditor of the company who was a creditor at the time the offer was made (or, if the offer was made over a period, at any time during that period), or

(c) the Secretary of State.

[S758]

NOTES

Commencement: to be appointed.

759 Enforcement of prohibition: remedial order

(1) A "remedial order" is an order for the purpose of putting a person affected by anything done in contravention of section 755 (prohibition of public offers by private company) in the position he would have been in if it had not been done.

(2) The following provisions are without prejudice to the generality of the power to make such an order.

(3) Where a private company has—

(a) allotted securities pursuant to an offer to the public, or

(b) allotted or agreed to allot securities with a view to their being offered to the public,

a remedial order may require any person knowingly concerned in the contravention of section 755 to offer to purchase any of those securities at such price and on such other terms as the court thinks fit.

(4) A remedial order may be made—

(a) against any person knowingly concerned in the contravention, whether or not an officer of the company;

(b) notwithstanding anything in the company's constitution (which includes, for this purpose, the terms on which any securities of the company are allotted or held);
(c) whether or not the holder of the securities subject to the order is the person to whom the company allotted or agreed to allot them.

(5) Where a remedial order is made against the company itself, the court may provide for the reduction of the company's capital accordingly.

[S759]

NOTES

Commencement: to be appointed.

760 Validity of allotment etc not affected

Nothing in this Chapter affects the validity of any allotment or sale of securities or of any agreement to allot or sell securities.

[S760]

NOTES

Commencement: to be appointed.

CHAPTER 2
MINIMUM SHARE CAPITAL REQUIREMENT FOR PUBLIC COMPANIES

761 Public company: requirement as to minimum share capital

(1) A company that is a public company (otherwise than by virtue of re-registration as a public company) must not do business or exercise any borrowing powers unless the registrar has issued it with a certificate under this section (a "trading certificate").

(2) The registrar shall issue a trading certificate if, on an application made in accordance with section 762, he is satisfied that the nominal value of the company's allotted share capital is not less than the authorised minimum.

(3) For this purpose a share allotted in pursuance of an employees' share scheme shall not be taken into account unless paid up as to—
(a) at least one-quarter of the nominal value of the share, and
(b) the whole of any premium on the share.

(4) A trading certificate has effect from the date on which it is issued and is conclusive evidence that the company is entitled to do business and exercise any borrowing powers.

[S761]

NOTES

Commencement: to be appointed.

762 Procedure for obtaining certificate

(1) An application for a certificate under section 761 must—
(a) state that the nominal value of the company's allotted share capital is not less than the authorised minimum,
(b) specify the amount, or estimated amount, of the company's preliminary expenses,
(c) specify any amount or benefit paid or given, or intended to be paid or given, to any promoter of the company, and the consideration for the payment or benefit, and
(d) be accompanied by a statement of compliance.

(2) The statement of compliance is a statement that the company meets the requirements for the issue of a certificate under section 761.

(3) The registrar may accept the statement of compliance as sufficient evidence of the matters stated in it.

[S762]

NOTES

Commencement: to be appointed.

763 The authorised minimum

(1) "The authorised minimum", in relation to the nominal value of a public company's allotted share capital is—

(a) £50,000, or

(b) the prescribed euro equivalent.

(2) The Secretary of State may by order prescribe the amount in euros that is for the time being to be treated as equivalent to the sterling amount of the authorised minimum.

(3) This power may be exercised from time to time as appears to the Secretary of State to be appropriate.

(4) The amount prescribed shall be determined by applying an appropriate spot rate of exchange to the sterling amount and rounding to the nearest 100 euros.

(5) An order under this section is subject to negative resolution procedure.

(6) This section has effect subject to any exercise of the power conferred by section 764 (power to alter authorised minimum).

[S763]

NOTES

Commencement: 20 January 2007 (for the purpose of enabling the exercise of powers to make Orders or Regulations by statutory instrument); to be appointed (otherwise).

764 Power to alter authorised minimum

(1) The Secretary of State may by order—

(a) alter the sterling amount of the authorised minimum, and

(b) make a corresponding alteration of the prescribed euro equivalent.

(2) The amount of the prescribed euro equivalent shall be determined by applying an appropriate spot rate of exchange to the sterling amount and rounding to the nearest 100 euros.

(3) An order under this section that increases the authorised minimum may—

(a) require a public company having an allotted share capital of which the nominal value is less than the amount specified in the order to—

(i) increase that value to not less than that amount, or

(ii) re-register as a private company;

(b) make provision in connection with any such requirement for any of the matters for which provision is made by this Act relating to—

(i) a company's registration, re-registration or change of name,

(ii) payment for shares comprised in a company's share capital, and

(iii) offers to the public of shares in or debentures of a company,

including provision as to the consequences (in criminal law or otherwise) of a failure to comply with any requirement of the order;

(c) provide for any provision of the order to come into force on different days for different purposes.

(4) An order under this section is subject to affirmative resolution procedure.

[S764]

NOTES

Commencement: 20 January 2007 (for the purpose of enabling the exercise of powers to make Orders or Regulations by statutory instrument); to be appointed (otherwise).

765 Authorised minimum: application of initial requirement

(1) The initial requirement for a public company to have allotted share capital of a nominal value not less than the authorised minimum, that is—

(a) the requirement in section 761(2) for the issue of a trading certificate, or

(b) the requirement in section 91(1)(a) for re-registration as a public company,

must be met either by reference to allotted share capital denominated in sterling or by reference to allotted share capital denominated in euros (but not partly in one and partly in the other).

(2) Whether the requirement is met is determined in the first case by reference to the sterling amount and in the second case by reference to the prescribed euro equivalent.

(3) No account is to be taken of any allotted share capital of the company denominated in a currency other than sterling or, as the case may be, euros.

(4) If the company could meet the requirement either by reference to share capital denominated in sterling or by reference to share capital denominated in euros, it must elect in its application for a trading certificate or, as the case may be, for re-registration as a public company which is to be the currency by reference to which the matter is determined.

[S765]

NOTES

Commencement: to be appointed.

766 Authorised minimum: application where shares denominated in different currencies etc

(1) The Secretary of State may make provision by regulations as to the application of the authorised minimum in relation to a public company that—

(a) has shares denominated in more than one currency,
(b) redenominates the whole or part of its allotted share capital, or
(c) allots new shares.

(2) The regulations may make provision as to the currencies, exchange rates and dates by reference to which it is to be determined whether the nominal value of the company's allotted share capital is less than the authorised minimum.

(3) The regulations may provide that where—

(a) a company has redenominated the whole or part of its allotted share capital, and
(b) the effect of the redenomination is that the nominal value of the company's allotted share capital is less than the authorised minimum,

the company must re-register as a private company.

(4) Regulations under subsection (3) may make provision corresponding to any provision made by sections 664 to 667 (re-registration as private company in consequence of cancellation of shares).

(5) Any regulations under this section have effect subject to section 765 (authorised minimum: application of initial requirement).

(6) Regulations under this section are subject to negative resolution procedure.

[S766]

NOTES

Commencement: 20 January 2007 (for the purpose of enabling the exercise of powers to make Orders or Regulations by statutory instrument); to be appointed (otherwise).

767 Consequences of doing business etc without a trading certificate

(1) If a company does business or exercises any borrowing powers in contravention of section 761, an offence is committed by—

(a) the company, and
(b) every officer of the company who is in default.

(2) A person guilty of an offence under subsection (1) is liable—

(a) on conviction on indictment, to a fine;
(b) on summary conviction, to a fine not exceeding the statutory maximum.

(3) A contravention of section 761 does not affect the validity of a transaction entered into by the company, but if a company—

(a) enters into a transaction in contravention of that section, and
(b) fails to comply with its obligations in connection with the transaction within 21 days from being called on to do so,

the directors of the company are jointly and severally liable to indemnify any other party to the transaction in respect of any loss or damage suffered by him by reason of the company's failure to comply with its obligations.

(4) The directors who are so liable are those who were directors at the time the company entered into the transaction.

[S767]

NOTES

Commencement: to be appointed.

PART 21
CERTIFICATION AND TRANSFER OF SECURITIES

CHAPTER 1
CERTIFICATION AND TRANSFER OF SECURITIES: GENERAL

Share certificates

768 Share certificate to be evidence of title

(1) In the case of a company registered in England and Wales or Northern Ireland, a certificate under the common seal of the company specifying any shares held by a member is prima facie evidence of his title to the shares.

(2) In the case of a company registered in Scotland—

(a) a certificate under the common seal of the company specifying any shares held by a member, or

(b) a certificate specifying any shares held by a member and subscribed by the company in accordance with the Requirements of Writing (Scotland) Act 1995 (c 7),

is sufficient evidence, unless the contrary is shown, of his title to the shares.

[S768]

NOTES

Commencement: to be appointed.

Issue of certificates etc on allotment

769 Duty of company as to issue of certificates etc on allotment

(1) A company must, within two months after the allotment of any of its shares, debentures or debenture stock, complete and have ready for delivery—

(a) the certificates of the shares allotted,

(b) the debentures allotted, or

(c) the certificates of the debenture stock allotted.

(2) Subsection (1) does not apply—

(a) if the conditions of issue of the shares, debentures or debenture stock provide otherwise,

(b) in the case of allotment to a financial institution (see section 778), or

(c) in the case of an allotment of shares if, following the allotment, the company has issued a share warrant in respect of the shares (see section 779).

(3) If default is made in complying with subsection (1) an offence is committed by every officer of the company who is in default.

(4) A person guilty of an offence under subsection (3) is liable on summary conviction to a fine not exceeding level 3 on the standard scale and, for continued contravention, a daily default fine not exceeding one-tenth of level 3 on the standard scale.

[S769]

NOTES

Commencement: to be appointed.

Transfer of securities

770 Registration of transfer

(1) A company may not register a transfer of shares in or debentures of the company unless—

(a) a proper instrument of transfer has been delivered to it, or

(b) the transfer—

(i) is an exempt transfer within the Stock Transfer Act 1982 (c 41), or

(ii) is in accordance with regulations under Chapter 2 of this Part.

(2) Subsection (1) does not affect any power of the company to register as shareholder or debenture holder a person to whom the right to any shares in or debentures of the company has been transmitted by operation of law.

[S770]

NOTES

Commencement: to be appointed.

771 Procedure on transfer being lodged

(1) When a transfer of shares in or debentures of a company has been lodged with the company, the company must either—

(a) register the transfer, or

(b) give the transferee notice of refusal to register the transfer, together with its reasons for the refusal,

as soon as practicable and in any event within two months after the date on which the transfer is lodged with it.

(2) If the company refuses to register the transfer, it must provide the transferee with such further information about the reasons for the refusal as the transferee may reasonably request.

This does not include copies of minutes of meetings of directors.

(3) If a company fails to comply with this section, an offence is committed by—

(a) the company, and

(b) every officer of the company who is in default.

(4) A person guilty of an offence under this section is liable on summary conviction to a fine not exceeding level 3 on the standard scale and, for continued contravention, a daily default fine not exceeding one-tenth of level 3 on the standard scale.

(5) This section does not apply—

(a) in relation to a transfer of shares if the company has issued a share warrant in respect of the shares (see section 779);

(b) in relation to the transmission of shares or debentures by operation of law.

[S771]

NOTES

Commencement: to be appointed.

772 Transfer of shares on application of transferor

On the application of the transferor of any share or interest in a company, the company shall enter in its register of members the name of the transferee in the same manner and subject to the same conditions as if the application for the entry were made by the transferee.

[S772]

NOTES

Commencement: to be appointed.

773 Execution of share transfer by personal representative

An instrument of transfer of the share or other interest of a deceased member of a company—

(a) may be made by his personal representative although the personal representative is not himself a member of the company, and

(b) is as effective as if the personal representative had been such a member at the time of the execution of the instrument.

[S773]

NOTES

Commencement: to be appointed.

774 Evidence of grant of probate etc

The production to a company of any document that is by law sufficient evidence of the grant of—

(a) probate of the will of a deceased person,

(b) letters of administration of the estate of a deceased person, or

(c) confirmation as executor of a deceased person,

shall be accepted by the company as sufficient evidence of the grant.

[S774]

NOTES

Commencement: to be appointed.

775 Certification of instrument of transfer

(1) The certification by a company of an instrument of transfer of any shares in, or debentures of, the company is to be taken as a representation by the company to any person acting on the faith of the certification that there have been produced to the company such documents as on their face show a prima facie title to the shares or debentures in the transferor named in the instrument.

(2) The certification is not to be taken as a representation that the transferor has any title to the shares or debentures.

(3) Where a person acts on the faith of a false certification by a company made negligently, the company is under the same liability to him as if the certification had been made fraudulently.

(4) For the purposes of this section—

(a) an instrument of transfer is certificated if it bears the words "certificate lodged" (or words to the like effect);

(b) the certification of an instrument of transfer is made by a company if—

(i) the person issuing the instrument is a person authorised to issue certificated instruments of transfer on the company's behalf, and

(ii) the certification is signed by a person authorised to certificate transfers on the company's behalf or by an officer or employee either of the company or of a body corporate so authorised;

(c) a certification is treated as signed by a person if—

(i) it purports to be authenticated by his signature or initials (whether handwritten or not), and

(ii) it is not shown that the signature or initials was or were placed there neither by himself nor by a person authorised to use the signature or initials for the purpose of certificating transfers on the company's behalf.

[S775]

NOTES

Commencement: to be appointed.

Issue of certificates etc on transfer

776 Duty of company as to issue of certificates etc on transfer

(1) A company must, within two months after the date on which a transfer of any of its shares, debentures or debenture stock is lodged with the company, complete and have ready for delivery—

(a) the certificates of the shares transferred,
(b) the debentures transferred, or
(c) the certificates of the debenture stock transferred.

(2) For this purpose a "transfer" means—
(a) a transfer duly stamped and otherwise valid, or
(b) an exempt transfer within the Stock Transfer Act 1982 (c 41),

but does not include a transfer that the company is for any reason entitled to refuse to register and does not register.

(3) Subsection (1) does not apply—
(a) if the conditions of issue of the shares, debentures or debenture stock provide otherwise,
(b) in the case of a transfer to a financial institution (see section 778), or
(c) in the case of a transfer of shares if, following the transfer, the company has issued a share warrant in respect of the shares (see section 779).

(4) Subsection (1) has effect subject to section 777 (cases where the Stock Transfer Act 1982 applies).

(5) If default is made in complying with subsection (1) an offence is committed by every officer of the company who is in default.

(6) A person guilty of an offence under this section is liable on summary conviction to a fine not exceeding level 3 on the standard scale and, for continued contravention, a daily default fine not exceeding one-tenth of level 3 on the standard scale.

[S776]

NOTES

Commencement: to be appointed.

777 Issue of certificates etc: cases within the Stock Transfer Act 1982

(1) Section 776(1) (duty of company as to issue of certificates etc on transfer) does not apply in the case of a transfer to a person where, by virtue of regulations under section 3 of the Stock Transfer Act 1982, he is not entitled to a certificate or other document of or evidencing title in respect of the securities transferred.

(2) But if in such a case the transferee—
(a) subsequently becomes entitled to such a certificate or other document by virtue of any provision of those regulations, and
(b) gives notice in writing of that fact to the company,

section 776 (duty to company as to issue of certificates etc) has effect as if the reference in subsection (1) of that section to the date of the lodging of the transfer were a reference to the date of the notice.

[S777]

NOTES

Commencement: to be appointed.

Issue of certificates etc on allotment or transfer to financial institution

778 Issue of certificates etc: allotment or transfer to financial institution

(1) A company—
(a) of which shares or debentures are allotted to a financial institution,
(b) of which debenture stock is allotted to a financial institution, or
(c) with which a transfer for transferring shares, debentures or debenture stock to a financial institution is lodged,

is not required in consequence of that allotment or transfer to comply with section 769(1) or 776(1) (duty of company as to issue of certificates etc).

(2) A "financial institution" means—
(a) a recognised clearing house acting in relation to a recognised investment exchange, or

(b) a nominee of—
  (i) a recognised clearing house acting in that way, or
  (ii) a recognised investment exchange,

designated for the purposes of this section in the rules of the recognised investment exchange in question.

(3) Expressions used in subsection (2) have the same meaning as in Part 18 of the Financial Services and Markets Act 2000 (c 8).

[S778]

NOTES

Commencement: to be appointed.

Share warrants

779 Issue and effect of share warrant to bearer

(1) A company limited by shares may, if so authorised by its articles, issue with respect to any fully paid shares a warrant (a "share warrant") stating that the bearer of the warrant is entitled to the shares specified in it.

(2) A share warrant issued under the company's common seal or (in the case of a company registered in Scotland) subscribed in accordance with the Requirements of Writing (Scotland) Act 1995 (c 7) entitles the bearer to the shares specified in it and the shares may be transferred by delivery of the warrant.

(3) A company that issues a share warrant may, if so authorised by its articles, provide (by coupons or otherwise) for the payment of the future dividends on the shares included in the warrant.

[S779]

NOTES

Commencement: to be appointed.

780 Duty of company as to issue of certificates on surrender of share warrant

(1) A company must, within two months of the surrender of a share warrant for cancellation, complete and have ready for delivery the certificates of the shares specified in the warrant.

(2) Subsection (1) does not apply if the company's articles provide otherwise.

(3) If default is made in complying with subsection (1) an offence is committed by every officer of the company who is in default.

(4) A person guilty of an offence under subsection (3) is liable on summary conviction to a fine not exceeding level 3 on the standard scale and, for continued contravention, a daily default fine not exceeding one-tenth of level 3 on the standard scale.

[S780]

NOTES

Commencement: to be appointed.

781 Offences in connection with share warrants (Scotland)

(1) If in Scotland a person—

(a) with intent to defraud, forges or alters, or offers, utters, disposes of, or puts off, knowing the same to be forged or altered, any share warrant or coupon, or any document purporting to be a share warrant or coupon issued in pursuance of this Act, or

(b) by means of any such forged or altered share warrant, coupon or document—
  (i) demands or endeavours to obtain or receive any share or interest in a company under this Act, or
  (ii) demands or endeavours to receive any dividend or money payment in respect of any such share or interest,

knowing the warrant, coupon or document to be forged or altered,

he commits an offence.

(2) If in Scotland a person without lawful authority or excuse (of which proof lies on him)—

(a) engraves or makes on any plate, wood, stone, or other material, any share warrant or coupon purporting to be—

(i) a share warrant or coupon issued or made by any particular company in pursuance of this Act, or

(ii) a blank share warrant or coupon so issued or made, or

(iii) a part of such a share warrant or coupon, or

(b) uses any such plate, wood, stone, or other material, for the making or printing of any such share warrant or coupon, or of any such blank share warrant or coupon or of any part of such a share warrant or coupon, or

(c) knowingly has in his custody or possession any such plate, wood, stone, or other material,

he commits an offence.

(3) A person guilty of an offence under subsection (1) is liable on summary conviction to imprisonment for a term not exceeding six months or to a fine not exceeding level 5 on the standard scale (or both).

(4) A person guilty of an offence under subsection (2) is liable—

(a) on conviction on indictment, to imprisonment for a term not exceeding seven years or a fine (or both);

(b) on summary conviction, to imprisonment for a term not exceeding six months or a fine not exceeding the statutory maximum (or both).

[S781]

NOTES

Commencement: to be appointed.

Supplementary provisions

782 Issue of certificates etc: court order to make good default

(1) If a company on which a notice has been served requiring it to make good any default in complying with—

(a) section 769(1) (duty of company as to issue of certificates etc on allotment),

(b) section 776(1) (duty of company as to issue of certificates etc on transfer), or

(c) section 780(1) (duty of company as to issue of certificates etc on surrender of share warrant),

fails to make good the default within ten days after service of the notice, the person entitled to have the certificates or the debentures delivered to him may apply to the court.

(2) The court may on such an application make an order directing the company and any officer of it to make good the default within such time as may be specified in the order.

(3) The order may provide that all costs (in Scotland, expenses) of and incidental to the application are to be borne by the company or by an officer of it responsible for the default.

[S782]

NOTES

Commencement: to be appointed.

CHAPTER 2
EVIDENCING AND TRANSFER OF TITLE TO SECURITIES WITHOUT WRITTEN INSTRUMENT

Introductory

783 Scope of this Chapter

In this Chapter—

(a) "securities" means shares, debentures, debenture stock, loan stock, bonds, units of a collective investment scheme within the meaning of the Financial Services and Markets Act 2000 (c 8) and other securities of any description;
(b) references to title to securities include any legal or equitable interest in securities;
(c) references to a transfer of title include a transfer by way of security;
(d) references to transfer without a written instrument include, in relation to bearer securities, transfer without delivery.

[S783]

NOTES

Commencement: to be appointed.

784 Power to make regulations

(1) The power to make regulations under this Chapter is exercisable by the Treasury and the Secretary of State, either jointly or concurrently.

(2) References in this Chapter to the authority having power to make regulations shall accordingly be read as references to both or either of them, as the case may require.

(3) Regulations under this Chapter are subject to affirmative resolution procedure.

[S784]

NOTES

Commencement: 20 January 2007 (for the purpose of enabling the exercise of powers to make Orders or Regulations by statutory instrument); to be appointed (otherwise).

Powers exercisable

785 Provision enabling procedures for evidencing and transferring title

(1) Provision may be made by regulations for enabling title to securities to be evidenced and transferred without a written instrument.

(2) The regulations may make provision—
(a) for procedures for recording and transferring title to securities, and
(b) for the regulation of those procedures and the persons responsible for or involved in their operation.

(3) The regulations must contain such safeguards as appear to the authority making the regulations appropriate for the protection of investors and for ensuring that competition is not restricted, distorted or prevented.

(4) The regulations may, for the purpose of enabling or facilitating the operation of the procedures provided for by the regulations, make provision with respect to the rights and obligations of persons in relation to securities dealt with under the procedures.

(5) The regulations may include provision for the purpose of giving effect to—
(a) the transmission of title to securities by operation of law;
(b) any restriction on the transfer of title to securities arising by virtue of the provisions of any enactment or instrument, court order or agreement;
(c) any power conferred by any such provision on a person to deal with securities on behalf of the person entitled.

(6) The regulations may make provision with respect to the persons responsible for the operation of the procedures provided for by the regulations—
(a) as to the consequences of their insolvency or incapacity, or
(b) as to the transfer from them to other persons of their functions in relation to those procedures.

[S785]

NOTES

Commencement: 20 January 2007 (for the purpose of enabling the exercise of powers to make Orders or Regulations by statutory instrument); to be appointed (otherwise).

786 Provision enabling or requiring arrangements to be adopted

(1) Regulations under this Chapter may make provision—
- (a) enabling the members of a company or of any designated class of companies to adopt, by ordinary resolution, arrangements under which title to securities is required to be evidenced or transferred (or both) without a written instrument; or
- (b) requiring companies, or any designated class of companies, to adopt such arrangements.

(2) The regulations may make such provision—
- (a) in respect of all securities issued by a company, or
- (b) in respect of all securities of a specified description.

(3) The arrangements provided for by regulations making such provision as is mentioned in subsection (1)—
- (a) must not be such that a person who but for the arrangements would be entitled to have his name entered in the company's register of members ceases to be so entitled, and
- (b) must be such that a person who but for the arrangements would be entitled to exercise any rights in respect of the securities continues to be able effectively to control the exercise of those rights.

(4) The regulations may—
- (a) prohibit the issue of any certificate by the company in respect of the issue or transfer of securities,
- (b) require the provision by the company to holders of securities of statements (at specified intervals or on specified occasions) of the securities held in their name, and
- (c) make provision as to the matters of which any such certificate or statement is, or is not, evidence.

(5) In this section—
- (a) references to a designated class of companies are to a class designated in the regulations or by order under section 787; and
- (b) "specified" means specified in the regulations.

[S786]

NOTES

Commencement: 20 January 2007 (for the purpose of enabling the exercise of powers to make Orders or Regulations by statutory instrument); to be appointed (otherwise).

787 Provision enabling or requiring arrangements to be adopted: order-making powers

(1) The authority having power to make regulations under this Chapter may by order—
- (a) designate classes of companies for the purposes of section 786 (provision enabling or requiring arrangements to be adopted);
- (b) provide that, in relation to securities of a specified description—
  - (i) in a designated class of companies, or
  - (ii) in a specified company or class of companies,

specified provisions of regulations made under this Chapter by virtue of that section either do not apply or apply subject to specified modifications.

(2) In subsection (1) "specified" means specified in the order.

(3) An order under this section is subject to negative resolution procedure.

[S787]

NOTES

Commencement: 20 January 2007 (for the purpose of enabling the exercise of powers to make Orders or Regulations by statutory instrument); to be appointed (otherwise).

Supplementary

788 Provision that may be included in regulations

Regulations under this Chapter may—

(a) modify or exclude any provision of any enactment or instrument, or any rule of law;
(b) apply, with such modifications as may be appropriate, the provisions of any enactment or instrument (including provisions creating criminal offences);
(c) require the payment of fees, or enable persons to require the payment of fees, of such amounts as may be specified in the regulations or determined in accordance with them;
(d) empower the authority making the regulations to delegate to any person willing and able to discharge them any functions of the authority under the regulations.

[S788]

NOTES

Commencement: 20 January 2007 (for the purpose of enabling the exercise of powers to make Orders or Regulations by statutory instrument); to be appointed (otherwise).

789 Duty to consult

Before making—
(a) regulations under this Chapter, or
(b) any order under section 787,

the authority having power to make regulations under this Chapter must carry out such consultation as appears to it to be appropriate.

[S789]

NOTES

Commencement: 20 January 2007 (for the purpose of enabling the exercise of powers to make Orders or Regulations by statutory instrument); to be appointed (otherwise).

790 Resolutions to be forwarded to registrar

Chapter 3 of Part 3 (resolutions affecting a company's constitution) applies to a resolution passed by virtue of regulations under this Chapter.

[S790]

NOTES

Commencement: to be appointed.

PART 22
INFORMATION ABOUT INTERESTS IN A COMPANY'S SHARES

Introductory

791 Companies to which this Part applies

This Part applies only to public companies.

[S791]

NOTES

Commencement: 20 January 2007.

792 Shares to which this Part applies

(1) References in this Part to a company's shares are to the company's issued shares of a class carrying rights to vote in all circumstances at general meetings of the company (including any shares held as treasury shares).

(2) The temporary suspension of voting rights in respect of any shares does not affect the application of this Part in relation to interests in those or any other shares.

[S792]

NOTES

Commencement: 20 January 2007.

Notice requiring information about interests in shares

793 Notice by company requiring information about interests in its shares

(1) A public company may give notice under this section to any person whom the company knows or has reasonable cause to believe—

(a) to be interested in the company's shares, or

(b) to have been so interested at any time during the three years immediately preceding the date on which the notice is issued.

(2) The notice may require the person—

(a) to confirm that fact or (as the case may be) to state whether or not it is the case, and

(b) if he holds, or has during that time held, any such interest, to give such further information as may be required in accordance with the following provisions of this section.

(3) The notice may require the person to whom it is addressed to give particulars of his own present or past interest in the company's shares (held by him at any time during the three year period mentioned in subsection (1)(b)).

(4) The notice may require the person to whom it is addressed, where—

(a) his interest is a present interest and another interest in the shares subsists, or

(b) another interest in the shares subsisted during that three year period at a time when his interest subsisted,

to give, so far as lies within his knowledge, such particulars with respect to that other interest as may be required by the notice.

(5) The particulars referred to in subsections (3) and (4) include—

(a) the identity of persons interested in the shares in question, and

(b) whether persons interested in the same shares are or were parties to—

(i) an agreement to which section 824 applies (certain share acquisition agreements), or

(ii) an agreement or arrangement relating to the exercise of any rights conferred by the holding of the shares.

(6) The notice may require the person to whom it is addressed, where his interest is a past interest, to give (so far as lies within his knowledge) particulars of the identity of the person who held that interest immediately upon his ceasing to hold it.

(7) The information required by the notice must be given within such reasonable time as may be specified in the notice.

[S793]

NOTES

Commencement: 20 January 2007.

794 Notice requiring information: order imposing restrictions on shares

(1) Where—

(a) a notice under section 793 (notice requiring information about interests in company's shares) is served by a company on a person who is or was interested in shares in the company, and

(b) that person fails to give the company the information required by the notice within the time specified in it,

the company may apply to the court for an order directing that the shares in question be subject to restrictions.

For the effect of such an order see section 797.

(2) If the court is satisfied that such an order may unfairly affect the rights of third parties in respect of the shares, the court may, for the purpose of protecting those rights and subject to such terms as it thinks fit, direct that such acts by such persons or descriptions of persons and for such purposes as may be set out in the order shall not constitute a breach of the restrictions.

(3) On an application under this section the court may make an interim order. Any such order may be made unconditionally or on such terms as the court thinks fit.

(4) Sections 798 to 802 make further provision about orders under this section.

[S794]

NOTES

Commencement: 20 January 2007.

795 Notice requiring information: offences

(1) A person who—

(a) fails to comply with a notice under section 793 (notice requiring information about interests in company's shares), or

(b) in purported compliance with such a notice—

(i) makes a statement that he knows to be false in a material particular, or

(ii) recklessly makes a statement that is false in a material particular,

commits an offence.

(2) A person does not commit an offence under subsection (1)(a) if he proves that the requirement to give information was frivolous or vexatious.

(3) A person guilty of an offence under this section is liable—

(a) on conviction on indictment, to imprisonment for a term not exceeding two years or a fine (or both);

(b) on summary conviction—

(i) in England and Wales, to imprisonment for a term not exceeding twelve months or to a fine not exceeding the statutory maximum (or both);

(ii) in Scotland or Northern Ireland, to imprisonment for a term not exceeding six months, or to a fine not exceeding the statutory maximum (or both).

[S795]

NOTES

Commencement: 20 January 2007.

796 Notice requiring information: persons exempted from obligation to comply

(1) A person is not obliged to comply with a notice under section 793 (notice requiring information about interests in company's shares) if he is for the time being exempted by the Secretary of State from the operation of that section.

(2) The Secretary of State must not grant any such exemption unless—

(a) he has consulted the Governor of the Bank of England, and

(b) he (the Secretary of State) is satisfied that, having regard to any undertaking given by the person in question with respect to any interest held or to be held by him in any shares, there are special reasons why that person should not be subject to the obligations imposed by that section.

[S796]

NOTES

Commencement: 20 January 2007.

Orders imposing restrictions on shares

797 Consequences of order imposing restrictions

(1) The effect of an order under section 794 that shares are subject to restrictions is as follows—

(a) any transfer of the shares is void;

(b) no voting rights are exercisable in respect of the shares;

(c) no further shares may be issued in right of the shares or in pursuance of an offer made to their holder;

(d) except in a liquidation, no payment may be made of sums due from the company on the shares, whether in respect of capital or otherwise.

(2) Where shares are subject to the restriction in subsection (1)(a), an agreement to transfer the shares is void.

This does not apply to an agreement to transfer the shares on the making of an order under section 800 made by virtue of subsection (3)(b) (removal of restrictions in case of court-approved transfer).

(3) Where shares are subject to the restriction in subsection (1)(c) or (d), an agreement to transfer any right to be issued with other shares in right of those shares, or to receive any payment on them (otherwise than in a liquidation), is void.

This does not apply to an agreement to transfer any such right on the making of an order under section 800 made by virtue of subsection (3)(b) (removal of restrictions in case of court-approved transfer).

(4) The provisions of this section are subject—

(a) to any directions under section 794(2) or section 799(3) (directions for protection of third parties), and

(b) in the case of an interim order under section 794(3), to the terms of the order.

[S797]

NOTES

Commencement: 20 January 2007.

798 Penalty for attempted evasion of restrictions

(1) This section applies where shares are subject to restrictions by virtue of an order under section 794.

(2) A person commits an offence if he—

(a) exercises or purports to exercise any right—

(i) to dispose of shares that to his knowledge, are for the time being subject to restrictions, or

(ii) to dispose of any right to be issued with any such shares, or

(b) votes in respect of any such shares (whether as holder or proxy), or appoints a proxy to vote in respect of them, or

(c) being the holder of any such shares, fails to notify of their being subject to those restrictions a person whom he does not know to be aware of that fact but does know to be entitled (apart from the restrictions) to vote in respect of those shares whether as holder or as proxy, or

(d) being the holder of any such shares, or being entitled to a right to be issued with other shares in right of them, or to receive any payment on them (otherwise than in a liquidation), enters into an agreement which is void under section 797(2) or (3).

(3) If shares in a company are issued in contravention of the restrictions, an offence is committed by—

(a) the company, and

(b) every officer of the company who is in default.

(4) A person guilty of an offence under this section is liable—

(a) on conviction on indictment, to a fine;

(b) on summary conviction, to a fine not exceeding the statutory maximum.

(5) The provisions of this section are subject—

(a) to any directions under—
section 794(2) (directions for protection of third parties), or
section 799 or 800 (relaxation or removal of restrictions), and

(b) in the case of an interim order under section 794(3), to the terms of the order.

[S798]

NOTES

Commencement: 20 January 2007.

799 Relaxation of restrictions

(1) An application may be made to the court on the ground that an order directing that shares shall be subject to restrictions unfairly affects the rights of third parties in respect of the shares.

(2) An application for an order under this section may be made by the company or by any person aggrieved.

(3) If the court is satisfied that the application is well-founded, it may, for the purpose of protecting the rights of third parties in respect of the shares, and subject to such terms as it thinks fit, direct that such acts by such persons or descriptions of persons and for such purposes as may be set out in the order do not constitute a breach of the restrictions.

[S799]

NOTES

Commencement: 20 January 2007.

800 Removal of restrictions

(1) An application may be made to the court for an order directing that the shares shall cease to be subject to restrictions.

(2) An application for an order under this section may be made by the company or by any person aggrieved.

(3) The court must not make an order under this section unless—

(a) it is satisfied that the relevant facts about the shares have been disclosed to the company and no unfair advantage has accrued to any person as a result of the earlier failure to make that disclosure, or

(b) the shares are to be transferred for valuable consideration and the court approves the transfer.

(4) An order under this section made by virtue of subsection (3)(b) may continue, in whole or in part, the restrictions mentioned in section 797(1)(c) and (d) (restrictions on issue of further shares or making of payments) so far as they relate to a right acquired or offer made before the transfer.

(5) Where any restrictions continue in force under subsection (4)—

(a) an application may be made under this section for an order directing that the shares shall cease to be subject to those restrictions, and

(b) subsection (3) does not apply in relation to the making of such an order.

[S800]

NOTES

Commencement: 20 January 2007.

801 Order for sale of shares

(1) The court may order that the shares subject to restrictions be sold, subject to the court's approval as to the sale.

(2) An application for an order under subsection (1) may only be made by the company.

(3) Where the court has made an order under this section, it may make such further order relating to the sale or transfer of the shares as it thinks fit.

(4) An application for an order under subsection (3) may be made—

(a) by the company,

(b) by the person appointed by or in pursuance of the order to effect the sale, or

(c) by any person interested in the shares.

(5) On making an order under subsection (1) or (3) the court may order that the applicant's costs (in Scotland, expenses) be paid out of the proceeds of sale.

[S801]

NOTES

Commencement: 20 January 2007.

802 Application of proceeds of sale under court order

(1) Where shares are sold in pursuance of an order of the court under section 801, the proceeds of the sale, less the costs of the sale, must be paid into court for the benefit of the persons who are beneficially interested in the shares.

(2) A person who is beneficially interested in the shares may apply to the court for the whole or part of those proceeds to be paid to him.

(3) On such an application the court shall order the payment to the applicant of—

(a) the whole of the proceeds of sale together with any interest on them, or

(b) if another person had a beneficial interest in the shares at the time of their sale, such proportion of the proceeds and interest as the value of the applicant's interest in the shares bears to the total value of the shares.

This is subject to the following qualification.

(4) If the court has ordered under section 801(5) that the costs (in Scotland, expenses) of an applicant under that section are to be paid out of the proceeds of sale, the applicant is entitled to payment of his costs (or expenses) out of those proceeds before any person interested in the shares receives any part of those proceeds.

[S802]

NOTES

Commencement: 20 January 2007.

Power of members to require company to act

803 Power of members to require company to act

(1) The members of a company may require it to exercise its powers under section 793 (notice requiring information about interests in shares).

(2) A company is required to do so once it has received requests (to the same effect) from members of the company holding at least 10% of such of the paid-up capital of the company as carries a right to vote at general meetings of the company (excluding any voting rights attached to any shares in the company held as treasury shares).

(3) A request—

(a) may be in hard copy form or in electronic form,

(b) must—

(i) state that the company is requested to exercise its powers under section 793,

(ii) specify the manner in which the company is requested to act, and

(iii) give reasonable grounds for requiring the company to exercise those powers in the manner specified, and

(c) must be authenticated by the person or persons making it.

[S803]

NOTES

Commencement: 20 January 2007.

804 Duty of company to comply with requirement

(1) A company that is required under section 803 to exercise its powers under section 793 (notice requiring information about interests in company's shares) must exercise those powers in the manner specified in the requests.

(2) If default is made in complying with subsection (1) an offence is committed by every officer of the company who is in default.

(3) A person guilty of an offence under this section is liable—

(a) on conviction on indictment, to a fine;

(b) on summary conviction, to a fine not exceeding the statutory maximum.

[S804]

NOTES

Commencement: 20 January 2007.

805 Report to members on outcome of investigation

(1) On the conclusion of an investigation carried out by a company in pursuance of a requirement under section 803 the company must cause a report of the information received in pursuance of the investigation to be prepared.

The report must be made available for inspection within a reasonable period (not more than 15 days) after the conclusion of the investigation.

(2) Where—

(a) a company undertakes an investigation in pursuance of a requirement under section 803, and

(b) the investigation is not concluded within three months after the date on which the company became subject to the requirement,

the company must cause to be prepared in respect of that period, and in respect of each succeeding period of three months ending before the conclusion of the investigation, an interim report of the information received during that period in pursuance of the investigation.

(3) Each such report must be made available for inspection within a reasonable period (not more than 15 days) after the end of the period to which it relates.

(4) The reports must be retained by the company for at least six years from the date on which they are first made available for inspection and must be kept available for inspection during that time—

(a) at the company's registered office, or

(b) at a place specified in regulations under section 1136.

(5) The company must give notice to the registrar—

(a) of the place at which the reports are kept available for inspection, and

(b) of any change in that place,

unless they have at all times been kept at the company's registered office.

(6) The company must within three days of making any report prepared under this section available for inspection, notify the members who made the requests under section 803 where the report is so available.

(7) For the purposes of this section an investigation carried out by a company in pursuance of a requirement under section 803 is concluded when—

(a) the company has made all such inquiries as are necessary or expedient for the purposes of the requirement, and

(b) in the case of each such inquiry—

(i) a response has been received by the company, or

(ii) the time allowed for a response has elapsed.

[S805]

NOTES

Commencement: 20 January 2007.

806 Report to members: offences

(1) If default is made for 14 days in complying with section 805(5) (notice to registrar of place at which reports made available for inspection) an offence is committed by—

(a) the company, and

(b) every officer of the company who is in default.

(2) A person guilty of an offence under subsection (1) is liable on summary conviction to a fine not exceeding level 3 on the standard scale and, for continued contravention, a daily default fine not exceeding one-tenth of level 3 on the standard scale.

(3) If default is made in complying with any other provision of section 805 (report to members on outcome of investigation), an offence is committed by every officer of the company who is in default.

(4) A person guilty of an offence under subsection (3) is liable—

(a) on conviction on indictment, to a fine;

(b) on summary conviction, to a fine not exceeding the statutory maximum.

[S806]

NOTES

Commencement: 20 January 2007.

807 Right to inspect and request copy of reports

(1) Any report prepared under section 805 must be open to inspection by any person without charge.

(2) Any person is entitled, on request and on payment of such fee as may be prescribed, to be provided with a copy of any such report or any part of it. The copy must be provided within ten days after the request is received by the company.

(3) If an inspection required under subsection (1) is refused, or default is made in complying with subsection (2), an offence is committed by—

(a) the company, and

(b) every officer of the company who is in default.

(4) A person guilty of an offence under this section is liable on summary conviction to a fine not exceeding level 3 on the standard scale and, for continued contravention, a daily default fine not exceeding one-tenth of level 3 on the standard scale.

(5) In the case of any such refusal or default the court may by order compel an immediate inspection or, as the case may be, direct that the copy required be sent to the person requiring it.

[S807]

NOTES

Commencement: 20 January 2007.

Register of interests disclosed

808 Register of interests disclosed

(1) The company must keep a register of information received by it in pursuance of a requirement imposed under section 793 (notice requiring information about interests in company's shares).

(2) A company which receives any such information must, within three days of the receipt, enter in the register—

(a) the fact that the requirement was imposed and the date on which it was imposed, and

(b) the information received in pursuance of the requirement.

(3) The information must be entered against the name of the present holder of the shares in question or, if there is no present holder or the present holder is not known, against the name of the person holding the interest.

(4) The register must be made up so that the entries against the names entered in it appear in chronological order.

(5) If default is made in complying with this section an offence is committed by—

(a) the company, and

(b) every officer of the company who is in default.

(6) A person guilty of an offence under this section is liable on summary conviction to a fine not exceeding level 3 on the standard scale and, for continued contravention, a daily default fine not exceeding one-tenth of level 3 on the standard scale.

(7) The company is not by virtue of anything done for the purposes of this section affected with notice of, or put upon inquiry as to, the rights of any person in relation to any shares.

[S808]

NOTES

Commencement: 20 January 2007.

See also the Companies Act 2006 (Commencement No 1, Transitional Provisions and Savings) Order 2006, SI 2006/3428, Sch 5, Pt 2, para 2 (Information about interests in a company's shares) at **[7590]**.

809 Register to be kept available for inspection

(1) The register kept under section 808 (register of interests disclosed) must be kept available for inspection—

(a) at the company's registered office, or

(b) at a place specified in regulations under section 1136.

(2) A company must give notice to the registrar of companies of the place where the register is kept available for inspection and of any change in that place.

(3) No such notice is required if the register has at all times been kept available for inspection at the company's registered office.

(4) If default is made in complying with subsection (1), or a company makes default for 14 days in complying with subsection (2), an offence is committed by—

(a) the company, and

(b) every officer of the company who is in default.

(5) A person guilty of an offence under this section is liable on summary conviction to a fine not exceeding level 3 on the standard scale and, for continued contravention, a daily default fine not exceeding one-tenth of level 3 on the standard scale.

[S809]

NOTES

Commencement: 20 January 2007.

See also the Companies Act 2006 (Commencement No 1, Transitional Provisions and Savings) Order 2006, SI 2006/3428, Sch 5, Pt 2, para 2 (Information about interests in a company's shares) at **[7590]**.

810 Associated index

(1) Unless the register kept under section 808 (register of interests disclosed) is kept in such a form as itself to constitute an index, the company must keep an index of the names entered in it.

(2) The company must make any necessary entry or alteration in the index within ten days after the date on which any entry or alteration is made in the register.

(3) The index must contain, in respect of each name, a sufficient indication to enable the information entered against it to be readily found.

(4) The index must be at all times kept available for inspection at the same place as the register.

(5) If default is made in complying with this section, an offence is committed by—

(a) the company, and

(b) every officer of the company who is in default.

(6) A person guilty of an offence under this section is liable on summary conviction to a fine not exceeding level 3 on the standard scale and, for continued contravention, a daily default fine not exceeding one-tenth of level 3 on the standard scale.

[S810]

NOTES

Commencement: 20 January 2007.

811 Rights to inspect and require copy of entries

(1) The register required to be kept under section 808 (register of interests disclosed), and any associated index, must be open to inspection by any person without charge.

(2) Any person is entitled, on request and on payment of such fee as may be prescribed, to be provided with a copy of any entry in the register.

(3) A person seeking to exercise either of the rights conferred by this section must make a request to the company to that effect.

(4) The request must contain the following information—
(a) in the case of an individual, his name and address;
(b) in the case of an organisation, the name and address of an individual responsible for making the request on behalf of the organisation;
(c) the purpose for which the information is to be used; and
(d) whether the information will be disclosed to any other person, and if so—
(i) where that person is an individual, his name and address,
(ii) where that person is an organisation, the name and address of an individual responsible for receiving the information on its behalf, and
(iii) the purpose for which the information is to be used by that person.

[S811]

NOTES

Commencement: 20 January 2007 (sub-ss (1)–(3)); to be appointed (otherwise).

812 Court supervision of purpose for which rights may be exercised

(1) Where a company receives a request under section 811 (register of interests disclosed: right to inspect and require copy), it must—
(a) comply with the request if it is satisfied that it is made for a proper purpose, and
(b) refuse the request if it is not so satisfied.

(2) If the company refuses the request, it must inform the person making the request, stating the reason why it is not satisfied.

(3) A person whose request is refused may apply to the court.

(4) If an application is made to the court—
(a) the person who made the request must notify the company, and
(b) the company must use its best endeavours to notify any persons whose details would be disclosed if the company were required to comply with the request.

(5) If the court is not satisfied that the inspection or copy is sought for a proper purpose, it shall direct the company not to comply with the request.

(6) If the court makes such a direction and it appears to the court that the company is or may be subject to other requests made for a similar purpose (whether made by the same person or different persons), it may direct that the company is not to comply with any such request.

The order must contain such provision as appears to the court appropriate to identify the requests to which it applies.

(7) If the court does not direct the company not to comply with the request, the company must comply with the request immediately upon the court giving its decision or, as the case may be, the proceedings being discontinued.

[S812]

NOTES

Commencement: to be appointed.

813 Register of interests disclosed: refusal of inspection or default in providing copy

(1) If an inspection required under section 811 (register of interests disclosed: right to inspect and require copy) is refused or default is made in providing a copy required under that section, otherwise than in accordance with an order of the court, an offence is committed by—
(a) the company, and
(b) every officer of the company who is in default.

(2) A person guilty of an offence under this section is liable on summary conviction to a fine not exceeding level 3 on the standard scale and, for continued contravention, a daily default fine not exceeding one-tenth of level 3 on the standard scale.

(3) In the case of any such refusal or default the court may by order compel an immediate inspection or, as the case may be, direct that the copy required be sent to the person requesting it.

[S813]

NOTES

Commencement: 20 January 2007.

Transitional adaptations: art 5 of the Companies Act 2006 (Commencement No 1, Transitional Provisions and Savings) Order 2006, SI 2006/3428 provides that the provisions brought into force by arts 2–4 of 2006 Order shall have effect subject to any transitional adaptations specified in Sch 1 to that Order. Schedule 1, para 2 to the Order (at **[7582]**) provides as follows—

"**2.**—(1) Section 813 (register of interests disclosed: refusal of inspection or default in providing copy) has effect with the following adaptation.

(2) In subsection (1) omit ", otherwise than in accordance with an order of the court,".".

814 Register of interests disclosed: offences in connection with request for or disclosure of information

(1) It is an offence for a person knowingly or recklessly to make in a request under section 811 (register of interests disclosed: right to inspect or require copy) a statement that is misleading, false or deceptive in a material particular.

(2) It is an offence for a person in possession of information obtained by exercise of either of the rights conferred by that section—

(a) to do anything that results in the information being disclosed to another person, or

(b) to fail to do anything with the result that the information is disclosed to another person,

knowing, or having reason to suspect, that person may use the information for a purpose that is not a proper purpose.

(3) A person guilty of an offence under this section is liable—

(a) on conviction on indictment, to imprisonment for a term not exceeding two years or a fine (or both);

(b) on summary conviction—

(i) in England and Wales, to imprisonment for a term not exceeding twelve months or to a fine not exceeding the statutory maximum (or both);

(ii) in Scotland or Northern Ireland, to imprisonment for a term not exceeding six months, or to a fine not exceeding the statutory maximum (or both).

[S814]

NOTES

Commencement: to be appointed.

815 Entries not to be removed from register

(1) Entries in the register kept under section 808 (register of interests disclosed) must not be deleted except in accordance with—

section 816 (old entries), or

section 817 (incorrect entry relating to third party).

(2) If an entry is deleted in contravention of subsection (1), the company must restore it as soon as reasonably practicable.

(3) If default is made in complying with subsection (1) or (2), an offence is committed by—

(a) the company, and

(b) every officer of the company who is in default.

(4) A person guilty of an offence under this section is liable on summary conviction to a fine not exceeding level 3 on the standard scale and, for continued contravention of subsection (2), a daily default fine not exceeding one-tenth of level 3 on the standard scale.

[S815]

NOTES

Commencement: 20 January 2007.

816 Removal of entries from register: old entries

A company may remove an entry from the register kept under section 808 (register of interests disclosed) if more than six years have elapsed since the entry was made.

[S816]

NOTES

Commencement: 20 January 2007.

817 Removal of entries from register: incorrect entry relating to third party

(1) This section applies where in pursuance of an obligation imposed by a notice under section 793 (notice requiring information about interests in company's shares) a person gives to a company the name and address of another person as being interested in shares in the company.

(2) That other person may apply to the company for the removal of the entry from the register.

(3) If the company is satisfied that the information in pursuance of which the entry was made is incorrect, it shall remove the entry.

(4) If an application under subsection (3) is refused, the applicant may apply to the court for an order directing the company to remove the entry in question from the register.

The court may make such an order if it thinks fit.

[S817]

NOTES

Commencement: 20 January 2007.

818 Adjustment of entry relating to share acquisition agreement

(1) If a person who is identified in the register kept by a company under section 808 (register of interests disclosed) as being a party to an agreement to which section 824 applies (certain share acquisition agreements) ceases to be a party to the agreement, he may apply to the company for the inclusion of that information in the register.

(2) If the company is satisfied that he has ceased to be a party to the agreement, it shall record that information (if not already recorded) in every place where his name appears in the register as a party to the agreement.

(3) If an application under this section is refused (otherwise than on the ground that the information has already been recorded), the applicant may apply to the court for an order directing the company to include the information in question in the register.

The court may make such an order if it thinks fit.

[S818]

NOTES

Commencement: 20 January 2007.

819 Duty of company ceasing to be public company

(1) If a company ceases to be a public company, it must continue to keep any register kept under section 808 (register of interests disclosed), and any associated index, until the end of the period of six years after it ceased to be such a company.

(2) If default is made in complying with this section, an offence is committed by—

(a) the company, and

(b) every officer of the company who is in default.

(3) A person guilty of an offence under this section is liable on summary conviction to a fine not exceeding level 3 on the standard scale and, for continued contravention, a daily default fine not exceeding one-tenth of level 3 on the standard scale.

[S819]

NOTES

Commencement: 20 January 2007.

Meaning of interest in shares

820 Interest in shares: general

(1) This section applies to determine for the purposes of this Part whether a person has an interest in shares.

(2) In this Part—

(a) a reference to an interest in shares includes an interest of any kind whatsoever in the shares, and

(b) any restraints or restrictions to which the exercise of any right attached to the interest is or may be subject shall be disregarded.

(3) Where an interest in shares is comprised in property held on trust, every beneficiary of the trust is treated as having an interest in the shares.

(4) A person is treated as having an interest in shares if—

(a) he enters into a contract to acquire them, or

(b) not being the registered holder, he is entitled—

(i) to exercise any right conferred by the holding of the shares, or

(ii) to control the exercise of any such right.

(5) For the purposes of subsection (4)(b) a person is entitled to exercise or control the exercise of a right conferred by the holding of shares if he—

(a) has a right (whether subject to conditions or not) the exercise of which would make him so entitled, or

(b) is under an obligation (whether subject to conditions or not) the fulfilment of which would make him so entitled.

(6) A person is treated as having an interest in shares if—

(a) he has a right to call for delivery of the shares to himself or to his order, or

(b) he has a right to acquire an interest in shares or is under an obligation to take an interest in shares.

This applies whether the right or obligation is conditional or absolute.

(7) Persons having a joint interest are treated as each having that interest.

(8) It is immaterial that shares in which a person has an interest are unidentifiable.

[S820]

NOTES

Commencement: 20 January 2007.

821 Interest in shares: right to subscribe for shares

(1) Section 793 (notice by company requiring information about interests in its shares) applies in relation to a person who has, or previously had, or is or was entitled to acquire, a right to subscribe for shares in the company as it applies in relation to a person who is or was interested in shares in that company.

(2) References in that section to an interest in shares shall be read accordingly.

[S821]

NOTES

Commencement: 20 January 2007.

822 Interest in shares: family interests

(1) For the purposes of this Part a person is taken to be interested in shares in which—

(a) his spouse or civil partner, or

(b) any infant child or step-child of his,

is interested.

(2) In relation to Scotland "infant" means a person under the age of 18 years.

[S822]

NOTES

Commencement: 20 January 2007.

823 Interest in shares: corporate interests

(1) For the purposes of this Part a person is taken to be interested in shares if a body corporate is interested in them and—

(a) the body or its directors are accustomed to act in accordance with his directions or instructions, or

(b) he is entitled to exercise or control the exercise of one-third or more of the voting power at general meetings of the body.

(2) For the purposes of this section a person is treated as entitled to exercise or control the exercise of voting power if—

(a) another body corporate is entitled to exercise or control the exercise of that voting power, and

(b) he is entitled to exercise or control the exercise of one-third or more of the voting power at general meetings of that body corporate.

(3) For the purposes of this section a person is treated as entitled to exercise or control the exercise of voting power if—

(a) he has a right (whether or not subject to conditions) the exercise of which would make him so entitled, or

(b) he is under an obligation (whether or not subject to conditions) the fulfilment of which would make him so entitled.

[S823]

NOTES

Commencement: 20 January 2007.

824 Interest in shares: agreement to acquire interests in a particular company

(1) For the purposes of this Part an interest in shares may arise from an agreement between two or more persons that includes provision for the acquisition by any one or more of them of interests in shares of a particular public company (the "target company" for that agreement).

(2) This section applies to such an agreement if—

(a) the agreement includes provision imposing obligations or restrictions on any one or more of the parties to it with respect to their use, retention or disposal of their interests in the shares of the target company acquired in pursuance of the agreement (whether or not together with any other interests of theirs in the company's shares to which the agreement relates), and

(b) an interest in the target company's shares is in fact acquired by any of the parties in pursuance of the agreement.

(3) The reference in subsection (2) to the use of interests in shares in the target company is to the exercise of any rights or of any control or influence arising from those interests (including the right to enter into an agreement for the exercise, or for control of the exercise, of any of those rights by another person).

(4) Once an interest in shares in the target company has been acquired in pursuance of the agreement, this section continues to apply to the agreement so long as the agreement continues to include provisions of any description mentioned in subsection (2).

This applies irrespective of—

(a) whether or not any further acquisitions of interests in the company's shares take place in pursuance of the agreement;

(b) any change in the persons who are for the time being parties to it;

(c) any variation of the agreement.

References in this subsection to the agreement include any agreement having effect (whether directly or indirectly) in substitution for the original agreement.

(5) In this section—

(a) "agreement" includes any agreement or arrangement, and

(b) references to provisions of an agreement include—
   (i) undertakings, expectations or understandings operative under an arrangement, and
   (ii) any provision whether express or implied and whether absolute or not.

References elsewhere in this Part to an agreement to which this section applies have a corresponding meaning.

(6) This section does not apply—
(a) to an agreement that is not legally binding unless it involves mutuality in the undertakings, expectations or understandings of the parties to it; or
(b) to an agreement to underwrite or sub-underwrite an offer of shares in a company, provided the agreement is confined to that purpose and any matters incidental to it.

[S824]

NOTES

Commencement: 20 January 2007.

825 Extent of obligation in case of share acquisition agreement

(1) For the purposes of this Part each party to an agreement to which section 824 applies is treated as interested in all shares in the target company in which any other party to the agreement is interested apart from the agreement (whether or not the interest of the other party was acquired, or includes any interest that was acquired, in pursuance of the agreement).

(2) For those purposes an interest of a party to such an agreement in shares in the target company is an interest apart from the agreement if he is interested in those shares otherwise than by virtue of the application of section 824 (and this section) in relation to the agreement.

(3) Accordingly, any such interest of the person (apart from the agreement) includes for those purposes any interest treated as his under section 822 or 823 (family or corporate interests) or by the application of section 824 (and this section) in relation to any other agreement with respect to shares in the target company to which he is a party.

(4) A notification with respect to his interest in shares in the target company made to the company under this Part by a person who is for the time being a party to an agreement to which section 824 applies must—
(a) state that the person making the notification is a party to such an agreement,
(b) include the names and (so far as known to him) the addresses of the other parties to the agreement, identifying them as such, and
(c) state whether or not any of the shares to which the notification relates are shares in which he is interested by virtue of section 824 (and this section) and, if so, the number of those shares.

[S825]

NOTES

Commencement: 20 January 2007.

Other supplementary provisions

826 Information protected from wider disclosure

(1) Information in respect of which a company is for the time being entitled to any exemption conferred by regulations under section 409(3) (information about related undertakings to be given in notes to accounts: exemption where disclosure harmful to company's business)—
(a) must not be included in a report under section 805 (report to members on outcome of investigation), and
(b) must not be made available under section 811 (right to inspect and request copy of entries).

(2) Where any such information is omitted from a report under section 805, that fact must be stated in the report.

[S826]

NOTES

Commencement: 20 January 2007.

Transitional adaptations: art 5 of the Companies Act 2006 (Commencement No 1, Transitional Provisions and Savings) Order 2006, SI 2006/3428 provides that the provisions brought into force by arts 2–4 of 2006 Order shall have effect subject to any transitional adaptations specified in Sch 1 to that Order. Schedule 1, para 3 to the Order (at **[7582]**) provides as follows—

"**3.**—(1) Section 826 (information about interests in a company's shares protected from wider disclosure) has effect with the following adaptation.

(2) In subsection (1) for "regulations under section 409(3)" substitute "section 231(3) of the Companies Act 1985 or Article 239(3) of the Companies (Northern Ireland) Order 1986".".

827 Reckoning of periods for fulfilling obligations

Where the period allowed by any provision of this Part for fulfilling an obligation is expressed as a number of days, any day that is not a working day shall be disregarded in reckoning that period.

[S827]

NOTES

Commencement: 20 January 2007.

828 Power to make further provision by regulations

(1) The Secretary of State may by regulations amend—

- (a) the definition of shares to which this Part applies (section 792),
- (b) the provisions as to notice by a company requiring information about interests in its shares (section 793), and
- (c) the provisions as to what is taken to be an interest in shares (sections 820 and 821).

(2) The regulations may amend, repeal or replace those provisions and make such other consequential amendments or repeals of provisions of this Part as appear to the Secretary of State to be appropriate.

(3) Regulations under this section are subject to affirmative resolution procedure.

[S828]

NOTES

Commencement: 20 January 2007.

PART 23
DISTRIBUTIONS

CHAPTER 1
RESTRICTIONS ON WHEN DISTRIBUTIONS MAY BE MADE

Introductory

829 Meaning of "distribution"

(1) In this Part "distribution" means every description of distribution of a company's assets to its members, whether in cash or otherwise, subject to the following exceptions.

(2) The following are not distributions for the purposes of this Part—

- (a) an issue of shares as fully or partly paid bonus shares;
- (b) the reduction of share capital—
  - (i) by extinguishing or reducing the liability of any of the members on any of the company's shares in respect of share capital not paid up, or
  - (ii) by repaying paid-up share capital;

(c) the redemption or purchase of any of the company's own shares out of capital (including the proceeds of any fresh issue of shares) or out of unrealised profits in accordance with Chapter 3, 4 or 5 of Part 18;

(d) a distribution of assets to members of the company on its winding up.

[S829]

NOTES

Commencement: to be appointed.

General rules

830 Distributions to be made only out of profits available for the purpose

(1) A company may only make a distribution out of profits available for the purpose.

(2) A company's profits available for distribution are its accumulated, realised profits, so far as not previously utilised by distribution or capitalisation, less its accumulated, realised losses, so far as not previously written off in a reduction or reorganisation of capital duly made.

(3) Subsection (2) has effect subject to sections 832 and 835 (investment companies etc: distributions out of accumulated revenue profits).

[S830]

NOTES

Commencement: to be appointed.

831 Net asset restriction on distributions by public companies

(1) A public company may only make a distribution—

(a) if the amount of its net assets is not less than the aggregate of its called-up share capital and undistributable reserves, and

(b) if, and to the extent that, the distribution does not reduce the amount of those assets to less than that aggregate.

(2) For this purpose a company's "net assets" means the aggregate of the company's assets less the aggregate of its liabilities.

(3) "Liabilities" here includes—

(a) where the relevant accounts are Companies Act accounts, provisions of a kind specified for the purposes of this subsection by regulations under section 396;

(b) where the relevant accounts are IAS accounts, provisions of any kind.

(4) A company's undistributable reserves are—

(a) its share premium account;

(b) its capital redemption reserve;

(c) the amount by which its accumulated, unrealised profits (so far as not previously utilised by capitalisation) exceed its accumulated, unrealised losses (so far as not previously written off in a reduction or reorganisation of capital duly made);

(d) any other reserve that the company is prohibited from distributing—

(i) by any enactment (other than one contained in this Part), or

(ii) by its articles.

The reference in paragraph (c) to capitalisation does not include a transfer of profits of the company to its capital redemption reserve.

(5) A public company must not include any uncalled share capital as an asset in any accounts relevant for purposes of this section.

(6) Subsection (1) has effect subject to sections 832 and 835 (investment companies etc: distributions out of accumulated revenue profits).

[S831]

NOTES

Commencement: to be appointed.

Distributions by investment companies

832 Distributions by investment companies out of accumulated revenue profits

(1) An investment company may make a distribution out of its accumulated, realised revenue profits if the following conditions are met.

(2) It may make such a distribution only if, and to the extent that, its accumulated, realised revenue profits, so far as not previously utilised by a distribution or capitalisation, exceed its accumulated revenue losses (whether realised or unrealised), so far as not previously written off in a reduction or reorganisation of capital duly made.

(3) It may make such a distribution only—
- (a) if the amount of its assets is at least equal to one and a half times the aggregate of its liabilities to creditors, and
- (b) if, and to the extent that, the distribution does not reduce that amount to less than one and a half times that aggregate.

(4) For this purpose a company's liabilities to creditors include—
- (a) in the case of Companies Act accounts, provisions of a kind specified for the purposes of this subsection by regulations under section 396;
- (b) in the case of IAS accounts, provisions for liabilities to creditors.

(5) The following conditions must also be met—
- (a) the company's shares must be listed on a recognised UK investment exchange;
- (b) during the relevant period it must not have—
  - (i) distributed any capital profits otherwise than by way of the redemption or purchase of any of the company's own shares in accordance with Chapter 3 or 4 of Part 18, or
  - (ii) applied any unrealised profits or any capital profits (realised or unrealised) in paying up debentures or amounts unpaid on its issued shares;
- (c) it must have given notice to the registrar under section 833(1) (notice of intention to carry on business as an investment company)—
  - (i) before the beginning of the relevant period, or
  - (ii) as soon as reasonably practicable after the date of its incorporation.

(6) For the purposes of this section—
- (a) "recognised UK investment exchange" means a recognised investment exchange within the meaning of Part 18 of the Financial Services and Markets Act 2000 (c 8), other than an overseas investment exchange within the meaning of that Part; and
- (b) the "relevant period" is the period beginning with—
  - (i) the first day of the accounting reference period immediately preceding that in which the proposed distribution is to be made, or
  - (ii) where the distribution is to be made in the company's first accounting reference period, the first day of that period,

and ending with the date of the distribution.

(7) The company must not include any uncalled share capital as an asset in any accounts relevant for purposes of this section.

[S832]

NOTES

Commencement: to be appointed.

833 Meaning of "investment company"

(1) In this Part an "investment company" means a public company that—
- (a) has given notice (which has not been revoked) to the registrar of its intention to carry on business as an investment company, and
- (b) since the date of that notice has complied with the following requirements.

(2) Those requirements are—
- (a) that the business of the company consists of investing its funds mainly in securities, with the aim of spreading investment risk and giving members of the company the benefit of the results of the management of its funds;
- (b) that the condition in section 834 is met as regards holdings in other companies;
- (c) that distribution of the company's capital profits is prohibited by its articles;

(d) that the company has not retained, otherwise than in compliance with this Part, in respect of any accounting reference period more than 15% of the income it derives from securities.

(3) Subsection (2)(c) does not require an investment company to be prohibited by its articles from redeeming or purchasing its own shares in accordance with Chapter 3 or 4 of Part 18 out of its capital profits.

(4) Notice to the registrar under this section may be revoked at any time by the company on giving notice to the registrar that it no longer wishes to be an investment company within the meaning of this section.

(5) On giving such a notice, the company ceases to be such a company.

[S833]

NOTES

Commencement: to be appointed.

834 Investment company: condition as to holdings in other companies

(1) The condition referred to in section 833(2)(b) (requirements to be complied with by investment company) is that none of the company's holdings in companies (other than those that are for the time being investment companies) represents more than 15% by value of the company's investments.

(2) For this purpose—

(a) holdings in companies that—

(i) are members of a group (whether or not including the investing company), and

(ii) are not for the time being investment companies,

are treated as holdings in a single company; and

(b) where the investing company is a member of a group, money owed to it by another member of the group—

(i) is treated as a security of the latter held by the investing company, and

(ii) is accordingly treated as, or as part of, the holding of the investing company in the company owing the money.

(3) The condition does not apply—

(a) to a holding in a company acquired before 6th April 1965 that on that date represented not more than 25% by value of the investing company's investments, or

(b) to a holding in a company that, when it was acquired, represented not more than 15% by value of the investing company's investments,

so long as no addition is made to the holding.

(4) For the purposes of subsection (3)—

(a) "holding" means the shares or securities (whether or one class or more than one class) held in any one company;

(b) an addition is made to a holding whenever the investing company acquires shares or securities of that one company, otherwise than by being allotted shares or securities without becoming liable to give any consideration, and if an addition is made to a holding that holding is acquired when the addition or latest addition is made to the holding; and

(c) where in connection with a scheme of reconstruction a company issues shares or securities to persons holding shares or securities in a second company in respect of and in proportion to (or as nearly as may be in proportion to) their holdings in the second company, without those persons becoming liable to give any consideration, a holding of the shares or securities in the second company and a corresponding holding of the shares or securities so issued shall be regarded as the same holding.

(5) In this section—

"company" and "shares" shall be construed in accordance with sections 99 and 288 of the Taxation of Chargeable Gains Act 1992 (c 12);

"group" means a company and all companies that are its 51% subsidiaries (within the meaning of section 838 of the Income and Corporation Taxes Act 1988 (c 1)); and "scheme of reconstruction" has the same meaning as in section 136 of the Taxation of Chargeable Gains Act 1992.

[S834]

NOTES

Commencement: to be appointed.

835 Power to extend provisions relating to investment companies

(1) The Secretary of State may by regulations extend the provisions of sections 832 to 834 (distributions by investment companies out of accumulated profits), with or without modifications, to other companies whose principal business consists of investing their funds in securities, land or other assets with the aim of spreading investment risk and giving their members the benefit of the results of the management of the assets.

(2) Regulations under this section are subject to affirmative resolution procedure.

[S835]

NOTES

Commencement: 20 January 2007 (for the purpose of enabling the exercise of powers to make Orders or Regulations by statutory instrument); to be appointed (otherwise).

CHAPTER 2
JUSTIFICATION OF DISTRIBUTION BY REFERENCE TO ACCOUNTS

Justification of distribution by reference to accounts

836 Justification of distribution by reference to relevant accounts

(1) Whether a distribution may be made by a company without contravening this Part is determined by reference to the following items as stated in the relevant accounts—

(a) profits, losses, assets and liabilities;

(b) provisions of the following kinds—

(i) where the relevant accounts are Companies Act accounts, provisions of a kind specified for the purposes of this subsection by regulations under section 396;

(ii) where the relevant accounts are IAS accounts, provisions of any kind;

(c) share capital and reserves (including undistributable reserves).

(2) The relevant accounts are the company's last annual accounts, except that—

(a) where the distribution would be found to contravene this Part by reference to the company's last annual accounts, it may be justified by reference to interim accounts, and

(b) where the distribution is proposed to be declared during the company's first accounting reference period, or before any accounts have been circulated in respect of that period, it may be justified by reference to initial accounts.

(3) The requirements of—

section 837 (as regards the company's last annual accounts),

section 838 (as regards interim accounts), and

section 839 (as regards initial accounts),

must be complied with, as and where applicable.

(4) If any applicable requirement of those sections is not complied with, the accounts may not be relied on for the purposes of this Part and the distribution is accordingly treated as contravening this Part.

[S836]

NOTES

Commencement: to be appointed.

Requirements applicable in relation to relevant accounts

837 Requirements where last annual accounts used

(1) The company's last annual accounts means the company's individual accounts—

(a) that were last circulated to members in accordance with section 423 (duty to circulate copies of annual accounts and reports), or

(b) if in accordance with section 426 the company provided a summary financial statement instead, that formed the basis of that statement.

(2) The accounts must have been properly prepared in accordance with this Act, or have been so prepared subject only to matters that are not material for determining (by reference to the items mentioned in section 836(1)) whether the distribution would contravene this Part.

(3) Unless the company is exempt from audit and the directors take advantage of that exemption, the auditor must have made his report on the accounts.

(4) If that report was qualified—

(a) the auditor must have stated in writing (either at the time of his report or subsequently) whether in his opinion the matters in respect of which his report is qualified are material for determining whether a distribution would contravene this Part, and

(b) a copy of that statement must—

(i) in the case of a private company, have been circulated to members in accordance with section 423, or

(ii) in the case of a public company, have been laid before the company in general meeting.

(5) An auditor's statement is sufficient for the purposes of a distribution if it relates to distributions of a description that includes the distribution in question, even if at the time of the statement it had not been proposed.

[S837]

NOTES

Commencement: to be appointed.

838 Requirements where interim accounts used

(1) Interim accounts must be accounts that enable a reasonable judgment to be made as to the amounts of the items mentioned in section 836(1).

(2) Where interim accounts are prepared for a proposed distribution by a public company, the following requirements apply.

(3) The accounts must have been properly prepared, or have been so prepared subject to matters that are not material for determining (by reference to the items mentioned in section 836(1)) whether the distribution would contravene this Part.

(4) "Properly prepared" means prepared in accordance with sections 395 to 397 (requirements for company individual accounts), applying those requirements with such modifications as are necessary because the accounts are prepared otherwise than in respect of an accounting reference period.

(5) The balance sheet comprised in the accounts must have been signed in accordance with section 414.

(6) A copy of the accounts must have been delivered to the registrar.

Any requirement of Part 35 of this Act as to the delivery of a certified translation into English of any document forming part of the accounts must also have been met.

[S838]

NOTES

Commencement: to be appointed.

839 Requirements where initial accounts used

(1) Initial accounts must be accounts that enable a reasonable judgment to be made as to the amounts of the items mentioned in section 836(1).

(2) Where initial accounts are prepared for a proposed distribution by a public company, the following requirements apply.

(3) The accounts must have been properly prepared, or have been so prepared subject to matters that are not material for determining (by reference to the items mentioned in section 836(1)) whether the distribution would contravene this Part.

(4) "Properly prepared" means prepared in accordance with sections 395 to 397 (requirements for company individual accounts), applying those requirements with such modifications as are necessary because the accounts are prepared otherwise than in respect of an accounting reference period.

(5) The company's auditor must have made a report stating whether, in his opinion, the accounts have been properly prepared.

(6) If that report was qualified—
- (a) the auditor must have stated in writing (either at the time of his report or subsequently) whether in his opinion the matters in respect of which his report is qualified are material for determining whether a distribution would contravene this Part, and
- (b) a copy of that statement must—
  - (i) in the case of a private company, have been circulated to members in accordance with section 423, or
  - (ii) in the case of a public company, have been laid before the company in general meeting.

(7) A copy of the accounts, of the auditor's report and of any auditor's statement must have been delivered to the registrar.

Any requirement of Part 35 of this Act as to the delivery of a certified translation into English of any of those documents must also have been met.

[S839]

NOTES

Commencement: to be appointed.

Application of provisions to successive distributions etc

840 Successive distributions etc by reference to the same accounts

(1) In determining whether a proposed distribution may be made by a company in a case where—
- (a) one or more previous distributions have been made in pursuance of a determination made by reference to the same relevant accounts, or
- (b) relevant financial assistance has been given, or other relevant payments have been made, since those accounts were prepared,

the provisions of this Part apply as if the amount of the proposed distribution was increased by the amount of the previous distributions, financial assistance and other payments.

(2) The financial assistance and other payments that are relevant for this purpose are—
- (a) financial assistance lawfully given by the company out of its distributable profits;
- (b) financial assistance given by the company in contravention of section 678 or 679 (prohibited financial assistance) in a case where the giving of that assistance reduces the company's net assets or increases its net liabilities;
- (c) payments made by the company in respect of the purchase by it of shares in the company, except a payment lawfully made otherwise than out of distributable profits;
- (d) payments of any description specified in section 705 (payments apart from purchase price of shares to be made out of distributable profits).

(3) In this section "financial assistance" has the same meaning as in Chapter 2 of Part 18 (see section 677).

(4) For the purpose of applying subsection (2)(b) in relation to any financial assistance—
- (a) "net assets" means the amount by which the aggregate amount of the company's assets exceeds the aggregate amount of its liabilities, and

(b) "net liabilities" means the amount by which the aggregate amount of the company's liabilities exceeds the aggregate amount of its assets,

taking the amount of the assets and liabilities to be as stated in the company's accounting records immediately before the financial assistance is given.

(5) For this purpose a company's liabilities include any amount retained as reasonably necessary for the purposes of providing for any liability—

(a) the nature of which is clearly defined, and

(b) which is either likely to be incurred or certain to be incurred but uncertain as to amount or as to the date on which it will arise.

[S840]

NOTES

Commencement: to be appointed.

CHAPTER 3
SUPPLEMENTARY PROVISIONS

Accounting matters

841 Realised losses and profits and revaluation of fixed assets

(1) The following provisions have effect for the purposes of this Part.

(2) The following are treated as realised losses—

(a) in the case of Companies Act accounts, provisions of a kind specified for the purposes of this paragraph by regulations under section 396 (except revaluation provisions);

(b) in the case of IAS accounts, provisions of any kind (except revaluation provisions).

(3) A "revaluation provision" means a provision in respect of a diminution in value of a fixed asset appearing on a revaluation of all the fixed assets of the company, or of all of its fixed assets other than goodwill.

(4) For the purpose of subsections (2) and (3) any consideration by the directors of the value at a particular time of a fixed asset is treated as a revaluation provided—

(a) the directors are satisfied that the aggregate value at that time of the fixed assets of the company that have not actually been revalued is not less than the aggregate amount at which they are then stated in the company's accounts, and

(b) it is stated in a note to the accounts—

(i) that the directors have considered the value of some or all of the fixed assets of the company without actually revaluing them,

(ii) that they are satisfied that the aggregate value of those assets at the time of their consideration was not less than the aggregate amount at which they were then stated in the company's accounts, and

(iii) that accordingly, by virtue of this subsection, amounts are stated in the accounts on the basis that a revaluation of fixed assets of the company is treated as having taken place at that time.

(5) Where—

(a) on the revaluation of a fixed asset, an unrealised profit is shown to have been made, and

(b) on or after the revaluation, a sum is written off or retained for depreciation of that asset over a period,

an amount equal to the amount by which that sum exceeds the sum which would have been so written off or retained for the depreciation of that asset over that period, if that profit had not been made, is treated as a realised profit made over that period.

[S841]

NOTES

Commencement: to be appointed.

842 Determination of profit or loss in respect of asset where records incomplete

In determining for the purposes of this Part whether a company has made a profit or loss in respect of an asset where—

(a) there is no record of the original cost of the asset, or

(b) a record cannot be obtained without unreasonable expense or delay,

its cost is taken to be the value ascribed to it in the earliest available record of its value made on or after its acquisition by the company.

[S842]

NOTES

Commencement: to be appointed.

843 Realised profits and losses of long-term insurance business

(1) The provisions of this section have effect for the purposes of this Part as it applies in relation to an authorised insurance company carrying on long-term business.

(2) An amount included in the relevant part of the company's balance sheet that—

(a) represents a surplus in the fund or funds maintained by it in respect of its long-term business, and

(b) has not been allocated to policy holders or, as the case may be, carried forward unappropriated in accordance with asset identification rules made under section 142(2) of the Financial Services and Markets Act 2000 (c 8),

is treated as a realised profit.

(3) For the purposes of subsection (2)—

(a) the relevant part of the balance sheet is that part of the balance sheet that represents accumulated profit or loss;

(b) a surplus in the fund or funds maintained by the company in respect of its long-term business means an excess of the assets representing that fund or those funds over the liabilities of the company attributable to its long-term business, as shown by an actuarial investigation.

(4) A deficit in the fund or funds maintained by the company in respect of its long-term business is treated as a realised loss.

For this purpose a deficit in any such fund or funds means an excess of the liabilities of the company attributable to its long-term business over the assets representing that fund or those funds, as shown by an actuarial investigation.

(5) Subject to subsections (2) and (4), any profit or loss arising in the company's long-term business is to be left out of account.

(6) For the purposes of this section an "actuarial investigation" means an investigation made into the financial condition of an authorised insurance company in respect of its long-term business—

(a) carried out once in every period of twelve months in accordance with rules made under Part 10 of the Financial Services and Markets Act 2000, or

(b) carried out in accordance with a requirement imposed under section 166 of that Act,

by an actuary appointed as actuary to the company.

(7) In this section "long-term business" means business that consists of effecting or carrying out contracts of long-term insurance.

This definition must be read with section 22 of the Financial Services and Markets Act 2000, any relevant order under that section and Schedule 2 to that Act.

[S843]

NOTES

Commencement: to be appointed.

844 Treatment of development costs

(1) Where development costs are shown or included as an asset in a company's accounts, any amount shown or included in respect of those costs is treated—

(a) for the purposes of section 830 (distributions to be made out of profits available for the purpose) as a realised loss, and
(b) for the purposes of section 832 (distributions by investment companies out of accumulated revenue profits) as a realised revenue loss.

This is subject to the following exceptions.

(2) Subsection (1) does not apply to any part of that amount representing an unrealised profit made on revaluation of those costs.

(3) Subsection (1) does not apply if—
(a) there are special circumstances in the company's case justifying the directors in deciding that the amount there mentioned is not to be treated as required by subsection (1),
(b) it is stated—
(i) in the case of Companies Act accounts, in the note required by regulations under section 396 as to the reasons for showing development costs as an asset, or
(ii) in the case of IAS accounts, in any note to the accounts,
that the amount is not to be so treated, and
(c) the note explains the circumstances relied upon to justify the decision of the directors to that effect.

[S844]

NOTES
Commencement: to be appointed.

Distributions in kind

845 Distributions in kind: determination of amount

(1) This section applies for determining the amount of a distribution consisting of or including, or treated as arising in consequence of, the sale, transfer or other disposition by a company of a non-cash asset where—
(a) at the time of the distribution the company has profits available for distribution, and
(b) if the amount of the distribution were to be determined in accordance with this section, the company could make the distribution without contravening this Part.

(2) The amount of the distribution (or the relevant part of it) is taken to be—
(a) in a case where the amount or value of the consideration for the disposition is not less than the book value of the asset, zero;
(b) in any other case, the amount by which the book value of the asset exceeds the amount or value of any consideration for the disposition.

(3) For the purposes of subsection (1)(a) the company's profits available for distribution are treated as increased by the amount (if any) by which the amount or value of any consideration for the disposition exceeds the book value of the asset.

(4) In this section "book value", in relation to an asset, means—
(a) the amount at which the asset is stated in the relevant accounts, or
(b) where the asset is not stated in those accounts at any amount, zero.

(5) The provisions of Chapter 2 (justification of distribution by reference to accounts) have effect subject to this section.

[S845]

NOTES
Commencement: to be appointed.

846 Distributions in kind: treatment of unrealised profits

(1) This section applies where—
(a) a company makes a distribution consisting of or including, or treated as arising in consequence of, the sale, transfer or other disposition by the company of a non-cash asset, and

(b) any part of the amount at which that asset is stated in the relevant accounts represents an unrealised profit.

(2) That profit is treated as a realised profit—

(a) for the purpose of determining the lawfulness of the distribution in accordance with this Part (whether before or after the distribution takes place), and

(b) for the purpose of the application, in relation to anything done with a view to or in connection with the making of the distribution, of any provision of regulations under section 396 under which only realised profits are to be included in or transferred to the profit and loss account.

[S846]

NOTES

Commencement: to be appointed.

Consequences of unlawful distribution

847 Consequences of unlawful distribution

(1) This section applies where a distribution, or part of one, made by a company to one of its members is made in contravention of this Part.

(2) If at the time of the distribution the member knows or has reasonable grounds for believing that it is so made, he is liable—

(a) to repay it (or that part of it, as the case may be) to the company, or

(b) in the case of a distribution made otherwise than in cash, to pay the company a sum equal to the value of the distribution (or part) at that time.

(3) This is without prejudice to any obligation imposed apart from this section on a member of a company to repay a distribution unlawfully made to him.

(4) This section does not apply in relation to—

(a) financial assistance given by a company in contravention of section 678 or 679, or

(b) any payment made by a company in respect of the redemption or purchase by the company of shares in itself.

[S847]

NOTES

Commencement: to be appointed.

Other matters

848 Saving for certain older provisions in articles

(1) Where immediately before the relevant date a company was authorised by a provision of its articles to apply its unrealised profits in paying up in full or in part unissued shares to be allotted to members of the company as fully or partly paid bonus shares, that provision continues (subject to any alteration of the articles) as authority for those profits to be so applied after that date.

(2) For this purpose the relevant date is—

(a) for companies registered in Great Britain, 22nd December 1980;

(b) for companies registered in Northern Ireland, 1st July 1983.

[S848]

NOTES

Commencement: to be appointed.

849 Restriction on application of unrealised profits

A company must not apply an unrealised profit in paying up debentures or any amounts unpaid on its issued shares.

[S849]

NOTES

Commencement: to be appointed.

850 Treatment of certain older profits or losses

(1) Where the directors of a company are, after making all reasonable enquiries, unable to determine whether a particular profit made before the relevant date is realised or unrealised, they may treat the profit as realised.

(2) Where the directors of a company, after making all reasonable enquiries, are unable to determine whether a particular loss made before the relevant date is realised or unrealised, they may treat the loss as unrealised.

(3) For the purposes of this section the relevant date is—

(a) for companies registered in Great Britain, 22nd December 1980;

(b) for companies registered in Northern Ireland, 1st July 1983.

[S850]

NOTES

Commencement: to be appointed.

851 Application of rules of law restricting distributions

(1) Except as provided in this section, the provisions of this Part are without prejudice to any rule of law restricting the sums out of which, or the cases in which, a distribution may be made.

(2) For the purposes of any rule of law requiring distributions to be paid out of profits or restricting the return of capital to members—

(a) section 845 (distributions in kind: determination of amount) applies to determine the amount of any distribution or return of capital consisting of or including, or treated as arising in consequence of the sale, transfer or other disposition by a company of a non-cash asset; and

(b) section 846 (distributions in kind: treatment of unrealised profits) applies as it applies for the purposes of this Part.

(3) In this section references to distributions are to amounts regarded as distributions for the purposes of any such rule of law as is referred to in subsection (1).

[S851]

NOTES

Commencement: to be appointed.

852 Saving for other restrictions on distributions

The provisions of this Part are without prejudice to any enactment, or any provision of a company's articles, restricting the sums out of which, or the cases in which, a distribution may be made.

[S852]

NOTES

Commencement: to be appointed.

853 Minor definitions

(1) The following provisions apply for the purposes of this Part.

(2) References to profit or losses of any description—

(a) are to profits or losses of that description made at any time, and

(b) except where the context otherwise requires, are to profits or losses of a revenue or capital character.

(3) "Capitalisation", in relation to a company's profits, means any of the following operations (whenever carried out)—

(a) applying the profits in wholly or partly paying up unissued shares in the company to be allotted to members of the company as fully or partly paid bonus shares, or
(b) transferring the profits to capital redemption reserve.

(4) References to "realised profits" and "realised losses", in relation to a company's accounts, are to such profits or losses of the company as fall to be treated as realised in accordance with principles generally accepted at the time when the accounts are prepared, with respect to the determination for accounting purposes of realised profits or losses.

(5) Subsection (4) is without prejudice to—
(a) the construction of any other expression (where appropriate) by reference to accepted accounting principles or practice, or
(b) any specific provision for the treatment of profits or losses of any description as realised.

(6) "Fixed assets" means assets of a company which are intended for use on a continuing basis in the company's activities.

[S853]

NOTES

Commencement: to be appointed.

PART 24
A COMPANY'S ANNUAL RETURN

854 Duty to deliver annual returns

(1) Every company must deliver to the registrar successive annual returns each of which is made up to a date not later than the date that is from time to time the company's return date.

(2) The company's return date is—
(a) the anniversary of the company's incorporation, or
(b) if the company's last return delivered in accordance with this Part was made up to a different date, the anniversary of that date.

(3) Each return must—
(a) contain the information required by or under the following provisions of this Part, and
(b) be delivered to the registrar within 28 days after the date to which it is made up.

[S854]

NOTES

Commencement: to be appointed.

855 Contents of annual return: general

(1) Every annual return must state the date to which it is made up and contain the following information—
(a) the address of the company's registered office;
(b) the type of company it is and its principal business activities;
(c) the prescribed particulars of—
(i) the directors of the company, and
(ii) in the case of a private company with a secretary or a public company, the secretary or joint secretaries;
(d) if the register of members is not kept available for inspection at the company's registered office, the address of the place where it is kept available for inspection;
(e) if any register of debenture holders (or a duplicate of any such register or a part of it) is not kept available for inspection at the company's registered office, the address of the place where it is kept available for inspection.

(2) The information as to the company's type must be given by reference to the classification scheme prescribed for the purposes of this section.

(3) The information as to the company's principal business activities may be given by reference to one or more categories of any prescribed system of classifying business activities.

[S855]

NOTES

Commencement: 20 January 2007 (for the purpose of enabling the exercise of powers to make Orders or Regulations by statutory instrument); to be appointed (otherwise).

856 Contents of annual return: information about share capital and shareholders

(1) The annual return of a company having a share capital must also contain—

(a) a statement of capital, and

(b) the particulars required by subsections (3) to (6) about the members of the company.

(2) The statement of capital must state with respect to the company's share capital at the date to which the return is made up—

(a) the total number of shares of the company,

(b) the aggregate nominal value of those shares,

(c) for each class of shares—

(i) prescribed particulars of the rights attached to the shares,

(ii) the total number of shares of that class, and

(iii) the aggregate nominal value of shares of that class, and

(d) the amount paid up and the amount (if any) unpaid on each share (whether on account of the nominal value of the share or by way of premium).

(3) The return must contain the prescribed particulars of every person who—

(a) is a member of the company on the date to which the return is made up, or

(b) has ceased to be a member of the company since the date to which the last return was made up (or, in the case of the first return, since the incorporation of the company).

The return must conform to such requirements as may be prescribed for the purpose of enabling the entries relating to any given person to be easily found.

(4) The return must also state—

(a) the number of shares of each class held by each member of the company at the date to which the return is made up,

(b) the number of shares of each class transferred—

(i) since the date to which the last return was made up, or

(ii) in the case of the first return, since the incorporation of the company,

by each member or person who has ceased to be a member, and

(c) the dates of registration of the transfers.

(5) If either of the two immediately preceding returns has given the full particulars required by subsections (3) and (4), the return need only give such particulars as relate—

(a) to persons ceasing to be or becoming members since the date of the last return, and

(b) to shares transferred since that date.

(6) Where the company has converted any of its shares into stock, the return must give the corresponding information in relation to that stock, stating the amount of stock instead of the number or nominal value of shares.

[S856]

NOTES

Commencement: 20 January 2007 (for the purpose of enabling the exercise of powers to make Orders or Regulations by statutory instrument); to be appointed (otherwise).

857 Contents of annual return: power to make further provision by regulations

(1) The Secretary of State may by regulations make further provision as to the information to be given in a company's annual return.

(2) The regulations may—

(a) amend or repeal the provisions of sections 855 and 856, and

(b) provide for exceptions from the requirements of those sections as they have effect from time to time.

(3) Regulations under this section are subject to negative resolution procedure.

[S857]

NOTES

Commencement: 20 January 2007 (for the purpose of enabling the exercise of powers to make Orders or Regulations by statutory instrument); to be appointed (otherwise).

858 Failure to deliver annual return

(1) If a company fails to deliver an annual return before the end of the period of 28 days after a return date, an offence is committed by—
- (a) the company,
- (b) subject to subsection (4)—
  - (i) every director of the company, and
  - (ii) in the case of a private company with a secretary or a public company, every secretary of the company, and
- (c) every other officer of the company who is in default.

(2) A person guilty of an offence under subsection (1) is liable on summary conviction to a fine not exceeding level 5 on the standard scale and, for continued contravention, a daily default fine not exceeding one-tenth of level 5 on the standard scale.

(3) The contravention continues until such time as an annual return made up to that return date is delivered by the company to the registrar.

(4) It is a defence for a director or secretary charged with an offence under subsection (1)(b) to prove that he took all reasonable steps to avoid the commission or continuation of the offence.

(5) In the case of continued contravention, an offence is also committed by every officer of the company who did not commit an offence under subsection (1) in relation to the initial contravention but is in default in relation to the continued contravention.

A person guilty of an offence under this subsection is liable on summary conviction to a fine not exceeding one-tenth of level 5 on the standard scale for each day on which the contravention continues and he is in default.

[S858]

NOTES

Commencement: to be appointed.

859 Application of provisions to shadow directors

For the purposes of this Part a shadow director is treated as a director.

[S859]

NOTES

Commencement: to be appointed.

PART 25
COMPANY CHARGES

CHAPTER 1
COMPANIES REGISTERED IN ENGLAND AND WALES OR IN NORTHERN IRELAND

Requirement to register company charges

860 Charges created by a company

(1) A company that creates a charge to which this section applies must deliver the prescribed particulars of the charge, together with the instrument (if any) by which the charge is created or evidenced, to the registrar for registration before the end of the period allowed for registration.

(2) Registration of a charge to which this section applies may instead be effected on the application of a person interested in it.

(3) Where registration is effected on the application of some person other than the company, that person is entitled to recover from the company the amount of any fees properly paid by him to the registrar on registration.

(4) If a company fails to comply with subsection (1), an offence is committed by—
  (a) the company, and
  (b) every officer of it who is in default.

(5) A person guilty of an offence under this section is liable—
  (a) on conviction on indictment, to a fine;
  (b) on summary conviction, to a fine not exceeding the statutory maximum.

(6) Subsection (4) does not apply if registration of the charge has been effected on the application of some other person.

(7) This section applies to the following charges—
  (a) a charge on land or any interest in land, other than a charge for any rent or other periodical sum issuing out of land,
  (b) a charge created or evidenced by an instrument which, if executed by an individual, would require registration as a bill of sale,
  (c) a charge for the purposes of securing any issue of debentures,
  (d) a charge on uncalled share capital of the company,
  (e) a charge on calls made but not paid,
  (f) a charge on book debts of the company,
  (g) a floating charge on the company's property or undertaking,
  (h) a charge on a ship or aircraft, or any share in a ship,
  (i) a charge on goodwill or on any intellectual property.

[S860]

NOTES

Commencement: 20 January 2007 (for the purpose of enabling the exercise of powers to make Orders or Regulations by statutory instrument); to be appointed (otherwise).

861 Charges which have to be registered: supplementary

(1) The holding of debentures entitling the holder to a charge on land is not, for the purposes of section 860(7)(a), an interest in the land.

(2) It is immaterial for the purposes of this Chapter where land subject to a charge is situated.

(3) The deposit by way of security of a negotiable instrument given to secure the payment of book debts is not, for the purposes of section 860(7)(f), a charge on those book debts.

(4) For the purposes of section 860(7)(i), "intellectual property" means—
  (a) any patent, trade mark, registered design, copyright or design right;
  (b) any licence under or in respect of any such right.

(5) In this Chapter—
"charge" includes mortgage, and
"company" means a company registered in England and Wales or in Northern Ireland.

[S861]

NOTES

Commencement: to be appointed.

862 Charges existing on property acquired

(1) This section applies where a company acquires property which is subject to a charge of a kind which would, if it had been created by the company after the acquisition of the property, have been required to be registered under this Chapter.

(2) The company must deliver the prescribed particulars of the charge, together with a certified copy of the instrument (if any) by which the charge is created or evidenced, to the registrar for registration.

(3) Subsection (2) must be complied with before the end of the period allowed for registration.

(4) If default is made in complying with this section, an offence is committed by—
- (a) the company, and
- (b) every officer of it who is in default.

(5) A person guilty of an offence under this section is liable—
- (a) on conviction on indictment, to a fine;
- (b) on summary conviction, to a fine not exceeding the statutory maximum.

[S862]

NOTES

Commencement: 20 January 2007 (for the purpose of enabling the exercise of powers to make Orders or Regulations by statutory instrument); to be appointed (otherwise).

Special rules about debentures

863 Charge in series of debentures

(1) Where a series of debentures containing, or giving by reference to another instrument, any charge to the benefit of which debenture holders of that series are entitled *pari passu* is created by a company, it is for the purposes of section 860(1) sufficient if the required particulars, together with the deed containing the charge (or, if there is no such deed, one of the debentures of the series), are delivered to the registrar before the end of the period allowed for registration.

(2) The following are the required particulars—
- (a) the total amount secured by the whole series, and
- (b) the dates of the resolutions authorising the issue of the series and the date of the covering deed (if any) by which the series is created or defined, and
- (c) a general description of the property charged, and
- (d) the names of the trustees (if any) for the debenture holders.

(3) Particulars of the date and amount of each issue of debentures of a series of the kind mentioned in subsection (1) must be sent to the registrar for entry in the register of charges.

(4) Failure to comply with subsection (3) does not affect the validity of the debentures issued.

(5) Subsections (2) to (6) of section 860 apply for the purposes of this section as they apply for the purposes of that section, but as if references to the registration of a charge were references to the registration of a series of debentures.

[S863]

NOTES

Commencement: to be appointed.

864 Additional registration requirement for commission etc in relation to debentures

(1) Where any commission, allowance or discount has been paid or made either directly or indirectly by a company to a person in consideration of his—
- (a) subscribing or agreeing to subscribe, whether absolutely or conditionally, for debentures in a company, or
- (b) procuring or agreeing to procure subscriptions, whether absolute or conditional, for such debentures,

the particulars required to be sent for registration under section 860 shall include particulars as to the amount or rate per cent. of the commission, discount or allowance so paid or made.

(2) The deposit of debentures as security for a debt of the company is not, for the purposes of this section, treated as the issue of debentures at a discount.

(3) Failure to comply with this section does not affect the validity of the debentures issued.

[S864]

NOTES

Commencement: to be appointed.

865 Endorsement of certificate on debentures

(1) The company shall cause a copy of every certificate of registration given under section 869 to be endorsed on every debenture or certificate of debenture stock which is issued by the company, and the payment of which is secured by the charge so registered.

(2) But this does not require a company to cause a certificate of registration of any charge so given to be endorsed on any debenture or certificate of debenture stock issued by the company before the charge was created.

(3) If a person knowingly and wilfully authorises or permits the delivery of a debenture or certificate of debenture stock which under this section is required to have endorsed on it a copy of a certificate of registration, without the copy being so endorsed upon it, he commits an offence.

(4) A person guilty of an offence under this section is liable on summary conviction to a fine not exceeding level 3 on the standard scale.

[S865]

NOTES

Commencement: to be appointed.

Charges in other jurisdictions

866 Charges created in, or over property in, jurisdictions outside the United Kingdom

(1) Where a charge is created outside the United Kingdom comprising property situated outside the United Kingdom, the delivery to the registrar of a verified copy of the instrument by which the charge is created or evidenced has the same effect for the purposes of this Chapter as the delivery of the instrument itself.

(2) Where a charge is created in the United Kingdom but comprises property outside the United Kingdom, the instrument creating or purporting to create the charge may be sent for registration under section 860 even if further proceedings may be necessary to make the charge valid or effectual according to the law of the country in which the property is situated.

[S866]

NOTES

Commencement: to be appointed.

867 Charges created in, or over property in, another United Kingdom jurisdiction

(1) Subsection (2) applies where—

(a) a charge comprises property situated in a part of the United Kingdom other than the part in which the company is registered, and

(b) registration in that other part is necessary to make the charge valid or effectual under the law of that part of the United Kingdom.

(2) The delivery to the registrar of a verified copy of the instrument by which the charge is created or evidenced, together with a certificate stating that the charge was presented for registration in that other part of the United Kingdom on the date on which it was so presented has, for the purposes of this Chapter, the same effect as the delivery of the instrument itself.

[S867]

NOTES

Commencement: to be appointed.

Orders charging land: Northern Ireland

868 Northern Ireland: registration of certain charges etc affecting land

(1) Where a charge imposed by an order under Article 46 of the 1981 Order or notice of such a charge is registered in the Land Registry against registered land or any estate in

registered land of a company, the Registrar of Titles shall as soon as may be cause two copies of the order made under Article 46 of that Order or of any notice under Article 48 of that Order to be delivered to the registrar.

(2) Where a charge imposed by an order under Article 46 of the 1981 Order is registered in the Registry of Deeds against any unregistered land or estate in land of a company, the Registrar of Deeds shall as soon as may be cause two copies of the order to be delivered to the registrar.

(3) On delivery of copies under this section, the registrar shall—
- (a) register one of them in accordance with section 869, and
- (b) not later than 7 days from that date of delivery, cause the other copy together with a certificate of registration under section 869(5) to be sent to the company against which judgment was given.

(4) Where a charge to which subsection (1) or (2) applies is vacated, the Registrar of Titles or, as the case may be, the Registrar of Deeds shall cause a certified copy of the certificate of satisfaction lodged under Article 132(1) of the 1981 Order to be delivered to the registrar for entry of a memorandum of satisfaction in accordance with section 872.

(5) In this section—

"the 1981 Order" means the Judgments Enforcement (Northern Ireland) Order 1981 (SI 1981/226 (NI 6));

"the Registrar of Deeds" means the registrar appointed under the Registration of Deeds Act (Northern Ireland) 1970 (c 25);

"Registry of Deeds" has the same meaning as in the Registration of Deeds Acts;

"Registration of Deeds Acts" means the Registration of Deeds Act (Northern Ireland) 1970 and every statutory provision for the time being in force amending that Act or otherwise relating to the registry of deeds, or the registration of deeds, orders or other instruments or documents in such registry;

"the Land Registry" and "the Registrar of Titles" are to be construed in accordance with section 1 of the Land Registration Act (Northern Ireland) 1970 (c 18);

"registered land" and "unregistered land" have the same meaning as in Part 3 of the Land Registration Act (Northern Ireland) 1970.

[S868]

NOTES

Commencement: to be appointed.

The register of charges

869 Register of charges to be kept by registrar

(1) The registrar shall keep, with respect to each company, a register of all the charges requiring registration under this Chapter.

(2) In the case of a charge to the benefit of which holders of a series of debentures are entitled, the registrar shall enter in the register the required particulars specified in section 863(2).

(3) In the case of a charge imposed by the Enforcement of Judgments Office under Article 46 of the Judgments Enforcement (Northern Ireland) Order 1981, the registrar shall enter in the register the date on which the charge became effective.

(4) In the case of any other charge, the registrar shall enter in the register the following particulars—
- (a) if it is a charge created by a company, the date of its creation and, if it is a charge which was existing on property acquired by the company, the date of the acquisition,
- (b) the amount secured by the charge,
- (c) short particulars of the property charged, and
- (d) the persons entitled to the charge.

(5) The registrar shall give a certificate of the registration of any charge registered in pursuance of this Chapter, stating the amount secured by the charge.

(6) The certificate—

(a) shall be signed by the registrar or authenticated by the registrar's official seal, and

(b) is conclusive evidence that the requirements of this Chapter as to registration have been satisfied.

(7) The register kept in pursuance of this section shall be open to inspection by any person.

[S869]

NOTES

Commencement: to be appointed.

870 The period allowed for registration

(1) The period allowed for registration of a charge created by a company is—

(a) 21 days beginning with the day after the day on which the charge is created, or

(b) if the charge is created outside the United Kingdom, 21 days beginning with the day after the day on which the instrument by which the charge is created or evidenced (or a copy of it) could, in due course of post (and if despatched with due diligence) have been received in the United Kingdom.

(2) The period allowed for registration of a charge to which property acquired by a company is subject is—

(a) 21 days beginning with the day after the day on which the acquisition is completed, or

(b) if the property is situated and the charge was created outside the United Kingdom, 21 days beginning with the day after the day on which the instrument by which the charge is created or evidenced (or a copy of it) could, in due course of post (and if despatched with due diligence) have been received in the United Kingdom.

(3) The period allowed for registration of particulars of a series of debentures as a result of section 863 is—

(a) if there is a deed containing the charge mentioned in section 863(1), 21 days beginning with the day after the day on which that deed is executed, or

(b) if there is no such deed, 21 days beginning with the day after the day on which the first debenture of the series is executed.

[S870]

NOTES

Commencement: to be appointed.

871 Registration of enforcement of security

(1) If a person obtains an order for the appointment of a receiver or manager of a company's property, or appoints such a receiver or manager under powers contained in an instrument, he shall within 7 days of the order or of the appointment under those powers, give notice of the fact to the registrar.

(2) Where a person appointed receiver or manager of a company's property under powers contained in an instrument ceases to act as such receiver or manager, he shall, on so ceasing, give the registrar notice to that effect.

(3) The registrar must enter a fact of which he is given notice under this section in the register of charges.

(4) A person who makes default in complying with the requirements of this section commits an offence.

(5) A person guilty of an offence under this section is liable on summary conviction to a fine not exceeding level 3 on the standard scale and, for continued contravention, a daily default fine not exceeding one-tenth of level 3 on the standard scale.

[S871]

NOTES

Commencement: to be appointed.

872 Entries of satisfaction and release

(1) Subsection (2) applies if a statement is delivered to the registrar verifying with respect to a registered charge—

(a) that the debt for which the charge was given has been paid or satisfied in whole or in part, or

(b) that part of the property or undertaking charged has been released from the charge or has ceased to form part of the company's property or undertaking.

(2) The registrar may enter on the register a memorandum of satisfaction in whole or in part, or of the fact part of the property or undertaking has been released from the charge or has ceased to form part of the company's property or undertaking (as the case may be).

(3) Where the registrar enters a memorandum of satisfaction in whole, the registrar shall if required send the company a copy of it.

[S872]

NOTES

Commencement: to be appointed.

873 Rectification of register of charges

(1) Subsection (2) applies if the court is satisfied—

(a) that the failure to register a charge before the end of the period allowed for registration, or the omission or mis-statement of any particular with respect to any such charge or in a memorandum of satisfaction—

(i) was accidental or due to inadvertence or to some other sufficient cause, or

(ii) is not of a nature to prejudice the position of creditors or shareholders of the company, or

(b) that on other grounds it is just and equitable to grant relief.

(2) The court may, on the application of the company or a person interested, and on such terms and conditions as seem to the court just and expedient, order that the period allowed for registration shall be extended or, as the case may be, that the omission or mis-statement shall be rectified.

[S873]

NOTES

Commencement: to be appointed.

Avoidance of certain charges

874 Consequence of failure to register charges created by a company

(1) If a company creates a charge to which section 860 applies, the charge is void (so far as any security on the company's property or undertaking is conferred by it) against—

(a) a liquidator of the company,

(b) an administrator of the company, and

(c) a creditor of the company,

unless that section is complied with.

(2) Subsection (1) is subject to the provisions of this Chapter.

(3) Subsection (1) is without prejudice to any contract or obligation for repayment of the money secured by the charge; and when a charge becomes void under this section, the money secured by it immediately becomes payable.

[S874]

NOTES

Commencement: to be appointed.

Companies' records and registers

875 Companies to keep copies of instruments creating charges

(1) A company must keep available for inspection a copy of every instrument creating a charge requiring registration under this Chapter, including any document delivered to the company under section 868(3)(b) (Northern Ireland: orders imposing charges affecting land).

(2) In the case of a series of uniform debentures, a copy of one of the debentures of the series is sufficient.

[S875]

NOTES

Commencement: to be appointed.

876 Company's register of charges

(1) Every limited company shall keep available for inspection a register of charges and enter in it—

(a) all charges specifically affecting property of the company, and

(b) all floating charges on the whole or part of the company's property or undertaking.

(2) The entry shall in each case give a short description of the property charged, the amount of the charge and, except in the cases of securities to bearer, the names of the persons entitled to it.

(3) If an officer of the company knowingly and wilfully authorises or permits the omission of an entry required to be made in pursuance of this section, he commits an offence.

(4) A person guilty of an offence under this section is liable—

(a) on conviction on indictment, to a fine;

(b) on summary conviction, to a fine not exceeding the statutory maximum.

[S876]

NOTES

Commencement: to be appointed.

877 Instruments creating charges and register of charges to be available for inspection

(1) This section applies to—

(a) documents required to be kept available for inspection under section 875 (copies of instruments creating charges), and

(b) a company's register of charges kept in pursuance of section 876.

(2) The documents and register must be kept available for inspection—

(a) at the company's registered office, or

(b) at a place specified in regulations under section 1136.

(3) The company must give notice to the registrar—

(a) of the place at which the documents and register are kept available for inspection, and

(b) of any change in that place,

unless they have at all times been kept at the company's registered office.

(4) The documents and register shall be open to the inspection—

(a) of any creditor or member of the company without charge, and

(b) of any other person on payment of such fee as may be prescribed.

(5) If default is made for 14 days in complying with subsection (3) or an inspection required under subsection (4) is refused, an offence is committed by—

(a) the company, and

(b) every officer of the company who is in default.

(6) A person guilty of an offence under this section is liable on summary conviction to a fine not exceeding level 3 on the standard scale and, for continued contravention, a daily default fine not exceeding one-tenth of level 3 on the standard scale.

(7) If an inspection required under subsection (4) is refused the court may by order compel an immediate inspection.

[S877]

NOTES

Commencement: 20 January 2007 (for the purpose of enabling the exercise of powers to make Orders or Regulations by statutory instrument); to be appointed (otherwise).

CHAPTER 2
COMPANIES REGISTERED IN SCOTLAND

Charges requiring registration

878 Charges created by a company

(1) A company that creates a charge to which this section applies must deliver the prescribed particulars of the charge, together with a copy certified as a correct copy of the instrument (if any) by which the charge is created or evidenced, to the registrar for registration before the end of the period allowed for registration.

(2) Registration of a charge to which this section applies may instead be effected on the application of a person interested in it.

(3) Where registration is effected on the application of some person other than the company, that person is entitled to recover from the company the amount of any fees properly paid by him to the registrar on the registration.

(4) If a company fails to comply with subsection (1), an offence is committed by—

(a) the company, and

(b) every officer of the company who is in default.

(5) A person guilty of an offence under this section is liable—

(a) on conviction on indictment, to a fine;

(b) on summary conviction, to a fine not exceeding the statutory maximum.

(6) Subsection (4) does not apply if registration of the charge has been effected on the application of some other person.

(7) This section applies to the following charges—

(a) a charge on land or any interest in such land, other than a charge for any rent or other periodical sum payable in respect of the land,

(b) a security over incorporeal moveable property of any of the following categories—

(i) goodwill,

(ii) a patent or a licence under a patent,

(iii) a trademark,

(iv) a copyright or a licence under a copyright,

(v) a registered design or a licence in respect of such a design,

(vi) a design right or a licence under a design right,

(vii) the book debts (whether book debts of the company or assigned to it), and

(viii) uncalled share capital of the company or calls made but not paid,

(c) a security over a ship or aircraft or any share in a ship,

(d) a floating charge.

[S878]

NOTES

Commencement: 20 January 2007 (for the purpose of enabling the exercise of powers to make Orders or Regulations by statutory instrument); to be appointed (otherwise).

879 Charges which have to be registered: supplementary

(1) A charge on land, for the purposes of section 878(7)(a), includes a charge created by a heritable security within the meaning of section 9(8) of the Conveyancing and Feudal Reform (Scotland) Act 1970 (c 35).

(2) The holding of debentures entitling the holder to a charge on land is not, for the purposes of section 878(7)(a), deemed to be an interest in land.

(3) It is immaterial for the purposes of this Chapter where land subject to a charge is situated.

(4) The deposit by way of security of a negotiable instrument given to secure the payment of book debts is not, for the purposes of section 878(7)(b)(vii), to be treated as a charge on those book debts.

(5) References in this Chapter to the date of the creation of a charge are—
- (a) in the case of a floating charge, the date on which the instrument creating the floating charge was executed by the company creating the charge, and
- (b) in any other case, the date on which the right of the person entitled to the benefit of the charge was constituted as a real right.

(6) In this Chapter "company" means an incorporated company registered in Scotland.

[S879]

NOTES

Commencement: to be appointed.

880 Duty to register charges existing on property acquired

(1) Subsection (2) applies where a company acquires any property which is subject to a charge of any kind as would, if it had been created by the company after the acquisition of the property, have been required to be registered under this Chapter.

(2) The company must deliver the prescribed particulars of the charge, together with a copy (certified to be a correct copy) of the instrument (if any) by which the charge was created or is evidenced, to the registrar for registration before the end of the period allowed for registration.

(3) If default is made in complying with this section, an offence is committed by—
- (a) the company, and
- (b) every officer of it who is in default.

(4) A person guilty of an offence under this section is liable—
- (a) on conviction on indictment, to a fine;
- (b) on summary conviction, to a fine not exceeding the statutory maximum.

[S880]

NOTES

Commencement: 20 January 2007 (for the purpose of enabling the exercise of powers to make Orders or Regulations by statutory instrument); to be appointed (otherwise).

881 Charge by way of ex facie absolute disposition, etc

(1) For the avoidance of doubt, it is hereby declared that, in the case of a charge created by way of an *ex facie* absolute disposition or assignation qualified by a back letter or other agreement, or by a standard security qualified by an agreement, compliance with section 878(1) does not of itself render the charge unavailable as security for indebtedness incurred after the date of compliance.

(2) Where the amount secured by a charge so created is purported to be increased by a further back letter or agreement, a further charge is held to have been created by the *ex facie* absolute disposition or assignation or (as the case may be) by the standard security, as qualified by the further back letter or agreement.

(3) In that case, the provisions of this Chapter apply to the further charge as if—
- (a) references in this Chapter (other than in this section) to a charge were references to the further charge, and
- (b) references to the date of the creation of a charge were references to the date on which the further back letter or agreement was executed.

[S881]

NOTES

Commencement: to be appointed.

Special rules about debentures

882 Charge in series of debentures

(1) Where a series of debentures containing, or giving by reference to any other instrument, any charge to the benefit of which the debenture-holders of that series are entitled *pari passu*, is created by a company, it is sufficient for purposes of section 878 if the required particulars, together with a copy of the deed containing the charge (or, if there is no such deed, of one of the debentures of the series) are delivered to the registrar before the end of the period allowed for registration.

(2) The following are the required particulars—
- (a) the total amount secured by the whole series,
- (b) the dates of the resolutions authorising the issue of the series and the date of the covering deed (if any) by which the security is created or defined,
- (c) a general description of the property charged,
- (d) the names of the trustees (if any) for the debenture-holders, and
- (e) in the case of a floating charge, a statement of any provisions of the charge and of any instrument relating to it which prohibit or restrict or regulate the power of the company to grant further securities ranking in priority to, or *pari passu* with, the floating charge, or which vary or otherwise regulate the order of ranking of the floating charge in relation to subsisting securities.

(3) Where more than one issue is made of debentures in the series, particulars of the date and amount of each issue of debentures of the series must be sent to the registrar for entry in the register of charges.

(4) Failure to comply with subsection (3) does not affect the validity of any of those debentures.

(5) Subsections (2) to (6) of section 878 apply for the purposes of this section as they apply for the purposes of that section but as if for the reference to the registration of the charge there was substituted a reference to the registration of the series of debentures.

[S882]

NOTES

Commencement: to be appointed.

883 Additional registration requirement for commission etc in relation to debentures

(1) Where any commission, allowance or discount has been paid or made either directly or indirectly by a company to a person in consideration of his—
- (a) subscribing or agreeing to subscribe, whether absolutely or conditionally, for debentures in a company, or
- (b) procuring or agreeing to procure subscriptions, whether absolute or conditional, for such debentures,

the particulars required to be sent for registration under section 878 shall include particulars as to the amount or rate per cent. of the commission, discount or allowance so paid or made.

(2) The deposit of debentures as security for a debt of the company is not, for the purposes of this section, treated as the issue of debentures at a discount.

(3) Failure to comply with this section does not affect the validity of the debentures issued.

[S883]

NOTES

Commencement: to be appointed.

Charges on property outside the United Kingdom

884 Charges on property outside United Kingdom

Where a charge is created in the United Kingdom but comprises property outside the United Kingdom, the copy of the instrument creating or purporting to create the charge may be sent for registration under section 878 even if further proceedings may be necessary to make the charge valid or effectual according to the law of the country in which the property is situated.

[S884]

NOTES

Commencement: to be appointed.

The register of charges

885 Register of charges to be kept by registrar

(1) The registrar shall keep, with respect to each company, a register of all the charges requiring registration under this Chapter.

(2) In the case of a charge to the benefit of which holders of a series of debentures are entitled, the registrar shall enter in the register the required particulars specified in section 882(2).

(3) In the case of any other charge, the registrar shall enter in the register the following particulars—

(a) if it is a charge created by a company, the date of its creation and, if it is a charge which was existing on property acquired by the company, the date of the acquisition,

(b) the amount secured by the charge,

(c) short particulars of the property charged,

(d) the persons entitled to the charge, and

(e) in the case of a floating charge, a statement of any of the provisions of the charge and of any instrument relating to it which prohibit or restrict or regulate the company's power to grant further securities ranking in

priority to, or *pari passu* with, the floating charge, or which vary or otherwise regulate the order of ranking of the floating charge in relation to subsisting securities.

(4) The registrar shall give a certificate of the registration of any charge registered in pursuance of this Chapter, stating—

(a) the name of the company and the person first-named in the charge among those entitled to the benefit of the charge (or, in the case of a series of debentures, the name of the holder of the first such debenture issued), and

(b) the amount secured by the charge.

(5) The certificate—

(a) shall be signed by the registrar or authenticated by the registrar's official seal, and

(b) is conclusive evidence that the requirements of this Chapter as to registration have been satisfied.

(6) The register kept in pursuance of this section shall be open to inspection by any person.

[S885]

NOTES

Commencement: to be appointed.

886 The period allowed for registration

(1) The period allowed for registration of a charge created by a company is—

(a) 21 days beginning with the day after the day on which the charge is created, or

(b) if the charge is created outside the United Kingdom, 21 days beginning with the day after the day on which a copy of the instrument by which the charge is created or evidenced could, in due course of post (and if despatched with due diligence) have been received in the United Kingdom.

(2) The period allowed for registration of a charge to which property acquired by a company is subject is—

(a) 21 days beginning with the day after the day on which the transaction is settled, or

(b) if the property is situated and the charge was created outside the United Kingdom, 21 days beginning with the day after the day on which a copy of the instrument by which the charge is created or evidenced could, in due course of post (and if despatched with due diligence) have been received in the United Kingdom.

(3) The period allowed for registration of particulars of a series of debentures as a result of section 882 is—

(a) if there is a deed containing the charge mentioned in section 882(1), 21 days beginning with the day after the day on which that deed is executed, or

(b) if there is no such deed, 21 days beginning with the day after the day on which the first debenture of the series is executed.

[S886]

NOTES

Commencement: to be appointed.

887 Entries of satisfaction and relief

(1) Subsection (2) applies if a statement is delivered to the registrar verifying with respect to any registered charge—

(a) that the debt for which the charge was given has been paid or satisfied in whole or in part, or

(b) that part of the property charged has been released from the charge or has ceased to form part of the company's property.

(2) If the charge is a floating charge, the statement must be accompanied by either—

(a) a statement by the creditor entitled to the benefit of the charge, or a person authorised by him for the purpose, verifying that the statement mentioned in subsection (1) is correct, or

(b) a direction obtained from the court, on the ground that the statement by the creditor mentioned in paragraph (a) could not be readily obtained, dispensing with the need for that statement.

(3) The registrar may enter on the register a memorandum of satisfaction (in whole or in part) regarding the fact contained in the statement mentioned in subsection (1).

(4) Where the registrar enters a memorandum of satisfaction in whole, he shall, if required, furnish the company with a copy of the memorandum.

(5) Nothing in this section requires the company to submit particulars with respect to the entry in the register of a memorandum of satisfaction where the company, having created a floating charge over all or any part of its property, disposes of part of the property subject to the floating charge.

[S887]

NOTES

Commencement: to be appointed.

888 Rectification of register of charges

(1) Subsection (2) applies if the court is satisfied—

(a) that the failure to register a charge before the end of the period allowed for registration, or the omission or mis-statement of any particular with respect to any such charge or in a memorandum of satisfaction—

(i) was accidental or due to inadvertence or to some other sufficient cause, or

(ii) is not of a nature to prejudice the position of creditors or shareholders of the company, or

(b) that on other grounds it is just and equitable to grant relief.

(2) The court may, on the application of the company or a person interested, and on such terms and conditions as seem to the court just and expedient, order that the period allowed for registration shall be extended or, as the case may be, that the omission or mis-statement shall be rectified.

[S888]

NOTES

Commencement: to be appointed.

Avoidance of certain charges

889 Charges void unless registered

(1) If a company creates a charge to which section 878 applies, the charge is void (so far as any security on the company's property or any part of it is conferred by the charge) against—

(a) the liquidator of the company,
(b) an administrator of the company, and
(c) any creditor of the company

unless that section is complied with.

(2) Subsection (1) is without prejudice to any contract or obligation for repayment of the money secured by the charge; and when a charge becomes void under this section the money secured by it immediately becomes payable.

[S889]

NOTES

Commencement: to be appointed.

Companies' records and registers

890 Copies of instruments creating charges to be kept by company

(1) Every company shall cause a copy of every instrument creating a charge requiring registration under this Chapter to be kept available for inspection.

(2) In the case of a series of uniform debentures, a copy of one debenture of the series is sufficient.

[S890]

NOTES

Commencement: to be appointed.

891 Company's register of charges

(1) Every company shall keep available for inspection a register of charges and enter in it all charges specifically affecting property of the company, and all floating charges on any property of the company.

(2) There shall be given in each case a short description of the property charged, the amount of the charge and, except in the case of securities to bearer, the names of the persons entitled to it.

(3) If an officer of the company knowingly and wilfully authorises or permits the omission of an entry required to be made in pursuance of this section, he commits an offence.

(4) A person guilty of an offence under this section is liable—

(a) on conviction on indictment, to a fine;
(b) on summary conviction, to a fine not exceeding the statutory maximum.

[S891]

NOTES

Commencement: to be appointed.

892 Instruments creating charges and register of charges to be available for inspection

(1) This section applies to—

(a) documents required to be kept available for inspection under section 890 (copies of instruments creating charges), and
(b) a company's register of charges kept in pursuance of section 891.

(2) The documents and register must be kept available for inspection—

(a) at the company's registered office, or
(b) at a place specified in regulations under section 1136.

(3) The company must give notice to the registrar—
(a) of the place at which the documents and register are kept available for inspection, and
(b) of any change in that place,

unless they have at all times been kept at the company's registered office.

(4) The documents and register shall be open to the inspection—
(a) of any creditor or member of the company without charge, and
(b) of any other person on payment of such fee as may be prescribed.

(5) If default is made for 14 days in complying with subsection (3) or an inspection required under subsection (4) is refused, an offence is committed by—
(a) the company, and
(b) every officer of the company who is in default.

(6) A person guilty of an offence under this section is liable on summary conviction to a fine not exceeding level 3 on the standard scale and, for continued contravention, a daily default fine not exceeding one-tenth of level 3 on the standard scale.

(7) If an inspection required under subsection (4) is refused the court may by order compel an immediate inspection.

[S892]

NOTES

Commencement: 20 January 2007 (for the purpose of enabling the exercise of powers to make Orders or Regulations by statutory instrument); to be appointed (otherwise).

CHAPTER 3
POWERS OF THE SECRETARY OF STATE

893 Power to make provision for effect of registration in special register

(1) In this section a "special register" means a register, other than the register of charges kept under this Part, in which a charge to which Chapter 1 or Chapter 2 applies is required or authorised to be registered.

(2) The Secretary of State may by order make provision for facilitating the making of information-sharing arrangements between the person responsible for maintaining a special register ("the responsible person") and the registrar that meet the requirement in subsection (4).

"Information-sharing arrangements" are arrangements to share and make use of information held by the registrar or by the responsible person.

(3) If the Secretary of State is satisfied that appropriate information-sharing arrangements have been made, he may by order provide that—
(a) the registrar is authorised not to register a charge of a specified description under Chapter 1 or Chapter 2,
(b) a charge of a specified description that is registered in the special register within a specified period is to be treated as if it had been registered (and certified by the registrar as registered) in accordance with the requirements of Chapter 1 or, as the case may be, Chapter 2, and
(c) the other provisions of Chapter 1 or, as the case may be, Chapter 2 apply to a charge so treated with specified modifications.

(4) The information-sharing arrangements must ensure that persons inspecting the register of charges—
(a) are made aware, in a manner appropriate to the inspection, of the existence of charges in the special register which are treated in accordance with provision so made, and
(b) are able to obtain information from the special register about any such charge.

(5) An order under this section may—
(a) modify any enactment or rule of law which would otherwise restrict or prevent the responsible person from entering into or giving effect to information-sharing arrangements,
(b) authorise the responsible person to require information to be provided to him for the purposes of the arrangements,

(c) make provision about—
  (i) the charging by the responsible person of fees in connection with the arrangements and the destination of such fees (including provision modifying any enactment which would otherwise apply in relation to fees payable to the responsible person), and
  (ii) the making of payments under the arrangements by the registrar to the responsible person,

(d) require the registrar to make copies of the arrangements available to the public (in hard copy or electronic form).

(6) In this section "specified" means specified in an order under this section.

(7) A description of charge may be specified, in particular, by reference to one or more of the following—
(a) the type of company by which it is created,
(b) the form of charge which it is,
(c) the description of assets over which it is granted,
(d) the length of the period between the date of its registration in the special register and the date of its creation.

(8) Provision may be made under this section relating to registers maintained under the law of a country or territory outside the United Kingdom.

(9) An order under this section is subject to negative resolution procedure.

[S893]

NOTES

Commencement: 20 January 2007 (for the purpose of enabling the exercise of powers to make Orders or Regulations by statutory instrument); to be appointed (otherwise).

894 General power to make amendments to this Part

(1) The Secretary of State may by regulations under this section—
(a) amend this Part by altering, adding or repealing provisions,
(b) make consequential amendments or repeals in this Act or any other enactment (whether passed or made before or after this Act).

(2) Regulations under this section are subject to affirmative resolution procedure.

[S894]

NOTES

Commencement: 20 January 2007 (for the purpose of enabling the exercise of powers to make Orders or Regulations by statutory instrument); to be appointed (otherwise).

PART 26
ARRANGEMENTS AND RECONSTRUCTIONS

Application of this Part

895 Application of this Part

(1) The provisions of this Part apply where a compromise or arrangement is proposed between a company and—
(a) its creditors, or any class of them, or
(b) its members, or any class of them.

(2) In this Part—

"arrangement" includes a reorganisation of the company's share capital by the consolidation of shares of different classes or by the division of shares into shares of different classes, or by both of those methods; and "company"—
  (a) in section 900 (powers of court to facilitate reconstruction or amalgamation) means a company within the meaning of this Act, and
  (b) elsewhere in this Part means any company liable to be wound up under the Insolvency Act 1986 (c 45) or the Insolvency (Northern Ireland) Order 1989 (SI 1989/2405 (NI 19)).

(3) The provisions of this Part have effect subject to Part 27 (mergers and divisions of public companies) where that Part applies (see sections 902 and 903).

[S895]

NOTES
Commencement: to be appointed.

Meeting of creditors or members

896 Court order for holding of meeting

(1) The court may, on an application under this section, order a meeting of the creditors or class of creditors, or of the members of the company or class of members (as the case may be), to be summoned in such manner as the court directs.

(2) An application under this section may be made by—
 (a) the company,
 (b) any creditor or member of the company, or
 (c) if the company is being wound up or an administration order is in force in relation to it, the liquidator or administrator.

[S896]

NOTES
Commencement: to be appointed.

897 Statement to be circulated or made available

(1) Where a meeting is summoned under section 896—
 (a) every notice summoning the meeting that is sent to a creditor or member must be accompanied by a statement complying with this section, and
 (b) every notice summoning the meeting that is given by advertisement must either—
  (i) include such a statement, or
  (ii) state where and how creditors or members entitled to attend the meeting may obtain copies of such a statement.

(2) The statement must—
 (a) explain the effect of the compromise or arrangement, and
 (b) in particular, state—
  (i) any material interests of the directors of the company (whether as directors or as members or as creditors of the company or otherwise), and
  (ii) the effect on those interests of the compromise or arrangement, in so far as it is different from the effect on the like interests of other persons.

(3) Where the compromise or arrangement affects the rights of debenture holders of the company, the statement must give the like explanation as respects the trustees of any deed for securing the issue of the debentures as it is required to give as respects the company's directors.

(4) Where a notice given by advertisement states that copies of an explanatory statement can be obtained by creditors or members entitled to attend the meeting, every such creditor or member is entitled, on making application in the manner indicated by the notice, to be provided by the company with a copy of the statement free of charge.

(5) If a company makes default in complying with any requirement of this section, an offence is committed by—
 (a) the company, and
 (b) every officer of the company who is in default.

This is subject to subsection (7) below.

(6) For this purpose the following are treated as officers of the company—
 (a) a liquidator or administrator of the company, and
 (b) a trustee of a deed for securing the issue of debentures of the company.

(7) A person is not guilty of an offence under this section if he shows that the default was due to the refusal of a director or trustee for debenture holders to supply the necessary particulars of his interests.

(8) A person guilty of an offence under this section is liable—
(a) on conviction on indictment, to a fine;
(b) on summary conviction, to a fine not exceeding the statutory maximum.

[S897]

NOTES

Commencement: to be appointed.

898 Duty of directors and trustees to provide information

(1) It is the duty of—
(a) any director of the company, and
(b) any trustee for its debenture holders,

to give notice to the company of such matters relating to himself as may be necessary for the purposes of section 897 (explanatory statement to be circulated or made available).

(2) Any person who makes default in complying with this section commits an offence.

(3) A person guilty of an offence under this section is liable on summary conviction to a fine not exceeding level 3 on the standard scale.

[S898]

NOTES

Commencement: to be appointed.

Court sanction for compromise or arrangement

899 Court sanction for compromise or arrangement

(1) If a majority in number representing 75% in value of the creditors or class of creditors or members or class of members (as the case may be), present and voting either in person or by proxy at the meeting summoned under section 896, agree a compromise or arrangement, the court may, on an application under this section, sanction the compromise or arrangement.

(2) An application under this section may be made by—
(a) the company,
(b) any creditor or member of the company, or
(c) if the company is being wound up or an administration order is in force in relation it, the liquidator or administrator.

(3) A compromise or agreement sanctioned by the court is binding on—
(a) all creditors or the class of creditors or on the members or class of members (as the case may be), and
(b) the company or, in the case of a company in the course of being wound up, the liquidator and contributories of the company.

(4) The court's order has no effect until a copy of it has been delivered to the registrar.

[S899]

NOTES

Commencement: to be appointed.

Reconstructions and amalgamations

900 Powers of court to facilitate reconstruction or amalgamation

(1) This section applies where application is made to the court under section 899 to sanction a compromise or arrangement and it is shown that—
(a) the compromise or arrangement is proposed for the purposes of, or in connection with, a scheme for the reconstruction of any company or companies, or the amalgamation of any two or more companies, and
(b) under the scheme the whole or any part of the undertaking or the property of any

company concerned in the scheme ("a transferor company") is to be transferred to another company ("the transferee company").

(2) The court may, either by the order sanctioning the compromise or arrangement or by a subsequent order, make provision for all or any of the following matters—

(a) the transfer to the transferee company of the whole or any part of the undertaking and of the property or liabilities of any transferor company;

(b) the allotting or appropriation by the transferee company of any shares, debentures, policies or other like interests in that company which under the compromise or arrangement are to be allotted or appropriated by that company to or for any person;

(c) the continuation by or against the transferee company of any legal proceedings pending by or against any transferor company;

(d) the dissolution, without winding up, of any transferor company;

(e) the provision to be made for any persons who, within such time and in such manner as the court directs, dissent from the compromise or arrangement;

(f) such incidental, consequential and supplemental matters as are necessary to secure that the reconstruction or amalgamation is fully and effectively carried out.

(3) If an order under this section provides for the transfer of property or liabilities—

(a) the property is by virtue of the order transferred to, and vests in, the transferee company, and

(b) the liabilities are, by virtue of the order, transferred to and become liabilities of that company.

(4) The property (if the order so directs) vests freed from any charge that is by virtue of the compromise or arrangement to cease to have effect.

(5) In this section—

"property" includes property, rights and powers of every description; and

"liabilities" includes duties.

(6) Every company in relation to which an order is made under this section must cause a copy of the order to be delivered to the registrar within seven days after its making.

(7) If default is made in complying with subsection (6) an offence is committed by—

(a) the company, and

(b) every officer of the company who is in default.

(8) A person guilty of an offence under subsection (7) is liable on summary conviction to a fine not exceeding level 3 on the standard scale and, for continued contravention, a daily default fine not exceeding one-tenth of level 3 on the standard scale.

[S900]

NOTES

Commencement: to be appointed.

Obligations of company with respect to articles etc

901 Obligations of company with respect to articles etc

(1) This section applies—

(a) to any order under section 899 (order sanctioning compromise or arrangement), and

(b) to any order under section 900 (order facilitating reconstruction or amalgamation) that alters the company's constitution.

(2) If the order amends—

(a) the company's articles, or

(b) any resolution or agreement to which Chapter 3 of Part 3 applies (resolution or agreement affecting a company's constitution),

the copy of the order delivered to the registrar by the company under section 899(4) or section 900(6) must be accompanied by a copy of the company's articles, or the resolution or agreement in question, as amended.

(3) Every copy of the company's articles issued by the company after the order is made must be accompanied by a copy of the order, unless the effect of the order has been incorporated into the articles by amendment.

(4) In this section—

(a) references to the effect of the order include the effect of the compromise or arrangement to which the order relates; and

(b) in the case of a company not having articles, references to its articles shall be read as references to the instrument constituting the company or defining its constitution.

(5) If a company makes default in complying with this section an offence is committed by—

(a) the company, and

(b) every officer of the company who is in default.

(6) A person guilty of an offence under this section is liable on summary conviction to a fine not exceeding level 3 on the standard scale.

[S901]

NOTES

Commencement: to be appointed.

PART 27
MERGERS AND DIVISIONS OF PUBLIC COMPANIES

CHAPTER 1
INTRODUCTORY

902 Application of this Part

(1) This Part applies where—

(a) a compromise or arrangement is proposed between a public company and—

(i) its creditors or any class of them, or

(ii) its members or any class of them,

for the purposes of, or in connection with, a scheme for the reconstruction of any company or companies or the amalgamation of any two or more companies,

(b) the scheme involves—

(i) a merger (as defined in section 904), or

(ii) a division (as defined in section 919), and

(c) the consideration for the transfer (or each of the transfers) envisaged is to be shares in the transferee company (or one or more of the transferee companies) receivable by members of the transferor company (or transferor companies), with or without any cash payment to members.

(2) In this Part—

(a) a "new company" means a company formed for the purposes of, or in connection with, the scheme, and

(b) an "existing company" means a company other than one formed for the purposes of, or in connection with, the scheme.

(3) This Part does not apply where the company in respect of which the compromise or arrangement is proposed is being wound up.

[S902]

NOTES

Commencement: to be appointed.

903 Relationship of this Part to Part 26

(1) The court must not sanction the compromise or arrangement under Part 26 (arrangements and reconstructions) unless the relevant requirements of this Part have been complied with.

(2) The requirements applicable to a merger are specified in sections 905 to 914. Certain of those requirements, and certain general requirements of Part 26, are modified or excluded by the provisions of sections 915 to 918.

(3) The requirements applicable to a division are specified in sections 920 to 930. Certain of those requirements, and certain general requirements of Part 26, are modified or excluded by the provisions of sections 931 to 934.

[S903]

NOTES

Commencement: to be appointed.

CHAPTER 2
MERGER

Introductory

904 Mergers and merging companies

(1) The scheme involves a merger where under the scheme—

(a) the undertaking, property and liabilities of one or more public companies, including the company in respect of which the compromise or arrangement is proposed, are to be transferred to another existing public company (a "merger by absorption"), or

(b) the undertaking, property and liabilities of two or more public companies, including the company in respect of which the compromise or arrangement is proposed, are to be transferred to a new company, whether or not a public company, (a "merger by formation of a new company").

(2) References in this Part to "the merging companies" are—

(a) in relation to a merger by absorption, to the transferor and transferee companies;

(b) in relation to a merger by formation of a new company, to the transferor companies.

[S904]

NOTES

Commencement: to be appointed.

Requirements applicable to merger

905 Draft terms of scheme (merger)

(1) A draft of the proposed terms of the scheme must be drawn up and adopted by the directors of the merging companies.

(2) The draft terms must give particulars of at least the following matters—

(a) in respect of each transferor company and the transferee company—

(i) its name,

(ii) the address of its registered office, and

(iii) whether it is a company limited by shares or a company limited by guarantee and having a share capital;

(b) the number of shares in the transferee company to be allotted to members of a transferor company for a given number of their shares (the "share exchange ratio") and the amount of any cash payment;

(c) the terms relating to the allotment of shares in the transferee company;

(d) the date from which the holding of shares in the transferee company will entitle the holders to participate in profits, and any special conditions affecting that entitlement;

(e) the date from which the transactions of a transferor company are to be treated for accounting purposes as being those of the transferee company;

(f) any rights or restrictions attaching to shares or other securities in the transferee company to be allotted under the scheme to the holders of shares or other securities in a transferor company to which any special rights or restrictions attach, or the measures proposed concerning them;

(g) any amount of benefit paid or given or intended to be paid or given—
(i) to any of the experts referred to in section 909 (expert's report), or
(ii) to any director of a merging company,
and the consideration for the payment of benefit.

(3) The requirements in subsection (2)(b), (c) and (d) are subject to section 915 (circumstances in which certain particulars not required).

[S905]

NOTES

Commencement: to be appointed.

906 Publication of draft terms (merger)

(1) The directors of each of the merging companies must deliver a copy of the draft terms to the registrar.

(2) The registrar must publish in the Gazette notice of receipt by him from that company of a copy of the draft terms.

(3) That notice must be published at least one month before the date of any meeting of that company summoned for the purpose of approving the scheme.

[S906]

NOTES

Commencement: to be appointed.

907 Approval of members of merging companies

(1) The scheme must be approved by a majority in number, representing 75% in value, of each class of members of each of the merging companies, present and voting either in person or by proxy at a meeting.

(2) This requirement is subject to sections 916, 917 and 918 (circumstances in which meetings of members not required).

[S907]

NOTES

Commencement: to be appointed.

908 Directors' explanatory report (merger)

(1) The directors of each of the merging companies must draw up and adopt a report.

(2) The report must consist of—
(a) the statement required by section 897 (statement explaining effect of compromise or arrangement), and
(b) insofar as that statement does not deal with the following matters, a further statement—
(i) setting out the legal and economic grounds for the draft terms, and in particular for the share exchange ratio, and
(ii) specifying any special valuation difficulties.

(3) The requirement in this section is subject to section 915 (circumstances in which reports not required).

[S908]

NOTES

Commencement: to be appointed.

909 Expert's report (merger)

(1) An expert's report must be drawn up on behalf of each of the merging companies.

(2) The report required is a written report on the draft terms to the members of the company.

(3) The court may on the joint application of all the merging companies approve the appointment of a joint expert to draw up a single report on behalf of all those companies.

If no such appointment is made, there must be a separate expert's report to the members of each merging company drawn up by a separate expert appointed on behalf of that company.

(4) The expert must be a person who—
- (a) is eligible for appointment as a statutory auditor (see section 1212), and
- (b) meets the independence requirement in section 936.

(5) The expert's report must—
- (a) indicate the method or methods used to arrive at the share exchange ratio;
- (b) give an opinion as to whether the method or methods used are reasonable in all the circumstances of the case, indicate the values arrived at using each such method and (if there is more than one method) give an opinion on the relative importance attributed to such methods in arriving at the value decided on;
- (c) describe any special valuation difficulties that have arisen;
- (d) state whether in the expert's opinion the share exchange ratio is reasonable; and
- (e) in the case of a valuation made by a person other than himself (see section 935), state that it appeared to him reasonable to arrange for it to be so made or to accept a valuation so made.

(6) The expert (or each of them) has—
- (a) the right of access to all such documents of all the merging companies, and
- (b) the right to require from the companies' officers all such information,

as he thinks necessary for the purposes of making his report.

(7) The requirement in this section is subject to section 915 (circumstances in which reports not required).

[S909]

NOTES
Commencement: to be appointed.

910 Supplementary accounting statement (merger)

(1) If the last annual accounts of any of the merging companies relate to a financial year ending more than seven months before the first meeting of the company summoned for the purposes of approving the scheme, the directors of that company must prepare a supplementary accounting statement.

(2) That statement must consist of—
- (a) a balance sheet dealing with the state of affairs of the company as at a date not more than three months before the draft terms were adopted by the directors, and
- (b) where the company would be required under section 399 to prepare group accounts if that date were the last day of a financial year, a consolidated balance sheet dealing with the state of affairs of the company and the undertakings that would be included in such a consolidation.

(3) The requirements of this Act (and where relevant Article 4 of the IAS Regulation) as to the balance sheet forming part of a company's annual accounts, and the matters to be included in notes to it, apply to the balance sheet required for an accounting statement under this section, with such modifications as are necessary by reason of its being prepared otherwise than as at the last day of a financial year.

(4) The provisions of section 414 as to the approval and signing of accounts apply to the balance sheet required for an accounting statement under this section.

[S910]

NOTES
Commencement: to be appointed.

911 Inspection of documents (merger)

(1) The members of each of the merging companies must be able, during the period specified below—
- (a) to inspect at the registered office of that company copies of the documents listed below relating to that company and every other merging company, and

(b) to obtain copies of those documents or any part of them on request free of charge.

(2) The period referred to above is the period—

(a) beginning one month before, and

(b) ending on the date of,

the first meeting of the members, or any class of members, of the company for the purposes of approving the scheme.

(3) The documents referred to above are—

(a) the draft terms;

(b) the directors' explanatory report;

(c) the expert's report;

(d) the company's annual accounts and reports for the last three financial years ending on or before the first meeting of the members, or any class of members, of the company summoned for the purposes of approving the scheme; and

(e) any supplementary accounting statement required by section 910.

(4) The requirements of subsection (3)(b) and (c) are subject to section 915 (circumstances in which reports not required).

[S911]

NOTES

Commencement: to be appointed.

912 Approval of articles of new transferee company (merger)

In the case of a merger by formation of a new company, the articles of the transferee company, or a draft of them, must be approved by ordinary resolution of the transferor company or, as the case may be, each of the transferor companies.

[S912]

NOTES

Commencement: to be appointed.

913 Protection of holders of securities to which special rights attached (merger)

(1) The scheme must provide that where any securities of a transferor company (other than shares) to which special rights are attached are held by a person otherwise than as a member or creditor of the company, that person is to receive rights in the transferee company of equivalent value.

(2) Subsection (1) does not apply if—

(a) the holder has agreed otherwise, or

(b) the holder is, or under the scheme is to be, entitled to have the securities purchased by the transferee company on terms that the court considers reasonable.

[S913]

NOTES

Commencement: to be appointed.

914 No allotment of shares to transferor company or its nominee (merger)

The scheme must not provide for shares in the transferee company to be allotted to a transferor company (or its nominee) in respect of shares in the transferor company held by it (or its nominee).

[S914]

NOTES

Commencement: to be appointed.

Exceptions where shares of transferor company held by transferee company

915 Circumstances in which certain particulars and reports not required (merger)

(1) This section applies in the case of a merger by absorption where all of the relevant securities of the transferor company (or, if there is more than one transferor company, of each of them) are held by or on behalf of the transferee company.

(2) The draft terms of the scheme need not give the particulars mentioned in section 905(2)(b), (c) or (d) (particulars relating to allotment of shares to members of transferor company).

(3) Section 897 (explanatory statement to be circulated or made available) does not apply.

(4) The requirements of the following sections do not apply—

section 908 (directors' explanatory report),
section 909 (expert's report).

(5) The requirements of section 911 (inspection of documents) so far as relating to any document required to be drawn up under the provisions mentioned in subsection (3) above do not apply.

(6) In this section "relevant securities", in relation to a company, means shares or other securities carrying the right to vote at general meetings of the company.

[S915]

NOTES

Commencement: to be appointed.

916 Circumstances in which meeting of members of transferee company not required (merger)

(1) This section applies in the case of a merger by absorption where 90% or more (but not all) of the relevant securities of the transferor company (or, if there is more than one transferor company, of each of them) are held by or on behalf of the transferee company.

(2) It is not necessary for the scheme to be approved at a meeting of the members, or any class of members, of the transferee company if the court is satisfied that the following conditions have been complied with.

(3) The first condition is that publication of notice of receipt of the draft terms by the registrar took place in respect of the transferee company at least one month before the date of the first meeting of members, or any class of members, of the transferor company summoned for the purpose of agreeing to the scheme.

(4) The second condition is that the members of the transferee company were able during the period beginning one month before, and ending on, that date—

(a) to inspect at the registered office of the transferee company copies of the documents listed in section 911(3)(a), (d) and (e) relating to that company and the transferor company (or, if there is more than one transferor company, each of them), and

(b) to obtain copies of those documents or any part of them on request free of charge.

(5) The third condition is that—

(a) one or more members of the transferee company, who together held not less than 5% of the paid-up capital of the company which carried the right to vote at general meetings of the company (excluding any shares in the company held as treasury shares) would have been able, during that period, to require a meeting of each class of members to be called for the purpose of deciding whether or not to agree to the scheme, and

(b) no such requirement was made.

(6) In this section "relevant securities", in relation to a company, means shares or other securities carrying the right to vote at general meetings of the company.

[S916]

NOTES

Commencement: to be appointed.

917 Circumstances in which no meetings required (merger)

(1) This section applies in the case of a merger by absorption where all of the relevant securities of the transferor company (or, if there is more than one transferor company, of each of them) are held by or on behalf of the transferee company.

(2) It is not necessary for the scheme to be approved at a meeting of the members, or any class of members, of any of the merging companies if the court is satisfied that the following conditions have been complied with.

(3) The first condition is that publication of notice of receipt of the draft terms by the registrar took place in respect of all the merging companies at least one month before the date of the court's order.

(4) The second condition is that the members of the transferee company were able during the period beginning one month before, and ending on, that date—

- (a) to inspect at the registered office of that company copies of the documents listed in section 911(3) relating to that company and the transferor company (or, if there is more than one transferor company, each of them), and
- (b) to obtain copies of those documents or any part of them on request free of charge.

(5) The third condition is that—

- (a) one or more members of the transferee company, who together held not less than 5% of the paid-up capital of the company which carried the right to vote at general meetings of the company (excluding any shares in the company held as treasury shares) would have been able, during that period, to require a meeting of each class of members to be called for the purpose of deciding whether or not to agree to the scheme, and
- (b) no such requirement was made.

(6) In this section "relevant securities", in relation to a company, means shares or other securities carrying the right to vote at general meetings of the company.

[S917]

NOTES

Commencement: to be appointed.

Other exceptions

918 Other circumstances in which meeting of members of transferee company not required (merger)

(1) In the case of any merger by absorption, it is not necessary for the scheme to be approved by the members of the transferee company if the court is satisfied that the following conditions have been complied with.

(2) The first condition is that publication of notice of receipt of the draft terms by the registrar took place in respect of that company at least one month before the date of the first meeting of members, or any class of members, of the transferor company (or, if there is more than one transferor company, any of them) summoned for the purposes of agreeing to the scheme.

(3) The second condition is that the members of that company were able during the period beginning one month before, and ending on, the date of any such meeting—

- (a) to inspect at the registered office of that company copies of the documents specified in section 911(3) relating to that company and the transferor company (or, if there is more than one transferor company, each of them), and
- (b) to obtain copies of those documents or any part of them on request free of charge.

(4) The third condition is that—

- (a) one or more members of that company, who together held not less than 5% of the paid-up capital of the company which carried the right to vote at general meetings of the company (excluding any shares in the company held as treasury shares) would have been able, during that period, to require a meeting of each class of members to be called for the purpose of deciding whether or not to agree to the scheme, and

(b) no such requirement was made.

[S918]

NOTES

Commencement: to be appointed.

CHAPTER 3
DIVISION

Introductory

919 Divisions and companies involved in a division

(1) The scheme involves a division where under the scheme the undertaking, property and liabilities of the company in respect of which the compromise or arrangement is proposed are to be divided among and transferred to two or more companies each of which is either—

(a) an existing public company, or

(b) a new company (whether or not a public company).

(2) References in this Part to the companies involved in the division are to the transferor company and any existing transferee companies.

[S919]

NOTES

Commencement: to be appointed.

Requirements to be complied with in case of division

920 Draft terms of scheme (division)

(1) A draft of the proposed terms of the scheme must be drawn up and adopted by the directors of each of the companies involved in the division.

(2) The draft terms must give particulars of at least the following matters—

(a) in respect of the transferor company and each transferee company—

(i) its name,

(ii) the address of its registered office, and

(iii) whether it is a company limited by shares or a company limited by guarantee and having a share capital;

(b) the number of shares in a transferee company to be allotted to members of the transferor company for a given number of their shares (the "share exchange ratio") and the amount of any cash payment;

(c) the terms relating to the allotment of shares in a transferee company;

(d) the date from which the holding of shares in a transferee company will entitle the holders to participate in profits, and any special conditions affecting that entitlement;

(e) the date from which the transactions of the transferor company are to be treated for accounting purposes as being those of a transferee company;

(f) any rights or restrictions attaching to shares or other securities in a transferee company to be allotted under the scheme to the holders of shares or other securities in the transferor company to which any special rights or restrictions attach, or the measures proposed concerning them;

(g) any amount of benefit paid or given or intended to be paid or given—

(i) to any of the experts referred to in section 924 (expert's report), or

(ii) to any director of a company involved in the division,

and the consideration for the payment of benefit.

(3) The draft terms must also—

(a) give particulars of the property and liabilities to be transferred (to the extent that these are known to the transferor company) and their allocation among the transferee companies;

(b) make provision for the allocation among and transfer to the transferee companies of any other property and liabilities that the transferor company has acquired or may subsequently acquire; and

(c) specify the allocation to members of the transferor company of shares in the transferee companies and the criteria upon which that allocation is based.

[S920]

NOTES

Commencement: to be appointed.

921 Publication of draft terms (division)

(1) The directors of each company involved in the division must deliver a copy of the draft terms to the registrar.

(2) The registrar must publish in the Gazette notice of receipt by him from that company of a copy of the draft terms.

(3) That notice must be published at least one month before the date of any meeting of that company summoned for the purposes of approving the scheme.

(4) The requirements in this section are subject to section 934 (power of court to exclude certain requirements).

[S921]

NOTES

Commencement: to be appointed.

922 Approval of members of companies involved in the division

(1) The compromise or arrangement must be approved by a majority in number, representing 75% in value, of each class of members of each of the companies involved in the division, present and voting either in person or by proxy at a meeting.

(2) This requirement is subject to sections 931 and 932 (circumstances in which meeting of members not required).

[S922]

NOTES

Commencement: to be appointed.

923 Directors' explanatory report (division)

(1) The directors of the transferor and each existing transferee company must draw up and adopt a report.

(2) The report must consist of—

(a) the statement required by section 897 (statement explaining effect of compromise or arrangement), and

(b) insofar as that statement does not deal with the following matters, a further statement—

(i) setting out the legal and economic grounds for the draft terms, and in particular for the share exchange ratio and for the criteria on which the allocation to the members of the transferor company of shares in the transferee companies was based, and

(ii) specifying any special valuation difficulties.

(3) The report must also state—

(a) whether a report has been made to any transferee company under section 593 (valuation of non-cash consideration for shares), and

(b) if so, whether that report has been delivered to the registrar of companies.

(4) The requirement in this section is subject to section 933 (agreement to dispense with reports etc).

[S923]

NOTES

Commencement: to be appointed.

924 Expert's report (division)

(1) An expert's report must be drawn up on behalf of each company involved in the division.

(2) The report required is a written report on the draft terms to the members of the company.

(3) The court may on the joint application of the companies involved in the division approve the appointment of a joint expert to draw up a single report on behalf of all those companies.

If no such appointment is made, there must be a separate expert's report to the members of each company involved in the division drawn up by a separate expert appointed on behalf of that company.

(4) The expert must be a person who—

(a) is eligible for appointment as a statutory auditor (see section 1212), and

(b) meets the independence requirement in section 936.

(5) The expert's report must—

(a) indicate the method or methods used to arrive at the share exchange ratio;

(b) give an opinion as to whether the method or methods used are reasonable in all the circumstances of the case, indicate the values arrived at using each such method and (if there is more than one method) give an opinion on the relative importance attributed to such methods in arriving at the value decided on;

(c) describe any special valuation difficulties that have arisen;

(d) state whether in the expert's opinion the share exchange ratio is reasonable; and

(e) in the case of a valuation made by a person other than himself (see section 935), state that it appeared to him reasonable to arrange for it to be so made or to accept a valuation so made.

(6) The expert (or each of them) has—

(a) the right of access to all such documents of the companies involved in the division, and

(b) the right to require from the companies' officers all such information,

as he thinks necessary for the purposes of making his report.

(7) The requirement in this section is subject to section 933 (agreement to dispense with reports etc).

[S924]

NOTES

Commencement: to be appointed.

925 Supplementary accounting statement (division)

(1) If the last annual accounts of a company involved in the division relate to a financial year ending more than seven months before the first meeting of the company summoned for the purposes of approving the scheme, the directors of that company must prepare a supplementary accounting statement.

(2) That statement must consist of—

(a) a balance sheet dealing with the state of affairs of the company as at a date not more than three months before the draft terms were adopted by the directors, and

(b) where the company would be required under section 399 to prepare group accounts if that date were the last day of a financial year, a consolidated balance sheet dealing with the state of affairs of the company and the undertakings that would be included in such a consolidation.

(3) The requirements of this Act (and where relevant Article 4 of the IAS Regulation) as to the balance sheet forming part of a company's annual accounts, and the matters to be included in notes to it, apply to the balance sheet required for an accounting statement under

this section, with such modifications as are necessary by reason of its being prepared otherwise than as at the last day of a financial year.

(4) The provisions of section 414 as to the approval and signing of accounts apply to the balance sheet required for an accounting statement under this section.

(5) The requirement in this section is subject to section 933 (agreement to dispense with reports etc).

[S925]

NOTES

Commencement: to be appointed.

926 Inspection of documents (division)

(1) The members of each company involved in the division must be able, during the period specified below—

(a) to inspect at the registered office of that company copies of the documents listed below relating to that company and every other company involved in the division, and

(b) to obtain copies of those documents or any part of them on request free of charge.

(2) The period referred to above is the period—

(a) beginning one month before, and

(b) ending on the date of,

the first meeting of the members, or any class of members, of the company for the purposes of approving the scheme.

(3) The documents referred to above are—

(a) the draft terms;

(b) the directors' explanatory report;

(c) the expert's report;

(d) the company's annual accounts and reports for the last three financial years ending on or before the first meeting of the members, or any class of members, of the company summoned for the purposes of approving the scheme; and

(e) any supplementary accounting statement required by section 925.

(4) The requirements in subsection (3)(b), (c) and (e) are subject to section 933 (agreement to dispense with reports etc) and section 934 (power of court to exclude certain requirements).

[S926]

NOTES

Commencement: to be appointed.

927 Report on material changes of assets of transferor company (division)

(1) The directors of the transferor company must report—

(a) to every meeting of the members, or any class of members, of that company summoned for the purpose of agreeing to the scheme, and

(b) to the directors of each existing transferee company,

any material changes in the property and liabilities of the transferor company between the date when the draft terms were adopted and the date of the meeting in question.

(2) The directors of each existing transferee company must in turn—

(a) report those matters to every meeting of the members, or any class of members, of that company summoned for the purpose of agreeing to the scheme, or

(b) send a report of those matters to every member entitled to receive notice of such a meeting.

(3) The requirement in this section is subject to section 933 (agreement to dispense with reports etc).

[S927]

NOTES

Commencement: to be appointed.

928 Approval of articles of new transferee company (division)

The articles of every new transferee company, or a draft of them, must be approved by ordinary resolution of the transferor company.

[S928]

NOTES

Commencement: to be appointed.

929 Protection of holders of securities to which special rights attached (division)

(1) The scheme must provide that where any securities of the transferor company (other than shares) to which special rights are attached are held by a person otherwise than as a member or creditor of the company, that person is to receive rights in a transferee company of equivalent value.

(2) Subsection (1) does not apply if—

(a) the holder has agreed otherwise, or

(b) the holder is, or under the scheme is to be, entitled to have the securities purchased by a transferee company on terms that the court considers reasonable.

[S929]

NOTES

Commencement: to be appointed.

930 No allotment of shares to transferor company or its nominee (division)

The scheme must not provide for shares in a transferee company to be allotted to the transferor company (or its nominee) in respect of shares in the transferor company held by it (or its nominee).

[S930]

NOTES

Commencement: to be appointed.

Exceptions where shares of transferor company held by transferee company

931 Circumstances in which meeting of members of transferor company not required (division)

(1) This section applies in the case of a division where all of the shares or other securities of the transferor company carrying the right to vote at general meetings of the company are held by or on behalf of one or more existing transferee companies.

(2) It is not necessary for the scheme to be approved by a meeting of the members, or any class of members, of the transferor company if the court is satisfied that the following conditions have been complied with.

(3) The first condition is that publication of notice of receipt of the draft terms by the registrar took place in respect of all the companies involved in the division at least one month before the date of the court's order.

(4) The second condition is that the members of every company involved in the division were able during the period beginning one month before, and ending on, that date—

(a) to inspect at the registered office of their company copies of the documents listed in section 926(3) relating to every company involved in the division, and

(b) to obtain copies of those documents or any part of them on request free of charge.

(5) The third condition is that—

(a) one or more members of the transferor company, who together held not less than 5% of the paid-up capital of the company (excluding any shares in the company held as treasury shares) would have been able, during that period, to require a meeting of each class of members to be called for the purpose of deciding whether or not to agree to the scheme, and

(b) no such requirement was made.

(6) The fourth condition is that the directors of the transferor company have sent—

(a) to every member who would have been entitled to receive notice of a meeting to agree to the scheme (had any such meeting been called), and

(b) to the directors of every existing transferee company,

a report of any material change in the property and liabilities of the transferor company between the date when the terms were adopted by the directors and the date one month before the date of the court's order.

[S931]

NOTES

Commencement: to be appointed.

Other exceptions

932 Circumstances in which meeting of members of transferee company not required (division)

(1) In the case of a division, it is not necessary for the scheme to be approved by the members of a transferee company if the court is satisfied that the following conditions have been complied with in relation to that company.

(2) The first condition is that publication of notice of receipt of the draft terms by the registrar took place in respect of that company at least one month before the date of the first meeting of members of the transferor company summoned for the purposes of agreeing to the scheme.

(3) The second condition is that the members of that company were able during the period beginning one month before, and ending on, that date—

(a) to inspect at the registered office of that company copies of the documents specified in section 926(3) relating to that company and every other company involved in the division, and

(b) to obtain copies of those documents or any part of them on request free of charge.

(4) The third condition is that—

(a) one or more members of that company, who together held not less than 5% of the paid-up capital of the company which carried the right to vote at general meetings of the company (excluding any shares in the company held as treasury shares) would have been able, during that period, to require a meeting of each class of members to be called for the purpose of deciding whether or not to agree to the scheme, and

(b) no such requirement was made.

(5) The first and second conditions above are subject to section 934 (power of court to exclude certain requirements).

[S932]

NOTES

Commencement: to be appointed.

933 Agreement to dispense with reports etc (division)

(1) If all members holding shares in, and all persons holding other securities of, the companies involved in the division, being shares or securities that carry a right to vote in general meetings of the company in question, so agree, the following requirements do not apply.

(2) The requirements that may be dispensed with under this section are—

(a) the requirements of—

(i) section 923 (directors' explanatory report),

(ii) section 924 (expert's report),

(iii) section 925 (supplementary accounting statement), and

(iv) section 927 (report on material changes in assets of transferor company); and

(b) the requirements of section 926 (inspection of documents) so far as relating to any document required to be drawn up under the provisions mentioned in paragraph (a)(i), (ii) or (iii) above.

(3) For the purposes of this section—
- (a) the members, or holders of other securities, of a company, and
- (b) whether shares or other securities carry a right to vote in general meetings of the company,

are determined as at the date of the application to the court under section 896.

[S933]

NOTES

Commencement: to be appointed.

934 Power of court to exclude certain requirements (division)

(1) In the case of a division, the court may by order direct that—
- (a) in relation to any company involved in the division, the requirements of—
  - (i) section 921 (publication of draft terms), and
  - (ii) section 926 (inspection of documents),

  do not apply, and
- (b) in relation to an existing transferee company, section 932 (circumstances in which meeting of members of transferee company not required) has effect with the omission of the first and second conditions specified in that section,

if the court is satisfied that the following conditions will be fulfilled in relation to that company.

(2) The first condition is that the members of that company will have received, or will have been able to obtain free of charge, copies of the documents listed in section 926—
- (a) in time to examine them before the date of the first meeting of the members, or any class of members, of that company summoned for the purposes of agreeing to the scheme, or
- (b) in the case of an existing transferee company where in the circumstances described in section 932 no meeting is held, in time to require a meeting as mentioned in subsection (4) of that section.

(3) The second condition is that the creditors of that company will have received or will have been able to obtain free of charge copies of the draft terms in time to examine them—
- (a) before the date of the first meeting of the members, or any class of members, of the company summoned for the purposes of agreeing to the scheme, or
- (b) in the circumstances mentioned in subsection (2)(b) above, at the same time as the members of the company.

(4) The third condition is that no prejudice would be caused to the members or creditors of the transferor company or any transferee company by making the order in question.

[S934]

NOTES

Commencement: to be appointed.

CHAPTER 4
SUPPLEMENTARY PROVISIONS

Expert's report and related matters

935 Expert's report: valuation by another person

(1) Where it appears to an expert—
- (a) that a valuation is reasonably necessary to enable him to draw up his report, and
- (b) that it is reasonable for that valuation, or part of it, to be made by (or for him to accept a valuation made by) another person who—
  - (i) appears to him to have the requisite knowledge and experience to make the valuation or that part of it, and
  - (ii) meets the independence requirement in section 936,

he may arrange for or accept such a valuation, together with a report which will enable him to make his own report under section 909 or 924.

(2) Where any valuation is made by a person other than the expert himself, the latter's report must state that fact and must also—

(a) state the former's name and what knowledge and experience he has to carry out the valuation, and

(b) describe so much of the undertaking, property and liabilities as was valued by the other person, and the method used to value them, and specify the date of the valuation.

[S935]

NOTES

Commencement: to be appointed.

936 Experts and valuers: independence requirement

(1) A person meets the independence requirement for the purposes of section 909 or 924 (expert's report) or section 935 (valuation by another person) only if—

(a) he is not—

(i) an officer or employee of any of the companies concerned in the scheme, or

(ii) a partner or employee of such a person, or a partnership of which such a person is a partner;

(b) he is not—

(i) an officer or employee of an associated undertaking of any of the companies concerned in the scheme, or

(ii) a partner or employee of such a person, or a partnership of which such a person is a partner; and

(c) there does not exist between—

(i) the person or an associate of his, and

(ii) any of the companies concerned in the scheme or an associated undertaking of such a company,

a connection of any such description as may be specified by regulations made by the Secretary of State.

(2) An auditor of a company is not regarded as an officer or employee of the company for this purpose.

(3) For the purposes of this section—

(a) the "companies concerned in the scheme" means every transferor and existing transferee company;

(b) "associated undertaking", in relation to a company, means—

(i) a parent undertaking or subsidiary undertaking of the company, or

(ii) a subsidiary undertaking of a parent undertaking of the company; and

(c) "associate" has the meaning given by section 937.

(4) Regulations under this section are subject to negative resolution procedure.

[S936]

NOTES

Commencement: 20 January 2007 (for the purpose of enabling the exercise of powers to make Orders or Regulations by statutory instrument); to be appointed (otherwise).

937 Experts and valuers: meaning of "associate"

(1) This section defines "associate" for the purposes of section 936 (experts and valuers: independence requirement).

(2) In relation to an individual, "associate" means—

(a) that individual's spouse or civil partner or minor child or step-child,

(b) any body corporate of which that individual is a director, and

(c) any employee or partner of that individual.

(3) In relation to a body corporate, "associate" means—

(a) any body corporate of which that body is a director,

(b) any body corporate in the same group as that body, and

(c) any employee or partner of that body or of any body corporate in the same group.

(4) In relation to a partnership that is a legal person under the law by which it is governed, "associate" means—

(a) any body corporate of which that partnership is a director,

(b) any employee of or partner in that partnership, and

(c) any person who is an associate of a partner in that partnership.

(5) In relation to a partnership that is not a legal person under the law by which it is governed, "associate" means any person who is an associate of any of the partners.

(6) In this section, in relation to a limited liability partnership, for "director" read "member".

[S937]

NOTES

Commencement: to be appointed.

Powers of the court

938 Power of court to summon meeting of members or creditors of existing transferee company

(1) The court may order a meeting of—

(a) the members of an existing transferee company, or any class of them, or

(b) the creditors of an existing transferee company, or any class of them, to be summoned in such manner as the court directs.

(2) An application for such an order may be made by—

(a) the company concerned,

(b) a member or creditor of the company, or

(c) if an administration order is in force in relation to the company, the administrator.

[S938]

NOTES

Commencement: to be appointed.

939 Court to fix date for transfer of undertaking etc of transferor company

(1) Where the court sanctions the compromise or arrangement, it must—

(a) in the order sanctioning the compromise or arrangement, or

(b) in a subsequent order under section 900 (powers of court to facilitate reconstruction or amalgamation),

fix a date on which the transfer (or transfers) to the transferee company (or transferee companies) of the undertaking, property and liabilities of the transferor company is (or are) to take place.

(2) Any such order that provides for the dissolution of the transferor company must fix the same date for the dissolution.

(3) If it is necessary for the transferor company to take steps to ensure that the undertaking, property and liabilities are fully transferred, the court must fix a date, not later than six months after the date fixed under subsection (1), by which such steps must be taken.

(4) In that case, the court may postpone the dissolution of the transferor company until that date.

(5) The court may postpone or further postpone the date fixed under subsection (3) if it is satisfied that the steps mentioned cannot be completed by the date (or latest date) fixed under that subsection.

[S939]

NOTES

Commencement: to be appointed.

Liability of transferee companies

940 Liability of transferee companies for each other's defaults

(1) In the case of a division, each transferee company is jointly and severally liable for any liability transferred to any other transferee company under the scheme to the extent that the other company has made default in satisfying that liability.

This is subject to the following provisions.

(2) If a majority in number representing 75% in value of the creditors or any class of creditors of the transferor company, present and voting either in person or by proxy at a meeting summoned for the purposes of agreeing to the scheme, so agree, subsection (1) does not apply in relation to the liabilities owed to the creditors or that class of creditors.

(3) A transferee company is not liable under this section for an amount greater than the net value transferred to it under the scheme.

The "net value transferred" is the value at the time of the transfer of the property transferred to it under the scheme less the amount at that date of the liabilities so transferred.
[S940]

NOTES

Commencement: to be appointed.

Interpretation

941 Meaning of "liabilities" and "property"

In this Part—
"liabilities" includes duties;
"property" includes property, rights and powers of every description.
[S941]

NOTES

Commencement: to be appointed.

PART 28
TAKEOVERS ETC

NOTES

The Takeovers Directive (at **[9592]**) had to be implemented by 20 May 2006 and, as this Act had not completed Parliamentary passage by that date, this was achieved by means of the Takeovers Directive (Interim Implementation) Regulations 2006, SI 2006/1183 (at **[7509]**). The 2006 Regulations were revoked by the Companies Act 2006 (Commencement No 2, Consequential Amendments, Transitional Provisions and Savings) Order 2007, SI 2007/1093, art 7, Sch 5, as from 6 April 2007 (the same date as this Part came into force). The revocation of SI 2006/1183 is subject to certain savings contained in Sch 6, paras 2, 3 to the 2007 Order at **[7629]**.

CHAPTER 1
THE TAKEOVER PANEL

The Panel and its rules

942 The Panel

(1) The body known as the Panel on Takeovers and Mergers ("the Panel") is to have the functions conferred on it by or under this Chapter.

(2) The Panel may do anything that it considers necessary or expedient for the purposes of, or in connection with, its functions.

(3) The Panel may make arrangements for any of its functions to be discharged by—
(a) a committee or sub-committee of the Panel, or

(b) an officer or member of staff of the Panel, or a person acting as such.

This is subject to section 943(4) and (5).

[S942]

NOTES

Commencement: 6 April 2007.

943 Rules

(1) The Panel must make rules giving effect to Articles 3.1, 4.2, 5, 6.1 to 6.3, 7 to 9 and 13 of the Takeovers Directive.

(2) Rules made by the Panel may also make other provision—

(a) for or in connection with the regulation of—

(i) takeover bids,

(ii) merger transactions, and

(iii) transactions (not falling within sub-paragraph (i) or (ii)) that have or may have, directly or indirectly, an effect on the ownership or control of companies;

(b) for or in connection with the regulation of things done in consequence of, or otherwise in relation to, any such bid or transaction;

(c) about cases where—

(i) any such bid or transaction is, or has been, contemplated or apprehended, or

(ii) an announcement is made denying that any such bid or transaction is intended.

(3) The provision that may be made under subsection (2) includes, in particular, provision for a matter that is, or is similar to, a matter provided for by the Panel in the City Code on Takeovers and Mergers as it had effect immediately before the passing of this Act.

(4) In relation to rules made by virtue of section 957 (fees and charges), functions under this section may be discharged either by the Panel itself or by a committee of the Panel (but not otherwise).

(5) In relation to rules of any other description, the Panel must discharge its functions under this section by a committee of the Panel.

(6) Section 1 (meaning of "company") does not apply for the purposes of this section.

(7) In this section "takeover bid" includes a takeover bid within the meaning of the Takeovers Directive.

(8) In this Chapter "the Takeovers Directive" means Directive 2004/25/EC of the European Parliament and of the Council.

(9) A reference to rules in the following provisions of this Chapter is to rules under this section.

[S943]

NOTES

Commencement: 6 April 2007.

Transitional adaptations: art 3 of the Companies Act 2006 (Commencement No 2, Consequential Amendments, Transitional Provisions and Savings) Order 2007, SI 2007/1093 provides that the provisions brought into force by art 2 of 2007 Order shall have effect subject to any transitional adaptations specified in Sch 1 to that Order. Schedule 1, para 2 to the Order (at **[7625]**) provides as follows—

"**2.**—(1) Section 943 (power of Takeover Panel to make rules) has effect with the following adaptation.

(2) For subsection (6) substitute—

"(6) Section 735(1) of the Companies Act 1985 and Article 2(3) of the Companies (Northern Ireland) Order 1986 (meaning of "company") do not apply for the purposes of this section."."

As to Rules made by the Takeover Panel under this section, see: http:/www.thetakeoverpanel.org.uk/new/

944 Further provisions about rules

(1) Rules may—

(a) make different provision for different purposes;

(b) make provision subject to exceptions or exemptions;

(c) contain incidental, supplemental, consequential or transitional provision;

(d) authorise the Panel to dispense with or modify the application of rules in particular cases and by reference to any circumstances.

Rules made by virtue of paragraph (d) must require the Panel to give reasons for acting as mentioned in that paragraph.

(2) Rules must be made by an instrument in writing.

(3) Immediately after an instrument containing rules is made, the text must be made available to the public, with or without payment, in whatever way the Panel thinks appropriate.

(4) A person is not to be taken to have contravened a rule if he shows that at the time of the alleged contravention the text of the rule had not been made available as required by subsection (3).

(5) The production of a printed copy of an instrument purporting to be made by the Panel on which is endorsed a certificate signed by an officer of the Panel authorised by it for that purpose and stating—

(a) that the instrument was made by the Panel,

(b) that the copy is a true copy of the instrument, and

(c) that on a specified date the text of the instrument was made available to the public as required by subsection (3),

is evidence (or in Scotland sufficient evidence) of the facts stated in the certificate.

(6) A certificate purporting to be signed as mentioned in subsection (5) is to be treated as having been properly signed unless the contrary is shown.

(7) A person who wishes in any legal proceedings to rely on an instrument by which rules are made may require the Panel to endorse a copy of the instrument with a certificate of the kind mentioned in subsection (5).

[S944]

NOTES

Commencement: 6 April 2007.

945 Rulings

(1) The Panel may give rulings on the interpretation, application or effect of rules.

(2) To the extent and in the circumstances specified in rules, and subject to any review or appeal, a ruling has binding effect.

[S945]

NOTES

Commencement: 6 April 2007.

946 Directions

Rules may contain provision conferring power on the Panel to give any direction that appears to the Panel to be necessary in order—

(a) to restrain a person from acting (or continuing to act) in breach of rules;

(b) to restrain a person from doing (or continuing to do) a particular thing, pending determination of whether that or any other conduct of his is or would be a breach of rules;

(c) otherwise to secure compliance with rules.

[S946]

NOTES

Commencement: 6 April 2007.

Information

947 Power to require documents and information

(1) The Panel may by notice in writing require a person—

(a) to produce any documents that are specified or described in the notice;

(b) to provide, in the form and manner specified in the notice, such information as may be specified or described in the notice.

(2) A requirement under subsection (1) must be complied with—

(a) at a place specified in the notice, and

(b) before the end of such reasonable period as may be so specified.

(3) This section applies only to documents and information reasonably required in connection with the exercise by the Panel of its functions.

(4) The Panel may require—

(a) any document produced to be authenticated, or

(b) any information provided (whether in a document or otherwise) to be verified,

in such manner as it may reasonably require.

(5) The Panel may authorise a person to exercise any of its powers under this section.

(6) A person exercising a power by virtue of subsection (5) must, if required to do so, produce evidence of his authority to exercise the power.

(7) The production of a document in pursuance of this section does not affect any lien that a person has on the document.

(8) The Panel may take copies of or extracts from a document produced in pursuance of this section.

(9) A reference in this section to the production of a document includes a reference to the production of—

(a) a hard copy of information recorded otherwise than in hard copy form, or

(b) information in a form from which a hard copy can be readily obtained.

(10) A person is not required by this section to disclose documents or information in respect of which a claim to legal professional privilege (in Scotland, to confidentiality of communications) could be maintained in legal proceedings.

[S947]

NOTES

Commencement: 6 April 2007.

948 Restrictions on disclosure

(1) This section applies to information (in whatever form)—

(a) relating to the private affairs of an individual, or

(b) relating to any particular business,

that is provided to the Panel in connection with the exercise of its functions.

(2) No such information may, during the lifetime of the individual or so long as the business continues to be carried on, be disclosed without the consent of that individual or (as the case may be) the person for the time being carrying on that business.

(3) Subsection (2) does not apply to any disclosure of information that—

(a) is made for the purpose of facilitating the carrying out by the Panel of any of its functions,

(b) is made to a person specified in Part 1 of Schedule 2,

(c) is of a description specified in Part 2 of that Schedule, or

(d) is made in accordance with Part 3 of that Schedule.

(4) The Secretary of State may amend Schedule 2 by order subject to negative resolution procedure.

(5) An order under subsection (4) must not—

(a) amend Part 1 of Schedule 2 by specifying a person unless the person exercises functions of a public nature (whether or not he exercises any other function);

(b) amend Part 2 of Schedule 2 by adding or modifying a description of disclosure unless the purpose for which the disclosure is permitted is likely to facilitate the exercise of a function of a public nature;

(c) amend Part 3 of Schedule 2 so as to have the effect of permitting disclosures to be made to a body other than one that exercises functions of a public nature in a country or territory outside the United Kingdom.

(6) Subsection (2) does not apply to—

(a) the disclosure by an authority within subsection (7) of information disclosed to it by the Panel in reliance on subsection (3);

(b) the disclosure of such information by anyone who has obtained it directly or indirectly from an authority within subsection (7).

(7) The authorities within this subsection are—

(a) the Financial Services Authority;

(b) an authority designated as a supervisory authority for the purposes of Article 4.1 of the Takeovers Directive;

(c) any other person or body that exercises functions of a public nature, under legislation in an EEA State other than the United Kingdom, that are similar to the Panel's functions or those of the Financial Services Authority.

(8) This section does not prohibit the disclosure of information if the information is or has been available to the public from any other source.

(9) Nothing in this section authorises the making of a disclosure in contravention of the Data Protection Act 1998 (c 29).

[S948]

NOTES

Commencement: 20 January 2007 (for the purpose of enabling the exercise of powers to make Orders or Regulations by statutory instrument); 6 April 2007 (otherwise).

949 Offence of disclosure in contravention of section 948

(1) A person who discloses information in contravention of section 948 is guilty of an offence, unless—

(a) he did not know, and had no reason to suspect, that the information had been provided as mentioned in section 948(1), or

(b) he took all reasonable steps and exercised all due diligence to avoid the commission of the offence.

(2) A person guilty of an offence under this section is liable—

(a) on conviction on indictment, to imprisonment for a term not exceeding two years or a fine (or both);

(b) on summary conviction—

(i) in England and Wales, to imprisonment for a term not exceeding twelve months or to a fine not exceeding the statutory maximum (or both);

(ii) in Scotland or Northern Ireland, to imprisonment for a term not exceeding six months, or to a fine not exceeding the statutory maximum (or both).

(3) Where a company or other body corporate commits an offence under this section, an offence is also committed by every officer of the company or other body corporate who is in default.

[S949]

NOTES

Commencement: 6 April 2007.

Co-operation

950 Panel's duty of co-operation

(1) The Panel must take such steps as it considers appropriate to co-operate with—

(a) the Financial Services Authority;

(b) an authority designated as a supervisory authority for the purposes of Article 4.1 of the Takeovers Directive;

(c) any other person or body that exercises functions of a public nature, under legislation in any country or territory outside the United Kingdom, that appear to the Panel to be similar to its own functions or those of the Financial Services Authority.

(2) Co-operation may include the sharing of information that the Panel is not prevented from disclosing.

[S950]

NOTES

Commencement: 6 April 2007.

Hearings and appeals

951 Hearings and appeals

(1) Rules must provide for a decision of the Panel to be subject to review by a committee of the Panel (the "Hearings Committee") at the instance of such persons affected by the decision as are specified in the rules.

(2) Rules may also confer other functions on the Hearings Committee.

(3) Rules must provide for there to be a right of appeal against a decision of the Hearings Committee to an independent tribunal (the "Takeover Appeal Board") in such circumstances and subject to such conditions as are specified in the rules.

(4) Rules may contain—

(a) provision as to matters of procedure in relation to proceedings before the Hearings Committee (including provision imposing time limits);

(b) provision about evidence in such proceedings;

(c) provision as to the powers of the Hearings Committee dealing with a matter referred to it;

(d) provision about enforcement of decisions of the Hearings Committee and the Takeover Appeal Board.

(5) Rules must contain provision—

(a) requiring the Panel, when acting in relation to any proceedings before the Hearings Committee or the Takeover Appeal Board, to do so by an officer or member of staff of the Panel (or a person acting as such);

(b) preventing a person who is or has been a member of the committee mentioned in section 943(5) from being a member of the Hearings Committee or the Takeover Appeal Board;

(c) preventing a person who is a member of the committee mentioned in section 943(5), of the Hearings Committee or of the Takeover Appeal Board from acting as mentioned in paragraph (a).

[S951]

NOTES

Commencement: 6 April 2007.

Contravention of rules etc

952 Sanctions

(1) Rules may contain provision conferring power on the Panel to impose sanctions on a person who has—

(a) acted in breach of rules, or

(b) failed to comply with a direction given by virtue of section 946.

(2) Subsection (3) applies where rules made by virtue of subsection (1) confer power on the Panel to impose a sanction of a kind not provided for by the City Code on Takeovers and Mergers as it had effect immediately before the passing of this Act.

(3) The Panel must prepare a statement (a "policy statement") of its policy with respect to—

(a) the imposition of the sanction in question, and
(b) where the sanction is in the nature of a financial penalty, the amount of the penalty that may be imposed.

An element of the policy must be that, in making a decision about any such matter, the Panel has regard to the factors mentioned in subsection (4).

(4) The factors are—
(a) the seriousness of the breach or failure in question in relation to the nature of the rule or direction contravened;
(b) the extent to which the breach or failure was deliberate or reckless;
(c) whether the person on whom the sanction is to be imposed is an individual.

(5) The Panel may at any time revise a policy statement.

(6) The Panel must prepare a draft of any proposed policy statement (or revised policy statement) and consult such persons about the draft as the Panel considers appropriate.

(7) The Panel must publish, in whatever way it considers appropriate, any policy statement (or revised policy statement) that it prepares.

(8) In exercising, or deciding whether to exercise, its power to impose a sanction within subsection (2) in the case of any particular breach or failure, the Panel must have regard to any relevant policy statement published and in force at the time when the breach or failure occurred.

[S952]

NOTES

Commencement: 6 April 2007.

953 Failure to comply with rules about bid documentation

(1) This section applies where a takeover bid is made for a company that has securities carrying voting rights admitted to trading on a regulated market in the United Kingdom.

(2) Where an offer document published in respect of the bid does not comply with offer document rules, an offence is committed by—
(a) the person making the bid, and
(b) where the person making the bid is a body of persons, any director, officer or member of that body who caused the document to be published.

(3) A person commits an offence under subsection (2) only if—
(a) he knew that the offer document did not comply, or was reckless as to whether it complied, and
(b) he failed to take all reasonable steps to secure that it did comply.

(4) Where a response document published in respect of the bid does not comply with response document rules, an offence is committed by any director or other officer of the company referred to in subsection (1) who—
(a) knew that the response document did not comply, or was reckless as to whether it complied, and
(b) failed to take all reasonable steps to secure that it did comply.

(5) Where an offence is committed under subsection (2)(b) or (4) by a company or other body corporate ("the relevant body")—
(a) subsection (2)(b) has effect as if the reference to a director, officer or member of the person making the bid included a reference to a director, officer or member of the relevant body;
(b) subsection (4) has effect as if the reference to a director or other officer of the company referred to in subsection (1) included a reference to a director, officer or member of the relevant body.

(6) A person guilty of an offence under this section is liable—
(a) on conviction on indictment, to a fine;
(b) on summary conviction, to a fine not exceeding the statutory maximum.

(7) Nothing in this section affects any power of the Panel in relation to the enforcement of its rules.

(8) Section 1 (meaning of "company") does not apply for the purposes of this section.

(9) In this section—

"designated" means designated in rules;

"offer document" means a document required to be published by rules giving effect to Article 6.2 of the Takeovers Directive;

"offer document rules" means rules designated as rules that give effect to Article 6.3 of that Directive;

"response document" means a document required to be published by rules giving effect to Article 9.5 of that Directive;

"response document rules" means rules designated as rules that give effect to the first sentence of Article 9.5 of that Directive;

"securities" means shares or debentures;

"takeover bid" has the same meaning as in that Directive;

"voting rights" means rights to vote at general meetings of the company in question, including rights that arise only in certain circumstances.

[S953]

NOTES

Commencement: 6 April 2007.

Transitional adaptations: art 3 of the Companies Act 2006 (Commencement No 2, Consequential Amendments, Transitional Provisions and Savings) Order 2007, SI 2007/1093 provides that the provisions brought into force by art 2 of 2007 Order shall have effect subject to any transitional adaptations specified in Sch 1 to that Order. Schedule 1, para 3 to the Order (at **[7625]**) provides as follows—

"**3.**—(1) Section 953 (failure to comply with rules about bid documentation) has effect with the following adaptation.

(2) For subsection (8) substitute—

"(8) Section 735(1) of the Companies Act 1985 and Article 2(3) of the Companies (Northern Ireland) Order 1986 (meaning of "company") do not apply for the purposes of this section."."

954 Compensation

(1) Rules may confer power on the Panel to order a person to pay such compensation as it thinks just and reasonable if he is in breach of a rule the effect of which is to require the payment of money.

(2) Rules made by virtue of this section may include provision for the payment of interest (including compound interest).

[S954]

NOTES

Commencement: 6 April 2007.

955 Enforcement by the court

(1) If, on the application of the Panel, the court is satisfied—

(a) that there is a reasonable likelihood that a person will contravene a rule-based requirement, or

(b) that a person has contravened a rule-based requirement or a disclosure requirement,

the court may make any order it thinks fit to secure compliance with the requirement.

(2) In subsection (1) "the court" means the High Court or, in Scotland, the Court of Session.

(3) Except as provided by subsection (1), no person—

(a) has a right to seek an injunction, or

(b) in Scotland, has title or interest to seek an interdict or an order for specific performance,

to prevent a person from contravening (or continuing to contravene) a rule-based requirement or a disclosure requirement.

(4) In this section—

"contravene" includes fail to comply;

"disclosure requirement" means a requirement imposed under section 947;
"rule-based requirement" means a requirement imposed by or under rules.

[S955]

NOTES

Commencement: 6 April 2007.

956 No action for breach of statutory duty etc

(1) Contravention of a rule-based requirement or a disclosure requirement does not give rise to any right of action for breach of statutory duty.

(2) Contravention of a rule-based requirement does not make any transaction void or unenforceable or (subject to any provision made by rules) affect the validity of any other thing.

(3) In this section—
- (a) "contravention" includes failure to comply;
- (b) "disclosure requirement" and "rule-based requirement" have the same meaning as in section 955.

[S956]

NOTES

Commencement: 6 April 2007.

Funding

957 Fees and charges

(1) Rules may provide for fees or charges to be payable to the Panel for the purpose of meeting any part of its expenses.

(2) A reference in this section or section 958 to expenses of the Panel is to any expenses that have been or are to be incurred by the Panel in, or in connection with, the discharge of its functions, including in particular—
- (a) payments in respect of the expenses of the Takeover Appeal Board;
- (b) the cost of repaying the principal of, and of paying any interest on, any money borrowed by the Panel;
- (c) the cost of maintaining adequate reserves.

[S957]

NOTES

Commencement: 6 April 2007.

958 Levy

(1) For the purpose of meeting any part of the expenses of the Panel, the Secretary of State may by regulations provide for a levy to be payable to the Panel—
- (a) by specified persons or bodies, or persons or bodies of a specified description, or
- (b) on transactions, of a specified description, in securities on specified markets.

In this subsection "specified" means specified in the regulations.

(2) The power to specify (or to specify descriptions of) persons or bodies must be exercised in such a way that the levy is payable only by persons or bodies that appear to the Secretary of State—
- (a) to be capable of being directly affected by the exercise of any of the functions of the Panel, or
- (b) otherwise to have a substantial interest in the exercise of any of those functions.

(3) Regulations under this section may in particular—
- (a) specify the rate of the levy and the period in respect of which it is payable at that rate;
- (b) make provision as to the times when, and the manner in which, payments are to be made in respect of the levy.

(4) In determining the rate of the levy payable in respect of a particular period, the Secretary of State—

(a) must take into account any other income received or expected by the Panel in respect of that period;

(b) may take into account estimated as well as actual expenses of the Panel in respect of that period.

(5) The Panel must—

(a) keep proper accounts in respect of any amounts of levy received by virtue of this section;

(b) prepare, in relation to each period in respect of which any such amounts are received, a statement of account relating to those amounts in such form and manner as is specified in the regulations.

Those accounts must be audited, and the statement certified, by persons appointed by the Secretary of State.

(6) Regulations under this section—

(a) are subject to affirmative resolution procedure if subsection (7) applies to them;

(b) otherwise, are subject to negative resolution procedure.

(7) This subsection applies to—

(a) the first regulations under this section;

(b) any other regulations under this section that would result in a change in the persons or bodies by whom, or the transactions on which, the levy is payable.

(8) If a draft of an instrument containing regulations under this section would, apart from this subsection, be treated for the purposes of the Standing Orders of either House of Parliament as a hybrid instrument, it is to proceed in that House as if it were not such an instrument.

[S958]

NOTES

Commencement: 20 January 2007 (for the purpose of enabling the exercise of powers to make Orders or Regulations by statutory instrument); 6 April 2007 (otherwise).

959 Recovery of fees, charges or levy

An amount payable by any person or body by virtue of section 957 or 958 is a debt due from that person or body to the Panel, and is recoverable accordingly.

[S959]

NOTES

Commencement: 6 April 2007.

Miscellaneous and supplementary

960 Panel as party to proceedings

The Panel is capable (despite being an unincorporated body) of—

(a) bringing proceedings under this Chapter in its own name;

(b) bringing or defending any other proceedings in its own name.

[S960]

NOTES

Commencement: 6 April 2007.

961 Exemption from liability in damages

(1) Neither the Panel, nor any person within subsection (2), is to be liable in damages for anything done (or omitted to be done) in, or in connection with, the discharge or purported discharge of the Panel's functions.

(2) A person is within this subsection if—

(a) he is (or is acting as) a member, officer or member of staff of the Panel, or

(b) he is a person authorised under section 947(5).

(3) Subsection (1) does not apply—

(a) if the act or omission is shown to have been in bad faith, or

(b) so as to prevent an award of damages in respect of the act or omission on the ground that it was unlawful as a result of section 6(1) of the Human Rights Act 1998 (c 42) (acts of public authorities incompatible with Convention rights).

[S961]

NOTES

Commencement: 6 April 2007.

962 Privilege against self-incrimination

(1) A statement made by a person in response to—

(a) a requirement under section 947(1), or

(b) an order made by the court under section 955 to secure compliance with such a requirement,

may not be used against him in criminal proceedings in which he is charged with an offence to which this subsection applies.

(2) Subsection (1) applies to any offence other than an offence under one of the following provisions (which concern false statements made otherwise than on oath)—

(a) section 5 of the Perjury Act 1911 (c 6);

(b) section 44(2) of the Criminal Law (Consolidation) (Scotland) Act 1995 (c 39);

(c) Article 10 of the Perjury (Northern Ireland) Order 1979 (SI 1979/1714 (NI 19)).

[S962]

NOTES

Commencement: 6 April 2007.

963 Annual reports

(1) After the end of each financial year the Panel must publish a report.

(2) The report must—

(a) set out how the Panel's functions were discharged in the year in question;

(b) include the Panel's accounts for that year;

(c) mention any matters the Panel considers to be of relevance to the discharge of its functions.

[S963]

NOTES

Commencement: 6 April 2007.

964 Amendments to Financial Services and Markets Act 2000

(*Amends FSMA 2000, ss 144, 349, 354, 417 at* **[2144]**, **[2347]**, **[2352]**, **[2414]**, *and repeals s 143* (*power to make rules endorsing the City Code on Takeovers and Mergers etc*).)

[S964]

NOTES

Commencement: 6 April 2007.

965 Power to extend to Isle of Man and Channel Islands

Her Majesty may by Order in Council direct that any of the provisions of this Chapter extend, with such modifications as may be specified in the Order, to the Isle of Man or any of the Channel Islands.

[S965]

NOTES

Commencement: 20 January 2007 (for the purpose of enabling the exercise of powers to make Orders or Regulations by statutory instrument); 6 April 2007 (otherwise).

CHAPTER 2
IMPEDIMENTS TO TAKEOVERS

Opting in and opting out

966 Opting in and opting out

(1) A company may by special resolution (an "opting-in resolution") opt in for the purposes of this Chapter if the following three conditions are met in relation to the company.

(2) The first condition is that the company has voting shares admitted to trading on a regulated market.

(3) The second condition is that—
- (a) the company's articles of association—
  - (i) do not contain any such restrictions as are mentioned in Article 11 of the Takeovers Directive, or
  - (ii) if they do contain any such restrictions, provide for the restrictions not to apply at a time when, or in circumstances in which, they would be disapplied by that Article,

  and
- (b) those articles do not contain any other provision which would be incompatible with that Article.

(4) The third condition is that—
- (a) no shares conferring special rights in the company are held by—
  - (i) a minister,
  - (ii) a nominee of, or any other person acting on behalf of, a minister, or
  - (iii) a company directly or indirectly controlled by a minister,

  and
- (b) no such rights are exercisable by or on behalf of a minister under any enactment.

(5) A company may revoke an opting-in resolution by a further special resolution (an "opting-out resolution").

(6) For the purposes of subsection (3), a reference in Article 11 of the Takeovers Directive to Article 7.1 or 9 of that Directive is to be read as referring to rules under section 943(1) giving effect to the relevant Article.

(7) In subsection (4) "minister" means—
- (a) the holder of an office in Her Majesty's Government in the United Kingdom;
- (b) the Scottish Ministers;
- (c) a Minister within the meaning given by section 7(3) of the Northern Ireland Act 1998 (c 47);
- [(d) the Welsh Ministers;]

and for the purposes of that subsection "minister" also includes the Treasury, the Board of Trade [and] the Defence Council …

(8) The Secretary of State may by order subject to negative resolution procedure provide that subsection (4) applies in relation to a specified person or body that exercises functions of a public nature as it applies in relation to a minister. "Specified" means specified in the order.

[S966]

NOTES

Commencement: 20 January 2007 (for the purpose of enabling the exercise of powers to make Orders or Regulations by statutory instrument); 6 April 2007 (otherwise).

Sub-s (7): para (d) inserted, word in second pair of square brackets inserted, and words omitted repealed, by the Government of Wales Act 2006 (Consequential Modifications and Transitional Provisions) Order 2007, SI 2007/1388, art 3, Sch 1, para 142, as from 25 May 2007.

Application to unregistered companies: see the Companies Acts (Unregistered Companies) Regulations 2007, SI 2007/318 at **[7606]**.

967 Further provision about opting-in and opting-out resolutions

(1) An opting-in resolution or an opting-out resolution must specify the date from which it is to have effect (the "effective date").

(2) The effective date of an opting-in resolution may not be earlier than the date on which the resolution is passed.

(3) The second and third conditions in section 966 must be met at the time when an opting-in resolution is passed, but the first one does not need to be met until the effective date.

(4) An opting-in resolution passed before the time when voting shares of the company are admitted to trading on a regulated market complies with the requirement in subsection (1) if, instead of specifying a particular date, it provides for the resolution to have effect from that time.

(5) An opting-in resolution passed before the commencement of this section complies with the requirement in subsection (1) if, instead of specifying a particular date, it provides for the resolution to have effect from that commencement.

(6) The effective date of an opting-out resolution may not be earlier than the first anniversary of the date on which a copy of the opting-in resolution was forwarded to the registrar.

(7) Where a company has passed an opting-in resolution, any alteration of its articles of association that would prevent the second condition in section 966 from being met is of no effect until the effective date of an opting-out resolution passed by the company.

[S967]

NOTES

Commencement: 6 April 2007.

Application to unregistered companies: see the Companies Acts (Unregistered Companies) Regulations 2007, SI 2007/318 at **[7606]**.

Consequences of opting in

968 Effect on contractual restrictions

(1) The following provisions have effect where a takeover bid is made for an opted-in company.

(2) An agreement to which this section applies is invalid in so far as it places any restriction—

- (a) on the transfer to the offeror, or at his direction to another person, of shares in the company during the offer period;
- (b) on the transfer to any person of shares in the company at a time during the offer period when the offeror holds shares amounting to not less than 75% in value of all the voting shares in the company;
- (c) on rights to vote at a general meeting of the company that decides whether to take any action which might result in the frustration of the bid;
- (d) on rights to vote at a general meeting of the company that—
  - (i) is the first such meeting to be held after the end of the offer period, and
  - (ii) is held at a time when the offeror holds shares amounting to not less than 75% in value of all the voting shares in the company.

(3) This section applies to an agreement—

- (a) entered into between a person holding shares in the company and another such person on or after 21st April 2004, or
- (b) entered into at any time between such a person and the company,

and it applies to such an agreement even if the law applicable to the agreement (apart from this section) is not the law of a part of the United Kingdom.

(4) The reference in subsection (2)(c) to rights to vote at a general meeting of the company that decides whether to take any action which might result in the frustration of the bid includes a reference to rights to vote on a written resolution concerned with that question.

(5) For the purposes of subsection (2)(c), action which might result in the frustration of a bid is any action of that kind specified in rules under section 943(1) giving effect to Article 9 of the Takeovers Directive.

(6) If a person suffers loss as a result of any act or omission that would (but for this section) be a breach of an agreement to which this section applies, he is entitled to

compensation, of such amount as the court considers just and equitable, from any person who would (but for this section) be liable to him for committing or inducing the breach.

(7) In subsection (6) "the court" means the High Court or, in Scotland, the Court of Session.

(8) A reference in this section to voting shares in the company does not include—

(a) debentures, or

(b) shares that, under the company's articles of association, do not normally carry rights to vote at its general meetings (for example, shares carrying rights to vote that, under those articles, arise only where specified pecuniary advantages are not provided).

[S968]

NOTES

Commencement: 6 April 2007.

Transitional adaptations: art 3 of the Companies Act 2006 (Commencement No 2, Consequential Amendments, Transitional Provisions and Savings) Order 2007, SI 2007/1093 provides that the provisions brought into force by art 2 of 2007 Order shall have effect subject to any transitional adaptations specified in Sch 1 to that Order. Schedule 1, para 1 to the Order (at **[7625]**) provides as follows—

"**4.**—(1) Section 968 (consequences of opting-in in relation to contractual restrictions on voting rights) has effect with the following adaptation.

(2) In subsection (4), at the end add "A "written resolution" means a resolution in writing agreed to in accordance with sections 381A to 381C of the Companies Act 1985, or Articles 389A to 389C of the Companies (Northern Ireland) Order 1986, or in accordance with the company's articles."."

Note that para 4 as set out above is revoked by the draft Companies Act 2006 (Commencement No 3, Consequential Amendments, Transitional Provisions and Savings) Order 2007, art 10(2), as from 1 October 2007 (see **[A12]**).

Application to unregistered companies: see the Companies Acts (Unregistered Companies) Regulations 2007, SI 2007/318 at **[7606]**.

969 Power of offeror to require general meeting to be called

(1) Where a takeover bid is made for an opted-in company, the offeror may by making a request to the directors of the company require them to call a general meeting of the company if, at the date at which the request is made, he holds shares amounting to not less than 75% in value of all the voting shares in the company.

(2) The reference in subsection (1) to voting shares in the company does not include—

(a) debentures, or

(b) shares that, under the company's articles of association, do not normally carry rights to vote at its general meetings (for example, shares carrying rights to vote that, under those articles, arise only where specified pecuniary advantages are not provided).

(3) Sections 303 to 305 (members' power to require general meetings to be called) apply as they would do if subsection (1) above were substituted for subsections (1) to (3) of section 303, and with any other necessary modifications.

[S969]

NOTES

Commencement: 6 April 2007.

Application to unregistered companies: see the Companies Acts (Unregistered Companies) Regulations 2007, SI 2007/318 at **[7606]**.

Supplementary

970 Communication of decisions

(1) A company that has passed an opting-in resolution or an opting-out resolution must notify—

(a) the Panel, and

(b) where the company—

(i) has voting shares admitted to trading on a regulated market in an EEA State other than the United Kingdom, or

(ii) has requested such admission,

the authority designated by that state as the supervisory authority for the purposes of Article 4.1 of the Takeovers Directive.

(2) Notification must be given within 15 days after the resolution is passed and, if any admission or request such as is mentioned in subsection (1)(b) occurs at a later time, within 15 days after that time.

(3) If a company fails to comply with this section, an offence is committed by—

(a) the company, and

(b) every officer of it who is in default.

(4) A person guilty of an offence under this section is liable on summary conviction to a fine not exceeding level 3 on the standard scale and, for continued contravention, a daily default fine not exceeding one-tenth of level 3 on the standard scale.

[S970]

NOTES

Commencement: 6 April 2007.

Application to unregistered companies: see the Companies Acts (Unregistered Companies) Regulations 2007, SI 2007/318 at **[7606]**.

971 Interpretation of this Chapter

(1) In this Chapter—

"offeror" and "takeover bid" have the same meaning as in the Takeovers Directive;

"offer period", in relation to a takeover bid, means the time allowed for acceptance of the bid by—

(a) rules under section 943(1) giving effect to Article 7.1 of the Takeovers Directive, or

(b) where the rules giving effect to that Article which apply to the bid are those of an EEA State other than the United Kingdom, those rules;

"opted-in company" means a company in relation to which—

(a) an opting-in resolution has effect, and

(b) the conditions in section 966(2) and (4) continue to be met;

"opting-in resolution" has the meaning given by section 966(1);

"opting-out resolution" has the meaning given by section 966(5);

"the Takeovers Directive" means Directive 2004/25/EC of the European Parliament and of the Council;

"voting rights" means rights to vote at general meetings of the company in question, including rights that arise only in certain circumstances;

"voting shares" means shares carrying voting rights.

(2) For the purposes of this Chapter—

(a) securities of a company are treated as shares in the company if they are convertible into or entitle the holder to subscribe for such shares;

(b) debentures issued by a company are treated as shares in the company if they carry voting rights.

[S971]

NOTES

Commencement: 6 April 2007.

Application to unregistered companies: see the Companies Acts (Unregistered Companies) Regulations 2007, SI 2007/318 at **[7606]**.

972 Transitory provision

(1) Where a takeover bid is made for an opted-in company, section 368 of the Companies Act 1985 (c 6) (extraordinary general meeting on members' requisition) and section 378 of that Act (extraordinary and special resolutions) have effect as follows until their repeal by this Act.

(2) Section 368 has effect as if a members' requisition included a requisition of a person who—

(a) is the offeror in relation to the takeover bid, and
(b) holds at the date of the deposit of the requisition shares amounting to not less than 75% in value of all the voting shares in the company.

(3) In relation to a general meeting of the company that—
(a) is the first such meeting to be held after the end of the offer period, and
(b) is held at a time when the offeror holds shares amounting to not less than 75% in value of all the voting shares in the company,

section 378(2) (meaning of "special resolution") has effect as if "14 days' notice" were substituted for "21 days' notice".

(4) A reference in this section to voting shares in the company does not include—
(a) debentures, or
(b) shares that, under the company's articles of association, do not normally carry rights to vote at its general meetings (for example, shares carrying rights to vote that, under those articles, arise only where specified pecuniary advantages are not provided).

[S972]

NOTES

Commencement: 6 April 2007.

Application to unregistered companies: see the Companies Acts (Unregistered Companies) Regulations 2007, SI 2007/318 at **[7606]**.

973 Power to extend to Isle of Man and Channel Islands

Her Majesty may by Order in Council direct that any of the provisions of this Chapter extend, with such modifications as may be specified in the Order, to the Isle of Man or any of the Channel Islands.

[S973]

NOTES

Commencement: 20 January 2007 (for the purpose of enabling the exercise of powers to make Orders or Regulations by statutory instrument); 6 April 2007 (otherwise).

Application to unregistered companies: see the Companies Acts (Unregistered Companies) Regulations 2007, SI 2007/318 at **[7606]**.

CHAPTER 3
"SQUEEZE-OUT" AND "SELL-OUT"

Takeover offers

974 Meaning of "takeover offer"

(1) For the purposes of this Chapter an offer to acquire shares in a company is a "takeover offer" if the following two conditions are satisfied in relation to the offer.

(2) The first condition is that it is an offer to acquire—
(a) all the shares in a company, or
(b) where there is more than one class of shares in a company, all the shares of one or more classes,

other than shares that at the date of the offer are already held by the offeror. Section 975 contains provision supplementing this subsection.

(3) The second condition is that the terms of the offer are the same—
(a) in relation to all the shares to which the offer relates, or
(b) where the shares to which the offer relates include shares of different classes, in relation to all the shares of each class.

Section 976 contains provision treating this condition as satisfied in certain circumstances.

(4) In subsections (1) to (3) "shares" means shares, other than relevant treasury shares, that have been allotted on the date of the offer (but see subsection (5)).

(5) A takeover offer may include among the shares to which it relates—

(a) all or any shares that are allotted after the date of the offer but before a specified date;
(b) all or any relevant treasury shares that cease to be held as treasury shares before a specified date;
(c) all or any other relevant treasury shares.

(6) In this section—
"relevant treasury shares" means shares that—
(a) are held by the company as treasury shares on the date of the offer, or
(b) become shares held by the company as treasury shares after that date but before a specified date;
"specified date" means a date specified in or determined in accordance with the terms of the offer.

(7) Where the terms of an offer make provision for their revision and for acceptances on the previous terms to be treated as acceptances on the revised terms, then, if the terms of the offer are revised in accordance with that provision—
(a) the revision is not to be regarded for the purposes of this Chapter as the making of a fresh offer, and
(b) references in this Chapter to the date of the offer are accordingly to be read as references to the date of the original offer.

[S974]

NOTES

Commencement: 6 April 2007.

Application to unregistered companies: see the Companies Acts (Unregistered Companies) Regulations 2007, SI 2007/318 at **[7606]**.

975 Shares already held by the offeror etc

(1) The reference in section 974(2) to shares already held by the offeror includes a reference to shares that he has contracted to acquire, whether unconditionally or subject to conditions being met.

This is subject to subsection (2).

(2) The reference in section 974(2) to shares already held by the offeror does not include a reference to shares that are the subject of a contract—
(a) intended to secure that the holder of the shares will accept the offer when it is made, and
(b) entered into—
(i) by deed and for no consideration,
(ii) for consideration of negligible value, or
(iii) for consideration consisting of a promise by the offeror to make the offer.

(3) In relation to Scotland, this section applies as if the words "by deed and" in subsection (2)(b)(i) were omitted.

(4) The condition in section 974(2) is treated as satisfied where—
(a) the offer does not extend to shares that associates of the offeror hold or have contracted to acquire (whether unconditionally or subject to conditions being met), and
(b) the condition would be satisfied if the offer did extend to those shares.

(For further provision about such shares, see section 977(2)).

[S975]

NOTES

Commencement: 6 April 2007.

Application to unregistered companies: see the Companies Acts (Unregistered Companies) Regulations 2007, SI 2007/318 at **[7606]**.

976 Cases where offer treated as being on same terms

(1) The condition in section 974(3) (terms of offer to be the same for all shares or all shares of particular classes) is treated as satisfied where subsection (2) or (3) below applies.

(2) This subsection applies where—

(a) shares carry an entitlement to a particular dividend which other shares of the same class, by reason of being allotted later, do not carry,
(b) there is a difference in the value of consideration offered for the shares allotted earlier as against that offered for those allotted later,
(c) that difference merely reflects the difference in entitlement to the dividend, and
(d) the condition in section 974(3) would be satisfied but for that difference.

(3) This subsection applies where—
(a) the law of a country or territory outside the United Kingdom—
(i) precludes an offer of consideration in the form, or any of the forms, specified in the terms of the offer ("the specified form"), or
(ii) precludes it except after compliance by the offeror with conditions with which he is unable to comply or which he regards as unduly onerous,
(b) the persons to whom an offer of consideration in the specified form is precluded are able to receive consideration in another form that is of substantially equivalent value, and
(c) the condition in section 974(3) would be satisfied but for the fact that an offer of consideration in the specified form to those persons is precluded.

[S976]

NOTES

Commencement: 6 April 2007.

Application to unregistered companies: see the Companies Acts (Unregistered Companies) Regulations 2007, SI 2007/318 at **[7606]**.

977 Shares to which an offer relates

(1) Where a takeover offer is made and, during the period beginning with the date of the offer and ending when the offer can no longer be accepted, the offeror—
(a) acquires or unconditionally contracts to acquire any of the shares to which the offer relates, but
(b) does not do so by virtue of acceptances of the offer,

those shares are treated for the purposes of this Chapter as excluded from those to which the offer relates.

(2) For the purposes of this Chapter shares that an associate of the offeror holds or has contracted to acquire, whether at the date of the offer or subsequently, are not treated as shares to which the offer relates, even if the offer extends to such shares.

In this subsection "contracted" means contracted unconditionally or subject to conditions being met.

(3) This section is subject to section 979(8) and (9).

[S977]

NOTES

Commencement: 6 April 2007.

Application to unregistered companies: see the Companies Acts (Unregistered Companies) Regulations 2007, SI 2007/318 at **[7606]**.

978 Effect of impossibility etc of communicating or accepting offer

(1) Where there are holders of shares in a company to whom an offer to acquire shares in the company is not communicated, that does not prevent the offer from being a takeover offer for the purposes of this Chapter if—
(a) those shareholders have no registered address in the United Kingdom,
(b) the offer was not communicated to those shareholders in order not to contravene the law of a country or territory outside the United Kingdom, and
(c) either—
(i) the offer is published in the Gazette, or
(ii) the offer can be inspected, or a copy of it obtained, at a place in an EEA State or on a website, and a notice is published in the Gazette specifying the address of that place or website.

(2) Where an offer is made to acquire shares in a company and there are persons for whom, by reason of the law of a country or territory outside the United Kingdom, it is

impossible to accept the offer, or more difficult to do so, that does not prevent the offer from being a takeover offer for the purposes of this Chapter.

(3) It is not to be inferred—

(a) that an offer which is not communicated to every holder of shares in the company cannot be a takeover offer for the purposes of this Chapter unless the requirements of paragraphs (a) to (c) of subsection (1) are met, or

(b) that an offer which is impossible, or more difficult, for certain persons to accept cannot be a takeover offer for those purposes unless the reason for the impossibility or difficulty is the one mentioned in subsection (2).

[S978]

NOTES

Commencement: 6 April 2007.

Application to unregistered companies: see the Companies Acts (Unregistered Companies) Regulations 2007, SI 2007/318 at **[7606]**.

"Squeeze-out"

979 Right of offeror to buy out minority shareholder

(1) Subsection (2) applies in a case where a takeover offer does not relate to shares of different classes.

(2) If the offeror has, by virtue of acceptances of the offer, acquired or unconditionally contracted to acquire—

(a) not less than 90% in value of the shares to which the offer relates, and

(b) in a case where the shares to which the offer relates are voting shares, not less than 90% of the voting rights carried by those shares,

he may give notice to the holder of any shares to which the offer relates which the offeror has not acquired or unconditionally contracted to acquire that he desires to acquire those shares.

(3) Subsection (4) applies in a case where a takeover offer relates to shares of different classes.

(4) If the offeror has, by virtue of acceptances of the offer, acquired or unconditionally contracted to acquire—

(a) not less than 90% in value of the shares of any class to which the offer relates, and

(b) in a case where the shares of that class are voting shares, not less than 90% of the voting rights carried by those shares,

he may give notice to the holder of any shares of that class to which the offer relates which the offeror has not acquired or unconditionally contracted to acquire that he desires to acquire those shares.

(5) In the case of a takeover offer which includes among the shares to which it relates—

(a) shares that are allotted after the date of the offer, or

(b) relevant treasury shares (within the meaning of section 974) that cease to be held as treasury shares after the date of the offer,

the offeror's entitlement to give a notice under subsection (2) or (4) on any particular date shall be determined as if the shares to which the offer relates did not include any allotted, or ceasing to be held as treasury shares, on or after that date.

(6) Subsection (7) applies where—

(a) the requirements for the giving of a notice under subsection (2) or (4) are satisfied, and

(b) there are shares in the company which the offeror, or an associate of his, has contracted to acquire subject to conditions being met, and in relation to which the contract has not become unconditional.

(7) The offeror's entitlement to give a notice under subsection (2) or (4) shall be determined as if—

(a) the shares to which the offer relates included shares falling within paragraph (b) of subsection (6), and

(b) in relation to shares falling within that paragraph, the words "by virtue of acceptances of the offer" in subsection (2) or (4) were omitted.

(8) Where—
(a) a takeover offer is made,
(b) during the period beginning with the date of the offer and ending when the offer can no longer be accepted, the offeror—
(i) acquires or unconditionally contracts to acquire any of the shares to which the offer relates, but
(ii) does not do so by virtue of acceptances of the offer, and
(c) subsection (10) applies,

then for the purposes of this section those shares are not excluded by section 977(1) from those to which the offer relates, and the offeror is treated as having acquired or contracted to acquire them by virtue of acceptances of the offer.

(9) Where—
(a) a takeover offer is made,
(b) during the period beginning with the date of the offer and ending when the offer can no longer be accepted, an associate of the offeror acquires or unconditionally contracts to acquire any of the shares to which the offer relates, and
(c) subsection (10) applies,

then for the purposes of this section those shares are not excluded by section 977(2) from those to which the offer relates.

(10) This subsection applies if—
(a) at the time the shares are acquired or contracted to be acquired as mentioned in subsection (8) or (9) (as the case may be), the value of the consideration for which they are acquired or contracted to be acquired ("the acquisition consideration") does not exceed the value of the consideration specified in the terms of the offer, or
(b) those terms are subsequently revised so that when the revision is announced the value of the acquisition consideration, at the time mentioned in paragraph (a), no longer exceeds the value of the consideration specified in those terms.

[S979]

NOTES

Commencement: 6 April 2007.

Application to unregistered companies: see the Companies Acts (Unregistered Companies) Regulations 2007, SI 2007/318 at **[7606]**.

980 Further provision about notices given under section 979

(1) A notice under section 979 must be given in the prescribed manner.

(2) No notice may be given under section 979(2) or (4) after the end of—
(a) the period of three months beginning with the day after the last day on which the offer can be accepted, or
(b) the period of six months beginning with the date of the offer, where that period ends earlier and the offer is one to which subsection (3) below applies.

(3) This subsection applies to an offer if the time allowed for acceptance of the offer is not governed by rules under section 943(1) that give effect to Article 7 of the Takeovers Directive.

In this subsection "the Takeovers Directive" has the same meaning as in section 943.

(4) At the time when the offeror first gives a notice under section 979 in relation to an offer, he must send to the company—
(a) a copy of the notice, and
(b) a statutory declaration by him in the prescribed form, stating that the conditions for the giving of the notice are satisfied.

(5) Where the offeror is a company (whether or not a company within the meaning of this Act) the statutory declaration must be signed by a director.

(6) A person commits an offence if—
(a) he fails to send a copy of a notice or a statutory declaration as required by subsection (4), or
(b) he makes such a declaration for the purposes of that subsection knowing it to be false or without having reasonable grounds for believing it to be true.

(7) It is a defence for a person charged with an offence for failing to send a copy of a notice as required by subsection (4) to prove that he took reasonable steps for securing compliance with that subsection.

(8) A person guilty of an offence under this section is liable—

(a) on conviction on indictment, to imprisonment for a term not exceeding two years or a fine (or both);

(b) on summary conviction—

(i) in England and Wales, to imprisonment for a term not exceeding twelve months or to a fine not exceeding the statutory maximum (or both) and, for continued contravention, a daily default fine not exceeding one-fiftieth of the statutory maximum;

(ii) in Scotland or Northern Ireland, to imprisonment for a term not exceeding six months, or to a fine not exceeding the statutory maximum (or both) and, for continued contravention, a daily default fine not exceeding one-fiftieth of the statutory maximum.

[S980]

NOTES

Commencement: 20 January 2007 (for the purpose of enabling the exercise of powers to make Orders or Regulations by statutory instrument); 6 April 2007 (otherwise).

Application to unregistered companies: see the Companies Acts (Unregistered Companies) Regulations 2007, SI 2007/318 at **[7606]**.

981 Effect of notice under section 979

(1) Subject to section 986 (applications to the court), this section applies where the offeror gives a shareholder a notice under section 979.

(2) The offeror is entitled and bound to acquire the shares to which the notice relates on the terms of the offer.

(3) Where the terms of an offer are such as to give the shareholder a choice of consideration, the notice must give particulars of the choice and state—

(a) that the shareholder may, within six weeks from the date of the notice, indicate his choice by a written communication sent to the offeror at an address specified in the notice, and

(b) which consideration specified in the offer will apply if he does not indicate a choice.

The reference in subsection (2) to the terms of the offer is to be read accordingly.

(4) Subsection (3) applies whether or not any time-limit or other conditions applicable to the choice under the terms of the offer can still be complied with.

(5) If the consideration offered to or (as the case may be) chosen by the shareholder—

(a) is not cash and the offeror is no longer able to provide it, or

(b) was to have been provided by a third party who is no longer bound or able to provide it,

the consideration is to be taken to consist of an amount of cash, payable by the offeror, which at the date of the notice is equivalent to the consideration offered or (as the case may be) chosen.

(6) At the end of six weeks from the date of the notice the offeror must immediately—

(a) send a copy of the notice to the company, and

(b) pay or transfer to the company the consideration for the shares to which the notice relates.

Where the consideration consists of shares or securities to be allotted by the offeror, the reference in paragraph (b) to the transfer of the consideration is to be read as a reference to the allotment of the shares or securities to the company.

(7) If the shares to which the notice relates are registered, the copy of the notice sent to the company under subsection (6)(a) must be accompanied by an instrument of transfer executed on behalf of the holder of the shares by a person appointed by the offeror.

On receipt of that instrument the company must register the offeror as the holder of those shares.

(8) If the shares to which the notice relates are transferable by the delivery of warrants or other instruments, the copy of the notice sent to the company under subsection (6)(a) must be accompanied by a statement to that effect. On receipt of that statement the company must issue the offeror with warrants or other instruments in respect of the shares, and those already in issue in respect of the shares become void.

(9) The company must hold any money or other consideration received by it under subsection (6)(b) on trust for the person who, before the offeror acquired them, was entitled to the shares in respect of which the money or other consideration was received.

Section 982 contains further provision about how the company should deal with such money or other consideration.

[S981]

NOTES

Commencement: 6 April 2007.

Application to unregistered companies: see the Companies Acts (Unregistered Companies) Regulations 2007, SI 2007/318 at **[7606]**.

982 Further provision about consideration held on trust under section 981(9)

(1) This section applies where an offeror pays or transfers consideration to the company under section 981(6).

(2) The company must pay into a separate bank account that complies with subsection (3)—

(a) any money it receives under paragraph (b) of section 981(6), and

(b) any dividend or other sum accruing from any other consideration it receives under that paragraph.

(3) A bank account complies with this subsection if the balance on the account—

(a) bears interest at an appropriate rate, and

(b) can be withdrawn by such notice (if any) as is appropriate.

(4) If—

(a) the person entitled to the consideration held on trust by virtue of section 981(9) cannot be found, and

(b) subsection (5) applies,

the consideration (together with any interest, dividend or other benefit that has accrued from it) must be paid into court.

(5) This subsection applies where—

(a) reasonable enquiries have been made at reasonable intervals to find the person, and

(b) twelve years have elapsed since the consideration was received, or the company is wound up.

(6) In relation to a company registered in Scotland, subsections (7) and (8) apply instead of subsection (4).

(7) If the person entitled to the consideration held on trust by virtue of section 981(9) cannot be found and subsection (5) applies—

(a) the trust terminates,

(b) the company or (if the company is wound up) the liquidator must sell any consideration other than cash and any benefit other than cash that has accrued from the consideration, and

(c) a sum representing—

(i) the consideration so far as it is cash,

(ii) the proceeds of any sale under paragraph (b), and

(iii) any interest, dividend or other benefit that has accrued from the consideration,

must be deposited in the name of the Accountant of Court in a separate bank account complying with subsection (3) and the receipt for the deposit must be transmitted to the Accountant of Court.

(8) Section 58 of the Bankruptcy (Scotland) Act 1985 (c 66) (so far as consistent with this Act) applies (with any necessary modifications) to sums deposited under subsection (7) as it applies to sums deposited under section 57(1)(a) of that Act.

(9) The expenses of any such enquiries as are mentioned in subsection (5) may be paid out of the money or other property held on trust for the person to whom the enquiry relates. **[S982]**

NOTES

Commencement: 6 April 2007.

Application to unregistered companies: see the Companies Acts (Unregistered Companies) Regulations 2007, SI 2007/318 at **[7606]**.

"Sell-out"

983 Right of minority shareholder to be bought out by offeror

(1) Subsections (2) and (3) apply in a case where a takeover offer relates to all the shares in a company.

For this purpose a takeover offer relates to all the shares in a company if it is an offer to acquire all the shares in the company within the meaning of section 974.

(2) The holder of any voting shares to which the offer relates who has not accepted the offer may require the offeror to acquire those shares if, at any time before the end of the period within which the offer can be accepted—

(a) the offeror has by virtue of acceptances of the offer acquired or unconditionally contracted to acquire some (but not all) of the shares to which the offer relates, and

(b) those shares, with or without any other shares in the company which he has acquired or contracted to acquire (whether unconditionally or subject to conditions being met)—

(i) amount to not less than 90% in value of all the voting shares in the company (or would do so but for section 990(1)), and

(ii) carry not less than 90% of the voting rights in the company (or would do so but for section 990(1)).

(3) The holder of any non-voting shares to which the offer relates who has not accepted the offer may require the offeror to acquire those shares if, at any time before the end of the period within which the offer can be accepted—

(a) the offeror has by virtue of acceptances of the offer acquired or unconditionally contracted to acquire some (but not all) of the shares to which the offer relates, and

(b) those shares, with or without any other shares in the company which he has acquired or contracted to acquire (whether unconditionally or subject to conditions being met), amount to not less than 90% in value of all the shares in the company (or would do so but for section 990(1)).

(4) If a takeover offer relates to shares of one or more classes and at any time before the end of the period within which the offer can be accepted—

(a) the offeror has by virtue of acceptances of the offer acquired or unconditionally contracted to acquire some (but not all) of the shares of any class to which the offer relates, and

(b) those shares, with or without any other shares of that class which he has acquired or contracted to acquire (whether unconditionally or subject to conditions being met)—

(i) amount to not less than 90% in value of all the shares of that class, and

(ii) in a case where the shares of that class are voting shares, carry not less than 90% of the voting rights carried by the shares of that class,

the holder of any shares of that class to which the offer relates who has not accepted the offer may require the offeror to acquire those shares.

(5) For the purposes of subsections (2) to (4), in calculating 90% of the value of any shares, shares held by the company as treasury shares are to be treated as having been acquired by the offeror.

(6) Subsection (7) applies where—

(a) a shareholder exercises rights conferred on him by subsection (2), (3) or (4),

(b) at the time when he does so, there are shares in the company which the offeror has contracted to acquire subject to conditions being met, and in relation to which the contract has not become unconditional, and

(c) the requirement imposed by subsection (2)(b), (3)(b) or (4)(b) (as the case may be) would not be satisfied if those shares were not taken into account.

(7) The shareholder is treated for the purposes of section 985 as not having exercised his rights under this section unless the requirement imposed by paragraph (b) of subsection (2), (3) or (4) (as the case may be) would be satisfied if—

(a) the reference in that paragraph to other shares in the company which the offeror has contracted to acquire unconditionally or subject to conditions being met were a reference to such shares which he has unconditionally contracted to acquire, and

(b) the reference in that subsection to the period within which the offer can be accepted were a reference to the period referred to in section 984(2).

(8) A reference in subsection (2)(b), (3)(b), (4)(b), (6) or (7) to shares which the offeror has acquired or contracted to acquire includes a reference to shares which an associate of his has acquired or contracted to acquire.

[S983]

NOTES

Commencement: 6 April 2007.

Application to unregistered companies: see the Companies Acts (Unregistered Companies) Regulations 2007, SI 2007/318 at **[7606]**.

984 Further provision about rights conferred by section 983

(1) Rights conferred on a shareholder by subsection (2), (3) or (4) of section 983 are exercisable by a written communication addressed to the offeror.

(2) Rights conferred on a shareholder by subsection (2), (3) or (4) of that section are not exercisable after the end of the period of three months from—

(a) the end of the period within which the offer can be accepted, or

(b) if later, the date of the notice that must be given under subsection (3) below.

(3) Within one month of the time specified in subsection (2), (3) or (4) (as the case may be) of that section, the offeror must give any shareholder who has not accepted the offer notice in the prescribed manner of—

(a) the rights that are exercisable by the shareholder under that subsection, and

(b) the period within which the rights are exercisable.

If the notice is given before the end of the period within which the offer can be accepted, it must state that the offer is still open for acceptance.

(4) Subsection (3) does not apply if the offeror has given the shareholder a notice in respect of the shares in question under section 979.

(5) An offeror who fails to comply with subsection (3) commits an offence.

If the offeror is a company, every officer of that company who is in default or to whose neglect the failure is attributable also commits an offence.

(6) If an offeror other than a company is charged with an offence for failing to comply with subsection (3), it is a defence for him to prove that he took all reasonable steps for securing compliance with that subsection.

(7) A person guilty of an offence under this section is liable—

(a) on conviction on indictment, to a fine;

(b) on summary conviction, to a fine not exceeding the statutory maximum and, for continued contravention, a daily default fine not exceeding one-fiftieth of the statutory maximum.

[S984]

NOTES

Commencement: 20 January 2007 (for the purpose of enabling the exercise of powers to make Orders or Regulations by statutory instrument); 6 April 2007 (otherwise).

Application to unregistered companies: see the Companies Acts (Unregistered Companies) Regulations 2007, SI 2007/318 at **[7606]**.

985 Effect of requirement under section 983

(1) Subject to section 986, this section applies where a shareholder exercises his rights under section 983 in respect of any shares held by him.

(2) The offeror is entitled and bound to acquire those shares on the terms of the offer or on such other terms as may be agreed.

(3) Where the terms of an offer are such as to give the shareholder a choice of consideration—

(a) the shareholder may indicate his choice when requiring the offeror to acquire the shares, and

(b) the notice given to the shareholder under section 984(3)—

(i) must give particulars of the choice and of the rights conferred by this subsection, and

(ii) may state which consideration specified in the offer will apply if he does not indicate a choice.

The reference in subsection (2) to the terms of the offer is to be read accordingly.

(4) Subsection (3) applies whether or not any time-limit or other conditions applicable to the choice under the terms of the offer can still be complied with.

(5) If the consideration offered to or (as the case may be) chosen by the shareholder—

(a) is not cash and the offeror is no longer able to provide it, or

(b) was to have been provided by a third party who is no longer bound or able to provide it,

the consideration is to be taken to consist of an amount of cash, payable by the offeror, which at the date when the shareholder requires the offeror to acquire the shares is equivalent to the consideration offered or (as the case may be) chosen.

[S985]

NOTES

Commencement: 6 April 2007.

Application to unregistered companies: see the Companies Acts (Unregistered Companies) Regulations 2007, SI 2007/318 at **[7606]**.

Supplementary

986 Applications to the court

(1) Where a notice is given under section 979 to a shareholder the court may, on an application made by him, order—

(a) that the offeror is not entitled and bound to acquire the shares to which the notice relates, or

(b) that the terms on which the offeror is entitled and bound to acquire the shares shall be such as the court thinks fit.

(2) An application under subsection (1) must be made within six weeks from the date on which the notice referred to in that subsection was given.

If an application to the court under subsection (1) is pending at the end of that period, section 981(6) does not have effect until the application has been disposed of.

(3) Where a shareholder exercises his rights under section 983 in respect of any shares held by him, the court may, on an application made by him or the offeror, order that the terms on which the offeror is entitled and bound to acquire the shares shall be such as the court thinks fit.

(4) On an application under subsection (1) or (3)—

(a) the court may not require consideration of a higher value than that specified in the terms of the offer ("the offer value") to be given for the shares to which the application relates unless the holder of the shares shows that the offer value would be unfair;

(b) the court may not require consideration of a lower value than the offer value to be given for the shares.

(5) No order for costs or expenses may be made against a shareholder making an application under subsection (1) or (3) unless the court considers that—

(a) the application was unnecessary, improper or vexatious,
(b) there has been unreasonable delay in making the application, or
(c) there has been unreasonable conduct on the shareholder's part in conducting the proceedings on the application.

(6) A shareholder who has made an application under subsection (1) or (3) must give notice of the application to the offeror.

(7) An offeror who is given notice of an application under subsection (1) or (3) must give a copy of the notice to—
(a) any person (other than the applicant) to whom a notice has been given under section 979;
(b) any person who has exercised his rights under section 983.

(8) An offeror who makes an application under subsection (3) must give notice of the application to—
(a) any person to whom a notice has been given under section 979;
(b) any person who has exercised his rights under section 983.

(9) Where a takeover offer has not been accepted to the extent necessary for entitling the offeror to give notices under subsection (2) or (4) of section 979 the court may, on an application made by him, make an order authorising him to give notices under that subsection if it is satisfied that—
(a) the offeror has after reasonable enquiry been unable to trace one or more of the persons holding shares to which the offer relates,
(b) the requirements of that subsection would have been met if the person, or all the persons, mentioned in paragraph (a) above had accepted the offer, and
(c) the consideration offered is fair and reasonable.

This is subject to subsection (10).

(10) The court may not make an order under subsection (9) unless it considers that it is just and equitable to do so having regard, in particular, to the number of shareholders who have been traced but who have not accepted the offer.

[S986]

NOTES

Commencement: 6 April 2007.

Application to unregistered companies: see the Companies Acts (Unregistered Companies) Regulations 2007, SI 2007/318 at **[7606]**.

987 Joint offers

(1) In the case of a takeover offer made by two or more persons jointly, this Chapter has effect as follows.

(2) The conditions for the exercise of the rights conferred by section 979 are satisfied—
(a) in the case of acquisitions by virtue of acceptances of the offer, by the joint offerors acquiring or unconditionally contracting to acquire the necessary shares jointly;
(b) in other cases, by the joint offerors acquiring or unconditionally contracting to acquire the necessary shares either jointly or separately.

(3) The conditions for the exercise of the rights conferred by section 983 are satisfied—
(a) in the case of acquisitions by virtue of acceptances of the offer, by the joint offerors acquiring or unconditionally contracting to acquire the necessary shares jointly;
(b) in other cases, by the joint offerors acquiring or contracting (whether unconditionally or subject to conditions being met) to acquire the necessary shares either jointly or separately.

(4) Subject to the following provisions, the rights and obligations of the offeror under sections 979 to 985 are respectively joint rights and joint and several obligations of the joint offerors.

(5) A provision of sections 979 to 986 that requires or authorises a notice or other document to be given or sent by or to the joint offerors is complied with if the notice or document is given or sent by or to any of them (but see subsection (6)).

(6) The statutory declaration required by section 980(4) must be made by all of the joint offerors and, where one or more of them is a company, signed by a director of that company.

(7) In sections 974 to 977, 979(9), 981(6), 983(8) and 988 references to the offeror are to be read as references to the joint offerors or any of them.

(8) In section 981(7) and (8) references to the offeror are to be read as references to the joint offerors or such of them as they may determine.

(9) In sections 981(5)(a) and 985(5)(a) references to the offeror being no longer able to provide the relevant consideration are to be read as references to none of the joint offerors being able to do so.

(10) In section 986 references to the offeror are to be read as references to the joint offerors, except that—

(a) an application under subsection (3) or (9) may be made by any of them, and
(b) the reference in subsection (9)(a) to the offeror having been unable to trace one or more of the persons holding shares is to be read as a reference to none of the offerors having been able to do so.

[S987]

NOTES

Commencement: 6 April 2007.

Application to unregistered companies: see the Companies Acts (Unregistered Companies) Regulations 2007, SI 2007/318 at **[7606]**.

Interpretation

988 Associates

(1) In this Chapter "associate", in relation to an offeror, means—

(a) a nominee of the offeror,
(b) a holding company, subsidiary or fellow subsidiary of the offeror or a nominee of such a holding company, subsidiary or fellow subsidiary,
(c) a body corporate in which the offeror is substantially interested,
(d) a person who is, or is a nominee of, a party to a share acquisition agreement with the offeror, or
(e) (where the offeror is an individual) his spouse or civil partner and any minor child or step-child of his.

(2) For the purposes of subsection (1)(b) a company is a fellow subsidiary of another body corporate if both are subsidiaries of the same body corporate but neither is a subsidiary of the other.

(3) For the purposes of subsection (1)(c) an offeror has a substantial interest in a body corporate if—

(a) the body or its directors are accustomed to act in accordance with his directions or instructions, or
(b) he is entitled to exercise or control the exercise of one-third or more of the voting power at general meetings of the body.

Subsections (2) and (3) of section 823 (which contain provision about when a person is treated as entitled to exercise or control the exercise of voting power) apply for the purposes of this subsection as they apply for the purposes of that section.

(4) For the purposes of subsection (1)(d) an agreement is a share acquisition agreement if—

(a) it is an agreement for the acquisition of, or of an interest in, shares to which the offer relates,
(b) it includes provisions imposing obligations or restrictions on any one or more of the parties to it with respect to their use, retention or disposal of such shares, or their interests in such shares, acquired in pursuance of the agreement (whether or not together with any other shares to which the offer relates or any other interests of theirs in such shares), and
(c) it is not an excluded agreement (see subsection (5)).

(5) An agreement is an "excluded agreement"—

(a) if it is not legally binding, unless it involves mutuality in the undertakings, expectations or understandings of the parties to it, or
(b) if it is an agreement to underwrite or sub-underwrite an offer of shares in a company, provided the agreement is confined to that purpose and any matters incidental to it.

(6) The reference in subsection (4)(b) to the use of interests in shares is to the exercise of any rights or of any control or influence arising from those interests (including the right to enter into an agreement for the exercise, or for control of the exercise, of any of those rights by another person).

(7) In this section—
(a) "agreement" includes any agreement or arrangement;
(b) references to provisions of an agreement include—
(i) undertakings, expectations or understandings operative under an arrangement, and
(ii) any provision whether express or implied and whether absolute or not.

[S988]

NOTES

Commencement: 6 April 2007.

Application to unregistered companies: see the Companies Acts (Unregistered Companies) Regulations 2007, SI 2007/318 at **[7606]**.

989 Convertible securities

(1) For the purposes of this Chapter securities of a company are treated as shares in the company if they are convertible into or entitle the holder to subscribe for such shares.

References to the holder of shares or a shareholder are to be read accordingly.

(2) Subsection (1) is not to be read as requiring any securities to be treated—
(a) as shares of the same class as those into which they are convertible or for which the holder is entitled to subscribe, or
(b) as shares of the same class as other securities by reason only that the shares into which they are convertible or for which the holder is entitled to subscribe are of the same class.

[S989]

NOTES

Commencement: 6 April 2007.

Application to unregistered companies: see the Companies Acts (Unregistered Companies) Regulations 2007, SI 2007/318 at **[7606]**.

990 Debentures carrying voting rights

(1) For the purposes of this Chapter debentures issued by a company to which subsection (2) applies are treated as shares in the company if they carry voting rights.

(2) This subsection applies to a company that has voting shares, or debentures carrying voting rights, which are admitted to trading on a regulated market.

(3) In this Chapter, in relation to debentures treated as shares by virtue of subsection (1)—
(a) references to the holder of shares or a shareholder are to be read accordingly;
(b) references to shares being allotted are to be read as references to debentures being issued.

[S990]

NOTES

Commencement: 6 April 2007.

Application to unregistered companies: see the Companies Acts (Unregistered Companies) Regulations 2007, SI 2007/318 at **[7606]**.

991 Interpretation

(1) In this Chapter—

"the company" means the company whose shares are the subject of a takeover offer;

"date of the offer" means—

(a) where the offer is published, the date of publication;

(b) where the offer is not published, or where any notices of the offer are given before the date of publication, the date when notices of the offer (or the first such notices) are given;

and references to the date of the offer are to be read in accordance with section 974(7) (revision of offer terms) where that applies;

"non-voting shares" means shares that are not voting shares;

"offeror" means (subject to section 987) the person making a takeover offer;

"voting rights" means rights to vote at general meetings of the company, including rights that arise only in certain circumstances;

"voting shares" means shares carrying voting rights.

(2) For the purposes of this Chapter a person contracts unconditionally to acquire shares if his entitlement under the contract to acquire them is not (or is no longer) subject to conditions or if all conditions to which it was subject have been met.

A reference to a contract becoming unconditional is to be read accordingly.

[S991]

NOTES

Commencement: 6 April 2007.

Application to unregistered companies: see the Companies Acts (Unregistered Companies) Regulations 2007, SI 2007/318 at **[7606]**.

CHAPTER 4
AMENDMENTS TO PART 7 OF THE COMPANIES ACT 1985

992 Matters to be dealt with in directors' report

(1)–(5) (*Amend CA 1985, ss 234ZZA, 251 at* **[220ZA]**, **[252]** *and add Sch 7, Pt 7 to that Act at* **[653AA]**.)

(6) The amendments made by this section apply in relation to directors' reports for financial years beginning on or after 20th May 2006.

[S992]

NOTES

Commencement: 6 April 2007.

As to the application of this section to the Companies (Northern Ireland) Order 1986, see the Companies Act 2006 (Commencement No 2, Consequential Amendments, Transitional Provisions and Savings) Order 2007, SI 2007/1093, art 9 at **[7622]**.

PART 29
FRAUDULENT TRADING

993 Offence of fraudulent trading

(1) If any business of a company is carried on with intent to defraud creditors of the company or creditors of any other person, or for any fraudulent purpose, every person who is knowingly a party to the carrying on of the business in that manner commits an offence.

(2) This applies whether or not the company has been, or is in the course of being, wound up.

(3) A person guilty of an offence under this section is liable—

(a) on conviction on indictment, to imprisonment for a term not exceeding ten years or a fine (or both);

(b) on summary conviction—

(i) in England and Wales, to imprisonment for a term not exceeding twelve months or a fine not exceeding the statutory maximum (or both);

(ii) in Scotland or Northern Ireland, to imprisonment for a term not exceeding six months or a fine not exceeding the statutory maximum (or both).

[S993]

NOTES

Commencement: 1 October 2007 (for transitional provisions see the note below).

Transitional provisions, etc: Sch 3, para 46 to the draft Companies Act 2006 (Commencement No 3, Consequential Amendments, Transitional Provisions and Savings) Order 2007 (at **[A12]**) provides as follows—

"46 Fraudulent trading (**s 993**)

(1) Section 458 of the 1985 Act or Article 451 of the 1986 Order (offences of fraudulent trading) continues to apply to offences completed before 1st October 2007.

(2) Where, in the case of an offence—

(a) a relevant event occurs before 1st October 2007, and

(b) another relevant event occurs on or after 1st October 2007,

the offence must be charged under section 993 of the Companies Act 2006 (and not under section 458 of the 1985 Act or Article 451 of the 1986 Order).

(3) If in the case of any such offence a relevant event occurred before 15th January 2007 section 993(3)(a) applies with the substitution of "seven years" for "ten years".

(4) "Relevant event" means an act, omission or other event (including any result of one or more acts or omissions) proof of which is required for conviction of the offence.".

PART 30
PROTECTION OF MEMBERS AGAINST UNFAIR PREJUDICE

Main provisions

994 Petition by company member

(1) A member of a company may apply to the court by petition for an order under this Part on the ground—

(a) that the company's affairs are being or have been conducted in a manner that is unfairly prejudicial to the interests of members generally or of some part of its members (including at least himself), or

(b) that an actual or proposed act or omission of the company (including an act or omission on its behalf) is or would be so prejudicial.

(2) The provisions of this Part apply to a person who is not a member of a company but to whom shares in the company have been transferred or transmitted by operation of law as they apply to a member of a company.

(3) In this section, and so far as applicable for the purposes of this section in the other provisions of this Part, "company" means—

(a) a company within the meaning of this Act, or

(b) a company that is not such a company but is a statutory water company within the meaning of the Statutory Water Companies Act 1991 (c 58).

[S994]

NOTES

Commencement: 1 October 2007 (for transitional adaptations see the note below).

Transitional adaptations: art 6 of the draft Companies Act 2006 (Commencement No 3, Consequential Amendments, Transitional Provisions and Savings) Order 2007 provides that the provisions brought into force by that Order shall have effect subject to any transitional adaptations specified in Sch 1 to that Order. Schedule 1, para 19 to the Order (at **[A12]**) provides as follows—

"19 Protection of members against unfair prejudice (**ss 994 to 999**)

(1) Section 994(3) (meaning of "company") has effect with the following adaptation.

(2) For paragraph (a) substitute—

"(a) a company within the meaning of the Companies Act 1985 or the Companies (Northern Ireland) Order 1986;".".

995 Petition by Secretary of State

(1) This section applies to a company in respect of which—

(a) the Secretary of State has received a report under section 437 of the Companies Act 1985 (c 6) (inspector's report);
(b) the Secretary of State has exercised his powers under section 447 or 448 of that Act (powers to require documents and information or to enter and search premises);
(c) the Secretary of State or the Financial Services Authority has exercised his or its powers under Part 11 of the Financial Services and Markets Act 2000 (c 8) (information gathering and investigations); or
(d) the Secretary of State has received a report from an investigator appointed by him or the Financial Services Authority under that Part.

(2) If it appears to the Secretary of State that in the case of such a company—
(a) the company's affairs are being or have been conducted in a manner that is unfairly prejudicial to the interests of members generally or of some part of its members, or
(b) an actual or proposed act or omission of the company (including an act or omission on its behalf) is or would be so prejudicial,
he may apply to the court by petition for an order under this Part.

(3) The Secretary of State may do this in addition to, or instead of, presenting a petition for the winding up of the company.

(4) In this section, and so far as applicable for the purposes of this section in the other provisions of this Part, "company" means any body corporate that is liable to be wound up under the Insolvency Act 1986 (c 45) or the Insolvency (Northern Ireland) Order 1989 (SI 1989/2405 (NI 19)).

[S995]

NOTES

Commencement: 1 October 2007.

996 Powers of the court under this Part

(1) If the court is satisfied that a petition under this Part is well founded, it may make such order as it thinks fit for giving relief in respect of the matters complained of.

(2) Without prejudice to the generality of subsection (1), the court's order may—
(a) regulate the conduct of the company's affairs in the future;
(b) require the company—
(i) to refrain from doing or continuing an act complained of, or
(ii) to do an act that the petitioner has complained it has omitted to do;
(c) authorise civil proceedings to be brought in the name and on behalf of the company by such person or persons and on such terms as the court may direct;
(d) require the company not to make any, or any specified, alterations in its articles without the leave of the court;
(e) provide for the purchase of the shares of any members of the company by other members or by the company itself and, in the case of a purchase by the company itself, the reduction of the company's capital accordingly.

[S996]

NOTES

Commencement: 1 October 2007.

Supplementary provisions

997 Application of general rule-making powers

The power to make rules under section 411 of the Insolvency Act 1986 (c 45) or Article 359 of the Insolvency (Northern Ireland) Order 1989 (SI 1989/2405 (NI 19)), so far as relating to a winding-up petition, applies for the purposes of a petition under this Part.

[S997]

NOTES

Commencement: 1 October 2007.

998 Copy of order affecting company's constitution to be delivered to registrar

(1) Where an order of the court under this Part—

(a) alters the company's constitution, or

(b) gives leave for the company to make any, or any specified, alterations to its constitution,

the company must deliver a copy of the order to the registrar.

(2) It must do so within 14 days from the making of the order or such longer period as the court may allow.

(3) If a company makes default in complying with this section, an offence is committed by—

(a) the company, and

(b) every officer of the company who is in default.

(4) A person guilty of an offence under this section is liable on summary conviction to a fine not exceeding level 3 on the standard scale and, for continued contravention, a daily default fine not exceeding one-tenth of level 3 on the standard scale.

[S998]

NOTES

Commencement: 1 October 2007.

999 Supplementary provisions where company's constitution altered

(1) This section applies where an order under this Part alters a company's constitution.

(2) If the order amends—

(a) a company's articles, or

(b) any resolution or agreement to which Chapter 3 of Part 3 applies (resolution or agreement affecting a company's constitution),

the copy of the order delivered to the registrar by the company under section 998 must be accompanied by a copy of the company's articles, or the resolution or agreement in question, as amended.

(3) Every copy of a company's articles issued by the company after the order is made must be accompanied by a copy of the order, unless the effect of the order has been incorporated into the articles by amendment.

(4) If a company makes default in complying with this section an offence is committed by—

(a) the company, and

(b) every officer of the company who is in default.

(5) A person guilty of an offence under this section is liable on summary conviction to a fine not exceeding level 3 on the standard scale.

[S999]

NOTES

Commencement: 1 October 2007 (for transitional provisions see the note below).

Transitional provisions, etc: Sch 3, para 47 to the draft Companies Act 2006 (Commencement No 3, Consequential Amendments, Transitional Provisions and Savings) Order 2007 (at **[A12]**) provides as follows—

"47 Protection of members against unfair prejudice (ss 994 to 999)

Section 999 of the Companies Act 2006 (provisions applying where court order alters a company's constitution) does not apply (by virtue of section 1297 of that Act) to an order of the court made before 1st October 2007.".

PART 31
DISSOLUTION AND RESTORATION TO THE REGISTER

CHAPTER 1
STRIKING OFF

Registrar's power to strike off defunct company

1000 Power to strike off company not carrying on business or in operation

(1) If the registrar has reasonable cause to believe that a company is not carrying on business or in operation, the registrar may send to the company by post a letter inquiring whether the company is carrying on business or in operation.

(2) If the registrar does not within one month of sending the letter receive any answer to it, the registrar must within 14 days after the expiration of that month send to the company by post a registered letter referring to the first letter, and stating—

(a) that no answer to it has been received, and

(b) that if an answer is not received to the second letter within one month from its date, a notice will be published in the Gazette with a view to striking the company's name off the register.

(3) If the registrar—

(a) receives an answer to the effect that the company is not carrying on business or in operation, or

(b) does not within one month after sending the second letter receive any answer,

the registrar may publish in the Gazette, and send to the company by post, a notice that at the expiration of three months from the date of the notice the name of the company mentioned in it will, unless cause is shown to the contrary, be struck off the register and the company will be dissolved.

(4) At the expiration of the time mentioned in the notice the registrar may, unless cause to the contrary is previously shown by the company, strike its name off the register.

(5) The registrar must publish notice in the Gazette of the company's name having been struck off the register.

(6) On the publication of the notice in the Gazette the company is dissolved.

(7) However—

(a) the liability (if any) of every director, managing officer and member of the company continues and may be enforced as if the company had not been dissolved, and

(b) nothing in this section affects the power of the court to wind up a company the name of which has been struck off the register.

[S1000]

NOTES

Commencement: to be appointed.

1001 Duty to act in case of company being wound up

(1) If, in a case where a company is being wound up—

(a) the registrar has reasonable cause to believe—

(i) that no liquidator is acting, or

(ii) that the affairs of the company are fully wound up, and

(b) the returns required to be made by the liquidator have not been made for a period of six consecutive months,

the registrar must publish in the Gazette and send to the company or the liquidator (if any) a notice that at the expiration of three months from the date of the notice the name of the company mentioned in it will, unless cause is shown to the contrary, be struck off the register and the company will be dissolved.

(2) At the expiration of the time mentioned in the notice the registrar may, unless cause to the contrary is previously shown by the company, strike its name off the register.

(3) The registrar must publish notice in the Gazette of the company's name having been struck off the register.

(4) On the publication of the notice in the Gazette the company is dissolved.

(5) However—

(a) the liability (if any) of every director, managing officer and member of the company continues and may be enforced as if the company had not been dissolved, and

(b) nothing in this section affects the power of the court to wind up a company the name of which has been struck off the register.

[S1001]

NOTES

Commencement: to be appointed.

1002 Supplementary provisions as to service of letter or notice

(1) A letter or notice to be sent under section 1000 or 1001 to a company may be addressed to the company at its registered office or, if no office has been registered, to the care of some officer of the company.

(2) If there is no officer of the company whose name and address are known to the registrar, the letter or notice may be sent to each of the persons who subscribed the memorandum (if their addresses are known to the registrar).

(3) A notice to be sent to a liquidator under section 1001 may be addressed to him at his last known place of business.

[S1002]

NOTES

Commencement: to be appointed.

Voluntary striking off

1003 Striking off on application by company

(1) On application by a company, the registrar of companies may strike the company's name off the register.

(2) The application—

(a) must be made on the company's behalf by its directors or by a majority of them, and

(b) must contain the prescribed information.

(3) The registrar may not strike a company off under this section until after the expiration of three months from the publication by the registrar in the Gazette of a notice—

(a) stating that the registrar may exercise the power under this section in relation to the company, and

(b) inviting any person to show cause why that should not be done.

(4) The registrar must publish notice in the Gazette of the company's name having been struck off.

(5) On the publication of the notice in the Gazette the company is dissolved.

(6) However—

(a) the liability (if any) of every director, managing officer and member of the company continues and may be enforced as if the company had not been dissolved, and

(b) nothing in this section affects the power of the court to wind up a company the name of which has been struck off the register.

[S1003]

NOTES

Commencement: 20 January 2007 (for the purpose of enabling the exercise of powers to make Orders or Regulations by statutory instrument); to be appointed (otherwise).

1004 Circumstances in which application not to be made: activities of company

(1) An application under section 1003 (application for voluntary striking off) on behalf of a company must not be made if, at any time in the previous three months, the company has—

(a) changed its name,
(b) traded or otherwise carried on business,
(c) made a disposal for value of property or rights that, immediately before ceasing to trade or otherwise carry on business, it held for the purpose of disposal for gain in the normal course of trading or otherwise carrying on business, or
(d) engaged in any other activity, except one which is—
  (i) necessary or expedient for the purpose of making an application under that section, or deciding whether to do so,
  (ii) necessary or expedient for the purpose of concluding the affairs of the company,
  (iii) necessary or expedient for the purpose of complying with any statutory requirement, or
  (iv) specified by the Secretary of State by order for the purposes of this sub-paragraph.

(2) For the purposes of this section, a company is not to be treated as trading or otherwise carrying on business by virtue only of the fact that it makes a payment in respect of a liability incurred in the course of trading or otherwise carrying on business.

(3) The Secretary of State may by order amend subsection (1) for the purpose of altering the period in relation to which the doing of the things mentioned in paragraphs (a) to (d) of that subsection is relevant.

(4) An order under this section is subject to negative resolution procedure.

(5) It is an offence for a person to make an application in contravention of this section.

(6) In proceedings for such an offence it is a defence for the accused to prove that he did not know, and could not reasonably have known, of the existence of the facts that led to the contravention.

(7) A person guilty of an offence under this section is liable—

(a) on conviction on indictment, to a fine;
(b) on summary conviction, to a fine not exceeding the statutory maximum.

[S1004]

NOTES

Commencement: 20 January 2007 (for the purpose of enabling the exercise of powers to make Orders or Regulations by statutory instrument); to be appointed (otherwise).

1005 Circumstances in which application not to be made: other proceedings not concluded

(1) An application under section 1003 (application for voluntary striking off) on behalf of a company must not be made at a time when—

(a) an application to the court under Part 26 has been made on behalf of the company for the sanctioning of a compromise or arrangement and the matter has not been finally concluded;
(b) a voluntary arrangement in relation to the company has been proposed under Part 1 of the Insolvency Act 1986 (c 45) or Part 2 of the Insolvency (Northern Ireland) Order 1989 (SI 1989/2405 (NI 19)) and the matter has not been finally concluded;
(c) the company is in administration under Part 2 of that Act or Part 3 of that Order;
(d) paragraph 44 of Schedule B1 to that Act or paragraph 45 of Schedule B1 to that Order applies (interim moratorium on proceedings where application to the court for an administration order has been made or notice of intention to appoint administrator has been filed);
(e) the company is being wound up under Part 4 of that Act or Part 5 of that Order, whether voluntarily or by the court, or a petition under that Part for winding up of the company by the court has been presented and not finally dealt with or withdrawn;
(f) there is a receiver or manager of the company's property;

(g) the company's estate is being administered by a judicial factor.

(2) For the purposes of subsection (1)(a), the matter is finally concluded if—

(a) the application has been withdrawn,

(b) the application has been finally dealt with without a compromise or arrangement being sanctioned by the court, or

(c) a compromise or arrangement has been sanctioned by the court and has, together with anything required to be done under any provision made in relation to the matter by order of the court, been fully carried out.

(3) For the purposes of subsection (1)(b), the matter is finally concluded if—

(a) no meetings are to be summoned under section 3 of the Insolvency Act 1986 (c 45) or Article 16 of the Insolvency (Northern Ireland) Order 1989,

(b) meetings summoned under that section or Article fail to approve the arrangement with no, or the same, modifications,

(c) an arrangement approved by meetings summoned under that section, or in consequence of a direction under section 6(4)(b) of that Act or Article 19(4)(b) of that Order, has been fully implemented, or

(d) the court makes an order under section 6(5) of that Act or Article 19(5) of that Order revoking approval given at previous meetings and, if the court gives any directions under section 6(6) of that Act or Article 19(6) of that Order, the company has done whatever it is required to do under those directions.

(4) It is an offence for a person to make an application in contravention of this section.

(5) In proceedings for such an offence it is a defence for the accused to prove that he did not know, and could not reasonably have known, of the existence of the facts that led to the contravention.

(6) A person guilty of an offence under this section is liable—

(a) on conviction on indictment, to a fine;

(b) on summary conviction, to a fine not exceeding the statutory maximum.

[S1005]

NOTES

Commencement: to be appointed.

1006 Copy of application to be given to members, employees, etc

(1) A person who makes an application under section 1003 (application for voluntary striking off) on behalf of a company must secure that, within seven days from the day on which the application is made, a copy of it is given to every person who at any time on that day is—

(a) a member of the company,

(b) an employee of the company,

(c) a creditor of the company,

(d) a director of the company,

(e) a manager or trustee of any pension fund established for the benefit of employees of the company, or

(f) a person of a description specified for the purposes of this paragraph by regulations made by the Secretary of State.

Regulations under paragraph (f) are subject to negative resolution procedure.

(2) Subsection (1) does not require a copy of the application to be given to a director who is a party to the application.

(3) The duty imposed by this section ceases to apply if the application is withdrawn before the end of the period for giving the copy application.

(4) A person who fails to perform the duty imposed on him by this section commits an offence.

If he does so with the intention of concealing the making of the application from the person concerned, he commits an aggravated offence.

(5) In proceedings for an offence under this section it is a defence for the accused to prove that he took all reasonable steps to perform the duty.

(6) A person guilty of an offence under this section (other than an aggravated offence) is liable—

(a) on conviction on indictment, to a fine;

(b) on summary conviction, to a fine not exceeding the statutory maximum.

(7) A person guilty of an aggravated offence under this section is liable—

(a) on conviction on indictment, to imprisonment for a term not exceeding seven years or a fine (or both);

(b) on summary conviction—

(i) in England and Wales, to imprisonment for a term not exceeding twelve months or to a fine not exceeding the statutory maximum (or both);

(ii) in Scotland or Northern Ireland, to imprisonment for a term not exceeding six months, or to a fine not exceeding the statutory maximum (or both).

[S1006]

NOTES

Commencement: 20 January 2007 (for the purpose of enabling the exercise of powers to make Orders or Regulations by statutory instrument); to be appointed (otherwise).

1007 Copy of application to be given to new members, employees, etc

(1) This section applies in relation to any time after the day on which a company makes an application under section 1003 (application for voluntary striking off) and before the day on which the application is finally dealt with or withdrawn.

(2) A person who is a director of the company at the end of a day on which a person (other than himself) becomes—

(a) a member of the company,

(b) an employee of the company,

(c) a creditor of the company,

(d) a director of the company,

(e) a manager or trustee of any pension fund established for the benefit of employees of the company, or

(f) a person of a description specified for the purposes of this paragraph by regulations made by the Secretary of State,

must secure that a copy of the application is given to that person within seven days from that day.

Regulations under paragraph (f) are subject to negative resolution procedure.

(3) The duty imposed by this section ceases to apply if the application is finally dealt with or withdrawn before the end of the period for giving the copy application.

(4) A person who fails to perform the duty imposed on him by this section commits an offence.

If he does so with the intention of concealing the making of the application from the person concerned, he commits an aggravated offence.

(5) In proceedings for an offence under this section it is a defence for the accused to prove—

(a) that at the time of the failure he was not aware of the fact that the company had made an application under section 1003, or

(b) that he took all reasonable steps to perform the duty.

(6) A person guilty of an offence under this section (other than an aggravated offence) is liable—

(a) on conviction on indictment, to a fine;

(b) on summary conviction, to a fine not exceeding the statutory maximum.

(7) A person guilty of an aggravated offence under this section is liable—

(a) on conviction on indictment, to imprisonment for a term not exceeding seven years or a fine (or both);

(b) on summary conviction—

(i) in England and Wales, to imprisonment for a term not exceeding twelve months or to a fine not exceeding the statutory maximum (or both);

(ii) in Scotland or Northern Ireland, to imprisonment for a term not exceeding six months, or to a fine not exceeding the statutory maximum (or both).

[S1007]

NOTES

Commencement: 20 January 2007 (for the purpose of enabling the exercise of powers to make Orders or Regulations by statutory instrument); to be appointed (otherwise).

1008 Copy of application: provisions as to service of documents

(1) The following provisions have effect for the purposes of—

section 1006 (copy of application to be given to members, employees, etc), and
section 1007 (copy of application to be given to new members, employees, etc).

(2) A document is treated as given to a person if it is—

(a) delivered to him, or
(b) left at his proper address, or
(c) sent by post to him at that address.

(3) For the purposes of subsection (2) and section 7 of the Interpretation Act 1978 (c 30) (service of documents by post) as it applies in relation to that subsection, the proper address of a person is—

(a) in the case of a firm incorporated or formed in the United Kingdom, its registered or principal office;
(b) in the case of a firm incorporated or formed outside the United Kingdom—
 (i) if it has a place of business in the United Kingdom, its principal office in the United Kingdom, or
 (ii) if it does not have a place of business in the United Kingdom, its registered or principal office;
(c) in the case of an individual, his last known address.

(4) In the case of a creditor of the company a document is treated as given to him if it is left or sent by post to him—

(a) at the place of business of his with which the company has had dealings by virtue of which he is a creditor of the company, or
(b) if there is more than one such place of business, at each of them.

[S1008]

NOTES

Commencement: to be appointed.

1009 Circumstances in which application to be withdrawn

(1) This section applies where, at any time on or after the day on which a company makes an application under section 1003 (application for voluntary striking off) and before the day on which the application is finally dealt with or withdrawn—

(a) the company—
 (i) changes its name,
 (ii) trades or otherwise carries on business,
 (iii) makes a disposal for value of any property or rights other than those which it was necessary or expedient for it to hold for the purpose of making, or proceeding with, an application under that section, or
 (iv) engages in any activity, except one to which subsection (4) applies;
(b) an application is made to the court under Part 26 on behalf of the company for the sanctioning of a compromise or arrangement;
(c) a voluntary arrangement in relation to the company is proposed under Part 1 of the Insolvency Act 1986 (c 45) or Part 2 of the Insolvency (Northern Ireland) Order 1989 (SI 1989/2405 (NI 19));
(d) an application to the court for an administration order in respect of the company is made under paragraph 12 of Schedule B1 to that Act or paragraph 13 of Schedule B1 to that Order;
(e) an administrator is appointed in respect of the company under paragraph 14 or 22 of Schedule B1 to that Act or paragraph 15 or 23 of Schedule B1 to that Order, or a copy of notice of intention to appoint an administrator of the company under any of those provisions is filed with the court;

(f) there arise any of the circumstances in which, under section 84(1) of that Act or Article 70 of that Order, the company may be voluntarily wound up;

(g) a petition is presented for the winding up of the company by the court under Part 4 of that Act or Part 5 of that Order;

(h) a receiver or manager of the company's property is appointed; or

(i) a judicial factor is appointed to administer the company's estate.

(2) A person who, at the end of a day on which any of the events mentioned in subsection (1) occurs, is a director of the company must secure that the company's application is withdrawn forthwith.

(3) For the purposes of subsection (1)(a), a company is not treated as trading or otherwise carrying on business by virtue only of the fact that it makes a payment in respect of a liability incurred in the course of trading or otherwise carrying on business.

(4) The excepted activities referred to in subsection (1)(a)(iv) are—

(a) any activity necessary or expedient for the purposes of—
   (i) making, or proceeding with, an application under section 1003 (application for voluntary striking off),
   (ii) concluding affairs of the company that are outstanding because of what has been necessary or expedient for the purpose of making, or proceeding with, such an application, or
   (iii) complying with any statutory requirement;

(b) any activity specified by the Secretary of State by order for the purposes of this subsection.

An order under paragraph (b) is subject to negative resolution procedure.

(5) A person who fails to perform the duty imposed on him by this section commits an offence.

(6) In proceedings for an offence under this section it is a defence for the accused to prove—

(a) that at the time of the failure he was not aware of the fact that the company had made an application under section 1003, or

(b) that he took all reasonable steps to perform the duty.

(7) A person guilty of an offence under this section is liable—

(a) on conviction on indictment, to a fine;

(b) on summary conviction, to a fine not exceeding the statutory maximum.

[S1009]

NOTES

Commencement: 20 January 2007 (for the purpose of enabling the exercise of powers to make Orders or Regulations by statutory instrument); to be appointed (otherwise).

1010 Withdrawal of application

An application under section 1003 is withdrawn by notice to the registrar.

[S1010]

NOTES

Commencement: to be appointed.

1011 Meaning of "creditor"

In this Chapter "creditor" includes a contingent or prospective creditor.

[S1011]

NOTES

Commencement: to be appointed.

CHAPTER 2
PROPERTY OF DISSOLVED COMPANY

Property vesting as bona vacantia

1012 Property of dissolved company to be bona vacantia

(1) When a company is dissolved, all property and rights whatsoever vested in or held on trust for the company immediately before its dissolution (including leasehold property, but not including property held by the company on trust for another person) are deemed to be *bona vacantia* and—

(a) accordingly belong to the Crown, or to the Duchy of Lancaster or to the Duke of Cornwall for the time being (as the case may be), and

(b) vest and may be dealt with in the same manner as other *bona vacantia* accruing to the Crown, to the Duchy of Lancaster or to the Duke of Cornwall.

(2) Subsection (1) has effect subject to the possible restoration of the company to the register under Chapter 3 (see section 1034).

[S1012]

NOTES

Commencement: to be appointed.

1013 Crown disclaimer of property vesting as bona vacantia

(1) Where property vests in the Crown under section 1012, the Crown's title to it under that section may be disclaimed by a notice signed by the Crown representative, that is to say the Treasury Solicitor, or, in relation to property in Scotland, the Queen's and Lord Treasurer's Remembrancer.

(2) The right to execute a notice of disclaimer under this section may be waived by or on behalf of the Crown either expressly or by taking possession.

(3) A notice of disclaimer must be executed within three years after—

(a) the date on which the fact that the property may have vested in the Crown under section 1012 first comes to the notice of the Crown representative, or

(b) if ownership of the property is not established at that date, the end of the period reasonably necessary for the Crown representative to establish the ownership of the property.

(4) If an application in writing is made to the Crown representative by a person interested in the property requiring him to decide whether he will or will not disclaim, any notice of disclaimer must be executed within twelve months after the making of the application or such further period as may be allowed by the court.

(5) A notice of disclaimer under this section is of no effect if it is shown to have been executed after the end of the period specified by subsection (3) or (4).

(6) A notice of disclaimer under this section must be delivered to the registrar and retained and registered by him.

(7) Copies of it must be published in the Gazette and sent to any persons who have given the Crown representative notice that they claim to be interested in the property.

(8) This section applies to property vested in the Duchy of Lancaster or the Duke of Cornwall under section 1012 as if for references to the Crown and the Crown representative there were respectively substituted references to the Duchy of Lancaster and to the Solicitor to that Duchy, or to the Duke of Cornwall and to the Solicitor to the Duchy of Cornwall, as the case may be.

[S1013]

NOTES

Commencement: to be appointed.

1014 Effect of Crown disclaimer

(1) Where notice of disclaimer is executed under section 1013 as respects any property, that property is deemed not to have vested in the Crown under section 1012.

(2) The following sections contain provisions as to the effect of the Crown disclaimer—
sections 1015 to 1019 apply in relation to property in England and Wales or Northern Ireland;
sections 1020 to 1022 apply in relation to property in Scotland.

[S1014]

NOTES

Commencement: to be appointed.

Effect of Crown disclaimer: England and Wales and Northern Ireland

1015 General effect of disclaimer

(1) The Crown's disclaimer operates so as to terminate, as from the date of the disclaimer, the rights, interests and liabilities of the company in or in respect of the property disclaimed.

(2) It does not, except so far as is necessary for the purpose of releasing the company from any liability, affect the rights or liabilities of any other person.

[S1015]

NOTES

Commencement: to be appointed.

1016 Disclaimer of leaseholds

(1) The disclaimer of any property of a leasehold character does not take effect unless a copy of the disclaimer has been served (so far as the Crown representative is aware of their addresses) on every person claiming under the company as underlessee or mortgagee, and either—

- (a) no application under section 1017 (power of court to make vesting order) is made with respect to that property before the end of the period of 14 days beginning with the day on which the last notice under this paragraph was served, or
- (b) where such an application has been made, the court directs that the disclaimer shall take effect.

(2) Where the court gives a direction under subsection (1)(b) it may also, instead of or in addition to any order it makes under section 1017, make such order as it thinks fit with respect to fixtures, tenant's improvements and other matters arising out of the lease.

(3) In this section the "Crown representative" means—

- (a) in relation to property vested in the Duchy of Lancaster, the Solicitor to that Duchy;
- (b) in relation to property vested in the Duke of Cornwall, the Solicitor to the Duchy of Cornwall;
- (c) in relation to property in Scotland, the Queen's and Lord Treasurer's Remembrancer;
- (d) in relation to other property, the Treasury Solicitor.

[S1016]

NOTES

Commencement: to be appointed.

1017 Power of court to make vesting order

(1) The court may on application by a person who—

- (a) claims an interest in the disclaimed property, or
- (b) is under a liability in respect of the disclaimed property that is not discharged by the disclaimer,

make an order under this section in respect of the property.

(2) An order under this section is an order for the vesting of the disclaimed property in, or its delivery to—

- (a) a person entitled to it (or a trustee for such a person), or

(b) a person subject to such a liability as is mentioned in subsection (1)(b) (or a trustee for such a person).

(3) An order under subsection (2)(b) may only be made where it appears to the court that it would be just to do so for the purpose of compensating the person subject to the liability in respect of the disclaimer.

(4) An order under this section may be made on such terms as the court thinks fit.

(5) On a vesting order being made under this section, the property comprised in it vests in the person named in that behalf in the order without conveyance, assignment or transfer.

[S1017]

NOTES

Commencement: to be appointed.

1018 Protection of persons holding under a lease

(1) The court must not make an order under section 1017 vesting property of a leasehold nature in a person claiming under the company as underlessee or mortgagee except on terms making that person—

(a) subject to the same liabilities and obligations as those to which the company was subject under the lease, or

(b) if the court thinks fit, subject to the same liabilities and obligations as if the lease had been assigned to him.

(2) Where the order relates to only part of the property comprised in the lease, subsection (1) applies as if the lease had comprised only the property comprised in the vesting order.

(3) A person claiming under the company as underlessee or mortgagee who declines to accept a vesting order on such terms is excluded from all interest in the property.

(4) If there is no person claiming under the company who is willing to accept an order on such terms, the court has power to vest the company's estate and interest in the property in any person who is liable (whether personally or in a representative character, and whether alone or jointly with the company) to perform the lessee's covenants in the lease.

(5) The court may vest that estate and interest in such a person freed and discharged from all estates, incumbrances and interests created by the company.

[S1018]

NOTES

Commencement: to be appointed.

1019 Land subject to rentcharge

Where in consequence of the disclaimer land that is subject to a rentcharge vests in any person, neither he nor his successors in title are subject to any personal liability in respect of sums becoming due under the rentcharge, except sums becoming due after he, or some person claiming under or through him, has taken possession or control of the land or has entered into occupation of it.

[S1019]

NOTES

Commencement: to be appointed.

Effect of Crown disclaimer: Scotland

1020 General effect of disclaimer

(1) The Crown's disclaimer operates to determine, as from the date of the disclaimer, the rights, interests and liabilities of the company, and the property of the company, in or in respect of the property disclaimed.

(2) It does not (except so far as is necessary for the purpose of releasing the company and its property from liability) affect the rights or liabilities of any other person.

[S1020]

NOTES

Commencement: to be appointed.

1021 Power of court to make vesting order

(1) The court may—

(a) on application by a person who either claims an interest in disclaimed property or is under a liability not discharged by this Act in respect of disclaimed property, and

(b) on hearing such persons as it thinks fit,

make an order for the vesting of the property in or its delivery to any persons entitled to it, or to whom it may seem just that the property should be delivered by way of compensation for such liability, or a trustee for him.

(2) The order may be made on such terms as the court thinks fit.

(3) On a vesting order being made under this section, the property comprised in it vests accordingly in the person named in that behalf in the order, without conveyance or assignation for that purpose.

[S1021]

NOTES

Commencement: to be appointed.

1022 Protection of persons holding under a lease

(1) Where the property disclaimed is held under a lease the court must not make a vesting order in favour of a person claiming under the company, whether—

(a) as sub-lessee, or

(b) as creditor in a duly registered or (as the case may be) recorded heritable security over a lease,

except on the following terms.

(2) The person must by the order be made subject—

(a) to the same liabilities and obligations as those to which the company was subject under the lease in respect of the property, or

(b) if the court thinks fit, only to the same liabilities and obligations as if the lease had been assigned to him.

In either event (if the case so requires) the liabilities and obligations must be as if the lease had comprised only the property comprised in the vesting order.

(3) A sub-lessee or creditor declining to accept a vesting order on such terms is excluded from all interest in and security over the property.

(4) If there is no person claiming under the company who is willing to accept an order on such terms, the court has power to vest the company's estate and interest in the property in any person liable (either personally or in a representative character, and either alone or jointly with the company) to perform the lessee's obligations under the lease.

(5) The court may vest that estate and interest in such a person freed and discharged from all interests, rights and obligations created by the company in the lease or in relation to the lease.

(6) For the purposes of this section a heritable security—

(a) is duly recorded if it is recorded in the Register of Sasines, and

(b) is duly registered if registered in accordance with the Land Registration (Scotland) Act 1979 (c 33).

[S1022]

NOTES

Commencement: to be appointed.

Supplementary provisions

1023 Liability for rentcharge on company's land after dissolution

(1) This section applies where on the dissolution of a company land in England and Wales or Northern Ireland that is subject to a rentcharge vests by operation of law in the Crown or any other person ("the proprietor").

(2) Neither the proprietor nor his successors in title are subject to any personal liability in respect of sums becoming due under the rentcharge, except sums becoming due after the proprietor, or some person claiming under or through him, has taken possession or control of the land or has entered into occupation of it.

(3) In this section "company" includes any body corporate.

[S1023]

NOTES

Commencement: to be appointed.

CHAPTER 3
RESTORATION TO THE REGISTER

Administrative restoration to the register

1024 Application for administrative restoration to the register

(1) An application may be made to the registrar to restore to the register a company that has been struck off the register under section 1000 or 1001 (power of registrar to strike off defunct company).

(2) An application under this section may be made whether or not the company has in consequence been dissolved.

(3) An application under this section may only be made by a former director or former member of the company.

(4) An application under this section may not be made after the end of the period of six years from the date of the dissolution of the company.

For this purpose an application is made when it is received by the registrar.

[S1024]

NOTES

Commencement: to be appointed.

1025 Requirements for administrative restoration

(1) On an application under section 1024 the registrar shall restore the company to the register if, and only if, the following conditions are met.

(2) The first condition is that the company was carrying on business or in operation at the time of its striking off.

(3) The second condition is that, if any property or right previously vested in or held on trust for the company has vested as *bona vacantia*, the Crown representative has signified to the registrar in writing consent to the company's restoration to the register.

(4) It is the applicant's responsibility to obtain that consent and to pay any costs (in Scotland, expenses) of the Crown representative—

(a) in dealing with the property during the period of dissolution, or

(b) in connection with the proceedings on the application,

that may be demanded as a condition of giving consent.

(5) The third condition is that the applicant has—

(a) delivered to the registrar such documents relating to the company as are necessary to bring up to date the records kept by the registrar, and

(b) paid any penalties under section 453 or corresponding earlier provisions (civil penalty for failure to deliver accounts) that were outstanding at the date of dissolution or striking off.

(6) In this section the "Crown representative" means—

(a) in relation to property vested in the Duchy of Lancaster, the Solicitor to that Duchy;

(b) in relation to property vested in the Duke of Cornwall, the Solicitor to the Duchy of Cornwall;

(c) in relation to property in Scotland, the Queen's and Lord Treasurer's Remembrancer;

(d) in relation to other property, the Treasury Solicitor.

[S1025]

NOTES

Commencement: to be appointed.

1026 Application to be accompanied by statement of compliance

(1) An application under section 1024 (application for administrative restoration to the register) must be accompanied by a statement of compliance.

(2) The statement of compliance required is a statement—

(a) that the person making the application has standing to apply (see subsection (3) of that section), and

(b) that the requirements for administrative restoration (see section 1025) are met.

(3) The registrar may accept the statement of compliance as sufficient evidence of those matters.

[S1026]

NOTES

Commencement: to be appointed.

1027 Registrar's decision on application for administrative restoration

(1) The registrar must give notice to the applicant of the decision on an application under section 1024 (application for administrative restoration to the register).

(2) If the decision is that the company should be restored to the register, the restoration takes effect as from the date that notice is sent.

(3) In the case of such a decision, the registrar must—

(a) enter on the register a note of the date as from which the company's restoration to the register takes effect, and

(b) cause notice of the restoration to be published in the Gazette.

(4) The notice under subsection (3)(b) must state—

(a) the name of the company or, if the company is restored to the register under a different name (see section 1033), that name and its former name,

(b) the company's registered number, and

(c) the date as from which the restoration of the company to the register takes effect.

[S1027]

NOTES

Commencement: to be appointed.

1028 Effect of administrative restoration

(1) The general effect of administrative restoration to the register is that the company is deemed to have continued in existence as if it had not been dissolved or struck off the register.

(2) The company is not liable to a penalty under section 453 or any corresponding earlier provision (civil penalty for failure to deliver accounts) for a financial year in relation to which the period for filing accounts and reports ended—

(a) after the date of dissolution or striking off, and

(b) before the restoration of the company to the register.

(3) The court may give such directions and make such provision as seems just for placing the company and all other persons in the same position (as nearly as may be) as if the company had not been dissolved or struck off the register.

(4) An application to the court for such directions or provision may be made any time within three years after the date of restoration of the company to the register.

[S1028]

NOTES

Commencement: to be appointed.

Restoration to the register by the court

1029 Application to court for restoration to the register

(1) An application may be made to the court to restore to the register a company—

(a) that has been dissolved under Chapter 9 of Part 4 of the Insolvency Act 1986 (c 45) or Chapter 9 of Part 5 of the Insolvency (Northern Ireland) Order 1989 (SI 1989/2405 (NI 19)) (dissolution of company after winding up),

(b) that is deemed to have been dissolved under paragraph 84(6) of Schedule B1 to that Act or paragraph 85(6) of Schedule B1 to that Order (dissolution of company following administration), or

(c) that has been struck off the register—

(i) under section 1000 or 1001 (power of registrar to strike off defunct company), or

(ii) under section 1003 (voluntary striking off),

whether or not the company has in consequence been dissolved.

(2) An application under this section may be made by—

(a) the Secretary of State,

(b) any former director of the company,

(c) any person having an interest in land in which the company had a superior or derivative interest,

(d) any person having an interest in land or other property—

(i) that was subject to rights vested in the company, or

(ii) that was benefited by obligations owed by the company,

(e) any person who but for the company's dissolution would have been in a contractual relationship with it,

(f) any person with a potential legal claim against the company,

(g) any manager or trustee of a pension fund established for the benefit of employees of the company,

(h) any former member of the company (or the personal representatives of such a person),

(i) any person who was a creditor of the company at the time of its striking off or dissolution,

(j) any former liquidator of the company,

(k) where the company was struck off the register under section 1003 (voluntary striking off), any person of a description specified by regulations under section 1006(1)(f) or 1007(2)(f) (persons entitled to notice of application for voluntary striking off),

or by any other person appearing to the court to have an interest in the matter.

[S1029]

NOTES

Commencement: to be appointed.

1030 When application to the court may be made

(1) An application to the court for restoration of a company to the register may be made at any time for the purpose of bringing proceedings against the company for damages for personal injury.

(2) No order shall be made on such an application if it appears to the court that the proceedings would fail by virtue of any enactment as to the time within which proceedings must be brought.

(3) In making that decision the court must have regard to its power under section 1032(3) (power to give consequential directions etc) to direct that the period between the dissolution (or striking off) of the company and the making of the order is not to count for the purposes of any such enactment.

(4) In any other case an application to the court for restoration of a company to the register may not be made after the end of the period of six years from the date of the dissolution of the company, subject as follows.

(5) In a case where—

(a) the company has been struck off the register under section 1000 or 1001 (power of registrar to strike off defunct company),

(b) an application to the registrar has been made under section 1024 (application for administrative restoration to the register) within the time allowed for making such an application, and

(c) the registrar has refused the application,

an application to the court under this section may be made within 28 days of notice of the registrar's decision being issued by the registrar, even if the period of six years mentioned in subsection (4) above has expired.

(6) For the purposes of this section—

(a) "personal injury" includes any disease and any impairment of a person's physical or mental condition; and

(b) references to damages for personal injury include—

(i) any sum claimed by virtue of section 1(2)(c) of the Law Reform (Miscellaneous Provisions) Act 1934 (c 41) or section 14(2)(c) of the Law Reform (Miscellaneous Provisions) Act (Northern Ireland) 1937 (1937 c 9 (NI)) (funeral expenses)), and

(ii) damages under the Fatal Accidents Act 1976 (c 30), the Damages (Scotland) Act 1976 (c 13) or the Fatal Accidents (Northern Ireland) Order 1977 (SI 1977/1251 (NI 18)).

[S1030]

NOTES

Commencement: to be appointed.

1031 Decision on application for restoration by the court

(1) On an application under section 1029 the court may order the restoration of the company to the register—

(a) if the company was struck off the register under section 1000 or 1001 (power of registrar to strike off defunct companies) and the company was, at the time of the striking off, carrying on business or in operation;

(b) if the company was struck off the register under section 1003 (voluntary striking off) and any of the requirements of sections 1004 to 1009 was not complied with;

(c) if in any other case the court considers it just to do so.

(2) If the court orders restoration of the company to the register, the restoration takes effect on a copy of the court's order being delivered to the registrar.

(3) The registrar must cause to be published in the Gazette notice of the restoration of the company to the register.

(4) The notice must state—

(a) the name of the company or, if the company is restored to the register under a different name (see section 1033), that name and its former name,

(b) the company's registered number, and

(c) the date on which the restoration took effect.

[S1031]

NOTES

Commencement: to be appointed.

1032 Effect of court order for restoration to the register

(1) The general effect of an order by the court for restoration to the register is that the company is deemed to have continued in existence as if it had not been dissolved or struck off the register.

(2) The company is not liable to a penalty under section 453 or any corresponding earlier provision (civil penalty for failure to deliver accounts) for a financial year in relation to which the period for filing accounts and reports ended—

(a) after the date of dissolution or striking off, and

(b) before the restoration of the company to the register.

(3) The court may give such directions and make such provision as seems just for placing the company and all other persons in the same position (as nearly as may be) as if the company had not been dissolved or struck off the register.

(4) The court may also give directions as to—

(a) the delivery to the registrar of such documents relating to the company as are necessary to bring up to date the records kept by the registrar,

(b) the payment of the costs (in Scotland, expenses) of the registrar in connection with the proceedings for the restoration of the company to the register,

(c) where any property or right previously vested in or held on trust for the company has vested as *bona vacantia*, the payment of the costs (in Scotland, expenses) of the Crown representative—

(i) in dealing with the property during the period of dissolution, or

(ii) in connection with the proceedings on the application.

(5) In this section the "Crown representative" means—

(a) in relation to property vested in the Duchy of Lancaster, the Solicitor to that Duchy;

(b) in relation to property vested in the Duke of Cornwall, the Solicitor to the Duchy of Cornwall;

(c) in relation to property in Scotland, the Queen's and Lord Treasurer's Remembrancer;

(d) in relation to other property, the Treasury Solicitor.

[S1032]

NOTES

Commencement: to be appointed.

Supplementary provisions

1033 Company's name on restoration

(1) A company is restored to the register with the name it had before it was dissolved or struck off the register, subject to the following provisions.

(2) If at the date of restoration the company could not be registered under its former name without contravening section 66 (name not to be the same as another in the registrar's index of company names), it must be restored to the register—

(a) under another name specified—

(i) in the case of administrative restoration, in the application to the registrar, or

(ii) in the case of restoration under a court order, in the court's order, or

(b) as if its registered number was also its name.

References to a company's being registered in a name, and to registration in that context, shall be read as including the company's being restored to the register.

(3) If a company is restored to the register under a name specified in the application to the registrar, the provisions of—

section 80 (change of name: registration and issue of new certificate of incorporation), and

section 81 (change of name: effect),

apply as if the application to the registrar were notice of a change of name.

(4) If a company is restored to the register under a name specified in the court's order, the provisions of—

section 80 (change of name: registration and issue of new certificate of incorporation), and

section 81 (change of name: effect),

apply as if the copy of the court order delivered to the registrar were notice of a change a name.

(5) If the company is restored to the register as if its registered number was also its name—

(a) the company must change its name within 14 days after the date of the restoration,

(b) the change may be made by resolution of the directors (without prejudice to any other method of changing the company's name),

(c) the company must give notice to the registrar of the change, and

(d) sections 80 and 81 apply as regards the registration and effect of the change.

(6) If the company fails to comply with subsection (5)(a) or (c) an offence is committed by—

(a) the company, and

(b) every officer of the company who is in default.

(7) A person guilty of an offence under subsection (6) is liable on summary conviction to a fine not exceeding level 5 on the standard scale and, for continued contravention, a daily default fine not exceeding one-tenth of level 5 on the standard scale.

[S1033]

NOTES

Commencement: to be appointed.

1034 Effect of restoration to the register where property has vested as bona vacantia

(1) The person in whom any property or right is vested by section 1012 (property of dissolved company to be *bona vacantia*) may dispose of, or of an interest in, that property or right despite the fact that the company may be restored to the register under this Chapter.

(2) If the company is restored to the register—

(a) the restoration does not affect the disposition (but without prejudice to its effect in relation to any other property or right previously vested in or held on trust for the company), and

(b) the Crown or, as the case may be, the Duke of Cornwall shall pay to the company an amount equal to—

(i) the amount of any consideration received for the property or right or, as the case may be, the interest in it, or

(ii) the value of any such consideration at the time of the disposition,

or, if no consideration was received an amount equal to the value of the property, right or interest disposed of, as at the date of the disposition.

(3) There may be deducted from the amount payable under subsection (2)(b) the reasonable costs of the Crown representative in connection with the disposition (to the extent that they have not been paid as a condition of administrative restoration or pursuant to a court order for restoration).

(4) Where a liability accrues under subsection (2) in respect of any property or right which before the restoration of the company to the register had accrued as *bona vacantia* to the Duchy of Lancaster, the Attorney General of that Duchy shall represent Her Majesty in any proceedings arising in connection with that liability.

(5) Where a liability accrues under subsection (2) in respect of any property or right which before the restoration of the company to the register had accrued as *bona vacantia* to the Duchy of Cornwall, such persons as the Duke of Cornwall (or other possessor for the time being of the Duchy) may appoint shall represent the Duke (or other possessor) in any proceedings arising out of that liability.

(6) In this section the "Crown representative" means—

(a) in relation to property vested in the Duchy of Lancaster, the Solicitor to that Duchy;

(b) in relation to property vested in the Duke of Cornwall, the Solicitor to the Duchy of Cornwall;

(c) in relation to property in Scotland, the Queen's and Lord Treasurer's Remembrancer;

(d) in relation to other property, the Treasury Solicitor.

[S1034]

NOTES

Commencement: to be appointed.

PART 32
COMPANY INVESTIGATIONS: AMENDMENTS

1035 Powers of Secretary of State to give directions to inspectors

(*This section inserts CA 1986, ss 446A, 446B at* **[479A]**, **[479B]** *and amends ss 431, 432, 437 and 442 at* **[467]**, **[468]**, **[471]** *and* **[475]**.)

[S1035]

NOTES

Commencement: 1 October 2007 (for transitional provisions see the note below).

Transitional provisions, etc: Sch 3, para 48 to the draft Companies Act 2006 (Commencement No 3, Consequential Amendments, Transitional Provisions and Savings) Order 2007 (at **[A12]**) provides as follows—

"48 Company investigations (ss 1035 to 1039)

Sections 1035 to 1039 of the Companies Act 2006 (company investigations: amendments) apply where an inspector is appointed under a provision of Part 14 of the 1985 Act on or after 1st October 2007.".

1036 Resignation, removal and replacement of inspectors

(*This section inserts CA 1986, ss 446C, 446D at* **[479C]**, **[479D]**.)

[S1036]

NOTES

Commencement: 1 October 2007 (for transitional provisions see the note to s 1035).

1037 Power to obtain information from former inspectors etc

(*This section inserts CA 1986, s 446E at* **[479E]** *and amends ss 451A and 452 at* **[485]** *and* **[486]**.)

[S1037]

NOTES

Commencement: 1 October 2007 (for transitional provisions see the note to s 1035).

1038 Power to require production of documents

(*This section substitutes CA 1985, ss 434(6) and 447(9) at* **[469]**, **[480]**.)

[S1038]

NOTES

Commencement: 1 October 2007 (for transitional provisions see the note to s 1035).

1039 Disqualification orders: consequential amendments

(*This section amends the Company Directors Disqualification Act 1986, s 8(1A) at* **[744]**.)

[S1039]

NOTES

Commencement: 1 October 2007 (for transitional provisions see the note to s 1035).

PART 33
UK COMPANIES NOT FORMED UNDER COMPANIES LEGISLATION

CHAPTER 1
COMPANIES NOT FORMED UNDER COMPANIES LEGISLATION BUT AUTHORISED TO REGISTER

1040 Companies authorised to register under this Act

(1) This section applies to—

(a) any company that was in existence on 2nd November 1862 (including any company registered under the Joint Stock Companies Acts), and

(b) any company formed after that date (whether before or after the commencement of this Act)—

(i) in pursuance of an Act of Parliament other than this Act or any of the former Companies Acts,

(ii) in pursuance of letters patent, or

(iii) that is otherwise duly constituted according to law.

(2) Any such company may on making application register under this Act.

(3) Subject to the following provisions, it may register as an unlimited company, as a company limited by shares or as a company limited by guarantee.

(4) A company having the liability of its members limited by Act of Parliament or letters patent—

(a) may not register under this section unless it is a joint stock company, and

(b) may not register under this section as an unlimited company or a company limited by guarantee.

(5) A company that is not a joint stock company may not register under this section as a company limited by shares.

(6) The registration of a company under this section is not invalid by reason that it has taken place with a view to the company's being wound up.

[S1040]

NOTES

Commencement: to be appointed.

1041 Definition of "joint stock company"

(1) For the purposes of section 1040 (companies authorised to register under this Act) "joint stock company" means a company—

(a) having a permanent paid-up or nominal share capital of fixed amount divided into shares, also of fixed amount, or held and transferable as stock, or divided and held partly in one way and partly in the other, and

(b) formed on the principle of having for its members the holders of those shares or that stock, and no other persons.

(2) Such a company when registered with limited liability under this Act is deemed a company limited by shares.

[S1041]

NOTES

Commencement: to be appointed.

1042 Power to make provision by regulations

(1) The Secretary of State may make provision by regulations—

(a) for and in connection with registration under section 1040 (companies authorised to register under this Act), and

(b) as to the application to companies so registered of the provisions of the Companies Acts.

(2) Without prejudice to the generality of that power, regulations under this section may make provision corresponding to any provision formerly made by Chapter 2 of Part 22 of the Companies Act 1985 (c 6).

(3) Regulations under this section are subject to negative resolution procedure.

[S1042]

NOTES

Commencement: 20 January 2007 (for the purpose of enabling the exercise of powers to make Orders or Regulations by statutory instrument); to be appointed (otherwise).

CHAPTER 2
UNREGISTERED COMPANIES

1043 Unregistered companies

(1) This section applies to bodies corporate incorporated in and having a principal place of business in the United Kingdom, other than—

- (a) bodies incorporated by, or registered under, a public general Act of Parliament;
- (b) bodies not formed for the purpose of carrying on a business that has for its object the acquisition of gain by the body or its individual members;
- (c) bodies for the time being exempted from this section by direction of the Secretary of State;
- (d) open-ended investment companies.

(2) The Secretary of State may make provision by regulations applying specified provisions of the Companies Acts to all, or any specified description of, the bodies to which this section applies.

(3) The regulations may provide that the specified provisions of the Companies Acts apply subject to any specified limitations and to such adaptations and modifications (if any) as may be specified.

(4) This section does not—

- (a) repeal or revoke in whole or in part any enactment, royal charter or other instrument constituting or regulating any body in relation to which provisions of the Companies Acts are applied by regulations under this section, or
- (b) restrict the power of Her Majesty to grant a charter in lieu or supplementary to any such charter.

But in relation to any such body the operation of any such enactment, charter or instrument is suspended in so far as it is inconsistent with any of those provisions as they apply for the time being to that body.

(5) In this section "specified" means specified in the regulations.

(6) Regulations under this section are subject to negative resolution procedure.

[S1043]

NOTES

Commencement: 20 January 2007 (for the purpose of enabling the exercise of powers to make Orders or Regulations by statutory instrument); 6 April 2007 (otherwise).

Regulations: the Companies Acts (Unregistered Companies) Regulations 2007, SI 2007/318 at **[7607]**.

PART 34
OVERSEAS COMPANIES

Introductory

1044 Overseas companies

In the Companies Acts an "overseas company" means a company incorporated outside the United Kingdom.

[S1044]

NOTES

Commencement: to be appointed.

1045 Company contracts and execution of documents by companies

(1) The Secretary of State may make provision by regulations applying sections 43 to 52 (formalities of doing business and other matters) to overseas companies, subject to such exceptions, adaptations or modifications as may be specified in the regulations.

(2) Regulations under this section are subject to negative resolution procedure.

[S1045]

NOTES

Commencement: 20 January 2007 (for the purpose of enabling the exercise of powers to make Orders or Regulations by statutory instrument); to be appointed (otherwise).

Registration of particulars

1046 Duty to register particulars

(1) The Secretary of State may make provision by regulations requiring an overseas company—

(a) to deliver to the registrar for registration a return containing specified particulars, and

(b) to deliver to the registrar with the return specified documents.

(2) The regulations—

(a) must, in the case of a company other than a Gibraltar company, require the company to register particulars if the company opens a branch in the United Kingdom, and

(b) may, in the case of a Gibraltar company, require the company to register particulars if the company opens a branch in the United Kingdom, and

(c) may, in any case, require the registration of particulars in such other circumstances as may be specified.

(3) In subsection (2)—

"branch" means a branch within the meaning of the Eleventh Company Law Directive (89/666/EEC);

"Gibraltar company" means a company incorporated in Gibraltar.

(4) The regulations may provide that where a company has registered particulars under this section and any alteration is made—

(a) in the specified particulars, or

(b) in any document delivered with the return,

the company must deliver to the registrar for registration a return containing specified particulars of the alteration.

(5) The regulations may make provision—

(a) requiring the return under this section to be delivered for registration to the registrar for a specified part of the United Kingdom, and

(b) requiring it to be so delivered before the end of a specified period.

(6) The regulations may make different provision according to—

(a) the place where the company is incorporated, and

(b) the activities carried on (or proposed to be carried on) by it.

This is without prejudice to the general power to make different provision for different cases.

(7) In this section "specified" means specified in the regulations.

(8) Regulations under this section are subject to affirmative resolution procedure.

[S1046]

NOTES

Commencement: 20 January 2007 (for the purpose of enabling the exercise of powers to make Orders or Regulations by statutory instrument); to be appointed (otherwise).

1047 Registered name of overseas company

(1) Regulations under section 1046 (duty to register particulars) must require an overseas company that is required to register particulars to register its name.

(2) This may be—

(a) the company's corporate name (that is, its name under the law of the country or territory in which it is incorporated) or

(b) an alternative name specified in accordance with section 1048.

(3) Subject only to subsection (5), an EEA company may always register its corporate name.

(4) In any other case, the following provisions of Part 5 (a company's name) apply in relation to the registration of the name of an overseas company—

(a) section 53 (prohibited names);

(b) sections 54 to 56 (sensitive words and expressions);

(c) section 65 (inappropriate use of indications of company type or legal form);

(d) sections 66 to 74 (similarity to other names);

(e) section 75 (provision of misleading information etc);

(f) section 76 (misleading indication of activities).

(5) The provisions of section 57 (permitted characters etc) apply in every case.

(6) Any reference in the provisions mentioned in subsection (4) or (5) to a change of name shall be read as a reference to registration of a different name under section 1048.

[S1047]

NOTES

Commencement: to be appointed.

1048 Registration under alternative name

(1) An overseas company that is required to register particulars under section 1046 may at any time deliver to the registrar for registration a statement specifying a name, other than its corporate name, under which it proposes to carry on business in the United Kingdom.

(2) An overseas company that has registered an alternative name may at any time deliver to the registrar of companies for registration a statement specifying a different name under which it proposes to carry on business in the United Kingdom (which may be its corporate name or a further alternative) in substitution for the name previously registered.

(3) The alternative name for the time being registered under this section is treated for all purposes of the law applying in the United Kingdom as the company's corporate name.

(4) This does not—

(a) affect the references in this section or section 1047 to the company's corporate name,

(b) affect any rights or obligation of the company, or

(c) render defective any legal proceedings by or against the company.

(5) Any legal proceedings that might have been continued or commenced against the company by its corporate name, or any name previously registered under this section, may be continued or commenced against it by its name for the time being so registered.

[S1048]

NOTES

Commencement: to be appointed.

Other requirements

1049 Accounts and reports: general

(1) The Secretary of State may make provision by regulations requiring an overseas company that is required to register particulars under section 1046—

(a) to prepare the like accounts and directors' report, and
(b) to cause to be prepared such an auditor's report,

as would be required if the company were formed and registered under this Act.

(2) The regulations may for this purpose apply, with or without modifications, all or any of the provisions of—

Part 15 (accounts and reports), and
Part 16 (audit).

(3) The Secretary of State may make provision by regulations requiring an overseas company to deliver to the registrar copies of—

(a) the accounts and reports prepared in accordance with the regulations, or
(b) the accounts and reports that it is required to prepare and have audited under the law of the country in which it is incorporated.

(4) Regulations under this section are subject to negative resolution procedure.

[S1049]

NOTES

Commencement: 20 January 2007 (for the purpose of enabling the exercise of powers to make Orders or Regulations by statutory instrument); to be appointed (otherwise).

1050 Accounts and reports: credit or financial institutions

(1) This section applies to a credit or financial institution—

(a) that is incorporated or otherwise formed outside the United Kingdom and Gibraltar,
(b) whose head office is outside the United Kingdom and Gibraltar, and
(c) that has a branch in the United Kingdom.

(2) In subsection (1) "branch" means a place of business that forms a legally dependent part of the institution and conducts directly all or some of the operations inherent in its business.

(3) The Secretary of State may make provision by regulations requiring an institution to which this section applies—

(a) to prepare the like accounts and directors' report, and
(b) to cause to be prepared such an auditor's report,

as would be required if the institution were a company formed and registered under this Act.

(4) The regulations may for this purpose apply, with or without modifications, all or any of the provisions of—

Part 15 (accounts and reports), and
Part 16 (audit).

(5) The Secretary of State may make provision by regulations requiring an institution to which this section applies to deliver to the registrar copies of—

(a) accounts and reports prepared in accordance with the regulations, or
(b) accounts and reports that it is required to prepare and have audited under the law of the country in which the institution has its head office.

(6) Regulations under this section are subject to negative resolution procedure.

[S1050]

NOTES

Commencement: 20 January 2007 (for the purpose of enabling the exercise of powers to make Orders or Regulations by statutory instrument); to be appointed (otherwise).

1051 Trading disclosures

(1) The Secretary of State may by regulations make provision requiring overseas companies carrying on business in the United Kingdom—

(a) to display specified information in specified locations,
(b) to state specified information in specified descriptions of document or communication, and
(c) to provide specified information on request to those they deal with in the course of their business.

(2) The regulations—
(a) shall in every case require a company that has registered particulars under section 1046 to disclose the name registered by it under section 1047, and
(b) may make provision as to the manner in which any specified information is to be displayed, stated or provided.

(3) The regulations may make provision corresponding to that made by—
section 83 (civil consequences of failure to make required disclosure), and
section 84 (criminal consequences of failure to make required disclosure).

(4) In this section "specified" means specified in the regulations.

(5) Regulations under this section are subject to affirmative resolution procedure.

[S1051]

NOTES

Commencement: 20 January 2007 (for the purpose of enabling the exercise of powers to make Orders or Regulations by statutory instrument); to be appointed (otherwise).

1052 Company charges

(1) The Secretary of State may by regulations make provision about the registration of specified charges over property in the United Kingdom of a registered overseas company.

(2) The power in subsection (1) includes power to make provision about—
(a) a registered overseas company that—
(i) has particulars registered in more than one part of the United Kingdom;
(ii) has property in more than one part of the United Kingdom;
(b) the circumstances in which property is to be regarded, for the purposes of the regulations, as being, or not being, in the United Kingdom or in a particular part of the United Kingdom;
(c) the keeping by a registered overseas company of records and registers about specified charges and their inspection;
(d) the consequences of a failure to register a charge in accordance with the regulations;
(e) the circumstances in which a registered overseas company ceases to be subject to the regulations.

(3) The regulations may for this purpose apply, with or without modifications, any of the provisions of Part 25 (company charges).

(4) The regulations may modify any reference in an enactment to Part 25, or to a particular provision of that Part, so as to include a reference to the regulations or to a specified provision of the regulations.

(5) Regulations under this section are subject to negative resolution procedure.

(6) In this section—
"registered overseas company" means an overseas company that has registered particulars under section 1046(1), and
"specified" means specified in the regulations.

[S1052]

NOTES

Commencement: 20 January 2007 (for the purpose of enabling the exercise of powers to make Orders or Regulations by statutory instrument); to be appointed (otherwise).

1053 Other returns etc

(1) This section applies to overseas companies that are required to register particulars under section 1046.

(2) The Secretary of State may make provision by regulations requiring the delivery to the registrar of returns—

(a) by a company to which this section applies that—

(i) is being wound up, or

(ii) becomes or ceases to be subject to insolvency proceedings, or an arrangement or composition or any analogous proceedings;

(b) by the liquidator of a company to which this section applies.

(3) The regulations may specify—

(a) the circumstances in which a return is to be made,

(b) the particulars to be given in it, and

(c) the period within which it is to be made.

(4) The Secretary of State may make provision by regulations requiring notice to be given to the registrar of the appointment in relation to a company to which this section applies of a judicial factor (in Scotland).

(5) The regulations may include provision corresponding to any provision made by section 1154 of this Act (duty to notify registrar of certain appointments).

(6) Regulations under this section are subject to affirmative resolution procedure.

[S1053]

NOTES

Commencement: 20 January 2007 (for the purpose of enabling the exercise of powers to make Orders or Regulations by statutory instrument); to be appointed (otherwise).

Supplementary

1054 Offences

(1) Regulations under this Part may specify the person or persons responsible for complying with any specified requirement of the regulations.

(2) Regulations under this Part may make provision for offences, including provision as to—

(a) the person or persons liable in the case of any specified contravention of the regulations, and

(b) circumstances that are, or are not, to be a defence on a charge of such an offence.

(3) The regulations must not provide—

(a) for imprisonment, or

(b) for the imposition on summary conviction of a fine exceeding level 5 on the standard scale and, for continued contravention, a daily default fine not exceeding one-tenth of level 5 on the standard scale.

(4) In this section "specified" means specified in the regulations.

[S1054]

NOTES

Commencement: 20 January 2007 (for the purpose of enabling the exercise of powers to make Orders or Regulations by statutory instrument); to be appointed (otherwise).

1055 Disclosure of individual's residential address: protection from disclosure

Where regulations under section 1046 (overseas companies: duty to register particulars) require an overseas company to register particulars of an individual's usual residential address, they must contain provision corresponding to that made by Chapter 8 of Part 10 (directors' residential addresses: protection from disclosure).

[S1055]

NOTES

Commencement: 20 January 2007 (for the purpose of enabling the exercise of powers to make Orders or Regulations by statutory instrument); to be appointed (otherwise).

1056 Requirement to identify persons authorised to accept service of documents

Regulations under section 1046 (overseas companies: duty to register particulars) must require an overseas company to register—

(a) particulars identifying every person resident in the United Kingdom authorised to accept service of documents on behalf of the company, or

(b) a statement that there is no such person.

[S1056]

NOTES

Commencement: 20 January 2007 (for the purpose of enabling the exercise of powers to make Orders or Regulations by statutory instrument); to be appointed (otherwise).

1057 Registrar to whom returns, notices etc to be delivered

(1) This section applies to an overseas company that is required to register or has registered particulars under section 1046 in more than one part of the United Kingdom.

(2) The Secretary of State may provide by regulations that, in the case of such a company, anything authorised or required to be delivered to the registrar under this Part is to be delivered—

(a) to the registrar for each part of the United Kingdom in which the company is required to register or has registered particulars, or

(b) to the registrar for such part or parts of the United Kingdom as may be specified in or determined in accordance with the regulations.

(3) Regulations under this section are subject to negative resolution procedure.

[S1057]

NOTES

Commencement: 20 January 2007 (for the purpose of enabling the exercise of powers to make Orders or Regulations by statutory instrument); to be appointed (otherwise).

1058 Duty to give notice of ceasing to have registrable presence

(1) The Secretary of State may make provision by regulations requiring an overseas company—

(a) if it has registered particulars following the opening of a branch, in accordance with regulations under section 1046(2)(a) or (b), to give notice to the registrar if it closes that branch;

(b) if it has registered particulars in other circumstances, in accordance with regulations under section 1046(2)(c), to give notice to the registrar if the circumstances that gave rise to the obligation to register particulars cease to obtain.

(2) The regulations must provide for the notice to be given to the registrar for the part of the United Kingdom to which the original return of particulars was delivered.

(3) The regulations may specify the period within which notice must be given.

(4) Regulations under this section are subject to negative resolution procedure.

[S1058]

NOTES

Commencement: 20 January 2007 (for the purpose of enabling the exercise of powers to make Orders or Regulations by statutory instrument); to be appointed (otherwise).

1059 Application of provisions in case of relocation of branch

For the purposes of this Part—

(a) the relocation of a branch from one part of the United Kingdom to another counts as the closing of one branch and the opening of another;

(b) the relocation of a branch within the same part of the United Kingdom does not.

[S1059]

NOTES

Commencement: to be appointed.

PART 35
THE REGISTRAR OF COMPANIES

The registrar

1060 The registrar

(1) There shall continue to be—

(a) a registrar of companies for England and Wales,

(b) a registrar of companies for Scotland, and

(c) a registrar of companies for Northern Ireland.

(2) The registrars shall be appointed by the Secretary of State.

(3) In the Companies Acts "the registrar of companies" and "the registrar" mean the registrar of companies for England and Wales, Scotland or Northern Ireland, as the case may require.

(4) References in the Companies Acts to registration in a particular part of the United Kingdom are to registration by the registrar for that part of the United Kingdom.

[S1060]

NOTES

Commencement: 6 April 2007 (certain purposes); to be appointed (otherwise) (see the note below).

Note: the Companies Act 2006 (Commencement No 1, Transitional Provisions and Savings) Order 2006, SI 2006/3428, art 4(3) provides that this section shall come into force on 6 April 2007 so far as is necessary for the purposes of the provisions of this Act brought into force on that date by art 4(1), (2) of that Order (see **[7577]**).

1061 The registrar's functions

(1) The registrar shall continue—

(a) to perform the functions conferred on the registrar—

(i) under the Companies Acts, and

(ii) under the enactments listed in subsection (2), and

(b) to perform such functions on behalf of the Secretary of State, in relation to the registration of companies or other matters, as the Secretary of State may from time to time direct.

(2) The enactments are—

the Joint Stock Companies Acts;

the Newspaper Libel and Registration Act 1881 (c 60);

the Limited Partnerships Act 1907 (c 24);

section 53 of the Industrial and Provident Societies Act 1965 (c 12) or, for Northern Ireland, section 62 of the Industrial and Provident Societies Act (Northern Ireland) 1969 (c 24 (NI));

the Insolvency Act 1986 (c 45) or, for Northern Ireland, the Insolvency (Northern Ireland) Order 1989 (SI 1989/2405 (NI 19));

section 12 of the Statutory Water Companies Act 1991 (c 58);

sections 3, 4, 6, 63 and 64 of, and Schedule 1 to, the Housing Act 1996 (c 52) or, for Northern Ireland, Articles 3 and 16 to 32 of the Housing (Northern Ireland) Order 1992 (SI 1992/1725 (NI 15));

sections 2, 4 and 26 of the Commonwealth Development Corporation Act 1999 (c 20);

Part 6 and section 366 of the Financial Services and Markets Act 2000 (c 8);

the Limited Liability Partnerships Act 2000 (c 12);

section 14 of the Insolvency Act 2000 (c 39) or, for Northern Ireland, Article 11 of the Insolvency (Northern Ireland) Order 2002 (SI 2002/ 3152 (NI 6));

section 121 of the Land Registration Act 2002 (c 9);

section 1248 of this Act.

(3) References in this Act to the functions of the registrar are to functions within subsection (1)(a) or (b).

[S1061]

NOTES

Commencement: 6 April 2007 (certain purposes); to be appointed (otherwise) (see the note below).

Note: the Companies Act 2006 (Commencement No 1, Transitional Provisions and Savings) Order 2006, SI 2006/3428, art 4(3) provides that this section shall come into force on 6 April 2007 so far as is necessary for the purposes of the provisions of this Act brought into force on that date by art 4(1), (2) of that Order (see **[7577]**).

1062 The registrar's official seal

The registrar shall have an official seal for the authentication of documents in connection with the performance of the registrar's functions.

[S1062]

NOTES

Commencement: to be appointed.

1063 Fees payable to registrar

(1) The Secretary of State may make provision by regulations requiring the payment to the registrar of fees in respect of—

(a) the performance of any of the registrar's functions, or

(b) the provision by the registrar of services or facilities for purposes incidental to, or otherwise connected with, the performance of any of the registrar's functions.

(2) The matters for which fees may be charged include—

(a) the performance of a duty imposed on the registrar or the Secretary of State,

(b) the receipt of documents delivered to the registrar, and

(c) the inspection, or provision of copies, of documents kept by the registrar.

(3) The regulations may—

(a) provide for the amount of the fees to be fixed by or determined under the regulations;

(b) provide for different fees to be payable in respect of the same matter in different circumstances;

(c) specify the person by whom any fee payable under the regulations is to be paid;

(d) specify when and how fees are to be paid.

(4) Regulations under this section are subject to negative resolution procedure.

(5) In respect of the performance of functions or the provision of services or facilities—

(a) for which fees are not provided for by regulations, or

(b) in circumstances other than those for which fees are provided for by regulations,

the registrar may determine from time to time what fees (if any) are chargeable.

(6) Fees received by the registrar are to be paid into the Consolidated Fund.

(7) (*Amends the Limited Partnerships Act 1907, ss 16, 17 at* **[3067]**, **[3068]**.)

[S1063]

NOTES

Commencement: 20 January 2007 (for the purpose of enabling the exercise of powers to make Orders or Regulations by statutory instrument); 6 April 2007 (otherwise (except in relation to Northern Ireland)).

Transitional provisions: the Companies Act 2006 (Commencement No 1, Transitional Provisions and Savings) Order 2006, SI 2006/3428, Sch 5, para 6(1), (2) (at **[7591]**) provides as follows—

"6 Saving for existing provisions relating to fees

(1) The coming into force of section 1063 of the Companies Act 2006 (fees payable to the registrar) does not affect the continued operation of any other provision under which the payment of fees to the registrar of companies may be required until—

(a) the coming into force of the repeal of the other provision; or

(b) the exercise of the power in section 1063 in a manner inconsistent with its continued operation.

(2) Notwithstanding the coming into force of the repeals in section 16 of the Limited Partnerships Act 1907 and the repeal of section 17(a) of that Act, the fees appointed under the said section 16 and having effect immediately before 6th April 2007 shall continue to be payable, and the rules in force under the said section 17(a) immediately before 6th April 2007 shall continue to have effect.".

Note: the commencement of this section on 6 April 2007 by SI 2006/3428 does not extend to Northern Ireland (see art 4(4) of that Order at **[7577]**).

Certificates of incorporation

1064 Public notice of issue of certificate of incorporation

(1) The registrar must cause to be published—

(a) in the Gazette, or

(b) in accordance with section 1116 (alternative means of giving public notice),

notice of the issue by the registrar of any certificate of incorporation of a company.

(2) The notice must state the name and registered number of the company and the date of issue of the certificate.

(3) This section applies to a certificate of incorporation issued under—

(a) section 80 (change of name),

(b) section 88 (Welsh companies), or

(c) any provision of Part 7 (re-registration),

as well as to the certificate issued on a company's formation.

[S1064]

NOTES

Commencement: to be appointed.

1065 Right to certificate of incorporation

Any person may require the registrar to provide him with a copy of any certificate of incorporation of a company, signed by the registrar or authenticated by the registrar's seal.

[S1065]

NOTES

Commencement: to be appointed.

Registered numbers

1066 Company's registered numbers

(1) The registrar shall allocate to every company a number, which shall be known as the company's registered number.

(2) Companies' registered numbers shall be in such form, consisting of one or more sequences of figures or letters, as the registrar may determine.

(3) The registrar may on adopting a new form of registered number make such changes of existing registered numbers as appear necessary.

(4) A change of a company's registered number has effect from the date on which the company is notified by the registrar of the change.

(5) For a period of three years beginning with that date any requirement to disclose the company's registered number imposed by regulations under section 82 or section 1051 (trading disclosures) is satisfied by the use of either the old number or the new.

(6) In this section "company" includes an overseas company whose particulars have been registered under section 1046, other than a company that appears to the registrar not to be required to register particulars under that section.

[S1066]

NOTES

Commencement: to be appointed.

1067 Registered numbers of branches of overseas company

(1) The registrar shall allocate to every branch of an overseas company whose particulars are registered under section 1046 a number, which shall be known as the branch's registered number.

(2) Branches' registered numbers shall be in such form, consisting of one or more sequences of figures or letters, as the registrar may determine.

(3) The registrar may on adopting a new form of registered number make such changes of existing registered numbers as appear necessary.

(4) A change of a branch's registered number has effect from the date on which the company is notified by the registrar of the change.

(5) For a period of three years beginning with that date any requirement to disclose the branch's registered number imposed by regulations under section 1051 (trading disclosures) is satisfied by the use of either the old number or the new.

[S1067]

NOTES

Commencement: to be appointed.

Delivery of documents to the registrar

1068 Registrar's requirements as to form, authentication and manner of delivery

(1) The registrar may impose requirements as to the form, authentication and manner of delivery of documents required or authorised to be delivered to the registrar under any enactment.

(2) As regards the form of the document, the registrar may—

(a) require the contents of the document to be in a standard form;
(b) impose requirements for the purpose of enabling the document to be scanned or copied.

(3) As regards authentication, the registrar may—

(a) require the document to be authenticated by a particular person or a person of a particular description;
(b) specify the means of authentication;
(c) require the document to contain or be accompanied by the name or registered number of the company to which it relates (or both).

(4) As regards the manner of delivery, the registrar may specify requirements as to—

(a) the physical form of the document (for example, hard copy or electronic form);
(b) the means to be used for delivering the document (for example, by post or electronic means);
(c) the address to which the document is to be sent;
(d) in the case of a document to be delivered by electronic means, the hardware and software to be used, and technical specifications (for example, matters relating to protocol, security, anti-virus protection or encryption).

(5) The registrar must secure that as from 1st January 2007 all documents subject to the Directive disclosure requirements (see section 1078) may be delivered to the registrar by electronic means.

(6) The power conferred by this section does not authorise the registrar to require documents to be delivered by electronic means (see section 1069).

(7) Requirements imposed under this section must not be inconsistent with requirements imposed by any enactment with respect to the form, authentication or manner of delivery of the document concerned.

[S1068]

NOTES

Commencement: 1 January 2007 (sub-s (5), and sub-ss (1)–(4), (6), (7) for certain purposes); 15 December 2007 (sub-ss (1)–(4), (6), (7) for certain purposes); to be appointed (otherwise) (see the notes below).

Note: the Companies Act 2006 (Commencement No 1, Transitional Provisions and Savings) Order 2006, SI 2006/3428, art 2(2) provides that that sub-ss (1)–(4), (6), (7) shall come into force on 1 January 2007 so far as is necessary for the purposes of the provisions of this Act brought into force on that date by art 2(1) of that Order (see **[7575]**).

Note: the draft Companies Act 2006 (Commencement No 3, Consequential Amendments, Transitional Provisions and Savings) Order 2007, art 4(1) provides that sub-ss (1)–(4), (6), (7) shall come into force on

15 December 2007 so far as necessary for the purposes of any Regulations made before that date in implementation of Directive 2005/56/EC of the European Parliament and of the Council on cross-border mergers of limited liability companies (see **[A12]**).

1069 Power to require delivery by electronic means

(1) The Secretary of State may make regulations requiring documents that are authorised or required to be delivered to the registrar to be delivered by electronic means.

(2) Any such requirement to deliver documents by electronic means is effective only if registrar's rules have been published with respect to the detailed requirements for such delivery.

(3) Regulations under this section are subject to affirmative resolution procedure.

[S1069]

NOTES

Commencement: 20 January 2007 (for the purpose of enabling the exercise of powers to make Orders or Regulations by statutory instrument); to be appointed (otherwise).

1070 Agreement for delivery by electronic means

(1) The registrar may agree with a company that documents relating to the company that are required or authorised to be delivered to the registrar—

- (a) will be delivered by electronic means, except as provided for in the agreement, and
- (b) will conform to such requirements as may be specified in the agreement or specified by the registrar in accordance with the agreement.

(2) An agreement under this section may relate to all or any description of documents to be delivered to the registrar.

(3) Documents in relation to which an agreement is in force under this section must be delivered in accordance with the agreement.

[S1070]

NOTES

Commencement: to be appointed.

1071 Document not delivered until received

(1) A document is not delivered to the registrar until it is received by the registrar.

(2) Provision may be made by registrar's rules as to when a document is to be regarded as received.

[S1071]

NOTES

Commencement: to be appointed.

Requirements for proper delivery

1072 Requirements for proper delivery

(1) A document delivered to the registrar is not properly delivered unless all the following requirements are met—

- (a) the requirements of the provision under which the document is to be delivered to the registrar as regards—
  - (i) the contents of the document, and
  - (ii) form, authentication and manner of delivery;
- (b) any applicable requirements under—

  section 1068 (registrar's requirements as to form, authentication and manner of delivery),

  section 1069 (power to require delivery by electronic means), or

  section 1070 (agreement for delivery by electronic means);

(c) any requirements of this Part as to the language in which the document is drawn up and delivered or as to its being accompanied on delivery by a certified translation into English;
(d) in so far as it consists of or includes names and addresses, any requirements of this Part as to permitted characters, letters or symbols or as to its being accompanied on delivery by a certificate as to the transliteration of any element;
(e) any applicable requirements under section 1111 (registrar's requirements as to certification or verification);
(f) any requirement of regulations under section 1082 (use of unique identifiers);
(g) any requirements as regards payment of a fee in respect of its receipt by the registrar.

(2) A document that is not properly delivered is treated for the purposes of the provision requiring or authorising it to be delivered as not having been delivered, subject to the provisions of section 1073 (power to accept documents not meeting requirements for proper delivery).

[S1072]

NOTES

Commencement: to be appointed.

1073 Power to accept documents not meeting requirements for proper delivery

(1) The registrar may accept (and register) a document that does not comply with the requirements for proper delivery.

(2) A document accepted by the registrar under this section is treated as received by the registrar for the purposes of section 1077 (public notice of receipt of certain documents).

(3) No objection may be taken to the legal consequences of a document's being accepted (or registered) by the registrar under this section on the ground that the requirements for proper delivery were not met.

(4) The acceptance of a document by the registrar under this section does not affect—
(a) the continuing obligation to comply with the requirements for proper delivery, or
(b) subject as follows, any liability for failure to comply with those requirements.

(5) For the purposes of—
(a) section 453 (civil penalty for failure to file accounts and reports), and
(b) any enactment imposing a daily default fine for failure to deliver the document,

the period after the document is accepted does not count as a period during which there is default in complying with the requirements for proper delivery.

(6) But if, subsequently—
(a) the registrar issues a notice under section 1094(4) in respect of the document (notice of administrative removal from the register), and
(b) the requirements for proper delivery are not complied with before the end of the period of 14 days after the issue of that notice,

any subsequent period of default does count for the purposes of those provisions.

[S1073]

NOTES

Commencement: to be appointed.

1074 Documents containing unnecessary material

(1) This section applies where a document delivered to the registrar contains unnecessary material.

(2) "Unnecessary material" means material that—
(a) is not necessary in order to comply with an obligation under any enactment, and
(b) is not specifically authorised to be delivered to the registrar.

(3) For this purpose an obligation to deliver a document of a particular description, or conforming to certain requirements, is regarded as not extending to anything that is not needed for a document of that description or, as the case may be, conforming to those requirements.

(4) If the unnecessary material cannot readily be separated from the rest of the document, the document is treated as not meeting the requirements for proper delivery.

(5) If the unnecessary material can readily be separated from the rest of the document, the registrar may register the document either—

(a) with the omission of the unnecessary material, or

(b) as delivered.

[S1074]

NOTES

Commencement: to be appointed.

1075 Informal correction of document

(1) A document delivered to the registrar may be corrected by the registrar if it appears to the registrar to be incomplete or internally inconsistent.

(2) This power is exercisable only—

(a) on instructions, and

(b) if the company has given (and has not withdrawn) its consent to instructions being given under this section.

(3) The following requirements must be met as regards the instructions—

(a) the instructions must be given in response to an enquiry by the registrar;

(b) the registrar must be satisfied that the person giving the instructions is authorised to do so—

(i) by the person by whom the document was delivered, or

(ii) by the company to which the document relates;

(c) the instructions must meet any requirements of registrar's rules as to—

(i) the form and manner in which they are given, and

(ii) authentication.

(4) The company's consent to instructions being given under this section (and any withdrawal of such consent)—

(a) may be in hard copy or electronic form, and

(b) must be notified to the registrar.

(5) This section applies in relation to documents delivered under Part 25 (company charges) by a person other than the company as if the references to the company were to the company or the person by whom the document was delivered.

(6) A document that is corrected under this section is treated, for the purposes of any enactment relating to its delivery, as having been delivered when the correction is made.

(7) The power conferred by this section is not exercisable if the document has been registered under section 1073 (power to accept documents not meeting requirements for proper delivery).

[S1075]

NOTES

Commencement: to be appointed.

1076 Replacement of document not meeting requirements for proper delivery

(1) The registrar may accept a replacement for a document previously delivered that—

(a) did not comply with the requirements for proper delivery, or

(b) contained unnecessary material (within the meaning of section 1074).

(2) A replacement document must not be accepted unless the registrar is satisfied that it is delivered by—

(a) the person by whom the original document was delivered, or

(b) the company to which the original document relates, and that it complies with the requirements for proper delivery.

(3) The power of the registrar to impose requirements as to the form and manner of delivery includes power to impose requirements as to the identification of the original document and the delivery of the replacement in a form and manner enabling it to be associated with the original.

(4) This section does not apply where the original document was delivered under Part 25 (company charges) (but see sections 873 and 888 (rectification of register of charges)).
[S1076]

NOTES

Commencement: to be appointed.

Public notice of receipt of certain documents

1077 Public notice of receipt of certain documents

(1) The registrar must cause to be published—

(a) in the Gazette, or

(b) in accordance with section 1116 (alternative means of giving public notice),

notice of the receipt by the registrar of any document that, on receipt, is subject to the Directive disclosure requirements (see section 1078).

(2) The notice must state the name and registered number of the company, the description of document and the date of receipt.

(3) The registrar is not required to cause notice of the receipt of a document to be published before the date of incorporation of the company to which the document relates.
[S1077]

NOTES

Commencement: 1 January 2007.

Transitional adaptations: art 5 of the Companies Act 2006 (Commencement No 1, Transitional Provisions and Savings) Order 2006, SI 2006/3428 provides that the provisions brought into force by arts 2–4 of 2006 Order shall have effect subject to any transitional adaptations specified in Sch 1 to that Order. Schedule 1, para 4 to the Order (at **[7582]**) provides as follows—

"**4.**—(1) Section 1077 (public notice of receipt of certain documents) has effect with the following adaptation.

(2) Omit subsection (1)(b).".

1078 Documents subject to Directive disclosure requirements

(1) The documents subject to the "Directive disclosure requirements" are as follows.

The requirements referred to are those of Article 3 of the First Company Law Directive (68/151/EEC), as amended, extended and applied.

(2) In the case of every company—

Constitutional documents

1. The company's memorandum and articles.
2. Any amendment of the company's articles (including every resolution or agreement required to be embodied in or annexed to copies of the company's articles issued by the company).
3. After any amendment of the company's articles, the text of the articles as amended.
4. Any notice of a change of the company's name.

Directors

1. The statement of proposed officers required on formation of the company.
2. Notification of any change among the company's directors.
3. Notification of any change in the particulars of directors required to be delivered to the registrar.

Accounts, reports and returns

1. All documents required to be delivered to the registrar under section 441 (annual accounts and reports).
2. The company's annual return.

Registered office

Notification of any change of the company's registered office.

Winding up

1. Copy of any winding-up order in respect of the company.

2. Notice of the appointment of liquidators.
3. Order for the dissolution of a company on a winding up.
4. Return by a liquidator of the final meeting of a company on a winding up.

(3) In the case of a public company—

Share capital

1. Any statement of capital and initial shareholdings.
2. Any return of allotment and the statement of capital accompanying it.
3. Copy of any resolution under section 570 or 571 (disapplication of pre-emption rights).
4. Copy of any report under section 593 or 599 as to the value of a non-cash asset.
5. Statement of capital accompanying notice given under section 625 (notice by company of redenomination of shares).
6. Statement of capital accompanying notice given under section 627 (notice by company of reduction of capital in connection with redenomination of shares).
7. Notice delivered under section 636 (notice of new name of class of shares) or 637 (notice of variation of rights attached to shares).
8. Statement of capital accompanying order delivered under section 649 (order of court confirming reduction of capital).
9. Notification (under section 689) of the redemption of shares and the statement of capital accompanying it.
10. Statement of capital accompanying return delivered under section 708 (notice of cancellation of shares on purchase of own shares) or 730 (notice of cancellation of shares held as treasury shares).
11. Any statement of compliance delivered under section 762 (statement that company meets conditions for issue of trading certificate).

Mergers and divisions

1. Copy of any draft of the terms of a scheme required to be delivered to the registrar under section 906 or 921.
2. Copy of any order under section 899 or 900 in respect of a compromise or arrangement to which Part 27 (mergers and divisions of public companies) applies.

(4) Where a private company re-registers as a public company (see section 96)—

(a) the last statement of capital relating to the company received by the registrar under any provision of the Companies Acts becomes subject to the Directive disclosure requirements, and

(b) section 1077 (public notice of receipt of certain documents) applies as if the statement had been received by the registrar when the re-registration takes effect.

(5) In the case of an overseas company, such particulars, returns and other documents required to be delivered under Part 34 as may be specified by the Secretary of State by regulations.

(6) Regulations under subsection (5) are subject to negative resolution procedure.

[S1078]

NOTES

Commencement: 1 January 2007.

Transitional adaptations: art 5 of the Companies Act 2006 (Commencement No 1, Transitional Provisions and Savings) Order 2006, SI 2006/3428 provides that the provisions brought into force by arts 2–4 of 2006 Order shall have effect subject to any transitional adaptations specified in Sch 1 to that Order. Schedule 1, para 5 to the Order (at **[7582]**) provides as follows—

"**5.**—(1) Section 1078 (documents subject to Directive disclosure requirements) has effect with the following adaptations.

(2) In subsection (2) (documents relating to any company)—

(a) under the heading "*Constitutional documents*"—

(i) in item 2 for "Any amendment of the company's articles" substitute "Any amendment of the company's memorandum or articles";

(ii) for item 3 substitute—

"3. After any amendment of the company's memorandum or articles, the text of the document as amended.";

(iii) omit item 4;

(b) under the heading "*Accounts, reports and returns*", in item 1 for "441" substitute "242 of the Companies Act 1985 or Article 250 of the Companies (Northern Ireland) Order 1986".

(3) In subsection (3) (documents relating to public company)—

(a) under the heading "*Share capital*"—

(i) in item 2 omit "and the statement of capital accompanying it";

(ii) in item 3 for "section 570 or 571" substitute "section 95(1), (2) or (3) of the Companies Act 1985 or Article 105(1), (2) or (3) of the Companies (Northern Ireland) Order 1986";

(iii) in item 4 for "section 593 or 599" substitute "section 103 or 104 of the Companies Act 1985 or Article 113 or 114 of the Companies (Northern Ireland) Order 1986";

(iv) omit items 5 and 6;

(v) for item 7 substitute—

"7. Statement or notice delivered under section 128 of the Companies Act 1985 or Article 138 of the Companies (Northern Ireland) Order 1986 (registration of particulars of special rights).";

(vi) omit item 8;

(vii) in item 9 for "section 689" substitute "section 122 of the Companies Act 1985 or Article 132 of the Companies (Northern Ireland) Order 1986" and omit "and the statement of capital accompanying it";

(viii) omit item 10;

(ix) for item 11 substitute—

"11. Any statutory declaration or statement delivered under section 117 of the Companies Act 1985 or Article 127 of the Companies (Northern Ireland) Order 1986 (public company share capital requirements).";

(b) under the heading "*Mergers and divisions*"—

(i) in item 1 for "section 906 or 921" substitute "paragraph 2(1) of Schedule 15B to the Companies Act 1985 or paragraph 2(1) of Schedule 15B to the Companies (Northern Ireland) Order 1986";

(ii) in item 2 for "section 899 or 900 in respect of a compromise or arrangement to which Part 27 (mergers and divisions of public companies) applies" substitute "section 425(2) or 427 of that Act in respect of a compromise or arrangement to which section 427A of that Act applies or under Article 418(2) or 420 of that Order in respect of a compromise or arrangement to which Article 420A of that Order applies".

(4) Omit subsection (4).

(5) For subsections (5) and (6) (power to make provision for documents relating to overseas company) substitute—

"(5) In the case of a company incorporated outside the United Kingdom or a credit or financial institution to which section 699A of the Companies Act 1985 or Article 648A of the Companies (Northern Ireland) Order 1986 applies—

1. Any return delivered under paragraph 1, 7 or 8 of Schedule 21A to that Act or paragraph 1, 7 or 8 of Schedule 20A to that Order (branch registration).
2. Any document delivered under paragraph 1 or 8 of Schedule 21A to that Act or under paragraph 1 or 8 of Schedule 20A to that Order.
3. Any notice under section 695A(3) of that Act or Article 645A of that Order of the closure of a branch.
4. Any document delivered under Schedule 21C to that Act or Schedule 20C to that Order (accounts and reports of foreign credit and financial institutions).
5. Any document delivered under Schedule 21D to that Act or Schedule 20D to that Order (accounts and reports of companies subject to branch registration, other than credit and financial institutions).
6. Any return delivered under section 703P of that Act or Article 652O of that Order (particulars on winding up).".

1079 Effect of failure to give public notice

(1) A company is not entitled to rely against other persons on the happening of any event to which this section applies unless—

(a) the event has been officially notified at the material time, or

(b) the company shows that the person concerned knew of the event at the material time.

(2) The events to which this section applies are—

(a) an amendment of the company's articles,

(b) a change among the company's directors,

(c) (as regards service of any document on the company) a change of the company's registered office,

(d) the making of a winding-up order in respect of the company, or

(e) the appointment of a liquidator in a voluntary winding up of the company.

(3) If the material time falls—

(a) on or before the 15th day after the date of official notification, or

(b) where the 15th day was not a working day, on or before the next day that was, the company is not entitled to rely on the happening of the event as against a person who shows that he was unavoidably prevented from knowing of the event at that time.

(4) "Official notification" means—

(a) in relation to an amendment of the company's articles, notification in accordance with section 1077 (public notice of receipt by registrar of certain documents) of the amendment and the amended text of the articles;

(b) in relation to anything else stated in a document subject to the Directive disclosure requirements, notification of that document in accordance with that section;

(c) in relation to the appointment of a liquidator in a voluntary winding up, notification of that event in accordance with section 109 of the Insolvency Act 1986 (c 45) or Article 95 of the Insolvency (Northern Ireland) Order 1989 (SI 1989/2405 (NI 19)).

[S1079]

NOTES

Commencement: 1 January 2007.

Transitional adaptations: art 5 of the Companies Act 2006 (Commencement No 1, Transitional Provisions and Savings) Order 2006, SI 2006/3428 provides that the provisions brought into force by arts 2–4 of 2006 Order shall have effect subject to any transitional adaptations specified in Sch 1 to that Order. Schedule 1, para 6 to the Order (at **[7582]**) provides as follows—

"**6.**—(1) Section 1079 (effect of failure to give public notice) has effect with the following adaptations.

(2) In subsection (2)(a) and subsection (4)(a) for "amendment of the company's articles" substitute "amendment of the company's memorandum or articles".".

The register

1080 The register

(1) The registrar shall continue to keep records of—

(a) the information contained in documents delivered to the registrar under any enactment,

(b) certificates of incorporation issued by the registrar, and

(c) certificates issued by the registrar under section 869(5) or 885(4) (certificates of registration of charge).

(2) The records relating to companies are referred to collectively in the Companies Acts as "the register".

(3) Information deriving from documents subject to the Directive disclosure requirements (see section 1078) that are delivered to the registrar on or after 1st January 2007 must be kept by the registrar in electronic form.

(4) Subject to that, information contained in documents delivered to the registrar may be recorded and kept in any form the registrar thinks fit, provided it is possible to inspect it and produce a copy of it.

This is sufficient compliance with any duty of the registrar to keep, file or register the document or to record the information contained in it.

(5) The records kept by the registrar must be such that information relating to a company is associated with that company, in such manner as the registrar may determine, so as to enable all the information relating to the company to be retrieved.

[S1080]

NOTES

Commencement: 1 January 2007.

Transitional adaptations: art 5 of the Companies Act 2006 (Commencement No 1, Transitional Provisions and Savings) Order 2006, SI 2006/3428 provides that the provisions brought into force by arts 2–4 of 2006 Order shall have effect subject to any transitional adaptations specified in Sch 1 to that Order. Schedule 1, para 7 to the Order (at **[7582]**) provides as follows—

"**7.**—(1) Section 1080 (the register) has effect with the following adaptation.

(2) In subsection (1)(c), for "section 869(5) or 885(4)" substitute "section 401(2) or 418 of the Companies Act 1985 or Article 409(3) of the Companies (Northern Ireland) Order 1986".".

1081 Annotation of the register

(1) The registrar must place a note in the register recording—

(a) the date on which a document is delivered to the registrar;

(b) if a document is corrected under section 1075, the nature and date of the correction;

(c) if a document is replaced (whether or not material derived from it is removed), the fact that it has been replaced and the date of delivery of the replacement;

(d) if material is removed—

(i) what was removed (giving a general description of its contents),

(ii) under what power, and

(iii) the date on which that was done.

(2) The Secretary of State may make provision by regulations—

(a) authorising or requiring the registrar to annotate the register in such other circumstances as may be specified in the regulations, and

(b) as to the contents of any such annotation.

(3) No annotation is required in the case of a document that by virtue of section 1072(2) (documents not meeting requirements for proper delivery) is treated as not having been delivered.

(4) A note may be removed if it no longer serves any useful purpose.

(5) Any duty or power of the registrar with respect to annotation of the register is subject to the court's power under section 1097 (powers of court on ordering removal of material from the register) to direct—

(a) that a note be removed from the register, or

(b) that no note shall be made of the removal of material that is the subject of the court's order.

(6) Notes placed in the register in accordance with subsection (1), or in pursuance of regulations under subsection (2), are part of the register for all purposes of the Companies Acts.

(7) Regulations under this section are subject to negative resolution procedure.

[S1081]

NOTES

Commencement: 20 January 2007 (for the purpose of enabling the exercise of powers to make Orders or Regulations by statutory instrument); to be appointed (otherwise).

1082 Allocation of unique identifiers

(1) The Secretary of State may make provision for the use, in connection with the register, of reference numbers ("unique identifiers") to identify each person who—

(a) is a director of a company,

(b) is secretary (or a joint secretary) of a company, or

(c) in the case of an overseas company whose particulars are registered under section 1046, holds any such position as may be specified for the purposes of this section by regulations under that section.

(2) The regulations may—

(a) provide that a unique identifier may be in such form, consisting of one or more sequences of letters or numbers, as the registrar may from time to time determine;

(b) make provision for the allocation of unique identifiers by the registrar;

(c) require there to be included, in any specified description of documents delivered to the registrar, as well as a statement of the person's name—

(i) a statement of the person's unique identifier, or

(ii) a statement that the person has not been allocated a unique identifier;

(d) enable the registrar to take steps where a person appears to have more than one unique identifier to discontinue the use of all but one of them.

(3) The regulations may contain provision for the application of the scheme in relation to persons appointed, and documents registered, before the commencement of this Act.

(4) The regulations may make different provision for different descriptions of person and different descriptions of document.

(5) Regulations under this section are subject to affirmative resolution procedure.

[S1082]

NOTES

Commencement: 20 January 2007 (for the purpose of enabling the exercise of powers to make Orders or Regulations by statutory instrument); to be appointed (otherwise).

1083 Preservation of original documents

(1) The originals of documents delivered to the registrar in hard copy form must be kept for three years after they are received by the registrar, after which they may be destroyed provided the information contained in them has been recorded in the register.

This is subject to section 1087(3) (extent of obligation to retain material not available for public inspection).

(2) The registrar is under no obligation to keep the originals of documents delivered in electronic form, provided the information contained in them has been recorded in the register.

(3) This section applies to documents held by the registrar when this section comes into force as well as to documents subsequently received.

[S1083]

NOTES

Commencement: to be appointed.

1084 Records relating to companies that have been dissolved etc

(1) This section applies where—

(a) a company is dissolved,

(b) an overseas company ceases to have any connection with the United Kingdom by virtue of which it is required to register particulars under section 1046, or

(c) a credit or financial institution ceases to be within section 1050 (overseas institutions required to file accounts with the registrar).

(2) At any time after two years from the date on which it appears to the registrar that—

(a) the company has been dissolved,

(b) the overseas company has ceased to have any connection with the United Kingdom by virtue of which it is required to register particulars under section 1046, or

(c) the credit or financial institution has ceased to be within section 1050 (overseas institutions required to file accounts with the registrar),

the registrar may direct that records relating to the company or institution may be removed to the Public Record Office or, as the case may be, the Public Record Office of Northern Ireland.

(3) Records in respect of which such a direction is given shall be disposed of under the enactments relating to that Office and the rules made under them.

(4) In subsection (1)(a) "company" includes a company provisionally or completely registered under the Joint Stock Companies Act 1844 (c 110).

(5) This section does not extend to Scotland.

[S1084]

NOTES

Commencement: to be appointed.

Inspection etc of the register

1085 Inspection of the register

(1) Any person may inspect the register.

(2) The right of inspection extends to the originals of documents delivered to the registrar in hard copy form if, and only if, the record kept by the registrar of the contents of the document is illegible or unavailable.

The period for which such originals are to be kept is limited by section 1083(1).

(3) This section has effect subject to section 1087 (material not available for public inspection).

[S1085]

NOTES

Commencement: 1 January 2007.

Transitional adaptations: art 5 of the Companies Act 2006 (Commencement No 1, Transitional Provisions and Savings) Order 2006, SI 2006/3428 provides that the provisions brought into force by arts 2–4 of 2006 Order shall have effect subject to any transitional adaptations specified in Sch 1 to that Order. Schedule 1, para 8 to the Order (at **[7582]**) provides as follows—

"**8.—**(1) Section 1085 (inspection of the register) has effect with the following adaptation.

(2) In subsection (2) for "section 1083(1)" substitute "section 707A(2) of the Companies Act 1985 or Article 656A(2) of the Companies (Northern Ireland) Order 1986".".

1086 Right to copy of material on the register

(1) Any person may require a copy of any material on the register.

(2) The fee for any such copy of material derived from a document subject to the Directive disclosure requirements (see section 1078), whether in hard copy or electronic form, must not exceed the administrative cost of providing it.

(3) This section has effect subject to section 1087 (material not available for public inspection).

[S1086]

NOTES

Commencement: 1 January 2007.

1087 Material not available for public inspection

(1) The following material must not be made available by the registrar for public inspection—

(a) the contents of any document sent to the registrar containing views expressed pursuant to section 56 (comments on proposal by company to use certain words or expressions in company name);

(b) protected information within section 242(1) (directors' residential addresses: restriction on disclosure by registrar) or any corresponding provision of regulations under section 1046 (overseas companies);

(c) any application to the registrar under section 1024 (application for administrative restoration to the register) that has not yet been determined or was not successful;

(d) any document received by the registrar in connection with the giving or withdrawal of consent under section 1075 (informal correction of documents);

(e) any application or other document delivered to the registrar under section 1088 (application to make address unavailable for public inspection) and any address in respect of which such an application is successful;

(f) any application or other document delivered to the registrar under section 1095 (application for rectification of register);

(g) any court order under section 1096 (rectification of the register under court order) that the court has directed under section 1097 (powers of court on ordering removal of material from the register) is not to be made available for public inspection;

(h) the contents of—

(i) any instrument creating or evidencing a charge and delivered to the registrar under section 860 (registration of company charges: England and Wales or Northern Ireland), or

(ii) any certified copy of an instrument creating or evidencing a charge and delivered to the registrar under section 878 (registration of company charges: Scotland);

(i) any e-mail address, identification code or password deriving from a document delivered for the purpose of authorising or facilitating electronic filing procedures or providing information by telephone;

(j) the contents of any documents held by the registrar pending a decision of the Regulator of Community Interest Companies under section 36 or 38 of the Companies (Audit, Investigations and Community Enterprise) Act 2004 (c 27) (decision on eligibility for registration as community interest company) and that the registrar is not later required to record;
(k) any other material excluded from public inspection by or under any other enactment.

(2) A restriction applying by reference to material deriving from a particular description of document does not affect the availability for public inspection of the same information contained in material derived from another description of document in relation to which no such restriction applies.

(3) Material to which this section applies need not be retained by the registrar for longer than appears to the registrar reasonably necessary for the purposes for which the material was delivered to the registrar.

[S1087]

NOTES

Commencement: 1 January 2007.

Transitional adaptations: art 5 of the Companies Act 2006 (Commencement No 1, Transitional Provisions and Savings) Order 2006, SI 2006/3428 provides that the provisions brought into force by arts 2–4 of 2006 Order shall have effect subject to any transitional adaptations specified in Sch 1 to that Order. Schedule 1, para 9 to the Order (at **[7582]**) provides as follows—

"**9.**—(1) Section 1087 (material not available for public inspection) has effect with the following adaptations.

(2) In subsection (1)(a) for "views expressed pursuant to section 56" substitute "a statement that a request has been made pursuant to section 29(2) of the Companies Act 1985 or Article 39(2) of the Companies (Northern Ireland) Order 1986 or any response to such a request".

(3) For subsection (1)(b) substitute—

"(b) at any time when an order made under section 723B of the Companies Act 1985 is in force in relation to an individual, so much of any record kept by the registrar as contains information which is recorded as particulars of the individual's residential address that were contained in a document delivered to the registrar after the order came into force;".

(4) Omit subsection (1)(c) to (g).

(5) In subsection (1)(h)(i), for "section 860" substitute "section 395 of the Companies Act 1985 or Article 402 of the Companies (Northern Ireland) Order 1986".

(6) In subsection (1)(h)(ii), for "section 878" substitute "section 410 of the Companies Act 1985".".

1088 Application to registrar to make address unavailable for public inspection

(1) The Secretary of State may make provision by regulations requiring the registrar, on application, to make an address on the register unavailable for public inspection.

(2) The regulations may make provision as to—
(a) who may make an application,
(b) the grounds on which an application may be made,
(c) the information to be included in and documents to accompany an application,
(d) the notice to be given of an application and of its outcome, and
(e) how an application is to be determined.

(3) Provision under subsection (2)(e) may in particular—
(a) confer a discretion on the registrar;
(b) provide for a question to be referred to a person other than the registrar for the purposes of determining the application.

(4) An application must specify the address to be removed from the register and indicate where on the register it is.

(5) The regulations may provide—
(a) that an address is not to be made unavailable for public inspection under this section unless replaced by a service address, and
(b) that in such a case the application must specify a service address.

(6) Regulations under this section are subject to affirmative resolution procedure.

[S1088]

NOTES

Commencement: 1 January 2007.

1089 Form of application for inspection or copy

(1) The registrar may specify the form and manner in which application is to be made for—

(a) inspection under section 1085, or

(b) a copy under section 1086.

(2) As from 1st January 2007, applications in respect of documents subject to the Directive disclosure requirements may be submitted to the registrar in hard copy or electronic form, as the applicant chooses.

This does not affect the registrar's power under subsection (1) above to impose requirements in respect of other matters.

[S1089]

NOTES

Commencement: 1 January 2007.

1090 Form and manner in which copies to be provided

(1) The following provisions apply as regards the form and manner in which copies are to be provided under section 1086.

(2) As from 1st January 2007, copies of documents subject to the Directive disclosure requirements must be provided in hard copy or electronic form, as the applicant chooses.

This is subject to the following proviso.

(3) The registrar is not obliged by subsection (2) to provide copies in electronic form of a document that was delivered to the registrar in hard copy form if—

(a) the document was delivered to the registrar on or before 31st December 1996, or

(b) the document was delivered to the registrar on or before 31st December 2006 and ten years or more elapsed between the date of delivery and the date of receipt of the first application for a copy on or after 1st January 2007.

(4) Subject to the preceding provisions of this section, the registrar may determine the form and manner in which copies are to be provided.

[S1090]

NOTES

Commencement: 1 January 2007.

1091 Certification of copies as accurate

(1) Copies provided under section 1086 in hard copy form must be certified as true copies unless the applicant dispenses with such certification.

(2) Copies so provided in electronic form must not be certified as true copies unless the applicant expressly requests such certification.

(3) A copy provided under section 1086, certified by the registrar (whose official position it is unnecessary to prove) to be an accurate record of the contents of the original document, is in all legal proceedings admissible in evidence—

(a) as of equal validity with the original document, and

(b) as evidence (in Scotland, sufficient evidence) of any fact stated in the original document of which direct oral evidence would be admissible.

(4) The Secretary of State may make provision by regulations as to the manner in which such a certificate is to be provided in a case where the copy is provided in electronic form.

(5) Except in the case of documents that are subject to the Directive disclosure requirements (see section 1078), copies provided by the registrar may, instead of being certified in writing to be an accurate record, be sealed with the registrar's official seal.

[S1091]

NOTES

Commencement: 1 January 2007.

Regulations: the Companies (Registrar, Languages and Trading Disclosures) Regulations 2006, SI 2006/3429.

1092 Issue of process for production of records kept by the registrar

(1) No process for compelling the production of a record kept by the registrar shall issue from any court except with the permission of the court.

(2) Any such process shall bear on it a statement that it is issued with the permission of the court.

[S1092]

NOTES

Commencement: 1 January 2007.

Correction or removal of material on the register

1093 Registrar's notice to resolve inconsistency on the register

(1) Where it appears to the registrar that the information contained in a document delivered to the registrar is inconsistent with other information on the register, the registrar may give notice to the company to which the document relates—

(a) stating in what respects the information contained in it appears to be inconsistent with other information on the register, and
(b) requiring the company to take steps to resolve the inconsistency.

(2) The notice must—

(a) state the date on which it is issued, and
(b) require the delivery to the registrar, within 14 days after that date, of such replacement or additional documents as may be required to resolve the inconsistency.

(3) If the necessary documents are not delivered within the period specified, an offence is committed by—

(a) the company, and
(b) every officer of the company who is in default.

(4) A person guilty of an offence under subsection (3) is liable on summary conviction to a fine not exceeding level 5 on the standard scale and, for continued contravention, a daily default fine not exceeding one-tenth of level 5 on the standard scale.

[S1093]

NOTES

Commencement: to be appointed.

1094 Administrative removal of material from the register

(1) The registrar may remove from the register anything that there was power, but no duty, to include.

(2) This power is exercisable, in particular, so as to remove—

(a) unnecessary material within the meaning of section 1074, and
(b) material derived from a document that has been replaced under—
section 1076 (replacement of document not meeting requirements for proper delivery), or
section 1093 (notice to remedy inconsistency on the register).

(3) This section does not authorise the removal from the register of—

(a) anything whose registration has had legal consequences in relation to the company as regards—
(i) its formation,
(ii) a change of name,

(iii) its re-registration,
(iv) its becoming or ceasing to be a community interest company,
(v) a reduction of capital,
(vi) a change of registered office,
(vii) the registration of a charge, or
(viii) its dissolution;

(b) an address that is a person's registered address for the purposes of section 1140 (service of documents on directors, secretaries and others).

(4) On or before removing any material under this section (otherwise than at the request of the company) the registrar must give notice—

(a) to the person by whom the material was delivered (if the identity, and name and address of that person are known), or

(b) to the company to which the material relates (if notice cannot be given under paragraph (a) and the identity of that company is known).

(5) The notice must—

(a) state what material the registrar proposes to remove, or has removed, and on what grounds, and

(b) state the date on which it is issued.

[S1094]

NOTES

Commencement: to be appointed.

1095 Rectification of register on application to registrar

(1) The Secretary of State may make provision by regulations requiring the registrar, on application, to remove from the register material of a description specified in the regulations that—

(a) derives from anything invalid or ineffective or that was done without the authority of the company, or

(b) is factually inaccurate, or is derived from something that is factually inaccurate or forged.

(2) The regulations may make provision as to—

(a) who may make an application,
(b) the information to be included in and documents to accompany an application,
(c) the notice to be given of an application and of its outcome,
(d) a period in which objections to an application may be made, and
(e) how an application is to be determined.

(3) An application must—

(a) specify what is to be removed from the register and indicate where on the register it is, and

(b) be accompanied by a statement that the material specified in the application complies with this section and the regulations.

(4) If no objections are made to the application, the registrar may accept the statement as sufficient evidence that the material specified in the application should be removed from the register.

(5) Where anything is removed from the register under this section the registration of which had legal consequences as mentioned in section 1094(3), any person appearing to the court to have a sufficient interest may apply to the court for such consequential orders as appear just with respect to the legal effect (if any) to be accorded to the material by virtue of its having appeared on the register.

(6) Regulations under this section are subject to affirmative resolution procedure.

[S1095]

NOTES

Commencement: 20 January 2007 (for the purpose of enabling the exercise of powers to make Orders or Regulations by statutory instrument); to be appointed (otherwise).

1096 Rectification of the register under court order

(1) The registrar shall remove from the register any material—

(a) that derives from anything that the court has declared to be invalid or ineffective, or to have been done without the authority of the company, or

(b) that a court declares to be factually inaccurate, or to be derived from something that is factually inaccurate, or forged,

and that the court directs should be removed from the register.

(2) The court order must specify what is to be removed from the register and indicate where on the register it is.

(3) The court must not make an order for the removal from the register of anything the registration of which had legal consequences as mentioned in section 1094(3) unless satisfied—

(a) that the presence of the material on the register has caused, or may cause, damage to the company, and

(b) that the company's interest in removing the material outweighs any interest of other persons in the material continuing to appear on the register.

(4) Where in such a case the court does make an order for removal, it may make such consequential orders as appear just with respect to the legal effect (if any) to be accorded to the material by virtue of its having appeared on the register.

(5) A copy of the court's order must be sent to the registrar for registration.

(6) This section does not apply where the court has other, specific, powers to deal with the matter, for example under—

(a) the provisions of Part 15 relating to the revision of defective accounts and reports, or

(b) section 873 or 888 (rectification of the register of charges).

[S1096]

NOTES

Commencement: to be appointed.

1097 Powers of court on ordering removal of material from the register

(1) Where the court makes an order for the removal of anything from the register under section 1096 (rectification of the register), it may give directions under this section.

(2) It may direct that any note on the register that is related to the material that is the subject of the court's order shall be removed from the register.

(3) It may direct that its order shall not be available for public inspection as part of the register.

(4) It may direct—

(a) that no note shall be made on the register as a result of its order, or

(b) that any such note shall be restricted to such matters as may be specified by the court.

(5) The court shall not give any direction under this section unless it is satisfied—

(a) that—

(i) the presence on the register of the note or, as the case may be, of an unrestricted note, or

(ii) the availability for public inspection of the court's order,

may cause damage to the company, and

(b) that the company's interest in non-disclosure outweighs any interest of other persons in disclosure.

[S1097]

NOTES

Commencement: to be appointed.

1098 Public notice of removal of certain material from the register

(1) The registrar must cause to be published—

(a) in the Gazette, or
(b) in accordance with section 1116 (alternative means of giving public notice),

notice of the removal from the register of any document subject to the Directive disclosure requirements (see section 1078) or of any material derived from such a document.

(2) The notice must state the name and registered number of the company, the description of document and the date of receipt.

[S1098]

NOTES

Commencement: to be appointed.

The registrar's index of company names

1099 The registrar's index of company names

(1) The registrar of companies must keep an index of the names of the companies and other bodies to which this section applies.

This is "the registrar's index of company names".

(2) This section applies to—
(a) UK-registered companies;
(b) any body to which any provision of the Companies Acts applies by virtue of regulations under section 1043 (unregistered companies); and
(c) overseas companies that have registered particulars with the registrar under section 1046, other than companies that appear to the registrar not to be required to do so.

(3) This section also applies to—
(a) limited partnerships registered in the United Kingdom;
(b) limited liability partnerships incorporated in the United Kingdom;
(c) European Economic Interest Groupings registered in the United Kingdom;
(d) open-ended investment companies authorised in the United Kingdom;
(e) societies registered under the Industrial and Provident Societies Act 1965 (c 12) or the Industrial and Provident Societies Act (Northern Ireland) 1969 (c 24 (NI)).

(4) The Secretary of State may by order amend subsection (3)—
(a) by the addition of any description of body;
(b) by the deletion of any description of body.

(5) Any such order is subject to negative resolution procedure.

[S1099]

NOTES

Commencement: 20 January 2007 (for the purpose of enabling the exercise of powers to make Orders or Regulations by statutory instrument); to be appointed (otherwise).

1100 Right to inspect index

Any person may inspect the registrar's index of company names.

[S1100]

NOTES

Commencement: to be appointed.

1101 Power to amend enactments relating to bodies other than companies

(1) The Secretary of State may by regulations amend the enactments relating to any description of body for the time being within section 1099(3) (bodies other than companies whose names are to be entered in the registrar's index), so as to—
(a) require the registrar to be provided with information as to the names of bodies registered, incorporated, authorised or otherwise regulated under those enactments, and
(b) make provision in relation to such bodies corresponding to that made by—

section 66 (company name not to be the same as another in the index), and
sections 67 and 68 (power to direct change of company name in case of similarity to existing name).

(2) Regulations under this section are subject to affirmative resolution procedure.

[S1101]

NOTES

Commencement: 20 January 2007 (for the purpose of enabling the exercise of powers to make Orders or Regulations by statutory instrument); to be appointed (otherwise).

Language requirements: translation

1102 Application of language requirements

(1) The provisions listed below apply to all documents required to be delivered to the registrar under any provision of—

(a) the Companies Acts, or

(b) the Insolvency Act 1986 (c 45) or the Insolvency (Northern Ireland) Order 1989 (SI 1989/2405 (NI 19)).

(2) The Secretary of State may make provision by regulations applying all or any of the listed provisions, with or without modifications, in relation to documents delivered to the registrar under any other enactment.

(3) The provisions are—

section 1103 (documents to be drawn up and delivered in English),
section 1104 (documents relating to Welsh companies),
section 1105 (documents that may be drawn up and delivered in other languages),
section 1107 (certified translations).

(4) Regulations under this section are subject to negative resolution procedure.

[S1102]

NOTES

Commencement: 1 January 2007.

1103 Documents to be drawn up and delivered in English

(1) The general rule is that all documents required to be delivered to the registrar must be drawn up and delivered in English.

(2) This is subject to—

section 1104 (documents relating to Welsh companies) and
section 1105 (documents that may be drawn up and delivered in other languages).

[S1103]

NOTES

Commencement: 1 January 2007.

Transitional adaptations: art 5 of the Companies Act 2006 (Commencement No 1, Transitional Provisions and Savings) Order 2006, SI 2006/3428 provides that the provisions brought into force by arts 2–4 of 2006 Order shall have effect subject to any transitional adaptations specified in Sch 1 to that Order. Schedule 1, para 10 to the Order (at **[7582]**) provides as follows—

"10.—(1) Section 1103 (documents to be drawn up and delivered in English) has effect with the following adaptation.

(2) After subsection (2) insert—

"(3) This section does not affect the operation of the following provisions (under which documents may be delivered in a language other than English if a certified translation is delivered)—

(a) section 228(2)(f) or 228A(2)(g) of the Companies Act 1985 or Article 236(2)(f) of the Companies (Northern Ireland) Order 1986 (conditions for exemption from duty to prepare group accounts: delivery of certain accounts and reports);

(b) section 242(1) of that Act or Article 250(1) of that Order (main requirements as to accounts and reports);

(c) section 272(5) of that Act or Article 280(5) of that Order (interim accounts prepared for a proposed distribution by a public company);
(d) section 273(7) of that Act or Article 281(7) of that Order (initial accounts prepared for a proposed distribution by a public company);
(e) paragraph 7(3) of Part 2 of Schedule 9 to that Act or paragraph 7(3) of Part 2 of Schedule 9 to that Order (information as to undertaking in which shares held as a result of financial assistance operation).".".

1104 Documents relating to Welsh companies

(1) Documents relating to a Welsh company may be drawn up and delivered to the registrar in Welsh.

(2) On delivery to the registrar any such document must be accompanied by a certified translation into English, unless it is—

(a) of a description excepted from that requirement by regulations made by the Secretary of State, or
(b) in a form prescribed in Welsh (or partly in Welsh and partly in English) by virtue of section 26 of the Welsh Language Act 1993 (c 38).

(3) Where a document is properly delivered to the registrar in Welsh without a certified translation into English, the registrar must obtain such a translation if the document is to be available for public inspection.

The translation is treated as if delivered to the registrar in accordance with the same provision as the original.

(4) A Welsh company may deliver to the registrar a certified translation into Welsh of any document in English that relates to the company and is or has been delivered to the registrar.

(5) Section 1105 (which requires certified translations into English of documents delivered to the registrar in another language) does not apply to a document relating to a Welsh company that is drawn up and delivered in Welsh.

[S1104]

NOTES

Commencement: 1 January 2007.

Transitional adaptations: art 5 of the Companies Act 2006 (Commencement No 1, Transitional Provisions and Savings) Order 2006, SI 2006/3428 provides that the provisions brought into force by arts 2–4 of 2006 Order shall have effect subject to any transitional adaptations specified in Sch 1 to that Order. Schedule 1, para 11 to the Order (at **[7582]**) provides as follows—

"11.—(1) Section 1104 (documents relating to Welsh companies) has effect with the following adaptations.

(2) For subsection (5) substitute—

"(5) None of the following provisions (which require certified translations into English of documents delivered to the registrar in another language) applies to a document relating to a Welsh company that is drawn up and delivered in Welsh—

(a) section 228(2)(f) and section 228A(2)(g) of the Companies Act 1985;
(b) section 242(1) of that Act;
(c) section 272(5) of that Act;
(d) section 273(7) of that Act;
(e) paragraph 7(3) of Part 2 of Schedule 9 to that Act;
(f) section 1105 of this Act.".

(3) After that subsection insert—

"(6) In this section, "a Welsh company" means a company whose memorandum states that its registered office is to be situated in Wales.".".

See also SI 2006/3428, art 8(1), Sch 5, Pt 1, para 1, which provides that regs 4 and 5 of the Companies (Welsh Language Forms and Documents) Regulations 1994, SI 1994/117 continue to have effect (notwithstanding the repeal of CA 1985, s 710B) as if reg 4 were made under sub-s (2) above, and reg 5 has effect as if the requirements imposed by it were requirements imposed by the registrar under CA 2006, s 1111 by means of rules under s 1117 of that Act.

1105 Documents that may be drawn up and delivered in other languages

(1) Documents to which this section applies may be drawn up and delivered to the registrar in a language other than English, but when delivered to the registrar they must be accompanied by a certified translation into English.

(2) This section applies to—

(a) agreements required to be forwarded to the registrar under Chapter 3 of Part 3 (agreements affecting the company's constitution);

(b) documents required to be delivered under section 400(2)(e) or section 401(2)(f) (company included in accounts of larger group: required to deliver copy of group accounts);

(c) instruments or copy instruments required to be delivered under Part 25 (company charges);

(d) documents of any other description specified in regulations made by the Secretary of State.

(3) Regulations under this section are subject to negative resolution procedure.

[S1105]

NOTES

Commencement: 1 January 2007.

Transitional adaptations: art 5 of the Companies Act 2006 (Commencement No 1, Transitional Provisions and Savings) Order 2006, SI 2006/3428 provides that the provisions brought into force by arts 2–4 of 2006 Order shall have effect subject to any transitional adaptations specified in Sch 1 to that Order. Schedule 1, para 12 to the Order (at **[7582]**) provides as follows—

"**12.**—(1) Section 1105 (documents that may be drawn up and delivered in other languages) has effect with the following adaptations.

(2) *In subsection (2)(a) for "Chapter 3 of Part 3" substitute "section 380 of the Companies Act 1985 or Article 388 of the Companies (Northern Ireland) Order 1986".*

(3) In subsection (2)(b) for "section 400(2)(e) or section 401(2)(f)" substitute "section 228(2)(e) or section 228A(2)(f) of the Companies Act 1985 or Article 236(2)(e) of the Companies (Northern Ireland) Order 1986".

(4) In subsection (2)(c) for "Part 25" substitute "Part 12 of the Companies Act 1985 or Part 13 of the Companies (Northern Ireland) Order 1986".".

Note that para 12(2) as set out above is revoked by the draft Companies Act 2006 (Commencement No 3, Consequential Amendments, Transitional Provisions and Savings) Order 2007, art 10(1), as from 1 October 2007 (see **[A12]**).

Regulations: the Companies (Registrar, Languages and Trading Disclosures) Regulations 2006, SI 2006/3429.

1106 Voluntary filing of translations

(1) A company may deliver to the registrar one or more certified translations of any document relating to the company that is or has been delivered to the registrar.

(2) The Secretary of State may by regulations specify—

(a) the languages, and

(b) the descriptions of document,

in relation to which this facility is available.

(3) The regulations must provide that it is available as from 1st January 2007—

(a) in relation to all the official languages of the European Union, and

(b) in relation to all documents subject to the Directive disclosure requirements (see section 1078).

(4) The power of the registrar to impose requirements as to the form and manner of delivery includes power to impose requirements as to the identification of the original document and the delivery of the translation in a form and manner enabling it to be associated with the original.

(5) Regulations under this section are subject to negative resolution procedure.

(6) This section does not apply where the original document was delivered to the registrar before this section came into force.

[S1106]

NOTES

Commencement: 1 January 2007.

Regulations: the Companies (Registrar, Languages and Trading Disclosures) Regulations 2006, SI 2006/3429.

1107 Certified translations

(1) In this Part a "certified translation" means a translation certified to be a correct translation.

(2) In the case of any discrepancy between the original language version of a document and a certified translation—

(a) the company may not rely on the translation as against a third party, but
(b) a third party may rely on the translation unless the company shows that the third party had knowledge of the original.

(3) A "third party" means a person other than the company or the registrar.

[S1107]

NOTES

Commencement: 1 January 2007.

Language requirements: transliteration

1108 Transliteration of names and addresses: permitted characters

(1) Names and addresses in a document delivered to the registrar must contain only letters, characters and symbols (including accents and other diacritical marks) that are permitted.

(2) The Secretary of State may make provision by regulations—

(a) as to the letters, characters and symbols (including accents and other diacritical marks) that are permitted, and
(b) permitting or requiring the delivery of documents in which names and addresses have not been transliterated into a permitted form.

(3) Regulations under this section are subject to negative resolution procedure.

[S1108]

NOTES

Commencement: 20 January 2007 (for the purpose of enabling the exercise of powers to make Orders or Regulations by statutory instrument); to be appointed (otherwise).

1109 Transliteration of names and addresses: voluntary transliteration into Roman characters

(1) Where a name or address is or has been delivered to the registrar in a permitted form using other than Roman characters, the company may deliver to the registrar a transliteration into Roman characters.

(2) The power of the registrar to impose requirements as to the form and manner of delivery includes power to impose requirements as to the identification of the original document and the delivery of the transliteration in a form and manner enabling it to be associated with the original.

[S1109]

NOTES

Commencement: to be appointed.

1110 Transliteration of names and addresses: certification

(1) The Secretary of State may make provision by regulations requiring the certification of transliterations and prescribing the form of certification.

(2) Different provision may be made for compulsory and voluntary transliterations.

(3) Regulations under this section are subject to negative resolution procedure.

[S1110]

NOTES

Commencement: 20 January 2007 (for the purpose of enabling the exercise of powers to make Orders or Regulations by statutory instrument); to be appointed (otherwise).

Supplementary provisions

1111 Registrar's requirements as to certification or verification

(1) Where a document required or authorised to be delivered to the registrar under any enactment is required—

(a) to be certified as an accurate translation or transliteration, or

(b) to be certified as a correct copy or verified,

the registrar may impose requirements as to the person, or description of person, by whom the certificate or verification is to be given.

(2) The power conferred by section 1068 (registrar's requirements as to form, authentication and manner of delivery) is exercisable in relation to the certificate or verification as if it were a separate document.

(3) Requirements imposed under this section must not be inconsistent with requirements imposed by any enactment with respect to the certification or verification of the document concerned.

[S1111]

NOTES

Commencement: 1 January 2007.
See also the final note to s 1104 at **[S1104]**.

1112 General false statement offence

(1) It is an offence for a person knowingly or recklessly—

(a) to deliver or cause to be delivered to the registrar, for any purpose of the Companies Acts, a document, or

(b) to make to the registrar, for any such purpose, a statement,

that is misleading, false or deceptive in a material particular.

(2) A person guilty of an offence under this section is liable—

(a) on conviction on indictment, to imprisonment for a term not exceeding two years or a fine (or both);

(b) on summary conviction—

(i) in England and Wales, to imprisonment for a term not exceeding twelve months or to a fine not exceeding the statutory maximum (or both);

(ii) in Scotland or Northern Ireland, to imprisonment for a term not exceeding six months, or to a fine not exceeding the statutory maximum (or both).

[S1112]

NOTES

Commencement: to be appointed.

1113 Enforcement of company's filing obligations

(1) This section applies where a company has made default in complying with any obligation under the Companies Acts—

(a) to deliver a document to the registrar, or

(b) to give notice to the registrar of any matter.

(2) The registrar, or any member or creditor of the company, may give notice to the company requiring it to comply with the obligation.

(3) If the company fails to make good the default within 14 days after service of the notice, the registrar, or any member or creditor of the company, may apply to the court for an order directing the company, and any specified officer of it, to make good the default within a specified time.

(4) The court's order may provide that all costs (in Scotland, expenses) of or incidental to the application are to be borne by the company or by any officers of it responsible for the default.

(5) This section does not affect the operation of any enactment making it an offence, or imposing a civil penalty, for the default.

[S1113]

NOTES

Commencement: to be appointed.

1114 Application of provisions about documents and delivery

(1) In this Part—

(a) "document" means information recorded in any form, and

(b) references to delivering a document include forwarding, lodging, registering, sending, producing or submitting it or (in the case of a notice) giving it.

(2) Except as otherwise provided, this Part applies in relation to the supply to the registrar of information otherwise than in documentary form as it applies in relation to the delivery of a document.

[S1114]

NOTES

Commencement: 1 January 2007 (certain purposes); to be appointed (otherwise) (see the note below).

Note: the Companies Act 2006 (Commencement No 1, Transitional Provisions and Savings) Order 2006, SI 2006/3428, art 2(2) provides that this section shall come into force on 1 January 2007 so far as is necessary for the purposes of the provisions of this Act brought into force on that date by art 2(1) of that Order (see **[7575]**).

1115 Supplementary provisions relating to electronic communications

(1) Registrar's rules may require a company to give any necessary consents to the use of electronic means for communications by the registrar to the company as a condition of making use of any facility to deliver material to the registrar by electronic means.

(2) A document that is required to be signed by the registrar or authenticated by the registrar's seal shall, if sent by electronic means, be authenticated in such manner as may be specified by registrar's rules.

[S1115]

NOTES

Commencement: to be appointed.

1116 Alternative to publication in the Gazette

(1) Notices that would otherwise need to be published by the registrar in the Gazette may instead be published by such means as may from time to time be approved by the registrar in accordance with regulations made by the Secretary of State.

(2) The Secretary of State may make provision by regulations as to what alternative means may be approved.

(3) The regulations may, in particular—

(a) require the use of electronic means;

(b) require the same means to be used—

(i) for all notices or for all notices of specified descriptions, and

(ii) whether the company is registered in England and Wales, Scotland or Northern Ireland;

(c) impose conditions as to the manner in which access to the notices is to be made available.

(4) Regulations under this section are subject to negative resolution procedure.

(5) Before starting to publish notices by means approved under this section the registrar must publish at least one notice to that effect in the Gazette.

(6) Nothing in this section prevents the registrar from giving public notice both in the Gazette and by means approved under this section.

In that case, the requirement of public notice is met when notice is first given by either means.

[S1116]

NOTES

Commencement: 20 January 2007 (for the purpose of enabling the exercise of powers to make Orders or Regulations by statutory instrument); to be appointed (otherwise).

1117 Registrar's rules

(1) Where any provision of this Part enables the registrar to make provision, or impose requirements, as to any matter, the registrar may make such provision or impose such requirements by means of rules under this section.

This is without prejudice to the making of such provision or the imposing of such requirements by other means.

(2) Registrar's rules—

(a) may make different provision for different cases, and

(b) may allow the registrar to disapply or modify any of the rules.

(3) The registrar must—

(a) publicise the rules in a manner appropriate to bring them to the notice of persons affected by them, and

(b) make copies of the rules available to the public (in hard copy or electronic form).

[S1117]

NOTES

Commencement: 1 January 2007 (certain purposes); to be appointed (otherwise) (see the note below).

Note: the Companies Act 2006 (Commencement No 1, Transitional Provisions and Savings) Order 2006, SI 2006/3428, art 2(2) provides that this section shall come into force on 1 January 2007 so far as is necessary for the purposes of the provisions of this Act brought into force on that date by art 2(1) of that Order (see **[7575]**).

See also the final note to s 1104 at **[S1104]**.

1118 Payments into the Consolidated Fund

Nothing in the Companies Acts or any other enactment as to the payment of receipts into the Consolidated Fund shall be read as affecting the operation in relation to the registrar of section 3(1) of the Government Trading Funds Act 1973 (c 63).

[S1118]

NOTES

Commencement: to be appointed.

1119 Contracting out of registrar's functions

(1) Where by virtue of an order made under section 69 of the Deregulation and Contracting Out Act 1994 (c 40) a person is authorised by the registrar to accept delivery of any class of documents that are under any enactment to be delivered to the registrar, the registrar may direct that documents of that class shall be delivered to a specified address of the authorised person.

Any such direction must be printed and made available to the public (with or without payment).

(2) A document of that class that is delivered to an address other than the specified address is treated as not having been delivered.

(3) Registrar's rules are not subordinate legislation for the purposes of section 71 of the Deregulation and Contracting Out Act 1994 (functions excluded from contracting out).

[S1119]

NOTES

Commencement: to be appointed.

1120 Application of this Part to overseas companies

Unless the context otherwise requires, the provisions of this Part apply to an overseas company as they apply to a company as defined in section 1.

[S1120]

NOTES

Commencement: 1 January 2007 (certain purposes); to be appointed (otherwise) (see the note below).

Note: the Companies Act 2006 (Commencement No 1, Transitional Provisions and Savings) Order 2006, SI 2006/3428, art 2(2) provides that this section shall come into force on 1 January 2007 so far as is necessary for the purposes of the provisions of this Act brought into force on that date by art 2(1) of that Order (see **[7575]**).

Transitional adaptations: art 5 of the Companies Act 2006 (Commencement No 1, Transitional Provisions and Savings) Order 2006, SI 2006/3428 provides that the provisions brought into force by arts 2–4 of 2006 Order shall have effect subject to any transitional adaptations specified in Sch 1 to that Order. Schedule 1, para 13 to the Order (at **[7582]**) provides as follows—

"**13.**—(1) Section 1120 (application of Part 35 to overseas companies) has effect with the following adaptations.

(2) For "an overseas company" substitute "an oversea company (as defined in section 744 of the Companies Act 1985) or a Part 23 company (as defined in Article 640 of the Companies (Northern Ireland) Order 1986)".

(3) For "a company as defined in section 1" substitute "a company as defined in section 735(1) of that Act or Article 3(1) of that Order".".

PART 36
OFFENCES UNDER THE COMPANIES ACTS

Liability of officer in default

1121 Liability of officer in default

(1) This section has effect for the purposes of any provision of the Companies Acts to the effect that, in the event of contravention of an enactment in relation to a company, an offence is committed by every officer of the company who is in default.

(2) For this purpose "officer" includes—

(a) any director, manager or secretary, and

(b) any person who is to be treated as an officer of the company for the purposes of the provision in question.

(3) An officer is "in default" for the purposes of the provision if he authorises or permits, participates in, or fails to take all reasonable steps to prevent, the contravention.

[S1121]

NOTES

Commencement: 20 January 2007 (certain purposes); 6 April 2007 (certain purposes); 1 October 2007 (certain purposes); to be appointed (otherwise) (see the notes below).

Note: the Companies Act 2006 (Commencement No 1, Transitional Provisions and Savings) Order 2006, SI 2006/3428, art 3(2) provides that this section shall come into force on 20 January 2007 so far as is necessary for the purposes of the provisions of this Act brought into force on that date by art 3(1) of that Order (see **[7576]**).

Note: the Companies Act 2006 (Commencement No 2, Consequential Amendments, Transitional Provisions and Savings) Order 2007, SI 2007/1093, art 2(2) provides that this section shall come into force on 6 April 2007 so far as is necessary for the purposes of the provisions of this Act brought into force on that date by art 2(1) of that Order (see **[7615]**).

Note: the draft Companies Act 2006 (Commencement No 3, Consequential Amendments, Transitional Provisions and Savings) Order 2007, art 2(1)(l) provides that this section shall come into force on 1 October 2007 in so far as it applies to offences under Parts XIV, XV of the Companies Act 1985 (see **[A12]**).

Note: the draft Companies Act 2006 (Commencement No 3, Consequential Amendments, Transitional Provisions and Savings) Order 2007, art 2(3) provides that this section shall come into force on 1 October 2007 so far as is necessary for the purposes of the provisions of this Act brought into force on that date by art 2(1), (2) of that Order (see **[A12]**).

1122 Liability of company as officer in default

(1) Where a company is an officer of another company, it does not commit an offence as an officer in default unless one of its officers is in default.

(2) Where any such offence is committed by a company the officer in question also commits the offence and is liable to be proceeded against and punished accordingly.

(3) In this section "officer" and "in default" have the meanings given by section 1121.

[S1122]

NOTES

Commencement: 20 January 2007 (certain purposes); 6 April 2007 (certain purposes); 1 October 2007 (certain purposes); to be appointed (otherwise) (see the notes below).

Note: the Companies Act 2006 (Commencement No 1, Transitional Provisions and Savings) Order 2006, SI 2006/3428, art 3(2) provides that this section shall come into force on 20 January 2007 so far as is necessary for the purposes of the provisions of this Act brought into force on that date by art 3(1) of that Order (see **[7576]**).

Note: the Companies Act 2006 (Commencement No 2, Consequential Amendments, Transitional Provisions and Savings) Order 2007, SI 2007/1093, art 2(2) provides that this section shall come into force on 6 April 2007 so far as is necessary for the purposes of the provisions of this Act brought into force on that date by art 2(1) of that Order (see **[7615]**).

Note: the draft Companies Act 2006 (Commencement No 3, Consequential Amendments, Transitional Provisions and Savings) Order 2007, art 2(1)(l) provides that this section shall come into force on 1 October 2007 in so far as it applies to offences under Parts XIV, XV of the Companies Act 1985 (see **[A12]**).

Note: the draft Companies Act 2006 (Commencement No 3, Consequential Amendments, Transitional Provisions and Savings) Order 2007, art 2(3) provides that this section shall come into force on 1 October 2007 so far as is necessary for the purposes of the provisions of this Act brought into force on that date by art 2(1), (2) of that Order (see **[A12]**).

Application to unregistered companies: see the Companies Acts (Unregistered Companies) Regulations 2007, SI 2007/318 at **[7606]**.

1123 Application to bodies other than companies

(1) Section 1121 (liability of officers in default) applies to a body other than a company as it applies to a company.

(2) As it applies in relation to a body corporate other than a company—

- (a) the reference to a director of the company shall be read as referring—
  - (i) where the body's affairs are managed by its members, to a member of the body,
  - (ii) in any other case, to any corresponding officer of the body, and
- (b) the reference to a manager or secretary of the company shall be read as referring to any manager, secretary or similar officer of the body.

(3) As it applies in relation to a partnership—

- (a) the reference to a director of the company shall be read as referring to a member of the partnership, and
- (b) the reference to a manager or secretary of the company shall be read as referring to any manager, secretary or similar officer of the partnership.

(4) As it applies in relation to an unincorporated body other than a partnership—

- (a) the reference to a director of the company shall be read as referring—
  - (i) where the body's affairs are managed by its members, to a member of the body,
  - (ii) in any other case, to a member of the governing body, and
- (b) the reference to a manager or secretary of the company shall be read as referring to any manager, secretary or similar officer of the body.

[S1123]

NOTES

Commencement: 6 April 2007 (certain purposes); 1 October 2007 (certain purposes); to be appointed (otherwise) (see the note below).

Note: the Companies Act 2006 (Commencement No 2, Consequential Amendments, Transitional Provisions and Savings) Order 2007, SI 2007/1093, art 2(2) provides that this section shall come into force on 6 April 2007 so far as is necessary for the purposes of the provisions of this Act brought into force on that date by art 2(1) of that Order (see **[7615]**).

Note: the draft Companies Act 2006 (Commencement No 3, Consequential Amendments, Transitional Provisions and Savings) Order 2007, art 2(1)(l) provides that this section shall come into force on 1 October 2007 in so far as it applies to offences under Parts XIV, XV of the Companies Act 1985 (see **[A12]**).

Offences under the Companies Act 1985

1124 Amendments of the Companies Act 1985

Schedule 3 contains amendments of the Companies Act 1985 (c 6) relating to offences.

[S1124]

NOTES

Commencement: 1 October 2007.

General provisions

1125 Meaning of "daily default fine"

(1) This section defines what is meant in the Companies Acts where it is provided that a person guilty of an offence is liable on summary conviction to a fine not exceeding a specified amount "and, for continued contravention, a daily default fine" not exceeding a specified amount.

(2) This means that the person is liable on a second or subsequent summary conviction of the offence to a fine not exceeding the latter amount for each day on which the contravention is continued (instead of being liable to a fine not exceeding the former amount).

[S1125]

NOTES

Commencement: 20 January 2007 (certain purposes); 6 April 2007 (certain purposes); 1 October 2007 (certain purposes); to be appointed (otherwise) (see the notes below).

Note: the Companies Act 2006 (Commencement No 1, Transitional Provisions and Savings) Order 2006, SI 2006/3428, art 3(2) provides that this section shall come into force on 20 January 2007 so far as is necessary for the purposes of the provisions of this Act brought into force on that date by art 3(1) of that Order (see **[7576]**).

Note: the Companies Act 2006 (Commencement No 2, Consequential Amendments, Transitional Provisions and Savings) Order 2007, SI 2007/1093, art 2(2) provides that this section shall come into force on 6 April 2007 so far as is necessary for the purposes of the provisions of this Act brought into force on that date by art 2(1) of that Order (see **[7615]**).

Note: the draft Companies Act 2006 (Commencement No 3, Consequential Amendments, Transitional Provisions and Savings) Order 2007, art 2(1)(l) provides that this section shall come into force on 1 October 2007 in so far as it applies to offences under Parts XIV, XV of the Companies Act 1985 (see **[A12]**).

Note: the draft Companies Act 2006 (Commencement No 3, Consequential Amendments, Transitional Provisions and Savings) Order 2007, art 2(3) provides that this section shall come into force on 1 October 2007 so far as is necessary for the purposes of the provisions of this Act brought into force on that date by art 2(1), (2) of that Order (see **[A12]**).

1126 Consents required for certain prosecutions

(1) This section applies to proceedings for an offence under any of the following provisions—

section 458, 460 or 949 of this Act (offences of unauthorised disclosure of information);
section 953 of this Act (failure to comply with rules about takeover bid documents);
section 448, 449, 450, 451 or 453A of the Companies Act 1985 (c 6) (offences in connection with company investigations);
section 798 of this Act or section 455 of the Companies Act 1985 (offence of attempting to evade restrictions on shares).

(2) No such proceedings are to be brought in England and Wales except by or with the consent of—

(a) in the case of an offence under—
  (i) section 458, 460 or 949 of this Act,
  (ii) section 953 of this Act, or
  (iii) section 448, 449, 450, 451 or 453A of the Companies Act 1985,

the Secretary of State or the Director of Public Prosecutions;

(b) in the case of an offence under section 798 of this Act or section 455 of the Companies Act 1985, the Secretary of State.

(3) No such proceedings are to be brought in Northern Ireland except by or with the consent of—

(a) in the case of an offence under—
(i) section 458, 460 or 949 of this Act,
(ii) section 953 of this Act, or
(iii) section 448, 449, 450, 451 or 453A of the Companies Act 1985,
the Secretary of State or the Director of Public Prosecutions for Northern Ireland;
(b) in the case of an offence under section 798 of this Act or section 455 of the Companies Act 1985, the Secretary of State.

[S1126]

NOTES

Commencement: 20 January 2007 (certain purposes); 6 April 2007 (certain purposes); 1 October 2007 (certain purposes); to be appointed (otherwise) (see the notes below).

Note: the Companies Act 2006 (Commencement No 1, Transitional Provisions and Savings) Order 2006, SI 2006/3428, art 3(2) provides that this section shall come into force on 20 January 2007 so far as is necessary for the purposes of the provisions of this Act brought into force on that date by art 3(1) of that Order (see **[7576]**).

Note: the Companies Act 2006 (Commencement No 2, Consequential Amendments, Transitional Provisions and Savings) Order 2007, SI 2007/1093, art 2(2) provides that this section shall come into force on 6 April 2007 so far as is necessary for the purposes of the provisions of this Act brought into force on that date by art 2(1) of that Order (see **[7615]**).

Note: the draft Companies Act 2006 (Commencement No 3, Consequential Amendments, Transitional Provisions and Savings) Order 2007, art 2(1)(l) provides that this section shall come into force on 1 October 2007 in so far as it applies to offences under Parts XIV, XV of the Companies Act 1985 (see **[A12]**).

1127 Summary proceedings: venue

(1) Summary proceedings for any offence under the Companies Acts may be taken—
(a) against a body corporate, at any place at which the body has a place of business, and
(b) against any other person, at any place at which he is for the time being.

(2) This is without prejudice to any jurisdiction exercisable apart from this section.

[S1127]

NOTES

Commencement: 20 January 2007 (certain purposes); 6 April 2007 (certain purposes); 1 October 2007 (certain purposes); to be appointed (otherwise) (see the notes below).

Note: the Companies Act 2006 (Commencement No 1, Transitional Provisions and Savings) Order 2006, SI 2006/3428, art 3(2) provides that this section shall come into force on 20 January 2007 so far as is necessary for the purposes of the provisions of this Act brought into force on that date by art 3(1) of that Order (see **[7576]**).

Note: the Companies Act 2006 (Commencement No 2, Consequential Amendments, Transitional Provisions and Savings) Order 2007, SI 2007/1093, art 2(2) provides that this section shall come into force on 6 April 2007 so far as is necessary for the purposes of the provisions of this Act brought into force on that date by art 2(1) of that Order (see **[7615]**).

Note: the draft Companies Act 2006 (Commencement No 3, Consequential Amendments, Transitional Provisions and Savings) Order 2007, art 2(1)(l) provides that this section shall come into force on 1 October 2007 in so far as it applies to offences under Parts XIV, XV of the Companies Act 1985 (see **[A12]**).

Note: the draft Companies Act 2006 (Commencement No 3, Consequential Amendments, Transitional Provisions and Savings) Order 2007, art 2(3) provides that this section shall come into force on 1 October 2007 so far as is necessary for the purposes of the provisions of this Act brought into force on that date by art 2(1), (2) of that Order (see **[A12]**).

1128 Summary proceedings: time limit for proceedings

(1) An information relating to an offence under the Companies Acts that is triable by a magistrates' court in England and Wales may be so tried if it is laid—
(a) at any time within three years after the commission of the offence, and
(b) within twelve months after the date on which evidence sufficient in the opinion of the Director of Public Prosecutions or the Secretary of State (as the case may be) to justify the proceedings comes to his knowledge.

(2) Summary proceedings in Scotland for an offence under the Companies Acts—
(a) must not be commenced after the expiration of three years from the commission of the offence;
(b) subject to that, may be commenced at any time—

(i) within twelve months after the date on which evidence sufficient in the Lord Advocate's opinion to justify the proceedings came to his knowledge, or

(ii) where such evidence was reported to him by the Secretary of State, within twelve months after the date on which it came to the knowledge of the latter.

Section 136(3) of the Criminal Procedure (Scotland) Act 1995 (c 46) (date when proceedings deemed to be commenced) applies for the purposes of this subsection as for the purposes of that section.

(3) A magistrates' court in Northern Ireland has jurisdiction to hear and determine a complaint charging the commission of a summary offence under the Companies Acts provided that the complaint is made—

(a) within three years from the time when the offence was committed, and

(b) within twelve months from the date on which evidence sufficient in the opinion of the Director of Public Prosecutions for Northern Ireland or the Secretary of State (as the case may be) to justify the proceedings comes to his knowledge.

(4) For the purposes of this section a certificate of the Director of Public Prosecutions, the Lord Advocate, the Director of Public Prosecutions for Northern Ireland or the Secretary of State (as the case may be) as to the date on which such evidence as is referred to above came to his notice is conclusive evidence.

[S1128]

NOTES

Commencement: 20 January 2007 (certain purposes); 6 April 2007 (certain purposes); 1 October 2007 (certain purposes); to be appointed (otherwise) (see the notes below).

Note: the Companies Act 2006 (Commencement No 1, Transitional Provisions and Savings) Order 2006, SI 2006/3428, art 3(2) provides that this section shall come into force on 20 January 2007 so far as is necessary for the purposes of the provisions of this Act brought into force on that date by art 3(1) of that Order (see **[7576]**).

Note: the Companies Act 2006 (Commencement No 2, Consequential Amendments, Transitional Provisions and Savings) Order 2007, SI 2007/1093, art 2(2) provides that this section shall come into force on 6 April 2007 so far as is necessary for the purposes of the provisions of this Act brought into force on that date by art 2(1) of that Order (see **[7615]**).

Note: the draft Companies Act 2006 (Commencement No 3, Consequential Amendments, Transitional Provisions and Savings) Order 2007, art 2(1)(l) provides that this section shall come into force on 1 October 2007 in so far as it applies to offences under Parts XIV, XV of the Companies Act 1985 (see **[A12]**).

Note: the draft Companies Act 2006 (Commencement No 3, Consequential Amendments, Transitional Provisions and Savings) Order 2007, art 2(3) provides that this section shall come into force on 1 October 2007 so far as is necessary for the purposes of the provisions of this Act brought into force on that date by art 2(1), (2) of that Order (see **[A12]**).

1129 Legal professional privilege

In proceedings against a person for an offence under the Companies Acts, nothing in those Acts is to be taken to require any person to disclose any information that he is entitled to refuse to disclose on grounds of legal professional privilege (in Scotland, confidentiality of communications).

[S1129]

NOTES

Commencement: 20 January 2007 (certain purposes); 6 April 2007 (certain purposes); 1 October 2007 (certain purposes); to be appointed (otherwise) (see the notes below).

Note: the Companies Act 2006 (Commencement No 1, Transitional Provisions and Savings) Order 2006, SI 2006/3428, art 3(2) provides that this section shall come into force on 20 January 2007 so far as is necessary for the purposes of the provisions of this Act brought into force on that date by art 3(1) of that Order (see **[7576]**).

Note: the Companies Act 2006 (Commencement No 2, Consequential Amendments, Transitional Provisions and Savings) Order 2007, SI 2007/1093, art 2(2) provides that this section shall come into force on 6 April 2007 so far as is necessary for the purposes of the provisions of this Act brought into force on that date by art 2(1) of that Order (see **[7615]**).

Note: the draft Companies Act 2006 (Commencement No 3, Consequential Amendments, Transitional Provisions and Savings) Order 2007, art 2(1)(l) provides that this section shall come into force on 1 October 2007 in so far as it applies to offences under Parts XIV, XV of the Companies Act 1985 (see **[A12]**).

Note: the draft Companies Act 2006 (Commencement No 3, Consequential Amendments, Transitional Provisions and Savings) Order 2007, art 2(3) provides that this section shall come into force on 1 October 2007 so far as is necessary for the purposes of the provisions of this Act brought into force on that date by art 2(1), (2) of that Order (see **[A12]**).

1130 Proceedings against unincorporated bodies

(1) Proceedings for an offence under the Companies Acts alleged to have been committed by an unincorporated body must be brought in the name of the body (and not in that of any of its members).

(2) For the purposes of such proceedings—

(a) any rules of court relating to the service of documents have effect as if the body were a body corporate, and

(b) the following provisions apply as they apply in relation to a body corporate—

(i) in England and Wales, section 33 of the Criminal Justice Act 1925 (c 86) and Schedule 3 to the Magistrates' Courts Act 1980 (c 43),

(ii) in Scotland, sections 70 and 143 of the Criminal Procedure (Scotland) Act 1995 (c 46),

(iii) in Northern Ireland, section 18 of the Criminal Justice Act (Northern Ireland) 1945 (c 15 (NI)) and Article 166 of and Schedule 4 to the Magistrates' Courts (Northern Ireland) Order 1981 (SI 1981/1675 (NI 26)).

(3) A fine imposed on an unincorporated body on its conviction of an offence under the Companies Acts must be paid out of the funds of the body.

[S1130]

NOTES

Commencement: 20 January 2007 (certain purposes); 6 April 2007 (certain purposes); 1 October 2007 (certain purposes); to be appointed (otherwise) (see the notes below).

Note: the Companies Act 2006 (Commencement No 1, Transitional Provisions and Savings) Order 2006, SI 2006/3428, art 3(2) provides that this section shall come into force on 20 January 2007 so far as is necessary for the purposes of the provisions of this Act brought into force on that date by art 3(1) of that Order (see **[7576]**).

Note: the Companies Act 2006 (Commencement No 2, Consequential Amendments, Transitional Provisions and Savings) Order 2007, SI 2007/1093, art 2(2) provides that this section shall come into force on 6 April 2007 so far as is necessary for the purposes of the provisions of this Act brought into force on that date by art 2(1) of that Order (see **[7615]**).

Note: the draft Companies Act 2006 (Commencement No 3, Consequential Amendments, Transitional Provisions and Savings) Order 2007, art 2(1)(l) provides that this section shall come into force on 1 October 2007 in so far as it applies to offences under Parts XIV, XV of the Companies Act 1985 (see **[A12]**).

Note: the draft Companies Act 2006 (Commencement No 3, Consequential Amendments, Transitional Provisions and Savings) Order 2007, art 2(3) provides that this section shall come into force on 1 October 2007 so far as is necessary for the purposes of the provisions of this Act brought into force on that date by art 2(1), (2) of that Order (see **[A12]**).

1131 Imprisonment on summary conviction in England and Wales: transitory provision

(1) This section applies to any provision of the Companies Acts that provides that a person guilty of an offence is liable on summary conviction in England and Wales to imprisonment for a term not exceeding twelve months.

(2) In relation to an offence committed before the commencement of section 154(1) of the Criminal Justice Act 2003 (c 44), for "twelve months" substitute "six months".

[S1131]

NOTES

Commencement: 20 January 2007 (certain purposes); 6 April 2007 (certain purposes); 1 October 2007 (certain purposes); to be appointed (otherwise) (see the notes below).

Note: the Companies Act 2006 (Commencement No 1, Transitional Provisions and Savings) Order 2006, SI 2006/3428, art 3(2) provides that this section shall come into force on 20 January 2007 so far as is necessary for the purposes of the provisions of this Act brought into force on that date by art 3(1) of that Order (see **[7576]**).

Note: the Companies Act 2006 (Commencement No 2, Consequential Amendments, Transitional Provisions and Savings) Order 2007, SI 2007/1093, art 2(2) provides that this section shall come into force on 6 April 2007 so far as is necessary for the purposes of the provisions of this Act brought into force on that date by art 2(1) of that Order (see **[7615]**).

Note: the draft Companies Act 2006 (Commencement No 3, Consequential Amendments, Transitional Provisions and Savings) Order 2007, art 2(1)(l) provides that this section shall come into force on 1 October 2007 in so far as it applies to offences under Parts XIV, XV of the Companies Act 1985 (see **[A12]**).

Note: the draft Companies Act 2006 (Commencement No 3, Consequential Amendments, Transitional Provisions and Savings) Order 2007, art 2(3) provides that this section shall come into force on 1 October 2007 so far as is necessary for the purposes of the provisions of this Act brought into force on that date by art 2(1), (2) of that Order (see **[A12]**).

Production and inspection of documents

1132 Production and inspection of documents where offence suspected

(1) An application under this section may be made—

(a) in England and Wales, to a judge of the High Court by the Director of Public Prosecutions, the Secretary of State or a chief officer of police;

(b) in Scotland, to one of the Lords Commissioners of Justiciary by the Lord Advocate;

(c) in Northern Ireland, to the High Court by the Director of Public Prosecutions for Northern Ireland, the Department of Enterprise, Trade and Investment or a chief superintendent of the Police Service of Northern Ireland.

(2) If on an application under this section there is shown to be reasonable cause to believe—

(a) that any person has, while an officer of a company, committed an offence in connection with the management of the company's affairs, and

(b) that evidence of the commission of the offence is to be found in any documents in the possession or control of the company,

an order under this section may be made.

(3) The order may—

(a) authorise any person named in it to inspect the documents in question, or any of them, for the purpose of investigating and obtaining evidence of the offence, or

(b) require the secretary of the company, or such other officer of it as may be named in the order, to produce the documents (or any of them) to a person named in the order at a place so named.

(4) This section applies also in relation to documents in the possession or control of a person carrying on the business of banking, so far as they relate to the company's affairs, as it applies to documents in the possession or control of the company, except that no such order as is referred to in subsection (3)(b) may be made by virtue of this subsection.

(5) The decision under this section of a judge of the High Court, any of the Lords Commissioners of Justiciary or the High Court is not appealable.

(6) In this section "document" includes information recorded in any form.

[S1132]

NOTES

Commencement: 6 April 2007 (certain purposes); 1 October 2007 (certain purposes); to be appointed (otherwise) (see the note below).

Note: the Companies Act 2006 (Commencement No 2, Consequential Amendments, Transitional Provisions and Savings) Order 2007, SI 2007/1093, art 2(2) provides that this section shall come into force on 6 April 2007 so far as is necessary for the purposes of the provisions of this Act brought into force on that date by art 2(1) of that Order (see **[7615]**).

Note: the draft Companies Act 2006 (Commencement No 3, Consequential Amendments, Transitional Provisions and Savings) Order 2007, art 2(1)(l) provides that this section shall come into force on 1 October 2007 in so far as it applies to offences under Parts XIV, XV of the Companies Act 1985 (see **[A12]**).

Note: the draft Companies Act 2006 (Commencement No 3, Consequential Amendments, Transitional Provisions and Savings) Order 2007, art 2(3) provides that this section shall come into force on 1 October 2007 so far as is necessary for the purposes of the provisions of this Act brought into force on that date by art 2(1), (2) of that Order (see **[A12]**).

Application to unregistered companies: see the Companies Acts (Unregistered Companies) Regulations 2007, SI 2007/318 at **[7606]**.

Supplementary

1133 Transitional provision

The provisions of this Part except section 1132 do not apply to offences committed before the commencement of the relevant provision.

[S1133]

NOTES

Commencement: 20 January 2007 (certain purposes); 6 April 2007 (certain purposes); 1 October 2007 (certain purposes); to be appointed (otherwise) (see the notes below).

Note: the Companies Act 2006 (Commencement No 1, Transitional Provisions and Savings) Order 2006, SI 2006/3428, art 3(2) provides that this section shall come into force on 20 January 2007 so far as is necessary for the purposes of the provisions of this Act brought into force on that date by art 3(1) of that Order (see **[7576]**).

Note: the Companies Act 2006 (Commencement No 2, Consequential Amendments, Transitional Provisions and Savings) Order 2007, SI 2007/1093, art 2(2) provides that this section shall come into force on 6 April 2007 so far as is necessary for the purposes of the provisions of this Act brought into force on that date by art 2(1) of that Order (see **[7615]**).

Note: the draft Companies Act 2006 (Commencement No 3, Consequential Amendments, Transitional Provisions and Savings) Order 2007, art 2(1)(l) provides that this section shall come into force on 1 October 2007 in so far as it applies to offences under Parts XIV, XV of the Companies Act 1985 (see **[A12]**).

Note: the draft Companies Act 2006 (Commencement No 3, Consequential Amendments, Transitional Provisions and Savings) Order 2007, art 2(3) provides that this section shall come into force on 1 October 2007 so far as is necessary for the purposes of the provisions of this Act brought into force on that date by art 2(1), (2) of that Order (see **[A12]**).

PART 37
COMPANIES: SUPPLEMENTARY PROVISIONS

Company records

1134 Meaning of "company records"

In this Part "company records" means—

(a) any register, index, accounting records, agreement, memorandum, minutes or other document required by the Companies Acts to be kept by a company, and

(b) any register kept by a company of its debenture holders.

[S1134]

NOTES

Commencement: 6 April 2007 (certain purposes); to be appointed (otherwise) (see the note below).

Note: the Companies Act 2006 (Commencement No 2, Consequential Amendments, Transitional Provisions and Savings) Order 2007, SI 2007/1093, art 2(2) provides that this section shall come into force on 6 April 2007 so far as is necessary for the purposes of the provisions of this Act brought into force on that date by art 2(1) of that Order (see **[7615]**).

Application to unregistered companies: see the Companies Acts (Unregistered Companies) Regulations 2007, SI 2007/318 at **[7606]**.

1135 Form of company records

(1) Company records—

(a) may be kept in hard copy or electronic form, and

(b) may be arranged in such manner as the directors of the company think fit,

provided the information in question is adequately recorded for future reference.

(2) Where the records are kept in electronic form, they must be capable of being reproduced in hard copy form.

(3) If a company fails to comply with this section, an offence is committed by every officer of the company who is in default.

(4) A person guilty of an offence under this section is liable on summary conviction to a fine not exceeding level 3 on the standard scale and, for continued contravention, a daily default fine not exceeding one-tenth of level 3 on the standard scale.

(5) Any provision of an instrument made by a company before 12th February 1979 that requires a register of holders of the company's debentures to be kept in hard copy form is to be read as requiring it to be kept in hard copy or electronic form.

[S1135]

NOTES

Commencement: 6 April 2007 (certain purposes); to be appointed (otherwise) (see the note below).

Note: the Companies Act 2006 (Commencement No 2, Consequential Amendments, Transitional Provisions and Savings) Order 2007, SI 2007/1093, art 2(2) provides that this section shall come into force on 6 April 2007 so far as is necessary for the purposes of the provisions of this Act brought into force on that date by art 2(1) of that Order (see **[7615]**).

Application to unregistered companies: see the Companies Acts (Unregistered Companies) Regulations 2007, SI 2007/318 at **[7606]**.

1136 Regulations about where certain company records to be kept available for inspection

(1) The Secretary of State may make provision by regulations specifying places other than a company's registered office at which company records required to be kept available for inspection under a relevant provision may be so kept in compliance with that provision.

(2) The "relevant provisions" are—
section 114 (register of members);
section 162 (register of directors);
section 228 (directors' service contracts);
section 237 (directors' indemnities);
section 275 (register of secretaries);
section 358 (records of resolutions etc);
section 702 (contracts relating to purchase of own shares);
section 720 (documents relating to redemption or purchase of own shares out of capital by private company);
section 743 (register of debenture holders);
section 805 (report to members of outcome of investigation by public company into interests in its shares);
section 809 (register of interests in shares disclosed to public company);
section 877 (instruments creating charges and register of charges: England and Wales);
section 892 (instruments creating charges and register of charges: Scotland).

(3) The regulations may specify a place by reference to the company's principal place of business, the part of the United Kingdom in which the company is registered, the place at which the company keeps any other records available for inspection or in any other way.

(4) The regulations may provide that a company does not comply with a relevant provision by keeping company records available for inspection at a place specified in the regulations unless conditions specified in the regulations are met.

(5) The regulations—
(a) need not specify a place in relation to each relevant provision;
(b) may specify more than one place in relation to a relevant provision.

(6) A requirement under a relevant provision to keep company records available for inspection is not complied with by keeping them available for inspection at a place specified in the regulations unless all the company's records subject to the requirement are kept there.

(7) Regulations under this section are subject to negative resolution procedure.

[S1136]

NOTES

Commencement: 20 January 2007 (for the purpose of enabling the exercise of powers to make Orders or Regulations by statutory instrument); to be appointed (otherwise).

1137 Regulations about inspection of records and provision of copies

(1) The Secretary of State may make provision by regulations as to the obligations of a company that is required by any provision of the Companies Acts—
(a) to keep available for inspection any company records, or
(b) to provide copies of any company records.

(2) A company that fails to comply with the regulations is treated as having refused inspection or, as the case may be, having failed to provide a copy.

(3) The regulations may—

(a) make provision as to the time, duration and manner of inspection, including the circumstances in which and extent to which the copying of information is permitted in the course of inspection, and

(b) define what may be required of the company as regards the nature, extent and manner of extracting or presenting any information for the purposes of inspection or the provision of copies.

(4) Where there is power to charge a fee, the regulations may make provision as to the amount of the fee and the basis of its calculation.

(5) Nothing in any provision of this Act or in the regulations shall be read as preventing a company—

(a) from affording more extensive facilities than are required by the regulations, or

(b) where a fee may be charged, from charging a lesser fee than that prescribed or none at all.

(6) Regulations under this section are subject to negative resolution procedure.

[S1137]

NOTES

Commencement: 20 January 2007 (for the purpose of enabling the exercise of powers to make Orders or Regulations by statutory instrument); to be appointed (otherwise).

1138 Duty to take precautions against falsification

(1) Where company records are kept otherwise than in bound books, adequate precautions must be taken—

(a) to guard against falsification, and

(b) to facilitate the discovery of falsification.

(2) If a company fails to comply with this section, an offence is committed by every officer of the company who is in default.

(3) A person guilty of an offence under this section is liable on summary conviction to a fine not exceeding level 3 on the standard scale and, for continued contravention, a daily default fine not exceeding one-tenth of level 3 on the standard scale.

(4) This section does not apply to the documents required to be kept under—

(a) section 228 (copy of director's service contract or memorandum of its terms); or

(b) section 237 (qualifying indemnity provision).

[S1138]

NOTES

Commencement: 6 April 2007 (certain purposes); to be appointed (otherwise) (see the note below).

Note: the Companies Act 2006 (Commencement No 2, Consequential Amendments, Transitional Provisions and Savings) Order 2007, SI 2007/1093, art 2(2) provides that this section shall come into force on 6 April 2007 so far as is necessary for the purposes of the provisions of this Act brought into force on that date by art 2(1) of that Order (see **[7615]**).

Application to unregistered companies: see the Companies Acts (Unregistered Companies) Regulations 2007, SI 2007/318 at **[7606]**.

Service addresses

1139 Service of documents on company

(1) A document may be served on a company registered under this Act by leaving it at, or sending it by post to, the company's registered office.

(2) A document may be served on an overseas company whose particulars are registered under section 1046—

(a) by leaving it at, or sending it by post to, the registered address of any person resident in the United Kingdom who is authorised to accept service of documents on the company's behalf, or

(b) if there is no such person, or if any such person refuses service or service cannot for any other reason be effected, by leaving it at or sending by post to any place of business of the company in the United Kingdom.

(3) For the purposes of this section a person's "registered address" means any address for the time being shown as a current address in relation to that person in the part of the register available for public inspection.

(4) Where a company registered in Scotland or Northern Ireland carries on business in England and Wales, the process of any court in England and Wales may be served on the company by leaving it at, or sending it by post to, the company's principal place of business in England and Wales, addressed to the manager or other head officer in England and Wales of the company.

Where process is served on a company under this subsection, the person issuing out the process must send a copy of it by post to the company's registered office.

(5) Further provision as to service and other matters is made in the company communications provisions (see section 1143).

[S1139]

NOTES

Commencement: 6 April 2007 (certain purposes); to be appointed (otherwise) (see the note below).

Note: the Companies Act 2006 (Commencement No 2, Consequential Amendments, Transitional Provisions and Savings) Order 2007, SI 2007/1093, art 2(2) provides that this section shall come into force on 6 April 2007 so far as is necessary for the purposes of the provisions of this Act brought into force on that date by art 2(1) of that Order (see **[7615]**).

Transitional adaptations: art 3 of the Companies Act 2006 (Commencement No 2, Consequential Amendments, Transitional Provisions and Savings) Order 2007, SI 2007/1093 provides that the provisions brought into force by art 2 of 2007 Order shall have effect subject to any transitional adaptations specified in Sch 1 to that Order. Schedule 1, para 5 to the Order (at **[7625]**) provides as follows—

"**5.**—(1) Section 1139 has effect with the following adaptation.

(2) In subsection (1) for "under this Act" substitute "under the Companies Act 1985 or the Companies (Northern Ireland) Order 1986".".

Application to unregistered companies: see the Companies Acts (Unregistered Companies) Regulations 2007, SI 2007/318 at **[7606]**.

1140 Service of documents on directors, secretaries and others

(1) A document may be served on a person to whom this section applies by leaving it at, or sending it by post to, the person's registered address.

(2) This section applies to—

(a) a director or secretary of a company;

(b) in the case of an overseas company whose particulars are registered under section 1046, a person holding any such position as may be specified for the purposes of this section by regulations under that section;

(c) a person appointed in relation to a company as—

(i) a judicial factor (in Scotland),

(ii) a receiver and manager appointed under section 18 of the Charities Act 1993 (c 10), or

(iii) a manager appointed under section 47 of the Companies (Audit, Investigations and Community Enterprise) Act 2004 (c 27).

(3) This section applies whatever the purpose of the document in question.

It is not restricted to service for purposes arising out of or in connection with the appointment or position mentioned in subsection (2) or in connection with the company concerned.

(4) For the purposes of this section a person's "registered address" means any address for the time being shown as a current address in relation to that person in the part of the register available for public inspection.

(5) If notice of a change of that address is given to the registrar, a person may validly serve a document at the address previously registered until the end of the period of 14 days beginning with the date on which notice of the change is registered.

(6) Service may not be effected by virtue of this section at an address—

(a) if notice has been registered of the termination of the appointment in relation to which the address was registered and the address is not a registered address of the person concerned in relation to any other appointment;

(b) in the case of a person holding any such position as is mentioned in subsection (2)(b), if the overseas company has ceased to have any connection with the United Kingdom by virtue of which it is required to register particulars under section 1046.

(7) Further provision as to service and other matters is made in the company communications provisions (see section 1143).

(8) Nothing in this section shall be read as affecting any enactment or rule of law under which permission is required for service out of the jurisdiction.

[S1140]

NOTES

Commencement: 6 April 2007 (certain purposes); to be appointed (otherwise) (see the note below).

Note: the Companies Act 2006 (Commencement No 2, Consequential Amendments, Transitional Provisions and Savings) Order 2007, SI 2007/1093, art 2(2) provides that this section shall come into force on 6 April 2007 so far as is necessary for the purposes of the provisions of this Act brought into force on that date by art 2(1) of that Order (see **[7615]**).

Application to unregistered companies: see the Companies Acts (Unregistered Companies) Regulations 2007, SI 2007/318 at **[7606]**.

1141 Service addresses

(1) In the Companies Acts a "service address", in relation to a person, means an address at which documents may be effectively served on that person.

(2) The Secretary of State may by regulations specify conditions with which a service address must comply.

(3) Regulations under this section are subject to negative resolution procedure.

[S1141]

NOTES

Commencement: 20 January 2007 (for the purpose of enabling the exercise of powers to make Orders or Regulations by statutory instrument); to be appointed (otherwise).

1142 Requirement to give service address

Any obligation under the Companies Acts to give a person's address is, unless otherwise expressly provided, to give a service address for that person.

[S1142]

NOTES

Commencement: to be appointed.

Sending or supplying documents or information

1143 The company communications provisions

(1) The provisions of sections 1144 to 1148 and Schedules 4 and 5 ("the company communications provisions") have effect for the purposes of any provision of the Companies Acts that authorises or requires documents or information to be sent or supplied by or to a company.

(2) The company communications provisions have effect subject to any requirements imposed, or contrary provision made, by or under any enactment.

(3) In particular, in their application in relation to documents or information to be sent or supplied to the registrar, they have effect subject to the provisions of Part 35.

(4) For the purposes of subsection (2), provision is not to be regarded as contrary to the company communications provisions by reason only of the fact that it expressly authorises a document or information to be sent or supplied in hard copy form, in electronic form or by means of a website.

[S1143]

NOTES

Commencement: 20 January 2007.

Transitional adaptations: art 5 of the Companies Act 2006 (Commencement No 1, Transitional Provisions and Savings) Order 2006, SI 2006/3428 provides that the provisions brought into force by arts 2–4 of 2006 Order shall have effect subject to any transitional adaptations specified in Sch 1 to that Order. Schedule 1, para 14 to the Order (at **[7582]**) provides as follows—

"14 The company communications provisions

(1) Section 1143 (the company communications provisions) has effect with the following adaptation.

(2) In subsection (3), after "Part 35" insert "and, to the extent that they remain in force, Part 24 of the Companies Act 1985 and Part 24 of the Companies (Northern Ireland) Order 1986".".

1144 Sending or supplying documents or information

(1) Documents or information to be sent or supplied to a company must be sent or supplied in accordance with the provisions of Schedule 4.

(2) Documents or information to be sent or supplied by a company must be sent or supplied in accordance with the provisions of Schedule 5.

(3) The provisions referred to in subsection (2) apply (and those referred to in subsection (1) do not apply) in relation to documents or information that are to be sent or supplied by one company to another.

[S1144]

NOTES

Commencement: 20 January 2007.

1145 Right to hard copy version

(1) Where a member of a company or a holder of a company's debentures has received a document or information from the company otherwise than in hard copy form, he is entitled to require the company to send him a version of the document or information in hard copy form.

(2) The company must send the document or information in hard copy form within 21 days of receipt of the request from the member or debenture holder.

(3) The company may not make a charge for providing the document or information in that form.

(4) If a company fails to comply with this section, an offence is committed by the company and every officer of it who is in default.

(5) A person guilty of an offence under this section is liable on summary conviction to a fine not exceeding level 3 on the standard scale and, for continued contravention, a daily default fine not exceeding one-tenth of level 3 on the standard scale.

[S1145]

NOTES

Commencement: 20 January 2007.

1146 Requirement of authentication

(1) This section applies in relation to the authentication of a document or information sent or supplied by a person to a company.

(2) A document or information sent or supplied in hard copy form is sufficiently authenticated if it is signed by the person sending or supplying it.

(3) A document or information sent or supplied in electronic form is sufficiently authenticated—

(a) if the identity of the sender is confirmed in a manner specified by the company, or
(b) where no such manner has been specified by the company, if the communication contains or is accompanied by a statement of the

identity of the sender and the company has no reason to doubt the truth of that statement.

(4) Where a document or information is sent or supplied by one person on behalf of another, nothing in this section affects any provision of the company's articles under which the company may require reasonable evidence of the authority of the former to act on behalf of the latter.

[S1146]

NOTES

Commencement: 20 January 2007.

1147 Deemed delivery of documents and information

(1) This section applies in relation to documents and information sent or supplied by a company.

(2) Where—

(a) the document or information is sent by post (whether in hard copy or electronic form) to an address in the United Kingdom, and
(b) the company is able to show that it was properly addressed, prepaid and posted,

it is deemed to have been received by the intended recipient 48 hours after it was posted.

(3) Where—

(a) the document or information is sent or supplied by electronic means, and
(b) the company is able to show that it was properly addressed,

it is deemed to have been received by the intended recipient 48 hours after it was sent.

(4) Where the document or information is sent or supplied by means of a website, it is deemed to have been received by the intended recipient—

(a) when the material was first made available on the website, or
(b) if later, when the recipient received (or is deemed to have received) notice of the fact that the material was available on the website.

(5) In calculating a period of hours for the purposes of this section, no account shall be taken of any part of a day that is not a working day.

(6) This section has effect subject to—

(a) in its application to documents or information sent or supplied by a company to its members, any contrary provision of the company's articles;
(b) in its application to documents or information sent or supplied by a company to its debentures holders, any contrary provision in the instrument constituting the debentures;
(c) in its application to documents or information sent or supplied by a company to a person otherwise than in his capacity as a member or debenture holder, any contrary provision in an agreement between the company and that person.

[S1147]

NOTES

Commencement: 20 January 2007.

1148 Interpretation of company communications provisions

(1) In the company communications provisions—

"address" includes a number or address used for the purposes of sending or receiving documents or information by electronic means;

"company" includes any body corporate;

"document" includes summons, notice, order or other legal process and registers.

(2) References in the company communications provisions to provisions of the Companies Acts authorising or requiring a document or information to be sent or supplied include all such provisions, whatever expression is used, and references to documents or information being sent or supplied shall be construed accordingly.

(3) References in the company communications provisions to documents or information being sent or supplied by or to a company include references to documents or information being sent or supplied by or to the directors of a company acting on behalf of the company.

[S1148]

NOTES

Commencement: 20 January 2007.

Requirements as to independent valuation

1149 Application of valuation requirements

The provisions of sections 1150 to 1153 apply to the valuation and report required by—

section 93 (re-registration as public company: recent allotment of shares for non-cash consideration);

section 593 (allotment of shares of public company in consideration of non-cash asset);

section 599 (transfer of non-cash asset to public company).

[S1149]

NOTES

Commencement: to be appointed.

1150 Valuation by qualified independent person

(1) The valuation and report must be made by a person ("the valuer") who—

(a) is eligible for appointment as a statutory auditor (see section 1212), and

(b) meets the independence requirement in section 1151.

(2) However, where it appears to the valuer to be reasonable for the valuation of the consideration, or part of it, to be made by (or for him to accept a valuation made by) another person who—

(a) appears to him to have the requisite knowledge and experience to value the consideration or that part of it, and

(b) is not an officer or employee of—

(i) the company, or

(ii) any other body corporate that is that company's subsidiary or holding company or a subsidiary of that company's holding company,

or a partner of or employed by any such officer or employee,

he may arrange for or accept such a valuation, together with a report which will enable him to make his own report under this section.

(3) The references in subsection (2)(b) to an officer or employee do not include an auditor.

(4) Where the consideration or part of it is valued by a person other than the valuer himself, the latter's report must state that fact and shall also—

(a) state the former's name and what knowledge and experience he has to carry out the valuation, and

(b) describe so much of the consideration as was valued by the other person, and the method used to value it, and specify the date of that valuation.

[S1150]

NOTES

Commencement: to be appointed.

1151 The independence requirement

(1) A person meets the independence requirement for the purposes of section 1150 only if—

(a) he is not—

(i) an officer or employee of the company, or

(ii) a partner or employee of such a person, or a partnership of which such a person is a partner;

(b) he is not—
 (i) an officer or employee of an associated undertaking of the company, or
 (ii) a partner or employee of such a person, or a partnership of which such a person is a partner; and

(c) there does not exist between—
 (i) the person or an associate of his, and
 (ii) the company or an associated undertaking of the company,

a connection of any such description as may be specified by regulations made by the Secretary of State.

(2) An auditor of the company is not regarded as an officer or employee of the company for this purpose.

(3) In this section—

"associated undertaking" means—
 (a) a parent undertaking or subsidiary undertaking of the company, or
 (b) a subsidiary undertaking of a parent undertaking of the company; and

"associate" has the meaning given by section 1152.

(4) Regulations under this section are subject to negative resolution procedure.

[S1151]

NOTES

Commencement: 20 January 2007 (for the purpose of enabling the exercise of powers to make Orders or Regulations by statutory instrument); to be appointed (otherwise).

1152 Meaning of "associate"

(1) This section defines "associate" for the purposes of section 1151 (valuation: independence requirement).

(2) In relation to an individual, "associate" means—
 (a) that individual's spouse or civil partner or minor child or step-child,
 (b) any body corporate of which that individual is a director, and
 (c) any employee or partner of that individual.

(3) In relation to a body corporate, "associate" means—
 (a) any body corporate of which that body is a director,
 (b) any body corporate in the same group as that body, and
 (c) any employee or partner of that body or of any body corporate in the same group.

(4) In relation to a partnership that is a legal person under the law by which it is governed, "associate" means—
 (a) any body corporate of which that partnership is a director,
 (b) any employee of or partner in that partnership, and
 (c) any person who is an associate of a partner in that partnership.

(5) In relation to a partnership that is not a legal person under the law by which it is governed, "associate" means any person who is an associate of any of the partners.

(6) In this section, in relation to a limited liability partnership, for "director" read "member".

[S1152]

NOTES

Commencement: to be appointed.

1153 Valuer entitled to full disclosure

(1) A person carrying out a valuation or making a report with respect to any consideration proposed to be accepted or given by a company, is entitled to require from the officers of the company such information and explanation as he thinks necessary to enable him to—
 (a) carry out the valuation or make the report, and
 (b) provide any note required by section 596(3) or 600(3) (note required where valuation carried out by another person).

(2) A person who knowingly or recklessly makes a statement to which this subsection applies that is misleading, false or deceptive in a material particular commits an offence.

(3) Subsection (2) applies to a statement—
- (a) made (whether orally or in writing) to a person carrying out a valuation or making a report, and
- (b) conveying or purporting to convey any information or explanation which that person requires, or is entitled to require, under subsection (1).

(4) A person guilty of an offence under subsection (2) is liable—
- (a) on conviction on indictment, to imprisonment for a term not exceeding two years or a fine (or both);
- (b) on summary conviction—
  - (i) in England and Wales, to imprisonment for a term not exceeding twelve months or to a fine not exceeding the statutory maximum (or both);
  - (ii) in Scotland or Northern Ireland, to imprisonment for a term not exceeding six months, or to a fine not exceeding the statutory maximum (or both).

[S1153]

NOTES

Commencement: to be appointed.

Notice of appointment of certain officers

1154 Duty to notify registrar of certain appointments etc

(1) Notice must be given to the registrar of the appointment in relation to a company of—
- (a) a judicial factor (in Scotland),
- (b) a receiver and manager appointed under section 18 of the Charities Act 1993 (c 10), or
- (c) a manager appointed under section 47 of the Companies (Audit, Investigations and Community Enterprise) Act 2004 (c 27).

(2) The notice must be given—
- (a) in the case of appointment of a judicial factor, by the judicial factor;
- (b) in the case of appointment of a receiver and manager under section 18 of the Charities Act 1993 (c 10), by the Charity Commission;
- (c) in the case of appointment of a manager under section 47 of the Companies (Audit, Investigations and Community Enterprise) Act 2004, by the Regulator of Community Interest Companies.

(3) The notice must specify an address at which service of documents (including legal process) may be effected on the person appointed.

Notice of a change in the address for service may be given to the registrar by the person appointed.

(4) Where notice has been given under this section of the appointment of a person, notice must also be given to the registrar of the termination of the appointment. This notice must be given by the person specified in subsection (2).

[S1154]

NOTES

Commencement: to be appointed.

1155 Offence of failure to give notice

(1) If a judicial factor fails to give notice of his appointment in accordance with section 1154 within the period of 14 days after the appointment he commits an offence.

(2) A person guilty of an offence under this section is liable on summary conviction to a fine not exceeding level 5 on the standard scale and, for continued contravention, a daily default fine not exceeding one-tenth of level 5 on the standard scale.

[S1155]

NOTES

Commencement: to be appointed.

Courts and legal proceedings

1156 Meaning of "the court"

(1) Except as otherwise provided, in the Companies Acts "the court" means—

(a) in England and Wales, the High Court or (subject to subsection (3)) a county court;

(b) in Scotland, the Court of Session or the sheriff court;

(c) in Northern Ireland, the High Court.

(2) The provisions of the Companies Acts conferring jurisdiction on "the court" as defined above have effect subject to any enactment or rule of law relating to the allocation of jurisdiction or distribution of business between courts in any part of the United Kingdom.

(3) The Lord Chancellor may, with the concurrence of the Lord Chief Justice, by order—

(a) exclude a county court from having jurisdiction under the Companies Acts, and

(b) for the purposes of that jurisdiction attach that court's district, or any part of it, to another county court.

(4) The Lord Chief Justice may nominate a judicial office holder (as defined in section 109(4) of the Constitutional Reform Act 2005 (c 4)) to exercise his functions under subsection (3).

[S1156]

NOTES

Commencement: 20 January 2007 (for the purpose of enabling the exercise of powers to make Orders or Regulations by statutory instrument); to be appointed (otherwise).

1157 Power of court to grant relief in certain cases

(1) If in proceedings for negligence, default, breach of duty or breach of trust against—

(a) an officer of a company, or

(b) a person employed by a company as auditor (whether he is or is not an officer of the company),

it appears to the court hearing the case that the officer or person is or may be liable but that he acted honestly and reasonably, and that having regard to all the circumstances of the case (including those connected with his appointment) he ought fairly to be excused, the court may relieve him, either wholly or in part, from his liability on such terms as it thinks fit.

(2) If any such officer or person has reason to apprehend that a claim will or might be made against him in respect of negligence, default, breach of duty or breach of trust—

(a) he may apply to the court for relief, and

(b) the court has the same power to relieve him as it would have had if it had been a court before which proceedings against him for negligence, default, breach of duty or breach of trust had been brought.

(3) Where a case to which subsection (1) applies is being tried by a judge with a jury, the judge, after hearing the evidence, may, if he is satisfied that the defendant (in Scotland, the defender) ought in pursuance of that subsection to be relieved either in whole or in part from the liability sought to be enforced against him, withdraw the case from the jury and forthwith direct judgment to be entered for the defendant (in Scotland, grant decree of absolvitor) on such terms as to costs (in Scotland, expenses) or otherwise as the judge may think proper.

[S1157]

NOTES

Commencement: to be appointed.

PART 38
COMPANIES: INTERPRETATION

Meaning of "UK-registered company"

1158 Meaning of "UK-registered company"

In the Companies Acts "UK-registered company" means a company registered under this Act.

The expression does not include an overseas company that has registered particulars under section 1046.

[S1158]

NOTES

Commencement: 1 October 2007 (certain purposes); 1 November 2007 (certain purposes); to be appointed (otherwise) (for transitional adaptations see the notes below).

Note: the draft Companies Act 2006 (Commencement No 3, Consequential Amendments, Transitional Provisions and Savings) Order 2007, arts 2(3) and 3(2) provide that this section shall come into force on 1 October 2007 and 1 November 2007 so far as is necessary for the purposes of the provisions of this Act brought into force on those dates by arts 2(1), (2) and 3(2) of that Order respectively (see **[A12]**).

Transitional adaptations: art 6 of the draft Companies Act 2006 (Commencement No 3, Consequential Amendments, Transitional Provisions and Savings) Order 2007 provides that the provisions brought into force by that Order shall have effect subject to any transitional adaptations specified in Sch 1 to that Order. Schedule 1, para 21 to the Order (at **[A12]**) provides as follows—

"21 Meaning of "UK-registered company" (s 1158)

(1) Section 1158 (meaning of "UK-registered company") has effect with the following adaptations.

(2) For "a company registered under this Act" substitute "a company within the meaning of the Companies Act 1985 or the Companies (Northern Ireland) Order 1986 or a company registered under section 680 of that Act or Article 629 of that Order.".

(3) For "an overseas company that has registered particulars under section 1046" substitute "an oversea company within the meaning of that Act or a Part 23 company within the meaning of that Order".".

Meaning of "subsidiary" and related expressions

1159 Meaning of "subsidiary" etc

(1) A company is a "subsidiary" of another company, its "holding company", if that other company—

(a) holds a majority of the voting rights in it, or

(b) is a member of it and has the right to appoint or remove a majority of its board of directors, or

(c) is a member of it and controls alone, pursuant to an agreement with other members, a majority of the voting rights in it,

or if it is a subsidiary of a company that is itself a subsidiary of that other company.

(2) A company is a "wholly-owned subsidiary" of another company if it has no members except that other and that other's wholly-owned subsidiaries or persons acting on behalf of that other or its wholly-owned subsidiaries.

(3) Schedule 6 contains provisions explaining expressions used in this section and otherwise supplementing this section.

(4) In this section and that Schedule "company" includes any body corporate.

[S1159]

NOTES

Commencement: to be appointed.

1160 Meaning of "subsidiary" etc: power to amend

(1) The Secretary of State may by regulations amend the provisions of section 1159 (meaning of "subsidiary" etc) and Schedule 6 (meaning of "subsidiary" etc: supplementary provisions) so as to alter the meaning of the expressions "subsidiary", "holding company" or "wholly-owned subsidiary".

(2) Regulations under this section are subject to negative resolution procedure.

(3) Any amendment made by regulations under this section does not apply for the purposes of enactments outside the Companies Acts unless the regulations so provide.

(4) So much of section 23(3) of the Interpretation Act 1978 (c 30) as applies section 17(2)(a) of that Act (effect of repeal and re-enactment) to deeds, instruments and documents other than enactments does not apply in relation to any repeal and re-enactment effected by regulations under this section.

[S1160]

NOTES

Commencement: 20 January 2007 (for the purpose of enabling the exercise of powers to make Orders or Regulations by statutory instrument); to be appointed (otherwise).

Meaning of "undertaking" and related expressions

1161 Meaning of "undertaking" and related expressions

(1) In the Companies Acts "undertaking" means—

(a) a body corporate or partnership, or

(b) an unincorporated association carrying on a trade or business, with or without a view to profit.

(2) In the Companies Acts references to shares—

(a) in relation to an undertaking with capital but no share capital, are to rights to share in the capital of the undertaking; and

(b) in relation to an undertaking without capital, are to interests—

(i) conferring any right to share in the profits or liability to contribute to the losses of the undertaking, or

(ii) giving rise to an obligation to contribute to the debts or expenses of the undertaking in the event of a winding up.

(3) Other expressions appropriate to companies shall be construed, in relation to an undertaking which is not a company, as references to the corresponding persons, officers, documents or organs, as the case may be, appropriate to undertakings of that description.

This is subject to provision in any specific context providing for the translation of such expressions.

(4) References in the Companies Acts to "fellow subsidiary undertakings" are to undertakings which are subsidiary undertakings of the same parent undertaking but are not parent undertakings or subsidiary undertakings of each other.

(5) In the Companies Acts "group undertaking", in relation to an undertaking, means an undertaking which is—

(a) a parent undertaking or subsidiary undertaking of that undertaking, or

(b) a subsidiary undertaking of any parent undertaking of that undertaking.

[S1161]

NOTES

Commencement: to be appointed.

1162 Parent and subsidiary undertakings

(1) This section (together with Schedule 7) defines "parent undertaking" and "subsidiary undertaking" for the purposes of the Companies Acts.

(2) An undertaking is a parent undertaking in relation to another undertaking, a subsidiary undertaking, if—

(a) it holds a majority of the voting rights in the undertaking, or

(b) it is a member of the undertaking and has the right to appoint or remove a majority of its board of directors, or

(c) it has the right to exercise a dominant influence over the undertaking—

(i) by virtue of provisions contained in the undertaking's articles, or

(ii) by virtue of a control contract, or

(d) it is a member of the undertaking and controls alone, pursuant to an agreement with other shareholders or members, a majority of the voting rights in the undertaking.

(3) For the purposes of subsection (2) an undertaking shall be treated as a member of another undertaking—

(a) if any of its subsidiary undertakings is a member of that undertaking, or

(b) if any shares in that other undertaking are held by a person acting on behalf of the undertaking or any of its subsidiary undertakings.

(4) An undertaking is also a parent undertaking in relation to another undertaking, a subsidiary undertaking, if—

(a) it has the power to exercise, or actually exercises, dominant influence or control over it, or

(b) it and the subsidiary undertaking are managed on a unified basis.

(5) A parent undertaking shall be treated as the parent undertaking of undertakings in relation to which any of its subsidiary undertakings are, or are to be treated as, parent undertakings; and references to its subsidiary undertakings shall be construed accordingly.

(6) Schedule 7 contains provisions explaining expressions used in this section and otherwise supplementing this section.

(7) In this section and that Schedule references to shares, in relation to an undertaking, are to allotted shares.

[S1162]

NOTES

Commencement: to be appointed.

Other definitions

1163 "Non-cash asset"

(1) In the Companies Acts "non-cash asset" means any property or interest in property, other than cash.

For this purpose "cash" includes foreign currency.

(2) A reference to the transfer or acquisition of a non-cash asset includes—

(a) the creation or extinction of an estate or interest in, or a right over, any property, and

(b) the discharge of a liability of any person, other than a liability for a liquidated sum.

[S1163]

NOTES

Commencement: to be appointed.

1164 Meaning of "banking company" and "banking group"

(1) This section defines "banking company" and "banking group" for the purposes of the Companies Acts.

(2) "Banking company" means a person who has permission under Part 4 of the Financial Services and Markets Act 2000 (c 8) to accept deposits, other than—

(a) a person who is not a company, and

(b) a person who has such permission only for the purpose of carrying on another regulated activity in accordance with permission under that Part.

(3) The definition in subsection (2) must be read with section 22 of that Act, any relevant order under that section and Schedule 2 to that Act.

(4) References to a banking group are to a group where the parent company is a banking company or where—

(a) the parent company's principal subsidiary undertakings are wholly or mainly credit institutions, and

(b) the parent company does not itself carry on any material business apart from the acquisition, management and disposal of interests in subsidiary undertakings.

"Group" here means a parent undertaking and its subsidiary undertakings.

(5) For the purposes of subsection (4)—

(a) a parent company's principal subsidiary undertakings are the subsidiary undertakings of the company whose results or financial position would principally affect the figures shown in the group accounts, and

(b) the management of interests in subsidiary undertakings includes the provision of services to such undertakings.

[S1164]

NOTES

Commencement: to be appointed.

1165 Meaning of "insurance company" and related expressions

(1) This section defines "insurance company", "authorised insurance company", "insurance group" and "insurance market activity" for the purposes of the Companies Acts.

(2) An "authorised insurance company" means a person (whether incorporated or not) who has permission under Part 4 of the Financial Services and Markets Act 2000 (c 8) to effect or carry out contracts of insurance.

(3) An "insurance company" means—

(a) an authorised insurance company, or

(b) any other person (whether incorporated or not) who—

(i) carries on insurance market activity, or

(ii) may effect or carry out contracts of insurance under which the benefits provided by that person are exclusively or primarily benefits in kind in the event of accident to or breakdown of a vehicle.

(4) Neither expression includes a friendly society within the meaning of the Friendly Societies Act 1992 (c 40).

(5) References to an insurance group are to a group where the parent company is an insurance company or where—

(a) the parent company's principal subsidiary undertakings are wholly or mainly insurance companies, and

(b) the parent company does not itself carry on any material business apart from the acquisition, management and disposal of interests in subsidiary undertakings.

"Group" here means a parent undertaking and its subsidiary undertakings.

(6) For the purposes of subsection (5)—

(a) a parent company's principal subsidiary undertakings are the subsidiary undertakings of the company whose results or financial position would principally affect the figures shown in the group accounts, and

(b) the management of interests in subsidiary undertakings includes the provision of services to such undertakings.

(7) "Insurance market activity" has the meaning given in section 316(3) of the Financial Services and Markets Act 2000.

(8) References in this section to contracts of insurance and to the effecting or carrying out of such contracts must be read with section 22 of that Act, any relevant order under that section and Schedule 2 to that Act.

[S1165]

NOTES

Commencement: to be appointed.

1166 "Employees' share scheme"

For the purposes of the Companies Acts an employees' share scheme is a scheme for encouraging or facilitating the holding of shares in or debentures of a company by or for the benefit of—

(a) the bona fide employees or former employees of—
(i) the company,
(ii) any subsidiary of the company, or
(iii) the company's holding company or any subsidiary of the company's holding company, or
(b) the spouses, civil partners, surviving spouses, surviving civil partners, or minor children or step-children of such employees or former employees.

[S1166]

NOTES

Commencement: to be appointed.

1167 Meaning of "prescribed"

In the Companies Acts "prescribed" means prescribed (by order or by regulations) by the Secretary of State.

[S1167]

NOTES

Commencement: 20 January 2007 (for the purpose of enabling the exercise of powers to make Orders or Regulations by statutory instrument); to be appointed (otherwise).

1168 Hard copy and electronic form and related expressions

(1) The following provisions apply for the purposes of the Companies Acts.

(2) A document or information is sent or supplied in hard copy form if it is sent or supplied in a paper copy or similar form capable of being read.

References to hard copy have a corresponding meaning.

(3) A document or information is sent or supplied in electronic form if it is sent or supplied—
(a) by electronic means (for example, by e-mail or fax), or
(b) by any other means while in an electronic form (for example, sending a disk by post).

References to electronic copy have a corresponding meaning.

(4) A document or information is sent or supplied by electronic means if it is—
(a) sent initially and received at its destination by means of electronic equipment for the processing (which expression includes digital compression) or storage of data, and
(b) entirely transmitted, conveyed and received by wire, by radio, by optical means or by other electromagnetic means.

References to electronic means have a corresponding meaning.

(5) A document or information authorised or required to be sent or supplied in electronic form must be sent or supplied in a form, and by a means, that the sender or supplier reasonably considers will enable the recipient—
(a) to read it, and
(b) to retain a copy of it.

(6) For the purposes of this section, a document or information can be read only if—
(a) it can be read with the naked eye, or
(b) to the extent that it consists of images (for example photographs, pictures, maps, plans or drawings), it can be seen with the naked eye.

(7) The provisions of this section apply whether the provision of the Companies Acts in question uses the words "sent" or "supplied" or uses other words (such as "deliver", "provide", "produce" or, in the case of a notice, "give") to refer to the sending or supplying of a document or information.

[S1168]

NOTES

Commencement: 1 January 2007 (certain purposes); 20 January 2007 (certain purposes); 6 April 2007 (certain purposes); 1 October 2007 (certain purposes); 15 December 2007 (certain purposes); to be appointed (otherwise) (see the notes below).

Note: the Companies Act 2006 (Commencement No 1, Transitional Provisions and Savings) Order 2006, SI 2006/3428, arts 2(2), 3(2) provide that this section shall come into force on 1 January 2007 and 20 January 2007 respectively so far as is necessary for the purposes of the provisions of this Act brought into force on those dates by arts 2(1), 3(1) of that Order (see **[7575]**, **[7576]**).

Note: the Companies Act 2006 (Commencement No 2, Consequential Amendments, Transitional Provisions and Savings) Order 2007, SI 2007/1093, art 2(2) provides that this section shall come into force on 6 April 2007 so far as is necessary for the purposes of the provisions of this Act brought into force on that date by art 2(1) of that Order (see **[7615]**).

Note: the draft Companies Act 2006 (Commencement No 3, Consequential Amendments, Transitional Provisions and Savings) Order 2007, art 2(3) provides that this section shall come into force on 1 October 2007 so far as is necessary for the purposes of the provisions of this Act brought into force on that date by art 2(1), (2) of that Order (see **[A12]**).

Note: the draft Companies Act 2006 (Commencement No 3, Consequential Amendments, Transitional Provisions and Savings) Order 2007, art 4(2) provides that this section shall come into force on 15 December 2007 so far as is necessary for the purposes of the provisions of this Act brought into force on that date by art 4(1) of that Order (see **[A12]**).

1169 Dormant companies

(1) For the purposes of the Companies Acts a company is "dormant" during any period in which it has no significant accounting transaction.

(2) A "significant accounting transaction" means a transaction that is required by section 386 to be entered in the company's accounting records.

(3) In determining whether or when a company is dormant, there shall be disregarded—

(a) any transaction arising from the taking of shares in the company by a subscriber to the memorandum as a result of an undertaking of his in connection with the formation of the company;

(b) any transaction consisting of the payment of—

(i) a fee to the registrar on a change of the company's name,

(ii) a fee to the registrar on the re-registration of the company,

(iii) a penalty under section 453 (penalty for failure to file accounts), or

(iv) a fee to the registrar for the registration of an annual return.

(4) Any reference in the Companies Acts to a body corporate other than a company being dormant has a corresponding meaning.

[S1169]

NOTES

Commencement: to be appointed.

1170 Meaning of "EEA State" and related expressions

In the Companies Acts—

["EEA State" has the meaning given by Schedule 1 to the Interpretation Act 1978;]

"EEA company" and "EEA undertaking" mean a company or undertaking governed by the law of an EEA State.

[S1170]

NOTES

Commencement: 6 April 2007.

Definition "EEA State" substituted by the Companies (EEA State) Regulations 2007, SI 2007/732, reg 3, as from 9 March 2007.

1171 The former Companies Acts

In the Companies Acts—

"the former Companies Acts" means—

(a) the Joint Stock Companies Acts, the Companies Act 1862 (c 89), the Companies (Consolidation) Act 1908 (c 69), the Companies Act 1929 (c 23), the Companies Act (Northern Ireland) 1932 (c 7 (NI)), the Companies Acts 1948 to 1983, the Companies Act (Northern Ireland) 1960 (c 22 (NI)), the Companies (Northern Ireland) Order 1986 (SI 1986/1032 (NI 6)) and the Companies Consolidation (Consequential Provisions) (Northern Ireland) Order 1986 (SI 1986/1035 (NI 9)), and

(b) the provisions of the Companies Act 1985 (c 6) and the Companies Consolidation (Consequential Provisions) Act 1985 (c 9) that are no longer in force;

"the Joint Stock Companies Acts" means the Joint Stock Companies Act 1856 (c 47), the Joint Stock Companies Acts 1856, 1857 (20 & 21 Vict c 14), the Joint Stock Banking Companies Act 1857 (c 49), and the Act to enable Joint Stock Banking Companies to be formed on the principle of limited liability (1858 c 91), but does not include the Joint Stock Companies Act 1844 (c 110).

[S1171]

NOTES

Commencement: to be appointed.

General

1172 References to requirements of this Act

References in the company law provisions of this Act to the requirements of this Act include the requirements of regulations and orders made under it.

[S1172]

NOTES

Commencement: to be appointed.

1173 Minor definitions: general

(1) In the Companies Acts—

"body corporate" and "corporation" include a body incorporated outside the United Kingdom, but do not include—

(a) a corporation sole, or

(b) a partnership that, whether or not a legal person, is not regarded as a body corporate under the law by which it is governed;

"credit institution" means a credit institution as defined in Article 4.1(a) of Directive 2006/48/EC of the European Parliament and of the Council relating to the taking up and pursuit of the business of credit institutions;

"financial institution" means a financial institution within the meaning of Article 1.1 of the Council Directive on the obligations of branches established in a Member State of credit and financial institutions having their head offices outside that Member State regarding the publication of annual accounting documents (the Bank Branches Directive, 89/ 117/EEC);

"firm" means any entity, whether or not a legal person, that is not an individual and includes a body corporate, a corporation sole and a partnership or other unincorporated association;

"the Gazette" means—

(a) as respects companies registered in England and Wales, the London Gazette,

(b) as respects companies registered in Scotland, the Edinburgh Gazette, and

(c) as respects companies registered in Northern Ireland, the Belfast Gazette;

"hire-purchase agreement" has the same meaning as in the Consumer Credit Act 1974 (c 39);

"officer", in relation to a body corporate, includes a director, manager or secretary;

"parent company" means a company that is a parent undertaking (see section 1162 and Schedule 7);

"regulated activity" has the meaning given in section 22 of the Financial Services and Markets Act 2000 (c 8);

"regulated market" has the same meaning as in Directive 2004/39/EC of the European Parliament and of the Council on markets in financial instruments (see Article 4.1(14));

"working day", in relation to a company, means a day that is not a Saturday or Sunday, Christmas Day, Good Friday or any day that is a bank holiday under the Banking and Financial Dealings Act 1971 (c 80) in the part of the United Kingdom where the company is registered.

(2) In relation to an EEA State that has not implemented Directive 2004/39/EC of the European Parliament and of the Council on markets in financial instruments, the following definition of "regulated market" has effect in place of that in subsection (1)—

"regulated market" has the same meaning as it has in Council Directive 93/22/EEC on investment services in the securities field.

[S1173]

NOTES

Commencement: 1 January 2007 (certain purposes); 20 January 2007 (certain purposes); 6 April 2007 (certain purposes); 1 October 2007 (certain purposes); 1 November 2007 (certain purposes); to be appointed (otherwise) (see the notes below).

Note: the Companies Act 2006 (Commencement No 1, Transitional Provisions and Savings) Order 2006, SI 2006/3428, art 2(2) provides that the definitions "the Gazette" and "working day" shall come into force on 1 January 2007 so far as is necessary for the purposes of the provisions of this Act brought into force on that date by art 2(1) of that Order (see **[7575]**).

Note: the Companies Act 2006 (Commencement No 1, Transitional Provisions and Savings) Order 2006, SI 2006/3428, art 3(2) provides that the definition "working day" shall come into force on 20 January 2007 so far as is necessary for the purposes of the provisions of this Act brought into force on that date by art 3(1) of that Order (see **[7576]**).

Note: the Companies Act 2006 (Commencement No 2, Consequential Amendments, Transitional Provisions and Savings) Order 2007, SI 2007/1093, art 2(2) provides that the definitions "body corporate", "the Gazette" and "regulated market" shall come into force on 6 April 2007 so far as is necessary for the purposes of the provisions of this Act brought into force on that date by art 2(1) of that Order (see **[7615]**).

Note: the draft Companies Act 2006 (Commencement No 3, Consequential Amendments, Transitional Provisions and Savings) Order 2007, art 2(3) provides that the definitions of "body corporate" (and "corporation"), "firm" and "working day" shall come into force on 1 October 2007 so far as is necessary for the purposes of the provisions of this Act brought into force on that date by art 2(1), (2) of that Order (see **[A12]**).

Note: the draft Companies Act 2006 (Commencement No 3, Consequential Amendments, Transitional Provisions and Savings) Order 2007, art 3(2) provides that the definition of "body corporate" shall come into force on 1 November 2007 so far as is necessary for the purposes of the provisions of this Act brought into force on that date by art 3(1) of that Order (see **[A12]**).

Application to unregistered companies: see the Companies Acts (Unregistered Companies) Regulations 2007, SI 2007/318 at **[7606]**.

1174 Index of defined expressions

Schedule 8 contains an index of provisions defining or otherwise explaining expressions used in the Companies Acts.

[S1174]

NOTES

Commencement: to be appointed.

PART 39
COMPANIES: MINOR AMENDMENTS

1175 Removal of special provisions about accounts and audit of charitable companies

(1) Part 7 of the Companies Act 1985 (c 6) and Part 8 of the Companies (Northern Ireland) Order 1986 (accounts and audit) are amended in accordance with Schedule 9 to this Act so as to remove the special provisions about companies that are charities.

(2) In that Schedule—

Part 1 contains repeals and consequential amendments of provisions of the Companies Act 1985;

Part 2 contains repeals and consequential amendments of provisions of the Companies (Northern Ireland) Order 1986.

[S1175]

NOTES

Commencement: to be appointed.

1176 Power of Secretary of State to bring civil proceedings on company's behalf

(1)–(3) (*Repeal CA 1985, s 438 at* **[472]**, *and amend ss 439, 453 of that Act at* **[473]**, **[487]**.)

(4) Nothing in this section affects proceedings brought under section 438 before the commencement of this section.

[S1176]

NOTES

Commencement: 6 April 2007.

1177 Repeal of certain provisions about company directors

The following provisions of Part 10 of the Companies Act 1985 shall cease to have effect—

section 311 (prohibition on tax-free payments to directors);

sections 323 and 327 (prohibition on directors dealing in share options);

sections 324 to 326 and 328 to 329, and Parts 2 to 4 of Schedule 13 (register of directors' interests);

sections 343 and 344 (special procedure for disclosure by banks).

[S1177]

NOTES

Commencement: 6 April 2007.

1178 Repeal of requirement that certain companies publish periodical statement

The following provisions shall cease to have effect—

section 720 of the Companies Act 1985 (c 6) (certain companies to publish periodical statement), and

Schedule 23 to that Act (form of statement under section 720).

[S1178]

NOTES

Commencement: 6 April 2007.

1179 Repeal of requirement that Secretary of State prepare annual report

Section 729 of the Companies Act 1985 (annual report to Parliament by Secretary of State on matters within the Companies Acts) shall cease to have effect.

[S1179]

NOTES

Commencement: 6 April 2007.

1180 Repeal of certain provisions about company charges

Part 4 of the Companies Act 1989 (c 40) (registration of company charges), which has not been brought into force, is repealed.

[S1180]

NOTES

Commencement: to be appointed.

1181 Access to constitutional documents of RTE and RTM companies

(1) The Secretary of State may by order—

(a) amend Chapter 1 of Part 1 of the Leasehold Reform, Housing and Urban Development Act 1993 (c 28) for the purpose of facilitating access to the provisions of the articles or any other constitutional document of RTE companies;

(b) amend Chapter 1 of Part 2 of the Commonhold and Leasehold Reform Act 2002 (c 15) (leasehold reform) for the purpose of facilitating access to the provisions of the articles or any other constitutional document of RTM companies.

(2) References in subsection (1) to provisions of a company's articles or any other constitutional document include any provisions included in those documents by virtue of any enactment.

(3) An order under this section is subject to negative resolution procedure.

(4) In this section—

"RTE companies" has the same meaning as in Chapter 1 of Part 1 of the Leasehold Reform, Housing and Urban Development Act 1993;

"RTM companies" has the same meaning as in Chapter 1 of Part 2 of the Commonhold and Leasehold Reform Act 2002.

[S1181]

NOTES

Commencement: 20 January 2007 (for the purpose of enabling the exercise of powers to make Orders or Regulations by statutory instrument); to be appointed (otherwise).

PART 40
COMPANY DIRECTORS: FOREIGN DISQUALIFICATION ETC

Introductory

1182 Persons subject to foreign restrictions

(1) This section defines what is meant by references in this Part to a person being subject to foreign restrictions.

(2) A person is subject to foreign restrictions if under the law of a country or territory outside the United Kingdom—

(a) he is, by reason of misconduct or unfitness, disqualified to any extent from acting in connection with the affairs of a company,

(b) he is, by reason of misconduct or unfitness, required—

(i) to obtain permission from a court or other authority, or

(ii) to meet any other condition,

before acting in connection with the affairs of a company, or

(c) he has, by reason of misconduct or unfitness, given undertakings to a court or other authority of a country or territory outside the United Kingdom—

(i) not to act in connection with the affairs of a company, or

(ii) restricting the extent to which, or the way in which, he may do so.

(3) The references in subsection (2) to acting in connection with the affairs of a company are to doing any of the following—

(a) being a director of a company,

(b) acting as receiver of a company's property, or

(c) being concerned or taking part in the promotion, formation or management of a company.

(4) In this section—

(a) "company" means a company incorporated or formed under the law of the country or territory in question, and

(b) in relation to such a company—

"director" means the holder of an office corresponding to that of director of a UK company; and

"receiver" includes any corresponding officer under the law of that country or territory.

[S1182]

NOTES

Commencement: to be appointed.

1183 Meaning of "the court" and "UK company"

In this Part—

"the court" means—

(a) in England and Wales, the High Court or a county court;

(b) in Scotland, the Court of Session or the sheriff court;

(c) in Northern Ireland, the High Court;

"UK company" means a company registered under this Act.

[S1183]

NOTES

Commencement: to be appointed.

Power to disqualify

1184 Disqualification of persons subject to foreign restrictions

(1) The Secretary of State may make provision by regulations disqualifying a person subject to foreign restrictions from—

(a) being a director of a UK company,

(b) acting as receiver of a UK company's property, or

(c) in any way, whether directly or indirectly, being concerned or taking part in the promotion, formation or management of a UK company.

(2) The regulations may provide that a person subject to foreign restrictions—

(a) is disqualified automatically by virtue of the regulations, or

(b) may be disqualified by order of the court on the application of the Secretary of State.

(3) The regulations may provide that the Secretary of State may accept an undertaking (a "disqualification undertaking") from a person subject to foreign restrictions that he will not do anything which would be in breach of a disqualification under subsection (1).

(4) In this Part—

(a) a "person disqualified under this Part" is a person—

(i) disqualified as mentioned in subsection (2)(a) or (b), or

(ii) who has given and is subject to a disqualification undertaking;

(b) references to a breach of a disqualification include a breach of a disqualification undertaking.

(5) The regulations may provide for applications to the court by persons disqualified under this Part for permission to act in a way which would otherwise be in breach of the disqualification.

(6) The regulations must provide that a person ceases to be disqualified under this Part on his ceasing to be subject to foreign restrictions.

(7) Regulations under this section are subject to affirmative resolution procedure.

[S1184]

NOTES

Commencement: 20 January 2007 (for the purpose of enabling the exercise of powers to make Orders or Regulations by statutory instrument); to be appointed (otherwise).

1185 Disqualification regulations: supplementary

(1) Regulations under section 1184 may make different provision for different cases and may in particular distinguish between cases by reference to—

(a) the conduct on the basis of which the person became subject to foreign restrictions;

(b) the nature of the foreign restrictions;

(c) the country or territory under whose law the foreign restrictions were imposed.

(2) Regulations under section 1184(2)(b) or (5) (provision for applications to the court)—

(a) must specify the grounds on which an application may be made;

(b) may specify factors to which the court shall have regard in determining an application.

(3) The regulations may, in particular, require the court to have regard to the following factors—

(a) whether the conduct on the basis of which the person became subject to foreign restrictions would, if done in relation to a UK company, have led a court to make a disqualification order on an application under the Company Directors Disqualification Act 1986 (c 46) or the Company Directors Disqualification (Northern Ireland) Order 2002 (SI 2002/3150 (NI 4));

(b) in a case in which the conduct on the basis of which the person became subject to foreign restrictions would not be unlawful if done in relation to a UK company, the fact that the person acted unlawfully under foreign law;

(c) whether the person's activities in relation to UK companies began after he became subject to foreign restrictions;

(d) whether the person's activities (or proposed activities) in relation to UK companies are undertaken (or are proposed to be undertaken) outside the United Kingdom.

(4) Regulations under section 1184(3) (provision as to undertakings given to the Secretary of State) may include provision allowing the Secretary of State, in determining whether to accept an undertaking, to take into account matters other than criminal convictions notwithstanding that the person may be criminally liable in respect of those matters.

(5) Regulations under section 1184(5) (provision for application to court for permission to act) may include provision—

(a) entitling the Secretary of State to be represented at the hearing of the application, and

(b) as to the giving of evidence or the calling of witnesses by the Secretary of State at the hearing of the application.

[S1185]

NOTES

Commencement: 20 January 2007 (for the purpose of enabling the exercise of powers to make Orders or Regulations by statutory instrument); to be appointed (otherwise).

1186 Offence of breach of disqualification

(1) Regulations under section 1184 may provide that a person disqualified under this Part who acts in breach of the disqualification commits an offence.

(2) The regulations may provide that a person guilty of such an offence is liable—

(a) on conviction on indictment, to imprisonment for a term not exceeding two years or a fine (or both);

(b) on summary conviction—

(i) in England and Wales, to imprisonment for a term not exceeding twelve months or to a fine not exceeding the statutory maximum (or both);

(ii) in Scotland or Northern Ireland, to imprisonment for a term not exceeding six months, or to a fine not exceeding the statutory maximum (or both).

(3) In relation to an offence committed before the commencement of section 154(1) of the Criminal Justice Act 2003 (c 44), for "twelve months" in subsection (2)(b)(i) substitute "six months".

[S1186]

NOTES

Commencement: 20 January 2007 (for the purpose of enabling the exercise of powers to make Orders or Regulations by statutory instrument); to be appointed (otherwise).

Power to make persons liable for company's debts

1187 Personal liability for debts of company

(1) The Secretary of State may provide by regulations that a person who, at a time when he is subject to foreign restrictions—

(a) is a director of a UK company, or

(b) is involved in the management of a UK company,

is personally responsible for all debts and other liabilities of the company incurred during that time.

(2) A person who is personally responsible by virtue of this section for debts and other liabilities of a company is jointly and severally liable in respect of those debts and liabilities with—

(a) the company, and
(b) any other person who (whether by virtue of this section or otherwise) is so liable.

(3) For the purposes of this section a person is involved in the management of a company if he is concerned, whether directly or indirectly, or takes part, in the management of the company.

(4) The regulations may make different provision for different cases and may in particular distinguish between cases by reference to—
(a) the conduct on the basis of which the person became subject to foreign restrictions;
(b) the nature of the foreign restrictions;
(c) the country or territory under whose law the foreign restrictions were imposed.

(5) Regulations under this section are subject to affirmative resolution procedure.

[S1187]

NOTES

Commencement: 20 January 2007 (for the purpose of enabling the exercise of powers to make Orders or Regulations by statutory instrument); to be appointed (otherwise).

Power to require statements to be sent to the registrar of companies

1188 Statements from persons subject to foreign restrictions

(1) The Secretary of State may make provision by regulations requiring a person who—
(a) is subject to foreign restrictions, and
(b) is not disqualified under this Part,

to send a statement to the registrar if he does anything that, if done by a person disqualified under this Part, would be in breach of the disqualification.

(2) The statement must include such information as may be specified in the regulations relating to—
(a) the person's activities in relation to UK companies, and
(b) the foreign restrictions to which the person is subject.

(3) The statement must be sent to the registrar within such period as may be specified in the regulations.

(4) The regulations may make different provision for different cases and may in particular distinguish between cases by reference to—
(a) the conduct on the basis of which the person became subject to foreign restrictions;
(b) the nature of the foreign restrictions;
(c) the country or territory under whose law the foreign restrictions were imposed.

(5) Regulations under this section are subject to affirmative resolution procedure.

[S1188]

NOTES

Commencement: 20 January 2007 (for the purpose of enabling the exercise of powers to make Orders or Regulations by statutory instrument); to be appointed (otherwise).

1189 Statements from persons disqualified

(1) The Secretary of State may make provision by regulations requiring a statement or notice sent to the registrar of companies under any of the provisions listed below that relates (wholly or partly) to a person who—
(a) is a person disqualified under this Part, or
(b) is subject to a disqualification order or disqualification undertaking under the Company Directors Disqualification Act 1986 (c 46) or the Company Directors Disqualification (Northern Ireland) Order 2002 (SI 2002/3150 (NI 4)),

to be accompanied by an additional statement.

(2) The provisions referred to above are—
(a) section 12 (statement of a company's proposed officers),

(b) section 167(2) (notice of person having become director), and

(c) section 276 (notice of a person having become secretary or one of joint secretaries).

(3) The additional statement is a statement that the person has obtained permission from a court, on an application under section 1184(5) or (as the case may be) for the purposes of section 1(1)(a) of the Company Directors Disqualification Act 1986 (c 46) or Article 3(1) of the Company Directors Disqualification (Northern Ireland) Order 2002 (SI 2002/3150 (NI 4)), to act in the capacity in question.

(4) Regulations under this section are subject to affirmative resolution procedure.

[S1189]

NOTES

Commencement: 20 January 2007 (for the purpose of enabling the exercise of powers to make Orders or Regulations by statutory instrument); to be appointed (otherwise).

1190 Statements: whether to be made public

(1) Regulations under section 1188 or 1189 (statements required to be sent to registrar) may provide that a statement sent to the registrar of companies under the regulations is to be treated as a record relating to a company for the purposes of section 1080 (the companies register).

(2) The regulations may make provision as to the circumstances in which such a statement is to be, or may be—

(a) withheld from public inspection, or

(b) removed from the register.

(3) The regulations may, in particular, provide that a statement is not to be withheld from public inspection or removed from the register unless the person to whom it relates provides such information, and satisfies such other conditions, as may be specified.

(4) The regulations may provide that section 1081 (note of removal of material from the register) does not apply, or applies with such modifications as may be specified, in the case of material removed from the register under the regulations.

(5) In this section "specified" means specified in the regulations.

[S1190]

NOTES

Commencement: to be appointed.

1191 Offences

(1) Regulations under section 1188 or 1189 may provide that it is an offence for a person—

(a) to fail to comply with a requirement under the regulations to send a statement to the registrar;

(b) knowingly or recklessly to send a statement under the regulations to the registrar that is misleading, false or deceptive in a material particular.

(2) The regulations may provide that a person guilty of such an offence is liable—

(a) on conviction on indictment, to imprisonment for a term not exceeding two years or a fine (or both);

(b) on summary conviction—

(i) in England and Wales, to imprisonment for a term not exceeding twelve months or to a fine not exceeding the statutory maximum (or both);

(ii) in Scotland or Northern Ireland, to imprisonment for a term not exceeding six months, or to a fine not exceeding the statutory maximum (or both).

(3) In relation to an offence committed before the commencement of section 154(1) of the Criminal Justice Act 2003 (c 44), for "twelve months" in subsection (2)(b)(i) substitute "six months".

[S1191]

NOTES

Commencement: 20 January 2007 (for the purpose of enabling the exercise of powers to make Orders or Regulations by statutory instrument); to be appointed (otherwise).

PART 41
BUSINESS NAMES

CHAPTER 1
RESTRICTED OR PROHIBITED NAMES

Introductory

1192 Application of this Chapter

(1) This Chapter applies to any person carrying on business in the United Kingdom.

(2) The provisions of this Chapter do not prevent—

(a) an individual carrying on business under a name consisting of his surname without any addition other than a permitted addition, or

(b) individuals carrying on business in partnership under a name consisting of the surnames of all the partners without any addition other than a permitted addition.

(3) The following are the permitted additions—

(a) in the case of an individual, his forename or initial;

(b) in the case of a partnership—

(i) the forenames of individual partners or the initials of those forenames, or

(ii) where two or more individual partners have the same surname, the addition of "s" at the end of that surname;

(c) in either case, an addition merely indicating that the business is carried on in succession to a former owner of the business.

[S1192]

NOTES

Commencement: to be appointed.

Sensitive words or expressions

1193 Name suggesting connection with government or public authority

(1) A person must not, without the approval of the Secretary of State, carry on business in the United Kingdom under a name that would be likely to give the impression that the business is connected with—

(a) Her Majesty's Government, any part of the Scottish administration or Her Majesty's Government in Northern Ireland,

(b) any local authority, or

(c) any public authority specified for the purposes of this section by regulations made by the Secretary of State.

(2) For the purposes of this section—

"local authority" means—

(a) a local authority within the meaning of the Local Government Act 1972 (c 70), the Common Council of the City of London or the Council of the Isles of Scilly,

(b) a council constituted under section 2 of the Local Government etc (Scotland) Act 1994 (c 39), or

(c) a district council in Northern Ireland;

"public authority" includes any person or body having functions of a public nature.

(3) Regulations under this section are subject to affirmative resolution procedure.

(4) A person who contravenes this section commits an offence.

(5) Where an offence under this section is committed by a body corporate, an offence is also committed by every officer of the body who is in default.

(6) A person guilty of an offence under this section is liable on summary conviction to a fine not exceeding level 3 on the standard scale and, for continued contravention, a daily default fine not exceeding one-tenth of level 3 on the standard scale.

[S1193]

NOTES

Commencement: 20 January 2007 (for the purpose of enabling the exercise of powers to make Orders or Regulations by statutory instrument); to be appointed (otherwise).

1194 Other sensitive words or expressions

(1) A person must not, without the approval of the Secretary of State, carry on business in the United Kingdom under a name that includes a word or expression for the time being specified in regulations made by the Secretary of State under this section.

(2) Regulations under this section are subject to approval after being made.

(3) A person who contravenes this section commits an offence.

(4) Where an offence under this section is committed by a body corporate, an offence is also committed by every officer of the body who is in default.

(5) A person guilty of an offence under this section is liable on summary conviction to a fine not exceeding level 3 on the standard scale and, for continued contravention, a daily default fine not exceeding one-tenth of level 3 on the standard scale.

[S1194]

NOTES

Commencement: 20 January 2007 (for the purpose of enabling the exercise of powers to make Orders or Regulations by statutory instrument); to be appointed (otherwise).

1195 Requirement to seek comments of government department or other relevant body

(1) The Secretary of State may by regulations under—

(a) section 1193 (name suggesting connection with government or public authority), or

(b) section 1194 (other sensitive words or expressions),

require that, in connection with an application for the approval of the Secretary of State under that section, the applicant must seek the view of a specified Government department or other body.

(2) Where such a requirement applies, the applicant must request the specified department or other body (in writing) to indicate whether (and if so why) it has any objections to the proposed name.

(3) He must submit to the Secretary of State a statement that such a request has been made and a copy of any response received from the specified body.

(4) If these requirements are not complied with, the Secretary of State may refuse to consider the application for approval.

(5) In this section "specified" means specified in the regulations.

[S1195]

NOTES

Commencement: 20 January 2007 (for the purpose of enabling the exercise of powers to make Orders or Regulations by statutory instrument); to be appointed (otherwise).

1196 Withdrawal of Secretary of State's approval

(1) This section applies to approval given for the purposes of—

section 1193 (name suggesting connection with government or public authority), or

section 1194 (other sensitive words or expressions).

(2) If it appears to the Secretary of State that there are overriding considerations of public policy that require such approval to be withdrawn, the approval may be withdrawn by notice in writing given to the person concerned.

(3) The notice must state the date as from which approval is withdrawn.

[S1196]

NOTES

Commencement: to be appointed.

Misleading names

1197 Name containing inappropriate indication of company type or legal form

(1) The Secretary of State may make provision by regulations prohibiting a person from carrying on business in the United Kingdom under a name consisting of or containing specified words, expressions or other indications—

(a) that are associated with a particular type of company or form of organisation, or

(b) that are similar to words, expressions or other indications associated with a particular type of company or form of organisation.

(2) The regulations may prohibit the use of words, expressions or other indications—

(a) in a specified part, or otherwise than in a specified part, of a name;

(b) in conjunction with, or otherwise than in conjunction with, such other words, expressions or indications as may be specified.

(3) In this section "specified" means specified in the regulations.

(4) Regulations under this section are subject to negative resolution procedure.

(5) A person who uses a name in contravention of regulations under this section commits an offence.

(6) Where an offence under this section is committed by a body corporate, an offence is also committed by every officer of the body who is in default.

(7) A person guilty of an offence under this section is liable on summary conviction to a fine not exceeding level 3 on the standard scale and, for continued contravention, a daily default fine not exceeding one-tenth of level 3 on the standard scale.

[S1197]

NOTES

Commencement: 20 January 2007 (for the purpose of enabling the exercise of powers to make Orders or Regulations by statutory instrument); to be appointed (otherwise).

1198 Name giving misleading indication of activities

(1) A person must not carry on business in the United Kingdom under a name that gives so misleading an indication of the nature of the activities of the business as to be likely to cause harm to the public.

(2) A person who uses a name in contravention of this section commits an offence.

(3) Where an offence under this section is committed by a body corporate, an offence is also committed by every officer of the body who is in default.

(4) A person guilty of an offence under this section is liable on summary conviction to a fine not exceeding level 3 on the standard scale and, for continued contravention, a daily default fine not exceeding one-tenth of level 3 on the standard scale.

[S1198]

NOTES

Commencement: to be appointed.

Supplementary

1199 Savings for existing lawful business names

(1) This section has effect in relation to—
sections 1192 to 1196 (sensitive words or expressions), and
section 1197 (inappropriate indication of company type or legal form).

(2) Those sections do not apply to the carrying on of a business by a person who—
(a) carried on the business immediately before the date on which this Chapter came into force, and
(b) continues to carry it on under the name that immediately before that date was its lawful business name.

(3) Where—
(a) a business is transferred to a person on or after the date on which this Chapter came into force, and
(b) that person carries on the business under the name that was its lawful business name immediately before the transfer,

those sections do not apply in relation to the carrying on of the business under that name during the period of twelve months beginning with the date of the transfer.

(4) In this section "lawful business name", in relation to a business, means a name under which the business was carried on without contravening—
(a) section 2(1) of the Business Names Act 1985 (c 7) or Article 4(1) of the Business Names (Northern Ireland) Order 1986 (SI 1986/1033 NI 7)), or
(b) after this Chapter has come into force, the provisions of this Chapter.

[S1199]

NOTES

Commencement: to be appointed.

CHAPTER 2
DISCLOSURE REQUIRED IN CASE OF INDIVIDUAL OR PARTNERSHIP

Introductory

1200 Application of this Chapter

(1) This Chapter applies to an individual or partnership carrying on business in the United Kingdom under a business name.

References in this Chapter to "a person to whom this Chapter applies" are to such an individual or partnership.

(2) For the purposes of this Chapter a "business name" means a name other than—
(a) in the case of an individual, his surname without any addition other than a permitted addition;
(b) in the case of a partnership—
(i) the surnames of all partners who are individuals, and
(ii) the corporate names of all partners who are bodies corporate,

without any addition other than a permitted addition.

(3) The following are the permitted additions—
(a) in the case of an individual, his forename or initial;
(b) in the case of a partnership—
(i) the forenames of individual partners or the initials of those forenames, or
(ii) where two or more individual partners have the same surname, the addition of "s" at the end of that surname;
(c) in either case, an addition merely indicating that the business is carried on in succession to a former owner of the business.

[S1200]

NOTES

Commencement: to be appointed.

1201 Information required to be disclosed

The "information required by this Chapter" is—

(a) in the case of an individual, his name;

(b) in the case of a partnership, the name of each member of the partnership;

and in relation to each person so named, an address in the United Kingdom at which service of any document relating in any way to the business will be effective.

[S1201]

NOTES

Commencement: to be appointed.

Disclosure requirements

1202 Disclosure required: business documents etc

(1) A person to whom this Chapter applies must state the information required by this Chapter, in legible characters, on all—

(a) business letters,

(b) written orders for goods or services to be supplied to the business,

(c) invoices and receipts issued in the course of the business, and

(d) written demands for payment of debts arising in the course of the business.

This subsection has effect subject to section 1203 (exemption for large partnerships if certain conditions met).

(2) A person to whom this Chapter applies must secure that the information required by this Chapter is immediately given, by written notice, to any person with whom anything is done or discussed in the course of the business and who asks for that information.

(3) The Secretary of State may by regulations require that such notices be given in a specified form.

(4) Regulations under this section are subject to negative resolution procedure.

[S1202]

NOTES

Commencement: 20 January 2007 (for the purpose of enabling the exercise of powers to make Orders or Regulations by statutory instrument); to be appointed (otherwise).

1203 Exemption for large partnerships if certain conditions met

(1) Section 1202(1) (disclosure required in business documents) does not apply in relation to a document issued by a partnership of more than 20 persons if the following conditions are met.

(2) The conditions are that—

(a) the partnership maintains at its principal place of business a list of the names of all the partners,

(b) no partner's name appears in the document, except in the text or as a signatory, and

(c) the document states in legible characters the address of the partnership's principal place of business and that the list of the partners' names is open to inspection there.

(3) Where a partnership maintains a list of the partners' names for the purposes of this section, any person may inspect the list during office hours.

(4) Where an inspection required by a person in accordance with this section is refused, an offence is committed by any member of the partnership concerned who without reasonable excuse refused the inspection or permitted it to be refused.

(5) A person guilty of an offence under subsection (4) is liable on summary conviction to a fine not exceeding level 3 on the standard scale and, for continued contravention, a daily default fine not exceeding one-tenth of level 3 on the standard scale.

[S1203]

NOTES

Commencement: to be appointed.

1204 Disclosure required: business premises

(1) A person to whom this Chapter applies must, in any premises—

(a) where the business is carried on, and

(b) to which customers of the business or suppliers of goods or services to the business have access,

display in a prominent position, so that it may easily be read by such customers or suppliers, a notice containing the information required by this Chapter.

(2) The Secretary of State may by regulations require that such notices be displayed in a specified form.

(3) Regulations under this section are subject to negative resolution procedure.

[S1204]

NOTES

Commencement: 20 January 2007 (for the purpose of enabling the exercise of powers to make Orders or Regulations by statutory instrument); to be appointed (otherwise).

Consequences of failure to make required disclosure

1205 Criminal consequences of failure to make required disclosure

(1) A person who without reasonable excuse fails to comply with the requirements of—

section 1202 (disclosure required: business documents etc), or

section 1204 (disclosure required: business premises),

commits an offence.

(2) Where an offence under this section is committed by a body corporate, an offence is also committed by every officer of the body who is in default.

(3) A person guilty of an offence under this section is liable on summary conviction to a fine not exceeding level 3 on the standard scale and, for continued contravention, a daily default fine not exceeding one-tenth of level 3 on the standard scale.

(4) References in this section to the requirements of section 1202 or 1204 include the requirements of regulations under that section.

[S1205]

NOTES

Commencement: to be appointed.

1206 Civil consequences of failure to make required disclosure

(1) This section applies to any legal proceedings brought by a person to whom this Chapter applies to enforce a right arising out of a contract made in the course of a business in respect of which he was, at the time the contract was made, in breach of section 1202(1) or (2) (disclosure in business documents etc) or section 1204(1) (disclosure at business premises).

(2) The proceedings shall be dismissed if the defendant (in Scotland, the defender) to the proceedings shows—

(a) that he has a claim against the claimant (pursuer) arising out of the contract that he has been unable to pursue by reason of the latter's breach of the requirements of this Chapter, or

(b) that he has suffered some financial loss in connection with the contract by reason of the claimant's (pursuer's) breach of those requirements,

unless the court before which the proceedings are brought is satisfied that it is just and equitable to permit the proceedings to continue.

(3) References in this section to the requirements of this Chapter include the requirements of regulations under this Chapter.

(4) This section does not affect the right of any person to enforce such rights as he may have against another person in any proceedings brought by that person.

[S1206]

NOTES

Commencement: to be appointed.

CHAPTER 3
SUPPLEMENTARY

1207 Application of general provisions about offences

The provisions of sections 1121 to 1123 (liability of officer in default) and 1125 to 1131 (general provisions about offences) apply in relation to offences under this Part as in relation to offences under the Companies Acts.

[S1207]

NOTES

Commencement: to be appointed.

1208 Interpretation

In this Part—

"business" includes a profession;

"initial" includes any recognised abbreviation of a name;

"partnership" means—

(a) a partnership within the Partnership Act 1890 (c 39), or

(b) a limited partnership registered under the Limited Partnerships Act 1907 (c 24),

or a firm or entity of a similar character formed under the law of a country or territory outside the United Kingdom;

"surname", in relation to a peer or person usually known by a British title different from his surname, means the title by which he is known.

[S1208]

NOTES

Commencement: to be appointed.

PART 42
STATUTORY AUDITORS

CHAPTER 1
INTRODUCTORY

1209 Main purposes of Part

The main purposes of this Part are—

(a) to secure that only persons who are properly supervised and appropriately qualified are appointed as statutory auditors, and

(b) to secure that audits by persons so appointed are carried out properly, with integrity and with a proper degree of independence.

[S1209]

NOTES

Commencement: to be appointed.

1210 Meaning of "statutory auditor" etc

(1) In this Part "statutory auditor" means—

(a) a person appointed as auditor under Part 16 of this Act,

(b) a person appointed as auditor under section 77 of or Schedule 11 to the Building Societies Act 1986 (c 53),

(c) a person appointed as auditor of an insurer that is a friendly society under section 72 of or Schedule 14 to the Friendly Societies Act 1992 (c 40),

(d) a person appointed as auditor of an insurer that is an industrial and provident society under section 4 of the Friendly and Industrial and Provident Societies Act 1968 (c 55) or under section 38 of the Industrial and Provident Societies Act (Northern Ireland) 1969 (c 24 (NI)),

(e) a person appointed as auditor for the purposes of regulation 3 of the Insurance Accounts Directive (Lloyd's Syndicate and Aggregate Accounts) Regulations 2004 (SI 2004/3219) or appointed to report on the "aggregate accounts" within the meaning of those Regulations,

(f) a person appointed as auditor of an insurer for the purposes of regulation 3 of the Insurance Accounts Directive (Miscellaneous Insurance Undertakings) Regulations 1993 (SI 1993/3245),

(g) a person appointed as auditor of a bank for the purposes of regulation 4 of the Bank Accounts Directive (Miscellaneous Banks) Regulations 1991 (SI 1991/2704), and

(h) a person appointed as auditor of a prescribed person under a prescribed enactment authorising or requiring the appointment;

and the expressions "statutory audit" and "statutory audit work" are to be construed accordingly.

(2) In this Part "audited person" means the person in respect of whom a statutory audit is conducted.

(3) In subsection (1)—

"bank" means a person who—

(a) is a credit institution within the meaning given by Article 4.1(a) of Directive 2006/48/EC of the European Parliament and of the Council relating to the taking up and pursuit of the business of credit institutions, and

(b) is a company or a firm as defined in Article 48 of the Treaty establishing the European Community;

"friendly society" means a friendly society within the meaning of the Friendly Societies Act 1992 (c 40);

"industrial and provident society" means—

(a) a society registered under the Industrial and Provident Societies Act 1965 (c 12) or a society deemed by virtue of section 4 of that Act to be so registered, or

(b) a society registered under the Industrial and Provident Societies Act (Northern Ireland) 1969 or a society deemed by virtue of section 4 of that Act to be so registered;

"insurer" means a person who is an insurance undertaking within the meaning given by Article 2.1 of Council Directive 1991/674/EEC on the annual accounts and consolidated accounts of insurance undertakings;

"prescribed" means prescribed, or of a description prescribed, by order made by the Secretary of State for the purposes of subsection (1)(h).

(4) An order under this section is subject to negative resolution procedure.

[S1210]

NOTES

Commencement: 20 January 2007 (for the purpose of enabling the exercise of powers to make Orders or Regulations by statutory instrument); to be appointed (otherwise).

1211 Eligibility for appointment as a statutory auditor: overview

A person is eligible for appointment as a statutory auditor only if the person is so eligible—

(a) by virtue of Chapter 2 (individuals and firms), or

(b) by virtue of Chapter 3 (Comptroller and Auditor General, etc).

[S1211]

NOTES

Commencement: to be appointed.

CHAPTER 2
INDIVIDUALS AND FIRMS

Eligibility for appointment

1212 Individuals and firms: eligibility for appointment as a statutory auditor

(1) An individual or firm is eligible for appointment as a statutory auditor if the individual or firm—

(a) is a member of a recognised supervisory body, and

(b) is eligible for appointment under the rules of that body.

(2) In the cases to which section 1222 applies (individuals retaining only 1967 Act authorisation) a person's eligibility for appointment as a statutory auditor is restricted as mentioned in that section.

[S1212]

NOTES

Commencement: to be appointed.

1213 Effect of ineligibility

(1) No person may act as statutory auditor of an audited person if he is ineligible for appointment as a statutory auditor.

(2) If at any time during his term of office a statutory auditor becomes ineligible for appointment as a statutory auditor, he must immediately—

(a) resign his office (with immediate effect), and

(b) give notice in writing to the audited person that he has resigned by reason of his becoming ineligible for appointment.

(3) A person is guilty of an offence if—

(a) he acts as a statutory auditor in contravention of subsection (1), or

(b) he fails to give the notice mentioned in paragraph (b) of subsection (2) in accordance with that subsection.

(4) A person guilty of an offence under subsection (3) is liable—

(a) on conviction on indictment, to a fine;

(b) on summary conviction, to a fine not exceeding the statutory maximum.

(5) A person is guilty of an offence if—

(a) he has been convicted of an offence under subsection (3)(a) or this subsection, and

(b) he continues to act as a statutory auditor in contravention of subsection (1) after the conviction.

(6) A person is guilty of an offence if—

(a) he has been convicted of an offence under subsection (3)(b) or this subsection, and

(b) he continues, after the conviction, to fail to give the notice mentioned in subsection (2)(b).

(7) A person guilty of an offence under subsection (5) or (6) is liable—

(a) on conviction on indictment, to a fine;

(b) on summary conviction, to a fine not exceeding one-tenth of the statutory maximum for each day on which the act or the failure continues.

(8) In proceedings against a person for an offence under this section it is a defence for him to show that he did not know and had no reason to believe that he was, or had become, ineligible for appointment as a statutory auditor.

[S1213]

NOTES

Commencement: to be appointed.

Independence requirement

1214 Independence requirement

(1) A person may not act as statutory auditor of an audited person if one or more of subsections (2), (3) and (4) apply to him.

(2) This subsection applies if the person is—

(a) an officer or employee of the audited person, or

(b) a partner or employee of such a person, or a partnership of which such a person is a partner.

(3) This subsection applies if the person is—

(a) an officer or employee of an associated undertaking of the audited person, or

(b) a partner or employee of such a person, or a partnership of which such a person is a partner.

(4) This subsection applies if there exists, between—

(a) the person or an associate of his, and

(b) the audited person or an associated undertaking of the audited person,

a connection of any such description as may be specified by regulations made by the Secretary of State.

(5) An auditor of an audited person is not to be regarded as an officer or employee of the person for the purposes of subsections (2) and (3).

(6) In this section "associated undertaking", in relation to an audited person, means—

(a) a parent undertaking or subsidiary undertaking of the audited person, or

(b) a subsidiary undertaking of a parent undertaking of the audited person.

(7) Regulations under subsection (4) are subject to negative resolution procedure.

[S1214]

NOTES

Commencement: 20 January 2007 (for the purpose of enabling the exercise of powers to make Orders or Regulations by statutory instrument); to be appointed (otherwise).

1215 Effect of lack of independence

(1) If at any time during his term of office a statutory auditor becomes prohibited from acting by section 1214(1), he must immediately—

(a) resign his office (with immediate effect), and

(b) give notice in writing to the audited person that he has resigned by reason of his lack of independence.

(2) A person is guilty of an offence if—

(a) he acts as a statutory auditor in contravention of section 1214(1), or

(b) he fails to give the notice mentioned in paragraph (b) of subsection (1) in accordance with that subsection.

(3) A person guilty of an offence under subsection (2) is liable—

(a) on conviction on indictment, to a fine;

(b) on summary conviction, to a fine not exceeding the statutory maximum.

(4) A person is guilty of an offence if—

(a) he has been convicted of an offence under subsection (2)(a) or this subsection, and

(b) he continues to act as a statutory auditor in contravention of section 1214(1) after the conviction.

(5) A person is guilty of an offence if—

(a) he has been convicted of an offence under subsection (2)(b) or this subsection, and

(b) after the conviction, he continues to fail to give the notice mentioned in subsection (1)(b).

(6) A person guilty of an offence under subsection (4) or (5) is liable—

(a) on conviction on indictment, to a fine;

(b) on summary conviction, to a fine not exceeding one-tenth of the statutory maximum for each day on which the act or the failure continues.

(7) In proceedings against a person for an offence under this section it is a defence for him to show that he did not know and had no reason to believe that he was, or had become, prohibited from acting as statutory auditor of the audited person by section 1214(1).

[S1215]

NOTES

Commencement: to be appointed.

Effect of appointment of a partnership

1216 Effect of appointment of a partnership

(1) This section applies where a partnership constituted under the law of—

(a) England and Wales,

(b) Northern Ireland, or

(c) any other country or territory in which a partnership is not a legal person,

is by virtue of this Chapter appointed as statutory auditor of an audited person.

(2) Unless a contrary intention appears, the appointment is an appointment of the partnership as such and not of the partners.

(3) Where the partnership ceases, the appointment is to be treated as extending to—

(a) any appropriate partnership which succeeds to the practice of that partnership, or

(b) any other appropriate person who succeeds to that practice having previously carried it on in partnership.

(4) For the purposes of subsection (3)—

(a) a partnership is to be regarded as succeeding to the practice of another partnership only if the members of the successor partnership are substantially the same as those of the former partnership, and

(b) a partnership or other person is to be regarded as succeeding to the practice of a partnership only if it or he succeeds to the whole or substantially the whole of the business of the former partnership.

(5) Where the partnership ceases and the appointment is not treated under subsection (3) as extending to any partnership or other person, the appointment may with the consent of the audited person be treated as extending to an appropriate partnership, or other appropriate person, who succeeds to—

(a) the business of the former partnership, or

(b) such part of it as is agreed by the audited person is to be treated as comprising the appointment.

(6) For the purposes of this section, a partnership or other person is "appropriate" if it or he—

(a) is eligible for appointment as a statutory auditor by virtue of this Chapter, and

(b) is not prohibited by section 1214(1) from acting as statutory auditor of the audited person.

[S1216]

NOTES

Commencement: to be appointed.

Supervisory bodies

1217 Supervisory bodies

(1) In this Part a "supervisory body" means a body established in the United Kingdom (whether a body corporate or an unincorporated association) which maintains and enforces rules as to—

(a) the eligibility of persons for appointment as a statutory auditor, and

(b) the conduct of statutory audit work,

which are binding on persons seeking appointment or acting as a statutory auditor either because they are members of that body or because they are otherwise subject to its control.

(2) In this Part references to the members of a supervisory body are to the persons who, whether or not members of the body, are subject to its rules in seeking appointment or acting as a statutory auditor.

(3) In this Part references to the rules of a supervisory body are to the rules (whether or not laid down by the body itself) which the body has power to enforce and which are relevant for the purposes of this Part.

This includes rules relating to the admission or expulsion of members of the body, so far as relevant for the purposes of this Part.

(4) Schedule 10 has effect with respect to the recognition of supervisory bodies for the purposes of this Part.

[S1217]

NOTES

Commencement: to be appointed.

1218 Exemption from liability for damages

(1) No person within subsection (2) is to be liable in damages for anything done or omitted in the discharge or purported discharge of functions to which this subsection applies.

(2) The persons within this subsection are—
- (a) any recognised supervisory body,
- (b) any officer or employee of a recognised supervisory body, and
- (c) any member of the governing body of a recognised supervisory body.

(3) Subsection (1) applies to the functions of a recognised supervisory body so far as relating to, or to matters arising out of, any of the following—
- (a) rules, practices, powers and arrangements of the body to which the requirements of Part 2 of Schedule 10 apply;
- (b) the obligations with which paragraph 20 of that Schedule requires the body to comply;
- (c) any guidance issued by the body;
- (d) the obligations imposed on the body by or by virtue of this Part.

(4) The reference in subsection (3)(c) to guidance issued by a recognised supervisory body is a reference to any guidance or recommendation which is—
- (a) issued or made by it to all or any class of its members or persons seeking to become members, and
- (b) relevant for the purposes of this Part,

including any guidance or recommendation relating to the admission or expulsion of members of the body, so far as relevant for the purposes of this Part.

(5) Subsection (1) does not apply—
- (a) if the act or omission is shown to have been in bad faith, or
- (b) so as to prevent an award of damages in respect of the act or omission on the ground that it was unlawful as a result of section 6(1) of the Human Rights Act 1998 (c 42) (acts of public authorities incompatible with Convention rights).

[S1218]

NOTES

Commencement: to be appointed.

Professional qualifications

1219 Appropriate qualifications

(1) A person holds an appropriate qualification for the purposes of this Chapter if and only if—
- (a) he holds a recognised professional qualification obtained in the United Kingdom,
- (b) immediately before the commencement of this Chapter, he—
  - (i) held an appropriate qualification for the purposes of Part 2 of the Companies Act 1989 (c 40) (eligibility for appointment as company auditor) by virtue of section 31(1)(a) or (c) of that Act, or

(ii) was treated as holding an appropriate qualification for those purposes by virtue of section 31(2), (3) or (4) of that Act,

(c) immediately before the commencement of this Chapter, he—

(i) held an appropriate qualification for the purposes of Part III of the Companies (Northern Ireland) Order 1990 (SI 1990/593 (NI 5)) by virtue of Article 34(1)(a) or (c) of that Order, or

(ii) was treated as holding an appropriate qualification for those purposes by virtue of Article 34(2), (3) or (4) of that Order,

(d) he is within subsection (2),

(e) he has been authorised to practise the profession of statutory auditor pursuant to the European Communities (Recognition of Professional Qualifications) (First General System) Regulations 2005 (SI 2005/18) and has fulfilled any requirements imposed pursuant to regulation 6 of those Regulations, or

(f) subject to any direction under section 1221(5), he is regarded for the purposes of this Chapter as holding an approved overseas qualification.

(2) A person is within this subsection if—

(a) before 1st January 1990, he began a course of study or practical training leading to a professional qualification in accountancy offered by a body established in the United Kingdom,

(b) he obtained that qualification on or after 1st January 1990 and before 1st January 1996, and

(c) the Secretary of State approves his qualification as an appropriate qualification for the purposes of this Chapter.

(3) The Secretary of State may approve a qualification under subsection (2)(c) only if he is satisfied that, at the time the qualification was awarded, the body concerned had adequate arrangements to ensure that the qualification was awarded only to persons educated and trained to a standard equivalent to that required, at that time, in the case of a recognised professional qualification under Part 2 of the Companies Act 1989 (c 40) (eligibility for appointment as company auditor).

[S1219]

NOTES

Commencement: to be appointed.

1220 Qualifying bodies and recognised professional qualifications

(1) In this Part a "qualifying body" means a body established in the United Kingdom (whether a body corporate or an unincorporated association) which offers a professional qualification in accountancy.

(2) In this Part references to the rules of a qualifying body are to the rules (whether or not laid down by the body itself) which the body has power to enforce and which are relevant for the purposes of this Part.

This includes, so far as so relevant, rules relating to—

(a) admission to or expulsion from a course of study leading to a qualification,

(b) the award or deprivation of a qualification, or

(c) the approval of a person for the purposes of giving practical training or the withdrawal of such approval.

(3) Schedule 11 has effect with respect to the recognition for the purposes of this Part of a professional qualification offered by a qualifying body.

[S1220]

NOTES

Commencement: to be appointed.

1221 Approval of overseas qualifications

(1) The Secretary of State may declare that the following are to be regarded for the purposes of this Chapter as holding an approved overseas qualification—

(a) persons who are qualified to audit accounts under the law of a specified foreign country, or

(b) persons who hold a specified professional qualification in accountancy obtained in a specified foreign country.

(2) A declaration under subsection (1)(b) may be expressed to be subject to the satisfaction of any specified requirement or requirements.

(3) The Secretary of State may make a declaration under subsection (1) only if he is satisfied that—

(a) in the case of a declaration under subsection (1)(a), the fact that the persons in question are qualified to audit accounts under the law of the specified foreign country, or

(b) in the case of a declaration under subsection (1)(b), the specified professional qualification taken with any requirement or requirements to be specified under subsection (2),

affords an assurance of professional competence equivalent to that afforded by a recognised professional qualification.

(4) The Secretary of State may make a declaration under subsection (1) only if he is satisfied that the treatment that the persons who are the subject of the declaration will receive as a result of it is comparable to the treatment which is, or is likely to be, afforded in the specified foreign country or a part of it to—

(a) in the case of a declaration under subsection (1)(a), some or all persons who are eligible to be appointed as a statutory auditor, and

(b) in the case of a declaration under subsection (1)(b), some or all persons who hold a corresponding recognised professional qualification.

(5) The Secretary of State may direct that persons holding an approved overseas qualification are not to be treated as holding an appropriate qualification for the purposes of this Chapter unless they hold such additional educational qualifications as the Secretary of State may specify for the purpose of ensuring that such persons have an adequate knowledge of the law and practice in the United Kingdom relevant to the audit of accounts.

(6) The Secretary of State may give different directions in relation to different approved overseas qualifications.

(7) The Secretary of State may, if he thinks fit, having regard to the considerations mentioned in subsections (3) and (4), withdraw a declaration under subsection (1) in relation to—

(a) persons becoming qualified to audit accounts under the law of the specified foreign country after such date as he may specify, or

(b) persons obtaining the specified professional qualification after such date as he may specify.

(8) The Secretary of State may, if he thinks fit, having regard to the considerations mentioned in subsections (3) and (4), vary or revoke a requirement specified under subsection (2) from such date as he may specify.

(9) In this section "foreign country", in relation to any time, means a country or territory that, at that time, is not a "relevant State" within the meaning of the European Communities (Recognition of Professional Qualifications) (First General System) Regulations 2005 (SI 2005/18) or part of such a State.

[S1221]

NOTES

Commencement: to be appointed.

1222 Eligibility of individuals retaining only 1967 Act authorisation

(1) A person whose only appropriate qualification is based on his retention of an authorisation originally granted by the Board of Trade or the Secretary of State under section 13(1) of the Companies Act 1967 (c 81) is eligible only for appointment as auditor of an unquoted company.

(2) A company is "unquoted" if, at the time of the person's appointment, neither the company, nor any parent undertaking of which it is a subsidiary undertaking, is a quoted company within the meaning of section 385(2).

(3) References to a person eligible for appointment as a statutory auditor by virtue of this Part in enactments relating to eligibility for appointment as auditor of a person other than a company do not include a person to whom this section applies.

[S1222]

NOTES

Commencement: to be appointed.

Information

1223 Matters to be notified to the Secretary of State

(1) The Secretary of State may require a recognised supervisory body or a recognised qualifying body—

(a) to notify him immediately of the occurrence of such events as he may specify in writing and to give him such information in respect of those events as is so specified;

(b) to give him, at such times or in respect of such periods as he may specify in writing, such information as is so specified.

(2) The notices and information required to be given must be such as the Secretary of State may reasonably require for the exercise of his functions under this Part.

(3) The Secretary of State may require information given under this section to be given in a specified form or verified in a specified manner.

(4) Any notice or information required to be given under this section must be given in writing unless the Secretary of State specifies or approves some other manner.

[S1223]

NOTES

Commencement: to be appointed.

1224 The Secretary of State's power to call for information

(1) The Secretary of State may by notice in writing require a person within subsection (2) to give him such information as he may reasonably require for the exercise of his functions under this Part.

(2) The persons within this subsection are—

(a) any recognised supervisory body,

(b) any recognised qualifying body, and

(c) any person eligible for appointment as a statutory auditor by virtue of this Chapter.

(3) The Secretary of State may require that any information which he requires under this section is to be given within such reasonable time and verified in such manner as he may specify.

[S1224]

NOTES

Commencement: to be appointed.

Enforcement

1225 Compliance orders

(1) If at any time it appears to the Secretary of State—

(a) in the case of a recognised supervisory body, that any requirement of Schedule 10 is not satisfied,

(b) in the case of a recognised professional qualification, that any requirement of Schedule 11 is not satisfied, or

(c) that a recognised supervisory body or a recognised qualifying body has failed to comply with an obligation to which it is subject under or by virtue of this Part, he may, instead of revoking the relevant recognition order, make an application to the court under this section.

(2) If on an application under this section the court decides that the requirement in question is not satisfied or, as the case may be, that the body has failed to comply with the obligation in question, it may order the body to take such steps as the court directs for securing that the requirement is satisfied or that the obligation is complied with.

(3) In this section "the court" means the High Court or, in Scotland, the Court of Session.
[S1225]

NOTES
Commencement: to be appointed.

CHAPTER 3
AUDITORS GENERAL

Eligibility for appointment

1226 Auditors General: eligibility for appointment as a statutory auditor

(1) In this Part "Auditor General" means—
- (a) the Comptroller and Auditor General,
- (b) the Auditor General for Scotland,
- (c) the Auditor General for Wales, or
- (d) the Comptroller and Auditor General for Northern Ireland.

(2) An Auditor General is eligible for appointment as a statutory auditor.

(3) Subsection (2) is subject to any suspension notice having effect under section 1234 (notices suspending eligibility for appointment as a statutory auditor).
[S1226]

NOTES
Commencement: to be appointed.

Conduct of audits

1227 Individuals responsible for audit work on behalf of Auditors General

An Auditor General must secure that each individual responsible for statutory audit work on behalf of that Auditor General is eligible for appointment as a statutory auditor by virtue of Chapter 2.
[S1227]

NOTES
Commencement: to be appointed.

The Independent Supervisor

1228 Appointment of the Independent Supervisor

(1) The Secretary of State must appoint a body ("the Independent Supervisor") to discharge the function mentioned in section 1229(1) ("the supervision function").

(2) An appointment under this section must be made by order.

(3) The order has the effect of making the body appointed under subsection (1) designated under section 5 of the Freedom of Information Act 2000 (c 36) (further powers to designate public authorities).

(4) A body may be appointed under this section only if it is a body corporate or an unincorporated association which appears to the Secretary of State—

(a) to be willing and able to discharge the supervision function, and
(b) to have arrangements in place relating to the discharge of that function which are such as to be likely to ensure that the conditions in subsection (5) are met.

(5) The conditions are—
(a) that the supervision function will be exercised effectively, and
(b) where the order is to contain any requirements or other provisions specified under subsection (6), that that function will be exercised in accordance with any such requirements or provisions.

(6) An order under this section may contain such requirements or other provisions relating to the exercise of the supervision function by the Independent Supervisor as appear to the Secretary of State to be appropriate.

(7) An order under this section is subject to negative resolution procedure.

[S1228]

NOTES
Commencement: 20 January 2007 (for the purpose of enabling the exercise of powers to make Orders or Regulations by statutory instrument); to be appointed (otherwise).

Supervision of Auditors General

1229 Supervision of Auditors General by the Independent Supervisor

(1) The Independent Supervisor must supervise the performance by each Auditor General of his functions as a statutory auditor.

(2) The Independent Supervisor must discharge that duty by—
(a) entering into supervision arrangements with one or more bodies, and
(b) overseeing the effective operation of any supervision arrangements entered into by it.

(3) For this purpose "supervision arrangements" are arrangements entered into by the Independent Supervisor with a body, for the purposes of this section, in accordance with which the body does one or more of the following—
(a) determines standards relating to professional integrity and independence which must be applied by an Auditor General in statutory audit work;
(b) determines technical standards which must be applied by an Auditor General in statutory audit work and the manner in which those standards are to be applied in practice;
(c) monitors the performance of statutory audits carried out by an Auditor General;
(d) investigates any matter arising from the performance by an Auditor General of a statutory audit;
(e) holds disciplinary hearings in respect of an Auditor General which appear to be desirable following the conclusion of such investigations;
(f) decides whether (and, if so, what) disciplinary action should be taken against an Auditor General to whom such a hearing related.

(4) The Independent Supervisor may enter into supervision arrangements with a body despite any relationship that may exist between the Independent Supervisor and that body.

(5) The Independent Supervisor must notify each Auditor General in writing of any supervision arrangements that it enters into under this section.

(6) Supervision arrangements within subsection (3)(f) may, in particular, provide for the payment by an Auditor General of a fine to any person.

(7) Any fine received by the Independent Supervisor under supervision arrangements is to be paid into the Consolidated Fund.

[S1229]

NOTES
Commencement: to be appointed.

1230 Duties of Auditors General in relation to supervision arrangements

(1) Each Auditor General must—

(a) comply with any standards of the kind mentioned in subsection (3)(a) or (b) of section 1229 determined under the supervision arrangements,
(b) take such steps as may be reasonably required of that Auditor General to enable his performance of statutory audits to be monitored by means of inspections carried out under the supervision arrangements, and
(c) comply with any decision of the kind mentioned in subsection (3)(f) of that section made under the supervision arrangements.

(2) Each Auditor General must pay to the body or bodies with which the Independent Supervisor enters into the supervision arrangements such proportion of the costs incurred by the body or bodies for the purposes of the arrangements as the Independent Supervisor may notify to him in writing.

(3) Expenditure under subsection (2) is—
(a) in the case of expenditure of the Comptroller and Auditor General, to be regarded as expenditure of the National Audit Office for the purposes of section 4(1) of the National Audit Act 1983 (c 44);
(b) in the case of expenditure of the Comptroller and Auditor General for Northern Ireland, to be regarded as expenditure of the Northern Ireland Audit Office for the purposes of Article 6(1) of the Audit (Northern Ireland) Order 1987 (SI 1987/460 (NI 5)).

(4) In this section "the supervision arrangements" means the arrangements entered into under section 1229.

[S1230]

NOTES

Commencement: to be appointed.

Reporting requirement

1231 Reports by the Independent Supervisor

(1) The Independent Supervisor must, at least once in each calendar year, prepare a report on the discharge of its functions.

(2) The Independent Supervisor must give a copy of each report prepared under subsection (1) to—
(a) the Secretary of State;
(b) the First Minister in Scotland;
(c) the First Minister and the deputy First Minister in Northern Ireland;
(d) the Assembly First Secretary in Wales.

(3) The Secretary of State must lay before each House of Parliament a copy of each report received by him under subsection (2)(a).

(4) In relation to a calendar year during which an appointment of a body as the Independent Supervisor is made or revoked by an order under section 1228, this section applies with such modifications as may be specified in the order.

[S1231]

NOTES

Commencement: 20 January 2007 (for the purpose of enabling the exercise of powers to make Orders or Regulations by statutory instrument); to be appointed (otherwise).

Information

1232 Matters to be notified to the Independent Supervisor

(1) The Independent Supervisor may require an Auditor General—
(a) to notify the Independent Supervisor immediately of the occurrence of such events as it may specify in writing and to give it such information in respect of those events as is so specified;
(b) to give the Independent Supervisor, at such times or in respect of such periods as it may specify in writing, such information as is so specified.

(2) The notices and information required to be given must be such as the Independent Supervisor may reasonably require for the exercise of the functions conferred on it by or by virtue of this Part.

(3) The Independent Supervisor may require information given under this section to be given in a specified form or verified in a specified manner.

(4) Any notice or information required to be given under this section must be given in writing unless the Independent Supervisor specifies or approves some other manner.

[S1232]

NOTES

Commencement: to be appointed.

1233 The Independent Supervisor's power to call for information

(1) The Independent Supervisor may by notice in writing require an Auditor General to give it such information as it may reasonably require for the exercise of the functions conferred on it by or by virtue of this Part.

(2) The Independent Supervisor may require that any information which it requires under this section is to be given within such reasonable time and verified in such manner as it may specify.

[S1233]

NOTES

Commencement: to be appointed.

Enforcement

1234 Suspension notices

(1) The Independent Supervisor may issue—

(a) a notice (a "suspension notice") suspending an Auditor General's eligibility for appointment as a statutory auditor in relation to all persons, or any specified person or persons, indefinitely or until a date specified in the notice;

(b) a notice amending or revoking a suspension notice previously issued to an Auditor General.

(2) In determining whether it is appropriate to issue a notice under subsection (1), the Independent Supervisor must have regard to—

(a) the Auditor General's performance of the obligations imposed on him by or by virtue of this Part, and

(b) the Auditor General's performance of his functions as a statutory auditor.

(3) A notice under subsection (1) must—

(a) be in writing, and

(b) state the date on which it takes effect (which must be after the period of three months beginning with the date on which it is issued).

(4) Before issuing a notice under subsection (1), the Independent Supervisor must—

(a) give written notice of its intention to do so to the Auditor General, and

(b) publish the notice mentioned in paragraph (a) in such manner as it thinks appropriate for bringing it to the attention of any other persons who are likely to be affected.

(5) A notice under subsection (4) must—

(a) state the reasons for which the Independent Supervisor proposes to act, and

(b) give particulars of the rights conferred by subsection (6).

(6) A person within subsection (7) may, within the period of three months beginning with the date of service or publication of the notice under subsection (4) or such longer period as the Independent Supervisor may allow, make written representations to the Independent Supervisor and, if desired, oral representations to a person appointed for that purpose by the Independent Supervisor.

(7) The persons within this subsection are—

(a) the Auditor General, and

(b) any other person who appears to the Independent Supervisor to be affected.

(8) The Independent Supervisor must have regard to any representations made in accordance with subsection (6) in determining—

(a) whether to issue a notice under subsection (1), and

(b) the terms of any such notice.

(9) If in any case the Independent Supervisor considers it appropriate to do so in the public interest it may issue a notice under subsection (1), without regard to the restriction in subsection (3)(b), even if—

(a) no notice has been given or published under subsection (4), or

(b) the period of time for making representations in pursuance of such a notice has not expired.

(10) On issuing a notice under subsection (1), the Independent Supervisor must—

(a) give a copy of the notice to the Auditor General, and

(b) publish the notice in such manner as it thinks appropriate for bringing it to the attention of persons likely to be affected.

(11) In this section "specified" means specified in, or of a description specified in, the suspension notice in question.

[S1234]

NOTES

Commencement: to be appointed.

1235 Effect of suspension notices

(1) An Auditor General must not act as a statutory auditor at any time when a suspension notice issued to him in respect of the audited person has effect.

(2) If at any time during an Auditor General's term of office as a statutory auditor a suspension notice issued to him in respect of the audited person takes effect, he must immediately—

(a) resign his office (with immediate effect), and

(b) give notice in writing to the audited person that he has resigned by reason of his becoming ineligible for appointment.

(3) A suspension notice does not make an Auditor General ineligible for appointment as a statutory auditor for the purposes of section 1213 (effect of ineligibility: criminal offences).

[S1235]

NOTES

Commencement: to be appointed.

1236 Compliance orders

(1) If at any time it appears to the Independent Supervisor that an Auditor General has failed to comply with an obligation imposed on him by or by virtue of this Part, the Independent Supervisor may make an application to the court under this section.

(2) If on an application under this section the court decides that the Auditor General has failed to comply with the obligation in question, it may order the Auditor General to take such steps as the court directs for securing that the obligation is complied with.

(3) In this section "the court" means the High Court or, in Scotland, the Court of Session.

[S1236]

NOTES

Commencement: to be appointed.

Proceedings

1237 Proceedings involving the Independent Supervisor

(1) If the Independent Supervisor is an unincorporated association, any relevant proceedings may be brought by or against it in the name of any body corporate whose constitution provides for the establishment of the body.

(2) For this purpose "relevant proceedings" means proceedings brought in or in connection with the exercise of any function by the body as the Independent Supervisor.

(3) Where an appointment under section 1228 is revoked, the revoking order may make such provision as the Secretary of State thinks fit with respect to pending proceedings.

[S1237]

NOTES

Commencement: 20 January 2007 (for the purpose of enabling the exercise of powers to make Orders or Regulations by statutory instrument); to be appointed (otherwise).

Grants

1238 Grants to the Independent Supervisor

(*Inserts the Companies (Audit, Investigations and Community Enterprise) Act 2004, s 16(2)(ka) at* **[896]**.)

[S1238]

NOTES

Commencement: to be appointed.

CHAPTER 4
THE REGISTER OF AUDITORS ETC

1239 The register of auditors

(1) The Secretary of State must make regulations requiring the keeping of a register of—

(a) the persons eligible for appointment as a statutory auditor, and

(b) third country auditors (see Chapter 5) who apply to be registered in the specified manner and in relation to whom specified requirements are met.

(2) The regulations must require each person's entry in the register to contain—

(a) his name and address,

(b) in the case of an individual eligible for appointment as a statutory auditor, the specified information relating to any firm on whose behalf he is responsible for statutory audit work,

(c) in the case of a firm eligible for appointment as a statutory auditor, the specified information relating to the individuals responsible for statutory audit work on its behalf,

(d) in the case of an individual or firm eligible for appointment as a statutory auditor by virtue of Chapter 2, the name of the relevant supervisory body, and

(e) in the case of a firm eligible for appointment as a statutory auditor by virtue of Chapter 2 or a third country auditor, the information mentioned in subsection (3),

and may require each person's entry to contain other specified information.

(3) The information referred to in subsection (2)(e) is—

(a) in relation to a body corporate, except where paragraph (b) applies, the name and address of each person who is a director of the body or holds any shares in it;

(b) in relation to a limited liability partnership, the name and address of each member of the partnership;

(c) in relation to a corporation sole, the name and address of the individual for the time being holding the office by the name of which he is the corporation sole;

(d) in relation to a partnership, the name and address of each partner.

(4) The regulations may provide that different parts of the register are to be kept by different persons.

(5) The regulations may impose such obligations as the Secretary of State thinks fit on—

(a) recognised supervisory bodies,

(b) any body designated by order under section 1252 (delegation of Secretary of State's functions),

(c) persons eligible for appointment as a statutory auditor,

(d) third country auditors,

(e) any person with whom arrangements are made by one or more recognised supervisory bodies, or by any body designated by order under section 1252, with respect to the keeping of the register, or

(f) the Independent Supervisor appointed under section 1228.

(6) The regulations may include—

(a) provision requiring that specified entries in the register be open to inspection at times and places specified or determined in accordance with the regulations;

(b) provision enabling a person to require a certified copy of specified entries in the register;

(c) provision authorising the charging of fees for inspection, or the provision of copies, of such reasonable amount as may be specified or determined in accordance with the regulations.

(7) The Secretary of State may direct in writing that the requirements imposed by the regulations in accordance with subsections (2)(e) and (3), or such of those requirements as are specified in the direction, are not to apply, in whole or in part, in relation to a particular registered third country auditor or class of registered third country auditors.

(8) The obligations imposed by regulations under this section on such persons as are mentioned in subsection (5)(b) or (e) are enforceable on the application of the Secretary of State by injunction or, in Scotland, by an order under section 45 of the Court of Session Act 1988 (c 36).

(9) In this section "specified" means specified by regulations under this section.

(10) Regulations under this section are subject to negative resolution procedure.

[S1239]

NOTES

Commencement: 20 January 2007 (for the purpose of enabling the exercise of powers to make Orders or Regulations by statutory instrument); to be appointed (otherwise).

1240 Information to be made available to public

(1) The Secretary of State may make regulations requiring a person eligible for appointment as a statutory auditor, or a member of a specified class of such persons, to keep and make available to the public specified information, including information regarding—

(a) the person's ownership and governance,

(b) the person's internal controls with respect to the quality and independence of its audit work,

(c) the person's turnover, and

(d) the audited persons of whom the person has acted as statutory auditor.

(2) Regulations under this section may—

(a) impose such obligations as the Secretary of State thinks fit on persons eligible for appointment as a statutory auditor;

(b) require the information to be made available to the public in a specified manner.

(3) In this section "specified" means specified by regulations under this section.

(4) Regulations under this section are subject to negative resolution procedure.

[S1240]

NOTES

Commencement: 20 January 2007 (for the purpose of enabling the exercise of powers to make Orders or Regulations by statutory instrument); to be appointed (otherwise).

CHAPTER 5
REGISTERED THIRD COUNTRY AUDITORS

Introductory

1241 Meaning of "third country auditor", "registered third country auditor" etc

(1) In this Part—

"third country auditor" means the auditor of the accounts of a traded non-Community company, and the expressions "third country audit" and "third country audit work" are to be construed accordingly;

"registered third country auditor" means a third country auditor who is entered in the register kept in accordance with regulations under section 1239(1).

(2) In subsection (1) "traded non-Community company" means a body corporate—

(a) which is incorporated or formed under the law of a country or territory which is not a member State or part of a member State,

(b) whose transferable securities are admitted to trading on a regulated market situated or operating in the United Kingdom, and

(c) which has not been excluded, or is not of a description of bodies corporate which has been excluded, from this definition by an order made by the Secretary of State.

(3) For this purpose—

"regulated market" has the meaning given by Article 4.1(14) of Directive 2004/39/EC of the European Parliament and of the Council on markets in financial instruments;

"transferable securities" has the meaning given by Article 4.1(18) of that Directive.

(4) An order under this section is subject to negative resolution procedure.

[S1241]

NOTES

Commencement: 20 January 2007 (for the purpose of enabling the exercise of powers to make Orders or Regulations by statutory instrument); to be appointed (otherwise).

Duties

1242 Duties of registered third country auditors

(1) A registered third country auditor must participate in—

(a) arrangements within paragraph 1 of Schedule 12 (arrangements for independent monitoring of audits of traded non-Community companies), and

(b) arrangements within paragraph 2 of that Schedule (arrangements for independent investigation for disciplinary purposes of public interest cases).

(2) A registered third country auditor must—

(a) take such steps as may be reasonably required of it to enable its performance of third country audits to be monitored by means of inspections carried out under the arrangements mentioned in subsection (1)(a), and

(b) comply with any decision as to disciplinary action to be taken against it made under the arrangements mentioned in subsection (1)(b).

(3) Schedule 12 makes further provision with respect to the arrangements in which registered third country auditors are required to participate.

(4) The Secretary of State may direct in writing that subsections (1) to (3) are not to apply, in whole or in part, in relation to a particular registered third country auditor or class of registered third country auditors.

[S1242]

NOTES

Commencement: to be appointed.

Information

1243 Matters to be notified to the Secretary of State

(1) The Secretary of State may require a registered third country auditor—

(a) to notify him immediately of the occurrence of such events as he may specify in writing and to give him such information in respect of those events as is so specified;

(b) to give him, at such times or in respect of such periods as he may specify in writing, such information as is so specified.

(2) The notices and information required to be given must be such as the Secretary of State may reasonably require for the exercise of his functions under this Part.

(3) The Secretary of State may require information given under this section to be given in a specified form or verified in a specified manner.

(4) Any notice or information required to be given under this section must be given in writing unless the Secretary of State specifies or approves some other manner.

[S1243]

NOTES

Commencement: to be appointed.

1244 The Secretary of State's power to call for information

(1) The Secretary of State may by notice in writing require a registered third country auditor to give him such information as he may reasonably require for the exercise of his functions under this Part.

(2) The Secretary of State may require that any information which he requires under this section is to be given within such reasonable time and verified in such manner as he may specify.

[S1244]

NOTES

Commencement: to be appointed.

Enforcement

1245 Compliance orders

(1) If at any time it appears to the Secretary of State that a registered third country auditor has failed to comply with an obligation imposed on him by or by virtue of this Part, the Secretary of State may make an application to the court under this section.

(2) If on an application under this section the court decides that the auditor has failed to comply with the obligation in question, it may order the auditor to take such steps as the court directs for securing that the obligation is complied with.

(3) In this section "the court" means the High Court or, in Scotland, the Court of Session.

[S1245]

NOTES

Commencement: to be appointed.

1246 Removal of third country auditors from the register of auditors

(1) The Secretary of State may, by regulations, confer on the person keeping the register in accordance with regulations under section 1239(1) power to remove a third country auditor from the register.

(2) Regulations under this section must require the person keeping the register, in determining whether to remove a third country auditor from the register, to have regard to the auditor's compliance with obligations imposed on him by or by virtue of this Part.

(3) Where provision is made under section 1239(4) (different parts of the register to be kept by different persons), references in this section to the person keeping the register are to the person keeping that part of the register which relates to third country auditors.

(4) Regulations under this section are subject to negative resolution procedure.

[S1246]

NOTES

Commencement: 20 January 2007 (for the purpose of enabling the exercise of powers to make Orders or Regulations by statutory instrument); to be appointed (otherwise).

1247 Grants to bodies concerned with arrangements under Schedule 12

(*Inserts the Companies* (*Audit, Investigations and Community Enterprise*) *Act 2004, s 16*(*2*)(*kb*) *at* **[896]**.)

[S1247]

NOTES

Commencement: to be appointed.

CHAPTER 6
SUPPLEMENTARY AND GENERAL

Power to require second company audit

1248 Secretary of State's power to require second audit of a company

(1) This section applies where a person appointed as statutory auditor of a company was not an appropriate person for any part of the period during which the audit was conducted.

(2) The Secretary of State may direct the company concerned to retain an appropriate person—

- (a) to conduct a second audit of the relevant accounts, or
- (b) to review the first audit and to report (giving his reasons) whether a second audit is needed.

(3) For the purposes of subsections (1) and (2) a person is "appropriate" if he—

- (a) is eligible for appointment as a statutory auditor or, if the person is an Auditor General, for appointment as statutory auditor of the company, and
- (b) is not prohibited by section 1214(1) (independence requirement) from acting as statutory auditor of the company.

(4) The Secretary of State must send a copy of a direction under subsection (2) to the registrar of companies.

(5) The company is guilty of an offence if—

- (a) it fails to comply with a direction under subsection (2) within the period of 21 days beginning with the date on which it is given, or
- (b) it has been convicted of a previous offence under this subsection and the failure to comply with the direction which led to the conviction continues after the conviction.

(6) The company must—

- (a) send a copy of a report under subsection (2)(b) to the registrar of companies, and
- (b) if the report states that a second audit is needed, take such steps as are necessary for the carrying out of that audit.

(7) The company is guilty of an offence if—

- (a) it fails to send a copy of a report under subsection (2)(b) to the registrar within the period of 21 days beginning with the date on which it receives it,
- (b) in a case within subsection (6)(b), it fails to take the steps mentioned immediately it receives the report, or
- (c) it has been convicted of a previous offence under this subsection and the failure to send a copy of the report, or take the steps, which led to the conviction continues after the conviction.

(8) A company guilty of an offence under this section is liable on summary conviction—

(a) in a case within subsection (5)(a) or (7)(a) or (b), to a fine not exceeding level 5 on the standard scale, and

(b) in a case within subsection (5)(b) or (7)(c), to a fine not exceeding one-tenth of level 5 on the standard scale for each day on which the failure continues.

(9) In this section "registrar of companies" has the meaning given by section 1060.

[S1248]

NOTES

Commencement: to be appointed.

1249 Supplementary provision about second audits

(1) If a person accepts an appointment, or continues to act, as statutory auditor of a company at a time when he knows he is not an appropriate person, the company may recover from him any costs incurred by it in complying with the requirements of section 1248.

For this purpose "appropriate" is to be construed in accordance with subsection (3) of that section.

(2) Where a second audit is carried out under section 1248, any statutory or other provision applying in relation to the first audit applies also, in so far as practicable, in relation to the second audit.

(3) A direction under section 1248(2) is, on the application of the Secretary of State, enforceable by injunction or, in Scotland, by an order under section 45 of the Court of Session Act 1988 (c 36).

[S1249]

NOTES

Commencement: to be appointed.

False and misleading statements

1250 Misleading, false and deceptive statements

(1) A person is guilty of an offence if—

(a) for the purposes of or in connection with any application under this Part, or

(b) in purported compliance with any requirement imposed on him by or by virtue of this Part,

he knowingly or recklessly furnishes information which is misleading, false or deceptive in a material particular.

(2) It is an offence for a person whose name does not appear on the register of auditors kept under regulations under section 1239 in an entry made under subsection (1)(a) of that section to describe himself as a registered auditor or so to hold himself out as to indicate, or be reasonably understood to indicate, that he is a registered auditor.

(3) It is an offence for a person whose name does not appear on the register of auditors kept under regulations under that section in an entry made under subsection (1)(b) of that section to describe himself as a registered third country auditor or so to hold himself out as to indicate, or be reasonably understood to indicate, that he is a registered third country auditor.

(4) It is an offence for a body which is not a recognised supervisory body or a recognised qualifying body to describe itself as so recognised or so to describe itself or hold itself out as to indicate, or be reasonably understood to indicate, that it is so recognised.

(5) A person guilty of an offence under subsection (1) is liable—

(a) on conviction on indictment, to imprisonment for a term not exceeding two years or to a fine (or both);

(b) on summary conviction—

(i) in England and Wales, to imprisonment for a term not exceeding twelve months or to a fine not exceeding the statutory maximum (or both),

(ii) in Scotland or Northern Ireland, to imprisonment for a term not exceeding six months or to a fine not exceeding the statutory maximum (or both).

In relation to an offence committed before the commencement of section 154(1) of the Criminal Justice Act 2003 (c 44), for "twelve months" in paragraph (b)(i) substitute "six months".

(6) Subject to subsection (7), a person guilty of an offence under subsection (2), (3) or (4) is liable on summary conviction—

(a) in England and Wales, to imprisonment for a term not exceeding 51 weeks or to a fine not exceeding level 5 on the standard scale (or both),

(b) in Scotland or Northern Ireland, to imprisonment for a term not exceeding six months or to a fine not exceeding level 5 on the standard scale (or both).

In relation to an offence committed before the commencement of section 281(5) of the Criminal Justice Act 2003, for "51 weeks" in paragraph (a) substitute "six months".

(7) Where a contravention of subsection (2), (3) or (4) involves a public display of the offending description, the maximum fine that may be imposed is an amount equal to level 5 on the standard scale multiplied by the number of days for which the display has continued.

(8) It is a defence for a person charged with an offence under subsection (2), (3) or (4) to show that he took all reasonable precautions and exercised all due diligence to avoid the commission of the offence.

[S1250]

NOTES

Commencement: to be appointed.

Fees

1251 Fees

(1) An applicant for a recognition order under this Part must pay such fee in respect of his application as the Secretary of State may by regulations prescribe; and no application is to be regarded as duly made unless this subsection is complied with.

(2) The Secretary of State may by regulations prescribe periodical fees to be paid by—

(a) every recognised supervisory body,

(b) every recognised qualifying body,

(c) every Auditor General, and

(d) every registered third country auditor.

(3) Fees received by the Secretary of State by virtue of this Part are to be paid into the Consolidated Fund.

(4) Regulations under this section are subject to negative resolution procedure.

[S1251]

NOTES

Commencement: 20 January 2007 (for the purpose of enabling the exercise of powers to make Orders or Regulations by statutory instrument); to be appointed (otherwise).

Delegation of Secretary of State's functions

1252 Delegation of the Secretary of State's functions

(1) The Secretary of State may make an order under this section (a "delegation order") for the purpose of enabling functions of the Secretary of State under this Part to be exercised by a body designated by the order.

(2) The body designated by a delegation order may be either—

(a) a body corporate which is established by the order, or

(b) subject to section 1253, a body (whether a body corporate or an unincorporated association) which is already in existence ("an existing body").

(3) A delegation order has the effect of making the body designated by the order designated under section 5 of the Freedom of Information Act 2000 (c 36) (further powers to designate public authorities).

(4) A delegation order has the effect of transferring to the body designated by it all functions of the Secretary of State under this Part—

(a) subject to such exceptions and reservations as may be specified in the order, and

(b) except—

(i) his functions in relation to the body itself, and

(ii) his functions under section 1228 (appointment of Independent Supervisor).

(5) A delegation order may confer on the body designated by it such other functions supplementary or incidental to those transferred as appear to the Secretary of State to be appropriate.

(6) Any transfer of functions under the following provisions must be subject to the reservation that the functions remain exercisable concurrently by the Secretary of State—

(a) section 1224 (power to call for information from recognised bodies etc);

(b) section 1244 (power to call for information from registered third country auditors);

(c) section 1254 (directions to comply with international obligations).

(7) Any transfer of—

(a) the function of refusing to make a declaration under section 1221(1) (approval of overseas qualifications) on the grounds referred to in section 1221(4) (lack of comparable treatment), or

(b) the function of withdrawing such a declaration under section 1221(7) on those grounds,

must be subject to the reservation that the function is exercisable only with the consent of the Secretary of State.

(8) A delegation order may be amended or, if it appears to the Secretary of State that it is no longer in the public interest that the order should remain in force, revoked by a further order under this section.

(9) Where functions are transferred or resumed, the Secretary of State may by order confer or, as the case may be, take away such other functions supplementary or incidental to those transferred or resumed as appear to him to be appropriate.

(10) Where a delegation order is made, Schedule 13 has effect with respect to—

(a) the status of the body designated by the order in exercising functions of the Secretary of State under this Part,

(b) the constitution and proceedings of the body where it is established by the order,

(c) the exercise by the body of certain functions transferred to it, and

(d) other supplementary matters.

(11) An order under this section which has the effect of transferring or resuming any functions is subject to affirmative resolution procedure.

(12) Any other order under this section is subject to negative resolution procedure.

[S1252]

NOTES

Commencement: 20 January 2007 (for the purpose of enabling the exercise of powers to make Orders or Regulations by statutory instrument); to be appointed (otherwise).

1253 Delegation of functions to an existing body

(1) The Secretary of State's power to make a delegation order under section 1252 which designates an existing body is exercisable in accordance with this section.

(2) The Secretary of State may make such a delegation order if it appears to him that—

(a) the body is able and willing to exercise the functions that would be transferred by the order, and

(b) the body has arrangements in place relating to the exercise of those functions which are such as to be likely to ensure that the conditions in subsection (3) are met.

(3) The conditions are—

(a) that the functions in question will be exercised effectively, and

(b) where the delegation order is to contain any requirements or other provisions specified under subsection (4), that those functions will be exercised in accordance with any such requirements or provisions.

(4) The delegation order may contain such requirements or other provision relating to the exercise of the functions by the designated body as appear to the Secretary of State to be appropriate.

(5) An existing body—

(a) may be designated by a delegation order under section 1252, and

(b) may accordingly exercise functions of the Secretary of State in pursuance of the order,

despite any involvement of the body in the exercise of any functions under arrangements within paragraph 21, 22, 23(1) or 24(1) of Schedule 10 or paragraph 1 or 2 of Schedule 12.

[S1253]

NOTES

Commencement: 20 January 2007 (for the purpose of enabling the exercise of powers to make Orders or Regulations by statutory instrument); to be appointed (otherwise).

International obligations

1254 Directions to comply with international obligations

(1) If it appears to the Secretary of State—

(a) that any action proposed to be taken by a recognised supervisory body or a recognised qualifying body, or a body designated by order under section 1252, would be incompatible with Community obligations or any other international obligations of the United Kingdom, or

(b) that any action which that body has power to take is required for the purpose of implementing any such obligations,

he may direct the body not to take or, as the case may be, to take the action in question.

(2) A direction may include such supplementary or incidental requirements as the Secretary of State thinks necessary or expedient.

(3) A direction under this section given to a body designated by order under section 1252 is enforceable on the application of the Secretary of State by injunction or, in Scotland, by an order under section 45 of the Court of Session Act 1988 (c 36).

[S1254]

NOTES

Commencement: to be appointed.

General provision relating to offences

1255 Offences by bodies corporate, partnerships and unincorporated associations

(1) Where an offence under this Part committed by a body corporate is proved to have been committed with the consent or connivance of, or to be attributable to any neglect on the part of, an officer of the body, or a person purporting to act in any such capacity, he as well as the body corporate is guilty of the offence and liable to be proceeded against and punished accordingly.

(2) Where an offence under this Part committed by a partnership is proved to have been committed with the consent or connivance of, or to be attributable to any neglect on the part of, a partner, he as well as the partnership is guilty of the offence and liable to be proceeded against and punished accordingly.

(3) Where an offence under this Part committed by an unincorporated association (other than a partnership) is proved to have been committed with the consent or connivance of, or to be attributable to any neglect on the part of, any officer of the association or any member of its governing body, he as well as the association is guilty of the offence and liable to be proceeded against and punished accordingly.

[S1255]

NOTES

Commencement: to be appointed.

1256 Time limits for prosecution of offences

(1) An information relating to an offence under this Part which is triable by a magistrates' court in England and Wales may be so tried if it is laid at any time within the period of twelve months beginning with the date on which evidence sufficient in the opinion of the Director of Public Prosecutions or the Secretary of State to justify the proceedings comes to his knowledge.

(2) Proceedings in Scotland for an offence under this Part may be commenced at any time within the period of twelve months beginning with the date on which evidence sufficient in the Lord Advocate's opinion to justify proceedings came to his knowledge or, where such evidence was reported to him by the Secretary of State, within the period of twelve months beginning with the date on which it came to the knowledge of the Secretary of State.

(3) For the purposes of subsection (2) proceedings are to be deemed to be commenced on the date on which a warrant to apprehend or cite the accused is granted, if the warrant is executed without undue delay.

(4) A complaint charging an offence under this Part which is triable by a magistrates' court in Northern Ireland may be so tried if it is made at any time within the period of twelve months beginning with the date on which evidence sufficient in the opinion of the Director of Public Prosecutions for Northern Ireland or the Secretary of State to justify the proceedings comes to his knowledge.

(5) This section does not authorise—

(a) in the case of proceedings in England and Wales, the trial of an information laid,

(b) in the case of proceedings in Scotland, the commencement of proceedings, or

(c) in the case of proceedings in Northern Ireland, the trial of a complaint made,

more than three years after the commission of the offence.

(6) For the purposes of this section a certificate of the Director of Public Prosecutions, the Lord Advocate, the Director of Public Prosecutions for Northern Ireland or the Secretary of State as to the date on which such evidence as is referred to above came to his knowledge is conclusive evidence.

(7) Nothing in this section affects proceedings within the time limits prescribed by section 127(1) of the Magistrates' Courts Act 1980 (c 43), section 331 of the Criminal Procedure (Scotland) Act 1975 or Article 19 of the Magistrates' Courts (Northern Ireland) Order 1981 (SI 1981/1675 (NI 26)) (the usual time limits for criminal proceedings).

[S1256]

NOTES

Commencement: to be appointed.

1257 Jurisdiction and procedure in respect of offences

(1) Summary proceedings for an offence under this Part may, without prejudice to any jurisdiction exercisable apart from this section, be taken—

(a) against a body corporate or unincorporated association at any place at which it has a place of business, and

(b) against an individual at any place where he is for the time being.

(2) Proceedings for an offence alleged to have been committed under this Part by an unincorporated association must be brought in the name of the association (and not in that of any of its members), and for the purposes of any such proceedings any rules of court relating to the service of documents apply as in relation to a body corporate.

(3) Section 33 of the Criminal Justice Act 1925 (c 86) and Schedule 3 to the Magistrates' Courts Act 1980 (c 43) (procedure on charge of offence against a corporation) apply in a case in which an unincorporated association is charged in England and Wales with an offence under this Part as they apply in the case of a corporation.

(4) Section 18 of the Criminal Justice Act (Northern Ireland) 1945 (c 15 (NI)) and Article 166 and Schedule 4 to the Magistrates' Courts (Northern Ireland) Order 1981 (SI 1981/1675 (NI 26)) (procedure on charge of offence against a corporation) apply in a case in which an unincorporated association is charged in Northern Ireland with an offence under this Part as they apply in the case of a corporation.

(5) In relation to proceedings on indictment in Scotland for an offence alleged to have been committed under this Part by an unincorporated association, section 70 of the Criminal Procedure (Scotland) Act 1995 (proceedings on indictment against bodies corporate) applies as if the association were a body corporate.

(6) A fine imposed on an unincorporated association on its conviction of such an offence must be paid out of the funds of the association.

[S1257]

NOTES

Commencement: to be appointed.

Notices etc

1258 Service of notices

(1) This section has effect in relation to any notice, direction or other document required or authorised by or by virtue of this Part to be given to or served on any person other than the Secretary of State.

(2) Any such document may be given to or served on the person in question—
- (a) by delivering it to him,
- (b) by leaving it at his proper address, or
- (c) by sending it by post to him at that address.

(3) Any such document may—
- (a) in the case of a body corporate, be given to or served on an officer of that body;
- (b) in the case of a partnership, be given to or served on any partner;
- (c) in the case of an unincorporated association other than a partnership, be given to or served on any member of the governing body of that association.

(4) For the purposes of this section and section 7 of the Interpretation Act 1978 (c 30) (service of documents by post) in its application to this section, the proper address of any person is his last known address (whether of his residence or of a place where he carries on business or is employed) and also—
- (a) in the case of a person who is eligible under the rules of a recognised supervisory body for appointment as a statutory auditor and who does not have a place of business in the United Kingdom, the address of that body;
- (b) in the case of a body corporate or an officer of that body, the address of the registered or principal office of that body in the United Kingdom;
- (c) in the case of an unincorporated association other than a partnership or a member of its governing body, its principal office in the United Kingdom.

[S1258]

NOTES

Commencement: to be appointed.

1259 Documents in electronic form

(1) This section applies where—
- (a) section 1258 authorises the giving or sending of a notice, direction or other document by its delivery to a particular person ("the recipient"), and
- (b) the notice, direction or other document is transmitted to the recipient—
  - (i) by means of an electronic communications network, or
  - (ii) by other means but in a form that requires the use of apparatus by the recipient to render it intelligible.

(2) The transmission has effect for the purposes of this Part as a delivery of the notice, direction or other document to the recipient, but only if the recipient has indicated to the person making the transmission his willingness to receive the notice, direction or other document in the form and manner used.

(3) An indication to a person for the purposes of subsection (2)—
- (a) must be given to the person in such manner as he may require,
- (b) may be a general indication or an indication that is limited to notices, directions or other documents of a particular description,

(c) must state the address to be used,
(d) must be accompanied by such other information as the person requires for the making of the transmission, and
(e) may be modified or withdrawn at any time by a notice given to the person in such manner as he may require.

(4) In this section "electronic communications network" has the same meaning as in the Communications Act 2003 (c 21).

[S1259]

NOTES

Commencement: to be appointed.

Interpretation

1260 Meaning of "associate"

(1) In this Part "associate", in relation to a person, is to be construed as follows.

(2) In relation to an individual, "associate" means—
(a) that individual's spouse, civil partner or minor child or step-child,
(b) any body corporate of which that individual is a director, and
(c) any employee or partner of that individual.

(3) In relation to a body corporate, "associate" means—
(a) any body corporate of which that body is a director,
(b) any body corporate in the same group as that body, and
(c) any employee or partner of that body or of any body corporate in the same group.

(4) In relation to a partnership constituted under the law of Scotland, or any other country or territory in which a partnership is a legal person, "associate" means—
(a) any body corporate of which that partnership is a director,
(b) any employee of or partner in that partnership, and
(c) any person who is an associate of a partner in that partnership.

(5) In relation to a partnership constituted under the law of England and Wales or Northern Ireland, or the law of any other country or territory in which a partnership is not a legal person, "associate" means any person who is an associate of any of the partners.

(6) In subsections (2)(b), (3)(a) and (4)(a), in the case of a body corporate which is a limited liability partnership, "director" is to be read as "member".

[S1260]

NOTES

Commencement: to be appointed.

1261 Minor definitions

(1) In this Part, unless a contrary intention appears—

"address" means—
(a) in relation to an individual, his usual residential or business address;
(b) in relation to a firm, its registered or principal office in the United Kingdom;

"company" means any company or other body the accounts of which must be audited in accordance with Part 16;

"director", in relation to a body corporate, includes any person occupying in relation to it the position of a director (by whatever name called) and any person in accordance with whose directions or instructions (not being advice given in a professional capacity) the directors of the body are accustomed to act;

"firm" means any entity, whether or not a legal person, which is not an individual and includes a body corporate, a corporation sole and a partnership or other unincorporated association;

"group", in relation to a body corporate, means the body corporate, any other body corporate which is its holding company or subsidiary and any other body corporate which is a subsidiary of that holding company;

"holding company" and "subsidiary" are to be read in accordance with section 1159 and Schedule 6;

"officer", in relation to a body corporate, includes a director, a manager, a secretary or, where the affairs of the body are managed by its members, a member;

"parent undertaking" and "subsidiary undertaking" are to be read in accordance with section 1162 and Schedule 7.

(2) For the purposes of this Part a body is to be regarded as "established in the United Kingdom" if and only if—

(a) it is incorporated or formed under the law of the United Kingdom or a part of the United Kingdom, or

(b) its central management and control are exercised in the United Kingdom;

and any reference to a qualification "obtained in the United Kingdom" is to a qualification obtained from such a body.

(3) The Secretary of State may by regulations make such modifications of this Part as appear to him to be necessary or appropriate for the purposes of its application in relation to any firm, or description of firm, which is not a body corporate or a partnership.

(4) Regulations under subsection (3) are subject to negative resolution procedure.

[S1261]

NOTES

Commencement: 20 January 2007 (for the purpose of enabling the exercise of powers to make Orders or Regulations by statutory instrument); to be appointed (otherwise).

1262 Index of defined expressions

The following Table shows provisions defining or otherwise explaining expressions used in this Part (other than provisions defining or explaining an expression used only in the same section)—

Expression	*Provision*
address	section 1261(1)
appropriate qualification	section 1219
associate	section 1260
audited person	section 1210(2)
Auditor General	section 1226(1)
company	section 1261(1)
delegation order	section 1252(1)
director (of a body corporate)	section 1261(1)
enactment	section 1293
established in the United Kingdom	section 1261(2)
firm	section 1261(1)
group (in relation to a body corporate)	section 1261(1)
holding company	section 1261(1)
main purposes of this Part	section 1209
member (of a supervisory body)	section 1217(2)
obtained in the United Kingdom	section 1261(2)
officer	section 1261(1)
parent undertaking	section 1261(1)
qualifying body	section 1220(1)
recognised, in relation to a professional qualification	section 1220(3) and Schedule 11

Expression	*Provision*
recognised, in relation to a qualifying body	paragraph 1(2) of Schedule 11
recognised, in relation to a supervisory body	section 1217(4) and Schedule 10
registered third country auditor	section 1241(1)
rules of a qualifying body	section 1220(2)
rules of a supervisory body	section 1217(3)
statutory auditor, statutory audit and statutory audit work	section 1210(1)
subsidiary	section 1261(1)
supervisory body	section 1217(1)
subsidiary undertaking	section 1261(1)
third country auditor, third country audit and third country audit work	section 1241(1)

[S1262]

NOTES

Commencement: to be appointed.

Miscellaneous and general

1263 Power to make provision in consequence of changes affecting accountancy bodies

(1) The Secretary of State may by regulations make such amendments of enactments as appear to him to be necessary or expedient in consequence of any change of name, merger or transfer of engagements affecting—

(a) a recognised supervisory body or recognised qualifying body, or

(b) a body of accountants referred to in, or approved, authorised or otherwise recognised for the purposes of, any other enactment.

(2) Regulations under this section are subject to negative resolution procedure.

[S1263]

NOTES

Commencement: 20 January 2007 (for the purpose of enabling the exercise of powers to make Orders or Regulations by statutory instrument); to be appointed (otherwise).

1264 Consequential amendments

Schedule 14 contains consequential amendments relating to this Part.

[S1264]

NOTES

Commencement: to be appointed.

PART 43
TRANSPARENCY OBLIGATIONS AND RELATED MATTERS

Introductory

1265 The transparency obligations directive

(*Amends FSMA 2000, s 103 at* **[2103]**.)

[S1265]

NOTES

Commencement: 8 November 2006.

Transparency obligations

1266 Transparency rules

(1) (*Inserts FSMA 2000, ss 89A–89G at* **[2089A]** *et seq.*)

(2) The effectiveness for the purposes of section 155 of the Financial Services and Markets Act 2000 (c 8) (consultation on proposed rules) of things done by the Financial Services Authority before this section comes into force with a view to making transparency rules (as defined in the provisions to be inserted in that Act by subsection (1) above) is not affected by the fact that those provisions were not then in force.

[S1266]

NOTES

Commencement: 8 November 2006.

1267 Competent authority's power to call for information

(*Inserts FSMA 2000, ss 89H–89J at* **[2089H]** *et seq.*)

[S1267]

NOTES

Commencement: 8 November 2006.

1268 Powers exercisable in case of infringement of transparency obligation

(*Inserts FSMA 2000, ss 89K–89N at* **[2089K]** *et seq.*)

[S1268]

NOTES

Commencement: 8 November 2006.

Other matters

1269 Corporate governance rules

(*Inserts FSMA 2000, s 89O at* **[2089O]**.)

[S1269]

NOTES

Commencement: 8 November 2006.

1270 Liability for false or misleading statements in certain publications

(*Inserts FSMA 2000, ss 90A, 90B at* **[2090A]** *et seq.*)

[S1270]

NOTES

Commencement: 8 November 2006.

1271 Exercise of powers where UK is host member State

(*Inserts FSMA 2000, s 100A at* **[2100A]**.)

[S1271]

NOTES

Commencement: 8 November 2006.

1272 Transparency obligations and related matters: minor and consequential amendments

(1) Schedule 15 to this Act makes minor and consequential amendments in connection with the provision made by this Part.

(2) In that Schedule-

Part 1 contains amendments of the Financial Services and Markets Act 2000 (c 8);

Part 2 contains amendments of the Companies (Audit, Investigations and Community Enterprise) Act 2004 (c 27).

[S1272]

NOTES

Commencement: 8 November 2006 (except in so far as relating to the amendment in Sch 15, para 11(2) to this Act); to be appointed (otherwise).

1273 Corporate governance regulations

(1) The Secretary of State may make regulations—

(a) for the purpose of implementing, enabling the implementation of or dealing with matters arising out of or related to, any Community obligation relating to the corporate governance of issuers who have requested or approved admission of their securities to trading on a regulated market;

(b) about corporate governance in relation to such issuers for the purpose of implementing, or dealing with matters arising out of or related to, any Community obligation.

(2) "Corporate governance", in relation to an issuer, includes—

(a) the nature, constitution or functions of the organs of the issuer;

(b) the manner in which organs of the issuer conduct themselves;

(c) the requirements imposed on organs of the issuer;

(d) the relationship between different organs of the issuer;

(e) the relationship between the organs of the issuer and the members of the issuer or holders of the issuer's securities.

(3) The regulations may—

(a) make provision by reference to any specified code on corporate governance that may be issued from time to time by a specified body;

(b) create new criminal offences (subject to subsection (4));

(c) make provision excluding liability in damages in respect of things done or omitted for the purposes of, or in connection with, the carrying on, or purported carrying on, of any specified activities.

"Specified" here means specified in the regulations.

(4) The regulations may not create a criminal offence punishable by a greater penalty than—

(a) on indictment, a fine;

(b) on summary conviction, a fine not exceeding the statutory maximum or (if calculated on a daily basis) £100 a day.

(5) Regulations under this section are subject to negative resolution procedure.

(6) In this section "issuer", "securities" and "regulated market" have the same meaning as in Part 6 of the Financial Services and Markets Act 2000 (c 8).

[S1273]

NOTES

Commencement: 8 November 2006.

PART 44
MISCELLANEOUS PROVISIONS

Regulation of actuaries etc

1274 Grants to bodies concerned with actuarial standards etc

(*Substitutes the Companies* (*Audit, Investigations and Community Enterprise*) *Act 2004, s 16*(2)(*l*)–(*t*) (*for the original para* (*l*)) *and amends sub-s* (5) *at* **[896]**.)

[S1274]

NOTES

Commencement: 8 November 2006.

1275 Levy to pay expenses of bodies concerned with actuarial standards etc

(1)–(5) (*Amend the Companies* (*Audit, Investigations and Community Enterprise*) *Act 2004, s 17 at* **[897]**)

(6) The above amendments have effect in relation to any exercise of the power to make regulations under section 17 of the Companies (Audit, Investigations and Community Enterprise) Act 2004 after this section comes into force, regardless of when the expenses to be met by the levy in respect of which the regulations are made were incurred.

(7) (*Amends the Pensions Act 2004, Sch 3* (*outside the scope of this work*).)

[S1275]

NOTES

Commencement: to be appointed.

1276 Application of provisions to Scotland and Northern Ireland

(*Amends the Companies* (*Audit, Investigations and Community Enterprise*) *Act 2004, ss 16, 66 at* **[896]**, **[939]**.)

[S1276]

NOTES

Commencement: 8 November 2006.

Information as to exercise of voting rights by institutional investors

1277 Power to require information about exercise of voting rights

(1) The Treasury or the Secretary of State may make provision by regulations requiring institutions to which this section applies to provide information about the exercise of voting rights attached to shares to which this section applies.

(2) This power is exercisable in accordance with—
section 1278 (institutions to which information provisions apply),
section 1279 (shares to which information provisions apply), and
section 1280 (obligations with respect to provision of information).

(3) In this section and the sections mentioned above—

(a) references to a person acting on behalf of an institution include—
  (i) any person to whom authority has been delegated by the institution to take decisions as to any matter relevant to the subject matter of the regulations, and
  (ii) such other persons as may be specified; and

(b) "specified" means specified in the regulations.

(4) The obligation imposed by regulations under this section is enforceable by civil proceedings brought by—

(a) any person to whom the information should have been provided, or
(b) a specified regulatory authority.

(5) Regulations under this section may make different provision for different descriptions of institution, different descriptions of shares and for other different circumstances.

(6) Regulations under this section are subject to affirmative resolution procedure.

[S1277]

NOTES

Commencement: 20 January 2007 (for the purpose of enabling the exercise of powers to make Orders or Regulations by statutory instrument); to be appointed (otherwise).

1278 Institutions to which information provisions apply

(1) The institutions to which section 1277 applies are—

(a) unit trust schemes within the meaning of the Financial Services and Markets Act 2000 (c 8) in respect of which an order is in force under section 243 of that Act;

(b) open-ended investment companies incorporated by virtue of regulations under section 262 of that Act;

(c) companies approved for the purposes of section 842 of the Income and Corporation Taxes Act 1988 (c 1) (investment trusts);

(d) pension schemes as defined in section 1(5) of the Pension Schemes Act 1993 (c 48) or the Pension Schemes (Northern Ireland) Act 1993 (c 49);

(e) undertakings authorised under the Financial Services and Markets Act 2000 to carry on long-term insurance business (that is, the activity of effecting or carrying out contracts of long-term insurance within the meaning of the Financial Services and Markets (Regulated Activities) Order 2001 (SI 2001/544);

(f) collective investment schemes that are recognised by virtue of section 270 of that Act (schemes authorised in designated countries or territories).

(2) Regulations under that section may—

(a) provide that the section applies to other descriptions of institution;

(b) provide that the section does not apply to a specified description of institution.

(3) The regulations must specify by whom, in the case of any description of institution, the duty imposed by the regulations is to be fulfilled.

[S1278]

NOTES

Commencement: 20 January 2007 (for the purpose of enabling the exercise of powers to make Orders or Regulations by statutory instrument); to be appointed (otherwise).

1279 Shares to which information provisions apply

(1) The shares to which section 1277 applies are shares—

(a) of a description traded on a specified market, and

(b) in which the institution has, or is taken to have, an interest.

Regulations under that section may provide that the section does not apply to shares of a specified description.

(2) For this purpose an institution has an interest in shares if the shares, or a depositary certificate in respect of them, are held by it, or on its behalf.

A "depositary certificate" means an instrument conferring rights (other than options)—

(a) in respect of shares held by another person, and

(b) the transfer of which may be effected without the consent of that person.

(3) Where an institution has an interest—

(a) in a specified description of collective investment scheme (within the meaning of the Financial Services and Markets Act 2000 (c 8)), or

(b) in any other specified description of scheme or collective investment vehicle,

it is taken to have an interest in any shares in which that scheme or vehicle has or is taken to have an interest.

(4) For this purpose a scheme or vehicle is taken to have an interest in shares if it would be regarded as having such an interest in accordance with subsection (2) if it was an institution to which section 1277 applied.

[S1279]

NOTES

Commencement: 20 January 2007 (for the purpose of enabling the exercise of powers to make Orders or Regulations by statutory instrument); to be appointed (otherwise).

1280 Obligations with respect to provision of information

(1) Regulations under section 1277 may require the provision of specified information about—

(a) the exercise or non-exercise of voting rights by the institution or any person acting on its behalf,

(b) any instructions given by the institution or any person acting on its behalf as to the exercise or non-exercise of voting rights, and

(c) any delegation by the institution or any person acting on its behalf of any functions in relation to the exercise or non-exercise of voting rights or the giving of such instructions.

(2) The regulations may require information to be provided in respect of specified occasions or specified periods.

(3) Where instructions are given to act on the recommendations or advice of another person, the regulations may require the provision of information about what recommendations or advice were given.

(4) The regulations may require information to be provided—

(a) in such manner as may be specified, and

(b) to such persons as may be specified, or to the public, or both.

(5) The regulations may provide—

(a) that an institution may discharge its obligations under the regulations by referring to information disclosed by a person acting on its behalf, and

(b) that in such a case it is sufficient, where that other person acts on behalf of more than one institution, that the reference is to information given in aggregated form, that is—

(i) relating to the exercise or non-exercise by that person of voting rights on behalf of more than one institution, or

(ii) relating to the instructions given by that person in respect of the exercise or non-exercise of voting rights on behalf of more than one institution, or

(iii) relating to the delegation by that person of functions in relation to the exercise or non-exercise of voting rights, or the giving of instructions in respect of the exercise or non-exercise of voting rights, on behalf of more than one institution.

(6) References in this section to instructions are to instructions of any description, whether general or specific, whether binding or not and whether or not acted upon.

[S1280]

NOTES

Commencement: 20 January 2007 (for the purpose of enabling the exercise of powers to make Orders or Regulations by statutory instrument); to be appointed (otherwise).

Disclosure of information under the Enterprise Act 2002

1281 Disclosure of information under the Enterprise Act 2002

(*Inserts the Enterprise Act 2002, s 241A (outside the scope of this work).*)

[S1281]

NOTES

Commencement: 6 April 2007.

Expenses of winding up

1282 Payment of expenses of winding up

(*Inserts the Insolvency Act 1986, s 176ZA at* **[3333ZA]** *and makes a corresponding amendment to the Insolvency* (*Northern Ireland*) *Order 1989, SI 1989/2405* (*outside the scope of this work*).)

[S1282]

NOTES

Commencement: to be appointed.

Commonhold associations

1283 Amendment of memorandum or articles of commonhold association

(*Amends the Commonhold and Leasehold Reform Act 2002, Sch 3* (*outside the scope of this work*).)

[S1283]

NOTES

Commencement: to be appointed.

PART 45
NORTHERN IRELAND

1284 Extension of Companies Acts to Northern Ireland

(1) The Companies Acts as defined by this Act (see section 2) extend to Northern Ireland.

(2) The Companies (Northern Ireland) Order 1986 (SI 1986/1032 (NI 6)), the Companies Consolidation (Consequential Provisions) (Northern Ireland) Order 1986 (SI 1986/1035 (NI 9)) and Part 3 of the Companies (Audit, Investigations and Community Enterprise) Order 2005 (SI 2005/1967 (NI 17)) shall cease to have effect accordingly.

[S1284]

NOTES

Commencement: 1 January 2007 (certain purposes); 20 January 2007 (certain purposes); 6 April 2007 (certain purposes); 1 October 2007 (certain purposes); 1 November 2007 (certain purposes); 15 December 2007 (certain purposes); 1 October 2008 (certain purposes); to be appointed (otherwise) (see the notes below).

Note: the Companies Act 2006 (Commencement No 1, Transitional Provisions and Savings) Order 2006, SI 2006/3428, arts 2(2), 3(2), 4(3) provide that this section shall come into force on 1 January 2007, 20 January 2007, and 6 April 2007 respectively so far as is necessary for the purposes of the provisions of this Act brought into force on those dates by arts 2(1), 3(1), 4(1), (2) of that Order (see **[7575]**, **[7576]**, **[7577]**).

Note: the Companies Act 2006 (Commencement No 2, Consequential Amendments, Transitional Provisions and Savings) Order 2007, SI 2007/1093, art 2(1)(e) provides that sub-s (1) shall come into force on 6 April 2007 so far as is necessary for the purposes of the provisions of this Act brought into force on that date by art 2(1)(a)–(c) of that Order, and so far as is necessary for the purposes of Part 2 of the Companies (Audit, Investigations and Community Enterprise) Act 2004 (see **[7615]**). Article 5 of that Order (at **[7618]**) further provides that sub-s (2) comes into force on 6 April 2007 in so far as relating to the repeals specified in Sch 2 to that Order.

Note: the draft Companies Act 2006 (Commencement No 3, Consequential Amendments, Transitional Provisions and Savings) Order 2007, arts 2(4), 3(2), 4(2) and 5(2) provide that this section shall come into force on 1 October 2007, 1 November 2007, 15 December 2007 and 1 October 2008 respectively so far as is necessary for the purposes of the provisions of this Act brought into force on those dates by arts 2(1)(a)–(j), 3(1), 4(1) and 5(1) of that Order (see **[A12]**). Article 8 of that Order further provides that sub-s (2) comes into force on 1 October 2007 in so far as relating to the repeals specified in Sch 2 to that Order.

Transitional adaptations: art 5 of the Companies Act 2006 (Commencement No 1, Transitional Provisions and Savings) Order 2006, SI 2006/3428 provides that the provisions brought into force by arts 2–4 of 2006 Order shall have effect subject to any transitional adaptations specified in Sch 1 to that Order. Schedule 1, para 15 to the Order (at **[7582]**) provides as follows—

"**15.**—(1) Section 1284 (extension of Companies Acts to Northern Ireland) has effect with the following adaptations.

(2) In subsection (1) for "The Companies Acts as defined by this Act (see section 2)" substitute "The company law provisions of this Act that are for the time being in force".

(3) For subsection (2) substitute—

"(2) The corresponding provisions of the Companies (Northern Ireland) Order 1986 shall cease to have effect accordingly."".

1285 Extension of GB enactments relating to SEs

(1) The enactments in force in Great Britain relating to SEs extend to Northern Ireland.

(2) The following enactments shall cease to have effect accordingly—

(a) the European Public Limited-Liability Company Regulations (Northern Ireland) 2004 (SR 2004/417), and

(b) the European Public Limited-Liability Company (Fees) Regulations (Northern Ireland) 2004 (SR 2004/418).

(3) In this section "SE" means a European Public Limited-Liability Company (or Societas Europaea) within the meaning of Council Regulation 2157/2001/EC of 8 October 2001 on the Statute for a European Company.

[S1285]

NOTES

Commencement: to be appointed.

1286 Extension of GB enactments relating to certain other forms of business organisation

(1) The enactments in force in Great Britain relating to—

(a) limited liability partnerships,

(b) limited partnerships,

(c) open-ended investment companies, and

(d) European Economic Interest Groupings,

extend to Northern Ireland.

(2) The following enactments shall cease to have effect accordingly—

(a) the Limited Liability Partnerships Act (Northern Ireland) 2002 (c 12 (NI));

(b) the Limited Partnerships Act 1907 (c 24) as it formerly had effect in Northern Ireland;

(c) the Open-Ended Investment Companies Act (Northern Ireland) 2002 (c 13 (NI));

(d) the European Economic Interest Groupings Regulations (Northern Ireland) 1989 (SR 1989/216).

[S1286]

NOTES

Commencement: to be appointed.

1287 Extension of enactments relating to business names

(1) The provisions of Part 41 of this Act (business names) extend to Northern Ireland.

(2) The Business Names (Northern Ireland) Order 1986 (SI 1986/1033 (NI 7)) shall cease to have effect accordingly.

[S1287]

NOTES

Commencement: to be appointed.

PART 46
GENERAL SUPPLEMENTARY PROVISIONS

Regulations and orders

1288 Regulations and orders: statutory instrument

Except as otherwise provided, regulations and orders under this Act shall be made by statutory instrument.

[S1288]

NOTES

Commencement: 8 November 2006.

Application of this Part to unregistered companies: see the Companies Acts (Unregistered Companies) Regulations 2007, SI 2007/318 at **[7606]**.

1289 Regulations and orders: negative resolution procedure

Where regulations or orders under this Act are subject to "negative resolution procedure" the statutory instrument containing the regulations or order shall be subject to annulment in pursuance of a resolution of either House of Parliament.

[S1289]

NOTES

Commencement: 8 November 2006.

Application of this Part to unregistered companies: see the Companies Acts (Unregistered Companies) Regulations 2007, SI 2007/318 at **[7606]**.

1290 Regulations and orders: affirmative resolution procedure

Where regulations or orders under this Act are subject to "affirmative resolution procedure" the regulations or order must not be made unless a draft of the statutory instrument containing them has been laid before Parliament and approved by a resolution of each House of Parliament.

[S1290]

NOTES

Commencement: 8 November 2006.

Application of this Part to unregistered companies: see the Companies Acts (Unregistered Companies) Regulations 2007, SI 2007/318 at **[7606]**.

1291 Regulations and orders: approval after being made

(1) Regulations or orders under this Act that are subject to "approval after being made"—

(a) must be laid before Parliament after being made, and

(b) cease to have effect at the end of 28 days beginning with the day on which they were made unless during that period they are approved by resolution of each House.

(2) In reckoning the period of 28 days no account shall be taken of any time during which Parliament is dissolved or prorogued or during which both Houses are adjourned for more than four days.

(3) The regulations or order ceasing to have effect does not affect—

(a) anything previously done under them or it, or

(b) the making of new regulations or a new order.

[S1291]

NOTES

Commencement: 8 November 2006.

Application of this Part to unregistered companies: see the Companies Acts (Unregistered Companies) Regulations 2007, SI 2007/318 at **[7606]**.

1292 Regulations and orders: supplementary

(1) Regulations or orders under this Act may—

(a) make different provision for different cases or circumstances,

(b) include supplementary, incidental and consequential provision, and

(c) make transitional provision and savings.

(2) Any provision that may be made by regulations under this Act may be made by order; and any provision that may be made by order under this Act may be made by regulations.

(3) Any provision that may be made by regulations or order under this Act for which no Parliamentary procedure is prescribed may be made by regulations or order subject to negative or affirmative resolution procedure.

(4) Any provision that may be made by regulations or order under this Act subject to negative resolution procedure may be made by regulations or order subject to affirmative resolution procedure.

[S1292]

NOTES

Commencement: 8 November 2006.

Application of this Part to unregistered companies: see the Companies Acts (Unregistered Companies) Regulations 2007, SI 2007/318 at **[7606]**.

Meaning of "enactment"

1293 Meaning of "enactment"

In this Act, unless the context otherwise requires, "enactment" includes—

(a) an enactment contained in subordinate legislation within the meaning of the Interpretation Act 1978 (c 30),

(b) an enactment contained in, or in an instrument made under, an Act of the Scottish Parliament, and

(c) an enactment contained in, or in an instrument made under, Northern Ireland legislation within the meaning of the Interpretation Act 1978.

[S1293]

NOTES

Commencement: 8 November 2006.

Application of this Part to unregistered companies: see the Companies Acts (Unregistered Companies) Regulations 2007, SI 2007/318 at **[7606]**.

Consequential and transitional provisions

1294 Power to make consequential amendments etc

(1) The Secretary of State or the Treasury may by order make such provision amending, repealing or revoking any enactment to which this section applies as they consider necessary or expedient in consequence of any provision made by or under this Act.

(2) This section applies to—

(a) any enactment passed or made before the passing of this Act,

(b) any enactment contained in this Act or in subordinate legislation made under it, and

(c) any enactment passed or made before the end of the session after that in which this Act is passed.

(3) Without prejudice to the generality of the power conferred by subsection (1), orders under this section may—

(a) make provision extending to other forms of organisation any provision made by or under this Act in relation to companies, or

(b) make provision corresponding to that made by or under this Act in relation to companies,

in either case with such adaptations or other modifications as appear to the Secretary of State or the Treasury to be necessary or expedient.

(4) The references in subsection (3) to provision made by this Act include provision conferring power to make provision by regulations, orders or other subordinate legislation.

(5) Amendments and repeals made under this section are additional, and without prejudice, to those made by or under any other provision of this Act.

(6) Orders under this section are subject to affirmative resolution procedure.

[S1294]

NOTES

Commencement: 8 November 2006.

Orders: the Companies Act 2006 (Commencement No 2, Consequential Amendments, Transitional Provisions and Savings) Order 2007, SI 2007/1093 at **[7614]**. See also the draft Companies Act 2006 (Commencement No 3, Consequential Amendments, Transitional Provisions and Savings) Order 2007 at **[A12]**.

Application of this Part to unregistered companies: see the Companies Acts (Unregistered Companies) Regulations 2007, SI 2007/318 at **[7606]**.

1295 Repeals

The enactments specified in Schedule 16, which include enactments that are no longer of practical utility, are repealed to the extent specified.

[S1295]

NOTES

Commencement: see Sch 16 at **[S1331]**.

Application of this Part to unregistered companies: see the Companies Acts (Unregistered Companies) Regulations 2007, SI 2007/318 at **[7606]**.

1296 Power to make transitional provision and savings

(1) The Secretary of State or the Treasury may by order make such transitional provision and savings as they consider necessary or expedient in connection with the commencement of any provision made by or under this Act.

(2) An order may, in particular, make such adaptations of provisions brought into force as appear to be necessary or expedient in consequence of other provisions of this Act not yet having come into force.

(3) Transitional provision and savings made under this section are additional, and without prejudice, to those made by or under any other provision of this Act.

(4) Orders under this section are subject to negative resolution procedure.

[S1296]

NOTES

Commencement: 8 November 2006.

Application of this Part to unregistered companies: see the Companies Acts (Unregistered Companies) Regulations 2007, SI 2007/318 at **[7606]**.

Orders: the Companies Act 2006 (Commencement No 1, Transitional Provisions and Savings) Order 2006, SI 2006/3428 at **[7574]**; the Companies Act 2006 (Commencement No 2, Consequential Amendments, Transitional Provisions and Savings) Order 2007, SI 2007/1093 at **[7614]**. See also the draft Companies Act 2006 (Commencement No 3, Consequential Amendments, Transitional Provisions and Savings) Order 2007 at **[A12]**.

1297 Continuity of the law

(1) This section applies where any provision of this Act re-enacts (with or without modification) an enactment repealed by this Act.

(2) The repeal and re-enactment does not affect the continuity of the law.

(3) Anything done (including subordinate legislation made), or having effect as if done, under or for the purposes of the repealed provision that could have been done under or for the purposes of the corresponding provision of this Act, if in force or effective immediately before the commencement of that corresponding provision, has effect thereafter as if done under or for the purposes of that corresponding provision.

(4) Any reference (express or implied) in this Act or any other enactment, instrument or document to a provision of this Act shall be construed (so far as the context permits) as

including, as respects times, circumstances or purposes in relation to which the corresponding repealed provision had effect, a reference to that corresponding provision.

(5) Any reference (express or implied) in any enactment, instrument or document to a repealed provision shall be construed (so far as the context permits), as respects times, circumstances and purposes in relation to which the corresponding provision of this Act has effect, as being or (according to the context) including a reference to the corresponding provision of this Act.

(6) This section has effect subject to any specific transitional provision or saving contained in this Act.

(7) References in this section to this Act include subordinate legislation made under this Act.

(8) In this section "subordinate legislation" has the same meaning as in the Interpretation Act 1978 (c 30).

[S1297]

NOTES

Commencement: 8 November 2006.

Note: the Companies Act 2006 (Commencement No 2, Consequential Amendments, Transitional Provisions and Savings) Order 2007, SI 2007/1093, art 10 at **[7623]** provides as follows (note that by virtue of art 1(2) "the Interim Regulations" means the Takeovers Directive (Interim Implementation) Regulations 2006)—

"10. Section 1297 of the Companies Act 2006 (continuity of the law) has effect as if, for the purpose of section 1297(1), the Interim Regulations were an enactment repealed and re-enacted by that Act.".

See also the draft Companies Act 2006 (Commencement No 3, Consequential Amendments, Transitional Provisions and Savings) Order 2007, art 12(1) at **[A12]** which provides that the amendments and repeals made by that Order do not affect the operation of this section.

Application of this Part to unregistered companies: see the Companies Acts (Unregistered Companies) Regulations 2007, SI 2007/318 at **[7606]**.

PART 47
FINAL PROVISIONS

1298 Short title

The short title of this Act is the Companies Act 2006.

[S1298]

NOTES

Commencement: 8 November 2006.

Application of this Part to unregistered companies: see the Companies Acts (Unregistered Companies) Regulations 2007, SI 2007/318 at **[7606]**.

1299 Extent

Except as otherwise provided (or the context otherwise requires), the provisions of this Act extend to the whole of the United Kingdom.

[S1299]

NOTES

Commencement: 8 November 2006.

Application of this Part to unregistered companies: see the Companies Acts (Unregistered Companies) Regulations 2007, SI 2007/318 at **[7606]**.

1300 Commencement

(1) The following provisions come into force on the day this Act is passed—

(a) Part 43 (transparency obligations and related matters), except the amendment in paragraph 11(2) of Schedule 15 of the definition of "regulated market" in Part 6 of the Financial Services and Markets Act 2000 (c 8),

(b) in Part 44 (miscellaneous provisions)—
section 1274 (grants to bodies concerned with actuarial standards etc), and

section 1276 (application of provisions to Scotland and Northern Ireland),

(c) Part 46 (general supplementary provisions), except section 1295 and Schedule 16 (repeals), and

(d) this Part.

(2) The other provisions of this Act come into force on such day as may be appointed by order of the Secretary of State or the Treasury.

[S1300]

NOTES

Commencement: 8 November 2006.

Application of this Part to unregistered companies: see the Companies Acts (Unregistered Companies) Regulations 2007, SI 2007/318 at **[7606]**.

Orders: the Companies Act 2006 (Commencement No 1, Transitional Provisions and Savings) Order 2006, SI 2006/3428 at **[7574]**; the Companies Act 2006 (Commencement No 2, Consequential Amendments, Transitional Provisions and Savings) Order 2007, SI 2007/1093 at **[7614]**. See also the draft Companies Act 2006 (Commencement No 3, Consequential Amendments, Transitional Provisions and Savings) Order 2007 at **[A12]**.

SCHEDULES

SCHEDULE 1
CONNECTED PERSONS: REFERENCES TO AN INTEREST IN SHARES OR DEBENTURES

Sections 254 and 255

Introduction

1.—(1) The provisions of this Schedule have effect for the interpretation of references in sections 254 and 255 (directors connected with or controlling a body corporate) to an interest in shares or debentures.

(2) The provisions are expressed in relation to shares but apply to debentures as they apply to shares.

General provisions

2.—(1) A reference to an interest in shares includes any interest of any kind whatsoever in shares.

(2) Any restraints or restrictions to which the exercise of any right attached to the interest is or may be subject shall be disregarded.

(3) It is immaterial that the shares in which a person has an interest are not identifiable.

(4) Persons having a joint interest in shares are deemed each of them to have that interest.

Rights to acquire shares

3.—(1) A person is taken to have an interest in shares if he enters into a contract to acquire them.

(2) A person is taken to have an interest in shares if—

(a) he has a right to call for delivery of the shares to himself or to his order, or

(b) he has a right to acquire an interest in shares or is under an obligation to take an interest in shares,

whether the right or obligation is conditional or absolute.

(3) Rights or obligations to subscribe for shares are not to be taken for the purposes of sub-paragraph (2) to be rights to acquire or obligations to take an interest in shares.

(4) A person ceases to have an interest in shares by virtue of this paragraph—

(a) on the shares being delivered to another person at his order—

(i) in fulfilment of a contract for their acquisition by him, or

(ii) in satisfaction of a right of his to call for their delivery;

(b) on a failure to deliver the shares in accordance with the terms of such a contract or on which such a right falls to be satisfied;
(c) on the lapse of his right to call for the delivery of shares.

Right to exercise or control exercise of rights

4.—(1) A person is taken to have an interest in shares if, not being the registered holder, he is entitled—
(a) to exercise any right conferred by the holding of the shares, or
(b) to control the exercise of any such right.

(2) For this purpose a person is taken to be entitled to exercise or control the exercise of a right conferred by the holding of shares if he—
(a) has a right (whether subject to conditions or not) the exercise of which would make him so entitled, or
(b) is under an obligation (whether or not so subject) the fulfilment of which would make him so entitled.

(3) A person is not by virtue of this paragraph taken to be interested in shares by reason only that—
(a) he has been appointed a proxy to exercise any of the rights attached to the shares, or
(b) he has been appointed by a body corporate to act as its representative at any meeting of a company or of any class of its members.

Bodies corporate

5.—(1) A person is taken to be interested in shares if a body corporate is interested in them and—
(a) the body corporate or its directors are accustomed to act in accordance with his directions or instructions, or
(b) he is entitled to exercise or control the exercise of more than one-half of the voting power at general meetings of the body corporate.

(2) For the purposes of sub-paragraph (1)(b) where—
(a) a person is entitled to exercise or control the exercise of more than one-half of the voting power at general meetings of a body corporate, and
(b) that body corporate is entitled to exercise or control the exercise of any of the voting power at general meetings of another body corporate,

the voting power mentioned in paragraph (b) above is taken to be exercisable by that person.

Trusts

6.—(1) Where an interest in shares is comprised in property held on trust, every beneficiary of the trust is taken to have an interest in shares, subject as follows.

(2) So long as a person is entitled to receive, during the lifetime of himself or another, income from trust property comprising shares, an interest in the shares in reversion or remainder or (as regards Scotland) in fee shall be disregarded.

(3) A person is treated as not interested in shares if and so long as he holds them—
(a) under the law in force in any part of the United Kingdom, as a bare trustee or as a custodian trustee, or
(b) under the law in force in Scotland, as a simple trustee.

(4) There shall be disregarded any interest of a person subsisting by virtue of—
(a) an authorised unit trust scheme (within the meaning of section 237 of the Financial Services and Markets Act 2000 (c 8));
(b) a scheme made under section 22 or 22A of the Charities Act 1960 (c 58), section 25 of the Charities Act (Northern Ireland) 1964 (c 33 (NI)) or section 24 or 25 of the Charities Act 1993 (c 10), section 11 of the Trustee Investments Act 1961 (c 62) or section 42 of the Administration of Justice Act 1982 (c 53); or
(c) the scheme set out in the Schedule to the Church Funds Investment Measure 1958 (1958 No 1).

(5) There shall be disregarded any interest—

(a) of the Church of Scotland General Trustees or of the Church of Scotland Trust in shares held by them;

(b) of any other person in shares held by those Trustees or that Trust otherwise than as simple trustees.

"The Church of Scotland General Trustees" are the body incorporated by the order confirmed by the Church of Scotland (General Trustees) Order Confirmation Act 1921 (1921 c xxv), and "the Church of Scotland Trust" is the body incorporated by the order confirmed by the Church of Scotland Trust Order Confirmation Act 1932 (1932 c xxi).

[S1301]

NOTES

Commencement: 1 October 2007.

SCHEDULE 2
SPECIFIED PERSONS, DESCRIPTIONS OF DISCLOSURES ETC FOR THE PURPOSES OF SECTION 948

Section 948

PART 1
SPECIFIED PERSONS

1. The Secretary of State.

2. The Department of Enterprise, Trade and Investment for Northern Ireland.

3. The Treasury.

4. The Bank of England.

5. The Financial Services Authority.

6. The Commissioners for Her Majesty's Revenue and Customs.

7. The Lord Advocate.

8. The Director of Public Prosecutions.

9. The Director of Public Prosecutions for Northern Ireland.

10. A constable.

11. A procurator fiscal.

12. The Scottish Ministers.

[S1302]

NOTES

Commencement: 6 April 2007.

PART 2
SPECIFIED DESCRIPTIONS OF DISCLOSURES

13. A disclosure for the purpose of enabling or assisting a person authorised under section 457 of this Act (persons authorised to apply to court) to exercise his functions.

Until the coming into force of section 457, the reference to that section is to be read as a reference to section 245C of the Companies Act 1985 (c 6).

14. A disclosure for the purpose of enabling or assisting an inspector appointed under Part 14 of the Companies Act 1985 (investigation of companies and their affairs, etc) to exercise his functions.

15. A disclosure for the purpose of enabling or assisting a person authorised under section 447 of the Companies Act 1985 (power to require production of documents) or section 84 of the Companies Act 1989 (c 40) (exercise of powers by officer etc) to exercise his functions.

16. A disclosure for the purpose of enabling or assisting a person appointed under section 167 of the Financial Services and Markets Act 2000 (c 8) (general investigations) to conduct an investigation to exercise his functions.

17. A disclosure for the purpose of enabling or assisting a person appointed under section 168 of the Financial Services and Markets Act 2000 (investigations in particular cases) to conduct an investigation to exercise his functions.

18. A disclosure for the purpose of enabling or assisting a person appointed under section 169(1)(b) of the Financial Services and Markets Act 2000 (investigation in support of overseas regulator) to conduct an investigation to exercise his functions.

19. A disclosure for the purpose of enabling or assisting the body corporate responsible for administering the scheme referred to in section 225 of the Financial Services and Markets Act 2000 (the ombudsman scheme) to exercise its functions.

20. A disclosure for the purpose of enabling or assisting a person appointed under paragraph 4 (the panel of ombudsmen) or 5 (the Chief Ombudsman) of Schedule 17 to the Financial Services and Markets Act 2000 to exercise his functions.

21. A disclosure for the purpose of enabling or assisting a person appointed under regulations made under section 262(1) and (2)(k) of the Financial Services and Markets Act 2000 (investigations into open-ended investment companies) to conduct an investigation to exercise his functions.

22. A disclosure for the purpose of enabling or assisting a person appointed under section 284 of the Financial Services and Markets Act 2000 (investigations into affairs of certain collective investment schemes) to conduct an investigation to exercise his functions.

23. A disclosure for the purpose of enabling or assisting the investigator appointed under paragraph 7 of Schedule 1 to the Financial Services and Markets Act 2000 (arrangements for investigation of complaints) to exercise his functions.

24. A disclosure for the purpose of enabling or assisting a person appointed by the Treasury to hold an inquiry into matters relating to financial services (including an inquiry under section 15 of the Financial Services and Markets Act 2000 (c 8)) to exercise his functions.

25. A disclosure for the purpose of enabling or assisting the Secretary of State or the Treasury to exercise any of their functions under any of the following—

(a) the Companies Acts;

(b) Part 5 of the Criminal Justice Act 1993 (c 36) (insider dealing);

(c) the Insolvency Act 1986 (c 45);

(d) the Company Directors Disqualification Act 1986 (c 46);

(e) Part 42 of this Act (statutory auditors);

(f) Part 3 (investigations and powers to obtain information) or 7 (financial markets and insolvency) of the Companies Act 1989 (c 40);

(g) the Financial Services and Markets Act 2000.

Until the coming into force of Part 42 of this Act, the reference to it in paragraph (e) is to be read as a reference to Part 2 of the Companies Act 1989.

26. A disclosure for the purpose of enabling or assisting the Scottish Ministers to exercise their functions under the enactments relating to insolvency.

27. A disclosure for the purpose of enabling or assisting the Department of Enterprise, Trade and Investment for Northern Ireland to exercise any powers conferred on it by the enactments relating to companies or insolvency.

28. A disclosure for the purpose of enabling or assisting a person appointed or authorised by the Department of Enterprise, Trade and Investment for Northern Ireland under the enactments relating to companies or insolvency to exercise his functions.

29. A disclosure for the purpose of enabling or assisting the Pensions Regulator to exercise the functions conferred on it by or by virtue of any of the following—
(a) the Pension Schemes Act 1993 (c 48);
(b) the Pensions Act 1995 (c 26);
(c) the Welfare Reform and Pensions Act 1999 (c 30);
(d) the Pensions Act 2004 (c 35);
(e) any enactment in force in Northern Ireland corresponding to any of those enactments.

30. A disclosure for the purpose of enabling or assisting the Board of the Pension Protection Fund to exercise the functions conferred on it by or by virtue of Part 2 of the Pensions Act 2004 or any enactment in force in Northern Ireland corresponding to that Part.

31. A disclosure for the purpose of enabling or assisting—
(a) the Bank of England,
(b) the European Central Bank, or
(c) the central bank of any country or territory outside the United Kingdom,
to exercise its functions.

32. A disclosure for the purpose of enabling or assisting the Commissioners for Her Majesty's Revenue and Customs to exercise their functions.

33. A disclosure for the purpose of enabling or assisting organs of the Society of Lloyd's (being organs constituted by or under the Lloyd's Act 1982 (c xiv)) to exercise their functions under or by virtue of the Lloyd's Acts 1871 to 1982.

34. A disclosure for the purpose of enabling or assisting the Office of Fair Trading to exercise its functions under any of the following—
(a) the Fair Trading Act 1973 (c 41);
(b) the Consumer Credit Act 1974 (c 39);
(c) the Estate Agents Act 1979 (c 38);
(d) the Competition Act 1980 (c 21);
(e) the Competition Act 1998 (c 41);
(f) the Financial Services and Markets Act 2000 (c 8);
(g) the Enterprise Act 2002 (c 40);
(h) the Control of Misleading Advertisements Regulations 1988 (SI 1988/915);
(i) the Unfair Terms in Consumer Contracts Regulations 1999 (SI 1999/2083).

35. A disclosure for the purpose of enabling or assisting the Competition Commission to exercise its functions under any of the following—
(a) the Fair Trading Act 1973;
(b) the Competition Act 1980;
(c) the Competition Act 1998;
(d) the Enterprise Act 2002.

36. A disclosure with a view to the institution of, or otherwise for the purposes of, proceedings before the Competition Appeal Tribunal.

37. A disclosure for the purpose of enabling or assisting an enforcer under Part 8 of the Enterprise Act 2002 (enforcement of consumer legislation) to exercise its functions under that Part.

38. A disclosure for the purpose of enabling or assisting the Charity Commission to exercise its functions.

39. A disclosure for the purpose of enabling or assisting the Attorney General to exercise his functions in connection with charities.

40. A disclosure for the purpose of enabling or assisting the National Lottery Commission to exercise its functions under sections 5 to 10 (licensing) and 15 (power of Secretary of State to require information) of the National Lottery etc Act 1993 (c 39).

41. A disclosure by the National Lottery Commission to the National Audit Office for the purpose of enabling or assisting the Comptroller and Auditor General to carry out an examination under Part 2 of the National Audit Act 1983 (c 44) into the economy, effectiveness and efficiency with which the National Lottery Commission has used its resources in discharging its functions under sections 5 to 10 of the National Lottery etc Act 1993.

42. A disclosure for the purpose of enabling or assisting a qualifying body under the Unfair Terms in Consumer Contracts Regulations 1999 (SI 1999/ 2083) to exercise its functions under those Regulations.

43. A disclosure for the purpose of enabling or assisting an enforcement authority under the Consumer Protection (Distance Selling) Regulations 2000 (SI 2000/2334) to exercise its functions under those Regulations.

44. A disclosure for the purpose of enabling or assisting an enforcement authority under the Financial Services (Distance Marketing) Regulations 2004 (SI 2004/2095) to exercise its functions under those Regulations.

45. A disclosure for the purpose of enabling or assisting a local weights and measures authority in England and Wales to exercise its functions under section 230(2) of the Enterprise Act 2002 (c 40) (notice of intention to prosecute, etc).

46. A disclosure for the purpose of enabling or assisting the Financial Services Authority to exercise its functions under any of the following—

(a) the legislation relating to friendly societies or to industrial and provident societies;

(b) the Building Societies Act 1986 (c 53);

(c) Part 7 of the Companies Act 1989 (c 40) (financial markets and insolvency);

(d) the Financial Services and Markets Act 2000 (c 8).

47. A disclosure for the purpose of enabling or assisting the competent authority for the purposes of Part 6 of the Financial Services and Markets Act 2000 (official listing) to exercise its functions under that Part.

48. A disclosure for the purpose of enabling or assisting a body corporate established in accordance with section 212(1) of the Financial Services and Markets Act 2000 (compensation scheme manager) to exercise its functions.

49. A disclosure for the purpose of enabling or assisting a recognised investment exchange or a recognised clearing house to exercise its functions as such.

"Recognised investment exchange" and "recognised clearing house" have the same meaning as in section 285 of the Financial Services and Markets Act 2000.

50. A disclosure for the purpose of enabling or assisting a person approved under the Uncertificated Securities Regulations 2001 (SI 2001/3755) as an operator of a relevant system (within the meaning of those regulations) to exercise his functions.

51. A disclosure for the purpose of enabling or assisting a body designated under section 326(1) of the Financial Services and Markets Act 2000 (designated professional bodies) to exercise its functions in its capacity as a body designated under that section.

52. A disclosure with a view to the institution of, or otherwise for the purposes of, civil proceedings arising under or by virtue of the Financial Services and Markets Act 2000.

53. A disclosure for the purpose of enabling or assisting a body designated by order under section 1252 of this Act (delegation of functions of Secretary of State) to exercise its functions under Part 42 of this Act (statutory auditors).

Until the coming into force of that Part, the references to section 1252 and Part 42 are to be read as references to section 46 of the Companies Act 1989 (c 40) and Part 2 of that Act respectively.

54. A disclosure for the purpose of enabling or assisting a recognised supervisory or qualifying body, within the meaning of Part 42 of this Act, to exercise its functions as such.

Until the coming into force of that Part, the reference to it is to be read as a reference to Part 2 of the Companies Act 1989.

55. A disclosure for the purpose of enabling or assisting an official receiver (including the Accountant in Bankruptcy in Scotland and the Official Assignee in Northern Ireland) to exercise his functions under the enactments relating to insolvency.

56. A disclosure for the purpose of enabling or assisting the Insolvency Practitioners Tribunal to exercise its functions under the Insolvency Act 1986 (c 45).

57. A disclosure for the purpose of enabling or assisting a body that is for the time being a recognised professional body for the purposes of section 391 of the Insolvency Act 1986 (recognised professional bodies) to exercise its functions as such.

58. A disclosure for the purpose of enabling or assisting an overseas regulatory authority to exercise its regulatory functions.

"Overseas regulatory authority" and "regulatory functions" have the same meaning as in section 82 of the Companies Act 1989.

59. A disclosure for the purpose of enabling or assisting the Regulator of Community Interest Companies to exercise functions under the Companies (Audit, Investigations and Community Enterprise) Act 2004 (c 27).

60. A disclosure with a view to the institution of, or otherwise for the purposes of, criminal proceedings.

61. A disclosure for the purpose of enabling or assisting a person authorised by the Secretary of State under Part 2, 3 or 4 of the Proceeds of Crime Act 2002 (c 29) to exercise his functions.

62. A disclosure with a view to the institution of, or otherwise for the purposes of, proceedings on an application under section 6, 7 or 8 of the Company Directors Disqualification Act 1986 (c 46) (disqualification for unfitness).

63. A disclosure with a view to the institution of, or otherwise for the purposes of, proceedings before the Financial Services and Markets Tribunal.

64. A disclosure for the purposes of proceedings before the Financial Services Tribunal by virtue of the Financial Services and Markets Act 2000 (Transitional Provisions) (Partly Completed Procedures) Order 2001 (SI 2001/3592).

65. A disclosure for the purposes of proceedings before the Pensions Regulator Tribunal.

66. A disclosure for the purpose of enabling or assisting a body appointed under section 14 of the Companies (Audit, Investigations and Community Enterprise) Act 2004 (supervision of periodic accounts and reports of issuers of listed securities) to exercise functions mentioned in subsection (2) of that section.

67. A disclosure with a view to the institution of, or otherwise for the purposes of, disciplinary proceedings relating to the performance by a solicitor, barrister, advocate, foreign lawyer, auditor, accountant, valuer or actuary of his professional duties.

"Foreign lawyer" has the meaning given by section 89(9) of the Courts and Legal Services Act 1990 (c 41).

68. A disclosure with a view to the institution of, or otherwise for the purposes of, disciplinary proceedings relating to the performance by a public servant of his duties.

"Public servant" means an officer or employee of the Crown or of any public or other authority for the time being designated for the purposes of this paragraph by the Secretary of State by order subject to negative resolution procedure.

69. A disclosure for the purpose of the provision of a summary or collection of information framed in such a way as not to enable the identity of any person to whom the information relates to be ascertained.

70. A disclosure in pursuance of any Community obligation.

[S1303]

NOTES

Commencement: 20 January 2007 (for the purpose of enabling the exercise of powers to make Orders or Regulations by statutory instrument); 6 April 2007 (otherwise).

PART 3
OVERSEAS REGULATORY BODIES

71. A disclosure is made in accordance with this Part of this Schedule if—

(a) it is made to a person or body within paragraph 72, and

(b) it is made for the purpose of enabling or assisting that person or body to exercise the functions mentioned in that paragraph.

72. The persons or bodies that are within this paragraph are those exercising functions of a public nature, under legislation in any country or territory outside the United Kingdom, that appear to the Panel to be similar to its own functions or those of the Financial Services Authority.

73. In determining whether to disclose information to a person or body in accordance with this Part of this Schedule, the Panel must have regard to the following considerations—

(a) whether the use that the person or body is likely to make of the information is sufficiently important to justify making the disclosure;

(b) whether the person or body has adequate arrangements to prevent the information from being used or further disclosed otherwise than for the purposes of carrying out the functions mentioned in paragraph 72 or any other purposes substantially similar to those for which information disclosed to the Panel could be used or further disclosed.

[S1304]

NOTES

Commencement: 6 April 2007.

SCHEDULE 3
AMENDMENTS OF REMAINING PROVISIONS OF THE COMPANIES ACT 1985 RELATING TO OFFENCES

Section 1124

(*This Schedule amends CA 1985, ss 444, 448, 449, 450, 451, 453A and 455 at* **[477]**, **[481]**, **[482]**, **[483]**, **[484]**, **[487A]** *and* **[489]**.)

[S1305]

NOTES

Commencement: 1 October 2007 (for transitional adaptations see the note below).

Transitional adaptations: art 6 of the draft Companies Act 2006 (Commencement No 3, Consequential Amendments, Transitional Provisions and Savings) Order 2007 provides that the provisions brought into force by that Order shall have effect subject to any transitional adaptations specified in Sch 1 to that Order. Schedule 1, para 20 to the Order provides for transitional adaptations of this Schedule (see that paragraph at **[A12]**) and see the notes to the amended ss 444, 449, 450 and 451 of the 1985 Act.

SCHEDULE 4
DOCUMENTS AND INFORMATION SENT OR SUPPLIED TO A COMPANY

Section 1144(1)

PART 1
INTRODUCTION

Application of Schedule

1.—(1) This Schedule applies to documents or information sent or supplied to a company.

(2) It does not apply to documents or information sent or supplied by another company (see section 1144(3) and Schedule 5).

[S1306]

NOTES

Commencement: 20 January 2007.

PART 2
COMMUNICATIONS IN HARD COPY FORM

Introduction

2. A document or information is validly sent or supplied to a company if it is sent or supplied in hard copy form in accordance with this Part of this Schedule.

Method of communication in hard copy form

3.—(1) A document or information in hard copy form may be sent or supplied by hand or by post to an address (in accordance with paragraph 4).

(2) For the purposes of this Schedule, a person sends a document or information by post if he posts a prepaid envelope containing the document or information.

Address for communications in hard copy form

4. A document or information in hard copy form may be sent or supplied—

(a) to an address specified by the company for the purpose;

(b) to the company's registered office;

(c) to an address to which any provision of the Companies Acts authorises the document or information to be sent or supplied.

[S1307]

NOTES

Commencement: 20 January 2007.

PART 3
COMMUNICATIONS IN ELECTRONIC FORM

Introduction

5. A document or information is validly sent or supplied to a company if it is sent or supplied in electronic form in accordance with this Part of this Schedule.

Conditions for use of communications in electronic form

6. A document or information may only be sent or supplied to a company in electronic form if—

(a) the company has agreed (generally or specifically) that the document or information may be sent or supplied in that form (and has not revoked that agreement), or
(b) the company is deemed to have so agreed by a provision in the Companies Acts.

Address for communications in electronic form

7.—(1) Where the document or information is sent or supplied by electronic means, it may only be sent or supplied to an address—
(a) specified for the purpose by the company (generally or specifically), or
(b) deemed by a provision in the Companies Acts to have been so specified.

(2) Where the document or information is sent or supplied in electronic form by hand or by post, it must be sent or supplied to an address to which it could be validly sent if it were in hard copy form.

[S1308]

NOTES
Commencement: 20 January 2007.

PART 4
OTHER AGREED FORMS OF COMMUNICATION

8. A document or information that is sent or supplied to a company otherwise than in hard copy form or electronic form is validly sent or supplied if it is sent or supplied in a form or manner that has been agreed by the company.

[S1309]

NOTES
Commencement: 20 January 2007.

SCHEDULE 5
COMMUNICATIONS BY A COMPANY
Section 1144(2)

PART 1
INTRODUCTION

Application of this Schedule

1. This Schedule applies to documents or information sent or supplied by a company.

[S1310]

NOTES
Commencement: 20 January 2007.

PART 2
COMMUNICATIONS IN HARD COPY FORM

Introduction

2. A document or information is validly sent or supplied by a company if it is sent or supplied in hard copy form in accordance with this Part of this Schedule.

Method of communication in hard copy form

3.—(1) A document or information in hard copy form must be—

(a) handed to the intended recipient, or
(b) sent or supplied by hand or by post to an address (in accordance with paragraph 4).

(2) For the purposes of this Schedule, a person sends a document or information by post if he posts a prepaid envelope containing the document or information.

Address for communications in hard copy form

4.—(1) A document or information in hard copy form may be sent or supplied by the company—
(a) to an address specified for the purpose by the intended recipient;
(b) to a company at its registered office;
(c) to a person in his capacity as a member of the company at his address as shown in the company's register of members;
(d) to a person in his capacity as a director of the company at his address as shown in the company's register of directors;
(e) to an address to which any provision of the Companies Acts authorises the document or information to be sent or supplied.

(2) Where the company is unable to obtain an address falling within sub-paragraph (1), the document or information may be sent or supplied to the intended recipient's last address known to the company.

[S1311]

NOTES
Commencement: 20 January 2007.

PART 3
COMMUNICATIONS IN ELECTRONIC FORM

Introduction

5. A document or information is validly sent or supplied by a company if it is sent in electronic form in accordance with this Part of this Schedule.

Agreement to communications in electronic form

6. A document or information may only be sent or supplied by a company in electronic form—
(a) to a person who has agreed (generally or specifically) that the document or information may be sent or supplied in that form (and has not revoked that agreement), or
(b) to a company that is deemed to have so agreed by a provision in the Companies Acts.

Address for communications in electronic form

7.—(1) Where the document or information is sent or supplied by electronic means, it may only be sent or supplied to an address—
(a) specified for the purpose by the intended recipient (generally or specifically), or
(b) where the intended recipient is a company, deemed by a provision of the Companies Acts to have been so specified.

(2) Where the document or information is sent or supplied in electronic form by hand or by post, it must be—
(a) handed to the intended recipient, or
(b) sent or supplied to an address to which it could be validly sent if it were in hard copy form.

[S1312]

NOTES

Commencement: 20 January 2007.

Transitional provisions: see the Companies Act 2006 (Commencement No 1, Transitional Provisions and Savings) Order 2006, SI 2006/3428, Sch 5, Pt 2, para 4 at **[7590]** (Existing agreements to communication by electronic means).

PART 4
COMMUNICATIONS BY MEANS OF A WEBSITE

Use of website

8. A document or information is validly sent or supplied by a company if it is made available on a website in accordance with this Part of this Schedule.

Agreement to use of website

9. A document or information may only be sent or supplied by the company to a person by being made available on a website if the person—

(a) has agreed (generally or specifically) that the document or information may be sent or supplied to him in that manner, or

(b) is taken to have so agreed under—

(i) paragraph 10 (members of the company etc), or

(ii) paragraph 11 (debenture holders),

and has not revoked that agreement.

Deemed agreement of members of company etc to use of website

10.—(1) This paragraph applies to a document or information to be sent or supplied to a person—

(a) as a member of the company, or

(b) as a person nominated by a member in accordance with the company's articles to enjoy or exercise all or any specified rights of the member in relation to the company, or

(c) as a person nominated by a member under section 146 to enjoy information rights.

(2) To the extent that—

(a) the members of the company have resolved that the company may send or supply documents or information to members by making them available on a website, or

(b) the company's articles contain provision to that effect,

a person in relation to whom the following conditions are met is taken to have agreed that the company may send or supply documents or information to him in that manner.

(3) The conditions are that—

(a) the person has been asked individually by the company to agree that the company may send or supply documents or information generally, or the documents or information in question, to him by means of a website, and

(b) the company has not received a response within the period of 28 days beginning with the date on which the company's request was sent.

(4) A person is not taken to have so agreed if the company's request—

(a) did not state clearly what the effect of a failure to respond would be, or

(b) was sent less than twelve months after a previous request made to him for the purposes of this paragraph in respect of the same or a similar class of documents or information.

(5) Chapter 3 of Part 3 (resolutions affecting a company's constitution) applies to a resolution under this paragraph.

Deemed agreement of debenture holders to use of website

11.—(1) This paragraph applies to a document or information to be sent or supplied to a person as holder of a company's debentures.

(2) To the extent that—
(a) the relevant debenture holders have duly resolved that the company may send or supply documents or information to them by making them available on a website, or
(b) the instrument creating the debenture in question contains provision to that effect,

a debenture holder in relation to whom the following conditions are met is taken to have agreed that the company may send or supply documents or information to him in that manner.

(3) The conditions are that—
(a) the debenture holder has been asked individually by the company to agree that the company may send or supply documents or information generally, or the documents or information in question, to him by means of a website, and
(b) the company has not received a response within the period of 28 days beginning with the date on which the company's request was sent.

(4) A person is not taken to have so agreed if the company's request—
(a) did not state clearly what the effect of a failure to respond would be, or
(b) was sent less than twelve months after a previous request made to him for the purposes of this paragraph in respect of the same or a similar class of documents or information.

(5) For the purposes of this paragraph—
(a) the relevant debenture holders are the holders of debentures of the company ranking *pari passu* for all purposes with the intended recipient, and
(b) a resolution of the relevant debenture holders is duly passed if they agree in accordance with the provisions of the instruments creating the debentures.

Availability of document or information

12.—(1) A document or information authorised or required to be sent or supplied by means of a website must be made available in a form, and by a means, that the company reasonably considers will enable the recipient—
(a) to read it, and
(b) to retain a copy of it.

(2) For this purpose a document or information can be read only if—
(a) it can be read with the naked eye, or
(b) to the extent that it consists of images (for example photographs, pictures, maps, plans or drawings), it can be seen with the naked eye.

Notification of availability

13.—(1) The company must notify the intended recipient of—
(a) the presence of the document or information on the website,
(b) the address of the website,
(c) the place on the website where it may be accessed, and
(d) how to access the document or information.

(2) The document or information is taken to be sent—
(a) on the date on which the notification required by this paragraph is sent, or
(b) if later, the date on which the document or information first appears on the website after that notification is sent.

Period of availability on website

14.—(1) The company must make the document or information available on the website throughout—
(a) the period specified by any applicable provision of the Companies Acts, or
(b) if no such period is specified, the period of 28 days beginning with the date on which the notification required under paragraph 13 is sent to the person in question.

(2) For the purposes of this paragraph, a failure to make a document or information available on a website throughout the period mentioned in sub-paragraph (1) shall be disregarded if—

(a) it is made available on the website for part of that period, and
(b) the failure to make it available throughout that period is wholly attributable to circumstances that it would not be reasonable to have expected the company to prevent or avoid.

[S1313]

NOTES

Commencement: 20 January 2007.

Transitional adaptations: art 5 of the Companies Act 2006 (Commencement No 1, Transitional Provisions and Savings) Order 2006, SI 2006/3428 provides that the provisions brought into force by arts 2–4 of 2006 Order shall have effect subject to any transitional adaptations specified in Sch 1 to that Order. Schedule 1, para 16 to the Order (at **[7582]**) provides as follows—

"16 Communications by a company

(1) Schedule 5 (communications by a company) has effect with the following adaptation.

(2) In paragraph 10(5), for "Chapter 3 of Part 3" substitute "section 380 of the Companies Act 1985 or Article 388 of the Companies (Northern Ireland) Order 1986".".

Note that para 16 as set out above is revoked by the draft Companies Act 2006 (Commencement No 3, Consequential Amendments, Transitional Provisions and Savings) Order 2007, art 10(1), as from 1 October 2007 (see **[A12]**).

Transitional provisions: see the Companies Act 2006 (Commencement No 1, Transitional Provisions and Savings) Order 2006, SI 2006/3428, Sch 5, Pt 2, para 5 at **[7590]** (Existing agreements to communication by electronic means).

PART 5
OTHER AGREED FORMS OF COMMUNICATION

15. A document or information that is sent or supplied otherwise than in hard copy or electronic form or by means of a website is validly sent or supplied if it is sent or supplied in a form or manner that has been agreed by the intended recipient.

[S1314]

NOTES

Commencement: 20 January 2007.

PART 6
SUPPLEMENTARY PROVISIONS

Joint holders of shares or debentures

16.—(1) This paragraph applies in relation to documents or information to be sent or supplied to joint holders of shares or debentures of a company.

(2) Anything to be agreed or specified by the holder must be agreed or specified by all the joint holders.

(3) Anything authorised or required to be sent or supplied to the holder may be sent or supplied either—
(a) to each of the joint holders, or
(b) to the holder whose name appears first in the register of members or the relevant register of debenture holders.

(4) This paragraph has effect subject to anything in the company's articles.

Death or bankruptcy of holder of shares

17.—(1) This paragraph has effect in the case of the death or bankruptcy of a holder of a company's shares.

(2) Documents or information required or authorised to be sent or supplied to the member may be sent or supplied to the persons claiming to be entitled to the shares in consequence of the death or bankruptcy—

(a) by name, or

(b) by the title of representatives of the deceased, or trustee of the bankrupt, or by any like description,

at the address in the United Kingdom supplied for the purpose by those so claiming.

(3) Until such an address has been so supplied, a document or information may be sent or supplied in any manner in which it might have been sent or supplied if the death or bankruptcy had not occurred.

(4) This paragraph has effect subject to anything in the company's articles.

(5) References in this paragraph to the bankruptcy of a person include—

(a) the sequestration of the estate of a person;

(b) a person's estate being the subject of a protected trust deed (within the meaning of the Bankruptcy (Scotland) Act 1985 (c 66)).

In such a case the reference in sub-paragraph (2)(b) to the trustee of the bankrupt is to be read as the permanent or interim trustee (within the meaning of that Act) on the sequestrated estate or, as the case may be, the trustee under the protected deed.

[S1315]

NOTES

Commencement: 20 January 2007.

SCHEDULE 6

MEANING OF "SUBSIDIARY" ETC: SUPPLEMENTARY PROVISIONS

Section 1159

Introduction

1. The provisions of this Part of this Schedule explain expressions used in section 1159 (meaning of "subsidiary" etc) and otherwise supplement that section.

Voting rights in a company

2. In section 1159(1)(a) and (c) the references to the voting rights in a company are to the rights conferred on shareholders in respect of their shares or, in the case of a company not having a share capital, on members, to vote at general meetings of the company on all, or substantially all, matters.

Right to appoint or remove a majority of the directors

3.—(1) In section 1159(1)(b) the reference to the right to appoint or remove a majority of the board of directors is to the right to appoint or remove directors holding a majority of the voting rights at meetings of the board on all, or substantially all, matters.

(2) A company shall be treated as having the right to appoint to a directorship if—

(a) a person's appointment to it follows necessarily from his appointment as director of the company, or

(b) the directorship is held by the company itself.

(3) A right to appoint or remove which is exercisable only with the consent or concurrence of another person shall be left out of account unless no other person has a right to appoint or, as the case may be, remove in relation to that directorship.

Rights exercisable only in certain circumstances or temporarily incapable of exercise

4.—(1) Rights which are exercisable only in certain circumstances shall be taken into account only—

(a) when the circumstances have arisen, and for so long as they continue to obtain, or

(b) when the circumstances are within the control of the person having the rights.

(2) Rights which are normally exercisable but are temporarily incapable of exercise shall continue to be taken into account.

Rights held by one person on behalf of another

5. Rights held by a person in a fiduciary capacity shall be treated as not held by him.

6.—(1) Rights held by a person as nominee for another shall be treated as held by the other.

(2) Rights shall be regarded as held as nominee for another if they are exercisable only on his instructions or with his consent or concurrence.

Rights attached to shares held by way of security

7. Rights attached to shares held by way of security shall be treated as held by the person providing the security—

(a) where apart from the right to exercise them for the purpose of preserving the value of the security, or of realising it, the rights are exercisable only in accordance with his instructions, and

(b) where the shares are held in connection with the granting of loans as part of normal business activities and apart from the right to exercise them for the purpose of preserving the value of the security, or of realising it, the rights are exercisable only in his interests.

Rights attributed to holding company

8.—(1) Rights shall be treated as held by a holding company if they are held by any of its subsidiary companies.

(2) Nothing in paragraph 6 or 7 shall be construed as requiring rights held by a holding company to be treated as held by any of its subsidiaries.

(3) For the purposes of paragraph 7 rights shall be treated as being exercisable in accordance with the instructions or in the interests of a company if they are exercisable in accordance with the instructions of or, as the case may be, in the interests of—

(a) any subsidiary or holding company of that company, or

(b) any subsidiary of a holding company of that company.

Disregard of certain rights

9. The voting rights in a company shall be reduced by any rights held by the company itself.

Supplementary

10. References in any provision of paragraphs 5 to 9 to rights held by a person include rights falling to be treated as held by him by virtue of any other provision of those paragraphs but not rights which by virtue of any such provision are to be treated as not held by him.

[S1316]

NOTES

Commencement: to be appointed.

SCHEDULE 7

PARENT AND SUBSIDIARY UNDERTAKINGS: SUPPLEMENTARY PROVISIONS

Section 1162

Introduction

1. The provisions of this Schedule explain expressions used in section 1162 (parent and subsidiary undertakings) and otherwise supplement that section.

Voting rights in an undertaking

2.—(1) In section 1162(2)(a) and (d) the references to the voting rights in an undertaking are to the rights conferred on shareholders in respect of their shares or, in the case of an undertaking not having a share capital, on members, to vote at general meetings of the undertaking on all, or substantially all, matters.

(2) In relation to an undertaking which does not have general meetings at which matters are decided by the exercise of voting rights the references to holding a majority of the voting rights in the undertaking shall be construed as references to having the right under the constitution of the undertaking to direct the overall policy of the undertaking or to alter the terms of its constitution.

Right to appoint or remove a majority of the directors

3.—(1) In section 1162(2)(b) the reference to the right to appoint or remove a majority of the board of directors is to the right to appoint or remove directors holding a majority of the voting rights at meetings of the board on all, or substantially all, matters.

(2) An undertaking shall be treated as having the right to appoint to a directorship if—

(a) a person's appointment to it follows necessarily from his appointment as director of the undertaking, or

(b) the directorship is held by the undertaking itself.

(3) A right to appoint or remove which is exercisable only with the consent or concurrence of another person shall be left out of account unless no other person has a right to appoint or, as the case may be, remove in relation to that directorship.

Right to exercise dominant influence

4.—(1) For the purposes of section 1162(2)(c) an undertaking shall not be regarded as having the right to exercise a dominant influence over another undertaking unless it has a right to give directions with respect to the operating and financial policies of that other undertaking which its directors are obliged to comply with whether or not they are for the benefit of that other undertaking.

(2) A "control contract" means a contract in writing conferring such a right which—

(a) is of a kind authorised by the articles of the undertaking in relation to which the right is exercisable, and

(b) is permitted by the law under which that undertaking is established.

(3) This paragraph shall not be read as affecting the construction of section 1162(4)(a).

Rights exercisable only in certain circumstances or temporarily incapable of exercise

5.—(1) Rights which are exercisable only in certain circumstances shall be taken into account only—

(a) when the circumstances have arisen, and for so long as they continue to obtain, or

(b) when the circumstances are within the control of the person having the rights.

(2) Rights which are normally exercisable but are temporarily incapable of exercise shall continue to be taken into account.

Rights held by one person on behalf of another

6. Rights held by a person in a fiduciary capacity shall be treated as not held by him.

7.—(1) Rights held by a person as nominee for another shall be treated as held by the other.

(2) Rights shall be regarded as held as nominee for another if they are exercisable only on his instructions or with his consent or concurrence.

Rights attached to shares held by way of security

8. Rights attached to shares held by way of security shall be treated as held by the person providing the security—

(a) where apart from the right to exercise them for the purpose of preserving the value of the security, or of realising it, the rights are exercisable only in accordance with his instructions, and

(b) where the shares are held in connection with the granting of loans as part of normal business activities and apart from the right to exercise them for the purpose of preserving the value of the security, or of realising it, the rights are exercisable only in his interests.

Rights attributed to parent undertaking

9.—(1) Rights shall be treated as held by a parent undertaking if they are held by any of its subsidiary undertakings.

(2) Nothing in paragraph 7 or 8 shall be construed as requiring rights held by a parent undertaking to be treated as held by any of its subsidiary undertakings.

(3) For the purposes of paragraph 8 rights shall be treated as being exercisable in accordance with the instructions or in the interests of an undertaking if they are exercisable in accordance with the instructions of or, as the case may be, in the interests of any group undertaking.

Disregard of certain rights

10. The voting rights in an undertaking shall be reduced by any rights held by the undertaking itself.

Supplementary

11. References in any provision of paragraphs 6 to 10 to rights held by a person include rights falling to be treated as held by him by virtue of any other provision of those paragraphs but not rights which by virtue of any such provision are to be treated as not held by him.
[S1317]

NOTES

Commencement: to be appointed.

SCHEDULE 8
INDEX OF DEFINED EXPRESSIONS

Section 1174

abbreviated accounts (in Part 15)	sections 444(4) and 445(3)
accounting reference date and accounting reference period	section 391
accounting standards (in Part 15)	section 464
accounts meeting	section 437(3)
acquisition, in relation to a non-cash asset	section 1163(2)
address	
— generally in the Companies Acts	section 1142
— in the company communications provisions	section 1148(1)
affirmative resolution procedure, in relation to regulations and orders	section 1290

allotment (time of)	section 558
allotment of equity securities (in Chapter 3 of Part 17)	section 560(2)
allotted share capital and allotted shares	section 546(1)(b) and (2)
annual accounts (in Part 15)	section 471
annual accounts and reports (in Part 15)	section 471
annual general meeting	section 336
annual return	section 854
appropriate audit authority (in sections 522, 523 and 524)	section 525(1)
appropriate rate of interest	
— in Chapter 5 of Part 17	section 592
— in Chapter 6 of Part 17	section 609
approval after being made, in relation to regulations and orders	section 1291
arrangement	
— in Chapter 7 of Part 17	section 616(1)
— in Part 26	section 895(2)
articles	section 18
associate (in Chapter 3 of Part 28)	section 988
associated bodies corporate and associated company (in Part 10)	section 256
authenticated, in relation to a document or information sent or supplied to a company	section 1146
authorised group, of members of a company (in Part 14)	section 370(3)
authorised insurance company	section 1165(2)
authorised minimum (in relation to share capital of public company)	section 763
available profits (in Chapter 5 of Part 18)	sections 711 and 712
banking company and banking group	section 1164
body corporate	section 1173(1)
called-up share capital	section 547
capital redemption reserve	section 733
capitalisation in relation to a company's profits (in Part 23)	section 853(3)
cash (in relation to paying up or allotting shares)	section 583
cause of action, in relation to derivative proceedings (in Chapter 2 of Part 11)	section 265(7)
certified translation (in Part 35)	section 1107
charge (in Chapter 1 of Part 25)	section 861(5)
circulation date, in relation to a written resolution (in Part 13)	section 290
class of shares	section 629
the Companies Acts	section 2
Companies Act accounts	sections 395(1)(a) and 403(2)(a)
Companies Act group accounts	section 403(2)(a)

Companies Act individual accounts	section 395(1)(a)
companies involved in the division (in Part 27)	section 919(2)
company	
— generally in the Companies Acts	section 1
— in Chapter 7 of Part 17	section 616(1)
— in Chapter 1 of Part 25	section 861(5)
— in Chapter 2 of Part 25	section 879(6)
— in Part 26	section 895(2)
— in Chapter 3 of Part 28	section 991(1)
— in the company communications provisions	section 1148(1)
the company communications provisions	section 1143
the company law provisions of this Act	section 2(2)
company records (in Part 37)	section 1134
connected with, in relation to a director (in Part 10)	sections 252 to 254
constitution, of a company	
— generally in the Companies Acts	section 17
— in Part 10	section 257
controlling, of a body corporate by a director (in Part 10)	section 255
corporation	section 1173(1)
the court	section 1156
credit institution	section 1173(1)
credit transaction (in Chapter 4 of Part 10)	section 202
creditor (in Chapter 1 of Part 31)	section 1011
daily default fine	section 1125
date of the offer (in Chapter 3 of Part 28)	section 991(1)
debenture	section 738
derivative claim (in Chapter 1 of Part 11)	section 260
derivative proceedings (in Chapter 2 of Part 11)	section 265
Directive disclosure requirements	section 1078
director	
— generally in the Companies Acts	section 250
— in Chapter 8 of Part 10	section 240(3)
— in Chapter 1 of Part 11	section 260(5)
— in Chapter 2 of Part 11	section 265(7)
— in Part 14	section 379(1)
directors' remuneration report	section 420
directors' report	section 415
distributable profits	
— in Chapter 2 of Part 18	section 683(1)
— elsewhere in Part 18	section 736
distribution	
— in Chapter 2 of Part 18	section 683(1)

— in Part 23	section 829
division (in Part 27)	section 919
document	
— in Part 35	section 1114(1)
— in the company communications provisions	section 1148(1)
dormant, in relation to a company or other body corporate	section 1169
EEA State and related expressions	section 1170
electronic form, electronic copy, electronic means	
— generally in the Companies Acts	section 1168(3) and (4)
— in relation to communications to a company	Part 3 of Schedule 4
— in relation to communications by a company	Part 3 of Schedule 5
eligible members, in relation to a written resolution	section 289
e-money issuer	
— in Part 15	section 474(1)
— in Part 16	section 539
employees' share scheme	section 1166
employer and employee (in Chapter 1 of Part 18)	section 676
enactment	section 1293
equity securities (in Chapter 3 of Part 17)	section 560(1)
equity share capital	section 548
equity shares (in Chapter 7 of Part 17)	section 616(1)
existing company (in Part 27)	section 902(2)
fellow subsidiary undertakings	section 1161(4)
financial assistance (in Chapter 2 of Part 18)	section 677
financial institution	section 1173(1)
financial year, of a company	section 390
firm	section 1173(1)
fixed assets (in Part 23)	section 853
the former Companies Acts	section 1171
the Gazette	section 1173(1)
group (in Part 15)	section 474(1)
group undertaking	section 1161(5)
hard copy form and hard copy	
— generally in the Companies Acts	section 1168(2)
— in relation to communications to a company	Part 2 of Schedule 4
— in relation to communications by a company	Part 2 of Schedule 5
hire-purchase agreement	section 1173(1)
holder of shares (in Chapter 3 of Part 17)	section 574

holding company	section 1159 (and see section 1160 and Schedule 6)
IAS accounts	sections 395(1)(b) and 403(1) and (2)(b)
IAS group accounts	section 403(1) and (2)(b)
IAS individual accounts	section 395(1)(b)
IAS Regulation (in Part 15)	section 474(1)
included in the consolidation, in relation to group accounts (in Part 15)	section 474(1)
individual accounts	section 394
information rights (in Part 9)	section 146(3)
insurance company	section 1165(3)
insurance group	section 1165(5)
insurance market activity	section 1165(7)
interest in shares (for the purposes of Part 22)	sections 820 to 825
international accounting standards (in Part 15)	section 474(1)
investment company (in Part 23)	section 833
ISD investment firm	
— in Part 15	section 474(1)
— in Part 16	section 539
issued share capital and issued shares	section 546(1)(a) and (2)
the issuing company (in Chapter 7 of Part 17)	section 610(6)
the Joint Stock Companies Acts	section 1171
liabilities (in Part 27)	section 941
liability, references to incurring, reducing or discharging (in Chapter 2 of Part 18)	section 683(2)
limited by guarantee	section 3(3)
limited by shares	section 3(2)
limited company	section 3
the main register (of members) (in Chapter 3 of Part 8)	section 131(1)
major audit (in sections 522 and 525)	section 525(2)
market purchase, by a company of its own shares (in Chapter 4 of Part 18)	section 693(4)
member, of a company	
— generally in the Companies Acts	section 112
— in Chapter 1 of Part 11	section 260(5)
— in Chapter 2 of Part 11	section 265(7)
memorandum of association	section 8
merger (in Part 27)	section 904
merging companies (in Part 27)	section 904(2)
merger by absorption (in Part 27)	section 904(1)(a)
merger by formation of a new company (in Part 27)	section 904(1)(b)
negative resolution procedure, in relation to regulations and orders	section 1289
net assets (in Part 7)	section 92

new company (in Part 27)	section 902(2)
non-cash asset	section 1163
non-voting shares (in Chapter 3 of Part 28)	section 991(1)
number, in relation to shares	section 540(4)(b)
off-market purchase, by a company of its own shares (in Chapter 4 of Part 18)	section 693(2)
offer period (in Chapter 2 of Part 28)	section 971(1)
offer to the public (in Chapter 1 of Part 20)	section 756
offeror	
— in Chapter 2 of Part 28	section 971(1)
— in Chapter 3 of Part 28	section 991(1)
officer, in relation to a body corporate	section 1173(1)
officer in default	section 1121
official seal, of registrar	section 1062
opted-in company (in Chapter 2 of Part 28)	section 971(1)
opting-in resolution (in Chapter 2 of Part 28)	section 966(1)
opting-out resolution (in Chapter 2 of Part 28)	section 966(5)
ordinary resolution	section 282
ordinary shares (in Chapter 3 of Part 17)	section 560(1)
organisation (in Part 14)	section 379(1)
other relevant transactions or arrangements (in Chapter 4 of Part 10)	section 210
overseas company	section 1044
overseas branch register	section 129(1)
paid up	section 583
the Panel (in Part 28)	section 942
parent company	section 1173(1)
parent undertaking	section 1162 (and see Schedule 7)
payment for loss of office (in Chapter 4 of Part 10)	section 215
pension scheme (in Chapter 1 of Part 18)	section 675
period for appointing auditors, in relation to a private company	section 485(2)
period for filing, in relation to accounts and reports for a financial year	section 442
permissible capital payment (in Chapter 5 of Part 18)	section 710
political donation (in Part 14)	section 364
political expenditure (in Part 14)	section 365
political organisation (in Part 14)	section 363(2)
prescribed	section 1167
private company	section 4
profit and loss account (in Part 15)	section 474(1) and (2)
profits and losses (in Part 23)	section 853(2)
profits available for distribution (for the purposes of Part 23)	section 830(2)

property (in Part 27)	section 941
protected information (in Chapter 8 of Part 10)	section 240
provision for entrenchment, in relation to a company's articles	section 22
public company	section 4
publication, in relation to accounts and reports (in sections 433 to 435)	section 436
qualified, in relation to an auditor's report etc (in Part 16)	section 539
qualifying shares (in Chapter 6 of Part 18)	section 724(2)
qualifying third party indemnity provision (in Chapter 7 of Part 10)	section 234
qualifying pension scheme indemnity provision (in Chapter 7 of Part 10)	section 235
quasi-loan (in Chapter 4 of Part 10)	section 199
quoted company	
— in Part 13	section 361
— in Part 15	section 385
— in Chapter 5 of Part 16	section 531 (and section 385)
realised profits and losses (in Part 23)	section 853(4)
redeemable shares	section 684(1)
redenominate	section 622(1)
redenomination reserve	section 628
the register	section 1080
register of charges, kept by registrar	
— in England and Wales and Northern Ireland	section 869
— in Scotland	section 885
register of directors	section 162
register of directors' residential addresses	section 165
register of members	section 113
register of secretaries	section 275
registered number, of a branch of an overseas company	section 1067
registered number, of a company	section 1066
registered office, of a company	section 86
registrar and registrar of companies	section 1060
registrar's index of company names	section 1099
registrar's rules	section 1117
registration in a particular part of the United Kingdom	section 1060(4)
regulated activity	
— generally in the Companies Acts	section 1173(1)
— in Part 15	section 474(1)
regulated market	section 1173(1)
relevant accounts (in Part 23)	section 836(2)
requirements for proper delivery (in Part 35)	section 1072 (and see section 1073)

requirements of this Act	section 1172
securities (and related expressions)	
— in Chapter 1 of Part 20	section 755(5)
— in Chapter 2 of Part 21	section 783
senior statutory auditor	section 504
sent or supplied, in relation to documents or information (in the company communications provisions)	section 1148(2) and (3)
service address	section 1141
service contract, of a director (in Part 10)	section 227
shadow director	section 251
share	
— generally in the Companies Acts	section 540 (and see section 1161(2))
— in Part 22	section 792
— in section 1162 and Schedule 7	section 1162(7)
share capital, company having a	section 545
share exchange ratio	
— in Chapter 2 of Part 27	section 905(2)
— in Chapter 3 of Part 27	section 920(2)
share premium account	section 610(1)
share warrant	section 779(1)
small companies regime, for accounts and reports	section 381
solvency statement (in sections 641 to 644)	section 643
special notice, in relation to a resolution	section 312
special resolution	section 283
statutory accounts	section 434(3)
subsidiary	section 1159 (and see section 1160 and Schedule 6)
subsidiary undertaking	section 1162 (and see Schedule 7)
summary financial statement	section 426
takeover bid (in Chapter 2 of Part 28)	section 971(1)
takeover offer (in Chapter 3 of Part 28)	section 974
the Takeovers Directive	
— in Chapter 1 of Part 28	section 943(8)
— in Chapter 2 of Part 28	section 971(1)
trading certificate	section 761(1)
transfer, in relation to a non-cash asset	section 1163(2)
treasury shares	section 724(5)
turnover	
— in Part 15	section 474(1)
— in Part 16	section 539
UCITS management company	
— in Part 15	section 474(1)
— in Part 16	section 539

UK-registered company	section 1158
uncalled share capital	section 547
unconditional, in relation to a contract to acquire shares (in Chapter 3 of Part 28)	section 991(2)
undistributable reserves	section 831(4)
undertaking	section 1161(1)
unique identifier	section 1082
unlimited company	section 3
unquoted company (in Part 15)	section 385
voting rights	
— in Chapter 2 of Part 28	section 971(1)
— in Chapter 3 of Part 28	section 991(1)
— in section 1159 and Schedule 6	paragraph 2 of Schedule 6
— in section 1162 and Schedule 7	paragraph 2 of Schedule 7
voting shares	
— in Chapter 2 of Part 28	section 971(1)
— in Chapter 3 of Part 28	section 991(1)
website, communication by a company by means of	Part 4 of Schedule 5
Welsh company	section 88
wholly-owned subsidiary	section 1159(2) (and see section 1160 and Schedule 6)
working day, in relation to a company	section 1173(1)
written resolution	section 288

[S1318]

NOTES

Commencement: to be appointed.

SCHEDULE 9
REMOVAL OF SPECIAL PROVISIONS ABOUT ACCOUNTS AND AUDIT OF CHARITABLE COMPANIES

Section 1175

PART 1
THE COMPANIES ACT 1985 (C 6)

(*Amends CA 1985, ss 240, 245, 249A, 249B, 249E, 262A at* **[227]**, **[234]**, **[246]**, **[248]**, **[251]**, **[267]**, *and repeals ss 249C, 249D at* **[249]**, **[250]**.)

[S1319]

NOTES

Commencement: to be appointed.

PART 2
THE COMPANIES (NORTHERN IRELAND) ORDER 1986 (SI 1986/1032 (NI 6)

(*Contains amendments to the Companies* (*Northern Ireland*) *Order 1986, SI 1986/1032* (*outside the scope of this work*).)

[S1320]

NOTES
Commencement: to be appointed.

SCHEDULE 10
RECOGNISED SUPERVISORY BODIES

Section 1217

PART 1
GRANT AND REVOCATION OF RECOGNITION OF A SUPERVISORY BODY

Application for recognition of supervisory body

1.—(1) A supervisory body may apply to the Secretary of State for an order declaring it to be a recognised supervisory body for the purposes of this Part of this Act ("a recognition order").

(2) Any such application must be—
(a) made in such manner as the Secretary of State may direct, and
(b) accompanied by such information as the Secretary of State may reasonably require for the purpose of determining the application.

(3) At any time after receiving an application and before determining it the Secretary of State may require the applicant to furnish additional information.

(4) The directions and requirements given or imposed under sub-paragraphs (2) and (3) may differ as between different applications.

(5) The Secretary of State may require any information to be furnished under this paragraph to be in such form or verified in such manner as he may specify.

(6) Every application must be accompanied by—
(a) a copy of the applicant's rules, and
(b) a copy of any guidance issued by the applicant in writing.

(7) The reference in sub-paragraph (6)(b) to guidance issued by the applicant is a reference to any guidance or recommendation—
(a) issued or made by it to all or any class of its members or persons seeking to become members,
(b) relevant for the purposes of this Part, and
(c) intended to have continuing effect,

including any guidance or recommendation relating to the admission or expulsion of members of the body, so far as relevant for the purposes of this Part.

Grant and refusal of recognition

2.—(1) The Secretary of State may, on an application duly made in accordance with paragraph 1 and after being furnished with all such information as he may require under that paragraph, make or refuse to make a recognition order in respect of the applicant.

(2) The Secretary of State may make a recognition order only if it appears to him, from the information furnished by the body and having regard to any other information in his possession, that the requirements of Part 2 of this Schedule are satisfied in the case of that body.

(3) The Secretary of State may refuse to make a recognition order in respect of a body if he considers that its recognition is unnecessary having regard to the existence of one or more other bodies which—
(a) maintain and enforce rules as to the appointment and conduct of statutory auditors, and
(b) have been or are likely to be recognised.

(4) Where the Secretary of State refuses an application for a recognition order he must give the applicant a written notice to that effect—
(a) specifying which requirements, in the opinion of the Secretary of State, are not satisfied, or

(b) stating that the application is refused on the ground mentioned in sub-paragraph (3).

(5) A recognition order must state the date on which it takes effect.

Revocation of recognition

3.—(1) A recognition order may be revoked by a further order made by the Secretary of State if at any time it appears to him—

(a) that any requirement of Part 2 of this Schedule is not satisfied in the case of the body to which the recognition order relates ("the recognised body"),

(b) that the body has failed to comply with any obligation imposed on it by or by virtue of this Part of this Act, or

(c) that the continued recognition of the body is undesirable having regard to the existence of one or more other bodies which have been or are to be recognised.

(2) An order revoking a recognition order must state the date on which it takes effect, which must be after the period of three months beginning with the date on which the revocation order is made.

(3) Before revoking a recognition order the Secretary of State must—

(a) give written notice of his intention to do so to the recognised body,

(b) take such steps as he considers reasonably practicable for bringing the notice to the attention of the members of the body, and

(c) publish the notice in such manner as he thinks appropriate for bringing it to the attention of any other persons who are in his opinion likely to be affected.

(4) A notice under sub-paragraph (3) must—

(a) state the reasons for which the Secretary of State proposes to act, and

(b) give particulars of the rights conferred by sub-paragraph (5).

(5) A person within sub-paragraph (6) may, within the period of three months beginning with the date of service or publication of the notice under sub-paragraph (3) or such longer period as the Secretary of State may allow, make written representations to the Secretary of State and, if desired, oral representations to a person appointed for that purpose by the Secretary of State.

(6) The persons within this sub-paragraph are—

(a) the recognised body on which a notice is served under sub-paragraph (3),

(b) any member of the body, and

(c) any other person who appears to the Secretary of State to be affected.

(7) The Secretary of State must have regard to any representations made in accordance with sub-paragraph (5) in determining whether to revoke the recognition order.

(8) If in any case the Secretary of State considers it essential to do so in the public interest he may revoke a recognition order without regard to the restriction imposed by sub-paragraph (2), even if—

(a) no notice has been given or published under sub-paragraph (3), or

(b) the period of time for making representations in pursuance of such a notice has not expired.

(9) An order revoking a recognition order may contain such transitional provision as the Secretary of State thinks necessary or expedient.

(10) A recognition order may be revoked at the request or with the consent of the recognised body and any such revocation is not subject to—

(a) the restrictions imposed by sub-paragraphs (1) and (2), or

(b) the requirements of sub-paragraphs (3) to (5) and (7).

(11) On making an order revoking a recognition order in respect of a body the Secretary of State must—

(a) give written notice of the making of the order to the body,

(b) take such steps as he considers reasonably practicable for bringing the making of the order to the attention of the members of the body, and

(c) publish a notice of the making of the order in such manner as he thinks appropriate for bringing it to the attention of any other persons who are in his opinion likely to be affected.

Transitional provision

4. A recognition order made and not revoked under—
   (a) paragraph 2(1) of Schedule 11 to the Companies Act 1989 (c 40), or
   (b) paragraph 2(1) of Schedule 11 to the Companies (Northern Ireland) Order 1990 (SI 1990/593 (NI 5)),

before the commencement of this Chapter of this Part of this Act is to have effect after the commencement of this Chapter as a recognition order made under paragraph 2(1) of this Schedule.

Orders not statutory instruments

5. Orders under this Part of this Schedule shall not be made by statutory instrument.

[S1321]

NOTES

Commencement: to be appointed.

PART 2
REQUIREMENTS FOR RECOGNITION OF A SUPERVISORY BODY

Holding of appropriate qualification

6.—(1) The body must have rules to the effect that a person is not eligible for appointment as a statutory auditor unless—
   (a) in the case of an individual, he holds an appropriate qualification,
   (b) in the case of a firm—
      (i) each individual responsible for statutory audit work on behalf of the firm is eligible for appointment as a statutory auditor, and
      (ii) the firm is controlled by qualified persons (see paragraph 7 below).

(2) Sub-paragraph (1) does not prevent the body from imposing more stringent requirements.

(3) A firm which has ceased to comply with the conditions mentioned in sub-paragraph (1)(b) may be permitted to remain eligible for appointment as a statutory auditor for a period of not more than three months.

7.—(1) This paragraph explains what is meant in paragraph 6(1)(b) by a firm being "controlled by qualified persons".

(2) In this paragraph references to a person being qualified are—
   (a) in relation to an individual, to his holding—
      (i) an appropriate qualification, or
      (ii) a corresponding qualification to audit accounts under the law of a member State, or part of a member State, other than the United Kingdom;
   (b) in relation to a firm, to its—
      (i) being eligible for appointment as a statutory auditor, or
      (ii) being eligible for a corresponding appointment as an auditor under the law of a member State, or part of a member State, other than the United Kingdom.

(3) A firm is to be treated as controlled by qualified persons if, and only if—
   (a) a majority of the members of the firm are qualified persons, and
   (b) where the firm's affairs are managed by a board of directors, committee or other management body, a majority of that body are qualified persons or, if the body consists of two persons only, at least one of them is a qualified person.

(4) A majority of the members of a firm means—
   (a) where under the firm's constitution matters are decided upon by the exercise of voting rights, members holding a majority of the rights to vote on all, or substantially all, matters;
   (b) in any other case, members having such rights under the constitution of the firm as enable them to direct its overall policy or alter its constitution.

(5) A majority of the members of the management body of a firm means—
- (a) where matters are decided at meetings of the management body by the exercise of voting rights, members holding a majority of the rights to vote on all, or substantially all, matters at such meetings;
- (b) in any other case, members having such rights under the constitution of the firm as enable them to direct its overall policy or alter its constitution.

(6) Paragraphs 5 to 11 of Schedule 7 to this Act (rights to be taken into account and attribution of rights) apply for the purposes of this paragraph.

Auditors to be fit and proper persons

8.—(1) The body must have adequate rules and practices designed to ensure that the persons eligible under its rules for appointment as a statutory auditor are fit and proper persons to be so appointed.

(2) The matters which the body may take into account for this purpose in relation to a person must include—
- (a) any matter relating to any person who is or will be employed by or associated with him for the purposes of or in connection with statutory audit work;
- (b) in the case of a body corporate, any matter relating to—
  - (i) any director or controller of the body,
  - (ii) any other body corporate in the same group, or
  - (iii) any director or controller of any such other body; and
- (c) in the case of a partnership, any matter relating to—
  - (i) any of the partners,
  - (ii) any director or controller of any of the partners,
  - (iii) any body corporate in the same group as any of the partners, or
  - (iv) any director or controller of any such other body.

(3) Where the person is a limited liability partnership, in sub-paragraph (2)(b) "director" is to be read as "member".

(4) In sub-paragraph (2)(b) and (c) "controller", in relation to a body corporate, means a person who either alone or with an associate or associates is entitled to exercise or control the exercise of 15% or more of the rights to vote on all, or substantially all, matters at general meetings of the body or another body corporate of which it is a subsidiary.

Professional integrity and independence

9.—(1) The body must have adequate rules and practices designed to ensure that—
- (a) statutory audit work is conducted properly and with integrity, and
- (b) persons are not appointed as statutory auditors in circumstances in which they have an interest likely to conflict with the proper conduct of the audit.

(2) The body must participate in arrangements within paragraph 21, and the rules and practices mentioned in sub-paragraph (1) must include provision requiring compliance with any standards for the time being determined under such arrangements.

(3) The body must also have adequate rules and practices designed to ensure that no firm is eligible under its rules for appointment as a statutory auditor unless the firm has arrangements to prevent a person to whom sub-paragraph (4) applies from being able to exert any influence over the way in which a statutory audit is conducted in circumstances in which that influence would be likely to affect the independence or integrity of the audit.

(4) This sub-paragraph applies to—
- (a) any individual who is not a qualified person within the meaning of paragraph 7, and
- (b) any person who is not a member of the firm.

Technical standards

10.—(1) The body must have rules and practices as to—
- (a) the technical standards to be applied in statutory audit work, and
- (b) the manner in which those standards are to be applied in practice.

(2) The body must participate in arrangements within paragraph 22, and the rules and practices mentioned in sub-paragraph (1) must include provision requiring compliance with any standards for the time being determined under such arrangements.

Procedures for maintaining competence

11. The body must have rules and practices designed to ensure that persons eligible under its rules for appointment as a statutory auditor continue to maintain an appropriate level of competence in the conduct of statutory audits.

Monitoring and enforcement

12.—(1) The body must have adequate arrangements and resources for the effective monitoring and enforcement of compliance with its rules.

(2) The arrangements for monitoring may make provision for that function to be performed on behalf of the body (and without affecting its responsibility) by any other body or person who is able and willing to perform it.

Independent monitoring of audits of listed companies and other major bodies

13.—(1) The body must—

(a) participate in arrangements within paragraph 23(1), and

(b) have rules designed to ensure that members of the body who perform any statutory audit functions in respect of major audits take such steps as may be reasonably required of them to enable their performance of any such functions to be monitored by means of inspections carried out under the arrangements.

(2) Any monitoring of such persons under the arrangements is to be regarded (so far as their performance of statutory audit functions in respect of major audits is concerned) as monitoring of compliance with the body's rules for the purposes of paragraph 12(1).

(3) In this paragraph—

"major audit" means a statutory audit conducted in respect of—

(a) a company any of whose securities have been admitted to the official list (within the meaning of Part 6 of the Financial Services and Markets Act 2000 (c 8)), or

(b) any other person in whose financial condition there is a major public interest;

"statutory audit function" means any function performed as a statutory auditor.

Membership, eligibility and discipline

14. The rules and practices of the body relating to—

(a) the admission and expulsion of members,

(b) the grant and withdrawal of eligibility for appointment as a statutory auditor, and

(c) the discipline it exercises over its members,

must be fair and reasonable and include adequate provision for appeals.

Investigation of complaints

15.—(1) The body must have effective arrangements for the investigation of complaints against—

(a) persons who are eligible under its rules for appointment as a statutory auditor, and

(b) the body in respect of matters arising out of its functions as a supervisory body.

(2) The arrangements mentioned in sub-paragraph (1) may make provision for the whole or part of that function to be performed by and to be the responsibility of a body or person independent of the body itself.

Independent investigation for disciplinary purposes of public interest cases

16.—(1) The body must—
- (a) participate in arrangements within paragraph 24(1), and
- (b) have rules and practices designed to ensure that, where the designated persons have decided that any particular disciplinary action should be taken against a member of the body following the conclusion of an investigation under such arrangements, that decision is to be treated as if it were a decision made by the body in disciplinary proceedings against the member.

(2) In sub-paragraph (1) "the designated persons" means the persons who, under the arrangements, have the function of deciding whether (and if so, what) disciplinary action should be taken against a member of the body in the light of an investigation carried out under the arrangements.

Meeting of claims arising out of audit work

17.—(1) The body must have adequate rules or arrangements designed to ensure that persons eligible under its rules for appointment as a statutory auditor take such steps as may reasonably be expected of them to secure that they are able to meet claims against them arising out of statutory audit work.

(2) This may be achieved by professional indemnity insurance or other appropriate arrangements.

Register of auditors and other information to be made available

18. The body must have rules requiring persons eligible under its rules for appointment as a statutory auditor to comply with any obligations imposed on them by—
- (a) requirements under section 1224 (Secretary of State's power to call for information);
- (b) regulations under section 1239 (the register of auditors);
- (c) regulations under section 1240 (information to be made available to the public).

Taking account of costs of compliance

19. The body must have satisfactory arrangements for taking account, in framing its rules, of the cost to those to whom the rules would apply of complying with those rules and any other controls to which they are subject.

Promotion and maintenance of standards

20. The body must be able and willing—
- (a) to promote and maintain high standards of integrity in the conduct of statutory audit work, and
- (b) to co-operate, by the sharing of information and otherwise, with the Secretary of State and any other authority, body or person having responsibility in the United Kingdom for the qualification, supervision or regulation of auditors.

[S1322]

NOTES

Commencement: to be appointed.

PART 3
ARRANGEMENTS IN WHICH RECOGNISED SUPERVISORY BODIES ARE REQUIRED TO PARTICIPATE

Arrangements for setting standards relating to professional integrity and independence

21. The arrangements referred to in paragraph 9(2) are appropriate arrangements—

(a) for the determining of standards for the purposes of the rules and practices mentioned in paragraph 9(1), and
(b) for ensuring that the determination of those standards is done independently of the body.

Arrangements for setting technical standards

22. The arrangements referred to in paragraph 10(2) are appropriate arrangements—
(a) for the determining of standards for the purposes of the rules and practices mentioned in paragraph 10(1), and
(b) for ensuring that the determination of those standards is done independently of the body.

Arrangements for independent monitoring of audits of listed companies and other major bodies

23.—(1) The arrangements referred to in paragraph 13(1) are appropriate arrangements—
(a) for enabling the performance by members of the body of statutory audit functions in respect of major audits to be monitored by means of inspections carried out under the arrangements, and
(b) for ensuring that the carrying out of such monitoring and inspections is done independently of the body.

(2) In this paragraph "major audit" and "statutory audit function" have the same meaning as in paragraph 13.

Arrangements for independent investigation for disciplinary purposes of public interest cases

24.—(1) The arrangements referred to in paragraph 16(1) are appropriate arrangements—
(a) for the carrying out of investigations into public interest cases arising in connection with the performance of statutory audit functions by members of the body,
(b) for the holding of disciplinary hearings relating to members of the body which appear to be desirable following the conclusion of such investigations,
(c) for requiring such hearings to be held in public except where the interests of justice otherwise require,
(d) for the persons before whom such hearings have taken place to decide whether (and, if so, what) disciplinary action should be taken against the members to whom the hearings related, and
(e) for ensuring that the carrying out of those investigations, the holding of those hearings and the taking of those decisions are done independently of the body.

(2) In this paragraph—
"public interest cases" means matters which raise or appear to raise important issues affecting the public interest;
"statutory audit function" means any function performed as a statutory auditor.

Supplementary: arrangements to operate independently of body

25.—(1) This paragraph applies for the purposes of—
(a) paragraph 21(b),
(b) paragraph 22(b),
(c) paragraph 23(1)(b), or
(d) paragraph 24(1)(e).

(2) Arrangements are not to be regarded as appropriate for the purpose of ensuring that a thing is done independently of the body unless they are designed to ensure that the body—
(a) will have no involvement in the appointment or selection of any of the persons who are to be responsible for doing that thing, and
(b) will not otherwise be involved in the doing of that thing.

(3) Sub-paragraph (2) imposes a minimum requirement and does not preclude the possibility that additional criteria may need to be satisfied in order for the arrangements to be regarded as appropriate for the purpose in question.

Supplementary: funding of arrangements

26. The body must pay any of the costs of maintaining any arrangements within paragraph 21, 22, 23 or 24 which the arrangements provide are to be paid by it.

Supplementary: scope of arrangement

27. Arrangements may qualify as arrangements within any of paragraphs 21, 22, 23 and 24 even though the matters for which they provide are more extensive in any respect than those mentioned in the applicable paragraph.

[S1323]

NOTES

Commencement: to be appointed.

SCHEDULE 11
RECOGNISED PROFESSIONAL QUALIFICATIONS

Section 1220

PART 1
GRANT AND REVOCATION OF RECOGNITION OF A PROFESSIONAL QUALIFICATION

Application for recognition of professional qualification

1.—(1) A qualifying body may apply to the Secretary of State for an order declaring a qualification offered by it to be a recognised professional qualification for the purposes of this Part of this Act ("a recognition order").

(2) In this Part of this Act "a recognised qualifying body" means a qualifying body offering a recognised professional qualification.

(3) Any application must be—
- (a) made in such manner as the Secretary of State may direct, and
- (b) accompanied by such information as the Secretary of State may reasonably require for the purpose of determining the application.

(4) At any time after receiving an application and before determining it the Secretary of State may require the applicant to furnish additional information.

(5) The directions and requirements given or imposed under sub-paragraphs (3) and (4) may differ as between different applications.

(6) The Secretary of State may require any information to be furnished under this paragraph to be in such form or verified in such manner as he may specify.

(7) In the case of examination standards, the verification required may include independent moderation of the examinations over such a period as the Secretary of State considers necessary.

(8) Every application must be accompanied by—
- (a) a copy of the applicant's rules, and
- (b) a copy of any guidance issued by the applicant in writing.

(9) The reference in sub-paragraph (8)(b) to guidance issued by the applicant is a reference to any guidance or recommendation—
- (a) issued or made by it to all or any class of persons holding or seeking to hold a qualification, or approved or seeking to be approved by the body for the purposes of giving practical training,
- (b) relevant for the purposes of this Part of this Act, and

(c) intended to have continuing effect,

including any guidance or recommendation relating to a matter within sub-paragraph (10).

(10) The matters within this sub-paragraph are—

(a) admission to or expulsion from a course of study leading to a qualification,

(b) the award or deprivation of a qualification, and

(c) the approval of a person for the purposes of giving practical training or the withdrawal of such an approval,

so far as relevant for the purposes of this Part of this Act.

Grant and refusal of recognition

2.—(1) The Secretary of State may, on an application duly made in accordance with paragraph 1 and after being furnished with all such information as he may require under that paragraph, make or refuse to make a recognition order in respect of the qualification in relation to which the application was made.

(2) The Secretary of State may make a recognition order only if it appears to him, from the information furnished by the applicant and having regard to any other information in his possession, that the requirements of Part 2 of this Schedule are satisfied in relation to the qualification.

(3) Where the Secretary of State refuses an application for a recognition order he must give the applicant a written notice to that effect specifying which requirements, in his opinion, are not satisfied.

(4) A recognition order must state the date on which it takes effect.

Revocation of recognition

3.—(1) A recognition order may be revoked by a further order made by the Secretary of State if at any time it appears to him—

(a) that any requirement of Part 2 of this Schedule is not satisfied in relation to the qualification to which the recognition order relates, or

(b) that the qualifying body has failed to comply with any obligation imposed on it by or by virtue of this Part of this Act.

(2) An order revoking a recognition order must state the date on which it takes effect, which must be after the period of three months beginning with the date on which the revocation order is made.

(3) Before revoking a recognition order the Secretary of State must—

(a) give written notice of his intention to do so to the qualifying body,

(b) take such steps as he considers reasonably practicable for bringing the notice to the attention of persons holding the qualification or in the course of studying for it, and

(c) publish the notice in such manner as he thinks appropriate for bringing it to the attention of any other persons who are in his opinion likely to be affected.

(4) A notice under sub-paragraph (3) must—

(a) state the reasons for which the Secretary of State proposes to act, and

(b) give particulars of the rights conferred by sub-paragraph (5).

(5) A person within sub-paragraph (6) may, within the period of three months beginning with the date of service or publication or such longer period as the Secretary of State may allow, make written representations to the Secretary of State and, if desired, oral representations to a person appointed for that purpose by the Secretary of State.

(6) The persons within this sub-paragraph are—

(a) the qualifying body on which a notice is served under sub-paragraph (3),

(b) any person holding the qualification or in the course of studying for it, and

(c) any other person who appears to the Secretary of State to be affected.

(7) The Secretary of State must have regard to any representations made in accordance with sub-paragraph (5) in determining whether to revoke the recognition order.

(8) If in any case the Secretary of State considers it essential to do so in the public interest he may revoke a recognition order without regard to the restriction imposed by sub-paragraph (2), even if—
(a) no notice has been given or published under sub-paragraph (3), or
(b) the period of time for making representations in pursuance of such a notice has not expired.

(9) An order revoking a recognition order may contain such transitional provision as the Secretary of State thinks necessary or expedient.

(10) A recognition order may be revoked at the request or with the consent of the qualifying body and any such revocation is not subject to—
(a) the restrictions imposed by sub-paragraphs (1) and (2), or
(b) the requirements of sub-paragraphs (3) to (5) and (7).

(11) On making an order revoking a recognition order the Secretary of State must—
(a) give written notice of the making of the order to the qualifying body,
(b) take such steps as he considers reasonably practicable for bringing the making of the order to the attention of persons holding the qualification or in the course of studying for it, and
(c) publish a notice of the making of the order in such manner as he thinks appropriate for bringing it to the attention of any other persons who are in his opinion likely to be affected.

Transitional provision

4. A recognition order made and not revoked under—
(a) paragraph 2(1) of Schedule 12 to the Companies Act 1989 (c 40), or
(b) paragraph 2(1) of Schedule 12 to the Companies (Northern Ireland) Order 1990 (SI 1990/593 (NI 5)),

before the commencement of this Chapter of this Part of this Act is to have effect after the commencement of this Chapter as a recognition order made under paragraph 2(1) of this Schedule.

Orders not statutory instruments

5. Orders under this Part of this Schedule shall not be made by statutory instrument.

[S1324]

NOTES

Commencement: 20 January 2007 (for the purpose of enabling the exercise of powers to make Orders or Regulations by statutory instrument); to be appointed (otherwise).

PART 2
REQUIREMENTS FOR RECOGNITION OF A PROFESSIONAL QUALIFICATION

Entry requirements

6.—(1) The qualification must only be open to persons who—
(a) have attained university entrance level, or
(b) have a sufficient period of professional experience.

(2) In relation to a person who has not been admitted to a university or other similar establishment in the United Kingdom, "attaining university entrance level" means—
(a) being educated to such a standard as would entitle him to be considered for such admission on the basis of—
(i) academic or professional qualifications obtained in the United Kingdom and recognised by the Secretary of State to be of an appropriate standard, or
(ii) academic or professional qualifications obtained outside the United Kingdom which the Secretary of State considers to be of an equivalent standard, or
(b) being assessed, on the basis of written tests of a kind appearing to the Secretary of

State to be adequate for the purpose (with or without oral examination), as of such a standard of ability as would entitle him to be considered for such admission.

(3) The assessment, tests and oral examination referred to in sub-paragraph (2)(b) may be conducted by—

(a) the qualifying body, or
(b) some other body approved by the Secretary of State.

(4) The reference in sub-paragraph (1)(b) to "a sufficient period of professional experience" is to not less than seven years' experience in a professional capacity in the fields of finance, law and accountancy.

Requirement for theoretical instruction or professional experience

7.—(1) The qualification must be restricted to persons who—

(a) have completed a course of theoretical instruction in the subjects prescribed for the purposes of paragraph 8, or
(b) have a sufficient period of professional experience.

(2) The reference in sub-paragraph (1)(b) to "a sufficient period of professional experience" is to not less than seven years' experience in a professional capacity in the fields of finance, law and accountancy.

Examination

8.—(1) The qualification must be restricted to persons who have passed an examination (at least part of which is in writing) testing—

(a) theoretical knowledge of the subjects prescribed for the purposes of this paragraph by regulations made by the Secretary of State, and
(b) ability to apply that knowledge in practice,

and requiring a standard of attainment at least equivalent to that required to obtain a degree from a university or similar establishment in the United Kingdom.

(2) The qualification may be awarded to a person without his theoretical knowledge of a subject being tested by examination if he has passed a university or other examination of equivalent standard in that subject or holds a university degree or equivalent qualification in it.

(3) The qualification may be awarded to a person without his ability to apply his theoretical knowledge of a subject in practice being tested by examination if he has received practical training in that subject which is attested by an examination or diploma recognised by the Secretary of State for the purposes of this paragraph.

(4) Regulations under this paragraph are subject to negative resolution procedure.

Practical training

9.—(1) The qualification must be restricted to persons who have completed at least three years' practical training of which—

(a) part was spent being trained in statutory audit work, and
(b) a substantial part was spent being trained in statutory audit work or other audit work of a description approved by the Secretary of State as being similar to statutory audit work.

(2) For the purpose of sub-paragraph (1) "statutory audit work" includes the work of a person appointed as the auditor of a person under the law of a country or territory outside the United Kingdom where it appears to the Secretary of State that the law and practice with respect to the audit of accounts is similar to that in the United Kingdom.

(3) The training must be given by persons approved by the body offering the qualification as persons whom the body is satisfied, in the light of undertakings given by them and the supervision to which they are subject (whether by the body itself or some other body or organisation), will provide adequate training.

(4) At least two-thirds of the training must be given by a person—

(a) eligible for appointment as a statutory auditor, or

(b) eligible for a corresponding appointment as an auditor under the law of a member State, or part of a member State, other than the United Kingdom.

Supplementary provision with respect to a sufficient period of professional experience

10.—(1) Periods of theoretical instruction in the fields of finance, law and accountancy may be deducted from the required period of professional experience, provided the instruction—

(a) lasted at least one year, and

(b) is attested by an examination recognised by the Secretary of State for the purposes of this paragraph;

but the period of professional experience may not be so reduced by more than four years.

(2) The period of professional experience together with the practical training required in the case of persons satisfying the requirement in paragraph 7 by virtue of having a sufficient period of professional experience must not be shorter than the course of theoretical instruction referred to in that paragraph and the practical training required in the case of persons satisfying the requirement of that paragraph by virtue of having completed such a course.

The body offering the qualification

11.—(1) The body offering the qualification must have—

(a) rules and arrangements adequate to ensure compliance with the requirements of paragraphs 6 to 10, and

(b) adequate arrangements for the effective monitoring of its continued compliance with those requirements.

(2) The arrangements must include arrangements for monitoring—

(a) the standard of the body's examinations, and

(b) the adequacy of the practical training given by the persons approved by it for that purpose.

[S1325]

NOTES

Commencement: 20 January 2007 (for the purpose of enabling the exercise of powers to make Orders or Regulations by statutory instrument); to be appointed (otherwise).

SCHEDULE 12
ARRANGEMENTS IN WHICH REGISTERED THIRD COUNTRY AUDITORS ARE REQUIRED TO PARTICIPATE

Section 1242

Arrangements for independent monitoring of audits of traded non-Community companies

1.—(1) The arrangements referred to in section 1242(1)(a) are appropriate arrangements—

(a) for enabling the performance by the registered third country auditor of third country audit functions to be monitored by means of inspections carried out under the arrangements, and

(b) for ensuring that the carrying out of such monitoring and inspections is done independently of the registered third country auditor.

(2) In this paragraph "third country audit function" means any function performed as a third country auditor.

Arrangements for independent investigations for disciplinary purposes

2.—(1) The arrangements referred to in section 1242(1)(b) are appropriate arrangements—

(a) for the carrying out of investigations into matters arising in connection with the performance of third country audit functions by the registered third country auditor,

(b) for the holding of disciplinary hearings relating to the registered third country auditor which appear to be desirable following the conclusion of such investigations,

(c) for requiring such hearings to be held in public except where the interests of justice otherwise require,

(d) for the persons before whom such hearings have taken place to decide whether (and, if so, what) disciplinary action should be taken against the registered third country auditor, and

(e) for ensuring that the carrying out of those investigations, the holding of those hearings and the taking of those decisions are done independently of the registered third country auditor.

(2) In this paragraph—

"disciplinary action" includes the imposition of a fine; and

"third country audit function" means any function performed as a third country auditor.

Supplementary: arrangements to operate independently of third country auditor

3.—(1) This paragraph applies for the purposes of—

(a) paragraph 1(1)(b), or

(b) paragraph 2(1)(e).

(2) Arrangements are not to be regarded as appropriate for the purpose of ensuring that a thing is done independently of the registered third country auditor unless they are designed to ensure that the registered third country auditor—

(a) will have no involvement in the appointment or selection of any of the persons who are to be responsible for doing that thing, and

(b) will not otherwise be involved in the doing of that thing.

(3) Sub-paragraph (2) imposes a minimum requirement and does not preclude the possibility that additional criteria may need to be satisfied in order for the arrangements to be regarded as appropriate for the purpose in question.

Supplementary: funding of arrangements

4.—(1) The registered third country auditor must pay any of the costs of maintaining any relevant arrangements which the arrangements provide are to be paid by it.

(2) For this purpose "relevant arrangements" are arrangements within paragraph 1 or 2 in which the registered third country auditor is obliged to participate.

Supplementary: scope of arrangements

5. Arrangements may qualify as arrangements within either of paragraphs 1 and 2 even though the matters for which they provide are more extensive in any respect than those mentioned in the applicable paragraph.

Specification of particular arrangements by the Secretary of State

6.—(1) If there exist two or more sets of arrangements within paragraph 1 or within paragraph 2, the obligation of a registered third country auditor under section 1242(1)(a) or (b), as the case may be, is to participate in such set of arrangements as the Secretary of State may by order specify.

(2) An order under sub-paragraph (1) is subject to negative resolution procedure.

[S1326]

NOTES

Commencement: 20 January 2007 (for the purpose of enabling the exercise of powers to make Orders or Regulations by statutory instrument); to be appointed (otherwise).

SCHEDULE 13
SUPPLEMENTARY PROVISIONS WITH RESPECT TO DELEGATION ORDER

Section 1252

Operation of this Schedule

1.—(1) This Schedule has effect in relation to a body designated by a delegation order under section 1252 as follows—

(a) paragraphs 2 to 12 have effect in relation to the body where it is established by the order;

(b) paragraphs 2 and 6 to 11 have effect in relation to the body where it is an existing body;

(c) paragraph 13 has effect in relation to the body where it is an existing body that is an unincorporated association.

(2) In their operation in accordance with sub-paragraph (1)(b), paragraphs 2 and 6 apply only in relation to—

(a) things done by or in relation to the body in or in connection with the exercise of functions transferred to it by the delegation order, and

(b) functions of the body which are functions so transferred.

(3) Any power conferred by this Schedule to make provision by order is a power to make provision by an order under section 1252.

Status

2. The body is not to be regarded as acting on behalf of the Crown and its members, officers and employees are not to be regarded as Crown servants.

Name, members and chairman

3.—(1) The body is to be known by such name as may be specified in the delegation order.

(2) The body is to consist of such persons (not being less than eight) as the Secretary of State may appoint after such consultation as he thinks appropriate.

(3) The chairman of the body is to be such person as the Secretary of State may appoint from among its members.

(4) The Secretary of State may make provision by order as to—

(a) the terms on which the members of the body are to hold and vacate office;

(b) the terms on which a person appointed as chairman is to hold and vacate the office of chairman.

Financial provisions

4.—(1) The body must pay to its chairman and members such remuneration, and such allowances in respect of expenses properly incurred by them in the performance of their duties, as the Secretary of State may determine.

(2) As regards any chairman or member in whose case the Secretary of State so determines, the body must pay or make provision for the payment of—

(a) such pension, allowance or gratuity to or in respect of that person on his retirement or death, or

(b) such contributions or other payment towards the provision of such a pension, allowance or gratuity,

as the Secretary of State may determine.

(3) Where—

(a) a person ceases to be a member of the body otherwise than on the expiry of his term of office, and

(b) it appears to the Secretary of State that there are special circumstances which make it right for that person to receive compensation, the body must make a payment to him by way of compensation of such amount as the Secretary of State may determine.

Proceedings

5.—(1) The delegation order may contain such provision as the Secretary of State considers appropriate with respect to the proceedings of the body.

(2) The delegation order may, in particular—
(a) authorise the body to discharge any functions by means of committees consisting wholly or partly of members of the body;
(b) provide that the validity of proceedings of the body, or of any such committee, is not affected by any vacancy among the members or any defect in the appointment of any member.

Fees

6.—(1) The body may retain fees payable to it.

(2) The fees must be applied for—
(a) meeting the expenses of the body in discharging its functions, and
(b) any purposes incidental to those functions.

(3) Those expenses include any expenses incurred by the body on such staff, accommodation, services and other facilities as appear to it to be necessary or expedient for the proper performance of its functions.

(4) In prescribing the amount of fees in the exercise of the functions transferred to it the body must prescribe such fees as appear to it sufficient to defray those expenses, taking one year with another.

(5) Any exercise by the body of the power to prescribe fees requires the approval of the Secretary of State.

(6) The Secretary of State may, after consultation with the body, by order vary or revoke any regulations prescribing fees made by the body.

Legislative functions

7.—(1) Regulations or an order made by the body in the exercise of the functions transferred to it must be made by instrument in writing, but not by statutory instrument.

(2) The instrument must specify the provision of this Part of this Act under which it is made.

(3) The Secretary of State may by order impose such requirements as he thinks necessary or expedient as to the circumstances and manner in which the body must consult on any regulations or order it proposes to make.

(4) Nothing in this Part applies to make regulations or an order made by the body subject to negative resolution procedure or affirmative resolution procedure.

8.—(1) Immediately after an instrument is made it must be printed and made available to the public with or without payment.

(2) A person is not to be taken to have contravened any regulation or order if he shows that at the time of the alleged contravention the instrument containing the regulation or order had not been made available as required by this paragraph.

9.—(1) The production of a printed copy of an instrument purporting to be made by the body on which is endorsed a certificate signed by an officer of the body authorised by it for the purpose and stating—
(a) that the instrument was made by the body,
(b) that the copy is a true copy of the instrument, and
(c) that on a specified date the instrument was made available to the public as required by paragraph 8,

is evidence (or, in Scotland, sufficient evidence) of the facts stated in the certificate.

(2) A certificate purporting to be signed as mentioned in sub-paragraph (1) is to be deemed to have been duly signed unless the contrary is shown.

(3) Any person wishing in any legal proceedings to cite an instrument made by the body may require the body to cause a copy of it to be endorsed with such a certificate as is mentioned in this paragraph.

Report and accounts

10.—(1) The body must, at least once in each calendar year for which the delegation order is in force, make a report to the Secretary of State on—

(a) the discharge of the functions transferred to it, and
(b) such other matters as the Secretary of State may by order require.

(2) The delegation order may modify sub-paragraph (1) as it has effect in relation to the calendar year in which the order comes into force or is revoked.

(3) The Secretary of State must lay before Parliament copies of each report received by him under this paragraph.

(4) The following provisions of this paragraph apply as follows—

(a) sub-paragraphs (5) and (6) apply only where the body is established by the order, and
(b) sub-paragraphs (7) and (8) apply only where the body is an existing body.

(5) The Secretary of State may, with the consent of the Treasury, give directions to the body with respect to its accounts and the audit of its accounts.

(6) A person may only be appointed as auditor of the body if he is eligible for appointment as a statutory auditor.

(7) Unless the body is a company to which section 394 (duty to prepare individual company accounts) applies, the Secretary of State may, with the consent of the Treasury, give directions to the body with respect to its accounts and the audit of its accounts.

(8) Whether or not the body is a company to which section 394 applies, the Secretary of State may direct that any provisions of this Act specified in the directions are to apply to the body, with or without any modifications so specified.

Other supplementary provisions

11.—(1) The transfer of a function to a body designated by a delegation order does not affect anything previously done in the exercise of the function transferred; and the resumption of a function so transferred does not affect anything previously done in exercise of the function resumed.

(2) The Secretary of State may by order make such transitional and other supplementary provision as he thinks necessary or expedient in relation to the transfer or resumption of a function.

(3) The provision that may be made in connection with the transfer of a function includes, in particular, provision—

(a) for modifying or excluding any provision of this Part of this Act in its application to the function transferred;
(b) for applying to the body designated by the delegation order, in connection with the function transferred, any provision applying to the Secretary of State which is contained in or made under any other enactment;
(c) for the transfer of any property, rights or liabilities from the Secretary of State to that body;
(d) for the carrying on and completion by that body of anything in the process of being done by the Secretary of State when the order takes effect;
(e) for the substitution of that body for the Secretary of State in any instrument, contract or legal proceedings.

(4) The provision that may be made in connection with the resumption of a function includes, in particular, provision—

(a) for the transfer of any property, rights or liabilities from that body to the Secretary of State;
(b) for the carrying on and completion by the Secretary of State of anything in the process of being done by that body when the order takes effect;
(c) for the substitution of the Secretary of State for that body in any instrument, contract or legal proceedings.

12. Where a delegation order is revoked, the Secretary of State may by order make provision—
(a) for the payment of compensation to persons ceasing to be employed by the body established by the delegation order;
(b) as to the winding up and dissolution of the body.

13.—(1) This paragraph applies where the body is an unincorporated association.

(2) Any relevant proceedings may be brought by or against the body in the name of any body corporate whose constitution provides for the establishment of the body.

(3) In sub-paragraph (2) "relevant proceedings" means proceedings brought in or in connection with the exercise of any transferred function.

(4) In relation to proceedings brought as mentioned in sub-paragraph (2), any reference in paragraph 11(3)(e) or (4)(c) to the body replacing or being replaced by the Secretary of State in any legal proceedings is to be read with the appropriate modifications.

[S1327]

NOTES

Commencement: 20 January 2007 (for the purpose of enabling the exercise of powers to make Orders or Regulations by statutory instrument); to be appointed (otherwise).

SCHEDULE 14
STATUTORY AUDITORS: CONSEQUENTIAL AMENDMENTS

Section 1264

(*Amends the Companies* (*Audit, Investigations and Community Enterprise*) *Act 2004, s 16 at* **[896]**.)

[S1328]

NOTES

Commencement: to be appointed.

SCHEDULE 15
TRANSPARENCY OBLIGATIONS AND RELATED MATTERS: MINOR AND CONSEQUENTIAL AMENDMENTS

Section 1272

PART 1
AMENDMENTS OF THE FINANCIAL SERVICES AND MARKETS ACT 2000

(*Amends FSMA 2000, ss 73, 73A, 90* (*and the preceding heading*)*, 91, 96B, 97, 99, 102A, 103, 429 at* **[2073]**, **[2073A]**, **[2090]**, **[2091]**, **[2096B]**, **[2097]**, **[2099]**, **[2102A]**, **[2103]**, **[2426]**.)

[S1329]

NOTES

Commencement: 8 November 2006 (except in so far as relating to the amendment in para 11(2) to the definition of "regulated market" in s 103 of the 2000 Act); to be appointed (otherwise).

PART 2
AMENDMENTS OF THE COMPANIES (AUDIT, INVESTIGATIONS AND COMMUNITY ENTERPRISE) ACT 2004

(*Amends the Companies* (*Audit, Investigations and Community Enterprise*) *Act 2004, ss 14, 15 at* **[894]**, **[895]**.)

[S1330]

NOTES

Commencement: 8 November 2006.

SCHEDULE 16
REPEALS

Section 1295

COMPANY LAW REPEALS (GREAT BRITAIN)

Short title and chapter	*Extent of repeal*
Companies Act 1985 (c 6)	Sections 1 to 430F.
	In section 437—
	(a) in subsection (1), the second sentence, and
	(b) subsections (1B) and (1C).
	Section 438.
	In section 439—
	(a) in subsection (2), ", or is ordered to pay the whole or any part of the costs of proceedings brought under section 438",
	(b) subsections (3) and (7), and
	(c) in subsection (8), "; and any such liability imposed by subsection (2) is (subject as mentioned above) a liability also to indemnify all persons against liability under subsection (3)".
	Section 442(2).
	Section 446.
	In section 448(7), the words "and liable to a fine." to the end.
	Section 449(7).
	Section 450(4).
	Section 451(3).
	In section 453(1A)—
	(a) paragraph (b), and
	(b) paragraph (d) and the word "and" preceding it.
	Section 453A(6).
	Sections 458 to 461.
	Sections 651 to 746.
	Schedules 1 to 15B.
	Schedules 20 to 25.
Insolvency Act 1985 (c 65)	Schedule 6.
Insolvency Act 1986 (c 45)	In Schedule 13, in Part 1, the entries relating to the following provisions of the Companies Act 1985—
	(a) section 13(4),
	(b) section 44(7),
	(c) section 103(7),

Short title and chapter	*Extent of repeal*
	(d) section 131(7),
	(e) section 140(2),
	(f) section 156(3),
	(g) section 173(4),
	(h) section 196,
	(i) section 380(4),
	(j) section 461(6),
	(k) section 462(5),
	(l) section 463(2),
	(m) section 463(3),
	(n) section 464(6),
	(o) section 657(2),
	(p) section 658(1), and
	(q) section 711(2).
Building Societies Act 1986 (c 53)	Section 102C(5).
Finance Act 1988 (c 39)	In section 117(3), from the beginning to "that section";".
	In section 117(4), the words "and (3)".
Water Act 1989 (c 15)	In Schedule 25, paragraph 71(3).
Companies Act 1989 (c 40)	Sections 1 to 22.
	Section 56(5).
	Sections 57 and 58.
	Section 64(2).
	Section 66(3).
	Section 71.
	Sections 92 to 110.
	Sections 113 to 138.
	Section 139(1) to (3).
	Sections 141 to 143.
	Section 144(1) to (3) and (6).
	Section 207.
	Schedules 1 to 9.
	In Schedule 10, paragraphs 1 to 24.
	Schedules 15 to 17.
	In Schedule 18, paragraphs 32 to 38.
	In Schedule 19, paragraphs 1 to 9 and 11 to 21.
Age of Legal Capacity (Scotland) Act 1991 (c 50)	In Schedule 1, paragraph 39.
Water Consolidation (Consequential Provisions) Act 1991 (c 60)	In Schedule 1, paragraph 40(2).
Charities Act 1992 (c 41)	In Schedule 6, paragraph 11.
Charities Act 1993 (c 10)	In Schedule 6, paragraph 20.
Criminal Justice Act 1993 (c 36)	In Schedule 5, paragraph 4.

Short title and chapter	*Extent of repeal*
Welsh Language Act 1993 (c 38)	Section 30.
Pension Schemes Act 1993 (c 48)	In Schedule 8, paragraph 16.
Trade Marks Act 1994 (c 26)	In Schedule 4, in paragraph 1(2), the reference to the Companies Act 1985.
Deregulation and Contracting Out Act 1994 (c 40)	Section 13(1).
	Schedule 5.
	In Schedule 16, paragraphs 8 to 10.
Requirements of Writing (Scotland) Act 1995 (c 7)	In Schedule 4, paragraphs 51 to 56.
Criminal Procedure (Consequential Provisions) (Scotland) Act 1995 (c 40)	In Schedule 4, paragraph 56(3) and (4).
Disability Discrimination Act 1995 (c 50)	In Schedule 6, paragraph 4.
Financial Services and Markets Act 2000 (c 8)	Section 143.
	Section 263.
Limited Liability Partnerships Act 2000 (c 12)	In the Schedule, paragraph 1.
Political Parties, Elections and Referendums Act 2000 (c 41)	Sections 139 and 140.
	Schedule 19.
	In Schedule 23, paragraphs 12 and 13.
Criminal Justice and Police Act 2001 (c 16)	Section 45.
	In Schedule 2, paragraph 17.
Enterprise Act 2002 (c 40)	In Schedule 17, paragraphs 3 to 8.
Companies (Audit, Investigations and Community Enterprise) Act 2004 (c 27)	Sections 7 to 10.
	Section 11(1).
	Sections 12 and 13.
	Sections 19 and 20.
	Schedule 1.
	In Schedule 2, paragraphs 5 to 10, 22 to 24 and 26.
	In Schedule 6, paragraphs 1 to 9.
Civil Partnership Act 2004 (c 33)	In Schedule 27, paragraphs 99 to 105.
Constitutional Reform Act 2005 (c 4)	In Schedule 11, in paragraph 4(3), the reference to the Companies Act 1985.

REPEALS AND REVOCATIONS RELATING TO NORTHERN IRELAND

Short title and chapter	*Extent of repeal or revocation*
Companies (Northern Ireland) Order 1986 (SI 1986/1032 (NI 6))	The whole Order.
Companies Consolidation (Consequential Provisions) (Northern Ireland) Order 1986 (SI 1986/1035 (NI 9))	The whole Order.
Business Names (Northern Ireland) Order 1986 (SI 1986/1033 (NI 7))	The whole Order.
Industrial Relations (Northern Ireland) Order 1987 (SI 1987/936 NI 9))	Article 3.
Finance Act 1988 (c 39)	In section 117(3), the words from "and for" to the end.
Companies (Northern Ireland) Order 1989 (SI 1989/2404 (NI 18))	The whole Order.
Insolvency (Northern Ireland) Order 1989 (SI 1989/2405 (NI 19))	In Schedule 7, in the entry relating to Article 166(4), the word "office". In Schedule 9, Part I.
European Economic Interest Groupings Regulations (Northern Ireland) 1989 (SR 1989/216)	The whole Regulations.
Companies (Northern Ireland) Order 1990 (SI 1990/593 (NI 5))	The whole Order.
Companies (No 2) (Northern Ireland) Order 1990 (SI 1990/1504 (NI 10))	Parts II to IV.
	Part VI.
	Schedules 1 to 6.
Criminal Justice Act 1993 (c 36)	In Schedule 5, Part 2.
	Schedule 6.
Financial Provisions (Northern Ireland) Order 1993 (SI 1993/1252 (NI 5))	Article 15.
Deregulation and Contracting Out Act 1994 (c 40)	Section 13(2).
	Schedule 6.
Pensions (Northern Ireland) Order 1995 (SI 1995/3213 (NI 22))	In Schedule 3, paragraph 7.
Deregulation and Contracting Out (Northern Ireland) Order 1996 (SI 1996/1632 (NI 11))	Article 11.
	Schedule 2.
	In Schedule 5, paragraph 4.
Youth Justice and Criminal Evidence Act 1999 (c 23)	In Schedule 4, paragraph 18.
Limited Liability Partnerships Act (Northern Ireland) 2002 (c 12 (NI))	The whole Act.

Short title and chapter	*Extent of repeal or revocation*
Open-Ended Investment Companies Act (Northern Ireland) 2002 (c 13)	The whole Act.
Company Directors Disqualification (Northern Ireland) Order 2002 (SI 2002/3150 (NI 4))	In Schedule 3, paragraphs 3 to 5.
Companies (Audit, Investigations and Community Enterprise) Act 2004 (c 27)	Section 11(2). In Schedule 2, paragraphs 11 to 15.
Law Reform (Miscellaneous Provisions) (Northern Ireland) Order 2005 (SI 2005/1452 (NI 7))	Article 4(2).
Companies (Audit, Investigations and Community Enterprise) (Northern Ireland) Order 2005 (SI 2005/1967 (NI 17))	The whole Order.

OTHER REPEALS

Short title and chapter	*Extent of repeal or revocation*
Limited Partnerships Act 1907 (c 24)	In section 16(1)—
	(a) the words ", and there shall be paid for such inspection such fees as may be appointed by the Board of Trade, not exceeding 5p for each inspection", and
	(b) the words from "and there shall be paid for such certificate" to the end.
	In section 17—
	(a) the words "(but as to fees with the concurrence of the Treasury)", and
	(b) paragraph (a).
Business Names Act 1985 (c 7)	The whole Act.
Companies Act 1989 (c 40)	Sections 24 to 54.
	Schedules 11 to 13.
Criminal Procedure (Consequential Provisions) (Scotland) Act 1995 (c 40)	In Schedule 4, paragraph 74(2).
Companies (Audit, Investigations and Community Enterprise) Act 2004 (c 27)	Sections 1 to 6.
	In Schedule 2, Part 1.
Civil Partnership Act 2004 (c 33)	In Schedule 27, paragraph 128.

[S1331]

NOTES

Commencement: 1 January 2007 (in part); 20 January 2007 (in part); 6 April 2007 (in part); to be appointed (otherwise) (for more detail see the notes below).

SI 2006/3428, art 7(a)–(c) (at **[7580]**) provide that this Schedule comes into force on 1 January 2007, 20 January 2007, and 6 April 2007 respectively, in so far as relating to the repeals specified in Schs 2–4 to that Order (at **[7583]**–**[7588]**).

SI 2006/3428, art 4(2) (at **[7577]**) provides that this Schedule comes into force on 6 April 2007, in so far as relating to the repeals specified in sub-paras (a)–(c) of that paragraph.

SI 2007/1093, art 5 (at **[7618]**) provides that this Schedule comes into force on 6 April 2007, in so far as relating to the repeals specified in Sch 2 to that Order (at **[7626]**).

The draft Companies Act 2006 (Commencement No 3, Consequential Amendments, Transitional Provisions and Savings) Order 2007, art 8 (see **[A12]**) provides that this Schedule comes into force on 1 October 2007 in so far as relating to the repeals specified in Sch 2 to that Order.

COMPANIES ACT 2006 EXPLANATORY NOTES

NOTES

The Explanatory Notes to the 2006 Act are not reproduced in this Edition of the *Company Law Handbook* because space is limited. They were printed in full in the Supplement to the 20th Edition of this work and are included in the CD version (which may be ordered from the LexisNexis Butterworths Customer Services Department) and can be accessed in the online version of the *Company Law Handbook* which is updated fortnightly (at www.lexisnexis.com/uk/legal).

[S1332]–[S1382]

C. Table of Origins for the Companies Act 2006

TABLE OF ORIGINS FOR THE COMPANIES ACT 2006

NOTES

1. This table shows the origin of the company law provisions of the Companies Act 2006 by reference to the enactments in force on the date that Act received Royal assent (subject to the note to the origins for Part 28). The Act received Royal Assent on 8 November 2006. Where an enactment had been amended before that date, the reference is to the text at that date; the table does not show the source of such amendments. [Editorial note: the "company law provisions of the Companies Act 2006" is defined by s 2 of the 2006 Act at **[S2]**, ie, "(a) the provisions of Parts 1 to 39 of this Act, and (b) the provisions of Parts 45 to 47 of this Act so far as they apply for the purposes of those Parts"].

2. The origin of a provision of the Companies Act 2006 in the Companies (Northern Ireland) Order 1986 is acknowledged where it makes significantly different provision in relation to Northern Ireland than in relation to England and Wales or, as the case may be, Great Britain.

3. In the table—
"1985" means the Companies Act 1985 (c 6);
"IA 1986" means the Insolvency Act 1986 (c 45);
"1986" means the Companies (Northern Ireland) Order 1986, SI 1096/1032 (NI 6);
"ICTA" means the Income and Corporation Taxes Act 1988 (c 1);
"1989" means the Companies Act 1989 (c 40).

4. The entry "drafting" indicates a new provision of a mechanical or editorial nature – for example, a provision defining an expression to avoid repetition or indicating where other relevant provisions are to be found.

5. A reference followed by "(changed)" means that the provision referred to has been re-enacted with one or more changes In general, a change is noted only in the primary context affected and not in every provision where a consequential change results The table does not show changes in the maximum penalties for offences.

6. The entry "new" indicates a provision which has no predecessor in the repealed legislation or which is fundamentally different from its predecessor.

7. The entries in the table are intended only as a general indication of what has changed and what is new. They should not be read as expressing any view as to the application or otherwise of any provision relating to enactments repealed and re-enacted.

CA 2006	*Origin*
PART 1 GENERAL INTRODUCTORY PROVISIONS	
1(1)	1985, s 735(1)(a), (b)
(2), (3)	drafting
2(1), (2)	1985, s 744 (changed)
3(1)–(4)	1985, s 1(2)
4(1), (2)	1985, s 1(3)
(3)	1985, s 1(3), 1986 art 12(3)
(4)	drafting
5(1)	1985, s 1(4)
(2)	1985, s 1(4), 1986 art 12(4)
(3)	1985, s 15(2)
6(1), (2)	drafting
PART 2 COMPANY FORMATION	
7(1), (2)	1985, s 1(1) (changed)
8(1)	new
(2)	1985, s 3(1)
9(1)	1985, s 10(1) (changed)
(2)	1985, s 2(1)(a), (b), (2), (3) (changed)
PART 2 COMPANY FORMATION	
(3)	1985, s 10(4)
(4)	new
(5)	1985, s 10(1), (6)
(6)	1985, s 10(1)
10(1)–(5)	new
11(1)	drafting
(2)	new
(3)	1985, s 2(4) (changed)
12(1)	1985, s 10(2) (changed)
(2)	new
(3), first sentence	1985, s 10(3)
(3), second sentence	new
13(1), (2)	1985, s 12(3), (3A) (changed)
14	1985, s 12(1), (2)
15(1)	1985, s 13(1)
(2)	new
(3)	1985, s 13(2)
(4)	1985, s 13(7)(a)

CA 2006	*Origin*
PART 2 COMPANY FORMATION	
16(1)	drafting
(2)	1985, s 13(3) (changed)
(3)	1985, s 13(4)
(4)	new
(5)	new
(6)	1985, s 13(5)
PART 3 A COMPANY'S CONSTITUTION	
Chapter 1 Introductory	
17	new
Chapter 2 Articles of association	
18(1)	new
(2)	1985, s 7(1) (changed)
(3)	1985, s 7(3) (changed)
(4)	1985, s 744
19(1)–(3)	1985, s 8(1), (4) (changed)
(4)	1985, s 8(3)
(5)	1985, s 8(5)
20(1), (2)	1985, s 8(2) (changed)
21(1)	1985, s 9(1)
(2), (3)	drafting
22(1)–(3)	new
23(1), (2)	new
24(1)–(4)	new
25(1)	1985, s 16(1)
(2)	1985, s 16(2)
26(1)	1985, s 18(2) (changed)
(2)	new
(3), (4)	1985, s 18(3) and Sch 24
27(1)–(5)	new
28(1)–(3)	new
Chapter 3 Resolutions and agreements affecting a company's constitution	
29(1)	1985, s 380(4) (changed)
(2)	1985, s 380(4A)
30(1)	1985, s 380(1)
(2), (3)	1985, s 380(5) and Sch 24
(4)	1985, s 380(7)
Chapter 4 Miscellaneous and supplementary provisions	
31(1)–(5)	new
32(1)	1985, s 19(1) (changed)
(2)	new

CA 2006	*Origin*
PART 3 A COMPANY'S CONSTITUTION	
Chapter 4 Miscellaneous and supplementary provisions	
(3), (4)	1985, s 19(2) (changed) and Sch 24
33(1)	1985, s 14(1) (changed)
(2)	1985, s 14(2) (changed)
34(1)	drafting
(2)	1985, s 18(1) (changed)
(3)	1985, s 18(2) (changed)
(4)	new
(5), (6)	1985, s 18(3) and Sch 24
35(1)–(5)	new
36(1), (2)	1985, s 380(2) (changed)
(3), (4)	1985, s 380(6) (changed) and Sch 24
(5)	1985, s 380(7)
37	1985, s 15(1)
38	Companies (Single Member Private Limited Companies) Regulations 1992 (SI 1992/1699) (changed)
PART 4 A COMPANY'S CAPACITY AND RELATED MATTERS	
39(1)	1985, s 35(1) (changed)
(2)	1985, s 35(4)
40(1)	1985, s 35A(1)
(2)	1985, s 35A(2) and 35B
(3)	1985, s 35A(3)
(4)	1985, s 35A(4)
(5)	1985, s 35A(5)
(6)	1985, s 35A(6)
41(1)	1985, s 322A(1), (4)
(2)	1985, s 322A(1), (2)
(3)	1985, s 322A(3)
(4)	1985, s 322A(5)
(5)	1985, s 322A(6)
(6)	1985, s 322A(7)
(7)	1985, s 322A(8)
42(1)	Charities Act 1993, s 65(1)
(2)	Charities Act 1993, s 65(2)
(3)	Charities Act 1993, s 65(3)
(4)	Charities Act 1993, s 65(4)

CA 2006	*Origin*
PART 4 A COMPANY'S CAPACITY AND RELATED MATTERS	
(5)	drafting
43(1), (2)	1985, s 36
44(1)	1985, s 36A(1)–(3)
(2)(a), (3), (4)	1985, s 36A(4)
(2)(b)	new
(5)	1985, s 36A(6) (changed)
(6)	1985, s 36A(4A)
(7)	1985, s 36A(8)
(8)	1985, s 36A(7)
45(1)	1985, s 36A(3)
(2)	1985, s 350(1)
(3)	1985, s 350(1) (changed)
(4), (5)	1985, s 350(2) and Sch 24
(6)	drafting
46(1)	1985, s 36AA(1)
(2)	1985, s 36AA(2)
47(1)	1985, s 38(1) (changed), (3)
(2)	1985, s 38(2) (changed)
48(1)	Requirements of Writing (Scotland) Act 1995 (c 7), s 15(3)
(2)	1985, s 36B(1)
(3)	1985, s 36B(2)
49(1)	1985, s 39(1) (changed)
(2)	1985, s 39(1)
(3)	1985, s 39(2), (2A)
(4)	1985, s 39(3)
(5)	1985, s 39(4)
(6)	1985, s 39(5)
50(1), (2)	1985, s 40(1)
51(1)	1985, s 36C(1)
(2)	1985, s 36C(2)
52	1985, s 37
PART 5 A COMPANY'S NAME	
Chapter 1 General requirements	
53	1985, s 26(1)(d), (e)
54(1)–(3)	1985, s 26(2)(a) and second sentence (changed)
55(1)	1985, s 26(2)(b) and 29(1)(a)
(2)	1985, s 29(6)
56(1)	1985, s 29(1)(b) (changed)

CA 2006	*Origin*
PART 5 A COMPANY'S NAME	
Chapter 1 General requirements	
(2)	1985, s 29(2)
(3), (4)	1985, s 29(3) (changed)
(5)	drafting
57(1)–(5)	new
Chapter 2 Indications of company type or legal form	
58(1)	1985, s 25(1) and 27(4)(b)
(2)	1985, s 25(1) and 27(4)(d)
(3)	drafting
59(1)	1985, s 25(2) (opening words) and 27(4)(a)
(2)	1985, s 25(2)(b) and 27(4)(c)
(3)	1985, s 25(2)(a)
(4)	drafting
60(1)(a), (b)	new
(1)(c)	drafting
(2)	1985, s 30(5B)
(3)	1985, s 30(4)
(4)	new
61(1)	1985, s 30(2), 1986 art 40(2)
(2)–(4)	1985, s 30(2), (3) (changed)
62(1)–(3)	1985, s 30(2), (3) (changed)
63(1)	1985, s 31(1)
(2), (3)	1985, s 31(5) and Sch 24
(4), (5)	new
64(1)–(3)	1985, s 31(2) first sentence
(4)	1985, s 31(2) second sentence (changed)
(5), (6)	1985, s 31(6) and Sch 24
(7)	1985, s 31(3)
65(1)–(5)	1985, s 26(1)(a), (b), (bb), (bbb) (changed)
Chapter 3 Similarity to other names	
66(1)	1985, s 26(1)(c)
(2), (3)	1985, s 26(3) (changed)
(4)–(6)	new
67(1)	1985, s 28(2)
(2)–(6)	new
68(1)	drafting
(2)	1985, s 28(2) full out

PART I COMPANIES LEGISLATION

CA 2006	Origin
PART 5 A COMPANY'S NAME	
Chapter 3 Similarity to other names	
(3)	1985, s 28(4)
(4)	1985, s 28(2) full out and (4)
(5), (6)	1985, s 28(5) and Sch 24
69(1)–(7)	new
70(1)–(6)	new
71(1)–(4)	new
72(1), (2)	new
73(1)–(6)	new
74(1)–(5)	new
Chapter 4 Other powers of the Secretary of State	
75(1), (2)	1985, s 28(3)
(3)	1985, s 28(4)
(4)	1985, s 28(3)
(5), (6)	1985, s 28(5) and Sch 24
76(1)	1985, s 32(1)
(2)	new
(3)	1985, s 32(2)
(4), (5)	1985, s 32(3)
(6), (7)	1985, s 32(4) (changed) and Sch 24
Chapter 5 Change of name	
77(1)(a)	1985, s 28(1)
(1)(b)	new
(2)	drafting
78(1)–(3)	new
79(1), (2)	new
80(1), (2)	1985, s 28(6) and 32(5) (changed)
(3)	1985, s 28(6) and 32(5)
81(1)	1985, s 28(6) and 32(5)
(2), (3)	1985, s 28(7) and 32(6)
Chapter 6 Trading disclosures	
82(1), (2)	1985, ss 348(1), 349(1), 351(1), (2), Business Names Act 1985, s 4(1) (changed)
(3)–(5)	new
83(1), (2)	Business Names Act 1985, s 5(1)
(3)	Business Names Act 1985, s 5(2)
84(1), (2)	1985, ss 348(2), 349(2), (3), 351(5), Business Names Act 1985, s 7 (changed)

CA 2006	Origin
PART 5 A COMPANY'S NAME	
Chapter 6 Trading disclosures	
(3)	new
85(1), (2)	new
PART 6 A COMPANY'S REGISTERED OFFICE	
86	1985, s 287(1)
87(1)	1985, s 287(3)
(2)	1985, s 287(4)
(3)	1985, s 287(5)
(4)	1985, s 287(6)
88(1)	drafting
(2)	1985, s 2(2)
(3), (4)	new
PART 7 RE-REGISTRATION AS A MEANS OF ALTERING A COMPANY'S STATUS	
89	drafting
90(1)	1985, s 43(1) (changed)
(2)	1985, s 43(1); drafting
(3)	1985, s 43(2)
(4)	1985, s 48(1), (2)
91(1)	1985, s 45(1)–(4)
(2)	1985, s 45(5), 1986 art 55(5)
(3)	1985, s 45(6)
(4)	1985, s 45(7)
(5)	1985, s 47(3) (changed)
92(1)	1985, s 43(3)(b), (c), (4)
(2)	1985, s 43(e)(ii)
(3), (4)	1985, s 46(2), (3)
(5), (6)	1985, s 46(4)
93(1)	1985, s 44(1)
(2)	1985, s 44(2), drafting
(3)–(5)	1985, s 44(4), (5)
(6)	1985, s 44(6), (7)(b)
(7)	1985, s 44(2), (7)(a)
94(1)	new
(2)	1985, s 43(3)(a)–(d)
(3)	1985, s 43(e)(i)
(4)	1985, s 47(2)
95(1)–(3)	new
96(1), (2)	1985, s 47(1)
(3)	new
(4), (5)	1985, s 47(4), (5)
97(1)	1985, s 53(1) (changed)
(2)	new

CA 2006	*Origin*
PART 7 RE-REGISTRATION AS A MEANS OF ALTERING A COMPANY'S STATUS	
(3)	1985, s 53(2)
98(1)	1985, s 54(1), (2)
(2)	1985, s 54(3)
(3), (4)	1985, s 54(5)
(5)	1985, s 54(6)
(6)	1985, s 54(8)
99(1), (2)	1985, s 54(4) (changed)
(3)	1985, s 54(7)
(4), (5)	1985, s 54(10), Sch 24
100(1)	new
(2)	1985, s 53(1)(b) (changed)
(3), (4)	new
101(1), (2)	1985, s 55(1)
(3)	new
(4), (5)	1985, s 55(2), (3)
102(1)	1985, s 49(1), (4), (8)(a) (changed)
(2)	1985, s 49(2)
(3)	1985, s 49(5)–(7) (changed)
(4)	1985, s 49(9)
(5)	new
103(1)	new
(2)	1985, s 49(8)(a), (c), (d)
(3), (4)	1985, s 49(8)(b), (8A) (changed)
(5)	new
104(1), (2)	1985, s 50(1)(b)
(3)	new
(4), (5)	1985, s 50(2), (3)
105(1)	1985, s 51(1) (changed)
(2)	1985, s 51(2)
(3), (4)	1985, s 51(3)
106(1)	new
(2)	1985, s 51(5) (changed)
(3)–(5)	new
107(1), (2)	1985, s 52(1)
(3)	new
(4), (5)	1985, s 52(2), (3)
108(1)–(5)	new
109(1)–(5)	new
110(1)–(5)	new
111(1)–(5)	new

CA 2006	*Origin*
PART 8 A COMPANY'S MEMBERS	
Chapter 1 The members of a company	
112(1)	1985, s 22(1) (changed)
(2)	1985, s 22(2)
Chapter 2 Register of members	
113(1), (2)	1985, s 352(1), (2)
(3), (4)	1985, s 352(3)
(5)	new
(6)	1985, s 352(4)
(7), (8)	1985, s 352(5), Sch 24
114(1)	1985, s 353(1) (changed)
(2)	1985, s 353(2)
(3)	1985, s 353(3)
(4)	1985, s 353(3), 1986 art 361(3)
(5), (6)	1985, s 353(4), Sch 24
115(1), (2)	1985, s 354(1)
(3)	1985, s 354(2)
(4)	1985, s 354(3) (changed)
(5), (6)	1985, s 354(4), Sch 24
116(1)	1985, s 356(1) (changed)
(2)	1985, s 356(3) first branch
(3), (4)	new
117(1)–(5)	new
118(1), (2)	1985, s 356(5), Sch 24 (changed)
(3)	1985, s 356(6)
119(1)–(3)	new
120(1)–(4)	new
121	1985, s 352(6) (changed)
122(1)	1985, s 355(1) (changed)
(2)	1985, s 355(4)
(3)	1985, s 355(5)
(4), (5)	1985, s 355(2), (3)
(6)	1985, s 355(4)
123(1)	new
(2), (3)	1985, s 352A(1), (2) (changed)
(4), (5)	1985, s 352A(3), Sch 24
124(1), (2)	1985, s 352(3A)
125(1)–(4)	1985, s 359(1)–(4)
126	1985, s 360
127	1985, s 361
128(1), (2)	1985, s 352(7)

CA 2006	Origin
PART 8 A COMPANY'S MEMBERS	
Chapter 3 Overseas branch registers	
129(1)	1985, s 362(1), (2) opening words
(2)	1985, Sch 14, Pt 1
(3), (4)	new
(5)	1985, s 362(2)(b), (c)
130(1)	1985, s 362(3), Sch 14, Pt 2, para 1(1), (2)
(2), (3)	1985, s 362(3), Sch 14, Pt 2, para 1(3), Sch 24
131(1)	1985, s 362(3), Sch 14, Pt 2, para 2(1)
(2), (3)	new
(4)	1985, s 362(3), Sch 14, Pt 2, para 7
132(1), (2)	1985, s 362(3), Sch 14, Pt 2, para 4(1) (changed)
(3), (4)	1985, s 362(3), Sch 14, Pt 2, para 4(2), Sch 24
133(1), (2)	1985, s 362(3), Sch 14, Pt 2, para 5
(3)	1985, s 362(3), Sch 14, Pt 2, para 8
134(1), (2)	1985, s 362(3), Sch 14, Pt 2, para 3(1) (changed)
(3)	1985, s 362(3), Sch 14, Pt 2, para 3(2)
135(1), (2)	1985, s 362(3), Sch 14, Pt 2, para 6
(3)	1985, s 362(3), Sch 14, Pt 2, para 1(1), (2)
(4), (5)	1985, s 362(3), Sch 14, Pt 2, para 1(3), Sch 24
Chapter 4 Prohibition on subsidiary being member of its holding company	
136(1)	1985, s 23(1)
(2)	drafting
137(1)	1985, s 23(4), (5)
(2)	1985, s 23(4), 1986 art 33(4)
(3), (4)	1985, s 23(6)
138(1), (2)	1985, s 23(2), Sch 2, para 4(1), (2); drafting
139(1)–(4)	1985, Sch 2, para 1(1)–(4)
(5)	1985, Sch 2, para 5(2)
(6)	1985, Sch 2, para 5(2), (3)
140(1), (2)	1985, Sch 2, para 3(1), (2)

CA 2006	Origin
PART 8 A COMPANY'S MEMBERS	
Chapter 4 Prohibition on subsidiary being member of its holding company	
(3), (4)	1985, Sch 2, para 5(2), (3)
141(1), (2)	1985, s 23(3)
141(3), (4)	1985, s 23(3A), (3B)
(5)	1985, s 23(3BA)
142(1), (2)	1985, s 23(3C)
143	1985, s 23(8)
144	1985, s 23(7)
PART 9 EXERCISE OF MEMBERS' RIGHTS	
145(1)–(4)	new
146(1)–(5)	new
147(1)–(6)	new
148(1)–(8)	new
149(1)–(3)	new
150(1)–(7)	new
151(1)–(3)	new
152(1)–(4)	new
153(1), (2)	new
PART 10 A COMPANY'S DIRECTORS	
Chapter 1 Appointment and removal of directors	
154(1)	1985, s 282(3)
(2)	1985, s 282(1) (changed)
155(1), (2)	new
156(1)–(7)	new
157(1)–(6)	new
158(1)–(5)	new
159(1)–(4)	new
160(1)–(4)	1985, s 292(1)–(4)
161(1), (2)	1985, s 285 (changed)
162(1)–(3)	1985, s 288(1) (changed)
(4)	new
(5)	1985, s 288(3)
(6)	1985, s 288(4), (6)
(7)	1985, s 288(4), Sch 24
(8)	1985, s 288(5)
163(1)	1985, s 289(1)(a) (changed)
(2)	1985, s 289(2)(a)
(3)	new
(4)	1985, s 289(2)(b) (changed)
(5)	new

CA 2006	*Origin*
PART 10 A COMPANY'S DIRECTORS	
Chapter 1 Appointment and removal of directors	
164	1985, s 289(1)(b) (changed)
165(1)–(6)	new
166(1), (2)	new
167(1), (2)	1985, s 288(2) (changed)
(3)	new
(4)	1985, s 288(4), (6)
(5)	1985, s 288(4), Sch 24
168(1)	1985, s 303(1) (changed)
(2)–(5)	1985, s 303(2)–(5)
169(1), (2)	1985, s 304(1)
(3), (4)	1985, s 304(2), (3)
(5)	1985, s 304(4) (changed)
(6)	1985, s 304(5)
Chapter 2 General duties of directors	
170(1)–(5)	new
171	new
172(1)	1985, s 309(1) (changed)
(2), (3)	new
173(1), (2)	new
174(1), (2)	new
175(1)–(7)	new
176(1)–(5)	new
177(1)–(6)	new
178(1), (2)	new
179	new
180(1)–(5)	new
181(1)–(5)	new
Chapter 3 Declaration of interest in existing transaction or arrangement	
182(1)	1985, s 317(1), (5) (changed)
(2)	1985, s 317(2) (changed)
(3)–(6)	new
183(1)	1985, s 317(7)
(2)	1985, s 317(7), Sch 24
184(1)–(5)	new
185(1), (2)	1985, s 317(3) (changed)
(3)	new
(4)	1985, s 317(4)
186(1), (2)	new
187(1)–(4)	1985, s 317(8) (changed)

CA 2006	*Origin*
PART 10 A COMPANY'S DIRECTORS	
Chapter 4 Transactions with directors requiring approval of members	
188(1)	1985, s 319(1) (changed)
(2)	1985, s 319(3) (changed)
(3)	1985, s 319(1) (changed)
(4)	1985, s 319(2) (changed)
(5)	1985, s 319(5), para 7 of Sch 15A (changed)
(6)	1985, s 319(4)
(7)	1985, s 319(7)(a)
189	1985, s 319(6)
190(1), (2)	1985, s 320(1) (changed)
(3)	new
(4)	1985, s 321(1)
(5), (6)	new
191(1)–(5)	1985, s 320(2) (changed)
192	1985, s 321(2)(a), (3) (changed)
193(1), (2)	1985, s 321(2)(b) (changed)
194(1), (2)	1985, s 321(4)
195(1)	1985, s 322(1), (3)
(2)	1985, s 322(1), (2)(a), (b)
(3)	1985, s 322(3), (4)
(4)	1985, s 322(3)
(5)	1985, s 322(4)
(6)	1985, s 322(5)
(7)	1985, s 322(6)
(8)	1985, s 322(4)
196	1985, s 322(2)(c)
197(1)	1985, s 330(2) (changed)
(2)–(5)	new
198(1)	1985, s 330(3), s 331(6)
(2)	1985, s 330(3)(a), (c) (changed)
(3)–(6)	new
199(1)	1985, s 331(3)
(2), (3)	1985, s 331(4)
200(1)	1985, s 330(3), s 331(6)
(2)	1985, s 330(3)(b), (c) (changed)
(3)–(6)	new
201(1)	1985, s 330(4), s 331(6)
(2)	1985, s 330(4) (changed)
(3)–(6)	new
202(1)	1985, s 331(7)

CA 2006	*Origin*
PART 10 A COMPANY'S DIRECTORS	
Chapter 4 Transactions with directors requiring approval of members	
(2)	1985, s 331(9)(b)
(3)	1985, s 331(8), (10)
203(1)	1985, s 330(6), (7) (changed)
(2)–(5)	new
(6)	1985, s 330(6)
204(1)	1985, s 337(1), (2) (changed)
(2)	1985, s 337(3), s 339(1), (2) (changed)
205(1)	1985, s 337A(1), (3) (changed)
(2)	1985, s 337A(4)
(3)	1985, s 337A(5)
(4)	1985, s 337A(6)
(5)	1985, s 337A(2)
206	new
207(1)	1985, s 334, s 339(1), (2) (changed)
(2)	1985, s 335(1), s 339(1), (2) (changed)
(3)	1985, s 335(2)
208(1)	1985, s 333, s 336(a) (changed)
(2)	1985, s 336(b) (changed)
209(1)	1985, s 338(1), (3)
(2)	1985, s 338(2)
(3), (4)	1985, s 338(6) (changed)
210(1)	1985, s 339(1)
(2)	1985, s 339(2)
(3)	1985, s 339(2), (3)
(4)	1985, s 339(2), (3)
(5)	1985, s 339(5)
211(1)	1985, s 339(6) and, s 340(1)
(2)	1985, s 340(2)
(3)	1985, s 340(3)
(4)	1985, s 340(6)
(5)	1985, s 340(4)
(6)	1985, s 340(5)
(7)	1985, s 340(7) (changed)
212	1985, s 331(9)(a)–(d)
213(1), (2)	1985, s 341(1)
(3), (4)	1985, s 341(2)
(5)	1985, s 341(3)

CA 2006	*Origin*
PART 10 A COMPANY'S DIRECTORS	
Chapter 4 Transactions with directors requiring approval of members	
(6)	1985, s 341(4)
(7)	1985, s 341(5)
(8)	1985, s 341(3)
214	new
215(1)	1985, s 312, s 313(1), s 314(1) (changed)
(2)–(4)	new
216(1), (2)	1985, s 316(2) (changed)
217(1)	1985, s 312
(2)	new
(3)	1985, s 312 (changed)
(4)	new
218(1)	1985, s 313(1)
(2)	new
(3)	1985, s 313(1) (changed)
(4)	new
(5)	1985, s 316(1)
219(1)	1985, s 314(1), s 315(1)(b) (changed)
(2)	1985, s 315(1)(b)
(3), (4)	new
(5)	1985, s 315(3)
(6)	new
(7)	1985, s 316(1)
220(1)	1985, s 316(3) (changed)
(2)–(5)	new
221(1)–(4)	new
222(1)	new
(2)	1985, s 313(2)
(3)	1985, s 315(1)
(4), (5)	new
223(1)	1985, s 319(6), 320(3), 330(5)
(2)	new
224(1) and (2)	new
225(1)–(3)	new
226	new
Chapter 5 Directors' service contracts	
227	new
228(1)	1985, s 318(1)
(2)	1985, s 318(2), (3) (changed)
(3)	new
(4)	1985, s 318(4)

CA 2006	Origin
PART 10 A COMPANY'S DIRECTORS	
Chapter 5 Directors' service contracts	
(5)	1985, s 318(8) (changed)
(6)	1985, s 318(8), Sch 24
(7)	1985, s 318(10)
229(1)	1985, s 318(7)
(2)	new
(3)	1985, s 318(8) (changed)
(4)	1985, s 318(8), Sch 24
(5)	1985, s 318(9) (changed)
230	1985, s 318(6)
Chapter 6 Contracts with sole members who are directors	
231(1)	1985, s 322B(1), (2) (changed)
(2)	1985, s 322B(1)
(3)	1985, s 322B(4) (changed)
(4)	1985, s 322B(4), Sch 24
(5)	1985, s 322B(3)
(6)	1985, s 322B(6)
(7)	1985, s 322B(5)
Chapter 7 Directors' liabilities	
232(1)	1985, s 309A(1), (2)
(2)	1985, s 309A(1), (3) (changed)
(3)	1985, s 309A(6)
(4)	new
233	1985, s 309A(5)
234(1)	1985, s 309A(4)
(2)	1985, s 309B(1), (2)
(3)	1985, s 309B(3), (4)
(4)	1985, s 309B(5)
(5)	1985, s 309B(6), (7)
(6)	1985, s 309B(4)(c)
235(1)–(6)	new
236(1)	1985, s 309C(1) (changed)
(2), (3)	1985, s 309C(2)
(4), (5)	1985, s 309C(3)
237(1)	1985, s 309C(4), (5)
(2)	1985, s 309C(5), s 318(1)
(3)	1985, s 309C(5), s 318(2), (3) (changed)
(4)	new
(5)	1985, s 309C(5), s 318(4)

CA 2006	Origin
PART 10 A COMPANY'S DIRECTORS	
Chapter 7 Directors' liabilities	
(6)	1985, s 309C(5), s 318(8) (changed).
(7)	1985, s 309C(5), s 318(8), Sch 24
(8)	1985, s 309C(5), s 318(10)
(9)	new
238(1)	1985, s 309C(5), s 318(7)
(2)	new
(3)	1985, s 309C(5), s 318(8) (changed)
(4)	1985, s 309C(5), 1985, s 318(8), Sch 24
(5)	1985, s 309C(5), s 318(9) (changed)
239(1)–(7)	new
Chapter 8 Directors' residential addresses: protection from disclosure	
240(1)–(3)	new
241(1), (2)	new
242(1)–(3)	new
243(1)–(8)	new
244(1)–(4)	new
245(1)–(6)	new
246(1)–(7)	new
Chapter 9 Supplementary provisions	
247(1)	1985, s 719(1)
(2)	1985, s 719(2) (changed)
(3)	new
(4)	1985, s 719(3)
(5)	1985, s 719(3) (changed)
(6)	1985, s 719(3)
(7)	1985, s 719(4) (changed)
248(1)	1985, s 382(1)
(2)	new
(3)	1985, s 382(5) (changed)
(4)	1985, s 382(5), Sch 24
249(1)	1985, s 382(2)
(2)	1985, s 382(4)
250	1985, s 741(1)
251(1), (2)	1985, s 741(2)
(3)	1985, s 741(3)
252(1)	1985, s 346(1)
(2)	1985, s 346(2), (3) (changed)
(3)	1985, s 346(2)

CA 2006	*Origin*
PART 10 A COMPANY'S DIRECTORS	
Chapter 9 Supplementary provisions	
253(1)	drafting
(2)	1985, s 346(2), (3) (changed)
(3)	new
254(1)	1985, s 346(1)
(2)	1985, s 346(4)
(3)	1985, s 346(7)
(4)	1985, s 346(8)
(5)	1985, s 346(4)
(6)	1985, s 346(6)
255(1)	1985, s 346(1)
(2)	1985, s 346(5)
(3)	1985, s 346(7)
(4)	1985, s 346(8)
(5)	1985, s 346(5)
(6)	1985, s 346(6)
256	new
257(1), (2)	new
258(1)	1985, s 345(1)
(2)	1985, s 345(2)
(3)	1985, s 345(3)
259	1985, s 347
PART 11 DERIVATIVE CLAIMS AND PROCEEDINGS BY MEMBERS	
Chapter 1 Derivative claims in England and Wales or Northern Ireland	
260(1)–(5)	new
261(1)–(4)	new
262(1)–(5)	new
263(1)–(7)	new
264(1)–(5)	new
Chapter 2 Derivative proceedings in Scotland	
265(1)–(7)	new
266(1)–(5)	new
267(1)–(5)	new
268(1)–(6)	new
269(1)–(5)	new
PART 12 COMPANY SECRETARIES	
270(1), (2)	new
(3)	1985, s 283(3) (changed)
271	1985, s 283(1) (changed)
272(1)–(7)	new
273(1), (2)	1985, s 286(1) (changed)
(3)	1985, s 286(2)

CA 2006	*Origin*
PART 12 COMPANY SECRETARIES	
274	1985, s 283(3) (changed)
275(1)–(3)	1985, s 288(1) (changed)
(4)	new
(5)	1985, s 288(3)
(6)	1985, s 288(4), (6)
(7)	1985, s 288(4), Sch 24
(8)	1985, s 288(5)
276(1), (2)	1985, s 288(2)
(3)	1985, s 288(4), (6) (changed)
(4)	1985, s 288(4), Sch 24
277(1)	1985, s 290(1)(a) (changed)
(2)	1985, s 289(2)(a), s 290(3)
(3)	new
(4)	1985, s 289(2)(b), s 290(3) (changed)
(5)	new
278(1)	1985, s 290(1)(b) (changed)
(2)	1985, s 290(2)
279(1), (2)	new
280	1985, s 284
PART 13 RESOLUTIONS AND MEETINGS	
Chapter 1 General provisions about resolutions	
281(1)–(4)	new
282(1)–(5)	new
283(1)	1985, s 378(1), (2) (changed)
(2), (3)	new
(4)	1985, s 378(1), (2) (changed)
(5)	1985, s 378(1), (2), (5) (changed)
(6)	1985, s 378(2) (changed)
284(1)	1985, s 370(6)
(2)	Table A, para 54 (changed)
(3)	1985, s 370(6), Table A, para 54 (changed)
(4)	1985, s 370(1), Table A, para 54
285(1)–(3)	new
286(1)–(3)	Table A, para 55
287	new

CA 2006	*Origin*
PART 13 RESOLUTIONS AND MEETINGS	
Chapter 2 Written resolutions	
288(1)	new
(2)	1985, s 381A(7), Sch 15A, para 1
(3)	new
(4)	1985, s 381A(1) (changed)
(5)	1985, s 381A(4)
289(1)	1985, s 381A(1) (changed)
(2)	new
290	new
291(1)–(7)	new
292(1)–(6)	new
293(1)–(7)	new
294(1), (2)	new
295(1), (2)	new
296(1)	1985, s 381A(2) (changed)
(2)–(4)	new
297(1), (2)	new
298(1), (2)	new
299(1), (2)	new
300	1985, s 381C(1)
Chapter 3 Resolutions at meetings	
301	1985, s 378(6) (changed)
302	Table A, para 37
303(1)	1985, s 368(1)
(2)	1985, s 368(1), (2), (2A)
(3)	1985, s 368(2) (changed)
(4)	1985, s 368(3) (changed)
(5)	new
(6)	1985, s 368(3) (changed)
304(1)	1985, s 368(4), (8)
(2), (3)	new
(4)	1985, s 368(7)
305(1)	1985, s 368(4)
(2)	new
(3)	1985, s 368(4)
(4)	1985, s 368(5)
(5)	new
(6), (7)	1985, s 368(6)
306(1), (2)	1985, s 371(1)
(3), (4)	1985, s 371(2)
(5)	1985, s 371(3)

CA 2006	*Origin*
PART 13 RESOLUTIONS AND MEETINGS	
Chapter 3 Resolutions at meetings	
307(1)	new
(2)	1985, s 369(1), (2) (changed)
(3)	1985, s 369(1), (2)
(4)	1985, s 369(3) (changed)
(5), (6)	1985, s 369(4) (changed)
(7)	drafting
308	1985, s 369(4A), (4B) (changed)
309(1)	1985, s 369(4B)
(2)	1985, s 369(4C) (changed)
(3)	1985, s 369(4B)(d)
310(1)	1985, s 370(2), Table A, para 38 (changed)
(2)	Table A, para 38 (changed)
(3)	new
(4)	1985, s 370(1), Table A, para 38
311(1), (2)	Table A, para 38
312(1)	1985, s 379(1)
(2)	1985, s 379(2)
(3)	1985, s 379(2) (changed)
(4)	1985, s 379(3)
313(1), (2)	1985 Table A, para 39 (changed)
314(1)	1985, s 376(1)(b)
(2), (3)	1985, s 376(2) (changed)
(4)	1985, s 376(1), s 377(1)(a) (changed)
315(1)	1985, s 376(3), (5)
(2)	1985, s 376(1)
(3)	1985, s 376(7)
(4)	1985, s 376(7), Sch 24
316(1)	new
(2)	1985, s 376(1), s 377(1)(b) (changed)
317(1)	1985, s 377(3) (changed)
(2)	1985, s 377(3)
318(1)	1985, s 370A
(2)	1985, s 370(1), (4) (changed)
(3)	1985, s 370A (changed)
319(1)	1985, s 370(5)
(2)	1985, s 370(1)

CA 2006	Origin
PART 13 RESOLUTIONS AND MEETINGS	
Chapter 3 Resolutions at meetings	
320(1)	1985, s 378(4), Table A, para 47
(2)	Table A, para 47
(3)	1985, s 378(4), Table A, paras 47 and 48 (changed)
321(1)	1985, s 373(1)(a)
(2)	1985, s 373(1)(b) (changed)
322	1985, s 374
323(1)	1985, s 375(1)(a)
(2), (3)	1985, s 375(2) (changed)
(4)	new
324(1)	1985, s 372(1) (changed)
(2)	1985, s 372(2)(b) (changed)
325(1)	1985, s 372(3) (changed)
(2)	new
(3)	1985, s 372(4)
(4)	1985, s 372(4), Sch 24
326(1), (2)	1985, s 372(6)
(3)	1985, s 372(6) (changed)
(4)	1985, s 372(6), Sch 24
327(1)	1985, s 372(5)
(2)	1985, s 372(5) (changed)
(3)	new
328(1), (2)	new
329(1)	1985, s 373(2)
(2)	1985, s 373(2) (changed)
330(1)–(7)	Table A, para 63 (changed)
331	new
332	1985, s 381
333(1)–(4)	new
334(1)–(3)	1985, s 125(6) (changed)
(4)	1985, s 125(6)(a)
(5)	new
(6)	1985, s 125(6)(b)
(7)	1985, s 125(7), (8)
335(1)–(6)	new
Chapter 4 Public companies: additional requirements for AGMs	
336(1)	1985, s 366(1) (changed)
(2)	new
(3)	1985, s 366(4) (changed)

CA 2006	Origin
PART 13 RESOLUTIONS AND MEETINGS	
Chapter 4 Public companies: additional requirements for AGMs	
(4)	1985, s 366(4), Sch 24
337(1)	1985, s 366(1)
(2)	1985, s 369(3)(a)
338(1)	1985, s 376(1)(b)
(2)	new
(3)	1985, s 376(2) (changed)
(4)	1985, s 376(1), s 377(1)(a), (2) (changed)
339(1)	1985, s 376(3), (5)
(2)	1985, s 376(1)
(3)	1985, s 376(6)
(4)	1985, s 376(7)
(5)	1985, s 376(7), Sch 24
340(1)	new
(2)	1985, s 376(1), s 377(1)(b) (changed)
Chapter 5 Additional requirements for quoted companies	
341(1)–(6)	new
342(1)–(4)	new
343(1)–(6)	new
344(1)–(4)	new
345(1)–(6)	new
346(1)–(5)	new
347(1)–(4)	new
348(1)–(4)	new
349(1)–(5)	new
350(1)–(5)	new
351(1)–(5)	new
352(1), (2)	new
353(1)–(5)	new
354(1)–(4)	new
Chapter 6 Records of resolutions and meetings	
355(1)	1985, s 382(1), s 382A(1) (changed)
(2)	new
(3)	1985, s 382(5) (changed)
(4)	1985, s 382(5), Sch 24
356(1)	drafting
(2), (3)	1985, s 382A(2)
(4)	1985, s 382(2)
(5)	1985, s 382(4)

CA 2006	Origin
PART 13 RESOLUTIONS AND MEETINGS	
Chapter 6 Records of resolutions and meetings	
357(1), (2)	1985, s 382B(1)
(3)	1985, s 382B(2)
(4)	1985, s 382B(2), Sch 24
(5)	1985, s 382B(3)
358(1)	1985, s 383(1) (changed)
(2)	new
(3)	1985, s 383(1)
(4)	1985, s 383(3) (changed)
(5)	1985, s 383(4) (changed)
(6)	1985, s 383(4), Sch 24
(7)	1985, s 383(5)
359	new
Chapter 7 Supplementary provisions	
360(1), (2)	new
361	new
PART 14 CONTROL OF POLITICAL DONATIONS AND EXPENDITURE	
362	1985, s 347A(1) (changed)
363(1)	1985, s 347A(6), (7)(a), (9)
(2)	1985, s 347A(6)(b), (7)(b), (c) (changed)
(3)	new
(4)	drafting
364(1)	drafting
(2)	1985, s 347A(4)
(3)	new
(4)	new
365(1)	1985, s 347A(5) (changed)
(2)	new
366(1)	1985, s 347C(1) (changed)
(2)	1985, s 347C(1), 347D(1), (2), (3) (changed)
(3)	1985, s 347D(3) (changed)
(4)	new
(5)	1985, s 347A(10), s 347C(1), s 347D(2), (3)
(6)	1985, s 347C(6), s 347D(9)
367(1), (2)	new

CA 2006	Origin
PART 14 CONTROL OF POLITICAL DONATIONS AND EXPENDITURE	
(3)	1985, s 347C(2), s 347D(4) (changed)
(4)	new
(5)	1985, s 347C(4), s 347D(6)
(6)	1985, s 347C(2), s 347D(4) (changed)
(7)	new
368(1)	1985, s 347C(3)(b), s 347D(5)
(2)	1985, s 347C(3), s 347D(5)
369(1)	1985, s 347F(1)
(2)	1985, s 347F(2), (3), (4)
(3)	1985, s 347F(2), (6) (changed)
(4)	new
(5)	1985, s 347F(3)
(6)	1985, s 347F(5)
370(1)	1985, s 347I(1) (changed)
(2)	1985, s 347I(1)
(3)	1985, s 54(2), s 347I(2) (changed)
(4)	1985, s 347I(3)
(5)	new
371(1)	1985, s 347I(3)
(2)	1985, s 347I(4), (5)
(3)	1985, s 347I(6)
(4)	1985, s 347I(7)
(5)	1985, s 347I(8)
372(1)	1985, s 347J(1)
(2)	1985, s 347J(2)
(3)	1985, s 347J(3)
(4)	1985, s 347J(4), (5)
(5)	1985, s 347J(6)
373(1)	1985, s 347K(1)
(2)	1985, s 347K(2)
374(1)–(3)	new
375(1)	1985, s 347B(1)
(2)	1985, s 347B(2) (changed)
376(1), (2)	1985, s 347B(3)
377(1)	1985, s 347B(8)
(2)	1985, s 347B(10)
(3)	1985, s 347B(9)
(4)	1985, s 347B(11)

PART I COMPANIES LEGISLATION

CA 2006	Origin
PART 14 CONTROL OF POLITICAL DONATIONS AND EXPENDITURE	
378(1)	1985, ss 347B(4), (6), (7) (changed)
(2)	new
(3)	1985, s 347B(5)
379(1)	1985, s 347A(3), (8)
(2)	1985, s 347A(10)
PART 15 ACCOUNTS AND REPORTS	
Chapter 1 Introduction	
380(1)–(4)	drafting
381	drafting
382(1)	1985, s 247(1)(a)
(2)	1985, s 247(1)(b), (2)
(3), (4)	1985, s 247(3), (4)
(5)	1985, s 247(5) (changed)
(6)	1985, s 247(6), Sch 4, para 56(2), (3)
(7)	drafting
383(1)	1985, s 247A(3)
(2)	1985, s 249(1)(a)
(3)	1985, s 249(1)(b), (2)
(4)	1985, s 249(3)
(5), (6)	1985, s 249(4)
(7)	1985, s 249(5), (6)
384(1)	1985, s 247A(1)–(1B)
(2)	1985, s 247A(2) (changed)
(3)	1985, s 247A(2A)
385(1)	new
(2)	1985, s 262(1) "quoted company"
(3)	drafting
(4)–(6)	new
Chapter 2 Accounting records	
386(1), (2)	1985, s 221(1)
(3)–(5)	1985, s 221(2)–(4)
387(1), (2)	1985, s 221(5)
(3)	1985, s 221(6), Sch 24
388(1)–(3)	1985, s 222(1)–(3)
(4), (5)	1985, s 222(5)
389(1), (2)	1985, s 222(4)
(3)	1985, s 222(6)
(4)	1985, s 222(4), (6), Sch 24
Chapter 3 A company's financial year	
390(1)–(5)	1985, s 223(1)–(5)

CA 2006	Origin
PART 15 ACCOUNTS AND REPORTS	
Chapter 3 A company's financial year	
391(1)	1985, s 224(1)
(2)	1985, s 224(2), (3)
(3)	1986 art 232(2), (3)
(4)	1985, s 224(3A), 1986 art 232(3A)
(5)–(7)	1985, s 224(4)–(6)
392(1)	1985, s 225(1)
(2)–(6)	1985, s 225(3)–(7)
Chapter 4 Annual accounts	
393(1), (2)	new
394	1985, s 226(1)
395(1)–(5)	1985, s 226(2)–(6)
396(1), (2)	1985, s 226A(1), (2)
(3)	1985, s 226A(3) (changed)
(4)	1985, s 226A(4)
(5)	1985, s 226A(5), (6)
397	1985, s 226B
398	1985, ss 227(8), 248(1) (changed)
399(1), (2)	1985, ss 227(1), (8), 248(1), (2) (changed)
(3)	1985, s 227(8)
(4)	new
400(1), (2)	1985, s 228(1), (2)
(3)	1985, s 228(5)
(4)	1985, s 228(3)
(5)	1985, s 228(4)
(6)	1985, s 228(6)
401(1), (2)	1985, s 228A(1), (2)
(3)	1985, s 228A(5)
(4)	1985, s 228A(3)
(5)	1985, s 228A(4)
(6)	1985, s 228A(6)
402	1985, s 229(5)
403(1)–(6)	1985, s 227(2)–(7)
404(1), (2)	1985, s 227A(1), (2)
(3)	1985, s 227A(3) (changed)
(4)	1985, s 227A(4)
(5)	1985, s 227A(5), (6)
405(1), (2)	1985, s 229(1), (2)
(3), (4)	1985, s 229(3)
406	1985, s 227B
407(1)–(5)	1985, s 227C(1)–(5)

CA 2006	Origin
PART 15 ACCOUNTS AND REPORTS	
Chapter 4 Annual accounts	
408(1)	1985, s 230(1) (changed)
(2)	1985, s 230(2) (changed)
(3), (4)	1985, s 230(3), (4)
409(1), (2)	1985, s 231(1), (2) (changed)
(3), (4)	1985, s 231(3) (changed)
(5)	1985, s 231(4)
410(1), (2)	1985, s 231(5)
(3)	1985, s 231(6)
(4), (5)	1985, s 231(7), Sch 24
411(1)	1985, ss 231A(1), 246(3)(b)(ai)
(2)	1985, s 231A(5)
(3)–(5)	1985, s 231A(2)–(4)
(6)	1985, s 231A(7), Sch 4, para 94(1), (2)
(7)	1985, s 231A(6)
412(1)–(4)	new
(5)	1985, s 232(3)
(6)	1985, s 232(4), Sch 24
413(1)–(8)	new
414(1), (2)	1985, s 233(1), (2)
(3)	1985, s 246(8)
(4), (5)	1985, s 233(5) (changed), Sch 24
Chapter 5 Directors' report	
415(1)	1985, s 234(1)
(2), (3)	1985, s 234(2), (3)
(4), (5)	1985, s 234(5), Sch 24
416(1)	1985, s 234ZZA(1)(a), (b)
(2)	1985, s 234ZZA(2)
(3)	1985, ss 234ZZA(1)(c), 246(4)(a)
(4)	1985, s 234ZZA(3), (4) (changed)
417(1)	1985, ss 234(1)(a), 246(4)(a)
(2)	new
(3), (4)	1985, s 234ZZB(1), (2)
(5)	new
(6)	1985, s 234ZZB(3), (5)
(7)	1985, s 246A(2A)
(8)	1985, s 234ZZB(4)
(9)	1985, s 234ZZB(6)
(10), (11)	new

CA 2006	Origin
PART 15 ACCOUNTS AND REPORTS	
Chapter 5 Directors' report	
418(1)	1985, s 234ZA(1)
(2)	1985, ss 234(1)(b), 234ZA(2)
(3), (4)	1985, s 234ZA(3), (4)
(5), (6)	1985, s 234ZA(6), Sch 24
419(1)	1985, s 234A(1)
(2)	1985, s 246(8)(b)
(3), (4)	1985, ss 234(5), 234A(4) (changed), Sch 24
Chapter 6 Quoted companies: directors' remuneration report	
420(1)	1985, s 421(1)
(2)	1985, s 234B(3), (4) (changed)
(3)	1985, s 234B(3), Sch 24
421(1), (2)	1985, s 234B(1), (2) (changed)
(3)	1985, s 234B(5), (6)
(4)	1985, s 234B(6), Sch 24
422(1)	1985, s 234C(1)
(2), (3)	1985, s 234C(4) (changed), Sch 24
Chapter 7 Publication of accounts and reports	
423(1)	1985, s 238(1), (1A)
(2), (3)	new
(4)	1985, s 238(3)
(5)	1985, s 238(6)
(6)	drafting
424(1)–(3)	1985, s 238(1) (changed)
(4)	1985, s 238(4) (changed)
(5)	new
(6)	drafting
425(1), (2)	1985, s 238(5), Sch 24
426(1)	1985, s 251(1)
(2), (3)	1985, s 251(2)
(4)	drafting
(5)	new
(6)	1985, s 251(5)
427(1)	1985, s 251(1) "summary financial statement"
(2)	1985, s 251(3)
(3)	1985, s 251(3A)
(4)	1985, s 251(4)
(5)	new
(6)	1985, s 251(5)

CA 2006	Origin
PART 15 ACCOUNTS AND REPORTS	
Chapter 7 Publication of accounts and reports	
428(1)	1985, s 251(1) "summary financial statement"
(2)	1985, s 251(3)
(3)	1985, s 251(3A)
(4)	1985, s 251(4)
(5)	new
(6)	1985, s 251(5)
429(1), (2)	1985, s 251(6), Sch 24
430(1)–(7)	new
431(1), (2)	1985, s 239(1), (2)
(3), (4)	1985, s 239(3), Sch 24
432(1), (2)	1985, s 239(1), (2)
(3), (4)	1985, s 239(3), Sch 24
433(1)–(3)	1985, ss 233(3), 234A(2) and 234C(2)
(4), (5)	1985, ss 233(6)(a), 234A(4)(a) and 234C(4)(a), Sch 24
434(1)	1985, s 240(1) (changed)
(2)	1985, s 240(2) (changed)
(3)	1985, s 240(5)
(4), (5)	1985, s 240(6), Sch 24
(6)	1985, s 251(7)
435(1), (2)	1985, s 240(3) (changed)
(3)	1985, s 240(5) (changed)
(4)	new
(5), (6)	1985, s 240(6), Sch 24
(7)	1985, s 251(7)
436(1), (2)	1985, ss 233(3), 234A(2), 234C(2), 240(4) (changed)
Chapter 8 Public companies: laying of accounts and reports before general meeting	
437(1)	1985, s 241(1) (changed)
(2)	1985, s 241(2)
(3)	drafting
438(1)–(3)	1985, s 241(2)–(4)
(4)	1985, s 241(2), Sch 24
Chapter 9 Quoted companies: members' approval of directors' remuneration report	
439(1)	1985, s 241A(1), (3)
(2)	1985, s 241A(4)
(3)	1985, s 241A(5), (7)
(4)	1985, s 241A(6)

CA 2006	Origin
PART 15 ACCOUNTS AND REPORTS	
Chapter 9 Quoted companies: members' approval of directors' remuneration report	
(5)	1985, s 241A(8)
(6)	1985, s 241A(2), (12)
440(1)	1985, s 241A(9)
(2), (3)	1985, s 241A(10), (11)
(4)	1985, s 241A(9), (10), Sch 24
(5)	1985, s 241A(2), (12)
Chapter 10 Filing of accounts and reports	
441(1)	1985, s 242(1)
(2)	drafting
442(1)	drafting
(2), (3)	1985, s 244(1), (2) (changed)
(4), (5)	1985, s 244(4), (5)
(6)	new
(7)	1985, s 244(6)
443(1)–(5)	new
444(1)	1985, ss 242(1)(a), (b), 246(5)
(2)	1985, ss 242(1)(d), 249E(1)(b) (changed)
(3)	1985, s 246(5), (6) (changed)
(4)	1985, s 247B(2)
(5)	1985, s 246(8)
(6)	1985, ss 233(4), 234A(3), 246(7)
(7)	1985, s 236(3)
445(1)	1985, ss 242(1)(a), (b), 246A(1)
(2)	1985, ss 242(1)(d), 249E(1)(b) (changed)
(3)	1985, s 246A(2), (3) (changed)
(4)	1985, s 247B(2)
(5)	1985, ss 233(4), 234A(3) (changed)
(6)	new
(7)	drafting
446(1)	1985, s 242(1)(a), (b)
(2)	1985, ss 242(1)(d), 249E(1)(b)
(3)	1985, ss 233(4), 234A(3) (changed)
(4)	new
(5)	drafting

CA 2006	*Origin*
PART 15 ACCOUNTS AND REPORTS	
Chapter 10 Filing of accounts and reports	
447(1)	1985, s 242(1)(a), (b), (c)
(2)	1985, ss 242(1)(d)
(3)	1985, ss 233(4), 234A(3), 234C(3) (changed)
(4)	new
448(1)–(3)	1985, s 254(1)–(3)
(4)	1985, s 254(4)
(5)	1985, s 244(6)
449(1)–(5)	1985, s 247B(1)–(5)
450(1), (2)	1985, ss 233(1), (2), 246(7)
(3)	1985, s 246(8), 246A(4)
(4), (5)	1985, s 233(5), Sch 24
451(1)	1985, s 242(2)
(2), (3)	1985, s 242(4), (5)
(4)	1985, s 242(2), Sch 24
452(1), (2)	1985, s 242(3)
453(1)	1985, s 242A(1)
(2)	1985, s 242A(2) (changed)
(3), (4)	1985, s 242A(3), (4)
(5)	new
Chapter 11 Revision of defective accounts and reports	
454(1)–(3)	1985, s 245(1)–(3)
(4)	1985, s 245(4) (changed)
(5)	1985, s 245(5)
455(1), (2)	1985, s 245A(1)
(3)–(5)	1985, s 245A(2)–(4)
456(1)–(3)	1985, s 245B(1)–(3)
(4)	1985, s 245B(3A)
(5)–(8)	1985, s 245B(4)–(7)
457(1)	1985, s 245C(1)
(2), (3)	1985, s 245C(2), (3)
(4)	1985, s 245C(4B)
(5)	1985, s 245C(1A), (4A)
(6)	1985, s 245C(5)
(7)	1985, s 245C(4)
458(1)	1985, s 245D(1), (3)
(2)	1985, s 245D(2)
(3)	1985, s 245E(1), (2)
(4)	1985, s 245E(3), (4) (changed)
(5)	1985, s 245E(3), Sch 24
459(1)–(8)	1985, s 245F(1)–(8)

CA 2006	*Origin*
PART 15 ACCOUNTS AND REPORTS	
Chapter 11 Revision of defective accounts and reports	
460(1), (2)	1985, s 245G(1), (2)
(3)	drafting; 1985, s 245G(3), (10)
(4)	1985, s 245G(7)(a), (8)
(5)	1985, s 245G(7)(b), Sch 24
461(1)	1985, s 245G(3)
(2)	1985, s 245G(3)(a)
(3)	1985, s 245G(3)(b), Sch 7B, Pt 1
(4)	1985, s 245G(3)(c), Sch 7B, Pt 2
(5), (6)	1985, s 245G(3)(d), Sch 7B, Pt 3
(7)	1985, s 245G(11)
462(1)–(3)	1985, s 245G(4)–(6)
Chapter 12 Supplementary provisions	
463(1)–(6)	new
464(1), (2)	1985, s 256(1), (2)
(3)	1985, s 256(4)
465(1)	1985, s 247(1)(a)
(2)	1985, s 247(1)(b), (2)
(3), (4)	1985, s 247(3), (4)
(5)	1985, s 247(5) (changed)
(6)	1985, s 247(6), Sch 4, para 56(2), (3)
(7)	drafting
466(1)	1985, s 247A(3)
(2)	1985, s 249(1)(a)
(3)	1985, s 249(1)(b), (2)
(4)	1985, s 249(3)
(5), (6)	1985, s 249(4)
(7)	1985, s 249(5), (6)
467(1)	1985, s 247A(1)–(1B)
(2)	1985, s 247A(2)
(3)	1985, s 247A(2A)
468(1)–(5)	new
469(1)–(4)	1985, s 242B(1)–(4) (changed)
470(1)	1985, s 255D(1)
(2)	1985, s 255D(2), (2A)
(3)	1985, s 255D(5)
(4)	1985, s 255D(4)
471(1)	1985, s 262(1) "annual accounts"

CA 2006	*Origin*
PART 15 ACCOUNTS AND REPORTS	
Chapter 12 Supplementary provisions	
(2), (3)	1985, s 238(1A); drafting
472(1), (2)	1985, s 261(1), (2)
473(1)–(4)	1985, s 257(2), (3) (changed)
474(1)	1985, ss 262(1), 744 "regulated activity"
(2)	1985, s 262(2)
PART 16 AUDIT	
Chapter 1 Requirement for audited accounts	
475(1)	1985, s 235(1) (changed)
(2), (3)	1985, s 249B(4)
(4)	1985, s 249B(5)
476(1)–(3)	1985, s 249B(2)
477(1)	1985, s 249A(1)
(2)	1985, s 249A(3)
(3)	1985, s 249A(6)
(4)	1985, s 249A(3)(a), (7)
(5)	drafting
478	1985, s 249B(1)(a)–(e)
479(1)–(3)	1985, s 249B(1)(f), (1A)–(1C)
(4)	drafting
(5), (6)	1985, s 249B(1)(C)
480(1), (2)	1985, s 249AA(1), (2)
(3)	drafting
481	1985, s 249AA(3)
482(1)–(4)	new
483(1)–(5)	new
484(1)	1985, s 257(1)
484(2)	1985, s 257(4)(c)
484(3)	1985, s 257 (2)(b), (d)
484(4)	1985, s 257 (3)
Chapter 2 Appointment of auditors	
485(1)	1985, s 384(1)
(2)–(5)	new
486(1), (2)	1985, s 387(1), (2)
(3), (4)	1985, s 387(2), Sch 24
487(1)–(4)	new
488(1)–(3)	new
489(1)	1985, s 384(1) (changed)
(2)	1985, ss 384(2), 385(2)
(3)	1985, ss 385(3), 388(1) (changed)

CA 2006	*Origin*
PART 16 AUDIT	
Chapter 2 Appointment of auditors	
(4)	1985, s 385(2), (4) (changed)
(5)	drafting
490(1), (2)	1985, s 387(1), (2)
(3), (4)	1985, s 387(2), Sch 24
491(1)	1985, s 385(2) (changed)
(2)	drafting
492(1)	1985, s 390A(1)
(2), (3)	1985, s 390A(2)
(4), (5)	1985, s 390A(4), (5)
493(1)–(4)	new
494(1)	1985, s 390B(1), (8)
(2)–(4)	1985, s 390B(2)–(4)
(5)	1985, s 390B(5)(a)
(6)	1985, s 390B(9)
Chapter 3 Functions of auditor	
495(1)	1985, s 235(1); drafting
(2)	1985, s 235(1A)
(3)	1985, s 235(1B), (2)
(4)	1985, s 235(2A)
496	1985, s 235(3)
497(1), (2)	1985, s 235(4), (5)
498(1)–(4)	1985, s 237(1)–(4)
(5)	1985, s 237(4A)
499(1), (2)	1985, s 389A(1), (2)
(3)	1985, s 389A(6)
(4)	1985, s 389A(7)
500(1)–(3)	1985, s 389A(3)–(5)
(4)	1985, s 389A(6)
(5)	1985, s 389A(7)
501(1)	1985, s 389B(1)
(2)	1985, s 389B(1), Sch 24
(3)	1985, s 389B(2), (3) (changed)
(4)	1985, s 389B(4)
(5)	1985, s 389B(4), Sch 24
(6)	1985, s 389B(5)
502(1)	1985, s 390(2)
(2)	1985, s 390(1)
(3)	1985, s 390(3)
503(1), (2)	1985, s 236(1)
(3)	new
504(1)–(4)	new

CA 2006	*Origin*
PART 16 AUDIT	
Chapter 3 Functions of auditor	
505(1), (2)	1985, s 236(2) (changed)
(3), (4)	1985, s 236(4), Sch 24
506(1), (2)	new
507(1)–(4)	new
508(1)–(4)	new
509(1)–(4)	new
Chapter 4 Removal, resignation, etc of auditors	
510(1), (2)	1985, s 391(1); drafting
(3)	1985, s 391(3)
(4)	drafting
511(1)	1985, s 391A(1)(a)
(2)–(6)	1985, s 391A(2)–(6)
512(1)	1985, s 391(2)
(2), (3)	1985, s 391(2), Sch 24
513(1), (2)	1985, s 391(4)
514(1)–(8)	new
515(1)	1985, s 391A(1)(b)
(2)	1985, s 391A(1) opening words (changed)
(3)–(7)	1985, s 391A(2)–(6)
516(1), (2)	1985, s 392(1)
(3)	1985, s 392(2)
517(1)	1985, s 392(3)
(2), (3)	1985, s 392(3), Sch 24
518(1)–(4)	1985, s 392A(1)–(4)
(5)	1985, s 392A(5)
(6), (7)	1985, s 392(5), Sch 24
(8)–(10)	1985, s 392A(6)–(8)
519(1)–(3)	1985, s 394(1) (changed)
(4)	1985, s 394(2) (changed)
(5), (6)	1985, s 394A(1), (2)
(7)	1985, s 394(1), Sch 24
520(1)	drafting
(2), (3)	1985, s 394(3), (4)
(4)	1985, s 394(6)
(5)	1985, s 394(7) (changed)
(6)	1985, s 394A(4)
(7)	new
(8)	1985, s 394A(4), Sch 24 (changed)
521(1)	1985, s 394(5)
(2)	1985, s 394(7)
(3), (4)	1985, s 394A(1), (2)

CA 2006	*Origin*
PART 16 AUDIT	
Chapter 4 Removal, resignation, etc of auditors	
(5)	1985, s 394A(1), Sch 24
522(1)–(8)	new
523(1)–(6)	new
524(1)–(4)	new
525(1)–(3)	new
526	1985, s 388(2)
Chapter 5 Quoted companies: right of members to raise audit concerns at accounts meeting	
527(1)–(6)	new
528(1)–(5)	new
529(1)–(4)	new
530(1), (2)	new
531(1), (2)	new
Chapter 6 Auditors' liability	
532(1)	1985, s 310(1) (changed)
(2)	1985, s 310(2), drafting
(3)	1985, s 310(1)
(4)	new
533	1985, s 310(3)(b)
534(1)–(3)	new
535(1)–(5)	new
536(1)–(5)	new
537(1)–(3)	new
538(1)–(3)	new
Chapter 7 Supplementary provisions	
539	1985, ss 262(1)
PART 17 A COMPANY'S SHARE CAPITAL	
Chapter 1 Shares and share capital of a company	
540(1)	1985, s 744 ("share")
(2), (3)	new
(4)	1985, s 744 ("share"), drafting
541	1985, s 182(1)(a)
542(1)–(5)	new
543(1), (2)	1985, s 182(2)
544(1), (2)	1985, s 182(1)(b)
(3)	drafting
545	new
546(1), (2)	new
547	1985, s 737(1), (2)

CA 2006	*Origin*
PART 17 A COMPANY'S SHARE CAPITAL	
Chapter 1 Shares and share capital of a company	
548	1985, s 744 ("equity share capital")
Chapter 2 Allotment of shares: general provisions	
549(1)	1985, s 80(1), (2) (changed)
(2), (3)	1985, s 80(2)
(4)	1985, s 80(9)
(5)	1985, s 80(9), Sch 24
(6)	1985, s 80(10) (changed)
550	new
551(1)	1985, s 80(1), (2)
(2)	1985, s 80(3)
(3)	1985, s 80(4)
(4)	1985, s 80(4), (5)
(5)	1985, s 80(5)
(6)	1985, s 80(6)
(7)	1985, s 80(7)
(8)	1985, s 80(8)
(9)	drafting
552(1)	1985, s 98(1)
(2)	1985, s 98(2)
(3)	1985, s 98(3)
553(1)	1985, s 97(1)
(2)	1985, s 97(2)(a)
(3)	1985, s 98(4)
554(1)–(5)	new
555(1)	1985, s 88(1)
(2)	1985, s 88(2) (changed)
(3), (4)	new
556(1)	1985, s 128(1), (2) (changed)
(2), (3)	1985, s 128(1)
(4)	1985, s 128(2)
557(1)	1985, s 88(5), s 128(5) (changed)
(2)	1985, s 88(5), s 128(5), Sch 24
(3)	1985, s 88(6) (changed)
558	1985, s 738(1)
559	1985, s 80(2)(a)
Chapter 3 Allotment of equity securities: existing shareholders' right of pre-emption	
560(1)	1985, s 94(2), (5)

CA 2006	*Origin*
PART 17 A COMPANY'S SHARE CAPITAL	
Chapter 3 Allotment of equity securities: existing shareholders' right of pre-emption	
(2)	1985, s 94(3), (3A)
561(1)	1985, s 89(1)
(2)	1985, s 89(4)
(3)	1985, s 94(3)
(4)	1985, s 89(6)
(5)	drafting
562(1)	1985, s 90(1)
(2)	new
(3)	1985, s 90(5) (changed)
(4)	1985, s 90(6)
(5)	1985, s 90(6) (changed)
(6), (7)	new
563(1), (2)	1985, s 92(1)
(3)	1985, s 92(2)
564	1985, s 94(2)
565	1985, s 89(4)
566	1985, s 89(5)
567(1), (2)	1985, s 91(1)
(3), (4)	1985, s 91(2)
568(1)	1985, s 89(2), (3)
(2)	1985, s 89(3)
(3)	1985, s 90(1)
(4)	1985, s 92(1)
(5)	1985, s 92(2)
569(1), (2)	new
570(1), (2)	1985, s 95(1)
(3)	1985, s 95(3)
(4)	1985, s 95(4)
571(1), (2)	1985, s 95(2)
(3)	1985, s 95(3)
(4)	1985, s 95(4)
(5), (6)	1985, s 95(5)
(7)	1985, s 95(5), Sch 15A, para 3(1), (2)
572(1), (2)	1985, s 95(6)
(3)	1985, s 95(6), Sch 24
573(1)	1985, s 95(2A)
(2)	1985, s 95(1), (2A)
(3)	1985, s 95(1), (2A), (4)
(4)	1985, s 95(2), (2A)
(5)	1985, s 95(1), (2A), (4), (5), Sch 15A, para 3(1), (2)

CA 2006	Origin
PART 17 A COMPANY'S SHARE CAPITAL	
Chapter 3 Allotment of equity securities: existing shareholders' right of pre-emption	
574(1), (2)	1985, s 94(7)
575(1)	1985, s 93(1)
(2)	1985, s 93(2)
576(1)	1985, s 96(1), (2)
(2)	1985, s 96(3)
(3)	1985, s 96(4)
577	1985, s 94(2)
Chapter 4 Public companies: allotment where issue not fully subscribed	
578(1)	1985, s 84(1)
(2)	1985, s 84(2)
(3)	1985, s 84(3) (changed)
(4)	1985, s 84(4)
(5)	1985, s 84(4), (5)
(6)	1985, s 84(6)
579(1), (2)	1985, s 85(1)
(3)	1985, s 85(2)
(4)	1985, s 85(3)
Chapter 5 Payment for shares	
580(1)	1985, s 100(1)
(2)	1985, s 100(2)
581	1985, s 119
582(1)	1985, s 99(1)
(2)	1985, s 99(4)
(3)	1985, s 99(1)
583(1)	drafting
(2)–(3)(d)	1985, s 738(2)
(3)(e), (4)	new
(4)	new
(5)	1985, s 738(3)
(6)	1985, s 738(4)
(7)	new
584	1985, s 106
585(1)	1985, s 99(2)
(2)	1985, s 99(3)
(3)	1985, s 99(5)
586(1)	1985, s 101(1)
(2)	1985, s 101(2)
(3)	1985, s 101(3), (4)
(4)	1985, s 101(5)
587(1)	1985, s 102(1)
(2)	1985, s 102(2)

CA 2006	Origin
PART 17 A COMPANY'S SHARE CAPITAL	
Chapter 5 Payment for shares	
(3)	1985, s 102(3), (4)
(4)	1985, s 102(5), (6)
(5)	1985, s 102(7)
588(1)	1985, s 112(1), (5)(a)
(2)	1985, s 112(3)
(3)	1985, s 112(4)
(4)	1985, s 112(5)(b)
589(1), (2)	1985, s 113(1)
(3)	1985, s 113(2), (3) (changed)
(4)	1985, s 113(4)
(5)	1985, s 113(5)
(6)	1985, s 113(6), (7)
590(1)	1985, s 114
(2)	1985, s 114., Sch 24
591(1), (2)	1985, s 115(1)
592(1), (2)	1985, s 107
Chapter 6 Public companies: independent valuation of non-cash consideration	
593(1)	1985, s 103(1)
(2)	1985, s 103(2)
(3)	1985, s 103(6)
(4)	drafting
594(1)–(3)	1985, s 103(3)
(4), (5)	1985, s 103(4)
(6)	1985, s 103(7)
595(1), (2)	1985, s 103(5)
(3)	1985, s 103(7)(b)
596(1)	drafting
(2)	1985, s 108(4)
(3)	1985, s 108(6)
(4), (5)	1985, s 108(7)
597(1), (2)	1985, s 111(1)
(3), (4)	1985, s 111(3), Sch 24
(5), (6)	1985, ss 88(6), 111(3)
598(1)	1985, s 104(1)
(2)	1985, s 104(2)
(3)	drafting
(4)	1985, s 104(6)(a)
(5)	1985, s 104(6)(b)
599(1)	1985, s 104(4)(a), (b), (d)
(2)	1985, s 104(5)(a)
(3)	1985, s 104(4)(d)

PART I COMPANIES LEGISLATION

CA 2006	Origin
PART 17 A COMPANY'S SHARE CAPITAL	
Chapter 6 Public companies: independent valuation of non-cash consideration	
(4)	1985, s 104(5)(b)
600(1)	drafting
(2)	1985, s 109(2)(a), (b)
(3)	1985, s 108(6)(a), (b), (c), 109(2)(c), (d)
(4), (5)	1985, s 109(3)
601(1), (2)	1985, s 104(4)(c), (d)
(3)	1985, s 104(4)(c) (changed)
602(1)	1985, s 111(2)
(2), (3)	1985, s 111(4), Sch 24
603	1985, s 104(3)
604(1)	1985, s 105(1)
(2)	1985, s 105(2)
(3)	1985, s 105(3)
605(1)	1985, s 112(1)
(2)	1985, s 112(2)
(3)	1985, s 112(3)
(4)	1985, s 112(4)
606(1)	1985, s 113(1)
(2)	1985, s 113(2), (3) (changed)
(3)	1985, s 113(4)
(4)	1985, s 113(5)
(5)	1986, s 113(6), (7)
(6)	1986, s 113(8)
607(1)	drafting
(2)	1985, s 114
(3)	1985, s 114, Sch 24
608(1), (2)	1985, s 115(1)
609(1), (2)	1985, s 107
Chapter 7 Share premiums	
610(1)	1985, s 130(1)
(2), (3)	1985, s 130(2) (changed)
(4)	1985, s 130(3)
(5), (6)	1985, s 130(4)
611(1)	1985, s 132(1)
(2)	1985, s 132(2)
(3)	1985, s 132(3)
(4)	1985, s 132(4)
(5)	1985, s 132(5)
612(1)	1985, s 131(1)
(2)	1985, s 131(2)

CA 2006	Origin
PART 17 A COMPANY'S SHARE CAPITAL	
Chapter 7 Share premiums	
(3)	1985, s 131(3)
(4)	1985, s 131(1), 132(8)
613(1)	drafting
(2), (3)	1985, s 131(4)
(4)	1985, s 131(5)
(5)	1985, s 131(6)
614(1)	1985, s 134(1)
(2)	1985, s 134(3)
615	1985, s 133(1)
616(1)	1985, s 131(7), 133(4)
(2)	1985, s 133(2)
(3)	1985, s 133(3)
Chapter 8 Alteration of share capital	
617(1)	1985, s 121(1) (changed)
(2)	1985, s 121(2)(a) (changed)
(3)	1985, s 121(2)(b), (c), (d) (changed)
(4), (5)	new
618(1)	1985, s 121(2)(b), (d)
(2)	1985, s 121(3) (changed)
(3)	1985, s 121(4) (changed)
(4), (5)	new
619(1)	1985, s 122(1)(a), (d)
(2), (3)	1985, s 122(1) (changed)
(4)	1985, s 122(2)
(5)	1985, s 122(2), Sch 24
620(1)	1985, s 121(2)(c) (changed)
(2)	1985, s 121(4) (changed)
(3)	new
621(1)	1985, s 122(1)(c)
(2), (3)	new
(4)	1985, s 122(2)
(5)	1985, s 122(2), Sch 24
622(1)–(8)	new
623	new
624(1)–(3)	new
625(1)–(5)	new
626(1)–(6)	new
627(1)–(8)	new
628(1)–(3)	new
Chapter 9 Classes of share and class rights	
629(1)	new

CA 2006	Origin
PART 17 A COMPANY'S SHARE CAPITAL	
Chapter 9 Classes of share and class rights	
(2)	1985, s 128(2)
630(1)	1985, s 125(1)
(2)–(4)	1985, s 125(2) (changed)
(5)	1985, s 125(7)
(6)	1985, s 125(8)
631(1)–(6)	new
632	1985, s 126 (changed)
633(1)	1985, s 127(1)(b)
(2)	1985, s 127(2), (2A)
(3)	1985, s 127(2)
(4)	1985, s 127(3)
(5)	1985, s 127(4)
(6)	1985, s 127(6)
634(1)–(6)	new
635(1)–(3)	1985, s 127(5)
636(1)	1985, s 128(4) (changed)
(2)	1985, s 128(5)
(3)	1985, s 128(5), Sch 24
637(1)	1985, s 128(3) (changed)
(2)	1985, s 128(5)
(3)	1985, s 128(5), Sch 24
638(1)	1985, s 129(1) (changed)
(2)	1985, s 129(4)
(3)	1985, s 129(4), Sch 24
639(1)	1985, s 129(3) (changed)
(2)	1985, s 129(4)
(3)	1985, s 129(4), Sch 24
640(1)	1985, s 129(2) (changed)
(2)	1985, s 129(4)
(3)	1985, s 129(4), Sch 24
Chapter 10 Reduction of share capital	
641(1)–(3)	1985, s 135(1) (changed)
(4)	1985, s 135(2)
(5), (6)	new
642(1)–(4)	new
643(1)–(5)	new
644(1)–(9)	new
645(1)	1985, s 136(1)
(2)	1985, s 136(2), (6)
(3)	1985, s 136(6)
(4)	1985, s 136(2)
646(1)	1985, s 136(3)
(2), (3)	1985, s 136(4)

CA 2006	Origin
PART 17 A COMPANY'S SHARE CAPITAL	
Chapter 10 Reduction of share capital	
(4), (5)	1985, s 136(5)
647(1)	1985, s 141 (changed)
(2)	1985, s 141, Sch 24
648(1), (2)	1985, s 137(1)
(3)	1985, s 137(2)(b)
(4)	1985, s 137(2)(a), (3)
649(1)	1985, s 138(1) (changed)
(2)	new
(3)	1985, s 138(2) (changed)
(4)	1985, s 138(3) (changed)
(5)	1985, s 138(4) (changed)
(6)	1985, s 138(4)
650(1)	1985, s 139(1)
(2)	1985, s 139(2)
(3)	drafting
651(1), (2)	1985, s 139(3)
(3)	1985, s 139(4) (changed)
(4)	1985, s 139(5)
(5)	new
(6)	1985, s 139(5)(a)
(7)	1985, s 139(5)(b)
652(1)	1985, s 140(1) (changed)
(2)	drafting
(3)	1985, s 140(5)
653(1)	1985, s 140(2)
(2)	1985, s 140(3)
(3)	1985, s 140(4)
(4)	drafting
Chapter 11 Miscellaneous and supplementary provisions	
654(1)–(3)	new
655	1985, s 111A
656(1)–(3)	1985, s 142(1)
(4)	1985, s 142(2) (changed)
(5)	1985, s 142(2), Sch 24
(6)	1985, s 142(3)
657(1)–(4)	new
PART 18 ACQUISITION BY LIMITED COMPANY OF ITS OWN SHARES	
Chapter 1 General provisions	
658(1)	1985, s 143(1)
(2)	1985, s 143(2)
(3)	1985, s 143(2), Sch 24

CA 2006	Origin
PART 18 ACQUISITION BY LIMITED COMPANY OF ITS OWN SHARES	
Chapter 1 General provisions	
659(1), (2)	1985, s 143(3)
660(1), (2)	1985, s 144(1) (changed)
(3)	1985, s 145(1), (2)(a)
661(1), (2)	1985, s 144(2) (changed)
(3)	1985, s 144(3)
(4)	1985, s 144(4)
(5)	1985, s 145(2)(a)
662(1)	1985, s 146(1)
(2)	1985, s 146(2)
(3)	1985, s 146(2), (3)
(4)	1985, s 147(1)
(5), (6)	1985, s 146(4)
663(1)	1985, s 122(1)(f)
(2), (3)	new
(4)	1985, s 122(2)
(5)	1985, s 122(2), Sch 24
664(1), (2)	1985, s 147(2) (changed)
(3)	new
(4)	1985, s 147(3) (changed)
(5), (6)	new
665(1), (2)	1985, s 147(4)
(3)	new
(4)	1985, s 147(4)(a) (changed)
(5)	1985, s 147(4)(b)
666(1), (2)	1985, s 149(1)
667(1), (2)	1985, s 149(2)
(3)	1985, s 149(2), Sch 24
668(1), (2)	1985, s 148(1)
(3)	1985, s 148(2)
669(1), (2)	1985, s 148(4)
670(1)	1985, s 150(1)
(2)	1985, s 150(2)
(3)	1985, s 150(3)
(4)	1985, s 150(4)
671	1985, s 145(3), s 146(1), s 148(3)
672(1)	1985, Sch 2, para 1(1)
(2)	1985, Sch 2, para 1(2)
(3)	1985, Sch 2, para 1(3)
(4)	1985, Sch 2, para 1(4)
(5)	1985, Sch 2, para 2(3)
(6)	1985, Sch 2, para 2(4)

CA 2006	Origin
PART 18 ACQUISITION BY LIMITED COMPANY OF ITS OWN SHARES	
Chapter 1 General provisions	
673(1)	1985, Sch 2, para 3(1)(a), (2)
(2)	1985, Sch 2, para 3(1)(b), (2)(a)
674	1985, Sch 2, para 4(1), (3)
675(1), (2)	1985, Sch 2, para 5(1), (2)
676	1985, Sch 2, para 5(1), (3)
Chapter 2 Financial assistance for purchase of own shares	
677(1)	1985, s 152(1)(a)
(2), (3)	1985, s 152(2)
678(1)	1985, s 151(1) (changed)
(2)	1985, s 153(1)
(3)	1985, s 151(2) (changed)
(4)	1985, s 153(2)
(5)	drafting
679(1)	1985, s 151(1) (changed)
(2)	1985, s 153(1) (changed)
(3)	1985, s 151(2) (changed)
(4)	1985, s 153(2) (changed)
(5)	drafting
680(1)	1985, s 151(3)
(2)	1985, s 151(3), Sch 24
681(1), (2)	1985, s 153(3)
682(1)	1985, s 153(4), s 154(1)
(2)	1985, s 153(4)
(3), (4)	1985, s 154(2)
(5)	1985, s 153(5)
683(1)	1985, s 152(1)(b), (c)
(2)	1985, s 152(3)
Chapter 3 Redeemable shares	
684(1)	1985, s 159(1) (changed)
(2)	new
(3)	1985, s 159(1) (changed)
(4)	1985, s 159(2)
685(1)–(4)	new
686(1)–(3)	1985, s 159(3) (changed)
687(1)–(3)	1985, s 160(1)
(4), (5)	1985, s 160(2)
(6)	1985, s 160(1)
688	1985, s 160(4) (changed)

CA 2006	*Origin*
PART 18 ACQUISITION BY LIMITED COMPANY OF ITS OWN SHARES	
Chapter 3 Redeemable shares	
689(1)	1985, s 122(1)(e)
(2), (3)	new
(4)	1985, s 122(2)
(5)	1985, s 122(2), Sch 24
Chapter 4 Purchase of own shares	
690(1)	1985, s 162(1) (changed)
(2)	1985, s 162(3)
691(1), (2)	1985, s 159(3), s 162(2)
692(1), (2)	1985, s 160(1), s 162(2)
(3), (4)	1985, s 160(2), s 162(2)
(5)	1985, s 160(1), s 162(2)
693(1)	1985, s 164(1), s 166(1)
(2)	1985, s 163(1)
(3)	1985, s 163(2)
(4)	1985, s 163(3)
(5)	1985, s 163(4), (5)
694(1)	1985, s 164(1)
(2)	1985, s 164(2), s 165(2) (changed)
(3)	1985, s 165(1)
(4)	1985, s 164(3), 165(2)
(5)	1985, s 164(4), 165(2)
(6)	drafting
695(1)	1985, s 164(5), 165(2)
(2)	1985, Sch 15A, para 5(1), (2)
(3), (4)	1985, s 164(5), s 165(2)
696(1)	1985, s 164(6), s 165(2)
(2)	1985, s 164(6), s 165(2), Sch 15A, para 5(3), (4)
(3)–(5)	1985, s 164(6), s 165(2)
697(1), (2)	1985, s 164(7)
(3)	1985, s 164(3), (7)
(4)	1985, s 164(4), (7)
(5)	drafting
698(1)	1985, s 164(5), (7)
(2)	1985, Sch 15A, para 5(1), (2)
(3), (4)	1985, s 164(5), (7)
699(1)	1985, s 164(6), (7)
(2)	1985, s 164(6), (7), Sch 15A, para 5(3)
(3)–(6)	1985, s 164(6), (7)
700(1), (2)	1985, s 167(2)

CA 2006	*Origin*
PART 18 ACQUISITION BY LIMITED COMPANY OF ITS OWN SHARES	
Chapter 4 Purchase of own shares	
(3)	1985, s 164(3), (7), s 167(2)
(4)	1985, s 164(4), (7), s 167(2)
(5)	1985, s 164(5), (6), (7), s 167(2)
701(1)	1985, s 166(1)
(2)	1985, s 166(2)
(3)	1985, s 166(3)(a), (b)
(4)	1985, s 166(4)
(5)	1985, s 166(3)(c), (4)
(6)	1985, s 166(5)
(7)	1985, s 166(6)
(8)	1985, s 166(7)
702(1)–(4)	1985, s 169(4) (changed)
(5)	new
(6)	1985, s 169(5)
(7)	1985, s 169(9)
703(1)	1985, s 169(7) (changed)
(2)	1985, s 169(7), Sch 24
(3)	1985, s 169(8)
704	1985, s 167(1)
705(1)	1985, s 168(1)
(2)	1985, s 168(2)
706	1985, s 160(4), s 162(2), (2B)
707(1)–(3)	1985, s 169(1), (1A), (1B) (changed)
(4)	1985, s 169(2)
(5)	1985, s 169(3)
(6)	1985, s 169(6)
(7)	1985, s 169(6), Sch 24
708(1)	1985, s 169(1), (1A), (1B) (changed)
(2), (3)	new
(4)	1985, s 169(6)
(5)	1985, s 169(6), Sch 24
Chapter 5 Redemption or purchase by private company out of capital	
709(1)	1985, s 171(1) (changed)
(2)	1985, s 171(2)
710(1), (2)	1985, s 171(3)
711(1), (2)	1985, s 172(1)
712(1)	drafting
(2)	1985, s 172(2)

CA 2006	Origin
PART 18 ACQUISITION BY LIMITED COMPANY OF ITS OWN SHARES	
Chapter 5 Redemption or purchase by private company out of capital	
(3)	1985, s 172(4)
(4)	1985, s 172(5)
(5)	drafting
(6)	1985, s 172(3)
(7)	1985, s 172(6)
713(1), (2)	1985, s 173(1)
714(1)–(3)	1985, s 173(3) (changed)
(4)	1985, s 173(4) (changed)
(5), (6)	1985, s 173(5) (changed)
715(1)	1985, s 173(6)
(2)	1985, s 173(6), Sch 24
716(1)	1985, s 173(2)
(2)	1985, s 174(1)
(3)	drafting
717(1)	drafting
(2)	1985, Sch 15A, para 6(1), (2)
(3)	1985, s 174(2)
(4)	1985, s 174(3), (5)
718(1)	drafting
(2)	1985, s 174(4), Sch 15A, para 6(1), (3)
(3)	1985, s 174(4)
719(1)	1985, s 175(1)
(2)	1985, s 175(2)
(3)	1985, s 175(3)
(4)	1985, s 175(4), (5)
720(1)	1985, s 175(4), (6)(a)
(2)	1985, s 175(6)(a) (changed)
(3)	new
(4)	1985, s 175(6)(b)
(5)	1985, s 175(7) (changed)
(6)	1985, s 175(7), Sch 24
(7)	1985, s 175(8)
721(1)	1985, s 176(1)
(2)	1985, s 176(1), (2)
(3)	1985, s 177(1)
(4), (5)	1985, s 177(2)
(6)	1985, s 177(3)
(7)	1985, s 177(4)
722(1)	new
(2)	1985, s 176(3)(a)

CA 2006	Origin
PART 18 ACQUISITION BY LIMITED COMPANY OF ITS OWN SHARES	
Chapter 5 Redemption or purchase by private company out of capital	
(3)	1985, s 176(3)(b)
(4)	1985, s 176(4)
(5)	1985, s 176(4), Sch 24
723(1)	1985, s 174(1)
(2)	drafting
Chapter 6 Treasury shares	
724(1)	1985, s 162(2B)
(2)	1985, s 162(4)
(3)	1985, s 162A(1)
(4)	1985, s 162A(2)
(5)	1985, s 162A(3)
725(1)	1985, s 162B(1)
(2)	1985, s 162B(2)
(3)	1985, s 162B(3)
(4)	1985, s 143(2A)
726(1)	1985, s 162C(1)
(2)	1985, s 162C(2), (3)
(3)	1985, s 162C(4)
(4)	1985, s 162C(5)
(5)	1985, s 162C(6)
727(1)	1985, s 162D(1)(a), (b)
(2)	1985, s 162D(2) (changed)
(3)	1985, s 162D(3)
(4), (5)	new
728(1)	1985, s 169A(1)(b)(ii), (2)
(2)	1985, s 169A(2)
(3)	1985, s 169A(3)
(4)	1985, s 169A(4)
(5)	1985, s 169A(4), Sch 24
729(1)	1985, s 162D(1)(c)
(2)	1985, s 162E(1)
(3)	1985, s 162E(2)
(4)	1985, s 162D(4)
(5)	1985, s 162D(5)
730(1)	1985, s 169A(1)(b)(i), (2)
(2)	1985, s 169A(2)
(3)	1985, s 169A(3)
(4), (5)	new
(6)	1985, s 169A(4)
(7)	1985, s 169A(4), Sch 24
731(1)	1985, s 162F(1)

CA 2006	*Origin*
PART 18 ACQUISITION BY LIMITED COMPANY OF ITS OWN SHARES	
Chapter 6 Treasury shares	
(2)	1985, s 162F(2)
(3)	1985, s 162F(3)
(4)	1985, s 162F(4), (5)
732(1)	1985, s 162G (changed)
(2)	1985, s 162G
Chapter 7 Supplementary provisions	
733(1), (2)	1985, s 170(1)
(3)	1985, s 170(2), (3)
(4)	1985, s 170(1)
(5), (6)	1985, s 170(4)
734(1)	drafting
(2)	1985, s 171(4)
(3)	1985, s 171(5)
(4)	1985, s 171(6)
735(1)	1985, s 178(1)
(2)	1985, s 178(2), (3)
(3)	1985, s 178(3)
(4)	1985, s 178(4)
(5)	1985, s 178(5)
(6)	1985, s 178(6)
736	1985, s 181(a)
737(1)–(4)	new
PART 19 DEBENTURES	
738	1985, s 744 ("debenture")
739(1), (2)	1985, s 193
740	1985, s 195
741(1)–(4)	new
742	1985, s 197
743(1)	new
(2)	1985, s 190(5) (changed)
(3)	1985, s 190(6)
(4), (5)	new
(6)	1985, s 190(1), (5)
744(1)	1985, s 191(1)
(2)	1985, s 191(2)
(3), (4)	new
(5)	1985, s 191(6)
(6)	new
745(1)–(5)	new
746(1)	1985, s 191(4) (changed)
(2)	1985, s 191(4), Sch 24
(3)	1985, s 191(5)
747(1)–(3)	new

CA 2006	*Origin*
PART 19 DEBENTURES	
748(1)	1985, s 191(7) (changed)
(2)	1985, s 191(7)
749(1)	1985, s 191(3)
(2)	1985, s 191(4)
(3)	1985, s 191(4), Sch 24
(4)	1985, s 191(5)
750(1)	1985, s 192(1)
(2)	1985, s 192(2)
(3)	1985, s 192(1)
751(1)	1985, s 192(3)
(2)	1985, s 192(3), 1986 art 201(3)
(3), (4)	1985, s 192(4)
752(1)	1985, s 194(1)
(2)	1985, s 194(2)
(3)	1985, s 194(4)
(4)	1985, s 194(5)
753	1985, s 194(3)
754(1)	1985, s 196(1)
(2)	1985, s 196(2)
(3)	1985, s 196(3)
(4)	1985, s 196(4)
PART 20 PUBLIC AND PRIVATE COMPANIES	
Chapter 1 Prohibition of public offers by private companies	
755(1)	1985, s 81(1) (changed)
(2)	1985, s 58(3)
(3), (4)	new
(5)	drafting
756(1), (2)	1985, s 742A(1)
(3)	1985, s 742A(2)
(4)	1985, s 742A(3), (4), and (5)
(5)	1985, s 742A(3)(a), (6)(b) (changed)
(6)	1985, s 742A(6)(a)
757(1)–(3)	new
758(1)–(4)	new
759(1)–(5)	new
760	1985, s 81(3)
Chapter 2 Minimum share capital requirement for public companies	
761(1)	1985, s 117(1)
(2)	1985, s 117(2) (changed)
(3)	1985, s 117(4)

CA 2006	Origin
PART 20 PUBLIC AND PRIVATE COMPANIES	
Chapter 2 Minimum share capital requirement for public companies	
(4)	1985, s 117(6) (changed)
762(1)	1985, s 117(3) (changed)
(2)	new
(3)	1985, s 117(5)
763(1)	1985, s 118(1) (changed)
(2)–(6)	new
764(1)	1985, s 118(1) (changed)
(2)	new
(3)	1985, s 118(2)
(4)	1985, s 118(3)
765(1)–(4)	new
766(1)–(6)	new
767(1)	1985, s 117(7)
(2)	1985, s 117(7), Sch 24
(3)	1985, s 117(8)
(4)	new
PART 21 CERTIFICATION AND TRANSFER OF SECURITIES	
Chapter 1 Certification and transfer of securities: general	
768(1)	1985, s 186(1)(a)
(2)	1985, s 186(1)(b), (2)
769(1)	1985, s 185(1)(a)
(2)	1985, s 185(1), (4)(a), (b)
(3)	1985, s 185(5)
(4)	1985, s 185(5), Sch 24
770(1)	1985, s 183(1)
(2)	1985, s 183(2)
771(1)–(6)	new
772	1985, s 183(4)
773	1985, s 183(3)
774	1985, s 187
775(1), (2)	1985, s 184(1)
(3)	1985, s 184(2)
(4)	1985, s 184(3)
776(1)	1985, s 185(1)(b)
(2)	1985, s 185(2)
(3)	1985, s 185(1), (4)(c)
(4)	drafting
(5)	1985, s 185(5)
(6)	1985, s 185(5), Sch 24
777(1), (2)	1985, s 185(3)
778(1)	1985, s 185(4), (4A)

CA 2006	Origin
PART 21 CERTIFICATION AND TRANSFER OF SECURITIES	
Chapter 1 Certification and transfer of securities: general	
(2)	1985, s 185(4B), (4C)
(3)	1985, s 185(4D)
779(1)	1985, s 188(1)
(2)	1985, s 188(2)
(3)	1985, s 188(3)
780(1)–(4)	new
781(1)	1985, s 189(1)
(2)	1985, s 189(2)
(3)	1985, s 189(1), Sch 24
(4)	1985, s 189(2), Sch 24
782(1)	1985, s 185(6)
(2), (3)	1985, s 185(7)
Chapter 2 Evidencing and transfer of title to securities without written instrument	
783	1989, s 207(1), (10)
784(1), (2)	new
(3)	1989, s 207(9)
785(1)	1989, s 207(1)
(2)	1989, s 207(2)
(3)	1989, s 207(3)
(4)	1989, s 207(4)
(5)	1989, s 207(5)
(6)	1989, s 207(6)
786(1)–(5)	new
787(1)–(3)	new
788	1989, s 207(7)
789	new
790	new
PART 22 INFORMATION ABOUT INTERESTS IN A COMPANY'S SHARES	
791	new
792(1)	1985, s 198(2) (changed)
(2)	1985, s 198(2)(b)
793(1), (2)	1985, s 212(1) (changed)
(3)	1985, s 212(2)(a)
(4)	1985, s 212(2)(b)
(5)	1985, s 212(3)
(6)	1985, s 212(2)(c)
(7)	1985, s 212(4)
794(1)	1985, s 216(1)
(2)	1985, s 216(1B)
(3)	1985, s 216(1A)
(4)	drafting

CA 2006	*Origin*
PART 22 INFORMATION ABOUT INTERESTS IN A COMPANY'S SHARES	
795(1)	1985, s 216(3)
(2)	1985, s 216(4)
(3)	1985, s 216(3), Sch 24
796(1), (2)	1985, s 216(5)
797(1)	1985, s 454(1)
(2)	1985, s 454(2)
(3)	1985, s 454(3)
(4)	1985, s 454(2), (3)
798(1), (2)	1985, s 455(1)
(3)	1985, s 455(2)
(4)	1985, s 455(2), Sch 24
(5)	1985, s 455(1), (2)
799(1)	1985, s 456(1A)
(2)	1985, s 456(2)
(3)	1985, s 456(1A)
800(1)	1985, s 456(1)
(2)	1985, s 456(2)
(3)	1985, s 456(3)
(4)	1985, s 456(6)
(5)	1985, s 456(7)
801(1), (2)	1985, s 456(4)
(3), (4)	1985, s 456(5)
(5)	1985, s 457(3)
802(1), (2)	1985, s 457(1)
(3)	1985, s 457(2)
(4)	1985, s 457(3)
803(1), (2)	1985, s 214(1) (changed)
(3)	1985, s 214(2) (changed)
804(1)	1985, s 214(4)
(2)	1985, s 214(5) (changed)
(3)	1985, s 214(5), Sch 24
805(1)	1985, s 215(1), (3)
(2)	1985, s 215(2)
(3)	1985, s 215(2), (3)
(4)	1985, s 215(7) (changed)
(5)	new
(6)	1985, s 215(5)
(7)	1985, s 215(6)
806(1), (2)	new
(3)	1985, s 215(8) (changed)
(4)	1985, s 215(8), Sch 24
807(1)	1985, s 215(7)(b), s 219(1)

CA 2006	*Origin*
PART 22 INFORMATION ABOUT INTERESTS IN A COMPANY'S SHARES	
(2)	1985, s 215(7)(b), s 219(2)
(3)	1985, s 215(7)(b), s 219(3)
(4)	1985, s 215(7)(b), s 219(3), Sch 24
(5)	1985, s 215(7)(b), s 219(4)
808(1)	1985, s 213(1)
(2)	1985, s 211(3), s 213(1), (3)
(3)	1985, s 213(1) (changed)
(4)	1985, s 211(5), s 213(3)
(5)	1985, s 211(10), s 213(3)
(6)	1985, s 211(10), s 213(3), Sch 24
(7)	1985, s 211(4), s 213(3)
809(1)	1985, s 211(8), s 213(3) (changed)
(2), (3)	1985, s 211(8), s 213(3), s 325(5), Sch 13, para 27
(4), (5)	new
810(1)–(3)	1985, s 211(6), s 213(3)
(4)	1985, s 211(8), s 213(3)
(5), (6)	new
811(1)	1985, s 211(8)(b), s 213(3), s 219(1)
(2)	1985, s 211(8)(b), s 213(3), s 219(2) (changed)
(3)	new
(4)	new
812(1)–(7)	new
813(1)	1985, s 211(8)(b), s 213(3), s 219(3) (changed)
(2)	1985, s 211(8)(b), s 213(3), s 219(3), Sch 24
(3)	1985, s 211(8)(b), s 213(3), s 219(4)
814(1)–(3)	new
815(1)	1985, s 218(1)
(2)	1985, s 218(2)
(3)	1985, s 218(3)
(4)	1985, s 218(3), Sch 24
816	1985, s 217(1) (changed)
817(1)	1985, s 217(2) (changed)
(2), (3)	1985, s 217(3)

CA 2006	*Origin*
PART 22 INFORMATION ABOUT INTERESTS IN A COMPANY'S SHARES	
(4)	1985, s 217(5)
818(1), (2)	1985, s 217(4)
(3)	1985, s 217(5)
819(1)	1985, s 211(7), s 213(3)
(2)	1985, s 211(10), s 213(3)
(3)	1985, s 211(10), s 213(3), Sch 24
820(1)	1985, s 208(1), s 212(5)
(2)	1985, s 208(2), s 212(5)
(3)	1985, s 208(3), s 212(5)
(4)	1985, s 208(4), s 212(5)
(5)	1985, s 208(6), s 212(5)
(6)	1985, s 208(5), s 212(5)
(7)	1985, s 208(7), s 212(5)
(8)	1985, s 208(8), s 212(5)
821(1), (2)	1985, s 212(6)
822(1), (2)	1985, s 203(1), s 212(5)
823(1)	1985, s 203(2), s 212(5)
(2)	1985, s 203(3), s 212(5)
(3)	1985, s 203(4), s 212(5)
824(1)	1985, s 204(1), (2), s 212(5)
(2)	1985, s 204(2), s 212(5)
(3)	1985, s 204(3), s 212(5)
(4)	1985, s 204(4), s 212(5)
(5)	1985, s 204(5), s 212(5)
(6)	1985, s 204(6), s 212(5)
825(1)	1985, s 205(1), s 212(5)
(2)	1985, s 205(2), s 212(5)
(3)	1985, s 205(3), s 212(5)
(4)	1985, s 205(4), s 212(5)
826(1)	1985, s 211(9), s 213(3), s 215(4)
(2)	1985, s 215(4)
827	1985, s 220(2) (changed)
828(1), (2)	1985, s 210A(1)
(3)	1985, s 210A(5)
PART 23 DISTRIBUTIONS	
Chapter 1 Restrictions on when distributions may be made	
829(1), (2)	1985, s 263(2)
830(1)	1985, s 263(1)
(2), (3)	1985, s 263(3)
831(1)	1985, s 264(1)

CA 2006	*Origin*
PART 23 DISTRIBUTIONS	
Chapter 1 Restrictions on when distributions may be made	
(2), (3)	1985, s 264(2)
(4)	1985, s 264(3)
(5)	1985, s 264(4)
(6)	1985, s 264(1)
832(1)–(3)	1985, s 265(1)
(4)	1985, s 265(2)
(5)	1985, s 265(4), (6)
(6)	1985, s 265(4A), (5)
(7)	1985, s 265(3)
833(1)	1985, s 266(1)
(2)	1985, s 266(2)
(3)	1985, s 266(2A)
(4), (5)	1985, s 266(3)
834(1)	1985, s 266(2)(b)
(2)	1985, s 266(4), ICTA, s 842(1A)
(3)	1985, s 266(4), ICTA, s 842(2)
(4)	1985, s 266(4), ICTA, s 842(3)
(5)	1985, s 266(4), ICTA, s 838, s 842(1A), (4)
835(1)	1985, s 267(1)
(2)	1985, s 267(2)(b)
Chapter 2 Justification of distribution by reference to accounts	
836(1)	1985, s 270(1), (2)
(2)	1985, s 270(3), (4)
(3), (4)	1985, s 270(5)
837(1)	1985, s 270(3)
(2)	1985, s 271(2)
(3)	1985, s 271(3)
(4)	1985, s 271(3), (4)
(5)	1985, s 271(5)
838(1)	1985, s 270(4)
(2)	1985, s 272(1)
(3)	1985, s 272(2)
(4), (5)	1985, s 272(3)
(6)	1985, s 272(4), (5)
839(1)	1985, s 270(4)
(2)	1985, s 273(1)
(3)	1985, s 273(2)
(4)	1985, s 272(3), s 273(3)

CA 2006	Origin
PART 23 DISTRIBUTIONS	
Chapter 2 Justification of distribution by reference to accounts	
(5)	1985, s 273(4)
(6)	1985, s 273(4), (5)
(7)	1985, s 273(6), (7)
840(1)	1985, s 274(1), (2)
(2)	1985, s 274(2)
(3)	1985, s 274(3) ("financial assistance")
(4)	1985, s 154(2)(a), s 274(3) ("net assets" and "net liabilities")
(5)	1985, s 154(2)(b), s 274(3) ("net liabilities")
Chapter 3 Supplementary provisions	
841(1), (2)	1985, s 275(1)
(3)	1985, s 275(1A)
(4)	1985, s 275(4), (5), (6)
(5)	1985, s 275(2)
842	1985, s 275(3)
843(1)	1985, s 268(1)
(2)	1985, s 268(1)(a)
(3)	1985, s 268(2)(aa), (a)
(4)	1985, s 268(1)(b), (2)(b)
(5)	1985, s 268(1)
(6)	1985, s 268(3)(a)
(7)	1985, s 268(3)(b), (4)
844(1)	1985, s 269(1)
(2), (3)	1985, s 269(2)
845(1)–(5)	new
846(1), (2)	1985, s 276 (changed)
847(1), (2)	1985, s 277(1)
(3), (4)	1985, s 277(2)
848(1)	1985, s 278
(2)	1985, s 278, 1986 art 286
849	1985, s 263(4)
850(1), (2)	1985, s 263(5)
(3)	1985, s 263(5), 1986 art 271(5)
851(1)	1985, s 281 (changed)
(2), (3)	new
852	1985, s 281
853(1)	1985, s 280(1)
(2)	1985, s 280(3)

CA 2006	Origin
PART 23 DISTRIBUTIONS	
Chapter 3 Supplementary provisions	
(3)	1985, s 280(2)
(4), (5)	1985, s 262(3), s 742(2)
(6)	1985, s 262(1), s 742(1)
PART 24 A COMPANY'S ANNUAL RETURN	
854(1), (2)	1985, s 363(1)
(3)	1985, s 363(2) (changed)
855(1)	1985, s 364(1) (changed)
(2)	1985, s 364(2)
(3)	1985, s 364(3)
856(1)	1985, s 364A(1)
(2)	1985, s 364A(2), (3) (changed)
(3)	1985, s 364A(4) (changed)
(4)	1985, s 364A(5)
(5)	1985, s 364A(6)
(6)	1985, s 364A(8)
857(1), (2)	1985, s 365(1)
(3)	1985, s 365(2)
858(1)	1985, s 363(3), (4) (changed)
(2)	1985, s 363(3), (4), Sch 24
(3)	1985, s 363(3)
(4)	1985, s 363(4)
(5)	new
859	1985, s 365(3)
PART 25 COMPANY CHARGES	
Chapter 1 Companies registered in England and Wales or in Northern Ireland	
860(1)	1985, ss 395(1), 399(1)
(2)	1985, s 399(1)
(3)	1985, s 399(2)
(4)–(6)	1985, s 399(3), Sch 24 (changed)
(7)	1985, s 396(1)
861(1)	1985, s 396(3)
(2)	1985, s 396(1)(d)
(3)	1985, s 396(2)
(4)	1985, s 396(3A)
(5)	1985, ss 395(1) ("company"), 396(4) ("charge"), 400(1) ("company")
862(1)	1985, s 400(1)

CA 2006	Origin
PART 25 COMPANY CHARGES	
Chapter 1 Companies registered in England and Wales or in Northern Ireland	
(2), (3)	1985, s 400(2)
(4), (5)	1985, s 400(4), Sch 24 (changed)
863(1)–(4)	1985, s 397(1)
(5)	1985, s 399(1)–(3)
864(1)	1985, s 397(2)
(2)	1985, s 397(3)
(3)	1985, s 397(2)
865(1)	1985, s 402(1)
(2)	1985, s 402(2)
(3), (4)	1985, s 402(3), Sch 24
866(1)	1985, s 398(1)
(2)	1985, s 398(3)
867(1), (2)	1985, s 398(4)
868(1), (2)	1986 art 408(1)
(3)	1986 art 408(2)
(4)	1986 art 408(3)
(5)	Drafting
869(1)	1985, s 401(1) (opening words)
(2)	1985, s 401(1)(a)
(3)	1986 art 409(2)(b)
(4)	1985, s 401(1)(b)
(5), (6)	1985, s 401(2)
(7)	1985, s 401(3)
870(1)	1985, ss 395(1), 398(2)
(2)	1985, s 400(2), (3)
(3)	1985, s 397(1)
871(1)	1985, s 405(1)
(2)	1985, s 405(2)
(3)	1985, s 405(1), (2)
(4), (5)	1985, s 405(4), Sch 24
872(1), (2)	1985, s 403(1) (changed)
(3)	1985, s 403(2)
873(1)	1985, s 404(1)
(2)	1985, s 404(2)
874(1), (2)	1985, s 395(1)
(3)	1985, s 395(2)
875(1)	1985, s 406(1), 1986 art 414(1)
(2)	1985, s 406(2)
876(1)	1985, s 407(1)
(2)	1985, s 407(2)
(3), (4)	1985, s 407(3), Sch 24

CA 2006	Origin
PART 25 COMPANY CHARGES	
Chapter 1 Companies registered in England and Wales or in Northern Ireland	
877(1)	1985, s 408(1)
(2)	1985, ss 406(1), 407(1), 408(1) (changed)
(3)	new
(4)	1985, s 408(1), (2) (changed)
(5), (6)	1985, s 408(3), Sch 24 (changed)
(7)	1985, s 408(4)
Chapter 2 Companies registered in Scotland	
878(1)	1985, ss 410(2), 415(1)
(2)	1985, s 415(1)
(3)	1985, s 415(2)
(4)–(6)	1985, s 415(3), Sch 24 (changed)
(7)	1985, s 410(4)
879(1)	1985, s 410(4)(a)
(2)	1985, s 413(1)
(3)	1985, s 410(4)(a)
(4)	1985, s 412
(5)	1985, s 410(5)
(6)	1985, s 410(5) ("company")
880(1), (2)	1985, s 416(1)
(3), (4)	1985, s 416(3), Sch 24 (changed)
881(1)	1985, s 414(1)
(2), (3)	1985, s 414(2)
882(1)–(4)	1985, s 413(2)
(5)	1985, s 415(1)–(3)
883(1)–(3)	1985, s 413(3)
884	1985, s 411(2)
885(1)	1985, s 417(1)
(2)	1985, s 417(2)
(3)	1985, s 417(3)
(4)	1985, s 418(1), (2)(b)
(5)	1985, s 418(2)(a), (c)
(6)	1985, s 417(4)
886(1)	1985, ss 410(2), 411(1)
(2)	1985, s 416(1), (2)
(3)	1985, s 413(2)
887(1)	1985, s 419(1) (changed)
(2)	1985, s 419(1B)(a), (c), (3) (changed)

CA 2006	*Origin*
PART 25 COMPANY CHARGES	
Chapter 2 Companies registered in Scotland	
(3)	1985, s 419(1)
(4)	1985, s 419(2)
(5)	1985, s 419(4)
888(1), (2)	1985, s 420
889(1)	1985, s 410(2)
(2)	1985, s 410(3)
890(1)	1985, s 421(1)
(2)	1985, s 421(2)
891(1)	1985, s 422(1)
(2)	1985, s 422(2)
(3), (4)	1985, s 422(3), Sch 24
892(1)	1985, s 423(1)
(2)	1985, ss 421(1), 422(1), 423(1) (changed)
(3)	new
(4)	1985, s 423(1), (2) (changed)
(5), (6)	1985, s 423(3), Sch 24 (changed)
(7)	1985, s 423(4)
Chapter 3 Powers of the Secretary of State	
893(1)–(9)	new
894(1), (2)	new
PART 26 ARRANGEMENTS AND RECONSTRUCTIONS	
895(1)	1985, s 425(1)
(2)	1985, ss 425(6), 427(6)
(3)	drafting
896(1), (2)	1985, s 425(1)
897(1)	1985, s 426(1), (2), (3)
(2)	1985, s 426(2)
(3)	1985, s 426(4)
(4)	1985, s 426(5)
(5)–(8)	1985, s 426(6), Sch 24
898(1)–(3)	1985, s 426(7), Sch 24
899(1)	1985, s 425(2)
(2)	new
(3)	1985, s 425(2)
(4)	1985, s 425(3)
900(1)	1985, s 427(1), (2)
(2)	1985, s 427(2), (3)
(3), (4)	1985, s 427(4)
(5)	1985, s 427(6)
(6)–(8)	1985, s 427(5), Sch 24

CA 2006	*Origin*
PART 26 ARRANGEMENTS AND RECONSTRUCTIONS	
901(1), (2)	new
(3), (4)	1985, s 425(3) (changed)
(5), (6)	1985, s 425(4), Sch 24
PART 27 MERGERS AND DIVISIONS OF PUBLIC COMPANIES	
Chapter 1 Introductory	
902(1)	1985, s 427A(1)
(2)	drafting
(3)	1985, s 427A(4)
903(1)	1985, s 427A(1)
(2), (3)	drafting
Chapter 2 Merger	
904(1)	1985, s 427A(2) Cases 1 and 2
(2)	drafting
905(1)	1985, Sch 15B, para 2(1)(a)
(2), (3)	1985, Sch 15B, para 2(2)
906(1), (2)	1985, Sch 15B, para 2(1)(b)
(3)	1985, Sch 15B, para 2(1)(c)
907(1)	1985, s 425(2), Sch 15B, para 1
(2)	1985, s 427A(1) closing words, Sch 15B, para 1 opening words
908(1)	1985, Sch 15B, para 3(a)
(2)	1985, Sch 15B, para 4(1)
(3)	1985, Sch 15B, para 3 opening words
909(1)	1985, Sch 15B, para 3(d)
(2)	1985, Sch 15B, para 5(1)
(3)	1985, Sch 15B, para 5(1), (2)
(4)	1985, Sch 15B, para 5(3)
(5)	1985, Sch 15B, para 5(7)
(6)	1985, Sch 15B, para 5(8)
(7)	1985, Sch 15B, para 3 opening words
910(1)	1985, Sch 15B, para 6(1)(e)
(2)	1985, Sch 15B, para 6(2)
(3)	1985, Sch 15B, para 6(3) (changed)
(4)	1985, Sch 15B, para 6(4)
911(1), (2)	1985, Sch 15B, para 3(e)

CA 2006	Origin
PART 27 MERGERS AND DIVISIONS OF PUBLIC COMPANIES	
Chapter 2 Merger	
(3)	1985, Sch 15B, para 6(1)
(4)	1985, Sch 15B, para 3 opening words
912	1985, Sch 15B, para 3(f)
913(1)	1985, Sch 15B, para 8(1)
(2)	1985, Sch 15B, para 8(2)
914	1985, Sch 15B, para 7
915(1)	1985, Sch 15B, para 12(1)
(2)	1985, Sch 15B, para 12(2)
(3)–(5)	1985, Sch 15B, para 12(3)
(6)	1985, Sch 15B, para 12(1)(a), (b)
916(1)	1985, Sch 15B, para 14(1)
(2)	1985, Sch 15B, para 14(2)
(3)–(5)	1985, Sch 15B paras 10(2), 14(3)
(6)	1985, Sch 15B para14(1)(a), (b)
917(1)	1985, Sch 15B, para 12(1)
(2)	1985, Sch 15B, para 12(4)
(3)–(5)	1985, Sch 15B, para 12(5)
(6)	1985, Sch 15B, para 12(1)(a), (b)
918(1)	1985, Sch 15B, para 10(1)
(2)–(4)	1985, Sch 15B, para 10(2)
Chapter 3 Division	
919(1)	1985, s 427A(2) Case 3
(2)	drafting
920(1)	1985, Sch 15B, para 2(1)(a)
(2)	1985, Sch 15B, para 2(2)
(3)	1985, Sch 15B, para 2(3)
921(1), (2)	1985, Sch 15B, para 2(1)(b)
(3)	1985, Sch 15B, para 2(1)(c)

CA 2006	Origin
PART 27 MERGERS AND DIVISIONS OF PUBLIC COMPANIES	
Chapter 3 Division	
(4)	1985, Sch 15B, para 2(1)(b), (c) opening words
922(1)	1985, s 425(2), Sch 15B, para 1
(2)	1985, s 427A(1) closing words, Sch 15B, para 1 opening words
923(1)	1985, Sch 15B, para 3(a)
(2)	1985, Sch 15B, para 4(1)
(3)	1985, Sch 15B, para 4(2)
(4)	1985, Sch 15B, para 3 opening words
924(1)	1985, Sch 15B, para 3(d)
(2)	1985, Sch 15B, para 5(1)
(3)	1985, Sch 15B, para 5(1), (2)
(4)	1985, Sch 15B, para 5(3)
(5)	1985, Sch 15B, para 5(7)
(6)	1985, Sch 15B, para 5(8)
(7)	1985, Sch 15B, para 3 opening words
925(1)	1985, Sch 15B, para 6(1)(e)
(2)	1985, Sch 15B, para 6(2)
(3)	1985, Sch 15B, para 6(3) (changed)
(4)	1985, Sch 15B, para 6(4)
(5)	1985, Sch 15B, para 3 opening words
926(1), (2)	1985, Sch 15B, para 3(e)
(3)	1985, Sch 15B, para 6(1)
(4)	1985, Sch 15B, para 3 opening words
927(1)	1985, Sch 15B, para 3(b)
(2)	1985, Sch 15B, para 3(c)
(3)	1985, Sch 15B, para 3 opening words
928	1985, Sch 15B, para 3(f)
929(1)	1985, Sch 15B, para 8(1)
(2)	1985, Sch 15B, para 8(2)
930	1985, Sch 15B, para 7
931(1)	1985, Sch 15B, para 13(1)
(2)	1985, Sch 15B, para 13(2)

CA 2006	*Origin*
PART 27 MERGERS AND DIVISIONS OF PUBLIC COMPANIES	
Chapter 3 Division	
(3)	1985, Sch 15B paras 12(5)(a), 13(3)(a)
(4)	1985, Sch 15B, para 13(3)(b)
(5)	1985, Sch 15B paras 12(5)(c), 13(3)(a)
(6)	1985, Sch 15B, para 13(3)(c)
932(1)	1985, Sch 15B, para 10(1)
(2)–(4)	1985, Sch 15B, para 10(2)
(5)	1985, Sch 15B, para 10(2) opening words
933(1)–(3)	1985, Sch 15B, para 11(1), (2)
934(1)	1985, Sch 15B, para 11(1), (3)
(2)	1985, Sch 15B, para 11(4)(a), (b)
(3)	1985, Sch 15B, para 11(4)(c)
(4)	1985, Sch 15B, para 11(4)(d)
Chapter 4 Supplementary provisions	
935(1)	1985, Sch 15B, para 5(4) (changed)
(2)	1985, Sch 15B, para 5(6)
936(1)–(4)	new
937(1)–(6)	new
938(1), (2)	1985, s 427A(3)
939(1)	1985, Sch 15B, para 9(1), (2)
(2)	1985, Sch 15B, para 9(2)
(3), (4)	1985, Sch 15B, para 9(3)
(5)	1985, Sch 15B, para 9(4)
940(1)	1985, Sch 15B, para 15(1)
(2)	1985, Sch 15B, para 15(2)
(3)	1985, Sch 15B, para 15(1)
941	1985, ss 427(6), 427A(8)

CA 2006	*Origin*
PART 28 TAKEOVERS ETC	
[Note: The Takeovers Directive (Interim Implementation) Regulations 2006, SI 2006/1183 are based on the provisions of this Part. So although the regulations came into force on 20 May 2006 and so before the date of Royal assent to the Companies Act 2006, they are not cited as origins for those provisions].	
Chapter 1 The Takeover Panel	
942(1)–(3)	new
943(1)–(9)	new
944(1)–(7)	new
945(1), (2)	new
946	new
947(1)–(10)	new
948(1)–(9)	new
949(1)–(3)	new
950(1), (2)	new
951(1)–(5)	new
952(1)–(8)	new
953(1)–(9)	new
954(1), (2)	new
955(1)–(4)	new
956(1)–(3)	new
957(1), (2)	new
958(1)–(8)	new
959	new
960	new
961(1)–(3)	new
962(1), (2)	new
963(1), (2)	new
964(1)–(6)	new
965	new
Chapter 2 Impediments to takeovers	
966(1)–(8)	new
967(1)–(7)	new
968(1)–(8)	new
969(1)–(3)	new
970(1)–(4)	new
971(1), (2)	new
972(1)–(4)	new
973	new
Chapter 3 "Squeeze-out" and "sell-out"	
974(1)–(3)	1985, s 428(1), drafting
(4), (5)	1985, s 428(2)
(6)	1985, s 428(2A)

CA 2006	*Origin*
PART 28 TAKEOVERS ETC	
Chapter 3 "Squeeze-out" and "sell-out"	
(7)	1985, s 428(7)
975(1), (2)	1985, s 428(5) (changed)
(3)	1985, s 428(6) (changed)
(4)	1985, s 430E(1)
976(1)	1985, s 428(3)
(2)	new
(3)	1985, s 428(4)
977(1)	1985, s 429(8) (changed)
(2)	1985, s 430E(1) (changed)
(3)	drafting
978(1)–(3)	new
979(1), (2)	1985, s 429(1) (changed)
(3), (4)	1985, s 429(2) (changed)
(5)–(7)	new
(8)	1985, s 429(8) (changed)
(9)	1985, ss 429(8), 430E(2) (changed)
(10)	1985, s 429(8) (changed)
980(1)	1985, s 429(4)
(2)	1985, s 429(3) (changed)
(3)	new
(4)	1985, s 429(4)
(5)	1985, s 429(5)
(6)	1985, s 429(6)
(7)	1985, s 429(7)
(8)	1985, s 429(6), Sch 24
981(1)	1985, s 430(1)
(2)	1985, s 430(2)
(3)	1985, s 430(3)
(4)	1985, s 430(4)
(5)	1985, s 430(4) (changed)
(6)	1985, s 430(5), (8)
(7)	1985, s 430(6)
(8)	1985, s 430(7)
(9)	1985, s 430(9), drafting
982(1)	drafting
(2), (3)	1985, s 430(10)
(4), (5)	1985, s 430(11)
(6)	1985, s 430(12)
(7)	1985, s 430(13)
(8)	1985, s 430(14)
(9)	1985, s 430(15)
983(1)	1985, s 430A(1), (1A)

CA 2006	*Origin*
PART 28 TAKEOVERS ETC	
Chapter 3 "Squeeze-out" and "sell-out"	
(2), (3)	1985, s 430A(1) (changed)
(4)	1985, s 430A(2) (changed)
(5)	1985, s 430A(2A)
(6), (7)	new
(8)	1985, s 430E(3)
984(1)	1985, s 430A(1)
(2)	1985, s 430A(4) (changed)
(3)	1985, s 430A(3)
(4)	1985, s 430A(5)
(5)	1985, s 430A(6)
(6)	1985, s 430A(7)
(7)	1985, s 430A(6), Sch 24
985(1)	1985, s 430B(1)
(2)	1985, s 430B(2)
(3)	1985, s 430B(3)
(4)	1985, s 430B(4)
(5)	1985, s 430B(4) (changed)
986(1)	1985, s 430C(1)
(2)	1985, s 430C(1), (2)
(3)	1985, s 430C(3)
(4)	new
(5)	1985, s 430C(4)
(6)–(8)	new
(9), (10)	1985, s 430C(5)
987(1)	1985, s 430D(1)
(2), (3)	1985, s 430D(2) (changed)
(4)	1985, s 430D(4) (changed)
(5), (6)	1985, s 430D(3)
(7)	1985, s 430D(4)
(8)	1985, s 430D(5)
(9)	1985, s 430D(6)
(10)	1985, s 430D(7)
988(1)	1985, s 430E(4), (8)
(2)	1985, s 430E(5)
(3)	1985, s 430E(6), (7)
(4)	1985, ss 204(2)(a), 430E(4)(d)
(5)	1985, ss 204(6), 430E(7)
(6)	1985, s 204(3)

CA 2006	*Origin*
PART 28 TAKEOVERS ETC	
Chapter 3 "Squeeze-out" and "sell-out"	
(7)	1985, ss 204(5), 430E(7)
989(1)	1985, s 430F(1)
(2)	1985, s 430F(2)
990(1)–(3)	new
991(1)	1985, s 428(8) ("the company" and "the offeror"), new ("date of the offer", "non-voting shares", "voting rights" and "voting shares")
(2)	new
Chapter 4 Amendments to Part 7 of the Companies Act 1985	
992(1)–(6)	new (amends 1985 Pt 7)
PART 29 FRAUDULENT TRADING	
993(1)–(3)	1985, s 458, Sch 24
PART 30 PROTECTION OF MEMBERS AGAINST UNFAIR PREJUDICE	
994(1)	1985, s 459(1)
(2)	1985, s 459(2)
(3)	1985, s 459(3)
995(1)	1985, s 460(1A)
(2), (3)	1985, s 460(1)
(4)	1985, s 460(2)
996(1)	1985, s 461(1)
(2)	1985, s 461(2), (3)
997	1985, s 461(6)
998(1)–(4)	1985, s 461(5)
999(1)–(5)	new
PART 31 DISSOLUTION AND RESTORATION TO THE REGISTER	
Chapter 1 Striking off	
1000(1)	1985, s 652(1)
(2)	1985, s 652(2)
(3)	1985, s 652(3)
(4)–(6)	1985, s 652(5)
(7)	1985, s 652(6)
1001(1)	1985, s 652(4)
(2)–(4)	1985, s 652(5)
(5)	1985, s 652(6)
1002(1)–(3)	1985, s 652(7)
1003(1)	1985, s 652A(1) (changed)
(2)	1985, s 652A(2) (changed)
(3)	1985, s 652A(3)

CA 2006	*Origin*
PART 31 DISSOLUTION AND RESTORATION TO THE REGISTER	
Chapter 1 Striking off	
(4)	1985, s 652A(4)
(5)	1985, s 652A(5)
(6)	1985, s 652A(6), (7)
1004(1)	1985, s 652B(1)
(2)	1985, s 652B(2)
(3)	1985, s 652B(9)
(4)	1985, s 652D(5)(c)
(5)	1985, s 652E(1)
(6)	1985, s 652E(3)
(7)	1985, s 652E(1), Sch 24
1005(1)	1985, s 652B(3)
(2)	1985, s 652B(4)
(3)	1985, s 652B(5)
(4)	1985, s 652E(1)
(5)	1985, s 652E(3)
(6)	1985, s 652E(1), Sch 24
1006(1)	1985, ss 652B(6), 652D(5)(c)
(2)	1985, s 652B(7)
(3)	1985, s 652B(8)
(4)	1985, s 652E(1), (2)
(5)	1985, s 652E(4)
(6)	1985, s 652E(1), Sch 24
(7)	1985, s 652E(2), Sch 24
1007(1)	1985, s 652C(1)
(2)	1985, ss 652C(2), 652D(5)(c)
(3)	1985, s 652C(3)
(4)	1985, s 652E(1), (2)
(5)	1985, s 652E(5)
(6)	1985, s 652E(1), Sch 24
(7)	1985, s 652E(2), Sch 24
1008(1), (2)	1985, s 652D(1)
(3)	1985, s 652D(2), (3)
(4)	1985, s 652D(4)
1009(1)	1985, s 652C(4)
(2)	1985, s 652C(5)
(3)	1985, s 652C(7)
(4)	1985, ss 652C(6), 652D(5)(c)
(5)	1985, s 652E(1)
(6)	1985, s 652E(5)
(7)	1985, s 652E(1), Sch 24
1010	1985, s 652D(6)

CA 2006	Origin
PART 31 DISSOLUTION AND RESTORATION TO THE REGISTER	
Chapter 1 Striking off	
1011	1985, s 652D(8)
Chapter 2 Property of dissolved company	
1012(1)	1985, s 654(1)
(2)	1985, s 654(2)
1013(1)	1985, s 656(1)
(2)	1985, s 656(2) (changed)
(3)–(5)	1985, s 656(3) (changed)
(6), (7)	1985, s 656(5)
(8)	1985, s 656(6)
1014(1)	1985, s 657(1)
(2)	drafting
1015(1), (2)	1985, s 657(2), IA 1986, s 178(4)
1016(1)	1985, s 657(2), IA 1986, s 179(1)
(2)	1985, s 657(2), IA 1986, s 179(2)
(3)	drafting
1017(1)	1985, s 657(2), 1A 1986, s 181(2), (3)
(2)	1985, s 657(2), 1A 1986, s 181(3)
(3)	1985, s 657(2), 1A 1986, s 181(4)
(4)	1985, s 657(2), 1A 1986, s 181(3)
(5)	1985, s 657(2), 1A 1986, s 181(6)
1018(1)	1985, s 657(2), 1A 1986, s 182(1)
(2)	1985, s 657(2), 1A 1986, s 182(2)
(3)	1985, s 657(2), 1A 1986, s 182(4)
(4), (5)	1985, s 657(2), 1A 1986, s 182(3)
1019	1985, s 657(2), 1A 1986, s 180(1), (2)
1020(1), (2)	1985, s 657(4)
1021(1), (2)	1985, s 657(5)
(3)	1985, s 657(6)
1022(1)	1985, Sch 20, para 5
(2)	1985, Sch 20, para 6
(3)	1985, Sch 20, para 7
(4), (5)	1985, Sch 20, para 8
(6)	1985, Sch 20, para 9

CA 2006	Origin
PART 31 DISSOLUTION AND RESTORATION TO THE REGISTER	
Chapter 2 Property of dissolved company	
1023(1)	1985, s 658(1), IA, s 180(1)
(2)	1985, s 658(1), IA, s 180(2)
(3)	1985, s 658(2)
Chapter 3 Restoration to the register	
1024(1)–(4)	new
1025(1)–(6)	new
1026(1)–(3)	new
1027(1)–(4)	new
1028(1)–(4)	new
1029(1), (2)	new
1030(1)–(6)	new
1031(1)–(4)	new
1032(1)–(5)	new
1033(1)–(7)	new
1034(1)	1985, s 655(1)
(2)	1985, s 655(2)
(3)	new
(4)	1985, s 655(3)
(5)	1985, s 655(4)
(6)	drafting
PART 32 COMPANY INVESTIGATIONS: AMENDMENTS	
1035(1)–(5)	new (inserts 1985, ss 446A and 446B; amends 1985 s, s 431, 432, 437 and 442)
1036	new (inserts 1985, ss 446C and 446D)
1037(1)–(3)	new (inserts 1985, s 446E; amends 1985, ss 451A and 452)
1038(1), (2)	new (amends 1985, ss 434 and 447)
1039	new (amends Company Directors Disqualification Act 1986, s 8)
PART 33 UK COMPANIES NOT FORMED UNDER THE COMPANIES LEGISLATION	
Chapter 1 Companies not formed under companies legislation but authorised to register	
1040(1)	1985, s 680(1)(a), (b), (1A), (2)
(2), (3)	1985, s 680(1) (closing words)

CA 2006	*Origin*
PART 33 UK COMPANIES NOT FORMED UNDER THE COMPANIES LEGISLATION	
Chapter 1 Companies not formed under companies legislation but authorised to register	
(4)	1985, s 680(3), (4)
(5)	1985, s 680(5)
(6)	1985, s 680(1) (closing words)
1041(1)	1985, s 683(1)
(2)	1985, s 683(2)
1042(1)–(3)	new
Chapter 2 Unregistered companies	
1043(1)	1985, s 718(1), (2)
(2)	1985, s 718(3) (changed)
(3)	1985, s 718(1) (changed)
(4)	1985, s 718(5)
(5)	1985, s 718(1), (3)
(6)	1985, s 718(6)
PART 34 OVERSEAS COMPANIES	
1044	1985, s 744 ("overseas company") (changed)
1045(1), (2)	1989, s 130(6)
1046(1)–(8)	new
1047(1)–(6)	new
1048(1), (2)	1985, s 694(4) (changed)
(3)–(5)	1985, s 694(5)
1049(1)–(4)	new
1050(1)–(6)	new
1051(1)–(5)	new
1052(1)–(6)	new
1053(1)–(6)	new
1054(1)–(4)	new
1055	new
1056	new
1057(1)–(3)	new
1058(1)–(4)	new
1059	1985, s 695A(4)
PART 35 THE REGISTRAR OF COMPANIES	
1060(1), (2)	1985, s 704(2)
(3)	1985, s 744 ("the registrar of companies" and "the registrar")
(4)	drafting
1061(1)–(3)	drafting
1062	1985, s 704(4) (changed)

CA 2006	*Origin*
PART 35 THE REGISTRAR OF COMPANIES	
1063(1)–(3)	1985, s 708(1) (changed)
(4)	1985, s 708(2), (3) (changed)
(5)	1985, s 708(5) (changed)
(6)	1985, s 708(4)
(7)	new
1064(1)–(3)	1985, s 711(1)(a) (changed)
1065	1985, s 710
1066(1)–(3)	1985, s 705(1)–(3)
(4), (5)	1985, s 705(4)
(6)	1985, s 705(5)(za)
1067(1)	1985, s 705A(1), (2) (changed)
(2)	1985, s 705A(3)
(3)	1985, s 705A(4)
(4), (5)	1985, s 705A(5)
1068(1)–(7)	new
1069(1)–(3)	new
1070(1)–(3)	new
1071(1), (2)	new
1072(1), (2)	new
1073(1)–(6)	new
1074(1)–(5)	new
1075(1)–(7)	new
1076(1)–(4)	new
1077(1)	1985, s 711(1) opening words
(2), (3)	new
1078(1)	drafting
(2), (3)	1985, s 711(1) (changed)
(4)	new
(5), (6)	new
1079(1)–(3)	1985, s 42(1)
(4)	1985, s 711(2) (changed)
1080(1), (2)	drafting
(3)	new
(4)	1985, s 707A(1)
(5)	new
1081(1)–(7)	new
1082(1)–(5)	new
1083(1)	1985, s 707A(2) (changed)
(2), (3)	new

CA 2006	Origin
PART 35 THE REGISTRAR OF COMPANIES	
1084(1)–(3)	1985, s 707A(3) (changed)
(4)	1985, s 707A(4)
(5)	1985, s 707A(3)
1085(1)	1985, s 709(1) opening words
(2)	1985, s 709(2) (changed)
(3)	drafting
1086(1)	1985, s 709(1)(a), (b)
(2)	new
(3)	drafting
1087(1)–(3)	new
1088(1)–(6)	new
1089(1), (2)	new
1090(1)–(4)	new
1091(1), (2)	new
(3)	1985, s 709(3)
(4)	new
(5)	1985, s 709(4)
1092(1), (2)	1985, s 709(5)
1093(1)–(4)	new
1094(1)–(5)	new
1095(1)–(6)	new
1096(1)–(6)	new
1097(1)–(5)	new
1098(1), (2)	new
1099(1)–(3)	1985, s 714(1) (changed)
(4), (5)	1985, s 714(2)
1100	1985, s 709(1) opening words
1101(1), (2)	new
1102(1)–(4)	new
1103(1), (2)	new
1104(1), (2)	1985, s 710B(1)–(3)
(3)	1985, s 710B(4)
(4)	1985, s 710B(5)
(5)	drafting
1105(1)–(3)	new
1106(1)–(6)	new
1107(1)	drafting
1107(2), (3)	new
1108(1)–(3)	new
1109(1), (2)	new
1110(1)–(3)	new
1111(1)–(3)	new

CA 2006	Origin
PART 35 THE REGISTRAR OF COMPANIES	
1112(1), (2)	new
1113(1)–(3)	1985, s 713(1)
(4), (5)	1985, s 713(2), (3)
1114(1)	1985, s 715A(1) "document", (2)
(2)	new
1115(1)	new
(2)	1985, s 710A(2)
1116(1)–(6)	new
1117(1)–(3)	new
1118	drafting
1119(1), (2)	1985, s 704(7), (8)
(3)	new
1120	new
PART 36 OFFENCES UNDER THE COMPANIES ACTS	
1121(1)	1985, s 730(5)
(2)	1985, s 744 "officer"
(3)	1985, s 730(5) (changed)
1122(1)–(3)	new
1123(1)–(4)	new
1124 and Sch 3	new (amend 1985 Act)
1125(1)	drafting
(2)	1985, s 730(4)
1126(1)	1985, s 732(1)
(2)	1985, s 732(2) (changed)
(3)	1986 art 680(2) (changed)
1127(1), (2)	1985, s 731(1)
1128(1)	1985, s 731(2)
(2)	1985, s 731(3)
(3)	1986 art 679(2)
(4)	1985, s 731(4), 1986 art 679(3)
1129	1985, s 732(3) (changed)
1130(1)	1985, s 734(1) (changed)
(2)	1985, s 734(1), (3), (4)
(3)	1985, s 734(2)
1131(1), (2)	new
1132(1), (2)	1985, s 721(1)
(3)–(5)	1985, s 721(2)–(4)
(6)	drafting
1133	new
PART 37 COMPANIES: SUPPLEMENTARY PROVISIONS	
1134	1985, s 722(1) (changed)

CA 2006	*Origin*
PART 37 COMPANIES: SUPPLEMENTARY PROVISIONS	
1135(1)	1985, ss 722(1), 723(1) (changed)
(2)	new
(3), (4)	new
(5)	1985, s 723(2)
1136(1)–(7)	new
1137(1), (2)	1985, s 723A(1)
(3)	1985, s 723A(2), (3)
(4)	1985, s 723A(4)
(5), (6)	1985, s 723A(6), (7)
1138(1)	1985, s 722(2)
(2), (3)	1985, s 722(3), Sch 24
(4)	new
1139(1)	1985, s 725(1)
(2)	1985, s 695(1), (2) (changed)
(3)	new
(4)	1985, s 725(2), (3)
(5)	drafting
1140(1)–(8)	new
1141(1)	drafting
(2), (3)	new
1142	new
1143(1)–(4), Schs 4 and 5	new
1144(1)–(3)	new
1145(1)–(5)	new
1146(1)–(4)	new
1147(1)–(6)	new
1148(1)–(3)	new
1149	drafting
1150(1)	1985, s 108(1) (changed)
(2), (3)	1985, s 108(2), (3)
(4)	1985, s 108(5)
1151(1)–(4)	new
1152(1)–(6)	new
1153(1)	1985, s 110(1)
(2), (3)	1985, s 110(2), (3)
(4)	1985, s 110(2), Sch 24
1154(1)–(4)	new
1155(1), (2)	new
1156(1)–(3)	1985, s 744 "the court", IA 1986, s 117 (changed)
1157(1)–(3)	1985, s 727(1)–(3)

CA 2006	*Origin*
PART 38 COMPANIES: INTERPRETATION	
1158	drafting
1159(1), (2)	1985, s 736(1), (2)
(3) and Sch 6	1985, s 736A(1)–(11)
(4)	1985, ss 736(3), 736A(12)
1160(1)	1985, s 736B(1)
(2)–(4)	1985, s 736B(3)–(5)
1161(1)–(5)	1985, s 259(1)–(5)
1162(1)–(5)	1985, s 258(1)–(5)
(6) and Sch 7	1985, s 258(6) and Sch 10A
1163(1), (2)	1985, s 739(1), (2)
1164(1)–(3)	1985, s 742B(1)–(3)
(4)	1985, s 255A(4)
(5)	1985, s 255A(5A)
1165(1)	drafting
(2)–(4)	1985, s 742C(1)–(4)
(5)	1985, s 255A(5)
(6)	1985, s 255A(5A)
(7)	1985, s 744 "insurance market activity"
(8)	1985, s 742C(5)
1166	1985, s 743
1167	1985, s 744 "prescribed"
1168(1)–(7)	new
1169(1)	1985, s 249AA(4)
(2), (3)	1985, s 249AA(5)–(7)
(4)	drafting
1170	1985, s 744 "EEA State", drafting
1171 "the former Companies Acts"	1985, s 735(1)(c) (changed)
"the Joint Stock Companies Acts"	1985, s 735(3)
1172	drafting
1173(1) "body corporate" and "corporation"	new
"credit institution"	1985, s 262 "credit institution" (changed)
"financial institution"	1985, s 699A(3) "financial institution"
"firm"	new
"the Gazette"	1985, s 744 "the Gazette"

PART I COMPANIES LEGISLATION

CA 2006	*Origin*
PART 38 COMPANIES: INTERPRETATION	
"hire-purchase agreement"	1985, s 744 "hire purchase agreement"
"officer"	1985, s 744 "officer"
"parent company"	1985, ss 258(1) and 742(1)
"regulated activity"	1985, s 744 "regulated activity"
"regulated market"	1985 passim (changed)
"working day"	drafting
(2)	drafting
1174 and Sch 8	drafting

CA 2006	*Origin*
PART 39 COMPANIES: MINOR AMENDMENTS	
1175(1), (2), Sch 9	new (amend 1985, Pt 7 and 1986, Pt 8)
1176(1)–(3)	new (repeals 1985, s 438, amends 1985, ss 439 and 453)
1177	new (repeals 1985, ss 311, 323 and 327, 324–326, 328, 329, Pts 2–4 of Sch 13 and ss 343 and 344)
1178	new (repeals 1985, s 720 and Sch 23)
1179	new (repeals 1985, s 729)
1180	new (repeals 1985, Pt 4)
1181(1)–(4)	new (power to amend)

[S1383]

D. Tables of Destinations (Companies Acts 1985 and 1989)

TABLES OF DESTINATIONS (COMPANIES ACTS 1985 AND 1989)

NOTES

1. The table identifies the provisions of the Companies Act 1985 (c 6) that are repealed and re-enacted (with or without changes) by the Companies Act 2006 and identifies the corresponding provisions in that Act.
2. The table is based on the table of origins. So it only shows a provision of the Companies Act 2006 as a destination of a provision of the Companies Act 1985 if the latter is cited in that table as an origin for the new provision.
3. A repealed provision of the Companies Act 1985 may not be listed in this table because the provision is spent or it is otherwise unnecessary to re-enact it, because the new provision is fundamentally different from the existing provision or because as a matter of policy it has been decided to repeal the existing provision without replacing it.
4. There is no entry for Schedule 24 to the Companies Act 1985 (punishment of offences) in the table. This is cited in the table of origins as the origin for a large number of provisions in the Companies Act 2006.
5. A section at the end of the table identifies the substantive provisions of the Companies Act 1989 (c 40) that are repealed and re-enacted by the Companies Act 2006.

COMPANIES ACT 1985

CA 1985	*CA 2006*
1 Mode of forming incorporated company	
(1)	s 7(1), (2) (changed)
(2)	s 3(1)–(4)
(3)	s 4(1)–(3)
(4)	s 5(1), (2)
2 Requirements with respect to memorandum	
(1)	s 9(2)
(2)	ss 9(2), 88(2)
(3)	s 9(2) (changed)
(4)	s 11(3) (changed)
3 Forms of memorandum	
(1)	s 8(2)
7 Articles prescribing regulations for companies	
(1)	s 18(2) (changed)
(3)	s 18(3) (changed)
8 Tables A, C, D and E	
(1)	s 19(1)–(3) (changed)
(2)	s 20(1), (2) (changed)
(3)	s 19(4)
(4)	s 19(1)–(3) (changed)
(5)	s 19(5)
9 Alteration of articles by special resolution	
(1), (2)	s 21(1)
10 Documents to be sent to registrar	
(1)	s 9(1), (5), (6) (changed)
(2)	s 12(1) (changed)
(3)	s 12(3)
(4)	s 9(3)
(6)	s 9(5)
12 Duty of registrar	
(1), (2)	s 14
(3), (3A)	s 13(1), (2) (changed)
13 Effect of registration	
(1)	s 15(1)
(2)	s 15(3)
(3)	s 16(2) (changed)
(4)	s 16(3)
(5)	s 16(6)
(7)	s 15(4)
14 Effect of memorandum and articles	
(1)	s 33(1) (changed)
(2)	s 33(2) (changed)
15 Memorandum and articles of company limited by guarantee	
(1)	s 37
(2)	s 5(3)

CA 1985	CA 2006
16 Effect of alteration on company's members	
(1)	s 25(1)
(2)	s 25(2)
18 Amendments of memorandum or articles to be registered	
(1)	s 34(2) (changed)
(2)	ss 26(1), 34(3) (changed)
(3)	ss 26(3), (4), 34(5), (6)
19 Copies of memorandum and articles to be given to members	
(1)	s 32(1) (changed)
(2)	s 32(3), (4) (changed)
22 Definition of "member"	
(1)	s 112(1) (changed)
(2)	s 112(2)
23 Membership of holding company	
(1)	s 136(1)
(2)	s 138(1), (2)
(3)	s 141(1), (2)
(3A)	s 141(3)
(3B)	s 141(4)
(3BA)	s 141(5)
(3C)	s 142(1), (2)
(4), (5)	s 137(1), (2)
(6)	s 137(3), (4)
(7)	s 144
(8)	s 143
25 Name as stated in memorandum	
(1)	s 58(1), (2)
(2)	s 59(1), (2), (3)
26 Prohibition on registration of certain names	
(1)	ss 53, 65(1)–(5), 66(1) (changed)
(2)	ss 54(1)–(3) and 55(1) (changed)
(3)	s 66(2), (3) (changed)
27 Alternatives of statutory designations	
(4)	ss 58(1), (2), 59(1), (2)
28 Change of name	
(1)	s 77(1)
(2)	ss 67(1), 68(2), (3)
(3)	s 75(1), (2), (4)

CA 1985	CA 2006
28 Change of name	
(4)	ss 68(3), 75(3)
(5)	ss 68(5), (6), 75(5), (6)
(6)	ss 80(1)–(3), 81(1)
(7)	s 81(2), (3)
29 Regulations about names	
(1)	ss 55(1), 56(1)
(2)	s 56(2)
(3)	s 56(3), (4) (changed)
(6)	s 55(2)
30 Exemption from requirement of "limited" as part of the name	
(2), (3)	ss 61(1)–(4), 62(1)–(3) (changed)
(4)	s 60(3)
(5B)	s 60(2)
31 Provisions applying to company exempt under s 30	
(1)	s 63(1)
(2)	s 64(1)–(4) (changed)
(3)	s 64(7)
(5)	s 63(2), (3)
(6)	s 64(5), (6)
32 Power to require company to abandon misleading name	
(1)	s 76(1)
(2)	s 76(3)
(3)	s 76(4), (5)
(4)	s 76(6), (7) (changed)
(5)	ss 80(1)–(3), 81(1)
(6)	s 81(2), (3)
35 A company's capacity not limited by its memorandum	
(1)	s 39(1) (changed)
(4)	s 39(2)
35A Power of directors to bind the company	
(1)	s 40(1)
(2)	s 40(2)
(3)	s 40(3)
(4)	s 40(4)
(5)	s 40(5)
(6)	s 40(6)

CA 1985	*CA 2006*
35B No duty to enquire as to capacity of company or authority of directors	
	s 40(2)
36 Company contracts: England and Wales	
(1), (2)	s 43(1), (2)
36A Execution of documents: England and Wales	
(2)	ss 44(1)
(3)	s 45(1)
(4)	s 44(2), (3), (4)
(4A)	s 44(6)
(6)	s 44(5)
(7)	s 44(8)
(8)	s 44(7)
36AA Execution of deeds: England and Wales	
(1)	s 46(1)
(2)	s 46(2)
36B Execution of documents by companies	
(1)	s 48(2)
(2)	s 48(3)
36C Pre-incorporation contracts, deeds and obligations	
(1)	s 51(1)
(2)	s 51(2)
37 Bills of exchange and promissory notes	
	s 52
38 Execution of deeds abroad	
(1)	s 47(1) (changed)
(2)	s 47(2)
(3)	s 47(1)
39 Power of company to have official seal for use abroad	
(1)	s 49(1), (2) (changed)
(2), (2A)	s 49(3)
(3)	s 49(4)
(4)	s 49(5)
(5)	s 49(6)
40 Official seal for share certificates, etc	
(1)	s 50(1), (2)
42 Events affecting a company's status	
(1)	s 1079(1)–(3)
43 Re-registration of private company as public	
(1)	s 90(1), (2) (changed)
(2)	s 90(3)

CA 1985	*CA 2006*
43 Re-registration of private company as public	
(3)	ss 92(1), (2), 94(2), (3)
(4)	s 92(1)
44 Consideration for shares recently allotted to be valued	
(1)	s 93(1)
(2)	s 93(2), (7)
(4), (5)	s 93(3)–(5)
(6)	s 93(6)
(7)	s 93(6), (7)
45 Additional requirements relating to share capital	
(1)–(4)	s 91(1)
46 Meaning of "unqualified report" in s 43(3)	
(2)	s 92(3)
(3)	s 92(4)
(4)	s 92(5), (6)
47 Certificate of re-registration under s 43	
(1)	s 96(1), (2)
(2)	s 94(4)
(3)	s 91(5) (changed)
(4)	s 96(4)
(5)	s 96(5)
48 Modification for unlimited company re-registering	
(1), (2)	s 90(4)
(5)	s 91(2)
(6)	s 91(3)
(7)	s 91(4)
49 Re-registration of limited company as unlimited	
(1)	s 102(1)
(2)	s 102(2)
(4)	s 102(1)
(5)–(7)	s 102(3)
(8)	ss 102(1), 103(2)–(4) (changed)
(8A)	s 103(3), (4) (changed)
(9)	s 102(4)
50 Certificate of re-registration under s 49	
(1)	s 104(1), (2)
(2)	s 104(4)
(3)	s 104(5)

CA 1985	CA 2006
51 Re-registration of unlimited company as limited	
(1)	s 105(1) (changed)
(2)	s 105(2)
(3)	s 105(3), (4)
(5)	s 106(2)
52 Certificate of re-registration under s 51	
(1)	s 107(1), (2)
(2)	s 107(4)
(3)	s 107(5)
53 Re-registration of public company as private	
(1)	ss 97(1), 100(2) (changed)
(2)	s 97(3)
54 Litigated objection to resolution under s 53	
(1)	s 98(1)
(2)	ss 98(1), 370(3) (changed)
(3)	s 98(2)
(4)	s 99(1), (2) (changed)
(5)	s 98(3), (4)
(6)	s 98(5), (6)
(7)	s 99(3)
(8)	s 98(6)
(10)	s 99(4), (5)
55 Certificate of re-registration under s 53	
(1)	s 101(1), (2)
(2)	s 101(4)
(3)	s 101(5)
58 Document offering shares etc for sale deemed a prospectus	
(3)	s 755(2)
80 Authority of company required for certain allotments	
(1)	s 549(1),s 551(1) (changed)
(2)	ss 549(1)–(3), 551(1), 559
(3)	s 551(2)
(4)	s 551(3), (4)
(5)	s 551(5)
(6)	s 551(6)
(7)	s 551(7)
(8)	s 551(8)
(9)	s 549(4), (5)

CA 1985	CA 2006
80 Authority of company required for certain allotments	
(10)	s 549(6) (changed)
81 Restriction on public offers by private company	
(1)	s 755(1)
(3)	s 760
84 Allotment where issue not fully subscribed	
(1)	s 578(1)
(2)	s 578(2)
(3)	s 578(3) (changed)
(4)	s 578(4), (5)
(5)	s 578(5)
(6)	s 578(6)
85 Effect of irregular allotment	
(1)	s 579(1), (2)
(2)	s 579(3)
(3)	s 579(4)
88 Return as to allotments, etc	
(1)	s 555(1)
(2)	s 555(2) (changed)
(5)	s 557(1), (2)
(6)	ss 557(3), 597(5), (6)
89 Offers to shareholders to be on pre-emptive basis	
(1)	s 561(1)
(2)	s 568(1)
(3)	s 568(1), (2)
(4)	ss 561(2), 565
(5)	s 566
(6)	s 561(4)
90 Communication of pre-emption offers to shareholders	
(1)	s 562(1)
(2)	s 568(3)
(5)	s 562(3) (changed)
(6)	s 562(4), (5) (changed)
91 Exclusion of ss 89, 90 by private company	
(1)	s 567(1), (2)
(2)	s 567(3), (4)
92 Consequences of contravening ss 89, 90	
(1)	ss 563(1), (2), 568(4)
(2)	ss 563(3), 568(5)

CA 1985	*CA 2006*
93 Saving for other restrictions as to offers	
(1)	s 575(1)
(2)	s 575(2)
94 Definitions for ss 89–96	
(2)	ss 560(1), 564, 577
(3)	ss 560(2), 561(3)
(3A)	s 560(2)
(5)	s 560(1)
(7)	s 574(1), (2)
95 Disapplication of pre-emption rights	
(1)	ss 570(1), (2), 573(2), (3), (5)
(2)	ss 571(1), (2), 573(4)
(2A)	s 573(1)–(5l)
(3)	ss 570(3), 571(3)
(4)	ss 570(4), 571(4), 573(3), (5)
(5)	ss 571(5)–(7), 573(5) (changed)
(6)	s 572(1)–(3)
96 Saving for company's pre-emption procedure operative before 1982	
(1), (2)	s 576(1)
(3)	s 576(2)
(4)	s 576(3)
97 Power of company to pay commissions	
(1)	s 553(1)
(2)	s 553(2)
98 Apart from s 97, commissions and discounts barred	
(1)	s 552(1)
(2)	s 552(2)
(3)	s 552(3)
(4)	s 553(3)
99 General rules as to payment for shares on allotment	
(1)	s 582(1), (3)
(2)	s 585(1)
(3)	s 585(2)
(4)	s 582(2)
(5)	s 585(3)
100 Prohibition on allotment of shares at a discount	
(1)	s 580(1)
(2)	s 580(2)

CA 1985	*CA 2006*
101 Shares to be allotted as at least one-quarter paid-up	
(1)	s 586(1)
(2)	s 586(2)
(3), (4)	s 586(3)
(5)	s 586(4)
102 Restriction on payment by long-term undertaking	
(1)	s 587(1)
(2)	s 587(2)
(3), (4)	s 587(3)
(5), (6)	s 587(4)
(7)	s 587(5)
103 Non-cash consideration to be valued before allotment	
(1)	s 593(1)
(2)	s 593(2)
(3)	s 594(1)–(3)
(4)	s 594(4), (5)
(5)	s 595(1), (2)
(6)	s 593(3)
(7)	ss 594(6), 595(3)
104 Transfer to public company of non-cash asset in initial period	
(1)	s 598(1)
(2)	s 598(2)
(3)	s 603
(4)	ss 599(1), (3), 601(1)–(3) (changed)
(5)	s 599(2), (4)
(6)	s 598(4), (5)
105 Agreements contravening s 104	
(1)	s 604(1)
(2)	s 604(2)
(3)	s 604(3)
106 Shares issued to subscribers of memorandum	
	s 584
107 Meaning of "the appropriate rate"	
	ss 592(1), (2), 609(1), (2)
108 Valuation and report (s 103)	
(1)	s 1150(1) (changed)
(2)	s 1150(2)
(3)	s 1150(3)
(4)	s 596(2)
(5)	s 1150(4)

PART I
COMPANIES LEGISLATION

CA 1985	CA 2006
108 Valuation and report (s 103)	
(6)	ss 596(3), 600(3)
(7)	s 596(4), (5)
109 Valuation and report (s 104)	
(2)	s 600(2), (3)
(3)	s 600(4), (5)
110 Entitlement of valuer to full disclosure	
(1)	s 1153(1)
(2)	s 1153(2), (4)
(3)	s 1153(3)
111 Matters to be communicated to registrar	
(1)	s 597(1), (2)
(2)	s 602(1)
(3)	s 597(3)–(6)
(4)	s 602(2), (3)
111A Right to damages, &c not affected	
	s 655
112 Liability of subsequent holders of shares allotted	
(1)	ss 588(1), 605(1)
(2)	s 605(2)
(3)	ss 588(2), 605(3)
(4)	ss 588(3), 605(4)
(5)	s 588(1), (4)
113 Relief in respect of certain liabilities under ss 99 ff	
(1)	ss 589(1), (2), 606(1)
(2)	ss 589(3), 606(2) (changed)
(3)	ss 589(3), 606(2)
(4)	ss 589(4), 606(3)
(5)	ss 589(5), 606(4)
(6), (7)	ss 589(6), 606(5)
(8)	s 606(6)
114 Penalty for contravention	
	ss 590(1), (2), 607(2), (3)
115 Undertakings to do work, etc	
(1)	ss 591(1), (2), 608(1), (2)
117 Public company share capital requirements	
(1)	s 761(1)
(2)	s 761(2) (changed)
(3)	s 762(1) (changed)
(4)	s 761(3)

CA 1985	CA 2006
117 Public company share capital requirements	
(5)	s 762(3)
(6)	s 761(4) (changed)
(7)	s 767(1), (2)
(8)	s 767(3)
118 The authorised minimum	
(1)	ss 763(1), 764(1) (changed)
(2)	s 764(3)
(3)	s 764(4)
119 Provision for different amounts to be paid on shares	
	s 581
121 Alteration of share capital (limited companies)	
(1)	s 617(1) (changed)
(2)	ss 617(2), (3), 618(1), 620(1) (changed)
(3)	s 618(2)
(4)	ss 618(3), 620(2) (changed)
122 Notice to registrar of alteration	
(1)	ss 619(1)–(3), 621(1), 663(1), 689(1) (changed)
(2)	ss 619(4), (5), 621(4), (5), 663(4), (5), 689(4), (5)
125 Variation of class rights	
(1)	s 630(1)
(2)	s 630(2)–(4) (changed)
(6)	s 334(1)–(4), (6) (changed)
(7)	ss 334(7), 630(5)
(8)	s 630(6)
126 Saving for court's powers under other provisions	
	s 632
127 Shareholders' right to object to variation	
(1)	s 633(1)
(2)	s 633(2), (3)
(2A)	s 633(2)
(3)	s 633(4)
(4)	s 633(5)
(5)	s 635(1)–(3)

CA 1985	*CA 2006*
127 Shareholders' right to object to variation	
(6)	s 633(6)
128 Registration of particulars of special rights	
(1)	s 556(1)–(3) (changed)
(2)	ss 556(1), (4), 629(2)
(3)	s 637(1) (changed)
(4)	s 636(1) (changed)
(5)	ss 557(1), (2), 636(2), (3), 637(2), (3) (changed)
129 Registration of newly created class rights	
(1)	s 638(1) (changed)
(2)	s 640(1) (changed)
(3)	s 639(1) (changed)
(4)	ss 638(2), (3), 639(2), (3), 640(2), (3)
130 Application of share premiums	
(1)	s 610(1)
(2)	s 610(2), (2) (changed)
(3)	s 610(4)
(4)	s 610(5), (6)
131 Merger relief	
(1)	s 612(1), (4)
(2)	s 612(2)
(3)	s 612(3)
(4)	s 613(2), (3)
(5)	s 613(4)
(6)	s 613(5)
(7)	s 616(1)
132 Relief in respect of group reconstructions	
(1)	s 611(1)
(2)	s 611(2)
(3)	s 611(3)
(4)	s 611(4)
(5)	s 611(5)
(8)	s 612(4)
133 Provisions supplementing ss 131, 132	
(1)	s 615
(2)	s 616(2)
(3)	s 616(3)

CA 1985	*CA 2006*
133 Provisions supplementing ss 131, 132	
(4)	s 616(1)
134 Provision for extending or restricting relief from s 130	
(1)	s 614(1)
(3)	s 614(2)
135 Special resolution for reduction of share capital	
(1)	s 641(1)–(3) (changed)
(2)	s 641(4)
136 Application to court for order of confirmation	
(1)	s 645(1)
(2)	ss 645(2), (4), 646(4)
(3)	s 646(1)
(4)	s 646(2), (3)
(5)	s 646(4), (5)
(6)	s 645(2), (3)
137 Court order confirming reduction	
(1)	s 648(1), (2)
(2)	s 648(3), (4)
(3)	s 648(4)
138 Registration of order and minute of reduction	
(1)	s 649(1) (changed)
(2)	s 649(3) (changed)
(3)	s 649(4) (changed)
(4)	s 649(5), (6) (changed)
139 Public company reducing capital below authorised minimum	
(1)	s 650(1)
(2)	s 650(2)
(3)	s 651(1), (2)
(4)	s 651(3) (changed)
(5)	s 651(4), (6), (7)
140 Liability of members on reduced shares	
(1)	s 652(1) (changed)
(2)	s 653(1)
(3)	s 653(2)
(4)	s 653(3)
(5)	s 653(3)
141 Penalty for concealing name of creditor, etc	
	s 647(1), (2) (changed)

CA 1985	*CA 2006*
142 Duty of directors on serious loss of capital	
(1)	s 656(1)–(3)
(2)	s 656(4), (5) (changed)
(3)	s 656(6)
143 General rule against company acquiring own shares	
(1)	s 658(1)
(2)	s 658(2), (3)
(2A)	s 725(4)
(3)	s 659(1), (2)
144 Acquisition of shares by company's nominee	
(1)	s 660(1), (2) (changed)
(2)	s 661(1), (2) (changed)
(3)	s 661(3)
(4)	s 661(4)
145 Exceptions from s 144	
(1)	s 660(3)
(2)	ss 660(3), 661(5)
(3)	s 671
146 Treatment of shares held by or for public company	
(1)	ss 662(1), 671
(2)	s 662(2), (3)
(3)	s 662(3)
(4)	s 662(5), (6)
147 Matters arising out of compliance with s 146(2)	
(2)	s 664(1), (2)
(3)	s 664(4) (changed)
(4)	s 665(1), (2), (4), (5) (changed)
148 Further provisions supplementing ss 146, 147	
(1)	s 668(1), (2)
(2)	s 668(3)
(3)	s 671
(4)	s 669(1), (2)
149 Sanctions for non-compliance	
(1)	s 666(1), (2)
(2)	s 667(1)–(3)
150 Charges of public companies on own shares	
(1)	s 670(1)
(2)	s 670(2)

CA 1985	*CA 2006*
150 Charges of public companies on own shares	
(3)	s 670(3)
(4)	s 670(4)
151 Financial assistance generally prohibited	
(1)	ss 678(1), 679(1) (changed)
(2)	ss 678(3), 679(3) (changed)
(3)	s 680(1), (2)
152 Definitions for this Chapter	
(1)	ss 677(1), 683(1)
(2)	s 677(2), (3)
(3)	s 683(2)
153 Transactions not prohibited by s 151	
(1)	ss 678(2), 679(2) (changed)
(2)	ss 678(4), 679(4)
(3)	s 681(1), (2)
(4)	s 682(1), (2)
(5)	s 682(5)
154 Special restriction for public companies	
(1)	s 682(1)
(2)	ss 682(3), (4), 840(4), (5)
159 Power to issue redeemable shares	
(1)	s 684(1), (3) (changed)
(2)	s 684(4)
(3)	ss 686(1)–(3) (changed), 691(1), (2)
160 Financing etc of redemption	
(1)	ss 687(1)–(3), (6), 692(1), (2), (5)
(2)	ss 687(4), (5), 692(3), (4)
(4)	ss 688, 706 (changed)
162 Power of company to purchase own shares	
(1)	s 690(1) (changed)
(2)	ss 691(1), (2), 692(1)–(5)
(2A)	s 706
(2B)	ss 706, 724(1)
(3)	s 690(2)
(4)	s 724(2)

CA 1985	*CA 2006*
162A Treasury shares	
(1)	s 724(3)
(2)	s 724(4)
(3)	s 724(5)
162B Treasury shares: maximum holdings	
(1)	s 725(1)
(2)	s 725(2)
(3)	s 725(4)
162C Treasury shares: voting and other rights	
(1)	s 726(1)
(2), (3)	s 726(2)
(4)	s 726(3)
(5)	s 726(4)
(6)	s 726(5)
162D Treasury shares: disposal and cancellation	
(1)	ss 727(1), 729(1)
(2)	s 727(2) (changed)
(3)	s 727(3)
(4)	s 729(4)
(5)	s 729(5)
162E Treasury shares: mandatory cancellation	
(1)	s 729(2)
(2)	s 729(3)
162F Treasury shares: proceeds of sale	
(1)	s 731(1)
(2)	s 731(2)
(3)	s 731(3)
(4), (5)	s 731(4)
162G Treasury shares: penalty for contravention	
	s 732(1), (2) (changed)
163 Definitions of "off-market" and "market" purchase	
(1)	s 693(2)
(2)	s 693(3)
(3)	s 693(4)
(4), (5)	s 693(5)
164 Authority for off-market purchase	
(1)	ss 693(1), 694(1)
(2)	s 694(2) (changed)
(3)	ss 694(4), 697(3), 700(3)
(4)	ss 694(5), 697(4), 700(4)
164 Authority for off-market purchase	
(5)	ss 694(1), (3), (4), 698(1), (3), (4), 700(5)
(6)	ss 696(1)–(5), 699(1)–(6), 700(5) (changed)
(7)	ss 697(1)–(4), 698(1), (3), (4), 699(1)–(6), 700(3)–(5)
165 Authority for contingent purchase contract	
(1)	s 694(3)
(2)	ss 694(2), (4), (5), 695(1), (3), (5), 696(1)–(5)
166 Authority for market purchase	
(1)	ss 693(1), 701(1)
(2)	s 701(2)
(3)	s 701(3), (5)
(4)	s 701(4), (5)
(5)	s 701(6)
(6)	s 701(7)
(7)	s 701(8)
167 Assignment or release of company's right to purchase own shares	
(1)	s 704
(2)	s 700(1)–(5)
168 Payments apart from purchase price to be made out of distributable profits	
(1)	s 705(1)
(2)	s 705(2)
169 Disclosure by company of purchase of own shares	
(1)	ss 707(1)–(3), 708(1) (changed)
(1A)	ss 707(1)–(3), 708(1) (changed)
(1B)	ss 707(1)–(3), 708(1) (changed)
(2)	s 707(4)
(3)	s 707(5)
(4)	s 702(1)–(4) (changed)
(5)	s 702(6)
(6)	ss 707(6), (7), 708(4), (5)
(7)	s 703(1), (2) (changed)
(8)	s 703(3)

CA 1985	CA 2006
169 Disclosure by company of purchase of own shares	
(9)	s 702(7)
169A Disclosure by company of cancellation or disposal of treasury shares	
(1)	ss 728(1), 730(1)
(2)	ss 728(2), 730(2)
(3)	ss 728(3), 730(3)
(4)	ss 728(4), (5), 730(6), (7)
170 The capital redemption reserve	
(1)	s 733(1), (2), (4)
(2), (3)	s 733(3)
(4)	s 733(5), (6)
171 Power of private companies to redeem or purchase own shares out of capital	
(1)	s 709(1) (changed)
(2)	s 709(2)
(3)	s 710(1), (2)
(4)	s 734(2)
(5)	s 734(3)
(6)	s 734(4)
172 Availability of profits for purposes of s 171	
(1)	s 711(1), (2)
(2)	s 712(2)
(3)	s 712(6)
(4)	s 712(3)
(5)	s 712(4)
(6)	s 712(7)
173 Conditions for payment out of capital	
(1)	s 713(1), (2)
(2)	s 716(1)
(3)	s 714(1)–(3)
(4)	s 714(4) (changed)
(5)	s 714(5), (6) (changed)
(6)	s 715(1), (2)
174 Procedure for special resolution under s 173	
(1)	ss 716(2), 723(1)
(2)	s 717(3)
(3)	s 717(4)
(4)	s 718(2), (3) (changed)
(5)	s 717(5)

CA 1985	CA 2006
175 Publicity for proposed payment out of capital	
(1)	s 719(1)
(2)	s 719(2)
(3)	s 719(3)
(4)	ss 719(4), 720(1)
(5)	s 719(4)
(6)	s 720(1), (2), (4) (changed)
(7)	s 720(5), (6)
(8)	s 720(7)
176 Objections by company's members or creditors	
(1)	s 721(1), (2)
(2)	s 721(2)
(3)	s 722(2), (3)
(4)	s 722(4), (5)
177 Powers of court on application under s 176	
(1)	s 721(3)
(2)	s 721(4), (5)
(3)	s 721(6)
(4)	s 721(7)
178 Effect of company's failure to redeem or purchase	
(1)	s 735(1)
(2)	s 735(2)
(3)	s 735(2), (3)
(4)	s 735(4)
(5)	s 735(5)
(6)	s 735(6)
181 Definitions for Chapter VII	
	s 736
182 Nature, transfer and numbering of shares	
(1)	ss 541, 544(1), (2)
(2)	s 543(1), (2)
183 Transfer and registration	
(1)	s 770(1)
(2)	s 770(2)
(3)	s 773
(4)	s 772
184 Certification of transfers	
(1)	s 775(1), (2)
(2)	s 775(3)
(3)	s 775(4)

CA 1985	*CA 2006*
185 Duty of company as to issue of certificates	
(1)	ss 769(1), (2), 776(1), (3)
(2)	s 776(2)
(3)	s 777(1), (2)
(4)	ss 769(2), 776(3), 778(1)
(4A)	s 778(1)
(4B), (4C)	s 778(2)
(4D)	s 778(3)
(5)	ss 769(3), (4), 776(5), (6)
(6)	s 782(1)
(7)	s 782(2), (3)
186 Certificate to be evidence of title	
(1)	s 768(1), (2)
(2)	s 768(2)
187 Evidence of grant of probate or confirmation as executor	
	s 774
188 Issue and effect of share warrant to bearer	
(1)	s 779(1)
(2)	s 779(2)
(3)	s 779(3)
189 Offences in connections with share warrants (Scotland)	
(1)	s 781(1), (3)
(2)	s 781(2), (4)
190 Register of debenture holders	
(1)	s 743(6)
(5)	s 743(2), (6) (changed)
(6)	s 743(3)
191 Right to inspect register	
(1)	s 744(1)
(2)	s 744(2)
(3)	s 749(1)
(4)	ss 746(1), (2), 749(2), (3)
(5)	ss 746(3), 749(4)
(6)	s 744(5)
(7)	s 748(1), (2) (changed)
192 Liability of trustees of debentures	
(1)	s 750(1), (3)
(2)	s 750(2)

CA 1985	*CA 2006*
192 Liability of trustees of debentures	
(3)	s 751(1), (2)
(4)	s 751(3), (4)
193 Perpetual debentures	
	s 739(1), (2)
194 Power to re-issue redeemed debentures	
(1)	s 752(1)
(2)	s 752(2)
(3)	s 753
(4)	s 752(3)
(5)	s 752(4)
195 Contract to subscribe for debentures	
	s 740
196 Payment of debts out of assets subject to floating charge (England and Wales)	
(1)	s 754(1)
(2)	s 754(2)
(3)	s 754(3)
(4)	s 754(4)
197 Debentures to bearer (Scotland)	
	s 742
198 Obligation of disclosure: the cases in which it may arise and "the relevant time"	
(2)	s 792(1), (2) (changed)
203 Notification of family and corporate interests	
(1)	s 822(1), (2)
(2)	s 823(1)
(3)	s 832(2)
(4)	s 823(3)
204 Agreement to acquire interests in a particular company	
(1)	s 824(1)
(2)	ss 824(1), (2), 988(4)
(3)	ss 824(3), 988(6)
(4)	s 824(4)
(5)	ss 824(5), 988(7)
(6)	ss 824(6), 988(5)
205 Obligation of disclosure arising under s 204	
(1)	s 825(1)
(2)	s 825(2)
(3)	s 825(3)
(4)	s 825(4)

CA 1985	*CA 2006*
207 Interests in shares by attribution	
(1)	ss 783, 785(1)
(2)	s 785(2)
(3)	s 785(3)
(4)	s 785(4)
(5)	s 785(5)
(6)	s 785(6)
(7)	s 788
(9)	s 784(3)
(10)	s 783
208 Interests in shares which are to be notified	
(1)	s 820(1)
(2)	s 820(2)
(3)	s 820(3)
(4)	s 820(4)
(5)	s 820(6)
(6)	s 820(5)
(7)	s 820(7)
(8)	s 820(8)
210A Power to make further provision by regulations	
(1)	s 828(1), (2)
(5)	s 828(3)
211 Register of interests in shares	
(3)	s 808(2)
(4)	s 808(7)
(5)	s 808(4)
(6)	s 810(1)–(3)
(7)	s 819(1)
(8)	ss 809(1), 810(4), 811(1), (2), 813(1)–(3) (changed)
(9)	s 826(1)
(10)	ss 808(5), (6), 819(2), (3)
212 Company investigations	
(1)	s 793(1), (2) (changed)
(2)	s 793(3), (4), (6)
(3)	s 793(5)
(4)	s 793(7)
(5)	ss 820(1)–(8), 822(1), (2), 823(1)–(3), 824(1)–(6), 825(1)–(4)
(6)	s 821(1), (2)

CA 1985	*CA 2006*
213 Registration of interests disclosed under s 212	
(1)	s 808(1)–(3) (changed)
(3)	ss 808(2), (4)–(7), 809(1), 810(1)–(4), 811(1), (2), 813(1)–(3), 819(1)–(3), 826(1)
214 Company investigation on requisition by members	
(1)	s 803(1), (2) (changed)
(2)	s 803(3) (changed)
(4)	s 804(1)
(5)	s 804(2), (3) (changed)
215 Company report to members	
(1)	s 805(1)
(2)	s 805(2), (3)
(3)	s 805(1), (3)
(4)	s 826(1), (2)
(5)	s 805(6)
(6)	s 805(7)
(7)	ss 805(4), 807(1)–(5)
(8)	s 806(3), (4)
216 Penalty for failure to provide information	
(1)	s 794(1)
(1A)	s 794(3)
(1B)	s 794(2)
(3)	s 795(1), (3)
(4)	s 795(2)
(5)	s 796(1), (2)
217 Removal of entries from register	
(1)	s 816 (changed)
(2)	s 817(1) (changed)
(3)	s 817(2), (3)
(4)	s 818(1), (2)
(5)	ss 817(4), 818(3)
218 Otherwise, entries not to be removed	
(1)	s 815(1)
(2)	s 815(2)
(3)	s 815(3), (4)
219 Inspection of register and reports	
(1)	s 807(1), 811(1)
(2)	s 807(2), 811(2)

CA 1985	*CA 2006*
219 Inspection of register and reports	
(3)	ss 807(3), (4), 813(1), (2) (changed)
(4)	ss 807(5), 813(3)
220 Definitions for Part VI	
(2)	s 827
221 Duty to keep accounting records	
(1)	s 386(1), (2)
(2)–(4)	s 386(3)–(5)
(5)	s 387(1), (2)
(6)	s 387(3)
222 Where and for how long records to be kept	
(1)–(3)	s 388(1)–(3)
(4)	s 389(1), (2), (4)
(5)	s 388(4), (5)
(6)	s 389(3), (4)
223 A company's financial year	
(1)–(5)	s 390(1)–(5)
224 Accounting reference periods and accounting reference date	
(1)	s 391(1)
(2), (3)	s 391(2)
(3A)	s 391(4)
(4)–(6)	s 391(5)–(7)
225 Alteration of accounting reference date	
(1)	s 392(1)
(3)–(7)	s 392(2)–(6)
226 Duty to prepare individual accounts	
(1)	s 394
(2)–(6)	s 395(1)–(5)
226A Companies Act individual accounts	
(1), (2)	s 396(1), (2)
(3)	s 396(3) (changed)
(4)	s 396(4)
(5), (6)	s 396(5)
226B IAS individual accounts	
	s 397
227 Duty to prepare group accounts	
(1)	s 399(2)
(2)–(7)	s 403(1)–(6)
(8)	s 399(2), (3)
227A Companies Act group accounts	
(1), (2)	s 404(1), (2)
(3)	s 404(3) (changed)
(4)	s 404(4)

CA 1985	*CA 2006*
227A Companies Act group accounts	
(5), (6)	s 404(5)
227B IAS group accounts	
	s 406
227C Consistency of accounts	
(1)–(5)	s 407(1)–(5)
228 Exemption for parent companies included in accounts of larger group	
(1), (2)	s 400(1), (2)
(3)	s 400(4)
(4)	s 400(5)
(5)	s 400(3)
(6)	s 400(6)
228A Exemption for parent companies included in non-EEA group accounts	
(1), (2)	s 401(1), (2)
(3)	s 401(4)
(4)	s 401(5)
(5)	s 401(3)
(6)	s 401(6)
229 Subsidiary undertakings included in the consolidation	
(1), (2)	s 405(1), (2)
(3)	s 405(3), (4)
(5)	s 402
230 Treatment of individual profit and loss account where group accounts prepared	
(1)	s 408(1) (changed)
(2)	s 408(2) (changed)
(3), (40	s 408(3), (4)
231 Disclosure required in notes to accounts: related undertakings	
(1), (2)	s 409(1), (2) (changed)
(3)	s 409(3), (4) (changed)
(4)	s 409(5)
(5)	s 410(1), (2)
(6)	s 410(3)
(7)	s 410(4), (5)
231A Disclosure required in notes to annual accounts: particulars of staff	
(1)	s 411(1)
(2)–(4)	s 411(3)–(5)
(5)	s 411(2)
(6)	s 411(7)
(7)	s 411(6)

CA 1985	CA 2006
232 Disclosure required in notes to accounts: emoluments and other benefits of directors and others	
(3)	s 412(5)
(4)	s 412(6)
233 Approval and signing of accounts	
(1), (2)	ss 414(1), (2), 450(1), (2)
(3)	ss 433(1)–(3), 436(1), (2),
(4)	ss 444(6), 445(5), 446(3), 447(3) (changed)
(5)	s 414(4), (5) (changed)
(6)(a)	s 433(4), (5),
234 Duty to prepare directors' report	
(1)	ss 415(1), 417(1), 418(2)
(2), (3)	s 415(2), (3)
(5)	ss 415(4), (5), 419(3), (4)
234ZZA Directors' report: general requirements	
(1)	s 416(1), (3)
(2)	s 416(2)
(3), (4)	s 416(4) (changed)
234ZZB Directors' report: business review	
(1), (2)	s 417(3), (4)
(3)	s 417(6)
(4)	s 417(8)
(5)	s 417(6)
(6)	s 417(9)
234ZA Statement as to disclosure of information to auditors	
(1)–(4)	s 418(1)–(4)
(6)	s 418(5), (6)
234A Approval and signing of directors' report	
(1)	s 419(1)
(2)	ss 433(1)–(3), 436(1), (2)
(3)	ss 444(6), 445(5), 446(3), 447(3)
(4)	ss 419(3), (4), 433(4), (5)
234B Duty to prepare directors' remuneration report	
(1)	ss 420(1), 421(1), (2)

CA 1985	CA 2006
234B Duty to prepare directors' remuneration report	
(2)	s 421(1), (2)
(3), (4)	s 420(2), (3)
(5), (6)	s 421(3), (4)
234C Approval and signing of directors' remuneration report	
(1)	s 422(1)
(2)	ss 433(1)–(3), 436(1), (2)
(3)	s 447(3)
(4)	s 422(2), (3)
235 Auditors' report	
(1)	ss 475(1), 495(1)
(1A)	s 495(2)
(1B), (2)	s 495(3)
(2A)	s 495(4)
(3)	s 496
(4), (5)	s 497(1), (2)
236 Signature of auditors' report	
(1)	s 503(1), (2)
(2)	s 505(1), (2) (changed)
(3)	s 444(7) (changed)
(4)	s 505(3), (4)
237 Duties of auditors	
(1)–(4)	s 498(1)–(4)
(4A)	s 498(5)
238 Persons entitled to receive copies of accounts and reports	
(1), (1A)	ss 423(1), 424(1)–(3) (changed)
(3)	s 423(4)
(4)	s 424(4) (changed)
(5)	s 425(1), (2)
(6)	s 423(5)
239 Right to demand copies of accounts and reports	
(1), (2)	ss 431(1), (2), 432(1), (2)
(3)	ss 431(3), (4), 432(3), (4)
240 Requirements in connection with publication of accounts	
(1)	s 434(1) (changed)
(2)	s 434(2) (changed)
(3)	s 435(1), (2) (changed)

CA 1985	*CA 2006*
240 Requirements in connection with publication of accounts	
(4)	s 436(1), (2) (changed)
(5)	ss 434(3), 435(3) (changed)
(6)	s 435(5), (6)
241 Accounts and reports to be laid before company in general meeting	
(1)	s 437(1) (changed)
(2)	ss 437(2), 438(1), (4)
(3), (4)	s 438(2), (3)
241A Members' approval of directors' remuneration report	
(1), (3)	s 439(1)
(4)	s 439(2)
(5)	s 439(3)
(6)	s 439(4)
(7)	s 439(3)
(8)	s 439(5)
(9)	s 440(1), (4)
(10)	s 440(2)–(4)
(11)	s 440(2), (3)
(12)	s 439(6)
242 Accounts and reports to be delivered to the registrar	
(1)	ss 441(1), 444(1), (2), 445(1), (2), 446(1), (2), 447(1), (2) (changed)
(2)	s 451(1)
(3)	s 452(1), (2)
(4), (5)	s 451(2), (3)
242A Civil penalty for failure to deliver accounts	
(1)	s 453(1)
(2)	s 453(2) (changed)
(3), (4)	s 453(3), (4)
242B Delivery and publication of accounts in ECUs	
(1)–(4)	s 469(1)–(4)
244 Period allowed for laying and delivering accounts and reports	
(1), (2)	s 442(2), (3) (changed)
(4), (5)	s 442(4), (5)
(6)	s 442(7)

CA 1985	*CA 2006*
245 Voluntary revision of annual accounts or directors' report	
(1)–(3)	s 454(1)–(3)
(4)	s 454(4) (changed)
(5)	s 454(5)
245A Secretary of State's notice in respect of annual accounts	
(1)	s 455(1), (2)
(2)–(4)	s 455(3)–(5)
245B Application to court in respect of defective accounts	
(1)–(3)	s 456(1)–(3)
(3A)	s 456(4)
(4)–(7)	s 456(5)–(8)
245C Other persons authorised to apply to court	
(1)	s 457(1)
(1A)	s 457(5)
(2), (3)	s 457(2), (3)
(4)	s 457(7)
(4A)	s 457(5)
(4B)	s 457(4)
(5)	s 457(6)
245D Disclosure of information held by Inland Revenue to persons authorised to apply to court	
(1)	s 458(1)
(2)	s 458(2)
(3)	s 458(1)
245E Restrictions on use and further disclosure of information disclosed under section 245D	
(1), (2)	s 458(3)
(3)	s 458(4), (5)
(4)	s 458(4) (changed)
(5)	ss 1126, 1130
245F Power of authorised persons to require documents, information and explanations	
(1)–(8)	s 459(1)–(8)
245G Restrictions on further disclosure of information obtained under section 245F	
(1), (2)	s 460(1), (2)
(3)	ss 460(3), 461(1)–(6)
(4)–(6)	s 462(1)–(3)
(7)	s 460(4), (5)
(8)	s 460(4)
(9)	ss 1126, 1130
(10)	s 460(3)

CA 1985	CA 2006
245G Restrictions on further disclosure of information obtained under section 245F	
(11)	s 461(7)
246 Special provisions for small companies	
(3)	s 411(1)
(4)	ss 416(3), 417(1)
(5)	s 444(1), (3) (changed)
(6)	s 444(3) (changed)
(7)	ss 444(6), 450(1), (2)
(8)	ss 414(3), 419(2), 444(5), 450(3)
246A Special provisions for medium-sized companies	
(1)	s 445(1)
(2)	s 445(3) (changed)
(2A)	s 417(7)
(3)	s 445(3) (changed)
(4)	s 450(3)
247 Qualification of company as small or medium-sized	
(1)(a)	ss 382(1), 465(1)
(1)(b), (2)	ss 382(2), 465(2)
(3), (4)	ss 382(3), (4), 465(3), (4)
(5)	ss 382(5), 465(5) (changed)
(6)	ss 382(6), 465(6)
247A Cases in which special provisions do not apply	
(1)–(1B)	ss 384(1), 467(1)
(2)	ss 384(2), 467(2) (changed)
(2A)	ss 384(3), 467(3)
(3)	ss 383(1), 466(1)
247B Special auditors' report	
(1)	s 449(1)
(2)	ss 444(4), 445(4), 449(2)
(3)–(5)	s 449(3)–(5)
248 Exemption for small and medium-sized groups	
(1), (2)	ss 398, 399(1), (2) (changed)
249 Qualification of group as small or medium-sized	
(1)(a)	s 466(2)
(1)(b), (2)	s 466(3)

CA 1985	CA 2006
249 Qualification of group as small or medium-sized	
(3)	s 466(4)
(4)	s 466(5), (6)
(5), (6)	s 466(7)
249A Exemptions from audit	
(1)	s 477(1)
(3)	s 477(2), (4)
(6)	s 477(3)
(7)	s 477(4)
249AA Dormant companies	
(1), (2)	s 480(1), (2)
(3)	s 481
(4)	s 1169(1)
(5)–(7)	s 1169(2), (3)
249B Cases where exemptions not available	
(1)	ss 478, 479(1)–(3)
(1A)	s 479(3)
(1B)	s 479(1)–(3)
(1C)	s 479(2), (5), (6)
(2), (3)	s 476(1)–(3)
(4)	s 475(2), (3)
(5)	s 475(4)
249E Effect of exemptions	
(1)(b)	ss 444(2), 445(2), 446(2) (changed)
251 Provision of summary financial statement to shareholders	
(1)	ss 426(1), 427(1)
(2)	s 426(2), (3)
(3)	ss 427(2), 428(2)
(3A)	ss 427(3), 428(3)
(4)	ss 427(4), 428(4)
(5)	ss 427(6), 428(6)
(6)	s 429(1), (2)
(7)	ss 434(6), 435(7)
254 Exemption from requirement to deliver accounts and reports	
(1)–(3)	s 448(1)–(3)
(4)	s 448(4)
255A Special provisions for banking and insurance groups	
(4)	s 1164(5)
(5)	s 1165(5)
(5A)	ss 1164(5), 1165(6)

CA 1985	*CA 2006*
255D Power to apply provisions to banking partnerships	
(1)	s 470(1)
(2), (2A)	s 470(2)
(4)	s 470(4)
(5)	s 470(3)
256 Accounting standards	
(1), (2)	s 464(1), (2)
(4)	s 464(3)
257 Power of Secretary of State to alter accounting requirements	
(1)	s 484(1)
(2)	ss 473(1)–(4) (changed), 484(3)
(3)	s 484(4)
(4)(c)	s 484(2)
258 Parent and subsidiary undertakings	
(1)–(6)	s 1162(1)–(6)
259 Meaning of "undertaking" and related expressions	
(1)	ss 1161(1), 1173 "parent company"
(2)–(5)	s 1161(2)–(5)
261 Notes to the accounts	
(1), (2)	s 472(1), (2)
262 Minor definitions	
(1)	ss 474(1), 539, 835(6), 1173 "credit institution" (changed)
(2)	s 474(2)
(3)	s 853(4), (5)
263 Certain distributions prohibited	
(1)	s 830(1)
(2)	s 829(1), (2)
(3)	s 830(2), (3)
(4)	s 849
(5)	s 850(1)–(3)
264 Restriction on distribution of assets	
(1)	s 831(1), (6)
(2)	s 831(2), (3)
(3)	s 831(4)
(4)	s 831(5)
265 Other distributions by investment companies	
(1)	s 832(1)–(3)
(2)	s 832(4)
(3)	s 832(7)

CA 1985	*CA 2006*
265 Other distributions by investment companies	
(4)	s 832(5)
(4A)	s 832(6)
(5)	s 832(6)
(6)	s 832(5)
266 Meaning of "investment company"	
(1)	s 833(1)
(2)	ss 833(2), 834(1)
(2A)	s 833(3)
(3)	s 833(4), (5)
(4)	s 834(2)–(5)
267 Extension of ss 265, 266 to other companies	
(1)	s 835(1)
(2)	s 835(2)
268 Realised profits of insurance company with long term business	
(1)	s 843(1), (2), (4), (5)
(2)	s 843(3), (4)
(3)	s 843(6), (7)
(4)	s 843(7)
269 Treatment of development costs	
(1)	s 844(1)
(2)	s 844(2), (3)
270 Distribution to be justified by reference to company's accounts	
(1), (2)	s 836(1)
(3)	ss 836(2), 837(1)
(4)	ss 836(2), 838(1), 839(1)
(5)	s 836(3), (4)
271 Requirements for last annual accounts	
(2)	s 837(2)
(3)	s 837(3), (4)
(4)	s 837(4)
(5)	s 837(5)
272 Requirements for interim accounts	
(1)	s 838(2)
(2)	s 838(3)
(3)	ss 838(4), (5), 839(4)
(4), (5)	s 838(6)
273 Requirements for initial accounts	
(1)	s 839(2)
(2)	s 839(3)
(3)	s 839(4)

CA 1985	CA 2006
273 Requirements for initial accounts	
(4)	s 839(5), (6)
(5)	s 839(6)
(6), (7)	s 839(7)
274 Method of applying s 270 to successive distributions	
(1)	s 840(1)
(2)	s 840(1), (2)
(3)	s 840(3)–(5)
275 Treatment of assets in the relevant accounts	
(1)	s 841(1), (2)
(1A)	s 841(3)
(2)	s 841(5)
(3)	s 842
(4)–(6)	s 841(4)
276 Distributions in kind	
	s 846(1), (2) (changed)
277 Consequences of unlawful distribution	
(1)	s 847(1), (2)
(2)	s 847(3), (4)
278 Saving for provision in articles operative before Act of 1980	
	s 848(1), (2)
280 Definitions for Part VIII	
(1)	s 853(1)
(2)	s 853(2)
(3)	s 853(3)
281 Saving for other restraints on distribution	
	ss 851, 852 (changed)
282 Directors	
(1)	s 154(2) (changed)
(3)	s 154(1)
283 Secretary	
(1)	s 271 (changed)
(3)	ss 270(3), 274 (changed)
284 Acts done by person in dual capacity	
	s 280
285 Validity of acts of directors	
	s 161(1), (2) (changed)
286 Qualifications of company secretaries	
(1)	s 273(1), (2) (changed)

CA 1985	CA 2006
286 Qualifications of company secretaries	
(2)	s 273(3)
287 Registered office	
(1)	s 86
(3)	s 87(1)
(4)	s 87(2)
(5)	s 87(3)
(6)	s 87(4)
288 Register of directors and secretaries	
(1)	ss 162(1)–(3), 275(1)–(3) (changed)
(2)	ss 167(1), (2), 276(1), (2)
(3)	ss 162(5), 275(5)
(4)	ss 162(6), (7), 167(4), (5), 275(6), (7), 276(3), (4)
(5)	ss 162(8), 275(8)
(6)	ss 162(6), 167(4), 275(6), 276(3)
289 Particulars of directors to be registered under s 288	
(1)	ss 163(1), 164 (changed)
(2)	ss 163(2), (4), 277(2), (4) (changed)
290 Particulars of secretaries to be registered under s 288	
(1)	ss 277(1), 278(1) (changed)
(2)	s 278(2)
(3)	s 277(2), (4)
292 Appointment of directors to be voted on individually	
(1)	s 160(1)
(2)	s 160(2)
(3)	s 160(3)
(4)	s 160(4)
303 Resolution to remove director	
(1)	s 168(1) (changed)
(2)	s 168(2)
(3)	s 168(3)
(4)	s 168(4)
(5)	s 168(5)
304 Director's right to protest removal	
(1)	s 169(1), (2)

CA 1985	*CA 2006*
304 Director's right to protest removal	
(2)	s 169(3)
(3)	s 169(4)
(4)	s 169(5)
(5)	s 169(6)
309 Directors to have regard to interests of employees	
(1)	s 172(1)
309A Provisions protecting directors from liability	
(1)	s 232(1), (2)
(2)	s 232(1)
(3)	s 232(2)
(4)	s 234(1)
(5)	s 233
(6)	s 232(3)
309B Qualifying third party indemnity provisions	
(1), (2)	s 234(2)
(3)	s 234(3)
(4)	s 234(3), (6)
(5)	s 234(4)
(6), (7)	s 234(5)
309C Disclosure of qualifying third party indemnity provisions	
(1)	s 236(1) (changed)
(2)	s 236(2), (3)
(3)	s 236(4), (5) (changed)
(4)	s 237(1)
(5)	ss 237(1)–(3), (5)–(8), 238(1), (3)–(5)
310 Provisions protecting auditors from liability	
(1)	s 532(1), (3) (changed)
(2)	s 532(2)
(3)	s 533
312 Payment to director for loss of office, etc	
	ss 215(1), 217(1), (3) (changed)
313 Company approval for property transfer	
(1)	ss 215(1), 218(1), (3) (changed)
(2)	s 222(2)

CA 1985	*CA 2006*
314 Director's duty of disclosure on takeover, etc	
(1)	ss 215(1), 219(1) (changed)
315 Consequences of non-compliance with s 314	
(1)	ss 219(1), (2), 222(3) (changed)
(3)	s 219(5)
316 Provisions supplementing ss 312 to 315	
(1)	ss 218(5), 219(7)
(2)	s 216(1), (2) (changed)
(3)	s 220(1)
317 Directors to disclose interest in contracts	
(1)	s 182(1) (changed)
(2)	s 182(2) (changed)
(3)	s 185(1), (2) (changed)
(4)	s 185(4)
(5)	s 185(1) (changed)
(7)	s 183(1), (2)
(8)	s 187(1)–(4)
318 Director's service contracts to be open to inspection	
(1)	ss 228(1), 237(2)
(2), (3)	ss 228(2), 237(3) (changed)
(4)	ss 228(4), 237(5)
(6)	s 230
(7)	ss 229(1), 238(1)
(8)	ss 228(5), (6), 229(3), (4), 237(6), (7), 238(3), (4) (changed)
(9)	ss 229(5), 238(5) (changed)
(10)	ss 228(7), 237(8)
319 Director's contract of employment for more than 5 years	
(1)	s 188(1), (3) (changed)
(2)	s 188(4) (changed)
(3)	s 188(2) (changed)
(4)	s 188(6)
(5)	s 188(5)
(6)	s 189
(7)	ss 188(7), 223(1)

CA 1985	CA 2006
320 Substantial property transactions involving directors, etc	
(1)	s 190(1), (2) (changed)
(2)	s 191(1)–(5) (changed)
(3)	s 223(1)
321 Exceptions from s 320	
(1)	s 190(4)
(2)	ss 192, 193(1), (2) (changed)
(3)	s 192
(4)	s 194(1), (2)
322 Liabilities arising from contravention of s 320	
(1)	s 195(1), (2)
(2)	ss 195(2) and 196
(3)	s 195(1), (3), (4)
(4)	s 195(3), (5), (8)
(5)	s 195(6)
(6)	s 195(7)
322A Invalidity of certain transactions involving directors, etc	
(1)	s 41(1), (2)
(2)	s 41(2)
(3)	s 41(3)
(4)	s 41(1)
(5)	s 41(4)
(6)	s 41(5)
(7)	s 41(6)
(8)	s 41(7)
322B Contracts with sole members who are directors	
(1)	s 231(1), (2) (changed)
(2)	s 231(1)
(3)	s 231(5)
(4)	s 231(3), (4) (changed)
(5)	s 231(7)
(6)	s 231(6)
325 Register of directors' interests notified under s 324	
(5)	s 809(2), (3)
330 General restriction on loans etc to directors and persons connected with them	
(2)	s 197(1) (changed)

CA 1985	CA 2006
330 General restriction on loans etc to directors and persons connected with them	
(3)	ss 198(1), (2) (changed), 200(1), (2)
(4)	s 201(1), (2) (changed)
(5)	s 223(1)
(6)	s 203(1), (6) (changed)
(7)	s 203(1) (changed)
331 Definitions for ss 330 ff	
(3)	s 199(1)
(4)	s 199(2), (3)
(6)	ss 198(1), 200(1), 201(1)
(7)	s 202(1)
(8)	s 202(3)
(9)	ss 202(2), 212
(10)	s 202(3)
333 Inter-company loans in same group	
	s 208(1) (changed)
334 Loans of small amounts	
	s 207(1) (changed)
335 Minor and business transactions	
(1)	s 207(2) (changed)
(2)	s 207(3)
336 Transactions at behest of holding company	
	208(1), (2) (changed)
337 Funding of director's expenditure on duty to company	
(1), (2)	s 204(1) (changed)
(3)	s 204(2) (changed)
337A Funding of director's expenditure on defending proceedings	
(1)	s 205(1) (changed)
(2)	s 205(5)
(3)	s 205(1) (changed)
(4)	s 205(2)
(5)	s 205(3)
(6)	s 205(4)
338 Loan or quasi-loan by money-lending company	
(1)	s 209(1)
(2)	s 209(2)
(3)	s 209(1)
(6)	s 209(3), (4)

CA 1985	*CA 2006*
339 "Relevant amounts" for purposes of ss 334 ff	
(1)	ss 204(2), 207(1), (2), 210(1)
(2)	ss 204(2), 207(1), (2), 210(2)–(4)
(3)	s 210(3), (4)
(5)	s 210(5)
(6)	s 211(1)
340 "Value" of transactions and arrangements	
(2)	s 211(2)
(3)	s 211(3)
(4)	s 211(5)
(5)	s 211(6)
(6)	s 211(4)
(7)	s 211(7) (changed)
341 Civil remedies for breach of s 330	
(1)	s 213(1), (2)
(2)	s 213(3), (4)
(3)	s 213(5), (8)
(4)	s 213(6)
(5)	s 213(7)
345 Power to increase financial limits	
(1)	s 258(1)
(2)	s 258(2)
(3)	s 258(3)
346 "Connected persons", etc	
(1)	ss 252(1), 254(1), 255(1)
(2), (3)	ss 252(2), (3), 253(2) (changed)
(4)	s 254(2), (5)
(5)	s 255(2), (5)
(6)	ss 254(6), 255(6)
(7)	ss 254(3), 255(3)
(8)	ss 254(4), 255(4)
347 Transactions under foreign law	
	s 259
347A Introductory provisions	
(1)	s 362 (changed)
(3)	s 379(1)
(4)	s 364(2)
(5)	s 365(1) (changed)
(6)	s 363(1), (2)
(7)	s 363(1), (2) (changed)

CA 1985	*CA 2006*
347A Introductory provisions	
(8)	s 379(1)
(9)	s 363(1)
(10)	ss 366(5), 379(2)
347B Exemptions	
(1)	s 375(1)
(2)	s 375(2) (changed)
(3)	s 376(1), (2)
(4)	s 378(1) (changed)
(5)	s 378(3)
(6), (7)	s 378(1) (changed)
(8)	s 377(1)
(9)	s 377(3)
(10)	s 377(2)
(11)	s 377(4)
347C Prohibition on donations and political expenditure by companies	
(1)	s 366(1), (2), (5) (changed)
(2)	s 367(3), (6) (changed)
(3)	s 368(1), (2)
(4)	s 367(5)
(6)	s 366(6)
347D Special rules for subsidiaries	
(1)	s 366(2)
(2)	s 366(2), (5) (changed)
(3)	s 366(2), (3), (5) (changed)
(4)	s 367(3), (6) (changed)
(5)	s 368(1), (2)
(6)	s 367(5)
(9)	s 366(6)
347F Remedies for breach of prohibitions on company donations etc	
(1)	s 369(1)
(2)	s 369(2), (3) (changed)
(3)	s 369(2), (5)
(4)	s 369(2)
(5)	s 369(6)
(6)	s 369(3) (changed)
347I Enforcement of directors' liabilities by shareholder action	
(1)	s 370(1), (2) (changed)

PART I COMPANIES LEGISLATION

CA 1985	CA 2006
347I Enforcement of directors' liabilities by shareholder action	
(2)	s 370(3)
(3)	ss 370(4), 371(1)
(4), (5)	s 371(2)
(6)	s 371(3)
(7)	s 371(4)
(8)	s 371(5)
347J Costs of shareholder action	
(1)	s 372(1)
(2)	s 372(2)
(3)	s 372(3)
(4), (5)	s 372(4)
(6)	s 372(5)
347K Information for purposes of shareholder action	
(1)	s 373(1)
(2)	s 373(2)
348 Company name to appear outside place of business	
(1)	s 82(1), (2)
(2)	s 84(1), (2)
349 Company's name to appear in its correspondence, etc	
(1)	s 82(1), (2)
(2), (3)	s 84(1), (2)
350 Company seal	
(1)	s 45(2), (3) (changed)
(2)	s 45(4), (5)
351 Particulars in correspondence etc	
(1), (2)	s 82(1), (2)
(5)	s 84(1), (2)
352 Obligation to keep and enter up register	
(1)	s 113(1)
(2)	s 113(2)
(3)	s 113(3), (4)
(4)	s 113(6)
(5)	s 113(7), (8)
(6)	s 121 (changed)
(7)	s 128(1), (2)
352A Statement that company has only one member	
(1)	s 123(2) (changed)
(2)	s 123(3) (changed)
(3)	s 123(4), (5)

CA 1985	CA 2006
352A Statement that company has only one member	
(3A)	s 124(1), (2)
353 Location of register	
(1)	s 114(1) (changed)
(2)	s 114(2)
(3)	s 114(3), (4)
(4)	s 114(5), (6)
354 Index of members	
(1)	s 115(1), (2)
(2)	s 115(3)
(3)	s 115(4) (changed)
(4)	s 115(5), (6)
355 Entries in register in relation to share warrants	
(1)	s 122(1) (changed)
(2)	s 122(4)
(3)	s 122(5)
(4)	s 122(2), (6)
(5)	s 122(3)
356 Inspection of register and index	
(1)	s 116(1) (changed)
(3)	s 116(2)
(5)	s 118(1), (2) (changed)
(6)	s 118(3)
359 Power of court to rectify register	
(1)	s 125(1)
(2)	s 125(2)
(3)	s 125(3)
(4)	s 125(4)
360 Trusts not to be entered on register in England and Wales	
	s 126
361 Register to be evidence	
	s 127
362 Overseas branch registers	
(1)	s 129(1)
(2)	s 129(1), (5)
(3)	ss 130(1)–(3), 131(1), (4), 132(1)–(4), 133(1)–(3), 134(1)–(3), 135(1)–(5)
363 Duty to deliver annual returns	
(1)	s 854(1), (2)
(2)	s 854(3) (changed)
(3)	s 858(1)–(3)

CA 1985	*CA 2006*
363 Duty to deliver annual returns	
(4)	s 858(1), (2), (4) (changed)
364 Contents of annual return: general	
(1)	s 855(1) (changed)
(2)	s 855(2)
(3)	s 855(3)
364A Contents of annual return: particulars of share capital and shareholders	
(1)	s 856(1)
(2)	s 856(2)
(3)	s 856(2) (changed)
(4)	s 856(3)
(5)	s 856(4)
(6)	s 856(5)
(8)	s 856(6)
365 Supplementary provisions: regulations and interpretation	
(1)	s 857(1), (2)
(2)	s 857(3)
(3)	s 859
366 Annual general meeting	
(1)	ss 336(1), 337(1)
(4)	s 336(3), (4)
368 Extraordinary general meeting on members' requisition	
(1)	s 303(1), (2)
(2)	s 303(2), (3) (changed)
(2A)	s 303(2)
(3)	s 303(4), (6) (changed)
(4)	ss 304(1), 305(1), (3)
(5)	s 305(4)
(6)	s 305(6), (7)
(7)	s 304(4)
(8)	s 304(1)
369 Length of notice for calling meetings	
(1), (2)	s 307(2), (3) (changed)
(3)	ss 307(4), 337(2) (changed)
(4)	s 307(5), (6) (changed)
(4A)	s 308 (changed)
(4B)	ss 308, 309(1), (3) (changed)

CA 1985	*CA 2006*
369 Length of notice for calling meetings	
(4C)	s 309(2)
370 General provisions as to meetings and votes	
(1)	ss 284(4), 310(4), 318(2), 319(2)
(2)	s 310(1)
(4)	s 318(2) (changed)
(5)	s 319(1)
(6)	s 284(1), (3)
370A Quorum at meetings of the sole member	
	s 318(1), (3) (changed)
371 Power of court to order meeting	
(1)	s 306(1), (2)
(2)	s 306(3), (4)
(3)	s 306(5)
372 Proxies	
(1)	s 324(1)
(2)	s 324(2) (changed)
(3)	s 325(1) (changed)
(4)	s 325(3), (4)
(5)	s 327(1), (2) (changed)
(6)	s 326(1)–(4) (changed)
373 Right to demand a poll	
(1)	s 321(1), (2) (changed)
(2)	s 329(1), (2) (changed)
374 Voting on a poll	
	s 322
375 Representation of corporations at meetings	
(1)	s 323(1)
(2)	s 323(2), (3) (changed)
376 Circulation of members' resolutions	
(1)	ss 314(1), (4), 315(2), 316(2), 338(1), (4), 339(2), 340(2)
(2)	ss 314(2), (3), 338(3)
(3)	ss 315(1), 339(1)
(5)	ss 315(1), 339(1)
(6)	s 339(3)

PART I COMPANIES LEGISLATION

CA 1985	CA 2006
376 Circulation of members' resolutions	
(7)	ss 315(3), (4), 339(4), (5)
377 In certain cases, compliance with s 376 not required	
(1)	ss 314(4), 316(2), 338(4), 340(2) (changed)
(3)	s 317(1), (2) (changed)
378 Extraordinary and special resolutions	
(1)	s 283(1), (4), (5) (changed)
(2)	s 283(1), (4)–(6) (changed)
(4)	s 320(1), (3)
(5)	s 283(5) (changed)
(6)	s 301 (changed)
379 Resolution requiring special notice	
(1)	s 312(1)
(2)	s 312(2), (3) (changed)
(3)	s 312(4)
380 Registration, etc of resolutions and agreements	
(1)	s 30(1)
(2)	s 36(1), (2) (changed)
(4)	s 29(1) (changed)
(4A)	s 29(2)
(5)	s 30(2), (3)
(6)	s 36(3), (4) (changed)
(7)	ss 30(4), 36(5)
381 Resolution passed at adjourned meeting	
	s 332
381A Written resolutions of private companies	
(1)	ss 288(1), 289(1) (changed)
(2)	s 296(1) (changed)
(4)	s 288(5)
(7)	s 288(2)
381C Written resolutions: supplementary provisions	
(1)	s 300
382 Minutes of meetings	
(1)	ss 248(1), 355(1)
(2)	ss 249(1), 356(4)

CA 1985	CA 2006
382 Minutes of meetings	
(4)	ss 249(2), 356(5)
(5)	ss 248(3), (4), 355(3), (4) (changed)
382A Recording of written resolutions	
(1)	s 355(1) (changed)
(2)	s 356(2), (3)
382B Recording of decisions by the sole member	
(1)	s 357(1), (2)
(2)	s 357(3), (4)
(3)	s 357(5)
383 Inspection of minute books	
(1)	s 358(1), (3) (changed)
(3)	s 358(4) (changed)
(4)	s 358(5), (6) (changed)
(5)	s 358(7)
384 Duty to appoint auditors	
(1)	ss 485(1), 489(1) (changed)
(2)	s 489(2)
385 Appointment at general meeting at which accounts laid	
(2)	ss 489(2), (4), 491(1) (changed)
(3)	s 489(3) (changed)
(4)	s 489(4) (changed)
387 Appointment by Secretary of State in default of appointment by company	
(1)	ss 486(1), 490(1)
(2)	ss 486(2)–(4), 490(2)–(4)
388 Filling of casual vacancies	
(1)	ss 489(3), 526
389A Rights to information	
(1)	s 499(1)
(2)	s 499(2)
(3)	s 500(1)
(4)	s 500(2)
(5)	s 500(3)
(6)	ss 499(3), 500(4)
(7)	ss 499(4) 500(5)
389B Offences relating to the provision of information to auditors	
(1)	s 501(1), (2)
(2)	s 501(3)

CA 1985	*CA 2006*
389B Offences relating to the provision of information to auditors	
(3)	s 501(3) (changed)
(4)	s 501(4), (5)
(5)	s 501(6)
390 Right to attend company meetings, &c	
(1)	s 502(2)
(2)	s 502(1)
(3)	s 502(2)
390A Remuneration of auditors	
(1)	s 492(1)
(2)	s 492(2), (3)
(4)	s 492(4)
(5)	s 492(5)
390B Disclosure of services provided by auditors or associates and related remuneration	
(1)	ss 494(1), 501(1), (2)
(2)	s 494(2)
(3)	s 494(3)
(4)	s 494(4)
(5)	s 494(5)
(8)	s 494(1)
(9)	s 494(6)
391 Removal of auditors	
(1)	s 510(1), (2)
(2)	s 512(1)–(3)
(3)	s 510(3)
(4)	s 513(1), (2)
391A Rights of auditors who are removed or not re-appointed	
(1)	ss 511(1), 515(1), (2) (changed)
(2)	ss 511(2), 515(3)
(3)	ss 511(3), 515(4)
(4)	ss 511(4), 515(5)
(5)	ss 511(5), 515(6)
(6)	ss 511(6), 515(7)
392 Resignation of auditors	
(1)	s 516(1), (2)
(2)	s 516(3)
(3)	s 517(1)–(3)
392A Rights of resigning auditors	
(1)	s 518(1)
(2)	s 518(2)

CA 1985	*CA 2006*
392A Rights of resigning auditors	
(3)	s 518(3)
(4)	s 518(4)
(5)	s 518(5)–(7)
(6)	s 518(8)
(7)	s 518(9)
(8)	s 518(10)
394 Statement by person ceasing to hold office as auditor	
(1)	s 519(1)–(3), (7) (changed)
(2)	s 519(4) (changed)
(3)	s 520(2)
(4)	s 520(3)
(5)	s 521(1)
(6)	s 520(4)
(7)	ss 520(5), 521(2) (changed)
394A Offences of failing to comply with s 394	
(1)	ss 519(5), 521(3)–(5)
(2)	ss 519(6), 521(4)
(4)	s 520(6), (8) (changed)
395 Certain charges void if not registered	
(1)	ss 860(1), 861(5), 870(1), 874(1), (2)
(2)	s 874(3)
396 Charges which have to be registered	
(1)	ss 860(7), 861(2)
(2)	s 861(3)
(3)	s 861(1)
(3A)	s 861(4)
(4)	s 861(5)
397 Formalities of registration (debentures)	
(1)	ss 863(1)–(4), 870(3)
(2)	s 864(1), (3)
(3)	s 864(2)
398 Verification of charge on property outside United Kingdom	
(1)	s 866(1)
(2)	s 870(1)
(3)	s 866(2)
(4)	s 867(1), (2)
399 Company's duty to register charges it creates	
(1)	ss 860(1), (2), 863(5)

CA 1985	*CA 2006*
399 Company's duty to register charges it creates	
(2)	ss 860(3), 863(5)
(3)	ss 860(4)–(6), 863(5)
400 Charges existing on property acquired	
(1)	ss 861(5), 862(1)
(2)	ss 862(2), (3), 870(2)
(3)	s 870(2)
(4)	s 862(4), (5) (changed)
401 Register of charges to be kept by registrar of companies	
(1)	s 869(1), (2), (4)
(2)	s 869(5), (6)
(3)	s 869(7)
402 Endorsement of certificate on debentures	
(1)	s 865(1)
(2)	s 865(2)
(3)	s 865(3), (4)
403 Entries of satisfaction and release	
(1)	s 872(1), (2) (changed)
(2)	s 872(3)
404 Rectification of register of charges	
(1)	s 873(1)
(2)	s 873(2)
405 Registration of enforcement of security	
(1)	s 871(1), (3)
(2)	s 871(2), (3)
(4)	s 871(4), (5)
406 Companies to keep copies of instrument creating charges	
(1)	ss 875(1), 877(2) (changed)
(2)	s 875(2)
407 Company's register of charges	
(1)	ss 876(1), 877(2) (changed)
(2)	s 876(2)
(3)	s 876(3), (4)
408 Right to inspect instruments which create charges, etc	
(1)	s 877(1), (2), (4) (changed)
(2)	s 877(2) (changed)
(3)	s 877(5), (6)
(4)	s 877(7)

CA 1985	*CA 2006*
410 Charges void unless registered	
(1)	s 878(1)
(2)	ss 886(1), 889(1)
(3)	s 889(2)
(4)	ss 878(7), 879(1), (3)
(5)	s 879(5), (6)
411 Charges on property outside United Kingdom	
(1)	s 886(1)
(2)	s 884
412 Negotiable instrument to secure book debts	
	s 879(4)
413 Charges associated with debentures	
(1)	s 879(2)
(2)	ss 882(1)–(4), 886(3)
(3)	s 883(1)–(3)
414 Charge by way of ex facie absolute disposition, etc	
(1)	s 881(1)
(2)	s 881(2), (3)
415 Company's duty to register charges created by it	
(1)	ss 878(1), (2), 882(5)
(2)	s 878(3), 882(5)
(3)	s 878(4)–(6), 882(5)
416 Duty to register charges existing on property acquired	
(1)	ss 880(1), (2), 886(2)
(2)	s 886(2)
(3)	s 880(3), (4) (changed)
417 Register of charges to be kept by registrar of companies	
(1)	s 885(1)
(2)	s 885(2)
(3)	s 885(3)
(4)	s 886(6)
418 Certificate of registration to be issued	
(1)	s 885(4)
(2)	s 885(4), (5)
419 Entries of satisfaction and release	
(1)	s 887(1), (3) (changed)
(1B)	s 887(2)
(2)	s 887(4)

CA 1985	CA 2006
419 Entries of satisfaction and release	
(3)	s 887(2) (changed)
(4)	s 887(5)
420 Rectification of register	
	s 888(1), (2)
421 Copies of instruments creating charges to be kept by company	
(1)	ss 890(1), 892(2) (changed)
(2)	s 890(2)
422 Company's register of charges	
(1)	ss 891(1), 892(2) (changed)
(2)	s 891(2)
(3)	s 891(3), (4)
423 Right to inspect copies of instruments, and company's register	
(1)	s 892(1), (2), (4) (changed)
(2)	s 892(4) (changed)
(3)	s 892(5), (6)
(4)	s 892(7)
425 Power of company to compromise with creditors and members	
(1)	ss 895(1), 896(1), (2)
(2)	ss 899(1), (3), 907(1), 922(1)
(3)	s 899(4), 901(3), (4) (changed)
(4)	s 901(5) and 96)
(6)	s 895(2)
426 Information as to compromise to be circulated	
(1)	s 897(1)
(2)	s 897(1), (2)
(3)	s 897(1)
(4)	s 897(3)
(5)	s 897(4)
(6)	ss 895(1), 897(5)–(8)
(7)	s 898(1)–(3)
427 Provisions for facilitating company reconstruction or amalgamation	
(1)	s 900(1)
(2)	s 900(1), (2)
(3)	s 900(2)
(4)	s 900(3), (4)
(5)	s 900(6)–(8)
(6)	ss 900(5), 941

CA 1985	CA 2006
427A Application of ss 425–427 to mergers and divisions of public companies	
(1)	ss 902(1), 903(1), 907(2), 922(2)
(2)	ss 904(1), 919(1)
(3)	s 938(1), (2)
(4)	s 902(3)
(8)	s 941
428 Takeover offers	
(1)	s 974(1)–(3)
(2)	s 974(4), (5)
(2A)	s 974(6)
(3)	s 976(1)
(4)	s 976(3)
(5)	s 975(1), (2) (changed)
(6)	s 975(3) (changed)
(7)	s 974(7)
(8)	s 991(1)
429 Right of offeror to buy out minority shareholders	
(1)	s 979(1), (2) (changed)
(2)	s 979(3), (4) (changed)
(3)	s 980(2) (changed)
(4)	s 980(1), (4)
(5)	s 980(5)
(6)	s 980(6), (8)
(7)	s 980(7)
(8)	ss 977(1), 979(8)–(10) (changed)
430 Effect of notice under s 429	
(1)	s 981(1)
(2)	s 981(2)
(3)	s 981(3)
(4)	s 981(4), (5) (changed)
(5)	s 981(6)
(6)	s 981(7)
(7)	s 981(8)
(8)	s 981(6)
(9)	s 981(9)
(10)	s 982(2), (3)
(11)	s 982(4), (5)
(12)	s 982(6)
(13)	s 982(7)
(14)	s 982(8)

CA 1985	*CA 2006*
430 Effect of notice under s 429	
(15)	s 982(9)
430A Right of minority shareholder to be bought out by offeror	
(1)	ss 983(1)–(3), 984(1)
(1A)	s 983(1)
(2)	s 983(4)
(2A)	s 983(5)
(3)	s 984(3)
(4)	s 984(2)
(5)	s 984(4)
(6)	s 984(5), (7)
(7)	s 984(6)
430B Effect of requirement under s 430A	
(1)	s 985(1)
(2)	s 985(2)
(3)	s 985(3)
(4)	s 985(4), (5) (changed)
430C Applications to the court	
(1)	s 986(1), (2)
(2)	s 986(2)
(3)	s 986(3)
(4)	s 986(5)
(5)	s 986(9), (10)
430D Joint offers	
(1)	s 987(1)
(2)	s 987(2), (3) (changed)
(3)	s 987(5), (6)
(4)	s 987(4), (7)
(5)	s 987(8)
(6)	s 987(9)
(7)	s 987(10)
430E Associates	
(1)	ss 975(4), 977(2) (changed)
(2)	s 979(9)
(3)	s 983(8)
(4)	s 988(1), (4)
(5)	s 988(2)
(6)	s 988(3)
(7)	s 988(3), (5), (7)
(8)	s 988(1)
430F Convertible securities	
(1)	s 989(1)
(2)	s 989(2)

CA 1985	*CA 2006*
458 Punishment for fraudulent trading	
	s 993(1)–(3)
459 Order on application of company member	
(1)	s 994(1)
(2)	s 994(2)
(3)	s 994(3)
460 Order on application of Secretary of State	
(1)	s 995(2), (3)
(1A)	s 995(1)
(2)	s 995(4)
461 Provisions as to petitions and orders under this Part	
(1)	s 996(1)
(2)	s 996(2)
(3)	s 996(2)
(5)	s 998(1)–(4)
(6)	s 997
652 Registrar may strike defunct company off register	
(1)	s 1000(1)
(2)	s 1000(2)
(3)	s 1000(3)
(4)	s 1001(1)
(5)	ss 1000(4)–(6), 1001(2)–(4)
(6)	ss 1000(7), 1001(5)
(7)	s 1002(1)–(3)
652A Registrar may strike private company off register on application	
(1)	s 1003(1) (changed)
(2)	s 1003(2) (changed)
(3)	s 1003(3)
(4)	s 1003(4)
(5)	s 1003(5)
(6)	s 1003(6)
(7)	s 1003(6)
652B Duties in connection with making application under section 652A	
(1)	s 1004(1)
(2)	s 1004(2)
(3)	s 1005(1)
(4)	s 1005(2)
(5)	s 1005(3)
(6)	s 1006(1)
(7)	s 1006(2)

CA 1985	*CA 2006*
652B Duties in connection with making application under section 652A	
(8)	s 1006(3)
(9)	s 1004(3)
652C Directors' duties following application under section 652A	
(1)	s 1007(1)
(2)	s 1007(2)
(3)	s 1007(3)
(4)	s 1009(1)
(5)	s 1009(2)
(6)	s 1009(4)
(7)	s 1009(3)
652D Sections 652B and 652C: supplementary provisions	
(1)	s 1008(1), (2)
(2)	s 1008(3)
(3)	s 1008(3)
(4)	s 1008(4)
(5)(c)	ss 1004(4), 1006(1), 1007(2), 1009(4)
(6)	s 1010
(8)	s 1011
652E Sections 652B and 652C: enforcement	
(1)	ss 1004(5), (7), 1005(4), (6), 1006(4), (6), 1007(4), (6), 1009(5), (7)
(2)	ss 1006(4), (7), 1007(4), (7)
(3)	ss 1004(6), 1005(5)
(4)	s 1006(5)
(5)	ss 1007(5), 1009(6)
654 Property of dissolved company to be bona vacantia	
(1)	s 1012(1)
(2)	s 1012(2)
655 Effect on s 654 of company's revival after dissolution	
(1)	s 1034(1)
(2)	s 1034(2)
(3)	s 1034(4)
(4)	s 1034(5)
656 Crown disclaimer of property vesting as bona vacantia	
(1)	s 1013(1)
(2)	s 1013(2) (changed)

CA 1985	*CA 2006*
656 Crown disclaimer of property vesting as bona vacantia	
(3)	s 1013(3)–(5) (changed)
(5)	s 1013(6), (7)
(6)	s 1013(8)
657 Effect of Crown disclaimer under s 656	
(1)	s 1014(1)
(2)	ss 1015(1), (2), 1016(1), (2), 1017(1)–(5), 1018(1)–(5), 1019
(4)	s 1020(1), (2)
(5)	s 1021(1), (2)
(6)	s 1021(3)
658 Liability for rentcharge on company's land after dissolution	
(1)	s 1023(1), (2)
(2)	s 1023(3)
680 Companies capable of being registered under this Chapter	
(1)(a), (b)	s 1040(1)
(1) (closing words)	s 1040(2), (3), (6)
(1A)	s 1040(1)
(2)	s 1040(1)
(3)	s 1040(4)
(4)	s 1040(4)
(5)	s 1040(5)
683 Definition of "joint stock company"	
(1)	s 1041(1)
(2)	s 1041(2)
694 Regulation of oversea companies in respect of their names	
(4)	s 1048(1), (2) (changed)
(5)	s 1048(3)–(5)
695 Service of documents on oversea company	
(1), (2)	s 1139(2) (changed)
695A Registrar to whom documents to be delivered: companies to which section 690A applies	
(4)	s 1059
699A Credit and financial institutions to which the Bank Branches Directive (89/117/ EEC) applies	
(3) ("financial institution")	s 1173(1)

CA 1985	CA 2006
704 Registration offices	
(2)	s 1060(1), (2)
(4)	s 1062 (changed)
(7), (8)	s 1119(1), (2)
705 Companies' registered numbers	
(1)–(3)	s 1066(1)–(3)
(4)	s 1066(4), (5)
(5)(za)	s 1066(6)
705A Registration of branches of oversea companies	
(1)	s 1067(1) (changed)
(2)	s 1067(1)
(3)	s 1067(2)
(4)	s 1067(3)
(5)	s 1067(4), (5)
707A The keeping of company records by the registrar	
(1)	s 1080(4)
(2)	s 1083(1) (changed)
(3)	s 1084(1)–(3) (changed), (5)
(4)	s 1084(4)
708 Fees payable to registrar	
(1)	s 1063(1)–(3) (changed)
(2), (3)	s 1063(4) (changed)
(4)	s 1063(6)
(5)	s 1063(5) (changed)
709 Inspection, &c. of records kept by the registrar	
(1) opening words	s 1085(1) ands 1100
(1)(a), (b)	s 1086(1)
(2)	s 1085(2) (changed)
(3)	s 1091(3)
(4)	s 1091(5)
(5)	s 1092(1), (2)
710 Certificate of incorporation	
	s 1065
710A Provision and authentication by registrar of documents in non-legible form	
(2)	s 1115(2)
710B Documents relating to Welsh companies	
(1)–(3)	s 1104(1), (2)
(4)	s 1104(3)
(5)	s 1104(4)

CA 1985	CA 2006
711 Public notice by registrar of receipt and issue of certain documents	
(1)	ss 1064(1)–(3), 1077(1)–(3), 1078(2), (3) (changed)
(2)	s 1079(4) (changed)
713 Enforcement of company's duty to make returns	
(1)	s 1113(1)–(3)
(2), (3)	s 1113(4), (5)
714 Registrar's index of company and corporate names	
(1)	s 1099(1)–(3) (changed)
(2)	s 1099(4), (5)
715A Interpretation	
(1) ("document"), (2)	s 1114(1)
718 Unregistered companies	
(1)	s 1043(1), (3), (5) (changed)
(2)	s 1043(1)
(3)	s 1043(2), (5) (changed)
(5)	s 1043(4)
(6)	s 1043(6)
719 Power of company to provide for employees on cessation or transfer of business	
(1)	s 247(1)
(2)	s 247(2) (changed)
(3)	s 247(4)–(6) (changed)
(4)	s 247(7) (changed)
721 Production and inspection of books where offence suspected	
(1)	s 1132(1), (2)
(2)–(4)	s 1132(3)–(5)
722 Form of company registers, etc	
(1)	ss 1134 and 1135(1) (changed)
(2)	s 1138(1)
(3)	s 1138(2), (3)
723 Use of computers for company records	
(1)	s 1135(1) (changed)
(2)	s 1135(5)
723A Obligations of company as to inspections of registers, &c.	
(1)	s 1137(1), (2)

CA 1985	*CA 2006*
723A Obligations of company as to inspections of registers, &c.	
(2)	s 1137(3)
(3)	s 1137(3)
(4)	s 1137(4)
(6), (7)	s 1137(5), (6)
725 Service of documents	
(1)	s 1139(1)
(2)	s 1139(4)
(3)	s 1139(4)
727 Power of court to grant relief in certain cases	
(1)–(3)	s 1157(1)–(3)
730 Punishment of offences	
(4)	s 1125(2)
(5)	s 1121(1), (3) (changed)
731 Summary proceedings	
(1)	s 1127(1), (2)
(2)	s 1128(1)
(3)	s 1128(2)
(4)	s 1128(4)
732 Prosecution by public authorities	
(1)	s 1126(1)
(2)	s 1126(2) (changed)
(3)	s 1129 (changed)
734 Criminal proceedings against unincorporated bodies	
(1)	s 1130(1), (2) (changed)
(2)	s 1130(3)
(3)	s 1130(2)
(4)	s 1130(2)
735 "Company", etc	
(1)(a), (b)	s 1(1)
(1)(c)	s 1171 (changed)
(3)	s 1171
736 "Subsidiary"; "holding company" and "wholly-owned subsidiary"	
(1), (2)	s 1159(1), (2)
(3)	s 1159(4)
736A Provisions supplementing s 736	
(1)–(11)	s 1159(3), Sch 6
736B Power to amend ss 736 and 736A	
(1)	s 1160(1)
(3)–(5)	s 1160(2)–(4)

CA 1985	*CA 2006*
737 "Called-up share capital"	
(1), (2)	s 547
738 "Allotment" and "paid up"	
(1)	s 558
(2)	s 583(2)–(3)(d)
(3)	s 583(5)
(4)	s 583(6)
739 "Non-cash asset"	
(1), (2)	s 1163(1), (2)
741 "Director" and "shadow director"	
(1)	s 250
(2)	s 251(1), (2)
(3)	s 251(3)
742 Expressions used in connection with accounts	
(1) ("fixed assets")	s 853(6)
(1) ("parent company")	s 1173(1)
(2)	s 853(4), (5)
742A Meaning of "offer to the public"	
(1)	s 756(1), (2)
(2)	s 756(3)
(3)	s 756(4), (5)(a)–(d) (changed)
(4)	s 756(4)
(5)	s 756(4)
(6)	s 756(5)(e), (6)
742B Meaning of "banking company"	
(1)–(3)	s 1164(1)–(3)
742C Meaning of "insurance company" and "authorised insurance company"	
(1)–(4)	s 1165(2)–(4)
(5)	s 1165(8)
743 "Employees' share scheme"	
	s 1166
744 Expressions used generally in this Act	
"articles"	s 18(4)
"the Companies Acts"	s 2(1), (2) (changed)
"the court"	s 1156(1)–(3) (changed)
"debenture"	s 738
"EEA State"	s 1170
"equity share capital"	s 548
"the Gazette"	s 1173(1)
"hire-purchase agreement"	s 1173(1)

CA 1985	CA 2006
744 Expressions used generally in this Act	
"insurance market activity"	s 1165(7)
"officer"	ss 1121(2), 1173(1)
"oversea company"	s 1044 (changed)
"prescribed"	s 1167
"the registrar of companies" and "the registrar"	s 1060(3)
"regulated activity"	s 1173(1)
"share"	s 540(1), (4)
744A Index of defined expressions	
	Sch 8
Sch 2 Interpretation of references to "beneficial interest"	
Part 1 References in sections 23, 145, 146 and 148	
para 1(1)	ss 139(1), 672(1)
para 1(2)	ss 139(2), 672(2)
para 1(3)	ss 139(3), 672(3)
para 1(4)	ss 139(4), 672(4)
para 2(3)	s 672(5)
para 2(4)	s 672(6)
para 3(1), (2)	ss 140(1), (2), 673(1), (2)
para 4(1)	ss 138(1), (2), 674
para 4(2)	s 138(1)
para 4(3)	s 674
para 5(1)	ss 675(1), (2), 676
para 5(2)	ss 139(5), (6), 140(3), 675(1), (2)
para 5(3)	ss 139(6), 140(4), 676
Sch 4 Form and content of company accounts	
Part 3 Notes to the accounts	
para 56(2), (3)	ss 382(6), 465(6)
Part 7 Interpretation of Schedule	
para 94(1), (2)	s 411(6)
Sch 7B Specified persons, descriptions of disclosures etc for the purposes of section 245G	
Part 1 Specified persons	
	s 461(1)
Part 2 Specified descriptions of disclosures	
	s 461(4)
Part 3 Overseas regulatory bodies	
	s 461(5), (6)

CA 1985	CA 2006
Sch 10A Parent and subsidiary undertakings: supplementary provisions	
para 1	Sch 7, para 1
para 2(1)	Sch 7, para 2(1)
para 2(2)	Sch 7, para 2(2)
para 3(1)	Sch 7, para 3(1)
para 3(2)	Sch 7, para 3(2)
para 3(2)	Sch 7, para 3(3)
para 4(1)	Sch 7, para 4(1)
para 4(2)	Sch 7, para 4(2)
para 4(3)	Sch 7, para 4(3)
para 5(1)	Sch 7, para 5(1)
para 5(2)	Sch 7, para 5(2)
para 6	Sch 7, para 6
para 7(1)	Sch 7, para 7(1)
para 7(2)	Sch 7, para 7(2)
para 8	Sch 7, para 8
para 9(1)	Sch 7, para 9(1)
para 9(2)	Sch 7, para 9(2)
para 9(3)	Sch 7, para 9(3)
para 10	Sch 7, para 10
para 11	Sch 7, para 11
Sch 13 Provisions supplementing and interpreting sections 324 to 328	
Part 4 Provisions with respect to register of directors' interests to be kept under section 325	
para 27	s 809(2), (3)
Sch 14 Overseas branch registers	
Part 1 Countries and territories in which overseas branch register may be kept	
	s 129(2)
Part 2 General provisions with respect to overseas branch registers	
para 1(1), (2)	ss 130(1), 135(3)
para 1(3)	ss 130(2), (3), 135(4), (5)
para 2(1)	s 131(1)
para 3(1)	s 134(1), (2) (changed)
para 3(2)	s 134(3)
para 4(1)	s 132(1), (2) (changed)
para 4(2)	s 132(3), (4)
para 5	s 133(1), (2)
para 6	s 135(1), (2)
para 7	s 131(4)

CA 1985	CA 2006
Sch 15A Written resolutions of private companies	
Part 1 Exceptions	
para 1	s 288(2)
Part 2 Adaptation of procedural requirements	
para 3(1), (2)	ss 571(7), 573(5)
para 5(1), (2)	ss 695(2), 698(2)
para 5(3), (4)	ss 696(2), 699(2)
para 6(1)	ss 717(2), 718(2)
para 6(2)	s 717(2)
para 6(3)	s 718(2)
para 7	s 188(5)
Sch 15B Provisions subject to which ss 425–427 have effect in their application to mergers and divisions of public companies	
para 1	ss 907(1), (2), 922(1), (2)
para 2(1)	ss 905(1), 906(1)–(3), 920(1), 921(1)–(4)
para 2(2)	ss 905(2), (3), 920(2)
para 2(3)	s 920(3)
para 3	ss 908(1), (3), 909(1), (7), 911(1), (2), (4), 912, 923(1), (4), 924(1), (7), 925(5), 926(1), (2), (4), 927(1)–(3), 928
para 4(1)	ss 908(2), 923(2)
para 4(2)	s 923(3)
para 5(1)	ss 909(2), (3), 924(2), (3)
para 5(2)	ss 909(3), 924(3)
para 5(3)	ss 909(4), 924(4)
para 5(4)	s 935(1) (changed)
para 5(6)	s 935(2)
para 5(7)	ss 909(5), 924(5)
para 5(8)	ss 909(6), 924(6)
para 6(1)	ss 910(1), 911(3), 925(1), 926(3)
para 6(2)	ss 910(2), 925(2)
para 6(3)	ss 910(3), 925(3) (changed)
para 6(4)	ss 910(4), 925(4),

CA 1985	CA 2006
Sch 15B Provisions subject to which ss 425–427 have effect in their application to mergers and divisions of public companies	
para 7	ss 914, 930
para 8(1)	ss 913(1), 929(1)
para 8(2)	ss 913(2), 929(2)
para 9(1)	s 939(1)
para 9(2)	s 939(1), (2)
para 9(3)	s 939(3), (4)
para 9(4)	s 939(5)
para 10(1)	ss 918(1), 932(1)
para 10(2)	ss 916(3)–(5), 918(2)–(4), 932(2)–(5)
para 11(1)	s 933(1)–(3), 934(1)
para 11(2)	s 933(1)–(3)
para 11(3)	s 934(1)
para 11(4)	s 934(2)–(4)
para 12(1)	ss 915(1), (6), 917(1), (6)
para 12(2)	s 915(2)
para 12(3)	s 915(3)–(5)
para 12(4)	s 917(2)
para 12(5)	ss 917(3)–(5), 931(3), (5)
para 13(1)	s 931(1)
para 13(2)	s 931(2)
para 13(3)	s 931(3), (4), (6)
para 14(1)	s 916(1)
para 14(2)	s 916(2)
para 14(3)	s 916(3)–(5)
para 15(1)	s 940(1)
para 15(2)	s 940(2)
para 15(3)	s 940(3)
Sch 20 Vesting of disclaimed property; protection of third parties	
Part 2 Crown disclaimer under section 656 (Scotland only)	
para 5	s 1022(1)
para 6	s 1022(2)
para 7	s 1022(3)
para 8	s 1022(4), (5)
para 9	s 1022(6)

COMPANIES ACT 1989

1. Section 130(6) of the Companies Act 1989 (power by regulations to apply provisions relating to company contracts and execution of documents by companies to overseas companies) is re-enacted in section 1045 of the Companies Act 2006.

2. Section 207 of the Companies Act 1989 (transfer of securities) is re-enacted in sections 783, 784(3), 785 and 788 of the Companies Act 2006.

[S1384]

PART II
FINANCIAL SERVICES AND MARKETS ACT 2000

FINANCIAL SERVICES AND MARKETS ACT 2000

(2000 c 8)

NOTES

This Act is reproduced as amended by the following Acts:

2000	Insolvency Act 2000; Regulation of Investigatory Powers Act 2000.
2001	Criminal Justice and Police Act 2001.
2002	Enterprise Act 2002; Proceeds of Crime Act 2002.
2003	Communications Act 2003.
2004	Civil Partnership Act 2004.
2005	Constitutional Reform Act 2005; Inquiries Act 2005; Gambling Act 2005; Regulation of Financial Services (Land Transactions) Act 2005.
2006	Consumer Credit Act 2006; Companies Act 2006; Investment Exchanges and Clearing Houses Act 2006.

This Act is reproduced as amended by the following SIs:

2000	Banking Consolidation Directive (Consequential Amendments) Regulations 2000, SI 2000/2952.
2001	Financial Services and Markets Act 2000 (Regulated Activities) Order 2001, SI 2001/544; Limited Liability Partnerships Regulations 2001, SI 2001/1090; Financial Services (EEA Passport Rights) Regulations 2001, SI 2001/1376; Financial Services and Markets Act 2000 (Variation of Threshold Conditions) Order 2001, SI 2001/2507; Public Offers of Securities (Exemptions) Regulations 2001, SI 2001/2955.
2002	Financial Services and Markets Act 2000 (Regulated Activities) (Amendment) Order 2002, SI 2002/682; Electronic Money (Miscellaneous Amendments) Regulations 2002, SI 2002/765; Electronic Commerce Directive (Financial Services and Markets) Regulations 2002, SI 2002/1775; Financial Services and Markets Act 2000 (Variation of Threshold Conditions) Order 2002, SI 2002/2707.
2003	Insurance Mediation Directive (Miscellaneous Amendments) Regulations 2003, SI 2003/1473; Financial Services and Markets Act 2000 (Regulated Activities) (Amendment) (No 2) Order 2003, SI 2003/1476; Collective Investment Schemes (Miscellaneous Amendments) Regulations 2003, SI 2003/2066.
2004	Life Assurance Consolidation Directive (Consequential Amendments) Regulations 2004, SI 2004/3379.
2005	Financial Services and Markets Act 2000 (Market Abuse) Regulations 2005, SI 2005/381; Prospectus Regulations 2005, SI 2005/1433; Insolvency (Northern Ireland) Order 2005, SI 2005/1455.
2006	Charities and Trustee Investment (Scotland) Act 2005 (Consequential Provisions and Modifications) Order 2006, SI 2006/242; Taxation of Pension Schemes (Consequential Amendments) Order 2006, SI 2006/745; the Takeovers Directive (Interim Implementation) Regulations 2006, SI 2006/1183; Financial Services and Markets Act 2000 (Regulated Activities) (Amendment) (No 2) Order 2006, SI 2006/2383; Financial Services and Markets Act 2000 (Markets in Financial Instruments) (Modification of Powers) Regulations 2006, SI 2006/2975; the Capital Requirements Regulations 2006, SI 2006/3221.
2007	Financial Services (EEA State) Regulations 2007, SI 2007/108; Financial Services and Markets Act 2000 (Markets in Financial Instruments) Regulations 2007, SI 2007/126; Companies Act 2006 (Commencement No 2, Consequential Amendments, Transitional Provisions and Savings) Order 2007, SI 2007/1093; the Regulatory Reform (Financial Services and Markets Act 2000) Order 2007, SI 2007/1973.

See also the prospective amendments made to this Act by the draft Companies Act 2006 (Commencement No 3, Consequential Amendments, Transitional Provisions and Savings) Order 2007 (see **[A12]**).

PART II
FSMA 2000

ARRANGEMENT OF SECTIONS

PART I
THE REGULATOR

PART II
REGULATED AND PROHIBITED ACTIVITIES

PART III
AUTHORISATION AND EXEMPTION

Authorisation

Ending of authorisation

Exercise of EEA rights by UK firms

Exemption

PART IV
PERMISSION TO CARRY ON REGULATED ACTIVITIES

Application for permission

Permission

Variation and cancellation of Part IV permission

Connected persons

Additional permissions

Procedure

References to the Tribunal

PART V
PERFORMANCE OF REGULATED ACTIVITIES

Prohibition orders

Approval

Transferable securities: powers of competent authority

Rights of investors

Registered investors

Sponsors

Transparency obligations

Power of competent authority to call for information

Powers exercisable in case of infringement of transparency obligation

Corporate governance

Compensation for false or misleading statements etc

Penalties

Competition

Miscellaneous

PART II
FSMA 2000

PART IX
HEARINGS AND APPEALS

Legal assistance before the Tribunal

Appeals

PART X
RULES AND GUIDANCE

CHAPTER I
RULE-MAKING POWERS

Specific rules

Modification or waiver

Contravention of rules

Procedural provisions

CHAPTER II
GUIDANCE

CHAPTER III
COMPETITION SCRUTINY

PART XI
INFORMATION GATHERING AND INVESTIGATIONS

Powers to gather information

PART II
FSMA 2000

Role of the Treasury

PART XX
PROVISION OF FINANCIAL SERVICES BY MEMBERS OF THE PROFESSIONS

PART XXI
MUTUAL SOCIETIES

Friendly societies

Building societies

Industrial and provident societies and credit unions

Supplemental

PART XXII
AUDITORS AND ACTUARIES

Appointment

Information

Disqualification

Offence

PART XXIII
PUBLIC RECORD, DISCLOSURE OF INFORMATION AND CO-OPERATION

The public record

Disclosure of information

Co-operation

PART XXIV
INSOLVENCY

Interpretation

Voluntary arrangements

Administration orders

Receivership

Voluntary winding up

Winding up by the court

Bankruptcy

Provisions against debt avoidance

Supplemental provisions concerning insurers

PART XXV
INJUNCTIONS AND RESTITUTION

Injunctions

Restitution orders

Restitution required by Authority

PART XXVI
NOTICES

Warning notices

Decision notices

Conclusion of proceedings

Publication

Third party rights and access to evidence

The Authority's procedures

PART XXVII
OFFENCES

Miscellaneous offences

Bodies corporate and partnerships

Institution of proceedings

PART XXVIII
MISCELLANEOUS

Schemes for reviewing past business

Third countries

International obligations

Gaming contracts

Trade-matching and reporting systems

An Act to make provision about the regulation of financial services and markets; to provide for the transfer of certain statutory functions relating to building societies, friendly societies, industrial and provident societies and certain other mutual societies; and for connected purposes

[14 June 2000]

NOTES

Commencement: see s 432 at **[2428]**. The main provisions of this Act came into force on 1 December 2001, ie, the date on which s 19 (the general prohibition) came into force. Where any provision in this work (including any inserted or substituted provision) came into force for all purposes on or before 1 July 2005, commencement information is not noted at provision level.

Transitional provisions and savings: a number of instruments have been made under this Act making various transitional provisions and savings which are not reproduced in this edition. These instruments are listed under the note "Orders" to s 426 and Sch 21.

Limited liability partnerships: ss 215(3), (4), (6), 356, 359(1)–(4), 361–365, 367, 370, and 371 of this Act apply to limited liability partnerships (except where the context otherwise requires and subject to certain modifications); see the Limited Liability Partnerships Regulations 2001, SI 2001/1090, reg 6 at **[6987]**.

Application of Act to certain overseas investment exchanges and clearing houses: see the Companies Act 1989, s 170 at **[841]**.

Exemption from requirement for contract for sale etc of land to be in writing: a contract regulated under this Act, other than a regulated mortgage contract, a regulated home reversion plan or a regulated home purchase plan, is exempt from the Law of Property (Miscellaneous Provisions) Act 1989, s 2 (contracts for sale etc of land to be made by writing); see s 2(5) of that Act.

Transfer of functions – mutual societies: the Financial Services and Markets Act 2000 (Mutual Societies) Order 2001, SI 2001/2617, art 4(2) transfers to the Financial Services Authority certain functions which, immediately before 1 December 2001, were functions of: (a) the Chief Registrar of friendly societies, assistant registrars of friendly societies or the central office of the registry of friendly societies; (b) the Friendly Societies Commission; or (c) the Building Societies Commission. Sch 2 to the 2001 Order makes provisions concerning the application of this Act in relation to functions transferred (or to be transferred) to the Authority by the said art 4(2).

Offences under this Act: generally, see Pt XXVII at **[2395]** et seq. As to offences committed by bodies corporate etc, see s 400 at **[2398]**; as to proceedings for offences, see s 401 at **[2399]**; and as to jurisdiction and procedure in respect of offences, see s 403 at **[2401]**. See also s 28(9) at **[2028]**, as to the illegality or invalidity of agreements.

PART I
THE REGULATOR

1 The Financial Services Authority

(1) The body corporate known as the Financial Services Authority ("the Authority") is to have the functions conferred on it by or under this Act.

(2) The Authority must comply with the requirements as to its constitution set out in Schedule 1.

(3) Schedule 1 also makes provision about the status of the Authority and the exercise of certain of its functions.

[2001]

NOTES

Note: the FSA is the same corporate entity as the former Securities and Investments Board and later assumed functions under the Banking Act 1985 and exercised other functions on behalf of the Treasury under other financial services legislation.

The self regulating bodies (the Securities and Futures Authority, the Investment Management Regulatory Organisation and the Personal Investment Authority) established under the Financial Services Act 1986 were constituted as companies limited by guarantee and were wound up on the designated dates specified under the Financial Services and Markets Act 2000 (Transitional Provisions) (Designated Date for The Securities and Futures Authority) Order 2001, SI 2001/2255, and the Financial Services and Markets (Transitional Provisions) (Designated Date for Certain Self-Regulating Organisations) Order 2000, SI 2000/1734.

The Authority's general duties

2 The Authority's general duties

(1) In discharging its general functions the Authority must, so far as is reasonably possible, act in a way—

(a) which is compatible with the regulatory objectives; and

(b) which the Authority considers most appropriate for the purpose of meeting those objectives.

(2) The regulatory objectives are—

(a) market confidence;

(b) public awareness;

(c) the protection of consumers; and

(d) the reduction of financial crime.

(3) In discharging its general functions the Authority must have regard to—

(a) the need to use its resources in the most efficient and economic way;

(b) the responsibilities of those who manage the affairs of authorised persons;

(c) the principle that a burden or restriction which is imposed on a person, or on the carrying on of an activity, should be proportionate to the benefits, considered in general terms, which are expected to result from the imposition of that burden or restriction;

(d) the desirability of facilitating innovation in connection with regulated activities;

(e) the international character of financial services and markets and the desirability of maintaining the competitive position of the United Kingdom;

(f) the need to minimise the adverse effects on competition that may arise from anything done in the discharge of those functions;

(g) the desirability of facilitating competition between those who are subject to any form of regulation by the Authority.

(4) The Authority's general functions are—

(a) its function of making rules under this Act (considered as a whole);

(b) its function of preparing and issuing codes under this Act (considered as a whole);

(c) its functions in relation to the giving of general guidance (considered as a whole); and

(d) its function of determining the general policy and principles by reference to which it performs particular functions.

(5) "General guidance" has the meaning given in section 158(5).

[2002]

The regulatory objectives

3 Market confidence

(1) The market confidence objective is: maintaining confidence in the financial system.

(2) "The financial system" means the financial system operating in the United Kingdom and includes—

(a) financial markets and exchanges;

(b) regulated activities; and
(c) other activities connected with financial markets and exchanges.

[2003]

4 Public awareness

(1) The public awareness objective is: promoting public understanding of the financial system.

(2) It includes, in particular—

(a) promoting awareness of the benefits and risks associated with different kinds of investment or other financial dealing; and
(b) the provision of appropriate information and advice.

(3) "The financial system" has the same meaning as in section 3.

[2004]

5 The protection of consumers

(1) The protection of consumers objective is: securing the appropriate degree of protection for consumers.

(2) In considering what degree of protection may be appropriate, the Authority must have regard to—

(a) the differing degrees of risk involved in different kinds of investment or other transaction;
(b) the differing degrees of experience and expertise that different consumers may have in relation to different kinds of regulated activity;
(c) the needs that consumers may have for advice and accurate information; and
(d) the general principle that consumers should take responsibility for their decisions.

(3) "Consumers" means persons—

(a) who are consumers for the purposes of section 138; or
(b) who, in relation to regulated activities carried on otherwise than by authorised persons, would be consumers for those purposes if the activities were carried on by authorised persons.

[2005]

6 The reduction of financial crime

(1) The reduction of financial crime objective is: reducing the extent to which it is possible for a business carried on—

(a) by a regulated person, or
(b) in contravention of the general prohibition,

to be used for a purpose connected with financial crime.

(2) In considering that objective the Authority must, in particular, have regard to the desirability of—

(a) regulated persons being aware of the risk of their businesses being used in connection with the commission of financial crime;
(b) regulated persons taking appropriate measures (in relation to their administration and employment practices, the conduct of transactions by them and otherwise) to prevent financial crime, facilitate its detection and monitor its incidence;
(c) regulated persons devoting adequate resources to the matters mentioned in paragraph (b).

(3) "Financial crime" includes any offence involving—

(a) fraud or dishonesty;
(b) misconduct in, or misuse of information relating to, a financial market; or
(c) handling the proceeds of crime.

(4) "Offence" includes an act or omission which would be an offence if it had taken place in the United Kingdom.

(5) "Regulated person" means an authorised person, a recognised investment exchange or a recognised clearing house.

[2006]

NOTES

Note: a "regulated person" for these purposes includes an authorised person, a recognised investment exchange and a recognised clearing house, but the position of exempt persons under s 38 (exemption orders) or s 39 (appointed representatives) is not clear.

Corporate governance

7 Duty of Authority to follow principles of good governance

In managing its affairs, the Authority must have regard to such generally accepted principles of good corporate governance as it is reasonable to regard as applicable to it.

[2007]

Arrangements for consulting practitioners and consumers

8 The Authority's general duty to consult

The Authority must make and maintain effective arrangements for consulting practitioners and consumers on the extent to which its general policies and practices are consistent with its general duties under section 2.

[2008]

NOTES

See further s 396 at **[2394]**.

9 The Practitioner Panel

(1) Arrangements under section 8 must include the establishment and maintenance of a panel of persons (to be known as "the Practitioner Panel") to represent the interests of practitioners.

(2) The Authority must appoint one of the members of the Practitioner Panel to be its chairman.

(3) The Treasury's approval is required for the appointment or dismissal of the chairman.

(4) The Authority must have regard to any representations made to it by the Practitioner Panel.

(5) The Authority must appoint to the Practitioner Panel such—

(a) individuals who are authorised persons,

(b) persons representing authorised persons,

(c) persons representing recognised investment exchanges, and

(d) persons representing recognised clearing houses,

as it considers appropriate.

[2009]

NOTES

Note: Information regarding the Practitioner Panel can be obtained through its website at www.fs-pp.org.uk.

10 The Consumer Panel

(1) Arrangements under section 8 must include the establishment and maintenance of a panel of persons (to be known as "the Consumer Panel") to represent the interests of consumers.

(2) The Authority must appoint one of the members of the Consumer Panel to be its chairman.

(3) The Treasury's approval is required for the appointment or dismissal of the chairman.

(4) The Authority must have regard to any representations made to it by the Consumer Panel.

(5) The Authority must appoint to the Consumer Panel such consumers, or persons representing the interests of consumers, as it considers appropriate.

(6) The Authority must secure that the membership of the Consumer Panel is such as to give a fair degree of representation to those who are using, or are or may be contemplating using, services otherwise than in connection with businesses carried on by them.

(7) "Consumers" means persons, other than authorised persons—
 (a) who are consumers for the purposes of section 138; or
 (b) who, in relation to regulated activities carried on otherwise than by authorised persons, would be consumers for those purposes if the activities were carried on by authorised persons.

[2010]

NOTES

Note: Information regarding the Consumer Panel can be obtained through its website at www.fs-cp.org.uk.

11 Duty to consider representations by the Panels

(1) This section applies to a representation made, in accordance with arrangements made under section 8, by the Practitioner Panel or by the Consumer Panel.

(2) The Authority must consider the representation.

(3) If the Authority disagrees with a view expressed, or proposal made, in the representation, it must give the Panel a statement in writing of its reasons for disagreeing.

[2011]

Reviews

12 Reviews

(1) The Treasury may appoint an independent person to conduct a review of the economy, efficiency and effectiveness with which the Authority has used its resources in discharging its functions.

(2) A review may be limited by the Treasury to such functions of the Authority (however described) as the Treasury may specify in appointing the person to conduct it.

(3) A review is not to be concerned with the merits of the Authority's general policy or principles in pursuing regulatory objectives or in exercising functions under Part VI.

(4) On completion of a review, the person conducting it must make a written report to the Treasury—
 (a) setting out the result of the review; and
 (b) making such recommendations (if any) as he considers appropriate.

(5) A copy of the report must be—
 (a) laid before each House of Parliament; and
 (b) published in such manner as the Treasury consider appropriate.

(6) Any expenses reasonably incurred in the conduct of a review are to be met by the Treasury out of money provided by Parliament.

(7) "Independent" means appearing to the Treasury to be independent of the Authority.

[2012]

13 Right to obtain documents and information

(1) A person conducting a review under section 12—
 (a) has a right of access at any reasonable time to all such documents as he may reasonably require for purposes of the review; and
 (b) may require any person holding or accountable for any such document to provide such information and explanation as are reasonably necessary for that purpose.

(2) Subsection (1) applies only to documents in the custody or under the control of the Authority.

(3) An obligation imposed on a person as a result of the exercise of powers conferred by subsection (1) is enforceable by injunction or, in Scotland, by an order for specific performance under section 45 of the Court of Session Act 1988.

[2013]

Inquiries

14 Cases in which the Treasury may arrange independent inquiries

(1) This section applies in two cases.

(2) The first is where it appears to the Treasury that—

(a) events have occurred in relation to—

(i) a collective investment scheme, or

(ii) a person who is, or was at the time of the events, carrying on a regulated activity (whether or not as an authorised person),

which posed or could have posed a grave risk to the financial system or caused or risked causing significant damage to the interests of consumers; and

(b) those events might not have occurred, or the risk or damage might have been reduced, but for a serious failure in—

(i) the system established by this Act[, or by any previous statutory provision,] for the regulation of such schemes or of such persons and their activities; or

(ii) the operation of that system.

(3) The second is where it appears to the Treasury that—

(a) events have occurred in relation to listed securities or an issuer of listed securities which caused or could have caused significant damage to holders of listed securities; and

(b) those events might not have occurred but for a serious failure [in—

(i) the regulatory system established by Part 6 or by any previous statutory provision concerned with the official listing of securities; or

(ii) the operation of that system].

(4) If the Treasury consider that it is in the public interest that there should be an independent inquiry into the events and the circumstances surrounding them, they may arrange for an inquiry to be held under section 15.

(5) "Consumers" means persons—

(a) who are consumers for the purposes of section 138; or

(b) who, in relation to regulated activities carried on otherwise than by authorised persons, would be consumers for those purposes if the activities were carried on by authorised persons.

[(5A) "Event" does not include any event occurring before 1st December 2001 (but no such limitation applies to the reference in subsection (4) to surrounding circumstances).]

(6) "The financial system" has the same meaning as in section 3.

(7) "Listed securities" means anything which has been admitted to the official list under Part VI.

[2014]

NOTES

Sub-s (2): words in square brackets inserted by the Inquiries Act 2005, s 46(1), (2), as from 7 June 2005.

Sub-s (3): words in square brackets substituted by the Inquiries Act 2005, s 46(1), (3), as from 7 June 2005.

Sub-s (5A): inserted by the Inquiries Act 2005, s 46(1), (4), as from 7 June 2005.

15 Power to appoint person to hold an inquiry

(1) If the Treasury decide to arrange for an inquiry to be held under this section, they may appoint such person as they consider appropriate to hold the inquiry.

(2) The Treasury may, by a direction to the appointed person, control—

(a) the scope of the inquiry;

(b) the period during which the inquiry is to be held;

(c) the conduct of the inquiry; and

PART II FSMA 2000

(d) the making of reports.

(3) A direction may, in particular—
(a) confine the inquiry to particular matters;
(b) extend the inquiry to additional matters;
(c) require the appointed person to discontinue the inquiry or to take only such steps as are specified in the direction;
(d) require the appointed person to make such interim reports as are so specified.

[2015]

16 Powers of appointed person and procedure

(1) The person appointed to hold an inquiry under section 15 may—
(a) obtain such information from such persons and in such manner as he thinks fit;
(b) make such inquiries as he thinks fit; and
(c) determine the procedure to be followed in connection with the inquiry.

(2) The appointed person may require any person who, in his opinion, is able to provide any information, or produce any document, which is relevant to the inquiry to provide any such information or produce any such document.

(3) For the purposes of an inquiry, the appointed person has the same powers as the court in respect of the attendance and examination of witnesses (including the examination of witnesses abroad) and in respect of the production of documents.

(4) "Court" means—
(a) the High Court; or
(b) in Scotland, the Court of Session.

[2016]

17 Conclusion of inquiry

(1) On completion of an inquiry under section 15, the person holding the inquiry must make a written report to the Treasury—
(a) setting out the result of the inquiry; and
(b) making such recommendations (if any) as he considers appropriate.

(2) The Treasury may publish the whole, or any part, of the report and may do so in such manner as they consider appropriate.

(3) Subsection (4) applies if the Treasury propose to publish a report but consider that it contains material—
(a) which relates to the affairs of a particular person whose interests would, in the opinion of the Treasury, be seriously prejudiced by publication of the material; or
(b) the disclosure of which would be incompatible with an international obligation of the United Kingdom.

(4) The Treasury must ensure that the material is removed before publication.

(5) The Treasury must lay before each House of Parliament a copy of any report or part of a report published under subsection (2).

(6) Any expenses reasonably incurred in holding an inquiry are to be met by the Treasury out of money provided by Parliament.

[2017]

18 Obstruction and contempt

(1) If a person ("A")—
(a) fails to comply with a requirement imposed on him by a person holding an inquiry under section 15, or
(b) otherwise obstructs such an inquiry,

the person holding the inquiry may certify the matter to the High Court (or, in Scotland, the Court of Session).

(2) The court may enquire into the matter.

(3) If, after hearing—
(a) any witnesses who may be produced against or on behalf of A, and
(b) any statement made by or on behalf of A,

the court is satisfied that A would have been in contempt of court if the inquiry had been proceedings before the court, it may deal with him as if he were in contempt.

[2018]

PART II
REGULATED AND PROHIBITED ACTIVITIES

The general prohibition

19 The general prohibition

(1) No person may carry on a regulated activity in the United Kingdom, or purport to do so, unless he is—

(a) an authorised person; or
(b) an exempt person.

(2) The prohibition is referred to in this Act as the general prohibition.

[2019]

Requirement for permission

20 Authorised persons acting without permission

(1) If an authorised person carries on a regulated activity in the United Kingdom, or purports to do so, otherwise than in accordance with permission—

(a) given to him by the Authority under Part IV, or
(b) resulting from any other provision of this Act,

he is to be taken to have contravened a requirement imposed on him by the Authority under this Act.

(2) The contravention does not—

(a) make a person guilty of an offence;
(b) make any transaction void or unenforceable; or
(c) (subject to subsection (3)) give rise to any right of action for breach of statutory duty.

(3) In prescribed cases the contravention is actionable at the suit of a person who suffers loss as a result of the contravention, subject to the defences and other incidents applying to actions for breach of statutory duty.

[2020]

NOTES

Regulations: the Financial Services and Markets Act 2000 (Rights of Action) Regulations 2001, SI 2001/2256 at **[4395]**.

Financial promotion

21 Restrictions on financial promotion

(1) A person ("A") must not, in the course of business, communicate an invitation or inducement to engage in investment activity.

(2) But subsection (1) does not apply if—

(a) A is an authorised person; or
(b) the content of the communication is approved for the purposes of this section by an authorised person.

(3) In the case of a communication originating outside the United Kingdom, subsection (1) applies only if the communication is capable of having an effect in the United Kingdom.

(4) The Treasury may by order specify circumstances in which a person is to be regarded for the purposes of subsection (1) as—

(a) acting in the course of business;

PART II FSMA 2000

(b) not acting in the course of business.

(5) The Treasury may by order specify circumstances (which may include compliance with financial promotion rules) in which subsection (1) does not apply.

(6) An order under subsection (5) may, in particular, provide that subsection (1) does not apply in relation to communications—

(a) of a specified description;

(b) originating in a specified country or territory outside the United Kingdom;

(c) originating in a country or territory which falls within a specified description of country or territory outside the United Kingdom; or

(d) originating outside the United Kingdom.

(7) The Treasury may by order repeal subsection (3).

(8) "Engaging in investment activity" means—

(a) entering or offering to enter into an agreement the making or performance of which by either party constitutes a controlled activity; or

(b) exercising any rights conferred by a controlled investment to acquire, dispose of, underwrite or convert a controlled investment.

(9) An activity is a controlled activity if—

(a) it is an activity of a specified kind or one which falls within a specified class of activity; and

(b) it relates to an investment of a specified kind, or to one which falls within a specified class of investment.

(10) An investment is a controlled investment if it is an investment of a specified kind or one which falls within a specified class of investment.

(11) Schedule 2 (except paragraph 26) applies for the purposes of subsections (9) and (10) with references to section 22 being read as references to each of those subsections.

(12) Nothing in Schedule 2, as applied by subsection (11), limits the powers conferred by subsection (9) or (10).

(13) "Communicate" includes causing a communication to be made.

(14) "Investment" includes any asset, right or interest.

(15) "Specified" means specified in an order made by the Treasury.

[2021]

NOTES

Orders: the Financial Services and Markets Act 2000 (Miscellaneous Provisions) Order 2001, SI 2001/3650; the Financial Services and Markets Act 2000 (Financial Promotion) Order 2005, SI 2005/1529 at **[4717]**.

Note that the following amending Orders have also been made under this section: the Financial Services and Markets Act 2000 (Financial Promotion and Miscellaneous Amendments) Order 2002, SI 2002/1310; the Financial Services and Markets Act 2000 (Commencement of Mortgage Regulation) (Amendment) Order 2002, SI 2002/1777; the Financial Services and Markets Act 2000 (Promotion of Collective Investment Schemes etc) (Exemptions) (Amendment) Order 2003, SI 2003/2067; the Financial Services and Markets Act 2000 (Financial Promotion and Promotion of Collective Investment Schemes) (Miscellaneous Amendments) Order 2005, SI 2005/270; the Financial Services and Markets Act 2000 (Financial Promotion) (Amendment) Order 2005, SI 2005/3392; the Financial Services and Markets Act 2000 (Financial Promotion) (Amendment) Order 2007, SI 2007/1083.

Regulated activities

22 The classes of activity and categories of investment

(1) An activity is a regulated activity for the purposes of this Act if it is an activity of a specified kind which is carried on by way of business and—

(a) relates to an investment of a specified kind; or

(b) in the case of an activity of a kind which is also specified for the purposes of this paragraph, is carried on in relation to property of any kind.

(2) Schedule 2 makes provision supplementing this section.

(3) Nothing in Schedule 2 limits the powers conferred by subsection (1).

(4) "Investment" includes any asset, right or interest.

(5) "Specified" means specified in an order made by the Treasury.

[2022]

NOTES

See further, the Gambling Act 2005, s 10(2) which provides that an order under this section which has the effect that a class of bet becomes or ceases to be a regulated activity may, in particular, include transitional provision relating to the application of the 2005 Act to that class of bet.

Orders: the Financial Services and Markets Act 2000 (Regulated Activities) Order 2001, SI 2001/544 at **[4001]**.

Note that the following amending Orders have also been made under this section: the Financial Services and Markets Act 2000 (Regulated Activities) (Amendment) Order 2001, SI 2001/3544; the Financial Services and Markets Act 2000 (Regulated Activities) (Amendment) Order 2002, SI 2002/682; the Financial Services and Markets Act 2000 (Financial Promotion and Miscellaneous Amendments) Order 2002, SI 2002/1310; the Financial Services and Markets Act 2000 (Regulated Activities) (Amendment) (No 2) Order 2002, SI 2002/1776; the Financial Services and Markets Act 2000 (Commencement of Mortgage Regulation) (Amendment) Order 2002, SI 2002/1777; the Financial Services and Markets Act 2000 (Regulated Activities) (Amendment) (No 1) Order 2003, SI 2003/1475; the Financial Services and Markets Act 2000 (Regulated Activities) (Amendment) (No 2) Order 2003, SI 2003/1476; the Financial Services and Markets Act 2000 (Regulated Activities) (Amendment) (No 3) Order 2003, SI 2003/2822; the Financial Services and Markets Act 2000 (Regulated Activities) (Amendment) Order 2004, SI 2004/1610; the Financial Services and Markets Act 2000 (Regulated Activities) (Amendment) (No 2) Order 2004, SI 2004/2737; the Financial Services and Markets Act 2000 (Regulated Activities) (Amendment) Order 2005, SI 2005/593; the Financial Services and Markets Act 2000 (Regulated Activities) (Amendment) (No 2) Order 2005, SI 2005/1518; the Financial Services and Markets Act 2000 (Regulated Activities) (Amendment) Order 2006, SI 2006/1969 at **[4813]**; the Financial Services and Markets Act 2000 (Regulated Activities) (Amendment) (No 2) Order 2006, SI 2006/2383 at **[4820]**; the Financial Services and Markets Act 2000 (Regulated Activities) (Amendment No 3) Order 2006, SI 2006/3384; the Financial Services and Markets Act 2000 (Regulated Activities) (Amendment) Order 2007, SI 2007/1339.

Offences

23 Contravention of the general prohibition

(1) A person who contravenes the general prohibition is guilty of an offence and liable—

(a) on summary conviction, to imprisonment for a term not exceeding six months or a fine not exceeding the statutory maximum, or both;

(b) on conviction on indictment, to imprisonment for a term not exceeding two years or a fine, or both.

(2) In this Act "an authorisation offence" means an offence under this section.

(3) In proceedings for an authorisation offence it is a defence for the accused to show that he took all reasonable precautions and exercised all due diligence to avoid committing the offence.

[2023]

24 False claims to be authorised or exempt

(1) A person who is neither an authorised person nor, in relation to the regulated activity in question, an exempt person is guilty of an offence if he—

(a) describes himself (in whatever terms) as an authorised person;

(b) describes himself (in whatever terms) as an exempt person in relation to the regulated activity; or

(c) behaves, or otherwise holds himself out, in a manner which indicates (or which is reasonably likely to be understood as indicating) that he is—

(i) an authorised person; or

(ii) an exempt person in relation to the regulated activity.

(2) In proceedings for an offence under this section it is a defence for the accused to show that he took all reasonable precautions and exercised all due diligence to avoid committing the offence.

(3) A person guilty of an offence under this section is liable on summary conviction to imprisonment for a term not exceeding six months or a fine not exceeding level 5 on the standard scale, or both.

(4) But where the conduct constituting the offence involved or included the public display of any material, the maximum fine for the offence is level 5 on the standard scale multiplied by the number of days for which the display continued.

[2024]

25 Contravention of section 21

(1) A person who contravenes section 21(1) is guilty of an offence and liable—

(a) on summary conviction, to imprisonment for a term not exceeding six months or a fine not exceeding the statutory maximum, or both;

(b) on conviction on indictment, to imprisonment for a term not exceeding two years or a fine, or both.

(2) In proceedings for an offence under this section it is a defence for the accused to show—

(a) that he believed on reasonable grounds that the content of the communication was prepared, or approved for the purposes of section 21, by an authorised person; or

(b) that he took all reasonable precautions and exercised all due diligence to avoid committing the offence.

[2025]

Enforceability of agreements

26 Agreements made by unauthorised persons

(1) An agreement made by a person in the course of carrying on a regulated activity in contravention of the general prohibition is unenforceable against the other party.

(2) The other party is entitled to recover—

(a) any money or other property paid or transferred by him under the agreement; and

(b) compensation for any loss sustained by him as a result of having parted with it.

(3) "Agreement" means an agreement—

(a) made after this section comes into force; and

(b) the making or performance of which constitutes, or is part of, the regulated activity in question.

(4) This section does not apply if the regulated activity is accepting deposits.

[2026]

NOTES

Application to certain agreements: sub-ss (1), (2) above (and, subject to certain modifications, s 28 below) apply to certain agreements entered into in contravention of the Financial Services Act 1986, s 3 (repealed by the Financial Services and Markets Act 2000 (Consequential Amendments and Repeals) Order 2001, SI 2001/3649, art 3(1)(c)), or the Insurance Companies Act 1982, s 2 (repealed by art 3(1)(b) of that Order) as they apply to an agreement in contravention of the general prohibition; see the Financial Services and Markets Act 2000 (Transitional Provisions and Savings) (Civil Remedies, Discipline, Criminal Offences etc) (No 2) Order 2001, SI 2001/3083, art 5(1), (3), (4).

27 Agreements made through unauthorised persons

(1) An agreement made by an authorised person ("the provider")—

(a) in the course of carrying on a regulated activity (not in contravention of the general prohibition), but

(b) in consequence of something said or done by another person ("the third party") in the course of a regulated activity carried on by the third party in contravention of the general prohibition,

is unenforceable against the other party.

(2) The other party is entitled to recover—

(a) any money or other property paid or transferred by him under the agreement; and

(b) compensation for any loss sustained by him as a result of having parted with it.

(3) "Agreement" means an agreement—

(a) made after this section comes into force; and

(b) the making or performance of which constitutes, or is part of, the regulated activity in question carried on by the provider.

(4) This section does not apply if the regulated activity is accepting deposits.

[2027]

NOTES

Application to certain agreements: sub-ss (1), (2) above (and, subject to certain modifications, s 28 below) apply to certain agreements entered into in contravention of the Financial Services Act 1986, s 3 (repealed by the Financial Services and Markets Act 2000 (Consequential Amendments and Repeals) Order 2001, SI 2001/3649, art 3(1)(c)) as they apply to an agreement in contravention of the general prohibition; see the Financial Services and Markets Act 2000 (Transitional Provisions and Savings) (Civil Remedies, Discipline, Criminal Offences etc) (No 2) Order 2001, SI 2001/3083, art 5(2), (3), (5).

28 Agreements made unenforceable by section 26 or 27

(1) This section applies to an agreement which is unenforceable because of section 26 or 27.

(2) The amount of compensation recoverable as a result of that section is—

(a) the amount agreed by the parties; or

(b) on the application of either party, the amount determined by the court.

(3) If the court is satisfied that it is just and equitable in the circumstances of the case, it may allow—

(a) the agreement to be enforced; or

(b) money and property paid or transferred under the agreement to be retained.

(4) In considering whether to allow the agreement to be enforced or (as the case may be) the money or property paid or transferred under the agreement to be retained the court must—

(a) if the case arises as a result of section 26, have regard to the issue mentioned in subsection (5); or

(b) if the case arises as a result of section 27, have regard to the issue mentioned in subsection (6).

(5) The issue is whether the person carrying on the regulated activity concerned reasonably believed that he was not contravening the general prohibition by making the agreement.

(6) The issue is whether the provider knew that the third party was (in carrying on the regulated activity) contravening the general prohibition.

(7) If the person against whom the agreement is unenforceable—

(a) elects not to perform the agreement, or

(b) as a result of this section, recovers money paid or other property transferred by him under the agreement,

he must repay any money and return any other property received by him under the agreement.

(8) If property transferred under the agreement has passed to a third party, a reference in section 26 or 27 or this section to that property is to be read as a reference to its value at the time of its transfer under the agreement.

(9) The commission of an authorisation offence does not make the agreement concerned illegal or invalid to any greater extent than is provided by section 26 or 27.

[2028]

NOTES

Application to certain agreements: see the notes to ss 26 and 27 at **[2026]** and **[2027]**.

29 Accepting deposits in breach of general prohibition

(1) This section applies to an agreement between a person ("the depositor") and another person ("the deposit-taker") made in the course of the carrying on by the deposit-taker of accepting deposits in contravention of the general prohibition.

(2) If the depositor is not entitled under the agreement to recover without delay any money deposited by him, he may apply to the court for an order directing the deposit-taker to return the money to him.

(3) The court need not make such an order if it is satisfied that it would not be just and equitable for the money deposited to be returned, having regard to the issue mentioned in subsection (4).

(4) The issue is whether the deposit-taker reasonably believed that he was not contravening the general prohibition by making the agreement.

(5) "Agreement" means an agreement—

(a) made after this section comes into force; and

(b) the making or performance of which constitutes, or is part of, accepting deposits.

[2029]

30 Enforceability of agreements resulting from unlawful communications

(1) In this section—

"unlawful communication" means a communication in relation to which there has been a contravention of section 21(1);

"controlled agreement" means an agreement the making or performance of which by either party constitutes a controlled activity for the purposes of that section; and

"controlled investment" has the same meaning as in section 21.

(2) If in consequence of an unlawful communication a person enters as a customer into a controlled agreement, it is unenforceable against him and he is entitled to recover—

(a) any money or other property paid or transferred by him under the agreement; and

(b) compensation for any loss sustained by him as a result of having parted with it.

(3) If in consequence of an unlawful communication a person exercises any rights conferred by a controlled investment, no obligation to which he is subject as a result of exercising them is enforceable against him and he is entitled to recover—

(a) any money or other property paid or transferred by him under the obligation; and

(b) compensation for any loss sustained by him as a result of having parted with it.

(4) But the court may allow—

(a) the agreement or obligation to be enforced, or

(b) money or property paid or transferred under the agreement or obligation to be retained,

if it is satisfied that it is just and equitable in the circumstances of the case.

(5) In considering whether to allow the agreement or obligation to be enforced or (as the case may be) the money or property paid or transferred under the agreement to be retained the court must have regard to the issues mentioned in subsections (6) and (7).

(6) If the applicant made the unlawful communication, the issue is whether he reasonably believed that he was not making such a communication.

(7) If the applicant did not make the unlawful communication, the issue is whether he knew that the agreement was entered into in consequence of such a communication.

(8) "Applicant" means the person seeking to enforce the agreement or obligation or retain the money or property paid or transferred.

(9) Any reference to making a communication includes causing a communication to be made.

(10) The amount of compensation recoverable as a result of subsection (2) or (3) is—

(a) the amount agreed between the parties; or

(b) on the application of either party, the amount determined by the court.

(11) If a person elects not to perform an agreement or an obligation which (by virtue of subsection (2) or (3)) is unenforceable against him, he must repay any money and return any other property received by him under the agreement.

(12) If (by virtue of subsection (2) or (3)) a person recovers money paid or property transferred by him under an agreement or obligation, he must repay any money and return any other property received by him as a result of exercising the rights in question.

(13) If any property required to be returned under this section has passed to a third party, references to that property are to be read as references to its value at the time of its receipt by the person required to return it.

[2030]

PART III
AUTHORISATION AND EXEMPTION

NOTES

Transitional provisions: see the Financial Services and Markets Act 2000 (Transitional Provisions) (Authorised Persons etc) Order 2001, SI 2001/2636. That Order sets out the transitional arrangements for ensuring that people who have been authorised to carry on particular business under the various regulatory regimes replaced by this Act are treated as authorised persons with the appropriate permission for the purposes of this Act. The regulatory regimes covered by the Order are the Financial Services Act 1986, the Banking Act 1987, the Insurance Companies Act 1982, the Friendly Societies Act 1992, the Building Societies Act 1986, the Banking Coordination (Second Council Directive) Regulations 1992 (SI 1992/3218) and the Investment Services Regulations 1995 (SI 1995/3275).

Authorisation

31 Authorised persons

(1) The following persons are authorised for the purposes of this Act—
- (a) a person who has a Part IV permission to carry on one or more regulated activities;
- (b) an EEA firm qualifying for authorisation under Schedule 3;
- (c) a Treaty firm qualifying for authorisation under Schedule 4;
- (d) a person who is otherwise authorised by a provision of, or made under, this Act.

(2) In this Act "authorised person" means a person who is authorised for the purposes of this Act.

[2031]

32 Partnerships and unincorporated associations

(1) If a firm is authorised—
- (a) it is authorised to carry on the regulated activities concerned in the name of the firm; and
- (b) its authorisation is not affected by any change in its membership.

(2) If an authorised firm is dissolved, its authorisation continues to have effect in relation to any [individual or] firm which succeeds to the business of the dissolved firm.

[(3) For the purposes of this section, an individual or firm is to be regarded as succeeding to the business of a dissolved firm only if succession is to the whole or substantially the whole of the business of the former firm.]

(4) "Firm" means—
- (a) a partnership; or
- (b) an unincorporated association of persons.

(5) "Partnership" does not include a partnership which is constituted under the law of any place outside the United Kingdom and is a body corporate.

[2032]

NOTES

Para (2): words in square brackets inserted by the Regulatory Reform (Financial Services and Markets Act 2000) Order 2007, SI 2007/1973, arts 2, 3(a), as from 12 July 2007.

Para (3): substituted by SI 2007/1973, arts 2, 3(b), as from 12 July 2007.

Ending of authorisation

33 Withdrawal of authorisation by the Authority

(1) This section applies if—
- (a) an authorised person's Part IV permission is cancelled; and
- (b) as a result, there is no regulated activity for which he has permission.

(2) The Authority must give a direction withdrawing that person's status as an authorised person.

[2033]

34 EEA firms

(1) An EEA firm ceases to qualify for authorisation under Part II of Schedule 3 if it ceases to be an EEA firm as a result of—

(a) having its EEA authorisation withdrawn; or
(b) ceasing to have an EEA right in circumstances in which EEA authorisation is not required.

(2) At the request of an EEA firm, the Authority may give a direction cancelling its authorisation under Part II of Schedule 3.

(3) If an EEA firm has a Part IV permission, it does not cease to be an authorised person merely because it ceases to qualify for authorisation under Part II of Schedule 3.

[2034]

NOTES

Note: "EEA firm" is defined in Sch 3, Pt I, para 5, and "EEA right" is defined in Sch 3, Pt I, para 7 (see **[2438]**).

35 Treaty firms

(1) A Treaty firm ceases to qualify for authorisation under Schedule 4 if its home State authorisation is withdrawn.

(2) At the request of a Treaty firm, the Authority may give a direction cancelling its Schedule 4 authorisation.

(3) If a Treaty firm has a Part IV permission, it does not cease to be an authorised person merely because it ceases to qualify for authorisation under Schedule 4.

[2035]

NOTES

Note: "Treaty firm" is defined in Sch 4, para 1 at **[2441]**.

36 Persons authorised as a result of paragraph 1(1) of Schedule 5

(1) At the request of a person authorised as a result of paragraph 1(1) of Schedule 5, the Authority may give a direction cancelling his authorisation as such a person.

(2) If a person authorised as a result of paragraph 1(1) of Schedule 5 has a Part IV permission, he does not cease to be an authorised person merely because he ceases to be a person so authorised.

[2036]

NOTES

Note: under Sch 5, para 1(1) the FSA may cancel the automatic authorisation of managers and depositaries of UCITS schemes at their request. The operator, trustee or depositary of a collective investment scheme recognised by virtue of s 264 is deemed to be an authorised person (Sch 5, para 1(1), (2)) in so far as it is carrying on a regulated activity, any activity appropriate to the capacity in which he acts in relation to the scheme of the kind described in Sch 2, para 8, or any activity in connection with, or for the purposes of, the scheme. In the case of an authorised OEIC, the OEIC is an authorised person by virtue of Sch 5, para 1(3) in so far as it is carrying on a regulated activity, the operation of the scheme or any other activity in connection with, or for the purposes of, the operation of the scheme.

Exercise of EEA rights by UK firms

37 Exercise of EEA rights by UK firms

Part III of Schedule 3 makes provision in relation to the exercise outside the United Kingdom of EEA rights by UK firms.

[2037]

NOTES

Note: "UK firm" is defined in Sch 3, Pt I, para 10 at **[2438]**.

Exemption

38 Exemption orders

(1) The Treasury may by order ("an exemption order") provide for—

(a) specified persons, or

(b) persons falling within a specified class,

to be exempt from the general prohibition.

(2) But a person cannot be an exempt person as a result of an exemption order if he has a Part IV permission.

(3) An exemption order may provide for an exemption to have effect—

(a) in respect of all regulated activities;

(b) in respect of one or more specified regulated activities;

(c) only in specified circumstances;

(d) only in relation to specified functions;

(e) subject to conditions.

(4) "Specified" means specified by the exemption order.

[2038]

NOTES

Orders: the Financial Services and Markets Act 2000 (Exemption) Order 2001, SI 2001/1201 at **[4149]**. Note that the following amending Orders have also been made under this section: the Financial Services and Markets Act 2000 (Exemption) (Amendment) Order 2001, SI 2001/3623; the Financial Services and Markets Act 2000 (Financial Promotion and Miscellaneous Amendments) Order 2002, SI 2002/1310; the Financial Services and Markets Act 2000 (Exemption) (Amendment) Order 2003, SI 2003/47; the Financial Services and Markets Act 2000 (Exemption) (Amendment) (No 2) Order 2003, SI 2003/1675; the Financial Services and Markets Act 2000 (Exemption) (Amendment) Order 2005, SI 2005/592; the Financial Services and Markets Act 2000 (Exemption) (Amendment) Order 2007, SI 2007/125; the Financial Services and Markets Act 2000 (Exemption) (Amendment No 2) Order 2007, SI 2007/1821.

39 Exemption of appointed representatives

(1) If a person (other than an authorised person)—

(a) is a party to a contract with an authorised person ("his principal") which—

(i) permits or requires him to carry on business of a prescribed description, and

(ii) complies with such requirements as may be prescribed, and

(b) is someone for whose activities in carrying on the whole or part of that business his principal has accepted responsibility in writing,

he is exempt from the general prohibition in relation to any regulated activity comprised in the carrying on of that business for which his principal has accepted responsibility.

[(1A) But a person is not exempt as a result of subsection (1)—

(a) if his principal is an investment firm or a credit institution, and

(b) so far as the business for which his principal has accepted responsibility is investment services business,

unless he is entered on the applicable register.

(1B) The "applicable register" is—

(a) in the case of a person established in an EEA State (other than the United Kingdom) which permits investment firms authorised by the competent authority of that State to appoint tied agents, the register of tied agents maintained in that State pursuant to Article 23 of the markets in financial instruments directive;

(b) in the case of a person established in an EEA State which does not permit investment firms authorised as mentioned in paragraph (a) to appoint tied agents—

(i) if his principal has his relevant office in the United Kingdom, the record maintained by the Authority by virtue of section 347(1)(ha), and

(ii) if his principal is established in an EEA State (other than the United Kingdom) which permits investment firms authorised by the competent authority of the State to appoint tied agents, the register of tied agents maintained by that State pursuant to Article 23 of the markets in financial instruments directive; and

PART II FSMA 2000

(c) in any other case, the record maintained by the Authority by virtue of section 347(1)(ha).]

(2) A person who is exempt as a result of subsection (1) is referred to in this Act as an appointed representative.

(3) The principal of an appointed representative is responsible, to the same extent as if he had expressly permitted it, for anything done or omitted by the representative in carrying on the business for which he has accepted responsibility.

(4) In determining whether an authorised person has complied with a provision contained in or made under this Act, [or with a provision contained in any directly applicable Community regulation made under the markets in financial instruments directive,] anything which a relevant person has done or omitted as respects business for which the authorised person has accepted responsibility is to be treated as having been done or omitted by the authorised person.

(5) "Relevant person" means a person who at the material time is or was an appointed representative by virtue of being a party to a contract with the authorised person.

(6) Nothing in subsection (4) is to cause the knowledge or intentions of an appointed representative to be attributed to his principal for the purpose of determining whether the principal has committed an offence, unless in all the circumstances it is reasonable for them to be attributed to him.

[(7) A person carries on "investment services business" if—
(a) the business includes providing services or carrying on activities of the kind mentioned in Article 4.1.25 of the markets in financial instruments directive, and
(b) as a result of providing such services or carrying on such activities he is a tied agent or would be if he were established in an EEA State.

(8) In this section—
"competent authority" has the meaning given in Article 4.1.22 of the markets in financial instruments directive;
"credit institution" means—
(a) a credit institution authorised under the banking consolidation directive, or
(b) an institution which would satisfy the requirements for authorisation as a credit institution under that directive if it had its relevant office in an EEA State;
"relevant office" means—
(a) in relation to a body corporate, its registered office or, if it has no registered office, its head office, and
(b) in relation to a person other than a body corporate, the person's head office.]

[2039]

NOTES

Sub-s (1A), (1B), (7), (8): inserted and added respectively by the Financial Services and Markets Act 2000 (Markets in Financial Instruments) Regulations 2007, SI 2007/126, reg 3(5), Sch 5, paras 1, 2(a), (c), as from 1 April 2007 (certain purposes (see reg 1(2) at **[7596]**)), and as from 1 November 2007 (otherwise).

Sub-s (4): words in square brackets inserted by SI 2007/126, reg 3(5), Sch 5, paras 1, 2(b), as from 1 April 2007 (certain purposes (see reg 1(2) at **[7596]**)), and as from 1 November 2007 (otherwise).

Transitional provisions: see the Financial Services and Markets Act 2000 (Markets in Financial Instruments) Regulations 2007, SI 2007/126, reg 9 (at **[7604]**).

Regulations: the Financial Services and Markets Act 2000 (Appointed Representatives) Regulations 2001, SI 2001/1217 at **[4159]**.

Note that the following amending Regulations have also been made under this section: the Financial Services and Markets Act 2000 (Appointed Representatives) (Amendment) Regulations 2001, SI 2001/2508; the Financial Services and Markets Act 2000 (Appointed Representatives) (Amendment) Regulations 2004, SI 2004/453; the Financial Services and Markets Act 2000 (Appointed Representatives) (Amendment) Regulations 2006, SI 2006/3414; the Financial Services and Markets Act 2000 (Markets in Financial Instruments) (Amendment) Regulations 2007, SI 2007/763.

[39A Certain tied agents operating outside United Kingdom

(1) This section applies to an authorised person whose relevant office is in the United Kingdom if—
(a) he is a party to a contract with a person (other than an authorised person) who is established—

(i) in the United Kingdom, or

(ii) in an EEA State which does not permit investment firms authorised by the competent authority of the State to appoint tied agents; and

(b) the contract is a relevant contract.

(2) A contract is a "relevant contract" if it satisfies conditions A to C

(3) Condition A is that the contract permits or requires the person mentioned in subsection (1)(a) (the "agent") to carry on investment services business.

(4) Condition B is that either—

(a) it is a condition of the contract that such business may only be carried on by the agent in an EEA State other than the United Kingdom; or

(b) in a case not falling within paragraph (a), the Authority is satisfied that no such business is, or is likely to be, carried on by the agent in the United Kingdom.

(5) Condition C is that the business is of a description that, if carried on in the United Kingdom, would be prescribed for the purposes of section 39(1)(a)(i).

(6) An authorised person to whom this section applies who—

(a) enters into or continues to perform a relevant contract with an agent which does not comply with the applicable requirements,

(b) enters into or continues to perform a relevant contract without accepting or having accepted responsibility in writing for the agent's activities in carrying on investment services business,

(c) enters into a relevant contract with an agent who is not entered on the record maintained by the Authority by virtue of section 347(1)(ha), or

(d) continues to perform a relevant contract with an agent when he knows or ought to know that the agent is not entered on that record,

is to be taken for the purposes of this Act to have contravened a requirement imposed on him by or under this Act.

(7) The "applicable requirements" are the requirements prescribed for the purposes of subsection (1)(a)(ii) of section 39 which have effect in the case of a person to whom subsection (1A) of that section applies.

(8) A person carries on "investment services business" if—

(a) his business includes providing services or carrying on activities of the kind mentioned in Article 4.1.25 of the markets in financial instruments directive, and

(b) as a result of providing such services or carrying on such activities he is a tied agent.

(9) In this section—

"competent authority" has the meaning given in Article 4.1.22 of the markets in financial instruments directive;

"relevant office" means—

(a) in relation to a body corporate, its registered office or, if it has no registered office, its head office, and

(b) in relation to a person other than a body corporate, the person's head office.]

[2039A]

NOTES

Commencement: see the note below.

Inserted by the Financial Services and Markets Act 2000 (Markets in Financial Instruments) Regulations 2007, SI 2007/126, reg 3(5), Sch 5, paras 1, 3, as from 1 April 2007 (certain purposes (see reg 1(2) at **[7596]**)), and as from 1 November 2007 (otherwise).

Transitional provisions: see the Financial Services and Markets Act 2000 (Markets in Financial Instruments) Regulations 2007, SI 2007/126, reg 9 (at **[7604]**).

PART IV
PERMISSION TO CARRY ON REGULATED ACTIVITIES

NOTES

Investment firms: see the Financial Services and Markets Act 2000 (Markets in Financial Instruments) Regulations 2007, SI 2007/126, reg 4 (at **[7599]**) which requires the FSA to be satisfied that the authorisation requirements of MiFID (as to which see Chapter I of Title II of MiFID (at **[9621]**) and

Commission Regulation 1287/2006 (at **[9887]**)) are met before giving permission under this Part to an investment firm (as defined in s 424A) or varying the permission of such a firm.

Transitional provisions: the Financial Services and Markets Act 2000 (Transitional Provisions) (Authorised Persons etc) Order 2001, SI 2001/2636, Pt II, Ch I provides that persons who are authorised or exempted from the need for authorisation under provisions of the previous regulatory regimes are treated, as from 1 December 2001, as having permission under Pt IV of this Act to carry on the activities they were lawfully able to carry on immediately before that date by reason of that authorisation or exemption. Pt II of SI 2001/2636 applies to: (a) persons authorised or exempted under the Financial Services Act 1986 (repealed by the Financial Services and Markets Act 2000 (Consequential Amendments and Repeals) Order 2001, SI 2001/3649, art 3(1)(c)); (b) persons authorised under the Banking Act 1987 (repealed by SI 2001/3649, art 3(1)(d)); (c) insurance companies; (d) friendly societies; and (e) building societies.

Pt III of SI 2001/2636 provides that restrictions and prohibitions imposed under provisions of the previous regulatory regimes on authorised persons are to have effect after 1 December 2001 as if they were requirements imposed under s 43 (in relation to persons with a permission under Pt IV of this Act). Pt III of SI 2001/2636 applies to: (a) prohibitions and requirements under the Financial Services Act 1986 (repealed as noted above); (b) restrictions and directions under the Banking Act 1987 (repealed as noted above); (c) directions and requirements under the Insurance Companies Act 1982 (repealed by SI 2001/3649, art 3(1)(b)); (d) conditions and directions under the Friendly Societies Act 1992; (e) conditions and directions under the Building Societies Act 1986; and (f) prohibitions and restrictions under the Banking Coordination (Second Council Directive) Regulations 1992, SI 1992/3218 (revoked by SI 2001/3649, art 3(2)(a)) and the Investment Services Regulations 1995, SI 1995/3275 (revoked by SI 2001/3649, art 3(2)(c)).

As to transitional modifications to ss 45–48, 50, 52–55, see the Financial Services and Markets Act 2000 (Interim Permissions) Order 2001, SI 2001/3374. This Order confers an interim permission on certain applicants who applied to the Financial Services Authority for permission under this Part and whose application was still pending on the date when the main provisions of this Act came into force (1 December 2001). The scope of the Order is limited to those applicants who were lawfully carrying on the activity which was regulated for the first time under this Act

See also the Financial Services and Markets Act 2000 (Transitional Provisions) (Mortgages) Order 2004, SI 2004/2615 at **[4695]**, the Financial Services and Markets Act 2000 (Transitional Provisions) (General Insurance Intermediaries) Order 2004, SI 2004/3351 at **[4710]**, the Financial Services and Markets Act 2000 (Regulated Activities) (Amendment) Order 2006, SI 2006/1969 at **[4813]**, the Financial Services and Markets Act 2000 (Regulated Activities) (Amendment) (No 2) Order 2006, SI 2006/2383 at **[4820]**, and the Financial Services and Markets Act 2000 (Markets in Financial Instruments) Regulations 2007, SI 2007/126 at **[7596]**.

Application for permission

40 Application for permission

(1) An application for permission to carry on one or more regulated activities may be made to the Authority by—

(a) an individual;

(b) a body corporate;

(c) a partnership; or

(d) an unincorporated association.

(2) An authorised person may not apply for permission under this section if he has a permission—

(a) given to him by the Authority under this Part, or

(b) having effect as if so given,

which is in force.

(3) An EEA firm may not apply for permission under this section to carry on a regulated activity which it is, or would be, entitled to carry on in exercise of an EEA right, whether through a United Kingdom branch or by providing services in the United Kingdom.

(4) A permission given by the Authority under this Part or having effect as if so given is referred to in this Act as "a Part IV permission".

[2040]

NOTES

Note: as to interim permission in respect of regulated mortgage business, see the Financial Services and Markets Act 2000 (Transitional Provisions) (Mortgages) Order 2004, SI 2004/2615 at **[4695]**.

Note: as to interim permission in respect of general insurance intermediaries, see the Financial Services and Markets Act 2000 (Transitional Provisions) (General Insurance Intermediaries) Order 2004, SI 2004/3351 at **[4710]**.

Note: as to interim permission in respect of the activity of establishing, operating or winding up a personal pension scheme or in respect of the specified investment of rights under a personal pension scheme, see the Financial Services and Markets Act 2000 (Regulated Activities) (Amendment) Order 2006, SI 2006/1969, art 4 at **[4815]**.

Note: as to interim permission in respect of the activities of entering into, administering, arranging and advising on regulated home reversion plans and regulated home purchase plans, see the Financial Services and Markets Act 2000 (Regulated Activities) (Amendment) (No 2) Order 2006, SI 2006/2383, art 37 at **[4822]**.

41 The threshold conditions

(1) "The threshold conditions", in relation to a regulated activity, means the conditions set out in Schedule 6.

(2) In giving or varying permission, or imposing or varying any requirement, under this Part the Authority must ensure that the person concerned will satisfy, and continue to satisfy, the threshold conditions in relation to all of the regulated activities for which he has or will have permission.

(3) But the duty imposed by subsection (2) does not prevent the Authority, having due regard to that duty, from taking such steps as it considers are necessary, in relation to a particular authorised person, in order to secure its regulatory objective of the protection of consumers.

[2041]

Permission

42 Giving permission

(1) "The applicant" means an applicant for permission under section 40.

(2) The Authority may give permission for the applicant to carry on the regulated activity or activities to which his application relates or such of them as may be specified in the permission.

(3) If the applicant—

(a) in relation to a particular regulated activity, is exempt from the general prohibition as a result of section 39(1) or an order made under section 38(1), but

(b) has applied for permission in relation to another regulated activity,

the application is to be treated as relating to all the regulated activities which, if permission is given, he will carry on.

(4) If the applicant—

(a) in relation to a particular regulated activity, is exempt from the general prohibition as a result of section 285(2) or (3), but

(b) has applied for permission in relation to another regulated activity,

the application is to be treated as relating only to that other regulated activity.

(5) If the applicant—

(a) is a person to whom, in relation to a particular regulated activity, the general prohibition does not apply as a result of Part XIX, but

(b) has applied for permission in relation to another regulated activity,

the application is to be treated as relating only to that other regulated activity.

(6) If it gives permission, the Authority must specify the permitted regulated activity or activities, described in such manner as the Authority considers appropriate.

(7) The Authority may—

(a) incorporate in the description of a regulated activity such limitations (for example as to circumstances in which the activity may, or may not, be carried on) as it considers appropriate;

(b) specify a narrower or wider description of regulated activity than that to which the application relates;

(c) give permission for the carrying on of a regulated activity which is not included among those to which the application relates.

[2042]

PART II FSMA 2000

43 Imposition of requirements

(1) A Part IV permission may include such requirements as the Authority considers appropriate.

(2) A requirement may, in particular, be imposed—

(a) so as to require the person concerned to take specified action; or

(b) so as to require him to refrain from taking specified action.

(3) A requirement may extend to activities which are not regulated activities.

(4) A requirement may be imposed by reference to the person's relationship with—

(a) his group; or

(b) other members of his group.

(5) A requirement expires at the end of such period as the Authority may specify in the permission.

(6) But subsection (5) does not affect the Authority's powers under section 44 or 45.

[2043]

Variation and cancellation of Part IV permission

44 Variation etc at request of authorised person

(1) The Authority may, on the application of an authorised person with a Part IV permission, vary the permission by—

(a) adding a regulated activity to those for which it gives permission;

(b) removing a regulated activity from those for which it gives permission;

(c) varying the description of a regulated activity for which it gives permission;

(d) cancelling a requirement imposed under section 43; or

(e) varying such a requirement.

(2) The Authority may, on the application of an authorised person with a Part IV permission, cancel the permission.

(3) The Authority may refuse an application under this section if it appears to it—

(a) that the interests of consumers, or potential consumers, would be adversely affected if the application were to be granted; and

(b) that it is desirable in the interests of consumers, or potential consumers, for the application to be refused.

(4) If, as a result of a variation of a Part IV permission under this section, there are no longer any regulated activities for which the authorised person concerned has permission, the Authority must, once it is satisfied that it is no longer necessary to keep the permission in force, cancel it.

(5) The Authority's power to vary a Part IV permission under this section extends to including any provision in the permission as varied that could be included if a fresh permission were being given in response to an application under section 40.

[2044]

45 Variation etc on the Authority's own initiative

(1) The Authority may exercise its power under this section in relation to an authorised person if it appears to it that—

(a) he is failing, or is likely to fail, to satisfy the threshold conditions;

(b) he has failed, during a period of at least 12 months, to carry on a regulated activity for which he has a Part IV permission; or

(c) it is desirable to exercise that power in order to protect the interests of consumers or potential consumers.

(2) The Authority's power under this section is the power to vary a Part IV permission in any of the ways mentioned in section 44(1) or to cancel it.

[(2A) Without prejudice to the generality of subsections (1) and (2), the Authority may, in relation to an authorised person who is an investment firm, exercise its power under this section to cancel the Part IV permission of the firm if it appears to it that—

(a) the firm has failed, during a period of at least six months, to carry on a regulated activity which is an investment service or activity for which it has a Part IV permission;

(b) the firm obtained the Part IV permission by making a false statement or by other irregular means;

(c) the firm no longer satisfies the requirements for authorisation pursuant to Chapter I of Title II of the markets in financial instruments directive, or pursuant to or contained in any Community legislation made under that Chapter, in relation to a regulated activity which is an investment service or activity for which it has a Part IV permission; or

(d) the firm has seriously and systematically infringed the operating conditions pursuant to Chapter II of Title II of the markets in financial instruments directive, or pursuant to or contained in any Community legislation made under that Chapter, in relation to a regulated activity which is an investment service or activity for which it has a Part IV permission.

(2B) For the purposes of subsection (2A) a regulated activity is an investment service or activity if it falls within the definition of "investment services and activities" in section 417(1).]

(3) If, as a result of a variation of a Part IV permission under this section, there are no longer any regulated activities for which the authorised person concerned has permission, the Authority must, once it is satisfied that it is no longer necessary to keep the permission in force, cancel it.

(4) The Authority's power to vary a Part IV permission under this section extends to including any provision in the permission as varied that could be included if a fresh permission were being given in response to an application under section 40.

(5) The Authority's power under this section is referred to in this Part as its own-initiative power.

[2045]

NOTES

Sub-ss (2A), (2B): inserted by the Financial Services and Markets Act 2000 (Markets in Financial Instruments) Regulations 2007, SI 2007/126, reg 3(5), Sch 5, paras 1, 4, as from 1 April 2007 (certain purposes (see reg 1(2) at **[7596]**)), and as from 1 November 2007 (otherwise).

46 Variation of permission on acquisition of control

(1) This section applies if it appears to the Authority that—

(a) a person has acquired control over a UK authorised person who has a Part IV permission; but

(b) there are no grounds for exercising its own-initiative power.

(2) If it appears to the Authority that the likely effect of the acquisition of control on the authorised person, or on any of its activities, is uncertain the Authority may vary the authorised person's permission by—

(a) imposing a requirement of a kind that could be imposed under section 43 on giving permission; or

(b) varying a requirement included in the authorised person's permission under that section.

(3) Any reference to a person having acquired control is to be read in accordance with Part XII.

[2046]

47 Exercise of power in support of overseas regulator

(1) The Authority's own-initiative power may be exercised in respect of an authorised person at the request of, or for the purpose of assisting, a regulator who is—

(a) outside the United Kingdom; and

(b) of a prescribed kind.

(2) Subsection (1) applies whether or not the Authority has powers which are exercisable in relation to the authorised person by virtue of any provision of Part XIII.

(3) If a request to the Authority for the exercise of its own-initiative power has been made by a regulator who is—

(a) outside the United Kingdom,
(b) of a prescribed kind, and
(c) acting in pursuance of provisions of a prescribed kind,

the Authority must, in deciding whether or not to exercise that power in response to the request, consider whether it is necessary to do so in order to comply with a Community obligation.

(4) In deciding in any case in which the Authority does not consider that the exercise of its own-initiative power is necessary in order to comply with a Community obligation, it may take into account in particular—

(a) whether in the country or territory of the regulator concerned, corresponding assistance would be given to a United Kingdom regulatory authority;
(b) whether the case concerns the breach of a law, or other requirement, which has no close parallel in the United Kingdom or involves the assertion of a jurisdiction not recognised by the United Kingdom;
(c) the seriousness of the case and its importance to persons in the United Kingdom;
(d) whether it is otherwise appropriate in the public interest to give the assistance sought.

(5) The Authority may decide not to exercise its own-initiative power, in response to a request, unless the regulator concerned undertakes to make such contribution towards the cost of its exercise as the Authority considers appropriate.

(6) Subsection (5) does not apply if the Authority decides that it is necessary for it to exercise its own-initiative power in order to comply with a Community obligation.

(7) In subsections (4) and (5) "request" means a request of a kind mentioned in subsection (1).

[2047]

NOTES

Regulations: the Financial Services and Markets Act 2000 (Own-initiative Power) (Overseas Regulators) Regulations 2001, SI 2001/2639 at **[4475]**.

48 Prohibitions and restrictions

(1) This section applies if the Authority—

(a) on giving a person a Part IV permission, imposes an assets requirement on him; or
(b) varies an authorised person's Part IV permission so as to alter an assets requirement imposed on him or impose such a requirement on him.

(2) A person on whom an assets requirement is imposed is referred to in this section as "A".

(3) "Assets requirement" means a requirement under section 43—

(a) prohibiting the disposal of, or other dealing with, any of A's assets (whether in the United Kingdom or elsewhere) or restricting such disposals or dealings; or
(b) that all or any of A's assets, or all or any assets belonging to consumers but held by A or to his order, must be transferred to and held by a trustee approved by the Authority.

(4) If the Authority—

(a) imposes a requirement of the kind mentioned in subsection (3)(a), and
(b) gives notice of the requirement to any institution with whom A keeps an account,

the notice has the effects mentioned in subsection (5).

(5) Those effects are that—

(a) the institution does not act in breach of any contract with A if, having been instructed by A (or on his behalf) to transfer any sum or otherwise make any payment out of A's account, it refuses to do so in the reasonably held belief that complying with the instruction would be incompatible with the requirement; and
(b) if the institution complies with such an instruction, it is liable to pay to the Authority an amount equal to the amount transferred from, or otherwise paid out of, A's account in contravention of the requirement.

(6) If the Authority imposes a requirement of the kind mentioned in subsection (3)(b), no assets held by a person as trustee in accordance with the requirement may, while the requirement is in force, be released or dealt with except with the consent of the Authority.

(7) If, while a requirement of the kind mentioned in subsection (3)(b) is in force, A creates a charge over any assets of his held in accordance with the requirement, the charge is (to the extent that it confers security over the assets) void against the liquidator and any of A's creditors.

(8) Assets held by a person as trustee ("T") are to be taken to be held by T in accordance with a requirement mentioned in subsection (3)(b) only if—

(a) A has given T written notice that those assets are to be held by T in accordance with the requirement; or

(b) they are assets into which assets to which paragraph (a) applies have been transposed by T on the instructions of A.

(9) A person who contravenes subsection (6) is guilty of an offence and liable on summary conviction to a fine not exceeding level 5 on the standard scale.

(10) "Charge" includes a mortgage (or in Scotland a security over property).

(11) Subsections (6) and (8) do not affect any equitable interest or remedy in favour of a person who is a beneficiary of a trust as a result of a requirement of the kind mentioned in subsection (3)(b).

[2048]

Connected persons

49 Persons connected with an applicant

(1) In considering—

(a) an application for a Part IV permission, or

(b) whether to vary or cancel a Part IV permission,

the Authority may have regard to any person appearing to it to be, or likely to be, in a relationship with the applicant or person given permission which is relevant.

(2) Before—

(a) giving permission in response to an application made by a person who is connected with an EEA firm [(other than an EEA firm falling within paragraph 5(e) of Schedule 3 (insurance and reinsurance intermediaries))], or

[(b) varying any permission given by the Authority to such a person, where the effect of the variation is to grant permission for the purposes of a single market directive other than the one for the purposes of which the existing permission was granted,]

the Authority must consult the firm's home state regulator.

[(2A) But subsection (2) does not apply to the extent that the permission relates to—

(a) an insurance mediation activity (within the meaning given by paragraph 2(5) of Schedule 6); or

(b) a regulated activity involving a regulated mortgage contract[, a regulated home reversion plan or a regulated home purchase plan].]

(3) A person ("A") is connected with an EEA firm if—

(a) A is a subsidiary undertaking of the firm; or

(b) A is a subsidiary undertaking of a parent undertaking of the firm.

[2049]

PART II
FSMA 2000

NOTES

Sub-s (2): words in square brackets in para (a) inserted by the Financial Services and Markets Act 2000 (Regulated Activities) (Amendment) (No 2) Order 2003, SI 2003/1476, art 20(1), (2), as from 31 October 2004 (in so far as relating to contracts of long-term care insurance), and as from 14 January 2005 (otherwise); for transitional provisions see arts 22–27 of that Order at **[4665]** et seq; para (b) substituted by the Regulatory Reform (Financial Services and Markets Act 2000) Order 2007, SI 2007/1973, arts 2, 4, as from 12 July 2007.

Sub-s (2A): inserted by the Financial Services and Markets Act 2000 (Regulated Activities) Order 2001, SI 2001/544, art 97, as from 15 July 2004 (see further the note below); words in square brackets inserted by the Financial Services and Markets Act 2000 (Regulated Activities) (Amendment) (No 2) Order 2006, SI 2006/2383, art 28, as from 6 April 2007 (for the full commencement details of SI 2006/2383, see art 1 of that Order at **[4820]**).

Note: sub-s (2A) was originally inserted by the Financial Services and Markets Act 2000 (Regulated Activities) (Amendment) (No 2) Order 2003, SI 2003/1476, art 20(1), (3), as from 31 October 2004 (in so far as relating to contracts of long-term care insurance), and as from 14 January 2005 (otherwise), subject to transitional provisions as noted to sub-s (2) above. Article 20(3) of SI 2003/1476 was subsequently revoked by the Financial Services and Markets Act 2000 (Regulated Activities) (Amendment)

Order 2004, SI 2004/1610, art 2, as from 15 July 2004. Article 3 of SI 2004/1610 also amended the Financial Services and Markets Act 2000 (Regulated Activities) Order 2001, SI 2001/544 by adding a new art 97 which, in turn, inserted the new sub-s (2A) as noted above.

Note: s 49(2) does not apply where the FSA is considering varying the Part IV permission of any person where that person is a member of a financial conglomerate where the FSA is acting in the course of carrying on supplemental supervision for the purposes of any provision (other than Articles 11, 12, 16, 17 or 18(3) of the Conglomerates Directive.

Note: "parent undertaking" and "subsidiary undertaking" are defined in s 420 at **[2417]**.

Additional permissions

50 Authority's duty to consider other permissions etc

(1) "Additional Part IV permission" means a Part IV permission which is in force in relation to an EEA firm, a Treaty firm or a person authorised as a result of paragraph 1(1) of Schedule 5.

(2) If the Authority is considering whether, and if so how, to exercise its own-initiative power under this Part in relation to an additional Part IV permission, it must take into account—

(a) the home State authorisation of the authorised person concerned;
(b) any relevant directive; and
(c) relevant provisions of the Treaty.

[2050]

Procedure

51 Applications under this Part

(1) An application for a Part IV permission must—

(a) contain a statement of the regulated activity or regulated activities which the applicant proposes to carry on and for which he wishes to have permission; and
(b) give the address of a place in the United Kingdom for service on the applicant of any notice or other document which is required or authorised to be served on him under this Act.

(2) An application for the variation of a Part IV permission must contain a statement—

(a) of the desired variation; and
(b) of the regulated activity or regulated activities which the applicant proposes to carry on if his permission is varied.

(3) Any application under this Part must—

(a) be made in such manner as the Authority may direct; and
(b) contain, or be accompanied by, such other information as the Authority may reasonably require.

(4) At any time after receiving an application and before determining it, the Authority may require the applicant to provide it with such further information as it reasonably considers necessary to enable it to determine the application.

(5) Different directions may be given, and different requirements imposed, in relation to different applications or categories of application.

(6) The Authority may require an applicant to provide information which he is required to provide under this section in such form, or to verify it in such a way, as the Authority may direct.

[2051]

52 Determination of applications

(1) An application under this Part must be determined by the Authority before the end of the period of six months beginning with the date on which it received the completed application.

(2) The Authority may determine an incomplete application if it considers it appropriate to do so; and it must in any event determine such an application within twelve months beginning with the date on which it received the application.

(3) The applicant may withdraw his application, by giving the Authority written notice, at any time before the Authority determines it.

(4) If the Authority grants an application for, or for variation of, a Part IV permission, it must give the applicant written notice.

(5) The notice must state the date from which the permission, or the variation, has effect.

(6) If the Authority proposes—

(a) to give a Part IV permission but to exercise its power under section 42(7)(a) or (b) or 43(1), or

(b) to vary a Part IV permission on the application of an authorised person but to exercise its power under any of those provisions (as a result of section 44(5)),

it must give the applicant a warning notice.

(7) If the Authority proposes to refuse an application made under this Part, it must (unless subsection (8) applies) give the applicant a warning notice.

(8) This subsection applies if it appears to the Authority that—

(a) the applicant is an EEA firm; and

(b) the application is made with a view to carrying on a regulated activity in a manner in which the applicant is, or would be, entitled to carry on that activity in the exercise of an EEA right whether through a United Kingdom branch or by providing services in the United Kingdom.

(9) If the Authority decides—

(a) to give a Part IV permission but to exercise its power under section 42(7)(a) or (b) or 43(1),

(b) to vary a Part IV permission on the application of an authorised person but to exercise its power under any of those provisions (as a result of section 44(5)), or

(c) to refuse an application under this Part,

it must give the applicant a decision notice.

[2052]

53 Exercise of own-initiative power: procedure

(1) This section applies to an exercise of the Authority's own-initiative power to vary an authorised person's Part IV permission.

(2) A variation takes effect—

(a) immediately, if the notice given under subsection (4) states that that is the case;

(b) on such date as may be specified in the notice; or

(c) if no date is specified in the notice, when the matter to which the notice relates is no longer open to review.

(3) A variation may be expressed to take effect immediately (or on a specified date) only if the Authority, having regard to the ground on which it is exercising its own-initiative power, reasonably considers that it is necessary for the variation to take effect immediately (or on that date).

(4) If the Authority proposes to vary the Part IV permission, or varies it with immediate effect, it must give the authorised person written notice.

(5) The notice must—

(a) give details of the variation;

(b) state the Authority's reasons for the variation and for its determination as to when the variation takes effect;

(c) inform the authorised person that he may make representations to the Authority within such period as may be specified in the notice (whether or not he has referred the matter to the Tribunal);

(d) inform him of when the variation takes effect; and

(e) inform him of his right to refer the matter to the Tribunal.

(6) The Authority may extend the period allowed under the notice for making representations.

(7) If, having considered any representations made by the authorised person, the Authority decides—

(a) to vary the permission in the way proposed, or

(b) if the permission has been varied, not to rescind the variation, it must give him written notice.

(8) If, having considered any representations made by the authorised person, the Authority decides—

(a) not to vary the permission in the way proposed,
(b) to vary the permission in a different way, or
(c) to rescind a variation which has effect,

it must give him written notice.

(9) A notice given under subsection (7) must inform the authorised person of his right to refer the matter to the Tribunal.

(10) A notice under subsection (8)(b) must comply with subsection (5).

(11) If a notice informs a person of his right to refer a matter to the Tribunal, it must give an indication of the procedure on such a reference.

(12) For the purposes of subsection (2)(c), whether a matter is open to review is to be determined in accordance with section 391(8).

[2053]

54 Cancellation of Part IV permission: procedure

(1) If the Authority proposes to cancel an authorised person's Part IV permission otherwise than at his request, it must give him a warning notice.

(2) If the Authority decides to cancel an authorised person's Part IV permission otherwise than at his request, it must give him a decision notice.

[2054]

References to the Tribunal

55 Right to refer matters to the Tribunal

(1) An applicant who is aggrieved by the determination of an application made under this Part may refer the matter to the Tribunal.

(2) An authorised person who is aggrieved by the exercise of the Authority's own-initiative power may refer the matter to the Tribunal.

[2055]

PART V
PERFORMANCE OF REGULATED ACTIVITIES

Prohibition orders

56 Prohibition orders

(1) Subsection (2) applies if it appears to the Authority that an individual is not a fit and proper person to perform functions in relation to a regulated activity carried on by an authorised person.

(2) The Authority may make an order ("a prohibition order") prohibiting the individual from performing a specified function, any function falling within a specified description or any function.

(3) A prohibition order may relate to—

(a) a specified regulated activity, any regulated activity falling within a specified description or all regulated activities;
(b) authorised persons generally or any person within a specified class of authorised person.

(4) An individual who performs or agrees to perform a function in breach of a prohibition order is guilty of an offence and liable on summary conviction to a fine not exceeding level 5 on the standard scale.

(5) In proceedings for an offence under subsection (4) it is a defence for the accused to show that he took all reasonable precautions and exercised all due diligence to avoid committing the offence.

(6) An authorised person must take reasonable care to ensure that no function of his, in relation to the carrying on of a regulated activity, is performed by a person who is prohibited from performing that function by a prohibition order.

(7) The Authority may, on the application of the individual named in a prohibition order, vary or revoke it.

(8) This section applies to the performance of functions in relation to a regulated activity carried on by—

(a) a person who is an exempt person in relation to that activity, and

(b) a person to whom, as a result of Part XX, the general prohibition does not apply in relation to that activity,

as it applies to the performance of functions in relation to a regulated activity carried on by an authorised person.

(9) "Specified" means specified in the prohibition order.

[2056]

NOTES

Transitional provisions: the Financial Services and Markets Act 2000 (Transitional Provisions) (Authorised Persons etc) Order 2001, SI 2001/2636, art 79 provides that where, on 1 December 2001, a person is the subject of a disqualification direction made under the Financial Services Act 1986, s 59, the direction has effect after that date as a prohibition order made under this section. The 1986 Act was repealed by the Financial Services and Markets Act 2000 (Consequential Amendments and Repeals) Order 2001, SI 2001/3649, art 3(1)(c).

57 Prohibition orders: procedure and right to refer to Tribunal

(1) If the Authority proposes to make a prohibition order it must give the individual concerned a warning notice.

(2) The warning notice must set out the terms of the prohibition.

(3) If the Authority decides to make a prohibition order it must give the individual concerned a decision notice.

(4) The decision notice must—

(a) name the individual to whom the prohibition order applies;

(b) set out the terms of the order; and

(c) be given to the individual named in the order.

(5) A person against whom a decision to make a prohibition order is made may refer the matter to the Tribunal.

[2057]

58 Applications relating to prohibitions: procedure and right to refer to Tribunal

(1) This section applies to an application for the variation or revocation of a prohibition order.

(2) If the Authority decides to grant the application, it must give the applicant written notice of its decision.

(3) If the Authority proposes to refuse the application, it must give the applicant a warning notice.

(4) If the Authority decides to refuse the application, it must give the applicant a decision notice.

(5) If the Authority gives the applicant a decision notice, he may refer the matter to the Tribunal.

[2058]

Approval

59 Approval for particular arrangements

(1) An authorised person ("A") must take reasonable care to ensure that no person performs a controlled function under an arrangement entered into by A in relation to the

carrying on by A of a regulated activity, unless the Authority approves the performance by that person of the controlled function to which the arrangement relates.

(2) An authorised person ("A") must take reasonable care to ensure that no person performs a controlled function under an arrangement entered into by a contractor of A in relation to the carrying on by A of a regulated activity, unless the Authority approves the performance by that person of the controlled function to which the arrangement relates.

(3) "Controlled function" means a function of a description specified in rules.

(4) The Authority may specify a description of function under subsection (3) only if, in relation to the carrying on of a regulated activity by an authorised person, it is satisfied that the first, second or third condition is met.

(5) The first condition is that the function is likely to enable the person responsible for its performance to exercise a significant influence on the conduct of the authorised person's affairs, so far as relating to the regulated activity.

(6) The second condition is that the function will involve the person performing it in dealing with customers of the authorised person in a manner substantially connected with the carrying on of the regulated activity.

(7) The third condition is that the function will involve the person performing it in dealing with property of customers of the authorised person in a manner substantially connected with the carrying on of the regulated activity.

(8) Neither subsection (1) nor subsection (2) applies to an arrangement which allows a person to perform a function if the question of whether he is a fit and proper person to perform the function is reserved under any of the single market directives to an authority in a country or territory outside the United Kingdom.

(9) In determining whether the first condition is met, the Authority may take into account the likely consequences of a failure to discharge that function properly.

(10) "Arrangement"—
- (a) means any kind of arrangement for the performance of a function of A which is entered into by A or any contractor of his with another person; and
- (b) includes, in particular, that other person's appointment to an office, his becoming a partner or his employment (whether under a contract of service or otherwise).

(11) "Customer", in relation to an authorised person, means a person who is using, or who is or may be contemplating using, any of the services provided by the authorised person.

[2059]

NOTES

Transitional provisions: the Financial Services and Markets Act 2000 (Transitional Provisions) (Authorised Persons etc) Order 2001, SI 2001/2636, Pt VI applies where a person is performing a function for another person at 1 December 2001, and provides for the continued performance of that function after that date to be taken to be approved by the Authority for the purposes of this section.

Note: "person" includes both individuals (natural persons) and bodies corporate or unincorporate; see the Interpretation Act 1978, Sch 1.

60 Applications for approval

(1) An application for the Authority's approval under section 59 may be made by the authorised person concerned.

(2) The application must—
- (a) be made in such manner as the Authority may direct; and
- (b) contain, or be accompanied by, such information as the Authority may reasonably require.

(3) At any time after receiving the application and before determining it, the Authority may require the applicant to provide it with such further information as it reasonably considers necessary to enable it to determine the application.

(4) The Authority may require an applicant to present information which he is required to give under this section in such form, or to verify it in such a way, as the Authority may direct.

(5) Different directions may be given, and different requirements imposed, in relation to different applications or categories of application.

(6) "The authorised person concerned" includes a person who has applied for permission under Part IV and will be the authorised person concerned if permission is given.

[2060]

NOTES

The authorised person concerned: as to the meaning of this, see also the Financial Services and Markets Act 2000 (EEA Passport Rights) Regulations 2001, SI 2001/2511, reg 10 at **[4457]**.

Note: as to interim approval in respect of regulated mortgage business, see the Financial Services and Markets Act 2000 (Transitional Provisions) (Mortgages) Order 2004, SI 2004/2615 at **[4695]**.

Note: as to interim approval in respect of general insurance intermediaries, see the Financial Services and Markets Act 2000 (Transitional Provisions) (General Insurance Intermediaries) Order 2004, SI 2004/3351 at **[4710]**.

Note: as to interim approval in respect of the activity of establishing, operating or winding up a personal pension scheme or in respect of the specified investment of rights under a personal pension scheme, see the Financial Services and Markets Act 2000 (Regulated Activities) (Amendment) Order 2006, SI 2006/1969, art 5 at **[4816]**.

Note: as to interim approval in respect of the activities of entering into, administering, arranging and advising on regulated home reversion plans and regulated home purchase plans, see the Financial Services and Markets Act 2000 (Regulated Activities) (Amendment) (No 2) Order 2006, SI 2006/2383, art 38 at **[4823]**.

61 Determination of applications

(1) The Authority may grant an application made under section 60 only if it is satisfied that the person in respect of whom the application is made ("the candidate") is a fit and proper person to perform the function to which the application relates.

(2) In deciding that question, the Authority may have regard (among other things) to whether the candidate, or any person who may perform a function on his behalf—

(a) has obtained a qualification,

(b) has undergone, or is undergoing, training, or

(c) possesses a level of competence,

required by general rules in relation to persons performing functions of the kind to which the application relates.

(3) The Authority must, before the end of the period of three months beginning with the date on which it receives an application made under section 60 ("the period for consideration"), determine whether—

(a) to grant the application; or

(b) to give a warning notice under section 62(2).

(4) If the Authority imposes a requirement under section 60(3), the period for consideration stops running on the day on which the requirement is imposed but starts running again—

(a) on the day on which the required information is received by the Authority; or

(b) if the information is not provided on a single day, on the last of the days on which it is received by the Authority.

(5) A person who makes an application under section 60 may withdraw his application by giving written notice to the Authority at any time before the Authority determines it, but only with the consent of—

(a) the candidate; and

(b) the person by whom the candidate is to be retained to perform the function concerned, if not the applicant.

[2061]

62 Applications for approval: procedure and right to refer to Tribunal

(1) If the Authority decides to grant an application made under section 60 ("an application"), it must give written notice of its decision to each of the interested parties.

(2) If the Authority proposes to refuse an application, it must give a warning notice to each of the interested parties.

(3) If the Authority decides to refuse an application, it must give a decision notice to each of the interested parties.

(4) If the Authority decides to refuse an application, each of the interested parties may refer the matter to the Tribunal.

(5) "The interested parties", in relation to an application, are—
(a) the applicant;
(b) the person in respect of whom the application is made ("A"); and
(c) the person by whom A's services are to be retained, if not the applicant.

[2062]

63 Withdrawal of approval

(1) The Authority may withdraw an approval given under section 59 if it considers that the person in respect of whom it was given is not a fit and proper person to perform the function to which the approval relates.

(2) When considering whether to withdraw its approval, the Authority may take into account any matter which it could take into account if it were considering an application made under section 60 in respect of the performance of the function to which the approval relates.

(3) If the Authority proposes to withdraw its approval, it must give each of the interested parties a warning notice.

(4) If the Authority decides to withdraw its approval, it must give each of the interested parties a decision notice.

(5) If the Authority decides to withdraw its approval, each of the interested parties may refer the matter to the Tribunal.

(6) "The interested parties", in relation to an approval, are—
(a) the person on whose application it was given ("A");
(b) the person in respect of whom it was given ("B"); and
(c) the person by whom B's services are retained, if not A.

[2063]

Conduct

64 Conduct: statements and codes

(1) The Authority may issue statements of principle with respect to the conduct expected of approved persons.

(2) If the Authority issues a statement of principle under subsection (1), it must also issue a code of practice for the purpose of helping to determine whether or not a person's conduct complies with the statement of principle.

(3) A code issued under subsection (2) may specify—
(a) descriptions of conduct which, in the opinion of the Authority, comply with a statement of principle;
(b) descriptions of conduct which, in the opinion of the Authority, do not comply with a statement of principle;
(c) factors which, in the opinion of the Authority, are to be taken into account in determining whether or not a person's conduct complies with a statement of principle.

(4) The Authority may at any time alter or replace a statement or code issued under this section.

(5) If a statement or code is altered or replaced, the altered or replacement statement or code must be issued by the Authority.

(6) A statement or code issued under this section must be published by the Authority in the way appearing to the Authority to be best calculated to bring it to the attention of the public.

(7) A code published under this section and in force at the time when any particular conduct takes place may be relied on so far as it tends to establish whether or not that conduct complies with a statement of principle.

(8) Failure to comply with a statement of principle under this section does not of itself give rise to any right of action by persons affected or affect the validity of any transaction.

(9) A person is not to be taken to have failed to comply with a statement of principle if he shows that, at the time of the alleged failure, it or its associated code of practice had not been published.

(10) The Authority must, without delay, give the Treasury a copy of any statement or code which it publishes under this section.

(11) The power under this section to issue statements of principle and codes of practice—
(a) includes power to make different provision in relation to persons, cases or circumstances of different descriptions; and
(b) is to be treated for the purposes of section 2(4)(a) as part of the Authority's rule-making functions.

(12) The Authority may charge a reasonable fee for providing a person with a copy of a statement or code published under this section.

(13) "Approved person" means a person in relation to whom the Authority has given its approval under section 59.

[2064]

65 Statements and codes: procedure

(1) Before issuing a statement or code under section 64, the Authority must publish a draft of it in the way appearing to the Authority to be best calculated to bring it to the attention of the public.

(2) The draft must be accompanied by—
(a) a cost benefit analysis; and
(b) notice that representations about the proposal may be made to the Authority within a specified time.

(3) Before issuing the proposed statement or code, the Authority must have regard to any representations made to it in accordance with subsection (2)(b).

(4) If the Authority issues the proposed statement or code it must publish an account, in general terms, of—
(a) the representations made to it in accordance with subsection (2)(b); and
(b) its response to them.

(5) If the statement or code differs from the draft published under subsection (1) in a way which is, in the opinion of the Authority, significant—
(a) the Authority must (in addition to complying with subsection (4)) publish details of the difference; and
(b) those details must be accompanied by a cost benefit analysis.

(6) Neither subsection (2)(a) nor subsection (5)(b) applies if the Authority considers—
(a) that, making the appropriate comparison, there will be no increase in costs; or
(b) that, making that comparison, there will be an increase in costs but the increase will be of minimal significance.

(7) Subsections (1) to (6) do not apply if the Authority considers that the delay involved in complying with them would prejudice the interests of consumers.

(8) A statement or code must state that it is issued under section 64.

(9) The Authority may charge a reasonable fee for providing a copy of a draft published under subsection (1).

(10) This section also applies to a proposal to alter or replace a statement or code.

(11) "Cost benefit analysis" means an estimate of the costs together with an analysis of the benefits that will arise—
(a) if the proposed statement or code is issued; or
(b) if subsection (5)(b) applies, from the statement or code that has been issued.

(12) "The appropriate comparison" means—
(a) in relation to subsection (2)(a), a comparison between the overall position if the statement or code is issued and the overall position if it is not issued;
(b) in relation to subsection (5)(b), a comparison between the overall position after the issuing of the statement or code and the overall position before it was issued.

[2065]

66 Disciplinary powers

(1) The Authority may take action against a person under this section if—

PART II
FSMA 2000

(a) it appears to the Authority that he is guilty of misconduct; and
(b) the Authority is satisfied that it is appropriate in all the circumstances to take action against him.

(2) A person is guilty of misconduct if, while an approved person—
(a) he has failed to comply with a statement of principle issued under section 64; or
(b) he has been knowingly concerned in a contravention by the relevant authorised person of a requirement imposed on that authorised person by or under this Act [or by any directly applicable Community regulation made under the markets in financial instruments directive].

(3) If the Authority is entitled to take action under this section against a person, it may—
(a) impose a penalty on him of such amount as it considers appropriate; or
(b) publish a statement of his misconduct.

(4) The Authority may not take action under this section after the end of the period of two years beginning with the first day on which the Authority knew of the misconduct, unless proceedings in respect of it against the person concerned were begun before the end of that period.

(5) For the purposes of subsection (4)—
(a) the Authority is to be treated as knowing of misconduct if it has information from which the misconduct can reasonably be inferred; and
(b) proceedings against a person in respect of misconduct are to be treated as begun when a warning notice is given to him under section 67(1).

(6) "Approved person" has the same meaning as in section 64.

(7) "Relevant authorised person", in relation to an approved person, means the person on whose application approval under section 59 was given.

[2066]

NOTES

Sub-s (2): words in square brackets inserted by the Financial Services and Markets Act 2000 (Markets in Financial Instruments) Regulations 2007, SI 2007/126, reg 3(5), Sch 5, paras 1, 5, as from 1 April 2007 (certain purposes (see reg 1(2) at **[7596]**)), and as from 1 November 2007 (otherwise).

As to the power of the Financial Services Authority to take action under this section in relation to persons who were formerly registered individuals (or registered persons) under the rules of a self-regulating organisation, in the case of a failure to comply with, or an act of misconduct or a contravention under, those rules, see the Financial Services and Markets Act 2000 (Transitional Provisions and Savings) (Civil Remedies, Discipline, Criminal Offences etc) (No 2) Order 2001, SI 2001/3083, art 9.

67 Disciplinary measures: procedure and right to refer to Tribunal

(1) If the Authority proposes to take action against a person under section 66, it must give him a warning notice.

(2) A warning notice about a proposal to impose a penalty must state the amount of the penalty.

(3) A warning notice about a proposal to publish a statement must set out the terms of the statement.

(4) If the Authority decides to take action against a person under section 66, it must give him a decision notice.

(5) A decision notice about the imposition of a penalty must state the amount of the penalty.

(6) A decision notice about the publication of a statement must set out the terms of the statement.

(7) If the Authority decides to take action against a person under section 66, he may refer the matter to the Tribunal.

[2067]

68 Publication

After a statement under section 66 is published, the Authority must send a copy of it to the person concerned and to any person to whom a copy of the decision notice was given.

[2068]

69 Statement of policy

(1) The Authority must prepare and issue a statement of its policy with respect to—

(a) the imposition of penalties under section 66; and

(b) the amount of penalties under that section.

(2) The Authority's policy in determining what the amount of a penalty should be must include having regard to—

(a) the seriousness of the misconduct in question in relation to the nature of the principle or requirement concerned;

(b) the extent to which that misconduct was deliberate or reckless; and

(c) whether the person on whom the penalty is to be imposed is an individual.

(3) The Authority may at any time alter or replace a statement issued under this section.

(4) If a statement issued under this section is altered or replaced, the Authority must issue the altered or replacement statement.

(5) The Authority must, without delay, give the Treasury a copy of any statement which it publishes under this section.

(6) A statement issued under this section must be published by the Authority in the way appearing to the Authority to be best calculated to bring it to the attention of the public.

(7) The Authority may charge a reasonable fee for providing a person with a copy of the statement.

(8) In exercising, or deciding whether to exercise, its power under section 66 in the case of any particular misconduct, the Authority must have regard to any statement of policy published under this section and in force at the time when the misconduct in question occurred.

[2069]

70 Statements of policy: procedure

(1) Before issuing a statement under section 69, the Authority must publish a draft of the proposed statement in the way appearing to the Authority to be best calculated to bring it to the attention of the public.

(2) The draft must be accompanied by notice that representations about the proposal may be made to the Authority within a specified time.

(3) Before issuing the proposed statement, the Authority must have regard to any representations made to it in accordance with subsection (2).

(4) If the Authority issues the proposed statement it must publish an account, in general terms, of—

(a) the representations made to it in accordance with subsection (2); and

(b) its response to them.

(5) If the statement differs from the draft published under subsection (1) in a way which is, in the opinion of the Authority, significant, the Authority must (in addition to complying with subsection (4)) publish details of the difference.

(6) The Authority may charge a reasonable fee for providing a person with a copy of a draft published under subsection (1).

(7) This section also applies to a proposal to alter or replace a statement.

[2070]

Breach of statutory duty

71 Actions for damages

(1) A contravention of section 56(6) or 59(1) or (2) is actionable at the suit of a private person who suffers loss as a result of the contravention, subject to the defences and other incidents applying to actions for breach of statutory duty.

(2) In prescribed cases, a contravention of that kind which would be actionable at the suit of a private person is actionable at the suit of a person who is not a private person, subject to the defences and other incidents applying to actions for breach of statutory duty.

(3) "Private person" has such meaning as may be prescribed.

[2071]

NOTES

Regulations: the Financial Services and Markets Act 2000 (Rights of Action) Regulations 2001, SI 2001/2256 at **[4395]**.

PART VI
OFFICIAL LISTING

NOTES

Transitional provisions: see the Financial Services and Markets Act 2000 (Official Listing of Securities) (Transitional Provisions) Order 2001, SI 2001/2957 which makes transitional provisions in relation to the listing if securities under this Act instead of the Financial Services Act 1986 (repealed).

The competent authority

72 The competent authority

(1) On the coming into force of this section, the functions conferred on the competent authority by this Part are to be exercised by the Authority.

(2) Schedule 7 modifies this Act in its application to the Authority when it acts as the competent authority.

(3) But provision is made by Schedule 8 allowing some or all of those functions to be transferred by the Treasury so as to be exercisable by another person.

[2072]

73 General duty of the competent authority

(1) In discharging its general functions the competent authority must have regard to—

(a) the need to use its resources in the most efficient and economic way;

(b) the principle that a burden or restriction which is imposed on a person should be proportionate to the benefits, considered in general terms, which are expected to arise from the imposition of that burden or restriction;

[(c) the desirability of facilitating innovation in respect of listed securities and in respect of financial instruments which have otherwise been admitted to trading on a regulated market or for which a request for admission to trading on such a market has been made;]

(d) the international character of capital markets and the desirability of maintaining the competitive position of the United Kingdom;

(e) the need to minimise the adverse effects on competition of anything done in the discharge of those functions;

[(f) the desirability of facilitating competition in relation to listed securities and in relation to financial instruments which have otherwise been admitted to trading on a regulated market or for which a request for admission to trading on such a market has been made.]

[(1A) To the extent that those general functions are functions under or relating to transparency rules, subsection (1)(c) and (f) have effect as if the references to a regulated market were references to a market.]

(2) The competent authority's general functions are—

(a) its function of making rules under this Part (considered as a whole);

(b) its functions in relation to the giving of general guidance in relation to this Part (considered as a whole);

(c) its function of determining the general policy and principles by reference to which it performs particular functions under this Part.

[2073]

NOTES

Sub-s (1): paras (c), (f) substituted by the Financial Services and Markets Act 2000 (Market Abuse) Regulations 2005, SI 2005/381, reg 4, Sch 1, para 1, as from 1 July 2005.

Sub-s (1A): inserted by the Companies Act 2006, s 1272, Sch 15, Pt 1, paras 1, 2, as from 8 November 2006.

[73A Part 6 Rules

(1) The competent authority may make rules ("Part 6 rules") for the purposes of this Part.

(2) Provisions of Part 6 rules expressed to relate to the official list are referred to in this Part as "listing rules".

(3) Provisions of Part 6 rules expressed to relate to disclosure of information in respect of financial instruments which have been admitted to trading on a regulated market or for which a request for admission to trading on such a market has been made, are referred to in this Part as "disclosure rules".

[(4) Provisions of Part 6 rules expressed to relate to transferable securities are referred to in this Part as "prospectus rules".

(5) In relation to prospectus rules, the purposes of this Part include the purposes of the prospectus directive.]

[(6) Transparency rules and corporate governance rules are not listing rules, disclosure rules or prospectus rules, but are Part 6 rules.]]

[2073A]

NOTES

Inserted by the Financial Services and Markets Act 2000 (Market Abuse) Regulations 2005, SI 2005/381, reg 4, Sch 1, para 2, as from 17 March 2005.

Sub-ss (4), (5): added by the Prospectus Regulations 2005, SI 2005/1433, reg 2(1), Sch 1, para 1, as from 1 July 2005.

Sub-s (6): added by the Companies Act 2006, s 1272, Sch 15, Pt 1, paras 1, 3, as from 8 November 2006.

PART II FSMA 2000

The official list

74 The official list

(1) The competent authority must maintain the official list.

(2) The competent authority may admit to the official list such securities and other things as it considers appropriate.

(3) But—

(a) nothing may be admitted to the official list except in accordance with this Part; and

(b) the Treasury may by order provide that anything which falls within a description or category specified in the order may not be admitted to the official list.

(4) …

(5) In the following provisions of this Part—

.....

"listing" means being included in the official list in accordance with this Part.

[2074]

NOTES

Sub-s (4): repealed by the Financial Services and Markets Act 2000 (Market Abuse) Regulations 2005, SI 2005/381, reg 4, Sch 1, para 3, as from 17 March 2005.

Sub-s (5): definition "security" repealed by the Prospectus Regulations 2005, SI 2005/1433, reg 2(1), Sch 1, para 2, as from 1 July 2005.

Note: the Financial Services and Markets Act 2000 (Official Listing of Securities) Regulations 2001, SI 2001/2956 at **[4478]** prescribes certain bodies whose securities may not be considered for listing under this Part.

Listing

75 Applications for listing

(1) Admission to the official list may be granted only on an application made to the competent authority in such manner as may be required by listing rules.

(2) No application for listing may be entertained by the competent authority unless it is made by, or with the consent of, the issuer of the securities concerned.

(3) No application for listing may be entertained by the competent authority in respect of securities which are to be issued by a body of a prescribed kind.

(4) The competent authority may not grant an application for listing unless it is satisfied that—

(a) the requirements of listing rules (so far as they apply to the application), and
(b) any other requirements imposed by the authority in relation to the application,

are complied with.

(5) An application for listing may be refused if, for a reason relating to the issuer, the competent authority considers that granting it would be detrimental to the interests of investors.

(6) An application for listing securities which are already officially listed in another EEA State may be refused if the issuer has failed to comply with any obligations to which he is subject as a result of that listing.

[2075]

NOTES

Regulations: the Financial Services and Markets Act 2000 (Official Listing of Securities) Regulations 2001, SI 2001/2956 at **[4478]**.

Note that the following amending Regulations have also been made under this section: the Financial Services and Markets Act 2000 (Official Listing of Securities) (Amendment) Regulations 2001, SI 2001/3439.

76 Decision on application

(1) The competent authority must notify the applicant of its decision on an application for listing—

(a) before the end of the period of six months beginning with the date on which the application is received; or
(b) if within that period the authority has required the applicant to provide further information in connection with the application, before the end of the period of six months beginning with the date on which that information is provided.

(2) If the competent authority fails to comply with subsection (1), it is to be taken to have decided to refuse the application.

(3) If the competent authority decides to grant an application for listing, it must give the applicant written notice.

(4) If the competent authority proposes to refuse an application for listing, it must give the applicant a warning notice.

(5) If the competent authority decides to refuse an application for listing, it must give the applicant a decision notice.

(6) If the competent authority decides to refuse an application for listing, the applicant may refer the matter to the Tribunal.

(7) If securities are admitted to the official list, their admission may not be called in question on the ground that any requirement or condition for their admission has not been complied with.

[2076]

77 Discontinuance and suspension of listing

(1) The competent authority may, in accordance with listing rules, discontinue the listing of any securities if satisfied that there are special circumstances which preclude normal regular dealings in them.

(2) The competent authority may, in accordance with listing rules, suspend the listing of any securities.

[(2A) The competent authority may discontinue under subsection (1) or suspend under subsection (2) the listing of any securities on its own initiative or on the application of the issuer of those securities.]

(3) If securities are suspended under subsection (2) they are to be treated, for the purposes of sections 96 and 99, as still being listed.

(4) This section applies to securities whenever they were admitted to the official list.

(5) If the competent authority discontinues or suspends the listing of any securities, [on its own initiative,] the issuer may refer the matter to the Tribunal.

[2077]

NOTES

Sub-s (2A): inserted by the Regulatory Reform (Financial Services and Markets Act 2000) Order 2007, SI 2007/1973, arts 2, 5(a), as from 12 July 2007.

Sub-s (5): words in square brackets inserted by SI 2007/1973, arts 2, 5(b), as from 12 July 2007.

78 Discontinuance or suspension: procedure

(1) A discontinuance or suspension [by the competent authority on its own initiative] takes effect—

(a) immediately, if the notice under subsection (2) states that that is the case;
(b) in any other case, on such date as may be specified in that notice.

(2) If [on its own initiative] the competent authority—

(a) proposes to discontinue or suspend the listing of securities, or
(b) discontinues or suspends the listing of securities with immediate effect,

it must give the issuer of the securities written notice.

(3) The notice must—

(a) give details of the discontinuance or suspension;
(b) state the competent authority's reasons for the discontinuance or suspension and for choosing the date on which it took effect or takes effect;
(c) inform the issuer of the securities that he may make representations to the competent authority within such period as may be specified in the notice (whether or not he has referred the matter to the Tribunal);
(d) inform him of the date on which the discontinuance or suspension took effect or will take effect; and
(e) inform him of his right to refer the matter to the Tribunal.

(4) The competent authority may extend the period within which representations may be made to it.

(5) If, having considered any representations made by the issuer of the securities, the competent authority decides—

(a) to discontinue or suspend the listing of the securities, or
(b) if the discontinuance or suspension has taken effect, not to cancel it,

the competent authority must give the issuer of the securities written notice.

(6) A notice given under subsection (5) must inform the issuer of the securities of his right to refer the matter to the Tribunal.

(7) If a notice informs a person of his right to refer a matter to the Tribunal, it must give an indication of the procedure on such a reference.

(8) If the competent authority decides—

(a) not to discontinue or suspend the listing of the securities, or
(b) if the discontinuance or suspension has taken effect, to cancel it,

the competent authority must give the issuer of the securities written notice.

(9) The effect of cancelling a discontinuance is that the securities concerned are to be readmitted, without more, to the official list.

(10) If the competent authority has suspended the listing of securities [on its own initiative] and proposes to refuse an application by the issuer of the securities for the cancellation of the suspension, it must give him a warning notice.

PART II
FSMA 2000

(11) The competent authority must, having considered any representations made in response to the warning notice—

(a) if it decides to refuse the application, give the issuer of the securities a decision notice;

(b) if it grants the application, give him written notice of its decision.

(12) If the competent authority decides to refuse an application for the cancellation of the suspension of listed securities, the applicant may refer the matter to the Tribunal.

(13) "Discontinuance" means a discontinuance of listing under section 77(1).

(14) "Suspension" means a suspension of listing under section 77(2).

[2078]

NOTES

Sub-ss (1), (2), (10): words in square brackets inserted by the Regulatory Reform (Financial Services and Markets Act 2000) Order 2007, SI 2007/1973, arts 2, 6, as from 12 July 2007.

[78A Discontinuance or suspension at the request of the issuer: procedure

(1) A discontinuance or suspension by the competent authority on the application of the issuer of the securities takes effect—

(a) immediately, if the notice under subsection (2) states that this is the case;

(b) in any other case, on such date as may be specified in that notice.

(2) If the competent authority discontinues or suspends the listing of securities on the application of the issuer of the securities it must give him written notice.

(3) The notice must—

(a) give details of the discontinuance or suspension;

(b) inform the issuer of the securities of the date on which the discontinuance or suspension took effect or will take effect; and

(c) inform the issuer of his right to apply for the cancellation of the suspension.

(4) If the competent authority proposes to refuse an application by the issuer of the securities for the discontinuance or suspension of the listing of the securities, it must give him a warning notice.

(5) The competent authority must, having considered any representations made in response to the warning notice, if it decides to refuse the application, give the issuer of the securities a decision notice.

(6) If the competent authority decides to refuse an application by the issuer of the securities for the discontinuance or suspension of the listing of the securities, the issuer may refer the matter to the Tribunal.

(7) If the competent authority has suspended the listing of securities on the application of the issuer of the securities and proposes to refuse an application by the issuer for the cancellation of the suspension, it must give him a warning notice.

(8) The competent authority must, having considered any representations made in response to the warning notice—

(a) if it decides to refuse the application for the cancellation of the suspension, give the issuer of the securities a decision notice;

(b) if it grants the application, give him written notice of its decision.

(9) If the competent authority decides to refuse an application for the cancellation of the suspension of listed securities, the applicant may refer the matter to the Tribunal.

(10) "Discontinuance" means a discontinuance of listing under section 77(1).

(11) "Suspension" means a suspension of listing under section 77(2).]

[2078A]

NOTES

Commencement: 12 July 2007.

Inserted by the Regulatory Reform (Financial Services and Markets Act 2000) Order 2007, SI 2007/1973, arts 2, 7, as from 12 July 2007.

Listing particulars

79 Listing particulars and other documents

(1) Listing rules may provide that securities … of a kind specified in the rules may not be admitted to the official list unless—

(a) listing particulars have been submitted to, and approved by, the competent authority and published; or

(b) in such cases as may be specified by listing rules, such document (other than listing particulars or a prospectus of a kind required by listing rules) as may be so specified has been published.

(2) "Listing particulars" means a document in such form and containing such information as may be specified in listing rules.

(3) For the purposes of this Part, the persons responsible for listing particulars are to be determined in accordance with regulations made by the Treasury.

[(3A) Listing rules made under subsection (1) may not specify securities of a kind for which an approved prospectus is required as a result of section 85.]

(4) Nothing in this section affects the competent authority's general power to make listing rules.

[2079]

NOTES

Sub-s (1): words omitted repealed by the Prospectus Regulations 2005, SI 2005/1433, reg 2(1), Sch 1, para 3(1), (2), as from 1 July 2005.

Sub-s (3A): inserted by SI 2005/1433, reg 2(1), Sch 1, para 3(1), (3), as from 1 July 2005.

Regulations: the Financial Services and Markets Act 2000 (Official Listing of Securities) Regulations 2001, SI 2001/2956 at **[4478]**.

80 General duty of disclosure in listing particulars

(1) Listing particulars submitted to the competent authority under section 79 must contain all such information as investors and their professional advisers would reasonably require, and reasonably expect to find there, for the purpose of making an informed assessment of—

(a) the assets and liabilities, financial position, profits and losses, and prospects of the issuer of the securities; and

(b) the rights attaching to the securities.

(2) That information is required in addition to any information required by—

(a) listing rules, or

(b) the competent authority,

as a condition of the admission of the securities to the official list.

(3) Subsection (1) applies only to information—

(a) within the knowledge of any person responsible for the listing particulars; or

(b) which it would be reasonable for him to obtain by making enquiries.

(4) In determining what information subsection (1) requires to be included in listing particulars, regard must be had (in particular) to—

(a) the nature of the securities and their issuer;

(b) the nature of the persons likely to consider acquiring them;

(c) the fact that certain matters may reasonably be expected to be within the knowledge of professional advisers of a kind which persons likely to acquire the securities may reasonably be expected to consult; and

(d) any information available to investors or their professional advisers as a result of requirements imposed on the issuer of the securities by a recognised investment exchange, by listing rules or by or under any other enactment.

[2080]

81 Supplementary listing particulars

(1) If at any time after the preparation of listing particulars which have been submitted to the competent authority under section 79 and before the commencement of dealings in the securities concerned following their admission to the official list—

PART II
FSMA 2000

(a) there is a significant change affecting any matter contained in those particulars the inclusion of which was required by—
  (i) section 80,
  (ii) listing rules, or
  (iii) the competent authority, or

(b) a significant new matter arises, the inclusion of information in respect of which would have been so required if it had arisen when the particulars were prepared,

the issuer must, in accordance with listing rules, submit supplementary listing particulars of the change or new matter to the competent authority, for its approval and, if they are approved, publish them.

(2) "Significant" means significant for the purpose of making an informed assessment of the kind mentioned in section 80(1).

(3) If the issuer of the securities is not aware of the change or new matter in question, he is not under a duty to comply with subsection (1) unless he is notified of the change or new matter by a person responsible for the listing particulars.

(4) But it is the duty of any person responsible for those particulars who is aware of such a change or new matter to give notice of it to the issuer.

(5) Subsection (1) applies also as respects matters contained in any supplementary listing particulars previously published under this section in respect of the securities in question.

[2081]

82 Exemptions from disclosure

(1) The competent authority may authorise the omission from listing particulars of any information, the inclusion of which would otherwise be required by section 80 or 81, on the ground—

(a) that its disclosure would be contrary to the public interest;
(b) that its disclosure would be seriously detrimental to the issuer; or
(c) in the case of securities of a kind specified in listing rules, that its disclosure is unnecessary for persons of the kind who may be expected normally to buy or deal in securities of that kind.

(2) But—

(a) no authority may be granted under subsection (1)(b) in respect of essential information; and
(b) no authority granted under subsection (1)(b) extends to any such information.

(3) The Secretary of State or the Treasury may issue a certificate to the effect that the disclosure of any information (including information that would otherwise have to be included in listing particulars for which they are themselves responsible) would be contrary to the public interest.

(4) The competent authority is entitled to act on any such certificate in exercising its powers under subsection (1)(a).

(5) This section does not affect any powers of the competent authority under listing rules made as a result of section 101(2).

(6) "Essential information" means information which a person considering acquiring securities of the kind in question would be likely to need in order not to be misled about any facts which it is essential for him to know in order to make an informed assessment.

(7) "Listing particulars" includes supplementary listing particulars.

[2082]–[2083]

83 (*Repealed by the Prospectus Regulations 2005, SI 2005/1433, reg 2(1), Sch 1, para 4, as from 1 July 2005.*)

[Transferable securities: public offers and admission to trading

84 Matters which may be dealt with by prospectus rules

(1) Prospectus rules may make provision as to—

(a) the required form and content of a prospectus (including a summary);
(b) the cases in which a summary need not be included in a prospectus;

(c) the languages which may be used in a prospectus (including a summary);
(d) the determination of the persons responsible for a prospectus;
(e) the manner in which applications to the competent authority for the approval of a prospectus are to be made.

(2) Prospectus rules may also make provision as to—
(a) the period of validity of a prospectus;
(b) the disclosure of the maximum price or of the criteria or conditions according to which the final offer price is to be determined, if that information is not contained in a prospectus;
(c) the disclosure of the amount of the transferable securities which are to be offered to the public or of the criteria or conditions according to which that amount is to be determined, if that information is not contained in a prospectus;
(d) the required form and content of other summary documents (including the languages which may be used in such a document);
(e) the ways in which a prospectus that has been approved by the competent authority may be made available to the public;
(f) the disclosure, publication or other communication of such information as the competent authority may reasonably stipulate;
(g) the principles to be observed in relation to advertisements in connection with an offer of transferable securities to the public or admission of transferable securities to trading on a regulated market and the enforcement of those principles;
(h) the suspension of trading in transferable securities where continued trading would be detrimental to the interests of investors;
(i) elections under section 87 or under Article 2.1(m)(iii) of the prospectus directive as applied for the purposes of this Part by section 102C

(3) Prospectus rules may also make provision as to—
(a) access to the register of investors maintained under section 87R; and
(b) the supply of information from that register.

(4) Prospectus rules may make provision for the purpose of dealing with matters arising out of or related to any provision of the prospectus directive.

(5) In relation to cases where the home State in relation to an issuer of transferable securities is an EEA State other than the United Kingdom, prospectus rules may make provision for the recognition of elections made in relation to such securities under the law of that State in accordance with Article 1.3 or 2.1(m)(iii) of the prospectus directive.

(6) In relation to a document relating to transferable securities issued by an issuer incorporated in a non-EEA State and drawn up in accordance with the law of that State, prospectus rules may make provision as to the approval of that document as a prospectus.

(7) Nothing in this section affects the competent authority's general power to make prospectus rules.]

[2084]

NOTES

Sections 84–87, 87A–87R substituted (together with the preceding heading) for original ss 84–87, by the Prospectus Regulations 2005, SI 2005/1433, reg 2(1), Sch 1, para 5, as from 1 July 2005.

[85 Prohibition of dealing etc in transferable securities without approved prospectus

(1) It is unlawful for transferable securities to which this subsection applies to be offered to the public in the United Kingdom unless an approved prospectus has been made available to the public before the offer is made.

(2) It is unlawful to request the admission of transferable securities to which this subsection applies to trading on a regulated market situated or operating in the United Kingdom unless an approved prospectus has been made available to the public before the request is made.

(3) A person who contravenes subsection (1) or (2) is guilty of an offence and liable—
(a) on summary conviction, to imprisonment for a term not exceeding 3 months or a fine not exceeding the statutory maximum or both;
(b) on conviction on indictment, to imprisonment for a term not exceeding 2 years or a fine or both.

PART II
FSMA 2000

(4) A contravention of subsection (1) or (2) is actionable, at the suit of a person who suffers loss as a result of the contravention, subject to the defences and other incidents applying to actions for breach of statutory duty.

(5) Subsection (1) applies to all transferable securities other than—
- (a) those listed in Schedule 11A;
- (b) such other transferable securities as may be specified in prospectus rules.

(6) Subsection (2) applies to all transferable securities other than—
- (a) those listed in Part 1 of Schedule 11A;
- (b) such other transferable securities as may be specified in prospectus rules.

(7) "Approved prospectus" means, in relation to transferable securities to which this section applies, a prospectus approved by the competent authority of the home State in relation to the issuer of the securities.]

[2085]

NOTES

Substituted as noted to s 84 at **[2084]**.

[86 Exempt offers to the public

(1) A person does not contravene section 85(1) if—
- (a) the offer is made to or directed at qualified investors only;
- (b) the offer is made to or directed at fewer than 100 persons, other than qualified investors, per EEA State;
- (c) the minimum consideration which may be paid by any person for transferable securities acquired by him pursuant to the offer is at least 50,000 euros (or an equivalent amount);
- (d) the transferable securities being offered are denominated in amounts of at least 50,000 euros (or equivalent amounts); or
- (e) the total consideration for the transferable securities being offered cannot exceed 100,000 euros (or an equivalent amount).

(2) Where—
- (a) a person who is not a qualified investor ("the client") has engaged a qualified investor falling within Article 2.1(e)(i) of the prospectus directive to act as his agent, and
- (b) the terms on which the qualified investor is engaged enable him to make decisions concerning the acceptance of offers of transferable securities on the client's behalf without reference to the client,

an offer made to or directed at the qualified investor is not to be regarded for the purposes of subsection (1) as also having been made to or directed at the client.

(3) For the purposes of subsection (1)(b), the making of an offer of transferable securities to—
- (a) trustees of a trust,
- (b) members of a partnership in their capacity as such, or
- (c) two or more persons jointly,

is to be treated as the making of an offer to a single person.

(4) In determining whether subsection (1)(e) is satisfied in relation to an offer ("offer A"), offer A is to be taken together with any other offer of transferable securities of the same class made by the same person which—
- (a) was open at any time within the period of 12 months ending with the date on which offer A is first made; and
- (b) had previously satisfied subsection (1)(e).

(5) For the purposes of this section, an amount (in relation to an amount denominated in euros) is an "equivalent amount" if it is an amount of equal value denominated wholly or partly in another currency or unit of account.

(6) The equivalent is to be calculated at the latest practicable date before (but in any event not more than 3 working days before) the date on which the offer is first made.

(7) "Qualified investor" means—
- (a) an entity falling within Article 2.1(e)(i), (ii) or (iii) of the prospectus directive;

(b) an investor registered on the register maintained by the competent authority under section 87R;

(c) an investor authorised by an EEA State other than the United Kingdom to be considered as a qualified investor for the purposes of the prospectus directive.]

[2086]

NOTES

Substituted as noted to s 84 at **[2084]**.

[87 Election to have prospectus

(1) A person who proposes—

(a) to issue transferable securities to which this section applies,

(b) to offer to the public transferable securities to which this section applies, or

(c) to request the admission to a regulated market of transferable securities to which this section applies,

may elect, in accordance with prospectus rules, to have a prospectus in relation to the securities.

(2) If a person makes such an election, the provisions of this Part and of prospectus rules apply in relation to those transferable securities as if, in relation to an offer of the securities to the public or the admission of the securities to trading on a regulated market, they were transferable securities for which an approved prospectus would be required as a result of section 85.

(3) Listing rules made under section 79 do not apply to securities which are the subject of an election.

(4) The transferable securities to which this section applies are those which fall within any of the following paragraphs of Schedule 11A—

(a) paragraph 2,

(b) paragraph 4,

(c) paragraph 8, or

(d) paragraph 9,

where the United Kingdom is the home State in relation to the issuer of the securities.]

[2087]

NOTES

Substituted as noted to s 84 at **[2084]**.

[Approval of prospectus

87A Criteria for approval of prospectus by competent authority

(1) The competent authority may not approve a prospectus unless it is satisfied that—

(a) the United Kingdom is the home State in relation to the issuer of the transferable securities to which it relates,

(b) the prospectus contains the necessary information, and

(c) all of the other requirements imposed by or in accordance with this Part or the prospectus directive have been complied with (so far as those requirements apply to a prospectus for the transferable securities in question).

(2) The necessary information is the information necessary to enable investors to make an informed assessment of—

(a) the assets and liabilities, financial position, profits and losses, and prospects of the issuer of the transferable securities and of any guarantor; and

(b) the rights attaching to the transferable securities.

(3) The necessary information must be presented in a form which is comprehensible and easy to analyse.

(4) The necessary information must be prepared having regard to the particular nature of the transferable securities and their issuer.

(5) The prospectus must include a summary (unless the transferable securities in question are ones in relation to which prospectus rules provide that a summary is not required).

(6) The summary must, briefly and in non-technical language, convey the essential characteristics of, and risks associated with, the issuer, any guarantor and the transferable securities to which the prospectus relates.

(7) Where the prospectus for which approval is sought does not include the final offer price or the amount of transferable securities to be offered to the public, the applicant must inform the competent authority in writing of that information as soon as that element is finalised.

(8) "Prospectus" (except in subsection (5)) includes a supplementary prospectus.]

[2087A]

NOTES

Substituted as noted to s 84 at **[2084]**.

[87B Exemptions from disclosure

(1) The competent authority may authorise the omission from a prospectus of any information, the inclusion of which would otherwise be required, on the ground—

(a) that its disclosure would be contrary to the public interest;

(b) that its disclosure would be seriously detrimental to the issuer, provided that the omission would be unlikely to mislead the public with regard to any facts or circumstances which are essential for an informed assessment of the kind mentioned in section 87A(2); or

(c) that the information is only of minor importance for a specific offer to the public or admission to trading on a regulated market and unlikely to influence an informed assessment of the kind mentioned in section 87A(2).

(2) The Secretary of State or the Treasury may issue a certificate to the effect that the disclosure of any information would be contrary to the public interest.

(3) The competent authority is entitled to act on any such certificate in exercising its powers under subsection (1)(a).

(4) This section does not affect any powers of the competent authority under prospectus rules.

(5) "Prospectus" includes a supplementary prospectus.]

[2087B]

NOTES

Substituted as noted to s 84 at **[2084]**.

[87C Consideration of application for approval

(1) The competent authority must notify the applicant of its decision on an application for approval of a prospectus before the end of the period for consideration.

(2) The period for consideration—

(a) begins with the first working day after the date on which the application is received; but

(b) if the competent authority gives a notice under subsection (4), is to be treated as beginning with the first working day after the date on which the notice is complied with.

(3) The period for consideration is—

(a) except in the case of a new issuer, 10 working days; or

(b) in that case, 20 working days.

(4) The competent authority may by notice in writing require a person who has applied for approval of a prospectus to provide—

(a) specified documents or documents of a specified description, or

(b) specified information or information of a specified description.

(5) No notice under subsection (4) may be given after the end of the period, beginning with the first working day after the date on which the application is received, of—

(a) except in the case of a new issuer, 10 working days; or

(b) in that case, 20 working days.

(6) Subsection (4) applies only to information and documents reasonably required in connection with the exercise by the competent authority of its functions in relation to the application.

(7) The competent authority may require any information provided under this section to be provided in such form as it may reasonably require.

(8) The competent authority may require—

(a) any information provided, whether in a document or otherwise, to be verified in such manner, or

(b) any document produced to be authenticated in such manner,

as it may reasonably require.

(9) The competent authority must notify the applicant of its decision on an application for approval of a supplementary prospectus before the end of the period of 7 working days beginning with the date on which the application is received; and subsections (4) and (6) to (8) apply to such an application as they apply to an application for approval of a prospectus.

(10) The competent authority's failure to comply with subsection (1) or (9) does not constitute approval of the application in question.

(11) "New issuer" means an issuer of transferable securities which—

(a) does not have transferable securities admitted to trading on any regulated market; and

(b) has not previously offered transferable securities to the public.]

[2087C]

NOTES

Substituted as noted to s 84 at **[2084]**.

[87D Procedure for decision on application for approval

(1) If the competent authority approves a prospectus, it must give the applicant written notice.

(2) If the competent authority proposes to refuse to approve a prospectus, it must give the applicant written notice.

(3) The notice must state the competent authority's reasons for the proposed refusal.

(4) If the competent authority decides to refuse to approve a prospectus, it must give the applicant written notice.

(5) The notice must—

(a) give the competent authority's reasons for refusing the application; and

(b) inform the applicant of his right to refer the matter to the Tribunal.

(6) If the competent authority refuses to approve a prospectus, the applicant may refer the matter to the Tribunal.

(7) In this section "prospectus" includes a supplementary prospectus.]

[2087D]

NOTES

Substituted as noted to s 84 at **[2084]**.

[Transfer of application for approval of a prospectus

87E Transfer by competent authority of application for approval

(1) The competent authority may transfer an application for the approval of a prospectus or a supplementary prospectus to the competent authority of another EEA State ("the transferee authority").

(2) Before doing so, the competent authority must obtain the agreement of the transferee authority.

(3) The competent authority must inform the applicant of the transfer within 3 working days beginning with the first working day after the date of the transfer.

(4) On making a transfer under subsection (1), the competent authority ceases to have functions under this Part in relation to the application transferred.]

[2087E]

NOTES

Substituted as noted to s 84 at **[2084]**.

[87F Transfer to competent authority of application for approval

(1) Where the competent authority agrees to the transfer to it of an application for the approval of a prospectus made to the competent authority of another EEA State—

(a) the United Kingdom is to be treated for the purposes of this Part as the home State in relation to the issuer of the transferable securities to which the prospectus relates, and

(b) this Part applies to the application as if it had been made to the competent authority but with the modification in subsection (2).

(2) Section 87C applies as if the date of the transfer were the date on which the application was received by the competent authority.]

[2087F]

NOTES

Substituted as noted to s 84 at **[2084]**.

[Supplementary prospectus

87G Supplementary prospectus

(1) Subsection (2) applies if, during the relevant period, there arises or is noted a significant new factor, material mistake or inaccuracy relating to the information included in a prospectus approved by the competent authority.

(2) The person on whose application the prospectus was approved must, in accordance with prospectus rules, submit a supplementary prospectus containing details of the new factor, mistake or inaccuracy to the competent authority for its approval.

(3) The relevant period begins when the prospectus is approved and ends—

(a) with the closure of the offer of the transferable securities to which the prospectus relates; or

(b) when trading in those securities on a regulated market begins.

(4) "Significant" means significant for the purposes of making an informed assessment of the kind mentioned in section 87A(2).

(5) Any person responsible for the prospectus who is aware of any new factor, mistake or inaccuracy which may require the submission of a supplementary prospectus in accordance with subsection (2) must give notice of it to—

(a) the issuer of the transferable securities to which the prospectus relates, and

(b) the person on whose application the prospectus was approved.

(6) A supplementary prospectus must provide sufficient information to correct any mistake or inaccuracy which gave rise to the need for it.

(7) Subsection (1) applies also to information contained in any supplementary prospectus published under this section.]

[2087G]

NOTES

Substituted as noted to s 84 at **[2084]**.

[Passporting

87H Prospectus approved in another EEA State

(1) A prospectus approved by the competent authority of an EEA State other than the United Kingdom is not an approved prospectus for the purposes of section 85 unless that authority has provided the competent authority with—

(a) a certificate of approval;

(b) a copy of the prospectus as approved; and

(c) if requested by the competent authority, a translation of the summary of the prospectus.

(2) A document is not a certificate of approval unless it states that the prospectus—

(a) has been drawn up in accordance with the prospectus directive; and

(b) has been approved, in accordance with that directive, by the competent authority providing the certificate.

(3) A document is not a certificate of approval unless it states whether (and, if so, why) the competent authority providing it authorised, in accordance with the prospectus directive, the omission from the prospectus of information which would otherwise have been required to be included.

(4) "Prospectus" includes a supplementary prospectus.]

[2087H]

NOTES

Substituted as noted to s 84 at **[2084]**.

[87I Provision of information to host Member State

(1) The competent authority must, if requested to do so, supply the competent authority of a specified EEA State with—

(a) a certificate of approval;

(b) a copy of the specified prospectus (as approved by the competent authority); and

(c) a translation of the summary of the specified prospectus (if the request states that one has been requested by the other competent authority).

(2) Only the following may make a request under this section—

(a) the issuer of the transferable securities to which the specified prospectus relates;

(b) a person who wishes to offer the transferable securities to which the specified prospectus relates to the public in an EEA State other than (or as well as) the United Kingdom;

(c) a person requesting the admission of the transferable securities to which the specified prospectus relates to a regulated market situated or operating in an EEA State other than (or as well as) the United Kingdom.

(3) A certificate of approval must state that the prospectus—

(a) has been drawn up in accordance with this Part and the prospectus directive; and

(b) has been approved, in accordance with those provisions, by the competent authority.

(4) A certificate of approval must state whether (and, if so, why) the competent authority authorised, in accordance with section 87B, the omission from the prospectus of information which would otherwise have been required to be included.

(5) The competent authority must comply with a request under this section—

(a) if the prospectus has been approved before the request is made, within 3 working days beginning with the date of the request; or

(b) if the request is submitted with an application for the approval of the prospectus, on the first working day after the date on which it approves the prospectus.

(6) "Prospectus" includes a supplementary prospectus.

(7) "Specified" means specified in a request made for the purposes of this section.]

[2087I]

NOTES

Substituted as noted to s 84 at **[2084]**.

[Transferable securities: powers of competent authority

87J Requirements imposed as condition of approval

(1) As a condition of approving a prospectus, the competent authority may by notice in writing—

(a) require the inclusion in the prospectus of such supplementary information necessary for investor protection as the competent authority may specify;

(b) require a person controlling, or controlled by, the applicant to provide specified information or documents;

(c) require an auditor or manager of the applicant to provide specified information or documents;

(d) require a financial intermediary commissioned to assist either in carrying out the offer to the public of the transferable securities to which the prospectus relates or in requesting their admission to trading on a regulated market, to provide specified information or documents.

(2) "Specified" means specified in the notice.

(3) "Prospectus" includes a supplementary prospectus.]

[2087J]

NOTES

Substituted as noted to s 84 at **[2084]**.

[87K Power to suspend or prohibit offer to the public

(1) This section applies where a person ("the offeror") has made an offer of transferable securities to the public in the United Kingdom ("the offer").

(2) If the competent authority has reasonable grounds for suspecting that an applicable provision has been infringed, it may—

(a) require the offeror to suspend the offer for a period not exceeding 10 working days;

(b) require a person not to advertise the offer, or to take such steps as the authority may specify to suspend any existing advertisement of the offer, for a period not exceeding 10 working days.

(3) If the competent authority has reasonable grounds for suspecting that it is likely that an applicable provision will be infringed, it may require the offeror to withdraw the offer.

(4) If the competent authority finds that an applicable provision has been infringed, it may require the offeror to withdraw the offer.

(5) "An applicable provision" means—

(a) a provision of this Part,

(b) a provision contained in prospectus rules,

(c) any other provision made in accordance with the prospectus directive,

applicable in relation to the offer.]

[2087K]

NOTES

Substituted as noted to s 84 at **[2084]**.

[87L Power to suspend or prohibit admission to trading on a regulated market

(1) This section applies where a person has requested the admission of transferable securities to trading on a regulated market situated or operating in the United Kingdom.

(2) If the competent authority has reasonable grounds for suspecting that an applicable provision has been infringed and the securities have not yet been admitted to trading on the regulated market in question, it may—

(a) require the person requesting admission to suspend the request for a period not exceeding 10 working days;

(b) require a person not to advertise the securities to which it relates, or to take such steps as the authority may specify to suspend any existing advertisement in connection with those securities, for a period not exceeding 10 working days.

(3) If the competent authority has reasonable grounds for suspecting that an applicable provision has been infringed and the securities have been admitted to trading on the regulated market in question, it may—

(a) require the market operator to suspend trading in the securities for a period not exceeding 10 working days;

(b) require a person not to advertise the securities, or to take such steps as the authority may specify to suspend any existing advertisement in connection with those securities, for a period not exceeding 10 working days.

(4) If the competent authority finds that an applicable provision has been infringed, it may require the market operator to prohibit trading in the securities on the regulated market in question.

(5) "An applicable provision" means—

(a) a provision of this Part,

(b) a provision contained in prospectus rules,

(c) any other provision made in accordance with the prospectus directive,

applicable in relation to the admission of the transferable securities to trading on the regulated market in question.]

[2087L]

NOTES

Substituted as noted to s 84 at **[2084]**.

[87M Public censure of issuer

(1) If the competent authority finds that—

(a) an issuer of transferable securities,

(b) a person offering transferable securities to the public, or

(c) a person requesting the admission of transferable securities to trading on a regulated market,

is failing or has failed to comply with his obligations under an applicable provision, it may publish a statement to that effect.

(2) If the competent authority proposes to publish a statement, it must give the person a warning notice setting out the terms of the proposed statement.

(3) If, after considering any representations made in response to the warning notice, the competent authority decides to make the proposed statement, it must give the person a decision notice setting out the terms of the statement.

(4) "An applicable provision" means—

(a) a provision of this Part,

(b) a provision contained in prospectus rules,

(c) any other provision made in accordance with the prospectus directive,

applicable to a prospectus in relation to the transferable securities in question.

(5) "Prospectus" includes a supplementary prospectus.]

[2087M]

NOTES

Substituted as noted to s 84 at **[2084]**.

[87N Right to refer matters to the Tribunal

(1) A person to whom a decision notice is given under section 87M may refer the matter to the Tribunal.

(2) A person to whom a notice is given under section 87O may refer the matter to the Tribunal.]

[2087N]

NOTES

Substituted as noted to s 84 at **[2084]**.

[87O Procedure under sections 87K and 87L

(1) A requirement under section 87K or 87L takes effect—

(a) immediately, if the notice under subsection (2) states that that is the case;

(b) in any other case, on such date as may be specified in that notice.

(2) If the competent authority—

(a) proposes to exercise the powers in section 87K or 87L in relation to a person, or

(b) exercises any of those powers in relation to a person with immediate effect,

it must give that person written notice.

(3) The notice must—

(a) give details of the competent authority's action or proposed action;

(b) state the competent authority's reasons for taking the action in question and choosing the date on which it took effect or takes effect;

(c) inform the recipient that he may make representations to the competent authority within such period as may be specified by the notice (whether or not he has referred the matter to the Tribunal);

(d) inform him of the date on which the action took effect or takes effect; and

(e) inform him of his right to refer the matter to the Tribunal.

(4) The competent authority may extend the period within which representations may be made to it.

(5) If, having considered any representations made to it, the competent authority decides to maintain, vary or revoke its earlier decision, it must give written notice to that effect to the person mentioned in subsection (2).

(6) A notice given under subsection (5) must inform that person, where relevant, of his right to refer the matter to the Tribunal.

(7) If a notice informs a person of his right to refer a matter to the Tribunal, it must give an indication of the procedure on such a reference.

(8) If a notice under this section relates to the exercise of the power conferred by section 87L(3), the notice must also be given to the person at whose request the transferable securities were admitted to trading on the regulated market.]

[2087O]

NOTES

Substituted as noted to s 84 at **[2084]**.

[87P Exercise of powers at request of competent authority of another EEA State

(1) This section applies if—

(a) the competent authority of an EEA State other than the United Kingdom has approved a prospectus,

(b) the transferable securities to which the prospectus relates have been offered to the public in the United Kingdom or their admission to trading on a regulated market has been requested, and

(c) that competent authority makes a request that the competent authority assist it in the performance of its functions under the law of that State in connection with the prospectus directive.

(2) For the purpose of complying with the request mentioned in subsection (1)(c), the powers conferred by sections 87K and 87L may be exercised as if the prospectus were one which had been approved by the competent authority.

(3) Section 87N does not apply to an exercise of those powers as a result of this section.

(4) Section 87O does apply to such an exercise of those powers but with the omission of subsections (3)(e), (6) and (7).]

[2087P]

NOTES

Substituted as noted to s 84 at **[2084]**.

[Rights of investors

87Q Right of investor to withdraw

(1) Where a person agrees to buy or subscribe for transferable securities in circumstances where the final offer price or the amount of transferable securities to be offered to the public is not included in the prospectus, he may withdraw his acceptance before the end of the withdrawal period.

(2) The withdrawal period—

(a) begins with the investor's acceptance; and

(b) ends at the end of the second working day after the date on which the competent authority is informed of the information in accordance with section 87A(7).

(3) Subsection (1) does not apply if the prospectus contains—

(a) in the case of the amount of transferable securities to be offered to the public, the criteria or conditions (or both) according to which that element will be determined, or

(b) in the case of price, the criteria or conditions (or both) according to which that element will be determined or the maximum price.

(4) Where a supplementary prospectus has been published and, prior to the publication, a person agreed to buy or subscribe for transferable securities to which it relates, he may withdraw his acceptance before the end of the period of 2 working days beginning with the first working day after the date on which the supplementary prospectus was published.]

[2087Q]

NOTES

Substituted as noted to s 84 at **[2084]**.

[Registered investors

87R Register of investors

(1) The competent authority must establish and maintain, in accordance with this section and prospectus rules, a register of investors for the purposes of section 86.

(2) An individual may not be entered in the register unless—

(a) he is resident in the United Kingdom; and

(b) he meets at least two of the criteria mentioned in Article 2.2 of the prospectus directive.

(3) A company may not be entered in the register unless—

(a) it falls within the meaning of "small and medium-sized enterprises" in Article 2.1 of the prospectus directive; and

(b) its registered office is in the United Kingdom.

(4) A person who does not fall within subsection (2) or (3) may not be entered in the register.]

[2087R]

NOTES

Substituted as noted to s 84 at **[2084]**.

Sponsors

88 Sponsors

(1) Listing rules may require a person to make arrangements with a sponsor for the performance by the sponsor of such services in relation to him as may be specified in the rules.

(2) "Sponsor" means a person approved by the competent authority for the purposes of the rules.

(3) Listing rules made by virtue of subsection (1) may—

(a) provide for the competent authority to maintain a list of sponsors;
(b) specify services which must be performed by a sponsor;
(c) impose requirements on a sponsor in relation to the provision of services or specified services;
(d) specify the circumstances in which a person is qualified for being approved as a sponsor.

(4) If the competent authority proposes—
(a) to refuse a person's application for approval as a sponsor, or
(b) to cancel a person's approval as a sponsor [otherwise than at his request],
it must give him a warning notice.

(5) If, after considering any representations made in response to the warning notice, the competent authority decides—
(a) to grant the application for approval, or
(b) not to cancel the approval,
it must give the person concerned, and any person to whom a copy of the warning notice was given, written notice of its decision.

(6) If, after considering any representations made in response to the warning notice, the competent authority decides—
(a) to refuse to grant the application for approval, or
(b) to cancel the approval,
it must give the person concerned a decision notice.

(7) A person to whom a decision notice is given under this section may refer the matter to the Tribunal.

[2088]

NOTES

Sub-s (4): words in square brackets inserted by the Regulatory Reform (Financial Services and Markets Act 2000) Order 2007, SI 2007/1973, arts 2, 9, as from 12 July 2007.

89 Public censure of sponsor

(1) Listing rules may make provision for the competent authority, if it considers that a sponsor has contravened a requirement imposed on him by rules made as a result of section 88(3)(c), to publish a statement to that effect.

(2) If the competent authority proposes to publish a statement it must give the sponsor a warning notice setting out the terms of the proposed statement.

(3) If, after considering any representations made in response to the warning notice, the competent authority decides to make the proposed statement, it must give the sponsor a decision notice setting out the terms of the statement.

(4) A sponsor to whom a decision notice is given under this section may refer the matter to the Tribunal.

[2089]

[Transparency obligations

89A Transparency rules

(1) The competent authority may make rules for the purposes of the transparency obligations directive.

(2) The rules may include provision for dealing with any matters arising out of or related to any provision of the transparency obligations directive.

(3) The competent authority may also make rules—
(a) for the purpose of ensuring that voteholder information in respect of voting shares traded on a UK market other than a regulated market is made public or notified to the competent authority;
(b) providing for persons who hold comparable instruments (see section 89F(1)(c)) in respect of voting shares to be treated, in the circumstances specified in the rules, as holding some or all of the voting rights in respect of those shares.

(4) Rules under this section may, in particular, make provision—

(a) specifying how the proportion of—

(i) the total voting rights in respect of shares in an issuer, or

(ii) the total voting rights in respect of a particular class of shares in an issuer,

held by a person is to be determined;

(b) specifying the circumstances in which, for the purposes of any determination of the voting rights held by a person ("P") in respect of voting shares in an issuer, any voting rights held, or treated by virtue of subsection (3)(b) as held, by another person in respect of voting shares in the issuer are to be regarded as held by P;

(c) specifying the nature of the information which must be included in any notification;

(d) about the form of any notification;

(e) requiring any notification to be given within a specified period;

(f) specifying the manner in which any information is to be made public and the period within which it must be made public;

(g) specifying circumstances in which any of the requirements imposed by rules under this section does not apply.

(5) Rules under this section are referred to in this Part as "transparency rules".

(6) Nothing in sections 89B to 89G affects the generality of the power to make rules under this section.]

[2089A]

NOTES

Commencement: 8 November 2006.

Inserted, together with the preceding heading and ss 89B–89G, by the Companies Act 2006, s 1266(1), as from 8 November 2006. See further, the note below.

Section 1266(2) of the 2006 Act provides as follows—

"(2) The effectiveness for the purposes of section 155 of the Financial Services and Markets Act 2000 (c 8) (consultation on proposed rules) of things done by the Financial Services Authority before this section comes into force with a view to making transparency rules (as defined in the provisions to be inserted in that Act by subsection (1) above) is not affected by the fact that those provisions were not then in force.".

[89B Provision of voteholder information

(1) Transparency rules may make provision for voteholder information in respect of voting shares to be notified, in circumstances specified in the rules—

(a) to the issuer, or

(b) to the public,

or to both.

(2) Transparency rules may make provision for voteholder information notified to the issuer to be notified at the same time to the competent authority.

(3) In this Part "voteholder information" in respect of voting shares means information relating to the proportion of voting rights held by a person in respect of the shares.

(4) Transparency rules may require notification of voteholder information relating to a person—

(a) initially, not later than such date as may be specified in the rules for the purposes of the first indent of Article 30.2 of the transparency obligations directive, and

(b) subsequently, in accordance with the following provisions.

(5) Transparency rules under subsection (4)(b) may require notification of voteholder information relating to a person only where there is a notifiable change in the proportion of—

(a) the total voting rights in respect of shares in the issuer, or

(b) the total voting rights in respect of a particular class of share in the issuer,

held by the person.

(6) For this purpose there is a "notifiable change" in the proportion of voting rights held by a person when the proportion changes—

(a) from being a proportion less than a designated proportion to a proportion equal to or greater than that designated proportion,

(b) from being a proportion equal to a designated proportion to a proportion greater or less than that designated proportion, or

PART II FSMA 2000

(c) from being a proportion greater than a designated proportion to a proportion equal to or less than that designated proportion.

(7) In subsection (6) "designated" means designated by the rules.]

[2089B]

NOTES

Commencement: 8 November 2006.
Inserted as noted to s 89A at **[2089A]**.

[89C Provision of information by issuers of transferable securities

(1) Transparency rules may make provision requiring the issuer of transferable securities, in circumstances specified in the rules—

(a) to make public information to which this section applies, or
(b) to notify to the competent authority information to which this section applies,

or to do both.

(2) In the case of every issuer, this section applies to—

(a) information required by Article 4 of the transparency obligations directive;
(b) information relating to the rights attached to the transferable securities, including information about the terms and conditions of those securities which could indirectly affect those rights; and
(c) information about new loan issues and about any guarantee or security in connection with any such issue.

(3) In the case of an issuer of debt securities, this section also applies to information required by Article 5 of the transparency obligations directive.

(4) In the case of an issuer of shares, this section also applies to—

(a) information required by Article 5 of the transparency obligations directive;
(b) information required by Article 6 of that directive;
(c) voteholder information—
 (i) notified to the issuer, or
 (ii) relating to the proportion of voting rights held by the issuer in respect of shares in the issuer;
(d) information relating to the issuer's capital; and
(e) information relating to the total number of voting rights in respect of shares or shares of a particular class.]

[2089C]

NOTES

Commencement: 8 November 2006.
Inserted as noted to s 89A at **[2089A]**.

[89D Notification of voting rights held by issuer

(1) Transparency rules may require notification of voteholder information relating to the proportion of voting rights held by an issuer in respect of voting shares in the issuer—

(a) initially, not later than such date as may be specified in the rules for the purposes of the second indent of Article 30.2 of the transparency obligations directive, and
(b) subsequently, in accordance with the following provisions.

(2) Transparency rules under subsection (1)(b) may require notification of voteholder information relating to the proportion of voting rights held by an issuer in respect of voting shares in the issuer only where there is a notifiable change in the proportion of—

(a) the total voting rights in respect of shares in the issuer, or
(b) the total voting rights in respect of a particular class of share in the issuer,

held by the issuer.

(3) For this purpose there is a "notifiable change" in the proportion of voting rights held by a person when the proportion changes—

(a) from being a proportion less than a designated proportion to a proportion equal to or greater than that designated proportion,
(b) from being a proportion equal to a designated proportion to a proportion greater or less than that designated proportion, or

(c) from being a proportion greater than a designated proportion to a proportion equal to or less than that designated proportion.

(4) In subsection (3) "designated" means designated by the rules.]

[2089D]

NOTES

Commencement: 8 November 2006.
Inserted as noted to s 89A at **[2089A]**.

[89E Notification of proposed amendment of issuer's constitution

Transparency rules may make provision requiring an issuer of transferable securities that are admitted to trading on a regulated market to notify a proposed amendment to its constitution—

(a) to the competent authority, and
(b) to the market on which the issuer's securities are admitted,

at times and in circumstances specified in the rules.]

[2089E]

NOTES

Commencement: 8 November 2006.
Inserted as noted to s 89A at **[2089A]**.

[89F Transparency rules: interpretation etc

(1) For the purposes of sections 89A to 89G—

(a) the voting rights in respect of any voting shares are the voting rights attached to those shares,
(b) a person is to be regarded as holding the voting rights in respect of the shares—
  (i) if, by virtue of those shares, he is a shareholder within the meaning of Article 2.1(e) of the transparency obligations directive;
  (ii) if, and to the extent that, he is entitled to acquire, dispose of or exercise those voting rights in one or more of the cases mentioned in Article 10(a) to (h) of the transparency obligations directive;
  (iii) if he holds, directly or indirectly, a financial instrument which results in an entitlement to acquire the shares and is an Article 13 instrument, and
(c) a person holds a "comparable instrument" in respect of voting shares if he holds, directly or indirectly, a financial instrument in relation to the shares which has similar economic effects to an Article 13 instrument (whether or not the financial instrument results in an entitlement to acquire the shares).

(2) Transparency rules under section 89A(3)(b) may make different provision for different descriptions of comparable instrument.

(3) For the purposes of sections 89A to 89G two or more persons may, at the same time, each be regarded as holding the same voting rights.

(4) In those sections—

"Article 13 instrument" means a financial instrument of a type determined by the European Commission under Article 13.2 of the transparency obligations directive;

"UK market" means a market that is situated or operating in the United Kingdom;

"voting shares" means shares of an issuer to which voting rights are attached.]

[2089F]

NOTES

Commencement: 8 November 2006.
Inserted as noted to s 89A at **[2089A]**.

[89G Transparency rules: other supplementary provisions

(1) Transparency rules may impose the same obligations on a person who has applied for the admission of transferable securities to trading on a regulated market without the issuer's consent as they impose on an issuer of transferable securities.

PART II
FSMA 2000

(2) Transparency rules that require a person to make information public may include provision authorising the competent authority to make the information public in the event that the person fails to do so.

(3) The competent authority may make public any information notified to the authority in accordance with transparency rules.

(4) Transparency rules may make provision by reference to any provision of any rules made by the Panel on Takeovers and Mergers under Part 28 of the Companies Act 2006.

(5) Sections 89A to 89F and this section are without prejudice to any other power conferred by this Part to make Part 6 rules.]

[2089G]

NOTES

Commencement: 8 November 2006.
Inserted as noted to s 89A at **[2089A]**.

[Power of competent authority to call for information

89H Competent authority's power to call for information

(1) The competent authority may by notice in writing given to a person to whom this section applies require him—

(a) to provide specified information or information of a specified description, or
(b) to produce specified documents or documents of a specified description.

(2) This section applies to—

(a) an issuer in respect of whom transparency rules have effect;
(b) a voteholder;
(c) an auditor of—
  (i) an issuer to whom this section applies, or
  (ii) a voteholder;
(d) a person who controls a voteholder;
(e) a person controlled by a voteholder;
(f) a director or other similar officer of an issuer to whom this section applies;
(g) a director or other similar officer of a voteholder or, where the affairs of a voteholder are managed by its members, a member of the voteholder.

(3) This section applies only to information and documents reasonably required in connection with the exercise by the competent authority of functions conferred on it by or under sections 89A to 89G (transparency rules).

(4) Information or documents required under this section must be provided or produced—

(a) before the end of such reasonable period as may be specified, and
(b) at such place as may be specified.

(5) If a person claims a lien on a document, its production under this section does not affect the lien.]

[2089H]

NOTES

Commencement: 8 November 2006.
Inserted, together with the preceding heading and ss 89I, 89J, by the Companies Act 2006, s 1267, as from 8 November 2006.

[89I Requirements in connection with call for information

(1) The competent authority may require any information provided under section 89H to be provided in such form as it may reasonably require.

(2) The competent authority may require—

(a) any information provided, whether in a document or otherwise, to be verified in such manner as it may reasonably require;
(b) any document produced to be authenticated in such manner as it may reasonably require.

(3) If a document is produced in response to a requirement imposed under section 89H, the competent authority may—

(a) take copies of or extracts from the document; or

(b) require the person producing the document, or any relevant person, to provide an explanation of the document.

(4) In subsection (3)(b) "relevant person", in relation to a person who is required to produce a document, means a person who—

(a) has been or is a director or controller of that person;

(b) has been or is an auditor of that person;

(c) has been or is an actuary, accountant or lawyer appointed or instructed by that person; or

(d) has been or is an employee of that person.

(5) If a person who is required under section 89H to produce a document fails to do so, the competent authority may require him to state, to the best of his knowledge and belief, where the document is.]

[2089I]

NOTES

Commencement: 8 November 2006.
Inserted as noted to s 89H at **[2089H]**.

[89J Power to call for information: supplementary provisions

(1) The competent authority may require an issuer to make public any information provided to the authority under section 89H.

(2) If the issuer fails to comply with a requirement under subsection (1), the competent authority may, after seeking representations from the issuer, make the information public.

(3) In sections 89H and 89I (power of competent authority to call for information)—

"control" and "controlled" have the meaning given by subsection (4) below;

"specified" means specified in the notice;

"voteholder" means a person who—

(a) holds voting rights in respect of any voting shares for the purposes of sections 89A to 89G (transparency rules), or

(b) is treated as holding such rights by virtue of rules under section 89A(3)(b).

(4) For the purposes of those sections a person ("A") controls another person ("B") if—

(a) A holds a majority of the voting rights in B,

(b) A is a member of B and has the right to appoint or remove a majority of the members of the board of directors (or, if there is no such board, the equivalent management body) of B,

(c) A is a member of B and controls alone, pursuant to an agreement with other shareholders or members, a majority of the voting rights in B, or

(d) A has the right to exercise, or actually exercises, dominant influence or control over B.

(5) For the purposes of subsection (4)(b)—

(a) any rights of a person controlled by A, and

(b) any rights of a person acting on behalf of A or a person controlled by A,

are treated as held by A.]

[2089J]

NOTES

Commencement: 8 November 2006.
Inserted as noted to s 89H at **[2089H]**.

[Powers exercisable in case of infringement of transparency obligation

89K Public censure of issuer

(1) If the competent authority finds that an issuer of securities admitted to trading on a regulated market is failing or has failed to comply with an applicable transparency obligation, it may publish a statement to that effect.

(2) If the competent authority proposes to publish a statement, it must give the issuer a warning notice setting out the terms of the proposed statement.

(3) If, after considering any representations made in response to the warning notice, the competent authority decides to make the proposed statement, it must give the issuer a decision notice setting out the terms of the statement.

(4) A notice under this section must inform the issuer of his right to refer the matter to the Tribunal (see section 89N) and give an indication of the procedure on such a reference.

(5) In this section "transparency obligation" means an obligation under—

(a) a provision of transparency rules, or

(b) any other provision made in accordance with the transparency obligations directive.

(6) In relation to an issuer whose home State is a member State other than the United Kingdom, any reference to an applicable transparency obligation must be read subject to section 100A(2).]

[2089K]

NOTES

Commencement: 8 November 2006.

Inserted, together with the preceding heading and ss 89L–89N, by the Companies Act 2006, s 1268, as from 8 November 2006.

[89L Power to suspend or prohibit trading of securities

(1) This section applies to securities admitted to trading on a regulated market.

(2) If the competent authority has reasonable grounds for suspecting that an applicable transparency obligation has been infringed by an issuer, it may—

(a) suspend trading in the securities for a period not exceeding 10 days,

(b) prohibit trading in the securities, or

(c) make a request to the operator of the market on which the issuer's securities are traded—

(i) to suspend trading in the securities for a period not exceeding 10 days, or

(ii) to prohibit trading in the securities.

(3) If the competent authority has reasonable grounds for suspecting that a provision required by the transparency obligations directive has been infringed by a voteholder of an issuer, it may—

(a) prohibit trading in the securities, or

(b) make a request to the operator of the market on which the issuer's securities are traded to prohibit trading in the securities.

(4) If the competent authority finds that an applicable transparency obligation has been infringed, it may require the market operator to prohibit trading in the securities.

(5) In this section "transparency obligation" means an obligation under—

(a) a provision contained in transparency rules, or

(b) any other provision made in accordance with the transparency obligations directive.

(6) In relation to an issuer whose home State is a member State other than the United Kingdom, any reference to an applicable transparency obligation must be read subject to section 100A(2).]

[2089L]

NOTES

Commencement: 8 November 2006.

Inserted as noted to s 89K at **[2089K]**.

[89M Procedure under section 89L

(1) A requirement under section 89L takes effect—

(a) immediately, if the notice under subsection (2) states that that is the case;

(b) in any other case, on such date as may be specified in the notice.

(2) If the competent authority—

(a) proposes to exercise the powers in section 89L in relation to a person, or

(b) exercises any of those powers in relation to a person with immediate effect,

it must give that person written notice.

(3) The notice must—

(a) give details of the competent authority's action or proposed action;

(b) state the competent authority's reasons for taking the action in question and choosing the date on which it took effect or takes effect;

(c) inform the recipient that he may make representations to the competent authority within such period as may be specified by the notice (whether or not he had referred the matter to the Tribunal);

(d) inform him of the date on which the action took effect or takes effect;

(e) inform him of his right to refer the matter to the Tribunal (see section 89N) and give an indication of the procedure on such a reference.

(4) The competent authority may extend the period within which representations may be made to it.

(5) If, having considered any representations made to it, the competent authority decides to maintain, vary or revoke its earlier decision, it must give written notice to that effect to the person mentioned in subsection (2).]

[2089M]

NOTES

Commencement: 8 November 2006.
Inserted as noted to s 89K at **[2089K]**.

[89N Right to refer matters to the Tribunal

A person—

(a) to whom a decision notice is given under section 89K (public censure), or

(b) to whom a notice is given under section 89M (procedure in connection with suspension or prohibition of trading),

may refer the matter to the Tribunal.]

[2089N]

NOTES

Commencement: 8 November 2006.
Inserted as noted to s 89K at **[2089K]**.

[Corporate governance

89O Corporate governance rules

(1) The competent authority may make rules ("corporate governance rules")—

(a) for the purpose of implementing, enabling the implementation of or dealing with matters arising out of or related to, any Community obligation relating to the corporate governance of issuers who have requested or approved admission of their securities to trading on a regulated market;

(b) about corporate governance in relation to such issuers for the purpose of implementing, or dealing with matters arising out of or related to, any Community obligation.

(2) "Corporate governance", in relation to an issuer, includes—

(a) the nature, constitution or functions of the organs of the issuer;

(b) the manner in which organs of the issuer conduct themselves;

(c) the requirements imposed on organs of the issuer;

(d) the relationship between the different organs of the issuer;

PART II FSMA 2000

(e) the relationship between the organs of the issuer and the members of the issuer or holders of the issuer's securities.

(3) The burdens and restrictions imposed by rules under this section on foreign-traded issuers must not be greater than the burdens and restrictions imposed on UK-traded issuers by—

(a) rules under this section, and
(b) listing rules.

(4) For this purpose—

"foreign-traded issuer" means an issuer who has requested or approved admission of the issuer's securities to trading on a regulated market situated or operating outside the United Kingdom;

"UK-traded issuer" means an issuer who has requested or approved admission of the issuer's securities to trading on a regulated market situated or operating in the United Kingdom.

(5) This section is without prejudice to any other power conferred by this Part to make Part 6 rules.]

[2089O]

NOTES

Commencement: 8 November 2006.

Inserted, together with the preceding heading, by the Companies Act 2006, s 1269, as from 8 November 2006.

[Compensation for false or misleading statements etc]

90 [Compensation for statements in listing particulars or prospectus]

(1) Any person responsible for listing particulars is liable to pay compensation to a person who has—

(a) acquired securities to which the particulars apply; and
(b) suffered loss in respect of them as a result of—
 (i) any untrue or misleading statement in the particulars; or
 (ii) the omission from the particulars of any matter required to be included by section 80 or 81.

(2) Subsection (1) is subject to exemptions provided by Schedule 10.

(3) If listing particulars are required to include information about the absence of a particular matter, the omission from the particulars of that information is to be treated as a statement in the listing particulars that there is no such matter.

(4) Any person who fails to comply with section 81 is liable to pay compensation to any person who has—

(a) acquired securities of the kind in question; and
(b) suffered loss in respect of them as a result of the failure.

(5) Subsection (4) is subject to exemptions provided by Schedule 10.

(6) This section does not affect any liability which may be incurred apart from this section.

(7) References in this section to the acquisition by a person of securities include references to his contracting to acquire them or any interest in them.

(8) No person shall, by reason of being a promoter of a company or otherwise, incur any liability for failing to disclose information which he would not be required to disclose in listing particulars in respect of a company's securities—

(a) if he were responsible for those particulars; or
(b) if he is responsible for them, which he is entitled to omit by virtue of section 82.

(9) The reference in subsection (8) to a person incurring liability includes a reference to any other person being entitled as against that person to be granted any civil remedy or to rescind or repudiate an agreement.

(10) "Listing particulars", in subsection (1) and Schedule 10, includes supplementary listing particulars.

[(11) This section applies in relation to a prospectus as it applies to listing particulars, with the following modifications—

(a) references in this section or in Schedule 10 to listing particulars, supplementary listing particulars or sections 80, 81 or 82 are to be read, respectively, as references to a prospectus, supplementary prospectus and sections 87A, 87G and 87B;

(b) references in Schedule 10 to admission to the official list are to be read as references to admission to trading on a regulated market;

(c) in relation to a prospectus, "securities" means "transferable securities".

(12) A person is not to be subject to civil liability solely on the basis of a summary in a prospectus unless the summary is misleading, inaccurate or inconsistent when read with the rest of the prospectus; and, in this subsection, a summary includes any translation of it.]

[2090]

NOTES

The section heading and the heading preceding this section were substituted by the Companies Act 2006, s 1272, Sch 15, Pt 1, paras 1, 4, 5, as from 8 November 2006.

Sub-ss (11), (12): added by SI 2005/1433, reg 2(1), Sch 1, para 6(1), (2), as from 1 July 2005.

[90A Compensation for statements in certain publications

(1) The publications to which this section applies are—

(a) any reports and statements published in response to a requirement imposed by a provision implementing Article 4, 5 or 6 of the transparency obligations directive, and

(b) any preliminary statement made in advance of a report or statement to be published in response to a requirement imposed by a provision implementing Article 4 of that directive, to the extent that it contains information that it is intended—

(i) will appear in the report or statement, and

(ii) will be presented in the report or statement in substantially the same form as that in which it is presented in the preliminary statement.

(2) The securities to which this section applies are—

(a) securities that are traded on a regulated market situated or operating in the United Kingdom, and

(b) securities that—

(i) are traded on a regulated market situated or operating outside the United Kingdom, and

(ii) are issued by an issuer for which the United Kingdom is the home Member State within the meaning of Article 2.1(i) of the transparency obligations directive.

(3) The issuer of securities to which this section applies is liable to pay compensation to a person who has—

(a) acquired such securities issued by it, and

(b) suffered loss in respect of them as a result of—

(i) any untrue or misleading statement in a publication to which this section applies, or

(ii) the omission from any such publication of any matter required to be included in it.

(4) The issuer is so liable only if a person discharging managerial responsibilities within the issuer in relation to the publication—

(a) knew the statement to be untrue or misleading or was reckless as to whether it was untrue or misleading, or

(b) knew the omission to be dishonest concealment of a material fact.

(5) A loss is not regarded as suffered as a result of the statement or omission in the publication unless the person suffering it acquired the relevant securities—

(a) in reliance on the information in the publication, and

(b) at a time when, and in circumstances in which, it was reasonable for him to rely on that information.

(6) Except as mentioned in subsection (8)—

PART II
FSMA 2000

(a) the issuer is not subject to any other liability than that provided for by this section in respect of loss suffered as a result of reliance by any person on—
(i) an untrue or misleading statement in a publication to which this section applies, or
(ii) the omission from any such publication of any matter required to be included in it, and
(b) a person other than the issuer is not subject to any liability, other than to the issuer, in respect of any such loss.

(7) Any reference in subsection (6) to a person being subject to a liability includes a reference to another person being entitled as against him to be granted any civil remedy or to rescind or repudiate an agreement.

(8) This section does not affect—
(a) the powers conferred by section 382 and 384 (powers of the court to make a restitution order and of the Authority to require restitution);
(b) liability for a civil penalty;
(c) liability for a criminal offence.

(9) For the purposes of this section—
(a) the following are persons "discharging managerial responsibilities" in relation to a publication—
(i) any director of the issuer (or person occupying the position of director, by whatever name called),
(ii) in the case of an issuer whose affairs are managed by its members, any member of the issuer,
(iii) in the case of an issuer that has no persons within sub- paragraph (i) or (ii), any senior executive of the issuer having responsibilities in relation to the publication;
(b) references to the acquisition by a person of securities include his contracting to acquire them or any interest in them.]

[2090A]

NOTES

Commencement: 8 November 2006.
Inserted, together with s 90B, by the Companies Act 2006, s 1270, as from 8 November 2006.

[90B Power to make further provision about liability for published information

(1) The Treasury may by regulations make provision about the liability of issuers of securities traded on a regulated market, and other persons, in respect of information published to holders of securities, to the market or to the public generally.

(2) Regulations under this section may amend any primary or subordinate legislation, including any provision of, or made under, this Act.]

[2090B]

NOTES

Commencement: 8 November 2006.
Inserted as noted to s 90A at **[2090A]**.

Penalties

91 [Penalties for breach of Part 6 rules]

[[(1) If the competent authority considers that—
(a) an issuer of listed securities, or
(b) an applicant for listing,

has contravened any provision of listing rules, it may impose on him a penalty of such amount as it considers appropriate.

(1ZA) If the competent authority considers that—
(a) an issuer who has requested or approved the admission of a financial instrument to trading on a regulated market,
(b) a person discharging managerial responsibilities within such an issuer, or

(c) a person connected with such a person discharging managerial responsibilities,

has contravened any provision of disclosure rules, it may impose on him a penalty of such amount as it considers appropriate.]]

[(1A) If the competent authority considers that—

(a) an issuer of transferable securities,

(b) a person offering transferable securities to the public or requesting their admission to trading on a regulated market,

(c) an applicant for the approval of a prospectus in relation to transferable securities,

(d) a person on whom a requirement has been imposed under section 87K or 87L, or

(e) any other person to whom a provision of the prospectus directive applies,

has contravened a provision of this Part or of prospectus rules, or a provision otherwise made in accordance with the prospectus directive or a requirement imposed on him under such a provision, it may impose on him a penalty of such amount as it considers appropriate.]

[(1B) If the competent authority considers—

(a) that a person has contravened—

(i) a provision of transparency rules or a provision otherwise made in accordance with the transparency obligations directive, or

(ii) a provision of corporate governance rules, or

(b) that a person on whom a requirement has been imposed under section 89L (power to suspend or prohibit trading of securities in case of infringement of applicable transparency obligation), has contravened that requirement,

it may impose on the person a penalty of such amount as it considers appropriate.]

(2) If, in the case of a contravention [by a person] referred to in subsection [[(1), (1ZA)(a), (1A) or (1B)] ("P")], the competent authority considers that [another person] who was at the material time a director of [P] was knowingly concerned in the contravention, it may impose upon him a penalty of such amount as it considers appropriate.]

(3) If the competent authority is entitled to impose a penalty on a person under this section in respect of a particular matter it may, instead of imposing a penalty on him in respect of that matter, publish a statement censuring him.

(4) Nothing in this section prevents the competent authority from taking any other steps which it has power to take under this Part.

(5) A penalty under this section is payable to the competent authority.

(6) The competent authority may not take action against a person under this section after the end of the period of two years beginning with the first day on which it knew of the contravention unless proceedings against that person, in respect of the contravention, were begun before the end of that period.

(7) For the purposes of subsection (6)—

(a) the competent authority is to be treated as knowing of a contravention if it has information from which the contravention can reasonably be inferred; and

(b) proceedings against a person in respect of a contravention are to be treated as begun when a warning notice is given to him under section 92.

[2091]

NOTES

Section heading: substituted by the Prospectus Regulations 2005, SI 2005/1433, reg 2(1), Sch 1, para 7(1), (4), as from 1 July 2005.

Sub-s (1): originally substituted (by a new sub-s (1) and (2)) by the Financial Services and Markets Act 2000 (Market Abuse) Regulations 2005, SI 2005/381, reg 4, Sch 1, para 4, as from 1 July 2005; further substituted (by a new sub-s (1) and (1ZA)) by the Companies Act 2006, s 1272, Sch 15, Pt 1, paras 1, 6(1), (2), as from 8 November 2006.

Sub-s (1ZA): substituted as noted above.

Sub-s (1A): inserted by SI 2005/1433, reg 2(1), Sch 1, para 7(1), (2), as from 1 July 2005.

Sub-s (1B): inserted by the Companies Act 2006, s 1272, Sch 15, Pt 1, paras 1, 6(1), (3), as from 8 November 2006.

Sub-s (2): substituted as noted above; words "(1), (1ZA)(a), (1A) or (1B)" in square brackets substituted by the Companies Act 2006, s 1272, Sch 15, Pt 1, paras 1, 6(1), (4), as from 8 November 2006; other words in square brackets substituted by SI 2005/1433, reg 2(1), Sch 1, para 6(1), (3), as from 1 July 2005.

92 Procedure

(1) If the competent authority proposes to take action against a person under section 91, it must give him a warning notice.

(2) A warning notice about a proposal to impose a penalty must state the amount of the proposed penalty.

(3) A warning notice about a proposal to publish a statement must set out the terms of the proposed statement.

(4) If the competent authority decides to take action against a person under section 91, it must give him a decision notice.

(5) A decision notice about the imposition of a penalty must state the amount of the penalty.

(6) A decision notice about the publication of a statement must set out the terms of the statement.

(7) If the competent authority decides to take action against a person under section 91, he may refer the matter to the Tribunal.

[2092]

93 Statement of policy

(1) The competent authority must prepare and issue a statement ("its policy statement") of its policy with respect to—

(a) the imposition of penalties under section 91; and
(b) the amount of penalties under that section.

(2) The competent authority's policy in determining what the amount of a penalty should be must include having regard to—

(a) the seriousness of the contravention in question in relation to the nature of the requirement contravened;
(b) the extent to which that contravention was deliberate or reckless; and
(c) whether the person on whom the penalty is to be imposed is an individual.

(3) The competent authority may at any time alter or replace its policy statement.

(4) If its policy statement is altered or replaced, the competent authority must issue the altered or replacement statement.

(5) In exercising, or deciding whether to exercise, its power under section 91 in the case of any particular contravention, the competent authority must have regard to any policy statement published under this section and in force at the time when the contravention in question occurred.

(6) The competent authority must publish a statement issued under this section in the way appearing to the competent authority to be best calculated to bring it to the attention of the public.

(7) The competent authority may charge a reasonable fee for providing a person with a copy of the statement.

(8) The competent authority must, without delay, give the Treasury a copy of any policy statement which it publishes under this section.

[2093]

94 Statements of policy: procedure

(1) Before issuing a statement under section 93, the competent authority must publish a draft of the proposed statement in the way appearing to the competent authority to be best calculated to bring it to the attention of the public.

(2) The draft must be accompanied by notice that representations about the proposal may be made to the competent authority within a specified time.

(3) Before issuing the proposed statement, the competent authority must have regard to any representations made to it in accordance with subsection (2).

(4) If the competent authority issues the proposed statement it must publish an account, in general terms, of—

(a) the representations made to it in accordance with subsection (2); and
(b) its response to them.

(5) If the statement differs from the draft published under subsection (1) in a way which is, in the opinion of the competent authority, significant, the competent authority must (in addition to complying with subsection (4)) publish details of the difference.

(6) The competent authority may charge a reasonable fee for providing a person with a copy of a draft published under subsection (1).

(7) This section also applies to a proposal to alter or replace a statement.

[2094]

Competition

95 Competition scrutiny

(1) The Treasury may by order provide for—
(a) regulating provisions, and
(b) the practices of the competent authority in exercising its functions under this Part ("practices"),

to be kept under review.

(2) Provision made as a result of subsection (1) must require the person responsible for keeping regulating provisions and practices under review to consider—
(a) whether any regulating provision or practice has a significantly adverse effect on competition; or
(b) whether two or more regulating provisions or practices taken together have, or a particular combination of regulating provisions and practices has, such an effect.

(3) An order under this section may include provision corresponding to that made by any provision of Chapter III of Part X.

(4) Subsection (3) is not to be read as in any way restricting the power conferred by subsection (1).

(5) Subsections (6) to (8) apply for the purposes of provision made by or under this section.

(6) Regulating provisions or practices have a significantly adverse effect on competition if—
(a) they have, or are intended or likely to have, that effect; or
(b) the effect that they have, or are intended or likely to have, is to require or encourage behaviour which has, or is intended or likely to have, a significantly adverse effect on competition.

(7) If regulating provisions or practices have, or are intended or likely to have, the effect of requiring or encouraging exploitation of the strength of a market position they are to be taken to have, or be intended or be likely to have, an adverse effect on competition.

(8) In determining whether any of the regulating provisions or practices have, or are intended or likely to have, a particular effect, it may be assumed that the persons to whom the provisions concerned are addressed will act in accordance with them.

(9) "Regulating provisions" means—
(a) [Part 6 rules],
(b) general guidance given by the competent authority in connection with its functions under this Part.

[2095]

NOTES

Sub-s (9): words in square brackets substituted by the Financial Services and Markets Act 2000 (Market Abuse) Regulations 2005, SI 2005/381, reg 4, Sch 1, para 5, as from 1 July 2005.

Miscellaneous

96 Obligations of issuers of listed securities

(1) Listing rules may—

PART II FSMA 2000

(a) specify requirements to be complied with by issuers of listed securities; and
(b) make provision with respect to the action that may be taken by the competent authority in the event of non-compliance.

(2) If the rules require an issuer to publish information, they may include provision authorising the competent authority to publish it in the event of his failure to do so.

(3) This section applies whenever the listed securities were admitted to the official list.

[2096]

[96A Disclosure of information requirements

(1) Disclosure rules must include provision specifying the disclosure of information requirements to be complied with by—

(a) issuers who have requested or approved admission of their financial instruments to trading on a regulated market in the United Kingdom;
(b) persons acting on behalf of or for the account of such issuers;
(c) persons discharging managerial responsibilities within an issuer—
  (i) who is registered in the United Kingdom and who has requested or approved admission of its shares to trading on a regulated market; or
  (ii) who is not registered in the United Kingdom or any other EEA State but who has requested or approved admission of its shares to trading on a regulated market and who is required to file annual information in relation to the shares in the United Kingdom in accordance with Article 10 of the prospectus directive;
(d) persons connected to such persons discharging managerial responsibilities.

(2) The rules must in particular—

(a) require an issuer to publish specified inside information;
(b) require an issuer to publish any significant change concerning information it has already published in accordance with paragraph (a);
(c) allow an issuer to delay the publication of inside information in specified circumstances;
(d) require an issuer (or a person acting on his behalf or for his account) who discloses inside information to a third party to publish that information without delay in specified circumstances;
(e) require an issuer (or person acting on his behalf or for his account) to draw up a list of those persons working for him who have access to inside information relating directly or indirectly to that issuer; and
(f) require persons discharging managerial responsibilities within an issuer falling within subsection (1)(c)(i) or (ii), and persons connected to such persons discharging managerial responsibilities, to disclose transactions conducted on their own account in shares of the issuer, or derivatives or any other financial instrument relating to those shares.

(3) Disclosure rules may make provision with respect to the action that may be taken by the competent authority in respect of non-compliance.]

[2096A]

NOTES

Inserted, together with ss 96B, 96C, by the Financial Services and Markets Act 2000 (Market Abuse) Regulations 2005, SI 2005/381, reg 4, Sch 1, para 6, as from 17 March 2005.

[96B [Disclosure rules: persons responsible for compliance]

(1) [For the purposes of the provisions of this Part relating to disclosure rules], a "person discharging managerial responsibilities within an issuer" means—

(a) a director of an issuer falling within section 96A(1)(c)(i) or (ii); or
(b) a senior executive of such an issuer who—
  (i) has regular access to inside information relating, directly or indirectly, to the issuer, and
  (ii) has power to make managerial decisions affecting the future development and business prospects of the issuer.

(2) A person "connected" with a person discharging managerial responsibilities within an issuer means—

(a) a "connected person" within the meaning in section 346 of the Companies

Act 1985 (reading that section as if any reference to a director of a company were a reference to a person discharging managerial responsibilities within an issuer);

(b) a relative of a person discharging managerial responsibilities within an issuer, who, on the date of the transaction in question, has shared the same household as that person for at least 12 months;

(c) a body corporate in which—

(i) a person discharging managerial responsibilities within an issuer, or

(ii) any person connected with him by virtue of subsection (a) or (b),

is a director or a senior executive who has the power to make management decisions affecting the future development and business prospects of that body corporate.]

[2096B]

NOTES

Inserted as noted to s 96A at **[2096A]**.

Section heading: substituted by the Companies Act 2006, s 1272, Sch 15, Pt 1, paras 1, 7(a), as from 8 November 2006.

Sub-s (1): words in square brackets substituted by the Companies Act 2006, s 1272, Sch 15, Pt 1, paras 1, 7(b), as from 8 November 2006.

Note: the repeal of s 346 of, and Sch 13 to, the Companies Act 1985 (meaning of "connected person") does not affect sub-s (2)(a) above; see the draft Companies Act 2006 (Commencement No 3, Consequential Amendments, Transitional Provisions and Savings) Order 2007, Sch 3, para 50 (at **[A12]**).

PART II
FSMA 2000

[96C Suspension of trading

(1) The competent authority may, in accordance with disclosure rules, suspend trading in a financial instrument.

(2) If the competent authority does so, the issuer of that financial instrument may refer the matter to the Tribunal.

(3) The provisions relating to suspension of listing of securities in section 78 apply to the suspension of trading in a financial instrument and the references to listing and securities are to be read as references to trading and financial instruments respectively for the purposes of this section.]

[2096C]

NOTES

Inserted as noted to s 96A at **[2096A]**.

97 Appointment by competent authority of persons to carry out investigations

(1) Subsection (2) applies if it appears to the competent authority that there are circumstances suggesting that—

[(a) there may have been a contravention of—

(i) a provision of this Part or of Part 6 rules, or

(ii) a provision otherwise made in accordance with the prospectus directive or the transparency obligations directive;

(b) a person who was at the material time a director of a person mentioned in section 91(1), (1ZA)(a), (1A) or (1B) has been knowingly concerned in a contravention by that person of—

(i) a provision of this Part or of Part 6 rules, or

(ii) a provision otherwise made in accordance with the prospectus directive or the transparency obligations directive;]

(c) …

(d) there may have been a contravention of section 83, 85[, 87G] or 98.

(2) The competent authority may appoint one or more competent persons to conduct an investigation on its behalf.

(3) Part XI applies to an investigation under subsection (2) as if—

(a) the investigator were appointed under section 167(1);

(b) references to the investigating authority in relation to him were to the competent authority;

(c) references to the offences mentioned in section 168 were to those mentioned in subsection (1)(d);

(d) references to an authorised person were references to the person under investigation.

[2097]–[2098]

NOTES

Sub-s (1): paras (a), (b) substituted by the Companies Act 2006, s 1272, Sch 15, Pt 1, paras 1, 8, as from 8 November 2006; para (c) repealed by the Financial Services and Markets Act 2000 (Market Abuse) Regulations 2005, SI 2005/381, reg 4, Sch 1, para 7, as from 1 July 2005; figure in square brackets in para (d) inserted by the Prospectus Regulations 2005, SI 2005/1433, reg 2(1), Sch 1, para 8, as from 1 July 2005.

98 (*Repealed by the Prospectus Regulations 2005, SI 2005/1433, reg 2(1), Sch 1, para 9, as from 1 July 2005.*)

99 Fees

(1) Listing rules may require the payment of fees to the competent authority in respect of—

(a) applications for listing;
(b) the continued inclusion of securities in the official list;
(c) applications under section 88 for approval as a sponsor; and
(d) continued inclusion of sponsors in the list of sponsors.

[(1A) Disclosure rules may require the payment of fees to the competent authority in respect of the continued admission of financial instruments to trading on a regulated market.]

[(1B) Prospectus rules may require the payment of fees to the competent authority in respect of—

(a) applications for approval of a prospectus or a supplementary prospectus;
(b) applications for inclusion in the register of investors;
(c) the continued inclusion of investors in that register;
(d) access to that register.]

[(1C) Transparency rules may require the payment of fees to the competent authority in respect of the continued admission of financial instruments to trading on a regulated market.]

(2) In exercising its powers under subsection (1), the competent authority may set such fees as it considers will (taking account of the income it expects as the competent authority) enable it—

(a) to meet expenses incurred in carrying out its functions under this Part or for any incidental purpose;
(b) to maintain adequate reserves; and
(c) in the case of the Authority, to repay the principal of, and pay any interest on, any money which it has borrowed and which has been used for the purpose of meeting expenses incurred in relation to—
  (i) its assumption of functions from the London Stock Exchange Limited in relation to the official list; and
  (ii) its assumption of functions under this Part.

(3) In fixing the amount of any fee which is to be payable to the competent authority, no account is to be taken of any sums which it receives, or expects to receive, by way of penalties imposed by it under this Part.

(4) Subsection (2)(c) applies whether expenses were incurred before or after the coming into force of this Part.

(5) Any fee which is owed to the competent authority under any provision made by or under this Part may be recovered as a debt due to it.

[2099]

NOTES

Sub-s (1A): inserted by the Financial Services and Markets Act 2000 (Market Abuse) Regulations 2005, SI 2005/381, reg 4, Sch 1, para 8, as from 1 July 2005.

Sub-s (1B): inserted by the Prospectus Regulations 2005, SI 2005/1433, reg 2(1), Sch 1, para 10, as from 1 July 2005.

Sub-s (1C): inserted by the Companies Act 2006, s 1272, Sch 15, Pt 1, paras 1, 9, as from 8 November 2006.

100 Penalties

(1) In determining its policy with respect to the amount of penalties to be imposed by it under this Part, the competent authority must take no account of the expenses which it incurs, or expects to incur, in discharging its functions under this Part.

(2) The competent authority must prepare and operate a scheme for ensuring that the amounts paid to it by way of penalties imposed under this Part are applied for the benefit of issuers of securities admitted to the official list[, and issuers who have requested or approved the admission of financial instruments to trading on a regulated market].

(3) The scheme may, in particular, make different provision with respect to different classes of issuer.

(4) Up to date details of the scheme must be set out in a document ("the scheme details").

(5) The scheme details must be published by the competent authority in the way appearing to it to be best calculated to bring them to the attention of the public.

(6) Before making the scheme, the competent authority must publish a draft of the proposed scheme in the way appearing to it to be best calculated to bring it to the attention of the public.

(7) The draft must be accompanied by notice that representations about the proposals may be made to the competent authority within a specified time.

(8) Before making the scheme, the competent authority must have regard to any representations made to it under subsection (7).

(9) If the competent authority makes the proposed scheme, it must publish an account, in general terms, of—

(a) the representations made to it in accordance with subsection (7); and
(b) its response to them.

(10) If the scheme differs from the draft published under subsection (6) in a way which is, in the opinion of the competent authority, significant the competent authority must (in addition to complying with subsection (9)) publish details of the difference.

(11) The competent authority must, without delay, give the Treasury a copy of any scheme details published by it.

(12) The competent authority may charge a reasonable fee for providing a person with a copy of—

(a) a draft published under subsection (6);
(b) scheme details.

(13) Subsections (6) to (10) and (12) apply also to a proposal to alter or replace the scheme.

[2100]

NOTES

Sub-s (2): words in square brackets added by the Financial Services and Markets Act 2000 (Market Abuse) Regulations 2005, SI 2005/381, reg 4, Sch 1, para 9, as from 1 July 2005.

[100A Exercise of powers where UK is host member state

(1) This section applies to the exercise by the competent authority of any power under this Part exercisable in case of infringement of—

(a) a provision of prospectus rules or any other provision made in accordance with the prospectus directive, or

(b) a provision of transparency rules or any other provision made in accordance with the transparency obligations directive,

in relation to an issuer whose home State is a member State other than the United Kingdom.

(2) The competent authority may act in such a case only in respect of the infringement of a provision required by the relevant directive.

Any reference to an applicable provision or applicable transparency obligation shall be read accordingly.

PART II
FSMA 2000

(3) If the authority finds that there has been such an infringement, it must give a notice to that effect to the competent authority of the person's home State requesting it—

(a) to take all appropriate measures for the purpose of ensuring that the person remedies the situation that has given rise to the notice, and

(b) to inform the authority of the measures it proposes to take or has taken or the reasons for not taking such measures.

(4) The authority may not act further unless satisfied—

(a) that the competent authority of the person's home State has failed or refused to take measures for the purpose mentioned in subsection (3)(a), or

(b) that the measures taken by that authority have proved inadequate for that purpose.

This does not affect exercise of the powers under section 87K(2), 87L(2) or (3) or 89L(2) or (3) (powers to protect market).

(5) If the authority is so satisfied, it must, after informing the competent authority of the person's home State, take all appropriate measures to protect investors.

(6) In such a case the authority must inform the Commission of the measures at the earliest opportunity.]

[2100A]

NOTES

Commencement: 8 November 2006.
Inserted by the Companies Act 2006, s 1271, as from 8 November 2006.

101 [Part 6 rules]: general provisions

(1) [Part 6 rules] may make different provision for different cases.

(2) [Part 6 rules] may authorise the competent authority to dispense with or modify the application of the rules in particular cases and by reference to any circumstances.

(3) [Part 6 rules] must be made by an instrument in writing.

(4) Immediately after an instrument containing [Part 6 rules] is made, it must be printed and made available to the public with or without payment.

(5) A person is not to be taken to have contravened [any Part 6 rule] if he shows that at the time of the alleged contravention the instrument containing the rule had not been made available as required by subsection (4).

(6) The production of a printed copy of an instrument purporting to be made by the competent authority on which is endorsed a certificate signed by an officer of the authority authorised by it for that purpose and stating—

(a) that the instrument was made by the authority,

(b) that the copy is a true copy of the instrument, and

(c) that on a specified date the instrument was made available to the public as required by subsection (4),

is evidence (or in Scotland sufficient evidence) of the facts stated in the certificate.

(7) A certificate purporting to be signed as mentioned in subsection (6) is to be treated as having been properly signed unless the contrary is shown.

(8) A person who wishes in any legal proceedings to rely on a rule-making instrument may require the Authority to endorse a copy of the instrument with a certificate of the kind mentioned in subsection (6).

[2101]

NOTES

Section heading: words in square brackets substituted by virtue of the Financial Services and Markets Act 2000 (Market Abuse) Regulations 2005, SI 2005/381, reg 4, Sch 1, para 10, as from 1 July 2005. Note that SI 2005/381 makes no provision for the section name to be amended, but in consequence of the amendments noted below, it is believed that it should be.

Sub-ss (1)–(5): words in square brackets substituted by SI 2005/381, reg 4, Sch 1, para 10, as from 1 July 2005.

102 Exemption from liability in damages

(1) Neither the competent authority nor any person who is, or is acting as, a member, officer or member of staff of the competent authority is to be liable in damages for anything done or omitted in the discharge, or purported discharge, of the authority's functions.

(2) Subsection (1) does not apply—
- (a) if the act or omission is shown to have been in bad faith; or
- (b) so as to prevent an award of damages made in respect of an act or omission on the ground that the act or omission was unlawful as a result of section 6(1) of the Human Rights Act 1998.

[2102]

[Interpretative provisions

102A Meaning of "securities" etc

(1) This section applies for the purposes of this Part.

(2) "Securities" means (except in section 74(2) and the expression "transferable securities") anything which has been, or may be, admitted to the official list.

(3) "Transferable securities" means anything which is a transferable security for the purposes of [Directive 2004/39/EC of the European Parliament and of the Council on markets in financial instruments], other than money-market instruments for the purposes of that directive which have a maturity of less than 12 months.

[(3A) "Debt securities" has the meaning given in Article 2.1(b) of the transparency obligations directive.]

(4) "Financial instrument" has the meaning given in Article 1.3 of Directive 2003/6/EC of the European Parliament and of the Council of 28 January 2003 on insider dealing and market manipulation.

(5) "Non-equity transferable securities" means all transferable securities that are not equity securities; and for this purpose "equity securities" has the meaning given in Article 2.1(b) of the prospectus directive.

(6) "Issuer"—
- (a) in relation to an offer of transferable securities to the public or admission of transferable securities to trading on a regulated market for which an approved prospectus is required as a result of section 85, means a legal person who issues or proposes to issue the transferable securities in question,
- [(aa) in relation to transparency rules, means a legal person whose securities are admitted to trading on a regulated market or whose voting shares are admitted to trading on a UK market other than a regulated market, and in the case of depository receipts representing securities, the issuer is the issuer of the securities represented,]
- (b) in relation to anything else which is or may be admitted to the official list, has such meaning as may be prescribed by the Treasury, and
- (c) in any other case, means a person who issues financial instruments.]

[2102A]

PART II FSMA 2000

NOTES

Sections 102A–102C, 103 substituted (together with the preceding heading) for original s 103, by the Prospectus Regulations 2005, SI 2005/1433, reg 2(1), Sch 1, para 11, as from 1 July 2005.

Sub-s (3): words in square brackets substituted by the Companies Act 2006, s 1272, Sch 15, Pt 1, paras 1, 10(1), (3), as from 8 November 2006.

Sub-s (3A): inserted by the Companies Act 2006, s 1272, Sch 15, Pt 1, paras 1, 10(1), (2), as from 8 November 2006.

Sub-s (6): para (aa) inserted by the Companies Act 2006, s 1272, Sch 15, Pt 1, paras 1, 10(1), (4), as from 8 November 2006.

[102B Meaning of "offer of transferable securities to the public" etc

(1) For the purposes of this Part there is an offer of transferable securities to the public if there is a communication to any person which presents sufficient information on—
- (a) the transferable securities to be offered, and

(b) the terms on which they are offered,

to enable an investor to decide to buy or subscribe for the securities in question.

(2) For the purposes of this Part, to the extent that an offer of transferable securities is made to a person in the United Kingdom it is an offer of transferable securities to the public in the United Kingdom.

(3) The communication may be made—

(a) in any form;
(b) by any means.

(4) Subsection (1) includes the placing of securities through a financial intermediary.

(5) Subsection (1) does not include a communication in connection with trading on—

(a) a regulated market;
(b) a multilateral trading facility; or
(c) a market prescribed by an order under section 130A(3).

(6) "Multilateral trading facility" means a multilateral system, operated by an investment firm (*within the meaning of Article 1.2 of the investment services directive*) or a market operator, which brings together multiple third-party buying and selling interests in financial instruments in accordance with non-discretionary rules so as to result in a contract.]

[2102B]

NOTES

Substituted as noted to s 102A at **[2102A]**.

Sub-s (6): words in italics repealed by the Financial Services and Markets Act 2000 (Markets in Financial Instruments) Regulations 2007, SI 2007/126, reg 3(5), Sch 5, paras 1, 6, as from 1 April 2007 (certain purposes (see reg 1(2) at **[7596]**)), and as from 1 November 2007 (otherwise).

[102C Meaning of "home State" in relation to transferable securities

In this Part, in relation to an issuer of transferable securities, the "home-State" is the EEA State which is the "home Member State" for the purposes of the prospectus directive (which is to be determined in accordance with Article 2.1(m) of that directive).]

[2102C]

NOTES

Substituted as noted to s 102A at **[2102A]**.

[103 Interpretation of this Part

(1) In this Part, save where the context otherwise requires—

"disclosure rules" has the meaning given in section 73A;

"inside information" has the meaning given in section 118C;

"listed securities" means anything which has been admitted to the official list;

"listing" has the meaning given in section 74(5);

"listing particulars" has the meaning given in section 79(2);

"listing rules" has the meaning given in section 73A;

"market operator" means a person who manages or operates the business of a regulated market;

"offer of transferable securities to the public" has the meaning given in section 102B;

"the official list" means the list maintained by the competent authority as that list has effect for the time being;

"Part 6 rules" has the meaning given in section 73A;

"the prospectus directive" means Directive 2003/71/EC of the European Parliament and of the Council of 4 November 2003 on the prospectus to be published when securities are offered to the public or admitted to trading;

"prospectus rules" has the meaning given in section 73A;

"regulated market" has the meaning given in *Article 1.13 of the investment services directive*;

"supplementary prospectus" has the meaning given in section 87G;

["the transparency obligations directive" means Directive 2004/ 109/EC of the European Parliament and of the Council relating to the harmonisation of transparency requirements in relation to information about issuers whose securities are admitted to trading on a regulated market;]

["transparency rules" has the meaning given by section 89A(5);
"voteholder information" has the meaning given by section 89B(3);]
"working day" means any day other that a Saturday, a Sunday, Christmas Day, Good Friday or a day which is a bank holiday under the Banking and Financial Dealings Act 1971 (c 80) in any part of the United Kingdom.

(2) In relation to any function conferred on the competent authority by this Part, any reference in this Part to the competent authority is to be read as a reference to the person by whom that function is for the time being exercisable.

(3) If, as a result of an order under Schedule 8, different functions conferred on the competent authority by this Part are exercisable by different persons, the powers conferred by section 91 are exercisable by such person as may be determined in accordance with the provisions of the order.]

[2103]

NOTES

Substituted as noted to s 102A at **[2102A]**.

Sub-s (1) is amended as follows:

In definition "regulated market" for the words in italics there are substituted the words "Article 4.1(14) of Directive 2004/39/EC of the European Parliament and of the Council on markets in financial instruments" by the Companies Act 2006, s 1272, Sch 15, Pt 1, paras 1, 11(1), (2), as from a day to be appointed.

Definitions "the transparency obligations directive", "transparency rules", and "voteholder information" inserted by the Companies Act 2006, ss 1265, 1272, Sch 15, Pt 1, paras 1, 11(1), (3), as from 8 November 2006.

PART II
FSMA 2000

PART VII
CONTROL OF BUSINESS TRANSFERS

104 Control of business transfers

No insurance business transfer scheme or banking business transfer scheme is to have effect unless an order has been made in relation to it under section 111(1).

[2104]

NOTES

Commencement: 1 December 2001 (for the purpose of insurance business transfer schemes); to be appointed (otherwise).

105 Insurance business transfer schemes

(1) A scheme is an insurance business transfer scheme if it—

(a) satisfies one of the conditions set out in subsection (2);
(b) results in the business transferred being carried on from an establishment of the transferee in an EEA State; and
(c) is not an excluded scheme.

(2) The conditions are that—

(a) the whole or part of the business carried on in one or more member States by a UK authorised person who has permission to effect or carry out contracts of insurance ("the authorised person concerned") is to be transferred to another body ("the transferee");
(b) the whole or part of the business, so far as it consists of reinsurance, carried on in the United Kingdom through an establishment there by an EEA firm qualifying for authorisation under Schedule 3 which has permission to effect or carry out contracts of insurance ("the authorised person concerned") is to be transferred to another body ("the transferee");
(c) the whole or part of the business carried on in the United Kingdom by an authorised person who is neither a UK authorised person nor an EEA firm but who has permission to effect or carry out contracts of insurance ("the authorised person concerned") is to be transferred to another body ("the transferee").

(3) A scheme is an excluded scheme for the purposes of this section if it falls within any of the following cases:

CASE 1

Where the authorised person concerned is a friendly society.

CASE 2

Where—

(a) the authorised person concerned is a UK authorised person;

(b) the business to be transferred under the scheme is business which consists of the effecting or carrying out of contracts of reinsurance in one or more EEA States other than the United Kingdom; and

(c) the scheme has been approved by a court in an EEA State other than the United Kingdom or by the host state regulator.

CASE 3

Where—

(a) the authorised person concerned is a UK authorised person;

(b) the business to be transferred under the scheme is carried on in one or more countries or territories (none of which is an EEA State) and does not include policies of insurance (other than reinsurance) against risks arising in an EEA State; and

(c) the scheme has been approved by a court in a country or territory other than an EEA State or by the authority responsible for the supervision of that business in a country or territory in which it is carried on.

CASE 4

Where the business to be transferred under the scheme is the whole of the business of the authorised person concerned and—

(a) consists solely of the effecting or carrying out of contracts of reinsurance, or

(b) all the policyholders are controllers of the firm or of firms within the same group as the firm which is the transferee,

and, in either case, all of the policyholders who will be affected by the transfer have consented to it.

(4) The parties to a scheme which falls within Case 2, 3 or 4 may apply to the court for an order sanctioning the scheme as if it were an insurance business transfer scheme.

(5) Subsection (6) applies if the scheme involves a compromise or arrangement falling within section 427A of the Companies Act 1985 (or Article 420A of the Companies (Northern Ireland) Order 1986).

(6) Sections 425 to 427 of that Act (or Articles 418 to 420 of that Order) have effect as modified by section 427A of that Act (or Article 420A of that Order) in relation to that compromise or arrangement.

(7) But subsection (6) does not affect the operation of this Part in relation to the scheme.

(8) "UK authorised person" means a body which is an authorised person and which—

(a) is incorporated in the United Kingdom; or

(b) is an unincorporated association formed under the law of any part of the United Kingdom.

(9) "Establishment" means, in relation to a person, his head office or a branch of his.

[2105]

NOTES

Transitional provisions: see the Financial Services and Markets Act 2000 (Transitional Provisions and Savings) (Business Transfers) Order 2001, SI 2001/3639. That Order makes savings and transitional provision for applications under the Insurance Companies Act 1982, Sch 2C (repealed) for approval of a transfer of the whole or part of the long term business carried on by an insurance company or approval of the transfer of rights and obligations under contracts of general insurance (including transfers of business to or from members of Lloyd's). In relation to any application that has been made but not determined before 1 December 2001, the relevant provisions of Sch 2C are saved, subject to the general modifications in art 2 of the Order and the specific modifications in arts 3 and 5.

106 Banking business transfer schemes

(1) A scheme is a banking business transfer scheme if it—

(a) satisfies one of the conditions set out in subsection (2);

(b) is one under which the whole or part of the business to be transferred includes the accepting of deposits; and

(c) is not an excluded scheme.

(2) The conditions are that—

(a) the whole or part of the business carried on by a UK authorised person who has permission to accept deposits ("the authorised person concerned") is to be transferred to another body ("the transferee");

(b) the whole or part of the business carried on in the United Kingdom by an authorised person who is not a UK authorised person but who has permission to accept deposits ("the authorised person concerned") is to be transferred to another body which will carry it on in the United Kingdom ("the transferee").

(3) A scheme is an excluded scheme for the purposes of this section if—

(a) the authorised person concerned is a building society or a credit union; or

(b) the scheme is a compromise or arrangement to which section 427A(1) of the Companies Act 1985 or Article 420A of the Companies (Northern Ireland) Order 1986 (mergers and divisions of public companies) applies.

(4) For the purposes of subsection (2)(a) it is immaterial whether or not the business to be transferred is carried on in the United Kingdom.

(5) "UK authorised person" has the same meaning as in section 105.

(6) "Building society" has the meaning given in the Building Societies Act 1986.

(7) "Credit union" means a credit union within the meaning of—

(a) the Credit Unions Act 1979;

(b) the Credit Unions (Northern Ireland) Order 1985.

[2106]

107 Application for order sanctioning transfer scheme

(1) An application may be made to the court for an order sanctioning an insurance business transfer scheme or a banking business transfer scheme.

(2) An application may be made by—

(a) the authorised person concerned;

(b) the transferee; or

(c) both.

(3) The application must be made—

(a) if the authorised person concerned and the transferee are registered or have their head offices in the same jurisdiction, to the court in that jurisdiction;

(b) if the authorised person concerned and the transferee are registered or have their head offices in different jurisdictions, to the court in either jurisdiction;

(c) if the transferee is not registered in the United Kingdom and does not have his head office there, to the court which has jurisdiction in relation to the authorised person concerned.

(4) "Court" means—

(a) the High Court; or

(b) in Scotland, the Court of Session.

[2107]

108 Requirements on applicants

(1) The Treasury may by regulations impose requirements on applicants under section 107.

(2) The court may not determine an application under that section if the applicant has failed to comply with a prescribed requirement.

(3) The regulations may, in particular, include provision—

(a) as to the persons to whom, and periods within which, notice of an application must be given;

(b) enabling the court to waive a requirement of the regulations in prescribed circumstances.

[2108]

NOTES

Regulations: the Financial Services and Markets Act 2000 (Control of Business Transfers) (Requirements on Applicants) Regulations 2001, SI 2001/3625 at **[4511]**.

109 Scheme reports

(1) An application under section 107 in respect of an insurance business transfer scheme must be accompanied by a report on the terms of the scheme ("a scheme report").

(2) A scheme report may be made only by a person—

(a) appearing to the Authority to have the skills necessary to enable him to make a proper report; and

(b) nominated or approved for the purpose by the Authority.

(3) A scheme report must be made in a form approved by the Authority.

[2109]

110 Right to participate in proceedings

On an application under section 107, the following are also entitled to be heard—

(a) the Authority, and

(b) any person (including an employee of the authorised person concerned or of the transferee) who alleges that he would be adversely affected by the carrying out of the scheme.

[2110]

111 Sanction of the court for business transfer schemes

(1) This section sets out the conditions which must be satisfied before the court may make an order under this section sanctioning an insurance business transfer scheme or a banking business transfer scheme.

(2) The court must be satisfied that—

(a) the appropriate certificates have been obtained (as to which see Parts I and II of Schedule 12);

(b) the transferee has the authorisation required (if any) to enable the business, or part, which is to be transferred to be carried on in the place to which it is to be transferred (or will have it before the scheme takes effect).

(3) The court must consider that, in all the circumstances of the case, it is appropriate to sanction the scheme.

[2111]

112 Effect of order sanctioning business transfer scheme

(1) If the court makes an order under section 111(1), it may by that or any subsequent order make such provision (if any) as it thinks fit—

(a) for the transfer to the transferee of the whole or any part of the undertaking concerned and of any property or liabilities of the authorised person concerned;

(b) for the allotment or appropriation by the transferee of any shares, debentures, policies or other similar interests in the transferee which under the scheme are to be allotted or appropriated to or for any other person;

(c) for the continuation by (or against) the transferee of any pending legal proceedings by (or against) the authorised person concerned;

(d) with respect to such incidental, consequential and supplementary matters as are, in its opinion, necessary to secure that the scheme is fully and effectively carried out.

(2) An order under subsection (1)(a) may—

(a) transfer property or liabilities whether or not the authorised person concerned otherwise has the capacity to effect the transfer in question;

(b) make provision in relation to property which was held by the authorised person concerned as trustee;

(c) make provision as to future or contingent rights or liabilities of the authorised person concerned, including provision as to the construction of instruments (including wills) under which such rights or liabilities may arise;

(d) make provision as to the consequences of the transfer in relation to any [occupational pension scheme (within the meaning of section 150(5) of the Finance Act 2004)] operated by or on behalf of the authorised person concerned.

(3) If an order under subsection (1) makes provision for the transfer of property or liabilities—

(a) the property is transferred to and vests in, and

(b) the liabilities are transferred to and become liabilities of,

the transferee as a result of the order.

(4) But if any property or liability included in the order is governed by the law of any country or territory outside the United Kingdom, the order may require the authorised person concerned, if the transferee so requires, to take all necessary steps for securing that the transfer to the transferee of the property or liability is fully effective under the law of that country or territory.

(5) Property transferred as the result of an order under subsection (1) may, if the court so directs, vest in the transferee free from any charge which is (as a result of the scheme) to cease to have effect.

(6) An order under subsection (1) which makes provision for the transfer of property is to be treated as an instrument of transfer for the purposes of the provisions mentioned in subsection (7) and any other enactment requiring the delivery of an instrument of transfer for the registration of property.

(7) The provisions are—

(a) section 183(1) of the Companies Act 1985;

(b) Article 193(1) and (2) of the Companies (Northern Ireland) Order 1986.

(8) If the court makes an order under section 111(1) in relation to an insurance business transfer scheme, it may by that or any subsequent order make such provision (if any) as it thinks fit—

(a) for dealing with the interests of any person who, within such time and in such manner as the court may direct, objects to the scheme;

(b) for the dissolution, without winding up, of the authorised person concerned;

(c) for the reduction, on such terms and subject to such conditions (if any) as it thinks fit, of the benefits payable under—

(i) any description of policy, or

(ii) policies generally,

entered into by the authorised person concerned and transferred as a result of the scheme.

(9) If, in the case of an insurance business transfer scheme, the authorised person concerned is not an EEA firm, it is immaterial for the purposes of subsection (1)(a), (c) or (d) or subsection (2), (3) or (4) that the law applicable to any of the contracts of insurance included in the transfer is the law of an EEA State other than the United Kingdom.

(10) The transferee must, if an insurance or banking business transfer scheme is sanctioned by the court, deposit two office copies of the order made under subsection (1) with the Authority within 10 days of the making of the order.

(11) But the Authority may extend that period.

(12) "Property" includes property, rights and powers of any description.

(13) "Liabilities" includes duties.

(14) "Shares" and "debentures" have the same meaning as in—

(a) the Companies Act 1985; or

(b) in Northern Ireland, the Companies (Northern Ireland) Order 1986.

(15) "Charge" includes a mortgage (or, in Scotland, a security over property).

[2112]

NOTES

Sub-s (2): words in square brackets substituted by the Taxation of Pension Schemes (Consequential Amendments) Order 2006, SI 2006/745, art 17, as from 6 April 2006.

Income and Corporation Taxes Act 1988, s 611: repealed by the Finance Act 2004, s 326, Sch 42, Pt 3, as from 6 April 2006.

PART II FSMA 2000

113 Appointment of actuary in relation to reduction of benefits

(1) This section applies if an order has been made under section 111(1).

(2) The court making the order may, on the application of the Authority, appoint an independent actuary—

(a) to investigate the business transferred under the scheme; and

(b) to report to the Authority on any reduction in the benefits payable under policies entered into by the authorised person concerned that, in the opinion of the actuary, ought to be made.

[2113]

114 Rights of certain policyholders

(1) This section applies in relation to an insurance business transfer scheme if—

(a) the authorised person concerned is an authorised person other than an EEA firm qualifying for authorisation under Schedule 3;

(b) the court has made an order under section 111 in relation to the scheme; and

(c) an EEA State other than the United Kingdom is, as regards any policy included in the transfer which evidences a contract of insurance, the State of the commitment or the EEA State in which the risk is situated ("the EEA State concerned").

(2) The court must direct that notice of the making of the order, or the execution of any instrument, giving effect to the transfer must be published by the transferee in the EEA State concerned.

(3) A notice under subsection (2) must specify such period as the court may direct as the period during which the policyholder may exercise any right which he has to cancel the policy.

(4) The order or instrument mentioned in subsection (2) does not bind the policyholder if—

(a) the notice required under that subsection is not published; or

(b) the policyholder cancels the policy during the period specified in the notice given under that subsection.

(5) The law of the EEA State concerned governs—

(a) whether the policyholder has a right to cancel the policy; and

(b) the conditions, if any, subject to which any such right may be exercised.

(6) Paragraph 6 of Schedule 12 applies for the purposes of this section as it applies for the purposes of that Schedule.

[2114]

Business transfers outside the United Kingdom

115 Certificates for purposes of insurance business transfers overseas

Part III of Schedule 12 makes provision about certificates which the Authority may issue in relation to insurance business transfers taking place outside the United Kingdom.

[2115]

116 Effect of insurance business transfers authorised in other EEA States

(1) This section applies if, as a result of an authorised transfer, an EEA firm falling within paragraph 5(d) of Schedule 3 transfers to another body all its rights and obligations under any UK policies.

(2) This section also applies if, as a result of an authorised transfer, a company authorised in an EEA State other than the United Kingdom under [Article 51 of the life assurance consolidation directive], or Article 23 of the first non-life insurance directive, transfers to another body all its rights and obligations under any UK policies.

(3) If appropriate notice of the execution of an instrument giving effect to the transfer is published, the instrument has the effect in law—

(a) of transferring to the transferee all the transferor's rights and obligations under the UK policies to which the instrument applies, and

(b) if the instrument so provides, of securing the continuation by or against the transferee of any legal proceedings by or against the transferor which relate to those rights and obligations.

(4) No agreement or consent is required before subsection (3) has the effects mentioned.

(5) "Authorised transfer" means—

(a) in subsection (1), a transfer authorised in the home State of the EEA firm in accordance with—

[(i) Article 14 of the life assurance consolidation directive; or]

(ii) Article 12 of the third non-life directive; and

(b) in subsection (2), a transfer authorised in an EEA State other than the United Kingdom in accordance with—

[(i) Article 53 of the life assurance consolidation directive; or]

(ii) Article 28a of the first non-life directive.

(6) "UK policy" means a policy evidencing a contract of insurance (other than a contract of reinsurance) to which the applicable law is the law of any part of the United Kingdom.

(7) "Appropriate notice" means—

(a) if the UK policy evidences a contract of insurance in relation to which an EEA State other than the United Kingdom is the State of the commitment, notice given in accordance with the law of that State;

(b) if the UK policy evidences a contract of insurance where the risk is situated in an EEA State other than the United Kingdom, notice given in accordance with the law of that EEA State;

(c) in any other case, notice given in accordance with the applicable law.

(8) Paragraph 6 of Schedule 12 applies for the purposes of this section as it applies for the purposes of that Schedule.

[2116]

PART II FSMA 2000

NOTES

Sub-ss (2), (5): words in square brackets substituted by the Life Assurance Consolidation Directive (Consequential Amendments) Regulations 2004, SI 2004/3379, reg 6(1), (2), as from 11 January 2005.

Modifications

117 Power to modify this Part

The Treasury may by regulations—

(a) provide for prescribed provisions of this Part to have effect in relation to prescribed cases with such modifications as may be prescribed;

(b) make such amendments to any provision of this Part as they consider appropriate for the more effective operation of that or any other provision of this Part.

[2117]

PART VIII
PENALTIES FOR MARKET ABUSE

NOTES

Note: this Part, and other provisions of this Act (particularly in Part VI) are amended by Regulations bringing into effect European Parliament and Council Directive 2003/6/EC on insider dealing and market manipulation (market abuse). By Article 18 of that Directive, Member States were required to bring into force the laws, regulations and administration provisions necessary to comply with the Directive not later than 12 October 2004. The Market Abuse Directive is implemented, in part, by the Financial Services and Markets Act 2000 (Market Abuse) Regulations 2005, SI 2005/381, in part by the Investment Recommendation (Media) Regulations 2005, SI 2005/382, and in part by the FSA using its powers to make rules under this Act. The amendments made by the Financial Services and Markets Act 2000 (Market Abuse) Regulations 2005 come into force on 17 March 2005 for certain purposes and on 1 July 2005 otherwise. The amendments made by those Regulations are noted to the appropriate sections of this Act.

Market abuse

[118 Market abuse

(1) For the purposes of this Act, market abuse is behaviour (whether by one person alone or by two or more persons jointly or in concert) which—

(a) occurs in relation to—
(i) qualifying investments admitted to trading on a prescribed market,
(ii) qualifying investments in respect of which a request for admission to trading on such a market has been made, or
(iii) in the case of subsection (2) or (3) behaviour, investments which are related investments in relation to such qualifying investments, and
(b) falls within any one or more of the types of behaviour set out in subsections (2) to (8).

(2) The first type of behaviour is where an insider deals, or attempts to deal, in a qualifying investment or related investment on the basis of inside information relating to the investment in question.

(3) The second is where an insider discloses inside information to another person otherwise than in the proper course of the exercise of his employment, profession or duties.

(4) The third is where the behaviour (not falling within subsection (2) or (3))—
(a) is based on information which is not generally available to those using the market but which, if available to a regular user of the market, would be, or would be likely to be, regarded by him as relevant when deciding the terms on which transactions in qualifying investments should be effected, and
(b) is likely to be regarded by a regular user of the market as a failure on the part of the person concerned to observe the standard of behaviour reasonably expected of a person in his position in relation to the market.

(5) The fourth is where the behaviour consists of effecting transactions or orders to trade (otherwise than for legitimate reasons and in conformity with accepted market practices on the relevant market) which—
(a) give, or are likely to give, a false or misleading impression as to the supply of, or demand for, or as to the price of, one or more qualifying investments, or
(b) secure the price of one or more such investments at an abnormal or artificial level.

(6) The fifth is where the behaviour consists of effecting transactions or orders to trade which employ fictitious devices or any other form of deception or contrivance.

(7) The sixth is where the behaviour consists of the dissemination of information by any means which gives, or is likely to give, a false or misleading impression as to a qualifying investment by a person who knew or could reasonably be expected to have known that the information was false or misleading.

(8) The seventh is where the behaviour (not falling within subsection (5), (6) or (7))—
(a) is likely to give a regular user of the market a false or misleading impression as to the supply of, demand for or price or value of, qualifying investments, or
(b) would be, or would be likely to be, regarded by a regular user of the market as behaviour that would distort, or would be likely to distort, the market in such an investment,

and the behaviour is likely to be regarded by a regular user of the market as a failure on the part of the person concerned to observe the standard of behaviour reasonably expected of a person in his position in relation to the market.

(9) Subsections (4) and (8) and the definition of "regular user" in section 130A(3) cease to have effect on 30 June 2008 and subsection (1)(b) is then to be read as no longer referring to those subsections.]

[2118]

NOTES

Substituted, together with ss 118B–118C for original s 118, by the Financial Services and Markets Act 2000 (Market Abuse) Regulations 2005, SI 2005/381, reg 5, Sch 2, para 1, as from 1 July 2005.

Orders: the Financial Services and Markets Act 2000 (Prescribed Markets and Qualifying Investments) Order 2001, SI 2001/996 at **[4106]**. Note, the 2001 Order was originally made under s 118(3) but, following the substitution of this section as noted above, now has effect as if made under s 130A(1) at **[2130A]**.

[118A Supplementary provision about certain behaviour

(1) Behaviour is to be taken into account for the purposes of this Part only if it occurs—
(a) in the United Kingdom, or
(b) in relation to—

(i) qualifying investments which are admitted to trading on a prescribed market situated in, or operating in, the United Kingdom,

(ii) qualifying investments for which a request for admission to trading on such a prescribed market has been made, or

(iii) in the case of section 118(2) and (3), investments which are related investments in relation to such qualifying investments.

(2) For the purposes of subsection (1), as it applies in relation to section 118(4) and (8), a prescribed market accessible electronically in the United Kingdom is to be treated as operating in the United Kingdom.

(3) For the purposes of section 118(4) and (8), the behaviour that is to be regarded as occurring in relation to qualifying investments includes behaviour which—

(a) occurs in relation to anything that is the subject matter, or whose price or value is expressed by reference to the price or value of the qualifying investments, or

(b) occurs in relation to investments (whether or not they are qualifying investments) whose subject matter is the qualifying investments.

(4) For the purposes of section 118(7), the dissemination of information by a person acting in the capacity of a journalist is to be assessed taking into account the codes governing his profession unless he derives, directly or indirectly, any advantage or profits from the dissemination of the information.

(5) Behaviour does not amount to market abuse for the purposes of this Act if—

(a) it conforms with a rule which includes a provision to the effect that behaviour conforming with the rule does not amount to market abuse,

(b) it conforms with the relevant provisions of Commission Regulation (EC) No 2273/2003 of 22 December 2003 implementing Directive 2003/6/EC of the European Parliament and of the Council as regards exemptions for buy-back programmes and stabilisation of financial instruments, or

(c) it is done by a person acting on behalf of a public authority in pursuit of monetary policies or policies with respect to exchange rates or the management of public debt or foreign exchange reserves.

(6) Subsections (2) and (3) cease to have effect on 30 June 2008.]

[2118A]

NOTES

Substituted as noted to s 118 at **[2118]**.

[118B Insiders

For the purposes of this Part an insider is any person who has inside information—

(a) as a result of his membership of an administrative, management or supervisory body of an issuer of qualifying investments,

(b) as a result of his holding in the capital of an issuer of qualifying investments,

(c) as a result of having access to the information through the exercise of his employment, profession or duties,

(d) as a result of his criminal activities, or

(e) which he has obtained by other means and which he knows, or could reasonably be expected to know, is inside information.]

[2118B]

NOTES

Substituted as noted to s 118 at **[2118]**.

[118C Inside information

(1) This section defines "inside information" for the purposes of this Part.

(2) In relation to qualifying investments, or related investments, which are not commodity derivatives, inside information is information of a precise nature which—

(a) is not generally available,

(b) relates, directly or indirectly, to one or more issuers of the qualifying investments or to one or more of the qualifying investments, and

(c) would, if generally available, be likely to have a significant effect on the price of the qualifying investments or on the price of related investments.

(3) In relation to qualifying investments or related investments which are commodity derivatives, inside information is information of a precise nature which—

(a) is not generally available,
(b) relates, directly or indirectly, to one or more such derivatives, and
(c) users of markets on which the derivatives are traded would expect to receive in accordance with any accepted market practices on those markets.

(4) In relation to a person charged with the execution of orders concerning any qualifying investments or related investments, inside information includes information conveyed by a client and related to the client's pending orders which—

(a) is of a precise nature,
(b) is not generally available,
(c) relates, directly or indirectly, to one or more issuers of qualifying investments or to one or more qualifying investments, and
(d) would, if generally available, be likely to have a significant effect on the price of those qualifying investments or the price of related investments.

(5) Information is precise if it—

(a) indicates circumstances that exist or may reasonably be expected to come into existence or an event that has occurred or may reasonably be expected to occur, and
(b) is specific enough to enable a conclusion to be drawn as to the possible effect of those circumstances or that event on the price of qualifying investments or related investments.

(6) Information would be likely to have a significant effect on price if and only if it is information of a kind which a reasonable investor would be likely to use as part of the basis of his investment decisions.

(7) For the purposes of subsection (3)(c), users of markets on which investments in commodity derivatives are traded are to be treated as expecting to receive information relating directly or indirectly to one or more such derivatives in accordance with any accepted market practices, which is—

(a) routinely made available to the users of those markets, or
(b) required to be disclosed in accordance with any statutory provision, market rules, or contracts or customs on the relevant underlying commodity market or commodity derivatives market.

(8) Information which can be obtained by research or analysis conducted by, or on behalf of, users of a market is to be regarded, for the purposes of this Part, as being generally available to them.]

[2118C]

NOTES

Substituted as noted to s 118 at **[2118]**.

The code

119 The code

(1) The Authority must prepare and issue a code containing such provisions as the Authority considers will give appropriate guidance to those determining whether or not behaviour amounts to market abuse.

(2) The code may among other things specify—

(a) descriptions of behaviour that, in the opinion of the Authority, amount to market abuse;
(b) descriptions of behaviour that, in the opinion of the Authority, do not amount to market abuse;
(c) factors that, in the opinion of the Authority, are to be taken into account in determining whether or not behaviour amounts to market abuse;
[(d) descriptions of behaviour that are accepted market practices in relation to one or more specified markets;
(e) descriptions of behaviour that are not accepted market practices in relation to one or more specified markets].

[(2A) In determining, for the purposes of subsections (2)(d) and (2)(e) or otherwise, what are and what are not accepted market practices, the Authority must have regard to the factors and procedures laid down in Articles 2 and 3 respectively of Commission Directive 2004/72/EC of 29 April 2004 implementing Directive 2003/6/EC of the European Parliament and of the Council.]

(3) The code may make different provision in relation to persons, cases or circumstances of different descriptions.

(4) The Authority may at any time alter or replace the code.

(5) If the code is altered or replaced, the altered or replacement code must be issued by the Authority.

(6) A code issued under this section must be published by the Authority in the way appearing to the Authority to be best calculated to bring it to the attention of the public.

(7) The Authority must, without delay, give the Treasury a copy of any code published under this section.

(8) The Authority may charge a reasonable fee for providing a person with a copy of the code.

[2119]

NOTES

Sub-s (2): paras (d), (e) added by the Financial Services and Markets Act 2000 (Market Abuse) Regulations 2005, SI 2005/381, reg 5, Sch 2, para 2(1), (2), as from 1 July 2005.

Sub-s (2A): inserted by SI 2005/381, reg 5, Sch 2, para 2(1), (3), as from 1 July 2005.

120 Provisions included in the Authority's code by reference to the City Code

(1) The Authority may include in a code issued by it under section 119 ("the Authority's code") provision to the effect that in its opinion behaviour conforming with the City Code—

(a) does not amount to market abuse;
(b) does not amount to market abuse in specified circumstances; or
(c) does not amount to market abuse if engaged in by a specified description of person.

(2) But the Treasury's approval is required before any such provision may be included in the Authority's code.

(3) If the Authority's code includes provision of a kind authorised by subsection (1), the Authority must keep itself informed of the way in which the Panel on Takeovers and Mergers interprets and administers the relevant provisions of the City Code.

(4) "City Code" means the City Code on Takeovers and Mergers issued by the Panel as it has effect at the time when the behaviour occurs.

(5) "Specified" means specified in the Authority's code.

[2120]

121 Codes: procedure

(1) Before issuing a code under section 119, the Authority must publish a draft of the proposed code in the way appearing to the Authority to be best calculated to bring it to the attention of the public.

(2) The draft must be accompanied by—

(a) a cost benefit analysis; and
(b) notice that representations about the proposal may be made to the Authority within a specified time.

(3) Before issuing the proposed code, the Authority must have regard to any representations made to it in accordance with subsection (2)(b).

(4) If the Authority issues the proposed code it must publish an account, in general terms, of—

(a) the representations made to it in accordance with subsection (2)(b); and
(b) its response to them.

(5) If the code differs from the draft published under subsection (1) in a way which is, in the opinion of the Authority, significant—

(a) the Authority must (in addition to complying with subsection (4)) publish details of the difference; and

(b) those details must be accompanied by a cost benefit analysis.

(6) Subsections (1) to (5) do not apply if the Authority considers that there is an urgent need to publish the code.

(7) Neither subsection (2)(a) nor subsection (5)(b) applies if the Authority considers—

(a) that, making the appropriate comparison, there will be no increase in costs; or

(b) that, making that comparison, there will be an increase in costs but the increase will be of minimal significance.

(8) The Authority may charge a reasonable fee for providing a person with a copy of a draft published under subsection (1).

(9) This section also applies to a proposal to alter or replace a code.

(10) "Cost benefit analysis" means an estimate of the costs together with an analysis of the benefits that will arise—

(a) if the proposed code is issued; or

(b) if subsection (5)(b) applies, from the code that has been issued.

(11) "The appropriate comparison" means—

(a) in relation to subsection (2)(a), a comparison between the overall position if the code is issued and the overall position if it is not issued;

(b) in relation to subsection (5)(b), a comparison between the overall position after the issuing of the code and the overall position before it was issued.

[2121]

122 Effect of the code

(1) If a person behaves in a way which is described (in the code in force under section 119 at the time of the behaviour) as behaviour that, in the Authority's opinion, does not amount to market abuse that behaviour of his is to be taken, for the purposes of this Act, as not amounting to market abuse.

(2) Otherwise, the code in force under section 119 at the time when particular behaviour occurs may be relied on so far as it indicates whether or not that behaviour should be taken to amount to market abuse.

[2122]

Power to impose penalties

123 Power to impose penalties in cases of market abuse

(1) If the Authority is satisfied that a person ("A")—

(a) is or has engaged in market abuse, or

(b) by taking or refraining from taking any action has required or encouraged another person or persons to engage in behaviour which, if engaged in by A, would amount to market abuse,

it may impose on him a penalty of such amount as it considers appropriate.

(2) But the Authority may not impose a penalty on a person if, having considered any representations made to it in response to a warning notice, there are reasonable grounds for it to be satisfied that—

(a) he believed, on reasonable grounds, that his behaviour did not fall within paragraph (a) or (b) of subsection (1), or

(b) he took all reasonable precautions and exercised all due diligence to avoid behaving in a way which fell within paragraph (a) or (b) of that subsection.

(3) If the Authority is entitled to impose a penalty on a person under this section it may, instead of imposing a penalty on him, publish a statement to the effect that he has engaged in market abuse.

[2123]

Statement of policy

124 Statement of policy

(1) The Authority must prepare and issue a statement of its policy with respect to—
(a) the imposition of penalties under section 123; and
(b) the amount of penalties under that section.

(2) The Authority's policy in determining what the amount of a penalty should be must include having regard to—
(a) whether the behaviour in respect of which the penalty is to be imposed had an adverse effect on the market in question and, if it did, how serious that effect was;
(b) the extent to which that behaviour was deliberate or reckless; and
(c) whether the person on whom the penalty is to be imposed is an individual.

(3) A statement issued under this section must include an indication of the circumstances in which the Authority is to be expected to regard a person as—
(a) having a reasonable belief that his behaviour did not amount to market abuse; or
(b) having taken reasonable precautions and exercised due diligence to avoid engaging in market abuse.

(4) The Authority may at any time alter or replace a statement issued under this section.

(5) If a statement issued under this section is altered or replaced, the Authority must issue the altered or replacement statement.

(6) In exercising, or deciding whether to exercise, its power under section 123 in the case of any particular behaviour, the Authority must have regard to any statement published under this section and in force at the time when the behaviour concerned occurred.

(7) A statement issued under this section must be published by the Authority in the way appearing to the Authority to be best calculated to bring it to the attention of the public.

(8) The Authority may charge a reasonable fee for providing a person with a copy of a statement published under this section.

(9) The Authority must, without delay, give the Treasury a copy of any statement which it publishes under this section.

[2124]

125 Statement of policy: procedure

(1) Before issuing a statement of policy under section 124, the Authority must publish a draft of the proposed statement in the way appearing to the Authority to be best calculated to bring it to the attention of the public.

(2) The draft must be accompanied by notice that representations about the proposal may be made to the Authority within a specified time.

(3) Before issuing the proposed statement, the Authority must have regard to any representations made to it in accordance with subsection (2).

(4) If the Authority issues the proposed statement it must publish an account, in general terms, of—
(a) the representations made to it in accordance with subsection (2); and
(b) its response to them.

(5) If the statement differs from the draft published under subsection (1) in a way which is, in the opinion of the Authority, significant, the Authority must (in addition to complying with subsection (4)) publish details of the difference.

(6) The Authority may charge a reasonable fee for providing a person with a copy of a draft published under subsection (1).

(7) This section also applies to a proposal to alter or replace a statement.

[2125]

Procedure

126 Warning notices

(1) If the Authority proposes to take action against a person under section 123, it must give him a warning notice.

(2) A warning notice about a proposal to impose a penalty must state the amount of the proposed penalty.

(3) A warning notice about a proposal to publish a statement must set out the terms of the proposed statement.

[2126]

127 Decision notices and right to refer to Tribunal

(1) If the Authority decides to take action against a person under section 123, it must give him a decision notice.

(2) A decision notice about the imposition of a penalty must state the amount of the penalty.

(3) A decision notice about the publication of a statement must set out the terms of the statement.

(4) If the Authority decides to take action against a person under section 123, that person may refer the matter to the Tribunal.

[2127]

Miscellaneous

128 Suspension of investigations

(1) If the Authority considers it desirable or expedient because of the exercise or possible exercise of a power relating to market abuse, it may direct a recognised investment exchange or recognised clearing house—

(a) to terminate, suspend or limit the scope of any inquiry which the exchange or clearing house is conducting under its rules; or

(b) not to conduct an inquiry which the exchange or clearing house proposes to conduct under its rules.

(2) A direction under this section—

(a) must be given to the exchange or clearing house concerned by notice in writing; and

(b) is enforceable, on the application of the Authority, by injunction or, in Scotland, by an order under section 45 of the Court of Session Act 1988.

(3) The Authority's powers relating to market abuse are its powers—

(a) to impose penalties under section 123; or

(b) to appoint a person to conduct an investigation under section 168 in a case falling within subsection (2)(d) of that section.

[2128]

129 Power of court to impose penalty in cases of market abuse

(1) The Authority may on an application to the court under section 381 or 383 request the court to consider whether the circumstances are such that a penalty should be imposed on the person to whom the application relates.

(2) The court may, if it considers it appropriate, make an order requiring the person concerned to pay to the Authority a penalty of such amount as it considers appropriate.

[2129]

130 Guidance

(1) The Treasury may from time to time issue written guidance for the purpose of helping relevant authorities to determine the action to be taken in cases where behaviour occurs which is behaviour—

(a) with respect to which the power in section 123 appears to be exercisable; and

(b) which appears to involve the commission of an offence under section 397 of this Act or Part V of the Criminal Justice Act 1993 (insider dealing).

(2) The Treasury must obtain the consent of the Attorney General and the Secretary of State before issuing any guidance under this section.

(3) In this section "relevant authorities"—

(a) in relation to England and Wales, means the Secretary of State, the Authority, the Director of the Serious Fraud Office and the Director of Public Prosecutions;

(b) in relation to Northern Ireland, means the Secretary of State, the Authority, the Director of the Serious Fraud Office and the Director of Public Prosecutions for Northern Ireland.

(4) Subsections (1) to (3) do not apply to Scotland.

(5) In relation to Scotland, the Lord Advocate may from time to time, after consultation with the Treasury, issue written guidance for the purpose of helping the Authority to determine the action to be taken in cases where behaviour mentioned in subsection (1) occurs.

[2130]

NOTES

Attorney General: any function of the Attorney General may be exercised by the Solicitor General; see the Law Officers Act 1997, s 1.

[130A Interpretation and supplementary provision

(1) The Treasury may by order specify (whether by name or description)—

(a) the markets which are prescribed markets for the purposes of specified provisions of this Part, and

(b) the investments that are qualifying investments in relation to the prescribed markets.

(2) An order may prescribe different investments or descriptions of investment in relation to different markets or descriptions of market.

(3) In this Part—

"accepted market practices" means practices that are reasonably expected in the financial market or markets in question and are accepted by the Authority or, in the case of a market situated in another EEA State, the competent authority of that EEA State within the meaning of Directive 2003/6/EC of the European Parliament and of the Council of 28 January 2003 on insider dealing and market manipulation (market abuse),

"behaviour" includes action or inaction,

"dealing", in relation to an investment, means acquiring or disposing of the investment whether as principal or agent or directly or indirectly, and includes agreeing to acquire or dispose of the investment, and entering into and bringing to an end a contract creating it,

"investment" is to be read with section 22 and Schedule 2,

"regular user", in relation to a particular market, means a reasonable person who regularly deals on that market in investments of the kind in question,

"related investment", in relation to a qualifying investment, means an investment whose price or value depends on the price or value of the qualifying investment.

(4) Any reference in this Act to a person engaged in market abuse is to a person engaged in market abuse either alone or with one or more other persons.]

[2130A]

NOTES

Inserted by the Financial Services and Markets Act 2000 (Market Abuse) Regulations 2005, SI 2005/381, reg 5, Sch 2, para 3, as from 1 July 2005.

Orders: the Financial Services and Markets Act 2000 (Prescribed Markets and Qualifying Investments) Order 2001, SI 2001/996 at **[4106]**. Note that the 2001 Order was originally made under s 118(3) of this Act but, following the substitution of that section as noted thereto, now has effect as if made under sub-s (1) above.

131 Effect on transactions

The imposition of a penalty under this Part does not make any transaction void or unenforceable.

[2131]

[131A Protected Disclosures

(1) A disclosure which satisfies the following three conditions is not to be taken to breach any restriction on the disclosure of information (however imposed).

PART II
FSMA 2000

(2) The first condition is that the information or other matter—

(a) causes the person making the disclosure (the discloser) to know or suspect, or

(b) gives him reasonable grounds for knowing or suspecting, that another person has engaged in market abuse.

(3) The second condition is that the information or other matter disclosed came to the discloser in the course of his trade, profession, business or employment.

(4) The third condition is that the disclosure is made to the Authority or to a nominated officer as soon as is practicable after the information or other matter comes to the discloser.

(5) A disclosure to a nominated officer is a disclosure which is made to a person nominated by the discloser's employer to receive disclosures under this section, and is made in the course of the discloser's employment and in accordance with the procedure established by the employer for the purpose.

(6) For the purposes of this section, references to a person's employer include any body, association or organisation (including a voluntary organisation) in connection with whose activities the person exercises a function (whether or not for gain or reward) and references to employment must be construed accordingly.]

[2131A]

NOTES

Inserted by the Financial Services and Markets Act 2000 (Market Abuse) Regulations 2005, SI 2005/381, reg 5, Sch 2, para 4, as from 1 July 2005.

PART IX
HEARINGS AND APPEALS

132 The Financial Services and Markets Tribunal

(1) For the purposes of this Act, there is to be a tribunal known as the Financial Services and Markets Tribunal (but referred to in this Act as "the Tribunal").

(2) The Tribunal is to have the functions conferred on it by or under this Act.

(3) The Lord Chancellor may by rules make such provision as appears to him to be necessary or expedient in respect of the conduct of proceedings before the Tribunal.

(4) Schedule 13 is to have effect as respects the Tribunal and its proceedings (but does not limit the Lord Chancellor's powers under this section).

[2132]

NOTES

Note: a reference in this section to this Act includes a reference to the Electronic Commerce Directive (Financial Services and Markets) Regulations 2002, SI 2002/1775; see reg 12(4) of those Regulations at **[4650]**.

Rules: the Financial Services and Markets Tribunal Rules 2001, SI 2001/2476 at **[4409]**.

133 Proceedings: general provision

(1) A reference to the Tribunal under this Act must be made before the end of—

(a) the period of 28 days beginning with the date on which the decision notice or supervisory notice in question is given; or

(b) such other period as may be specified in rules made under section 132.

(2) Subject to rules made under section 132, the Tribunal may allow a reference to be made after the end of that period.

(3) On a reference the Tribunal may consider any evidence relating to the subject-matter of the reference, whether or not it was available to the Authority at the material time.

(4) On a reference the Tribunal must determine what (if any) is the appropriate action for the Authority to take in relation to the matter referred to it.

(5) On determining a reference, the Tribunal must remit the matter to the Authority with such directions (if any) as the Tribunal considers appropriate for giving effect to its determination.

(6) In determining a reference made as a result of a decision notice, the Tribunal may not direct the Authority to take action which the Authority would not, as a result of section 388(2), have had power to take when giving the decision notice.

(7) In determining a reference made as a result of a supervisory notice, the Tribunal may not direct the Authority to take action which would have otherwise required the giving of a decision notice.

(8) The Tribunal may, on determining a reference, make recommendations as to the Authority's regulating provisions or its procedures.

(9) The Authority must not take the action specified in a decision notice—
(a) during the period within which the matter to which the decision notice relates may be referred to the Tribunal; and
(b) if the matter is so referred, until the reference, and any appeal against the Tribunal's determination, has been finally disposed of.

(10) The Authority must act in accordance with the determination of, and any direction given by, the Tribunal.

(11) An order of the Tribunal may be enforced—
(a) as if it were an order of a county court; or
(b) in Scotland, as if it were an order of the Court of Session.

(12) "Supervisory notice" has the same meaning as in section 395.

[2133]

NOTES

Note: a reference in this section to this Act includes a reference to the Electronic Commerce Directive (Financial Services and Markets) Regulations 2002, SI 2002/1775; see reg 12(3)(c) of those Regulations at **[4650]**.

References to the Tribunal: may be made under the following provisions of this Act: ss 53(7) (read together with s 53(9)), 55(1), (2), 57(5), 58(5), 62(4), 63(5), 67(7), 76(6), 77(5), 78(3) (read together with s 78(6)), 87N (in relation to notices given under ss 87M and 87O), 89(4), 92(7), 127(4), 185(7), 186(5), 187(4), 197(6) (read together with 197(8)), 200(5)(b), 208(4), 245(2)(b), 252(4), 255(2), 256(5), 259(6) (read together with 259(10)), 260(2)(b), 268(3) (read together with 268(4)), 269(3), 271(3)(b), 276(2)(b), 280(2)(b), 282(3) (read together with 282(4)), 282(6) (read together with 282(8)), 320(4), 321(10), (11), 331(9), 345(5), 386(3), 388(5), 393(9), (11), Sch 3, para 15A(6), Sch 3, para 19(7A), (12), Sch 3, para 20(4A), Sch 3, para 22(3)(b).

Legal assistance before the Tribunal

134 Legal assistance scheme

(1) The Lord Chancellor may by regulations establish a scheme governing the provision of legal assistance in connection with proceedings before the Tribunal.

(2) If the Lord Chancellor establishes a scheme under subsection (1), it must provide that a person is eligible for assistance only if—
(a) he falls within subsection (3); and
(b) he fulfils such other criteria (if any) as may be prescribed as a result of section 135(1)(d).

(3) A person falls within this subsection if he is an individual who has referred a matter to the Tribunal under section 127(4).

(4) In this Part of this Act "the legal assistance scheme" means any scheme in force under subsection (1).

[2134]

NOTES

Regulations: the Financial Services and Markets Tribunal (Legal Assistance) Regulations 2001, SI 2001/3632 at **[4517]**; the Financial Services and Markets Tribunal (Legal Assistance Scheme—Costs) Regulations 2001, SI 2001/3633 at **[4560]**.

135 Provisions of the legal assistance scheme

(1) The legal assistance scheme may, in particular, make provision as to—
(a) the kinds of legal assistance that may be provided;

(b) the persons by whom legal assistance may be provided;
(c) the manner in which applications for legal assistance are to be made;
(d) the criteria on which eligibility for legal assistance is to be determined;
(e) the persons or bodies by whom applications are to be determined;
(f) appeals against refusals of applications;
(g) the revocation or variation of decisions;
(h) its administration and the enforcement of its provisions.

(2) Legal assistance under the legal assistance scheme may be provided subject to conditions or restrictions, including conditions as to the making of contributions by the person to whom it is provided.

[2135]

NOTES

Regulations: the Financial Services and Markets Tribunal (Legal Assistance) Regulations 2001, SI 2001/3632 at **[4517]**; the Financial Services and Markets Tribunal (Legal Assistance Scheme—Costs) Regulations 2001, SI 2001/3633 at **[4560]**.

136 Funding of the legal assistance scheme

(1) The Authority must pay to the Lord Chancellor such sums at such times as he may, from time to time, determine in respect of the anticipated or actual cost of legal assistance provided in connection with proceedings before the Tribunal under the legal assistance scheme.

(2) In order to enable it to pay any sum which it is obliged to pay under subsection (1), the Authority must make rules requiring the payment to it by authorised persons or any class of authorised person of specified amounts or amounts calculated in a specified way.

(3) Sums received by the Lord Chancellor under subsection (1) must be paid into the Consolidated Fund.

(4) The Lord Chancellor must, out of money provided by Parliament fund the cost of legal assistance provided in connection with proceedings before the Tribunal under the legal assistance scheme.

(5) Subsection (6) applies if, as respects a period determined by the Lord Chancellor, the amount paid to him under subsection (1) as respects that period exceeds the amount he has expended in that period under subsection (4).

(6) The Lord Chancellor must—
(a) repay, out of money provided by Parliament, the excess to the Authority; or
(b) take the excess into account on the next occasion on which he makes a determination under subsection (1).

(7) The Authority must make provision for any sum repaid to it under subsection (6)(a)—
(a) to be distributed among—
(i) the authorised persons on whom a levy was imposed in the period in question as a result of rules made under subsection (2); or
(ii) such of those persons as it may determine;
(b) to be applied in order to reduce any amounts which those persons, or such of them as it may determine, are or will be liable to pay to the Authority, whether under rules made under subsection (2) or otherwise; or
(c) to be partly so distributed and partly so applied.

(8) If the Authority considers that it is not practicable to deal with any part of a sum repaid to it under subsection (6)(a) in accordance with provision made by it as a result of subsection (7), it may, with the consent the Lord Chancellor, apply or dispose of that part of that sum in such manner as it considers appropriate.

(9) "Specified" means specified in the rules.

[2136]

Appeals

137 Appeal on a point of law

(1) A party to a reference to the Tribunal may with permission appeal—

(a) to the Court of Appeal, or
(b) in Scotland, to the Court of Session,

on a point of law arising from a decision of the Tribunal disposing of the reference.

(2) "Permission" means permission given by the Tribunal or by the Court of Appeal or (in Scotland) the Court of Session.

(3) If, on an appeal under subsection (1), the court considers that the decision of the Tribunal was wrong in law, it may—

(a) remit the matter to the Tribunal for rehearing and determination by it; or
(b) itself make a determination.

(4) An appeal may not be brought from a decision of the Court of Appeal under subsection (3) except with the leave of—

(a) the Court of Appeal; or
(b) the House of Lords.

(5) An appeal lies, with the leave of the Court of Session or the *House of Lords*, from any decision of the Court of Session under this section, and such leave may be given on such terms as to costs, expenses or otherwise as the Court of Session or the *House of Lords* may determine.

(6) Rules made under section 132 may make provision for regulating or prescribing any matters incidental to or consequential on an appeal under this section.

[2137]

NOTES

Sub-s (4): para (b) substituted by the Constitutional Reform Act 2005, s 40, Sch 9, Pt 1, para 70(a), as from a day to be appointed, as follows—

"(b) the Supreme Court.".

Sub-s (5): for the words in italics there are substituted the words "Supreme Court" by the Constitutional Reform Act 2005, s 40, Sch 9, Pt 1, para 70(b), as from a day to be appointed.

Rules made under section 132: see that section at **[2132]**.

PART X
RULES AND GUIDANCE

CHAPTER I
RULE-MAKING POWERS

138 General rule-making power

(1) The Authority may make such rules applying to authorised persons—

(a) with respect to the carrying on by them of regulated activities, or
(b) with respect to the carrying on by them of activities which are not regulated activities,

as appear to it to be necessary or expedient for the purpose of protecting the interests of consumers.

[(1A) The Authority may also make such rules applying to authorised persons who are investment firms or credit institutions, with respect to the provision by them of a relevant ancillary service, as appear to the Authority to be necessary or expedient for the purpose of protecting the interests of consumers.

(1B) "Credit institution" means—

(a) a credit institution authorised under the banking consolidation directive, or
(b) an institution which would satisfy the requirements for authorisation as a credit institution under that directive if it had its registered office (or if it does not have a registered office, its head office) in an EEA State.

(1C) "Relevant ancillary service" means any service of a kind mentioned in Section B of Annex I to the markets in financial instruments directive the provision of which does not involve the carrying on of a regulated activity.]

(2) Rules made under this section are referred to in this Act as the Authority's general rules.

(3) The Authority's power to make general rules is not limited by any other power which it has to make regulating provisions.

(4) The Authority's general rules may make provision applying to authorised persons even though there is no relationship between the authorised persons to whom the rules will apply and the persons whose interests will be protected by the rules.

(5) General rules may contain requirements which take into account, in the case of an authorised person who is a member of a group, any activity of another member of the group.

(6) General rules may not—

(a) make provision prohibiting an EEA firm from carrying on, or holding itself out as carrying on, any activity which it has permission conferred by Part II of Schedule 3 to carry on in the United Kingdom;

(b) make provision, as respects an EEA firm, about any matter responsibility for which is, under any of the single market directives, reserved to the firm's home state regulator.

(7) "Consumers" means persons—

(a) who use, have used, or are or may be contemplating using, any of the services provided by—

(i) authorised persons in carrying on regulated activities; ...

[(ia) authorised persons who are investment firms or credit institutions in providing a relevant ancillary service; or]

(ii) persons acting as appointed representatives;

(b) who have rights or interests which are derived from, or are otherwise attributable to, the use of any such services by other persons; or

(c) who have rights or interests which may be adversely affected by the use of any such services by persons acting on their behalf or in a fiduciary capacity in relation to them.

(8) If an authorised person is carrying on a regulated activity in his capacity as a trustee, the persons who are, have been or may be beneficiaries of the trust are to be treated as persons who use, have used or are or may be contemplating using services provided by the authorised person in his carrying on of that activity.

(9) For the purposes of subsection (7) a person who deals with an authorised person in the course of the authorised person's carrying on of a regulated activity is to be treated as using services provided by the authorised person in carrying on those activities.

[2138]

NOTES

Sub-ss (1A)–(1C): inserted by the Financial Services and Markets Act 2000 (Markets in Financial Instruments) (Modification of Powers) Regulations 2006, SI 2006/2975, regs 2, 3(a), as from 6 December 2006, subject to transitional provisions as noted below.

Sub-s (7): word omitted from sub-para (a)(i) repealed, and sub-para (a)(ia) inserted, by SI 2006/2975, regs 2, 3(b), as from 6 December 2006, subject to transitional provisions as noted below.

Transitional provisions: the Financial Services and Markets Act 2000 (Markets in Financial Instruments) (Modification of Powers) Regulations 2006, SI 2006/2975, reg 14 provides as follows:

"14 Transitional provision: rules under sections 138 and 145 of the Act

If, before these Regulations come into force—

(a) the Authority has taken any step mentioned in section 155 of the Act in relation to rules proposed to be made under section 138 or 145 of the Act as amended by these Regulations; and

(b) that step would have satisfied a requirement of section 155 in relation to those rules had it been taken after these Regulations come into force,

the step shall be treated as having satisfied that requirement of section 155.".

Modification of the meaning of "Consumers": the definition of "Consumers" in sub-s (7) has been extended by the Financial Services and Markets Act 2000 (Consequential and Transitional Provisions) (Miscellaneous) Order 2001, SI 2001/1821, art 3 (to include users of regulated services before commencement); and by the Financial Services and Markets Act 2000 (Consequential Amendments and Transitional Provisions) (Credit Unions) Order 2002, SI 2002/1501, art 4 (to include customers of credit unions before commencement). The extended definition applies for the purposes of the provisions of this Act specified in SI 2001/1821, art 3 and SI 2002/1501, art 4 and does not apply for the purposes of Sch 4, para 1 (Treaty rights).

Rules: the Industrial Assurance (Premium Receipt Books) Regulations 1948, SI 1948/2770 have effect as if made as rules under this section by virtue of the Industrial Assurance and Friendly Societies Act 1948, s 8(2) and the Financial Services and Markets Act 2000 (Transitional Provisions and Savings) (Rules) Order 2001, SI 2001/1534.

139 Miscellaneous ancillary matters

(1) Rules relating to the handling of money held by an authorised person in specified circumstances ("clients' money") may—

- (a) make provision which results in that clients' money being held on trust in accordance with the rules;
- (b) treat two or more accounts as a single account for specified purposes (which may include the distribution of money held in the accounts);
- (c) authorise the retention by the authorised person of interest accruing on the clients' money; and
- (d) make provision as to the distribution of such interest which is not to be retained by him.

(2) An institution with which an account is kept in pursuance of rules relating to the handling of clients' money does not incur any liability as constructive trustee if money is wrongfully paid from the account, unless the institution permits the payment—

- (a) with knowledge that it is wrongful; or
- (b) having deliberately failed to make enquiries in circumstances in which a reasonable and honest person would have done so.

(3) In the application of subsection (1) to Scotland, the reference to money being held on trust is to be read as a reference to its being held as agent for the person who is entitled to call for it to be paid over to him or to be paid on his direction or to have it otherwise credited to him.

(4) Rules may—

- (a) confer rights on persons to rescind agreements with, or withdraw offers to, authorised persons within a specified period; and
- (b) make provision, in respect of authorised persons and persons exercising those rights, for the restitution of property and the making or recovery of payments where those rights are exercised.

(5) "Rules" means general rules.

(6) "Specified" means specified in the rules.

[2139]

140 Restriction on managers of [certain collective investment schemes]

[(1) The Authority may make rules prohibiting an authorised person who has permission to act as—

- (a) the manager of an authorised unit trust scheme, or
- (b) the management company of an authorised UCITS open-ended investment company, from carrying on a specified activity.]

(2) Such rules may specify an activity which is not a regulated activity.

[(3) In this section—

- (a) "authorised UCITS open-ended investment company" means an authorised open-ended investment company to which the UCITS directive applies; and
- (b) "management company" has the meaning given by Article 1a.2 of the UCITS directive.]

[2140]

NOTES

Section heading: words in square brackets substituted by the Collective Investment Schemes (Miscellaneous Amendments) Regulations 2003, SI 2003/2066, reg 5(a), as from 13 February 2004.

Sub-s (1): substituted by SI 2003/2066, reg 5(b), as from 13 February 2004.

Sub-s (3): added by SI 2003/2066, reg 5(c), as from 13 February 2004.

Note: Rules made by the Authority under this section do not apply to incoming providers to the extent that they specify an activity which is an incoming electronic commerce activity; see the Electronic Commerce Directive (Financial Services and Markets) Regulations 2002, SI 2002/1775, reg 5.

PART II FSMA 2000

141 Insurance business rules

(1) The Authority may make rules prohibiting an authorised person who has permission to effect or carry out contracts of insurance from carrying on a specified activity.

(2) Such rules may specify an activity which is not a regulated activity.

(3) The Authority may make rules in relation to contracts entered into by an authorised person in the course of carrying on business which consists of the effecting or carrying out of contracts of long-term insurance.

(4) Such rules may, in particular—

(a) restrict the descriptions of property or indices of the value of property by reference to which the benefits under such contracts may be determined;

(b) make provision, in the interests of the protection of policyholders, for the substitution of one description of property, or index of value, by reference to which the benefits under a contract are to be determined for another such description of property or index.

(5) Rules made under this section are referred to in this Act as insurance business rules.

[2141]

NOTES

Note: Rules made by the Authority under this section do not apply to incoming providers to the extent that they specify an activity which is an incoming electronic commerce activity; see the Electronic Commerce Directive (Financial Services and Markets) Regulations 2002, SI.2002/1775, reg 5.

142 Insurance business: regulations supplementing Authority's rules

(1) The Treasury may make regulations for the purpose of preventing a person who is not an authorised person but who—

(a) is a parent undertaking of an authorised person who has permission to effect or carry out contracts of insurance, and

(b) falls within a prescribed class,

from doing anything to lessen the effectiveness of asset identification rules.

(2) "Asset identification rules" means rules made by the Authority which require an authorised person who has permission to effect or carry out contracts of insurance to identify assets which belong to him and which are maintained in respect of a particular aspect of his business.

(3) The regulations may, in particular, include provision—

(a) prohibiting the payment of dividends;

(b) prohibiting the creation of charges;

(c) making charges created in contravention of the regulations void.

(4) The Treasury may by regulations provide that, in prescribed circumstances, charges created in contravention of asset identification rules are void.

(5) A person who contravenes regulations under subsection (1) is guilty of an offence and liable on summary conviction to a fine not exceeding level 5 on the standard scale.

(6) "Charges" includes mortgages (or in Scotland securities over property).

[2142]–[2143]

143 (*Repealed by the Companies Act 2006, ss 964(1), (2), 1295, Sch 16, as from a 6 April 2007.*)

Specific rules

144 Price stabilising rules

(1) The Authority may make rules ("price stabilising rules") as to—

(a) the circumstances and manner in which,

(b) the conditions subject to which, and

(c) the time when or the period during which,

action may be taken for the purpose of stabilising the price of investments of specified kinds.

(2) Price stabilising rules—

(a) are to be made so as to apply only to authorised persons;
(b) may make different provision in relation to different kinds of investment.

(3) The Authority may make rules which, for the purposes of section 397(5)(b), treat a person who acts or engages in conduct—
(a) for the purpose of stabilising the price of investments, and
(b) in conformity with such provisions corresponding to price stabilising rules and made by a body or authority outside the United Kingdom as may be specified in the rules under this subsection,

as acting, or engaging in that conduct, for that purpose and in conformity with price stabilising rules.

(4) The Treasury may by order impose limitations on the power to make rules under this section.

(5) Such an order may, in particular—
(a) specify the kinds of investment in relation to which price stabilising rules may make provision;
(b) specify the kinds of investment in relation to which rules made under subsection (3) may make provision;
(c) provide for price stabilising rules to make provision for action to be taken for the purpose of stabilising the price of investments only in such circumstances as the order may specify;
(d) provide for price stabilising rules to make provision for action to be taken for that purpose only at such times or during such periods as the order may specify.

(6) If provisions specified in rules made under subsection (3) are altered, the rules continue to apply to those provisions as altered, but only if before the alteration the Authority has notified the body or authority concerned (and has not withdrawn its notification) that it is satisfied with its consultation procedures.

[(7) "Consultation procedures" means procedures designed to provide an opportunity for persons likely to be affected by alterations to those provisions to make representations about proposed alterations to any of those provisions.]

[2144]

NOTES

Sub-s (7): substituted by the Companies Act 2006, s 964(1), (3), as from 6 April 2007.

145 Financial promotion rules

(1) The Authority may make rules applying to authorised persons about the communication by them, or their approval of the communication by others, of invitations or inducements—
(a) to engage in investment activity; or
(b) to participate in a collective investment scheme.

(2) Rules under this section may, in particular, make provision about the form and content of communications.

(3) Subsection (1) applies only to communications which—
(a) if made by a person other than an authorised person, without the approval of an authorised person, would contravene section 21(1);
(b) may be made by an authorised person without contravening section 238(1).

[(3A) But subsection (3) does not prevent the Authority from making rules under subsection (1) in relation to a communication that would not contravene section 21(1) if made by a person other than an authorised person, without the approval of an authorised person, if the conditions set out in subsection (3B) are satisfied.

(3B) Those conditions are—
(a) that the communication would not contravene subsection (1) of section 21 because it is a communication to which that subsection does not apply as a result of an order under subsection (5) of that section;
(b) that the Authority considers that any of the requirements of—
(i) paragraphs 1 to 8 of Article 19 of the markets in financial instruments directive; or
(ii) any implementing measure made under paragraph 10 of that Article,

apply to the communication; and

(c) that the Authority considers that the rules are necessary to secure that the communication satisfies such of the requirements mentioned in paragraph (b) as the Authority considers apply to the communication.]

(4) "Engage in investment activity" has the same meaning as in section 21.

(5) The Treasury may by order impose limitations on the power to make rules under this section.

[2145]

NOTES

Sub-ss (3A), (3B): inserted by the Financial Services and Markets Act 2000 (Markets in Financial Instruments) (Modification of Powers) Regulations 2006, SI 2006/2975, regs 2, 4, as from 6 December 2006, subject to transitional provisions as noted to s 138 at **[2138]**.

Note: The FSA has made a number of legal instruments under this section which are reflected in its Handbook.

146 Money laundering rules

The Authority may make rules in relation to the prevention and detection of money laundering in connection with the carrying on of regulated activities by authorised persons.

[2146]

NOTES

Note: From 2001–2005 the FSA made a number of legal instruments under this section which were reflected in its Handbook. However, with effect from 31 August 2006, the FSA has repealed these instruments, and the Money Laundering Sourcebook has been revoked in its entirety.

147 Control of information rules

(1) The Authority may make rules ("control of information rules") about the disclosure and use of information held by an authorised person ("A").

(2) Control of information rules may—

(a) require the withholding of information which A would otherwise have to disclose to a person ("B") for or with whom A does business in the course of carrying on any regulated or other activity;

(b) specify circumstances in which A may withhold information which he would otherwise have to disclose to B;

(c) require A not to use for the benefit of B information A holds which A would otherwise have to use in that way;

(d) specify circumstances in which A may decide not to use for the benefit of B information A holds which A would otherwise have to use in that way.

[2147]

NOTES

Note: The FSA has made a number of legal instruments under this section which are reflected in its Handbook.

Modification or waiver

148 Modification or waiver of rules

(1) …

[(2) The Authority may, on the application or with the consent of a person who is subject to rules made by the Authority, direct that all or any of those rules (other than rules made under section 247 (trust scheme rules) or section 248 (scheme particulars rules))—

(a) are not to apply to that person; or

(b) are to apply to him with such modifications as may be specified in the direction.]

(3) An application must be made in such manner as the Authority may direct.

(4) The Authority may not give a direction unless it is satisfied that—

(a) compliance by the … person with the rules, or with the rules as unmodified, would be unduly burdensome or would not achieve the purpose for which the rules were made; and

(b) the direction would not result in undue risk to persons whose interests the rules are intended to protect.

(5) A direction may be given subject to conditions.

(6) Unless it is satisfied that it is inappropriate or unnecessary to do so, a direction must be published by the Authority in such a way as it thinks most suitable for bringing the direction to the attention of—

(a) those likely to be affected by it; and

(b) others who may be likely to make an application for a similar direction.

(7) In deciding whether it is satisfied as mentioned in subsection (6), the Authority must—

(a) take into account whether the direction relates to a rule contravention of which is actionable in accordance with section 150;

(b) consider whether its publication would prejudice, to an unreasonable degree, the commercial interests of the … person concerned or any other member of his immediate group; and

(c) consider whether its publication would be contrary to an international obligation of the United Kingdom.

(8) For the purposes of paragraphs (b) and (c) of subsection (7), the Authority must consider whether it would be possible to publish the direction without either of the consequences mentioned in those paragraphs by publishing it without disclosing the identity of the … person concerned.

(9) The Authority may—

(a) revoke a direction; or

(b) vary it on the application, or with the consent, of the … person to whom it relates.

(10) "Direction" means a direction under subsection (2).

(11) "Immediate group", in relation to [a person] ("A"), means—

(a) A;

(b) a parent undertaking of A;

(c) a subsidiary undertaking of A;

(d) a subsidiary undertaking of a parent undertaking of A;

(e) a parent undertaking of a subsidiary undertaking of A.

[2148]

NOTES

Sub-s (1): repealed by the Regulatory Reform (Financial Services and Markets Act 2000) Order 2007, SI 2007/1973, arts 2, 10(a), as from 12 July 2007.

Sub-s (2): substituted by SI 2007/1973, arts 2, 10(b), as from 12 July 2007.

Sub-ss (4), (7), (8), (9): words omitted repealed by SI 2007/1973, arts 2, 10(c), as from 12 July 2007.

Sub-s (11): words in square brackets substituted by SI 2007/1973, arts 2, 10(d), as from 12 July 2007.

Transitional provisions: see the Financial Services and Markets Act 2000 (Transitional Provisions and Savings) (Rules) Order 2001, SI 2001/1534, Pt II, art 8. That Part concerns the power of the FSA to designate rules and legislative provisions which were repealed or lapsed at commencement so that they continue in effect after commencement as if they were rules made by the FSA. Art 8 carries forward any waiver or modification of the pre-commencement provision that was granted before commencement. See also the Financial Services and Markets Act 2000 (Consequential and Transitional Provisions) (Miscellaneous) (No 2) Order 2001, SI 2001/2659, art 3 which makes transitional modifications of certain provisions of this Act (including this one). For example, references to "authorised persons" are treated as referring to persons who will be authorised at commencement.

Application of this section to financial conglomerates: see the Financial Conglomerates and Other Financial Groups Regulations 2004, SI 2004/1862, reg 4 at **[4686]**.

Application of this section to open-ended investment companies: see the Open-Ended Investment Companies Regulations 2001, SI 2001/1228, reg 7.

See also the Capital Requirements Regulations 2006, SI 2006/3221, regs 8, 9 at **[7552]**, **[7553]** (Exercise of functions under this section for the purpose of applying a decision or a joint decision).

Contravention of rules

149 Evidential provisions

(1) If a particular rule so provides, contravention of the rule does not give rise to any of the consequences provided for by other provisions of this Act.

(2) A rule which so provides must also provide—
- (a) that contravention may be relied on as tending to establish contravention of such other rule as may be specified; or
- (b) that compliance may be relied on as tending to establish compliance with such other rule as may be specified.

(3) A rule may include the provision mentioned in subsection (1) only if the Authority considers that it is appropriate for it also to include the provision required by subsection (2).

[2149]

NOTES

Transitional provisions: as to the consequences of contravention of continued rules, see the Financial Services and Markets Act 2000 (Transitional Provisions and Savings) (Rules) Order 2001, SI 2001/1534, art 6.

150 Actions for damages

(1) A contravention by an authorised person of a rule is actionable at the suit of a private person who suffers loss as a result of the contravention, subject to the defences and other incidents applying to actions for breach of statutory duty.

(2) If rules so provide, subsection (1) does not apply to contravention of a specified provision of those rules.

(3) In prescribed cases, a contravention of a rule which would be actionable at the suit of a private person is actionable at the suit of a person who is not a private person, subject to the defences and other incidents applying to actions for breach of statutory duty.

(4) In subsections (1) and (3) "rule" does not include—
- (a) [Part 6 rules]; or
- (b) a rule requiring an authorised person to have or maintain financial resources.

(5) "Private person" has such meaning as may be prescribed.

[2150]

NOTES

Sub-s (4): words in square brackets substituted by the Financial Services and Markets Act 2000 (Market Abuse) Regulations 2005, SI 2005/381, reg 6, as from 1 July 2005.

Regulations: the Financial Services and Markets Act 2000 (Rights of Action) Regulations 2001, SI 2001/2256 at **[4395]**; the Financial Services and Markets Act 2000 (Fourth Motor Insurance Directive) Regulations 2002, SI 2002/2706.

151 Limits on effect of contravening rules

(1) A person is not guilty of an offence by reason of a contravention of a rule made by the Authority.

(2) No such contravention makes any transaction void or unenforceable.

[2151]

NOTES

Note: "Rule" is defined as a rule made by the FSA under this Act; see s 417 at **[2414]**.

Procedural provisions

152 Notification of rules to the Treasury

(1) If the Authority makes any rules, it must give a copy to the Treasury without delay.

(2) If the Authority alters or revokes any rules, it must give written notice to the Treasury without delay.

(3) Notice of an alteration must include details of the alteration.

[2152]

153 Rule-making instruments

(1) Any power conferred on the Authority to make rules is exercisable in writing.

(2) An instrument by which rules are made by the Authority ("a rule-making instrument") must specify the provision under which the rules are made.

(3) To the extent to which a rule-making instrument does not comply with subsection (2), it is void.

(4) A rule-making instrument must be published by the Authority in the way appearing to the Authority to be best calculated to bring it to the attention of the public.

(5) The Authority may charge a reasonable fee for providing a person with a copy of a rule-making instrument.

(6) A person is not to be taken to have contravened any rule made by the Authority if he shows that at the time of the alleged contravention the rule-making instrument concerned had not been made available in accordance with this section.

[2153]

154 Verification of rules

(1) The production of a printed copy of a rule-making instrument purporting to be made by the Authority—

- (a) on which is endorsed a certificate signed by a member of the Authority's staff authorised by it for that purpose, and
- (b) which contains the required statements,

is evidence (or in Scotland sufficient evidence) of the facts stated in the certificate.

(2) The required statements are—

- (a) that the instrument was made by the Authority;
- (b) that the copy is a true copy of the instrument; and
- (c) that on a specified date the instrument was made available to the public in accordance with section 153(4).

(3) A certificate purporting to be signed as mentioned in subsection (1) is to be taken to have been properly signed unless the contrary is shown.

(4) A person who wishes in any legal proceedings to rely on a rule-making instrument may require the Authority to endorse a copy of the instrument with a certificate of the kind mentioned in subsection (1).

[2154]

155 Consultation

(1) If the Authority proposes to make any rules, it must publish a draft of the proposed rules in the way appearing to it to be best calculated to bring them to the attention of the public.

(2) The draft must be accompanied by—

- (a) a cost benefit analysis;
- (b) an explanation of the purpose of the proposed rules;
- (c) an explanation of the Authority's reasons for believing that making the proposed rules is compatible with its general duties under section 2; and
- (d) notice that representations about the proposals may be made to the Authority within a specified time.

(3) In the case of a proposal to make rules under a provision mentioned in subsection (9), the draft must also be accompanied by details of the expected expenditure by reference to which the proposal is made.

(4) Before making the proposed rules, the Authority must have regard to any representations made to it in accordance with subsection (2)(d).

(5) If the Authority makes the proposed rules, it must publish an account, in general terms, of—

- (a) the representations made to it in accordance with subsection (2)(d); and

(b) its response to them.

(6) If the rules differ from the draft published under subsection (1) in a way which is, in the opinion of the Authority, significant—

(a) the Authority must (in addition to complying with subsection (5)) publish details of the difference; and

(b) those details must be accompanied by a cost benefit analysis.

(7) Subsections (1) to (6) do not apply if the Authority considers that the delay involved in complying with them would be prejudicial to the interests of consumers.

(8) Neither subsection (2)(a) nor subsection (6)(b) applies if the Authority considers—

(a) that, making the appropriate comparison, there will be no increase in costs; or

(b) that, making that comparison, there will be an increase in costs but the increase will be of minimal significance.

(9) Neither subsection (2)(a) nor subsection (6)(b) requires a cost benefit analysis to be carried out in relation to rules made under—

(a) section 136(2);

(b) subsection (1) of section 213 as a result of subsection (4) of that section;

(c) section 234;

(d) paragraph 17 of Schedule 1.

(10) "Cost benefit analysis" means an estimate of the costs together with an analysis of the benefits that will arise—

(a) if the proposed rules are made; or

(b) if subsection (6) applies, from the rules that have been made.

(11) "The appropriate comparison" means—

(a) in relation to subsection (2)(a), a comparison between the overall position if the rules are made and the overall position if they are not made;

(b) in relation to subsection (6)(b), a comparison between the overall position after the making of the rules and the overall position before they were made.

(12) The Authority may charge a reasonable fee for providing a person with a copy of a draft published under subsection (1).

[2155]

NOTES

Transitional provisions: see further as to the application of this section to persons with interim permission or interim approval, the Financial Services and Markets Act 2000 (Mutual Societies) Order 2001, SI 2001/2617, art 4(3), Sch 2, paras 11(b), 14(b); the Financial Services and Markets Act 2000 (Transitional Provisions) (Complaints relating to General Insurance and Mortgages) (Amendment) Order 2004, SI 2004/1609, art 6; the Financial Services and Markets Act 2000 (Transitional Provisions) (Mortgages) Order 2004, SI 2004/2615, arts 1(3), 2, 3, 4(2); and the Financial Services and Markets Act 2000 (Transitional Provisions) (General Insurance Intermediaries) Order 2004, SI 2004/3351, art 4. See also the Compensation Act 2006 (Contribution for Mesothelioma Claims) Regulations 2006, SI 206/3259, reg 4 (disapplication of this section in relation to the first occasion that the FSA makes rules or guidance in relation to mesothelioma claims)

156 General supplementary powers

(1) Rules made by the Authority may make different provision for different cases and may, in particular, make different provision in respect of different descriptions of authorised person, activity or investment.

(2) Rules made by the Authority may contain such incidental, supplemental, consequential and transitional provision as the Authority considers appropriate.

[2156]

CHAPTER II
GUIDANCE

157 Guidance

(1) The Authority may give guidance consisting of such information and advice as it considers appropriate—

(a) with respect to the operation of this Act and of any rules made under it;

(b) with respect to any matters relating to functions of the Authority;

(c) for the purpose of meeting the regulatory objectives;

(d) with respect to any other matters about which it appears to the Authority to be desirable to give information or advice.

(2) The Authority may give financial or other assistance to persons giving information or advice of a kind which the Authority could give under this section.

(3) If the Authority proposes to give guidance to regulated persons generally, or to a class of regulated person, in relation to rules to which those persons are subject, [subsections (1), (2)(d) and (4) of section 155 apply to the proposed guidance as they apply to proposed rules, unless the Authority considers that the delay in complying with them would be prejudicial to the interests of consumers].

(4) The Authority may—

(a) publish its guidance;

(b) offer copies of its published guidance for sale at a reasonable price; and

(c) if it gives guidance in response to a request made by any person, make a reasonable charge for that guidance.

(5) In this Chapter [(except in section 158A)], references to guidance given by the Authority include references to any recommendation made by the Authority to persons generally, to regulated persons generally or to any class of regulated person.

(6) "Regulated person" means any—

(a) authorised person;

(b) person who is otherwise subject to rules made by the Authority.

[2157]

NOTES

Sub-s (3): words in square brackets substituted by the Regulatory Reform (Financial Services and Markets Act 2000) Order 2007, SI 2007/1973, arts 2, 13, as from 12 July 2007.

Sub-s (5): words in square brackets inserted by the Financial Services and Markets Act 2000 (Markets in Financial Instruments) (Modification of Powers) Regulations 2006, SI 2006/2975, regs 2, 5, as from 6 December 2006.

Regulated person: for the purposes of sub-s (3) above and s 158(5) (guidance to regulated persons generally), guidance given to building societies, friendly societies and industrial and provident societies generally or to a class of such societies is to be treated as if given to regulated persons generally or to a class of regulated persons, whether or not those societies would otherwise be "regulated persons" within the meaning of this section; see the Financial Services and Markets Act 2000 (Mutual Societies) Order 2001, SI 2001/2617, Sch 2, para 12 et seq.

Transitional provisions: see further as to the application of this section to persons with interim permission or interim approval, the Financial Services and Markets Act 2000 (Mutual Societies) Order 2001, SI 2001/2617, art 4(3), Sch 2, paras 11(b), 14(b); the Financial Services and Markets Act 2000 (Transitional Provisions) (Complaints relating to General Insurance and Mortgages) (Amendment) Order 2004, SI 2004/1609, art 6; the Financial Services and Markets Act 2000 (Transitional Provisions) (Mortgages) Order 2004, SI 2004/2615, arts 1(3), 2, 3, 4(2); and the Financial Services and Markets Act 2000 (Transitional Provisions) (General Insurance Intermediaries) Order 2004, SI 2004/3351, art 4. See also the Compensation Act 2006 (Contribution for Mesothelioma Claims) Regulations 2006, SI 206/3259, reg 4 (disapplication of sub-s (3) in relation to the first occasion that the FSA makes rules or guidance in relation to mesothelioma claims)

158 Notification of guidance to the Treasury

(1) On giving any general guidance, the Authority must give the Treasury a copy of the guidance without delay.

(2) If the Authority alters any of its general guidance, it must give written notice to the Treasury without delay.

(3) The notice must include details of the alteration.

(4) If the Authority revokes any of its general guidance, it must give written notice to the Treasury without delay.

(5) "General guidance" means guidance given by the Authority under section 157 which is—

(a) given to persons generally, to regulated persons generally or to a class of regulated person;

(b) intended to have continuing effect; and
(c) given in writing or other legible form.

(6) "Regulated person" has the same meaning as in section 157.

[2158]

NOTES

Regulated person: see the note to s 157 at **[2157]**.

[158A Guidance on outsourcing by investment firms and credit institutions

(1) Without prejudice to the generality of section 157, the Authority must give guidance in the terms required by Article 15(3) of Commission Directive 2006/73/EC of 10 August 2006 (requirement to publish statement of policy on outsourcing of investment services by investment firms and credit institutions).

(2) Subsections (1), (2)(b) and (d), (4), (5), (6)(a) and (7) of section 155 apply to guidance which the Authority is required to give under this section as they apply to proposed rules.

(3) The Authority must publish its guidance under this section.

(4) The Authority may offer copies of the published guidance for sale at a reasonable price.

(5) Subsections (1) to (4) of section 158 apply to guidance under this section as they apply to general guidance (as defined by section 158(5)).]

[2158A]

NOTES

Commencement: 6 December 2006.

Inserted by the Financial Services and Markets Act 2000 (Markets in Financial Instruments) (Modification of Powers) Regulations 2006, SI 2006/2975, regs 2, 6, as from 6 December 2006, subject to transitional provisions as noted below.

Transitional provisions: the Financial Services and Markets Act 2000 (Markets in Financial Instruments) (Modification of Powers) Regulations 2006, SI 2006/2975, reg 15 provides as follows:

"15 Transitional provision: guidance on outsourcing by investment firms and credit institutions

If, before these Regulations come into force—

(a) the Authority has taken any step mentioned in subsection (2) of section 158A of the Act (inserted by these Regulations) in relation to guidance of the sort referred to in subsection (1) of that section; and
(b) that step would have satisfied a requirement of section 158A(2) in relation to that guidance had it been taken after these Regulations come into force,

the step shall be treated as having satisfied that requirement."

CHAPTER III
COMPETITION SCRUTINY

159 Interpretation

(1) In this Chapter—

["OFT" means the Office of Fair Trading;]

"practices", in relation to the Authority, means practices adopted by the Authority in the exercise of functions under this Act;

"regulating provisions" means any—

(a) rules;
(b) general guidance (as defined by section 158(5)) [or guidance under section 158A];
(c) statement issued by the Authority under section 64;
(d) code issued by the Authority under section 64 or 119.

(2) For the purposes of this Chapter, regulating provisions or practices have a significantly adverse effect on competition if—

(a) they have, or are intended or likely to have, that effect; or
(b) the effect that they have, or are intended or likely to have, is to require or encourage behaviour which has, or is intended or likely to have, a significantly adverse effect on competition.

(3) If regulating provisions or practices have, or are intended or likely to have, the effect of requiring or encouraging exploitation of the strength of a market position they are to be taken, for the purposes of this Chapter, to have an adverse effect on competition.

(4) In determining under this Chapter whether any of the regulating provisions have, or are likely to have, a particular effect, it may be assumed that the persons to whom the provisions concerned are addressed will act in accordance with them.

[2159]

NOTES

Sub-s (1): definition in square brackets substituted by the Enterprise Act 2002, s 278(1), Sch 25, para 40(1), (2), as from 1 April 2003; words in square brackets in para (b) of definition "regulating provisions" inserted by the Financial Services and Markets Act 2000 (Markets in Financial Instruments) (Modification of Powers) Regulations 2006, SI 2006/2975, regs 2, 7, as from 6 December 2006.

160 Reports by [OFT]

(1) The [OFT] must keep the regulating provisions and the Authority's practices under review.

(2) If at any time the [OFT] considers that—

(a) a regulating provision or practice has a significantly adverse effect on competition, or

(b) two or more regulating provisions or practices taken together, or a particular combination of regulating provisions and practices, have such an effect,

[the OFT] must make a report to that effect.

(3) If at any time the [OFT] considers that—

(a) a regulating provision or practice does not have a significantly adverse effect on competition, or

(b) two or more regulating provisions or practices taken together, or a particular combination of regulating provisions and practices, do not have any such effect,

[the OFT] may make a report to that effect.

(4) A report under subsection (2) must include details of the adverse effect on competition.

(5) If the [OFT] makes a report under subsection (2) [the OFT] must—

(a) send a copy of it to the Treasury, the Competition Commission and the Authority; and

(b) publish it in the way appearing to [it] to be best calculated to bring it to the attention of the public.

(6) If the [OFT] makes a report under subsection (3)—

(a) [the OFT] must send a copy of it to the Treasury, the Competition Commission and the Authority; and

(b) [the OFT] may publish it.

(7) Before publishing a report under this section the [OFT] must, so far as practicable, exclude any matter which relates to the private affairs of a particular individual the publication of which, in the opinion of the [OFT], would or might seriously and prejudicially affect his interests.

(8) Before publishing such a report the [OFT] must, so far as practicable, exclude any matter which relates to the affairs of a particular body the publication of which, in the opinion of the [OFT], would or might seriously and prejudicially affect its interests.

(9) Subsections (7) and (8) do not apply in relation to copies of a report which the [OFT] is required to send under subsection (5)(a) or (6)(a).

(10) For the purposes of the law of defamation, absolute privilege attaches to any report of the [OFT] under this section.

[2160]

NOTES

Words in square brackets substituted by the Enterprise Act 2002, s 278(1), Sch 25, para 40(1), (3), as from 1 April 2003.

PART II FSMA 2000

161 Power of [OFT] to request information

(1) For the purpose of investigating any matter with a view to its consideration under section 160, the [OFT] may exercise the powers conferred on [it] by this section.

(2) The [OFT] may by notice in writing require any person to produce to [it] or to a person appointed by [it] for the purpose, at a time and place specified in the notice, any document which—

(a) is specified or described in the notice; and
(b) is a document in that person's custody or under his control.

(3) The [OFT] may by notice in writing—

(a) require any person carrying on any business to provide [it] with such information as may be specified or described in the notice; and
(b) specify the time within which, and the manner and form in which, any such information is to be provided.

(4) A requirement may be imposed under subsection (2) or (3)(a) only in respect of documents or information which relate to any matter relevant to the investigation.

(5) If a person ("the defaulter") refuses, or otherwise fails, to comply with a notice under this section, the [OFT] may certify that fact in writing to the court and the court may enquire into the case.

(6) If, after hearing any witness who may be produced against or on behalf of the defaulter and any statement which may be offered in defence, the court is satisfied that the defaulter did not have a reasonable excuse for refusing or otherwise failing to comply with the notice, the court may deal with the defaulter as if he were in contempt.

(7) "Court" means—

(a) the High Court; or
(b) in relation to Scotland, the Court of Session.

[2161]

NOTES

Words in square brackets substituted by the Enterprise Act 2002, s 278(1), Sch 25, para 40(1), (4), as from 1 April 2003.

162 Consideration by Competition Commission

(1) If the [OFT]—

(a) makes a report under section 160(2), or
(b) asks the Commission to consider a report that [the OFT] has made under section 160(3),

the Commission must investigate the matter.

(2) The Commission must then make its own report on the matter unless it considers that, as a result of a change of circumstances, no useful purpose would be served by a report.

(3) If the Commission decides in accordance with subsection (2) not to make a report, it must make a statement setting out the change of circumstances which resulted in that decision.

(4) A report made under this section must state the Commission's conclusion as to whether—

(a) the regulating provision or practice which is the subject of the report has a significantly adverse effect on competition; or
(b) the regulating provisions or practices, or combination of regulating provisions and practices, which are the subject of the report have such an effect.

(5) A report under this section stating the Commission's conclusion that there is a significantly adverse effect on competition must also—

(a) state whether the Commission considers that that effect is justified; and
(b) if it states that the Commission considers that it is not justified, state its conclusion as to what action, if any, ought to be taken by the Authority.

(6) Subsection (7) applies whenever the Commission is considering, for the purposes of this section, whether a particular adverse effect on competition is justified.

(7) The Commission must ensure, so far as that is reasonably possible, that the conclusion it reaches is compatible with the functions conferred, and obligations imposed, on the Authority by or under this Act.

(8) A report under this section must contain such an account of the Commission's reasons for its conclusions as is expedient, in the opinion of the Commission, for facilitating proper understanding of them.

(9) Schedule 14 supplements this section.

(10) If the Commission makes a report under this section it must send a copy to the Treasury, the Authority and the [OFT].

[2162]

NOTES

Sub-ss (1), (10): words in square brackets substituted by the Enterprise Act 2002, s 278(1), Sch 25, para 40(1), (5), as from 1 April 2003.

163 Role of the Treasury

(1) This section applies if the Competition Commission makes a report under section 162(2) which states its conclusion that there is a significantly adverse effect on competition.

(2) If the Commission's conclusion, as stated in the report, is that the adverse effect on competition is not justified, the Treasury must give a direction to the Authority requiring it to take such action as may be specified in the direction.

(3) But subsection (2) does not apply if the Treasury consider—

- (a) that, as a result of action taken by the Authority in response to the Commission's report, it is unnecessary for them to give a direction; or
- (b) that the exceptional circumstances of the case make it inappropriate or unnecessary for them to do so.

(4) In considering the action to be specified in a direction under subsection (2), the Treasury must have regard to any conclusion of the Commission included in the report because of section 162(5)(b).

(5) Subsection (6) applies if—

- (a) the Commission's conclusion, as stated in its report, is that the adverse effect on competition is justified; but
- (b) the Treasury consider that the exceptional circumstances of the case require them to act.

(6) The Treasury may give a direction to the Authority requiring it to take such action—

- (a) as they consider to be necessary in the light of the exceptional circumstances of the case; and
- (b) as may be specified in the direction.

(7) The Authority may not be required as a result of this section to take any action—

- (a) that it would not have power to take in the absence of a direction under this section; or
- (b) that would otherwise be incompatible with any of the functions conferred, or obligations imposed, on it by or under this Act.

(8) Subsection (9) applies if the Treasury are considering—

- (a) whether subsection (2) applies and, if so, what action is to be specified in a direction under that subsection; or
- (b) whether to give a direction under subsection (6).

(9) The Treasury must—

- (a) do what they consider appropriate to allow the Authority, and any other person appearing to the Treasury to be affected, an opportunity to make representations; and
- (b) have regard to any such representations.

(10) If, in reliance on subsection (3)(a) or (b), the Treasury decline to act under subsection (2), they must make a statement to that effect, giving their reasons.

PART II
FSMA 2000

(11) If the Treasury give a direction under this section they must make a statement giving—

(a) details of the direction; and

(b) if the direction is given under subsection (6), their reasons for giving it.

(12) The Treasury must—

(a) publish any statement made under this section in the way appearing to them best calculated to bring it to the attention of the public; and

(b) lay a copy of it before Parliament.

[2163]

164 The Competition Act 1998

(1) The Chapter I prohibition does not apply to an agreement the parties to which consist of or include—

(a) an authorised person, or

(b) a person who is otherwise subject to the Authority's regulating provisions,

to the extent to which the agreement consists of provisions the inclusion of which in the agreement is encouraged by any of the Authority's regulating provisions.

(2) The Chapter I prohibition does not apply to the practices of an authorised person or a person who is otherwise subject to the regulating provisions to the extent to which the practices are encouraged by any of the Authority's regulating provisions.

(3) The Chapter II prohibition does not apply to conduct of—

(a) an authorised person, or

(b) a person who is otherwise subject to the Authority's regulating provisions,

to the extent to which the conduct is encouraged by any of the Authority's regulating provisions.

(4) "The Chapter I prohibition" means the prohibition imposed by section 2(1) of the Competition Act 1998.

(5) "The Chapter II prohibition" means the prohibition imposed by section 18(1) of that Act.

[2164]

PART XI
INFORMATION GATHERING AND INVESTIGATIONS

Powers to gather information

165 Authority's power to require information

(1) The Authority may, by notice in writing given to an authorised person, require him—

(a) to provide specified information or information of a specified description; or

(b) to produce specified documents or documents of a specified description.

(2) The information or documents must be provided or produced—

(a) before the end of such reasonable period as may be specified; and

(b) at such place as may be specified.

(3) An officer who has written authorisation from the Authority to do so may require an authorised person without delay—

(a) to provide the officer with specified information or information of a specified description; or

(b) to produce to him specified documents or documents of a specified description.

(4) This section applies only to information and documents reasonably required in connection with the exercise by the Authority of functions conferred on it by or under this Act.

(5) The Authority may require any information provided under this section to be provided in such form as it may reasonably require.

(6) The Authority may require—

(a) any information provided, whether in a document or otherwise, to be verified in such manner, or

(b) any document produced to be authenticated in such manner,

as it may reasonably require.

(7) The powers conferred by subsections (1) and (3) may also be exercised to impose requirements on—

(a) a person who is connected with an authorised person;
(b) an operator, trustee or depositary of a scheme recognised under section 270 or 272 who is not an authorised person;
(c) a recognised investment exchange or recognised clearing house.

(8) "Authorised person" includes a person who was at any time an authorised person but who has ceased to be an authorised person.

(9) "Officer" means an officer of the Authority and includes a member of the Authority's staff or an agent of the Authority.

(10) "Specified" means—

(a) in subsections (1) and (2), specified in the notice; and
(b) in subsection (3), specified in the authorisation.

(11) For the purposes of this section, a person is connected with an authorised person ("A") if he is or has at any relevant time been—

(a) a member of A's group;
(b) a controller of A;
(c) any other member of a partnership of which A is a member; or
(d) in relation to A, a person mentioned in Part I of Schedule 15.

[2165]

NOTES

Transitional provisions: this section and ss 166, 167 are modified by the Financial Services and Markets Act 2000 (Transitional Provisions and Savings) (Civil Remedies, Discipline, Criminal Offences etc) (No 2) Order 2001, SI 2001/3083, arts 15–17, so that the powers conferred by ss 165–167 are exercisable in respect of any person who was, before 1 December 2001, a regulated person but who is not, and never has been, an authorised person under this Act.

Note: any reference in this section, and in ss 166–168 and 176 to an authorised person includes a reference to an unauthorised incoming provider; see the Electronic Commerce Directive (Financial Services and Markets) Regulations 2002, SI 2002/1775, reg 12(3) at **[4650]**.

166 Reports by skilled persons

(1) The Authority may, by notice in writing given to a person to whom subsection (2) applies, require him to provide the Authority with a report on any matter about which the Authority has required or could require the provision of information or production of documents under section 165.

(2) This subsection applies to—

(a) an authorised person ("A"),
(b) any other member of A's group,
(c) a partnership of which A is a member, or
(d) a person who has at any relevant time been a person falling within paragraph (a), (b) or (c),

who is, or was at the relevant time, carrying on a business.

(3) The Authority may require the report to be in such form as may be specified in the notice.

(4) The person appointed to make a report required by subsection (1) must be a person—

(a) nominated or approved by the Authority; and
(b) appearing to the Authority to have the skills necessary to make a report on the matter concerned.

(5) It is the duty of any person who is providing (or who at any time has provided) services to a person to whom subsection (2) applies in relation to a matter on which a report is required under subsection (1) to give a person appointed to provide such a report all such assistance as the appointed person may reasonably require.

(6) The obligation imposed by subsection (5) is enforceable, on the application of the Authority, by an injunction or, in Scotland, by an order for specific performance under section 45 of the Court of Session Act 1988.

[2166]

NOTES

Transitional provisions; authorised person: see the notes to s 165 at **[2165]**.

Appointment of investigators

167 Appointment of persons to carry out general investigations

(1) If it appears to the Authority or the Secretary of State ("the investigating authority") that there is good reason for doing so, the investigating authority may appoint one or more competent persons to conduct an investigation on its behalf into—

(a) the nature, conduct or state of the business of [a recognised investment exchange or] an authorised person or of an appointed representative;

(b) a particular aspect of that business; or

(c) the ownership or control of [a recognised investment exchange or] an authorised person.

(2) If a person appointed under subsection (1) thinks it necessary for the purposes of his investigation, he may also investigate the business of a person who is or has at any relevant time been—

(a) a member of the group of which the person under investigation ("A") is part; or

(b) a partnership of which A is a member.

(3) If a person appointed under subsection (1) decides to investigate the business of any person under subsection (2) he must give that person written notice of his decision.

(4) The power conferred by this section may be exercised in relation to a former authorised person (or appointed representative) but only in relation to—

(a) business carried on at any time when he was an authorised person (or appointed representative); or

(b) the ownership or control of a former authorised person at any time when he was an authorised person.

(5) "Business" includes any part of a business even if it does not consist of carrying on regulated activities.

[(6) References in subsection (1) to a recognised investment exchange do not include references to an overseas investment exchange (as defined by section 313(1)).]

[2167]

NOTES

Sub-s (1): words in square brackets inserted by the Financial Services and Markets Act 2000 (Markets in Financial Instruments) Regulations 2007, SI 2007/126, reg 3(5), Sch 5, paras 1, 7(a), as from 1 April 2007 (certain purposes (see reg 1(2) at **[7596]**)), and as from 1 November 2007 (otherwise).

Sub-s (6): added by SI 2007/126, reg 3(5), Sch 5, paras 1, 7(b), as from 1 April 2007 (certain purposes (see reg 1(2) at **[7596]**)), and as from 1 November 2007 (otherwise).

Transitional provisions; authorised person: see the notes to s 165 at **[2165]**.

168 Appointment of persons to carry out investigations in particular cases

(1) Subsection (3) applies if it appears to an investigating authority that there are circumstances suggesting that—

(a) a person may have contravened any regulation made under section 142; or

(b) a person may be guilty of an offence under section 177, 191, 346 or 398(1) or under Schedule 4.

(2) Subsection (3) also applies if it appears to an investigating authority that there are circumstances suggesting that—

(a) an offence under section 24(1) or 397 or under Part V of the Criminal Justice Act 1993 may have been committed;

(b) there may have been a breach of the general prohibition;

(c) there may have been a contravention of section 21 or 238; or

(d) market abuse may have taken place.

(3) The investigating authority may appoint one or more competent persons to conduct an investigation on its behalf.

(4) Subsection (5) applies if it appears to the Authority that there are circumstances suggesting that—

(a) a person may have contravened section 20;

(b) a person may be guilty of an offence under prescribed regulations relating to money laundering;

(c) an authorised person may have contravened a rule made by the Authority;

(d) an individual may not be a fit and proper person to perform functions in relation to a regulated activity carried on by an authorised or exempt person;

(e) an individual may have performed or agreed to perform a function in breach of a prohibition order;

(f) an authorised or exempt person may have failed to comply with section 56(6);

(g) an authorised person may have failed to comply with section 59(1) or (2);

(h) a person in relation to whom the Authority has given its approval under section 59 may not be a fit and proper person to perform the function to which that approval relates; *or*

(i) a person may be guilty of misconduct for the purposes of section 66[; or

(j) a person may have contravened any provision made by or under this Act for the purpose of implementing the markets in financial instruments directive or by any directly applicable Community regulation made under that directive].

(5) The Authority may appoint one or more competent persons to conduct an investigation on its behalf.

(6) "Investigating authority" means the Authority or the Secretary of State.

[2168]

PART II FSMA 2000

NOTES

Sub-s (4): word in italics in para (h) repealed, and para (j) and the word immediately preceding it inserted, by the Financial Services and Markets Act 2000 (Markets in Financial Instruments) Regulations 2007, SI 2007/126, reg 3(5), Sch 5, paras 1, 8, as from 1 April 2007 (certain purposes (see reg 1(2) at **[7596]**)), and as from 1 November 2007 (otherwise).

Transitional provisions: see the Financial Services and Markets Act 2000 (Transitional Provisions and Savings) (Civil Remedies, Discipline, Criminal Offences etc) (No 2) Order 2001, SI 2001/3083, art 18 which modifies this section so it applies where there are circumstances suggesting that a person has contravened, or committed an offence under, certain enactments, provisions or rules before commencement.

Note: the Money Laundering Regulations 2003, SI 2003/3075 have been prescribed for the purposes of sub-s (4)(b) above by reg 1(3) of those Regulations.

Note: the reference in sub-s (4)(c) above to a rule made by the Authority includes a reference to a requirement imposed by the Authority under the Electronic Commerce Directive (Financial Services and Markets) Regulations 2002, SI 2002/1775; see reg 12(5) of those Regulations at **[4650]**.

Authorised person: see the note to s 165 at **[2165]**.

Regulations: the Money Laundering Regulations 2003, SI 2003/3075.

Assistance to overseas regulators

169 Investigations etc in support of overseas regulator

(1) At the request of an overseas regulator, the Authority may—

(a) exercise the power conferred by section 165; or

(b) appoint one or more competent persons to investigate any matter.

(2) An investigator has the same powers as an investigator appointed under section 168(3) (as a result of subsection (1) of that section).

(3) If the request has been made by a competent authority in pursuance of any Community obligation the Authority must, in deciding whether or not to exercise its investigative power, consider whether its exercise is necessary to comply with any such obligation.

(4) In deciding whether or not to exercise its investigative power, the Authority may take into account in particular—

(a) whether in the country or territory of the overseas regulator concerned, corresponding assistance would be given to a United Kingdom regulatory authority;

(b) whether the case concerns the breach of a law, or other requirement, which has no close parallel in the United Kingdom or involves the assertion of a jurisdiction not recognised by the United Kingdom;

(c) the seriousness of the case and its importance to persons in the United Kingdom;
(d) whether it is otherwise appropriate in the public interest to give the assistance sought.

(5) The Authority may decide that it will not exercise its investigative power unless the overseas regulator undertakes to make such contribution towards the cost of its exercise as the Authority considers appropriate.

(6) Subsections (4) and (5) do not apply if the Authority considers that the exercise of its investigative power is necessary to comply with a Community obligation.

(7) If the Authority has appointed an investigator in response to a request from an overseas regulator, it may direct the investigator to permit a representative of that regulator to attend, and take part in, any interview conducted for the purposes of the investigation.

(8) A direction under subsection (7) is not to be given unless the Authority is satisfied that any information obtained by an overseas regulator as a result of the interview will be subject to safeguards equivalent to those contained in Part XXIII.

(9) The Authority must prepare a statement of its policy with respect to the conduct of interviews in relation to which a direction under subsection (7) has been given.

(10) The statement requires the approval of the Treasury.

(11) If the Treasury approve the statement, the Authority must publish it.

(12) No direction may be given under subsection (7) before the statement has been published.

(13) "Overseas regulator" has the same meaning as in section 195.

(14) "Investigative power" means one of the powers mentioned in subsection (1).

(15) "Investigator" means a person appointed under subsection (1)(b).

[2169]

Conduct of investigations

170 Investigations: general

(1) This section applies if an investigating authority appoints one or more competent persons ("investigators") under section 167 or 168(3) or (5) to conduct an investigation on its behalf.

(2) The investigating authority must give written notice of the appointment of an investigator to the person who is the subject of the investigation ("the person under investigation").

(3) Subsections (2) and (9) do not apply if—
(a) the investigator is appointed as a result of section 168(1) or (4) and the investigating authority believes that the notice required by subsection (2) or (9) would be likely to result in the investigation being frustrated; or
(b) the investigator is appointed as a result of subsection (2) of section 168.

(4) A notice under subsection (2) must—
(a) specify the provisions under which, and as a result of which, the investigator was appointed; and
(b) state the reason for his appointment.

(5) Nothing prevents the investigating authority from appointing a person who is a member of its staff as an investigator.

(6) An investigator must make a report of his investigation to the investigating authority.

(7) The investigating authority may, by a direction to an investigator, control—
(a) the scope of the investigation;
(b) the period during which the investigation is to be conducted;
(c) the conduct of the investigation; and
(d) the reporting of the investigation.

(8) A direction may, in particular—
(a) confine the investigation to particular matters;

(b) extend the investigation to additional matters;
(c) require the investigator to discontinue the investigation or to take only such steps as are specified in the direction;
(d) require the investigator to make such interim reports as are so specified.

(9) If there is a change in the scope or conduct of the investigation and, in the opinion of the investigating authority, the person subject to investigation is likely to be significantly prejudiced by not being made aware of it, that person must be given written notice of the change.

(10) "Investigating authority", in relation to an investigator, means—
(a) the Authority, if the Authority appointed him;
(b) the Secretary of State, if the Secretary of State appointed him.

[2170]

171 Powers of persons appointed under section 167

(1) An investigator may require the person who is the subject of the investigation ("the person under investigation") or any person connected with the person under investigation—
(a) to attend before the investigator at a specified time and place and answer questions; or
(b) otherwise to provide such information as the investigator may require.

(2) An investigator may also require any person to produce at a specified time and place any specified documents or documents of a specified description.

(3) A requirement under subsection (1) or (2) may be imposed only so far as the investigator concerned reasonably considers the question, provision of information or production of the document to be relevant to the purposes of the investigation.

[(3A) Where the investigation relates to a recognised investment exchange, an investigator has the additional powers conferred by sections 172 and 173 (and for this purpose references in those sections to an investigator are to be read accordingly).]

(4) For the purposes of this section and section 172, a person is connected with the person under investigation ("A") if he is or has at any relevant time been—
(a) a member of A's group;
(b) a controller of A;
(c) a partnership of which A is a member; or
(d) in relation to A, a person mentioned in Part I or II of Schedule 15.

(5) "Investigator" means a person conducting an investigation under section 167.

(6) "Specified" means specified in a notice in writing.

[(7) The reference in subsection (3A) to a recognised investment exchange does not include a reference to an overseas investment exchange (as defined by section 313(1)).]

[2171]

NOTES

Sub-ss (3A), (7): inserted and added respectively by the Financial Services and Markets Act 2000 (Markets in Financial Instruments) Regulations 2007, SI 2007/126, reg 3(5), Sch 5, paras 1, 9, as from 1 April 2007 (certain purposes (see reg 1(2) at **[7596]**)), and as from 1 November 2007 (otherwise).

172 Additional power of persons appointed as a result of section 168(1) or (4)

(1) An investigator has the powers conferred by section 171.

(2) An investigator may also require a person who is neither the subject of the investigation ("the person under investigation") nor a person connected with the person under investigation—
(a) to attend before the investigator at a specified time and place and answer questions; or
(b) otherwise to provide such information as the investigator may require for the purposes of the investigation.

(3) A requirement may only be imposed under subsection (2) if the investigator is satisfied that the requirement is necessary or expedient for the purposes of the investigation.

PART II FSMA 2000

(4) "Investigator" means a person appointed as a result of subsection (1) or (4) of section 168.

(5) "Specified" means specified in a notice in writing.

[2172]

173 Powers of persons appointed as a result of section 168(2)

(1) Subsections (2) to (4) apply if an investigator considers that any person ("A") is or may be able to give information which is or may be relevant to the investigation.

(2) The investigator may require A—

(a) to attend before him at a specified time and place and answer questions; or

(b) otherwise to provide such information as he may require for the purposes of the investigation.

(3) The investigator may also require A to produce at a specified time and place any specified documents or documents of a specified description which appear to the investigator to relate to any matter relevant to the investigation.

(4) The investigator may also otherwise require A to give him all assistance in connection with the investigation which A is reasonably able to give.

(5) "Investigator" means a person appointed under subsection (3) of section 168 (as a result of subsection (2) of that section).

[2173]

174 Admissibility of statements made to investigators

(1) A statement made to an investigator by a person in compliance with an information requirement is admissible in evidence in any proceedings, so long as it also complies with any requirements governing the admissibility of evidence in the circumstances in question.

(2) But in criminal proceedings in which that person is charged with an offence to which this subsection applies or in proceedings in relation to action to be taken against that person under section 123—

(a) no evidence relating to the statement may be adduced, and

(b) no question relating to it may be asked,

by or on behalf of the prosecution or (as the case may be) the Authority, unless evidence relating to it is adduced, or a question relating to it is asked, in the proceedings by or on behalf of that person.

(3) Subsection (2) applies to any offence other than one—

(a) under section 177(4) or 398;

(b) under section 5 of the Perjury Act 1911 (false statements made otherwise than on oath);

(c) under section 44(2) of the Criminal Law (Consolidation) (Scotland) Act 1995 (false statements made otherwise than on oath); or

(d) under Article 10 of the Perjury (Northern Ireland) Order 1979.

(4) "Investigator" means a person appointed under section 167 or 168(3) or (5).

(5) "Information requirement" means a requirement imposed by an investigator under section 171, 172, 173 or 175.

[2174]

175 Information and documents: supplemental provisions

(1) If the Authority or an investigator has power under this Part to require a person to produce a document but it appears that the document is in the possession of a third person, that power may be exercised in relation to the third person.

(2) If a document is produced in response to a requirement imposed under this Part, the person to whom it is produced may—

(a) take copies or extracts from the document; or

(b) require the person producing the document, or any relevant person, to provide an explanation of the document.

(3) If a person who is required under this Part to produce a document fails to do so, the Authority or an investigator may require him to state, to the best of his knowledge and belief, where the document is.

(4) A lawyer may be required under this Part to furnish the name and address of his client.

(5) No person may be required under this Part to disclose information or produce a document in respect of which he owes an obligation of confidence by virtue of carrying on the business of banking unless—
- (a) he is the person under investigation or a member of that person's group;
- (b) the person to whom the obligation of confidence is owed is the person under investigation or a member of that person's group;
- (c) the person to whom the obligation of confidence is owed consents to the disclosure or production; or
- (d) the imposing on him of a requirement with respect to such information or document has been specifically authorised by the investigating authority.

(6) If a person claims a lien on a document, its production under this Part does not affect the lien.

(7) "Relevant person", in relation to a person who is required to produce a document, means a person who—
- (a) has been or is or is proposed to be a director or controller of that person;
- (b) has been or is an auditor of that person;
- (c) has been or is an actuary, accountant or lawyer appointed or instructed by that person; or
- (d) has been or is an employee of that person.

(8) "Investigator" means a person appointed under section 167 or 168(3) or (5).

[2175]

NOTES

Open-ended investment companies: sub-ss (2)–(4), (6) above have effect as if the Open-ended Investment Companies Regulations 2001, SI 2001/1228, reg 30 was contained in Pt XI (ss 165–177 and Sch 15) of this Act; see reg 30(6) of the 2001 Regulations.

176 Entry of premises under warrant

(1) A justice of the peace may issue a warrant under this section if satisfied on information on oath given by or on behalf of the Secretary of State, the Authority or an investigator that there are reasonable grounds for believing that the first, second or third set of conditions is satisfied.

(2) The first set of conditions is—
- (a) that a person on whom an information requirement has been imposed has failed (wholly or in part) to comply with it; and
- (b) that on the premises specified in the warrant—
  - (i) there are documents which have been required; or
  - (ii) there is information which has been required.

(3) The second set of conditions is—
- (a) that the premises specified in the warrant are premises of an authorised person or an appointed representative;
- (b) that there are on the premises documents or information in relation to which an information requirement could be imposed; and
- (c) that if such a requirement were to be imposed—
  - (i) it would not be complied with; or
  - (ii) the documents or information to which it related would be removed, tampered with or destroyed.

(4) The third set of conditions is—
- (a) that an offence mentioned in section 168 for which the maximum sentence on conviction on indictment is two years or more has been (or is being) committed by any person;
- (b) that there are on the premises specified in the warrant documents or information relevant to whether that offence has been (or is being) committed;
- (c) that an information requirement could be imposed in relation to those documents or information; and
- (d) that if such a requirement were to be imposed—
  - (i) it would not be complied with; or

(ii) the documents or information to which it related would be removed, tampered with or destroyed.

(5) A warrant under this section shall authorise a constable—

(a) to enter the premises specified in the warrant;

(b) to search the premises and take possession of any documents or information appearing to be documents or information of a kind in respect of which a warrant under this section was issued ("the relevant kind") or to take, in relation to any such documents or information, any other steps which may appear to be necessary for preserving them or preventing interference with them;

(c) to take copies of, or extracts from, any documents or information appearing to be of the relevant kind;

(d) to require any person on the premises to provide an explanation of any document or information appearing to be of the relevant kind or to state where it may be found; and

(e) to use such force as may be reasonably necessary.

(6) In England and Wales, sections 15(5) to (8) and section 16 of the Police and Criminal Evidence Act 1984 (execution of search warrants and safeguards) apply to warrants issued under this section.

(7) In Northern Ireland, Articles 17(5) to (8) and 18 of the Police and Criminal Evidence (Northern Ireland) Order 1989 apply to warrants issued under this section.

(8) Any document of which possession is taken under this section may be retained—

(a) for a period of three months; or

(b) if within that period proceedings to which the document is relevant are commenced against any person for any criminal offence, until the conclusion of those proceedings.

(9) In the application of this section to Scotland—

(a) for the references to a justice of the peace substitute references to a justice of the peace or a sheriff; and

(b) for the references to information on oath substitute references to evidence on oath.

(10) "Investigator" means a person appointed under section 167 or 168(3) or (5).

(11) "Information requirement" means a requirement imposed—

(a) by the Authority under section [87C, 87J,] 165 or 175; or

(b) by an investigator under section 171, 172, 173 or 175.

[2176]

NOTES

Sub-s (11): figures in square brackets inserted by the Prospectus Regulations 2005, SI 2005/1433, reg 2(1), Sch 1, para 12, as from 1 July 2005.

Authorised person: see the note to s 165 at **[2165]**.

Additional powers of seizure: the power of seizure conferred by sub-s (5) above is a power of seizure to which the Criminal Justice and Police Act 2001, s 50 (additional powers of seizure from premises) applies; see s 50 of, and Sch 1, Pt 1, para 69 to, the 2001 Act.

Offences

177 Offences

(1) If a person other than the investigator ("the defaulter") fails to comply with a requirement imposed on him under this Part the person imposing the requirement may certify that fact in writing to the court.

(2) If the court is satisfied that the defaulter failed without reasonable excuse to comply with the requirement, it may deal with the defaulter (and in the case of a body corporate, any director or officer) as if he were in contempt[; and "officer", in relation to a limited liability partnership, means a member of the limited liability partnership].

(3) A person who knows or suspects that an investigation is being or is likely to be conducted under this Part is guilty of an offence if—

(a) he falsifies, conceals, destroys or otherwise disposes of a document which he knows or suspects is or would be relevant to such an investigation, or

(b) he causes or permits the falsification, concealment, destruction or disposal of such a document,

unless he shows that he had no intention of concealing facts disclosed by the documents from the investigator.

(4) A person who, in purported compliance with a requirement imposed on him under this Part—

(a) provides information which he knows to be false or misleading in a material particular, or

(b) recklessly provides information which is false or misleading in a material particular,

is guilty of an offence.

(5) A person guilty of an offence under subsection (3) or (4) is liable—

(a) on summary conviction, to imprisonment for a term not exceeding six months or a fine not exceeding the statutory maximum, or both;

(b) on conviction on indictment, to imprisonment for a term not exceeding two years or a fine, or both.

(6) Any person who intentionally obstructs the exercise of any rights conferred by a warrant under section 176 is guilty of an offence and liable on summary conviction to imprisonment for a term not exceeding *three months* or a fine not exceeding level 5 on the standard scale, or both.

(7) "Court" means—

(a) the High Court;

(b) in Scotland, the Court of Session.

[2177]

NOTES

Sub-s (2): words in square brackets added by the Limited Liability Partnerships Regulations 2001, SI 2001/1090, reg 9, Sch 5, para 21, as from 6 April 2001.

Sub-s (6): for the words in italics there are substituted the words "51 weeks" by the Criminal Justice Act 2003, Sch 26, para 54(2), as from a day to be appointed.

Open-ended investment companies: this section has effect as if the Open-ended Investment Companies Regulations 2001, SI 2001/1228, reg 30 was contained in Pt XI (ss 165–177 and Sch 15) of this Act; see reg 30(6) of the 2001 Regulations.

PART XII
CONTROL OVER AUTHORISED PERSONS

NOTES

Transitional provisions: see the Financial Services and Markets Act 2000 (Transitional Provisions) (Controllers) Order 2001, SI 2001/2637 which makes transitional provisions for people who are subject to a regime requiring them to notify a significant shareholding in an authorised person and who will fall within this Part. The Order deals both with the status after commencement of people who have been approved as shareholder controllers under existing regimes and with partly completed procedures. It also provides that the FSA can exercise its powers under this Act in respect of a person who has failed to comply with obligations under the pre-existing regimes, in circumstances where that person would have been subject to an equivalent obligation under this Part after commencement.

See also s 192 at **[2192]** with regard to the Treasury's power to change the definition of "control".

Notice of control

178 Obligation to notify the Authority

(1) If a step which a person proposes to take would result in his acquiring—

(a) control over a UK authorised person,

(b) an additional kind of control over a UK authorised person, or

(c) an increase in a relevant kind of control which he already has over a UK authorised person,

he must notify the Authority of his proposal.

(2) A person who, without himself taking any such step, acquires any such control or additional or increased control must notify the Authority before the end of the period of 14 days beginning with the day on which he first becomes aware that he has acquired it.

(3) A person who is under the duty to notify the Authority imposed by subsection (1) must also give notice to the Authority on acquiring, or increasing, the control in question.

(4) In this Part "UK authorised person" means an authorised person who—

(a) is a body incorporated in, or an unincorporated association formed under the law of, any part of the United Kingdom; and

(b) is not a person authorised as a result of paragraph 1 of Schedule 5.

(5) A notice under subsection (1) or (2) is referred to in this Part as "a notice of control".

[2178]

Acquiring, increasing and reducing control

179 Acquiring control

(1) For the purposes of this Part, a person ("the acquirer") acquires control over a UK authorised person ("A") on first falling within any of the cases in subsection (2).

(2) The cases are where the acquirer—

(a) holds 10% or more of the shares in A;

(b) is able to exercise significant influence over the management of A by virtue of his shareholding in A;

(c) holds 10% or more of the shares in a parent undertaking ("P") of A;

(d) is able to exercise significant influence over the management of P by virtue of his shareholding in P;

(e) is entitled to exercise, or control the exercise of, 10% or more of the voting power in A;

(f) is able to exercise significant influence over the management of A by virtue of his voting power in A;

(g) is entitled to exercise, or control the exercise of, 10% or more of the voting power in P; or

(h) is able to exercise significant influence over the management of P by virtue of his voting power in P.

(3) In subsection (2) "the acquirer" means—

(a) the acquirer;

(b) any of the acquirer's associates; or

(c) the acquirer and any of his associates.

(4) For the purposes of this Part, each of the following is to be regarded as a kind of control—

(a) control arising as a result of the holding of shares in A;

(b) control arising as a result of the holding of shares in P;

(c) control arising as a result of the entitlement to exercise, or control the exercise of, voting power in A;

(d) control arising as a result of the entitlement to exercise, or control the exercise of, voting power in P.

(5) For the purposes of this section and sections 180 and 181, "associate", "shares" and "voting power" have the same meaning as in section 422.

[2179]

180 Increasing control

(1) For the purposes of this Part, a controller of a person ("A") who is a UK authorised person increases his control over A if—

(a) the percentage of shares held by the controller in A increases by any of the steps mentioned in subsection (2);

(b) the percentage of shares held by the controller in a parent undertaking ("P") of A increases by any of the steps mentioned in subsection (2);

(c) the percentage of voting power which the controller is entitled to exercise, or control the exercise of, in A increases by any of the steps mentioned in subsection (2);

(d) the percentage of voting power which the controller is entitled to exercise, or control the exercise of, in P increases by any of the steps mentioned in subsection (2); or

(e) the controller becomes a parent undertaking of A.

(2) The steps are—
(a) from below 10% to 10% or more but less than 20%;
(b) from below 20% to 20% or more but less than 33%;
(c) from below 33% to 33% or more but less than 50%;
(d) from below 50% to 50% or more.

(3) In paragraphs (a) to (d) of subsection (1) "the controller" means—
(a) the controller;
(b) any of the controller's associates; or
(c) the controller and any of his associates.

(4) In the rest of this Part "acquiring control" or "having control" includes—
(a) acquiring or having an additional kind of control; or
(b) acquiring an increase in a relevant kind of control, or having increased control of a relevant kind.

[2180]

181 Reducing control

(1) For the purposes of this Part, a controller of a person ("A") who is a UK authorised person reduces his control over A if—
(a) the percentage of shares held by the controller in A decreases by any of the steps mentioned in subsection (2),
(b) the percentage of shares held by the controller in a parent undertaking ("P") of A decreases by any of the steps mentioned in subsection (2),
(c) the percentage of voting power which the controller is entitled to exercise, or control the exercise of, in A decreases by any of the steps mentioned in subsection (2),
(d) the percentage of voting power which the controller is entitled to exercise, or control the exercise of, in P decreases by any of the steps mentioned in subsection (2), or
(e) the controller ceases to be a parent undertaking of A,

unless the controller ceases to have the kind of control concerned over A as a result.

(2) The steps are—
(a) from 50% or more to 33% or more but less than 50%;
(b) from 33% or more to 20% or more but less than 33%;
(c) from 20% or more to 10% or more but less than 20%;
(d) from 10% or more to less than 10%.

(3) In paragraphs (a) to (d) of subsection (1) "the controller" means—
(a) the controller;
(b) any of the controller's associates; or
(c) the controller and any of his associates.

[2181]

Acquiring or increasing control: procedure

182 Notification

(1) A notice of control must—
(a) be given to the Authority in writing; and
(b) include such information and be accompanied by such documents as the Authority may reasonably require.

(2) The Authority may require the person giving a notice of control to provide such additional information or documents as it reasonably considers necessary in order to enable it to determine what action it is to take in response to the notice.

(3) Different requirements may be imposed in different circumstances.

[2182]

183 Duty of Authority in relation to notice of control

(1) The Authority must, before the end of the period of three months beginning with the date on which it receives a notice of control ("the period for consideration"), determine whether—

(a) to approve of the person concerned having the control to which the notice relates; or

(b) to serve a warning notice under subsection (3) or section 185(3).

(2) Before doing so, the Authority must comply with such requirements as to consultation with competent authorities outside the United Kingdom as may be prescribed.

(3) If the Authority proposes to give the person concerned a notice of objection under section 186(1), it must give him a warning notice.

[2183]

NOTES

Regulations: the Financial Services and Markets Act 2000 (Consultation with Competent Authorities) Regulations 2001, SI 2001/2509 at **[4440]**; the Financial Conglomerates and Other Financial Groups Regulations 2004, SI 2004/1862 at **[4683]**.

Note that the following amending Regulations have also been made under this section: the Collective Investment Schemes (Miscellaneous Amendments) Regulations 2003, SI 2003/2066.

184 Approval of acquisition of control

(1) If the Authority decides to approve of the person concerned having the control to which the notice relates it must notify that person of its approval in writing without delay.

(2) If the Authority fails to comply with subsection (1) of section 183 it is to be treated as having given its approval and notified the person concerned at the end of the period fixed by that subsection.

(3) The Authority's approval remains effective only if the person to whom it relates acquires the control in question—

(a) before the end of such period as may be specified in the notice; or

(b) if no period is specified, before the end of the period of one year beginning with the date—

(i) of the notice of approval;

(ii) on which the Authority is treated as having given approval under subsection (2); or

(iii) of a decision on a reference to the Tribunal which results in the person concerned receiving approval.

[2184]

185 Conditions attached to approval

(1) The Authority's approval under section 184 may be given unconditionally or subject to such conditions as the Authority considers appropriate.

(2) In imposing any conditions, the Authority must have regard to its duty under section 41.

(3) If the Authority proposes to impose conditions on a person it must give him a warning notice.

(4) If the Authority decides to impose conditions on a person it must give him a decision notice.

(5) A person who is subject to a condition imposed under this section may apply to the Authority—

(a) for the condition to be varied; or

(b) for the condition to be cancelled.

(6) The Authority may, on its own initiative, cancel a condition imposed under this section.

(7) If the Authority has given its approval to a person subject to a condition, he may refer to the Tribunal—

(a) the imposition of the condition; or

(b) the Authority's decision to refuse an application made by him under subsection (5).

[2185]

186 Objection to acquisition of control

(1) On considering a notice of control, the Authority may give a decision notice under this section to the person acquiring control ("the acquirer") unless it is satisfied that the approval requirements are met.

(2) The approval requirements are that—
(a) the acquirer is a fit and proper person to have the control over the authorised person that he has or would have if he acquired the control in question; and
(b) the interests of consumers would not be threatened by the acquirer's control or by his acquiring that control.

(3) In deciding whether the approval requirements are met, the Authority must have regard, in relation to the control that the acquirer—
(a) has over the authorised person concerned ("A"), or
(b) will have over A if the proposal to which the notice of control relates is carried into effect,

to its duty under section 41 in relation to each regulated activity carried on by A.

(4) If the Authority gives a notice under this section but considers that the approval requirements would be met if the person to whom a notice is given were to take, or refrain from taking, a particular step, the notice must identify that step.

(5) A person to whom a notice under this section is given may refer the matter to the Tribunal.

(6) "Consumers" means persons who are consumers for the purposes of section 138.

[2186]

187 Objection to existing control

(1) If the Authority is not satisfied that the approval requirements are met, it may give a decision notice under this section to a person if he has failed to comply with a duty to notify imposed by section 178.

(2) If the failure relates to subsection (1) or (2) of that section, the Authority may (instead of giving a notice under subsection (1)) approve the acquisition of the control in question by the person concerned as if he had given it a notice of control.

(3) The Authority may also give a decision notice under this section to a person who is a controller of a UK authorised person if the Authority becomes aware of matters as a result of which it is satisfied that—
(a) the approval requirements are not met with respect to the controller; or
(b) a condition imposed under section 185 required that person to do (or refrain from doing) a particular thing and the condition has been breached as a result of his failing to do (or doing) that thing.

(4) A person to whom a notice under this section is given may refer the matter to the Tribunal.

(5) "Approval requirements" has the same meaning as in section 186.

[2187]

NOTES

Note: the Financial Services and Markets Act 2000 (Consultation with Competent Authorities) Regulations 2001, SI 2001/2509, reg 4 (at **[4443]**) prescribes the same circumstances that are prescribed for the purposes of s 183.

188 Notices of objection under section 187: procedure

(1) If the Authority proposes to give a notice of objection to a person under section 187, it must give him a warning notice.

(2) Before doing so, the Authority must comply with such requirements as to consultation with competent authorities outside the United Kingdom as may be prescribed.

(3) If the Authority decides to give a warning notice under this section, it must do so before the end of the period of three months beginning—
(a) in the case of a notice to be given under section 187(1), with the date on which it became aware of the failure to comply with the duty in question;

(b) in the case of a notice to be given under section 187(3), with the date on which it became aware of the matters in question.

(4) The Authority may require the person concerned to provide such additional information or documents as it considers reasonable.

(5) Different requirements may be imposed in different circumstances.

(6) In this Part "notice of objection" means a notice under section 186 or 187.

[2188]

NOTES

Regulations: the Financial Services and Markets Act 2000 (Consultation with Competent Authorities) Regulations 2001, SI 2001/2509 at **[4440]**; the Financial Conglomerates and Other Financial Groups Regulations 2004, SI 2004/1862 at **[4683]**.

Note that the following amending Regulations have also been made under this section: the Collective Investment Schemes (Miscellaneous Amendments) Regulations 2003, SI 2003/2066.

Improperly acquired shares

189 Improperly acquired shares

(1) The powers conferred by this section are exercisable if a person has acquired, or has continued to hold, any shares in contravention of—

(a) a notice of objection; or
(b) a condition imposed on the Authority's approval.

(2) The Authority may by notice in writing served on the person concerned ("a restriction notice") direct that any such shares which are specified in the notice are, until further notice, subject to one or more of the following restrictions—

(a) a transfer of (or agreement to transfer) those shares, or in the case of unissued shares any transfer of (or agreement to transfer) the right to be issued with them, is void;
(b) no voting rights are to be exercisable in respect of the shares;
(c) no further shares are to be issued in right of them or in pursuance of any offer made to their holder;
(d) except in a liquidation, no payment is to be made of any sums due from the body corporate on the shares, whether in respect of capital or otherwise.

(3) The court may, on the application of the Authority, order the sale of any shares to which this section applies and, if they are for the time being subject to any restriction under subsection (2), that they are to cease to be subject to that restriction.

(4) No order may be made under subsection (3)—

(a) until the end of the period within which a reference may be made to the Tribunal in respect of the notice of objection; and
(b) if a reference is made, until the matter has been determined or the reference withdrawn.

(5) If an order has been made under subsection (3), the court may, on the application of the Authority, make such further order relating to the sale or transfer of the shares as it thinks fit.

(6) If shares are sold in pursuance of an order under this section, the proceeds of sale, less the costs of the sale, must be paid into court for the benefit of the persons beneficially interested in them; and any such person may apply to the court for the whole or part of the proceeds to be paid to him.

(7) This section applies—

(a) in the case of an acquirer falling within section 178(1), to all the shares—
  (i) in the authorised person which the acquirer has acquired;
  (ii) which are held by him or an associate of his; and
  (iii) which were not so held immediately before he became a person with control over the authorised person;
(b) in the case of an acquirer falling within section 178(2), to all the shares held by him or an associate of his at the time when he first became aware that he had acquired control over the authorised person; and
(c) to all the shares in an undertaking ("C")—

(i) which are held by the acquirer or an associate of his, and
(ii) which were not so held before he became a person with control in relation to the authorised person,

where C is the undertaking in which shares were acquired by the acquirer (or an associate of his) and, as a result, he became a person with control in relation to that authorised person.

(8) A copy of the restriction notice must be served on—
(a) the authorised person to whose shares it relates; and
(b) if it relates to shares held by an associate of that authorised person, on that associate.

(9) The jurisdiction conferred by this section may be exercised by the High Court and the Court of Session.

[2189]

Reducing control: procedure

190 Notification

(1) If a step which a controller of a UK authorised person proposes to take would result in his—
(a) ceasing to have control of a relevant kind over the authorised person, or
(b) reducing a relevant kind of control over that person,

he must notify the Authority of his proposal.

(2) A controller of a UK authorised person who, without himself taking any such step, ceases to have that control or reduces that control must notify the Authority before the end of the period of 14 days beginning with the day on which he first becomes aware that—
(a) he has ceased to have the control in question; or
(b) he has reduced that control.

(3) A person who is under the duty to notify the Authority imposed by subsection (1) must also give a notice to the Authority—
(a) on ceasing to have the control in question; or
(b) on reducing that control.

(4) A notice under this section must—
(a) be given to the Authority in writing; and
(b) include details of the extent of the control (if any) which the person concerned will retain (or still retains) over the authorised person concerned.

[2190]

Offences

191 Offences under this Part

(1) A person who fails to comply with the duty to notify the Authority imposed on him by section 178(1) or 190(1) is guilty of an offence.

(2) A person who fails to comply with the duty to notify the Authority imposed on him by section 178(2) or 190(2) is guilty of an offence.

(3) If a person who has given a notice of control to the Authority carries out the proposal to which the notice relates, he is guilty of an offence if—
(a) the period of three months beginning with the date on which the Authority received the notice is still running; and
(b) the Authority has not responded to the notice by either giving its approval or giving him a warning notice under section 183(3) or 185(3).

(4) A person to whom the Authority has given a warning notice under section 183(3) is guilty of an offence if he carries out the proposal to which the notice relates before the Authority has decided whether to give him a notice of objection.

(5) A person to whom a notice of objection has been given is guilty of an offence if he acquires the control to which the notice applies at a time when the notice is still in force.

PART II FSMA 2000

(6) A person guilty of an offence under subsection (1), (2), (3) or (4) is liable on summary conviction to a fine not exceeding level 5 on the standard scale.

(7) A person guilty of an offence under subsection (5) is liable—

(a) on summary conviction, to a fine not exceeding the statutory maximum; and

(b) on conviction on indictment, to imprisonment for a term not exceeding two years or a fine, or both.

(8) A person guilty of an offence under subsection (5) is also liable on summary conviction to a fine not exceeding one tenth of the statutory maximum for each day on which the offence has continued.

(9) It is a defence for a person charged with an offence under subsection (1) to show that he had, at the time of the alleged offence, no knowledge of the act or circumstances by virtue of which the duty to notify the Authority arose.

(10) If a person—

(a) was under the duty to notify the Authority imposed by section 178(1) or 190(1) but had no knowledge of the act or circumstances by virtue of which that duty arose, but

(b) subsequently becomes aware of that act or those circumstances,

he must notify the Authority before the end of the period of 14 days beginning with the day on which he first became so aware.

(11) A person who fails to comply with the duty to notify the Authority imposed by subsection (10) is guilty of an offence and liable, on summary conviction, to a fine not exceeding level 5 on the standard scale.

[2191]

Miscellaneous

192 Power to change definitions of control etc

The Treasury may by order—

(a) provide for exemptions from the obligations to notify imposed by sections 178 and 190;

(b) amend section 179 by varying, or removing, any of the cases in which a person is treated as having control over a UK authorised person or by adding a case;

(c) amend section 180 by varying, or removing, any of the cases in which a person is treated as increasing control over a UK authorised person or by adding a case;

(d) amend section 181 by varying, or removing, any of the cases in which a person is treated as reducing his control over a UK authorised person or by adding a case;

(e) amend section 422 by varying, or removing, any of the cases in which a person is treated as being a controller of a person or by adding a case.

[2192]

NOTES

Orders: the Financial Services and Markets Act 2000 (Controllers) (Exemption) Order 2001, SI 2001/2638 at **[4473]**; the Financial Services and Markets Act 2000 (Controllers) (Exemption) (No 2) Order 2001, SI 2001/3338 at **[4508]**.

Note that the following amending Orders have also been made under this section: the Financial Services and Markets Act 2000 (Regulated Activities) (Amendment) (No 2) Order 2003, SI 2003/1476 at **[4663]**.

PART XIII
INCOMING FIRMS: INTERVENTION BY AUTHORITY

NOTES

Transitional provisions: The Financial Services and Markets Act 2000 (Transitional Provisions) (Authorised Persons etc) Order 2001, SI 2001/2636, Pt III provides that restrictions and prohibitions imposed under provisions of the previous regulatory regimes on authorised persons are to have effect as from 1 December 2001 as if they were requirements imposed under s 196 (in relation to persons with a permission under Sch 3 or 4). As to the restrictions and prohibitions to which Pt III of the 2001 Order applies, see the note "Transitional provisions" to Pt IV of this Act (preceding s 40 at **[2040]**).

Interpretation

193 Interpretation of this Part

(1) In this Part—

"additional procedure" means the procedure described in section 199;

"incoming firm" means—

(a) an EEA firm which is exercising, or has exercised, its right to carry on a regulated activity in the United Kingdom in accordance with Schedule 3; or

(b) a Treaty firm which is exercising, or has exercised, its right to carry on a regulated activity in the United Kingdom in accordance with Schedule 4; and

"power of intervention" means the power conferred on the Authority by section 196.

(2) In relation to an incoming firm which is an EEA firm, expressions used in this Part and in Schedule 3 have the same meaning in this Part as they have in that Schedule.

[2193]

194 General grounds on which power of intervention is exercisable

(1) The Authority may exercise its power of intervention in respect of an incoming firm if it appears to it that—

(a) the firm has contravened, or is likely to contravene, a requirement which is imposed on it by or under this Act (in a case where the Authority is responsible for enforcing compliance in the United Kingdom);

(b) the firm has, in purported compliance with any requirement imposed by or under this Act, knowingly or recklessly given the Authority information which is false or misleading in a material particular; or

(c) it is desirable to exercise the power in order to protect the interests of actual or potential customers.

(2) Subsection (3) applies to an incoming EEA firm falling within sub-paragraph (a) or (b) of paragraph 5 of Schedule 3 which is exercising an EEA right to carry on any Consumer Credit Act business in the United Kingdom.

(3) The Authority may exercise its power of intervention in respect of the firm if [the Office of Fair Trading] has informed the Authority that—

(a) the firm,

(b) any of the firm's employees, agents or associates (whether past or present), or

(c) if the firm is a body corporate, a controller of the firm or an associate of such a controller,

has done any of the things specified in paragraphs *(a) to (d) of section 25(2)* of the Consumer Credit Act 1974.

(4) "Associate", "Consumer Credit Act business" and "controller" have the same meaning as in section 203.

[2194]

NOTES

Sub-s (3): words in square brackets substituted by the Enterprise Act 2002, s 278(1), Sch 25, para 40(1), (6), as from 1 April 2003; for the words in italics there are substituted the words "(a) to (e) of section 25(2A)" by the Consumer Credit Act 2006, s 33(7), as from a day to be appointed.

Note: "customer" is defined in s 59(11) at **[2059]**.

[194A Contravention by relevant EEA firm with UK branch of requirement under markets in financial instruments directive: Authority primarily responsible for securing compliance

(1) This section applies if—

(a) a relevant EEA firm has a branch in the United Kingdom; and

(b) the Authority ascertains that the firm has contravened, or is contravening, a requirement falling within subsection (3) (in a case to which Article 62.2 of the markets in financial instruments directive applies).

(2) "Relevant EEA firm" means an EEA firm falling within paragraph 5(a) or (b) of Schedule 3 which is exercising in the United Kingdom an EEA right deriving from the markets in financial instruments directive.

(3) A requirement falls within this subsection if it is imposed on the firm—

(a) by any provision of or made under this Act which implements the markets in financial instruments directive; or

(b) by any directly applicable Community regulation made under that directive.

(4) The Authority must give the firm written notice which—

(a) requires the firm to put an end to the contravention;

(b) states that the Authority's power of intervention will become exercisable in relation to the firm if the firm continues the contravention; and

(c) indicates any requirements that the Authority proposes to impose on the firm in exercise of its power of intervention in the event of the power becoming exercisable.

(5) The Authority may exercise its power of intervention in respect of the firm if—

(a) a reasonable time has expired since the giving of the notice under subsection (4);

(b) the firm has failed to put an end to the contravention within that time; and

(c) the Authority has informed the firm's home state regulator of its intention to exercise its power of intervention in respect of the firm.

(6) Subsection (5) applies whether or not the Authority's power of intervention is also exercisable as a result of section 194.

(7) If the Authority exercises its power of intervention in respect of a relevant EEA firm by virtue of subsection (5), it must at the earliest opportunity inform the firm's home state regulator and the Commission of—

(a) the fact that the Authority has exercised that power in respect of the firm; and

(b) any requirements it has imposed on the firm in exercise of the power.]

[2194A]

NOTES

Commencement: see the note below.

Inserted by the Financial Services and Markets Act 2000 (Markets in Financial Instruments) Regulations 2007, SI 2007/126, reg 3(1), Sch 1, paras 1, 2, as from 1 April 2007 (certain purposes (see reg 1(2) at **[7596]**)), and as from 1 November 2007 (otherwise).

195 Exercise of power in support of overseas regulator

(1) The Authority may exercise its power of intervention in respect of an incoming firm at the request of, or for the purpose of assisting, an overseas regulator.

(2) Subsection (1) applies whether or not the Authority's power of intervention is also exercisable as a result of section 194.

(3) "An overseas regulator" means an authority in a country or territory outside the United Kingdom—

(a) which is a home state regulator; or

(b) which exercises any function of a kind mentioned in subsection (4).

(4) The functions are—

(a) a function corresponding to any function of the Authority under this Act;

(b) a function corresponding to any function exercised by the competent authority under Part VI . . .;

(c) a function corresponding to any function exercised by the Secretary of State under the Companies Act 1985;

(d) a function in connection with—

(i) the investigation of conduct of the kind prohibited by Part V of the Criminal Justice Act 1993 (insider dealing); or

(ii) the enforcement of rules (whether or not having the force of law) relating to such conduct;

(e) a function prescribed by regulations made for the purposes of this subsection which, in the opinion of the Treasury, relates to companies or financial services.

(5) If—

(a) a request to the Authority for the exercise of its power of intervention has been made by a home state regulator in pursuance of a Community obligation, or

(b) a home state regulator has notified the Authority that an EEA firm's EEA authorisation has been withdrawn, the Authority must, in deciding whether or not to exercise its power of intervention, consider whether exercising it is necessary in order to comply with a Community obligation.

(6) In deciding in any case in which the Authority does not consider that the exercise of its power of intervention is necessary in order to comply with a Community obligation, it may take into account in particular—

- (a) whether in the country or territory of the overseas regulator concerned, corresponding assistance would be given to a United Kingdom regulatory authority;
- (b) whether the case concerns the breach of a law, or other requirement, which has no close parallel in the United Kingdom or involves the assertion of a jurisdiction not recognised by the United Kingdom;
- (c) the seriousness of the case and its importance to persons in the United Kingdom;
- (d) whether it is otherwise appropriate in the public interest to give the assistance sought.

(7) The Authority may decide not to exercise its power of intervention, in response to a request, unless the regulator concerned undertakes to make such contribution to the cost of its exercise as the Authority considers appropriate.

(8) Subsection (7) does not apply if the Authority decides that it is necessary for it to exercise its power of intervention in order to comply with a Community obligation.

[2195]

NOTES

Sub-s (4): words omitted from para (b) repealed by the Prospectus Regulations 2005, SI 2005/1433, reg 2(1), Sch 1, para 13, as from 1 July 2005.

Community obligation: this term is not defined in this Act but has the meaning given by the European Communities Act 1972, Sch 1, Pt II, ie "any obligation created or arising by or under the Treaties, whether an enforceable Community obligation or not". See also the Interpretation Act 1978, Sch 1.

[195A Contravention by relevant EEA firm of requirement under markets in financial instruments directive: home state regulator primarily responsible for securing compliance

(1) This section applies if the Authority has clear and demonstrable grounds for believing that a relevant EEA firm has contravened, or is contravening, a requirement falling within subsection (2) (in a case to which Article 62.1 or 62.3 of the markets in financial instruments directive applies).

(2) A requirement falls within this subsection if it is imposed on the firm—

- (a) by or under any provision adopted in the firm's home state for the purpose of implementing the markets in financial instruments directive; or
- (b) by any directly applicable Community regulation made under that directive.

(3) The Authority must notify the firm's home state regulator of the situation mentioned in subsection (1).

(4) The notice under subsection (3) must—

- (a) request that the home state regulator take all appropriate measures for the purpose of ensuring that the firm puts an end to the contravention;
- (b) state that the Authority's power of intervention is likely to become exercisable in relation to the firm if the firm continues the contravention; and
- (c) indicate any requirements that the Authority proposes to impose on the firm in exercise of its power of intervention in the event of the power becoming exercisable.

(5) The Authority may exercise its power of intervention in respect of the firm if—

- (a) a reasonable time has expired since the giving of the notice under subsection (3); and
- (b) conditions A to C are satisfied.

(6) Condition A is that—

- (a) the firm's home state regulator has failed or refused to take measures for the purpose mentioned in subsection (4)(a); or
- (b) any measures taken by the home state regulator have proved inadequate for that purpose.

PART II
FSMA 2000

(7) Condition B is that the firm is acting in a manner which is clearly prejudicial to the interests of investors in the United Kingdom or the orderly functioning of the markets.

(8) Condition C is that the Authority has informed the firm's home state regulator of its intention to exercise its power of intervention in respect of the firm.

(9) Subsection (5) applies whether or not the Authority's power of intervention is also exercisable as a result of section 194 or 195.

(10) If the Authority exercises its power of intervention in respect of a relevant EEA firm by virtue of subsection (5), it must at the earliest opportunity inform the Commission of—

(a) the fact that the Authority has exercised that power in respect of the firm; and

(b) any requirements it has imposed on the firm in exercise of the power.

(11) In this section—

"home state", in relation to a relevant EEA firm, means—

(a) in the case of a firm which is a body corporate, the EEA State in which the firm has its registered office or, if it has no registered office, its head office; and

(b) in any other case, the EEA State in which the firm has its head office;

"relevant EEA firm" has the same meaning as in section 194A.]

[2195A]

NOTES

Commencement: see the note below.

Inserted by the Financial Services and Markets Act 2000 (Markets in Financial Instruments) Regulations 2007, SI 2007/126, reg 3(1), Sch 1, paras 1, 3, as from 1 April 2007 (certain purposes (see reg 1(2) at **[7596]**)), and as from 1 November 2007 (otherwise).

196 The power of intervention

If the Authority is entitled to exercise its power of intervention in respect of an incoming firm under this Part, it may impose any requirement in relation to the firm which it could impose if—

(a) the firm's permission was a Part IV permission; and

(b) the Authority was entitled to exercise its power under that Part to vary that permission.

[2196]

Exercise of power of intervention

197 Procedure on exercise of power of intervention

(1) A requirement takes effect—

(a) immediately, if the notice given under subsection (3) states that that is the case;

(b) on such date as may be specified in the notice; or

(c) if no date is specified in the notice, when the matter to which it relates is no longer open to review.

(2) A requirement may be expressed to take effect immediately (or on a specified date) only if the Authority, having regard to the ground on which it is exercising its power of intervention, considers that it is necessary for the requirement to take effect immediately (or on that date).

(3) If the Authority proposes to impose a requirement under section 196 on an incoming firm, or imposes such a requirement with immediate effect, it must give the firm written notice.

(4) The notice must—

(a) give details of the requirement;

(b) inform the firm of when the requirement takes effect;

(c) state the Authority's reasons for imposing the requirement and for its determination as to when the requirement takes effect;

(d) inform the firm that it may make representations to the Authority within such period as may be specified in the notice (whether or not it has referred the matter to the Tribunal); and

(e) inform it of its right to refer the matter to the Tribunal.

(5) The Authority may extend the period allowed under the notice for making representations.

(6) If, having considered any representations made by the firm, the Authority decides—
- (a) to impose the requirement proposed, or
- (b) if it has been imposed, not to rescind the requirement,

it must give it written notice.

(7) If, having considered any representations made by the firm, the Authority decides—
- (a) not to impose the requirement proposed,
- (b) to impose a different requirement from that proposed, or
- (c) to rescind a requirement which has effect,

it must give it written notice.

(8) A notice given under subsection (6) must inform the firm of its right to refer the matter to the Tribunal.

(9) A notice under subsection (7)(b) must comply with subsection (4).

(10) If a notice informs a person of his right to refer a matter to the Tribunal, it must give an indication of the procedure on such a reference.

[2197]

198 Power to apply to court for injunction in respect of certain overseas insurance companies

(1) This section applies if the Authority has received a request made in respect of an incoming EEA firm in accordance with—
- (a) Article 20.5 of the first non-life insurance directive; or
- [(b) Article 37.5 of the life assurance consolidation directive].

(2) The court may, on an application made to it by the Authority with respect to the firm, grant an injunction restraining (or in Scotland an interdict prohibiting) the firm disposing of or otherwise dealing with any of its assets.

(3) If the court grants an injunction, it may by subsequent orders make provision for such incidental, consequential and supplementary matters as it considers necessary to enable the Authority to perform any of its functions under this Act.

(4) "The court" means—
- (a) the High Court; or
- (b) in Scotland, the Court of Session.

[2198]

NOTES

Sub-s (1): para (b) substituted by the Life Assurance Consolidation Directive (Consequential Amendments) Regulations 2004, SI 2004/3379, reg 6(1), (3), as from 11 January 2005.

199 Additional procedure for EEA firms in certain cases

(1) This section applies if it appears to the Authority that its power of intervention is exercisable in relation to an EEA firm exercising EEA rights in the United Kingdom ("an incoming EEA firm") in respect of the contravention of a relevant requirement.

(2) A requirement is relevant if—
- (a) it is imposed by the Authority under this Act; and
- (b) as respects its contravention, any of the single market directives [(other than the markets in financial instruments directive)] provides that a procedure of the kind set out in the following provisions of this section is to apply.

(3) The Authority must, in writing, require the firm to remedy the situation.

(4) If the firm fails to comply with the requirement under subsection (3) within a reasonable time, the Authority must give a notice to that effect to the firm's home state regulator requesting it—
- (a) to take all appropriate measures for the purpose of ensuring that the firm remedies the situation which has given rise to the notice; and
- (b) to inform the Authority of the measures it proposes to take or has taken or the reasons for not taking such measures.

PART II FSMA 2000

(5) Except as mentioned in subsection (6), the Authority may not exercise its power of intervention unless satisfied—

(a) that the firm's home state regulator has failed or refused to take measures for the purpose mentioned in subsection (4)(a); or

(b) that the measures taken by the home state regulator have proved inadequate for that purpose.

(6) If the Authority decides that it should exercise its power of intervention in respect of the incoming EEA firm as a matter of urgency in order to protect the interests of consumers, it may exercise that power—

(a) before complying with subsections (3) and (4); or

(b) where it has complied with those subsections, before it is satisfied as mentioned in subsection (5).

(7) In such a case the Authority must at the earliest opportunity inform the firm's home state regulator and the Commission.

(8) If—

(a) the Authority has (by virtue of subsection (6)) exercised its power of intervention before complying with subsections (3) and (4) or before it is satisfied as mentioned in subsection (5), and

(b) the Commission decides under any of the single market directives [(other than the markets in financial instruments directive)] that the Authority must rescind or vary any requirement imposed in the exercise of its power of intervention,

the Authority must in accordance with the decision rescind or vary the requirement.

[2199]

NOTES

Sub-ss (2), (8): words in square brackets inserted by the Financial Services and Markets Act 2000 (Markets in Financial Instruments) Regulations 2007, SI 2007/126, reg 3(1), Sch 1, paras 1, 4, as from 1 April 2007 (certain purposes (see reg 1(2) at **[7596]**)), and as from 1 November 2007 (otherwise).

Supplemental

200 Rescission and variation of requirements

(1) The Authority may rescind or vary a requirement imposed in exercise of its power of intervention on its own initiative or on the application of the person subject to the requirement.

(2) The power of the Authority on its own initiative to rescind a requirement is exercisable by written notice given by the Authority to the person concerned, which takes effect on the date specified in the notice.

(3) Section 197 applies to the exercise of the power of the Authority on its own initiative to vary a requirement as it applies to the imposition of a requirement.

(4) If the Authority proposes to refuse an application for the variation or rescission of a requirement, it must give the applicant a warning notice.

(5) If the Authority decides to refuse an application for the variation or rescission of a requirement—

(a) the Authority must give the applicant a decision notice; and

(b) that person may refer the matter to the Tribunal.

[2200]

201 Effect of certain requirements on other persons

If the Authority, in exercising its power of intervention, imposes on an incoming firm a requirement of a kind mentioned in subsection (3) of section 48, the requirement has the same effect in relation to the firm as it would have in relation to an authorised person if it had been imposed on the authorised person by the Authority acting under section 45.

[2201]

202 Contravention of requirement imposed under this Part

(1) Contravention of a requirement imposed by the Authority under this Part does not—

(a) make a person guilty of an offence;
(b) make any transaction void or unenforceable; or
(c) (subject to subsection (2)) give rise to any right of action for breach of statutory duty.

(2) In prescribed cases the contravention is actionable at the suit of a person who suffers loss as a result of the contravention, subject to the defences and other incidents applying to actions for breach of statutory duty.

[2202]

NOTES

Regulations: the Financial Services and Markets Act 2000 (Rights of Action) Regulations 2001, SI 2001/2256 at **[4395]**.

Powers of [Office of Fair Trading]

203 Power to prohibit the carrying on of Consumer Credit Act business

(1) If it appears to [the Office of Fair Trading ("the OFT")] that subsection (4) has been, or is likely to be, contravened as respects a consumer credit EEA firm, [it] may by written notice given to the firm impose on the firm a consumer credit prohibition.

(2) If it appears to the [OFT] that a restriction imposed under section 204 on an EEA consumer credit firm has not been complied with, [it] may by written notice given to the firm impose a consumer credit prohibition.

(3) "Consumer credit prohibition" means a prohibition on carrying on, or purporting to carry on, in the United Kingdom any Consumer Credit Act business which consists of or includes carrying on one or more listed activities.

(4) This subsection is contravened as respects a firm if—
(a) the firm or any of its employees, agents or associates (whether past or present), or
(b) if the firm is a body corporate, any controller of the firm or an associate of any such controller,

does any of the things specified in paragraphs *(a) to (d) of section 25(2)* of the Consumer Credit Act 1974.

(5) A consumer credit prohibition may be absolute or may be imposed—
(a) for such period,
(b) until the occurrence of such event, or
(c) until such conditions are complied with,

as may be specified in the notice given under subsection (1) or (2).

(6) Any period, event or condition so specified may be varied by the [OFT] on the application of the firm concerned.

(7) A consumer credit prohibition may be withdrawn by written notice served by the [OFT] on the firm concerned, and any such notice takes effect on such date as is specified in the notice.

(8) Schedule 16 has effect as respects consumer credit prohibitions and restrictions under section 204.

(9) A firm contravening a prohibition under this section is guilty of an offence and liable—
(a) on summary conviction, to a fine not exceeding the statutory maximum;
(b) on conviction on indictment, to a fine.

(10) In this section and section 204—

"a consumer credit EEA firm" means an EEA firm falling within any of paragraphs (a) to (c) of paragraph 5 of Schedule 3 whose EEA authorisation covers any Consumer Credit Act business;

"Consumer Credit Act business" means consumer credit business, consumer hire business or ancillary credit business;

"consumer credit business", "consumer hire business" and "ancillary credit business" have the same meaning as in the Consumer Credit Act 1974;

"listed activity" means an activity listed in [Annex 1 to the banking consolidation directive] or the Annex to the investment services directive;

PART II
FSMA 2000

"associate" has the same meaning as in section *25(2)* of the Consumer Credit Act 1974;
"controller" has the meaning given by section 189(1) of that Act.

[2203]

NOTES

In the heading preceding this section words in square brackets substituted by the Enterprise Act 2002, s 278(1), Sch 25, para 40(1), (7), as from 1 April 2003.

Sub-ss (1), (2), (6), (7): words in square brackets substituted by the Enterprise Act 2002, s 278(1), Sch 25, para 40(1), (7), as from 1 April 2003.

Sub-s (4): for the words in italics there are substituted the words "(a) to (e) of section 25(2A)" by the Consumer Credit Act 2006, s 33(7), as from a day to be appointed.

Sub-s (10): words in square brackets in definition "listed activity" substituted by the Banking Consolidation Directive (Consequential Amendments) Regulations 2000, SI 2000/2952, reg 8(1), (2), as from 22 November 2000; for the figure in italics in the definition "associate" there is substituted "25(2A)" by the Consumer Credit Act 2006, s 33(8), as from a day to be appointed.

204 Power to restrict the carrying on of Consumer Credit Act business

(1) In this section "restriction" means a direction that a consumer credit EEA firm may not carry on in the United Kingdom, otherwise than in accordance with such condition or conditions as may be specified in the direction, any Consumer Credit Act business which—

(a) consists of or includes carrying on any listed activity; and
(b) is specified in the direction.

(2) If it appears to the [OFT] that the situation as respects a consumer credit EEA firm is such that the powers conferred by section 203(1) are exercisable, the [OFT] may, instead of imposing a prohibition, impose such restriction as appears to [it] desirable.

(3) A restriction—

(a) may be withdrawn, or
(b) may be varied with the agreement of the firm concerned,

by written notice served by the [OFT] on the firm, and any such notice takes effect on such date as is specified in the notice.

(4) A firm contravening a restriction is guilty of an offence and liable—

(a) on summary conviction, to a fine not exceeding the statutory maximum;
(b) on conviction on indictment, to a fine.

[2204]

NOTES

Sub-ss (2), (3): words in square brackets substituted by the Enterprise Act 2002, s 278(1), Sch 25, para 40(1), (8), as from 1 April 2003.

PART XIV
DISCIPLINARY MEASURES

205 Public censure

If the Authority considers that an authorised person has contravened a requirement imposed on him by or under this Act, [or by any directly applicable Community regulation made under the markets in financial instruments directive,] the Authority may publish a statement to that effect.

[2205]

NOTES

Words in square brackets inserted by the Financial Services and Markets Act 2000 (Markets in Financial Instruments) Regulations 2007, SI 2007/126, reg 3(5), Sch 5, paras 1, 10, as from 1 April 2007 (certain purposes (see reg 1(2) at **[7596]**)), and as from 1 November 2007 (otherwise).

Transitional provisions: as to the exercise of the power conferred by this section in respect of: (a) certain contraventions of the Financial Services Act 1986, before 1 December 2001; and (b) contraventions of the rules of self-regulating organisations before that date, see the Financial Services and Markets Act 2000 (Transitional Provisions and Savings) (Civil Remedies, Discipline, Criminal Offences etc) (No 2) Order 2001, SI 2001/3083, arts 6, 7.

Requirements imposed by the FSA: note that for the purposes of this section a requirement imposed by the FSA under the Electronic Commerce Directive (Financial Services and Markets) Regulations 2002, SI 2002/1775 upon an authorised incoming provider is to be treated as imposed on him by or under this Act; see reg 12(1) of those Regulations at **[4650]**.

206 Financial penalties

(1) If the Authority considers that an authorised person has contravened a requirement imposed on him by or under this Act, [or by any directly applicable Community regulation made under the markets in financial instruments directive,] it may impose on him a penalty, in respect of the contravention, of such amount as it considers appropriate.

(2) The Authority may not in respect of any contravention both require a person to pay a penalty under this section and withdraw his authorisation under section 33.

(3) A penalty under this section is payable to the Authority.

[2206]

NOTES

Sub-s (1): words in square brackets inserted by the Financial Services and Markets Act 2000 (Markets in Financial Instruments) Regulations 2007, SI 2007/126, reg 3(5), Sch 5, paras 1, 11, as from 1 April 2007 (certain purposes (see reg 1(2) at **[7596]**)), and as from 1 November 2007 (otherwise).

Transitional provisions: as to the exercise of the power conferred by this section in respect of contraventions of the rules of self-regulating organisations before 1 December 2001, see the Financial Services and Markets Act 2000 (Transitional Provisions and Savings) (Civil Remedies, Discipline, Criminal Offences etc) (No 2) Order 2001, SI 2001/3083, art 8.

Requirements imposed by the FSA: see the note to s 205 at **[2205]**.

207 Proposal to take disciplinary measures

(1) If the Authority proposes—

(a) to publish a statement in respect of an authorised person (under section 205), or

(b) to impose a penalty on an authorised person (under section 206),

it must give the authorised person a warning notice.

(2) A warning notice about a proposal to publish a statement must set out the terms of the statement.

(3) A warning notice about a proposal to impose a penalty, must state the amount of the penalty.

[2207]

NOTES

Requirements imposed by the FSA: see the note to s 205 at **[2205]**.

208 Decision notice

(1) If the Authority decides—

(a) to publish a statement under section 205 (whether or not in the terms proposed), or

(b) to impose a penalty under section 206 (whether or not of the amount proposed),

it must without delay give the authorised person concerned a decision notice.

(2) In the case of a statement, the decision notice must set out the terms of the statement.

(3) In the case of a penalty, the decision notice must state the amount of the penalty.

(4) If the Authority decides to—

(a) publish a statement in respect of an authorised person under section 205, or

(b) impose a penalty on an authorised person under section 206,

the authorised person may refer the matter to the Tribunal.

[2208]

NOTES

Requirements imposed by the FSA: see the note to s 205 at **[2205]**.

209 Publication

After a statement under section 205 is published, the Authority must send a copy of it to the authorised person and to any person on whom a copy of the decision notice was given under section 393(4).

[2209]

NOTES

Requirements imposed by the FSA: see the note to s 205 at **[2205]**.

210 Statements of policy

(1) The Authority must prepare and issue a statement of its policy with respect to—

(a) the imposition of penalties under this Part; and

(b) the amount of penalties under this Part.

(2) The Authority's policy in determining what the amount of a penalty should be must include having regard to—

(a) the seriousness of the contravention in question in relation to the nature of the requirement contravened;

(b) the extent to which that contravention was deliberate or reckless; and

(c) whether the person on whom the penalty is to be imposed is an individual.

(3) The Authority may at any time alter or replace a statement issued under this section.

(4) If a statement issued under this section is altered or replaced, the Authority must issue the altered or replacement statement.

(5) The Authority must, without delay, give the Treasury a copy of any statement which it publishes under this section.

(6) A statement issued under this section must be published by the Authority in the way appearing to the Authority to be best calculated to bring it to the attention of the public.

(7) In exercising, or deciding whether to exercise, its power under section 206 in the case of any particular contravention, the Authority must have regard to any statement published under this section and in force at the time when the contravention in question occurred.

(8) The Authority may charge a reasonable fee for providing a person with a copy of the statement.

[2210]

211 Statements of policy: procedure

(1) Before issuing a statement under section 210, the Authority must publish a draft of the proposed statement in the way appearing to the Authority to be best calculated to bring it to the attention of the public.

(2) The draft must be accompanied by notice that representations about the proposal may be made to the Authority within a specified time.

(3) Before issuing the proposed statement, the Authority must have regard to any representations made to it in accordance with subsection (2).

(4) If the Authority issues the proposed statement it must publish an account, in general terms, of—

(a) the representations made to it in accordance with subsection (2); and

(b) its response to them.

(5) If the statement differs from the draft published under subsection (1) in a way which is, in the opinion of the Authority, significant, the Authority must (in addition to complying with subsection (4)) publish details of the difference.

(6) The Authority may charge a reasonable fee for providing a person with a copy of a draft published under subsection (1).

(7) This section also applies to a proposal to alter or replace a statement.

[2211]

PART XV
THE FINANCIAL SERVICES COMPENSATION SCHEME

The scheme manager

212 The scheme manager

(1) The Authority must establish a body corporate ("the scheme manager") to exercise the functions conferred on the scheme manager by or under this Part.

(2) The Authority must take such steps as are necessary to ensure that the scheme manager is, at all times, capable of exercising those functions.

(3) The constitution of the scheme manager must provide for it to have—
- (a) a chairman; and
- (b) a board (which must include the chairman) whose members are the scheme manager's directors.

(4) The chairman and other members of the board must be persons appointed, and liable to removal from office, by the Authority (acting, in the case of the chairman, with the approval of the Treasury).

(5) But the terms of their appointment (and in particular those governing removal from office) must be such as to secure their independence from the Authority in the operation of the compensation scheme.

(6) The scheme manager is not to be regarded as exercising functions on behalf of the Crown.

(7) The scheme manager's board members, officers and staff are not to be regarded as Crown servants.

[2212]

The scheme

213 The compensation scheme

(1) The Authority must by rules establish a scheme for compensating persons in cases where relevant persons are unable, or are likely to be unable, to satisfy claims against them.

(2) The rules are to be known as the Financial Services Compensation Scheme (but are referred to in this Act as "the compensation scheme").

(3) The compensation scheme must, in particular, provide for the scheme manager—
- (a) to assess and pay compensation, in accordance with the scheme, to claimants in respect of claims made in connection with regulated activities carried on (whether or not with permission) by relevant persons; and
- (b) to have power to impose levies on authorised persons, or any class of authorised person, for the purpose of meeting its expenses (including in particular expenses incurred, or expected to be incurred, in paying compensation, borrowing or insuring risks).

(4) The compensation scheme may provide for the scheme manager to have power to impose levies on authorised persons, or any class of authorised person, for the purpose of recovering the cost (whenever incurred) of establishing the scheme.

(5) In making any provision of the scheme by virtue of subsection (3)(b), the Authority must take account of the desirability of ensuring that the amount of the levies imposed on a particular class of authorised person reflects, so far as practicable, the amount of the claims made, or likely to be made, in respect of that class of person.

(6) An amount payable to the scheme manager as a result of any provision of the scheme made by virtue of subsection (3)(b) or (4) may be recovered as a debt due to the scheme manager.

(7) Sections 214 to 217 make further provision about the scheme but are not to be taken as limiting the power conferred on the Authority by subsection (1).

(8) In those sections "specified" means specified in the scheme.

(9) In this Part (except in sections 219, 220 or 224) "relevant person" means a person who was—

(a) an authorised person at the time the act or omission giving rise to the claim against him took place; or
(b) an appointed representative at that time.

(10) But a person who, at that time—
(a) qualified for authorisation under Schedule 3, and
(b) fell within a prescribed category,

is not to be regarded as a relevant person in relation to any activities for which he had permission as a result of any provision of, or made under, that Schedule unless he had elected to participate in the scheme in relation to those activities at that time.

[2213]

NOTES

Note: membership of the scheme is voluntary for those who qualify for authorisation under Sch 3 to this Act (ie, incoming EEA firms authorised under Sch 3). The compensation scheme may provide that incoming EEA firms can elect to participate in relation to some or all the activities for which it has permission under Sch 3 (see s 214(5)). The Financial Services and Markets Act 2000 (Compensation Scheme: Electing Participants) Regulations 2001, SI 2001/1783, reg 3 (as amended) prescribes the categories of firms to which this applies (see **[4364]**).

Note: this section did not apply in relation to persons who were relevant persons, within the meaning of this section, only by virtue of having an interim permission, or appointed representatives of such persons. See, as to interim permission in respect of regulated mortgage business, the Financial Services and Markets Act 2000 (Transitional Provisions) (Mortgages) Order 2004, SI 2004/2615 at **[4695]** et seq, and, as to interim permission in respect of general insurance intermediaries, the Financial Services and Markets Act 2000 (Transitional Provisions) (General Insurance Intermediaries) Order 2004, SI 2004/3351 at **[4710]** et seq. These provisions lapsed with effect from 31 October 2005.

Regulations: the Financial Services and Markets Act 2000 (Compensation Scheme: Electing Participants) Regulations 2001, SI 2001/1783 at **[4362]**.

Note that the following amending Regulations have also been made under this section: the Collective Investment Schemes (Miscellaneous Amendments) Regulations 2003, SI 2003/2066.

Provisions of the scheme

214 General

(1) The compensation scheme may, in particular, make provision—
(a) as to the circumstances in which a relevant person is to be taken (for the purposes of the scheme) to be unable, or likely to be unable, to satisfy claims made against him;
(b) for the establishment of different funds for meeting different kinds of claim;
(c) for the imposition of different levies in different cases;
(d) limiting the levy payable by a person in respect of a specified period;
(e) for repayment of the whole or part of a levy in specified circumstances;
(f) for a claim to be entertained only if it is made by a specified kind of claimant;
(g) for a claim to be entertained only if it falls within a specified kind of claim;
(h) as to the procedure to be followed in making a claim;
(i) for the making of interim payments before a claim is finally determined;
(j) limiting the amount payable on a claim to a specified maximum amount or a maximum amount calculated in a specified manner;
(k) for payment to be made, in specified circumstances, to a person other than the claimant.

(2) Different provision may be made with respect to different kinds of claim.

(3) The scheme may provide for the determination and regulation of matters relating to the scheme by the scheme manager.

(4) The scheme, or particular provisions of the scheme, may be made so as to apply only in relation to—
(a) activities carried on,
(b) claimants,
(c) matters arising, or
(d) events occurring,

in specified territories, areas or localities.

(5) The scheme may provide for a person who—
(a) qualifies for authorisation under Schedule 3, and

(b) falls within a prescribed category,

to elect to participate in the scheme in relation to some or all of the activities for which he has permission as a result of any provision of, or made under, that Schedule.

(6) The scheme may provide for the scheme manager to have power—

(a) in specified circumstances,

(b) but only if the scheme manager is satisfied that the claimant is entitled to receive a payment in respect of his claim—

(i) under a scheme which is comparable to the compensation scheme, or

(ii) as the result of a guarantee given by a government or other authority,

to make a full payment of compensation to the claimant and recover the whole or part of the amount of that payment from the other scheme or under that guarantee.

[2214]

NOTES

Regulations: the Financial Services and Markets Act 2000 (Compensation Scheme: Electing Participants) Regulations 2001, SI 2001/1783 at **[4362]**.

Note that the following amending Regulations have also been made under this section: the Collective Investment Schemes (Miscellaneous Amendments) Regulations 2003, SI 2003/2066.

215 Rights of the scheme in relevant person's insolvency

(1) The compensation scheme may, in particular, make provision—

(a) as to the effect of a payment of compensation under the scheme in relation to rights or obligations arising out of the claim against a relevant person in respect of which the payment was made;

(b) for conferring on the scheme manager a right of recovery against that person.

(2) Such a right of recovery conferred by the scheme does not, in the event of the relevant person's insolvency, exceed such right (if any) as the claimant would have had in that event.

(3) If a person other than the scheme manager [makes an administration application under Schedule B1 to the 1986 Act or [Schedule B1 to] the 1989 Order] in relation to a company or partnership which is a relevant person, the scheme manager has the same rights as are conferred on the Authority by section 362.

[(3A) In subsection (3) the reference to making an administration application includes a reference to—

(a) appointing an administrator under paragraph 14 or 22 of Schedule B1 to the 1986 Act [or paragraph 15 or 23 of Schedule B1 to the 1989 Order], or

(b) filing with the court a copy of notice of intention to appoint an administrator under [any] of those paragraphs.]

(4) If a person other than the scheme manager presents a petition for the winding up of a body which is a relevant person, the scheme manager has the same rights as are conferred on the Authority by section 371.

(5) If a person other than the scheme manager presents a bankruptcy petition to the court in relation to an individual who, or an entity which, is a relevant person, the scheme manager has the same rights as are conferred on the Authority by section 374.

(6) Insolvency rules may be made for the purpose of integrating any procedure for which provision is made as a result of subsection (1) into the general procedure on the administration of a company or partnership or on a winding-up, bankruptcy or sequestration.

(7) "Bankruptcy petition" means a petition to the court—

(a) under section 264 of the 1986 Act or Article 238 of the 1989 Order for a bankruptcy order to be made against an individual;

(b) under section 5 of the 1985 Act for the sequestration of the estate of an individual; or

(c) under section 6 of the 1985 Act for the sequestration of the estate belonging to or held for or jointly by the members of an entity mentioned in subsection (1) of that section.

(8) "Insolvency rules" are—

(a) for England and Wales, rules made under sections 411 and 412 of the 1986 Act;

(b) for Scotland, rules made by order by the Treasury, after consultation with the Scottish Ministers, for the purposes of this section; and

(c) for Northern Ireland, rules made under Article 359 of the 1989 Order and section 55 of the Judicature (Northern Ireland) Act 1978.

(9) "The 1985 Act", "the 1986 Act", "the 1989 Order" and "court" have the same meaning as in Part XXIV.

[2215]

NOTES

Sub-s (3): words in first pair of square brackets substituted by the Enterprise Act 2002, s 248(3), Sch 17, paras 53, 54(1), (2), as from 15 September 2003 (for savings and transitional provisions, see the note to the Insolvency Act 1986, s 8 at **[3164]**); words in second pair of square brackets substituted by the Insolvency (Northern Ireland) Order 2005, SI 2005/1455, art 3(3), Sch 2, paras 56, 57(1), (2), as from 27 March 2006.

Sub-s (3A): inserted by the Enterprise Act 2002, s 248(3), Sch 17, paras 53, 54(1), (3), as from 15 September 2003 (for savings and transitional provisions, see the note to the Insolvency Act 1986, s 8 at **[3164]**); words in square brackets in para (a) inserted, and word in square brackets in para (b) substituted, by SI 2005/1455, art 3(3), Sch 2, paras 56, 57(1), (3), as from 27 March 2006.

Application to limited liability partnerships: see the Limited Liability Partnerships Regulations 2001, SI 2001/1090, reg 6 at **[6987]**.

216 Continuity of long-term insurance policies

(1) The compensation scheme may, in particular, include provision requiring the scheme manager to make arrangements for securing continuity of insurance for policyholders, or policyholders of a specified class, of relevant long-term insurers.

(2) "Relevant long-term insurers" means relevant persons who—

(a) have permission to effect or carry out contracts of long-term insurance; and

(b) are unable, or likely to be unable, to satisfy claims made against them.

(3) The scheme may provide for the scheme manager to take such measures as appear to him to be appropriate—

(a) for securing or facilitating the transfer of a relevant long-term insurer's business so far as it consists of the carrying out of contracts of long-term insurance, or of any part of that business, to another authorised person;

(b) for securing the issue by another authorised person to the policyholders concerned of policies in substitution for their existing policies.

(4) The scheme may also provide for the scheme manager to make payments to the policyholders concerned—

(a) during any period while he is seeking to make arrangements mentioned in subsection (1);

(b) if it appears to him that it is not reasonably practicable to make such arrangements.

(5) A provision of the scheme made by virtue of section 213(3)(b) may include power to impose levies for the purpose of meeting expenses of the scheme manager incurred in—

(a) taking measures as a result of any provision of the scheme made by virtue of subsection (3);

(b) making payments as a result of any such provision made by virtue of subsection (4).

[2216]

217 Insurers in financial difficulties

(1) The compensation scheme may, in particular, include provision for the scheme manager to have power to take measures for safeguarding policyholders, or policyholders of a specified class, of relevant insurers.

(2) "Relevant insurers" means relevant persons who—

(a) have permission to effect or carry out contracts of insurance; and

(b) are in financial difficulties.

(3) The measures may include such measures as the scheme manager considers appropriate for—

(a) securing or facilitating the transfer of a relevant insurer's business so far as it consists of the carrying out of contracts of insurance, or of any part of that business, to another authorised person;

(b) giving assistance to the relevant insurer to enable it to continue to effect or carry out contracts of insurance.

(4) The scheme may provide—

(a) that if measures of a kind mentioned in subsection (3)(a) are to be taken, they should be on terms appearing to the scheme manager to be appropriate, including terms reducing, or deferring payment of, any of the things to which any of those who are eligible policyholders in relation to the relevant insurer are entitled in their capacity as such;

(b) that if measures of a kind mentioned in subsection (3)(b) are to be taken, they should be conditional on the reduction of, or the deferment of the payment of, the things to which any of those who are eligible policyholders in relation to the relevant insurer are entitled in their capacity as such;

(c) for ensuring that measures of a kind mentioned in subsection (3)(b) do not benefit to any material extent persons who were members of a relevant insurer when it began to be in financial difficulties or who had any responsibility for, or who may have profited from, the circumstances giving rise to its financial difficulties, except in specified circumstances;

(d) for requiring the scheme manager to be satisfied that any measures he proposes to take are likely to cost less than it would cost to pay compensation under the scheme if the relevant insurer became unable, or likely to be unable, to satisfy claims made against him.

(5) The scheme may provide for the Authority to have power—

(a) to give such assistance to the scheme manager as it considers appropriate for assisting the scheme manager to determine what measures are practicable or desirable in the case of a particular relevant insurer;

(b) to impose constraints on the taking of measures by the scheme manager in the case of a particular relevant insurer;

(c) to require the scheme manager to provide it with information about any particular measures which the scheme manager is proposing to take.

(6) The scheme may include provision for the scheme manager to have power—

(a) to make interim payments in respect of eligible policyholders of a relevant insurer;

(b) to indemnify any person making payments to eligible policyholders of a relevant insurer.

(7) A provision of the scheme made by virtue of section 213(3)(b) may include power to impose levies for the purpose of meeting expenses of the scheme manager incurred in—

(a) taking measures as a result of any provision of the scheme made by virtue of subsection (1);

(b) making payments or giving indemnities as a result of any such provision made by virtue of subsection (6).

(8) "Financial difficulties" and "eligible policyholders" have such meanings as may be specified.

[2217]

Annual report

218 Annual report

(1) At least once a year, the scheme manager must make a report to the Authority on the discharge of its functions.

(2) The report must—

(a) include a statement setting out the value of each of the funds established by the compensation scheme; and

(b) comply with any requirements specified in rules made by the Authority.

(3) The scheme manager must publish each report in the way it considers appropriate.

[2218]

PART II FSMA 2000

Information and documents

219 Scheme manager's power to require information

(1) The scheme manager may, by notice in writing given to the relevant person in respect of whom a claim is made under the scheme or to a person otherwise involved, require that person—

(a) to provide specified information or information of a specified description; or

(b) to produce specified documents or documents of a specified description.

(2) The information or documents must be provided or produced—

(a) before the end of such reasonable period as may be specified; and

(b) in the case of information, in such manner or form as may be specified.

(3) This section applies only to information and documents the provision or production of which the scheme manager considers—

(a) to be necessary for the fair determination of the claim; or

(b) to be necessary (or likely to be necessary) for the fair determination of other claims made (or which it expects may be made) in respect of the relevant person concerned.

(4) If a document is produced in response to a requirement imposed under this section, the scheme manager may—

(a) take copies or extracts from the document; or

(b) require the person producing the document to provide an explanation of the document.

(5) If a person who is required under this section to produce a document fails to do so, the scheme manager may require the person to state, to the best of his knowledge and belief, where the document is.

(6) If the relevant person is insolvent, no requirement may be imposed under this section on a person to whom section 220 or 224 applies.

(7) If a person claims a lien on a document, its production under this Part does not affect the lien.

(8) "Relevant person" has the same meaning as in section 224.

(9) "Specified" means specified in the notice given under subsection (1).

(10) A person is involved in a claim made under the scheme if he was knowingly involved in the act or omission giving rise to the claim.

[2219]

220 Scheme manager's power to inspect information held by liquidator etc

(1) For the purpose of assisting the scheme manager to discharge its functions in relation to a claim made in respect of an insolvent relevant person, a person to whom this section applies must permit a person authorised by the scheme manager to inspect relevant documents.

(2) A person inspecting a document under this section may take copies of, or extracts from, the document.

(3) This section applies to—

(a) the administrative receiver, administrator, liquidator or trustee in bankruptcy of an insolvent relevant person;

(b) the permanent trustee, within the meaning of the Bankruptcy (Scotland) Act 1985, on the estate of an insolvent relevant person.

(4) This section does not apply to a liquidator, administrator or trustee in bankruptcy who is—

(a) the Official Receiver;

(b) the Official Receiver for Northern Ireland; or

(c) the Accountant in Bankruptcy.

(5) "Relevant person" has the same meaning as in section 224.

[2220]

221 Powers of court where information required

(1) If a person ("the defaulter")—

(a) fails to comply with a requirement imposed under section 219, or

(b) fails to permit documents to be inspected under section 220,

the scheme manager may certify that fact in writing to the court and the court may enquire into the case.

(2) If the court is satisfied that the defaulter failed without reasonable excuse to comply with the requirement (or to permit the documents to be inspected), it may deal with the defaulter (and, in the case of a body corporate, any director or officer) as if he were in contempt[; and "officer", in relation to a limited liability partnership, means a member of the limited liability partnership].

(3) "Court" means—

(a) the High Court;

(b) in Scotland, the Court of Session.

[2221]

NOTES

Sub-s (2): words in square brackets added by the Limited Liability Partnerships Regulations 2001, SI 2001/1090, reg 9, Sch 5, para 21, as from 6 April 2001.

Miscellaneous

222 Statutory immunity

(1) Neither the scheme manager nor any person who is, or is acting as, its board member, officer or member of staff is to be liable in damages for anything done or omitted in the discharge, or purported discharge, of the scheme manager's functions.

(2) Subsection (1) does not apply—

(a) if the act or omission is shown to have been in bad faith; or

(b) so as to prevent an award of damages made in respect of an act or omission on the ground that the act or omission was unlawful as a result of section 6(1) of the Human Rights Act 1998.

[2222]

223 Management expenses

(1) The amount which the scheme manager may recover, from the sums levied under the scheme, as management expenses attributable to a particular period may not exceed such amount as may be fixed by the scheme as the limit applicable to that period.

(2) In calculating the amount of any levy to be imposed by the scheme manager, no amount may be included to reflect management expenses unless the limit mentioned in subsection (1) has been fixed by the scheme.

(3) "Management expenses" means expenses incurred, or expected to be incurred, by the scheme manager in connection with its functions under this Act other than those incurred—

(a) in paying compensation;

(b) as a result of any provision of the scheme made by virtue of section 216(3) or (4) or 217(1) or (6).

[2223]

224 Scheme manager's power to inspect documents held by Official Receiver etc

(1) If, as a result of the insolvency or bankruptcy of a relevant person, any documents have come into the possession of a person to whom this section applies, he must permit any person authorised by the scheme manager to inspect the documents for the purpose of establishing—

(a) the identity of persons to whom the scheme manager may be liable to make a payment in accordance with the compensation scheme; or

(b) the amount of any payment which the scheme manager may be liable to make.

(2) A person inspecting a document under this section may take copies or extracts from the document.

PART II FSMA 2000

(3) In this section "relevant person" means a person who was—
(a) an authorised person at the time the act or omission which may give rise to the liability mentioned in subsection (1)(a) took place; or
(b) an appointed representative at that time.

(4) But a person who, at that time—
(a) qualified for authorisation under Schedule 3, and
(b) fell within a prescribed category,
is not to be regarded as a relevant person for the purposes of this section in relation to any activities for which he had permission as a result of any provision of, or made under, that Schedule unless he had elected to participate in the scheme in relation to those activities at that time.

(5) This section applies to—
(a) the Official Receiver;
(b) the Official Receiver for Northern Ireland; and
(c) the Accountant in Bankruptcy.

[2224]

NOTES

Regulations: the Financial Services and Markets Act 2000 (Compensation Scheme: Electing Participants) Regulations 2001, SI 2001/1783 at **[4362]**.

Note that the following amending Regulations have also been made under this section: the Collective Investment Schemes (Miscellaneous Amendments) Regulations 2003, SI 2003/2066.

PART XVI
THE OMBUDSMAN SCHEME

NOTES

Transitional provisions: see the Financial Services and Markets Act 2000 (Transitional Provisions) (Ombudsman Scheme and Complaints Scheme) Order 2001, SI 2001/2326. Arts 2–17 of that Order make transitional provisions in relation to the establishment of the ombudsman scheme by this Part. The Order provides for certain complaints relating to acts or omissions occurring before the commencement of this Part, which fell (or would have fallen) within the scope of one of the "former schemes", to be dealt with under the new scheme, subject to specified modifications set out in arts 4–7. Arts 8–10 make provision for appeals against certain determinations made before commencement under the IMRO scheme, the SFA scheme and the building societies scheme. Art 16 provides that where consultation on rules for the new scheme was undertaken before 19 July 2001, that consultation is to be taken to satisfy the requirements in Sch 17 to this Act to the extent that it would have done so if undertaken after that date. Art 17 provides for liabilities of the former schemes arising from the handling of complaints to become liabilities of the operator of the new scheme. Arts 18–20 are concerned with complaints relating to certain matters occurring before the coming into force of s 19 of this Act. Art 18 empowers the FSA to make arrangements for the investigation of such complaints and supplements the Authority's duty, under Sch 1, paras 7 and 8, to make arrangements for the investigation of complaints relating to the exercise of (or failure to exercise) its functions under the Act. Art 19 makes provision about anticipatory consultation with respect to any "transitional complaints scheme" made under art 18. Art 20 confers exemption from liability in damages on those investigating "transitional complaints" under art 18.

See also the Financial Services and Markets Act 2000 (Transitional Provisions) (Complaints Relating to General Insurance and Mortgages) Order 2004, SI 2004/454 at **[4671]** et seq. The 2004 Order makes further provision in relation to the inclusion of the activities of arranging and advising on regulated mortgage contracts, and insurance mediation activities, as regulated activities for the purposes of this Act. It modifies this Part and provides that certain complaints relating to acts or omissions which would have fallen within the Mortgage Code Arbitration Scheme or the Dispute Resolution Facility established by the General Insurance Standards Council can be dealt with under the new scheme established by this Part.

Disputes relating to mutual societies: nothing in the Friendly Societies Act 1992, s 80(1) (determination of certain disputes by arbitration), or in rules of a kind mentioned in that subsection, prevents any person from having a complaint dealt with under the ombudsman scheme under this Part before, or instead of, arbitration; see s 80(1A) of the 1992 Act. Similarly, nothing in the Industrial and Provident Societies Act 1965, s 60(1) (decision of disputes), or in rules of a kind mentioned in that subsection, prevents any person from having a complaint dealt with under the ombudsman scheme under this Part before, or instead of, determination in the manner directed in the rules; see s 60(1A) of the 1965 Act.

The scheme

225 The scheme and the scheme operator

(1) This Part provides for a scheme under which certain disputes may be resolved quickly and with minimum formality by an independent person.

(2) The scheme is to be administered by a body corporate ("the scheme operator").

(3) The scheme is to be operated under a name chosen by the scheme operator but is referred to in this Act as "the ombudsman scheme".

(4) Schedule 17 makes provision in connection with the ombudsman scheme and the scheme operator.

[2225]

226 Compulsory jurisdiction

(1) A complaint which relates to an act or omission of a person ("the respondent") in carrying on an activity to which compulsory jurisdiction rules apply is to be dealt with under the ombudsman scheme if the conditions mentioned in subsection (2) are satisfied.

(2) The conditions are that—

(a) the complainant is eligible and wishes to have the complaint dealt with under the scheme;

(b) the respondent was an authorised person at the time of the act or omission to which the complaint relates; and

(c) the act or omission to which the complaint relates occurred at a time when compulsory jurisdiction rules were in force in relation to the activity in question.

(3) "Compulsory jurisdiction rules" means rules—

(a) made by the Authority for the purposes of this section; and

(b) specifying the activities to which they apply.

(4) Only activities which are regulated activities, or which could be made regulated activities by an order under section 22, may be specified.

(5) Activities may be specified by reference to specified categories (however described).

(6) A complainant is eligible, in relation to the compulsory jurisdiction of the ombudsman scheme, if he falls within a class of person specified in the rules as eligible.

(7) The rules—

(a) may include provision for persons other than individuals to be eligible; but

(b) may not provide for authorised persons to be eligible except in specified circumstances or in relation to complaints of a specified kind.

(8) The jurisdiction of the scheme which results from this section is referred to in this Act as the "compulsory jurisdiction".

[2226]

PART II
FSMA 2000

NOTES

Transitional provisions: see the Financial Services and Markets Act 2000 (Transitional Provisions) (Ombudsman Scheme and Complaints Scheme) Order 2001, SI 2001/2326 in relation to complaints first arising before N2 or relating to acts or omissions occurring before N2. See also the Financial Services and Markets Act 2000 (Transitional Provisions) (Complaints relating to General Insurance and Mortgages) Order 2004, SI 2004/454, art 2 (at **[4671]**) for application of compulsory jurisdiction to a complaint referred to the new scheme on or after the relevant commencement date.

[226A Consumer credit jurisdiction

(1) A complaint which relates to an act or omission of a person ("the respondent") is to be dealt with under the ombudsman scheme if the conditions mentioned in subsection (2) are satisfied.

(2) The conditions are that—

(a) the complainant is eligible and wishes to have the complaint dealt with under the scheme;

(b) the complaint falls within a description specified in consumer credit rules;

(c) at the time of the act or omission the respondent was the licensee under a standard licence or was authorised to carry on an activity by virtue of section 34A of the Consumer Credit Act 1974;
(d) the act or omission occurred in the course of a business being carried on by the respondent which was of a type mentioned in subsection (3);
(e) at the time of the act or omission that type of business was specified in an order made by the Secretary of State; and
(f) the complaint cannot be dealt with under the compulsory jurisdiction.

(3) The types of business referred to in subsection (2)(d) are—
(a) a consumer credit business;
(b) a consumer hire business;
(c) a business so far as it comprises or relates to credit brokerage;
(d) a business so far as it comprises or relates to debt-adjusting;
(e) a business so far as it comprises or relates to debt-counselling;
(f) a business so far as it comprises or relates to debt-collecting;
(g) a business so far as it comprises or relates to debt administration;
(h) a business so far as it comprises or relates to the provision of credit information services;
(i) a business so far as it comprises or relates to the operation of a credit reference agency.

(4) A complainant is eligible if—
(a) he is—
(i) an individual; or
(ii) a surety in relation to a security provided to the respondent in connection with the business mentioned in subsection (2)(d); and
(b) he falls within a class of person specified in consumer credit rules.

(5) The approval of the Treasury is required for an order under subsection (2)(e).

(6) The jurisdiction of the scheme which results from this section is referred to in this Act as the "consumer credit jurisdiction".

(7) In this Act "consumer credit rules" means rules made by the scheme operator with the approval of the Authority for the purposes of the consumer credit jurisdiction.

(8) Consumer credit rules under this section may make different provision for different cases.

(9) Expressions used in the Consumer Credit Act 1974 have the same meaning in this section as they have in that Act.]

[2226A]

NOTES

Commencement: 16 June 2006.

Inserted by the Consumer Credit Act 2006, s 59(1), as from 16 June 2006.

Transitional provisions: see the Consumer Credit Act 2006, Sch 3, para 29 which provides that "Section 1 of this Act (substitution of definition of "individual" in the Consumer Credit Act 1974, s 189) shall have no effect for the purposes of section 226A(4)(a) of the 2000 Act in relation to a complaint which relates to an act or omission occurring before the commencement of section 1".

Orders: the Financial Services and Markets Act 2000 (Ombudsman Scheme) (Consumer Credit Jurisdiction) Order 2007, SI 2007/383 at **[4827]**.

227 Voluntary jurisdiction

(1) A complaint which relates to an act or omission of a person ("the respondent") in carrying on an activity to which voluntary jurisdiction rules apply is to be dealt with under the ombudsman scheme if the conditions mentioned in subsection (2) are satisfied.

(2) The conditions are that—
(a) the complainant is eligible and wishes to have the complaint dealt with under the scheme;
(b) at the time of the act or omission to which the complaint relates, the respondent was participating in the scheme;
(c) at the time when the complaint is referred under the scheme, the respondent has not withdrawn from the scheme in accordance with its provisions;
(d) the act or omission to which the complaint relates occurred at a time when voluntary jurisdiction rules were in force in relation to the activity in question; and

(e) the complaint cannot be dealt with under the compulsory jurisdiction [or the consumer credit jurisdiction].

(3) "Voluntary jurisdiction rules" means rules—
(a) made by the scheme operator for the purposes of this section; and
(b) specifying the activities to which they apply.

(4) The only activities which may be specified in the rules are activities which are, or could be, specified in compulsory jurisdiction rules.

(5) Activities may be specified by reference to specified categories (however described).

(6) The rules require the Authority's approval.

(7) A complainant is eligible, in relation to the voluntary jurisdiction of the ombudsman scheme, if he falls within a class of person specified in the rules as eligible.

(8) The rules may include provision for persons other than individuals to be eligible.

(9) A person qualifies for participation in the ombudsman scheme if he falls within a class of person specified in the rules in relation to the activity in question.

(10) Provision may be made in the rules for persons other than authorised persons to participate in the ombudsman scheme.

(11) The rules may make different provision in relation to complaints arising from different activities.

(12) The jurisdiction of the scheme which results from this section is referred to in this Act as the "voluntary jurisdiction".

(13) In such circumstances as may be specified in voluntary jurisdiction rules, a complaint—
(a) which relates to an act or omission occurring at a time before the rules came into force, and
(b) which could have been dealt with under a scheme which has to any extent been replaced by the voluntary jurisdiction,

is to be dealt with under the ombudsman scheme even though paragraph (b) or (d) of subsection (2) would otherwise prevent that.

(14) In such circumstances as may be specified in voluntary jurisdiction rules, a complaint is to be dealt with under the ombudsman scheme even though—
(a) paragraph (b) or (d) of subsection (2) would otherwise prevent that, and
(b) the complaint is not brought within the scheme as a result of subsection (13),

but only if the respondent has agreed that complaints of that kind were to be dealt with under the scheme.

[2227]

NOTES

Sub-s (2): words in square brackets inserted by the Consumer Credit Act 2006, s 61(2), as from 16 June 2006.

PART II
FSMA 2000

Determination of complaints

228 Determination under the compulsory jurisdiction

(1) This section applies only in relation to the compulsory jurisdiction [and to the consumer credit jurisdiction].

(2) A complaint is to be determined by reference to what is, in the opinion of the ombudsman, fair and reasonable in all the circumstances of the case.

(3) When the ombudsman has determined a complaint he must give a written statement of his determination to the respondent and to the complainant.

(4) The statement must—
(a) give the ombudsman's reasons for his determination;
(b) be signed by him; and
(c) require the complainant to notify him in writing, before a date specified in the statement, whether he accepts or rejects the determination.

(5) If the complainant notifies the ombudsman that he accepts the determination, it is binding on the respondent and the complainant and final.

(6) If, by the specified date, the complainant has not notified the ombudsman of his acceptance or rejection of the determination he is to be treated as having rejected it.

(7) The ombudsman must notify the respondent of the outcome.

(8) A copy of the determination on which appears a certificate signed by an ombudsman is evidence (or in Scotland sufficient evidence) that the determination was made under the scheme.

(9) Such a certificate purporting to be signed by an ombudsman is to be taken to have been duly signed unless the contrary is shown.

[2228]

NOTES

Sub-s (1): words in square brackets inserted by the Consumer Credit Act 2006, s 61(3), as from 16 June 2006.

Transitional provisions: ss 228–232 of this Act apply in relation to a relevant transitional complaint as they apply in relation to a complaint of the kind mentioned in s 226(1), subject to transitional provisions; see the Financial Services and Markets Act 2000 (Transitional Provisions) (Complaints relating to General Insurance and Mortgages) Order 2004, SI 2004/454, art 5 at **[4675]**.

229 Awards

(1) This section applies only in relation to the compulsory jurisdiction [and to the consumer credit jurisdiction].

(2) If a complaint which has been dealt with under the scheme is determined in favour of the complainant, the determination may include—

(a) an award against the respondent of such amount as the ombudsman considers fair compensation for loss or damage (of a kind falling within subsection (3)) suffered by the complainant ("a money award");

(b) a direction that the respondent take such steps in relation to the complainant as the ombudsman considers just and appropriate (whether or not a court could order those steps to be taken).

(3) A money award may compensate for—

(a) financial loss; or

(b) any other loss, or any damage, of a specified kind.

(4) The Authority may specify [for the purposes of the compulsory jurisdiction] the maximum amount which may be regarded as fair compensation for a particular kind of loss or damage specified under subsection (3)(b).

[(4A) The scheme operator may specify for the purposes of the consumer credit jurisdiction the maximum amount which may be regarded as fair compensation for a particular kind of loss or damage specified under subsection (3)(b).]

(5) A money award may not exceed the monetary limit; but the ombudsman may, if he considers that fair compensation requires payment of a larger amount, recommend that the respondent pay the complainant the balance.

(6) The monetary limit is such amount as may be specified.

(7) Different amounts may be specified in relation to different kinds of complaint.

(8) A money award—

(a) may provide for the amount payable under the award to bear interest at a rate and as from a date specified in the award; and

(b) is enforceable by the complainant in accordance with Part III of Schedule 17 [or (as the case may be) Part 3A of that Schedule].

(9) Compliance with a direction under subsection (2)(b)—

(a) is enforceable by an injunction; or

(b) in Scotland, is enforceable by an order under section 45 of the Court of Session Act 1988.

(10) Only the complainant may bring proceedings for an injunction or proceedings for an order.

[(11) "Specified" means—

(a) for the purposes of the compulsory jurisdiction, specified in compulsory jurisdiction rules;

(b) for the purposes of the consumer credit jurisdiction, specified in consumer credit rules.

(12) Consumer credit rules under this section may make different provision for different cases.]

[2229]

NOTES

Sub-ss (1), (4), (8): words in square brackets inserted by the Consumer Credit Act 2006, s 61(3), (4), (6), as from 16 June 2006.

Sub-s (4A): inserted by the Consumer Credit Act 2006, s 61(5), as from 16 June 2006.

Sub-ss (11), (12): substituted, for original sub-s (11), by the Consumer Credit Act 2006, s 61(7), as from 16 June 2006.

Transitional provisions: see the note to s 228 at **[2228]**.

230 Costs

(1) The scheme operator may by rules ("costs rules") provide for an ombudsman to have power, on determining a complaint under the compulsory jurisdiction [or the consumer credit jurisdiction], to award costs in accordance with the provisions of the rules.

(2) Costs rules require the approval of the Authority.

(3) Costs rules may not provide for the making of an award against the complainant in respect of the respondent's costs.

(4) But they may provide for the making of an award against the complainant in favour of the scheme operator, for the purpose of providing a contribution to resources deployed in dealing with the complaint, if in the opinion of the ombudsman—

(a) the complainant's conduct was improper or unreasonable; or

(b) the complainant was responsible for an unreasonable delay.

(5) Costs rules may authorise an ombudsman making an award in accordance with the rules to order that the amount payable under the award bears interest at a rate and as from a date specified in the order.

(6) An amount due under an award made in favour of the scheme operator is recoverable as a debt due to the scheme operator.

(7) Any other award made against the respondent is to be treated as a money award for the purposes of paragraph 16 of Schedule 17 [or (as the case may be) paragraph 16D of that Schedule].

[2230]

NOTES

Sub-ss (1), (7): words in square brackets inserted by the Consumer Credit Act 2006, s 61(8), as from 16 June 2006.

Transitional provisions: see the note to s 228 at **[2228]**.

Information

231 Ombudsman's power to require information

(1) An ombudsman may, by notice in writing given to a party to a complaint, require that party—

(a) to provide specified information or information of a specified description; or

(b) to produce specified documents or documents of a specified description.

(2) The information or documents must be provided or produced—

(a) before the end of such reasonable period as may be specified; and

(b) in the case of information, in such manner or form as may be specified.

(3) This section applies only to information and documents the production of which the ombudsman considers necessary for the determination of the complaint.

(4) If a document is produced in response to a requirement imposed under this section, the ombudsman may—
(a) take copies or extracts from the document; or
(b) require the person producing the document to provide an explanation of the document.

(5) If a person who is required under this section to produce a document fails to do so, the ombudsman may require him to state, to the best of his knowledge and belief, where the document is.

(6) If a person claims a lien on a document, its production under this Part does not affect the lien.

(7) "Specified" means specified in the notice given under subsection (1).

[2231]

NOTES

Transitional provisions: see the note to s 228 at **[2228]**.

232 Powers of court where information required

(1) If a person ("the defaulter") fails to comply with a requirement imposed under section 231, the ombudsman may certify that fact in writing to the court and the court may enquire into the case.

(2) If the court is satisfied that the defaulter failed without reasonable excuse to comply with the requirement, it may deal with the defaulter (and, in the case of a body corporate, any director or officer) as if he were in contempt[; and "officer", in relation to a limited liability partnership, means a member of the limited liability partnership].

(3) "Court" means—
(a) the High Court;
(b) in Scotland, the Court of Session.

[2232]

NOTES

Sub-s (2): words in square brackets added by the Limited Liability Partnerships Regulations 2001, SI 2001/1090, reg 9, Sch 5, para 21, as from 6 April 2001.

Transitional provisions: see the note to s 228 at **[2228]**.

233 (*Inserts the Data Protection Act 1998, s 31(4A), which provides that the scheme operator is to be one of those persons specified in s 31 of the 1998 Act who is not required to disclose information if that disclosure, obtained when considering a complaint brought under the scheme, would prejudice legal professional privilege (see the Data Protection Act 1998, s 7, Sch 7, para 10).*)

Funding

234 Industry funding

(1) For the purpose of funding—
(a) the establishment of the ombudsman scheme (whenever any relevant expense is incurred), and
(b) its operation in relation to the compulsory jurisdiction,

the Authority may make rules requiring the payment to it or to the scheme operator, by authorised persons or any class of authorised person of specified amounts (or amounts calculated in a specified way).

(2) "Specified" means specified in the rules.

[2233]

[234A Funding by consumer credit licensees etc

(1) For the purpose of funding—
(a) the establishment of the ombudsman scheme so far as it relates to the consumer credit jurisdiction (whenever any relevant expense is incurred), and

(b) its operation in relation to the consumer credit jurisdiction,

the scheme operator may from time to time with the approval of the Authority determine a sum which is to be raised by way of contributions under this section.

(2) A sum determined under subsection (1) may include a component to cover the costs of the collection of contributions to that sum ("collection costs") under this section.

(3) The scheme operator must notify the OFT of every determination under subsection (1).

(4) The OFT must give general notice of every determination so notified.

(5) The OFT may by general notice impose requirements on—

(a) licensees to whom this section applies, or

(b) persons who make applications to which this section applies,

to pay contributions to the OFT for the purpose of raising sums determined under subsection (1).

(6) The amount of the contribution payable by a person under such a requirement—

(a) shall be the amount specified in or determined under the general notice; and

(b) shall be paid before the end of the period or at the time so specified or determined.

(7) A general notice under subsection (5) may—

(a) impose requirements only on descriptions of licensees or applicants specified in the notice;

(b) provide for exceptions from any requirement imposed on a description of licensees or applicants;

(c) impose different requirements on different descriptions of licensees or applicants;

(d) make provision for refunds in specified circumstances.

(8) Contributions received by the OFT must be paid to the scheme operator.

(9) As soon as practicable after the end of—

(a) each financial year of the scheme operator, or

(b) if the OFT and the scheme operator agree that this paragraph is to apply instead of paragraph (a) for the time being, each period agreed by them,

the scheme operator must pay to the OFT an amount representing the extent to which collection costs are covered in accordance with subsection (2) by the total amount of the contributions paid by the OFT to it during the year or (as the case may be) the agreed period.

(10) Amounts received by the OFT from the scheme operator are to be retained by it for the purpose of meeting its costs.

(11) The Secretary of State may by order provide that the functions of the OFT under this section are for the time being to be carried out by the scheme operator.

(12) An order under subsection (11) may provide that while the order is in force this section shall have effect subject to such modifications as may be set out in the order.

(13) The licensees to whom this section applies are licensees under standard licences which cover to any extent the carrying on of a type of business specified in an order under section 226A(2)(e).

(14) The applications to which this section applies are applications for—

(a) standard licences covering to any extent the carrying on of a business of such a type;

(b) the renewal of standard licences on terms covering to any extent the carrying on of a business of such a type.

(15) Expressions used in the Consumer Credit Act 1974 have the same meaning in this section as they have in that Act.]

[2233A]

NOTES

Commencement: 16 June 2006.
Inserted by the Consumer Credit Act 2006, s 60, as from 16 June 2006.

PART II FSMA 2000

PART XVII
COLLECTIVE INVESTMENT SCHEMES

NOTES

Transitional provisions: the Financial Services and Markets Act 2000 (Transitional Provisions) (Authorised Persons etc) Order 2001, SI 2001/2636, Pt V, provides that collective investment schemes which were authorised or recognised under the Financial Services Act 1986, Pt I, Chapter VIII immediately before 1 December 2001 are to be treated as from that date as if authorised and recognised under Pt XVII of this Act. Directions imposed on schemes under the 1986 Act have effect, as from 1 December 2001, as directions imposed under Pt XVII of this Act. The 1986 Act was repealed by the Financial Services and Markets Act 2000 (Consequential Amendments and Repeals) Order 2001, SI 2001/3649, art 3(1)(c).

CHAPTER I
INTERPRETATION

235 Collective investment schemes

(1) In this Part "collective investment scheme" means any arrangements with respect to property of any description, including money, the purpose or effect of which is to enable persons taking part in the arrangements (whether by becoming owners of the property or any part of it or otherwise) to participate in or receive profits or income arising from the acquisition, holding, management or disposal of the property or sums paid out of such profits or income.

(2) The arrangements must be such that the persons who are to participate ("participants") do not have day-to-day control over the management of the property, whether or not they have the right to be consulted or to give directions.

(3) The arrangements must also have either or both of the following characteristics—

(a) the contributions of the participants and the profits or income out of which payments are to be made to them are pooled;

(b) the property is managed as a whole by or on behalf of the operator of the scheme.

(4) If arrangements provide for such pooling as is mentioned in subsection (3)(a) in relation to separate parts of the property, the arrangements are not to be regarded as constituting a single collective investment scheme unless the participants are entitled to exchange rights in one part for rights in another.

(5) The Treasury may by order provide that arrangements do not amount to a collective investment scheme—

(a) in specified circumstances; or

(b) if the arrangements fall within a specified category of arrangement.

[2234]

NOTES

Orders: the Financial Services and Markets Act 2000 (Collective Investment Schemes) Order 2001, SI 2001/1062 at **[4141]**; the Financial Services and Markets Act 2000 (Miscellaneous Provisions) Order 2001, SI 2001/3650.

Note that the following amending Orders have also been made under this section: the Financial Services and Markets Act 2000 (Collective Investment Schemes) (Amendment) Order 2005, SI 2005/57; the Financial Services and Markets Act 2000 (Collective Investment Schemes) (Amendment) Order 2007, SI 2007/800.

236 Open-ended investment companies

(1) In this Part "an open-ended investment company" means a collective investment scheme which satisfies both the property condition and the investment condition.

(2) The property condition is that the property belongs beneficially to, and is managed by or on behalf of, a body corporate ("BC") having as its purpose the investment of its funds with the aim of—

(a) spreading investment risk; and

(b) giving its members the benefit of the results of the management of those funds by or on behalf of that body.

(3) The investment condition is that, in relation to BC, a reasonable investor would, if he were to participate in the scheme—

(a) expect that he would be able to realize, within a period appearing to him to be reasonable, his investment in the scheme (represented, at any given time, by the value of shares in, or securities of, BC held by him as a participant in the scheme); and

(b) be satisfied that his investment would be realized on a basis calculated wholly or mainly by reference to the value of property in respect of which the scheme makes arrangements.

(4) In determining whether the investment condition is satisfied, no account is to be taken of any actual or potential redemption or repurchase of shares or securities under—

(a) Chapter VII of Part V of the Companies Act 1985;

(b) Chapter VII of Part VI of the Companies (Northern Ireland) Order 1986;

(c) corresponding provisions in force in another EEA State; or

(d) provisions in force in a country or territory other than an EEA state which the Treasury have, by order, designated as corresponding provisions.

(5) The Treasury may by order amend the definition of "an open-ended investment company" for the purposes of this Part.

[2235]

237 Other definitions

(1) In this Part "unit trust scheme" means a collective investment scheme under which the property is held on trust for the participants.

(2) In this Part—

"trustee", in relation to a unit trust scheme, means the person holding the property in question on trust for the participants;

"depositary", in relation to—

(a) a collective investment scheme which is constituted by a body incorporated by virtue of regulations under section 262, or

(b) any other collective investment scheme which is not a unit trust scheme,

means any person to whom the property subject to the scheme is entrusted for safekeeping;

"the operator", in relation to a unit trust scheme with a separate trustee, means the manager and in relation to an open-ended investment company, means that company;

"units" means the rights or interests (however described) of the participants in a collective investment scheme.

(3) In this Part—

"an authorised unit trust scheme" means a unit trust scheme which is authorised for the purposes of this Act by an authorisation order in force under section 243;

"an authorised open-ended investment company" means a body incorporated by virtue of regulations under section 262 in respect of which an authorisation order is in force under any provision made in such regulations by virtue of subsection (2)(l) of that section;

"a recognised scheme" means a scheme recognised under section 264, 270 or 272.

[2236]

CHAPTER II
RESTRICTIONS ON PROMOTION

238 Restrictions on promotion

(1) An authorised person must not communicate an invitation or inducement to participate in a collective investment scheme.

(2) But that is subject to the following provisions of this section and to section 239.

(3) Subsection (1) applies in the case of a communication originating outside the United Kingdom only if the communication is capable of having an effect in the United Kingdom.

(4) Subsection (1) does not apply in relation to—

(a) an authorised unit trust scheme;

(b) a scheme constituted by an authorised open-ended investment company; or

(c) a recognised scheme.

(5) Subsection (1) does not apply to anything done in accordance with rules made by the Authority for the purpose of exempting from that subsection the promotion otherwise than to the general public of schemes of specified descriptions.

(6) The Treasury may by order specify circumstances in which subsection (1) does not apply.

(7) An order under subsection (6) may, in particular, provide that subsection (1) does not apply in relation to communications—

(a) of a specified description;
(b) originating in a specified country or territory outside the United Kingdom;
(c) originating in a country or territory which falls within a specified description of country or territory outside the United Kingdom; or
(d) originating outside the United Kingdom.

(8) The Treasury may by order repeal subsection (3).

(9) "Communicate" includes causing a communication to be made.

(10) "Promotion otherwise than to the general public" includes promotion in a way designed to reduce, so far as possible, the risk of participation by persons for whom participation would be unsuitable.

(11) "Participate", in relation to a collective investment scheme, means become a participant (within the meaning given by section 235(2)) in the scheme.

[2237]

NOTES

Orders: the Financial Services and Markets Act 2000 (Promotion of Collective Investment Schemes) (Exemptions) Order 2001, SI 2001/1060 at **[4112]**.

Note that the following amending Orders have also been made under this section: the Financial Services and Markets Act 2000 (Financial Promotion and Miscellaneous Amendments) Order 2002, SI 2002/1310; the Financial Services and Markets Act 2000 (Promotion of Collective Investment Schemes etc) (Exemptions) (Amendment) Order 2003, SI 2003/2067; the Financial Services and Markets Act 2000 (Financial Promotion and Promotion of Collective Investment Schemes) (Miscellaneous Amendments) Order 2005, SI 2005/270; the Financial Services and Markets Act 2000 (Promotion of Collective Investment Schemes) (Exemptions) (Amendment) Order 2005, SI 2005/1532.

239 Single property schemes

(1) The Treasury may by regulations make provision for exempting single property schemes from section 238(1).

(2) For the purposes of subsection (1) a single property scheme is a scheme which has the characteristics mentioned in subsection (3) and satisfies such other requirements as are prescribed by the regulations conferring the exemption.

(3) The characteristics are—

(a) that the property subject to the scheme (apart from cash or other assets held for management purposes) consists of—
  (i) a single building (or a single building with ancillary buildings) managed by or on behalf of the operator of the scheme, or
  (ii) a group of adjacent or contiguous buildings managed by him or on his behalf as a single enterprise,

with or without ancillary land and with or without furniture, fittings or other contents of the building or buildings in question; and

(b) that the units of the participants in the scheme are either dealt in on a recognised investment exchange or offered on terms such that any agreement for their acquisition is conditional on their admission to dealings on such an exchange.

(4) If regulations are made under subsection (1), the Authority may make rules imposing duties or liabilities on the operator and (if any) the trustee or depositary of a scheme exempted by the regulations.

(5) The rules may include, to such extent as the Authority thinks appropriate, provision for purposes corresponding to those for which provision can be made under section 248 in relation to authorised unit trust schemes.

[2238]

240 Restriction on approval of promotion

(1) An authorised person may not approve for the purposes of section 21 the content of a communication relating to a collective investment scheme if he would be prohibited by section 238(1) from effecting the communication himself or from causing it to be communicated.

(2) For the purposes of determining in any case whether there has been a contravention of section 21(1), an approval given in contravention of subsection (1) is to be regarded as not having been given.

[2239]

241 Actions for damages

If an authorised person contravenes a requirement imposed on him by section 238 or 240, section 150 applies to the contravention as it applies to a contravention mentioned in that section.

[2240]

CHAPTER III
AUTHORISED UNIT TRUST SCHEMES

Applications for authorisation

242 Applications for authorisation of unit trust schemes

(1) Any application for an order declaring a unit trust scheme to be an authorised unit trust scheme must be made to the Authority by the manager and trustee, or proposed manager and trustee, of the scheme.

(2) The manager and trustee (or proposed manager and trustee) must be different persons.

(3) The application—
(a) must be made in such manner as the Authority may direct; and
(b) must contain or be accompanied by such information as the Authority may reasonably require for the purpose of determining the application.

(4) At any time after receiving an application and before determining it, the Authority may require the applicants to provide it with such further information as it reasonably considers necessary to enable it to determine the application.

(5) Different directions may be given, and different requirements imposed, in relation to different applications.

(6) The Authority may require applicants to present information which they are required to give under this section in such form, or to verify it in such a way, as the Authority may direct.

[2241]

243 Authorisation orders

(1) If, on an application under section 242 in respect of a unit trust scheme, the Authority—
(a) is satisfied that the scheme complies with the requirements set out in this section,
(b) is satisfied that the scheme complies with the requirements of the trust scheme rules, and
(c) has been provided with a copy of the trust deed and a certificate signed by a solicitor to the effect that it complies with such of the requirements of this section or those rules as relate to its contents,

the Authority may make an order declaring the scheme to be an authorised unit trust scheme.

(2) If the Authority makes an order under subsection (1), it must give written notice of the order to the applicant.

(3) In this Chapter "authorisation order" means an order under subsection (1).

(4) The manager and the trustee must be persons who are independent of each other.

(5) The manager and the trustee must each—

(a) be a body corporate incorporated in the United Kingdom or another EEA State, and

(b) have a place of business in the United Kingdom,

and the affairs of each must be administered in the country in which it is incorporated.

(6) If the manager is incorporated in another EEA State, the scheme must not be one which satisfies the requirements prescribed for the purposes of section 264.

(7) The manager and the trustee must each be an authorised person and the manager must have permission to act as manager and the trustee must have permission to act as trustee.

(8) The name of the scheme must not be undesirable or misleading.

(9) The purposes of the scheme must be reasonably capable of being successfully carried into effect.

(10) The participants must be entitled to have their units redeemed in accordance with the scheme at a price—

(a) related to the net value of the property to which the units relate; and

(b) determined in accordance with the scheme.

(11) But a scheme is to be treated as complying with subsection (10) if it requires the manager to ensure that a participant is able to sell his units on an investment exchange at a price not significantly different from that mentioned in that subsection.

[2242]

NOTES

Transitional provisions: schemes that were authorised under the Financial Services Act 1986 regime were treated as authorised (subject to certain conditions) under the Financial Services and Markets Act 2000 (Transitional Provisions) (Authorised Persons etc) Order 2001, SI 2001/2636, art 65.

References to solicitors, etc: a registered European lawyer may provide professional activities by way of legal advice and assistance or legal aid under this Act and references to a solicitor, counsel or legal representative shall be interpreted accordingly: see the European Communities (Lawyer's Practice) Regulations 2000, SI 2000/1119, reg 14, Sch 3, Pt 1 (as amended by the European Communities (Lawyer's Practice) (Amendment) Regulations 2004, SI 2004/1628).

244 Determination of applications

(1) An application under section 242 must be determined by the Authority before the end of the period of six months beginning with the date on which it receives the completed application.

(2) The Authority may determine an incomplete application if it considers it appropriate to do so; and it must in any event determine such an application within twelve months beginning with the date on which it first receives the application.

(3) The applicant may withdraw his application, by giving the Authority written notice, at any time before the Authority determines it.

[2243]

Applications refused

245 Procedure when refusing an application

(1) If the Authority proposes to refuse an application made under section 242 it must give each of the applicants a warning notice.

(2) If the Authority decides to refuse the application—

(a) it must give each of the applicants a decision notice; and

(b) either applicant may refer the matter to the Tribunal.

[2244]

Certificates

246 Certificates

(1) If the manager or trustee of a unit trust scheme which complies with the conditions necessary for it to enjoy the rights conferred by any relevant Community instrument so requests, the Authority may issue a certificate to the effect that the scheme complies with those conditions.

(2) Such a certificate may be issued on the making of an authorisation order in respect of the scheme or at any subsequent time.

[2245]

Rules

247 Trust scheme rules

(1) The Authority may make rules ("trust scheme rules") as to—

(a) the constitution, management and operation of authorised unit trust schemes;
(b) the powers, duties, rights and liabilities of the manager and trustee of any such scheme;
(c) the rights and duties of the participants in any such scheme; and
(d) the winding up of any such scheme.

(2) Trust scheme rules may, in particular, make provision—

(a) as to the issue and redemption of the units under the scheme;
(b) as to the expenses of the scheme and the means of meeting them;
(c) for the appointment, removal, powers and duties of an auditor for the scheme;
(d) for restricting or regulating the investment and borrowing powers exercisable in relation to the scheme;
(e) requiring the keeping of records with respect to the transactions and financial position of the scheme and for the inspection of those records;
(f) requiring the preparation of periodical reports with respect to the scheme and the provision of those reports to the participants and to the Authority; and
(g) with respect to the amendment of the scheme.

(3) Trust scheme rules may make provision as to the contents of the trust deed, including provision requiring any of the matters mentioned in subsection (2) to be dealt with in the deed.

(4) But trust scheme rules are binding on the manager, trustee and participants independently of the contents of the trust deed and, in the case of the participants, have effect as if contained in it.

(5) If—

(a) a modification is made of the statutory provisions in force in Great Britain or Northern Ireland relating to companies,
(b) the modification relates to the rights and duties of persons who hold the beneficial title to any shares in a company without also holding the legal title, and
(c) it appears to the Treasury that, for the purpose of assimilating the law relating to authorised unit trust schemes to the law relating to companies as so modified, it is expedient to modify the rule-making powers conferred on the Authority by this section,

the Treasury may by order make such modifications of those powers as they consider appropriate.

[2246]

248 Scheme particulars rules

(1) The Authority may make rules ("scheme particulars rules") requiring the manager of an authorised unit trust scheme—

(a) to submit scheme particulars to the Authority; and
(b) to publish scheme particulars or make them available to the public on request.

(2) "Scheme particulars" means particulars in such form, containing such information about the scheme and complying with such requirements, as are specified in scheme particulars rules.

PART II FSMA 2000

(3) Scheme particulars rules may require the manager of an authorised unit trust scheme to submit, and to publish or make available, revised or further scheme particulars if there is a significant change affecting any matter—

(a) which is contained in scheme particulars previously published or made available; and

(b) whose inclusion in those particulars was required by the rules.

(4) Scheme particulars rules may require the manager of an authorised unit trust scheme to submit, and to publish or make available, revised or further scheme particulars if—

(a) a significant new matter arises; and

(b) the inclusion of information in respect of that matter would have been required in previous particulars if it had arisen when those particulars were prepared.

(5) Scheme particulars rules may provide for the payment, by the person or persons who in accordance with the rules are treated as responsible for any scheme particulars, of compensation to any qualifying person who has suffered loss as a result of—

(a) any untrue or misleading statement in the particulars; or

(b) the omission from them of any matter required by the rules to be included.

(6) "Qualifying person" means a person who—

(a) has become or agreed to become a participant in the scheme; or

(b) although not being a participant, has a beneficial interest in units in the scheme.

(7) Scheme particulars rules do not affect any liability which any person may incur apart from the rules.

[2247]

249 Disqualification of auditor for breach of trust scheme rules

(1) If it appears to the Authority that an auditor has failed to comply with a duty imposed on him by trust scheme rules, it may disqualify him from being the auditor for any authorised unit trust scheme or authorised open-ended investment company.

(2) Subsections (2) to (5) of section 345 have effect in relation to disqualification under subsection (1) as they have effect in relation to disqualification under subsection (1) of that section.

[2248]

NOTES

Open-ended investment companies: sub-s (1) above applies to a failure by an auditor to comply with a duty imposed on him by any rules made by the Financial Services Authority under the Open-Ended Investment Companies Regulations 2001, SI 2001/1228, reg 6(1) as it applies to a breach of trust scheme rules; see reg 69 of, and Sch 5, para 20 to, the 2001 Regulations.

250 Modification or waiver of rules

(1) In this section "rules" means—

(a) trust scheme rules; or

(b) scheme particulars rules.

(2) The Authority may, on the application or with the consent of any person to whom any rules apply, direct that all or any of the rules—

(a) are not to apply to him as respects a particular scheme; or

(b) are to apply to him, as respects a particular scheme, with such modifications as may be specified in the direction.

(3) The Authority may, on the application or with the consent of the manager and trustee of a particular scheme acting jointly, direct that all or any of the rules—

(a) are not to apply to the scheme; or

(b) are to apply to the scheme with such modifications as may be specified in the direction.

(4) Subsections (3) to (9) and (11) of section 148 have effect in relation to a direction under subsection (2) as they have effect in relation to a direction under section 148(2) but with the following modifications—

(a) ...

(b) any reference to the [person] is to be read as a reference to the person mentioned in subsection (2); and

(c) subsection (7)(b) is to be read, in relation to a participant of the scheme, as if the word "commercial" were omitted.

(5) Subsections (3) to (9) and (11) of section 148 have effect in relation to a direction under subsection (3) as they have effect in relation to a direction under section 148(2) but with the following modifications—

(a) subsection (4)(a) is to be read as if the words "by the … person" were omitted;

(b) subsections (7)(b) and (11) are to be read as if references to the … person were references to each of the manager and the trustee of the scheme;

(c) subsection (7)(b) is to be read, in relation to a participant of the scheme, as if the word "commercial" were omitted;

(d) subsection (8) is to be read as if the reference to the … person concerned were a reference to the scheme concerned and to its manager and trustee; and

(e) subsection (9) is to be read as if the reference to the … person were a reference to the manager and trustee of the scheme acting jointly.

[2249]

NOTES

Sub-s (4): para (a) repealed, and word in square brackets in para (b) substituted, by the Regulatory Reform (Financial Services and Markets Act 2000) Order 2007, SI 2007/1973, arts 2, 11(a), (b), as from 12 July 2007.

Sub-s (5): words omitted repealed by SI 2007/1973, arts 2, 11(c), as from 12 July 2007.

Alterations

251 Alteration of schemes and changes of manager or trustee

(1) The manager of an authorised unit trust scheme must give written notice to the Authority of any proposal to alter the scheme or to replace its trustee.

(2) Any notice given in respect of a proposal to alter the scheme involving a change in the trust deed must be accompanied by a certificate signed by a solicitor to the effect that the change will not affect the compliance of the deed with the trust scheme rules.

(3) The trustee of an authorised unit trust scheme must give written notice to the Authority of any proposal to replace the manager of the scheme.

(4) Effect is not to be given to any proposal of which notice has been given under subsection (1) or (3) unless—

(a) the Authority, by written notice, has given its approval to the proposal; or

(b) one month, beginning with the date on which the notice was given, has expired without the manager or trustee having received from the Authority a warning notice under section 252 in respect of the proposal.

(5) The Authority must not approve a proposal to replace the manager or the trustee of an authorised unit trust scheme unless it is satisfied that, if the proposed replacement is made, the scheme will continue to comply with the requirements of section 243(4) to (7).

[2250]

NOTES

References to solicitors, etc: see the note to s 242 at **[2243]**.

252 Procedure when refusing approval of change of manager or trustee

(1) If the Authority proposes to refuse approval of a proposal to replace the trustee or manager of an authorised unit trust scheme, it must give a warning notice to the person by whom notice of the proposal was given under section 251(1) or (3).

(2) If the Authority proposes to refuse approval of a proposal to alter an authorised unit trust scheme it must give separate warning notices to the manager and the trustee of the scheme.

(3) To be valid the warning notice must be received by that person before the end of one month beginning with the date on which notice of the proposal was given.

(4) If, having given a warning notice to a person, the Authority decides to refuse approval—

PART II FSMA 2000

(a) it must give him a decision notice; and
(b) he may refer the matter to the Tribunal.

[2251]

Exclusion clauses

253 Avoidance of exclusion clauses

Any provision of the trust deed of an authorised unit trust scheme is void in so far as it would have the effect of exempting the manager or trustee from liability for any failure to exercise due care and diligence in the discharge of his functions in respect of the scheme.

[2252]

Ending of authorisation

254 Revocation of authorisation order otherwise than by consent

(1) An authorisation order may be revoked by an order made by the Authority if it appears to the Authority that—

(a) one or more of the requirements for the making of the order are no longer satisfied;
(b) the manager or trustee of the scheme concerned has contravened a requirement imposed on him by or under this Act;
(c) the manager or trustee of the scheme has, in purported compliance with any such requirement, knowingly or recklessly given the Authority information which is false or misleading in a material particular;
(d) no regulated activity is being carried on in relation to the scheme and the period of that inactivity began at least twelve months earlier; or
(e) none of paragraphs (a) to (d) applies, but it is desirable to revoke the authorisation order in order to protect the interests of participants or potential participants in the scheme.

(2) For the purposes of subsection (1)(e), the Authority may take into account any matter relating to—

(a) the scheme;
(b) the manager or trustee;
(c) any person employed by or associated with the manager or trustee in connection with the scheme;
(d) any director of the manager or trustee;
(e) any person exercising influence over the manager or trustee;
(f) any body corporate in the same group as the manager or trustee;
(g) any director of any such body corporate;
(h) any person exercising influence over any such body corporate.

[2253]

255 Procedure

(1) If the Authority proposes to make an order under section 254 revoking an authorisation order ("a revoking order"), it must give separate warning notices to the manager and the trustee of the scheme.

(2) If the Authority decides to make a revoking order, it must without delay give each of them a decision notice and either of them may refer the matter to the Tribunal.

[2254]

256 Requests for revocation of authorisation order

(1) An authorisation order may be revoked by an order made by the Authority at the request of the manager or trustee of the scheme concerned.

(2) If the Authority makes an order under subsection (1), it must give written notice of the order to the manager and trustee of the scheme concerned.

(3) The Authority may refuse a request to make an order under this section if it considers that—

(a) the public interest requires that any matter concerning the scheme should be investigated before a decision is taken as to whether the authorisation order should be revoked; or

(b) revocation would not be in the interests of the participants or would be incompatible with a Community obligation.

(4) If the Authority proposes to refuse a request under this section, it must give separate warning notices to the manager and the trustee of the scheme.

(5) If the Authority decides to refuse the request, it must without delay give each of them a decision notice and either of them may refer the matter to the Tribunal.

[2255]

Powers of intervention

257 Directions

(1) The Authority may give a direction under this section if it appears to the Authority that—

(a) one or more of the requirements for the making of an authorisation order are no longer satisfied;

(b) the manager or trustee of an authorised unit trust scheme has contravened, or is likely to contravene, a requirement imposed on him by or under this Act;

(c) the manager or trustee of such a scheme has, in purported compliance with any such requirement, knowingly or recklessly given the Authority information which is false or misleading in a material particular; or

(d) none of paragraphs (a) to (c) applies, but it is desirable to give a direction in order to protect the interests of participants or potential participants in such a scheme.

(2) A direction under this section may—

(a) require the manager of the scheme to cease the issue or redemption, or both the issue and redemption, of units under the scheme;

(b) require the manager and trustee of the scheme to wind it up.

(3) If the authorisation order is revoked, the revocation does not affect any direction under this section which is then in force.

(4) A direction may be given under this section in relation to a scheme in the case of which the authorisation order has been revoked if a direction under this section was already in force at the time of revocation.

(5) If a person contravenes a direction under this section, section 150 applies to the contravention as it applies to a contravention mentioned in that section.

(6) The Authority may, either on its own initiative or on the application of the manager or trustee of the scheme concerned, revoke or vary a direction given under this section if it appears to the Authority—

(a) in the case of revocation, that it is no longer necessary for the direction to take effect or continue in force;

(b) in the case of variation, that the direction should take effect or continue in force in a different form.

[2256]

258 Applications to the court

(1) If the Authority could give a direction under section 257, it may also apply to the court for an order—

(a) removing the manager or the trustee, or both the manager and the trustee, of the scheme; and

(b) replacing the person or persons removed with a suitable person or persons nominated by the Authority.

(2) The Authority may nominate a person for the purposes of subsection (1)(b) only if it is satisfied that, if the order was made, the requirements of section 243(4) to (7) would be complied with.

(3) If it appears to the Authority that there is no person it can nominate for the purposes of subsection (1)(b), it may apply to the court for an order—

PART II
FSMA 2000

(a) removing the manager or the trustee, or both the manager and the trustee, of the scheme; and
(b) appointing an authorised person to wind up the scheme.

(4) On an application under this section the court may make such order as it thinks fit.

(5) The court may, on the application of the Authority, rescind any such order as is mentioned in subsection (3) and substitute such an order as is mentioned in subsection (1).

(6) The Authority must give written notice of the making of an application under this section to the manager and trustee of the scheme concerned.

(7) The jurisdiction conferred by this section may be exercised by—
(a) the High Court;
(b) in Scotland, the Court of Session.

[2257]

259 Procedure on giving directions under section 257 and varying them on Authority's own initiative

(1) A direction takes effect—
(a) immediately, if the notice given under subsection (3) states that that is the case;
(b) on such date as may be specified in the notice; or
(c) if no date is specified in the notice, when the matter to which it relates is no longer open to review.

(2) A direction may be expressed to take effect immediately (or on a specified date) only if the Authority, having regard to the ground on which it is exercising its power under section 257, considers that it is necessary for the direction to take effect immediately (or on that date).

(3) If the Authority proposes to give a direction under section 257, or gives such a direction with immediate effect, it must give separate written notice to the manager and the trustee of the scheme concerned.

(4) The notice must—
(a) give details of the direction;
(b) inform the person to whom it is given of when the direction takes effect;
(c) state the Authority's reasons for giving the direction and for its determination as to when the direction takes effect;
(d) inform the person to whom it is given that he may make representations to the Authority within such period as may be specified in it (whether or not he has referred the matter to the Tribunal); and
(e) inform him of his right to refer the matter to the Tribunal.

(5) If the direction imposes a requirement under section 257(2)(a), the notice must state that the requirement has effect until—
(a) a specified date; or
(b) a further direction.

(6) If the direction imposes a requirement under section 257(2)(b), the scheme must be wound up—
(a) by a date specified in the notice; or
(b) if no date is specified, as soon as practicable.

(7) The Authority may extend the period allowed under the notice for making representations.

(8) If, having considered any representations made by a person to whom the notice was given, the Authority decides—
(a) to give the direction in the way proposed, or
(b) if it has been given, not to revoke the direction,

it must give separate written notice to the manager and the trustee of the scheme concerned.

(9) If, having considered any representations made by a person to whom the notice was given, the Authority decides—
(a) not to give the direction in the way proposed,
(b) to give the direction in a way other than that proposed, or
(c) to revoke a direction which has effect,

it must give separate written notice to the manager and the trustee of the scheme concerned.

(10) A notice given under subsection (8) must inform the person to whom it is given of his right to refer the matter to the Tribunal.

(11) A notice under subsection (9)(b) must comply with subsection (4).

(12) If a notice informs a person of his right to refer a matter to the Tribunal, it must give an indication of the procedure on such a reference.

(13) This section applies to the variation of a direction on the Authority's own initiative as it applies to the giving of a direction.

(14) For the purposes of subsection (1)(c), whether a matter is open to review is to be determined in accordance with section 391(8).

[2258]

260 Procedure: refusal to revoke or vary direction

(1) If on an application under section 257(6) for a direction to be revoked or varied the Authority proposes—

(a) to vary the direction otherwise than in accordance with the application, or

(b) to refuse to revoke or vary the direction,

it must give the applicant a warning notice.

(2) If the Authority decides to refuse to revoke or vary the direction—

(a) it must give the applicant a decision notice; and

(b) the applicant may refer the matter to the Tribunal.

[2259]

261 Procedure: revocation of direction and grant of request for variation

(1) If the Authority decides on its own initiative to revoke a direction under section 257 it must give separate written notices of its decision to the manager and trustee of the scheme.

(2) If on an application under section 257(6) for a direction to be revoked or varied the Authority decides to revoke the direction or vary it in accordance with the application, it must give the applicant written notice of its decision.

(3) A notice under this section must specify the date on which the decision takes effect.

(4) The Authority may publish such information about the revocation or variation, in such way, as it considers appropriate.

[2260]

CHAPTER IV
OPEN-ENDED INVESTMENT COMPANIES

262 Open-ended investment companies

(1) The Treasury may by regulations make provision for—

(a) facilitating the carrying on of collective investment by means of open-ended investment companies;

(b) regulating such companies.

(2) The regulations may, in particular, make provision—

(a) for the incorporation and registration in Great Britain of bodies corporate;

(b) for a body incorporated by virtue of the regulations to take such form as may be determined in accordance with the regulations;

(c) as to the purposes for which such a body may exist, the investments which it may issue and otherwise as to its constitution;

(d) as to the management and operation of such a body and the management of its property;

(e) as to the powers, duties, rights and liabilities of such a body and of other persons, including—

(i) the directors or sole director of such a body;

(ii) its depositary (if any);

(iii) its shareholders, and persons who hold the beneficial title to shares in it without holding the legal title;

(iv) its auditor; and

(v) any persons who act or purport to act on its behalf;

PART II
FSMA 2000

(f) as to the merger of one or more such bodies and the division of such a body;
(g) for the appointment and removal of an auditor for such a body;
(h) as to the winding up and dissolution of such a body;
(i) for such a body, or any director or depositary of such a body, to be required to comply with directions given by the Authority;
(j) enabling the Authority to apply to a court for an order removing and replacing any director or depositary of such a body;
(k) for the carrying out of investigations by persons appointed by the Authority or the Secretary of State;
(l) corresponding to any provision made in relation to unit trust schemes by Chapter III of this Part.

(3) Regulations under this section may—
(a) impose criminal liability;
(b) confer functions on the Authority;
(c) in the case of provision made by virtue of subsection (2)(l), authorise the making of rules by the Authority;
(d) confer jurisdiction on any court or on the Tribunal;
(e) provide for fees to be charged by the Authority in connection with the carrying out of any of its functions under the regulations (including fees payable on a periodical basis);
(f) modify, exclude or apply (with or without modifications) any primary or subordinate legislation (including any provision of, or made under, this Act);
(g) make consequential amendments, repeals and revocations of any such legislation;
(h) modify or exclude any rule of law.

(4) The provision that may be made by virtue of subsection (3)(f) includes provision extending or adapting any power to make subordinate legislation.

(5) Regulations under this section may, in particular—
(a) revoke the Open-Ended Investment Companies (Investment Companies with Variable Capital) Regulations 1996; and
(b) provide for things done under or in accordance with those regulations to be treated as if they had been done under or in accordance with regulations under this section.

[2261]

NOTES

Open-Ended Investment Companies (Investment Companies with Variable Capital) Regulations 1996: SI 1996/2827: revoked, subject to transitional provisions and savings, by the Open-Ended Investment Companies Regulations 2001, SI 2001/1228, reg 85.

Regulations: the Open-Ended Investment Companies Regulations 2001, SI 2001/1228.

Note that the following amending Regulations have also been made under this section: the Open-Ended Investment Companies (Amendment) Regulations 2005, SI 2005/923.

263 (*Spent; this section amended the Companies Act 1985, s 716* (*s 716 was repealed by the Regulatory Reform* (*Removal of 20 Member Limit in Partnerships etc*) *Order 2002, SI 2002/3203, art 2, as from 21 December 2002*) *This section is also repealed by the Companies Act 2006, s 1295, Sch 16, as from a day to be appointed.*)

CHAPTER V
RECOGNISED OVERSEAS SCHEMES

Schemes constituted in other EEA States

264 Schemes constituted in other EEA States

(1) A collective investment scheme constituted in another EEA State is a recognised scheme if—
(a) it satisfies such requirements as are prescribed for the purposes of this section; and
(b) not less than two months before inviting persons in the United Kingdom to become participants in the scheme, the operator of the scheme gives notice to the Authority of his intention to do so, specifying the way in which the invitation is to be made.

(2) But this section does not make the scheme a recognised scheme if within two months of receiving the notice under subsection (1) the Authority notifies—

(a) the operator of the scheme, and

(b) the authorities of the State in question who are responsible for the authorisation of collective investment schemes,

that the way in which the invitation is to be made does not comply with the law in force in the United Kingdom.

(3) The notice to be given to the Authority under subsection (1)—

(a) must be accompanied by a certificate from the authorities mentioned in subsection (2)(b) to the effect that the scheme complies with the conditions necessary for it to enjoy the rights conferred by any relevant Community instrument;

(b) must contain the address of a place in the United Kingdom for the service on the operator of notices or other documents required or authorised to be served on him under this Act; and

(c) must contain or be accompanied by such other information and documents as may be prescribed.

(4) A notice given by the Authority under subsection (2) must—

(a) give the reasons for which the Authority considers that the law in force in the United Kingdom will not be complied with; and

(b) specify a reasonable period (which may not be less than 28 days) within which any person to whom it is given may make representations to the Authority.

(5) For the purposes of this section a collective investment scheme is constituted in another EEA State if—

(a) it is constituted under the law of that State by a contract or under a trust and is managed by a body corporate incorporated under that law; or

(b) it takes the form of an open-ended investment company incorporated under that law.

(6) The operator of a recognised scheme may give written notice to the Authority that he desires the scheme to be no longer recognised by virtue of this section.

(7) On the giving of notice under subsection (6), the scheme ceases to be a recognised scheme.

[2262]

NOTES

Regulations: the Financial Services and Markets Act 2000 (Collective Investment Schemes Constituted in Other EEA States) Regulations 2001, SI 2001/2383 at **[4405]**.

Note that the following amending Regulations have also been made under this section: the Collective Investment Schemes (Miscellaneous Amendments) Regulations 2003, SI 2003/2066.

265 Representations and references to the Tribunal

(1) This section applies if any representations are made to the Authority, before the period for making representations has ended, by a person to whom a notice was given by the Authority under section 264(2).

(2) The Authority must, within a reasonable period, decide in the light of those representations whether or not to withdraw its notice.

(3) If the Authority withdraws its notice the scheme is a recognised scheme from the date on which the notice is withdrawn.

(4) If the Authority decides not to withdraw its notice, it must give a decision notice to each person to whom the notice under section 264(2) was given.

(5) The operator of the scheme to whom the decision notice is given may refer the matter to the Tribunal.

[2263]

266 Disapplication of rules

(1) Apart from—

(a) financial promotion rules, and

(b) rules under section 283(1),

rules made by the Authority under this Act do not apply to the operator, trustee or depositary of a scheme in relation to the carrying on by him of regulated activities for which he has permission in that capacity.

[(1A) But subsection (1) does not affect the application of rules to an operator of a scheme if the operator is an EEA firm falling within paragraph 5(f) of Schedule 3 who qualifies for authorisation under that Schedule.]

(2) "Scheme" means a scheme which is a recognised scheme by virtue of section 264.

[2264]

NOTES

Sub-s (1A): inserted by the Collective Investment Schemes (Miscellaneous Amendments) Regulations 2003, SI 2003/2066, reg 9, as from 13 February 2004.

267 Power of Authority to suspend promotion of scheme

(1) Subsection (2) applies if it appears to the Authority that the operator of a scheme has communicated an invitation or inducement in relation to the scheme in a manner contrary to financial promotion rules.

(2) The Authority may direct that—

(a) the exemption from subsection (1) of section 238 provided by subsection (4)(c) of that section is not to apply in relation to the scheme; and

(b) subsection (5) of that section does not apply with respect to things done in relation to the scheme.

(3) A direction under subsection (2) has effect—

(a) for a specified period;

(b) until the occurrence of a specified event; or

(c) until specified conditions are complied with.

(4) The Authority may, either on its own initiative or on the application of the operator of the scheme concerned, vary a direction given under subsection (2) if it appears to the Authority that the direction should take effect or continue in force in a different form.

(5) The Authority may, either on its own initiative or on the application of the operator of the recognised scheme concerned, revoke a direction given under subsection (2) if it appears to the Authority—

(a) that the conditions specified in the direction have been complied with; or

(b) that it is no longer necessary for the direction to take effect or continue in force.

(6) If an event is specified, the direction ceases to have effect (unless revoked earlier) on the occurrence of that event.

(7) For the purposes of this section and sections 268 and 269—

(a) the scheme's home State is the EEA State in which the scheme is constituted (within the meaning given by section 264);

(b) the competent authorities in the scheme's home State are the authorities in that State who are responsible for the authorisation of collective investment schemes.

(8) "Scheme" means a scheme which is a recognised scheme by virtue of section 264.

(9) "Specified", in relation to a direction, means specified in it.

[2265]

268 Procedure on giving directions under section 267 and varying them on Authority's own initiative

(1) A direction under section 267 takes effect—

(a) immediately, if the notice given under subsection (3)(a) states that that is the case;

(b) on such date as may be specified in the notice; or

(c) if no date is specified in the notice, when the matter to which it relates is no longer open to review.

(2) A direction may be expressed to take effect immediately (or on a specified date) only if the Authority, having regard to its reasons for exercising its power under section 267, considers that it is necessary for the direction to take effect immediately (or on that date).

(3) If the Authority proposes to give a direction under section 267, or gives such a direction with immediate effect, it must—

(a) give the operator of the scheme concerned written notice; and

(b) inform the competent authorities in the scheme's home State of its proposal or (as the case may be) of the direction.

(4) The notice must—

(a) give details of the direction;

(b) inform the operator of when the direction takes effect;

(c) state the Authority's reasons for giving the direction and for its determination as to when the direction takes effect;

(d) inform the operator that he may make representations to the Authority within such period as may be specified in it (whether or not he has referred the matter to the Tribunal); and

(e) inform him of his right to refer the matter to the Tribunal.

(5) The Authority may extend the period allowed under the notice for making representations.

(6) Subsection (7) applies if, having considered any representations made by the operator, the Authority decides—

(a) to give the direction in the way proposed, or

(b) if it has been given, not to revoke the direction.

(7) The Authority must—

(a) give the operator of the scheme concerned written notice; and

(b) inform the competent authorities in the scheme's home State of the direction.

(8) Subsection (9) applies if, having considered any representations made by a person to whom the notice was given, the Authority decides—

(a) not to give the direction in the way proposed,

(b) to give the direction in a way other than that proposed, or

(c) to revoke a direction which has effect.

(9) The Authority must—

(a) give the operator of the scheme concerned written notice; and

(b) inform the competent authorities in the scheme's home State of its decision.

(10) A notice given under subsection (7)(a) must inform the operator of his right to refer the matter to the Tribunal.

(11) A notice under subsection (9)(a) given as a result of subsection (8)(b) must comply with subsection (4).

(12) If a notice informs a person of his right to refer a matter to the Tribunal, it must give an indication of the procedure on such a reference.

(13) This section applies to the variation of a direction on the Authority's own initiative as it applies to the giving of a direction.

(14) For the purposes of subsection (1)(c), whether a matter is open to review is to be determined in accordance with section 391(8).

[2266]

269 Procedure on application for variation or revocation of direction

(1) If, on an application under subsection (4) or (5) of section 267, the Authority proposes—

(a) to vary a direction otherwise than in accordance with the application, or

(b) to refuse the application,

it must give the operator of the scheme concerned a warning notice.

(2) If, on such an application, the Authority decides—

(a) to vary a direction otherwise than in accordance with the application, or

(b) to refuse the application,

it must give the operator of the scheme concerned a decision notice.

(3) If the application is refused, the operator of the scheme may refer the matter to the Tribunal.

(4) If, on such an application, the Authority decides to grant the application it must give the operator of the scheme concerned written notice.

(5) If the Authority decides on its own initiative to revoke a direction given under section 267 it must give the operator of the scheme concerned written notice.

(6) The Authority must inform the competent authorities in the scheme's home State of any notice given under this section.

[2267]

Schemes authorised in designated countries or territories

270 Schemes authorised in designated countries or territories

(1) A collective investment scheme which is not a recognised scheme by virtue of section 264 but is managed in, and authorised under the law of, a country or territory outside the United Kingdom is a recognised scheme if—

(a) that country or territory is designated for the purposes of this section by an order made by the Treasury;

(b) the scheme is of a class specified by the order;

(c) the operator of the scheme has given written notice to the Authority that he wishes it to be recognised; and

(d) either—

(i) the Authority, by written notice, has given its approval to the scheme's being recognised; or

(ii) two months, beginning with the date on which notice was given under paragraph (c), have expired without the operator receiving a warning notice from the Authority under section 271.

(2) The Treasury may not make an order designating any country or territory for the purposes of this section unless satisfied—

(a) that the law and practice under which relevant collective investment schemes are authorised and supervised in that country or territory affords to investors in the United Kingdom protection at least equivalent to that provided for them by or under this Part in the case of comparable authorised schemes; and

(b) that adequate arrangements exist, or will exist, for co-operation between the authorities of the country or territory responsible for the authorisation and supervision of relevant collective investment schemes and the Authority.

(3) "Relevant collective investment schemes" means collective investment schemes of the class or classes to be specified by the order.

(4) "Comparable authorised schemes" means whichever of the following the Treasury consider to be the most appropriate, having regard to the class or classes of scheme to be specified by the order—

(a) authorised unit trust schemes;

(b) authorised open-ended investment companies;

(c) both such unit trust schemes and such companies.

(5) If the Treasury are considering whether to make an order designating a country or territory for the purposes of this section—

(a) the Treasury must ask the Authority for a report—

(i) on the law and practice of that country or territory in relation to the authorisation and supervision of relevant collective investment schemes,

(ii) on any existing or proposed arrangements for co-operation between it and the authorities responsible in that country or territory for the authorisation and supervision of relevant collective investment schemes,

having regard to the Treasury's need to be satisfied as mentioned in subsection (2);

(b) the Authority must provide the Treasury with such a report; and

(c) the Treasury must have regard to it in deciding whether to make the order.

(6) The notice to be given by the operator under subsection (1)(c)—

(a) must contain the address of a place in the United Kingdom for the service on the operator of notices or other documents required or authorised to be served on him under this Act; and

(b) must contain or be accompanied by such information and documents as may be specified by the Authority.

[2268]

NOTES

Orders: the Financial Services and Markets Act 2000 (Collective Investment Schemes) (Designated Countries and Territories) Order 2003, SI 2003/1181 (which designates Jersey, Guernsey and the Isle of Man). Also, the Financial Services (Designated Countries and Territories) (Overseas Collective Investment Schemes) (Bermuda) Order 1988, SI 1988/2284 (made under FSA 1986, s 87(1)) which continues in force and has effect as if made under sub-s (1)(a) above by virtue of the Financial Services and Markets Act 2000 (Transitional Provisions) (Authorised Persons etc) Order 2001, SI 2001/2636, art 67(1).

271 Procedure

(1) If the Authority proposes to refuse approval of a scheme's being a recognised scheme by virtue of section 270, it must give the operator of the scheme a warning notice.

(2) To be valid the warning notice must be received by the operator before the end of two months beginning with the date on which notice was given under section 270(1)(c).

(3) If, having given a warning notice, the Authority decides to refuse approval—

(a) it must give the operator of the scheme a decision notice; and

(b) the operator may refer the matter to the Tribunal.

[2269]

Individually recognised overseas schemes

272 Individually recognised overseas schemes

(1) The Authority may, on the application of the operator of a collective investment scheme which—

(a) is managed in a country or territory outside the United Kingdom,

(b) does not satisfy the requirements prescribed for the purposes of section 264,

(c) is not managed in a country or territory designated for the purposes of section 270 or, if it is so managed, is of a class not specified by the designation order, and

(d) appears to the Authority to satisfy the requirements set out in the following provisions of this section,

make an order declaring the scheme to be a recognised scheme.

(2) Adequate protection must be afforded to participants in the scheme.

(3) The arrangements for the scheme's constitution and management must be adequate.

(4) The powers and duties of the operator and, if the scheme has a trustee or depositary, of the trustee or depositary must be adequate.

(5) In deciding whether the matters mentioned in subsection (3) or (4) are adequate, the Authority must have regard to—

(a) any rule of law, and

(b) any matters which are, or could be, the subject of rules,

applicable in relation to comparable authorised schemes.

(6) "Comparable authorised schemes" means whichever of the following the Authority considers the most appropriate, having regard to the nature of scheme in respect of which the application is made—

(a) authorised unit trust schemes;

(b) authorised open-ended investment companies;

(c) both such unit trust schemes and such companies.

(7) The scheme must take the form of an open-ended investment company or (if it does not take that form) the operator must be a body corporate.

(8) The operator of the scheme must—

(a) if an authorised person, have permission to act as operator;

(b) if not an authorised person, be a fit and proper person to act as operator.

(9) The trustee or depositary (if any) of the scheme must—

(a) if an authorised person, have permission to act as trustee or depositary;

(b) if not an authorised person, be a fit and proper person to act as trustee or depositary.

(10) The operator and the trustee or depositary (if any) of the scheme must be able and willing to co-operate with the Authority by the sharing of information and in other ways.

(11) The name of the scheme must not be undesirable or misleading.

(12) The purposes of the scheme must be reasonably capable of being successfully carried into effect.

(13) The participants must be entitled to have their units redeemed in accordance with the scheme at a price related to the net value of the property to which the units relate and determined in accordance with the scheme.

(14) But a scheme is to be treated as complying with subsection (13) if it requires the operator to ensure that a participant is able to sell his units on an investment exchange at a price not significantly different from that mentioned in that subsection.

(15) Subsection (13) is not to be read as imposing a requirement that the participants must be entitled to have their units redeemed (or sold as mentioned in subsection (14)) immediately following a demand to that effect.

[2270]

273 Matters that may be taken into account

For the purposes of subsections (8)(b) and (9)(b) of section 272, the Authority may take into account any matter relating to—

(a) any person who is or will be employed by or associated with the operator, trustee or depositary in connection with the scheme;
(b) any director of the operator, trustee or depositary;
(c) any person exercising influence over the operator, trustee or depositary;
(d) any body corporate in the same group as the operator, trustee or depositary;
(e) any director of any such body corporate;
(f) any person exercising influence over any such body corporate.

[2271]

274 Applications for recognition of individual schemes

(1) An application under section 272 for an order declaring a scheme to be a recognised scheme must be made to the Authority by the operator of the scheme.

(2) The application—

(a) must be made in such manner as the Authority may direct;
(b) must contain the address of a place in the United Kingdom for the service on the operator of notices or other documents required or authorised to be served on him under this Act;
(c) must contain or be accompanied by such information as the Authority may reasonably require for the purpose of determining the application.

(3) At any time after receiving an application and before determining it, the Authority may require the applicant to provide it with such further information as it reasonably considers necessary to enable it to determine the application.

(4) Different directions may be given, and different requirements imposed, in relation to different applications.

(5) The Authority may require an applicant to present information which he is required to give under this section in such form, or to verify it in such a way, as the Authority may direct.

[2272]

275 Determination of applications

(1) An application under section 272 must be determined by the Authority before the end of the period of six months beginning with the date on which it receives the completed application.

(2) The Authority may determine an incomplete application if it considers it appropriate to do so; and it must in any event determine such an application within twelve months beginning with the date on which it first receives the application.

(3) If the Authority makes an order under section 272(1), it must give written notice of the order to the applicant.

[2273]

276 Procedure when refusing an application

(1) If the Authority proposes to refuse an application made under section 272 it must give the applicant a warning notice.

(2) If the Authority decides to refuse the application—

(a) it must give the applicant a decision notice; and

(b) the applicant may refer the matter to the Tribunal.

[2274]

277 Alteration of schemes and changes of operator, trustee or depositary

(1) The operator of a scheme recognised by virtue of section 272 must give written notice to the Authority of any proposed alteration to the scheme.

(2) Effect is not to be given to any such proposal unless—

(a) the Authority, by written notice, has given its approval to the proposal; or

(b) one month, beginning with the date on which notice was given under subsection (1), has expired without the Authority having given written notice to the operator that it has decided to refuse approval.

(3) At least one month before any replacement of the operator, trustee or depositary of such a scheme, notice of the proposed replacement must be given to the Authority—

(a) by the operator, trustee or depositary (as the case may be); or

(b) by the person who is to replace him.

[2275]

Schemes recognised under sections 270 and 272

278 Rules as to scheme particulars

The Authority may make rules imposing duties or liabilities on the operator of a scheme recognised under section 270 or 272 for purposes corresponding to those for which rules may be made under section 248 in relation to authorised unit trust schemes.

[2276]

279 Revocation of recognition

The Authority may direct that a scheme is to cease to be recognised by virtue of section 270 or revoke an order under section 272 if it appears to the Authority—

(a) that the operator, trustee or depositary of the scheme has contravened a requirement imposed on him by or under this Act;

(b) that the operator, trustee or depositary of the scheme has, in purported compliance with any such requirement, knowingly or recklessly given the Authority information which is false or misleading in a material particular;

(c) in the case of an order under section 272, that one or more of the requirements for the making of the order are no longer satisfied; or

(d) that none of paragraphs (a) to (c) applies, but it is undesirable in the interests of the participants or potential participants that the scheme should continue to be recognised.

[2277]

280 Procedure

(1) If the Authority proposes to give a direction under section 279 or to make an order under that section revoking a recognition order, it must give a warning notice to the operator and (if any) the trustee or depositary of the scheme.

(2) If the Authority decides to give a direction or make an order under that section—

(a) it must without delay give a decision notice to the operator and (if any) the trustee or depositary of the scheme; and

(b) the operator or the trustee or depositary may refer the matter to the Tribunal.

[2278]

281 Directions

(1) In this section a "relevant recognised scheme" means a scheme recognised under section 270 or 272.

(2) If it appears to the Authority that—
(a) the operator, trustee or depositary of a relevant recognised scheme has contravened, or is likely to contravene, a requirement imposed on him by or under this Act,
(b) the operator, trustee or depositary of such a scheme has, in purported compliance with any such requirement, knowingly or recklessly given the Authority information which is false or misleading in a material particular,
(c) one or more of the requirements for the recognition of a scheme under section 272 are no longer satisfied, or
(d) none of paragraphs (a) to (c) applies, but the exercise of the power conferred by this section is desirable in order to protect the interests of participants or potential participants in a relevant recognised scheme who are in the United Kingdom,

it may direct that the scheme is not to be a recognised scheme for a specified period or until the occurrence of a specified event or until specified conditions are complied with.

[2279]

282 Procedure on giving directions under section 281 and varying them otherwise than as requested

(1) A direction takes effect—
(a) immediately, if the notice given under subsection (3) states that that is the case;
(b) on such date as may be specified in the notice; or
(c) if no date is specified in the notice, when the matter to which it relates is no longer open to review.

(2) A direction may be expressed to take effect immediately (or on a specified date) only if the Authority, having regard to the ground on which it is exercising its power under section 281, considers that it is necessary for the direction to take effect immediately (or on that date).

(3) If the Authority proposes to give a direction under section 281, or gives such a direction with immediate effect, it must give separate written notice to the operator and (if any) the trustee or depositary of the scheme concerned.

(4) The notice must—
(a) give details of the direction;
(b) inform the person to whom it is given of when the direction takes effect;
(c) state the Authority's reasons for giving the direction and for its determination as to when the direction takes effect;
(d) inform the person to whom it is given that he may make representations to the Authority within such period as may be specified in it (whether or not he has referred the matter to the Tribunal); and
(e) inform him of his right to refer the matter to the Tribunal.

(5) The Authority may extend the period allowed under the notice for making representations.

(6) If, having considered any representations made by a person to whom the notice was given, the Authority decides—
(a) to give the direction in the way proposed, or
(b) if it has been given, not to revoke the direction,

it must give separate written notice to the operator and (if any) the trustee or depositary of the scheme concerned.

(7) If, having considered any representations made by a person to whom the notice was given, the Authority decides—
(a) not to give the direction in the way proposed,
(b) to give the direction in a way other than that proposed, or
(c) to revoke a direction which has effect,

it must give separate written notice to the operator and (if any) the trustee or depositary of the scheme concerned.

(8) A notice given under subsection (6) must inform the person to whom it is given of his right to refer the matter to the Tribunal.

(9) A notice under subsection (7)(b) must comply with subsection (4).

(10) If a notice informs a person of his right to refer a matter to the Tribunal, it must give an indication of the procedure on such a reference.

(11) This section applies to the variation of a direction on the Authority's own initiative as it applies to the giving of a direction.

(12) For the purposes of subsection (1)(c), whether a matter is open to review is to be determined in accordance with section 391(8).

[2280]

Facilities and information in UK

283 Facilities and information in UK

(1) The Authority may make rules requiring operators of recognised schemes to maintain in the United Kingdom, or in such part or parts of it as may be specified, such facilities as the Authority thinks desirable in the interests of participants and as are specified in rules.

(2) The Authority may by notice in writing require the operator of any recognised scheme to include such explanatory information as is specified in the notice in any communication of his which—

(a) is a communication of an invitation or inducement of a kind mentioned in section 21(1); and

(b) names the scheme.

(3) In the case of a communication originating outside the United Kingdom, subsection (2) only applies if the communication is capable of having an effect in the United Kingdom.

[2281]

CHAPTER VI
INVESTIGATIONS

284 Power to investigate

(1) An investigating authority may appoint one or more competent persons to investigate on its behalf—

(a) the affairs of, or of the manager or trustee of, any authorised unit trust scheme,

(b) the affairs of, or of the operator, trustee or depositary of, any recognised scheme so far as relating to activities carried on in the United Kingdom, or

(c) the affairs of, or of the operator, trustee or depositary of, any other collective investment scheme except a body incorporated by virtue of regulations under section 262,

if it appears to the investigating authority that it is in the interests of the participants or potential participants to do so or that the matter is of public concern.

(2) A person appointed under subsection (1) to investigate the affairs of, or of the manager, trustee, operator or depositary of, any scheme (scheme "A"), may also, if he thinks it necessary for the purposes of that investigation, investigate—

(a) the affairs of, or of the manager, trustee, operator or depositary of, any other such scheme as is mentioned in subsection (1) whose manager, trustee, operator or depositary is the same person as the manager, trustee, operator or depositary of scheme A;

(b) the affairs of such other schemes and persons (including bodies incorporated by virtue of regulations under section 262 and the directors and depositaries of such bodies) as may be prescribed.

(3) If the person appointed to conduct an investigation under this section ("B") considers that a person ("C") is or may be able to give information which is relevant to the investigation, B may require C—

(a) to produce to B any documents in C's possession or under his control which appear to B to be relevant to the investigation,

(b) to attend before B, and

(c) otherwise to give B all assistance in connection with the investigation which C is reasonably able to give,

and it is C's duty to comply with that requirement.

(4) Subsections (5) to (9) of section 170 apply if an investigating authority appoints a person under this section to conduct an investigation on its behalf as they apply in the case mentioned in subsection (1) of that section.

(5) Section 174 applies to a statement made by a person in compliance with a requirement imposed under this section as it applies to a statement mentioned in that section.

(6) Subsections (2) to (4) and (6) of section 175 and section 177 have effect as if this section were contained in Part XI.

(7) Subsections (1) to (9) of section 176 apply in relation to a person appointed under subsection (1) as if—

(a) references to an investigator were references to a person so appointed;

(b) references to an information requirement were references to a requirement imposed under section 175 or under subsection (3) by a person so appointed;

(c) the premises mentioned in subsection (3)(a) were the premises of a person whose affairs are the subject of an investigation under this section or of an appointed representative of such a person.

(8) No person may be required under this section to disclose information or produce a document in respect of which he owes an obligation of confidence by virtue of carrying on the business of banking unless subsection (9) or (10) applies.

(9) This subsection applies if—

(a) the person to whom the obligation of confidence is owed consents to the disclosure or production; or

(b) the imposing on the person concerned of a requirement with respect to information or a document of a kind mentioned in subsection (8) has been specifically authorised by the investigating authority.

(10) This subsection applies if the person owing the obligation of confidence or the person to whom it is owed is—

(a) the manager, trustee, operator or depositary of any collective investment scheme which is under investigation;

(b) the director of a body incorporated by virtue of regulations under section 262 which is under investigation;

(c) any other person whose own affairs are under investigation.

(11) "Investigating authority" means the Authority or the Secretary of State.

[2282]

NOTES

The business of banking: this phrase is not defined in this Act and it is not clear whether it applies to all those who have permission or authorisation to accept deposits.

PART XVIII
RECOGNISED INVESTMENT EXCHANGES AND CLEARING HOUSES

CHAPTER I
EXEMPTION

General

285 Exemption for recognised investment exchanges and clearing houses

(1) In this Act—

(a) "recognised investment exchange" means an investment exchange in relation to which a recognition order is in force; and

(b) "recognised clearing house" means a clearing house in relation to which a recognition order is in force.

(2) A recognised investment exchange is exempt from the general prohibition as respects any regulated activity—

(a) which is carried on as a part of the exchange's business as an investment exchange; or

(b) which is carried on for the purposes of, or in connection with, the provision of clearing services by the exchange.

(3) A recognised clearing house is exempt from the general prohibition as respects any regulated activity which is carried on for the purposes of, or in connection with, the provision of clearing services by the clearing house.

[2283]

286 Qualification for recognition

(1) The Treasury may make regulations setting out the requirements—

(a) which must be satisfied by an investment exchange or clearing house if it is to qualify as a body in respect of which the Authority may make a recognition order under this Part; and

(b) which, if a recognition order is made, it must continue to satisfy if it is to remain a recognised body.

(2) But if regulations contain provision as to the default rules of an investment exchange or clearing house, or as to proceedings taken under such rules by such a body, they require the approval of the Secretary of State.

(3) "Default rules" means rules of an investment exchange or clearing house which provide for the taking of action in the event of a person's appearing to be unable, or likely to become unable, to meet his obligations in respect of one or more market contracts connected with the exchange or clearing house.

(4) "Market contract" means—

(a) a contract to which Part VII of the Companies Act 1989 applies as a result of section 155 of that Act or a contract to which Part V of the Companies (No 2) (Northern Ireland) Order 1990 applies as a result of Article 80 of that Order; and

(b) such other kind of contract as may be prescribed.

[(4A) If regulations under subsection (1) require an investment exchange to make information available to the public in accordance with—

(a) Article 29.1 of the markets in financial instruments directive and the Commission Regulation, or

(b) Article 44.1 of that directive and that Regulation,

the regulations may authorise the Authority to waive the requirement in the circumstances specified in the relevant provisions.

(4B) The "relevant provisions" for the purposes of subsection (4A) are—

(a) in a case falling within paragraph (a) of that subsection, Article 29.2 of the markets in financial instruments directive and the Commission Regulation, and

(b) in a case falling within paragraph (b) of that subsection, Article 44.2 of that directive and that Regulation.

(4C) If regulations under subsection (1) require an investment exchange to make information available to the public in accordance with—

(a) Article 30.1 of the markets in financial instruments directive and the Commission Regulation, or

(b) Article 45.1 of that directive and that Regulation,

the regulations may authorise the Authority to defer the requirement in the circumstances specified, and subject to the requirements contained, in the relevant provisions.

(4D) The "relevant provisions" for the purposes of subsection (4C) are—

(a) in a case falling within paragraph (a) of that subsection, Article 30.2 of the markets in financial instruments directive and the Commission Regulation, and

(b) in a case falling within paragraph (b) of that subsection, Article 45.2 of that directive and that Regulation.

(4E) "The Commission Regulation" means Commission Regulation 1287/2006 of 10 August 2006.]

(5) Requirements resulting from this section are referred to in this Part as "recognition requirements".

[(6) In the case of an investment exchange, requirements resulting from this section are in addition to requirements which must be satisfied by the exchange as a result of section 290(1A) before the Authority may make a recognition order declaring the exchange to be a recognised investment exchange.]

[2284]

PART II
FSMA 2000

NOTES

Sub-ss (4A)–(4E): inserted by the Financial Services and Markets Act 2000 (Markets in Financial Instruments) (Modification of Powers) Regulations 2006, SI 2006/2975, regs 2, 8, as from 6 December 2006.

Sub-s (6): added by the Financial Services and Markets Act 2000 (Markets in Financial Instruments) Regulations 2007, SI 2007/126, reg 3(2), Sch 2, paras 1, 2, as from 1 April 2007 (certain purposes (see reg 1(2) at **[7596]**)), and as from 1 November 2007 (otherwise).

Regulations: the Financial Services and Markets Act 2000 (Recognition Requirements for Investment Exchanges and Clearing Houses) Regulations 2001, SI 2001/995.

Note that the following amending Regulations have also been made under this section: the Financial Services and Markets Act 2000 (Recognition Requirements for Investment Exchanges and Clearing Houses) (Amendment) Regulations 2006, SI 2006/3386.

Applications for recognition

287 Application by an investment exchange

(1) Any body corporate or unincorporated association may apply to the Authority for an order declaring it to be a recognised investment exchange for the purposes of this Act.

(2) The application must be made in such manner as the Authority may direct and must be accompanied by—

(a) a copy of the applicant's rules;
(b) a copy of any guidance issued by the applicant;
(c) the required particulars; and
(d) such other information as the Authority may reasonably require for the purpose of determining the application.

(3) The required particulars are—

(a) particulars of any arrangements which the applicant has made, or proposes to make, for the provision of clearing services in respect of transactions effected on the exchange;
(b) if the applicant proposes to provide clearing services in respect of transactions other than those effected on the exchange, particulars of the criteria which the applicant will apply when determining to whom it will provide those services[;
(c) a programme of operations which includes the types of business the applicant proposes to undertake and the applicant's proposed organisational structure;
(d) such particulars of the persons who effectively direct the business and operations of the exchange as the Authority may reasonably require;
(e) such particulars of the ownership of the exchange, and in particular of the identity and scale of interests of the persons who are in a position to exercise significant influence over the management of the exchange, whether directly or indirectly, as the Authority may reasonably require].

[(4) Subsection (3)(c) to (e) does not apply to an application by an overseas applicant.]

[2285]

NOTES

Sub-s (3): paras (c)–(e) added by the Financial Services and Markets Act 2000 (Markets in Financial Instruments) Regulations 2007, SI 2007/126, reg 3(2), Sch 2, paras 1, 3(a), as from 1 April 2007 (certain purposes (see reg 1(2) at **[7596]**)), and as from 1 November 2007 (otherwise).

Sub-s (4): added by SI 2007/126, reg 3(2), Sch 2, paras 1, 3(b), as from 1 April 2007 (certain purposes (see reg 1(2) at **[7596]**)), and as from 1 November 2007 (otherwise).

288 Application by a clearing house

(1) Any body corporate or unincorporated association may apply to the Authority for an order declaring it to be a recognised clearing house for the purposes of this Act.

(2) The application must be made in such manner as the Authority may direct and must be accompanied by—

(a) a copy of the applicant's rules;
(b) a copy of any guidance issued by the applicant;
(c) the required particulars; and
(d) such other information as the Authority may reasonably require for the purpose of determining the application.

(3) The required particulars are—

(a) if the applicant makes, or proposes to make, clearing arrangements with a recognised investment exchange, particulars of those arrangements;

(b) if the applicant proposes to provide clearing services for persons other than recognised investment exchanges, particulars of the criteria which it will apply when determining to whom it will provide those services.

[2286]

289 Applications: supplementary

(1) At any time after receiving an application and before determining it, the Authority may require the applicant to provide such further information as it reasonably considers necessary to enable it to determine the application.

(2) Information which the Authority requires in connection with an application must be provided in such form, or verified in such manner, as the Authority may direct.

(3) Different directions may be given, or requirements imposed, by the Authority with respect to different applications.

[2287]

290 Recognition orders

(1) If it appears to the Authority that the applicant satisfies the recognition requirements applicable in its case, the Authority may make a recognition order declaring the applicant to be—

(a) a recognised investment exchange, if the application is made under section 287;

(b) a recognised clearing house, if it is made under section 288.

[(1A) In the case of an application for an order declaring the applicant to be a recognised investment exchange, the reference in subsection (1) to the recognition requirements applicable in its case includes a reference to requirements contained in any directly applicable Community regulation made under the markets in financial instruments directive.

(1B) In the case mentioned in subsection (1A), the application must be determined by the Authority before the end of the period of six months beginning with the date on which it receives the completed application.

(1C) Subsection (1B) does not apply in the case of an application by an overseas applicant.]

(2) The Treasury's approval of the making of a recognition order is required under section 307.

(3) In considering an application, the Authority may have regard to any information which it considers is relevant to the application.

(4) A recognition order must specify a date on which it is to take effect.

(5) Section 298 has effect in relation to a decision to refuse to make a recognition order—

(a) as it has effect in relation to a decision to revoke such an order; and

(b) as if references to a recognised body were references to the applicant.

(6) Subsection (5) does not apply in a case in which the Treasury have failed to give their approval under section 307.

[2288]

NOTES

Sub-ss (1A)–(1C): inserted by the Financial Services and Markets Act 2000 (Markets in Financial Instruments) Regulations 2007, SI 2007/126, reg 3(2), Sch 2, paras 1, 4, as from 1 April 2007 (certain purposes (see reg 1(2) at **[7596]**)), and as from 1 November 2007 (otherwise).

[290A Refusal of recognition on ground of excessive regulatory provision

(1) The Authority must not make a recognition order if it appears to the Authority that an existing or proposed regulatory provision of the applicant in connection with—

(a) the applicant's business as an investment exchange, or

(b) the provision by the applicant of clearing services,

imposes or will impose an excessive requirement on the persons affected (directly or indirectly) by it.

(2) The reference in section 290(1) (making of recognition order) to satisfying the applicable recognition requirements shall be read accordingly.

(3) Expressions used in subsection (1) above that are defined for the purposes of section 300A (power of Authority to disallow excessive regulatory provision) have the same meaning as in that section.

(4) The provisions of section 300A(3) and (4) (determination whether regulatory provision excessive) apply for the purposes of this section as for the purposes of section 300A.

(5) Section 298 has effect in relation to a decision under this section to refuse a recognition order—

(a) as it has effect in relation to a decision to revoke such an order, and

(b) as if references to a recognised body were references to the applicant.

(6) This section does not apply to an application for recognition as an overseas investment exchange or overseas clearing house.]

[2288A]

NOTES

Commencement: 20 December 2006.

Inserted by the Investment Exchanges and Clearing Houses Act 2006, s 4, as from 20 December 2006.

291 Liability in relation to recognised body's regulatory functions

(1) A recognised body and its officers and staff are not to be liable in damages for anything done or omitted in the discharge of the recognised body's regulatory functions unless it is shown that the act or omission was in bad faith.

(2) But subsection (1) does not prevent an award of damages made in respect of an act or omission on the ground that the act or omission was unlawful as a result of section 6(1) of the Human Rights Act 1998.

(3) "Regulatory functions" means the functions of the recognised body so far as relating to, or to matters arising out of, the obligations to which the body is subject under or by virtue of this Act.

[2289]

292 Overseas investment exchanges and overseas clearing houses

(1) An application under section 287 or 288 by an overseas applicant must contain the address of a place in the United Kingdom for the service on the applicant of notices or other documents required or authorised to be served on it under this Act.

(2) If it appears to the Authority that an overseas applicant satisfies the requirements of subsection (3) it may make a recognition order declaring the applicant to be—

(a) a recognised investment exchange;

(b) a recognised clearing house.

(3) The requirements are that—

(a) investors are afforded protection equivalent to that which they would be afforded if the body concerned were required to comply with recognition requirements[, other than any such requirements which are expressed in regulations under section 286 not to apply for the purposes of this paragraph];

(b) there are adequate procedures for dealing with a person who is unable, or likely to become unable, to meet his obligations in respect of one or more market contracts connected with the investment exchange or clearing house;

(c) the applicant is able and willing to co-operate with the Authority by the sharing of information and in other ways;

(d) adequate arrangements exist for co-operation between the Authority and those responsible for the supervision of the applicant in the country or territory in which the applicant's head office is situated.

(4) In considering whether it is satisfied as to the requirements mentioned in subsection (3)(a) and (b), the Authority is to have regard to—

(a) the relevant law and practice of the country or territory in which the applicant's head office is situated;
(b) the rules and practices of the applicant.

(5) In relation to an overseas applicant and a body or association declared to be a recognised investment exchange or recognised clearing house by a recognition order made by virtue of subsection (2)—
(a) the reference in section 313(2) to recognition requirements is to be read as a reference to matters corresponding to the matters in respect of which provision is made in the recognition requirements;
(b) sections 296(1) and 297(2) have effect as if the requirements mentioned in section 296(1)(a) and section 297(2)(a) were those of subsection (3)(a), (b), and (c) of this section;
(c) section 297(2) has effect as if the grounds on which a recognition order may be revoked under that provision included the ground that in the opinion of the Authority arrangements of the kind mentioned in subsection (3)(d) no longer exist.

[2290]

NOTES

Sub-s (3): words in square brackets in para (a) inserted by the Financial Services and Markets Act 2000 (Markets in Financial Instruments) (Modification of Powers) Regulations 2006, SI 2006/2975, regs 2, 9, as from 6 December 2006.

Regulations under section 286: see that section at **[2284]**.

[Publication of information by recognised investment exchange

292A Publication of information by recognised investment exchange

(1) A recognised investment exchange must as soon as practicable after a recognition order is made in respect of it publish such particulars of the ownership of the exchange as the Authority may reasonably require.

(2) The particulars published under subsection (1) must include particulars of the identity and scale of interests of the persons who are in a position to exercise significant influence over the management of the exchange, whether directly or indirectly.

(3) If an ownership transfer takes place in relation to a recognised investment exchange, the exchange must as soon as practicable after becoming aware of the transfer publish such particulars relating to the transfer as the Authority may reasonably require.

(4) "Ownership transfer", in relation to an exchange, means a transfer of ownership which gives rise to a change in the persons who are in a position to exercise significant influence over the management of the exchange, whether directly or indirectly.

(5) A recognised investment exchange must publish such particulars of any decision it makes to suspend or remove a financial instrument from trading on a regulated market operated by it as the Authority may reasonably require.

(6) The Authority may determine the manner of publication under subsections (1), (3) and (5) and the timing of publication under subsection (5).

(7) This section does not apply to an overseas investment exchange.]

[2290A]

NOTES

Commencement: see the note below.

Inserted, together with the preceding heading, by the Financial Services and Markets Act 2000 (Markets in Financial Instruments) Regulations 2007, SI 2007/126, reg 3(2), Sch 2, paras 1, 5, as from 1 April 2007 (certain purposes (see reg 1(2) at **[7596]**)), and as from 1 November 2007 (otherwise).

Supervision

293 Notification requirements

(1) The Authority may make rules requiring a recognised body to give it—

(a) notice of such events relating to the body as may be specified; and
(b) such information in respect of those events as may be specified.

(2) The rules may also require a recognised body to give the Authority, at such times or in respect of such periods as may be specified, such information relating to the body as may be specified.

(3) An obligation imposed by the rules extends only to a notice or information which the Authority may reasonably require for the exercise of its functions under this Act.

(4) The rules may require information to be given in a specified form and to be verified in a specified manner.

(5) If a recognised body—
(a) alters or revokes any of its rules or guidance, or
(b) makes new rules or issues new guidance,
it must give written notice to the Authority without delay.

(6) If a recognised investment exchange makes a change—
(a) in the arrangements it makes for the provision of clearing services in respect of transactions effected on the exchange, or
(b) in the criteria which it applies when determining to whom it will provide clearing services,
it must give written notice to the Authority without delay.

(7) If a recognised clearing house makes a change—
(a) in the recognised investment exchanges for whom it provides clearing services, or
(b) in the criteria which it applies when determining to whom (other than recognised investment exchanges) it will provide clearing services,
it must give written notice to the Authority without delay.

(8) Subsections (5) to (7) do not apply to an overseas investment exchange or an overseas clearing house.

(9) "Specified" means specified in the Authority's rules.

[2291]

[293A Information: compliance of recognised investment exchanges with directly applicable Community regulations

The Authority may require a recognised investment exchange to give the Authority such information as it reasonably requires in order to satisfy itself that the exchange is complying with any directly applicable Community regulation made under the markets in financial instruments directive.]

[2291A]

NOTES

Commencement: see the note below.

Inserted by the Financial Services and Markets Act 2000 (Markets in Financial Instruments) Regulations 2007, SI 2007/126, reg 3(2), Sch 2, paras 1, 6, as from 1 April 2007 (certain purposes (see reg 1(2) at **[7596]**)), and as from 1 November 2007 (otherwise).

294 Modification or waiver of rules

(1) The Authority may, on the application or with the consent of a recognised body, direct that rules made under section 293 or 295—
(a) are not to apply to the body; or
(b) are to apply to the body with such modifications as may be specified in the direction.

(2) An application must be made in such manner as the Authority may direct.

(3) Subsections (4) to (6) apply to a direction given under subsection (1).

(4) The Authority may not give a direction unless it is satisfied that—
(a) compliance by the recognised body with the rules, or with the rules as unmodified, would be unduly burdensome or would not achieve the purpose for which the rules were made; and

(b) the direction would not result in undue risk to persons whose interests the rules are intended to protect.

(5) A direction may be given subject to conditions.

(6) The Authority may—

(a) revoke a direction; or

(b) vary it on the application, or with the consent, of the recognised body to which it relates.

[2292]

295 Notification: overseas investment exchanges and overseas clearing houses

(1) At least once a year, every overseas investment exchange and overseas clearing house must provide the Authority with a report.

(2) The report must contain a statement as to whether any events have occurred which are likely—

(a) to affect the Authority's assessment of whether it is satisfied as to the requirements set out in section 292(3); or

(b) to have any effect on competition.

(3) The report must also contain such information as may be specified in rules made by the Authority.

(4) The investment exchange or clearing house must provide the Treasury and the [OFT] with a copy of the report.

[2293]

NOTES

Sub-s (4): word in square brackets substituted by the Enterprise Act 2002, s 278(1), Sch 25, para 40(1), (9), as from 1 April 2003.

296 Authority's power to give directions

(1) This section applies if it appears to the Authority that a recognised body—

(a) has failed, or is likely to fail, to satisfy the recognition requirements; or

(b) has failed to comply with any other obligation imposed on it by or under this Act.

[(1A) This section also applies in the case of a recognised body which is a recognised investment exchange if it appears to the Authority that the body has failed, or is likely to fail, to comply with any obligation imposed on it by any directly applicable Community regulation made under the markets in financial instruments directive.]

(2) The Authority may direct the body to take specified steps for the purpose of securing the body's compliance with—

(a) the recognition requirements; or

(b) any obligation of the kind in question.

[(2A) In the case of a recognised investment exchange other than an overseas investment exchange, those steps may include—

(a) the granting to the Authority of access to the premises of the exchange for the purpose of inspecting—

(i) those premises; or

(ii) any documents on the premises which appear to the Authority to be relevant for the purpose mentioned in subsection (2);

(b) the suspension of the carrying on of any regulated activity by the exchange for the period specified in the direction.]

(3) A direction under this section is enforceable, on the application of the Authority, by an injunction or, in Scotland, by an order for specific performance under section 45 of the Court of Session Act 1988.

(4) The fact that a rule made by a recognised body has been altered in response to a direction given by the Authority does not prevent it from being subsequently altered or revoked by the recognised body.

[2294]

PART II
FSMA 2000

NOTES

Sub-ss (1A), (2A): inserted by the Financial Services and Markets Act 2000 (Markets in Financial Instruments) Regulations 2007, SI 2007/126, reg 3(2), Sch 2, paras 1, 7, as from 1 April 2007 (certain purposes (see reg 1(2) at **[7596]**)), and as from 1 November 2007 (otherwise).

Application: this section and s 297 apply in relation to a failure by a recognised investment exchange or recognised clearing house to comply with an obligation under the CA 1989, Pt VII, as to a failure to comply with an obligation under this Act; see s 169(2) of the 1989 Act at **[840]**.

297 Revoking recognition

(1) A recognition order may be revoked by an order made by the Authority at the request, or with the consent, of the recognised body concerned.

(2) If it appears to the Authority that a recognised body—

(a) is failing, or has failed, to satisfy the recognition requirements, or

(b) is failing, or has failed, to comply with any other obligation imposed on it by or under this Act,

it may make an order revoking the recognition order for that body even though the body does not wish the order to be made.

[(2A) If it appears to the Authority that a recognised body which is a recognised investment exchange—

(a) has not carried on the business of an investment exchange during the period of twelve months beginning with the day on which the recognition order took effect in relation to it,

(b) has not carried on the business of an investment exchange at any time during the period of six months ending with the relevant day, or

(c) has failed, or is likely to fail, to comply with any obligation imposed on it by a directly applicable Community regulation made under the markets in financial instruments directive,

it may make an order revoking the recognition order for that body even though the body does not wish the order to be made.

(2B) The "relevant day", for the purposes of paragraph (b) of subsection (2A), is the day on which the power to make an order under that subsection is exercised.

(2C) Subsection (2A) does not apply to an overseas investment exchange.]

(3) An order under this section ("a revocation order") must specify the date on which it is to take effect.

(4) In the case of a revocation order made under subsection (2) [or (2A)], the specified date must not be earlier than the end of the period of three months beginning with the day on which the order is made.

(5) A revocation order may contain such transitional provisions as the Authority thinks necessary or expedient.

[2295]

NOTES

Sub-ss (2A)–(2C): inserted by the Financial Services and Markets Act 2000 (Markets in Financial Instruments) Regulations 2007, SI 2007/126, reg 3(2), Sch 2, paras 1, 8(a), as from 1 April 2007 (certain purposes (see reg 1(2) at **[7596]**)), and as from 1 November 2007 (otherwise).

Sub-s (4): words in square brackets inserted by SI 2007/126, reg 3(2), Sch 2, paras 1, 8(b), as from 1 April 2007 (certain purposes (see reg 1(2) at **[7596]**)), and as from 1 November 2007 (otherwise).

Application: see the note to s 296 at **[2294]**.

298 Directions and revocation: procedure

(1) Before giving a direction under section 296, or making a revocation order under section 297(2) [or (2A)], the Authority must—

(a) give written notice of its intention to do so to the recognised body concerned;

(b) take such steps as it considers reasonably practicable to bring the notice to the attention of members (if any) of that body; and

(c) publish the notice in such manner as it thinks appropriate for bringing it to the attention of other persons who are, in its opinion, likely to be affected.

(2) A notice under subsection (1) must—
(a) state why the Authority intends to give the direction or make the order; and
(b) draw attention to the right to make representations conferred by subsection (3).

(3) Before the end of the period for making representations—
(a) the recognised body,
(b) any member of that body, and
(c) any other person who is likely to be affected by the proposed direction or revocation order,

may make representations to the Authority.

(4) The period for making representations is—
(a) two months beginning—
(i) with the date on which the notice is served on the recognised body; or
(ii) if later, with the date on which the notice is published; or
(b) such longer period as the Authority may allow in the particular case.

(5) In deciding whether to—
(a) give a direction, or
(b) make a revocation order,

the Authority must have regard to any representations made in accordance with subsection (3).

(6) When the Authority has decided whether to give a direction under section 296 or to make the proposed revocation order, it must—
(a) give the recognised body written notice of its decision; and
(b) if it has decided to give a direction or make an order, take such steps as it considers reasonably practicable for bringing its decision to the attention of members of the body or of other persons who are, in the Authority's opinion, likely to be affected.

(7) If the Authority considers it essential to do so, it may give a direction under section 296—
(a) without following the procedure set out in this section; or
(b) if the Authority has begun to follow that procedure, regardless of whether the period for making representations has expired.

(8) If the Authority has, in relation to a particular matter, followed the procedure set out in subsections (1) to (5), it need not follow it again if, in relation to that matter, it decides to take action other than that specified in its notice under subsection (1).

[2296]

NOTES

Sub-s (1): words in square brackets inserted by the Financial Services and Markets Act 2000 (Markets in Financial Instruments) Regulations 2007, SI 2007/126, reg 3(2), Sch 2, paras 1, 9, as from 1 April 2007 (certain purposes (see reg 1(2) at **[7596]**)), and as from 1 November 2007 (otherwise).

299 Complaints about recognised bodies

(1) The Authority must make arrangements for the investigation of any relevant complaint about a recognised body.

(2) "Relevant complaint" means a complaint which the Authority considers is relevant to the question of whether the body concerned should remain a recognised body.

[2297]

300 Extension of functions of Tribunal

(1) If the Treasury are satisfied that the condition mentioned in subsection (2) is satisfied, they may by order confer functions on the Tribunal with respect to disciplinary proceedings—
(a) of one or more investment exchanges in relation to which a recognition order under section 290 is in force or of such investment exchanges generally, or
(b) of one or more clearing houses in relation to which a recognition order under that section is in force or of such clearing houses generally.

(2) The condition is that it is desirable to exercise the power conferred under subsection (1) with a view to ensuring that—
(a) decisions taken in disciplinary proceedings with respect to which functions are to be conferred on the Tribunal are consistent with—

PART II FSMA 2000

(i) decisions of the Tribunal in cases arising under Part VIII; and
(ii) decisions taken in other disciplinary proceedings with respect to which the Tribunal has functions as a result of an order under this section; or
(b) the disciplinary proceedings are in accordance with the Convention rights.

(3) An order under this section may modify or exclude any provision made by or under this Act with respect to proceedings before the Tribunal.

(4) "Disciplinary proceedings" means proceedings under the rules of an investment exchange or clearing house in relation to market abuse by persons subject to the rules.

(5) "The Convention rights" has the meaning given in section 1 of the Human Rights Act 1998.

[2298]

[Power to disallow excessive regulatory provision

300A Power of Authority to disallow excessive regulatory provision

(1) This section applies where a recognised body proposes to make any regulatory provision in connection with its business as an investment exchange or the provision by it of clearing services.

(2) If it appears to the Authority—
(a) that the proposed provision will impose a requirement on persons affected (directly or indirectly) by it, and
(b) that the requirement is excessive,
the Authority may direct that the proposed provision must not be made.

(3) A requirement is excessive if—
(a) it is not required under Community law or any enactment or rule of law in the United Kingdom, and
(b) either—
(i) it is not justified as pursuing a reasonable regulatory objective, or
(ii) it is disproportionate to the end to be achieved.

(4) In considering whether a requirement is excessive the Authority must have regard to all the relevant circumstances, including—
(a) the effect of existing legal and other requirements,
(b) the global character of financial services and markets and the international mobility of activity,
(c) the desirability of facilitating innovation, and
(d) the impact of the proposed provision on market confidence.

(5) In this section "requirement" includes any obligation or burden.

(6) Any provision made in contravention of a direction under this section is of no effect.]

[2298A]

NOTES

Commencement: 20 December 2006.

Inserted, together with the preceding heading, by the Investment Exchanges and Clearing Houses Act 2006, s 1, as from 20 December 2006. Note that by virtue of s 5(3) of the 2006 Act, this section (a) does not apply to regulatory provision made before that day, and (b) applies to regulatory provision proposed on or after that day, whenever originally proposed.

[300B Duty to notify proposal to make regulatory provision

(1) A recognised body that proposes to make any regulatory provision must give written notice of the proposal to the Authority without delay.

(2) The Authority may by rules under section 293 (notification requirements)—
(a) specify descriptions of regulatory provision in relation to which, or circumstances in which, the duty in subsection (1) above does not apply, or
(b) provide that the duty applies only to specified descriptions of regulatory provision or in specified circumstances.

(3) The Authority may also by rules under that section—

(a) make provision as to the form and contents of the notice required, and
(b) require the body to provide such information relating to the proposal as may be specified in the rules or as the Authority may reasonably require.]

[2298B]

NOTES

Commencement: 20 December 2006.

Inserted, together with ss 300C–300E, by the Investment Exchanges and Clearing Houses Act 2006, s 2, as from 20 December 2006. Note that by virtue of s 5(3) of the 2006 Act, this section (a) does not apply to regulatory provision made before that day, and (b) applies to regulatory provision proposed on or after that day, whenever originally proposed.

Note that the Investment Exchanges and Clearing Houses Act 2006, s 3 provides as follows—

"3 Interim power to give directions about notification

(1) The Authority may, on the application or with the consent of a recognised body, direct that the obligation under section 300B(1) of the Financial Services and Markets Act 2000 (c 8) (duty to notify Authority of proposal to make regulatory provision) does not apply—
(a) to specified provision proposed to be made by that body, or
(b) to any provision proposed to be made by that body that is of a specified description or is made in specified circumstances.

(2) An application must be made in such manner as the Authority may require.

(3) The Authority may give a direction if it thinks it appropriate to do so.

(4) A direction may be given subject to conditions.

(5) The effect of a direction is that the provisions of sections 300B to 300D of that Act (provisions requiring notification and restricting the making of regulatory provision of which notification is required) do not apply or, as the case may be, cease to apply to regulatory provision to which the direction relates.

(6) The Authority may—
(a) revoke a direction, or
(b) vary it on the application or with the consent of the recognised body to which it relates.

(7) Expressions used in this section that are defined for the purposes of sections 300A to 300E of that Act have the same meaning as in those sections.

(8) This section shall cease to have effect twelve months after the passing of this Act.".

[300C Restriction on making provision before Authority decides whether to act

(1) Where notice of a proposal to make regulatory provision is required to be given to the Authority under section 300B, the provision must not be made—
(a) before that notice is given, or
(b) subject to the following provisions of this section, before the end of the initial period.

(2) The initial period is—
(a) the period of 30 days beginning with the day on which the Authority receives notice of the proposal, or
(b) if any consultation period announced by the body in relation to the proposal ends after that 30-day period, the end of the consultation period.

(3) If before the end of the initial period the Authority notifies the body that it is calling in the proposal, the provisions of section 300D (consideration by Authority whether to disallow proposed provision) apply as to when the provision may be made.

(4) If—
(a) before the end of the initial period the Authority notifies the body that it is not calling in the proposal, or
(b) the initial period ends without the Authority having notified the body that it is calling in the proposal,

the body may then make the proposed provision.

(5) Any provision made in contravention of this section is of no effect.]

[2298C]

NOTES

Commencement: 20 December 2006.

Inserted as noted to s 300B at **[2298B]**.

PART II
FSMA 2000

[300D Consideration by Authority whether to disallow proposed provision

(1) This section applies where the Authority notifies a recognised body that it is calling in a proposal to make regulatory provision.

(2) The Authority must publish a notice—

(a) giving details of the proposed provision,

(b) stating that it has called in the proposal in order to consider whether to disallow it, and

(c) specifying a period during which representations with respect to that question may be made to it.

(3) The Authority may extend the period for making representations.

(4) The Authority must notify the body of its decision whether to disallow the provision not later than 30 days after the end of the period for making representations, and must publish the decision and the reasons for it.

(5) The body must not make the provision unless and until—

(a) the Authority notifies it of its decision not to disallow it, or

(b) the 30-day period specified in subsection (4) ends without the Authority having notified any decision.

(6) If the Authority notifies the body of its decision to disallow the provision and that decision is questioned in legal proceedings—

(a) the body must not make the provision until those proceedings, and any proceedings on appeal, are finally determined,

(b) if the Authority's decision is quashed and the matter is remitted to it for reconsideration, the court may give directions as to the period within which the Authority is to complete its reconsideration, and

(c) the body must not make the provision until—

(i) the Authority notifies it of its decision on reconsideration not to disallow the provision, or

(ii) the period specified by the court ends without the Authority having notified any decision.

(7) Any provision made in contravention of subsection (5) or (6) is of no effect.]

[2298D]

NOTES

Commencement: 20 December 2006.
Inserted as noted to s 300B at **[2298B]**.

[300E Power to disallow excessive regulatory provision: supplementary

(1) In sections 300A to 300D—

(a) "regulatory provision" means any rule, guidance, arrangements, policy or practice, and

(b) references to making provision shall be read accordingly as including, as the case may require, issuing guidance, entering into arrangements or adopting a policy or practice.

(2) For the purposes of those sections a variation of a proposal is treated as a new proposal.

(3) Those sections do not apply to an overseas investment exchange or overseas clearing house.]

[2298E]

NOTES

Commencement: 20 December 2006.
Inserted as noted to s 300B at **[2298B]**.

Other matters

301 Supervision of certain contracts

(1) The Secretary of State and the Treasury, acting jointly, may by regulations provide for—

(a) Part VII of the Companies Act 1989 (financial markets and insolvency), and
(b) Part V of the Companies (No 2) (Northern Ireland) Order 1990,

to apply to relevant contracts as it applies to contracts connected with a recognised body.

(2) "Relevant contracts" means contracts of a prescribed description in relation to which settlement arrangements are provided by a person for the time being included in a list ("the list") maintained by the Authority for the purposes of this section.

(3) Regulations may be made under this section only if the Secretary of State and the Treasury are satisfied, having regard to the extent to which the relevant contracts concerned are contracts of a kind dealt in by persons supervised by the Authority, that it is appropriate for the arrangements mentioned in subsection (2) to be supervised by the Authority.

(4) The approval of the Treasury is required for—

(a) the conditions set by the Authority for admission to the list; and
(b) the arrangements for admission to, and removal from, the list.

(5) If the Treasury withdraw an approval given by them under subsection (4), all regulations made under this section and then in force are to be treated as suspended.

(6) But if—

(a) the Authority changes the conditions or arrangements (or both), and
(b) the Treasury give a fresh approval under subsection (4),

the suspension of the regulations ends on such date as the Treasury may, in giving the fresh approval, specify.

(7) The Authority must—

(a) publish the list as for the time being in force; and
(b) provide a certified copy of it to any person who wishes to refer to it in legal proceedings.

(8) A certified copy of the list is evidence (or in Scotland sufficient evidence) of the contents of the list.

(9) A copy of the list which purports to be certified by or on behalf of the Authority is to be taken to have been duly certified unless the contrary is shown.

(10) Regulations under this section may, in relation to a person included in the list—

(a) apply (with such exceptions, additions and modifications as appear to the Secretary of State and the Treasury to be necessary or expedient) such provisions of, or made under, this Act as they consider appropriate;
(b) provide for the provisions of Part VII of the Companies Act 1989 and Part V of the Companies (No 2)(Northern Ireland) Order 1990 to apply (with such exceptions, additions or modifications as appear to the Secretary of State and the Treasury to be necessary or expedient).

[2299]

[CHAPTER 1A
CONTROL OVER RECOGNISED INVESTMENT EXCHANGE

Notice of control

301A Obligation to notify the Authority of acquisition of or increase in control

(1) If a step which a person proposes to take would result in his acquiring—

(a) control over a recognised investment exchange,
(b) an additional kind of control over an exchange, or
(c) an increase in a relevant kind of control which he already has over an exchange,

he must notify the Authority of his proposal.

(2) A person who, without himself taking any such step, acquires any such control or additional or increased control must notify the Authority before the end of the period of 14 days beginning with the day on which he first becomes aware that he has acquired it.

(3) A person who is under the duty to notify the Authority imposed by subsection (1) must also give notice to the Authority on acquiring, or increasing, the control in question.

(4) A notice under subsection (1) or (2) is referred to in this Chapter as a "notice of control".

(5) Section 182 applies to a notice of control under this Chapter as it applies to a notice of control under Part 12.

(6) Nothing in this Chapter applies to an overseas investment exchange.]

[2299A]

NOTES

Commencement: see the note below

Chapter 1A (ss 301A–301G) was inserted by the Financial Services and Markets Act 2000 (Markets in Financial Instruments) Regulations 2007, SI 2007/126, reg 3(2), Sch 2, paras 1, 10, as from 1 April 2007 (certain purposes (see reg 1(2) at **[7596]**)), and as from 1 November 2007 (otherwise).

[Acquiring and increasing control

301B Acquiring and increasing control

(1) For the purposes of this Chapter, a person ("the acquirer") acquires control over a recognised investment exchange ("E") on first falling within any of the cases in subsection (2).

(2) The cases are where the acquirer—
- (a) holds 20% or more of the shares in E;
- (b) is able to exercise significant influence over the management of E by virtue of his shareholding in E;
- (c) holds 20% or more shares in a parent undertaking ("P") of E;
- (d) is able to exercise significant influence over the management of P by virtue of his shareholding in P;
- (e) is entitled to exercise, or control the exercise of, 20% or more of the voting power in E;
- (f) is able to exercise significant influence over the management of E by virtue of his voting power in E;
- (g) is entitled to exercise, or to control the exercise of, 20% or more of the voting power in P; or
- (h) is able to exercise significant influence over the management of P by virtue of his voting power in P.

(3) In subsection (2) "the acquirer" means—
- (a) the acquirer,
- (b) any of his associates, or
- (c) the acquirer and any of his associates.

(4) For the purposes of this Chapter, each of the following is to be regarded as a kind of control—
- (a) control arising as a result of the holding of shares in E;
- (b) control arising as a result of the holding of shares in P;
- (c) control arising as a result of the entitlement to exercise, or control the exercise of, voting power in E;
- (d) control arising as a result of the entitlement to exercise, or control the exercise of, voting power in P.

(5) For the purposes of this Chapter, a controller of E increases his control over E if—
- (a) the percentage of shares held by the controller in E increases by the step mentioned in subsection (6);
- (b) the percentage of shares held by the controller in P increases by the step mentioned in subsection (6);
- (c) the percentage of voting power which the controller is entitled to exercise, or control the exercise of, in E increases by the step mentioned in subsection (6);
- (d) the percentage of voting power which the controller is entitled to exercise, or control the exercise of, in P increases by the step mentioned in subsection (6); or
- (e) the controller becomes a parent undertaking of E.

(6) The step is from 20% or more (but less than 50%) to 50% or more.

(7) In the rest of this Chapter "acquiring control" or "having control" includes—

(a) acquiring or having an additional kind of control; or

(b) acquiring an increase in a relevant kind of control, or having increased control of a relevant kind.]

[2299B]

NOTES

Commencement: see the note below

Chapter 1A (ss 301A–301G) was inserted by the Financial Services and Markets Act 2000 (Markets in Financial Instruments) Regulations 2007, SI 2007/126, reg 3(2), Sch 2, paras 1, 10, as from 1 April 2007 (certain purposes (see reg 1(2) at **[7596]**)), and as from 1 November 2007 (otherwise).

[Acquiring or increasing control: procedure

301C Duty of Authority in relation to notice of control

(1) The Authority must, before the end of the period of three months beginning with the date on which it receives a notice of control, determine whether—

(a) to approve of the person concerned having the control to which the notice relates; or

(b) to give a warning notice under subsection (7).

(2) If the Authority decides to approve of the person concerned having the control to which the notice relates it must notify that person of its approval in writing without delay.

(3) If the Authority fails to comply with subsection (1) it is to be treated as having given its approval and notified the person concerned at the end of the period fixed by that subsection.

(4) The Authority's approval remains effective only if the person to whom it relates acquires the control in question—

(a) before the end of such period as may be specified in the notice of approval under subsection (2); or

(b) if no period is specified, before the end of the period of one year beginning with the date—

(i) of the notice of approval under subsection (2);

(ii) on which the Authority is treated as having given approval under subsection (3); or

(iii) of a decision on a reference to the Tribunal which results in the person concerned receiving approval.

(5) The Authority may give a decision notice under this subsection unless it is satisfied that the approval requirement is met.

(6) The approval requirement is that the acquisition of control by the person who gave the notice of control does not pose a threat to the sound and prudent management of any financial market operated by the recognised investment exchange.

(7) If the Authority proposes to give the person concerned a decision notice under subsection (5), it must give him a warning notice.

(8) A person to whom a decision notice is given under subsection (5) may refer the matter to the Tribunal.]

[2299C]

NOTES

Commencement: see the note below

Chapter 1A (ss 301A–301G) was inserted by the Financial Services and Markets Act 2000 (Markets in Financial Instruments) Regulations 2007, SI 2007/126, reg 3(2), Sch 2, paras 1, 10, as from 1 April 2007 (certain purposes (see reg 1(2) at **[7596]**)), and as from 1 November 2007 (otherwise).

[301D Objection to existing control

(1) If the Authority is not satisfied that the approval requirement is met, it may give a decision notice under this section to a person if he has failed to comply with a duty to notify imposed by section 301A.

PART II FSMA 2000

(2) If the failure relates to subsection (1) or (2) of that section, the Authority may (instead of giving a notice under subsection (1)) approve the acquisition of control in question by the person concerned as if he had given it a notice of control.

(3) The Authority may also give a decision notice under this section to a person who is a controller of a recognised investment exchange if the Authority becomes aware of matters as a result of which it is satisfied that the approval requirement is not met with respect to the controller.

(4) If the Authority proposes to give a decision notice under subsection (1) or (3) to a person, it must give him a warning notice before the end of the period of three months beginning—

- (a) in the case of a notice to be given under subsection (1), with the date on which it became aware of the failure to comply with the duty in question;
- (b) in the case of a notice to be given under subsection (3), with the date on which it became aware of the matters in question.

(5) A person to whom a decision notice is given under this section may refer the matter to the Tribunal.

(6) "Approval requirement" has the same meaning as in section 301C.]

[2299D]

NOTES

Commencement: see the note below

Chapter 1A (ss 301A–301G) was inserted by the Financial Services and Markets Act 2000 (Markets in Financial Instruments) Regulations 2007, SI 2007/126, reg 3(2), Sch 2, paras 1, 10, as from 1 April 2007 (certain purposes (see reg 1(2) at **[7596]**)), and as from 1 November 2007 (otherwise).

[Improperly acquired shares

301E Improperly acquired shares

(1) The powers conferred by this section are exercisable if a person has acquired, or has continued to hold, any shares in contravention of a decision notice given under section 301C(5) or 301D(1) or (3).

(2) The Authority may by notice in writing given to the person concerned ("a restriction notice") direct that any such shares which are specified in the notice are, until further notice, subject to one or more of the following restrictions—

- (a) a transfer of (or agreement to transfer) those shares, or in the case of unissued shares any transfer of (or agreement to transfer) the right to be issued with them, is void;
- (b) no voting rights are to be exercisable in respect of the shares;
- (c) no further shares are to be issued in right of them or in pursuance of any offer made to their holder;
- (d) except in a liquidation, no payment is to be made of any sums due from the body corporate on the shares, whether in respect of capital or otherwise.

(3) The court may, on the application of the Authority, order the sale of any shares to which this section applies and, if they are for the time being subject to any restriction under subsection (2), that they are to cease to be subject to that restriction.

(4) No order may be made under subsection (3)—

- (a) until the end of the period within which a reference may be made to the Tribunal in respect of the decision notice in question; and
- (b) if a reference is made, until the matter has been determined or the reference withdrawn.

(5) If an order has been made under subsection (3), the court may, on the application of the Authority, make such further order relating to the sale or transfer of the shares as it thinks fit.

(6) If shares are sold in pursuance of an order under this section, the proceeds of sale, less the costs of the sale, must be paid into court for the benefit of the persons beneficially interested in them; and any such person may apply to the court for the whole or part of the proceeds to be paid to him.

(7) This section applies—

(a) in the case of an acquirer falling within section 301A(1), to all the shares—

(i) in the recognised investment exchange which the acquirer has acquired,

(ii) which are held by him or an associate of his, and

(iii) which were not so held immediately before he became a person having control over the exchange;

(b) in the case of an acquirer falling within section 301A(2), to all the shares held by him or an associate of his at the time when he first became aware that he had acquired control over the exchange; and

(c) to all the shares in an undertaking ("C")—

(i) which are held by the acquirer or an associate of his, and

(ii) which were not so held before he became a person with control in relation to the exchange,

where C is the undertaking in which shares were acquired by the acquirer (or an associate of his) and, as a result, he became a person with control in relation to that exchange.

(8) A copy of the restriction notice must be given to—

(a) the recognised investment exchange to whose shares it relates; and

(b) if it relates to shares held by an associate of that exchange, that associate.

(9) The jurisdiction conferred by this section may be exercised by the High Court and the Court of Session.]

[2299E]

NOTES

Commencement: see the note below

Chapter 1A (ss 301A–301G) was inserted by the Financial Services and Markets Act 2000 (Markets in Financial Instruments) Regulations 2007, SI 2007/126, reg 3(2), Sch 2, paras 1, 10, as from 1 April 2007 (certain purposes (see reg 1(2) at **[7596]**)), and as from 1 November 2007 (otherwise).

PART II
FSMA 2000

[Offences

301F Offences in relation to acquisition of control

(1) A person who fails to comply with the duty to notify the Authority imposed on him by section 301A(1) is guilty of an offence.

(2) A person who fails to comply with the duty to notify the Authority imposed on him by section 301A(2) is guilty of an offence.

(3) If a person who has given a notice of control to the Authority carries out the proposal to which the notice relates, he is guilty of an offence if—

(a) the period of three months beginning with the date on which the Authority received the notice is still running; and

(b) the Authority has not responded to the notice by either giving its approval or giving him a warning notice under section 301C(7).

(4) A person to whom the Authority has given a warning notice under subsection (7) of section 301C is guilty of an offence if he carries out the proposal to which the notice relates before the Authority has decided whether to give him a decision notice under subsection (5) of that section.

(5) A person to whom a decision notice under section 301C(5) or 301D(1) or (3) has been given is guilty of an offence if he acquires or retains the control to which the notice applies at a time when the notice is still in force.

(6) A person guilty of an offence under subsection (1), (2), (3) or (4) is liable on summary conviction to a fine not exceeding level 5 on the standard scale.

(7) A person guilty of an offence under subsection (5) is liable—

(a) on summary conviction, to a fine not exceeding the statutory maximum; and

(b) on conviction on indictment, to imprisonment for a term not exceeding two years, or to a fine, or both.

(8) It is a defence for a person charged with an offence under subsection (1) to show that he had, at the time of the alleged offence, no knowledge of the act or circumstances by virtue of which the duty to notify the Authority arose.

(9) If a person—

(a) was under the duty to notify the Authority imposed by section 301A(1) but had no knowledge of the act or circumstances by virtue of which that duty arose, but

(b) subsequently becomes aware of that act or those circumstances,

he must notify the Authority before the end of the period of 14 days beginning with the day on which he first became so aware.

(10) A person who fails to comply with the duty to notify the Authority imposed by subsection (9) is guilty of an offence and liable, on summary conviction, to a fine not exceeding level 5 on the standard scale.]

[2299F]

NOTES

Commencement: see the note below

Chapter 1A (ss 301A–301G) was inserted by the Financial Services and Markets Act 2000 (Markets in Financial Instruments) Regulations 2007, SI 2007/126, reg 3(2), Sch 2, paras 1, 10, as from 1 April 2007 (certain purposes (see reg 1(2) at **[7596]**)), and as from 1 November 2007 (otherwise).

[Interpretation

301G Interpretation of Chapter 1A

In this Chapter—

"associate", "shares" and "voting power" have the same meaning as in section 422;

"controller", in relation to a recognised investment exchange, means a person who falls within any of the cases in section 301B(2);

"notice of control" has the meaning given in section 301A(4).]

[2299G]

NOTES

Commencement: see the note below

Chapter 1A (ss 301A–301G) was inserted by the Financial Services and Markets Act 2000 (Markets in Financial Instruments) Regulations 2007, SI 2007/126, reg 3(2), Sch 2, paras 1, 10, as from 1 April 2007 (certain purposes (see reg 1(2) at **[7596]**)), and as from 1 November 2007 (otherwise).

CHAPTER II
COMPETITION SCRUTINY

302 Interpretation

(1) In this Chapter and Chapter III—

"practices" means—

(a) in relation to a recognised investment exchange, the practices of the exchange in its capacity as such; and

(b) in relation to a recognised clearing house, the practices of the clearing house in respect of its clearing arrangements;

"regulatory provisions" means—

(a) the rules of an investment exchange or a clearing house;

(b) any guidance issued by an investment exchange or clearing house;

(c) in the case of an investment exchange, the arrangements and criteria mentioned in section *287(3)*;

(d) in the case of a clearing house, the arrangements and criteria mentioned in section 288(3).

(2) For the purposes of this Chapter, regulatory provisions or practices have a significantly adverse effect on competition if—

(a) they have, or are intended or likely to have, that effect; or

(b) the effect that they have, or are intended or likely to have, is to require or encourage behaviour which has, or is intended or likely to have, a significantly adverse effect on competition.

(3) If regulatory provisions or practices have, or are intended or likely to have, the effect of requiring or encouraging exploitation of the strength of a market position they are to be taken, for the purposes of this Chapter, to have an adverse effect on competition.

(4) In determining under this Chapter whether any regulatory provisions have, or are intended or likely to have, a particular effect, it may be assumed that persons to whom the provisions concerned are addressed will act in accordance with them.

[2300]

NOTES

Sub-s (1): for the words in italics in the definition "regulatory provisions" there are substituted the words "287(3)(a) and (b)" by the Financial Services and Markets Act 2000 (Markets in Financial Instruments) Regulations 2007, SI 2007/126, reg 3(2), Sch 2, paras 1, 11, as from 1 April 2007 (certain purposes (see reg 1(2) at **[7596]**)), and as from 1 November 2007 (otherwise).

Role of [Office of Fair Trading]

303 Initial report by [OFT]

(1) The Authority must send to the Treasury and to the [OFT] a copy of any regulatory provisions with which it is provided on an application for recognition under section 287 or 288.

(2) The Authority must send to the [OFT] such information in its possession as a result of the application for recognition as it considers will assist [the OFT] in discharging [its] functions in connection with the application.

(3) The [OFT] must issue a report as to whether—

(a) a regulatory provision of which a copy has been sent to [it] under subsection (1) has a significantly adverse effect on competition; or

(b) a combination of regulatory provisions so copied to [it] have such an effect.

(4) If the [OFT's] conclusion is that one or more provisions have a significantly adverse effect on competition, [it] must state [its] reasons for that conclusion.

(5) When the [OFT] issues a report under subsection (3), [the OFT] must send a copy of it to the Authority, the Competition Commission and the Treasury.

[(6) In the case of an application for recognition under section 287, the OFT must issue its report under subsection (3) before the end of the period of 12 weeks beginning with the date on which it receives the copy sent to it under subsection (1).

(7) Subsection (6) does not apply if the application is made by an overseas investment exchange.]

[2301]

NOTES

Sub-ss (6), (7): added by the Financial Services and Markets Act 2000 (Markets in Financial Instruments) Regulations 2007, SI 2007/126, reg 3(2), Sch 2, paras 1, 12, as from 1 April 2007 (certain purposes (see reg 1(2) at **[7596]**)), and as from 1 November 2007 (otherwise).

All other words in square brackets (including the words in the heading preceding this section) substituted by the Enterprise Act 2002, s 278(1), Sch 25, para 40(1), (10), as from 1 April 2003.

304 Further reports by [OFT]

(1) The [OFT] must keep under review the regulatory provisions and practices of recognised bodies.

(2) If at any time the [OFT] considers that—

(a) a regulatory provision or practice has a significantly adverse effect on competition, or

(b) regulatory provisions or practices, or a combination of regulating provisions and practices have such an effect,

[the OFT] must make a report.

(3) If at any time the [OFT] considers that—

(a) a regulatory provision or practice does not have a significantly adverse effect on competition, or

(b) regulatory provisions or practices, or a combination of regulatory provisions and practices do not have any such effect,

[the OFT] may make a report to that effect.

(4) A report under subsection (2) must contain details of the adverse effect on competition.

(5) If the [OFT] makes a report under subsection (2), [the OFT] must—

(a) send a copy of it to the Treasury, to the Competition Commission and to the Authority; and

(b) publish it in the way appearing to [the OFT] to be best calculated to bring it to the attention of the public.

(6) If the [OFT] makes a report under subsection (3)—

(a) [the OFT] must send a copy of it to the Treasury, to the Competition Commission and to the Authority; and

(b) [the OFT] may publish it.

(7) Before publishing a report under this section, the [OFT] must, so far as practicable, exclude any matter which relates to the private affairs of a particular individual the publication of which, in the opinion of the [OFT], would or might seriously and prejudicially affect his interests.

(8) Before publishing such a report, the [OFT] must exclude any matter which relates to the affairs of a particular body the publication of which, in the opinion of the [OFT], would or might seriously and prejudicially affect its interests.

(9) Subsections (7) and (8) do not apply to the copy of a report which the [OFT] is required to send to the Treasury, the Competition Commission and the Authority under subsection (5)(a) or (6)(a).

(10) For the purposes of the law of defamation, absolute privilege attaches to any report of the [OFT] under this section.

[2302]

NOTES

Words in square brackets substituted by the Enterprise Act 2002, s 278(1), Sch 25, para 40(1), (11), as from 1 April 2003.

305 Investigations by [OFT]

(1) For the purpose of investigating any matter with a view to its consideration under section 303 or 304, the [OFT] may exercise the powers conferred on [it] by this section.

(2) The [OFT] may by notice in writing require any person to produce to [it] or to a person appointed by [it] for the purpose, at a time and place specified in the notice, any document which—

(a) is specified or described in the notice; and

(b) is a document in that person's custody or under his control.

(3) The [OFT] may by notice in writing—

(a) require any person carrying on any business to provide [it] with such information as may be specified or described in the notice; and

(b) specify the time within which, and the manner and form in which, any such information is to be provided.

(4) A requirement may be imposed under subsection (2) or (3)(a) only in respect of documents or information which relate to any matter relevant to the investigation.

(5) If a person ("the defaulter") refuses, or otherwise fails, to comply with a notice under this section, the [OFT] may certify that fact in writing to the court and the court may enquire into the case.

(6) If, after hearing any witness who may be produced against or on behalf of the defaulter and any statement which may be offered in defence, the court is satisfied that the defaulter did not have a reasonable excuse for refusing or otherwise failing to comply with the notice, the court may deal with the defaulter as if he were in contempt.

(7) In this section, "the court" means—

(a) the High Court; or

(b) in Scotland, the Court of Session.

[2303]

NOTES

Words in square brackets substituted by the Enterprise Act 2002, s 278(1), Sch 25, para 40(1), (12), as from 1 April 2003.

Role of Competition Commission

306 Consideration by Competition Commission

(1) If subsection (2) or (3) applies, the Commission must investigate the matter which is the subject of the [OFT's] report.

(2) This subsection applies if the [OFT] sends to the Competition Commission a report—

(a) issued by [the OFT] under section 303(3) which concludes that one or more regulatory provisions have a significantly adverse effect on competition, or

(b) made by [the OFT] under section 304(2).

(3) This subsection applies if the [OFT] asks the Commission to consider a report—

(a) issued by [the OFT] under section 303(3) which concludes that one or more regulatory provisions do not have a significantly adverse effect on competition, or

(b) made by [the OFT] under section 304(3).

(4) The Commission must then make its own report on the matter unless it considers that, as a result of a change of circumstances, no useful purpose would be served by a report.

(5) If the Commission decides in accordance with subsection (4) not to make a report, it must make a statement setting out the change of circumstances which resulted in that decision.

(6) A report made under this section must state the Commission's conclusion as to whether—

(a) the regulatory provision or practice which is the subject of the report has a significantly adverse effect on competition, or

(b) the regulatory provisions or practices or combination of regulatory provisions and practices which are the subject of the report have such an effect.

(7) A report under this section stating the Commission's conclusion that there is a significantly adverse effect on competition must also—

(a) state whether the Commission considers that that effect is justified; and

(b) if it states that the Commission considers that it is not justified, state its conclusion as to what action, if any, the Treasury ought to direct the Authority to take.

(8) Subsection (9) applies whenever the Commission is considering, for the purposes of this section, whether a particular adverse effect on competition is justified.

(9) The Commission must ensure, so far as that is reasonably possible, that the conclusion it reaches is compatible with the obligations imposed on the recognised body concerned by or under this Act.

(10) A report under this section must contain such an account of the Commission's reasons for its conclusions as is expedient, in the opinion of the Commission, for facilitating proper understanding of them.

(11) The provisions of Schedule 14 (except paragraph 2(b)) apply for the purposes of this section as they apply for the purposes of section 162.

(12) If the Commission makes a report under this section it must send a copy to the Treasury, the Authority and the [OFT].

[(13) Subsection (14) applies if—

(a) the case relates to an application for recognition under section 287, other than an application by an overseas applicant; and

(b) subsection (2)(a) or (3)(a) of this section applies.

(14) The Commission must—

(a) make a report under this section, or a statement under subsection (5), before the end of the period of 12 weeks beginning with the date on which it receives a copy of the OFT's report under section 303(3); and

PART II FSMA 2000

(b) if it makes a statement under subsection (5), send a copy to the Authority and the Treasury.]

[2304]

NOTES

Sub-ss (13), (14): added by the Financial Services and Markets Act 2000 (Markets in Financial Instruments) Regulations 2007, SI 2007/126, reg 3(2), Sch 2, paras 1, 13, as from 1 April 2007 (certain purposes (see reg 1(2) at **[7596]**)), and as from 1 November 2007 (otherwise).

All other words in square brackets substituted by the Enterprise Act 2002, s 278(1), Sch 25, para 40(1), (13), as from 1 April 2003.

Role of the Treasury

307 Recognition orders: role of the Treasury

(1) Subsection (2) applies if, on an application for a recognition order—

(a) the [OFT] makes a report under section 303 but does not ask the Competition Commission to consider it under section 306;

(b) the Competition Commission concludes—

(i) that the applicant's regulatory provisions do not have a significantly adverse effect on competition; or

(ii) that if those provisions do have that effect, the effect is justified.

(2) The Treasury may refuse to approve the making of the recognition order only if they consider that the exceptional circumstances of the case make it inappropriate for them to give their approval.

(3) Subsection (4) applies if, on an application for a recognition order, the Competition Commission concludes—

(a) that the applicant's regulatory provisions have a significantly adverse effect on competition; and

(b) that that effect is not justified.

(4) The Treasury must refuse to approve the making of the recognition order unless they consider that the exceptional circumstances of the case make it inappropriate for them to refuse their approval.

[(5) Subsection (6) applies in the case of an application for recognition under section 287, other than an application by an overseas applicant.

(6) The Treasury must decide whether to approve the application before the end of the period of 10 days beginning with—

(a) in a case falling within subsection (2)(a) or (3)(a) of section 306, the date on which they receive a copy of the report under that section or, if no such report was made, of the statement under subsection (5) of that section;

(b) in any other case, the date on which they receive a copy of the report from the OFT under section 303.]

[2305]

NOTES

Sub-s (1): word in square brackets substituted by the Enterprise Act 2002, s 278(1), Sch 25, para 40(1), (14)(a), as from 1 April 2003.

Sub-ss (5), (6): added by the Financial Services and Markets Act 2000 (Markets in Financial Instruments) Regulations 2007, SI 2007/126, reg 3(2), Sch 2, paras 1, 14, as from 1 April 2007 (certain purposes (see reg 1(2) at **[7596]**)), and as from 1 November 2007 (otherwise).

308 Directions by the Treasury

(1) This section applies if the Competition Commission makes a report under section 306(4) (other than a report on an application for a recognition order) which states the Commission's conclusion that there is a significantly adverse effect on competition.

(2) If the Commission's conclusion, as stated in the report, is that the adverse effect on competition is not justified, the Treasury must give a remedial direction to the Authority.

(3) But subsection (2) does not apply if the Treasury consider—

(a) that, as a result of action taken by the Authority or the recognised body concerned in response to the Commission's report, it is unnecessary for them to give a direction; or

(b) that the exceptional circumstances of the case make it inappropriate or unnecessary for them to do so.

(4) In considering the action to be specified in a remedial direction, the Treasury must have regard to any conclusion of the Commission included in the report because of section 306(7)(b).

(5) Subsection (6) applies if—

(a) the Commission's conclusion, as stated in its report, is that the adverse effect on competition is justified; but

(b) the Treasury consider that the exceptional circumstances of the case require them to act.

(6) The Treasury may give a direction to the Authority requiring it to take such action—

(a) as they consider to be necessary in the light of the exceptional circumstances of the case; and

(b) as may be specified in the direction.

(7) If the action specified in a remedial direction is the giving by the Authority of a direction—

(a) the direction to be given must be compatible with the recognition requirements applicable to the recognised body in relation to which it is given; and

(b) subsections (3) and (4) of section 296 apply to it as if it were a direction given under that section.

(8) "Remedial direction" means a direction requiring the Authority—

(a) to revoke the recognition order for the body concerned; or

(b) to give such directions to the body concerned as may be specified in it.

[2306]

309 Statements by the Treasury

(1) If, in reliance on subsection (3)(a) or (b) of section 308, the Treasury decline to act under subsection (2) of that section, they must make a statement to that effect, giving their reasons.

(2) If the Treasury give a direction under section 308 they must make a statement giving—

(a) details of the direction; and

(b) if the direction is given under subsection (6) of that section, their reasons for giving it.

(3) The Treasury must—

(a) publish any statement made under this section in the way appearing to them best calculated to bring it to the attention of the public; and

(b) lay a copy of it before Parliament.

[2307]

310 Procedure on exercise of certain powers by the Treasury

(1) Subsection (2) applies if the Treasury are considering—

(a) whether to refuse their approval under section 307;

(b) whether section 308(2) applies; or

(c) whether to give a direction under section 308(6).

(2) The Treasury must—

(a) take such steps as they consider appropriate to allow the exchange or clearing house concerned, and any other person appearing to the Treasury to be affected, an opportunity to make representations—

(i) about any report made by the [OFT] under section 303 or 304 or by the Competition Commission under section 306;

(ii) as to whether, and if so how, the Treasury should exercise their powers under section 307 or 308; and

(b) have regard to any such representations.

[2308]

NOTES

Sub-s (2): word in square brackets substituted by the Enterprise Act 2002, s 278(1), Sch 25, para 40(1), (14)(b), as from 1 April 2003.

CHAPTER III
EXCLUSION FROM THE COMPETITION ACT 1998

311 The Chapter I prohibition

(1) The Chapter I prohibition does not apply to an agreement for the constitution of a recognised body to the extent to which the agreement relates to the regulatory provisions of that body.

(2) If the conditions set out in subsection (3) are satisfied, the Chapter I prohibition does not apply to an agreement for the constitution of—

(a) an investment exchange which is not a recognised investment exchange, or
(b) a clearing house which is not a recognised clearing house,

to the extent to which the agreement relates to the regulatory provisions of that body.

(3) The conditions are that—

(a) the body has applied for a recognition order in accordance with the provisions of this Act; and
(b) the application has not been determined.

(4) The Chapter I prohibition does not apply to a recognised body's regulatory provisions.

(5) The Chapter I prohibition does not apply to a decision made by a recognised body to the extent to which the decision relates to any of that body's regulatory provisions or practices.

(6) The Chapter I prohibition does not apply to practices of a recognised body.

(7) The Chapter I prohibition does not apply to an agreement the parties to which consist of or include—

(a) a recognised body, or
(b) a person who is subject to the rules of a recognised body,

to the extent to which the agreement consists of provisions the inclusion of which is required or encouraged by any of the body's regulatory provisions or practices.

(8) If a recognised body's recognition order is revoked, this section is to have effect as if that body had continued to be recognised until the end of the period of six months beginning with the day on which the revocation took effect.

(9) "The Chapter I prohibition" means the prohibition imposed by section 2(1) of the Competition Act 1998.

(10) Expressions used in this section which are also used in Part I of the Competition Act 1998 are to be interpreted in the same way as for the purposes of that Part of that Act.

[2309]

312 The Chapter II prohibition

(1) The Chapter II prohibition does not apply to—

(a) practices of a recognised body;
(b) the adoption or enforcement of such a body's regulatory provisions;
(c) any conduct which is engaged in by such a body or by a person who is subject to the rules of such a body to the extent to which it is encouraged or required by the regulatory provisions of the body.

(2) The Chapter II prohibition means the prohibition imposed by section 18(1) of the Competition Act 1998.

[2310]

NOTES

Note: "regulatory provisions" is defined in s 302(1) at **[2300]**.

[CHAPTER 3A
PASSPORT RIGHTS

EEA market operators in United Kingdom

312A Exercise of passport rights by EEA market operator

(1) An EEA market operator may, in pursuance of the right under the applicable provision, make arrangements in the United Kingdom to facilitate access to, or use of, a specified regulated market or specified multilateral trading facility operated by it if—

(a) the operator has given its home state regulator notice of its intention to make such arrangements; and

(b) the home state regulator has given the Authority notice of the operator's intention.

(2) In making arrangements under subsection (1), the operator is exempt from the general prohibition as respects any regulated activity which is carried on as a part of its business of operating the market or facility in question, or in connection with, or for the purposes of, that business.

(3) "Specified" means specified in the notice referred to in subsection (1)(a).

(4) This section does not apply to an overseas investment exchange.]

[2310A]

NOTES

Commencement: see the note below

Chapter 3A (ss 312A–312D) was inserted by the Financial Services and Markets Act 2000 (Markets in Financial Instruments) Regulations 2007, SI 2007/126, reg 3(2), Sch 2, paras 1, 15, as from 1 April 2007 (certain purposes (see reg 1(2) at **[7596]**)), and as from 1 November 2007 (otherwise).

Transitional provisions: the Financial Services and Markets Act 2000 (Markets in Financial Instruments) Regulations 2007, SI 2007/126, reg 5(1) (at **[7600]**) provides that sub-s (2) above applies to arrangements made on or before 31 October 2007, in the UK, by an EEA market operator to facilitate access to, or use of, a regulated market or multilateral trading facility operated by it as it applies to arrangements under sub-s (1) above.

[312B Removal of passport rights from EEA market operator

(1) The Authority may prohibit an EEA market operator from making or, as the case may be, continuing arrangements in the United Kingdom, in pursuance of the applicable provision, to facilitate access to, or use of, a regulated market or multilateral trading facility operated by the operator if—

(a) the Authority has clear and demonstrable grounds for believing that the operator has contravened a relevant requirement, and

(b) the Authority has first complied with subsections (3) to (9).

(2) A requirement is relevant if it is imposed—

(a) by the operator's home state regulator in the implementation of the markets in financial instruments directive or any Community legislation made under that directive;

(b) by provision implementing that directive, or any Community legislation made under it, in the operator's home state; or

(c) by any directly applicable Community regulation made under that directive.

(3) The Authority must notify the operator and its home state regulator of its finding under subsection (1)(a).

(4) The notice to the home state regulator under subsection (3) must—

(a) request that the home state regulator take all appropriate measures for the purpose of ensuring that the operator puts an end to the contravention; and

(b) state that the Authority proposes to exercise the power under subsection (1) if the operator continues the contravention.

(5) The Authority may not exercise the power under subsection (1) unless satisfied—

(a) either—

(i) that the home state regulator has failed or refused to take measures for the purpose mentioned in subsection (4)(a); or

(ii) that the measures taken by the home state regulator have proved inadequate for that purpose; and

PART II
FSMA 2000

(b) that the operator is acting in a manner which is clearly prejudicial to the interests of investors in the United Kingdom or the orderly functioning of the financial markets.

(6) If the Authority is satisfied as mentioned in subsection (5), it must give written notice to—

(a) the operator, and

(b) the home state regulator,

of its intention to exercise the power under subsection (1).

(7) A notice under subsection (6) must—

(a) state why the Authority intends to exercise its power under subsection (1), and

(b) in the case of the notice to the operator, inform the operator that it may make representations to the Authority before the end of the representation period.

(8) The representation period is—

(a) the period of two months beginning with the date on which the notice is given to the operator; or

(b) such longer period as the Authority may allow in a particular case.

(9) If, having considered any representations made by the operator, the Authority decides to exercise the power under subsection (1), it must—

(a) notify the operator in writing that it will be prohibited from making or, as the case may be, continuing the arrangements mentioned in that subsection from the date specified in the notice; and

(b) notify the home state regulator of the action to be taken in relation to the operator.

(10) If the Authority exercises the power under subsection (1) it must at the earliest opportunity notify the Commission of the action taken in relation to the operator.

(11) The exemption conferred on an operator by section 312A(2) ceases to apply if the Authority exercises the power under subsection (1) in relation to the operator.

(12) The right to make the arrangements mentioned in subsection (1) may be reinstated in relation to the operator (together with the exemption mentioned in subsection (11)) if the Authority is satisfied that the contravention which led to the Authority exercising the power under subsection (1) has been remedied.]

[2310B]

NOTES

Commencement: see the note below

Chapter 3A (ss 312A–312D) was inserted by the Financial Services and Markets Act 2000 (Markets in Financial Instruments) Regulations 2007, SI 2007/126, reg 3(2), Sch 2, paras 1, 15, as from 1 April 2007 (certain purposes (see reg 1(2) at **[7596]**)), and as from 1 November 2007 (otherwise).

[Recognised investment exchanges operating in EEA States (other than the United Kingdom)

312C Exercise of passport rights by recognised investment exchange

(1) Subject to subsection (4), a recognised investment exchange may, in pursuance of the right under the applicable provision, make arrangements in an EEA State (other than the United Kingdom) to facilitate access to, or use of, a regulated market or multilateral trading facility operated by the exchange ("the relevant arrangements").

(2) The exchange must give the Authority written notice of its intention to make the relevant arrangements which—

(a) describes the arrangements, and

(b) identifies the EEA State in which it intends to make them.

(3) The Authority must, within one month of receiving a notice under subsection (2), send a copy of it to the host state regulator.

(4) The exchange may not make the relevant arrangements until the Authority has complied with subsection (3).

(5) Subsection (6) applies if the Authority receives a request for information—

(a) under the second sub-paragraph of Article 31.6 of the markets in financial instruments directive (in the case of relevant arrangements relating to a multilateral trading facility), or

(b) under the third sub-paragraph of Article 42.6 of that directive (in the case of relevant arrangements relating to a regulated market),

from the host state regulator.

(6) The Authority must, as soon as reasonably practicable, comply with the request.

(7) "Host state regulator" means the competent authority (within the meaning of Article 4.1.22 of the markets in financial instruments directive) of the EEA State in which the exchange intends to make, or has made, the relevant arrangements.

(8) This section does not apply to an overseas investment exchange.]

[2310C]

NOTES

Commencement: see the note below

Chapter 3A (ss 312A–312D) was inserted by the Financial Services and Markets Act 2000 (Markets in Financial Instruments) Regulations 2007, SI 2007/126, reg 3(2), Sch 2, paras 1, 15, as from 1 April 2007 (certain purposes (see reg 1(2) at **[7596]**)), and as from 1 November 2007 (otherwise).

Transitional provisions: the Financial Services and Markets Act 2000 (Markets in Financial Instruments) Regulations 2007, SI 2007/126, reg 5(2) (at **[7600]**) provides that sub-ss (2), (4) above do not apply in relation to arrangements made by a recognised investment exchange on or before 31 October 2007 in the territory of another EEA State to facilitate access to, or use of, a regulated market or multilateral trading facility operated by it by persons established in that State.

[Interpretation

312D Interpretation of Chapter 3A

In this Chapter—

"the applicable provision" means—

(a) in the case of arrangements relating to a multilateral trading facility, Article 31.5 of the markets in financial instruments directive; and

(b) in the case of arrangements relating to a regulated market, the first sub-paragraph of Article 42.6 of that directive;

"EEA market operator" means a person who is a market operator (within the meaning of Article 4.1.13 of the markets in financial instruments directive) whose home state is an EEA State other than the United Kingdom;

"home state", in relation to an EEA market operator, means the EEA State in which it has its registered office, or if it has no registered office, its head office;

"home state regulator" means the competent authority (within the meaning of Article 4.1.22 of the markets in financial instruments directive) of the EEA State which is the home state in relation to the EEA market operator concerned.]

[2310D]

NOTES

Commencement: see the note below

Chapter 3A (ss 312A–312D) was inserted by the Financial Services and Markets Act 2000 (Markets in Financial Instruments) Regulations 2007, SI 2007/126, reg 3(2), Sch 2, paras 1, 15, as from 1 April 2007 (certain purposes (see reg 1(2) at **[7596]**)), and as from 1 November 2007 (otherwise).

CHAPTER IV

Interpretation

313 Interpretation of Part XVIII

(1) In this Part—

"application" means an application for a recognition order made under section 287 or 288;

"applicant" means a body corporate or unincorporated association which has applied for a recognition order;

PART II FSMA 2000

["multilateral trading facility" has the meaning given in Article 4.1.15 of the markets in financial instruments directive;]
["OFT" means the Office of Fair Trading;]
"overseas applicant" means a body corporate or association which has neither its head office nor its registered office in the United Kingdom and which has applied for a recognition order;
"overseas investment exchange" means a body corporate or association which has neither its head office nor its registered office in the United Kingdom and in relation to which a recognition order is in force;
"overseas clearing house" means a body corporate or association which has neither its head office nor its registered office in the United Kingdom and in relation to which a recognition order is in force;
"recognised body" means a recognised investment exchange or a recognised clearing house;
"recognised clearing house" has the meaning given in section 285;
"recognised investment exchange" has the meaning given in section 285;
"recognition order" means an order made under section 290 or 292;
"recognition requirements" has the meaning given by section 286;
["regulated market" has the meaning given in Article 4.1.14 of the markets in financial instruments directive;]
"remedial direction" has the meaning given in section 308(8);
"revocation order" has the meaning given in section 297.

(2) References in this Part to rules of an investment exchange (or a clearing house) are to rules made, or conditions imposed, by the investment exchange (or the clearing house) with respect to—
(a) recognition requirements;
(b) admission of persons to, or their exclusion from the use of, its facilities; or
(c) matters relating to its constitution.

(3) References in this Part to guidance issued by an investment exchange are references to guidance issued, or any recommendation made, in writing or other legible form and intended to have continuing effect, by the investment exchange to—
(a) all or any class of its members or users, or
(b) persons seeking to become members of the investment exchange or to use its facilities,
with respect to any of the matters mentioned in subsection (2)(a) to (c).

(4) References in this Part to guidance issued by a clearing house are to guidance issued, or any recommendation made, in writing or other legible form and intended to have continuing effect, by the clearing house to—
(a) all or any class of its members, or
(b) persons using or seeking to use its services,
with respect to the provision by it or its members of clearing services.

[2311]

NOTES

Sub-s (1): definition "OFT" substituted by the Enterprise Act 2002, s 278(1), Sch 25, para 40(1), (15), as from 1 April 2003; definitions "multilateral trading facility" and "regulated market" inserted by the Financial Services and Markets Act 2000 (Markets in Financial Instruments) Regulations 2007, SI 2007/126, reg 3(2), Sch 2, paras 1, 16, as from 1 April 2007 (certain purposes (see reg 1(2) at **[7596]**)), and as from 1 November 2007 (otherwise).

[PART 18A
SUSPENSION AND REMOVAL OF FINANCIAL INSTRUMENTS FROM TRADING

313A Authority's power to require suspension or removal of financial instruments from trading

(1) The Authority may, for the purpose of protecting—
(a) the interests of investors, or
(b) the orderly functioning of the financial markets,
require an institution to suspend or remove a financial instrument from trading.

(2) If the Authority exercises the power conferred by subsection (1), the institution concerned or, if any, the issuer of the financial instrument concerned may refer the matter to the Tribunal.

(3) In this section, "trading" includes trading otherwise than on a regulated market or a multilateral trading facility.]

[2311A]

NOTES

Commencement: see the note below

Part 18A (ss 313A–313D) was inserted by the Financial Services and Markets Act 2000 (Markets in Financial Instruments) Regulations 2007, SI 2007/126, reg 3(3), Sch 3, as from 1 April 2007 (certain purposes (see reg 1(2) at **[7596]**)), and as from 1 November 2007 (otherwise).

[313B Suspension or removal of financial instruments from trading: procedure

(1) A requirement imposed on an institution under section 313A (a "relevant requirement") takes effect—

- (a) immediately, if the notice given under subsection (2) states that this is the case;
- (b) in any other case, on such date as may be specified in the notice.

(2) If the Authority proposes to impose a relevant requirement on an institution, or imposes such a requirement with immediate effect, it must give written notice to—

- (a) the institution, and
- (b) if any, the issuer of the financial instrument in question.

(3) The notice must—

- (a) give details of the relevant requirement;
- (b) state the Authority's reasons for imposing the requirement and choosing the date on which it took effect or takes effect;
- (c) inform the recipient that he may make representations to the Authority within such period as may be specified by the notice (whether or not he has referred the matter to the Tribunal);
- (d) inform him of the date on which the requirement took effect or takes effect; and
- (e) inform him of his right to refer the matter to the Tribunal and give an indication of the procedure on such a reference.

(4) The Authority may extend the period within which representations may be made to it.

(5) If, having considered any representations made to it by the institution or any issuer, the Authority decides—

- (a) to impose the relevant requirement proposed, or
- (b) if it has been imposed, not to revoke it,

it must give the institution and any issuer written notice.

(6) If, having considered any representations made to it by the institution or any issuer, the Authority decides—

- (a) not to impose the relevant requirement proposed, or
- (b) to revoke a requirement which has been imposed,

it must give the institution and any issuer written notice.

(7) A notice given under subsection (5) must inform the recipient of his right to refer the matter to the Tribunal.

(8) Subsections (9) and (10) apply if—

- (a) the Authority has imposed a relevant requirement on an institution, and
- (b) the institution or any issuer of the financial instrument in question has applied for the revocation of the requirement.

(9) If the Authority decides to grant the application, it must give the institution and any issuer written notice of its decision.

(10) If the Authority proposes to refuse the application, it must give the institution and any issuer a warning notice.

(11) If, having considered any representations made in response to the warning notice, the Authority decides to refuse the application, it must give the institution and any issuer a decision notice.

PART II
FSMA 2000

(12) If the Authority gives a decision notice under subsection (11), the recipient may refer the matter to the Tribunal.]

[2311B]

NOTES

Commencement: see the note below

Part 18A (ss 313A–313D) was inserted by the Financial Services and Markets Act 2000 (Markets in Financial Instruments) Regulations 2007, SI 2007/126, reg 3(3), Sch 3, as from 1 April 2007 (certain purposes (see reg 1(2) at **[7596]**)), and as from 1 November 2007 (otherwise).

[313C Notification in relation to suspension or removal of a financial instrument from trading

(1) If the Authority exercises the power under section 313A(1) in relation to a financial instrument traded on a regulated market, it must as soon as reasonably practicable—

(a) publish its decision in such manner as it considers appropriate, and
(b) inform the competent authorities of all other EEA States of its decision.

(2) If the Authority receives notice from a recognised investment exchange that the exchange has suspended or removed a financial instrument from trading on a regulated market operated by it, the Authority must inform the competent authorities of all other EEA States of the action taken by the exchange.

(3) Subsections (4) and (5) apply if the Authority receives notice from the competent authority of another EEA State that that authority, pursuant to Article 41.2 of the markets in financial instruments directive—

(a) has required the suspension of a financial instrument from trading, or
(b) has required the removal of a financial instrument from trading.

(4) In the case of a notice under subsection (3)(a), the Authority—

(a) must require each recognised investment exchange to suspend the instrument from trading on any regulated market operated by the exchange, and
(b) must require each institution operating a multilateral trading facility to suspend the instrument from trading on that facility,

unless such a step would be likely to cause significant damage to the interests of investors or the orderly functioning of the financial markets.

(5) In the case of a notice under subsection (3)(b), the Authority—

(a) must require each recognised investment exchange to remove the instrument from trading on any regulated market operated by the exchange, and
(b) must require each institution operating a multilateral trading facility to remove the instrument from trading on that facility,

unless such a step would be likely to cause significant damage to the interests of investors or the orderly functioning of the financial markets.

(6) "Competent authority" has the meaning given in Article 4.1.22 of the markets in financial instruments directive.]

[2311C]

NOTES

Commencement: see the note below

Part 18A (ss 313A–313D) was inserted by the Financial Services and Markets Act 2000 (Markets in Financial Instruments) Regulations 2007, SI 2007/126, reg 3(3), Sch 3, as from 1 April 2007 (certain purposes (see reg 1(2) at **[7596]**)), and as from 1 November 2007 (otherwise).

[313D Interpretation of Part 18A

In this Part—

"financial instrument" has the meaning given in Article 4.1.17 of the markets in financial instruments directive;

"institution" means—

(a) a recognised investment exchange, other than an overseas investment exchange (within the meaning of Part 18);
(b) an investment firm;
(c) a credit institution authorised under the banking consolidation directive, when carrying on investment services and activities; or

(d) an institution which would satisfy the requirements for authorisation as a credit institution under that directive if it had its registered office (or if it does not have a registered office, its head office) in an EEA State,

but does not include an EEA firm qualifying for authorisation under Schedule 3;

"issuer", in relation to a financial instrument, means the person who issued the instrument;

"multilateral trading facility" has the meaning given in Article 4.1.15 of the markets in financial instruments directive;

"regulated market" has the meaning given in Article 4.1.14 of the markets in financial instruments directive.]

[2311D]

NOTES

Commencement: see the note below

Part 18A (ss 313A–313D) was inserted by the Financial Services and Markets Act 2000 (Markets in Financial Instruments) Regulations 2007, SI 2007/126, reg 3(3), Sch 3, as from 1 April 2007 (certain purposes (see reg 1(2) at **[7596]**)), and as from 1 November 2007 (otherwise).

PART XIX
LLOYD'S

General

314 Authority's general duty

(1) The Authority must keep itself informed about—

(a) the way in which the Council supervises and regulates the market at Lloyd's; and

(b) the way in which regulated activities are being carried on in that market.

(2) The Authority must keep under review the desirability of exercising—

(a) any of its powers under this Part;

(b) any powers which it has in relation to the Society as a result of section 315.

[2312]

The Society

315 The Society: authorisation and permission

(1) The Society is an authorised person.

(2) The Society has permission to carry on a regulated activity of any of the following kinds—

(a) arranging deals in contracts of insurance written at Lloyd's ("the basic market activity");

(b) arranging deals in participation in Lloyd's syndicates ("the secondary market activity"); and

(c) an activity carried on in connection with, or for the purposes of, the basic or secondary market activity.

(3) For the purposes of Part IV, the Society's permission is to be treated as if it had been given on an application for permission under that Part.

(4) The power conferred on the Authority by section 45 may be exercised in anticipation of the coming into force of the Society's permission (or at any other time).

(5) The Society is not subject to any requirement of this Act concerning the registered office of a body corporate.

[2313]

Power to apply Act to Lloyd's underwriting

316 Direction by Authority

(1) The general prohibition or (if the general prohibition is not applied under this section) a core provision applies to the carrying on of an insurance market activity by—

(a) a member of the Society, or
(b) the members of the Society taken together,

only if the Authority so directs.

(2) A direction given under subsection (1) which applies a core provision is referred to in this Part as "an insurance market direction".

(3) In subsection (1)—

"core provision" means a provision of this Act mentioned in section 317; and
"insurance market activity" means a regulated activity relating to contracts of insurance written at Lloyd's.

(4) In deciding whether to give a direction under subsection (1), the Authority must have particular regard to—

(a) the interests of policyholders and potential policyholders;
(b) any failure by the Society to satisfy an obligation to which it is subject as a result of a provision of the law of another EEA State which—
  (i) gives effect to any of the insurance directives; and
  (ii) is applicable to an activity carried on in that State by a person to whom this section applies;
(c) the need to ensure the effective exercise of the functions which the Authority has in relation to the Society as a result of section 315.

(5) A direction under subsection (1) must be in writing.

(6) A direction under subsection (1) applying the general prohibition may apply it in relation to different classes of person.

(7) An insurance market direction—

(a) must specify each core provision, class of person and kind of activity to which it applies;
(b) may apply different provisions in relation to different classes of person and different kinds of activity.

(8) A direction under subsection (1) has effect from the date specified in it, which may not be earlier than the date on which it is made.

(9) A direction under subsection (1) must be published in the way appearing to the Authority to be best calculated to bring it to the attention of the public.

(10) The Authority may charge a reasonable fee for providing a person with a copy of the direction.

(11) The Authority must, without delay, give the Treasury a copy of any direction which it gives under this section.

[2314]

317 The core provisions

(1) The core provisions are Parts V, X, XI, XII, XIV, XV, XVI, XXII and XXIV, sections 384 to 386 and Part XXVI.

(2) References in an applied core provision to an authorised person are (where necessary) to be read as references to a person in the class to which the insurance market direction applies.

(3) An insurance market direction may provide that a core provision is to have effect, in relation to persons to whom the provision is applied by the direction, with modifications.

[2315]

318 Exercise of powers through Council

(1) The Authority may give a direction under this subsection to the Council or to the Society (acting through the Council) or to both.

(2) A direction under subsection (1) is one given to the body concerned—

(a) in relation to the exercise of its powers generally with a view to achieving, or in support of, a specified objective; or
(b) in relation to the exercise of a specified power which it has, whether in a specified manner or with a view to achieving, or in support of, a specified objective.

(3) "Specified" means specified in the direction.

(4) A direction under subsection (1) may be given—
(a) instead of giving a direction under section 316(1); or
(b) if the Authority considers it necessary or expedient to do so, at the same time as, or following, the giving of such a direction.

(5) A direction may also be given under subsection (1) in respect of underwriting agents as if they were among the persons mentioned in section 316(1).

(6) A direction under this section—
(a) does not, at any time, prevent the exercise by the Authority of any of its powers;
(b) must be in writing.

(7) A direction under subsection (1) must be published in the way appearing to the Authority to be best calculated to bring it to the attention of the public.

(8) The Authority may charge a reasonable fee for providing a person with a copy of the direction.

(9) The Authority must, without delay, give the Treasury a copy of any direction which it gives under this section.

[2316]

319 Consultation

(1) Before giving a direction under section 316 or 318, the Authority must publish a draft of the proposed direction.

(2) The draft must be accompanied by—
(a) a cost benefit analysis; and
(b) notice that representations about the proposed direction may be made to the Authority within a specified time.

(3) Before giving the proposed direction, the Authority must have regard to any representations made to it in accordance with subsection (2)(b).

(4) If the Authority gives the proposed direction it must publish an account, in general terms, of—
(a) the representations made to it in accordance with subsection (2)(b); and
(b) its response to them.

(5) If the direction differs from the draft published under subsection (1) in a way which is, in the opinion of the Authority, significant—
(a) the Authority must (in addition to complying with subsection (4)) publish details of the difference; and
(b) those details must be accompanied by a cost benefit analysis.

(6) Subsections (1) to (5) do not apply if the Authority considers that the delay involved in complying with them would be prejudicial to the interests of consumers.

(7) Neither subsection (2)(a) nor subsection (5)(b) applies if the Authority considers—
(a) that, making the appropriate comparison, there will be no increase in costs; or
(b) that, making that comparison, there will be an increase in costs but the increase will be of minimal significance.

(8) The Authority may charge a reasonable fee for providing a person with a copy of a draft published under subsection (1).

(9) When the Authority is required to publish a document under this section it must do so in the way appearing to it to be best calculated to bring it to the attention of the public.

(10) "Cost benefit analysis" means an estimate of the costs together with an analysis of the benefits that will arise—
(a) if the proposed direction is given; or
(b) if subsection (5)(b) applies, from the direction that has been given.

(11) "The appropriate comparison" means—
(a) in relation to subsection (2)(a), a comparison between the overall position if the direction is given and the overall position if it is not given;
(b) in relation to subsection (5)(b), a comparison between the overall position after the giving of the direction and the overall position before it was given.

[2317]

Former underwriting members

320 Former underwriting members

(1) A former underwriting member may carry out each contract of insurance that he has underwritten at Lloyd's whether or not he is an authorised person.

(2) If he is an authorised person, any Part IV permission that he has does not extend to his activities in carrying out any of those contracts.

(3) The Authority may impose on a former underwriting member such requirements as appear to it to be appropriate for the purpose of protecting policyholders against the risk that he may not be able to meet his liabilities.

(4) A person on whom a requirement is imposed may refer the matter to the Tribunal.

[2318]

321 Requirements imposed under section 320

(1) A requirement imposed under section 320 takes effect—

(a) immediately, if the notice given under subsection (2) states that that is the case;

(b) in any other case, on such date as may be specified in that notice.

(2) If the Authority proposes to impose a requirement on a former underwriting member ("A") under section 320, or imposes such a requirement on him which takes effect immediately, it must give him written notice.

(3) The notice must—

(a) give details of the requirement;

(b) state the Authority's reasons for imposing it;

(c) inform A that he may make representations to the Authority within such period as may be specified in the notice (whether or not he has referred the matter to the Tribunal);

(d) inform him of the date on which the requirement took effect or will take effect; and

(e) inform him of his right to refer the matter to the Tribunal.

(4) The Authority may extend the period allowed under the notice for making representations.

(5) If, having considered any representations made by A, the Authority decides—

(a) to impose the proposed requirement, or

(b) if it has been imposed, not to revoke it,

it must give him written notice.

(6) If the Authority decides—

(a) not to impose a proposed requirement, or

(b) to revoke a requirement that has been imposed,

it must give A written notice.

(7) If the Authority decides to grant an application by A for the variation or revocation of a requirement, it must give him written notice of its decision.

(8) If the Authority proposes to refuse an application by A for the variation or revocation of a requirement it must give him a warning notice.

(9) If the Authority, having considered any representations made in response to the warning notice, decides to refuse the application, it must give A a decision notice.

(10) A notice given under—

(a) subsection (5), or

(b) subsection (9) in the case of a decision to refuse the application,

must inform A of his right to refer the matter to the Tribunal.

(11) If the Authority decides to refuse an application for a variation or revocation of the requirement, the applicant may refer the matter to the Tribunal.

(12) If a notice informs a person of his right to refer a matter to the Tribunal, it must give an indication of the procedure on such a reference.

[2319]

322 Rules applicable to former underwriting members

(1) The Authority may make rules imposing such requirements on persons to whom the rules apply as appear to it to be appropriate for protecting policyholders against the risk that those persons may not be able to meet their liabilities.

(2) The rules may apply to—

(a) former underwriting members generally; or

(b) to a class of former underwriting member specified in them.

(3) Section 319 applies to the making of proposed rules under this section as it applies to the giving of a proposed direction under section 316.

(4) Part X (except sections 152 to 154) does not apply to rules made under this section. **[2320]**

Transfers of business done at Lloyd's

323 Transfer schemes

The Treasury may by order provide for the application of any provision of Part VII (with or without modification) in relation to schemes for the transfer of the whole or any part of the business carried on by one or more members of the Society or former underwriting members. **[2321]**

NOTES

Orders: the Financial Services and Markets Act 2000 (Control of Transfers of Business Done at Lloyd's) Order 2001, SI 2001/3626.

Supplemental

324 Interpretation of this Part

(1) In this Part—

"arranging deals", in relation to the investments to which this Part applies, has the same meaning as in paragraph 3 of Schedule 2;

"former underwriting member" means a person ceasing to be an underwriting member of the Society on, or at any time after, 24 December 1996; and

"participation in Lloyd's syndicates", in relation to the secondary market activity, means the investment described in sub-paragraph (1) of paragraph 21 of Schedule 2.

(2) A term used in this Part which is defined in Lloyd's Act 1982 has the same meaning as in that Act. **[2322]**

PART XX
PROVISION OF FINANCIAL SERVICES BY MEMBERS OF THE PROFESSIONS

325 Authority's general duty

(1) The Authority must keep itself informed about—

(a) the way in which designated professional bodies supervise and regulate the carrying on of exempt regulated activities by members of the professions in relation to which they are established;

(b) the way in which such members are carrying on exempt regulated activities.

(2) In this Part—

"exempt regulated activities" means regulated activities which may, as a result of this Part, be carried on by members of a profession which is supervised and regulated by a designated professional body without breaching the general prohibition; and

"members", in relation to a profession, means persons who are entitled to practise the profession in question and, in practising it, are subject to the rules of the body designated in relation to that profession, whether or not they are members of that body.

PART II
FSMA 2000

(3) The Authority must keep under review the desirability of exercising any of its powers under this Part.

(4) Each designated professional body must co-operate with the Authority, by the sharing of information and in other ways, in order to enable the Authority to perform its functions under this Part.

[2323]

326 Designation of professional bodies

(1) The Treasury may by order designate bodies for the purposes of this Part.

(2) A body designated under subsection (1) is referred to in this Part as a designated professional body.

(3) The Treasury may designate a body under subsection (1) only if they are satisfied that—

(a) the basic condition, and
(b) one or more of the additional conditions,

are met in relation to it.

(4) The basic condition is that the body has rules applicable to the carrying on by members of the profession in relation to which it is established of regulated activities which, if the body were to be designated, would be exempt regulated activities.

(5) The additional conditions are that—

(a) the body has power under any enactment to regulate the practice of the profession;
(b) being a member of the profession is a requirement under any enactment for the exercise of particular functions or the holding of a particular office;
(c) the body has been recognised for the purpose of any enactment other than this Act and the recognition has not been withdrawn;
(d) the body is established in an EEA State other than the United Kingdom and in that State—
 (i) the body has power corresponding to that mentioned in paragraph (a);
 (ii) there is a requirement in relation to the body corresponding to that mentioned in paragraph (b); or
 (iii) the body is recognised in a manner corresponding to that mentioned in paragraph (c).

(6) "Enactment" includes an Act of the Scottish Parliament, Northern Ireland legislation and subordinate legislation (whether made under an Act, an Act of the Scottish Parliament or Northern Ireland legislation).

(7) "Recognised" means recognised by—

(a) a Minister of the Crown;
(b) the Scottish Ministers;
(c) a Northern Ireland Minister;
(d) a Northern Ireland department or its head.

[2324]

NOTES

Orders: the Financial Services and Markets Act 2000 (Designated Professional Bodies) Order 2001, SI 2001/1226 at **[4162]** which, at the date of publication, designates the following bodies for the purposes of this Part: the Law Society, the Law Society of Scotland, the Law Society of Northern Ireland, the Institute of Chartered Accountants in England and Wales, the Institute of Chartered Accountants of Scotland, the Institute of Chartered Accountants in Ireland, the Association of Chartered Certified Accountants, the Institute of Actuaries, the Council for Licensed Conveyancers, and the Royal Institution of Chartered Surveyors. Note that the Council for Licensed Conveyancers was added by the Financial Services and Markets Act 2000 (Designated Professional Bodies) (Amendment) Order 2004, SI 2004/3352, as from 14 January 2005, and the Royal Institution of Chartered Surveyors was added by the Financial Services and Markets Act 2000 (Designated Professional Bodies) (Amendment) Order 2006, SI 2006/58, as from 10 February 2006 (both amending Orders also made under this section).

---

327 Exemption from the general prohibition

(1) The general prohibition does not apply to the carrying on of a regulated activity by a person ("P") if—

(a) the conditions set out in subsections (2) to (7) are satisfied; and
(b) there is not in force—

(i) a direction under section 328, or
(ii) an order under section 329,
which prevents this subsection from applying to the carrying on of that activity by him.

(2) P must be—
(a) a member of a profession; or
(b) controlled or managed by one or more such members.

(3) P must not receive from a person other than his client any pecuniary reward or other advantage, for which he does not account to his client, arising out of his carrying on of any of the activities.

(4) The manner of the provision by P of any service in the course of carrying on the activities must be incidental to the provision by him of professional services.

(5) P must not carry on, or hold himself out as carrying on, a regulated activity other than—
(a) one which rules made as a result of section 332(3) allow him to carry on; or
(b) one in relation to which he is an exempt person.

(6) The activities must not be of a description, or relate to an investment of a description, specified in an order made by the Treasury for the purposes of this subsection.

(7) The activities must be the only regulated activities carried on by P (other than regulated activities in relation to which he is an exempt person).

(8) "Professional services" means services—
(a) which do not constitute carrying on a regulated activity, and
(b) the provision of which is supervised and regulated by a designated professional body.

[2325]

NOTES

Orders: the Financial Services and Markets Act 2000 (Professions) (Non-Exempt Activities) Order 2001, SI 2001/1227 at **[4164]**; the Financial Services and Markets Act 2000 (Miscellaneous Provisions) Order 2001, SI 2001/3650.

Note that the following amending Orders have also been made under this section: the Financial Services and Markets Act 2000 (Commencement of Mortgage Regulation) (Amendment) Order 2002, SI 2002/1777.

328 Directions in relation to the general prohibition

(1) The Authority may direct that section 327(1) is not to apply to the extent specified in the direction.

(2) A direction under subsection (1)—
(a) must be in writing;
(b) may be given in relation to different classes of person or different descriptions of regulated activity.

(3) A direction under subsection (1) must be published in the way appearing to the Authority to be best calculated to bring it to the attention of the public.

(4) The Authority may charge a reasonable fee for providing a person with a copy of the direction.

(5) The Authority must, without delay, give the Treasury a copy of any direction which it gives under this section.

[(6) The Authority may exercise the power conferred by subsection (1) only if it is satisfied either—
(a) that it is desirable to do so in order to protect the interests of clients; or
(b) that it is necessary to do so in order to comply with a Community obligation imposed by the insurance mediation directive.]

(7) In considering whether it is [satisfied of the matter specified in subsection (6)(a)], the Authority must have regard amongst other things to the effectiveness of any arrangements made by any designated professional body—
(a) for securing compliance with rules made under section 332(1);
(b) for dealing with complaints against its members in relation to the carrying on by them of exempt regulated activities;

PART II FSMA 2000

(c) in order to offer redress to clients who suffer, or claim to have suffered, loss as a result of misconduct by its members in their carrying on of exempt regulated activities;
(d) for co-operating with the Authority under section 325(4).

(8) In this Part "clients" means—
(a) persons who use, have used or are or may be contemplating using, any of the services provided by a member of a profession in the course of carrying on exempt regulated activities;
(b) persons who have rights or interests which are derived from, or otherwise attributable to, the use of any such services by other persons; or
(c) persons who have rights or interests which may be adversely affected by the use of any such services by persons acting on their behalf or in a fiduciary capacity in relation to them.

(9) If a member of a profession is carrying on an exempt regulated activity in his capacity as a trustee, the persons who are, have been or may be beneficiaries of the trust are to be treated as persons who use, have used or are or may be contemplating using services provided by that person in his carrying on of that activity.

[2326]

NOTES

Sub-s (6): substituted by the Insurance Mediation Directive (Miscellaneous Amendments) Regulations 2003, SI 2003/1473, reg 9(a), as from 14 January 2005.

Sub-s (7): words in square brackets substituted by SI 2003/1473, reg 9(b), as from 14 January 2005.

329 Orders in relation to the general prohibition

(1) Subsection (2) applies if it appears to the Authority that a person to whom, as a result of section 327(1), the general prohibition does not apply is not a fit and proper person to carry on regulated activities in accordance with that section.

(2) The Authority may make an order disapplying section 327(1) in relation to that person to the extent specified in the order.

(3) The Authority may, on the application of the person named in an order under subsection (1), vary or revoke it.

(4) "Specified" means specified in the order.

(5) If a partnership is named in an order under this section, the order is not affected by any change in its membership.

(6) If a partnership named in an order under this section is dissolved, the order continues to have effect in relation to any partnership which succeeds to the business of the dissolved partnership.

(7) For the purposes of subsection (6), a partnership is to be regarded as succeeding to the business of another partnership only if—
(a) the members of the resulting partnership are substantially the same as those of the former partnership; and
(b) succession is to the whole or substantially the whole of the business of the former partnership.

[2327]

330 Consultation

(1) Before giving a direction under section 328(1), the Authority must publish a draft of the proposed direction.

(2) The draft must be accompanied by—
(a) a cost benefit analysis; and
(b) notice that representations about the proposed direction may be made to the Authority within a specified time.

(3) Before giving the proposed direction, the Authority must have regard to any representations made to it in accordance with subsection (2)(b).

(4) If the Authority gives the proposed direction it must publish an account, in general terms, of—

(a) the representations made to it in accordance with subsection (2)(b); and

(b) its response to them.

(5) If the direction differs from the draft published under subsection (1) in a way which is, in the opinion of the Authority, significant—

(a) the Authority must (in addition to complying with subsection (4)) publish details of the difference; and

(b) those details must be accompanied by a cost benefit analysis.

(6) Subsections (1) to (5) do not apply if the Authority considers that the delay involved in complying with them would prejudice the interests of consumers.

(7) Neither subsection (2)(a) nor subsection (5)(b) applies if the Authority considers—

(a) that, making the appropriate comparison, there will be no increase in costs; or

(b) that, making that comparison, there will be an increase in costs but the increase will be of minimal significance.

(8) The Authority may charge a reasonable fee for providing a person with a copy of a draft published under subsection (1).

(9) When the Authority is required to publish a document under this section it must do so in the way appearing to it to be best calculated to bring it to the attention of the public.

(10) "Cost benefit analysis" means an estimate of the costs together with an analysis of the benefits that will arise—

(a) if the proposed direction is given; or

(b) if subsection (5)(b) applies, from the direction that has been given.

(11) "The appropriate comparison" means—

(a) in relation to subsection (2)(a), a comparison between the overall position if the direction is given and the overall position if it is not given;

(b) in relation to subsection (5)(b), a comparison between the overall position after the giving of the direction and the overall position before it was given.

[2328]

331 Procedure on making or varying orders under section 329

(1) If the Authority proposes to make an order under section 329, it must give the person concerned a warning notice.

(2) The warning notice must set out the terms of the proposed order.

(3) If the Authority decides to make an order under section 329, it must give the person concerned a decision notice.

(4) The decision notice must—

(a) name the person to whom the order applies;

(b) set out the terms of the order; and

(c) be given to the person named in the order.

(5) Subsections (6) to (8) apply to an application for the variation or revocation of an order under section 329.

(6) If the Authority decides to grant the application, it must give the applicant written notice of its decision.

(7) If the Authority proposes to refuse the application, it must give the applicant a warning notice.

(8) If the Authority decides to refuse the application, it must give the applicant a decision notice.

(9) A person—

(a) against whom the Authority have decided to make an order under section 329, or

(b) whose application for the variation or revocation of such an order the Authority had decided to refuse,

may refer the matter to the Tribunal.

(10) The Authority may not make an order under section 329 unless—

(a) the period within which the decision to make to the order may be referred to the Tribunal has expired and no such reference has been made; or

(b) if such a reference has been made, the reference has been determined.

[2329]

332 Rules in relation to persons to whom the general prohibition does not apply

(1) The Authority may make rules applicable to persons to whom, as a result of section 327(1), the general prohibition does not apply.

(2) The power conferred by subsection (1) is to be exercised for the purpose of ensuring that clients are aware that such persons are not authorised persons.

(3) A designated professional body must make rules—

(a) applicable to members of the profession in relation to which it is established who are not authorised persons; and

(b) governing the carrying on by those members of regulated activities (other than regulated activities in relation to which they are exempt persons).

(4) Rules made in compliance with subsection (3) must be designed to secure that, in providing a particular professional service to a particular client, the member carries on only regulated activities which arise out of, or are complementary to, the provision by him of that service to that client.

(5) Rules made by a designated professional body under subsection (3) require the approval of the Authority.

[2330]

333 False claims to be a person to whom the general prohibition does not apply

(1) A person who—

(a) describes himself (in whatever terms) as a person to whom the general prohibition does not apply, in relation to a particular regulated activity, as a result of this Part, or

(b) behaves, or otherwise holds himself out, in a manner which indicates (or which is reasonably likely to be understood as indicating) that he is such a person,

is guilty of an offence if he is not such a person.

(2) In proceedings for an offence under this section it is a defence for the accused to show that he took all reasonable precautions and exercised all due diligence to avoid committing the offence.

(3) A person guilty of an offence under this section is liable on summary conviction to imprisonment for a term not exceeding six months or a fine not exceeding level 5 on the standard scale, or both.

(4) But where the conduct constituting the offence involved or included the public display of any material, the maximum fine for the offence is level 5 on the standard scale multiplied by the number of days for which the display continued.

[2331]

PART XXI
MUTUAL SOCIETIES

Friendly societies

334 The Friendly Societies Commission

(1) The Treasury may by order provide—

(a) for any functions of the Friendly Societies Commission to be transferred to the Authority;

(b) for any functions of the Friendly Societies Commission which have not been, or are not being, transferred to the Authority to be transferred to the Treasury.

(2) If the Treasury consider it appropriate to do so, they may by order provide for the Friendly Societies Commission to cease to exist on a day specified in or determined in accordance with the order.

(3) The enactments relating to friendly societies which are mentioned in Part I of Schedule 18 are amended as set out in that Part.

(4) Part II of Schedule 18—

(a) removes certain restrictions on the ability of incorporated friendly societies to form subsidiaries and control corporate bodies; and

(b) makes connected amendments.

[2332]

NOTES

Friendly Societies Commission: the Commission was established by the Friendly Societies Act 1992, s 1, Sch 1, as originally enacted. Section 1 of the 1992 Act (together with ss 2–4) was substituted by a new s 1 (functions of the Financial Services Authority in relation to friendly societies), and Sch 1 was repealed by the Financial Services and Markets Act 2000 (Mutual Societies) Order 2001, SI 2001/2617, art 13(1), (2), Sch 3, Pt I, paras 53, 54, 119, Sch 4, subject to transitional provisions and savings in art 13(3) of, and Sch 5, paras 8, 9, 16 to, that Order. Provision for the Commission to cease to exist is made by art 10 of the 2001 Order.

Orders: the Financial Services and Markets Act 2000 (Mutual Societies) Order 2001, SI 2001/2617.

335 The Registry of Friendly Societies

(1) The Treasury may by order provide—

(a) for any functions of the Chief Registrar of Friendly Societies, or of an assistant registrar of friendly societies for the central registration area, to be transferred to the Authority;

(b) for any of their functions which have not been, or are not being, transferred to the Authority to be transferred to the Treasury.

(2) The Treasury may by order provide—

(a) for any functions of the central office of the registry of friendly societies to be transferred to the Authority;

(b) for any functions of that office which have not been, or are not being, transferred to the Authority to be transferred to the Treasury.

(3) The Treasury may by order provide—

(a) for any functions of the assistant registrar of friendly societies for Scotland to be transferred to the Authority;

(b) for any functions of the assistant registrar which have not been, or are not being, transferred to the Authority to be transferred to the Treasury.

(4) If the Treasury consider it appropriate to do so, they may by order provide for—

(a) the office of Chief Registrar of Friendly Societies,

(b) the office of assistant registrar of friendly societies for the central registration area,

(c) the central office, or

(d) the office of assistant registrar of friendly societies for Scotland,

to cease to exist on a day specified in or determined in accordance with the order.

[2333]

NOTES

The Registry of Friendly Societies: the offices of Chief Registrar of Friendly Societies, Assistant Registrar of Friendly Societies, and Assistant registrar of Friendly Societies for Scotland were continued by the Friendly Societies Act 1974, s 1. That section was repealed by the Financial Services and Markets Act 2000 (Mutual Societies) Order 2001, SI 2001/2617, art 13(1), (2), Sch 3, Pt I, paras 1, 2, Sch 4, subject to transitional provisions and savings in art 13(3), Sch 5, paras 3, 4 thereof. Provision for these offices to cease to exist is made by art 12 of the 2001 Order.

Orders: the Financial Services and Markets Act 2000 (Mutual Societies) Order 2001, SI 2001/2617.

Building societies

336 The Building Societies Commission

(1) The Treasury may by order provide—

(a) for any functions of the Building Societies Commission to be transferred to the Authority;

(b) for any functions of the Building Societies Commission which have not been, or are not being, transferred to the Authority to be transferred to the Treasury.

PART II FSMA 2000

(2) If the Treasury consider it appropriate to do so, they may by order provide for the Building Societies Commission to cease to exist on a day specified in or determined in accordance with the order.

(3) The enactments relating to building societies which are mentioned in Part III of Schedule 18 are amended as set out in that Part.

[2334]

NOTES

Building Societies Commission: the Commission was established by the Building Societies Act 1986, s 1, Sch 1, as originally enacted. Section 1 of the 1986 Act (together with ss 2–4) was substituted by a new s 1 (functions of the Financial Services Authority in relation to building societies), and Sch 1 was repealed by the Financial Services and Markets Act 2000 (Mutual Societies) Order 2001, SI 2001/2617, art 13(1), (2), Sch 3, Pt II, paras 131, 132, 199, Sch 4, subject to transitional provisions and savings in art 13(3) of, and Sch 5, paras 17, 18, 27 to, that Order. Provision for the Commission to cease to exist is made by art 9 of the 2001 Order.

Orders: the Financial Services and Markets Act 2000 (Mutual Societies) Order 2001, SI 2001/2617.

337 The Building Societies Investor Protection Board

The Treasury may by order provide for the Building Societies Investor Protection Board to cease to exist on a day specified in or determined in accordance with the order.

[2335]

NOTES

Building Societies Investor Protection Board: the Board was established by the Building Societies Act 1986, s 24, Sch 5 (repealed by the Financial Services and Markets Act 2000 (Mutual Societies) Order 2001, SI 2001/2617, art 13(1), (2), Sch 3, Pt II, paras 131, 139, 202, Sch 4, subject to transitional provisions and savings in art 13(3) of, and Sch 5, paras 17, 19, 29 thereof). Provision for the Board to cease to exist is made by art 11 of the 2001 Order.

Orders: the Financial Services and Markets Act 2000 (Mutual Societies) Order 2001, SI 2001/2617.

Industrial and provident societies and credit unions

338 Industrial and provident societies and credit unions

(1) The Treasury may by order provide for the transfer to the Authority of any functions conferred by—

(a) the Industrial and Provident Societies Act 1965;

(b) the Industrial and Provident Societies Act 1967;

(c) the Friendly and Industrial and Provident Societies Act 1968;

(d) the Industrial and Provident Societies Act 1975;

(e) the Industrial and Provident Societies Act 1978;

(f) the Credit Unions Act 1979.

(2) The Treasury may by order provide for the transfer to the Treasury of any functions under those enactments which have not been, or are not being, transferred to the Authority.

(3) The enactments relating to industrial and provident societies which are mentioned in Part IV of Schedule 18 are amended as set out in that Part.

(4) The enactments relating to credit unions which are mentioned in Part V of Schedule 18 are amended as set out in that Part.

[2336]

NOTES

Note: credit unions in Northern Ireland have not been brought within this Act's regime and remain under the jurisdiction of the Registrar of Friendly Societies in Northern Ireland. A transitional exemption in the Financial Services and Markets Act 2000 (Exemption) Order 2001, SI 2001/1201, art 6 was made permanent in respect of credit unions within the meaning of Credit Unions (Northern Ireland) Order 1985 by the Financial Services and Markets Act 2000 (Exemption) (Amendment) Order 2001, SI 2001/3623, arts 3, 4, which adds a new para 24A to this effect to the Schedule of SI 2001/1201.

Orders: the Financial Services and Markets Act 2000 (Mutual Societies) Order 2001, SI 2001/2617.

Supplemental

339 Supplemental provisions

(1) The additional powers conferred by section 428 on a person making an order under this Act include power for the Treasury, when making an order under section 334, 335, 336 or 338 which transfers functions, to include provision—

(a) for the transfer of any functions of a member of the body, or servant or agent of the body or person, whose functions are transferred by the order;

(b) for the transfer of any property, rights or liabilities held, enjoyed or incurred by any person in connection with transferred functions;

(c) for the carrying on and completion by or under the authority of the person to whom functions are transferred of any proceedings, investigations or other matters commenced, before the order takes effect, by or under the authority of the person from whom the functions are transferred;

(d) amending any enactment relating to transferred functions in connection with their exercise by, or under the authority of, the person to whom they are transferred;

(e) for the substitution of the person to whom functions are transferred for the person from whom they are transferred, in any instrument, contract or legal proceedings made or begun before the order takes effect.

(2) The additional powers conferred by section 428 on a person making an order under this Act include power for the Treasury, when making an order under section 334(2), 335(4), 336(2) or 337, to include provision—

(a) for the transfer of any property, rights or liabilities held, enjoyed or incurred by any person in connection with the office or body which ceases to have effect as a result of the order;

(b) for the carrying on and completion by or under the authority of such person as may be specified in the order of any proceedings, investigations or other matters commenced, before the order takes effect, by or under the authority of the person whose office, or the body which, ceases to exist as a result of the order;

(c) amending any enactment which makes provision with respect to that office or body;

(d) for the substitution of the Authority, the Treasury or such other body as may be specified in the order in any instrument, contract or legal proceedings made or begun before the order takes effect.

(3) On or after the making of an order under any of sections 334 to 338 ("the original order"), the Treasury may by order make any incidental, supplemental, consequential or transitional provision which they had power to include in the original order.

(4) A certificate issued by the Treasury that property vested in a person immediately before an order under this Part takes effect has been transferred as a result of the order is conclusive evidence of the transfer.

(5) Subsections (1) and (2) are not to be read as affecting in any way the powers conferred by section 428.

[2337]

NOTES

Orders: the Financial Services and Markets Act 2000 (Mutual Societies) Order 2001, SI 2001/2617; the Financial Services and Markets Act 2000 (Transitional Provisions, Repeals and Savings) (Financial Services Compensation Scheme) Order 2001, SI 2001/2967; the Financial Services and Markets Act 2000 (Consequential Amendments and Savings) (Industrial Assurance) Order 2001, SI 2001/3647.

PART XXII
AUDITORS AND ACTUARIES

Appointment

340 Appointment

(1) Rules may require an authorised person, or an authorised person falling within a specified class—

(a) to appoint an auditor, or

(b) to appoint an actuary,

if he is not already under an obligation to do so imposed by another enactment.

(2) Rules may require an authorised person, or an authorised person falling within a specified class—

(a) to produce periodic financial reports; and

(b) to have them reported on by an auditor or an actuary.

(3) Rules may impose such other duties on auditors of, or actuaries acting for, authorised persons as may be specified.

(4) Rules under subsection (1) may make provision—

(a) specifying the manner in which and time within which an auditor or actuary is to be appointed;

(b) requiring the Authority to be notified of an appointment;

(c) enabling the Authority to make an appointment if no appointment has been made or notified;

(d) as to remuneration;

(e) as to the term of office, removal and resignation of an auditor or actuary.

(5) An auditor or actuary appointed as a result of rules under subsection (1), or on whom duties are imposed by rules under subsection (3)—

(a) must act in accordance with such provision as may be made by rules; and

(b) is to have such powers in connection with the discharge of his functions as may be provided by rules.

(6) In subsections (1) to (3) "auditor" or "actuary" means an auditor, or actuary, who satisfies such requirements as to qualifications, experience and other matters (if any) as may be specified.

(7) "Specified" means specified in rules.

[2338]

Information

341 Access to books etc

(1) An appointed auditor of, or an appointed actuary acting for, an authorised person—

(a) has a right of access at all times to the authorised person's books, accounts and vouchers; and

(b) is entitled to require from the authorised person's officers such information and explanations as he reasonably considers necessary for the performance of his duties as auditor or actuary.

(2) "Appointed" means appointed under or as a result of this Act.

[2339]

342 Information given by auditor or actuary to the Authority

(1) This section applies to a person who is, or has been, an auditor of an authorised person appointed under or as a result of a statutory provision.

(2) This section also applies to a person who is, or has been, an actuary acting for an authorised person and appointed under or as a result of a statutory provision.

(3) An auditor or actuary does not contravene any duty to which he is subject merely because he gives to the Authority—

(a) information on a matter of which he has, or had, become aware in his capacity as auditor of, or actuary acting for, the authorised person, or

(b) his opinion on such a matter,

if he is acting in good faith and he reasonably believes that the information or opinion is relevant to any functions of the Authority.

(4) Subsection (3) applies whether or not the auditor or actuary is responding to a request from the Authority.

(5) The Treasury may make regulations prescribing circumstances in which an auditor or actuary must communicate matters to the Authority as mentioned in subsection (3).

(6) It is the duty of an auditor or actuary to whom any such regulations apply to communicate a matter to the Authority in the circumstances prescribed by the regulations.

(7) The matters to be communicated to the Authority in accordance with the regulations may include matters relating to persons other than the authorised person concerned.

[2340]

NOTES

Regulations: the Financial Services and Markets Act 2000 (Communications by Auditors) Regulations 2001, SI 2001/2587 at **[4469]**; the Financial Services and Markets Act 2000 (Communications by Actuaries) Regulations 2003, SI 2003/1294 at **[4655]**.

343 Information given by auditor or actuary to the Authority: persons with close links

(1) This section applies to a person who—

(a) is, or has been, an auditor of an authorised person appointed under or as a result of a statutory provision; and

(b) is, or has been, an auditor of a person ("CL") who has close links with the authorised person.

(2) This section also applies to a person who—

(a) is, or has been, an actuary acting for an authorised person and appointed under or as a result of a statutory provision; and

(b) is, or has been, an actuary acting for a person ("CL") who has close links with the authorised person.

(3) An auditor or actuary does not contravene any duty to which he is subject merely because he gives to the Authority—

(a) information on a matter concerning the authorised person of which he has, or had, become aware in his capacity as auditor of, or actuary acting for, CL, or

(b) his opinion on such a matter,

if he is acting in good faith and he reasonably believes that the information or opinion is relevant to any functions of the Authority.

(4) Subsection (3) applies whether or not the auditor or actuary is responding to a request from the Authority.

(5) The Treasury may make regulations prescribing circumstances in which an auditor or actuary must communicate matters to the Authority as mentioned in subsection (3).

(6) It is the duty of an auditor or actuary to whom any such regulations apply to communicate a matter to the Authority in the circumstances prescribed by the regulations.

(7) The matters to be communicated to the Authority in accordance with the regulations may include matters relating to persons other than the authorised person concerned.

(8) CL has close links with the authorised person concerned ("A") if CL is—

(a) a parent undertaking of A;

(b) a subsidiary undertaking of A;

(c) a parent undertaking of a subsidiary undertaking of A; or

(d) a subsidiary undertaking of a parent undertaking of A.

(9) "Subsidiary undertaking" includes all the instances mentioned in Article 1(1) and (2) of the Seventh Company Law Directive in which an entity may be a subsidiary of an undertaking.

[2341]

NOTES

Regulations: the Financial Services and Markets Act 2000 (Communications by Auditors) Regulations 2001, SI 2001/2587 at **[4469]**; the Financial Services and Markets Act 2000 (Communications by Actuaries) Regulations 2003, SI 2003/1294 at **[4655]**.

344 Duty of auditor or actuary resigning etc to give notice

(1) This section applies to an auditor or actuary to whom section 342 applies.

(2) He must without delay notify the Authority if he—

(a) is removed from office by an authorised person;

(b) resigns before the expiry of his term of office with such a person; or
(c) is not re-appointed by such a person.

(3) If he ceases to be an auditor of, or actuary acting for, such a person, he must without delay notify the Authority—
(a) of any matter connected with his so ceasing which he thinks ought to be drawn to the Authority's attention; or
(b) that there is no such matter.

[2342]

Disqualification

345 Disqualification

(1) If it appears to the Authority that an auditor or actuary to whom section 342 applies has failed to comply with a duty imposed on him under this Act, it may disqualify him from being the auditor of, or (as the case may be) from acting as an actuary for, any authorised person or any particular class of authorised person.

(2) If the Authority proposes to disqualify a person under this section it must give him a warning notice.

(3) If it decides to disqualify him it must give him a decision notice.

(4) The Authority may remove any disqualification imposed under this section if satisfied that the disqualified person will in future comply with the duty in question.

(5) A person who has been disqualified under this section may refer the matter to the Tribunal.

[2343]

NOTES

Transitional provisions: the Financial Services and Markets Act 2000 (Transitional Provisions) (Authorised Persons etc) Order 2001, SI 2001/2636, art 78, provides for the disqualification under this section of an auditor who, at 1 December 2001, has been disqualified pursuant to the Financial Services Act 1986, s 111(3) (repealed by the Financial Services and Markets Act 2000 (Consequential Amendments and Repeals) Order 2001, SI 2001/3649, art 3(1)(c), or the Insurance Companies Act 1982, s 21A(5) (repealed by art 3(1)(b) of that Order).

Offence

346 Provision of false or misleading information to auditor or actuary

(1) An authorised person who knowingly or recklessly gives an appointed auditor or actuary information which is false or misleading in a material particular is guilty of an offence and liable—
(a) on summary conviction, to imprisonment for a term not exceeding six months or a fine not exceeding the statutory maximum, or both;
(b) on conviction on indictment, to imprisonment for a term not exceeding two years or a fine, or both.

(2) Subsection (1) applies equally to an officer, controller or manager of an authorised person.

(3) "Appointed" means appointed under or as a result of this Act.

[2344]

PART XXIII
PUBLIC RECORD, DISCLOSURE OF INFORMATION AND CO-OPERATION

The public record

347 The record of authorised persons etc

(1) The Authority must maintain a record of every—
(a) person who appears to the Authority to be an authorised person;

(b) authorised unit trust scheme;
(c) authorised open-ended investment company;
(d) recognised scheme;
(e) recognised investment exchange;
(f) recognised clearing house;
(g) individual to whom a prohibition order relates;
(h) approved person; *and*
[(ha) person to whom subsection (2A) applies; and]
(i) person falling within such other class (if any) as the Authority may determine.

(2) The record must include such information as the Authority considers appropriate and at least the following information—

(a) in the case of a person appearing to the Authority to be an authorised person—
  (i) information as to the services which he holds himself out as able to provide; and
  (ii) any address of which the Authority is aware at which a notice or other document may be served on him;
(b) in the case of an authorised unit trust scheme, the name and address of the manager and trustee of the scheme;
(c) in the case of an authorised open-ended investment company, the name and address of—
  (i) the company;
  (ii) if it has only one director, the director; and
  (iii) its depositary (if any);
(d) in the case of a recognised scheme, the name and address of—
  (i) the operator of the scheme; and
  (ii) any representative of the operator in the United Kingdom;
(e) in the case of a recognised investment exchange or recognised clearing house, the name and address of the exchange or clearing house;
(f) in the case of an individual to whom a prohibition order relates—
  (i) his name; and
  (ii) details of the effect of the order;
(g) in the case of a person who is an approved person—
  (i) his name;
  (ii) the name of the relevant authorised person;
  (iii) if the approved person is performing a controlled function under an arrangement with a contractor of the relevant authorised person, the name of the contractor.

[(2A) This subsection applies to—

(a) an appointed representative to whom subsection (1A) of section 39 applies for whom the applicable register (as defined by subsection (1B) of that section) is the record maintained by virtue of subsection (1)(ha) above;
(b) a person mentioned in subsection (1)(a) of section 39A if—
  (i) the contract with an authorised person to which he is party complies with the applicable requirements (as defined by subsection (7) of that section), and
  (ii) the authorised person has accepted responsibility in writing for the person's activities in carrying on investment services business (as defined by subsection (8) of that section); and
(c) any person not falling within paragraph (a) or (b) in respect of whom the Authority considers that a record must be maintained for the purpose of securing compliance with Article 23.3 of the markets in financial instruments directive (registration of tied agents).]

(3) If it appears to the Authority that a person in respect of whom there is an entry in the record as a result of one of the paragraphs of subsection (1) has ceased to be a person to whom that paragraph applies, the Authority may remove the entry from the record.

(4) But if the Authority decides not to remove the entry, it must—

(a) make a note to that effect in the record; and
(b) state why it considers that the person has ceased to be a person to whom that paragraph applies.

(5) The Authority must—

PART II FSMA 2000

(a) make the record available for inspection by members of the public in a legible form at such times and in such place or places as the Authority may determine; and

(b) provide a certified copy of the record, or any part of it, to any person who asks for it—

(i) on payment of the fee (if any) fixed by the Authority; and

(ii) in a form (either written or electronic) in which it is legible to the person asking for it.

(6) The Authority may—

(a) publish the record, or any part of it;

(b) exploit commercially the information contained in the record, or any part of that information.

(7) "Authorised unit trust scheme", "authorised open-ended investment company" and "recognised scheme" have the same meaning as in Part XVII, and associated expressions are to be read accordingly.

(8) "Approved person" means a person in relation to whom the Authority has given its approval under section 59 and "controlled function" and "arrangement" have the same meaning as in that section.

(9) "Relevant authorised person" has the meaning given in section 66.

[2345]

NOTES

Sub-s (1): word in italics in para (h) repealed, and para (ha) inserted, by the Financial Services and Markets Act 2000 (Markets in Financial Instruments) Regulations 2007, SI 2007/126, reg 3(5), Sch 5, paras 1, 12(a), (b), as from 1 April 2007 (certain purposes (see reg 1(2) at **[7596]**)), and as from 1 November 2007 (otherwise).

Sub-s (2A): inserted by SI 2007/126, reg 3(5), Sch 5, paras 1, 12(c), as from 1 April 2007 (certain purposes (see reg 1(2) at **[7596]**)), and as from 1 November 2007 (otherwise).

Transitional provisions: see the note to s 39 at **[2039]**.

Disclosure of information

348 Restrictions on disclosure of confidential information by Authority etc

(1) Confidential information must not be disclosed by a primary recipient, or by any person obtaining the information directly or indirectly from a primary recipient, without the consent of—

(a) the person from whom the primary recipient obtained the information; and

(b) if different, the person to whom it relates.

(2) In this Part "confidential information" means information which—

(a) relates to the business or other affairs of any person;

(b) was received by the primary recipient for the purposes of, or in the discharge of, any functions of the Authority, the competent authority for the purposes of Part VI or the Secretary of State under any provision made by or under this Act; and

(c) is not prevented from being confidential information by subsection (4).

(3) It is immaterial for the purposes of subsection (2) whether or not the information was received—

(a) by virtue of a requirement to provide it imposed by or under this Act;

(b) for other purposes as well as purposes mentioned in that subsection.

(4) Information is not confidential information if—

(a) it has been made available to the public by virtue of being disclosed in any circumstances in which, or for any purposes for which, disclosure is not precluded by this section; or

(b) it is in the form of a summary or collection of information so framed that it is not possible to ascertain from it information relating to any particular person.

(5) Each of the following is a primary recipient for the purposes of this Part—

(a) the Authority;

(b) any person exercising functions conferred by Part VI on the competent authority;

(c) the Secretary of State;

(d) a person appointed to make a report under section 166;

(e) any person who is or has been employed by a person mentioned in paragraphs (a) to (c);
(f) any auditor or expert instructed by a person mentioned in those paragraphs.

(6) In subsection (5)(f) "expert" includes—
(a) a competent person appointed by the competent authority under section 97;
(b) a competent person appointed by the Authority or the Secretary of State to conduct an investigation under Part XI;
(c) any body or person appointed under paragraph 6 of Schedule 1 to perform a function on behalf of the Authority.

[2346]

NOTES

Disapplication of this section: as to the circumstances in which this section is disapplied, see the Takeovers Directive (Interim Implementation) Regulations 2006, SI 2006/1183, reg 18 at **[7526]** (revoked subject to savings).

Note: "primary recipient" includes the Bank of England for the purposes of the Financial Services and Markets Act 2000 (Confidential Information) (Bank of England) (Consequential Provisions) Order 2001, SI 2001/3648, art 3(4), and any person upon whom functions are conferred by, or under, the Financial Services and Markets Act 2000 (Disclosure of Confidential Information) (Amendment) (No 2) Regulations 2003, SI 2003/2174, with effect from 23 August 2003.

Information relating to mutual societies: the following information is to be treated as confidential information for the purposes of this section and ss 349–353: (a) certain information relating to the business or other affairs of a building society or other body (see the Building Societies Act 1986, s 53A (disclosure of information)); (b) certain information relating to the business or other affairs of a friendly society, a registered branch of a friendly society or any other person (see the Friendly Societies Act 1992, s 63A (disclosure of information)).

PART II FSMA 2000

349 Exceptions from section 348

(1) Section 348 does not prevent a disclosure of confidential information which is—
(a) made for the purpose of facilitating the carrying out of a public function; and
(b) permitted by regulations made by the Treasury under this section.

(2) The regulations may, in particular, make provision permitting the disclosure of confidential information or of confidential information of a prescribed kind—
(a) by prescribed recipients, or recipients of a prescribed description, to any person for the purpose of enabling or assisting the recipient to discharge prescribed public functions;
(b) by prescribed recipients, or recipients of a prescribed description, to prescribed persons, or persons of prescribed descriptions, for the purpose of enabling or assisting those persons to discharge prescribed public functions;
(c) by the Authority to the Treasury or the Secretary of State for any purpose;
(d) by any recipient if the disclosure is with a view to or in connection with prescribed proceedings.

(3) The regulations may also include provision—
(a) making any permission to disclose confidential information subject to conditions (which may relate to the obtaining of consents or any other matter);
(b) restricting the uses to which confidential information disclosed under the regulations may be put.

[(3A) Section 348 does not apply to—
(a) the disclosure by a recipient to which subsection (3B) applies of confidential information disclosed to it by the Authority in reliance on subsection (1);
(b) the disclosure of such information by a person obtaining it directly or indirectly from a recipient to which subsection (3B) applies.

(3B) This subsection applies to—
(a) the Panel on Takeovers and Mergers;
(b) an authority designated as a supervisory authority for the purposes of Article 4.1 of the Takeovers Directive;
(c) any other person or body that exercises public functions, under legislation in an EEA State other than the United Kingdom, that are similar to the Authority's functions or those of the Panel on Takeovers and Mergers.]

(4) In relation to confidential information, each of the following is a "recipient"—
(a) a primary recipient;
(b) a person obtaining the information directly or indirectly from a primary recipient.

(5) "Public functions" includes—
(a) functions conferred by or in accordance with any provision contained in any enactment or subordinate legislation;
(b) functions conferred by or in accordance with any provision contained in the Community Treaties or any Community instrument;
(c) similar functions conferred on persons by or under provisions having effect as part of the law of a country or territory outside the United Kingdom;
(d) functions exercisable in relation to prescribed disciplinary proceedings.

(6) "Enactment" includes—
(a) an Act of the Scottish Parliament;
(b) Northern Ireland legislation.

(7) "Subordinate legislation" has the meaning given in the Interpretation Act 1978 and also includes an instrument made under an Act of the Scottish Parliament or under Northern Ireland legislation.

[(8) …]

[2347]

NOTES

Sub-ss (3A), (3B): inserted by the Companies Act 2006, s 964(1), (4), as from 6 April 2007.

Sub-s (8): added by the Takeovers Directive (Interim Implementation) Regulations 2006, SI 2006/1183, reg 18(3), (5), as from 20 May 2006; repealed by the Companies Act 2006 (Commencement No 2, Consequential Amendments, Transitional Provisions and Savings) Order 2007, SI 2007/1093, art 7, Sch 5, as from 6 April 2007.

Transitional provisions: in relation to the Financial Services and Markets Act 2000 (Disclosure of Confidential Information) Regulations 2001, SI 2001/2188, see the Financial Services and Markets Act 2000 (Consequential and Transitional Provisions) (Miscellaneous) (No 2) Order 2001, SI 2001/2659, art 7.

Information relating to mutual societies: see the note to s 348 at **[2346]**.

Regulations: the Financial Services and Markets Act 2000 (Disclosure of Confidential Information) Regulations 2001, SI 2001/2188 at **[4372]**; the Electronic Commerce Directive (Financial Services and Markets) Regulations 2002, SI 2002/1775 at **[4639]**.

Note that the following amending Regulations have also been made under this section: the Financial Services and Markets Act 2000 (Disclosure of Confidential Information) (Amendment) Regulations 2001, SI 2001/3437; the Financial Services and Markets Act 2000 (Disclosure of Confidential Information) (Amendment) (No 2) Regulations 2001, SI 2001/3624; the Financial Services and Markets Act 2000 (Disclosure of Confidential Information) (Amendment) Regulations 2003, SI 2003/693; the Insurance Mediation Directive (Miscellaneous Amendments) Regulations 2003, SI 2003/1473; the Collective Investment Schemes (Miscellaneous Amendments) Regulations 2003, SI 2003/2066; the Financial Services and Markets Act 2000 (Disclosure of Confidential Information) (Amendment) (No 2) Regulations 2003, SI 2003/2174; the Financial Services and Markets Act 2000 (Disclosure of Confidential Information) (Amendment) (No 3) Regulations 2003, SI 2003/2817; the Financial Services and Markets Act 2000 (Disclosure of Confidential Information) (Amendment) Regulations 2005, SI 2005/3071; the Financial Services and Markets Act 2000 (Disclosure of Confidential Information) (Amendment) Regulations 2006, SI 2006/3413; the Financial Services and Markets Act 2000 (Markets in Financial Instruments) (Amendment) Regulations 2007, SI 2007/763.

350 Disclosure of information by the Inland Revenue

(1) No obligation as to secrecy imposed by statute or otherwise prevents the disclosure of Revenue information to—
(a) the Authority, or
(b) the Secretary of State,

if the disclosure is made for the purpose of assisting in the investigation of a matter under section 168 or with a view to the appointment of an investigator under that section.

(2) A disclosure may only be made under subsection (1) by or under the authority of the Commissioners of Inland Revenue.

(3) Section 348 does not apply to Revenue information.

(4) Information obtained as a result of subsection (1) may not be used except—
(a) for the purpose of deciding whether to appoint an investigator under section 168;
(b) in the conduct of an investigation under section 168;
(c) in criminal proceedings brought against a person under this Act or the Criminal Justice Act 1993 as a result of an investigation under section 168;
(d) for the purpose of taking action under this Act against a person as a result of an investigation under section 168;

(e) in proceedings before the Tribunal as a result of action taken as mentioned in paragraph (d).

(5) Information obtained as a result of subsection (1) may not be disclosed except—

(a) by or under the authority of the Commissioners of Inland Revenue;

(b) in proceedings mentioned in subsection (4)(c) or (e) or with a view to their institution.

(6) Subsection (5) does not prevent the disclosure of information obtained as a result of subsection (1) to a person to whom it could have been disclosed under subsection (1).

(7) "Revenue information" means information held by a person which it would be an offence under section 182 of the Finance Act 1989 for him to disclose.

[2348]

NOTES

Commissioners of Inland Revenue: a reference to the Commissioners of Inland Revenue is now to be taken as a reference to the Commissioners for Her Majesty's Revenue and Customs; see the Commissioners for Revenue and Customs Act 2005, s 50(1), (7).

Application: the Commissioners for Her Majesty's Revenue and Customs may supply information in accordance with this section only if the information was obtained or is held in the exercise of a function relating to matters to which the Commissioners for Revenue and Customs Act 2005, s 7 applies; see s 17(6) of, Sch 2, Pt 2, para 18 to, that Act

351 Competition information

(1)–(3) …

(4) Section 348 does not apply to competition information.

(5) "Competition information" means information which—

(a) relates to the affairs of a particular individual or body;

(b) is not otherwise in the public domain; and

(c) was obtained under or by virtue of a competition provision.

(6) "Competition provision" means any provision of—

(a) an order made under section 95;

(b) Chapter III of Part X; or

(c) Chapter II of Part XVIII.

(7) …

[2349]

NOTES

Sub-ss (1)–(3), (7): repealed by the Enterprise Act 2002, ss 247(k), 278(2), Sch 26, as from 20 June 2003.

Information relating to mutual societies: see the note to s 348 at **[2346]**.

352 Offences

(1) A person who discloses information in contravention of section 348 or 350(5) is guilty of an offence.

(2) A person guilty of an offence under subsection (1) is liable—

(a) on summary conviction, to imprisonment for a term not exceeding three months or a fine not exceeding the statutory maximum, or both;

(b) on conviction on indictment, to imprisonment for a term not exceeding two years or a fine, or both.

(3) A person is guilty of an offence if, in contravention of any provision of regulations made under section 349, he uses information which has been disclosed to him in accordance with the regulations.

(4) A person is guilty of an offence if, in contravention of subsection (4) of section 350, he uses information which has been disclosed to him in accordance with that section.

(5) A person guilty of an offence under subsection (3) or (4) is liable on summary conviction to imprisonment for a term not exceeding *three months* or a fine not exceeding level 5 on the standard scale, or both.

(6) In proceedings for an offence under this section it is a defence for the accused to prove—

(a) that he did not know and had no reason to suspect that the information was confidential information or that it had been disclosed in accordance with section 350;

(b) that he took all reasonable precautions and exercised all due diligence to avoid committing the offence.

[2350]

NOTES

Sub-s (5): for the words in italics there are substituted the words "51 weeks" by the Criminal Justice Act 2003, Sch 26, para 54(3), as from a day to be appointed.

Information relating to mutual societies: see the note to s 348 at **[2346]**.

353 Removal of other restrictions on disclosure

(1) The Treasury may make regulations permitting the disclosure of any information, or of information of a prescribed kind—

(a) by prescribed persons for the purpose of assisting or enabling them to discharge prescribed functions under this Act or any rules or regulations made under it;

(b) by prescribed persons, or persons of a prescribed description, to the Authority for the purpose of assisting or enabling the Authority to discharge prescribed functions;

[(c) by the scheme operator to the Office of Fair Trading for the purpose of assisting or enabling that Office to discharge prescribed functions under the Consumer Credit Act 1974].

(2) Regulations under this section may not make any provision in relation to the disclosure of confidential information by primary recipients or by any person obtaining confidential information directly or indirectly from a primary recipient.

(3) If a person discloses any information as permitted by regulations under this section the disclosure is not to be taken as a contravention of any duty to which he is subject.

[2351]

NOTES

Sub-s (1): para (c) inserted by the Consumer Credit Act 2006, s 61(9), as from 16 June 2006.

Information relating to mutual societies: see the note to s 348 at **[2346]**.

Regulations: the Financial Services and Markets Act 2000 (Disclosure of Information by Prescribed Persons) Regulations 2001, SI 2001/1857 at **[4368]**.

Note that the following amending Regulations have also been made under this section: the Financial Services and Markets Act 2000 (Disclosure of Information by Prescribed Persons) (Amendment) Regulations 2005, SI 2005/272.

Co-operation

354 Authority's duty to co-operate with others

(1) The Authority must take such steps as it considers appropriate to co-operate with other persons (whether in the United Kingdom or elsewhere) who have functions—

(a) similar to those of the Authority; or

(b) in relation to the prevention or detection of financial crime.

[(1A) The Authority must take such steps as it considers appropriate to co- operate with—

(a) the Panel on Takeovers and Mergers;

(b) an authority designated as a supervisory authority for the purposes of Article 4.1 of the Takeovers Directive;

(c) any other person or body that exercises functions of a public nature, under legislation in any country or territory outside the United Kingdom, that appear to the Authority to be similar to those of the Panel on Takeovers and Mergers.]

(2) Co-operation may include the sharing of information which the Authority is not prevented from disclosing.

(3) "Financial crime" has the same meaning as in section 6.

[2352]

NOTES

Sub-s (1A): inserted by the Companies Act 2006, s 964(1), (5), as from 6 April 2007.

PART XXIV
INSOLVENCY

Interpretation

355 Interpretation of this Part

(1) In this Part—

"the 1985 Act" means the Bankruptcy (Scotland) Act 1985;

"the 1986 Act" means the Insolvency Act 1986;

"the 1989 Order" means the Insolvency (Northern Ireland) Order 1989;

"body" means a body of persons—

(a) over which the court has jurisdiction under any provision of, or made under, the 1986 Act (or the 1989 Order); but

(b) which is not a building society, a friendly society or an industrial and provident society; and

"court" means—

(a) the court having jurisdiction for the purposes of the 1985 Act or the 1986 Act; or

(b) in Northern Ireland, the High Court.

(2) In this Part "insurer" has such meaning as may be specified in an order made by the Treasury.

[2353]

NOTES

Orders: the Financial Services and Markets Act 2000 (Insolvency) (Definition of "Insurer") Order 2001, SI 2001/2634 at **[4471]**; the Financial Services and Markets Act 2000 (Administration Orders Relating to Insurers) Order 2002, SI 2002/1242.

Voluntary arrangements

356 Authority's powers to participate in proceedings: company voluntary arrangements

[(1) Where a voluntary arrangement has effect under Part I of the 1986 Act in respect of a company or insolvent partnership which is an authorised person, the Authority may apply to the court under section 6 or 7 of that Act.]

[(2) Where a voluntary arrangement has been approved under Part II of the 1989 Order in respect of a company or insolvent partnership which is an authorised person, the Authority may apply to the court under Article 19 or 20 of that Order.]

(3) If a person other than the Authority makes an application to the court in relation to the company or insolvent partnership under [any] of those provisions, the Authority is entitled to be heard at any hearing relating to the application.

[2354]

NOTES

Sub-ss (1), (2): substituted by the Insolvency Act 2000, s 15(3)(a), (b), as from 1 January 2003.

Sub-s (3): word in square brackets substituted by the Insolvency Act 2000, s 15(3)(c), as from 1 January 2003.

Application to limited liability partnerships: see the Limited Liability Partnerships Regulations 2001, SI 2001/1090, reg 6 at **[6987]**.

357 Authority's powers to participate in proceedings: individual voluntary arrangements

(1) The Authority is entitled to be heard on an application by an individual who is an authorised person under section 253 of the 1986 Act (or Article 227 of the 1989 Order).

(2) Subsections (3) to (6) apply if such an order is made on the application of such a person.

(3) A person appointed for the purpose by the Authority is entitled to attend any meeting of creditors of the debtor summoned under section 257 of the 1986 Act (or Article 231 of the 1989 Order).

(4) Notice of the result of a meeting so summoned is to be given to the Authority by the chairman of the meeting.

(5) The Authority may apply to the court—

(a) under section 262 of the 1986 Act (or Article 236 of the 1989 Order); or

(b) under section 263 of the 1986 Act (or Article 237 of the 1989 Order).

(6) If a person other than the Authority makes an application to the court under any provision mentioned in subsection (5), the Authority is entitled to be heard at any hearing relating to the application.

[2355]

358 Authority's powers to participate in proceedings: trust deeds for creditors in Scotland

(1) This section applies where a trust deed has been granted by or on behalf of a debtor who is an authorised person.

(2) The trustee must, as soon as practicable after he becomes aware that the debtor is an authorised person, send to the Authority—

(a) in every case, a copy of the trust deed;

(b) where any other document or information is sent to every creditor known to the trustee in pursuance of paragraph 5(1)(c) of Schedule 5 to the 1985 Act, a copy of such document or information.

(3) Paragraph 7 of that Schedule applies to the Authority as if it were a qualified creditor who has not been sent a copy of the notice as mentioned in paragraph 5(1)(c) of the Schedule.

(4) The Authority must be given the same notice as the creditors of any meeting of creditors held in relation to the trust deed.

(5) A person appointed for the purpose by the Authority is entitled to attend and participate in (but not to vote at) any such meeting of creditors as if the Authority were a creditor under the deed.

(6) This section does not affect any right the Authority has as a creditor of a debtor who is an authorised person.

(7) Expressions used in this section and in the 1985 Act have the same meaning in this section as in that Act.

[2356]

Administration orders

[359 Administration order

(1) The Authority may make an administration application under Schedule B1 to the 1986 Act [or Schedule B1 to the 1989 Order] in relation to a company or insolvent partnership which—

(a) is or has been an authorised person,

(b) is or has been an appointed representative, or

(c) is carrying on or has carried on a regulated activity in contravention of the general prohibition.

(2) Subsection (3) applies in relation to an administration application made (or a petition presented) by the Authority by virtue of this section.

(3) Any of the following shall be treated for the purpose of paragraph 11(a) of Schedule B1 to the 1986 Act [or paragraph 12(a) of Schedule B1 to the 1989 Order] as unable to pay its debts—

(a) a company or partnership in default on an obligation to pay a sum due and payable under an agreement, and

(b) an authorised deposit taker in default on an obligation to pay a sum due and payable in respect of a relevant deposit.

(4) In this section—

"agreement" means an agreement the making or performance of which constitutes or is part of a regulated activity carried on by the company or partnership,

"authorised deposit taker" means a person with a Part IV permission to accept deposits (but not a person who has a Part IV permission to accept deposits only for the purpose of carrying on another regulated activity in accordance with that permission),

"company" means a company—

(a) in respect of which an administrator may be appointed under Schedule B1 to the 1986 Act, or

[(b) in respect of which an administrator may be appointed under Schedule B1 to the 1989 Order,] and

"relevant deposit" shall, ignoring any restriction on the meaning of deposit arising from the identity of the person making the deposit, be construed in accordance with—

(a) section 22,

(b) any relevant order under that section, and

(c) Schedule 2.

(5) The definition of "authorised deposit taker" in subsection (4) shall be construed in accordance with—

(a) section 22,

(b) any relevant order under that section, and

(c) Schedule 2.]

[2357]

NOTES

Substituted by the Enterprise Act 2002, s 248(3), Sch 17, paras 53, 55, as from 15 September 2003 (for savings and transitional provisions, see the note to the Insolvency Act 1986, s 8 at **[3164]**).

Sub-ss (1), (3), (4): words in square brackets substituted by the Insolvency (Northern Ireland) Order 2005, SI 2005/1455, art 3(3), Sch 2, paras 56, 58, as from 27 March 2006.

Application to limited liability partnerships: see the Limited Liability Partnerships Regulations 2001, SI 2001/1090, reg 6 at **[6987]**.

360 Insurers

(1) The Treasury may by order provide that such provisions of Part II of the 1986 Act (or Part III of the 1989 Order) as may be specified are to apply in relation to insurers with such modifications as may be specified.

(2) An order under this section—

(a) may provide that such provisions of this Part as may be specified are to apply in relation to the administration of insurers in accordance with the order with such modifications as may be specified; and

(b) requires the consent of the Secretary of State.

(3) "Specified" means specified in the order.

[2358]

NOTES

Orders: the Financial Services and Markets Act 2000 (Administration Orders Relating to Insurers) Order 2002, SI 2002/1242; the Financial Services and Markets Act 2000 (Administration Orders Relating to Insurers) (Northern Ireland) Order 2005, SI 2005/1644 (revoked by SI 2007/846 as from 6 April 2007 subject to savings); the Financial Services and Markets Act 2000 (Administration Orders Relating to Insurers) (Northern Ireland) Order 2007, SI 2007/846.

Note that the following amending Orders have also been made under this section: the Financial Services and Markets Act 2000 (Administration Orders Relating to Insurers) (Amendment) Order 2003, SI 2003/2134; the Financial Services and Markets Act 2000 (Transitional Provisions, Repeals and Savings) (Financial Services Compensation Scheme) (Amendment) Order 2004, SI 2004/952.

[361 Administrator's duty to report to Authority

(1) This section applies where a company or partnership is—

(a) in administration within the meaning of Schedule B1 to the 1986 Act, or

[(b) in administration within the meaning of Schedule B1 to the 1989 Order].

(2) If the administrator thinks that the company or partnership is carrying on or has carried on a regulated activity in contravention of the general prohibition, he must report to the Authority without delay.

(3) Subsection (2) does not apply where the administration arises out of an administration order made on an application made or petition presented by the Authority.]

[2359]

NOTES

Substituted by the Enterprise Act 2002, s 248(3), Sch 17, paras 53, 56, as from 15 September 2003 (for savings and transitional provisions, see the note to the Insolvency Act 1986, s 8 at **[3164]**).

Sub-s (1): para (b) substituted by the Insolvency (Northern Ireland) Order 2005, SI 2005/1455, art 3(3), Sch 2, paras 56, 59, as from 27 March 2006.

Application to limited liability partnerships: see the Limited Liability Partnerships Regulations 2001, SI 2001/1090, reg 6 at **[6987]**.

362 Authority's powers to participate in proceedings

(1) This section applies if a person other than the Authority [makes an administration application under Schedule B1 to the 1986 Act] [or Schedule B1 to the 1989 Order] in relation to a company or partnership which—

(a) is, or has been, an authorised person;

(b) is, or has been, an appointed representative; or

(c) is carrying on, or has carried on, a regulated activity in contravention of the general prohibition.

[(1A) This section also applies in relation to—

(a) the appointment under paragraph 14 or 22 of Schedule B1 to the 1986 Act [or paragraph 15 or 23 of Schedule B1 to the 1989 Order] of an administrator of a company of a kind described in subsection (1)(a) to (c), or

(b) the filing with the court of a copy of notice of intention to appoint an administrator under [any] of those paragraphs.]

(2) The Authority is entitled to be heard—

(a) at the hearing of the [administration application …]; and

(b) at any other hearing of the court in relation to the company or partnership under Part II of the 1986 Act (or Part III of the 1989 Order).

(3) Any notice or other document required to be sent to a creditor of the company or partnership must also be sent to the Authority.

[(4) The Authority may apply to the court under paragraph 74 of Schedule B1 to the 1986 Act [or paragraph 75 of Schedule B1 to the 1989 Order].

(4A) In respect of an application under subsection (4)—

(a) paragraph 74(1)(a) and (b) shall have effect as if for the words "harm the interests of the applicant (whether alone or in common with some or all other members or creditors)" there were substituted the words "harm the interests of some or all members or creditors", and

[(b) paragraph 75(1)(a) and (b) of Schedule B1 to the 1989 Order shall have effect as if for the words "harm the interests of the applicant (whether alone or in common with some or all other members or creditors)" there were substituted the words "harm the interests of some or all members or creditors".]]

(5) A person appointed for the purpose by the Authority is entitled—

(a) to attend any meeting of creditors of the company or partnership summoned under any enactment;

(b) to attend any meeting of a committee established under [paragraph 57 of Schedule B1 to the 1986 Act] [or paragraph 58 of Schedule B1 to the 1989 Order]; and

(c) to make representations as to any matter for decision at such a meeting.

(6) If, during the course of the administration of a company, a compromise or arrangement is proposed between the company and its creditors, or any class of them, the Authority may apply to the court under section 425 of the Companies Act 1985 (or Article 418 of the Companies (Northern Ireland) Order 1986).

[2360]

NOTES

Sub-s (1): words in first pair of square brackets substituted by the Enterprise Act 2002, s 248(3), Sch 17, paras 53, 57(a), as from 15 September 2003 (for savings and transitional provisions, see the note to the Insolvency Act 1986, s 8 at **[3164]**); words in second pair of square brackets substituted by the Insolvency (Northern Ireland) Order 2005, SI 2005/1455, art 3(3), Sch 2, paras 56, 60(1), (2), as from 27 March 2006.

Sub-s (1A): inserted by the Enterprise Act 2002, s 248(3), Sch 17, paras 53, 57(b), as from 15 September 2003 (for savings and transitional provisions, see the note to the Insolvency Act 1986, s 8 at **[3164]**); words in square brackets in para (a) inserted, and word in square brackets in para (b) substituted, by SI 2005/1455, art 3(3), Sch 2, paras 56, 60(1), (3), as from 27 March 2006.

Sub-s (2): words in square brackets substituted by the Enterprise Act 2002, s 248(3), Sch 17, paras 53, 57(c), as from 15 September 2003 (for savings and transitional provisions, see the note to the Insolvency Act 1986, s 8 at **[3164]**); words omitted repealed by SI 2005/1455, arts 3(3), 31, Sch 2, paras 56, 60(1), (4), Sch 9, as from 27 March 2006.

Sub-s (4): substituted, together with sub-s (4A) for original sub-s (4), by the Enterprise Act 2002, s 248(3), Sch 17, paras 53, 57(d), as from 15 September 2003 (for savings and transitional provisions, see the note to the Insolvency Act 1986, s 8 at **[3164]**); words in square brackets substituted by SI 2005/1455, art 3(3), Sch 2, paras 56, 60(1), (5), as from 27 March 2006.

Sub-s (4A): substituted as noted above; para (b) substituted by SI 2005/1455, art 3(3), Sch 2, paras 56, 60(1), (6), as from 27 March 2006.

Sub-s (5): words in first pair of square brackets substituted by the Enterprise Act 2002, s 248(3), Sch 17, paras 53, 57(e), as from 15 September 2003 (for savings and transitional provisions, see the note to the Insolvency Act 1986, s 8 at **[3164]**); words in second pair of square brackets substituted by SI 2005/1455, art 3(3), Sch 2, paras 56, 60(1), (7), as from 27 March 2006.

Application to limited liability partnerships: see the Limited Liability Partnerships Regulations 2001, SI 2001/1090, reg 6 at **[6987]**.

[362A Administrator appointed by company or directors

(1) This section applies in relation to a company of a kind described in section 362(1)(a) to (c).

(2) An administrator of the company may not be appointed under paragraph 22 of Schedule B1 to the 1986 Act [or paragraph 23 of Schedule B1 to the 1989 Order] without the consent of the Authority.

(3) Consent under subsection (2)—

(a) must be in writing, and

(b) must be filed with the court along with the notice of intention to appoint under paragraph 27 of [Schedule B1 to the 1986 Act or paragraph 28 of Schedule B1 to the 1989 Order].

(4) In a case where no notice of intention to appoint is required—

(a) subsection (3)(b) shall not apply, but

(b) consent under subsection (2) must accompany the notice of appointment filed under paragraph 29 of [Schedule B1 to the 1986 Act or paragraph 30 of Schedule B1 to the 1989 Order].]

[2360A]

NOTES

Inserted by the Enterprise Act 2002, s 248(3), Sch 17, paras 53, 58, as from 15 September 2003 (for savings and transitional provisions, see the note to the Insolvency Act 1986, s 8 at **[3164]**).

Sub-s (2): words in square brackets inserted by the Insolvency (Northern Ireland) Order 2005, SI 2005/1455, art 3(3), Sch 2, paras 56, 61(1), (2), as from 27 March 2006.

Sub-ss (3), (4): words in square brackets substituted by the SI 2005/1455, art 3(3), Sch 2, paras 56, 61(1), (3), (4), as from 27 March 2006.

Application to limited liability partnerships: see the Limited Liability Partnerships Regulations 2001, SI 2001/1090, reg 6 at **[6987]**.

Receivership

363 Authority's powers to participate in proceedings

(1) This section applies if a receiver has been appointed in relation to a company which—

(a) is, or has been, an authorised person;

(b) is, or has been, an appointed representative; or

(c) is carrying on, or has carried on, a regulated activity in contravention of the general prohibition.

(2) The Authority is entitled to be heard on an application made under section 35 or 63 of the 1986 Act (or Article 45 of the 1989 Order).

(3) The Authority is entitled to make an application under section 41(1)(a) or 69(1)(a) of the 1986 Act (or Article 51(1)(a) of the 1989 Order).

(4) A report under section 48(1) or 67(1) of the 1986 Act (or Article 58(1) of the 1989 Order) must be sent by the person making it to the Authority.

(5) A person appointed for the purpose by the Authority is entitled—

(a) to attend any meeting of creditors of the company summoned under any enactment;

(b) to attend any meeting of a committee established under section 49 or 68 of the 1986 Act (or Article 59 of the 1989 Order); and

(c) to make representations as to any matter for decision at such a meeting.

[2361]

NOTES

Application to limited liability partnerships: see the Limited Liability Partnerships Regulations 2001, SI 2001/1090, reg 6 at **[6987]**.

364 Receiver's duty to report to Authority

If—

(a) a receiver has been appointed in relation to a company, and

(b) it appears to the receiver that the company is carrying on, or has carried on, a regulated activity in contravention of the general prohibition,

the receiver must report the matter to the Authority without delay.

[2362]

NOTES

Application to limited liability partnerships: see the Limited Liability Partnerships Regulations 2001, SI 2001/1090, reg 6 at **[6987]**.

Voluntary winding up

365 Authority's powers to participate in proceedings

(1) This section applies in relation to a company which—

(a) is being wound up voluntarily;

(b) is an authorised person; and

(c) is not an insurer effecting or carrying out contracts of long-term insurance.

(2) The Authority may apply to the court under section 112 of the 1986 Act (or Article 98 of the 1989 Order) in respect of the company.

(3) The Authority is entitled to be heard at any hearing of the court in relation to the voluntary winding up of the company.

(4) Any notice or other document required to be sent to a creditor of the company must also be sent to the Authority.

(5) A person appointed for the purpose by the Authority is entitled—

(a) to attend any meeting of creditors of the company summoned under any enactment;

(b) to attend any meeting of a committee established under section 101 of the 1986 Act (or Article 87 of the 1989 Order); and

(c) to make representations as to any matter for decision at such a meeting.

(6) The voluntary winding up of the company does not bar the right of the Authority to have it wound up by the court.

(7) If, during the course of the winding up of the company, a compromise or arrangement is proposed between the company and its creditors, or any class of them, the Authority may apply to the court under section 425 of the Companies Act 1985 (or Article 418 of the Companies (Northern Ireland) Order 1986).

[2363]

NOTES

Application to limited liability partnerships: see the Limited Liability Partnerships Regulations 2001, SI 2001/1090, reg 6 at **[6987]**.

366 Insurers effecting or carrying out long-term contracts or insurance

(1) An insurer effecting or carrying out contracts of long-term insurance may not be wound up voluntarily without the consent of the Authority.

(2) If notice of a general meeting of such an insurer is given, specifying the intention to propose a resolution for voluntary winding up of the insurer, a director of the insurer must notify the Authority as soon as practicable after he becomes aware of it.

(3) A person who fails to comply with subsection (2) is guilty of an offence and liable on summary conviction to a fine not exceeding level 5 on the standard scale.

(4) The following provisions do not apply in relation to a winding-up resolution—

(a) sections 378(3) and 381A of the Companies Act 1985 ("the 1985 Act"); and

(b) Articles 386(3) and 389A of the Companies (Northern Ireland) Order 1986 ("the 1986 Order").

(5) A copy of a winding-up resolution forwarded to the registrar of companies in accordance with section 380 of the 1985 Act (or Article 388 of the 1986 Order) must be accompanied by a certificate issued by the Authority stating that it consents to the voluntary winding up of the insurer.

(6) If subsection (5) is complied with, the voluntary winding up is to be treated as having commenced at the time the resolution was passed.

(7) If subsection (5) is not complied with, the resolution has no effect.

(8) "Winding-up resolution" means a resolution for voluntary winding up of an insurer effecting or carrying out contracts of long-term insurance.

[2364]

Winding up by the court

367 Winding-up petitions

(1) The Authority may present a petition to the court for the winding up of a body which—

(a) is, or has been, an authorised person;

(b) is, or has been, an appointed representative; or

(c) is carrying on, or has carried on, a regulated activity in contravention of the general prohibition.

(2) In subsection (1) "body" includes any partnership.

(3) On such a petition, the court may wind up the body if—

(a) the body is unable to pay its debts within the meaning of section 123 or 221 of the 1986 Act (or Article 103 or 185 of the 1989 Order); or

(b) the court is of the opinion that it is just and equitable that it should be wound up.

(4) If a body is in default on an obligation to pay a sum due and payable under an agreement, it is to be treated for the purpose of subsection (3)(a) as unable to pay its debts.

(5) "Agreement" means an agreement the making or performance of which constitutes or is part of a regulated activity carried on by the body concerned.

(6) Subsection (7) applies if a petition is presented under subsection (1) for the winding up of a partnership—

(a) on the ground mentioned in subsection (3)(b); or

(b) in Scotland, on a ground mentioned in subsection (3)(a) or (b).

(7) The court has jurisdiction, and the 1986 Act (or the 1989 Order) has effect, as if the partnership were an unregistered company as defined by section 220 of that Act (or Article 184 of that Order).

[2365]

NOTES

Transitional provisions: as to the application of this section to a body which has been an authorised institution within the meaning of the Banking Act 1987 (repealed by the Financial Services and Markets Act 2000 (Consequential Amendments and Repeals) Order 2001, SI 2001/3649, art 3(1)(d), or which, before 1 December 2001, contravened s 3 of the 1987 Act (restriction on acceptance of deposits), see the Financial Services and Markets Act 2000 (Transitional Provisions and Savings) (Civil Remedies, Discipline, Criminal Offences etc) (No 2) Order 2001, SI 2001/3083, art 12.

Application to limited liability partnerships: see the Limited Liability Partnerships Regulations 2001, SI 2001/1090, reg 6 at **[6987]**.

368 Winding-up petitions: EEA and Treaty firms

The Authority may not present a petition to the court under section 367 for the winding up of—

(a) an EEA firm which qualifies for authorisation under Schedule 3, or

(b) a Treaty firm which qualifies for authorisation under Schedule 4,

unless it has been asked to do so by the home state regulator of the firm concerned.

[2366]

369 Insurers: service of petition etc on Authority

(1) If a person other than the Authority presents a petition for the winding up of an authorised person with permission to effect or carry out contracts of insurance, the petitioner must serve a copy of the petition on the Authority.

(2) If a person other than the Authority applies to have a provisional liquidator appointed under section 135 of the 1986 Act (or Article 115 of the 1989 Order) in respect of an authorised person with permission to effect or carry out contracts of insurance, the applicant must serve a copy of the application on the Authority.

[2367]

370 Liquidator's duty to report to Authority

If—

(a) a company is being wound up voluntarily or a body is being wound up on a petition presented by a person other than the Authority, and

(b) it appears to the liquidator that the company or body is carrying on, or has carried on, a regulated activity in contravention of the general prohibition,

the liquidator must report the matter to the Authority without delay.

[2368]

NOTES

Application to limited liability partnerships: see the Limited Liability Partnerships Regulations 2001, SI 2001/1090, reg 6 at **[6987]**.

371 Authority's powers to participate in proceedings

(1) This section applies if a person other than the Authority presents a petition for the winding up of a body which—

(a) is, or has been, an authorised person;

(b) is, or has been, an appointed representative; or

(c) is carrying on, or has carried on, a regulated activity in contravention of the general prohibition.

(2) The Authority is entitled to be heard—

(a) at the hearing of the petition; and

(b) at any other hearing of the court in relation to the body under or by virtue of Part IV or V of the 1986 Act (or Part V or VI of the 1989 Order).

(3) Any notice or other document required to be sent to a creditor of the body must also be sent to the Authority.

(4) A person appointed for the purpose by the Authority is entitled—

(a) to attend any meeting of creditors of the body;

(b) to attend any meeting of a committee established for the purposes of Part IV or V of the 1986 Act under section 101 of that Act or under section 141 or 142 of that Act;

(c) to attend any meeting of a committee established for the purposes of Part V or VI of the 1989 Order under Article 87 of that Order or under Article 120 of that Order; and

(d) to make representations as to any matter for decision at such a meeting.

(5) If, during the course of the winding up of a company, a compromise or arrangement is proposed between the company and its creditors, or any class of them, the Authority may apply to the court under section 425 of the Companies Act 1985 (or Article 418 of the Companies (Northern Ireland) Order 1986).

[2369]

NOTES

Application to limited liability partnerships: see the Limited Liability Partnerships Regulations 2001, SI 2001/1090, reg 6 at **[6987]**.

Bankruptcy

372 Petitions

(1) The Authority may present a petition to the court—

(a) under section 264 of the 1986 Act (or Article 238 of the 1989 Order) for a bankruptcy order to be made against an individual; or

(b) under section 5 of the 1985 Act for the sequestration of the estate of an individual.

(2) But such a petition may be presented only on the ground that—

(a) the individual appears to be unable to pay a regulated activity debt; or

(b) the individual appears to have no reasonable prospect of being able to pay a regulated activity debt.

(3) An individual appears to be unable to pay a regulated activity debt if he is in default on an obligation to pay a sum due and payable under an agreement.

(4) An individual appears to have no reasonable prospect of being able to pay a regulated activity debt if—

(a) the Authority has served on him a demand requiring him to establish to the satisfaction of the Authority that there is a reasonable prospect that he will be able to pay a sum payable under an agreement when it falls due;

(b) at least three weeks have elapsed since the demand was served; and

(c) the demand has been neither complied with nor set aside in accordance with rules.

(5) A demand made under subsection (4)(a) is to be treated for the purposes of the 1986 Act (or the 1989 Order) as if it were a statutory demand under section 268 of that Act (or Article 242 of that Order).

(6) For the purposes of a petition presented in accordance with subsection (1)(b)—

(a) the Authority is to be treated as a qualified creditor; and

(b) a ground mentioned in subsection (2) constitutes apparent insolvency.

(7) "Individual" means an individual—

(a) who is, or has been, an authorised person; or

(b) who is carrying on, or has carried on, a regulated activity in contravention of the general prohibition.

(8) "Agreement" means an agreement the making or performance of which constitutes or is part of a regulated activity carried on by the individual concerned.

(9) "Rules" means—

(a) in England and Wales, rules made under section 412 of the 1986 Act;

(b) in Scotland, rules made by order by the Treasury, after consultation with the Scottish Ministers, for the purposes of this section; and

(c) in Northern Ireland, rules made under Article 359 of the 1989 Order.

[2370]

NOTES

Rules: the Bankruptcy (Financial Services and Markets Act 2000) (Scotland) Rules 2001, SI 2001/3591.

373 Insolvency practitioner's duty to report to Authority

(1) If—

(a) a bankruptcy order or sequestration award is in force in relation to an individual by virtue of a petition presented by a person other than the Authority, and

(b) it appears to the insolvency practitioner that the individual is carrying on, or has carried on, a regulated activity in contravention of the general prohibition,

the insolvency practitioner must report the matter to the Authority without delay.

(2) "Bankruptcy order" means a bankruptcy order under Part IX of the 1986 Act (or Part IX of the 1989 Order).

(3) "Sequestration award" means an award of sequestration under section 12 of the 1985 Act.

(4) "Individual" includes an entity mentioned in section 374(1)(c).

[2371]

374 Authority's powers to participate in proceedings

(1) This section applies if a person other than the Authority presents a petition to the court—

(a) under section 264 of the 1986 Act (or Article 238 of the 1989 Order) for a bankruptcy order to be made against an individual;

(b) under section 5 of the 1985 Act for the sequestration of the estate of an individual; or

(c) under section 6 of the 1985 Act for the sequestration of the estate belonging to or held for or jointly by the members of an entity mentioned in subsection (1) of that section.

(2) The Authority is entitled to be heard—

(a) at the hearing of the petition; and

(b) at any other hearing in relation to the individual or entity under—

(i) Part IX of the 1986 Act;

(ii) Part IX of the 1989 Order; or

(iii) the 1985 Act.

(3) A copy of the report prepared under section 274 of the 1986 Act (or Article 248 of the 1989 Order) must also be sent to the Authority.

(4) A person appointed for the purpose by the Authority is entitled—

(a) to attend any meeting of creditors of the individual or entity;

(b) to attend any meeting of a committee established under section 301 of the 1986 Act (or Article 274 of the 1989 Order);

(c) to attend any meeting of commissioners held under paragraph 17 or 18 of Schedule 6 to the 1985 Act; and

(d) to make representations as to any matter for decision at such a meeting.

(5) "Individual" means an individual who—

(a) is, or has been, an authorised person; or

(b) is carrying on, or has carried on, a regulated activity in contravention of the general prohibition.

(6) "Entity" means an entity which—

(a) is, or has been, an authorised person; or

(b) is carrying on, or has carried on, a regulated activity in contravention of the general prohibition.

[2372]

Provisions against debt avoidance

375 Authority's right to apply for an order

(1) The Authority may apply for an order under section 423 of the 1986 Act (or Article 367 of the 1989 Order) in relation to a debtor if—

(a) at the time the transaction at an undervalue was entered into, the debtor was carrying on a regulated activity (whether or not in contravention of the general prohibition); and

(b) a victim of the transaction is or was party to an agreement entered into with the debtor, the making or performance of which constituted or was part of a regulated activity carried on by the debtor.

(2) An application made under this section is to be treated as made on behalf of every victim of the transaction to whom subsection (1)(b) applies.

(3) Expressions which are given a meaning in Part XVI of the 1986 Act (or Article 367, 368 or 369 of the 1989 Order) have the same meaning when used in this section.

[2373]

Supplemental provisions concerning insurers

376 Continuation of contracts of long-term insurance where insurer in liquidation

(1) This section applies in relation to the winding up of an insurer which effects or carries out contracts of long-term insurance.

(2) Unless the court otherwise orders, the liquidator must carry on the insurer's business so far as it consists of carrying out the insurer's contracts of long-term insurance with a view to its being transferred as a going concern to a person who may lawfully carry out those contracts.

(3) In carrying on the business, the liquidator—

(a) may agree to the variation of any contracts of insurance in existence when the winding up order is made; but

(b) must not effect any new contracts of insurance.

(4) If the liquidator is satisfied that the interests of the creditors in respect of liabilities of the insurer attributable to contracts of long-term insurance effected by it require the appointment of a special manager, he may apply to the court.

(5) On such an application, the court may appoint a special manager to act during such time as the court may direct.

(6) The special manager is to have such powers, including any of the powers of a receiver or manager, as the court may direct.

(7) Section 177(5) of the 1986 Act (or Article 151(5) of the 1989 Order) applies to a special manager appointed under subsection (5) as it applies to a special manager appointed under section 177 of the 1986 Act (or Article 151 of the 1989 Order).

(8) If the court thinks fit, it may reduce the value of one or more of the contracts of long-term insurance effected by the insurer.

(9) Any reduction is to be on such terms and subject to such conditions (if any) as the court thinks fit.

(10) The court may, on the application of an official, appoint an independent actuary to investigate the insurer's business so far as it consists of carrying out its contracts of long-term insurance and to report to the official—

(a) on the desirability or otherwise of that part of the insurer's business being continued; and

(b) on any reduction in the contracts of long-term insurance effected by the insurer that may be necessary for successful continuation of that part of the insurer's business.

(11) "Official" means—
(a) the liquidator;
(b) a special manager appointed under subsection (5); or
(c) the Authority.

(12) The liquidator may make an application in the name of the insurer and on its behalf under Part VII without obtaining the permission that would otherwise be required by section 167 of, and Schedule 4 to, the 1986 Act (or Article 142 of, and Schedule 2 to, the 1989 Order).

[2374]

377 Reducing the value of contracts instead of winding up

(1) This section applies in relation to an insurer which has been proved to be unable to pay its debts.

(2) If the court thinks fit, it may reduce the value of one or more of the insurer's contracts instead of making a winding up order.

(3) Any reduction is to be on such terms and subject to such conditions (if any) as the court thinks fit.

[2375]

NOTES

EEA insurers: this section does not apply in relation to an EEA insurer; see the Insurers (Reorganisation and Winding Up) Regulations 2004, SI 2004/353, reg 4.

378 Treatment of assets on winding up

(1) The Treasury may by regulations provide for the treatment of the assets of an insurer on its winding up.

(2) The regulations may, in particular, provide for—
(a) assets representing a particular part of the insurer's business to be available only for meeting liabilities attributable to that part of the insurer's business;
(b) separate general meetings of the creditors to be held in respect of liabilities attributable to a particular part of the insurer's business.

[2376]

379 Winding-up rules

(1) Winding-up rules may include provision—
(a) for determining the amount of the liabilities of an insurer to policyholders of any class or description for the purpose of proof in a winding up; and
(b) generally for carrying into effect the provisions of this Part with respect to the winding up of insurers.

(2) Winding-up rules may, in particular, make provision for all or any of the following matters—
(a) the identification of assets and liabilities;
(b) the apportionment, between assets of different classes or descriptions, of—
(i) the costs, charges and expenses of the winding up; and
(ii) any debts of the insurer of a specified class or description;
(c) the determination of the amount of liabilities of a specified description;
(d) the application of assets for meeting liabilities of a specified description;
(e) the application of assets representing any excess of a specified description.

(3) "Specified" means specified in winding-up rules.

(4) "Winding-up rules" means rules made under section 411 of the 1986 Act (or Article 359 of the 1989 Order).

(5) Nothing in this section affects the power to make winding-up rules under the 1986 Act or the 1989 Order.

[2377]

NOTES

Rules: the Insurers (Winding Up) Rules 2001, SI 2001/3635 at **[4585]**; the Insurers (Winding Up) (Scotland) Rules 2001, SI 2001/4040.

PART XXV
INJUNCTIONS AND RESTITUTION

Injunctions

380 Injunctions

(1) If, on the application of the Authority or the Secretary of State, the court is satisfied—

(a) that there is a reasonable likelihood that any person will contravene a relevant requirement, or

(b) that any person has contravened a relevant requirement and that there is a reasonable likelihood that the contravention will continue or be repeated,

the court may make an order restraining (or in Scotland an interdict prohibiting) the contravention.

(2) If on the application of the Authority or the Secretary of State the court is satisfied—

(a) that any person has contravened a relevant requirement, and

(b) that there are steps which could be taken for remedying the contravention,

the court may make an order requiring that person, and any other person who appears to have been knowingly concerned in the contravention, to take such steps as the court may direct to remedy it.

(3) If, on the application of the Authority or the Secretary of State, the court is satisfied that any person may have—

(a) contravened a relevant requirement, or

(b) been knowingly concerned in the contravention of such a requirement,

it may make an order restraining (or in Scotland an interdict prohibiting) him from disposing of, or otherwise dealing with, any assets of his which it is satisfied he is reasonably likely to dispose of or otherwise deal with.

(4) The jurisdiction conferred by this section is exercisable by the High Court and the Court of Session.

(5) In subsection (2), references to remedying a contravention include references to mitigating its effect.

(6) "Relevant requirement"—

(a) in relation to an application by the Authority, means a requirement—

(i) which is imposed by or under this Act [or by any directly applicable Community regulation made under the markets in financial instruments directive]; or

(ii) which is imposed by or under any other Act and whose contravention constitutes an offence which the Authority has power to prosecute under this Act;

(b) in relation to an application by the Secretary of State, means a requirement which is imposed by or under this Act and whose contravention constitutes an offence which the Secretary of State has power to prosecute under this Act.

(7) In the application of subsection (6) to Scotland—

(a) in paragraph (a)(ii) for "which the Authority has power to prosecute under this Act" substitute "mentioned in paragraph (a) or (b) of section 402(1)"; and

(b) in paragraph (b) omit "which the Secretary of State has power to prosecute under this Act".

[2378]

NOTES

Sub-s (6): words in square brackets inserted by the Financial Services and Markets Act 2000 (Markets in Financial Instruments) Regulations 2007, SI 2007/126, reg 3(5), Sch 5, paras 1, 13, as from 1 April 2007 (certain purposes (see reg 1(2) at **[7596]**)), and as from 1 November 2007 (otherwise).

Transitional provisions: any requirement, condition or prohibition imposed before 1 December 2001 by or under certain specified provisions is to be treated as a relevant requirement for the purposes of sub-s (2) above, and any restriction or requirement imposed by or under certain other provisions is to be treated as a relevant requirement for the purposes of sub-s (3)(a) above; see, in general, the Financial Services and Markets Act 2000 (Transitional Provisions and Savings) (Civil Remedies, Discipline, Criminal Offences etc) (No 2) Order 2001, SI 2001/3083, arts 2, 4. The specified provisions for the purposes of sub-ss (2), (3)(a) are listed in arts 2(3), 4(3) of the 2001 Order.

Note: for the purposes of this section a requirement imposed by the FSA under the Electronic Commerce Directive (Financial Services and Markets) Regulations 2002, SI 2002/1775 upon an incoming provider is to be treated as imposed on him by or under this Act; see reg 12(2) of those Regulations at **[4650]**.

381 Injunctions in cases of market abuse

(1) If, on the application of the Authority, the court is satisfied—

(a) that there is a reasonable likelihood that any person will engage in market abuse, or

(b) that any person is or has engaged in market abuse and that there is a reasonable likelihood that the market abuse will continue or be repeated,

the court may make an order restraining (or in Scotland an interdict prohibiting) the market abuse.

(2) If on the application of the Authority the court is satisfied—

(a) that any person is or has engaged in market abuse, and

(b) that there are steps which could be taken for remedying the market abuse,

the court may make an order requiring him to take such steps as the court may direct to remedy it.

(3) Subsection (4) applies if, on the application of the Authority, the court is satisfied that any person—

(a) may be engaged in market abuse; or

(b) may have been engaged in market abuse.

(4) The court make an order restraining (or in Scotland an interdict prohibiting) the person concerned from disposing of, or otherwise dealing with, any assets of his which it is satisfied that he is reasonably likely to dispose of, or otherwise deal with.

(5) The jurisdiction conferred by this section is exercisable by the High Court and the Court of Session.

(6) In subsection (2), references to remedying any market abuse include references to mitigating its effect.

[2379]

Restitution orders

382 Restitution orders

(1) The court may, on the application of the Authority or the Secretary of State, make an order under subsection (2) if it is satisfied that a person has contravened a relevant requirement, or been knowingly concerned in the contravention of such a requirement, and—

(a) that profits have accrued to him as a result of the contravention; or

(b) that one or more persons have suffered loss or been otherwise adversely affected as a result of the contravention.

(2) The court may order the person concerned to pay to the Authority such sum as appears to the court to be just having regard—

(a) in a case within paragraph (a) of subsection (1), to the profits appearing to the court to have accrued;

(b) in a case within paragraph (b) of that subsection, to the extent of the loss or other adverse effect;

(c) in a case within both of those paragraphs, to the profits appearing to the court to have accrued and to the extent of the loss or other adverse effect.

(3) Any amount paid to the Authority in pursuance of an order under subsection (2) must be paid by it to such qualifying person or distributed by it among such qualifying persons as the court may direct.

(4) On an application under subsection (1) the court may require the person concerned to supply it with such accounts or other information as it may require for any one or more of the following purposes—

(a) establishing whether any and, if so, what profits have accrued to him as mentioned in paragraph (a) of that subsection;

(b) establishing whether any person or persons have suffered any loss or adverse effect as mentioned in paragraph (b) of that subsection and, if so, the extent of that loss or adverse effect; and

(c) determining how any amounts are to be paid or distributed under subsection (3).

(5) The court may require any accounts or other information supplied under subsection (4) to be verified in such manner as it may direct.

(6) The jurisdiction conferred by this section is exercisable by the High Court and the Court of Session.

(7) Nothing in this section affects the right of any person other than the Authority or the Secretary of State to bring proceedings in respect of the matters to which this section applies.

(8) "Qualifying person" means a person appearing to the court to be someone—

(a) to whom the profits mentioned in subsection (1)(a) are attributable; or

(b) who has suffered the loss or adverse effect mentioned in subsection (1)(b).

(9) "Relevant requirement"—

(a) in relation to an application by the Authority, means a requirement—

(i) which is imposed by or under this Act [or by any directly applicable Community regulation made under the markets in financial instruments directive]; or

(ii) which is imposed by or under any other Act and whose contravention constitutes an offence which the Authority has power to prosecute under this Act;

(b) in relation to an application by the Secretary of State, means a requirement which is imposed by or under this Act and whose contravention constitutes an offence which the Secretary of State has power to prosecute under this Act.

(10) In the application of subsection (9) to Scotland—

(a) in paragraph (a)(ii) for "which the Authority has power to prosecute under this Act" substitute "mentioned in paragraph (a) or (b) of section 402(1); and

(b) in paragraph (b) omit "which the Secretary of State has power to prosecute under this Act".

[2380]

NOTES

Sub-s (9): words in square brackets inserted by the Financial Services and Markets Act 2000 (Markets in Financial Instruments) Regulations 2007, SI 2007/126, reg 3(5), Sch 5, paras 1, 14, as from 1 April 2007 (certain purposes (see reg 1(2) at **[7596]**)), and as from 1 November 2007 (otherwise).

Transitional provisions: any requirement, condition or prohibition imposed before 1 December 2001 by or under certain specified provisions is to be treated as a relevant requirement for the purposes of this section; see the Financial Services and Markets Act 2000 (Transitional Provisions and Savings) (Civil Remedies, Discipline, Criminal Offences etc) (No 2) Order 2001, SI 2001/3083, art 2. The specified provisions are listed in art 2(3) of the 2001 Order.

Note: for the purposes of this section a requirement imposed by the FSA under the Electronic Commerce Directive (Financial Services and Markets) Regulations 2002, SI 2002/1775 upon an incoming provider is to be treated as imposed on him by or under this Act; see reg 12(2) of those Regulations at **[4650]**.

383 Restitution orders in cases of market abuse

(1) The court may, on the application of the Authority, make an order under subsection (4) if it is satisfied that a person ("the person concerned")—

(a) has engaged in market abuse, or

(b) by taking or refraining from taking any action has required or encouraged another person or persons to engage in behaviour which, if engaged in by the person concerned, would amount to market abuse,

and the condition mentioned in subsection (2) is fulfilled.

(2) The condition is—

(a) that profits have accrued to the person concerned as a result; or

(b) that one or more persons have suffered loss or been otherwise adversely affected as a result.

(3) But the court may not make an order under subsection (4) if it is satisfied that—

(a) the person concerned believed, on reasonable grounds, that his behaviour did not fall within paragraph (a) or (b) of subsection (1); or

(b) he took all reasonable precautions and exercised all due diligence to avoid behaving in a way which fell within paragraph (a) or (b) of subsection (1).

(4) The court may order the person concerned to pay to the Authority such sum as appears to the court to be just having regard—

(a) in a case within paragraph (a) of subsection (2), to the profits appearing to the court to have accrued;

(b) in a case within paragraph (b) of that subsection, to the extent of the loss or other adverse effect;

(c) in a case within both of those paragraphs, to the profits appearing to the court to have accrued and to the extent of the loss or other adverse effect.

(5) Any amount paid to the Authority in pursuance of an order under subsection (4) must be paid by it to such qualifying person or distributed by it among such qualifying persons as the court may direct.

(6) On an application under subsection (1) the court may require the person concerned to supply it with such accounts or other information as it may require for any one or more of the following purposes—

(a) establishing whether any and, if so, what profits have accrued to him as mentioned in subsection (2)(a);

(b) establishing whether any person or persons have suffered any loss or adverse effect as mentioned in subsection (2)(b) and, if so, the extent of that loss or adverse effect; and

(c) determining how any amounts are to be paid or distributed under subsection (5).

(7) The court may require any accounts or other information supplied under subsection (6) to be verified in such manner as it may direct.

(8) The jurisdiction conferred by this section is exercisable by the High Court and the Court of Session.

(9) Nothing in this section affects the right of any person other than the Authority to bring proceedings in respect of the matters to which this section applies.

(10) "Qualifying person" means a person appearing to the court to be someone—

(a) to whom the profits mentioned in paragraph (a) of subsection (2) are attributable; or

(b) who has suffered the loss or adverse effect mentioned in paragraph (b) of that subsection.

[2381]

Restitution required by Authority

384 Power of Authority to require restitution

(1) The Authority may exercise the power in subsection (5) if it is satisfied that an authorised person ("the person concerned") has contravened a relevant requirement, or been knowingly concerned in the contravention of such a requirement, and—

(a) that profits have accrued to him as a result of the contravention; or

(b) that one or more persons have suffered loss or been otherwise adversely affected as a result of the contravention.

(2) The Authority may exercise the power in subsection (5) if it is satisfied that a person ("the person concerned")—

(a) has engaged in market abuse, or

(b) by taking or refraining from taking any action has required or encouraged another person or persons to engage in behaviour which, if engaged in by the person concerned, would amount to market abuse,

and the condition mentioned in subsection (3) is fulfilled.

(3) The condition is—

(a) that profits have accrued to the person concerned as a result of the market abuse; or

(b) that one or more persons have suffered loss or been otherwise adversely affected as a result of the market abuse.

(4) But the Authority may not exercise that power as a result of subsection (2) if, having considered any representations made to it in response to a warning notice, there are reasonable grounds for it to be satisfied that—

(a) the person concerned believed, on reasonable grounds, that his behaviour did not fall within paragraph (a) or (b) of that subsection; or

(b) he took all reasonable precautions and exercised all due diligence to avoid behaving in a way which fell within paragraph (a) or (b) of that subsection.

(5) The power referred to in subsections (1) and (2) is a power to require the person concerned, in accordance with such arrangements as the Authority considers appropriate, to pay to the appropriate person or distribute among the appropriate persons such amount as appears to the Authority to be just having regard—

(a) in a case within paragraph (a) of subsection (1) or (3), to the profits appearing to the Authority to have accrued;

(b) in a case within paragraph (b) of subsection (1) or (3), to the extent of the loss or other adverse effect;

(c) in a case within paragraphs (a) and (b) of subsection (1) or (3), to the profits appearing to the Authority to have accrued and to the extent of the loss or other adverse effect.

(6) "Appropriate person" means a person appearing to the Authority to be someone—

(a) to whom the profits mentioned in paragraph (a) of subsection (1) or (3) are attributable; or

(b) who has suffered the loss or adverse effect mentioned in paragraph (b) of subsection (1) or (3).

(7) "Relevant requirement" means—

(a) a requirement imposed by or under this Act [or by any directly applicable Community regulation made under the markets in financial instruments directive]; and

(b) a requirement which is imposed by or under any other Act and whose contravention constitutes an offence in relation to which this Act confers power to prosecute on the Authority.

(8) In the application of subsection (7) to Scotland, in paragraph (b) for "in relation to which this Act confers power to prosecute on the Authority" substitute "mentioned in paragraph (a) or (b) of section 402(1)".

[2382]

PART II
FSMA 2000

NOTES

Sub-s (7): words in square brackets inserted by the Financial Services and Markets Act 2000 (Markets in Financial Instruments) Regulations 2007, SI 2007/126, reg 3(5), Sch 5, paras 1, 15, as from 1 April 2007 (certain purposes (see reg 1(2) at **[7596]**)), and as from 1 November 2007 (otherwise).

Transitional provisions: as to the power of the Authority under sub-s (5) in relation to certain conduct before 1 December 2001, see the Financial Services and Markets Act 2000 (Transitional Provisions and Savings) (Civil Remedies, Discipline, Criminal Offences etc) (No 2) Order 2001, SI 2001/3083, art 3.

Note: for the purposes of this section a requirement imposed by the FSA under the Electronic Commerce Directive (Financial Services and Markets) Regulations 2002, SI 2002/1775 upon an authorised incoming provider is to be treated as imposed on him by or under this Act; see reg 12(1) of those Regulations at **[4650]**.

385 Warning notices

(1) If the Authority proposes to exercise the power under section 384(5) in relation to a person, it must give him a warning notice.

(2) A warning notice under this section must specify the amount which the Authority proposes to require the person concerned to pay or distribute as mentioned in section 384(5).

[2383]

386 Decision notices

(1) If the Authority decides to exercise the power under section 384(5), it must give a decision notice to the person in relation to whom the power is exercised.

(2) The decision notice must—

(a) state the amount that he is to pay or distribute as mentioned in section 384(5);

(b) identify the person or persons to whom that amount is to be paid or among whom that amount is to be distributed; and

(c) state the arrangements in accordance with which the payment or distribution is to be made.

(3) If the Authority decides to exercise the power under section 384(5), the person in relation to whom it is exercised may refer the matter to the Tribunal.

[2384]

PART XXVI
NOTICES

Warning notices

387 Warning notices

(1) A warning notice must—

(a) state the action which the Authority proposes to take;

(b) be in writing;

(c) give reasons for the proposed action;

(d) state whether section 394 applies; and

(e) if that section applies, describe its effect and state whether any secondary material exists to which the person concerned must be allowed access under it.

(2) The warning notice must specify a reasonable period (which may not be less than 28 days) within which the person to whom it is given may make representations to the Authority.

(3) The Authority may extend the period specified in the notice.

(4) The Authority must then decide, within a reasonable period, whether to give the person concerned a decision notice.

[2385]

NOTES

Note: "secondary material" is defined in s 394 at **[2392]**.

Decision notices

388 Decision notices

(1) A decision notice must—

(a) be in writing;

(b) give the Authority's reasons for the decision to take the action to which the notice relates;

(c) state whether section 394 applies;

(d) if that section applies, describe its effect and state whether any secondary material exists to which the person concerned must be allowed access under it; and

(e) give an indication of—

(i) any right to have the matter referred to the Tribunal which is given by this Act; and

(ii) the procedure on such a reference.

(2) If the decision notice was preceded by a warning notice, the action to which the decision notice relates must be action under the same Part as the action proposed in the warning notice.

(3) The Authority may, before it takes the action to which a decision notice ("the original notice") relates, give the person concerned a further decision notice which relates to different action in respect of the same matter.

(4) The Authority may give a further decision notice as a result of subsection (3) only if the person to whom the original notice was given consents.

(5) If the person to whom a decision notice is given under subsection (3) had the right to refer the matter to which the original decision notice related to the Tribunal, he has that right as respects the decision notice under subsection (3).

[2386]

Conclusion of proceedings

389 Notices of discontinuance

(1) If the Authority decides not to take—
(a) the action proposed in a warning notice, or
(b) the action to which a decision notice relates,
it must give a notice of discontinuance to the person to whom the warning notice or decision notice was given.

(2) But subsection (1) does not apply if the discontinuance of the proceedings concerned results in the granting of an application made by the person to whom the warning or decision notice was given.

(3) A notice of discontinuance must identify the proceedings which are being discontinued.

[2387]

390 Final notices

(1) If the Authority has given a person a decision notice and the matter was not referred to the Tribunal within the period mentioned in section 133(1), the Authority must, on taking the action to which the decision notice relates, give the person concerned and any person to whom the decision notice was copied a final notice.

(2) If the Authority has given a person a decision notice and the matter was referred to the Tribunal, the Authority must, on taking action in accordance with any directions given by—
(a) the Tribunal, or
(b) the court under section 137,
give that person and any person to whom the decision notice was copied a final notice.

(3) A final notice about a statement must—
(a) set out the terms of the statement;
(b) give details of the manner in which, and the date on which, the statement will be published.

(4) A final notice about an order must—
(a) set out the terms of the order;
(b) state the date from which the order has effect.

(5) A final notice about a penalty must—
(a) state the amount of the penalty;
(b) state the manner in which, and the period within which, the penalty is to be paid;
(c) give details of the way in which the penalty will be recovered if it is not paid by the date stated in the notice.

(6) A final notice about a requirement to make a payment or distribution in accordance with section 384(5) must state—
(a) the persons to whom,
(b) the manner in which, and
(c) the period within which,
it must be made.

(7) In any other case, the final notice must—
(a) give details of the action being taken;
(b) state the date on which the action is to be taken.

(8) The period stated under subsection (5)(b) or (6)(c) may not be less than 14 days beginning with the date on which the final notice is given.

(9) If all or any of the amount of a penalty payable under a final notice is outstanding at the end of the period stated under subsection (5)(b), the Authority may recover the outstanding amount as a debt due to it.

(10) If all or any of a required payment or distribution has not been made at the end of a period stated in a final notice under subsection (6)(c), the obligation to make the payment is enforceable, on the application of the Authority, by injunction or, in Scotland, by an order under section 45 of the Court of Session Act 1988.

[2388]

Publication

391 Publication

(1) Neither the Authority nor a person to whom a warning notice or decision notice is given or copied may publish the notice or any details concerning it.

(2) A notice of discontinuance must state that, if the person to whom the notice is given consents, the Authority may publish such information as it considers appropriate about the matter to which the discontinued proceedings related.

(3) A copy of a notice of discontinuance must be accompanied by a statement that, if the person to whom the notice is copied consents, the Authority may publish such information as it considers appropriate about the matter to which the discontinued proceedings related, so far as relevant to that person.

(4) The Authority must publish such information about the matter to which a final notice relates as it considers appropriate.

(5) When a supervisory notice takes effect, the Authority must publish such information about the matter to which the notice relates as it considers appropriate.

(6) But the Authority may not publish information under this section if publication of it would, in its opinion, be unfair to the person with respect to whom the action was taken or prejudicial to the interests of consumers.

(7) Information is to be published under this section in such manner as the Authority considers appropriate.

(8) For the purposes of determining when a supervisory notice takes effect, a matter to which the notice relates is open to review if—

(a) the period during which any person may refer the matter to the Tribunal is still running;

(b) the matter has been referred to the Tribunal but has not been dealt with;

(c) the matter has been referred to the Tribunal and dealt with but the period during which an appeal may be brought against the Tribunal's decision is still running; or

(d) such an appeal has been brought but has not been determined.

(9) "Notice of discontinuance" means a notice given under section 389.

(10) "Supervisory notice" has the same meaning as in section 395.

(11) "Consumers" means persons who are consumers for the purposes of section 138.

[2389]

Third party rights and access to evidence

392 Application of sections 393 and 394

Sections 393 and 394 apply to—

(a) a warning notice given in accordance with section 54(1), 57(1), 63(3), 67(1), 88(4)(b), 89(2), 92(1), 126(1), 207(1), 255(1), 280(1), 331(1), 345(2) (whether as a result of subsection (1) of that section or section 249(1)) *or 385(1)*;

(b) a decision notice given in accordance with section 54(2), 57(3), 63(4), 67(4), 88(6)(b), 89(3), 92(4), 127(1), 208(1), 255(2), 280(2), 331(3), 345(3) (whether as a result of subsection (1) of that section or section 249(1)) *or 386(1)*.

[2390]

NOTES

For the words in italics in para (a) there are substituted the words ", 385(1) or 412B(4) or (8)", and for the words in italics in para (b) there are substituted the words ", 386(1) or 412B(5) or (9)", by the Financial Services and Markets Act 2000 (Markets in Financial Instruments) Regulations 2007, SI 2007/126, reg 3(5), Sch 5, paras 1, 16, as from 1 April 2007 (certain purposes (see reg 1(2) at **[7596]**)), and as from 1 November 2007 (otherwise).

393 Third party rights

(1) If any of the reasons contained in a warning notice to which this section applies relates to a matter which—

(a) identifies a person ("the third party") other than the person to whom the notice is given, and

(b) in the opinion of the Authority, is prejudicial to the third party,

a copy of the notice must be given to the third party.

(2) Subsection (1) does not require a copy to be given to the third party if the Authority—

(a) has given him a separate warning notice in relation to the same matter; or

(b) gives him such a notice at the same time as it gives the warning notice which identifies him.

(3) The notice copied to a third party under subsection (1) must specify a reasonable period (which may not be less than 28 days) within which he may make representations to the Authority.

(4) If any of the reasons contained in a decision notice to which this section applies relates to a matter which—

(a) identifies a person ("the third party") other than the person to whom the decision notice is given, and

(b) in the opinion of the Authority, is prejudicial to the third party,

a copy of the notice must be given to the third party.

(5) If the decision notice was preceded by a warning notice, a copy of the decision notice must (unless it has been given under subsection (4)) be given to each person to whom the warning notice was copied.

(6) Subsection (4) does not require a copy to be given to the third party if the Authority—

(a) has given him a separate decision notice in relation to the same matter; or

(b) gives him such a notice at the same time as it gives the decision notice which identifies him.

(7) Neither subsection (1) nor subsection (4) requires a copy of a notice to be given to a third party if the Authority considers it impracticable to do so.

(8) Subsections (9) to (11) apply if the person to whom a decision notice is given has a right to refer the matter to the Tribunal.

(9) A person to whom a copy of the notice is given under this section may refer to the Tribunal—

(a) the decision in question, so far as it is based on a reason of the kind mentioned in subsection (4); or

(b) any opinion expressed by the Authority in relation to him.

(10) The copy must be accompanied by an indication of the third party's right to make a reference under subsection (9) and of the procedure on such a reference.

(11) A person who alleges that a copy of the notice should have been given to him, but was not, may refer to the Tribunal the alleged failure and—

(a) the decision in question, so far as it is based on a reason of the kind mentioned in subsection (4); or

(b) any opinion expressed by the Authority in relation to him.

(12) Section 394 applies to a third party as it applies to the person to whom the notice to which this section applies was given, in so far as the material which the Authority must disclose under that section relates to the matter which identifies the third party.

(13) A copy of a notice given to a third party under this section must be accompanied by a description of the effect of section 394 as it applies to him.

(14) Any person to whom a warning notice or decision notice was copied under this section must be given a copy of a notice of discontinuance applicable to the proceedings to which the warning notice or decision notice related.

[2391]

394 Access to Authority material

(1) If the Authority gives a person ("A") a notice to which this section applies, it must—

(a) allow him access to the material on which it relied in taking the decision which gave rise to the obligation to give the notice;

PART II FSMA 2000

(b) allow him access to any secondary material which, in the opinion of the Authority, might undermine that decision.

(2) But the Authority does not have to allow A access to material under subsection (1) if the material is excluded material or it—

(a) relates to a case involving a person other than A; and
(b) was taken into account by the Authority in A's case only for purposes of comparison with other cases.

(3) The Authority may refuse A access to particular material which it would otherwise have to allow him access to if, in its opinion, allowing him access to the material—

(a) would not be in the public interest; or
(b) would not be fair, having regard to—
(i) the likely significance of the material to A in relation to the matter in respect of which he has been given a notice to which this section applies; and
(ii) the potential prejudice to the commercial interests of a person other than A which would be caused by the material's disclosure.

(4) If the Authority does not allow A access to material because it is excluded material consisting of a protected item, it must give A written notice of—

(a) the existence of the protected item; and
(b) the Authority's decision not to allow him access to it.

(5) If the Authority refuses under subsection (3) to allow A access to material, it must give him written notice of—

(a) the refusal; and
(b) the reasons for it.

(6) "Secondary material" means material, other than material falling within paragraph (a) of subsection (1) which—

(a) was considered by the Authority in reaching the decision mentioned in that paragraph; or
(b) was obtained by the Authority in connection with the matter to which the notice to which this section applies relates but which was not considered by it in reaching that decision.

(7) "Excluded material" means material which—

[(a) is material the disclosure of which for the purposes of or in connection with any legal proceedings is prohibited by section 17 of the Regulation of Investigatory Powers Act 2000; or]
(c) is a protected item (as defined in section 413).

[2392]

NOTES

Sub-s (7): para (a) substituted, for original paras (a), (b), by the Regulation of Investigatory Powers Act 2000, s 82(1), Sch 4, para 11, as from 2 October 2000.

The Authority's procedures

395 The Authority's procedures

(1) The Authority must determine the procedure that it proposes to follow in relation to the giving of—

(a) supervisory notices; and
(b) warning notices and decision notices.

(2) That procedure must be designed to secure, among other things, that the decision which gives rise to the obligation to give any such notice is taken by a person not directly involved in establishing the evidence on which that decision is based.

(3) But the procedure may permit a decision which gives rise to an obligation to give a supervisory notice to be taken by a person other than a person mentioned in subsection (2) if—

(a) the Authority considers that, in the particular case, it is necessary in order to protect the interests of consumers; and
(b) the person taking the decision is of a level of seniority laid down by the procedure.

(4) A level of seniority laid down by the procedure for the purposes of subsection (3)(b) must be appropriate to the importance of the decision.

(5) The Authority must issue a statement of the procedure.

(6) The statement must be published in the way appearing to the Authority to be best calculated to bring it to the attention of the public.

(7) The Authority may charge a reasonable fee for providing a person with a copy of the statement.

(8) The Authority must, without delay, give the Treasury a copy of any statement which it issues under this section.

(9) When giving a supervisory notice, or a warning notice or decision notice, the Authority must follow its stated procedure.

(10) If the Authority changes the procedure in a material way, it must publish a revised statement.

(11) The Authority's failure in a particular case to follow its procedure as set out in the latest published statement does not affect the validity of a notice given in that case.

(12) But subsection (11) does not prevent the Tribunal from taking into account any such failure in considering a matter referred to it.

(13) "Supervisory notice" means a notice given in accordance with section—

(a) 53(4), (7) or (8)(b);
(b) 78(2) or (5);
[(bza) 78A(2) or (8)(b);]
[(ba) 96C;]
[(bb) 87O(2) or (5);]
(c) 197(3), (6) or (7)(b);
(d) 259(3), (8) or (9)(b);
(e) 268(3), (7)(a) or (9)(a) (as a result of subsection (8)(b));
(f) 282(3), (6) or (7)(b);
(g) 321(2) or (5).

[2393]

NOTES

Sub-s (13): para (bza) inserted by the Regulatory Reform (Financial Services and Markets Act 2000) Order 2007, SI 2007/1973, arts 2, 8, as from 12 July 2007; para (ba) inserted by the Financial Services and Markets Act 2000 (Market Abuse) Regulations 2005, SI 2005/381, reg 7, as from 1 July 2005; para (bb) inserted by the Prospectus Regulations 2005, SI 2005/1433, reg 2(1), Sch 1, para 14, as from 1 July 2005.

Open-Ended Investment Companies: this section has effect as if sub-s (13) included a reference to a notice given in accordance with the Open-Ended Investment Companies Regulations 2001, SI 2001/1228, reg 27(3), (8) or (9)(b); see reg 27(15) of the 2001 Regulations.

396 Statements under section 395: consultation

(1) Before issuing a statement of procedure under section 395, the Authority must publish a draft of the proposed statement in the way appearing to the Authority to be best calculated to bring it to the attention of the public.

(2) The draft must be accompanied by notice that representations about the proposal may be made to the Authority within a specified time.

(3) Before issuing the proposed statement of procedure, the Authority must have regard to any representations made to it in accordance with subsection (2).

(4) If the Authority issues the proposed statement of procedure it must publish an account, in general terms, of—

(a) the representations made to it in accordance with subsection (2); and

(b) its response to them.

(5) If the statement of procedure differs from the draft published under subsection (1) in a way which is, in the opinion of the Authority, significant, the Authority must (in addition to complying with subsection (4)) publish details of the difference.

(6) The Authority may charge a reasonable fee for providing a person with a copy of a draft published under subsection (1).

(7) This section also applies to a proposal to revise a statement of policy.

[2394]

PART XXVII
OFFENCES

Miscellaneous offences

397 Misleading statements and practices

(1) This subsection applies to a person who—

(a) makes a statement, promise or forecast which he knows to be misleading, false or deceptive in a material particular;

(b) dishonestly conceals any material facts whether in connection with a statement, promise or forecast made by him or otherwise; or

(c) recklessly makes (dishonestly or otherwise) a statement, promise or forecast which is misleading, false or deceptive in a material particular.

(2) A person to whom subsection (1) applies is guilty of an offence if he makes the statement, promise or forecast or conceals the facts for the purpose of inducing, or is reckless as to whether it may induce, another person (whether or not the person to whom the statement, promise or forecast is made)—

(a) to enter or offer to enter into, or to refrain from entering or offering to enter into, a relevant agreement; or

(b) to exercise, or refrain from exercising, any rights conferred by a relevant investment.

(3) Any person who does any act or engages in any course of conduct which creates a false or misleading impression as to the market in or the price or value of any relevant investments is guilty of an offence if he does so for the purpose of creating that impression and of thereby inducing another person to acquire, dispose of, subscribe for or underwrite those investments or to refrain from doing so or to exercise, or refrain from exercising, any rights conferred by those investments.

(4) In proceedings for an offence under subsection (2) brought against a person to whom subsection (1) applies as a result of paragraph (a) of that subsection, it is a defence for him to show that the statement, promise or forecast was made in conformity with[—

(a) price stabilising rules;

(b) control of information rules; or

(c) the relevant provisions of Commission Regulation (EC) No 2273/2003 of 22 December 2003 implementing Directive 2003/6/EC of the European Parliament and of the Council as regards exemptions for buy-back programmes and stabilisation of financial instruments].

(5) In proceedings brought against any person for an offence under subsection (3) it is a defence for him to show—

(a) that he reasonably believed that his act or conduct would not create an impression that was false or misleading as to the matters mentioned in that subsection;

(b) that he acted or engaged in the conduct—

  (i) for the purpose of stabilising the price of investments; and

  (ii) in conformity with price stabilising rules; …

(c) that he acted or engaged in the conduct in conformity with control of information rules[; or

(d) that he acted or engaged in the conduct in conformity with the relevant provisions of Commission Regulation (EC) No 2273/2003 of 22 December 2003 implementing Directive 2003/6/EC of the European Parliament and of the Council as regards exemptions for buy-back programmes and stabilisation of financial instruments].

(6) Subsections (1) and (2) do not apply unless—

(a) the statement, promise or forecast is made in or from, or the facts are concealed in or from, the United Kingdom or arrangements are made in or from the United Kingdom for the statement, promise or forecast to be made or the facts to be concealed;

(b) the person on whom the inducement is intended to or may have effect is in the United Kingdom; or

(c) the agreement is or would be entered into or the rights are or would be exercised in the United Kingdom.

(7) Subsection (3) does not apply unless—

(a) the act is done, or the course of conduct is engaged in, in the United Kingdom; or

(b) the false or misleading impression is created there.

(8) A person guilty of an offence under this section is liable—

(a) on summary conviction, to imprisonment for a term not exceeding six months or a fine not exceeding the statutory maximum, or both;

(b) on conviction on indictment, to imprisonment for a term not exceeding seven years or a fine, or both.

(9) "Relevant agreement" means an agreement—

(a) the entering into or performance of which by either party constitutes an activity of a specified kind or one which falls within a specified class of activity; and

(b) which relates to a relevant investment.

(10) "Relevant investment" means an investment of a specified kind or one which falls within a prescribed class of investment.

(11) Schedule 2 (except paragraphs 25 and 26) applies for the purposes of subsections (9) and (10) with references to section 22 being read as references to each of those subsections.

(12) Nothing in Schedule 2, as applied by subsection (11), limits the power conferred by subsection (9) or (10).

(13) "Investment" includes any asset, right or interest.

(14) "Specified" means specified in an order made by the Treasury.

[2395]

PART II
FSMA 2000

NOTES

Sub-s (4): words in square brackets substituted by the Financial Services and Markets Act 2000 (Market Abuse) Regulations 2005, SI 2005/381, reg 8(1), (2), as from 17 March 2005.

Sub-s (5): word omitted from para (b) repealed, and para (d) and the word immediately preceding it added, by SI 2005/381, reg 8(1), (3), as from 17 March 2005.

Orders: Financial Services and Markets Act 2000 (Misleading Statements and Practices) Order 2001, SI 2001/3645 at **[4620]**.

Note that the following amending Orders have also been made under this section: the Financial Services and Markets Act 2000 (Commencement of Mortgage Regulation) (Amendment) Order 2002, SI 2002/1777; the Financial Services and Markets Act 2000 (Misleading Statements and Practices) (Amendment) Order 2003, SI 2003/1474.

398 Misleading the Authority: residual cases

(1) A person who, in purported compliance with any requirement imposed by or under this Act, knowingly or recklessly gives the Authority information which is false or misleading in a material particular is guilty of an offence.

(2) Subsection (1) applies only to a requirement in relation to which no other provision of this Act creates an offence in connection with the giving of information.

(3) A person guilty of an offence under this section is liable—

(a) on summary conviction, to a fine not exceeding the statutory maximum;

(b) on conviction on indictment, to a fine.

[2396]

NOTES

Note: for the purposes of this section a requirement imposed by the FSA under the Electronic Commerce Directive (Financial Services and Markets) Regulations 2002, SI 2002/1775 upon an incoming provider is to be treated as imposed on him by or under this Act; see reg 12(2) of those Regulations at **[4650]**.

399 Misleading [the OFT]

Section 44 of the Competition Act 1998 (offences connected with the provision of false or misleading information) applies in relation to any function of [the Office of Fair Trading] under this Act as if it were a function under Part I of that Act.

[2397]

NOTES

Words in square brackets substituted by the Enterprise Act 2002, s 278(1), Sch 25, para 40(1), (16), as from 1 April 2003.

Bodies corporate and partnerships

400 Offences by bodies corporate etc

(1) If an offence under this Act committed by a body corporate is shown—

(a) to have been committed with the consent or connivance of an officer, or

(b) to be attributable to any neglect on his part,

the officer as well as the body corporate is guilty of the offence and liable to be proceeded against and punished accordingly.

(2) If the affairs of a body corporate are managed by its members, subsection (1) applies in relation to the acts and defaults of a member in connection with his functions of management as if he were a director of the body.

(3) If an offence under this Act committed by a partnership is shown—

(a) to have been committed with the consent or connivance of a partner, or

(b) to be attributable to any neglect on his part,

the partner as well as the partnership is guilty of the offence and liable to be proceeded against and punished accordingly.

(4) In subsection (3) "partner" includes a person purporting to act as a partner.

(5) "Officer", in relation to a body corporate, means—

(a) a director, member of the committee of management, chief executive, manager, secretary or other similar officer of the body, or a person purporting to act in any such capacity; and

(b) an individual who is a controller of the body.

(6) If an offence under this Act committed by an unincorporated association (other than a partnership) is shown—

(a) to have been committed with the consent or connivance of an officer of the association or a member of its governing body, or

(b) to be attributable to any neglect on the part of such an officer or member,

that officer or member as well as the association is guilty of the offence and liable to be proceeded against and punished accordingly.

(7) Regulations may provide for the application of any provision of this section, with such modifications as the Treasury consider appropriate, to a body corporate or unincorporated association formed or recognised under the law of a territory outside the United Kingdom.

[2398]

Institution of proceedings

401 Proceedings for offences

(1) In this section "offence" means an offence under this Act or subordinate legislation made under this Act.

(2) Proceedings for an offence may be instituted in England and Wales only—

(a) by the Authority or the Secretary of State; or

(b) by or with the consent of the Director of Public Prosecutions.

(3) Proceedings for an offence may be instituted in Northern Ireland only—

(a) by the Authority or the Secretary of State; or

(b) by or with the consent of the Director of Public Prosecutions for Northern Ireland.

(4) Except in Scotland, proceedings for an offence under section 203 may also be instituted by [the Office of Fair Trading].

(5) In exercising its power to institute proceedings for an offence, the Authority must comply with any conditions or restrictions imposed in writing by the Treasury.

(6) Conditions or restrictions may be imposed under subsection (5) in relation to—

(a) proceedings generally; or

(b) such proceedings, or categories of proceedings, as the Treasury may direct.

[2399]

NOTES

Sub-s (4): words in square brackets substituted by the Enterprise Act 2002, s 278(1), Sch 25, para 40(1), (17), as from 1 April 2003.

Transitional provisions: this section and s 403 have effect as if offences committed before 1 December 2001 under certain provisions (the Insurance Companies Act 1982, the Financial Services Act 1986, the Banking Act 1987, and certain related provisions) were an offence under this Act; see the Financial Services and Markets Act 2000 (Transitional Provisions and Savings) (Civil Remedies, Discipline, Criminal Offences etc) (No 2) Order 2001, SI 2001/3083, art 13. The 1982, 1986 and 1987 Acts were repealed by the Financial Services and Markets Act 2000 (Consequential Amendments and Repeals) Order 2001, SI 2001/3649, art 3(1)(b)–(d).

402 Power of the Authority to institute proceedings for certain other offences

(1) Except in Scotland, the Authority may institute proceedings for an offence under—

(a) Part V of the Criminal Justice Act 1993 (insider dealing); or

(b) prescribed regulations relating to money laundering.

(2) In exercising its power to institute proceedings for any such offence, the Authority must comply with any conditions or restrictions imposed in writing by the Treasury.

(3) Conditions or restrictions may be imposed under subsection (2) in relation to—

(a) proceedings generally; or

(b) such proceedings, or categories of proceedings, as the Treasury may direct.

[2400]

NOTES

Note: the Money Laundering Regulations 2003, SI 2003/3075 have been prescribed for the purposes of sub-s (1)(b) above by reg 1(3) of those Regulations.

Regulations: the Money Laundering Regulations 2003, SI 2003/3075.

403 Jurisdiction and procedure in respect of offences

(1) A fine imposed on an unincorporated association on its conviction of an offence is to be paid out of the funds of the association.

(2) Proceedings for an offence alleged to have been committed by an unincorporated association must be brought in the name of the association (and not in that of any of its members).

(3) Rules of court relating to the service of documents are to have effect as if the association were a body corporate.

(4) In proceedings for an offence brought against an unincorporated association—

(a) section 33 of the Criminal Justice Act 1925 and Schedule 3 to the Magistrates' Courts Act 1980 (procedure) apply as they do in relation to a body corporate;

(b) section 70 of the Criminal Procedure (Scotland) Act 1995 (procedure) applies as if the association were a body corporate;

(c) section 18 of the Criminal Justice (Northern Ireland) Act 1945 and Schedule 4 to the Magistrates' Courts (Northern Ireland) Order 1981 (procedure) apply as they do in relation to a body corporate.

(5) Summary proceedings for an offence may be taken—

(a) against a body corporate or unincorporated association at any place at which it has a place of business;

(b) against an individual at any place where he is for the time being.

(6) Subsection (5) does not affect any jurisdiction exercisable apart from this section.

(7) "Offence" means an offence under this Act.

[2401]

NOTES

Transitional provisions: See the note to s 401 at **[2399]**.

PART XXVIII
MISCELLANEOUS

Schemes for reviewing past business

404 Schemes for reviewing past business

(1) Subsection (2) applies if the Treasury are satisfied that there is evidence suggesting—

(a) that there has been a widespread or regular failure on the part of authorised persons to comply with rules relating to a particular kind of activity; and

(b) that, as a result, private persons have suffered (or will suffer) loss in respect of which authorised persons are (or will be) liable to make payments ("compensation payments").

(2) The Treasury may by order ("a scheme order") authorise the Authority to establish and operate a scheme for—

(a) determining the nature and extent of the failure;

(b) establishing the liability of authorised persons to make compensation payments; and

(c) determining the amounts payable by way of compensation payments.

(3) An authorised scheme must be made so as to comply with specified requirements.

(4) A scheme order may be made only if—

(a) the Authority has given the Treasury a report about the alleged failure and asked them to make a scheme order;

(b) the report contains details of the scheme which the Authority propose to make; and

(c) the Treasury are satisfied that the proposed scheme is an appropriate way of dealing with the failure.

(5) A scheme order may provide for specified provisions of or made under this Act to apply in relation to any provision of, or determination made under, the resulting authorised scheme subject to such modifications (if any) as may be specified.

(6) For the purposes of this Act, failure on the part of an authorised person to comply with any provision of an authorised scheme is to be treated (subject to any provision made by the scheme order concerned) as a failure on his part to comply with rules.

(7) The Treasury may prescribe circumstances in which loss suffered by a person ("A") acting in a fiduciary or other prescribed capacity is to be treated, for the purposes of an authorised scheme, as suffered by a private person in relation to whom A was acting in that capacity.

(8) This section applies whenever the failure in question occurred.

(9) "Authorised scheme" means a scheme authorised by a scheme order.

(10) "Private person" has such meaning as may be prescribed.

(11) "Specified" means specified in a scheme order.

[2402]

NOTES

"Private person": no regulations have been made under sub-s (10). It is not clear whether the definition of "private person" for this section will be the same as may be specified for the purposes of other provisions of this Act; see, for example, s 71 at **[2071]**, and the Financial Services and Markets Act 2000 (Rights of Action) Regulations 2001, SI 2001/2256, reg 3 at **[4397]** (made under s 71(2), (3)).

Transitional provisions: certain transitional provisions were made concerning the pensions mis-selling and FSAVC reviews conducted under FSA 1986 to treat them as a scheme made under this Act; see the Financial Services and Markets Act 2000 (Transitional Provisions) (Reviews of Pensions Business) Order 2001, SI 2001/2512.

Third countries

405 Directions

(1) For the purpose of implementing a third country decision, the Treasury may direct the Authority to—

(a) refuse an application for permission under Part IV made by a body incorporated in, or formed under the law of, any part of the United Kingdom;
(b) defer its decision on such an application either indefinitely or for such period as may be specified in the direction;
(c) give a notice of objection to a person who has served a notice of control to the effect that he proposes to acquire a 50% stake in a UK authorised person; or
(d) give a notice of objection to a person who has acquired a 50% stake in a UK authorised person without having served the required notice of control.

(2) A direction may also be given in relation to—

(a) any person falling within a class specified in the direction;
(b) future applications, notices of control or acquisitions.

(3) The Treasury may revoke a direction at any time.

(4) But revocation does not affect anything done in accordance with the direction before it was revoked.

(5) "Third country decision" means a decision of the Council or the Commission under—

(a) Article 7(5) of the investment services directive;
(b) …
(c) Article 29b(4) of the first non-life insurance directive; or
[(d) Article 59(4) of the life assurance consolidation directive.]

[2403]

NOTES

Sub-s (5): para (b) repealed by the Capital Requirements Regulations 2006, SI 2006/3221, reg 29(1), Sch 3, para 1, as from 1 January 2007; para (d) substituted by the Life Assurance Consolidation Directive (Consequential Amendments) Regulations 2004, SI 2004/3379, reg 6(1), (4), as from 11 January 2005; para (a) substituted by the Financial Services and Markets Act 2000 (Markets in Financial Instruments) Regulations 2007, SI 2007/126, reg 3(5), Sch 5, paras 1, 17, as from 1 April 2007 (certain purposes (see reg 1(2) at **[7596]**)), and as from 1 November 2007 (otherwise), as follows—

"(a) Article 15(3) of the markets in financial instruments directive;".

406 Interpretation of section 405

(1) For the purposes of section 405, a person ("the acquirer") acquires a 50% stake in a UK authorised person ("A") on first falling within any of the cases set out in subsection (2).

(2) The cases are where the acquirer—

(a) holds 50% or more of the shares in A;
(b) holds 50% or more of the shares in a parent undertaking ("P") of A;
(c) is entitled to exercise, or control the exercise of, 50% or more of the voting power in A; or
(d) is entitled to exercise, or control the exercise of, 50% or more of the voting power in P.

(3) In subsection (2) "the acquirer" means—

(a) the acquirer;
(b) any of the acquirer's associates; or
(c) the acquirer and any of his associates.

(4) "Associate", "shares" and "voting power" have the same meaning as in section 422.

[2404]

407 Consequences of a direction under section 405

(1) If the Authority refuses an application for permission as a result of a direction under section 405(1)(a)—

(a) subsections (7) to (9) of section 52 do not apply in relation to the refusal; but
(b) the Authority must notify the applicant of the refusal and the reasons for it.

(2) If the Authority defers its decision on an application for permission as a result of a direction under section 405(1)(b)—

(a) the time limit for determining the application mentioned in section 52(1) or (2) stops running on the day of the deferral and starts running again (if at all) on the day the period specified in the direction (if any) ends or the day the direction is revoked; and
(b) the Authority must notify the applicant of the deferral and the reasons for it.

(3) If the Authority gives a notice of objection to a person as a result of a direction under section 405(1)(c) or (d)—

(a) sections 189 and 191 have effect as if the notice was a notice of objection within the meaning of Part XII; and
(b) the Authority must state in the notice the reasons for it.

[2405]

408 EFTA firms

(1) If a third country decision has been taken, the Treasury may make a determination in relation to an EFTA firm which is a subsidiary undertaking of a parent undertaking which is governed by the law of the country to which the decision relates.

(2) "Determination" means a determination that the firm concerned does not qualify for authorisation under Schedule 3 even if it satisfies the conditions in paragraph 13 or 14 of that Schedule.

(3) A determination may also be made in relation to any firm falling within a class specified in the determination.

(4) The Treasury may withdraw a determination at any time.

(5) But withdrawal does not affect anything done in accordance with the determination before it was withdrawn.

(6) If the Treasury make a determination in respect of a particular firm, or withdraw such a determination, they must give written notice to that firm.

(7) The Treasury must publish notice of any determination (or the withdrawal of any determination)—

(a) in such a way as they think most suitable for bringing the determination (or withdrawal) to the attention of those likely to be affected by it; and
(b) on, or as soon as practicable after, the date of the determination (or withdrawal).

(8) "EFTA firm" means a firm, institution or undertaking which—

(a) is an EEA firm as a result of paragraph 5(a), (b) or (d) of Schedule 3; and
(b) is incorporated in, or formed under the law of, an EEA State which is not a member State.

(9) "Third country decision" has the same meaning as in section 405.

[2406]

409 Gibraltar

(1) The Treasury may by order—

(a) modify Schedule 3 so as to provide for Gibraltar firms of a specified description to qualify for authorisation under that Schedule in specified circumstances;
(b) modify Schedule 3 so as to make provision in relation to the exercise by UK firms of rights under the law of Gibraltar which correspond to EEA rights;
(c) modify Schedule 4 so as to provide for Gibraltar firms of a specified description to qualify for authorisation under that Schedule in specified circumstances;
(d) modify section 264 so as to make provision in relation to collective investment schemes constituted under the law of Gibraltar;
(e) provide for the Authority to be able to give notice under section 264(2) on grounds relating to the law of Gibraltar;

(f) provide for this Act to apply to a Gibraltar recognised scheme as if the scheme were a scheme recognised under section 264.

(2) The fact that a firm may qualify for authorisation under Schedule 3 as a result of an order under subsection (1) does not prevent it from applying for a Part IV permission.

(3) "Gibraltar firm" means a firm which has its head office in Gibraltar or is otherwise connected with Gibraltar.

(4) "Gibraltar recognised scheme" means a collective investment scheme—

(a) constituted in an EEA State other than the United Kingdom, and

(b) recognised in Gibraltar under provisions which appear to the Treasury to give effect to the provisions of a relevant Community instrument.

(5) "Specified" means specified in the order.

(6) "UK firm" and "EEA right" have the same meaning as in Schedule 3.

[2407]

NOTES

Orders: the Financial Services and Markets Act 2000 (Gibraltar) Order 2001, SI 2001/3084 at **[4504]**.

Note that the following amending Orders have also been made under this section: the Financial Services and Markets Act 2000 (Gibraltar) (Amendment) Order 2005, SI 2005/1; the Financial Services and Markets Act 2000 (Gibraltar) (Amendment) Order 2006, SI 2006/1805.

International obligations

410 International obligations

(1) If it appears to the Treasury that any action proposed to be taken by a relevant person would be incompatible with Community obligations or any other international obligations of the United Kingdom, they may direct that person not to take that action.

(2) If it appears to the Treasury that any action which a relevant person has power to take is required for the purpose of implementing any such obligations, they may direct that person to take that action.

(3) A direction under this section—

(a) may include such supplemental or incidental requirements as the Treasury consider necessary or expedient; and

(b) is enforceable, on an application made by the Treasury, by injunction or, in Scotland, by an order for specific performance under section 45 of the Court of Session Act 1988.

(4) "Relevant person" means—

(a) the Authority;

(b) any person exercising functions conferred by Part VI on the competent authority;

(c) any recognised investment exchange (other than one which is an overseas investment exchange);

(d) any recognised clearing house (other than one which is an overseas clearing house);

(e) a person included in the list maintained under section 301; or

(f) the scheme operator of the ombudsman scheme.

[2408]

411 (*Sub-s* (*1*) *repealed by the Financial Services and Markets Act 2000* (*Consequential Amendments*) (*Taxes*) *Order 2001, SI 2001/3629, art 109, Schedule, as from 1 December 2001; sub-s* (*2*) *inserts the Income and Corporations Taxes Act 1988, ss 76A, 76B.*)

Gaming contracts

412 Gaming contracts

(1) No contract to which this section applies is void or unenforceable because of—

(a) *section 18 of the Gaming Act 1845, section 1 of the Gaming Act 1892 or* Article 170 of the Betting, Gaming, Lotteries and Amusements (Northern Ireland) Order 1985; or (*b*) *any rule of the law of Scotland under which a contract by way of gaming or wagering is not legally enforceable.*

(2) This section applies to a contract if—

(a) it is entered into by either or each party by way of business;

(b) the entering into or performance of it by either party constitutes an activity of a specified kind or one which falls within a specified class of activity; and

(c) it relates to an investment of a specified kind or one which falls within a specified class of investment.

(3) Part II of Schedule 2 applies for the purposes of subsection (2)(c), with the references to section 22 being read as references to that subsection.

(4) Nothing in Part II of Schedule 2, as applied by subsection (3), limits the power conferred by subsection (2)(c).

(5) "Investment" includes any asset, right or interest.

(6) "Specified" means specified in an order made by the Treasury.

[2409]

NOTES

Sub-s (1): words in italics in para (a), and the whole of para (b), repealed by the Gambling Act 2005, ss 334(1)(e), 356, (2), Sch 17, as from 1 September 2007 (and this repeal does not permit enforcement of a right which is created, or which emanates from an agreement made, before that date).

Gaming Act 1845, s 18; Gaming Act 1892, s 1: repealed by the Gambling Act 2005, ss 334(1)(c), (d), 356(3)(d), (e), (4), Sch 17, as from 1 September 2007.

Orders: the Financial Services and Markets Act 2000 (Gaming Contracts) Order 2001, SI 2001/2510 at **[4446]**.

[Trade-matching and reporting systems

412A Approval and monitoring of trade-matching and reporting systems

(1) A relevant system is an approved relevant system if it is approved by the Authority under subsection (2) for the purposes of Article 25.5 of the markets in financial instruments directive; and references in this section and section 412B to an "approved relevant system" are to be read accordingly.

(2) The Authority must approve a relevant system if, on an application by the operator of the system, it is satisfied that the arrangements established by the system for reporting transactions comply with Article 12(1) of Commission Regulation 1287/2006 of 10 August 2006 ("the Regulation").

(3) Section 51(3) and (4) applies to an application under this section as it applies to an application under Part 4.

(4) If, at any time after approving a relevant system under subsection (2), the Authority is not satisfied as mentioned in that subsection, it may suspend or withdraw the approval.

(5) The Authority must keep under review the arrangements established by an approved relevant system for reporting transactions for the purpose of ensuring that the arrangements comply with Article 12(1) of the Regulation; and for the purposes of this subsection the Authority must have regard to information provided to it under subsections (6) and (7).

(6) The operator of an approved relevant system must make reports to the Authority at specified intervals containing specified information relating to—

(a) the system,

(b) the reports made by the system in accordance with Article 25 of the markets in financial instruments directive and the Regulation, and

(c) the transactions to which those reports relate.

"Specified" means specified by the Authority.

(7) The Authority may by written notice require the operator of an approved relevant system to provide such additional information as may be specified in the notice, by such reasonable time as may be so specified, about any of the matters mentioned in subsection (6).

(8) The recipient of a notice under subsection (7) must provide the information by the time specified in the notice.

(9) In this section and section 412B, "relevant system" means a trade-matching or reporting system of a kind described in Article 12 of the Regulation.]

[2409A]

NOTES

Commencement: see the note below.

Inserted, together with the preceding heading and s 412B, by the Financial Services and Markets Act 2000 (Markets in Financial Instruments) Regulations 2007, SI 2007/126, reg 3(5), Sch 5, paras 1, 18, as from 1 April 2007 (certain purposes (see reg 1(2) at **[7596]**)), and as from 1 November 2007 (otherwise).

[412B Procedure for approval and suspension or withdrawal of approval

(1) If the Authority approves a relevant system, it must give the operator of the system written notice specifying the date from which the approval has effect.

(2) If the Authority proposes to refuse to approve a relevant system, it must give the operator of the system a warning notice.

(3) If the Authority decides to refuse to approve a relevant system, it must give the operator of the system a decision notice.

(4) If the Authority proposes to suspend or withdraw its approval in relation to an approved relevant system, it must give the operator of the system a warning notice.

(5) If the Authority decides to suspend or withdraw its approval in relation to an approved relevant system, it must give the operator of the system a decision notice specifying the date from which the suspension or withdrawal is to take effect.

(6) Subsections (7) to (9) apply if—

(a) the Authority has suspended its approval in relation to an approved relevant system, and

(b) the operator of the system has applied for the suspension to be cancelled.

(7) The Authority must grant the application if it is satisfied as mentioned in section 412A(2); and in such a case the Authority must give written notice to the operator that the suspension is to be cancelled from the date specified in the notice.

(8) If the Authority proposes to refuse the application, it must give the operator a warning notice.

(9) If the Authority decides to refuse the application, it must give the operator a decision notice.

(10) A person who receives a decision notice under subsection (3), (5) or (9) may refer the matter to the Tribunal.]

[2409A]

NOTES

Commencement: see the note below.

Inserted, together with s 412A, by the Financial Services and Markets Act 2000 (Markets in Financial Instruments) Regulations 2007, SI 2007/126, reg 3(5), Sch 5, paras 1, 18, as from 1 April 2007 (certain purposes (see reg 1(2) at **[7596]**)), and as from 1 November 2007 (otherwise).

Limitation on powers to require documents

413 Protected items

(1) A person may not be required under this Act to produce, disclose or permit the inspection of protected items.

(2) "Protected items" means—

(a) communications between a professional legal adviser and his client or any person representing his client which fall within subsection (3);

(b) communications between a professional legal adviser, his client or any person representing his client and any other person which fall within subsection (3) (as a result of paragraph (b) of that subsection);

(c) items which—

PART II FSMA 2000

(i) are enclosed with, or referred to in, such communications;
(ii) fall within subsection (3); and
(iii) are in the possession of a person entitled to possession of them.

(3) A communication or item falls within this subsection if it is made—

(a) in connection with the giving of legal advice to the client; or
(b) in connection with, or in contemplation of, legal proceedings and for the purposes of those proceedings.

(4) A communication or item is not a protected item if it is held with the intention of furthering a criminal purpose.

[2410]

Service of notices

414 Service of notices

(1) The Treasury may by regulations make provision with respect to the procedure to be followed, or rules to be applied, when a provision of or made under this Act requires a notice, direction or document of any kind to be given or authorises the imposition of a requirement.

(2) The regulations may, in particular, make provision—

(a) as to the manner in which a document must be given;
(b) as to the address to which a document must be sent;
(c) requiring, or allowing, a document to be sent electronically;
(d) for treating a document as having been given, or as having been received, on a date or at a time determined in accordance with the regulations;
(e) as to what must, or may, be done if the person to whom a document is required to be given is not an individual;
(f) as to what must, or may, be done if the intended recipient of a document is outside the United Kingdom.

(3) Subsection (1) applies however the obligation to give a document is expressed (and so, in particular, includes a provision which requires a document to be served or sent).

(4) Section 7 of the Interpretation Act 1978 (service of notice by post) has effect in relation to provisions made by or under this Act subject to any provision made by regulations under this section.

[2411]

NOTES

Regulations: the Financial Services and Markets Act 2000 (Service of Notices) Regulations 2001, SI 2001/1420 at **[4351]**; the Electronic Commerce Directive (Financial Services and Markets) Regulations 2002, SI 2002/1775 at **[4639]**.

Note that the following amending Regulations have also been made under this section: the Financial Services and Markets Act 2000 (Service of Notices) (Amendment) Regulations 2005, SI 2005/274.

Jurisdiction

415 Jurisdiction in civil proceedings

(1) Proceedings arising out of any act or omission (or proposed act or omission) of—

(a) the Authority,
(b) the competent authority for the purposes of Part VI,
(c) the scheme manager, or
(d) the scheme operator,

in the discharge or purported discharge of any of its functions under this Act may be brought before the High Court or the Court of Session.

(2) The jurisdiction conferred by subsection (1) is in addition to any other jurisdiction exercisable by those courts.

[2412]

Removal of certain unnecessary provisions

416 Provisions relating to industrial assurance and certain other enactments

(1) The following enactments are to cease to have effect—
(a) the Industrial Assurance Act 1923;
(b) the Industrial Assurance and Friendly Societies Act 1948;
(c) the Insurance Brokers (Registration) Act 1977.

(2) The Industrial Assurance (Northern Ireland) Order 1979 is revoked.

(3) The following bodies are to cease to exist—
(a) the Insurance Brokers Registration Council;
(b) the Policyholders Protection Board;
(c) the Deposit Protection Board;
(d) the Board of Banking Supervision.

(4) If the Treasury consider that, as a consequence of any provision of this section, it is appropriate to do so, they may by order make any provision of a kind that they could make under this Act (and in particular any provision of a kind mentioned in section 339) with respect to anything done by or under any provision of Part XXI.

(5) Subsection (4) is not to be read as affecting in any way any other power conferred on the Treasury by this Act.

[2413]

NOTES

Orders: the Financial Services and Markets Act 2000 (Dissolution of the Insurance Brokers Registration Council) (Consequential Provisions) Order 2001, SI 2001/1283; the Financial Services and Markets Act 2000 (Transitional Provisions, Repeals and Savings) (Financial Services Compensation Scheme) Order 2001, SI 2001/2967; the Financial Services and Markets Act 2000 (Consequential Amendments and Savings) (Industrial Assurance) Order 2001, SI 2001/3647.

Note that the following amending Orders have also been made under this section: the Financial Services and Markets Act 2000 (Consequential Amendments) Order 2002, SI 2002/1555.

PART XXIX
INTERPRETATION

417 Definitions

(1) In this Act—

"appointed representative" has the meaning given in section 39(2);

"auditors and actuaries rules" means rules made under section 340;

"authorisation offence" has the meaning given in section 23(2);

"authorised open-ended investment company" has the meaning given in section 237(3);

"authorised person" has the meaning given in section 31(2);

"the Authority" means the Financial Services Authority;

"body corporate" includes a body corporate constituted under the law of a country or territory outside the United Kingdom;

"chief executive"—
(a) in relation to a body corporate whose principal place of business is within the United Kingdom, means an employee of that body who, alone or jointly with one or more others, is responsible under the immediate authority of the directors, for the conduct of the whole of the business of that body; and
(b) in relation to a body corporate whose principal place of business is outside the United Kingdom, means the person who, alone or jointly with one or more others, is responsible for the conduct of its business within the United Kingdom;

"collective investment scheme" has the meaning given in section 235;

"the Commission" means the European Commission (except in provisions relating to the Competition Commission);

"the compensation scheme" has the meaning given in section 213(2);

"control of information rules" has the meaning given in section 147(1);

"director", in relation to a body corporate, includes—
(a) a person occupying in relation to it the position of a director (by whatever name called); and

(b) a person in accordance with whose directions or instructions (not being advice given in a professional capacity) the directors of that body are accustomed to act;

"documents" includes information recorded in any form and, in relation to information recorded otherwise than in legible form, references to its production include references to producing a copy of the information in legible form[, or in a form from which it can readily be produced in visible and legible form];

["electronic commerce directive" means Directive 2000/31/EC of the European Parliament and the Council of 8 June 2000 on certain legal aspects of information society services, in particular electronic commerce, in the Internal Market (Directive on electronic commerce);]

"exempt person", in relation to a regulated activity, means a person who is exempt from the general prohibition in relation to that activity as a result of an exemption order made under section 38(1) or as a result of section 39(1) or 285(2) or (3);

"financial promotion rules" means rules made under section 145;

"friendly society" means an incorporated or registered friendly society;

"general prohibition" has the meaning given in section 19(2);

"general rules" has the meaning given in section 138(2);

"incorporated friendly society" means a society incorporated under the Friendly Societies Act 1992;

"industrial and provident society" means a society registered or deemed to be registered under the Industrial and Provident Societies Act 1965 or the Industrial and Provident Societies Act (Northern Ireland) 1969;

["information society service" means an information society service within the meaning of Article 2(a) of the electronic commerce directive;]

["investment services and activities" has the meaning given in Article 4.1.2 of the markets in financial instruments directive, read with—

(a) Chapter VI of Commission Regulation 1287/2006 of 10 August 2006, and

(b) Article 52 of Commission Directive 2006/73/EC of 10 August 2006;]

"market abuse" has the meaning given in section 118;

"Minister of the Crown" has the same meaning as in the Ministers of the Crown Act 1975;

"money laundering rules" means rules made under section 146;

"notice of control" [(except in Chapter 1A of Part 18)] has the meaning given in section 178(5);

"the ombudsman scheme" has the meaning given in section 225(3);

"open-ended investment company" has the meaning given in section 236;

"Part IV permission" has the meaning given in section 40(4);

"partnership" includes a partnership constituted under the law of a country or territory outside the United Kingdom;

"prescribed" (where not otherwise defined) means prescribed in regulations made by the Treasury;

"price stabilising rules" means rules made under section 144;

"private company" has the meaning given in section 1(3) of the Companies Act 1985 or in Article 12(3) of the Companies (Northern Ireland) Order 1986;

"prohibition order" has the meaning given in section 56(2);

"recognised clearing house" and "recognised investment exchange" have the meaning given in section 285;

"registered friendly society" means a society which is—

(a) a friendly society within the meaning of section 7(1)(a) of the Friendly Societies Act 1974; and

(b) registered within the meaning of that Act;

"regulated activity" has the meaning given in section 22;

"regulating provisions" has the meaning given in section 159(1);

"regulatory objectives" means the objectives mentioned in section 2;

"regulatory provisions" has the meaning given in section 302;

"rule" means a rule made by the Authority under this Act;

"rule-making instrument" has the meaning given in section 153;

"the scheme manager" has the meaning given in section 212(1);

"the scheme operator" has the meaning given in section 225(2);

"scheme particulars rules" has the meaning given in section 248(1);

"Seventh Company Law Directive" means the European Council Seventh Company Law Directive of 13 June 1983 on consolidated accounts (No 83/349/EEC);

["Takeovers Directive" means Directive 2004/25/EC of the European Parliament and of the Council;]

"threshold conditions", in relation to a regulated activity, has the meaning given in section 41;
"the Treaty" means the treaty establishing the European Community;
"trust scheme rules" has the meaning given in section 247(1);
"UK authorised person" has the meaning given in section 178(4); and
"unit trust scheme" has the meaning given in section 237.

(2) In the application of this Act to Scotland, references to a matter being actionable at the suit of a person are to be read as references to the matter being actionable at the instance of that person.

(3) For the purposes of any provision of this Act [(other than a provision of Part 6)] authorising or requiring a person to do anything within a specified number of days no account is to be taken of any day which is a public holiday in any part of the United Kingdom.

[(4) For the purposes of this Act—
(a) an information society service is provided from an EEA State if it is provided from an establishment in that State;
(b) an establishment, in connection with an information society service, is the place at which the provider of the service (being a national of an EEA State or a company or firm as mentioned in Article 48 of the Treaty) effectively pursues an economic activity for an indefinite period;
(c) the presence or use in a particular place of equipment or other technical means of providing an information society service does not, of itself, constitute that place as an establishment of the kind mentioned in paragraph (b);
(d) where it cannot be determined from which of a number of establishments a given information society service is provided, that service is to be regarded as provided from the establishment where the provider has the centre of his activities relating to the service.]

[2414]

PART II
FSMA 2000

NOTES

Sub-s (1): words in square brackets in definition "documents" inserted by the Criminal Justice and Police Act 2001, s 70, Sch 2, Pt 2, para 16(1), (2)(f), as from 1 April 2003; definitions "electronic commerce directive" and "information society service" inserted by the Electronic Commerce Directive (Financial Services and Markets) Regulations 2002, SI 2002/1775, reg 13(1), (2)(a), (b) as from 21 August 2002; definition "investment services and activities" inserted, and words in square brackets in definition "notice of control" inserted, by the Financial Services and Markets Act 2000 (Markets in Financial Instruments) Regulations 2007, SI 2007/126, reg 3(5), Sch 5, paras 1, 19, as from 1 April 2007 (certain purposes (see reg 1(2) at **[7596]**)), and as from 1 November 2007 (otherwise); definition "Takeovers Directive" inserted by the Companies Act 2006, s 964(1), (6), as from 6 April 2007.

Sub-s (3): words in square brackets inserted by the Prospectus Regulations 2005, SI 2005/1433, reg 2(1), Sch 1, para 15, as from 1 July 2005.

Sub-s (4): added by SI 2002/1775, reg 13(1), (2)(c), as from 21 August 2002.

Seventh Company Law Directive (83/349/EEC): OJ L193 18.7.1983 p 1.

418 Carrying on regulated activities in the United Kingdom

(1) In the [five] cases described in this section, a person who—
(a) is carrying on a regulated activity, but
(b) would not otherwise be regarded as carrying it on in the United Kingdom,

is, for the purposes of this Act, to be regarded as carrying it on in the United Kingdom.

(2) The first case is where—
(a) his registered office (or if he does not have a registered office his head office) is in the United Kingdom;
(b) he is entitled to exercise rights under a single market directive as a UK firm; and
(c) he is carrying on in another EEA State a regulated activity to which that directive applies.

(3) The second case is where—
(a) his registered office (or if he does not have a registered office his head office) is in the United Kingdom;
(b) he is the manager of a scheme which is entitled to enjoy the rights conferred by an instrument which is a relevant Community instrument for the purposes of section 264; and
(c) persons in another EEA State are invited to become participants in the scheme.

(4) The third case is where—

(a) his registered office (or if he does not have a registered office his head office) is in the United Kingdom;

(b) the day-to-day management of the carrying on of the regulated activity is the responsibility of—

(i) his registered office (or head office); or

(ii) another establishment maintained by him in the United Kingdom.

(5) The fourth case is where—

(a) his head office is not in the United Kingdom; but

(b) the activity is carried on from an establishment maintained by him in the United Kingdom.

[(5A) The fifth case is any other case where the activity—

(a) consists of the provision of an information society service to a person or persons in one or more EEA States; and

(b) is carried on from an establishment in the United Kingdom.]

(6) For the purposes of subsections (2) to [(5A)] it is irrelevant where the person with whom the activity is carried on is situated.

[2415]

NOTES

Sub-s (1): word in square brackets substituted by the Electronic Commerce Directive (Financial Services and Markets) Regulations 2002, SI 2002/1775, reg 13(1), (3)(a), as from 21 August 2002.

Sub-s (5A): inserted by SI 2002/1775, reg 13(1), (3)(b), as from 21 August 2002.

Sub-s (6): number in square brackets substituted by SI 2002/1775, reg 13(1), (3)(c), as from 21 August 2002.

419 Carrying on regulated activities by way of business

(1) The Treasury may by order make provision—

(a) as to the circumstances in which a person who would otherwise not be regarded as carrying on a regulated activity by way of business is to be regarded as doing so;

(b) as to the circumstances in which a person who would otherwise be regarded as carrying on a regulated activity by way of business is to be regarded as not doing so.

(2) An order under subsection (1) may be made so as to apply—

(a) generally in relation to all regulated activities;

(b) in relation to a specified category of regulated activity; or

(c) in relation to a particular regulated activity.

(3) An order under subsection (1) may be made so as to apply—

(a) for the purposes of all provisions;

(b) for a specified group of provisions; or

(c) for a specified provision.

(4) "Provision" means a provision of, or made under, this Act.

(5) Nothing in this section is to be read as affecting the provisions of section 428(3).

[2416]

NOTES

Orders: the Financial Services and Markets Act 2000 (Carrying on Regulated Activities by Way of Business) Order 2001, SI 2001/1177 at **[4145]**.

Note that the following amending Orders have also been made under this section: the Financial Services and Markets Act 2000 (Carrying on Regulated Activities by Way of Business) (Amendment) Order 2005, SI 2005/922.

420 Parent and subsidiary undertaking

(1) In this Act, except in relation to an incorporated friendly society, "parent undertaking" and "subsidiary undertaking" have the same meaning as in Part VII of the Companies Act 1985 (or Part VIII of the Companies (Northern Ireland) Order 1986).

(2) But—

(a) "parent undertaking" also includes an individual who would be a parent undertaking for the purposes of those provisions if he were taken to be an undertaking (and "subsidiary undertaking" is to be read accordingly);

(b) "subsidiary undertaking" also includes, in relation to a body incorporated in or formed under the law of an EEA State other than the United Kingdom, an undertaking which is a subsidiary undertaking within the meaning of any rule of law in force in that State for purposes connected with implementation of the Seventh Company Law Directive (and "parent undertaking" is to be read accordingly).

(3) In this Act "subsidiary undertaking", in relation to an incorporated friendly society, means a body corporate of which the society has control within the meaning of section 13(9)(a) or (aa) of the Friendly Societies Act 1992 (and "parent undertaking" is to be read accordingly).

[2417]

421 Group

(1) In this Act "group", in relation to a person ("A"), means A and any person who is—

(a) a parent undertaking of A;
(b) a subsidiary undertaking of A;
(c) a subsidiary undertaking of a parent undertaking of A;
(d) a parent undertaking of a subsidiary undertaking of A;
(e) an undertaking in which A or an undertaking mentioned in paragraph (a), (b), (c) or (d) has a participating interest;
(f) if A or an undertaking mentioned in paragraph (a) or (d) is a building society, an associated undertaking of the society; or
(g) if A or an undertaking mentioned in paragraph (a) or (d) is an incorporated friendly society, a body corporate of which the society has joint control (within the meaning of section 13(9)(c) or (cc) of the Friendly Societies Act 1992).

(2) "Participating interest" has the same meaning as in Part VII of the Companies Act 1985 or Part VIII of the Companies (Northern Ireland) Order 1986; but also includes an interest held by an individual which would be a participating interest for the purposes of those provisions if he were taken to be an undertaking.

(3) "Associated undertaking" has the meaning given in section 119(1) of the Building Societies Act 1986.

[2418]

422 Controller

(1) In this Act[, except in Chapter 1A of Part 18,] "controller", in relation to an undertaking ("A"), means a person who falls within any of the cases in subsection (2).

(2) The cases are where the person—

(a) holds 10% or more of the shares in A;
(b) is able to exercise significant influence over the management of A by virtue of his shareholding in A;
(c) holds 10% or more of the shares in a parent undertaking ("P") of A;
(d) is able to exercise significant influence over the management of P by virtue of his shareholding in P;
(e) is entitled to exercise, or control the exercise of, 10% or more of the voting power in A;
(f) is able to exercise significant influence over the management of A by virtue of his voting power in A;
(g) is entitled to exercise, or control the exercise of, 10% or more of the voting power in P; or
(h) is able to exercise significant influence over the management of P by virtue of his voting power in P.

(3) In subsection (2) "the person" means—

(a) the person;
(b) any of the person's associates; or
(c) the person and any of his associates.

(4) "Associate", in relation to a person ("H") holding shares in an undertaking ("C") or entitled to exercise or control the exercise of voting power in relation to another undertaking ("D"), means—

PART II
FSMA 2000

(a) the spouse [or civil partner] of H;
(b) a child or stepchild of H (if under 18);
(c) the trustee of any settlement under which H has a life interest in possession (or in Scotland a life interest);
(d) an undertaking of which H is a director;
(e) a person who is an employee or partner of H;
(f) if H is an undertaking—
  (i) a director of H;
  (ii) a subsidiary undertaking of H;
  (iii) a director or employee of such a subsidiary undertaking; and
(g) if H has with any other person an agreement or arrangement with respect to the acquisition, holding or disposal of shares or other interests in C or D or under which they undertake to act together in exercising their voting power in relation to C or D, that other person.

(5) "Settlement", in subsection (4)(c), includes any disposition or arrangement under which property is held on trust (or subject to a comparable obligation).

(6) "Shares"—
(a) in relation to an undertaking with a share capital, means allotted shares;
(b) in relation to an undertaking with capital but no share capital, means rights to share in the capital of the undertaking;
(c) in relation to an undertaking without capital, means interests—
  (i) conferring any right to share in the profits, or liability to contribute to the losses, of the undertaking; or
  (ii) giving rise to an obligation to contribute to the debts or expenses of the undertaking in the event of a winding up.

(7) "Voting power", in relation to an undertaking which does not have general meetings at which matters are decided by the exercise of voting rights, means the right under the constitution of the undertaking to direct the overall policy of the undertaking or alter the terms of its constitution.

[2419]

NOTES

Sub-s (1): words in square brackets inserted by the Financial Services and Markets Act 2000 (Markets in Financial Instruments) Regulations 2007, SI 2007/126, reg 3(5), Sch 5, paras 1, 20, as from 1 April 2007 (certain purposes (see reg 1(2) at **[7596]**)), and as from 1 November 2007 (otherwise).

Sub-s (4): words in square brackets inserted by the Civil Partnership Act 2004, s 261(1), Sch 27, para 165, as from 5 December 2005.

Stepchild: this includes relationships arising through civil partnerships; see the Civil Partnership Act 2004, ss 246, 247, Sch 21.

423 Manager

(1) In this Act, except in relation to a unit trust scheme or a registered friendly society, "manager" means an employee who—
(a) under the immediate authority of his employer is responsible, either alone or jointly with one or more other persons, for the conduct of his employer's business; or
(b) under the immediate authority of his employer or of a person who is a manager by virtue of paragraph (a) exercises managerial functions or is responsible for maintaining accounts or other records of his employer.

(2) If the employer is not an individual, references in subsection (1) to the authority of the employer are references to the authority—
(a) in the case of a body corporate, of the directors;
(b) in the case of a partnership, of the partners; and
(c) in the case of an unincorporated association, of its officers or the members of its governing body.

(3) "Manager", in relation to a body corporate, means a person (other than an employee of the body) who is appointed by the body to manage any part of its business and includes an employee of the body corporate (other than the chief executive) who, under the immediate authority of a director or chief executive of the body corporate, exercises managerial functions or is responsible for maintaining accounts or other records of the body corporate.

[2420]

424 Insurance

(1) In this Act, references to—

(a) contracts of insurance,

(b) reinsurance,

(c) contracts of long-term insurance,

(d) contracts of general insurance,

are to be read with section 22 and Schedule 2.

(2) In this Act "policy" and "policyholder", in relation to a contract of insurance, have such meaning as the Treasury may by order specify.

(3) The law applicable to a contract of insurance, the effecting of which constitutes the carrying on of a regulated activity, is to be determined, if it is of a prescribed description, in accordance with regulations made by the Treasury.

[2421]

NOTES

Regulations: the Financial Services and Markets Act 2000 (Law Applicable to Contracts of Insurance) Regulations 2001, SI 2001/2635.

Orders: the Financial Services and Markets Act 2000 (Meaning of "Policy" and "Policyholder") Order 2001, SI 2001/2361 at **[4402]**.

Note that the following amending Regulations have also been made under this section: the Financial Services and Markets Act 2000 (Law Applicable to Contracts of Insurance) (Amendment) Regulations 2001, SI 2001/3542.

[424A Investment firm

(1) In this Act, "investment firm" has the meaning given in Article 4.1.1 of the markets in financial instruments directive.

(2) Subsection (1) is subject to subsections (3) to (5).

(3) References in this Act to an "investment firm" include references to a person who would be an investment firm (within the meaning of Article 4.1.1 of the markets in financial instruments directive) if—

(a) his registered office, or

(b) in the case of an individual or a body corporate with no registered office, his head office,

were in an EEA State.

(4) But subsection (3) does not apply if the person in question is one to whom the markets in financial instruments directive would not apply by virtue of Article 2 of that directive.

(5) References in this Act to an "investment firm" do not include references to—

(a) a person to whom the markets in financial instruments directive does not apply by virtue of Article 2 of the directive; or

(b) a person whose home Member State (within the meaning of Article 4.1.20 of the markets in financial instruments directive) is an EEA State and to whom, by reason of the fact that the State has given effect to Article 3 of that directive, that directive does not apply by virtue of that Article.]

[2421A]

NOTES

Commencement: 6 December 2006.

Inserted by the Financial Services and Markets Act 2000 (Markets in Financial Instruments) (Modification of Powers) Regulations 2006, SI 2006/2975, regs 2, 10, as from 6 December 2006.

Sub-s (3): substituted by the Financial Services and Markets Act 2000 (Markets in Financial Instruments) Regulations 2007, SI 2007/126, reg 3(5), Sch 5, paras 1, 21, as from 1 April 2007 (certain purposes (see reg 1(2) at **[7596]**)), and as from 1 November 2007 (otherwise), as follows—

"(3) References in this Act to an "investment firm" include references to a person who would be an investment firm (within the meaning of Article 4.1.1 of the markets in financial instruments directive) if—

(a) in the case of a body corporate, his registered office or, if he has no registered office, his head office, and

(b) in the case of a person other than a body corporate, his head office,

were in an EEA State.".

PART II
FSMA 2000

425 Expressions relating to authorisation elsewhere in the single market

(1) In this Act—

[(a) "banking consolidation directive", ["life assurance consolidation directive",] "EEA authorisation", "EEA firm", "EEA right", "EEA State", … , "first non-life insurance directive", "insurance directives", "insurance mediation directive", *"investment services directive"*, ["markets in financial instruments directive",] "single market directives"[, " tied agent"] and "UCITS directive" have the meaning given in Schedule 3; and]

(b) "home state regulator", in relation to an EEA firm, has the meaning given in Schedule 3.

(2) In this Act—

(a) "home state authorisation" has the meaning given in Schedule 4;

(b) "Treaty firm" has the meaning given in Schedule 4; and

(c) "home state regulator", in relation to a Treaty firm, has the meaning given in Schedule 4.

[2422]

NOTES

Sub-s (1): para (a) substituted by the Collective Investment Schemes (Miscellaneous Amendments) Regulations 2003, SI 2003/2066, reg 2(1), as from 13 February 2004; words in first pair of square brackets in para (a) inserted, and words omitted from that paragraph repealed, by the Life Assurance Consolidation Directive (Consequential Amendments) Regulations 2004, SI 2004/3379, reg 6(1), (5), as from 11 January 2005; words in second pair of square brackets in para (a) inserted by the Financial Services and Markets Act 2000 (Markets in Financial Instruments) (Modification of Powers) Regulations 2006, SI 2006/2975, regs 2, 11, as from 6 December 2006; words in italics in para (a) repealed, and words in final pair of square brackets in that paragraph inserted, by the Financial Services and Markets Act 2000 (Markets in Financial Instruments) Regulations 2007, SI 2007/126, reg 3(5), Sch 5, paras 1, 22, as from 1 April 2007 (certain purposes (see reg 1(2) at **[7596]**)), and as from 1 November 2007 (otherwise).

PART XXX
SUPPLEMENTAL

426 Consequential and supplementary provision

(1) A Minister of the Crown may by order make such incidental, consequential, transitional or supplemental provision as he considers necessary or expedient for the general purposes, or any particular purpose, of this Act or in consequence of any provision made by or under this Act or for giving full effect to this Act or any such provision.

(2) An order under subsection (1) may, in particular, make provision—

(a) for enabling any person by whom any powers will become exercisable, on a date set by or under this Act, by virtue of any provision made by or under this Act to take before that date any steps which are necessary as a preliminary to the exercise of those powers;

(b) for applying (with or without modifications) or amending, repealing or revoking any provision of or made under an Act passed before this Act or in the same Session;

(c) dissolving any body corporate established by any Act passed, or instrument made, before the passing of this Act;

(d) for making savings, or additional savings, from the effect of any repeal or revocation made by or under this Act.

(3) Amendments made under this section are additional, and without prejudice, to those made by or under any other provision of this Act.

(4) No other provision of this Act restricts the powers conferred by this section.

[2423]

NOTES

Modification: this section shall have effect as if the provisions referred to in sub-s (2)(b) above included the provisions of the Criminal Justice and Police Act 2001, Pt 2: see Sch 2, Pt 2, para 26 to the 2001 Act.

Regulations: the Financial Services and Markets Act 2000 (Recognition Requirements for Investment Exchanges and Clearing Houses) Regulations 2001, SI 2001/995; the Financial Services and Markets

Act 2000 (Disclosure of Confidential Information) Regulations 2001, SI 2001/2188 at **[4372]**; the Financial Services and Markets Act 2000 (EEA Passport Rights) Regulations 2001, SI 2001/2511 at **[4448]**.

Orders: the Financial Services and Markets Act 2000 (Regulated Activities) Order 2001, SI 2001/544 at **[4001]**; the Financial Services and Markets Act 2000 (Transitional Provisions and Savings) (Rules) Order 2001, SI 2001/1534; the Financial Services and Markets Act 2000 (Consequential and Transitional Provisions) (Miscellaneous) Order 2001, SI 2001/1821; the Financial Services and Markets Act 2000 (Transitional Provisions) (Ombudsman Scheme and Complaints Scheme) Order 2001, SI 2001/2326; the Financial Services and Markets Act 2000 (Transitional Provisions) (Reviews of Pensions Business) Order 2001, SI 2001/2512; the Financial Services and Markets Act 2000 (Mutual Societies) Order 2001, SI 2001/2617; the Financial Services and Markets Act 2000 (Transitional Provisions) (Authorised Persons etc) Order 2001, SI 2001/2636; the Financial Services and Markets Act 2000 (Transitional Provisions) (Controllers) Order 2001, SI 2001/2637; the Financial Services and Markets Act 2000 (Consequential and Transitional Provisions) (Miscellaneous) (No 2) Order 2001, SI 2001/2659; the Financial Services and Markets Act 2000 (Official Listing of Securities) (Transitional Provisions) Order 2001, SI 2001/2957; the Financial Services and Markets Act 2000 (Consequential Amendments) (Pre-Commencement Modifications) Order 2001, SI 2001/2966; the Financial Services and Markets Act 2000 (Transitional Provisions, Repeals and Savings) (Financial Services Compensation Scheme) Order 2001, SI 2001/2967; the Financial Services and Markets Act 2000 (Transitional Provisions and Savings) (Civil Remedies, Discipline, Criminal Offences etc) (No 2) Order 2001, SI 2001/3083; the Financial Services and Markets Act 2000 (Interim Permissions) Order 2001, SI 2001/3374; the Financial Services and Markets Act 2000 (Dissolution of the Board of Banking Supervision) (Transitional Provisions) Order 2001, SI 2001/3582; the Financial Services and Markets Act 2000 (Transitional Provisions) (Partly Completed Procedures) Order 2001, SI 2001/3592; the Financial Services and Markets Act 2000 (Disclosure of Confidential Information) (Amendment) (No 2) Regulations 2001, SI 2001/3624; the Financial Services and Markets Act 2000 (Consequential Amendments) (Taxes) Order 2001, SI 2001/3629; the Financial Services and Markets Act 2000 (Transitional Provisions and Savings) (Business Transfers) Order 2001, SI 2001/3639; the Financial Services and Markets Act 2000 (Savings, Modifications and Consequential Provisions) (Rehabilitation of Offenders) (Scotland) Order 2001, SI 2001/3640; the Financial Services and Markets Act 2000 (Transitional Provisions and Savings) (Information Requirements and Investigations) Order 2001, SI 2001/3646; the Financial Services and Markets Act 2000 (Consequential Amendments and Savings) (Industrial Assurance) Order 2001, SI 2001/3647; the Financial Services and Markets Act 2000 (Confidential Information) (Bank of England) (Consequential Provisions) Order 2001, SI 2001/3648 at **[4624]**; the Financial Services and Markets Act 2000 (Consequential Amendments and Repeals) Order 2001, SI 2001/3649; the Financial Services and Markets Act 2000 (Miscellaneous Provisions) Order 2001, SI 2001/3650; the Financial Services and Markets Act 2000 (Scope of Permission Notices) Order 2001, SI 2001/3771 at **[4632]**; the Financial Services and Markets Act 2000 (Consequential Amendments) (No 2) Order 2001, SI 2001/3801; the Financial Services and Markets Act 2000 (Permission and Applications) (Credit Unions etc) Order 2002, SI 2002/704; the Financial Services and Markets Act 2000 (Administration Orders Relating to Insurers) Order 2002, SI 2002/1242; the Financial Services and Markets Act 2000 (Consequential Amendments) (Taxes) Order 2002, SI 2002/1409; the Financial Services and Markets Act 2000 (Consequential Amendments and Transitional Provisions) (Credit Unions) Order 2002, SI 2002/1501; the Financial Services and Markets Act 2000 (Consequential Amendments) Order 2002, SI 2002/1555; the Financial Services and Markets Act 2000 (Collective Investment Schemes) (Designated Countries and Territories) Order 2003, SI 2003/1181; the Financial Services and Markets Act 2000 (Regulated Activities) (Amendment) (No 1) Order 2003, SI 2003/1475 at **[4657]**; the Financial Services and Markets Act 2000 (Regulated Activities) (Amendment) (No 2) Order 2003, SI 2003/1476 at **[4663]**; the Financial Services and Markets Act 2000 (Administration Orders Relating to Insurers) (Amendment) Order 2003, SI 2003/2134; the Financial Services and Markets Act 2000 (Consequential Amendments) Order 2004, SI 2004/355; the Financial Services and Markets Act 2000 (Transitional Provisions) (Complaints Relating to General Insurance and Mortgages) Order 2004, SI 2004/454 at **[4671]**; the Financial Services and Markets Act 2000 (Transitional Provisions, Repeals and Savings) (Financial Services Compensation Scheme) (Amendment) Order 2004, SI 2004/952; the Financial Services and Markets Act 2000 (Transitional Provisions) (Complaints Relating to General Insurance and Mortgages) (Amendment) Order 2004, SI 2004/1609; the Financial Services and Markets Act 2000 (Transitional Provisions) (Mortgages) Order 2004, SI 2004/2615 at **[4695]**; the Financial Services and Markets Act 2000 (Transitional Provisions) (General Insurance Intermediaries) Order 2004, SI 2004/3351 at **[4710]**; the Financial Services and Markets Act 2000 (Administration Orders Relating to Insurers) (Northern Ireland) Order 2005, SI 2005/1644 (revoked by SI 2007/846 as from 6 April 2007 subject to savings); the Financial Services and Markets Act 2000 (Consequential Amendments) Order 2005, SI 2005/2967; the Financial Services and Markets Act 2000 (Regulated Activities) (Amendment) Order 2006, SI 2006/1969; the Financial Services and Markets Act 2000 (Regulated Activities) (Amendment) (No 2) Order 2006, SI 2006/2383; the Lloyd's Sourcebook (Finance Act 1993 and Finance Act 1994) (Amendment) Order 2006, SI 2006/3273; the Financial Services and Markets Act 2000 (Administration Orders Relating to Insurers) (Northern Ireland) Order 2007, SI 2007/846.

PART II
FSMA 2000

427 Transitional provisions

(1) Subsections (2) and (3) apply to an order under section 426 which makes transitional provisions or savings.

(2) The order may, in particular—

(a) if it makes provision about the authorisation and permission of persons who before commencement were entitled to carry on any activities, also include provision for such persons not to be treated as having any authorisation or permission (whether on an application to the Authority or otherwise);

(b) make provision enabling the Authority to require persons of such descriptions as it may direct to re-apply for permissions having effect by virtue of the order;

(c) make provision for the continuation as rules of such provisions (including primary and subordinate legislation) as may be designated in accordance with the order by the Authority, including provision for the modification by the Authority of provisions designated;

(d) make provision about the effect of requirements imposed, liabilities incurred and any other things done before commencement, including provision for and about investigations, penalties and the taking or continuing of any other action in respect of contraventions;

(e) make provision for the continuation of disciplinary and other proceedings begun before commencement, including provision about the decisions available to bodies before which such proceedings take place and the effect of their decisions;

(f) make provision as regards the Authority's obligation to maintain a record under section 347 as respects persons in relation to whom provision is made by the order.

(3) The order may—

(a) confer functions on the Treasury, the Secretary of State, the Authority, the scheme manager, the scheme operator, members of the panel established under paragraph 4 of Schedule 17, the Competition Commission or [the Office of Fair Trading];

(b) confer jurisdiction on the Tribunal;

(c) provide for fees to be charged in connection with the carrying out of functions conferred under the order;

(d) modify, exclude or apply (with or without modifications) any primary or subordinate legislation (including any provision of, or made under, this Act).

(4) In subsection (2) "commencement" means the commencement of such provisions of this Act as may be specified by the order.

[2424]

NOTES

Sub-s (3): words in square brackets substituted by the Enterprise Act 2002, s 278(1), Sch 25, para 40(1), (18), as from 1 April 2003.

Note: in accordance with the Financial Services and Markets Act 2000 (Transitional Provisions) (Mortgages) Order 2004, SI 2004/2615 at **[4695]** and the Financial Services and Markets Act 2000 (Transitional Provisions) (General Insurance Intermediaries) Order 2004, SI 2004/3351 at **[4710]**, certain firms carrying on regulated mortgage business and insurance mediation business whose applications for permission were still pending prior to the relevant dates on which these activities became regulated activities received interim permission or interim approval to carry on these regulated activities. Generally, firms with interim permission or approval were subject to FSA's rules as well as its supervisory jurisdiction and its associated sanctions and enforcement regime. Such firms were not, however, covered by the Financial Services Compensation Scheme. Interim permission or interim approval continued until the firm's application was determined and permission granted, or until the applicant withdrew their application, or until the Financial Services Tribunal confirmed the FSA's decision to refuse the application for permission. In any event, interim permission and interim approval ended on 31 October 2005 for regulated mortgage firms and on 14 January 2006 for insurance mediation activities and after this date no firms have interim permission to carry on these activities.

Order under section 426: see that section at **[2423]**.

428 Regulations and orders

(1) Any power to make an order which is conferred on a Minister of the Crown by this Act and any power to make regulations which is conferred by this Act is exercisable by statutory instrument.

(2) The Lord Chancellor's power to make rules under section 132 is exercisable by statutory instrument.

(3) Any statutory instrument made under this Act may—

(a) contain such incidental, supplemental, consequential and transitional provision as the person making it considers appropriate; and

(b) make different provision for different cases.

[2425]

429 Parliamentary control of statutory instruments

(1) No order is to be made under—
- (a) section 144(4), 192(b) or (e), 236(5), 404 or 419, or
- (b) paragraph 1 of Schedule 8,

unless a draft of the order has been laid before Parliament and approved by a resolution of each House.

(2) No regulations are to be made under section [90B or] 262 unless a draft of the regulations has been laid before Parliament and approved by a resolution of each House.

(3) An order to which, if it is made, subsection (4) or (5) will apply is not to be made unless a draft of the order has been laid before Parliament and approved by a resolution of each House.

(4) This subsection applies to an order under section 21 if—
- (a) it is the first order to be made, or to contain provisions made, under section 21(4);
- (b) it varies an order made under section 21(4) so as to make section 21(1) apply in circumstances in which it did not previously apply;
- (c) it is the first order to be made, or to contain provision made, under section 21(5);
- (d) it varies a previous order made under section 21(5) so as to make section 21(1) apply in circumstances in which it did not, as a result of that previous order, apply;
- (e) it is the first order to be made, or to contain provisions made, under section 21(9) or (10);
- (f) it adds one or more activities to those that are controlled activities for the purposes of section 21; or
- (g) it adds one or more investments to those which are controlled investments for the purposes of section 21.

(5) This subsection applies to an order under section 38 if—
- (a) it is the first order to be made, or to contain provisions made, under that section; or
- (b) it contains provisions restricting or removing an exemption provided by an earlier order made under that section.

(6) An order containing a provision to which, if the order is made, subsection (7) will apply is not to be made unless a draft of the order has been laid before Parliament and approved by a resolution of each House.

(7) This subsection applies to a provision contained in an order if—
- (a) it is the first to be made in the exercise of the power conferred by subsection (1) of section 326 or it removes a body from those for the time being designated under that subsection; or
- (b) it is the first to be made in the exercise of the power conferred by subsection (6) of section 327 or it adds a description of regulated activity or investment to those for the time being specified for the purposes of that subsection.

(8) Any other statutory instrument made under this Act, apart from one made under section 431(2) or to which paragraph 26 of Schedule 2 applies, shall be subject to annulment in pursuance of a resolution of either House of Parliament.

[2426]

NOTES

Sub-s (2): words in square brackets inserted by the Companies Act 2006, s 1272, Sch 15, Pt 1, paras 1, 12, as from 8 November 2006.

430 Extent

(1) This Act, except Chapter IV of Part XVII, extends to Northern Ireland.

(2) Except where Her Majesty by Order in Council provides otherwise, the extent of any amendment or repeal made by or under this Act is the same as the extent of the provision amended or repealed.

(3) Her Majesty may by Order in Council provide for any provision of or made under this Act relating to a matter which is the subject of other legislation which extends to any of the Channel Islands or the Isle of Man to extend there with such modifications (if any) as may be specified in the Order.

[2427]

431 Commencement

(1) The following provisions come into force on the passing of this Act—
(a) this section;
(b) sections 428, 430 and 433;
(c) paragraphs 1 and 2 of Schedule 21.

(2) The other provisions of this Act come into force on such day as the Treasury may by order appoint; and different days may be appointed for different purposes.

[2428]

NOTES

Orders: the Financial Services and Markets Act 2000 (Commencement No 1) Order 2001, SI 2001/516; the Financial Services and Markets Act 2000 (Commencement No 2) Order 2001, SI 2001/1282; the Financial Services and Markets Act 2000 (Commencement No 3) Order 2001, SI 2001/1820; the Financial Services and Markets Act 2000 (Commencement No 4 and Transitional Provision) Order 2001, SI 2001/2364; the Financial Services and Markets Act 2000 (Commencement No 5) Order 2001, SI 2001/2632; the Financial Services and Markets Act 2000 (Commencement No 6) Order 2001, SI 2001/3436; the Financial Services and Markets Act 2000 (Commencement No 7) Order 2001, SI 2001/3538.

432 Minor and consequential amendments, transitional provisions and repeals

(1) Schedule 20 makes minor and consequential amendments.
(2) Schedule 21 makes transitional provisions.
(3) The enactments set out in Schedule 22 are repealed.

[2429]

433 Short title

This Act may be cited as the Financial Services and Markets Act 2000.

[2430]

SCHEDULES

SCHEDULE 1
THE FINANCIAL SERVICES AUTHORITY

Section 1

PART I
GENERAL

Interpretation

1.—(1) In this Schedule—
"the 1985 Act" means the Companies Act 1985;
"non-executive committee" means the committee maintained under paragraph 3;
"functions", in relation to the Authority, means functions conferred on the Authority by or under any provision of this Act.

(2) For the purposes of this Schedule, the following are the Authority's legislative functions—
(a) making rules;
(b) issuing codes under section 64 or 119;
(c) issuing statements under section 64, 69, 124 or 210;
(d) giving directions under section 316, 318 or 328;
(e) issuing general guidance (as defined by section 158(5)) [or guidance under section 158A].

Constitution

2.—(1) The constitution of the Authority must continue to provide for the Authority to have—
(a) a chairman; and

(b) a governing body.

(2) The governing body must include the chairman.

(3) The chairman and other members of the governing body must be appointed, and be liable to removal from office, by the Treasury.

(4) The validity of any act of the Authority is not affected—
(a) by a vacancy in the office of chairman; or
(b) by a defect in the appointment of a person as a member of the governing body or as chairman.

Non-executive members of the governing body

3.—(1) The Authority must secure—
(a) that the majority of the members of its governing body are non-executive members; and
(b) that a committee of its governing body, consisting solely of the non-executive members, is set up and maintained for the purposes of discharging the functions conferred on the committee by this Schedule.

(2) The members of the non-executive committee are to be appointed by the Authority.

(3) The non-executive committee is to have a chairman appointed by the Treasury from among its members.

Functions of the non-executive committee

4.—(1) In this paragraph "the committee" means the non-executive committee.

(2) The non-executive functions are functions of the Authority but must be discharged by the committee.

(3) The non-executive functions are—
(a) keeping under review the question whether the Authority is, in discharging its functions in accordance with decisions of its governing body, using its resources in the most efficient and economic way;
(b) keeping under review the question whether the Authority's internal financial controls secure the proper conduct of its financial affairs; and
(c) determining the remuneration of—
(i) the chairman of the Authority's governing body; and
(ii) the executive members of that body.

(4) The function mentioned in sub-paragraph (3)(b) and those mentioned in sub-paragraph (3)(c) may be discharged on behalf of the committee by a sub-committee.

(5) Any sub-committee of the committee—
(a) must have as its chairman the chairman of the committee; but
(b) may include persons other than members of the committee.

(6) The committee must prepare a report on the discharge of its functions for inclusion in the Authority's annual report to the Treasury under paragraph 10.

(7) The committee's report must relate to the same period as that covered by the Authority's report.

Arrangements for discharging functions

5.—(1) The Authority may make arrangements for any of its functions to be discharged by a committee, sub-committee, officer or member of staff of the Authority.

[(2) But—
(a) in exercising the legislative functions mentioned in paragraph 1(2)(a) to (d), the Authority must act through its governing body; and
(b) the legislative function mentioned in paragraph 1(2)(e) may not be discharged by an officer or member of staff of the Authority.]

(3) Sub-paragraph (1) does not apply to the non-executive functions.

PART II
FSMA 2000

Monitoring and enforcement

6.—(1) The Authority must maintain arrangements designed to enable it to determine whether persons on whom requirements are imposed by or under this Act[, or by any directly applicable Community regulation made under the markets in financial instruments directive,] are complying with them.

(2) Those arrangements may provide for functions to be performed on behalf of the Authority by any body or person who, in its opinion, is competent to perform them.

(3) The Authority must also maintain arrangements for enforcing the provisions of, or made under, this Act [or of any directly applicable Community regulation made under the markets in financial instruments directive].

(4) Sub-paragraph (2) does not affect the Authority's duty under sub-paragraph (1).

Arrangements for the investigation of complaints

7.—(1) The Authority must—
- (a) make arrangements ("the complaints scheme") for the investigation of complaints arising in connection with the exercise of, or failure to exercise, any of its functions (other than its legislative functions); and
- (b) appoint an independent person ("the investigator") to be responsible for the conduct of investigations in accordance with the complaints scheme.

(2) The complaints scheme must be designed so that, as far as reasonably practicable, complaints are investigated quickly.

(3) The Treasury's approval is required for the appointment or dismissal of the investigator.

(4) The terms and conditions on which the investigator is appointed must be such as, in the opinion of the Authority, are reasonably designed to secure—
- (a) that he will be free at all times to act independently of the Authority; and
- (b) that complaints will be investigated under the complaints scheme without favouring the Authority.

(5) Before making the complaints scheme, the Authority must publish a draft of the proposed scheme in the way appearing to the Authority best calculated to bring it to the attention of the public.

(6) The draft must be accompanied by notice that representations about it may be made to the Authority within a specified time.

(7) Before making the proposed complaints scheme, the Authority must have regard to any representations made to it in accordance with sub-paragraph (6).

(8) If the Authority makes the proposed complaints scheme, it must publish an account, in general terms, of—
- (a) the representations made to it in accordance with sub-paragraph (6); and
- (b) its response to them.

(9) If the complaints scheme differs from the draft published under sub-paragraph (5) in a way which is, in the opinion of the Authority, significant the Authority must (in addition to complying with sub-paragraph (8)) publish details of the difference.

(10) The Authority must publish up-to-date details of the complaints scheme including, in particular, details of—
- (a) the provision made under paragraph 8(5); and
- (b) the powers which the investigator has to investigate a complaint.

(11) Those details must be published in the way appearing to the Authority to be best calculated to bring them to the attention of the public.

(12) The Authority must, without delay, give the Treasury a copy of any details published by it under this paragraph.

(13) The Authority may charge a reasonable fee for providing a person with a copy of—
- (a) a draft published under sub-paragraph (5);
- (b) details published under sub-paragraph (10).

(14) Sub-paragraphs (5) to (9) and (13)(a) also apply to a proposal to alter or replace the complaints scheme.

Investigation of complaints

8.—(1) The Authority is not obliged to investigate a complaint in accordance with the complaints scheme which it reasonably considers would be more appropriately dealt with in another way (for example by referring the matter to the Tribunal or by the institution of other legal proceedings).

(2) The complaints scheme must provide—
- (a) for reference to the investigator of any complaint which the Authority is investigating; and
- (b) for him—
  - (i) to have the means to conduct a full investigation of the complaint;
  - (ii) to report on the result of his investigation to the Authority and the complainant; and
  - (iii) to be able to publish his report (or any part of it) if he considers that it (or the part) ought to be brought to the attention of the public.

(3) If the Authority has decided not to investigate a complaint, it must notify the investigator.

(4) If the investigator considers that a complaint of which he has been notified under sub-paragraph (3) ought to be investigated, he may proceed as if the complaint had been referred to him under the complaints scheme.

(5) The complaints scheme must confer on the investigator the power to recommend, if he thinks it appropriate, that the Authority—
- (a) makes a compensatory payment to the complainant,
- (b) remedies the matter complained of,

or takes both of those steps.

(6) The complaints scheme must require the Authority, in a case where the investigator—
- (a) has reported that a complaint is well-founded, or
- (b) has criticised the Authority in his report,

to inform the investigator and the complainant of the steps which it proposes to take in response to the report.

(7) The investigator may require the Authority to publish the whole or a specified part of the response.

(8) The investigator may appoint a person to conduct the investigation on his behalf but subject to his direction.

(9) Neither an officer nor an employee of the Authority may be appointed under sub-paragraph (8).

(10) Sub-paragraph (2) is not to be taken as preventing the Authority from making arrangements for the initial investigation of a complaint to be conducted by the Authority.

Records

9. The Authority must maintain satisfactory arrangements for—
- (a) recording decisions made in the exercise of its functions; and
- (b) the safe-keeping of those records which it considers ought to be preserved.

Annual report

10.—(1) At least once a year the Authority must make a report to the Treasury on—
- (a) the discharge of its functions;
- (b) the extent to which, in its opinion, the regulatory objectives have been met;
- (c) its consideration of the matters mentioned in section 2(3); and
- (d) such other matters as the Treasury may from time to time direct.

(2) The report must be accompanied by—

PART II FSMA 2000

(a) the report prepared by the non-executive committee under paragraph 4(6); and
(b) such other reports or information, prepared by such persons, as the Treasury may from time to time direct.

(3) The Treasury must lay before Parliament a copy of each report received by them under this paragraph.

(4) The Treasury may—
(a) require the Authority to comply with any provisions of the 1985 Act about accounts and their audit which would not otherwise apply to it; or
(b) direct that any such provision of that Act is to apply to the Authority with such modifications as are specified in the direction.

(5) Compliance with any requirement imposed under sub-paragraph (4)(a) or (b) is enforceable by injunction or, in Scotland, an order under section 45(b) of the Court of Session Act 1988.

(6) Proceedings under sub-paragraph (5) may be brought only by the Treasury.

Annual public meeting

11.—(1) Not later than three months after making a report under paragraph 10, the Authority must hold a public meeting ("the annual meeting") for the purposes of enabling that report to be considered.

(2) The Authority must organise the annual meeting so as to allow—
(a) a general discussion of the contents of the report which is being considered; and
(b) a reasonable opportunity for those attending the meeting to put questions to the Authority about the way in which it discharged, or failed to discharge, its functions during the period to which the report relates.

(3) But otherwise the annual meeting is to be organised and conducted in such a way as the Authority considers appropriate.

(4) The Authority must give reasonable notice of its annual meeting.

(5) That notice must—
(a) give details of the time and place at which the meeting is to be held;
(b) set out the proposed agenda for the meeting;
(c) indicate the proposed duration of the meeting;
(d) give details of the Authority's arrangements for enabling persons to attend; and
(e) be published by the Authority in the way appearing to it to be most suitable for bringing the notice to the attention of the public.

(6) If the Authority proposes to alter any of the arrangements which have been included in the notice given under sub-paragraph (4) it must—
(a) give reasonable notice of the alteration; and
(b) publish that notice in the way appearing to the Authority to be best calculated to bring it to the attention of the public.

Report of annual meeting

12. Not later than one month after its annual meeting, the Authority must publish a report of the proceedings of the meeting.

[2431]

NOTES

Para 1: words in square brackets in sub-para (2)(e) inserted by the Financial Services and Markets Act 2000 (Markets in Financial Instruments) (Modification of Powers) Regulations 2006, SI 2006/2975, regs 2, 12, as from 6 December 2006.

Para 5: sub-para (2) substituted by the Regulatory Reform (Financial Services and Markets Act 2000) Order 2007, SI 2007/1973, arts 2, 14, as from 12 July 2007.

Para 6: words in square brackets inserted by the Financial Services and Markets Act 2000 (Markets in Financial Instruments) Regulations 2007, SI 2007/126, reg 3(5), Sch 5, paras 1, 23, as from 1 April 2007 (certain purposes (see reg 1(2) at **[7596]**)), and as from 1 November 2007 (otherwise).

Transitional provisions: see the Financial Services and Markets Act 2000 (Transitional Provisions and Savings) (Rules) Order 2001, SI 2001/1534, art 4(7), the Financial Services and Markets Act 2000 (Transitional Provisions) (Reviews of Pensions Business) Order 2001, SI 2001/2512, and the Financial Services and Markets Act 2000 (Interim Permissions) Order 2001, SI 2001/3374, art 12(3). Note also that the reference to the Authority's functions includes its functions as a designated agency under the Financial Services Act 1986 (repealed by the Financial Services and Markets Act 2000 (Consequential Amendments and Repeals) Order 2001, SI 2001/3649, art 3(1)(c)) and the reference to the Authority's legislative functions includes its functions of issuing statements of principle, rules, regulations and codes of practice under that Act; see the Financial Services and Markets Act 2000 (Consequential and Transitional Provisions) (Miscellaneous) Order 2001, SI 2001/1821, art 2(1)(b), (c).

Note: for the purposes of para 6 a requirement imposed by the FSA under the Electronic Commerce Directive (Financial Services and Markets) Regulations 2002, SI 2002/1775 upon an incoming provider is to be treated as imposed on him by or under this Act; see reg 12(2) of those Regulations at **[4650]**.

Note: FSA 1986, s 190 was repealed by the Data Protection Act 1998, s 74(2), Sch 16, Pt I, as from 1 March 2000. Section 31(1) of the 1998 Act provides that personal data processed for the purposes of discharging functions to which that subsection applies are exempt from the subject information provisions in any case to the extent to which the application of those provisions to the data would be likely to prejudice the proper discharge of those functions.

PART II
STATUS

13. In relation to any of its functions—

(a) the Authority is not to be regarded as acting on behalf of the Crown; and

(b) its members, officers and staff are not to be regarded as Crown servants.

Exemption from requirement of "limited" in Authority's name

14. The Authority is to continue to be exempt from the requirements of the 1985 Act relating to the use of "limited" as part of its name.

15. If the Secretary of State is satisfied that any action taken by the Authority makes it inappropriate for the exemption given by paragraph 14 to continue he may, after consulting the Treasury, give a direction removing it.

[2432]

NOTES

Transitional provisions: see the note to Pt I of this Schedule at **[2431]**.

PART II
FSMA 2000

PART III
PENALTIES AND FEES

Penalties

16.—(1) In determining its policy with respect to the amounts of penalties to be imposed by it under this Act, the Authority must take no account of the expenses which it incurs, or expects to incur, in discharging its functions.

(2) The Authority must prepare and operate a scheme for ensuring that the amounts paid to the Authority by way of penalties imposed under this Act are applied for the benefit of authorised persons.

(3) The scheme may, in particular, make different provision with respect to different classes of authorised person.

(4) Up to date details of the scheme must be set out in a document ("the scheme details").

(5) The scheme details must be published by the Authority in the way appearing to it to be best calculated to bring them to the attention of the public.

(6) Before making the scheme, the Authority must publish a draft of the proposed scheme in the way appearing to the Authority to be best calculated to bring it to the attention of the public.

(7) The draft must be accompanied by notice that representations about the proposals may be made to the Authority within a specified time.

(8) Before making the scheme, the Authority must have regard to any representations made to it in accordance with sub-paragraph (7).

(9) If the Authority makes the proposed scheme, it must publish an account, in general terms, of—

(a) the representations made to it in accordance with sub-paragraph (7); and

(b) its response to them.

(10) If the scheme differs from the draft published under sub-paragraph (6) in a way which is, in the opinion of the Authority, significant the Authority must (in addition to complying with sub-paragraph (9)) publish details of the difference.

(11) The Authority must, without delay, give the Treasury a copy of any scheme details published by it.

(12) The Authority may charge a reasonable fee for providing a person with a copy of—

(a) a draft published under sub-paragraph (6);

(b) scheme details.

(13) Sub-paragraphs (6) to (10) and (12)(a) also apply to a proposal to alter or replace the complaints scheme.

Fees

17.—(1) The Authority may make rules providing for the payment to it of such fees, in connection with the discharge of any of its functions under or as a result of this Act, as it considers will (taking account of its expected income from fees and charges provided for by any other provision of this Act) enable it—

(a) to meet expenses incurred in carrying out its functions or for any incidental purpose;

(b) to repay the principal of, and pay any interest on, any money which it has borrowed and which has been used for the purpose of meeting expenses incurred in relation to its assumption of functions under this Act or the Bank of England Act 1998; and

(c) to maintain adequate reserves.

(2) In fixing the amount of any fee which is to be payable to the Authority, no account is to be taken of any sums which the Authority receives, or expects to receive, by way of penalties imposed by it under this Act.

(3) Sub-paragraph (1)(b) applies whether expenses were incurred before or after the coming into force of this Act or the Bank of England Act 1998.

(4) Any fee which is owed to the Authority under any provision made by or under this Act may be recovered as a debt due to the Authority.

Services for which fees may not be charged

18. The power conferred by paragraph 17 may not be used to require—

(a) a fee to be paid in respect of the discharge of any of the Authority's functions under paragraphs 13, 14, 19 or 20 of Schedule 3; or

(b) a fee to be paid by any person whose application for approval under section 59 has been granted.

[2433]

NOTES

Transitional provisions: see the note to Pt I of this Schedule at **[2431]**.

PART IV
MISCELLANEOUS

Exemption from liability in damages

19.—(1) Neither the Authority nor any person who is, or is acting as, a member, officer or member of staff of the Authority is to be liable in damages for anything done or omitted in the discharge, or purported discharge, of the Authority's functions.

(2) Neither the investigator appointed under paragraph 7 nor a person appointed to conduct an investigation on his behalf under paragraph 8(8) is to be liable in damages for anything done or omitted in the discharge, or purported discharge, of his functions in relation to the investigation of a complaint.

(3) Neither sub-paragraph (1) nor sub-paragraph (2) applies—

(a) if the act or omission is shown to have been in bad faith; or

(b) so as to prevent an award of damages made in respect of an act or omission on the ground that the act or omission was unlawful as a result of section 6(1) of the Human Rights Act 1998.

[19A. For the purposes of this Act anything done by an accredited financial investigator within the meaning of the Proceeds of Crime Act 2002 who is—

(a) a member of the staff of the Authority, or

(b) a person appointed by the Authority under section 97, 167 or 168 to conduct an investigation,

must be treated as done in the exercise or discharge of a function of the Authority.]

20, 21. …

[2434]

NOTES

Para 19A: inserted by the Proceeds of Crime Act 2002, s 456, Sch 11, para 38, as from 24 February 2003.

Paras 20, 21: amend the House of Commons Disqualification Act 1975, Sch 1, Pt III, and the Northern Ireland Assembly Disqualification Act 1975, Sch 1, Pt III.

Transitional provisions: see the note to Pt I of this Schedule at **[2431]**.

PART II
FSMA 2000

SCHEDULE 2
REGULATED ACTIVITIES

Section 22(2)

NOTES

The regulated activities for the purposes of s 22 of this Act are set out in the Financial Services and Markets Act 2000 (Regulated Activities) Order 2001, SI 2001/544 at **[4001]**.

PART I
REGULATED ACTIVITIES

General

1. The matters with respect to which provision may be made under section 22(1) in respect of activities include, in particular, those described in general terms in this Part of this Schedule.

Dealing in investments

2.—(1) Buying, selling, subscribing for or underwriting investments or offering or agreeing to do so, either as a principal or as an agent.

(2) In the case of an investment which is a contract of insurance, that includes carrying out the contract.

Arranging deals in investments

3. Making, or offering or agreeing to make—

(a) arrangements with a view to another person buying, selling, subscribing for or underwriting a particular investment;

(b) arrangements with a view to a person who participates in the arrangements buying, selling, subscribing for or underwriting investments.

Deposit taking

4. Accepting deposits.

Safekeeping and administration of assets

5.—(1) Safeguarding and administering assets belonging to another which consist of or include investments or offering or agreeing to do so.

(2) Arranging for the safeguarding and administration of assets belonging to another, or offering or agreeing to do so.

Managing investments

6. Managing, or offering or agreeing to manage, assets belonging to another person where—

(a) the assets consist of or include investments; or

(b) the arrangements for their management are such that the assets may consist of or include investments at the discretion of the person managing or offering or agreeing to manage them.

Investment advice

7. Giving or offering or agreeing to give advice to persons on—

(a) buying, selling, subscribing for or underwriting an investment; or

(b) exercising any right conferred by an investment to acquire, dispose of, underwrite or convert an investment.

Establishing collective investment schemes

8. Establishing, operating or winding up a collective investment scheme, including acting as—

(a) trustee of a unit trust scheme;

(b) depositary of a collective investment scheme other than a unit trust scheme; or

(c) sole director of a body incorporated by virtue of regulations under section 262.

Using computer-based systems for giving investment instructions

9.—(1) Sending on behalf of another person instructions relating to an investment by means of a computer-based system which enables investments to be transferred without a written instrument.

(2) Offering or agreeing to send such instructions by such means on behalf of another person.

(3) Causing such instructions to be sent by such means on behalf of another person.

(4) Offering or agreeing to cause such instructions to be sent by such means on behalf of another person.

[2435]

PART II
INVESTMENTS

General

10. The matters with respect to which provision may be made under section 22(1) in respect of investments include, in particular, those described in general terms in this Part of this Schedule.

Securities

11.—(1) Shares or stock in the share capital of a company.

(2) "Company" includes—
(a) any body corporate (wherever incorporated), and
(b) any unincorporated body constituted under the law of a country or territory outside the United Kingdom,

other than an open-ended investment company.

Instruments creating or acknowledging indebtedness

12. Any of the following—
(a) debentures;
(b) debenture stock;
(c) loan stock;
(d) bonds;
(e) certificates of deposit;
(f) any other instruments creating or acknowledging a present or future indebtedness.

Government and public securities

13.—(1) Loan stock, bonds and other instruments—
(a) creating or acknowledging indebtedness; and
(b) issued by or on behalf of a government, local authority or public authority.

(2) "Government, local authority or public authority" means—
(a) the government of the United Kingdom, of Northern Ireland, or of any country or territory outside the United Kingdom;
(b) a local authority in the United Kingdom or elsewhere;
(c) any international organisation the members of which include the United Kingdom or another member State.

Instruments giving entitlement to investments

14.—(1) Warrants or other instruments entitling the holder to subscribe for any investment.

(2) It is immaterial whether the investment is in existence or identifiable.

Certificates representing securities

15. Certificates or other instruments which confer contractual or property rights—
(a) in respect of any investment held by someone other than the person on whom the rights are conferred by the certificate or other instrument; and
(b) the transfer of which may be effected without requiring the consent of that person.

Units in collective investment schemes

16.—(1) Shares in or securities of an open-ended investment company.

(2) Any right to participate in a collective investment scheme.

Options

17. Options to acquire or dispose of property.

Futures

18. Rights under a contract for the sale of a commodity or property of any other description under which delivery is to be made at a future date.

Contracts for differences

19. Rights under—
(a) a contract for differences; or
(b) any other contract the purpose or pretended purpose of which is to secure a profit or avoid a loss by reference to fluctuations in—
(i) the value or price of property of any description; or
(ii) an index or other factor designated for that purpose in the contract.

Contracts of insurance

20. Rights under a contract of insurance, including rights under contracts falling within head C of Schedule 2 to the Friendly Societies Act 1992.

Participation in Lloyd's syndicates

21.—(1) The underwriting capacity of a Lloyd's syndicate.

(2) A person's membership (or prospective membership) of a Lloyd's syndicate.

Deposits

22. Rights under any contract under which a sum of money (whether or not denominated in a currency) is paid on terms under which it will be repaid, with or without interest or a premium, and either on demand or at a time or in circumstances agreed by or on behalf of the person making the payment and the person receiving it.

Loans secured on land

23.—(1) Rights under any contract under which—
(a) one person provides another with credit; and
(b) the obligation of the borrower to repay is secured on land.

(2) "Credit" includes any cash loan or other financial accommodation.

(3) "Cash" includes money in any form.

[Other finance arrangements involving land

23A.—(1) Rights under any arrangement for the provision of finance under which the person providing the finance either—
(a) acquires a major interest in land from the person to whom the finance is provided, or
(b) disposes of a major interest in land to that person,
as part of the arrangement.

(2) References in sub-paragraph (1) to a "major interest" in land are to—
(a) in relation to land in England or Wales—
(i) an estate in fee simple absolute, or
(ii) a term of years absolute,
whether subsisting at law or in equity;
(b) in relation to land in Scotland—
(i) the interest of an owner of land, or
(ii) the tenant's right over or interest in a property subject to a lease;
(c) in relation to land in Northern Ireland—
(i) any freehold estate, or
(ii) any leasehold estate,
whether subsisting at law or in equity.

(3) It is immaterial for the purposes of sub-paragraph (1) whether either party acquires or (as the case may be) disposes of the interest in land—
(a) directly, or
(b) indirectly.]

Rights in investments

24. Any right or interest in anything which is an investment as a result of any other provision made under section 22(1).

[2436]

NOTES

Para 23A: inserted by the Regulation of Financial Services (Land Transactions) Act 2005, s 1, as from 19 February 2006.

Modifications to para 12(e): (i) a reference to a certificate of deposit includes a reference to uncertificated units of an eligible debt security where the issue of those units corresponds, in accordance with the current terms of issue of the security, to the issue of a certificate of deposit which is a certificate of deposit for the purposes of that enactment; (ii) a reference to an amount stated in a certificate of deposit includes a reference to a principal amount stated in, or determined in accordance with, the current terms of issue of an eligible debt security of the kind referred to in (i) above; see the Uncertificated Securities (Amendment) (Eligible Debt Securities) Regulations 2003, SI 2003/1633, reg 15, Sch 2, para 6.

Modifications to para 12(f): the reference to securities, instruments or investments creating or acknowledging indebtedness (or creating or acknowledging a present or future indebtedness) includes a reference to uncertificated units of eligible debt securities; see SI 2003/1633, reg 15, Sch 2, para 8.

PART III
SUPPLEMENTAL PROVISIONS

The order-making power

25.—(1) An order under section 22(1) may—

(a) provide for exemptions;

(b) confer powers on the Treasury or the Authority;

(c) authorise the making of regulations or other instruments by the Treasury for purposes of, or connected with, any relevant provision;

(d) authorise the making of rules or other instruments by the Authority for purposes of, or connected with, any relevant provision;

(e) make provision in respect of any information or document which, in the opinion of the Treasury or the Authority, is relevant for purposes of, or connected with, any relevant provision;

(f) make such consequential, transitional or supplemental provision as the Treasury consider appropriate for purposes of, or connected with, any relevant provision.

(2) Provision made as a result of sub-paragraph (1)(f) may amend any primary or subordinate legislation, including any provision of, or made under, this Act.

(3) "Relevant provision" means any provision—

(a) of section 22 or this Schedule; or

(b) made under that section or this Schedule.

Parliamentary control

26.—(1) This paragraph applies to the first order made under section 22(1).

(2) This paragraph also applies to any subsequent order made under section 22(1) which contains a statement by the Treasury that, in their opinion, the effect (or one of the effects) of the proposed order would be that an activity which is not a regulated activity would become a regulated activity.

(3) An order to which this paragraph applies—

(a) must be laid before Parliament after being made; and

(b) ceases to have effect at the end of the relevant period unless before the end of that period the order is approved by a resolution of each House of Parliament (but without that affecting anything done under the order or the power to make a new order).

(4) "Relevant period" means a period of twenty-eight days beginning with the day on which the order is made.

(5) In calculating the relevant period no account is to be taken of any time during which Parliament is dissolved or prorogued or during which both Houses are adjourned for more than four days.

Interpretation

27.—(1) In this Schedule—

"buying" includes acquiring for valuable consideration;

"offering" includes inviting to treat;

"property" includes currency of the United Kingdom or any other country or territory; and

"selling" includes disposing for valuable consideration.

(2) In sub-paragraph (1) "disposing" includes—

(a) in the case of an investment consisting of rights under a contract—

(i) surrendering, assigning or converting those rights; or

(ii) assuming the corresponding liabilities under the contract;

(b) in the case of an investment consisting of rights under other arrangements, assuming the corresponding liabilities under the contract or arrangements;

(c) in the case of any other investment, issuing or creating the investment or granting the rights or interests of which it consists.

(3) In this Schedule references to an instrument include references to any record (whether or not in the form of a document).

[2437]

NOTES

Order under section 22: see that section at **[2022]**.

SCHEDULE 3
EEA PASSPORT RIGHTS

Sections 31(1)(b) and 37

NOTES

Transitional provisions: the Financial Services and Markets Act 2000 (Transitional Provisions) (Authorised Persons etc) Order 2001, SI 2001/2636, Pt II, Chapter II, provides that EEA firms with "passports" before 1 December 2001 under the Insurance Companies Act 1982, the Banking Coordination (Second Council Directive) Regulations 1992, SI 1992/3218, or the Investment Services Regulations 1995, SI 1995/3275, are to be treated after that date as having complied with the procedures in this Schedule. In relation to UK firms with "passports" before 1 December 2001, see art 77 of the 2001 Order. The 1982 Act was repealed, and SI 1992/3218 and SI 1995/3275 were revoked, by the Financial Services and Markets Act 2000 (Consequential Amendments and Repeals) Order 2001, SI 2001/3649, art 3(1)(b), (2)(a), (c).

PART I
DEFINED TERMS

The single market directives

1. "The single market directives" means—

[(a) the banking consolidation directive;]

(c) the insurance directives; …

(d) the *investment services directive*[; …

(e) the insurance mediation directive][; and

(f) the UCITS directive.]

The banking [consolidation directive]

[2. The banking consolidation directive" means Directive 2006/48/EC of the European Parliament and of the Council of 14 June 2006 relating to the taking up and pursuit of the business of credit institutions.]

The insurance directives

3.—(1) "The insurance directives" means the first, second and third non-life insurance directives and the [life assurance consolidation directive].

(2) "First non-life insurance directive" means the Council Directive of 24 July 1973 on the co-ordination of laws, regulations and administrative provisions relating to the taking up and pursuit of the business of direct insurance other than life assurance (No 73/239/EEC).

(3) "Second non-life insurance directive" means the Council Directive of 22 June 1988 on the co-ordination of laws, etc, and laying down provisions to facilitate the effective exercise of freedom to provide services and amending Directive 73/239/EEC (No 88/357/EEC).

(4) "Third non-life insurance directive" means the Council Directive of 18 June 1992 on the co-ordination of laws, etc, and amending Directives 73/239/EEC and 88/357/EEC (No 92/49/EEC).

[(8) "Life assurance consolidation directive" means Directive 2002/83/EC of the European Parliament and of the Council of 5th November 2002 concerning life assurance.]

The investment services directive

4. "The investment services directive" means the Council Directive of 10 May 1993 on investment services in the securities field (No 93/22/EEC).

[The insurance mediation directive

4A. "The insurance mediation directive" means the European Parliament and Council Directive of 9th December 2002 on insurance mediation (No 2002/92/EC).]

[The UCITS directive

4B. "The UCITS directive" means the Council Directive of 20 December 1985 on the coordination of laws, regulations and administrative provisions relating to undertakings for collective investment in transferable securities (No 85/611/EEC).]

[The markets in financial instruments directive

4C. "The markets in financial instruments directive" means Directive 2004/39/EC of the European Parliament and of the Council of 21 April 2004 on markets in financial instruments.]

EEA firm

5. "EEA firm" means any of the following if it does not have its [relevant office] in the United Kingdom—

(a) an investment firm (as defined in *Article 1.2 of the investment services directive*) which is authorised (within the meaning of *Article 3*) by its home state regulator;

[(b) a credit institution (as defined in Article 4.1 of the banking consolidation directive) which is authorised (within the meaning of Article 4.2) by its home state regulator,

(c) a financial institution (as defined in Article 4.5 of the banking consolidation directive) which is a subsidiary of the kind mentioned in Article 24 and which fulfils the conditions in that Article;]

(d) an undertaking pursuing the activity of direct insurance (within the meaning of [Article 2 of the life assurance consolidation directive or Article 1 of the first non-life insurance directive]) which has received authorisation under [Article 4 of the life assurance consolidation directive or Article 6 of the first non-life insurance directive] from its home state regulator[; …

(e) an insurance intermediary (as defined in Article 2.5 of the insurance mediation

PART II
FSMA 2000

directive), or a reinsurance intermediary (as defined in Article 2.6) which is registered with its home state regulator under Article 3][; or
(f) a management company (as defined in Article 1a.2 of the UCITS directive) which is authorised (within the meaning of Article 5) by its home state regulator.]

[5A. In paragraph 5, "relevant office" means—
(a) in relation to a firm falling within sub-paragraph (e) of that paragraph which has a registered office, its registered office;
(b) in relation to any other firm, its head office.]

EEA authorisation

[6. "EEA authorisation" means—
(a) in relation to an EEA firm falling within paragraph 5(e), registration with its home state regulator under Article 3 of the insurance mediation directive;
(b) in relation to any other EEA firm, authorisation granted to an EEA firm by its home state regulator for the purpose of the relevant single market directive.]

EEA right

7. "EEA right" means the entitlement of a person to establish a branch, or provide services, in an EEA State other than that in which he has his [relevant office]—
(a) in accordance with the Treaty as applied in the EEA; and
(b) subject to the conditions of the relevant single market directive.

[7A. In paragraph 7, "relevant office" means—
(a) in relation to a person who has a registered office and whose entitlement is subject to the conditions of the insurance mediation directive, his registered office;
(b) in relation to any other person, his head office.]

EEA State

[8. "EEA State" has the meaning given by Schedule 1 to the Interpretation Act 1978.]

Home state regulator

9. "Home state regulator" means the competent authority (within the meaning of the relevant single market directive) of an EEA State (other than the United Kingdom) in relation to the EEA firm concerned.

UK firm

10. "UK firm" means a person whose [relevant office] is in the UK and who has an EEA right to carry on activity in an EEA State other than the United Kingdom.

[10A. In paragraph 10, "relevant office" means—
(a) in relation to a firm whose EEA right derives from the insurance mediation directive and which has a registered office, its registered office;
(b) in relation to any other firm, its head office.]

[UK investment firm

10B. "UK investment firm" means a UK firm—
(a) which is an investment firm, and
(b) whose EEA right derives from the markets in financial instruments directive.]

11. "Host state regulator" means the competent authority (within the meaning of the relevant single market directive) of an EEA State (other than the United Kingdom) in relation to a UK firm's exercise of EEA rights there.

[Tied agent

11A. "Tied agent" has the meaning given in Article 4.1.25 of the markets in financial instruments directive.]

[2438]

NOTES

Para 1: sub-para (a) substituted, for original sub-paras (a), (b), by the Banking Consolidation Directive (Consequential Amendments) Regulations 2000, SI 2000/2952, reg 8(1), (5)(a), as from 22 November 2000; word omitted from sub-para (c) repealed, and sub-para (e) and the word immediately preceding it inserted, by the Insurance Mediation Directive (Miscellaneous Amendments) Regulations 2003, SI 2003/1473, reg 2(2)(a), as from 14 January 2005; for the words in italics in sub-para (d) there are substituted the words "markets in financial instruments directive" by the Financial Services and Markets Act 2000 (Markets in Financial Instruments) Regulations 2007, SI 2007/126, reg 3(4), Sch 4, paras 1, 2, as from 1 April 2007 (certain purposes (see reg 1(2) at **[7596]**)), and as from 1 November 2007 (otherwise); word omitted from sub-para (d) repealed, and sub-para (f) and the word immediately preceding it inserted, by the Collective Investment Schemes (Miscellaneous Amendments) Regulations 2003, SI 2003/2066, reg 2(2)(a), as from 13 February 2004.

Para 2: substituted by the Capital Requirements Regulations 2006, SI 2006/3221, reg 29(1), Sch 3, para 2(1), (2), as from 1 January 2007; words in square brackets in the heading preceding para 2 substituted by virtue of SI 2000/2952, reg 8(1), (5)(b), as from 22 November 2000.

Para 3: words in square brackets in sub-para (1) substituted, and sub-para (8) substituted for the original sub-paras (5)–(7), by the Life Assurance Consolidation Directive (Consequential Amendments) Regulations 2004, SI 2004/3379, reg 6(1), (6)(a), as from 11 January 2005.

Para 4: repealed by SI 2007/126, reg 3(4), Sch 4, paras 1, 3, as from 1 April 2007 (certain purposes (see reg 1(2) at **[7596]**)), and as from 1 November 2007 (otherwise).

Paras 4A, 5A, 7A, 10A: inserted by SI 2003/1473, reg 2(2)(b), (d), (g), (i), as from 14 January 2005.

Para 4B: inserted by SI 2003/2066, reg 2(2)(b), as from 13 February 2004.

Para 4C: inserted by the Financial Services and Markets Act 2000 (Markets in Financial Instruments) (Modification of Powers) Regulations 2006, SI 2006/2975, regs 2, 13, as from 6 December 2006.

Para 5: words in first pair of square brackets substituted, and sub-para (e) and the word immediately preceding it inserted, by SI 2003/1473, reg 2(2)(c), as from 14 January 2005; for the words in italics in sub-para (a) there are substituted the words "Article 4.1.1 of the markets in financial instruments directive" and "Article 5" respectively by SI 2007/126, reg 3(4), Sch 4, paras 1, 4, as from 1 April 2007 (certain purposes (see reg 1(2) at **[7596]**)), and as from 1 November 2007 (otherwise); sub-paras (b), (c) substituted by SI 2006/3221, reg 29(1), Sch 3, para 2(1), (3), as from 1 January 2007; words in square brackets in sub-para (d) substituted by SI 2004/3379, reg 6(1), (6)(b), as from 11 January 2005; word omitted from sub-para (d) repealed, and sub-para (f) and the word immediately preceding it inserted, by SI 2003/2066, reg 2(2)(c), as from 13 February 2004.

Para 6: substituted by SI 2003/1473, reg 2(2)(e), as from 14 January 2005.

Paras 7, 10: words in square brackets substituted by SI 2003/1473, reg 2(2)(f), (h), as from 14 January 2005.

Para 8: substituted by the Financial Services (EEA State) Regulations 2007, SI 2007/108, reg 2, as from 13 February 2007.

Paras 10B, 11A: inserted by SI 2007/126, reg 3(4), Sch 4, paras 1, 5, 6, as from 1 April 2007 (certain purposes (see reg 1(2) at **[7596]**)), and as from 1 November 2007 (otherwise).

EEA firm (para 5): regulations made under the Income Tax (Trading and Other Income) Act 2005, s 694, may provide that an EEA firm of the kind mentioned in para 5(a)–(c) of this Schedule that qualifies for authorisation under para 12 *post* may only be an individual investment plan manager if certain requirements specified in those regulations are met; see ss 697, 698 of the 2005 Act.

"The banking consolidation directive", ie, Directive 2000/12/EC: repealed and replaced by European Parliament and Council Directive 2006/48/EC relating to the taking up and pursuit of the business of credit institutions (recast).

"The investment services directive", ie, Directive 93/22/EEC: repealed by European Parliament and Council Directive 2004/39/EC on markets in financial instruments amending Council Directives 85/611/EEC and 93/6/EEC and Directive 2000/12/EC of the European Parliament and of the Council and repealing Council Directive 93/22/EEC, as from 1 November 2007 (the MiFID Directive).

PART II
EXERCISE OF PASSPORT RIGHTS BY EEA FIRMS

Firms qualifying for authorisation

12.—(1) Once an EEA firm which is seeking to establish a branch in the United Kingdom in exercise of an EEA right satisfies the establishment conditions, it qualifies for authorisation.

(2) Once an EEA firm which is seeking to provide services in the United Kingdom in exercise of an EEA right satisfies the service conditions, it qualifies for authorisation.

PART II FSMA 2000

[(3) If an EEA firm falling within paragraph 5(a) is seeking to use a tied agent established in the United Kingdom in connection with the exercise of an EEA right deriving from the markets in financial instruments directive, this Part of this Schedule applies as if the firm were seeking to establish a branch in the United Kingdom.

(4) But if—

(a) an EEA firm already qualifies for authorisation by virtue of sub-paragraph (1); and

(b) the EEA right which it is exercising derives from the markets in financial instruments directive,

sub-paragraph (3) does not require the firm to satisfy the establishment conditions in respect of its use of the tied agent in question.]

Establishment

13.—(1) [If the firm falls within paragraph 5(a), (b), [(c), (d) or (f)],] The establishment conditions are that—

(a) the Authority has received notice ("a consent notice") from the firm's home state regulator that it has given the firm consent to establish a branch in the United Kingdom;

(b) the consent notice—

(i) is given in accordance with the relevant single market directive;

(ii) identifies the activities to which consent relates; and

(iii) includes such other information as may be prescribed; *and*

[(ba) in the case of a firm falling within paragraph 5(a), the Authority has given the firm notice for the purposes of this paragraph or two months have elapsed beginning with the date when the home state regulator gave the consent notice; and"]

(c) [in the case of a firm falling within paragraph 5(b), (c), (d) or (f),] the firm has been informed of the applicable provisions or two months have elapsed beginning with the date when the Authority received the consent notice.

[(1A) If the firm falls within paragraph 5(e), the establishment conditions are that—

(a) the firm has given its home state regulator notice of its intention to establish a branch in the United Kingdom;

(b) the Authority has received notice ("a regulator's notice") from the firm's home state regulator that the firm intends to establish a branch in the United Kingdom;

(c) the firm's home state regulator has informed the firm that the regulator's notice has been sent to the Authority; and

(d) one month has elapsed beginning with the date on which the firm's home state regulator informed the firm that the regulator's notice has been sent to the Authority.]

(2) If the Authority has received a consent notice, it must—

(a) prepare for the firm's supervision;

(b) [except if the firm falls within paragraph 5(a),] notify the firm of the applicable provisions (if any); and

(c) if the firm falls within paragraph 5(d), notify its home state regulator of the applicable provisions (if any).

(3) A notice under sub-paragraph (2)(b) or (c) must be given before the end of the period of two months beginning with the day on which the Authority received the consent notice.

(4) For the purposes of this paragraph—

"applicable provisions" means the host state rules with which the firm is required to comply when carrying on a permitted activity through a branch in the United Kingdom;

"host state rules" means rules—

(a) made in accordance with the relevant single market directive; and

(b) which are the responsibility of the United Kingdom (both as to implementation and as to supervision of compliance) in accordance with that directive; and

"permitted activity" means an activity identified in the consent notice [or regulator's notice, as the case may be].

Services

14.—(1) The service conditions are that—

(a) the firm has given its home state regulator notice of its intention to provide services in the United Kingdom ("a notice of intention");

(b) if the firm falls within [paragraph 5(a), [(d), (e) or (f)]], the Authority has received notice ("a regulator's notice") from the firm's home state regulator containing such information as may be prescribed; …

[(ba) if the firm falls within paragraph 5(b) and is seeking to provide services in exercise of the right under Article 31.5 of the markets in financial instruments directive, the Authority has received notice ("a regulator's notice") from the firm's home state regulator stating that the firm intends to exercise that right in the United Kingdom;]

(c) if the firm falls within [paragraph 5(d) or (e)], its home state regulator has informed it that the regulator's notice has been sent to the Authority[; and

(d) if the firm falls within paragraph 5(e), one month has elapsed beginning with the date on which the firm's home state regulator informed the firm that the regulator's notice has been sent to the Authority].

(2) If the Authority has received a regulator's notice or, where none is required by sub-paragraph (1), has been informed of the firm's intention to provide services in the United Kingdom, it must[, unless the firm falls within paragraph 5(e),]—

(a) prepare for the firm's supervision; and

(b) notify the firm of the applicable provisions (if any).

[(2A) Sub-paragraph (2)(b) does not apply in the case of a firm falling within paragraph 5(a).]

(3) A notice under sub-paragraph (2)(b) must be given before the end of the period of two months beginning on the day on which the Authority received the regulator's notice, or was informed of the firm's intention.

(4) For the purposes of this paragraph—

"applicable provisions" means the host state rules with which the firm is required to comply when carrying on a permitted activity by providing services in the United Kingdom;

"host state rules" means rules—

(a) made in accordance with the relevant single market directive; and

(b) which are the responsibility of the United Kingdom (both as to implementation and as to supervision of compliance) in accordance with that directive; and

"permitted activity" means an activity identified in—

(a) the regulator's notice; or

(b) where none is required by sub-paragraph (1), the notice of intention.

Grant of permission

15.—(1) On qualifying for authorisation as a result of paragraph 12, a firm has, in respect of each permitted activity which is a regulated activity, permission to carry it on through its United Kingdom branch (if it satisfies the establishment conditions) or by providing services in the United Kingdom (if it satisfies the service conditions).

[(1A) Sub-paragraph (1) is to be read subject to paragraph 15A(3).]

(2) The permission is to be treated as being on terms equivalent to those appearing from the consent notice, regulator's notice or notice of intention.

(3) Sections *21, 39(1) and 147(1)* of the Consumer Credit Act 1974 (business requiring a licence under that Act) do not apply in relation to the carrying on of a permitted activity which is Consumer Credit Act business by a firm which qualifies for authorisation as a result of paragraph 12, unless [the Office of Fair Trading] has exercised the power conferred on [it] by section 203 in relation to the firm.

(4) "Consumer Credit Act business" has the same meaning as in section 203.

[Power to restrict permission of management companies

15A.—(1) Sub-paragraph (2) applies if—

PART II
FSMA 2000

(a) a firm falling within paragraph 5(f) qualifies for authorisation as a result of paragraph 12(1) (establishment conditions satisfied); but
(b) the Authority determines that the way in which the firm intends to invite persons in the United Kingdom to become participants in any collective investment scheme which that firm manages does not comply with the law in force in the United Kingdom.

(2) The Authority may give a notice to the firm and the firm's home state regulator of the Authority's determination under sub-paragraph (1)(b).

(3) Paragraph 15(1) does not give a firm to which the Authority has given (and not withdrawn) a notice under sub-paragraph (2) permission to carry on through the firm's United Kingdom branch the regulated activity of dealing in units in the collective investment schemes which the firm manages.

(4) Any notice given under sub-paragraph (2) must be given before the end of the period of two months beginning with the day on which the Authority received the consent notice.

(5) Sections 264(4) and 265(1), (2) and (4) apply to a notice given under sub-paragraph (2) as they apply to a notice given by the Authority under section 264(2).

(6) If a decision notice is given to the firm under section 265(4), by virtue of sub-paragraph (5), the firm may refer the matter to the Tribunal.

(7) In sub-paragraph (3)—
(a) "units" has the meaning given by section 237(2); and
(b) the reference to "dealing in" units in a collective investment scheme must be read with—
(i) section 22;
(ii) any relevant order under that section; and
(iii) Schedule 2.]

Effect of carrying on regulated activity when not qualified for authorisation

16.—(1) This paragraph applies to an EEA firm which is not qualified for authorisation under paragraph 12.

(2) Section 26 does not apply to an agreement entered into by the firm.

(3) Section 27 does not apply to an agreement in relation to which the firm is a third party for the purposes of that section.

(4) Section 29 does not apply to an agreement in relation to which the firm is the deposit-taker.

Continuing regulation of EEA firms

17. Regulations may—
(a) modify any provision of this Act which is an applicable provision (within the meaning of paragraph 13 or 14) in its application to an EEA firm qualifying for authorisation;
(b) make provision as to any change (or proposed change) of a prescribed kind relating to an EEA firm or to an activity that it carries on in the United Kingdom and as to the procedure to be followed in relation to such cases;
(c) provide that the Authority may treat an EEA firm's notification that it is to cease to carry on regulated activity in the United Kingdom as a request for cancellation of its qualification for authorisation under this Schedule.

Giving up right to authorisation

18. Regulations may provide that in prescribed circumstances an EEA firm falling within paragraph 5(c) may, on following the prescribed procedure—
(a) have its qualification for authorisation under this Schedule cancelled; and
(b) seek to become an authorised person by applying for a Part IV permission.

[2439]

NOTES

Para 12: sub-paras (3), (4) added by the Financial Services and Markets Act 2000 (Markets in Financial Instruments) Regulations 2007, SI 2007/126, reg 3(4), Sch 4, paras 1, 7, as from 1 April 2007 (certain purposes (see reg 1(2) at **[7596]**)), and as from 1 November 2007 (otherwise).

Para 13: words in first (outer) pair of square brackets in sub-para (1), words in square brackets in sub-para (4), and the whole of sub-para (1A), inserted by the Insurance Mediation Directive (Miscellaneous Amendments) Regulations 2003, SI 2003/1473, reg 3, as from 14 January 2005; words in second (inner) pair of square brackets in sub-para (1) substituted by the Collective Investment Schemes (Miscellaneous Amendments) Regulations 2003, SI 2003/2066, reg 3(1)(a), as from 13 February 2004; word in italics in sub-para (1)(b)(iii) repealed, and sub-para (1)(ba) and the words in square brackets in sub-paras (1)(c), (2)(a) inserted, by SI 2007/126, reg 3(4), Sch 4, paras 1, 8, as from 1 April 2007 (certain purposes (see reg 1(2) at **[7596]**)), and as from 1 November 2007 (otherwise) (for transitional provisions, see the note below).

Para 14: words in first (outer) pair of square brackets in sub-para (1)(b) substituted, and word omitted from that paragraph repealed, by SI 2003/1473, reg 4(1), (2)(a), (b), as from 14 January 2005; words in second (inner) pair of square brackets in sub-para (1)(b) substituted by SI 2003/2066, reg 3(1)(b), as from 13 February 2004; sub-paras (1)(ba), (2A) inserted by SI 2007/126, reg 3(4), Sch 4, paras 1, 9, as from 1 April 2007 (certain purposes (see reg 1(2) at **[7596]**)), and as from 1 November 2007 (otherwise); words in square brackets in sub-para (1)(c) substituted, sub-para (1)(d) and the word immediately preceding it inserted, and words in square brackets in sub-para (2) inserted, by SI 2003/1473, reg 4(1), (2)(c), (d), (3), as from 14 January 2005.

Para 15: sub-para (1A) inserted by SI 2003/2066, reg 3(1)(c), as from 13 February 2004; for the words in italics in sub-para (3) there are substituted the words "21 and 39(1)" by the Consumer Credit Act 2006, s 33(9), as from a day to be appointed; words in square brackets in sub-para (3) substituted by the Enterprise Act 2002, s 278(1), Sch 25, para 40(1), (19)(a), as from 1 April 2003.

Para 15A: inserted by SI 2003/2066, reg 3(1)(d), as from 13 February 2004.

Transitional provisions: the Financial Services and Markets Act 2000 (Markets in Financial Instruments) Regulations 2007, SI 2007/126 provide for various transitional provisions in connection with the amendments made by those Regulations to this Schedule. For transitional provisions in connection with para 13 above, see reg 6 of the 2007 Regulations at **[7601]**.

Establishment (para 13): see further the Financial Services and Markets Act 2000 (EEA Passport Rights) Regulations 2001, SI 2001/2511, reg 2 at **[4449]**.

Services (para 14): see further the Financial Services and Markets Act 2000 (EEA Passport Rights) Regulations 2001, SI 2001/2511, reg 3 at **[4450]**.

See also the note "EEA firm" to Pt I of this Schedule at **[2438]**.

Regulations: the Financial Services and Markets Act 2000 (EEA Passport Rights) Regulations 2001, SI 2001/2511 at **[4448]**.

Note that the following amending Regulations have also been made under this Part: the Electronic Money (Miscellaneous Amendments) Regulations 2002, SI 2002/765; the Insurance Mediation Directive (Miscellaneous Amendments) Regulations 2003, SI 2003/1473; the Collective Investment Schemes (Miscellaneous Amendments) Regulations 2003, SI 2003/2066; the Financial Services and Markets Act 2000 (EEA Passport Rights) (Amendment) Regulations 2006, SI 2006/3385.

PART III
EXERCISE OF PASSPORT RIGHTS BY UK FIRMS

Establishment

19.—(1) [Subject to sub-paragraph (5A),] A UK firm may not exercise an EEA right to establish a branch unless three conditions are satisfied.

(2) The first is that the firm has given the Authority, in the specified way, notice of its intention to establish a branch ("a notice of intention") which—

(a) identifies the activities which it seeks to carry on through the branch; and
(b) includes such other information as may be specified.

(3) *The* activities identified in a notice of intention may include activities which are not regulated activities.

(4) The second is that the Authority has given notice in specified terms ("a consent notice") to the host state regulator.

[(5) The third is—

(a) if the EEA right in question derives from the insurance mediation directive, that one month has elapsed beginning with the date on which the firm received notice, in accordance with sub-paragraph (11), that the Authority has given a consent notice;
(b) in any other case, that either—

PART II FSMA 2000

(i) the host state regulator has notified the firm (or, where the EEA right in question derives from any of the insurance directives, the Authority) of the applicable provisions; or

(ii) two months have elapsed beginning with the date on which the Authority gave the consent notice.]

[(5A) If—

(a) the EEA right in question derives from the insurance mediation directive, and

(b) the EEA State in which the firm intends to establish a branch has not notified the Commission, in accordance with Article 6(2) of that directive, of its wish to be informed of the intention of any UK firm to establish a branch in its territory,

the second and third conditions do not apply (and so the firm may establish the branch to which its notice of intention relates as soon as the first condition is satisfied).]

[(5B) If the firm is a UK investment firm, a notice of intention may not include ancillary services unless such services are to be provided in connection with the carrying on of one or more investment services and activities.

(5C) In sub-paragraph (5B) "ancillary services" has the meaning given in Article 4.1.3 of the markets in financial instruments directive.]

(6) If the firm's EEA right derives from [the banking consolidation directive, *the investment services directive or the UCITS directive]* and the first condition is satisfied, the Authority must give a consent notice to the host state regulator unless it has reason to doubt the adequacy of the firm's resources or its administrative structure.

(7) If the firm's EEA right derives from any of the insurance directives and the first condition is satisfied, the Authority must give a consent notice unless it has reason—

(a) to doubt the adequacy of the firm's resources or its administrative structure, or

(b) to question the reputation, qualifications or experience of the directors or managers of the firm or the person proposed as the branch's authorised agent for the purposes of those directives,

in relation to the business to be conducted through the proposed branch.

[(7A) If—

(a) the firm's EEA right derives from the insurance mediation directive,

(b) the first condition is satisfied, and

(c) the second condition applies,

the Authority must give a consent notice, and must do so within one month beginning with the date on which it received the firm's notice of intention.]

[(7B) If the firm is a UK investment firm and the first condition is satisfied, the Authority must give a consent notice to the host state regulator within three months beginning with the date on which it received the firm's notice of intention unless the Authority has reason to doubt the adequacy of the firm's resources or its administrative structure.]

(8) If the Authority proposes to refuse to give a consent notice it must give the firm concerned a warning notice.

(9) If the firm's EEA right derives from any of the insurance directives and the host state regulator has notified it of the applicable provisions, the Authority must inform the firm of those provisions.

(10) Rules may specify the procedure to be followed by the Authority in exercising its functions under this paragraph.

(11) If the Authority gives a consent notice it must give written notice that it has done so to the firm concerned.

(12) If the Authority decides to refuse to give a consent notice—

(a) it must, [within the relevant period], give the person who gave that notice a decision notice to that effect; and

(b) that person may refer the matter to the Tribunal.

[(12A) In sub-paragraph (12), "the relevant period" means—

(a) if the firm's EEA right derives from the UCITS directive, two months beginning with the date on which the Authority received the notice of intention;

(b) in any other case, three months beginning with that date.]

(13) In this paragraph, "applicable provisions" means the host state rules with which the firm will be required to comply when conducting business through the proposed branch in the EEA State concerned.

(14) In sub-paragraph (13), "host state rules" means rules—
(a) made in accordance with the relevant single market directive; and
(b) which are the responsibility of the EEA State concerned (both as to implementation and as to supervision of compliance) in accordance with that directive.

(15) "Specified" means specified in rules.

Services

20.—(1) A UK firm may not exercise an EEA right to provide services unless the firm has given the Authority, in the specified way, notice of its intention to provide services ("a notice of intention") which—
(a) identifies the activities which it seeks to carry out by way of provision of services; and
(b) includes such other information as may be specified.

(2) *The* activities identified in a notice of intention may include activities which are not regulated activities.

[(2A) If the firm is a UK investment firm, a notice of intention may not include ancillary services unless such services are to be provided in connection with the carrying on of one or more investment services and activities.

(2B) In sub-paragraph (2A) "ancillary services" has the meaning given in Article 4.1.3 of the markets in financial instruments directive.]

(3) If the firm's EEA right derives from [the banking consolidation directive, the *investment services directive* or the UCITS directive], the Authority must, within one month of receiving a notice of intention, send a copy of it to the host state regulator [with such other information as may be specified].

[(3A) If the firm's EEA right derives from any of the insurance directives, the Authority must, within one month of receiving the notice of intention—
(a) give notice in specified terms ("a consent notice") to the host state regulator; or
(b) give written notice to the firm of—
(i) its refusal to give a consent notice; and
(ii) its reasons for that refusal.]

[(3B) If the firm's EEA right derives from the insurance mediation directive and the EEA State in which the firm intends to provide services has notified the Commission, in accordance with Article 6(2) of that directive, of its wish to be informed of the intention of any UK firm to provide services in its territory—
(a) the Authority must, within one month of receiving the notice of intention, send a copy of it to the host state regulator;
(b) the Authority, when it sends the copy in accordance with sub-paragraph (a), must give written notice to the firm concerned that it has done so; and
(c) the firm concerned must not provide the services to which its notice of intention relates until one month, beginning with the date on which it receives the notice under sub-paragraph (b), has elapsed.]

(4) When the Authority sends the copy under sub-paragraph (3) [or gives a consent notice], it must give written notice to the firm concerned.

[(4A) If the firm is given notice under sub-paragraph (3A)(b), it may refer the matter to the Tribunal.

(4B) If the firm's EEA right derives from any of the insurance directives [or from the markets in financial instruments directive], it must not provide the services to which its notice of intention relates until it has received written notice under sub-paragraph (4).

[(4BA) If the firm's EEA right derives from the markets in financial instruments directive, the Authority must comply as soon as reasonably practicable with a request for information under the second sub-paragraph of Article 31.6 of that directive from the host state regulator.]

(4C) Rules may specify the procedure to be followed by the Authority under this paragraph.]

(5) …

PART II FSMA 2000

(6) "Specified" means specified in rules.

[Tied agents

20A.—(1) If a UK investment firm is seeking to use a tied agent established in an EEA State (other than the United Kingdom) in connection with the exercise of an EEA right deriving from the markets in financial instruments directive, this Part of this Schedule applies as if the firm were seeking to establish a branch in that State.

(2) But if—

(a) a UK investment firm has already established a branch in an EEA State other than the United Kingdom in accordance with paragraph 19; and

(b) the EEA right which it is exercising derives from the markets in financial instruments directive,

paragraph 19 does not apply in respect of its use of the tied agent in question.]

Offence relating to exercise of passport rights

21.—(1) If a UK firm which is not an authorised person contravenes the prohibition imposed by—

(a) sub-paragraph (1) of paragraph 19, or

(b) [sub-paragraph (1), (3B)(c) or (4B)] of paragraph 20,

it is guilty of an offence.

(2) A firm guilty of an offence under sub-paragraph (1) is liable—

(a) on summary conviction, to a fine not exceeding the statutory maximum; or

(b) on conviction on indictment, to a fine.

(3) In proceedings for an offence under sub-paragraph (1), it is a defence for the firm to show that it took all reasonable precautions and exercised all due diligence to avoid committing the offence.

Continuing regulation of UK firms

22.—(1) Regulations may make such provision as the Treasury consider appropriate in relation to a UK firm's exercise of EEA rights, and may in particular provide for the application (with or without modification) of any provision of, or made under, this Act in relation to an activity of a UK firm.

(2) Regulations may—

(a) make provision as to any change (or proposed change) of a prescribed kind relating to a UK firm or to an activity that it carries on and as to the procedure to be followed in relation to such cases;

(b) make provision with respect to the consequences of the firm's failure to comply with a provision of the regulations.

(3) Where a provision of the kind mentioned in sub-paragraph (2) requires the Authority's consent to a change (or proposed change)—

(a) consent may be refused only on prescribed grounds; and

(b) if the Authority decides to refuse consent, the firm concerned may refer the matter to the Tribunal.

23.—(1) *Sub-paragraph* (2) *applies* if a UK firm—

(a) has a Part IV permission; and

(b) is exercising an EEA right to carry on any Consumer Credit Act business in an EEA State other than the United Kingdom.

(2) The Authority may exercise its power under section 45 in respect of the firm if [the Office of Fair Trading] has informed the Authority that—

(a) the firm,

(b) any of the firm's employees, agents or associates (whether past or present), or

(c) if the firm is a body corporate, a controller of the firm or an associate of such a controller, has done any of the things specified in paragraphs *(a) to (d) of section 25(2)* of the Consumer Credit Act 1974.

[(2A) The Authority may also exercise its power under section 45 in respect of the firm if the Office of Fair Trading has informed the Authority that it has concerns about any of the following—

(a) the firm's skills, knowledge and experience in relation to Consumer Credit Act businesses;

(b) such skills, knowledge and experience of other persons who are participating in any Consumer Credit Act business being carried on by the firm;

(c) practices and procedures that the firm is implementing in connection with any such business.]

(3) "Associate", "Consumer Credit Act business" and "controller" have the same meaning as in section 203.

24.—(1) Sub-paragraph (2) applies if a UK firm—

(a) is not required to have a Part IV permission in relation to the business which it is carrying on; and

(b) is exercising the right conferred by [[Article 24] of the banking consolidation directive] to carry on that business in an EEA State other than the United Kingdom.

(2) If requested to do so by the host state regulator in the EEA State in which the UK firm's business is being carried on, the Authority may impose any requirement in relation to the firm which it could impose if—

(a) the firm had a Part IV permission in relation to the business which it is carrying on; and

(b) the Authority was entitled to exercise its power under that Part to vary that permission.

[Information to be included in the public record

25. The Authority must include in the record that it maintains under section 347 in relation to any UK firm whose EEA right derives from the insurance mediation directive information as to each EEA State in which the UK firm, in accordance with such a right—

(a) has established a branch; or

(b) is providing services.]

[2440]

NOTES

Para 19: words in square brackets in sub-para (1), and the whole of sub-paras (5A), (7A) inserted, and sub-para (5) substituted, by the Insurance Mediation Directive (Miscellaneous Amendments) Regulations 2003, SI 2003/1473, reg 5, as from 14 January 2005; for the words in italics in sub-paras (3), (6) there are substituted the words "Subject to sub-paragraph (5B), the" and "the UCITS directive or, in the case of a credit institution authorised under the banking consolidation directive, the markets in financial instruments directive" respectively, and sub-paras (5B), (5C), (7B) inserted, by SI 2007/126, reg 3(4), Sch 4, paras 1, 10, as from 1 April 2007 (certain purposes (see reg 1(2) at **[7596]**)), and as from 1 November 2007 (otherwise) (for transitional provisions, see the note below); words in square brackets in sub-paras (6), (12) substituted, and sub-para (12A) inserted, by the Collective Investment Schemes (Miscellaneous Amendments) Regulations 2003, SI 2003/2066, reg 4(1)(a), as from 13 February 2004.

Para 20: for the words in italics in sub-paras (2), (3) there are substituted the words "Subject to sub-paragraph (2A), the" and "markets in financial instruments directive" respectively, sub-pars (2A), (2B), (4BA) inserted, and words in square brackets in sub-para (4B) inserted, by SI 2007/126, reg 3(4), Sch 4, paras 1, 11, as from 1 April 2007 (certain purposes (see reg 1(2) at **[7596]**)), and as from 1 November 2007 (otherwise) (for transitional provisions, see the note below); words in first pair of square brackets in sub-para (3) substituted, and words in second pair of square brackets in that paragraph added, by SI 2003/2066, reg 4(1)(b), as from 13 February 2004; sub-paras (3A), (4A)–(4C) inserted, words in square brackets in sub-para (4) inserted, and sub-para (5) repealed, by the Financial Services (EEA Passport Rights) Regulations 2001, SI 2001/1376, reg 2(1)–(5), as from 30 April 2001; sub-para (3B) inserted by SI 2003/1473, reg 6(1), as from 14 January 2005.

Para 20A: inserted by SI 2007/126, reg 3(4), Sch 4, paras 1, 12, as from 1 April 2007 (certain purposes (see reg 1(2) at **[7596]**)), and as from 1 November 2007 (otherwise).

Para 21: words in square brackets substituted by SI 2003/1473, reg 6(2), as from 14 January 2005.

Para 23: for the words in italics in sub-para (1) there are substituted the words "Sub-paragraphs (2) and (2A) apply", for the words in italics in sub-para (2) there are substituted the words "(a) to (e) of section 25(2A)", and sub-para (2A) is inserted, by the Consumer Credit Act 2006, s 33(10)–(12), as from a day to be appointed; words in square brackets in sub-para (2) substituted by the Enterprise Act 2002, s 278(1), Sch 25, para 40(1), (19)(b), as from 1 April 2003.

Para 24: words in first (outer) pair of square brackets substituted by the Banking Consolidation Directive (Consequential Amendments) Regulations 2000, SI 2000/2952, reg 8(1), (5)(f), as from 22 November 2000; words in second (inner) pair of square brackets substituted by the Capital Requirements Regulations 2006, SI 2006/3221, reg 29(1), Sch 3, para 2(1), (4), as from 1 January 2007.

Para 25: inserted, together with preceding heading, by SI 2003/1473, reg 7, as from 14 January 2005.

Transitional provisions: the Financial Services and Markets Act 2000 (Markets in Financial Instruments) Regulations 2007, SI 2007/126 provide for various transitional provisions in connection with the amendments made by those Regulations to this Schedule. For transitional provisions in connection with paras 19, 20 above, see regs 7, 8 of the 2007 Regulations at **[7602]**, **[7603]**.

Exercise of passport rights by UK firms: see further the Financial Services and Markets Act 2000 (EEA Passport Rights) Regulations 2001, SI 2001/2511, Pt III (regs 11–18) at **[4458]** et seq.

Regulations: the Financial Services and Markets Act 2000 (EEA Passport Rights) Regulations 2001, SI 2001/2511 at **[4448]**.

Note that the following amending Regulations have also been made under this Part: the Collective Investment Schemes (Miscellaneous Amendments) Regulations 2003, SI 2003/2066; the Financial Services and Markets Act 2000 (EEA Passport Rights) (Amendment) Regulations 2006, SI 2006/3385; the Financial Services and Markets Act 2000 (Markets in Financial Instruments) (Amendment) Regulations 2007, SI 2007/763.

SCHEDULE 4
TREATY RIGHTS

Section 31(1)(c)

NOTES

Transitional provisions: the Financial Services and Markets Act 2000 (Transitional Provisions) (Authorised Persons etc) Order 2001, SI 2001/2636, Pt II, Chapter III, provides that treaty firms authorised before 1 December 2001 under the Financial Services Act 1986, s 31 and certain treaty firms which were authorised insurance companies before that date are to be treated after 1 December 2001 as having complied with the procedures of this Schedule. The 1986 Act was repealed by the Financial Services and Markets Act 2000 (Consequential Amendments and Repeals) Order 2001, SI 2001/3649, art 3(1)(c).

Definitions

1. In this Schedule—

"consumers" means persons who are consumers for the purposes of section 138;

"Treaty firm" means a person—

(a) whose head office is situated in an EEA State (its "home state") other than the United Kingdom; and

(b) which is recognised under the law of that State as its national; and

"home state regulator", in relation to a Treaty firm, means the competent authority of the firm's home state for the purpose of its home state authorisation (as to which see paragraph 3(1)(a)).

Firms qualifying for authorisation

2. Once a Treaty firm which is seeking to carry on a regulated activity satisfies the conditions set out in paragraph 3(1), it qualifies for authorisation.

Exercise of Treaty rights

3.—(1) The conditions are that—

(a) the firm has received authorisation ("home state authorisation") under the law of its home state to carry on the regulated activity in question ("the permitted activity");

(b) the relevant provisions of the law of the firm's home state—

(i) afford equivalent protection; or

(ii) satisfy the conditions laid down by a Community instrument for the co-ordination or approximation of laws, regulations or administrative provisions of member States relating to the carrying on of that activity; and

(c) the firm has no EEA right to carry on that activity in the manner in which it is seeking to carry it on.

(2) A firm is not to be regarded as having home state authorisation unless its home state regulator has so informed the Authority in writing.

(3) Provisions afford equivalent protection if, in relation to the firm's carrying on of the permitted activity, they afford consumers protection which is at least equivalent to that afforded by or under this Act in relation to that activity.

(4) A certificate issued by the Treasury that the provisions of the law of a particular EEA State afford equivalent protection in relation to the activities specified in the certificate is conclusive evidence of that fact.

Permission

4.—(1) On qualifying for authorisation under this Schedule, a Treaty firm has permission to carry on each permitted activity through its United Kingdom branch or by providing services in the United Kingdom.

(2) The permission is to be treated as being on terms equivalent to those to which the firm's home state authorisation is subject.

(3) If, on qualifying for authorisation under this Schedule, a firm has a Part IV permission which includes permission to carry on a permitted activity, the Authority must give a direction cancelling the permission so far as it relates to that activity.

(4) The Authority need not give a direction under sub-paragraph (3) if it considers that there are good reasons for not doing so.

Notice to Authority

5.—(1) Sub-paragraph (2) applies to a Treaty firm which—
- (a) qualifies for authorisation under this Schedule, but
- (b) is not carrying on in the United Kingdom the regulated activity, or any of the regulated activities, which it has permission to carry on there.

(2) At least seven days before it begins to carry on such a regulated activity, the firm must give the Authority written notice of its intention to do so.

(3) If a Treaty firm to which sub-paragraph (2) applies has given notice under that sub-paragraph, it need not give such a notice if it again becomes a firm to which that sub-paragraph applies.

(4) Subsections (1), (3) and (6) of section 51 apply to a notice under sub-paragraph (2) as they apply to an application for a Part IV permission.

Offences

6.—(1) A person who contravenes paragraph 5(2) is guilty of an offence.

(2) In proceedings against a person for an offence under sub-paragraph (1) it is a defence for him to show that he took all reasonable precautions and exercised all due diligence to avoid committing the offence.

(3) A person is guilty of an offence if in, or in connection with, a notice given by him under paragraph 5(2) he—
- (a) provides information which he knows to be false or misleading in a material particular; or
- (b) recklessly provides information which is false or misleading in a material particular.

(4) A person guilty of an offence under this paragraph is liable—
- (a) on summary conviction, to a fine not exceeding the statutory maximum;
- (b) on conviction on indictment, to a fine.

[2441]

NOTES

Qualifies for authorisation (para 2): regulations made under the Income Tax (Trading and Other Income) Act 2005, s 694, may provide that a firm which is an authorised person as a result of qualifying for authorisation under para 2 of this Schedule may only be a plan manager if certain requirements specified in those regulations are met; see ss 697, 698 of the 2005 Act.

SCHEDULE 5
PERSONS CONCERNED IN COLLECTIVE INVESTMENT SCHEMES

Section 36

Authorisation

1.—(1) A person who for the time being is an operator, trustee or depositary of a recognised collective investment scheme is an authorised person.

(2) "Recognised" means recognised by virtue of section 264.

(3) An authorised open-ended investment company is an authorised person.

[(4) A body—

(a) incorporated by virtue of regulations made under section 1 of the Open-Ended Investment Companies Act (Northern Ireland) 2002 in respect of which an authorisation order is in force, and

(b) to which the UCITS directive applies,

is an authorised person.

(5) "Authorisation order" means an order made under (or having effect as made under) any provision of those regulations which is made by virtue of section 1(2)(l) of that Act (provision corresponding to Chapter 3 of Part 17 of the Act).]

Permission

2.—(1) A person authorised as a result of paragraph 1(1) has permission to carry on, so far as it is a regulated activity—

(a) any activity, appropriate to the capacity in which he acts in relation to the scheme, of the kind described in paragraph 8 of Schedule 2;

(b) any activity in connection with, or for the purposes of, the scheme.

(2) A person authorised as a result of paragraph 1(3) [or (4)] has permission to carry on, so far as it is a regulated activity—

(a) the operation of the scheme;

(b) any activity in connection with, or for the purposes of, the operation of the scheme.

[2442]

NOTES

Para 1: sub-paras (4), (5) added by the Collective Investment Schemes (Miscellaneous Amendments) Regulations 2003, SI 2003/2066, reg 10(a), as from 13 February 2004.

Para 2: words in square brackets inserted by SI 2003/2066, reg 10(b), as from 13 February 2004.

SCHEDULE 6
THRESHOLD CONDITIONS

Section 41

PART I
PART IV PERMISSION

Legal status

1.—(1) If the regulated activity concerned is the effecting or carrying out of contracts of insurance the authorised person must be a body corporate [(other than a limited liability partnership)], a registered friendly society or a member of Lloyd's.

(2) If the person concerned appears to the Authority to be seeking to carry on, or to be carrying on, a regulated activity constituting accepting deposits [or issuing electronic money], it must be—

(a) a body corporate; or
(b) a partnership.

Location of offices

2.—(1) [Subject to *sub-paragraph* (*3*),] If the person concerned is a body corporate constituted under the law of any part of the United Kingdom—
(a) its head office, and
(b) if it has a registered office, that office,

must be in the United Kingdom.

(2) If the person concerned has its head office in the United Kingdom but is not a body corporate, it must carry on business in the United Kingdom.

[(2A) If—
(a) the regulated activity concerned is any of the investment services and activities, and
(b) the person concerned is a body corporate with no registered office,

sub-paragraph (2B) applies in place of sub-paragraph (1).

(2B) If the person concerned has its head office in the United Kingdom, it must carry on business in the United Kingdom.]

[(3) If the regulated activity concerned is an insurance mediation activity, sub-paragraph (1) does not apply.

(4) If the regulated activity concerned is an insurance mediation activity, the person concerned—
(a) if he is a body corporate constituted under the law of any part of the United Kingdom, must have its registered office, or if it has no registered office, its head office, in the United Kingdom;
(b) if he is a natural person, is to be treated for the purposes of sub-paragraph (2), as having his head office in the United Kingdom if his residence is situated there.

(5) "Insurance mediation activity" means any of the following activities—
(a) dealing in rights under a contract of insurance as agent;
(b) arranging deals in rights under a contract of insurance;
(c) assisting in the administration and performance of a contract of insurance;
(d) advising on buying or selling rights under a contract of insurance;
(e) agreeing to do any of the activities specified in sub-paragraph (a) to (d).

(6) Paragraph (5) must be read with—
(a) section 22;
(b) any relevant order under that section; and
(c) Schedule 2.]

[Appointment of claims representatives

2A.—(1) If it appears to the Authority that—
(a) the regulated activity that the person concerned is carrying on, or is seeking to carry on, is the effecting or carrying out of contracts of insurance, and
(b) contracts of insurance against damage arising out of or in connection with the use of motor vehicles on land (other than carrier's liability) are being, or will be, effected or carried out by the person concerned,

that person must have a claims representative in each EEA State other than the United Kingdom.

(2) For the purposes of sub-paragraph (1)(b), contracts of reinsurance are to be disregarded.

(3) A claims representative is a person with responsibility for handling and settling claims arising from accidents of the kind mentioned in Article 1(2) of the fourth motor insurance directive.

(4) In this paragraph "fourth motor insurance directive" means Directive 2000/26/EC of the European Parliament and of the Council of 16th May 2000 on the approximation of the

laws of the Member States relating to insurance against civil liability in respect of the use of motor vehicles and amending Council Directives 73/239/EEC and 88/357/EEC.]

Close links

3.—(1) If the person concerned ("A") has close links with another person ("CL") the Authority must be satisfied—

(a) that those links are not likely to prevent the Authority's effective supervision of A; and

(b) if it appears to the Authority that CL is subject to the laws, regulations or administrative provisions of a territory which is not an EEA State ("the foreign provisions"), that neither the foreign provisions, nor any deficiency in their enforcement, would prevent the Authority's effective supervision of A.

(2) A has close links with CL if—

(a) CL is a parent undertaking of A;

(b) CL is a subsidiary undertaking of A;

(c) CL is a parent undertaking of a subsidiary undertaking of A;

(d) CL is a subsidiary undertaking of a parent undertaking of A;

(e) CL owns or controls 20% or more of the voting rights or capital of A; or

(f) A owns or controls 20% or more of the voting rights or capital of CL.

(3) "Subsidiary undertaking" includes all the instances mentioned in Article 1(1) and (2) of the Seventh Company Law Directive in which an entity may be a subsidiary of an undertaking.

Adequate resources

4.—(1) The resources of the person concerned must, in the opinion of the Authority, be adequate in relation to the regulated activities that he seeks to carry on, or carries on.

(2) In reaching that opinion, the Authority may—

(a) take into account the person's membership of a group and any effect which that membership may have; and

(b) have regard to—

(i) the provision he makes and, if he is a member of a group, which other members of the group make in respect of liabilities (including contingent and future liabilities); and

(ii) the means by which he manages and, if he is a member of a group, which other members of the group manage the incidence of risk in connection with his business.

Suitability

5. The person concerned must satisfy the Authority that he is a fit and proper person having regard to all the circumstances, including—

(a) his connection with any person;

(b) the nature of any regulated activity that he carries on or seeks to carry on; and

(c) the need to ensure that his affairs are conducted soundly and prudently.

[2443]

NOTES

Para 1: words in first pair of square brackets inserted by the Financial Services and Markets Act 2000 (Variation of Threshold Conditions) Order 2001, SI 2001/2507, art 2, as from 3 September 2001; words in second pair of square brackets inserted by the Financial Services and Markets Act 2000 (Regulated Activities) (Amendment) Order 2002, SI 2002/682, art 8, as from 27 April 2002.

Para 2: words in square brackets in sub-para (1), and the whole of sub-paras (3)–(6) inserted by the Financial Services and Markets Act 2000 (Regulated Activities) (Amendment) (No 2) Order 2003, SI 2003/1476, art 19, as from 31 October 2004 (in so far as relating to contracts of long-term care insurance), and as from 14 January 2005 (otherwise) (for transitional provisions see arts 22–27 of that Order at **[4665]** et seq); for the words in italics in sub-para (1) there are substituted the words "sub-paragraphs (2A) and (3)", and sub-paras (2A), (2B) inserted, by the Financial Services and Markets Act 2000 (Markets in Financial Instruments) Regulations 2007, SI 2007/126, reg 3(5), Sch 5, paras 1, 24, as from 1 April 2007 (certain purposes (see reg 1(2) at **[7596]**)), and as from 1 November 2007 (otherwise).

Para 2A: inserted by the Financial Services and Markets Act 2000 (Variation of Threshold Conditions) Order 2002, SI 2002/2707, art 2, as from 19 January 2003.

Swiss general insurance companies: the conditions in paras 4, 5 have been removed in relation to a Swiss general insurance company; see the Financial Services and Markets Act 2000 (Variation of Threshold Conditions) Order 2001, SI 2001/2507, art 3(3) (as substituted by the Financial Services and Markets Act 2000 (Variation of Threshold Conditions) (Amendment) Order 2005, SI 2005/680). See also art 4 of that Order for additional conditions imposed on such companies.

PART II
AUTHORISATION

Authorisation under Schedule 3

6. In relation to an EEA firm qualifying for authorisation under Schedule 3, the conditions set out in paragraphs 1 and 3 to 5 apply, so far as relevant, to—

(a) an application for permission under Part IV;

(b) exercise of the Authority's own-initiative power under section 45 in relation to a Part IV permission.

Authorisation under Schedule 4

7. In relation to a person who qualifies for authorisation under Schedule 4, the conditions set out in paragraphs 1 and 3 to 5 apply, so far as relevant, to—

(a) an application for an additional permission;

(b) the exercise of the Authority's own-initiative power under section 45 in relation to additional permission.

[2444]

PART II
FSMA 2000

PART III
ADDITIONAL CONDITIONS

8.—(1) If this paragraph applies to the person concerned, he must, for the purposes of such provisions of this Act as may be specified, satisfy specified additional conditions.

(2) This paragraph applies to a person who—

(a) has his head office outside the EEA; and

(b) appears to the Authority to be seeking to carry on a regulated activity relating to insurance business.

(3) "Specified" means specified in, or in accordance with, an order made by the Treasury.

9. The Treasury may by order—

(a) vary or remove any of the conditions set out in Parts I and II;

(b) add to those conditions.

[2445]

NOTES

Orders: the Financial Services and Markets Act 2000 (Variation of Threshold Conditions) Order 2001, SI 2001/2507.

Note that the following amending Orders have also been made under this Part: the Financial Services and Markets Act 2000 (Variation of Threshold Conditions) Order 2002, SI 2002/2707; the Financial Services and Markets Act 2000 (Variation of Threshold Conditions) (Amendment) Order 2005, SI 2005/680.

SCHEDULE 7
THE AUTHORITY AS COMPETENT AUTHORITY FOR PART VI

Section 72(2)

General

1. This Act applies in relation to the Authority when it is exercising functions under Part VI as the competent authority subject to the following modifications.

The Authority's general functions

2. In section 2—
   (a) subsection (4)(a) does not apply to [Part 6 rules];
   (b) subsection (4)(c) does not apply to general guidance given in relation to Part VI; and
   (c) subsection (4)(d) does not apply to functions under Part VI.

Duty to consult

3. Section 8 does not apply.

Rules

4.—(1) Sections 149, 153, 154 and 156 do not apply.

(2) Section 155 has effect as if—
   (a) the reference in subsection (2)(c) to the general duties of the Authority under section 2 were a reference to its duty under section 73; and
   (b) section 99 were included in the provisions referred to in subsection (9).

Statements of policy

5.—(1) Paragraph 5 of Schedule 1 has effect as if the requirement to act through the Authority's governing body applied also to the exercise of its functions of publishing statements under section 93.

(2) Paragraph 1 of Schedule 1 has effect as if section 93 were included in the provisions referred to in sub-paragraph (2)(d).

Penalties

6. Paragraph 16 of Schedule 1 does not apply in relation to penalties under Part VI (for which separate provision is made by section 100).

Fees

7. Paragraph 17 of Schedule 1 does not apply in relation to fees payable under Part VI (for which separate provision is made by section 99).

Exemption from liability in damages

8. Schedule 1 has effect as if—
   (a) sub-paragraph (1) of paragraph 19 were omitted (similar provision being made in relation to the competent authority by section 102); and
   (b) for the words from the beginning to "(a)" in sub-paragraph (3) of that paragraph, there were substituted "Sub-paragraph (2) does not apply".

[2446]

NOTES

Para 2: words in square brackets in sub-para (a) substituted by the Financial Services and Markets Act 2000 (Market Abuse) Regulations 2005, SI 2005/381, reg 4, Sch 1, para 12, as from 1 July 2005.

SCHEDULE 8
TRANSFER OF FUNCTIONS UNDER PART VI

Section 72(3)

The power to transfer

1.—(1) The Treasury may by order provide for any function conferred on the competent authority which is exercisable for the time being by a particular person to be transferred so as to be exercisable by another person.

(2) An order may be made under this paragraph only if—
- (a) the person from whom the relevant functions are to be transferred has agreed in writing that the order should be made;
- (b) the Treasury are satisfied that the manner in which, or efficiency with which, the functions are discharged would be significantly improved if they were transferred to the transferee; or
- (c) the Treasury are satisfied that it is otherwise in the public interest that the order should be made.

Supplemental

2.—(1) An order under this Schedule does not affect anything previously done by any person ("the previous authority") in the exercise of functions which are transferred by the order to another person ("the new authority").

(2) Such an order may, in particular, include provision—
- (a) modifying or excluding any provision of Part VI, IX or XXVI in its application to any such functions;
- (b) for reviews similar to that made, in relation to the Authority, by section 12;
- (c) imposing on the new authority requirements similar to those imposed, in relation to the Authority, by sections 152, 155 and 354;
- (d) as to the giving of guidance by the new authority;
- (e) for the delegation by the new authority of the exercise of functions under Part VI and as to the consequences of delegation;
- (f) for the transfer of any property, rights or liabilities relating to any such functions from the previous authority to the new authority;
- (g) for the carrying on and completion by the new authority of anything in the process of being done by the previous authority when the order takes effect;
- (h) for the substitution of the new authority for the previous authority in any instrument, contract or legal proceedings;
- (i) for the transfer of persons employed by the previous authority to the new authority and as to the terms on which they are to transfer;
- (j) making such amendments to any primary or subordinate legislation (including any provision of, or made under, this Act) as the Treasury consider appropriate in consequence of the transfer of functions effected by the order.

(3) Nothing in this paragraph is to be taken as restricting the powers conferred by section 428.

3. If the Treasury have made an order under paragraph 1 ("the transfer order") they may, by a separate order made under this paragraph, make any provision of a kind that could have been included in the transfer order.

[2447]–[2448]

(*Sch 9 repealed by the Prospectus Regulations 2005, SI 2005/1433, reg 2(1), Sch 1, para 16, as from 1 July 2005.*)

SCHEDULE 10
COMPENSATION: EXEMPTIONS

Section 90(2) and (5)

Statements believed to be true

1.—(1) In this paragraph "statement" means—
- (a) any untrue or misleading statement in listing particulars; or

PART II FSMA 2000

(b) the omission from listing particulars of any matter required to be included by section 80 or 81.

(2) A person does not incur any liability under section 90(1) for loss caused by a statement if he satisfies the court that, at the time when the listing particulars were submitted to the competent authority, he reasonably believed (having made such enquiries, if any, as were reasonable) that—

(a) the statement was true and not misleading, or
(b) the matter whose omission caused the loss was properly omitted,

and that one or more of the conditions set out in sub-paragraph (3) are satisfied.

(3) The conditions are that—

(a) he continued in his belief until the time when the securities in question were acquired;
(b) they were acquired before it was reasonably practicable to bring a correction to the attention of persons likely to acquire them;
(c) before the securities were acquired, he had taken all such steps as it was reasonable for him to have taken to secure that a correction was brought to the attention of those persons;
(d) he continued in his belief until after the commencement of dealings in the securities following their admission to the official list and they were acquired after such a lapse of time that he ought in the circumstances to be reasonably excused.

Statements by experts

2.—(1) In this paragraph "statement" means a statement included in listing particulars which—

(a) purports to be made by, or on the authority of, another person as an expert; and
(b) is stated to be included in the listing particulars with that other person's consent.

(2) A person does not incur any liability under section 90(1) for loss in respect of any securities caused by a statement if he satisfies the court that, at the time when the listing particulars were submitted to the competent authority, he reasonably believed that the other person—

(a) was competent to make or authorise the statement, and
(b) had consented to its inclusion in the form and context in which it was included,

and that one or more of the conditions set out in sub-paragraph (3) are satisfied.

(3) The conditions are that—

(a) he continued in his belief until the time when the securities were acquired;
(b) they were acquired before it was reasonably practicable to bring the fact that the expert was not competent, or had not consented, to the attention of persons likely to acquire the securities in question;
(c) before the securities were acquired he had taken all such steps as it was reasonable for him to have taken to secure that that fact was brought to the attention of those persons;
(d) he continued in his belief until after the commencement of dealings in the securities following their admission to the official list and they were acquired after such a lapse of time that he ought in the circumstances to be reasonably excused.

Corrections of statements

3.—(1) In this paragraph "statement" has the same meaning as in paragraph 1.

(2) A person does not incur liability under section 90(1) for loss caused by a statement if he satisfies the court—

(a) that before the securities in question were acquired, a correction had been published in a manner calculated to bring it to the attention of persons likely to acquire the securities; or
(b) that he took all such steps as it was reasonable for him to take to secure such publication and reasonably believed that it had taken place before the securities were acquired.

(3) Nothing in this paragraph is to be taken as affecting paragraph 1.

Corrections of statements by experts

4.—(1) In this paragraph "statement" has the same meaning as in paragraph 2.

(2) A person does not incur liability under section 90(1) for loss caused by a statement if he satisfies the court—

(a) that before the securities in question were acquired, the fact that the expert was not competent or had not consented had been published in a manner calculated to bring it to the attention of persons likely to acquire the securities; or

(b) that he took all such steps as it was reasonable for him to take to secure such publication and reasonably believed that it had taken place before the securities were acquired.

(3) Nothing in this paragraph is to be taken as affecting paragraph 2.

Official statements

5. A person does not incur any liability under section 90(1) for loss resulting from—

(a) a statement made by an official person which is included in the listing particulars, or

(b) a statement contained in a public official document which is included in the listing particulars,

if he satisfies the court that the statement is accurately and fairly reproduced.

False or misleading information known about

6. A person does not incur any liability under section 90(1) or (4) if he satisfies the court that the person suffering the loss acquired the securities in question with knowledge—

(a) that the statement was false or misleading,

(b) of the omitted matter, or

(c) of the change or new matter,

as the case may be.

Belief that supplementary listing particulars not called for

7. A person does not incur any liability under section 90(4) if he satisfies the court that he reasonably believed that the change or new matter in question was not such as to call for supplementary listing particulars.

Meaning of "expert"

8. "Expert" includes any engineer, valuer, accountant or other person whose profession, qualifications or experience give authority to a statement made by him.

[2449]–[2450]

(*Sch 11 repealed by the Prospectus Regulations 2005, SI 2005/1433, reg 2(1), Sch 1, para 16, as from 1 July 2005.*)

[SCHEDULE 11A
TRANSFERABLE SECURITIES

Section 85(5)(a)

PART 1

1. Units (within the meaning in section 237(2)) in an open-ended collective investment scheme.

2. Non-equity transferable securities issued by

(a) the government of an EEA State;

(b) a local or regional authority of an EEA State;

(c) a public international body of which an EEA State is a member;

(d) the European Central Bank;
(e) the central bank of an EEA State.

3. Shares in the share capital of the central bank of an EEA State.

4. Transferable securities unconditionally and irrevocably guaranteed by the government, or a local or regional authority, of an EEA State.

5.—(1) Non-equity transferable securities, issued in a continuous or repeated manner by a credit institution, which satisfy the conditions in sub-paragraph (2).

(2) The conditions are that the transferable securities—
(a) are not subordinated, convertible or exchangeable;
(b) do not give a right to subscribe to or acquire other types of securities and are not linked to a derivative instrument;
(c) materialise reception of repayable deposits; and
(d) are covered by a deposit guarantee under directive 94/19/EC of the European Parliament and of the Council on deposit-guarantee schemes.

6. Non-fungible shares of capital—
(a) the main purpose of which is to provide the holder with a right to occupy any immoveable property, and
(b) which cannot be sold without that right being given up.]

[2450A]

NOTES

Inserted by the Prospectus Regulations 2005, SI 2005/1433, reg 2(2), Sch 2, as from 1 July 2005.

[PART 2

7.—(1) Transferable securities issued by a body specified in sub-paragraph (2) if, and only if, the proceeds of the offer of the transferable securities to the public will be used solely for the purposes of the issuer's objectives.

(2) The bodies are
(a) a charity within the meaning of—
(i) section 96(1) of the Charities Act 1993 (c 10), or
(ii) section 35 of the Charities Act (Northern Ireland) 1964 (c 33 (NI));
[(b) a body entered in the Scottish Charity Register;]
(c) a housing association within the meaning of—
(i) section 5(1) of the Housing Act 1985 (c 68),
(ii) section 1 of the Housing Associations Act 1985 (c 69), or
(iii) Article 3 of the Housing (Northern Ireland) Order 1992 (SI 1992/1725 (NI 15));
(d) an industrial and provident society registered in accordance with—
(i) section 1(2)(b) of the Industrial and Provident Societies Act 1965 (c 12), or
(ii) section 1(2)(b) of the Industrial and Provident Societies Act (Northern Ireland) 1969 (c 24 (NI));
(e) a non-profit making association or body recognised by an EEA State with objectives similar to those of a body falling within any of sub-paragraphs (a) to (d).

8.—(1) Non-equity transferable securities, issued in a continuous or repeated manner by a credit institution, which satisfy the conditions in sub-paragraph (2).

(2) The conditions are—
(a) that the total consideration of the offer is less than 50,000,000 euros (or an equivalent amount); and
(b) those mentioned in paragraph 5(2)(a) and (b).

(3) In determining whether sub-paragraph (2)(a) is satisfied in relation to an offer ("offer A"), offer A is to be taken together with any other offer of transferable securities of the same class made by the same person which—
(a) was open at any time within the period of 12 months ending with the date on which offer A is first made; and

(b) had previously satisfied sub-paragraph (2)(a).

(4) For the purposes of this paragraph, an amount (in relation to an amount denominated in euros) is an "equivalent amount" if it is an amount of equal value denominated wholly or partly in another currency or unit of account.

(5) The equivalent is to be calculated at the latest practicable date before (but in any event not more than 3 working days before) the date on which the offer is first made.

(6) "Credit institution" means a credit institution as defined in [Article 4(1)(a)] of the banking consolidation directive.

9.—(1) Transferable securities included in an offer where the total consideration of the offer is less than 2,500,000 euros (or an equivalent amount).

(2) Sub-paragraphs (3) to (5) of paragraph 8 apply for the purposes of this paragraph but with the references in sub-paragraph (3) to "sub-paragraph (2)(a)" being read as references to "paragraph 9(1)".]

[2450B]

NOTES

Inserted by the Prospectus Regulations 2005, SI 2005/1433, reg 2(2), Sch 2, as from 1 July 2005.

Para 7: sub-para (2)(b) substituted by the Charities and Trustee Investment (Scotland) Act 2005 (Consequential Provisions and Modifications) Order 2006, SI 2006/242, art 5, Schedule, Pt 1, para 7, as from 1 April 2006.

Para 8: words in square brackets in sub-para (6) substituted by the Capital Requirements Regulations 2006, SI 2006/3221, reg 29(1), Sch 3, para 3, as from 1 January 2007.

SCHEDULE 12
TRANSFER SCHEMES: CERTIFICATES

Sections 111(2) and 115

PART I
INSURANCE BUSINESS TRANSFER SCHEMES

1.—(1) For the purposes of section 111(2) the appropriate certificates, in relation to an insurance business transfer scheme, are—

(a) a certificate under paragraph 2;
(b) if sub-paragraph (2) applies, a certificate under paragraph 3;
(c) if sub-paragraph (3) applies, a certificate under paragraph 4;
(d) if sub-paragraph (4) applies, a certificate under paragraph 5.

(2) This sub-paragraph applies if—

(a) the authorised person concerned is a UK authorised person which has received authorisation under [Article 4 of the life assurance consolidation directive or Article 6] of the first non-life insurance directive from the Authority; and
(b) the establishment from which the business is to be transferred under the proposed insurance business transfer scheme is in an EEA State other than the United Kingdom.

(3) This sub-paragraph applies if—

(a) the authorised person concerned has received authorisation under [Article 4 of the life assurance consolidation directive] from the Authority;
(b) the proposed transfer relates to business which consists of the effecting or carrying out of contracts of long-term insurance; and
(c) as regards any policy which is included in the proposed transfer and which evidences a contract of insurance (other than reinsurance), an EEA State other than the United Kingdom is the State of the commitment.

(4) This sub-paragraph applies if—

(a) the authorised person concerned has received authorisation under Article 6 of the first non-life insurance directive from the Authority;
(b) the business to which the proposed insurance business transfer scheme relates is business which consists of the effecting or carrying out of contracts of general insurance; and
(c) as regards any policy which is included in the proposed transfer and which

PART II
FSMA 2000

evidences a contract of insurance (other than reinsurance), the risk is situated in an EEA State other than the United Kingdom.

Certificates as to margin of solvency

2.—(1) A certificate under this paragraph is to be given—
(a) by the relevant authority; or
(b) in a case in which there is no relevant authority, by the Authority.

(2) A certificate given under sub-paragraph (1)(a) is one certifying that, taking the proposed transfer into account—
(a) the transferee possesses, or will possess before the scheme takes effect, the necessary margin of solvency; or
(b) there is no necessary margin of solvency applicable to the transferee.

(3) A certificate under sub-paragraph (1)(b) is one certifying that the Authority has received from the authority which it considers to be the authority responsible for supervising persons who effect or carry out contracts of insurance in the place to which the business is to be transferred that, taking the proposed transfer into account—
(a) the transferee possesses or will possess before the scheme takes effect the margin of solvency required under the law applicable in that place; or
(b) there is no such margin of solvency applicable to the transferee.

(4) "Necessary margin of solvency" means the margin of solvency required in relation to the transferee, taking the proposed transfer into account, under the law which it is the responsibility of the relevant authority to apply.

(5) "Margin of solvency" means the excess of the value of the assets of the transferee over the amount of its liabilities.

(6) "Relevant authority" means—
(a) if the transferee is an EEA firm falling within paragraph 5(d) of Schedule 3, its home state regulator;
(b) if the transferee is a Swiss general insurer, the authority responsible in Switzerland for supervising persons who effect or carry out contracts of insurance;
(c) if the transferee is an authorised person not falling within paragraph (a) or (b), the Authority.

(7) In sub-paragraph (6), any reference to a transferee of a particular description includes a reference to a transferee who will be of that description if the proposed scheme takes effect.

(8) "Swiss general insurer" means a body—
(a) whose head office is in Switzerland;
(b) which has permission to carry on regulated activities consisting of the effecting and carrying out of contracts of general insurance; and
(c) whose permission is not restricted to the effecting or carrying out of contracts of reinsurance.

Certificates as to consent

3. A certificate under this paragraph is one given by the Authority and certifying that the host State regulator has been notified of the proposed scheme and that—
(a) that regulator has responded to the notification; or
(b) that it has not responded but the period of three months beginning with the notification has elapsed.

Certificates as to long-term business

4. A certificate under this paragraph is one given by the Authority and certifying that the authority responsible for supervising persons who effect or carry out contracts of insurance in the State of the commitment has been notified of the proposed scheme and that—
(a) that authority has consented to the proposed scheme; or
(b) the period of three months beginning with the notification has elapsed and that authority has not refused its consent.

Certificates as to general business

5. A certificate under this paragraph is one given by the Authority and certifying that the authority responsible for supervising persons who effect or carry out contracts of insurance in the EEA State in which the risk is situated has been notified of the proposed scheme and that—

(a) that authority has consented to the proposed scheme; or

(b) the period of three months beginning with the notification has elapsed and that authority has not refused its consent.

Interpretation of Part I

6.—(1) "State of the commitment", in relation to a commitment entered into at any date, means—

(a) if the policyholder is an individual, the State in which he had his habitual residence at that date;

(b) if the policyholder is not an individual, the State in which the establishment of the policyholder to which the commitment relates was situated at that date.

(2) "Commitment" means a commitment represented by contracts of insurance of a prescribed class.

(3) References to the EEA State in which a risk is situated are—

(a) if the insurance relates to a building or to a building and its contents (so far as the contents are covered by the same policy), to the EEA State in which the building is situated;

(b) if the insurance relates to a vehicle of any type, to the EEA State of registration;

(c) in the case of policies of a duration of four months or less covering travel or holiday risks (whatever the class concerned), to the EEA State in which the policyholder took out the policy;

(d) in a case not covered by paragraphs (a) to (c)—

(i) if the policyholder is an individual, to the EEA State in which he has his habitual residence at the date when the contract is entered into; and

(ii) otherwise, to the EEA State in which the establishment of the policyholder to which the policy relates is situated at that date.

[2451]

NOTES

Para 1: words in square brackets substituted by the Life Assurance Consolidation Directive (Consequential Amendments) Regulations 2004, SI 2004/3379, reg 6(1), (7)(a), as from 11 January 2005.

Regulations: the Financial Services and Markets Act 2000 (Control of Business Transfers) (Requirements on Applicants) Regulations 2001, SI 2001/3625 at **[4511]**.

PART II

BANKING BUSINESS TRANSFER SCHEMES

7.—(1) For the purposes of section 111(2) the appropriate certificates, in relation to a banking business transfer scheme, are—

(a) a certificate under paragraph 8; and

(b) if sub-paragraph (2) applies, a certificate under paragraph 9.

(2) This sub-paragraph applies if the authorised person concerned or the transferee is an EEA firm falling within paragraph 5(b) of Schedule 3.

Certificates as to financial resources

8.—(1) A certificate under this paragraph is one given by the relevant authority and certifying that, taking the proposed transfer into account, the transferee possesses, or will possess before the scheme takes effect, adequate financial resources.

(2) "Relevant authority" means—

(a) if the transferee is a person with a Part IV permission or with permission under Schedule 4, the Authority;

(b) if the transferee is an EEA firm falling within paragraph 5(b) of Schedule 3, its home state regulator;
(c) if the transferee does not fall within paragraph (a) or (b), the authority responsible for the supervision of the transferee's business in the place in which the transferee has its head office.

(3) In sub-paragraph (2), any reference to a transferee of a particular description of person includes a reference to a transferee who will be of that description if the proposed banking business transfer scheme takes effect.

Certificates as to consent of home state regulator

9. A certificate under this paragraph is one given by the Authority and certifying that the home State regulator of the authorised person concerned or of the transferee has been notified of the proposed scheme and that—
(a) the home State regulator has responded to the notification; or
(b) the period of three months beginning with the notification has elapsed.

[2452]

PART III
INSURANCE BUSINESS TRANSFERS EFFECTED OUTSIDE THE UNITED KINGDOM

10.—(1) This paragraph applies to a proposal to execute under provisions corresponding to Part VII in a country or territory other than the United Kingdom an instrument transferring all the rights and obligations of the transferor under general or long-term insurance policies, or under such descriptions of such policies as may be specified in the instrument, to the transferee if any of the conditions in sub-paragraphs (2), (3) or (4) is met in relation to it.

(2) The transferor is an EEA firm falling within paragraph 5(d) of Schedule 3 and the transferee is an authorised person whose margin of solvency is supervised by the Authority.

(3) The transferor is a company authorised in an EEA State other than the United Kingdom under [Article 51 of the life assurance consolidation directive], or Article 23 of the first non-life insurance directive and the transferee is a UK authorised person which has received authorisation under [Article 4 of the life assurance consolidation directive or Article 6 of the first non-life insurance directive].

(4) The transferor is a Swiss general insurer and the transferee is a UK authorised person which has received authorisation under [Article 4 of the life assurance consolidation directive or Article 6 of the first non-life insurance directive].

(5) In relation to a proposed transfer to which this paragraph applies, the Authority may, if it is satisfied that the transferee possesses the necessary margin of solvency, issue a certificate to that effect.

(6) "Necessary margin of solvency" means the margin of solvency which the transferee, taking the proposed transfer into account, is required by the Authority to maintain.

(7) "Swiss general insurer" has the same meaning as in paragraph 2.

(8) "General policy" means a policy evidencing a contract which, if it had been effected by the transferee, would have constituted the carrying on of a regulated activity consisting of the effecting of contracts of general insurance.

(9) "Long-term policy" means a policy evidencing a contract which, if it had been effected by the transferee, would have constituted the carrying on of a regulated activity consisting of the effecting of contracts of long-term insurance.

[2453]

NOTES

Para 10: words in square brackets substituted by the Life Assurance Consolidation Directive (Consequential Amendments) Regulations 2004, SI 2004/3379, reg 6(1), (7)(b), (c), as from 11 January 2005.

SCHEDULE 13
THE FINANCIAL SERVICES AND MARKETS TRIBUNAL

Section 132(4)

PART I
GENERAL

Interpretation

1. In this Schedule—
"panel of chairmen" means the panel established under paragraph 3(1);
"lay panel" means the panel established under paragraph 3(4);
"rules" means rules made by the Lord Chancellor under section 132.

[2454]

PART II
THE TRIBUNAL

President

2.—(1) The Lord Chancellor must appoint one of the members of the panel of chairmen to preside over the discharge of the Tribunal's functions.

(2) The member so appointed is to be known as the President of the Financial Services and Markets Tribunal (but is referred to in this Act as "the President").

(3) The Lord Chancellor may appoint one of the members of the panel of chairmen to be Deputy President.

(4) The Deputy President is to have such functions in relation to the Tribunal as the President may assign to him.

(5) The Lord Chancellor may not appoint a person to be the President or Deputy President unless that person—
- (a) has a ten year general qualification within the meaning of section 71 of the Courts and Legal Services Act 1990;
- (b) is an advocate or solicitor in Scotland of at least ten years' standing; or
- (c) is—
  - (i) a member of the Bar of Northern Ireland of at least ten years' standing; or
  - (ii) a *solicitor of the Supreme Court of Northern Ireland* of at least ten years' standing.

(6) If the President (or Deputy President) ceases to be a member of the panel of chairmen, he also ceases to be the President (or Deputy President).

(7) The functions of the President may, if he is absent or is otherwise unable to act, be discharged—
- (a) by the Deputy President; or
- (b) if there is no Deputy President or he too is absent or otherwise unable to act, by a person appointed for that purpose from the panel of chairmen by the Lord Chancellor.

[(8) The Lord Chancellor may appoint a person under sub-paragraph (7)(b) only after consulting the following—
- (a) the Lord Chief Justice of England and Wales;
- (b) the Lord President of the Court of Session;
- (c) the Lord Chief Justice of Northern Ireland.

(9) The Lord Chief Justice of England and Wales may nominate a judicial office holder (as defined in section 109(4) of the Constitutional Reform Act 2005) to exercise his functions under this paragraph.

(10) The Lord President of the Court of Session may nominate a judge of the Court of Session who is a member of the First or Second Division of the Inner House of that Court to exercise his functions under this paragraph.

(11) The Lord Chief Justice of Northern Ireland may nominate any of the following to exercise his functions under this paragraph—

(a) the holder of one of the offices listed in Schedule 1 to the Justice (Northern Ireland) Act 2002;

(b) a Lord Justice of Appeal (as defined in section 88 of that Act).]

Panels

3.—(1) The Lord Chancellor must appoint a panel of persons for the purposes of serving as chairmen of the Tribunal.

(2) A person is qualified for membership of the panel of chairmen if—

(a) he has a seven year general qualification within the meaning of section 71 of the Courts and Legal Services Act 1990;

(b) he is an advocate or solicitor in Scotland of at least seven years' standing; or

(c) he is—

(i) a member of the Bar of Northern Ireland of at least seven years' standing; or

(ii) a *solicitor of the Supreme Court of Northern Ireland* of at least seven years' standing.

(3) The panel of chairmen must include at least one member who is a person of the kind mentioned in sub-paragraph (2)(b).

(4) The Lord Chancellor must also appoint a panel of persons who appear to him to be qualified by experience or otherwise to deal with matters of the kind that may be referred to the Tribunal.

Terms of office etc

4.—(1) Subject to the provisions of this Schedule, each member of the panel of chairmen and the lay panel is to hold and vacate office in accordance with the terms of his appointment.

(2) The Lord Chancellor may remove a member of either panel (including the President) on the ground of incapacity or misbehaviour.

[(2A) The Lord Chancellor may remove a person under sub-paragraph (2) only with the concurrence of the appropriate senior judge.

(2B) The appropriate senior judge is the Lord Chief Justice of England and Wales, unless—

(a) the person to be removed exercises functions wholly or mainly in Scotland, in which case it is the Lord President of the Court of Session, or

(b) the person to be removed exercises functions wholly or mainly in Northern Ireland, in which case it is the Lord Chief Justice of Northern Ireland.]

(3) A member of either panel—

(a) may at any time resign office by notice in writing to the Lord Chancellor;

(b) is eligible for re-appointment if he ceases to hold office.

Remuneration and expenses

5. The Lord Chancellor may pay to any person, in respect of his service—

(a) as a member of the Tribunal (including service as the President or Deputy President), or

(b) as a person appointed under paragraph 7(4),

such remuneration and allowances as he may determine.

Staff

6.—(1) The Lord Chancellor may appoint such staff for the Tribunal as he may determine.

(2) The remuneration of the Tribunal's staff is to be defrayed by the Lord Chancellor.

(3) Such expenses of the Tribunal as the Lord Chancellor may determine are to be defrayed by the Lord Chancellor.

[2455]

NOTES

Para 2: for the words in italics in sub-para (5)(c)(ii) there are substituted the words "solicitor of the Court of Judicature of Northern Ireland" by the Constitutional Reform Act 2005, s 59(5), Sch 11, Pt 3, para 5, as from a day to be appointed; sub-paras (8)–(11) added by the Constitutional Reform Act 2005, s 15, Sch 4, Pt 1, para 286(1), (2), as from 3 April 2006.

Para 3: for the words in italics in sub-para (2)(c)(ii) there are substituted the words "solicitor of the Court of Judicature of Northern Ireland" by the Constitutional Reform Act 2005, s 59(5), Sch 11, Pt 3, para 5, as from a day to be appointed.

Para 4: sub-paras (2A), (2B) inserted by the Constitutional Reform Act 2005, s 15, Sch 4, Pt 1, para 286(1), (3), as from 3 April 2006.

PART III
CONSTITUTION OF TRIBUNAL

7.—(1) On a reference to the Tribunal, the persons to act as members of the Tribunal for the purposes of the reference are to be selected from the panel of chairmen or the lay panel in accordance with arrangements made by the President for the purposes of this paragraph ("the standing arrangements").

(2) The standing arrangements must provide for at least one member to be selected from the panel of chairmen.

(3) If while a reference is being dealt with, a person serving as member of the Tribunal in respect of the reference becomes unable to act, the reference may be dealt with by—

(a) the other members selected in respect of that reference; or
(b) if it is being dealt with by a single member, such other member of the panel of chairmen as may be selected in accordance with the standing arrangements for the purposes of the reference.

(4) If it appears to the Tribunal that a matter before it involves a question of fact of special difficulty, it may appoint one or more experts to provide assistance.

[2456]

PART IV
TRIBUNAL PROCEDURE

8. For the purpose of dealing with references, or any matter preliminary or incidental to a reference, the Tribunal must sit at such times and in such place or places as the Lord Chancellor may[, after consulting the President of the Financial Services and Markets Tribunal,] direct.

9. Rules made by the Lord Chancellor under section 132 may, in particular, include provision—

(a) as to the manner in which references are to be instituted;
(b) for the holding of hearings in private in such circumstances as may be specified in the rules;
(c) as to the persons who may appear on behalf of the parties;
(d) for a member of the panel of chairmen to hear and determine interlocutory matters arising on a reference;
(e) for the suspension of decisions of the Authority which have taken effect;
(f) as to the withdrawal of references;
(g) as to the registration, publication and proof of decisions and orders.

Practice directions

10. The President of the Tribunal may give directions as to the practice and procedure to be followed by the Tribunal in relation to references to it.

PART II
FSMA 2000

Evidence

11.—(1) The Tribunal may by summons require any person to attend, at such time and place as is specified in the summons, to give evidence or to produce any document in his custody or under his control which the Tribunal considers it necessary to examine.

(2) The Tribunal may—
(a) take evidence on oath and for that purpose administer oaths; or
(b) instead of administering an oath, require the person examined to make and subscribe a declaration of the truth of the matters in respect of which he is examined.

(3) A person who without reasonable excuse—
(a) refuses or fails—
(i) to attend following the issue of a summons by the Tribunal, or
(ii) to give evidence, or
(b) alters, suppresses, conceals or destroys, or refuses to produce a document which he may be required to produce for the purposes of proceedings before the Tribunal,

is guilty of an offence.

(4) A person guilty of an offence under sub-paragraph (3)(a) is liable on summary conviction to a fine not exceeding the statutory maximum.

(5) A person guilty of an offence under sub-paragraph (3)(b) is liable—
(a) on summary conviction, to a fine not exceeding the statutory maximum;
(b) on conviction on indictment, to imprisonment for a term not exceeding two years or a fine or both.

Decisions of Tribunal

12.—(1) A decision of the Tribunal may be taken by a majority.

(2) The decision must—
(a) state whether it was unanimous or taken by a majority;
(b) be recorded in a document which—
(i) contains a statement of the reasons for the decision; and
(ii) is signed and dated by the member of the panel of chairmen dealing with the reference.

(3) The Tribunal must—
(a) inform each party of its decision; and
(b) as soon as reasonably practicable, send to each party and, if different, to any authorised person concerned, a copy of the document mentioned in sub-paragraph (2).

(4) The Tribunal must send the Treasury a copy of its decision.

Costs

13.—(1) If the Tribunal considers that a party to any proceedings on a reference has acted vexatiously, frivolously or unreasonably it may order that party to pay to another party to the proceedings the whole or part of the costs or expenses incurred by the other party in connection with the proceedings.

(2) If, in any proceedings on a reference, the Tribunal considers that a decision of the Authority which is the subject of the reference was unreasonable it may order the Authority to pay to another party to the proceedings the whole or part of the costs or expenses incurred by the other party in connection with the proceedings.

[2457]

NOTES

Para 8: words in square brackets inserted by the Constitutional Reform Act 2005, s 15, Sch 4, Pt 1, para 286(1), (4), as from 3 April 2006.

Rules: see the notes to s 132 at **[2132]**.

SCHEDULE 14
ROLE OF THE COMPETITION COMMISSION

Section 162

Provision of information by Treasury

1.—(1) The Treasury's powers under this paragraph are to be exercised only for the purpose of assisting the Commission in carrying out an investigation under section 162.

(2) The Treasury may give to the Commission—

(a) any information in their possession which relates to matters falling within the scope of the investigation; and

(b) other assistance in relation to any such matters.

(3) In carrying out an investigation under section 162, the Commission must have regard to any information given to it under this paragraph.

Consideration of matters arising on a report

2. In considering any matter arising from a report made by the [OFT] under section 160, the Commission must have regard to—

(a) any representations made to [the Commission] in connection with the matter by any person appearing to the Commission to have a substantial interest in the matter; and

(b) any cost benefit analysis prepared by the Authority (at any time) in connection with the regulatory provision or practice, or any of the regulatory provisions or practices, which are the subject of the report.

[Investigations under section 162: application of Enterprise Act 2002

2A.—(1) The following sections of Part 3 of the Enterprise Act 2002 shall apply, with the modifications mentioned in sub-paragraphs (2) and (3), for the purposes of any investigation by the Commission under section 162 of this Act as they apply for the purposes of references under that Part—

(a) section 109 (attendance of witnesses and production of documents etc);

(b) section 110 (enforcement of powers under section 109: general);

(c) section 111 (penalties);

(d) section 112 (penalties: main procedural requirements);

(e) section 113 (payments and interest by instalments);

(f) section 114 (appeals in relation to penalties);

(g) section 115 (recovery of penalties); and

(h) section 116 (statement of policy).

(2) Section 110 shall, in its application by virtue of sub-paragraph (1), have effect as if—

(a) subsection (2) were omitted; and

(b) in subsection (9) the words from "or section" to "section 65(3))" were omitted.

(3) Section 111(5)(b) shall, in its application by virtue of sub-paragraph (1), have effect as if for sub-paragraph (ii) there were substituted—

"(ii) if earlier, the day on which the report of the Commission on the investigation concerned is made or, if the Commission decides not to make a report, the day on which the Commission makes the statement required by section 162(3) of the Financial Services and Markets Act 2000."

(4) Section 117 of the Enterprise Act 2002 (false or misleading information) shall apply in relation to functions of the Commission in connection with an investigation under section 162 of this Act as it applies in relation to its functions under Part 3 of that Act but as if, in subsections (1)(a) and (2), the words ["the OFT, OFCOM,] "and "or the Secretary of State" were omitted.

(5) Provisions of Part 3 of the Enterprise Act 2002 which have effect for the purposes of sections 109 to 117 of that Act (including, in particular, provisions relating to offences and the making of orders) shall, for the purposes of the application of those sections by virtue of sub-paragraph (1) or (4) above, have effect in relation to those sections as applied by virtue of those sub-paragraphs.

(6) Accordingly, corresponding provisions of this Act shall not have effect in relation to those sections as applied by virtue of those sub-paragraphs.

Section 162: modification of Schedule 7 to the Competition Act 1998

2B. For the purposes of its application in relation to the function of the Commission of deciding in accordance with section 162(2) of this Act not to make a report, paragraph 15(7) of Schedule 7 to the Competition Act 1998 (power of the Chairman to act on his own while a group is being constituted) has effect as if, after paragraph (a), there were inserted

"; or

(aa) in the case of an investigation under section 162 of the Financial Services and Markets Act 2000, decide not to make a report in accordance with subsection (2) of that section (decision not to make a report where no useful purpose would be served).

Reports under section 162: further provision

2C.—(1) For the purposes of section 163 of this Act, a conclusion contained in a report of the Commission is to be disregarded if the conclusion is not that of at least two-thirds of the members of the group constituted in connection with the investigation concerned in pursuance of paragraph 15 of Schedule 7 to the Competition Act 1998.

(2) If a member of a group so constituted disagrees with any conclusions contained in a report made under section 162 of this Act as the conclusions of the Commission, the report shall, if the member so wishes, include a statement of his disagreement and of his reasons for disagreeing.

(3) For the purposes of the law relating to defamation, absolute privilege attaches to any report made by the Commission under section 162.]

...

3. ...

Publication of reports

4.—(1) If the Commission makes a report under section 162, it must publish it in such a way as appears to it to be best calculated to bring it to the attention of the public.

(2) Before publishing the report the Commission must, so far as practicable, exclude any matter which relates to the private affairs of a particular individual the publication of which, in the opinion of the Commission, would or might seriously and prejudicially affect his interests.

(3) Before publishing the report the Commission must, so far as practicable, also exclude any matter which relates to the affairs of a particular body the publication of which, in the opinion of the Commission, would or might seriously and prejudicially affect its interests.

(4) Sub-paragraphs (2) and (3) do not apply in relation to copies of a report which the Commission is required to send under section 162(10).

[2458]

NOTES

Para 2: words in square brackets substituted by the Enterprise Act 2002, s 278(1), Sch 25, para 40(1), (20)(a), as from 1 April 2003.

Paras 2A–2C: inserted by the Enterprise Act 2002, s 278(1), Sch 25, para 40(1), (20)(b), as from 20 June 2003, except in relation to any investigation commenced before that date under ss 162 or 306 of this Act; words in square brackets in para 2A(4) substituted by the Communications Act 2003, s 389, Sch 16, para 5, as from 29 December 2003 (subject to transitional provisions in Sch 18 thereto).

Para 3: repealed by the Enterprise Act 2002, s 278, Sch 25, para 40(1), (20)(c), Sch 26, as from 20 June 2003, except in relation to any investigation commenced before that date under ss 162 or 306 of this Act.

SCHEDULE 15
INFORMATION AND INVESTIGATIONS: CONNECTED PERSONS

Sections 165(11) and 171(4)

PART I
RULES FOR SPECIFIC BODIES

Corporate bodies

1. If the authorised person ("BC") is a body corporate, a person who is or has been—
   (a) an officer or manager of BC or of a parent undertaking of BC;
   (b) an employee of BC;
   (c) an agent of BC or of a parent undertaking of BC.

Partnerships

2. If the authorised person ("PP") is a partnership, a person who is or has been a member, manager, employee or agent of PP.

Unincorporated associations

3. If the authorised person ("UA") is an unincorporated association of persons which is neither a partnership nor an unincorporated friendly society, a person who is or has been an officer, manager, employee or agent of UA.

Friendly societies

4.—(1) If the authorised person ("FS") is a friendly society, a person who is or has been an officer, manager or employee of FS.

(2) In relation to FS, "officer" and "manager" have the same meaning as in section 119(1) of the Friendly Societies Act 1992.

Building societies

5.—(1) If the authorised person ("BS") is a building society, a person who is or has been an officer or employee of BS.

(2) In relation to BS, "officer" has the same meaning as it has in section 119(1) of the Building Societies Act 1986.

Individuals

6. If the authorised person ("IP") is an individual, a person who is or has been an employee or agent of IP.

Application to sections 171 and 172

7. For the purposes of sections 171 and 172, if the person under investigation is not an authorised person the references in this Part of this Schedule to an authorised person are to be taken to be references to the person under investigation.

[2459]

PART II
ADDITIONAL RULES

8. A person who is, or at the relevant time was, the partner, manager, employee, agent, appointed representative, banker, auditor, actuary or solicitor of—
   - (a) the person under investigation ("A");
   - (b) a parent undertaking of A;
   - (c) a subsidiary undertaking of A;
   - (d) a subsidiary undertaking of a parent undertaking of A; or
   - (e) a parent undertaking of a subsidiary undertaking of A.

[2460]

SCHEDULE 16
PROHIBITIONS AND RESTRICTIONS IMPOSED BY [OFFICE OF FAIR TRADING]

Section 203(8)

Preliminary

1. In this Schedule—

"appeal period" has the same meaning as in the Consumer Credit Act 1974;
"prohibition" means a consumer credit prohibition under section 203;
"restriction" means a restriction under section 204.

Notice of prohibition or restriction

2.—(1) This paragraph applies if the [OFT] proposes, in relation to a firm—
   - (a) to impose a prohibition;
   - (b) to impose a restriction; or
   - (c) to vary a restriction otherwise than with the agreement of the firm.

(2) The [OFT] must by notice—
   - (a) inform the firm of [its] proposal, stating [its] reasons; and
   - (b) invite the firm to submit representations in accordance with paragraph 4.

(3) If [the OFT] imposes the prohibition or restriction or varies the restriction, the [OFT] may give directions authorising the firm to carry into effect agreements made before the coming into force of the prohibition, restriction or variation.

(4) A prohibition, restriction or variation is not to come into force before the end of the appeal period.

(5) If the [OFT] imposes a prohibition or restriction or varies a restriction, [the OFT] must serve a copy of the prohibition, restriction or variation—
   - (a) on the Authority; and
   - (b) on the firm's home state regulator.

Application to revoke prohibition or restriction

3.—(1) This paragraph applies if the [OFT] proposes to refuse an application made by a firm for the revocation of a prohibition or restriction.

(2) The [OFT] must by notice—
   - (a) inform the firm of the proposed refusal, stating [its] reasons; and
   - (b) invite the firm to submit representations in accordance with paragraph 4.

Representations to [OFT]

4.—(1) If this paragraph applies to an invitation to submit representations, the [OFT] must invite the firm, within 21 days after the notice containing the invitation is given to it or such longer period as [the OFT] may allow—
   - (a) to submit its representations in writing to [the OFT]; and
   - (b) to give notice to [the OFT], if the firm thinks fit, that it wishes to make representations orally.

(2) If notice is given under sub-paragraph (1)(b), the [OFT] must arrange for the oral representations to be heard.

(3) The [OFT] must give the firm notice of [its] determination.

Appeals

5. Section 41 of the Consumer Credit Act 1974 (appeals to the Secretary of State) has effect as if—

(a) the following determinations were mentioned in column 1 of the table set out at the end of that section—

(i) imposition of a prohibition or restriction or the variation of a restriction; and

(ii) refusal of an application for the revocation of a prohibition or restriction; and

(b) the firm concerned were mentioned in column 2 of that table in relation to those determinations.

[2461]

NOTES

Words in square brackets substituted by the Enterprise Act 2002, s 278(1), Sch 25, para 40(1), (21), as from 1 April 2003.

SCHEDULE 17
THE OMBUDSMAN SCHEME

Section 225(4)

NOTES

Transitional provisions: see the note preceding s 225 at **[2225]**.

PART I
GENERAL

Interpretation

1. In this Schedule—

"ombudsman" means a person who is a member of the panel; and

"the panel" means the panel established under paragraph 4.

[2462]

PART II
THE SCHEME OPERATOR

Establishment by the Authority

2.—(1) The Authority must establish a body corporate to exercise the functions conferred on the scheme operator by or under this Act.

(2) The Authority must take such steps as are necessary to ensure that the scheme operator is, at all times, capable of exercising those functions.

Constitution

3.—(1) The constitution of the scheme operator must provide for it to have—

(a) a chairman; and

(b) a board (which must include the chairman) whose members are the scheme operator's directors.

PART II FSMA 2000

(2) The chairman and other members of the board must be persons appointed, and liable to removal from office, by the Authority (acting, in the case of the chairman, with the approval of the Treasury).

(3) But the terms of their appointment (and in particular those governing removal from office) must be such as to secure their independence from the Authority in the operation of the scheme.

(4) The function of making voluntary jurisdiction rules under section 227[, the function of making consumer credit rules, the function of making determinations under section 234A(1)] and the functions conferred by paragraphs 4, 5, 7, 9 or 14 may be exercised only by the board.

(5) The validity of any act of the scheme operator is unaffected by—
(a) a vacancy in the office of chairman; or
(b) a defect in the appointment of a person as chairman or as a member of the board.

The panel of ombudsmen

4.—(1) The scheme operator must appoint and maintain a panel of persons, appearing to it to have appropriate qualifications and experience, to act as ombudsmen for the purposes of the scheme.

(2) A person's appointment to the panel is to be on such terms (including terms as to the duration and termination of his appointment and as to remuneration) as the scheme operator considers—
(a) consistent with the independence of the person appointed; and
(b) otherwise appropriate.

The Chief Ombudsman

5.—(1) The scheme operator must appoint one member of the panel to act as Chief Ombudsman.

(2) The Chief Ombudsman is to be appointed on such terms (including terms as to the duration and termination of his appointment) as the scheme operator considers appropriate.

Status

6.—(1) The scheme operator is not to be regarded as exercising functions on behalf of the Crown.

(2) The scheme operator's board members, officers and staff are not to be regarded as Crown servants.

(3) Appointment as Chief Ombudsman or to the panel or as a deputy ombudsman does not confer the status of Crown servant.

Annual reports

7.—(1) At least once a year—
(a) the scheme operator must make a report to the Authority on the discharge of its functions; and
(b) the Chief Ombudsman must make a report to the Authority on the discharge of his functions.

(2) Each report must distinguish between functions in relation to the scheme's compulsory jurisdiction[, functions in relation to its consumer credit jurisdiction] and functions in relation to its voluntary jurisdiction.

(3) Each report must also comply with any requirements specified in rules made by the Authority.

(4) The scheme operator must publish each report in the way it considers appropriate.

Guidance

8. The scheme operator may publish guidance consisting of such information and advice as it considers appropriate and may charge for it or distribute it free of charge.

Budget

9.—(1) The scheme operator must, before the start of each of its financial years, adopt an annual budget which has been approved by the Authority.

(2) The scheme operator may, with the approval of the Authority, vary the budget for a financial year at any time after its adoption.

(3) The annual budget must include an indication of—

(a) the distribution of resources deployed in the operation of the scheme, and

(b) the amounts of income of the scheme operator arising or expected to arise from the operation of the scheme,

distinguishing between the scheme's compulsory[, consumer credit] and voluntary jurisdiction.

Exemption from liability in damages

10.—(1) No person is to be liable in damages for anything done or omitted in the discharge, or purported discharge, of any functions under this Act in relation to the compulsory jurisdiction [or to the consumer credit jurisdiction].

(2) Sub-paragraph (1) does not apply—

(a) if the act or omission is shown to have been in bad faith; or

(b) so as to prevent an award of damages made in respect of an act or omission on the ground that the act or omission was unlawful as a result of section 6(1) of the Human Rights Act 1998.

Privilege

11. For the purposes of the law relating to defamation, proceedings in relation to a complaint which is subject to the compulsory jurisdiction [or to the consumer credit jurisdiction] are to be treated as if they were proceedings before a court.

[2463]

NOTES

Paras 3, 7, 9–11: words in square brackets inserted by the Consumer Credit Act 2006, s 61(10), as from 16 June 2006.

Para 9(3) above does not apply to the scheme operator's first budget (ie, its budget for the financial year during which 18 June 2001 occurs); see the Financial Services and Markets Act 2000 (Consequential and Transitional Provisions) (Miscellaneous) Order 2001, SI 2001/1821, art 4.

PART III
THE COMPULSORY JURISDICTION

Introduction

12. This Part of this Schedule applies only in relation to the compulsory jurisdiction.

Authority's procedural rules

13.—(1) The Authority must make rules providing that a complaint is not to be entertained unless the complainant has referred it under the ombudsman scheme before the applicable time limit (determined in accordance with the rules) has expired.

(2) The rules may provide that an ombudsman may extend that time limit in specified circumstances.

(3) The Authority may make rules providing that a complaint is not to be entertained (except in specified circumstances) if the complainant has not previously communicated its substance to the respondent and given him a reasonable opportunity to deal with it.

(4) The Authority may make rules requiring an authorised person who may become subject to the compulsory jurisdiction as a respondent to establish such procedures as the Authority considers appropriate for the resolution of complaints which—
- (a) may be referred to the scheme; and
- (b) arise out of activity to which the Authority's powers under Part X do not apply.

The scheme operator's rules

14.—(1) The scheme operator must make rules, to be known as "scheme rules", which are to set out the procedure for reference of complaints and for their investigation, consideration and determination by an ombudsman.

(2) Scheme rules may, among other things—
- (a) specify matters which are to be taken into account in determining whether an act or omission was fair and reasonable;
- (b) provide that a complaint may, in specified circumstances, be dismissed without consideration of its merits;
- (c) provide for the reference of a complaint, in specified circumstances and with the consent of the complainant, to another body with a view to its being determined by that body instead of by an ombudsman;
- (d) make provision as to the evidence which may be required or admitted, the extent to which it should be oral or written and the consequences of a person's failure to produce any information or document which he has been required (under section 231 or otherwise) to produce;
- (e) allow an ombudsman to fix time limits for any aspect of the proceedings and to extend a time limit;
- (f) provide for certain things in relation to the reference, investigation or consideration (but not determination) of a complaint to be done by a member of the scheme operator's staff instead of by an ombudsman;
- (g) make different provision in relation to different kinds of complaint.

(3) The circumstances specified under sub-paragraph (2)(b) may include the following—
- (a) the ombudsman considers the complaint frivolous or vexatious;
- (b) legal proceedings have been brought concerning the subject-matter of the complaint and the ombudsman considers that the complaint is best dealt with in those proceedings; or
- (c) the ombudsman is satisfied that there are other compelling reasons why it is inappropriate for the complaint to be dealt with under the ombudsman scheme.

(4) If the scheme operator proposes to make any scheme rules it must publish a draft of the proposed rules in the way appearing to it to be best calculated to bring them to the attention of persons appearing to it to be likely to be affected.

(5) The draft must be accompanied by a statement that representations about the proposals may be made to the scheme operator within a time specified in the statement.

(6) Before making the proposed scheme rules, the scheme operator must have regard to any representations made to it under sub-paragraph (5).

(7) The consent of the Authority is required before any scheme rules may be made.

Fees

15.—(1) Scheme rules may require a respondent to pay to the scheme operator such fees as may be specified in the rules.

(2) The rules may, among other things—
- (a) provide for the scheme operator to reduce or waive a fee in a particular case;
- (b) set different fees for different stages of the proceedings on a complaint;
- (c) provide for fees to be refunded in specified circumstances;
- (d) make different provision for different kinds of complaint.

Enforcement of money awards

16. A money award, including interest, which has been registered in accordance with scheme rules may—
   (a) if a county court so orders in England and Wales, be recovered by execution issued from the county court (or otherwise) as if it were payable under an order of that court;
   (b) be enforced in Northern Ireland as a money judgment under the Judgments Enforcement (Northern Ireland) Order 1981;
   (c) be enforced in Scotland by the sheriff, as if it were a judgment or order of the sheriff and whether or not the sheriff could himself have granted such judgment or order.

[2464]

[PART 3A
THE CONSUMER CREDIT JURISDICTION

Introduction

16A. This Part of this Schedule applies only in relation to the consumer credit jurisdiction.

Procedure for complaints etc

16B.—(1) Consumer credit rules—
   (a) must provide that a complaint is not to be entertained unless the complainant has referred it under the ombudsman scheme before the applicable time limit (determined in accordance with the rules) has expired;
   (b) may provide that an ombudsman may extend that time limit in specified circumstances;
   (c) may provide that a complaint is not to be entertained (except in specified circumstances) if the complainant has not previously communicated its substance to the respondent and given him a reasonable opportunity to deal with it;
   (d) may make provision about the procedure for the reference of complaints and for their investigation, consideration and determination by an ombudsman.

(2) Sub-paragraphs (2) and (3) of paragraph 14 apply in relation to consumer credit rules under sub-paragraph (1) of this paragraph as they apply in relation to scheme rules under that paragraph.

(3) Consumer credit rules may require persons falling within sub-paragraph (6) to establish such procedures as the scheme operator considers appropriate for the resolution of complaints which may be referred to the scheme.

(4) Consumer credit rules under sub-paragraph (3) may make different provision in relation to persons of different descriptions or to complaints of different descriptions.

(5) Consumer credit rules under sub-paragraph (3) may authorise the scheme operator to dispense with or modify the application of such rules in particular cases where the scheme operator—
   (a) considers it appropriate to do so; and
   (b) is satisfied that the specified conditions (if any) are met.

(6) A person falls within this sub-paragraph if he is licensed by a standard licence (within the meaning of the Consumer Credit Act 1974) to carry on to any extent a business of a type specified in an order under section 226A(2)(e) of this Act.

Fees

16C.—(1) Consumer credit rules may require a respondent to pay to the scheme operator such fees as may be specified in the rules.

(2) Sub-paragraph (2) of paragraph 15 applies in relation to consumer credit rules under this paragraph as it applies in relation to scheme rules under that paragraph.

Enforcement of money awards

16D. A money award, including interest, which has been registered in accordance with consumer credit rules may—

(a) if a county court so orders in England and Wales, be recovered by execution issued from the county court (or otherwise) as if it were payable under an order of that court;

(b) be enforced in Northern Ireland as a money judgment under the Judgments Enforcement (Northern Ireland) Order 1981;

(c) be enforced in Scotland as if it were a decree of the sheriff and whether or not the sheriff could himself have granted such a decree.

Procedure for consumer credit rules

16E.—(1) If the scheme operator makes any consumer credit rules, it must give a copy of them to the Authority without delay.

(2) If the scheme operator revokes any such rules, it must give written notice to the Authority without delay.

(3) The power to make such rules is exercisable in writing.

(4) Immediately after the making of such rules, the scheme operator must arrange for them to be printed and made available to the public.

(5) The scheme operator may charge a reasonable fee for providing a person with a copy of any such rules.

Verification of consumer credit rules

16F.—(1) The production of a printed copy of consumer credit rules purporting to be made by the scheme operator—

(a) on which there is endorsed a certificate signed by a member of the scheme operator's staff authorised by the scheme operator for that purpose, and

(b) which contains the required statements,

is evidence (or in Scotland sufficient evidence) of the facts stated in the certificate.

(2) The required statements are—

(a) that the rules were made by the scheme operator;

(b) that the copy is a true copy of the rules; and

(c) that on a specified date the rules were made available to the public in accordance with paragraph 16E(4).

(3) A certificate purporting to be signed as mentioned in sub-paragraph (1) is to be taken to have been duly signed unless the contrary is shown.

Consultation

16G.—(1) If the scheme operator proposes to make consumer credit rules, it must publish a draft of the proposed rules in the way appearing to it to be best calculated to bring the draft to the attention of the public.

(2) The draft must be accompanied by—

(a) an explanation of the proposed rules; and

(b) a statement that representations about the proposals may be made to the scheme operator within a specified time.

(3) Before making any consumer credit rules, the scheme operator must have regard to any representations made to it in accordance with sub-paragraph (2)(b).

(4) If consumer credit rules made by the scheme operator differ from the draft published under sub-paragraph (1) in a way which the scheme operator considers significant, the scheme operator must publish a statement of the difference.]

[2464A]

NOTES

Commencement: 16 June 2006.
Inserted by the Consumer Credit Act 2006, s 59(2), Sch 2, as from 16 June 2006.

PART IV
THE VOLUNTARY JURISDICTION

Introduction

17. This Part of this Schedule applies only in relation to the voluntary jurisdiction.

Terms of reference to the scheme

18.—(1) Complaints are to be dealt with and determined under the voluntary jurisdiction on standard terms fixed by the scheme operator with the approval of the Authority.

(2) Different standard terms may be fixed with respect to different matters or in relation to different cases.

(3) The standard terms may, in particular—
(a) require the making of payments to the scheme operator by participants in the scheme of such amounts, and at such times, as may be determined by the scheme operator;
(b) make provision as to the award of costs on the determination of a complaint.

(4) The scheme operator may not vary any of the standard terms or add or remove terms without the approval of the Authority.

(5) The standard terms may include provision to the effect that (unless acting in bad faith) none of the following is to be liable in damages for anything done or omitted in the discharge or purported discharge of functions in connection with the voluntary jurisdiction—
(a) the scheme operator;
(b) any member of its governing body;
(c) any member of its staff;
(d) any person acting as an ombudsman for the purposes of the scheme.

Delegation by and to other schemes

19.—(1) The scheme operator may make arrangements with a relevant body—
(a) for the exercise by that body of any part of the voluntary jurisdiction of the ombudsman scheme on behalf of the scheme; or
(b) for the exercise by the scheme of any function of that body as if it were part of the voluntary jurisdiction of the scheme.

(2) A "relevant body" is one which the scheme operator is satisfied—
(a) is responsible for the operation of a broadly comparable scheme (whether or not established by statute) for the resolution of disputes; and
(b) in the case of arrangements under sub-paragraph (1)(a), will exercise the jurisdiction in question in a way compatible with the requirements imposed by or under this Act in relation to complaints of the kind concerned.

(3) Such arrangements require the approval of the Authority.

Voluntary jurisdiction rules: procedure

20.—(1) If the scheme operator makes voluntary jurisdiction rules, it must give a copy to the Authority without delay.

(2) If the scheme operator revokes any such rules, it must give written notice to the Authority without delay.

(3) The power to make voluntary jurisdiction rules is exercisable in writing.

PART II
FSMA 2000

(4) Immediately after making voluntary jurisdiction rules, the scheme operator must arrange for them to be printed and made available to the public.

(5) The scheme operator may charge a reasonable fee for providing a person with a copy of any voluntary jurisdiction rules.

Verification of the rules

21.—(1) The production of a printed copy of voluntary jurisdiction rules purporting to be made by the scheme operator—

(a) on which is endorsed a certificate signed by a member of the scheme operator's staff authorised by the scheme operator for that purpose, and

(b) which contains the required statements,

is evidence (or in Scotland sufficient evidence) of the facts stated in the certificate.

(2) The required statements are—

(a) that the rules were made by the scheme operator;

(b) that the copy is a true copy of the rules; and

(c) that on a specified date the rules were made available to the public in accordance with paragraph 20(4).

(3) A certificate purporting to be signed as mentioned in sub-paragraph (1) is to be taken to have been duly signed unless the contrary is shown.

Consultation

22.—(1) If the scheme operator proposes to make voluntary jurisdiction rules, it must publish a draft of the proposed rules in the way appearing to it to be best calculated to bring them to the attention of the public.

(2) The draft must be accompanied by—

(a) an explanation of the proposed rules; and

(b) a statement that representations about the proposals may be made to the scheme operator within a specified time.

(3) Before making any voluntary jurisdiction rules, the scheme operator must have regard to any representations made to it in accordance with sub-paragraph (2)(b).

(4) If voluntary jurisdiction rules made by the scheme operator differ from the draft published under sub-paragraph (1) in a way which the scheme operator considers significant, the scheme operator must publish a statement of the difference.

[2465]–[2466]

SCHEDULE 18
MUTUALS

Sections 334, 336 and 338

(Sch 18, Pt I repeals the Friendly Societies Act 1974, ss 4, 10, 31–36A, 37(1), (1A), (7A)–(9), 38–50, and amends the Friendly Societies Act 1974, ss 7, 11, 99(4).)

PART II
FRIENDLY SOCIETIES: SUBSIDIARIES AND CONTROLLED BODIES

Interpretation

9. In this Part of this Schedule—

"the 1992 Act" means the Friendly Societies Act 1992; and
"section 13" means section 13 of that Act.

10–15. …

References in other enactments

16. References in any provision of, or made under, any enactment to subsidiaries of, or bodies jointly controlled by, an incorporated friendly society are to be read as including references to bodies which are such subsidiaries or bodies as a result of any provision of this Part of this Schedule.

[2467]–[2473]

NOTES

Paras 10–15: amend the Friendly Societies Act 1992; ss 13, 52, Sch 8, and repeal Sch 7 to that Act.

(Sch 18, Pt III repeals the Building Societies Act 1986, s 9, Sch 3; Sch 18, Pt IV repeals the Industrial and Provident Societies Act 1965, ss 8, 70; Sch 18, Pt V repeals the Credit Unions Act 1979, ss 6(2)–(6), 11(2)–(6), 11B–11D, 12(4), (5), 14(2), (3), (5), (6), 28(2); Sch 19 repealed by the Enterprise Act 2002, ss 247(k), 278(2), Sch 26, as from 20 June 2003; Sch 20 contains minor and consequential amendments to legislation not reproduced in this Handbook.)

SCHEDULE 21
TRANSITIONAL PROVISIONS AND SAVINGS

Section 432(2)

Self-regulating organisations

1.—(1) No new application under section 9 of the 1986 Act (application for recognition) may be entertained.

(2) No outstanding application made under that section before the passing of this Act may continue to be entertained.

(3) After the date which is the designated date for a recognised self-regulating organisation—

(a) the recognition order for that organisation may not be revoked under section 11 of the 1986 Act (revocation of recognition);

(b) no application may be made to the court under section 12 of the 1986 Act (compliance orders) with respect to that organisation.

(4) The powers conferred by section 13 of the 1986 Act (alteration of rules for protection of investors) may not be exercised.

(5) "Designated date" means such date as the Treasury may by order designate.

(6) Sub-paragraph (3) does not apply to a recognised self-regulating organisation in respect of which a notice of intention to revoke its recognition order was given under section 11(3) of the 1986 Act before the passing of this Act if that notice has not been withdrawn.

(7) Expenditure incurred by the Authority in connection with the winding up of any body which was, immediately before the passing of this Act, a recognised self-regulating organisation is to be treated as having been incurred in connection with the discharge by the Authority of functions under this Act.

(8) "Recognised self-regulating organisation" means an organisation which, immediately before the passing of this Act, was such an organisation for the purposes of the 1986 Act.

(9) "The 1986 Act" means the Financial Services Act 1986.

Self-regulating organisations for friendly societies

2.—(1) No new application under paragraph 2 of Schedule 11 to the 1986 Act (application for recognition) may be entertained.

(2) No outstanding application made under that paragraph before the passing of this Act may continue to be entertained.

(3) After the date which is the designated date for a recognised self-regulating organisation for friendly societies—

(a) the recognition order for that organisation may not be revoked under paragraph 5 of Schedule 11 to the 1986 Act (revocation of recognition);

(b) no application may be made to the court under paragraph 6 of that Schedule (compliance orders) with respect to that organisation.

(4) "Designated date" means such date as the Treasury may by order designate.

(5) Sub-paragraph (3) does not apply to a recognised self-regulating organisation for friendly societies in respect of which a notice of intention to revoke its recognition order was given under section 11(3) of the 1986 Act (as applied by paragraph 5(2) of that Schedule) before the passing of this Act if that notice has not been withdrawn.

(6) Expenditure incurred by the Authority in connection with the winding up of any body which was, immediately before the passing of this Act, a recognised self-regulating organisation for friendly societies is to be treated as having been incurred in connection with the discharge by the Authority of functions under this Act.

(7) "Recognised self-regulating organisation for friendly societies" means an organisation which, immediately before the passing of this Act, was such an organisation for the purposes of the 1986 Act.

(8) "The 1986 Act" means the Financial Services Act 1986.

[2474]–[3000]

NOTES

Financial Services Act 1986: repealed by the Financial Services and Markets Act 2000 (Consequential Amendments and Repeals) Order 2001, SI 2001/3649, art 3(1)(c).

Orders: the Financial Services and Markets (Transitional Provisions) (Designated Date for Certain Self-Regulating Organisations) Order 2000, SI 2000/1734 (art 2 of which provides that for the purposes of paras 1, 2 of this Schedule, 25 July 2000 shall be the designated date for the Personal Investment Authority Limited and the Investment Management Regulatory Organisation Limited); the Financial Services and Markets (Transitional Provisions) (Designated Date for The Securities and Futures Authority) Order 2001, SI 2001/2255 (art 2 of which provides that for the purposes of para 1(5) of this Schedule, 13 July 2001 shall be the designated date for The Securities and Futures Authority Limited).

(Sch 22 (Repeals) contains repeals of, or in, the following Acts: the Industrial Assurance Act 1923, the Industrial Assurance and Friendly Societies Act 1948, the Industrial and Provident Societies Act 1965, the Friendly Societies Act 1974, the House of Commons Disqualification Act 1975, the Northern Ireland Assembly Disqualification Act 1975, the Insurance Brokers (Registration) Act 1977, the Credit Unions Act 1979, the Building Societies Act 1986, ICTA 1988, FA 1991, the Friendly Societies Act 1992, and the Judicial Pensions and Retirement Act 1993.)

PART III
OTHER LEGISLATION

PART III
OTHER LEGISLATION

PARTNERSHIP ACT 1890

(1890 c 39)

NOTES

This Act is reproduced as amended by: the Statute Law Revision Act 1908; the Mental Health Act 1959; the Decimal Currency Act 1969; the Courts Act 1971; the Trusts of Land and Appointment of Trustees Act 1996; the Statute Law (Repeals) Act 1998; the Civil Partnership Act 2004.

ARRANGEMENT OF SECTIONS

An Act to declare and amend the Law of Partnership

[14 August 1890]

Nature of Partnership

1 Definition of Partnership

(1) Partnership is the relation which subsists between persons carrying on a business in common with a view of profit.

(2) But the relation between members of any company or association which is—

(a) Registered as a Company under the Companies Act 1862 or any other Act of Parliament for the time being in force and relating to the registration of joint stock companies; or

(b) Formed or incorporated by or in pursuance of any other Act of Parliament or letters patent, or Royal Charter …

(c) …

is not a partnership within the meaning of this Act.

[3001]

NOTES

Sub-s (2): para (c) and word immediately preceding it repealed by the Statute Law (Repeals) Act 1998, as from 19 November 1998.

Companies Act 1862: repealed by the Companies (Consolidation) Act 1908, s 286, Sch 6, Pt I; see now the Companies Act 1985.

2 Rules for determining existence of partnership

In determining whether a partnership does or does not exist, regard shall be had to the following rules—

(1) Joint tenancy, tenancy in common, joint property, common property, or part ownership does not of itself create a partnership as to anything so held or owned, whether the tenants or owners do or do not share any profits made by the use thereof.

(2) The sharing of gross returns does not of itself create a partnership, whether the persons sharing such returns have or have not a joint or common right or interest in any property from which or from the use of which the returns are derived.

(3) The receipt by a person of a share of the profits of a business is *prima facie* evidence that he is a partner in the business, but receipt of such a share, or of a payment contingent on or varying with the profits of a business, does not of itself make him a partner in the business; and in particular—

(a) The receipt by a person of a debt or other liquidated amount by instalments or otherwise out of the accruing profits of a business does not of itself make him a partner in the business or liable as such:

(b) A contract for the remuneration of a servant or agent of a person engaged in a business by a share of the profits of the business does not of itself make the servant or agent a partner in the business or liable as such:

(c) A person being the widow[, widower, surviving civil partner] or child of a deceased partner, and receiving by way of annuity a portion of the profits made in the business in which the deceased person was a partner, is not by reason only of such receipt a partner in the business or liable as such:

(d) The advance of money by way of loan to a person engaged or about to engage in any business on a contract with that person that the lender shall receive a rate of interest varying with the profits, or shall receive a share of the profits arising from carrying on the business, does not of itself make the lender a partner with the person or persons carrying on the business or liable as such. Provided that the contract is in writing, and signed by or on behalf of all the parties thereto:

(e) A person receiving by way of annuity or otherwise a portion of the profits of a business in consideration of the sale by him of the goodwill of the business is not by reason only of such receipt a partner in the business or liable as such.

[3002]

Words in square brackets inserted by the Civil Partnership Act 2004, s 261(1), Sch 27, para 2, as from 5 December 2005.

3 Postponement of rights of person lending or selling in consideration of share of profits in case of insolvency

In the event of any person to whom money has been advanced by way of loan upon such a contract as is mentioned in the last foregoing section, or of any buyer of a goodwill in consideration of a share of the profits of the business, being adjudged a bankrupt, entering into an arrangement to pay his creditors less than [100p] in the pound, or dying in insolvent circumstances, the lender of the loan shall not be entitled to recover anything in respect of his loan, and the seller of the goodwill shall not be entitled to recover anything in respect of the share of profits contracted for, until the claims of the other creditors of the borrower or buyer for valuable consideration in money or money's worth have been satisfied.

[3003]

NOTES

Sum in square brackets substituted by virtue of the Decimal Currency Act 1969, s 10(1), as from 16 May 1969.

4 Meaning of firm

(1) Persons who have entered into partnership with one another are for the purposes of this Act called collectively a firm, and the name under which their business is carried on is called the firm-name.

(2) In Scotland a firm is a legal person distinct from the partners of whom it is composed, but an individual partner may be charged on a decree or diligence directed against the firm, and on payment of the debts is entitled to relief pro rata from the firm and its other members.

[3004]

Relations of Partners to persons dealing with them

5 Power of partner to bind the firm

Every partner is an agent of the firm and his other partners for the purpose of the business of the partnership; and the acts of every partner who does any act for carrying on in the usual way business of the kind carried on by the firm of which he is a member bind the firm and his partners, unless the partner so acting has in fact no authority to act for the firm in the particular matter, and the person with whom he is dealing either knows that he has no authority, or does not know or believe him to be a partner.

[3005]

6 Partners bound by acts on behalf of firm

An act or instrument relating to the business of the firm done or executed in the firm-name, or in any other manner showing an intention to bind the firm, by any person thereto authorised, whether a partner or not, is binding on the firm and all the partners.

Provided that this section shall not affect any general rule of law relating to the execution of deeds or negotiable instruments.

[3006]

7 Partner using credit of firm for private purposes

Where one partner pledges the credit of the firm for a purpose apparently not connected with the firm's ordinary course of business, the firm is not bound, unless he is in fact specially authorised by the other partners; but this section does not affect any personal liability incurred by an individual partner.

[3007]

8 Effect of notice that firm will not be bound by acts of partner

If it has been agreed between the partners that any restriction shall be placed on the power of any one or more of them to bind the firm, no act done in contravention of the agreement is binding on the firm with respect to persons having notice of the agreement.

[3008]

9 Liability of partners

Every partner in a firm is liable jointly with the other partners, and in Scotland severally also, for all debts and obligations of the firm incurred while he is a partner; and after his death his estate is also severally liable in a due course of administration for such debts and obligations, so far as they remain unsatisfied, but subject in England or Ireland to the prior payment of his separate debts.

[3009]

10 Liability of the firm for wrongs

Where, by any wrongful act or omission of any partner acting in the ordinary course of the business of the firm, or with the authority of his co-partners, loss or injury is caused to any person not being a partner in the firm, or any penalty is incurred, the firm is liable therefor to the same extent as the partner so acting or omitting to act.

[3010]

11 Misapplication of money or property received for or in custody of the firm

In the following cases; namely—

(a) Where one partner acting within the scope of his apparent authority receives the money or property of a third person and misapplies it; and

(b) Where a firm in the course of its business receives money or property of a third person, and the money or property so received is misapplied by one or more of the partners while it is in the custody of the firm;

the firm is liable to make good the loss.

[3011]

12 Liability for wrongs joint and several

Every partner is liable jointly with his co-partners and also severally for everything for which the firm while he is a partner therein becomes liable under either of the two last preceding sections.

[3012]

13 Improper employment of trust-property for partnership purposes

If a partner, being a trustee, improperly employs trust-property in the business or on the account of the partnership, no other partner is liable for the trust property to the persons beneficially interested therein:

Provided as follows—

(1) This section shall not affect any liability incurred by any partner by reason of his having notice of a breach of trust; and

(2) Nothing in this section shall prevent trust money from being followed and recovered from the firm if still in its possession or under its control.

[3013]

14 Persons liable by "holding out"

(1) Every one who by words spoken or written or by conduct represents himself, or who knowingly suffers himself to be represented, as a partner in a particular firm, is liable as a partner to any one who has on the faith of any such representation given credit to the firm, whether the representation has or has not been made or communicated to the person so giving credit by or with the knowledge of the apparent partner making the representation or suffering it to be made.

(2) Provided that where after a partner's death the partnership business is continued in the old firm's name, the continued use of that name or of the deceased partner's name as part thereof shall not of itself make his executors or administrators estate or effects liable for any partnership debts contracted after his death.

[3014]

15 Admissions and representation of partners

An admission or representation made by any partner concerning the partnership affairs, and in the ordinary course of its business, is evidence against the firm.

[3015]

16 Notice to acting partner to be notice to the firm

Notice to any partner who habitually acts in the partnership business of any matter relating to partnership affairs operates as notice to the firm, except in the case of a fraud on the firm committed by or with the consent of that partner.

[3016]

17 Liabilities of incoming and outgoing partners

(1) A person who is admitted as a partner into an existing firm does not thereby become liable to the creditors of the firm for anything done before he became a partner.

(2) A partner who retires from a firm does not thereby cease to be liable for partnership debts or obligations incurred before his retirement.

(3) A retiring partner may be discharged from any existing liabilities, by an agreement to that effect between himself and the members of the firm as newly constituted and the creditors, and this agreement may be either expressed or inferred as a fact from the course of dealing between the creditors and the firm as newly constituted.

[3017]

18 Revocation of continuing guaranty by change in firm

A continuing guaranty or cautionary obligation given either to a firm or to a third person in respect of the transactions of a firm is, in the absence of agreement to the contrary, revoked as to future transactions by any change in the constitution of the firm to which, or of the firm in respect of the transactions of which, the guaranty or obligation was given.

[3018]

Relations of Partners to one another

19 Variation by consent of terms of partnership

The mutual rights and duties of partners, whether ascertained by agreement or defined by this Act, may be varied by the consent of all the partners, and such consent may be either express or inferred from a course of dealing.

[3019]

20 Partnership property

(1) All property and rights and interests in property originally brought into the partnership stock or acquired, whether by purchase or otherwise, on account of the firm, or for the purposes and in the course of the partnership business, are called in this Act partnership property, and must be held and applied by the partners exclusively for the purposes of the partnership and in accordance with the partnership agreement.

(2) Provided that the legal estate or interest in any land, or in Scotland the title to and interest in any heritable estate, which belongs to the partnership shall devolve according to the nature and tenure thereof, and the general rules of law thereto applicable, but in trust, so far as necessary, for the persons beneficially interested in the land under this section.

(3) Where co-owners of an estate or interest in any land, or in Scotland of any heritable estate, not being itself partnership property, are partners as to profits made by the use of that land or estate, and purchase other land or estate out of the profits to be used in like manner, the land or estate so purchased belongs to them, in the absence of an agreement to the contrary, not as partners, but as co-owners for the same respective estates and interests as are held by them in the land or estate first mentioned at the date of the purchase.

[3020]

21 Property bought with partnership money

Unless the contrary intention appears, property bought with money belonging to the firm is deemed to have been bought on account of the firm.

[3021]

22 (*Repealed by the Trusts of Land and Appointment of Trustees Act 1996, s 25(2), (5), Sch 4, except in relation to any circumstances involving the personal representatives of a partner who died before 1 July 1997.*)

23 Procedure against partnership property for a partner's separate judgement debt

(1) … A writ of execution shall not issue against any partnership property except on a judgment against the firm.

(2) The High Court, or a judge thereof, … , or a county court, may, on the application by summons of any judgment creditor of a partner, make an order charging that partner's interest in the partnership property and profits with payment of the amount of the judgment debt and interest thereon, and may by the same or a subsequent order appoint a receiver of that partner's share of profits (whether already declared or accruing), and of any other money which may be coming to him in respect of the partnership, and direct all accounts and inquiries, and give all other orders and directions which might have been directed or given if the charge had been made in favour of the judgment creditor by the partner, or which the circumstances of the case may require.

(3) The other partner or partners shall be at liberty at any time to redeem the interest charged, or in case of a sale being directed, to purchase the same.

(4) …

(5) This section shall not apply to Scotland.

[3022]

NOTES

Sub-s (1): words omitted repealed by the Statute Law Revision Act 1908, as from 21 December 1908.

Sub-s (2): words omitted repealed by the Courts Act 1971, s 56(4), Sch 11, Pt II, as from 1 January 1972.

Sub-s (4): repealed by the Statute Law (Repeals) Act 1998, as from 19 November 1998.

24 Rules as to interests and duties of partners subject to special agreement

The interests of partners in the partnership property and their rights and duties in relation to the partnership shall be determined, subject to any agreement express or implied between the partners, by the following rules—

(1) All the partners are entitled to share equally in the capital and profits of the business, and must contribute equally towards the losses whether of capital or otherwise sustained by the firm.

(2) The firm must indemnify every partner in respect of payments made and personal liabilities incurred by him—

- (a) In the ordinary and proper conduct of the business of the firm; or,
- (b) In or about anything necessarily done for the preservation of the business or property of the firm.

(3) A partner making, for the purpose of the partnership, any actual payment or advance beyond the amount of capital which he has agreed to subscribe, is entitled to interest at the rate of five per cent per annum from the date of the payment or advance.

(4) A partner is not entitled, before the ascertainment of profits, to interest on the capital subscribed by him.

(5) Every partner may take part in the management of the partnership business.

(6) No partner shall be entitled to remuneration for acting in the partnership business.

(7) No person may be introduced as a partner without the consent of all existing partners.

(8) Any difference arising as to ordinary matters connected with the partnership business may be decided by a majority of the partners, but no change may be made in the nature of the partnership business without the consent of all existing partners.

(9) The partnership books are to be kept at the place of business of the partnership (or the principal place, if there is more than one), and every partner may, when he thinks fit, have access to and inspect and copy any of them.

[3023]

25 Expulsion of partner

No majority of the partners can expel any partner unless a power to do so has been conferred by express agreement between the partners.

[3024]

26 Retirement from partnership at will

(1) Where no fixed term has been agreed upon for the duration of the partnership, any partner may determine the partnership at any time on giving notice of his intention so to do to all the other partners.

(2) Where the partnership has originally been constituted by deed, a notice in writing, signed by the partner giving it, shall be sufficient for this purpose.

[3025]

27 Where partnership for term is continued over, continuance on old terms presumed

(1) Where a partnership entered into for a fixed term is continued after the term has expired, and without any express new agreement, the rights and duties of the partners remain the same as they were at the expiration of the term, so far as is consistent with the incidents of a partnership at will.

(2) A continuance of the business by the partners or such of them as habitually acted therein during the term, without any settlement or liquidation of the partnership affairs, is presumed to be a continuance of the partnership.

[3026]

28 Duty of partners to render accounts, etc

Partners are bound to render true accounts and full information of all things affecting the partnership to any partner or his legal representatives.

[3027]

29 Accountability of partners for private profits

(1) Every partner must account to the firm for any benefit derived by him without the consent of the other partners from any transaction concerning the partnership, or from any use by him of the partnership property name or business connexion.

(2) This section applies also to transactions undertaken after a partnership has been dissolved by the death of a partner, and before the affairs thereof have been completely wound up, either by any surviving partner or by the representatives of the deceased partner.

[3028]

30 Duty of partner not to compete with firm

If a partner, without the consent of the other partners, carries on any business of the same nature as and competing with that of the firm, he must account for and pay over to the firm all profits made by him in that business.

[3029]

31 Rights of assignee of share in partnership

(1) An assignment by any partner of his share in the partnership, either absolute or by way of mortgage or redeemable charge, does not, as against the other partners, entitle the assignee, during the continuance of the partnership, to interfere in the management or administration of the partnership business or affairs, or to require any accounts of the partnership transactions, or to inspect the partnership books, but entitles the assignee only to receive the share of profits to which the assigning partner would otherwise be entitled, and the assignee must accept the account of profits agreed to by the partners.

(2) In case of a dissolution of the partnership, whether as respects all the partners or as respects the assigning partner, the assignee is entitled to receive the share of the partnership assets to which the assigning partner is entitled as between himself and the other partners, and, for the purpose of ascertaining that share, to an account as from the date of the dissolution.

[3030]

Dissolution of Partnership, and its consequences

32 Dissolution by expiration or notice

Subject to any agreement between the partners, a partnership is dissolved—

(a) If entered into for a fixed term, by the expiration of that term:

(b) If entered into for a single adventure or undertaking, by the termination of that adventure or undertaking:

(c) If entered into for an undefined time, by any partner giving notice to the other or others of his intention to dissolve the partnership.

In the last-mentioned case the partnership is dissolved as from the date mentioned in the notice as the date of dissolution, or, if no date is so mentioned, as from the date of the communication of the notice.

[3031]

33 Dissolution by bankruptcy, death or charge

(1) Subject to any agreement between the partners, every partnership is dissolved as regards all the partners by the death or bankruptcy of any partner.

(2) A partnership may, at the option of the other partners, be dissolved if any partner suffers his share of the partnership property to be charged under this Act for his separate debt.

[3032]

34 Dissolution by illegality of partnership

A partnership is in every case dissolved by the happening of any event which makes it unlawful for the business of the firm to be carried on or for the members of the firm to carry it on in partnership.

[3033]

35 Dissolution by the Court

On application by a partner the Court may decree a dissolution of the partnership in any of the following cases—

(a) ...

(b) When a partner, other than the partner suing, becomes in any other way permanently incapable of performing his part of the partnership contract;

(c) When a partner, other than the partner suing, has been guilty of such conduct as, in the opinion of the Court, regard being had to the nature of the business, is calculated to prejudicially affect the carrying on of the business;

(d) When a partner, other than the partner suing, wilfully or persistently commits a breach of the partnership agreement, or otherwise so conducts himself in matters relating to the partnership business that it is not reasonably practicable for the other partner or partners to carry on the business in partnership with him;

(e) When the business of the partnership can only be carried on at a loss;

(f) Whenever in any case circumstances have arisen which, in the opinion of the Court, render it just and equitable that the partnership be dissolved.

[3034]

NOTES

Para (a) repealed by the Mental Health Act 1959, s 149(2), Sch 8, as from 1 November 1960.

36 Rights of persons dealing with firm against apparent members of firm

(1) Where a person deals with a firm after a change in its constitution he is entitled to treat all apparent members of the old firm as still being members of the firm until he has notice of the change.

(2) An advertisement in the London Gazette as to a firm whose principal place of business is in England or Wales, in the Edinburgh Gazette as to a firm whose principal place of business is in Scotland, and in the Dublin Gazette as to a firm whose principal place of business is in Ireland, shall be notice as to persons who had not dealings with the firm before the date of the dissolution or change so advertised.

(3) The estate of a partner who dies, or who becomes bankrupt, or of a partner who, not having been known to the person dealing with the firm to be a partner, retires from the firm, is not liable for partnership debts contracted after the date of the death, bankruptcy, or retirement respectively.

[3035]

NOTES

Dublin Gazette: this should now be construed as a reference to the Belfast Gazette: see the General Adaptation of Enactments (Northern Ireland) Order 1921, SR & O 1921/1804.

37 Right of partners to notify dissolution

On the dissolution of a partnership or retirement of a partner any partner may publicly notify the same, and may require the other partner or partners to concur for that purpose in all necessary or proper acts, if any, which cannot be done without his or their concurrence.

[3036]

38 Continuing authority of partners for purposes of winding up

After the dissolution of a partnership the authority of each partner to bind the firm, and the other rights and obligations of the partners, continue notwithstanding the dissolution so far as may be necessary to wind up the affairs of the partnership, and to complete transactions begun but unfinished at the time of the dissolution, but not otherwise.

Provided that the firm is in no case bound by the acts of a partner who has become bankrupt; but this proviso does not affect the liability of any person who has after the bankruptcy represented himself or knowingly suffered himself to be represented as a partner of the bankrupt.

[3037]

39 Rights of partners as to application of partnership property

On the dissolution of a partnership every partner is entitled, as against the other partners in the firm, and all persons claiming through them in respect of their interests as partners, to have the property of the partnership applied in payment of the debts and liabilities of the firm, and to have the surplus assets after such payment applied in payment of what may be due to the partners respectively after deducting what may be due from them as partners to the firm; and for that purpose any partner or his representatives may on the termination of the partnership apply to the Court to wind up the business and affairs of the firm.

[3038]

40 Apportionment of premium where partnership prematurely dissolved

Where one partner has paid a premium to another on entering into a partnership for a fixed term, and the partnership is dissolved before the expiration of that term otherwise than by the death of a partner, the Court may order the repayment of the premium, or of such part thereof as it thinks just, having regard to the terms of the partnership contract and to the length of time during which the partnership has continued; unless—

(a) the dissolution is, in the judgment of the Court, wholly or chiefly due to the misconduct of the partner who paid the premium; or

(b) the partnership has been dissolved by an agreement containing no provision for a return of any part of the premium.

[3039]

41 Rights where partnership dissolved for fraud or misrepresentation

Where a partnership contract is rescinded on the ground of the fraud or misrepresentation of one of the parties thereto, the party entitled to rescind is, without prejudice to any other right, entitled—

(a) to a lien on, or right of retention of, the surplus of the partnership assets, after satisfying the partnership liabilities, for any sum of money paid by him for the purchase of a share in the partnership and for any capital contributed by him, and is

(b) to stand in the place of the creditors of the firm for any payments made by him in respect of the partnership liabilities, and

(c) to be indemnified by the person guilty of the fraud or making the representation against all the debts and liabilities of the firm.

[3040]

42 Right of outgoing partner in certain cases to share profits made after dissolution

(1) Where any member of a firm has died or otherwise ceased to be a partner, and the surviving or continuing partners carry on the business of the firm with its capital or assets without any final settlement of accounts as between the firm and the outgoing partner or his estate, then, in the absence of any agreement to the contrary, the outgoing partner or his estate is entitled at the option of himself or his representatives to such share of the profits made since the dissolution as the Court may find to be attributable to the use of his share of the partnership assets, or to interest at the rate of five per cent per annum on the amount of his share of the partnership assets.

(2) Provided that where by the partnership contract an option is given to surviving or continuing partners to purchase the interest of a deceased or outgoing partner, and that option is duly exercised, the estate of the deceased partner, or the outgoing partner or his estate, as the case may be, is not entitled to any further or other share of profits; but if any partner assuming to act in exercise of the option does not in all material respects comply with the terms thereof, he is liable to account under the foregoing provisions of this section.

[3041]

43 Retiring or deceased partner's share to be a debt

Subject to any agreement between the partners, the amount due from surviving or continuing partners to an outgoing partner or the representatives of a deceased partner in respect of the outgoing or deceased partner's share is a debt accruing at the date of the dissolution or death.

[3042]

44 Rule for distribution of assets on final settlement of accounts

In settling accounts between the partners after a dissolution of partnership, the following rules shall, subject to any agreement, be observed—

(a) Losses, including losses and deficiencies of capital, shall be paid first out of profits, next out of capital, and lastly, if necessary, by the partners individually in the proportion in which they were entitled to share profits;

(b) The assets of the firm including the sums, if any, contributed by the partners to make up losses or deficiencies of capital, shall be applied in the following manner and order—

1. In paying the debts and liabilities of the firm to persons who are not partners therein:
2. In paying to each partner rateably what is due from the firm to him for advances as distinguished from capital:
3. In paying to each partner rateably what is due from the firm to him in respect of capital:
4. The ultimate residue, if any, shall be divided among the partners in the proportion in which profits are divisible.

[3043]

Supplemental

45 Definitions of "court" and "business"

In this Act, unless the contrary intention appears,—

The expression "court" includes every court and judge having jurisdiction in the case;

The expression "business" includes every trade, occupation, or profession.

[3044]

46 Saving for rules of equity and common law

The rules of equity and of common law applicable to partnership shall continue in force except so far as they are inconsistent with the express provisions of this Act.

[3045]

47 Provision as to bankruptcy in Scotland

(1) In the application of this Act to Scotland the bankruptcy of a firm or of an individual shall mean sequestration under the Bankruptcy (Scotland) Acts, and also in the case of an individual the issue against him of a decree of cessio bonorum.

(2) Nothing in this Act shall alter the rules of the law of Scotland relating to the bankruptcy of a firm or of the individual partners thereof.

[3046]

48, 49 (*Repealed by the Statute Law Revision Act 1908.*)

50 Short title

This Act may be cited as the Partnership Act 1890.

[3047]

(*Schedule repealed by the Statute Law Revision Act 1908.*)

FORGED TRANSFERS ACT 1891 (NOTE)

(54 & 55 Vict c 43)

NOTES

This Act has been omitted from this Edition of the *Company Law Handbook* in order to create space for other legislation (ie, the Companies Act 2006 and the associated destination and derivation tables). It was printed in the 20th Edition of this work (at p 1145 et seq) and, as of 1 July 2007, it had not been amended since the publication of that Edition. This Act is, however, included in the CD version of this work (which may be ordered from the LexisNexis Butterworths Customer Services Department) and can be accessed in the online version of the *Company Law Handbook* which is updated fortnightly (at www.lexisnexis.com/uk/legal).

[3048]–[3052]

FORGED TRANSFERS ACT 1892 (NOTE)

(55 & 56 Vict c 36)

NOTES

This Act has been omitted from this Edition of the *Company Law Handbook* in order to create space for other legislation (ie, the Companies Act 2006 and the associated destination and derivation tables). It was printed in the 20th Edition of this work (at p 1147) and, as of 1 July 2007, it had not been amended since the publication of that Edition. This Act is, however, included in the CD version of this work (which may be ordered from the LexisNexis Butterworths Customer Services Department) and can be accessed in the online version of the *Company Law Handbook* which is updated fortnightly (at www.lexisnexis.com/uk/legal).

[3053]–[3054]

LIMITED PARTNERSHIPS ACT 1907

(1907 c 24)

NOTES

This Act is reproduced as amended by: the Companies (Consolidation) Act 1908; the Perjury Act 1911; the Statute Law Revision Act 1927; the Perjury Act (Northern Ireland) 1946; the Decimal Currency Act 1969; the Finance Act 1973; the Banking Act 1979; the Companies Act 2006; the Finance (Miscellaneous Provisions) (Northern Ireland) Order 1973, SI 1973/1323; the Regulatory Reform (Removal of 20 Member Limit in Partnerships etc) Order 2002, SI 2002/3203.

As to the repeal of this Act in relation to Northern Ireland, see the Companies Act 2006, s 1286(2) at **[S1286]**.

ARRANGEMENT OF SECTIONS

An Act to establish Limited Partnership

[28 August 1907]

1 Short title

This Act may be cited for all purposes as the Limited Partnerships Act 1907.

[3055]

2 (*Repealed by the Statute Law Revision Act 1927.*)

3 Interpretation of terms

In the construction of this Act the following words and expressions shall have the meanings respectively assigned to them in this section, unless there be something in the subject or context repugnant to such construction—

"Firm," "firm name," and "business" have the same meanings as in the Partnership Act 1890;

"General partner" shall mean any partner who is not a limited partner as defined by this Act.

[3056]

4 Definition and constitution of limited partnership

(1) … Limited partnerships may be formed in the manner and subject to the conditions by this Act provided.

(2) A limited partnership … must consist of one or more persons called general partners, who shall be liable for all debts and obligations of the firm, and one or more persons to be called limited partners, who shall at the time of entering into such partnership contribute thereto a sum or sums as capital or property valued at a stated amount, and who shall not be liable for the debts or obligations of the firm beyond the amount so contributed.

(3) A limited partner shall not during the continuance of the partnership, either directly or indirectly, draw out or receive back any part of his contribution, and if he does so draw out or receive back any such part shall be liable for the debts and obligations of the firm up to the amount so drawn out or received back.

(4) A body corporate may be a limited partner.

[3057]

NOTES

Sub-s (1): words omitted repealed by the Statute Law Revision Act 1927, as from 22 December 1927.

Sub-s (2): words omitted repealed by a combination of the Banking Act 1979, ss 46(b), 51(2), Sch 7, as from 19 February 1982, the Regulatory Reform (Removal of 20 Member Limit in Partnerships etc) Order 2002, SI 2002/3203, art 3, as from 21 December 2002, and the Partnerships etc (Removal of Twenty Member Limit) (Northern Ireland) Order 2003, SI 2003/2904, arts 3(1), 4, Schedule, as from 13 January 2004.

Note: the Regulatory Reform (Removal of 20 Member Limit in Partnerships etc) Order 2002, SI 2002/3203 reforms the law relating to the maximum limit of 20 on the numbers of persons who can be members of partnerships (including limited partnerships), and of certain companies or associations. It does so by repealing CA 1985, ss 716, 717 and amending sub-s (2) above, thereby removing the maximum limits on the number of members in a partnership or limited partnership, company or association.

5 Registration of limited partnership required

Every limited partnership must be registered as such in accordance with the provisions of this Act, or in default thereof it shall be deemed to be a general partnership, and every limited partner shall be deemed to be a general partner.

[3058]

6 Modifications of general law in case of limited partnerships

(1) A limited partner shall not take part in the management of the partnership business, and shall not have power to bind the firm—

Provided that a limited partner may by himself or his agent at any time inspect the books of the firm and examine into the state and prospects of the partnership business, and may advise with the partners thereon.

If a limited partner takes part in the management of the partnership business he shall be liable for all debts and obligations of the firm incurred while he so takes part in the management as though he were a general partner.

(2) A limited partnership shall not be dissolved by the death or bankruptcy of a limited partner, and the lunacy of a limited partner shall not be a ground for dissolution of the partnership by the court unless the lunatic's share cannot be otherwise ascertained and realised.

(3) In the event of the dissolution of a limited partnership its affairs shall be wound up by the general partners unless the court otherwise orders.

(4) …

(5) Subject to any agreement expressed or implied between the partners—

(a) Any difference arising as to ordinary matters connected with the partnership business may be decided by a majority of the general partners;

(b) A limited partner may, with the consent of the general partners, assign his share in the partnership, and upon such an assignment the assignee shall become a limited partner with all the rights of the assignor;

(c) The other partners shall not be entitled to dissolve the partnership by reason of any limited partner suffering his share to be charged for his separate debt;

(d) A person may be introduced as a partner without the consent of the existing limited partners;

(e) A limited partner shall not be entitled to dissolve the partnership by notice.

[3059]

NOTES

Sub-s (4): repealed by the Companies (Consolidation) Act 1908, s 286, Sch 6, Pt I, as from 21 December 1908.

7 Law as to private partnerships to apply where not excluded by this Act

Subject to the provisions of this Act, the Partnership Act 1890 and the rules of equity and of common law applicable to partnerships, except so far as they are inconsistent with the express provisions of the last-mentioned Act, shall apply to limited partnerships.

[3060]

8 Manner and particulars of registration

The registration of a limited partnership shall be effected by sending by post or delivering to the registrar at the register office in that part of the United Kingdom in which the principal place of business of the limited partnership is situated or proposed to be situated a statement signed by the partners containing the following particulars—

(a) The firm name;

(b) The general nature of the business;

(c) The principal place of business;

(d) The full name of each of the partners;

(e) The term, if any, for which the partnership is entered into, and the date of its commencement;

(f) A statement that the partnership is limited, and the description of every limited partner as such;

(g) The sum contributed by each limited partner, and whether paid in cash or how otherwise.

[3061]

9 Registration of changes in partnerships

(1) If during the continuance of a limited partnership any change is made or occurs in—

(a) the firm name,

(b) the general nature of the business,

(c) the principal place of business,

(d) the partners or the name of any partner,

(e) the term or character of the partnership,

(f) the sum contributed by any limited partner,

(g) the liability of any partner by reason of his becoming a limited instead of a general partner or a general instead of a limited partner,

a statement, signed by the firm, specifying the nature of the change shall within seven days be sent by post or delivered to the registrar at the register office in that part of the United Kingdom in which the partnership is registered.

(2) If default is made in compliance with the requirements of this section each of the general partners shall, on conviction under the Summary Jurisdiction Acts, be liable to a fine not exceeding one pound for each day during which the default continues.

[3062]

10 Advertisement in Gazette of statement of general partner becoming a limited partner and of assignment of share of limited partner

(1) Notice of any arrangement or transaction under which any person will cease to be a general partner in any firm, and will become a limited partner in that firm, or under which the share of a limited partner in a firm will be assigned to any person, shall be forthwith advertised in the Gazette, and until notice of the arrangement or transaction is so advertised the arrangement or transaction shall, for the purposes of this Act, be deemed to be of no effect.

(2) For the purposes of this section, the expression "the Gazette" means—

In the case of a limited partnership registered in England, the London Gazette.

In the case of a limited partnership registered in Scotland, the Edinburgh Gazette.

In the case of a limited partnership registered in Ireland, the Dublin Gazette.

[3063]

NOTES

Dublin Gazette: this should now be construed as a reference to the Belfast Gazette: see the General Adaptation of Enactments (Northern Ireland) Order 1921, SR & O 1921/1804.

11, 12 *(S 11 repealed by the Finance Act 1973, s 59(7), Sch 22, Pt V and the Finance (Miscellaneous Provisions) (Northern Ireland) Order 1973, SI 1973/1323, art 10(1), Sch 4, as from 1 August 1973; s 12 repealed by the Perjury Act 1911, s 17, Schedule and the Perjury Act (Northern Ireland) 1946, s 16(3), Schedule, as from 1 January 1912.)*

13 Registrar to file statement and issue certificate of registration

On receiving any statement made in pursuance of this Act the registrar shall cause the same to be filed, and he shall send by post to the firm from whom such statement shall have been received a certificate of the registration thereof.

[3064]

14 Register and index to be kept

At each of the register offices herein-after referred to the registrar shall keep, in proper books to be provided for the purpose, a register and an index of all the limited partnerships registered as aforesaid, and of all the statements registered in relation to such partnerships.

[3065]

15 Registrar of joint stock companies to be registrar under Act

The registrar of joint stock companies shall be the registrar of limited partnerships, and the several offices for the registration of joint stock companies in London, Edinburgh, and Dublin shall be the offices for the registration of limited partnerships carrying on business within those parts of the United Kingdom in which they are respectively situated.

[3066]

16 Inspection of statements registered

(1) Any person may inspect the statements filed by the registrar in the register offices aforesaid, *and there shall be paid for such inspection such fees as may be appointed by the Board of Trade, not exceeding [5p] for each inspection*; and any person may require a certificate of the registration of any limited partnership, or a copy of or extract from any registered statement, to be certified by the registrar, *and there shall be paid for such certificate of registration, certified copy, or extract such fees as the Board of Trade may appoint, not exceeding [10p] for the certificate of registration, and not exceeding [2p] for each folio of seventy-two words, or in Scotland for each sheet of two hundred words.*

(2) A certificate of registration or a copy of or extract from any statement registered under this Act, if duly certified to be a true copy under the hand of the registrar or one of the assistant registrars (whom it shall not be necessary to prove to be the registrar or assistant registrar) shall, in all legal proceedings, civil or criminal, and in all cases whatsoever be received in evidence.

[3067]

NOTES

Sub-s (1): words in italics repealed by the Companies Act 2006, ss 1063(7)(a), 1295, Sch 16, as from 6 April 2007 (for transitional provisions see the note below); sums in square brackets substituted by virtue of the Decimal Currency Act 1969, s 10(1), as from 16 May 1969.

Transitional provisions: the Companies Act 2006 (Commencement No 1, Transitional Provisions and Savings) Order 2006, SI 2006/3428, Sch 5, para 6(2) provides as follows—

"(2) Notwithstanding the coming into force of the repeals in section 16 of the Limited Partnerships Act 1907 and the repeal of section 17(a) of that Act, the fees appointed under the said section 16 and having effect immediately before 6th April 2007 shall continue to be payable, and the rules in force under the said section 17(a) immediately before 6th April 2007 shall continue to have effect."

Note also that SI 2006/3428, art 4(4) provides that the commencement of CA 2006, s 1063 does not extend to Northern Ireland.

17 Power to Board of Trade to make rules

The Board of Trade may make rules (*but as to fees with the concurrence of the Treasury*) concerning any of the following matters:—

(*a*) *The fees to be paid to the registrar under this Act, so that they do not exceed in the case of the original registration of a limited partnership the sum of two pounds, and in any other case the sum of [25p];*

(b) The duties or additional duties to be performed by the registrar for the purposes of this Act;

(c) The performance by assistant registrars and other officers of acts by this Act required to be done by the registrar;

(d) The forms to be used for the purposes of this Act;

(e) Generally, the conduct and regulation of registration under this Act and any matters incidental thereto.

[3068]–[3077]

NOTES

Words in italics repealed by the Companies Act 2006, ss 1063(7)(b), 1295, Sch 16, as from 6 April 2007 (for transitional provisions see the note to s 16 at **[3067]**); sum in square brackets in para (a) substituted by virtue of the Decimal Currency Act 1969, s 10(1).

Rules: the Limited Partnerships Rules 1907, SR & O 1907/1020.

STOCK TRANSFER ACT 1963 (NOTE)

(1963 c 18)

NOTES

This Act has been omitted from this Edition of the *Company Law Handbook* in order to create space for other legislation (ie, the Companies Act 2006 and the associated destination and derivation tables). It was printed in the 20th Edition of this work (at p 1151 et seq) and, as of 1 July 2007, it had not been amended since the publication of that Edition. This Act is, however, included in the CD version of this work (which may be ordered from the LexisNexis Butterworths Customer Services Department) and can be accessed in the online version of the *Company Law Handbook* which is updated fortnightly (at www.lexisnexis.com/uk/legal).

[3078]–[3086]

THEFT ACT 1968 (NOTE)

(1968 c 60)

NOTES

This Act has been omitted from this Edition of the *Company Law Handbook* in order to create space for other legislation (ie, the Companies Act 2006 and the associated destination and derivation tables). It was printed in the 20th Edition of this work (at p 1159 et seq). Since publication of the 20th Edition, this Act has been amended by the Fraud Act 2006 (at **[3634]** et seq). The 2006 Act repealed the 'deception offences' in this Act (ie, ss 15, 15A, 15B, 16, 20(2)) and made a consequential amendment to s 18. The repeal of these provisions came into effect on 15 January 2007, but was subject to savings and transitional provisions in relation to any liability, investigation, legal proceeding or penalty for or in respect of any offence partly committed before that date (see Sch 2, para 3 to the 2006 Act). This Act is, however, included in the CD version of this work (which may be ordered from the LexisNexis Butterworths Customer Services Department) and can be accessed in the online version of the *Company Law Handbook* which is updated fortnightly (at www.lexisnexis.com/uk/legal).

[3087]–[3103]

FAIR TRADING ACT 1973 (NOTE)

(1973 c 41)

NOTES

Part V of this Act (Mergers) has now been completely repealed. Sections 57–62 (newspaper mergers) were repealed by the Communications Act 2003, ss 373, 406, Sch 19, as from 29 December 2003 (subject to transitional provisions contained in Sch 18, paras 59–62 to that Act). Sections 63–75 (other merger references) and ss 75A–75K (restriction on power to make merger reference where prior notice has been given) were repealed by the Enterprise Act 2002, s 278(2), Sch 26, as from 20 June 2003 (subject to savings in relation to cases where two or more enterprises ceased to be distinct enterprises before that date; see Sch 24, para 13 to the 2002 Act at **[3632]**). Note also that the Enterprise Act 2002 (Commencement No 3, Transitional and Transitory Provisions and Savings) Order 2003, SI 2003/1397, art 3(1) provided for savings, etc, in relation to the merger of water and sewerage undertakers (and see also the Enterprise Act 2002 (Commencement No 7 and Transitional Provisions and Savings) Order 2004, SI 2004/3233). Sections 76, 77 (supplementary) were repealed by the Enterprise Act 2002, s 278(2), Sch 26, as from 20 June 2003 (subject to savings, etc, as noted above) and the Enterprise Act 2002 and Media Mergers (Consequential Amendments) Order 2003, SI 2003/3180, art 2, Schedule, para 1(3), as from 29 December 2003 (subject to transitional provisions contained in art 3 thereof). In so far as other provisions of this Act are still in force, they are outside the scope of this work.

[3104]–[3136]

INDUSTRY ACT 1975 (NOTE)

(1975 c 68)

NOTES

This Act has been omitted from this Edition of the *Company Law Handbook* in order to create space for other legislation (ie, the Companies Act 2006 and the associated destination and derivation tables). It was printed in the 20th Edition of this work (at p 1166 et seq) and, as of 1 July 2007, it had not been amended since the publication of that Edition. This Act is, however, included in the CD version of this work (which may be ordered from the LexisNexis Butterworths Customer Services Department) and can be accessed in the online version of the *Company Law Handbook* which is updated fortnightly (at www.lexisnexis.com/uk/legal).

[3137]–[3151]

INSOLVENCY ACT 1986

(1986 c 45)

NOTES

This Act is reproduced as amended by the following Acts:

1988	Court of Session Act 1988; Criminal Justice Act 1988; ICTA 1988.
1989	CA 1989; Water Act 1989.
1990	Broadcasting Act 1990; Courts and Legal Services Act 1990; Law Reform (Miscellaneous Provisions) (Scotland) Act 1990.
1991	FA 1991; Water Consolidation (Consequential Provisions) Act 1991.
1992	F (No 2) A 1992; Social Security (Consequential Provisions) Act 1992; Transport and Works Act 1992; Tribunals and Inquiries Act 1992.
1993	Bankruptcy (Scotland) Act 1993; FA 1993; Pension Schemes Act 1993; Railways Act 1993; Statute Law (Repeals) Act 1993.
1994	FA 1994; Insolvency Act 1994; Insolvency (No 2) Act 1994; Value Added Tax Act 1994.
1995	Criminal Procedure (Consequential Provisions) (Scotland) Act 1995; FA 1995; Gas Act 1995; Requirements of Writing (Scotland) Act 1995.
1996	Employment Rights Act 1996; FA 1996.
1997	FA 1997.
1998	Bank of England Act 1998; Government of Wales Act 1998; Northern Ireland Act 1998; Scotland Act 1998.
1999	Access to Justice Act 1999; Youth Justice and Criminal Evidence Act 1999.
2000	Abolition of Feudal Tenure etc (Scotland) Act 2000; Adults with Incapacity (Scotland) Act 2000; FA 2000; Insolvency Act 2000; Utilities Act 2000.
2001	FA 2001.
2002	Commonhold and Leasehold Reform Act 2002; Enterprise Act 2002; Income Tax (Earnings and Pensions) Act 2003.
2003	Communications Act 2003; Courts Act 2003.
2004	Companies (Audit, Investigations and Community Enterprise) Act 2004; Civil Partnership Act 2004.
2005	Constitutional Reform Act 2005; Mental Capacity Act 2005.
2006	Government of Wales Act 2006; the Companies Act 2006.
2007	Bankruptcy and Diligence etc (Scotland) Act 2007.

This Act is reproduced as amended by the following SIs:

1986	Insolvency Proceedings (Monetary Limits) Order 1986, SI 1986/1996.
1987	Insolvency (ECSC Levy Debts) Regulations 1987, SI 1987/2093.
1989	Companies (Northern Ireland) Order 1989, SI 1989/2404; Insolvency (Northern Ireland) Order 1989, SI 1989/2405.
1992	Companies (Single Member Private Limited Companies) Regulations 1992, SI 1992/1699.
1994	Insolvent Partnerships Order 1994, SI 1994/2421.
1999	Scotland Act 1998 (Consequential Modifications) (No 2) Order 1999, SI 1999/1820.

2001	Limited Liability Partnerships (Scotland) Regulations 2001, SSI 2001/128; Limited Liability Partnerships Regulations 2001, SI 2001/1090; Financial Services and Markets Act 2000 (Consequential Amendments and Repeals) Order 2001, SI 2001/3649.
2002	Insolvency Act 1986 (Amendment) Regulations 2002, SI 2002/1037; Insolvency Act 1986 (Amendment) (No 2) Regulations 2002, SI 2002/1240; Financial Services and Markets Act 2000 (Consequential Amendments) Order 2002, SI 2002/1555; Insolvency Act 1986 (Amendment) (No 3) Regulations 2002, SI 2002/1990; Insolvent Partnerships (Amendment) (No 2) Order 2002, SI 2002/2708; Company Directors Disqualification (Northern Ireland) Order 2002, SI 2002/3150.
2003	Insolvency Act 1986 (Amendment) (Administrative Receivership and Capital Market Arrangements) Order 2003, SI 2003/1468; Insolvency Act 1986 (Amendment) (Administrative Receivership and Urban Regeneration etc) Order 2003, SI 2003/1832; Enterprise Act 2002 (Insolvency) Order 2003, SI 2003/2096.
2004	Water Industry (Scotland) Act 2002 (Consequential Modifications) Order 2004, SI 2004/1822; Insolvency Act 2000 (Company Directors Disqualification Undertakings) Order 2004, SI 2004/1941; Enterprise Act 2002 (Insolvency) Order 2004, SI 2004/2312; European Public Limited-Liability Company Regulations 2004, SI 2004/2326.
2005	Insolvency Act 1986 (Amendment) Regulations 2005, SI 2005/879; Mental Health (Care and Treatment) (Scotland) Act 2003 (Consequential Provisions) Order 2005, SI 2005/2078; Mental Health (Care and Treatment) (Scotland) Act 2003 (Modification of Enactments) Order 2005, SSI 2005/486; Railway (Licensing of Railway Undertakings) Regulations 2005, SI 2005/3050; Civil Partnership Act 2004 (Overseas Relationships and Consequential, etc Amendments) Order 2005, SI 2005/3129.
2006	European Cooperative Society Regulations 2006, SI 2006/2078; Companies (Registrar, Languages and Trading Disclosures) Regulations 2006, SI 2006/3429.

See also the prospective amendments made to this Act by the draft Companies Act 2006 (Commencement No 3, Consequential Amendments, Transitional Provisions and Savings) Order 2007 (see **[A12]**).

ARRANGEMENT OF SECTIONS

THE FIRST GROUP OF PARTS
COMPANY INSOLVENCY; COMPANIES WINDING UP

PART I
COMPANY VOLUNTARY ARRANGEMENTS

The proposal

Consideration and implementation of proposal

PART II
ADMINISTRATION

PART III
RECEIVERSHIP

CHAPTER I
RECEIVERS AND MANAGERS (ENGLAND AND WALES)

Preliminary and general provisions

Receivers and managers appointed out of court

Provisions applicable to every receivership

Administrative receivers: general

Administrative receivers: ascertainment and investigation of company's affairs

CHAPTER II
RECEIVERS (SCOTLAND)

CHAPTER III
RECEIVERS' POWERS IN GREAT BRITAIN AS A WHOLE

CHAPTER IV
PROHIBITION OF APPOINTMENT OF ADMINISTRATIVE RECEIVER

PART IV
WINDING UP OF COMPANIES REGISTERED UNDER THE COMPANIES ACTS

CHAPTER I
PRELIMINARY

Modes of winding up

Contributories

CHAPTER II
VOLUNTARY WINDING UP (INTRODUCTORY AND GENERAL)

Resolutions for, and commencement of, voluntary winding up

Consequences of resolution to wind up

Declaration of solvency

CHAPTER III
MEMBERS' VOLUNTARY WINDING UP

CHAPTER IV
CREDITORS' VOLUNTARY WINDING UP

CHAPTER V
PROVISIONS APPLYING TO BOTH KINDS OF VOLUNTARY WINDING UP

CHAPTER VI
WINDING UP BY THE COURT

Jurisdiction (England and Wales)

Jurisdiction (Scotland)

Grounds and effect of winding-up petition

Commencement of winding up

Investigation procedures

Appointment of liquidator

Liquidation committees

The liquidator's functions

General powers of court

Enforcement of, and appeal from, orders

CHAPTER VII
LIQUIDATORS

Preliminary

Liquidator's powers and duties

Removal; vacation of office

Release of liquidator

CHAPTER VIII
PROVISIONS OF GENERAL APPLICATION IN WINDING UP

Preferential debts

Property subject to floating charge

Special managers

Disclaimer (England and Wales only)

PART VI
MISCELLANEOUS PROVISIONS APPLYING TO COMPANIES WHICH ARE INSOLVENT OR IN LIQUIDATION

Office-holders

Management by administrators, liquidators, etc

Adjustment of prior transactions (administration and liquidation)

PART VII
INTERPRETATION FOR FIRST GROUP OF PARTS

THE THIRD GROUP OF PARTS
MISCELLANEOUS MATTERS BEARING ON BOTH COMPANY AND INDIVIDUAL INSOLVENCY;
GENERAL INTERPRETATION; FINAL PROVISIONS

PART XII
PREFERENTIAL DEBTS IN COMPANY AND INDIVIDUAL INSOLVENCY

PART XIII
INSOLVENCY PRACTITIONERS AND THEIR QUALIFICATION

Restrictions on unqualified persons acting as liquidator, trustee in bankruptcy, etc

The requisite qualification, and the means of obtaining it

PART XVIII
INTERPRETATION

PART XIX
FINAL PROVISIONS

SCHEDULES

An Act to consolidate the enactments relating to company insolvency and winding up (including the winding up of companies that are not insolvent, and of unregistered companies); enactments relating to the insolvency and bankruptcy of individuals; and other enactments bearing on those two subject matters, including the functions and qualification of insolvency practitioners, the public administration of insolvency, the penalisation and redress of malpractice and wrongdoing, and the avoidance of certain transactions at an undervalue

[25 July 1986]

NOTES

Commencement:

This Act came into force on 29 December 1986 by virtue of s 443 and the Insolvency Act 1985 (Commencement No 5) Order 1986, SI 1986/1924. Where any provision in this work (including any

inserted or substituted provision) came into force for all purposes on or before 1 July 2005, commencement information is not noted at provision level.

Application of this Act:

This Act is applied, with certain modifications, to various types of business and financial sectors, etc, as follows:

Limited liability partnerships: Parts I, II, III, IV, VI and VII of the First Group of Parts, and the whole of the Third Group of Parts, apply to limited liability partnerships; see the Limited Liability Partnerships Regulations 2001, SI 2001/1090, reg 5(1) at **[6986]**. For general modifications of this Act in its application to LLPs see reg 5(2) of those Regulations, and for specific modifications see Sch 3 (at **[6995]**). See also reg 5(3) of, and Sch 4 to, those Regulations (disapplication to Scotland), and the Limited Liability Partnerships (Scotland) Regulations 2001, SSI 2001/128, reg 4, Schs 2, 3 (at **[6977]**, **[6980A]**, **[6980B]**). Cross-references are provided throughout this Act on the provisions affected by the Regulations noted above.

Insurers: as to the application of this Act to insurers, see the Financial Services and Markets Act 2000 (Administration Orders Relating to Insurers) Order 2002, SI 2002/1242, and the Insurers (Reorganisation and Winding Up) Regulations 2004, SI 2004/353 at **[7200A]**.

EEA credit institutions: as to the application of this Act to EEA credit institutions or any branch of an EEA credit institution, see the Credit Institutions (Reorganisation and Winding up) Regulations 2004, SI 2004/1045 at **[7211]**.

European Economic Interest Groupings: as to the application of this Act to European Economic Interest Groupings, see the European Economic Interest Grouping Regulations 1989, SI 1989/638, reg 19 at **[6620]**.

Open-ended investment companies: as to the application of this Act to open-ended investment companies, see the Open-Ended Investment Companies Regulations 2001, SI 2001/1228, reg 31.

Companies incorporated outside Great Britain: the Enterprise Act 2002, s 254 provides that the Secretary of State may by order provide for a provision of this Act to apply (with or without modification) in relation to a company incorporated outside Great Britain. As of 1 July 2007 no Orders had been made under that section.

Non-companies: the Enterprise Act 2002, s 255 provides that the Treasury may with the concurrence of the Secretary of State by order provide for a company arrangement or administration provision to apply (ie, Pts I, II) in relation to (a) a society registered under the Industrial and Provident Societies Act 1965; (b) a society registered under the Friendly Societies Act 1974, s 7(1)(b), (c), (d), (e) or (f); (c) a friendly society within the meaning of the Friendly Societies Act 1992; (d) an unregistered friendly society. As of 1 July 2007 no Orders had been made under that section.

Former authorised institutions: see the Banks (Former Authorised Institutions) (Insolvency) Order 2006, SI 2006/3107 as to the application of Part II of, and Sch B1 to, this Act, to any company within the meaning of s 735(1) of the Companies Act 1985 that (a) has a liability in respect of a deposit which it accepted in accordance with the Banking Act 1979 or Banking Act 1987, but (b) does not have permission under Part IV of the Financial Services and Markets Act 2000 to accept deposits.

Special administration regimes: see (i) the Water Industry Act 1991, ss 23–25, Sch 3 (application to water or sewerage undertakers and qualifying licensed water suppliers); (ii) the Building Societies Act 1986, ss 90, 90A, Schs 15, 15A (application to building societies); (iii) the Railways Act 1993, ss 59–62, 65, Sch 6 and the Channel Tunnel Rail Link Act 1996, s 19 (application to protected railway companies); (iv) the Transport Act 2000, ss 26–32, Sch 1 (application to air traffic services); (v) the Greater London Authority Act 1999, ss 220–224, Sch 14 (application to public-private partnership companies carrying out certain railway works). See also the Enterprise Act 2002, s 249 (reproduced in the notes to s 8 of this Act at **[3164]**); and, with regard to companies which hold a licence under the Electricity Act 1989, s 6(1)(b) or (c) (transmission and distribution licences for electricity) or the Gas Act 1986, s 7 (licensing of gas transporters), see the Energy Act 2004, ss 154–171, Schs 20, 21

Other bodies etc: see (i) the Friendly Societies Act 1992, ss 23, 52, Sch 10 (application to incorporated and registered friendly societies) (see also the note 'Non companies' above); (ii) the Industrial and Provident Societies Act 1965, ss 55–58 (application to industrial and provident societies) (see also the note 'Non companies' above); (iii) the Agricultural Marketing Act 1958, s 3(3), Sch 2, para 4 (application to agricultural marketing boards); (iv) the European Public Limited-Liability Company Regulations 2004, SI 2004/2326 at **[7249]** (application to Societas Europaea); (v) CA 1989, s 182 at **[852]** (application to certain proceedings begun before the commencement of that section in respect of insolvency proceedings regarding members of recognised investment exchanges and clearing houses and persons to whom market charges have been granted); (vi) the Solicitors' Incorporated Practices Order 1991, SI 1991/2684, arts 2–5, Sch 1 (application to a "recognised body" within the meaning of the Administration of Justice Act 1985, s 9); (vi) the National Health Service Act 2006, ss 52–55 (application to NHS foundation trusts).

European Grouping of Territorial Cooperation: see the European Grouping of Territorial Cooperation Regulations 2007, SI 2007/1949.

See also the powers to apply this Act in s 420 at **[3441A]** (insolvent partnerships) and s 422 at **[3442]** (formerly authorised banks).

Other Modifications, etc:

Cross-Border insolvency proceedings: British insolvency law (as defined in Article 2 of the UNCITRAL Model Law as set out in Schedule 1 to the Cross-Border Insolvency Regulations 2006, SI 2006/1030) and Part III of this Act shall apply with such modifications as the context requires for the purpose of giving effect to the provisions of the 2006 Regulations; see reg 2 of the 2006 Regulations at **[7484]**.

Scotland: by virtue of the Scotland Act 1998, s 125, Sch 8, para 23, (i) anything directed to be done, or which may be done, to or by the registrar of companies in Scotland by virtue of ss 53(1), 54(3), 61(6), 62(5) (so far as relating to the giving of notice), 67(1), 69(2), 84(3), 94(3), 106(3) and (5), 112(3), 130(1), 147(3), 170(2) and 172(8), or the assistant registrar of friendly societies for Scotland by virtue of any of those provisions as applied (with or without modification) in relation to friendly societies, industrial and provident societies or building societies, shall, or (as the case may be) may, also be done to or by the Accountant in Bankruptcy, and (ii) anything directed to be done to or by the registrar of companies in Scotland by virtue of ss 89(3), 109(1), 171(5) and (6), 173(2)(a) and 192(1), or the assistant registrar of friendly societies for Scotland by virtue of any of those provisions as applied (with or without modification) in relation to friendly societies, industrial and provident societies or building societies, shall instead be done to or by the Accountant in Bankruptcy.

Miscellaneous:

Registrar of companies: as to the contracting out of certain functions of the registrar of companies in relation to Scotland conferred by or under this Act, see the Contracting Out (Functions in relation to the Registration of Companies) Order 1995, SI 1995/1013, art 4, Sch 2 at **[6839]**, **[6842]**.

Official Receiver: as to the contracting out of functions of the Official Receiver conferred by or under this Act, see the Contracting Out (Functions of the Official Receiver) Order 1995, SI 1995/1386 at **[6844]**.

Proceeds of crime: if an order for the winding up of a company is made or it passes a resolution for its voluntary winding up, the functions of the liquidator (or any provisional liquidator) are not exercisable in relation to property deemed to be the proceeds of crime; see the Proceeds of Crime Act 2002, Pt 9 (ss 426–434).

Interaction with Companies Act 1985: as to the relationship of CA 1985, to this Act, see s 735A of the 1985 Act at **[613]** (repealed by CA 2006, as from a day to be appointed).

Companies Act: references in this Act to the Companies Act are to the Companies Act 1985 (see s 436 at **[3454]**).

Only those provisions of this Act relating to company law are reproduced. Provisions not reproduced are not annotated.

THE FIRST GROUP OF PARTS
COMPANY INSOLVENCY; COMPANIES WINDING UP

PART I
COMPANY VOLUNTARY ARRANGEMENTS

The proposal

1 Those who may propose an arrangement

(1) The directors of a company [(other than one which is in administration or being wound up)] may make a proposal under this Part to the company and to its creditors for a composition in satisfaction of its debts or a scheme of arrangement of its affairs (from here on referred to, in either case, as a "voluntary arrangement").

(2) A proposal under this Part is one which provides for some person ("the nominee") to act in relation to the voluntary arrangement either as trustee or otherwise for the purpose of supervising its implementation; and the nominee must be a person who is qualified to act as an insolvency practitioner [or authorised to act as nominee, in relation to the voluntary arrangement].

(3) Such a proposal may also be made—

[(a) where the company is in administration, by the administrator,] and

(b) where the company is being wound up, by the liquidator.

[(4) In this Part "company" means—

(a) a company within the meaning of section 735(1) of the Companies Act 1985,

(b) a company incorporated in an EEA State other than the United Kingdom; or

(c) a company not incorporated in an EEA State but having its centre of main interests in a member State other than Denmark.

(5) In subsection (4), in relation to a company, "centre of main interests" has the same meaning as in the EC Regulation and, in the absence of proof to the contrary, is presumed to be the place of its registered office (within the meaning of that Regulation).

(6) If a company incorporated outside the United Kingdom has a principal place of business in Northern Ireland, no proposal under this Part shall be made in relation to it unless it also has a principal place of business in England and Wales or Scotland (or both in England and Wales or Scotland).]

[3152]

NOTES

Sub-s (1): words in square brackets substituted by the Enterprise Act 2002, s 248(3), Sch 17, paras 9, 10(a), as from 15 September 2003 (for savings and transitional provisions, see the note to s 8 at **[3164]**).

Sub-s (2): words in square brackets substituted by the Insolvency Act 2000, s 2, Sch 2, Pt I, paras 1, 2, as from 1 January 2003 (for transitional provisions see the note below).

Sub-s (3): para (a) substituted by the Enterprise Act 2002, s 248(3), Sch 17, paras 9, 10(b), as from 15 September 2003 (for savings and transitional provisions, see the note to s 8 at **[3164]**).

Sub-ss (4)–(6): substituted (for the original sub-s (4) as added by the Insolvency Act 1986 (Amendment) (No 2) Regulations 2002, SI 2002/1240, regs 3, 4, as from 31 May 2002) by the Insolvency Act 1986 (Amendment) Regulations 2005, SI 2005/879, reg 2(1), (2), as from 13 April 2005, except in relation to any voluntary arrangement under this Part that took effect before that date.

Transitional provisions: the Insolvency Act 2000 (Commencement No 3 and Transitional Provisions) Order 2002, SI 2002/2711, art 3 provides for the following transitional provisions (note that by virtue of arts 1, 2, the "appointed day" means 1 January 2003):

"(1) In a case where—

(a) a proposal is made by the directors of a company and before the appointed day the intended nominee has endorsed a copy of the written notice of the proposal under Rule 1.4(3) of the Insolvency Rules, or, in Scotland, under Rule 1.4(3) of the Insolvency (Scotland) Rules;

(b) a proposal is made by the liquidator or the administrator (acting as nominee) and before the appointed day the liquidator or administrator (as the case may be) has sent out a notice summoning the meetings under section 3 of the Act as required by Rule 1.11 of the Insolvency Rules, or, in Scotland, by Rule 1.11 of the Insolvency (Scotland) Rules; or

(c) a proposal is made by the liquidator or the administrator of a company (not acting as the nominee) and before the appointed day the intended nominee has endorsed a copy of the written notice of the proposal under Rule 1.12(2) of the Insolvency Rules, or, in Scotland, Rule 1.12(2) of the Insolvency (Scotland) Rules,

the amendments made to the Act by Part I of Schedule 2 and the repeal made by section 15(1) and Schedule 5 in respect of section 5(2) and (3) of the Act shall not apply and the provisions of the Act as they have effect immediately before the appointed day shall continue to have effect.

(2) The provisions of paragraph (1) shall—

(a) apply in relation to building societies as they apply in relation to companies; and

(b) in their application to building societies, have effect with the substitution for "company" of "building society".

(3) In this article "proposal" has the same meaning as it has in section 1(2) of the Act.".

Application to limited liability partnerships: see the introductory note to this Act and the Limited Liability Partnerships Regulations 2001, SI 2001/1090, reg 5, Sch 3 at **[6986]**, **[6995]**.

[1A Moratorium

(1) Where the directors of an eligible company intend to make a proposal for a voluntary arrangement, they may take steps to obtain a moratorium for the company.

(2) The provisions of Schedule A1 to this Act have effect with respect to—

(a) companies eligible for a moratorium under this section,

(b) the procedure for obtaining such a moratorium,

(c) the effects of such a moratorium, and

(d) the procedure applicable (in place of sections 2 to 6 and 7) in relation to the approval and implementation of a voluntary arrangement where such a moratorium is or has been in force.]

[3153]

PART III OTHER LEGISLATION

NOTES

Inserted by the Insolvency Act 2000, s 1, Sch 1, paras 1, 2, as from 1 January 2003.

Application to limited liability partnerships: see the introductory note to this Act and the Limited Liability Partnerships Regulations 2001, SI 2001/1090, reg 5, Sch 3 at **[6986]**, **[6995]**.

2 Procedure where nominee is not the liquidator or administrator

(1) This section applies where the nominee under section 1 is not the liquidator or administrator of the company [and the directors do not propose to take steps to obtain a moratorium under section 1A for the company].

(2) The nominee shall, within 28 days (or such longer period as the court may allow) after he is given notice of the proposal for a voluntary arrangement, submit a report to the court stating—

(a) [whether, in his opinion, the proposed voluntary arrangement has a reasonable prospect of being approved and implemented,

(aa)] whether, in his opinion, meetings of the company and of its creditors should be summoned to consider the proposal, and

(b) if in his opinion such meetings should be summoned, the date on which, and time and place at which, he proposes the meetings should be held.

(3) For the purposes of enabling the nominee to prepare his report, the person intending to make the proposal shall submit to the nominee—

(a) a document setting out the terms of the proposed voluntary arrangement, and

(b) a statement of the company's affairs containing—

(i) such particulars of its creditors and of its debts and other liabilities and of its assets as may be prescribed, and

(ii) such other information as may be prescribed.

[(4) The court may—

(a) on an application made by the person intending to make the proposal, in a case where the nominee has failed to submit the report required by this section or has died, or

(b) on an application made by that person or the nominee, in a case where it is impracticable or inappropriate for the nominee to continue to act as such,

direct that the nominee be replaced as such by another person qualified to act as an insolvency practitioner, or authorised to act as nominee, in relation to the voluntary arrangement.]

[3154]

NOTES

Sub-s (1): words in square brackets added by the Insolvency Act 2000, s 1, Sch 1, paras 1, 3, as from 1 January 2003.

Sub-s (2): words in square brackets inserted by the Insolvency Act 2000, s 2, Sch 2, Pt I, paras 1, 3(a), as from 1 January 2003 (for transitional provisions see the note to s 1 at **[3152]**).

Sub-s (4): substituted by the Insolvency Act 2000, s 2, Sch 2, Pt I, paras 1, 3(b), as from 1 January 2003 (for transitional provisions see the note to s 1 at **[3152]**).

Application to limited liability partnerships: see the introductory note to this Act and the Limited Liability Partnerships Regulations 2001, SI 2001/1090, reg 5, Sch 3 at **[6986]**, **[6995]**.

3 Summoning of meetings

(1) Where the nominee under section 1 is not the liquidator or administrator, and it has been reported to the court that such meetings as are mentioned in section 2(2) should be summoned, the person making the report shall (unless the court otherwise directs) summon those meetings for the time, date and place proposed in the report.

(2) Where the nominee is the liquidator or administrator, he shall summon meetings of the company and of its creditors to consider the proposal for such a time, date and place as he thinks fit.

(3) The persons to be summoned to a creditors' meeting under this section are every creditor of the company of whose claim and address the person summoning the meeting is aware.

[3155]

NOTES

Application to limited liability partnerships: see the introductory note to this Act and the Limited Liability Partnerships Regulations 2001, SI 2001/1090, reg 5, Sch 3 at **[6986]**, **[6995]**.

Consideration and implementation of proposal

4 Decisions of meetings

(1) The meetings summoned under section 3 shall decide whether to approve the proposed voluntary arrangement (with or without modifications).

(2) The modifications may include one conferring the functions proposed to be conferred on the nominee on another person qualified to act as an insolvency practitioner [or authorised to act as nominee, in relation to the voluntary arrangement].

But they shall not include any modification by virtue of which the proposal ceases to be a proposal such as is mentioned in section 1.

(3) A meeting so summoned shall not approve any proposal or modification which affects the right of a secured creditor of the company to enforce his security, except with the concurrence of the creditor concerned.

(4) Subject as follows, a meeting so summoned shall not approve any proposal or modification under which—

(a) any preferential debt of the company is to be paid otherwise than in priority to such of its debts as are not preferential debts, or

(b) a preferential creditor of the company is to be paid an amount in respect of a preferential debt that bears to that debt a smaller proportion than is borne to another preferential debt by the amount that is to be paid in respect of that other debt.

However, the meeting may approve such a proposal or modification with the concurrence of the preferential creditor concerned.

(5) Subject as above, each of the meetings shall be conducted in accordance with the rules.

(6) After the conclusion of either meeting in accordance with the rules, the chairman of the meeting shall report the result of the meeting to the court, and, immediately after reporting to the court, shall give notice of the result of the meeting to such persons as may be prescribed.

(7) References in this section to preferential debts and preferential creditors are to be read in accordance with section 386 in Part XII of this Act.

[3156]

NOTES

Sub-s (2): words in square brackets substituted by the Insolvency Act 2000, s 2, Sch 2, Pt I, paras 1, 4, as from 1 January 2003 (for transitional provisions see the note to s 1 at **[3152]**).

Application to limited liability partnerships: see the introductory note to this Act and the Limited Liability Partnerships Regulations 2001, SI 2001/1090, reg 5, Sch 3 at **[6986]**, **[6995]**.

[4A Approval of arrangement

(1) This section applies to a decision, under section 4, with respect to the approval of a proposed voluntary arrangement.

(2) The decision has effect if, in accordance with the rules—

(a) it has been taken by both meetings summoned under section 3, or

(b) (subject to any order made under subsection (4)) it has been taken by the creditors' meeting summoned under that section.

(3) If the decision taken by the creditors' meeting differs from that taken by the company meeting, a member of the company may apply to the court.

(4) An application under subsection (3) shall not be made after the end of the period of 28 days beginning with—

(a) the day on which the decision was taken by the creditors' meeting, or

(b) where the decision of the company meeting was taken on a later day, that day.

(5) Where a member of a regulated company, within the meaning given by paragraph 44 of Schedule A1, applies to the court under subsection (3), the Financial Services Authority is entitled to be heard on the application.

(6) On an application under subsection (3), the court may—

(a) order the decision of the company meeting to have effect instead of the decision of the creditors' meeting, or

(b) make such other order as it thinks fit.]

[3157]

NOTES

Inserted by the Insolvency Act 2000, s 2, Sch 2, Pt I, paras 1, 5, as from 1 January 2003 (for transitional provisions see the note to s 1 at **[3152]**).

Application to limited liability partnerships: see the introductory note to this Act and the Limited Liability Partnerships Regulations 2001, SI 2001/1090, reg 5, Sch 3 at **[6986]**, **[6995]**.

5 Effect of approval

[(1) This section applies where a decision approving a voluntary arrangement has effect under section 4A.]

(2) The … voluntary arrangement—

(a) takes effect as if made by the company at the creditors' meeting, and

[(b) binds every person who in accordance with the rules—

(i) was entitled to vote at that meeting (whether or not he was present or represented at it), or

(ii) would have been so entitled if he had had notice of it,

as if he were a party to the voluntary arrangement.]

[(2A) If—

(a) when the arrangement ceases to have effect any amount payable under the arrangement to a person bound by virtue of subsection (2)(b)(ii) has not been paid, and

(b) the arrangement did not come to an end prematurely,

the company shall at that time become liable to pay to that person the amount payable under the arrangement.]

(3) Subject as follows, if the company is being wound up or [is in administration], the court may do one or both of the following, namely—

(a) by order stay or sist all proceedings in the winding up or [provide for the appointment of the administrator to cease to have effect];

(b) give such directions with respect to the conduct of the winding up or the administration as it thinks appropriate for facilitating the implementation of the … voluntary arrangement.

(4) The court shall not make an order under subsection (3)(a)—

(a) at any time before the end of the period of 28 days beginning with the first day on which each of the reports required by section 4(6) has been made to the court, or

(b) at any time when an application under the next section or an appeal in respect of such an application is pending, or at any time in the period within which such an appeal may be brought.

[3158]

NOTES

Sub-s (1): substituted by the Insolvency Act 2000, s 2, Sch 2, Pt I, paras 1, 6(a), as from 1 January 2003 (for transitional provisions see the note to s 1 at **[3152]**).

Sub-s (2): word omitted repealed, and para (b) substituted (together with sub-s (2A) for original para (b)), by the Insolvency Act 2000, ss 2, 15(1), Sch 2, Pt I, paras 1, 6(b), (c), Sch 5, as from 1 January 2003 (for transitional provisions see the note to s 1 at **[3152]**).

Sub-s (2A): substituted as noted above.

Sub-s (3): words in square brackets substituted by the Enterprise Act 2002, s 248(3), Sch 17, paras 9, 11, as from 15 September 2003 (for savings and transitional provisions, see the note to s 8 at **[3164]**); word omitted repealed by the Insolvency Act 2000, ss 2, 15(1), Sch 2, Pt I, paras 1, 6(b), Sch 5, as from 1 January 2003 (for transitional provisions see the note to s 1 at **[3152]**).

Application to limited liability partnerships: see the introductory note to this Act and the Limited Liability Partnerships Regulations 2001, SI 2001/1090, reg 5, Sch 3 at **[6986]**, **[6995]**.

6 Challenge of decisions

(1) Subject to this section, an application to the court may be made, by any of the persons specified below, on one or both of the following grounds, namely—

(a) that a voluntary arrangement [which has effect under section 4A] unfairly prejudices the interests of a creditor, member or contributory of the company;

(b) that there has been some material irregularity at or in relation to either of the meetings.

(2) The persons who may apply under this section are—

(a) a person entitled, in accordance with the rules, to vote at either of the meetings;

[(aa) a person who would have been entitled, in accordance with the rules, to vote at the creditors' meeting if he had had notice of it]

(b) the nominee or any person who has replaced him under section 2(4) or 4(2); and

(c) if the company is being wound up or [is in administration], the liquidator or administrator.

(3) An application under this section shall not be made

[(a)] after the end of the period of 28 days beginning with the first day on which each of the reports required by section 4(6) has been made to the court [or

(b) in the case of a person who was not given notice of the creditors' meeting, after the end of the period of 28 days beginning with the day on which he became aware that the meeting had taken place,

but (subject to that) an application made by a person within subsection (2)(aa) on the ground that the voluntary arrangement prejudices his interests may be made after the arrangement has ceased to have effect, unless it came to an end prematurely.]

(4) Where on such an application the court is satisfied as to either of the grounds mentioned in subsection (1), it may do one or both of the following, namely—

(a) revoke or suspend [any decision approving the voluntary arrangement which has effect under section 4A] or, in a case falling within subsection (1)(b), any [decision taken by the meeting in question which has effect under that section];

(b) give a direction to any person for the summoning of further meetings to consider any revised proposal the person who made the original proposal may make or, in a case falling within subsection (1)(b), a further company or (as the case may be) creditors' meeting to reconsider the original proposal.

(5) Where at any time after giving a direction under subsection (4)(b) for the summoning of meetings to consider a revised proposal the court is satisfied that the person who made the original proposal does not intend to submit a revised proposal, the court shall revoke the direction and revoke or suspend any [decision approving the voluntary arrangement which has effect under section 4A].

(6) In a case where the court, on an application under this section with respect to any meeting—

(a) gives a direction under subsection (4)(b), or

(b) revokes or suspends an approval under subsection (4)(a) or (5),

the court may give such supplemental directions as it thinks fit and, in particular, directions with respect to things done [under the voluntary arrangement since it took effect].

(7) Except in pursuance of the preceding provisions of this section, [a decision taken] at a meeting summoned under section 3 is not invalidated by any irregularity at or in relation to the meeting.

[3159]

NOTES

Sub-ss (1), (4)–(7): words in square brackets substituted by the Insolvency Act 2000, s 2, Sch 2, Pt I, paras 1, 7(1), (2), (5)–(8), as from 1 January 2003 (for transitional provisions see the note to s 1 at **[3152]**).

Sub-s (2): para (aa) inserted by the Insolvency Act 2000, s 2, Sch 2, Pt I, paras 1, 7(1), (3), as from 1 January 2003 (for transitional provisions see the note to s 1 at **[3152]**); words in square brackets in para (c) substituted by the Enterprise Act 2002, s 248(3), Sch 17, paras 9, 12, as from 15 September 2003 (for savings and transitional provisions, see the note to s 8 at **[3164]**).

Sub-s (3): words in square brackets inserted by the Insolvency Act 2000, s 2, Sch 2, Pt I, paras 1, 7(1), (4), as from 1 January 2003 (for transitional provisions see the note to s 1 at **[3152]**).

Application to limited liability partnerships: see the introductory note to this Act and the Limited Liability Partnerships Regulations 2001, SI 2001/1090, reg 5, Sch 3 at **[6986]**, **[6995]**.

[6A False representations, etc

(1) If, for the purpose of obtaining the approval of the members or creditors of a company to a proposal for a voluntary arrangement, a person who is an officer of the company—

(a) makes any false representation, or

(b) fraudulently does, or omits to do, anything,

he commits an offence.

(2) Subsection (1) applies even if the proposal is not approved.

(3) For purposes of this section "officer" includes a shadow director.

(4) A person guilty of an offence under this section is liable to imprisonment or a fine, or both.]

[3160]

NOTES

Inserted by the Insolvency Act 2000, s 2, Sch 2, Pt I, paras 1, 8, as from 1 January 2003 (for transitional provisions see the note to s 1 at **[3152]**).

Application to limited liability partnerships: see the introductory note to this Act and the Limited Liability Partnerships Regulations 2001, SI 2001/1090, reg 5, Sch 3 at **[6986]**, **[6995]**.

7 Implementation of proposal

(1) This section applies where a voluntary arrangement [has effect under section 4A].

(2) The person who is for the time being carrying out in relation to the voluntary arrangement the functions conferred—

[(a) on the nominee by virtue of the approval given at one or both of the meetings summoned under section 3]

(b) by virtue of section 2(4) or 4(2) on a person other than the nominee,

shall be known as the supervisor of the voluntary arrangement.

(3) If any of the company's creditors or any other person is dissatisfied by any act, omission or decision of the supervisor, he may apply to the court; and on the application the court may—

(a) confirm, reverse or modify any act or decision of the supervisor,

(b) give him directions, or

(c) make such other order as it thinks fit.

(4) The supervisor—

(a) may apply to the court for directions in relation to any particular matter arising under the voluntary arrangement, and

(b) is included among the persons who may apply to the court for the winding up of the company or for an administration order to be made in relation to it.

(5) The court may, whenever—

(a) it is expedient to appoint a person to carry out the functions of the supervisor, and

(b) it is inexpedient, difficult or impracticable for an appointment to be made without the assistance of the court,

make an order appointing a person who is qualified to act as an insolvency practitioner [or authorised to act as supervisor, in relation to the voluntary arrangement] either in substitution for the existing supervisor or to fill a vacancy.

(6) The power conferred by subsection (5) is exercisable so as to increase the number of persons exercising the functions of supervisor or, where there is more than one person exercising those functions, so as to replace one or more of those persons.

[3161]

NOTES

Sub-ss (1), (5): words in square brackets substituted by the Insolvency Act 2000, s 2, Sch 2, Pt I, paras 1, 9(a), (c), as from 1 January 2003 (for transitional provisions see the note to s 1 at **[3152]**).

Sub-s (2): para (a) substituted by the Insolvency Act 2000, s 2, Sch 2, Pt I, paras 1, 9(b), as from 1 January 2003 (for transitional provisions see the note to s 1 at **[3152]**).

Application to limited liability partnerships: see the introductory note to this Act and the Limited Liability Partnerships Regulations 2001, SI 2001/1090, reg 5, Sch 3 at **[6986]**, **[6995]**.

[7A Prosecution of delinquent officers of company

(1) This section applies where a moratorium under section 1A has been obtained for a company or the approval of a voluntary arrangement in relation to a company has taken effect under section 4A or paragraph 36 of Schedule A1.

(2) If it appears to the nominee or supervisor that any past or present officer of the company has been guilty of any offence in connection with the moratorium or, as the case may be, voluntary arrangement for which he is criminally liable, the nominee or supervisor shall forthwith—

(a) report the matter to the appropriate authority, and

(b) provide the appropriate authority with such information and give the authority such access to and facilities for inspecting and taking copies of documents (being information or documents in the possession or under the control of the nominee or supervisor and relating to the matter in question) as the authority requires.

In this subsection, "the appropriate authority" means—

(i) in the case of a company registered in England and Wales, the Secretary of State, and

(ii) in the case of a company registered in Scotland, the Lord Advocate.

(3) Where a report is made to the Secretary of State under subsection (2), he may, for the purpose of investigating the matter reported to him and such other matters relating to the affairs of the company as appear to him to require investigation, exercise any of the powers which are exercisable by inspectors appointed under section 431 or 432 of the Companies Act to investigate a company's affairs.

(4) For the purpose of such an investigation any obligation imposed on a person by any provision of the Companies Act to produce documents or give information to, or otherwise to assist, inspectors so appointed is to be regarded as an obligation similarly to assist the Secretary of State in his investigation.

(5) An answer given by a person to a question put to him in exercise of the powers conferred by subsection (3) may be used in evidence against him.

(6) However, in criminal proceedings in which that person is charged with an offence to which this subsection applies—

(a) no evidence relating to the answer may be adduced, and

(b) no question relating to it may be asked,

by or on behalf of the prosecution, unless evidence relating to it is adduced, or a question relating to it is asked, in the proceedings by or on behalf of that person.

(7) Subsection (6) applies to any offence other than—

(a) an offence under section 2 or 5 of the Perjury Act 1911 (false statements made on oath otherwise than in judicial proceedings or made otherwise than on oath), or

(b) an offence under section 44(1) or (2) of the Criminal Law (Consolidation) (Scotland) Act 1995 (false statements made on oath or otherwise than on oath).

(8) Where a prosecuting authority institutes criminal proceedings following any report under subsection (2), the nominee or supervisor, and every officer and agent of the company past and present (other than the defendant or defender), shall give the authority all assistance in connection with the prosecution which he is reasonably able to give.

For this purpose—

"agent" includes any banker or solicitor of the company and any person employed by the company as auditor, whether that person is or is not an officer of the company,

"prosecuting authority" means the Director of Public Prosecutions, the Lord Advocate or the Secretary of State.

(9) The court may, on the application of the prosecuting authority, direct any person referred to in subsection (8) to comply with that subsection if he has failed to do so.]

[3162]

NOTES

Inserted, together with s 7B, by the Insolvency Act 2000, s 2, Sch 2, Pt I, paras 1, 10, as from 1 January 2003 (for transitional provisions see the note to s 1 at **[3152]**).

Application to limited liability partnerships: see the introductory note to this Act and the Limited Liability Partnerships Regulations 2001, SI 2001/1090, reg 5, Sch 3 at **[6986]**, **[6995]**.

PART III OTHER LEGISLATION

[7B Arrangements coming to an end prematurely

For the purposes of this Part, a voluntary arrangement the approval of which has taken effect under section 4A or paragraph 36 of Schedule A1 comes to an end prematurely if, when it ceases to have effect, it has not been fully implemented in respect of all persons bound by the arrangement by virtue of section 5(2)(b)(i) or, as the case may be, paragraph 37(2)(b)(i) of Schedule A1.]

[3163]

NOTES

Inserted as noted to s 7A at **[3162]**.

Application to limited liability partnerships: see the introductory note to this Act and the Limited Liability Partnerships Regulations 2001, SI 2001/1090, reg 5, Sch 3 at **[6986]**, **[6995]**.

[PART II
ADMINISTRATION

8 Administration

Schedule B1 to this Act (which makes provision about the administration of companies) shall have effect.]

[3164]–[3183]

NOTES

This section was substituted for the original Pt II of this Act (ss 8–27) by the Enterprise Act 2002, s 248(1), as from 15 September 2003, subject to the following savings and transitional provisions.

Savings in relation to special administration regimes:

The Enterprise Act 2002, s 249(1), (2) (Special administration regimes) provides as follows—

"(1) Section 248 shall have no effect in relation to—

(a) a company holding an appointment under Chapter I of Part II of the Water Industry Act 1991 (c 56) (water and sewerage undertakers),

[(aa) a qualifying licensed water supplier within the meaning of subsection (6) of section 23 of the Water Industry Act 1991 (meaning and effect of special administration order),]

(b) a protected railway company within the meaning of section 59 of the Railways Act 1993 (c 43) (railway administration order) (including that section as it has effect by virtue of section 19 of the Channel Tunnel Rail Link Act 1996 (c 61) (administration)),

(c) a licence company within the meaning of section 26 of the Transport Act 2000 (c 38) (air traffic services),

(d) a public-private partnership company within the meaning of section 210 of the Greater London Authority Act 1999 (c 29) (public-private partnership agreement), or

(e) a building society within the meaning of section 119 of the Building Societies Act 1986 (c 53) (interpretation).

(2) A reference in an Act listed in subsection (1) to a provision of Part II of the Insolvency Act 1986 (or to a provision which has effect in relation to a provision of that Part of that Act) shall, in so far as it relates to a company or society listed in subsection (1), continue to have effect as if it referred to Part II as it had effect immediately before the coming into force of section 248.".

In s 249 as reproduced above, para (aa) was inserted by the Water Act 2003, s 101(1), Sch 8, para 55(1), (3), as from 1 December 2005.

As to special administration regimes, see also the Energy Act 2004, Pt 3, Chapter 3 (in particular, s 159 of, and Sch 20 to, that Act) and the introductory notes to this Act.

Transitional provisions:

The Enterprise Act 2002 (Commencement No 4 and Transitional Provisions and Savings) Order 2003, SI 2003/2093, art 3, provides as follows (note that by virtue of art 2(1) "the first commencement date" means 15 September 2003)—

"3 Administration—transitional provisions

(1) In this article "the former administration provisions" means the law relating to administration under Part II of the Insolvency Act 1986 and section 62(2)(a) of the Criminal Justice Act 1988 without the amendments and repeals made by the provisions of the Enterprise Act 2002 mentioned in paragraph (2).

(2) In a case where a petition for an administration order has been presented before the first commencement date—

(a) section 248 and Schedules 16 and 17; and

(b) section 278(2) and Schedule 26 as respects the repeals relating to sections 212, 230(1), 231, 232, 240(1) and 245(3) of the Insolvency Act 1986, the entries in Schedule 10 to the Insolvency Act 1986 in respect of sections 12(2), 15(8), 18(5), 21(3), 22(6), 23(3), 24(7) and 27(6) of that Act and section 62(2)(a) of the Criminal Justice Act 1988,

shall have no effect.

(3) The former administration provisions shall continue to apply insofar as is necessary to give effect to—

(a) the Insolvent Partnerships Order 1994;

(b) regulation 5 of the Limited Liability Partnerships Regulations 2001; and

(c) the Financial Services and Markets Act 2000 (Administration Orders relating to Insurers) Order 2002.".

The Enterprise Act 2002, Sch 17, para 1 provides that in any instrument made before s 248(1)–(3) of the 2002 Act comes into force: (a) a reference to the making of an administration order shall be treated as including a reference to the appointment of an administrator under Sch B1, para 14 or 22 to this Act (as inserted by s 248(2) of the 2002 Act), and (b) a reference to making an application for an administration order by petition shall be treated as including a reference to making an administration application under that Schedule, appointing an administrator under para 14 or 22 of that Schedule or giving notice under para 15 or 26 of that Schedule.

Application to limited liability partnerships: see the introductory note to this Act and the Limited Liability Partnerships Regulations 2001, SI 2001/1090, reg 5, Sch 3 at **[6986]**, **[6995]**.

PART III
RECEIVERSHIP

CHAPTER I
RECEIVERS AND MANAGERS (ENGLAND AND WALES)

Preliminary and general provisions

28 Extent of this Chapter

This Chapter does not apply to receivers appointed under Chapter II of this Part (Scotland).

[3184]

NOTES

Application to limited liability partnerships: see the introductory note to this Act and the Limited Liability Partnerships Regulations 2001, SI 2001/1090, reg 5, Sch 3 at **[6986]**, **[6995]**.

---

29 Definitions

(1) It is hereby declared that, except where the context otherwise requires—

(a) any reference in the Companies Act or this Act to a receiver or manager of the property of a company, or to a receiver of it, includes a receiver or manager, or (as the case may be) a receiver of part only of that property and a receiver only of the income arising from the property or from part of it; and

(b) any reference in the Companies Act or this Act to the appointment of a receiver or manager under powers contained in an instrument includes an appointment made under powers which, by virtue of an enactment, are implied in and have effect as if contained in an instrument.

(2) In this Chapter "administrative receiver" means—

(a) a receiver or manager of the whole (or substantially the whole) of a company's property appointed by or on behalf of the holders of any debentures of the company secured by a charge which, as created, was a floating charge, or by such a charge and one or more other securities; or

(b) a person who would be such a receiver or manager but for the appointment of some other person as the receiver of part of the company's property.

[3185]

NOTES

Application to limited liability partnerships: see the introductory note to this Act and the Limited Liability Partnerships Regulations 2001, SI 2001/1090, reg 5, Sch 3 at **[6986]**, **[6995]**.

---

30 Disqualification of body corporate from acting as receiver

A body corporate is not qualified for appointment as receiver of the property of a company, and any body corporate which acts as such a receiver is liable to a fine.

[3186]

NOTES

Application to limited liability partnerships: see the introductory note to this Act and the Limited Liability Partnerships Regulations 2001, SI 2001/1090, reg 5, Sch 3 at **[6986]**, **[6995]**.

[31 Disqualification of bankrupt

(1) A person commits an offence if he acts as receiver or manager of the property of a company on behalf of debenture holders while—

(a) he is an undischarged bankrupt, or

(b) a bankruptcy restrictions order is in force in respect of him.

(2) A person guilty of an offence under subsection (1) shall be liable to imprisonment, a fine or both.

(3) This section does not apply to a receiver or manager acting under an appointment made by the court.]

[3187]

NOTES

Substituted by the Enterprise Act 2002, s 257(3), Sch 21, para 1, as from 1 April 2004.

Application to limited liability partnerships: see the introductory note to this Act and the Limited Liability Partnerships Regulations 2001, SI 2001/1090, reg 5, Sch 3 at **[6986]**, **[6995]**.

32 Power for court to appoint official receiver

Where application is made to the court to appoint a receiver on behalf of the debenture holders or other creditors of a company which is being wound up by the court, the official receiver may be appointed.

[3188]

NOTES

Application to limited liability partnerships: see the introductory note to this Act and the Limited Liability Partnerships Regulations 2001, SI 2001/1090, reg 5, Sch 3 at **[6986]**, **[6995]**.

Receivers and managers appointed out of court

33 Time from which appointment is effective

(1) The appointment of a person as a receiver or manager of a company's property under powers contained in an instrument—

(a) is of no effect unless it is accepted by that person before the end of the business day next following that on which the instrument of appointment is received by him or on his behalf, and

(b) subject to this, is deemed to be made at the time at which the instrument of appointment is so received.

(2) This section applies to the appointment of two or more persons as joint receivers or managers of a company's property under powers contained in an instrument, subject to such modifications as may be prescribed by the rules.

[3189]

NOTES

Application to limited liability partnerships: see the introductory note to this Act and the Limited Liability Partnerships Regulations 2001, SI 2001/1090, reg 5, Sch 3 at **[6986]**, **[6995]**.

34 Liability for invalid appointment

Where the appointment of a person as the receiver or manager of a company's property under powers contained in an instrument is discovered to be invalid (whether by virtue of the invalidity of the instrument or otherwise), the court may order the person by whom or on whose behalf the appointment was made to indemnify the person appointed against any liability which arises solely by reason of the invalidity of the appointment.

[3190]

NOTES

Application to limited liability partnerships: see the introductory note to this Act and the Limited Liability Partnerships Regulations 2001, SI 2001/1090, reg 5, Sch 3 at **[6986]**, **[6995]**.

35 Application to court for directions

(1) A receiver or manager of the property of a company appointed under powers contained in an instrument, or the persons by whom or on whose behalf a receiver or manager has been so appointed, may apply to the court for directions in relation to any particular matter arising in connection with the performance of the functions of the receiver or manager.

(2) On such an application, the court may give such directions, or may make such order declaring the rights of persons before the court or otherwise, as it thinks just.

[3191]

NOTES

Application to limited liability partnerships: see the introductory note to this Act and the Limited Liability Partnerships Regulations 2001, SI 2001/1090, reg 5, Sch 3 at **[6986]**, **[6995]**.

36 Court's power to fix remuneration

(1) The court may, on an application made by the liquidator of a company, by order fix the amount to be paid by way of remuneration to a person who, under powers contained in an instrument, has been appointed receiver or manager of the company's property.

(2) The court's power under subsection (1), where no previous order has been made with respect thereto under the subsection—

(a) extends to fixing the remuneration for any period before the making of the order or the application for it,

(b) is exercisable notwithstanding that the receiver or manager has died or ceased to act before the making of the order or the application, and

(c) where the receiver or manager has been paid or has retained for his remuneration for any period before the making of the order any amount in excess of that so fixed for that period, extends to requiring him or his personal representatives to account for the excess or such part of it as may be specified in the order.

But the power conferred by paragraph (c) shall not be exercised as respects any period before the making of the application for the order under this section, unless in the court's opinion there are special circumstances making it proper for the power to be exercised.

(3) The court may from time to time on an application made either by the liquidator or by the receiver or manager, vary or amend an order made under subsection (1).

[3192]

NOTES

Application to limited liability partnerships: see the introductory note to this Act and the Limited Liability Partnerships Regulations 2001, SI 2001/1090, reg 5, Sch 3 at **[6986]**, **[6995]**.

37 Liability for contracts, etc

(1) A receiver or manager appointed under powers contained in an instrument (other than an administrative receiver) is, to the same extent as if he had been appointed by order of the court—

(a) personally liable on any contract entered into by him in the performance of his functions (except in so far as the contract otherwise provides) and on any contract of employment adopted by him in the performance of those functions, and

(b) entitled in respect of that liability to indemnity out of the assets.

(2) For the purposes of subsection (1)(a), the receiver or manager is not to be taken to have adopted a contract of employment by reason of anything done or omitted to be done within 14 days after his appointment.

(3) Subsection (1) does not limit any right to indemnity which the receiver or manager would have apart from it, nor limit his liability on contracts entered into without authority, nor confer any right to indemnity in respect of that liability.

(4) Where at any time the receiver or manager so appointed vacates office—

(a) his remuneration and any expenses properly incurred by him, and

(b) any indemnity to which he is entitled out of the assets of the company,

shall be charged on and paid out of any property of the company which is in his custody or under his control at that time in priority to any charge or other security held by the person by or on whose behalf he was appointed.

[3193]

NOTES

Application to limited liability partnerships: see the introductory note to this Act and the Limited Liability Partnerships Regulations 2001, SI 2001/1090, reg 5, Sch 3 at **[6986]**, **[6995]**.

38 Receivership accounts to be delivered to registrar

(1) Except in the case of an administrative receiver, every receiver or manager of a company's property who has been appointed under powers contained in an instrument shall deliver to the registrar of companies for registration the requisite accounts of his receipts and payments.

PART III OTHER LEGISLATION

(2) The accounts shall be delivered within one month (or such longer period as the registrar may allow) after the expiration of 12 months from the date of his appointment and of every subsequent period of 6 months, and also within one month after he ceases to act as receiver or manager.

(3) The requisite accounts shall be an abstract in the prescribed form showing—

(a) receipts and payments during the relevant period of 12 or 6 months, or

(b) where the receiver or manager ceases to act, receipts and payments during the period from the end of the period of 12 or 6 months to which the last preceding abstract related (or, if no preceding abstract has been delivered under this section, from the date of his appointment) up to the date of his so ceasing, and the aggregate amount of receipts and payments during all preceding periods since his appointment.

(4) In this section "prescribed" means prescribed by regulations made by statutory instrument by the Secretary of State.

(5) A receiver or manager who makes default in complying with this section is liable to a fine and, for continued contravention, to a daily default fine.

[3194]

NOTES

Application to limited liability partnerships: see the introductory note to this Act and the Limited Liability Partnerships Regulations 2001, SI 2001/1090, reg 5, Sch 3 at **[6986]**, **[6995]**.

Provisions applicable to every receivership

39 Notification that receiver or manager appointed

(1) When a receiver or manager of the property of a company has been appointed, every invoice, order for goods or business letter issued by or on behalf of the company or the receiver or manager or the liquidator of the company, being a document on or in which the company's name appears, shall contain a statement that a receiver or manager has been appointed.

(2) If default is made in complying with this section, the company and any of the following persons, who knowingly and wilfully authorises or permits the default, namely, any officer of the company, any liquidator of the company and any receiver or manager, is liable to a fine.

[3195]

NOTES

Application to limited liability partnerships: see the introductory note to this Act and the Limited Liability Partnerships Regulations 2001, SI 2001/1090, reg 5, Sch 3 at **[6986]**, **[6995]**.

40 Payment of debts out of assets subject to floating charge

(1) The following applies, in the case of a company, where a receiver is appointed on behalf of the holders of any debentures of the company secured by a charge which, as created, was a floating charge.

(2) If the company is not at the time in course of being wound up, its preferential debts (within the meaning given to that expression by section 386 in Part XII) shall be paid out of the assets coming to the hands of the receiver in priority to any claims for principal or interest in respect of the debentures.

(3) Payments made under this section shall be recouped, as far as may be, out of the assets of the company available for payment of general creditors.

[3196]

NOTES

Application to limited liability partnerships: see the introductory note to this Act and the Limited Liability Partnerships Regulations 2001, SI 2001/1090, reg 5, Sch 3 at **[6986]**, **[6995]**.

41 Enforcement of duty to make returns

(1) If a receiver or manager of a company's property—

(a) having made default in filing, delivering or making any return, account or other document, or in giving any notice, which a receiver or manager is by law required to file, deliver, make or give, fails to make good the default within 14 days after the service on him of a notice requiring him to do so, or

(b) having been appointed under powers contained in an instrument, has, after being required at any time by the liquidator of the company to do so, failed to render proper accounts of his receipts and payments and to vouch them and pay over to the liquidator the amount properly payable to him,

the court may, on an application made for the purpose, make an order directing the receiver or manager (as the case may be) to make good the default within such time as may be specified in the order.

(2) In the case of the default mentioned in subsection (1)(a), application to the court may be made by any member or creditor of the company or by the registrar of companies; and in the case of the default mentioned in subsection (1)(b), the application shall be made by the liquidator.

In either case the court's order may provide that all costs of and incidental to the application shall be borne by the receiver or manager, as the case may be.

(3) Nothing in this section prejudices the operation of any enactment imposing penalties on receivers in respect of any such default as is mentioned in subsection (1).

[3197]

NOTES

Application to limited liability partnerships: see the introductory note to this Act and the Limited Liability Partnerships Regulations 2001, SI 2001/1090, reg 5, Sch 3 at **[6986]**, **[6995]**.

Administrative receivers: general

42 General powers

(1) The powers conferred on the administrative receiver of a company by the debentures by virtue of which he was appointed are deemed to include (except in so far as they are inconsistent with any of the provisions of those debentures) the powers specified in Schedule 1 to this Act.

(2) In the application of Schedule 1 to the administrative receiver of a company—

(a) the words "he" and "him" refer to the administrative receiver, and

(b) references to the property of the company are to the property of which he is or, but for the appointment of some other person as the receiver of part of the company's property, would be the receiver or manager.

(3) A person dealing with the administrative receiver in good faith and for value is not concerned to inquire whether the receiver is acting within his powers.

[3198]

NOTES

Application to limited liability partnerships: see the introductory note to this Act and the Limited Liability Partnerships Regulations 2001, SI 2001/1090, reg 5, Sch 3 at **[6986]**, **[6995]**.

43 Power to dispose of charged property, etc

(1) Where, on an application by the administrative receiver, the court is satisfied that the disposal (with or without other assets) of any relevant property which is subject to a security would be likely to promote a more advantageous realisation of the company's assets than would otherwise be effected, the court may by order authorise the administrative receiver to dispose of the property as if it were not subject to the security.

(2) Subsection (1) does not apply in the case of any security held by the person by or on whose behalf the administrative receiver was appointed, or of any security to which a security so held has priority.

(3) It shall be a condition of an order under this section that—

(a) the net proceeds of the disposal, and

(b) where those proceeds are less than such amount as may be determined by the

PART III OTHER LEGISLATION

court to be the net amount which would be realised on a sale of the property in the open market by a willing vendor, such sums as may be required to make good the deficiency,

shall be applied towards discharging the sums secured by the security.

(4) Where a condition imposed in pursuance of subsection (3) relates to two or more securities, that condition shall require the net proceeds of the disposal and, where paragraph (b) of that subsection applies, the sums mentioned in that paragraph to be applied towards discharging the sums secured by those securities in the order of their priorities.

(5) An office copy of an order under this section shall, within 14 days of the making of the order, be sent by the administrative receiver to the registrar of companies.

(6) If the administrative receiver without reasonable excuse fails to comply with subsection (5), he is liable to a fine and, for continued contravention, to a daily default fine.

(7) In this section "relevant property", in relation to the administrative receiver, means the property of which he is or, but for the appointment of some other person as the receiver of part of the company's property, would be the receiver or manager.

[3199]

NOTES

Application to limited liability partnerships: see the introductory note to this Act and the Limited Liability Partnerships Regulations 2001, SI 2001/1090, reg 5, Sch 3 at **[6986]**, **[6995]**.

44 Agency and liability for contracts

(1) The administrative receiver of a company—

(a) is deemed to be the company's agent, unless and until the company goes into liquidation;

(b) is personally liable on any contract entered into by him in the carrying out of his functions (except in so far as the contract otherwise provides) and[, to the extent of any qualifying liability,] on any contract of employment adopted by him in the carrying out of those functions; and

(c) is entitled in respect of that liability to an indemnity out of the assets of the company.

(2) For the purposes of subsection (1)(b) the administrative receiver is not to be taken to have adopted a contract of employment by reason of anything done or omitted to be done within 14 days after his appointment.

[(2A) For the purposes of subsection (1)(b), a liability under a contract of employment is a qualifying liability if—

(a) it is a liability to pay a sum by way of wages or salary or contribution to an occupational pension scheme,

(b) it is incurred while the administrative receiver is in office, and

(c) it is in respect of services rendered wholly or partly after the adoption of the contract.

(2B) Where a sum payable in respect of a liability which is a qualifying liability for the purposes of subsection (1)(b) is payable in respect of services rendered partly before and partly after the adoption of the contract, liability under subsection (1)(b) shall only extend to so much of the sum as is payable in respect of services rendered after the adoption of the contract.

(2C) For the purposes of subsections (2A) and (2B)—

(a) wages or salary payable in respect of a period of holiday or absence from work through sickness or other good cause are deemed to be wages or (as the case may be) salary in respect of services rendered in that period, and

(b) a sum payable in lieu of holiday is deemed to be wages or (as the case may be) salary in respect of services rendered in the period by reference to which the holiday entitlement arose.

(2D) In subsection (2C)(a), the reference to wages or salary payable in respect of a period of holiday includes any sums which, if they had been paid, would have been treated for the purposes of the enactments relating to social security as earnings in respect of that period.]

(3) This section does not limit any right to indemnity which the administrative receiver would have apart from it, nor limit his liability on contracts entered into or adopted without authority, nor confer any right to indemnity in respect of that liability.

[3200]

NOTES

Sub-s (1): words in square brackets in para (b) inserted by the Insolvency Act 1994, s 2(1), (2), (4), in relation to contracts of employment adopted on or after 15 March 1994.

Sub-ss (2A)–(2D): inserted by the Insolvency Act 1994, s 2(1), (3), (4), in relation to contracts of employment adopted on or after 15 March 1994.

Application to limited liability partnerships: see the introductory note to this Act and the Limited Liability Partnerships Regulations 2001, SI 2001/1090, reg 5, Sch 3 at **[6986]**, **[6995]**.

45 Vacation of office

(1) An administrative receiver of a company may at any time be removed from office by order of the court (but not otherwise) and may resign his office by giving notice of his resignation in the prescribed manner to such persons as may be prescribed.

(2) An administrative receiver shall vacate office if he ceases to be qualified to act as an insolvency practitioner in relation to the company.

(3) Where at any time an administrative receiver vacates office—

(a) his remuneration and any expenses properly incurred by him, and

(b) any indemnity to which he is entitled out of the assets of the company,

shall be charged on and paid out of any property of the company which is in his custody or under his control at that time in priority to any security held by the person by or on whose behalf he was appointed.

(4) Where an administrative receiver vacates office otherwise than by death, he shall, within 14 days after his vacation of office, send a notice to that effect to the registrar of companies.

(5) If an administrative receiver without reasonable excuse fails to comply with subsection (4), he is liable to a fine *and, for continued contravention, to a daily default fine.*

[3201]

NOTES

Sub-s (5): words in italics repealed by CA 1989, ss 107, 212, Sch 16, para 3, Sch 24, as from a day to be appointed.

Application to limited liability partnerships: see the introductory note to this Act and the Limited Liability Partnerships Regulations 2001, SI 2001/1090, reg 5, Sch 3 at **[6986]**, **[6995]**.

Administrative receivers: ascertainment and investigation of company's affairs

46 Information to be given by administrative receiver

(1) Where an administrative receiver is appointed, he shall—

(a) forthwith send to the company and publish in the prescribed manner a notice of his appointment, and

(b) within 28 days after his appointment, unless the court otherwise directs, send such a notice to all the creditors of the company (so far as he is aware of their addresses).

(2) This section and the next do not apply in relation to the appointment of an administrative receiver to act—

(a) with an existing administrative receiver, or

(b) in place of an administrative receiver dying or ceasing to act,

except that, where they apply to an administrative receiver who dies or ceases to act before they have been fully complied with, the references in this section and the next to the administrative receiver include (subject to the next subsection) his successor and any continuing administrative receiver.

(3) If the company is being wound up, this section and the next apply notwithstanding that the administrative receiver and the liquidator are the same person, but with any necessary modifications arising from that fact.

(4) If the administrative receiver without reasonable excuse fails to comply with this section, he is liable to a fine and, for continued contravention, to a daily default fine.

[3202]

NOTES

Application to limited liability partnerships: see the introductory note to this Act and the Limited Liability Partnerships Regulations 2001, SI 2001/1090, reg 5, Sch 3 at **[6986]**, **[6995]**.

47 Statement of affairs to be submitted

(1) Where an administrative receiver is appointed, he shall forthwith require some or all of the persons mentioned below to make out and submit to him a statement in the prescribed form as to the affairs of the company.

(2) A statement submitted under this section shall be verified by affidavit by the persons required to submit it and shall show—

- (a) particulars of the company's assets, debts and liabilities;
- (b) the names and addresses of its creditors;
- (c) the securities held by them respectively;
- (d) the dates when the securities were respectively given; and
- (e) such further or other information as may be prescribed.

(3) The persons referred to in subsection (1) are—

- (a) those who are or have been officers of the company;
- (b) those who have taken part in the company's formation at any time within one year before the date of the appointment of the administrative receiver;
- (c) those who are in the company's employment, or have been in its employment within that year, and are in the administrative receiver's opinion capable of giving the information required;
- (d) those who are or have been within that year officers of or in the employment of a company which is, or within that year was, an officer of the company.

In this subsection "employment" includes employment under a contract for services.

(4) Where any persons are required under this section to submit a statement of affairs to the administrative receiver, they shall do so (subject to the next subsection) before the end of the period of 21 days beginning with the day after that on which the prescribed notice of the requirement is given to them by the administrative receiver.

(5) The administrative receiver, if he thinks fit, may—

- (a) at any time release a person from an obligation imposed on him under subsection (1) or (2), or
- (b) either when giving notice under subsection (4) or subsequently, extend the period so mentioned;

and where the administrative receiver has refused to exercise a power conferred by this subsection, the court, if it thinks fit, may exercise it.

(6) If a person without reasonable excuse fails to comply with any obligation imposed under this section, he is liable to a fine and, for continued contravention, to a daily default fine.

[3203]

NOTES

Application to limited liability partnerships: see the introductory note to this Act and the Limited Liability Partnerships Regulations 2001, SI 2001/1090, reg 5, Sch 3 at **[6986]**, **[6995]**.

48 Report by administrative receiver

(1) Where an administrative receiver is appointed, he shall, within 3 months (or such longer period as the court may allow) after his appointment, send to the registrar of companies, to any trustees for secured creditors of the company and (so far as he is aware of their addresses) to all such creditors a report as to the following matters, namely—

- (a) the events leading up to his appointment, so far as he is aware of them;
- (b) the disposal or proposed disposal by him of any property of the company and the carrying on or proposed carrying on by him of any business of the company;

(c) the amounts of principal and interest payable to the debenture holders by whom or on whose behalf he was appointed and the amounts payable to preferential creditors; and

(d) the amount (if any) likely to be available for the payment of other creditors.

(2) The administrative receiver shall also, within 3 months (or such longer period as the court may allow) after his appointment, either—

(a) send a copy of the report (so far as he is aware of their addresses) to all unsecured creditors of the company; or

(b) publish in the prescribed manner a notice stating an address to which unsecured creditors of the company should write for copies of the report to be sent to them free of charge,

and (in either case), unless the court otherwise directs, lay a copy of the report before a meeting of the company's unsecured creditors summoned for the purpose on not less than 14 days' notice.

(3) The court shall not give a direction under subsection (2) unless—

(a) the report states the intention of the administrative receiver to apply for the direction, and

(b) a copy of the report is sent to the persons mentioned in paragraph (a) of that subsection, or a notice is published as mentioned in paragraph (b) of that subsection, not less than 14 days before the hearing of the application.

(4) Where the company has gone or goes into liquidation, the administrative receiver—

(a) shall, within 7 days after his compliance with subsection (1) or, if later, the nomination or appointment of the liquidator, send a copy of the report to the liquidator, and

(b) where he does so within the time limited for compliance with subsection (2), is not required to comply with that subsection.

(5) A report under this section shall include a summary of the statement of affairs made out and submitted to the administrative receiver under section 47 and of his comments (if any) upon it.

(6) Nothing in this section is to be taken as requiring any such report to include any information the disclosure of which would seriously prejudice the carrying out by the administrative receiver of his functions.

(7) Section 46(2) applies for the purposes of this section also.

(8) If the administrative receiver without reasonable excuse fails to comply with this section, he is liable to a fine and, for continued contravention, to a daily default fine.

[3204]

NOTES

Application to limited liability partnerships: see the introductory note to this Act and the Limited Liability Partnerships Regulations 2001, SI 2001/1090, reg 5, Sch 3 at **[6986]**, **[6995]**.

49 Committee of creditors

(1) Where a meeting of creditors is summoned under section 48, the meeting may, if it thinks fit, establish a committee ("the creditors' committee") to exercise the functions conferred on it by or under this Act.

(2) If such a committee is established, the committee may, on giving not less than 7 days' notice, require the administrative receiver to attend before it at any reasonable time and furnish it with such information relating to the carrying out by him of his functions as it may reasonably require.

[3205]

NOTES

Application to limited liability partnerships: see the introductory note to this Act and the Limited Liability Partnerships Regulations 2001, SI 2001/1090, reg 5, Sch 3 at **[6986]**, **[6995]**.

CHAPTER II
RECEIVERS (SCOTLAND)

50 Extent of this Chapter

This Chapter extends to Scotland only.

[3206]

NOTES

Application to limited liability partnerships: see the introductory note to this Act, the Limited Liability Partnerships Regulations 2001, SI 2001/1090, reg 5, Sch 3 at **[6986]**, **[6995]**, and the Limited Liability Partnerships (Scotland) Regulations 2001, SSI 2001/128, reg 4, Schs 2, 3 at **[6977]**, **[6980A]**, **[6980B]**.

51 Power to appoint receiver

(1) It is competent under the law of Scotland for the holder of a floating charge over all or any part of the property (including uncalled capital), which may from time to time be comprised in the property and undertaking of an incorporated company (whether a company within the meaning of the Companies Act or not) which the Court of Session has jurisdiction to wind up, to appoint a receiver of such part of the property of the company as is subject to the charge.

(2) It is competent under the law of Scotland for the court, on the application of the holder of such a floating charge, to appoint a receiver of such part of the property of the company as is subject to the charge.

[(2A) Subsections (1) and (2) are subject to section 72A.]

(3) The following are disqualified from being appointed as receiver—

(a) a body corporate;
(b) an undischarged bankrupt; and
[(ba) a person subject to a bankruptcy restrictions order;]
(c) a firm according to the law of Scotland.

(4) A body corporate or a firm according to the law of Scotland which acts as a receiver is liable to a fine.

(5) An undischarged bankrupt [or a person subject to a bankruptcy restrictions order] who so acts is liable to imprisonment or a fine, or both.

(6) In this section, "receiver" includes joint receivers[; and

"bankruptcy restrictions order" means—

(a) a bankruptcy restrictions order made under section 56A of the Bankruptcy (Scotland) Act 1985 (c 66);
(b) a bankruptcy restrictions undertaking entered into under section 56G of that Act;
(c) a bankruptcy restrictions order made under paragraph 1 of Schedule 4A to this Act; or
(d) a bankruptcy restrictions undertaking entered into under paragraph 7 of that Schedule].

[3207]

NOTES

Sub-s (2A): inserted by the Enterprise Act 2002, s 248(3), Sch 17, paras 9, 13, as from 15 September 2003 (for savings and transitional provisions, see the note to s 8 at **[3164]**).

Sub-ss (3), (5), (6): words in square brackets inserted by the Bankruptcy and Diligence etc (Scotland) Act 2007, s 3, as from a day to be appointed.

Application to limited liability partnerships: see the introductory note to this Act, the Limited Liability Partnerships Regulations 2001, SI 2001/1090, reg 5, Sch 3 at **[6986]**, **[6995]**, and the Limited Liability Partnerships (Scotland) Regulations 2001, SSI 2001/128, reg 4, Schs 2, 3 at **[6977]**, **[6980A]**, **[6980B]**.

52 Circumstances justifying appointment

(1) A receiver may be appointed under section 51(1) by the holder of the floating charge on the occurrence of any event which, by the provisions of the instrument creating the charge, entitles the holder of the charge to make that appointment and, in so far as not otherwise provided for by the instrument, on the occurrence of any of the following events, namely—

(a) the expiry of a period of 21 days after the making of a demand for payment of the whole or any part of the principal sum secured by the charge, without payment having been made;

(b) the expiry of a period of 2 months during the whole of which interest due and payable under the charge has been in arrears;

(c) the making of an order or the passing of a resolution to wind up the company;

(d) the appointment of a receiver by virtue of any other floating charge created by the company.

(2) A receiver may be appointed by the court under section 51(2) on the occurrence of any event which, by the provisions of the instrument creating the floating charge, entitles the holder of the charge to make that appointment and, in so far as not otherwise provided for by the instrument on the occurrence of any of the following events, namely—

(a) where the court, on the application of the holder of the charge, pronounces itself satisfied that the position of the holder of the charge is likely to be prejudiced if no such appointment is made;

(b) any of the events referred to in paragraphs (a) to (c) of subsection (1).

[3208]

NOTES

Application to limited liability partnerships: see the introductory note to this Act, the Limited Liability Partnerships Regulations 2001, SI 2001/1090, reg 5, Sch 3 at **[6986]**, **[6995]**, and the Limited Liability Partnerships (Scotland) Regulations 2001, SSI 2001/128, reg 4, Schs 2, 3 at **[6977]**, **[6980A]**, **[6980B]**.

53 Mode of appointment by holder of charge

(1) The appointment of a receiver by the holder of the floating charge under section 51(1) shall be by means of [an instrument subscribed in accordance with the Requirements of Writing (Scotland) Act 1995] ("the instrument of appointment"), a copy (certified in the prescribed manner to be a correct copy) whereof shall be delivered by or on behalf of the person making the appointment to the registrar of companies for registration within 7 days of its execution and shall be accompanied by a notice in the prescribed form.

(2) If any person without reasonable excuse makes default in complying with the requirements of subsection (1), he is liable to a fine *and, for continued contravention, to a daily default fine*.

(3) …

[(4) If the receiver is to be appointed by the holders of a series of secured debentures, the instrument of appointment may be executed on behalf of the holders of the floating charge by any person authorised by resolution of the debenture-holders to execute the instrument.]

(5) On receipt of the certified copy of the instrument of appointment in accordance with subsection (1), the registrar shall, on payment of the prescribed fee, enter the particulars of the appointment in the register of charges.

(6) The appointment of a person as a receiver by an instrument of appointment in accordance with subsection (1)—

(a) is of no effect unless it is accepted by that person before the end of the business day next following that on which the instrument of appointment is received by him or on his behalf, and

(b) subject to paragraph (a), is deemed to be made on the day on and at the time at which the instrument of appointment is so received, as evidence by a written docquet by that person or on his behalf;

and this subsection applies to the appointment of joint receivers subject to such modifications as may be prescribed.

(7) On the appointment of a receiver under this section, the floating charge by virtue of which he was appointed attaches to the property then subject to the charge; and such attachment has effect as if the charge was a fixed security over the property to which it has attached.

[3209]

NOTES

Sub-s (1): words in square brackets substituted by the Requirements of Writing (Scotland) Act 1995, s 14(1), Sch 4, para 58(a), as from 1 August 1995.

Sub-s (2): words in italics repealed by CA 1989, ss 107, 212, Sch 16, para 3, Sch 24, as from a day to be appointed.

Sub-s (3): repealed by the Law Reform (Miscellaneous Provisions) (Scotland) Act 1990, s 74, Sch 8, Pt II, para 35, Sch 9, as from 1 December 1990.

Sub-s (4): substituted by the Requirements of Writing (Scotland) Act 1995, s 14(1), Sch 4, para 58(b), as from 1 August 1995.

Application to limited liability partnerships: see the introductory note to this Act, the Limited Liability Partnerships Regulations 2001, SI 2001/1090, reg 5, Sch 3 at **[6986]**, **[6995]**, and the Limited Liability Partnerships (Scotland) Regulations 2001, SSI 2001/128, reg 4, Schs 2, 3 at **[6977]**, **[6980A]**, **[6980B]**.

Modification (by virtue of the Scotland Act 1998): see the Note at the beginning of this Act.

Regulations: the Receivers (Scotland) Regulations 1986, SI 1986/1917.

54 Appointment by court

(1) Application for the appointment of a receiver by the court under section 51(2) shall be by petition to the court, which shall be served on the company.

(2) On such an application, the court shall, if it thinks fit, issue an interlocutor making the appointment of the receiver.

(3) A copy (certified by the clerk of the court to be a correct copy) of the court's interlocutor making the appointment shall be delivered by or on behalf of the petitioner to the registrar of companies for registration, accompanied by a notice in the prescribed form within 7 days of the date of the interlocutor or such longer period as the court may allow.

If any person without reasonable excuse makes default in complying with the requirements of this subsection, he is liable to a fine *and, for continued contravention, to a daily default fine*.

(4) On receipt of the certified copy interlocutor in accordance with subsection (3), the registrar shall, on payment of the prescribed fee, enter the particulars of the appointment in the register of charges.

(5) The receiver is to be regarded as having been appointed on the date of his being appointed by the court.

(6) On the appointment of a receiver under this section, the floating charge by virtue of which he was appointed attaches to the property then subject to the charge; and such attachment has effect as if the charge were a fixed security over the property to which it has attached.

(7) In making rules of court for the purposes of this section, the Court of Session shall have regard to the need for special provision for cases which appear to the court to require to be dealt with as a matter of urgency.

[3210]

NOTES

Sub-s (3): words in italics repealed by CA 1989, ss 107, 212, Sch 16, para 3, Sch 24, as from a day to be appointed.

Application to limited liability partnerships: see the introductory note to this Act, the Limited Liability Partnerships Regulations 2001, SI 2001/1090, reg 5, Sch 3 at **[6986]**, **[6995]**, and the Limited Liability Partnerships (Scotland) Regulations 2001, SSI 2001/128, reg 4, Schs 2, 3 at **[6977]**, **[6980A]**, **[6980B]**.

Modification (by virtue of the Scotland Act 1998): see the Note at the beginning of this Act.

Regulations: the Receivers (Scotland) Regulations 1986, SI 1986/1917.

55 Powers of receiver

(1) Subject to the next subsection, a receiver has in relation to such part of the property of the company as is attached by the floating charge by virtue of which he was appointed, the powers, if any, given to him by the instrument creating that charge.

(2) In addition, the receiver has under this Chapter the powers as respects that property (in so far as these are not inconsistent with any provision contained in that instrument) which are specified in Schedule 2 to this Act.

(3) Subsections (1) and (2) apply—

(a) subject to the rights of any person who has effectually executed diligence on all or any part of the property of the company prior to the appointment of the receiver, and

(b) subject to the rights of any person who holds over all or any part of the property of the company a fixed security or floating charge having priority over, or ranking pari passu with, the floating charge by virtue of which the receiver was appointed.

(4) A person dealing with a receiver in good faith and for value is not concerned to enquire whether the receiver is acting within his powers.

[3211]

NOTES

Application to limited liability partnerships: see the introductory note to this Act, the Limited Liability Partnerships Regulations 2001, SI 2001/1090, reg 5, Sch 3 at **[6986]**, **[6995]**, and the Limited Liability Partnerships (Scotland) Regulations 2001, SSI 2001/128, reg 4, Schs 2, 3 at **[6977]**, **[6980A]**, **[6980B]**.

56 Precedence among receivers

(1) Where there are two or more floating charges subsisting over all or any part of the property of the company, a receiver may be appointed under this Chapter by virtue of each such charge; but a receiver appointed by, or on the application of, the holder of a floating charge having priority of ranking over any other floating charge by virtue of which a receiver has been appointed has the powers given to a receiver by section 55 and Schedule 2 to the exclusion of any other receiver.

(2) Where two or more floating charges rank with one another equally, and two or more receivers have been appointed by virtue of such charges, the receivers so appointed are deemed to have been appointed as joint receivers.

(3) Receivers appointed, or deemed to have been appointed, as joint receivers shall act jointly unless the instrument of appointment or respective instruments of appointment otherwise provide.

(4) Subject to subsection (5) below, the powers of a receiver appointed by, or on the application of, the holder of a floating charge are suspended by, and as from the date of, the appointment of a receiver by, or on the application of, the holder of a floating charge having priority of ranking over that charge to such extent as may be necessary to enable the receiver second mentioned to exercise his powers under section 55 and Schedule 2; and any powers so suspended take effect again when the floating charge having priority of ranking ceases to attach to the property then subject to the charge, whether such cessation is by virtue of section 62(6) or otherwise.

(5) The suspension of the powers of a receiver under subsection (4) does not have the effect of requiring him to release any part of the property (including any letters or documents) of the company from his control until he receives from the receiver superseding him a valid indemnity (subject to the limit of the value of such part of the property of the company as is subject to the charge by virtue of which he was appointed) in respect of any expenses, charges and liabilities he may have incurred in the performance of his functions as receiver.

(6) The suspension of the powers of a receiver under subsection (4) does not cause the floating charge by virtue of which he was appointed to cease to attach to the property to which it attached by virtue of section 53(7) or 54(6).

(7) Nothing in this section prevents the same receiver being appointed by virtue of two or more floating charges.

[3212]

NOTES

Application to limited liability partnerships: see the introductory note to this Act, the Limited Liability Partnerships Regulations 2001, SI 2001/1090, reg 5, Sch 3 at **[6986]**, **[6995]**, and the Limited Liability Partnerships (Scotland) Regulations 2001, SSI 2001/128, reg 4, Schs 2, 3 at **[6977]**, **[6980A]**, **[6980B]**.

57 Agency and liability of receiver for contracts

(1) A receiver is deemed to be the agent of the company in relation to such property of the company as is attached by the floating charge by virtue of which he was appointed.

[(1A) Without prejudice to subsection (1), a receiver is deemed to be the agent of the company in relation to any contract of employment adopted by him in the carrying out of his functions.]

(2) A receiver (including a receiver whose powers are subsequently suspended under section 56) is personally liable on any contract entered into by him in the performance of his

functions, except in so far as the contract otherwise provides, and[, to the extent of any qualifying liability,] on any contract of employment adopted by him in the carrying out of those functions.

[(2A) For the purposes of subsection (2), a liability under a contract of employment is a qualifying liability if—

(a) it is a liability to pay a sum by way of wages or salary or contribution to an occupational pension scheme,

(b) it is incurred while the receiver is in office, and

(c) it is in respect of services rendered wholly or partly after the adoption of the contract.

(2B) Where a sum payable in respect of a liability which is a qualifying liability for the purposes of subsection (2) is payable in respect of services rendered partly before and partly after the adoption of the contract, liability under that subsection shall only extend to so much of the sum as is payable in respect of services rendered after the adoption of the contract.

(2C) For the purposes of subsections (2A) and (2B)—

(a) wages or salary payable in respect of a period of holiday or absence from work through sickness or other good cause are deemed to be wages or (as the case may be) salary in respect of services rendered in that period, and

(b) a sum payable in lieu of holiday is deemed to be wages or (as the case may be) salary in respect of services rendered in the period by reference to which the holiday entitlement arose.

(2D) In subsection (2C)(a), the reference to wages or salary payable in respect of a period of holiday includes any sums which, if they had been paid, would have been treated for the purposes of the enactments relating to social security as earnings in respect of that period.]

(3) A receiver who is personally liable by virtue of subsection (2) is entitled to be indemnified out of the property in respect of which he was appointed.

(4) Any contract entered into by or on behalf of the company prior to the appointment of a receiver continues in force (subject to its terms) notwithstanding that appointment, but the receiver does not by virtue only of his appointment incur any personal liability on any such contract.

(5) For the purposes of subsection (2), a receiver is not to be taken to have adopted a contract of employment by reason of anything done or omitted to be done within 14 days after his appointment.

(6) This section does not limit any right to indemnity which the receiver would have apart from it, nor limit his liability on contracts entered into or adopted without authority, nor confer any right to indemnity in respect of that liability.

(7) Any contract entered into by a receiver in the performance of his functions continues in force (subject to its terms) although the powers of the receiver are subsequently suspended under section 56.

[3213]

NOTES

Sub-ss (1A), (2A)–(2D): inserted by the Insolvency Act 1994, s 3(1), (2), (4), (5), in relation to contracts of employment adopted on or after 15 March 1994.

Sub-s (2): words in square brackets inserted by the Insolvency Act 1994, s 3(1), (3), (5), in relation to contracts of employment adopted on or after 15 March 1994.

Application to limited liability partnerships: see the introductory note to this Act, the Limited Liability Partnerships Regulations 2001, SI 2001/1090, reg 5, Sch 3 at **[6986]**, **[6995]**, and the Limited Liability Partnerships (Scotland) Regulations 2001, SSI 2001/128, reg 4, Schs 2, 3 at **[6977]**, **[6980A]**, **[6980B]**.

58 Remuneration of receiver

(1) The remuneration to be paid to a receiver is to be determined by agreement between the receiver and the holder of the floating charge by virtue of which he was appointed.

(2) Where the remuneration to be paid to the receiver has not been determined under subsection (1), or where it has been so determined but is disputed by any of the persons mentioned in paragraphs (a) to (d) below, it may be fixed instead by the Auditor of the Court of Session on application made to him by—

(a) the receiver;

(b) the holder of any floating charge or fixed security over all or any part of the property of the company;
(c) the company; or
(d) the liquidator of the company.

(3) Where the receiver has been paid or has retained for his remuneration for any period before the remuneration has been fixed by the Auditor of the Court of Session under subsection (2) any amount in excess of the remuneration so fixed for that period, the receiver or his personal representatives shall account for the excess.

[3214]

NOTES

Application to limited liability partnerships: see the introductory note to this Act, the Limited Liability Partnerships Regulations 2001, SI 2001/1090, reg 5, Sch 3 at **[6986]**, **[6995]**, and the Limited Liability Partnerships (Scotland) Regulations 2001, SSI 2001/128, reg 4, Schs 2, 3 at **[6977]**, **[6980A]**, **[6980B]**.

59 Priority of debts

(1) Where a receiver is appointed and the company is not at the time of the appointment in course of being wound up, the debts which fall under subsection (2) of this section shall be paid out of any assets coming to the hands of the receiver in priority to any claim for principal or interest by the holder of the floating charge by virtue of which the receiver was appointed.

(2) Debts falling under this subsection are preferential debts (within the meaning given by section 386 in Part XII) which, by the end of a period of 6 months after advertisement by the receiver for claims in the Edinburgh Gazette and in a newspaper circulating in the district where the company carries on business either—
(i) have been intimated to him, or
(ii) have become known to him.

(3) Any payments made under this section shall be recouped as far as may be out of the assets of the company available for payment of ordinary creditors.

[3215]

NOTES

Application to limited liability partnerships: see the introductory note to this Act and the Limited Liability Partnerships Regulations 2001, SI 2001/1090, reg 5, Sch 3 at **[6986]**, **[6995]**.

60 Distribution of moneys

(1) Subject to the next section, and to the rights of any of the following categories of persons (which rights shall, except to the extent otherwise provided in any instrument, have the following order of priority), namely—
(a) the holder of any fixed security which is over property subject to the floating charge and which ranks prior to, or pari passu with, the floating charge;
(b) all persons who have effectually executed diligence on any part of the property of the company which is subject to the charge by virtue of which the receiver was appointed;
(c) creditors in respect of all liabilities, charges and expenses incurred by or on behalf of the receiver;
(d) the receiver in respect of his liabilities, expenses and remuneration, and any indemnity to which he is entitled out of the property of the company; and
(e) the preferential creditors entitled to payment under section 59,

the receiver shall pay moneys received by him to the holder of the floating charge by virtue of which the receiver was appointed in or towards satisfaction of the debt secured by the floating charge.

(2) Any balance of moneys remaining after the provisions of subsection (1) and section 61 below have been satisfied shall be paid in accordance with their respective rights and interests to the following persons, as the case may require—
(a) any other receiver;
(b) the holder of a fixed security which is over property subject to the floating charge;
(c) the company or its liquidator, as the case may be.

(3) Where any question arises as to the person entitled to a payment under this section, or where a receipt or a discharge of a security cannot be obtained in respect of any such

PART III OTHER LEGISLATION

payment, the receiver shall consign the amount of such payment in any joint stock bank of issue in Scotland in name of the Accountant of Court for behoof of the person or persons entitled thereto.

[3216]

NOTES

Application to limited liability partnerships: see the introductory note to this Act, the Limited Liability Partnerships Regulations 2001, SI 2001/1090, reg 5, Sch 3 at **[6986]**, **[6995]**, and the Limited Liability Partnerships (Scotland) Regulations 2001, SSI 2001/128, reg 4, Schs 2, 3 at **[6977]**, **[6980A]**, **[6980B]**.

61 Disposal of interest in property

(1) Where the receiver sells or disposes, or is desirous of selling or disposing, of any property or interest in property of the company which is subject to the floating charge by virtue of which the receiver was appointed and which is—

(a) subject to any security or interest of, or burden or encumbrance in favour of, a creditor the ranking of which is prior to, or pari passu with, or postponed to the floating charge, or

(b) property or an interest in property affected or attached by effectual diligence executed by any person,

and the receiver is unable to obtain the consent of such creditor or, as the case may be, such person to such a sale or disposal, the receiver may apply to the court for authority to sell or dispose of the property or interest in property free of such security, interest, burden, encumbrance or diligence.

[(1A) For the purposes of subsection (1) above, an inhibition which takes effect after the creation of the floating charge by virtue of which the receiver was appointed is not an effectual diligence.]

[(1B) For the purposes of subsection (1) above, an arrestment is an effectual diligence only where it is executed before the floating charge, by virtue of which the receiver was appointed, attaches to the property comprised in the company's property and undertaking.]

(2) Subject to the next subsection, on such an application the court may, if it thinks fit, authorise the sale or disposal of the property or interest in question free of such security, interest, burden, encumbrance or diligence, and such authorisation may be on such terms or conditions as the court thinks fit.

(3) In the case of an application where a fixed security over the property or interest in question which ranks prior to the floating charge has not been met or provided for in full, the court shall not authorise the sale or disposal of the property or interest in question unless it is satisfied that the sale or disposal would be likely to provide a more advantageous realisation of the company's assets than would otherwise be effected.

(4) It shall be a condition of an authorisation to which subsection (3) applies that—

(a) the net proceeds of the disposal, and

(b) where those proceeds are less than such amount as may be determined by the court to be the net amount which would be realised on a sale of the property or interest in the open market by a willing seller, such sums as may be required to make good the deficiency,

shall be applied towards discharging the sums secured by the fixed security.

(5) Where a condition imposed in pursuance of subsection (4) relates to two or more such fixed securities, that condition shall require the net proceeds of the disposal and, where paragraph (b) of that subsection applies, the sums mentioned in that paragraph to be applied towards discharging the sums secured by those fixed securities in the order of their priorities.

(6) A copy of an authorisation under subsection (2) certified by the clerk of court shall, within 14 days of the granting of the authorisation, be sent by the receiver to the registrar of companies.

(7) If the receiver without reasonable excuse fails to comply with subsection (6), he is liable to a fine and, for continued contravention, to a daily default fine.

(8) Where any sale or disposal is effected in accordance with the authorisation of the court under subsection (2), the receiver shall grant to the purchaser or disponee an appropriate document of transfer or conveyance of the property or interest in question, and that document has the effect, or, where recording, intimation or registration of that document is a legal

requirement for completion of title to the property or interest, then that recording, intimation or registration (as the case may be) has the effect, of—

(a) disencumbering the property or interest of the security, interest, burden or encumbrance affecting it, and

(b) freeing the property or interest from the diligence executed upon it.

(9) Nothing in this section prejudices the right of any creditor of the company to rank for his debt in the winding up of the company.

[3217]

NOTES

Sub-s (1A): inserted by the Bankruptcy and Diligence etc (Scotland) Act 2007, s 155(1), (2), as from a day to be appointed.

Sub-s (1B): inserted by the Bankruptcy and Diligence etc (Scotland) Act 2007, s 226, Sch 5, para 14(1), (2), as from a day to be appointed (note that Sch 5, para 14 actually provides that this subsection should be inserted after sub-s (1)).

Application to limited liability partnerships: see the introductory note to this Act, the Limited Liability Partnerships Regulations 2001, SI 2001/1090, reg 5, Sch 3 at **[6986]**, **[6995]**, and the Limited Liability Partnerships (Scotland) Regulations 2001, SSI 2001/128, reg 4, Schs 2, 3 at **[6977]**, **[6980A]**, **[6980B]**.

Modification (by virtue of the Scotland Act 1998): see the Note at the beginning of this Act.

62 Cessation of appointment of receiver

(1) A receiver may be removed from office by the court under subsection (3) below and may resign his office by giving notice of his resignation in the prescribed manner to such persons as may be prescribed.

(2) A receiver shall vacate office if he ceases to be qualified to act as an insolvency practitioner in relation to the company.

(3) Subject to the next subsection, a receiver may, on application to the court by the holder of the floating charge by virtue of which he was appointed, be removed by the court on cause shown.

(4) Where at any time a receiver vacates office—

(a) his remuneration and any expenses properly incurred by him, and

(b) any indemnity to which he is entitled out of the property of the company,

shall be paid out of the property of the company which is subject to the floating charge and shall have priority as provided for in section 60(1).

(5) When a receiver ceases to act as such otherwise than by death he shall, and, when a receiver is removed by the court, the holder of the floating charge by virtue of which he was appointed shall, within 14 days of the cessation or removal (as the case may be) give the registrar of companies notice to that effect, and the registrar shall enter the notice in the register of charges.

If the receiver or the holder of the floating charge (as the case may require) makes default in complying with the requirements of this subsection, he is liable to a fine *and, for continued contravention, to a daily default fine*.

(6) If by the expiry of a period of one month following upon the removal of the receiver or his ceasing to act as such no other receiver has been appointed, the floating charge by virtue of which the receiver was appointed—

(a) thereupon ceases to attach to the property then subject to the charge, and

(b) again subsists as a floating charge;

and for the purposes of calculating the period of one month under this subsection no account shall be taken of any period during which [the company is in administration,] under Part II of this Act …

[3218]

NOTES

Sub-s (5): words in italics repealed by CA 1989, ss 107, 212, Sch 16, para 3, Sch 24, as from a day to be appointed.

Sub-s (6): words in square brackets substituted, and words omitted repealed, by the Enterprise Act 2002 (Insolvency) Order 2003, SI 2003/2096, arts 4, 6, Schedule, Pt 1, paras 8, 9, as from 15 September 2003, except in relation to any case where a petition for an administration order was presented before that date.

Application to limited liability partnerships: see the introductory note to this Act, the Limited Liability Partnerships Regulations 2001, SI 2001/1090, reg 5, Sch 3 at **[6986]**, **[6995]**, and the Limited Liability Partnerships (Scotland) Regulations 2001, SSI 2001/128, reg 4, Schs 2, 3 at **[6977]**, **[6980A]**, **[6980B]**.

Modification (by virtue of the Scotland Act 1998): see the Note at the beginning of this Act.
Regulations: the Receivers (Scotland) Regulations 1986, SI 1986/1917.

63 Powers of court

(1) The court on the application of—

(a) the holder of a floating charge by virtue of which a receiver was appointed, or

(b) a receiver appointed under section 51,

may give directions to the receiver in respect of any matter arising in connection with the performance by him of his functions.

(2) Where the appointment of a person as a receiver by the holder of a floating charge is discovered to be invalid (whether by virtue of the invalidity of the instrument or otherwise), the court may order the holder of the floating charge to indemnify the person appointed against any liability which arises solely by reason of the invalidity of the appointment.

[3219]

NOTES

Application to limited liability partnerships: see the introductory note to this Act, the Limited Liability Partnerships Regulations 2001, SI 2001/1090, reg 5, Sch 3 at **[6986]**, **[6995]**, and the Limited Liability Partnerships (Scotland) Regulations 2001, SSI 2001/128, reg 4, Schs 2, 3 at **[6977]**, **[6980A]**, **[6980B]**.

64 Notification that receiver appointed

(1) Where a receiver has been appointed, every invoice, order for goods or business letter issued by or on behalf of the company or the receiver or the liquidator of the company, being a document on or in which the name of the company appears, shall contain a statement that a receiver has been appointed.

(2) If default is made in complying with the requirements of this section, the company and any of the following persons who knowingly and wilfully authorises or permits the default, namely any officer of the company, any liquidator of the company and any receiver, is liable to a fine.

[3220]

NOTES

Application to limited liability partnerships: see the introductory note to this Act, the Limited Liability Partnerships Regulations 2001, SI 2001/1090, reg 5, Sch 3 at **[6986]**, **[6995]**, and the Limited Liability Partnerships (Scotland) Regulations 2001, SSI 2001/128, reg 4, Schs 2, 3 at **[6977]**, **[6980A]**, **[6980B]**.

65 Information to be given by receiver

(1) Where a receiver is appointed, he shall—

(a) forthwith send to the company and publish notice of his appointment, and

(b) within 28 days after his appointment, unless the court otherwise directs, send such notice to all the creditors of the company (so far as he is aware of their addresses).

(2) This section and the next do not apply in relation to the appointment of a receiver to act—

(a) with an existing receiver, or

(b) in place of a receiver who has died or ceased to act,

except that, where they apply to a receiver who dies or ceases to act before they have been fully complied with, the references in this section and the next to the receiver include (subject to subsection (3) of this section) his successor and any continuing receiver.

(3) If the company is being wound up, this section and the next apply notwithstanding that the receiver and the liquidator are the same person, but with any necessary modifications arising from that fact.

(4) If a person without reasonable excuse fails to comply with this section, he is liable to a fine and, for continued contravention, to a daily default fine.

[3221]

NOTES

Application to limited liability partnerships: see the introductory note to this Act, the Limited Liability Partnerships Regulations 2001, SI 2001/1090, reg 5, Sch 3 at **[6986]**, **[6995]**, and the Limited Liability Partnerships (Scotland) Regulations 2001, SSI 2001/128, reg 4, Schs 2, 3 at **[6977]**, **[6980A]**, **[6980B]**.

Regulations: the Receivers (Scotland) Regulations 1986, SI 1986/1917.

66 Company's statement of affairs

(1) Where a receiver of a company is appointed, the receiver shall forthwith require some or all of the persons mentioned in subsection (3) below to make out and submit to him a statement in the prescribed form as to the affairs of the company.

(2) A statement submitted under this section shall be verified by affidavit by the persons required to submit it and shall show—

(a) particulars of the company's assets, debts and liabilities;
(b) the names and addresses of its creditors;
(c) the securities held by them respectively;
(d) the dates when the securities were respectively given; and
(e) such further or other information as may be prescribed.

(3) The persons referred to in subsection (1) are—

(a) those who are or have been officers of the company;
(b) those who have taken part in the company's formation at any time within one year before the date of the appointment of the receiver;
(c) those who are in the company's employment or have been in its employment within that year, and are in the receiver's opinion capable of giving the information required;
(d) those who are or have been within that year officers of or in the employment of a company which is, or within that year was, an officer of the company.

In this subsection "employment" includes employment under a contract for services.

(4) Where any persons are required under this section to submit a statement of affairs to the receiver they shall do so (subject to the next subsection) before the end of the period of 21 days beginning with the day after that on which the prescribed notice of the requirement is given to them by the receiver.

(5) The receiver, if he thinks fit, may—

(a) at any time release a person from an obligation imposed on him under subsection (1) or (2), or
(b) either when giving the notice mentioned in subsection (4) or subsequently extend the period so mentioned,

and where the receiver has refused to exercise a power conferred by this subsection, the court, if it thinks fit, may exercise it.

(6) If a person without reasonable excuse fails to comply with any obligation imposed under this section, he is liable to a fine and, for continued contravention to a daily default fine. **[3222]**

NOTES

Application to limited liability partnerships: see the introductory note to this Act, the Limited Liability Partnerships Regulations 2001, SI 2001/1090, reg 5, Sch 3 at **[6986]**, **[6995]**, and the Limited Liability Partnerships (Scotland) Regulations 2001, SSI 2001/128, reg 4, Schs 2, 3 at **[6977]**, **[6980A]**, **[6980B]**.

Regulations: the Receivers (Scotland) Regulations 1986, SI 1986/1917.

67 Report by receiver

(1) Where a receiver is appointed under section 51, he shall within 3 months (or such longer period as the court may allow) after his appointment, send to the registrar of companies, to the holder of the floating charge by virtue of which he was appointed and to any trustees for secured creditors of the company and (so far as he is aware of their addresses) to all such creditors a report as to the following matters, namely—

(a) the events leading up to his appointment, so far as he is aware of them;
(b) the disposal or proposed disposal by him of any property of the company and the carrying on or proposed carrying on by him of any business of the company;

PART III OTHER LEGISLATION

(c) the amounts of principal and interest payable to the holder of the floating charge by virtue of which he was appointed and the amounts payable to preferential creditors; and

(d) the amount (if any) likely to be available for the payment of other creditors.

(2) The receiver shall also, within 3 months (or such longer period as the court may allow) after his appointment, either—

(a) send a copy of the report (so far as he is aware of their addresses) to all unsecured creditors of the company, or

(b) publish in the prescribed manner a notice stating an address to which unsecured creditors of the company should write for copies of the report to be sent to them free of charge,

and (in either case), unless the court otherwise directs, lay a copy of the report before a meeting of the company's unsecured creditors summoned for the purpose on not less than 14 days' notice.

(3) The court shall not give a direction under subsection (2) unless—

(a) the report states the intention of the receiver to apply for the direction, and

(b) a copy of the report is sent to the persons mentioned in paragraph (a) of that subsection, or a notice is published as mentioned in paragraph (b) of that subsection, not less than 14 days before the hearing of the application.

(4) Where the company has gone or goes into liquidation, the receiver—

(a) shall, within 7 days after his compliance with subsection (1) or, if later, the nomination or appointment of the liquidator, send a copy of the report to the liquidator, and

(b) where he does so within the time limited for compliance with subsection (2), is not required to comply with that subsection.

(5) A report under this section shall include a summary of the statement of affairs made out and submitted under section 66 and of his comments (if any) on it.

(6) Nothing in this section shall be taken as requiring any such report to include any information the disclosure of which would seriously prejudice the carrying out by the receiver of his functions.

(7) Section 65(2) applies for the purposes of this section also.

(8) If a person without reasonable excuse fails to comply with this section, he is liable to a fine and, for continued contravention, to a daily default fine.

(9) In this section "secured creditor", in relation to a company, means a creditor of the company who holds in respect of his debt a security over property of the company, and "unsecured creditor" shall be construed accordingly.

[3223]

NOTES

Application to limited liability partnerships: see the introductory note to this Act, the Limited Liability Partnerships Regulations 2001, SI 2001/1090, reg 5, Sch 3 at **[6986]**, **[6995]**, and the Limited Liability Partnerships (Scotland) Regulations 2001, SSI 2001/128, reg 4, Schs 2, 3 at **[6977]**, **[6980A]**, **[6980B]**.

Modification (by virtue of the Scotland Act 1998): see the Note at the beginning of this Act.

Regulations: the Receivers (Scotland) Regulations 1986, SI 1986/1917.

68 Committee of creditors

(1) Where a meeting of creditors is summoned under section 67, the meeting may, if it thinks fit, establish a committee ("the creditors' committee") to exercise the functions conferred on it by or under this Act.

(2) If such a committee is established, the committee may on giving not less than 7 days' notice require the receiver to attend before it at any reasonable time and furnish it with such information relating to the carrying out by him of his functions as it may reasonably require.

[3224]

NOTES

Application to limited liability partnerships: see the introductory note to this Act, the Limited Liability Partnerships Regulations 2001, SI 2001/1090, reg 5, Sch 3 at **[6986]**, **[6995]**, and the Limited Liability Partnerships (Scotland) Regulations 2001, SSI 2001/128, reg 4, Schs 2, 3 at **[6977]**, **[6980A]**, **[6980B]**.

69 Enforcement of receiver's duty to make returns, etc

(1) If any receiver—

(a) having made default in filing, delivering or making any return, account or other document, or in giving any notice, which a receiver is by law required to file, deliver, make or give, fails to make good the default within 14 days after the service on him of a notice requiring him to do so; or

(b) has, after being required at any time by the liquidator of the company so to do, failed to render proper accounts of his receipts and payments and to vouch the same and to pay over to the liquidator the amount properly payable to him,

the court may, on an application made for the purpose, make an order directing the receiver to make good the default within such time as may be specified in the order.

(2) In the case of any such default as is mentioned in subsection (1)(a), an application for the purposes of this section may be made by any member or creditor of the company or by the registrar of companies; and, in the case of any such default as is mentioned in subsection (1)(b), the application shall be made by the liquidator; and, in either case, the order may provide that all expenses of and incidental to the application shall be borne by the receiver.

(3) Nothing in this section prejudices the operation of any enactments imposing penalties on receivers in respect of any such default as is mentioned in subsection (1).

[3225]

NOTES

Application to limited liability partnerships: see the introductory note to this Act, the Limited Liability Partnerships Regulations 2001, SI 2001/1090, reg 5, Sch 3 at **[6986]**, **[6995]**, and the Limited Liability Partnerships (Scotland) Regulations 2001, SSI 2001/128, reg 4, Schs 2, 3 at **[6977]**, **[6980A]**, **[6980B]**.

Modification (by virtue of the Scotland Act 1998): see the Note at the beginning of this Act.

70 Interpretation for Chapter II

(1) In this Chapter, unless the contrary intention appears, the following expressions have the following meanings respectively assigned to them—

"company" means an incorporated company (whether or not a company within the meaning of the Companies Act) which the Court of Session has jurisdiction to wind up;

"fixed security", in relation to any property of a company, means any security, other than a floating charge or a charge having the nature of a floating charge, which on the winding up of the company in Scotland would be treated as an effective security over that property, and (without prejudice to that generality) includes a security over that property, being a heritable security within the meaning of the Conveyancing and Feudal Reform (Scotland) Act 1970;

"instrument of appointment" has the meaning given by section 53(1);

"prescribed" means prescribed by regulations made under this Chapter by the Secretary of State;

"receiver" means a receiver of such part of the property of the company as is subject to the floating charge by virtue of which he has been appointed under section 51;

"register of charges" means the register kept by the registrar of companies for the purposes of Chapter II of Part XII of the Companies Act;

"secured debenture" means a bond, debenture, debenture stock or other security which, either itself or by reference to any other instrument, creates a floating charge over all or any part of the property of the company, but does not include a security which creates no charge other than a fixed security; and

"series of secured debentures" means two or more secured debentures created as a series by the company in such a manner that the holders thereof are entitled pari passu to the benefit of the floating charge.

(2) Where a floating charge, secured debenture or series of secured debentures has been created by the company, then, except where the context otherwise requires, any reference in this Chapter to the holder of the floating charge shall—

(a) where the floating charge, secured debenture or series of secured debentures provides for a receiver to be appointed by any person or body, be construed as a reference to that person or body;

(b) where, in the case of a series of secured debentures, no such provision has been made therein but—

(i) there are trustees acting for the debenture-holders under and in accordance with a trust deed, be construed as a reference to those trustees, and

(ii) where no such trustees are acting, be construed as a reference to—

(aa) a majority in nominal value of those present or represented by proxy and voting at a meeting of debenture-holders at which the holders of at least one-third in nominal value of the outstanding debentures of the series are present or so represented, or

(bb) where no such meeting is held, the holders of at least one-half in nominal value of the outstanding debentures of the series.

(3) Any reference in this Chapter to a floating charge, secured debenture, series of secured debentures or instrument creating a charge includes, except where the context otherwise requires, a reference to that floating charge, debenture, series of debentures or instrument as varied by any instrument.

(4) References in this Chapter to the instrument by which a floating charge was created are, in the case of a floating charge created by words in a bond or other written acknowledgement, references to the bond or, as the case may be, the other written acknowledgement.

[3226]

NOTES

Application to limited liability partnerships: see the introductory note to this Act, the Limited Liability Partnerships Regulations 2001, SI 2001/1090, reg 5, Sch 3 at **[6986]**, **[6995]**, and the Limited Liability Partnerships (Scotland) Regulations 2001, SSI 2001/128, reg 4, Schs 2, 3 at **[6977]**, **[6980A]**, **[6980B]**.

71 Prescription of forms, etc; regulations

(1) The notice referred to in section 62(5), and the notice referred to in section 65(1)(a) shall be in such form as may be prescribed.

(2) Any power conferred by this Chapter on the Secretary of State to make regulations is exercisable by statutory instrument; and a statutory instrument made in the exercise of the power so conferred to prescribe a fee is subject to annulment in pursuance of a resolution of either House of Parliament.

[3227]

NOTES

Application to limited liability partnerships: see the introductory note to this Act, the Limited Liability Partnerships Regulations 2001, SI 2001/1090, reg 5, Sch 3 at **[6986]**, **[6995]**, and the Limited Liability Partnerships (Scotland) Regulations 2001, SSI 2001/128, reg 4, Schs 2, 3 at **[6977]**, **[6980A]**, **[6980B]**.

CHAPTER III
RECEIVERS' POWERS IN GREAT BRITAIN AS A WHOLE

72 Cross-border operation of receivership provisions

(1) A receiver appointed under the law of either part of Great Britain in respect of the whole or any part of any property or undertaking of a company and in consequence of the company having created a charge which, as created, was a floating charge may exercise his powers in the other part of Great Britain so far as their exercise is not inconsistent with the law applicable there.

(2) In subsection (1) "receiver" includes a manager and a person who is appointed both receiver and manager.

[3228]

NOTES

Application to limited liability partnerships: see the introductory note to this Act and the Limited Liability Partnerships Regulations 2001, SI 2001/1090, reg 5, Sch 3 at **[6986]**, **[6995]**.

[CHAPTER IV
PROHIBITION OF APPOINTMENT OF ADMINISTRATIVE RECEIVER

72A Floating charge holder not to appoint administrative receiver

(1) The holder of a qualifying floating charge in respect of a company's property may not appoint an administrative receiver of the company.

(2) In Scotland, the holder of a qualifying floating charge in respect of a company's property may not appoint or apply to the court for the appointment of a receiver who on appointment would be an administrative receiver of property of the company.

(3) In subsections (1) and (2)—

"holder of a qualifying floating charge in respect of a company's property" has the same meaning as in paragraph 14 of Schedule B1 to this Act, and

"administrative receiver" has the meaning given by section 251.

(4) This section applies—

(a) to a floating charge created on or after a date appointed by the Secretary of State by order made by statutory instrument, and

(b) in spite of any provision of an agreement or instrument which purports to empower a person to appoint an administrative receiver (by whatever name).

(5) An order under subsection (4)(a) may—

(a) make provision which applies generally or only for a specified purpose;

(b) make different provision for different purposes;

(c) make transitional provision.

(6) This section is subject to the exceptions specified in [sections 72B to 72GA].]

[3228A]

NOTES

Inserted, together with the preceding heading and ss 72B–72D, 72E–72G, 72H, by the Enterprise Act 2002, s 250(1), as from 15 September 2003.

Sub-s (6): words in square brackets substituted by the Insolvency Act 1986 (Amendment) (Administrative Receivership and Urban Regeneration etc) Order 2003, SI 2003/1832, art 2(a), as from 15 September 2003 (ie, immediately after the coming into force of ss 72A–72G of, and Sch 2A to, this Act).

Application to limited liability partnerships: see the introductory note to this Act and the Limited Liability Partnerships Regulations 2001, SI 2001/1090, reg 5, Sch 3 at **[6986]**, **[6995]**.

Orders: the Insolvency Act 1986, Section 72A (Appointed Date) Order 2003, SI 2003/2095, appointing 15 September 2003 for the purposes of sub-s (4)(a) above.

[72B First exception: capital market

(1) Section 72A does not prevent the appointment of an administrative receiver in pursuance of an agreement which is or forms part of a capital market arrangement if—

(a) a party incurs or, when the agreement was entered into was expected to incur, a debt of at least £50 million under the arrangement, and

(b) the arrangement involves the issue of a capital market investment.

(2) In subsection (1)—

"capital market arrangement" means an arrangement of a kind described in paragraph 1 of Schedule 2A, and

"capital market investment" means an investment of a kind described in paragraph 2 or 3 of that Schedule.]

[3228B]

NOTES

Inserted as noted to s 72A at **[3228A]**.

Application to limited liability partnerships: see the introductory note to this Act and the Limited Liability Partnerships Regulations 2001, SI 2001/1090, reg 5, Sch 3 at **[6986]**, **[6995]**.

[72C Second exception: public-private partnership

(1) Section 72A does not prevent the appointment of an administrative receiver of a project company of a project which—

(a) is a public-private partnership project, and

(b) includes step-in rights.

(2) In this section "public-private partnership project" means a project—

(a) the resources for which are provided partly by one or more public bodies and partly by one or more private persons, or

(b) which is designed wholly or mainly for the purpose of assisting a public body to discharge a function.

(3) In this section—

"step-in rights" has the meaning given by paragraph 6 of Schedule 2A, and

"project company" has the meaning given by paragraph 7 of that Schedule.]

[3228C]

NOTES

Inserted as noted to s 72A at **[3228A]**.

Application to limited liability partnerships: see the introductory note to this Act and the Limited Liability Partnerships Regulations 2001, SI 2001/1090, reg 5, Sch 3 at **[6986]**, **[6995]**.

[72D Third exception: utilities

(1) Section 72A does not prevent the appointment of an administrative receiver of a project company of a project which—

(a) is a utility project, and

(b) includes step-in rights.

(2) In this section—

(a) "utility project" means a project designed wholly or mainly for the purpose of a regulated business,

(b) "regulated business" means a business of a kind listed in paragraph 10 of Schedule 2A,

(c) "step-in rights" has the meaning given by paragraph 6 of that Schedule, and

(d) "project company" has the meaning given by paragraph 7 of that Schedule.]

[3228D]

NOTES

Inserted as noted to s 72A at **[3228A]**.

Application to limited liability partnerships: see the introductory note to this Act and the Limited Liability Partnerships Regulations 2001, SI 2001/1090, reg 5, Sch 3 at **[6986]**, **[6995]**.

[72DA Exception in respect of urban regeneration projects

(1) Section 72A does not prevent the appointment of an administrative receiver of a project company of a project which—

(a) is designed wholly or mainly to develop land which at the commencement of the project is wholly or partly in a designated disadvantaged area outside Northern Ireland, and

(b) includes step-in rights.

(2) In subsection (1) "develop" means to carry out—

(a) building operations,

(b) any operation for the removal of substances or waste from land and the levelling of the surface of the land, or

(c) engineering operations in connection with the activities mentioned in paragraph (a) or (b).

(3) In this section—

"building" includes any structure or erection, and any part of a building as so defined, but does not include plant and machinery comprised in a building,

"building operations" includes—

(a) demolition of buildings,

(b) filling in of trenches,

(c) rebuilding,

(d) structural alterations of, or additions to, buildings and

(e) other operations normally undertaken by a person carrying on business as a builder,

"designated disadvantaged area" means an area designated as a disadvantaged area under section 92 of the Finance Act 2001,

"engineering operations" includes the formation and laying out of means of access to highways,

"project company" has the meaning given by paragraph 7 of Schedule 2A,

"step-in rights" has the meaning given by paragraph 6 of that Schedule,

"substance" means any natural or artificial substance whether in solid or liquid form or in the form of a gas or vapour, and "waste" includes any waste materials, spoil, refuse or other matter deposited on land.]

[3228DA]

NOTES

Inserted by the Insolvency Act 1986 (Amendment) (Administrative Receivership and Urban Regeneration etc) Order 2003, SI 2003/1832, art 2(b), as from 15 September 2003 (ie, immediately after the coming into force of ss 72A–72G of, and Sch 2A to, this Act).

Application to limited liability partnerships: see the introductory note to this Act and the Limited Liability Partnerships Regulations 2001, SI 2001/1090, reg 5, Sch 3 at **[6986]**, **[6995]**.

[72E Fourth exception: project finance

(1) Section 72A does not prevent the appointment of an administrative receiver of a project company of a project which—

(a) is a financed project, and
(b) includes step-in rights.

(2) In this section—

(a) a project is "financed" if under an agreement relating to the project a project company incurs, or when the agreement is entered into is expected to incur, a debt of at least £50 million for the purposes of carrying out the project,
(b) "project company" has the meaning given by paragraph 7 of Schedule 2A, and
(c) "step-in rights" has the meaning given by paragraph 6 of that Schedule.]

[3228E]

NOTES

Inserted as noted to s 72A at **[3228A]**.

Application to limited liability partnerships: see the introductory note to this Act and the Limited Liability Partnerships Regulations 2001, SI 2001/1090, reg 5, Sch 3 at **[6986]**, **[6995]**.

[72F Fifth exception: financial market

Section 72A does not prevent the appointment of an administrative receiver of a company by virtue of—

(a) a market charge within the meaning of section 173 of the Companies Act 1989 (c 40),
(b) a system-charge within the meaning of the Financial Markets and Insolvency Regulations 1996 (SI 1996/1469),
(c) a collateral security charge within the meaning of the Financial Markets and Insolvency (Settlement Finality) Regulations 1999 (SI 1999/2979).]

[3228F]

NOTES

Inserted as noted to s 72A at **[3228A]**.

Application to limited liability partnerships: see the introductory note to this Act and the Limited Liability Partnerships Regulations 2001, SI 2001/1090, reg 5, Sch 3 at **[6986]**, **[6995]**.

[72G Sixth exception: registered social landlord

Section 72A does not prevent the appointment of an administrative receiver of a company which is registered as a social landlord under Part I of the Housing Act 1996 (c 52) or under Part 3 of the Housing (Scotland) Act 2001 (asp 10).]

[3228G]

NOTES

Inserted as noted to s 72A at **[3228A]**.

Application to limited liability partnerships: see the introductory note to this Act and the Limited Liability Partnerships Regulations 2001, SI 2001/1090, reg 5, Sch 3 at **[6986]**, **[6995]**.

[72GA Exception in relation to protected railway companies etc

Section 72A does not prevent the appointment of an administrative receiver of—

(a) a company holding an appointment under Chapter I of Part II of the Water Industry Act 1991,

(b) a protected railway company within the meaning of section 59 of the Railways Act 1993 (including that section as it has effect by virtue of section 19 of the Channel Tunnel Rail Link Act 1996, or

(c) a licence company within the meaning of section 26 of the Transport Act 2000.]

[3228GA]

NOTES

Inserted by the Insolvency Act 1986 (Amendment) (Administrative Receivership and Urban Regeneration etc) Order 2003, SI 2003/1832, art 2(c), as from 15 September 2003 (ie, immediately after the coming into force of ss 72A–72G of, and Sch 2A to, this Act).

Application to limited liability partnerships: see the introductory note to this Act and the Limited Liability Partnerships Regulations 2001, SI 2001/1090, reg 5, Sch 3 at **[6986]**, **[6995]**.

[72H Sections 72A to 72G: supplementary

(1) Schedule 2A (which supplements sections 72B to 72G) shall have effect.

(2) The Secretary of State may by order—

(a) insert into this Act provision creating an additional exception to section 72A(1) or (2);

(b) provide for a provision of this Act which creates an exception to section 72A(1) or (2) to cease to have effect;

(c) amend section 72A in consequence of provision made under paragraph (a) or (b);

(d) amend any of sections 72B to 72G;

(e) amend Schedule 2A.

(3) An order under subsection (2) must be made by statutory instrument.

(4) An order under subsection (2) may make—

(a) provision which applies generally or only for a specified purpose;

(b) different provision for different purposes;

(c) consequential or supplementary provision;

(d) transitional provision.

(5) An order under subsection (2)—

(a) in the case of an order under subsection (2)(e), shall be subject to annulment in pursuance of a resolution of either House of Parliament,

(b) in the case of an order under subsection (2)(d) varying the sum specified in section 72B(1)(a) or 72E(2)(a) (whether or not the order also makes consequential or transitional provision), shall be subject to annulment in pursuance of a resolution of either House of Parliament, and

(c) in the case of any other order under subsection (2)(a) to (d), may not be made unless a draft has been laid before and approved by resolution of each House of Parliament.]

[3228H]

NOTES

Inserted as noted to s 72A at **[3228A]**.

Application to limited liability partnerships: see the introductory note to this Act and the Limited Liability Partnerships Regulations 2001, SI 2001/1090, reg 5, Sch 3 at **[6986]**, **[6995]**.

Orders: the Insolvency Act 1986 (Amendment) (Administrative Receivership and Capital Market Arrangements) Order 2003, SI 2003/1468; the Insolvency Act 1986 (Amendment) (Administrative Receivership and Urban Regeneration etc) Order 2003, SI 2003/1832.

PART IV
WINDING UP OF COMPANIES REGISTERED UNDER THE COMPANIES ACTS

CHAPTER I
PRELIMINARY

Modes of winding up

73 Alternative modes of winding up

(1) The winding up of a company, within the meaning given to that expression by section 735 of the Companies Act, may be either voluntary (Chapters II, III, IV and V in this Part) or by the court (Chapter VI).

(2) This Chapter, and Chapters VII to X, relate to winding up generally, except where otherwise stated.

[3229]

NOTES

Application to limited liability partnerships: see the introductory note to this Act and the Limited Liability Partnerships Regulations 2001, SI 2001/1090, reg 5, Sch 3 at **[6986]**, **[6995]**.

Contributories

74 Liability as contributories of present and past members

(1) When a company is wound up, every present and past member is liable to contribute to its assets to any amount sufficient for payment of its debts and liabilities, and the expenses of the winding up, and for the adjustment of the rights of the contributories among themselves.

(2) This is subject as follows—

(a) a past member is not liable to contribute if he has ceased to be a member for one year or more before the commencement of the winding up;

(b) a past member is not liable to contribute in respect of any debt or liability of the company contracted after he ceased to be a member;

(c) a past member is not liable to contribute, unless it appears to the court that the existing members are unable to satisfy the contributions required to be made by them in pursuance of the Companies Act and this Act;

(d) in the case of a company limited by shares, no contribution is required from any member exceeding the amount (if any) unpaid on the shares in respect of which he is liable as a present or past member;

(e) nothing in the Companies Act or this Act invalidates any provision contained in a policy of insurance or other contract whereby the liability of individual members on the policy or contract is restricted, or whereby the funds of the company are alone made liable in respect of the policy or contract;

(f) a sum due to any member of the company (in his character of a member) by way of dividends, profits or otherwise is not deemed to be a debt of the company, payable to that member in a case of competition between himself and any other creditor not a member of the company, but any such sum may be taken into account for the purpose of the final adjustment of the rights of the contributories among themselves.

(3) In the case of a company limited by guarantee, no contribution is required from any member exceeding the amount undertaken to be contributed by him to the company's assets in the event of its being wound up; but if it is a company with a share capital, every member of it is liable (in addition to the amount so undertaken to be contributed to the assets), to contribute to the extent of any sums unpaid on shares held by him.

[3230]

NOTES

Application to limited liability partnerships: see the introductory note to this Act and the Limited Liability Partnerships Regulations 2001, SI 2001/1090, reg 5, Sch 3 at **[6986]**, **[6995]**.

75 Directors, etc with unlimited liability

(1) In the winding up of a limited company, any director or manager (whether past or present) whose liability is under the Companies Act unlimited is liable, in addition to his liability (if any) to contribute as an ordinary member, to make a further contribution as if he were at the commencement of the winding up a member of an unlimited company.

(2) However—

(a) a past director or manager is not liable to make such further contribution if he has ceased to hold office for a year or more before the commencement of the winding up;

(b) a past director or manager is not liable to make such further contribution in respect of any debt or liability of the company contracted after he ceased to hold office;

(c) subject to the company's articles, a director or manager is not liable to make such

PART III OTHER LEGISLATION

further contribution unless the court deems it necessary to require that contribution in order to satisfy the company's debts and liabilities, and the expenses of the winding up.

[3231]

NOTES

Application to limited liability partnerships: see the introductory note to this Act and the Limited Liability Partnerships Regulations 2001, SI 2001/1090, reg 5, Sch 3 at **[6986]**, **[6995]**.

76 Liability of past directors and shareholders

(1) This section applies where a company is being wound up and—

(a) it has under Chapter VII of Part V of the Companies Act (redeemable shares; purchase by a company of its own shares) made a payment out of capital in respect of the redemption or purchase of any of its own shares (the payment being referred to below as "the relevant payment"), and

(b) the aggregate amount of the company's assets and the amounts paid by way of contribution to its assets (apart from this section) is not sufficient for payment of its debts and liabilities, and the expenses of the winding up.

(2) If the winding up commenced within one year of the date on which the relevant payment was made, then—

(a) the person from whom the shares were redeemed or purchased, and

(b) the directors who signed the statutory declaration made in accordance with section 173(3) of the Companies Act for purposes of the redemption or purchase (except a director who shows that he had reasonable grounds for forming the opinion set out in the declaration),

are, so as to enable that insufficiency to be met, liable to contribute to the following extent to the company's assets.

(3) A person from whom any of the shares were redeemed or purchased is liable to contribute an amount not exceeding so much of the relevant payment as was made by the company in respect of his shares; and the directors are jointly and severally liable with that person to contribute that amount.

(4) A person who has contributed any amount to the assets in pursuance of this section may apply to the court for an order directing any other person jointly and severally liable in respect of that amount to pay him such amount as the court thinks just and equitable.

(5) Sections 74 and 75 do not apply in relation to liability accruing by virtue of this section.

(6) This section is deemed included in Chapter VII of Part V of the Companies Act for the purposes of the Secretary of State's power to make regulations under section 179 of that Act.

[3232]

NOTES

Application to limited liability partnerships: see the introductory note to this Act and the Limited Liability Partnerships Regulations 2001, SI 2001/1090, reg 5, Sch 3 at **[6986]**, **[6995]**.

77 Limited company formerly unlimited

(1) This section applies in the case of a company being wound up which was at some former time registered as unlimited but has re-registered—

(a) as a public company under section 43 of the Companies Act (or the former corresponding provision, section 5 of the Companies Act 1980), or

(b) as a limited company under section 51 of the Companies Act (or the former corresponding provision, section 44 of the Companies Act 1967).

(2) Notwithstanding section 74(2)(a) above, a past member of the company who was a member of it at the time of re-registration, if the winding up commences within the period of 3 years beginning with the day on which the company was re-registered, is liable to contribute to the assets of the company in respect of debts and liabilities contracted before that time.

(3) If no persons who were members of the company at that time are existing members of it, a person who at that time was a present or past member is liable to contribute as above

notwithstanding that the existing members have satisfied the contributions required to be made by them under the Companies Act and this Act.

This applies subject to section 74(2)(a) above and to subsection (2) of this section, but notwithstanding section 74(2)(c).

(4) Notwithstanding section 74(2)(d) and (3), there is no limit on the amount which a person who, at that time, was a past or present member of the company is liable to contribute as above.

[3233]

NOTES

Application to limited liability partnerships: see the introductory note to this Act and the Limited Liability Partnerships Regulations 2001, SI 2001/1090, reg 5, Sch 3 at **[6986]**, **[6995]**.

78 Unlimited company formerly limited

(1) This section applies in the case of a company being wound up which was at some former time registered as limited but has been re-registered as unlimited under section 49 of the Companies Act (or the former corresponding provision, section 43 of the Companies Act 1967).

(2) A person who, at the time when the application for the company to be re-registered was lodged, was a past member of the company and did not after that again become a member of it is not liable to contribute to the assets of the company more than he would have been liable to contribute had the company not been re-registered.

[3234]

NOTES

Application to limited liability partnerships: see the introductory note to this Act and the Limited Liability Partnerships Regulations 2001, SI 2001/1090, reg 5, Sch 3 at **[6986]**, **[6995]**.

79 Meaning of "contributory"

(1) In this Act and the Companies Act the expression "contributory" means every person liable to contribute to the assets of a company in the event of its being wound up, and for the purposes of all proceedings for determining, and all proceedings prior to the final determination of, the persons who are to be deemed contributories, includes any person alleged to be a contributory.

(2) The reference in subsection (1) to persons liable to contribute to the assets does not include a person so liable by virtue of a declaration by the court under section 213 (imputed responsibility for company's fraudulent trading) or section 214 (wrongful trading) in Chapter X of this Part.

(3) A reference in a company's articles to a contributory does not (unless the context requires) include a person who is a contributory only by virtue of section 76.

This subsection is deemed included in Chapter VII of Part V of the Companies Act for the purposes of the Secretary of State's power to make regulations under section 179 of that Act.

[3235]

NOTES

Application to limited liability partnerships: see the introductory note to this Act and the Limited Liability Partnerships Regulations 2001, SI 2001/1090, reg 5, Sch 3 at **[6986]**, **[6995]**.

80 Nature of contributory's liability

The liability of a contributory creates a debt (in England and Wales in the nature of a specialty) accruing due from him at the time when his liability commenced, but payable at the times when calls are made for enforcing the liability.

[3236]

NOTES

Application to limited liability partnerships: see the introductory note to this Act and the Limited Liability Partnerships Regulations 2001, SI 2001/1090, reg 5, Sch 3 at **[6986]**, **[6995]**.

81 Contributories in case of death of a member

(1) If a contributory dies either before or after he has been placed on the list of contributories, his personal representatives, and the heirs and legatees of heritage of his heritable estate in Scotland, are liable in a due course of administration to contribute to the assets of the company in discharge of his liability and are contributories accordingly.

(2) Where the personal representatives are placed on the list of contributories, the heirs or legatees of heritage need not be added, but they may be added as and when the court thinks fit.

(3) If in England and Wales the personal representatives make default in paying any money ordered to be paid by them, proceedings may be taken for administering the estate of the deceased contributory and for compelling payment out of it of the money due.

[3237]

NOTES

Application to limited liability partnerships: see the introductory note to this Act and the Limited Liability Partnerships Regulations 2001, SI 2001/1090, reg 5, Sch 3 at **[6986]**, **[6995]**.

82 Effect of contributory's bankruptcy

(1) The following applies if a contributory becomes bankrupt, either before or after he has been placed on the list of contributories.

(2) His trustee in bankruptcy represents him for all purposes of the winding up, and is a contributory accordingly.

(3) The trustee may be called on to admit to proof against the bankrupt's estate, or otherwise allow to be paid out of the bankrupt's assets in due course of law, any money due from the bankrupt in respect of his liability to contribute to the company's assets.

(4) There may be proved against the bankrupt's estate the estimated value of his liability to future calls as well as calls already made.

[3238]

NOTES

Application to limited liability partnerships: see the introductory note to this Act and the Limited Liability Partnerships Regulations 2001, SI 2001/1090, reg 5, Sch 3 at **[6986]**, **[6995]**.

83 Companies registered under Companies Act, Part XXII, Chapter II

(1) The following applies in the event of a company being wound up which has been registered under section 680 of the Companies Act (or previous corresponding provisions in the Companies Act 1948 or earlier Acts).

(2) Every person is a contributory, in respect of the company's debts and liabilities contracted before registration, who is liable—

(a) to pay, or contribute to the payment of, any debt or liability so contracted, or

(b) to pay, or contribute to the payment of, any sum for the adjustment of the rights of the members among themselves in respect of any such debt or liability, or

(c) to pay, or contribute to the amount of, the expenses of winding up the company, so far as relates to the debts or liabilities above-mentioned.

(3) Every contributory is liable to contribute to the assets of the company, in the course of the winding up, all sums due from him in respect of any such liability.

(4) In the event of the death, bankruptcy or insolvency of any contributory, provisions of this Act, with respect to the personal representatives, to the heirs and legatees of heritage of the heritable estate in Scotland of deceased contributories and to the trustees of bankrupt or insolvent contributories respectively, apply.

[3239]

NOTES

Application to limited liability partnerships: see the introductory note to this Act and the Limited Liability Partnerships Regulations 2001, SI 2001/1090, reg 5, Sch 3 at **[6986]**, **[6995]**.

CHAPTER II
VOLUNTARY WINDING UP (INTRODUCTORY AND GENERAL)

Resolutions for, and commencement of, voluntary winding up

84 Circumstances in which company may be wound up voluntarily

(1) A company may be wound up voluntarily—

(a) when the period (if any) fixed for the duration of the company by the articles expires, or the event (if any) occurs, on the occurrence of which the articles provide that the company is to be dissolved, and the company in general meeting has passed a resolution requiring it to be wound up voluntarily;

(b) if the company resolves by special resolution that it be wound up voluntarily;

(c) if the company resolves by extraordinary resolution to the effect that it cannot by reason of its liabilities continue its business, and that it is advisable to wind up.

(2) In this Act the expression "a resolution for voluntary winding up" means a resolution passed under any of the paragraphs of subsection (1).

[(2A) Before a company passes a resolution for voluntary winding up it must give written notice of the resolution to the holder of any qualifying floating charge to which section 72A applies.

(2B) Where notice is given under subsection (2A) a resolution for voluntary winding up may be passed only—

(a) after the end of the period of five business days beginning with the day on which the notice was given, or

(b) if the person to whom the notice was given has consented in writing to the passing of the resolution.]

(3) A resolution passed under paragraph (a) of subsection (1), as well as a special resolution under paragraph (b) and an extraordinary resolution under paragraph (c), is subject to section 380 of the Companies Act (copy of resolution to be forwarded to registrar of companies within 15 days).

[(4) This section has effect subject to section 43 of the Commonhold and Leasehold Reform Act 2002.]

[3240]

NOTES

Sub-s (1): para (c) repealed by the draft Companies Act 2006 (Commencement No 3, Consequential Amendments, Transitional Provisions and Savings) Order 2007, art 10(3), Sch 5, as from 1 October 2007 (see **[A12]**).

Sub-ss (2A), (2B): inserted by the Enterprise Act 2002 (Insolvency) Order 2003, SI 2003/2096, arts 4, 6, Schedule, Pt 1, paras 8, 10, as from 15 September 2003, except in relation to any case where a petition for an administration order was presented before that date.

Sub-s (4): added by the Commonhold and Leasehold Reform Act 2002, s 68, Sch 5, para 6, as from 27 September 2004, in relation to England and Wales only.

Application to limited liability partnerships: see the introductory note to this Act, the Limited Liability Partnerships Regulations 2001, SI 2001/1090, reg 5, Sch 3 at **[6986]**, **[6995]**, and the Limited Liability Partnerships (Scotland) Regulations 2001, SSI 2001/128, reg 4, Schs 2, 3 at **[6977]**, **[6980A]**, **[6980B]**.

Modification in relation to Scotland: see the Note at the beginning of this Act.

85 Notice of resolution to wind up

(1) When a company has passed a resolution for voluntary winding up, it shall, within 14 days after the passing of the resolution, give notice of the resolution by advertisement in the Gazette.

(2) If default is made in complying with this section, the company and every officer of it who is in default is liable to a fine and, for continued contravention, to a daily default fine.

For purposes of this subsection the liquidator is deemed an officer of the company.

[3241]

NOTES

Application to limited liability partnerships: see the introductory note to this Act and the Limited Liability Partnerships Regulations 2001, SI 2001/1090, reg 5, Sch 3 at **[6986]**, **[6995]**.

86 Commencement of winding up

A voluntary winding up is deemed to commence at the time of the passing of the resolution for voluntary winding up.

[3242]

NOTES

Application to limited liability partnerships: see the introductory note to this Act and the Limited Liability Partnerships Regulations 2001, SI 2001/1090, reg 5, Sch 3 at **[6986]**, **[6995]**.

Consequences of resolution to wind up

87 Effect on business and status of company

(1) In case of a voluntary winding up, the company shall from the commencement of the winding up cease to carry on its business, except so far as may be required for its beneficial winding up.

(2) However, the corporate state and corporate powers of the company, notwithstanding anything to the contrary in its articles, continue until the company is dissolved.

[3243]

NOTES

Application to limited liability partnerships: see the introductory note to this Act and the Limited Liability Partnerships Regulations 2001, SI 2001/1090, reg 5, Sch 3 at **[6986]**, **[6995]**.

88 Avoidance of share transfers, etc after winding-up resolution

Any transfer of shares, not being a transfer made to or with the sanction of the liquidator, and any alteration in the status of the company's members, made after the commencement of a voluntary winding up, is void.

[3244]

NOTES

Application to limited liability partnerships: see the introductory note to this Act and the Limited Liability Partnerships Regulations 2001, SI 2001/1090, reg 5, Sch 3 at **[6986]**, **[6995]**.

Declaration of solvency

89 Statutory declaration of solvency

(1) Where it is proposed to wind up a company voluntarily, the directors (or, in the case of a company having more than two directors, the majority of them) may at a directors' meeting make a statutory declaration to the effect that they have made a full inquiry into the company's affairs and that, having done so, they have formed the opinion that the company will be able to pay its debts in full, together with interest at the official rate (as defined in section 251), within such period, not exceeding 12 months from the commencement of the winding up, as may be specified in the declaration.

(2) Such a declaration by the directors has no effect for purposes of this Act unless—

(a) it is made within the 5 weeks immediately preceding the date of the passing of the resolution for winding up, or on that date but before the passing of the resolution, and

(b) it embodies a statement of the company's assets and liabilities as at the latest practicable date before the making of the declaration.

(3) The declaration shall be delivered to the registrar of companies before the expiration of 15 days immediately following the date on which the resolution for winding up is passed.

(4) A director making a declaration under this section without having reasonable grounds for the opinion that the company will be able to pay its debts in full, together with interest at the official rate, within the period specified is liable to imprisonment or a fine, or both.

(5) If the company is wound up in pursuance of a resolution passed within 5 weeks after the making of the declaration, and its debts (together with interest at the official rate) are not

paid or provided for in full within the period specified, it is to be presumed (unless the contrary is shown) that the director did not have reasonable grounds for his opinion.

(6) If a declaration required by subsection (3) to be delivered to the registrar is not so delivered within the time prescribed by that subsection, the company and every officer in default is liable to a fine and, for continued contravention, to a daily default fine.

[3245]

NOTES

Application to limited liability partnerships: see the introductory note to this Act and the Limited Liability Partnerships Regulations 2001, SI 2001/1090, reg 5, Sch 3 at **[6986]**, **[6995]**.

Modification in relation to Scotland: see the Note at the beginning of this Act.

90 Distinction between "members" ' and "creditors" ' voluntary winding up

A winding up in the case of which a directors' statutory declaration under section 89 has been made is a "members' voluntary winding up"; and a winding up in the case of which such a declaration has not been made is a "creditors' voluntary winding up".

[3246]

NOTES

Application to limited liability partnerships: see the introductory note to this Act and the Limited Liability Partnerships Regulations 2001, SI 2001/1090, reg 5, Sch 3 at **[6986]**, **[6995]**.

CHAPTER III
MEMBERS' VOLUNTARY WINDING UP

91 Appointment of liquidator

(1) In a members' voluntary winding up, the company in general meeting shall appoint one or more liquidators for the purpose of winding up the company's affairs and distributing its assets.

(2) On the appointment of a liquidator all the powers of the directors cease, except so far as the company in general meeting or the liquidator sanctions their continuance.

[3247]

NOTES

Application to limited liability partnerships: see the introductory note to this Act, the Limited Liability Partnerships Regulations 2001, SI 2001/1090, reg 5, Sch 3 at **[6986]**, **[6995]**, and the Limited Liability Partnerships (Scotland) Regulations 2001, SSI 2001/128, reg 4, Schs 2, 3 at **[6977]**, **[6980A]**, **[6980B]**.

92 Power to fill vacancy in office of liquidator

(1) If a vacancy occurs by death, resignation or otherwise in the office of liquidator appointed by the company, the company in general meeting may, subject to any arrangement with its creditors, fill the vacancy.

(2) For that purpose a general meeting may be convened by any contributory or, if there were more liquidators than one, by the continuing liquidators.

(3) The meeting shall be held in manner provided by this Act or by the articles, or in such manner as may, on application by any contributory or by the continuing liquidators, be determined by the court.

[3248]

NOTES

Application to limited liability partnerships: see the introductory note to this Act, the Limited Liability Partnerships Regulations 2001, SI 2001/1090, reg 5, Sch 3 at **[6986]**, **[6995]**, and the Limited Liability Partnerships (Scotland) Regulations 2001, SSI 2001/128, reg 4, Schs 2, 3 at **[6977]**, **[6980A]**, **[6980B]**.

Meeting held in manner provided by this Act: it is thought that the reference in sub-s (3) above to "this Act" should be a reference to CA 1985.

93 General company meeting at each year's end

(1) Subject to sections 96 and 102, in the event of the winding up continuing for more than one year, the liquidator shall summon a general meeting of the company at the end of the

first year from the commencement of the winding up, and of each succeeding year, or at the first convenient date within 3 months from the end of the year or such longer period as the Secretary of State may allow.

(2) The liquidator shall lay before the meeting an account of his acts and dealings, and of the conduct of the winding up, during the preceding year.

(3) If the liquidator fails to comply with this section, he is liable to a fine.

[3249]

NOTES

Application to limited liability partnerships: see the introductory note to this Act, the Limited Liability Partnerships Regulations 2001, SI 2001/1090, reg 5, Sch 3 at **[6986]**, **[6995]**, and the Limited Liability Partnerships (Scotland) Regulations 2001, SSI 2001/128, reg 4, Schs 2, 3 at **[6977]**, **[6980A]**, **[6980B]**.

94 Final meeting prior to dissolution

(1) As soon as the company's affairs are fully wound up, the liquidator shall make up an account of the winding up, showing how it has been conducted and the company's property has been disposed of, and thereupon shall call a general meeting of the company for the purpose of laying before it the account, and giving an explanation of it.

(2) The meeting shall be called by advertisement in the Gazette, specifying its time, place and object and published at least one month before the meeting.

(3) Within one week after the meeting, the liquidator shall send to the registrar of companies a copy of the account, and shall make a return to him of the holding of the meeting and of its date.

(4) If the copy is not sent or the return is not made in accordance with subsection (3), the liquidator is liable to a fine and, for continued contravention, to a daily default fine.

(5) If a quorum is not present at the meeting, the liquidator shall, in lieu of the return mentioned above, make a return that the meeting was duly summoned and that no quorum was present; and upon such a return being made, the provisions of subsection (3) as to the making of the return are deemed complied with.

(6) If the liquidator fails to call a general meeting of the company as required by subsection (1), he is liable to a fine.

[3250]

NOTES

Application to limited liability partnerships: see the introductory note to this Act, the Limited Liability Partnerships Regulations 2001, SI 2001/1090, reg 5, Sch 3 at **[6986]**, **[6995]**, and the Limited Liability Partnerships (Scotland) Regulations 2001, SSI 2001/128, reg 4, Schs 2, 3 at **[6977]**, **[6980A]**, **[6980B]**.

Modification in relation to Scotland: see the Note at the beginning of this Act.

95 Effect of company's insolvency

(1) This section applies where the liquidator is of the opinion that the company will be unable to pay its debts in full (together with interest at the official rate) within the period stated in the directors' declaration under section 89.

(2) The liquidator shall—

- (a) summon a meeting of creditors for a day not later than the 28th day after the day on which he formed that opinion;
- (b) send notices of the creditors' meeting to the creditors by post not less than 7 days before the day on which that meeting is to be held;
- (c) cause notice of the creditors' meeting to be advertised once in the Gazette and once at least in 2 newspapers circulating in the relevant locality (that is to say the locality in which the company's principal place of business in Great Britain was situated during the relevant period); and
- (d) during the period before the day on which the creditors' meeting is to be held, furnish creditors free of charge with such information concerning the affairs of the company as they may reasonably require;

and the notice of the creditors' meeting shall state the duty imposed by paragraph (d) above.

(3) The liquidator shall also—

(a) make out a statement in the prescribed form as to the affairs of the company;
(b) lay that statement before the creditors' meeting; and
(c) attend and preside at that meeting.

(4) The statement as to the affairs of the company shall be verified by affidavit by the liquidator and shall show—

(a) particulars of the company's assets, debts and liabilities;
(b) the names and addresses of the company's creditors;
(c) the securities held by them respectively;
(d) the dates when the securities were respectively given; and
(e) such further or other information as may be prescribed.

(5) Where the company's principal place of business in Great Britain was situated in different localities at different times during the relevant period, the duty imposed by subsection (2)(c) applies separately in relation to each of those localities.

(6) Where the company had no place of business in Great Britain during the relevant period, references in subsections (2)(c) and (5) to the company's principal place of business in Great Britain are replaced by references to its registered office.

(7) In this section "the relevant period" means the period of 6 months immediately preceding the day on which were sent the notices summoning the company meeting at which it was resolved that the company be wound up voluntarily.

(8) If the liquidator without reasonable excuse fails to comply with this section, he is liable to a fine.

[3251]

NOTES

Application to limited liability partnerships: see the introductory note to this Act, the Limited Liability Partnerships Regulations 2001, SI 2001/1090, reg 5, Sch 3 at **[6986]**, **[6995]**, and the Limited Liability Partnerships (Scotland) Regulations 2001, SSI 2001/128, reg 4, Schs 2, 3 at **[6977]**, **[6980A]**, **[6980B]**.

96 Conversion to creditors' voluntary winding up

As from the day on which the creditors' meeting is held under section 95, this Act has effect as if—

(a) the directors' declaration under section 89 had not been made; and
(b) the creditors' meeting and the company meeting at which it was resolved that the company be wound up voluntarily were the meetings mentioned in section 98 in the next Chapter;

and accordingly the winding up becomes a creditors' voluntary winding up.

[3252]

NOTES

Application to limited liability partnerships: see the introductory note to this Act and the Limited Liability Partnerships Regulations 2001, SI 2001/1090, reg 5, Sch 3 at **[6986]**, **[6995]**.

CHAPTER IV
CREDITORS' VOLUNTARY WINDING UP

97 Application of this Chapter

(1) Subject as follows, this Chapter applies in relation to a creditors' voluntary winding up.

(2) Sections 98 and 99 do not apply where, under section 96 in Chapter III, a members' voluntary winding up has become a creditors' voluntary winding up.

[3253]

NOTES

Application to limited liability partnerships: see the introductory note to this Act, the Limited Liability Partnerships Regulations 2001, SI 2001/1090, reg 5, Sch 3 at **[6986]**, **[6995]**, and the Limited Liability Partnerships (Scotland) Regulations 2001, SSI 2001/128, reg 4, Schs 2, 3 at **[6977]**, **[6980A]**, **[6980B]**.

98 Meeting of creditors

(1) The company shall—

(a) cause a meeting of its creditors to be summoned for a day not later than the 14th day after the day on which there is to be held the company meeting at which the resolution for voluntary winding up is to be proposed;

(b) cause the notices of the creditors' meeting to be sent by post to the creditors not less than 7 days before the day on which that meeting is to be held; and

(c) cause notice of the creditors' meeting to be advertised once in the Gazette and once at least in two newspapers circulating in the relevant locality (that is to say the locality in which the company's principal place of business in Great Britain was situated during the relevant period).

(2) The notice of the creditors' meeting shall state either—

(a) the name and address of a person qualified to act as an insolvency practitioner in relation to the company who, during the period before the day on which that meeting is to be held, will furnish creditors free of charge with such information concerning the company's affairs as they may reasonably require; or

(b) a place in the relevant locality where, on the two business days falling next before the day on which that meeting is to be held, a list of the names and addresses of the company's creditors will be available for inspection free of charge.

(3) Where the company's principal place of business in Great Britain was situated in different localities at different times during the relevant period, the duties imposed by subsections (1)(c) and (2)(b) above apply separately in relation to each of those localities.

(4) Where the company had no place of business in Great Britain during the relevant period, references in subsections (1)(c) and (3) to the company's principal place of business in Great Britain are replaced by references to its registered office.

(5) In this section "the relevant period" means the period of 6 months immediately preceding the day on which were sent the notices summoning the company meeting at which it was resolved that the company be wound up voluntarily.

(6) If the company without reasonable excuse fails to comply with subsection (1) or (2), it is guilty of an offence and liable to a fine.

[3254]

NOTES

Application to limited liability partnerships: see the introductory note to this Act and the Limited Liability Partnerships Regulations 2001, SI 2001/1090, reg 5, Sch 3 at **[6986]**, **[6995]**.

99 Directors to lay statement of affairs before creditors

(1) The directors of the company shall—

(a) make out a statement in the prescribed form as to the affairs of the company;

(b) cause that statement to be laid before the creditors' meeting under section 98; and

(c) appoint one of their number to preside at that meeting;

and it is the duty of the director so appointed to attend the meeting and preside over it.

(2) The statement as to the affairs of the company shall be verified by affidavit by some or all of the directors and shall show—

(a) particulars of the company's assets, debts and liabilities;

(b) the names and addresses of the company's creditors;

(c) the securities held by them respectively;

(d) the dates when the securities were respectively given; and

(e) such further or other information as may be prescribed.

(3) If—

(a) the directors without reasonable excuse fail to comply with subsection (1) or (2); or

(b) any director without reasonable excuse fails to comply with subsection (1), so far as requiring him to attend and preside at the creditors' meeting,

the directors are or (as the case may be) the director is guilty of an offence and liable to a fine.

[3255]

NOTES

Application to limited liability partnerships: see the introductory note to this Act and the Limited Liability Partnerships Regulations 2001, SI 2001/1090, reg 5, Sch 3 at **[6986]**, **[6995]**.

100 Appointment of liquidator

(1) The creditors and the company at their respective meetings mentioned in section 98 may nominate a person to be liquidator for the purpose of winding up the company's affairs and distributing its assets.

(2) The liquidator shall be the person nominated by the creditors or, where no person has been so nominated, the person (if any) nominated by the company.

(3) In the case of different persons being nominated, any director, member or creditor of the company may, within 7 days after the date on which the nomination was made by the creditors, apply to the court for an order either—

(a) directing that the person nominated as liquidator by the company shall be liquidator instead of or jointly with the person nominated by the creditors, or

(b) appointing some other person to be liquidator instead of the person nominated by the creditors.

[(4) The court shall grant an application under subsection (3) made by the holder of a qualifying floating charge in respect of the company's property (within the meaning of paragraph 14 of Schedule B1) unless the court thinks it right to refuse the application because of the particular circumstances of the case.]

[3256]

NOTES

Sub-s (4): added by the Enterprise Act 2002, s 248(3), Sch 17, paras 9, 14, as from a day to be appointed (for savings and transitional provisions, see the note to s 8 at **[3164]**).

Application to limited liability partnerships: see the introductory note to this Act, the Limited Liability Partnerships Regulations 2001, SI 2001/1090, reg 5, Sch 3 at **[6986]**, **[6995]**, and the Limited Liability Partnerships (Scotland) Regulations 2001, SSI 2001/128, reg 4, Schs 2, 3 at **[6977]**, **[6980A]**, **[6980B]**.

101 Appointment of liquidation committee

(1) The creditors at the meeting to be held under section 98 or at any subsequent meeting may, if they think fit, appoint a committee ("the liquidation committee") of not more than 5 persons to exercise the functions conferred on it by or under this Act.

(2) If such a committee is appointed, the company may, either at the meeting at which the resolution for voluntary winding up is passed or at any time subsequently in general meeting, appoint such number of persons as they think fit to act as members of the committee, not exceeding 5.

(3) However, the creditors may, if they think fit, resolve that all or any of the persons so appointed by the company ought not to be members of the liquidation committee; and if the creditors so resolve—

(a) the persons mentioned in the resolution are not then, unless the court otherwise directs, qualified to act as members of the committee; and

(b) on any application to the court under this provision the court may, if it thinks fit, appoint other persons to act as such members in place of the persons mentioned in the resolution.

(4) In Scotland, the liquidation committee has, in addition to the powers and duties conferred and imposed on it by this Act, such of the powers and duties of commissioners on a bankrupt estate as may be conferred and imposed on liquidation committees by the rules.

[3257]

NOTES

Application to limited liability partnerships: see the introductory note to this Act, the Limited Liability Partnerships Regulations 2001, SI 2001/1090, reg 5, Sch 3 at **[6986]**, **[6995]**, and the Limited Liability Partnerships (Scotland) Regulations 2001, SSI 2001/128, reg 4, Schs 2, 3 at **[6977]**, **[6980A]**, **[6980B]**.

102 Creditors' meeting where winding up converted under s 96

Where, in the case of a winding up which was, under section 96 in Chapter III, converted to a creditors' voluntary winding up, a creditors' meeting is held in accordance with section 95, any appointment made or committee established by that meeting is deemed to have been made or established by a meeting held in accordance with section 98 in this Chapter.

[3258]

NOTES

Application to limited liability partnerships: see the introductory note to this Act, the Limited Liability Partnerships Regulations 2001, SI 2001/1090, reg 5, Sch 3 at **[6986]**, **[6995]**, and the Limited Liability Partnerships (Scotland) Regulations 2001, SSI 2001/128, reg 4, Schs 2, 3 at **[6977]**, **[6980A]**, **[6980B]**.

103 Cesser of directors' powers

On the appointment of a liquidator, all the powers of the directors cease, except so far as the liquidation committee (or, if there is no such committee, the creditors) sanction their continuance.

[3259]

NOTES

Application to limited liability partnerships: see the introductory note to this Act and the Limited Liability Partnerships Regulations 2001, SI 2001/1090, reg 5, Sch 3 at **[6986]**, **[6995]**.

104 Vacancy in office of liquidator

If a vacancy occurs, by death, resignation or otherwise, in the office of a liquidator (other than a liquidator appointed by, or by the direction of, the court), the creditors may fill the vacancy.

[3260]

NOTES

Application to limited liability partnerships: see the introductory note to this Act, the Limited Liability Partnerships Regulations 2001, SI 2001/1090, reg 5, Sch 3 at **[6986]**, **[6995]**, and the Limited Liability Partnerships (Scotland) Regulations 2001, SSI 2001/128, reg 4, Schs 2, 3 at **[6977]**, **[6980A]**, **[6980B]**.

105 Meetings of company and creditors at each year's end

(1) If the winding up continues for more than one year, the liquidator shall summon a general meeting of the company and a meeting of the creditors at the end of the first year from the commencement of the winding up, and of each succeeding year, or at the first convenient date within 3 months from the end of the year or such longer period as the Secretary of State may allow.

(2) The liquidator shall lay before each of the meetings an account of his acts and dealings and of the conduct of the winding up during the preceding year.

(3) If the liquidator fails to comply with this section, he is liable to a fine.

(4) Where under section 96 a members' voluntary winding up has become a creditors' voluntary winding up, and the creditors' meeting under section 95 is held 3 months or less before the end of the first year from the commencement of the winding up, the liquidator is not required by this section to summon a meeting of creditors at the end of that year.

[3261]

NOTES

Application to limited liability partnerships: see the introductory note to this Act, the Limited Liability Partnerships Regulations 2001, SI 2001/1090, reg 5, Sch 3 at **[6986]**, **[6995]**, and the Limited Liability Partnerships (Scotland) Regulations 2001, SSI 2001/128, reg 4, Schs 2, 3 at **[6977]**, **[6980A]**, **[6980B]**.

106 Final meeting prior to dissolution

(1) As soon as the company's affairs are fully wound up, the liquidator shall make up an account of the winding up, showing how it has been conducted and the company's property has been disposed of, and thereupon shall call a general meeting of the company and a meeting of the creditors for the purpose of laying the account before the meetings and giving an explanation of it.

(2) Each such meeting shall be called by advertisement in the Gazette specifying the time, place and object of the meeting, and published at least one month before it.

(3) Within one week after the date of the meetings (or, if they are not held on the same date, after the date on the later one) the liquidator shall send to the registrar of companies a copy of the account, and shall make a return to him of the holding of the meetings and of their dates.

(4) If the copy is not sent or the return is not made in accordance with subsection (3), the liquidator is liable to a fine and, for continued contravention, to a daily default fine.

(5) However, if a quorum is not present at either such meeting, the liquidator shall, in lieu of the return required by subsection (3), make a return that the meeting was duly summoned and that no quorum was present; and upon such return being made the provisions of that subsection as to the making of the return are, in respect of that meeting, deemed complied with.

(6) If the liquidator fails to call a general meeting of the company or a meeting of the creditors as required by this section, he is liable to a fine.

[3262]

NOTES

Application to limited liability partnerships: see the introductory note to this Act, the Limited Liability Partnerships Regulations 2001, SI 2001/1090, reg 5, Sch 3 at **[6986]**, **[6995]**, and the Limited Liability Partnerships (Scotland) Regulations 2001, SSI 2001/128, reg 4, Schs 2, 3 at **[6977]**, **[6980A]**, **[6980B]**.

Modification in relation to Scotland: see the Note at the beginning of this Act.

CHAPTER V
PROVISIONS APPLYING TO BOTH KINDS OF VOLUNTARY WINDING UP

107 Distribution of company's property

Subject to the provisions of this Act as to preferential payments, the company's property in a voluntary winding up shall on the winding up be applied in satisfaction of the company's liabilities pari passu and, subject to that application, shall (unless the articles otherwise provide) be distributed among the members according to their rights and interests in the company.

[3263]

NOTES

Application to limited liability partnerships: see the introductory note to this Act and the Limited Liability Partnerships Regulations 2001, SI 2001/1090, reg 5, Sch 3 at **[6986]**, **[6995]**.

108 Appointment or removal of liquidator by the court

(1) If from any cause whatever there is no liquidator acting, the court may appoint a liquidator.

(2) The court may, on cause shown, remove a liquidator and appoint another.

[3264]

NOTES

Application to limited liability partnerships: see the introductory note to this Act and the Limited Liability Partnerships Regulations 2001, SI 2001/1090, reg 5, Sch 3 at **[6986]**, **[6995]**.

109 Notice by liquidator of his appointment

(1) The liquidator shall, within 14 days after his appointment, publish in the Gazette and deliver to the registrar of companies for registration a notice of his appointment in the form prescribed by statutory instrument made by the Secretary of State.

(2) If the liquidator fails to comply with this section, he is liable to a fine and, for continued contravention, to a daily default fine.

[3265]

NOTES

Application to limited liability partnerships: see the introductory note to this Act, the Limited Liability Partnerships Regulations 2001, SI 2001/1090, reg 5, Sch 3 at **[6986]**, **[6995]**, and the Limited Liability Partnerships (Scotland) Regulations 2001, SSI 2001/128, reg 4, Schs 2, 3 at **[6977]**, **[6980A]**, **[6980B]**.

Modification in relation to Scotland: see the Note at the beginning of this Act.

Deliver to the registrar of companies: the Accountant in Bankruptcy in Scotland must forward copies of notices of the appointment of a liquidator of a community interest company to the Regulator of Community Interest Companies (since in Scotland such notices are received by the Accountant in Bankruptcy and not the registrar of companies); see the Bankruptcy (Scotland) Act 1985, s 71A (as inserted by the Companies (Audit, Investigations and Community Enterprise) Act 2004, s 59(2)

Prescribed form: see Appendix 4 at **[A4]**.

110 Acceptance of shares, etc, as consideration for sale of company property

(1) This section applies, in the case of a company proposed to be, or being, wound up voluntarily, where the whole or part of the company's business or property is proposed to be transferred or sold

[(a)] to another company ("the transferee company"), whether or not the latter is a company within the meaning of the Companies Act[, or

(b) to a limited liability partnership (the "transferee limited liability partnership")].

(2) With the requisite sanction, the liquidator of the company being, or proposed to be, wound up ("the transferor company") may receive, in compensation or part compensation for the transfer or [sale—

(a) in the case of the transferee company, shares, policies or other like interests in the company for distribution among the members of the transferor company, or

(b) in the case of the transferee limited liability partnership, membership in the limited liability partnership for distribution among the members of the transferor company.]

(3) The sanction requisite under subsection (2) is—

(a) in the case of a members' voluntary winding up, that of a special resolution of the company, conferring either a general authority on the liquidator or an authority in respect of any particular arrangement, and

(b) in the case of a creditors' voluntary winding up, that of either the court or the liquidation committee.

(4) Alternatively to subsection (2), the liquidator may (with that sanction) enter into any other arrangement whereby the members of the transferor company [may—

(a) in the case of the transferee company, in lieu of receiving cash, shares, policies or other like interests (or in addition thereto) participate in the profits of, or receive any other benefit from, the company, or

(b) in the case of the transferee limited liability partnership, in lieu of receiving cash, or membership (or in addition thereto) participate in some other way in the profits of, or receive any other benefit from, the limited liability partnership.]

(5) A sale or arrangement in pursuance of this section is binding on members of the transferor company.

(6) A special resolution is not invalid for purposes of this section by reason that it is passed before or concurrently with a resolution for voluntary winding up or for appointing liquidators; but, if an order is made within a year for winding up the company by the court, the special resolution is not valid unless sanctioned by the court.

[3266]

NOTES

Sub-s (1): words in square brackets inserted, in relation to England and Wales, by the Limited Liability Partnerships Regulations 2001, SI 2001/1090, reg 9, Sch 5, para 15(1), (2), as from 6 April 2001, and in relation to Scotland, by the Limited Liability Partnerships (Scotland) Regulations 2001, SSI 2001/128, reg 5, Sch 4, para 1(1), (2), as from 6 April 2001.

Sub-ss (2), (4): words in square brackets substituted, in relation to England and Wales, by SI 2001/1090, reg 9, Sch 5, para 15(1), (3), (4), as from 6 April 2001, and in relation to Scotland, by SSI 2001/128, reg 5, Sch 4, para 1(1), (3), (4), as from 6 April 2001.

Application to limited liability partnerships: see the introductory note to this Act, the Limited Liability Partnerships Regulations 2001, SI 2001/1090, reg 5, Sch 3 at **[6986]**, **[6995]**, and the Limited Liability Partnerships (Scotland) Regulations 2001, SSI 2001/128, reg 4, Schs 2, 3 at **[6977]**, **[6980A]**, **[6980B]**.

111 Dissent from arrangement under s 110

(1) This section applies in the case of a voluntary winding up where, for the purposes of section 110(2) or (4), there has been passed a special resolution of the transferor company providing the sanction requisite for the liquidator under that section.

(2) If a member of the transferor company who did not vote in favour of the special resolution expresses his dissent from it in writing, addressed to the liquidator and left at the company's registered office within 7 days after the passing of the resolution, he may require the liquidator either to abstain from carrying the resolution into effect or to purchase his interest at a price to be determined by agreement or by arbitration under this section.

(3) If the liquidator elects to purchase the member's interest, the purchase money must be paid before the company is dissolved and be raised by the liquidator in such manner as may be determined by special resolution.

(4) For purposes of an arbitration under this section, the provisions of the Companies Clauses Consolidation Act 1845 or, in the case of a winding up in Scotland, the Companies Clauses Consolidation (Scotland) Act 1845 with respect to the settlement of disputes by arbitration are incorporated with this Act, and—

(a) in the construction of those provisions this Act is deemed the special Act and "the company" means the transferor company, and

(b) any appointment by the incorporated provisions directed to be made under the hand of the secretary or any two of the directors may be made in writing by the liquidator (or, if there is more than one liquidator, then any two or more of them).

[3267]

NOTES

Application to limited liability partnerships: see the introductory note to this Act, the Limited Liability Partnerships Regulations 2001, SI 2001/1090, reg 5, Sch 3 at **[6986]**, **[6995]**, and the Limited Liability Partnerships (Scotland) Regulations 2001, SSI 2001/128, reg 4, Schs 2, 3 at **[6977]**, **[6980A]**, **[6980B]**.

112 Reference of questions to court

(1) The liquidator or any contributory or creditor may apply to the court to determine any question arising in the winding up of a company, or to exercise, as respects the enforcing of calls or any other matter, all or any of the powers which the court might exercise if the company were being wound up by the court.

(2) The court, if satisfied that the determination of the question or the required exercise of power will be just and beneficial, may accede wholly or partially to the application on such terms and conditions as it thinks fit, or may make such other order on the application as it thinks just.

(3) A copy of an order made by virtue of this section staying the proceedings in the winding up shall forthwith be forwarded by the company, or otherwise as may be prescribed, to the registrar of companies, who shall enter it in his records relating to the company.

[3268]

NOTES

Application to limited liability partnerships: see the introductory note to this Act, the Limited Liability Partnerships Regulations 2001, SI 2001/1090, reg 5, Sch 3 at **[6986]**, **[6995]**, and the Limited Liability Partnerships (Scotland) Regulations 2001, SSI 2001/128, reg 4, Schs 2, 3 at **[6977]**, **[6980A]**, **[6980B]**.

Modification in relation to Scotland: see the Note at the beginning of this Act.

113 Court's power to control proceedings (Scotland)

If the court, on the application of the liquidator in the winding up of a company registered in Scotland, so directs, no action or proceeding shall be proceeded with or commenced against the company except by leave of the court and subject to such terms as the court may impose.

[3269]

NOTES

Application to limited liability partnerships: see the introductory note to this Act, the Limited Liability Partnerships Regulations 2001, SI 2001/1090, reg 5, Sch 3 at **[6986]**, **[6995]**, and the Limited Liability Partnerships (Scotland) Regulations 2001, SSI 2001/128, reg 4, Schs 2, 3 at **[6977]**, **[6980A]**, **[6980B]**.

114 No liquidator appointed or nominated by company

(1) This section applies where, in the case of a voluntary winding up, no liquidator has been appointed or nominated by the company.

(2) The powers of the directors shall not be exercised, except with the sanction of the court or (in the case of a creditors' voluntary winding up) so far as may be necessary to secure compliance with sections 98 (creditors' meeting) and 99 (statement of affairs), during the period before the appointment or nomination of a liquidator of the company.

(3) Subsection (2) does not apply in relation to the powers of the directors—

(a) to dispose of perishable goods and other goods the value of which is likely to diminish if they are not immediately disposed of, and

(b) to do all such other things as may be necessary for the protection of the company's assets.

(4) If the directors of the company without reasonable excuse fail to comply with this section, they are liable to a fine.

[3270]

NOTES

Application to limited liability partnerships: see the introductory note to this Act, the Limited Liability Partnerships Regulations 2001, SI 2001/1090, reg 5, Sch 3 at **[6986]**, **[6995]**, and the Limited Liability Partnerships (Scotland) Regulations 2001, SSI 2001/128, reg 4, Schs 2, 3 at **[6977]**, **[6980A]**, **[6980B]**.

115 Expenses of voluntary winding up

All expenses properly incurred in the winding up, including the remuneration of the liquidator, are payable out of the company's assets in priority to all other claims.

[3271]

NOTES

Application to limited liability partnerships: see the introductory note to this Act, the Limited Liability Partnerships Regulations 2001, SI 2001/1090, reg 5, Sch 3 at **[6986]**, **[6995]**, and the Limited Liability Partnerships (Scotland) Regulations 2001, SSI 2001/128, reg 4, Schs 2, 3 at **[6977]**, **[6980A]**, **[6980B]**.

116 Saving for certain rights

The voluntary winding up of a company does not bar the right of any creditor or contributory to have it wound up by the court; but in the case of an application by a contributory the court must be satisfied that the rights of the contributories will be prejudiced by a voluntary winding up.

[3272]

NOTES

Application to limited liability partnerships: see the introductory note to this Act and the Limited Liability Partnerships Regulations 2001, SI 2001/1090, reg 5, Sch 3 at **[6986]**, **[6995]**.

CHAPTER VI
WINDING UP BY THE COURT

Jurisdiction (England and Wales)

117 High Court and county court jurisdiction

(1) The High Court has jurisdiction to wind up any company registered in England and Wales.

(2) Where the amount of a company's share capital paid up or credited as paid up does not exceed £120,000, then (subject to this section) the county court of the district in which the company's registered office is situated has concurrent jurisdiction with the High Court to wind up the company.

(3) The money sum for the time being specified in subsection (2) is subject to increase or reduction by order under section 416 in Part XV.

(4) The Lord Chancellor [may, with the concurrence of the Lord Chief Justice, by order] in a statutory instrument exclude a county court from having winding-up jurisdiction, and for the purposes of that jurisdiction may attach its district, or any part thereof, to any other county court, and may by statutory instrument revoke or vary any such order.

In exercising the powers of this section, the Lord Chancellor shall provide that a county court is not to have winding-up jurisdiction unless it has for the time being jurisdiction for the purposes of Parts VIII to XI of this Act (individual insolvency).

(5) Every court in England and Wales having winding-up jurisdiction has for the purposes of that jurisdiction all the powers of the High Court; and every prescribed officer of the court shall perform any duties which an officer of the High Court may discharge by order of a judge of that court or otherwise in relation to winding up.

(6) For the purposes of this section, a company's "registered office" is the place which has longest been its registered office during the 6 months immediately preceding the presentation of the petition for winding up.

[(7) This section is subject to Article 3 of the EC Regulation (jurisdiction under EC Regulation).]

[(8) The Lord Chief Justice may nominate a judicial office holder (as defined in section 109(4) of the Constitutional Reform Act 2005) to exercise his functions under this section.]

[3273]

NOTES

Sub-s (4): words in square brackets substituted by the Constitutional Reform Act 2005, s 15, Sch 4, Pt 1, paras 185, 186(1), (2), as from 3 April 2006.

Sub-s (7): added by the Insolvency Act 1986 (Amendment) (No 2) Regulations 2002, SI 2002/1240, regs 3, 6, as from 31 May 2002.

Sub-s (8): added by the Constitutional Reform Act 2005, s 15, Sch 4, Pt 1, paras 185, 186(1), (3), as from 3 April 2006.

Application to limited liability partnerships: see the introductory note to this Act and the Limited Liability Partnerships Regulations 2001, SI 2001/1090, reg 5, Sch 3 at **[6986]**, **[6995]**.

Orders: the Civil Courts Order 1983, SI 1983/713.

118 Proceedings taken in wrong court

(1) Nothing in section 117 invalidates a proceeding by reason of its being taken in the wrong court.

(2) The winding up of a company by the court in England and Wales, or any proceedings in the winding up, may be retained in the court in which the proceedings were commenced, although it may not be the court in which they ought to have been commenced.

[3274]

NOTES

Application to limited liability partnerships: see the introductory note to this Act and the Limited Liability Partnerships Regulations 2001, SI 2001/1090, reg 5, Sch 3 at **[6986]**, **[6995]**.

119 Proceedings in county court; case stated for High Court

(1) If any question arises in any winding-up proceedings in a county court which all the parties to the proceedings, or which one of them and the judge of the court, desire to have determined in the first instance in the High Court, the judge shall state the facts in the form of a special case for the opinion of the High Court.

(2) Thereupon the special case and the proceedings (or such of them as may be required) shall be transmitted to the High Court for the purposes of the determination.

[3275]

NOTES

Application to limited liability partnerships: see the introductory note to this Act and the Limited Liability Partnerships Regulations 2001, SI 2001/1090, reg 5, Sch 3 at **[6986]**, **[6995]**.

Jurisdiction (Scotland)

120 Court of Session and sheriff court jurisdiction

(1) The Court of Session has jurisdiction to wind up any company registered in Scotland.

(2) When the Court of Session is in vacation, the jurisdiction conferred on that court by this section may (subject to the provisions of this Part) be exercised by the judge acting as vacation judge …

(3) Where the amount of a company's share capital paid up or credited as paid up does not exceed £120,000, the sheriff court of the sheriffdom in which the company's registered office is situated has concurrent jurisdiction with the Court of Session to wind up the company; but—

(a) the Court of Session may, if it thinks expedient having regard to the amount of the company's assets to do so—

(i) remit to a sheriff court any petition presented to the Court of Session for winding up such a company, or

(ii) require such a petition presented to a sheriff court to be remitted to the Court of Session; and

(b) the Court of Session may require any such petition as above-mentioned presented to one sheriff court to be remitted to another sheriff court; and

(c) in a winding up in the sheriff court the sheriff may submit a stated case for the opinion of the Court of Session on any question of law arising in that winding up.

(4) For purposes of this section, the expression "registered office" means the place which has longest been the company's registered office during the 6 months immediately preceding the presentation of the petition for winding up.

(5) The money sum for the time being specified in subsection (3) is subject to increase or reduction by order under section 416 in Part XV.

[(6) This section is subject to Article 3 of the EC Regulation (jurisdiction under EC Regulation).]

[3276]

NOTES

Sub-s (2): words omitted repealed by the Court of Session Act 1988, s 52(2), Sch 2, Pt III, as from 29 September 1988.

Sub-s (6): added by the Insolvency Act 1986 (Amendment) (No 2) Regulations 2002, SI 2002/1240, regs 3, 7, as from 31 May 2002.

Application to limited liability partnerships: see the introductory note to this Act and the Limited Liability Partnerships Regulations 2001, SI 2001/1090, reg 5, Sch 3 at **[6986]**, **[6995]**.

121 Power to remit winding up to Lord Ordinary

(1) The Court of Session may, by Act of Sederunt, make provision for the taking of proceedings in a winding up before one of the Lords Ordinary; and, where provision is so made, the Lord Ordinary has, for the purposes of the winding up, all the powers and jurisdiction of the court.

(2) However, the Lord Ordinary may report to the Inner House any matter which may arise in the course of a winding up.

[3277]

NOTES

Application to limited liability partnerships: see the introductory note to this Act and the Limited Liability Partnerships Regulations 2001, SI 2001/1090, reg 5, Sch 3 at **[6986]**, **[6995]**.

Grounds and effect of winding-up petition

122 Circumstances in which company may be wound up by the court

(1) A company may be wound up by the court if—

(a) the company has by special resolution resolved that the company be wound up by the court,

(b) being a public company which was registered as such on its original incorporation, the company has not been issued with a certificate under section 117 of the Companies Act (public company share capital requirements) and more than a year has expired since it was so registered,

(c) it is an old public company, within the meaning of the Consequential Provisions Act,

(d) the company does not commence its business within a year from its incorporation or suspends its business for a whole year,

(e) [except in the case of a private company limited by shares or by guarantee,] the number of members is reduced below 2,

(f) the company is unable to pay its debts,

[(fa) at the time at which a moratorium for the company under section 1A comes to an end, no voluntary arrangement approved under Part I has effect in relation to the company]

(g) the court is of the opinion that it is just and equitable that the company should be wound up.

(2) In Scotland, a company which the Court of Session has jurisdiction to wind up may be wound up by the Court if there is subsisting a floating charge over property comprised in the company's property and undertaking, and the court is satisfied that the security of the creditor entitled to the benefit of the floating charge is in jeopardy.

For this purpose a creditor's security is deemed to be in jeopardy if the Court is satisfied that events have occurred or are about to occur which render it unreasonable in the creditor's interests that the company should retain power to dispose of the property which is subject to the floating charge.

[3278]

NOTES

Sub-s (1): words in square brackets in para (e) inserted by the Companies (Single Member Private Limited Companies) Regulations 1992, SI 1992/1699, reg 2, Schedule, para 8, as from 15 July 1992; para (fa) inserted by the Insolvency Act 2000, s 1, Sch 1, paras 1, 6, as from 1 January 2003.

Application to limited liability partnerships: see the introductory note to this Act and the Limited Liability Partnerships Regulations 2001, SI 2001/1090, reg 5, Sch 3 at **[6986]**, **[6995]**.

123 Definition of inability to pay debts

(1) A company is deemed unable to pay its debts—

(a) if a creditor (by assignment or otherwise) to whom the company is indebted in a sum exceeding £750 then due has served on the company, by leaving it at the company's registered office, a written demand (in the prescribed form) requiring the company to pay the sum so due and the company has for 3 weeks thereafter neglected to pay the sum or to secure or compound for it to the reasonable satisfaction of the creditor, or

(b) if, in England and Wales, execution or other process issued on a judgment, decree or order of any court in favour of a creditor of the company is returned unsatisfied in whole or in part, or

(c) if, in Scotland, the induciae of a charge for payment on an extract decree, or an extract registered bond, or an extract registered protest, have expired without payment being made, or

(d) if, in Northern Ireland, a certificate of unenforceability has been granted in respect of a judgment against the company, or

(e) if it is proved to the satisfaction of the court that the company is unable to pay its debts as they fall due.

(2) A company is also deemed unable to pay its debts if it is proved to the satisfaction of the court that the value of the company's assets is less than the amount of its liabilities, taking into account its contingent and prospective liabilities.

(3) The money sum for the time being specified in subsection (1)(a) is subject to increase or reduction by order under section 416 in Part XV.

[3279]

NOTES

Application to limited liability partnerships: see the introductory note to this Act and the Limited Liability Partnerships Regulations 2001, SI 2001/1090, reg 5, Sch 3 at **[6986]**, **[6995]**.

124 Application for winding up

(1) Subject to the provisions of this section, an application to the court for the winding up of a company shall be by petition presented either by the company, or the directors, or by any creditor or creditors (including any contingent or prospective creditor or creditors), contributory or contributories[, or by a liquidator (within the meaning of Article 2(b) of the EC Regulation) appointed in proceedings by virtue of Article 3(1) of the EC Regulation or a temporary administrator (within the meaning of Article 38 of the EC Regulation)] [or by [the designated officer for a magistrates' court] in the exercise of the power conferred by section 87A of the Magistrates' Courts Act 1980 (enforcement of fines imposed on companies)], or by all or any of those parties, together or separately.

(2) Except as mentioned below, a contributory is not entitled to present a winding-up petition unless either—

(a) the number of members is reduced below 2, or

(b) the shares in respect of which he is a contributory, or some of them, either were originally allotted to him, or have been held by him, and registered in his name, for at least 6 months during the 18 months before the commencement of the winding up, or have devolved on him through the death of a former holder.

(3) A person who is liable under section 76 to contribute to a company's assets in the event of its being wound up may petition on either of the grounds set out in section 122(1)(f) and (g), and subsection (2) above does not then apply; but unless the person is a contributory otherwise than under section 76, he may not in his character as contributory petition on any other ground.

This subsection is deemed included in Chapter VII of Part V of the Companies Act (redeemable shares; purchase by a company of its own shares) for the purposes of the Secretary of State's power to make regulations under section 179 of that Act.

[(3A) A winding-up petition on the ground set out in section 122(1)(fa) may only be presented by one or more creditors.]

(4) A winding-up petition may be presented by the Secretary of State—

(a) if the ground of the petition is that in section 122(1)(b) or (c), or

[(b) in a case falling within section 124A [or 124B] below.]

[(4AA) A winding up petition may be presented by the Financial Services Authority in a case falling within section 124C(1) or (2).]

[(4A) A winding-up petition may be presented by the Regulator of Community Interest Companies in a case falling within section 50 of the Companies (Audit, Investigations and Community Enterprise) Act 2004.]

(5) Where a company is being wound up voluntarily in England and Wales, a winding-up petition may be presented by the official receiver attached to the court as well as by any other person authorised in that behalf under the other provisions of this section; but the court shall not make a winding-up order on the petition unless it is satisfied that the voluntary winding up cannot be continued with due regard to the interests of the creditors or contributories.

[3280]

NOTES

Sub-s (1): words in first pair of square brackets inserted by the Insolvency Act 1986 (Amendment) (No 2) Regulations 2002, SI 2002/1240, regs 3, 8, as from 31 May 2002; words in second (outer) pair of square brackets inserted by the Criminal Justice Act 1988, s 62(2)(b), as from 5 January 1989; words in third (inner) pair of square brackets substituted by the Courts Act 2003, s 109(1), Sch 8, para 294, as from 1 April 2005 (for transitional provisions and savings in connection with the commencement of the Courts Act 2003 and the continuity of functions, etc, see SI 2005/911).

Sub-s (3A): inserted by the Insolvency Act 2000, s 1, Sch 1, paras 1, 7, as from 1 January 2003.

Sub-s (4): para (b) substituted by CA 1989, s 60(2), as from 21 February 1990; words in square brackets in para (b) inserted by the European Public Limited-Liability Company Regulations 2004, SI 2004/2326, reg 73(4)(a), as from 8 October 2004.

Sub-s (4AA): inserted by the European Cooperative Society Regulations 2006, SI 2006/22078, reg 33(2), as from 18 August 2006.

Sub-s (4A): inserted by the Companies (Audit, Investigations and Community Enterprise) Act 2004, s 50(3), as from 1 July 2005.

Application to limited liability partnerships: see the introductory note to this Act and the Limited Liability Partnerships Regulations 2001, SI 2001/1090, reg 5, Sch 3 at **[6986]**, **[6995]**.

[124A Petition for winding up on grounds of public interest

(1) Where it appears to the Secretary of State from—

(a) any report made or information obtained under Part XIV [(except section 448A)] of the Companies Act 1985 (company investigations, &c),

[(b) any report made by inspectors under—

(i) section 167, 168, 169 or 284 of the Financial Services and Markets Act 2000, or

(ii) where the company is an open-ended investment company (within the meaning of that Act), regulations made as a result of section 262(2)(k) of that Act;

(bb) any information or documents obtained under section 165, 171, 172, 173 or 175 of that Act,]

(c) any information obtained under section 2 of the Criminal Justice Act 1987 or section 52 of the Criminal Justice (Scotland) Act 1987 (fraud investigations), or

(d) any information obtained under section 83 of the Companies Act 1989 (powers exercisable for purpose of assisting overseas regulatory authorities),

that it is expedient in the public interest that a company should be wound up, he may present a petition for it to be wound up if the court thinks it just and equitable for it to be so.

(2) This section does not apply if the company is already being wound up by the court.]

[3281]

NOTES

Inserted by CA 1989, s 60(3), as from 21 February 1990.

Sub-s (1): words in square brackets in para (a) inserted by the Companies (Audit, Investigations and Community Enterprise) Act 2004, s 25, Sch 2, Pt 3, para 27, as from 6 April 2005 (for transitional provisions see the Companies (Audit, Investigations and Community Enterprise) Act 2004 (Commencement) and Companies Act 1989 (Commencement No 18) Order 2004, SI 2004/3322, art 13 at **[7351]**); paras (b), (bb) substituted, for original para (b), by the Financial Services and Markets Act 2000 (Consequential Amendments and Repeals) Order 2001, SI 2001/3649, art 305, as from 1 December 2001.

Application to limited liability partnerships: see the introductory note to this Act and the Limited Liability Partnerships Regulations 2001, SI 2001/1090, reg 5, Sch 3 at **[6986]**, **[6995]**.

[124B Petition for winding up of SE

(1) Where—

(a) an SE whose registered office is in Great Britain is not in compliance with Article 7 of Council Regulation (EC) No 2157/2001 on the Statute for a European company (the "EC Regulation") (location of head office and registered office), and

(b) it appears to the Secretary of State that the SE should be wound up, he may present a petition for it to be wound up if the court thinks it is just and equitable for it to be so.

(2) This section does not apply if the SE is already being wound up by the court.

(3) In this section "SE" has the same meaning as in the EC Regulation.]

[3281A]

NOTES

Inserted by the European Public Limited-Liability Company Regulations 2004, SI 2004/2326, reg 73(3), as from 8 October 2004.

Application to limited liability partnerships: see the introductory note to this Act and the Limited Liability Partnerships Regulations 2001, SI 2001/1090, reg 5, Sch 3 at **[6986]**, **[6995]**.

[124C Petition for winding up of SCE

(1) Where, in the case of an SCE whose registered office is in Great Britain—

(a) there has been such a breach as is mentioned in Article 73(1) of Council Regulation (EC) No 1435/2003 on the Statute for a European Cooperative Society (SCE) (the "European Cooperative Society Regulation") (winding up by the court or other competent authority), and

(b) it appears to the Financial Services Authority that the SCE should be wound up,

the Authority may present a petition for the SCE to be wound up if the court thinks it is just and equitable for it to be so.

PART III OTHER LEGISLATION

(2) Where, in the case of an SCE whose registered office is in Great Britain—

(a) the SCE is not in compliance with Article 6 of the European Cooperative Society Regulation (location of head office and registered office, and

(b) it appears to the Financial Service Authority that the SCE should be wound up,

the Authority may present a petition for the SCE to be wound up if the court thinks it is just and equitable for it to be so.

(3) This section does not apply if the SCE is already being wound up by the court.

(4) In this section "SCE" has the same meaning as in the European Cooperative Society Regulation.]

[3281B]

NOTES

Commencement: 18 August 2006.

Inserted by the European Cooperative Society Regulations 2006, SI 2006/22078, reg 33(1), as from 18 August 2006.

Application to limited liability partnerships: see the introductory note to this Act and the Limited Liability Partnerships Regulations 2001, SI 2001/1090, reg 5, Sch 3 at **[6986]**, **[6995]**.

125 Powers of court on hearing of petition

(1) On hearing a winding-up petition the court may dismiss it, or adjourn the hearing conditionally or unconditionally, or make an interim order, or any other order that it thinks fit; but the court shall not refuse to make a winding-up order on the ground only that the company's assets have been mortgaged to an amount equal to or in excess of those assets, or that the company has no assets.

(2) If the petition is presented by members of the company as contributories on the ground that it is just and equitable that the company should be wound up, the court, if it is of opinion—

(a) that the petitioners are entitled to relief either by winding up the company or by some other means, and

(b) that in the absence of any other remedy it would be just and equitable that the company should be wound up,

shall make a winding-up order; but this does not apply if the court is also of the opinion both that some other remedy is available to the petitioners and that they are acting unreasonably in seeking to have the company wound up instead of pursuing that other remedy.

[3282]

NOTES

Application to limited liability partnerships: see the introductory note to this Act and the Limited Liability Partnerships Regulations 2001, SI 2001/1090, reg 5, Sch 3 at **[6986]**, **[6995]**.

126 Power to stay or restrain proceedings against company

(1) At any time after the presentation of a winding-up petition, and before a winding-up order has been made, the company, or any creditor or contributory, may—

(a) where any action or proceeding against the company is pending in the High Court or Court of Appeal in England and Wales or Northern Ireland, apply to the court in which the action or proceeding is pending for a stay of proceedings therein, and

(b) where any other action or proceeding is pending against the company, apply to the court having jurisdiction to wind up the company to restrain further proceedings in the action or proceeding;

and the court to which application is so made may (as the case may be) stay, sist or restrain the proceedings accordingly on such terms as it thinks fit.

(2) In the case of a company registered under section 680 of the Companies Act (pre-1862 companies; companies formed under legislation other than the Companies Acts) or the previous corresponding legislation, where the application to stay, sist or restrain is by a creditor, this section extends to actions and proceedings against any contributory of the company.

[3283]

NOTES

Application to limited liability partnerships: see the introductory note to this Act, the Limited Liability Partnerships Regulations 2001, SI 2001/1090, reg 5, Sch 3 at **[6986]**, **[6995]**, and the Limited Liability Partnerships (Scotland) Regulations 2001, SSI 2001/128, reg 4, Schs 2, 3 at **[6977]**, **[6980A]**, **[6980B]**.

127 Avoidance of property dispositions, etc

[(1)] In a winding up by the court, any disposition of the company's property, and any transfer of shares, or alteration in the status of the company's members, made after the commencement of the winding up is, unless the court otherwise orders, void.

[(2) This section has no effect in respect of anything done by an administrator of a company while a winding-up petition is suspended under paragraph 40 of Schedule B1.]

[3284]

NOTES

Sub-s (1) numbered as such, and sub-s (2) added, by the Enterprise Act 2002, s 248(3), Sch 17, paras 9, 15, as from 15 September 2003 (for savings and transitional provisions, see the note to s 8 at **[3164]**).

Application to limited liability partnerships: see the introductory note to this Act, the Limited Liability Partnerships Regulations 2001, SI 2001/1090, reg 5, Sch 3 at **[6986]**, **[6995]**, and the Limited Liability Partnerships (Scotland) Regulations 2001, SSI 2001/128, reg 4, Schs 2, 3 at **[6977]**, **[6980A]**, **[6980B]**.

128 Avoidance of attachments, etc

(1) Where a company registered in England and Wales is being wound up by the court, any attachment, sequestration, distress or execution put in force against the estate or effects of the company after the commencement of the winding up is void.

(2) This section, so far as relates to any estate or effects of the company situated in England and Wales, applies in the case of a company registered in Scotland as it applies in the case of a company registered in England and Wales.

[3285]

NOTES

Application to limited liability partnerships: see the introductory note to this Act, the Limited Liability Partnerships Regulations 2001, SI 2001/1090, reg 5, Sch 3 at **[6986]**, **[6995]**, and the Limited Liability Partnerships (Scotland) Regulations 2001, SSI 2001/128, reg 4, Schs 2, 3 at **[6977]**, **[6980A]**, **[6980B]**.

Commencement of winding up

129 Commencement of winding up by the court

(1) If, before the presentation of a petition for the winding up of a company by the court, a resolution has been passed by the company for voluntary winding up, the winding up of the company is deemed to have commenced at the time of the passing of the resolution; and unless the court, on proof of fraud or mistake, directs otherwise, all proceedings taken in the voluntary winding up are deemed to have been validly taken.

[(1A) Where the court makes a winding-up order by virtue of paragraph 13(1)(e) of Schedule B1, the winding up is deemed to commence on the making of the order.]

(2) In any other case, the winding up of a company by the court is deemed to commence at the time of the presentation of the petition for winding up.

[3286]

NOTES

Sub-s (1A): inserted by the Enterprise Act 2002, s 248(3), Sch 17, paras 9, 16, as from 15 September 2003 (for savings and transitional provisions, see the note to s 8 at **[3164]**).

Application to limited liability partnerships: see the introductory note to this Act and the Limited Liability Partnerships Regulations 2001, SI 2001/1090, reg 5, Sch 3 at **[6986]**, **[6995]**.

130 Consequences of winding-up order

(1) On the making of a winding-up order, a copy of the order must forthwith be forwarded by the company (or otherwise as may be prescribed) to the registrar of companies, who shall enter it in his records relating to the company.

(2) When a winding-up order has been made or a provisional liquidator has been appointed, no action or proceeding shall be proceeded with or commenced against the company or its property, except by leave of the court and subject to such terms as the court may impose.

(3) When an order has been made for winding up a company registered under section 680 of the Companies Act, no action or proceeding shall be commenced or proceeded with against the company or its property or any contributory of the company, in respect of any debt of the company, except by leave of the court, and subject to such terms as the court may impose.

(4) An order for winding up a company operates in favour of all the creditors and of all contributories of the company as if made on the joint petition of a creditor and of a contributory.

[3287]

NOTES

Application to limited liability partnerships: see the introductory note to this Act, the Limited Liability Partnerships Regulations 2001, SI 2001/1090, reg 5, Sch 3 at **[6986]**, **[6995]**, and the Limited Liability Partnerships (Scotland) Regulations 2001, SSI 2001/128, reg 4, Schs 2, 3 at **[6977]**, **[6980A]**, **[6980B]**.

Modification in relation to Scotland: see the Note at the beginning of this Act.

Investigation procedures

131 Company's statement of affairs

(1) Where the court has made a winding-up order or appointed a provisional liquidator, the official receiver may require some or all of the persons mentioned in subsection (3) below to make out and submit to him a statement in the prescribed form as to the affairs of the company.

(2) The statement shall be verified by affidavit by the persons required to submit it and shall show—

(a) particulars of the company's assets and liabilities;
(b) the names and addresses of the company's creditors;
(c) the securities held by them respectively;
(d) the dates when the securities were respectively given; and
(e) such further or other information as may be prescribed or as the official receiver may require.

(3) The persons referred to in subsection (1) are—

(a) those who are or have been officers of the company;
(b) those who have taken part in the formation of the company at any time within one year before the relevant date;
(c) those who are in the company's employment, or have been in its employment within that year, and are in the official receiver's opinion capable of giving the information required;
(d) those who are or have been within that year officers of, or in the employment of, a company which is, or within that year was, an officer of the company.

(4) Where any persons are required under this section to submit a statement of affairs to the official receiver, they shall do so (subject to the next subsection) before the end of the period of 21 days beginning with the day after that on which the prescribed notice of the requirement is given to them by the official receiver.

(5) The official receiver, if he thinks fit, may—

(a) at any time release a person from an obligation imposed on him under subsection (1) or (2) above; or
(b) either when giving the notice mentioned in subsection (4) or subsequently, extend the period so mentioned;

and where the official receiver has refused to exercise a power conferred by this subsection, the court, if it thinks fit, may exercise it.

(6) In this section—

"employment" includes employment under a contract for services; and

"the relevant date" means—

(a) in a case where a provisional liquidator is appointed, the date of his appointment; and
(b) in a case where no such appointment is made, the date of the winding-up order.

(7) If a person without reasonable excuse fails to comply with any obligation imposed under this section, he is liable to a fine and, for continued contravention, to a daily default fine.

(8) In the application of this section to Scotland references to the official receiver are to the liquidator or, in a case where a provisional liquidator is appointed, the provisional liquidator.

[3288]

NOTES

Application to limited liability partnerships: see the introductory note to this Act, the Limited Liability Partnerships Regulations 2001, SI 2001/1090, reg 5, Sch 3 at **[6986]**, **[6995]**, and the Limited Liability Partnerships (Scotland) Regulations 2001, SSI 2001/128, reg 4, Schs 2, 3 at **[6977]**, **[6980A]**, **[6980B]**.

132 Investigation by official receiver

(1) Where a winding-up order is made by the court in England and Wales, it is the duty of the official receiver to investigate—
(a) if the company has failed, the causes of the failure; and
(b) generally, the promotion, formation, business, dealings and affairs of the company,

and to make such report (if any) to the court as he thinks fit.

(2) The report is, in any proceedings, prima facie evidence of the facts stated in it.

[3289]

NOTES

Application to limited liability partnerships: see the introductory note to this Act and the Limited Liability Partnerships Regulations 2001, SI 2001/1090, reg 5, Sch 3 at **[6986]**, **[6995]**.

133 Public examination of officers

(1) Where a company is being wound up by the court, the official receiver or, in Scotland, the liquidator may at any time before the dissolution of the company apply to the court for the public examination of any person who—
(a) is or has been an officer of the company; or
(b) has acted as liquidator or administrator of the company or as receiver or manager or, in Scotland, receiver of its property; or
(c) not being a person falling within paragraph (a) or (b), is or has been concerned, or has taken part, in the promotion, formation or management of the company.

(2) Unless the court otherwise orders, the official receiver or, in Scotland, the liquidator shall make an application under subsection (1) if he is requested in accordance with the rules to do so by—
(a) one-half, in value, of the company's creditors; or
(b) three-quarters, in value, of the company's contributories.

(3) On an application under subsection (1), the court shall direct that a public examination of the person to whom the application relates shall be held on a day appointed by the court; and that person shall attend on that day and be publicly examined as to the promotion, formation or management of the company or as to the conduct of its business and affairs, or his conduct or dealings in relation to the company.

(4) The following may take part in the public examination of a person under this section and may question that person concerning the matters mentioned in subsection (3), namely—
(a) the official receiver;
(b) the liquidator of the company;
(c) any person who has been appointed as special manager of the company's property or business;

(d) any creditor of the company who has tendered a proof or, in Scotland, submitted a claim in the winding up;

(e) any contributory of the company.

[3290]

NOTES

Application to limited liability partnerships: see the introductory note to this Act, the Limited Liability Partnerships Regulations 2001, SI 2001/1090, reg 5, Sch 3 at **[6986]**, **[6995]**, and the Limited Liability Partnerships (Scotland) Regulations 2001, SSI 2001/128, reg 4, Schs 2, 3 at **[6977]**, **[6980A]**, **[6980B]**.

134 Enforcement of s 133

(1) If a person without reasonable excuse fails at any time to attend his public examination under section 133, he is guilty of a contempt of court and liable to be punished accordingly.

(2) In a case where a person without reasonable excuse fails at any time to attend his examination under section 133 or there are reasonable grounds for believing that a person has absconded, or is about to abscond, with a view to avoiding or delaying his examination under that section, the court may cause a warrant to be issued to a constable or prescribed officer of the court—

(a) for the arrest of that person; and

(b) for the seizure of any books, papers, records, money or goods in that person's possession.

(3) In such a case the court may authorise the person arrested under the warrant to be kept in custody, and anything seized under such a warrant to be held, in accordance with the rules, until such time as the court may order.

[3291]

NOTES

Application to limited liability partnerships: see the introductory note to this Act, the Limited Liability Partnerships Regulations 2001, SI 2001/1090, reg 5, Sch 3 at **[6986]**, **[6995]**, and the Limited Liability Partnerships (Scotland) Regulations 2001, SSI 2001/128, reg 4, Schs 2, 3 at **[6977]**, **[6980A]**, **[6980B]**.

Appointment of liquidator

135 Appointment and powers of provisional liquidator

(1) Subject to the provisions of this section, the court may, at any time after the presentation of a winding-up petition, appoint a liquidator provisionally.

(2) In England and Wales, the appointment of a provisional liquidator may be made at any time before the making of a winding-up order; and either the official receiver or any other fit person may be appointed.

(3) In Scotland, such an appointment may be made at any time before the first appointment of liquidators.

(4) The provisional liquidator shall carry out such functions as the court may confer on him.

(5) When a liquidator is provisionally appointed by the court, his powers may be limited by the order appointing him.

[3292]

NOTES

Application to limited liability partnerships: see the introductory note to this Act, the Limited Liability Partnerships Regulations 2001, SI 2001/1090, reg 5, Sch 3 at **[6986]**, **[6995]**, and the Limited Liability Partnerships (Scotland) Regulations 2001, SSI 2001/128, reg 4, Schs 2, 3 at **[6977]**, **[6980A]**, **[6980B]**.

136 Functions of official receiver in relation to office of liquidator

(1) The following provisions of this section have effect, subject to section 140 below, on a winding-up order being made by the court in England and Wales.

(2) The official receiver, by virtue of his office, becomes the liquidator of the company and continues in office until another person becomes liquidator under the provisions of this Part.

(3) The official receiver is, by virtue of his office, the liquidator during any vacancy.

(4) At any time when he is the liquidator of the company, the official receiver may summon separate meetings of the company's creditors and contributories for the purpose of choosing a person to be liquidator of the company in place of the official receiver.

(5) It is the duty of the official receiver—

(a) as soon as practicable in the period of 12 weeks beginning with the day on which the winding-up order was made, to decide whether to exercise his power under subsection (4) to summon meetings, and

(b) if in pursuance of paragraph (a) he decides not to exercise that power, to give notice of his decision, before the end of that period, to the court and to the company's creditors and contributories, and

(c) (whether or not he has decided to exercise that power) to exercise his power to summon meetings under subsection (4) if he is at any time requested, in accordance with the rules, to do so by one-quarter, in value, of the company's creditors;

and accordingly, where the duty imposed by paragraph (c) arises before the official receiver has performed a duty imposed by paragraph (a) or (b), he is not required to perform the latter duty.

(6) A notice given under subsection (5)(b) to the company's creditors shall contain an explanation of the creditors' power under subsection (5)(c) to require the official receiver to summon meetings of the company's creditors and contributories.

[3293]

NOTES

Application to limited liability partnerships: see the introductory note to this Act and the Limited Liability Partnerships Regulations 2001, SI 2001/1090, reg 5, Sch 3 at **[6986]**, **[6995]**.

137 Appointment by Secretary of State

(1) In a winding up by the court in England and Wales the official receiver may, at any time when he is the liquidator of the company, apply to the Secretary of State for the appointment of a person as liquidator in his place.

(2) If meetings are held in pursuance of a decision under section 136(5)(a), but no person is chosen to be liquidator as a result of those meetings, it is the duty of the official receiver to decide whether to refer the need for an appointment to the Secretary of State.

(3) On an application under subsection (1), or a reference made in pursuance of a decision under subsection (2), the Secretary of State shall either make an appointment or decline to make one.

(4) Where a liquidator has been appointed by the Secretary of State under subsection (3), the liquidator shall give notice of his appointment to the company's creditors or, if the court so allows, shall advertise his appointment in accordance with the directions of the court.

(5) In that notice or advertisement the liquidator shall—

(a) state whether he proposes to summon a general meeting of the company's creditors under section 141 below for the purpose of determining (together with any meeting of contributories) whether a liquidation committee should be established under that section, and

(b) if he does not propose to summon such a meeting, set out the power of the company's creditors under that section to require him to summon one.

[3294]

NOTES

Application to limited liability partnerships: see the introductory note to this Act and the Limited Liability Partnerships Regulations 2001, SI 2001/1090, reg 5, Sch 3 at **[6986]**, **[6995]**.

138 Appointment of liquidator in Scotland

(1) Where a winding-up order is made by the court in Scotland, a liquidator shall be appointed by the court at the time when the order is made.

(2) The liquidator so appointed (here referred to as "the interim liquidator") continues in office until another person becomes liquidator in his place under this section or the next.

(3) The interim liquidator shall (subject to the next subsection) as soon as practicable in the period of 28 days beginning with the day on which the winding-up order was made or such longer period as the court may allow, summon separate meetings of the company's creditors and contributories for the purpose of choosing a person (who may be the person who is the interim liquidator) to be liquidator of the company in place of the interim liquidator.

(4) If it appears to the interim liquidator, in any case where a company is being wound up on grounds including its inability to pay its debts, that it would be inappropriate to summon under subsection (3) a meeting of the company's contributories, he may summon only a meeting of the company's creditors for the purpose mentioned in that subsection.

(5) If one or more meetings are held in pursuance of this section but no person is appointed or nominated by the meeting or meetings, the interim liquidator shall make a report to the court which shall appoint either the interim liquidator or some other person to be liquidator of the company.

(6) A person who becomes liquidator of the company in place of the interim liquidator shall, unless he is appointed by the court, forthwith notify the court of that fact.

[3295]

NOTES

Application to limited liability partnerships: see the introductory note to this Act, the Limited Liability Partnerships Regulations 2001, SI 2001/1090, reg 5, Sch 3 at **[6986]**, **[6995]**, and the Limited Liability Partnerships (Scotland) Regulations 2001, SSI 2001/128, reg 4, Schs 2, 3 at **[6977]**, **[6980A]**, **[6980B]**.

139 Choice of liquidator at meetings of creditors and contributories

(1) This section applies where a company is being wound up by the court and separate meetings of the company's creditors and contributories are summoned for the purpose of choosing a person to be liquidator of the company.

(2) The creditors and the contributories at their respective meetings may nominate a person to be liquidator.

(3) The liquidator shall be the person nominated by the creditors or, where no person has been so nominated, the person (if any) nominated by the contributories.

(4) In the case of different persons being nominated, any contributory or creditor may, within 7 days after the date on which the nomination was made by the creditors, apply to the court for an order either—

- (a) appointing the person nominated as liquidator by the contributories to be a liquidator instead of, or jointly with, the person nominated by the creditors; or
- (b) appointing some other person to be liquidator instead of the person nominated by the creditors.

[3296]

NOTES

Application to limited liability partnerships: see the introductory note to this Act, the Limited Liability Partnerships Regulations 2001, SI 2001/1090, reg 5, Sch 3 at **[6986]**, **[6995]**, and the Limited Liability Partnerships (Scotland) Regulations 2001, SSI 2001/128, reg 4, Schs 2, 3 at **[6977]**, **[6980A]**, **[6980B]**.

140 Appointment by the court following administration or voluntary arrangement

[(1) Where a winding-up order is made immediately upon the appointment of an administrator ceasing to have effect, the court may appoint as liquidator of the company the person whose appointment as administrator has ceased to have effect.]

(2) Where a winding-up order is made at a time when there is a supervisor of a voluntary arrangement approved in relation to the company under Part I, the court may appoint as liquidator of the company the person who is the supervisor at the time when the winding-up order is made.

(3) Where the court makes an appointment under this section, the official receiver does not become the liquidator as otherwise provided by section 136(2), and he has no duty under section 136(5)(a) or (b) in respect of the summoning of creditors' or contributories' meetings.
[3297]

NOTES

Sub-s (1): substituted by the Enterprise Act 2002, s 248(3), Sch 17, paras 9, 17, as from 15 September 2003 (for savings and transitional provisions, see the note to s 8 at **[3164]**).

Application to limited liability partnerships: see the introductory note to this Act, the Limited Liability Partnerships Regulations 2001, SI 2001/1090, reg 5, Sch 3 at **[6986]**, **[6995]**, and the Limited Liability Partnerships (Scotland) Regulations 2001, SSI 2001/128, reg 4, Schs 2, 3 at **[6977]**, **[6980A]**, **[6980B]**.

Liquidation committees

141 Liquidation committee (England and Wales)

(1) Where a winding-up order has been made by the court in England and Wales and separate meetings of creditors and contributories have been summoned for the purpose of choosing a person to be liquidator, those meetings may establish a committee ("the liquidation committee") to exercise the functions conferred on it by or under this Act.

(2) The liquidator (not being the official receiver) may at any time, if he thinks fit, summon separate general meetings of the company's creditors and contributories for the purpose of determining whether such a committee should be established and, if it is so determined, of establishing it.

The liquidator (not being the official receiver) shall summon such a meeting if he is requested, in accordance with the rules, to do so by one-tenth, in value, of the company's creditors.

(3) Where meetings are summoned under this section, or for the purpose of choosing a person to be liquidator, and either the meeting of creditors or the meeting of contributories decides that a liquidation committee should be established, but the other meeting does not so decide or decides that a committee should not be established, the committee shall be established in accordance with the rules, unless the court otherwise orders.

(4) The liquidation committee is not to be able or required to carry out its functions at any time when the official receiver is liquidator; but at any such time its functions are vested in the Secretary of State except to the extent that the rules otherwise provide.

(5) Where there is for the time being no liquidation committee, and the liquidator is a person other than the official receiver, the functions of such a committee are vested in the Secretary of State except to the extent that the rules otherwise provide.
[3298]

NOTES

Application to limited liability partnerships: see the introductory note to this Act and the Limited Liability Partnerships Regulations 2001, SI 2001/1090, reg 5, Sch 3 at **[6986]**, **[6995]**.

142 Liquidation committee (Scotland)

(1) Where a winding-up order has been made by the court in Scotland and separate meetings of creditors and contributories have been summoned for the purpose of choosing a person to be liquidator or, under section 138(4), only a meeting of creditors has been summoned for that purpose, those meetings or (as the case may be) that meeting may establish a committee ("the liquidation committee") to exercise the functions conferred on it by or under this Act.

(2) The liquidator may at any time, if he thinks fit, summon separate general meetings of the company's creditors and contributories for the purpose of determining whether such a committee should be established and, if it is so determined, of establishing it.

(3) The liquidator, if appointed by the court otherwise than under section 139(4)(a), is required to summon meetings under subsection (2) if he is requested, in accordance with the rules, to do so by one-tenth, in value, of the company's creditors.

(4) Where meetings are summoned under this section, or for the purpose of choosing a person to be liquidator, and either the meeting of creditors or the meeting of contributories

decides that a liquidation committee should be established, but the other meeting does not so decide or decides that a committee should not be established, the committee shall be established in accordance with the rules, unless the court otherwise orders.

(5) Where in the case of any winding up there is for the time being no liquidation committee, the functions of such a committee are vested in the court except to the extent that the rules otherwise provide.

(6) In addition to the powers and duties conferred and imposed on it by this Act, a liquidation committee has such of the powers and duties of commissioners in a sequestration as may be conferred and imposed on such committees by the rules.

[3299]

NOTES

Application to limited liability partnerships: see the introductory note to this Act, the Limited Liability Partnerships Regulations 2001, SI 2001/1090, reg 5, Sch 3 at **[6986]**, **[6995]**, and the Limited Liability Partnerships (Scotland) Regulations 2001, SSI 2001/128, reg 4, Schs 2, 3 at **[6977]**, **[6980A]**, **[6980B]**.

The liquidator's functions

143 General functions in winding up by the court

(1) The functions of the liquidator of a company which is being wound up by the court are to secure that the assets of the company are got in, realised and distributed to the company's creditors and, if there is a surplus, to the persons entitled to it.

(2) It is the duty of the liquidator of a company which is being wound up by the court in England and Wales, if he is not the official receiver—

(a) to furnish the official receiver with such information,

(b) to produce to the official receiver, and permit inspection by the official receiver of, such books, papers and other records, and

(c) to give the official receiver such other assistance,

as the official receiver may reasonably require for the purposes of carrying out his functions in relation to the winding up.

[3300]

NOTES

Application to limited liability partnerships: see the introductory note to this Act, the Limited Liability Partnerships Regulations 2001, SI 2001/1090, reg 5, Sch 3 at **[6986]**, **[6995]**, and the Limited Liability Partnerships (Scotland) Regulations 2001, SSI 2001/128, reg 4, Schs 2, 3 at **[6977]**, **[6980A]**, **[6980B]**.

144 Custody of company's property

(1) When a winding-up order has been made, or where a provisional liquidator has been appointed, the liquidator or the provisional liquidator (as the case may be) shall take into his custody or under his control all the property and things in action to which the company is or appears to be entitled.

(2) In a winding up by the court in Scotland, if and so long as there is no liquidator, all the property of the company is deemed to be in the custody of the court.

[3301]

NOTES

Application to limited liability partnerships: see the introductory note to this Act, the Limited Liability Partnerships Regulations 2001, SI 2001/1090, reg 5, Sch 3 at **[6986]**, **[6995]**, and the Limited Liability Partnerships (Scotland) Regulations 2001, SSI 2001/128, reg 4, Schs 2, 3 at **[6977]**, **[6980A]**, **[6980B]**.

145 Vesting of company property in liquidator

(1) When a company is being wound up by the court, the court may on the application of the liquidator by order direct that all or any part of the property of whatsoever description belonging to the company or held by trustees on its behalf shall vest in the liquidator by his official name; and thereupon the property to which the order relates vests accordingly.

(2) The liquidator may, after giving such indemnity (if any) as the court may direct, bring or defend in his official name any action or other legal proceeding which relates to that property or which it is necessary to bring or defend for the purpose of effectually winding up the company and recovering its property.

[3302]

NOTES

Application to limited liability partnerships: see the introductory note to this Act, the Limited Liability Partnerships Regulations 2001, SI 2001/1090, reg 5, Sch 3 at **[6986]**, **[6995]**, and the Limited Liability Partnerships (Scotland) Regulations 2001, SSI 2001/128, reg 4, Schs 2, 3 at **[6977]**, **[6980A]**, **[6980B]**.

146 Duty to summon final meeting

(1) Subject to the next subsection, if it appears to the liquidator of a company which is being wound by the court that the winding up of the company is for practical purposes complete and the liquidator is not the official receiver, the liquidator shall summon a final general meeting of the company's creditors which—

(a) shall receive the liquidator's report of the winding up, and
(b) shall determine whether the liquidator should have his release under section 174 in Chapter VII of this Part.

(2) The liquidator may, if he thinks fit, give the notice summoning the final general meeting at the same time as giving notice of any final distribution of the company's property but, if summoned for an earlier date, that meeting shall be adjourned (and, if necessary, further adjourned) until a date on which the liquidator is able to report to the meeting that the winding up of the company is for practical purposes complete.

(3) In the carrying out of his functions in the winding up it is the duty of the liquidator to retain sufficient sums from the company's property to cover the expenses of summoning and holding the meeting required by this section.

[3303]

NOTES

Application to limited liability partnerships: see the introductory note to this Act, the Limited Liability Partnerships Regulations 2001, SI 2001/1090, reg 5, Sch 3 at **[6986]**, **[6995]**, and the Limited Liability Partnerships (Scotland) Regulations 2001, SSI 2001/128, reg 4, Schs 2, 3 at **[6977]**, **[6980A]**, **[6980B]**.

General powers of court

147 Power to stay or sist winding up

(1) The court may at any time after an order for winding up, on the application either of the liquidator or the official receiver or any creditor or contributory, and on proof to the satisfaction of the court that all proceedings in the winding up ought to be stayed or sisted, make an order staying or sisting the proceedings, either altogether or for a limited time, on such terms and conditions as the court thinks fit.

(2) The court may, before making an order, require the official receiver to furnish to it a report with respect to any facts or matters which are in his opinion relevant to the application.

(3) A copy of every order made under this section shall forthwith be forwarded by the company, or otherwise as may be prescribed, to the registrar of companies, who shall enter it in his records relating to the company.

[3304]

NOTES

Application to limited liability partnerships: see the introductory note to this Act, the Limited Liability Partnerships Regulations 2001, SI 2001/1090, reg 5, Sch 3 at **[6986]**, **[6995]**, and the Limited Liability Partnerships (Scotland) Regulations 2001, SSI 2001/128, reg 4, Schs 2, 3 at **[6977]**, **[6980A]**, **[6980B]**.

Modification in relation to Scotland: see the Note at the beginning of this Act.

148 Settlement of list of contributories and application of assets

(1) As soon as may be after making a winding-up order, the court shall settle a list of contributories, with power to rectify the register of members in all cases where rectification is

required in pursuance of the Companies Act or this Act, and shall cause the company's assets to be collected, and applied in discharge of its liabilities.

(2) If it appears to the court that it will not be necessary to make calls on or adjust the rights of contributories, the court may dispense with the settlement of a list of contributories.

(3) In settling the list, the court shall distinguish between persons who are contributories in their own right and persons who are contributories as being representatives of or liable for the debts of others.

[3305]

NOTES

Application to limited liability partnerships: see the introductory note to this Act and the Limited Liability Partnerships Regulations 2001, SI 2001/1090, reg 5, Sch 3 at **[6986]**, **[6995]**.

149 Debts due from contributory to company

(1) The court may, at any time after making a winding-up order, make an order on any contributory for the time being on the list of contributories to pay, in manner directed by the order, any money due from him (or from the estate of the person who he represents) to the company, exclusive of any money payable by him or the estate by virtue of any call in pursuance of the Companies Act or this Act.

(2) The court in making such an order may—

(a) in the case of an unlimited company, allow to the contributory by way of set-off any money due to him or the estate which he represents from the company on any independent dealing or contract with the company, but not any money due to him as a member of the company in respect of any dividend or profit, and

(b) in the case of a limited company, make to any director or manager whose liability is unlimited or to his estate the like allowance.

(3) In the case of any company, whether limited or unlimited, when all the creditors are paid in full (together with interest at the official rate), any money due on any account whatever to a contributory from the company may be allowed to him by way of set-off against any subsequent call.

[3306]

NOTES

Application to limited liability partnerships: see the introductory note to this Act and the Limited Liability Partnerships Regulations 2001, SI 2001/1090, reg 5, Sch 3 at **[6986]**, **[6995]**.

150 Power to make calls

(1) The court may, at any time after making a winding-up order, and either before or after it has ascertained the sufficiency of the company's assets, make calls on all or any of the contributories for the time being settled on the list of the contributories to the extent of their liability, for payment of any money which the court considers necessary to satisfy the company's debts and liabilities, and the expenses of winding up, and for the adjustment of the rights of the contributories among themselves, and make an order for payment of any calls so made.

(2) In making a call the court may take into consideration the probability that some of the contributories may partly or wholly fail to pay it.

[3307]

NOTES

Application to limited liability partnerships: see the introductory note to this Act and the Limited Liability Partnerships Regulations 2001, SI 2001/1090, reg 5, Sch 3 at **[6986]**, **[6995]**.

151 Payment into bank of money due to company

(1) The court may order any contributory, purchaser or other person from whom money is due to the company to pay the amount due into the Bank of England (or any branch of it) to the account of the liquidator instead of to the liquidator, and such an order may be enforced in the same manner as if it had directed payment to the liquidator.

(2) All money and securities paid or delivered into the Bank of England (or branch) in the event of a winding up by the court are subject in all respects to the orders of the court.

[3308]

NOTES

Application to limited liability partnerships: see the introductory note to this Act and the Limited Liability Partnerships Regulations 2001, SI 2001/1090, reg 5, Sch 3 at **[6986]**, **[6995]**.

152 Order on contributory to be conclusive evidence

(1) An order made by the court on a contributory is conclusive evidence that the money (if any) thereby appearing to be due or ordered to be paid is due, but subject to any right of appeal.

(2) All other pertinent matters stated in the order are to be taken as truly stated as against all persons and in all proceedings except proceedings in Scotland against the heritable estate of a deceased contributory; and in that case the order is only prima facie evidence for the purpose of charging his heritable estate, unless his heirs or legatees of heritage were on the list of contributories at the time of the order being made.

[3309]

NOTES

Application to limited liability partnerships: see the introductory note to this Act and the Limited Liability Partnerships Regulations 2001, SI 2001/1090, reg 5, Sch 3 at **[6986]**, **[6995]**.

153 Power to exclude creditors not proving in time

The court may fix a time or times within which creditors are to prove their debts or claims or to be excluded from the benefit of any distribution made before those debts are proved.

[3310]

NOTES

Application to limited liability partnerships: see the introductory note to this Act and the Limited Liability Partnerships Regulations 2001, SI 2001/1090, reg 5, Sch 3 at **[6986]**, **[6995]**.

154 Adjustment of rights of contributories

The court shall adjust the rights of the contributories among themselves and distribute any surplus among the persons entitled to it.

[3311]

NOTES

Application to limited liability partnerships: see the introductory note to this Act and the Limited Liability Partnerships Regulations 2001, SI 2001/1090, reg 5, Sch 3 at **[6986]**, **[6995]**.

155 Inspection of books by creditors, etc

(1) The court may, at any time after making a winding-up order, make such order for inspection of the company's books and papers by creditors and contributories as the court thinks just; and any books and papers in the company's possession may be inspected by creditors and contributories accordingly, but not further or otherwise.

(2) Nothing in this section excludes or restricts any statutory rights of a government department or person acting under the authority of a government department.

[(3) For the purposes of subsection (2) above, references to a government department shall be construed as including references to any part of the Scottish Administration.]

[3312]

NOTES

Sub-s (3): added by the Scotland Act 1998 (Consequential Modifications) (No 2) Order 1999, SI 1999/1820, art 4, Sch 2, Pt I, para 85, as from 1 July 1999.

Application to limited liability partnerships: see the introductory note to this Act and the Limited Liability Partnerships Regulations 2001, SI 2001/1090, reg 5, Sch 3 at **[6986]**, **[6995]**.

156 Payment of expenses of winding up

The court may, in the event of the assets being insufficient to satisfy the liabilities, make an order as to the payment out of the assets of the expenses incurred in the winding up in such order of priority as the court thinks just.

[3313]

NOTES

Application to limited liability partnerships: see the introductory note to this Act and the Limited Liability Partnerships Regulations 2001, SI 2001/1090, reg 5, Sch 3 at **[6986]**, **[6995]**.

157 Attendance at company meetings (Scotland)

In the winding up by the court of a company registered in Scotland, the court has power to require the attendance of any officer of the company at any meeting of creditors or of contributories, or of a liquidation committee, for the purpose of giving information as to the trade, dealings, affairs or property of the company.

[3314]

NOTES

Application to limited liability partnerships: see the introductory note to this Act and the Limited Liability Partnerships Regulations 2001, SI 2001/1090, reg 5, Sch 3 at **[6986]**, **[6995]**.

158 Power to arrest absconding contributory

The court, at any time either before or after making a winding-up order, on proof of probable cause for believing that a contributory is about to quit the United Kingdom or otherwise to abscond or to remove or conceal any of his property for the purpose of evading payment of calls, may cause the contributory to be arrested and his books and papers and moveable personal property to be seized and him and them to be kept safely until such time as the court may order.

[3315]

NOTES

Application to limited liability partnerships: see the introductory note to this Act and the Limited Liability Partnerships Regulations 2001, SI 2001/1090, reg 5, Sch 3 at **[6986]**, **[6995]**.

159 Powers of court to be cumulative

Powers conferred by this Act and the Companies Act on the court are in addition to, and not in restriction of, any existing powers of instituting proceedings against a contributory or debtor of the company, or the estate of any contributory or debtor, for the recovery of any call or other sums.

[3316]

NOTES

Application to limited liability partnerships: see the introductory note to this Act and the Limited Liability Partnerships Regulations 2001, SI 2001/1090, reg 5, Sch 3 at **[6986]**, **[6995]**.

160 Delegation of powers to liquidator (England and Wales)

(1) Provision may be made by rules for enabling or requiring all or any of the powers and duties conferred and imposed on the court in England and Wales by the Companies Act and this Act in respect of the following matters—

- (a) the holding and conducting of meetings to ascertain the wishes of creditors and contributories,
- (b) the settling of lists of contributories and the rectifying of the register of members where required, and the collection and application of the assets,
- (c) the payment, delivery, conveyance, surrender or transfer of money, property, books or papers to the liquidator,
- (d) the making of calls,
- (e) the fixing of a time within which debts and claims must be proved,

to be exercised or performed by the liquidator as an officer of the court, and subject to the court's control.

(2) But the liquidator shall not, without the special leave of the court, rectify the register of members, and shall not make any call without either that special leave or the sanction of the liquidation committee.

[3317]

NOTES

Application to limited liability partnerships: see the introductory note to this Act and the Limited Liability Partnerships Regulations 2001, SI 2001/1090, reg 5, Sch 3 at **[6986]**, **[6995]**.

Enforcement of, and appeal from, orders

161 Orders for calls on contributories (Scotland)

(1) In Scotland, where an order, interlocutor or decree has been made for winding up a company by the court, it is competent to the court, on production by the liquidators of a list certified by them of the names of the contributories liable in payment of any calls, and of the amount due by each contributory, and of the date when that amount became due, to pronounce forthwith a decree against those contributories for payment of the sums so certified to be due, with interest from that date until payment (at 5 per cent. per annum) in the same way and to the same effect as if they had severally consented to registration for execution, on a charge of 6 days, of a legal obligation to pay those calls and interest.

(2) The decree may be extracted immediately, and no suspension of it is competent, except on caution or consignation, unless with special leave of the court.

[3318]

NOTES

Application to limited liability partnerships: see the introductory note to this Act and the Limited Liability Partnerships Regulations 2001, SI 2001/1090, reg 5, Sch 3 at **[6986]**, **[6995]**.

162 Appeals from orders in Scotland

(1) Subject to the provisions of this section and to rules of court, an appeal from any order or decision made or given in the winding up of a company by the court in Scotland under this Act lies in the same manner and subject to the same conditions as an appeal from an order or decision of the court in cases within its ordinary jurisdiction.

(2) In regard to orders or judgments pronounced by the judge acting as vacation judge … —

- (a) none of the orders specified in Part I of Schedule 3 to this Act are subject to review, reduction, suspension or stay of execution, and
- (b) every other order or judgment (except as mentioned below) may be submitted to review by the Inner House by reclaiming motion enrolled within 14 days from the date of the order or judgment.

(3) However, an order being one of those specified in Part II of that Schedule shall, from the date of the order and notwithstanding that it has been submitted to review as above, be carried out and receive effect until the Inner House have disposed of the matter.

(4) In regard to orders or judgments pronounced in Scotland by a Lord Ordinary before whom proceedings in a winding up are being taken, any such order or judgment may be submitted to review by the Inner House by reclaiming motion enrolled within 14 days from its date; but should it not be so submitted to review during session, the provisions of this section in regard to orders or judgments pronounced by the judge acting as vacation judge apply.

(5) Nothing in this section affects provisions of the Companies Act or this Act in reference to decrees in Scotland for payment of calls in the winding up of companies, whether voluntary or by the court.

[3319]

NOTES

Sub-s (2): words omitted repealed by the Court of Session Act 1988, s 52(2), Sch 2, Pt III, as from 29 September 1988.

Application to limited liability partnerships: see the introductory note to this Act, the Limited Liability Partnerships Regulations 2001, SI 2001/1090, reg 5, Sch 3 at **[6986]**, **[6995]**, and the Limited Liability Partnerships (Scotland) Regulations 2001, SSI 2001/128, reg 4, Schs 2, 3 at **[6977]**, **[6980A]**, **[6980B]**.

CHAPTER VII
LIQUIDATORS

Preliminary

163 Style and title of liquidators

The liquidator of a company shall be described—

(a) where a person other than the official receiver is liquidator, by the style of "the liquidator" of the particular company, or

(b) where the official receiver is liquidator, by the style of "the official receiver and liquidator" of the particular company;

and in neither case shall he be described by an individual name.

[3320]

NOTES

Application to limited liability partnerships: see the introductory note to this Act, the Limited Liability Partnerships Regulations 2001, SI 2001/1090, reg 5, Sch 3 at **[6986]**, **[6995]**, and the Limited Liability Partnerships (Scotland) Regulations 2001, SSI 2001/128, reg 4, Schs 2, 3 at **[6977]**, **[6980A]**, **[6980B]**.

164 Corrupt inducement affecting appointment

A person who gives, or agrees or offers to give, to any member or creditor of a company any valuable consideration with a view to securing his own appointment or nomination, or to securing or preventing the appointment or nomination of some person other than himself, as the company's liquidator is liable to a fine.

[3321]

NOTES

Application to limited liability partnerships: see the introductory note to this Act, the Limited Liability Partnerships Regulations 2001, SI 2001/1090, reg 5, Sch 3 at **[6986]**, **[6995]**, and the Limited Liability Partnerships (Scotland) Regulations 2001, SSI 2001/128, reg 4, Schs 2, 3 at **[6977]**, **[6980A]**, **[6980B]**.

Liquidator's powers and duties

165 Voluntary winding up

(1) This section has effect where a company is being wound up voluntarily, but subject to section 166 below in the case of a creditors' voluntary winding up.

(2) The liquidator may—

(a) in the case of a members' voluntary winding up, with the sanction of an extraordinary resolution of the company, and

(b) in the case of a creditors' voluntary winding up, with the sanction of the court or the liquidation committee (or, if there is no such committee, a meeting of the company's creditors),

exercise any of the powers specified in Part I of Schedule 4 to this Act (payment of debts, compromise of claims, etc).

(3) The liquidator may, without sanction, exercise either of the powers specified in Part II of that Schedule (institution and defence of proceedings; carrying on the business of the company) and any of the general powers specified in Part III of that Schedule.

(4) The liquidator may—

(a) exercise the court's power of settling a list of contributories (which list is prima facie evidence of the liability of the persons named in it to be contributories),

(b) exercise the court's power of making calls,

(c) summon general meetings of the company for the purpose of obtaining its sanction by special or extraordinary resolution or for any other purpose he may think fit.

(5) The liquidator shall pay the company's debts and adjust the rights of the contributories among themselves.

(6) Where the liquidator in exercise of the powers conferred on him by this Act disposes of any property of the company to a person who is connected with the company (within the meaning of section 249 in Part VII), he shall, if there is for the time being a liquidation committee, give notice to the committee of that exercise of his powers.

[3322]

NOTES

Application to limited liability partnerships: see the introductory note to this Act, the Limited Liability Partnerships Regulations 2001, SI 2001/1090, reg 5, Sch 3 at **[6986]**, **[6995]**, and the Limited Liability Partnerships (Scotland) Regulations 2001, SSI 2001/128, reg 4, Schs 2, 3 at **[6977]**, **[6980A]**, **[6980B]**.

166 Creditors' voluntary winding up

(1) This section applies where, in the case of a creditors' voluntary winding up, a liquidator has been nominated by the company.

[(1A) The exercise by the liquidator of the power specified in paragraph 6 of Schedule 4 to this Act (power to sell any of the company's property) shall not be challengeable on the ground of any prior inhibition.]

(2) The powers conferred on the liquidator by section 165 shall not be exercised, except with the sanction of the court, during the period before the holding of the creditors' meeting under section 98 in Chapter IV.

(3) Subsection (2) does not apply in relation to the power of the liquidator—

(a) to take into his custody or under his control all the property to which the company is or appears to be entitled;

(b) to dispose of perishable goods and other goods the value of which is likely to diminish if they are not immediately disposed of; and

(c) to do all such other things as may be necessary for the protection of the company's assets.

(4) The liquidator shall attend the creditors' meeting held under section 98 and shall report to the meeting on any exercise by him of his powers (whether or not under this section or under section 112 or 165).

(5) If default is made—

(a) by the company in complying with subsection (1) or (2) of section 98, or

(b) by the directors in complying with subsection (1) or (2) of section 99,

the liquidator shall, within 7 days of the relevant day, apply to the court for directions as to the manner in which that default is to be remedied.

(6) "The relevant day" means the day on which the liquidator was nominated by the company or the day on which he first became aware of the default, whichever is the later.

(7) If the liquidator without reasonable excuse fails to comply with this section, he is liable to a fine.

[3323]

NOTES

Sub-s (1A): inserted by the Bankruptcy and Diligence etc (Scotland) Act 2007, s 155(1), (3), as from a day to be appointed.

Application to limited liability partnerships: see the introductory note to this Act, the Limited Liability Partnerships Regulations 2001, SI 2001/1090, reg 5, Sch 3 at **[6986]**, **[6995]**, and the Limited Liability Partnerships (Scotland) Regulations 2001, SSI 2001/128, reg 4, Schs 2, 3 at **[6977]**, **[6980A]**, **[6980B]**.

167 Winding up by the court

(1) Where a company is being wound up by the court, the liquidator may—

(a) with the sanction of the court or the liquidation committee, exercise any of the powers specified in Parts I and II of Schedule 4 to this Act (payment of debts; compromise of claims, etc; institution and defence of proceedings; carrying on of the business of the company), and

(b) with or without that sanction, exercise any of the general powers specified in Part III of that Schedule.

(2) Where the liquidator (not being the official receiver), in exercise of the powers conferred on him by this Act—

(a) disposes of any property of the company to a person who is connected with the company (within the meaning of section 249 in Part VII), or
(b) employs a solicitor to assist him in the carrying out of his functions,

he shall, if there is for the time being a liquidation committee, give notice to the committee of that exercise of his powers.

(3) The exercise by the liquidator in a winding up by the court of the powers conferred by this section is subject to the control of the court, and any creditor or contributory may apply to the court with respect to any exercise or proposed exercise of any of those powers.

[3324]

NOTES

Application to limited liability partnerships: see the introductory note to this Act, the Limited Liability Partnerships Regulations 2001, SI 2001/1090, reg 5, Sch 3 at **[6986]**, **[6995]**, and the Limited Liability Partnerships (Scotland) Regulations 2001, SSI 2001/128, reg 4, Schs 2, 3 at **[6977]**, **[6980A]**, **[6980B]**.

168 Supplementary powers (England and Wales)

(1) This section applies in the case of a company which is being wound up by the court in England and Wales.

(2) The liquidator may summon general meetings of the creditors or contributories for the purpose of ascertaining their wishes; and it is his duty to summon meetings at such times as the creditors or contributories by resolution (either at the meeting appointing the liquidator or otherwise) may direct, or whenever requested in writing to do so by one-tenth in value of the creditors or contributories (as the case may be).

(3) The liquidator may apply to the court (in the prescribed manner) for directions in relation to any particular matter arising in the winding up.

(4) Subject to the provisions of this Act, the liquidator shall use his own discretion in the management of the assets and their distribution among the creditors.

(5) If any person is aggrieved by an act or decision of the liquidator, that person may apply to the court; and the court may confirm, reverse or modify the act or decision complained of, and make such order in the case as it thinks just.

[(5A) Where at any time after a winding-up petition has been presented to the court against any person (including an insolvent partnership or other body which may be wound up under Part V of the Act as an unregistered company), whether by virtue of the provisions of the Insolvent Partnerships Order 1994 or not, the attention of the court is drawn to the fact that the person in question is a member of an insolvent partnership, the court may make an order as to the future conduct of the insolvency proceedings and any such order may apply any provisions of that Order with any necessary modifications.

(5B) Any order or directions under subsection (5A) may be made or given on the application of the official receiver, any responsible insolvency practitioner, the trustee of the partnership or any other interested person and may include provisions as to the administration of the joint estate of the partnership, and in particular how it and the separate estate of any member are to be administered.

[(5C) Where the court makes an order for the winding up of an insolvent partnership under—

(a) section 72(1)(a) of the Financial Services Act 1986;
(b) section 92(1)(a) of the Banking Act 1987; or
(c) section 367(3)(a) of the Financial Services and Markets Act 2000,

the court may make an order as to the future conduct of the winding up proceedings, and any such order may apply any provisions of the Insolvent Partnerships Order 1994 with any necessary modifications.]]

[3325]

NOTES

Sub-ss (5A), (5B): added, together with sub-s (5C), by the Insolvent Partnerships Order 1994, SI 1994/2421, art 14(1), as from 1 December 1994.

Sub-s (5C): added as noted above. It was repealed by the Financial Services and Markets Act 2000 (Consequential Amendments and Repeals) Order 2001, SI 2001/3649, art 306, as from 1 December 2001, but was subsequently substituted by the Financial Services and Markets Act 2000 (Consequential Amendments) Order 2002, SI 2002/1555, art 15, as from 3 July 2002, which further provided that the repeal by SI 2001/3649 was to be treated as if it had not been made.

Application to limited liability partnerships: see the introductory note to this Act and the Limited Liability Partnerships Regulations 2001, SI 2001/1090, reg 5, Sch 3 at **[6986]**, **[6995]**.

169 Supplementary powers (Scotland)

(1) In the case of a winding up in Scotland, the court may provide by order that the liquidator may, where there is no liquidation committee, exercise any of the following powers, namely—

(a) to bring or defend any action or other legal proceeding in the name and on behalf of the company, or

(b) to carry on the business of the company so far as may be necessary for its beneficial winding up,

without the sanction or intervention of the court.

(2) In a winding up by the court in Scotland, the liquidator has (subject to the rules) the same powers as a trustee on a bankrupt estate.

[3326]

NOTES

Application to limited liability partnerships: see the introductory note to this Act, the Limited Liability Partnerships Regulations 2001, SI 2001/1090, reg 5, Sch 3 at **[6986]**, **[6995]**, and the Limited Liability Partnerships (Scotland) Regulations 2001, SSI 2001/128, reg 4, Schs 2, 3 at **[6977]**, **[6980A]**, **[6980B]**.

170 Enforcement of liquidator's duty to make returns, etc

(1) If a liquidator who has made any default—

(a) in filing, delivering or making any return, account or other document, or

(b) in giving any notice which he is by law required to file, deliver, make or give,

fails to make good the default within 14 days after the service on him of a notice requiring him to do so, the court has the following powers.

(2) On an application made by any creditor or contributory of the company, or by the registrar of companies, the court may make an order directing the liquidator to make good the default within such time as may be specified in the order.

(3) The court's order may provide that all costs of and incidental to the application shall be borne by the liquidator.

(4) Nothing in this section prejudices the operation of any enactment imposing penalties on a liquidator in respect of any such default as is mentioned above.

[3327]

NOTES

Application to limited liability partnerships: see the introductory note to this Act, the Limited Liability Partnerships Regulations 2001, SI 2001/1090, reg 5, Sch 3 at **[6986]**, **[6995]**, and the Limited Liability Partnerships (Scotland) Regulations 2001, SSI 2001/128, reg 4, Schs 2, 3 at **[6977]**, **[6980A]**, **[6980B]**.

Modification in relation to Scotland: see the Note at the beginning of this Act.

Removal; vacation of office

171 Removal, etc (voluntary winding up)

(1) This section applies with respect to the removal from office and vacation of office of the liquidator of a company which is being wound up voluntarily.

(2) Subject to the next subsection, the liquidator may be removed from office only by an order of the court or—

(a) in the case of a members' voluntary winding up, by a general meeting of the company summoned specially for that purpose, or

(b) in the case of a creditors' voluntary winding up, by a general meeting of the company's creditors summoned specially for that purpose in accordance with the rules.

(3) Where the liquidator was appointed by the court under section 108 in Chapter V, a meeting such as is mentioned in subsection (2) above shall be summoned for the purpose of replacing him only if he thinks fit or the court so directs or the meeting is requested, in accordance with the rules—

(a) in the case of a members' voluntary winding up, by members representing not less than one-half of the total voting rights of all the members having at the date of the request a right to vote at the meeting, or

(b) in the case of a creditors' voluntary winding up, by not less than one-half, in value, of the company's creditors.

(4) A liquidator shall vacate office if he ceases to be a person who is qualified to act as an insolvency practitioner in relation to the company.

(5) A liquidator may, in the prescribed circumstances, resign his office by giving notice of his resignation to the registrar of companies.

(6) Where—

(a) in the case of a members' voluntary winding up, a final meeting of the company has been held under section 94 in Chapter III, or

(b) in the case of a creditors' voluntary winding up, final meetings of the company and of the creditors have been held under section 106 in Chapter IV,

the liquidator whose report was considered at the meeting or meetings shall vacate office as soon as he has complied with subsection (3) of that section and has given notice to the registrar of companies that the meeting or meetings have been held and of the decisions (if any) of the meeting or meetings.

[3328]

NOTES

Application to limited liability partnerships: see the introductory note to this Act, the Limited Liability Partnerships Regulations 2001, SI 2001/1090, reg 5, Sch 3 at **[6986]**, **[6995]**, and the Limited Liability Partnerships (Scotland) Regulations 2001, SSI 2001/128, reg 4, Schs 2, 3 at **[6977]**, **[6980A]**, **[6980B]**.

Modification in relation to Scotland: see the Note at the beginning of this Act.

172 Removal, etc (winding up by the court)

(1) This section applies with respect to the removal from office and vacation of office of the liquidator of a company which is being wound up by the court, or of a provisional liquidator.

(2) Subject as follows, the liquidator may be removed from office only by an order of the court or by a general meeting of the company's creditors summoned specially for that purpose in accordance with the rules; and a provisional liquidator may be removed from office only by an order of the court.

(3) Where—

(a) the official receiver is liquidator otherwise than in succession under section 136(3) to a person who held office as a result of a nomination by a meeting of the company's creditors or contributories, or

(b) the liquidator was appointed by the court otherwise than under section 139(4)(a) or 140(1), or was appointed by the Secretary of State,

a general meeting of the company's creditors shall be summoned for the purpose of replacing him only if he thinks fit, or the court so directs, or the meeting is requested, in accordance with the rules, by not less than one-quarter, in value, of the creditors.

(4) If appointed by the Secretary of State, the liquidator may be removed from office by a direction of the Secretary of State.

(5) A liquidator or provisional liquidator, not being the official receiver, shall vacate office if he ceases to be a person who is qualified to act as an insolvency practitioner in relation to the company.

(6) A liquidator may, in the prescribed circumstances, resign his office by giving notice of his resignation to the court.

(7) Where an order is made under section 204 (early dissolution in Scotland) for the dissolution of the company, the liquidator shall vacate office when the dissolution of the company takes effect in accordance with that section.

(8) Where a final meeting has been held under section 146 (liquidator's report on completion of winding up), the liquidator whose report was considered at the meeting shall vacate office as soon as he has given notice to the court and the registrar of companies that the meeting has been held and of the decisions (if any) of the meeting.

[3329]

NOTES

Application to limited liability partnerships: see the introductory note to this Act, the Limited Liability Partnerships Regulations 2001, SI 2001/1090, reg 5, Sch 3 at **[6986]**, **[6995]**, and the Limited Liability Partnerships (Scotland) Regulations 2001, SSI 2001/128, reg 4, Schs 2, 3 at **[6977]**, **[6980A]**, **[6980B]**.

Modification in relation to Scotland: see the Note at the beginning of this Act.

Release of liquidator

173 Release (voluntary winding up)

(1) This section applies with respect to the release of the liquidator of a company which is being wound up voluntarily.

(2) A person who has ceased to be a liquidator shall have his release with effect from the following time, that is to say—

(a) in the case of a person who has been removed from office by a general meeting of the company or by a general meeting of the company's creditors that has not resolved against his release or who has died, the time at which notice is given to the registrar of companies in accordance with the rules that that person has ceased to hold office;

(b) in the case of a person who has been removed from office by a general meeting of the company's creditors that has resolved against his release, or by the court, or who has vacated office under section 171(4) above, such time as the Secretary of State may, on the application of that person, determine;

(c) in the case of a person who has resigned, such time as may be prescribed;

(d) in the case of a person who has vacated office under subsection (6)(a) of section 171, the time at which he vacated office;

(e) in the case of a person who has vacated office under subsection (6)(b) of that section—

(i) if the final meeting of the creditors referred to in that subsection has resolved against that person's release, such time as the Secretary of State may, on an application by that person, determine, and

(ii) if that meeting has not resolved against that person's release, the time at which he vacated office.

(3) In the application of subsection (2) to the winding up of a company registered in Scotland, the references to a determination by the Secretary of State as to the time from which a person who has ceased to be liquidator shall have his release are to be read as references to such a determination by the Accountant of Court.

(4) Where a liquidator has his release under subsection (2), he is, with effect from the time specified in that subsection, discharged from all liability both in respect of acts or omissions of his in the winding up and otherwise in relation to his conduct as liquidator.

But nothing in this section prevents the exercise, in relation to a person who has had his release under subsection (2), of the court's powers under section 212 of this Act (summary remedy against delinquent directors, liquidators, etc).

[3330]

NOTES

Application to limited liability partnerships: see the introductory note to this Act, the Limited Liability Partnerships Regulations 2001, SI 2001/1090, reg 5, Sch 3 at **[6986]**, **[6995]**, and the Limited Liability Partnerships (Scotland) Regulations 2001, SSI 2001/128, reg 4, Schs 2, 3 at **[6977]**, **[6980A]**, **[6980B]**.

Modification in relation to Scotland: see the Note at the beginning of this Act.

174 Release (winding up by the court)

(1) This section applies with respect to the release of the liquidator of a company which is being wound up by the court, or of a provisional liquidator.

(2) Where the official receiver has ceased to be liquidator and a person becomes liquidator in his stead, the official receiver has his release with effect from the following time, that is to say—

(a) in a case where that person was nominated by a general meeting of creditors or contributories, or was appointed by the Secretary of State, the time at which the official receiver gives notice to the court that he has been replaced;

(b) in a case where that person is appointed by the court, such time as the court may determine.

(3) If the official receiver while he is a liquidator gives notice to the Secretary of State that the winding up is for practical purposes complete, he has his release with effect from such time as the Secretary of State may determine.

(4) A person other than the official receiver who has ceased to be a liquidator has his release with effect from the following time, that is to say—

(a) in the case of a person who has been removed from office by a general meeting of creditors that has not resolved against his release or who has died, the time at which notice is given to the court in accordance with the rules that that person has ceased to hold office;

(b) in the case of a person who has been removed from office by a general meeting of creditors that has resolved against his release, or by the court or the Secretary of State, or who has vacated office under section 172(5) or (7), such time as the Secretary of State may, on an application by that person, determine;

(c) in the case of a person who has resigned, such time as may be prescribed;

(d) in the case of a person who has vacated office under section 172(8)—

(i) if the final meeting referred to in that subsection has resolved against that person's release, such time as the Secretary of State may, on an application by that person, determine, and

(ii) if that meeting has not so resolved, the time at which that person vacated office.

(5) A person who has ceased to hold office as a provisional liquidator has his release with effect from such time as the court may, on an application by him, determine.

(6) Where the official receiver or a liquidator or provisional liquidator has his release under this section, he is, with effect from the time specified in the preceding provisions of this section, discharged from all liability both in respect of acts or omissions of his in the winding up and otherwise in relation to his conduct as liquidator or provisional liquidator.

But nothing in this section prevents the exercise, in relation to a person who has had his release under this section, of the court's powers under section 212 (summary remedy against delinquent directors, liquidators, etc).

(7) In the application of this section to a case where the order for winding up has been made by the court in Scotland, the references to a determination by the Secretary of State as to the time from which a person who has ceased to be liquidator has his release are to such a determination by the Accountant of Court.

[3331]

NOTES

Application to limited liability partnerships: see the introductory note to this Act, the Limited Liability Partnerships Regulations 2001, SI 2001/1090, reg 5, Sch 3 at **[6986]**, **[6995]**, and the Limited Liability Partnerships (Scotland) Regulations 2001, SSI 2001/128, reg 4, Schs 2, 3 at **[6977]**, **[6980A]**, **[6980B]**.

CHAPTER VIII
PROVISIONS OF GENERAL APPLICATION IN WINDING UP

Preferential debts

175 Preferential debts (general provision)

(1) In a winding up the company's preferential debts (within the meaning given by section 386 in Part XII) shall be paid in priority to all other debts.

(2) Preferential debts—

(a) rank equally among themselves after the expenses of the winding up and shall be paid in full, unless the assets are insufficient to meet them, in which case they abate in equal proportions; and

(b) so far as the assets of the company available for payment of general creditors are insufficient to meet them, have priority over the claims of holders of debentures secured by, or holders of, any floating charge created by the company, and shall be paid accordingly out of any property comprised in or subject to that charge.

[3332]

NOTES

Application to limited liability partnerships: see the introductory note to this Act and the Limited Liability Partnerships Regulations 2001, SI 2001/1090, reg 5, Sch 3 at **[6986]**, **[6995]**.

176 Preferential charge on goods distrained

(1) This section applies where a company is being wound up by the court in England and Wales, and is without prejudice to section 128 (avoidance of attachments, etc).

(2) Where any person (whether or not a landlord or person entitled to rent) has distrained upon the goods or effects of the company in the period of 3 months ending with the date of the winding-up order, those goods or effects, or the proceeds of their sale, shall be charged for the benefit of the company with the preferential debts of the company to the extent that the company's property is for the time being insufficient for meeting them.

(3) Where by virtue of a charge under subsection (2) any person surrenders any goods or effects to a company or makes a payment to a company, that person ranks, in respect of the amount of the proceeds of sale of those goods or effects by the liquidator or (as the case may be) the amount of the payment, as a preferential creditor of the company, except as against so much of the company's property as is available for the payment of preferential creditors by virtue of the surrender or payment.

[3333]

NOTES

Application to limited liability partnerships: see the introductory note to this Act and the Limited Liability Partnerships Regulations 2001, SI 2001/1090, reg 5, Sch 3 at **[6986]**, **[6995]**.

[Property subject to floating charge

NOTES

See further, as to the effect of floating charges on winding up, the Bankruptcy and Diligence etc (Scotland) Act 2007, s 45.

[176ZA Payment of expenses of winding up (England and Wales)

(1) The expenses of winding up in England and Wales, so far as the assets of the company available for payment of general creditors are insufficient to meet them, have priority over any claims to property comprised in or subject to any floating charge created by the company and shall be paid out of any such property accordingly.

(2) In subsection (1)—

(a) the reference to assets of the company available for payment of general creditors does not include any amount made available under section 176A(2)(a);

(b) the reference to claims to property comprised in or subject to a floating charge is to the claims of—

(i) the holders of debentures secured by, or holders of, the floating charge, and
(ii) any preferential creditors entitled to be paid out of that property in priority to them.

(3) Provision may be made by rules restricting the application of subsection (1), in such circumstances as may be prescribed, to expenses authorised or approved—

(a) by the holders of debentures secured by, or holders of, the floating charge and by any preferential creditors entitled to be paid in priority to them, or

(b) by the court.

(4) References in this section to the expenses of the winding up are to all expenses properly incurred in the winding up, including the remuneration of the liquidator.]

[3333ZA]

PART III OTHER LEGISLATION

NOTES

Commencement: to be appointed.

Inserted by the Companies Act 2006, s 1282(1), as from a day to be appointed.

176A Share of assets for unsecured creditors

(1) This section applies where a floating charge relates to property of a company—

(a) which has gone into liquidation,

(b) which is in administration,

(c) of which there is a provisional liquidator, or

(d) of which there is a receiver.

(2) The liquidator, administrator or receiver—

(a) shall make a prescribed part of the company's net property available for the satisfaction of unsecured debts, and

(b) shall not distribute that part to the proprietor of a floating charge except in so far as it exceeds the amount required for the satisfaction of unsecured debts.

(3) Subsection (2) shall not apply to a company if—

(a) the company's net property is less than the prescribed minimum, and

(b) the liquidator, administrator or receiver thinks that the cost of making a distribution to unsecured creditors would be disproportionate to the benefits.

(4) Subsection (2) shall also not apply to a company if or in so far as it is disapplied by—

(a) a voluntary arrangement in respect of the company, or

(b) a compromise or arrangement agreed under section 425 of the Companies Act (compromise with creditors and members).

(5) Subsection (2) shall also not apply to a company if—

(a) the liquidator, administrator or receiver applies to the court for an order under this subsection on the ground that the cost of making a distribution to unsecured creditors would be disproportionate to the benefits, and

(b) the court orders that subsection (2) shall not apply.

(6) In subsections (2) and (3) a company's net property is the amount of its property which would, but for this section, be available for satisfaction of claims of holders of debentures secured by, or holders of, any floating charge created by the company.

(7) An order under subsection (2) prescribing part of a company's net property may, in particular, provide for its calculation—

(a) as a percentage of the company's net property, or

(b) as an aggregate of different percentages of different parts of the company's net property.

(8) An order under this section—

(a) must be made by statutory instrument, and

(b) shall be subject to annulment pursuant to a resolution of either House of Parliament.

(9) In this section—

"floating charge" means a charge which is a floating charge on its creation and which is created after the first order under subsection (2)(a) comes into force, and

"prescribed" means prescribed by order by the Secretary of State.

(10) An order under this section may include transitional or incidental provision.]

[3333A]

NOTES

Inserted, together with the heading preceding s 176ZA, by the Enterprise Act 2002, s 252, as from 15 September 2003.

Application to limited liability partnerships: see the introductory note to this Act and the Limited Liability Partnerships Regulations 2001, SI 2001/1090, reg 5, Sch 3 at **[6986]**, **[6995]**.

Orders: the Insolvency Act 1986 (Prescribed Part) Order 2003, SI 2003/2097 at **[7192]**.

Special managers

177 Power to appoint special manager

(1) Where a company has gone into liquidation or a provisional liquidator has been appointed, the court may, on an application under this section, appoint any person to be the special manager of the business or property of the company.

(2) The application may be made by the liquidator or provisional liquidator in any case where it appears to him that the nature of the business or property of the company, or the interests of the company's creditors or contributories or members generally, require the appointment of another person to manage the company's business or property.

(3) The special manager has such powers as may be entrusted to him by the court.

(4) The court's power to entrust powers to the special manager includes power to direct that any provision of this Act that has effect in relation to the provisional liquidator or liquidator of a company shall have the like effect in relation to the special manager for the purposes of the carrying out by him of any of the functions of the provisional liquidator or liquidator.

(5) The special manager shall—

(a) give such security or, in Scotland, caution as may be prescribed;

(b) prepare and keep such accounts as may be prescribed; and

(c) produce those accounts in accordance with the rules to the Secretary of State or to such other persons as may be prescribed.

[3334]

NOTES

Application to limited liability partnerships: see the introductory note to this Act, the Limited Liability Partnerships Regulations 2001, SI 2001/1090, reg 5, Sch 3 at **[6986]**, **[6995]**, and the Limited Liability Partnerships (Scotland) Regulations 2001, SSI 2001/128, reg 4, Schs 2, 3 at **[6977]**, **[6980A]**, **[6980B]**.

Disclaimer (England and Wales only)

178 Power to disclaim onerous property

(1) This and the next two sections apply to a company that is being wound up in England and Wales.

(2) Subject as follows, the liquidator may, by the giving of the prescribed notice, disclaim any onerous property and may do so notwithstanding that he has taken possession of it, endeavoured to sell it, or otherwise exercised rights of ownership in relation to it.

(3) The following is onerous property for the purposes of this section—

(a) any unprofitable contract, and

(b) any other property of the company which is unsaleable or not readily saleable or is such that it may give rise to a liability to pay money or perform any other onerous act.

(4) A disclaimer under this section—

(a) operates so as to determine, as from the date of the disclaimer, the rights, interests and liabilities of the company in or in respect of the property disclaimed; but

(b) does not, except so far as is necessary for the purpose of releasing the company from any liability, affect the rights or liabilities of any other person.

(5) A notice of disclaimer shall not be given under this section in respect of any property if—

(a) a person interested in the property has applied in writing to the liquidator or one of his predecessors as liquidator requiring the liquidator or that predecessor to decide whether he will disclaim or not, and

(b) the period of 28 days beginning with the day on which that application was made, or such longer period as the court may allow, has expired without a notice of disclaimer having been given under this section in respect of that property.

(6) Any person sustaining loss or damage in consequence of the operation of a disclaimer under this section is deemed a creditor of the company to the extent of the loss or damage and accordingly may prove for the loss or damage in the winding up.

[3335]

NOTES

Application to limited liability partnerships: see the introductory note to this Act and the Limited Liability Partnerships Regulations 2001, SI 2001/1090, reg 5, Sch 3 at **[6986]**, **[6995]**.

179 Disclaimer of leaseholds

(1) The disclaimer under section 178 of any property of a leasehold nature does not take effect unless a copy of the disclaimer has been served (so far as the liquidator is aware of their addresses) on every person claiming under the company as underlessee or mortgagee and either—

(a) no application under section 181 below is made with respect to that property before the end of the period of 14 days beginning with the day on which the last notice served under this subsection was served; or

(b) where such an application has been made, the court directs that the disclaimer shall take effect.

(2) Where the court gives a direction under subsection (1)(b) it may also, instead of or in addition to any order it makes under section 181, make such orders with respect to fixtures, tenant's improvements and other matters arising out of the lease as it thinks fit.

[3336]

NOTES

Application to limited liability partnerships: see the introductory note to this Act and the Limited Liability Partnerships Regulations 2001, SI 2001/1090, reg 5, Sch 3 at **[6986]**, **[6995]**.

180 Land subject to rentcharge

(1) The following applies where, in consequence of the disclaimer under section 178 of any land subject to a rentcharge, that land vests by operation of law in the Crown or any other person (referred to in the next subsection as "the proprietor").

(2) The proprietor and the successors in title of the proprietor are not subject to any personal liability in respect of any sums becoming due under the rentcharge except sums becoming due after the proprietor, or some person claiming under or through the proprietor, has taken possession or control of the land or has entered into occupation of it.

[3337]

NOTES

Application to limited liability partnerships: see the introductory note to this Act and the Limited Liability Partnerships Regulations 2001, SI 2001/1090, reg 5, Sch 3 at **[6986]**, **[6995]**.

181 Powers of court (general)

(1) This section and the next apply where the liquidator has disclaimed property under section 178.

(2) An application under this section may be made to the court by—

(a) any person who claims an interest in the disclaimed property, or

(b) any person who is under any liability in respect of the disclaimed property, not being a liability discharged by the disclaimer.

(3) Subject as follows, the court may on the application make an order, on such terms as it thinks fit, for the vesting of the disclaimed property in, or for its delivery to—

(a) a person entitled to it or a trustee for such a person, or

(b) a person subject to such a liability as is mentioned in subsection (2)(b) or a trustee for such a person.

(4) The court shall not make an order under subsection (3)(b) except where it appears to the court that it would be just to do so for the purpose of compensating the person subject to the liability in respect of the disclaimer.

(5) The effect of any order under this section shall be taken into account in assessing for the purpose of section 178(6) the extent of any loss or damage sustained by any person in consequence of the disclaimer.

(6) An order under this section vesting property in any person need not be completed by conveyance, assignment or transfer.

[3338]

NOTES

Application to limited liability partnerships: see the introductory note to this Act and the Limited Liability Partnerships Regulations 2001, SI 2001/1090, reg 5, Sch 3 at **[6986]**, **[6995]**.

182 Powers of court (leaseholds)

(1) The court shall not make an order under section 181 vesting property of a leasehold nature in any person claiming under the company as underlessee or mortgagee except on terms making that person—

(a) subject to the same liabilities and obligations as the company was subject to under the lease at the commencement of the winding up, or

(b) if the court thinks fit, subject to the same liabilities and obligations as that person would be subject to if the lease had been assigned to him at the commencement of the winding up.

(2) For the purposes of an order under section 181 relating to only part of any property comprised in a lease, the requirements of subsection (1) apply as if the lease comprised only the property to which the order relates.

(3) Where subsection (1) applies and no person claiming under the company as underlessee or mortgagee is willing to accept an order under section 181 on the terms required by virtue of that subsection, the court may, by order under that section, vest the company's estate or interest in the property in any person who is liable (whether personally or in a representative capacity, and whether alone or jointly with the company) to perform the lessee's covenants in the lease.

The court may vest that estate and interest in such a person freed and discharged from all estates, incumbrances and interests created by the company.

(4) Where subsection (1) applies and a person claiming under the company as underlessee or mortgagee declines to accept an order under section 181, that person is excluded from all interest in the property.

[3339]

NOTES

Application to limited liability partnerships: see the introductory note to this Act and the Limited Liability Partnerships Regulations 2001, SI 2001/1090, reg 5, Sch 3 at **[6986]**, **[6995]**.

Execution, attachment and the Scottish equivalents

183 Effect of execution or attachment (England and Wales)

(1) Where a creditor has issued execution against the goods or land of a company or has attached any debt due to it, and the company is subsequently wound up, he is not entitled to retain the benefit of the execution or attachment against the liquidator unless he has completed the execution or attachment before the commencement of the winding up.

(2) However—

(a) if a creditor has had notice of a meeting having been called at which a resolution for voluntary winding up is to be proposed, the date on which he had notice is substituted, for the purpose of subsection (1), for the date of commencement of the winding up;

(b) a person who purchases in good faith under a sale by the [enforcement officer or other officer charged with the execution of the writ] any goods of a company on which execution has been levied in all cases acquires a good title to them against the liquidator; and

(c) the rights conferred by subsection (1) on the liquidator may be set aside by the court in favour of the creditor to such extent and subject to such terms as the court thinks fit.

(3) For purposes of this Act—

(a) an execution against goods is completed by seizure and sale, or by the making of a charging order under section 1 of the Charging Orders Act 1979;

(b) an attachment of a debt is completed by receipt of the debt; and

(c) an execution against land is completed by seizure, by the appointment of a receiver, or by the making of a charging order under section 1 of the Act above-mentioned.

(4) In this section, "goods" includes all chattels personal; and ["enforcement officer" means an individual who is authorised to act as an enforcement officer under the Courts Act 2003].

(5) This section does not apply in the case of a winding up in Scotland.

[3340]

NOTES

Sub-ss (2), (4): words in square brackets substituted by the Courts Act 2003, s 109(1), Sch 8, para 295, as from 15 March 2004.

Application to limited liability partnerships: see the introductory note to this Act and the Limited Liability Partnerships Regulations 2001, SI 2001/1090, reg 5, Sch 3 at **[6986]**, **[6995]**.

184 Duties of [officers charged with execution of writs and other processes] (England and Wales)

(1) The following applies where a company's goods are taken in execution and, before their sale or the completion of the execution (by the receipt or recovery of the full amount of the levy), notice is served on the [enforcement officer, or other officer, charged with execution of the writ or other process,] that a provisional liquidator has been appointed or that a winding-up order has been made, or that a resolution for voluntary winding up has been passed.

(2) The [enforcement officer or other officer] shall, on being so required, deliver the goods and any money seized or received in part satisfaction of the execution to the liquidator; but the costs of execution are a first charge on the goods or money so delivered, and the liquidator may sell the goods, or a sufficient part of them, for the purpose of satisfying the charge.

(3) If under an execution in respect of a judgment for a sum exceeding [£500] a company's goods are sold or money is paid in order to avoid sale, the [enforcement officer or other officer] shall deduct the costs of the execution from the proceeds of sale or the money paid and retain the balance for 14 days.

(4) If within that time notice is served on the [enforcement officer or other officer] of a petition for the winding up of the company having been presented, or of a meeting having been called at which there is to be proposed a resolution for voluntary winding up, and an order is made or a resolution passed (as the case may be), the [enforcement officer or other officer] shall pay the balance to the liquidator, who is entitled to retain it as against the execution creditor.

(5) The rights conferred by this section on the liquidator may be set aside by the court in favour of the creditor to such extent and subject to such terms as the court thinks fit.

(6) In this section, "goods" includes all chattels personal; and ["enforcement officer" means an individual who is authorised to act as an enforcement officer under the Courts Act 2003].

(7) The money sum for the time being specified in subsection (3) is subject to increase or reduction by order under section 416 in Part XV.

(8) This section does not apply in the case of a winding up in Scotland.

[3341]

NOTES

Section heading, sub-ss (1), (2), (4), (6): words in square brackets substituted by the Courts Act 2003, s 109(1), Sch 8, para 296, as from 15 March 2004.

Sub-s (3): sum in first pair of square brackets increased from £250 by the Insolvency Proceedings (Monetary Limits) Order 1986, SI 1986/1996, art 2, Schedule, Pt I (but this amendment is not to affect any case where the goods are sold or payment to avoid sale is made before 29 December 1986); words in second pair of square brackets substituted by the Courts Act 2003, s 109(1), Sch 8, para 296(1), (3), as from 15 March 2004.

Application to limited liability partnerships: see the introductory note to this Act and the Limited Liability Partnerships Regulations 2001, SI 2001/1090, reg 5, Sch 3 at **[6986]**, **[6995]**.

185 Effect of diligence (Scotland)

(1) In the winding up of a company registered in Scotland, the following provisions of the Bankruptcy (Scotland) Act 1985—

(a) subsections (1) to (6)[, (8A) to (8F) and (10)] of section 37 (effect of sequestration on diligence); and

(b) subsections (3), (4), (7) and (8) of section 39 (realisation of estate),

apply, so far as consistent with this Act, in like manner as they apply in the sequestration of a debtor's estate, with the substitutions specified below and with any other necessary modifications.

(2) The substitutions to be made in those sections of the Act of 1985 are as follows—

(a) for references to the debtor, substitute references to the company;

(b) for references to the sequestration, substitute references to the winding up;

(c) for references to the date of sequestration, substitute references to the commencement of the winding up of the company; and

(d) for references to the *permanent* trustee, substitute references to the liquidator.

(3) In this section, "the commencement of the winding up of the company" means, where it is being wound up by the court, the day on which the winding-up order is made.

(4) This section, so far as relating to any estate or effects of the company situated in Scotland, applies in the case of a company registered in England and Wales as in the case of one registered in Scotland.

[3342]

NOTES

Sub-s (1): words in square brackets inserted by the Bankruptcy and Diligence etc (Scotland) Act 2007, s 226, Sch 5, para 14(1), (3), as from a day to be appointed.

Sub-s (2): word in italics in para (d) repealed by the Bankruptcy and Diligence etc (Scotland) Act 2007, s 226, Sch 6, Pt 1, as from a day to be appointed.

Application to limited liability partnerships: see the introductory note to this Act, the Limited Liability Partnerships Regulations 2001, SI 2001/1090, reg 5, Sch 3 at **[6986]**, **[6995]**, and the Limited Liability Partnerships (Scotland) Regulations 2001, SSI 2001/128, reg 4, Schs 2, 3 at **[6977]**, **[6980A]**, **[6980B]**.

Miscellaneous matters

186 Rescission of contracts by the court

(1) The court may, on the application of a person who is, as against the liquidator, entitled to the benefit or subject to the burden of a contract made with the company, make an order rescinding the contract on such terms as to payment by or to either party of damages for the non-performance of the contract, or otherwise as the court thinks just.

(2) Any damages payable under the order to such a person may be proved by him as a debt in the winding up.

[3343]

NOTES

Application to limited liability partnerships: see the introductory note to this Act, the Limited Liability Partnerships Regulations 2001, SI 2001/1090, reg 5, Sch 3 at **[6986]**, **[6995]**, and the Limited Liability Partnerships (Scotland) Regulations 2001, SSI 2001/128, reg 4, Schs 2, 3 at **[6977]**, **[6980A]**, **[6980B]**.

187 Power to make over assets to employees

(1) On the winding up of a company (whether by the court or voluntarily), the liquidator may, subject to the following provisions of this section, make any payment which the company has, before the commencement of the winding up, decided to make under section 719 of the Companies Act (power to provide for employees or former employees on cessation or transfer of business).

(2) The power which a company may exercise by virtue only of that section may be exercised by the liquidator after the winding up has commenced if, after the company's

PART III OTHER LEGISLATION

liabilities have been fully satisfied and provision has been made for the expenses of the winding up, the exercise of that power has been sanctioned by such a resolution of the company as would be required of the company itself by section 719(3) before that commencement, if paragraph (b) of that subsection were omitted and any other requirement applicable to its exercise by the company had been met.

(3) Any payment which may be made by a company under this section (that is, a payment after the commencement of its winding up) may be made out of the company's assets which are available to the members on the winding up.

(4) On a winding up by the court, the exercise by the liquidator of his powers under this section is subject to the court's control, and any creditor or contributory may apply to the court with respect to any exercise or proposed exercise of the power.

(5) Subsections (1) and (2) above have effect notwithstanding anything in any rule of law or in section 107 of this Act (property of company after satisfaction of liabilities to be distributed among members).

[3344]

NOTES

Application to limited liability partnerships: see the introductory note to this Act, the Limited Liability Partnerships Regulations 2001, SI 2001/1090, reg 5, Sch 3 at **[6986]**, **[6995]**, and the Limited Liability Partnerships (Scotland) Regulations 2001, SSI 2001/128, reg 4, Schs 2, 3 at **[6977]**, **[6980A]**, **[6980B]**.

188 Notification that company is in liquidation

[(1) When a company is being wound up, whether by the court or voluntarily—

(a) every invoice, order for goods, business letter or order form (whether in hard copy, electronic or any other form) issued by or on behalf of the company, or a liquidator of the company or a receiver or manager of the company's property, being a document on or in which the name of the company appears, and

(b) all the company's websites,

must contain a statement that the company is being wound up.]

(2) If default is made in complying with this section, the company and any of the following persons who knowingly and wilfully authorises or permits the default, namely, any officer of the company, any liquidator of the company and any receiver or manager, is liable to a fine.

[3345]

NOTES

Sub-s (1): substituted by the Companies (Registrar, Languages and Trading Disclosures) Regulations 2006, SI 2006/3429, reg 7(1), as from 1 January 2007.

Application to limited liability partnerships: see the introductory note to this Act, the Limited Liability Partnerships Regulations 2001, SI 2001/1090, reg 5, Sch 3 at **[6986]**, **[6995]**, and the Limited Liability Partnerships (Scotland) Regulations 2001, SSI 2001/128, reg 4, Schs 2, 3 at **[6977]**, **[6980A]**, **[6980B]**.

189 Interest on debts

(1) In a winding up interest is payable in accordance with this section on any debt proved in the winding up, including so much of any such debt as represents interest on the remainder.

(2) Any surplus remaining after the payment of the debts proved in a winding up shall, before being applied for any other purpose, be applied in paying interest on those debts in respect of the periods during which they have been outstanding since the company went into liquidation.

(3) All interest under this section ranks equally, whether or not the debts on which it is payable rank equally.

(4) The rate of interest payable under this section in respect of any debt ("the official rate" for the purposes of any provision of this Act in which that expression is used) is whichever is the greater of—

(a) the rate specified in section 17 of the Judgments Act 1838 on the day on which the company went into liquidation, and

(b) the rate applicable to that debt apart from the winding up.

(5) In the application of this section to Scotland—

(a) references to a debt proved in a winding up have effect as references to a claim accepted in a winding up, and

(b) the reference to section 17 of the Judgments Act 1838 has effect as a reference to the rules.

[3346]

NOTES

Application to limited liability partnerships: see the introductory note to this Act, the Limited Liability Partnerships Regulations 2001, SI 2001/1090, reg 5, Sch 3 at **[6986]**, **[6995]**, and the Limited Liability Partnerships (Scotland) Regulations 2001, SSI 2001/128, reg 4, Schs 2, 3 at **[6977]**, **[6980A]**, **[6980B]**.

190 Documents exempt from stamp duty

(1) In the case of a winding up by the court, or of a creditors' voluntary winding up, the following has effect as regards exemption from duties chargeable under the enactments relating to stamp duties.

(2) If the company is registered in England and Wales, the following documents are exempt from stamp duty—

(a) every assurance relating solely to freehold or leasehold property, or to any estate, right or interest in, any real or personal property, which forms part of the company's assets and which, after the execution of the assurance, either at law or in equity, is or remains part of those assets, and

(b) every writ, order, certificate, or other instrument or writing relating solely to the property of any company which is being wound up as mentioned in subsection (1), or to any proceeding under such a winding up.

"Assurance" here includes deed, conveyance, assignment and surrender.

(3) If the company is registered in Scotland, the following documents are exempt from stamp duty—

(a) every conveyance relating solely to property which forms part of the company's assets and which, after the execution of the conveyance, is or remains the company's property for the benefit of its creditors,

(b) any article of roup or sale, submission and every other instrument and writing whatsoever relating solely to the company's property, and

(c) every deed or writing forming part of the proceedings in the winding up.

"Conveyance" here includes assignation, instrument, discharge, writing and deed.

[3347]

NOTES

Application to limited liability partnerships: see the introductory note to this Act and the Limited Liability Partnerships Regulations 2001, SI 2001/1090, reg 5, Sch 3 at **[6986]**, **[6995]**.

191 Company's books to be evidence

Where a company is being wound up, all books and papers of the company and of the liquidators are, as between the contributories of the company, prima facie evidence of the truth of all matters purporting to be recorded in them.

[3348]

NOTES

Application to limited liability partnerships: see the introductory note to this Act, the Limited Liability Partnerships Regulations 2001, SI 2001/1090, reg 5, Sch 3 at **[6986]**, **[6995]**, and the Limited Liability Partnerships (Scotland) Regulations 2001, SSI 2001/128, reg 4, Schs 2, 3 at **[6977]**, **[6980A]**, **[6980B]**.

192 Information as to pending liquidations

(1) If the winding up of a company is not concluded within one year after its commencement, the liquidator shall, at such intervals as may be prescribed, until the winding up is concluded, send to the registrar of companies a statement in the prescribed form and containing the prescribed particulars with respect to the proceedings in, and position of, the liquidation.

(2) If a liquidator fails to comply with this section, he is liable to a fine and, for continued contravention, to a daily default fine.

[3349]

NOTES

Application to limited liability partnerships: see the introductory note to this Act, the Limited Liability Partnerships Regulations 2001, SI 2001/1090, reg 5, Sch 3 at **[6986]**, **[6995]**, and the Limited Liability Partnerships (Scotland) Regulations 2001, SSI 2001/128, reg 4, Schs 2, 3 at **[6977]**, **[6980A]**, **[6980B]**.

Modification in relation to Scotland: see the Note at the beginning of this Act.

193 Unclaimed dividends (Scotland)

(1) The following applies where a company registered in Scotland has been wound up, and is about to be dissolved.

(2) The liquidator shall lodge in an appropriate bank or institution as defined in section 73(1) of the Bankruptcy (Scotland) Act 1985 (not being a bank or institution in or of which the liquidator is acting partner, manager, agent or cashier) in the name of the Accountant of Court the whole unclaimed dividends and unapplied or undistributable balances, and the deposit receipts shall be transmitted to the Accountant of Court.

(3) The provisions of section 58 of the Bankruptcy (Scotland) Act 1985 (so far as consistent with this Act and the Companies Act) apply with any necessary modifications to sums lodged in a bank or institution under this section as they apply to sums deposited under section 57 of the Act first mentioned.

[3350]

NOTES

Application to limited liability partnerships: see the introductory note to this Act, the Limited Liability Partnerships Regulations 2001, SI 2001/1090, reg 5, Sch 3 at **[6986]**, **[6995]**, and the Limited Liability Partnerships (Scotland) Regulations 2001, SSI 2001/128, reg 4, Schs 2, 3 at **[6977]**, **[6980A]**, **[6980B]**.

194 Resolutions passed at adjourned meetings

Where a resolution is passed at an adjourned meeting of a company's creditors or contributories, the resolution is treated for all purposes as having been passed on the date on which it was in fact passed, and not as having been passed on any earlier date.

[3351]

NOTES

Application to limited liability partnerships: see the introductory note to this Act, the Limited Liability Partnerships Regulations 2001, SI 2001/1090, reg 5, Sch 3 at **[6986]**, **[6995]**, and the Limited Liability Partnerships (Scotland) Regulations 2001, SSI 2001/128, reg 4, Schs 2, 3 at **[6977]**, **[6980A]**, **[6980B]**.

195 Meetings to ascertain wishes of creditors or contributories

(1) The court may—

(a) as to all matters relating to the winding up of a company, have regard to the wishes of the creditors or contributories (as proved to it by any sufficient evidence), and

(b) if it thinks fit, for the purpose of ascertaining those wishes, direct meetings of the creditors or contributories to be called, held and conducted in such manner as the court directs, and appoint a person to act as chairman of any such meeting and report the result of it to the court.

(2) In the case of creditors, regard shall be had to the value of each creditor's debt.

(3) In the case of contributories, regard shall be had to the number of votes conferred on each contributory by the Companies Act or the articles.

[3352]

NOTES

Application to limited liability partnerships: see the introductory note to this Act and the Limited Liability Partnerships Regulations 2001, SI 2001/1090, reg 5, Sch 3 at **[6986]**, **[6995]**.

196 Judicial notice of court documents

In all proceedings under this Part, all courts, judges and persons judicially acting, and all officers, judicial or ministerial, of any court, or employed in enforcing the process of any court shall take judicial notice—

(a) of the signature of any officer of the High Court or of a county court in England and Wales, or of the Court of Session or a sheriff court in Scotland, or of the High Court in Northern Ireland, and also

(b) of the official seal or stamp of the several offices of the High Court in England and Wales or Northern Ireland, or of the Court of Session, appended to or impressed on any document made, issued or signed under the provisions of this Act or the Companies Act, or any official copy of such a document.

[3353]

NOTES

Application to limited liability partnerships: see the introductory note to this Act, the Limited Liability Partnerships Regulations 2001, SI 2001/1090, reg 5, Sch 3 at **[6986]**, **[6995]**, and the Limited Liability Partnerships (Scotland) Regulations 2001, SSI 2001/128, reg 4, Schs 2, 3 at **[6977]**, **[6980A]**, **[6980B]**.

197 Commission for receiving evidence

(1) When a company is wound up in England and Wales or in Scotland, the court may refer the whole or any part of the examination of witnesses—

(a) to a specified county court in England and Wales, or

(b) to the sheriff principal for a specified sheriffdom in Scotland, or

(c) to the High Court in Northern Ireland or a specified Northern Ireland County Court,

("specified" meaning specified in the order of the winding-up court).

(2) Any person exercising jurisdiction as a judge of the court to which the reference is made (or, in Scotland, the sheriff principal to whom it is made) shall then, by virtue of this section, be a commissioner for the purpose of taking the evidence of those witnesses.

(3) The judge or sheriff principal has in the matter referred the same power of summoning and examining witnesses, of requiring the production and delivery of documents, of punishing defaults by witnesses, and of allowing costs and expenses to witnesses, as the court which made the winding-up order.

These powers are in addition to any which the judge or sheriff principal might lawfully exercise apart from this section.

(4) The examination so taken shall be returned or reported to that court which made the order in such manner as the court requests.

(5) This section extends to Northern Ireland.

[3354]

NOTES

Application to limited liability partnerships: see the introductory note to this Act and the Limited Liability Partnerships Regulations 2001, SI 2001/1090, reg 5, Sch 3 at **[6986]**, **[6995]**.

198 Court order for examination of persons in Scotland

(1) The court may direct the examination in Scotland of any person for the time being in Scotland (whether a contributory of the company or not), in regard to the trade, dealings, affairs or property of any company in course of being wound up, or of any person being a contributory of the company, so far as the company may be interested by reason of his being a contributory.

(2) The order or commission to take the examination shall be directed to the sheriff principal of the sheriffdom in which the person to be examined is residing or happens to be for the time; and the sheriff principal shall summon the person to appear before him at a time and place to be specified in the summons for examination on oath as a witness or as a haver, and to produce any books or papers called for which are in his possession or power.

(3) The sheriff principal may take the examination either orally or on written interrogatories, and shall report the same in writing in the usual form to the court, and shall

transmit with the report the books and papers produced, if the originals are required and specified by the order or commission, or otherwise copies or extracts authenticated by the sheriff.

(4) If a person so summoned fails to appear at the time and place specified, or refuses to be examined or to make the production required, the sheriff principal shall proceed against him as a witness or haver duly cited; and failing to appear or refusing to give evidence or make production may be proceeded against by the law of Scotland.

(5) The sheriff principal is entitled to such fees, and the witness is entitled to such allowances, as sheriffs principal when acting as commissioners under appointment from the Court of Session and as witnesses and havers are entitled to in the like cases according to the law and practice of Scotland.

(6) If any objection is stated to the sheriff principal by the witness, either on the ground of his incompetency as a witness, or as to the production required, or on any other ground, the sheriff principal may, if he thinks fit, report the objection to the court, and suspend the examination of the witness until it has been disposed of by the court.

[3355]

NOTES

Application to limited liability partnerships: see the introductory note to this Act and the Limited Liability Partnerships Regulations 2001, SI 2001/1090, reg 5, Sch 3 at **[6986]**, **[6995]**.

199 Costs of application for leave to proceed (Scottish companies)

Where a petition or application for leave to proceed with an action or proceeding against a company which is being wound up in Scotland is unopposed and is granted by the court, the costs of the petition or application shall, unless the court otherwise directs, be added to the amount of the petitioner's or applicant's claim against the company.

[3356]

NOTES

Application to limited liability partnerships: see the introductory note to this Act, the Limited Liability Partnerships Regulations 2001, SI 2001/1090, reg 5, Sch 3 at **[6986]**, **[6995]**, and the Limited Liability Partnerships (Scotland) Regulations 2001, SSI 2001/128, reg 4, Schs 2, 3 at **[6977]**, **[6980A]**, **[6980B]**.

200 Affidavits etc in United Kingdom and overseas

(1) An affidavit required to be sworn under or for the purposes of this Part may be sworn in the United Kingdom, or elsewhere in Her Majesty's dominions, before any court, judge or person lawfully authorised to take and receive affidavits, or before any of Her Majesty's consuls or vice-consuls in any place outside Her dominions.

(2) All courts, judges, justices, commissioners and persons acting judicially shall take judicial notice of the seal or stamp or signature (as the case may be) of any such court, judge, person, consul or vice-consul attached, appended or subscribed to any such affidavit, or to any other document to be used for the purposes of this Part.

[3357]

NOTES

Application to limited liability partnerships: see the introductory note to this Act, the Limited Liability Partnerships Regulations 2001, SI 2001/1090, reg 5, Sch 3 at **[6986]**, **[6995]**, and the Limited Liability Partnerships (Scotland) Regulations 2001, SSI 2001/128, reg 4, Schs 2, 3 at **[6977]**, **[6980A]**, **[6980B]**.

CHAPTER IX
DISSOLUTION OF COMPANIES AFTER WINDING UP

201 Dissolution (voluntary winding up)

(1) This section applies, in the case of a company wound up voluntarily, where the liquidator has sent to the registrar of companies his final account and return under section 94 (members' voluntary) or section 106 (creditors' voluntary).

(2) The registrar on receiving the account and return shall forthwith register them; and on the expiration of 3 months from the registration of the return the company is deemed to be dissolved.

(3) However, the court may, on the application of the liquidator or any other person who appears to the court to be interested, make an order deferring the date at which the dissolution of the company is to take effect for such time as the court thinks fit.

(4) It is the duty of the person on whose application an order of the court under this section is made within 7 days after the making of the order to deliver to the registrar [a copy] of the order for registration; and if that person fails to do so he is liable to a fine and, for continued contravention, to a daily default fine.

[3358]

NOTES

Sub-s (4): words in square brackets substituted by the Companies (Registrar, Languages and Trading Disclosures) Regulations 2006, SI 2006/3429, reg 3(1)(d), as from 1 January 2007.

Application to limited liability partnerships: see the introductory note to this Act and the Limited Liability Partnerships Regulations 2001, SI 2001/1090, reg 5, Sch 3 at **[6986]**, **[6995]**. Note also that in so far as this section applies to LLPs by virtue of the Limited Liability Partnerships Regulations 2001, SI 2001/1090, the substitution of the words "a copy" for the original words "an office copy" in sub-s (4) has no effect; see the Companies (Registrar, Languages and Trading Disclosures) Regulations 2006, SI 2006/3429, reg 3(3).

202 Early dissolution (England and Wales)

(1) This section applies where an order for the winding up of a company has been made by the court in England and Wales.

(2) The official receiver, if—

(a) he is the liquidator of the company, and

(b) it appears to him—

(i) that the realisable assets of the company are insufficient to cover the expenses of the winding up, and

(ii) that the affairs of the company do not require any further investigation,

may at any time apply to the registrar of companies for the early dissolution of the company.

(3) Before making that application, the official receiver shall give not less than 28 days' notice of his intention to do so to the company's creditors and contributories and, if there is an administrative receiver of the company, to that receiver.

(4) With the giving of that notice the official receiver ceases (subject to any directions under the next section) to be required to perform any duties imposed on him in relation to the company, its creditors or contributories by virtue of any provision of this Act, apart from a duty to make an application under subsection (2) of this section.

(5) On the receipt of the official receiver's application under subsection (2) the registrar shall forthwith register it and, at the end of the period of 3 months beginning with the day of the registration of the application, the company shall be dissolved.

However, the Secretary of State may, on the application of the official receiver or any other person who appears to the Secretary of State to be interested, give directions under section 203 at any time before the end of that period.

[3359]

NOTES

Application to limited liability partnerships: see the introductory note to this Act and the Limited Liability Partnerships Regulations 2001, SI 2001/1090, reg 5, Sch 3 at **[6986]**, **[6995]**.

203 Consequence of notice under s 202

(1) Where a notice has been given under section 202(3), the official receiver or any creditor or contributory of the company, or the administrative receiver of the company (if there is one) may apply to the Secretary of State for directions under this section.

(2) The grounds on which that application may be made are—

(a) that the realisable assets of the company are sufficient to cover the expenses of the winding up;

(b) that the affairs of the company do require further investigation; or

(c) that for any other reason the early dissolution of the company is inappropriate.

(3) Directions under this section—

PART III OTHER LEGISLATION

(a) are directions making such provision as the Secretary of State thinks fit for enabling the winding up of the company to proceed as if no notice had been given under section 202(3), and

(b) may, in the case of an application under section 202(5), include a direction deferring the date at which the dissolution of the company is to take effect for such period as the Secretary of State thinks fit.

(4) An appeal to the court lies from any decision of the Secretary of State on an application for directions under this section.

(5) It is the duty of the person on whose application any directions are given under this section, or in whose favour an appeal with respect to an application for such directions is determined, within 7 days after the giving of the directions or the determination of the appeal, to deliver to the registrar of companies for registration such a copy of the directions or determination as is prescribed.

(6) If a person without reasonable excuse fails to deliver a copy as required by subsection (5), he is liable to a fine and, for continued contravention, to a daily default fine.

[3360]

NOTES

Application to limited liability partnerships: see the introductory note to this Act and the Limited Liability Partnerships Regulations 2001, SI 2001/1090, reg 5, Sch 3 at **[6986]**, **[6995]**.

204 Early dissolution (Scotland)

(1) This section applies where a winding-up order has been made by the court in Scotland.

(2) If after a meeting or meetings under section 138 (appointment of liquidator in Scotland) it appears to the liquidator that the realisable assets of the company are insufficient to cover the expenses of the winding up, he may apply to the court for an order that the company be dissolved.

(3) Where the liquidator makes that application, if the court is satisfied that the realisable assets of the company are insufficient to cover the expenses of the winding up and it appears to the court appropriate to do so, the court shall make an order that the company be dissolved in accordance with this section.

(4) A copy of the order shall within 14 days from its date be forwarded by the liquidator to the registrar of companies, who shall forthwith register it; and, at the end of the period of 3 months beginning with the day of the registration of the order, the company shall be dissolved.

(5) The court may, on an application by any person who appears to the court to have an interest, order that the date at which the dissolution of the company is to take effect shall be deferred for such period as the court thinks fit.

(6) It is the duty of the person on whose application an order is made under subsection (5), within 7 days after the making of the order, to deliver to the registrar of companies such a copy of the order as is prescribed.

(7) If the liquidator without reasonable excuse fails to comply with the requirements of subsection (4), he is liable to a fine and, for continued contravention, to a daily default fine.

(8) If a person without reasonable excuse fails to deliver a copy as required by subsection (6), he is liable to a fine and, for continued contravention, to a daily default fine.

[3361]

NOTES

Application to limited liability partnerships: see the introductory note to this Act and the Limited Liability Partnerships Regulations 2001, SI 2001/1090, reg 5, Sch 3 at **[6986]**, **[6995]**.

205 Dissolution otherwise than under ss 202–204

(1) This section applies where the registrar of companies receives—

(a) a notice served for the purposes of section 172(8) (final meeting of creditors and vacation of office by liquidator), or

(b) a notice from the official receiver that the winding up of a company by the court is complete.

(2) The registrar shall, on receipt of the notice, forthwith register it; and, subject as follows, at the end of the period of 3 months beginning with the day of the registration of the notice, the company shall be dissolved.

(3) The Secretary of State may, on the application of the official receiver or any other person who appears to the Secretary of State to be interested, give a direction deferring the date at which the dissolution of the company is to take effect for such period as the Secretary of State thinks fit.

(4) An appeal to the court lies from any decision of the Secretary of State on an application for a direction under subsection (3).

(5) Subsection (3) does not apply in a case where the winding-up order was made by the court in Scotland, but in such a case the court may, on an application by any person appearing to the court to have an interest, order that the date at which the dissolution of the company is to take effect shall be deferred for such period as the court thinks fit.

(6) It is the duty of the person—

(a) on whose application a direction is given under subsection (3);

(b) in whose favour an appeal with respect to an application for such a direction is determined; or

(c) on whose application an order is made under subsection (5),

within 7 days after the giving of the direction, the determination of the appeal or the making of the order, to deliver to the registrar for registration such a copy of the direction, determination or order as is prescribed.

(7) If a person without reasonable excuse fails to deliver a copy as required by subsection (6), he is liable to a fine and, for continued contravention, to a daily default fine.

[3362]

NOTES

Application to limited liability partnerships: see the introductory note to this Act and the Limited Liability Partnerships Regulations 2001, SI 2001/1090, reg 5, Sch 3 at **[6986]**, **[6995]**.

CHAPTER X
MALPRACTICE BEFORE AND DURING LIQUIDATION; PENALISATION OF COMPANIES AND COMPANY OFFICERS; INVESTIGATIONS AND PROSECUTIONS

Offences of fraud, deception, etc

206 Fraud, etc in anticipation of winding up

(1) When a company is ordered to be wound up by the court, or passes a resolution for voluntary winding up, any person, being a past or present officer of the company, is deemed to have committed an offence if, within the 12 months immediately preceding the commencement of the winding up, he has—

(a) concealed any part of the company's property to the value of [£500] or more, or concealed any debt due to or from the company, or

(b) fraudulently removed any part of the company's property to the value of [£500] or more, or

(c) concealed, destroyed, mutilated or falsified any book or paper affecting or relating to the company's property or affairs, or

(d) made any false entry in any book or paper affecting or relating to the company's property or affairs, or

(e) fraudulently parted with, altered or made any omission in any document affecting or relating to the company's property or affairs, or

(f) pawned, pledged or disposed of any property of the company which has been obtained on credit and has not been paid for (unless the pawning, pledging or disposal was in the ordinary way of the company's business).

(2) Such a person is deemed to have committed an offence if within the period above mentioned he has been privy to the doing by others of any of the things mentioned in paragraphs (c), (d) and (e) of subsection (1); and he commits an offence if, at any time after

the commencement of the winding up, he does any of the things mentioned in paragraphs (a) to (f) of that subsection, or is privy to the doing by others of any of the things mentioned in paragraphs (c) to (e) of it.

(3) For purposes of this section, "officer" includes a shadow director.

(4) It is a defence—

(a) for a person charged under paragraph (a) or (f) of subsection (1) (or under subsection (2) in respect of the things mentioned in either of those two paragraphs) to prove that he had no intent to defraud, and

(b) for a person charged under paragraph (c) or (d) of subsection (1) (or under subsection (2) in respect of the things mentioned in either of those two paragraphs) to prove that he had no intent to conceal the state of affairs of the company or to defeat the law.

(5) Where a person pawns, pledges or disposes of any property in circumstances which amount to an offence under subsection (1)(f), every person who takes in pawn or pledge, or otherwise receives, the property knowing it to be pawned, pledged or disposed of in such circumstances, is guilty of an offence.

(6) A person guilty of an offence under this section is liable to imprisonment or a fine, or both.

(7) The money sums specified in paragraphs (a) and (b) of subsection (1) are subject to increase or reduction by order under section 416 in Part XV.

[3363]

NOTES

Sub-s (1): sums in square brackets in sub-paras (a), (b) increased from £120 by the Insolvency Proceedings (Monetary Limits) Order 1986, SI 1986/1996, art 2(1), Schedule, Pt I.

Application to limited liability partnerships: see the introductory note to this Act, the Limited Liability Partnerships Regulations 2001, SI 2001/1090, reg 5, Sch 3 at **[6986]**, **[6995]**, and the Limited Liability Partnerships (Scotland) Regulations 2001, SSI 2001/128, reg 4, Schs 2, 3 at **[6977]**, **[6980A]**, **[6980B]**.

207 Transactions in fraud of creditors

(1) When a company is ordered to be wound up by the court or passes a resolution for voluntary winding up, a person is deemed to have committed an offence if he, being at the time an officer of the company—

(a) has made or caused to be made any gift or transfer of, or charge on, or has caused or connived at the levying of any execution against, the company's property, or

(b) has concealed or removed any part of the company's property since, or within 2 months before, the date of any unsatisfied judgment or order for the payment of money obtained against the company.

(2) A person is not guilty of an offence under this section—

(a) by reason of conduct constituting an offence under subsection (1)(a) which occurred more than 5 years before the commencement of the winding up, or

(b) if he proves that, at the time of the conduct constituting the offence, he had no intent to defraud the company's creditors.

(3) A person guilty of an offence under this section is liable to imprisonment or a fine, or both.

[3364]

NOTES

Application to limited liability partnerships: see the introductory note to this Act, the Limited Liability Partnerships Regulations 2001, SI 2001/1090, reg 5, Sch 3 at **[6986]**, **[6995]**, and the Limited Liability Partnerships (Scotland) Regulations 2001, SSI 2001/128, reg 4, Schs 2, 3 at **[6977]**, **[6980A]**, **[6980B]**.

208 Misconduct in course of winding up

(1) When a company is being wound up, whether by the court or voluntarily, any person, being a past or present officer of the company, commits an offence if he—

(a) does not to the best of his knowledge and belief fully and truly discover to the liquidator all the company's property, and how and to whom and for what consideration and when the company disposed of any part of that property (except such part as has been disposed of in the ordinary way of the company's business), or

(b) does not deliver up to the liquidator (or as he directs) all such part of the company's property as is in his custody or under his control, and which he is required by law to deliver up, or

(c) does not deliver up to the liquidator (or as he directs) all books and papers in his custody or under his control belonging to the company and which he is required by law to deliver up, or

(d) knowing or believing that a false debt has been proved by any person in the winding up, fails to inform the liquidator as soon as practicable, or

(e) after the commencement of the winding up, prevents the production of any book or paper affecting or relating to the company's property or affairs.

(2) Such a person commits an offence if after the commencement of the winding up he attempts to account for any part of the company's property by fictitious losses or expenses; and he is deemed to have committed that offence if he has so attempted at any meeting of the company's creditors within the 12 months immediately preceding the commencement of the winding up.

(3) For purposes of this section, "officer" includes a shadow director.

(4) It is a defence—

(a) for a person charged under paragraph (a), (b) or (c) of subsection (1) to prove that he had no intent to defraud, and

(b) for a person charged under paragraph (e) of that subsection to prove that he had no intent to conceal the state of affairs of the company or to defeat the law.

(5) A person guilty of an offence under this section is liable to imprisonment or a fine, or both.

[3365]

NOTES

Application to limited liability partnerships: see the introductory note to this Act, the Limited Liability Partnerships Regulations 2001, SI 2001/1090, reg 5, Sch 3 at **[6986]**, **[6995]**, and the Limited Liability Partnerships (Scotland) Regulations 2001, SSI 2001/128, reg 4, Schs 2, 3 at **[6977]**, **[6980A]**, **[6980B]**.

209 Falsification of company's books

(1) When a company is being wound up, an officer or contributory of the company commits an offence if he destroys, mutilates, alters or falsifies any books, papers or securities, or makes or is privy to the making of any false or fraudulent entry in any register, book of account or document belonging to the company with intent to defraud or deceive any person.

(2) A person guilty of an offence under this section is liable to imprisonment or a fine, or both.

[3366]

NOTES

Application to limited liability partnerships: see the introductory note to this Act, the Limited Liability Partnerships Regulations 2001, SI 2001/1090, reg 5, Sch 3 at **[6986]**, **[6995]**, and the Limited Liability Partnerships (Scotland) Regulations 2001, SSI 2001/128, reg 4, Schs 2, 3 at **[6977]**, **[6980A]**, **[6980B]**.

210 Material omissions from statement relating to company's affairs

(1) When a company is being wound up, whether by the court or voluntarily, any person, being a past or present officer of the company, commits an offence if he makes any material omission in any statement relating to the company's affairs.

(2) When a company has been ordered to be wound up by the court, or has passed a resolution for voluntary winding up, any such person is deemed to have committed that offence if, prior to the winding up, he has made any material omission in any such statement.

(3) For purposes of this section, "officer" includes a shadow director.

(4) It is a defence for a person charged under this section to prove that he had no intent to defraud.

(5) A person guilty of an offence under this section is liable to imprisonment or a fine, or both.

[3367]

NOTES

Application to limited liability partnerships: see the introductory note to this Act, the Limited Liability Partnerships Regulations 2001, SI 2001/1090, reg 5, Sch 3 at **[6986]**, **[6995]**, and the Limited Liability Partnerships (Scotland) Regulations 2001, SSI 2001/128, reg 4, Schs 2, 3 at **[6977]**, **[6980A]**, **[6980B]**.

211 False representations to creditors

(1) When a company is being wound up, whether by the court or voluntarily, any person, being a past or present officer of the company—

(a) commits an offence if he makes any false representation or commits any other fraud for the purpose of obtaining the consent of the company's creditors or any of them to an agreement with reference to the company's affairs or to the winding up, and

(b) is deemed to have committed that offence if, prior to the winding up, he has made any false representation, or committed any other fraud, for that purpose.

(2) For purposes of this section, "officer" includes a shadow director.

(3) A person guilty of an offence under this section is liable to imprisonment or a fine, or both.

[3368]

NOTES

Application to limited liability partnerships: see the introductory note to this Act, the Limited Liability Partnerships Regulations 2001, SI 2001/1090, reg 5, Sch 3 at **[6986]**, **[6995]**, and the Limited Liability Partnerships (Scotland) Regulations 2001, SSI 2001/128, reg 4, Schs 2, 3 at **[6977]**, **[6980A]**, **[6980B]**.

Penalisation of directors and officers

212 Summary remedy against delinquent directors, liquidators, etc

(1) This section applies if in the course of the winding up of a company it appears that a person who—

(a) is or has been an officer of the company,

(b) has acted as liquidator … or administrative receiver of the company, or

(c) not being a person falling within paragraph (a) or (b), is or has been concerned, or has taken part, in the promotion, formation or management of the company,

has misapplied or retained, or become accountable for, any money or other property of the company, or been guilty of any misfeasance or breach of any fiduciary or other duty in relation to the company.

(2) The reference in subsection (1) to any misfeasance or breach of any fiduciary or other duty in relation to the company includes, in the case of a person who has acted as liquidator … of the company, any misfeasance or breach of any fiduciary or other duty in connection with the carrying out of his functions as liquidator … of the company.

(3) The court may, on the application of the official receiver or the liquidator, or of any creditor or contributory, examine into the conduct of the person falling within subsection (1) and compel him—

(a) to repay, restore or account for the money or property or any part of it, with interest at such rate as the court thinks just, or

(b) to contribute such sum to the company's assets by way of compensation in respect of the misfeasance or breach of fiduciary or other duty as the court thinks just.

(4) The power to make an application under subsection (3) in relation to a person who has acted as liquidator … of the company is not exercisable, except with the leave of the court, after [he] has had his release.

(5) The power of a contributory to make an application under subsection (3) is not exercisable except with the leave of the court, but is exercisable notwithstanding that he will not benefit from any order the court may make on the application.

[3369]

NOTES

Sub-ss (1), (2): words omitted repealed by the Enterprise Act 2002, ss 248(3), 278(2), Sch 17, paras 9, 18(a), (b), Sch 26, as from 15 September 2003 (for savings and transitional provisions, see the note to s 8 at **[3164]**).

Sub-s (4): words omitted repealed, and word in square brackets substituted, by the Enterprise Act 2002, ss 248(3), 278(2), Sch 17, paras 9, 18(c), Sch 26, as from 15 September 2003 (for savings and transitional provisions, see the note to s 8 at **[3164]**).

Application to limited liability partnerships: see the introductory note to this Act, the Limited Liability Partnerships Regulations 2001, SI 2001/1090, reg 5, Sch 3 at **[6986]**, **[6995]**, and the Limited Liability Partnerships (Scotland) Regulations 2001, SSI 2001/128, reg 4, Schs 2, 3 at **[6977]**, **[6980A]**, **[6980B]**.

213 Fraudulent trading

(1) If in the course of the winding up of a company it appears that any business of the company has been carried on with intent to defraud creditors of the company or creditors of any other person, or for any fraudulent purpose, the following has effect.

(2) The court, on the application of the liquidator may declare that any persons who were knowingly parties to the carrying on of the business in the manner above-mentioned are to be liable to make such contributions (if any) to the company's assets as the court thinks proper. **[3370]**

NOTES

Application to limited liability partnerships: see the introductory note to this Act, the Limited Liability Partnerships Regulations 2001, SI 2001/1090, reg 5, Sch 3 at **[6986]**, **[6995]**, and the Limited Liability Partnerships (Scotland) Regulations 2001, SSI 2001/128, reg 4, Schs 2, 3 at **[6977]**, **[6980A]**, **[6980B]**.

214 Wrongful trading

(1) Subject to subsection (3) below, if in the course of the winding up of a company it appears that subsection (2) of this section applies in relation to a person who is or has been a director of the company, the court, on the application of the liquidator, may declare that that person is to be liable to make such contribution (if any) to the company's assets as the court thinks proper.

(2) This subsection applies in relation to a person if—

(a) the company has gone into insolvent liquidation,

(b) at some time before the commencement of the winding up of the company, that person knew or ought to have concluded that there was no reasonable prospect that the company would avoid going into insolvent liquidation, and

(c) that person was a director of the company at that time;

but the court shall not make a declaration under this section in any case where the time mentioned in paragraph (b) above was before 28th April 1986.

(3) The court shall not make a declaration under this section with respect to any person if it is satisfied that after the condition specified in subsection (2)(b) was first satisfied in relation to him that person took every step with a view to minimising the potential loss to the company's creditors as (assuming him to have known that there was no reasonable prospect that the company would avoid going into insolvent liquidation) he ought to have taken.

(4) For the purposes of subsections (2) and (3), the facts which a director of a company ought to know or ascertain, the conclusions which he ought to reach and the steps which he ought to take are those which would be known or ascertained, or reached or taken, by a reasonably diligent person having both—

(a) the general knowledge, skill and experience that may reasonably be expected of a person carrying out the same functions as are carried out by that director in relation to the company, and

(b) the general knowledge, skill and experience that that director has.

(5) The reference in subsection (4) to the functions carried out in relation to a company by a director of the company includes any functions which he does not carry out but which have been entrusted to him.

(6) For the purposes of this section a company goes into insolvent liquidation if it goes into liquidation at a time when its assets are insufficient for the payment of its debts and other liabilities and the expenses of the winding up.

(7) In this section "director" includes a shadow director.

(8) This section is without prejudice to section 213.

[3371]

NOTES

Application to limited liability partnerships: see the introductory note to this Act, the Limited Liability Partnerships Regulations 2001, SI 2001/1090, reg 5, Sch 3 at **[6986]**, **[6995]**, and the Limited Liability Partnerships (Scotland) Regulations 2001, SSI 2001/128, reg 4, Schs 2, 3 at **[6977]**, **[6980A]**, **[6980B]**.

215 Proceedings under ss 213, 214

(1) On the hearing of an application under section 213 or 214, the liquidator may himself give evidence or call witnesses.

(2) Where under either section the court makes a declaration, it may give such further directions as it thinks proper for giving effect to the declaration; and in particular, the court may—

(a) provide for the liability of any person under the declaration to be a charge on any debt or obligation due from the company to him, or on any mortgage or charge or any interest in a mortgage or charge on assets of the company held by or vested in him, or any person on his behalf, or any person claiming as assignee from or through the person liable or any person acting on his behalf, and

(b) from time to time make such further order as may be necessary for enforcing any charge imposed under this subsection.

(3) For the purposes of subsection (2), "assignee"—

(a) includes a person to whom or in whose favour, by the directions of the person made liable, the debt, obligation, mortgage or charge was created, issued or transferred or the interest created, but

(b) does not include an assignee for valuable consideration (not including consideration by way of marriage [or the formation of a civil partnership]) given in good faith and without notice of any of the matters on the ground of which the declaration is made.

(4) Where the court makes a declaration under either section in relation to a person who is a creditor of the company, it may direct that the whole or any part of any debt owed by the company to that person and any interest thereon shall rank in priority after all other debts owed by the company and after any interest on those debts.

(5) Sections 213 and 214 have effect notwithstanding that the person concerned may be criminally liable in respect of matters on the ground of which the declaration under the section is to be made.

[3372]

NOTES

Sub-s (3): words in square brackets inserted by the Civil Partnership Act 2004, s 261(1), Sch 27, para 112, as from 5 December 2005.

Application to limited liability partnerships: see the introductory note to this Act, the Limited Liability Partnerships Regulations 2001, SI 2001/1090, reg 5, Sch 3 at **[6986]**, **[6995]**, and the Limited Liability Partnerships (Scotland) Regulations 2001, SSI 2001/128, reg 4, Schs 2, 3 at **[6977]**, **[6980A]**, **[6980B]**.

216 Restriction on re-use of company names

(1) This section applies to a person where a company ("the liquidating company") has gone into insolvent liquidation on or after the appointed day and he was a director or shadow director of the company at any time in the period of 12 months ending with the day before it went into liquidation.

(2) For the purposes of this section, a name is a prohibited name in relation to such a person if—

(a) it is a name by which the liquidating company was known at any time in that period of 12 months, or

(b) it is a name which is so similar to a name falling within paragraph (a) as to suggest an association with that company.

(3) Except with leave of the court or in such circumstances as may be prescribed, a person to whom this section applies shall not at any time in the period of 5 years beginning with the day on which the liquidating company went into liquidation—

(a) be a director of any other company that is known by a prohibited name, or

(b) in any way, whether directly or indirectly, be concerned or take part in the promotion, formation or management of any such company, or

(c) in any way, whether directly or indirectly, be concerned or take part in the carrying on of a business carried on (otherwise than by a company) under a prohibited name.

(4) If a person acts in contravention of this section, he is liable to imprisonment or a fine, or both.

(5) In subsection (3) "the court" means any court having jurisdiction to wind up companies; and on an application for leave under that subsection, the Secretary of State or the official receiver may appear and call the attention of the court to any matters which seem to him to be relevant.

(6) References in this section, in relation to any time, to a name by which a company is known are to the name of the company at that time or to any name under which the company carries on business at that time.

(7) For the purposes of this section a company goes into insolvent liquidation if it goes into liquidation at a time when its assets are insufficient for the payment of its debts and other liabilities and the expenses of the winding up.

(8) In this section "company" includes a company which may be wound up under Part V of this Act.

[3373]

NOTES

Application to limited liability partnerships: see the introductory note to this Act and the Limited Liability Partnerships Regulations 2001, SI 2001/1090, reg 5, Sch 3 at **[6986]**, **[6995]**.

217 Personal liability for debts, following contravention of s 216

(1) A person is personally responsible for all the relevant debts of a company if at any time—

(a) in contravention of section 216, he is involved in the management of the company, or

(b) as a person who is involved in the management of the company, he acts or is willing to act on instructions given (without the leave of the court) by a person whom he knows at that time to be in contravention in relation to the company of section 216.

(2) Where a person is personally responsible under this section for the relevant debts of a company, he is jointly and severally liable in respect of those debts with the company and any other person who, whether under this section or otherwise, is so liable.

(3) For the purposes of this section the relevant debts of a company are—

(a) in relation to a person who is personally responsible under paragraph (a) of subsection (1), such debts and other liabilities of the company as are incurred at a time when that person was involved in the management of the company, and

(b) in relation to a person who is personally responsible under paragraph (b) of that subsection, such debts and other liabilities of the company as are incurred at a time when that person was acting or was willing to act on instructions given as mentioned in that paragraph.

(4) For the purposes of this section, a person is involved in the management of a company if he is a director of the company or if he is concerned, whether directly or indirectly, or takes part, in the management of the company.

(5) For the purposes of this section a person who, as a person involved in the management of a company, has at any time acted on instructions given (without the leave of the court) by a person whom he knew at that time to be in contravention in relation to the company of section 216 is presumed, unless the contrary is shown, to have been willing at any time thereafter to act on any instructions given by that person.

(6) In this section "company" includes a company which may be wound up under Part V.

[3374]

NOTES

Application to limited liability partnerships: see the introductory note to this Act and the Limited Liability Partnerships Regulations 2001, SI 2001/1090, reg 5, Sch 3 at **[6986]**, **[6995]**.

Investigation and prosecution of malpractice

218 Prosecution of delinquent officers and members of company

(1) If it appears to the court in the course of a winding up by the court that any past or present officer, or any member, of the company has been guilty of any offence in relation to the company for which he is criminally liable, the court may (either on the application of a person interested in the winding up or of its own motion) direct the liquidator to refer the matter—

[(a) in the case of a winding up in England and Wales, to the Secretary of State, and

(b) in the case of a winding up in Scotland, to the Lord Advocate.]

(2) …

(3) If in the case of a winding up by the court in England and Wales it appears to the liquidator, not being the official receiver, that any past or present officer of the company, or any member of it, has been guilty of an offence in relation to the company for which he is criminally liable, the liquidator shall report the matter to the official receiver.

(4) If it appears to the liquidator in the course of a voluntary winding up that any past or present officer of the company, or any member of it, has been guilty of an offence in relation to the company for which he is criminally liable, he shall [forthwith report the matter—

(a) in the case of a winding up in England and Wales, to the Secretary of State, and

(b) in the case of a winding up in Scotland, to the Lord Advocate,

and shall furnish to the Secretary of State or (as the case may be) the Lord Advocate] such information and give to him such access to and facilities for inspecting and taking copies of documents (being information or documents in the possession or under the control of the liquidator and relating to the matter in question) as [the Secretary of State or (as the case may be) the Lord Advocate] requires.

[(5) Where a report is made to the Secretary of State under subsection (4) he may, for the purpose of investigating the matter reported to him and such other matters relating to the affairs of the company as appear to him to require investigation, exercise any of the powers which are exercisable by inspectors appointed under section 431 or 432 of the Companies Act to investigate a company's affairs.]

(6) If it appears to the court in the course of a voluntary winding up that—

(a) any past or present officer of the company, or any member of it, has been guilty as above-mentioned, and

(b) no report with respect to the matter has been made by the liquidator … under subsection (4),

the court may (on the application of any person interested in the winding up or of its own motion) direct the liquidator to make such a report.

On a report being made accordingly, this section has effect as though the report had been made in pursuance of subsection (4).

[3375]

NOTES

Sub-ss (1), (4): words in square brackets substituted by the Insolvency Act 2000, s 10(1), (2), (4), as from 2 April 2001.

Sub-s (2): repealed by the Insolvency Act 2000, ss 10(1), (3), 15(1), Sch 5, as from 2 April 2001.

Sub-s (5): substituted by the Insolvency Act 2000, s 10(1), (5), as from 2 April 2001.

Sub-s (6): words omitted repealed by the Insolvency Act 2000, ss 10(1), (6), 15(1), Sch 5, as from 2 April 2001.

Application to limited liability partnerships: see the introductory note to this Act, the Limited Liability Partnerships Regulations 2001, SI 2001/1090, reg 5, Sch 3 at **[6986]**, **[6995]**, and the Limited Liability Partnerships (Scotland) Regulations 2001, SSI 2001/128, reg 4, Schs 2, 3 at **[6977]**, **[6980A]**, **[6980B]**.

219 Obligations arising under s 218

(1) For the purpose of an investigation by the Secretary of State [in consequence of a report made to him under section 218(4)], any obligation imposed on a person by any provision of the Companies Act to produce documents or give information to, or otherwise to assist, inspectors appointed as mentioned in [section 218(5)] is to be regarded as an obligation similarly to assist the Secretary of State in his investigation.

(2) An answer given by a person to a question put to him in exercise of the powers conferred by section 218(5) may be used in evidence against him.

[(2A) However, in criminal proceedings in which that person is charged with an offence to which this subsection applies—

(a) no evidence relating to the answer may be adduced, and

(b) no question relating to it may be asked,

by or on behalf of the prosecution, unless evidence relating to it is adduced, or a question relating to it is asked, in the proceedings by or on behalf of that person.

(2B) Subsection (2A) applies to any offence other than—

(a) an offence under section 2 or 5 of the Perjury Act 1911 (false statements made on oath otherwise than in judicial proceedings or made otherwise than on oath), or

(b) an offence under section 44(1) or (2) of the Criminal Law (Consolidation) (Scotland) Act 1995 (false statements made on oath or otherwise than on oath).]

(3) Where criminal proceedings are instituted by [the Director of Public Prosecutions, the Lord Advocate] or the Secretary of State following any report or reference under section 218, it is the duty of the liquidator and every officer and agent of the company past and present (other than the defendant or defender) to give to [the Director of Public Prosecutions, the Lord Advocate] or the Secretary of State (as the case may be) all assistance in connection with the prosecution which he is reasonably able to give.

For this purpose "agent" includes any banker or solicitor of the company and any person employed by the company as auditor, whether that person is or is not an officer of the company.

(4) If a person fails or neglects to give assistance in the manner required by subsection (3), the court may, on the application of the [Director of Public Prosecutions, the Lord Advocate] or the Secretary of State (as the case may be) direct the person to comply with that subsection; and if the application is made with respect to a liquidator, the court may (unless it appears that the failure or neglect to comply was due to the liquidator not having in his hands sufficient assets of the company to enable him to do so) direct that the costs shall be borne by the liquidator personally.

[3376]

NOTES

Sub-ss (1), (3), (4): words in square brackets substituted by the Insolvency Act 2000, s 10(1), (7), as from 2 April 2001.

Sub-ss (2A), (2B): inserted by the Insolvency Act 2000, s 11, as from 2 April 2001.

Application to limited liability partnerships: see the introductory note to this Act and the Limited Liability Partnerships Regulations 2001, SI 2001/1090, reg 5, Sch 3 at **[6986]**, **[6995]**.

PART III
OTHER LEGISLATION

PART V
WINDING UP OF UNREGISTERED COMPANIES

220 Meaning of "unregistered company"

(1) For the purposes of this Part, the expression "unregistered company" includes *any trustee savings bank certified under the enactments relating to such banks*, any association and any company, with the following exceptions—

(a) …

(b) a company registered in any part of the United Kingdom under the Joint Stock Companies Acts or under the legislation (past or present) relating to companies in Great Britain.

(2) On such day as the Treasury appoints by order under section 4(3) of the Trustee Savings Banks Act 1985, the words in subsection (1) from "any trustee" to "banks" cease to have effect and are hereby repealed.

[3377]

NOTES

Sub-s (1): words in italics formerly in CA 1985, s 665(1), and an additional word "and" following the word "banks" which is not reproduced, were repealed by the Trustee Savings Banks Act 1985, ss 4(3), 7(3), Sch 4. The repeal of those words was brought into force on 21 July 1986 by virtue of the Trustee Savings Banks Act 1985 (Appointed Day) (No 4) Order 1986, SI 1986/1223 (made under s 4(3) of that Act). It is thought, therefore, that, as construed in accordance with s 437, Sch 11, para 27 post, the words specified in sub-s (1) above by sub-s (2) above have ceased to have effect and are thus repealed; para (a) repealed by the Transport and Works Act 1992, ss 65(1)(f), 68(1), Sch 4, Pt I, as from 1 January 1993.

221 Winding up of unregistered companies

(1) Subject to the provisions of this Part, any unregistered company may be wound up under this Act; and all the provisions of this Act and the Companies Act about winding up apply to an unregistered company with the exceptions and additions mentioned in the following subsections.

(2) If an unregistered company has a principal place of business situated in Northern Ireland, it shall not be wound up under this Part unless it has a principal place of business situated in England and Wales or Scotland, or in both England and Wales and Scotland.

(3) For the purpose of determining a court's winding-up jurisdiction, an unregistered company is deemed—

- (a) to be registered in England and Wales or Scotland, according as its principal place of business is situated in England and Wales or Scotland, or
- (b) if it has a principal place of business situated in both countries, to be registered in both countries;

and the principal place of business situated in that part of Great Britain in which proceedings are being instituted is, for all purposes of the winding up, deemed to be the registered office of the company.

(4) No unregistered company shall be wound up under this Act voluntarily[, except in accordance with the EC Regulation].

(5) The circumstances in which an unregistered company may be wound up are as follows—

- (a) if the company is dissolved, or has ceased to carry on business, or is carrying on business only for the purpose of winding up its affairs;
- (b) if the company is unable to pay its debts;
- (c) if the court is of opinion that it is just and equitable that the company should be wound up.

(6) A petition for winding up a trustee savings bank may be presented by the Trustee Savings Banks Central Board or by a commissioner appointed under section 35 of the Trustee Savings Banks Act 1981 as well as by any person authorised under Part IV of this Act to present a petition for the winding up of a company.

On such day as the Treasury appoints by order under section 4(3) of the Trustee Savings Banks Act 1985, this subsection ceases to have effect and is hereby repealed.

(7) In Scotland, an unregistered company which the Court of Session has jurisdiction to wind up may be wound up by the court if there is subsisting a floating charge over property comprised in the company's property and undertaking, and the court is satisfied that the security of the creditor entitled to the benefit of the floating charge is in jeopardy.

For this purpose a creditor's security is deemed to be in jeopardy if the court is satisfied that events have occurred or are about to occur which render it unreasonable in the creditor's interests that the company should retain power to dispose of the property which is subject to the floating charge.

[3378]

NOTES

Sub-s (4): words in square brackets added by the Insolvency Act 1986 (Amendment) (No 2) Regulations 2002, SI 2002/1240, regs 3, 9, as from 31 May 2002.

Sub-s (6): CA 1985, s 666(6), from which sub-s (6) above was principally derived, was repealed by the Trustee Savings Banks Act 1985, ss 4(3), 7(3), Sch 4, as from 21 July 1986 by virtue of the Trustee Savings Banks Act 1985 (Appointed Day) (No 4) Order 1986, SI 1986/1223 (made under s 4(3) of that Act). It is thought, therefore, that, as construed in accordance with s 437, Sch 11, para 27, sub-s (6) above has ceased to have effect and is thus repealed.

222 Inability to pay debts; unpaid creditor for £750 or more

(1) An unregistered company is deemed (for the purposes of section 221) unable to pay its debts if there is a creditor, by assignment or otherwise, to whom the company is indebted in a sum exceeding £750 then due and—

(a) the creditor has served on the company, by leaving at its principal place of business, or by delivering to the secretary or some director, manager or principal officer of the company, or by otherwise serving in such manner as the court may approve or direct, a written demand in the prescribed form requiring the company to pay the sum due, and

(b) the company has for 3 weeks after the service of the demand neglected to pay the sum or to secure or compound for it to the creditor's satisfaction.

(2) The money sum for the time being specified in subsection (1) is subject to increase or reduction by regulations under section 417 in Part XV; but no increase in the sum so specified affects any case in which the winding-up petition was presented before the coming into force of the increase.

[3379]

223 Inability to pay debts: debt remaining unsatisfied after action brought

An unregistered company is deemed (for the purposes of section 221) unable to pay its debts if an action or other proceeding has been instituted against any member for any debt or demand due, or claimed to be due, from the company, or from him in his character of member, and—

(a) notice in writing of the institution of the action or proceeding has been served on the company by leaving it at the company's principal place of business (or by delivering it to the secretary, or some director, manager or principal officer of the company, or by otherwise serving it in such manner as the court may approve or direct), and

(b) the company has not within 3 weeks after service of the notice paid, secured or compounded for the debt or demand, or procured the action or proceeding to be stayed or sisted, or indemnified the defendant or defender to his reasonable satisfaction against the action or proceeding, and against all costs, damages and expenses to be incurred by him because of it.

[3380]

224 Inability to pay debts: other cases

(1) An unregistered company is deemed (for purposes of section 221) unable to pay its debts—

(a) if in England and Wales execution or other process issued on a judgment, decree or order obtained in any court in favour of a creditor against the company, or any member of it as such, or any person authorised to be sued as nominal defendant on behalf of the company, is returned unsatisfied;

(b) if in Scotland the induciae of a charge for payment on an extract decree, or an extract registered bond, or an extract registered protest, have expired without payment being made;

(c) if in Northern Ireland a certificate of unenforceability has been granted in respect of any judgment, decree or order obtained as mentioned in paragraph (a);

(d) it is otherwise proved to the satisfaction of the court that the company is unable to pay its debts as they fall due.

(2) An unregistered company is also deemed unable to pay its debts if it is proved to the satisfaction of the court that the value of the company's assets is less than the amount of its liabilities, taking into account its contingent and prospective liabilities.

[3381]

225 Oversea company may be wound up though dissolved

[(1)] Where a company incorporated outside Great Britain which has been carrying on business in Great Britain ceases to carry on business in Great Britain, it may be wound up as an unregistered company under this Act, notwithstanding that it has been dissolved or otherwise ceased to exist as a company under or by virtue of the laws of the country under which it was incorporated.

[(2) This section is subject to the EC Regulation.]

[3382]

NOTES

Sub-s (1) numbered as such, and sub-s (2) added, by the Insolvency Act 1986 (Amendment) (No 2) Regulations 2002, SI 2002/1240, regs 3, 10, as from 31 May 2002.

226 Contributories in winding up of unregistered company

(1) In the event of an unregistered company being wound up, every person is deemed a contributory who is liable to pay or contribute to the payment of any debt or liability of the company, or to pay or contribute to the payment of any sum for the adjustment of the rights of members among themselves, or to pay or contribute to the payment of the expenses of winding up the company.

(2) Every contributory is liable to contribute to the company's assets all sums due from him in respect of any such liability as is mentioned above.

(3) In the case of an unregistered company engaged in or formed for working mines within the stannaries, a past member is not liable to contribute to the assets if he has ceased to be a member for 2 years or more either before the mine ceased to be worked or before the date of the winding-up order.

(4) In the event of the death, bankruptcy or insolvency of any contributory, the provisions of this Act with respect to the personal representatives, to the heirs and legatees of heritage of the heritable estate in Scotland of deceased contributories, and to the trustees of bankrupt or insolvent contributories, respectively apply.

[3383]

227 Power of court to stay, sist or restrain proceedings

The provisions of this Part with respect to staying, sisting or restraining actions and proceedings against a company at any time after the presentation of a petition for winding up and before the making of a winding-up order extend, in the case of an unregistered company, where the application to stay, sist or restrain is presented by a creditor, to actions and proceedings against any contributory of the company.

[3384]

228 Actions stayed on winding-up order

Where an order has been made for winding up an unregistered company, no action or proceeding shall be proceeded with or commenced against any contributory of the company in respect of any debt of the company, except by leave of the court, and subject to such terms as the court may impose.

[3385]

229 Provisions of this Part to be cumulative

(1) The provisions of this Part with respect to unregistered companies are in addition to and not in restriction of any provisions in Part IV with respect to winding up companies by the court; and the court or liquidator may exercise any powers or do any act in the case of unregistered companies which might be exercised or done by it or him in winding up companies formed and registered under the Companies Act.

(2) However, an unregistered company is not, except in the event of its being wound up, deemed to be a company under the Companies Act, and then only to the extent provided by this Part of this Act.

[3386]

PART VI
MISCELLANEOUS PROVISIONS APPLYING TO COMPANIES WHICH ARE INSOLVENT OR IN LIQUIDATION

Office-holders

230 Holders of office to be qualified insolvency practitioners

(1) …

(2) Where an administrative receiver of a company is appointed, he must be a person who is so qualified.

(3) Where a company goes into liquidation, the liquidator must be a person who is so qualified.

(4) Where a provisional liquidator is appointed, he must be a person who is so qualified.

(5) Subsections (3) and (4) are without prejudice to any enactment under which the official receiver is to be, or may be, liquidator or provisional liquidator.

[3387]

NOTES

Sub-s (1): repealed by the Enterprise Act 2002, ss 248(3), 287(2), Sch 17, paras 9, 19, Sch 26, as from 15 September 2003 (for savings and transitional provisions, see the note to s 8 at **[3164]**).

Application to limited liability partnerships: see the introductory note to this Act and the Limited Liability Partnerships Regulations 2001, SI 2001/1090, reg 5, Sch 3 at **[6986]**, **[6995]**.

231 Appointment to office of two or more persons

(1) This section applies if an appointment or nomination of any person to the office of … administrative receiver, liquidator or provisional liquidator—

(a) relates to more than one person, or

(b) has the effect that the office is to be held by more than one person.

(2) The appointment or nomination shall declare whether any act required or authorised under any enactment to be done by the … administrative receiver, liquidator or provisional liquidator is to be done by all or any one or more of the persons for the time being holding the office in question.

[3388]

NOTES

Sub-ss (1), (2): words omitted repealed by the Enterprise Act 2002, ss 248(3), 287(2), Sch 17, paras 9, 20, Sch 26, as from 15 September 2003 (for savings and transitional provisions, see the note to s 8 at **[3164]**).

Application to limited liability partnerships: see the introductory note to this Act, the Limited Liability Partnerships Regulations 2001, SI 2001/1090, reg 5, Sch 3 at **[6986]**, **[6995]**, and the Limited Liability Partnerships (Scotland) Regulations 2001, SSI 2001/128, reg 4, Schs 2, 3 at **[6977]**, **[6980A]**, **[6980B]**.

232 Validity of office-holder's acts

The acts of an individual as … administrative receiver, liquidator or provisional liquidator of a company are valid notwithstanding any defect in his appointment, nomination or qualifications.

[3389]

NOTES

Word omitted repealed by the Enterprise Act 2002, ss 248(3), 287(2), Sch 17, paras 9, 21, Sch 26, as from 15 September 2003 (for savings and transitional provisions, see the note to s 8 at **[3164]**).

Application to limited liability partnerships: see the introductory note to this Act, the Limited Liability Partnerships Regulations 2001, SI 2001/1090, reg 5, Sch 3 at **[6986]**, **[6995]**, and the Limited Liability Partnerships (Scotland) Regulations 2001, SSI 2001/128, reg 4, Schs 2, 3 at **[6977]**, **[6980A]**, **[6980B]**.

Management by administrators, liquidators, etc

233 Supplies of gas, water, electricity, etc

(1) This section applies in the case of a company where—

[(a) the company enters administration,]

(b) an administrative receiver is appointed, or

[(ba) a moratorium under section 1A is in force, or]

(c) a voluntary arrangement [approved under Part I], has taken effect, or

(d) the company goes into liquidation, or

(e) a provisional liquidator is appointed;

and "the office-holder" means the administrator, the administrative receiver, [the nominee,] the supervisor of the voluntary arrangement, the liquidator or the provisional liquidator, as the case may be.

(2) If a request is made by or with the concurrence of the office-holder for the giving, after the effective date, of any of the supplies mentioned in the next subsection, the supplier—

(a) may make it a condition of the giving of the supply that the office-holder personally guarantees the payment of any charges in respect of the supply, but

(b) shall not make it a condition of the giving of the supply, or do anything which has the effect of making it a condition of the giving of the supply, that any outstanding charges in respect of a supply given to the company before the effective date are paid.

(3) The supplies referred to in subsection (2) are—

[(a) a supply of gas by a gas supplier within the meaning of Part I of the Gas Act 1986;]

[(b) a supply of electricity by an electricity supplier within the meaning of Part I of the Electricity Act 1989;]

(c) a supply of water by [a water undertaker] or, in Scotland, [Scottish Water],

[(d) a supply of communications services by a provider of a public electronic communications service.]

(4) "The effective date" for the purposes of this section is whichever is applicable of the following dates—

[(a) the date on which the company entered administration,]

(b) the date on which the administrative receiver was appointed (or, if he was appointed in succession to another administrative receiver, the date on which the first of his predecessors was appointed),

[(ba) the date on which the moratorium came into force]

(c) the date on which the voluntary arrangement [took effect],

(d) the date on which the company went into liquidation,

(e) the date on which the provisional liquidator was appointed.

(5) The following applies to expressions used in subsection (3)—

(a)–(c) …

[(d) "communications services" do not include electronic communications services to the extent that they are used to broadcast or otherwise transmit programme services (within the meaning of the Communications Act 2003).]

[3390]

NOTES

Sub-s (1): para (a) substituted by the Enterprise Act 2002, s 248(3), Sch 17, paras 9, 22(a), as from 15 September 2003 (for savings and transitional provisions, see the note to s 8 at **[3164]**); para (ba) and final words in square brackets inserted, and second words in square brackets substituted, by the Insolvency Act 2000, s 1, Sch 1, paras 1, 8(1), (2), as from 1 January 2003.

Sub-s (3): para (a) substituted by the Gas Act 1995, s 16(1), Sch 4, para 14(1), as from 1 March 1996; para (b) substituted by the Utilities Act 2000, s 108, Sch 6, para 47(1), (2)(a), as from 1 October 2001; words in first pair of square brackets in para (c) substituted by the Water Act 1989, s 190(1), Sch 25, para 78(1), as from 1 September 1989; words in second pair of square brackets in para (c) substituted by the Water Industry (Scotland) Act 2002 (Consequential Modifications) Order 2004, SI 2004/1822, art 2, Schedule, Pt 1, para 14(a), as from 14 July 2004; para (d) substituted by the Communications Act 2003, s 406, Sch 17, para 82(1), (2)(a), as from 25 July 2003 (certain purposes), and as from 29 December 2003 (otherwise).

Sub-s (4): para (a) substituted by the Enterprise Act 2002, s 248(3), Sch 17, paras 9, 22(b), as from 15 September 2003 (for savings and transitional provisions, see the note to s 8 at **[3164]**); para (ba) inserted, and words in square brackets in para (c) substituted, by the Insolvency Act 2000, s 1, Sch 1, paras 1, 8(1), (3), as from 1 January 2003.

Sub-s (5): para (a) repealed by the Gas Act 1995, ss 16(1), 17(5), Sch 4, para 14(2), Sch 6, as from 1 March 1996; para (b) repealed by the Utilities Act 2000, s 108, Sch 6, para 47(1), (2)(b), Sch 8, as from 1 October 2001; para (c) repealed by SI 2004/1822, art 2, Schedule, Pt 1, para 14(b), as from 14 July 2004; para (d) substituted by the Communications Act 2003, s 406, Sch 17, para 82(1), (2)(b), as from 25 July 2003 (certain purposes), and as from 29 December 2003 (otherwise).

Application to limited liability partnerships: see the introductory note to this Act, the Limited Liability Partnerships Regulations 2001, SI 2001/1090, reg 5, Sch 3 at **[6986]**, **[6995]**, and the Limited Liability Partnerships (Scotland) Regulations 2001, SSI 2001/128, reg 4, Schs 2, 3 at **[6977]**, **[6980A]**, **[6980B]**.

234 Getting in the company's property

(1) This section applies in the case of a company where—

[(a) the company enters administration,] or
(b) an administrative receiver is appointed, or
(c) the company goes into liquidation, or
(d) a provisional liquidator is appointed;

and "the office-holder" means the administrator, the administrative receiver, the liquidator or the provisional liquidator, as the case may be.

(2) Where any person has in his possession or control any property, books, papers or records to which the company appears to be entitled, the court may require that person forthwith (or within such period as the court may direct) to pay, deliver convey, surrender or transfer the property, books, papers or records to the office-holder.

(3) Where the office-holder—

(a) seizes or disposes of any property which is not property of the company, and
(b) at the time of seizure or disposal believes, and has reasonable grounds for believing, that he is entitled (whether in pursuance of an order of the court or otherwise) to seize or dispose of that property,

the next subsection has effect.

(4) In that case the office-holder—

(a) is not liable to any person in respect of any loss or damage resulting from the seizure or disposal except in so far as that loss or damage is caused by the office-holder's own negligence, and
(b) has a lien on the property, or the proceeds of its sale, for such expenses as were incurred in connection with the seizure or disposal.

[3391]

NOTES

Sub-s (1): para (a) substituted by the Enterprise Act 2002, s 248(3), Sch 17, paras 9, 23, as from 15 September 2003 (for savings and transitional provisions, see the note to s 8 at **[3164]**).

Application to limited liability partnerships: see the introductory note to this Act, the Limited Liability Partnerships Regulations 2001, SI 2001/1090, reg 5, Sch 3 at **[6986]**, **[6995]**, and the Limited Liability Partnerships (Scotland) Regulations 2001, SSI 2001/128, reg 4, Schs 2, 3 at **[6977]**, **[6980A]**, **[6980B]**.

235 Duty to co-operate with office-holder

(1) This section applies as does section 234; and it also applies, in the case of a company in respect of which a winding-up order has been made by the court in England and Wales, as if references to the office-holder included the official receiver, whether or not he is the liquidator.

(2) Each of the persons mentioned in the next subsection shall—

(a) give to the office-holder such information concerning the company and its promotion, formation, business, dealings, affairs or property as the office-holder may at any time after the effective date reasonably require, and
(b) attend on the office-holder at such times as the latter may reasonably require.

(3) The persons referred to above are—

(a) those who are or have at any time been officers of the company,
(b) those who have taken part in the formation of the company at any time within one year before the effective date,
(c) those who are in the employment of the company, or have been in its employment (including employment under a contract for services) within that year, and are in the office-holder's opinion capable of giving information which he requires,
(d) those who are, or have within that year been, officers of, or in the employment (including employment under a contract for services) of, another company which is, or within that year was, an officer of the company in question, and
(e) in the case of a company being wound up by the court, any person who has acted as administrator, administrative receiver or liquidator of the company.

(4) For the purposes of subsections (2) and (3), "the effective date" is whichever is applicable of the following dates—

[(a) the date on which the company entered administration,]
(b) the date on which the administrative receiver was appointed or, if he was appointed in succession to another administrative receiver, the date on which the first of his predecessors was appointed,
(c) the date on which the provisional liquidator was appointed, and

(d) the date on which the company went into liquidation.

(5) If a person without reasonable excuse fails to comply with any obligation imposed by this section, he is liable to a fine and, for continued contravention, to a daily default fine.

[3392]

NOTES

Sub-s (4): para (a) substituted by the Enterprise Act 2002, s 248(3), Sch 17, paras 9, 24, as from 15 September 2003 (for savings and transitional provisions, see the note to s 8 at **[3164]**).

Application to limited liability partnerships: see the introductory note to this Act, the Limited Liability Partnerships Regulations 2001, SI 2001/1090, reg 5, Sch 3 at **[6986]**, **[6995]**, and the Limited Liability Partnerships (Scotland) Regulations 2001, SSI 2001/128, reg 4, Schs 2, 3 at **[6977]**, **[6980A]**, **[6980B]**.

236 Inquiry into company's dealings, etc

(1) This section applies as does section 234; and it also applies in the case of a company in respect of which a winding-up order has been made by the court in England and Wales as if references to the office-holder included the official receiver, whether or not he is the liquidator.

(2) The court may, on the application of the office-holder, summon to appear before it—

(a) any officer of the company,

(b) any person known or suspected to have in his possession any property of the company or supposed to be indebted to the company, or

(c) any person whom the court thinks capable of giving information concerning the promotion, formation, business, dealings, affairs or property of the company.

(3) The court may require any such person as is mentioned in subsection (2)(a) to (c) to submit an affidavit to the court containing an account of his dealings with the company or to produce any books, papers or other records in his possession or under his control relating to the company or the matters mentioned in paragraph (c) of the subsection.

(4) The following applies in a case where—

(a) a person without reasonable excuse fails to appear before the court when he is summoned to do so under this section, or

(b) there are reasonable grounds for believing that a person has absconded, or is about to abscond, with a view to avoiding his appearance before the court under this section.

(5) The court may, for the purpose of bringing that person and anything in his possession before the court, cause a warrant to be issued to a constable or prescribed officer of the court—

(a) for the arrest of that person, and

(b) for the seizure of any books, papers, records, money or goods in that person's possession.

(6) The court may authorise a person arrested under such a warrant to be kept in custody, and anything seized under such a warrant to be held, in accordance with the rules, until that person is brought before the court under the warrant or until such other time as the court may order.

[3393]

NOTES

Application to limited liability partnerships: see the introductory note to this Act, the Limited Liability Partnerships Regulations 2001, SI 2001/1090, reg 5, Sch 3 at **[6986]**, **[6995]**, and the Limited Liability Partnerships (Scotland) Regulations 2001, SSI 2001/128, reg 4, Schs 2, 3 at **[6977]**, **[6980A]**, **[6980B]**.

237 Court's enforcement powers under s 236

(1) If it appears to the court, on consideration of any evidence obtained under section 236 or this section, that any person has in his possession any property of the company, the court may, on the application of the office-holder, order that person to deliver the whole or any part of the property to the officer-holder at such time, in such manner and on such terms as the court thinks fit.

(2) If it appears to the court, on consideration of any evidence so obtained, that any person is indebted to the company, the court may, on the application of the office-holder,

order that person to pay to the office-holder, at such time and in such manner as the court may direct, the whole or any part of the amount due, whether in full discharge of the debt or otherwise, as the court thinks fit.

(3) The court may, if it thinks fit, order that any person who if within the jurisdiction of the court would be liable to be summoned to appear before it under section 236 or this section shall be examined in any part of the United Kingdom where he may for the time being be, or in a place outside the United Kingdom.

(4) Any person who appears or is brought before the court under section 236 or this section may be examined on oath, either orally or (except in Scotland) by interrogatories, concerning the company or the matters mentioned in section 236(2)(c).

[3394]

NOTES

Application to limited liability partnerships: see the introductory note to this Act, the Limited Liability Partnerships Regulations 2001, SI 2001/1090, reg 5, Sch 3 at **[6986]**, **[6995]**, and the Limited Liability Partnerships (Scotland) Regulations 2001, SSI 2001/128, reg 4, Schs 2, 3 at **[6977]**, **[6980A]**, **[6980B]**.

Adjustment of prior transactions (administration and liquidation)

238 Transactions at an undervalue (England and Wales)

(1) This section applies in the case of a company where—

[(a) the company enters administration,] or

(b) the company goes into liquidation;

and "the office-holder" means the administrator or the liquidator, as the case may be.

(2) Where the company has at a relevant time (defined in section 240) entered into a transaction with any person at an undervalue, the office-holder may apply to the court for an order under this section.

(3) Subject as follows, the court shall, on such an application, make such order as it thinks fit for restoring the position to what it would have been if the company had not entered into that transaction.

(4) For the purposes of this section and section 241, a company enters into a transaction with a person at an undervalue if—

(a) the company makes a gift to that person or otherwise enters into a transaction with that person on terms that provide for the company to receive no consideration, or

(b) the company enters into a transaction with that person for a consideration the value of which, in money or money's worth, is significantly less than the value, in money or money's worth, of the consideration provided by the company.

(5) The court shall not make an order under this section in respect of a transaction at an undervalue if it is satisfied—

(a) that the company which entered into the transaction did so in good faith and for the purpose of carrying on its business, and

(b) that at the time it did so there were reasonable grounds for believing that the transaction would benefit the company.

[3395]

NOTES

Sub-s (1): para (a) substituted by the Enterprise Act 2002, s 248(3), Sch 17, paras 9, 25, as from 15 September 2003 (for savings and transitional provisions, see the note to s 8 at **[3164]**).

Application to limited liability partnerships: see the introductory note to this Act and the Limited Liability Partnerships Regulations 2001, SI 2001/1090, reg 5, Sch 3 at **[6986]**, **[6995]**.

239 Preferences (England and Wales)

(1) This section applies as does section 238.

(2) Where the company has at a relevant time (defined in the next section) given a preference to any person, the office-holder may apply to the court for an order under this section.

(3) Subject as follows, the court shall, on such an application, make such order as it thinks fit for restoring the position to what it would have been if the company had not given that preference.

(4) For the purposes of this section and section 241, a company gives a preference to a person if—

(a) that person is one of the company's creditors or a surety or guarantor for any of the company's debts or other liabilities, and

(b) the company does anything or suffers anything to be done which (in either case) has the effect of putting that person into a position which, in the event of the company going into insolvent liquidation, will be better than the position he would have been in if that thing had not been done.

(5) The court shall not make an order under this section in respect of a preference given to any person unless the company which gave the preference was influenced in deciding to give it by a desire to produce in relation to that person the effect mentioned in subsection (4)(b).

(6) A company which has given a preference to a person connected with the company (otherwise than by reason only of being its employee) at the time the preference was given is presumed, unless the contrary is shown, to have been influenced in deciding to give it by such a desire as is mentioned in subsection (5).

(7) The fact that something has been done in pursuance of the order of a court does not, without more, prevent the doing or suffering of that thing from constituting the giving of a preference.

[3396]

NOTES

Application to limited liability partnerships: see the introductory note to this Act and the Limited Liability Partnerships Regulations 2001, SI 2001/1090, reg 5, Sch 3 at **[6986]**, **[6995]**.

240 "Relevant time" under ss 238, 239

(1) Subject to the next subsection, the time at which a company enters into a transaction at an undervalue or gives a preference is a relevant time if the transaction is entered into, or the preference given—

(a) in the case of a transaction at an undervalue or of a preference which is given to a person who is connected with the company (otherwise than by reason only of being its employee), at a time in the period of 2 years ending with the onset of insolvency (which expression is defined below),

(b) in the case of a preference which is not such a transaction and is not so given, at a time in the period of 6 months ending with the onset of insolvency, *and*

[(c) in either case, at a time between the making of an administration application in respect of the company and the making of an administration order on that application, and

(d) in either case, at a time between the filing with the court of a copy of notice of intention to appoint an administrator under paragraph 14 or 22 of Schedule B1 and the making of an appointment under that paragraph.]

(2) Where a company enters into a transaction at an undervalue or gives a preference at a time mentioned in subsection (1)(a) or (b), that time is not a relevant time for the purposes of section 238 or 239 unless the company—

(a) is at that time unable to pay its debts within the meaning of section 123 in Chapter VI of Part IV, or

(b) becomes unable to pay its debts within the meaning of that section in consequence of the transaction or preference;

but the requirements of this subsection are presumed to be satisfied, unless the contrary is shown, in relation to any transaction at an undervalue which is entered into by a company with a person who is connected with the company.

(3) For the purposes of subsection (1), the onset of insolvency is—

[(a) in a case where section 238 or 239 applies by reason of an administrator of a company being appointed by administration order, the date on which the administration application is made,

(b) in a case where section 238 or 239 applies by reason of an administrator of a company being appointed under paragraph 14 or 22 of Schedule B1 following filing with the court of a copy of a notice of intention to appoint under that paragraph, the date on which the copy of the notice is filed,

(c) in a case where section 238 or 239 applies by reason of an administrator of a company being appointed otherwise than as mentioned in paragraph (a) or (b), the date on which the appointment takes effect,

(d) in a case where section 238 or 239 applies by reason of a company going into liquidation either following conversion of administration into winding up by virtue of Article 37 of the EC Regulation or at the time when the appointment of an administrator ceases to have effect, the date on which the company entered administration (or, if relevant, the date on which the application for the administration order was made or a copy of the notice of intention to appoint was filed), and

(e) in a case where section 238 or 239 applies by reason of a company going into liquidation at any other time, the date of the commencement of the winding up.]

[3397]

NOTES

Sub-s (1): word omitted from para (b) repealed, and paras (c), (d) substituted for original para (c), by the Enterprise Act 2002, ss 248(3), 278(2), Sch 17, paras 9, 26(1)–(3), Sch 26, as from 15 September 2003 (for savings and transitional provisions, see the note to s 8 at **[3164]**).

Sub-s (3): paras (a)–(e) substituted, for paras (a), (aa), (b), by the Enterprise Act 2002, s 248(3), Sch 17, paras 9, 26(1), (4), as from 15 September 2003 (for savings and transitional provisions, see the note to s 8 at **[3164]**); the original para (aa) was inserted by the Insolvency Act 1986 (Amendment) (No 2) Regulations 2002, SI 2002/1240, regs 3, 11, as from 31 May 2002.

Application to limited liability partnerships: see the introductory note to this Act and the Limited Liability Partnerships Regulations 2001, SI 2001/1090, reg 5, Sch 3 at **[6986]**, **[6995]**.

241 Orders under ss 238, 239

(1) Without prejudice to the generality of sections 238(3) and 239(3), an order under either of those sections with respect to a transaction or preference entered into or given by a company may (subject to the next subsection)—

(a) require any property transferred as part of the transaction, or in connection with the giving of the preference, to be vested in the company,

(b) require any property to be so vested if it represents in any person's hands the application either of the proceeds of sale of property so transferred or of money so transferred,

(c) release or discharge (in whole or in part) any security given by the company,

(d) require any person to pay, in respect of benefits received by him from the company, such sums to the office-holder as the court may direct,

(e) provide for any surety or guarantor whose obligations to any person were released or discharged (in whole or in part) under the transaction, or by the giving of the preference, to be under such new or revived obligations to that person as the court thinks appropriate,

(f) provide for security to be provided for the discharge of any obligation imposed by or arising under the order, for such an obligation to be charged on any property and for the security or charge to have the same priority as a security or charge released or discharged (in whole or in part) under the transaction or by the giving of the preference, and

(g) provide for the extent to which any person whose property is vested by the order in the company, or on whom obligations are imposed by the order, is to be able to prove in the winding up of the company for debts or other liabilities which arose from, or were released or discharged (in whole or in part) under or by, the transaction or the giving of the preference.

(2) An order under section 238 or 239 may affect the property of, or impose any obligation on, any person whether or not he is the person with whom the company in question entered into the transaction or (as the case may be) the person to whom the preference was given; but such an order—

(a) shall not prejudice any interest in property which was acquired from a person other than the company and was acquired [in good faith and for value], or prejudice any interest deriving from such an interest, and

(b) shall not require a person who received a benefit from the transaction or preference [in good faith and for value] to pay a sum to the office-holder, except where that person was a party to the transaction or the payment is to be in respect of a preference given to that person at a time when he was a creditor of the company.

[(2A) Where a person has acquired an interest in property from a person other than the company in question, or has received a benefit from the transaction or preference, and at the time of that acquisition or receipt—

(a) he had notice of the relevant surrounding circumstances and of the relevant proceedings, or

(b) he was connected with, or was an associate of, either the company in question or the person with whom that company entered into the transaction or to whom that company gave the preference,

then, unless the contrary is shown, it shall be presumed for the purposes of paragraph (a) or (as the case may be) paragraph (b) of subsection (2) that the interest was acquired or the benefit was received otherwise than in good faith.]

[(3) For the purposes of subsection (2A)(a), the relevant surrounding circumstances are (as the case may require)—

(a) the fact that the company in question entered into the transaction at an undervalue; or

(b) the circumstances which amounted to the giving of the preference by the company in question;

and subsections (3A) to (3C) have effect to determine whether, for those purposes, a person has notice of the relevant proceedings.

[(3A) Where section 238 or 239 applies by reason of a company's entering administration, a person has notice of the relevant proceedings if he has notice that—

(a) an administration application has been made,

(b) an administration order has been made,

(c) a copy of a notice of intention to appoint an administrator under paragraph 14 or 22 of Schedule B1 has been filed, or

(d) notice of the appointment of an administrator has been filed under paragraph 18 or 29 of that Schedule.]

[(3B) Where section 238 or 239 applies by reason of a company's going into liquidation at the time when the appointment of an administrator of the company ceases to have effect, a person has notice of the relevant proceedings if he has notice that—

(a) an administration application has been made,

(b) an administration order has been made,

(c) a copy of a notice of intention to appoint an administrator under paragraph 14 or 22 of Schedule B1 has been filed,

(d) notice of the appointment of an administrator has been filed under paragraph 18 or 29 of that Schedule, or

(e) the company has gone into liquidation.]

(3C) In a case where section 238 or 239 applies by reason of the company in question going into liquidation at any other time, a person has notice of the relevant proceedings if he has notice—

(a) where the company goes into liquidation on the making of a winding-up order, of the fact that the petition on which the winding-up order is made has been presented or of the fact that the company has gone into liquidation;

(b) in any other case, of the fact that the company has gone into liquidation.]

(4) The provisions of sections 238 to 241 apply without prejudice to the availability of any other remedy, even in relation to a transaction or preference which the company had no power to enter into or give.

[3398]

NOTES

Sub-s (2): words in square brackets in paras (a), (b) substituted by the Insolvency (No 2) Act 1994, s 1(1), in relation to interests acquired and benefits received after 26 July 1994.

Sub-s (2A): inserted by the Insolvency (No 2) Act 1994, s 1(2), in relation to interests acquired and benefits received after 26 July 1994.

Sub-ss (3), (3C): substituted together with sub-ss (3A), (3B), for sub-s (3) as originally enacted, by the Insolvency (No 2) Act 1994, s 1(3), in relation to interests acquired and benefits received after 26 July 1994.

Sub-ss (3A), (3B): substituted as noted above; further substituted by the Enterprise Act 2002, s 248(3), Sch 17, paras 9, 27, as from 15 September 2003 (for savings and transitional provisions, see the note to s 8 at **[3164]**).

Application to limited liability partnerships: see the introductory note to this Act and the Limited Liability Partnerships Regulations 2001, SI 2001/1090, reg 5, Sch 3 at **[6986]**, **[6995]**.

242 Gratuitous alienations (Scotland)

(1) Where this subsection applies and—

(a) the winding up of a company has commenced, an alienation by the company is challengeable by—

(i) any creditor who is a creditor by virtue of a debt incurred on or before the date of such commencement, or

(ii) the liquidator;

(b) [a company enters administration], an alienation by the company is challengeable by the administrator.

(2) Subsection (1) applies where—

(a) by the alienation, whether before or after 1st April 1986 (the coming into force of section 75 of the Bankruptcy (Scotland) Act 1985), any part of the company's property is transferred or any claim or right of the company is discharged or renounced, and

(b) the alienation takes place on a relevant day.

(3) For the purposes of subsection (2)(b), the day on which an alienation takes place is the day on which it becomes completely effectual; and in that subsection "relevant day" means, if the alienation has the effect of favouring—

(a) a person who is an associate (within the meaning of the Bankruptcy (Scotland) Act 1985) of the company, a day not earlier than 5 years before the date on which—

(i) the winding up of the company commences, or

(ii) as the case may be, [the company enters administration]; or

(b) any other person, a day not earlier than 2 years before that date.

(4) On a challenge being brought under subsection (1), the court shall grant decree of reduction or for such restoration of property to the company's assets or other redress as may be appropriate; but the court shall not grant such a decree if the person seeking to uphold the alienation establishes—

(a) that immediately, or at any other time, after the alienation the company's assets were greater than its liabilities, or

(b) that the alienation was made for adequate consideration, or

(c) that the alienation—

(i) was a birthday, Christmas or other conventional gift, or

(ii) was a gift made, for a charitable purpose, to a person who is not an associate of the company,

which, having regard to all the circumstances, it was reasonable for the company to make:

Provided that this subsection is without prejudice to any right or interest acquired in good faith and for value from or through the transferee in the alienation.

(5) In subsection (4) above, "charitable purpose" means any charitable, benevolent or philanthropic purpose, whether or not it is charitable within the meaning of any rule of law.

(6) For the purposes of the foregoing provisions of this section, an alienation in implementation of a prior obligation is deemed to be one for which there was no consideration or no adequate consideration to the extent that the prior obligation was undertaken for no consideration or no adequate consideration.

(7) A liquidator and an administrator have the same right as a creditor has under any rule of law to challenge an alienation of a company made for no consideration or no adequate consideration.

(8) This section applies to Scotland only.

[3399]

NOTES

Sub-ss (1), (3): words in square brackets substituted by the Enterprise Act 2002, s 248(3), Sch 17, paras 9, 28, as from 15 September 2003 (for savings and transitional provisions, see the note to s 8 at **[3164]**).

Application to limited liability partnerships: see the introductory note to this Act, the Limited Liability Partnerships Regulations 2001, SI 2001/1090, reg 5, Sch 3 at **[6986]**, **[6995]**, and the Limited Liability Partnerships (Scotland) Regulations 2001, SSI 2001/128, reg 4, Schs 2, 3 at **[6977]**, **[6980A]**, **[6980B]**.

243 Unfair preferences (Scotland)

(1) Subject to subsection (2) below, subsection (4) below applies to a transaction entered into by a company, whether before or after 1st April 1986, which has the effect of creating a preference in favour of a creditor to the prejudice of the general body of creditors, being a preference created not earlier than 6 months before the commencement of the winding up of the company or [the company enters administration].

(2) Subsection (4) below does not apply to any of the following transactions—
- (a) a transaction in the ordinary course of trade or business;
- (b) a payment in cash for a debt which when it was paid had become payable, unless the transaction was collusive with the purpose of prejudicing the general body of creditors;
- (c) a transaction whereby the parties to it undertake reciprocal obligations (whether the performance by the parties of their respective obligations occurs at the same time or at different times) unless the transaction was collusive as aforesaid;
- (d) the granting of a mandate by a company authorising an arrestee to pay over the arrested funds or part thereof to the arrester where—
  - (i) there has been a decree for payment or a warrant for summary diligence, and
  - (ii) the decree or warrant has been preceded by an arrestment on the dependence of the action or followed by an arrestment in execution.

(3) For the purposes of subsection (1) above, the day on which a preference was created is the day on which the preference became completely effectual.

(4) A transaction to which this subsection applies is challengeable by—
- (a) in the case of a winding up—
  - (i) any creditor who is a creditor by virtue of a debt incurred on or before the date of commencement of the winding up, or
  - (ii) the liquidator; and
- (b) [where the company has entered administration], the administrator.

(5) On a challenge being brought under subsection (4) above, the court, if satisfied that the transaction challenged is a transaction to which this section applies, shall grant decree of reduction or for such restoration of property to the company's assets or other redress as may be appropriate:

Provided that this subsection is without prejudice to any right or interest acquired in good faith and for value from or through the creditor in whose favour the preference was created.

(6) A liquidator and an administrator have the same right as a creditor has under any rule of law to challenge a preference created by a debtor.

(7) This section applies to Scotland only.

[3400]

NOTES

Sub-ss (1), (4): words in square brackets substituted by the Enterprise Act 2002, s 248(3), Sch 17, paras 9, 29, as from 15 September 2003 (for savings and transitional provisions, see the note to s 8 at **[3164]**).

Application to limited liability partnerships: see the introductory note to this Act, the Limited Liability Partnerships Regulations 2001, SI 2001/1090, reg 5, Sch 3 at **[6986]**, **[6995]**, and the Limited Liability Partnerships (Scotland) Regulations 2001, SSI 2001/128, reg 4, Schs 2, 3 at **[6977]**, **[6980A]**, **[6980B]**.

244 Extortionate credit transactions

(1) This section applies as does section 238, and where the company is, or has been, a party to a transaction for, or involving, the provision of credit to the company.

(2) The court may, on the application of the office-holder, make an order with respect to the transaction if the transaction is or was extortionate and was entered into in the period of 3 years ending with [the day on which the company entered administration or went into liquidation].

(3) For the purposes of this section a transaction is extortionate if, having regard to the risk accepted by the person providing the credit—

(a) the terms of it are or were such as to require grossly exorbitant payments to be made (whether unconditionally or in certain contingencies) in respect of the provision of the credit, or

(b) it otherwise grossly contravened ordinary principles of fair dealing;

and it shall be presumed, unless the contrary is proved, that a transaction with respect to which an application is made under this section is or, as the case may be, was extortionate.

(4) An order under this section with respect to any transaction may contain such one or more of the following as the court thinks fit, that is to say—

(a) provision setting aside the whole or part of any obligation created by the transaction,

(b) provision otherwise varying the terms of the transaction or varying the terms on which any security for the purposes of the transaction is held,

(c) provision requiring any person who is or was a party to the transaction to pay to the office-holder any sums paid to that person, by virtue of the transaction, by the company,

(d) provision requiring any person to surrender to the office-holder any property held by him as security for the purposes of the transaction,

(e) provision directing accounts to be taken between any persons.

(5) The powers conferred by this section are exercisable in relation to any transaction concurrently with any powers exercisable in relation to that transaction as a transaction at an undervalue or under section 242 (gratuitous alienations in Scotland).

[3401]

NOTES

Sub-s (2): words in square brackets substituted by the Enterprise Act 2002, s 248(3), Sch 17, paras 9, 30, as from 15 September 2003 (for savings and transitional provisions, see the note to s 8 at **[3164]**).

Application to limited liability partnerships: see the introductory note to this Act, the Limited Liability Partnerships Regulations 2001, SI 2001/1090, reg 5, Sch 3 at **[6986]**, **[6995]**, and the Limited Liability Partnerships (Scotland) Regulations 2001, SSI 2001/128, reg 4, Schs 2, 3 at **[6977]**, **[6980A]**, **[6980B]**.

245 Avoidance of certain floating charges

(1) This section applies as does section 238, but applies to Scotland as well as to England and Wales.

(2) Subject as follows, a floating charge on the company's undertaking or property created at a relevant time is invalid except to the extent of the aggregate of—

(a) the value of so much of the consideration for the creation of the charge as consists of money paid, or goods or services supplied, to the company at the same time as, or after, the creation of the charge,

(b) the value of so much of that consideration as consists of the discharge or reduction, at the same time as, or after, the creation of the charge, of any debt of the company, and

(c) the amount of such interest (if any) as is payable on the amount falling within paragraph (a) or (b) in pursuance of any agreement under which the money was so paid, the goods or services were so supplied or the debt was so discharged or reduced.

(3) Subject to the next subsection, the time at which a floating charge is created by a company is a relevant time for the purposes of this section if the charge is created—

(a) in the case of a charge which is created in favour of a person who is connected with the company, at a time in the period of 2 years ending with the onset of insolvency,

(b) in the case of a charge which is created in favour of any other person, at a time in the period of 12 months ending with the onset of insolvency, …

[(c) in either case, at a time between the making of an administration application in respect of the company and the making of an administration order on that application, or

PART III OTHER LEGISLATION

(d) in either case, at a time between the filing with the court of a copy of notice of intention to appoint an administrator under paragraph 14 or 22 of Schedule B1 and the making of an appointment under that paragraph.]

(4) Where a company creates a floating charge at a time mentioned in subsection (3)(b) and the person in favour of whom the charge is created is not connected with the company, that time is not a relevant time for the purposes of this section unless the company—

(a) is at that time unable to pay its debts within the meaning of section 123 in Chapter VI of Part IV, or

(b) becomes unable to pay its debts within the meaning of that section in consequence of the transaction under which the charge is created.

(5) For the purposes of subsection (3), the onset of insolvency is—

[(a) in a case where this section applies by reason of an administrator of a company being appointed by administration order, the date on which the administration application is made,

(b) in a case where this section applies by reason of an administrator of a company being appointed under paragraph 14 or 22 of Schedule B1 following filing with the court of a copy of notice of intention to appoint under that paragraph, the date on which the copy of the notice is filed,

(c) in a case where this section applies by reason of an administrator of a company being appointed otherwise than as mentioned in paragraph (a) or (b), the date on which the appointment takes effect, and

(d) in a case where this section applies by reason of a company going into liquidation, the date of the commencement of the winding up.]

(6) For the purposes of subsection (2)(a) the value of any goods or services supplied by way of consideration for a floating charge is the amount in money which at the time they were supplied could reasonably have been expected to be obtained for supplying the goods or services in the ordinary course of business and on the same terms (apart from the consideration) as those on which they were supplied to the company.

[3402]

NOTES

Sub-s (3): word omitted from para (b) repealed, and paras (c), (d) substituted for original para (c), by the Enterprise Act 2002, ss 248(3), 278(2), Sch 17, paras 9, 31(1)–(3), Sch 26, as from 15 September 2003 (for savings and transitional provisions, see the note to s 8 at **[3164]**).

Sub-s (5): paras (a)–(d) substituted, for original paras (a), (b), by the Enterprise Act 2002, s 248(3), Sch 17, paras 9, 31(1), (4), as from 15 September 2003 (for savings and transitional provisions, see the note to s 8 at **[3164]**).

Application to limited liability partnerships: see the introductory note to this Act, the Limited Liability Partnerships Regulations 2001, SI 2001/1090, reg 5, Sch 3 at **[6986]**, **[6995]**, and the Limited Liability Partnerships (Scotland) Regulations 2001, SSI 2001/128, reg 4, Schs 2, 3 at **[6977]**, **[6980A]**, **[6980B]**.

246 Unenforceability of liens on books, etc

(1) This section applies in the case of a company where—

[(a) the company enters administration,] or

(b) the company goes into liquidation, or

(c) a provisional liquidator is appointed;

and "the office-holder" means the administrator, the liquidator or the provisional liquidator, as the case may be.

(2) Subject as follows, a lien or other right to retain possession of any of the books, papers or other records of the company is unenforceable to the extent that its enforcement would deny possession of any books, papers or other records to the office-holder.

(3) This does not apply to a lien on documents which give a title to property and are held as such.

[3403]

NOTES

Sub-s (1): para (a) substituted by the Enterprise Act 2002, s 248(3), Sch 17, paras 9, 32, as from 15 September 2003 (for savings and transitional provisions, see the note to s 8 at **[3164]**).

Application to limited liability partnerships: see the introductory note to this Act and the Limited Liability Partnerships Regulations 2001, SI 2001/1090, reg 5, Sch 3 at **[6986]**, **[6995]**.

PART VII
INTERPRETATION FOR FIRST GROUP OF PARTS

247 "Insolvency" and "go into liquidation"

(1) In this Group of Parts, except in so far as the context otherwise requires, "insolvency", in relation to a company, includes the approval of a voluntary arrangement under Part I, [or the appointment of an administrator or administrative receiver].

(2) For the purposes of any provision in this Group of Parts, a company goes into liquidation if it passes a resolution for voluntary winding up or an order for its winding up is made by the court at a time when it has not already gone into liquidation by passing such a resolution.

[(3) The reference to a resolution for voluntary winding up in subsection (2) includes a reference to a resolution which is deemed to occur by virtue of—

(a) paragraph 83(6)(b) of Schedule B1, or

(b) an order made following conversion of administration or a voluntary arrangement into winding up by virtue of Article 37 of the EC Regulation.]

[3404]

NOTES

Sub-s (1): words in square brackets substituted by the Enterprise Act 2002, s 248(3), Sch 17, paras 9, 33(1), (2), as from 15 September 2003 (for savings and transitional provisions, see the note to s 8 at **[3164]**).

Sub-s (3): added by the Insolvency Act 1986 (Amendment) (No 2) Regulations 2002, SI 2002/1240, regs 3, 12, as from 31 May 2002; substituted by the Enterprise Act 2002, s 248(3), Sch 17, paras 9, 33(1), (3), as from 15 September 2003 (for savings and transitional provisions, see the note to s 8 at **[3164]**).

Application to limited liability partnerships: see the introductory note to this Act and the Limited Liability Partnerships Regulations 2001, SI 2001/1090, reg 5, Sch 3 at **[6986]**, **[6995]**.

248 "Secured creditor", etc

In this Group of Parts, except in so far as the context otherwise requires—

(a) "secured creditor", in relation to a company, means a creditor of the company who holds in respect of his debt a security over property of the company, and "unsecured creditor" is to be read accordingly; and

(b) "security" means—

(i) in relation to England and Wales, any mortgage, charge, lien or other security, and

(ii) in relation to Scotland, any security (whether heritable or moveable), any floating charge and any right of lien or preference and any right of retention (other than a right of compensation or set off).

[3405]

NOTES

Application to limited liability partnerships: see the introductory note to this Act and the Limited Liability Partnerships Regulations 2001, SI 2001/1090, reg 5, Sch 3 at **[6986]**, **[6995]**.

249 "Connected" with a company

For the purposes of any provision in this Group of Parts, a person is connected with a company if—

(a) he is a director or shadow director of the company or an associate of such a director or shadow director, or

(b) he is an associate of the company;

and "associate" has the meaning given by section 435 in Part XVIII of this Act.

[3406]

NOTES

Application to limited liability partnerships: see the introductory note to this Act and the Limited Liability Partnerships Regulations 2001, SI 2001/1090, reg 5, Sch 3 at **[6986]**, **[6995]**.

250 "Member" of a company

For the purposes of any provision in this Group of Parts, a person who is not a member of a company but to whom shares in the company have been transferred, or transmitted by operation of law, is to be regarded as a member of the company, and references to a member or members are to be read accordingly.

[3407]

NOTES

Application to limited liability partnerships: see the introductory note to this Act and the Limited Liability Partnerships Regulations 2001, SI 2001/1090, reg 5, Sch 3 at **[6986]**, **[6995]**.

251 Expressions used generally

In this Group of Parts, except in so far as the context otherwise requires—

"administrative receiver" means—

(a) an administrative receiver as defined by section 29(2) in Chapter I of Part III, or

(b) a receiver appointed under section 51 in Chapter II of that Part in a case where the whole (or substantially the whole) of the company's property is attached by the floating charge;

"business day" means any day other than a Saturday, a Sunday, Christmas Day, Good Friday or a day which is a bank holiday in any part of Great Britain;

"chattel leasing agreement" means an agreement for the bailment or, in Scotland, the hiring of goods which is capable of subsisting for more than 3 months;

"contributory" has the meaning given by section 79;

"director" includes any person occupying the position of director, by whatever name called;

"floating charge" means a charge which, as created, was a floating charge and includes a floating charge within section 462 of the Companies Act (Scottish floating charges);

"office copy", in relation to Scotland, means a copy certified by the clerk of court;

"the official rate", in relation to interest, means the rate payable under section 189(4);

"prescribed" means prescribed by the rules;

"receiver", in the expression "receiver or manager", does not include a receiver appointed under section 51 in Chapter II of Part III;

"retention of title agreement" means an agreement for the sale of goods to a company, being an agreement—

(a) which does not constitute a charge on the goods, but

(b) under which, if the seller is not paid and the company is wound up, the seller will have priority over all other creditors of the company as respects the goods or any property representing the goods;

"the rules" means rules under section 411 in Part XV; and

"shadow director", in relation to a company, means a person in accordance with whose directions or instructions the directors of the company are accustomed to act (but so that a person is not deemed a shadow director by reason only that the directors act on advice given by him in a professional capacity);

and any expression for whose interpretation provision is made by Part XXVI of the Companies Act, other than an expression defined above in this section, is to be construed in accordance with that provision.

[3408]

NOTES

Application to limited liability partnerships: see the introductory note to this Act, the Limited Liability Partnerships Regulations 2001, SI 2001/1090, reg 5, Sch 3 at **[6986]**, **[6995]**, and the Limited Liability Partnerships (Scotland) Regulations 2001, SSI 2001/128, reg 4, Schs 2, 3 at **[6977]**, **[6980A]**, **[6980B]**.

THE THIRD GROUP OF PARTS
MISCELLANEOUS MATTERS BEARING ON BOTH COMPANY AND INDIVIDUAL INSOLVENCY;
GENERAL INTERPRETATION; FINAL PROVISIONS

PART XII
PREFERENTIAL DEBTS IN COMPANY AND INDIVIDUAL INSOLVENCY

386 Categories of preferential debts

(1) A reference in this Act to the preferential debts of a company or an individual is to the debts listed in Schedule 6 to this Act [(contributions to occupational pension schemes; remuneration, &c. of employees; levies on coal and steel production)]; and references to preferential creditors are to be read accordingly.

(2) In that Schedule "the debtor" means the company or the individual concerned.

(3) Schedule 6 is to be read with [Schedule 4 to the Pension Schemes Act 1993] (occupational pension scheme contributions).

[3409]

NOTES

Sub-s (1): words in square brackets substituted by the Enterprise Act 2002, s 251(3), as from 15 September 2003 (for savings and transitional provisions, see the note to Sch 6 at **[3477]**).

Sub-s (3): words in square brackets substituted by the Pension Schemes Act 1993, s 190, Sch 8, para 8, as from 7 February 1994.

Application to limited liability partnerships: see the introductory note to this Act and the Limited Liability Partnerships Regulations 2001, SI 2001/1090, reg 5, Sch 3 at **[6986]**, **[6995]**.

387 "The relevant date"

(1) This section explains references in Schedule 6 to the relevant date (being the date which determines the existence and amount of a preferential debt).

(2) For the purposes of section 4 in Part I (meetings to consider company voluntary arrangement), the relevant date in relation to a company which is not being wound up is—

[(a) if the company is in administration, the date on which it entered administration, and

(b) if the company is not in administration, the date on which the voluntary arrangement takes effect.]

[(2A) For the purposes of paragraph 31 of Schedule A1 (meetings to consider company voluntary arrangement where a moratorium under section 1A is in force), the relevant date in relation to a company is the date of filing.]

(3) In relation to a company which is being wound up, the following applies—

(a) if the winding up is by the court, and the winding-up order was made immediately upon the discharge of an administration order, the relevant date is [the date on which the company entered administration];

[(aa) if the winding up is by the court and the winding-up order was made following conversion of administration into winding up by virtue of Article 37 of the EC Regulation, the relevant date is [the date on which the company entered administration];

(ab) if the company is deemed to have passed a resolution for voluntary winding up by virtue of an order following conversion of administration into winding up under Article 37 of the EC Regulation, the relevant date is [the date on which the company entered administration];]

(b) if the case does not fall within paragraph (a)[, (aa) or (ab)] and the company—

(i) is being wound up by the court, and

(ii) had not commenced to be wound up voluntarily before the date of the making of the winding-up order,

the relevant date is the date of the appointment (or first appointment) of a provisional liquidator or, if no such appointment has been made, the date of the winding-up order;

[(ba) if the case does not fall within paragraph (a), (aa), (ab) or (b) and the company is being wound up following administration pursuant to paragraph 83 of Schedule B1, the relevant date is the date on which the company entered administration;]

PART III
OTHER LEGISLATION

(c) if the case does not fall within [paragraph (a), (aa), (ab), (b) or (ba)], the relevant date is the date of the passing of the resolution for the winding up of the company.

[(3A) In relation to a company which is in administration (and to which no other provision of this section applies) the relevant date is the date on which the company enters administration.]

(4) In relation to a company in receivership (where section 40 or, as the case may be, section 59 applies), the relevant date is—

(a) in England and Wales, the date of the appointment of the receiver by debenture-holders, and

(b) in Scotland, the date of the appointment of the receiver under section 53(6) or (as the case may be) 54(5).

(5) For the purposes of section 258 in Part VIII (individual voluntary arrangements), the relevant date is, in relation to a debtor who is not an undischarged bankrupt

[(a) where an interim order has been made under section 252 with respect to his proposal, the date of that order, and

(b) in any other case, the date on which the voluntary arrangement takes effect.]

(6) In relation to a bankrupt, the following applies—

(a) where at the time the bankruptcy order was made there was an interim receiver appointed under section 286, the relevant date is the date on which the interim receiver was first appointed after the presentation of the bankruptcy petition;

(b) otherwise, the relevant date is the date of the making of the bankruptcy order.

[3410]

NOTES

Sub-s (2): paras (a), (b) substituted by the Enterprise Act 2002, s 248(3), Sch 17, paras 9, 34(1), (2), as from 15 September 2003 (for savings and transitional provisions, see the note to s 8 at **[3164]**).

Sub-s (2A): inserted by the Insolvency Act 2000, s 1, Sch 1, paras 1, 9, as from 1 January 2003.

Sub-s (3): paras (aa), (ab) and words in square brackets in para (b) inserted by the Insolvency Act 1986 (Amendment) (No 2) Regulations 2002, SI 2002/1240, regs 3, 16, as from 31 May 2002; words in square brackets in paras (a), (aa), (ab) (c) substituted, and para (ba) inserted, by the Enterprise Act 2002, s 248(3), Sch 17, paras 9, 34(1), (3), as from 15 September 2003 (for savings and transitional provisions, see the note to s 8 at **[3164]**).

Sub-s (3A): inserted by the Enterprise Act 2002, s 248(3), Sch 17, paras 9, 34(1), (4), as from 15 September 2003 (for savings and transitional provisions, see the note to s 8 at **[3164]**).

Sub-s (5): words in square brackets substituted by the Insolvency Act 2000, s 3, Sch 3, paras 1, 15, as from 1 January 2003 (for transitional provisions see the note below).

Transitional provisions: the Insolvency Act 2000 (Commencement No 3 and Transitional Provisions) Order 2002, SI 2002/2711, art 4 provides for the following transitional provisions (note that by virtue of arts 1 and 2, the "appointed day" means 1 January 2003):

"(1) In a case where a proposal is made by a debtor and before the appointed day the intended nominee has endorsed a copy of the written notice of the proposal under Rule 5.4(3) of the Insolvency Rules the amendments made to the Act by section 3 and Schedule 3 and the repeal made by section 15(1) and Schedule 5 in respect of section 255(1)(d) of the Act shall not apply and the provisions of the Act as they have effect immediately before the appointed day shall continue to have effect.

(2) In this article, "proposal" has the same meaning as it has in section 253 of the Act.".

Application to limited liability partnerships: see the introductory note to this Act and the Limited Liability Partnerships Regulations 2001, SI 2001/1090, reg 5, Sch 3 at **[6986]**, **[6995]**.

PART XIII
INSOLVENCY PRACTITIONERS AND THEIR QUALIFICATION

Restrictions on unqualified persons acting as liquidator, trustee in bankruptcy, etc

388 Meaning of "act as insolvency practitioner"

(1) A person acts as an insolvency practitioner in relation to a company by acting—

(a) as its liquidator, provisional liquidator, administrator or administrative receiver, or

[(b) where a voluntary arrangement in relation to the company is proposed or approved under Part I, as nominee or supervisor].

(2) A person acts as an insolvency practitioner in relation to an individual by acting—

(a) as his trustee in bankruptcy or interim receiver of his property or as permanent or interim trustee in the sequestration of his estate; or

(b) as trustee under a deed which is a deed of arrangement made for the benefit of his creditors or, in Scotland, a trust deed for his creditors; or

[(c) where a voluntary arrangement in relation to the individual is proposed or approved under Part VIII, as nominee or supervisor]

(d) in the case of a deceased individual to the administration of whose estate this section applies by virtue of an order under section 421 (application of provisions of this Act to insolvent estates of deceased persons), as administrator of that estate.

[(2A) A person acts as an insolvency practitioner in relation to an insolvent partnership by acting—

(a) as its liquidator, provisional liquidator or administrator, or

(b) as trustee of the partnership under article 11 of the Insolvent Partnerships Order 1994, or

[(c) where a voluntary arrangement in relation to the insolvent partnership is proposed or approved under Part I of the Act, as nominee or supervisor].]

[(2B) In relation to a voluntary arrangement proposed under Part I or VIII, a person acts as nominee if he performs any of the functions conferred on nominees under the Part in question.]

(3) References in this section to an individual include, except in so far as the context otherwise requires, references … to any debtor within the meaning of the Bankruptcy (Scotland) Act 1985.

(4) In this section—

"administrative receiver" has the meaning given by section 251 in Part VII;

"company" means a company within the meaning given by section 735(1) of the Companies Act or a company which may be wound up under Part V of this Act (unregistered companies); and

"interim trustee" and "permanent trustee" mean the same as in the Bankruptcy (Scotland) Act 1985.

[(5) Nothing in this section applies to anything done by—

(a) the official receiver; or

(b) the Accountant in Bankruptcy (within the meaning of the Bankruptcy (Scotland) Act 1985).]

[(6) Nothing in this section applies to anything done (whether in the United Kingdom or elsewhere) in relation to insolvency proceedings under the EC Regulation in a member State other than the United Kingdom.]

[3411]

NOTES

Sub-s (1): para (b) substituted by the Insolvency Act 2000, s 4(1), (2)(a), as from 1 January 2003 (for transitional provisions see the note below).

Sub-s (2): para (c) substituted by the Insolvency Act 2000, s 4(1), (2)(b), as from 1 January 2003 (for transitional provisions see the note below).

Sub-s (2A): inserted by the Insolvent Partnerships Order 1994, SI 1994/2421, art 15(1), as from 1 December 1994; para (c) substituted by the Insolvent Partnerships (Amendment) (No 2) Order 2002, SI 2002/2708, art 3, as from 1 January 2003. Note: SI 2002/2708 (which also amends the Insolvent Partnerships Order 1994, SI 1994/2421) provides (in art 11) that "the amendments to the 1994 Order set out in articles 3, 4, 5, 6, 8, 9 and 10 of, and Schedules 1 and 2 to, this Order" do not apply where, in relation to a voluntary arrangement under the Insolvency Act 1986, Pt I, as the case may be, a proposal is made by (a) the members of a partnership and before 1 January 2003 the intended nominee has endorsed a copy of the written notice of the proposal under r 1.4(3) (of the Insolvency Rules 1986, SI 1986/1925), (b) the liquidator or the administrator (acting as nominee) and before 1 January 2003 the liquidator or administrator (as the case may be) has sent out a notice summoning the meetings under s 3 of the 1986 Act as required by r 1.11, or (c) the liquidator or the administrator of a partnership (not acting as the nominee) and before 1 January 2003 the intended nominee has endorsed a copy of the written notice of the proposal under rule 1.12(2). It should be noted that art 3 of the 2002 Order amends this section and not the Insolvent Partnerships Order 1994.

Sub-s (2B): inserted by the Insolvency Act 2000, s 4(1), (2)(c), as from 1 January 2003 (for transitional provisions see the note below).

Sub-s (3): words omitted repealed by SI 1994/2421, art 15(2), as from 1 December 1994.

Sub-s (5): substituted by the Bankruptcy (Scotland) Act 1993, s 11(1), as from 1 April 1993.

Sub-s (6): added by the Insolvency Act 1986 (Amendment) (No 2) Regulations 2002, SI 2002/1240, regs 3, 17, as from 31 May 2002.

Transitional provisions: the Insolvency Act 2000 (Commencement No 3 and Transitional Provisions) Order 2002, SI 2002/2711, art 5 provides for the following transitional provisions (note that by virtue of arts 1 and 2, the "appointed day" means 1 January 2003):

"(1) The amendments made by section 4(1) and 4(2) to section 388 of the Act shall not apply in any case where—

(a) a person acts as a nominee (within the meaning of section 1(2) of the Act) and that case falls within paragraph (1) of article 3; or

(b) a person acts as a nominee (within the meaning of section 253(2) of the Act) and that case falls within paragraph (1) of article 4,

and in such cases section 388 of the Act as it has effect immediately before the appointed day shall continue to have effect.".

Application to limited liability partnerships: see the introductory note to this Act and the Limited Liability Partnerships Regulations 2001, SI 2001/1090, reg 5, Sch 3 at **[6986]**, **[6995]**.

389 Acting without qualification an offence

(1) A person who acts as an insolvency practitioner in relation to a company or an individual at a time when he is not qualified to do so is liable to imprisonment or a fine, or to both.

[(1A) This section is subject to section 389A.]

(2) This section does not apply to the official receiver [or the Accountant in Bankruptcy (within the meaning of the Bankruptcy (Scotland) Act 1985)]. **[3412]**

NOTES

Sub-s (1A): inserted by the Insolvency Act 2000, s 4(1), (3), as from 1 January 2003.

Sub-s (2): words in square brackets added by the Bankruptcy (Scotland) Act 1993, s 11(2), as from 1 April 1993.

Application to limited liability partnerships: see the introductory note to this Act and the Limited Liability Partnerships Regulations 2001, SI 2001/1090, reg 5, Sch 3 at **[6986]**, **[6995]**.

[389A Authorisation of nominees and supervisors

(1) Section 389 does not apply to a person acting, in relation to a voluntary arrangement proposed or approved under Part I or Part VIII, as nominee or supervisor if he is authorised so to act.

(2) For the purposes of subsection (1) and those Parts, an individual to whom subsection (3) does not apply is authorised to act as nominee or supervisor in relation to such an arrangement if—

(a) he is a member of a body recognised for the purpose by the Secretary of State, and

(b) there is in force security (in Scotland, caution) for the proper performance of his functions and that security or caution meets the prescribed requirements with respect to his so acting in relation to the arrangement.

(3) This subsection applies to a person if—

(a) he has been adjudged bankrupt or sequestration of his estate has been awarded and (in either case) he has not been discharged,

(b) he is subject to a disqualification order made or a disqualification undertaking accepted under the Company Directors Disqualification Act 1986 or to a disqualification order made under Part II of the Companies (Northern Ireland) Order 1989 [or a disqualification undertaking accepted under the Company Directors Disqualification (Northern Ireland) Order 2002], *or*

(c) he is a patient within the meaning of *Part VII of the Mental Health Act 1983 or* [section 329(1) of the Mental Health (Care and Treatment) (Scotland) Act 2003][, or

(d) he lacks capacity (within the meaning of the Mental Capacity Act 2005) to act as nominee or supervisor].

(4) The Secretary of State may by order declare a body which appears to him to fall within subsection (5) to be a recognised body for the purposes of subsection (2)(a).

(5) A body may be recognised if it maintains and enforces rules for securing that its members—

(a) are fit and proper persons to act as nominees or supervisors, and

(b) meet acceptable requirements as to education and practical training and experience.

(6) For the purposes of this section, a person is a member of a body only if he is subject to its rules when acting as nominee or supervisor (whether or not he is in fact a member of the body).

(7) An order made under subsection (4) in relation to a body may be revoked by a further order if it appears to the Secretary of State that the body no longer falls within subsection (5).

(8) An order of the Secretary of State under this section has effect from such date as is specified in the order; and any such order revoking a previous order may make provision for members of the body in question to continue to be treated as members of a recognised body for a specified period after the revocation takes effect.]

[3413]

NOTES

Inserted by the Insolvency Act 2000, s 4(1), (4), as from 1 January 2003.

Sub-s (3): words in square brackets in para (b) inserted by the Insolvency Act 2000 (Company Directors Disqualification Undertakings) Order 2004, SI 2004/1941, art 3, Schedule, paras 1, 2, as from 1 September 2004, in relation to disqualification undertakings under the Company Directors Disqualification (Northern Ireland) Order 2002 accepted on or after that date; word "or" in italics in para (b), and words "Part VII of the Mental Health Act 1983 or" in italics in para (c) repealed, and para (d) and the word immediately preceding it inserted, by the Mental capacity Act 2005, s 67(1), (2), Sch 6, para 31(1), (2), Sch 7, as from 1 October 2007; words in square brackets in para (c) substituted, in relation to Scotland, by the Mental Health (Care and Treatment) (Scotland) Act 2003 (Modification of Enactments) Order 2005, SSI 2005/486, art 2, Sch 1, para 18(1), (2), as from 27 September 2005, and, in relation to England and Wales, by the Mental Health (Care and Treatment) (Scotland) Act 2003 (Consequential Provisions) Order 2005, SI 2005/2078, art 15, Sch 1, para 3(1), (2), as from 5 October 2005.

Application to limited liability partnerships: see the introductory note to this Act and the Limited Liability Partnerships Regulations 2001, SI 2001/1090, reg 5, Sch 3 at **[6986]**, **[6995]**.

[389B Official receiver as nominee or supervisor

(1) The official receiver is authorised to act as nominee or supervisor in relation to a voluntary arrangement approved under Part VIII provided that the debtor is an undischarged bankrupt when the arrangement is proposed.

(2) The Secretary of State may by order repeal the proviso in subsection (1).

(3) An order under subsection (2)—

(a) must be made by statutory instrument, and

(b) shall be subject to annulment in pursuance of a resolution of either House of Parliament.]

[3413A]

NOTES

Inserted, in relation to England and Wales only, by the Enterprise Act 2002, s 264(1), Sch 22, para 3, as from 1 April 2004.

Application to limited liability partnerships: see the introductory note to this Act and the Limited Liability Partnerships Regulations 2001, SI 2001/1090, reg 5, Sch 3 at **[6986]**, **[6995]**.

The requisite qualification, and the means of obtaining it

390 Persons not qualified to act as insolvency practitioners

(1) A person who is not an individual is not qualified to act as an insolvency practitioner.

(2) A person is not qualified to act as an insolvency practitioner at any time unless at that time—

(a) he is authorised so to act by virtue of membership of a professional body recognised under section 391 below, being permitted so to act by or under the rules of that body, or

(b) he holds an authorisation granted by a competent authority under section 393.

(3) A person is not qualified to act as an insolvency practitioner in relation to another person at any time unless—

(a) there is in force at that time security or, in Scotland, caution for the proper performance of his functions, and

(b) that security or caution meets the prescribed requirements with respect to his so acting in relation to that other person.

(4) A person is not qualified to act as an insolvency practitioner at any time if at that time—

(a) he has been adjudged bankrupt or sequestration of his estate has been awarded and (in either case) he has not been discharged,

(b) he is subject to a disqualification order made [or a disqualification undertaking accepted] under the Company Directors Disqualification Act 1986 [or to a disqualification order made under Part II of the Companies (Northern Ireland) Order 1989] [or to a disqualification undertaking accepted under the Company Directors Disqualification (Northern Ireland) Order 2002], *or*

(c) he is a patient within the meaning of *Part VII of the Mental Health Act 1983 or* [section 329(1) of the Mental Health (Care and Treatment) (Scotland) Act 2003] [or has had a guardian appointed to him under the Adults with Incapacity (Scotland) Act 2000 (asp 4)][, or

(d) he lacks capacity (within the meaning of the Mental Capacity Act 2005) to act as an insolvency practitioner].

[(5) A person is not qualified to act as an insolvency practitioner while a bankruptcy restrictions order is in force in respect of him.]

[3414]

NOTES

Sub-s (4): words in first and second pairs of square brackets in para (b) inserted by the Insolvency Act 2000, s 8, Sch 4, Pt II, para 16(1), (2), as from 2 April 2001; words in third pair of square brackets in para (b) inserted by the Insolvency Act 2000 (Company Directors Disqualification Undertakings) Order 2004, SI 2004/1941, art 3, Schedule, paras 1, 3, as from 1 September 2004, in relation to disqualification undertakings under the Company Directors Disqualification (Northern Ireland) Order 2002 accepted on or after that date; word "or" in italics in para (b), and words "Part VII of the Mental Health Act 1983 or" in italics in para (c) repealed, and para (d) and the word immediately preceding it inserted, by the Mental capacity Act 2005, s 67(1), (2), Sch 6, para 31(1), (3), Sch 7, as from 1 October 2007; words in first pair of square brackets in para (c) substituted, in relation to Scotland, by the Mental Health (Care and Treatment) (Scotland) Act 2003 (Modification of Enactments) Order 2005, SSI 2005/486, art 2, Sch 1, para 18(1), (3), as from 27 September 2005, and, in relation to England and Wales, by the Mental Health (Care and Treatment) (Scotland) Act 2003 (Consequential Provisions) Order 2005, SI 2005/2078, art 15, Sch 1, para 3(1), (3), as from 5 October 2005; words in second pair of square brackets in para (c) added by the Adults with Incapacity (Scotland) Act 2000, s 88(2), Sch 5, para 18, as from 1 April 2002.

Sub-s (5): added, in relation to England and Wales only, by the Enterprise Act 2002, s 257(3), Sch 21, para 4, as from 1 April 2004.

Application to limited liability partnerships: see the introductory note to this Act and the Limited Liability Partnerships Regulations 2001, SI 2001/1090, reg 5, Sch 3 at **[6986]**, **[6995]**.

Regulations: the Insolvency Practitioners Regulations 2005, SI 2005/524 at **[7369]**.

391 Recognised professional bodies

(1) The Secretary of State may by order declare a body which appears to him to fall within subsection (2) below to be a recognised professional body for the purposes of this section.

(2) A body may be recognised if it regulates the practice of a profession and maintains and enforces rules for securing that such of its members as are permitted by or under the rules to act as insolvency practitioners—

(a) are fit and proper persons so to act, and

(b) meet acceptable requirements as to education and practical training and experience.

(3) References to members of a recognised professional body are to persons who, whether members of that body or not, are subject to its rules in the practice of the profession in question.

The reference in section 390(2) above to membership of a professional body recognised under this section is to be read accordingly.

(4) An order made under subsection (1) in relation to a professional body may be revoked by a further order if it appears to the Secretary of State that the body no longer falls within subsection (2).

(5) An order of the Secretary of State under this section has effect from such date as is specified in the order; and any such order revoking a previous order may make provision

whereby members of the body in question continue to be treated as authorised to act as insolvency practitioners for a specified period after the revocation takes effect.

[3415]

NOTES

Application to limited liability partnerships: see the introductory note to this Act and the Limited Liability Partnerships Regulations 2001, SI 2001/1090, reg 5, Sch 3 at **[6986]**, **[6995]**.

Orders: the Insolvency Practitioners (Recognised Professional Bodies) Order 1986, SI 1986/1764 recognising the following bodies for the purposes of this section: the Chartered Association of Certified Accountants; the Insolvency Practitioners Association; the Institute of Chartered Accountants in England and Wales; the Institute of Chartered Accountants in Ireland; the Institute of Chartered Accountants of Scotland; the Law Society; the Law Society of Scotland.

392 Authorisation by competent authority

(1) Application may be made to a competent authority for authorisation to act as an insolvency practitioner.

(2) The competent authorities for this purpose are—

(a) in relation to a case of any description specified in directions given by the Secretary of State, the body or person so specified in relation to cases of that description, and

(b) in relation to a case not falling within paragraph (a), the Secretary of State.

(3) The application—

(a) shall be made in such manner as the competent authority may direct,

(b) shall contain or be accompanied by such information as that authority may reasonably require for the purpose of determining the application, and

(c) shall be accompanied by the prescribed fee;

and the authority may direct that notice of the making of the application shall be published in such manner as may be specified in the direction.

(4) At any time after receiving the application and before determining it the authority may require the applicant to furnish additional information.

(5) Directions and requirements given or imposed under subsection (3) or (4) may differ as between different applications.

(6) Any information to be furnished to the competent authority under this section shall, if it so requires, be in such form or verified in such manner as it may specify.

(7) An application may be withdrawn before it is granted or refused.

(8) Any sums received under this section by a competent authority other than the Secretary of State may be retained by the authority; and any sums so received by the Secretary of State shall be paid into the Consolidated Fund.

[(9) Subsection (3)(c) shall not have effect in respect of an application made to the Secretary of State (but this subsection is without prejudice to section 415A).]

[3416]

NOTES

Sub-s (9): added by the Enterprise Act 2002, s 270(3), as from 1 April 2004.

Application to limited liability partnerships: see the introductory note to this Act and the Limited Liability Partnerships Regulations 2001, SI 2001/1090, reg 5, Sch 3 at **[6986]**, **[6995]**.

Regulations: the Insolvency Practitioners Regulations 2005, SI 2005/524 at **[7369]**.

393 Grant, refusal and withdrawal of authorisation

(1) The competent authority may, on an application duly made in accordance with section 392 and after being furnished with all such information as it may require under that section, grant or refuse the application.

(2) The authority shall grant the application if it appears to it from the information furnished by the applicant and having regard to such other information, if any, as it may have—

(a) that the applicant is a fit and proper person to act as an insolvency practitioner, and

(b) that the applicant meets the prescribed requirements with respect to education and practical training and experience.

(3) An authorisation granted under this section, if not previously withdrawn, continues in force for such period not exceeding the prescribed maximum as may be specified in the authorisation.

(4) An authorisation so granted may be withdrawn by the competent authority if it appears to it—

(a) that the holder of the authorisation is no longer a fit and proper person to act as an insolvency practitioner, or

(b) without prejudice to paragraph (a), that the holder—

(i) has failed to comply with any provision of this Part or of any regulations made under this Part or Part XV, or

(ii) in purported compliance with any such provision, has furnished the competent authority with false, inaccurate or misleading information.

(5) An authorisation granted under this section may be withdrawn by the competent authority at the request or with the consent of the holder of the authorisation.

[3417]

NOTES

Application to limited liability partnerships: see the introductory note to this Act and the Limited Liability Partnerships Regulations 2001, SI 2001/1090, reg 5, Sch 3 at **[6986]**, **[6995]**.

Regulations: the Insolvency Practitioners Regulations 2005, SI 2005/524 at **[7369]**.

394 Notices

(1) Where a competent authority grants an authorisation under section 393, it shall give written notice of that fact to the applicant, specifying the date on which the authorisation takes effect.

(2) Where the authority proposes to refuse an application, or to withdraw an authorisation under section 393(4), it shall give the applicant or holder of the authorisation written notice of its intention to do so, setting out particulars of the grounds on which it proposes to act.

(3) In the case of a proposed withdrawal the notice shall state the date on which it is proposed that the withdrawal should take effect.

(4) A notice under subsection (2) shall give particulars of the rights exercisable under the next two sections by a person on whom the notice is served.

[3418]

NOTES

Application to limited liability partnerships: see the introductory note to this Act and the Limited Liability Partnerships Regulations 2001, SI 2001/1090, reg 5, Sch 3 at **[6986]**, **[6995]**.

395 Right to make representations

(1) A person on whom a notice is served under section 394(2) may within 14 days after the date of service make written representations to the competent authority.

(2) The competent authority shall have regard to any representations so made in determining whether to refuse the application or withdraw the authorisation, as the case may be.

[3419]

NOTES

Application to limited liability partnerships: see the introductory note to this Act and the Limited Liability Partnerships Regulations 2001, SI 2001/1090, reg 5, Sch 3 at **[6986]**, **[6995]**.

396 Reference to Tribunal

(1) The Insolvency Practitioners Tribunal ("the Tribunal") continues in being; and the provisions of Schedule 7 apply to it.

(2) Where a person is served with a notice under section 394(2), he may—

(a) at any time within 28 days after the date of service of the notice, or

(b) at any time after the making by him of representations under section 395 and before the end of the period of 28 days after the date of the service on him of a notice by the competent authority that the authority does not propose to alter its decision in consequence of the representations,

give written notice to the authority requiring the case to be referred to the Tribunal.

(3) Where a requirement is made under subsection (2), then, unless the competent authority—

(a) has decided or decides to grant the application or, as the case may be, not to withdraw the authorisation, and

(b) within 7 days after the date of the making of the requirement, gives written notice of that decision to the person by whom the requirement was made,

it shall refer the case to the Tribunal.

[3420]

NOTES

Application to limited liability partnerships: see the introductory note to this Act and the Limited Liability Partnerships Regulations 2001, SI 2001/1090, reg 5, Sch 3 at **[6986]**, **[6995]**.

Rules: the Insolvency Practitioners Tribunal (Conduct of Investigations) Rules 1986, SI 1986/952 at **[6044]**.

397 Action of Tribunal on reference

(1) On a reference under section 396 the Tribunal shall—

(a) investigate the case, and

(b) make a report to the competent authority stating what would in their opinion be the appropriate decision in the matter and the reasons for that opinion,

and it is the duty of the competent authority to decide the matter accordingly.

(2) The Tribunal shall send a copy of the report to the applicant or, as the case may be, the holder of the authorisation; and the competent authority shall serve him with a written notice of the decision made by it in accordance with the report.

(3) The competent authority may, if he thinks fit, publish the report of the Tribunal.

[3421]

NOTES

Application to limited liability partnerships: see the introductory note to this Act and the Limited Liability Partnerships Regulations 2001, SI 2001/1090, reg 5, Sch 3 at **[6986]**, **[6995]**.

398 Refusal or withdrawal without reference to Tribunal

Where in the case of any proposed refusal or withdrawal of an authorisation either—

(a) the period mentioned in section 396(2)(a) has expired without the making of any requirement under that subsection or of any representations under section 395, or

(b) the competent authority has given a notice such as is mentioned in section 396(2)(b) and the period so mentioned has expired without the making of any such requirement,

the competent authority may give written notice of the refusal or withdrawal to the person concerned in accordance with the proposal in the notice given under section 394(2).

[3422]

NOTES

Application to limited liability partnerships: see the introductory note to this Act and the Limited Liability Partnerships Regulations 2001, SI 2001/1090, reg 5, Sch 3 at **[6986]**, **[6995]**.

PART XIV
PUBLIC ADMINISTRATION (ENGLAND AND WALES)

Official Receivers

399 Appointment, etc of official receivers

(1) For the purposes of this Act the official receiver, in relation to any bankruptcy[, winding up or individual voluntary arrangement], is any person who by virtue of the following provisions of this section or section 401 below is authorised to act as the official receiver in relation to that bankruptcy[, winding up or individual voluntary arrangement]

(2) The Secretary of State may (subject to the approval of the Treasury as to numbers) appoint persons to the office of official receiver, and a person appointed to that office (whether under this section or section 70 of the Bankruptcy Act 1914)—

(a) shall be paid out of money provided by Parliament such salary as the Secretary of State may with the concurrence of the Treasury direct,

(b) shall hold office on such other terms and conditions as the Secretary of State may with the concurrence of the Treasury direct, and

(c) may be removed from office by a direction of the Secretary of State.

(3) Where a person holds the office of official receiver, the Secretary of State shall from time to time attach him either to the High Court or to a county court having jurisdiction for the purposes of the second Group of Parts of this Act.

(4) Subject to any directions under subsection (6) below, an official receiver attached to a particular court is the person authorised to act as the official receiver in relation to every bankruptcy[, winding up or individual voluntary arrangement] falling within the jurisdiction of that court.

(5) The Secretary of State shall ensure that there is, at all times, at least one official receiver attached to the High Court and at least one attached to each county court having jurisdiction for the purposes of the second Group of Parts; but he may attach the same official receiver to two or more different courts.

(6) The Secretary of State may give directions with respect to the disposal of the business of official receivers, and such directions may, in particular—

(a) authorise an official receiver attached to one court to act as the official receiver in relation to any case or description of cases falling within the jurisdiction of another court;

(b) provide, where there is more than one official receiver authorised to act as the official receiver in relation to cases falling within the jurisdiction of any court, for the distribution of their business between or among themselves.

(7) A person who at the coming into force of section 222 of the Insolvency Act 1985 (replaced by this section) is an official receiver attached to a court shall continue in office after the coming into force of that section as an official receiver attached to that court under this section.

[3423]

NOTES

Sub-ss (1), (4): words in square brackets substituted by the Enterprise Act 2002, s 269, Sch 23, paras 1, 14, as from 1 April 2004.

Application to limited liability partnerships: see the introductory note to this Act and the Limited Liability Partnerships Regulations 2001, SI 2001/1090, reg 5, Sch 3 at **[6986]**, **[6995]**.

400 Functions and status of official receivers

(1) In addition to any functions conferred on him by this Act, a person holding the office of official receiver shall carry out such other functions as may from time to time be conferred on him by the Secretary of State.

(2) In the exercise of the functions of his office a person holding the office of official receiver shall act under the general directions of the Secretary of State and shall also be an officer of the court in relation to which he exercises those functions.

(3) Any property vested in his official capacity in a person holding the office of official receiver shall, on his dying, ceasing to hold office or being otherwise succeeded in relation to

the bankruptcy or winding up in question by another official receiver, vest in his successor without any conveyance, assignment or transfer.

[3424]

NOTES

Application to limited liability partnerships: see the introductory note to this Act and the Limited Liability Partnerships Regulations 2001, SI 2001/1090, reg 5, Sch 3 at **[6986]**, **[6995]**.

401 Deputy official receivers and staff

(1) The Secretary of State may, if he thinks it expedient to do so in order to facilitate the disposal of the business of the official receiver attached to any court, appoint an officer of his department to act as deputy to that official receiver.

(2) Subject to any directions given by the Secretary of State under section 399 or 400, a person appointed to act as deputy to an official receiver has, on such conditions and for such period as may be specified in the terms of his appointment, the same status and functions as the official receiver to whom he is appointed deputy.

Accordingly, references in this Act (except section 399(1) to (5)) to an official receiver include a person appointed to act as his deputy.

(3) An appointment made under subsection (1) may be terminated at any time by the Secretary of State.

(4) The Secretary of State may, subject to the approval of the Treasury as to numbers and remuneration and as to the other terms and conditions of the appointments, appoint officers of his department to assist official receivers in the carrying out of their functions.

[3425]

NOTES

Application to limited liability partnerships: see the introductory note to this Act and the Limited Liability Partnerships Regulations 2001, SI 2001/1090, reg 5, Sch 3 at **[6986]**, **[6995]**.

The Official Petitioner

402 Official Petitioner

(1) There continues to be an officer known as the Official Petitioner for the purpose of discharging, in relation to cases in which a criminal bankruptcy order is made, the functions assigned to him by or under this Act; and the Director of Public Prosecutions continues, by virtue of his office, to be the Official Petitioner.

(2) The functions of the Official Petitioner include the following—

- *(a) to consider whether, in a case in which a criminal bankruptcy order is made, it is in the public interest that he should himself present a petition under section 264(1)(d) of this Act;*
- *(b) to present such a petition in any case where he determines that it is in the public interest for him to do so;*
- *(c) to make payments, in such cases as he may determine, towards expenses incurred by other persons in connection with proceedings in pursuance of such a petition; and*
- *(d) to exercise, so far as he considers it in the public interest to do so, any of the powers conferred on him by or under this Act.*

(3) Any functions of the Official Petitioner may be discharged on his behalf by any person acting with his authority.

(4) Neither the Official Petitioner nor any person acting with his authority is liable to any action or proceeding in respect of anything done or omitted to be done in the discharge, or purported discharge, of the functions of the Official Petitioner.

(5) In this section "criminal bankruptcy order" means an order under section 39(1) of the Powers of Criminal Courts Act 1973.

[3426]

NOTES

Repealed by the Criminal Justice Act 1988, s 170(2), Sch 16, as from a day to be appointed.

PART III
OTHER LEGISLATION

Application to limited liability partnerships: see the introductory note to this Act and the Limited Liability Partnerships Regulations 2001, SI 2001/1090, reg 5, Sch 3 at **[6986]**, **[6995]**.

Insolvency Service finance, accounting and investment

403 Insolvency Services Account

(1) All money received by the Secretary of State in respect of proceedings under this Act as it applies to England and Wales shall be paid into the Insolvency Services Account kept by the Secretary of State with the Bank of England; and all payments out of money standing to the credit of the Secretary of State in that account shall be made by the Bank of England in such manner as he may direct.

(2) Whenever the cash balance standing to the credit of the Insolvency Services Account is in excess of the amount which in the opinion of the Secretary of State is required for the time being to answer demands in respect of bankrupts' estates or companies' estates, the Secretary of State shall—

(a) notify the excess to the National Debt Commissioners, and

(b) pay into the Insolvency Services Investment Account ("the Investment Account") kept by the Commissioners with the Bank of England the whole or any part of the excess as the Commissioners may require for investment in accordance with the following provisions of this Part.

(3) Whenever any part of the money so invested is, in the opinion of the Secretary of State, required to answer any demand in respect of bankrupt's estates or companies' estates, he shall notify to the National Debt Commissioners the amount so required and the Commissioners—

(a) shall thereupon repay to the Secretary of State such sum as may be required to the credit of the Insolvency Services Account, and

(b) for that purpose may direct the sale of such part of the securities in which the money has been invested as may be necessary.

[3427]

NOTES

Application to limited liability partnerships: see the introductory note to this Act and the Limited Liability Partnerships Regulations 2001, SI 2001/1090, reg 5, Sch 3 at **[6986]**, **[6995]**.

404 Investment Account

Any money standing to the credit of the Investment Account (including any money received by the National Debt Commissioners by way of interest on or proceeds of any investment under this section) may be invested by the Commissioners, in accordance with such directions as may be given by the Treasury, in any manner for the time being specified in Part II of Schedule 1 to the Trustee Investments Act 1961.

[3428]–[3429]

NOTES

Application to limited liability partnerships: see the introductory note to this Act and the Limited Liability Partnerships Regulations 2001, SI 2001/1090, reg 5, Sch 3 at **[6986]**, **[6995]**.

405 (*Repealed by the Enterprise Act 2002, ss 272(1), 278(2), Sch 26, as from 1 April 2004.*)

406 [Interest on money received by liquidators or trustees in bankruptcy and invested]

Where under rules made by virtue of paragraph 16 of Schedule 8 to this Act (investment of money received by company liquidators) [or paragraph 21 of Schedule 9 to this Act (investment of money received by trustee in bankruptcy) a company or a bankrupt's estate] has become entitled to any sum by way of interest, the Secretary of State shall certify that sum and the amount of tax payable on it to the National Debt Commissioners; and the Commissioners shall pay, out of the Investment Account—

(a) into the Insolvency Services Account, the sum so certified less the amount of tax so certified, and

(b) to the Commissioners of Inland Revenue, the amount of tax so certified.

[3430]

NOTES

Words in square brackets substituted by the Insolvency Act 2000, s 13(2), as from 2 April 2001.

Application to limited liability partnerships: see the introductory note to this Act and the Limited Liability Partnerships Regulations 2001, SI 2001/1090, reg 5, Sch 3 at **[6986]**, **[6995]**.

Commissioners of Inland Revenue: a reference to the Commissioners of Inland Revenue is now to be taken as a reference to the Commissioners for Her Majesty's Revenue and Customs; see the Commissioners for Revenue and Customs Act 2005, s 50(1), (7).

407 Unclaimed dividends and undistributed balances

(1) The Secretary of State shall from time to time pay into the Consolidated Fund out of the Insolvency Services Account so much of the sums standing to the credit of that Account as represents—

- (a) dividends which were declared before such date as the Treasury may from time to time determine and have not been claimed, and
- (b) balances ascertained before that date which are too small to be divided among the persons entitled to them.

(2) For the purposes of this section the sums standing to the credit of the Insolvency Services Account are deemed to include any sums paid out of that Account and represented by any sums or securities standing to the credit of the Investment Account.

(3) The Secretary of State may require the National Debt Commissioners to pay out of the Investment Account into the Insolvency Services Account the whole or part of any sum which he is required to pay out of that account under subsection (1); and the Commissioners may direct the sale of such securities standing to the credit of the Investment Account as may be necessary for that purpose.

[3431]

NOTES

Application to limited liability partnerships: see the introductory note to this Act and the Limited Liability Partnerships Regulations 2001, SI 2001/1090, reg 5, Sch 3 at **[6986]**, **[6995]**.

[408 Adjustment of balances

(1) The Treasury may direct the payment out of the Consolidated Fund of sums into—

- (a) the Insolvency Services Account;
- (b) the Investment Account.

(2) The Treasury shall certify to the House of Commons the reason for any payment under subsection (1).

(3) The Secretary of State may pay sums out of the Insolvency Services Account into the Consolidated Fund.

(4) The National Debt Commissioners may pay sums out of the Investment Account into the Consolidated Fund.]

[3432]

NOTES

Substituted by the Enterprise Act 2002, s 272(2), as from 1 April 2004.

Application to limited liability partnerships: see the introductory note to this Act and the Limited Liability Partnerships Regulations 2001, SI 2001/1090, reg 5, Sch 3 at **[6986]**, **[6995]**.

409 Annual financial statement and audit

(1) The National Debt Commissioners shall for each year ending on 31st March prepare a statement of the sums credited and debited to the Investment Account in such form and manner as the Treasury may direct and shall transmit it to the Comptroller and Auditor General before the end of November next following the year.

(2) The Secretary of State shall for each year ending 31st March prepare a statement of the sums received or paid by him under section 403 above in such form and manner as the Treasury may direct and shall transmit each statement to the Comptroller and Auditor General before the end of November next following the year.

(3) Every such statement shall include such additional information as the Treasury may direct.

(4) The Comptroller and Auditor General shall examine, certify and report on every such statement and shall lay copies of it, and of his report, before Parliament.

[3433]

NOTES

Application to limited liability partnerships: see the introductory note to this Act and the Limited Liability Partnerships Regulations 2001, SI 2001/1090, reg 5, Sch 3 at **[6986]**, **[6995]**.

Supplementary

410 Extent of this Part

This Part of this Act extends to England and Wales only.

[3434]

NOTES

Application to limited liability partnerships: see the introductory note to this Act and the Limited Liability Partnerships Regulations 2001, SI 2001/1090, reg 5, Sch 3 at **[6986]**, **[6995]**.

PART XV
SUBORDINATE LEGISLATION

General insolvency rules

411 Company insolvency rules

(1) Rules may be made—

(a) in relation to England and Wales, by the Lord Chancellor with the concurrence of the Secretary of State [and, in the case of rules that affect court procedure, with the concurrence of the Lord Chief Justice], or

(b) in relation to Scotland, by the Secretary of State,

for the purpose of giving effect to Parts I to VII of this Act [or the EC Regulation].

(2) Without prejudice to the generality of subsection (1), or to any provision of those Parts by virtue of which rules under this section may be made with respect to any matter, rules under this section may contain—

(a) any such provision as is specified in Schedule 8 to this Act or corresponds to provision contained immediately before the coming into force of section 106 of the Insolvency Act 1985 in rules made, or having effect as if made, under section 663(1) or (2) of the Companies Act (old winding-up rules), and

(b) such incidental, supplemental and transitional provisions as may appear to the Lord Chancellor or, as the case may be, the Secretary of State necessary or expedient.

[(2A) For the purposes of subsection (2), a reference in Schedule 8 to this Act to doing anything under or for the purposes of a provision of this Act includes a reference to doing anything under or for the purposes of the EC Regulation (in so far as the provision of this Act relates to a matter to which the EC Regulation applies).

(2B) Rules under this section for the purpose of giving effect to the EC Regulation may not create an offence of a kind referred to in paragraph 1(1)(d) of Schedule 2 to the European Communities Act 1972.]

(3) In Schedule 8 to this Act "liquidator" includes a provisional liquidator; and references above in this section to Parts I to VII of this Act are to be read as including the Companies Act so far as relating to, and to matters connected with or arising out of, the insolvency or winding up of companies.

(4) Rules under this section shall be made by statutory instrument subject to annulment in pursuance of a resolution of either House of Parliament.

(5) Regulations made by the Secretary of State under a power conferred by rules under this section shall be made by statutory instrument and, after being made, shall be laid before each House of Parliament.

(6) Nothing in this section prejudices any power to make rules of court.

[(7) The Lord Chief Justice may nominate a judicial office holder (as defined in section 109(4) of the Constitutional Reform Act 2005) to exercise his functions under this section.]

[3435]

NOTES

Sub-s (1): words in square brackets in para (a) inserted by the Constitutional Reform Act 2005, s 15, Sch 4, Pt 1, paras 185, 188(1), (2), as from 3 April 2006; words in second pair of square brackets inserted by the Insolvency Act 1986 (Amendment) Regulations 2002, SI 2002/1037, regs 2, 3(1), as from 3 May 2002.

Sub-ss (2A), (2B): inserted by SI 2002/1037, regs 2, 3(2), as from 3 May 2002.

Sub-s (7): added by the Constitutional Reform Act 2005, s 15, Sch 4, Pt 1, paras 185, 188(1), (3), as from 3 April 2006.

Application to limited liability partnerships: see the introductory note to this Act and the Limited Liability Partnerships Regulations 2001, SI 2001/1090, reg 5, Sch 3 at **[6986]**, **[6995]**.

Rules: the Insolvency (Scotland) Rules 1986, SI 1986/1915; the Insolvency Rules 1986, SI 1986/1925 at **[6060]**; the Companies (Unfair Prejudice Applications) Proceedings Rules 1986, SI 1986/2000 at **[6574]**; the Insolvent Companies (Disqualification of Unfit Directors) Proceedings Rules 1987, SI 1987/2023 at **[6583]**; the Insolvent Companies (Reports on Conduct of Directors) Rules 1996, SI 1996/1909 at **[6916]**; the Insolvent Companies (Reports on Conduct of Directors) (Scotland) Rules 1996, SI 1996/1910 at **[6922]**; the Railway Administration Order Rules 2001, SI 2001/3352; the Insurers (Winding Up) Rules 2001, SI 2001/3635 at **[4585]**; the Insurers (Winding Up) (Scotland) Rules 2001, SI 2001/4040; the Energy Administration Rules 2005, SI 2005/2483; the Energy Administration (Scotland) Rules 2006, SI 2006/772.

Regulations: the Insolvency Regulations 1994, SI 1994/2507 at **[6794]**.

413 Insolvency Rules Committee

(1) The committee established under section 10 of the Insolvency Act 1976 (advisory committee on bankruptcy and winding-up rules) continues to exist for the purpose of being consulted under this section.

(2) The Lord Chancellor shall consult the committee before making any rules under section 411 or 412 [other than rules which contain a statement that the only provision made by the rules is provision applying rules made under section 411, with or without modifications, for the purposes of provision made by [any of sections 23 to 26 of the Water Industry Act 1991 or Schedule 3 to that Act]] [or by any of sections 59 to 65 of, or Schedule 6 or 7 to, the Railways Act 1993].

(3) Subject to the next subsection, the committee shall consist of—
- (a) a judge of the High Court attached to the Chancery Division;
- (b) a circuit judge;
- (c) a registrar in bankruptcy of the High Court;
- (d) the registrar of a county court;
- (e) a practising barrister;
- (f) a practising solicitor; and
- (g) a practising accountant;

and the appointment of any person as a member of the committee shall be made [in accordance with subsection (3A) or (3B)].

[(3A) The Lord Chief Justice must appoint the persons referred to in paragraphs (a) to (d) of subsection (3), after consulting the Lord Chancellor.

(3B) The Lord Chancellor must appoint the persons referred to in paragraphs (e) to (g) of subsection (3), after consulting the Lord Chief Justice.]

(4) The Lord Chancellor may appoint as additional members of the committee any persons appearing to him to have qualifications or experience that would be of value to the committee in considering any matter with which it is concerned.

[(5) The Lord Chief Justice may nominate a judicial office holder (as defined in section 109(4) of the Constitutional Reform Act 2005) to exercise his functions under this section.]

[3436]

NOTES

Sub-s (2): words in first (outer) pair of square brackets substituted by the Water Act 1989, s 190(1), Sch 25, para 78(2), as from 1 September 1989; words in second (inner) pair of square brackets substituted by the Water Consolidation (Consequential Provisions) Act 1991, s 2(1), Sch 1, para 46, as from 1 December 1991; words in third pair of square brackets added by the Railways Act 1993, s 152, Sch 12, para 25, as from 1 April 1994.

Sub-s (3): words in square brackets substituted by the Constitutional Reform Act 2005, s 15, Sch 4, Pt 1, paras 185, 190(1), (2), as from 3 April 2006.

Sub-ss (3A), (3B), (5): inserted and added respectively by the Constitutional Reform Act 2005, s 15, Sch 4, Pt 1, paras 185, 190(1), (3), (4), as from 3 April 2006.

Application to limited liability partnerships: see the introductory note to this Act and the Limited Liability Partnerships Regulations 2001, SI 2001/1090, reg 5, Sch 3 at **[6986]**, **[6995]**.

Fees orders

414 Fees orders (company insolvency proceedings)

(1) There shall be paid in respect of—

(a) proceedings under any of Parts I to VII of this Act, and

(b) the performance by the official receiver or the Secretary of State of functions under those Parts,

such fees as the competent authority may with the sanction of the Treasury by order direct.

(2) That authority is—

(a) in relation to England and Wales, the Lord Chancellor, and

(b) in relation to Scotland, the Secretary of State.

(3) The Treasury may by order direct by whom and in what manner the fees are to be collected and accounted for.

(4) The Lord Chancellor may, with the sanction of the Treasury, by order provide for sums to be deposited, by such persons, in such manner and in such circumstances as may be specified in the order, by way of security for fees payable by virtue of this section.

(5) An order under this section may contain such incidental, supplemental and transitional provisions as may appear to the Lord Chancellor, the Secretary of State or (as the case may be) the Treasury necessary or expedient.

(6) An order under this section shall be made by statutory instrument and, after being made, shall be laid before each House of Parliament.

(7) Fees payable by virtue of this section shall be paid into the Consolidated Fund.

(8) References in subsection (1) to Parts I to VII of this Act are to be read as including the Companies Act so far as relating to, and to matters connected with or arising out of, the insolvency or winding up of companies.

(9) Nothing in this section prejudices any power to make rules of court; and the application of this section to Scotland is without prejudice to section 2 of the Courts of Law Fees (Scotland) Act 1985.

[3437]

NOTES

Application to limited liability partnerships: see the introductory note to this Act and the Limited Liability Partnerships Regulations 2001, SI 2001/1090, reg 5, Sch 3 at **[6986]**, **[6995]**.

Orders: the Insolvency Proceedings (Fees) Order 2004, SI 2004/593; the Civil Proceedings Fees Order 2004, SI 2004/3121 (see Appendix 3 (Fees Instruments) at **[A3]**).

[415A Fees orders (general)

(1) The Secretary of State—

(a) may by order require a body to pay a fee in connection with the grant or maintenance of recognition of the body under section 391, and

(b) may refuse recognition, or revoke an order of recognition under section 391(1) by a further order, where a fee is not paid.

(2) The Secretary of State—

(a) may by order require a person to pay a fee in connection with the grant or maintenance of authorisation of the person under section 393, and
(b) may disregard an application or withdraw an authorisation where a fee is not paid.

(3) The Secretary of State may by order require the payment of fees in respect of—
(a) the operation of the Insolvency Services Account;
(b) payments into and out of that Account.

(4) The following provisions of section 414 apply to fees under this section as they apply to fees under that section—
(a) subsection (3) (manner of payment),
(b) subsection (5) (additional provision),
(c) subsection (6) (statutory instrument),
(d) subsection (7) (payment into Consolidated Fund), and
(e) subsection (9) (saving for rules of court).]

[3437A]

NOTES

Inserted by the Enterprise Act 2002, s 270(1), as from 18 December 2003, subject to s 270(2) of that Act which provides that an Order made under this section may relate to the maintenance of recognition or authorisation granted before that date.

Application to limited liability partnerships: see the introductory note to this Act and the Limited Liability Partnerships Regulations 2001, SI 2001/1090, reg 5, Sch 3 at **[6986]**, **[6995]**.

Orders: the Insolvency Practitioners and Insolvency Services Account (Fees) Order 2003, SI 2003/3363 (see Appendix 3 (Fees Instruments) at **[A3]**).

Specification, increase and reduction of money sums relevant in the operation of this Act

416 Monetary limits (companies winding up)

(1) The Secretary of State may by order in a statutory instrument increase or reduce any of the money sums for the time being specified in the following provisions in the first Group of Parts—

section 117(2) (amount of company's share capital determining whether county court has jurisdiction to wind it up);
section 120(3) (the equivalent as respects sheriff court jurisdiction in Scotland);
section 123(1)(a) (minimum debt for service of demand on company by unpaid creditor);
section 184(3) (minimum value of judgment, affecting sheriff's duties on levying execution);
section 206(1)(a) and (b) (minimum value of company property concealed or fraudulently removed, affecting criminal liability of company's officer).

(2) An order under this section may contain such transitional provisions as may appear to the Secretary of State necessary or expedient.

(3) No order under this section increasing or reducing any of the money sums for the time being specified in section 117(2), 120(3) or 123(1)(a) shall be made unless a draft of the order has been laid before and approved by a resolution of each House of Parliament.

(4) A statutory instrument containing an order under this section, other than an order to which subsection (3) applies, is subject to annulment in pursuance of a resolution of either House of Parliament.

[3438]

NOTES

Application to limited liability partnerships: see the introductory note to this Act, the Limited Liability Partnerships Regulations 2001, SI 2001/1090, reg 5, Sch 3 at **[6986]**, **[6995]**, and the Limited Liability Partnerships (Scotland) Regulations 2001, SSI 2001/128, reg 4, Schs 2, 3 at **[6977]**, **[6980A]**, **[6980B]**.

Orders: the Insolvency Proceedings (Monetary Limits) Order 1986, SI 1986/1996 (increasing the sums specified in ss 184(3), 206(1)(a), (b)).

417 Money sum in s 222

The Secretary of State may by regulations in a statutory instrument increase or reduce the money sum for the time being specified in section 222(1) (minimum debt for service of demand on unregistered company by unpaid creditor); but such regulations shall not be made unless a draft of the statutory instrument containing them has been approved by resolution of each House of Parliament.

[3439]

NOTES

Application to limited liability partnerships: see the introductory note to this Act and the Limited Liability Partnerships Regulations 2001, SI 2001/1090, reg 5, Sch 3 at **[6986]**, **[6995]**.

[417A Money sums (company moratorium)

(1) The Secretary of State may by order increase or reduce any of the money sums for the time being specified in the following provisions of Schedule A1 to this Act—

paragraph 17(1) (maximum amount of credit which company may obtain without disclosure of moratorium);

paragraph 41(4) (minimum value of company property concealed or fraudulently removed, affecting criminal liability of company's officer).

(2) An order under this section may contain such transitional provisions as may appear to the Secretary of State necessary or expedient.

(3) An order under this section shall be made by statutory instrument subject to annulment in pursuance of a resolution of either House of Parliament.]

[3440]

NOTES

Inserted by the Insolvency Act 2000, s 1, Sch 1, paras 1, 10, as from 1 January 2003.

Application to limited liability partnerships: see the introductory note to this Act and the Limited Liability Partnerships Regulations 2001, SI 2001/1090, reg 5, Sch 3 at **[6986]**, **[6995]**.

Insolvency practice

419 Regulations for purposes of Part XIII

(1) The Secretary of State may make regulations for the purpose of giving effect to Part XIII of this Act; and "prescribed" in that Part means prescribed by regulations made by the Secretary of State.

(2) Without prejudice to the generality of subsection (1) or to any provision of that Part by virtue of which regulations may be made with respect to any matter, regulations under this section may contain—

(a) provision as to the matters to be taken into account in determining whether a person is a fit and proper person to act as an insolvency practitioner;

(b) provision prohibiting a person from so acting in prescribed cases, being cases in which a conflict of interest will or may arise;

(c) provision imposing requirements with respect to—

(i) the preparation and keeping by a person who acts as an insolvency practitioner of prescribed books, accounts and other records, and

(ii) the production of those books, accounts and records to prescribed persons;

(d) provision conferring power on prescribed persons—

(i) to require any person who acts or has acted as an insolvency practitioner to answer any inquiry in relation to a case in which he is so acting or has so acted, and

(ii) to apply to a court to examine such a person or any other person on oath concerning such a case;

(e) provision making non-compliance with any of the regulations a criminal offence; and

(f) such incidental, supplemental and transitional provisions as may appear to the Secretary of State necessary or expedient.

(3) Any power conferred by Part XIII or this Part to make regulations, rules or orders is exercisable by statutory instrument subject to annulment by resolution of either House of Parliament.

(4) Any rule or regulation under Part XIII or this Part may make different provision with respect to different cases or descriptions of cases, including different provision for different areas.

[3441]

NOTES

Application to limited liability partnerships: see the introductory note to this Act and the Limited Liability Partnerships Regulations 2001, SI 2001/1090, reg 5, Sch 3 at **[6986]**, **[6995]**.

Regulations: the Insolvency Practitioners (Recognised Professional Bodies) Order 1986, SI 1986/1764; the Insolvency Practitioners Regulations 2005, SI 2005/524 at **[7369]**.

Other order making powers

420 Insolvent partnerships

(1) The Lord Chancellor may, by order made with the concurrence of the Secretary of State [and the Lord Chief Justice], provide that such provisions of this Act as may be specified in the order shall apply in relation to insolvent partnerships with such modifications as may be so specified.

[(1A) An order under this section may make provision in relation to the EC Regulation.

(1B) But provision made by virtue of this section in relation to the EC Regulation may not create an offence of a kind referred to in paragraph 1(1)(d) of Schedule 2 to the European Communities Act 1972.]

(2) An order under this section may make different provision for different cases and may contain such incidental, supplemental and transitional provisions as may appear to the Lord Chancellor [and the Lord Chief Justice] necessary or expedient.

(3) An order under this section shall be made by statutory instrument subject to annulment in pursuance of a resolution of either House of Parliament.

[(4) The Lord Chief Justice may nominate a judicial office holder (as defined in section 109(4) of the Constitutional Reform Act 2005) to exercise his functions under this section.]

[3441A]

NOTES

Sub-ss (1), (2): words in square brackets inserted by the Constitutional Reform Act 2005, s 15(1), Sch 4, Pt 1, paras 185, 191(1)–(3), as from 3 April 2006.

Sub-ss (1A), (1B): inserted by the Insolvency Act 1986 (Amendment) Regulations 2002, SI 2002/1037, regs 2, 3(5), as from 3 May 2002.

Sub-s (4): added by the Constitutional Reform Act 2005, s 15(1), Sch 4, Pt 1, paras 185, 191(1), (4), as from 3 April 2006.

Application to limited liability partnerships: see the introductory note to this Act and the Limited Liability Partnerships Regulations 2001, SI 2001/1090, reg 5, Sch 3 at **[6986]**, **[6995]**.

Orders: the Insolvent Partnerships Order 1994, SI 1994/2421.

422 [Formerly authorised banks]

[(1) The Secretary of State may by order made with the concurrence of the Treasury and after consultation with the Financial Services Authority provide that specified provisions in the first Group of Parts shall apply with specified modifications in relation to any person who—

(a) has a liability in respect of a deposit which he accepted in accordance with the Banking Act 1979 (c 37) or 1987 (c 22), but

(b) does not have permission under Part IV of the Financial Services and Markets Act 2000 (c 8) (regulated activities) to accept deposits.

(1A) Subsection (1)(b) shall be construed in accordance with—

(a) section 22 of the Financial Services and Markets Act 2000 (classes of regulated activity and categories of investment),

(b) any relevant order under that section, and

(c) Schedule 2 to that Act (regulated activities).]

[(1A) …]

(2) An order under this section may make different provision for different cases and may contain such incidental, supplemental and transitional provisions as may appear to the Secretary of State necessary or expedient.

(3) An order under this section shall be made by statutory instrument subject to annulment in pursuance of a resolution of either House of Parliament.

[3442]

NOTES

Section heading: substituted by the Financial Services and Markets Act 2000 (Consequential Amendments) Order 2002, SI 2002/1555, art 16(1), (2), as from 3 July 2002.

Sub-ss (1), (1A): substituted, for original sub-s (1), by the Enterprise Act 2002, s 248(3), Sch 17, paras 9, 35, as from 15 September 2003 (for savings and transitional provisions, see the note to s 8 at **[3164]**).

Second sub-s (1A): inserted by SI 2002/1555, art 16(1), (4), as from 3 July 2002; repealed by the Enterprise Act 2002 (Insolvency) Order 2003, SI 2003/2096, arts 4, 6, Schedule, Pt 1, paras 8, 11, as from 15 September 2003, except in relation to any case where a petition for an administration order was presented before that date.

Application to limited liability partnerships: see the introductory note to this Act and the Limited Liability Partnerships Regulations 2001, SI 2001/1090, reg 5, Sch 3 at **[6986]**, **[6995]**.

Banking Act 1987: repealed by SI 2001/3649, art 3(1)(d), as from 1 December 2001.

Orders: the Banks (Former Authorised Institutions) (Insolvency) Order 2006, SI 2006/3107.

PART XVI
PROVISIONS AGAINST DEBT AVOIDANCE
(ENGLAND AND WALES ONLY)

423 Transactions defrauding creditors

(1) This section relates to transactions entered into at an undervalue; and a person enters into such a transaction with another person if—

(a) he makes a gift to the other person or he otherwise enters into a transaction with the other on terms that provide for him to receive no consideration;

(b) he enters into a transaction with the other in consideration of marriage [or the formation of a civil partnership]; or

(c) he enters into a transaction with the other for a consideration the value of which, in money or money's worth, is significantly less than the value, in money or money's worth, of the consideration provided by himself.

(2) Where a person has entered into such a transaction, the court may, if satisfied under the next subsection, make such order as it thinks fit for—

(a) restoring the position to what it would have been if the transaction had not been entered into, and

(b) protecting the interests of persons who are victims of the transaction.

(3) In the case of a person entering into such a transaction, an order shall only be made if the court is satisfied that it was entered into by him for the purpose—

(a) of putting assets beyond the reach of a person who is making, or may at some time make, a claim against him, or

(b) of otherwise prejudicing the interests of such a person in relation to the claim which he is making or may make.

(4) In this section "the court" means the High Court or—

(a) if the person entering into the transaction is an individual, any other court which would have jurisdiction in relation to a bankruptcy petition relating to him;

(b) if that person is a body capable of being wound up under Part IV or V of this Act, any other court having jurisdiction to wind it up.

(5) In relation to a transaction at an undervalue, references here and below to a victim of the transaction are to a person who is, or is capable of being, prejudiced by it; and in the following two sections the person entering into the transaction is referred to as "the debtor".

[3443]

NOTES

Sub-s (1): words in square brackets inserted by the Civil Partnership Act 2004, s 261(1), Sch 27, para 121, as from 5 December 2005.

Application to limited liability partnerships: see the introductory note to this Act and the Limited Liability Partnerships Regulations 2001, SI 2001/1090, reg 5, Sch 3 at **[6986]**, **[6995]**.

424 Those who may apply for an order under s 423

(1) An application for an order under section 423 shall not be made in relation to a transaction except—

(a) in a case where the debtor has been adjudged bankrupt or is a body corporate which is being wound up or [is in administration], by the official receiver, by the trustee of the bankrupt's estate or the liquidator or administrator of the body corporate or (with the leave of the court) by a victim of the transaction;

(b) in a case where a victim of the transaction is bound by a voluntary arrangement approved under Part I or Part VIII of this Act, by the supervisor of the voluntary arrangement or by any person who (whether or not so bound) is such a victim; or

(c) in any other case, by a victim of the transaction.

(2) An application made under any of the paragraphs of subsection (1) is to be treated as made on behalf of every victim of the transaction.

[3444]

NOTES

Sub-s (1): words in square brackets substituted by the Enterprise Act 2002, s 248(3), Sch 17, paras 9, 36, as from 15 September 2003 (for savings and transitional provisions, see the note to s 8 at **[3164]**).

Application to limited liability partnerships: see the introductory note to this Act and the Limited Liability Partnerships Regulations 2001, SI 2001/1090, reg 5, Sch 3 at **[6986]**, **[6995]**.

425 Provision which may be made by order under s 423

(1) Without prejudice to the generality of section 423, an order made under that section with respect to a transaction may (subject as follows)—

(a) require any property transferred as part of the transaction to be vested in any person, either absolutely or for the benefit of all the persons on whose behalf the application for the order is treated as made;

(b) require any property to be so vested if it represents, in any person's hands, the application either of the proceeds of sale of property so transferred or of money so transferred;

(c) release or discharge (in whole or in part) any security given by the debtor;

(d) require any person to pay to any other person in respect of benefits received from the debtor such sums as the court may direct;

(e) provide for any surety or guarantor whose obligations to any person were released or discharged (in whole or in part) under the transaction to be under such new or revived obligations as the court thinks appropriate;

(f) provide for security to be provided for the discharge of any obligation imposed by or arising under the order, for such an obligation to be charged on any property and for such security or charge to have the same priority as a security or charge released or discharged (in whole or in part) under the transaction.

(2) An order under section 423 may affect the property of, or impose any obligation on, any person whether or not he is the person with whom the debtor entered into the transaction; but such an order—

(a) shall not prejudice any interest in property which was acquired from a person other than the debtor and was acquired in good faith, for value and without notice of the relevant circumstances, or prejudice any interest deriving from such an interest, and

(b) shall not require a person who received a benefit from the transaction in good faith, for value and without notice of the relevant circumstances to pay any sum unless he was a party to the transaction.

(3) For the purposes of this section the relevant circumstances in relation to a transaction are the circumstances by virtue of which an order under section 423 may be made in respect of the transaction.

(4) In this section "security" means any mortgage, charge, lien or other security.

[3445]

NOTES

Application to limited liability partnerships: see the introductory note to this Act and the Limited Liability Partnerships Regulations 2001, SI 2001/1090, reg 5, Sch 3 at **[6986]**, **[6995]**.

PART III
OTHER LEGISLATION

PART XVII
MISCELLANEOUS AND GENERAL

426 Co-operation between courts exercising jurisdiction in relation to insolvency

(1) An order made by a court in any part of the United Kingdom in the exercise of jurisdiction in relation to insolvency law shall be enforced in any other part of the United Kingdom as if it were made by a court exercising the corresponding jurisdiction in that other part.

(2) However, without prejudice to the following provisions of this section, nothing in subsection (1) requires a court in any part of the United Kingdom to enforce, in relation to property situated in that part, any order made by a court in any other part of the United Kingdom.

(3) The Secretary of State, with the concurrence in relation to property situated in England and Wales of the Lord Chancellor, may by order make provision for securing that a trustee or assignee under the insolvency law of any part of the United Kingdom has, with such modifications as may be specified in the order, the same rights in relation to any property situated in another part of the United Kingdom as he would have in the corresponding circumstances if he were a trustee or assignee under the insolvency law of that other part.

(4) The courts having jurisdiction in relation to insolvency law in any part of the United Kingdom shall assist the courts having the corresponding jurisdiction in any other part of the United Kingdom or any relevant country or territory.

(5) For the purposes of subsection (4) a request made to a court in any part of the United Kingdom by a court in any other part of the United Kingdom or in a relevant country or territory is authority for the court to which the request is made to apply, in relation to any matters specified in the request, the insolvency law which is applicable by either court in relation to comparable matters falling within its jurisdiction.

In exercising its discretion under this subsection, a court shall have regard in particular to the rules of private international law.

(6) Where a person who is a trustee or assignee under the insolvency law of any part of the United Kingdom claims property situated in any other part of the United Kingdom (whether by virtue of an order under subsection (3) or otherwise), the submission of that claim to the court exercising jurisdiction in relation to insolvency law in that other part shall be treated in the same manner as a request made by a court for the purpose of subsection (4).

(7) Section 38 of the Criminal Law Act 1977 (execution of warrant of arrest throughout the United Kingdom) applies to a warrant which, in exercise of any jurisdiction in relation to insolvency law, is issued in any part of the United Kingdom for the arrest of a person as it applies to a warrant issued in that part of the United Kingdom for the arrest of a person charged with an offence.

(8) Without prejudice to any power to make rules of court, any power to make provision by subordinate legislation for the purpose of giving effect in relation to companies or individuals to the insolvency law of any part of the United Kingdom includes power to make provisions for the purpose of giving effect in that part to any provision made by or under the preceding provisions of this section.

(9) An order under subsection (3) shall be made by statutory instrument subject to annulment in pursuance of a resolution of either House of Parliament.

(10) In this section "insolvency law" means—

(a) in relation to England and Wales, provision [extending to England and Wales and] made by or under this Act or sections [1A,] 6 to 10, [12 to 15], 19(c) and 20 (with Schedule 1) of the Company Directors Disqualification Act 1986 [and sections 1 to 17 of that Act as they apply for the purposes of those provisions of that Act];

(b) in relation to Scotland, provision extending to Scotland and made by or under this Act, sections [1A,] 6 to 10, [12 to 15], 19(c) and 20 (with Schedule 1) of the Company Directors Disqualification Act 1986 [and sections 1 to 17 of that Act as they apply for the purposes of those provisions of that Act], Part XVIII of the Companies Act or the Bankruptcy (Scotland) Act 1985;

(c) in relation to Northern Ireland, provision made by or under [the Insolvency (Northern Ireland) Order 1989] [or the Company Directors Disqualification (Northern Ireland) Order 2002];

(d) in relation to any relevant country or territory, so much of the law of that country or territory as corresponds to provisions falling within any of the foregoing paragraphs;

and references in this subsection to any enactment include, in relation to any time before the coming into force of that enactment the corresponding enactment in force at that time.

(11) In this section "relevant country or territory" means—

(a) any of the Channel Islands or the Isle of Man, or

(b) any country or territory designated for the purposes of this section by the Secretary of State by order made by statutory instrument.

[(12) In the application of this section to Northern Ireland—

(a) for any reference to the Secretary of State there is substituted a reference to the Department of Economic Development in Northern Ireland;

(b) in subsection (3) for the words "another part of the United Kingdom" and the words "that other part" there are substituted the words "Northern Ireland";

(c) for subsection (9) there is substituted the following subsection—

"(9) An order made under subsection (3) by the Department of Economic Development in Northern Ireland shall be a statutory rule for the purposes of the Statutory Rules (Northern Ireland) Order 1979 and shall be subject to negative resolution within the meaning of section 41(6) of the Interpretation Act (Northern Ireland) 1954.".]

[3446]

NOTES

Sub-s (10): words in square brackets in paras (a), (b) inserted or substituted by the Insolvency Act 2000, s 8, Sch 4, Pt II, para 16(1), (3), as from 2 April 2001; words in first pair of square brackets in para (c) substituted by the Insolvency (Northern Ireland) Order 1989, SI 1989/2405, art 381(2), Sch 9, Pt II, para 41(a); words in second pair of square brackets in para (c) added by the Companies (Northern Ireland) Order 1989, SI 1989/2404, arts 25(2), 36, Sch 4, Pt I, para 1, and substituted by the Company Directors Disqualification (Northern Ireland) Order 2002, SI 2002/3150, art 26(2), Sch 3, para 2.

Sub-s (12): added by SI 1989/2405, art 381(2), Sch 9, Pt II, para 41(b), but not yet in operation so far as amends sub-s (11)(b) to give the Department of Economic Development in Northern Ireland power to make an order designating relevant countries for the purposes of this section as it applies to Northern Ireland.

Application to limited liability partnerships: see the introductory note to this Act and the Limited Liability Partnerships Regulations 2001, SI 2001/1090, reg 5, Sch 3 at **[6986]**, **[6995]**.

Criminal Law Act 1977, s 38: repealed by the Criminal Justice and Public Order Act 1994, s 168(3), Sch 11.

Orders: the Co-operation of Insolvency Courts (Designation of Relevant Countries and Territories) Order 1986, SI 1986/2123 designating the following countries and territories for the purposes of this section: Anguilla; Australia; the Bahamas; Bermuda; Botswana; Canada; Cayman Islands; Falkland Islands; Gibraltar; Hong Kong; Republic of Ireland; Montserrat; New Zealand; St Helena; Turks and Caicos Islands; Tuvalu; Virgin Islands; the Co-operation of Insolvency Courts (Designation of Relevant Countries) Order 1996, SI 1996/253 designating Malaysia and the Republic of South Africa as relevant countries for the purposes of this section; the Co-operation of Insolvency Courts (Designation of Relevant Country) Order 1998, SI 1998/2766 designating Brunei Darussalam as a relevant country for the purposes of this section.

[426A Disqualification from Parliament (England and Wales)

(1) A person in respect of whom a bankruptcy restrictions order has effect shall be disqualified—

(a) from membership of the House of Commons,

(b) from sitting or voting in the House of Lords, and

(c) from sitting or voting in a committee of the House of Lords or a joint committee of both Houses.

(2) If a member of the House of Commons becomes disqualified under this section, his seat shall be vacated.

(3) If a person who is disqualified under this section is returned as a member of the House of Commons, his return shall be void.

(4) No writ of summons shall be issued to a member of the House of Lords who is disqualified under this section.

(5) If a court makes a bankruptcy restrictions order or interim order in respect of a member of the House of Commons or the House of Lords the court shall notify the Speaker of that House.

(6) If the Secretary of State accepts a bankruptcy restrictions undertaking made by a member of the House of Commons or the House of Lords, the Secretary of State shall notify the Speaker of that House.]

[3446A]

NOTES

Inserted, together with ss 426B, 426C, by the Enterprise Act 2002, s 266(1), as from 1 April 2004.

Application to limited liability partnerships: see the introductory note to this Act and the Limited Liability Partnerships Regulations 2001, SI 2001/1090, reg 5, Sch 3 at **[6986]**, **[6995]**.

[426B Devolution

(1) If a court makes a bankruptcy restrictions order or interim order in respect of a member of the Scottish Parliament, the Northern Ireland Assembly or the National Assembly for Wales, the court shall notify the presiding officer of that body.

(2) If the Secretary of State accepts a bankruptcy restrictions undertaking made by a member of the Scottish Parliament, the Northern Ireland Assembly or the National Assembly for Wales, the Secretary of State shall notify the presiding officer of that body.]

[3446B]

NOTES

Inserted as noted to s 426A at **[3446A]**.

Application to limited liability partnerships: see the introductory note to this Act and the Limited Liability Partnerships Regulations 2001, SI 2001/1090, reg 5, Sch 3 at **[6986]**, **[6995]**.

[426C Irrelevance of privilege

(1) An enactment about insolvency applies in relation to a member of the House of Commons or the House of Lords irrespective of any Parliamentary privilege.

(2) In this section "enactment" includes a provision made by or under—

(a) an Act of the Scottish Parliament, or

(b) Northern Ireland legislation.]

[3446C]

NOTES

Inserted as noted to s 426A at **[3446A]**.

Application to limited liability partnerships: see the introductory note to this Act and the Limited Liability Partnerships Regulations 2001, SI 2001/1090, reg 5, Sch 3 at **[6986]**, **[6995]**.

427 [Disqualification from Parliament (Scotland and Northern Ireland)]

(1) Where a court in … Northern Ireland adjudges an individual bankrupt or a court in Scotland awards sequestration of an individual's estate, the individual is disqualified—

(a) for sitting or voting in the House of Lords,

(b) for being elected to, or sitting or voting in, the House of Commons, and

(c) for sitting or voting in a committee of either House.

(2) Where an individual is disqualified under this section, the disqualification ceases—

(a) except where the adjudication is annulled or the award recalled or reduced without the individual having been first discharged, on the discharge of the individual, and

(b) in the excepted case, on the annulment, recall or reduction, as the case may be.

(3) No writ of summons shall be issued to any lord of Parliament who is for the time being disqualified under this section for sitting and voting in the House of Lords.

(4) Where a member of the House of Commons who is disqualified under this section continues to be so disqualified until the end of the period of 6 months beginning with the day of the adjudication or award, his seat shall be vacated at the end of that period.

(5) A court which makes an adjudication or award such as is mentioned in subsection (1) in relation to any lord of Parliament or member of the House of Commons shall forthwith certify the adjudication or award to the Speaker of the House of Lords or, as the case may be, to the Speaker of the House of Commons.

(6) Where a court has certified an adjudication or award to the Speaker of the House of Commons under subsection (5), then immediately after it becomes apparent which of the following certificates is applicable, the court shall certify to the Speaker of the House of Commons—

(a) that the period of 6 months beginning with the day of the adjudication or award has expired without the adjudication or award having been annulled, recalled or reduced, or

(b) that the adjudication or award has been annulled, recalled or reduced before the end of that period.

[(6A) Subsections (4) to (6) have effect in relation to a member of the Scottish Parliament but as if—

(a) references to the House of Commons were to the Parliament and references to the Speaker were to the Presiding Officer, and

(b) in subsection (4), for "under this section" there were substituted "under section 15(1)(b) of the Scotland Act 1998 by virtue of this section".]

[(6B) Subsections (4) to (6) have effect in relation to a member of the National Assembly for Wales but as if—

(a) references to the House of Commons were to the Assembly and references to the Speaker were to the presiding officer, and

(b) in subsection (4), for "under this section" there were substituted "under [section 16(2) of the Government of Wales Act 2006] by virtue of this section".]

[(6C) Subsection (1), as applied to a member of the Northern Ireland Assembly by virtue of section 36(4) of the Northern Ireland Act 1998, has effect as if "or Northern Ireland" were omitted; and subsections (4) to (6) have effect in relation to such a member as if—

(a) references to the House of Commons were to the Assembly and references to the Speaker were to the Presiding Officer; and

(b) in subsection (4), for "under this section" there were substituted "under section 36(4) of the Northern Ireland Act 1998 by virtue of this section".]

(7) …

[3447]

NOTES

Section heading: substituted by the Enterprise Act 2002, s 266(1), as from 1 April 2004.

Sub-s (1): words omitted repealed by the Enterprise Act 2002, ss 266(2)(a), 278(2), Sch 26, as from 1 April 2004.

Sub-s (6A): inserted by the Scotland Act 1998, s 125(1), Sch 8, para 23(1), (6), as from 19 November 1998.

Sub-s (6B): inserted by the Government of Wales Act 1998, s 125, Sch 12, para 24, as from 1 April 1999; words in square brackets substituted by the Government of Wales Act 2006, s 160(1), Sch 10, para 18, as from 25 May 2007.

Sub-s (6C): inserted by the Northern Ireland Act 1998, s 99, Sch 13, para 6, as from 2 December 1999.

Sub-s (7): repealed by the Enterprise Act 2002, ss 266(2)(b), 278(2), Sch 26, as from 1 April 2004.

Application to limited liability partnerships: see the introductory note to this Act and the Limited Liability Partnerships Regulations 2001, SI 2001/1090, reg 5, Sch 3 at **[6986]**, **[6995]**.

430 Provision introducing Schedule of punishments

(1) Schedule 10 to this Act has effect with respect to the way in which offences under this Act are punishable on conviction.

(2) In relation to an offence under a provision of this Act specified in the first column of the Schedule (the general nature of the offence being described in the second column), the third column shows whether the offence is punishable on conviction on indictment, or on summary conviction, or either in the one way or the other.

(3) The fourth column of the Schedule shows, in relation to an offence, the maximum punishment by way of fine or imprisonment under this Act which may be imposed on a person convicted of the offence in the way specified in relation to it in the third column (that is to say, on indictment or summarily), a reference to a period of years or months being to a term of imprisonment of that duration.

(4) The fifth column shows (in relation to an offence for which there is an entry in that column) that a person convicted of the offence after continued contravention is liable to a daily default fine; that is to say, he is liable on a second or subsequent conviction of the

offence to the fine specified in that column for each day on which the contravention is continued (instead of the penalty specified for the offence in the fourth column of the Schedule).

(5) For the purpose of any enactment in this Act whereby an officer of a company who is in default is liable to a fine or penalty, the expression "officer who is in default" means any officer of the company who knowingly and wilfully authorises or permits the default, refusal or contravention mentioned in the enactment.

[3448]

NOTES

Application to limited liability partnerships: see the introductory note to this Act, the Limited Liability Partnerships Regulations 2001, SI 2001/1090, reg 5, Sch 3 at **[6986]**, **[6995]**, and the Limited Liability Partnerships (Scotland) Regulations 2001, SSI 2001/128, reg 4, Schs 2, 3 at **[6977]**, **[6980A]**, **[6980B]**.

431 Summary proceedings

(1) Summary proceedings for any offence under any of Parts I to VII of this Act may (without prejudice to any jurisdiction exercisable apart from this subsection) be taken against a body corporate at any place at which the body has a place of business, and against any other person at any place at which he is for the time being.

(2) Notwithstanding anything in section 127(1) of the Magistrates' Courts Act 1980, an information relating to such an offence which is triable by a magistrates' court in England and Wales may be so tried if it is laid at any time within 3 years after the commission of the offence and within 12 months after the date on which evidence sufficient in the opinion of the Director of Public Prosecutions or the Secretary of State (as the case may be) to justify the proceedings comes to his knowledge.

(3) Summary proceedings in Scotland for such an offence shall not be commenced after the expiration of 3 years from the commission of the offence.

Subject to this (and notwithstanding anything in [section 136 of the Criminal Procedure (Scotland) Act 1995]), such proceedings may (in Scotland) be commenced at any time within 12 months after the date on which evidence sufficient in the Lord Advocate's opinion to justify the proceedings came to his knowledge or, where such evidence was reported to him by the Secretary of State, within 12 months after the date on which it came to the knowledge of the latter; and subsection (3) of that section applies for the purpose of this subsection as it applies for the purpose of that section.

(4) For purposes of this section, a certificate of the Director of Public Prosecutions, the Lord Advocate or the Secretary of State (as the case may be) as to the date on which such evidence as is referred to above came to his knowledge is conclusive evidence.

[3449]

NOTES

Sub-s (3): words in square brackets substituted by the Criminal Procedure (Consequential Provisions) (Scotland) Act 1995, s 5, Sch 4, para 61, as from 1 April 1996.

Application to limited liability partnerships: see the introductory note to this Act and the Limited Liability Partnerships Regulations 2001, SI 2001/1090, reg 5, Sch 3 at **[6986]**, **[6995]**.

432 Offences by bodies corporate

(1) This section applies to offences under this Act other than those excepted by subsection (4).

(2) Where a body corporate is guilty of an offence to which this section applies and the offence is proved to have been committed with the consent or connivance of, or to be attributable to any neglect on the part of, any director, manager, secretary or other similar officer of the body corporate or any person who was purporting to act in any such capacity he, as well as the body corporate, is guilty of the offence and liable to be proceeded against and punished accordingly.

(3) Where the affairs of a body corporate are managed by its members, subsection (2) applies in relation to the acts and defaults of a member in connection with his functions of management as if he were a director of the body corporate.

(4) The offences excepted from this section are those under sections 30, 39, 51, 53, 54, 62, 64, 66, 85, 89, 164, 188, 201, 206, 207, 208, 209, 210 and 211 [and those under paragraphs 16(2), 17(3)(a), 18(3)(a), 19(3)(a), 22(1) and 23(1)(a) of Schedule A1].

[3450]

NOTES

Sub-s (4): words in square brackets added by the Insolvency Act 2000, s 1, Sch 1, paras 1, 11, as from 1 January 2003.

Application to limited liability partnerships: see the introductory note to this Act and the Limited Liability Partnerships Regulations 2001, SI 2001/1090, reg 5, Sch 3 at **[6986]**, **[6995]**.

433 Admissibility in evidence of statements of affairs, etc

[(1)] In any proceedings (whether or not under this Act)—

(a) a statement of affairs prepared for the purposes of any provision of this Act which is derived from the Insolvency Act 1985, and

(b) any other statement made in pursuance of a requirement imposed by or under any such provision or by or under rules made under this Act,

may be used in evidence against any person making or concurring in making the statement.

[(2) However, in criminal proceedings in which any such person is charged with an offence to which this subsection applies—

(a) no evidence relating to the statement may be adduced, and

(b) no question relating to it may be asked,

by or on behalf of the prosecution, unless evidence relating to it is adduced, or a question relating to it is asked, in the proceedings by or on behalf of that person.

(3) Subsection (2) applies to any offence other than—

(a) an offence under section 22(6), 47(6), 48(8), 66(6), 67(8), 95(8), 98(6), 99(3)(a), 131(7), 192(2), 208(1)(a) or (d) or (2), 210, 235(5), 353(1), 354(1)(b) or (3) or 356(1) or (2)(a) or (b) or paragraph 4(3)(a) of Schedule 7;

(b) an offence which is—

   (i) created by rules made under this Act, and

   (ii) designated for the purposes of this subsection by such rules or by regulations made by the Secretary of State;

(c) an offence which is—

   (i) created by regulations made under any such rules, and

   (ii) designated for the purposes of this subsection by such regulations;

(d) an offence under section 1, 2 or 5 of the Perjury Act 1911 (false statements made on oath or made otherwise than on oath); or

(e) an offence under section 44(1) or (2) of the Criminal Law (Consolidation) (Scotland) Act 1995 (false statements made on oath or otherwise than on oath).

(4) Regulations under subsection (3)(b)(ii) shall be made by statutory instrument and, after being made, shall be laid before each House of Parliament.]

[3451]

NOTES

Sub-s (1) numbered as such and sub-ss (2)–(4) added by the Youth Justice and Criminal Evidence Act 1999, s 59, Sch 3, para 7, as from 14 April 2000 (in relation to England and Wales), and 1 January 2001 (in relation to Scotland).

Application to limited liability partnerships: see the introductory note to this Act and the Limited Liability Partnerships Regulations 2001, SI 2001/1090, reg 5, Sch 3 at **[6986]**, **[6995]**.

434 Crown application

For the avoidance of doubt it is hereby declared that provisions of this Act which derive from the Insolvency Act 1985 bind the Crown so far as affecting or relating to the following matters, namely—

(a) remedies against, or against the property of, companies or individuals;

(b) priorities of debts;

(c) transactions at an undervalue or preferences;

(d) voluntary arrangements approved under Part I or Part VIII, and

(e) discharge from bankruptcy.

[3452]

PART III OTHER LEGISLATION

NOTES

Application to limited liability partnerships: see the introductory note to this Act and the Limited Liability Partnerships Regulations 2001, SI 2001/1090, reg 5, Sch 3 at **[6986]**, **[6995]**.

PART XVIII
INTERPRETATION

435 Meaning of "associate"

(1) For the purposes of this Act any question whether a person is an associate of another person is to be determined in accordance with the following provisions of this section (any provision that a person is an associate of another person being taken to mean that they are associates of each other).

[(2) A person is an associate of an individual if that person is—
(a) the individual's husband or wife or civil partner,
(b) a relative of—
(i) the individual, or
(ii) the individual's husband or wife or civil partner, or
(c) the husband or wife or civil partner of a relative of—
(i) the individual, or
(ii) the individual's husband or wife or civil partner.]

(3) A person is an associate of any person with whom he is in partnership, and of the husband or wife [or civil partner] or a relative of any individual with whom he is in partnership; and a Scottish firm is an associate of any person who is a member of the firm.

(4) A person is an associate of any person whom he employs or by whom he is employed.

(5) A person in his capacity as trustee of a trust other than—
(a) a trust arising under any of the second Group of Parts or the Bankruptcy (Scotland) Act 1985, or
(b) a pension scheme or an employees' share scheme (within the meaning of the Companies Act),

is an associate of another person if the beneficiaries of the trust include, or the terms of the trust confer a power that may be exercised for the benefit of, that other person or an associate of that other person.

(6) A company is an associate of another company—
(a) if the same person has control of both, or a person has control of one and persons who are his associates, or he and persons who are his associates, have control of the other, or
(b) if a group of two or more persons has control of each company, and the groups either consist of the same persons or could be regarded as consisting of the same persons by treating (in one or more cases) a member of either group as replaced by a person of whom he is an associate.

(7) A company is an associate of another person if that person has control of it or if that person and persons who are his associates together have control of it.

(8) For the purposes of this section a person is a relative of an individual if he is that individual's brother, sister, uncle, aunt, nephew, niece, lineal ancestor or lineal descendant, treating—
(a) any relationship of the half blood as a relationship of the whole blood and the stepchild or adopted child of any person as his child, and
(b) an illegitimate child as the legitimate child of his mother and reputed father;

and references in this section to a husband or wife include a former husband or wife and a reputed husband or wife [and references to a civil partner include a former civil partner] [and a reputed civil partner].

(9) For the purposes of this section any director or other officer of a company is to be treated as employed by that company.

(10) For the purposes of this section a person is to be taken as having control of a company if—

(a) the directors of the company or of another company which has control of it (or any of them) are accustomed to act in accordance with his directions or instructions, or

(b) he is entitled to exercise, or control the exercise of, one third or more of the voting power at any general meeting of the company or of another company which has control of it;

and where two or more persons together satisfy either of the above conditions, they are to be taken as having control of the company.

(11) In this section "company" includes any body corporate (whether incorporated in Great Britain or elsewhere); and references to directors and other officers of a company and to voting power at any general meeting of a company have effect with any necessary modifications.

[3453]

NOTES

Sub-s (2): substituted by the Civil Partnership Act 2004, s 261(1), Sch 27, para 122(1), (2), as from 5 December 2005.

Sub-s (3): words in square brackets inserted by the Civil Partnership Act 2004, s 261(1), Sch 27, para 122(1), (3), as from 5 December 2005.

Sub-s (8): words in first pair of square brackets inserted by the Civil Partnership Act 2004, s 261(1), Sch 27, para 122(1), (4), as from 5 December 2005; words in second pair of square brackets inserted by the Civil Partnership Act 2004 (Overseas Relationships and Consequential, etc Amendments) Order 2005, SI 2005/3129, art 4(4), Sch 4, para 8, as from 5 December 2005.

Application to limited liability partnerships: see the introductory note to this Act and the Limited Liability Partnerships Regulations 2001, SI 2001/1090, reg 5, Sch 3 at **[6986]**, **[6995]**.

Stepchild: this includes relationships arising through civil partnerships; see the Civil Partnership Act 2004, ss 246, 247, Sch 21.

436 Expressions used generally

In this Act, except in so far as the context otherwise requires (and subject to Parts VII and XI)—

"the appointed day" means the day on which this Act comes into force under section 443;

"associate" has the meaning given by section 435;

"business" includes a trade or profession;

"the Companies Act" means the Companies Act 1985;

"conditional sale agreement" and "hire-purchase agreement" have the same meanings as in the Consumer Credit Act 1974;

["the EC Regulation" means Council Regulation (EC) No 1346/2000;]

["EEA State" means a state that is a Contracting Party to the Agreement on the European Economic Area signed at Oporto on 2nd May 1992 as adjusted by the Protocol signed at Brussels on 17th March 1993;]

"modifications" includes additions, alterations and omissions and cognate expressions shall be construed accordingly;

"property" includes money, goods, things in action, land and every description of property wherever situated and also obligations and every description of interest, whether present or future or vested or contingent, arising out of, or incidental to, property;

"records" includes computer records and other non-documentary records;

"subordinate legislation" has the same meaning as in the Interpretation Act 1978; and

"transaction" includes a gift, agreement or arrangement, and references to entering into a transaction shall be construed accordingly.

[3454]

NOTES

Definition "the EC Regulation" inserted by the Insolvency Act 1986 (Amendment) Regulations 2002, SI 2002/1037, regs 2, 4, as from 3 May 2002.

Definition "EEA State" inserted by the Insolvency Act 1986 (Amendment) Regulations 2005, SI 2005/879, reg 2(1), (3), as from 13 April 2005, except in relation to any voluntary arrangement under Part I, or the appointment of an administrator under Part II, that took effect before that date.

Application to limited liability partnerships: see the introductory note to this Act, the Limited Liability Partnerships Regulations 2001, SI 2001/1090, reg 5, Sch 3 at **[6986]**, **[6995]**, and the Limited Liability Partnerships (Scotland) Regulations 2001, SSI 2001/128, reg 4, Schs 2, 3 at **[6977]**, **[6980A]**, **[6980B]**.

[436A Proceedings under EC Regulation: modified definition of property

In the application of this Act to proceedings by virtue of Article 3 of the EC Regulation, a reference to property is a reference to property which may be dealt with in the proceedings.]

[3455]

NOTES

Inserted by the Insolvency Act 1986 (Amendment) (No 2) Regulations 2002, SI 2002/1240, regs 3, 18, as from 31 May 2002.

Application to limited liability partnerships: see the introductory note to this Act and the Limited Liability Partnerships Regulations 2001, SI 2001/1090, reg 5, Sch 3 at **[6986]**, **[6995]**.

PART XIX
FINAL PROVISIONS

NOTES

Application of this Part to limited liability partnerships: see the introductory note to this Act and the Limited Liability Partnerships Regulations 2001, SI 2001/1090, reg 5, Sch 3 at **[6986]**, **[6995]**.

437 Transitional provisions, and savings

The transitional provisions and savings set out in Schedule 11 to this Act shall have effect, the Schedule comprising the following Parts—

Part I: company insolvency and winding up (matters arising before appointed day, and continuance of proceedings in certain cases as before that day);

Part II: individual insolvency (matters so arising, and continuance of bankruptcy proceedings in certain cases as before that day);

Part III: transactions entered into before the appointed day and capable of being affected by orders of the court under Part XVI of this Act;

Part IV: insolvency practitioners acting as such before the appointed day; and

Part V: general transitional provisions and savings required consequentially on, and in connection with, the repeal and replacement by this Act and the Company Directors Disqualification Act 1986 of provisions of the Companies Act, the greater part of the Insolvency Act 1985 and other enactments.

[3456]

438 Repeals

The enactments specified in the second column of Schedule 12 to this Act are repealed to the extent specified in the third column of that Schedule.

[3457]

439 Amendment of enactments

(1) The Companies Act is amended as shown in Parts I and II of Schedule 13 to this Act, being amendments consequential on this Act and the Company Directors Disqualification Act 1986.

(2) The enactments specified in the first column of Schedule 14 to this Act (being enactments which refer, or otherwise relate, to those which are repealed and replaced by this Act or the Company Directors Disqualification Act 1986) are amended as shown in the second column of that Schedule.

(3) The Lord Chancellor may by order make such consequential modifications of any provision contained in any subordinate legislation made before the appointed day and such transitional provisions in connection with those modifications as appear to him necessary or expedient in respect of—

(a) any reference in that subordinate legislation to the Bankruptcy Act 1914;

(b) any reference in that subordinate legislation to any enactment repealed by Part III or IV of Schedule 10 to the Insolvency Act 1985; or

(c) any reference in that subordinate legislation to any matter provided for under the Act of 1914 or under any enactment so repealed.

(4) An order under this section shall be made by statutory instrument subject to annulment in pursuance of a resolution of either House of Parliament.

[3458]

NOTES

Orders: the Insolvency (Amendment of Subordinate Legislation) Order 1986, SI 1986/2001; the Insolvency (Land Registration Rules) Order 1986, SI 1986/2245; the Insolvency (Amendment of Subordinate Legislation) Order 1987, SI 1987/1398.

440 Extent (Scotland)

(1) Subject to the next subsection, provisions of this Act contained in the first Group of Parts extend to Scotland except where otherwise stated.

(2) The following provisions of this Act do not extend to Scotland—

(a) In the first Group of Parts—
section 43;
sections 238 to 241; and
section 246;

(b) the second Group of Parts;

(c) in the third Group of Parts—
sections 399 to 402,
sections 412, 413, 415, [415A(3),] 418, 420 and 421,
sections 423 to 425, and
section 429(1) and (2); and

(d) in the Schedules—
Parts II and III of Schedule 11; and
Schedules 12 and 14 so far as they repeal or amend enactments which extend to England and Wales only.

[3459]

NOTES

Sub-s (2): figure in square brackets inserted by the Enterprise Act 2002, s 270(4), as from 18 December 2003.

441 Extent (Northern Ireland)

(1) The following provisions of this Act extend to Northern Ireland—

(a) sections 197, 426, 427 and 428; and

(b) so much of section 439 and Schedule 14 as relates to enactments which extend to Northern Ireland.

(2) Subject as above, and to any provision expressly relating to companies incorporated elsewhere than in Great Britain, nothing in this Act extends to Northern Ireland or applies to or in relation to companies registered or incorporated in Northern Ireland.

[3460]

442 Extent (other territories)

Her Majesty may, by Order in Council, direct that such of the provisions of this Act as are specified in the Order, being provisions formerly contained in the Insolvency Act 1985, shall extend to any of the Channel Islands or any colony with such modifications as may be so specified.

[3461]

NOTES

Orders: the Insolvency Act 1986 (Guernsey) Order 1989, SI 1989/2409.

443 Commencement

This Act comes into force on the day appointed under section 236(2) of the Insolvency Act 1985 for the coming into force of Part III of that Act (individual insolvency and bankruptcy), immediately after that Part of that Act comes into force for England and Wales.

[3462]

NOTES

See the note "Commencement" at the beginning of this Act.

444 Citation

This Act may be cited as the Insolvency Act 1986.

[3463]

SCHEDULES

[SCHEDULE A1
MORATORIUM WHERE DIRECTORS PROPOSE VOLUNTARY ARRANGEMENT

Section 1A

PART I
INTRODUCTORY

Interpretation

1. In this Schedule—

"the beginning of the moratorium" has the meaning given by paragraph 8(1),

"the date of filing" means the date on which the documents for the time being referred to in paragraph 7(1) are filed or lodged with the court,

"hire-purchase agreement" includes a conditional sale agreement, a chattel leasing agreement and a retention of title agreement,

"market contract" and "market charge" have the meanings given by Part VII of the Companies Act 1989,

.....

"moratorium" means a moratorium under section 1A,

"the nominee" includes any person for the time being carrying out the functions of a nominee under this Schedule,

.....

"the settlement finality regulations" means the Financial Markets and Insolvency (Settlement Finality) Regulations 1999,

"system-charge" has the meaning given by the Financial Markets and Insolvency Regulations 1996.

Eligible companies

2.—(1) A company is eligible for a moratorium if it meets the requirements of paragraph 3, unless—

(a) it is excluded from being eligible by virtue of paragraph 4, or
(b) it falls within sub-paragraph (2).

(2) A company falls within this sub-paragraph if—

[(a) it effects or carries out contracts of insurance, but is not exempt from the general prohibition, within the meaning of section 19 of the Financial Services and Markets Act 2000, in relation to that activity,
(b) it has permission under Part IV of that Act to accept deposits,
(bb) it has a liability in respect of a deposit which it accepted in accordance with the Banking Act 1979 (c 37) or 1987 (c 22),]
(c) it is a party to a market contract … or any of its property is subject to a market charge … or a system-charge, or
(d) it is a participant (within the meaning of the settlement finality regulations) or any of its property is subject to a collateral security charge (within the meaning of those regulations).

[(3) Paragraphs (a), (b) and (bb) of sub-paragraph (2) must be read with—

(a) section 22 of the Financial Services and Markets Act 2000;
(b) any relevant order under that section; and
(c) Schedule 2 to that Act.]

3.—(1) A company meets the requirements of this paragraph if the qualifying conditions are met—

(a) in the year ending with the date of filing, or
(b) in the financial year of the company which ended last before that date.

(2) For the purposes of sub-paragraph (1)—

(a) the qualifying conditions are met by a company in a period if, in that period, it satisfies two or more of the requirements for being a small company specified for the time being in section 247(3) of the Companies Act 1985, and

(b) a company's financial year is to be determined in accordance with that Act.

(3) Subsections (4), (5) and (6) of section 247 of that Act apply for the purposes of this paragraph as they apply for the purposes of that section.

[(4) A company does not meet the requirements of this paragraph if it is a holding company of a group of companies which does not qualify as a small group or a medium-sized group in respect of the financial year of the company which ended last before the date of filing.

(5) For the purposes of sub-paragraph (4) "group" has the meaning given by section 262 of the Companies Act 1985 (c 6) (definitions for Part VII) and a group qualifies as small or medium-sized if it qualifies as such under section 249 of the Companies Act 1985 (qualification of group as small or medium-sized).]

4.—(1) A company is excluded from being eligible for a moratorium if, on the date of filing—

[(a) the company is in administration,]

(b) the company is being wound up,

(c) there is an administrative receiver of the company,

(d) a voluntary arrangement has effect in relation to the company,

(e) there is a provisional liquidator of the company,

(f) a moratorium has been in force for the company at any time during the period of 12 months ending with the date of filing and—

(i) no voluntary arrangement had effect at the time at which the moratorium came to an end, or

(ii) a voluntary arrangement which had effect at any time in that period has come to an end prematurely,

[(fa) an administrator appointed under paragraph 22 of Schedule B1 has held office in the period of 12 months ending with the date of filing,] or

(g) a voluntary arrangement in relation to the company which had effect in pursuance of a proposal under section 1(3) has come to an end prematurely and, during the period of 12 months ending with the date of filing, an order under section 5(3)(a) has been made.

(2) Sub-paragraph (1)(b) does not apply to a company which, by reason of a winding-up order made after the date of filing, is treated as being wound up on that date.

[Capital market arrangement

4A. A company is also excluded from being eligible for a moratorium if, on the date of filing, it is a party to an agreement which is or forms part of a capital market arrangement under which—

(i) a party has incurred, or when the agreement was entered into was expected to incur, a debt of at least £10 million under the arrangement, and

(ii) the arrangement involves the issue of a capital market investment.

Public private partnership

4B. A company is also excluded from being eligible for a moratorium if, on the date of filing, it is a project company of a project which—

(i) is a public-private partnership project, and

(ii) includes step-in rights.

Liability under an arrangement

4C.—(1) A company is also excluded from being eligible for a moratorium if, on the date of filing, it has incurred a liability under an agreement of £10 million or more.

(2) Where the liability in sub-paragraph (1) is a contingent liability under or by virtue of a guarantee or an indemnity or security provided on behalf of another person, the amount of that liability is the full amount of the liability in relation to which the guarantee, indemnity or security is provided.

(3) In this paragraph—

(a) the reference to "liability" includes a present or future liability whether, in either case, it is certain or contingent,

(b) the reference to "liability" includes a reference to a liability to be paid wholly or partly in foreign currency (in which case the sterling equivalent shall be calculated as at the time when the liability is incurred).

Interpretation of capital market arrangement

4D.—(1) For the purposes of paragraph 4A an arrangement is a capital market arrangement if—

(a) it involves a grant of security to a person holding it as trustee for a person who holds a capital market investment issued by a party to the arrangement, or

(b) at least one party guarantees the performance of obligations of another party, or

(c) at least one party provides security in respect of the performance of obligations of another party, or

(d) the arrangement involves an investment of a kind described in articles 83 to 85 of the Financial Services and Markets Act 2000 (Regulated Activities) Order 2001 (SI 2001/544) (options, futures and contracts for differences).

(2) For the purposes of sub-paragraph (1)—

(a) a reference to holding as trustee includes a reference to holding as nominee or agent,

(b) a reference to holding for a person who holds a capital market investment includes a reference to holding for a number of persons at least one of whom holds a capital market investment, and

(c) a person holds a capital market investment if he has a legal or beneficial interest in it.

(3) In paragraph 4A, 4C, 4J and this paragraph—

"agreement" includes an agreement or undertaking effected by—

(a) contract,

(b) deed, or

(c) any other instrument intended to have effect in accordance with the law of England and Wales, Scotland or another jurisdiction, and

"party" to an arrangement includes a party to an agreement which—

(a) forms part of the arrangement,

(b) provides for the raising of finance as part of the arrangement, or

(c) is necessary for the purposes of implementing the arrangement.

Capital market investment

4E.—(1) For the purposes of paragraphs 4A and 4D, an investment is a capital market investment if—

(a) it is within article 77 of the Financial Services and Markets Act 2000 (Regulated Activities) Order 2001 (SI 2001/544) (debt instruments) and

(b) it is rated, listed or traded or designed to be rated, listed or traded.

(2) In sub-paragraph (1)—

"listed" means admitted to the official list within the meaning given by section 103(1) of the Financial Services and Markets Act 2000 (c 8) (interpretation),

"rated" means rated for the purposes of investment by an internationally recognised rating agency,

"traded" means admitted to trading on a market established under the rules of a recognised investment exchange or on a foreign market.

(3) In sub-paragraph (2)—

"foreign market" has the same meaning as "relevant market" in article 67(2) of the Financial Services and Markets Act 2000 (Financial Promotion) Order 2001 (SI 2001/1335) (foreign markets), "recognised investment exchange" has the meaning given by section 285 of the Financial Services and Markets Act 2000 (recognised investment exchange).

4F.—(1) For the purposes of paragraphs 4A and 4D an investment is also a capital market investment if it consists of a bond or commercial paper issued to one or more of the following—

(a) an investment professional within the meaning of article 19(5) of the Financial Services and Markets Act 2000 (Financial Promotion) Order 2001,

(b) a person who is, when the agreement mentioned in paragraph 4A is entered into, a certified high net worth individual in relation to a communication within the meaning of article 48(2) of that order,

(c) a person to whom article 49(2) of that order applies (high net worth company, &c.),

(d) a person who is, when the agreement mentioned in paragraph 4A is entered into, a certified sophisticated investor in relation to a communication within the meaning of article 50(1) of that order, and

(e) a person in a State other than the United Kingdom who under the law of that State is not prohibited from investing in bonds or commercial paper.

(2) For the purposes of sub-paragraph (1)—

(a) in applying article 19(5) of the Financial Services and Markets Act 2000 (Financial Promotion) Order 2001 for the purposes of sub-paragraph (1)(a)—

(i) in article 19(5)(b), ignore the words after "exempt person",

(ii) in article 19(5)(c)(i), for the words from "the controlled activity" to the end substitute "a controlled activity", and

(iii) in article 19(5)(e) ignore the words from "where the communication" to the end, and

(b) in applying article 49(2) of that order for the purposes of sub-paragraph (1)(c), ignore article 49(2)(e).

(3) In sub-paragraph (1)—

"bond" shall be construed in accordance with article 77 of the Financial Services and Markets Act 2000 (Regulated Activities) Order 2001 (SI 2001/544), and

"commercial paper" has the meaning given by article 9(3) of that order.

Debt

4G. The debt of at least £10 million referred to in paragraph 4A—

(a) may be incurred at any time during the life of the capital market arrangement, and

(b) may be expressed wholly or partly in a foreign currency (in which case the sterling equivalent shall be calculated as at the time when the arrangement is entered into).

Interpretation of project company

4H.—(1) For the purposes of paragraph 4B a company is a "project company" of a project if—

(a) it holds property for the purpose of the project,

(b) it has sole or principal responsibility under an agreement for carrying out all or part of the project,

(c) it is one of a number of companies which together carry out the project,

(d) it has the purpose of supplying finance to enable the project to be carried out, or

(e) it is the holding company of a company within any of paragraphs (a) to (d).

(2) But a company is not a "project company" of a project if—

(a) it performs a function within sub-paragraph (1)(a) to (d) or is within sub-paragraph (1)(e), but

(b) it also performs a function which is not—

(i) within sub-paragraph (1)(a) to (d),

(ii) related to a function within sub-paragraph (1)(a) to (d), or

(iii) related to the project.

(3) For the purposes of this paragraph a company carries out all or part of a project whether or not it acts wholly or partly through agents.

Public-private partnership project

4I.—(1) In paragraph 4B "public-private partnership project" means a project—
(a) the resources for which are provided partly by one or more public bodies and partly by one or more private persons, or
(b) which is designed wholly or mainly for the purpose of assisting a public body to discharge a function.

(2) In sub-paragraph (1) "resources" includes—
(a) funds (including payment for the provision of services or facilities),
(b) assets,
(c) professional skill,
(d) the grant of a concession or franchise, and
(e) any other commercial resource.

(3) In sub-paragraph (1) "public body" means—
(a) a body which exercises public functions,
(b) a body specified for the purposes of this paragraph by the Secretary of State, and
(c) a body within a class specified for the purposes of this paragraph by the Secretary of State.

(4) A specification under sub-paragraph (3) may be—
(a) general, or
(b) for the purpose of the application of paragraph 4B to a specified case.

Step-in rights

4J.—(1) For the purposes of paragraph 4B a project has "step-in rights" if a person who provides finance in connection with the project has a conditional entitlement under an agreement to—
(i) assume sole or principal responsibility under an agreement for carrying out all or part of the project, or
(ii) make arrangements for carrying out all or part of the project.

(2) In sub-paragraph (1) a reference to the provision of finance includes a reference to the provision of an indemnity.

"Person"

4K. For the purposes of paragraphs 4A to 4J, a reference to a person includes a reference to a partnership or another unincorporated group of persons.]

5. The Secretary of State may by regulations modify the qualifications for eligibility of a company for a moratorium.]

[3464]

NOTES

Inserted by the Insolvency Act 2000, s 1, Sch 1, paras 1, 4, as from 11 May 2001 (para 5), and as from 1 January 2003 (otherwise).

Para 1: definitions omitted repealed by virtue of the Financial Services and Markets Act 2000 (Consequential Amendments) Order 2002, SI 2002/1555, art 28(1), (2), as from 3 July 2002.

Para 2: sub-paras (2)(a)–(bb) substituted for original sub-paras (2)(a), (b), words omitted from sub-para (2)(c) repealed, and sub-para (3) added, by virtue of SI 2002/1555, arts 28(1), (3), 29, as from 3 July 2002.

Para 3: sub-paras (4), (5) added by the Insolvency Act 1986 (Amendment) (No 3) Regulations 2002, SI 2002/1990, reg 3(1), (2), as from 1 January 2003 (being the day on which the Insolvency Act 2000, s 1 comes into force for the purpose of giving effect to para 4 of this Schedule; see reg 2 of the 2002 Regulations).

Para 4: sub-para (1)(a) substituted, and sub-para (1)(fa) inserted, by the Enterprise Act 2002, s 248(3), Sch 17, paras 9, 37(1), (2), as from 15 September 2003 (for savings and transitional provisions, see the note to s 8 at **[3164]**).

Paras 4A–4K: inserted by SI 2002/1990, reg 3(1), (3), as from 1 January 2003 (being the day on which the Insolvency Act 2000, s 1 comes into force for the purpose of giving effect to para 4 of this Schedule; see reg 2 of the 2002 Regulations).

Application to limited liability partnerships: see the introductory note to this Act and the Limited Liability Partnerships Regulations 2001, SI 2001/1090, reg 5, Sch 3 at **[6986]**, **[6995]**.

Modification: a reference to commercial paper in this Schedule includes a reference to uncertificated units of an eligible debt security where the issue of the units corresponds, in accordance with the current terms of issue of the security, to the issue of commercial paper within the meaning of the Financial Services and Markets Act 2000 (Regulated Activities) Order 2001, SI 2001/544, art 9(3); see the Uncertificated Securities (Amendment) (Eligible Debt Securities) Regulations 2003, SI 2003/1633, reg 15, Sch 2, para 7.

Banking Act 1987, Insurance Companies Act 1982: repealed by the Financial Services and Markets Act 2000 (Consequential Amendments and Repeals) Order 2001, SI 2001/3649, art 3(1)(b), (d), as from 1 December 2001.

Financial Services and Markets Act 2000 (Financial Promotion) Order 2001, SI 2001/1335: revoked and replaced by the Financial Services and Markets Act 2000 (Financial Promotion) Order 2005, SI 2005/1529.

Regulations: the Insolvency Act 1986 (Amendment) (No 3) Regulations 2002, SI 2002/1990.

[PART II
OBTAINING A MORATORIUM

Nominee's statement

6.—(1) Where the directors of a company wish to obtain a moratorium, they shall submit to the nominee—

(a) a document setting out the terms of the proposed voluntary arrangement,

(b) a statement of the company's affairs containing—

(i) such particulars of its creditors and of its debts and other liabilities and of its assets as may be prescribed, and

(ii) such other information as may be prescribed, and

(c) any other information necessary to enable the nominee to comply with sub-paragraph (2) which he requests from them.

(2) The nominee shall submit to the directors a statement in the prescribed form indicating whether or not, in his opinion—

(a) the proposed voluntary arrangement has a reasonable prospect of being approved and implemented,

(b) the company is likely to have sufficient funds available to it during the proposed moratorium to enable it to carry on its business, and

(c) meetings of the company and its creditors should be summoned to consider the proposed voluntary arrangement.

(3) In forming his opinion on the matters mentioned in sub-paragraph (2), the nominee is entitled to rely on the information submitted to him under sub-paragraph (1) unless he has reason to doubt its accuracy.

(4) The reference in sub-paragraph (2)(b) to the company's business is to that business as the company proposes to carry it on during the moratorium.

Documents to be submitted to court

7.—(1) To obtain a moratorium the directors of a company must file (in Scotland, lodge) with the court—

(a) a document setting out the terms of the proposed voluntary arrangement,

(b) a statement of the company's affairs containing—

(i) such particulars of its creditors and of its debts and other liabilities and of its assets as may be prescribed, and

(ii) such other information as may be prescribed,

(c) a statement that the company is eligible for a moratorium,

(d) a statement from the nominee that he has given his consent to act, and

(e) a statement from the nominee that, in his opinion—

(i) the proposed voluntary arrangement has a reasonable prospect of being approved and implemented,

(ii) the company is likely to have sufficient funds available to it during the proposed moratorium to enable it to carry on its business, and

(iii) meetings of the company and its creditors should be summoned to consider the proposed voluntary arrangement.

(2) Each of the statements mentioned in sub-paragraph (1)(b) to (e), except so far as it contains the particulars referred to in paragraph (b)(i), must be in the prescribed form.

(3) The reference in sub-paragraph (1)(e)(ii) to the company's business is to that business as the company proposes to carry it on during the moratorium.

(4) The Secretary of State may by regulations modify the requirements of this paragraph as to the documents required to be filed (in Scotland, lodged) with the court in order to obtain a moratorium.

Duration of moratorium

8.—(1) A moratorium comes into force when the documents for the time being referred to in paragraph 7(1) are filed or lodged with the court and references in this Schedule to "the beginning of the moratorium" shall be construed accordingly.

(2) A moratorium ends at the end of the day on which the meetings summoned under paragraph 29(1) are first held (or, if the meetings are held on different days, the later of those days), unless it is extended under paragraph 32.

(3) If either of those meetings has not first met before the end of the period of 28 days beginning with the day on which the moratorium comes into force, the moratorium ends at the end of the day on which those meetings were to be held (or, if those meetings were summoned to be held on different days, the later of those days), unless it is extended under paragraph 32.

(4) If the nominee fails to summon either meeting within the period required by paragraph 29(1), the moratorium ends at the end of the last day of that period.

(5) If the moratorium is extended (or further extended) under paragraph 32, it ends at the end of the day to which it is extended (or further extended).

(6) Sub-paragraphs (2) to (5) do not apply if the moratorium comes to an end before the time concerned by virtue of—
- (a) paragraph 25(4) (effect of withdrawal by nominee of consent to act),
- (b) an order under paragraph 26(3), 27(3) or 40 (challenge of actions of nominee or directors), or
- (c) a decision of one or both of the meetings summoned under paragraph 29.

(7) If the moratorium has not previously come to an end in accordance with sub-paragraphs (2) to (6), it ends at the end of the day on which a decision under paragraph 31 to approve a voluntary arrangement takes effect under paragraph 36.

(8) The Secretary of State may by order increase or reduce the period for the time being specified in sub-paragraph (3).

Notification of beginning of moratorium

9.—(1) When a moratorium comes into force, the directors shall notify the nominee of that fact forthwith.

(2) If the directors without reasonable excuse fail to comply with sub-paragraph (1), each of them is liable to imprisonment or a fine, or both.

10.—(1) When a moratorium comes into force, the nominee shall, in accordance with the rules—
- (a) advertise that fact forthwith, and
- (b) notify the registrar of companies, the company and any petitioning creditor of the company of whose claim he is aware of that fact.

(2) In sub-paragraph (1)(b), "petitioning creditor" means a creditor by whom a winding-up petition has been presented before the beginning of the moratorium, as long as the petition has not been dismissed or withdrawn.

(3) If the nominee without reasonable excuse fails to comply with sub-paragraph (1)(a) or (b), he is liable to a fine.

Notification of end of moratorium

11.—(1) When a moratorium comes to an end, the nominee shall, in accordance with the rules—

(a) advertise that fact forthwith, and

(b) notify the court, the registrar of companies, the company and any creditor of the company of whose claim he is aware of that fact.

(2) If the nominee without reasonable excuse fails to comply with sub-paragraph (1)(a) or (b), he is liable to a fine.]

[3465]

NOTES

Inserted as noted to Pt I of this Schedule at **[3464]**.

Application to limited liability partnerships: see the introductory note to this Act and the Limited Liability Partnerships Regulations 2001, SI 2001/1090, reg 5, Sch 3 at **[6986]**, **[6995]**.

[PART III
EFFECTS OF MORATORIUM

Effect on creditors, etc

12.—(1) During the period for which a moratorium is in force for a company—

(a) no petition may be presented for the winding up of the company,

(b) no meeting of the company may be called or requisitioned except with the consent of the nominee or the leave of the court and subject (where the court gives leave) to such terms as the court may impose,

(c) no resolution may be passed or order made for the winding up of the company,

[(d) no administration application may be made in respect of the company,

(da) no administrator of the company may be appointed under paragraph 14 or 22 of Schedule B1,]

(e) no administrative receiver of the company may be appointed,

(f) no landlord or other person to whom rent is payable may exercise any right of forfeiture by peaceable re-entry in relation to premises let to the company in respect of a failure by the company to comply with any term or condition of its tenancy of such premises, except with the leave of the court and subject to such terms as the court may impose,

(g) no other steps may be taken to enforce any security over the company's property, or to repossess goods in the company's possession under any hire-purchase agreement, except with the leave of the court and subject to such terms as the court may impose, and

(h) no other proceedings and no execution or other legal process may be commenced or continued, and no distress may be levied, against the company or its property except with the leave of the court and subject to such terms as the court may impose.

(2) Where a petition, other than an excepted petition, for the winding up of the company has been presented before the beginning of the moratorium, section 127 shall not apply in relation to any disposition of property, transfer of shares or alteration in status made during the moratorium or at a time mentioned in paragraph 37(5)(a).

(3) In the application of sub-paragraph (1)(h) to Scotland, the reference to execution being commenced or continued includes a reference to diligence being carried out or continued, and the reference to distress being levied is omitted.

(4) Paragraph (a) of sub-paragraph (1) does not apply to an excepted petition and, where such a petition has been presented before the beginning of the moratorium or is presented during the moratorium, paragraphs (b) and (c) of that sub-paragraph do not apply in relation to proceedings on the petition.

(5) For the purposes of this paragraph, "excepted petition" means a petition under—

(a) section 124A [or 124B] of this Act,

(b) section 72 of the Financial Services Act 1986 on the ground mentioned in subsection (1)(b) of that section, or

(c) section 92 of the Banking Act 1987 on the ground mentioned in subsection (1)(b) of that section,

PART III
OTHER LEGISLATION

[(d) section 367 of the Financial Services and Markets Act 2000 on the ground mentioned in subsection (3)(b) of that section.]

13.—(1) This paragraph applies where there is an uncrystallised floating charge on the property of a company for which a moratorium is in force.

(2) If the conditions for the holder of the charge to give a notice having the effect mentioned in sub-paragraph (4) are met at any time, the notice may not be given at that time but may instead be given as soon as practicable after the moratorium has come to an end.

(3) If any other event occurs at any time which (apart from this sub-paragraph) would have the effect mentioned in sub-paragraph (4), then—
- (a) the event shall not have the effect in question at that time, but
- (b) if notice of the event is given to the company by the holder of the charge as soon as is practicable after the moratorium has come to an end, the event is to be treated as if it had occurred when the notice was given.

(4) The effect referred to in sub-paragraphs (2) and (3) is—
- (a) causing the crystallisation of the floating charge, or
- (b) causing the imposition, by virtue of provision in the instrument creating the charge, of any restriction on the disposal of any property of the company.

(5) Application may not be made for leave under paragraph 12(1)(g) or (h) with a view to obtaining—
- (a) the crystallisation of the floating charge, or
- (b) the imposition, by virtue of provision in the instrument creating the charge, of any restriction on the disposal of any property of the company.

14. Security granted by a company at a time when a moratorium is in force in relation to the company may only be enforced if, at that time, there were reasonable grounds for believing that it would benefit the company.

Effect on company

15.—(1) Paragraphs 16 to 23 apply in relation to a company for which a moratorium is in force.

(2) The fact that a company enters into a transaction in contravention of any of paragraphs 16 to 22 does not—
- (a) make the transaction void, or
- (b) make it to any extent unenforceable against the company.

Company invoices, etc

16.—(1) Every invoice, order for goods or business letter which—
- (a) is issued by or on behalf of the company, and
- (b) on or in which the company's name appears,

shall also contain the nominee's name and a statement that the moratorium is in force for the company.

(2) If default is made in complying with sub-paragraph (1), the company and (subject to sub-paragraph (3)) any officer of the company is liable to a fine.

(3) An officer of the company is only liable under sub-paragraph (2) if, without reasonable excuse, he authorises or permits the default.

Obtaining credit during moratorium

17.—(1) The company may not obtain credit to the extent of £250 or more from a person who has not been informed that a moratorium is in force in relation to the company.

(2) The reference to the company obtaining credit includes the following cases—
- (a) where goods are bailed (in Scotland, hired) to the company under a hire-purchase agreement, or agreed to be sold to the company under a conditional sale agreement, and

(b) where the company is paid in advance (whether in money or otherwise) for the supply of goods or services.

(3) Where the company obtains credit in contravention of sub-paragraph (1)—
(a) the company is liable to a fine, and
(b) if any officer of the company knowingly and wilfully authorised or permitted the contravention, he is liable to imprisonment or a fine, or both.

(4) The money sum specified in sub-paragraph (1) is subject to increase or reduction by order under section 417A in Part XV.

Disposals and payments

18.—(1) Subject to sub-paragraph (2), the company may only dispose of any of its property if—
(a) there are reasonable grounds for believing that the disposal will benefit the company, and
(b) the disposal is approved by the committee established under paragraph 35(1) or, where there is no such committee, by the nominee.

(2) Sub-paragraph (1) does not apply to a disposal made in the ordinary way of the company's business.

(3) If the company makes a disposal in contravention of sub-paragraph (1) otherwise than in pursuance of an order of the court—
(a) the company is liable to a fine, and
(b) if any officer of the company authorised or permitted the contravention, without reasonable excuse, he is liable to imprisonment or a fine, or both.

19.—(1) Subject to sub-paragraph (2), the company may only make any payment in respect of any debt or other liability of the company in existence before the beginning of the moratorium if—
(a) there are reasonable grounds for believing that the payment will benefit the company, and
(b) the payment is approved by the committee established under paragraph 35(1) or, where there is no such committee, by the nominee.

(2) Sub-paragraph (1) does not apply to a payment required by paragraph 20(6).

(3) If the company makes a payment in contravention of sub-paragraph (1) otherwise than in pursuance of an order of the court—
(a) the company is liable to a fine, and
(b) if any officer of the company authorised or permitted the contravention, without reasonable excuse, he is liable to imprisonment or a fine, or both.

Disposal of charged property, etc

20.—(1) This paragraph applies where—
(a) any property of the company is subject to a security, or
(b) any goods are in the possession of the company under a hire-purchase agreement.

(2) If the holder of the security consents, or the court gives leave, the company may dispose of the property as if it were not subject to the security.

(3) If the owner of the goods consents, or the court gives leave, the company may dispose of the goods as if all rights of the owner under the hire-purchase agreement were vested in the company.

(4) Where property subject to a security which, as created, was a floating charge is disposed of under sub-paragraph (2), the holder of the security has the same priority in respect of any property of the company directly or indirectly representing the property disposed of as he would have had in respect of the property subject to the security.

(5) Sub-paragraph (6) applies to the disposal under sub-paragraph (2) or (as the case may be) sub-paragraph (3) of—
(a) any property subject to a security other than a security which, as created, was a floating charge, or
(b) any goods in the possession of the company under a hire-purchase agreement.

PART III
OTHER LEGISLATION

(6) It shall be a condition of any consent or leave under sub-paragraph (2) or (as the case may be) sub-paragraph (3) that—

(a) the net proceeds of the disposal, and

(b) where those proceeds are less than such amount as may be agreed, or determined by the court, to be the net amount which would be realised on a sale of the property or goods in the open market by a willing vendor, such sums as may be required to make good the deficiency,

shall be applied towards discharging the sums secured by the security or payable under the hire-purchase agreement.

(7) Where a condition imposed in pursuance of sub-paragraph (6) relates to two or more securities, that condition requires—

(a) the net proceeds of the disposal, and

(b) where paragraph (b) of sub-paragraph (6) applies, the sums mentioned in that paragraph,

to be applied towards discharging the sums secured by those securities in the order of their priorities.

(8) Where the court gives leave for a disposal under sub-paragraph (2) or (3), the directors shall, within 14 days after leave is given, send an office copy of the order giving leave to the registrar of companies.

(9) If the directors without reasonable excuse fail to comply with sub-paragraph (8), they are liable to a fine.

21.—(1) Where property is disposed of under paragraph 20 in its application to Scotland, the company shall grant to the disponee an appropriate document of transfer or conveyance of the property, and

(a) that document, or

(b) where any recording, intimation or registration of the document is a legal requirement for completion of title to the property, that recording, intimation or registration,

has the effect of disencumbering the property of, or (as the case may be) freeing the property from, the security.

(2) Where goods in the possession of the company under a hire-purchase agreement are disposed of under paragraph 20 in its application to Scotland, the disposal has the effect of extinguishing, as against the disponee, all rights of the owner of the goods under the agreement.

22.—(1) If the company—

(a) without any consent or leave under paragraph 20, disposes of any of its property which is subject to a security otherwise than in accordance with the terms of the security,

(b) without any consent or leave under paragraph 20, disposes of any goods in the possession of the company under a hire-purchase agreement otherwise than in accordance with the terms of the agreement, or

(c) fails to comply with any requirement imposed by paragraph 20 or 21,

it is liable to a fine.

(2) If any officer of the company, without reasonable excuse, authorises or permits any such disposal or failure to comply, he is liable to imprisonment or a fine, or both.

Market contracts, etc

23.—(1) If the company enters into any transaction to which this paragraph applies—

(a) the company is liable to a fine, and

(b) if any officer of the company, without reasonable excuse, authorised or permitted the company to enter into the transaction, he is liable to imprisonment or a fine, or both.

(2) A company enters into a transaction to which this paragraph applies if it—

(a) enters into a market contract, …

(b) gives a transfer order,

(c) grants a market charge … or a system-charge, or

(d) provides any collateral security.

(3) The fact that a company enters into a transaction in contravention of this paragraph does not—

(a) make the transaction void, or
(b) make it to any extent unenforceable by or against the company.

(4) Where during the moratorium a company enters into a transaction to which this paragraph applies, nothing done by or in pursuance of the transaction is to be treated as done in contravention of paragraphs 12(1)(g), 14 or 16 to 22.

(5) Paragraph 20 does not apply in relation to any property which is subject to a market charge, … a system-charge or a collateral security charge.

(6) In this paragraph, "transfer order", "collateral security" and "collateral security charge" have the same meanings as in the settlement finality regulations.]

[3466]

NOTES

Inserted as noted to Pt I of this Schedule at **[3464]**.

Para 12: sub-paras (1)(d), (da) substituted, for original sub-para (1)(d), by the Enterprise Act 2002, s 248(3), Sch 17, paras 9, 37(1), (3), as from 15 September 2003 (for savings and transitional provisions, see the note to s 8 at **[3164]**); words in square brackets in sub-para (5)(a) inserted by the European Public Limited-Liability Company Regulations 2004, SI 2004/2326, reg 73(4)(b), as from 8 October 2004; sub-para (5)(d) inserted by virtue of the Financial Services and Markets Act 2000 (Consequential Amendments) Order 2002, SI 2002/1555, art 30, as from 3 July 2002.

Para 23: words omitted from sub-paras (2), (5) repealed by virtue of SI 2002/1555, art 28(1), (4), as from 3 July 2002.

Application to limited liability partnerships: see the introductory note to this Act and the Limited Liability Partnerships Regulations 2001, SI 2001/1090, reg 5, Sch 3 at **[6986]**, **[6995]**.

Banking Act 1987, Financial Services Act 1986: repealed by the Financial Services and Markets Act 2000 (Consequential Amendments and Repeals) Order 2001, SI 2001/3649, art 3(1)(c), (d), as from 1 December 2001.

[PART IV NOMINEES

Monitoring of company's activities

24.—(1) During a moratorium, the nominee shall monitor the company's affairs for the purpose of forming an opinion as to whether—

(a) the proposed voluntary arrangement or, if he has received notice of proposed modifications under paragraph 31(7), the proposed arrangement with those modifications has a reasonable prospect of being approved and implemented, and
(b) the company is likely to have sufficient funds available to it during the remainder of the moratorium to enable it to continue to carry on its business.

(2) The directors shall submit to the nominee any information necessary to enable him to comply with sub-paragraph (1) which he requests from them.

(3) In forming his opinion on the matters mentioned in sub-paragraph (1), the nominee is entitled to rely on the information submitted to him under sub-paragraph (2) unless he has reason to doubt its accuracy.

(4) The reference in sub-paragraph (1)(b) to the company's business is to that business as the company proposes to carry it on during the remainder of the moratorium.

Withdrawal of consent to act

25.—(1) The nominee may only withdraw his consent to act in the circumstances mentioned in this paragraph.

(2) The nominee must withdraw his consent to act if, at any time during a moratorium—

(a) he forms the opinion that—
    (i) the proposed voluntary arrangement or, if he has received notice of proposed modifications under paragraph 31(7), the proposed arrangement with those modifications no longer has a reasonable prospect of being approved or implemented, or

(ii) the company will not have sufficient funds available to it during the remainder of the moratorium to enable it to continue to carry on its business,

(b) he becomes aware that, on the date of filing, the company was not eligible for a moratorium, or

(c) the directors fail to comply with their duty under paragraph 24(2).

(3) The reference in sub-paragraph (2)(a)(ii) to the company's business is to that business as the company proposes to carry it on during the remainder of the moratorium.

(4) If the nominee withdraws his consent to act, the moratorium comes to an end.

(5) If the nominee withdraws his consent to act he must, in accordance with the rules, notify the court, the registrar of companies, the company and any creditor of the company of whose claim he is aware of his withdrawal and the reason for it.

(6) If the nominee without reasonable excuse fails to comply with sub-paragraph (5), he is liable to a fine.

Challenge of nominee's actions, etc

26.—(1) If any creditor, director or member of the company, or any other person affected by a moratorium, is dissatisfied by any act, omission or decision of the nominee during the moratorium, he may apply to the court.

(2) An application under sub-paragraph (1) may be made during the moratorium or after it has ended.

(3) On an application under sub-paragraph (1) the court may—

(a) confirm, reverse or modify any act or decision of the nominee,

(b) give him directions, or

(c) make such other order as it thinks fit.

(4) An order under sub-paragraph (3) may (among other things) bring the moratorium to an end and make such consequential provision as the court thinks fit.

27.—(1) Where there are reasonable grounds for believing that—

(a) as a result of any act, omission or decision of the nominee during the moratorium, the company has suffered loss, but

(b) the company does not intend to pursue any claim it may have against the nominee,

any creditor of the company may apply to the court.

(2) An application under sub-paragraph (1) may be made during the moratorium or after it has ended.

(3) On an application under sub-paragraph (1) the court may—

(a) order the company to pursue any claim against the nominee,

(b) authorise any creditor to pursue such a claim in the name of the company, or

(c) make such other order with respect to such a claim as it thinks fit,

unless the court is satisfied that the act, omission or decision of the nominee was in all the circumstances reasonable.

(4) An order under sub-paragraph (3) may (among other things)—

(a) impose conditions on any authority given to pursue a claim,

(b) direct the company to assist in the pursuit of a claim,

(c) make directions with respect to the distribution of anything received as a result of the pursuit of a claim,

(d) bring the moratorium to an end and make such consequential provision as the court thinks fit.

(5) On an application under sub-paragraph (1) the court shall have regard to the interests of the members and creditors of the company generally.

Replacement of nominee by court

28.—(1) The court may—

(a) on an application made by the directors in a case where the nominee has failed to comply with any duty imposed on him under this Schedule or has died, or

(b) on an application made by the directors or the nominee in a case where it is impracticable or inappropriate for the nominee to continue to act as such,

direct that the nominee be replaced as such by another person qualified to act as an insolvency practitioner, or authorised to act as nominee, in relation to the voluntary arrangement.

(2) A person may only be appointed as a replacement nominee under this paragraph if he submits to the court a statement indicating his consent to act.]

[3467]

NOTES

Inserted as noted to Pt I of this Schedule at **[3464]**.

Application to limited liability partnerships: see the introductory note to this Act and the Limited Liability Partnerships Regulations 2001, SI 2001/1090, reg 5, Sch 3 at **[6986]**, **[6995]**.

[PART V
CONSIDERATION AND IMPLEMENTATION OF VOLUNTARY ARRANGEMENT

Summoning of meetings

29.—(1) Where a moratorium is in force, the nominee shall summon meetings of the company and its creditors for such a time, date (within the period for the time being specified in paragraph 8(3)) and place as he thinks fit.

(2) The persons to be summoned to a creditors' meeting under this paragraph are every creditor of the company of whose claim the nominee is aware.

Conduct of meetings

30.—(1) Subject to the provisions of paragraphs 31 to 35, the meetings summoned under paragraph 29 shall be conducted in accordance with the rules.

(2) A meeting so summoned may resolve that it be adjourned (or further adjourned).

(3) After the conclusion of either meeting in accordance with the rules, the chairman of the meeting shall report the result of the meeting to the court, and, immediately after reporting to the court, shall give notice of the result of the meeting to such persons as may be prescribed.

Approval of voluntary arrangement

31.—(1) The meetings summoned under paragraph 29 shall decide whether to approve the proposed voluntary arrangement (with or without modifications).

(2) The modifications may include one conferring the functions proposed to be conferred on the nominee on another person qualified to act as an insolvency practitioner, or authorised to act as nominee, in relation to the voluntary arrangement.

(3) The modifications shall not include one by virtue of which the proposal ceases to be a proposal such as is mentioned in section 1.

(4) A meeting summoned under paragraph 29 shall not approve any proposal or modification which affects the right of a secured creditor of the company to enforce his security, except with the concurrence of the creditor concerned.

(5) Subject to sub-paragraph (6), a meeting so summoned shall not approve any proposal or modification under which—

(a) any preferential debt of the company is to be paid otherwise than in priority to such of its debts as are not preferential debts, or

(b) a preferential creditor of the company is to be paid an amount in respect of a preferential debt that bears to that debt a smaller proportion than is borne to another preferential debt by the amount that is to be paid in respect of that other debt.

(6) The meeting may approve such a proposal or modification with the concurrence of the preferential creditor concerned.

(7) The directors of the company may, before the beginning of the period of seven days which ends with the meetings (or either of them) summoned under paragraph 29 being held, give notice to the nominee of any modifications of the proposal for which the directors intend to seek the approval of those meetings.

(8) References in this paragraph to preferential debts and preferential creditors are to be read in accordance with section 386 in Part XII of this Act.

Extension of moratorium

32.—(1) Subject to sub-paragraph (2), a meeting summoned under paragraph 29 which resolves that it be adjourned (or further adjourned) may resolve that the moratorium be extended (or further extended), with or without conditions.

(2) The moratorium may not be extended (or further extended) to a day later than the end of the period of two months which begins—

(a) where both meetings summoned under paragraph 29 are first held on the same day, with that day,

(b) in any other case, with the day on which the later of those meetings is first held.

(3) At any meeting where it is proposed to extend (or further extend) the moratorium, before a decision is taken with respect to that proposal, the nominee shall inform the meeting—

(a) of what he has done in order to comply with his duty under paragraph 24 and the cost of his actions for the company, and

(b) of what he intends to do to continue to comply with that duty if the moratorium is extended (or further extended) and the expected cost of his actions for the company.

(4) Where, in accordance with sub-paragraph (3)(b), the nominee informs a meeting of the expected cost of his intended actions, the meeting shall resolve whether or not to approve that expected cost.

(5) If a decision not to approve the expected cost of the nominee's intended actions has effect under paragraph 36, the moratorium comes to an end.

(6) A meeting may resolve that a moratorium which has been extended (or further extended) be brought to an end before the end of the period of the extension (or further extension).

(7) The Secretary of State may by order increase or reduce the period for the time being specified in sub-paragraph (2).

33.—(1) The conditions which may be imposed when a moratorium is extended (or further extended) include a requirement that the nominee be replaced as such by another person qualified to act as an insolvency practitioner, or authorised to act as nominee, in relation to the voluntary arrangement.

(2) A person may only be appointed as a replacement nominee by virtue of sub-paragraph (1) if he submits to the court a statement indicating his consent to act.

(3) At any meeting where it is proposed to appoint a replacement nominee as a condition of extending (or further extending) the moratorium—

(a) the duty imposed by paragraph 32(3)(b) on the nominee shall instead be imposed on the person proposed as the replacement nominee, and

(b) paragraphs 32(4) and (5) and 36(1)(e) apply as if the references to the nominee were to that person.

34.—(1) If a decision to extend, or further extend, the moratorium takes effect under paragraph 36, the nominee shall, in accordance with the rules, notify the registrar of companies and the court.

(2) If the moratorium is extended, or further extended, by virtue of an order under paragraph 36(5), the nominee shall, in accordance with the rules, send an office copy of the order to the registrar of companies.

(3) If the nominee without reasonable excuse fails to comply with this paragraph, he is liable to a fine.

Moratorium committee

35.—(1) A meeting summoned under paragraph 29 which resolves that the moratorium be extended (or further extended) may, with the consent of the nominee, resolve that a committee be established to exercise the functions conferred on it by the meeting.

(2) The meeting may not so resolve unless it has approved an estimate of the expenses to be incurred by the committee in the exercise of the proposed functions.

(3) Any expenses, not exceeding the amount of the estimate, incurred by the committee in the exercise of its functions shall be reimbursed by the nominee.

(4) The committee shall cease to exist when the moratorium comes to an end.

Effectiveness of decisions

36.—(1) Sub-paragraph (2) applies to references to one of the following decisions having effect, that is, a decision, under paragraph 31, 32 or 35, with respect to—

(a) the approval of a proposed voluntary arrangement,
(b) the extension (or further extension) of a moratorium,
(c) the bringing of a moratorium to an end,
(d) the establishment of a committee, or
(e) the approval of the expected cost of a nominee's intended actions.

(2) The decision has effect if, in accordance with the rules—

(a) it has been taken by both meetings summoned under paragraph 29, or
(b) (subject to any order made under sub-paragraph (5)) it has been taken by the creditors' meeting summoned under that paragraph.

(3) If a decision taken by the creditors' meeting under any of paragraphs 31, 32 or 35 with respect to any of the matters mentioned in sub-paragraph (1) differs from one so taken by the company meeting with respect to that matter, a member of the company may apply to the court.

(4) An application under sub-paragraph (3) shall not be made after the end of the period of 28 days beginning with—

(a) the day on which the decision was taken by the creditors' meeting, or
(b) where the decision of the company meeting was taken on a later day, that day.

(5) On an application under sub-paragraph (3), the court may—

(a) order the decision of the company meeting to have effect instead of the decision of the creditors' meeting, or
(b) make such other order as it thinks fit.

Effect of approval of voluntary arrangement

37.—(1) This paragraph applies where a decision approving a voluntary arrangement has effect under paragraph 36.

(2) The approved voluntary arrangement—

(a) takes effect as if made by the company at the creditors' meeting, and
(b) binds every person who in accordance with the rules—
  (i) was entitled to vote at that meeting (whether or not he was present or represented at it), or
  (ii) would have been so entitled if he had had notice of it,

as if he were a party to the voluntary arrangement.

(3) If—

(a) when the arrangement ceases to have effect any amount payable under the arrangement to a person bound by virtue of sub-paragraph (2)(b)(ii) has not been paid, and
(b) the arrangement did not come to an end prematurely,

the company shall at that time become liable to pay to that person the amount payable under the arrangement.

(4) Where a petition for the winding up of the company, other than an excepted petition within the meaning of paragraph 12, was presented before the beginning of the moratorium, the court shall dismiss the petition.

PART III
OTHER LEGISLATION

(5) The court shall not dismiss a petition under sub-paragraph (4)—

(a) at any time before the end of the period of 28 days beginning with the first day on which each of the reports of the meetings required by paragraph 30(3) has been made to the court, or

(b) at any time when an application under paragraph 38 or an appeal in respect of such an application is pending, or at any time in the period within which such an appeal may be brought.

Challenge of decisions

38.—(1) Subject to the following provisions of this paragraph, any of the persons mentioned in sub-paragraph (2) may apply to the court on one or both of the following grounds—

(a) that a voluntary arrangement approved at one or both of the meetings summoned under paragraph 29 and which has taken effect unfairly prejudices the interests of a creditor, member or contributory of the company,

(b) that there has been some material irregularity at or in relation to either of those meetings.

(2) The persons who may apply under this paragraph are—

(a) a person entitled, in accordance with the rules, to vote at either of the meetings,

(b) a person who would have been entitled, in accordance with the rules, to vote at the creditors' meeting if he had had notice of it, and

(c) the nominee.

(3) An application under this paragraph shall not be made—

(a) after the end of the period of 28 days beginning with the first day on which each of the reports required by paragraph 30(3) has been made to the court, or

(b) in the case of a person who was not given notice of the creditors' meeting, after the end of the period of 28 days beginning with the day on which he became aware that the meeting had taken place,

but (subject to that) an application made by a person within sub-paragraph (2)(b) on the ground that the arrangement prejudices his interests may be made after the arrangement has ceased to have effect, unless it came to an end prematurely.

(4) Where on an application under this paragraph the court is satisfied as to either of the grounds mentioned in sub-paragraph (1), it may do any of the following—

(a) revoke or suspend—

(i) any decision approving the voluntary arrangement which has effect under paragraph 36, or

(ii) in a case falling within sub-paragraph (1)(b), any decision taken by the meeting in question which has effect under that paragraph,

(b) give a direction to any person—

(i) for the summoning of further meetings to consider any revised proposal for a voluntary arrangement which the directors may make, or

(ii) in a case falling within sub-paragraph (1)(b), for the summoning of a further company or (as the case may be) creditors' meeting to reconsider the original proposal.

(5) Where at any time after giving a direction under sub-paragraph (4)(b)(i) the court is satisfied that the directors do not intend to submit a revised proposal, the court shall revoke the direction and revoke or suspend any decision approving the voluntary arrangement which has effect under paragraph 36.

(6) Where the court gives a direction under sub-paragraph (4)(b), it may also give a direction continuing or, as the case may require, renewing, for such period as may be specified in the direction, the effect of the moratorium.

(7) Sub-paragraph (8) applies in a case where the court, on an application under this paragraph—

(a) gives a direction under sub-paragraph (4)(b), or

(b) revokes or suspends a decision under sub-paragraph (4)(a) or (5).

(8) In such a case, the court may give such supplemental directions as it thinks fit and, in particular, directions with respect to—

(a) things done under the voluntary arrangement since it took effect, and

(b) such things done since that time as could not have been done if a moratorium had been in force in relation to the company when they were done.

(9) Except in pursuance of the preceding provisions of this paragraph, a decision taken at a meeting summoned under paragraph 29 is not invalidated by any irregularity at or in relation to the meeting.

Implementation of voluntary arrangement

39.—(1) This paragraph applies where a voluntary arrangement approved by one or both of the meetings summoned under paragraph 29 has taken effect.

(2) The person who is for the time being carrying out in relation to the voluntary arrangement the functions conferred—

(a) by virtue of the approval of the arrangement, on the nominee, or

(b) by virtue of paragraph 31(2), on a person other than the nominee,

shall be known as the supervisor of the voluntary arrangement.

(3) If any of the company's creditors or any other person is dissatisfied by any act, omission or decision of the supervisor, he may apply to the court.

(4) On an application under sub-paragraph (3) the court may—

(a) confirm, reverse or modify any act or decision of the supervisor,

(b) give him directions, or

(c) make such other order as it thinks fit.

(5) The supervisor—

(a) may apply to the court for directions in relation to any particular matter arising under the voluntary arrangement, and

(b) is included among the persons who may apply to the court for the winding up of the company or for an administration order to be made in relation to it.

(6) The court may, whenever—

(a) it is expedient to appoint a person to carry out the functions of the supervisor, and

(b) it is inexpedient, difficult or impracticable for an appointment to be made without the assistance of the court,

make an order appointing a person who is qualified to act as an insolvency practitioner, or authorised to act as supervisor, in relation to the voluntary arrangement, either in substitution for the existing supervisor or to fill a vacancy.

(7) The power conferred by sub-paragraph (6) is exercisable so as to increase the number of persons exercising the functions of supervisor or, where there is more than one person exercising those functions, so as to replace one or more of those persons.

[3468]

NOTES

Inserted as noted to Pt I of this Schedule at **[3464]**.

Application to limited liability partnerships: see the introductory note to this Act and the Limited Liability Partnerships Regulations 2001, SI 2001/1090, reg 5, Sch 3 at **[6986]**, **[6995]**.

[PART VI
MISCELLANEOUS

Challenge of directors' actions

40.—(1) This paragraph applies in relation to acts or omissions of the directors of a company during a moratorium.

(2) A creditor or member of the company may apply to the court for an order under this paragraph on the ground—

(a) that the company's affairs, business and property are being or have been managed by the directors in a manner which is unfairly prejudicial to the interests of its creditors or members generally, or of some part of its creditors or members (including at least the petitioner), or

(b) that any actual or proposed act or omission of the directors is or would be so prejudicial.

(3) An application for an order under this paragraph may be made during or after the moratorium.

(4) On an application for an order under this paragraph the court may—
(a) make such order as it thinks fit for giving relief in respect of the matters complained of,
(b) adjourn the hearing conditionally or unconditionally, or
(c) make an interim order or any other order that it thinks fit.

(5) An order under this paragraph may in particular—
(a) regulate the management by the directors of the company's affairs, business and property during the remainder of the moratorium,
(b) require the directors to refrain from doing or continuing an act complained of by the petitioner, or to do an act which the petitioner has complained they have omitted to do,
(c) require the summoning of a meeting of creditors or members for the purpose of considering such matters as the court may direct,
(d) bring the moratorium to an end and make such consequential provision as the court thinks fit.

(6) In making an order under this paragraph the court shall have regard to the need to safeguard the interests of persons who have dealt with the company in good faith and for value.

[(7) Sub-paragraph (8) applies where—
[(a) the appointment of an administrator has effect in relation to the company and that appointment was in pursuance of—
(i) an administration application made, or
(ii) a notice of intention to appoint filed,
before the moratorium came into force, or]
(b) the company is being wound up in pursuance of a petition presented before the moratorium came into force.

(8) No application for an order under this paragraph may be made by a creditor or member of the company; but such an application may be made instead by the administrator or (as the case may be) the liquidator.]

Offences

41.—(1) This paragraph applies where a moratorium has been obtained for a company.

(2) If, within the period of 12 months ending with the day on which the moratorium came into force, a person who was at the time an officer of the company—
(a) did any of the things mentioned in paragraphs (a) to (f) of sub-paragraph (4), or
(b) was privy to the doing by others of any of the things mentioned in paragraphs (c), (d) and (e) of that sub-paragraph,
he is to be treated as having committed an offence at that time.

(3) If, at any time during the moratorium, a person who is an officer of the company—
(a) does any of the things mentioned in paragraphs (a) to (f) of sub-paragraph (4), or
(b) is privy to the doing by others of any of the things mentioned in paragraphs (c), (d) and (e) of that sub-paragraph,
he commits an offence.

(4) Those things are—
(a) concealing any part of the company's property to the value of £500 or more, or concealing any debt due to or from the company, or
(b) fraudulently removing any part of the company's property to the value of £500 or more, or
(c) concealing, destroying, mutilating or falsifying any book or paper affecting or relating to the company's property or affairs, or
(d) making any false entry in any book or paper affecting or relating to the company's property or affairs, or
(e) fraudulently parting with, altering or making any omission in any document affecting or relating to the company's property or affairs, or
(f) pawning, pledging or disposing of any property of the company which has been obtained on credit and has not been paid for (unless the pawning, pledging or disposal was in the ordinary way of the company's business).

(5) For the purposes of this paragraph, "officer" includes a shadow director.

(6) It is a defence—

(a) for a person charged under sub-paragraph (2) or (3) in respect of the things mentioned in paragraph (a) or (f) of sub-paragraph (4) to prove that he had no intent to defraud, and

(b) for a person charged under sub-paragraph (2) or (3) in respect of the things mentioned in paragraph (c) or (d) of sub-paragraph (4) to prove that he had no intent to conceal the state of affairs of the company or to defeat the law.

(7) Where a person pawns, pledges or disposes of any property of a company in circumstances which amount to an offence under sub-paragraph (2) or (3), every person who takes in pawn or pledge, or otherwise receives, the property knowing it to be pawned, pledged or disposed of in circumstances which—

(a) would, if a moratorium were obtained for the company within the period of 12 months beginning with the day on which the pawning, pledging or disposal took place, amount to an offence under sub-paragraph (2), or

(b) amount to an offence under sub-paragraph (3),

commits an offence.

(8) A person guilty of an offence under this paragraph is liable to imprisonment or a fine, or both.

(9) The money sums specified in paragraphs (a) and (b) of sub-paragraph (4) are subject to increase or reduction by order under section 417A in Part XV.

42.—(1) If, for the purpose of obtaining a moratorium, or an extension of a moratorium, for a company, a person who is an officer of the company—

(a) makes any false representation, or

(b) fraudulently does, or omits to do, anything,

he commits an offence.

(2) Sub-paragraph (1) applies even if no moratorium or extension is obtained.

(3) For the purposes of this paragraph, "officer" includes a shadow director.

(4) A person guilty of an offence under this paragraph is liable to imprisonment or a fine, or both.

Void provisions in floating charge documents

43.—(1) A provision in an instrument creating a floating charge is void if it provides for—

(a) obtaining a moratorium, or

(b) anything done with a view to obtaining a moratorium (including any preliminary decision or investigation),

to be an event causing the floating charge to crystallise or causing restrictions which would not otherwise apply to be imposed on the disposal of property by the company or a ground for the appointment of a receiver.

(2) In sub-paragraph (1), "receiver" includes a manager and a person who is appointed both receiver and manager.

Functions of the Financial Services Authority

44.—(1) This Schedule has effect in relation to a moratorium for a regulated company with the modifications in sub-paragraphs (2) to (16) below.

(2) Any notice or other document required by virtue of this Schedule to be sent to a creditor of a regulated company must also be sent to the Authority.

(3) The Authority is entitled to be heard on any application to the court for leave under paragraph 20(2) or 20(3) (disposal of charged property, etc).

(4) Where paragraph 26(1) (challenge of nominee's actions, etc) applies, the persons who may apply to the court include the Authority.

(5) If a person other than the Authority applies to the court under that paragraph, the Authority is entitled to be heard on the application.

(6) Where paragraph 27(1) (challenge of nominee's actions, etc) applies, the persons who may apply to the court include the Authority.

(7) If a person other than the Authority applies to the court under that paragraph, the Authority is entitled to be heard on the application.

(8) The persons to be summoned to a creditors' meeting under paragraph 29 include the Authority.

(9) A person appointed for the purpose by the Authority is entitled to attend and participate in (but not to vote at)—
- (a) any creditors' meeting summoned under that paragraph,
- (b) any meeting of a committee established under paragraph 35 (moratorium committee).

(10) The Authority is entitled to be heard on any application under paragraph 36(3) (effectiveness of decisions).

(11) Where paragraph 38(1) (challenge of decisions) applies, the persons who may apply to the court include the Authority.

(12) If a person other than the Authority applies to the court under that paragraph, the Authority is entitled to be heard on the application.

(13) Where paragraph 39(3) (implementation of voluntary arrangement) applies, the persons who may apply to the court include the Authority.

(14) If a person other than the Authority applies to the court under that paragraph, the Authority is entitled to be heard on the application.

(15) Where paragraph 40(2) (challenge of directors' actions) applies, the persons who may apply to the court include the Authority.

(16) If a person other than the Authority applies to the court under that paragraph, the Authority is entitled to be heard on the application.

(17) This paragraph does not prejudice any right the Authority has (apart from this paragraph) as a creditor of a regulated company.

(18) In this paragraph—
"the Authority" means the Financial Services Authority, and
"regulated company" means a company which—
- (a) is, or has been, an authorised person within the meaning given by section 31 of the Financial Services and Markets Act 2000,
- (b) is, or has been, an appointed representative within the meaning given by section 39 of that Act, or
- (c) is carrying on, or has carried on, a regulated activity, within the meaning given by section 22 of that Act, in contravention of the general prohibition within the meaning given by section 19 of that Act.

Subordinate legislation

45.—(1) Regulations or an order made by the Secretary of State under this Schedule may make different provision for different cases.

(2) Regulations so made may make such consequential, incidental, supplemental and transitional provision as may appear to the Secretary of State necessary or expedient.

(3) Any power of the Secretary of State to make regulations under this Schedule may be exercised by amending or repealing any enactment contained in this Act (including one contained in this Schedule) or contained in the Company Directors Disqualification Act 1986.

(4) Regulations (except regulations under paragraph 5) or an order made by the Secretary of State under this Schedule shall be made by statutory instrument subject to annulment in pursuance of a resolution of either House of Parliament.

(5) Regulations under paragraph 5 of this Schedule are to be made by statutory instrument and shall only be made if a draft containing the regulations has been laid before and approved by resolution of each House of Parliament.]

[3469]

NOTES

Inserted as noted to Pt I of this Schedule at **[3464]**.

Para 40: sub-paras (7), (8) substituted, for original sub-para (7), by the Enterprise Act 2002, s 248(3), Sch 17, paras 9, 37(1), (4), as from 15 September 2003 (for savings and transitional provisions, see the note to s 8 at **[3164]**); sub-para (7)(a) further substituted by the Enterprise Act 2002 (Insolvency) Order 2004, SI 2004/2312, art 2, as from 15 October 2004.

Application to limited liability partnerships: see the introductory note to this Act and the Limited Liability Partnerships Regulations 2001, SI 2001/1090, reg 5, Sch 3 at **[6986]**, **[6995]**.

Regulations under paragraph 5: see Part I of this Schedule *ante*.

[SCHEDULE B1
ADMINISTRATION

Section 8

Arrangement of Schedule

PART III OTHER LEGISLATION

NATURE OF ADMINISTRATION

Administration

1.—(1) For the purposes of this Act “administrator” of a company means a person appointed under this Schedule to manage the company’s affairs, business and property.

(2) For the purposes of this Act—

(a) a company is “in administration” while the appointment of an administrator of the company has effect,

(b) a company “enters administration” when the appointment of an administrator takes effect,

(c) a company ceases to be in administration when the appointment of an administrator of the company ceases to have effect in accordance with this Schedule, and

(d) a company does not cease to be in administration merely because an administrator vacates office (by reason of resignation, death or otherwise) or is removed from office.

2. A person may be appointed as administrator of a company—

(a) by administration order of the court under paragraph 10,

(b) by the holder of a floating charge under paragraph 14, or

(c) by the company or its directors under paragraph 22.

Purpose of administration

3.—(1) The administrator of a company must perform his functions with the objective of—

(a) rescuing the company as a going concern, or
(b) achieving a better result for the company's creditors as a whole than would be likely if the company were wound up (without first being in administration), or
(c) realising property in order to make a distribution to one or more secured or preferential creditors.

(2) Subject to sub-paragraph (4), the administrator of a company must perform his functions in the interests of the company's creditors as a whole.

(3) The administrator must perform his functions with the objective specified in sub-paragraph (1)(a) unless he thinks either—
(a) that it is not reasonably practicable to achieve that objective, or
(b) that the objective specified in sub-paragraph (1)(b) would achieve a better result for the company's creditors as a whole.

(4) The administrator may perform his functions with the objective specified in sub-paragraph (1)(c) only if—
(a) he thinks that it is not reasonably practicable to achieve either of the objectives specified in sub-paragraph (1)(a) and (b), and
(b) he does not unnecessarily harm the interests of the creditors of the company as a whole.

4. The administrator of a company must perform his functions as quickly and efficiently as is reasonably practicable.

Status of administrator

5. An administrator is an officer of the court (whether or not he is appointed by the court).

General restrictions

6. A person may be appointed as administrator of a company only if he is qualified to act as an insolvency practitioner in relation to the company.

7. A person may not be appointed as administrator of a company which is in administration (subject to the provisions of paragraphs 90 to 97 and 100 to 103 about replacement and additional administrators).

8.—(1) A person may not be appointed as administrator of a company which is in liquidation by virtue of—
(a) a resolution for voluntary winding up, or
(b) a winding-up order.

(2) Sub-paragraph (1)(a) is subject to paragraph 38.

(3) Sub-paragraph (1)(b) is subject to paragraphs 37 and 38.

9.—(1) A person may not be appointed as administrator of a company which—
(a) has a liability in respect of a deposit which it accepted in accordance with the Banking Act 1979 (c 37) or 1987 (c 22), but
(b) is not an authorised deposit taker.

(2) A person may not be appointed as administrator of a company which effects or carries out contracts of insurance.

(3) But sub-paragraph (2) does not apply to a company which—
(a) is exempt from the general prohibition in relation to effecting or carrying out contracts of insurance, or
(b) is an authorised deposit taker effecting or carrying out contracts of insurance in the course of a banking business.

(4) In this paragraph—
"authorised deposit taker" means a person with permission under Part IV of the Financial Services and Markets Act 2000 (c 8) to accept deposits, and
"the general prohibition" has the meaning given by section 19 of that Act.

(5) This paragraph shall be construed in accordance with—

(a) section 22 of the Financial Services and Markets Act 2000 (classes of regulated activity and categories of investment),
(b) any relevant order under that section, and
(c) Schedule 2 to that Act (regulated activities).

APPOINTMENT OF ADMINISTRATOR BY COURT

Administration order

10. An administration order is an order appointing a person as the administrator of a company.

Conditions for making order

11. The court may make an administration order in relation to a company only if satisfied—
(a) that the company is or is likely to become unable to pay its debts, and
(b) that the administration order is reasonably likely to achieve the purpose of administration.

Administration application

12.—(1) An application to the court for an administration order in respect of a company (an "administration application") may be made only by—
(a) the company,
(b) the directors of the company,
(c) one or more creditors of the company,
(d) the [designated officer] for a magistrates' court in the exercise of the power conferred by section 87A of the Magistrates' Courts Act 1980 (c 43) (fine imposed on company), or
(e) a combination of persons listed in paragraphs (a) to (d).

(2) As soon as is reasonably practicable after the making of an administration application the applicant shall notify—
(a) any person who has appointed an administrative receiver of the company,
(b) any person who is or may be entitled to appoint an administrative receiver of the company,
(c) any person who is or may be entitled to appoint an administrator of the company under paragraph 14, and
(d) such other persons as may be prescribed.

(3) An administration application may not be withdrawn without the permission of the court.

(4) In sub-paragraph (1) "creditor" includes a contingent creditor and a prospective creditor.

[(5) Sub-paragraph (1) is without prejudice to section 7(4)(b).]

Powers of court

13.—(1) On hearing an administration application the court may—
(a) make the administration order sought;
(b) dismiss the application;
(c) adjourn the hearing conditionally or unconditionally;
(d) make an interim order;
(e) treat the application as a winding-up petition and make any order which the court could make under section 125;
(f) make any other order which the court thinks appropriate.

(2) An appointment of an administrator by administration order takes effect—
(a) at a time appointed by the order, or
(b) where no time is appointed by the order, when the order is made.

(3) An interim order under sub-paragraph (1)(d) may, in particular—

(a) restrict the exercise of a power of the directors or the company;
(b) make provision conferring a discretion on the court or on a person qualified to act as an insolvency practitioner in relation to the company.

(4) This paragraph is subject to paragraph 39.

APPOINTMENT OF ADMINISTRATOR BY HOLDER OF FLOATING CHARGE

Power to appoint

14.—(1) The holder of a qualifying floating charge in respect of a company's property may appoint an administrator of the company.

(2) For the purposes of sub-paragraph (1) a floating charge qualifies if created by an instrument which—
(a) states that this paragraph applies to the floating charge,
(b) purports to empower the holder of the floating charge to appoint an administrator of the company,
(c) purports to empower the holder of the floating charge to make an appointment which would be the appointment of an administrative receiver within the meaning given by section 29(2), or
(d) purports to empower the holder of a floating charge in Scotland to appoint a receiver who on appointment would be an administrative receiver.

(3) For the purposes of sub-paragraph (1) a person is the holder of a qualifying floating charge in respect of a company's property if he holds one or more debentures of the company secured—
(a) by a qualifying floating charge which relates to the whole or substantially the whole of the company's property,
(b) by a number of qualifying floating charges which together relate to the whole or substantially the whole of the company's property, or
(c) by charges and other forms of security which together relate to the whole or substantially the whole of the company's property and at least one of which is a qualifying floating charge.

Restrictions on power to appoint

15.—(1) A person may not appoint an administrator under paragraph 14 unless—
(a) he has given at least two business days' written notice to the holder of any prior floating charge which satisfies paragraph 14(2), or
(b) the holder of any prior floating charge which satisfies paragraph 14(2) has consented in writing to the making of the appointment.

(2) One floating charge is prior to another for the purposes of this paragraph if—
(a) it was created first, or
(b) it is to be treated as having priority in accordance with an agreement to which the holder of each floating charge was party.

(3) Sub-paragraph (2) shall have effect in relation to Scotland as if the following were substituted for paragraph (a)—
"(a) it has priority of ranking in accordance with section 464(4)(b) of the Companies Act 1985 (c 6),

16. An administrator may not be appointed under paragraph 14 while a floating charge on which the appointment relies is not enforceable.

17. An administrator of a company may not be appointed under paragraph 14 if—
(a) a provisional liquidator of the company has been appointed under section 135, or
(b) an administrative receiver of the company is in office.

Notice of appointment

18.—(1) A person who appoints an administrator of a company under paragraph 14 shall file with the court—

(a) a notice of appointment, and
(b) such other documents as may be prescribed.

(2) The notice of appointment must include a statutory declaration by or on behalf of the person who makes the appointment—
(a) that the person is the holder of a qualifying floating charge in respect of the company's property,
(b) that each floating charge relied on in making the appointment is (or was) enforceable on the date of the appointment, and
(c) that the appointment is in accordance with this Schedule.

(3) The notice of appointment must identify the administrator and must be accompanied by a statement by the administrator—
(a) that he consents to the appointment,
(b) that in his opinion the purpose of administration is reasonably likely to be achieved, and
(c) giving such other information and opinions as may be prescribed.

(4) For the purpose of a statement under sub-paragraph (3) an administrator may rely on information supplied by directors of the company (unless he has reason to doubt its accuracy).

(5) The notice of appointment and any document accompanying it must be in the prescribed form.

(6) A statutory declaration under sub-paragraph (2) must be made during the prescribed period.

(7) A person commits an offence if in a statutory declaration under sub-paragraph (2) he makes a statement—
(a) which is false, and
(b) which he does not reasonably believe to be true.

Commencement of appointment

19. The appointment of an administrator under paragraph 14 takes effect when the requirements of paragraph 18 are satisfied.

20. A person who appoints an administrator under paragraph 14—
(a) shall notify the administrator and such other persons as may be prescribed as soon as is reasonably practicable after the requirements of paragraph 18 are satisfied, and
(b) commits an offence if he fails without reasonable excuse to comply with paragraph (a).

Invalid appointment: indemnity

21.—(1) This paragraph applies where—
(a) a person purports to appoint an administrator under paragraph 14, and
(b) the appointment is discovered to be invalid.

(2) The court may order the person who purported to make the appointment to indemnify the person appointed against liability which arises solely by reason of the appointment's invalidity.

APPOINTMENT OF ADMINISTRATOR BY COMPANY OR DIRECTORS

Power to appoint

22.—(1) A company may appoint an administrator.

(2) The directors of a company may appoint an administrator.

Restrictions on power to appoint

23.—(1) This paragraph applies where an administrator of a company is appointed—

(a) under paragraph 22, or
(b) on an administration application made by the company or its directors.

(2) An administrator of the company may not be appointed under paragraph 22 during the period of 12 months beginning with the date on which the appointment referred to in sub-paragraph (1) ceases to have effect.

24.—(1) If a moratorium for a company under Schedule A1 ends on a date when no voluntary arrangement is in force in respect of the company, this paragraph applies for the period of 12 months beginning with that date.

(2) This paragraph also applies for the period of 12 months beginning with the date on which a voluntary arrangement in respect of a company ends if—
(a) the arrangement was made during a moratorium for the company under Schedule A1, and
(b) the arrangement ends prematurely (within the meaning of section 7B).

(3) While this paragraph applies, an administrator of the company may not be appointed under paragraph 22.

25. An administrator of a company may not be appointed under paragraph 22 if—
(a) a petition for the winding up of the company has been presented and is not yet disposed of,
(b) an administration application has been made and is not yet disposed of, or
(c) an administrative receiver of the company is in office.

Notice of intention to appoint

26.—(1) A person who proposes to make an appointment under paragraph 22 shall give at least five business days' written notice to—
(a) any person who is or may be entitled to appoint an administrative receiver of the company, and
(b) any person who is or may be entitled to appoint an administrator of the company under paragraph 14.

(2) A person who proposes to make an appointment under paragraph 22 shall also give such notice as may be prescribed to such other persons as may be prescribed.

(3) A notice under this paragraph must—
(a) identify the proposed administrator, and
(b) be in the prescribed form.

27.—(1) A person who gives notice of intention to appoint under paragraph 26 shall file with the court as soon as is reasonably practicable a copy of—
(a) the notice, and
(b) any document accompanying it.

(2) The copy filed under sub-paragraph (1) must be accompanied by a statutory declaration made by or on behalf of the person who proposes to make the appointment—
(a) that the company is or is likely to become unable to pay its debts,
(b) that the company is not in liquidation, and
(c) that, so far as the person making the statement is able to ascertain, the appointment is not prevented by paragraphs 23 to 25, and
(d) to such additional effect, and giving such information, as may be prescribed.

(3) A statutory declaration under sub-paragraph (2) must—
(a) be in the prescribed form, and
(b) be made during the prescribed period.

(4) A person commits an offence if in a statutory declaration under sub-paragraph (2) he makes a statement—
(a) which is false, and
(b) which he does not reasonably believe to be true.

28.—(1) An appointment may not be made under paragraph 22 unless the person who makes the appointment has complied with any requirement of paragraphs 26 and 27 and—
(a) the period of notice specified in paragraph 26(1) has expired, or

(b) each person to whom notice has been given under paragraph 26(1) has consented in writing to the making of the appointment.

(2) An appointment may not be made under paragraph 22 after the period of ten business days beginning with the date on which the notice of intention to appoint is filed under paragraph 27(1).

Notice of appointment

29.—(1) A person who appoints an administrator of a company under paragraph 22 shall file with the court—

(a) a notice of appointment, and
(b) such other documents as may be prescribed.

(2) The notice of appointment must include a statutory declaration by or on behalf of the person who makes the appointment—

(a) that the person is entitled to make an appointment under paragraph 22,
(b) that the appointment is in accordance with this Schedule, and
(c) that, so far as the person making the statement is able to ascertain, the statements made and information given in the statutory declaration filed with the notice of intention to appoint remain accurate.

(3) The notice of appointment must identify the administrator and must be accompanied by a statement by the administrator—

(a) that he consents to the appointment,
(b) that in his opinion the purpose of administration is reasonably likely to be achieved, and
(c) giving such other information and opinions as may be prescribed.

(4) For the purpose of a statement under sub-paragraph (3) an administrator may rely on information supplied by directors of the company (unless he has reason to doubt its accuracy).

(5) The notice of appointment and any document accompanying it must be in the prescribed form.

(6) A statutory declaration under sub-paragraph (2) must be made during the prescribed period.

(7) A person commits an offence if in a statutory declaration under sub-paragraph (2) he makes a statement—

(a) which is false, and
(b) which he does not reasonably believe to be true.

30. In a case in which no person is entitled to notice of intention to appoint under paragraph 26(1) (and paragraph 28 therefore does not apply)—

(a) the statutory declaration accompanying the notice of appointment must include the statements and information required under paragraph 27(2), and
(b) paragraph 29(2)(c) shall not apply.

Commencement of appointment

31. The appointment of an administrator under paragraph 22 takes effect when the requirements of paragraph 29 are satisfied.

32. A person who appoints an administrator under paragraph 22—

(a) shall notify the administrator and such other persons as may be prescribed as soon as is reasonably practicable after the requirements of paragraph 29 are satisfied, and
(b) commits an offence if he fails without reasonable excuse to comply with paragraph (a).

33. If before the requirements of paragraph 29 are satisfied the company enters administration by virtue of an administration order or an appointment under paragraph 14—

(a) the appointment under paragraph 22 shall not take effect, and
(b) paragraph 32 shall not apply.

Invalid appointment: indemnity

34.—(1) This paragraph applies where—
(a) a person purports to appoint an administrator under paragraph 22, and
(b) the appointment is discovered to be invalid.

(2) The court may order the person who purported to make the appointment to indemnify the person appointed against liability which arises solely by reason of the appointment's invalidity.

ADMINISTRATION APPLICATION—SPECIAL CASES

Application by holder of floating charge

35.—(1) This paragraph applies where an administration application in respect of a company—
(a) is made by the holder of a qualifying floating charge in respect of the company's property, and
(b) includes a statement that the application is made in reliance on this paragraph.

(2) The court may make an administration order—
(a) whether or not satisfied that the company is or is likely to become unable to pay its debts, but
(b) only if satisfied that the applicant could appoint an administrator under paragraph 14.

Intervention by holder of floating charge

36.—(1) This paragraph applies where—
(a) an administration application in respect of a company is made by a person who is not the holder of a qualifying floating charge in respect of the company's property, and
(b) the holder of a qualifying floating charge in respect of the company's property applies to the court to have a specified person appointed as administrator (and not the person specified by the administration applicant).

(2) The court shall grant an application under sub-paragraph (1)(b) unless the court thinks it right to refuse the application because of the particular circumstances of the case.

Application where company in liquidation

37.—(1) This paragraph applies where the holder of a qualifying floating charge in respect of a company's property could appoint an administrator under paragraph 14 but for paragraph 8(1)(b).

(2) The holder of the qualifying floating charge may make an administration application.

(3) If the court makes an administration order on hearing an application made by virtue of sub-paragraph (2)—
(a) the court shall discharge the winding-up order,
(b) the court shall make provision for such matters as may be prescribed,
(c) the court may make other consequential provision,
(d) the court shall specify which of the powers under this Schedule are to be exercisable by the administrator, and
(e) this Schedule shall have effect with such modifications as the court may specify.

38.—(1) The liquidator of a company may make an administration application.

(2) If the court makes an administration order on hearing an application made by virtue of sub-paragraph (1)—
(a) the court shall discharge any winding-up order in respect of the company,
(b) the court shall make provision for such matters as may be prescribed,
(c) the court may make other consequential provision,
(d) the court shall specify which of the powers under this Schedule are to be exercisable by the administrator, and

(e) this Schedule shall have effect with such modifications as the court may specify.

Effect of administrative receivership

39.—(1) Where there is an administrative receiver of a company the court must dismiss an administration application in respect of the company unless—

(a) the person by or on behalf of whom the receiver was appointed consents to the making of the administration order,

(b) the court thinks that the security by virtue of which the receiver was appointed would be liable to be released or discharged under sections 238 to 240 (transaction at undervalue and preference) if an administration order were made,

(c) the court thinks that the security by virtue of which the receiver was appointed would be avoided under section 245 (avoidance of floating charge) if an administration order were made, or

(d) the court thinks that the security by virtue of which the receiver was appointed would be challengeable under section 242 (gratuitous alienations) or 243 (unfair preferences) or under any rule of law in Scotland.

(2) Sub-paragraph (1) applies whether the administrative receiver is appointed before or after the making of the administration application.

EFFECT OF ADMINISTRATION

Dismissal of pending winding-up petition

40.—(1) A petition for the winding up of a company—

(a) shall be dismissed on the making of an administration order in respect of the company, and

(b) shall be suspended while the company is in administration following an appointment under paragraph 14.

(2) Sub-paragraph (1)(b) does not apply to a petition presented under—

(a) section 124A (public interest),

[(aa) section 124B (SEs),] or

(b) section 367 of the Financial Services and Markets Act 2000 (c 8) (petition by Financial Services Authority).

(3) Where an administrator becomes aware that a petition was presented under a provision referred to in sub-paragraph (2) before his appointment, he shall apply to the court for directions under paragraph 63.

Dismissal of administrative or other receiver

41.—(1) When an administration order takes effect in respect of a company any administrative receiver of the company shall vacate office.

(2) Where a company is in administration, any receiver of part of the company's property shall vacate office if the administrator requires him to.

(3) Where an administrative receiver or receiver vacates office under sub-paragraph (1) or (2)—

(a) his remuneration shall be charged on and paid out of any property of the company which was in his custody or under his control immediately before he vacated office, and

(b) he need not take any further steps under section 40 or 59.

(4) In the application of sub-paragraph (3)(a)—

(a) "remuneration" includes expenses properly incurred and any indemnity to which the administrative receiver or receiver is entitled out of the assets of the company,

(b) the charge imposed takes priority over security held by the person by whom or on whose behalf the administrative receiver or receiver was appointed, and

(c) the provision for payment is subject to paragraph 43.

Moratorium on insolvency proceedings

42.—(1) This paragraph applies to a company in administration.

(2) No resolution may be passed for the winding up of the company.

(3) No order may be made for the winding up of the company.

(4) Sub-paragraph (3) does not apply to an order made on a petition presented under—
(a) section 124A (public interest),
[(aa) section 124B (SEs),] or
(b) section 367 of the Financial Services and Markets Act 2000 (c 8) (petition by Financial Services Authority).

(5) If a petition presented under a provision referred to in sub-paragraph (4) comes to the attention of the administrator, he shall apply to the court for directions under paragraph 63.

Moratorium on other legal process

43.—(1) This paragraph applies to a company in administration.

(2) No step may be taken to enforce security over the company's property except—
(a) with the consent of the administrator, or
(b) with the permission of the court.

(3) No step may be taken to repossess goods in the company's possession under a hire-purchase agreement except—
(a) with the consent of the administrator, or
(b) with the permission of the court.

(4) A landlord may not exercise a right of forfeiture by peaceable re-entry in relation to premises let to the company except—
(a) with the consent of the administrator, or
(b) with the permission of the court.

(5) In Scotland, a landlord may not exercise a right of irritancy in relation to premises let to the company except—
(a) with the consent of the administrator, or
(b) with the permission of the court.

(6) No legal process (including legal proceedings, execution, distress and diligence) may be instituted or continued against the company or property of the company except—
(a) with the consent of the administrator, or
(b) with the permission of the court.

[(6A) An administrative receiver of the company may not be appointed.]

(7) Where the court gives permission for a transaction under this paragraph it may impose a condition on or a requirement in connection with the transaction.

(8) In this paragraph "landlord" includes a person to whom rent is payable.

Interim moratorium

44.—(1) This paragraph applies where an administration application in respect of a company has been made and—
(a) the application has not yet been granted or dismissed, or
(b) the application has been granted but the administration order has not yet taken effect.

(2) This paragraph also applies from the time when a copy of notice of intention to appoint an administrator under paragraph 14 is filed with the court until—
(a) the appointment of the administrator takes effect, or
(b) the period of five business days beginning with the date of filing expires without an administrator having been appointed.

(3) Sub-paragraph (2) has effect in relation to a notice of intention to appoint only if it is in the prescribed form.

(4) This paragraph also applies from the time when a copy of notice of intention to appoint an administrator is filed with the court under paragraph 27(1) until—

(a) the appointment of the administrator takes effect, or

(b) the period specified in paragraph 28(2) expires without an administrator having been appointed.

(5) The provisions of paragraphs 42 and 43 shall apply (ignoring any reference to the consent of the administrator).

(6) If there is an administrative receiver of the company when the administration application is made, the provisions of paragraphs 42 and 43 shall not begin to apply by virtue of this paragraph until the person by or on behalf of whom the receiver was appointed consents to the making of the administration order.

(7) This paragraph does not prevent or require the permission of the court for—

(a) the presentation of a petition for the winding up of the company under a provision mentioned in paragraph 42(4),

(b) the appointment of an administrator under paragraph 14,

(c) the appointment of an administrative receiver of the company, or

(d) the carrying out by an administrative receiver (whenever appointed) of his functions.

Publicity

45.—(1) While a company is in administration every business document issued by or on behalf of the company or the administrator must state—

(a) the name of the administrator, and

(b) that the affairs, business and property of the company are being managed by him.

(2) Any of the following commits an offence if without reasonable excuse he authorises or permits a contravention of sub-paragraph (1)—

(a) the administrator,

(b) an officer of the company, and

(c) the company.

(3) In sub-paragraph (1) "business document" means—

(a) an invoice,

(b) an order for goods or services, and

(c) a business letter.

PROCESS OF ADMINISTRATION

Announcement of administrator's appointment

46.—(1) This paragraph applies where a person becomes the administrator of a company.

(2) As soon as is reasonably practicable the administrator shall—

(a) send a notice of his appointment to the company, and

(b) publish a notice of his appointment in the prescribed manner.

(3) As soon as is reasonably practicable the administrator shall—

(a) obtain a list of the company's creditors, and

(b) send a notice of his appointment to each creditor of whose claim and address he is aware.

(4) The administrator shall send a notice of his appointment to the registrar of companies before the end of the period of 7 days beginning with the date specified in sub-paragraph (6).

(5) The administrator shall send a notice of his appointment to such persons as may be prescribed before the end of the prescribed period beginning with the date specified in sub-paragraph (6).

(6) The date for the purpose of sub-paragraphs (4) and (5) is—

(a) in the case of an administrator appointed by administration order, the date of the order,

(b) in the case of an administrator appointed under paragraph 14, the date on which he receives notice under paragraph 20, and

(c) in the case of an administrator appointed under paragraph 22, the date on which he receives notice under paragraph 32.

(7) The court may direct that sub-paragraph (3)(b) or (5)—
(a) shall not apply, or
(b) shall apply with the substitution of a different period.

(8) A notice under this paragraph must—
(a) contain the prescribed information, and
(b) be in the prescribed form.

(9) An administrator commits an offence if he fails without reasonable excuse to comply with a requirement of this paragraph.

Statement of company's affairs

47.—(1) As soon as is reasonably practicable after appointment the administrator of a company shall by notice in the prescribed form require one or more relevant persons to provide the administrator with a statement of the affairs of the company.

(2) The statement must—
(a) be verified by a statement of truth in accordance with Civil Procedure Rules,
(b) be in the prescribed form,
(c) give particulars of the company's property, debts and liabilities,
(d) give the names and addresses of the company's creditors,
(e) specify the security held by each creditor,
(f) give the date on which each security was granted, and
(g) contain such other information as may be prescribed.

(3) In sub-paragraph (1) "relevant person" means—
(a) a person who is or has been an officer of the company,
(b) a person who took part in the formation of the company during the period of one year ending with the date on which the company enters administration,
(c) a person employed by the company during that period, and
(d) a person who is or has been during that period an officer or employee of a company which is or has been during that year an officer of the company.

(4) For the purpose of sub-paragraph (3) a reference to employment is a reference to employment through a contract of employment or a contract for services.

(5) In Scotland, a statement of affairs under sub-paragraph (1) must be a statutory declaration made in accordance with the Statutory Declarations Act 1835 (c 62) (and sub-paragraph (2)(a) shall not apply).

48.—(1) A person required to submit a statement of affairs must do so before the end of the period of 11 days beginning with the day on which he receives notice of the requirement.

(2) The administrator may—
(a) revoke a requirement under paragraph 47(1), or
(b) extend the period specified in sub-paragraph (1) (whether before or after expiry).

(3) If the administrator refuses a request to act under sub-paragraph (2)—
(a) the person whose request is refused may apply to the court, and
(b) the court may take action of a kind specified in sub-paragraph (2).

(4) A person commits an offence if he fails without reasonable excuse to comply with a requirement under paragraph 47(1).

Administrator's proposals

49.—(1) The administrator of a company shall make a statement setting out proposals for achieving the purpose of administration.

(2) A statement under sub-paragraph (1) must, in particular—
(a) deal with such matters as may be prescribed, and
(b) where applicable, explain why the administrator thinks that the objective mentioned in paragraph 3(1)(a) or (b) cannot be achieved.

(3) Proposals under this paragraph may include—

(a) a proposal for a voluntary arrangement under Part I of this Act (although this paragraph is without prejudice to section 4(3));
(b) a proposal for a compromise or arrangement to be sanctioned under section 425 of the Companies Act (compromise with creditors or members).

(4) The administrator shall send a copy of the statement of his proposals—
(a) to the registrar of companies,
(b) to every creditor of the company of whose claim and address he is aware, and
(c) to every member of the company of whose address he is aware.

(5) The administrator shall comply with sub-paragraph (4)—
(a) as soon as is reasonably practicable after the company enters administration, and
(b) in any event, before the end of the period of eight weeks beginning with the day on which the company enters administration.

(6) The administrator shall be taken to comply with sub-paragraph (4)(c) if he publishes in the prescribed manner a notice undertaking to provide a copy of the statement of proposals free of charge to any member of the company who applies in writing to a specified address.

(7) An administrator commits an offence if he fails without reasonable excuse to comply with sub-paragraph (5).

(8) A period specified in this paragraph may be varied in accordance with paragraph 107.

Creditors' meeting

50.—(1) In this Schedule "creditors' meeting" means a meeting of creditors of a company summoned by the administrator—
(a) in the prescribed manner, and
(b) giving the prescribed period of notice to every creditor of the company of whose claim and address he is aware.

(2) A period prescribed under sub-paragraph (1)(b) may be varied in accordance with paragraph 107.

(3) A creditors' meeting shall be conducted in accordance with the rules.

Requirement for initial creditors' meeting

51.—(1) Each copy of an administrator's statement of proposals sent to a creditor under paragraph 49(4)(b) must be accompanied by an invitation to a creditors' meeting (an "initial creditors' meeting").

(2) The date set for an initial creditors' meeting must be—
(a) as soon as is reasonably practicable after the company enters administration, and
(b) in any event, within the period of ten weeks beginning with the date on which the company enters administration.

(3) An administrator shall present a copy of his statement of proposals to an initial creditors' meeting.

(4) A period specified in this paragraph may be varied in accordance with paragraph 107.

(5) An administrator commits an offence if he fails without reasonable excuse to comply with a requirement of this paragraph.

52.—(1) Paragraph 51(1) shall not apply where the statement of proposals states that the administrator thinks—
(a) that the company has sufficient property to enable each creditor of the company to be paid in full,
(b) that the company has insufficient property to enable a distribution to be made to unsecured creditors other than by virtue of section 176A(2)(a), or
(c) that neither of the objectives specified in paragraph 3(1)(a) and (b) can be achieved.

(2) But the administrator shall summon an initial creditors' meeting if it is requested—
(a) by creditors of the company whose debts amount to at least 10% of the total debts of the company,
(b) in the prescribed manner, and

(c) in the prescribed period.

(3) A meeting requested under sub-paragraph (2) must be summoned for a date in the prescribed period.

(4) The period prescribed under sub-paragraph (3) may be varied in accordance with paragraph 107.

Business and result of initial creditors' meeting

53.—(1) An initial creditors' meeting to which an administrator's proposals are presented shall consider them and may—
(a) approve them without modification, or
(b) approve them with modification to which the administrator consents.

(2) After the conclusion of an initial creditors' meeting the administrator shall as soon as is reasonably practicable report any decision taken to—
(a) the court,
(b) the registrar of companies, and
(c) such other persons as may be prescribed.

(3) An administrator commits an offence if he fails without reasonable excuse to comply with sub-paragraph (2).

Revision of administrator's proposals

54.—(1) This paragraph applies where—
(a) an administrator's proposals have been approved (with or without modification) at an initial creditors' meeting,
(b) the administrator proposes a revision to the proposals, and
(c) the administrator thinks that the proposed revision is substantial.

(2) The administrator shall—
(a) summon a creditors' meeting,
(b) send a statement in the prescribed form of the proposed revision with the notice of the meeting sent to each creditor,
(c) send a copy of the statement, within the prescribed period, to each member of the company of whose address he is aware, and
(d) present a copy of the statement to the meeting.

(3) The administrator shall be taken to have complied with sub-paragraph (2)(c) if he publishes a notice undertaking to provide a copy of the statement free of charge to any member of the company who applies in writing to a specified address.

(4) A notice under sub-paragraph (3) must be published—
(a) in the prescribed manner, and
(b) within the prescribed period.

(5) A creditors' meeting to which a proposed revision is presented shall consider it and may—
(a) approve it without modification, or
(b) approve it with modification to which the administrator consents.

(6) After the conclusion of a creditors' meeting the administrator shall as soon as is reasonably practicable report any decision taken to—
(a) the court,
(b) the registrar of companies, and
(c) such other persons as may be prescribed.

(7) An administrator commits an offence if he fails without reasonable excuse to comply with sub-paragraph (6).

Failure to obtain approval of administrator's proposals

55.—(1) This paragraph applies where an administrator reports to the court that—
(a) an initial creditors' meeting has failed to approve the administrator's proposals presented to it, or

(b) a creditors' meeting has failed to approve a revision of the administrator's proposals presented to it.

(2) The court may—

(a) provide that the appointment of an administrator shall cease to have effect from a specified time;

(b) adjourn the hearing conditionally or unconditionally;

(c) make an interim order;

(d) make an order on a petition for winding up suspended by virtue of paragraph 40(1)(b);

(e) make any other order (including an order making consequential provision) that the court thinks appropriate.

Further creditors' meetings

56.—(1) The administrator of a company shall summon a creditors' meeting if—

(a) it is requested in the prescribed manner by creditors of the company whose debts amount to at least 10% of the total debts of the company, or

(b) he is directed by the court to summon a creditors' meeting.

(2) An administrator commits an offence if he fails without reasonable excuse to summon a creditors' meeting as required by this paragraph.

Creditors' committee

57.—(1) A creditors' meeting may establish a creditors' committee.

(2) A creditors' committee shall carry out functions conferred on it by or under this Act.

(3) A creditors' committee may require the administrator—

(a) to attend on the committee at any reasonable time of which he is given at least seven days' notice, and

(b) to provide the committee with information about the exercise of his functions.

Correspondence instead of creditors' meeting

58.—(1) Anything which is required or permitted by or under this Schedule to be done at a creditors' meeting may be done by correspondence between the administrator and creditors—

(a) in accordance with the rules, and

(b) subject to any prescribed condition.

(2) A reference in this Schedule to anything done at a creditors' meeting includes a reference to anything done in the course of correspondence in reliance on sub-paragraph (1).

(3) A requirement to hold a creditors' meeting is satisfied by conducting correspondence in accordance with this paragraph.

FUNCTIONS OF ADMINISTRATOR

General powers

59.—(1) The administrator of a company may do anything necessary or expedient for the management of the affairs, business and property of the company.

(2) A provision of this Schedule which expressly permits the administrator to do a specified thing is without prejudice to the generality of sub-paragraph (1).

(3) A person who deals with the administrator of a company in good faith and for value need not inquire whether the administrator is acting within his powers.

60. The administrator of a company has the powers specified in Schedule 1 to this Act.

61. The administrator of a company—

(a) may remove a director of the company, and

(b) may appoint a director of the company (whether or not to fill a vacancy).

62. The administrator of a company may call a meeting of members or creditors of the company.

63. The administrator of a company may apply to the court for directions in connection with his functions.

64.—(1) A company in administration or an officer of a company in administration may not exercise a management power without the consent of the administrator.

(2) For the purpose of sub-paragraph (1)—

(a) "management power" means a power which could be exercised so as to interfere with the exercise of the administrator's powers,

(b) it is immaterial whether the power is conferred by an enactment or an instrument, and

(c) consent may be general or specific.

Distribution

65.—(1) The administrator of a company may make a distribution to a creditor of the company.

(2) Section 175 shall apply in relation to a distribution under this paragraph as it applies in relation to a winding up.

(3) A payment may not be made by way of distribution under this paragraph to a creditor of the company who is neither secured nor preferential unless the court gives permission.

66. The administrator of a company may make a payment otherwise than in accordance with paragraph 65 or paragraph 13 of Schedule 1 if he thinks it likely to assist achievement of the purpose of administration.

General duties

67. The administrator of a company shall on his appointment take custody or control of all the property to which he thinks the company is entitled.

68.—(1) Subject to sub-paragraph (2), the administrator of a company shall manage its affairs, business and property in accordance with—

(a) any proposals approved under paragraph 53,

(b) any revision of those proposals which is made by him and which he does not consider substantial, and

(c) any revision of those proposals approved under paragraph 54.

(2) If the court gives directions to the administrator of a company in connection with any aspect of his management of the company's affairs, business or property, the administrator shall comply with the directions.

(3) The court may give directions under sub-paragraph (2) only if—

(a) no proposals have been approved under paragraph 53,

(b) the directions are consistent with any proposals or revision approved under paragraph 53 or 54,

(c) the court thinks the directions are required in order to reflect a change in circumstances since the approval of proposals or a revision under paragraph 53 or 54, or

(d) the court thinks the directions are desirable because of a misunderstanding about proposals or a revision approved under paragraph 53 or 54.

Administrator as agent of company

69. In exercising his functions under this Schedule the administrator of a company acts as its agent.

Charged property: floating charge

70.—(1) The administrator of a company may dispose of or take action relating to property which is subject to a floating charge as if it were not subject to the charge.

(2) Where property is disposed of in reliance on sub-paragraph (1) the holder of the floating charge shall have the same priority in respect of acquired property as he had in respect of the property disposed of.

(3) In sub-paragraph (2) "acquired property" means property of the company which directly or indirectly represents the property disposed of.

Charged property: non-floating charge

71.—(1) The court may by order enable the administrator of a company to dispose of property which is subject to a security (other than a floating charge) as if it were not subject to the security.

(2) An order under sub-paragraph (1) may be made only—
- (a) on the application of the administrator, and
- (b) where the court thinks that disposal of the property would be likely to promote the purpose of administration in respect of the company.

(3) An order under this paragraph is subject to the condition that there be applied towards discharging the sums secured by the security—
- (a) the net proceeds of disposal of the property, and
- (b) any additional money required to be added to the net proceeds so as to produce the amount determined by the court as the net amount which would be realised on a sale of the property at market value.

(4) If an order under this paragraph relates to more than one security, application of money under sub-paragraph (3) shall be in the order of the priorities of the securities.

(5) An administrator who makes a successful application for an order under this paragraph shall send a copy of the order to the registrar of companies before the end of the period of 14 days starting with the date of the order.

(6) An administrator commits an offence if he fails to comply with sub-paragraph (5) without reasonable excuse.

Hire-purchase property

72.—(1) The court may by order enable the administrator of a company to dispose of goods which are in the possession of the company under a hire-purchase agreement as if all the rights of the owner under the agreement were vested in the company.

(2) An order under sub-paragraph (1) may be made only—
- (a) on the application of the administrator, and
- (b) where the court thinks that disposal of the goods would be likely to promote the purpose of administration in respect of the company.

(3) An order under this paragraph is subject to the condition that there be applied towards discharging the sums payable under the hire-purchase agreement—
- (a) the net proceeds of disposal of the goods, and
- (b) any additional money required to be added to the net proceeds so as to produce the amount determined by the court as the net amount which would be realised on a sale of the goods at market value.

(4) An administrator who makes a successful application for an order under this paragraph shall send a copy of the order to the registrar of companies before the end of the period of 14 days starting with the date of the order.

(5) An administrator commits an offence if he fails without reasonable excuse to comply with sub-paragraph (4).

Protection for secured or preferential creditor

73.—(1) An administrator's statement of proposals under paragraph 49 may not include any action which—

(a) affects the right of a secured creditor of the company to enforce his security,
(b) would result in a preferential debt of the company being paid otherwise than in priority to its non-preferential debts, or
(c) would result in one preferential creditor of the company being paid a smaller proportion of his debt than another.

(2) Sub-paragraph (1) does not apply to—
(a) action to which the relevant creditor consents,
(b) a proposal for a voluntary arrangement under Part I of this Act (although this sub-paragraph is without prejudice to section 4(3)), or
(c) a proposal for a compromise or arrangement to be sanctioned under section 425 of the Companies Act (compromise with creditors or members).

(3) The reference to a statement of proposals in sub-paragraph (1) includes a reference to a statement as revised or modified.

Challenge to administrator's conduct of company

74.—(1) A creditor or member of a company in administration may apply to the court claiming that—
(a) the administrator is acting or has acted so as unfairly to harm the interests of the applicant (whether alone or in common with some or all other members or creditors), or
(b) the administrator proposes to act in a way which would unfairly harm the interests of the applicant (whether alone or in common with some or all other members or creditors).

(2) A creditor or member of a company in administration may apply to the court claiming that the administrator is not performing his functions as quickly or as efficiently as is reasonably practicable.

(3) The court may—
(a) grant relief;
(b) dismiss the application;
(c) adjourn the hearing conditionally or unconditionally;
(d) make an interim order;
(e) make any other order it thinks appropriate.

(4) In particular, an order under this paragraph may—
(a) regulate the administrator's exercise of his functions;
(b) require the administrator to do or not do a specified thing;
(c) require a creditors' meeting to be held for a specified purpose;
(d) provide for the appointment of an administrator to cease to have effect;
(e) make consequential provision.

(5) An order may be made on a claim under sub-paragraph (1) whether or not the action complained of—
(a) is within the administrator's powers under this Schedule;
(b) was taken in reliance on an order under paragraph 71 or 72.

(6) An order may not be made under this paragraph if it would impede or prevent the implementation of—
(a) a voluntary arrangement approved under Part I,
(b) a compromise or arrangement sanctioned under section 425 of the Companies Act (compromise with creditors and members), or
(c) proposals or a revision approved under paragraph 53 or 54 more than 28 days before the day on which the application for the order under this paragraph is made.

Misfeasance

75.—(1) The court may examine the conduct of a person who—
(a) is or purports to be the administrator of a company, or
(b) has been or has purported to be the administrator of a company.

(2) An examination under this paragraph may be held only on the application of—
(a) the official receiver,

(b) the administrator of the company,
(c) the liquidator of the company,
(d) a creditor of the company, or
(e) a contributory of the company.

(3) An application under sub-paragraph (2) must allege that the administrator—
(a) has misapplied or retained money or other property of the company,
(b) has become accountable for money or other property of the company,
(c) has breached a fiduciary or other duty in relation to the company, or
(d) has been guilty of misfeasance.

(4) On an examination under this paragraph into a person's conduct the court may order him—
(a) to repay, restore or account for money or property;
(b) to pay interest;
(c) to contribute a sum to the company's property by way of compensation for breach of duty or misfeasance.

(5) In sub-paragraph (3) "administrator" includes a person who purports or has purported to be a company's administrator.

(6) An application under sub-paragraph (2) may be made in respect of an administrator who has been discharged under paragraph 98 only with the permission of the court.

ENDING ADMINISTRATION

Automatic end of administration

76.—(1) The appointment of an administrator shall cease to have effect at the end of the period of one year beginning with the date on which it takes effect.

(2) But—
(a) on the application of an administrator the court may by order extend his term of office for a specified period, and
(b) an administrator's term of office may be extended for a specified period not exceeding six months by consent.

77.—(1) An order of the court under paragraph 76—
(a) may be made in respect of an administrator whose term of office has already been extended by order or by consent, but
(b) may not be made after the expiry of the administrator's term of office.

(2) Where an order is made under paragraph 76 the administrator shall as soon as is reasonably practicable notify the registrar of companies.

(3) An administrator who fails without reasonable excuse to comply with sub-paragraph (2) commits an offence.

78.—(1) In paragraph 76(2)(b) "consent" means consent of—
(a) each secured creditor of the company, and
(b) if the company has unsecured debts, creditors whose debts amount to more than 50% of the company's unsecured debts, disregarding debts of any creditor who does not respond to an invitation to give or withhold consent.

(2) But where the administrator has made a statement under paragraph 52(1)(b) "consent" means—
(a) consent of each secured creditor of the company, or
(b) if the administrator thinks that a distribution may be made to preferential creditors, consent of—
(i) each secured creditor of the company, and
(ii) preferential creditors whose debts amount to more than 50% of the preferential debts of the company, disregarding debts of any creditor who does not respond to an invitation to give or withhold consent.

(3) Consent for the purposes of paragraph 76(2)(b) may be—
(a) written, or
(b) signified at a creditors' meeting.

(4) An administrator's term of office—

(a) may be extended by consent only once,
(b) may not be extended by consent after extension by order of the court, and
(c) may not be extended by consent after expiry.

(5) Where an administrator's term of office is extended by consent he shall as soon as is reasonably practicable—
(a) file notice of the extension with the court, and
(b) notify the registrar of companies.

(6) An administrator who fails without reasonable excuse to comply with sub-paragraph (5) commits an offence.

Court ending administration on application of administrator

79.—(1) On the application of the administrator of a company the court may provide for the appointment of an administrator of the company to cease to have effect from a specified time.

(2) The administrator of a company shall make an application under this paragraph if—
(a) he thinks the purpose of administration cannot be achieved in relation to the company,
(b) he thinks the company should not have entered administration, or
(c) a creditors' meeting requires him to make an application under this paragraph.

(3) The administrator of a company shall make an application under this paragraph if—
(a) the administration is pursuant to an administration order, and
(b) the administrator thinks that the purpose of administration has been sufficiently achieved in relation to the company.

(4) On an application under this paragraph the court may—
(a) adjourn the hearing conditionally or unconditionally;
(b) dismiss the application;
(c) make an interim order;
(d) make any order it thinks appropriate (whether in addition to, in consequence of or instead of the order applied for).

Termination of administration where objective achieved

80.—(1) This paragraph applies where an administrator of a company is appointed under paragraph 14 or 22.

(2) If the administrator thinks that the purpose of administration has been sufficiently achieved in relation to the company he may file a notice in the prescribed form—
(a) with the court, and
(b) with the registrar of companies.

(3) The administrator's appointment shall cease to have effect when the requirements of sub-paragraph (2) are satisfied.

(4) Where the administrator files a notice he shall within the prescribed period send a copy to every creditor of the company of whose claim and address he is aware.

(5) The rules may provide that the administrator is taken to have complied with sub-paragraph (4) if before the end of the prescribed period he publishes in the prescribed manner a notice undertaking to provide a copy of the notice under sub-paragraph (2) to any creditor of the company who applies in writing to a specified address.

(6) An administrator who fails without reasonable excuse to comply with sub-paragraph (4) commits an offence.

Court ending administration on application of creditor

81.—(1) On the application of a creditor of a company the court may provide for the appointment of an administrator of the company to cease to have effect at a specified time.

(2) An application under this paragraph must allege an improper motive—
(a) in the case of an administrator appointed by administration order, on the part of the applicant for the order, or

(b) in any other case, on the part of the person who appointed the administrator.

(3) On an application under this paragraph the court may—

(a) adjourn the hearing conditionally or unconditionally;

(b) dismiss the application;

(c) make an interim order;

(d) make any order it thinks appropriate (whether in addition to, in consequence of or instead of the order applied for).

Public interest winding-up

82.—(1) This paragraph applies where a winding-up order is made for the winding up of a company in administration on a petition presented under—

(a) section 124A (public interest),

[(aa) section 124B (SEs),] or

(b) section 367 of the Financial Services and Markets Act 2000 (c 8) (petition by Financial Services Authority).

(2) This paragraph also applies where a provisional liquidator of a company in administration is appointed following the presentation of a petition under any of the provisions listed in sub-paragraph (1).

(3) The court shall order—

(a) that the appointment of the administrator shall cease to have effect, or

(b) that the appointment of the administrator shall continue to have effect.

(4) If the court makes an order under sub-paragraph (3)(b) it may also—

(a) specify which of the powers under this Schedule are to be exercisable by the administrator, and

(b) order that this Schedule shall have effect in relation to the administrator with specified modifications.

Moving from administration to creditors' voluntary liquidation

83.—(1) This paragraph applies in England and Wales where the administrator of a company thinks—

(a) that the total amount which each secured creditor of the company is likely to receive has been paid to him or set aside for him, and

(b) that a distribution will be made to unsecured creditors of the company (if there are any).

(2) This paragraph applies in Scotland where the administrator of a company thinks—

(a) that each secured creditor of the company will receive payment in respect of his debt, and

(b) that a distribution will be made to unsecured creditors (if there are any).

(3) The administrator may send to the registrar of companies a notice that this paragraph applies.

(4) On receipt of a notice under sub-paragraph (3) the registrar shall register it.

(5) If an administrator sends a notice under sub-paragraph (3) he shall as soon as is reasonably practicable—

(a) file a copy of the notice with the court, and

(b) send a copy of the notice to each creditor of whose claim and address he is aware.

(6) On the registration of a notice under sub-paragraph (3)—

(a) the appointment of an administrator in respect of the company shall cease to have effect, and

(b) the company shall be wound up as if a resolution for voluntary winding up under section 84 were passed on the day on which the notice is registered.

(7) The liquidator for the purposes of the winding up shall be—

(a) a person nominated by the creditors of the company in the prescribed manner and within the prescribed period, or

(b) if no person is nominated under paragraph (a), the administrator.

(8) In the application of Part IV to a winding up by virtue of this paragraph—

(a) section 85 shall not apply,

(b) section 86 shall apply as if the reference to the time of the passing of the resolution for voluntary winding up were a reference to the beginning of the date of registration of the notice under sub-paragraph (3),
(c) section 89 does not apply,
(d) sections 98, 99 and 100 shall not apply,
(e) section 129 shall apply as if the reference to the time of the passing of the resolution for voluntary winding up were a reference to the beginning of the date of registration of the notice under sub-paragraph (3), and
(f) any creditors' committee which is in existence immediately before the company ceases to be in administration shall continue in existence after that time as if appointed as a liquidation committee under section 101.

Moving from administration to dissolution

84.—(1) If the administrator of a company thinks that the company has no property which might permit a distribution to its creditors, he shall send a notice to that effect to the registrar of companies.

(2) The court may on the application of the administrator of a company disapply sub-paragraph (1) in respect of the company.

(3) On receipt of a notice under sub-paragraph (1) the registrar shall register it.

(4) On the registration of a notice in respect of a company under sub-paragraph (1) the appointment of an administrator of the company shall cease to have effect.

(5) If an administrator sends a notice under sub-paragraph (1) he shall as soon as is reasonably practicable—
(a) file a copy of the notice with the court, and
(b) send a copy of the notice to each creditor of whose claim and address he is aware.

(6) At the end of the period of three months beginning with the date of registration of a notice in respect of a company under sub-paragraph (1) the company is deemed to be dissolved.

(7) On an application in respect of a company by the administrator or another interested person the court may—
(a) extend the period specified in sub-paragraph (6),
(b) suspend that period, or
(c) disapply sub-paragraph (6).

(8) Where an order is made under sub-paragraph (7) in respect of a company the administrator shall as soon as is reasonably practicable notify the registrar of companies.

(9) An administrator commits an offence if he fails without reasonable excuse to comply with sub-paragraph (5).

Discharge of administration order where administration ends

85.—(1) This paragraph applies where—
(a) the court makes an order under this Schedule providing for the appointment of an administrator of a company to cease to have effect, and
(b) the administrator was appointed by administration order.

(2) The court shall discharge the administration order.

Notice to Companies Registrar where administration ends

86.—(1) This paragraph applies where the court makes an order under this Schedule providing for the appointment of an administrator to cease to have effect.

(2) The administrator shall send a copy of the order to the registrar of companies within the period of 14 days beginning with the date of the order.

(3) An administrator who fails without reasonable excuse to comply with sub-paragraph (2) commits an offence.

REPLACING ADMINISTRATOR

Resignation of administrator

87.—(1) An administrator may resign only in prescribed circumstances.

(2) Where an administrator may resign he may do so only—

(a) in the case of an administrator appointed by administration order, by notice in writing to the court,

(b) in the case of an administrator appointed under paragraph 14, by notice in writing to the [holder of the floating charge by virtue of which the appointment was made],

(c) in the case of an administrator appointed under paragraph 22(1), by notice in writing to the company, or

(d) in the case of an administrator appointed under paragraph 22(2), by notice in writing to the directors of the company.

Removal of administrator from office

88. The court may by order remove an administrator from office.

Administrator ceasing to be qualified

89.—(1) The administrator of a company shall vacate office if he ceases to be qualified to act as an insolvency practitioner in relation to the company.

(2) Where an administrator vacates office by virtue of sub-paragraph (1) he shall give notice in writing—

(a) in the case of an administrator appointed by administration order, to the court,

(b) in the case of an administrator appointed under paragraph 14, to the [holder of the floating charge by virtue of which the appointment was made],

(c) in the case of an administrator appointed under paragraph 22(1), to the company, or

(d) in the case of an administrator appointed under paragraph 22(2), to the directors of the company.

(3) An administrator who fails without reasonable excuse to comply with sub-paragraph (2) commits an offence.

Supplying vacancy in office of administrator

90. Paragraphs 91 to 95 apply where an administrator—

(a) dies,

(b) resigns,

(c) is removed from office under paragraph 88, or

(d) vacates office under paragraph 89.

91.—(1) Where the administrator was appointed by administration order, the court may replace the administrator on an application under this sub-paragraph made by—

(a) a creditors' committee of the company,

(b) the company,

(c) the directors of the company,

(d) one or more creditors of the company, or

(e) where more than one person was appointed to act jointly or concurrently as the administrator, any of those persons who remains in office.

(2) But an application may be made in reliance on sub-paragraph (1)(b) to (d) only where—

(a) there is no creditors' committee of the company,

(b) the court is satisfied that the creditors' committee or a remaining administrator is not taking reasonable steps to make a replacement, or

(c) the court is satisfied that for another reason it is right for the application to be made.

92. Where the administrator was appointed under paragraph 14 the holder of the floating charge by virtue of which the appointment was made may replace the administrator.

93.—(1) Where the administrator was appointed under paragraph 22(1) by the company it may replace the administrator.

(2) A replacement under this paragraph may be made only—

(a) with the consent of each person who is the holder of a qualifying floating charge in respect of the company's property, or

(b) where consent is withheld, with the permission of the court.

94.—(1) Where the administrator was appointed under paragraph 22(2) the directors of the company may replace the administrator.

(2) A replacement under this paragraph may be made only—

(a) with the consent of each person who is the holder of a qualifying floating charge in respect of the company's property, or

(b) where consent is withheld, with the permission of the court.

95. The court may replace an administrator on the application of a person listed in paragraph 91(1) if the court—

(a) is satisfied that a person who is entitled to replace the administrator under any of paragraphs 92 to 94 is not taking reasonable steps to make a replacement, or

(b) that for another reason it is right for the court to make the replacement.

Substitution of administrator: competing floating charge-holder

96.—(1) This paragraph applies where an administrator of a company is appointed under paragraph 14 by the holder of a qualifying floating charge in respect of the company's property.

(2) The holder of a prior qualifying floating charge in respect of the company's property may apply to the court for the administrator to be replaced by an administrator nominated by the holder of the prior floating charge.

(3) One floating charge is prior to another for the purposes of this paragraph if—

(a) it was created first, or

(b) it is to be treated as having priority in accordance with an agreement to which the holder of each floating charge was party.

(4) Sub-paragraph (3) shall have effect in relation to Scotland as if the following were substituted for paragraph (a)—

"(a) it has priority of ranking in accordance with section 464(4)(b) of the Companies Act 1985 (c 6),

Substitution of administrator appointed by company or directors: creditors' meeting

97.—(1) This paragraph applies where—

(a) an administrator of a company is appointed by a company or directors under paragraph 22, and

(b) there is no holder of a qualifying floating charge in respect of the company's property.

(2) A creditors' meeting may replace the administrator.

(3) A creditors' meeting may act under sub-paragraph (2) only if the new administrator's written consent to act is presented to the meeting before the replacement is made.

Vacation of office: discharge from liability

98.—(1) Where a person ceases to be the administrator of a company (whether because he vacates office by reason of resignation, death or otherwise, because he is removed from office or because his appointment ceases to have effect) he is discharged from liability in respect of any action of his as administrator.

(2) The discharge provided by sub-paragraph (1) takes effect—

(a) in the case of an administrator who dies, on the filing with the court of notice of his death,
(b) in the case of an administrator appointed under paragraph 14 or 22, at a time appointed by resolution of the creditors' committee or, if there is no committee, by resolution of the creditors, or
(c) in any case, at a time specified by the court.

(3) For the purpose of the application of sub-paragraph (2)(b) in a case where the administrator has made a statement under paragraph 52(1)(b), a resolution shall be taken as passed if (and only if) passed with the approval of—
(a) each secured creditor of the company, or
(b) if the administrator has made a distribution to preferential creditors or thinks that a distribution may be made to preferential creditors—
(i) each secured creditor of the company, and
(ii) preferential creditors whose debts amount to more than 50% of the preferential debts of the company, disregarding debts of any creditor who does not respond to an invitation to give or withhold approval.

(4) Discharge—
(a) applies to liability accrued before the discharge takes effect, and
(b) does not prevent the exercise of the court's powers under paragraph 75.

Vacation of office: charges and liabilities

99.—(1) This paragraph applies where a person ceases to be the administrator of a company (whether because he vacates office by reason of resignation, death or otherwise, because he is removed from office or because his appointment ceases to have effect).

(2) In this paragraph—
"the former administrator" means the person referred to in sub-paragraph (1), and
"cessation" means the time when he ceases to be the company's administrator.

(3) The former administrator's remuneration and expenses shall be—
(a) charged on and payable out of property of which he had custody or control immediately before cessation, and
(b) payable in priority to any security to which paragraph 70 applies.

(4) A sum payable in respect of a debt or liability arising out of a contract entered into by the former administrator or a predecessor before cessation shall be—
(a) charged on and payable out of property of which the former administrator had custody or control immediately before cessation, and
(b) payable in priority to any charge arising under sub-paragraph (3).

(5) Sub-paragraph (4) shall apply to a liability arising under a contract of employment which was adopted by the former administrator or a predecessor before cessation; and for that purpose—
(a) action taken within the period of 14 days after an administrator's appointment shall not be taken to amount or contribute to the adoption of a contract,
(b) no account shall be taken of a liability which arises, or in so far as it arises, by reference to anything which is done or which occurs before the adoption of the contract of employment, and
(c) no account shall be taken of a liability to make a payment other than wages or salary.

(6) In sub-paragraph (5)(c) "wages or salary" includes—
(a) a sum payable in respect of a period of holiday (for which purpose the sum shall be treated as relating to the period by reference to which the entitlement to holiday accrued),
(b) a sum payable in respect of a period of absence through illness or other good cause,
(c) a sum payable in lieu of holiday,
(d) in respect of a period, a sum which would be treated as earnings for that period for the purposes of an enactment about social security, and
(e) a contribution to an occupational pension scheme.

GENERAL

Joint and concurrent administrators

100.—(1) In this Schedule—

(a) a reference to the appointment of an administrator of a company includes a reference to the appointment of a number of persons to act jointly or concurrently as the administrator of a company, and

(b) a reference to the appointment of a person as administrator of a company includes a reference to the appointment of a person as one of a number of persons to act jointly or concurrently as the administrator of a company.

(2) The appointment of a number of persons to act as administrator of a company must specify—

(a) which functions (if any) are to be exercised by the persons appointed acting jointly, and

(b) which functions (if any) are to be exercised by any or all of the persons appointed.

101.—(1) This paragraph applies where two or more persons are appointed to act jointly as the administrator of a company.

(2) A reference to the administrator of the company is a reference to those persons acting jointly.

(3) But a reference to the administrator of a company in paragraphs 87 to 99 of this Schedule is a reference to any or all of the persons appointed to act jointly.

(4) Where an offence of omission is committed by the administrator, each of the persons appointed to act jointly—

(a) commits the offence, and

(b) may be proceeded against and punished individually.

(5) The reference in paragraph 45(1)(a) to the name of the administrator is a reference to the name of each of the persons appointed to act jointly.

(6) Where persons are appointed to act jointly in respect of only some of the functions of the administrator of a company, this paragraph applies only in relation to those functions.

102.—(1) This paragraph applies where two or more persons are appointed to act concurrently as the administrator of a company.

(2) A reference to the administrator of a company in this Schedule is a reference to any of the persons appointed (or any combination of them).

103.—(1) Where a company is in administration, a person may be appointed to act as administrator jointly or concurrently with the person or persons acting as the administrator of the company.

(2) Where a company entered administration by administration order, an appointment under sub-paragraph (1) must be made by the court on the application of—

(a) a person or group listed in paragraph 12(1)(a) to (e), or

(b) the person or persons acting as the administrator of the company.

(3) Where a company entered administration by virtue of an appointment under paragraph 14, an appointment under sub-paragraph (1) must be made by—

(a) the holder of the floating charge by virtue of which the appointment was made, or

(b) the court on the application of the person or persons acting as the administrator of the company.

(4) Where a company entered administration by virtue of an appointment under paragraph 22(1), an appointment under sub-paragraph (1) above must be made either by the court on the application of the person or persons acting as the administrator of the company or—

(a) by the company, and

(b) with the consent of each person who is the holder of a qualifying floating charge in respect of the company's property or, where consent is withheld, with the permission of the court.

(5) Where a company entered administration by virtue of an appointment under paragraph 22(2), an appointment under sub-paragraph (1) must be made either by the court on the application of the person or persons acting as the administrator of the company or—

(a) by the directors of the company, and
(b) with the consent of each person who is the holder of a qualifying floating charge in respect of the company's property or, where consent is withheld, with the permission of the court.

(6) An appointment under sub-paragraph (1) may be made only with the consent of the person or persons acting as the administrator of the company.

Presumption of validity

104. An act of the administrator of a company is valid in spite of a defect in his appointment or qualification.

Majority decision of directors

105. A reference in this Schedule to something done by the directors of a company includes a reference to the same thing done by a majority of the directors of a company.

Penalties

106.—(1) A person who is guilty of an offence under this Schedule is liable to a fine (in accordance with section 430 and Schedule 10).

(2) A person who is guilty of an offence under any of the following paragraphs of this Schedule is liable to a daily default fine (in accordance with section 430 and Schedule 10)—

(a) paragraph 20,
(b) paragraph 32,
(c) paragraph 46,
(d) paragraph 48,
(e) paragraph 49,
(f) paragraph 51,
(g) paragraph 53,
(h) paragraph 54,
(i) paragraph 56,
(j) paragraph 71,
(k) paragraph 72,
(l) paragraph 77,
(m) paragraph 78,
(n) paragraph 80,
(o) paragraph 84,
(p) paragraph 86, and
(q) paragraph 89.

Extension of time limit

107.—(1) Where a provision of this Schedule provides that a period may be varied in accordance with this paragraph, the period may be varied in respect of a company—

(a) by the court, and
(b) on the application of the administrator.

(2) A time period may be extended in respect of a company under this paragraph—

(a) more than once, and
(b) after expiry.

108.—(1) A period specified in paragraph 49(5), 50(1)(b) or 51(2) may be varied in respect of a company by the administrator with consent.

(2) In sub-paragraph (1) "consent" means consent of—

(a) each secured creditor of the company, and
(b) if the company has unsecured debts, creditors whose debts amount to more than

50% of the company's unsecured debts, disregarding debts of any creditor who does not respond to an invitation to give or withhold consent.

(3) But where the administrator has made a statement under paragraph 52(1)(b) "consent" means—

(a) consent of each secured creditor of the company, or

(b) if the administrator thinks that a distribution may be made to preferential creditors, consent of—

(i) each secured creditor of the company, and

(ii) preferential creditors whose debts amount to more than 50% of the total preferential debts of the company, disregarding debts of any creditor who does not respond to an invitation to give or withhold consent.

(4) Consent for the purposes of sub-paragraph (1) may be—

(a) written, or

(b) signified at a creditors' meeting.

(5) The power to extend under sub-paragraph (1)—

(a) may be exercised in respect of a period only once,

(b) may not be used to extend a period by more than 28 days,

(c) may not be used to extend a period which has been extended by the court, and

(d) may not be used to extend a period after expiry.

109. Where a period is extended under paragraph 107 or 108, a reference to the period shall be taken as a reference to the period as extended.

Amendment of provision about time

110.—(1) The Secretary of State may by order amend a provision of this Schedule which—

(a) requires anything to be done within a specified period of time,

(b) prevents anything from being done after a specified time, or

(c) requires a specified minimum period of notice to be given.

(2) An order under this paragraph—

(a) must be made by statutory instrument, and

(b) shall be subject to annulment in pursuance of a resolution of either House of Parliament.

Interpretation

111.—(1) In this Schedule—

"administrative receiver" has the meaning given by section 251,

"administrator" has the meaning given by paragraph 1 and, where the context requires, includes a reference to a former administrator,

.....

"correspondence" includes correspondence by telephonic or other electronic means,

"creditors' meeting" has the meaning given by paragraph 50,

"enters administration" has the meaning given by paragraph 1,

"floating charge" means a charge which is a floating charge on its creation,

"in administration" has the meaning given by paragraph 1,

"hire-purchase agreement" includes a conditional sale agreement, a chattel leasing agreement and a retention of title agreement,

"holder of a qualifying floating charge" in respect of a company's property has the meaning given by paragraph 14,

"market value" means the amount which would be realised on a sale of property in the open market by a willing vendor,

"the purpose of administration" means an objective specified in paragraph 3, and

"unable to pay its debts" has the meaning given by section 123.

[(1A) In this Schedule, "company" means—

(a) a company within the meaning of section 735(1) of the Companies Act 1985,

(b) a company incorporated in an EEA State other than the United Kingdom, or

(c) a company not incorporated in an EEA State but having its centre of main interests in a member State other than Denmark.

(1B) In sub-paragraph (1A), in relation to a company, "centre of main interests" has the same meaning as in the EC Regulation and, in the absence of proof to the contrary, is presumed to be the place of its registered office (within the meaning of that Regulation).]

(2) A reference in this Schedule to a thing in writing includes a reference to a thing in electronic form.

(3) In this Schedule a reference to action includes a reference to inaction.

[Non-UK companies

111A. A company incorporated outside the United Kingdom that has a principal place of business in Northern Ireland may not enter administration under this Schedule unless it also has a principal place of business in England and Wales or Scotland (or both in England and Wales and in Scotland).]

Scotland

112. In the application of this Schedule to Scotland—

(a) a reference to filing with the court is a reference to lodging in court, and
(b) a reference to a charge is a reference to a right in security.

113. Where property in Scotland is disposed of under paragraph 70 or 71, the administrator shall grant to the disponee an appropriate document of transfer or conveyance of the property, and—

(a) that document, or
(b) recording, intimation or registration of that document (where recording, intimation or registration of the document is a legal requirement for completion of title to the property),

has the effect of disencumbering the property of or, as the case may be, freeing the property from, the security.

114. In Scotland, where goods in the possession of a company under a hire-purchase agreement are disposed of under paragraph 72, the disposal has the effect of extinguishing as against the disponee all rights of the owner of the goods under the agreement.

115.—(1) In Scotland, the administrator of a company may make, in or towards the satisfaction of the debt secured by the floating charge, a payment to the holder of a floating charge which has attached to the property subject to the charge.

(2) In Scotland, where the administrator thinks that the company has insufficient property to enable a distribution to be made to unsecured creditors other than by virtue of section 176A(2)(a), he may file a notice to that effect with the registrar of companies.

(3) On delivery of the notice to the registrar of companies, any floating charge granted by the company shall, unless it has already so attached, attach to the property which is subject to the charge and that attachment shall have effect as if each floating charge is a fixed security over the property to which it has attached.

116. In Scotland, the administrator in making any payment in accordance with paragraph 115 shall make such payment subject to the rights of any of the following categories of persons (which rights shall, except to the extent provided in any instrument, have the following order of priority)—

(a) the holder of any fixed security which is over property subject to the floating charge and which ranks prior to, or pari passu with, the floating charge,
(b) creditors in respect of all liabilities and expenses incurred by or on behalf of the administrator,
(c) the administrator in respect of his liabilities, expenses and remuneration and any indemnity to which he is entitled out of the property of the company,
(d) the preferential creditors entitled to payment in accordance with paragraph 65,
(e) the holder of the floating charge in accordance with the priority of that charge in relation to any other floating charge which has attached, and
(f) the holder of a fixed security, other than one referred to in paragraph (a), which is over property subject to the floating charge.]

[3469A]

PART III OTHER LEGISLATION

NOTES

Inserted by the Enterprise Act 2002, s 248(2), Sch 16, as from 15 September 2003 (for savings and transitional provisions, see the note to s 8 at **[3164]**).

Para 12: words in square brackets in sub-para (1)(d) substituted by the Courts Act 2003, s 109(1), Sch 8, para 299, as from 1 April 2005 (for transitional provisions and savings in connection with the commencement of the Courts Act 2003 and the continuity of functions, etc, see SI 2005/911); sub-para (5) added by the Enterprise Act 2002 (Insolvency) Order 2003, SI 2003/2096, arts 2(1), (2), 6, as from 15 September 2003, except in relation to any case where a petition for an administration order was presented before that date.

Para 40: sub-para (2)(aa) inserted by the European Public Limited-Liability Company Regulations 2004, SI 2004/2326, reg 73(4)(c), as from 8 October 2004.

Para 42: sub-para (4)(aa) inserted by SI 2004/2326, reg 73(4)(c), as from 8 October 2004.

Para 43: sub-para (6A) inserted by SI 2003/2096, art 2(1), (3) as from 15 September 2003, except in relation to any case where a petition for an administration order was presented before that date.

Para 82: sub-para (1)(aa) inserted by SI 2004/2326, reg 73(4)(c), as from 8 October 2004.

Paras 87, 89: words in square brackets in sub-para (2)(b) substituted by SI 2003/2096, arts 2(1), (4), (5), 6, as from 15 September 2003, except in relation to any case where a petition for an administration order was presented before that date.

Para 111: definition omitted from sub-para (1) repealed, and sub-paras (1A), (1B) inserted, by the Insolvency Act 1986 (Amendment) Regulations 2005, SI 2005/879, reg 2(1), (4)(a), (b), as from 13 April 2005, except in relation to the appointment of an administrator under Part II that took effect before that date.

Para 111A: inserted by SI 2005/879, reg 2(1), (4)(c), as from 13 April 2005, except in relation to the appointment of an administrator under Part II that took effect before that date.

Application to limited liability partnerships: see the introductory note to this Act and the Limited Liability Partnerships Regulations 2001, SI 2001/1090, reg 5, Sch 3 at **[6986]**, **[6995]**.

SCHEDULE 1
POWERS OF ADMINISTRATOR OR ADMINISTRATIVE RECEIVER

Sections 14, 42

1. Power to take possession of, collect and get in the property of the company and, for that purpose, to take such proceedings as may seem to him expedient.

2. Power to sell or otherwise dispose of the property of the company by public auction or private contract or, in Scotland, to sell, … hire out or otherwise dispose of the property of the company by public roup or private bargain.

3. Power to raise or borrow money and grant security therefor over the property of the company.

4. Power to appoint a solicitor or accountant or other professionally qualified person to assist him in the performance of his functions.

5. Power to bring or defend any action or other legal proceedings in the name and on behalf of the company.

6. Power to refer to arbitration any question affecting the company.

7. Power to effect and maintain insurances in respect of the business and property of the company.

8. Power to use the company's seal.

9. Power to do all acts and to execute in the name and on behalf of the company any deed, receipt or other document.

10. Power to draw, accept, make and endorse any bill of exchange or promissory note in the name and on behalf of the company.

11. Power to appoint any agent to do any business which he is unable to do himself or which can more conveniently be done by an agent and power to employ and dismiss employees.

12. Power to do all such things (including the carrying out of works) as may be necessary for the realisation of the property of the company.

13. Power to make any payment which is necessary or incidental to the performance of his functions.

14. Power to carry on the business of the company.

15. Power to establish subsidiaries of the company.

16. Power to transfer to subsidiaries of the company the whole or any part of the business and property of the company.

17. Power to grant or accept a surrender of a lease or tenancy of any of the property of the company, and to take a lease or tenancy of any property required or convenient for the business of the company.

18. Power to make any arrangement or compromise on behalf of the company.

19. Power to call up any uncalled capital of the company.

20. Power to rank and claim in the bankruptcy, insolvency, sequestration or liquidation of any person indebted to the company and to receive dividends, and to accede to trust deeds for the creditors of any such person.

21. Power to present or defend a petition for the winding up of the company.

22. Power to change the situation of the company's registered office.

23. Power to do all other things incidental to the exercise of the foregoing powers.

[3470]

NOTES

Para 2: word omitted repealed by the Abolition of Feudal Tenure etc (Scotland) Act 2000, s 76(2), Sch 13, Pt I, as from 28 November 2004.

Application to limited liability partnerships: see the introductory note to this Act and the Limited Liability Partnerships Regulations 2001, SI 2001/1090, reg 5, Sch 3 at **[6986]**, **[6995]**.

SCHEDULE 2
POWERS OF A SCOTTISH RECEIVER (ADDITIONAL TO THOSE CONFERRED ON HIM BY THE INSTRUMENT OF CHARGE)

Section 55

1. Power to take possession of, collect and get in the property from the company or a liquidator thereof or any other person, and for that purpose, to take such proceedings as may seem to him expedient.

2. Power to sell, … hire out or otherwise dispose of the property by public roup or private bargain and with or without advertisement.

3. Power to raise or borrow money and grant security therefor over the property.

4. Power to appoint a solicitor or accountant or other professionally qualified person to assist him in the performance of his functions.

5. Power to bring or defend any action or other legal proceedings in the name and on behalf of the company.

6. Power to refer to arbitration all questions affecting the company.

7. Power to effect and maintain insurances in respect of the business and property of the company.

PART III OTHER LEGISLATION

8. Power to use the company's seal.

9. Power to do all acts and to execute in the name and on behalf of the company any deed, receipt or other document.

10. Power to draw, accept, make and endorse any bill of exchange or promissory note in the name and on behalf of the company.

11. Power to appoint any agent to do any business which he is unable to do himself or which can more conveniently be done by an agent, and power to employ and dismiss employees.

12. Power to do all such things (including the carrying out of works), as may be necessary for the realisation of the property.

13. Power to make any payment which is necessary or incidental to the performance of his functions.

14. Power to carry on the business of the company or any part of it.

15. Power to grant or accept a surrender of a lease or tenancy of any of the property, and to take a lease or tenancy of any property required or convenient for the business of the company.

16. Power to make any arrangement or compromise on behalf of the company.

17. Power to call up any uncalled capital of the company.

18. Power to establish subsidiaries of the company.

19. Power to transfer to subsidiaries of the company the business of the company or any part of it and any of the property.

20. Power to rank and claim in the bankruptcy, insolvency, sequestration or liquidation of any person or company indebted to the company and to receive dividends, and to accede to trust deeds for creditors of any such person.

21. Power to present or defend a petition for the winding up of the company.

22. Power to change the situation of the company's registered office.

23. Power to do all other things incidental to the exercise of the powers mentioned in section 55(1) of this Act or above in this Schedule.

[3471]

NOTES

Para 2: word omitted repealed by the Abolition of Feudal Tenure etc (Scotland) Act 2000, s 76(2), Sch 13, Pt I, as from 28 November 2004.

Application to limited liability partnerships: see the introductory note to this Act, the Limited Liability Partnerships Regulations 2001, SI 2001/1090, reg 5, Sch 3 at **[6986]**, **[6995]**, and the Limited Liability Partnerships (Scotland) Regulations 2001, SSI 2001/128, reg 4, Schs 2, 3 at **[6977]**, **[6980A]**, **[6980B]**.

[SCHEDULE 2A
EXCEPTIONS TO PROHIBITION ON APPOINTMENT OF ADMINISTRATIVE RECEIVER: SUPPLEMENTARY PROVISIONS

Section 72H

Capital market arrangement

1.—(1) For the purposes of section 72B an arrangement is a capital market arrangement if—

(a) it involves a grant of security to a person holding it as trustee for a person who holds a capital market investment issued by a party to the arrangement, or

[(aa) it involves a grant of security to—
(i) a party to the arrangement who issues a capital market investment, or
(ii) a person who holds the security as trustee for a party to the arrangement in connection with the issue of a capital market investment, or
(ab) it involves a grant of security to a person who holds the security as trustee for a party to the arrangement who agrees to provide finance to another party, or]
(b) at least one party guarantees the performance of obligations of another party, or
(c) at least one party provides security in respect of the performance of obligations of another party, or
(d) the arrangement involves an investment of a kind described in articles 83 to 85 of the Financial Services and Markets Act 2000 (Regulated Activities) Order 2001 (SI 2001/544) (options, futures and contracts for differences).

(2) For the purposes of sub-paragraph (1)—
(a) a reference to holding as trustee includes a reference to holding as nominee or agent,
(b) a reference to holding for a person who holds a capital market investment includes a reference to holding for a number of persons at least one of whom holds a capital market investment, and
(c) a person holds a capital market investment if he has a legal or beneficial interest in it[; and
(d) the reference to the provision of finance includes the provision of an indemnity].

(3) In section 72B(1) and this paragraph "party" to an arrangement includes a party to an agreement which—
(a) forms part of the arrangement,
(b) provides for the raising of finance as part of the arrangement, or
(c) is necessary for the purposes of implementing the arrangement.

Capital market investment

2.—(1) For the purposes of section 72B an investment is a capital market investment if it—
(a) is within article 77 of the Financial Services and Markets Act 2000 (Regulated Activities) Order 2001 (SI 2001/544) (debt instruments), and
(b) is rated, listed or traded or designed to be rated, listed or traded.

(2) In sub-paragraph (1)—
"rated" means rated for the purposes of investment by an internationally recognised rating agency,
"listed" means admitted to the official list within the meaning given by section 103(1) of the Financial Services and Markets Act 2000 (c 8) (interpretation), and
"traded" means admitted to trading on a market established under the rules of a recognised investment exchange or on a foreign market.

(3) In sub-paragraph (2)—
"recognised investment exchange" has the meaning given by section 285 of the Financial Services and Markets Act 2000 (recognised investment exchange), and
"foreign market" has the same meaning as "relevant market" in article 67(2) of the Financial Services and Markets Act 2000 (Financial Promotion) Order 2001 (SI 2001/1335) (foreign markets).

3.—(1) An investment is also a capital market investment for the purposes of section 72B if it consists of a bond or commercial paper issued to one or more of the following—
(a) an investment professional within the meaning of article 19(5) of the Financial Services and Markets Act 2000 (Financial Promotion) Order 2001,
(b) a person who is, when the agreement mentioned in section 72B(1) is entered into, a certified high net worth individual in relation to a communication within the meaning of article 48(2) of that order,
(c) a person to whom article 49(2) of that order applies (high net worth company, &c),
(d) a person who is, when the agreement mentioned in section 72B(1) is entered into, a certified sophisticated investor in relation to a communication within the meaning of article 50(1) of that order, and
(e) a person in a State other than the United Kingdom who under the law of that State is not prohibited from investing in bonds or commercial paper.

(2) In sub-paragraph (1)—

"bond" shall be construed in accordance with article 77 of the Financial Services and Markets Act 2000 (Regulated Activities) Order 2001 (SI 2001/544), and
"commercial paper" has the meaning given by article 9(3) of that order.

(3) For the purposes of sub-paragraph (1)—
(a) in applying article 19(5) of the Financial Promotion Order for the purposes of sub-paragraph (1)(a)—
(i) in article 19(5)(b), ignore the words after "exempt person",
(ii) in article 19(5)(c)(i), for the words from "the controlled activity" to the end substitute "a controlled activity", and
(iii) in article 19(5)(e) ignore the words from "where the communication" to the end, and
(b) in applying article 49(2) of that order for the purposes of sub-paragraph (1)(c), ignore article 49(2)(e).

"Agreement"

4. For the purposes of sections 72B and 72E and this Schedule "agreement" includes an agreement or undertaking effected by—
(a) contract,
(b) deed, or
(c) any other instrument intended to have effect in accordance with the law of England and Wales, Scotland or another jurisdiction.

Debt

5. The debt of at least £50 million referred to in section 72B(1)(a) or 72E(2)(a)—
(a) may be incurred at any time during the life of the capital market arrangement or financed project, and
(b) may be expressed wholly or partly in foreign currency (in which case the sterling equivalent shall be calculated as at the time when the arrangement is entered into or the project begins).

Step-in rights

6.—(1) For the purposes of sections 72C to 72E a project has "step-in rights" if a person who provides finance in connection with the project has a conditional entitlement under an agreement to—
(a) assume sole or principal responsibility under an agreement for carrying out all or part of the project, or
(b) make arrangements for carrying out all or part of the project.

(2) In sub-paragraph (1) a reference to the provision of finance includes a reference to the provision of an indemnity.

Project company

7.—(1) For the purposes of sections 72C to 72E a company is a "project company" of a project if—
(a) it holds property for the purpose of the project,
(b) it has sole or principal responsibility under an agreement for carrying out all or part of the project,
(c) it is one of a number of companies which together carry out the project,
(d) it has the purpose of supplying finance to enable the project to be carried out, or
(e) it is the holding company of a company within any of paragraphs (a) to (d).

(2) But a company is not a "project company" of a project if—
(a) it performs a function within sub-paragraph (1)(a) to (d) or is within sub-paragraph (1)(e), but
(b) it also performs a function which is not—
(i) within sub-paragraph (1)(a) to (d),
(ii) related to a function within sub-paragraph (1)(a) to (d), or
(iii) related to the project.

(3) For the purposes of this paragraph a company carries out all or part of a project whether or not it acts wholly or partly through agents.

"Resources"

8. In section 72C "resources" includes—
(a) funds (including payment for the provision of services or facilities),
(b) assets,
(c) professional skill,
(d) the grant of a concession or franchise, and
(e) any other commercial resource.

"Public body"

9.—(1) In section 72C "public body" means—
(a) a body which exercises public functions,
(b) a body specified for the purposes of this paragraph by the Secretary of State, and
(c) a body within a class specified for the purposes of this paragraph by the Secretary of State.

(2) A specification under sub-paragraph (1) may be—
(a) general, or
(b) for the purpose of the application of section 72C to a specified case.

Regulated business

10.—(1) For the purposes of section 72D a business is regulated if it is carried on—
(a) …
(b) in reliance on a licence under section 7 or 7A of the Gas Act 1986 (c 44) (transport and supply of gas),
(c) in reliance on a licence granted by virtue of section 41C of that Act (power to prescribe additional licensable activity),
(d) in reliance on a licence under section 6 of the Electricity Act 1989 (c 29) (supply of electricity),
(e) by a water undertaker,
(f) by a sewerage undertaker,
(g) by a universal service provider within the meaning given by section 4(3) and (4) of the Postal Services Act 2000 (c 26),
(h) by the Post Office company within the meaning given by section 62 of that Act (transfer of property),
(i) by a relevant subsidiary of the Post Office Company within the meaning given by section 63 of that Act (government holding),
(j) in reliance on a licence under section 8 of the Railways Act 1993 (c 43) (railway services),
(k) in reliance on a licence exemption under section 7 of that Act (subject to sub-paragraph (2) below),
(l) by the operator of a system of transport which is deemed to be a railway for a purpose of Part I of that Act by virtue of section 81(2) of that Act (tramways, &c), …
(m) by the operator of a vehicle carried on flanged wheels along a system within paragraph (l); [or
(n) in reliance on a European licence granted pursuant to a provision contained in any instrument made for the purpose of implementing Council Directive 1995/18/EC dated 19th June 1995 on the licensing of railway undertakings, as amended by Directive 2001/13/EC dated 26th February 2001 and Directive 2004/49/EC dated 29th April 2004, both of the European Parliament and of the Council, or pursuant to any action taken by an EEA State for that purpose].

(2) Sub-paragraph (1)(k) does not apply to the operator of a railway asset on a railway unless on some part of the railway there is a permitted line speed exceeding 40 kilometres per hour.

PART III OTHER LEGISLATION

[(2A) For the purposes of section 72D a business is also regulated to the extent that it consists in the provision of a public electronic communications network or a public electronic communications service.]

[(2B) In sub-paragraph (1)(n), an "EEA State" means a member State, Norway, Iceland or Liechtenstein.]

"Person"

11. A reference to a person in this Schedule includes a reference to a partnership or another unincorporated group of persons.]

[3471A]

NOTES

Inserted by the Enterprise Act 2002, s 250(2), Sch 18, as from 15 September 2003.

Para 1: sub-paras (1)(aa), (ab), (2)(d) (and the word immediately preceding it) inserted by the Insolvency Act 1986 (Amendment) (Administrative Receivership and Capital Market Arrangements) Order 2003, SI 2003/1468, arts 2, 3, as from 15 September 2003 (ie, immediately after the coming into force of this Schedule and ss 72A–72G of this Act).

Para 10: sub-para (1)(a) repealed, and sub-para (2A) inserted, by the Communications Act 2003, s 406, Sch 17, para 82(1), (4), Sch 19, as from 25 July 2003 (certain purposes), and as from 29 December 2003 (otherwise); word omitted from sub-para (1)(l) repealed, and sub-para (1)(n) (and the word immediately preceding it) and sub-para (2B) inserted, the Railway (Licensing of Railway Undertakings) Regulations 2005, SI 2005/3050, as from 28 November 2005.

Modification: a reference to commercial paper in this Schedule includes a reference to uncertificated units of an eligible debt security where the issue of the units corresponds, in accordance with the current terms of issue of the security, to the issue of commercial paper within the meaning of the Financial Services and Markets Act 2000 (Regulated Activities) Order 2001, SI 2001/544, art 9(3); see the Uncertificated Securities (Amendment) (Eligible Debt Securities) Regulations 2003, SI 2003/1633, reg 15, Sch 2, para 7.

Application to limited liability partnerships: see the introductory note to this Act and the Limited Liability Partnerships Regulations 2001, SI 2001/1090, reg 5, Sch 3 at **[6986]**, **[6995]**.

Financial Services and Markets Act 2000 (Financial Promotion) Order 2001, SI 2001/1335: revoked and replaced by the Financial Services and Markets Act 2000 (Financial Promotion) Order 2005, SI 2005/1529.

SCHEDULE 3
ORDERS IN COURSE OF WINDING UP PRONOUNCED IN VACATION (SCOTLAND)

Section 162

PART I
ORDERS WHICH ARE TO BE FINAL

Orders under section 153, as to the time for proving debts and claims.

Orders under section 195 as to meetings for ascertaining wishes of creditors or contributories.

Orders under section 198, as to the examination of witnesses in regard to the property or affairs of a company.

[3472]

NOTES

Application to limited liability partnerships: see the introductory note to this Act, the Limited Liability Partnerships Regulations 2001, SI 2001/1090, reg 5, Sch 3 at **[6986]**, **[6995]**, and the Limited Liability Partnerships (Scotland) Regulations 2001, SSI 2001/128, reg 4, Schs 2, 3 at **[6977]**, **[6980A]**, **[6980B]**.

PART II
ORDERS WHICH ARE TO TAKE EFFECT UNTIL MATTER DISPOSED OF BY INNER HOUSE

Orders under section 126(1), 130(2) or (3), 147, 227 or 228, restraining or permitting the commencement or the continuance of legal proceedings.

Orders under section 135(5), limiting the powers of provisional liquidators.

Orders under section 108, appointing a liquidator to fill a vacancy.

Orders under section 167 or 169, sanctioning the exercise of any powers by a liquidator, other than the powers specified in paragraphs 1, 2 and 3 of Schedule 4 to this Act.

Orders under section 158, as to the arrest and detention of an absconding contributory and his property.

[3473]

NOTES

Application to limited liability partnerships: see the introductory note to this Act, the Limited Liability Partnerships Regulations 2001, SI 2001/1090, reg 5, Sch 3 at **[6986]**, **[6995]**, and the Limited Liability Partnerships (Scotland) Regulations 2001, SSI 2001/128, reg 4, Schs 2, 3 at **[6977]**, **[6980A]**, **[6980B]**.

SCHEDULE 4
POWERS OF LIQUIDATOR IN A WINDING UP

Sections 165, 167

PART I
POWERS EXERCISABLE WITH SANCTION

1. Power to pay any class of creditors in full.

2. Power to make any compromise or arrangement with creditors or persons claiming to be creditors, or having or alleging themselves to have any claim (present or future, certain or contingent, ascertained or sounding only in damages) against the company, or whereby the company may be rendered liable.

3. Power to compromise, on such terms as may be agreed—

(a) all calls and liabilities to calls, all debts and liabilities capable of resulting in debts, and all claims (present or future, certain or contingent, ascertained or sounding only in damages) subsisting or supposed to subsist between the company and a contributory or alleged contributory or other debtor or person apprehending liability to the company, and

(b) all questions in any way relating to or affecting the assets or the winding up of the company,

and take any security for the discharge of any such call, debt, liability or claim and give a complete discharge in respect of it.

[3A. Power to bring legal proceedings under section 213, 214, 238, 239, 242, 243 or 423.]

[3474]

NOTES

Para 3A: added by the Enterprise Act 2002, s 253, as from 15 September 2003, except in relation to any proceedings of a kind mentioned in para 3A which were commenced prior to that date.

Application to limited liability partnerships: see the introductory note to this Act, the Limited Liability Partnerships Regulations 2001, SI 2001/1090, reg 5, Sch 3 at **[6986]**, **[6995]**, and the Limited Liability Partnerships (Scotland) Regulations 2001, SSI 2001/128, reg 4, Schs 2, 3 at **[6977]**, **[6980A]**, **[6980B]**.

PART II
POWERS EXERCISABLE WITHOUT SANCTION IN VOLUNTARY WINDING UP, WITH SANCTION IN WINDING UP BY THE COURT

4. Power to bring or defend any action or other legal proceeding in the name and on behalf of the company.

5. Power to carry on the business of the company so far as may be necessary for its beneficial winding up.

[3475]

NOTES

Application to limited liability partnerships: see the introductory note to this Act, the Limited Liability Partnerships Regulations 2001, SI 2001/1090, reg 5, Sch 3 at **[6986]**, **[6995]**, and the Limited Liability Partnerships (Scotland) Regulations 2001, SSI 2001/128, reg 4, Schs 2, 3 at **[6977]**, **[6980A]**, **[6980B]**.

PART III
POWERS EXERCISABLE WITHOUT SANCTION IN ANY WINDING UP

6. Power to sell any of the company's property by public auction or private contract with power to transfer the whole of it to any person or to sell the same in parcels.

7. Power to do all acts and execute, in the name and on behalf of the company, all deeds, receipts and other documents and for that purpose to use, when necessary, the company's seal.

8. Power to prove, rank and claim in the bankruptcy, insolvency or sequestration of any contributory for any balance against his estate, and to receive dividends in the bankruptcy, insolvency or sequestration in respect of that balance, as a separate debt due from the bankrupt or insolvent, and rateably with the other separate creditors.

9. Power to draw, accept, make and indorse any bill of exchange or promissory note in the name and on behalf of the company, with the same effect with respect to the company's liability as if the bill or note had been drawn, accepted, made or indorsed by or on behalf of the company in the course of its business.

10. Power to raise on the security of the assets of the company any money requisite.

11. Power to take out in his official name letters of administration to any deceased contributory, and to do in his official name any other act necessary for obtaining payment of any money due from a contributory or his estate which cannot conveniently be done in the name of the company.

In all such cases the money due is deemed, for the purpose of enabling the liquidator to take out the letters of administration or recover the money, to be due to the liquidator himself.

12. Power to appoint an agent to do any business which the liquidator is unable to do himself.

13. Power to do all such other things as may be necessary for winding up the company's affairs and distributing its assets.

[3476]

NOTES

Application to limited liability partnerships: see the introductory note to this Act, the Limited Liability Partnerships Regulations 2001, SI 2001/1090, reg 5, Sch 3 at **[6986]**, **[6995]**, and the Limited Liability Partnerships (Scotland) Regulations 2001, SSI 2001/128, reg 4, Schs 2, 3 at **[6977]**, **[6980A]**, **[6980B]**.

SCHEDULE 6
THE CATEGORIES OF PREFERENTIAL DEBTS

Section 386

1–7. …

Category 4: Contributions to occupational pension schemes, etc

8. Any sum which is owed by the debtor and is a sum to which [Schedule 4 to the Pension Schemes Act 1993] applies (contributions to occupational pension schemes and state scheme premiums).

Category 5: Remuneration, etc, of employees

9. So much of any amount which—

(a) is owed by the debtor to a person who is or has been an employee of the debtor, and

(b) is payable by way of remuneration in respect of the whole or any part of the period of 4 months next before the relevant date,

as does not exceed so much as may be prescribed by order made by the Secretary of State.

10. An amount owed by way of accrued holiday remuneration, in respect of any period of employment before the relevant date, to a person whose employment by the debtor has been terminated, whether before, on or after that date.

11. So much of any sum owed in respect of money advanced for the purpose as has been applied for the payment of a debt which, if it had not been paid, would have been a debt falling within paragraph 9 or 10.

12. So much of any amount which—

(a) is ordered (whether before or after the relevant date) to be paid by the debtor under the Reserve Forces (Safeguard of Employment) Act 1985, and

(b) is so ordered in respect of a default made by the debtor before that date in the discharge of his obligations under that Act,

as does not exceed such amount as may be prescribed by order made by the Secretary of State.

Interpretation for Category 5

13.—(1) For the purposes of paragraphs 9 to 12, a sum is payable by the debtor to a person by way of remuneration in respect of any period if—

(a) it is paid as wages or salary (whether payable for time or for piece work or earned wholly or partly by way of commission) in respect of services rendered to the debtor in that period, or

(b) it is an amount falling within the following sub-paragraph and is payable by the debtor in respect of that period.

[(2) An amount falls within this sub-paragraph if it is—

(a) a guarantee payment under Part III of the Employment Rights Act 1996 (employee without work to do);

(b) any payment for time off under section 53 (time off to look for work or arrange training) or section 56 (time off for ante-natal care) of that Act or under section 169 of the Trade Union and Labour Relations (Consolidation) Act 1992 (time off for carrying out trade union duties etc);

(c) remuneration on suspension on medical grounds, or on maternity grounds, under Part VII of the Employment Rights Act 1996; or

(d) remuneration under a protective award under section 189 of the Trade Union and Labour Relations (Consolidation) Act 1992 (redundancy dismissal with compensation).]

14.—(1) This paragraph relates to a case in which a person's employment has been terminated by or in consequence of his employer going into liquidation or being adjudged bankrupt or (his employer being a company not in liquidation) by or in consequence of—

(a) a receiver being appointed as mentioned in section 40 of this Act (debenture-holders secured by floating charge), or

(b) the appointment of a receiver under section 53(6) or 54(5) of this Act (Scottish company with property subject to floating charge), or

(c) the taking of possession by debenture-holders (so secured), as mentioned in section 196 of the Companies Act.

(2) For the purposes of paragraphs 9 to 12, holiday remuneration is deemed to have accrued to that person in respect of any period of employment if, by virtue of his contract of employment or of any enactment that remuneration would have accrued in respect of that period if his employment had continued until he became entitled to be allowed the holiday.

(3) The reference in sub-paragraph (2) to any enactment includes an order or direction made under an enactment.

15. Without prejudice to paragraphs 13 and 14—

(a) any remuneration payable by the debtor to a person in respect of a period of

PART III OTHER LEGISLATION

holiday or of absence from work through sickness or other good cause is deemed to be wages or (as the case may be) salary in respect of services rendered to the debtor in that period, and

(b) references here and in those paragraphs to remuneration in respect of a period of holiday include any sums which, if they had been paid, would have been treated for the purposes of the enactments relating to social security as earnings in respect of that period.

[Category 6: Levies on coal and steel production

15A. Any sums due at the relevant date from the debtor in respect of:

(a) the levies on the production of coal and steel referred to in Articles 49 and 50 of the ECSC Treaty, or

(b) any surcharge for delay provided for in Article 50(3) of that Treaty and Article 6 of Decision 3/52 of the High Authority of the Coal and Steel Community.]

Orders

16. An order under paragraph 9 or 12—

(a) may contain such transitional provisions as may appear to the Secretary of State necessary or expedient;

(b) shall be made by statutory instrument subject to annulment in pursuance of a resolution of either House of Parliament.

[3477]

NOTES

Paras 1–7: repealed by the Enterprise Act 2002, ss 251(1), 278(2), Sch 26, as from 15 September 2003, subject to the following transitional provisions contained in the Enterprise Act 2002 (Commencement No 4 and Transitional Provisions and Savings) Order 2003, SI 2003/2093, art 4 (as amended by the Enterprise Act 2002 (Transitional Provisions) (Insolvency) Order 2003, SI 2003/2332)—

"4 Abolition of Crown preferences—transitional provisions

(1) This article applies to a case where before the first commencement date—

(a) a petition for an administration order pursuant to Part II of the Insolvency Act 1986 is presented;

(b) a voluntary arrangement under Part I of the Insolvency Act 1986 has effect;

(c) a receiver is appointed under the terms of a charge (which when created was a floating charge) in relation to the property of a company subject to the charge;

(d) a petition for a winding-up order is presented;

(e) a resolution for the winding up of the company is passed;

(f) a petition for a bankruptcy order (or, in Scotland, for sequestration) is presented; or

(g) a voluntary arrangement pursuant to Part VIII of the Insolvency Act 1986 has effect.

[(1A) This article also applies to a case where—

(a) an administration order under Part II of the Insolvency Act 1986 is made on a petition presented prior to the first commencement date;

(b) that order is discharged; and

(c) immediately on the discharge of that order—

(i) a winding-up order is made in respect of the company in question; or

(ii) a resolution for the winding up of the company is passed,

on or after the first commencement date.

(1B) This article also applies to a case where—

(a) a winding-up order is made on a petition presented prior to the first commencement date; and

(b) the company in question enters administration by virtue of an order made under paragraphs 37 or 38 of Schedule B1 to the Insolvency Act 1986.

(1C) This article also applies to a case where—

(a) a resolution for the winding up of a company is passed before the first commencement date; and

(b) the company enters administration by virtue of an order made under paragraph 38 of Schedule B1 to the Insolvency Act 1986.

(1D) This article also applies to a case where—

(a) a receiver is appointed before the first commencement date in respect of a company;

(b) the receiver vacates office; and

(c) the company in respect of which the receiver is appointed enters administration within the meaning of paragraph 1(2)(b) of Schedule B1 to the Insolvency Act 1986 during the period that the receiver is in office or immediately after the end of that period.]

(2) This article also applies to a case where proposals for a voluntary arrangement under Part I of the Insolvency Act 1986 are made (whether before or after the first commencement date) by—

(a) a liquidator in a winding up where the winding-up petition is presented or, as the case may be, the resolution for winding up is passed, before the first commencement date; or

(b) an administrator appointed in relation to an administration under Part II of the Insolvency Act 1986 where the administration order is made on a petition which is presented before the first commencement date.

(3) This article also applies to a case in which a proposal for a voluntary arrangement under Part VIII of the Insolvency Act 1986 is made (whether before or after the first commencement date) by a person who was adjudged bankrupt on a petition which was presented before the first commencement date.

(4) In a case to which this article applies—

(a) the provisions of section 251; and

(b) the provisions of section 278(2) and Schedule 26 as respects the repeals relating to paragraphs 1 to 3 and 8 to 8C in Schedule 3 to the Bankruptcy (Scotland) Act 1985, paragraphs 1 to 7 of Schedule 6 to the Insolvency Act 1986, the table in paragraph 32 of Schedule 29 to the Income and Corporation Taxes Act 1988, paragraphs 21A and 22 of Schedule 2 to the Finance Act 1991, paragraph 73 of Schedule 2 to the Social Security (Consequential Provisions) Act 1992, sections 36(1) to (3) of the Finance Act 1993, paragraphs 13(1) and 13(2) of Schedule 6 and paragraph 7(2) of Schedule 7 to the Finance Act 1994, paragraph 8 of Schedule 14 to the Value Added Tax Act 1994, section 17 of the Finance Act 1995, paragraphs 12(1) and 12(2) of Schedule 5 to the Finance Act 1996, sections 166(7)(a), 183(3)(a) and 189(4) of the Employment Rights Act 1996, paragraph 6 of Schedule 2 to the Finance Act 1997, paragraphs 2 and 3 of Schedule 7 to the Finance Act 2000 and paragraphs 17(1) and (2) and 18 of Schedule 5 to the Finance Act 2001,

shall not have effect.".

Para 8: words in square brackets substituted by the Pension Schemes Act 1993, s 190, Sch 8, para 18, as from 7 February 1994.

Para 13: sub-para (2) substituted by the Employment Rights Act 1996, s 240, Sch 1, para 29, as from 22 August 1996.

Para 15A: inserted by the Insolvency (ECSC Levy Debts) Regulations 1987, SI 1987/2093, reg 2(1), (3), as from 1 January 1988.

Application to limited liability partnerships: see the introductory note to this Act and the Limited Liability Partnerships Regulations 2001, SI 2001/1090, reg 5, Sch 3 at **[6986]**, **[6995]**.

Orders: the Insolvency Proceedings (Monetary Limits) Order 1986, SI 1986/1996 prescribing £800 for the purposes of paras 9, 12 above.

SCHEDULE 7
INSOLVENCY PRACTITIONERS TRIBUNAL

Section 396

Panels of members

1.—(1) The Secretary of State shall draw up and from time to time revise—

(a) a panel of persons who—

[(i) have a 7 year general qualification, within the meaning of section 71 of the Courts and Legal Services Act 1990;

(ii) are advocates or solicitors in Scotland of at least 7 years' standing],

and are nominated for the purpose by the Lord Chancellor or the Lord President of the Court of Session, and

(b) a panel of persons who are experienced in insolvency matters;

and the members of the Tribunal shall be selected from those panels in accordance with this Schedule.

(2) The power to revise the panels includes power to terminate a person's membership of either of them, and is accordingly to that extent subject to [section 7 of the Tribunals and Inquiries Act 1992] (which makes it necessary to obtain the concurrence of the Lord Chancellor and the Lord President of the Court of Session to dismissals in certain cases).

Remuneration of members

2. The Secretary of State may out of money provided by Parliament pay to members of the Tribunal such remuneration as he may with the approval of the Treasury determine; and such

PART III OTHER LEGISLATION

expenses of the Tribunal as the Secretary of State and the Treasury may approve shall be defrayed by the Secretary of State out of money so provided.

Sittings of Tribunal

3.—(1) For the purposes of carrying out their functions in relation to any cases referred to them, the Tribunal may sit either as a single tribunal or in two or more divisions.

(2) The functions of the Tribunal in relation to any case referred to them shall be exercised by three members consisting of—

(a) a chairman selected by the Secretary of State from the panel drawn up under paragraph 1(1)(a) above, and

(b) two other members selected by the Secretary of State from the panel drawn up under paragraph 1(1)(b).

Procedure of Tribunal

4.—(1) Any investigation by the Tribunal shall be so conducted as to afford a reasonable opportunity for representations to be made to the Tribunal by or on behalf of the person whose case is the subject of the investigation.

(2) For the purposes of any such investigation, the Tribunal—

(a) may by summons require any person to attend, at such time and place as is specified in the summons, to give evidence or to produce any books, papers and other records in his possession or under his control which the Tribunal consider it necessary for the purposes of the investigation to examine, and

(b) may take evidence on oath, and for the purpose administer oaths, or may, instead of administering an oath, require the person examined to make and subscribe a declaration of the truth of the matter respecting which he is examined;

but no person shall be required, in obedience to such a summons, to go more than ten miles from his place of residence, unless the necessary expenses of his attendance are paid or tendered to him.

(3) Every person who—

(a) without reasonable excuse fails to attend in obedience to a summons issued under this paragraph, or refuses to give evidence, or

(b) intentionally alters, suppresses, conceals or destroys or refuses to produce any document which he may be required to produce for the purpose of an investigation by the Tribunal,

is liable to a fine.

(4) Subject to the provisions of this paragraph, the Secretary of State may make rules for regulating the procedure on any investigation by the Tribunal.

(5) In their application to Scotland, sub-paragraphs (2) and (3) above have effect as if for any reference to a summons there were substituted a reference to a notice in writing.

[3478]

NOTES

Para 1: words in square brackets in sub-para (1)(a) substituted by the Courts and Legal Services Act 1990, s 71(2), Sch 10, para 67, as from 1 January 1991; words in square brackets in sub-para (2) substituted by the Tribunals and Inquiries Act 1992, s 18(1), Sch 3, para 19, as from 1 October 1992.

Application to limited liability partnerships: see the introductory note to this Act and the Limited Liability Partnerships Regulations 2001, SI 2001/1090, reg 5, Sch 3 at **[6986]**, **[6995]**.

Rules: by virtue of the Interpretation Act 1978, s 17(2)(b), the Insolvency Practitioners Tribunal (Conduct of Investigations) Rules 1986, SI 1986/952 at **[6044]** have effect as if made under this Schedule.

SCHEDULE 8
PROVISIONS CAPABLE OF INCLUSION IN COMPANY INSOLVENCY RULES

Section 411

Courts

1. Provision for supplementing, in relation to the insolvency or winding up of companies, any provision made by or under section 117 of this Act (jurisdiction in relation to winding up).

2.—[(1)] Provision for regulating the practice and procedure of any court exercising jurisdiction for the purposes of Parts I to VII of this Act or the Companies Act so far as relating to, and to matters connected with or arising out of, the insolvency or winding up of companies, being any provision that could be made by rules of court.

[(2) Rules made by virtue of this paragraph about the consequence of failure to comply with practice or procedure may, in particular, include provision about the termination of administration.]

Notices, etc

3. Provision requiring notice of any proceedings in connection with or arising out of the insolvency or winding up of a company to be given or published in the manner prescribed by the rules.

4. Provision with respect to the form, manner of serving, contents and proof of any petition, application, order, notice, statement or other document required to be presented, made, given, published or prepared under any enactment or subordinate legislation relating to, or to matters connected with or arising out of, the insolvency or winding up of companies.

5. Provision specifying the persons to whom any notice is to be given.

Registration of voluntary arrangements

6. Provision for the registration of voluntary arrangements approved under Part I of this Act, including provision for the keeping and inspection of a register.

Provisional liquidator

7. Provision as to the manner in which a provisional liquidator appointed under section 135 is to carry out his functions.

Conduct of insolvency

8. Provision with respect to the certification of any person as, and as to the proof that a person is, the liquidator, administrator or administrative receiver of a company.

9. The following provision with respect to meetings of a company's creditors, contributories or members—

(a) provision as to the manner of summoning a meeting (including provision as to how any power to require a meeting is to be exercised, provision as to the manner of determining the value of any debt or contribution for the purposes of any such power and provision making the exercise of any such power subject to the deposit of a sum sufficient to cover the expenses likely to be incurred in summoning and holding a meeting);

(b) provision specifying the time and place at which a meeting may be held and the period of notice required for a meeting;

(c) provision as to the procedure to be followed at a meeting (including the manner in which decisions may be reached by a meeting and the manner in which the value of any vote at a meeting is to be determined);

(d) provision for requiring a person who is or has been an officer of the company to attend a meeting;

(e) provision creating, in the prescribed circumstances, a presumption that a meeting has been duly summoned and held;

(f) provision as to the manner of proving the decisions of a meeting.

10.—(1) Provision as to the functions, membership and proceedings of a committee established under [section 49, 68, 101, 141 or 142 of, or paragraph 57 of Schedule B1 to, this Act].

(2) The following provision with respect to the establishment of a committee under section 101, 141 or 142 of this Act, that is to say—

PART III
OTHER LEGISLATION

(a) provision for resolving differences between a meeting of the company's creditors and a meeting of its contributories or members;

(b) provision authorising the establishment of the committee without a meeting of contributories in a case where a company is being wound up on grounds including its inability to pay its debts; and

(c) provision modifying the requirements of this Act with respect to the establishment of the committee in a case where a winding-up order has been made immediately upon the discharge of an administration order.

11. Provision as to the manner in which any requirement that may be imposed on a person under any of Parts I to VII of this Act by the official receiver, the liquidator, administrator or administrative receiver of a company or a special manager appointed under section 177 is to be so imposed.

12. Provision as to the debts that may be proved in a winding up, as to the manner and conditions of proving a debt and as to the manner and expenses of establishing the value of any debt or security.

13. Provision with respect to the manner of the distribution of the property of a company that is being wound up, including provision with respect to unclaimed funds and dividends.

14. Provision which, with or without modifications, applies in relation to the winding up of companies any enactment contained in Parts VIII to XI of this Act or in the Bankruptcy (Scotland) Act 1985.

[14A. Provision about the application of section 176A of this Act which may include, in particular—

(a) provision enabling a receiver to institute winding up proceedings;

(b) provision requiring a receiver to institute winding up proceedings.]

[Administration

14B. Provision which—

(a) applies in relation to administration, with or without modifications, a provision of Parts IV to VII of this Act, or

(b) serves a purpose in relation to administration similar to a purpose that may be served by the rules in relation to winding up by virtue of a provision of this Schedule.]

Financial provisions

15. Provision as to the amount, or manner of determining the amount, payable to the liquidator, administrator or administrative receiver of a company or a special manager appointed under section 177, by way of remuneration for the carrying out of functions in connection with or arising out of the insolvency or winding up of a company.

16. Provision with respect to the manner in which moneys received by the liquidator of a company in the course of carrying out his functions as such are to be invested or otherwise handled and with respect to the payment of interest on sums which, in pursuance of rules made by virtue of this paragraph, have been paid into the Insolvency Services Account.

[16A. Provision enabling the Secretary of State to set the rate of interest paid on sums which have been paid into the Insolvency Services Account.]

17. Provision as to the fees, costs, charges and other expenses that may be treated as the expenses of a winding up.

18. Provision as to the fees, costs, charges and other expenses that may be treated as properly incurred by the administrator or administrative receiver of a company.

19. Provision as to the fees, costs, charges and other expenses that may be incurred for any of the purposes of Part I of this Act or in the administration of any voluntary arrangement approved under that Part.

Information and records

20. Provision requiring registrars and other officers of courts having jurisdiction in England and Wales in relation to, or to matters connected with or arising out of, the insolvency or winding up of companies—

(a) to keep books and other records with respect to the exercise of that jurisdiction, and

(b) to make returns to the Secretary of State of the business of those courts.

21. Provision requiring a creditor, member or contributory, or such a committee as is mentioned in paragraph 10 above, to be supplied (on payment in prescribed cases of the prescribed fee) with such information and with copies of such documents as may be prescribed.

22. Provision as to the manner in which public examinations under sections 133 and 134 of this Act and proceedings under sections 236 and 237 are to be conducted, as to the circumstances in which records of such examinations or proceedings are to be made available to prescribed persons and as to the costs of such examinations and proceedings.

23. Provision imposing requirements with respect to—

(a) the preparation and keeping by the liquidator, administrator or administrative receiver of a company, or by the supervisor of a voluntary arrangement approved under Part I of this Act, of prescribed books, accounts and other records;

(b) the production of those books, accounts and records for inspection by prescribed persons;

(c) the auditing of accounts kept by the liquidator, administrator or administrative receiver of a company, or the supervisor of such a voluntary arrangement; and

(d) the issue by the administrator or administrative receiver of a company of such a certificate as is mentioned in section 22(3)(b) of the Value Added Tax Act 1983 (refund of tax in cases of bad debts) and the supply of copies of the certificate to creditors of the company.

24. Provision requiring the person who is the supervisor of a voluntary arrangement approved under Part I, when it appears to him that the voluntary arrangement has been fully implemented and that nothing remains to be done by him under the arrangement—

(a) to give notice of that fact to persons bound by the voluntary arrangement, and

(b) to report to those persons on the carrying out of the functions conferred on the supervisor of the arrangement.

25. Provision as to the manner in which the liquidator of a company is to act in relation to the books, papers and other records of the company, including provision authorising their disposal.

26. Provision imposing requirements in connection with the carrying out of functions under section 7(3) of the Company Directors Disqualification Act 1986 (including, in particular, requirements with respect to the making of periodic returns).

General

27. Provision conferring power on the Secretary of State to make regulations with respect to so much of any matter that may be provided for in the rules as relates to the carrying out of the functions of the liquidator, administrator or administrative receiver of a company.

28. Provision conferring a discretion on the court.

29. Provision conferring power on the court to make orders for the purpose of securing compliance with obligations imposed by or under [section 47, 66, 131, 143(2) or 235 of, or paragraph 47 of Schedule B1 to, this Act] or section 7(4) of the Company Directors Disqualification Act 1986.

30. Provision making non-compliance with any of the rules a criminal offence.

31. Provision making different provision for different cases or descriptions of cases, including different provisions for different areas.

[3479]

NOTES

Para 2: sub-para (1) numbered as such, and sub-para (2) added, by the Enterprise Act 2002, s 248(3), Sch 17, paras 9, 38(1), (2), as from 15 September 2003 (for savings and transitional provisions, see the note to s 8 at **[3164]**).

Paras 10, 29: words in square brackets substituted by the Enterprise Act 2002, s 248(3), Sch 17, paras 9, 38(1), (3), (6), as from 15 September 2003 (for savings and transitional provisions, see the note to s 8 at **[3164]**).

Paras 14A, 14B: inserted by the Enterprise Act 2002, s 248(3), Sch 17, paras 9, 38(1), (4), (5), as from 15 September 2003 (for savings and transitional provisions, see the note to s 8 at **[3164]**).

Paras 16A: inserted by the Enterprise Act 2002, s 271(1), as from 18 December 2003.

Application to limited liability partnerships: see the introductory note to this Act, the Limited Liability Partnerships Regulations 2001, SI 2001/1090, reg 5, Sch 3 at **[6986]**, **[6995]**, and the Limited Liability Partnerships (Scotland) Regulations 2001, SSI 2001/128, reg 4, Schs 2, 3 at **[6977]**, **[6980A]**, **[6980B]**.

Regulations: the Insolvency Regulations 1994, SI 1994/2507 at **[6794]**.

Section 430

SCHEDULE 10
PUNISHMENT OF OFFENCES UNDER THIS ACT

Section of Act creating offence	*General nature of offence*	*Mode of prosecution*	*Punishment*	*Daily default fine (where applicable)*
[6A(1).	False representation or fraud for purpose of obtaining members' or creditors' approval of proposed voluntary arrangement.	1. On indictment.	7 years or a fine, or both.	
		2. Summary.	6 months or the statutory maximum, or both.]	
…	…	…	…	…
30	Body corporate acting as receiver	1. On indictment	A fine	
		2. Summary	The statutory maximum	
31	… bankrupt acting as receiver or manager	1. On indictment	2 years or a fine, or both	
		2. Summary	6 months or the statutory maximum, or both	
38(5)	Receiver failing to deliver accounts to registrar	Summary	One-fifth of the statutory maximum	One-fiftieth of the statutory maximum.
39(2)	Company and others failing to state in correspondence that receiver appointed	Summary	One-fifth of the statutory maximum	
43(6)	Administrative receiver failing to file office copy of order permitting disposal of charged property	Summary	One-fifth of the statutory maximum	One-fiftieth of the statutory maximum.
45(5)	Administrative receiver failing to file notice of vacation of office	Summary	One-fifth of the statutory maximum	*One-fiftieth of the statutory maximum.*
46(4)	Administrative receiver failing to give notice of his appointment	Summary	One-fifth of the statutory maximum	One-fiftieth of the statutory maximum.

PART III
OTHER LEGISLATION

Section of Act creating offence	*General nature of offence*	*Mode of prosecution*	*Punishment*	*Daily default fine (where applicable)*
47(6)	Failure to comply with provisions relating to statement of affairs, where administrative receiver appointed	1. On indictment	A fine	
		2. Summary	The statutory maximum	One-tenth of the statutory maximum.
48(8)	Administrative receiver failing to comply with requirements as to his report	Summary	One-fifth of the statutory maximum	One-fiftieth of the statutory maximum.
51(4)	Body corporate or Scottish firm acting as receiver	1. On indictment	A fine	
		2. Summary	The statutory maximum	
51(5)	Undischarged bankrupt acting as receiver (Scotland)	1. On indictment	2 years or a fine, or both	
		2. Summary	6 months or the statutory maximum, or both	
53(2)	Failing to deliver to registrar copy of instrument of appointment of receiver	Summary	One-fifth of the statutory maximum	*One-fiftieth of the statutory maximum.*
54(3)	Failing to deliver to registrar the court's interlocutor appointing receiver	Summary	One-fifth of the statutory maximum	*One-fiftieth of the statutory maximum.*
61(7)	Receiver failing to send to registrar certified copy of court order authorising disposal of charged property	Summary	One-fifth of the statutory maximum	One-fiftieth of the statutory maximum.
62(5)	Failing to give notice to registrar of cessation or removal of receiver	Summary	One-fifth of the statutory maximum	*One-fiftieth of the statutory maximum.*
64(2)	Company and others failing to state on correspondence etc that receiver appointed	Summary	One-fifth of the statutory maximum	
65(4)	Receiver failing to send or publish notice of his appointment	Summary	One-fifth of the statutory maximum	One-fiftieth of the statutory maximum.

Section of Act creating offence	*General nature of offence*	*Mode of prosecution*	*Punishment*	*Daily default fine (where applicable)*
66(6)	Failing to comply with provisions concerning statement of affairs, where receiver appointed	1. On indictment	A fine	
		2. Summary	The statutory maximum	One-tenth of the statutory maximum.
67(8)	Receiver failing to comply with requirements as to his report	Summary	One-fifth of the statutory maximum	One-fiftieth of the statutory maximum.
85(2)	Company failing to give notice in Gazette of resolution for voluntary winding up	Summary	One-fifth of the statutory maximum	One-fiftieth of the statutory maximum.
89(4)	Director making statutory declaration of company's solvency without reasonable grounds for his opinion	1. On indictment	2 years or a fine, or both	
		2. Summary	6 months or the statutory maximum, or both	
89(6)	Declaration under section 89 not delivered to registrar within prescribed time	Summary	One-fifth of the statutory maximum	One-fiftieth of the statutory maximum.
93(3)	Liquidator failing to summon general meeting of company at each year's end	Summary	One-fifth of the statutory maximum	
94(4)	Liquidator failing to send to registrar a copy of account of winding up and return of final meeting	Summary	One-fifth of the statutory maximum	One-fiftieth of the statutory maximum.
94(6)	Liquidator failing to call final meeting	Summary	One-fifth of the statutory maximum	
95(8)	Liquidator failing to comply with s 95, where company insolvent	Summary	The statutory maximum	
98(6)	Company failing to comply with s 98 in respect of summoning and giving notice of creditors' meeting	1. On indictment	A fine	

Section of Act creating offence	*General nature of offence*	*Mode of prosecution*	*Punishment*	*Daily default fine (where applicable)*
		2. Summary	The statutory maximum	
99(3)	Directors failing to attend and lay statement in prescribed form before creditors' meeting	1. On indictment	A fine	
		2. Summary	The statutory maximum	
105(3)	Liquidator failing to summon company general meeting and creditors' meeting at each year's end	Summary	One-fifth of the statutory maximum	
106(4)	Liquidator failing to send to registrar account of winding up and return of final meetings	Summary	One-fifth of the statutory maximum	One-fiftieth of the statutory maximum.
106(6)	Liquidator failing to call final meeting of company or creditors	Summary	One-fifth of the statutory maximum	
109(2)	Liquidator failing to publish notice of his appointment	Summary	One-fifth of the statutory maximum	One-fiftieth of the statutory maximum.
114(4)	Directors exercising powers in breach of s 114, where no liquidator	Summary	The statutory maximum	
131(7)	Failing to comply with requirements as to statement of affairs, where liquidator appointed	1. On indictment	A fine	
		2. Summary	The statutory maximum	One-tenth of the statutory maximum.
164	Giving, offering etc corrupt inducement affecting appointment of liquidator	1. On indictment	A fine	
		2. Summary	The statutory maximum	
166(7)	Liquidator failing to comply with requirements of s 166 in creditors' voluntary winding up	Summary	The statutory maximum	
188(2)	Default in compliance with s 188 as to notification that company being wound up	Summary	One-fifth of the statutory maximum	

Section of Act creating offence	*General nature of offence*	*Mode of prosecution*	*Punishment*	*Daily default fine (where applicable)*
192(2)	Liquidator failing to notify registrar as to progress of winding up	Summary	One-fifth of the statutory maximum	One-fiftieth of the statutory maximum.
201(4)	Failing to deliver to registrar office copy of court order deferring dissolution	Summary	One-fifth of the statutory maximum	One-fiftieth of the statutory maximum.
203(6)	Failing to deliver to registrar copy of directions or result of appeal under s 203	Summary	One-fifth of the statutory maximum	One-fiftieth of the statutory maximum.
204(7)	Liquidator failing to deliver to registrar copy of court order for early dissolution	Summary	One-fifth of the statutory maximum	One-fiftieth of the statutory maximum.
204(8)	Failing to deliver to registrar copy of court order deferring early dissolution	Summary	One-fifth of the statutory maximum	One-fiftieth of the statutory maximum.
205(7)	Failing to deliver to registrar copy of Secretary of State's directions or court order deferring dissolution	Summary	One-fifth of the statutory maximum	One-fiftieth of the statutory maximum.
206(1)	Fraud etc in anticipation of winding up	1. On indictment	7 years or a fine, or both	
		2. Summary	6 months or the statutory maximum, or both	
206(2)	Privity to fraud in anticipation of winding up; fraud, or privity to fraud, after commencement of winding up	1. On indictment	7 years or a fine, or both	
		2. Summary	6 months or the statutory maximum, or both	
206(5)	Knowingly taking in pawn or pledge, or otherwise receiving, company property	1. On indictment	7 years or a fine, or both	
		2. Summary	6 months or the statutory maximum, or both	

PART III
OTHER LEGISLATION

Section of Act creating offence	*General nature of offence*	*Mode of prosecution*	*Punishment*	*Daily default fine (where applicable)*
207	Officer of company entering into transaction in fraud of company's creditors	1. On indictment	2 years or a fine, or both	
		2. Summary	6 months or the statutory maximum, or both	
208	Officer of company misconducting himself in course of winding up	1. On indictment	7 years or a fine, or both	
		2. Summary	6 months or the statutory maximum, or both	
209	Officer or contributory destroying, falsifying, etc company's books	1. On indictment	7 years or a fine, or both	
		2. Summary	6 months or the statutory maximum, or both	
210	Officer of company making material omission from statement relating to company's affairs	1. On indictment	7 years or a fine, or both	
		2. Summary	6 months or the statutory maximum, or both	
211	False representation or fraud for purpose of obtaining creditors' consent to an agreement in connection with winding up	1. On indictment	7 years or a fine, or both	
		2. Summary	6 months or the statutory maximum, or both	
216(4)	Contravening restrictions on re-use of name of company in insolvent liquidation	1. On indictment	2 years or a fine, or both	
		2. Summary	6 months or the statutory maximum, or both	
235(5)	Failing to co-operate with office-holder	1. On indictment	A fine	

Section of Act creating offence	*General nature of offence*	*Mode of prosecution*	*Punishment*	*Daily default fine (where applicable)*
		2. Summary	The statutory maximum	One-tenth of the statutory maximum.
389	Acting as insolvency practitioner when not qualified	1. On indictment	2 years or a fine, or both	
		2. Summary	6 months or the statutory maximum, or both	
[Sch A1, para 9(2).	Directors failing to notify nominee of beginning of moratorium.	1. On indictment.	2 years or a fine, or both.	
		2. Summary	6 months or the statutory maximum, or both.	
Sch A1, para 10(3).	Nominee failing to advertise or notify beginning of moratorium.	Summary.	One-fifth of the statutory maximum.	
Sch A1, para 11(2).	Nominee failing to advertise or notify end of moratorium.	Summary.	One-fifth of the statutory maximum.	
Sch A1, para 16(2).	Company and officers failing to state in correspondence etc that moratorium in force.	Summary.	One-fifth of the statutory maximum.	
Sch A1, para 17(3)(a)	Company obtaining credit without disclosing existence of moratorium.	1. On indictment.	A fine.	
		2. Summary.	The statutory maximum.	
Sch A1, para 17(3)(b).	Obtaining credit for company without disclosing existence of moratorium.	1. On indictment.	2 years or a fine, or both.	
		2. Summary.	6 months or the statutory maximum, or both.	
Sch A1, para 18(3)(a).	Company disposing of property otherwise than in ordinary way of business.	1. On indictment.	A fine.	

Section of Act creating offence	*General nature of offence*	*Mode of prosecution*	*Punishment*	*Daily default fine (where applicable)*
		2. Summary.	The statutory maximum.	
Sch A1, para 18(3)(b).	Authorising or permitting disposal of company property.	1. On indictment.	2 years or a fine, or both.	
		2. Summary.	6 months or the statutory maximum, or both.	
Sch A1, para 19(3)(a).	Company making payments in respect of liabilities existing before beginning of moratorium.	1. On indictment.	A fine.	
		2. Summary.	The statutory maximum.	
Sch A1, para 19(3)(b).	Authorising or permitting such a payment.	1. On indictment.	2 years or a fine, or both.	
		2. Summary.	6 months or the statutory maximum, or both.	
Sch A1, para 20(9).	Directors failing to send to registrar office copy of court order permitting disposal of charged property.	Summary.	One-fifth of the statutory maximum.	
Sch A1, para 22(1).	Company disposing of charged property.	1. On indictment.	A fine.	
		2. Summary.	The statutory maximum.	
Sch A1, para 22(2).	Authorising or permitting such a disposal.	1. On indictment.	2 years or a fine, or both.	
		2. Summary.	6 months or the statutory maximum, or both.	
Sch A1, para 23(1)(a).	Company entering into market contract, etc.	1. On indictment.	A fine.	

Section of Act creating offence	General nature of offence	Mode of prosecution	Punishment	Daily default fine (where applicable)
		2. Summary.	The statutory maximum.	
Sch A1, para 23(1)(b).	Authorising or permitting company to do so.	1. On indictment.	2 years or a fine, or both.	
		2. Summary.	6 months or the statutory maximum, or both.	
Sch A1, para 25(6).	Nominee failing to give notice of withdrawal of consent to act.	Summary.	One-fifth of the statutory maximum.	
Sch A1, para 34(3).	Nominee failing to give notice of extension of moratorium.	Summary.	One-fifth of the statutory maximum.	
Sch A1, para 41(2).	Fraud or privity to fraud in anticipation of moratorium.	1. On indictment.	7 years or a fine, or both.	
		2. Summary.	6 months or the statutory maximum, or both.	
Sch A1, para 41(3).	Fraud or privity to fraud during moratorium.	1. On indictment.	7 years or a fine, or both.	
		2. Summary.	6 months or the statutory maximum, or both.	
Sch A1, para 42(1).	False representation or fraud for purpose of obtaining or extending moratorium.	1. On indictment.	7 years or a fine, or both.	
		2. Summary.	6 months or the statutory maximum, or both.]	
[Sch B1, para 18(7).	Making false statement in statutory declaration where administrator appointed by holder of floating charge.	1. On indictment.	2 years, or a fine or both.	
		2. Summary.	6 months, or the statutory maximum or both.	

Section of Act creating offence	*General nature of offence*	*Mode of prosecution*	*Punishment*	*Daily default fine (where applicable)*
Sch B1, para 20.	Holder of floating charge failing to notify administrator or others of commencement of appointment.	1. On indictment.	2 years, or a fine or both.	
		2. Summary.	6 months, or the statutory maximum or both.	One-tenth of the statutory maximum.
Sch B1, para 27(4).	Making false statement in statutory declaration where appointment of administrator proposed by company or directors.	1. On indictment.	2 years, or a fine or both.	
		2. Summary.	6 months, or the statutory maximum or both.	
Sch B1, para 29(7).	Making false statement in statutory declaration where administrator appointed by company or directors.	1. On indictment.	2 years, or a fine or both.	
		2. Summary.	6 months, or the statutory maximum or both.	
Sch B1, para 32.	Company or directors failing to notify administrator or others of commencement of appointment.	1. On indictment.	2 years, or a fine or both.	
		2. Summary.	6 months, or the statutory maximum or both.	One-tenth of the statutory maximum.
Sch B1, para 45(2).	Administrator, company or officer failing to state in business document that administrator appointed.	Summary.	One-fifth of the statutory maximum.	
Sch B1, para 46(9).	Administrator failing to give notice of his appointment.	Summary.	One-fifth of the statutory maximum.	One-fiftieth of the statutory maximum.

Section of Act creating offence	General nature of offence	Mode of prosecution	Punishment	Daily default fine (where applicable)
Sch B1, para 48(4).	Failing to comply with provisions about statement of affairs where administrator appointed.	1. On indictment.	A fine.	
		2. Summary.	The statutory maximum.	One-tenth of the statutory maximum.
Sch B1, para 49(7).	Administrator failing to send out statement of his proposals.	Summary.	One-fifth of the statutory maximum.	One-fiftieth of the statutory maximum.
Sch B1, para 51(5).	Administrator failing to arrange initial creditors' meeting.	Summary.	One-fifth of the statutory maximum.	One-fiftieth of the statutory maximum.
Sch B1, para 53(3).	Administrator failing to report decision taken at initial creditors' meeting.	Summary.	One-fifth of the statutory maximum.	One-fiftieth of the statutory maximum.
Sch B1, para 54(7).	Administrator failing to report decision taken at creditors' meeting summoned to consider revised proposal.	Summary.	One-fifth of the statutory maximum.	One-fiftieth of the statutory maximum.
Sch B1, para 56(2).	Administrator failing to summon creditors' meeting.	Summary.	One-fifth of the statutory maximum.	One-fiftieth of the statutory maximum.
Sch B1, para 71(6).	Administrator failing to file court order enabling disposal of charged property.	Summary.	One-fifth of the statutory maximum.	One-fiftieth of the statutory maximum.
Sch B1, para 72(5).	Administrator failing to file court order enabling disposal of hire-purchase property.	Summary.	One-fifth of the statutory maximum.	One-fiftieth of the statutory maximum.
Sch B1, para 77(3).	Administrator failing to notify Registrar of Companies of automatic end of administration.	Summary.	One-fifth of the statutory maximum.	One-fiftieth of the statutory maximum.
Sch B1, para 78(6).	Administrator failing to give notice of extension by consent of term of office.	Summary.	One-fifth of the statutory maximum.	One-fiftieth of the statutory maximum.
Sch B1, para 80(6).	Administrator failing to give notice of termination of administration where objective achieved.	Summary.	One-fifth of the statutory maximum.	One-fiftieth of the statutory maximum.

Section of Act creating offence	*General nature of offence*	*Mode of prosecution*	*Punishment*	*Daily default fine (where applicable)*
Sch B1, para 84(9).	Administrator failing to comply with provisions where company moves to dissolution.	Summary.	One-fifth of the statutory maximum.	One-fiftieth of the statutory maximum.
Sch B1, para 86(3).	Administrator failing to notify Registrar of Companies where court terminates administration.	Summary.	One-fifth of the statutory maximum.	One-fiftieth of the statutory maximum.
Sch B1, para 89(3).	Administrator failing to give notice on ceasing to be qualified.	Summary.	One-fifth of the statutory maximum.	One-fiftieth of the statutory maximum.]
Sch 7, para 4(3)	Failure to attend and give evidence to Insolvency Practitioners Tribunal; suppressing, concealing, etc relevant documents	Summary	Level 3 on the standard scale within the meaning given by section 75 of the Criminal Justice Act 1982	

[3480]

NOTES

Certain provisions outside the scope of this work have been omitted from this Schedule.

Entry relating to section 6A inserted by the Insolvency Act 2000, s 2, Sch 2, Pt I, paras 1, 12, as from 1 January 2003 (for transitional provisions see the note to s 1 at **[3152]**).

Entries omitted relating to ss 12(2), 15(8), 18(5), 21(3), 22(6), 23(3), 24(7), 27(6) repealed by the Enterprise Act 2002, ss 248(3), 278(2), Sch 17, paras 9, 39(1), (3), Sch 26, as from 15 September 2003 (for savings and transitional provisions, see the note to s 8 at **[3164]**).

Word omitted from column 1 of entry relating to s 31 repealed by the Enterprise Act 2002, s 278(2), Sch 26, as from 1 April 2004.

Entries in italics in column 5 relating to ss 45(5), 53(2), 54(3), 62(5) repealed by CA 1989, s 212, Sch 24, as from a day to be appointed.

Entries relating to Schedule A1 inserted by the Insolvency Act 2000, s 1, Sch 1, paras 1, 12, as from 1 January 2003.

Entries relating to Schedule B1 inserted by the Enterprise Act 2002, s 248(3), Sch 17, paras 9, 39(1), (2), as from 15 September 2003 (for savings and transitional provisions, see the note to s 8 at **[3164]**).

The Note to this Schedule was repealed by the Statute Law (Repeals) Act 1993, as from 5 November 1993.

Application to limited liability partnerships: see the introductory note to this Act, the Limited Liability Partnerships Regulations 2001, SI 2001/1090, reg 5, Sch 3 at **[6986]**, **[6995]**, and the Limited Liability Partnerships (Scotland) Regulations 2001, SSI 2001/128, reg 4, Schs 2, 3 at **[6977]**, **[6980A]**, **[6980B]**.

SCHEDULE 11
TRANSITIONAL PROVISIONS AND SAVINGS

Section 437

PART I
COMPANY INSOLVENCY AND WINDING UP

Administration orders

1.—(1) Where any right to appoint an administrative receiver of a company is conferred by any debentures or floating charge created before the appointed day, the conditions precedent to the exercise of that right are deemed to include the presentation of a petition applying for an administration order to be made in relation to the company.

(2) "Administrative receiver" here has the meaning assigned by section 251.

Receivers and managers (England and Wales)

2.—(1) In relation to any receiver or manager of a company's property who was appointed before the appointed day, the new law does not apply; and the relevant provisions of the former law continue to have effect.

(2) "The new law" here means Chapter I of Part III, and Part VI, of this Act; and "the former law" means the Companies Act and so much of this Act as replaces provisions of that Act (without the amendments in paragraphs 15 to 17 of Schedule 6 to the Insolvency Act 1985, or the associated repeals made by that Act), and any provision of the Insolvency Act 1985 which was in force before the appointed day.

(3) This paragraph is without prejudice to the power conferred by this Act under which rules under section 411 may make transitional provision in connection with the coming into force of those rules; and such provision may apply those rules in relation to the receiver or manager of a company's property notwithstanding that he was appointed before the coming into force of the rules or section 411.

Receivers (Scotland)

3.—(1) In relation to any receiver appointed under section 467 of the Companies Act before the appointed day, the new law does not apply and the relevant provisions of the former law continue to have effect.

(2) "The new law" here means Chapter II of Part III, and Part VI, of this Act; and "the former law" means the Companies Act and so much of this Act as replaces provisions of that Act (without the amendments in paragraphs 18 to 22 of Schedule 6 to the Insolvency Act 1985 or the associated repeals made by that Act), and any provision of the Insolvency Act 1985 which was in force before the appointed day.

(3) This paragraph is without prejudice to the power conferred by this Act under which rules under section 411 may make transitional provision in connection with the coming into force of those rules; and such provision may apply those rules in relation to a receiver appointed under section 467 notwithstanding that he was appointed before the coming into force of the rules or section 411.

Winding up already in progress

4.—(1) In relation to any winding up which has commenced, or is treated as having commenced, before the appointed day, the new law does not apply, and the former law continues to have effect, subject to the following paragraphs.

(2) "The new law" here means any provisions in the first Group of Parts of this Act which replace sections 66 to 87 and 89 to 105 of the Insolvency Act 1985; and "the former law" means Parts XX and XXI of the Companies Act (without the amendments in paragraphs 23 to 52 of Schedule 6 to the Insolvency Act 1985, or the associated repeals made by that Act).

PART III
OTHER LEGISLATION

Statement of affairs

5.—(1) Where a winding up by the court in England and Wales has commenced, or is treated as having commenced, before the appointed day, the official receiver or (on appeal from a refusal by him) the court may, at any time on or after that day—

(a) release a person from an obligation imposed on him by or under section 528 of the Companies Act (statement of affairs), or

(b) extend the period specified in subsection (6) of that section.

(2) Accordingly, on and after the appointed day, section 528(6) has effect in relation to a winding up to which this paragraph applies with the omission of the words from "or within" onwards.

Provisions relating to liquidator

6.—(1) This paragraph applies as regards the liquidator in the case of a winding up by the court in England and Wales commenced, or treated as having commenced, before the appointed day.

(2) The official receiver may, at any time when he is liquidator of the company, apply to the Secretary of State for the appointment of a liquidator in his (the official receiver's) place; and on any such application the Secretary of State shall either make an appointment or decline to make one.

(3) Where immediately before the appointed day the liquidator of the company has not made an application under section 545 of the Companies Act (release of liquidators), then—

(a) except where the Secretary of State otherwise directs, sections 146(1) and (2) and 172(8) of this Act apply, and section 545 does not apply, in relation to any liquidator of that company who holds office on or at any time after the appointed day and is not the official receiver;

(b) section 146(3) applies in relation to the carrying out at any time after that day by any liquidator of the company of any of his functions; and

(c) a liquidator in relation to whom section 172(8) has effect by virtue of this paragraph has his release with effect from the time specified in section 174(4)(d) of this Act.

(4) Subsection (6) of section 174 of this Act has effect for the purposes of sub-paragraph (3)(c) above as it has for the purposes of that section, but as if the reference to section 212 were to section 631 of the Companies Act.

(5) The liquidator may employ a solicitor to assist him in the carrying out of his functions without the permission of the committee of inspection; but if he does so employ a solicitor he shall inform the committee of inspection that he has done so.

Winding up under supervision of the court

7. The repeals in Part II of Schedule 10 to the Insolvency Act 1985 of references (in the Companies Act and elsewhere) to a winding up under the supervision of the court do not affect the operation of the enactments in which the references are contained in relation to any case in which an order under section 606 of the Companies Act (power to order winding up under supervision) was made before the appointed day.

Saving for power to make rules

8.—(1) Paragraphs 4 to 7 are without prejudice to the power conferred by this Act under which rules made under section 411 may make transitional provision in connection with the coming into force of those rules.

(2) Such provision may apply those rules in relation to a winding up notwithstanding that the winding up commenced, or is treated as having commenced, before the coming into force of the rules or section 411.

Setting aside of preferences and other transactions

9.—(1) Where a provision in Part VI of this Act applies in relation to a winding up or in relation to a case in which an administration order has been made, a preference given, floating charge created or other transaction entered into before the appointed day shall not be set aside under that provision except to the extent that it could have been set aside under the law in force immediately before that day, assuming for this purpose that any relevant administration order had been a winding-up order.

(2) The references above to setting aside a preference, floating charge or other transaction include the making of an order which varies or reverses any effect of a preference, floating charge or other transaction.

[3481]

NOTES

Application to limited liability partnerships: see the introductory note to this Act and the Limited Liability Partnerships Regulations 2001, SI 2001/1090, reg 5, Sch 3 at **[6986]**, **[6995]**.

PART III
TRANSITIONAL EFFECT OF PART XVI

20.—(1) A transaction entered into before the appointed day shall not be set aside under Part XVI of this Act except to the extent that it could have been set aside under the law in force immediately before that day.

(2) References above to setting aside a transaction include the making of any order which varies or reverses any effect of a transaction.

[3482]

NOTES

Application to limited liability partnerships: see the introductory note to this Act and the Limited Liability Partnerships Regulations 2001, SI 2001/1090, reg 5, Sch 3 at **[6986]**, **[6995]**.

PART IV
INSOLVENCY PRACTITIONERS

21. Where an individual began to act as an insolvency practitioner in relation to any person before the appointed day, nothing in section 390(2) or (3) prevents that individual from being qualified to act as an insolvency practitioner in relation to that person.

[3483]

NOTES

Application to limited liability partnerships: see the introductory note to this Act and the Limited Liability Partnerships Regulations 2001, SI 2001/1090, reg 5, Sch 3 at **[6986]**, **[6995]**.

PART V
GENERAL TRANSITIONAL PROVISIONS AND SAVINGS

Interpretation for this Part

22. In this Part of this Schedule, "the former enactments" means so much of the Companies Act as is repealed and replaced by this Act, the Insolvency Act 1985 and the other enactments repealed by this Act.

General saving for past acts and events

23. So far as anything done or treated as done under or for the purposes of any provision of the former enactments could have been done under or for the purposes of the corresponding provision of this Act, it is not invalidated by the repeal of that provision but has effect as if done under or for the purposes of the corresponding provision; and any order, regulation, rule

or other instrument made or having effect under any provision of the former enactments shall, insofar as its effect is preserved by this paragraph, be treated for all purposes as made and having effect under the corresponding provision.

Periods of time

24. Where any period of time specified in a provision of the former enactments is current immediately before the appointed day, this Act has effect as if the corresponding provision had been in force when the period began to run; and (without prejudice to the foregoing) any period of time so specified and current is deemed for the purposes of this Act—

(a) to run from the date or event from which it was running immediately before the appointed day, and

(b) to expire (subject to any provision of this Act for its extension) whenever it would have expired if this Act had not been passed;

and any rights, priorities, liabilities, reliefs, obligations, requirements, powers, duties or exemptions dependent on the beginning, duration or end of such a period as above mentioned shall be under this Act as they were or would have been under the former enactments.

Internal cross-references in this Act

25. Where in any provision of this Act there is a reference to another such provision, and the first-mentioned provision operates, or is capable of operating, in relation to things done or omitted, or events occurring or not occurring, in the past (including in particular past acts of compliance with any enactment, failures of compliance, contraventions, offences and convictions of offences), the reference to the other provision is to be read as including a reference to the corresponding provision of the former enactments.

Punishment of offences

26.—(1) Offences committed before the appointed day under any provision of the former enactments may, notwithstanding any repeal by this Act, be prosecuted and punished after that day as if this Act had not passed.

(2) A contravention of any provision of the former enactments committed before the appointed day shall not be visited with any severer punishment under or by virtue of this Act than would have been applicable under that provision at the time of the contravention; but where an offence for the continuance of which a penalty was provided has been committed under any provision of the former enactments, proceedings may be taken under this Act in respect of the continuance of the offence on and after the appointed day in the like manner as if the offence had been committed under the corresponding provision of this Act.

References elsewhere to the former enactments

27.—(1) A reference in any enactment, instrument or document (whether express or implied, and in whatever phraseology) to a provision of the former enactments (including the corresponding provision of any yet earlier enactment) is to be read, where necessary to retain for the enactment, instrument or document the same force and effect as it would have had but for the passing of this Act, as, or as including, a reference to the corresponding provision by which it is replaced in this Act.

(2) The generality of the preceding sub-paragraph is not affected by any specific conversion of references made by this Act, nor by the inclusion in any provision of this Act of a reference (whether express or implied, and in whatever phraseology) to the provision of the former enactments corresponding to that provision, or to a provision of the former enactments which is replaced by a corresponding provision of this Act.

Saving for power to repeal provisions in section 51

28. The Secretary of State may by order in a statutory instrument repeal subsections (3) to (5) of section 51 of this Act and the entries in Schedule 10 relating to subsections (4) and (5) of that section.

Saving for Interpretation Act 1978 ss 16, 17

29. Nothing in this Schedule is to be taken as prejudicing sections 16 and 17 of the Interpretation Act 1978 (savings from, and effect of, repeals); and for the purposes of section 17(2) of that Act (construction of references to enactments repealed and replaced, etc), so much of section 18 of the Insolvency Act 1985 as is replaced by a provision of this Act is deemed to have been repealed by this Act and not by the Company Directors Disqualification Act 1986.

[3484]

NOTES

Application to limited liability partnerships: see the introductory note to this Act and the Limited Liability Partnerships Regulations 2001, SI 2001/1090, reg 5, Sch 3 at **[6986]**, **[6995]**.

BANK OF ENGLAND ACT 1998 (NOTE)

(1998 c 11)

NOTES

This Act has been omitted from this Edition of the *Company Law Handbook* in order to create space for other legislation (ie, the Companies Act 2006 and the associated destination and derivation tables). Relevant parts of it were printed in the 20th Edition of this work (at p 1414 et seq) and, as of 1 July 2007, those provisions had not been amended since the publication of that Edition. This Act is, however, included in the CD version of this work (which may be ordered from the LexisNexis Butterworths Customer Services Department) and can be accessed in the online version of the *Company Law Handbook* which is updated fortnightly (at www.lexisnexis.com/uk/legal).

[3485]–[3494]

COMPANY AND BUSINESS NAMES (CHAMBER OF COMMERCE, ETC) ACT 1999

(1999 c 19)

NOTES

As of 1 July 2007, this Act had not been amended.

An Act to make provision concerning the approval of company or business names containing the expression "chamber of commerce" or any related expression; and for connected purposes

[27 July 1999]

1 Approval to be required for company or business names including the expression "chamber of commerce"

It is the duty of the Secretary of State to secure that the expression "chamber of commerce" and its Welsh equivalent ("siambr fasnach") is specified—

(a) in regulations under section 29(1)(a) of the Companies Act 1985, and
(b) in regulations under section 3(1)(a) of the Business Names Act 1985,

as an expression for the registration of which as or as part of a company's name, or for the use of which as or as part of a business name, the approval of the Secretary of State is required.

[3495]

2 Approval of certain company names

(1) Before determining under section 26(2) of the Companies Act 1985 whether to approve the registration of a company under a name which includes—

(a) the expression "chamber of commerce" or "siambr fasnach", or
(b) any other expression for the time being specified in regulations under

PART III OTHER LEGISLATION

section 29(1)(a) of the Companies Act 1985 which begins with the words "chamber of" or "chambers of" (or the Welsh equivalents),

the Secretary of State must consult at least one relevant representative body.

(2) The Secretary of State may publish guidance with respect to factors which may be taken into account in determining whether to approve the registration of a name to which this section applies.

[3496]

3 Approval of certain business names

(1) Before determining under section 2(1) of the Business Names Act 1985 whether to approve the carrying on of a business under a name which includes—

(a) the expression "chamber of commerce" or "siambr fasnach", or

(b) any other expression for the time being specified in regulations under section 3(1)(a) of the Business Names Act 1985 which begins with the words "chamber of" or "chambers of" (or the Welsh equivalents),

the Secretary of State must consult at least one relevant representative body.

(2) The Secretary of State may publish guidance with respect to factors which may be taken into account in determining whether to approve the use of a business name to which this section applies.

[3497]

4 Relevant representative bodies

(1) The relevant representative bodies for the purposes of this Act are—

(a) British Chambers of Commerce;

(b) the body known as Scottish Chambers of Commerce.

(2) The Secretary of State may by order amend subsection (1) by adding to or deleting from it the name of any body (whether corporate or unincorporated).

(3) The power to make an order under this section is exercisable by statutory instrument which shall be liable to annulment in pursuance of a resolution of either House of Parliament.

[3498]

5 Citation, commencement and extent

(1) This Act may be cited as the Company and Business Names (Chamber of Commerce, Etc) Act 1999.

(2) This Act shall come into force on such day as the Secretary of State may by order made by statutory instrument appoint.

(3) This Act does not extend to Northern Ireland.

[3499]

NOTES

Orders: the Company and Business Names (Chamber of Commerce, etc) Act 1999 (Commencement) Order 2001, SI 2001/258 (bringing this Act into force on 10 May 2001).

LIMITED LIABILITY PARTNERSHIPS ACT 2000

(2000 c 12)

NOTES

This Act is reproduced as amended by: the Companies (Audit, Investigations and Community Enterprise) Act 2004; the Companies Act 2006; the Income Tax Act 2007; the Open-Ended Investment Companies Regulations 2001, SI 2001/1228; the Limited Liability Partnerships (Particulars of Usual Residential Address) (Confidentiality Orders) Regulations 2002, SI 2002/915.

ARRANGEMENT OF SECTIONS

Introductory

An Act to make provision for limited liability partnerships

[20 July 2000]

Introductory

1 Limited liability partnerships

(1) There shall be a new form of legal entity to be known as a limited liability partnership.

(2) A limited liability partnership is a body corporate (with legal personality separate from that of its members) which is formed by being incorporated under this Act; and—

(a) in the following provisions of this Act (except in the phrase "oversea limited liability partnership"), and

(b) in any other enactment (except where provision is made to the contrary or the context otherwise requires),

references to a limited liability partnership are to such a body corporate.

(3) A limited liability partnership has unlimited capacity.

(4) The members of a limited liability partnership have such liability to contribute to its assets in the event of its being wound up as is provided for by virtue of this Act.

(5) Accordingly, except as far as otherwise provided by this Act or any other enactment, the law relating to partnerships does not apply to a limited liability partnership.

(6) The Schedule (which makes provision about the names and registered offices of limited liability partnerships) has effect.

[3500]

Incorporation

2 Incorporation document etc

(1) For a limited liability partnership to be incorporated—

(a) two or more persons associated for carrying on a lawful business with a view to profit must have subscribed their names to an incorporation document,

PART III OTHER LEGISLATION

(b) there must have been delivered to the registrar either the incorporation document or a copy authenticated in a manner approved by him, and

(c) there must have been so delivered a statement in a form approved by the registrar, made by either a solicitor engaged in the formation of the limited liability partnership or anyone who subscribed his name to the incorporation document, that the requirement imposed by paragraph (a) has been complied with.

(2) The incorporation document must—

(a) be in a form approved by the registrar (or as near to such a form as circumstances allow),

(b) state the name of the limited liability partnership,

(c) state whether the registered office of the limited liability partnership is to be situated in England and Wales, in Wales or in Scotland,

(d) state the address of that registered office,

(e) state the name and address of each of the persons who are to be members of the limited liability partnership on incorporation, and

(f) either specify which of those persons are to be designated members or state that every person who from time to time is a member of the limited liability partnership is a designated member.

[(2A) Where a confidentiality order, made under section 723B of the Companies Act 1985 as applied to a limited liability partnerships, is in force in respect of any individual named as a member of a limited liability partnership under subsection (2) that subsection shall have effect as if the reference to the address of the individual were a reference to the address for the time being notified by him under the Limited Liability Partnerships (Particulars of Usual Residential Address) (Confidentiality Orders) Regulations 2002 to any limited liability partnership of which he is a member or if he is not such a member either the address specified in his application for a confidentiality order or the address last notified by him under such a confidentiality order as the case may be.

(2B) Where the incorporation document or a copy of such delivered under this section includes an address specified in reliance on subsection (2A) there shall be delivered with it or the copy of it a statement in a form approved by the registrar containing particulars of the usual residential address of the member whose address is so specified.]

(3) If a person makes a false statement under subsection (1)(c) which he—

(a) knows to be false, or

(b) does not believe to be true,

he commits an offence.

(4) A person guilty of an offence under subsection (3) is liable—

(a) on summary conviction, to imprisonment for a period not exceeding six months or a fine not exceeding the statutory maximum, or to both, or

(b) on conviction on indictment, to imprisonment for a period not exceeding two years or a fine, or to both.

[3501]

NOTES

Sub-ss (2A), (2B): inserted by the Limited Liability Partnerships (Particulars of Usual Residential Address) (Confidentiality Orders) Regulations 2002, SI 2002/915, reg 16, Sch 2, para 1, as from 2 April 2002.

3 Incorporation by registration

(1) When the requirements imposed by paragraphs (b) and (c) of subsection (1) of section 2 have been complied with, the registrar shall retain the incorporation document or copy delivered to him and, unless the requirement imposed by paragraph (a) of that subsection has not been complied with, he shall—

(a) register the incorporation document or copy, and

(b) give a certificate that the limited liability partnership is incorporated by the name specified in the incorporation document.

(2) The registrar may accept the statement delivered under paragraph (c) of subsection (1) of section 2 as sufficient evidence that the requirement imposed by paragraph (a) of that subsection has been complied with.

(3) The certificate shall either be signed by the registrar or be authenticated by his official seal.

(4) The certificate is conclusive evidence that the requirements of section 2 are complied with and that the limited liability partnership is incorporated by the name specified in the incorporation document.

[3502]

Membership

4 Members

(1) On the incorporation of a limited liability partnership its members are the persons who subscribed their names to the incorporation document (other than any who have died or been dissolved).

(2) Any other person may become a member of a limited liability partnership by and in accordance with an agreement with the existing members.

(3) A person may cease to be a member of a limited liability partnership (as well as by death or dissolution) in accordance with an agreement with the other members or, in the absence of agreement with the other members as to cessation of membership, by giving reasonable notice to the other members.

(4) A member of a limited liability partnership shall not be regarded for any purpose as employed by the limited liability partnership unless, if he and the other members were partners in a partnership, he would be regarded for that purpose as employed by the partnership.

[3503]

5 Relationship of members etc

(1) Except as far as otherwise provided by this Act or any other enactment, the mutual rights and duties of the members of a limited liability partnership, and the mutual rights and duties of a limited liability partnership and its members, shall be governed—

- (a) by agreement between the members, or between the limited liability partnership and its members, or
- (b) in the absence of agreement as to any matter, by any provision made in relation to that matter by regulations under section 15(c).

(2) An agreement made before the incorporation of a limited liability partnership between the persons who subscribe their names to the incorporation document may impose obligations on the limited liability partnership (to take effect at any time after its incorporation).

[3504]

6 Members as agents

(1) Every member of a limited liability partnership is the agent of the limited liability partnership.

(2) But a limited liability partnership is not bound by anything done by a member in dealing with a person if—

- (a) the member in fact has no authority to act for the limited liability partnership by doing that thing, and
- (b) the person knows that he has no authority or does not know or believe him to be a member of the limited liability partnership.

(3) Where a person has ceased to be a member of a limited liability partnership, the former member is to be regarded (in relation to any person dealing with the limited liability partnership) as still being a member of the limited liability partnership unless—

- (a) the person has notice that the former member has ceased to be a member of the limited liability partnership, or
- (b) notice that the former member has ceased to be a member of the limited liability partnership has been delivered to the registrar.

(4) Where a member of a limited liability partnership is liable to any person (other than another member of the limited liability partnership) as a result of a wrongful act or omission

of his in the course of the business of the limited liability partnership or with its authority, the limited liability partnership is liable to the same extent as the member.

[3505]

7 Ex-members

(1) This section applies where a member of a limited liability partnership has either ceased to be a member or—

(a) has died,

(b) has become bankrupt or had his estate sequestrated or has been wound up,

(c) has granted a trust deed for the benefit of his creditors, or

(d) has assigned the whole or any part of his share in the limited liability partnership (absolutely or by way of charge or security).

(2) In such an event the former member or—

(a) his personal representative,

(b) his trustee in bankruptcy or permanent or interim trustee (within the meaning of the Bankruptcy (Scotland) Act 1985) or liquidator,

(c) his trustee under the trust deed for the benefit of his creditors, or

(d) his assignee,

may not interfere in the management or administration of any business or affairs of the limited liability partnership.

(3) But subsection (2) does not affect any right to receive an amount from the limited liability partnership in that event.

[3506]

8 Designated members

(1) If the incorporation document specifies who are to be designated members—

(a) they are designated members on incorporation, and

(b) any member may become a designated member by and in accordance with an agreement with the other members,

and a member may cease to be a designated member in accordance with an agreement with the other members.

(2) But if there would otherwise be no designated members, or only one, every member is a designated member.

(3) If the incorporation document states that every person who from time to time is a member of the limited liability partnership is a designated member, every member is a designated member.

(4) A limited liability partnership may at any time deliver to the registrar—

(a) notice that specified members are to be designated members, or

(b) notice that every person who from time to time is a member of the limited liability partnership is a designated member,

and, once it is delivered, subsection (1) (apart from paragraph (a)) and subsection (2), or subsection (3), shall have effect as if that were stated in the incorporation document.

(5) A notice delivered under subsection (4)—

(a) shall be in a form approved by the registrar, and

(b) shall be signed by a designated member of the limited liability partnership or authenticated in a manner approved by the registrar.

(6) A person ceases to be a designated member if he ceases to be a member.

[3507]

9 Registration of membership changes

(1) A limited liability partnership must ensure that—

(a) where a person becomes or ceases to be a member or designated member, notice is delivered to the registrar within fourteen days, and

(b) where there is any change in the name or address of a member, notice is delivered to the registrar within 28 days.

(2) Where all the members from time to time of a limited liability partnership are designated members, subsection (1)(a) does not require notice that a person has become or ceased to be a designated member as well as a member.

(3) A notice delivered under subsection (1)—

(a) shall be in a form approved by the registrar, and

(b) shall be signed by a designated member of the limited liability partnership or authenticated in a manner approved by the registrar,

and, if it relates to a person becoming a member or designated member, shall contain a statement that he consents to becoming a member or designated member signed by him or authenticated in a manner approved by the registrar.

[(3A) Where a confidentiality order under section 723B of the Companies Act 1985 as applied to limited liability partnerships is made in respect of an existing member, the limited liability partnership must ensure that there is delivered within 28 days to the registrar notice in a form approved by the registrar containing the address for the time being notified to it by the member under the Limited Liability Partnerships (Particulars of Usual Residential Address) (Confidentiality Orders) Regulations 2002.

(3B) Where such a confidentiality order is in force in respect of a member the requirement in subsection (1)(b) to notify a change in the address of a member shall be read in relation to that member as a requirement to deliver to the registrar, within 28 days, notice of—

(a) any change in the usual residential address of that member; and

(b) any change in the address for the time being notified to the limited liability partnership by the member under the Limited Liability Partnerships (Particulars of Usual Residential Address) (Confidentiality Orders) Regulations 2002,

and the registrar may approve different forms for the notification of each kind of address.]

(4) If a limited liability partnership fails to comply with subsection (1), the partnership and every designated member commits an offence.

(5) But it is a defence for a designated member charged with an offence under subsection (4) to prove that he took all reasonable steps for securing that subsection (1) was complied with.

(6) A person guilty of an offence under subsection (4) is liable on summary conviction to a fine not exceeding level 5 on the standard scale.

[3508]

NOTES

Sub-ss (3A), (3B): inserted by the Limited Liability Partnerships (Particulars of Usual Residential Address) (Confidentiality Orders) Regulations 2002, SI 2002/915, reg 16, Sch 2, para 1, as from 2 April 2002.

Taxation

10, 11 *(S 10 inserts the Income and Corporation Taxes Act 1988, ss 118ZA, 118ZB, 118ZC, 118ZD, amends s 362 of the 1988 Act, and inserts the Taxation of Chargeable Gains Act 1992, ss 59A, 156A, and is repealed in part by the Income Tax Act 2007, s 1031, Sch 3; s 11 inserts the Inheritance Tax Act 1984, s 267A.)*

12 Stamp duty

(1) Stamp duty shall not be chargeable on an instrument by which property is conveyed or transferred by a person to a limited liability partnership in connection with its incorporation within the period of one year beginning with the date of incorporation if the following two conditions are satisfied.

(2) The first condition is that at the relevant time the person—

(a) is a partner in a partnership comprised of all the persons who are or are to be members of the limited liability partnership (and no-one else), or

(b) holds the property conveyed or transferred as nominee or bare trustee for one or more of the partners in such a partnership.

(3) The second condition is that—

(a) the proportions of the property conveyed or transferred to which the persons mentioned in subsection (2)(a) are entitled immediately after the conveyance or transfer are the same as those to which they were entitled at the relevant time, or

(b) none of the differences in those proportions has arisen as part of a scheme or arrangement of which the main purpose, or one of the main purposes, is avoidance of liability to any duty or tax.

(4) For the purposes of subsection (2) a person holds property as bare trustee for a partner if the partner has the exclusive right (subject only to satisfying any outstanding charge, lien or other right of the trustee to resort to the property for payment of duty, taxes, costs or other outgoings) to direct how the property shall be dealt with.

(5) In this section "the relevant time" means—
- (a) if the person who conveyed or transferred the property to the limited liability partnership acquired the property after its incorporation, immediately after he acquired the property, and
- (b) in any other case, immediately before its incorporation.

(6) An instrument in respect of which stamp duty is not chargeable by virtue of subsection (1) shall not be taken to be duly stamped unless—
- (a) it has, in accordance with section 12 of the Stamp Act 1891, been stamped with a particular stamp denoting that it is not chargeable with any duty or that it is duly stamped, or
- (b) it is stamped with the duty to which it would be liable apart from that subsection.

[3509]

13 (*Amends the Social Security Contributions and Benefits Act 1992, s 15 and the Social Security Contributions and Benefits* (*Northern Ireland*) *Act 1992, s 15*.)

Regulations

14 Insolvency and winding up

(1) Regulations shall make provision about the insolvency and winding up of limited liability partnerships by applying or incorporating, with such modifications as appear appropriate, Parts I to IV, VI and VII of the Insolvency Act 1986.

(2) Regulations may make other provision about the insolvency and winding up of limited liability partnerships, and provision about the insolvency and winding up of oversea limited liability partnerships, by—
- (a) applying or incorporating, with such modifications as appear appropriate, any law relating to the insolvency or winding up of companies or other corporations which would not otherwise have effect in relation to them, or
- (b) providing for any law relating to the insolvency or winding up of companies or other corporations which would otherwise have effect in relation to them not to apply to them or to apply to them with such modifications as appear appropriate.

(3) In this Act "oversea limited liability partnership" means a body incorporated or otherwise established outside Great Britain and having such connection with Great Britain, and such other features, as regulations may prescribe.

[3510]

NOTES

Regulations: the Limited Liability Partnerships (Scotland) Regulations 2001, SSI 2001/128 at **[6974]**; the Limited Liability Partnerships Regulations 2001, SI 2001/1090 at **[6982]**.

15 Application of company law etc

Regulations may make provision about limited liability partnerships and oversea limited liability partnerships (not being provision about insolvency or winding up) by—
- (a) applying or incorporating, with such modifications as appear appropriate, any law relating to companies or other corporations which would not otherwise have effect in relation to them,
- (b) providing for any law relating to companies or other corporations which would otherwise have effect in relation to them not to apply to them or to apply to them with such modifications as appear appropriate, or
- (c) applying or incorporating, with such modifications as appear appropriate, any law relating to partnerships.

[3511]

NOTES

Regulations: the Limited Liability Partnerships (Scotland) Regulations 2001, SSI 2001/128 at **[6974]**; the Limited Liability Partnerships Regulations 2001, SI 2001/1090 at **[6982]**; the Limited Liability

Partnerships (No 2) Regulations 2002, SI 2002/913 at **[7076]**; the Companies (Registrar, Languages and Trading Disclosures) Regulations 2006, SI 2006/3429 at **[7592]**.

16 Consequential amendments

(1) Regulations may make in any enactment such amendments or repeals as appear appropriate in consequence of this Act or regulations made under it.

(2) The regulations may, in particular, make amendments and repeals affecting companies or other corporations or partnerships.

[3512]

NOTES

Regulations: the Limited Liability Partnerships (Scotland) Regulations 2001, SSI 2001/128 at **[6974]**; the Limited Liability Partnerships Regulations 2001, SI 2001/1090 at **[6982]**; the Limited Liability Partnerships (No 2) Regulations 2002, SI 2002/913 at **[7076]**.

17 General

(1) In this Act "regulations" means regulations made by the Secretary of State by statutory instrument.

(2) Regulations under this Act may in particular—

(a) make provisions for dealing with non-compliance with any of the regulations (including the creation of criminal offences),
(b) impose fees (which shall be paid into the Consolidated Fund), and
(c) provide for the exercise of functions by persons prescribed by the regulations.

(3) Regulations under this Act may—

(a) contain any appropriate consequential, incidental, supplementary or transitional provisions or savings, and
(b) make different provision for different purposes.

(4) No regulations to which this subsection applies shall be made unless a draft of the statutory instrument containing the regulations (whether or not together with other provisions) has been laid before, and approved by a resolution of, each House of Parliament.

(5) Subsection (4) applies to—

(a) regulations under section 14(2) not consisting entirely of the application or incorporation (with or without modifications) of provisions contained in or made under the Insolvency Act 1986,
(b) regulations under section 15 not consisting entirely of the application or incorporation (with or without modifications) of provisions contained in or made under Part I, Chapter VIII of Part V, Part VII, Parts XI to XIII, Parts XVI to XVIII, Part XX or Parts XXIV to XXVI of the Companies Act 1985,
(c) regulations under section 14 or 15 making provision about oversea limited liability partnerships, and
(d) regulations under section 16.

(6) A statutory instrument containing regulations under this Act shall (unless a draft of it has been approved by a resolution of each House of Parliament) be subject to annulment in pursuance of a resolution of either House of Parliament.

[3513]

Supplementary

18 Interpretation

In this Act—

"address", in relation to a member of a limited liability partnership, means—
(a) if an individual, his usual residential address, and
(b) if a corporation or Scottish firm, its registered or principal office,

"business" includes every trade, profession and occupation,

"designated member" shall be construed in accordance with section 8,

"enactment" includes subordinate legislation (within the meaning of the Interpretation Act 1978),

"incorporation document" shall be construed in accordance with section 2,
"limited liability partnership" has the meaning given by section 1(2),
"member" shall be construed in accordance with section 4,
"modifications" includes additions and omissions,
"name", in relation to a member of a limited liability partnership, means—

(a) if an individual, his forename and surname (or, in the case of a peer or other person usually known by a title, his title instead of or in addition to either or both his forename and surname), and
(b) if a corporation or Scottish firm, its corporate or firm name,

"oversea limited liability partnership" has the meaning given by section 14(3),
"the registrar" means—

(a) if the registered office of the limited liability partnership is, or is to be, situated in England and Wales or in Wales, the registrar or other officer performing under the Companies Act 1985 the duty of registration of companies in England and Wales, and
(b) if its registered office is, or is to be, situated in Scotland, the registrar or other officer performing under that Act the duty of registration of companies in Scotland, and

"regulations" has the meaning given by section 17(1).

[3514]

19 Commencement, extent and short title

(1) The preceding provisions of this Act shall come into force on such day as the Secretary of State may by order made by statutory instrument appoint; and different days may be appointed for different purposes.

(2) The Secretary of State may by order made by statutory instrument make any transitional provisions and savings which appear appropriate in connection with the coming into force of any provision of this Act.

(3) For the purposes of the Scotland Act 1998 this Act shall be taken to be a pre-commencement enactment within the meaning of that Act.

(4) Apart from sections 10 to 13 (and this section), this Act does not extend to Northern Ireland.

(5) This Act may be cited as the Limited Liability Partnerships Act 2000.

[3515]

NOTES

Orders: the Limited Liability Partnerships Act 2000 (Commencement) Order 2000, SI 2000/3316 (bringing this Act (with the exception of this section which came into force on Royal assent) into force on 6 April 2001).

SCHEDULE
NAMES AND REGISTERED OFFICES

Section 1

PART I
NAMES

1. …

Name to indicate status

2.—(1) The name of a limited liability partnership must end with—

(a) the expression "limited liability partnership", or
(b) the abbreviation "llp" or "LLP".

(2) But if the incorporation document for a limited liability partnership states that the registered office is to be situated in Wales, its name must end with—

(a) one of the expressions "limited liability partnership" and "partneriaeth atebolrwydd cyfyngedig", or
(b) one of the abbreviations "llp", "LLP", "pac" and "PAC".

Registration of names

3.—(1) A limited liability partnership shall not be registered by a name—

(a) which includes, otherwise than at the end of the name, either of the expressions "limited liability partnership" and "partneriaeth atebolrwydd cyfyngedig" or any of the abbreviations "llp", "LLP", "pac" and "PAC",

(b) which is the same as a name appearing in the index kept under section 714(1) of the Companies Act 1985,

(c) the use of which by the limited liability partnership would in the opinion of the Secretary of State constitute a criminal offence, or

(d) which in the opinion of the Secretary of State is offensive.

(2) Except with the approval of the Secretary of State, a limited liability partnership shall not be registered by a name which—

(a) in the opinion of the Secretary of State would be likely to give the impression that it is connected in any way with Her Majesty's Government or with any local authority, or

(b) includes any word or expression for the time being specified in regulations under section 29 of the Companies Act 1985 (names needing approval),

and in paragraph (a) "local authority" means any local authority within the meaning of the Local Government Act 1972 or the Local Government etc (Scotland) Act 1994, the Common Council of the City of London or the Council of the Isles of Scilly.

Change of name

4.—(1) A limited liability partnership may change its name at any time.

(2) Where a limited liability partnership has been registered by a name which—

(a) is the same as or, in the opinion of the Secretary of State, too like a name appearing at the time of registration in the index kept under section 714(1) of the Companies Act 1985, or

(b) is the same as or, in the opinion of the Secretary of State, too like a name which should have appeared in the index at that time,

the Secretary of State may within twelve months of that time in writing direct the limited liability partnership to change its name within such period as he may specify.

(3) If it appears to the Secretary of State—

(a) that misleading information has been given for the purpose of the registration of a limited liability partnership by a particular name, or

(b) that undertakings or assurances have been given for that purpose and have not been fulfilled,

he may, within five years of the date of its registration by that name, in writing direct the limited liability partnership to change its name within such period as he may specify.

(4) If in the Secretary of State's opinion the name by which a limited liability partnership is registered gives so misleading an indication of the nature of its activities as to be likely to cause harm to the public, he may in writing direct the limited liability partnership to change its name within such period as he may specify.

(5) But the limited liability partnership may, within three weeks from the date of the direction apply to the court to set it aside and the court may set the direction aside or confirm it and, if it confirms it, shall specify the period within which it must be complied with.

(6) In sub-paragraph (5) "the court" means—

(a) if the registered office of the limited liability partnership is situated in England and Wales or in Wales, the High Court, and

(b) if it is situated in Scotland, the Court of Session.

(7) Where a direction has been given under sub-paragraph (2), (3) or (4) specifying a period within which a limited liability partnership is to change its name, the Secretary of State may at any time before that period ends extend it by a further direction in writing.

(8) If a limited liability partnership fails to comply with a direction under this paragraph—

(a) the limited liability partnership, and

(b) any designated member in default,

commits an offence.

(9) A person guilty of an offence under sub-paragraph (8) is liable on summary conviction to a fine not exceeding level 3 on the standard scale.

Notification of change of name

5.—(1) Where a limited liability partnership changes its name it shall deliver notice of the change to the registrar.

(2) A notice delivered under sub-paragraph (1)—

(a) shall be in a form approved by the registrar, and

(b) shall be signed by a designated member of the limited liability partnership or authenticated in a manner approved by the registrar.

(3) Where the registrar receives a notice under sub-paragraph (2) he shall (unless the new name is one by which a limited liability partnership may not be registered)—

(a) enter the new name in the index kept under section 714(1) of the Companies Act 1985, and

(b) issue a certificate of the change of name.

(4) The change of name has effect from the date on which the certificate is issued.

Effect of change of name

6. A change of name by a limited liability partnership does not—

(a) affect any of its rights or duties,

(b) render defective any legal proceedings by or against it,

and any legal proceedings that might have been commenced or continued against it by its former name may be commenced or continued against it by its new name.

Improper use of "limited liability partnership" etc

7.—(1) If any person carries on a business under a name or title which includes as the last words—

(a) the expression "limited liability partnership" or "partneriaeth atebolrwydd cyfyngedig", or

(b) any contraction or imitation of either of those expressions,

that person, unless a limited liability partnership or oversea limited liability partnership, commits an offence.

(2) A person guilty of an offence under sub-paragraph (1) is liable on summary conviction to a fine not exceeding level 3 on the standard scale.

Similarity of names

8. In determining for the purposes of this Part whether one name is the same as another there are to be disregarded—

(1) the definite article as the first word of the name,

(2) any of the following (or their Welsh equivalents or abbreviations of them or their Welsh equivalents) at the end of the name—
"limited liability partnership",
"company",
"and company",
"company limited"
"and company limited",
"limited",
"unlimited",
"public limited company", …
["community interest company",
"community interest public limited company",]
"investment company with variable capital", and
["open-ended investment company", and]

(3) type and case of letters, accents, spaces between letters and punctuation marks, and "and" and "&" are to be taken as the same.

[3516]

NOTES

Para 1: amends CA 1985, s 714(1) at **[586]** and is repealed by the Companies Act 2006, s 1295, Sch 16, as from a day to be appointed.

Para 8: word omitted from entry "public limited company" repealed, and entry "open-ended investment company" inserted, by the Open-Ended Investment Companies Regulations 2001, SI 2001/1228, reg 84, Sch 7, para 11, as from 1 December 2001; entries "community interest company" and "community interest public limited company" inserted by the Companies (Audit, Investigations and Community Enterprise) Act 2004, s 33, Sch 6, para 10, as from 1 July 2005.

PART II
REGISTERED OFFICES

Situation of registered office

9.—(1) A limited liability partnership shall—

(a) at all times have a registered office situated in England and Wales or in Wales, or

(b) at all times have a registered office situated in Scotland,

to which communications and notices may be addressed.

(2) On the incorporation of a limited liability partnership the situation of its registered office shall be that stated in the incorporation document.

(3) Where the registered office of a limited liability partnership is situated in Wales, but the incorporation document does not state that it is to be situated in Wales (as opposed to England and Wales), the limited liability partnership may deliver notice to the registrar stating that its registered office is to be situated in Wales.

(4) A notice delivered under sub-paragraph (3)—

(a) shall be in a form approved by the registrar, and

(b) shall be signed by a designated member of the limited liability partnership or authenticated in a manner approved by the registrar.

Change of registered office

10.—(1) A limited liability partnership may change its registered office by delivering notice of the change to the registrar.

(2) A notice delivered under sub-paragraph (1)—

(a) shall be in a form approved by the registrar, and

(b) shall be signed by a designated member of the limited liability partnership or authenticated in a manner approved by the registrar.

[3517]

ENTERPRISE ACT 2002

(2002 c 40)

NOTES

This Act is reproduced as amended by: the Communications Act 2003; the Civil Partnership Act 2004; the EC Merger Control (Consequential Amendments) Regulations 2004, SI 2004/1079.

ARRANGEMENT OF SECTIONS

PART 3
MERGERS

CHAPTER 1
DUTY TO MAKE REFERENCES

Duty to make references: completed mergers

CHAPTER 3
OTHER SPECIAL CASES

Special public interest cases

European mergers

CHAPTER 4
ENFORCEMENT

Powers exercisable before references under section 22 or 33

Interim restrictions and powers

Final powers

Public interest and special public interest cases

Undertakings and orders: general provisions

Enforcement functions of OFT

Other

CHAPTER 5
SUPPLEMENTARY

Merger notices

Establish and provide for the functions of the Office of Fair Trading, the Competition Appeal Tribunal and the Competition Service; to make provision about mergers and market structures and conduct; to amend the constitution and functions of the Competition Commission; to create an offence for those entering into certain anti-competitive agreements; to provide for the disqualification of directors of companies engaging in certain anti-competitive practices; to make other provision about competition law; to amend the law relating to the protection of the collective interests of consumers; to make further provision about the disclosure of information obtained under competition and consumer legislation; to amend the Insolvency Act 1986 and make other provision about insolvency; and for connected purposes

[7 November 2002]

1–20 (*Ss 1–11* (*Pt 1: the Office of Fair Trading*), *ss 12–20* (*Pt 2: the Competition Appeal Tribunal*) *outside the scope of this work.*)

PART 3
MERGERS

NOTES

Commencement: unless otherwise specified, this Part (including Schs 7, 8, 10) came into force on 23 June 2003 (see s 279 at **[3626]** and the Orders noted thereto). Where any provision in this work (including any inserted or substituted provision) came into force for all purposes on or before 1 July 2005, commencement information is not noted at provision level.

Transitional provisions and savings: for general savings and transitional provisions with regard to the operation of this Part, see Sch 24, para 13 to this Act (at **[3632]**), and the Enterprise Act 2002 (Commencement No 3, Transitional and Transitory Provisions and Savings) Order 2003, SI 2003/1397, art 4, which reads as follows—

"4 Transitional provisions relating to merger references

(1) Subject to paragraphs 15 to 18 of Schedule 24, the old law shall in particular continue to apply in relation to the enforcement, variation or release of any undertakings accepted before the appointed day under section 75G or 88 of the 1973 Act in relation to any relevant arrangements which are not otherwise dealt with by paragraph 13 of Schedule 24.

(2) The power of the decision-making authority under section 27(5) or 29(1) (including those provisions as applied by any enactment) in relation to events or transactions is exercisable in relation to a merger which has occurred before the appointed day where the merger forms part of successive events or a series of transactions which include at least one event or transaction to which the new law applies.

(3) Where the decision-making authority exercises its power as mentioned in paragraph (2) in relation to a merger which has occurred before the appointed day, paragraph 13(1) of Schedule 24 shall accordingly cease to apply in relation to the merger.

(4) In this article—

"appointed day", "relevant arrangements", "new law" and "old law" have the same meaning as in paragraph 13 of Schedule 24;

"enactment" has the meaning given by section 129(1); and

"merger" means a ceasing of two or more enterprises to be distinct enterprises (within the meaning of Part 5 of the 1973 Act).".

Mergers of Water enterprises: as to the application of this Part to such mergers, see the Water Industry Act 1991, ss 32–35, Sch 4ZA, and the Water Mergers (Modification of Enactments) Regulations 2004, SI 2004/3202 (made under Sch 4ZA to the 1991 Act). For transitional provisions in connection with the application of this Part to water and sewerage undertakers, see the Enterprise Act 2002 (Commencement No 3, Transitional and Transitory Provisions and Savings) Order 2003, SI 2003/1397, art 3, and the Enterprise Act 2002 (Commencement No 7 and Transitional Provisions and Savings) Order 2004, SI 2004/3233, arts 3–5. See also the Water Services etc (Scotland) Act 2005 (Consequential Provisions and Modifications) Order 2005, SI 2005/3172.

Review of media ownership: as to the duty of OFCOM to review the operation of the provisions of this Part of this Act (in so far as they relate to intervention by the Secretary of State in connection with newspapers or other media enterprises), see the Communications Act 2003, s 391.

Intervention to protect legitimate interests: the provisions of ss 23–32 of this Act (and related provisions) apply, with modifications, for the purposes of deciding whether a relevant merger situation has been created for the purpose of s 68(2)(a) of this Act; see the Enterprise Act 2002 (Protection of Legitimate Interests) Order 2003, SI 2003/1592 at **[7174]** et seq.

CHAPTER 1
DUTY TO MAKE REFERENCES

Duty to make references: completed mergers

22 Duty to make references in relation to completed mergers

(1) The OFT shall, subject to subsections (2) and (3), make a reference to the Commission if the OFT believes that it is or may be the case that—

(a) a relevant merger situation has been created; and

(b) the creation of that situation has resulted, or may be expected to result, in a substantial lessening of competition within any market or markets in the United Kingdom for goods or services.

(2) The OFT may decide not to make a reference under this section if it believes that—

(a) the market concerned is not, or the markets concerned are not, of sufficient importance to justify the making of a reference to the Commission; or

(b) any relevant customer benefits in relation to the creation of the relevant merger situation concerned outweigh the substantial lessening of competition concerned and any adverse effects of the substantial lessening of competition concerned.

(3) No reference shall be made under this section if—

(a) the making of the reference is prevented by section … 74(1) or 96(3) or paragraph 4 of Schedule 7;

(b) the OFT is considering whether to accept undertakings under section 73 instead of making such a reference;

(c) the relevant merger situation concerned is being, or has been, dealt with in connection with a reference made under section 33;

(d) a notice under section 42(2) is in force in relation to the matter or the matter to which such a notice relates has been finally determined under Chapter 2 otherwise than in circumstances in which a notice is then given to the OFT under section 56(1); …

(e) the European Commission is considering a request made, in relation to the matter concerned, by the United Kingdom (whether alone or with others) under article [22(1) of the EC Merger Regulation], is proceeding with the matter in pursuance of such a request or has dealt with the matter in pursuance of such a request[; or

(f) subject to subsection (3A), a reasoned submission requesting referral to the European Commission has been submitted to the European Commission under article 4(5) of the EC Merger Regulation].

[(3A) Subsection (3)(f) shall cease to apply if the OFT is informed that a Member State competent to examine the concentration under its national competition law has, within the time permitted by Article 4(5) of the EC Merger Regulation, expressed its disagreement as regards the request to refer the case to the European Commission; and this subsection shall be construed in accordance with that Regulation.]

(4) A reference under this section shall, in particular, specify—

(a) the enactment under which it is made; and

(b) the date on which it is made.

(5) The references in this section to the creation of a relevant merger situation shall be construed in accordance with section 23, the reference in subsection (2) of this section to relevant customer benefits shall be construed in accordance with section 30 and the reference in subsection (3) of this section to a matter to which a notice under section 42(2) relates being finally determined under Chapter 2 shall be construed in accordance with section 43(4) and (5).

(6) In this Part "market in the United Kingdom" includes—

(a) so far as it operates in the United Kingdom or a part of the United Kingdom, any market which operates there and in another country or territory or in a part of another country or territory; and

(b) any market which operates only in a part of the United Kingdom;

and references to a market for goods or services include references to a market for goods and services.

(7) In this Part "the decision-making authority" means—

(a) in the case of a reference or possible reference under this section or section 33, the OFT or (as the case may be) the Commission; and

(b) in the case of a notice or possible notice under section 42(2) or 59(2) or a reference or possible reference under section 45 or 62, the OFT, the Commission or (as the case may be) the Secretary of State.

[3518]

NOTES

Sub-s (3): figure omitted from para (a) repealed by the Communications Act 2003, s 406, Sch 19, as from 29 December 2003; word omitted from para (d) repealed, words in square brackets in para (e) substituted, and para (f) added, by the EC Merger Control (Consequential Amendments) Regulations 2004, SI 2004/1079, reg 2, Schedule, para 2(1)–(3), as from 1 May 2004.

Sub-s (3A): inserted by SI 2004/1079, reg 2, Schedule, para 2(1), (4), as from 1 May 2004.

23 Relevant merger situations

(1) For the purposes of this Part, a relevant merger situation has been created if—

(a) two or more enterprises have ceased to be distinct enterprises at a time or in circumstances falling within section 24; and

(b) the value of the turnover in the United Kingdom of the enterprise being taken over exceeds £70 million.

(2) For the purposes of this Part, a relevant merger situation has also been created if—

(a) two or more enterprises have ceased to be distinct enterprises at a time or in circumstances falling within section 24; and

(b) as a result, one or both of the conditions mentioned in subsections (3) and (4) below prevails or prevails to a greater extent.

(3) The condition mentioned in this subsection is that, in relation to the supply of goods of any description, at least one-quarter of all the goods of that description which are supplied in the United Kingdom, or in a substantial part of the United Kingdom—

(a) are supplied by one and the same person or are supplied to one and the same person; or

(b) are supplied by the persons by whom the enterprises concerned are carried on, or are supplied to those persons.

(4) The condition mentioned in this subsection is that, in relation to the supply of services of any description, the supply of services of that description in the United Kingdom, or in a substantial part of the United Kingdom, is to the extent of at least one-quarter—

(a) supply by one and the same person, or supply for one and the same person; or

(b) supply by the persons by whom the enterprises concerned are carried on, or supply for those persons.

(5) For the purpose of deciding whether the proportion of one-quarter mentioned in subsection (3) or (4) is fulfilled with respect to goods or (as the case may be) services of any description, the decision-making authority shall apply such criterion (whether value, cost, price, quantity, capacity, number of workers employed or some other criterion, of whatever nature), or such combination of criteria, as the decision-making authority considers appropriate.

(6) References in subsections (3) and (4) to the supply of goods or (as the case may be) services shall, in relation to goods or services of any description which are the subject of different forms of supply, be construed in whichever of the following ways the decision-making authority considers appropriate—

(a) as references to any of those forms of supply taken separately;

(b) as references to all those forms of supply taken together; or

(c) as references to any of those forms of supply taken in groups.

(7) For the purposes of subsection (6) the decision-making authority may treat goods or services as being the subject of different forms of supply whenever—

(a) the transactions concerned differ as to their nature, their parties, their terms or their surrounding circumstances; and

(b) the difference is one which, in the opinion of the decision-making authority, ought for the purposes of that subsection to be treated as a material difference.

(8) The criteria for deciding when goods or services can be treated, for the purposes of this section, as goods or services of a separate description shall be such as in any particular case the decision-making authority considers appropriate in the circumstances of that case.

(9) For the purposes of this Chapter, the question whether a relevant merger situation has been created shall be determined as at—

(a) in the case of a reference which is treated as having been made under section 22 by virtue of section 37(2), such time as the Commission may determine; and

(b) in any other case, immediately before the time when the reference has been, or is to be, made.

[3519]

24 Time-limits and prior notice

(1) For the purposes of section 23 two or more enterprises have ceased to be distinct enterprises at a time or in circumstances falling within this section if—

(a) the two or more enterprises ceased to be distinct enterprises before the day on which the reference relating to them is to be made and did so not more than four months before that day; or

(b) notice of material facts about the arrangements or transactions under or in consequence of which the enterprises have ceased to be distinct enterprises has not been given in accordance with subsection (2).

(2) Notice of material facts is given in accordance with this subsection if—

(a) it is given to the OFT prior to the entering into of the arrangements or transactions concerned or the facts are made public prior to the entering into of those arrangements or transactions; or

(b) it is given to the OFT, or the facts are made public, more than four months before the day on which the reference is to be made.

(3) In this section—

"made public" means so publicised as to be generally known or readily ascertainable; and

"notice" includes notice which is not in writing.

[3520]

25 Extension of time-limits

(1) The OFT and the persons carrying on the enterprises which have or may have ceased to be distinct enterprises may agree to extend by no more than 20 days the four month period mentioned in section 24(1)(a) or (2)(b).

(2) The OFT may by notice to the persons carrying on the enterprises which have or may have ceased to be distinct enterprises extend the four month period mentioned in section 24(1)(a) or (2)(b) if it considers that any of those persons has failed to provide, within the period stated in a notice under section 31 and in the manner authorised or required, information requested of him in that notice.

(3) An extension under subsection (2) shall be for the period beginning with the end of the period within which the information is to be provided and which is stated in the notice under section 31 and ending with—

(a) the provision of the information to the satisfaction of the OFT; or

(b) if earlier, the cancellation by the OFT of the extension.

(4) The OFT may by notice to the persons carrying on the enterprises which have or may have ceased to be distinct enterprises extend the four month period mentioned in section 24(1)(a) or (2)(b) if it is seeking undertakings from any of those persons under section 73.

(5) An extension under subsection (4) shall be for the period beginning with the receipt of the notice under that subsection and ending with the earliest of the following events—

(a) the giving of the undertakings concerned;

(b) the expiry of the period of 10 days beginning with the first day after the receipt by the OFT of a notice from the person who has been given a notice under subsection (4) and from whom the undertakings are being sought stating that he does not intend to give the undertakings; or

(c) the cancellation by the OFT of the extension.

(6) The OFT may by notice to the persons carrying on the enterprises which have or may have ceased to be distinct enterprises extend the four month period mentioned in section 24(1)(a) or (2)(b) if the European Commission is considering a request made, in

relation to the matter concerned, by the United Kingdom (whether alone or with others) under article [22(1) of the EC Merger Regulation] (but is not yet proceeding with the matter in pursuance of such a request).

(7) An extension under subsection (6) shall be for the period beginning with the receipt of the notice under that subsection and ending with the receipt of a notice under subsection (8).

(8) The OFT shall, in connection with any notice given by it under subsection (6), by notice inform the persons carrying on the enterprises which have or may have ceased to be distinct enterprises of the completion by the European Commission of its consideration of the request of the United Kingdom.

(9) Subject to subsections (10) and (11), where the four month period mentioned in section 24(1)(a) or (2)(b) is extended or further extended by virtue of this section in relation to a particular case, any reference to that period in section 24 or the preceding provisions of this section shall have effect in relation to that case as if it were a reference to a period equivalent to the aggregate of the period being extended and the period of the extension (whether or not those periods overlap in time).

(10) Subsection (11) applies where—

(a) the four month period mentioned in section 24(1)(a) or (2)(b) is further extended;

(b) the further extension and at least one previous extension is made under one or more of subsections (2), (4) and (6); and

(c) the same days or fractions of days are included in or comprise the further extension and are included in or comprise at least one such previous extension.

(11) In calculating the period of the further extension, any days or fractions of days of the kind mentioned in subsection (10)(c) shall be disregarded.

(12) No more than one extension is possible under subsection (1).

[3521]

NOTES

Sub-s (6): words in square brackets substituted by the EC Merger Control (Consequential Amendments) Regulations 2004, SI 2004/1079, reg 2, Schedule, para 2(1), (5), as from 1 May 2004.

26 Enterprises ceasing to be distinct enterprises

(1) For the purposes of this Part any two enterprises cease to be distinct enterprises if they are brought under common ownership or common control (whether or not the business to which either of them formerly belonged continues to be carried on under the same or different ownership or control).

(2) Enterprises shall, in particular, be treated as being under common control if they are—

(a) enterprises of interconnected bodies corporate;

(b) enterprises carried on by two or more bodies corporate of which one and the same person or group of persons has control; or

(c) an enterprise carried on by a body corporate and an enterprise carried on by a person or group of persons having control of that body corporate.

(3) A person or group of persons able, directly or indirectly, to control or materially to influence the policy of a body corporate, or the policy of any person in carrying on an enterprise but without having a controlling interest in that body corporate or in that enterprise, may, for the purposes of subsections (1) and (2), be treated as having control of it.

(4) For the purposes of subsection (1), in so far as it relates to bringing two or more enterprises under common control, a person or group of persons may be treated as bringing an enterprise under his or their control if—

(a) being already able to control or materially to influence the policy of the person carrying on the enterprise, that person or group of persons acquires a controlling interest in the enterprise or, in the case of an enterprise carried on by a body corporate, acquires a controlling interest in that body corporate; or

(b) being already able materially to influence the policy of the person carrying on the enterprise, that person or group of persons becomes able to control that policy.

[3522]

27 Time when enterprises cease to be distinct

(1) Subsection (2) applies in relation to any arrangements or transaction—

(a) not having immediate effect or having immediate effect only in part; but

(b) under or in consequence of which any two enterprises cease to be distinct enterprises.

(2) The time when the parties to any such arrangements or transaction become bound to such extent as will result, on effect being given to their obligations, in the enterprises ceasing to be distinct enterprises shall be taken to be the time at which the two enterprises cease to be distinct enterprises.

(3) In accordance with subsections (1) and (2) (but without prejudice to the generality of those subsections) for the purpose of determining the time at which any two enterprises cease to be distinct enterprises no account shall be taken of any option or other conditional right until the option is exercised or the condition is satisfied.

(4) Subsections (1) to (3) are subject to subsections (5) to (8) and section 29.

(5) The decision-making authority may, for the purposes of a reference, treat successive events to which this subsection applies as having occurred simultaneously on the date on which the latest of them occurred.

(6) Subsection (5) applies to successive events—

(a) which occur within a period of two years under or in consequence of the same arrangements or transaction, or successive arrangements or transactions between the same parties or interests; and

(b) by virtue of each of which, under or in consequence of the arrangements or the transaction or transactions concerned, any enterprises cease as between themselves to be distinct enterprises.

(7) The decision-making authority may, for the purposes of subsections (5) and (6), treat such arrangements or transactions as the decision-making authority considers appropriate as arrangements or transactions between the same interests.

(8) In deciding whether it is appropriate to treat arrangements or transactions as arrangements or transactions between the same interests the decision-making authority shall, in particular, have regard to the persons substantially concerned in the arrangements or transactions concerned.

[3523]

NOTES

Application in relation to anticipated mergers and public interest intervention notices relating to them: by the Enterprise Act 2002 (Anticipated Mergers) Order 2003, SI 2003/1595, art 3(a), this section is applied to such cases with the modification that for sub-ss (5), (6) there are substituted the following subsections—

"(5) The decision-making authority may, for the purposes of a reference, treat successive events to which this subsection applies as if they will occur simultaneously on the date on which the latest of the events will occur.

(6) Subsection (5) applies to successive events—

(a) which consist of—

(i) one or more than one event which has occurred within the period of two years before the date of the reference; and

(ii) one or more than one event which will occur;

(b) which are events which have occurred or will occur under or in consequence of the same arrangements or transactions, or successive arrangements or transactions between the same parties or interests; and

(c) by virtue of each of which, under or in consequence of the arrangements or the transaction or transactions concerned, any enterprises cease as between themselves to be distinct enterprises.".

28 Turnover test

(1) For the purposes of section 23 the value of the turnover in the United Kingdom of the enterprise being taken over shall be determined by taking the total value of the turnover in the United Kingdom of the enterprises which cease to be distinct enterprises and deducting—

(a) the turnover in the United Kingdom of any enterprise which continues to be carried on under the same ownership and control; or

(b) if no enterprise continues to be carried on under the same ownership and control, the turnover in the United Kingdom which, of all the turnovers concerned, is the turnover of the highest value.

(2) For the purposes of this Part (other than section 121(4)(c)(ii)) the turnover in the United Kingdom of an enterprise shall be determined in accordance with such provisions as may be specified in an order made by the Secretary of State.

(3) An order under subsection (2) may, in particular, make provision as to—

(a) the amounts which are, or which are not, to be treated as comprising an enterprise's turnover;

(b) the date or dates by reference to which an enterprise's turnover is to be determined;

(c) the connection with the United Kingdom by virtue of which an enterprise's turnover is turnover in the United Kingdom.

(4) An order under subsection (2) may, in particular, make provision enabling the decision-making authority to determine matters of a description specified in the order (including any of the matters mentioned in paragraphs (a) to (c) of subsection (3)).

(5) The OFT shall—

(a) keep under review the sum for the time being mentioned in section 23(1)(b); and

(b) from time to time advise the Secretary of State as to whether the sum is still appropriate.

(6) The Secretary of State may by order amend section 23(1)(b) so as to alter the sum for the time being mentioned there.

[3524]

NOTES

Orders: the Enterprise Act 2002 (Merger Fees and Determination of Turnover) Order 2003, SI 2003/1370 at **[7162]**.

29 Obtaining control by stages

(1) Where an enterprise is brought under the control of a person or group of persons in the course of two or more transactions (in this section a "series of transactions") to which subsection (2) applies, those transactions may, if the decision-making authority considers it appropriate, be treated for the purposes of a reference as having occurred simultaneously on the date on which the latest of them occurred.

(2) This subsection applies to—

(a) any transaction which—

(i) enables that person or group of persons directly or indirectly to control or materially to influence the policy of any person carrying on the enterprise;

(ii) enables that person or group of persons to do so to a greater degree; or

(iii) is a step (whether direct or indirect) towards enabling that person or group of persons to do so; and

(b) any transaction by virtue of which that person or group of persons acquires a controlling interest in the enterprise or, where the enterprise is carried on by a body corporate, in that body corporate.

(3) Where a series of transactions includes a transaction falling within subsection (2)(b), any transaction occurring after the occurrence of that transaction is to be disregarded for the purposes of subsection (1).

(4) Where the period within which a series of transactions occurs exceeds two years, the transactions that may be treated as mentioned in subsection (1) are any of those transactions that occur within a period of two years.

(5) Sections 26(2) to (4) and 127(1), (2) and (4) to (6) shall apply for the purposes of this section to determine—

(a) whether an enterprise is brought under the control of a person or group of persons; and

(b) whether a transaction is one to which subsection (2) applies;

as they apply for the purposes of section 26 to determine whether enterprises are brought under common control.

(6) In determining for the purposes of this section the time at which any transaction occurs, no account shall be taken of any option or other conditional right until the option is exercised or the condition is satisfied.

[3525]

NOTES

Application in relation to anticipated mergers and public interest intervention notices relating to them: by the Enterprise Act 2002 (Anticipated Mergers) Order 2003, SI 2003/1595, art 3(b), this section is applied to such cases with the modification that for sub-ss (1)–(4) there are substituted the following subsections—

"(1) Where an enterprise will be brought under the control of a person or group of persons in the course of two or more transactions (in this section a "series of transactions") to which subsection (2) applies, those transactions may, if the decision-making authority considers it appropriate, be treated for the purposes of a reference as if they will occur simultaneously on the date on which the latest of them will occur.

(2) This subsection applies to—

(a) any transaction which has occurred or which will occur and which—

(i) enables that person or group of persons directly or indirectly to control or materially to influence the policy of any person carrying on the enterprise;

(ii) enables that person or group of persons to do so to a greater degree; or

(iii) is a step (whether direct or indirect) towards enabling that person or group of persons to do so; and

(b) any transaction which has occurred or which will occur and by virtue of which that person or group of persons acquires a controlling interest in the enterprise or, where the enterprise is carried on by a body corporate, in that body corporate.

(3) Where a series of transactions includes a transaction falling within subsection (2)(b), any transaction occurring after the occurrence of that transaction is to be disregarded for the purposes of subsection (1).

(4) Where the period within which any relevant transactions have occurred exceeds two years before the date of the reference, the relevant transactions that may be treated as mentioned in subsection (1) are any of those transactions that have occurred within the period of two years.

(4A) In subsection (4) "relevant transactions" means transactions which have occurred and which are transactions in the series of transactions.".

30 Relevant customer benefits

(1) For the purposes of this Part a benefit is a relevant customer benefit if—

(a) it is a benefit to relevant customers in the form of—

(i) lower prices, higher quality or greater choice of goods or services in any market in the United Kingdom (whether or not the market or markets in which the substantial lessening of competition concerned has, or may have, occurred or (as the case may be) may occur); or

(ii) greater innovation in relation to such goods or services; and

(b) the decision-making authority believes—

(i) in the case of a reference or possible reference under section 22 or 45(2), as mentioned in subsection (2); and

(ii) in the case of a reference or possible reference under section 33 or 45(4), as mentioned in subsection (3).

(2) The belief, in the case of a reference or possible reference under section 22 or section 45(2), is that—

(a) the benefit has accrued as a result of the creation of the relevant merger situation concerned or may be expected to accrue within a reasonable period as a result of the creation of that situation; and

(b) the benefit was, or is, unlikely to accrue without the creation of that situation or a similar lessening of competition.

(3) The belief, in the case of a reference or possible reference under section 33 or 45(4), is that—

(a) the benefit may be expected to accrue within a reasonable period as a result of the creation of the relevant merger situation concerned; and

(b) the benefit is unlikely to accrue without the creation of that situation or a similar lessening of competition.

(4) In subsection (1) "relevant customers" means—

(a) customers of any person carrying on an enterprise which, in the creation of the relevant merger situation concerned, has ceased to be, or (as the case may be) will cease to be, a distinct enterprise;

(b) customers of such customers; and

(c) any other customers in a chain of customers beginning with the customers mentioned in paragraph (a);

and in this subsection "customers" includes future customers.

[3526]

31 Information powers in relation to completed mergers

(1) The OFT may by notice to any of the persons carrying on the enterprises which have or may have ceased to be distinct enterprises request him to provide the OFT with such information as the OFT may require for the purpose of deciding whether to make a reference under section 22.

(2) The notice shall state—

(a) the information required;

(b) the period within which the information is to be provided; and

(c) the possible consequences of not providing the information within the stated period and in the authorised or required manner.

[3527]

32 Supplementary provision for purposes of sections 25 and 31

(1) The Secretary of State may make regulations for the purposes of sections 25 and 31.

(2) The regulations may, in particular—

(a) provide for the manner in which any information requested by the OFT under section 31 is authorised or required to be provided, and the time at which such information is to be treated as provided (including the time at which it is to be treated as provided to the satisfaction of the OFT for the purposes of section 25(3));

(b) provide for the persons carrying on the enterprises which have or may have ceased to be distinct enterprises to be informed, in circumstances in which section 25(3) applies—

(i) of the fact that the OFT is satisfied as to the provision of the information requested by it or (as the case may be) of the OFT's decision to cancel the extension; and

(ii) of the time at which the OFT is to be treated as so satisfied or (as the case may be) of the time at which the cancellation is to be treated as having effect;

(c) provide for the persons carrying on the enterprises which have or may have ceased to be distinct enterprises to be informed, in circumstances in which section 25(5) applies—

(i) of the OFT's decision to cancel the extension; and

(ii) of the time at which the cancellation is to be treated as having effect;

(d) provide for the time at which any notice under section 25(4), (5)(b), (6) or (8) is to be treated as received;

(e) provide that a person is, or is not, to be treated, in such circumstances as may be specified in the regulations, as acting on behalf of a person carrying on an enterprise which has or may have ceased to be a distinct enterprise.

(3) A notice under section 25(2)—

(a) shall be given within 5 days of the end of the period within which the information is to be provided and which is stated in the notice under section 31; and

(b) shall inform the person to whom it is addressed of—

(i) the OFT's opinion as mentioned in section 25(2); and

(ii) the OFT's intention to extend the period for considering whether to make a reference.

(4) In determining for the purposes of section 25(1) or (5)(b) or subsection (3)(a) above any period which is expressed in the enactment concerned as a period of days or number of days no account shall be taken of—

(a) Saturday, Sunday, Good Friday and Christmas Day; and

(b) any day which is a bank holiday in England and Wales.

[3528]

Duty to make references: anticipated mergers

33 Duty to make references in relation to anticipated mergers

(1) The OFT shall, subject to subsections (2) and (3), make a reference to the Commission if the OFT believes that it is or may be the case that—

(a) arrangements are in progress or in contemplation which, if carried into effect, will result in the creation of a relevant merger situation; and

(b) the creation of that situation may be expected to result in a substantial lessening of competition within any market or markets in the United Kingdom for goods or services.

(2) The OFT may decide not to make a reference under this section if it believes that—

(a) the market concerned is not, or the markets concerned are not, of sufficient importance to justify the making of a reference to the Commission;

(b) the arrangements concerned are not sufficiently far advanced, or are not sufficiently likely to proceed, to justify the making of a reference to the Commission; or

(c) any relevant customer benefits in relation to the creation of the relevant merger situation concerned outweigh the substantial lessening of competition concerned and any adverse effects of the substantial lessening of competition concerned.

(3) No reference shall be made under this section if—

(a) the making of the reference is prevented by section … , 74(1) or 96(3) or paragraph 4 of Schedule 7;

(b) the OFT is considering whether to accept undertakings under section 73 instead of making such a reference;

(c) the arrangements concerned are being, or have been, dealt with in connection with a reference made under section 22;

(d) a notice under section 42(2) is in force in relation to the matter or the matter to which such a notice relates has been finally determined under Chapter 2 otherwise than in circumstances in which a notice is then given to the OFT under section 56(1); …

(e) the European Commission is considering a request made, in relation to the matter concerned, by the United Kingdom (whether alone or with others) under article [22(1) of the EC Merger Regulation], is proceeding with the matter in pursuance of such a request or has dealt with the matter in pursuance of such a request[; or

(f) subject to subsection (3A), a reasoned submission requesting referral to the European Commission has been submitted to the European Commission under article 4(5) of the EC Merger Regulation].

[(3A) Section 33(3)(f) shall cease to apply if the OFT is informed that a Member State competent to examine the concentration under its national competition law has, within the time permitted by Article 4(5) of the EC Merger Regulation, expressed its disagreement as regards the request to refer the case to the European Commission; and this subsection shall be construed in accordance with that Regulation.]

(4) A reference under this section shall, in particular, specify—

(a) the enactment under which it is made; and

(b) the date on which it is made.

[3529]

NOTES

Sub-s (3): figure omitted from para (a) repealed by the Communications Act 2003, s 406, Sch 19, as from 29 December 2003; word omitted from para (d) repealed, words in square brackets in para (e) substituted, and para (f) added, by the EC Merger Control (Consequential Amendments) Regulations 2004, SI 2004/1079, reg 2, Schedule, para 2(1), (6), (7), as from 1 May 2004.

Sub-s (3A): inserted by SI 2004/1079, reg 2, Schedule, para 2(1), (8), as from 1 May 2004.

---

34 Supplementary provision in relation to anticipated mergers

(1) The Secretary of State may by order make such provision as he considers appropriate about the operation of sections 27 and 29 in relation to—

(a) references under this Part which relate to arrangements which are in progress or in contemplation; or

(b) notices under section 42(2), 59(2) or 67(2) which relate to such arrangements.

(2) An order under subsection (1) may, in particular—

(a) provide for sections 27(5) to (8) and 29 to apply with modifications in relation to such references or notices or in relation to particular descriptions of such references or notices;

(b) enable particular descriptions of events, arrangements or transactions which have already occurred—

(i) to be taken into account for the purposes of deciding whether to make such references or such references of a particular description or whether to give such notices or such notices of a particular description;

(ii) to be dealt with under such references or such references of a particular description or under such notices or such notices of a particular description.

[3530]

NOTES

Orders: the Enterprise Act 2002 (Anticipated Mergers) Order 2003, SI 2003/1595.

[Cases referred by European Commission under EC Merger Regulation

34A Duty of OFT where case referred by the European Commission

(1) Subsection (2) applies if the European Commission has by a decision referred the whole or part of a case to the OFT under Article 4(4) or 9 of the EC Merger Regulation, or is deemed to have taken such a decision, unless an intervention notice is in force in relation to that case.

(2) Before the end of the preliminary assessment period, the OFT shall—

(a) decide whether to make a reference to the Commission under section 22 or 33; and

(b) inform the persons carrying on the enterprises concerned by notice of that decision and of the reasons for it.

(3) The OFT may, for the purposes of subsection (2), decide not to make a reference on the basis that it is considering whether to seek or accept undertakings under section 73 instead of making a reference; but a decision taken on that basis does not prevent the OFT from making a reference under section 22 or 33 in the event of no such undertakings being offered or accepted.

(4) In this section—

"the preliminary assessment period" means, subject to subsection (5), the period of 45 working days beginning with the day after the day on which the decision of the European Commission to refer the case is taken (or is deemed to have been taken); and

"working day" means any day which is not—

(a) a Saturday;

(b) a Sunday; or

(c) a day which is a European Commission holiday (as published in the Official Journal of the European Communities before the beginning of the year in which it occurs).

(5) If the OFT has imposed a requirement under section 34B and it considers that the person on whom that requirement was imposed has failed to comply with it, the OFT may, by notice to the persons carrying on the enterprises concerned, extend the preliminary assessment period.

(6) The period of an extension under subsection (5) shall—

(a) begin with the end of the period within which the requirement under section 34B could be complied with; and

(b) end with the earlier of either compliance with the requirement to the satisfaction of the OFT or cancellation by the OFT of the extension.

(7) A notice under subsection (6) shall—

(a) be given within 5 working days of the end of the period mentioned in paragraph (a) of that subsection; and

(b) inform the person to whom it is addressed that the OFT is of the opinion mentioned in subsection (5) and that it intends to extend the preliminary assessment period.]

[3530A]

NOTES

Inserted, together with the preceding heading and s 34B, by the EC Merger Control (Consequential Amendments) Regulations 2004, SI 2004/1079, reg 2, Schedule, para 2(1), (9), as from 1 May 2004.

[34B Power to request information in referred cases

(1) In a case mentioned in section 34A(1), the OFT may by notice to any of the persons carrying on the enterprises concerned request him to provide the OFT with such information as the OFT may require for the purpose of making a decision for the purposes of section 34A(2).

(2) The notice shall state—

(a) the information required;

(b) the period within which the information is to be provided;

(c) the manner (if any) in which the information is required to be provided; and

(d) the possible consequences—

(i) of not providing the information within the stated period; and

(ii) if a manner for its provision is stated in the notice, of not providing it in that manner.]

[3530B]

NOTES

Inserted as noted to s 34A at **[3530A]**.

Determination of references

35 Questions to be decided in relation to completed mergers

(1) Subject to subsections (6) and (7) and section 127(3), the Commission shall, on a reference under section 22, decide the following questions—

(a) whether a relevant merger situation has been created; and

(b) if so, whether the creation of that situation has resulted, or may be expected to result, in a substantial lessening of competition within any market or markets in the United Kingdom for goods or services.

(2) For the purposes of this Part there is an anti-competitive outcome if—

(a) a relevant merger situation has been created and the creation of that situation has resulted, or may be expected to result, in a substantial lessening of competition within any market or markets in the United Kingdom for goods or services; or

(b) arrangements are in progress or in contemplation which, if carried into effect, will result in the creation of a relevant merger situation and the creation of that situation may be expected to result in a substantial lessening of competition within any market or markets in the United Kingdom for goods or services.

(3) The Commission shall, if it has decided on a reference under section 22 that there is an anti-competitive outcome (within the meaning given by subsection (2)(a)), decide the following additional questions—

(a) whether action should be taken by it under section 41(2) for the purpose of remedying, mitigating or preventing the substantial lessening of competition concerned or any adverse effect which has resulted from, or may be expected to result from, the substantial lessening of competition;

(b) whether it should recommend the taking of action by others for the purpose of remedying, mitigating or preventing the substantial lessening of competition concerned or any adverse effect which has resulted from, or may be expected to result from, the substantial lessening of competition; and

(c) in either case, if action should be taken, what action should be taken and what is to be remedied, mitigated or prevented.

(4) In deciding the questions mentioned in subsection (3) the Commission shall, in particular, have regard to the need to achieve as comprehensive a solution as is reasonable and practicable to the substantial lessening of competition and any adverse effects resulting from it.

(5) In deciding the questions mentioned in subsection (3) the Commission may, in particular, have regard to the effect of any action on any relevant customer benefits in relation to the creation of the relevant merger situation concerned.

(6) In relation to the question whether a relevant merger situation has been created, a reference under section 22 may be framed so as to require the Commission to exclude from consideration—

(a) subsection (1) of section 23;

(b) subsection (2) of that section; or

(c) one of those subsections if the Commission finds that the other is satisfied.

(7) In relation to the question whether any such result as is mentioned in section 23(2)(b) has arisen, a reference under section 22 may be framed so as to require the Commission to confine its investigation to the supply of goods or services in a part of the United Kingdom specified in the reference.

[3531]

36 Questions to be decided in relation to anticipated mergers

(1) Subject to subsections (5) and (6) and section 127(3), the Commission shall, on a reference under section 33, decide the following questions—

(a) whether arrangements are in progress or in contemplation which, if carried into effect, will result in the creation of a relevant merger situation; and

(b) if so, whether the creation of that situation may be expected to result in a substantial lessening of competition within any market or markets in the United Kingdom for goods or services.

(2) The Commission shall, if it has decided on a reference under section 33 that there is an anti-competitive outcome (within the meaning given by section 35(2)(b)), decide the following additional questions—

(a) whether action should be taken by it under section 41(2) for the purpose of remedying, mitigating or preventing the substantial lessening of competition concerned or any adverse effect which may be expected to result from the substantial lessening of competition;

(b) whether it should recommend the taking of action by others for the purpose of remedying, mitigating or preventing the substantial lessening of competition concerned or any adverse effect which may be expected to result from the substantial lessening of competition; and

(c) in either case, if action should be taken, what action should be taken and what is to be remedied, mitigated or prevented.

(3) In deciding the questions mentioned in subsection (2) the Commission shall, in particular, have regard to the need to achieve as comprehensive a solution as is reasonable and practicable to the substantial lessening of competition and any adverse effects resulting from it.

(4) In deciding the questions mentioned in subsection (2) the Commission may, in particular, have regard to the effect of any action on any relevant customer benefits in relation to the creation of the relevant merger situation concerned.

(5) In relation to the question whether a relevant merger situation will be created, a reference under section 33 may be framed so as to require the Commission to exclude from consideration—

(a) subsection (1) of section 23;

(b) subsection (2) of that section; or

(c) one of those subsections if the Commission finds that the other is satisfied.

(6) In relation to the question whether any such result as is mentioned in section 23(2)(b) will arise, a reference under section 33 may be framed so as to require the Commission to confine its investigation to the supply of goods or services in a part of the United Kingdom specified in the reference.

[3532]

PART III OTHER LEGISLATION

NOTES

Application in relation to anticipated mergers and public interest intervention notices relating to them: in the case of any reference where the Competition Commission exercises its discretion under ss 27(5) or 29(1) of this Act (as modified by the Enterprise Act 2002 (Anticipated Mergers) Order 2003, SI 2003/1595) sub-s (2)(a) and (b) above have effect as if the words "or has resulted" were inserted after "result"; see art 4 of the 2003 Order.

37 Cancellation and variation of references under section 22 or 33

(1) The Commission shall cancel a reference under section 33 if it considers that the proposal to make arrangements of the kind mentioned in the reference has been abandoned.

(2) The Commission may, if it considers that doing so is justified by the facts (including events occurring on or after the making of the reference concerned), treat a reference made under section 22 or 33 as if it had been made under section 33 or (as the case may be) 22; and, in such cases, references in this Part to references under those sections shall, so far as may be necessary, be construed accordingly.

(3) Where, by virtue of subsection (2), the Commission treats a reference made under section 22 or 33 as if it had been made under section 33 or (as the case may be) 22, sections 77 to 81 shall, in particular, apply as if the reference had been made under section 33 or (as the case may be) 22 instead of under section 22 or 33.

(4) Subsection (5) applies in relation to any undertaking accepted under section 80, or any order made under section 81, which is in force immediately before the Commission, by virtue of subsection (2), treats a reference made under section 22 or 33 as if it had been made under section 33 or (as the case may be) 22.

(5) The undertaking or order shall, so far as applicable, continue in force as if—

(a) in the case of an undertaking or order which relates to a reference made under section 22, accepted or made in relation to a reference made under section 33; and

(b) in the case of an undertaking or order which relates to a reference made under section 33, accepted or made in relation to a reference made under section 22;

and the undertaking or order concerned may be varied, superseded, released or revoked accordingly.

(6) The OFT may at any time vary a reference under section 22 or 33.

(7) The OFT shall consult the Commission before varying any such reference.

(8) Subsection (7) shall not apply if the Commission has requested the variation concerned.

(9) No variation by the OFT under this section shall be capable of altering the period permitted by section 39 within which the report of the Commission under section 38 is to be prepared and published.

[3533]

38 Investigations and reports on references under section 22 or 33

(1) The Commission shall prepare and publish a report on a reference under section 22 or 33 within the period permitted by section 39.

(2) The report shall, in particular, contain—

(a) the decisions of the Commission on the questions which it is required to answer by virtue of section 35 or (as the case may be) 36;

(b) its reasons for its decisions; and

(c) such information as the Commission considers appropriate for facilitating a proper understanding of those questions and of its reasons for its decisions.

(3) The Commission shall carry out such investigations as it considers appropriate for the purposes of preparing a report under this section.

(4) The Commission shall, at the same time as a report prepared under this section is published, give it to the OFT.

[3534]

39 Time-limits for investigations and reports

(1) The Commission shall prepare and publish its report under section 38 within the period of 24 weeks beginning with the date of the reference concerned.

(2) …

(3) The Commission may extend, by no more than 8 weeks, the period within which a report under section 38 is to be prepared and published if it considers that there are special reasons why the report cannot be prepared and published within that period.

(4) The Commission may extend the period within which a report under section 38 is to be prepared and published if it considers that a relevant person has failed (whether with or without a reasonable excuse) to comply with any requirement of a notice under section 109.

(5) In subsection (4) "relevant person" means—
(a) any person carrying on any of the enterprises concerned;
(b) any person who (whether alone or as a member of a group) owns or has control of any such person; or
(c) any officer, employee or agent of any person mentioned in paragraph (a) or (b).

(6) For the purposes of subsection (5) a person or group of persons able, directly or indirectly, to control or materially to influence the policy of a body of persons corporate or unincorporate, but without having a controlling interest in that body of persons, may be treated as having control of it.

(7) An extension under subsection (3) or (4) shall come into force when published under section 107.

(8) An extension under subsection (4) shall continue in force until—
(a) the person concerned provides the information or documents to the satisfaction of the Commission or (as the case may be) appears as a witness in accordance with the requirements of the Commission; or
(b) the Commission publishes its decision to cancel the extension.

(9) References in this Part to the date of a reference shall be construed as references to the date specified in the reference as the date on which it is made.

(10) This section is subject to section 40.

[3535]

NOTES

Sub-s (2): repealed by the EC Merger Control (Consequential Amendments) Regulations 2004, SI 2004/1079, reg 2, Schedule, para 2(1), (10), as from 1 May 2004.

40 Section 39: supplementary

(1), (2) …

(3) A period extended under subsection (3) of section 39 may also be extended under subsection (4) of that section and a period extended under subsection (4) of that section may also be extended under subsection (3) of that section.

(4) No more than one extension is possible under section 39(3).

(5) Where a period within which a report under section 38 is to be prepared and published is extended or further extended under section 39(3) or (4), the period as extended or (as the case may be) further extended shall, subject to subsections (6) and (7), be calculated by taking the period being extended and adding to it the period of the extension (whether or not those periods overlap in time).

(6) Subsection (7) applies where—
(a) the period within which the report under section 38 is to be prepared and published is further extended;
(b) the further extension and at least one previous extension is made under section 39(4); and
(c) the same days or fractions of days are included in or comprise the further extension and are included in or comprise at least one such previous extension.

(7) In calculating the period of the further extension, any days or fractions of days of the kind mentioned in subsection (6)(c) shall be disregarded.

(8) The Secretary of State may by order amend section 39 so as to alter any one or more of the following periods—
(a) the period of 24 weeks mentioned in subsection (1) of that section or any period for the time being mentioned in that subsection in substitution for that period;

(b) …

(c) the period of 8 weeks mentioned in subsection (3) of that section or any period for the time being mentioned in that subsection in substitution for that period.

(9) No alteration shall be made by virtue of subsection (8) which results in the period for the time being mentioned in subsection (1) … of section 39 exceeding 24 weeks or the period for the time being mentioned in subsection (3) of that section exceeding 8 weeks.

(10) An order under subsection (8) shall not affect any period of time within which the Commission is under a duty to prepare and publish its report under section 38 in relation to a reference under section 22 or 33 if the Commission is already under that duty in relation to that reference when the order is made.

(11) Before making an order under subsection (8) the Secretary of State shall consult the Commission and such other persons as he considers appropriate.

(12) The Secretary of State may make regulations for the purposes of section 39(8).

(13) The regulations may, in particular—

(a) provide for the time at which information or documents are to be treated as provided (including the time at which they are to be treated as provided to the satisfaction of the Commission for the purposes of section 39(8));

(b) provide for the time at which a person is to be treated as appearing as a witness (including the time at which he is to be treated as appearing as a witness in accordance with the requirements of the Commission for the purposes of section 39(8));

(c) provide for the persons carrying on the enterprises which have or may have ceased to be, or may cease to be, distinct enterprises to be informed, in circumstances in which section 39(8) applies, of the fact that—

(i) the Commission is satisfied as to the provision of the information or documents required by it; or

(ii) the person concerned has appeared as a witness in accordance with the requirements of the Commission;

(d) provide for the persons carrying on the enterprises which have or may have ceased to be, or may cease to be, distinct enterprises to be informed, in circumstances in which section 39(8) applies, of the time at which the Commission is to be treated as satisfied as mentioned in paragraph (c)(i) above or the person concerned is to be treated as having appeared as mentioned in paragraph (c)(ii) above.

[3536]

NOTES

Sub-ss (1), (2): repealed by the EC Merger Control (Consequential Amendments) Regulations 2004, SI 2004/1079, reg 2, Schedule, para 2(1), (11)(a), as from 1 May 2004.

Sub-ss (8), (9): words omitted repealed by SI 2004/1079, reg 2, Schedule, para 2(1), (11)(a), (b), as from 1 May 2004.

41 Duty to remedy effects of completed or anticipated mergers

(1) Subsection (2) applies where a report of the Commission has been prepared and published under section 38 within the period permitted by section 39 and contains the decision that there is an anti-competitive outcome.

(2) The Commission shall take such action under section 82 or 84 as it considers to be reasonable and practicable—

(a) to remedy, mitigate or prevent the substantial lessening of competition concerned; and

(b) to remedy, mitigate or prevent any adverse effects which have resulted from, or may be expected to result from, the substantial lessening of competition.

(3) The decision of the Commission under subsection (2) shall be consistent with its decisions as included in its report by virtue of section 35(3) or (as the case may be) 36(2) unless there has been a material change of circumstances since the preparation of the report or the Commission otherwise has a special reason for deciding differently.

(4) In making a decision under subsection (2), the Commission shall, in particular, have regard to the need to achieve as comprehensive a solution as is reasonable and practicable to the substantial lessening of competition and any adverse effects resulting from it.

(5) In making a decision under subsection (2), the Commission may, in particular, have regard to the effect of any action on any relevant customer benefits in relation to the creation of the relevant merger situation concerned.

[3537]

CHAPTER 2
PUBLIC INTEREST CASES

Power to make references

42 Intervention by Secretary of State in certain public interest cases

(1) Subsection (2) applies where—

(a) the Secretary of State has reasonable grounds for suspecting that it is or may be the case that a relevant merger situation has been created or that arrangements are in progress or in contemplation which, if carried into effect, will result in the creation of a relevant merger situation;

(b) no reference under section 22 or 33 has been made in relation to the relevant merger situation concerned;

(c) no decision has been made not to make such a reference (other than a decision made by virtue of subsection (2)(b) of section 33 or a decision to accept undertakings under section 73 instead of making such a reference); and

(d) no reference is prevented from being made under section 22 or 33 by virtue of—

(i) section 22(3)(a) or (e) or (as the case may be) 33(3)(a) or (e); or

(ii) Community law or anything done under or in accordance with it.

(2) The Secretary of State may give a notice to the OFT (in this Part "an intervention notice") if he believes that it is or may be the case that one or more than one public interest consideration is relevant to a consideration of the relevant merger situation concerned.

(3) For the purposes of this Part a public interest consideration is a consideration which, at the time of the giving of the intervention notice concerned, is specified in section 58 or is not so specified but, in the opinion of the Secretary of State, ought to be so specified.

(4) No more than one intervention notice shall be given under subsection (2) in relation to the same relevant merger situation.

(5) For the purposes of deciding whether a relevant merger situation has been created or whether arrangements are in progress or in contemplation which, if carried into effect, will result in the creation of a relevant merger situation, sections 23 to 32 (read together with section 34) shall apply for the purposes of this Chapter as they do for the purposes of Chapter 1 but subject to subsection (6).

(6) In their application by virtue of subsection (5) sections 23 to 32 shall have effect as if—

(a) for paragraph (a) of section 23(9) there were substituted—

"(a) in relation to the giving of an intervention notice, the time when the notice is given;

(aa) in relation to the making of a report by the OFT under section 44, the time of the making of the report;

(ab) in the case of a reference which is treated as having been made under section 45(2) or (3) by virtue of section 49(1), such time as the Commission may determine; and";

(b) the references to the OFT in sections 25(1) to (3), (6) and (8) and 31 included references to the Secretary of State;

(c) the references to the OFT in section 25(4) and (5) were references to the Secretary of State;

(d) the reference in section 25(4) to section 73 were a reference to paragraph 3 of Schedule 7;

(e) after section 25(5) there were inserted—

"(5A) The Secretary of State may by notice to the persons carrying on the enterprises which have or may have ceased to be distinct enterprises extend the four month period mentioned in section 24(1)(a) or (2)(b) if, by virtue of section 46(5) or paragraph 3(6) of Schedule 7, he decides to delay a decision as to whether to make a reference under section 45.

(5B) An extension under subsection (5A) shall be for the period of the delay.";

PART III OTHER LEGISLATION

(f) in section 25(10)(b) after the word "(4)" there were inserted ", (5A)";
(g) the reference in section 25(12) to one extension were a reference to one extension by the OFT and one extension by the Secretary of State;
(h) the powers to extend time-limits under section 25 as applied by subsection (5) above, and the power to request information under section 31(1) as so applied, were not exercisable by the OFT or the Secretary of State before the giving of an intervention notice but the existing time-limits in relation to possible references under section 22 or 33 were applicable for the purposes of the giving of that notice;
(i) the existing time-limits in relation to possible references under section 22 or 33 (except for extensions under section 25(4)) remained applicable on and after the giving of an intervention notice as if any extensions were made under section 25 as applied by subsection (5) above but subject to further alteration by the OFT or the Secretary of State under section 25 as so applied;
(j) in subsection (1) of section 31 for the words "section 22" there were substituted "section 45(2) or (3)" and, in the application of that subsection to the OFT, for the word "deciding" there were substituted "enabling the Secretary of State to decide";
(k) in the case of the giving of intervention notices, the references in sections 23 to 32 to the making of a reference or a reference were, so far as necessary, references to the giving of an intervention notice or an intervention notice; and
(l) the references to the OFT in section 32(2)(a) to (c) and (3) were construed in accordance with the above modifications.

(7) Where the Secretary of State has given an intervention notice mentioning a public interest consideration which, at that time, is not finalised, he shall, as soon as practicable, take such action as is within his power to ensure that it is finalised.

(8) For the purposes of this Part a public interest consideration is finalised if—
(a) it is specified in section 58 otherwise than by virtue of an order under subsection (3) of that section; or
(b) it is specified in that section by virtue of an order under subsection (3) of that section and the order providing for it to be so specified has been laid before, and approved by, Parliament in accordance with subsection (7) of section 124 and within the period mentioned in that subsection.

[3538]

43 Intervention notices under section 42

(1) An intervention notice shall state—
(a) the relevant merger situation concerned;
(b) the public interest consideration or considerations which are, or may be, relevant to a consideration of the relevant merger situation concerned; and
(c) where any public interest consideration concerned is not finalised, the proposed timetable for finalising it.

(2) Where the Secretary of State believes that it is or may be the case that two or more public interest considerations are relevant to a consideration of the relevant merger situation concerned, he may decide not to mention in the intervention notice such of those considerations as he considers appropriate.

(3) An intervention notice shall come into force when it is given and shall cease to be in force when the matter to which it relates is finally determined under this Chapter.

(4) For the purposes of this Part, a matter to which an intervention notice relates is finally determined under this Chapter if—
(a) the time within which the OFT [or (if relevant) OFCOM] is to report to the Secretary of State under section 44 [or (as the case may be) 44A] has expired and no such report has been made;
(b) the Secretary of State decides to accept an undertaking or group of undertakings under paragraph 3 of Schedule 7 instead of making a reference under section 45;
(c) the Secretary of State otherwise decides not to make a reference under that section;
(d) the Commission cancels such a reference under section 48(1) or 53(1);
(e) the time within which the Commission is to prepare a report under section 50 and give it to the Secretary of State has expired and no such report has been prepared and given to the Secretary of State;

(f) the time within which the Secretary of State is to make and publish a decision under section 54(2) has expired and no such decision has been made and published;

(g) the Secretary of State decides under section 54(2) to make no finding at all in the matter;

(h) the Secretary of State otherwise decides under section 54(2) not to make an adverse public interest finding;

(i) the Secretary of State decides under section 54(2) to make an adverse public interest finding but decides neither to accept an undertaking under paragraph 9 of Schedule 7 nor to make an order under paragraph 11 of that Schedule; or

(j) the Secretary of State decides under section 54(2) to make an adverse public interest finding and accepts an undertaking under paragraph 9 of Schedule 7 or makes an order under paragraph 11 of that Schedule.

(5) For the purposes of this Part the time when a matter to which an intervention notice relates is finally determined under this Chapter is—

(a) in a case falling within subsection (4)(a), (e) or (f), the expiry of the time concerned;

(b) in a case falling within subsection (4)(b), the acceptance of the undertaking or group of undertakings concerned;

(c) in a case falling within subsection (4)(c), (d), (g) or (h), the making of the decision concerned;

(d) in a case falling within subsection (4)(i), the making of the decision neither to accept an undertaking under paragraph 9 of Schedule 7 nor to make an order under paragraph 11 of that Schedule; and

(e) in a case falling within subsection (4)(j), the acceptance of the undertaking concerned or (as the case may be) the making of the order concerned.

[(6) In this Part "OFCOM" means the Office of Communications.]

[3539]

NOTES

Sub-s (4): words in square brackets inserted by the Communications Act 2003, s 389, Sch 16, para 8(1), (2), as from 29 December 2003.

Sub-s (6): added by the Communications Act 2003, s 389, Sch 16, para 8(1), (3), as from 29 December 2003.

---

44 Investigation and report by OFT

(1) Subsection (2) applies where the Secretary of State has given an intervention notice in relation to a relevant merger situation.

(2) The OFT shall, within such period as the Secretary of State may require, give a report to the Secretary of State in relation to the case.

(3) The report shall contain—

(a) advice from the OFT on the considerations relevant to the making of a reference under section 22 or 33 which are also relevant to the Secretary of State's decision as to whether to make a reference under section 45; and

(b) a summary of any representations about the case which have been received by the OFT and which relate to any public interest consideration mentioned in the intervention notice concerned [(other than a media public interest consideration)] and which is or may be relevant to the Secretary of State's decision as to whether to make a reference under section 45.

(4) The report shall, in particular, include decisions as to whether the OFT believes that it is, or may be, the case that—

(a) a relevant merger situation has been created or arrangements are in progress or in contemplation which, if carried into effect, will result in the creation of a relevant merger situation;

(b) the creation of that situation has resulted, or may be expected to result, in a substantial lessening of competition within any market or markets in the United Kingdom for goods or services;

(c) the market or markets concerned would not be of sufficient importance to justify the making of a reference to the Commission under section 22 or 33;

(d) in the case of arrangements which are in progress or in contemplation, the arrangements are not sufficiently far advanced, or not sufficiently likely to proceed, to justify the making of such a reference;

(e) any relevant customer benefits in relation to the creation of the relevant merger situation concerned outweigh the substantial lessening of competition and any adverse effects of the substantial lessening of competition; or

(f) it would be appropriate to deal with the matter (disregarding any public interest considerations mentioned in the intervention notice concerned) by way of undertakings under paragraph 3 of Schedule 7.

(5) If the OFT believes that it is or may be the case that it would be appropriate to deal with the matter (disregarding any public interest considerations mentioned in the intervention notice concerned) by way of undertakings under paragraph 3 of Schedule 7, the report shall contain descriptions of the undertakings which the OFT believes are, or may be, appropriate.

[(5A) The report may, in particular, contain a summary of any representations about the case which have been received by the OFT and which relate to any media public interest consideration mentioned in the intervention notice concerned and which is or may be relevant to the Secretary of State's decision as to whether to make a reference under section 45.]

(6) The report may, in particular, include advice and recommendations on any public interest consideration mentioned in the intervention notice concerned and which is or may be relevant to the Secretary of State's decision as to whether to make a reference under section 45.

(7) The OFT shall carry out such investigations as it considers appropriate for the purposes of producing a report under this section.

[(8) In this Part 'media public interest consideration' means any consideration which, at the time of the giving of the intervention notice concerned—

(a) is specified in section 58(2A) to (2C); or

(b) in the opinion of the Secretary of State, is concerned with broadcasting or newspapers and ought to be specified in section 58.

(9) In this Part 'broadcasting' means the provision of services the provision of which—

(a) is required to be licensed under Part 1 or 3 of the Broadcasting Act 1990 or Part 1 or 2 of the Broadcasting Act 1996; or

(b) would be required to be so licensed if provided by a person subject to licensing under the Part in question.

(10) In this Part 'newspaper' means a daily, Sunday or local (other than daily or Sunday) newspaper circulating wholly or mainly in the United Kingdom or in a part of the United Kingdom.

(11) The Secretary of State may by order amend subsections (9) and (10).]

[3540]

NOTES

Sub-s (3): words in square brackets in para (b) inserted by the Communications Act 2003, s 376(1), as from 29 December 2003.

Sub-ss (5A), (8)–(11): inserted and added respectively by the Communications Act 2003, s 376(2), (3), as from 29 December 2003.

[44A Additional investigation and report by OFCOM: media mergers

(1) Subsection (2) applies where—

(a) the Secretary of State has given an intervention notice in relation to a relevant merger situation; and

(b) the intervention notice mentions any media public interest consideration.

(2) OFCOM shall, within such period as the Secretary of State may require, give a report to the Secretary of State on the effect of the consideration or considerations concerned on the case.

(3) The report shall contain—

(a) advice and recommendations on any media public interest consideration mentioned in the intervention notice concerned and which is or may be relevant to the Secretary of State's decision as to whether to make a reference under section 45; and

(b) a summary of any representations about the case which have been received by OFCOM and which relate to any such consideration.

(4) OFCOM shall carry out such investigations as they consider appropriate for the purposes of producing a report under this section.]

[3540A]

NOTES

Inserted by the Communications Act 2003, s 377, as from 29 December 2003.

45 Power of Secretary of State to refer matter to Commission

(1) Subsections (2) to (5) apply where the Secretary of State—

(a) has given an intervention notice in relation to a relevant merger situation; and

(b) has received a report of the OFT under section 44[, and any report of OFCOM which is required by virtue of section 44A,] in relation to the matter.

(2) The Secretary of State may make a reference to the Commission if he believes that it is or may be the case that—

(a) a relevant merger situation has been created;

(b) the creation of that situation has resulted, or may be expected to result, in a substantial lessening of competition within any market or markets in the United Kingdom for goods or services;

(c) one or more than one public interest consideration mentioned in the intervention notice is relevant to a consideration of the relevant merger situation concerned; and

(d) taking account only of the substantial lessening of competition and the relevant public interest consideration or considerations concerned, the creation of that situation operates or may be expected to operate against the public interest.

(3) The Secretary of State may make a reference to the Commission if he believes that it is or may be the case that—

(a) a relevant merger situation has been created;

(b) the creation of that situation has not resulted, and may be expected not to result, in a substantial lessening of competition within any market or markets in the United Kingdom for goods or services;

(c) one or more than one public interest consideration mentioned in the intervention notice is relevant to a consideration of the relevant merger situation concerned; and

(d) taking account only of the relevant public interest consideration or considerations concerned, the creation of that situation operates or may be expected to operate against the public interest.

(4) The Secretary of State may make a reference to the Commission if he believes that it is or may be the case that—

(a) arrangements are in progress or in contemplation which, if carried into effect, will result in the creation of a relevant merger situation;

(b) the creation of that situation may be expected to result in a substantial lessening of competition within any market or markets in the United Kingdom for goods or services;

(c) one or more than one public interest consideration mentioned in the intervention notice is relevant to a consideration of the relevant merger situation concerned; and

(d) taking account only of the substantial lessening of competition and the relevant public interest consideration or considerations concerned, the creation of the relevant merger situation may be expected to operate against the public interest.

(5) The Secretary of State may make a reference to the Commission if he believes that it is or may be the case that—

(a) arrangements are in progress or in contemplation which, if carried into effect, will result in the creation of a relevant merger situation;

(b) the creation of that situation may be expected not to result in a substantial lessening of competition within any market or markets in the United Kingdom for goods or services;

(c) one or more than one public interest consideration mentioned in the intervention notice is relevant to a consideration of the relevant merger situation concerned; and

(d) taking account only of the relevant public interest consideration or considerations concerned, the creation of the relevant merger situation may be expected to operate against the public interest.

(6) For the purposes of this Chapter any anti-competitive outcome shall be treated as being adverse to the public interest unless it is justified by one or more than one public interest consideration which is relevant.

(7) This section is subject to section 46.

[3541]

NOTES

Sub-s (1): words in square brackets in para (b) inserted by the Communications Act 2003, s 389, Sch 16, para 9, as from 29 December 2003.

46 References under section 45: supplementary

(1) No reference shall be made under section 45 if—

(a) the making of the reference is prevented by section … 74(1) or 96(3) or paragraph 4 of Schedule 7; …

(b) the European Commission is considering a request made, in relation to the matter concerned, by the United Kingdom (whether alone or with others) under article [22(1) of the EC Merger Regulation], is proceeding with the matter in pursuance of such a request or has dealt with the matter in pursuance of such a request[; or

(c) subject to subsection (1A), a reasoned submission requesting referral to the European Commission has been submitted to the European Commission under article 4(5) of the EC Merger Regulation].

[(1A) Subsection (1)(c) shall cease to apply if the Secretary of State is informed that a Member State competent to examine the concentration under its national competition law has, within the time permitted by Article 4(5) of the EC Merger Regulation, expressed its disagreement as regards the request to refer the case to the European Commission; and this subsection shall be construed in accordance with that Regulation.]

(2) The Secretary of State, in deciding whether to make a reference under section 45, shall accept the decisions of the OFT included in its report by virtue of subsection (4) of section 44 and any descriptions of undertakings as mentioned in subsection (5) of that section.

(3) Where the decision to make a reference under section 45 is made at any time on or after the end of the period of 24 weeks beginning with the giving of the intervention notice concerned, the Secretary of State shall, in deciding whether to make such a reference, disregard any public interest consideration which is mentioned in the intervention notice but which has not been finalised before the end of that period.

(4) Subject to subsection (5), where the decision to make a reference under section 45(2) or (4) is made at any time before the end of the period of 24 weeks beginning with the giving of the intervention notice concerned, the Secretary of State shall, in deciding whether to make such a reference, disregard any public interest consideration which is mentioned in the intervention notice but which has not been finalised if its effect would be to prevent, or to help to prevent, an anti-competitive outcome from being adverse to the public interest.

(5) The Secretary of State may, if he believes that there is a realistic prospect of the public interest consideration mentioned in subsection (4) being finalised within the period of 24 weeks beginning with the giving of the intervention notice concerned, delay deciding whether to make the reference concerned until the public interest consideration is finalised or, if earlier, the period expires.

(6) A reference under section 45 shall, in particular, specify—

(a) the subsection of that section under which it is made;

(b) the date on which it is made; and

(c) the public interest consideration or considerations mentioned in the intervention notice concerned which the Secretary of State is not under a duty to disregard by virtue of subsection (3) above and which he believes are or may be relevant to a consideration of the relevant merger situation concerned.

[3542]

NOTES

Sub-s (1): figure omitted from para (a) repealed by the Communications Act 2003, s 406, Sch 19, as from 29 December 2003; word omitted from the end of para (a) repealed, words in square brackets in para (b) substituted, and para (c) added, by the EC Merger Control (Consequential Amendments) Regulations 2004, SI 2004/1079, reg 2, Schedule, para 2(1), (12), (13), as from 1 May 2004.

Sub-s (1A): inserted by SI 2004/1079, reg 2, Schedule, para 2(1), (14), as from 1 May 2004.

[Cases referred by European Commission under the EC Merger Regulation

46A Cases referred by the European Commission where intervention notice is in force

(1) Subsection (2) applies if the European Commission has by a decision referred the whole or part of a case to the OFT under Article 4(4) or 9 of the EC Merger Regulation, or is deemed to have taken such a decision, and an intervention notice is in force in relation to that case.

(2) Before the end of the preliminary assessment period, the Secretary of State shall—

(a) decide whether to make a reference to the Commission under section 45; and

(b) inform the persons carrying on the enterprises concerned by notice of that decision and of the reasons for it.

(3) The Secretary of State may, for the purposes of subsection (2), decide not to make a reference on the basis that he is considering whether to seek or accept undertakings under paragraph 3 of Schedule 7 instead of making a reference; but a decision taken on that basis does not prevent the Secretary of State from making a reference under section 45 in the event of no such undertakings being offered or accepted.

(4) In this section—

"the preliminary assessment period" means, subject to section 46B, the period of 45 working days beginning with the day after the day on which the decision of the European Commission to refer the case is taken (or is deemed to have been taken); and

"working day" means any day which is not—

(a) a Saturday;

(b) a Sunday; or

(c) a day which is a European Commission holiday (as published in the Official Journal of the European Communities before the beginning of the year in which it occurs).]

[3542A]

PART III OTHER LEGISLATION

NOTES

Inserted, together with the preceding heading and ss 46B, 46C, by the EC Merger Control (Consequential Amendments) Regulations 2004, SI 2004/1079, reg 2, Schedule, para 2(1), (15), as from 1 May 2004.

[46B Extension of preliminary assessment period

(1) If the OFT has imposed a requirement under section 46C and it considers that the person on whom that requirement was imposed has failed to comply with it, the OFT may, by notice to the persons carrying on the enterprises concerned, extend the preliminary assessment period.

(2) If the Secretary of State has imposed a requirement under section 46C and he considers that the person on whom that requirement was imposed has failed to comply with it, he may, by notice to the persons carrying on the enterprises concerned, extend the preliminary assessment period.

(3) The period of an extension under this section shall—

(a) begin with the end of the period within which the requirement under section 46C could be complied with; and

(b) end with—

(i) in the case of a notice under subsection (1), the earlier of either compliance with the requirement to the satisfaction of the OFT or cancellation by the OFT of the extension.

(ii) in the case of a notice under subsection (2), the earlier of either compliance with the requirement to the satisfaction of the Secretary of State or cancellation by him of the extension.

(4) A notice under this section shall—

(a) be given within 5 working days of the end of the period mentioned in subsection (3)(a); and

(b) inform the person to whom it is addressed—

(i) in the case of a notice under subsection (1), that the OFT is of the opinion mentioned in that subsection and that it intends to extend the preliminary assessment period.

(ii) in the case of a notice under subsection (2), that the Secretary of State is of the opinion mentioned in that subsection and that he intends to extend the preliminary assessment period.]

[3542B]

NOTES

Inserted as noted to s 46A at **[3542A]**.

[46C Power to request information in referred cases

(1) In a case mentioned in section 46A(1), the OFT may by notice to any of the persons carrying on the enterprises concerned request him to provide the OFT with such information as the OFT may require for the purpose of enabling the Secretary of State to make a decision for the purposes of section 46A(2).

(2) In such a case, the Secretary of State may by notice to any of the persons carrying on the enterprises concerned request him to provide the Secretary of State with such information as he may require for the purpose of enabling him to make a decision for the purposes of section 46A(2).

(3) A notice under subsection (1) or (2) shall state—

(a) the information required;

(b) the period within which the information is to be provided; and

(c) the manner (if any) in which the information is required to be provided; and

(d) the possible consequences—

(i) of not providing the information within the stated period; and

(ii) if a manner for its provision is stated in the notice, of not providing it in that manner.]

[3542C]

NOTES

Inserted as noted to s 46A at **[3542A]**.

Reports on references

47 Questions to be decided on references under section 45

(1) The Commission shall, on a reference under section 45(2) or (3), decide whether a relevant merger situation has been created.

(2) If the Commission decides that such a situation has been created, it shall, on a reference under section 45(2), decide the following additional questions—

(a) whether the creation of that situation has resulted, or may be expected to result, in a substantial lessening of competition within any market or markets in the United Kingdom for goods or services; and

(b) whether, taking account only of any substantial lessening of competition and the admissible public interest consideration or considerations concerned, the creation of that situation operates or may be expected to operate against the public interest.

(3) If the Commission decides that a relevant merger situation has been created, it shall, on a reference under section 45(3), decide whether, taking account only of the admissible

public interest consideration or considerations concerned, the creation of that situation operates or may be expected to operate against the public interest.

(4) The Commission shall, on a reference under section 45(4) or (5), decide whether arrangements are in progress or in contemplation which, if carried into effect, will result in the creation of a relevant merger situation.

(5) If the Commission decides that such arrangements are in progress or in contemplation, it shall, on a reference under section 45(4), decide the following additional questions—

(a) whether the creation of that situation may be expected to result in a substantial lessening of competition within any market or markets in the United Kingdom for goods or services; and

(b) whether, taking account only of any substantial lessening of competition and the admissible public interest consideration or considerations concerned, the creation of that situation may be expected to operate against the public interest.

(6) If the Commission decides that arrangements are in progress or in contemplation which, if carried into effect, will result in the creation of a relevant merger situation, it shall, on a reference under section 45(5), decide whether, taking account only of the admissible public interest consideration or considerations concerned, the creation of that situation may be expected to operate against the public interest.

(7) The Commission shall, if it has decided on a reference under section 45 that the creation of a relevant merger situation operates or may be expected to operate against the public interest, decide the following additional questions—

(a) whether action should be taken by the Secretary of State under section 55 for the purpose of remedying, mitigating or preventing any of the effects adverse to the public interest which have resulted from, or may be expected to result from, the creation of the relevant merger situation;

(b) whether the Commission should recommend the taking of other action by the Secretary of State or action by persons other than itself and the Secretary of State for the purpose of remedying, mitigating or preventing any of the effects adverse to the public interest which have resulted from, or may be expected to result from, the creation of the relevant merger situation; and

(c) in either case, if action should be taken, what action should be taken and what is to be remedied, mitigated or prevented.

(8) Where the Commission has decided by virtue of subsection (2)(a) or (5)(a) that there is or will be a substantial lessening of competition within any market or markets in the United Kingdom for goods or services, it shall also decide separately the following questions (on the assumption that it is proceeding as mentioned in section 56(6))—

(a) whether action should be taken by it under section 41 for the purpose of remedying, mitigating or preventing the substantial lessening of competition concerned or any adverse effect which has resulted from, or may be expected to result from, the substantial lessening of competition;

(b) whether the Commission should recommend the taking of action by other persons for the purpose of remedying, mitigating or preventing the substantial lessening of competition concerned or any adverse effect which has resulted from, or may be expected to result from, the substantial lessening of competition; and

(c) in either case, if action should be taken, what action should be taken and what is to be remedied, mitigated or prevented.

(9) In deciding the questions mentioned in subsections (7) and (8) the Commission shall, in particular, have regard to the need to achieve as comprehensive a solution as is reasonable and practicable to—

(a) the adverse effects to the public interest; or

(b) (as the case may be) the substantial lessening of competition and any adverse effects resulting from it.

(10) In deciding the questions mentioned in subsections (7) and (8) in a case where it has decided by virtue of subsection (2)(a) or (5)(a) that there is or will be a substantial lessening of competition, the Commission may, in particular, have regard to the effect of any action on any relevant customer benefits in relation to the creation of the relevant merger situation concerned.

(11) In this section "admissible public interest consideration" means any public interest consideration which is specified in the reference under section 45 and which the Commission is not under a duty to disregard.

[3543]

48 Cases where references or certain questions need not be decided

(1) The Commission shall cancel a reference under section 45(4) or (5) if it considers that the proposal to make arrangements of the kind mentioned in that reference has been abandoned.

(2) In relation to the question whether a relevant merger situation has been created or the question whether a relevant merger situation will be created, a reference under section 45 may be framed so as to require the Commission to exclude from consideration—

(a) subsection (1) of section 23;
(b) subsection (2) of that section; or
(c) one of those subsections if the Commission finds that the other is satisfied.

(3) In relation to the question whether any such result as is mentioned in section 23(2)(b) has arisen or the question whether any such result will arise, a reference under section 45 may be framed so as to require the Commission to confine its investigation to the supply of goods or services in a part of the United Kingdom specified in the reference.

[3544]

49 Variation of references under section 45

(1) The Commission may, if it considers that doing so is justified by the facts (including events occurring on or after the making of the reference concerned), treat—

(a) a reference made under subsection (2) or (3) of section 45 as if it had been made under subsection (4) or (as the case may be) (5) of that section; or
(b) a reference made under subsection (4) or (5) of section 45 as if it had been made under subsection (2) or (as the case may be) (3) of that section;

and, in such cases, references in this Part to references under those enactments shall, so far as may be necessary, be construed accordingly.

(2) Where, by virtue of subsection (1), the Commission treats a reference made under subsection (2) or (3) of section 45 as if it had been made under subsection (4) or (as the case may be) (5) of that section, paragraphs 1, 2, 7 and 8 of Schedule 7 shall, in particular, apply as if the reference had been made under subsection (4) or (as the case may be) (5) of that section instead of under subsection (2) or (3) of that section.

(3) Where, by virtue of subsection (1), the Commission treats a reference made under subsection (4) or (5) of section 45 as if it had been made under subsection (2) or (as the case may be) (3) of that section, paragraphs 1, 2, 7 and 8 of Schedule 7 shall, in particular, apply as if the reference had been made under subsection (2) or (as the case may be) (3) of that section instead of under subsection (4) or (5) of that section.

(4) Subsection (5) applies in relation to any undertaking accepted under paragraph 1 of Schedule 7, or any order made under paragraph 2 of that Schedule, which is in force immediately before the Commission, by virtue of subsection (1), treats a reference as mentioned in subsection (1).

(5) The undertaking or order shall, so far as applicable, continue in force as if—

(a) in the case of an undertaking or order which relates to a reference under subsection (2) or (3) of section 45, accepted or made in relation to a reference made under subsection (4) or (as the case may be) (5) of that section; and
(b) in the case of an undertaking or order which relates to a reference made under subsection (4) or (5) of that section, accepted or made in relation to a reference made under subsection (2) or (as the case may be) (3) of that section;

and the undertaking or order concerned may be varied, superseded, released or revoked accordingly.

(6) The Secretary of State may at any time vary a reference under section 45.

(7) The Secretary of State shall consult the Commission before varying any such reference.

(8) Subsection (7) shall not apply if the Commission has requested the variation concerned.

(9) No variation by the Secretary of State under this section shall be capable of altering the public interest consideration or considerations specified in the reference or the period permitted by section 51 within which the report of the Commission under section 50 is to be prepared and given to the Secretary of State.

[3545]

50 Investigations and reports on references under section 45

(1) The Commission shall prepare a report on a reference under section 45 and give it to the Secretary of State within the period permitted by section 51.

(2) The report shall, in particular, contain—

(a) the decisions of the Commission on the questions which it is required to answer by virtue of section 47;

(b) its reasons for its decisions; and

(c) such information as the Commission considers appropriate for facilitating a proper understanding of those questions and of its reasons for its decisions.

[(2A) Where the report relates to a reference under section 45 which has been made after a report of OFCOM under section 44A, the Commission shall give a copy of its report (whether or not published) to OFCOM.]

(3) The Commission shall carry out such investigations as it considers appropriate for the purpose of producing a report under this section.

[3546]

NOTES

Sub-s (2A): inserted by the Communications Act 2003, s 389, Sch 16, para 10, as from 29 December 2003.

51 Time-limits for investigations and reports by Commission

(1) The Commission shall prepare its report under section 50 and give it to the Secretary of State under that section within the period of 24 weeks beginning with the date of the reference concerned.

(2) …

(3) The Commission may extend, by no more than 8 weeks, the period within which a report under section 50 is to be prepared and given to the Secretary of State if it considers that there are special reasons why the report cannot be prepared and given to the Secretary of State within that period.

(4) The Commission may extend the period within which a report under section 50 is to be prepared and given to the Secretary of State if it considers that a relevant person has failed (whether with or without a reasonable excuse) to comply with any requirement of a notice under section 109.

(5) In subsection (4) "relevant person" means—

(a) any person carrying on any of the enterprises concerned;

(b) any person who (whether alone or as a member of a group) owns or has control of any such person; or

(c) any officer, employee or agent of any person mentioned in paragraph (a) or (b).

(6) For the purposes of subsection (5) a person or group of persons able, directly or indirectly, to control or materially to influence the policy of a body of persons corporate or unincorporate, but without having a controlling interest in that body of persons, may be treated as having control of it.

(7) An extension under subsection (3) or (4) shall come into force when published under section 107.

(8) An extension under subsection (4) shall continue in force until—

(a) the person concerned provides the information or documents to the satisfaction of the Commission or (as the case may be) appears as a witness in accordance with the requirements of the Commission; or

(b) the Commission publishes its decision to cancel the extension.

(9) This section is subject to sections 52 and 53.

[3547]

NOTES

Sub-s (2): repealed by the EC Merger Control (Consequential Amendments) Regulations 2004, SI 2004/1079, reg 2, Schedule, para 2(1), (16), as from 1 May 2004.

52 Section 51: supplementary

(1), (2) …

(3) A period extended under subsection (3) of section 51 may also be extended under subsection (4) of that section and a period extended under subsection (4) of that section may also be extended under subsection (3) of that section.

(4) No more than one extension is possible under section 51(3).

(5) Where a period within which a report under section 50 is to be prepared and given to the Secretary of State is extended or further extended under section 51(3) or (4), the period as extended or (as the case may be) further extended shall, subject to subsections (6) and (7), be calculated by taking the period being extended and adding to it the period of the extension (whether or not those periods overlap in time).

(6) Subsection (7) applies where—

(a) the period within which the report under section 50 is to be prepared and given to the Secretary of State is further extended;

(b) the further extension and at least one previous extension is made under section 51(4); and

(c) the same days or fractions of days are included in or comprise the further extension and are included in or comprise at least one such previous extension.

(7) In calculating the period of the further extension, any days or fractions of days of the kind mentioned in subsection (6)(c) shall be disregarded.

(8) The Secretary of State may by order amend section 51 so as to alter any one or more of the following periods—

(a) the period of 24 weeks mentioned in subsection (1) of that section or any period for the time being mentioned in that subsection in substitution for that period;

(b) …

(c) the period of 8 weeks mentioned in subsection (3) of that section or any period for the time being mentioned in that subsection in substitution for that period.

(9) No alteration shall be made by virtue of subsection (8) which results in the period for the time being mentioned in subsection (1) … of section 51 exceeding 24 weeks or the period for the time being mentioned in subsection (3) of that section exceeding 8 weeks.

(10) An order under subsection (8) shall not affect any period of time within which the Commission is under a duty to prepare and give to the Secretary of State its report under section 50 in relation to a reference under section 45 if the Commission is already under that duty in relation to that reference when the order is made.

(11) Before making an order under subsection (8) the Secretary of State shall consult the Commission and such other persons as he considers appropriate.

(12) The Secretary of State may make regulations for the purposes of section 51(8).

(13) The regulations may, in particular—

(a) provide for the time at which information or documents are to be treated as provided (including the time at which they are to be treated as provided to the satisfaction of the Commission for the purposes of section 51(8));

(b) provide for the time at which a person is to be treated as appearing as a witness (including the time at which he is to be treated as appearing as a witness in accordance with the requirements of the Commission for the purposes of section 51(8));

(c) provide for the persons carrying on the enterprises which have or may have ceased to be, or may cease to be, distinct enterprises to be informed, in circumstances in which section 51(8) applies, of the fact that—

(i) the Commission is satisfied as to the provision of the information or documents required by it; or

(ii) the person concerned has appeared as a witness in accordance with the requirements of the Commission;

(d) provide for the persons carrying on the enterprises which have or may have ceased to be, or may cease to be, distinct enterprises to be informed, in circumstances in which section 51(8) applies, of the time at which the Commission is to be treated as satisfied as mentioned in paragraph (c)(i) above or the person concerned is to be treated as having appeared as mentioned in paragraph (c)(ii) above.

[3548]

NOTES

Sub-ss (1), (2): repealed by the EC Merger Control (Consequential Amendments) Regulations 2004, SI 2004/1079, reg 2, Schedule, para 2(1), (17)(a), as from 1 May 2004.

Sub-ss (8), (9): words omitted repealed by SI 2004/1079, reg 2, Schedule, para 2(1), (17)(a), (b), as from 1 May 2004.

53 Restrictions on action where public interest considerations not finalised

(1) The Commission shall cancel a reference under section 45 if—

(a) the intervention notice concerned mentions a public interest consideration which was not finalised on the giving of that notice or public interest considerations which, at that time, were not finalised;

(b) no other public interest consideration is mentioned in the notice;

(c) at least 24 weeks has elapsed since the giving of the notice; and

(d) the public interest consideration mentioned in the notice has not been finalised within that period of 24 weeks or (as the case may be) none of the public interest considerations mentioned in the notice has been finalised within that period of 24 weeks.

(2) Where a reference to the Commission under section 45 specifies a public interest consideration which has not been finalised before the making of the reference, the Commission shall not give its report to the Secretary of State under section 50 in relation to that reference unless—

(a) the period of 24 weeks beginning with the giving of the intervention notice concerned has expired; [or]

(b) the public interest consideration concerned has been finalised; …

(c) …

(3) The Commission shall, in reporting on any of the questions mentioned in section 47(2)(b), (3), (5)(b), (6) and (7), disregard any public interest consideration which has not been finalised before the giving of the report.

(4) The Commission shall, in reporting on any of the questions mentioned in section 47(2)(b), (3), (5)(b), (6) and (7), disregard any public interest consideration which was not finalised on the giving of the intervention notice concerned and has not been finalised within the period of 24 weeks beginning with the giving of the notice concerned.

(5) Subsections (1) to (4) are without prejudice to the power of the Commission to carry out investigations in relation to any public interest consideration to which it might be able to have regard in its report.

[3549]

NOTES

Sub-s (2): word in square brackets in para (a) added, and para (c) and the word immediately preceding it repealed, by the EC Merger Control (Consequential Amendments) Regulations 2004, SI 2004/1079, reg 2, Schedule, para 2(1), (18), as from 1 May 2004.

Decisions of the Secretary of State

54 Decision of Secretary of State in public interest cases

(1) Subsection (2) applies where the Secretary of State has received a report of the Commission under section 50 in relation to a relevant merger situation.

(2) The Secretary of State shall decide whether to make an adverse public interest finding in relation to the relevant merger situation and whether to make no finding at all in the matter.

(3) For the purposes of this Part the Secretary of State makes an adverse public interest finding in relation to a relevant merger situation if, in relation to that situation, he decides—

(a) in connection with a reference to the Commission under subsection (2) of section 45, that it is the case as mentioned in paragraphs (a) to (d) of that subsection or subsection (3) of that section;

(b) in connection with a reference to the Commission under subsection (3) of that section, that it is the case as mentioned in paragraphs (a) to (d) of that subsection;

(c) in connection with a reference to the Commission under subsection (4) of that section, that it is the case as mentioned in paragraphs (a) to (d) of that subsection or subsection (5) of that section; and

(d) in connection with a reference to the Commission under subsection (5) of that section, that it is the case as mentioned in paragraphs (a) to (d) of that subsection.

(4) The Secretary of State may make no finding at all in the matter only if he decides that there is no public interest consideration which is relevant to a consideration of the relevant merger situation concerned.

(5) The Secretary of State shall make and publish his decision under subsection (2) within the period of 30 days beginning with the receipt of the report of the Commission under section 50.

(6) In making a decision under subsections (2) to (4), the Secretary of State shall disregard any public interest consideration not specified in the reference under section 45 and any public interest consideration disregarded by the Commission for the purposes of its report.

(7) In deciding whether to make an adverse public interest finding under subsection (2), the Secretary of State shall accept—

(a) in connection with a reference to the Commission under section 45(2) or (4), the decision of the report of the Commission under section 50 as to whether there is an anti-competitive outcome; and

(b) in connection with a reference to the Commission under section 45(3) or (5)—

(i) the decision of the report of the Commission under section 50 as to whether a relevant merger situation has been created or (as the case may be) arrangements are in progress or in contemplation which, if carried into effect, will result in the creation of a relevant merger situation; and

(ii) the decision of the report of the OFT under section 44 as to the absence of a substantial lessening of competition.

(8) In determining for the purposes of subsection (5) the period of 30 days no account shall be taken of—

(a) Saturday, Sunday, Good Friday and Christmas Day; and

(b) any day which is a bank holiday in England and Wales.

[3550]

55 Enforcement action by Secretary of State

(1) Subsection (2) applies where the Secretary of State has decided under subsection (2) of section 54 within the period required by subsection (5) of that section to make an adverse public interest finding in relation to a relevant merger situation and has published his decision within the period so required.

(2) The Secretary of State may take such action under paragraph 9 or 11 of Schedule 7 as he considers to be reasonable and practicable to remedy, mitigate or prevent any of the effects adverse to the public interest which have resulted from, or may be expected to result from, the creation of the relevant merger situation concerned.

(3) In making a decision under subsection (2) the Secretary of State shall, in particular, have regard to the report of the Commission under section 50.

(4) In making a decision under subsection (2) in any case of a substantial lessening of competition, the Secretary of State may, in particular, have regard to the effect of any action on any relevant customer benefits in relation to the creation of the relevant merger situation concerned.

[3551]

Other

56 Competition cases where intervention on public interest grounds ceases

(1) Where the Secretary of State decides not to make a reference under section 45 on the ground that no public interest consideration to which he is able to have regard is relevant to a consideration of the relevant merger situation concerned, he shall by notice require the OFT to deal with the matter otherwise than under this Chapter.

(2) Where a notice is given to the OFT in the circumstances mentioned in subsection (1), the OFT shall decide whether to make a reference under section 22 or 33; and any time-limits in relation to the Secretary of State's decision whether to make a reference under section 45 (including any remaining powers of extension) shall apply in relation to the decision of the OFT whether to make a reference under section 22 or 33.

(3) Where the Commission cancels under section 53(1) a reference under section 45 and the report of the OFT under section 44 contains the decision that it is or may be the case that there is an anti-competitive outcome in relation to the relevant merger situation concerned, the Commission shall proceed under this Part as if a reference under section 22 or (as the case may be) 33 had been made to it by the OFT.

(4) In proceeding by virtue of subsection (3) to prepare and publish a report under section 38, the Commission shall proceed as if—

(a) the reference under section 22 or 33 had been made at the same time as the reference under section 45;

(b) the timetable for preparing and giving its report under section 50 (including any remaining powers of extension and as extended by an additional period of 20 days) were the timetable for preparing and publishing its report under section 38; and

(c) in relation to the question whether a relevant merger situation has been created or the question whether arrangements are in progress or in contemplation which, if carried into effect, will result in the creation of a relevant merger situation, the Commission were confined to the questions on the subject to be investigated by it under section 47.

(5) In determining the period of 20 days mentioned in subsection (4) no account shall be taken of—

(a) Saturday, Sunday, Good Friday and Christmas Day; and

(b) any day which is a bank holiday in England and Wales.

(6) Where the Secretary of State decides under section 54(2) to make no finding at all in the matter in connection with a reference under section 45(2) or (4), the Commission shall proceed under this Part as if a reference under section 22 or (as the case may be) 33 had been made to it instead of a reference under section 45 and as if its report to the Secretary of State under section 50 had been prepared and published by it under section 38 within the period permitted by section 39.

(7) In relation to proceedings by virtue of subsection (6), the reference in section 41(3) to decisions of the Commission as included in its report by virtue of section 35(3) or 36(2) shall be construed as a reference to decisions which were included in the report of the Commission by virtue of section 47(8).

(8) Where the Commission becomes under a duty to proceed as mentioned in subsection (3) or (6), references in this Part to references under sections 22 and 33 shall, so far as may be necessary, be construed accordingly; and, in particular, sections 77 to 81 shall apply as if a reference has been made to the Commission by the OFT under section 22 or (as the case may be) 33.

[3552]

57 Duties of OFT and Commission to inform Secretary of State

(1) The OFT shall, in considering whether to make a reference under section 22 or 33, bring to the attention of the Secretary of State any case which it believes raises any consideration specified in section 58 unless it believes that the Secretary of State would consider any such consideration immaterial in the context of the particular case.

(2) The OFT[, OFCOM] and the Commission shall bring to the attention of the Secretary of State any representations about exercising his powers under section 58(3) which have been made to the OFT[, OFCOM] or (as the case may be) the Commission.

[3553]

PART III OTHER LEGISLATION

NOTES

Sub-s (2): words in square brackets inserted by the Communications Act 2003, s 389, Sch 16, para 11, as from 29 December 2003.

58 Specified considerations

(1) The interests of national security are specified in this section.

(2) In subsection (1) "national security" includes public security; and in this subsection "public security" has the same meaning as in article [21(4) of the EC Merger Regulation].

[(2A) The need for—

(a) accurate presentation of news; and

(b) free expression of opinion;

in newspapers is specified in this section.

(2B) The need for, to the extent that it is reasonable and practicable, a sufficient plurality of views in newspapers in each market for newspapers in the United Kingdom or a part of the United Kingdom is specified in this section.

(2C) The following are specified in this section—

(a) the need, in relation to every different audience in the United Kingdom or in a particular area or locality of the United Kingdom, for there to be a sufficient plurality of persons with control of the media enterprises serving that audience;

(b) the need for the availability throughout the United Kingdom of a wide range of broadcasting which (taken as a whole) is both of high quality and calculated to appeal to a wide variety of tastes and interests; and

(c) the need for persons carrying on media enterprises, and for those with control of such enterprises, to have a genuine commitment to the attainment in relation to broadcasting of the standards objectives set out in section 319 of the Communications Act 2003.]

(3) The Secretary of State may by order modify this section for the purpose of specifying in this section a new consideration or removing or amending any consideration which is for the time being specified in this section.

(4) An order under this section may, in particular—

(a) provide for a consideration to be specified in this section for a particular purpose or purposes or for all purposes;

(b) apply in relation to cases under consideration by the OFT, [OFCOM,] the Commission or the Secretary of State before the making of the order as well as cases under consideration on or after the making of the order.

[3554]

NOTES

Sub-s (2): words in square brackets substituted by the EC Merger Control (Consequential Amendments) Regulations 2004, SI 2004/1079, reg 2, Schedule, para 2(1), (19), as from 1 May 2004.

Sub-ss (2A)–(2C): inserted by the Communications Act 2003, s 375(1), as from 29 December 2003.

Sub-s (4): word in square brackets in para (b) inserted by the Communications Act 2003, s 389, Sch 16, para 12, as from 29 December 2003.

[58A Construction of consideration specified in section 58(2C)

(1) For the purposes of section 58 and this section an enterprise is a media enterprise if it consists in or involves broadcasting.

(2) In the case of a merger situation in which at least one of the enterprises ceasing to be distinct consists in or involves broadcasting, the references in section 58(2C)(a) or this section to media enterprises include references to newspaper enterprises.

(3) In this Part "newspaper enterprise" means an enterprise consisting in or involving the supply of newspapers.

(4) Wherever in a merger situation two media enterprises serving the same audience cease to be distinct, the number of such enterprises serving that audience shall be assumed to be more immediately before they cease to be distinct than it is afterwards.

(5) For the purposes of section 58, where two or more media enterprises—

(a) would fall to be treated as under common ownership or common control for the purposes of section 26, or

(b) are otherwise in the same ownership or under the same control,

they shall be treated (subject to subsection (4)) as all under the control of only one person.

(6) A reference in section 58 or this section to an audience shall be construed in relation to a media enterprise in whichever of the following ways the decision-making authority considers appropriate—

(a) as a reference to any one of the audiences served by that enterprise, taking them separately;

(b) as a reference to all the audiences served by that enterprise, taking them together;

(c) as a reference to a number of those audiences taken together in such group as the decision-making authority considers appropriate; or

(d) as a reference to a part of anything that could be taken to be an audience under any of paragraphs (a) to (c) above.

(7) The criteria for deciding who can be treated for the purposes of this section as comprised in an audience, or as comprised in an audience served by a particular service—

(a) shall be such as the decision-making authority considers appropriate in the circumstances of the case; and

(b) may allow for persons to be treated as members of an audience if they are only potentially members of it.

(8) In this section 'audience' includes readership.

(9) The power under subsection (3) of section 58 to modify that section includes power to modify this section.]

[3554A]

NOTES

Inserted by the Communications Act 2003, s 375(2), as from 29 December 2003.

CHAPTER 3
OTHER SPECIAL CASES

Special public interest cases

59 Intervention by Secretary of State in special public interest cases

(1) Subsection (2) applies where the Secretary of State has reasonable grounds for suspecting that it is or may be the case that a special merger situation has been created or arrangements are in progress or in contemplation which, if carried into effect, will result in the creation of a special merger situation.

(2) The Secretary of State may give a notice to the OFT (in this Part "a special intervention notice") if he believes that it is or may be the case that one or more than one consideration specified in section 58 is relevant to a consideration of the special merger situation concerned.

[(3) For the purposes of this Part a special merger situation has been created if—

(a) the condition mentioned in subsection (3A) is satisfied; and

(b) immediately before the enterprises concerned ceased to be distinct—

(i) the conditions mentioned in subsection (3B) were satisfied;

(ii) the condition mentioned in subsection (3C) was satisfied; or

(iii) the condition mentioned in subsection (3D) was satisfied.

(3A) The condition mentioned in this subsection is that—

(a) no relevant merger situation has been created because of section 23(1)(b) and (2)(b); but

(b) a relevant merger situation would have been created if those enactments were disregarded.

(3B) The conditions mentioned in this subsection are that—

(a) at least one of the enterprises concerned was carried on in the United Kingdom or by or under the control of a body corporate incorporated in the United Kingdom; and

PART III OTHER LEGISLATION

(b) a person carrying on one or more of the enterprises concerned was a relevant government contractor.

(3C) The condition mentioned in this subsection is that, in relation to the supply of newspapers of any description, at least one-quarter of all the newspapers of that description which were supplied in the United Kingdom, or in a substantial part of the United Kingdom, were supplied by the person or persons by whom one of the enterprises concerned was carried on.

(3D) The condition mentioned in this subsection is that, in relation to the provision of broadcasting of any description, at least one-quarter of all broadcasting of that description provided in the United Kingdom, or in a substantial part of the United Kingdom, was provided by the person or persons by whom one of the enterprises concerned was carried on.]

(5) For the purposes of deciding whether a relevant merger situation has been created or whether arrangements are in progress or in contemplation which, if carried into effect, will result in the creation of a relevant merger situation, sections 23 to 32 (read together with section 34) shall apply for the purposes of this Chapter as they do for the purposes of Chapter 1 but subject to subsection (6).

(6) In their application by virtue of subsection (5) sections 23 to 32 shall have effect as if—

(a) for paragraph (a) of section 23(9) there were substituted—

"(a) in relation to the giving of a special intervention notice, the time when the notice is given;

(aa) in relation to the making of a report by the OFT under section 61, the time of the making of the report;

(ab) in the case of a reference which is treated as having been made under section 62(2) by virtue of section 64(2), such time as the Commission may determine; and";

(b) the references to the OFT in section 24(2)(a) and (b) included references to the Secretary of State;

(c) the references to the OFT in sections 25(1) to (3), (6) and (8) and 31 included references to the Secretary of State;

(d) the references to the OFT in section 25(4) and (5) were references to the Secretary of State;

(e) the reference in section 25(4) to section 73 were a reference to paragraph 3 of Schedule 7;

(f) the reference in section 25(12) to one extension were a reference to one extension by the OFT and one extension by the Secretary of State;

(g) the powers to extend time-limits under section 25 as applied by subsection (5) above, and the power to request information under section 31(1) as so applied, were not exercisable by the OFT or the Secretary of State before the giving of a special intervention notice;

(h) in subsection (1) of section 31 for the words "section 22" there were substituted "section 62(2)" and, in the application of that subsection to the OFT, for the word "deciding" there were substituted "enabling the Secretary of State to decide";

(i) in the case of the giving of special intervention notices, the references in sections 23 to 32 to the making of a reference or a reference were, so far as necessary, references to the giving of a special intervention notice or a special intervention notice; and

(j) the references to the OFT in section 32(2)(a) to (c) and (3) were construed in accordance with the above modifications.

[(6A) The Secretary of State may by order amend the conditions mentioned in subsection (3)(b)(ii) and (iii).]

(7) No more than one special intervention notice shall be given under subsection (2) in relation to the same special merger situation.

(8) In this section "relevant government contractor" means—

(a) a government contractor—

(i) who has been notified by or on behalf of the Secretary of State of information, documents or other articles relating to defence and of a confidential nature which the government contractor or an employee of his may hold or receive in connection with being such a contractor; and

(ii) whose notification has not been revoked by or on behalf of the Secretary of State; or

(b) a former government contractor who was so notified when he was a government contractor and whose notification has not been revoked by or on behalf of the Secretary of State.

(9) In this section—

"defence" has the same meaning as in section 2 of the Official Secrets Act 1989 (c 6); and

"government contractor" has the same meaning as in the Act of 1989 and includes any sub-contractor of a government contractor, any sub-contractor of that sub-contractor and any other sub-contractor in a chain of sub-contractors which begins with the sub-contractor of the government contractor.

[3555]

NOTES

Sub-ss (3), (3A)–(3D): substituted, for original sub-ss (3), (4), by the Communications Act 2003, s 378(1), as from 29 December 2003.

Sub-s (6A): inserted by the Communications Act 2003, s 378(2), as from 29 December 2003.

[59A Construction of conditions in section 59(3C) and (3D)

(1) For the purpose of deciding whether the proportion of one-quarter mentioned in section 59(3C) or (3D) is fulfilled with respect to—

(a) newspapers of any description, or

(b) broadcasting of any description,

the decision-making authority shall apply such criterion (whether value, cost, price, quantity, capacity, number of workers employed or some other criterion, of whatever nature), or such combination of criteria, as the decision-making authority considers appropriate.

(2) References in section 59(3C) to the supply of newspapers shall, in relation to newspapers of any description which are the subject of different forms of supply, be construed in whichever of the following ways the decision-making authority considers appropriate—

(a) as references to any of those forms of supply taken separately;

(b) as references to all those forms of supply taken together; or

(c) as references to any of those forms of supply taken in groups.

(3) For the purposes of subsection (2) the decision-making authority may treat newspapers as being the subject of different forms of supply whenever—

(a) the transactions concerned differ as to their nature, their parties, their terms or their surrounding circumstances; and

(b) the difference is one which, in the opinion of the decision-making authority, ought for the purposes of that subsection to be treated as a material difference.

(4) References in section 59(3D) to the provision of broadcasting shall, in relation to broadcasting of any description which is the subject of different forms of provision, be construed in whichever of the following ways the decision-making authority considers appropriate—

(a) as references to any of those forms of provision taken separately;

(b) as references to all those forms of provision taken together; or

(c) as references to any of those forms of provision taken in groups.

(5) For the purposes of subsection (4) the decision-making authority may treat broadcasting as being the subject of different forms of provision whenever—

(a) the transactions concerned differ as to their nature, their parties, their terms or their surrounding circumstances; and

(b) the difference is one which, in the opinion of the decision-making authority, ought for the purposes of that subsection to be treated as a material difference.

(6) The criteria for deciding when newspapers or broadcasting can be treated, for the purposes of section 59, as newspapers or broadcasting of a separate description shall be such as in any particular case the decision-making authority considers appropriate in the circumstances of that case.

(7) In section 59 and this section 'provision' and cognate expressions have the same meaning in relation to broadcasting as in Part 3 of the Communications Act 2003; but this subsection is subject to subsections (4) and (5) of this section.]

[3555A]

NOTES

Inserted by the Communications Act 2003, s 378(3), as from 29 December 2003.

60 Special intervention notices under section 59

(1) A special intervention notice shall state—

(a) the special merger situation concerned; and

(b) the consideration specified in section 58 or considerations so specified which are, or may be, relevant to the special merger situation concerned.

(2) Where the Secretary of State believes that it is or may be the case that two or more considerations specified in section 58 are relevant to a consideration of the special merger situation concerned, he may decide not to mention in the special intervention notice such of those considerations as he considers appropriate.

(3) A special intervention notice shall come into force when it is given and shall cease to be in force when the matter to which it relates is finally determined under this Chapter.

(4) For the purposes of this Part, a matter to which a special intervention notice relates is finally determined under this Chapter if—

(a) the time within which the OFT [or (if relevant) OFCOM] is to report to the Secretary of State under section 61 [or (as the case may be) 61A] has expired and no such report has been made;

(b) the Secretary of State decides to accept an undertaking or group of undertakings under paragraph 3 of Schedule 7 instead of making a reference under section 62;

(c) the Secretary of State otherwise decides not to make a reference under that section;

(d) the Commission cancels such a reference under section 64(1);

(e) the time within which the Commission is to prepare a report under section 65 and give it to the Secretary of State has expired and no such report has been prepared and given to the Secretary of State;

(f) the time within which the Secretary of State is to make and publish a decision under section 66(2) has expired and no such decision has been made and published;

(g) the Secretary of State decides under subsection (2) of section 66 otherwise than as mentioned in subsection (5) of that section;

(h) the Secretary of State decides under subsection (2) of section 66 as mentioned in subsection (5) of that section but decides neither to accept an undertaking under paragraph 9 of Schedule 7 nor to make an order under paragraph 11 of that Schedule; or

(i) the Secretary of State decides under subsection (2) of section 66 as mentioned in subsection (5) of that section and accepts an undertaking under paragraph 9 of Schedule 7 or makes an order under paragraph 11 of that Schedule.

(5) For the purposes of this Part the time when a matter to which a special intervention notice relates is finally determined under this Chapter is—

(a) in a case falling within subsection (4)(a), (e) or (f), the expiry of the time concerned;

(b) in a case falling within subsection (4)(b), the acceptance of the undertaking or group of undertakings concerned;

(c) in a case falling within subsection (4)(c), (d) or (g), the making of the decision concerned;

(d) in a case falling within subsection (4)(h), the making of the decision neither to accept an undertaking under paragraph 9 of Schedule 7 nor to make an order under paragraph 11 of that Schedule; and

(e) in a case falling within subsection (4)(i), the acceptance of the undertaking concerned or (as the case may be) the making of the order concerned.

[3556]

NOTES

Sub-s (4): words in square brackets in para (a) inserted by the Communications Act 2003, s 389, Sch 16, para 13, as from 29 December 2003.

61 Initial investigation and report by OFT

(1) Subsection (2) applies where the Secretary of State has given a special intervention notice in relation to a special merger situation.

(2) The OFT shall, within such period as the Secretary of State may require, give a report to the Secretary of State in relation to the case.

(3) The report shall contain—

(a) advice from the OFT on the considerations relevant to the making of a reference under section 22 or 33 which are also relevant to the Secretary of State's decision as to whether to make a reference under section 62; and

(b) a summary of any representations about the case which have been received by the OFT and which relate to any consideration mentioned in the special intervention notice concerned [(other than a consideration which, at the time of the giving of the notice, was specified in section 58(2A) to (2C))] and which is or may be relevant to the Secretary of State's decision as to whether to make a reference under section 62.

(4) The report shall include a decision as to whether the OFT believes (disregarding section [59(3B)(b)]) that it is, or may be, the case that a special merger situation has been created or (as the case may be) arrangements are in progress or in contemplation which, if carried into effect, will result in the creation of a special merger situation.

[(4A) The report may, in particular, contain a summary of any representations about the case which have been received by the OFT and which relate to any consideration which—

(a) is mentioned in the special intervention notice concerned and, at the time of the giving of that notice, was specified in section 58(2A) to (2C); and

(b) is or may be relevant to the Secretary of State's decision as to whether to make a reference under section 62.]

(5) The report may, in particular, include advice and recommendations on any consideration mentioned in the special intervention notice concerned and which is or may be relevant to the Secretary of State's decision as to whether to make a reference under section 62.

(6) The OFT shall carry out such investigations as it considers appropriate for the purposes of producing a report under this section.

[3557]

NOTES

Sub-s (3): words in square brackets inserted by the Communications Act 2003, s 379(1), (2), as from 29 December 2003.

Sub-s (4): number in square brackets substituted by the Communications Act 2003, s 379(1), (3), as from 29 December 2003.

Sub-s (4A): inserted by the Communications Act 2003, s 379(1), (4), as from 29 December 2003.

[61A Additional investigation and report by OFCOM: certain media mergers

(1) Subsection (2) applies where—

(a) the Secretary of State has given a special intervention notice in relation to a special merger situation; and

(b) the special intervention notice mentions any consideration which, at the time of the giving of the notice, was specified in section 58(2A) to (2C).

(2) OFCOM shall, within such period as the Secretary of State may require, give a report to the Secretary of State on the effect of the consideration or considerations concerned on the case.

(3) The report shall contain—

(a) advice and recommendations on any consideration which—

(i) is mentioned in the special intervention notice concerned and, at the time of the giving of that notice, was specified in section 58(2A) to (2C); and

(ii) is or may be relevant to the Secretary of State's decision as to whether to make a reference under section 62; and

(b) a summary of any representations about the case which have been received by OFCOM and which relate to any such consideration.

(4) OFCOM shall carry out such investigations as they consider appropriate for the purposes of producing a report under this section.]

[3557A]

NOTES

Inserted by the Communications Act 2003, s 380, as from 29 December 2003.

62 Power of Secretary of State to refer the matter

(1) Subsection (2) applies where the Secretary of State—

(a) has given a special intervention notice in relation to a special merger situation; and

(b) has received a report of the OFT under section 61[, and any report of OFCOM which is required by virtue of section 61A,] in relation to the matter.

(2) The Secretary of State may make a reference to the Commission if he believes that it is or may be the case that—

(a) a special merger situation has been created;

(b) one or more than one consideration mentioned in the special intervention notice is relevant to a consideration of the special merger situation concerned; and

(c) taking account only of the relevant consideration or considerations concerned, the creation of that situation operates or may be expected to operate against the public interest.

(3) The Secretary of State may make a reference to the Commission if he believes that it is or may be the case that—

(a) arrangements are in progress or in contemplation which, if carried into effect, will result in the creation of a special merger situation;

(b) one or more than one consideration mentioned in the special intervention notice is relevant to a consideration of the special merger situation concerned; and

(c) taking account only of the relevant consideration or considerations concerned, the creation of that situation may be expected to operate against the public interest.

(4) No reference shall be made under this section if the making of the reference is prevented by … paragraph 4 of Schedule 7.

(5) The Secretary of State, in deciding whether to make a reference under this section, shall accept the decision of the OFT included in its report under section 61 by virtue of subsection (4) of that section.

(6) A reference under this section shall, in particular, specify—

(a) the subsection of this section under which it is made;

(b) the date on which it is made; and

(c) the consideration or considerations mentioned in the special intervention notice which the Secretary of State believes are, or may be, relevant to a consideration of the special merger situation concerned.

[3558]

NOTES

Sub-s (1): words in square brackets in para (b) inserted by the Communications Act 2003, s 389, Sch 16, para 14, as from 29 December 2003.

Sub-s (4): words omitted repealed by the Communications Act 2003, s 406, Sch 19, as from 29 December 2003.

63 Questions to be decided on references under section 62

(1) The Commission shall, on a reference under section 62(2), decide whether a special merger situation has been created.

(2) The Commission shall, on a reference under section 62(3), decide whether arrangements are in progress or in contemplation which, if carried into effect, will result in the creation of a special merger situation.

(3) If the Commission decides that a special merger situation has been created or that arrangements are in progress or in contemplation which, if carried into effect, will result in the creation of a special merger situation, it shall, on a reference under section 62, decide

whether, taking account only of the consideration or considerations mentioned in the reference, the creation of that situation operates or may be expected to operate against the public interest.

(4) The Commission shall, if it has decided on a reference under section 62 that the creation of a special merger situation operates or may be expected to operate against the public interest, decide the following additional questions—

(a) whether action should be taken by the Secretary of State under section 66 for the purpose of remedying, mitigating or preventing any of the effects adverse to the public interest which have resulted from, or may be expected to result from, the creation of the special merger situation concerned;

(b) whether the Commission should recommend the taking of other action by the Secretary of State or action by persons other than itself and the Secretary of State for the purpose of remedying, mitigating or preventing any of the effects adverse to the public interest which have resulted from, or may be expected to result from, the creation of the special merger situation concerned; and

(c) in either case, if action should be taken, what action should be taken and what is to be remedied, mitigated or prevented.

[3559]

64 Cancellation and variation of references under section 62

(1) The Commission shall cancel a reference under section 62(3) if it considers that the proposal to make arrangements of the kind mentioned in that reference has been abandoned.

(2) The Commission may, if it considers that doing so is justified by the facts (including events occurring on or after the making of the reference concerned), treat a reference made under subsection (2) or (3) of section 62 as if it had been made under subsection (3) or (as the case may be) (2) of that section; and, in such cases, references in this Part to references under those enactments shall, so far as may be necessary, be construed accordingly.

(3) Where, by virtue of subsection (2), the Commission treats a reference made under subsection (2) or (3) of section 62 as if it had been made under subsection (3) or (as the case may be) (2) of that section, paragraphs 1, 2, 7 and 8 of Schedule 7 shall, in particular, apply as if the reference had been made under subsection (3) or (as the case may be) (2) of that section instead of under subsection (2) or (3) of that section.

(4) Subsection (5) applies in relation to any undertaking accepted under paragraph 1 of Schedule 7, or any order made under paragraph 2 of that Schedule, which is in force immediately before the Commission, by virtue of subsection (2), treats a reference made under subsection (2) or (3) of section 62 as if it had been made under subsection (3) or (as the case may be) (2) of that section.

(5) The undertaking or order shall, so far as applicable, continue in force as if—

(a) in the case of an undertaking or order which relates to a reference under subsection (2) of section 62, accepted or made in relation to a reference made under subsection (3) of that section; and

(b) in the case of an undertaking or order which relates to a reference made under subsection (3) of that section, accepted or made in relation to a reference made under subsection (2) of that section;

and the undertaking or order concerned may be varied, superseded, released or revoked accordingly.

(6) The Secretary of State may at any time vary a reference under section 62.

(7) The Secretary of State shall consult the Commission before varying any such reference.

(8) Subsection (7) shall not apply if the Commission has requested the variation concerned.

(9) No variation by the Secretary of State under this section shall be capable of altering the consideration or considerations specified in the reference or the period permitted by virtue of section 65 within which the report of the Commission under that section is to be prepared and given to the Secretary of State.

[3560]

65 Investigations and reports on references under section 62

(1) The Commission shall prepare a report on a reference under section 62 and give it to the Secretary of State within the period permitted by virtue of this section.

(2) The report shall, in particular, contain—

(a) the decisions of the Commission on the questions which it is required to answer by virtue of section 63;

(b) its reasons for its decisions; and

(c) such information as the Commission considers appropriate for facilitating a proper understanding of those questions and of its reasons for its decisions.

[(2A) Where the report relates to a reference under section 62 which has been made after a report of OFCOM under section 61A, the Commission shall give a copy of its report (whether or not published) to OFCOM.]

(3) Sections 51 and 52 (but not section 53) shall apply for the purposes of a report under this section as they apply for the purposes of a report under section 50.

(4) The Commission shall carry out such investigations as it considers appropriate for the purpose of producing a report under this section.

[3561]

NOTES

Sub-s (2A): inserted by the Communications Act 2003, s 389, Sch 16, para 15, as from 29 December 2003.

66 Decision and enforcement action by Secretary of State

(1) Subsection (2) applies where the Secretary of State has received a report of the Commission under section 65 in relation to a special merger situation.

(2) The Secretary of State shall, in connection with a reference under section 62(2) or (3), decide the questions which the Commission is required to decide by virtue of section 63(1) to (3).

(3) The Secretary of State shall make and publish his decision under subsection (2) within the period of 30 days beginning with the receipt of the report of the Commission under section 65; and subsection (8) of section 54 shall apply for the purposes of this subsection as it applies for the purposes of subsection (5) of that section.

(4) In making his decisions under subsection (2), the Secretary of State shall accept the decisions of the report of the Commission under section 65 as to whether a special merger situation has been created or whether arrangements are in progress or in contemplation which, if carried into effect, will result in the creation of a special merger situation.

(5) Subsection (6) applies where the Secretary of State has decided under subsection (2) that—

(a) a special merger situation has been created or arrangements are in progress or in contemplation which, if carried into effect, will result in the creation of a special merger situation;

(b) at least one consideration which is mentioned in the special intervention notice concerned is relevant to a consideration of the special merger situation concerned; and

(c) taking account only of the relevant consideration or considerations concerned, the creation of that situation operates or may be expected to operate against the public interest;

and has so decided, and published his decision, within the period required by subsection (3).

(6) The Secretary of State may take such action under paragraph 9 or 11 of Schedule 7 as he considers to be reasonable and practicable to remedy, mitigate or prevent any of the effects adverse to the public interest which have resulted from, or may be expected to result from, the creation of the special merger situation concerned.

(7) In making a decision under subsection (6), the Secretary of State shall, in particular, have regard to the report of the Commission under section 65.

[3562]

European mergers

67 Intervention to protect legitimate interests

(1) Subsection (2) applies where—

(a) the Secretary of State has reasonable grounds for suspecting that it is or may be the case that—

(i) a relevant merger situation has been created or that arrangements are in progress or in contemplation which, if carried into effect, will result in the creation of a relevant merger situation; and

(ii) a concentration with a Community dimension (within the meaning of the [EC Merger Regulation]), or a part of such a concentration, has thereby arisen or will thereby arise;

(b) a reference … is prevented from being made under [section 22 or 33] in relation to the relevant merger situation concerned [(whether or not there would otherwise have been a duty to make such a reference)] by virtue of Community law or anything done under or in accordance with it; and

(c) the Secretary of State is considering whether to take appropriate measures to protect legitimate interests as permitted by article [21(4) of the EC Merger Regulation].

(2) The Secretary of State may give a notice to the OFT (in this section "a European intervention notice") if he believes that it is or may be the case that one or more than one public interest consideration is relevant to a consideration of the relevant merger situation concerned.

(3) A European intervention notice shall state—

(a) the relevant merger situation concerned;

(b) the public interest consideration or considerations which are, or may be, relevant to a consideration of the relevant merger situation concerned; and

(c) where any public interest consideration concerned is not finalised, the proposed timetable for finalising it.

(4) Where the Secretary of State believes that it is or may be the case that two or more public interest considerations are relevant to a consideration of the relevant merger situation concerned, he may decide not to mention in the intervention notice such of those considerations as he considers appropriate.

(5) No more than one European intervention notice shall be given under subsection (2) in relation to the same relevant merger situation.

(6) Where the Secretary of State has given a European intervention notice mentioning a public interest consideration which, at that time, is not finalised, he shall, as soon as practicable, take such action as is within his power to ensure that it is finalised.

(7) For the purposes of deciding whether a relevant merger situation has been created or whether arrangements are in progress or in contemplation which, if carried into effect, will result in the creation of a relevant merger situation, sections 23 to 32 (read together with section 34) shall apply for the purposes of this section as they do for the purposes of Chapter 1 but subject to subsection (8).

(8) In their application by virtue of subsection (7) sections 23 to 32 shall have effect as if—

(a) references in those sections to the decision-making authority were references to the Secretary of State;

(b) for paragraphs (a) and (b) of section 23(9) there were substituted ", in relation to the giving of a European intervention notice, the time when the notice is given";

(c) the references to the OFT in section 24(2)(a) and (b) included references to the Secretary of State;

(d) sections 25, 31 and 32 were omitted; and

(e) the references in sections 23 to 29 to the making of a reference or a reference were, so far as necessary, references to the giving of a European intervention notice or a European intervention notice.

(9) Section 42(3) shall, in its application to this section and section 68, have effect as if for the words "intervention notice" there were substituted "European intervention notice".

[3563]

NOTES

Sub-s (1): words in square brackets in paras (a)(ii), (c) substituted by the EC Merger Control (Consequential Amendments) Regulations 2004, SI 2004/1079, reg 2, Schedule, para 2(1), (20), as from 1 May 2004; words omitted from para (b) repealed, words in first pair of square brackets in that paragraph substituted, and words in second pair of square brackets inserted, by the Communications Act 2003, ss 389(1), 406(7), Sch 16, para 16, Sch 19, as from 29 December 2003.

68 Scheme for protecting legitimate interests

(1) The Secretary of State may by order provide for the taking of action, where a European intervention notice has been given, to remedy, mitigate or prevent effects adverse to the public interest which have resulted from, or may be expected to result from, the creation of a European relevant merger situation.

(2) In subsection (1) "European relevant merger situation" means a relevant merger situation—

- (a) which has been created or will be created if arrangements which are in progress or in contemplation are carried into effect;
- (b) by virtue of which a concentration with a Community dimension (within the meaning of the [EC Merger Regulation]), or a part of such a concentration, has arisen or will arise; and
- (c) in relation to which a reference ... was prevented from being made under [section 22 or 33 (whether or not there would otherwise have been a duty to make such a reference)] by virtue of Community law or anything done under or in accordance with it.

(3) Provision made under subsection (1) shall include provision ensuring that considerations which are not public interest considerations mentioned in the European intervention notice concerned may not be taken into account in determining whether anything operates, or may be expected to operate, against the public interest.

(4) Provision made under subsection (1) shall include provision—

- (a) applying with modifications sections 23 to 32 for the purposes of deciding for the purposes of this section whether a relevant merger situation has been created or whether arrangements are in progress or in contemplation which, if carried into effect, will result in the creation of a relevant merger situation;
- (b) requiring the OFT to make a report to the Secretary of State before a reference is made;
- (c) enabling the Secretary of State to make a reference to the Commission;
- (d) requiring the Commission to investigate and report to the Secretary of State on such a reference;
- (e) enabling the taking of interim and final enforcement action.

(5) An order under this section may include provision (including provision for the creation of offences and penalties, the payment of fees and the delegation of functions) corresponding to any provision made in, or in connection with, this Part in relation to intervention notices or special intervention notices and the cases to which they relate.

(6) In this section "European intervention notice" has the same meaning as in section 67.

[3564]–[3565]

NOTES

Sub-s (2): words in square brackets in para (b) substituted by the EC Merger Control (Consequential Amendments) Regulations 2004, SI 2004/1079, reg 2, Schedule, para 2(1), (21), as from 1 May 2004; words omitted from para (c) repealed, and words in square brackets in that paragraph substituted, by the Communications Act 2003, ss 389, 406, Sch 16, para 17, Sch 19, as from 29 December 2003.

Orders: the Enterprise Act 2002 (Protection of Legitimate Interests) Order 2003, SI 2003/1592 at **[7174]**.

69, 70 (*S 69 (the merger regime contained in this Part did not, by virtue of s 69, apply to newspaper mergers and, as such, the provisions relating to such mergers in the Fair Trading Act 1973 continued to have effect. Section 69 of this Act, and ss 57–62 of the 1973 Act, were repealed by the Communications Act 2003, ss 374, 406, Sch 19, as from 29 December 2003 (for transitional provisions see Sch 18, paras 59–62 to the 2003 Act); s 70 amends the Water Industry Act 1991, and is outside the scope of this work.*)

CHAPTER 4
ENFORCEMENT

Powers exercisable before references under section 22 or 33

71 Initial undertakings: completed mergers

(1) Subsection (2) applies where the OFT is considering whether to make a reference under section 22.

(2) The OFT may, for the purpose of preventing pre-emptive action, accept from such of the parties concerned as it considers appropriate undertakings to take such action as it considers appropriate.

(3) No undertaking shall be accepted under subsection (2) unless the OFT has reasonable grounds for suspecting that it is or may be the case that a relevant merger situation has been created.

(4) An undertaking under this section—
- (a) shall come into force when accepted;
- (b) may be varied or superseded by another undertaking; and
- (c) may be released by the OFT.

(5) An undertaking which—
- (a) is in force under this section in relation to a possible reference or reference under section 22; and
- (b) has not been adopted under section 80 or paragraph 1 of Schedule 7;

shall cease to be in force if an order under section 72 or 81 comes into force in relation to that reference or an order under paragraph 2 of that Schedule comes into force in relation to the matter.

(6) An undertaking under this section shall, if it has not previously ceased to be in force and if it has not been adopted under section 80 or paragraph 1 of Schedule 7, cease to be in force—
- (a) where the OFT has decided to make the reference concerned under section 22, at the end of the period of 7 days beginning with the making of the reference;
- (b) where the OFT has decided to accept an undertaking under section 73 instead of making that reference, on the acceptance of that undertaking;
- (c) where an intervention notice is in force, at the end of the period of 7 days beginning with the giving of that notice; and
- (d) where the OFT has otherwise decided not to make the reference concerned under section 22, on the making of that decision.

(7) The OFT shall, as soon as reasonably practicable, consider any representations received by it in relation to varying or releasing an undertaking under this section.

(8) In this section and section 72 "pre-emptive action" means action which might prejudice the reference concerned or impede the taking of any action under this Part which may be justified by the Commission's decisions on the reference.

[3566]

72 Initial enforcement orders: completed mergers

(1) Subsection (2) applies where the OFT is considering whether to make a reference under section 22.

(2) The OFT may by order, for the purpose of preventing pre-emptive action—
- (a) prohibit or restrict the doing of things which the OFT considers would constitute pre-emptive action;
- (b) impose on any person concerned obligations as to the carrying on of any activities or the safeguarding of any assets;
- (c) provide for the carrying on of any activities or the safeguarding of any assets either by the appointment of a person to conduct or supervise the conduct of any activities (on such terms and with such powers as may be specified or described in the order) or in any other manner;
- (d) do anything which may be done by virtue of paragraph 19 of Schedule 8.

(3) No order shall be made under subsection (2) unless the OFT has reasonable grounds for suspecting that it is or may be the case that—

(a) a relevant merger situation has been created; and
(b) pre-emptive action is in progress or in contemplation.

(4) An order under this section—
(a) shall come into force at such time as is determined by or under the order; and
(b) may be varied or revoked by another order.

(5) An order which—
(a) is in force under this section in relation to a possible reference or a reference under section 22; and
(b) has not been adopted under section 81 or paragraph 2 of Schedule 7;

shall cease to be in force if an undertaking under section 71 or 80 comes into force in relation to that reference or an undertaking under paragraph 1 of that Schedule comes into force in relation to the matter.

(6) An order under this section shall, if it has not previously ceased to be in force and if it is not adopted under section 81 or paragraph 2 of Schedule 7, cease to be in force—
(a) where the OFT has decided to make the reference concerned under section 22, at the end of the period of 7 days beginning with the making of the reference;
(b) where the OFT has decided to accept an undertaking under section 73 instead of making that reference, on the acceptance of that undertaking;
(c) where an intervention notice is in force, at the end of the period of 7 days beginning with the giving of that notice; and
(d) where the OFT has otherwise decided not to make the reference concerned under section 22, on the making of that decision.

(7) The OFT shall, as soon as reasonably practicable, consider any representations received by it in relation to varying or revoking an order under this section.

[3567]

73 Undertakings in lieu of references under section 22 or 33

(1) Subsection (2) applies if the OFT considers that it is under a duty to make a reference under section 22 or 33 (disregarding the operation of section 22(3)(b) or (as the case may be) 33(3)(b) but taking account of the power of the OFT under section 22(2) or (as the case may be) 33(2) to decide not to make such a reference).

(2) The OFT may, instead of making such a reference and for the purpose of remedying, mitigating or preventing the substantial lessening of competition concerned or any adverse effect which has or may have resulted from it or may be expected to result from it, accept from such of the parties concerned as it considers appropriate undertakings to take such action as it considers appropriate.

(3) In proceeding under subsection (2), the OFT shall, in particular, have regard to the need to achieve as comprehensive a solution as is reasonable and practicable to the substantial lessening of competition and any adverse effects resulting from it.

(4) In proceeding under subsection (2), the OFT may, in particular, have regard to the effect of any action on any relevant customer benefits in relation to the creation of the relevant merger situation concerned.

(5) An undertaking under this section—
(a) shall come into force when accepted;
(b) may be varied or superseded by another undertaking; and
(c) may be released by the OFT.

(6) An undertaking under this section which is in force in relation to a relevant merger situation shall cease to be in force if an order comes into force under section 75 or 76 in relation to that undertaking.

(7) The OFT shall, as soon as reasonably practicable, consider any representations received by it in relation to varying or releasing an undertaking under this section.

[3568]

74 Effect of undertakings under section 73

(1) The relevant authority shall not make a reference under section 22, 33 or 45 in relation to the creation of a relevant merger situation if—
(a) the OFT has accepted an undertaking or group of undertakings under section 73; and

(b) the relevant merger situation is the situation by reference to which the undertaking or group of undertakings was accepted.

(2) Subsection (1) does not prevent the making of a reference if material facts about relevant arrangements or transactions, or relevant proposed arrangements or transactions, were not notified (whether in writing or otherwise) to the OFT or made public before any undertaking concerned was accepted.

(3) For the purposes of subsection (2) arrangements or transactions, or proposed arrangements or transactions, are relevant if they are the ones in consequence of which the enterprises concerned ceased or may have ceased, or may cease, to be distinct enterprises.

(4) In subsection (2) "made public" means so publicised as to be generally known or readily ascertainable.

(5) In this section "relevant authority" means—

(a) in relation to a possible reference under section 22 or 33, the OFT; and

(b) in relation to a possible reference under section 45, the Secretary of State.

[3569]

75 Order-making power where undertakings under section 73 not fulfilled etc

(1) Subsection (2) applies where the OFT considers that—

(a) an undertaking accepted by it under section 73 has not been, is not being or will not be fulfilled; or

(b) in relation to an undertaking accepted by it under that section, information which was false or misleading in a material respect was given to the OFT by the person giving the undertaking before the OFT decided to accept the undertaking.

(2) The OFT may, for any of the purposes mentioned in section 73(2), make an order under this section.

(3) Subsections (3) and (4) of section 73 shall apply for the purposes of subsection (2) above as they apply for the purposes of subsection (2) of that section.

(4) An order under this section may contain—

(a) anything permitted by Schedule 8; and

(b) such supplementary, consequential or incidental provision as the OFT considers appropriate.

(5) An order under this section—

(a) shall come into force at such time as is determined by or under the order;

(b) may contain provision which is different from the provision contained in the undertaking concerned; and

(c) may be varied or revoked by another order.

(6) The OFT shall, as soon as reasonably practicable, consider any representations received by it in relation to varying or revoking an order under this section.

[3570]

76 Supplementary interim order-making power

(1) Subsection (2) applies where—

(a) the OFT has the power to make an order under section 75 in relation to a particular undertaking and intends to make such an order; or

(b) the Commission has the power to make an order under section 83 in relation to a particular undertaking and intends to make such an order.

(2) The OFT or (as the case may be) the Commission may, for the purpose of preventing any action which might prejudice the making of that order, make an order under this section.

(3) No order shall be made under subsection (2) unless the OFT or (as the case may be) the Commission has reasonable grounds for suspecting that it is or may be the case that action which might prejudice the making of the order under section 75 or (as the case may be) 83 is in progress or in contemplation.

(4) An order under subsection (2) may—

(a) prohibit or restrict the doing of things which the OFT or (as the case may be) the Commission considers would prejudice the making of the order under section 75 or (as the case may be) 83;

(b) impose on any person concerned obligations as to the carrying on of any activities or the safeguarding of any assets;

(c) provide for the carrying on of any activities or the safeguarding of any assets either by the appointment of a person to conduct or supervise the conduct of any activities (on such terms and with such powers as may be specified or described in the order) or in any other manner;

(d) do anything which may be done by virtue of paragraph 19 of Schedule 8.

(5) An order under this section—

(a) shall come into force at such time as is determined by or under the order; and

(b) may be varied or revoked by another order.

(6) An order under this section shall, if it has not previously ceased to be in force, cease to be in force on—

(a) the coming into force of an order under section 75 or (as the case may be) 83 in relation to the undertaking concerned; or

(b) the making of the decision not to proceed with such an order.

(7) The OFT or (as the case may be) the Commission shall, as soon as reasonably practicable, consider any representations received by it in relation to varying or revoking an order under this section.

[3571]

Interim restrictions and powers

77 Restrictions on certain dealings: completed mergers

(1) Subsections (2) and (3) apply where—

(a) a reference has been made under section 22 but not finally determined; and

(b) no undertakings under section 71 or 80 are in force in relation to the relevant merger situation concerned and no orders under section 72 or 81 are in force in relation to that situation.

(2) No relevant person shall, without the consent of the Commission—

(a) complete any outstanding matters in connection with any arrangements which have resulted in the enterprises concerned ceasing to be distinct enterprises;

(b) make any further arrangements in consequence of that result (other than arrangements which reverse that result); or

(c) transfer the ownership or control of any enterprises to which the reference relates.

(3) No relevant person shall, without the consent of the Commission, assist in any of the activities mentioned in paragraphs (a) to (c) of subsection (2).

(4) The prohibitions in subsections (2) and (3) do not apply in relation to anything which the person concerned is required to do by virtue of any enactment.

(5) The consent of the Commission under subsection (2) or (3)—

(a) may be general or special;

(b) may be revoked by the Commission; and

(c) shall be published in such manner as the Commission considers appropriate for the purpose of bringing it to the attention of any person entitled to the benefit of it.

(6) Paragraph (c) of subsection (5) shall not apply if the Commission considers that publication is not necessary for the purpose mentioned in that paragraph.

(7) Subsections (2) and (3) shall apply to a person's conduct outside the United Kingdom if (and only if) he is—

(a) a United Kingdom national;

(b) a body incorporated under the law of the United Kingdom or of any part of the United Kingdom; or

(c) a person carrying on business in the United Kingdom.

(8) In this section "relevant person" means—

(a) any person who carries on any enterprise to which the reference relates or who has control of any such enterprise;

(b) any subsidiary of any person falling within paragraph (a); or

(c) any person associated with any person falling within paragraph (a) or any subsidiary of any person so associated.

[3572]

78 Restrictions on certain share dealings: anticipated mergers

(1) Subsection (2) applies where—

(a) a reference has been made under section 33; and

(b) no undertakings under section 80 are in force in relation to the relevant merger situation concerned and no orders under section 81 are in force in relation to that situation.

(2) No relevant person shall, without the consent of the Commission, directly or indirectly acquire during the relevant period an interest in shares in a company if any enterprise to which the reference relates is carried on by or under the control of that company.

(3) The consent of the Commission under subsection (2)—

(a) may be general or special;

(b) may be revoked by the Commission; and

(c) shall be published in such manner as the Commission considers appropriate for bringing it to the attention of any person entitled to the benefit of it.

(4) Paragraph (c) of subsection (3) shall not apply if the Commission considers that publication is not necessary for the purpose mentioned in that paragraph.

(5) Subsection (2) shall apply to a person's conduct outside the United Kingdom if (and only if) he is—

(a) a United Kingdom national;

(b) a body incorporated under the law of the United Kingdom or of any part of the United Kingdom; or

(c) a person carrying on business in the United Kingdom.

(6) In this section and section 79—

"company" includes any body corporate;

"relevant period" means the period beginning with the making of the reference concerned and ending when the reference is finally determined;

"relevant person" means—

(a) any person who carries on any enterprise to which the reference relates or who has control of any such enterprise;

(b) any subsidiary of any person falling within paragraph (a); or

(c) any person associated with any person falling within paragraph (a) or any subsidiary of any person so associated; and

"share" means share in the capital of a company, and includes stock.

[3573]

79 Sections 77 and 78: further interpretation provisions

(1) For the purposes of this Part a reference under section 22 or 33 is finally determined if—

(a) the reference is cancelled under section 37(1);

(b) the time within which the Commission is to prepare and publish a report under section 38 in relation to the reference has expired and no such report has been prepared and published;

(c) the report of the Commission under section 38 contains the decision that there is not an anti-competitive outcome;

(d) the report of the Commission under section 38 contains the decision that there is an anti-competitive outcome and the Commission has decided under section 41(2) neither to accept an undertaking under section 82 nor to make an order under section 84; or

(e) the report of the Commission under section 38 contains the decision that there is an anti-competitive outcome and the Commission has decided under section 41(2) to accept an undertaking under section 82 or to make an order under section 84.

(2) For the purposes of this Part the time when a reference under section 22 or 33 is finally determined is—

(a) in a case falling within subsection (1)(a), the making of the decision concerned;

(b) in a case falling within subsection (1)(b), the expiry of the time concerned;

(c) in a case falling within subsection (1)(c), the publication of the report;

(d) in a case falling within subsection (1)(d), the making of the decision under section 41(2); and

(e) in a case falling within subsection (1)(e), the acceptance of the undertaking concerned or (as the case may be) the making of the order concerned.

(3) For the purposes of section 78 and subject to subsection (4) below, the circumstances in which a person acquires an interest in shares include those where—

(a) he enters into a contract to acquire the shares (whether or not for cash);

(b) he is not the registered holder but acquires the right to exercise, or to control the exercise of, any right conferred by the holding of the shares; or

(c) he—

(i) acquires a right to call for delivery of the shares to himself or to his order or to acquire an interest in the shares; or

(ii) assumes an obligation to acquire such an interest.

(4) The circumstances in which a person acquires an interest in shares for the purposes of section 78 do not include those where he acquires an interest in pursuance of an obligation assumed before the publication by the OFT of the reference concerned.

(5) The circumstances in which a person acquires a right mentioned in subsection (3)—

(a) include those where he acquires a right, or assumes an obligation, whose exercise or fulfilment would give him that right; but

(b) do not include those where he is appointed as proxy to vote at a specified meeting of a company or of any class of its members or at any adjournment of the meeting or he is appointed by a corporation to act as its representative at any meeting of the company or of any class of its members.

(6) References to rights and obligations in subsections (3) to (5) include conditional rights and conditional obligations.

(7) References in sections 77 and 78 to a person carrying on or having control of any enterprise includes a group of persons carrying on or having control of an enterprise and any member of such a group.

(8) Sections 26(2) to (4) and 127(1), (2) and (4) to (6) shall apply for the purposes of sections 77 and 78 to determine whether any person or group of persons has control of any enterprise and whether persons are associated as they apply for the purposes of section 26 to determine whether enterprises are brought under common control.

(9) Sections 736 and 736A of the Companies Act 1985 (c 6) shall apply for the purposes of sections 77 and 78 to determine whether a company is a subsidiary of an individual or of a group of persons as they apply to determine whether it is a subsidiary of a company; and references to a subsidiary in subsections (8) and (9) of section 736A as so applied shall be construed accordingly.

[3574]

80 Interim undertakings

(1) Subsections (2) and (3) apply where a reference under section 22 or 33 has been made but is not finally determined.

(2) The Commission may, for the purpose of preventing pre-emptive action, accept from such of the parties concerned as it considers appropriate undertakings to take such action as it considers appropriate.

(3) The Commission may, for the purpose of preventing pre-emptive action, adopt an undertaking accepted by the OFT under section 71 if the undertaking is still in force when the Commission adopts it.

(4) An undertaking adopted under subsection (3)—

(a) shall continue in force, in accordance with its terms, when adopted;

(b) may be varied or superseded by an undertaking under this section; and

(c) may be released by the Commission.

(5) Any other undertaking under this section—

(a) shall come into force when accepted;

(b) may be varied or superseded by another undertaking; and

(c) may be released by the Commission.

(6) References in this Part to undertakings under this section shall, unless the context otherwise requires, include references to undertakings adopted under this section; and references to the acceptance or giving of undertakings under this section shall be construed accordingly.

(7) An undertaking which is in force under this section in relation to a reference under section 22 or 33 shall cease to be in force if an order under section 81 comes into force in relation to that reference.

(8) An undertaking under this section shall, if it has not previously ceased to be in force, cease to be in force when the reference under section 22 or 33 is finally determined.

(9) The Commission shall, as soon as reasonably practicable, consider any representations received by it in relation to varying or releasing an undertaking under this section.

(10) In this section and section 81 "pre-emptive action" means action which might prejudice the reference concerned or impede the taking of any action under this Part which may be justified by the Commission's decisions on the reference.

[3575]

81 Interim orders

(1) Subsections (2) and (3) apply where a reference has been made under section 22 or 33 but is not finally determined.

(2) The Commission may by order, for the purpose of preventing pre-emptive action—
- (a) prohibit or restrict the doing of things which the Commission considers would constitute pre-emptive action;
- (b) impose on any person concerned obligations as to the carrying on of any activities or the safeguarding of any assets;
- (c) provide for the carrying on of any activities or the safeguarding of any assets either by the appointment of a person to conduct or supervise the conduct of any activities (on such terms and with such powers as may be specified or described in the order) or in any other manner;
- (d) do anything which may be done by virtue of paragraph 19 of Schedule 8.

(3) The Commission may, for the purpose of preventing pre-emptive action, adopt an order made by the OFT under section 72 if the order is still in force when the Commission adopts it.

(4) An order adopted under subsection (3)—
- (a) shall continue in force, in accordance with its terms, when adopted; and
- (b) may be varied or revoked by an order under this section.

(5) Any other order under this section—
- (a) shall come into force at such time as is determined by or under the order; and
- (b) may be varied or revoked by another order.

(6) References in this Part to orders under this section shall, unless the context otherwise requires, include references to orders adopted under this section; and references to the making of orders under this section shall be construed accordingly.

(7) An order which is in force under this section in relation to a reference under section 22 or 33 shall cease to be in force if an undertaking under section 80 comes into force in relation to that reference.

(8) An order under this section shall, if it has not previously ceased to be in force, cease to be in force when the reference under section 22 or 33 is finally determined.

(9) The Commission shall, as soon as reasonably practicable, consider any representations received by it in relation to varying or revoking an order under this section.

[3576]

Final powers

82 Final undertakings

(1) The Commission may, in accordance with section 41, accept, from such persons as it considers appropriate, undertakings to take action specified or described in the undertakings.

(2) An undertaking under this section—
- (a) shall come into force when accepted;
- (b) may be varied or superseded by another undertaking; and
- (c) may be released by the Commission.

(3) An undertaking which is in force under this section in relation to a reference under section 22 or 33 shall cease to be in force if an order under section 76(1)(b) or 83 comes into force in relation to the subject-matter of the undertaking.

(4) No undertaking shall be accepted under this section in relation to a reference under section 22 or 33 if an order has been made under—

(a) section 76(1)(b) or 83 in relation to the subject-matter of the undertaking; or

(b) section 84 in relation to that reference.

(5) The Commission shall, as soon as reasonably practicable, consider any representations received by it in relation to varying or releasing an undertaking under this section.

[3577]

83 Order-making power where final undertakings not fulfilled

(1) Subsection (2) applies where the Commission considers that—

(a) an undertaking accepted by it under section 82 has not been, is not being or will not be fulfilled; or

(b) in relation to an undertaking accepted by it under that section, information which was false or misleading in a material respect was given to the Commission or the OFT by the person giving the undertaking before the Commission decided to accept the undertaking.

(2) The Commission may, for any of the purposes mentioned in section 41(2), make an order under this section.

(3) Subsections (3) to (5) of section 41 shall apply for the purposes of subsection (2) above as they apply for the purposes of subsection (2) of that section.

(4) An order under this section may contain—

(a) anything permitted by Schedule 8; and

(b) such supplementary, consequential or incidental provision as the Commission considers appropriate.

(5) An order under this section—

(a) shall come into force at such time as is determined by or under the order;

(b) may contain provision which is different from the provision contained in the undertaking concerned; and

(c) may be varied or revoked by another order.

(6) No order shall be varied or revoked under this section unless the OFT advises that such a variation or revocation is appropriate by reason of a change of circumstances.

[3578]

84 Final orders

(1) The Commission may, in accordance with section 41, make an order under this section.

(2) An order under this section may contain—

(a) anything permitted by Schedule 8; and

(b) such supplementary, consequential or incidental provision as the Commission considers appropriate.

(3) An order under this section—

(a) shall come into force at such time as is determined by or under the order; and

(b) may be varied or revoked by another order.

(4) No order shall be varied or revoked under this section unless the OFT advises that such a variation or revocation is appropriate by reason of a change of circumstances.

(5) No order shall be made under this section in relation to a reference under section 22 or 33 if an undertaking has been accepted under section 82 in relation to that reference.

[3579]

Public interest and special public interest cases

85 Enforcement regime for public interest and special public interest cases

(1) Schedule 7 (which provides for the enforcement regime in public interest and special public interest cases) shall have effect.

(2) The OFT may advise the Secretary of State in relation to the taking by him of enforcement action under Schedule 7.

[3580]

Undertakings and orders: general provisions

86 Enforcement orders: general provisions

(1) An enforcement order may extend to a person's conduct outside the United Kingdom if (and only if) he is—

(a) a United Kingdom national;
(b) a body incorporated under the law of the United Kingdom or of any part of the United Kingdom; or
(c) a person carrying on business in the United Kingdom.

(2) Nothing in an enforcement order shall have effect so as to—

(a) cancel or modify conditions in licences granted—
   (i) under a patent granted under the Patents Act 1977 (c 37) or a European patent (UK) (within the meaning of the Act of 1977); or
   (ii) in respect of a design registered under the Registered Designs Act 1949 (c 88);

by the proprietor of the patent or design; or

(b) require an entry to be made in the register of patents or the register of designs to the effect that licences under such a patent or such a design are to be available as of right.

(3) An enforcement order may prohibit the performance of an agreement already in existence when the order is made.

(4) Schedule 8 (which provides for the contents of certain enforcement orders) shall have effect.

(5) Part 1 of Schedule 9 (which enables certain enforcement orders to modify licence conditions etc in regulated markets) shall have effect.

(6) In this Part "enforcement order" means an order made under section 72, 75, 76, 81, 83 or 84 or under paragraph 2, 5, 6, 10 or 11 of Schedule 7.

[3581]

87 Delegated power of directions

(1) An enforcement order may authorise the person making the order to give directions falling within subsection (2) to—

(a) a person specified in the directions; or
(b) the holder for the time being of an office so specified in any body of persons corporate or unincorporate.

(2) Directions fall within this subsection if they are directions—

(a) to take such action as may be specified or described in the directions for the purpose of carrying out, or ensuring compliance with, the enforcement order concerned; or
(b) to do, or refrain from doing, anything so specified or described which the person might be required by that order to do or refrain from doing.

(3) An enforcement order may authorise the person making the order to vary or revoke any directions so given.

(4) The court may by order require any person who has failed to comply with directions given by virtue of this section to comply with them, or otherwise remedy his failure, within such time as may be specified in the order.

(5) Where the directions related to anything done in the management or administration of a body of persons corporate or unincorporate, the court may by order require the body of

PART III
OTHER LEGISLATION

persons concerned or any officer of it to comply with the directions, or otherwise remedy the failure to comply with them, within such time as may be specified in the order.

(6) An order under subsection (4) or (5) shall be made on the application of the person authorised by virtue of this section to give the directions concerned.

(7) An order under subsection (4) or (5) may provide for all the costs or expenses of, or incidental to, the application for the order to be met by any person in default or by any officers of a body of persons corporate or unincorporate who are responsible for its default.

(8) In this section "the court" means—

(a) in relation to England and Wales or Northern Ireland, the High Court; and

(b) in relation to Scotland, the Court of Session.

[3582]

88 Contents of certain enforcement orders

(1) This section applies in relation to any order under section 75, 83 or 84 or under paragraph 5, 10 or 11 of Schedule 7.

(2) The order or any explanatory material accompanying the order shall state—

(a) the actions that the persons or description of persons to whom the order is addressed must do or (as the case may be) refrain from doing;

(b) the date on which the order comes into force;

(c) the possible consequences of not complying with the order; and

(d) the section of this Part under which a review can be sought in relation to the order.

[3583]

89 Subject-matter of undertakings

(1) The provision which may be contained in an enforcement undertaking is not limited to the provision which is permitted by Schedule 8.

(2) In this Part "enforcement undertaking" means an undertaking under section 71, 73, 80 or 82 or under paragraph 1, 3 or 9 of Schedule 7.

[3584]

90 Procedural requirements for certain undertakings and orders

Schedule 10 (which provides for the procedure for accepting certain enforcement undertakings and making certain enforcement orders and for their termination) shall have effect.

[3585]

91 Register of undertakings and orders

(1) The OFT shall compile and maintain a register for the purposes of this Part.

(2) The register shall be kept in such form as the OFT considers appropriate.

(3) The OFT shall ensure that the following matters are entered in the register—

(a) the provisions of any enforcement undertaking accepted under this Part;

(b) the provisions of any enforcement order made under this Part;

(c) the details of any variation, release or revocation of such an undertaking or order; and

(d) the details of any consent given by the Commission under section 77(2) or (3) or 78(2) or by the Secretary of State under paragraph 7(2) or (3) or 8(2) of Schedule 7.

(4) The duty in subsection (3) does not extend to anything of which the OFT is unaware.

(5) The Commission and the Secretary of State shall inform the OFT of any matters which are to be included in the register by virtue of subsection (3) and which relate to enforcement undertakings accepted by them, enforcement orders made by them or consents given by them.

(6) The OFT shall ensure that the contents of the register are available to the public—

(a) during (as a minimum) such hours as may be specified in an order made by the Secretary of State; and

(b) subject to such reasonable fees (if any) as the OFT may determine.

(7) If requested by any person to do so and subject to such reasonable fees (if any) as the OFT may determine, the OFT shall supply the person concerned with a copy (certified to be true) of the register or of an extract from it.

[3586]

NOTES

Orders: the OFT Registers of Undertakings and Orders (Available Hours) Order 2003, SI 2003/1373 (which provides that the OFT shall ensure that the contents of the register are available to the public (as a minimum) between the hours of 10.00 am and 4.00 pm on any working day).

Enforcement functions of OFT

92 Duty of OFT to monitor undertakings and orders

(1) The OFT shall keep under review—

(a) the carrying out of any enforcement undertaking or any enforcement order; and

(b) compliance with the prohibitions in sections 77(2) and (3) and 78(2) and in paragraphs 7(2) and (3) and 8(2) of Schedule 7.

(2) The OFT shall, in particular, from time to time consider—

(a) whether an enforcement undertaking or enforcement order has been or is being complied with;

(b) whether, by reason of any change of circumstances, an enforcement undertaking is no longer appropriate and—

(i) one or more of the parties to it can be released from it; or

(ii) it needs to be varied or to be superseded by a new enforcement undertaking; and

(c) whether, by reason of any change of circumstances, an enforcement order is no longer appropriate and needs to be varied or revoked.

(3) The OFT shall give the Commission or (as the case may be) the Secretary of State such advice as it considers appropriate in relation to—

(a) any possible variation or release by the Commission or (as the case may be) the Secretary of State of an enforcement undertaking accepted by it or (as the case may be) him;

(b) any possible new enforcement undertaking to be accepted by the Commission or (as the case may be) the Secretary of State so as to supersede another enforcement undertaking given to the Commission or (as the case may be) the Secretary of State;

(c) any possible variation or revocation by the Commission or (as the case may be) the Secretary of State of an enforcement order made by the Commission or (as the case may be) the Secretary of State;

(d) any possible enforcement undertaking to be accepted by the Commission or (as the case may be) the Secretary of State instead of an enforcement order or any possible enforcement order to be made by the Commission or (as the case may be) the Secretary of State instead of an enforcement undertaking;

(e) the enforcement by virtue of section 94(6) to (8) of any enforcement undertaking or enforcement order; or

(f) the enforcement by virtue of section 95(4) and (5) of the prohibitions in sections 77(2) and (3) and 78(2) and in paragraphs 7(2) and (3) and 8(2) of Schedule 7.

(4) The OFT shall take such action as it considers appropriate in relation to—

(a) any possible variation or release by it of an enforcement undertaking accepted by it;

(b) any possible new enforcement undertaking to be accepted by it so as to supersede another enforcement undertaking given to it;

(c) any possible variation or revocation by it of an enforcement order made by it;

(d) any possible enforcement undertaking to be accepted by it instead of an enforcement order or any possible enforcement order to be made by it instead of an enforcement undertaking;

(e) the enforcement by it by virtue of section 94(6) of any enforcement undertaking or enforcement order; or

(f) the enforcement by it by virtue of section 95(4) and (5) of the prohibitions in sections 77(2) and (3) and 78(2) and in paragraphs 7(2) and (3) and 8(2) of Schedule 7.

(5) The OFT shall keep under review the effectiveness of enforcement undertakings accepted under this Part and enforcement orders made under this Part.

(6) The OFT shall, whenever requested to do so by the Secretary of State and otherwise from time to time, prepare a report of its findings under subsection (5).

(7) The OFT shall—

(a) give any report prepared by it under subsection (6) to the Commission;

(b) give a copy of the report to the Secretary of State; and

(c) publish the report.

[3587]

93 Further role of OFT in relation to undertakings and orders

(1) Subsections (2) and (3) apply where—

(a) the Commission is considering whether to accept undertakings under section 80 or 82; or

(b) the Secretary of State is considering whether to accept undertakings under paragraph 1, 3 or 9 of Schedule 7.

(2) The Commission or (as the case may be) the Secretary of State (in this section "the relevant authority") may require the OFT to consult with such persons as the relevant authority considers appropriate with a view to discovering whether they will offer undertakings which the relevant authority would be prepared to accept under section 80 or 82 or (as the case may be) paragraph 1, 3 or 9 of Schedule 7.

(3) The relevant authority may require the OFT to report to the relevant authority on the outcome of the OFT's consultations within such period as the relevant authority may require.

(4) A report under subsection (3) shall, in particular, contain advice from the OFT as to whether any undertakings offered should be accepted by the relevant authority under section 80 or 82 or (as the case may be) paragraph 1, 3 or 9 of Schedule 7.

(5) The powers conferred on the relevant authority by subsections (1) to (4) are without prejudice to the power of the relevant authority to consult the persons concerned itself.

(6) If asked by the relevant authority for advice in relation to the taking of enforcement action (whether or not by way of undertaking) in a particular case, the OFT shall give such advice as it considers appropriate.

[3588]

Other

94 Rights to enforce undertakings and orders

(1) This section applies to any enforcement undertaking or enforcement order.

(2) Any person to whom such an undertaking or order relates shall have a duty to comply with it.

(3) The duty shall be owed to any person who may be affected by a contravention of the undertaking or (as the case may be) order.

(4) Any breach of the duty which causes such a person to sustain loss or damage shall be actionable by him.

(5) In any proceedings brought under subsection (4) against a person to whom an enforcement undertaking or an enforcement order relates it shall be a defence for that person to show that he took all reasonable steps and exercised all due diligence to avoid contravening the undertaking or (as the case may be) order.

(6) Compliance with an enforcement undertaking or an enforcement order shall also be enforceable by civil proceedings brought by the OFT for an injunction or for interdict or for any other appropriate relief or remedy.

(7) Compliance with an undertaking under section 80 or 82, an order made by the Commission under section 76 or an order under section 81, 83 or 84, shall also be enforceable by civil proceedings brought by the Commission for an injunction or for interdict or for any other appropriate relief or remedy.

(8) Compliance with an undertaking under paragraph 1, 3 or 9 of Schedule 7, an order made by the Secretary of State under paragraph 2 of that Schedule or an order under paragraph 5, 6, 10 or 11 of that Schedule, shall also be enforceable by civil proceedings brought by the Secretary of State for an injunction or for interdict or for any other appropriate relief or remedy.

(9) Subsections (6) to (8) shall not prejudice any right that a person may have by virtue of subsection (4) to bring civil proceedings for contravention or apprehended contravention of an enforcement undertaking or an enforcement order.

[3589]

95 Rights to enforce statutory restrictions

(1) The obligation to comply with section 77(2) or (3) or 78(2) or paragraph 7(2) or (3) or 8(2) of Schedule 7 shall be a duty owed to any person who may be affected by a contravention of the enactment concerned.

(2) Any breach of the duty which causes such a person to sustain loss or damage shall be actionable by him.

(3) In any proceedings brought under subsection (2) against a person who has an obligation to comply with section 77(2) or (3) or 78(2) or paragraph 7(2) or (3) or 8(2) of Schedule 7 it shall be a defence for that person to show that he took all reasonable steps and exercised all due diligence to avoid contravening the enactment concerned.

(4) Compliance with section 77(2) or (3) or 78(2) shall also be enforceable by civil proceedings brought by the OFT or the Commission for an injunction or for interdict or for any other appropriate relief or remedy.

(5) Compliance with paragraph 7(2) or (3) or 8(2) of Schedule 7 shall also be enforceable by civil proceedings brought by the OFT or the Secretary of State for an injunction or for interdict or for any other appropriate relief or remedy.

(6) Subsections (4) and (5) shall not prejudice any right that a person may have by virtue of subsection (2) to bring civil proceedings for contravention or apprehended contravention of section 77(2) or (3) or 78(2) or paragraph 7(2) or (3) or 8(2) of Schedule 7.

[3590]

CHAPTER 5
SUPPLEMENTARY

Merger notices

96 Merger notices

(1) A person authorised to do so by regulations under section 101 may give notice to the OFT of proposed arrangements which might result in the creation of a relevant merger situation.

(2) Any such notice (in this Part a "merger notice")—

(a) shall be in the prescribed form; and
(b) shall state that the existence of the proposal has been made public.

(3) No reference shall be made under section 22, 33 or 45 in relation to—

(a) arrangements of which notice is given under subsection (1) above or arrangements which do not differ from them in any material respect; or
(b) the creation of any relevant merger situation which is, or may be, created in consequence of carrying such arrangements into effect;

if the period for considering the merger notice has expired without a reference being made under that section in relation to those arrangements.

(4) Subsection (3) is subject to section 100.

(5) In this section and sections 99(5)(c) and 100(1)(c) "prescribed" means prescribed by the OFT by notice having effect for the time being and published in the London, Edinburgh and Belfast Gazettes.

(6) In this Part "notified arrangements" means arrangements of which notice is given under subsection (1) above or arrangements not differing from them in any material respect.

[3591]

97 Period for considering merger notices

(1) The period for considering a merger notice is, subject as follows, the period of 20 days beginning with the first day after—

(a) the notice has been received by the OFT; and

(b) any fee payable by virtue of section 121 to the OFT in respect of the notice has been paid.

(2) Where no intervention notice is in force in relation to the matter concerned, the OFT may by notice to the person who gave the merger notice extend by a further 10 days the period for considering the merger notice.

(3) Where an intervention notice is in force in relation to the matter concerned and there has been no extension under subsection (2), the OFT may by notice to the person who gave the merger notice extend by a further 20 days the period for considering the merger notice.

(4) Where an intervention notice is in force in relation to the matter concerned and there has been an extension under subsection (2), the OFT may by notice to the person who gave the merger notice extend the period for considering the merger notice by a further number of days which, including any extension already made under subsection (2), does not exceed 20 days.

(5) The OFT may by notice to the person who gave the merger notice extend the period for considering a merger notice if the OFT considers that the person has failed to provide, within the period stated in a notice under section 99(2) and in the authorised or required manner, information requested of him in that notice.

(6) An extension under subsection (5) shall be for the period until the person concerned provides the information to the satisfaction of the OFT or, if earlier, the cancellation by the OFT of the extension.

(7) The OFT may by notice to the person who gave the merger notice extend the period for considering a merger notice if the OFT is seeking undertakings under section 73 or (as the case may be) the Secretary of State is seeking undertakings under paragraph 3 of Schedule 7.

(8) An extension under subsection (7) shall be for the period beginning with the receipt of the notice under that subsection and ending with the earliest of the following events—

(a) the giving of the undertakings concerned;

(b) the expiry of the period of 10 days beginning with the first day after the receipt by the OFT of a notice from the person from whom the undertakings are being sought stating that he does not intend to give the undertakings; or

(c) the cancellation by the OFT of the extension.

(9) The Secretary of State may by notice to the person who gave the merger notice extend the period for considering a merger notice if, by virtue of paragraph 3(6) of Schedule 7, he decides to delay a decision as to whether to make a reference under section 45.

(10) An extension under subsection (9) shall be for the period of the delay.

(11) The OFT may by notice to the person who gave the merger notice extend the period for considering a merger notice if the European Commission is considering a request made, in relation to the matter concerned, by the United Kingdom (whether alone or with others) under article [22(1) of the EC Merger Regulation] (but is not yet proceeding with the matter in pursuance of such a request).

(12) An extension under subsection (11) shall be for the period beginning with the receipt of the notice under that subsection and ending with the receipt of a notice under subsection (13).

(13) The OFT shall, in connection with any notice given by it under subsection (11), by notice inform the person who gave the merger notice of the completion by the European Commission of its consideration of the request of the United Kingdom.

[3592]

NOTES

Sub-s (11): words in square brackets substituted by the EC Merger Control (Consequential Amendments) Regulations 2004, SI 2004/1079, reg 2, Schedule, para 2(1), (22), as from 1 May 2004.

98 Section 97: supplementary

(1) A notice under section 97(2), (3), (4), (5), (7), (9) or (11) shall be given, before the end of the period for considering the merger notice, to the person who gave the merger notice.

(2) A notice under section 97(5)—

(a) shall also be given within 5 days of the end of the period within which the information is to be provided and which is stated in the notice under section 99(2); and

(b) shall also inform the person who gave the merger notice of—

(i) the OFT's opinion as mentioned in section 97(5); and

(ii) the OFT's intention to extend the period for considering a merger notice.

(3) In determining for the purposes of section 97(1), (2), (3), (4) or (8)(b) or subsection (2)(a) above any period which is expressed in the enactment concerned as a period of days or number of days no account shall be taken of—

(a) Saturday, Sunday, Good Friday and Christmas Day; and

(b) any day which is a bank holiday in England and Wales.

(4) Any reference in this Part (apart from in section 97(1) and section 99(1)) to the period for considering a merger notice shall, if that period is extended by virtue of any one or more of subsections (2), (3), (4) (5), (7), (9) and (11) of section 97 in relation to a particular case, be construed in relation to that case as a reference to that period as so extended; but only one extension is possible under section 97(2), (3) or (4).

(5) Where the period for considering a merger notice is extended or further extended by virtue of section 97, the period as extended or (as the case may be) further extended shall, subject to subsections (6) and (7), be calculated by taking the period being extended and adding to it the period of the extension (whether or not those periods overlap in time).

(6) Subsection (7) applies where—

(a) the period for considering a merger notice is further extended;

(b) the further extension and at least one previous extension is made under one or more of subsections (5), (7), (9) and (11) of section 97; and

(c) the same days or fractions of days are included in or comprise the further extension and are included in or comprise at least one such previous extension.

(7) In calculating the period of the further extension, any days or fractions of days of the kind mentioned in subsection (6)(c) shall be disregarded.

[3593]

99 Certain functions of OFT and Secretary of State in relation to merger notices

(1) The OFT shall, so far as practicable and when the period for considering any merger notice begins, take such action as the OFT considers appropriate to bring—

(a) the existence of the proposal;

(b) the fact that the merger notice has been given; and

(c) the date on which the period for considering the notice may expire;

to the attention of those whom the OFT considers would be affected if the arrangements were carried into effect.

(2) The OFT may by notice to the person who gave the merger notice request him to provide the OFT with such information as the OFT or (as the case may be) the Secretary of State may require for the purpose of carrying out its or (as the case may be) his functions in relation to the merger notice.

(3) A notice under subsection (2) shall state—

(a) the information required;

(b) the period within which the information is to be provided; and

(c) the possible consequences of not providing the information within the stated period and in the authorised or required manner.

(4) A notice by the OFT under subsection (2) shall be given, before the end of the period for considering the merger notice, to the person who gave the merger notice.

PART III OTHER LEGISLATION

(5) The OFT may, at any time before the end of the period for considering any merger notice, reject the notice if—

(a) the OFT suspects that any information given in respect of the notified arrangements (whether in the merger notice or otherwise) by the person who gave the notice or any connected person is in any material respect false or misleading;

(b) the OFT suspects that it is not proposed to carry the notified arrangements into effect;

(c) any prescribed information is not given in the merger notice or any information requested by notice under subsection (2) is not provided as required; or

(d) the OFT considers that the notified arrangements are, or if carried into effect would result in, a concentration with a Community dimension within the meaning of the [EC Merger Regulation].

(6) In this section and section 100 "connected person", in relation to the person who gave a merger notice, means—

(a) any person who, for the purposes of section 127, is associated with him; or

(b) any subsidiary of the person who gave the merger notice or of any person so associated with him.

[3594]

NOTES

Sub-s (5): words in square brackets substituted by the EC Merger Control (Consequential Amendments) Regulations 2004, SI 2004/1079, reg 2, Schedule, para 2(1), (23), as from 1 May 2004.

100 Exceptions to protection given by merger notices

(1) Section 96(3) does not prevent any reference being made to the Commission if—

(a) before the end of the period for considering the merger notice, the OFT rejects the notice under section 99(5);

(b) before the end of that period, any of the enterprises to which the notified arrangements relate cease to be distinct from each other;

(c) any information (whether prescribed information or not) that—

(i) is, or ought to be, known to the person who gave the merger notice or any connected person; and

(ii) is material to the notified arrangements;

is not disclosed to the OFT by such time before the end of that period as may be specified in regulations under section 101;

(d) at any time after the merger notice is given but before the enterprises to which the notified arrangements relate cease to be distinct from each other, any of those enterprises ceases to be distinct from any enterprise other than an enterprise to which those arrangements relate;

(e) the six months beginning with the end of the period for considering the merger notice expires without the enterprises to which the notified arrangements relate ceasing to be distinct from each other;

(f) the merger notice is withdrawn; or

(g) any information given in respect of the notified arrangements (whether in the merger notice or otherwise) by the person who gave the notice or any connected person is in any material respect false or misleading.

(2) Subsection (3) applies where—

(a) two or more transactions which have occurred, or, if any arrangements are carried into effect, will occur, may be treated for the purposes of a reference under section 22, 33 or 45 as having occurred simultaneously on a particular date; and

(b) section 96(3) does not prevent such a reference in relation to the last of those transactions.

(3) Section 96(3) does not prevent such a reference in relation to any of those transactions which actually occurred less than six months before—

(a) that date; or

(b) the actual occurrence of another of those transactions in relation to which such a reference may be made (whether or not by virtue of this subsection).

(4) In determining for the purposes of subsections (2) and (3) the time at which any transaction actually occurred, no account shall be taken of any option or other conditional right until the option is exercised or the condition is satisfied.

(5) In this section references to the enterprises to which the notified arrangements relate are references to those enterprises that would have ceased to be distinct from one another if the arrangements mentioned in the merger notice concerned had been carried into effect at the time when the notice was given.

[3595]

101 Merger notices: regulations

(1) The Secretary of State may make regulations for the purposes of sections 96 to 100.

(2) The regulations may, in particular—

(a) provide for section 97(1), (2), (3) or (4) or section 100(1)(e) to apply as if any reference to a period of days or months were a reference to a period specified in the regulations for the purposes of the enactment concerned;

(b) provide for the manner in which any merger notice is authorised or required to be rejected or withdrawn, and the time at which any merger notice is to be treated as received or rejected;

(c) provide for the time at which any notice under section 97(7), (8)(b), (11) or (13) is to be treated as received;

(d) provide for the manner in which any information requested by the OFT or any other material information is authorised or required to be provided or disclosed, and the time at which such information is to be treated as provided or disclosed (including the time at which it is to be treated as provided to the satisfaction of the OFT for the purposes of section 97(6));

(e) provide for the person who gave the merger notice to be informed, in circumstances in which section 97(6) applies—

(i) of the fact that the OFT is satisfied as to the provision of the information requested by the OFT or (as the case may be) of the OFT's decision to cancel the extension; and

(ii) of the time at which the OFT is to be treated as so satisfied or (as the case may be) of the time at which the cancellation is to be treated as having effect;

(f) provide for the person who gave the merger notice to be informed, in circumstances in which section 97(8) applies—

(i) of any decision by the OFT to cancel the extension; and

(ii) of the time at which such a cancellation is to be treated as having effect;

(g) provide for the time at which any fee is to be treated as paid;

(h) provide that a person is, or is not, to be treated, in such circumstances as may be specified in the regulations, as acting on behalf of a person authorised by regulations under this section to give a merger notice or a person who has given such a notice.

[3596]

NOTES

Regulations: the Enterprise Act 2002 (Merger Prenotification) Regulations 2003, SI 2003/1369 at **[7418]**.

102 Power to modify sections 97 to 101

The Secretary of State may, for the purposes of determining the effect of giving a merger notice and the action which may be or is to be taken by any person in connection with such a notice, by order modify sections 97 to 101.

[3597]

General duties in relation to references

103 Duty of expedition in relation to references

(1) In deciding whether to make a reference under section 22 or 33 the OFT shall have regard, with a view to the prevention or removal of uncertainty, to the need for making a decision as soon as reasonably practicable.

(2) In deciding whether to make a reference under section 45 or 62 the Secretary of State shall have regard, with a view to the prevention or removal of uncertainty, to the need for making a decision as soon as reasonably practicable.

[3598]

PART III OTHER LEGISLATION

104 Certain duties of relevant authorities to consult

(1) Subsection (2) applies where the relevant authority is proposing to make a relevant decision in a way which the relevant authority considers is likely to be adverse to the interests of a relevant party.

(2) The relevant authority shall, so far as practicable, consult that party about what is proposed before making that decision.

(3) In consulting the party concerned, the relevant authority shall, so far as practicable, give the reasons of the relevant authority for the proposed decision.

(4) In considering what is practicable for the purposes of this section the relevant authority shall, in particular, have regard to—

(a) any restrictions imposed by any timetable for making the decision; and

(b) any need to keep what is proposed, or the reasons for it, confidential.

(5) The duty under this section shall not apply in relation to the making of any decision so far as particular provision is made elsewhere by virtue of this Part for consultation before the making of that decision.

(6) In this section—

"the relevant authority" means the OFT, the Commission or the Secretary of State;

"relevant decision" means—

(a) in the case of the OFT, any decision by the OFT—

(i) as to whether to make a reference under section 22 or 33 or accept undertakings under section 73 instead of making such a reference; or

(ii) to vary under section 37 such a reference;

(b) in the case of the Commission, any decision on the questions mentioned in section 35(1) or (3), 36(1) or (2), 47 or 63; and

(c) in the case of the Secretary of State, any decision by the Secretary of State—

(i) as to whether to make a reference under section 45 or 62; or

(ii) to vary under section 49 or (as the case may be) 64 such a reference; and

"relevant party" means any person who appears to the relevant authority to control enterprises which are the subject of the reference or possible reference concerned.

[3599]

[104A Public consultation in relation to media mergers

(1) Subsection (2) applies where the Commission—

(a) is preparing—

(i) a report under section 50 on a reference which specifies a media public interest consideration; or

(ii) a report under section 65 on a reference which specifies a consideration specified in section 58(2A) to (2C); and

(b) is not under a duty to disregard the consideration concerned.

(2) The Commission shall have regard (among other things) to the need to consult the public so far as they might be affected by the creation of the relevant merger situation or special merger situation concerned and so far as such consultation is practicable.

(3) Any consultation of the kind mentioned in subsection (2) may be undertaken by the Commission by consulting such representative sample of the public or section of the public concerned as the Commission considers appropriate.]

[3599A]

NOTES

Inserted by the Communications Act 2003, s 381, as from 29 December 2003.

Information and publicity requirements

105 General information duties of OFT and Commission

(1) Where the OFT decides to investigate a matter so as to enable it to decide whether to make a reference under section 22 or 33, or so as to make a report under section 44 or 61, it

shall, so far as practicable, take such action as it considers appropriate to bring information about the investigation to the attention of those whom it considers might be affected by the creation of the relevant merger situation concerned or (as the case may be) the special merger situation concerned.

[(1A) Where OFCOM decide to investigate a matter so as to make a report under section 44A or 61A, they shall, so far as practicable, take such action as they consider appropriate to bring information about the investigation to the attention of those who they consider might be affected by the creation of the relevant merger situation concerned or (as the case may be) the special merger situation concerned.]

(2) [Subsections (1) and (1A) do] not apply in relation to arrangements which might result in the creation of a relevant merger situation if a merger notice has been given in relation to those arrangements under section 96.

(3) The OFT shall give the Commission [or OFCOM]—

(a) such information in its possession as the Commission [or (as the case may be) OFCOM] may reasonably require to enable the Commission [or (as the case may be) OFCOM] to carry out its functions under this Part; and

(b) any other assistance which the Commission [or (as the case may be) OFCOM] may reasonably require for the purpose of assisting it in carrying out its functions under this Part and which it is within the power of the OFT to give.

[(3A) OFCOM shall give the Commission or the OFT—

(a) such information in their possession as the Commission or (as the case may be) the OFT may reasonably require to enable the Commission or (as the case may be) the OFT to carry out its functions under this Part; and

(b) any other assistance which the Commission or (as the case may be) the OFT may reasonably require for the purpose of assisting it in carrying out its functions under this Part and which it is within the power of OFCOM to give.]

(4) The OFT shall give the Commission [or OFCOM] any information in its possession which has not been requested by the Commission [or (as the case may be) OFCOM] but which, in the opinion of the OFT, would be appropriate to give to the Commission [or (as the case may be) OFCOM] for the purpose of assisting it in carrying out its functions under this Part.

[(4A) OFCOM shall give the Commission or the OFT any information in their possession which has not been requested by the Commission or (as the case may be) the OFT but which, in the opinion of OFCOM, would be appropriate to give to the Commission or (as the case may be) the OFT for the purpose of assisting it in carrying out its functions under this Part.]

(5) The OFT[, OFCOM] and the Commission shall give the Secretary of State—

(a) such information in their possession as the Secretary of State may by direction reasonably require to enable him to carry out his functions under this Part; and

(b) any other assistance which the Secretary of State may by direction reasonably require for the purpose of assisting him in carrying out his functions under this Part and which it is within the power of the OFT[, OFCOM] or (as the case may be) the Commission to give.

(6) The OFT [and OFCOM] shall give the Secretary of State any information in [their] possession which has not been requested by the Secretary of State but which, in the opinion of the OFT [or (as the case may be) OFCOM], would be appropriate to give to the Secretary of State for the purpose of assisting him in carrying out his functions under this Part.

(7) The Commission shall have regard to any information given to it under subsection (3)[, (3A), (4) or (4A)]; and the Secretary of State shall have regard to any information given to him under subsection (5) or (6).

[(7A) OFCOM shall have regard to any information given to them under subsection (3) or (4); and the OFT shall have regard to any information given to it under subsection (3A) or (4A).]

(8) Any direction given under subsection (5)—

(a) shall be in writing; and

(b) may be varied or revoked by a subsequent direction.

[3600]

PART III OTHER LEGISLATION

NOTES

Sub-ss (1A), (3A), (4A), (7A): inserted by the Communications Act 2003, s 382(1), (2), (5), (7), (11), as from 29 December 2003.

Sub-ss (2), (7): words in square brackets substituted by the Communications Act 2003, s 382(1), (3), (10), as from 29 December 2003.

Sub-ss (3), (4), (5): words in square brackets inserted by the Communications Act 2003, s 382(1), (4), (6), (8), as from 29 December 2003.

Sub-s (6): words in first and third pairs of square brackets inserted, and word in second pair of square brackets substituted, by the Communications Act 2003, s 382(1), (9), as from 29 December 2003.

106 Advice and information about references under sections 22 and 33

(1) As soon as reasonably practicable after the passing of this Act, the OFT shall prepare and publish general advice and information about the making of references by it under section 22 or 33.

(2) The OFT may at any time publish revised, or new, advice or information.

(3) As soon as reasonably practicable after the passing of this Act, the Commission shall prepare and publish general advice and information about the consideration by it of references under section 22 or 33 and the way in which relevant customer benefits may affect the taking of enforcement action in relation to such references.

(4) The Commission may at any time publish revised, or new, advice or information.

(5) Advice and information published under this section shall be prepared with a view to—

(a) explaining relevant provisions of this Part to persons who are likely to be affected by them; and

(b) indicating how the OFT or (as the case may be) the Commission expects such provisions to operate.

(6) Advice (or information) published by virtue of subsection (1) or (3) may include advice (or information) about the factors which the OFT or (as the case may be) the Commission may take into account in considering whether, and if so how, to exercise a function conferred by this Part.

(7) Any advice or information published by the OFT or the Commission under this section shall be published in such manner as the OFT or (as the case may be) the Commission considers appropriate.

(8) In preparing any advice or information under this section, the OFT shall consult the Commission and such other persons as it considers appropriate.

(9) In preparing any advice or information under this section, the Commission shall consult the OFT and such other persons as it considers appropriate.

[3601]

[106A Advice and information in relation to media mergers

(1) The Secretary of State may prepare and publish general advice and information about the considerations specified in section 58(2A) to (2C).

(2) The Secretary of State may at any time publish revised, or new, advice or information.

(3) Advice or information published under this section shall be prepared with a view to—

(a) explaining the considerations specified in section 58(2A) to (2C) to persons who are likely to be affected by them; and

(b) indicating how the Secretary of State expects this Part to operate in relation to such considerations.

(4) Any advice or information published by the Secretary of State under this section shall be published in such manner as the Secretary of State considers appropriate.

(5) In preparing any advice or information under this section, the Secretary of State shall consult the OFT, OFCOM, the Commission and such other persons as he considers appropriate.]

[3601A]

NOTES

Inserted by the Communications Act 2003, s 383, as from 29 December 2003.

[106B General advisory functions of OFCOM

(1) OFCOM may, in connection with any case on which they are required to give a report by virtue of section 44A or 61A, give such advice as they consider appropriate to the Secretary of State in relation to—

(a) any report made in such a case by the Commission under section 50 or 65; and

(b) the taking by the Secretary of State of enforcement action under Schedule 7.

(2) OFCOM may, if requested to do so by the Secretary of State, give such other advice as they consider appropriate to the Secretary of State in connection with any case on which they are required to give a report by virtue of section 44A or 61A.

(3) OFCOM shall publish any advice given by them under this section but advice given by them in relation to a report of the Commission under section 50 or 65 or related enforcement action shall not be published before the report itself is published.]

[3601B]

NOTES

Inserted by the Communications Act 2003, s 384, as from 29 December 2003.

107 Further publicity requirements

(1) The OFT shall publish—

(a) any reference made by it under section 22 or 33 or any decision made by it not to make such a reference (other than a decision made by virtue of subsection (2)(b) of section 33);

(b) any variation made by it under section 37 of a reference under section 22 or 33;

(c) such information as it considers appropriate about any decision made by it under section 57(1) to bring a case to the attention of the Secretary of State;

(d) any enforcement undertaking accepted by it under section 71;

(e) any enforcement order made by it under section 72 or 76 or paragraph 2 of Schedule 7;

(f) any variation, release or revocation of such an undertaking or order;

(g) any decision made by it as mentioned in section 76(6)(b); and

(h) any decision made by it to dispense with the requirements of Schedule 10.

(2) The Commission shall publish—

(a) any cancellation by it under section 37(1) of a reference under section 33;

(b) any decision made by it under section 37(2) to treat a reference made under section 22 or 33 as if it had been made under section 32 or (as the case may be) 22;

(c) any extension by it under section 39 of the period within which a report under section 38 is to be prepared and published;

(d) any decision made by it to cancel an extension as mentioned in section 39(8)(b);

(e) any decision made by it under section 41(2) neither to accept an undertaking under section 82 nor to make an order under section 84;

(f) any decision made by it that there has been a material change of circumstances as mentioned in subsection (3) of section 41 or there is another special reason as mentioned in that subsection of that section;

(g) any cancellation by it under section 48(1) or 53(1) of a reference under section 45 or any cancellation by it under section 64(1) of a reference under section 62;

(h) any decision made by it under section 49(1) to treat—

  (i) a reference made under subsection (2) or (3) of section 45 as if it had been made under subsection (4) or (as the case may be) (5) of that section; or

  (ii) a reference made under subsection (4) or (5) of section 45 as if it had been made under subsection (2) or (as the case may be) (3) of that section;

(i) any extension by it under section 51 of the period within which a report under section 50 is to be prepared and published;

(j) any decision made by it under section 51(8)(b) to cancel such an extension;

(k) any extension by it under section 51 as applied by section 65(3) of the period within which a report under section 65 is to be prepared and published;

PART III
OTHER LEGISLATION

(l) any decision made by it under section 51(8)(b) as applied by section 65(3) to cancel such an extension;
(m) any decision made by it under section 64(2) to treat a reference made under subsection (2) or (3) of section 62 as if it had been made under subsection (3) or (as the case may be) (2) of that section;
(n) any decision made by it as mentioned in section 76(6)(b);
(o) any enforcement order made by it under section 76 or 81;
(p) any enforcement undertaking accepted by it under section 80;
(q) any variation, release or revocation of such an order or undertaking; and
(r) any decision made by it to dispense with the requirements of Schedule 10.

(3) The Secretary of State shall publish—
(a) any intervention notice or special intervention notice given by him;
(b) any report of the OFT under section 44 or 61 which has been received by him;
[(ba) any report of OFCOM under section 44A or 61A which has been received by him;]
(c) any reference made by him under section 45 or 62 or any decision made by him not to make such a reference;
(d) any variation made by him under section 49 of a reference under section 45 or under section 64 of a reference under section 62;
(e) any report of the Commission under section 50 or 65 which has been received by him;
(f) any decision made by him neither to accept an undertaking under paragraph 9 of Schedule 7 nor to make an order under paragraph 11 of that Schedule;
(g) any notice given by him under section 56(1);
(h) any enforcement undertaking accepted by him under paragraph 1 of Schedule 7;
(i) any variation or release of such an undertaking;
(j) any decision made by him as mentioned in paragraph 6(6)(b) of Schedule 7; and
(k) any decision made by him to dispense with the requirements of Schedule 10.

(4) Where any person is under a duty by virtue of subsection (1), (2) or (3) to publish the result of any action taken by that person or any decision made by that person, the person concerned shall, subject to subsections (5) and (6), also publish that person's reasons for the action concerned or (as the case may be) the decision concerned.

(5) Such reasons need not, if it is not reasonably practicable to do so, be published at the same time as the result of the action concerned or (as the case may be) as the decision concerned.

(6) Subsections (4) and (5) shall not apply in relation to any information published under subsection (1)(c).

(7) The Secretary of State shall publish his reasons for—
(a) any decision made by him under section 54(2) or 66(2); or
(b) any decision to make an order under section 58(3) or vary or revoke such an order.

(8) Such reasons may be published after—
(a) in the case of subsection (7)(a), the publication of the decision concerned; and
(b) in the case of subsection (7)(b), the making of the order or of the variation or revocation;

if it is not reasonably practicable to publish them at the same time as the publication of the decision or (as the case may be) the making of the order or variation or revocation.

(9) The Secretary of State shall publish—
(a) the report of the OFT under section 44[, and any report of OFCOM under section 44A,] in relation to a matter no later than publication of his decision as to whether to make a reference under section 45 in relation to that matter; and
(b) the report of the Commission under section 50 in relation to a matter no later than publication of his decision under section 54(2) in relation to that matter.

(10) The Secretary of State shall publish—
(a) the report of the OFT under section 61[, and any report of OFCOM under section 61A,] in relation to a matter no later than publication of his decision as to whether to make a reference under section 62 in relation to that matter; and
(b) the report of the Commission under section 65 in relation to a matter no later than publication of his decision under section 66(2) in relation to that matter.

(11) Where the Secretary of State has decided under section 55(2) or 66(6) to accept an undertaking under paragraph 9 of Schedule 7 or to make an order under paragraph 11 of that

Schedule, he shall (after the acceptance of the undertaking or (as the case may be) the making of the order) lay details of his decision and his reasons for it, and the Commission's report under section 50 or (as the case may be) 65, before each House of Parliament.

[3602]

NOTES

Sub-ss (3), (9), (10): words in square brackets inserted by the Communications Act 2003, s 389, Sch 16, para 18, as from 29 December 2003.

108 Defamation

For the purposes of the law relating to defamation, absolute privilege attaches to any advice, guidance, notice or direction given, or decision or report made, by the OFT, [OFCOM,] the Commission or the Secretary of State in the exercise of any of their functions under this Part.

[3603]

NOTES

Word in square brackets inserted by the Communications Act 2003, s 389, Sch 16, para 19, as from 29 December 2003.

Investigation powers

109 Attendance of witnesses and production of documents etc

(1) The Commission may, for the purpose of any investigation on a reference made to it under this Part, give notice to any person requiring him—

(a) to attend at a time and place specified in the notice; and

(b) to give evidence to the Commission or a person nominated by the Commission for the purpose.

(2) The Commission may, for the purpose of any investigation on a reference made to it under this Part, give notice to any person requiring him—

(a) to produce any documents which—

(i) are specified or described in the notice, or fall within a category of document which is specified or described in the notice; and

(ii) are in that person's custody or under his control; and

(b) to produce them at a time and place so specified and to a person so specified.

(3) The Commission may, for the purpose of any investigation on a reference made to it under this Part, give notice to any person who carries on any business requiring him—

(a) to supply to the Commission such estimates, forecasts, returns or other information as may be specified or described in the notice; and

(b) to supply it at a time and place, and in a form and manner, so specified and to a person so specified.

(4) A notice under this section shall include information about the possible consequences of not complying with the notice.

(5) The Commission or any person nominated by it for the purpose may, for the purpose of any investigation on a reference made to it under this Part, take evidence on oath, and for that purpose may administer oaths.

(6) The person to whom any document is produced in accordance with a notice under this section may, for the purpose of any investigation on a reference made to the Commission under this Part, copy the document so produced.

(7) No person shall be required under this section—

(a) to give any evidence or produce any documents which he could not be compelled to give or produce in civil proceedings before the court; or

(b) to supply any information which he could not be compelled to supply in evidence in such proceedings.

(8) No person shall be required, in compliance with a notice under this section, to go more than 10 miles from his place of residence unless his necessary travelling expenses are paid or offered to him.

(9) Any reference in this section to the production of a document includes a reference to the production of a legible and intelligible copy of information recorded otherwise than in legible form.

(10) In this section "the court" means—
- (a) in relation to England and Wales or Northern Ireland, the High Court; and
- (b) in relation to Scotland, the Court of Session.

[3604]

110 Enforcement of powers under section 109: general

(1) Where the Commission considers that a person has, without reasonable excuse, failed to comply with any requirement of a notice under section 109, it may impose a penalty in accordance with section 111.

(2) The Commission may proceed (whether at the same time or at different times) under subsection (1) and section 39(4) or (as the case may be) 51(4) (including that enactment as applied by section 65(3)) in relation to the same failure.

(3) Where the Commission considers that a person has intentionally obstructed or delayed another person in the exercise of his powers under section 109(6), it may impose a penalty in accordance with section 111.

(4) No penalty shall be imposed by virtue of subsection (1) or (3) if more than 4 weeks have passed since the publication of the report of the Commission on the reference concerned; but this subsection shall not apply in relation to any variation or substitution of the penalty which is permitted by virtue of this Part.

(5) A person, subject to subsection (6), commits an offence if he intentionally alters, suppresses or destroys any document which he has been required to produce by a notice under section 109.

(6) A person does not commit an offence under subsection (5) in relation to any act which constitutes a failure to comply with a notice under section 109 if the Commission has proceeded against that person under subsection (1) above in relation to that failure.

(7) A person who commits an offence under subsection (5) shall be liable—
- (a) on summary conviction, to a fine not exceeding the statutory maximum;
- (b) on conviction on indictment, to imprisonment for a term not exceeding two years or to a fine or to both.

(8) The Commission shall not proceed against a person under subsection (1) in relation to an act which constitutes an offence under subsection (5) if that person has been found guilty of that offence.

(9) In deciding whether and, if so, how to proceed under subsection (1) or (3) or section 39(4) or 51(4) (including that enactment as applied by section 65(3)), the Commission shall have regard to the statement of policy which was most recently published under section 116 at the time when the failure concerned or (as the case may be) the obstruction or delay concerned occurred.

(10) The reference in this section to the production of a document includes a reference to the production of a legible and intelligible copy of information recorded otherwise than in legible form; and the reference to suppressing a document includes a reference to destroying the means of reproducing information recorded otherwise than in legible form.

[3605]

111 Penalties

(1) A penalty imposed under section 110(1) or (3) shall be of such amount as the Commission considers appropriate.

(2) The amount may, in the case of a penalty imposed under section 110(1), be a fixed amount, an amount calculated by reference to a daily rate or a combination of a fixed amount and an amount calculated by reference to a daily rate.

(3) The amount shall, in the case of a penalty imposed under section 110(3), be a fixed amount.

(4) No penalty imposed under section 110(1) shall—
- (a) in the case of a fixed amount, exceed such amount as the Secretary of State may by order specify;

(b) in the case of an amount calculated by reference to a daily rate, exceed such amount per day as the Secretary of State may so specify; and
(c) in the case of a fixed amount and an amount calculated by reference to a daily rate, exceed such fixed amount and such amount per day as the Secretary of State may so specify.

(5) In imposing a penalty by reference to a daily rate—
(a) no account shall be taken of any days before the service of the notice under section 112 on the person concerned; and
(b) unless the Commission determines an earlier date (whether before or after the penalty is imposed), the amount payable shall cease to accumulate at the beginning of—
(i) the day on which the requirement of the notice concerned under section 109 is satisfied or (as the case may be) the obstruction or delay is removed; or
(ii) if earlier, the day on which the report of the Commission on the reference concerned is published (or, in the case of a report under section 50 or 65, given) or, if no such report is published (or given) within the period permitted for that purpose by this Part, the latest day on which the report may be published (or given) within the permitted period.

(6) No penalty imposed under section 110(3) shall exceed such amount as the Secretary of State may by order specify.

(7) An order under subsection (4) or (6) shall not specify—
(a) in the case of a fixed amount, an amount exceeding £30,000;
(b) in the case of an amount calculated by reference to a daily rate, an amount per day exceeding £15,000; and
(c) in the case of a fixed amount and an amount calculated by reference to a daily rate, a fixed amount exceeding £30,000 and an amount per day exceeding £15,000.

(8) Before making an order under subsection (4) or (6) the Secretary of State shall consult the Commission and such other persons as he considers appropriate.

[3606]

NOTES

Orders: the Competition Commission (Penalties) Order 2003, SI 2003/1371. This Order provides that the specified amount for the purposes of sub-ss (4)(a) and (6) above is £20,000; for the purposes of sub-s (4)(b) above is £5,000; and for the purposes of sub-s (4)(c) above the fixed amount specified shall be £20,000 and the amount per day specified shall be £5,000.

112 Penalties: main procedural requirements

(1) As soon as practicable after imposing a penalty under section 110(1) or (3), the Commission shall give notice of the penalty.

(2) The notice shall state—
(a) that the Commission has imposed a penalty on the person concerned;
(b) whether the penalty is of a fixed amount, of an amount calculated by reference to a daily rate or of both a fixed amount and an amount calculated by reference to a daily rate;
(c) the amount or amounts concerned and, in the case of an amount calculated by reference to a daily rate, the day on which the amount first starts to accumulate and the day or days on which it might cease to accumulate;
(d) the failure or (as the case may be) the obstruction or delay which the Commission considers gave it the power to impose the penalty;
(e) any other facts which the Commission considers justify the imposition of a penalty and the amount or amounts of the penalty;
(f) the manner in which, and place at which, the penalty is required to be paid to the Commission;
(g) the date or dates, no earlier than the end of the relevant period beginning with the date of service of the notice on the person concerned, by which the penalty or (as the case may be) different portions of it are required to be paid;
(h) that the penalty or (as the case may be) different portions of it may be paid earlier than the date or dates by which it or they are required to be paid; and
(i) that the person concerned has the right to apply under subsection (3) below or to appeal under section 114 and the main details of those rights.

PART III OTHER LEGISLATION

(3) The person against whom the penalty was imposed may, within 14 days of the date of service on him of a notice under subsection (1), apply to the Commission for it to specify a different date or (as the case may be) different dates by which the penalty or (as the case may be) different portions of it are to be paid.

(4) A notice under this section shall be given by—

(a) serving a copy of the notice on the person on whom the penalty was imposed; and

(b) publishing the notice.

(5) In this section "relevant period" means the period of 28 days mentioned in subsection (3) of section 114 or, if another period is specified by the Secretary of State under that subsection, that period.

[3607]

113 Payments and interest by instalments

(1) If the whole or any portion of a penalty is not paid by the date by which it is required to be paid, the unpaid balance from time to time shall carry interest at the rate for the time being specified in section 17 of the Judgments Act 1838 (c 110).

(2) Where an application has been made under section 112(3), the penalty shall not be required to be paid until the application has been determined, withdrawn or otherwise dealt with.

(3) If a portion of a penalty has not been paid by the date required for it, the Commission may, where it considers it appropriate to do so, require so much of the penalty as has not already been paid (and is capable of being paid immediately) to be paid immediately.

(4) Any sums received by the Commission in or towards the payment of a penalty, or interest on a penalty, shall be paid into the Consolidated Fund.

[3608]

114 Appeals in relation to penalties

(1) This section applies if a person on whom a penalty is imposed under section 110(1) or (3) is aggrieved by—

(a) the imposition or nature of the penalty;

(b) the amount or amounts of the penalty; or

(c) the date by which the penalty is required to be paid or (as the case may be) the different dates by which portions of the penalty are required to be paid.

(2) The person aggrieved may apply to the Competition Appeal Tribunal.

(3) If a copy of the notice under section 112(1) was served on the person on whom the penalty was imposed, the application to the Competition Appeal Tribunal shall, subject to subsection (4), be made within—

(a) the period of 28 days starting with the day on which the copy was served on the person concerned; or

(b) such other period as the Secretary of State may by order specify.

(4) If the application relates to a decision of the Commission on an application by the person on whom the penalty was imposed under section 112(3), the application to the Competition Appeal Tribunal shall be made within—

(a) the period of 28 days starting with the day on which the person concerned is notified of the decision; or

(b) such other period as the Secretary of State may by order specify.

(5) On an application under this section, the Competition Appeal Tribunal may—

(a) quash the penalty;

(b) substitute a penalty of a different nature or of such lesser amount or amounts as the Competition Appeal Tribunal considers appropriate; or

(c) in a case falling within subsection (1)(c), substitute for the date or dates imposed by the Commission an alternative date or dates;

if it considers it appropriate to do so.

(6) The Competition Appeal Tribunal shall not substitute a penalty of a different nature under subsection (5)(b) unless it considers that the person on whom the penalty is imposed will, or is likely to, pay less under the substituted penalty than he would have paid under the original penalty.

(7) Where an application has been made under this section—
(a) the penalty shall not be required to be paid until the application has been determined, withdrawn or otherwise dealt with; and
(b) the Commission may agree to reduce the amount or amounts of the penalty in settlement of the application.

(8) Where the Competition Appeal Tribunal substitutes a penalty of a different nature or of a lesser amount or amounts it may require the payment of interest on the substituted penalty at such rate or rates, and from such date or dates, as it considers appropriate.

(9) Where the Competition Appeal Tribunal specifies as a date by which the penalty, or a portion of the penalty, is to be paid a date before the determination of the application under this section it may require the payment of interest on the penalty, or portion, from that date at such rate as it considers appropriate.

(10) An appeal lies to the appropriate court—
(a) on a point of law arising from a decision of the Tribunal in proceedings under this section; or
(b) from a decision of the Tribunal in such proceedings as to the amount or amounts of a penalty.

(11) An appeal under subsection (10)—
(a) may be brought by a party to the proceedings before the Tribunal; and
(b) requires the permission of the Tribunal or the appropriate court.

(12) In this section "the appropriate court" means the Court of Appeal or, in the case of Tribunal proceedings in Scotland, the Court of Session.

[3609]

115 Recovery of penalties

Where a penalty imposed under section 110(1) or (3), or any portion of such a penalty, has not been paid by the date on which it is required to be paid and—
(a) no application relating to the penalty has been made under section 114 during the period within which such an application may be made, or
(b) any such application which has been made has been determined, withdrawn or otherwise dealt with,

the Commission may recover from the person on whom the penalty was imposed any of the penalty and any interest which has not been paid; and in England and Wales and Northern Ireland such penalty and interest may be recovered as a civil debt due to the Commission.

[3610]

116 Statement of policy

(1) The Commission shall prepare and publish a statement of policy in relation to the enforcement of notices under section 109.

(2) The statement shall, in particular, include a statement about the considerations relevant to the determination of the nature and amount of any penalty imposed under section 110(1) or (3).

(3) The Commission may revise its statement of policy and, where it does so, it shall publish the revised statement.

(4) The Commission shall consult such persons as it considers appropriate when preparing or revising its statement of policy.

[3611]

117 False or misleading information

(1) A person commits an offence if—
(a) he supplies any information to the OFT, [OFCOM,] the Commission or the Secretary of State in connection with any of their functions under this Part;
(b) the information is false or misleading in a material respect; and
(c) he knows that it is false or misleading in a material respect or is reckless as to whether it is false or misleading in a material respect.

(2) A person commits an offence if he—
(a) supplies any information to another person which he knows to be false or misleading in a material respect; or

PART III
OTHER LEGISLATION

(b) recklessly supplies any information to another person which is false or misleading in a material respect;

knowing that the information is to be used for the purpose of supplying information to the OFT, [OFCOM,] the Commission or the Secretary of State in connection with any of their functions under this Part.

(3) A person who commits an offence under subsection (1) or (2) shall be liable—

(a) on summary conviction, to a fine not exceeding the statutory maximum;

(b) on conviction on indictment, to imprisonment for a term not exceeding two years or to a fine or to both.

[3612]

NOTES

Sub-ss (1), (2): words in square brackets inserted by the Communications Act 2003, s 389, Sch 16, para 20, as from 29 December 2003.

See further, the EEC Merger Control (Distinct Market Investigations) Regulations 1990, SI 1990/1715 (as amended) which confer investigative powers upon the OFT for the purpose of furnishing information to the European Commission under the Merger Regulation. Article 5 of the Regulations provides that this section has effect as if those Regulations were contained in Part 3 of this Act.

Reports

118 Excisions from reports

(1) Subsection (2) applies where the Secretary of State is under a duty to publish—

(a) a report of the OFT under section 44 or 61;

[(aa) a report of OFCOM under section 44A or 61A;] or

(b) a report of the Commission under section 50 or 65.

(2) The Secretary of State may exclude a matter from the report concerned if he considers that publication of the matter would be inappropriate.

(3) In deciding what is inappropriate for the purposes of subsection (2) the Secretary of State shall have regard to the considerations mentioned in section 244.

(4) The body which has prepared the report shall advise the Secretary of State as to the matters (if any) which it considers should be excluded by him under subsection (2).

(5) References in sections 38(4) and 107(11) to the giving or laying of a report of the Commission shall be construed as references to the giving or laying of the report as published.

[3613]

NOTES

Sub-s (1): para (aa) inserted by the Communications Act 2003, s 389, Sch 16, para 21, as from 29 December 2003.

119 Minority reports of Commission

(1) Subsection (2) applies where, on a reference to the Commission under this Part, a member of a group constituted in connection with the reference in pursuance of paragraph 15 of Schedule 7 to the Competition Act 1998 (c 41), disagrees with any decisions contained in the report of the Commission under this Part as the decisions of the Commission.

(2) The report shall, if the member so wishes, include a statement of his disagreement and of his reasons for disagreeing.

[3614]

[Further provision about media mergers

119A Other general functions of OFCOM in relation to this Part

(1) OFCOM have the function of obtaining, compiling and keeping under review information about matters relating to the carrying out of their functions under this Part.

(2) That function is to be carried out with a view to (among other things) ensuring that OFCOM have sufficient information to take informed decisions and to carry out their other functions effectively.

(3) In carrying out that function OFCOM may carry out, commission or support (financially or otherwise) research.

(4) Section 3 of the Communications Act 2003 (general duties of OFCOM) shall not apply in relation to functions of OFCOM under this Part.]

[3614A]

NOTES

Inserted, together with the preceding heading, by the Communications Act 2003, s 385, as from 29 December 2003.

[119B Monitoring role for OFT in relation to media mergers

(1) The OFT has the function of obtaining, compiling and keeping under review information about matters which may be relevant to the Secretary of State in deciding whether to give a special intervention notice mentioning a consideration specified in section 58(2A) to (2C).

(2) That function is to be carried out with a view to (among other things) ensuring that the Secretary of State is aware of cases where, in the opinion of the OFT, he might wish to consider giving such a notice.

(3) That function does not extend to obtaining, compiling or keeping under review information with a view to carrying out a detailed analysis in each case of the operation in relation to that case of the consideration specified in section 58(2A) to (2C).]

[3614B]

NOTES

Inserted by the Communications Act 2003, s 386, as from 29 December 2003.

Miscellaneous

120 Review of decisions under Part 3

(1) Any person aggrieved by a decision of the OFT, [OFCOM,] the Secretary of State or the Commission under this Part in connection with a reference or possible reference in relation to a relevant merger situation or a special merger situation may apply to the Competition Appeal Tribunal for a review of that decision.

(2) For this purpose "decision"—

(a) does not include a decision to impose a penalty under section 110(1) or (3); but

(b) includes a failure to take a decision permitted or required by this Part in connection with a reference or possible reference.

(3) Except in so far as a direction to the contrary is given by the Competition Appeal Tribunal, the effect of the decision is not suspended by reason of the making of the application.

(4) In determining such an application the Competition Appeal Tribunal shall apply the same principles as would be applied by a court on an application for judicial review.

(5) The Competition Appeal Tribunal may—

(a) dismiss the application or quash the whole or part of the decision to which it relates; and

(b) where it quashes the whole or part of that decision, refer the matter back to the original decision maker with a direction to reconsider and make a new decision in accordance with the ruling of the Competition Appeal Tribunal.

(6) An appeal lies on any point of law arising from a decision of the Competition Appeal Tribunal under this section to the appropriate court.

(7) An appeal under subsection (6) requires the permission of the Tribunal or the appropriate court.

(8) In this section—

"the appropriate court" means the Court of Appeal or, in the case of Tribunal proceedings in Scotland, the Court of Session; and

"Tribunal rules" has the meaning given by section 15(1).

[3615]

NOTES

Sub-s (1): word in square brackets inserted by the Communications Act 2003, s 389, Sch 16, para 22, as from 29 December 2003.

121 Fees

(1) The Secretary of State may by order require the payment to him or the OFT of such fees as may be prescribed by the order in connection with the exercise by the Secretary of State, the OFT[, OFCOM] and the Commission of their functions under or by virtue of this Part, … and sections 32 to 34 of, and Schedule 4ZA to, the Water Industry Act 1991 (c 56).

(2) An order under this section may, in particular, provide for fees to be payable—

(a) in respect of a merger notice; [or]

(b) …

(c) on the occurrence of any event specified in the order.

(3) The events that may be specified in an order under this section by virtue of subsection (2)(c) include, in particular—

(a) the decision by the OFT in relation to a possible reference under section 22 or 33 that it is or may be the case that a relevant merger situation has been created or (as the case may be) that arrangements are in progress or in contemplation which, if carried into effect, will result in the creation of a relevant merger situation;

(b) the decision by the Secretary of State in relation to a possible reference under section 45 that it is or may be the case that a relevant merger situation has been created or (as the case may be) that arrangements are in progress or in contemplation which, if carried into effect, will result in the creation of a relevant merger situation;

(c) the decision by the Secretary of State in relation to a possible reference under section 62 that—

(i) it is or may be the case that a special merger situation has been created or (as the case may be) that arrangements are in progress or in contemplation which, if carried into effect, will result in the creation of a special merger situation; and

(ii) one or more than one consideration mentioned in the special intervention notice is relevant to a consideration of the special merger situation concerned; and

(d) the decision by the OFT in relation to a possible reference under section 32 of the Act of 1991 that it is or may be the case that arrangements are in progress which, if carried into effect, will result in a merger of any two or more water enterprises or that such a merger has taken place otherwise than as a result of the carrying into effect of arrangements that have been the subject of a reference by virtue of paragraph (a) of that section.

(4) An order under this section may, in particular, contain provision—

(a) for ascertaining the persons by whom fees are payable;

(b) specifying whether any fee is payable to the Secretary of State or the OFT;

(c) for the amount of any fee to be calculated by reference to matters which may include—

(i) …

(ii) … the value of the turnover of the enterprises concerned;

(d) as to the time when any fee is to be paid; and

(e) for the repayment by the Secretary of State or the OFT of the whole or part of any fee in specified circumstances.

(5) For the purposes of subsection (4)(c)(ii) the turnover of an enterprise shall be determined in accordance with such provisions as may be specified in an order under this section.

(6) Provision made by virtue of subsection (5) may, in particular, include provision—

(a) as to the amounts which are, or which are not, to be treated as comprising an enterprise's turnover;

(b) as to the date or dates by reference to which an enterprise's turnover is to be determined;

(c) restricting the turnover to be taken into consideration to turnover which has a connection of a particular description with the United Kingdom.

(7) An order under this section may, in particular, in connection with provisions of the kind mentioned in subsection (5) make provision enabling the Secretary of State or the OFT to determine matters of a description specified in the order (including any of the matters mentioned in paragraphs (a) to (c) of subsection (6)).

(8) In determining the amount of any fees to be prescribed by an order under this section, the Secretary of State may take into account all costs incurred by him and by the OFT in respect of the exercise by him, the OFT[, OFCOM] and the Commission of their respective functions under or by virtue of this Part, … and sections 32 to 34 of, and Schedule 4ZA to, the Act of 1991.

(9) Fees paid to the Secretary of State or the OFT under this section shall be paid into the Consolidated Fund.

(10) …

[3616]

NOTES

Sub-ss (1), (2), (8): words in square brackets inserted, and words omitted repealed, by the Communications Act 2003, ss 389, 406, Sch 16, para 23(1)–(3), (5), Sch 19, as from 29 December 2003.

Sub-s (4): words omitted from para (c) repealed by the Communications Act 2003, ss 389, 406, Sch 16, para 23(1), (4), Sch 19, as from 29 December 2003.

Sub-s (10): repealed by the Communications Act 2003, ss 389, 406, Sch 16, para 23(1), (6), Sch 19, as from 29 December 2003.

Orders: the Enterprise Act 2002 (Merger Fees and Determination of Turnover) Order 2003, SI 2003/1370 at **[7162]**.

122 Primacy of Community law

(1) Advice and information published by virtue of section 106(1) or (3) shall include such advice and information about the effect of Community law, and anything done under or in accordance with it, on the provisions of this Part as the OFT or (as the case may be) the Commission considers appropriate.

(2) Advice and information published by the OFT by virtue of section 106(1) shall, in particular, include advice and information about the circumstances in which the duties of the OFT under sections 22 and 33 do not apply as a result of the [EC Merger Regulation] or anything done under or in accordance with them.

(3) The duty or power to make a reference under section 22 or 45(2) or (3), and the power to give an intervention notice under section 42, shall apply in a case in which the relevant enterprises ceased to be distinct enterprises at a time or in circumstances not falling within section 24 if the condition mentioned in subsection (4) is satisfied.

(4) The condition mentioned in this subsection is that, because of the [EC Merger Regulation] or anything done under or in accordance with them, the reference, or (as the case may be) the reference under section 22 to which the intervention notice relates, could not have been made earlier than 4 months before the date on which it is to be made.

(5) Where the duty or power to make a reference under section 22 or 45(2) or (3), or the power to give an intervention notice under section 42, applies as mentioned in subsection (3), references in this Part to the creation of a relevant merger situation shall be construed accordingly.

[3617]

NOTES

Sub-ss (2), (4): words in square brackets substituted by the EC Merger Control (Consequential Amendments) Regulations 2004, SI 2004/1079, reg 2, Schedule, para 2(1), (24), as from 1 May 2004.

123 Power to alter share of supply test

(1) The Secretary of State may by order amend or replace the conditions which determine for the purposes of this Part whether a relevant merger situation has been created.

(2) The Secretary of State shall not exercise his power under subsection (1)—

(a) to amend or replace the conditions mentioned in paragraphs (a) and (b) of subsection (1) of section 23;
(b) to amend or replace the condition mentioned in paragraph (a) of subsection (2) of that section.

(3) In exercising his power under subsection (1) to amend or replace the condition mentioned in paragraph (b) of subsection (2) of section 23 or any condition which for the time being applies instead of it, the Secretary of State shall, in particular, have regard to the desirability of ensuring that any amended or new condition continues to operate by reference to the degree of commercial strength which results from the enterprises concerned having ceased to be distinct.

(4) Before making an order under this section the Secretary of State shall consult the OFT and the Commission.

(5) An order under this section may provide for the delegation of functions to the decision-making authority.

[3618]

Other

124 Orders and regulations under Part 3

(1) Any power of the Secretary of State to make an order or regulations under this Part shall be exercisable by statutory instrument.

(2) Any power of the Secretary of State to make an order or regulations under this Part—
(a) may be exercised so as to make different provision for different cases or different purposes; and
(b) includes power to make such incidental, supplementary, consequential, transitory, transitional or saving provision as the Secretary of State considers appropriate.

(3) The power of the Secretary of State under section 34[, 59(6A)] or 123 (including that power as extended by subsection (2) above) may be exercised by modifying any enactment comprised in or made under this Act, or any other enactment.

(4) The power of the Secretary of State under section 40(8), [44(11),] 52(8) (including that enactment as applied by section 65(3)), 58(3), 68 or 102 as extended by subsection (2) above may be exercised by modifying any enactment comprised in or made under this Act, or any other enactment.

(5) An order made by the Secretary of State under section 28 (including that enactment as applied by section 42(5), 59(5) and 67(7)), 40(8), 52(8) (including that enactment as applied by section 65(3)), 111(4) or (6), 114(3)(b) or (4)(b) or 121 or Schedule 7 shall be subject to annulment in pursuance of a resolution of either House of Parliament.

(6) No order shall be made by the Secretary of State under section 34, [44(11), 59(6A),] 68, 102, 123 or 128(6) unless a draft of it has been laid before, and approved by a resolution of, each House of Parliament.

(7) An order made by the Secretary of State under section 58(3) shall be laid before Parliament after being made and shall cease to have effect unless approved, within the period of 28 days beginning with the day on which it is made, by a resolution of each House of Parliament.

(8) In calculating the period of 28 days mentioned in subsection (7), no account shall be taken of any time during which Parliament is dissolved or prorogued or during which both Houses are adjourned for more than four days.

(9) If an order made by the Secretary of State ceases to have effect by virtue of subsection (7), any modification made by it of an enactment is repealed (and the previous enactment revived) but without prejudice to the validity of anything done in connection with that modification before the order ceased to have effect and without prejudice to the making of a new order.

(10) If, apart from this subsection, an order made by the Secretary of State under section 58(3) would be treated for the purposes of the standing orders of either House of Parliament as a hybrid instrument, it shall proceed in that House as if it were not such an instrument.

[3619]

NOTES

Sub-ss (3), (4), (6): figures in square brackets inserted by the Communications Act 2003, s 389, Sch 16, para 24, as from 29 December 2003.

125 Offences by bodies corporate

(1) Where an offence under this Part committed by a body corporate is proved to have been committed with the consent or connivance of, or to be attributable to any neglect on the part of—

(a) a director, manager, secretary or other similar officer of the body corporate, or

(b) a person purporting to act in such a capacity,

he as well as the body corporate commits the offence and shall be liable to be proceeded against and punished accordingly.

(2) Where the affairs of a body corporate are managed by its members, subsection (1) applies in relation to the acts and defaults of a member in connection with his functions of management as if he were a director of the body corporate.

(3) Where an offence under this Part is committed by a Scottish partnership and is proved to have been committed with the consent or connivance of a partner, or to be attributable to any neglect on the part of a partner, he as well as the partnership commits the offence and shall be liable to be proceeded against and punished accordingly.

(4) In subsection (3) "partner" includes a person purporting to act as a partner.

[3620]

126 Service of documents

(1) Any document required or authorised by virtue of this Part to be served on any person may be served—

(a) by delivering it to him or by leaving it at his proper address or by sending it by post to him at that address;

(b) if the person is a body corporate other than a limited liability partnership, by serving it in accordance with paragraph (a) on the secretary of the body;

(c) if the person is a limited liability partnership, by serving it in accordance with paragraph (a) on a member of the partnership; or

(d) if the person is a partnership, by serving it in accordance with paragraph (a) on a partner or a person having the control or management of the partnership business.

(2) For the purposes of this section and section 7 of the Interpretation Act 1978 (c 30) (service of documents by post) in its application to this section, the proper address of any person on whom a document is to be served shall be his last known address, except that—

(a) in the case of service on a body corporate (other than a limited liability partnership) or its secretary, it shall be the address of the registered or principal office of the body;

(b) in the case of service on a limited liability partnership or a member of the partnership, it shall be the address of the registered or principal office of the partnership;

(c) in the case of service on a partnership or a partner or a person having the control or management of a partnership business, it shall be the address of the principal office of the partnership.

(3) For the purposes of subsection (2) the principal office of a company constituted under the law of a country or territory outside the United Kingdom or of a partnership carrying on business outside the United Kingdom is its principal office within the United Kingdom.

(4) Subsection (5) applies if a person to be served under this Part with any document by another has specified to that other an address within the United Kingdom other than his proper address (as determined under subsection (2)) as the one at which he or someone on his behalf will accept documents of the same description as that document.

(5) In relation to that document, that address shall be treated as his proper address for the purposes of this section and section 7 of the Interpretation Act 1978 in its application to this section, instead of that determined under subsection (2).

(6) Any notice in writing or other document required or authorised by virtue of this Part to be served on any person may be served on that person by transmitting the text of the notice

or other document to him by means of [an electronic communications network] or by other means but while in electronic form provided the text is received by that person in legible form and is capable of being used for subsequent reference.

(7) This section does not apply to any document if rules of court make provision about its service.

(8) In this section references to serving include references to similar expressions (such as giving or sending).

[3621]

NOTES

Sub-s (6): words in square brackets substituted by the Communications Act 2003, s 406, Sch 17, para 174(1), (2), as from 25 July 2003 (certain purposes), and as from 29 December 2003 (otherwise).

127 Associated persons

(1) Associated persons, and any bodies corporate which they or any of them control, shall be treated as one person—

(a) for the purpose of deciding under section 26 whether any two enterprises have been brought under common ownership or common control;

[(aa) for the purposes of section 58(2C); and]

(b) for the purpose of determining what activities are carried on by way of business by any one person so far as that question arises in connection with paragraph 13(2) of Schedule 8.

(2) Subsection (1) shall not exclude from section 26 any case which would otherwise fall within that section.

(3) A reference under section 22, 33, 45 or 62 (whether or not made by virtue of this section) may be framed so as to exclude from consideration, either altogether or for a specified purpose or to a specified extent, any matter which, apart from this section, would not have been taken into account on that reference.

(4) For the purposes of this section—

(a) any individual and that individual's spouse[, civil partner] or partner and any relative, or spouse[, civil partner] or partner of a relative, of that individual or of that individual's spouse[, civil partner] or partner;

(b) any person in his capacity as trustee of a settlement and the settlor or grantor and any person associated with the settlor or grantor;

(c) persons carrying on business in partnership and the spouse[, civil partner] or partner and relatives of any of them; or

(d) two or more persons acting together to secure or exercise control of a body of persons corporate or unincorporate or to secure control of any enterprise or assets,

shall be regarded as associated with one another.

(5) The reference in subsection (1) to bodies corporate which associated persons control shall be construed in accordance with section 26(3) and (4).

(6) In this section "relative" means a brother, sister, uncle, aunt, nephew, niece, lineal ancestor or descendant (the step-child of any person, or anyone adopted by a person, whether legally or otherwise, as his child being regarded as a relative or taken into account to trace a relationship in the same way as that person's child); and references to a spouse[, civil partner] or partner shall include a former spouse or partner.

[3622]

NOTES

Sub-s (1): para (aa) substituted for the original word "and" at the end of para (a) by the Communications Act 2003, s 375(3), as from 29 December 2003.

Sub-ss (4), (6): words in square brackets inserted by the Civil Partnership Act 2004, s 261(1), Sch 27, para 168, as from 5 December 2005.

Step-child: this includes relationships arising through civil partnerships; see the Civil Partnership Act 2004, ss 246, 247, Sch 21.

128 Supply of services and market for services etc

(1) References in this Part to the supply of services shall be construed in accordance with this section; and references in this Part to a market for services and other related expressions shall be construed accordingly.

(2) The supply of services does not include the provision of services under a contract of service or of apprenticeship whether it is express or implied and (if it is express) whether it is oral or in writing.

(3) The supply of services includes—
- (a) performing for gain or reward any activity other than the supply of goods;
- (b) rendering services to order;
- (c) the provision of services by making them available to potential users.

(4) The supply of services includes making arrangements for the use of computer software or for granting access to data stored in any form which is not readily accessible.

(5) The supply of services includes making arrangements by means of a relevant agreement (within the meaning of [paragraph 29 of Schedule 2 to the Telecommunications Act 1984]) for sharing the use of telecommunications apparatus.

(6) The supply of services includes permitting or making arrangements to permit the use of land in such circumstances as the Secretary of State may by order specify.

[3623]

NOTES

Sub-s (5): words in square brackets substituted by the Communications Act 2003, s 406, Sch 17, para 174(1), (3), as from 29 December 2003.

Orders: the Enterprise Act 2002 (Supply of Services) Order 2003, SI 2003/1594. This Order specifies the circumstances in which permitting or making arrangements to permit the use of land will be regarded as a supply of services for the purposes of this Part. The arrangements specified relate to permitting the use of caravan sites, car parks, bus stations, the Channel Tunnel System and railway stations and networks.

129 Other interpretation provisions

(1) In this Part, unless the context otherwise requires—

"action" includes omission; and references to the taking of action include references to refraining from action;

"agreement" means any agreement or arrangement, in whatever way and whatever form it is made, and whether it is, or is intended to be, legally enforceable or not;

"business" includes a professional practice and includes any other undertaking which is carried on for gain or reward or which is an undertaking in the course of which goods or services are supplied otherwise than free of charge;

"change of circumstances" includes any discovery that information has been supplied which is false or misleading in a material respect;

"Community law" means—
- (a) all the rights, powers, liabilities, obligations and restrictions from time to time created or arising by or under the Community Treaties; and
- (b) all the remedies and procedures from time to time provided for by or under the Community Treaties;

"consumer" means any person who is—
- (a) a person to whom goods are or are sought to be supplied (whether by way of sale or otherwise) in the course of a business carried on by the person supplying or seeking to supply them; or
- (b) a person for whom services are or are sought to be supplied in the course of a business carried on by the person supplying or seeking to supply them;

and who does not receive or seek to receive the goods or services in the course of a business carried on by him;

"customer" includes a customer who is not a consumer;

["the EC Merger Regulation" means Council Regulation (EC) No 139/2004 of 20th January 2004 on the control of concentrations between undertakings;]

"enactment" includes an Act of the Scottish Parliament, Northern Ireland legislation and an enactment comprised in subordinate legislation, and includes an enactment whenever passed or made;

"enterprise" means the activities, or part of the activities, of a business;

.....

"goods" includes buildings and other structures, and also includes ships, aircraft and hovercraft;
"modify" includes amend or repeal;
"notice" means notice in writing;
"price" includes any charge or fee (however described);
"subordinate legislation" has the same meaning as in the Interpretation Act 1978 (c 30) and also includes an instrument made under an Act of the Scottish Parliament and an instrument made under Northern Ireland legislation;
"subsidiary" has the meaning given by section 736 of the Companies Act 1985 (c 6);
"supply", in relation to the supply of goods, includes supply by way of sale, lease, hire or hire-purchase, and, in relation to buildings or other structures, includes the construction of them by a person for another person; and
"United Kingdom national" means an individual who is—

(a) a British citizen, a British overseas territories citizen, a British National (Overseas) or a British Overseas citizen;
(b) a person who under the British Nationality Act 1981 (c 61) is a British subject; or
(c) a British protected person within the meaning of that Act.

(2) For the purposes of this Part any two bodies corporate are interconnected if—

(a) one of them is a body corporate of which the other is a subsidiary; or
(b) both of them are subsidiaries of one and the same body corporate;

and in this Part "interconnected bodies corporate" shall be construed accordingly and "group of interconnected bodies corporate" means a group consisting of two or more bodies corporate all of whom are interconnected with each other.

(3) References in this Part to a person carrying on business include references to a person carrying on business in partnership with one or more other persons.

(4) Any duty to publish which is imposed on a person by this Part shall, unless the context otherwise requires, be construed as a duty on that person to publish in such manner as he considers appropriate for the purpose of bringing the matter concerned to the attention of those likely to be affected by it.

[3624]

NOTES

Sub-s (1): definition "the EC Merger Regulation" inserted, and definition omitted repealed, by the EC Merger Control (Consequential Amendments) Regulations 2004, SI 2004/1079, reg 2, Schedule, para 2(1), (25), as from 1 May 2004.

130 Index of defined expressions

In this Part, the expressions listed in the left-hand column have the meaning given by, or are to be interpreted in accordance with, the provisions listed in the right-hand column.

Expression	*Provision of this Act*
Action (and the taking of action)	Section 129(1)
Adverse public interest finding	Section 54(3)
Agreement	Section 129(1)
Anti-competitive outcome	Section 35(2)
[Broadcasting	Section 44(9)]
Business (and carrying on business)	Section 129(1) and (3)
Change of circumstances	Section 129(1)
The Commission	Section 273
Community law	Section 129(1)
Consumer	Section 129(1)
Customer	Section 129(1)
Date of reference	Section 39(9)

Expression	*Provision of this Act*
The decision-making authority	Section 22(7)
[EC Merger Regulation	Section 129(1)]
Enactment	Section 129(1)
Enforcement order	Section 86(6)
Enforcement undertaking	Section 89(2)
Enterprise	Section 129(1)
Enterprises ceasing to be distinct	Section 26(1)
…	…
Final determination of matter to which intervention notice relates	Section 43(4) and (5)
Final determination of matter to which special intervention notice relates	Section 60(4) and (5)
Final determination of reference under section 22 or 33	Section 79(1) and (2)
Goods	Section 129(1)
Interconnected bodies corporate (and a group of interconnected bodies corporate)	Section 129(2)
Intervention notice	Section 42(2)
Market for goods or services	Section 22(6)
Market in the United Kingdom	Section 22(6)
[Media public interest consideration	Section 44(8)]
Merger notice	Section 96(2)
Modify	Section 129(1)
[Newspaper	Section 44(10)
[Newspaper enterprise	Section 58A(3)]
Notice	Section 129(1)
Notified arrangements	Section 96(6)
[OFCOM	Section 43(6)]
The OFT	Section 273
Orders under section 81	Section 81(6)
Orders under paragraph 2 of Schedule 7	Paragraph 2(7) of Schedule 7
The period for considering a merger notice	Sections 97 and 98
Price	Section 129(1)
Public interest consideration	Sections 42(3) and 67(9)
Public interest consideration being finalised	Section 42(8)
Publish	Section 129(4)
References under section 22, 33, 45 or 62	Sections 37(2), 49(1), 56(8) and 64(2)
Relevant customer benefit	Section 30
Relevant merger situation	Section 23 (as read with other enactments)
Reports of the Commission	Section 118(5)
Special intervention notice	Section 59(2)

PART III
OTHER LEGISLATION

Expression	Provision of this Act
Special merger situation	Section 59(3)
Subordinate legislation	Section 129(1)
Subsidiary	Section 129(1)
Supply (in relation to the supply of goods)	Section 129(1)
The supply of services (and a market for services etc)	Section 128
The turnover in the United Kingdom of an enterprise	Section 28(2)
Undertakings under section 80	Section 80(6)
Undertakings under paragraph 1 of Schedule 7	Paragraph 1(7) of Schedule 7
United Kingdom national	Section 129(1)

[3625]

NOTES

Entries "Broadcasting", "Media public interest consideration", "Newspaper", "Newspaper enterprise", and "OFCOM" inserted by the Communications Act 2003, s 389, Sch 16, para 25, as from 29 December 2003; entry "EC Merger Regulation" inserted, and entry omitted repealed, by the EC Merger Control (Consequential Amendments) Regulations 2004, SI 2004/1079, reg 2, Schedule, para 2(1), (26), as from 1 May 2004.

131–272 (*Ss 131–184 (Pt 4: Market Investigations), ss 185–187 (Pt 5: the Competition Commission), ss 188–202 (Pt 6: Cartel Offence), ss 203–209 (Pt 7: Miscellaneous Competition Provisions), ss 210–236 (Pt 8 Enforcement of certain consumer legislation), ss 237–247 (Pt 9: Information) outside the scope of this work; ss 248–272 (Pt 10: Insolvency) these sections are mostly amending and, in so far as the amendments are relevant to this work, they have been incorporated in the appropriate place (see the Insolvency Act 1986 at* **[3152]** *et seq). Note also s 254, which provides that the Secretary of State may by order provide for any provision of the Insolvency Act 1986 to apply (with or without modification) in relation to a company incorporated outside Great Britain.*)

PART 11
SUPPLEMENTARY

273 Interpretation

In this Act—

"the 1973 Act" means the Fair Trading Act 1973 (c 41);
"the 1998 Act" means the Competition Act 1998 (c 41);
"the Commission" means the Competition Commission;
"the Director" means the Director General of Fair Trading; and
"the OFT" means the Office of Fair Trading.

[3625A]

274, 275 (*Outside the scope of this work.*)

276 Transitional or transitory provisions and savings

(1) Schedule 24 (which makes transitional and transitory provisions and savings) has effect.

(2) The Secretary of State may by order made by statutory instrument make such transitional or transitory provisions and savings as he considers appropriate in connection with the coming into force of any provision of this Act.

(3) An order under subsection (2) may modify any Act or subordinate legislation.

(4) Schedule 24 does not restrict the power under subsection (2) to make other transitional or transitory provisions and savings.

[3625B]

NOTES

Orders: the Enterprise Act 2002 (Commencement No 2, Transitional and Transitory Provisions) Order 2003, SI 2003/766; the Enterprise Act 2002 (Commencement No 3, Transitional and Transitory Provisions and Savings) Order 2003, SI 2003/1397; the Enterprise Act 2002 (Part 8 Designated Enforcers: Criteria for Designation, Designation of Public Bodies as Designated Enforcers and Transitional Provisions) Order 2003, SI 2003/1399; the Enterprise Act 2002 (Commencement No 4 and Transitional Provisions and Savings) Order 2003. SI 2003/2093; the Enterprise Act 2002 (Transitional Provisions) (Insolvency) Order 2003, SI 2003/2332; the Enterprise Act 2002 (Commencement No 7 and Transitional Provisions and Savings) Order 2004, SI 2004/3233.

277, 278 (*Outside the scope of this work.*)

279 Commencement

The preceding provisions of this Act shall come into force on such day as the Secretary of State may by order made by statutory instrument appoint; and different days may be appointed for different purposes.

[3626]

NOTES

Orders: the Enterprise Act 2002 (Commencement No 1) Order 2003, SI 2003/765; the Enterprise Act 2002 (Commencement No 2, Transitional and Transitory Provisions) Order 2003, SI 2003/766; the Enterprise Act 2002 (Commencement No 3, Transitional and Transitory Provisions and Savings) Order 2003, SI 2003/1397; the Enterprise Act 2002 (Commencement No 4 and Transitional Provisions and Savings) Order 2003, SI 2003/2093; the Enterprise Act (Commencement No 5 and Amendment) Order 2003, SI 2003/3340; the Enterprise Act 2002 (Commencement No 6) Order 2004, SI 2004/1866; the Enterprise Act 2002 (Commencement No 7 and Transitional Provisions and Savings) Order 2004, SI 2004/3233.

280 Extent

(1) Sections 256 to 265, 267, 269 and 272 extend only to England and Wales.

(2) Sections 204, 248 to 255 and 270 extend only to England and Wales and Scotland (but subsection (3) of section 415A as inserted by section 270 extends only to England and Wales).

(3) Any other modifications by this Act of an enactment have the same extent as the enactment being modified.

(4) Otherwise, this Act extends to England and Wales, Scotland and Northern Ireland.

[3627]

281 Short title

This Act may be cited as the Enterprise Act 2002.

[3628]

SCHEDULES

(*Schs 1–6 outside the scope of this work.*)

SCHEDULE 7
ENFORCEMENT REGIME FOR PUBLIC INTEREST AND SPECIAL PUBLIC INTEREST CASES

Section 85

Pre-emptive undertakings and orders

1.—(1) Sub-paragraph (2) applies where an intervention notice or special intervention notice is in force.

(2) The Secretary of State may, for the purpose of preventing pre-emptive action, accept from such of the parties concerned as he considers appropriate undertakings to take such action as he considers appropriate.

(3) Sub-paragraph (4) applies where an intervention notice is in force.

(4) The Secretary of State may, for the purpose of preventing pre-emptive action, adopt an undertaking accepted by the OFT under section 71 if the undertaking is still in force when the Secretary of State adopts it.

(5) An undertaking adopted under sub-paragraph (4)—
(a) shall continue in force, in accordance with its terms, when adopted;
(b) may be varied or superseded by an undertaking under this paragraph; and
(c) may be released by the Secretary of State.

(6) Any other undertaking under this paragraph—
(a) shall come into force when accepted;
(b) may be varied or superseded by another undertaking; and
(c) may be released by the Secretary of State.

(7) References in this Part to undertakings under this paragraph shall, unless the context otherwise requires, include references to undertakings adopted under this paragraph; and references to the acceptance or giving of undertakings under this paragraph shall be construed accordingly.

(8) An undertaking which is in force under this paragraph in relation to a reference or possible reference under section 45 or (as the case may be) 62 shall cease to be in force if an order under paragraph 2 or an undertaking under paragraph 3 comes into force in relation to that reference.

(9) An undertaking under this paragraph shall, if it has not previously ceased to be in force, cease to be in force when the intervention notice concerned or (as the case may be) special intervention notice concerned ceases to be in force.

(10) No undertaking shall be accepted by the Secretary of State under this paragraph before the making of a reference under section 45 or (as the case may be) 62 unless the undertaking relates to a relevant merger situation which has been, or may have been, created or (as the case may be) a special merger situation which has been, or may have been, created.

(11) The Secretary of State shall, as soon as reasonably practicable, consider any representations received by him in relation to varying or releasing an undertaking under this paragraph.

(12) In this paragraph and paragraph 2 "pre-emptive action" means action which might prejudice the reference or possible reference concerned under section 45 or (as the case may be) 62 or impede the taking of any action under this Part which may be justified by the Secretary of State's decisions on the reference.

2.—(1) Sub-paragraph (2) applies where an intervention notice or special intervention notice is in force.

(2) The Secretary of State or the OFT may by order, for the purpose of preventing pre-emptive action—
(a) prohibit or restrict the doing of things which the Secretary of State or (as the case may be) the OFT considers would constitute pre-emptive action;
(b) impose on any person concerned obligations as to the carrying on of any activities or the safeguarding of any assets;
(c) provide for the carrying on of any activities or the safeguarding of any assets either by the appointment of a person to conduct or supervise the conduct of any activities (on such terms and with such powers as may be specified or described in the order) or in any other manner;
(d) do anything which may be done by virtue of paragraph 19 of Schedule 8.

(3) Sub-paragraph (4) applies where an intervention notice is in force.

(4) The Secretary of State or the OFT may, for the purpose of preventing pre-emptive action, adopt an order made by the OFT under section 72 if the order is still in force when the Secretary of State or (as the case may be) the OFT adopts it.

(5) An order adopted under sub-paragraph (4)—
(a) shall continue in force, in accordance with its terms, when adopted; and
(b) may be varied or revoked by an order under this paragraph.

(6) Any other order under this paragraph—
(a) shall come into force at such time as is determined by or under the order; and

(b) may be varied or revoked by another order.

(7) References in this Part to orders under this paragraph shall, unless the context otherwise requires, include references to orders adopted under this paragraph; and references to the making of orders under this paragraph shall be construed accordingly.

(8) An order which is in force under this paragraph in relation to a reference or possible reference under section 45 or (as the case may be) 62 shall cease to be in force if an undertaking under paragraph 1 or 3 comes into force in relation to that reference.

(9) An order under this paragraph shall, if it has not previously ceased to be in force, cease to be in force when the intervention notice concerned or (as the case may be) special intervention notice concerned ceases to be in force.

(10) No order shall be made by the Secretary of State or the OFT under this paragraph before the making of a reference under section 45 or (as the case may be) 62 unless the order relates to a relevant merger situation which has been, or may have been, created or (as the case may be) a special merger situation which has been, or may have been, created.

(11) The Secretary of State or (as the case may be) the OFT shall, as soon as reasonably practicable, consider any representations received by that person in relation to varying or revoking an order under this paragraph.

Undertakings in lieu of reference under section 45 or 62

3.—(1) Sub-paragraph (2) applies if the Secretary of State has power to make a reference to the Commission under section 45 or 62 and otherwise intends to make such a reference.

(2) The Secretary of State may, instead of making such a reference and for the purpose of remedying, mitigating or preventing any of the effects adverse to the public interest which have or may have resulted, or which may be expected to result, from the creation of the relevant merger situation concerned or (as the case may be) the special merger situation concerned, accept from such of the parties concerned as he considers appropriate undertakings to take such action as he considers appropriate.

(3) In proceeding under sub-paragraph (2), the Secretary of State shall, in particular—

(a) accept the decisions of the OFT included in its report under section 44 so far as they relate to the matters mentioned in subsections (4) and (5) of that section; or

(b) (as the case may be) accept the decisions of the OFT included in its report under section 61 so far as they relate to the matters mentioned in subsections (3)(a) and (4) of that section.

(4) In proceeding under sub-paragraph (2) in relation to an anti-competitive outcome, the Secretary of State may, in particular, have regard to the effect of any action on any relevant customer benefits in relation to the creation of the relevant merger situation concerned.

(5) No undertaking shall be accepted by the Secretary of State under this paragraph in connection with a possible reference under section 45 if a public interest consideration mentioned in the intervention notice concerned has not been finalised and the period of 24 weeks beginning with the giving of that notice has not expired.

(6) The Secretary of State may delay making a decision as to whether to accept any such undertaking (and any related decision as to whether to make a reference under section 45) if he considers that there is a realistic prospect of the public interest consideration being finalised within the period of 24 weeks beginning with the giving of the intervention notice concerned.

(7) A delay under sub-paragraph (6) shall not extend beyond—

(a) the time when the public interest consideration is finalised; or

(b) if earlier, the expiry of the period of 24 weeks mentioned in that sub-paragraph.

(8) An undertaking under this paragraph—

(a) shall come into force when accepted;

(b) may be varied or superseded by another undertaking; or

(c) may be released by the Secretary of State.

(9) An undertaking under this paragraph which is in force in relation to a relevant merger situation or (as the case may be) a special merger situation shall cease to be in force if an order comes into force under paragraph 5 or 6 in relation to that undertaking.

PART III
OTHER LEGISLATION

(10) The Secretary of State shall, as soon as reasonably practicable, consider any representations received by him in relation to varying or releasing an undertaking under this section.

4.—(1) The relevant authority shall not make a reference under section 22, 33 or 45 in relation to the creation of a relevant merger situation or (as the case may be) a reference under section 62 in relation to the creation of a special merger situation if—

(a) the Secretary of State has accepted an undertaking or group of undertakings under paragraph 3; and

(b) the relevant merger situation or (as the case may be) the special merger situation is the situation by reference to which the undertaking or group of undertakings was accepted.

(2) In sub-paragraph (1) "the relevant authority" means—

(a) in relation to a possible reference under section 22 or 33, the OFT; and

(b) in relation to a possible reference under section 45 or 62, the Secretary of State.

(3) Sub-paragraph (1) does not prevent the making of a reference if material facts about relevant arrangements or transactions, or relevant proposed arrangements or transactions, were not notified (whether in writing or otherwise) to the Secretary of State or the OFT or made public before any undertaking concerned was accepted.

(4) For the purposes of sub-paragraph (3) arrangements or transactions, or proposed arrangements or transactions, are relevant if they are the ones in consequence of which the enterprises concerned ceased or may have ceased, or may cease, to be distinct enterprises.

(5) In sub-paragraph (3) "made public" means so publicised as to be generally known or readily ascertainable.

5.—(1) Sub-paragraph (2) applies where the Secretary of State considers that—

(a) an undertaking accepted by him under paragraph 3 has not been, is not being or will not be fulfilled; or

(b) in relation to an undertaking accepted by him under that paragraph, information which was false or misleading in a material respect was given to him or the OFT by the person giving the undertaking before he decided to accept the undertaking.

(2) The Secretary of State may, for any of the purposes mentioned in paragraph 3(2), make an order under this paragraph.

(3) Sub-paragraphs (3) and (4) of paragraph 3 shall apply for the purposes of sub-paragraph (2) above as they apply for the purposes of sub-paragraph (2) of that paragraph.

(4) An order under this paragraph may contain—

(a) anything permitted by Schedule 8; and

(b) such supplementary, consequential or incidental provision as the Secretary of State considers appropriate.

(5) An order under this paragraph

(a) shall come into force at such time as is determined by or under the order; and

(b) may contain provision which is different from the provision contained in the undertaking concerned.

(6) No order shall be varied or revoked under this paragraph unless the OFT advises that such a variation or revocation is appropriate by reason of a change of circumstances.

6.—(1) Sub-paragraph (2) applies where—

(a) the Secretary of State has the power to make an order under paragraph 5 in relation to a particular undertaking and intends to make such an order; or

(b) the Secretary of State has the power to make an order under paragraph 10 in relation to a particular undertaking and intends to make such an order.

(2) The Secretary of State may, for the purpose of preventing any action which might prejudice the making of that order, make an order under this paragraph.

(3) No order shall be made under sub-paragraph (2) unless the Secretary of State has reasonable grounds for suspecting that it is or may be the case that action which might prejudice the making of the order under paragraph 5 or (as the case may be) 10 is in progress or in contemplation.

(4) An order under sub-paragraph (2) may—

(a) prohibit or restrict the doing of things which the Secretary of State considers would prejudice the making of the order under paragraph 5 or 10;

(b) impose on any person concerned obligations as to the carrying on of any activities or the safeguarding of any assets;

(c) provide for the carrying on of any activities or the safeguarding of any assets either by the appointment of a person to conduct or supervise the conduct of any activities (on such terms and with such powers as may be specified or described in the order) or in any other manner;

(d) do anything which may be done by virtue of paragraph 19 of Schedule 8.

(5) An order under this paragraph shall come into force at such time as is determined by or under the order.

(6) An order under this paragraph shall, if it has not previously ceased to be in force, cease to be in force on—

(a) the coming into force of an order under paragraph 5 or (as the case may be) 10 in relation to the undertaking concerned; or

(b) the making of the decision not to proceed with such an order.

(7) The Secretary of State shall, as soon as reasonably practicable, consider any representations received by him in relation to varying or revoking an order under this paragraph.

Statutory restrictions following reference under section 45 or 62

7.—(1) Sub-paragraphs (2) and (3) apply where—

(a) a reference has been made under section 45(2) or (3) or 62(2) but not finally determined; and

(b) no undertakings under paragraph 1 are in force in relation to the relevant merger situation concerned or (as the case may be) the special merger situation concerned and no orders under paragraph 2 are in force in relation to that situation.

(2) No relevant person shall, without the consent of the Secretary of State—

(a) complete any outstanding matters in connection with any arrangements which have resulted in the enterprises concerned ceasing to be distinct enterprises;

(b) make any further arrangements in consequence of that result (other than arrangements which reverse that result); or

(c) transfer the ownership or control of any enterprises to which the reference relates.

(3) No relevant person shall, without the consent of the Secretary of State, assist in any of the activities mentioned in paragraphs (a) to (c) of sub-paragraph (2).

(4) The prohibitions in sub-paragraphs (2) and (3) do not apply in relation to anything which the person concerned is required to do by virtue of any enactment.

(5) The consent of the Secretary of State under sub-paragraph (2) or (3)—

(a) may be general or specific;

(b) may be revoked by the Secretary of State; and

(c) shall be published in such manner as the Secretary of State considers appropriate for bringing it to the attention of any person entitled to the benefit of it.

(6) Paragraph (c) of sub-paragraph (5) shall not apply if the Secretary of State considers that publication is not necessary for the purpose mentioned in that paragraph.

(7) Sub-paragraphs (2) and (3) shall apply to a person's conduct outside the United Kingdom if (and only if) he is—

(a) a United Kingdom national;

(b) a body incorporated under the law of the United Kingdom or of any part of the United Kingdom; or

(c) a person carrying on business in the United Kingdom.

(8) For the purpose of this paragraph a reference under section 45(2) or (3) is finally determined if—

(a) the time within which the Commission is to prepare a report under section 50 in relation to the reference and give it to the Secretary of State has expired and no such report has been so prepared and given;

(b) the Commission decides to cancel the reference under section 53(1);

(c) the time within which the Secretary of State is to make and publish a decision under section 54(2) has expired and no such decision has been made and published;
(d) the Secretary of State decides under section 54(2) to make no finding at all in the matter;
(e) the Secretary of State otherwise decides under section 54(2) not to make an adverse public interest finding;
(f) the Secretary of State decides under section 54(2) to make an adverse public interest finding but decides neither to accept an undertaking under paragraph 9 of this Schedule nor to make an order under paragraph 11 of this Schedule; or
(g) the Secretary of State decides under section 54(2) to make an adverse public interest finding and accepts an undertaking under paragraph 9 of this Schedule or makes an order under paragraph 11 of this Schedule.

(9) For the purpose of this paragraph a reference under section 62(2) is finally determined if—
(a) the time within which the Commission is to prepare a report under section 65 in relation to the reference and give it to the Secretary of State has expired and no such report has been so prepared and given;
(b) the time within which the Secretary of State is to make and publish a decision under section 66(2) has expired and no such decision has been made and published;
(c) the Secretary of State decides under subsection (2) of section 66 otherwise than as mentioned in subsection (5) of that section;
(d) the Secretary of State decides under subsection (2) of section 66 as mentioned in subsection (5) of that section but decides neither to accept an undertaking under paragraph 9 of this Schedule nor to make an order under paragraph 11 of this Schedule; or
(e) the Secretary of State decides under subsection (2) of section 66 as mentioned in subsection (5) of that section and accepts an undertaking under paragraph 9 of this Schedule or makes an order under paragraph 11 of this Schedule.

(10) For the purposes of this paragraph the time when a reference under section 45(2) or (3) or (as the case may be) 62(2) is finally determined is—
(a) in a case falling within sub-paragraph (8)(a) or (c) or (as the case may be) (9)(a) or (b), the expiry of the time concerned;
(b) in a case falling within sub-paragraph (8)(b), (d) or (e) or (as the case may be) (9)(c), the making of the decision concerned;
(c) in a case falling within sub-paragraph (8)(f) or (as the case may be) (9)(d), the making of the decision neither to accept an undertaking under paragraph 9 of this Schedule nor to make an order under paragraph 11 of this Schedule; and
(d) in a case falling within sub-paragraph (8)(g) or (as the case may be) (9)(e), the acceptance of the undertaking concerned or (as the case may be) the making of the order concerned.

(11) In this paragraph "relevant person" means—
(a) any person who carries on any enterprise to which the reference relates or who has control of any such enterprise;
(b) any subsidiary of any person falling within paragraph (a); or
(c) any person associated with any person falling within paragraph (a) or any subsidiary of any person so associated.

8.—(1) Sub-paragraph (2) applies where—
(a) a reference has been made under section 45(4) or (5) or 62(3); and
(b) no undertakings under paragraph 1 are in force in relation to the relevant merger situation concerned or (as the case may be) special merger situation concerned and no orders under paragraph 2 are in force in relation to that situation.

(2) No relevant person shall, without the consent of the Secretary of State, directly or indirectly acquire during the relevant period an interest in shares in a company if any enterprise to which the reference relates is carried on by or under the control of that company.

(3) The consent of the Secretary of State under sub-paragraph (2)—
(a) may be general or specific;
(b) may be revoked by the Secretary of State; and
(c) shall be published in such manner as the Secretary of State considers appropriate for bringing it to the attention of any person entitled to the benefit of it.

(4) Paragraph (c) of sub-paragraph (3) shall not apply if the Secretary of State considers that publication is not necessary for the purpose mentioned in that paragraph.

(5) Sub-paragraph (2) shall apply to a person's conduct outside the United Kingdom if (and only if) he is—

(a) a United Kingdom national;

(b) a body incorporated under the law of the United Kingdom or of any part of the United Kingdom; or

(c) a person carrying on business in the United Kingdom.

(6) In this paragraph—

"company" includes any body corporate;

"relevant period" means the period beginning with the publication of the decision of the Secretary of State to make the reference concerned and ending when the reference is finally determined;

"relevant person" means—

(a) any person who carries on any enterprise to which the reference relates or who has control of any such enterprise;

(b) any subsidiary of any person falling within paragraph (a); or

(c) any person associated with any person falling within paragraph (a) or any subsidiary of any person so associated; and

"share" means share in the capital of a company, and includes stock.

(7) For the purposes of the definition of "relevant period" in sub-paragraph (6), a reference under section 45(4) or (5) is finally determined if—

(a) the Commission cancels the reference under section 48(1) or 53(1);

(b) the time within which the Commission is to prepare a report under section 50 in relation to the reference and give it to the Secretary of State has expired and no such report has been so prepared and given;

(c) the time within which the Secretary of State is to make and publish a decision under section 54(2) has expired and no such decision has been made and published;

(d) the Secretary of State decides under section 54(2) to make no finding at all in the matter;

(e) the Secretary of State otherwise decides under section 54(2) not to make an adverse public interest finding;

(f) the Secretary of State decides under section 54(2) to make an adverse public interest finding but decides neither to accept an undertaking under paragraph 9 of this Schedule nor to make an order under paragraph 11 of this Schedule; or

(g) the Secretary of State decides under section 54(2) to make an adverse public interest finding and accepts an undertaking under paragraph 9 of this Schedule or makes an order under paragraph 11 of this Schedule.

(8) For the purposes of the definition of "relevant period" in sub-paragraph (6), a reference under section 62(3) is finally determined if—

(a) the Commission cancels the reference under section 64(1);

(b) the time within which the Commission is to prepare a report under section 65 in relation to the reference and give it to the Secretary of State has expired and no such report has been so prepared and given;

(c) the time within which the Secretary of State is to make and publish a decision under section 66(2) has expired and no such decision has been made and published;

(d) the Secretary of State decides under subsection (2) of section 66 otherwise than as mentioned in subsection (5) of that section;

(e) the Secretary of State decides under subsection (2) of section 66 as mentioned in subsection (5) of that section but decides neither to accept an undertaking under paragraph 9 of this Schedule nor to make an order under paragraph 11 of this Schedule; or

(f) the Secretary of State decides under subsection (2) of section 66 as mentioned in subsection (5) of that section and accepts an undertaking under paragraph 9 of this Schedule or makes an order under paragraph 11 of this Schedule.

(9) For the purposes of the definition of "relevant period" in sub-paragraph (6) above, the time when a reference under section 45(4) or (5) or (as the case may be) 62(3) is finally determined is—

(a) in a case falling within sub-paragraph (7)(a), (d) or (e) or (as the case may be) (8)(a) or (d), the making of the decision concerned;

(b) in a case falling within sub-paragraph (7)(b) or (c) or (as the case may be) (8)(b) or (c), the expiry of the time concerned;

(c) in a case falling within sub-paragraph (7)(f) or (as the case may be) (8)(e), the making of the decision neither to accept an undertaking under paragraph 9 of this Schedule nor to make an order under paragraph 11 of this Schedule; and

(d) in a case falling within sub-paragraph (7)(g) or (as the case may be) (8)(f), the acceptance of the undertaking concerned or (as the case may be) the making of the order concerned.

(10) Section 79 shall apply for the purposes of paragraph 7 and this paragraph in relation to a reference under section 45 or 62 as it applies for the purposes of sections 77 and 78 in relation to a reference under section 22 or 33.

(11) In its application by virtue of sub-paragraph (10) section 79 shall have effect as if—

(a) subsections (1) and (2) were omitted; and

(b) for the reference in subsection (4) to the OFT there were substituted a reference to the Secretary of State.

Final undertakings and orders

9.—(1) The Secretary of State may, in accordance with section 55 or (as the case may be) 66(5) to (7), accept, from such persons as he considers appropriate, undertakings to take action specified or described in the undertakings.

(2) An undertaking under this paragraph—

(a) shall come into force when accepted;

(b) may be varied or superseded by another undertaking; and

(c) may be released by the Secretary of State.

(3) An undertaking which is in force under this paragraph in relation to a reference under section 45 or 62 shall cease to be in force if an order under paragraph 6(1)(b) or 10 comes into force in relation to the subject-matter of the undertaking.

(4) No undertaking shall be accepted under this paragraph in relation to a reference under section 45 or 62 if an order has been made under—

(a) paragraph 6(1)(b) or 10 in relation to the subject-matter of the undertaking; or

(b) paragraph 11 in relation to that reference.

(5) The Secretary of State shall, as soon as reasonably practicable, consider any representations received by him in relation to varying or releasing an undertaking under this section.

10.—(1) Sub-paragraph (2) applies where the Secretary of State considers that—

(a) an undertaking accepted by him under paragraph 9 has not been, is not being or will not be fulfilled; or

(b) in relation to an undertaking accepted by him under that paragraph, information which was false or misleading in a material respect was given to him or the OFT by the person giving the undertaking before he decided to accept the undertaking.

(2) The Secretary of State may, for any purpose mentioned in section 55(2) or (as the case may be) 66(6), make an order under this paragraph.

(3) Subsections (3) and (4) of section 55 or (as the case may be) subsection (7) of section 66 shall apply for the purposes of sub-paragraph (2) above as they or it applies for the purposes of section 55(2) or (as the case may be) 66(6).

(4) An order under this paragraph may contain—

(a) anything permitted by Schedule 8; and

(b) such supplementary, consequential or incidental provision as the Secretary of State considers appropriate.

(5) An order under this paragraph—

(a) shall come into force at such time as is determined by or under the order; and

(b) may contain provision which is different from the provision contained in the undertaking concerned.

(6) No order shall be varied or revoked under this paragraph unless the OFT advises that such a variation or revocation is appropriate by reason of a change of circumstances.

11.—(1) The Secretary of State may, in accordance with section 55 or (as the case may be) 66(5) to (7), make an order under this paragraph.

(2) An order under this paragraph may contain—

(a) anything permitted by Schedule 8; and

(b) such supplementary, consequential or incidental provision as the Secretary of State considers appropriate.

(3) An order under this paragraph shall come into force at such time as is determined by or under the order.

(4) No order shall be made under this paragraph in relation to a reference under section 45 or (as the case may be) 62 if an undertaking has been accepted under paragraph 9 in relation to that reference.

(5) No order shall be varied or revoked under this paragraph unless the OFT advises that such a variation or revocation is appropriate by reason of a change of circumstances.

[3629]

SCHEDULE 8
PROVISION THAT MAY BE CONTAINED IN CERTAIN ENFORCEMENT ORDERS

Section 86(4)

Introductory

1. This Schedule applies in relation to such orders, and to such extent, as is provided by this Part and Part 4 and any other enactment; and references in this Schedule to an order shall be construed accordingly.

General restrictions on conduct

2.—(1) An order may—

(a) prohibit the making or performance of an agreement;

(b) require any party to an agreement to terminate the agreement.

(2) An order made by virtue of sub-paragraph (1) shall not—

(a) prohibit the making or performance of; or

(b) require any person to terminate,

an agreement so far as, if made, the agreement would relate, or (as the case may be) so far as the agreement relates, to the terms and conditions of employment of any workers or to the physical conditions in which any workers are required to work.

3.—(1) An order may prohibit the withholding from any person of—

(a) any goods or services;

(b) any orders for any such goods or services.

(2) References in sub-paragraph (1) to withholding include references to—

(a) agreeing or threatening to withhold; and

(b) procuring others to withhold or to agree or threaten to withhold.

4. An order may prohibit requiring as a condition of the supply of goods or services to any person—

(a) the buying of any goods;

(b) the making of any payment in respect of services other than the goods or services supplied;

(c) the doing of any other such matter or the refraining from doing anything mentioned in paragraph (a) or (b) or any other such matter.

5. An order may prohibit—

(a) discrimination between persons in the prices charged for goods or services;

(b) anything which the relevant authority considers to be such discrimination;

(c) procuring others to do anything which is such discrimination or which the relevant authority considers to be such discrimination.

6. An order may prohibit—

(a) giving, or agreeing to give in other ways, any preference in respect of the supply of goods or services or in respect of the giving of orders for goods or services;
(b) giving, or agreeing to give in other ways, anything which the relevant authority considers to be a preference in respect of the supply of goods or services or in respect of the giving of orders for goods or services;
(c) procuring others to do anything mentioned in paragraph (a) or (b).

7. An order may prohibit—
(a) charging, for goods or services supplied, prices differing from those in any published list or notification;
(b) doing anything which the relevant authority considers to be charging such prices.

8.—(1) An order may regulate the prices to be charged for any goods or services.

(2) No order shall be made by virtue of sub-paragraph (1) unless the relevant report in relation to the matter concerned identifies the prices charged for the goods or services as requiring remedial action.

(3) In this paragraph "the relevant report" means the report of the Commission which is required by the enactment concerned before an order can be made under this Schedule.

9. An order may prohibit the exercise of any right to vote exercisable by virtue of the holding of any shares, stock or securities.

General obligations to be performed

10.—(1) An order may require a person to supply goods or services or to do anything which the relevant authority considers appropriate to facilitate the provision of goods or services.

(2) An order may require a person who is supplying, or is to supply, goods or services to supply such goods or services to a particular standard or in a particular manner or to do anything which the relevant authority considers appropriate to facilitate the provision of such goods or services to that standard or in that manner.

11. An order may require any activities to be carried on separately from any other activities.

Acquisitions and divisions

12.—(1) An order may prohibit or restrict—
(a) the acquisition by any person of the whole or part of the undertaking or assets of another person's business;
(b) the doing of anything which will or may result in two or more bodies corporate becoming interconnected bodies corporate.

(2) An order may require that if—
(a) an acquisition of the kind mentioned in sub-paragraph (1)(a) is made; or
(b) anything is done which results in two or more bodies corporate becoming interconnected bodies corporate;

the persons concerned or any of them shall observe any prohibitions or restrictions imposed by or under the order.

(3) This paragraph shall also apply to any result consisting in two or more enterprises ceasing to be distinct enterprises (other than any result consisting in two or more bodies corporate becoming interconnected bodies corporate).

13.—(1) An order may provide for—
(a) the division of any business (whether by the sale of any part of the undertaking or assets or otherwise);
(b) the division of any group of interconnected bodies corporate.

(2) For the purposes of sub-paragraph (1)(a) all the activities carried on by way of business by any one person or by any two or more interconnected bodies corporate may be treated as a single business.

(3) An order made by virtue of this paragraph may contain such provision as the relevant authority considers appropriate to effect or take account of the division, including, in particular, provision as to—

(a) the transfer or creation of property, rights, liabilities or obligations;

(b) the number of persons to whom the property, rights, liabilities or obligations are to be transferred or in whom they are to be vested;

(c) the time within which the property, rights, liabilities or obligations are to be transferred or vested;

(d) the adjustment of contracts (whether by discharge or reduction of any liability or obligation or otherwise);

(e) the creation, allotment, surrender or cancellation of any shares, stock or securities;

(f) the formation or winding up of any company or other body of persons corporate or unincorporate;

(g) the amendment of the memorandum and articles or other instruments regulating any such company or other body of persons;

(h) the extent to which, and the circumstances in which, provisions of the order affecting a company or other body of persons corporate or unincorporate in its share capital, constitution or other matters may be altered by the company or other body of persons concerned;

(i) the registration of the order under any enactment by a company or other body of persons corporate or unincorporate which is affected by it as mentioned in paragraph (h);

(j) the continuation, with any necessary change of parties, of any legal proceedings;

(k) the approval by the relevant authority or another person of anything required by virtue of the order to be done or of any person to whom anything is to be transferred, or in whom anything is to be vested, by virtue of the order; or

(l) the appointment of trustees or other persons to do anything on behalf of another person which is required of that person by virtue of the order or to monitor the doing by that person of any such thing.

14. The references in paragraph 13 to the division of a business as mentioned in sub-paragraph (1)(a) of that paragraph shall, in the case of an order under section 75, 83, 84, 160 or 161, or an order under paragraph 5, 10 or 11 of Schedule 7, be construed as including references to the separation, by the sale of any part of any undertaking or assets concerned or other means, of enterprises which are under common control (within the meaning of section 26) otherwise than by reason of their being enterprises of interconnected bodies corporate.

Supply and publication of information

15.—(1) An order may require a person supplying goods or services to publish a list of prices or otherwise notify prices.

(2) An order made by virtue of this paragraph may also require or prohibit the publication or other notification of further information.

16. An order may prohibit any person from notifying (whether by publication or otherwise) to persons supplying goods or services prices recommended or suggested as appropriate to be charged by those persons for those goods or services.

17.—(1) An order may require a person supplying goods or services to publish—

(a) accounting information in relation to the supply of the goods or services;

(b) information in relation to the quantities of goods or services supplied;

(c) information in relation to the geographical areas in which they are supplied.

(2) In sub-paragraph (1) "accounting information", in relation to a supply of goods or services, means information as to—

(a) the costs of the supply, including fixed costs and overheads;

(b) the manner in which fixed costs and overheads are calculated and apportioned for accounting purposes of the supplier; and

(c) the income attributable to the supply.

18. An order made by virtue of paragraph 15 or 17 may provide for the manner in which information is to be published or otherwise notified.

19. An order may—

(a) require any person to supply information to the relevant authority;

(b) where the OFT is not the relevant authority, require any person to supply information to the OFT;
(c) provide for the publication, by the person who has received information by virtue of paragraph (a) or (b), of that information.

National security

20.—(1) An order may make such provision as the person making the order considers to be appropriate in the interests of national security (within the meaning of section 58(1)).

(2) Such provision may, in particular, include provision requiring a person to do, or not to do, particular things.

[Newspaper mergers

20A.—(1) This paragraph applies in relation to any order—
(a) which is to be made following the giving of—
(i) an intervention notice which mentions a newspaper public interest consideration;
(ii) an intervention notice which mentions any other media public interest consideration in relation to a relevant merger situation in which one of the enterprises ceasing to be distinct is a newspaper enterprise;
(iii) a special intervention notice which mentions a consideration specified in section 58(2A) or (2B); or
(iv) a special intervention notice which, in relation to a special merger situation in which one of the enterprises ceasing to be distinct is a newspaper enterprise, mentions a consideration specified in section 58(2C); and
(b) to which the consideration concerned is still relevant.

(2) The order may make such provision as the person making the order considers to be appropriate in all circumstances of the case.

(3) Such provision may, in particular, include provision requiring a person to do, or not to do, particular things.

(4) Provision made by virtue of this paragraph may, in particular, include provision—
(a) altering the constitution of a body corporate (whether in connection with the appointment of directors, the establishment of an editorial board or otherwise);
(b) requiring the agreement of the relevant authority or another person before the taking of particular action (including the appointment or dismissal of an editor, journalists or directors or acting as a shadow director);
(c) attaching conditions to the operation of a newspaper;
(d) prohibiting consultation or co-operation between subsidiaries.

(5) In this paragraph 'newspaper public interest consideration' means a media public interest consideration other than one which is such a consideration—
(a) by virtue of section 58(2C); or
(b) by virtue of having been, in the opinion of the Secretary of State, concerned with broadcasting and a consideration that ought to have been specified in section 58.

(6) This paragraph is without prejudice to the operation of the other paragraphs of this Schedule in relation to the order concerned.]

Supplementary

21.—(1) An order, as well as making provision in relation to all cases to which it may extend, may make provision in relation to—
(a) those cases subject to specified exceptions; or
(b) any particular case or class of case.

(2) An order may, in relation to the cases in relation to which it applies, make the full provision which may be made by it or any less provision (whether by way of exception or otherwise).

(3) An order may make provision for matters to be determined under the order.

(4) An order may—

(a) make different provision for different cases or classes of case or different purposes;
(b) make such transitional, transitory or saving provision as the person making it considers appropriate.

22.—(1) An order which may prohibit the doing of anything (or the refraining from doing anything) may in particular by virtue of paragraph 21(2) prohibit the doing of that thing (or the refraining from doing of it) except to such extent and in such circumstances as may be provided by or under the order.

(2) Any such order may, in particular, prohibit the doing of that thing (or the refraining from doing of it)—
(a) without the agreement of the relevant authority or another person; or
(b) by or in relation to a person who has not been approved by the relevant authority or another person.

Interpretation

23. References in this Schedule to the notification of prices or other information are not limited to the notification in writing of prices or other information.

24. In this Schedule "the relevant authority" means—
(a) in the case of an order to be made by the OFT, the OFT;
(b) in the case of an order to be made by the Commission, the Commission; and
(c) in the case of an order to be made by the Secretary of State, the Secretary of State.
[3630]

NOTES

Para 20A: inserted by the Communications Act 2003, s 387, as from 29 December 2003.

(*Sch 9 outside the scope of this work.*)

SCHEDULE 10
PROCEDURAL REQUIREMENTS FOR CERTAIN ENFORCEMENT UNDERTAKINGS AND ORDERS

Section 90

Requirements for accepting undertakings and making orders

1. Paragraph 2 applies in relation to—
(a) any undertaking under section 73 or 82 or paragraph 3 or 9 of Schedule 7 (other than an undertaking under the enactment concerned which varies an undertaking under that enactment but not in any material respect); and
(b) any order under section 75, 83 or 84 or paragraph 5, 10 or 11 of Schedule 7 (other than an order under the enactment concerned which is a revoking order of the kind dealt with by paragraphs 6 to 8 below).

2.—(1) Before accepting an undertaking to which this paragraph applies or making an order to which this paragraph applies, the OFT, the Commission or (as the case may be) the Secretary of State (in this Schedule "the relevant authority") shall—
(a) give notice of the proposed undertaking or (as the case may be) order; and
(b) consider any representations made in accordance with the notice and not withdrawn.

(2) A notice under sub-paragraph (1) shall state—
(a) that the relevant authority proposes to accept the undertaking or (as the case may be) make the order;
(b) the purpose and effect of the undertaking or (as the case may be) order;
(c) the situation that the undertaking or (as the case may be) order is seeking to deal with;
(d) any other facts which the relevant authority considers justify the acceptance of the undertaking or (as the case may be) the making of the order;

PART III
OTHER LEGISLATION

(e) a means of gaining access to an accurate version of the proposed undertaking or (as the case may be) order at all reasonable times; and

(f) the period (not less than 15 days starting with the date of publication of the notice in the case of an undertaking and not less than 30 days starting with that date in the case of an order) within which representations may be made in relation to the proposed undertaking or (as the case may be) order.

(3) A notice under sub-paragraph (1) shall be given by—

(a) in the case of a proposed order, serving on any person identified in the order as a person on whom a copy of the order should be served a copy of the notice and a copy of the proposed order; and

(b) in every case, publishing the notice.

(4) The relevant authority shall not accept the undertaking with modifications or (as the case may be) make the order with modifications unless the relevant authority—

(a) gives notice of the proposed modifications; and

(b) considers any representations made in accordance with the notice and not withdrawn.

(5) A notice under sub-paragraph (4) shall state—

(a) the proposed modifications;

(b) the reasons for them; and

(c) the period (not less than 7 days starting with the date of the publication of the notice under sub-paragraph (4)) within which representations may be made in relation to the proposed modifications.

(6) A notice under sub-paragraph (4) shall be given by—

(a) in the case of a proposed order, serving a copy of the notice on any person identified in the order as a person on whom a copy of the order should be served; and

(b) in every case, publishing the notice.

3.—(1) If, after giving notice under paragraph 2(1) or (4), the relevant authority decides—

(a) not to accept the undertaking concerned or (as the case may be) make the order concerned; and

(b) not to proceed by virtue of paragraph 5;

the relevant authority shall give notice of that decision.

(2) A notice under sub-paragraph (1) shall be given by—

(a) in the case of a proposed order, serving a copy of the notice on any person identified in the order as a person on whom a copy of the order should be served; and

(b) in every case, publishing the notice.

4. As soon as practicable after accepting an undertaking to which paragraph 2 applies or (as the case may be) making an order to which that paragraph applies, the relevant authority shall (except in the case of an order which is a statutory instrument)—

(a) serve a copy of the undertaking on any person by whom it is given or (as the case may be) serve a copy of the order on any person identified in the order as a person on whom a copy of the order should be served; and

(b) publish the undertaking or (as the case may be) the order.

5.—(1) The requirements of paragraph 2(4) (and those of paragraph 2(1)) shall not apply if the relevant authority—

(a) has already given notice under paragraph 2(1) but not paragraph 2(4) in relation to the proposed undertaking or order; and

(b) considers that the modifications which are now being proposed are not material in any respect.

(2) The requirements of paragraph 2(4) (and those of paragraph 2(1)) shall not apply if the relevant authority—

(a) has already given notice under paragraphs 2(1) and (4) in relation to the matter concerned; and

(b) considers that the further modifications which are now being proposed do not differ in any material respect from the modifications in relation to which notice was last given under paragraph 2(4).

Termination of undertakings and orders

6. Paragraph 7 applies where the relevant authority is proposing to—
   (a) release any undertaking under section 73 or 82 or paragraph 3 or 9 of Schedule 7 (other than in connection with accepting an undertaking under the enactment concerned which varies or supersedes an undertaking under that enactment); or
   (b) revoke any order under section 75, 83 or 84 or paragraph 5, 10 or 11 of Schedule 7 (other than in connection with making an order under the enactment concerned which varies or supersedes an order under that enactment).

7.—(1) Before releasing an undertaking to which this paragraph applies or (as the case may be) revoking an order to which this paragraph applies, the relevant authority shall—
   (a) give notice of the proposed release or (as the case may be) revocation; and
   (b) consider any representations made in accordance with the notice and not withdrawn.

(2) A notice under sub-paragraph (1) shall state—
   (a) the fact that a release or (as the case may be) revocation is proposed;
   (b) the reasons for it; and
   (c) the period (not less than 15 days starting with the date of publication of the notice in the case of an undertaking and not less than 30 days starting with that date in the case of an order) within which representations may be made in relation to the proposed release or (as the case may be) revocation.

(3) If after giving notice under sub-paragraph (1) the relevant authority decides not to proceed with the release or (as the case may be) the revocation, the relevant authority shall give notice of that decision.

(4) A notice under sub-paragraph (1) or (3) shall be given by—
   (a) serving a copy of the notice on the person who gave the undertaking which is being released or (as the case may be) on any person identified in the order being revoked as a person on whom a copy of the order should be served; and
   (b) publishing the notice.

8. As soon as practicable after releasing the undertaking or making the revoking order, the relevant authority shall (except in the case of an order which is a statutory instrument)—
   (a) serve a copy of the release of the undertaking on the person who gave the undertaking or (as the case may be) serve a copy of the revoking order on any person identified in the order being revoked as a person on whom a copy of that order should be served; and
   (b) publish the release or (as the case may be) the revoking order.

Power to dispense with the requirements of the Schedule

9. The relevant authority may dispense with any or all of the requirements of this Schedule if the relevant authority considers that the relevant authority has special reasons for doing so.
[3631]

(*Schs 11–15 outside the scope of this work; Sch 16 inserts the Insolvency Act 1986, Sch B1 at* **[3469A]**; *Sch 17 contains minor and consequential amendments relating to administration and, in so far as relevant to this work, have been incorporated at the appropriate place; Sch 18 inserts the Insolvency Act 1986, Sch 2A at* **[3471A]**; *Schs 19–23 concern individual insolvency and are outside the scope of this work.*)

SCHEDULE 24
TRANSITIONAL AND TRANSITORY PROVISIONS AND SAVINGS

Section 276

1–12. (*Outside the scope of this work.*)

Merger references

13.—(1) Subject to paragraphs 15 to 18, the old law shall continue to apply where—
   (a) two or more enterprises have ceased to be distinct enterprises (within the meaning of Part 5 of the 1973 Act); and

PART III OTHER LEGISLATION

(b) the cessation has occurred before the appointed day.

(2) Subject to sub-paragraphs (3), (4) and (5) and paragraphs 15 to 18, the old law shall continue to apply in relation to any relevant arrangements which were in progress or in contemplation before the appointed day and are in progress or in contemplation on that day and (if events so require) the actual results of those arrangements where, before the appointed day—

(a) a merger notice was given, and not rejected under section 75B(7) of the 1973 Act or withdrawn, in relation to the arrangements;

(b) no merger notice was so given but, in relation to the arrangements—

(i) a reference was made under section 75 of the 1973 Act;

(ii) undertakings were accepted under section 75G of that Act; or

(iii) a decision was made by the Secretary of State neither to make a reference under section 75 of that Act nor to accept undertakings under section 75G of that Act; or

(c) a merger notice was so given, was rejected under section 75B(7) of the 1973 Act or withdrawn, paragraph (a) does not apply in relation to a different merger notice given in relation to the arrangements and, in relation to the arrangements, paragraph (b)(i), (ii) or (iii) applies.

(3) Subject to sub-paragraph (8), the new law shall, in a case of the kind mentioned in sub-paragraph (2)(a), apply in relation to any relevant arrangements and (if events so require) the actual results of those arrangements if, on or after the appointed day, a merger notice is rejected under section 75B(7) of the 1973 Act or withdrawn in relation to the arrangements.

(4) Subject to sub-paragraph (8), the new law shall, in a case of the kind mentioned in sub-paragraph (2)(a), apply in relation to any relevant arrangements and (if events so require) the actual results of those arrangements if—

(a) the making of a reference under section 64 or 75 of the 1973 Act in relation to those arrangements and (if events so require) the actual results of those arrangements was, immediately before the appointed day and by virtue of section 75C(1)(c), (e) or (g) of that Act, not prevented;

(b) the period for considering the merger notice has expired (whether before, on or after the appointed day); and

(c) no reference has been made under section 64 or 75 of the 1973 Act and no undertakings have been accepted under section 75G of that Act.

(5) Subject to sub-paragraph (8), the new law shall, in a case of the kind mentioned in sub-paragraph (2)(a), apply in relation to any relevant arrangements and (if events so require) the actual results of those arrangements if—

(a) the making of a reference under section 64 or 75 of the 1973 Act in relation to those arrangements and (if events so require) the actual results of those arrangements becomes, on or after the appointed day and by virtue of section 75C(1)(b), (c), (d), (e) or (g) of that Act, not prevented;

(b) the period for considering the merger notice has expired (whether before, on or after the appointed day); and

(c) no reference has been made under section 64 or 75 of the 1973 Act and no undertakings have been accepted under section 75G of that Act.

(6) Subject to sub-paragraph (8), the new law shall apply in relation to relevant arrangements and (if events so require) the actual results of those arrangements if—

(a) the arrangements were in progress or in contemplation before the appointed day and are in progress or in contemplation on that day;

(b) before the appointed day and in relation to the arrangements—

(i) no reference was made under section 75 of the 1973 Act;

(ii) no undertakings were accepted under section 75G of that Act; and

(iii) a decision neither to make a reference under section 75 of that Act nor to accept undertakings under section 75G of that Act was not made by the Secretary of State; and

(c) no merger notice was given to the Director or the OFT before that day in relation to the arrangements.

(7) Subject to sub-paragraph (8), the new law shall, in a case of the kind mentioned in sub-paragraph (2)(c) (excluding the words from "and" to the end), apply in relation to any relevant arrangements and (if events so require) the actual results of those arrangements if, in relation to the arrangements, sub-paragraph (2)(b)(i), (ii) and (iii) do not apply.

(8) Subject to paragraphs 15 to 18, the old law shall continue to apply in relation to concentrations with a Community dimension (within the meaning of the European Merger Regulations) notified before the appointed day to the European Commission under article 4 of those Regulations.

(9) In this paragraph references to relevant arrangements which are in progress or in contemplation on the appointed day include references to the actual results of those arrangements if the arrangements were in progress or in contemplation immediately before the appointed day and have, at the beginning of the appointed day, resulted in two or more enterprises ceasing to be distinct enterprises (within the meaning of Part 5 of the 1973 Act).

(10) In this paragraph—

"the European Merger Regulations" has the meaning given by section 129(1);

"merger notice" means a notice under section 75A(1) of the 1973 Act;

"the new law" means Part 3 of this Act and any related provision of law (including, in particular, any modification made under section 276(2) to that Part or any such provision);

"the old law" means sections 64 to 75K of the 1973 Act and any related provision of law (including, in particular, any modification made under section 276(2) to those sections or any such provision); and

"relevant arrangements" means arrangements which might result in two or more enterprises ceasing to be distinct enterprises (within the meaning of Part 5 of the 1973 Act).

14. (*Outside the scope of this work.*)

Enforcement undertakings and orders

15.—(1) Section 94(1) to (6) shall apply in relation to any undertaking—

(a) accepted (whether before, on or after the appointed day) by a Minister of the Crown—

(i) in pursuance of a proposal under section 56A of the 1973 Act; or

(ii) under section 56F, 75G or 88 of that Act; and

(b) of a description specified in an order made by the Secretary of State under this paragraph;

as it applies in relation to enforcement undertakings under Part 3.

(2) Section 94(1) to (6) shall apply in relation to any order made by a Minister of the Crown under section 56, 73, 74, 75K or 89 of the 1973 Act (whether before, on or after the appointed day) and of a description specified in an order made by the Secretary of State under this paragraph as it applies in relation to enforcement orders under Part 3.

(3) Compliance with—

(a) an undertaking accepted by a Minister of the Crown under section 88 of the 1973 Act (whether before, on or after the appointed day) and of a description specified in an order made by the Secretary of State under this paragraph; or

(b) an order made by a Minister of the Crown under section 56, 73, 74 or 89 of the 1973 Act (whether before, on or after the appointed day) and of a description specified in an order made by the Secretary of State under this paragraph;

shall also be enforceable by civil proceedings brought by the Commission for an injunction or for interdict or for any other appropriate relief or remedy.

(4) Sub-paragraph (3) and section 94(6) as applied by virtue of sub-paragraph (1) or (2) shall not prejudice any right that a person may have by virtue of section 94(4) as so applied to bring civil proceedings for contravention or apprehended contravention of an undertaking or order.

(5) Sections 93 and 93A of the 1973 Act shall accordingly cease to apply in relation to undertakings and orders to which sub-paragraphs (1) to (3) above apply.

16.—(1) Sub-paragraph (2) applies to any undertaking—

(a) accepted (whether before, on or after the appointed day) by a Minister of the Crown—

(i) in pursuance of a proposal under section 56A of the 1973 Act; or

(ii) under section 56F, 75G or 88 of that Act; and

(b) of a description specified in an order made by the Secretary of State under this paragraph.

PART III
OTHER LEGISLATION

(2) An undertaking to which this sub-paragraph applies may be—

(a) superseded by a new undertaking accepted by the relevant authority under this paragraph;

(b) varied by an undertaking accepted by the relevant authority under this paragraph; or

(c) released by the relevant authority.

(3) Subject to sub-paragraph (4) and any provision made under section 276(2), the power of the relevant authority under this paragraph to supersede, vary or release an undertaking is exercisable in the same circumstances, and on the same terms and conditions, as the power of the Minister concerned to supersede, vary or release the undertaking would be exercisable under the 1973 Act.

(4) The duty under section 75J(b) of the 1973 Act to give advice shall be a duty of the OFT to consider what action (if any) it should take.

(5) Where the relevant authority has the power by virtue of this paragraph to supersede, vary or release an undertaking accepted by a Minister of the Crown—

(a) in pursuance of a proposal under section 56A of the 1973 Act; or

(b) under section 56F, 75G or 88 of that Act;

the Minister concerned shall accordingly cease to have the power under that Act to supersede, vary or release the undertaking.

(6) In this paragraph "the relevant authority" means—

(a) in the case of an undertaking accepted in pursuance of a proposal under section 56A of the 1973 Act or an undertaking under section 56F or 75G of that Act, the OFT; and

(b) in the case of an undertaking accepted under section 88 of that Act, the Commission.

17.—(1) Any order made by a Minister of the Crown under section 56, 73, 74 or 89 of the 1973 Act (whether before, on or after the appointed day) and of a description specified in an order made by the Secretary of State under this paragraph may be varied or revoked by an order made by the Commission under this paragraph.

(2) Any order made by a Minister of the Crown under section 75K of the 1973 Act (whether before, on or after the appointed day) and of a description specified in an order made by the Secretary of State under this paragraph may be varied or revoked by an order made by the OFT under this paragraph.

(3) Subject to sub-paragraph (4) and any provision made under section 276(2), the power of the Commission to make an order under sub-paragraph (1), and the power of the OFT to make an order under sub-paragraph (2), is exercisable in the same circumstances, and on the same terms and conditions, as the power of the Minister concerned to make a corresponding varying or revoking order under the 1973 Act would be exercisable.

(4) The power of the Commission to make an order under sub-paragraph (1), and the power of the OFT to make an order under sub-paragraph (2), shall not be exercisable by statutory instrument and shall not be subject to the requirements of section 134(1) of the 1973 Act.

(5) Where the Commission or the OFT has the power by virtue of this paragraph to vary or revoke an order made by a Minister of the Crown under section 56, 73, 74, 75K or 89 of the 1973 Act, the Minister concerned shall accordingly cease to have the power to do so under that Act.

18.—(1) Section 94(1) to (6) shall apply in relation to undertakings accepted under paragraph 16 and orders made under paragraph 17 as it applies in relation to enforcement undertakings and enforcement orders under Part 3.

(2) Compliance with an undertaking accepted by the Commission under paragraph 16 or an order made by it under paragraph 17 shall also be enforceable by civil proceedings brought by the Commission for an injunction or for interdict or for any other appropriate relief or remedy.

(3) Sub-paragraph (2) and section 94(6) as applied by virtue of sub-paragraph (1) shall not prejudice any right that a person may have by virtue of section 94(4) as so applied to bring civil proceedings for contravention or apprehended contravention of an undertaking or order.

Paragraphs 13 to 18: supplementary provision

19.—(1) In paragraphs 13 to 18 "the appointed day" means such day as the Secretary of State may by order made by statutory instrument appoint; and different days may be appointed for different purposes.

(2) An order made by the Secretary of State under paragraph 15, 16 or 17—

(a) may make different provision for different purposes; and

(b) shall be made by statutory instrument which shall be subject to annulment in pursuance of a resolution of either House of Parliament.

20–22. (*Outside the scope of this work.*)

[3632]–[3633]

NOTES

Transitional provisions:

The Enterprise Act 2002 (Commencement No 3, Transitional and Transitory Provisions and Savings) Order 2003, SI 2003/1397, art 4(2) provides that the power of the decision-making authority under ss 27(5) or 29(1) of this Act (including those provisions as applied by any enactment) in relation to events or transactions is exercisable in relation to a merger which has occurred before the appointed day (20 June 2003) where the merger forms part of successive events or a series of transactions which include at least one event or transaction to which the new law applies. Art 4(3) of that Order further provides that where the decision-making authority exercises its power as mentioned above in relation to a merger which has occurred before the appointed day, para 13(1) of this Schedule shall cease to apply in relation to the merger.

See also the Enterprise Act 2002 (Commencement No 3, Transitional and Transitory Provisions and Savings) Order 2003, SI 2003/1397, art 3 for transitional provisions in relation to mergers of water or sewerage undertakers.

Orders: the Enterprise Act 2002 (Commencement No 3, Transitional and Transitory Provisions and Savings) Order 2003, SI 2003/1397 (specifying 20 June 2003 as the appointed day for the purposes of paras 13–18); the Enterprise Act 2002 (Enforcement Undertakings and Orders) Order 2004, SI 2004/2181; the Enterprise Act 2002 (Enforcement Undertakings) Order 2006, SI 2006/354; the Enterprise Act 2002 (Enforcement Undertakings and Orders) Order 2006, SI 2006/355; the Enterprise Act 2002 (Enforcement Undertakings) (No 2) Order 2006, SI 2006/3095

(Sch 25 contains minor and consequential amendments which, in so far as relevant to this work, have been incorporated at the appropriate place; Sch 26 contains repeals to specified provisions of (inter alia) the Fair Trading Act 1973, the Companies Consolidation (Consequential Provisions) Act 1985, the Insolvency Act 1986, the Companies Act 1989, and the Financial Services and Markets Act 2000 which, in so far as relevant to this work, have been incorporated at the appropriate place.)

FRAUD ACT 2006

(2006 c 35)

NOTES

As of 1 July 2007, this Act had not been amended. See, however, the prospective amendments made to s 9 (at **[3642]**) by the draft Companies Act 2006 (Commencement No 3, Consequential Amendments, Transitional Provisions and Savings) Order 2007 (see the draft Order in Appendix 12 at **[A12]**).

ARRANGEMENT OF SECTIONS

Fraud

An Act to make provision for, and in connection with, criminal liability for fraud and obtaining services dishonestly

[8 November 2006]

Fraud

1 Fraud

(1) A person is guilty of fraud if he is in breach of any of the sections listed in subsection (2) (which provide for different ways of committing the offence).

(2) The sections are—
- (a) section 2 (fraud by false representation),
- (b) section 3 (fraud by failing to disclose information), and
- (c) section 4 (fraud by abuse of position).

(3) A person who is guilty of fraud is liable—
- (a) on summary conviction, to imprisonment for a term not exceeding 12 months or to a fine not exceeding the statutory maximum (or to both);
- (b) on conviction on indictment, to imprisonment for a term not exceeding 10 years or to a fine (or to both).

(4) Subsection (3)(a) applies in relation to Northern Ireland as if the reference to 12 months were a reference to 6 months.

[3634]

NOTES

Commencement: 15 January 2007.

2 Fraud by false representation

(1) A person is in breach of this section if he—
- (a) dishonestly makes a false representation, and
- (b) intends, by making the representation—
  - (i) to make a gain for himself or another, or
  - (ii) to cause loss to another or to expose another to a risk of loss.

(2) A representation is false if—
- (a) it is untrue or misleading, and
- (b) the person making it knows that it is, or might be, untrue or misleading.

(3) "Representation" means any representation as to fact or law, including a representation as to the state of mind of—
- (a) the person making the representation, or
- (b) any other person.

(4) A representation may be express or implied.

(5) For the purposes of this section a representation may be regarded as made if it (or anything implying it) is submitted in any form to any system or device designed to receive, convey or respond to communications (with or without human intervention).

[3635]

NOTES
Commencement: 15 January 2007.

3 Fraud by failing to disclose information

A person is in breach of this section if he—

(a) dishonestly fails to disclose to another person information which he is under a legal duty to disclose, and
(b) intends, by failing to disclose the information—
  (i) to make a gain for himself or another, or
  (ii) to cause loss to another or to expose another to a risk of loss.

[3636]

NOTES
Commencement: 15 January 2007.

4 Fraud by abuse of position

(1) A person is in breach of this section if he—

(a) occupies a position in which he is expected to safeguard, or not to act against, the financial interests of another person,
(b) dishonestly abuses that position, and
(c) intends, by means of the abuse of that position—
  (i) to make a gain for himself or another, or
  (ii) to cause loss to another or to expose another to a risk of loss.

(2) A person may be regarded as having abused his position even though his conduct consisted of an omission rather than an act.

[3637]

NOTES
Commencement: 15 January 2007.

5 "Gain" and "loss"

(1) The references to gain and loss in sections 2 to 4 are to be read in accordance with this section.

(2) "Gain" and "loss"—

(a) extend only to gain or loss in money or other property;
(b) include any such gain or loss whether temporary or permanent;

and "property" means any property whether real or personal (including things in action and other intangible property).

(3) "Gain" includes a gain by keeping what one has, as well as a gain by getting what one does not have.

(4) "Loss" includes a loss by not getting what one might get, as well as a loss by parting with what one has.

[3638]

NOTES
Commencement: 15 January 2007.

6 Possession etc of articles for use in frauds

(1) A person is guilty of an offence if he has in his possession or under his control any article for use in the course of or in connection with any fraud.

(2) A person guilty of an offence under this section is liable—

(a) on summary conviction, to imprisonment for a term not exceeding 12 months or to a fine not exceeding the statutory maximum (or to both);
(b) on conviction on indictment, to imprisonment for a term not exceeding 5 years or to a fine (or to both).

(3) Subsection (2)(a) applies in relation to Northern Ireland as if the reference to 12 months were a reference to 6 months.

[3639]

NOTES

Commencement: 15 January 2007.

7 Making or supplying articles for use in frauds

(1) A person is guilty of an offence if he makes, adapts, supplies or offers to supply any article—

(a) knowing that it is designed or adapted for use in the course of or in connection with fraud, or

(b) intending it to be used to commit, or assist in the commission of, fraud.

(2) A person guilty of an offence under this section is liable—

(a) on summary conviction, to imprisonment for a term not exceeding 12 months or to a fine not exceeding the statutory maximum (or to both);

(b) on conviction on indictment, to imprisonment for a term not exceeding 10 years or to a fine (or to both).

(3) Subsection (2)(a) applies in relation to Northern Ireland as if the reference to 12 months were a reference to 6 months.

[3640]

NOTES

Commencement: 15 January 2007.

8 "Article"

(1) For the purposes of—

(a) sections 6 and 7, and

(b) the provisions listed in subsection (2), so far as they relate to articles for use in the course of or in connection with fraud,

"article" includes any program or data held in electronic form.

(2) The provisions are—

(a) section 1(7)(b) of the Police and Criminal Evidence Act 1984 (c 60),

(b) section 2(8)(b) of the Armed Forces Act 2001 (c 19), and

(c) Article 3(7)(b) of the Police and Criminal Evidence (Northern Ireland) Order 1989 (SI 1989/1341 (NI 12));

(meaning of "prohibited articles" for the purposes of stop and search powers).

[3641]

NOTES

Commencement: 15 January 2007.

9 Participating in fraudulent business carried on by sole trader etc

(1) A person is guilty of an offence if he is knowingly a party to the carrying on of a business to which this section applies.

(2) This section applies to a business which is carried on—

(a) by a person who is outside the reach of section 458 of the Companies Act 1985 (c 6) or Article 451 of the Companies (Northern Ireland) Order 1986 (SI 1986/1032) (NI 6)) (offence of fraudulent trading), and

(b) with intent to defraud creditors of any person or for any other fraudulent purpose.

(3) The following are within the reach of section 458 of the 1985 Act—

(a) a company (within the meaning of that Act);

(b) a person to whom that section applies (with or without adaptations or modifications) as if the person were a company;

(c) a person exempted from the application of that section.

(4) *The following are within the reach of Article 451 of the 1986 Order—*

(*a*) *a company (within the meaning of that Order);*

(*b*) *a person to whom that Article applies (with or without adaptations or modifications) as if the person were a company;*

(*c*) *a person exempted from the application of that Article.*

(5) "Fraudulent purpose" has the same meaning as in section 458 of the 1985 Act or Article 451 of the 1986 Order.

(6) A person guilty of an offence under this section is liable—

(a) on summary conviction, to imprisonment for a term not exceeding 12 months or to a fine not exceeding the statutory maximum (or to both);

(b) on conviction on indictment, to imprisonment for a term not exceeding 10 years or to a fine (or to both).

(7) Subsection (6)(a) applies in relation to Northern Ireland as if the reference to 12 months were a reference to 6 months.

[3642]

NOTES

Commencement: 15 January 2007.

Sub-s (4): repealed by the draft Companies Act 2006 (Commencement No 3, Consequential Amendments, Transitional Provisions and Savings) Order 2007, art 10(3), Sch 5, as from 1 October 2007 (see **[A12]**).

10 (*Amends the Companies Act 1985, Sch 24 at* **[689]**, *and the Companies* (*Northern Ireland*) *Order 1986, Sch 23.*)

Obtaining services dishonestly

11 Obtaining services dishonestly

(1) A person is guilty of an offence under this section if he obtains services for himself or another—

(a) by a dishonest act, and

(b) in breach of subsection (2).

(2) A person obtains services in breach of this subsection if—

(a) they are made available on the basis that payment has been, is being or will be made for or in respect of them,

(b) he obtains them without any payment having been made for or in respect of them or without payment having been made in full, and

(c) when he obtains them, he knows—

(i) that they are being made available on the basis described in paragraph (a), or

(ii) that they might be,

but intends that payment will not be made, or will not be made in full.

(3) A person guilty of an offence under this section is liable—

(a) on summary conviction, to imprisonment for a term not exceeding 12 months or to a fine not exceeding the statutory maximum (or to both);

(b) on conviction on indictment, to imprisonment for a term not exceeding 5 years or to a fine (or to both).

(4) Subsection (3)(a) applies in relation to Northern Ireland as if the reference to 12 months were a reference to 6 months.

[3643]

NOTES

Commencement: 15 January 2007.

PART III
OTHER LEGISLATION

Supplementary

12 Liability of company officers for offences by company

(1) Subsection (2) applies if an offence under this Act is committed by a body corporate.

(2) If the offence is proved to have been committed with the consent or connivance of—

(a) a director, manager, secretary or other similar officer of the body corporate, or

(b) a person who was purporting to act in any such capacity,

he (as well as the body corporate) is guilty of the offence and liable to be proceeded against and punished accordingly.

(3) If the affairs of a body corporate are managed by its members, subsection (2) applies in relation to the acts and defaults of a member in connection with his functions of management as if he were a director of the body corporate.

[3644]

NOTES

Commencement: 15 January 2007.

13 Evidence

(1) A person is not to be excused from—

(a) answering any question put to him in proceedings relating to property, or

(b) complying with any order made in proceedings relating to property,

on the ground that doing so may incriminate him or his spouse or civil partner of an offence under this Act or a related offence.

(2) But, in proceedings for an offence under this Act or a related offence, a statement or admission made by the person in—

(a) answering such a question, or

(b) complying with such an order,

is not admissible in evidence against him or (unless they married or became civil partners after the making of the statement or admission) his spouse or civil partner.

(3) "Proceedings relating to property" means any proceedings for—

(a) the recovery or administration of any property,

(b) the execution of a trust, or

(c) an account of any property or dealings with property,

and "property" means money or other property whether real or personal (including things in action and other intangible property).

(4) "Related offence" means—

(a) conspiracy to defraud;

(b) any other offence involving any form of fraudulent conduct or purpose.

[3645]

NOTES

Commencement: 15 January 2007.

14 (*Introduces Sch 1* (*minor and consequential amendments*), *Sch 2* (*transitional provisions and savings*), *and Sch 3* (*repeals and revocations*).)

15 Commencement and extent

(1) This Act (except this section and section 16) comes into force on such day as the Secretary of State may appoint by an order made by statutory instrument; and different days may be appointed for different purposes.

(2) Subject to subsection (3), sections 1 to 9 and 11 to 13 extend to England and Wales and Northern Ireland only.

(3) Section 8, so far as it relates to the Armed Forces Act 2001 (c 19), extends to any place to which that Act extends.

(4) Any amendment in section 10 or Schedule 1, and any related provision in section 14 or Schedule 2 or 3, extends to any place to which the provision which is the subject of the amendment extends.

[3646]

NOTES

Commencement: 8 November 2006.
Orders: the Fraud Act 2006 (Commencement) Order 2006, SI 2006/3200.

16 Short title

This Act may be cited as the Fraud Act 2006.

[3647]

NOTES

Commencement: 8 November 2006.

SCHEDULES

(Sch 1: para 1 repeals the Theft Act 1968, s 15, 15A, 16, 20(2) (the deception offences); paras 2–38 contain minor and consequential amendments which, in so far as relevant to this work, are incorporated at the appropriate place.)

SCHEDULE 2
TRANSITIONAL PROVISIONS AND SAVINGS

Section 14(2)

Maximum term of imprisonment for offences under this Act

1. In relation to an offence committed before the commencement of section 154(1) of the Criminal Justice Act 2003 (c 44), the references to 12 months in sections 1(3)(a), 6(2)(a), 7(2)(a), 9(6)(a) and 11(3)(a) are to be read as references to 6 months.

Increase in penalty for fraudulent trading

2. Section 10 does not affect the penalty for any offence committed before that section comes into force.

Abolition of deception offences

3.—(1) Paragraph 1 of Schedule 1 does not affect any liability, investigation, legal proceeding or penalty for or in respect of any offence partly committed before the commencement of that paragraph.

(2) An offence is partly committed before the commencement of paragraph 1 of Schedule 1 if—

(a) a relevant event occurs before its commencement, and

(b) another relevant event occurs on or after its commencement.

(3) "Relevant event", in relation to an offence, means any act, omission or other event (including any result of one or more acts or omissions) proof of which is required for conviction of the offence.

Scope of offences relating to stolen goods under the Theft Act 1968 (c 60)

4. Nothing in paragraph 6 of Schedule 1 affects the operation of section 24 of the Theft Act 1968 in relation to goods obtained in the circumstances described in section 15(1) of that Act where the obtaining is the result of a deception made before the commencement of that paragraph.

Dishonestly retaining a wrongful credit under the Theft Act 1968

5. Nothing in paragraph 7 of Schedule 1 affects the operation of section 24A(7) and (8) of the Theft Act 1968 in relation to credits falling within section 24A(3) or (4) of that Act and made before the commencement of that paragraph.

6–11. (*Outside the scope of this work.*)

[3648]

NOTES

Commencement: 15 January 2007.

(*Sch 3* (*repeals and revocations*) *omitted.*)

BANKRUPTCY AND DILIGENCE ETC (SCOTLAND) ACT 2007

(2007 asp 3)

NOTES

Only provisions of this Act relevant to company law are reproduced. Provisions not reproduced are not annotated.

As of 1 July 2007, this Act had not been amended.

ARRANGEMENT OF SECTIONS

PART 2
FLOATING CHARGES

Registration and creation etc

An Act of the Scottish Parliament to amend the law of sequestration and personal insolvency; to amend the law about floating charges; to establish a Scottish Civil Enforcement Commission and replace officers of court with judicial officers; to amend the law of diligence; and for connected purposes

[15 January 2007]

PART 2
FLOATING CHARGES

Registration and creation etc

37 Register of Floating Charges

(1) The Keeper of the Registers of Scotland (in this Part, the "Keeper") must establish and maintain a register to be known as the Register of Floating Charges.

(2) The Keeper must accept an application for registration of—

(a) any document delivered to the Keeper in pursuance of section 38, 41, 42, 43 or 44 of this Act; and

(b) any notice delivered to the Keeper in pursuance of section 39 or 45(2) of this Act,

provided that the application is accompanied by such information as the Keeper may require for the purposes of the registration.

(3) On receipt of such an application, the Keeper must note the date of receipt of the application; and, where the application is accepted by the Keeper, that date is to be treated for the purposes of this Part as the date of registration of the document or notice to which the application relates.

(4) The Keeper must, after accepting such an application, complete registration by registering in the Register of Floating Charges the document or notice to which the application relates.

(5) The Keeper must—

(a) make the Register of Floating Charges available for public inspection at all reasonable times;

(b) provide facilities for members of the public to obtain copies of the documents in the Register; and

(c) supply an extract of a document in the Register, certified as a true copy of the original, to any person requesting it.

(6) An extract certified as mentioned in subsection (5)(c) above is sufficient evidence of the original.

(7) The Keeper may charge such fees—

(a) for registering a document or notice in the Register of Floating Charges; or

(b) in relation to anything done under subsection (5) above,

as the Scottish Ministers may by regulations prescribe.

(8) The Scottish Ministers may by regulations make provision as to—

(a) the form and manner in which the Register of Floating Charges is to be maintained;

(b) the form of documents (including notices as mentioned in sections 39(1) and 45(2) of this Act) for registration in that Register, the particulars they are to contain and the manner in which they are to be delivered to the Keeper.

(9) Provision under subsection (8) above may, in particular, facilitate the use—

(a) of electronic communication;

(b) of documents in electronic form (and of certified electronic signatures in documents).

[3649]

NOTES

Commencement: to be appointed.

38 Creation of floating charges

(1) It continues to be competent, for the purpose of securing any obligation to which this subsection applies, for a company to grant in favour of the creditor in the obligation a charge (known as a "floating charge") over all or any part of the property which may from time to time be comprised in the company's property and undertaking.

(2) Subsection (1) above applies to any debt or other obligation incurred or to be incurred by, or binding upon, the company or any other person.

(3) From the coming into force of this section, a floating charge is (subject to section 39 of this Act) created only when a document—

(a) granting a floating charge; and

(b) subscribed by the company granting the charge,

is registered in the Register of Floating Charges.

(4) References in this Part to a document which grants a floating charge are to a document by means of which a floating charge is granted.

[3650]

NOTES

Commencement: to be appointed.

39 Advance notice of floating charges

(1) Where a company proposes to grant a floating charge, the company and the person in whose favour the charge is to be granted may apply to have joint notice of the proposed charge registered in the Register of Floating Charges.

(2) Subsection (3) below applies where—

(a) a notice under subsection (1) above is registered in the Register of Floating Charges; and

(b) within 21 days of the notice being so registered, a document—

(i) granting a floating charge conforming with the particulars contained in the notice; and

(ii) subscribed by the company granting the charge,

is registered in the Register of Floating Charges.

(3) Where this subsection applies, the floating charge so created is to be treated as having been created when the notice under subsection (1) above was so registered.

[3651]

NOTES

Commencement: to be appointed.

40 Ranking of floating charges

(1) Subject to subsections (4) and (5) below, a floating charge—

(a) created on or after the coming into force of this section; and

(b) which has attached to all or any part of the property of a company,

ranks as described in subsection (2) below.

(2) The floating charge referred to in subsection (1) above—

(a) ranks with—

(i) any other floating charge which has attached to that property or any part of it; or

(ii) any fixed security over that property or any part of it,

according to date of creation; and

(b) ranks equally with any floating charge or fixed security referred to in paragraph (a) above which was created on the same date as the floating charge referred to in subsection (1) above.

(3) For the purposes of subsection (2) above—

(a) the date of creation of a fixed security is the date on which the right to the security was constituted as a real right; and

(b) the date of creation of a floating charge subsisting before the coming into force of this section is the date on which the instrument creating the charge was executed by the company granting the charge.

(4) Where all or any part of the property of a company is subject to both—

(a) a floating charge; and

(b) a fixed security arising by operation of law,

the fixed security has priority over the floating charge.

(5) Where the holder of a floating charge over all or any part of the property of a company has received intimation in writing of the subsequent creation of—

(a) another floating charge over the same property or any part of it; or

(b) a fixed security over the same property or any part of it,

the priority of ranking of the first-mentioned charge is restricted to security for the matters referred to in subsection (6) below.

(6) Those matters are—

(a) the present debt incurred (whenever payable);

(b) any future debt which, under the contract to which the charge relates, the holder is required to allow the debtor to incur;

(c) any interest due or to become due on the debts referred to in paragraphs (a) and (b) above;
(d) any expenses or outlays which may be reasonably incurred by the holder; and
(e) in the case of a floating charge to secure a contingent liability (other than a liability arising under any further debts incurred from time to time), the maximum sum to which the contingent liability is capable of amounting, whether or not it is contractually limited.

(7) Subsections (1) to (6) above, and any provision made under section 41(1) of this Act, are subject to sections 175 and 176A (provision for preferential debts and share of assets) of the Insolvency Act 1986 (c 45).

[3652]

NOTES

Commencement: to be appointed.

41 Ranking clauses

(1) The document granting a floating charge over all or any part of the property of a company may make provision regulating the order in which the charge ranks with any other floating charge or any fixed security (including a future floating charge or fixed security) over that property or any part of it.

(2) Provision under subsection (1) above—
(a) may displace in whole or part—
(i) subsections (1) and (2) of section 40 of this Act;
(ii) subsections (5) and (6) of that section;
(b) may not affect the operation of subsection (4) of that section (whether as against subsections (1) and (2) of that section or other provision under subsection (1) above).

(3) Accordingly, subsections (1), (2), (5) and (6) of that section have effect subject to any provision made under subsection (1) above.

(4) Provision under subsection (1) above is not valid unless it is made with the consent of the holder of any subsisting floating charge, or any subsisting fixed security, which would be adversely affected by the provision.

(5) A document of consent for the purpose of subsection (4) above may be registered in the Register of Floating Charges.

[3653]

NOTES

Commencement: to be appointed.

42 Assignation of floating charges

(1) A floating charge may be assigned (and the rights under it vested in the assignee) by the registration in the Register of Floating Charges of a document of assignation subscribed by the holder of the charge.

(2) An assignation under subsection (1) above may be in whole or to such extent as may be specified in the document of assignation.

(3) This section is without prejudice to any other enactment, or any rule of law, by virtue of which a floating charge may be assigned.

[3654]

NOTES

Commencement: to be appointed.

43 Alteration of floating charges

(1) A document of alteration may alter (whether by addition, deletion or substitution of text or otherwise) the terms of a document granting a floating charge.

(2) If (and in so far as) an alteration to the terms of a document granting a floating charge concerns—

PART III OTHER LEGISLATION

(a) the ranking of the charge with any other floating charge or any fixed security; or

(b) the specification of—

(i) the property that is subject to the charge; or

(ii) the obligations that are secured by the charge,

the alteration is not valid unless subsection (3) below is satisfied.

(3) This subsection is satisfied if the alteration is made by a document of alteration which is—

(a) subscribed by—

(i) the company which granted the charge;

(ii) the holder of the charge; and

(iii) the holder of any other subsisting floating charge, or any subsisting fixed security, which would be adversely affected by the alteration; and

(b) registered in the Register of Floating Charges.

(4) But paragraph (a)(i) of subsection (3) above does not apply in respect of an alteration which—

(a) relates only to the ranking of the floating charge first-mentioned in that subsection with any other floating charge or any fixed security; and

(b) does not adversely affect the interests of the company which granted the charge.

(5) The granting, by the holder of a floating charge, of consent to the release from the scope of the charge of any particular property, or class of property, which is subject to the charge is to be treated as constituting an alteration—

(a) to the terms of the document granting the charge; and

(b) as to the specification of the property that is subject to the charge.

(6) For the purpose of subsection (5) above, property is not to be regarded as released from the scope of a floating charge by reason only of its ceasing to be the property of the company which granted the charge.

[3655]

NOTES

Commencement: to be appointed.

44 Discharge of floating charges

(1) A floating charge may be discharged by the registration in the Register of Floating Charges of a document of discharge subscribed by the holder of the charge.

(2) A discharge under subsection (1) above may be in whole or to such extent as may be specified in the document of discharge.

(3) This section is without prejudice to any other means by which a floating charge may be discharged or extinguished.

[3656]

NOTES

Commencement: to be appointed.

45 Effect of floating charges on winding up

(1) Where a company goes into liquidation, a floating charge created over property of the company attaches to the property to which it relates.

(2) But, in a case mentioned in subsection (7)(a) below, there is no attachment under subsection (1) above until such time as a notice of attachment is registered in the Register of Floating Charges on the application of the holder of the charge.

(3) The attachment of a floating charge to property under subsection (1) above is subject to the rights of any person who—

(a) has effectually executed diligence on the property to which the charge relates or any part of it;

(b) holds over that property or any part of it a fixed security ranking in priority to the floating charge; or

(c) holds over that property or any part of it another floating charge so ranking.

(4) Interest accrues in respect of a floating charge which has attached to property until payment is made of any sum due under the charge.

(5) Part IV, except section 185, of the Insolvency Act 1986 has (subject to subsection (1) above) effect in relation to a floating charge as if the charge were a fixed security over the property to which it has attached in respect of the principal of the debt or obligation to which it relates and any interest due or to become due on it.

(6) Subsections (1) to (5) above do not affect the operation of—
- (a) sections 53(7) and 54(6) (attachment of floating charge on appointment of receiver) of the Insolvency Act 1986;
- (b) sections 175 and 176A of that Act; or
- (c) paragraph 115(3) of Schedule B1 (attachment of floating charge on delivery of a notice by an administrator) to that Act.

(7) For the purposes of this section, reference to a company going into liquidation—
- (a) in a case where a court of a member State has under the EC Regulation jurisdiction as respects the company which granted the relevant floating charge, means the opening of insolvency proceedings in that State;
- (b) in any other case, is to be construed in accordance with section 247(2) and (3) of the Insolvency Act 1986 (c 45).

(8) In subsection (7)(a) above—

"the EC Regulation" is the Regulation of the Council of the European Union published as Council Regulation (EC) No 1346/2000 on insolvency proceedings;

"court" is to be construed in accordance with Article 2(d) of that Regulation;

"insolvency proceedings" is to be construed in accordance with Article 2(a) of that Regulation;

"member State" means a member State of the European Union apart from the United Kingdom.

[3657]

NOTES

Commencement: to be appointed.

46 Repeals, savings and transitional arrangements

(1) Part XVIII (floating charges: Scotland) of the Companies Act 1985 (c 6) is repealed.

(2) Nothing in this Part (except sections 40 and 41 so far as they concern the ranking of floating charges subsisting immediately before the coming into force of this section) affects the validity or operation of floating charges subsisting before the coming into force of this section.

(3) So, despite the repeal of Chapters I and III of Part XVIII of that Act by subsection (1) above, the provisions of those Chapters are to be treated as having effect for the purposes of floating charges subsisting immediately before the coming into force of this section.

(4) In particular—
- (a) floating charges subsisting immediately before the coming into force of this section rank with each other as they ranked with each other in accordance with section 464 of the Companies Act 1985 immediately before that section was repealed by subsection (1) above; and
- (b) a floating charge subsisting immediately before the coming into force of this section ranks with a fixed security so subsisting as it ranked with the security in accordance with section 464 of the Companies Act 1985 immediately before that section was repealed by subsection (1) above.

(5) Section 140 (floating charges (Scotland)) of the Companies Act 1989 (c 40) is repealed (but, despite being repealed, is to be treated as having effect for the purposes of subsections (3) and (4) above).

[3658]

NOTES

Commencement: to be appointed.

47 Interpretation

In this Part—

"company" means an incorporated company (whether or not a company within the meaning of the Companies Act 1985 (c 6));

"fixed security", in relation to any property of a company, means any security (other than a floating charge or a charge having the character of a floating charge) which on the winding up of the company in Scotland would be treated as an effective security over that property including, in particular, a heritable security (within the meaning of section 9(8) of the Conveyancing and Feudal Reform (Scotland) Act 1970 (c 35)).

[3659]

NOTES

Commencement: to be appointed.

48, 49 *(S 48 amends the Requirements of Writing (Scotland) Act 1995, s 6, the Conveyancing (Scotland) Act 1924, s 46, and the Law Reform (Miscellaneous Provisions) (Scotland) Act 1985, s 8; s 49 substitutes the Industrial and Provident Societies Act 1967, s 3, repeals s 4 of the 1967 Act, and amends s 5 of that Act.)*

PART 17
GENERAL AND MISCELLANEOUS

221 Interpretation

In this Act—

the "1985 Act" means the Bankruptcy (Scotland) Act 1985 (c 66);

the "1987 Act" means the Debtors (Scotland) Act 1987 (c 18);

the "2002 Act" means the Debt Arrangement and Attachment (Scotland) Act 2002 (asp 17);

"certified electronic signature" is to be read in accordance with section 7(2) and (3) of the Electronic Communications Act 2000 (c 7);

the "Commission" means the Scottish Civil Enforcement Commission;

"debt advice and information package" has the meaning given by section 81(8) of this Act;

"decree" means—

(a) a decree of the Court of Session, of the High Court of Justiciary or of the sheriff;
(b) a decree of the Court of Teinds;
(c) a summary warrant;
(d) a civil judgement granted outside Scotland by a court, tribunal or arbiter which, by virtue of any enactment or rule of law, is enforceable in Scotland;
(e) an order or determination which, by virtue of any enactment, is enforceable as if it were an extract registered decree arbitral bearing a warrant for execution granted by the sheriff;
(f) a warrant granted in criminal proceedings for enforcement by civil diligence;
(g) an order under section 114 of the Companies Clauses Consolidation (Scotland) Act 1845 (c 17);
(h) a determination under section 46 of the Harbours, Docks and Piers Clauses Act 1847 (c 27); or
(i) a liability order within the meaning of section 33(2) of the Child Support Act 1991 (c 48);

"document of debt" means—

(a) a document registered for execution in the Books of Council and Session or in the sheriff court books;
(b) a bill protested for non-payment by a notary public; or
(c) a document or settlement which, by virtue of an Order in Council made under section 13 of the Civil Jurisdiction and Judgments Act 1982 (c 27), is enforceable in Scotland;

"electronic communication" has the meaning given by section 15(1) of the Electronic Communications Act 2000 (c 7);

"judicial officer" shall be construed in accordance with section 57(1) of this Act; and "professional association" shall be construed in accordance with section 63(1)(a) of this Act.

[3660]

NOTES

Commencement: 8 March 2007.

227 Short title and commencement

(1) This Act may be cited as the Bankruptcy and Diligence etc (Scotland) Act 2007.

(2) Section 222 of this Act comes into force on the day after Royal Assent.

(3) The remaining provisions of this Act, except this section and sections 224 and 225, come into force on such day as the Scottish Ministers may, by order, appoint.

(4) Different days may, under subsection (3) above, be appointed for different purposes.

[3661]–[4000]

NOTES

Commencement: 15 January 2007.

Orders: the Bankruptcy and Diligence etc (Scotland) Act 2007 (Commencement No 1) Order 2007, SSI 2007/82 (not relevant to the provisions included in this work).

PART IV
STATUTORY INSTRUMENTS

A. FSMA 2000: STATUTORY INSTRUMENTS

FINANCIAL SERVICES AND MARKETS ACT 2000 (REGULATED ACTIVITIES) ORDER 2001

(SI 2001/544)

NOTES

Made: 26 February 2001.

Authority: Financial Services and Markets Act 2000, ss 22(1), (5), 426, 428(3), Sch 2, para 25.

Commencement: 1 December 2001 (being the date on which the Financial Services and Markets Act 2000, s 19 came into force) and subject as follows; 1 January 2002 (arts 59, 60, 87); 31 October 2004 (arts 61–63, 88, 90, 91); see art 2 at **[4002]**. Where any provision in this work (including any inserted or substituted provision) came into force for all purposes on or before 1 July 2005, commencement information is not noted at provision level.

This Order is reproduced as amended by: the Financial Services and Markets Act 2000 (Regulated Activities) (Amendment) Order 2001, SI 2001/3544; the Financial Services and Markets Act 2000 (Regulated Activities) (Amendment) Order 2002, SI 2002/682; the Financial Services and Markets Act 2000 (Financial Promotion and Miscellaneous Amendments) Order 2002, SI 2002/1310; the Financial Services and Markets Act 2000 (Regulated Activities) (Amendment) (No 2) Order 2002, SI 2002/1776; the Financial Services and Markets Act 2000 (Commencement of Mortgage Regulation) (Amendment) Order 2002, SI 2002/1777; the Financial Services and Markets Act 2000 (Regulated Activities) (Amendment) (No 1) Order 2003, SI 2003/1475; the Financial Services and Markets Act 2000 (Regulated Activities) (Amendment) (No 2) Order 2003, SI 2003/1476; the Financial Services and Markets Act 2000 (Regulated Activities) (Amendment) (No 3) Order 2003, SI 2003/2822; the Financial Services and Markets Act 2000 (Regulated Activities) (Amendment) Order 2004, SI 2004/1610; the Financial Services and Markets Act 2000 (Regulated Activities) (Amendment) (No 2) Order 2004, SI 2004/2737; the Life Assurance Consolidation Directive (Consequential Amendments) Regulations 2004, SI 2004/3379; the Financial Services and Markets Act 2000 (Regulated Activities) (Amendment) Order 2005, SI 2005/593; the Financial Services and Markets Act 2000 (Regulated Activities) (Amendment) (No 2) Order 2005, SI 2005/1518; the Civil Partnership Act 2004 (Amendments to Subordinate Legislation) Order 2005, SI 2005/2114; the Financial Services and Markets Act 2000 (Regulated Activities) (Amendment) Order 2006, SI 2006/1969; the Financial Services and Markets Act 2000 (Regulated Activities) (Amendment) (No 2) Order 2006, SI 2006/2383; the Capital Requirements Regulations 2006, SI 2006/3221; the Financial Services and Markets Act 2000 (Regulated Activities) (Amendment No 3) Order 2006, SI 2006/3384; the Companies Act 2006 (Commencement No 2, Consequential Amendments, Transitional Provisions and Savings) Order 2007, SI 2007/1093; the Financial Services and Markets Act 2000 (Regulated Activities) (Amendment) Order 2007, SI 2007/1339.

Transitional provisions: for transitional provisions relating to interim permissions and interim approvals in respect of regulated mortgage business, general insurance intermediaries, pension schemes, regulated home reversion plans and regulated home purchase plans, see the Financial Services and Markets Act 2000 (Transitional Provisions) (Mortgages) Order 2004, SI 2004/2615 at **[4695]**, the Financial Services and Markets Act 2000 (Transitional Provisions) (General Insurance Intermediaries) Order 2004, SI 2004/3351 at **[4710]**, the Financial Services and Markets Act 2000 (Regulated Activities) (Amendment) Order 2006, SI 2006/1969 at **[4813]**, and the Financial Services and Markets Act 2000 (Regulated Activities) (Amendment) (No 2) Order 2006, SI 2006/2383 at **[4820]**.

ARRANGEMENT OF ARTICLES

CHAPTER VI
ARRANGING DEALS IN INVESTMENTS

The activities

Exclusions

CHAPTER VII
MANAGING INVESTMENTS

The activity

Exclusions

CHAPTER VIIA
ASSISTING IN THE ADMINISTRATION AND PERFORMANCE OF A CONTRACT OF INSURANCE

The Activity

Exclusions

CHAPTER VIII
SAFEGUARDING AND ADMINISTERING INVESTMENTS

The activity

Exclusions

CHAPTER IX
SENDING DEMATERIALISED INSTRUCTIONS

The activities

Exclusions

CHAPTER X
COLLECTIVE INVESTMENT SCHEMES

The activities

Exclusion

CHAPTER XI
PENSION SCHEMES

The activities

Exclusion

CHAPTER XIA
PROVIDING BASIC ADVICE ON STAKEHOLDER PRODUCTS

The Activity

CHAPTER XII
ADVISING ON INVESTMENTS

The activity

Exclusions

CHAPTER XIII
LLOYD'S

The activities

Exclusion

CHAPTER XIV
FUNERAL PLAN CONTRACTS

The activity

Exclusions

CHAPTER XV
REGULATED MORTGAGE CONTRACTS

The activities

Exclusions

CHAPTER 15A
REGULATED HOME REVERSION PLANS

The activities

Exclusions

CHAPTER 15B
REGULATED HOME PURCHASE PLANS

The activities

Exclusions

CHAPTER XVI
AGREEING TO CARRY ON ACTIVITIES

The activity

Exclusions

CHAPTER XVII
EXCLUSIONS APPLYING TO SEVERAL SPECIFIED KINDS OF ACTIVITY

PART III
SPECIFIED INVESTMENTS

PART I
GENERAL

1 Citation

This Order may be cited as the Financial Services and Markets Act 2000 (Regulated Activities) Order 2001.

[4001]

2 Commencement

(1) Except as provided by paragraph (2), this Order comes into force on the day on which section 19 of the Act comes into force.

(2) This Order comes into force—

(a) for the purposes of articles 59, 60 and 87 (funeral plan contracts) on 1st January 2002; and

(b) for the purposes of articles 61 to 63, 88, 90 and 91 (regulated mortgage contracts) [on such a day as the Treasury may specify].

[(3) Any day specified under paragraph 2(b) must be caused to be notified in the London, Edinburgh and Belfast Gazettes published not later than one week before that day.]

[4002]

NOTES

Para (2): words in square brackets in sub-para (b) substituted by the Financial Services and Markets Act 2000 (Commencement of Mortgage Regulation) (Amendment) Order 2002, SI 2002/1777, art 2(1), (2), as from 30 August 2002.

Para (3): added by SI 2002/1777, art 2(1), (3), as from 30 August 2002.

FSMA 2000, s 19 came into force on 1 December 2001 (see the Financial Services and Markets Act 2000 (Commencement No 7) Order 2001, SI 2001/3538).

On such a day as the Treasury may specify: 31 October 2004 (see the London Gazette, 14 July 2003).

3 Interpretation

(1) In this Order—

"the Act" means the Financial Services and Markets Act 2000;

"annuities on human life" does not include superannuation allowances and annuities payable out of any fund applicable solely to the relief and maintenance of persons engaged, or who have been engaged, in any particular profession, trade or employment, or of the dependants of such persons;

"buying" includes acquiring for valuable consideration;

"close relative" in relation to a person means—

- (a) his spouse [or civil partner];
- (b) his children and step children, his parents and step-parents, his brothers and sisters and his step-brothers and step-sisters; and
- (c) the spouse [or civil partner] of any person within sub-paragraph (b);

["the Commission Regulation" means Commission Regulation 1287/2006 of 10 August 2006;]

"contract of general insurance" means any contract falling within Part I of Schedule 1;

"contract of insurance" means any contract of insurance which is a contract of long-term insurance or a contract of general insurance, and includes—

- (a) fidelity bonds, performance bonds, administration bonds, bail bonds, customs bonds or similar contracts of guarantee, where these are—
  - (i) effected or carried out by a person not carrying on a banking business;
  - (ii) not effected merely incidentally to some other business carried on by the person effecting them; and
  - (iii) effected in return for the payment of one or more premiums;
- (b) tontines;
- (c) capital redemption contracts or pension fund management contracts, where these are effected or carried out by a person who—
  - (i) does not carry on a banking business; and
  - (ii) otherwise carries on a regulated activity of the kind specified by article 10(1) or (2);
- (d) contracts to pay annuities on human life;
- (e) contracts of a kind referred to in article 1(2)(e) of the first life insurance directive (collective insurance etc); and
- (f) contracts of a kind referred to in article 1(3) of the first life insurance directive (social insurance);

but does not include a funeral plan contract (or a contract which would be a funeral plan contract but for the exclusion in article 60);

"contract of long-term insurance" means any contract falling within Part II of Schedule 1;

"contractually based investment" means—

- (a) rights under a qualifying contract of insurance;
- (b) any investment of the kind specified by any of articles 83, 84, 85 and 87; or
- (c) any investment of the kind specified by article 89 so far as relevant to an investment falling within (a) or (b);

["credit institution" means—

- (a) a credit institution authorised under the banking consolidation directive other than an institution to which Article 2.1 of the markets in financial instruments directive (the text of which is set out in Schedule 3) applies, or
- (b) an institution which would satisfy the requirements for authorisation as a credit institution under that directive (other than an institution to which Article 2.1 of the markets in financial instruments directive would apply) if it had its registered office (or if it does not have a registered office, its head office) in an EEA State;]

"deposit" has the meaning given by article 5;

["electronic money" means monetary value, as represented by a claim on the issuer, which is—

- (a) stored on an electronic device;
- (b) issued on receipt of funds; and
- (c) accepted as a means of payment by persons other than the issuer;]

["financial instrument" means any instrument listed in Section C of Annex I to the markets in financial instruments directive (the text of which is set out in Part 1 of Schedule 2) read with Chapter VI of the Commission Regulation (the text of which is set out in Part 2 of Schedule 2);]

"funeral plan contract" has the meaning given by article 59;

["home Member State", in relation to an investment firm, has the meaning given by Article 4.1.20 of the markets in financial instruments directive, and in relation to a credit institution, has the meaning given by Article 4.7 of the banking consolidation directive;]

["home purchase provider" has the meaning given by article 63F(3);

"home purchaser" has the meaning given by article 63F(3);]

"instrument" includes any record whether or not in the form of a document;

["investment firm" means a person whose regular occupation or business is the provision or performance of investment services and activities on a professional basis but does not include—

(a) a person to whom the markets in financial instruments directive does not apply by virtue of Article 2 of that directive (the text of which is set out in Schedule 3);

(b) a person whose home Member State is an EEA State other than the United Kingdom and to whom, by reason of the fact that the State has given effect to Article 3 of that directive, that directive does not apply by virtue of that Article;

(c) a person who does not have a home Member State and to whom (if he had his registered office in an EEA State, or, being a person other than a body corporate or a body corporate not having a registered office, if he had his head office in an EEA State) the markets in financial instruments directive would not apply by virtue of Article 2 of that directive;]

["investment services and activities" means—

(a) any service provided to third parties listed in Section A of Annex I to the markets in financial instruments directive (the text of which is set out in Part 3 of Schedule 2) read with Article 52 of Commission Directive 2006/73/EC of 10 August 2006 (the text of which is set out in Part 4 of Schedule 2), or

(b) any activity listed in Section A of Annex I to that directive,

relating to any financial instrument;]

"joint enterprise" means an enterprise into which two or more persons ("the participators") enter for commercial purposes related to a business or businesses (other than the business of engaging in a regulated activity) carried on by them; and, where a participator is a member of a group, each other member of the group is also to be regarded as a participator in the enterprise;

"local authority" means—

(a) in England and Wales, a local authority within the meaning of the Local Government Act 1972, the Greater London Authority, the Common Council of the City of London or the Council of the Isles of Scilly;

(b) in Scotland, a local authority within the meaning of the Local Government (Scotland) Act 1973;

(c) in Northern Ireland, a district council within the meaning of the Local Government Act (Northern Ireland) 1972;

["management company" has the meaning given by Article 1a.2 of the UCITS directive as amended by Directive 2001/107/EC;]

"managing agent" means a person who is permitted by the Council of Lloyd's in the conduct of his business as an underwriting agent to perform for a member of Lloyd's one or more of the following functions—

(a) underwriting contracts of insurance at Lloyd's;

(b) reinsuring such contracts in whole or in part;

(c) paying claims on such contracts;

["market operator" means a market operator within the meaning of Article 4.1.13 of the markets in financial instruments directive, or a person who would be a market operator if he had his registered office, or if he does not have a registered office his head office, in an EEA State, but does not include—

(a) a person to whom the markets in financial instruments directive does not apply by virtue of Article 2 of that directive (the text of which is set out in Schedule 3);

(b) a person who does not have a home Member State to whom (if he had his registered office, or if he does not have a registered office his head office, in an EEA State) the markets in financial instruments directive would not apply by virtue of Article 2 of that directive;]

["multilateral trading facility" means—

(a) a multilateral trading facility (within the meaning of Article 4.1.15 of the markets in financial instruments directive) operated by an investment firm, a credit institution or a market operator, or

(b) a facility which—

(i) is operated by an investment firm, a credit institution or market operator which does not have a home Member State, and

(ii) if its operator had a home Member State, would be a multilateral trading facility within the meaning of Article 4.1.15 of the markets in financial instruments directive;]

["occupational pension scheme" has the meaning given by section 1 of the Pension Schemes Act 1993 but with paragraph (b) of the definition omitted;]

"overseas person" means a person who—

(a) carries on activities of the kind specified by any of articles 14, 21, 25, [25A,] [25B, 25C,] [25D,] 37[, 39A], 40, 45, 51, 52[, 53, 53A [, 53B, 53C, 61, 63B and 63F]] or, so far as relevant to any of those articles, article 64 (or activities of a kind which would be so specified but for the exclusion in article 72); but

(b) does not carry on any such activities, or offer to do so, from a permanent place of business maintained by him in the United Kingdom;

"pension fund management contract" means a contract to manage the investments of pension funds (other than funds solely for the benefit of the officers or employees of the person effecting or carrying out the contract and their dependants or, in the case of a company, partly for the benefit of officers and employees and their dependants of its subsidiary or holding company or a subsidiary of its holding company); and for the purposes of this definition, "subsidiary" and "holding company" are to be construed in accordance with section 736 of the Companies Act 1985 or article 4 of the Companies (Northern Ireland) Order 1986;

["personal pension scheme" means a scheme or arrangement which is not an occupational pension scheme or a stakeholder pension scheme and which is comprised in one or more instruments or agreements, having or capable of having effect so as to provide benefits to or in respect of people—

(a) on retirement,

(b) on having reached a particular age, or

(c) on termination of service in an employment;]

["plan provider" has the meaning given by paragraph (3) of article 63B, read with paragraphs (7) and (8) of that article;]

"property" includes currency of the United Kingdom or any other country or territory;

"qualifying contract of insurance" means a contract of long-term insurance which is not—

(a) a reinsurance contract; nor

(b) a contract in respect of which the following conditions are met—

(i) the benefits under the contract are payable only on death or in respect of incapacity due to injury, sickness or infirmity;

(ii) . . .

(iii) the contract has no surrender value, or the consideration consists of a single premium and the surrender value does not exceed that premium; and

(iv) the contract makes no provision for its conversion or extension in a manner which would result in it ceasing to comply with any of the above conditions;

["regulated home purchase plan" has the meaning given by article 63F(3);

"regulated home reversion plan" has the meaning given by article 63B(3);]

"regulated mortgage contract" has the meaning given by article 61(3);

["relevant investment" means—

(a) rights under a qualifying contract of insurance;

(b) rights under any other contract of insurance;

(c) any investment of the kind specified by any of articles 83, 84, 85 and 87; or

(d) any investment of the kind specified by article 89 so far as relevant to an investment falling within (a) or (c);]

["reversion seller" has the meaning given by article 63B(3);]

"security" means (except where the context otherwise requires) any investment of the kind specified by any of articles 76 to 82 or, so far as relevant to any such investment, article 89;

"selling", in relation to any investment, includes disposing of the investment for valuable consideration, and for these purposes "disposing" includes—

(a) in the case of an investment consisting of rights under a contract—

(i) surrendering, assigning or converting those rights; or

(ii) assuming the corresponding liabilities under the contract;

(b) in the case of an investment consisting of rights under other arrangements, assuming the corresponding liabilities under the arrangements; and

(c) in the case of any other investment, issuing or creating the investment or granting the rights or interests of which it consists;

"stakeholder pension scheme" has the meaning given by section 1 of the Welfare Reform and Pensions Act 1999 [in relation to Great Britain and has the meaning given by article 3 of the Welfare Reform and Pensions (Northern Ireland) Order 1999 in relation to Northern Ireland];

"syndicate" means one or more persons, to whom a particular syndicate number has been assigned by or under the authority of the Council of Lloyd's, carrying out or effecting contracts of insurance written at Lloyd's;

"voting shares", in relation to a body corporate, means shares carrying voting rights attributable to share capital which are exercisable in all circumstances at any general meeting of that body corporate.

(2) For the purposes of this Order, a transaction is entered into through a person if he enters into it as agent or arranges, in a manner constituting the carrying on of an activity of the kind specified by article 25(1)[, 25A(1), 25B(1) or 25C(1)], for it to be entered into by another person as agent or principal.

(3) For the purposes of this Order, a contract of insurance is to be treated as falling within Part II of Schedule 1, notwithstanding the fact that it contains related and subsidiary provisions such that it might also be regarded as falling within Part I of that Schedule, if its principal object is that of a contract falling within Part II and it is effected or carried out by an authorised person who has permission to effect or carry out contracts falling within paragraph I of Part II of Schedule 1.

[4003]

NOTES

Para (1) is amended as follows:

Words in square brackets in definition "close relative" inserted by the Civil Partnership Act 2004 (Amendments to Subordinate Legislation) Order 2005, SI 2005/2114, art 2(16), Sch 16, Pt 1, para 1(1), (2), as from 5 December 2005.

Definitions "the Commission Regulation", "credit institution", "financial instrument", "home Member State", "investment firm", "investment services and activities", "management company", "market operator", and "multilateral trading facility" inserted by the Financial Services and Markets Act 2000 (Regulated Activities) (Amendment No 3) Order 2006, SI 2006/3384, arts 2, 3(b), as from 1 April 2007 (for the purposes of enabling applications to be made for (i) a Part IV permission, (ii) a variation of a Part IV permission, and (iii) the Authority's approval under s 59 of the 2000 Act, in relation to an activity of the kind specified by art 25D of this Order, or in relation to an investment of the kind specified by arts 83, 84 or 85 of this Order), and as from 1 November 2007 (otherwise).

Definition "electronic money" inserted by the Financial Services and Markets Act 2000 (Regulated Activities) (Amendment) Order 2002, SI 2002/682, art 2, as from 27 April 2002 (subject to transitional provisions in relation to persons issuing electronic money immediately before that date contained in art 9 at **[4637]**).

Definitions "home purchase provider", "home purchaser", "plan provider", "regulated home purchase plan", "regulated home reversion plan", and "reversion seller" inserted by the Financial Services and Markets Act 2000 (Regulated Activities) (Amendment) (No 2) Order 2006, SI 2006/2383, arts 2, 3(1)(a), (c)–(e), as from 6 November 2006 (for the purposes of enabling applications to be made for (i) a Pt IV permission, or a variation of a Pt IV permission, in relation to activities of the kind specified by arts 25B, 25C, 53B, 53C, 63B or 63F or, so far as relevant to any such activity, art 64 of this Order; or (ii) the Authority's approval under FSMA 2000, s 59 in relation to any of those activities), and as from 6 April 2007 (otherwise) (for transitional provisions and effect see arts 36–40 of, and the Schedule to, the 2006 Order at **[4821]** et seq).

Definition "occupational pension scheme" substituted by the Financial Services and Markets Act 2000 (Regulated Activities) (Amendment) Order 2006, SI 2006/1969, art 2(1), (2)(a), as from 1 October 2006 (for the purposes of enabling applications to be made for Part IV permission or for a variation of Part IV permission in relation to the regulated activity specified by art 52(b) of this Order (as amended by SI 2006/1969) or in relation to an investment specified by art 82(2) of this Order (as so amended)), and as from 6 April 2007 (otherwise); for transitional provisions and effect see arts 3–7 of, and the Schedule to, the 2006 Order at **[4814]**.

In definition "overseas person" first figure in square brackets inserted, and words in the penultimate (outer) pair of square brackets substituted, by the Financial Services and Markets Act 2000 (Regulated Activities) (Amendment) (No 1) Order 2003, SI 2003/1475, art 3, as from 31 October 2004 (for transitional provisions see arts 26–29 at **[4659]** et seq); second figures in square brackets inserted, and words in final (inner) pair of square brackets substituted, by SI 2006/2383, arts 2, 3(1)(b), as from 6 November 2006 (for the purposes of enabling applications to be made for (i) a Pt IV permission, or a variation of a Pt IV permission, in relation to activities of the kind specified by arts 25B, 25C, 53B, 53C, 63B or 63F or, so far as relevant to any such activity, art 64 of this Order; or (ii) the Authority's approval under FSMA 2000, s 59 in relation to any of those activities), and as from 6 April 2007 (otherwise) (for transitional provisions and effect see arts 36–40 of, and the Schedule to, the 2006 Order at **[4821]** et seq); third figure in square brackets inserted by SI 2006/3384, arts 2, 3(a), as from 1 April 2007 (for the purposes of enabling applications to be made for (i) a Part IV permission, (ii) a variation of a Part IV permission, and (iii) the Authority's approval under s 59 of the 2000 Act, in relation to an activity of the kind specified by art 25D of this Order, or in relation to an investment of the kind specified by arts 83, 84 or 85 of this Order), and as from 1 November 2007 (otherwise); fourth figure in square brackets inserted by the Financial Services and Markets Act 2000 (Regulated Activities) (Amendment) (No 2) Order 2003, SI 2003/1476, art 3(1)(a), as from 31 October 2004 (in so far as relating to contracts of long-term care insurance), and as from 14 January 2005 (otherwise) (for transitional provisions see arts 22–27 of that Order at **[4665]** et seq).

Definition "personal pension scheme" inserted by SI 2006/1969, art 2(1), (2)(a), as from 1 October 2006 (for the purposes of enabling applications to be made for Part IV permission or for a variation of Part IV permission in relation to the regulated activity specified by art 52(b) of this Order (as amended by SI 2006/1969) or in relation to an investment specified by art 82(2) of this Order (as so amended)), and as from 6 April 2007 (otherwise); for transitional provisions and effect see arts 3–7 of, and the Schedule to, the 2006 Order at **[4814]** et seq.

In definition "qualifying contract of insurance" sub-para (b)(ii) revoked by the Financial Services and Markets Act 2000 (Regulated Activities) (Amendment) Order 2007, SI 2007/1339, arts 2, 3, as from 6 June 2007.

Definition "relevant investment", inserted by SI 2003/1476, art 3(1)(b), as from 31 October 2004 (in so far as relating to contracts of long-term care insurance), and as from 14 January 2005 (otherwise) (for transitional provisions see arts 22–27 of that Order at **[4665]** et seq).

Words in square brackets in definition "stakeholder pension scheme" added by SI 2005/593, art 2(1), (2)(b), as from 6 April 2005.

Para (2): words in square brackets inserted by SI 2006/2383, arts 2, 3(2), as from 6 November 2006 (for the purposes of enabling applications to be made for (i) a Pt IV permission, or a variation of a Pt IV permission, in relation to activities of the kind specified by arts 25B, 25C, 53B, 53C, 63B or 63F or, so far as relevant to any such activity, art 64 of this Order; or (ii) the Authority's approval under FSMA 2000, s 59 in relation to any of those activities), and as from 6 April 2007 (otherwise) (for transitional provisions and effect see arts 36–40 of, and the Schedule to, the 2006 Order at **[4821]** et seq).

Close relative: as to the meaning of "step-children", and related expressions, see the Civil Partnership Act 2004, s 246 (as applied to this Order by the Civil Partnership Act 2004 (Relationships Arising Through Civil Partnership) Order 2005, SI 2005/3137, art 3, Schedule).

PART II
SPECIFIED ACTIVITIES

CHAPTER I
GENERAL

4 Specified activities: general

(1) The following provisions of this Part specify kinds of activity for the purposes of section 22 of the Act (and accordingly any activity of one of those kinds, which is carried on by way of business, and relates to an investment of a kind specified by any provision of Part III and applicable to that activity, is a regulated activity for the purposes of the Act).

(2) The kinds of activity specified by articles 51 and 52 are also specified for the purposes of section 22(1)(b) of the Act (and accordingly any activity of one of those kinds, when carried on by way of business, is a regulated activity when carried on in relation to property of any kind).

(3) Subject to paragraph (4), each provision specifying a kind of activity is subject to the exclusions applicable to that provision (and accordingly any reference in this Order to an activity of the kind specified by a particular provision is to be read subject to any such exclusions).

(4) Where an investment firm—

(a) provides core investment services to third parties on a professional basis, and

(b) in doing so would be treated as carrying on an activity of a kind specified by a provision of this Part but for an exclusion in any of [articles 15, 16, 19, 22, 23, 29, 38, 68, [69, 70 and 72E]],

that exclusion is to be disregarded (and accordingly the investment firm is to be treated as carrying on an activity of the kind specified by the provision in question).

[(4A) Where a person, other than a person specified by Article 1.2 of the insurance mediation directive (the text of which is set out in Part 1 of Schedule 4)—

(a) for remuneration, takes up or pursues insurance mediation or reinsurance mediation in relation to a risk or commitment located in an EEA State, and

(b) in doing so would be treated as carrying on an activity of a kind specified by a provision of this Part but for an exclusion in any of articles 30, 66 and 67,

that exclusion is to be disregarded (and accordingly that person is to be treated as carrying on an activity of the kind specified by the provision in question).]

(5) In this article—

"core investment service" means any service listed in section A of the Annex to the investment services directive, the text of which is set out in Schedule 2; ...

["insurance mediation" has the meaning given by Article 2.3 of the insurance mediation directive, the text of which is set out in Part II of Schedule 4;]

"investment firm" means a person whose regular occupation or business is the provision of core investment services to third parties on a professional basis, other than—

(a) a person to whom the investment services directive does not apply by virtue of Article 2.2 of that directive (the text of which is set out in Schedule 3); or

(b) a person to whom (if he were incorporated in or formed under the law of an EEA State or, being an individual, had his head office in an EEA State) that directive would not apply by virtue of Article 2.2 of that directive;

["reinsurance mediation" has the meaning given by Article 2.4 of the insurance mediation directive, the text of which is set out in Part III of Schedule 4.]

[4004]

NOTES

Para (4): words in first (outer) pair of square brackets in sub-para (b) substituted by the Financial Services and Markets Act 2000 (Regulated Activities) (Amendment) Order 2002, SI 2002/682, art 11, as from 27 April 2002; words in second (inner) pair of square brackets in sub-para (b) substituted by the Financial Services and Markets Act 2000 (Regulated Activities) (Amendment) (No 2) Order 2005, SI 2005/1518, art 2(1), (2), as from 1 October 2005; whole paragraph substituted by the Financial Services and Markets Act 2000 (Regulated Activities) (Amendment No 3) Order 2006, SI 2006/3384, arts 2, 4(a), as from 1 April 2007 (for the purposes of enabling applications to be made for (i) a Part IV permission, (ii) a variation of a Part IV permission, and (iii) the Authority's approval under s 59 of the 2000 Act, in relation to an activity of the kind specified by art 25D of this Order, or in relation to an investment of the kind specified by arts 83, 84 or 85 of this Order), and as from 1 November 2007 (otherwise), as follows—

"(4) Where an investment firm or credit institution—

(a) provides or performs investment services and activities on a professional basis, and

(b) in doing so would be treated as carrying on an activity of a kind specified by a provision of this Part but for an exclusion in any of articles 15, 16, 19, 22, 23, 29, 38, 67, 68, 69, 70 and 72E,

that exclusion is to be disregarded and, accordingly, the investment firm or credit institution is to be treated as carrying on an activity of the kind specified by the provision in question.".

Para (4A): inserted by the Financial Services and Markets Act 2000 (Regulated Activities) (Amendment) (No 2) Order 2003, SI 2003/1476, art 3(2)(a), as from 31 October 2004 (in so far as relating to contracts of long-term care insurance), and as from 14 January 2005 (otherwise), for transitional provisions see arts 22–27 of that Order at **[4665]** et seq.

Para (5): definitions "insurance mediation" and "reinsurance mediation" inserted, and word omitted from definition "core investment service" revoked, by SI 2003/1476, art 3(2)(b), as from 31 October 2004 (in so far as relating to contracts of long-term care insurance), and as from 14 January 2005 (otherwise), for transitional provisions see arts 22–27 of that Order at **[4665]** et seq; definitions "core investment service" and "investment firm" revoked by SI 2006/3384, arts 2, 4(a), as from 1 April 2007 (for the purposes of enabling applications to be made for (i) a Part IV permission, (ii) a variation of a Part IV permission, and (iii) the Authority's approval under s 59 of the 2000 Act, in relation to an activity of the kind specified by art 25D of this Order, or in relation to an investment of the kind specified by arts 83, 84 or 85 of this Order), and as from 1 November 2007 (otherwise).

CHAPTER II
ACCEPTING DEPOSITS

The activity

5 Accepting deposits

(1) Accepting deposits is a specified kind of activity if—

(a) money received by way of deposit is lent to others; or

(b) any other activity of the person accepting the deposit is financed wholly, or to a material extent, out of the capital of or interest on money received by way of deposit.

(2) In paragraph (1), "deposit" means a sum of money, other than one excluded by any of [articles 6 to 9A], paid on terms—

(a) under which it will be repaid, with or without interest or premium, and either on demand or at a time or in circumstances agreed by or on behalf of the person making the payment and the person receiving it; and

(b) which are not referable to the provision of property (other than currency) or services or the giving of security.

(3) For the purposes of paragraph (2), money is paid on terms which are referable to the provision of property or services or the giving of security if, and only if—

(a) it is paid by way of advance or part payment under a contract for the sale, hire or other provision of property or services, and is repayable only in the event that the property or services is or are not in fact sold, hired or otherwise provided;

(b) it is paid by way of security for the performance of a contract or by way of security in respect of loss which may result from the non-performance of a contract; or

(c) without prejudice to sub-paragraph (b), it is paid by way of security for the delivery up or return of any property, whether in a particular state of repair or otherwise.

[4005]

NOTES

Para (2): words in square brackets substituted by the Financial Services and Markets Act 2000 (Regulated Activities) (Amendment) Order 2002, SI 2002/682, art 3(1), as from 27 April 2002, subject to transitional provisions in relation to persons issuing electronic money immediately before that date contained in art 9 at **[4637]**.

See the Financial Services and Markets Act 2000 (Carrying on Regulated Activities by Way of Business) Order 2001, SI 2001/1177, art 2 at **[4146]** in relation to deposit taking business.

Exclusions

6 Sums paid by certain persons

(1) A sum is not a deposit for the purposes of article 5 if it is—

(a) paid by any of the following persons—

(i) the Bank of England, the central bank of an EEA State other than the United Kingdom, or the European Central Bank;

(ii) an authorised person who has permission to accept deposits, or to effect or carry out contracts of insurance;

(iii) an EEA firm falling within paragraph 5(b), (c) or (d) of Schedule 3 to the Act (other than one falling within paragraph (ii) above);

(iv) the National Savings Bank;

(v) a municipal bank, that is to say a company which was, immediately before the coming into force of this article, exempt from the prohibition in section 3 of the Banking Act 1987 by virtue of section 4(1) of, and paragraph 4 of Schedule 2 to, that Act;

(vi) Keesler Federal Credit Union;

(vii) a body of persons certified as a school bank by the National Savings Bank or by an authorised person who has permission to accept deposits;

(viii) a local authority;

(ix) any body which by virtue of any enactment has power to issue a precept to a local authority in England and Wales or a requisition to a local authority

in Scotland, or to the expenses of which, by virtue of any enactment, a local authority in the United Kingdom is or can be required to contribute (and in this paragraph, "enactment" includes an enactment comprised in, or in an instrument made under, an Act of the Scottish Parliament);
(x) the European Community, the European Atomic Energy Community or the European Coal and Steel Community;
(xi) the European Investment Bank;
(xii) the International Bank for Reconstruction and Development;
(xiii) the International Finance Corporation;
(xiv) the International Monetary Fund;
(xv) the African Development Bank;
(xvi) the Asian Development Bank;
(xvii) the Caribbean Development Bank;
(xviii) the Inter-American Development Bank;
(xix) the European Bank for Reconstruction and Development;
[(xx) the Council of Europe Development Bank;]

(b) paid by a person other than one mentioned in sub-paragraph (a) in the course of carrying on a business consisting wholly or to a significant extent of lending money;

(c) paid by one company to another at a time when both are members of the same group or when the same individual is a majority shareholder controller of both of them; or

(d) paid by a person who, at the time when it is paid, is a close relative of the person receiving it or who is, or is a close relative of, a director or manager of that person or who is, or is a close relative of, a controller of that person.

(2) For the purposes of paragraph (1)(c), an individual is a majority shareholder controller of a company if he is a controller of the company by virtue of paragraph (a), (c), (e) or (g) of section 422(2) of the Act, and if in his case the greatest percentage of those referred to in those paragraphs is 50 or more.

(3) In the application of sub-paragraph (d) of paragraph (1) to a sum paid by a partnership, that sub-paragraph is to have effect as if, for the reference to the person paying the sum, there were substituted a reference to each of the partners.

[4006]

NOTES

Para (1): sub-para (a)(xx) substituted by the Financial Services and Markets Act 2000 (Financial Promotion and Miscellaneous Amendments) Order 2002, SI 2002/1310, art 4(1), as from 5 June 2002.

7 Sums received by solicitors etc

(1) A sum is not a deposit for the purposes of article 5 if it is received by a practising solicitor acting in the course of his profession.

(2) In paragraph (1), "practising solicitor" means—

(a) a solicitor who is qualified to act as such under section 1 of the Solicitors Act 1974, article 4 of the Solicitors (Northern Ireland) Order 1976 or section 4 of the Solicitors (Scotland) Act 1980;

(b) a recognised body;

(c) a registered foreign lawyer in the course of providing professional services as a member of a multi-national partnership;

(d) a registered European lawyer; or

(e) a partner of a registered European lawyer who is providing professional services in accordance with—
(i) rules made under section 31 of the Solicitors Act 1974;
(ii) regulations made under article 26 of the Solicitors (Northern Ireland) Order 1976; or
(iii) rules made under section 34 of the Solicitors (Scotland) Act 1980.

(3) In this article—

(a) "a recognised body" means a body corporate recognised by—
(i) the Council of the Law Society under section 9 of the Administration of Justice Act 1985;
(ii) the Incorporated Law Society of Northern Ireland under article 26A of the Solicitors (Northern Ireland) Order 1976; or

(iii) the Council of the Law Society of Scotland under section 34 of the Solicitors (Scotland) Act 1980;

(b) "registered foreign lawyer" has the meaning given by section 89 of the Courts and Legal Services Act 1990 or, in Scotland, section 65 of the Solicitors (Scotland) Act 1980;

(c) "multi-national partnership" has the meaning given by section 89 of the Courts and Legal Services Act 1990 but, in Scotland, is a reference to a "multi-national practice" within the meaning of section 60A of the Solicitors (Scotland) Act 1980; and

(d) "registered European lawyer" has the meaning given by regulation 2(1) of the European Communities (Lawyer's Practice) Regulations 2000 or regulation 2(1) of the European Communities (Lawyer's Practice) (Scotland) Regulation 2000.

[4007]

8 Sums received by persons authorised to deal etc

A sum is not a deposit for the purposes of article 5 if it is received by a person who is—

(a) an authorised person with permission to carry on an activity of the kind specified by any of articles 14, 21, 25, 37, 51 and 52, or

(b) an exempt person in relation to any such activity,

in the course of, or for the purpose of, [carrying on any such activity (or any activity which would be such an activity but for any exclusion made by this Part)] with or on behalf of the person by or on behalf of whom the sum is paid.

[4008]

NOTES

Words in square brackets substituted by the Financial Services and Markets Act 2000 (Regulated Activities) (Amendment) Order 2001, SI 2001/3544, arts 2, 3, as from 1 December 2001.

9 Sums received in consideration for the issue of debt securities

(1) Subject to paragraph (2), a sum is not a deposit for the purposes of article 5 if it is received by a person as consideration for the issue by him of any investment of the kind specified by article 77 or 78.

(2) The exclusion in paragraph (1) does not apply to the receipt by a person of a sum as consideration for the issue by him of commercial paper unless—

(a) the commercial paper is issued to persons—

(i) whose ordinary activities involve them in acquiring, holding, managing or disposing of investments (as principal or agent) for the purposes of their businesses; or

(ii) who it is reasonable to expect will acquire, hold, manage or dispose of investments (as principal or agent) for the purposes of their businesses; and

(b) the redemption value of the commercial paper is not less than £100,000 (or an amount of equivalent value denominated wholly or partly in a currency other than sterling), and no part of the commercial paper may be transferred unless the redemption value of that part is not less than £100,000 (or such an equivalent amount).

[(3) In paragraph (2), "commercial paper" means an investment of the kind specified by article 77 or 78 having a maturity of less than one year from the date of issue.]

[4009]

NOTES

Para (3): substituted by the Financial Services and Markets Act 2000 (Regulated Activities) (Amendment) Order 2002, SI 2002/682, art 12, as from 27 April 2002.

[9A Sums received in exchange for electronic money

A sum is not a deposit for the purposes of article 5 if it is immediately exchanged for electronic money.]

[4010]

NOTES

Inserted by the Financial Services and Markets Act 2000 (Regulated Activities) (Amendment) Order 2002, SI 2002/682, art 3(2), as from 27 April 2002, subject to transitional provisions in relation to persons issuing electronic money immediately before that date contained in art 9 at **[4637]**.

[9AA Information society services

Article 5 is subject to the exclusion in article 72A (information society services).]

[4010A]

NOTES

Inserted by the Financial Services and Markets Act 2000 (Regulated Activities) (Amendment) (No 2) Order 2002, SI 2002/1776, art 3(1), (2), as from 21 August 2002.

[CHAPTER IIA
ELECTRONIC MONEY

The activity

9B Issuing electronic money

Issuing electronic money is a specified kind of activity.]

[4011]

NOTES

Chapter IIA (arts 9B–9K) inserted by the Financial Services and Markets Act 2000 (Regulated Activities) (Amendment) Order 2002, SI 2002/682, art 4, as from 11 April 2002 (for the purpose of making rules under arts 9G, 9H), and as from 27 April 2002 (otherwise); for transitional provisions in relation to persons issuing electronic money immediately before that date, see art 9 at **[4637]**.

[Exclusions

9C Persons certified as small issuers etc

(1) There is excluded from article 9B the issuing of electronic money by a person to whom the Authority has given a certificate under this article (provided the certificate has not been revoked).

(2) An application for a certificate may be made by—

(a) a body corporate, or

(b) a partnership,

(other than a credit institution as defined in [Article 4(1)(a)] of the banking consolidation directive) which has its head office in the United Kingdom.

(3) The authority must, on the application of such a person ("A"), give A a certificate if it appears to the Authority that paragraph (4), (5) or (6) applies.

(4) This paragraph applies if—

(a) A does not issue electronic money except on terms that the electronic device on which the monetary value is stored is subject to a maximum storage amount of not more than 150 euro; and

(b) A's total liabilities with respect to the issuing of electronic money do not (or will not) usually exceed 5 million euro and do not (or will not) ever exceed 6 million euro.

(5) This paragraph applies if—

(a) the condition in paragraph (4)(a) is met;

(b) A's total liabilities with respect to the issuing of electronic money do not (or will not) exceed 10 million euro; and

(c) electronic money issued by A is accepted as a means of payment only by—

(i) subsidiaries of A which perform operational or other ancillary functions related to electronic money issued or distributed by A; or

(ii) other members of the same group as A (other than subsidiaries of A).

(6) This paragraph applies if—

(a) the conditions in paragraphs (4)(a) and (5)(b) are met; and

(b) electronic money issued by A is accepted as a means of payment, in the course of business, by not more than one hundred persons where—

(i) those persons accept such electronic money only at locations within the same premises or limited local area; or

(ii) those persons have a close financial or business relationship with A, such as a common marketing or distribution scheme.

(7) For the purposes of paragraph (6)(b)(i), locations are to be treated as situated within the same premises or limited local area if they are situated within—

(a) a shopping centre, airport, railway station, bus station, or campus of a university, polytechnic, college, school or similar educational establishment; or

(b) an area which does not exceed four square kilometres;

but sub-paragraphs (a) and (b) are illustrative only and are not to be treated as limiting the scope of paragraph (6)(b)(i).

(8) For the purposes of paragraph (6)(b)(ii), persons are not to be treated as having a close financial or business relationship with A merely because they participate in arrangements for the acceptance of electronic money issued by A.

(9) In this article, references to amounts in euro include references to equivalent amounts in sterling.

(10) A person to whom a certificate has been given under this article (and whose certificate has not been revoked) is referred to in this Chapter as a "certified person".]

[4012]

NOTES

Inserted as noted to art 9B at **[4011]**.

Para (2): words in square brackets substituted the Capital Requirements Regulations 2006, SI 2006/3221, reg 29(4), Sch 6, para 6(1), (2), as from 1 January 2007.

[9D Applications for certificates

The following provisions of the Act apply to applications to the Authority for certificates under 9C (and the determination of such applications) as they apply to applications for Part IV permissions (and the determination of such applications)—

(a) section 51(1)(b) and (3) to (6);

(b) section 52, except subsections (6), (8) and (9)(a) and (b); and

(c) section 55(1).]

[4013]

NOTES

Inserted as noted to art 9B at **[4011]**.

[9E Revocation of certificate on Authority's own initiative

(1) The Authority may revoke a certificate given to a person ("A") under article 9C if—

(a) it appears to it that A does not meet the relevant conditions, or has failed to meet the relevant conditions at any time since the certificate was given; or

(b) the person to whom the certificate was given has contravened any rule or requirement to which he is subject as a result of article 9G.

(2) For the purposes of paragraph (1), A meets the relevant conditions at any time if, at that time, paragraph (4), (5) or (6) of article 9C applies.

(3) Sections 54 and 55(2) of the Act apply to the revocation of a certificate under paragraph (1) as they apply to the cancellation of a Part IV permission on the Authority's own initiative, as if references in those sections to an authorised person were references to a certified person.]

[4014]

NOTES

Inserted as noted to art 9B at **[4011]**.

[9F Revocation of certificate on request

(1) A certified person ("B") may apply to the Authority for his certificate to be revoked, and the Authority must then revoke the certificate and give B written notice that it has done so.

(2) An application under paragraph (1) must be made in such manner as the Authority may direct.

(3) If—

(a) B has made an application under Part IV of the Act for permission to carry on a regulated activity of the kind specified by article 9B (or for variation of an existing permission so as to add a regulated activity of that kind), and

(b) on making an application for revocation of his certificate under paragraph (1), he requests that the revocation be conditional on the granting of his application under Part IV of the Act,

the revocation of B's certificate is to be conditional on the granting of his application under Part IV of the Act.]

[4015]

NOTES

Inserted as noted to art 9B at **[4011]**.

[9G Obtaining information from certified persons etc

(1) The Authority may make rules requiring certified persons to provide information to the Authority about their activities so far as relating to the issuing of electronic money, including the amount of their liabilities with respect to the issuing of electronic money.

(2) Section 148 of the Act (modification or waiver of rules) applies in relation to rules made under paragraph (1) as if references in that section to an authorised person were references to a certified person.

(3) Section 150 of the Act (actions for damages) applies in relation to a rule made under paragraph (1) as if the reference in subsection (1) of that section to an authorised person were a reference to a certified person.

(4) The Authority may, by notice in writing given to a certified person, require him—

(a) to provide specified information or information of a specified description; or

(b) to produce specified documents or documents of a specified description.

(5) Paragraph (4) applies only to information or documents reasonably required for the purposes of determining whether the certified person meets, or has met, the relevant conditions.

(6) Subsections (2), (5) and (6) of section 165 of the Act (Authority's power to require information) apply to a requirement imposed under paragraph (4) as they apply to a requirement imposed under that section.

(7) Section 166 of the Act (reports by skilled persons) has effect as if—

(a) the reference in subsection (1) of that section to section 165 included a reference to paragraph (4) above; and

(b) the reference in section 166(2)(a) of the Act to an authorised person included a reference to a certified person.

(8) Subsection (4) of section 168 of the Act (appointment of persons to carry out investigations in particular cases) has effect as if it provided for subsection (5) of that section to apply if it appears to the Authority that there are circumstances suggesting that a certified person may not meet, or may not have met, the relevant conditions.

(9) Sections 175 (information and documents: supplemental provisions), 176 (entry of premises under warrant) and 177 (offences) of the Act apply to a requirement imposed under paragraph (4) as they apply to a requirement imposed under section 165 of the Act (the reference in section 176(3)(a) to an authorised person being read as a reference to a certified person).

(10) In this article—

(a) "specified", in paragraph (4), means specified in the notice mentioned in that paragraph;

(b) a certified person ("A") meets the relevant conditions at any time if, at that time, paragraph (4), (5) or (6) of article 9C applies.]

[4016]

NOTES

Inserted as noted to art 9B at **[4011]**.

[Supplemental

9H Rules prohibiting the issue of electronic money at a discount

(1) The Authority may make rules applying to authorised persons with permission to carry on an activity of the kind specified by article 9B, prohibiting the issue of electronic money having a monetary value greater than the funds received.

(2) Section 148 of the Act (modification or waiver of rules) applies in relation to rules made under paragraph (1).]

[4017]

NOTES

Inserted as noted to art 9B at **[4011]**.

[9I False claims to be a certified person

A person who is not a certified person is to be treated as guilty of an offence under section 24 of the Act (false claims to be authorised or exempt) if he—

(a) describes himself (in whatever terms) as a certified person;

(b) behaves, or otherwise holds himself out, in a manner which indicates (or which is reasonably likely to be understood as indicating) that he is a certified person.]

[4018]

NOTES

Inserted as noted to art 9B at **[4011]**.

[9J Exclusion of electronic money from the compensation scheme

The compensation scheme established under Part XV of the Act is not to provide for the compensation of persons in respect of claims made in connection with any activity of the kind specified by article 9B.]

[4019]

NOTES

Inserted as noted to art 9B at **[4011]**.

[9K Record of certified persons

The record maintained by the Authority under section 347 of the Act (public record of authorised persons etc) must include every certified person.]

[4020]

NOTES

Inserted as noted to art 9B at **[4011]**.

CHAPTER III
INSURANCE

The activities

10 Effecting and carrying out contracts of insurance

(1) Effecting a contract of insurance as principal is a specified kind of activity.

(2) Carrying out a contract of insurance as principal is a specified kind of activity.

[4021]

PART IV
STATUTORY INSTRUMENTS

Exclusions

11 Community co-insurers

(1) There is excluded from article 10(1) or (2) the effecting or carrying out of a contract of insurance by an EEA firm falling within paragraph 5(d) of Schedule 3 to the Act—

(a) other than through a branch in the United Kingdom; and

(b) pursuant to a Community co-insurance operation in which the firm is participating otherwise than as the leading insurer.

(2) In paragraph (1), "Community co-insurance operation" and "leading insurer" have the same meaning as in the Council Directive of 30 May 1978 on the co-ordination of laws, regulations and administrative provisions relating to Community co-insurance (No 78/473/EEC).

[4022]

12 Breakdown insurance

(1) There is excluded from article 10(1) or (2) the effecting or carrying out, by a person who does not otherwise carry on an activity of the kind specified by that article, of a contract of insurance which—

(a) is a contract under which the benefits provided by that person ("the provider") are exclusively or primarily benefits in kind in the event of accident to or breakdown of a vehicle; and

(b) contains the terms mentioned in paragraph (2).

(2) Those terms are that—

(a) the assistance takes either or both of the forms mentioned in paragraph (3)(a) and (b);

(b) the assistance is not available outside the United Kingdom and the Republic of Ireland except where it is provided without the payment of additional premium by a person in the country concerned with whom the provider has entered into a reciprocal agreement; and

(c) assistance provided in the case of an accident or breakdown occurring in the United Kingdom or the Republic of Ireland is, in most circumstances, provided by the provider's servants.

(3) The forms of assistance are—

(a) repairs to the relevant vehicle at the place where the accident or breakdown has occurred; this assistance may also include the delivery of parts, fuel, oil, water or keys to the relevant vehicle;

(b) removal of the relevant vehicle to the nearest or most appropriate place at which repairs may be carried out, or to—

(i) the home, point of departure or original destination within the United Kingdom of the driver and passengers, provided the accident or breakdown occurred within the United Kingdom;

(ii) the home, point of departure or original destination within the Republic of Ireland of the driver and passengers, provided the accident or breakdown occurred within the Republic of Ireland or within Northern Ireland;

(iii) the home, point of departure or original destination within Northern Ireland of the driver and passengers, provided the accident or breakdown occurred within the Republic of Ireland;

and this form of assistance may include the conveyance of the driver or passengers of the relevant vehicle, with the vehicle, or (where the vehicle is to be conveyed only to the nearest or most appropriate place at which repairs may be carried out) separately, to the nearest location from which they may continue their journey by other means.

(4) A contract does not fail to meet the condition in paragraph (1)(a) solely because the provider may reimburse the person entitled to the assistance for all or part of any sums paid by him in respect of assistance either because he failed to identify himself as a person entitled to the assistance or because he was unable to get in touch with the provider in order to claim the assistance.

(5) In this article—

"the assistance" means the benefits to be provided under a contract of the kind mentioned in paragraph (1);

"breakdown" means an event—

(a) which causes the driver of the relevant vehicle to be unable to start a journey in the vehicle or involuntarily to bring the vehicle to a halt on a journey because of some malfunction of the vehicle or failure of it to function, and

(b) after which the journey cannot reasonably be commenced or continued in the relevant vehicle;

"the relevant vehicle" means the vehicle (including a trailer or caravan) in respect of which the assistance is required.

[4023]

[12A Information society services

Article 10 is subject to the exclusion in article 72A (information society services), as qualified by paragraph (2) of that article.]

[4023A]

NOTES

Inserted by the Financial Services and Markets Act 2000 (Regulated Activities) (Amendment) (No 2) Order 2002, SI 2002/1776 art 3(1), (3), as from 21 August 2002.

Supplemental

13 Application of sections 327 and 332 of the Act to insurance market activities

(1) In sections 327(5) and (7) and 332(3)(b) of the Act (exemption from the general prohibition for members of the professions, and rules in relation to such persons), the references to "a regulated activity" and "regulated activities" do not include—

(a) any activity of the kind specified by article 10(1) or (2), where—
  (i) P is a member of the Society; and
  (ii) by virtue of section 316 of the Act (application of the Act to Lloyd's underwriting), the general prohibition does not apply to the carrying on by P of that activity; or

(b) any activity of the kind specified by article 10(2), where—
  (i) P is a former underwriting member; and
  (ii) the contract of insurance in question is one underwritten by P at Lloyd's.

(2) In paragraph (1)—

"member of the Society" has the same meaning as in Lloyd's Act 1982; and

"former underwriting member" has the meaning given by section 324(1) of the Act.

[4024]

CHAPTER IV

DEALING IN INVESTMENTS AS PRINCIPAL

The activity

14 Dealing in investments as principal

[(1)] Buying, selling, subscribing for or underwriting securities or contractually based investments (other than investments of the kind specified by article 87, or article 89 so far as relevant to that article) as principal is a specified kind of activity.

[(2) Paragraph (1) does not apply to a kind of activity to which article 25D applies.]

[4025]

NOTES

Para (1) numbered as such, and para (2) added, by the Financial Services and Markets Act 2000 (Regulated Activities) (Amendment No 3) Order 2006, SI 2006/3384, arts 2, 5, as from 1 April 2007 (for the purposes of enabling applications to be made for (i) a Part IV permission, (ii) a variation of a Part IV permission, and (iii) the Authority's approval under s 59 of the 2000 Act, in relation to an activity of the kind specified by art 25D of this Order, or in relation to an investment of the kind specified by arts 83, 84 or 85 of this Order), and as from 1 November 2007 (otherwise).

See the Financial Services and Markets Act 2000 (Carrying on Regulated Activities by Way of Business) Order 2001, SI 2001/1177, art 3 at **[4147]** in relation to investment business.

Exclusions

15 Absence of holding out etc

(1) Subject to paragraph (3), a person ("A") does not carry on an activity of the kind specified by article 14 by entering into a transaction which relates to a security or is the assignment (or, in Scotland, the assignation) of a qualifying contract of insurance (or an investment of the kind specified by article 89, so far as relevant to such a contract), unless—

- (a) A holds himself out as willing, as principal, to buy, sell or subscribe for investments of the kind to which the transaction relates at prices determined by him generally and continuously rather than in respect of each particular transaction;
- (b) A holds himself out as engaging in the business of buying investments of the kind to which the transaction relates, with a view to selling them;
- (c) A holds himself out as engaging in the business of underwriting investments of the kind to which the transaction relates; or
- (d) A regularly solicits members of the public with the purpose of inducing them, as principals or agents, to enter into transactions constituting activities of the kind specified by article 14, and the transaction is entered into as a result of his having solicited members of the public in that manner.

(2) In paragraph (1)(d), "members of the public" means any persons other than—

- (a) authorised persons or persons who are exempt persons in relation to activities of the kind specified by article 14;
- (b) members of the same group as A;
- (c) persons who are or who propose to become participators with A in a joint enterprise;
- (d) any person who is solicited by A with a view to the acquisition by A of 20 per cent or more of the voting shares in a body corporate;
- (e) if A (either alone or with members of the same group as himself) holds more than 20 per cent of the voting shares in a body corporate, any person who is solicited by A with a view to—
  - (i) the acquisition by A of further shares in the body corporate; or
  - (ii) the disposal by A of shares in the body corporate to the person solicited or to a member of the same group as the person solicited;
- (f) any person who—
  - (i) is solicited by A with a view to the disposal by A of shares in a body corporate to the person solicited or to a member of the same group as that person; and
  - (ii) either alone or with members of the same group holds 20 per cent or more of the voting shares in the body corporate;
- (g) any person whose head office is outside the United Kingdom, who is solicited by an approach made or directed to him at a place outside the United Kingdom and whose ordinary business involves him in carrying on activities of the kind specified by any of articles 14, 21, 25, 37, 40, 45, 51, 52 and 53 or (so far as relevant to any of those articles) article 64, or would do so apart from any exclusion from any of those articles made by this Order.

(3) This article does not apply where A enters into the transaction as bare trustee or, in Scotland, as nominee for another person and is acting on that other person's instructions (but the exclusion in article 66(1) applies if the conditions set out there are met).

[(4) This article is subject to article 4(4).]

[4026]

NOTES

Para (4): added by the Financial Services and Markets Act 2000 (Regulated Activities) (Amendment No 3) Order 2006, SI 2006/3384, arts 2, 6, as from 1 April 2007 (for the purposes of enabling applications to be made for (i) a Part IV permission, (ii) a variation of a Part IV permission, and (iii) the Authority's approval under s 59 of the 2000 Act, in relation to an activity of the kind specified by art 25D of this Order, or in relation to an investment of the kind specified by arts 83, 84 or 85 of this Order), and as from 1 November 2007 (otherwise).

16 Dealing in contractually based investments

[(1)] A person who is not an authorised person does not carry on an activity of the kind specified by article 14 by entering into a transaction relating to a contractually based investment—

(a) with or through an authorised person, or an exempt person acting in the course of a business comprising a regulated activity in relation to which he is exempt; or

(b) through an office outside the United Kingdom maintained by a party to the transaction, and with or through a person whose head office is situated outside the United Kingdom and whose ordinary business involves him in carrying on activities of the kind specified by any of articles 14, 21, 25, 37, 40, 45, 51, 52 and 53 or, so far as relevant to any of those articles, article 64 (or would do so apart from any exclusion from any of those articles made by this Order).

[(2) This article is subject to article 4(4).]

[4027]

NOTES

Para (1) numbered as such, and para (2) added, by the Financial Services and Markets Act 2000 (Regulated Activities) (Amendment No 3) Order 2006, SI 2006/3384, arts 2, 7, as from 1 April 2007 (for the purposes of enabling applications to be made for (i) a Part IV permission, (ii) a variation of a Part IV permission, and (iii) the Authority's approval under s 59 of the 2000 Act, in relation to an activity of the kind specified by art 25D of this Order, or in relation to an investment of the kind specified by arts 83, 84 or 85 of this Order), and as from 1 November 2007 (otherwise).

17 Acceptance of instruments creating or acknowledging indebtedness

(1) A person does not carry on an activity of the kind specified by article 14 by accepting an instrument creating or acknowledging indebtedness in respect of any loan, credit, guarantee or other similar financial accommodation or assurance which he has made, granted or provided.

(2) The reference in paragraph (1) to a person accepting an instrument includes a reference to a person becoming a party to an instrument otherwise than as a debtor or a surety.

[4028]

NOTES

Modification: references in para (1) to securities, instruments or investments creating or acknowledging indebtedness (or creating or acknowledging a present or future indebtedness) includes a reference to uncertificated units of eligible debt securities; see the Uncertificated Securities (Amendment) (Eligible Debt Securities) Regulations 2003, SI 2003/1633, reg 15, Sch 2, para 8.

Modification: references in para (2) to a person becoming party to an instrument includes a reference to a person assuming rights and obligations in respect of uncertificated units of an eligible debt security in accordance with its current terms of issue; see the Uncertificated Securities (Amendment) (Eligible Debt Securities) Regulations 2003, SI 2003/1633, reg 15, Sch 2, para 9.

18 Issue by a company of its own shares etc

(1) There is excluded from article 14 the issue by a company of its own shares or share warrants, and the issue by any person of his own debentures or debenture warrants.

(2) In this article—

(a) "company" means any body corporate other than an open-ended investment company;

(b) "shares" and "debentures" include any investment of the kind specified by article 76 or 77;

(c) "share warrants" and "debenture warrants" mean any investment of the kind specified by article 79 which relates to shares in the company concerned or, as the case may be, debentures issued by [the person concerned].

[4029]

NOTES

Para (2): words in square brackets substituted by the Financial Services and Markets Act 2000 (Regulated Activities) (Amendment) Order 2001, SI 2001/3544, arts 2, 4, as from 1 December 2001.

[18A Dealing by a company in its own shares

(1) A company does not carry on an activity of the kind specified by article 14 by purchasing its own shares where section 162A of the Companies Act 1985 (Treasury shares) applies to the shares purchased.

(2) A company does not carry on an activity of the kind specified by article 14 by dealing in its own shares held as treasury shares, in accordance with section 162D of that Act (Treasury shares: disposal and cancellation).

(3) In this article "shares held as treasury shares" has the same meaning as in that Act.]

[4029A]

NOTES

Inserted by the Financial Services and Markets Act 2000 (Regulated Activities) (Amendment) (No 3) Order 2003, SI 2003/2822, arts 2, 3, as from 1 December 2003.

19 Risk management

(1) A person ("B") does not carry on an activity of the kind specified by article 14 by entering as principal into a transaction with another person ("C") if—

(a) the transaction relates to investments of the kind specified by any of articles 83 to 85 (or article 89 so far as relevant to any of those articles);
(b) neither B nor C is an individual;
(c) the sole or main purpose for which B enters into the transaction (either by itself or in combination with other such transactions) is that of limiting the extent to which a relevant business will be affected by any identifiable risk arising otherwise than as a result of the carrying on of a regulated activity; and
(d) the relevant business consists mainly of activities other than—
  (i) regulated activities; or
  (ii) activities which would be regulated activities but for any exclusion made by this Part.

(2) In paragraph (1), "relevant business" means a business carried on by—

(a) B;
(b) a member of the same group as B; or
(c) where B and another person are, or propose to become, participators in a joint enterprise, that other person.

[(3) This article is subject to article 4(4).]

[4030]

NOTES

Para (3): added by the Financial Services and Markets Act 2000 (Regulated Activities) (Amendment No 3) Order 2006, SI 2006/3384, arts 2, 8, as from 1 April 2007 (for the purposes of enabling applications to be made for (i) a Part IV permission, (ii) a variation of a Part IV permission, and (iii) the Authority's approval under s 59 of the 2000 Act, in relation to an activity of the kind specified by art 25D of this Order, or in relation to an investment of the kind specified by arts 83, 84 or 85 of this Order), and as from 1 November 2007 (otherwise).

20 Other exclusions

Article 14 is also subject to the exclusions in articles 66 (trustees etc), 68 (sale of goods and supply of services), 69 (groups and joint enterprises), 70 (sale of body corporate), 71 (employee share schemes)[, 72 (overseas persons) and 72A (information society services)].

[4031]

NOTES

Words in square brackets substituted by the Financial Services and Markets Act 2000 (Regulated Activities) (Amendment) (No 2) Order 2002, SI 2002/1776, art 3(1), (4), as from 21 August 2002.

CHAPTER V
DEALING IN INVESTMENTS AS AGENT

The activity

21 Dealing in investments as agent

[(1)] Buying, selling, subscribing for or underwriting securities or [relevant investments] (other than investments of the kind specified by article 87, or article 89 so far as relevant to that article) as agent is a specified kind of activity.

[(2) Paragraph (1) does not apply to a kind of activity to which article 25D applies.]

[4032]

NOTES

Para (1) numbered as such, and para (2) added, by the Financial Services and Markets Act 2000 (Regulated Activities) (Amendment No 3) Order 2006, SI 2006/3384, arts 2, 9, as from 1 April 2007 (for the purposes of enabling applications to be made for (i) a Part IV permission, (ii) a variation of a Part IV permission, and (iii) the Authority's approval under s 59 of the 2000 Act, in relation to an activity of the kind specified by art 25D of this Order, or in relation to an investment of the kind specified by arts 83, 84 or 85 of this Order), and as from 1 November 2007 (otherwise).

Words in square brackets in para (1) substituted by the Financial Services and Markets Act 2000 (Regulated Activities) (Amendment) (No 2) Order 2003, SI 2003/1476, art 4(1), as from 31 October 2004 (in so far as relating to contracts of long-term care insurance), and as from 14 January 2005 (otherwise), for transitional provisions see arts 22–27 of that Order at **[4665]** et seq.

See the Financial Services and Markets Act 2000 (Carrying on Regulated Activities by Way of Business) Order 2001, SI 2001/1177, art 3 at **[4147]** in relation to investment business.

Exclusions

22 Deals with or through authorised persons

(1) A person who is not an authorised person does not carry on an activity of the kind specified by article 21 by entering into a transaction as agent for another person ("the client") with or through an authorised person if—

(a) the transaction is entered into on advice given to the client by an authorised person; or

(b) it is clear, in all the circumstances, that the client, in his capacity as an investor, is not seeking and has not sought advice from the agent as to the merits of the client's entering into the transaction (or, if the client has sought such advice, the agent has declined to give it but has recommended that the client seek such advice from an authorised person).

[(2) But the exclusion in paragraph (1) does not apply if—

(a) the transaction relates to a contract of insurance; or

(b) the agent receives from any person other than the client any pecuniary reward or other advantage, for which he does not account to the client, arising out of his entering into the transaction.]

[(3) This article is subject to article 4(4).]

[4033]

NOTES

Para (2): substituted by the Financial Services and Markets Act 2000 (Regulated Activities) (Amendment) (No 2) Order 2003, SI 2003/1476, art 4(2), as from 31 October 2004 (in so far as relating to contracts of long-term care insurance), and as from 14 January 2005 (otherwise), for transitional provisions see arts 22–27 of that Order at **[4665]**.

Para (3): added by the Financial Services and Markets Act 2000 (Regulated Activities) (Amendment No 3) Order 2006, SI 2006/3384, arts 2, 10, as from 1 April 2007 (for the purposes of enabling applications to be made for (i) a Part IV permission, (ii) a variation of a Part IV permission, and (iii) the Authority's approval under s 59 of the 2000 Act, in relation to an activity of the kind specified by art 25D of this Order, or in relation to an investment of the kind specified by arts 83, 84 or 85 of this Order), and as from 1 November 2007 (otherwise).

23 Risk management

(1) A person ("B") does not carry on an activity of the kind specified by article 21 by entering as agent for a relevant person into a transaction with another person ("C") if—

(a) the transaction relates to investments of the kind specified by any of articles 83 to 85 (or article 89 so far as relevant to any of those articles);

(b) neither B nor C is an individual;

(c) the sole or main purpose for which B enters into the transaction (either by itself or in combination with other such transactions) is that of limiting the extent to which a relevant business will be affected by any identifiable risk arising otherwise than as a result of the carrying on of a regulated activity; and

(d) the relevant business consists mainly of activities other than—

(i) regulated activities; or

(ii) activities which would be regulated activities but for any exclusion made by this Part.

(2) In paragraph (1), "relevant person" means—

(a) a member of the same group as B; or

(b) where B and another person are, or propose to become, participators in a joint enterprise, that other person;

and "relevant business" means a business carried on by a relevant person.

[(3) This article is subject to article 4(4).]

[4034]

NOTES

Para (3): added by the Financial Services and Markets Act 2000 (Regulated Activities) (Amendment No 3) Order 2006, SI 2006/3384, arts 2, 11, as from 1 April 2007 (for the purposes of enabling applications to be made for (i) a Part IV permission, (ii) a variation of a Part IV permission, and (iii) the Authority's approval under s 59 of the 2000 Act, in relation to an activity of the kind specified by art 25D of this Order, or in relation to an investment of the kind specified by arts 83, 84 or 85 of this Order), and as from 1 November 2007 (otherwise).

24 Other exclusions

Article 21 is also subject to the exclusions in articles 67 (profession or non-investment business), 68 (sale of goods and supply of services), 69 (groups and joint enterprises), 70 (sale of body corporate), 71 (employee share schemes)[, 72 (overseas persons)[, 72A (information society services), 72B (activities carried on by a provider of relevant goods or services) and 72D (large risks contracts where risk situated outside the EEA)]].

[4035]

NOTES

Words in first (outer) pair of square brackets substituted by the Financial Services and Markets Act 2000 (Regulated Activities) (Amendment) (No 2) Order 2002, SI 2002/1776, art 3(1), (5), as from 21 August 2002; words in second (inner) pair of square brackets substituted by the Financial Services and Markets Act 2000 (Regulated Activities) (Amendment) (No 2) Order 2003, SI 2003/1476, art 4(3), as from 31 October 2004 (in so far as relating to contracts of long-term care insurance), and as from 14 January 2005 (otherwise), for transitional provisions see arts 22–27 of that Order at **[4665]** et seq.

CHAPTER VI
ARRANGING DEALS IN INVESTMENTS

The activities

25 Arranging deals in investments

(1) Making arrangements for another person (whether as principal or agent) to buy, sell, subscribe for or underwrite a particular investment which is—

(a) a security,

(b) a [relevant investment], or

(c) an investment of the kind specified by article 86, or article 89 so far as relevant to that article,

is a specified kind of activity.

(2) Making arrangements with a view to a person who participates in the arrangements buying, selling, subscribing for or underwriting investments falling within paragraph (1)(a), (b) or (c) (whether as principal or agent) is also a specified kind of activity.

[(3) Paragraphs (1) and (2) do not apply to a kind of activity to which article 25D applies.]

[4036]

NOTES

Para (1): words in square brackets substituted by the Financial Services and Markets Act 2000 (Regulated Activities) (Amendment) (No 2) Order 2003, SI 2003/1476, art 5(1), as from 31 October 2004 (in so far as relating to contracts of long-term care insurance), and as from 14 January 2005 (otherwise); for transitional provisions see arts 22–27 of that Order at **[4665]** et seq.

Para (3): added by the Financial Services and Markets Act 2000 (Regulated Activities) (Amendment No 3) Order 2006, SI 2006/3384, arts 2, 12, as from 1 April 2007 (for the purposes of enabling applications to be made for (i) a Part IV permission, (ii) a variation of a Part IV permission, and (iii) the Authority's approval under s 59 of the 2000 Act, in relation to an activity of the kind specified by art 25D of this Order, or in relation to an investment of the kind specified by arts 83, 84 or 85 of this Order), and as from 1 November 2007 (otherwise).

See the Financial Services and Markets Act 2000 (Carrying on Regulated Activities by Way of Business) Order 2001, SI 2001/1177, art 3 at **[4147]** in relation to investment business, except in so far as that activity relates to investment of the kind specified by arts 86 or 89 of this order so far as relevant to that article.

[25A Arranging regulated mortgage contracts

(1) Making arrangements—

(a) for another person to enter into a regulated mortgage contract as borrower; or

(b) for another person to vary the terms of a regulated mortgage contract entered into by him as borrower after the coming into force of article 61, in such a way as to vary his obligations under that contract,

is a specified kind of activity.

(2) Making arrangements with a view to a person who participates in the arrangements entering into a regulated mortgage contract as borrower is also a specified kind of activity.

(3) In this article "borrower" has the meaning given by article 61(3)(a)(i).]

[4036A]

NOTES

Inserted by the Financial Services and Markets Act 2000 (Regulated Activities) (Amendment) (No 1) Order 2003, SI 2003/1475, art 4, as from 31 October 2004; for transitional provisions see arts 26–29 at **[4659]** et seq.

[25B Arranging regulated home reversion plans

(1) Making arrangements—

(a) for another person to enter into a regulated home reversion plan as reversion seller or as plan provider; or

(b) for another person to vary the terms of a regulated home reversion plan, entered into on or after 6th April 2007 by him as reversion seller or as plan provider, in such a way as to vary his obligations under that plan,

is a specified kind of activity.

(2) Making arrangements with a view to a person who participates in the arrangements entering into a regulated home reversion plan as reversion seller or as plan provider is also a specified kind of activity.]

[4036B]

NOTES

Commencement: 6 November 2006 (certain purposes); 6 April 2007 (otherwise) (for more information see the note below).

Inserted, together with art 25C, by the Financial Services and Markets Act 2000 (Regulated Activities) (Amendment) (No 2) Order 2006, SI 2006/2383, arts 2, 4, as from 6 November 2006 (for the purposes of enabling applications to be made for (i) a Pt IV permission, or a variation of a Pt IV permission, in relation to activities of the kind specified by arts 25B, 25C, 53B, 53C, 63B or 63F or, so far as relevant to any such activity, art 64 of this Order; or (ii) the Authority's approval under FSMA 2000, s 59 in relation to any of those activities), and as from 6 April 2007 (otherwise) (for transitional provisions and effect see arts 36–40 of, and the Schedule to, the 2006 Order at **[4821]** et seq).

[25C Arranging regulated home purchase plans

(1) Making arrangements—

(a) for another person to enter into a regulated home purchase plan as home purchaser; or

(b) for another person to vary the terms of a regulated home purchase plan, entered into on or after 6th April 2007 by him as home purchaser, in such a way as to vary his obligations under that plan,

is a specified kind of activity.

(2) Making arrangements with a view to a person who participates in the arrangements entering into a regulated home purchase plan as home purchaser is also a specified kind of activity.]

[4036C]

NOTES

Commencement: 6 November 2006 (certain purposes); 6 April 2007 (otherwise) (for more information see the note to art 25B at **[4036B]**).

Inserted as noted to art 25B at **[4036B]**.

[25D Operating a multilateral trading facility

(1) The operation of a multilateral trading facility on which MiFID instruments are traded is a specified kind of activity.

(2) In paragraph (1), "MiFID instrument" means any investment—

(a) of the kind specified by article 76, 77, 78, 79, 80, 81, 83, 84 or 85; or

(b) of the kind specified by article 89 so far as relevant to an investment falling within sub-paragraph (a),

that is a financial instrument.]

[4036D]

NOTES

Commencement: 1 April 2007 (certain purposes); 1 November 2007 (otherwise) (for more information see below).

Inserted by the Financial Services and Markets Act 2000 (Regulated Activities) (Amendment No 3) Order 2006, SI 2006/3384, arts 2, 13, as from 1 April 2007 (for the purposes of enabling applications to be made for (i) a Part IV permission, (ii) a variation of a Part IV permission, and (iii) the Authority's approval under s 59 of the 2000 Act, in relation to an activity of the kind specified by art 25D of this Order, or in relation to an investment of the kind specified by arts 83, 84 or 85 of this Order), and as from 1 November 2007 (otherwise).

Exclusions

26 Arrangements not causing a deal

There are excluded from [articles 25(1), 25A(1), 25B(1) and 25C(1)] arrangements which do not or would not bring about the transaction to which the arrangements relate.

[4037]

NOTES

Words in square brackets substituted by the Financial Services and Markets Act 2000 (Regulated Activities) (Amendment) (No 2) Order 2006, SI 2006/2383, arts 2, 5, as from 6 November 2006 (for the purposes of enabling applications to be made for (i) a Pt IV permission, or a variation of a Pt IV permission, in relation to activities of the kind specified by arts 25B, 25C, 53B, 53C, 63B or 63F or, so far as relevant to any such activity, art 64 of this Order; or (ii) the Authority's approval under FSMA 2000, s 59 in relation to any of those activities), and as from 6 April 2007 (otherwise) (for transitional provisions and effect see arts 36–40 of, and the Schedule to, the 2006 Order at **[4821]** et seq).

27 Enabling parties to communicate

A person does not carry on an activity of the kind specified by [article 25(2), 25A(2), 25B(2) or 25C(2)] merely by providing means by which one party to a transaction (or potential transaction) is able to communicate with other such parties.

[4038]

NOTES

Words in square brackets substituted by the Financial Services and Markets Act 2000 (Regulated Activities) (Amendment) (No 2) Order 2006, SI 2006/2383, arts 2, 6, as from 6 November 2006 (for the purposes of enabling applications to be made for (i) a Pt IV permission, or a variation of a Pt IV permission, in relation to activities of the kind specified by arts 25B, 25C, 53B, 53C, 63B or 63F or, so far as relevant to any such activity, art 64 of this Order; or (ii) the Authority's approval under FSMA 2000, s 59 in relation to any of those activities), and as from 6 April 2007 (otherwise) (for transitional provisions and effect see arts 36–40 of, and the Schedule to, the 2006 Order at **[4821]** et seq).

28 Arranging transactions to which the arranger is a party

(1) There are excluded from article 25(1) any arrangements for a transaction into which the person making the arrangements enters or is to enter as principal or as agent for some other person.

(2) There are excluded from article 25(2) any arrangements which a person makes with a view to transactions into which he enters or is to enter as principal or as agent for some other person.

[(3) But the exclusions in paragraphs (1) and (2) do not apply to arrangements made for or with a view to a transaction which relates to a contract of insurance, unless the person making the arrangements either—

(a) is the only policyholder; or

(b) as a result of the transaction, would become the only policyholder.]

[4039]

NOTES

Para (3): added by the Financial Services and Markets Act 2000 (Regulated Activities) (Amendment) (No 2) Order 2003, SI 2003/1476, art 5(2), as from 31 October 2004 (in so far as relating to contracts of long-term care insurance), and as from 14 January 2005 (otherwise), for transitional provisions see arts 22–27 of that Order at **[4665]** et seq.

[28A Arranging contracts [or plans] to which the arranger is a party

(1) There are excluded from [articles 25A(1), 25B(1) and 25C(1)] any arrangements—

(a) for a [contract or plan] into which the person making the arrangements enters or is to enter; or

(b) for a variation of a [contract or plan] to which that person is (or is to become) a party.

(2) There are excluded [articles 25A(2), 25B(2) and 25C(2)] any arrangements which a person makes with a view to contracts [or plans] into which he enters or is to enter.]

[4039A]

NOTES

Inserted by the Financial Services and Markets Act 2000 (Regulated Activities) (Amendment) (No 1) Order 2003, SI 2003/1475, art 7, as from 31 October 2004; for transitional provisions see arts 26–29 at **[4659]** et seq.

Article heading: words in square brackets inserted by the Financial Services and Markets Act 2000 (Regulated Activities) (Amendment) (No 2) Order 2006, SI 2006/2383, arts 2, 7(1), as from 6 November 2006 (for the purposes of enabling applications to be made for (i) a Pt IV permission, or a variation of a Pt IV permission, in relation to activities of the kind specified by arts 25B, 25C, 53B, 53C, 63B or 63F or, so far as relevant to any such activity, art 64 of this Order; or (ii) the Authority's approval under FSMA 2000, s 59 in relation to any of those activities), and as from 6 April 2007 (otherwise) (for transitional provisions and effect see arts 36–40 of, and the Schedule to, the 2006 Order at **[4821]** et seq).

Para (1): words in square brackets substituted by SI 2006/2383, arts 2, 7(1)(a), as from 6 November 2006 (certain purposes), and as from 6 April 2007 (otherwise) (for purposes, transitional provisions, and effect, see the note "Article heading" above).

Para (2): words in first pair of square brackets substituted, and words in second pair of square brackets inserted, by SI 2006/2383, arts 2, 7(1)(b), as from 6 November 2006 (certain purposes), and as from 6 April 2007 (otherwise) (for purposes, transitional provisions, and effect, see the note "Article heading" above).

29 Arranging deals with or through authorised persons

(1) There are excluded from [articles 25(1) and (2), 25A(1) and (2), 25B(1) and (2) and 25C(1) and (2)] arrangements made by a person ("A") who is not an authorised person for or with a view to a transaction which is or is to be entered into by a person ("the client") with or though an authorised person if—

(a) the transaction is or is to be entered into on advice to the client by an authorised person; or

(b) it is clear, in all the circumstances, that the client, in his capacity as an [investor, borrower, reversion seller, plan provider or (as the case may be) home purchaser], is not seeking and has not sought advice from A as to the merits of the client's entering into the transaction (or, if the client has sought such advice, A has declined to give it but has recommended that the client seek such advice from an authorised person).

[(2) But the exclusion in paragraph (1) does not apply if—

(a) the transaction relates, or would relate, to a contract of insurance; or

(b) A receives from any person other than the client any pecuniary reward or other advantage, for which he does not account to the client, arising out of his making the arrangements.]

[(3) This article is subject to article 4(4).]

[4040]

NOTES

Para (1): words in square brackets substituted by the Financial Services and Markets Act 2000 (Regulated Activities) (Amendment) (No 2) Order 2006, SI 2006/2383, arts 2, 8, as from 6 November 2006 (for the purposes of enabling applications to be made for (i) a Pt IV permission, or a variation of a Pt IV permission, in relation to activities of the kind specified by arts 25B, 25C, 53B, 53C, 63B or 63F or, so far as relevant to any such activity, art 64 of this Order; or (ii) the Authority's approval under FSMA 2000, s 59 in relation to any of those activities), and as from 6 April 2007 (otherwise) (for transitional provisions and effect see arts 36–40 of, and the Schedule to, the 2006 Order at **[4821]** et seq).

Para (2): substituted by the Financial Services and Markets Act 2000 (Regulated Activities) (Amendment) (No 2) Order 2003, SI 2003/1476, art 5(3), as from 31 October 2004 (in so far as relating to contracts of long-term care insurance), and as from 14 January 2005 (otherwise), for transitional provisions see arts 22–27 of that Order at **[4665]**.

Para (3): added by the Financial Services and Markets Act 2000 (Regulated Activities) (Amendment No 3) Order 2006, SI 2006/3384, arts 2, 14, as from 1 April 2007 (for the purposes of enabling applications to be made for (i) a Part IV permission, (ii) a variation of a Part IV permission, and (iii) the Authority's approval under s 59 of the 2000 Act, in relation to an activity of the kind specified by art 25D of this Order, or in relation to an investment of the kind specified by arts 83, 84 or 85 of this Order), and as from 1 November 2007 (otherwise).

[29A Arrangements made in the course of administration by authorised person

[(1)] A person who is not an authorised person ("A") does not carry on an activity of the kind specified by article 25A(1)(b) as a result of—

(a) anything done by an authorised person ("B") in relation to a regulated mortgage contract which B is administering pursuant to an arrangement of the kind mentioned in article 62(a); or

(b) anything A does in connection with the administration of a regulated mortgage contract in circumstances falling within article 62(b).]

[(2) A person who is not an authorised person ("A") does not carry on an activity of the kind specified by article 25B(1)(b) as a result of—

(a) anything done by an authorised person ("B") in relation to a regulated home reversion plan which B is administering pursuant to an arrangement of the kind mentioned in article 63C(a); or

(b) anything A does in connection with the administration of a regulated home reversion plan in circumstances falling within article 63C(b).

(3) A person who is not an authorised person ("A") does not carry on an activity of the kind specified by article 25C(1)(b) as a result of—

(a) anything done by an authorised person ("B") in relation to a regulated home purchase plan which B is administering pursuant to an arrangement of the kind mentioned in article 63G(a); or

(b) anything A does in connection with the administration of a regulated home purchase plan in circumstances falling within article 63G(b).]

[4040A]

NOTES

Inserted by the Financial Services and Markets Act 2000 (Regulated Activities) (Amendment) (No 1) Order 2003, SI 2003/1475, art 9, as from 31 October 2004; for transitional provisions see arts 26–29 at **[4659]** et seq.

Para (1) numbered as such, and paras (2), (3) added, by the Financial Services and Markets Act 2000 (Regulated Activities) (Amendment) (No 2) Order 2006, SI 2006/2383, arts 2, 9, as from 6 November 2006 (for the purposes of enabling applications to be made for (i) a Pt IV permission, or a variation of a Pt IV permission, in relation to activities of the kind specified by arts 25B, 25C, 53B, 53C, 63B or 63F or, so far as relevant to any such activity, art 64 of this Order; or (ii) the Authority's approval under FSMA 2000, s 59 in relation to any of those activities), and as from 6 April 2007 (otherwise) (for transitional provisions and effect see arts 36–40 of, and the Schedule to, the 2006 Order at **[4821]** et seq).

30 Arranging transactions in connection with lending on the security of insurance policies

(1) There are excluded from article 25(1) and (2) arrangements made by a money-lender under which either—

[(a) a relevant authorised person or a person acting on his behalf will introduce to the money-lender persons with whom the relevant authorised person has entered, or proposes to enter, into a relevant transaction, or will advise such persons to approach the money-lender, with a view to the money-lender lending money on the security of any contract effected pursuant to a relevant transaction;]

(b) a relevant authorised person gives an assurance to the money-lender as to the amount which, on the security of any contract effected pursuant to a relevant transaction, will or may be received by the money-lender should the money-lender lend money to a person introduced to him pursuant to the arrangements.

(2) In paragraph (1)—

"money-lender" means a person who is—

(a) a money-lending company within the meaning of section 338 of the Companies Act 1985;

(b) a body corporate incorporated under the law of, or of any part of, the United Kingdom relating to building societies; or

(c) a person whose ordinary business includes the making of loans or the giving of guarantees in connection with loans;

"relevant authorised person" means an authorised person who has permission to effect [contracts of insurance] or to sell investments of the kind specified by article 89, so far as relevant to such contracts;

"relevant transaction" means the effecting of a [contract of insurance] or the sale of an investment of the kind specified by article 89, so far as relevant to such contracts.

[(3) This article is subject to article 4(4A).]

[4041]

NOTES

Para (1): sub-para (a) substituted by the Financial Services and Markets Act 2000 (Regulated Activities) (Amendment) Order 2001, SI 2001/3544, arts 2, 5, as from 1 December 2001.

Para (2): words in square brackets in definitions "relevant authorised person" and "relevant transaction" substituted by the Financial Services and Markets Act 2000 (Regulated Activities) (Amendment) (No 2) Order 2003, SI 2003/1476, art 5(4), as from 31 October 2004 (in so far as relating to contracts of long-term care insurance), and as from 14 January 2005 (otherwise), for transitional provisions see arts 22–27 of that Order at **[4665]** et seq.

Para (3): added by the Financial Services and Markets Act 2000 (Regulated Activities) (Amendment No 3) Order 2006, SI 2006/3384, arts 2, 15, as from 1 April 2007 (for the purposes of enabling applications to be made for (i) a Part IV permission, (ii) a variation of a Part IV permission, and (iii) the Authority's approval under s 59 of the 2000 Act, in relation to an activity of the kind specified by art 25D of this Order, or in relation to an investment of the kind specified by arts 83, 84 or 85 of this Order), and as from 1 November 2007 (otherwise).

31 Arranging the acceptance of debentures in connection with loans

(1) There are excluded from article 25(1) and (2) arrangements under which a person accepts or is to accept, whether as principal or agent, an instrument creating or acknowledging indebtedness in respect of any loan, credit, guarantee or other similar financial accommodation or assurance which is, or is to be, made, granted or provided by that person or his principal.

(2) The reference in paragraph (1) to a person accepting an instrument includes a reference to a person becoming a party to an instrument otherwise than as a debtor or a surety.

[4042]

NOTES

Modification: references in para (1) to securities, instruments or investments creating or acknowledging indebtedness (or creating or acknowledging a present or future indebtedness) includes a reference to uncertificated units of eligible debt securities; see the Uncertificated Securities (Amendment) (Eligible Debt Securities) Regulations 2003, SI 2003/1633, reg 15, Sch 2, para 8.

Modification: references in para (2) to a person becoming party to an instrument includes a reference to a person assuming rights and obligations in respect of uncertificated units of an eligible debt security in accordance with its current terms of issue; see the Uncertificated Securities (Amendment) (Eligible Debt Securities) Regulations 2003, SI 2003/1633, reg 15, Sch 2, para 9.

32 Provision of finance

There are excluded from article 25(2) arrangements having as their sole purpose the provision of finance to enable a person to buy, sell, subscribe for or underwrite investments.

[4043]

33 Introducing

There are excluded from [articles 25(2), 25A(2), 25B(2) and 25C(2)] arrangements where—

(a) they are arrangements under which persons ("clients") will be introduced to another person;

(b) the person to whom introductions are to be made is—

(i) an authorised person;

(ii) an exempt person acting in the course of a business comprising a regulated activity in relation to which he is exempt; or

(iii) a person who is not unlawfully carrying on regulated activities in the United Kingdom and whose ordinary business involves him in engaging in an activity of the kind specified by any of articles 14, 21, 25, [25A,] [25B, 25C,] 37[, 39A], 40, 45, 51, [52, 53[, 53A, 53B and 53C]] (or, so far as relevant to any of those articles, article 64), or would do so apart from any exclusion from any of those articles made by this Order; …

(c) the introduction is made with a view to the provision of independent advice or the independent exercise of discretion in relation to investments generally or in relation to any class of investments to which the arrangements relate[; and

(d) the arrangements are made with a view to a person entering into a transaction which does not relate to a contract of insurance].

[4044]

NOTES

Words in first pair of square brackets substituted by the Financial Services and Markets Act 2000 (Regulated Activities) (Amendment) (No 2) Order 2006, SI 2006/2383, arts 2, 10(a), as from 6 November 2006 (for the purposes of enabling applications to be made for (i) a Pt IV permission, or a variation of a Pt IV permission, in relation to activities of the kind specified by arts 25B, 25C, 53B, 53C, 63B or 63F or, so far as relevant to any such activity, art 64 of this Order; or (ii) the Authority's approval under FSMA 2000, s 59 in relation to any of those activities), and as from 6 April 2007 (otherwise) (for transitional provisions and effect see arts 36–40 of, and the Schedule to, the 2006 Order at **[4821]** et seq).

Figure in first pair of square brackets in para (b)(iii) inserted, and words in the penultimate (outer) pair of square brackets in that paragraph substituted, by the Financial Services and Markets Act 2000 (Regulated Activities) (Amendment) (No 1) Order 2003, SI 2003/1475, art 10, as from 31 October 2004, for transitional provisions see arts 26–29 at **[4659]** et seq.

Figures in second pair of square brackets in para (b)(iii) inserted, and words in final (inner) pair of square brackets substituted, by SI 2006/2383, arts 2, 10(b), as from 6 November 2006 (certain purposes), and as from 6 April 2007 (otherwise) (for purposes, transitional provisions, and effect, see the note above).

Figure in third pair of square brackets in para (b)(iii) inserted, word omitted from that paragraph revoked, and para (d) and the word immediately preceding it added, by the Financial Services and Markets Act 2000 (Regulated Activities) (Amendment) (No 2) Order 2003, SI 2003/1476, art 5(5), as from 31 October 2004 (in so far as relating to contracts of long-term care insurance), and as from 14 January 2005 (otherwise), for transitional provisions see arts 22–27 of that Order at **[4665]** et seq.

[33A Introducing to authorised persons etc

(1) There are excluded from article 25A(2) arrangements where—

(a) they are arrangements under which a client is introduced to a person ("N") who is—

(i) an authorised person who has permission to carry on a regulated activity of the kind specified by any of articles 25A, 53A, and 61(1),

(ii) an appointed representative who may carry on a regulated activity of the kind specified by either of articles 25A and 53A without contravening the general prohibition, or

(iii) an overseas person who carries on activities specified by any of articles 25A, 53A and 61(1); and

(b) the conditions mentioned in paragraph (2) are satisfied.

[(1A) There are excluded from article 25B(2) arrangements where—

(a) they are arrangements under which a client is introduced to a person ("N") who is—

(i) an authorised person who has permission to carry on a regulated activity of the kind specified by any of articles 25B, 53B and 63B(1),

(ii) an appointed representative who may carry on a regulated activity of the kind specified by either of articles 25B and 53B without contravening the general prohibition, or

(iii) an overseas person who carries on activities specified by any of articles 25B, 53B and 63B(1); and

(b) the conditions mentioned in paragraph (2) are satisfied.

(1B) There are excluded from article 25C(2) arrangements where—

(a) they are arrangements under which a client is introduced to a person ("N") who is—

(i) an authorised person who has permission to carry on a regulated activity of the kind specified by any of articles 25C, 53C and 63F(1),

(ii) an appointed representative who may carry on a regulated activity of the kind specified by either of articles 25C and 53C without contravening the general prohibition, or

(iii) an overseas person who carries on activities specified by any of articles 25C, 53C and 63F(1); and

(b) the conditions mentioned in paragraph (2) are satisfied.]

(2) Those conditions are—

(a) that the person making the introduction ("P") does not receive any money, other than money payable to P on his own account, paid by the client for or in connection with any transaction which the client enters into with or through N as a result of the introduction; and

(b) that before making the introduction P discloses to the client such of the information mentioned in paragraph (3) as applies to P.

(3) That information is—

(a) that P is a member of the same group as N;

(b) details of any payment which P will receive from N, by way of fee or commission, for introducing the client to N;

(c) an indication of any other reward or advantage received or to be received by P that arises out of his introducing clients to N.

[(4) In this article, "client" means—

(a) for the purposes of paragraph (1), a borrower within the meaning given by article 61(3)(a)(i), or a person who is or may be contemplating entering into a regulated mortgage contract as such a borrower;

(b) for the purposes of paragraph (1A), a reversion seller, a plan provider or a person who is or may be contemplating entering into a regulated home reversion plan as a reversion seller or as a plan provider;

(c) for the purposes of paragraph (1B), a home purchaser or a person who is or may be contemplating entering into a regulated home purchase plan as a home purchaser.]

[4044A]

NOTES

Inserted by the Financial Services and Markets Act 2000 (Regulated Activities) (Amendment) (No 1) Order 2003, SI 2003/1475, art 11, as from 31 October 2004; for transitional provisions see arts 26–29 at **[4659]** et seq.

Paras (1A), (1B) inserted, and para (4) substituted, by the Financial Services and Markets Act 2000 (Regulated Activities) (Amendment) (No 2) Order 2006, SI 2006/2383, arts 2, 11, as from 6 November 2006 (for the purposes of enabling applications to be made for (i) a Pt IV permission, or a variation of a Pt IV permission, in relation to activities of the kind specified by arts 25B, 25C, 53B, 53C, 63B or 63F or, so far as relevant to any such activity, art 64 of this Order; or (ii) the Authority's approval under FSMA 2000, s 59 in relation to any of those activities), and as from 6 April 2007 (otherwise) (for transitional provisions and effect see arts 36–40 of, and the Schedule to, the 2006 Order at **[4821]** et seq).

34 Arrangements for the issue of shares etc

(1) There are excluded from article 25(1) and (2)—

(a) arrangements made by a company for the purposes of issuing its own shares or share warrants; and

(b) arrangements made by any person for the purposes of issuing his own debentures or debenture warrants;

and for the purposes of article 25(1) and (2), a company is not, by reason of issuing its own shares or share warrants, and a person is not, by reason of issuing his own debentures or debenture warrants, to be treated as selling them.

(2) In paragraph (1), "company", "shares", "debentures", "share warrants" and "debenture warrants" have the meanings given by article 18(2).

[4045]

35 International securities self-regulating organisations

(1) There are excluded from article 25(1) and (2) any arrangements made for the purposes of carrying out the functions of a body or association which is approved under this article as an international securities self-regulating organisation, whether the arrangements are made by the organisation itself or by a person acting on its behalf.

(2) The Treasury may approve as an international securities self-regulating organisation any body corporate or unincorporated association with respect to which the conditions mentioned in paragraph (3) appear to them to be met if, having regard to such matters affecting international trade, overseas earnings and the balance of payments or otherwise as they consider relevant, it appears to them that to do so would be desirable and not result in any undue risk to investors.

(3) The conditions are that—

(a) the body or association does not have its head office in the United Kingdom;

(b) the body or association is not eligible for recognition under section 287 or 288 of the Act (applications by investment exchanges and clearing houses) on the ground that (whether or not it has applied, and whether or not it would be eligible on other grounds) it is unable to satisfy the requirements of one or both of paragraphs (a) and (b) of section 292(3) of the Act (requirements for overseas investment exchanges and overseas clearing houses);

(c) the body or association is able and willing to co-operate with the Authority by the sharing of information and in other ways;

(d) adequate arrangements exist for co-operation between the Authority and those responsible for the supervision of the body or association in the country or territory in which its head office is situated;

(e) the body or association has a membership composed of persons falling within any of the following categories, that is to say, authorised persons, exempt persons, and persons whose head offices are outside the United Kingdom and whose ordinary business involves them in engaging in activities which are activities of a kind specified by this Order (or would be apart from any exclusion made by this Part); and

(f) the body or association facilitates and regulates the activity of its members in the conduct of international securities business.

(4) In paragraph (3)(f), "international securities business" means the business of buying, selling, subscribing for or underwriting investments (or agreeing to do so), either as principal or agent, where—

(a) the investments are securities or [relevant investments] and are of a kind which, by their nature, and the manner in which the business is conducted, may be expected normally to be bought or dealt in by persons sufficiently expert to understand the risks involved; and

(b) either the transaction is international or each of the parties may be expected to be indifferent to the location of the other;

and, for the purposes of this definition, it is irrelevant that the investments may ultimately be bought otherwise than in the course of such business by persons not so expert.

(5) Any approval under this article is to be given by notice in writing; and the Treasury may by a further notice in writing withdraw any such approval if for any reason it appears to them that it is not appropriate to it to continue in force.

[4046]

NOTES

Para (4): words in square brackets in sub-para (a) substituted by the Financial Services and Markets Act 2000 (Regulated Activities) (Amendment) (No 2) Order 2003, SI 2003/1476, art 5(6), as from 31 October 2004 (in so far as relating to contracts of long-term care insurance), and as from 14 January 2005 (otherwise), for transitional provisions see arts 22–27 of that Order at **[4665]** et seq.

36 Other exclusions

[(1)] Article 25 is also subject to the exclusions in articles 66 (trustees etc), 67 (profession or non-investment business), 68 (sale of goods and supply of services), 69 (groups and joint enterprises), 70 (sale of body corporate), 71 (employee share schemes)[, 72 (overseas persons)[, 72A (information society services), 72B (activities carried on by a provider of relevant goods or services), 72C (provision of information about contracts of insurance on an incidental basis) and 72D (large risks contracts where risk situated outside the EEA)]].

[(2) [Articles 25A, 25B and 25C are] also subject to the exclusions in articles 66 (trustees etc), 67 (profession or non-investment business), 72 (overseas persons) and 72A (information society services).]

[(3) Article 25D is also subject to the exclusion in article 72 (overseas persons).]

[4047]

NOTES

Para (1): numbered as such by the Financial Services and Markets Act 2000 (Regulated Activities) (Amendment) (No 1) Order 2003, SI 2003/1475, art 12(a), as from 31 October 2004 (for transitional provisions see arts 26–29 at **[4659]** et seq); words in first (outer) pair of square brackets substituted by the Financial Services and Markets Act 2000 (Regulated Activities) (Amendment) (No 2) Order 2002, SI 2002/1776, art 3(1), (6), as from 21 August 2002; words in second (inner) pair of square brackets substituted by the Financial Services and Markets Act 2000 (Regulated Activities) (Amendment) (No 2) Order 2003, SI 2003/1476, art 5(7), as from 31 October 2004 (in so far as relating to contracts of long-term care insurance), and as from 14 January 2005 (otherwise), for transitional provisions see arts 22–27 of that Order at **[4665]** et seq.

Para (2): added by SI 2003/1475, art 12(b), as from 31 October 2004, for transitional provisions see arts 26–29 at **[4659]** et seq; words in square brackets substituted by the Financial Services and Markets Act 2000 (Regulated Activities) (Amendment) (No 2) Order 2006, SI 2006/2383, arts 2, 12, as from 6 November 2006 (for the purposes of enabling applications to be made for (i) a Pt IV permission, or a variation of a Pt IV permission, in relation to activities of the kind specified by arts 25B, 25C, 53B, 53C, 63B or 63F or, so far as relevant to any such activity, art 64 of this Order; or (ii) the Authority's approval under FSMA 2000, s 59 in relation to any of those activities), and as from 6 April 2007 (otherwise) (for transitional provisions and effect see arts 36–40 of, and the Schedule to, the 2006 Order at **[4821]** et seq).

Para (3): added by the Financial Services and Markets Act 2000 (Regulated Activities) (Amendment No 3) Order 2006, SI 2006/3384, arts 2, 16, as from 1 April 2007 (for the purposes of enabling applications to be made for (i) a Part IV permission, (ii) a variation of a Part IV permission, and (iii) the Authority's approval under s 59 of the 2000 Act, in relation to an activity of the kind specified by art 25D of this Order, or in relation to an investment of the kind specified by arts 83, 84 or 85 of this Order), and as from 1 November 2007 (otherwise).

CHAPTER VII
MANAGING INVESTMENTS

The activity

37 Managing investments

Managing assets belonging to another person, in circumstances involving the exercise of discretion, is a specified kind of activity if—

(a) the assets consist of or include any investment which is a security or a contractually based investment; or

(b) the arrangements for their management are such that the assets may consist of or include such investments, and either the assets have at any time since 29th April 1988 done so, or the arrangements have at any time (whether before or after that date) been held out as arrangements under which the assets would do so.

[4048]

NOTES

See the Financial Services and Markets Act 2000 (Carrying on Regulated Activities by Way of Business) Order 2001, SI 2001/1177, art 3 at **[4147]** in relation to investment business, and art 4 at **[4148]** in respect of activities of managing investments where assets in question are held for the purposes of an occupational pension scheme.

Exclusions

38 Attorneys

[(1)] A person does not carry on an activity of the kind specified by article 37 if—

(a) he is a person appointed to manage the assets in question under a power of attorney; and

(b) all routine or day-to-day decisions, so far as relating to investments of a kind mentioned in article 37(a), are taken on behalf of that person by—

(i) an authorised person with permission to carry on activities of the kind specified by article 37; …

(ii) a person who is an exempt person in relation to activities of that kind[; or

(iii) an overseas person.]

[(2) This article is subject to article 4(4).]

[4049]

NOTES

Para (1) numbered as such, and para (2) added, by the Financial Services and Markets Act 2000 (Regulated Activities) (Amendment No 3) Order 2006, SI 2006/3384, arts 2, 17, as from 1 April 2007 (for the purposes of enabling applications to be made for (i) a Part IV permission, (ii) a variation of a Part IV permission, and (iii) the Authority's approval under s 59 of the 2000 Act, in relation to an activity of the kind specified by art 25D of this Order, or in relation to an investment of the kind specified by arts 83, 84 or 85 of this Order), and as from 1 November 2007 (otherwise). Note that the Queen's Printer's copy of SI 2006/3384 does not actually specify that the words "This article is subject to article 4(4)" should be numbered as paragraph (2) even though it does provide that the original text should be numbered as paragraph (1). It is assumed that this is an error.

Word omitted from para (1)(b)(i) revoked, and para (1)(b)(iii) and the word immediately preceding it added, by the Financial Services and Markets Act 2000 (Regulated Activities) (Amendment) Order 2001, SI 2001/3544, arts 2, 6, as from 1 December 2001.

39 Other exclusions

Article 37 is also subject to the exclusions in articles 66 (trustees etc), 68 (sale of goods and supply of services)[, 69 (groups and joint enterprises)[, 72A (information society services) and 72C (provision of information about contracts of insurance on an incidental basis)]].

[4050]

NOTES

Words in first (outer) pair of square brackets substituted by the Financial Services and Markets Act 2000 (Regulated Activities) (Amendment) (No 2) Order 2002, SI 2002/1776, art 3(1), (7), as from 21 August 2002; words in second (inner) pair of square brackets substituted by the Financial Services and Markets Act 2000 (Regulated Activities) (Amendment) (No 2) Order 2003, SI 2003/1476, art 6, as from 31 October 2004 (in so far as relating to contracts of long-term care insurance), and as from 14 January 2005 (otherwise), for transitional provisions see arts 22–27 of that Order at **[4665]** et seq.

[CHAPTER VIIA
ASSISTING IN THE ADMINISTRATION AND PERFORMANCE OF A CONTRACT OF INSURANCE

The Activity

39A Assisting in the administration and performance of a contract of insurance

Assisting in the administration and performance of a contract of insurance is a specified kind of activity.]

[4050A]

NOTES

Chapter VIIA (arts 39A–39C and the preceding headings) inserted by the Financial Services and Markets Act 2000 (Regulated Activities) (Amendment) (No 2) Order 2003, SI 2003/1476, art 7, as from 31 October 2004 (in so far as relating to contracts of long-term care insurance), and as from 14 January 2005 (otherwise); for transitional provisions see arts 22–27 of that Order at **[4665]** et seq.

[Exclusions

39B Claims management on behalf of an insurer etc

(1) A person does not carry on an activity of the kind specified by article 39A if he acts in the course of carrying on the activity of—
- (a) expert appraisal;
- (b) loss adjusting on behalf of a relevant insurer; or
- (c) managing claims on behalf of a relevant insurer,

and that activity is carried on in the course of carrying on any profession or business.

(2) In this article—
- (a) "relevant insurer" means—
  - (i) a person who has Part IV permission to carry on an activity of the kind specified by article 10;
  - (ii) a person to whom the general prohibition does not apply by virtue of section 316(1)(a) of the Act (members of the Society of Lloyd's);
  - (iii) an EEA firm falling within paragraph 5(d) of Schedule 3 to the Act (insurance undertaking); or
  - (iv) a relevant reinsurer;
- (b) "relevant reinsurer" means a person whose main business consists of accepting risks ceded by—
  - (i) a person falling within sub-paragraph (i), (ii) or (iii) of the definition of "relevant insurer"; or
  - (ii) a person who is established outside the United Kingdom who carries on an activity of the kind specified by article 10 by way of business.]

[4050B]

NOTES

Inserted as noted to art 39A at **[4050A]**.

[39C Other exclusions

Article 39A is also subject to the exclusions in articles 66 (trustees etc), 67 (profession or non-investment business), 72A (information society services), 72B (activities carried on by a provider of relevant goods or services), 72C (provision of information about contracts of insurance on an incidental basis) and 72D (large risks contracts where risk situated outside the EEA).]

[4050C]

NOTES

Inserted as noted to art 39A at **[4050A]**.

CHAPTER VIII
SAFEGUARDING AND ADMINISTERING INVESTMENTS

The activity

40 Safeguarding and administering investments

(1) The activity consisting of both—
- (a) the safeguarding of assets belonging to another, and
- (b) the administration of those assets,

or arranging for one or more other persons to carry on that activity, is a specified kind of activity if the condition in sub-paragraph (a) or (b) of paragraph (2) is met.

(2) The condition is that—
- (a) the assets consist of or include any investment which is a security or a contractually based investment; or
- (b) the arrangements for their safeguarding and administration are such that the assets may consist of or include such investments, and either the assets have at any time since 1st June 1997 done so, or the arrangements have at any time (whether before or after that date) been held out as ones under which such investments would be safeguarded and administered.

(3) For the purposes of this article—

(a) it is immaterial that title to the assets safeguarded and administered is held in uncertificated form;

(b) it is immaterial that the assets safeguarded and administered may be transferred to another person, subject to a commitment by the person safeguarding and administering them, or arranging for their safeguarding and administration, that they will be replaced by equivalent assets at some future date or when so requested by the person to whom they belong.

[4051]

NOTES

See the Financial Services and Markets Act 2000 (Carrying on Regulated Activities by Way of Business) Order 2001, SI 2001/1177, art 3 at **[4147]** in relation to investment business.

Exclusions

41 Acceptance of responsibility by third party

(1) There are excluded from article 40 any activities which a person carries on pursuant to arrangements which—

(a) are ones under which a qualifying custodian undertakes to the person to whom the assets belong a responsibility in respect of the assets which is no less onerous than the qualifying custodian would have if the qualifying custodian were safeguarding and administering the assets; and

(b) are operated by the qualifying custodian in the course of carrying on in the United Kingdom an activity of the kind specified by article 40.

(2) In paragraph (1), "qualifying custodian" means a person who is—

(a) an authorised person who has permission to carry on an activity of the kind specified by article 40, or

(b) an exempt person acting in the course of a business comprising a regulated activity in relation to which he is exempt.

[4052]

42 Introduction to qualifying custodians

(1) There are excluded from article 40 any arrangements pursuant to which introductions are made by a person ("P") to a qualifying custodian with a view to the qualifying custodian providing in the United Kingdom a service comprising an activity of the kind specified by article 40, where the qualifying person (or other person who is to safeguard and administer the assets in question) is not connected with P.

(2) For the purposes of paragraph (1)—

(a) "qualifying custodian" has the meaning given by article 41(2); and

(b) a person is connected with P if either he is a member of the same group as P, or P is remunerated by him.

[4053]

43 Activities not constituting administration

The following activities do not constitute the administration of assets for the purposes of article 40—

(a) providing information as to the number of units or the value of any assets safeguarded;

(b) converting currency;

(c) receiving documents relating to an investment solely for the purpose of onward transmission to, from or at the direction of the person to whom the investment belongs.

[4054]

44 Other exclusions

Article 40 is also subject to the exclusions in articles 66 (trustees etc), 67 (profession or non-investment business), 68 (sale of goods and supply of services), 69 (groups and joint enterprises)[, 71 (employee share schemes)[, 72A (information society services) and 72C (provision of information about contracts of insurance on an incidental basis)]].

[4055]

NOTES

Words in first (outer) pair of square brackets substituted by the Financial Services and Markets Act 2000 (Regulated Activities) (Amendment) (No 2) Order 2002, SI 2002/1776, art 3(1), (8), as from 21 August 2002; words in second (inner) pair of square brackets substituted by the Financial Services and Markets Act 2000 (Regulated Activities) (Amendment) (No 2) Order 2003, SI 2003/1476, art 8, as from 31 October 2004 (in so far as relating to contracts of long-term care insurance), and as from 14 January 2005 (otherwise), for transitional provisions see arts 22–27 of that Order at **[4665]** et seq.

CHAPTER IX
SENDING DEMATERIALISED INSTRUCTIONS

The activities

45 Sending dematerialised instructions

(1) Sending, on behalf of another person, dematerialised instructions relating to a security [or a contractually based investment] is a specified kind of activity, where those instructions are sent by means of a relevant system in respect of which an Operator is approved under the [2001] Regulations.

(2) Causing dematerialised instructions relating to a security [or a contractually based investment] to be sent [on behalf of another person] by means of such a system is also a specified kind of activity where the person causing them to be sent is a system-participant.

(3) In this Chapter—

[(a) "the 2001 Regulations" means the Uncertificated Securities Regulations 2001;]

(b) "dematerialised instruction", "Operator", "settlement bank" and "system-participant" have the meaning given by regulation 3 of the [2001] Regulations.

[4056]

NOTES

Para (1): words in first pair of square brackets inserted, and date in second pair of square brackets substituted, by the Financial Services and Markets Act 2000 (Regulated Activities) (Amendment) Order 2002, SI 2002/682, art 13(1), as from 27 April 2002.

Para (2): words in first pair of square brackets inserted by SI 2002/682, art 13(2), as from 27 April 2002; words in second pair of square brackets inserted by the Financial Services and Markets Act 2000 (Regulated Activities) (Amendment) Order 2001, SI 2001/3544, arts 2, 7, as from 1 December 2001.

Para (3): words in square brackets substituted by SI 2002/682, art 13(3), as from 27 April 2002.

See the Financial Services and Markets Act 2000 (Carrying on Regulated Activities by Way of Business) Order 2001, SI 2001/1177, art 3 at **[4147]** in relation to investment business.

Exclusions

46 Instructions on behalf of participating issuers

There is excluded from article 45 the act of sending, or causing to be sent, a dematerialised instruction where the person on whose behalf the instruction is sent or caused to be sent is a participating issuer within the meaning of the [2001] Regulations.

[4057]

NOTES

Date in square brackets substituted by the Financial Services and Markets Act 2000 (Regulated Activities) (Amendment) Order 2002, SI 2002/682, art 13(4), as from 27 April 2002.

47 Instructions on behalf of settlement banks

There is excluded from article 45 the act of sending, or causing to be sent, a dematerialised instruction where the person on whose behalf the instruction is sent or caused to be sent is a settlement bank in its capacity as such.

[4058]

48 Instructions in connection with takeover offers

(1) There is excluded from article 45 of the act of sending, or causing to be sent, a dematerialised instruction where the person on whose behalf the instruction is sent or caused to be sent is an offeror making a takeover offer.

(2) In this article—

(a) "offeror" means, in the case of a takeover offer made by two or more persons jointly, the joint offers or any of them;

(b) "takeover offer" means—

(i) an offer to acquire shares (which in this sub-paragraph has the same meaning as in [section 974 of the Companies Act 2006]) in a body corporate incorporated in the United Kingdom which is a takeover offer within the meaning of [Chapter 3 of Part 28] of that Act (or would be such an offer if that Part of that Act applied in relation to any body corporate);

(ii) an offer to acquire all or substantially all the shares, or all the shares of a particular class, in a body corporate incorporated outside the United Kingdom; or

(iii) an offer made to all the holders of shares, or shares of a particular class, in a body corporate to acquire a specified proportion of those shares;

but in determining whether an offer falls within paragraph (ii) there are to be disregarded any shares which the offeror or any associate of his (within the meaning of [section 988 of the Companies Act 2006]) holds or has contracted to acquire; and in determining whether an offer falls within paragraph (iii) the offeror, any such associate and any person whose shares the offeror or any such associate has contracted to acquire is not to be regarded as a holder of shares.

[4059]

NOTES

Para (2): words in square brackets in sub-para (b) substituted the Companies Act 2006 (Commencement No 2, Consequential Amendments, Transitional Provisions and Savings) Order 2007, SI 2007/1093, art 6(1), Sch 3, para 8, as from 6 April 2007.

49 Instructions in the course of providing a network

There is excluded from article 45 the act of sending, or causing to be sent, a dematerialised instruction as a necessary part of providing a network, the purpose of which is to carry dematerialised instructions which are at all time properly authenticated (within the meaning of the [2001] Regulations).

[4060]

NOTES

Date in square brackets substituted by the Financial Services and Markets Act 2000 (Regulated Activities) (Amendment) Order 2002, SI 2002/682, art 13(4), as from 27 April 2002.

50 Other exclusions

Article 45 is also subject to the exclusions in articles 66 (trustees etc)[, 69 (groups and joint enterprises) and 72A (information society services)].

[4061]

NOTES

Words in square brackets substituted by the Financial Services and Markets Act 2000 (Regulated Activities) (Amendment) (No 2) Order 2002, SI 2002/1776, art 3(1), (9), as from 21 August 2002.

CHAPTER X
COLLECTIVE INVESTMENT SCHEMES

The activities

51 Establishing etc a collective investment scheme

(1) The following are specified kinds of activity—

(a) establishing, operating or winding up a collective investment scheme;

(b) acting as trustee of an authorised unit trust scheme;

(c) acting as the depositary or sole director of an open-ended investment company.

(2) In this article, "trustee", "authorised unit trust scheme" and "depositary" have the meaning given by section 237 of the Act.

[4062]

NOTES

See the Financial Services and Markets Act 2000 (Carrying on Regulated Activities by Way of Business) Order 2001, SI 2001/1177, art 3 at **[4147]** in relation to investment business.

[Exclusion

51A Information society services

Article 51 is subject to the exclusion in article 72A (information society services).]

[4062A]

NOTES

Inserted, together with the preceding heading, by the Financial Services and Markets Act 2000 (Regulated Activities) (Amendment) (No 2) Order 2002, SI 2002/1776, art 3(1), (10), as from 21 August 2002.

CHAPTER XI
... PENSION SCHEMES

The activities

[52 Establishing etc a pension scheme

The following are specified kinds of activity—

(a) establishing, operating or winding up a stakeholder pension scheme;

(b) establishing, operating or winding up a personal pension scheme.]

[4063]

NOTES

Commencement: 1 October 2006 (certain purposes); 6 April 2007 (otherwise) (see below).

The word omitted from the Chapter heading preceding this article was revoked, and this article was substituted, by the Financial Services and Markets Act 2000 (Regulated Activities) (Amendment) Order 2006, SI 2006/1969, art 2(1), (3), (4), as from 1 October 2006 (for the purposes of enabling applications to be made for Part IV permission or for a variation of Part IV permission in relation to the regulated activity specified by art 52(b) of this Order (as so substituted)), and as from 6 April 2007 (otherwise); for transitional provisions and effect see arts 3–7 of, and the Schedule to, the 2006 Order at **[4814]** et seq.

See the Financial Services and Markets Act 2000 (Carrying on Regulated Activities by Way of Business) Order 2001, SI 2001/1177, art 3 at **[4147]** in relation to investment business.

[Exclusion

52A Information society services

Article 52 is subject to the exclusion in article 72A (information society services).]

[4063A]

NOTES

Inserted by the Financial Services and Markets Act 2000 (Regulated Activities) (Amendment) (No 2) Order 2002, SI 2002/1776, art 3(1), (11), as from 21 August 2002.

[CHAPTER XIA
PROVIDING BASIC ADVICE ON STAKEHOLDER PRODUCTS

The Activity

52B Providing basic advice on stakeholder products

(1) Providing basic advice to a retail consumer on a stakeholder product is a specified kind of activity.

(2) For the purposes of paragraph (1), a person ("P") provides basic advice when—
- (a) he asks a retail consumer questions to enable him to assess whether a stakeholder product is appropriate for that consumer; and
- (b) relying on the information provided by the retail consumer P assesses that a stakeholder product is appropriate for the retail consumer and—
  - (i) describes that product to that consumer;
  - (ii) gives a recommendation of that product to that consumer; and
- (c) the retail consumer has indicated to P that he has understood the description and the recommendation in sub-paragraph (b).

(3) In this article—

"retail consumer" means any person who is advised by P on the merits of opening or buying a stakeholder product in the course of a business carried on by P and who does not receive the advice in the course of a business carried on by him;

"stakeholder product" means—
- (a) an account which qualifies as a stakeholder child trust fund within the meaning given by the Child Trust Funds Regulations 2004;
- [(b) rights under a stakeholder pension scheme;]
- (c) an investment of a kind specified in regulations made by the Treasury.]

[4063B]

NOTES

Inserted, together with the preceding headings, by the Financial Services and Markets Act 2000 (Regulated Activities) (Amendment) (No 2) Order 2004, SI 2004/2737, arts, 2, 3, as from 6 April 2005. For transitional provisions, see the note below.

Para (3): in definition "stakeholder product", para (b) substituted by the Financial Services and Markets Act 2000 (Regulated Activities) (Amendment) Order 2005, SI 2005/593, art 2(3), as from 6 April 2005.

Transitional provisions: SI 2004/2737, art 4, provides as follows—

"4 Transitional provisions

(1) Part 4 of the Act shall apply in the case of persons who have permission at the date this Order comes into force to carry out the activity specified in article 53 of the principal Order and who wish to carry out the activity specified in article 52B of that Order as follows.

(2) Where P is a person to whom paragraph (1) applies—
- (a) the procedures established under sections 44 and 45 in respect of application for permission shall not apply in respect of permission to carry out the article 52B activity,
- (b) P shall be deemed to have such a permission if he has notified the Authority in writing of his wish to undertake the activity and the Authority has acknowledged receipt of P's notification in writing from the date of the acknowledgement.".

Regulations: the Financial Services and Markets 2000 (Stakeholder Products) Regulations 2004, SI 2004/2738 at **[4701]**.

CHAPTER XII
ADVISING ON INVESTMENTS

The activity

53 Advising on investments

Advising a person is a specified kind of activity if the advice is—
- (a) given to the person in his capacity as an investor or potential investor, or in his capacity as agent for an investor or a potential investor; and
- (b) advice on the merits of his doing any of the following (whether as principal or agent)—

(i) buying, selling, subscribing for or underwriting a particular investment which is a security or a [relevant investment], or

(ii) exercising any right conferred by such an investment to buy, sell, subscribe for or underwrite such an investment.

[4064]

NOTES

Words in square brackets substituted by the Financial Services and Markets Act 2000 (Regulated Activities) (Amendment) (No 2) Order 2003, SI 2003/1476, art 9(1), as from 31 October 2004 (in so far as relating to contracts of long-term care insurance), and as from 14 January 2005 (otherwise); for transitional provisions see arts 22–27 of that Order at **[4665]** et seq.

Transitional provisions: see the note to art 52B at **[4063B]**.

See the Financial Services and Markets Act 2000 (Carrying on Regulated Activities by Way of Business) Order 2001, SI 2001/1177, art 3 at **[4147]** in relation to investment business.

[53A Advising on regulated mortgage contracts

(1) Advising a person is a specified kind of activity if the advice—

(a) is given to the person in his capacity as a borrower or potential borrower; and

(b) is advice on the merits of his doing any of the following—

(i) entering into a particular regulated mortgage contract, or

(ii) varying the terms of a regulated mortgage contract entered into by him after the coming into force of article 61 in such a way as to vary his obligations under that contract.

(2) In this article, "borrower" has the meaning given by article 61(3)(a)(i).]

[4064A]

NOTES

Inserted by the Financial Services and Markets Act 2000 (Regulated Activities) (Amendment) (No 1) Order 2003, SI 2003/1475, art 13, as from 31 October 2004; for transitional provisions see arts 26–29 at **[4659]** et seq.

[53B Advising on regulated home reversion plans

Advising a person is a specified kind of activity if the advice—

(a) is given to the person in his capacity as—

(i) a reversion seller or potential reversion seller, or

(ii) a plan provider or potential plan provider; and

(b) is advice on the merits of his doing either of the following—

(i) entering into a particular regulated home reversion plan, or

(ii) varying the terms of a regulated home reversion plan, entered into on or after 6th April 2007 by him, in such a way as to vary his obligations under that plan.]

[4064B]

NOTES

Commencement: 6 November 2006 (certain purposes); 6 April 2007 (otherwise) (for more information see the note below).

Inserted, together with art 53C, by the Financial Services and Markets Act 2000 (Regulated Activities) (Amendment) (No 2) Order 2006, SI 2006/2383, arts 2, 13, as from 6 November 2006 (for the purposes of enabling applications to be made for (i) a Pt IV permission, or a variation of a Pt IV permission, in relation to activities of the kind specified by arts 25B, 25C, 53B, 53C, 63B or 63F or, so far as relevant to any such activity, art 64 of this Order; or (ii) the Authority's approval under FSMA 2000, s 59 in relation to any of those activities), and as from 6 April 2007 (otherwise) (for transitional provisions and effect see arts 36–40 of, and the Schedule to, the 2006 Order at **[4821]** et seq).

[53C Advising on regulated home purchase plans

Advising a person is a specified kind of activity if the advice—

(a) is given to the person in his capacity as a home purchaser or potential home purchaser; and

(b) is advice on the merits of his doing either of the following—

(i) entering into a particular regulated home purchase plan, or

(ii) varying the terms of a regulated home purchase plan, entered into on or after 6th April 2007 by him, in such a way as to vary his obligations under that plan.]

[4064C]

NOTES

Commencement: 6 November 2006 (certain purposes); 6 April 2007 (otherwise) (for more information see the note to art 53B at **[4064B]**).

Inserted as noted to art 53B at **[4064B]**.

Exclusions

54 Advice given in newspapers etc

(1) There is excluded from [articles 53, 53A, 53B and 53C] the giving of advice in writing or other legible form if the advice is contained in a newspaper, journal, magazine, or other periodical publication, or is given by way of a service comprising regularly updated news or information, if the principal purpose of the publication or service, taken as a whole and including any advertisements or other promotional material contained in it, is neither—

(a) that of giving advice of a kind mentioned in article 53[, 53A, 53B or 53C, as the case may be]; nor

[(b) that of leading or enabling persons—

(i) to buy, sell, subscribe for or underwrite securities or [relevant investments], or (as the case may be),

(ii) to enter as borrower into regulated mortgage contracts, or vary the terms of regulated mortgage contracts entered into by them as borrower;

[(iii) to enter as reversion seller or plan provider into regulated home reversion plans, or vary the terms of regulated home reversion plans entered into by them as reversion seller or plan provider,

(iv) to enter as home purchaser into regulated home purchase plans, or vary the terms of regulated home purchase plans entered into by them as home purchaser].]

(2) There is also excluded from [articles 53, 53A, 53B and 53C] the giving of advice in any service consisting of the broadcast or transmission of television or radio programmes, if the principal purpose of the service, taken as a whole and including any advertisements or other promotional material contained in it, is neither of those mentioned in paragraph (1)(a) and (b).

(3) The Authority may, on the application of the proprietor of any such publication or service as is mentioned in paragraph (1) or (2), certify that it is of the nature described in that paragraph, and may revoke any such certificate if it considers that it is no longer justified.

(4) A certificate given under paragraph (3) and not revoked is conclusive evidence of the matters certified.

[4065]

NOTES

Para (1) is amended as follows:

Words in first and second pairs of square brackets substituted by the Financial Services and Markets Act 2000 (Regulated Activities) (Amendment) (No 2) Order 2006, SI 2006/2383, arts 2, 14(a)(i), (ii), as from 6 November 2006 (for the purposes of enabling applications to be made for (i) a Pt IV permission, or a variation of a Pt IV permission, in relation to activities of the kind specified by arts 25B, 25C, 53B, 53C, 63B or 63F or, so far as relevant to any such activity, art 64 of this Order; or (ii) the Authority's approval under FSMA 2000, s 59 in relation to any of those activities), and as from 6 April 2007 (otherwise) (for transitional provisions and effect see arts 36–40 of, and the Schedule to, the 2006 Order at **[4821]** et seq).

Sub-para (b) substituted by the Financial Services and Markets Act 2000 (Regulated Activities) (Amendment) (No 1) Order 2003, SI 2003/1475, art 14, as from 31 October 2004 (for transitional provisions see arts 26–29 at **[4659]** et seq).

Words in square brackets in sub-para (b)(i) substituted by the Financial Services and Markets Act 2000 (Regulated Activities) (Amendment) (No 2) Order 2003, SI 2003/1476, art 9(2), as from 31 October 2004 (in so far as relating to contracts of long-term care insurance), and as from 14 January 2005 (otherwise) (for transitional provisions see arts 22–27 of that Order at **[4665]** et seq).

Sub-paras (b)(iii), (iv) inserted by SI 2006/2383, arts 2, 14(a)(iii), as from 6 November 2006 (certain purposes), and as from 6 April 2007 (otherwise) (for purposes, transitional provisions, and effect, see the note above).

Para (2): words in square brackets substituted by SI 2006/2383, arts 2, 14(b), as from 6 November 2006 (certain purposes), and as from 6 April 2007 (otherwise) (for purposes, transitional provisions, and effect, see the note above).

[54A Advice given in the course of administration by authorised person

[(1)] A person who is not an authorised person ("A") does not carry on an activity of the kind specified by article 53A by reason of—

(a) anything done by an authorised person ("B") in relation to a regulated mortgage contract which B is administering pursuant to arrangements of the kind mentioned in article 62(a); or

(b) anything A does in connection with the administration of a regulated mortgage contract in circumstances falling within article 62(b).]

[(2) A person who is not an authorised person ("A") does not carry on an activity of the kind specified by article 53B by reason of—

(a) anything done by an authorised person ("B") in relation to a regulated home reversion plan which B is administering pursuant to arrangements of the kind mentioned in article 63C(a); or

(b) anything A does in connection with the administration of a regulated home reversion plan in circumstances falling within article 63C(b).

(3) A person who is not an authorised person ("A") does not carry on an activity of the kind specified by article 53C by reason of—

(a) anything done by an authorised person ("B") in relation to a regulated home purchase plan which B is administering pursuant to arrangements of the kind mentioned in article 63G(a); or

(b) anything A does in connection with the administration of a regulated home purchase plan in circumstances falling within article 63G(b).]

[4065A]

NOTES

Inserted by the Financial Services and Markets Act 2000 (Regulated Activities) (Amendment) (No 1) Order 2003, SI 2003/1475, art 15, as from 31 October 2004; for transitional provisions see arts 26–29 at **[4659]** et seq.

Para (1) numbered as such, and paras (2), (3) added, by the Financial Services and Markets Act 2000 (Regulated Activities) (Amendment) (No 2) Order 2006, SI 2006/2383, arts 2, 15, as from 6 November 2006 (for the purposes of enabling applications to be made for (i) a Pt IV permission, or a variation of a Pt IV permission, in relation to activities of the kind specified by arts 25B, 25C, 53B, 53C, 63B or 63F or, so far as relevant to any such activity, art 64 of this Order; or (ii) the Authority's approval under FSMA 2000, s 59 in relation to any of those activities), and as from 6 April 2007 (otherwise) (for transitional provisions and effect see arts 36–40 of, and the Schedule to, the 2006 Order at **[4821]** et seq).

55 Other exclusions

[(1)] Article 53 is also subject to the exclusions in articles 66 (trustees etc), 67, (profession or non-investment business), 68 (sale of goods and supply of services), 69 (groups and joint enterprises), 70 (sale of body corporate)[, 72 (overseas persons)[, 72A (information society services), 72B (activities carried on by a provider of relevant goods or services) and 72D (large risks contracts where risk situated outside the EEA)]]

[(2) [Articles 53A, 53B and 53C are] also subject to the exclusions in articles 66 (trustees etc), 67 (profession or non-investment business) and 72A (information society services).]

[4066]

NOTES

Para (1): numbered as such by the Financial Services and Markets Act 2000 (Regulated Activities) (Amendment) (No 1) Order 2003, SI 2003/1475, art 16(a), as from 31 October 2004, for transitional provisions see arts 26–29 at **[4659]** et seq; words in first (outer) pair of square brackets substituted by the Financial Services and Markets Act 2000 (Regulated Activities) (Amendment) (No 2) Order 2002, SI 2002/1776, art 3(1), (12), as from 21 August 2002; words in second (inner) pair of square brackets substituted by the Financial Services and Markets Act 2000 (Regulated Activities) (Amendment) (No 2) Order 2003, SI 2003/1476, art 9(3), as from 31 October 2004 (in so far as relating to contracts of long-term care insurance), and as from 14 January 2005 (otherwise), for transitional provisions see arts 22–27 of that Order at **[4665]** et seq.

Para (2): added by SI 2003/1475, art 16(b), as from 31 October 2004 (for transitional provisions see arts 26–29 at **[4659]** et seq); words in square brackets substituted by the Financial Services and Markets Act 2000 (Regulated Activities) (Amendment) (No 2) Order 2006, SI 2006/2383, arts 2, 16, as from

6 November 2006 (for the purposes of enabling applications to be made for (i) a Pt IV permission, or a variation of a Pt IV permission, in relation to activities of the kind specified by arts 25B, 25C, 53B, 53C, 63B or 63F or, so far as relevant to any such activity, art 64 of this Order; or (ii) the Authority's approval under FSMA 2000, s 59 in relation to any of those activities), and as from 6 April 2007 (otherwise) (for transitional provisions and effect see arts 36–40 of, and the Schedule to, the 2006 Order at **[4821]** et seq).

CHAPTER XIII
LLOYD'S

The activities

56 Advice on syndicate participation at Lloyd's

Advising a person to become, or continue or cease to be, a member of a particular Lloyd's syndicate is a specified kind of activity.

[4067]

57 Managing the underwriting capacity of a Lloyd's syndicate

Managing the underwriting capacity of a Lloyd's syndicate as a managing agent at Lloyd's is a specified kind of activity.

[4068]

58 Arranging deals in contracts of insurance written at Lloyd's

The arranging, by the society incorporated by Lloyd's Act 1871 by the name of Lloyd's, of deals in contracts of insurance written at Lloyd's, is a specified kind of activity.

[4069]

[Exclusion

58A Information society services

Articles 56 to 58 are subject to the exclusion in article 72A (information society services).]

[4069A]

NOTES

Inserted, together with the preceding heading, by the Financial Services and Markets Act 2000 (Regulated Activities) (Amendment) (No 2) Order 2002, SI 2002/1776, art 3(1), (13), as from 21 August 2002.

CHAPTER XIV
FUNERAL PLAN CONTRACTS

The activity

59 Funeral plan contracts

(1) Entering as provider into a funeral plan contract is a specified kind of activity.

(2) A "funeral plan contract" is a contract (other than one excluded by article 60) under which—

(a) a person ("the customer") makes one or more payments to another person ("the provider"); and

(b) the provider undertakes to provide, or secure that another person provides, a funeral in the United Kingdom for the customer (or some other person who is living at the date when the contract is entered into) on his death;

unless, at the time of entering into the contract, the customer and the provider intend or expect the funeral to occur within one month.

[4070]

[Exclusions]

60 Plans covered by insurance or trust arrangements

(1) There is excluded from article 59 any contract under which—

(a) the provider undertakes to secure that sums paid by the customer under the contract will be applied towards a contract of whole life insurance on the life of the customer (or other person for whom the funeral is to be provided), effected and carried out by an authorised person who has permission to effect and carry out such contracts of insurance, for the purpose of providing the funeral; or

(b) the provider undertakes to secure that sums paid by the customer under the contract will be held on trust for the purpose of providing the funeral, and that the following requirements are or will be met with respect to the trust—

(i) the trust must be established by a written instrument;

(ii) more than half of the trustees must be unconnected with the provider;

(iii) the trustees must appoint, or have appointed, an independent fund manager who is an authorised person who has permission to carry on an activity of the kind specified by article 37, and who is a person who is unconnected with the provider, to manage the assets of the trust;

(iv) annual accounts must be prepared, and audited by a person who is eligible for appointment as a company auditor under section 25 of the Companies Act 1989, with respect to the assets and liabilities of the trust; and

(v) the assets and liabilities of the trust must, at least once every three years, be determined, calculated and verified by an actuary who is a Fellow of the Institute of Actuaries or of the Faculty of Actuaries.

(2) For the purposes of paragraph (1)(b)(ii) and (iii), a person is unconnected with the provider if he is a person other than—

(a) the provider;

(b) a member of the same group as the provider;

(c) a director, other officer or employee of the provider, or of any member of the same group as the provider;

(d) a partner of the provider;

(e) a close relative of a person falling within sub-paragraph (a), (c) or (d); or

(f) an agent of any person falling within sub-paragraphs (a) to (e).

[4071]

NOTES

The heading preceding this article was substituted by the Financial Services and Markets Act 2000 (Regulated Activities) (Amendment) (No 2) Order 2002, art 3(1), (14), as from 21 August 2002.

[60A Information society services

Article 59 is subject to the exclusion in article 72A (information society services).]

[4071A]

NOTES

Inserted by the Financial Services and Markets Act 2000 (Regulated Activities) (Amendment) (No 2) Order 2002, SI 2002/1776, art 3(1), (15), as from 21 August 2002.

CHAPTER XV
REGULATED MORTGAGE CONTRACTS

The activities

61 Regulated mortgage contracts

(1) Entering into a regulated mortgage contract as lender is a specified kind of activity.

(2) Administering a regulated mortgage contract is also a specified kind of activity, where the contract was entered into [by way of business] after the coming into force of this article.

(3) In this Chapter—

[(a) a contract is a "regulated mortgage contract" if, at the time it is entered into, the following conditions are met—

(i) the contract is one under which a person ("the lender") provides credit to an individual or to trustees ("the borrower");

(ii) the contract provides for the obligation of the borrower to repay to be secured by a first legal mortgage on land (other than timeshare accommodation) in the United Kingdom;

(iii) at least 40% of that land is used, or is intended to be used, as or in connection with a dwelling by the borrower or (in the case of credit provided to trustees) by an individual who is a beneficiary of the trust, or by a related person;

[but such a contract is not a regulated mortgage contract if it is a regulated home purchase plan;]]

(b) "administering" a regulated mortgage contract means either or both of—

(i) notifying the borrower of changes in interest rates or payments due under the contract, or of other matters of which the contract requires him to be notified; and

(ii) taking any necessary steps for the purposes of collecting or recovering payments due under the contract from the borrower;

but a person is not to be treated as administering a regulated mortgage contract merely because he has, or exercises, a right to take action for the purposes of enforcing the contract (or to require that such action is or is not taken);

(c) "credit" includes a cash loan, and any other form of financial accommodation.

(4) For the purposes of [paragraph 3(a)]—

(a) a "first legal mortgage" means a legal mortgage ranking in priority ahead of all other mortgages (if any) affecting the land in question, where "mortgage" includes charge and (in Scotland) a heritable security;

(b) the area of any land which comprises a building or other structure containing two or more storeys is to be taken to be the aggregate of the floor areas of each of those storeys;

(c) "related person", in relation to the borrower or (in the case of credit provided to trustees) a beneficiary of the trust, means—

(i) that person's spouse [or civil partner];

(ii) a person (whether or not of the opposite sex) whose relationship with that person has the characteristics of the relationship between husband and wife; or

(iii) that person's parent, brother, sister, child, grandparent or grandchild; and

(d) "timeshare accommodation" has the meaning given by section 1 of the Timeshare Act 1992.

[4072]

NOTES

Para (2): words in square brackets inserted by the Financial Services and Markets Act 2000 (Regulated Activities) (Amendment) Order 2001, SI 2001/3544, arts 2, 8(a), as from 1 September 2002.

Para (3): sub-para (a) substituted by SI 2001/3544, arts 2, 8(b), as from 1 September 2002; words in square brackets inserted by the Financial Services and Markets Act 2000 (Regulated Activities) (Amendment) (No 2) Order 2006, SI 2006/2383, arts 2, 17, as from 6 November 2006 (for the purposes of enabling applications to be made for (i) a Pt IV permission, or a variation of a Pt IV permission, in relation to activities of the kind specified by arts 25B, 25C, 53B, 53C, 63B or 63F or, so far as relevant to any such activity, art 64 of this Order; or (ii) the Authority's approval under FSMA 2000, s 59 in relation to any of those activities), and as from 6 April 2007 (otherwise) (for transitional provisions and effect see arts 36–40 of, and the Schedule to, the 2006 Order at **[4821]** et seq).

Para (4): words in first pair of square brackets substituted by SI 2001/3544, arts 2, 8(c), as from 1 September 2002; words in second pair of square brackets inserted by the Civil Partnership Act 2004 (Amendments to Subordinate Legislation) Order 2005, SI 2005/2114, art 2(16), Sch 16, Pt 1, para 1(1), (3), as from 5 December 2005.

Exclusions

62 Arranging administration by authorised person

A person who is not an authorised person does not carry on an activity of the kind specified by article 61(2) in relation to a regulated mortgage contract where he—

(a) arranges for another person, being an authorised person with permission to carry on an activity of that kind, to administer the contract; or

(b) administers the contract himself during a period of not more than one month beginning with the day on which any such arrangement comes to an end.

[4073]

63 Administration pursuant to agreement with authorised person

A person who is not an authorised person does not carry on an activity of the kind specified by article 61(2) in relation to a regulated mortgage contract where he administers the contract pursuant to an agreement with an authorised person who has permission to carry on an activity of that kind.

[4074]

[63A Other exclusions

Article 61 is also subject to the exclusions in articles 66 (trustees etc), 72 (overseas persons) and 72A (information society services).]

[4074A]

NOTES

Inserted by the Financial Services and Markets Act 2000 (Regulated Activities) (Amendment) (No 2) Order 2002, SI 2002/1776, art 3(1), (16), as from 21 August 2002; substituted by the Financial Services and Markets Act 2000 (Regulated Activities) (Amendment) (No 1) Order 2003, SI 2003/1475, art 17, as from 31 October 2004 (for transitional provisions see arts 26–29 at **[4659]** et seq).

[CHAPTER 15A
REGULATED HOME REVERSION PLANS

The activities

63B Entering into and administering regulated home reversion plans

(1) Entering into a regulated home reversion plan as plan provider is a specified kind of activity.

(2) Administering a regulated home reversion plan is also a specified kind of activity where the plan was entered into on or after 6th April 2007.

(3) In this Chapter—

(a) a "regulated home reversion plan" is an arrangement comprised in one or more instruments or agreements, in relation to which the following conditions are met at the time it is entered into—

(i) the arrangement is one under which a person (the "plan provider") buys all or part of a qualifying interest in land (other than timeshare accommodation) in the United Kingdom from an individual or trustees (the "reversion seller");

(ii) the reversion seller (if he is an individual) or an individual who is a beneficiary of the trust (if the reversion seller is a trustee), or a related person, is entitled under the arrangement to occupy at least 40% of the land in question as or in connection with a dwelling, and intends to do so; and

(iii) the arrangement specifies one or more qualifying termination events, on the occurrence of which that entitlement will end;

(b) "administering" a regulated home reversion plan means any of—

(i) notifying the reversion seller of changes in payments due under the plan, or of other matters of which the plan requires him to be notified;

(ii) taking any necessary steps for the purposes of making payments to the reversion seller under the plan; and

(iii) taking any necessary steps for the purposes of collecting or recovering payments due under the plan from the reversion seller,

but a person is not to be treated as administering a regulated home reversion plan merely because he has, or exercises, a right to take action for the purposes of enforcing the plan (or to require that such action is or is not taken).

(4) For the purposes of paragraph (3)—

(a) the reference to a "qualifying interest" in land—

(i) in relation to land in England or Wales, is to an estate in fee simple absolute or a term of years absolute, whether subsisting at law or in equity;

(ii) in relation to land in Scotland, is to the interest of an owner in land or the tenant's right over or interest in a property subject to a lease;

(iii) in relation to land in Northern Ireland, is to any freehold estate or any leasehold estate, whether subsisting at law or in equity;

(b) "timeshare accommodation" has the meaning given by section 1 of the Timeshare Act 1992;

(c) "related person" in relation to the reversion seller or, where the reversion seller is a trustee, a beneficiary of the trust, means—

(i) that person's spouse or civil partner;

(ii) a person (whether or not of the opposite sex) whose relationship with that person has the characteristics of the relationship between husband and wife; or

(iii) that person's parent, brother, sister, child, grandparent or grandchild; and

(d) "qualifying termination event", in relation to a person's entitlement to occupy land, means—

(i) the person becomes a resident of a care home;

(ii) the person dies;

(iii) the end of a specified period of at least twenty years beginning with the day on which the reversion seller entered into the arrangement.

(5) For the purposes of paragraph (3)(a)(ii), the area of any land which comprises a building or other structure containing two or more storeys is to be taken to be the aggregate of the floor areas of each of those storeys.

(6) For the purposes of the definition of "qualifying termination event" in paragraph (4), "care home"—

(a) in relation to England and Wales, has the meaning given by section 3 of the Care Standards Act 2000;

(b) in relation to Scotland, means accommodation provided by a "care home" within the meaning of section 2(3)of the Regulation of Care (Scotland) Act 2001;

(c) in relation to Northern Ireland, means—

(i) a residential care home within the meaning of article 10 of the Health and Personal Social Services (Quality, Improvement and Regulation) (Northern Ireland) Order 2003; or

(ii) a nursing home within the meaning of article 11 of that Order.

(7) In this Order—

(a) references to entering into a regulated home reversion plan as plan provider include acquiring any obligations or rights (including his interest in land) of the plan provider, under such a plan; but

(b) in relation to a person who acquires any such obligations or rights, an activity is a specified kind of activity for the purposes of articles 25B(1)(b) and 53B(b)(ii) and paragraph (2) only if the plan was entered into by the plan provider (rather than the obligations or rights acquired) on or after 6th April 2007.

(8) Accordingly, references in this Order to a plan provider, other than in paragraph (7), include a person who acquires any such obligations or rights.]

[4074B]

NOTES

Commencement: 6 November 2006 (certain purposes); 6 April 2007 (otherwise) (for more information see the note below).

Chapters 15A, 15B (arts 63B–63I and the preceding headings) inserted by the Financial Services and Markets Act 2000 (Regulated Activities) (Amendment) (No 2) Order 2006, SI 2006/2383, arts 2, 18, as from 6 November 2006 (for the purposes of enabling applications to be made for (i) a Pt IV permission, or a variation of a Pt IV permission, in relation to activities of the kind specified by arts 25B, 25C, 53B, 53C, 63B or 63F or, so far as relevant to any such activity, art 64 of this Order; or (ii) the Authority's approval under FSMA 2000, s 59 in relation to any of those activities), and as from 6 April 2007 (otherwise) (for transitional provisions and effect see arts 36–40 of, and the Schedule to, the 2006 Order at **[4821]** et seq).

[Exclusions

63C Arranging administration by authorised person

A person who is not an authorised person does not carry on an activity of the kind specified by article 63B(2) in relation to a regulated home reversion plan where he—

(a) arranges for another person, being an authorised person with permission to carry on an activity of that kind, to administer the plan; or

(b) administers the plan himself during a period of not more than one month beginning with the day on which any such arrangement comes to an end.]

[4074C]

NOTES

Commencement: 6 November 2006 (certain purposes); 6 April 2007 (otherwise) (for more information see the note to art 63B at **[4074B]**).

Inserted as noted to art 63B at **[4074B]**.

[63D Administration pursuant to agreement with authorised person

A person who is not an authorised person does not carry on an activity of the kind specified by article 63B(2) in relation to a regulated home reversion plan where he administers the plan pursuant to an agreement with an authorised person who has permission to carry on an activity of that kind.]

[4074D]

NOTES

Commencement: 6 November 2006 (certain purposes); 6 April 2007 (otherwise) (for more information see the note to art 63B at **[4074B]**).

Inserted as noted to art 63B at **[4074B]**.

[63E Other exclusions

Article 63B is also subject to the exclusions in articles 66 (trustees etc), 72 (overseas persons) and 72A (information society services).]

[4074E]

NOTES

Commencement: 6 November 2006 (certain purposes); 6 April 2007 (otherwise) (for more information see the note to art 63B at **[4074B]**).

Inserted as noted to art 63B at **[4074B]**.

[CHAPTER 15B
REGULATED HOME PURCHASE PLANS

The activities

63F Entering into and administering regulated home purchase plans

(1) Entering into a regulated home purchase plan as home purchase provider is a specified kind of activity.

(2) Administering a regulated home purchase plan is also a specified kind of activity where the plan was entered into by way of business on or after 6th April 2007.

(3) In this Chapter—

(a) a "regulated home purchase plan" is an arrangement comprised in one or more instruments or agreements, in relation to which the following conditions are met at the time it is entered into—

(i) the arrangement is one under which a person (the "home purchase provider") buys a qualifying interest or an undivided share of a qualifying interest in land (other than timeshare accommodation) in the United Kingdom;

(ii) where an undivided share of a qualifying interest in land is bought, the interest is held on trust for the home purchase provider and the individual or trustees mentioned in paragraph (iii) as beneficial tenants in common;

(iii) the arrangement provides for the obligation of an individual or trustees (the "home purchaser") to buy the interest bought by the home purchase provider over the course of or at the end of a specified period; and

(iv) the home purchaser (if he is an individual) or an individual who is a beneficiary of the trust (if the home purchaser is a trustee), or a related person, is entitled under the arrangement to occupy at least 40% of the land in question as or in connection with a dwelling during that period, and intends to do so;

(b) "administering" a regulated home purchase plan means either or both of—
  (i) notifying the home purchaser of changes in payments due under the plan, or of other matters of which the plan requires him to be notified; and
  (ii) taking any necessary steps for the purposes of collecting or recovering payments due under the plan from the home purchaser;

but a person is not to be treated as administering a regulated home purchase plan merely because he has, or exercises, a right to take action for the purposes of enforcing the plan or to require that such action is or is not taken.

(4) Article 63B(4)(a) to (c) applies for the purposes of paragraph (3)(a) with references to the "reversion seller" being read as references to the "home purchaser".

(5) Article 63B(5) applies for the purposes of paragraph (3)(a)(iv) with the reference to "paragraph (3)(a)(ii)" being read as a reference to "paragraph (3)(a)(iv)".]

[4074F]

NOTES

Commencement: 6 November 2006 (certain purposes); 6 April 2007 (otherwise) (for more information see the note to art 63B at **[4074B]**).

Inserted as noted to art 63B at **[4074B]**.

[Exclusions

63G Arranging administration by authorised person

A person who is not an authorised person does not carry on an activity of the kind specified by article 63F(2) in relation to a regulated home purchase plan where he—

(a) arranges for another person, being an authorised person with permission to carry on an activity of that kind, to administer the plan; or

(b) administers the plan himself during a period of not more than one month beginning with the day on which any such arrangement comes to an end.]

[4074G]

NOTES

Commencement: 6 November 2006 (certain purposes); 6 April 2007 (otherwise) (for more information see the note to art 63B at **[4074B]**).

Inserted as noted to art 63B at **[4074B]**.

[63H Administration pursuant to agreement with authorised person

A person who is not an authorised person does not carry on an activity of the kind specified by article 63F(2) in relation to a regulated home purchase plan where he administers the plan pursuant to an agreement with an authorised person who has permission to carry on an activity of that kind.]

[4074H]

NOTES

Commencement: 6 November 2006 (certain purposes); 6 April 2007 (otherwise) (for more information see the note to art 63B at **[4074B]**).

Inserted as noted to art 63B at **[4074B]**.

[63I Other exclusions

Article 63F is also subject to the exclusions in articles 66 (trustees etc), 72 (overseas persons) and 72A (information society services).]

[4074I]

NOTES

Commencement: 6 November 2006 (certain purposes); 6 April 2007 (otherwise) (for more information see the note to art 63B at **[4074B]**).

Inserted as noted to art 63B at **[4074B]**.

CHAPTER XVI
AGREEING TO CARRY ON ACTIVITIES

The activity

64 Agreeing to carry on specified kinds of activity

Agreeing to carry on an activity of the kind specified by any other provision of this Part (other than article 5, [9B,] 10, [25D,] 51 or 52) is a specified kind of activity.

[4075]

NOTES

First figure in square brackets inserted by the Financial Services and Markets Act 2000 (Regulated Activities) (Amendment) Order 2002, SI 2002/682, art 5, as from 27 April 2002, subject to transitional provisions in relation to persons issuing electronic money immediately before that date contained in art 9 at **[4637]**; second figure in square brackets inserted by the Financial Services and Markets Act 2000 (Regulated Activities) (Amendment No 3) Order 2006, SI 2006/3384, arts 2, 18, as from 1 April 2007 (for the purposes of enabling applications to be made for (i) a Part IV permission, (ii) a variation of a Part IV permission, and (iii) the Authority's approval under s 59 of the 2000 Act, in relation to an activity of the kind specified by art 25D of this Order, or in relation to an investment of the kind specified by arts 83, 84 or 85 of this Order), and as from 1 November 2007 (otherwise).

See the Financial Services and Markets Act 2000 (Carrying on Regulated Activities by Way of Business) Order 2001, SI 2001/1177, art 3 at **[4147]** in relation to investment business.

[Exclusions

65 Overseas persons etc

Article 64 is subject to the exclusions in articles 72 (overseas persons) and 72A (information society services).]

[4076]

NOTES

Substituted, together with the preceding heading, by the Financial Services and Markets Act 2000 (Regulated Activities) (Amendment) (No 2) Order 2002, SI 2002/1776, art 3(1), (17), as from 21 August 2002.

CHAPTER XVII
EXCLUSIONS APPLYING TO SEVERAL SPECIFIED KINDS OF ACTIVITY

66 Trustees, nominees and personal representatives

(1) A person ("X") does not carry on an activity of the kind specified by article 14 where he enters into a transaction as bare trustee or, in Scotland, as nominee for another person ("Y") and—

- (a) X is acting on Y's instructions; and
- (b) X does not hold himself out as providing a service of buying and selling securities or contractually based investments.

(2) Subject to paragraph (7), there are excluded from [articles 25(1) and (2)[, 25A(1) and (2), 25B(1) and (2) and 25C(1) and (2)]] arrangements made by a person acting as trustee or personal representative for or with a view to a transaction which is or is to be entered into—

- (a) by that person and a fellow trustee or personal representative (acting in their capacity as such); or
- (b) by a beneficiary under the trust, will or intestacy.

(3) Subject to paragraph (7), there is excluded from article 37 any activity carried on by a person acting as trustee or personal representative, unless—

- (a) he holds himself out as providing a service comprising an activity of the kind specified by article 37; or
- (b) the assets in question are held for the purposes of an occupational pension scheme, and, by virtue of article 4 of the Financial Services and Markets Act 2000 (Carrying on Regulated Activities by Way of Business) Order 2001, he is to be treated as carrying on that activity by way of business.

PART IV
STATUTORY INSTRUMENTS

[(3A) Subject to paragraph (7), there is excluded from article 39A any activity carried on by a person acting as trustee or personal representative, unless he holds himself out as providing a service comprising an activity of the kind specified by article 39A.]

(4) Subject to paragraph (7), there is excluded from article 40 any activity carried on by a person acting as trustee or personal representative, unless he holds himself out as providing a service comprising an activity of the kind specified by article 40.

[(4A) There is excluded from article 40 any activity carried on by a person acting as trustee which consists of arranging for one or more other persons to safeguard and administer trust assets where—

(a) that other person is a qualifying custodian; or
(b) that safeguarding and administration is also arranged by a qualifying custodian.

In this paragraph, "qualifying custodian" has the meaning given by article 41(2).]

(5) A person does not, by sending or causing to be sent a dematerialised instruction (within the meaning of article 45), carry on an activity of the kind specified by that article if the instruction relates to an investment which that person holds as trustee or personal representative.

(6) Subject to paragraph (7), there is excluded from [articles 53[, 53A, 53B and 53C]] the giving of advice by a person acting as trustee or personal representative where he gives the advice to—

(a) a fellow trustee or personal representative for the purposes of the trust or the estate; or
(b) a beneficiary under the trust, will or intestacy concerning his interest in the trust fund or estate.

[(6A) Subject to paragraph (7), a person acting as trustee or personal representative does not carry on an activity of the kind specified by article 61(1) or (2) where the borrower under the regulated mortgage contract in question is a beneficiary under the trust, will or intestacy.]

[(6B) Subject to paragraph (7), a person acting as trustee or personal representative does not carry on an activity of the kind specified by article 63B(1) or (2) where the reversion seller under the regulated home reversion plan in question is a beneficiary under the trust, will or intestacy.

(6C) Subject to paragraph (7), a person acting as trustee or personal representative does not carry on an activity of the kind specified by article 63F(1) or (2) where the home purchaser under the regulated home purchase plan in question is a beneficiary under the trust, will or intestacy.]

(7) Paragraphs (2), (3)[, (3A)], [(4), (6)[, (6A), (6B) and (6C)]] do not apply if the person carrying on the activity is remunerated for what he does in addition to any remuneration he receives as trustee or personal representative, and for these purposes a person is not to be regarded as receiving additional remuneration merely because his remuneration is calculated by reference to time spent.

[(8) This article is subject to article 4(4A).]

[4077]

NOTES

Para (2): words in first (outer) pair of square brackets substituted by the Financial Services and Markets Act 2000 (Regulated Activities) (Amendment) (No 1) Order 2003, SI 2003/1475, art 18(a), as from 31 October 2004 (for transitional provisions see arts 26–29 at **[4659]** et seq); words in second (inner) pair of square brackets substituted by the Financial Services and Markets Act 2000 (Regulated Activities) (Amendment) (No 2) Order 2006, SI 2006/2383, arts 2, 19(a), as from 6 November 2006 (for the purposes of enabling applications to be made for (i) a Pt IV permission, or a variation of a Pt IV permission, in relation to activities of the kind specified by arts 25B, 25C, 53B, 53C, 63B or 63F or, so far as relevant to any such activity, art 64 of this Order; or (ii) the Authority's approval under FSMA 2000, s 59 in relation to any of those activities), and as from 6 April 2007 (otherwise) (for transitional provisions and effect see arts 36–40 of, and the Schedule to, the 2006 Order at **[4821]** et seq).

Para (3A): inserted by the Financial Services and Markets Act 2000 (Regulated Activities) (Amendment) (No 2) Order 2003, SI 2003/1476, art 10(1)(a), as from 31 October 2004 (in so far as relating to contracts of long-term care insurance), and as from 14 January 2005 (otherwise); for transitional provisions see arts 22–27 of that Order at **[4665]** et seq.

Para (4A): inserted by the Financial Services and Markets Act 2000 (Regulated Activities) (Amendment) Order 2005, SI 2005/593, art 2(4), as from 6 April 2005.

Para (6): words in first (outer) pair of square brackets substituted by SI 2003/1475, art 18(b), as from 31 October 2004 (for transitional provisions see arts 26–29 at **[4659]** et seq); words in second (inner) pair of square brackets substituted by SI 2006/2383, arts 2, 19(b), as from 6 November 2006 (certain purposes), and as from 6 April 2007 (otherwise) (for purposes, transitional provisions, and effect, see the para (2) note above).

Para (6A): inserted by SI 2003/1475, art 18(c), as from 31 October 2004; for transitional provisions see arts 26–29 at **[4659]** et seq.

Paras (6B), (6C): inserted by SI 2006/2383, arts 2, 19(c), as from 6 November 2006 (certain purposes), and as from 6 April 2007 (otherwise) (for purposes, transitional provisions, and effect, see the para (2) note above).

Para (7): figure in first pair of square brackets inserted by SI 2003/1476, art 10(1)(b), as from 31 October 2004 (in so far as relating to contracts of long-term care insurance), and as from 14 January 2005 (otherwise), for transitional provisions see arts 22–27 of that Order at **[4665]** et seq; words in second (outer) pair of square brackets substituted by SI 2003/1475, art 18(d), as from 31 October 2004, for transitional provisions see arts 26–29 at **[4659]** et seq; words in third (inner) pair of square brackets substituted by SI 2006/2383, arts 2, 19(d), as from 6 November 2006 (certain purposes), and as from 6 April 2007 (otherwise) (for purposes, transitional provisions, and effect, see the para (2) note above).

Para (8): added by the Financial Services and Markets Act 2000 (Regulated Activities) (Amendment No 3) Order 2006, SI 2006/3384, arts 2, 19, as from 1 April 2007 (for the purposes of enabling applications to be made for (i) a Part IV permission, (ii) a variation of a Part IV permission, and (iii) the Authority's approval under s 59 of the 2000 Act, in relation to an activity of the kind specified by art 25D of this Order, or in relation to an investment of the kind specified by arts 83, 84 or 85 of this Order), and as from 1 November 2007 (otherwise).

67 Activities carried on in the course of a profession or non-investment business

(1) There is excluded from articles 21, 25(1) and (2)[, 25A], [25B, 25C,] [39A, 40], [53 [, 53A, 53B and 53C]] any activity which

(a) is carried on in the course of carrying on any profession or business which does not otherwise consist of [the carrying on of regulated activities in the United Kingdom]; and

(b) may reasonably be regarded as a necessary part of other services provided in the course of that profession or business.

(2) But the exclusion in paragraph (1) does not apply if the activity in question is remunerated separately from the other services.

[(3) This article is subject to article 4(4) and (4A).]

[4078]

NOTES

Para (1) is amended as follows:

Figure in first pair of square brackets inserted, and words in fourth (outer) pair of square brackets substituted, by the Financial Services and Markets Act 2000 (Regulated Activities) (Amendment) (No 1) Order 2003, SI 2003/1475, art 19, as from 31 October 2004, for transitional provisions see arts 26–29 at **[4659]** et seq.

Figures in second pair of square brackets inserted by the Financial Services and Markets Act 2000 (Regulated Activities) (Amendment) (No 2) Order 2006, SI 2006/2383, arts 2, 20(a), as from 6 November 2006 (for the purposes of enabling applications to be made for (i) a Pt IV permission, or a variation of a Pt IV permission, in relation to activities of the kind specified by arts 25B, 25C, 53B, 53C, 63B or 63F or, so far as relevant to any such activity, art 64 of this Order; or (ii) the Authority's approval under FSMA 2000, s 59 in relation to any of those activities), and as from 6 April 2007 (otherwise) (for transitional provisions and effect see arts 36–40 of, and the Schedule to, the 2006 Order at **[4821]** et seq).

Figures in third pair of square brackets substituted by the Financial Services and Markets Act 2000 (Regulated Activities) (Amendment) (No 2) Order 2003, SI 2003/1476, art 10(2), as from 31 October 2004 (in so far as relating to contracts of long-term care insurance), and as from 14 January 2005 (otherwise), for transitional provisions see arts 22–27 of that Order at **[4665]** et seq.

Words in fifth (inner) pair of square brackets substituted by SI 2006/2383, arts 2, 20(b), as from 6 November 2006 (certain purposes), and as from 6 April 2007 (otherwise) (for purposes, transitional provisions, and effect, see the note above).

Words in square brackets in sub-para (a) substituted by the Financial Services and Markets Act 2000 (Regulated Activities) (Amendment) Order 2001, SI 2001/3544, arts 2, 9, as from 1 December 2001.

Para (3): added by the Financial Services and Markets Act 2000 (Regulated Activities) (Amendment No 3) Order 2006, SI 2006/3384, arts 2, 20, as from 1 April 2007 (for the purposes of enabling applications to be made for (i) a Part IV permission, (ii) a variation of a Part IV permission, and (iii) the Authority's approval under s 59 of the 2000 Act, in relation to an activity of the kind specified by art 25D of this Order, or in relation to an investment of the kind specified by arts 83, 84 or 85 of this Order), and as from 1 November 2007 (otherwise).

68 Activities carried on in connection with the sale of goods or supply of services

(1) Subject to paragraphs (9), (10) and (11), this article concerns certain activities carried on for the purposes of or in connection with the sale of goods or supply of services by a supplier to a customer, where—

"supplier" means a person whose main business is to sell goods or supply services and not to carry on any activities of the kind specified by any of articles 14, 21, 25, 37[, 39A], 40, 45, 51, 52 and 53 and, where the supplier is a member of a group, also means any other member of that group; and

"customer" means a person, other than an individual, to whom a supplier sells goods or supplies services, or agrees to do so, and, where the customer is a member of a group, also means any other member of that group;

and in this article "related sale or supply" means a sale of goods or supply of services to the customer otherwise than by the supplier, but for or in connection with the same purpose as the sale or supply mentioned above.

(2) There is excluded from article 14 any transaction entered into by a supplier with a customer, if the transaction is entered into for the purposes of or in connection with the sale of goods or supply of services, or a related sale or supply.

(3) There is excluded from article 21 any transaction entered into [by a supplier as agent for a customer], if the transaction is entered into for the purposes of or in connection with the sale of goods or supply of services, or a related sale or supply, and provided that—

(a) where the investment to which the transaction relates is a security, the supplier does not hold himself out (other than to the customer) as engaging in the business of buying securities of the kind to which the transaction relates with a view to selling them, and does not regularly solicit members of the public for the purpose of inducing them (as principals or agents) to buy, sell, subscribe for or underwrite securities;

(b) where the investment to which the transaction relates is a contractually based investment, the supplier enters into the transaction—

(i) with or through an authorised person, or an exempt person acting in the course of a business comprising a regulated activity in relation to which he is exempt; or

(ii) through an office outside the United Kingdom maintained by a party to the transaction, and with or through a person whose head office is situated outside the United Kingdom and whose ordinary business involves him in carrying on activities of the kind specified by any of articles 14, 21, 25, 37, 40, 45, 51, 52 and 53 or, so far as relevant to any of those articles, article 64, or would do so apart from any exclusion from any of those articles made by this Order.

(4) In paragraph (3)(a), "members of the public" has the meaning given by article 15(2), references to "A" being read as references to the supplier.

(5) There are excluded from article 25(1) and (2) arrangements made by a supplier for, or with a view to, a transaction which is or is to be entered into by a customer for the purposes of or in connection with the sale of goods or supply of services, or a related sale or supply.

(6) There is excluded from article 37 any activity carried on by a supplier where the assets in question—

(a) are those of a customer; and

(b) are managed for the purposes of or in connection with the sale of goods or supply of services, or a related sale or supply.

(7) There is excluded from article 40 any activity carried on by a supplier where the assets in question are or are to be safeguarded and administered for the purposes of or in connection with the sale of goods or supply of services, or a related sale or supply.

(8) There is excluded from article 53 the giving of advice by a supplier to a customer for the purposes of or in connection with the sale of goods or supply of services, or a related sale or supply, or to a person with whom the customer proposes to enter into a transaction for the purposes of or in connection with such a sale or supply or related sale or supply.

(9) Paragraphs (2), (3) and (5) do not apply in the case of a transaction for the sale or purchase of a [contract of insurance], an investment of the kind specified by article 81, or an investment of the kind specified by article 89 so far as relevant to such a contract or such an investment.

(10) Paragraph (6) does not apply where the assets managed consist of qualifying contracts of insurance, investments of the kind specified by article 81, or investments of the kind specified by article 89 so far as relevant to such contracts or such investments.

(11) Paragraph (8) does not apply in the case of advice in relation to an investment which is a [contract of insurance], is of the kind specified by article 81, or is of the kind specified by article 89 so far as relevant to such a contract or such an investment.

[(12) This article is subject to article 4(4).]

[4079]

NOTES

Para (1): figure in square brackets in definition "supplier" inserted by the Financial Services and Markets Act 2000 (Regulated Activities) (Amendment) (No 2) Order 2003, SI 2003/1476, art 10(3)(a), as from 31 October 2004 (in so far as relating to contracts of long-term care insurance), and as from 14 January 2005 (otherwise); for transitional provisions see arts 22–27 of that Order at **[4665]** et seq.

Para (3): words in square brackets substituted by the Financial Services and Markets Act 2000 (Regulated Activities) (Amendment) Order 2001, SI 2001/3544, arts 2, 10, as from 1 December 2001.

Paras (9), (11): words in square brackets substituted by SI 2003/1476, art 10(3)(b), (c), as from 31 October 2004 (in so far as relating to contracts of long-term care insurance), and as from 14 January 2005 (otherwise); for transitional provisions see arts 22–27 of that Order at **[4665]** et seq.

Para (12): added by the Financial Services and Markets Act 2000 (Regulated Activities) (Amendment No 3) Order 2006, SI 2006/3384, arts 2, 21, as from 1 April 2007 (for the purposes of enabling applications to be made for (i) a Part IV permission, (ii) a variation of a Part IV permission, and (iii) the Authority's approval under s 59 of the 2000 Act, in relation to an activity of the kind specified by art 25D of this Order, or in relation to an investment of the kind specified by arts 83, 84 or 85 of this Order), and as from 1 November 2007 (otherwise).

69 Groups and joint enterprises

(1) There is excluded from article 14 any transaction into which a person enters as principal with another person if that other person is also acting as principal and—

(a) they are members of the same group; or

(b) they are, or propose to become, participators in a joint enterprise and the transaction is entered into for the purposes of or in connection with that enterprise.

(2) There is excluded from article 21 any transaction into which a person enters as agent for another person if that other person is acting as principal, and the condition in paragraph (1)(a) or (b) is met, provided that—

(a) where the investment to which the transaction relates is a security, the agent does not hold himself out (other than to members of the same group or persons who are or propose to become participators with him in a joint enterprise) as engaging in the business of buying securities of the kind to which the transaction relates with a view to selling them, and does not regularly solicit members of the public for the purpose of inducing them (as principals or agents) to buy, sell, subscribe for or underwrite securities;

(b) where the investment to which the transaction relates is a contractually based investment, the agent enters into the transaction—

(i) with or through an authorised person, or an exempt person acting in the course of a business comprising a regulated activity in relation to which he is exempt; or

(ii) through an office outside the United Kingdom maintained by a party to the transaction, and with or through a person whose head office is situated outside the United Kingdom and whose ordinary business involves him in carrying on activities of the kind specified by any of articles 14, 21, 25, 37, 40, 45, 51, 52 and 53 or, so far as relevant to any of those articles, article 64, or would do so apart from any exclusion from any of those articles made by this Order.

(3) In paragraph (2)(a), "members of the public" has the meaning given by article 15(2), references to "A" being read as references to the agent.

(4) There are excluded from article 25(1) and (2) arrangements made by a person if—

(a) he is a member of a group and the arrangements in question are for, or with a view to, a transaction which is or is to be entered into, as principal, by another member of the same group; or

(b) he is or proposes to become a participator in a joint enterprise, and the arrangements in question are for, or with a view to, a transaction which is or is to be entered into, as principal, by another person who is or proposes to become a participator in that enterprise, for the purposes of or in connection with that enterprise.

(5) There is excluded from article 37 any activity carried on by a person if—
(a) he is a member of a group and the assets in question belong to another member of the same group; or
(b) he is or proposes to become a participator in a joint enterprise with the person to whom the assets belong, and the assets are managed for the purposes of or in connection with that enterprise.

(6) There is excluded from article 40 any activity carried on by a person if—
(a) he is a member of a group and the assets in question belong to another member of the same group; or
(b) he is or proposes to become a participator in a joint enterprise, and the assets in question—
(i) belong to another person who is or proposes to become a participator in that joint enterprise; and
(ii) are or are to be safeguarded and administered for the purposes of or in connection with that enterprise.

(7) A person who is a member of a group does not carry on an activity of the kind specified by article 45 where he sends a dematerialised instruction, or causes one to be sent, on behalf of another member of the same group, if the investment to which the instruction relates is one in respect of which a member of the same group is registered as holder in the appropriate register of securities, or will be so registered as a result of the instruction.

(8) In paragraph (7), "dematerialised instruction" and "register of securities" have the meaning given by regulation 3 of the Uncertificated Securities Regulations [2001].

(9) There is excluded from article 53 the giving of advice by a person if—
(a) he is a member of a group and gives the advice in question to another member of the same group; or
(b) he is, or proposes to become, a participator in a joint enterprise and the advice in question is given to another person who is, or proposes to become, a participator in that enterprise for the purposes of or in connection with that enterprise.

[(10) Paragraph (2) does not apply to a transaction for the sale or purchase of a contract of insurance.

(11) Paragraph (4) does not apply to arrangements for, or with a view to, a transaction for the sale or purchase of a contract of insurance.

(12) Paragraph (9) does not apply where the advice relates to a transaction for the sale or purchase of a contract of insurance.]

[(13) This article is subject to article 4(4).]

[4080]

NOTES

Para (8): date in square brackets substituted by the Financial Services and Markets Act 2000 (Regulated Activities) (Amendment) Order 2002, SI 2002/682, art 13(4), as from 27 April 2002.

Paras (10)–(12): added by the Financial Services and Markets Act 2000 (Regulated Activities) (Amendment) (No 2) Order 2003, SI 2003/1476, art 10(4), as from 31 October 2004 (in so far as relating to contracts of long-term care insurance), and as from 14 January 2005 (otherwise); for transitional provisions see arts 22–27 of that Order at **[4665]** et seq.

Para (13): added by the Financial Services and Markets Act 2000 (Regulated Activities) (Amendment No 3) Order 2006, SI 2006/3384, arts 2, 22, as from 1 April 2007 (for the purposes of enabling applications to be made for (i) a Part IV permission, (ii) a variation of a Part IV permission, and (iii) the Authority's approval under s 59 of the 2000 Act, in relation to an activity of the kind specified by art 25D of this Order, or in relation to an investment of the kind specified by arts 83, 84 or 85 of this Order), and as from 1 November 2007 (otherwise).

70 Activities carried on in connection with the sale of a body corporate

(1) A person does not carry on an activity of the kind specified by article 14 by entering as principal into a transaction if—
(a) the transaction is one to acquire or dispose of shares in a body corporate other than an open-ended investment company, or is entered into for the purposes of such an acquisition or disposal; and
(b) either—
(i) the conditions set out in paragraph (2) are met; or
(ii) those conditions are not met, but the object of the transaction may

nevertheless reasonably be regarded as being the acquisition of day to day control of the affairs of the body corporate.

(2) The conditions mentioned in paragraph (1)(b) are that—

(a) the shares consist of or include 50 per cent or more of the voting shares in the body corporate; or

(b) the shares, together with any already held by the person acquiring them, consist of or include at least that percentage of such shares; and

(c) in either case, the acquisition or disposal is between parties each of whom is a body corporate, a partnership, a single individual or a group of connected individuals.

(3) In paragraph (2)(c), "a group of connected individuals" means—

(a) in relation to a party disposing of shares in a body corporate, a single group of persons each of whom is—
  (i) a director or manager of the body corporate;
  (ii) a close relative of any such director or manager;
  (iii) a person acting as trustee for any person falling within paragraph (i) or (ii); and

(b) in relation to a party acquiring shares in a body corporate, a single group of persons each of whom is—
  (i) a person who is or is to be a director or manager of the body corporate;
  (ii) a close relative of any such person; or
  (iii) a person acting as trustee for any person falling within paragraph (i) or (ii).

(4) A person does not carry on an activity of the kind specified by article 21 by entering as agent into a transaction of the kind described in paragraph (1).

(5) There are excluded from article 25(1) and (2) arrangements made for, or with a view to, a transaction of the kind described in paragraph (1).

(6) There is excluded from article 53 the giving of advice in connection with a transaction (or proposed transaction) of the kind described in paragraph (1).

[(7) Paragraphs (4), (5) and (6) do not apply in the case of a transaction for the sale or purchase of a contract of insurance.]

[(8) This article is subject to article 4(4).]

[4081]

NOTES

Para (7): added by the Financial Services and Markets Act 2000 (Regulated Activities) (Amendment) (No 2) Order 2003, SI 2003/1476, art 10(5), as from 31 October 2004 (in so far as relating to contracts of long-term care insurance), and as from 14 January 2005 (otherwise); for transitional provisions see arts 22–27 of that Order at **[4665]** et seq.

Para (8): added by the Financial Services and Markets Act 2000 (Regulated Activities) (Amendment No 3) Order 2006, SI 2006/3384, arts 2, 23, as from 1 April 2007 (for the purposes of enabling applications to be made for (i) a Part IV permission, (ii) a variation of a Part IV permission, and (iii) the Authority's approval under s 59 of the 2000 Act, in relation to an activity of the kind specified by art 25D of this Order, or in relation to an investment of the kind specified by arts 83, 84 or 85 of this Order), and as from 1 November 2007 (otherwise).

71 Activities carried on in connection with employee share schemes

(1) A person ("C"), a member of the same group as C or a relevant trustee does not carry on an activity of the kind specified by article 14 by entering as principal into a transaction the purpose of which is to enable or facilitate—

(a) transactions in shares in, or debentures issued by, C between, or for the benefit of, any of the persons mentioned in paragraph (2); or

(b) the holding of such shares or debentures by, or for the benefit of, such persons.

(2) The persons referred to in paragraph (1) are—

(a) the bona fide employees or former employees of C or of another member of the same group as C;

(b) the wives, husbands, widows, widowers, [civil partners, surviving civil partners,] or children or step-children under the age of eighteen of such employees or former employees.

(3) C, a member of the same group as C or a relevant trustee does not carry on an activity of the kind specified by article 21 by entering as agent into a transaction of the kind described in paragraph (1).

(4) There are excluded from article 25(1) or (2) arrangements made by C, a member of the same group as C or a relevant trustee if the arrangements in question are for, or with a view to, a transaction of the kind described in paragraph (1).

(5) There is excluded from article 40 any activity if the assets in question are, or are to be, safeguarded and administered by C, a member of the same group as C or a relevant trustee for the purpose of enabling or facilitating transactions of the kind described in paragraph (1).

(6) In this article—

(a) "shares" and "debentures" include—

(i) any investment of the kind specified by article 76 or 77;

(ii) any investment of the kind specified by article 79 or 80 so far as relevant to articles 76 and 77; and

(iii) any investment of the kind specified by article 89 so far as relevant to investments of the kind mentioned in paragraph (i) or (ii);

(b) "relevant trustee" means a person who, in pursuance of the arrangements made for the purpose mentioned in paragraph (1), holds, as trustee, shares in or debentures issued by C.

[4082]

NOTES

Para (2): words in square brackets in sub-para (b) inserted by the Civil Partnership Act 2004 (Amendments to Subordinate Legislation) Order 2005, SI 2005/2114, art 2(16), Sch 16, Pt 1, para 1(1), (4), as from 5 December 2005.

Step-children, etc: as to the meaning of this, and related expressions, see the Civil Partnership Act 2004, s 246 (as applied to this Order by the Civil Partnership Act 2004 (Relationships Arising Through Civil Partnership) Order 2005, SI 2005/3137, art 3, Schedule).

72 Overseas persons

(1) An overseas person does not carry on an activity of the kind specified by article 14 [or 25D] by—

(a) entering into a transaction as principal with or though an authorised person, or an exempt person acting in the course of a business comprising a regulated activity in relation to which he is exempt; or

(b) entering into a transaction as principal with a person in the United Kingdom, if the transaction is the result of a legitimate approach.

(2) An overseas person does not carry on an activity of the kind specified by article 21 [or 25D] by—

(a) entering into a transaction as agent for any person with or through an authorised person or an exempt person acting in the course of a business comprising a regulated activity in relation to which he is exempt; or

(b) entering into a transaction with another party ("X") as agent for any person ("Y"), other than with or through an authorised person or such an exempt person, unless—

(i) either X or Y is in the United Kingdom; and

(ii) the transaction is the result of an approach (other than a legitimate approach) made by or on behalf of, or to, whichever of X or Y is in the United Kingdom.

(3) There are excluded from article 25(1) [or 25D] arrangements made by an overseas person with an authorised person, or an exempt person acting in the course of a business comprising a regulated activity in relation to which he is exempt.

(4) There are excluded from article 25(2) [or 25D] arrangements made by an overseas person with a view to transactions which are, as respects transactions in the United Kingdom, confined to—

(a) transactions entered into by authorised persons as principal or agent; and

(b) transactions entered into by exempt persons, as principal or agent, in the course of business comprising regulated activities in relation to which they are exempt.

(5) There is excluded from article 53 the giving of advice by an overseas person as a result of a legitimate approach.

[(5A) An overseas person does not carry on an activity of the kind specified by article 25A(1)(a), 25B(1)(a) or 25C(1)(a) if each person who may be contemplating entering into the relevant type of agreement in the relevant capacity is non-resident.

(5B) There are excluded from articles 25A(1)(b), 25B(1)(b) and 25C(1)(b) arrangements made by an overseas person to vary the terms of a qualifying agreement.

(5C) There are excluded from articles 25A(2), 25B(2) and 25C(2), arrangements made by an overseas person which are made solely with a view to non-resident persons who participate in those arrangements entering, in the relevant capacity, into the relevant type of agreement.

(5D) An overseas person does not carry on an activity of the kind specified in article 61(1), 63B(1) or 63F(1) by entering into a qualifying agreement.

(5E) An overseas person does not carry on an activity of the kind specified in article 61(2), 63B(2) or 63F(2) where he administers a qualifying agreement.

(5F) In paragraphs (5A) to (5E)—

- (a) "non-resident" means not normally resident in the United Kingdom;
- (b) "qualifying agreement" means—
  - (i) in relation to articles 25A and 61, a regulated mortgage contract where the borrower (or each borrower) is non-resident when he enters into it;
  - (ii) in relation to articles 25B and 63B, a regulated home reversion plan where the reversion seller (or each reversion seller) is non-resident when he enters into it;
  - (iii) in relation to articles 25C and 63F, a regulated home purchase plan where the home purchaser (or each home purchaser) is non-resident when he enters into it;
- (c) "the relevant capacity" means—
  - (i) in the case of a regulated mortgage contract, as borrower;
  - (ii) in the case of a regulated home reversion plan, as reversion seller or plan provider;
  - (iii) in the case of a regulated home purchase plan, as home purchaser;
- (d) "the relevant type of agreement" means—
  - (i) in relation to article 25A, a regulated mortgage contract;
  - (ii) in relation to article 25B, a regulated home reversion plan;
  - (iii) in relation to article 25C, a regulated home purchase plan.]

(6) There is excluded from article 64 any agreement made by an overseas person to carry on an activity of the kind specified by article 25(1) or (2), 37[, 39A], 40 or 45 if the agreement is the result of a legitimate approach.

(7) In this article, "legitimate approach" means—

- (a) an approach made to the overseas person which has not been solicited by him in any way, or has been solicited by him in a way which does not contravene section 21 of the Act; or
- (b) an approach made by or on behalf of the overseas person in a way which does not contravene that section.

[(8) Paragraphs (1) to (5) do not apply where the overseas person is an investment firm or credit institution—

- (a) who is providing or performing investment services and activities on a professional basis; and
- (b) whose home Member State is the United Kingdom.]

[4083]

NOTES

Paras (1)–(4): figures in square brackets inserted by the Financial Services and Markets Act 2000 (Regulated Activities) (Amendment No 3) Order 2006, SI 2006/3384, arts 2, 24(a)–(d), as from 1 April 2007 (for the purposes of enabling applications to be made for (i) a Part IV permission, (ii) a variation of a Part IV permission, and (iii) the Authority's approval under s 59 of the 2000 Act, in relation to an activity of the kind specified by art 25D of this Order, or in relation to an investment of the kind specified by arts 83, 84 or 85 of this Order), and as from 1 November 2007 (otherwise).

Paras (5A)–(5F): inserted by the Financial Services and Markets Act 2000 (Regulated Activities) (Amendment) (No 1) Order 2003, SI 2003/1475, art 20, as from 31 October 2004 (for transitional provisions see arts 26–29 at **[4659]** et seq); and substituted by the Financial Services and Markets Act 2000 (Regulated Activities) (Amendment) (No 2) Order 2006, SI 2006/2383, arts 2, 21, as from 6 November 2006 (for the purposes of enabling applications to be made for (i) a Pt IV permission, or a variation of a Pt IV permission, in relation to activities of the kind specified by arts 25B, 25C, 53B, 53C,

PART IV STATUTORY INSTRUMENTS

63B or 63F or, so far as relevant to any such activity, art 64 of this Order; or (ii) the Authority's approval under FSMA 2000, s 59 in relation to any of those activities), and as from 6 April 2007 (otherwise) (for transitional provisions and effect see arts 36–40 of, and the Schedule to, the 2006 Order at **[4821]** et seq).

Para (6): figure in square brackets inserted by the Financial Services and Markets Act 2000 (Regulated Activities) (Amendment) (No 2) Order 2003, SI 2003/1476, art 10(6), as from 31 October 2004 (in so far as relating to contracts of long-term care insurance), and as from 14 January 2005 (otherwise); for transitional provisions see arts 22–27 of that Order at **[4665]** et seq.

Para (8): added by SI 2006/3384, arts 2, 24(e), as from 1 April 2007 (for the purposes of enabling applications to be made for (i) a Part IV permission, (ii) a variation of a Part IV permission, and (iii) the Authority's approval under s 59 of the 2000 Act, in relation to an activity of the kind specified by art 25D of this Order, or in relation to an investment of the kind specified by arts 83, 84 or 85 of this Order), and as from 1 November 2007 (otherwise).

[72A Information society services

(1) There is excluded from this Part any activity consisting of the provision of an information society service from an EEA State other than the United Kingdom.

(2) The exclusion in paragraph (1) does not apply to the activity of effecting or carrying out a contract of insurance as principal, where—

(a) the activity is carried on by an undertaking which has received official authorisation in accordance with [Article 4 of the life assurance consolidation directive] or the first non-life insurance directive, and

(b) the insurance falls within the scope of any of the insurance directives.]

[4083A]

NOTES

Inserted by the Financial Services and Markets Act 2000 (Regulated Activities) (Amendment) (No 2) Order 2002, SI 2002/1776, art 2, as from 21 August 2002.

Para (2): words in square brackets substituted by the Life Assurance Consolidation Directive (Consequential Amendments) Regulations 2004, SI 2004/3379, reg 17, as from 11 January 2005.

[72B Activities carried on by a provider of relevant goods or services

(1) In this article—

"connected contract of insurance" means a contract of insurance which—

(a) is not a contract of long-term insurance;

(b) has a total duration (or would have a total duration were any right to renew conferred by the contract exercised) of five years or less;

(c) has an annual premium (or, where the premium is paid otherwise than by way of annual premium, the equivalent of an annual premium) of 500 euro or less, or the equivalent amount in sterling or other currency;

(d) covers the risk of—

(i) breakdown, loss of, or damage to, non-motor goods supplied by the provider; or

(ii) damage to, or loss of, baggage and other risks linked to the travel booked with the provider ("travel risks");

(e) does not cover any liability risks (except, in the case of a contract which covers travel risks, where that cover is ancillary to the main cover provided by the contract);

(f) is complementary to the non-motor goods being supplied or service being provided by the provider; and

(g) is of such a nature that the only information that a person requires in order to carry on an activity of the kind specified by article 21, 25, 39A or 53 in relation to it is the cover provided by the contract;

"non-motor goods" means goods which are not mechanically propelled road vehicles;

"provider" means a person who supplies non-motor goods or provides services related to travel in the course of carrying on a profession or business which does not otherwise consist of the carrying on of regulated activities.

(2) There is excluded from article 21 any transaction for the sale or purchase of a connected contract of insurance into which a provider enters as agent.

(3) There are excluded from article 25(1) and (2) any arrangements made by a provider for, or with a view to, a transaction for the sale or purchase of a connected contract of insurance.

(4) There is excluded from article 39A any activity carried on by a provider where the contract of insurance in question is a connected contract of insurance.

(5) There is excluded from article 53 the giving of advice by a provider in relation to a transaction for the sale or purchase of a connected contract of insurance.

(6) For the purposes of this article, a contract of insurance which covers travel risks is not to be treated as a contract of long-term insurance, notwithstanding the fact that it contains related and subsidiary provisions such that it might be regarded as a contract of long-term insurance, if the cover to which those provisions relate is ancillary to the main cover provided by the contract.]

[4083B]

NOTES

Inserted, together with arts 72C, 72D, by the Financial Services and Markets Act 2000 (Regulated Activities) (Amendment) (No 2) Order 2003, SI 2003/1476, art 11, as from 31 October 2004 (in so far as relating to contracts of long-term care insurance), and as from 14 January 2005 (otherwise); for transitional provisions see arts 22–27 of that Order at **[4665]** et seq.

[72C Provision of information on an incidental basis

(1) There is excluded from articles 25(1) and (2) the making of arrangements for, or with a view to, a transaction for the sale or purchase of a contract of insurance or an investment of the kind specified by article 89, so far as relevant to such a contract, where that activity meets the conditions specified in paragraph (4).

(2) There is excluded from articles 37 and 40 any activity—

(a) where the assets in question are rights under a contract of insurance or an investment of the kind specified by article 89, so far as relevant to such a contract; and

(b) which meets the conditions specified in paragraph (4).

(3) There is excluded from article 39A any activity which meets the conditions specified in paragraph (4).

(4) The conditions specified in this paragraph are that the activity—

(a) consists of the provision of information to the policyholder or potential policyholder;

(b) is carried on by a person in the course of carrying on a profession or business which does not otherwise consist of the carrying on of regulated activities; and

(c) may reasonably be regarded as being incidental to that profession or business.]

[4083C]

NOTES

Inserted as noted to art 72B at **[4083B]**.

[72D Large risks contracts where risk situated outside the EEA

(1) There is excluded from articles 21, 25(1) and (2), 39A and 53 any activity which is carried on in relation to a large risks contract of insurance, to the extent that the risk or commitment covered by the contract is not situated in an EEA State.

(2) In this article, a "large risks contract of insurance" is a contract of insurance the principal object of which is to cover—

(a) risks falling within paragraph 4 (railway rolling stock), 5 (aircraft), 6 (ships), 7 (goods in transit), 11 (aircraft liability) or 12 (liability of ships) of Part 1 of Schedule 1;

(b) risks falling within paragraph 14 (credit) or 15 (suretyship) of that Part provided that the risks relate to a business carried on by the policyholder; or

(c) risks falling within paragraph 3 (land vehicles), 8 (fire and natural forces), 9 (damage to property), 10 (motor vehicle liability), 13 (general liability) or 16 (miscellaneous financial loss) of that Part provided that the risks relate to a business carried on by the policyholder and that the condition specified in paragraph (3) is met in relation to that business.

(3) The condition specified in this paragraph is that at least two of the three following criteria were met in the most recent financial year for which information is available—

(a) the balance sheet total of the business (within the meaning of section 247(5) of the Companies Act 1985 or article 255(5) of the Companies (Northern Ireland) Order 1986) exceeded 6.2 million euro,

(b) the net turnover (within the meaning given to "turnover" by section 262(1) of that Act or article 270(1) of that Order) exceeded 12.8 million euro,

(c) the number of employees (within the meaning given by section 247(6) of that Act or article 255(6) of that Order) exceeded 250,

and for a financial year which is a company's financial year but not in fact a year, the net turnover of the policyholder shall be proportionately adjusted.

(4) For the purposes of paragraph (3), where the policyholder is a member of a group for which consolidated accounts (within the meaning of the Seventh Company Law Directive) are drawn up, the question whether the condition specified by that paragraph is met is to be determined by reference to those accounts.]

[4083D]

NOTES

Inserted as noted to art 72B at **[4083B]**.

[72E Business Angel-led Enterprise Capital Funds

(1) A body corporate of a type specified in paragraph (7) does not carry on the activity of the kind specified by article 21 by entering as agent into a transaction on behalf of the participants of a Business Angel-led Enterprise Capital Fund.

(2) There are excluded from article 25(1) and (2) arrangements, made by a body corporate of a type specified in paragraph (7), for or with a view to a transaction which is or is to be entered into by or on behalf of the participants in a Business Angel-led Enterprise Capital Fund.

(3) There is excluded from article 37 any activity, carried on by a body corporate of a type specified in paragraph (7), which consists in the managing of assets belonging to the participants in a Business Angel-led Enterprise Capital Fund.

(4) There is excluded from article 40 any activity, carried on by a body corporate of a type specified in paragraph (7), in respect of assets belonging to the participants in a Business Angel-led Enterprise Capital Fund.

(5) A body corporate of a type specified in paragraph (7) does not carry on the activity of the kind specified in article 51(1)(a) where it carries on the activity of establishing, operating or winding up a Business Angel-led Enterprise Capital Fund.

(6) A body corporate of a type specified in paragraph (7) does not carry on the activity of the kind specified in article 53 where it is advising the participants in a Business Angel-led Enterprise Capital Fund on investments to be made by or on behalf of the participants of that Business Angel-led Enterprise Capital Fund.

(7) The type of body corporate specified is a limited company—

(i) which operates a Business Angel-led Enterprise Capital Fund; and

(ii) the members of which are participants in the Business Angel-led Enterprise Capital Fund operated by that limited company and between them have invested at least 50 per cent of the total investment in that Business Angel-led Enterprise Capital Fund excluding any investment made by the Secretary of State.

(8) For the purposes of paragraph (7), "a limited company" means a body corporate with limited liability which is a company or firm formed in accordance with the law of an EEA State and having its registered office, central administration or principal place of business within the territory of an EEA State.

(9) Nothing in this article has the effect of excluding a body corporate from the application of the Money Laundering Regulations 2003, in so far as those Regulations would have applied to it but for this article.

(10) Nothing in this article has the effect of excluding a body corporate from the application of section 397 of the Act (misleading statements and practices), in so far as that section would have applied to it but for this article.]

[(11) This article is subject to article 4(4).]

[4083E]

NOTES

Commencement: 1 October 2005.

Inserted, together with art 72F, by the Financial Services and Markets Act 2000 (Regulated Activities) (Amendment) (No 2) Order 2005, SI 2005/1518, art 2(1), (3), as from 1 October 2005.

Para (11): added by SI 2006/3384, arts 2, 25, as from 1 April 2007 (for the purposes of enabling applications to be made for (i) a Part IV permission, (ii) a variation of a Part IV permission, and (iii) the Authority's approval under s 59 of the 2000 Act, in relation to an activity of the kind specified by art 25D of this Order, or in relation to an investment of the kind specified by arts 83, 84 or 85 of this Order), and as from 1 November 2007 (otherwise).

[72F Interpretation

(1) For the purposes of this article and of article 72E—

"Business Angel-led Enterprise Capital Fund" means a collective investment scheme which—

(a) is established for the purpose of enabling participants to participate in or receive profits or income arising from the acquisition, holding, management or disposal of investments falling within one or more of—

(i) article 76, being shares in an unlisted company;

(ii) article 77, being instruments creating or acknowledging indebtedness in respect of an unlisted company; and

(iii) article 79, being warrants or other instruments entitling the holder to subscribe for shares in an unlisted company;

(b) has only the following as its participants—

(i) the Secretary of State;

(ii) a body corporate of a type specified in article 72E(7); and

(iii) one or more persons each of whom at the time they became a participant was—

(aa) a sophisticated investor;

(bb) a high net worth individual;

(cc) a high net worth company;

(dd) a high net worth unincorporated association;

(ee) a trustee of a high value trust; or

(ff) a self-certified sophisticated investor;

(c) is prevented, by the arrangements by which it is established, from—

(i) acquiring investments, other than those falling within paragraphs (i) to (iii) of sub-paragraph (a); and

(ii) acquiring investments falling within paragraphs (i) to (iii) of sub-paragraph (a) in an unlisted company, where the aggregated cost of those investments exceeds £2 million, unless that acquisition is necessary to prevent or reduce the dilution of an existing shareholding in that unlisted company;

"high net worth company" means a body corporate which—

(a) falls within article 49(2)(a) of the Financial Services and Markets Act 2000 (Financial Promotion) Order 2001 (high net worth companies, unincorporated associations etc); and

(b) has executed a document [(in a manner which binds the company)] in the following terms:

"This company is a high net worth company and falls within article 49(2)(a) of the Financial Services and Markets Act 2000 (Financial Promotion) Order 2001. We understand that any Business Angel-led Enterprise Capital Fund (within the meaning of article 72F of the Financial Services and Markets Act 2000 (Regulated Activities) Order 2001), in which this company participates, or any person who operates that Business Angel-led Enterprise Capital Fund, in which this company participates, will not be authorised under the Financial Services and Markets Act 2000 (and so will not have to satisfy the threshold conditions set out in Part I of Schedule 6 to that Act and will not be subject to Financial Services Authority rules such as those on holding client money). We understand that this means that redress through the Financial Services Authority, the Financial Ombudsman Scheme or the Financial Services Compensation Scheme will not be available. We also understand the risks associated in investing in a Business Angel-led Enterprise Capital Fund and are aware that it is open to us to seek advice from someone who is authorised under the Financial Services and Markets Act 2000 and who specialises in advising on this kind of investment."

PART IV STATUTORY INSTRUMENTS

"high net worth individual" means an individual who—

(a) is a "certified high net worth individual" within the meaning of article 48(2) of the Financial Services and Markets Act 2000 (Financial Promotion) Order 2001 (certified high net worth individuals); and

(b) has signed a statement in the following terms:

"I declare that I am a certified high net worth individual within the meaning of article 48(2) of the Financial Services and Markets Act 2000 (Financial Promotion) Order 2001 and that I understand that any Business Angel-led Enterprise Capital Fund (within the meaning of article 72F of the Financial Services and Markets Act 2000 (Regulated Activities) Order 2001), in which I participate, or any person who operates that Business Angel-led Enterprise Capital Fund, in which I participate, will not be authorised under the Financial Services and Markets Act 2000 (and so will not have to satisfy the threshold conditions set out in Part I of Schedule 6 to that Act and will not be subject to Financial Services Authority rules such as those on holding client money). I understand that this means that redress through the Financial Services Authority, the Financial Ombudsman Scheme or the Financial Services Compensation Scheme will not be available. I also understand the risks associated in investing in a Business Angel-led Enterprise Capital Fund and am aware that it is open to me to seek advice from someone who is authorised under the Financial Services and Markets Act 2000 and who specialises in advising on this kind of investment.";

"high net worth unincorporated association" means an unincorporated association—

(a) which falls within article 49(2)(b) of the Financial Services and Markets Act 2000 (Financial Promotion) Order 2001; and

(b) on behalf of which an officer of that association or a member of its governing body has signed a statement in the following terms:

"This unincorporated association is a high net worth unincorporated association and falls within article 49(2)(b) of the Financial Services and Markets Act 2000 (Financial Promotion) Order 2001. I understand that any Business Angel-led Enterprise Capital Fund (within the meaning of article 72F of the Financial Services and Markets Act 2000 (Regulated Activities) Order 2001), in which this association participates, or any person who operates that Business Angel-led Enterprise Capital Fund, in which this association participates, will not be authorised under the Financial Services and Markets Act 2000 (and so will not have to satisfy the threshold conditions set out in Part I of Schedule 6 to that Act and will not be subject to Financial Services Authority rules such as those on holding client money). I understand that this means that redress through the Financial Services Authority, the Financial Ombudsman Scheme or the Financial Services Compensation Scheme will not be available. I also understand the risks associated in investing in a Business Angel-led Enterprise Capital Fund and am aware that it is open to the association to seek advice from someone who is authorised under the Financial Services and Markets Act 2000 and who specialises in advising on this kind of investment.";

"high value trust" means a trust—

(a) where the aggregate value of the cash and investments which form a part of the trust's assets (before deducting the amount of its liabilities) is £10 million or more;

(b) on behalf of which a trustee has signed a statement in the following terms:

"This trust is a high value trust. I understand that any Business Angel-led Enterprise Capital Fund (within the meaning of article 72F of the Financial Services and Markets Act 2000 (Regulated Activities) Order 2001), in which this trust participates, or any person who operates that Business Angel-led Enterprise Capital Fund, in which this trust participates, will not be authorised under the Financial Services and Markets Act 2000 (and so will not have to satisfy the threshold conditions set out in Part I of Schedule 6 to that Act and will not be subject to Financial Services Authority rules such as those on holding client money). I understand that this means that redress through the Financial Services Authority, the Financial Ombudsman Scheme or the Financial Services Compensation Scheme will not be available. I also understand the risks associated in investing in a Business Angel-led Enterprise Capital Fund and am aware that it is open to the trust to seek advice from someone who is authorised under the Financial Services and Markets Act 2000 and who specialises in advising on this kind of investment.";

"self-certified sophisticated investor" means an individual who—

(a) is a "self-certified sophisticated investor" within the meaning of article 50A of the Financial Services and Markets Act 2000 (Financial Promotion) Order 2001;

(b) has signed a statement in the following terms:

"I declare that I am a self-certified sophisticated investor within the meaning of article 50A of the Financial Services and Markets Act 2000 (Financial Promotion) Order 2001 and that I understand that any Business Angel-led Enterprise Capital Fund (within the meaning of article 72F of the Financial Services and Markets Act 2000 (Regulated Activities) Order 2001), in which I participate, or any person who operates that Business Angel-led Enterprise Capital Fund, in which I participate, will not be authorised under the Financial Services and Markets Act 2000 (and so will not have to satisfy the threshold conditions set out in Part I of Schedule 6 to that Act and will not be subject to Financial Services Authority rules such as those on holding client money). I understand that this means that redress through the Financial Services Authority, the Financial Ombudsman Scheme or the Financial Services Compensation Scheme will not be available. I also understand the risks associated in investing in a Business Angel-led Enterprise Capital Fund and am aware that it is open to me to seek advice from someone who is authorised under the Financial Services and Markets Act 2000 and who specialises in advising on this kind of investment.";

"sophisticated investor" means an individual who—

(a) is a "certified sophisticated investor" within the meaning of article 50(1) of the Financial Services and Markets Act 2000 (Financial Promotion) Order 2001; and

(b) has signed a statement in the following terms:

"I declare that I am a certified sophisticated investor within the meaning of article 50(1) of the Financial Services and Markets Act 2000 (Financial Promotion) Order 2001 and that I understand that any Business Angel-led Enterprise Capital Fund (within the meaning of article 72F of the Financial Services and Markets Act 2000 (Regulated Activities) Order 2001), in which I participate, or any person who operates that Business Angel-led Enterprise Capital Fund, in which I participate, will not be authorised under the Financial Services and Markets Act 2000 (and so will not have to satisfy the threshold conditions set out in Part I of Schedule 6 to that Act and will not be subject to Financial Services Authority rules such as those on holding client money). I understand that this means that redress through the Financial Services Authority, the Financial Ombudsman Scheme or the Financial Services Compensation Scheme will not be available. I also understand the risks associated in investing in a Business Angel-led Enterprise Capital Fund and am aware that it is open to me to seek advice from someone who is authorised under the Financial Services and Markets Act 2000 and who specialises in advising on this kind of investment.";

"unlisted company" has the meaning given by article 3 of the Financial Services and Markets Act 2000 (Financial Promotion) Order 2001.

(2) References in this Article and in Article 72E to a participant in a Business Angel-led Enterprise Capital Fund, doing things on behalf of such a participant and property belonging to such a participant are, respectively, references to that participant in that capacity, to doing things on behalf of that participant in that capacity or to the property of that participant held in that capacity.]

[4083F]

NOTES

Commencement: 1 October 2005.

Inserted as noted to art 72E at **[4083E]**.

Para (1): words in square brackets in definition "high net worth company" substituted by the Financial Services and Markets Act 2000 (Regulated Activities) (Amendment) (No 2) Order 2006, SI 2006/2383, arts 2, 22, as from 6 April 2007 (for the full commencement details of SI 2006/2383, see art 1 of that Order at **[4820]**).

PART III
SPECIFIED INVESTMENTS

73 Investments: general

The following kinds of investment are specified for the purposes of section 22 of the Act.

[4084]

74 Deposits

A deposit.

[4085]

[74A Electronic money

Electronic money.]

[4086]

NOTES

Inserted by the Financial Services and Markets Act 2000 (Regulated Activities) (Amendment) Order 2002, SI 2002/682, art 6, as from 27 April 2002, subject to transitional provisions in relation to persons issuing electronic money immediately before that date contained in art 9 at **[4637]**.

75 Contracts of insurance

Rights under a contract of insurance.

[4087]

76 Shares etc

(1) Shares or stock in the share capital of—

(a) any body corporate (wherever incorporated), and

(b) any unincorporated body constituted under the law of a country or territory outside the United Kingdom.

(2) Paragraph (1) includes—

(a) any shares of a class defined as deferred shares for the purposes of section 119 of the Building Societies Act 1986; and

(b) any transferable shares in a body incorporated under the law of, or any part of, the United Kingdom relating to industrial and provident societies or credit unions, or in a body constituted under the law of another EEA State for purposes equivalent to those of such a body.

(3) But subject to paragraph (2) there are excluded from paragraph (1) shares or stock in the share capital of—

(a) an open-ended investment company;

(b) a building society incorporated under the law of, or any part of, the United Kingdom;

(c) a body incorporated under the law of, or any part of, the United Kingdom relating to industrial and provident societies or credit unions;

(d) any body constituted under the law of an EEA State for purposes equivalent to those of a body falling within sub-paragraph (b) or (c).

[4088]

77 Instruments creating or acknowledging indebtedness

(1) Subject to paragraph (2), such of the following as do not fall within article 78—

(a) debentures;

(b) debenture stock;

(c) loan stock;

(d) bonds;

(e) certificates of deposit;

(f) any other instrument creating or acknowledging indebtedness.

(2) If and to the extent that they would otherwise fall within paragraph (1), there are excluded from that paragraph—

(a) an instrument acknowledging or creating indebtedness for, or for money borrowed to defray, the consideration payable under a contract for the supply of goods or services;
(b) a cheque or other bill of exchange, a banker's draft or a letter of credit (but not a bill of exchange accepted by a banker);
(c) a banknote, a statement showing a balance on a current, deposit or savings account, a lease or other disposition of property, or a heritable security; and
(d) a contract of insurance.

(3) An instrument excluded from paragraph (1) of article 78 by paragraph (2)(b) of that article is not thereby to be taken to fall within paragraph (1) of this article.

[4089]

NOTES

Modification: references in para (1) to securities, instruments or investments creating or acknowledging indebtedness (or creating or acknowledging a present or future indebtedness) includes a reference to uncertificated units of eligible debt securities; see the Uncertificated Securities (Amendment) (Eligible Debt Securities) Regulations 2003, SI 2003/1633, reg 15, Sch 2, para 8.

78 Government and public securities

(1) Subject to paragraph (2), loan stock, bonds and other instruments creating or acknowledging indebtedness, issued by or on behalf of any of the following—
(a) the government of the United Kingdom;
(b) the Scottish Administration;
(c) the Executive Committee of the Northern Ireland Assembly;
(d) the National Assembly for Wales;
(e) the government of any country or territory outside the United Kingdom;
(f) a local authority in the United Kingdom or elsewhere; or
(g) a body the members of which comprise—
(i) states including the United Kingdom or another EEA State; or
(ii) bodies whose members comprise states including the United Kingdom or another EEA State.

(2) There are excluded from paragraph (1)—
(a) so far as applicable, the instruments mentioned in article 77(2)(a) to (d);
(b) any instrument creating or acknowledging indebtedness in respect of—
(i) money received by the Director of Savings as deposits or otherwise in connection with the business of the National Savings Bank;
(ii) money raised under the National Loans Act 1968 under the auspices of the Director of Savings or treated as so raised by virtue of section 11(3) of the National Debt Act 1972.

[4090]

NOTES

Modification: references in this article to securities, instruments or investments creating or acknowledging indebtedness (or creating or acknowledging a present or future indebtedness) includes a reference to uncertificated units of eligible debt securities; see the Uncertificated Securities (Amendment) (Eligible Debt Securities) Regulations 2003, SI 2003/1633, reg 15, Sch 2, para 8.

79 Instruments giving entitlements to investments

(1) Warrants and other instruments entitling the holder to subscribe for any investment of the kind specified by article 76, 77 or 78.

(2) It is immaterial whether the investment to which the entitlement relates is in existence or identifiable.

(3) An investment of the kind specified by this article is not to be regarded as falling within article 83, 84 or 85.

[4091]

80 Certificates representing certain securities

(1) Subject to paragraph (2), certificates or other instruments which confer contractual or property rights (other than rights consisting of an investment of the kind specified by article 83)—

(a) in respect of any investment of the kind specified by any of articles 76 to 79, being an investment held by a person other than the person on whom the rights are conferred by the certificate or instrument; and
(b) the transfer of which may be effected without the consent of that person.

(2) There is excluded from paragraph (1) any certificate or other instrument which confers rights in respect of two or more investments issued by different persons, or in respect of two or more different investments of the kind specified by article 78 and issued by the same person.

[4092]

81 Units in a collective investment scheme

Units in a collective investment scheme (within the meaning of Part XVII of the Act).

[4093]

[82 Rights under a pension scheme

(1) Rights under a stakeholder pension scheme.

(2) Rights under a personal pension scheme.]

[4094]

NOTES

Commencement: 1 October 2006 (certain purposes); 6 April 2007 (otherwise) (see below).

Substituted by the Financial Services and Markets Act 2000 (Regulated Activities) (Amendment) Order 2006, SI 2006/1969, art 2(1), (5), as from 1 October 2006 (for the purposes of enabling applications to be made for Part IV permission or for a variation of Part IV permission in relation to an investment specified by art 82(2) of this Order (as so substituted)), and as from 6 April 2007 (otherwise); for transitional provisions and effect see arts 3–7 of, and the Schedule to, the 2006 Order at **[4814]** et seq.

83 Options

[(1)] Options to acquire or dispose of—
(a) a security or contractually based investment (other than one of a kind specified by this article);
(b) currency of the United Kingdom or any other country or territory;
(c) palladium, platinum, gold or silver; *or*
(d) an option to acquire or dispose of an investment of the kind specified by this article by virtue of paragraph (a), (b) or (c)[;
(e) subject to paragraph (4), an option to acquire or dispose of an option to which paragraph 5, 6, 7 or 10 of Section C of Annex I to the markets in financial instruments directive (the text of which is set out in Part I of Schedule 2) applies].

[(2) Subject to paragraph (4), options—
(a) to which paragraph (1) does not apply;
(b) which relate to commodities;
(c) which may be settled physically; and
(d) either—
(i) to which paragraph 5 or 6 of Section C of Annex I to the markets in financial instruments directive, the text of which is set out in Part 1 of Schedule 2, applies, or
(ii) which in accordance with Article 38 of the Commission Regulation (the text of which is set out in Part 2 of Schedule 2) are to be considered as having the characteristics of other derivative financial instruments and not being for commercial purposes, and to which paragraph 7 of Section C of Annex I to the markets in financial instruments directive applies.

(3) Subject to paragraph (4), options—
(a) to which paragraph (1) does not apply;
(b) which may be settled physically; and
(c) to which paragraph 10 of Section C of Annex I to the markets in financial instruments directive (read with the Commission Regulation) applies.

(4) Paragraphs (1)(e), (2) and (3) only apply to options in relation to which—
(a) an investment firm or credit institution is providing or performing investment services and activities on a professional basis,
(b) a management company is providing, in accordance with Article 5(3) of the

UCITS directive, the investment service specified in paragraph 4 or 5 of Section A, or the ancillary service specified in paragraph 1 of Section B, of Annex I to the markets in financial instruments directive, or

(c) a market operator is providing the investment service specified in paragraph 8 of Section A of Annex I to the markets in financial instruments directive.

(5) Expressions used in paragraphs (1)(e), (2) and (3) and in the markets in financial instruments directive have the same meaning as in that directive.]

[4095]

NOTES

Para (1): numbered as such, word in italics in sub-para (c) revoked, and sub-para (e) inserted, by the Financial Services and Markets Act 2000 (Regulated Activities) (Amendment No 3) Order 2006, SI 2006/3384, arts 2, 26(a), (b), as from 1 April 2007 (for the purposes of enabling applications to be made for (i) a Part IV permission, (ii) a variation of a Part IV permission, and (iii) the Authority's approval under s 59 of the 2000 Act, in relation to an activity of the kind specified by art 25D of this Order, or in relation to an investment of the kind specified by arts 83, 84 or 85 of this Order), and as from 1 November 2007 (otherwise).

Paras (2)–(5): added by SI 2006/3384, arts 2, 26(c), as from the same dates and for the same purposes as noted above.

84 Futures

(1) Subject to paragraph (2), rights under a contract for the sale of a commodity or property of any other description under which delivery is to be made at a future date and at a price agreed on when the contract is made.

[(1A) Subject to paragraph (1D), futures—

(a) to which paragraph (1) does not apply;

(b) which relate to commodities;

(c) which may be settled physically; and

(d) to which paragraph 5 or 6 of Section C of Annex I to the markets in financial instruments directive applies.

(1B) Subject to paragraph (1D), futures and forwards—

(a) to which paragraph (1) does not apply;

(b) which relate to commodities;

(c) which may be settled physically;

(d) which in accordance with Article 38 of the Commission Regulation (the text of which is set out in Part 2 of Schedule 2) are to be considered as having the characteristics of other derivative financial instruments and not being for commercial purposes; and

(e) to which paragraph 7 of Section C of Annex I to the markets in financial instruments directive applies.

(1C) Subject to paragraph (1D), futures—

(a) to which paragraph (1) does not apply;

(b) which may be settled physically; and

(c) to which paragraph 10 of Section C of Annex I to the markets in financial instruments directive (read with the Commission Regulation) applies.

(1D) Paragraph (1A), (1B) and (1C) only apply to futures or forwards in relation to which—

(a) an investment firm or credit institution is providing or performing investment services and activities on a professional basis,

(b) a management company is providing, in accordance with Article 5(3) of the UCITS directive, the investment service specified in paragraph 4 or 5 of Section A, or the ancillary service specified in paragraph 1 of Section B, of Annex I to the markets in financial instruments directive, or

(c) a market operator is providing the investment service specified in paragraph 8 of Section A of Annex I to the markets in financial instruments directive.

(1E) Expressions used in paragraphs (1A) to (1C) and in the markets in financial instruments directive have the same meaning as in that directive.]

(2) There are excluded from paragraph (1) rights under any contract which is made for commercial and not investment purposes.

PART IV STATUTORY INSTRUMENTS

(3) A contract is to be regarded as made for investment purposes if it is made or traded on a recognised investment exchange, or is made otherwise than on a recognised investment exchange but is expressed to be as traded on such an exchange or on the same terms as those on which an equivalent contract would be made on such an exchange.

(4) A contract not falling within paragraph (3) is to be regarded as made for commercial purposes if under the terms of the contract delivery is to be made within seven days, unless it can be shown that there existed an understanding that (notwithstanding the express terms of the contract) delivery would not be made within seven days.

(5) The following are indications that a contract not falling within paragraph (3) or (4) is made for commercial purposes and the absence of them is an indication that it is made for investment purposes—

(a) one or more of the parties is a producer of the commodity or other property, or uses it in his business;

(b) the seller delivers or intends to deliver the property or the purchaser takes or intends to take delivery of it.

(6) It is an indication that a contract is made for commercial purposes that the prices, the lot, the delivery date or other terms are determined by the parties for the purposes of the particular contract and not by reference (or not solely by reference) to regularly published prices, to standard lots or delivery dates or to standard terms.

(7) The following are indications that a contract is made for investment purposes—

(a) it is expressed to be as traded on an investment exchange;

(b) performance of the contract is ensured by an investment exchange or a clearing house;

(c) there are arrangements for the payment or provision of margin.

(8) For the purposes of paragraph (1), a price is to be taken to be agreed on when a contract is made—

(a) notwithstanding that it is left to be determined by reference to the price at which a contract is to be entered into on a market or exchange or could be entered into at a time and place specified in the contract; or

(b) in a case where the contract is expressed to be by reference to a standard lot and quality, notwithstanding that provision is made for a variation in the price to take account of any variation in quantity or quality on delivery.

[4096]

NOTES

Paras (1A)–(1E): inserted by the Financial Services and Markets Act 2000 (Regulated Activities) (Amendment No 3) Order 2006, SI 2006/3384, arts 2, 27, as from 1 April 2007 (for the purposes of enabling applications to be made for (i) a Part IV permission, (ii) a variation of a Part IV permission, and (iii) the Authority's approval under s 59 of the 2000 Act, in relation to an activity of the kind specified by art 25D of this Order, or in relation to an investment of the kind specified by arts 83, 84 or 85 of this Order), and as from 1 November 2007 (otherwise).

85 Contracts for differences etc

(1) Subject to paragraph (2), rights under—

(a) a contract for differences; or

(b) any other contract the purpose or pretended purpose of which is to secure a profit or avoid a loss by reference to fluctuations in—

(i) the value or price of property of any description; or

(ii) an index or other factor designated for that purpose in the contract.

(2) There are excluded from paragraph (1)—

(a) rights under a contract if the parties intend that the profit is to be secured or the loss is to be avoided by one or more of the parties taking delivery of any property to which the contract relates;

(b) rights under a contract under which money is received by way of deposit on terms that any interest or other return to be paid on the sum deposited will be calculated by reference to fluctuations in an index or other factor;

(c) rights under any contract under which—

(i) money is received by the Director of Savings as deposits or otherwise in connection with the business of the National Savings Bank; or

(ii) money is raised under the National Loans Act 1968 under the auspices of the Director of Savings or treated as so raised by virtue of section 11(3) of the National Debt Act 1972;

(d) rights under a qualifying contract of insurance.

[(3) Subject to paragraph (4), derivative instruments for the transfer of credit risk—

(a) to which neither article 83 nor paragraph (1) applies; and

(b) to which paragraph 8 of Section C of Annex I to the markets in financial instruments directive applies.

(4) Paragraph (3) only applies to derivatives in relation to which—

(a) an investment firm or credit institution is providing or performing investment services and activities on a professional basis,

(b) a management company is providing, in accordance with Article 5(3) of the UCITS directive, the investment service specified in paragraph 4 or 5 of Section A, or the ancillary service specified in paragraph 1 of Section B, of Annex I to the markets in financial instruments directive, or

(c) a market operator is providing the investment service specified in paragraph 8 of Section A of Annex I to the markets in financial instruments directive.

(5) "Derivative instruments for the transfer of credit risk" has the same meaning as in the markets in financial instruments directive.]

[4097]

NOTES

Paras (3)–(5): added by the Financial Services and Markets Act 2000 (Regulated Activities) (Amendment No 3) Order 2006, SI 2006/3384, arts 2, 28, as from 1 April 2007 (for the purposes of enabling applications to be made for (i) a Part IV permission, (ii) a variation of a Part IV permission, and (iii) the Authority's approval under s 59 of the 2000 Act, in relation to an activity of the kind specified by art 25D of this Order, or in relation to an investment of the kind specified by arts 83, 84 or 85 of this Order), and as from 1 November 2007 (otherwise).

86 Lloyd's syndicate capacity and syndicate membership

(1) The underwriting capacity of a Lloyd's syndicate.

(2) A person's membership (or prospective membership) of a Lloyd's syndicate.

[4098]

87 Funeral plan contracts

Rights under a funeral plan contract.

[4099]

88 Regulated mortgage contracts

Rights under a regulated mortgage contract.

[4100]

[88A Regulated home reversion plans

Rights under a regulated home reversion plan.]

[4100A]

NOTES

Commencement: 6 November 2006 (certain purposes); 6 April 2007 (otherwise) (for more information see the note below).

Inserted, together with art 88B, by the Financial Services and Markets Act 2000 (Regulated Activities) (Amendment) (No 2) Order 2006, SI 2006/2383, arts 2, 23, as from 6 November 2006 (for the purposes of enabling applications to be made for (i) a Pt IV permission, or a variation of a Pt IV permission, in relation to activities of the kind specified by arts 25B, 25C, 53B, 53C, 63B or 63F or, so far as relevant to any such activity, art 64 of this Order; or (ii) the Authority's approval under FSMA 2000, s 59 in relation to any of those activities), and as from 6 April 2007 (otherwise) (for transitional provisions and effect see arts 36–40 of, and the Schedule to, the 2006 Order at **[4821]** et seq).

[88B Regulated home purchase plans

Rights under a regulated home purchase plan.]

[4100B]

NOTES

Commencement: 6 November 2006 (certain purposes); 6 April 2007 (otherwise) (for more information see the note to art 88A at **[4100A]**).

Inserted as noted to art 88A at **[4100A]**.

89 Rights to or interests in investments

(1) Subject to paragraphs (2) to (4), any right to or interest in anything which is specified by any other provision of this Part (other than [article 88, 88A or 88B]).

(2) Paragraph (1) does not include interests under the trusts of an occupational pension scheme.

(3) Paragraph (1) does not include—

(a) rights to or interests in a contract of insurance of the kind referred to in paragraph (1)(a) of article 60; or

(b) interests under a trust of the kind referred to in paragraph (1)(b) of that article.

(4) Paragraph (1) does not include anything which is specified by any other provision of this Part.

[4101]

NOTES

Para (1): words in square brackets substituted by the Financial Services and Markets Act 2000 (Regulated Activities) (Amendment) (No 2) Order 2006, SI 2006/2383, arts 2, 24, as from 6 November 2006 (for the purposes of enabling applications to be made for (i) a Pt IV permission, or a variation of a Pt IV permission, in relation to activities of the kind specified by arts 25B, 25C, 53B, 53C, 63B or 63F or, so far as relevant to any such activity, art 64 of this Order; or (ii) the Authority's approval under FSMA 2000, s 59 in relation to any of those activities), and as from 6 April 2007 (otherwise) (for transitional provisions and effect see arts 36–40 of, and the Schedule to, the 2006 Order at **[4821]** et seq).

90, 91 *((Pt IV) reg 90 amends the Consumer Credit Act 1974, ss 16, 43, 52, 53, 137, 151; reg 91 amends the Consumer Credit (Advertisements) Regulations 1989, SI 1989/1125, reg 9 and the Consumer Credit (Content of Quotations) and Consumer Credit (Advertisements) (Amendment) Regulations 1999, SI 1999/2725, reg 2.)*

[PART V
UNAUTHORISED PERSONS CARRYING ON INSURANCE MEDIATION ACTIVITIES

92 Interpretation

In this Part—

"designated professional body" means a body which is for the time being designated by the Treasury under section 326 of the Act (designation of professional bodies);

"insurance mediation activity" means any regulated activity of the kind specified by article 21, 25(1) or (2), 39A or 53, or, so far as relevant to any of those articles, article 64, which is carried on in relation to a contract of insurance;

"the record" means the record maintained by the Authority under section 347 of the Act (public record of authorised persons etc);

"recorded insurance intermediary" has the meaning given by article 93(4);

"a relevant member", in relation to a designated professional body, means a member (within the meaning of section 325(2) of the Act) of the profession in relation to which that designated professional body is established, or a person who is controlled or managed by one or more such members.]

[4101A]

NOTES

Added, together with the preceding heading and arts 93–96, by the Financial Services and Markets Act 2000 (Regulated Activities) (Amendment) (No 2) Order 2003, SI 2003/1476, art 13, as from 31 October 2004 (in so far as relating to contracts of long-term care insurance), and as from 14 January 2005 (otherwise); for transitional provisions see arts 22–27 of that Order at **[4665]** et seq.

[93 Duty to maintain a record of persons carrying on insurance mediation activities

(1) Subject to articles 95 and 96, the Authority must include in the record every person who—

(a) as a result of information obtained by virtue of its rules or by virtue of a direction given, or requirement imposed, under section 51(3) of the Act (procedure for applications under Part IV), appears to the Authority to fall within paragraph (2); or

(b) as a result of information obtained by virtue of article 94, appears to the Authority to fall within paragraph (3).

(2) A person falls within this paragraph if he is, or has entered into a contract by virtue of which he will be, an appointed representative who carries on any insurance mediation activity.

(3) A person falls within this paragraph if—

(a) he is a relevant member of a designated professional body who carries on, or is proposing to carry on, any insurance mediation activity; and

(b) the general prohibition does not (or will not) apply to the carrying on of those activities by virtue of section 327 of the Act (exemption from the general prohibition).

(4) In this Part, "recorded insurance intermediary" means a person who is included in the record by virtue of paragraph (1).

(5) The record must include—

(a) in the case of any recorded insurance intermediary, its address; and

(b) in the case of a recorded insurance intermediary which is not an individual, the name of the individuals who are responsible for the management of the business carried on by the intermediary, so far as it relates to insurance mediation activities.]

[4101B]

NOTES

Added as noted to art 92 at **[4101A]**.

[94 Members of designated professional bodies

(1) A designated professional body must, by notice in writing, inform the Authority of—

(a) the name,

(b) the address, and

(c) in the case of a relevant member which is not an individual, the name of the individuals who are responsible for the management of the business carried on by the member, so far as it relates to insurance mediation activities,

of any relevant member who falls within paragraph (2).

(2) A relevant member of a designated professional body falls within this paragraph if, in accordance with the rules of that body, he carries on, or proposes to carry on any insurance mediation activity but does not have, and does not propose to apply for, Part IV permission on the basis that the general prohibition does not (or will not) apply to the carrying on of that activity by virtue of section 327 of the Act.

(3) A designated professional body must also, by notice in writing, inform the Authority of any change in relation to the matters specified in sub-paragraphs (a) to (c) of paragraph (1).

(4) A designated professional body must inform the Authority when a relevant member to whom paragraph (2) applies ceases, for whatever reason, to carry on insurance mediation activities.

(5) The Authority may give directions to a designated professional body as to the manner in which the information referred to in paragraphs (1), (3) and (4) must be provided.]

[4101C]

NOTES

Added as noted to art 92 at **[4101A]**.

[95 Exclusion from record where not fit and proper to carry on insurance mediation activities

(1) If it appears to the Authority that a person who falls within article 93(2) (appointed representatives) ("AR") is not a fit and proper person to carry on insurance mediation activities, it may decide not to include him in the record or, if that person is already included in the record, to remove him from the record.

(2) Where the Authority proposes to make a determination under paragraph (1), it must give AR a warning notice.

(3) If the Authority makes a determination under paragraph (1), it must give AR a decision notice.

(4) If the Authority gives AR a decision notice under paragraph (3), AR may refer the matter to the Tribunal.

(5) The Authority may, on the application of AR, revoke a determination under paragraph (1).

(6) If the Authority decides to grant the application, it must give AR written notice of its decision.

(7) If the Authority proposes to refuse the application, it must give AR a warning notice.

(8) If the Authority decides to refuse the application, it must give AR a decision notice.

(9) If the Authority gives AR a decision notice under paragraph (8), AR may refer the matter to the Tribunal.

(10) Sections 393 and 394 of the Act (third party rights and access to Authority material) apply to a warning notice given in accordance with paragraph (2) or (7) and to a decision notice given in accordance with paragraph (3) or (8).]

[4101D]

NOTES

Added as noted to art 92 at **[4101A]**.

[96 Exclusion from the record where Authority has exercised its powers under Part XX of the Act

(1) If a person who appears to the Authority to fall within article 93(3) (member of a designated professional body) falls within paragraph (2) or (3), the Authority must not include him in the record or, if that person is already included in the record, must remove him from the record.

(2) A person falls within this paragraph if, by virtue of a direction given by the Authority under section 328(1) of the Act (directions in relation to the general prohibition), section 327(1) of the Act does not apply in relation to the carrying on by him of any insurance mediation activity.

(3) A person falls within this paragraph if the Authority has made an order under section 329(2) of the Act (orders in relation to the general prohibition) disapplying section 327(1) of the Act in relation to the carrying on by him of any insurance mediation activity.]

[4101E]

NOTES

Added as noted to art 92 at **[4101A]**.

97 *(Art 97 (Pt VI) added by the Financial Services and Markets Act 2000 (Regulated Activities) (Amendment) Order 2004, SI 2004/1610, art 3, as from 15 July 2004, and inserts the Financial Services and Markets Act 2000, s 49(2A) at* **[2049]**.)

SCHEDULES

SCHEDULE 1
CONTRACTS OF INSURANCE

Article 3(1)

PART I
CONTRACTS OF GENERAL INSURANCE

1 Accident

Contracts of insurance providing fixed pecuniary benefits or benefits in the nature of indemnity (or a combination of both) against risks of the person insured or, in the case of a contract made by virtue of section 140, 140A or 140B of the Local Government Act 1972 (or, in Scotland, section 86(1) of the Local Government (Scotland) Act 1973), a person for whose benefit the contract is made—

(a) sustaining injury as the result of an accident or of an accident of a specified class; or

(b) dying as a result of an accident or of an accident of a specified class; or

(c) becoming incapacitated in consequence of disease or of disease of a specified class,

including contracts relating to industrial injury and occupational disease but excluding contracts falling within paragraph 2 of Part I of, or paragraph IV of Part II of, this Schedule.

2 Sickness

Contracts of insurance providing fixed pecuniary benefits or benefits in the nature of indemnity (or a combination of both) against risks of loss to the persons insured attributable to sickness or infirmity but excluding contracts falling within paragraph IV of Part II of this Schedule.

3 Land vehicles

Contracts of insurance against loss of or damage to vehicles used on land, including motor vehicles but excluding railway rolling stock.

4 Railway rolling stock

Contract of insurance against loss of or damage to railway rolling stock.

5 Aircraft

Contracts of insurance upon aircraft or upon the machinery, tackle, furniture or equipment of aircraft.

6 Ships

Contracts of insurance upon vessels used on the sea or on inland water, or upon the machinery, tackle, furniture or equipment of such vessels.

7 Goods in transit

Contracts of insurance against loss of or damage to merchandise, baggage and all other goods in transit, irrespective of the form of transport.

8 Fire and natural forces

Contracts of insurance against loss of or damage to property (other than property to which paragraphs 3 to 7 relate) due to fire, explosion, storm, natural forces other than storm, nuclear energy or land subsidence.

9 Damage to property

Contracts of insurance against loss of or damage to property (other than property to which paragraphs 3 to 7 relate) due to hail or frost or any other event (such as theft) other than those mentioned in paragraph 8.

10 Motor vehicle liability

Contracts of insurance against damage arising out of or in connection with the use of motor vehicles on land, including third-party risks and carrier's liability.

11 Aircraft liability

Contracts of insurance against damage arising out of or in connection with the use of aircraft, including third-party risks and carrier's liability.

12 Liability of ships

Contracts of insurance against damage arising out of or in connection with the use of vessels on the sea or on inland water, including third party risks and carrier's liability.

13 General liability

Contracts of insurance against risks of the persons insured incurring liabilities to third parties, the risks in question not being risks to which paragraph 10, 11 or 12 relates.

14 Credit

Contracts of insurance against risks of loss to the persons insured arising from the insolvency of debtors of theirs or from the failure (otherwise than through insolvency) of debtors of theirs to pay their debts when due.

15 Suretyship

(1) Contracts of insurance against the risks of loss to the persons insured arising from their having to perform contracts of guarantee entered into by them.

(2) Fidelity bonds, performance bonds, administration bonds, bail bonds or customs bonds or similar contracts of guarantee, where these are—
- (a) effected or carried out by a person not carrying on a banking business;
- (b) not effected merely incidentally to some other business carried on by the person effecting them; and
- (c) effected in return for the payment of one or more premiums.

16 Miscellaneous financial loss

Contracts of insurance against any of the following risks, namely—
- (a) risks of loss to the persons insured attributable to interruptions of the carrying on of business carried on by them or to reduction of the scope of business so carried on;
- (b) risks of loss to the persons insured attributable to their incurring unforeseen expense (other than loss such as is covered by contracts falling within paragraph 18);
- (c) risks which do not fall within sub-paragraph (a) or (b) and which are not of a kind such that contracts of insurance against them fall within any other provision of this Schedule.

17 Legal expenses

Contracts of insurance against risks of loss to the persons insured attributable to their incurring legal expenses (including costs of litigation).

18 Assistance

Contracts of insurance providing either or both of the following benefits, namely—
- (a) assistance (whether in cash or in kind) for persons who get into difficulties while travelling, while away from home or while away from their permanent residence; or
- (b) assistance (whether in cash or in kind) for persons who get into difficulties otherwise than as mentioned in sub-paragraph (a).

[4102]

NOTES

Note: see also the FSA Authorisation Handbook, Appendix 6, for guidance on the identification of contracts of insurance.

PART II
CONTRACTS OF LONG-TERM INSURANCE

I Life and annuity

Contracts of insurance on human life or contracts to pay annuities on human life, but excluding (in each case) contracts within paragraph III.

II Marriage and birth

Contract of insurance to provide a sum on marriage [or the formation of a civil partnership] or on the birth of a child, being contracts expressed to be in effect for a period of more than one year.

III Linked long term

Contracts of insurance on human life or contracts to pay annuities on human life where the benefits are wholly or party to be determined by references to the value of, or the income from, property of any description (whether or not specified in the contracts) or by reference to fluctuations in, or in an index of, the value of property of any description (whether or not so specified).

IV Permanent health

Contracts of insurance providing specified benefits against risks of persons becoming incapacitated in consequence of sustaining injury as a result of an accident or of an accident of a specified class or of sickness or infirmity, being contracts that—

(a) are expressed to be in effect for a period of not less than five years, or until the normal retirement age for the persons concerned, or without limit of time; and

(b) either are not expressed to be terminable by the insurer, or are expressed to be so terminable only in special circumstances mentioned in the contract.

V Tontines

Tontines.

VI Capital redemption contracts

Capital redemption contracts, where effected or carried out by a person who does not carry on a banking business, and otherwise carries on a regulated activity of the kind specified by article 10(1) or (2).

VII Pension fund management

(a) Pension fund management contracts, and

(b) pension fund management contracts which are combined with contracts of insurance covering either conservation of capital or payment of a minimum interest, where effected or carried out by a person who does not carry on a banking business, and otherwise carries on a regulated activity of the kind specified by article 10(1) or (2).

VIII Collective insurance etc

Contracts of a kind referred to in article 1(2)(e) of the first life insurance directive.

IX Social insurance

Contracts of a kind referred to in article 1(3) of the first life insurance directive.

[4103]

NOTES

II Marriage and birth: words in square brackets inserted by the Civil Partnership Act 2004 (Amendments to Subordinate Legislation) Order 2005, SI 2005/2114, art 2(16), Sch 16, Pt 1, para 1(1), (5), as from 5 December 2005. Note it is unclear whether these words should also be inserted after the word "Marriage" in the heading to this paragraph.

SCHEDULE 2
ANNEX TO THE INVESTMENT SERVICES DIRECTIVE

Article 4

"ANNEX

SECTION A

Services

1.—(a) Reception and transmission, on behalf of investors, of orders in relation to one or more instruments listed in Section B.

(*b*) *Execution of such orders other than for own account.*

2. *Dealing in any of the instruments listed in Section B for own account.*

3. *Managing portfolios of investments in accordance with mandates given by investors on a discretionary, client-by-client basis where such portfolios include one or more of the instruments listed in Section B.*

4. *Underwriting in respect of issues of any of the instruments listed in Section B and/or the placing of such issues.*

SECTION B

Investments

1.—(*a*) *Transferable securities.*

(*b*) *Units in collective investment undertakings.*

2. *Money-market instruments.*

3. *Financial-futures contracts, including equivalent cash-settled instruments.*

4. *Forward interest-rate agreements* (*FRAs*).

5. *Interest-rate, currency and equity swaps.*

6. *Options to acquire or dispose of any instruments falling within this section of the Annex, including equivalent cash-settled instruments. This category includes in particular options on currency and on interest rates.*

SECTION C

Non-core services

1. *Safekeeping and administration in relation to one or more of the instruments listed in Section B.*

2. *Safe custody services.*

3. *Granting credits or loans to an investor to allow him to carry out a transaction in one or more of the instruments listed in Section B, where the firm granting the credit or loan is involved in the transaction.*

4. *Advice to undertakings on capital structure, industrial strategy and related matters and advice and service relating to mergers and the purchase of undertakings.*

5. *Services related to underwriting.*

6. *Investment advice concerning one or more of the instruments listed in Section B.*

7. *Foreign-exchange services where these are connected with the provision of investment services."*

[4104]

NOTES

Substituted by the Financial Services and Markets Act 2000 (Regulated Activities) (Amendment No 3) Order 2006, SI 2006/3384, arts 2, 29, as from 1 April 2007 (for the purposes of enabling applications to be made for (i) a Part IV permission, (ii) a variation of a Part IV permission, and (iii) the Authority's approval under s 59 of the 2000 Act, in relation to an activity of the kind specified by art 25D of this Order, or in relation to an investment of the kind specified by arts 83, 84 or 85 of this Order), and as from 1 November 2007 (otherwise), as follows—

"SCHEDULE 2

SECTIONS A AND C OF ANNEX I TO THE MARKETS IN FINANCIAL INSTRUMENTS DIRECTIVE AND RELATED COMMUNITY SUBORDINATE LEGISLATION

Article 3(1)

PART 1

SECTION C OF ANNEX I TO THE MARKETS IN FINANCIAL INSTRUMENTS DIRECTIVE

FINANCIAL INSTRUMENTS

1. Transferable securities;

2. Money-market instruments;

3. Units in collective investment undertakings;

4. Options, futures, swaps, forward rate agreements and any other derivative contracts relating to securities, currencies, interest rates or yields, or other derivatives instruments, financial indices or financial measures which may be settled physically or in cash;

5. Options, futures, swaps, forward rate agreements and any other derivative contracts relating to commodities that must be settled in cash or may be settled in cash at the option of one of the parties (otherwise than by reason of a default or other termination event);

6. Options, futures, swaps, and any other derivative contracts relating to commodities that can be physically settled provided that they are traded on a regulated market and/or an MTF;

7. Options, futures, swaps, forwards and any other derivative contracts relating to commodities, that can be physically settled not otherwise mentioned in C6 and not being for commercial purposes, which have the characteristics of other derivative financial instruments, having regard to whether, inter alia, they are cleared and settled through recognised clearing houses or are subject to regular margin calls;

8. Derivative instruments for the transfer of credit risk;

9. Financial contracts for differences;

10. Options, futures, swaps, forward rate agreements and any other derivative contracts relating to climatic variables, freight rates, emission allowances or inflation rates or other official economic statistics that must be settled in cash or may be settled in cash at the option of one of the parties (otherwise than by reason of a default or other termination event), as well as any other derivative contracts relating to assets, rights, obligations, indices and measures not otherwise mentioned in this Section, which have the characteristics of other derivative financial instruments, having regard to whether, inter alia, they are traded on a regulated market or an MTF, are cleared and settled through recognised clearing houses or are subject to regular margin calls.

PART 2
CHAPTER VI OF THE COMMISSION REGULATION

DERIVATIVE FINANCIAL INSTRUMENTS
ARTICLE 38

Characteristics of other derivative financial instruments

1. For the purposes of Section C(7) of Annex I to Directive 2004/39/EC, a contract which is not a spot contract within the meaning of paragraph 2 of this Article and which is not covered by paragraph 4 shall be considered as having the characteristics of other derivative financial instruments and not being for commercial purposes if it satisfies the following conditions:

(a) it meets one of the following sets of criteria:
   - (i) it is traded on a third country trading facility that performs a similar function to a regulated market or an MTF;
   - (ii) it is expressly stated to be traded on, or is subject to the rules of, a regulated market, an MTF or such a third country trading facility;
   - (iii) it is expressly stated to be equivalent to a contract traded on a regulated market, MTF or such a third country trading facility;

(b) it is cleared by a clearing house or other entity carrying out the same functions as a central counterparty, or there are arrangements for the payment or provision of margin in relation to the contract;

(c) it is standardised so that, in particular, the price, the lot, the delivery date or other terms are determined principally by reference to regularly published prices, standard lots or standard delivery dates.

2. A spot contract for the purposes of paragraph 1 means a contract for the sale of a commodity, asset or right, under the terms of which delivery is scheduled to be made within the longer of the following periods:

(a) two trading days;

(b) the period generally accepted in the market for that commodity, asset or right as the standard delivery period.

However, a contract is not a spot contract if, irrespective of its explicit terms, there is an understanding between the parties to the contract that delivery of the underlying is to be postponed and not to be performed within the period mentioned in the first subparagraph.

3. For the purposes of Section C(10) of Annex I to Directive 2004/39/EC, a derivative contract relating to an underlying referred to in that Section or in Article 39 shall be considered to have the characteristics of other derivative financial instruments if one of the following conditions is satisfied:

(a) that contract is settled in cash or may be settled in cash at the option of one or more of the parties, otherwise than by reason of a default or other termination event;

(b) that contract is traded on a regulated market or an MTF;

(c) the conditions laid down in paragraph 1 are satisfied in relation to that contract.

4. A contract shall be considered to be for commercial purposes for the purposes of Section C(7) of Annex I to Directive 2004/39/EC, and as not having the characteristics of other derivative financial instruments for the purposes of Sections C(7) and (10) of that Annex, if it is entered into with or by an operator or administrator of an energy transmission grid, energy balancing mechanism or pipeline network, and it is necessary to keep in balance the supplies and uses of energy at a given time.

ARTICLE 39
DERIVATIVES WITHIN SECTION C(10) OF ANNEX I TO DIRECTIVE 2004/39/EC

In addition to derivative contracts of a kind referred to in Section C(10) of Annex I to Directive 2004/39/EC, a derivative contract relating to any of the following shall fall within that Section if it meets the criteria set out in that Section and in Article 38(3):

(a) telecommunications bandwidth;

(b) commodity storage capacity;

(c) transmission or transportation capacity relating to commodities, whether cable, pipeline or other means;

(d) an allowance, credit, permit, right or similar asset which is directly linked to the supply, distribution or consumption of energy derived from renewable resources;

(e) a geological, environmental or other physical variable;

(f) any other asset or right of a fungible nature, other than a right to receive a service, that is capable of being transferred;

(g) an index or measure related to the price or value of, or volume of transactions in any asset, right, service or obligation.

PART 3
SECTION A OF ANNEX I TO THE MARKETS IN FINANCIAL INSTRUMENTS DIRECTIVE

INVESTMENT SERVICES AND ACTIVITIES

1. Reception and transmission of orders in relation to one or more financial instruments.

2. Execution of orders on behalf of clients.

3. Dealing on own account.

4. Portfolio management.

5. Investment advice.

6. Underwriting of financial instruments and/or placing of financial instruments on a firm commitment basis.

7. Placing of financial instruments without a firm commitment basis.

8. Operation of Multilateral Trading Facilities.

PART 4
ARTICLE 52 OF COMMISSION DIRECTIVE 2006/73/EC

ARTICLE 52
INVESTMENT ADVICE

For the purposes of the definition of "investment advice" in Article 4(1)(4) of Directive 2004/39/EC, a personal recommendation is a recommendation that is made to a person in his capacity as an investor or potential investor, or in his capacity as an agent for an investor or potential investor.

That recommendation must be presented as suitable for that person, or must be based on a consideration of the circumstances of that person, and must constitute a recommendation to take one of the following sets of steps:

(a) to buy, sell, subscribe for, exchange, redeem, hold or underwrite a particular financial instrument;

(b) to exercise or not to exercise any right conferred by a particular financial instrument to buy, sell, subscribe for, exchange, or redeem a financial instrument.

A recommendation is not a personal recommendation if it is issued exclusively through distribution channels or to the public.".

Note: the Investment Services Directive (Council Directive 93/22/EEC on investment services in the securities field) is set out in full at **[9144]** et seq. As to its prospective repeal, see the note at the beginning of that Directive.

SCHEDULE 3
ARTICLE 2.2 OF THE INVESTMENT SERVICES DIRECTIVE

Article 4

"This Directive shall not apply to—

(*a*) *insurance undertakings as defined in Article 1 of Directive 73/239/EEC or Article 1 of Directive 79/267/EEC or undertakings carrying on the reinsurance and retrocession activities referred to in Directive 64/225/EEC;*

(*b*) *firms which provide investment services exclusively for their parent undertakings, for their subsidiaries or for other subsidiaries of their parent undertakings;*

(*c*) *persons providing an investment service where that service is provided in an incidental manner in the course of a professional activity and that activity is regulated by legal or regulatory provisions or a code of ethics governing the profession which do not exclude the provision of that service;*

(*d*) *firms that provide investment services consisting exclusively in the administration of employee participation schemes;*

(*e*) *firms that provide investment services that consist in providing both the services referred to in (b) and those referred to in (d);*

(*f*) *the central banks of Member States and other national bodies performing similar functions and other public bodies charged with or intervening in the management of the public debt;*

(*g*) *firms*

— *which may not hold clients' funds or securities and which for that reason may not at any time place themselves in debit with their clients, and*

— *which may not provide any investment service except the reception and transmission of orders in transferable securities and units in collective investment undertakings, and*

— *which in the course of providing that service may transmit orders only to*

(*i*) *investment firms authorised in accordance with this Directive;*

PART IV
STATUTORY INSTRUMENTS

(ii) *credit institutions authorised in accordance with Directives 77/80/EEC and 89/646/EEC;*

(iii) *branches of investment firms or of credit institutions which are authorised in a third country and which are subject to and comply with prudential rules considered by the competent authorities as at least as stringent as those laid down in this Directive, in Directive 89/646/EEC or in [Directive 2006/49/EC];*

(iv) *collective investment undertakings authorised under the law of a Member State to market units to the public and to the managers of such undertakings;*

(v) *investment companies with fixed capital, as defined in Article 15(4) of Directive 79/91/EEC, the securities of which are listed or dealt in on a regulated market in a Member State;*

— *the activities of which are governed at national level by rules or by a code of ethics;*

(*h*) *collective investment undertakings whether coordinated at Community level or not and the depositaries and managers of such undertakings;*

(*i*) *person whose main business is trading in commodities amongst themselves or with producers or professional users of such products and who provide investment services only for such producers and professional users to the extent necessary for their main business;*

(*j*) *firms that provide investment services consisting exclusively in dealing for their own account on financial-futures or options markets or which deal for the accounts of other members of those markets or make prices for them and which are guaranteed by clearing members of the same markets. Responsibility for ensuring the performance of contracts entered into by such firms must be assumed by clearing members of the same markets;*

(*k*) *associations set up by Danish pension funds with the sole aim of managing the assets of pension funds that are members of those associations;*

(*l*) *"agenti di cambio" whose activities and functions are governed by Italian Royal Decree No 222 of 7 March 1925 and subsequent provisions amending it, and who are authorised to carry on their activities under Article 19 of Italian Law No 1 of 2 January 1991."*

[4105]

NOTES

Substituted by the Financial Services and Markets Act 2000 (Regulated Activities) (Amendment No 3) Order 2006, SI 2006/3384, arts 2, 30, as from 1 April 2007 (for the purposes of enabling applications to be made for (i) a Part IV permission, (ii) a variation of a Part IV permission, and (iii) the Authority's approval under s 59 of the 2000 Act, in relation to an activity of the kind specified by art 25D of this Order, or in relation to an investment of the kind specified by arts 83, 84 or 85 of this Order), and as from 1 November 2007 (otherwise), as follows—

"SCHEDULE 3
ARTICLE 2 OF THE MARKETS IN FINANCIAL INSTRUMENTS DIRECTIVE

ARTICLE 2
EXEMPTIONS

1. This Directive shall not apply to:

(a) insurance undertakings as defined in Article 1 of Directive 73/239/EEC or assurance undertakings as defined in Article 1 of Directive 2002/83/EC or undertakings carrying on the reinsurance and retrocession activities referred to in Directive 64/225/EEC;

(b) persons which provide investment services exclusively for their parent undertakings, for their subsidiaries or for other subsidiaries of their parent undertakings;

(c) persons providing an investment service where that service is provided in an incidental manner in the course of a professional activity and that activity is regulated by legal or regulatory provisions or a code of ethics governing the profession which do not exclude the provision of that service;

(d) persons who do not provide any investment services or activities other than dealing on own account unless they are market makers or deal on own account outside a regulated market or an MTF on an organised, frequent and systematic basis by providing a system accessible to third parties in order to engage in dealings with them;

(e) persons which provide investment services consisting exclusively in the administration of employee-participation schemes;

(f) persons which provide investment services which only involve both administration of employee-participation schemes and the provision of investment services exclusively for their parent undertakings, for their subsidiaries or for other subsidiaries of their parent undertakings;

(g) the members of the European System of Central Banks and other national bodies performing similar functions and other public bodies charged with or intervening in the management of the public debt;

(h) collective investment undertakings and pension funds whether coordinated at Community level or not and the depositaries and managers of such undertakings;

(i) persons dealing on own account in financial instruments, or providing investment services in commodity derivatives or derivative contracts included in Annex I, Section C10 to the clients of their main business, provided this is an ancillary activity to their main business, when considered on a group basis, and that main business is not the provision of investment services within the meaning of this Directive or banking services under Directive 2000/12/EC;

(j) persons providing investment advice in the course of providing another professional activity not covered by this Directive provided that the provision of such advice is not specifically remunerated;

(k) persons whose main business consists of dealing on own account in commodities and/or commodity derivatives. This exception shall not apply where the persons that deal on own account in commodities and/or commodity derivatives are part of a group the main business of which is the provision of other investment services within the meaning of this Directive or banking services under Directive 2000/12/EC;

(l) firms which provide investment services and/or perform investment activities consisting exclusively in dealing on own account on markets in financial futures or options or other derivatives and on cash markets for the sole purpose of hedging positions on derivatives markets or which deal for the accounts of other members of those markets or make prices for them and which are guaranteed by clearing members of the same markets, where responsibility for ensuring the performance of contracts entered into by such firms is assumed by clearing members of the same markets;

(m) associations set up by Danish and Finnish pensions funds with the sole aim of managing the assets of pension funds that are members of those associations;

(n) 'agenti di cambio' whose activities and functions are governed by Article 201 of Italian Legislative Decree No 58 of 24 February 1998.

2. The rights conferred by this Directive shall not extend to the provision of services as counterparty in transactions carried out by public bodies dealing with public debt or by members of the European System of Central Banks performing their tasks as provided for by the Treaty and the Statute of the European System of Central Banks and of the European Central Bank or performing equivalent functions under national provisions.

3. In order to take account of developments on financial markets, and to ensure the uniform application of this Directive, the Commission, acting in accordance with the procedure referred to in Article 64(2), may, in respect of exemptions (c), (i) and (k) define the criteria for determining when an activity is to be considered as ancillary to the main business on a group level as well as for determining when an activity is provided in an incidental manner.".

Words in square brackets in para (g)(iii) substituted the Capital Requirements Regulations 2006, SI 2006/3221, reg 29(4), Sch 6, para 6(1), (3), as from 1 January 2007.

Note: the Investment Services Directive (Council Directive 93/22/EEC on investment services in the securities field) is set out in full at **[9144]** et seq. As to its prospective repeal, see the note at the beginning of that Directive.

[SCHEDULE 4
RELEVANT TEXT OF THE INSURANCE MEDIATION DIRECTIVE

Article 4

PART I
ARTICLE 1.2

"This Directive shall not apply to persons providing mediation services for insurance contracts if all the following conditions are met:

(a) the insurance contract only requires knowledge of the insurance cover that is provided;

(b) the insurance contract is not a life assurance contract;

(c) the insurance contract does not cover any liability risks;

(d) the principal professional activity of the person is other than insurance mediation;

(e) the insurance is complementary to the product or service supplied by any provider, where such insurance covers:

(i) the risk of breakdown, loss of or damage to goods supplied by that provider; or

(ii) damage to or loss of baggage and other risks linked to the travel booked with that provider, even if the insurance covers life assurance or liability risks, provided that the cover is ancillary to the main cover for the risks linked to that travel;

(f) the amount of the annual premium does not exceed EUR 500 and the total duration of the insurance contract, including any renewals, does not exceed five years."]

[4105A]

NOTES

Inserted by the Financial Services and Markets Act 2000 (Regulated Activities) (Amendment) (No 2) Order 2003, SI 2003/1476, art 12, as from 31 October 2004 (in so far as relating to contracts of long-term care insurance), and as from 14 January 2005 (otherwise); for transitional provisions see arts 22–27 of that Order at **[4665]** et seq.

[PART II
ARTICLE 2.3

""Insurance mediation" means the activities of introducing, proposing or carrying out other work preparatory to the conclusion of contracts of insurance, or of concluding such contracts, or of assisting in the administration and performance of such contracts, in particular in the event of a claim.

These activities when undertaken by an insurance undertaking or an employee of an insurance undertaking who is acting under the responsibility of the insurance undertaking shall not be considered as insurance mediation.

The provision of information on an incidental basis in the context of another professional activity provided that the purpose of that activity is not to assist the customer in concluding or performing an insurance contract, the management of claims of an insurance undertaking on a professional basis, and loss adjusting and expert appraisal of claims shall also not be considered as insurance mediation."]

[4105B]

NOTES

Inserted as noted to Sch 4, Pt I at **[4105A]**.

[PART III
ARTICLE 2.4

""Reinsurance mediation" means the activities of introducing, proposing or carrying out other work preparatory to the conclusion of contracts of reinsurance, or of concluding such contracts, or of assisting in the administration and performance of such contracts, in particular in the event of a claim.

These activities when undertaken by a reinsurance undertaking or an employee of a reinsurance undertaking who is acting under the responsibility of the reinsurance undertaking are not considered as reinsurance mediation.

The provision of information on an incidental basis in the context of another professional activity provided that the purpose of that activity is not to assist the customer in concluding or performing a reinsurance contract, the management of claims of a reinsurance undertaking on a professional basis, and loss adjusting and expert appraisal of claims shall also not be considered as reinsurance mediation."]

[4105C]

NOTES

NOTES

Inserted as noted to Sch 4, Pt I at **[4105A]**.

FINANCIAL SERVICES AND MARKETS ACT 2000 (PRESCRIBED MARKETS AND QUALIFYING INVESTMENTS) ORDER 2001

(SI 2001/996)

NOTES

Made: 15 March 2001.

Authority: Financial Services and Markets Act 2000, s 118(3).

Commencement: 1 December 2001 (being the date on which the Financial Services and Markets Act 2000, s 123 came into force); see art 2 at **[4107]**. Where any provision in this work (including any inserted or substituted provision) came into force for all purposes on or before 1 July 2005, commencement information is not noted at provision level.

This Order is reproduced as amended by: the Financial Services and Markets Act 2000 (Prescribed Markets and Qualifying Investments) (Amendment) Order 2001, SI 2001/3681; the Financial Services and Markets Act 2000 (Market Abuse) Regulations 2005, SI 2005/381; the Financial Services and Markets Act 2000 (Markets in Financial Instruments) Regulations 2007, SI 2007/126.

1 Citation

This Order may be cited as the Financial Services and Markets Act 2000 (Prescribed Markets and Qualifying Investments) Order 2001.

[4106]

2 Commencement

This Order comes into force on the day on which section 123 of the Act (power to impose penalties in cases of market abuse) comes into force.

[4107]

NOTES

FSMA 2000, s 123 came into force on 1 December 2001 (see the Financial Services and Markets Act 2000 (Commencement No 7) Order 2001, SI 2001/3538).

3 Interpretation

In this Order—

"the Act" means the Financial Services and Markets Act 2000; and

["regulated market" has the meaning given in *Article 1(13) of the investment services directive*;]

"UK recognised investment exchange" means a body corporate or unincorporated association in respect of which there is in effect a recognition order made under section 290(1)(a) of the Act (recognition orders in respect of investment exchanges other than overseas investment exchanges).

[4108]

NOTES

Definition "regulated market" inserted by the Financial Services and Markets Act 2000 (Market Abuse) Regulations 2005, SI 2005/381, reg 10(1), as from 1 July 2005; for the words in italics in that definition there are substituted the words "Article 4.1.14 of the markets in financial instruments directive" by the Financial Services and Markets Act 2000 (Markets in Financial Instruments) Regulations 2007, SI 2007/126, reg 3(6), Sch 6, Pt 2, para 15, as from 1 November 2007 (for the full commencement details of SI 2007/126, see reg 1 of those Regulations at **[7596]**).

[4 Prescribed Markets

(1) There are prescribed, as markets to which subsections (2), (3), (5), (6) and (7) of section 118 apply—

(a) all markets which are established under the rules of a UK recognised investment exchange,

(b) the market known as OFEX,

(c) all other markets which are regulated markets.

(2) There are prescribed, as markets to which subsections (4) and (8) of section 118 apply—

(a) all markets which are established under the rules of a UK recognised investment exchange;
(b) the market known as OFEX.]

[4109]–[4110]

NOTES

Articles 4, 5 substituted for original arts 4, 4A, 5, by the Financial Services and Markets Act 2000 (Market Abuse) Regulations 2005, SI 2005/381, reg 10(2), as from 1 July 2005. Art 4A was previously inserted by the Financial Services and Markets Act 2000 (Prescribed Markets and Qualifying Investments) (Amendment) Order 2001, SI 2001/3681, art 2, as from 5 December 2001.

4A (*See the note to art 4 at* **[4109]**.)

[5 Qualifying Investments

There are prescribed, as qualifying investments in relation to the markets prescribed by article 4, all financial instruments within the meaning given in Article 1(3) of Directive 2003/6/EC of the European Parliament and the Council of 28 January 2003 on insider dealing and market manipulation (market abuse).]

[4111]

NOTES

Substituted as noted to art 4 at **[4109]**.

FINANCIAL SERVICES AND MARKETS ACT 2000 (PROMOTION OF COLLECTIVE INVESTMENT SCHEMES) (EXEMPTIONS) ORDER 2001

(SI 2001/1060)

NOTES

Made: 19 March 2001.
Authority: Financial Services and Markets Act 2000, s 238(6), (7).
Commencement: 1 December 2001 (being the date on which the Financial Services and Markets Act 2000, s 19 came into force). See art 1 at **[4112]**. Where any provision in this work (including any inserted or substituted provision) came into force for all purposes on or before 1 July 2005, commencement information is not noted at provision level.

This Order is reproduced as amended by: the Financial Services and Markets Act 2000 (Financial Promotion) (Amendment) Order 2001, SI 2001/2633; the Financial Services and Markets Act 2000 (Financial Promotion and Miscellaneous Amendments) Order 2002, SI 2002/1310; the Financial Services and Markets Act 2000 (Financial Promotion) (Amendment) (Electronic Commerce Directive) Order 2002, SI 2002/2157; the Financial Services and Markets Act 2000 (Promotion of Collective Investment Schemes etc) (Exemptions) (Amendment) Order 2003, SI 2003/2067; the Financial Services and Markets Act 2000 (Financial Promotion and Promotion of Collective Investment Schemes) (Miscellaneous Amendments) Order 2005, SI 2005/270; the Financial Services and Markets Act 2000 (Promotion of Collective Investment Schemes) (Exemptions) (Amendment) Order 2005, SI 2005/1532; the Civil Partnership Act 2004 (Amendments to Subordinate Legislation) Order 2005, SI 2005/2114.

ARRANGEMENT OF ARTICLES

PART I
GENERAL AND INTERPRETATION

PART I
GENERAL AND INTERPRETATION

1 Citation and commencement

(1) This Order may be cited as the Financial Services and Markets Act 2000 (Promotion of Collective Investment Schemes) (Exemptions) Order 2001.

(2) This Order comes into force on the day on which section 19 of the Act comes into force.

[4112]

NOTES

FSMA 2000, s 19 came into force on 1 December 2001 (see the Financial Services and Markets Act 2000 (Commencement No 7) Order 2001, SI 2001/3538).

2 Interpretation: general

(1) In this Order—

"the Act" means the Financial Services and Markets Act 2000;

"authorised unit trust scheme" has the meaning given by section 237 of the Act;

"close relative", in relation to a person means—

(a) his spouse [or civil partner];

(b) his children and step-children, his parents and step-parents, his brothers and sisters and his step-brothers and step-sisters; and

(c) the spouse [or civil partner] of any person within sub-paragraph (b);

"overseas scheme" means an unregulated scheme which is operated and managed in a country or territory outside the United Kingdom;

"publication" means—

PART IV
STATUTORY INSTRUMENTS

(a) a newspaper, journal, magazine or other periodical publication;
(b) a web site [or similar system for the electronic display of information];
(c) any programme forming part of a service consisting of the broadcast or transmission of television or radio programmes; and
(d) any teletext service, that is to say a service consisting of television transmissions consisting of a succession of visual displays (with or without accompanying sound) capable of being selected and held for separate viewing or other use;

"qualifying contract of insurance" has the meaning given in the Regulated Activities Order;

"the Regulated Activities Order" means the Financial Services and Markets Act 2000 (Regulated Activities) Order 2001;

"relevant scheme activities" means—
(i) the activity specified by article 51 of the Regulated Activities Order; or
(ii) any activity specified by article 14, 21, 25, 37 or 53 of that Order when carried on in relation to units;

"solicited real time communication" has the meaning given by article 5;

"units" has the meaning given by section 237(2) of the Act;

"unregulated scheme" means a collective investment scheme which is not an authorised unit trust scheme nor a scheme constituted by an authorised open-ended investment company nor a recognised scheme for the purposes of Part XVII of the Act;

"unsolicited real time communication" has the meaning given by article 5.

(2) In this Order, any reference to the "scheme promotion restriction" means the restriction imposed by section 238(1) of the Act.

[4113]

NOTES

Para (1): in definition "close relative" words in square brackets inserted by the Civil Partnership Act 2004 (Amendments to Subordinate Legislation) Order 2005, SI 2005/2114, art 2(16), Sch 16, Pt 1, para 2, as from 5 December 2005; in definition "publication" words in square brackets inserted by the Financial Services and Markets Act 2000 (Financial Promotion and Miscellaneous Amendments) Order 2002, SI 2002/1310, art 3(1), (2), as from 5 June 2002.

Close relative: as to the meaning of "step-children", and related expressions, see the Civil Partnership Act 2004, s 246 (as applied to this Order by the Civil Partnership Act 2004 (Relationships Arising Through Civil Partnership) Order 2005, SI 2005/3137, art 3, Schedule).

3 Interpretation: communications

In this Order—

(a) any reference to a communication is a reference to the communication, by an authorised person in the course of business, of an invitation or inducement to participate in an unregulated scheme;
(b) any reference to a communication being made to another person is a reference to a communication being addressed, whether verbally or in legible form, to a particular person or persons (for example where it is contained in a telephone call or letter);
(c) any reference to a communication being directed at persons is a reference to a communication being addressed to persons generally (for example where it is contained in a television broadcast or web site);
(d) "communicate" includes causing a communication to be made;
(e) a "recipient" of a communication is a person to whom the communication is made or, in the case of a non-real time communication which is directed at persons generally, any person who reads or hears the communication;
[(f) "electronic commerce communication" means a communication, the making of which constitutes the provision of an information society service;
(g) "incoming electronic commerce communication" means an electronic commerce communication made from an establishment in an EEA State other than the United Kingdom;
(h) "outgoing electronic commerce communication" means an electronic commerce communication made from an establishment in the United Kingdom to a person in an EEA State other than the United Kingdom.]

[4114]

NOTES

Paras (f)–(h) added by the Financial Services and Markets Act 2000 (Financial Promotion) (Amendment) (Electronic Commerce Directive) Order 2002, SI 2002/2157, arts 7, 8(1), as from 21 August 2002.

4 Interpretation: real time communications

(1) In this Order, references to a real time communication are references to any communication made in the course of a personal visit, telephone conversation or other interactive dialogue.

(2) A non-real time communication is a communication not falling within paragraph (1).

(3) For the purposes of this Order, non-real time communications include communications made by letter or e-mail or contained in a publication.

(4) For the purposes of this Order, the factors in paragraph (5) are to be treated as indications that a communication is a non-real time communication.

(5) The factors are that—

(a) the communication is made to or directed at more than one recipient in identical terms (save for details of the recipient's identity);

(b) the communication is made or directed by way of a system which in the normal course constitutes or creates a record of the communication which is available to the recipient to refer to at a later time;

(c) the communication is made or directed by way of a system which in the normal course does not enable or require the recipient to respond immediately to it.

[4115]

5 Interpretation: solicited and unsolicited real time communications

(1) A real time communication is solicited where it is made in the course of a personal visit, telephone call or other interactive dialogue if that call, visit or dialogue—

(a) was initiated by the recipient of the communication; or

(b) takes place in response to an express request from the recipient of the communication.

(2) A real time communication is unsolicited where it is made otherwise than as described in paragraph (1).

(3) For the purposes of paragraph (1)—

(a) a person is not to be treated as expressly requesting a call, visit or dialogue—

(i) because he omits to indicate that he does not wish to receive any or any further visits or calls or to engage in any or any further dialogue;

(ii) because he agrees to standard terms that state that such visits, calls or dialogue will take place, unless he has signified clearly that, in addition to agreeing to the terms, he is willing for them to take place;

(b) a communication is solicited only if it is clear from all the circumstances when the call, visit or dialogue is initiated or requested that during the course of the visit, call or dialogue communications will be made concerning the kind of activities or investments to which the communications in fact made relate;

(c) it is immaterial whether the express request is made before or after this Order comes into force.

(4) Where a real time communication is solicited by a recipient ("R"), it is treated as having also been solicited by any other person to whom it is made at the same time as it is made to R if that other recipient is—

(a) a close relative of R; or

(b) expected to participate in the unregulated scheme jointly with R.

[4116]

[5A Interpretation: outgoing electronic commerce communications

(1) For the purposes of the application of those articles to outgoing electronic commerce communications—

(a) any reference in article 21(4)(d) or 23(1)(a) or (3)(d) to an authorised person includes a reference to a person who is entitled, under the law of an EEA State other than the United Kingdom, to carry on regulated activities in that State;

(b) any reference in article 21 or 22 to an amount in pounds sterling includes a reference to an equivalent amount in another currency.

(2) For the purposes of the application of article 22 to outgoing electronic commerce communications, any reference in section 737 or 264(2) of the Companies Act 1985 (or the equivalent provision in the Companies (Northern Ireland) Order 1986) to a company includes a reference to a company registered under the law of an EEA State other than the United Kingdom.]

[4116A]

NOTES

Inserted by the Financial Services and Markets Act 2000 (Financial Promotion) (Amendment) (Electronic Commerce Directive) Order 2002, SI 2002/2157, arts 7, 8(2), as from 21 August 2002.

6 Degree of prominence to be given to required indications

Where a communication must, if it is to fall within any provision of this Order, be accompanied by an indication of any matter, the indication must be presented to the recipient—

(a) in a way that can be easily understood; and
(b) in such manner as, depending on the means by which the communication is made or directed, is best calculated to bring the matter in question to the attention of the recipient and to allow him to consider it.

[4117]

7 Combination of different exemptions

Nothing in this Order is to be construed as preventing a person from relying on more than one exemption in respect of the same communication.

[4118]

PART II
TERRITORIAL SCOPE

8 Communications to overseas recipients

(1) Subject to [paragraphs (2) and (7)], the scheme promotion restriction does not apply to any communication—

(a) which is made (whether from inside or outside the United Kingdom) to a person who receives the communication outside the United Kingdom; or
(b) which is directed (whether from inside or outside the United Kingdom) only at persons outside the United Kingdom.

(2) Paragraph (1) does not apply to an unsolicited real time communication unless—

(a) it is made from a place outside the United Kingdom; and
(b) it relates to an overseas scheme.

(3) For the purposes of paragraph (1)(b)—

(a) if the conditions set out in paragraph (4)(a), (b), (c) and (d) are met, a communication directed from a place inside the United Kingdom is to be regarded as directed only at persons outside the United Kingdom;
(b) if the conditions set out in paragraph (4)(c) and (d) are met, a communication directed from a place outside the United Kingdom is to be regarded as directed only at persons outside the United Kingdom;
(c) in any other case where one or more of the conditions in paragraph (4)(a) to (e) are met, that fact shall be taken into account in determining whether the communication is to be regarded as directed only at persons outside the United Kingdom (but a communication may still be regarded as directed only at persons outside the United Kingdom even if none of the conditions in paragraph (4) is met).

(4) The conditions are that—

(a) the communication is accompanied by an indication that it is directed only at persons outside the United Kingdom;
(b) the communication is accompanied by an indication that it must not be acted upon by persons in the United Kingdom;

(c) the communication is not referred to in, or directly accessible from, any other communication which is made to a person or directed at persons in the United Kingdom by or on behalf of the same person;
(d) there are in place proper systems and procedures to prevent recipients in the United Kingdom (other than those to whom the communication might otherwise lawfully have been made or directed) acquiring from the person directing the communication, a close relative of his or a company in the same group, units in the scheme to which the communication relates;
(e) the communication is included in—
  (i) a web site, newspaper, journal, magazine or periodical publication which is principally accessed in or intended for a market outside the United Kingdom;
  (ii) a radio or television broadcast or teletext service transmitted principally for reception outside the United Kingdom.

(5) For the purposes of paragraph (1)(b), a communication may be treated as directed only at persons outside the United Kingdom even if—
(a) it is also directed, for the purposes of article 14(1)(b), at investment professionals falling within article 14(5) (but disregarding paragraph (6) of that article for this purpose);
(b) it is also directed, for the purposes of article 22(1)(b), at high net worth persons to whom article 22 applies (but disregarding paragraph (2)(e) of that article for this purpose).

(6) Where a communication falls within paragraph (5)—
(a) the condition in paragraph (4)(a) is to be construed as requiring an indication that the communication is directed only at persons outside the United Kingdom or persons having professional experience in matters relating to investments or high net worth persons (as the case may be);
(b) the condition in paragraph (4)(b) is to be construed as requiring an indication that the communication must not be acted upon by persons in the United Kingdom or by persons who do not have professional experience in matters relating to investments or who are not high net worth persons (as the case may be).

[(7) Paragraph (1) does not apply to an outgoing electronic commerce communication.]

[4119]

NOTES

Para (1): words in square brackets substituted by the Financial Services and Markets Act 2000 (Financial Promotion) (Amendment) (Electronic Commerce Directive) Order 2002, SI 2002/2157, arts 7, 9(a), as from 21 August 2002.

Para (7): added by SI 2002/2157, arts 7, 9(b), as from 21 August 2002.

9 Solicited real time communications from overseas

The scheme promotion restriction does not apply to any solicited real time communication which is made from outside the United Kingdom and which relates to units in an overseas scheme.

[4120]

10 Communications from overseas to previously overseas customers

(1) The scheme promotion restriction does not apply to a non-real time or unsolicited real time communication which—
(a) is made from outside the United Kingdom by an authorised person to a previously overseas customer of his; and
(b) relates to units in an overseas scheme.

(2) In this article—

"previously overseas customer" means a person with whom the authorised person has done business within the period of twelve months ending with the day on which the communication was made ("the earlier business") and where—
  (a) at the time that the earlier business was done, the customer was neither resident in the United Kingdom nor had a place of business there; or
  (b) at the time the earlier business was done, the authorised person had on a former occasion done business with the customer, being business of the same description as the business to which the communication relates, and

on that former occasion the customer was neither resident in the United Kingdom nor had a place of business there.

(3) For the purposes of this article, an authorised person has done business with a customer if, in the course of his overseas business, he has—

(a) effected a transaction, or arranged for a transaction to be effected, with the customer in respect of units in an overseas scheme; or

(b) given, outside the United Kingdom, any advice on the merits of the customer buying or selling units in an overseas scheme.

[4121]

[10A Incoming electronic commerce communications

(1) The scheme promotion restriction does not apply to an incoming electronic commerce communication.

(2) Paragraph (1) does not apply to—

(a) a communication which constitutes an advertisement by the operator of a UCITS Directive scheme of units in that scheme; or

(b) an unsolicited communication made by electronic mail.

(3) In this article, "UCITS Directive scheme" means an undertaking for collective investment in transferable securities which is subject to [the UCITS directive], and has been authorised in accordance with Article 4 of that Directive.

(4) For the purposes of this article, a communication by electronic mail is to be regarded as unsolicited, unless it is made in response to an express request from the recipient of the communication.]

[4121A]

NOTES

Inserted by the Financial Services and Markets Act 2000 (Financial Promotion) (Amendment) (Electronic Commerce Directive) Order 2002, SI 2002/2157, arts 7, 10, as from 21 August 2002.

Para (3): words in square brackets substituted by the Financial Services and Markets Act 2000 (Promotion of Collective Investment Schemes etc) (Exemptions) (Amendment) Order 2003, SI 2003/2067, art 2(1), (2), as from 13 February 2004.

PART III
OTHER EXEMPTIONS

11 Follow up non-real time communications and solicited real time communications

(1) Where an authorised person makes or directs a communication ("the first communication") which is exempt from the scheme promotion restriction because, in compliance with the requirements of another provision of this Order, it is accompanied by certain indications or contains certain information, then the scheme promotion restriction does not apply to any subsequent communication which complies with the requirements of paragraph (2).

(2) The requirements of this paragraph are that the subsequent communication—

(a) is a non-real time communication or a solicited real time communication;

(b) is made by the same person who made the first communication;

(c) is made to a recipient of the first communication;

(d) relates to the same unregulated scheme as the first communication; and

(e) is made within 12 months of the recipient receiving the first communication.

(3) A communication made or directed before this Order comes into force is to be treated as a first communication falling within paragraph (1) if it would have fallen within that paragraph had it been made or directed after this Order comes into force.

[4122]

12 Introductions

(1) If the requirements of paragraph (2) are met, the scheme promotion restriction does not apply to any real time communication which is made with a view to or for the purposes of introducing the recipient to—

(a) an authorised person who carries on one or more relevant scheme activities in relation to units in unregulated schemes; or

(b) a person who is exempt, as a result of an exemption order made under section 38(1) of the Act, in relation to one or more relevant scheme activities.

(2) The requirements of this paragraph are that—

(a) the maker of the communication ("A") is not a close relative of, nor a member of the same group as, the person to whom the introduction is, or is to be, made;

(b) A does not carry on business in relevant scheme activities in relation to units in unregulated schemes;

(c) A does not receive from any person other than the recipient any pecuniary reward or other advantage arising out of his making the introduction; and

(d) it is clear in all the circumstances that the recipient, in his capacity as an investor, is not seeking and has not sought advice from A as to the merits of participating in an unregulated scheme (or, if the client has sought such advice, A has declined to give it, but has recommended that the recipient seek such advice from an authorised person specialising in that kind of investment).

[4123]

13 Generic promotions

The scheme promotion restriction does not apply to any communication which—

(a) does not relate to units of a particular unregulated scheme identified (directly or indirectly) in the communication; and

(b) does not identify (directly or indirectly) any person who operates a collective investment scheme or sells units.

[4124]

14 Investment professionals

(1) The scheme promotion restriction does not apply to any communication which—

(a) is made only to recipients whom the person making the communication believes on reasonable grounds to be investment professionals; or

(b) may reasonably be regarded as directed only at such recipients.

(2) For the purposes of paragraph (1)(b), if all the conditions set out in paragraph (4)(a) to (c) are met in relation to the communication, it is to be regarded as directed only at investment professionals.

(3) In any other case in which one or more of the conditions set out in paragraph (4)(a) to (c) are met, that fact shall be taken into account in determining whether the communication is directed only at investment professionals (but a communication may still be regarded as so directed even if none of the conditions in paragraph (4) is met).

(4) The conditions are that—

(a) the communication is accompanied by an indication that it is directed at persons having professional experience of participating in unregulated schemes and that the units to which the communication relates are available only to such persons;

(b) the communication is accompanied by an indication that persons who do not have professional experience in participating in unregulated schemes should not rely on it;

(c) there are in place proper systems and procedures to prevent recipients other than investment professionals from acquiring from the person directing the communication, a close relative of his or a company in the same group, units in the scheme to which the communication relates.

(5) "Investment professionals" means—

(a) an authorised person;

(b) a person who is exempt, as a result of an exemption order made under section 38(1) of the Act, in relation to one or more relevant scheme activities;

(c) any other person—

(i) whose ordinary activities involve him in participating in unregulated schemes for the purposes of a business carried on by him; or

(ii) who it is reasonable to expect will so participate for the purposes of a business carried on by him;

(d) a government, local authority (whether in the United Kingdom or elsewhere) or an international organisation;

(e) a person ("A") who is a director, officer or employee of a person ("B") falling within any of sub-paragraphs (a) to (d), when the communication is made to A in that capacity and where A's responsibilities when acting in that capacity involve him in B's participation in unregulated schemes.

(6) For the purposes of paragraph (1), a communication is to be treated as made only to or directed only at investment professionals even if it also made to or directed at other persons to whom it may lawfully be communicated.

(7) In this article—

"government" means the government of the United Kingdom, the Scottish Administration, the Executive Committee of the Northern Ireland Assembly, the National Assembly for Wales and any government of any country or territory outside the United Kingdom;

"international organisation" means any body the members of which comprise—

(a) states including the United Kingdom or another EEA State; or

(b) bodies whose members comprise states including the United Kingdom or another EEA State.

[4125]

15 One off non-real time communications and solicited real time communications

(1) The scheme promotion restriction does not apply to a one off communication which is either a non-real time communication or a solicited real time communication.

(2) If both the conditions set out in paragraph (3) are met in relation to a communication it is to be regarded as a one off communication. In any other case in which either of those conditions is met, that fact is to be taken into account in determining whether the communication is a one off communication (but a communication may still be regarded as a one off communication even if neither of the conditions in paragraph (3) is met).

(3) The conditions are that—

(a) the communication is made only to one recipient or only to one group of recipients in the expectation that they would engage in any investment activity jointly;

(b) the communication is not part of an organised marketing campaign.

[4126]

[15A One off unsolicited real time communications

(1) The scheme promotion restriction does not apply to an unsolicited real time communication if the conditions in paragraph (2) are met.

(2) The conditions in this paragraph are that—

(a) the communication is a one off communication;

(b) the communicator believes on reasonable grounds that the recipient understands the risks associated with engaging in the investment activity to which the communication relates;

(c) at the time the communication is made, the communicator believes on reasonable grounds that the recipient would expect to be contacted by him in relation to the investment activity to which the communication relates.

(3) Paragraphs (2) and (3) of article 15 apply in determining whether a communication is a one off communication for the purposes of this article as they apply for the purposes of article 15.]

[4127]

NOTES

Inserted by the Financial Services and Markets Act 2000 (Financial Promotion) (Amendment) Order 2001, SI 2001/2633, art 3, as from 1 December 2001.

16 Communications required or authorised by enactments

The scheme promotion restriction does not apply to any communication which is required or authorised to be communicated by or under any enactment other than the Act.

[4128]

17 Persons in the business of placing promotional material

The scheme promotion restriction does not apply to any communication which is made to a person whose business it is to place, or arrange for the placing of, promotional material provided that it is communicated so that he can place or arrange for placing it.

[4129]

18 Existing participants in an unregulated scheme

The scheme promotion restriction does not apply to any communication which is—

(a) a non-real time communication or a solicited real time communication;
(b) communicated by the operator of an unregulated scheme; and
(c) communicated to persons whom the person making the communication believes on reasonable grounds to be persons who are entitled to units in that scheme.

[4130]

19 Group companies

The scheme promotion restriction does not apply to any communication made by one body corporate in a group to another body corporate in the same group.

[4131]

20 Persons in the business of disseminating information

(1) The scheme promotion restriction does not apply to any communication which is made only to recipients whom the person making the communication believes on reasonable grounds to be persons to whom paragraph (2) applies.

(2) This paragraph applies to—

(a) a person who receives the communication in the course of a business which involves the dissemination through a publication of information concerning investments;
(b) a person whilst acting in the capacity of director, officer or employee of a person falling within sub-paragraph (a) being a person whose responsibilities when acting in that capacity involve him in the business referred to in that sub-paragraph;
(c) any person to whom the communication may otherwise lawfully be made.

[4132]

[21 Certified high net worth individuals

(1) If the requirements of paragraphs (4) and (7) are met, the scheme promotion restriction does not apply to any communication which—

(a) is a non-real time communication or a solicited real time communication;
(b) is made to an individual whom the person making the communication believes on reasonable grounds to be a certified high net worth individual;
(c) relates only to units falling within paragraph (8); and
(d) does not invite or induce the recipient to enter into an agreement under the terms of which he can incur a liability or obligation to pay or contribute more than he commits by way of investment.

(2) "Certified high net worth individual" means an individual who has signed, within the period of twelve months ending with the day on which the communication is made, a statement complying with Part I of the Schedule.

(3) The validity of a statement signed for the purposes of paragraph (2) is not affected by a defect in the form or wording of the statement, provided that the defect does not alter the statement's meaning and that the words shown in bold type in Part I of the Schedule are so shown in the statement.

(4) The requirements of this paragraph are that either the communication is accompanied by the giving of a warning in accordance with paragraphs (5) and (6) or, where because of the nature of the communication this is not reasonably practicable,—

(a) a warning in accordance with paragraph (5) is given to the recipient orally at the beginning of the communication together with an indication that he will receive the warning in legible form and that, before receipt of that warning, he should consider carefully any decision to participate in a collective investment scheme to which the communication relates; and

(b) a warning in accordance with paragraphs (5) and (6) (d) to (h) is sent to the recipient of the communication within two business days of the day on which the communication is made.

(5) The warning must be in the following terms—

"Reliance on this promotion for the purpose of buying the units to which the promotion relates may expose an individual to a significant risk of losing all of the property or other assets invested.".

But, where a warning is sent pursuant to paragraph (4)(b), for the words "this promotion" in both places where they occur there must be substituted wording which clearly identifies the promotion which is the subject of the warning.

(6) The warning must—

(a) be given at the beginning of the communication;

(b) precede any other written or pictorial matter;

(c) be in a font size consistent with the text forming the remainder of the communication;

(d) be indelible;

(e) be legible;

(f) be printed in black, bold type;

(g) be surrounded by a black border which does not interfere with the text of the warning; and

(h) not be hidden, obscured or interrupted by any other written or pictorial matter.

(7) The requirements of this paragraph are that the communication is accompanied by an indication—

(a) that it is exempt from the restriction on the promotion of unregulated schemes (in section 238 of the Act) on the grounds that the communication is made to a certified high net worth individual;

(b) of the requirements that must be met for an individual to qualify as a certified high net worth individual;

(c) that any individual who is in any doubt about the units to which the communication relates should consult an authorised person specialising in advising in participation in unregulated schemes.

(8) A unit falls within this paragraph if it is in an unregulated scheme which invests wholly or predominantly in the shares in or debentures of one or more unlisted companies.

(9) "Business day" means any day except a Saturday, a Sunday, Christmas Day, Good Friday or a day which is a bank holiday under the Banking and Financial Dealings Act 1971 in any part of the United Kingdom.

(10) "Unlisted company" has the meaning given in the Financial Services and Markets Act 2000 (Financial Promotion) Order 2001.]

[4133]

NOTES

Substituted by the Financial Services and Markets Act 2000 (Financial Promotion and Promotion of Collective Investment Schemes) (Miscellaneous Amendments) Order 2005, SI 2005/270, art 3, Sch 2, para 1, as from 3 March 2005, subject to transitional provisions as noted below.

Transitional provisions: SI 2005/270, art 5 provides as follows (note that by virtue of art 1, the 2005 Order came into force on 3 March 2005)—

"5 Transitional provision: CIS Exemptions Order

(1) Paragraph (2) applies where, immediately before the coming into force of this Order, an individual is a certified high net worth individual within the meaning of article 21 of the CIS Exemptions Order.

(2) That individual must, for so long as he holds a current certificate of high net worth, be treated as a certified high net worth individual for the purpose of article 21 of the CIS Exemptions Order as substituted by this Order.

(3) For the purposes of this article, a certificate of high net worth—

(a) means a certificate of high net worth which, immediately before the coming into force of this Order, satisfies the criteria in article 21(3)(a), (c) and (d) of the CIS Exemptions Order; and

(b) is current if it is signed and dated—

(i) within the period of twelve months ending with the day on which the communication (referred to in article 21 of the CIS Exemptions Order) is made; and

(ii) prior to this Order coming into force.".

22 High net worth companies, unincorporated associations etc

(1) The scheme promotion restriction does not apply to any communication which—

(a) is made only to recipients whom the person making the communication believes on reasonable grounds to be persons to whom paragraph (2) applies; or

(b) may reasonably be regarded as directed only at persons to whom paragraph (2) applies.

(2) This paragraph applies to—

[(a) any body corporate which has, or which is a member of the same group as an undertaking which has, a called-up share capital or net assets of not less than—

(i) if the body corporate has more than 20 members or is a subsidiary undertaking of an undertaking which has more than 20 members, £500,000;

(ii) otherwise, £5 million;]

(b) any unincorporated association or partnership which has net assets of not less than £5 million;

(c) the trustee of a high value trust;

(d) any person ("A") whilst acting in the capacity of director, officer or employee of a person ("B") falling within any of sub-paragraphs (a) to (c), where A's responsibilities, when acting in that capacity, involve him in B's participation in unregulated schemes;

(e) any person to whom the communication might otherwise lawfully be made.

(3) For the purposes of paragraph (1)(b)—

(a) if all the conditions set out in paragraph (4)(a) to (c) are met in relation to the communication, it is to be regarded as directed at persons to whom paragraph (2) applies;

(b) in any other case in which one or more of those conditions are met, that fact is to be taken into account in determining whether the communication is directed at persons to whom paragraph (2) applies (but a communication may still be regarded as so directed even if none of the conditions in paragraph (4) is met).

(4) The conditions are that—

(a) the communication includes an indication of the description of persons to whom it is directed and an indication of the fact that the units to which it relates are available only to such persons;

(b) the communication includes an indication that persons of any other description should not rely upon it;

(c) there are in place proper systems and procedures to prevent recipients other than persons to whom paragraph (2) applies from acquiring from the person directing the communication, a close relative of his or a company in the same group, units in the scheme to which the communication relates.

(5) In this article—

"called-up share capital" has the meaning given in the Companies Act 1985 or in the Companies (Northern Ireland) Order 1986;

"high value trust" means a trust where the aggregate value of the cash and investments which form part of the trust's assets (before deducing the amount of its liabilities)—

(a) is £10 million or more; or

(b) has been £10 million or more at any time during the year immediately preceding the date on which communication in question was first made or directed;

"net assets" has the meaning given in section 264 of the Companies Act 1985 or the equivalent provision of the Companies (Northern Ireland) Order 1986.

[4134]

NOTES

Para (2): sub-para (a) substituted by the Financial Services and Markets Act 2000 (Financial Promotion and Miscellaneous Amendments) Order 2002, SI 2002/1310, art 3(1), (3), as from 5 June 2002.

PART IV STATUTORY INSTRUMENTS

23 Sophisticated investors

(1) "Certified sophisticated investor" means a person—

(a) who has a current certificate in writing or other legible form signed by an authorised person to the effect that he is sufficiently knowledgeable to understand the risks associated with participating in unregulated schemes; and

(b) who has signed, within the period of twelve months ending with the day on which the communication is made, a statement in the following terms—

"I make this statement so that I can receive promotions which are exempt from the restriction on promotion of unregulated schemes in the Financial Services and Markets Act 2000. The exemption relates to certified sophisticated investors and I declare that I qualify as such. I accept that the schemes to which the promotions will relate are not authorised or recognised for the purposes of that Act. I am aware that it is open to me to seek advice from an authorised person who specialises in advising on this kind of investment".

[(1A) The validity of a statement signed in accordance with paragraph (1)(b) is not affected by a defect in the wording of the statement, provided that the defect does not alter the statement's meaning.]

(2) If the requirements of paragraph (3) are met, the scheme promotion restriction does not apply to any communication which—

(a) is made to a certified sophisticated investor; and

(b) does not invite or induce the recipient to participate in an unregulated scheme operated by the person who has signed the certificate referred to in paragraph (1)(a) or to acquire units from that person.

(3) The requirements of this paragraph are that the communication is accompanied by an indication—

(a) that it is exempt from the scheme promotion restriction (in section 238 of the Financial Services and Markets Act 2000) on the communication of invitations or inducements to participate in unregulated schemes on the ground that it is made to a certified sophisticated investor;

(b) of the requirements that must be met for a person to qualify as a certified sophisticated investor;

(c) that buying the units to which the communication relates may expose the individual to a significant risk of losing all of the property invested;

(d) that any individual who is in any doubt about the investment to which the invitation or inducement relates should consult an authorised person specialising in advising on investments of the kind in question.

(4) For the purposes of paragraph (1)(a), a certificate is current if it is signed and dated not more than three years before the date on which the communication is made.

[4135]

NOTES

Para (1A): inserted by the Financial Services and Markets Act 2000 (Financial Promotion and Promotion of Collective Investment Schemes) (Miscellaneous Amendments) Order 2005, SI 2005/270, art 3, Sch 2, para 2, as from 3 March 2005.

[23A Self-certified sophisticated investors

(1) "Self-certified sophisticated investor" means an individual who has signed, within the period of twelve months ending with the day on which the communication is made, a statement complying with Part II of the Schedule.

(2) The validity of a statement signed for the purposes of paragraph (1) is not affected by a defect in the form or wording of the statement, provided that the defect does not alter the statement's meaning and that the words shown in bold type in Part II of the Schedule are so shown in the statement.

(3) If the requirements of paragraphs (4) and (7) are met, the scheme promotion restriction does not apply to any communication which—

(a) is made to an individual whom the person making the communication believes on reasonable grounds to be a self-certified sophisticated investor;

(b) relates only to units falling within paragraph (8); and

(c) does not invite or induce the recipient to enter into an agreement under the terms of which he can incur a liability or obligation to pay or contribute more than he commits by way of investment.

(4) The requirements of this paragraph are—

(a) …

(b) … that either the communication is accompanied by the giving of a warning in accordance with paragraphs (5) and (6) or, where because of the nature of the communication this is not reasonably practicable,—

(i) a warning in accordance with paragraph (5) is given to the recipient orally at the beginning of the communication together with an indication that he will receive the warning in legible form and that, before receipt of that warning, he should consider carefully any decision to participate in a collective investment scheme to which the communication relates; and

(ii) a warning in accordance with paragraphs (5) and (6) (d) to (h) is sent to the recipient of the communication within two business days of the day on which the communication is made.

(5) The warning must be in the following terms—

"Reliance on this promotion for the purpose of buying [the] units to which the promotion relates may expose an individual to a significant risk of losing all of the property or other assets invested.".

But, where a warning is sent pursuant to paragraph (4)(b), for the words "this promotion" in both places where they occur there must be substituted wording which clearly identifies the promotion which is the subject of the warning.

(6) The warning must—

(a) be given at the beginning of the communication;

(b) precede any other written or pictorial matter;

(c) be in a font size consistent with the text forming the remainder of the communication;

(d) be indelible;

(e) be legible;

(f) be printed in black, bold type;

(g) be surrounded by a black border which does not interfere with the text of the warning; and

(h) not be hidden, obscured or interrupted by any other written or pictorial matter.

(7) The requirements of this paragraph are that the communication is accompanied by an indication—

(a) that it is exempt from the scheme promotion restriction (in section 238 of the Act) on the communication of invitations or inducements to participate in unregulated schemes on the ground that it is made to a self-certified sophisticated investor;

(b) of the requirements that must be met for an individual to qualify as a self-certified sophisticated investor;

(c) that any individual who is in any doubt about the investment to which the invitation or inducement relates should consult an authorised person specialising in advising on investments of the kind in question.

(8) A unit falls within this paragraph if it is in an unregulated scheme which invests wholly or predominantly in the shares in or debentures of one or more an unlisted companies.

(9) "Business day" means any day except a Saturday, a Sunday, Christmas Day, Good Friday or a day which is a bank holiday under the Banking and Financial Dealings Act 1971 in any part of the United Kingdom.

(10) "Unlisted company" has the meaning given in the Financial Services and Markets Act 2000 (Financial Promotion) Order 2001.]

[4135A]

NOTES

Inserted by the Financial Services and Markets Act 2000 (Financial Promotion and Promotion of Collective Investment Schemes) (Miscellaneous Amendments) Order 2005, SI 2005/270, art 3, Sch 2, para 3, as from 3 March 2005.

Para (4): words omitted revoked by the Financial Services and Markets Act 2000 (Promotion of Collective Investment Schemes) (Exemptions) (Amendment) Order 2005, SI 2005/1532, art 2(1), (2)(a), (b), as from 1 July 2005.

Para (5): word in square brackets substituted by SI 2005/1532, art 2(1), (2)(c), as from 1 July 2005.

24 Associations of high net worth or sophisticated investors

The scheme promotion restriction does not apply to any non-real time communication or solicited real time communication which—

(a) is made to an association[, or to a member of an association,] the membership of which the person making the communication believes on reasonable grounds comprises wholly or predominantly persons who are—

(i) certified high net worth individuals within the meaning of article 21;

(ii) high net worth persons falling within article 22(2)(a) to (d);

(iii) certified sophisticated investors within the meaning of article 23 [or 23A]; and

(b) does not invite or induce the recipient to enter into an agreement under the terms of which he can incur a liability or obligation to pay or contribute more than he commits by way of investment.

[4136]

NOTES

Words in square brackets inserted by the Financial Services and Markets Act 2000 (Promotion of Collective Investment Schemes) (Exemptions) (Amendment) Order 2005, SI 2005/1532, art 2(1), (3), as from 1 July 2005.

25 Settlors, trustees and personal representatives

The scheme promotion restriction does not apply to any communication which is made—

(a) by an authorised person when acting as a settlor or grantor of a trust, a trustee or a personal representative;

(b) to a trustee of the trust, a fellow trustee or a fellow personal representative (as the case may be),

if the communication is made for the purposes of the trust or estate.

[4137]

26 Beneficiaries of trust, will or intestacy

The scheme promotion restriction does not apply to any communication which is made—

(a) by an authorised person when acting as a settlor of a trust, trustee or personal representative to a beneficiary under the trust, will or intestacy; or

(b) by an authorised person who is a beneficiary under a trust, will or intestacy to another beneficiary under the same trust, will or intestacy,

if the communication relates to the management or distribution of that trust fund or estate.

[4138]

27 Remedy following report by Parliamentary Commissioner for Administration

The scheme promotion restriction does not apply to any communication made or directed by a person for the purpose of enabling any injustice, stated by the Parliamentary Commissioner for Administration in a report under section 10 of the Parliamentary Commissioner Act 1967 to have occurred, to be remedied with respect to the recipient.

[4139]

28 Persons placing promotional material in particular publications

The scheme promotion restriction does not apply to any communication received by a person who receives the publication in which the communication is contained because he has himself placed an advertisement in that publication.

[4140]

[29 Open-ended investment companies authorised in Northern Ireland

(1) The scheme promotion restriction does not apply in relation to a scheme constituted by an authorised Northern Ireland open-ended investment company.

(2) In this article—

(a) "authorised Northern Ireland open-ended investment company" means a body incorporated by virtue of regulations made under section 1 of the Open-Ended Investment Companies Act (Northern Ireland) 2002 in respect of which an authorisation order is in force; and

(b) "authorisation order" means an order made under (or having effect as made under) any provision of those regulations which is made by virtue of section 1(2)(1) of that Act (provision corresponding to Chapter 3 of Part 17 of the Act).]

[4140A]

NOTES

Added by the Financial Services and Markets Act 2000 (Promotion of Collective Investment Schemes etc) (Exemptions) (Amendment) Order 2003, SI 2003/2067, art 2(1), (3), as from 5 September 2003.

[30 EEA management companies

The scheme promotion restriction does not apply to any communication which is made by an EEA firm which—

(a) falls within paragraph 5(f) of Schedule 3 to the Act (management companies of UCITS), and

(b) qualifies for authorisation by virtue of paragraph 12 of that Schedule,

unless the Authority has given (and not withdrawn) a notice to that firm under paragraph 15A(2) of that Schedule (notice indicating that the way in which the firm intends to invite persons in the United Kingdom to become participants in any collective investment scheme which that firm manages does not comply with the law in force in the United Kingdom).]

[4140B]

NOTES

Added by the Financial Services and Markets Act 2000 (Promotion of Collective Investment Schemes etc) (Exemptions) (Amendment) Order 2003, SI 2003/2067, art 2(1), (4), as from 13 February 2004.

[SCHEDULE
STATEMENTS FOR CERTIFIED HIGH NET WORTH INDIVIDUALS AND SELF-CERTIFIED SOPHISTICATED INVESTORS

Articles 21 and 23A

PART I
STATEMENT FOR CERTIFIED HIGH NET WORTH INDIVIDUALS

1. The statement to be signed for the purposes of article 21(2) (definition of high net worth individual) must be in the following form and contain the following content—

"STATEMENT FOR CERTIFIED HIGH NET WORTH INDIVIDUAL

I declare that I am a certified high net worth individual for the purposes of the Financial Services and Markets Act 2000 (Promotion of Collective Investment Schemes) (Exemptions) Order 2001.

I understand that this means—

(a) I can receive promotions, made by a person who is authorised by the Financial Services Authority, which relate to units in unregulated collective investment schemes that invest wholly or predominantly in unlisted companies;

(b) the schemes to which the promotions will relate are not authorised or recognised for the purposes of the Financial Services and Markets Act 2000.

I am a certified high net worth individual because **at least one of the following applies**—

(a) I had, during the financial year immediately preceding the date below, an annual income to the value of £100,000 or more;

(b) I held, throughout the financial year immediately preceding the date below, net assets to the value of £250,000 or more. Net assets for these purposes do not include—

PART IV
STATUTORY INSTRUMENTS

(i) the property which is my primary residence or any loan secured on that residence;
(ii) any rights of mine under a qualifying contract of insurance within the meaning of the Financial Services and Markets Act 2000 (Regulated Activities) Order 2001; or
(iii) any benefits (in the form of pensions or otherwise) which are payable on the termination of my service or on my death or retirement and to which I am (or my dependants are), or may be, entitled.

I accept that I can lose my property and other assets from making investment decisions based on financial promotions.

I am aware that it is open to me to seek advice from someone who specialises in advising on unregulated collective investment schemes.

Signature..

Date ....”]

[4140C]

NOTES

Added by the Financial Services and Markets Act 2000 (Financial Promotion and Promotion of Collective Investment Schemes) (Miscellaneous Amendments) Order 2005, SI 2005/270, art 3, Sch 2, para 4, as from 3 March 2005.

[PART II
STATEMENT FOR SELF-CERTIFIED SOPHISTICATED INVESTORS

2. The statement to be signed for the purposes of article 23A(1) (definition of self-certified sophisticated investor) must be in the following form and contain the following content—

“STATEMENT FOR SELF-CERTIFIED SOPHISTICATED INVESTOR

I declare that I am a self-certified sophisticated investor for the purposes of the Financial Services and Markets Act 2000 (Promotion of Collective Investment Schemes) (Exemptions) Order 2001.

I understand that this means—

(a) I can receive promotions, made by a person who is authorised by the Financial Services Authority, which relate to units in unregulated collective investment schemes that invest wholly or predominantly in unlisted companies;
(b) the schemes to which the promotions will relate are not authorised or recognised for the purposes of the Financial Services and Markets Act 2000.

I am a self-certified sophisticated investor because **at least one of the following applies**—

(a) I am a member of a network or syndicate of business angels and have been so for at least the last six months prior to the date below;
(b) I have made more than one investment in an unlisted company in the two years prior to the date below;
(c) I am working, or have worked in the two years prior to the date below, in a professional capacity in the private equity sector, or in the provision of finance for small and medium enterprises;
(d) I am currently, or have been in the two years prior to the date below, a director of a company with an annual turnover of at least £1 million.

I accept that I can lose my property and other assets from making investment decisions based on financial promotions.

I am aware that it is open to me to seek advice from someone who specialises in advising on unregulated collective investment schemes.

Signature..

Date ....”]

[4140D]

NOTES

Added as noted to Pt I at **[4140C]**.

FINANCIAL SERVICES AND MARKETS ACT 2000 (COLLECTIVE INVESTMENT SCHEMES) ORDER 2001

(SI 2001/1062)

NOTES

Made: 19 March 2001.

Authority: Financial Services and Markets Act 2000, s 235(5).

Commencement: 1 December 2001 (being the date on which the Financial Services and Markets Act 2000, s 19 came into force); see art 1 at **[4141]**. Where any provision in this work (including any inserted or substituted provision) came into force for all purposes on or before 1 July 2005, commencement information is not noted at provision level.

This Order is reproduced as amended by: the Financial Services and Markets Act 2000 (Miscellaneous Provisions) Order 2001, SI 2001/3650; the Financial Services and Markets Act 2000 (Collective Investment Schemes) (Amendment) Order 2005, SI 2005/57; the Civil Partnership Act 2004 (Amendments to Subordinate Legislation) Order 2005, SI 2005/2114; the Financial Services and Markets Act 2000 (Regulated Activities) (Amendment) Order 2006, SI 2006/1969; the Financial Services and Markets Act 2000 (Regulated Activities) (Amendment No 3) Order 2006, SI 2006/3384; the Financial Services and Markets Act 2000 (Collective Investment Schemes) (Amendment) Order 2007, SI 2007/800.

1 Citation and commencement

This Order may be cited as the Financial Services and Markets Act 2000 (Collective Investment Schemes) Order 2001 and comes into force on the day on which section 19 of the Act comes into force.

[4141]

NOTES

FSMA 2000, s 19 came into force on 1 December 2001 (see the Financial Services and Markets Act 2000 (Commencement No 7) Order 2001, SI 2001/3538).

2 Interpretation

In this Order—

"the Act" means the Financial Services and Markets Act 2000;

"the 1988 Act" means the Income and Corporation Taxes Act 1988;

"authorised unit trust scheme" has the meaning given by section 237(3) of the Act;

"contract of insurance" and "contract of long term insurance" have the meaning given by article 3(1) of the Regulated Activities Order;

"feeder fund" means an authorised unit trust scheme the sole object of which is investment in units of a single authorised unit trust scheme or shares in a single open-ended investment company;

"franchise arrangements" means arrangements under which a person earns profits or income by exploiting a right conferred by the arrangements to use a trade mark or design or other intellectual property or the good-will attached to it;

"funeral plan contract" has the meaning given by article 59 of the Regulated Activities Order;

"individual pension account" has the meaning given by regulation 4 of the Personal Pension Schemes (Restriction on Discretion to Approve) (Permitted Investments) Regulations 2001;

. . . .

["occupational pension scheme" has the meaning given by section 1 of the Pension Schemes Act 1993 but with paragraph (b) of the definition omitted;]

"the operator" has the meaning given by section 237(2) of the Act;

["personal pension scheme" means a scheme or arrangement which is not an occupational pension scheme and which is comprised in one or more instruments or agreements, having or capable of having effect so as to provide benefits to or in respect of people—

(a) on retirement,
(b) on having reached a particular age, or
(c) on termination of service in an employment;]

"personal pension unit trust" means a personal pension scheme which is an authorised unit trust scheme of a kind mentioned in Part I of Schedule 1 to the Personal Pension Schemes (Appropriate Schemes) Regulations 1997;

"recognised scheme" has the meaning given by section 237(3) of the Act;

"the Regulated Activities Order" means the Financial Services and Markets Act 2000 (Regulated Activities) Order 2001;

"timeshare rights" has the meaning given by section 1 of the Timeshare Act 1992.

[4142]

NOTES

Original (joint) definition "occupational pension scheme" and "personal pension scheme" revoked, and new (separate) definitions "occupational pension scheme" and "personal pension scheme" inserted, by the Financial Services and Markets Act 2000 (Regulated Activities) (Amendment) Order 2006, SI 2006/1969, art 8, as from 6 April 2007.

3 Arrangements not amounting to a collective investment scheme

Arrangements of the kind specified by the Schedule to this Order do not amount to a collective investment scheme.

[4143]

SCHEDULE

ARRANGEMENTS NOT AMOUNTING TO A COLLECTIVE INVESTMENT SCHEME

Article 3

1 Individual investment management arrangements

Arrangements do not amount to a collective investment scheme if—

(a) the property to which the arrangements relate (other than cash awaiting investment) consists of investments of one or more of the following kinds:
  (i) an investment of the kind specified by any of articles 76 to 80 of the Regulated Activities Order;
  (ii) an investment of the kind specified by article 81 of that Order (units in a collective investment scheme) so far as relating to authorised unit trust schemes, recognised schemes or shares in an open-ended investment company; or
  (iii) a contract of long term insurance;
(b) each participant is entitled to a part of that property and to withdraw that part at any time; and
(c) the arrangements do not have the characteristics mentioned in section 235(3)(a) of the Act and have those mentioned in section 235(3)(b) only because the parts of the property to which different participants are entitled are not bought and sold separately except where a person becomes or ceases to be a participant.

2 Enterprise initiative schemes

(1) Arrangements do not amount to a collective investment scheme if—
(a) the property to which the arrangements relate (other than cash awaiting investment) consists of shares;
(b) the arrangements constitute a complying fund;
(c) each participant is entitled to a part of the property to which the arrangements relate and—
  (i) to the extent that the property to which he is entitled comprises relevant shares of a class which are admitted to official listing in an EEA State or to dealings on a recognised investment exchange, he is entitled to withdraw it at any time after the end of the period of five years beginning with the date on which the shares in question were issued;
  (ii) to the extent that the property to which he is entitled comprises other relevant shares, he is entitled to withdraw it at any time after the end of the period of seven years beginning with the date on which the shares in question were issued;
  (iii) to the extent that the property to which he is entitled comprises shares other than relevant shares, he is entitled to withdraw it at any time after the end of

the period of six months beginning with the date on which the shares in question ceased to be relevant shares; and

(iv) to the extent that the property comprises cash which the operator has agreed (conditionally or unconditionally) to apply in subscribing for shares, he is entitled to withdraw it at any time; and

(d) the arrangements would meet the conditions described in paragraph 1(c) were it not for the fact that the operator is entitled to exercise all or any of the rights conferred by shares included in the property to which the arrangements relate.

(2) In sub-paragraph (1)—

(a) "shares" means investments of the kind specified by article 76 of the Regulated Activities Order (shares etc) and shares are to be regarded as relevant shares if and so long as they are shares in respect of which neither—

(i) a claim for relief made in accordance with section 306 of the 1988 Act has been disallowed; nor

(ii) an assessment has been made pursuant to section 307 of the 1988 Act withdrawing or refusing relief by reason of the body corporate in which the shares are held having ceased to be a body corporate which is a qualifying company for the purposes of that Act;

(b) "complying fund" means arrangements which provide that—

(i) the operator will, so far as is practicable, make investments each of which, subject to each participant's individual circumstances, qualify for relief by virtue of Chapter III of Part VII of the 1988 Act; and

(ii) the minimum contribution to the arrangements which each participant must make is not less than £2000.

3 Pure deposit based schemes

Arrangements do not amount to a collective investment scheme if the whole amount of each participant's contribution is a deposit which is accepted by an authorised person with permission to carry on an activity of the kind specified by article 5 of the Regulated Activities Order (accepting deposits) or a person who is an exempt person in relation to such an activity.

4 Schemes not operated by way of business

Arrangements do not amount to a collective investment scheme if they are operated otherwise than by way of business.

5 Debt issues

(1) Arrangements do not amount to a collective investment scheme if they are arrangements under which the rights or interests of participants are, except as provided in sub-paragraph (2), represented by investments of one, and only one, of the following descriptions:

(a) investments of the kind specified by article 77 of the Regulated Activities Order (instruments creating or acknowledging indebtedness) which are—

(i) issued by a single body corporate other than an open-ended investment company; or

(ii) issued by a single issuer who is not a body corporate and which are guaranteed by the government of the United Kingdom, the Scottish Administration, the Executive Committee of the Northern Ireland Assembly, the National Assembly for Wales or the government of any country or territory outside the United Kingdom;

and which are not convertible into or exchangeable for investments of any other description;

(b) investments falling within sub-paragraph (a)(i) or (ii) ("the former investments") which are convertible into or exchangeable for investments of the kind specified by article 76 of the Regulated Activities Order ("the latter investments") provided that the latter investments are issued by the same person who issued the former investments or are issued by a single other issuer;

(c) investments of the kind specified by article 78 of the Regulated Activities Order (government and public securities) which are issued by a single issuer; or

(d) investments of the kind specified by article 79 of the Regulated Activities Order (instruments giving entitlement to investments) which are issued otherwise than by an open-ended investment company and which confer rights in respect of investments, issued by the same issuer, of the kind specified by article 76 of that Order or within any of paragraphs (a) to (c).

(2) Arrangements which would otherwise not amount to a collective investment scheme by virtue of the provisions of sub-paragraph (1) are not to be regarded as amounting to such a scheme by reason only that one or more of the participants ("the counterparty") is a person—

(a) whose ordinary business involves him in carrying on activities of the kind specified by any of articles 14 (dealing in investments as principal), 21 (dealing in investments as agent), 25 (arranging deals in investments), [25D (operating a multilateral trading facility),] 37 (managing investments), 40 (safeguarding and administering investments), 45 (sending dematerialised instructions), 51 (establishing etc a collective investment scheme), 52 (establishing etc a stakeholder pension scheme) and 53 (advising on investments) or, so far as relevant to any of those articles, article 64 of the Regulated Activities Order (agreeing to carry on specified kinds of activities), or would do so apart from any exclusion from any of those articles made by that Order; and

(b) whose rights or interests in the arrangements are or include rights or interests under a swap arrangement.

(3) In sub-paragraph (2), "swap arrangement" means an arrangement the purpose of which is to facilitate the making of payments to participants whether in a particular amount or currency or at a particular time or rate of interest or all or any combination of those things, being an arrangement under which the counterparty—

(a) is entitled to receive amounts, whether representing principal or interest, payable in respect of any property subject to the arrangements or sums determined by reference to such amounts; and

(b) makes payments, whether or not of the same amount or in the same currency as the amounts or sums referred to in paragraph (a), which are calculated in accordance with an agreed formula by reference to those amounts or sums.

6 Common accounts

Arrangements do not amount to a collective investment scheme if—

(a) they are arrangements under which the rights or interests of participants are rights to or interests in money held in a common account; and

(b) that money is held in the account on the understanding that an amount representing the contribution of each participant is to be applied—

(i) in making payments to him;

(ii) in satisfaction of sums owed by him; or

(iii) in the acquisition of property for him or the provision of services to him.

[7 Certain funds relating to leasehold property

Arrangements do not amount to a collective investment scheme if the rights or interests of the participants are rights or interests—

(a) in a fund which is a trust fund within the meaning of section 42(1) of the Landlord and Tenant Act 1987 or which would be such a trust fund if the landlord were not an exempt landlord within the meaning of section 58(1) of that Act; or

(b) in money held in a designated account by the scheme administrator under a tenancy deposit scheme within the meaning of section 212(2) of the Housing Act 2004.]

8 Certain employee share schemes

(1) Arrangements do not amount to a collective investment scheme if they are operated by a person ("A"), a member of the same group as A or a relevant trustee for the purpose of enabling or facilitating—

(a) transactions in shares in, or debentures issued by, A between, or for the benefit of, any of the persons mentioned in sub-paragraph (2); or

(b) the holding of such shares or debentures by, or for the benefit of, any such persons.

(2) The persons referred to in sub-paragraph (1) are—

(a) the bona fide employees or former employees of A or of another member of the same group; or

(b) the wives, husbands, widows, widowers, [civil partners, surviving civil partners,] or children or step-children under the age of eighteen of such employees or former employees.

(3) For the purposes of this paragraph—

(a) "shares" and "debentures" have the meaning given by article 71(6)(a) of the Regulated Activities Order:

(b) "relevant trustee" means a person who, in pursuance of the arrangements, holds shares in or debentures issued by A.

9 Schemes entered into for commercial purposes related to existing business

(1) Subject to sub-paragraph (2), arrangements do not amount to a collective investment scheme if each of the participants—

[(a) carries on a business other than the business of engaging in any regulated activity of the kind specified by any of articles 14, 21, 25[, 25D], 37, 40, 45, 51 to 53 or, so far as relevant to any of those articles, article 64 of the Regulated Activities Order;]

(b) enters into the arrangements for commercial purposes related to that business.

(2) Sub-paragraph (1) does not apply where the person will carry on the business in question by virtue of being a participant in the arrangements.

10 Group schemes

Arrangements do not amount to a collective investment scheme if each of the participants is a body corporate in the same group as the operator.

11 Franchise arrangements

Franchise arrangements do not amount to a collective investment scheme.

12 Trading schemes

Arrangements do not amount to a collective investment scheme if—

(a) the purpose of the arrangements is that participants should receive, by way of reward, payments or other benefits in respect of the introduction by any person of other persons who become participants;

(b) the arrangements are such that the payments or other benefits referred to in paragraph (a) are to be wholly or mainly funded out of the contributions of other participants; and

(c) the only reason why the arrangements have either or both of the characteristics mentioned in section 235(3) of the Act is because, pending their being used to fund those payments or other benefits, contributions of participants are managed as a whole by or on behalf of the operator of the scheme.

13 Timeshare schemes

Arrangements do not amount to a collective investment scheme if the rights or interests of the participants are timeshare rights.

14 Other schemes relating to use or enjoyment of property

Arrangements do not amount to a collective investment scheme if—

(a) the predominant purpose of the arrangements is to enable the participants to share in the use or enjoyment of property or to make its use or enjoyment available gratuitously to others; and

(b) the property to which the arrangements relate does not consist of the currency of any country or territory and does not consist of or include any investment of the kind specified by Part III of the Regulated Activities Order or which would be of such a kind apart from any exclusion made by that Part of the Order.

15 Schemes involving the issue of certificates representing investments

Arrangements do not amount to a collective investment scheme if the rights or interests of the participants are investments of the kind specified by article 80 of the Regulated Activities Order (certificates representing certain securities).

16 Clearing services

Arrangements do not amount to a collective investment scheme if their purpose is the provision of clearing services and they are operated by an authorised person, a recognised clearing house or a recognised investment exchange.

17 Contracts of insurance

A contract of insurance does not amount to a collective investment scheme.

[18 Funeral plan contracts

Arrangements do not amount to a collective investment scheme if they consist of, or are made pursuant to—

(a) a funeral plan contract; or

(b) a contract which would be a funeral plan contract but for—

(i) the proviso to article 59(2) of the Regulated Activities Order, or

(ii) the exclusion in article 60 of that Order.]

19 Individual pension accounts

An individual pension account does not amount to a collective investment scheme.

20 Occupational and personal pension schemes

(1) An occupational pension scheme does not amount to a collective investment scheme.

(2) A personal pension scheme does not amount to a collective investment scheme.

(3) Sub-paragraph (2) does not extend to a personal pension unit trust which is constituted as a feeder fund or comprises feeder funds.

[21 Bodies corporate etc

(1) Subject to sub-paragraph (2), no body incorporated under the law of, or any part of, the United Kingdom relating to building societies or industrial and provident societies or registered under any such law relating to friendly societies, and no other body corporate other than an open-ended investment company, amounts to a collective investment scheme.

(2) Sub-paragraph (1) does not apply to any body incorporated as a limited liability partnership.]

[4144]

NOTES

Para 5: words in square brackets in sub-para (2)(a) inserted by the Financial Services and Markets Act 2000 (Regulated Activities) (Amendment No 3) Order 2006, SI 2006/3384, art 36(1), (2), as from 1 November 2007 (for the full commencement details of SI 2006/3384, see the Note for that Order at **[4826A]**).

Para 7: substituted by the Financial Services and Markets Act 2000 (Collective Investment Schemes) (Amendment) Order 2007, SI 2007/800, art 2, as from 6 April 2007.

Para 8: words in square brackets in sub-para (2)(b) inserted by the Civil Partnership Act 2004 (Amendments to Subordinate Legislation) Order 2005, SI 2005/2114, art 2(16), Sch 16, Pt 1, para 3, as from 5 December 2005.

Para 9: sub-para (1)(a) substituted by the Financial Services and Markets Act 2000 (Miscellaneous Provisions) Order 2001, SI 2001/3650, art 2(1), (2), as from 1 December 2001; figure in square brackets in sub-para (1)(a) inserted by SI 2006/3384, art 36(1), (3), as from 1 November 2007 (for the full commencement details of SI 2006/3384, see the Note for that Order at **[4826A]**).

Paras 18, 21: substituted by SI 2001/3650, art 2(1), (3), (4), as from 1 December 2001.

Step-children, etc: as to the meaning of this, and related expressions, see the Civil Partnership Act 2004, s 246 (as applied to this Order by the Civil Partnership Act 2004 (Relationships Arising Through Civil Partnership) Order 2005, SI 2005/3137, art 3, Schedule).

FINANCIAL SERVICES AND MARKETS ACT 2000 (CARRYING ON REGULATED ACTIVITIES BY WAY OF BUSINESS) ORDER 2001

(SI 2001/1177)

NOTES

Made: 26 March 2001.

Authority: Financial Services and Markets Act 2000, ss 419, 428(3).

Commencement: 1 December 2001 (being the date on which the Financial Services and Markets Act 2000, s 19 came into force); see art 1 at **[4145]**. Where any provision in this work (including any

inserted or substituted provision) came into force for all purposes on or before 1 July 2005, commencement information is not noted at provision level.

This Order is reproduced as amended by: the Financial Services and Markets Act 2000 (Regulated Activities) (Amendment) (No 1) Order 2003, SI 2003/1475; the Financial Services and Markets Act 2000 (Regulated Activities) (Amendment) (No 2) Order 2003, SI 2003/1476; the Financial Services and Markets Act 2000 (Carrying on Regulated Activities by Way of Business) (Amendment) Order 2005, SI 2005/922; the Financial Services and Markets Act 2000 (Regulated Activities) (Amendment) Order 2006, SI 2006/1969; the Financial Services and Markets Act 2000 (Regulated Activities) (Amendment) (No 2) Order 2006, SI 2006/2383; the Financial Services and Markets Act 2000 (Regulated Activities) (Amendment No 3) Order 2006, SI 2006/3384.

ARRANGEMENT OF ARTICLES

1 Citation, commencement and interpretation

(1) This Order may be cited as the Financial Services and Markets Act 2000 (Carrying on Regulated Activities by Way of Business) Order 2001, and comes into force on the day on which section 19 of the Financial Services and Markets Act 2000 comes into force.

(2) In this Order—

(a) the "Regulated Activities Order" means the Financial Services and Markets Act 2000 (Regulated Activities) Order 2001;

(b) ["contract of insurance",] "contractually based investment", "deposit", "overseas person" and "security" have the same meaning as in that Order;

(c) "shares" and "debentures" mean any investment of the kind specified by article 76 or 77 of that Order;

(d) "units in a collective investment scheme" means any investment of the kind specified by article 81 of that Order;

(e) "warrants" means any investment of the kind specified by article 79 of that Order.

[4145]

NOTES

Para (2): words in square brackets in sub-para (b) inserted by the Financial Services and Markets Act 2000 (Regulated Activities) (Amendment) (No 2) Order 2003, SI 2003/1476, art 18(1), (2), as from 31 October 2004 (in so far as relating to contracts of long-term care insurance), and as from 14 January 2005 (otherwise); for transitional provisions see arts 22–27 of that Order at **[4665]** et seq.

FSMA 2000, s 19 came into force on 1 December 2001 (see the Financial Services and Markets Act 2000 (Commencement No 7) Order 2001, SI 2001/3538).

2 Deposit taking business

(1) A person who carries on an activity of the kind specified by article 5 of the Regulated Activities Order (accepting deposits) is not to be regarded as doing so by way of business if—

(a) he does not hold himself out as accepting deposits on a day to day basis; and

(b) any deposits which he accepts are accepted only on particular occasions, whether or not involving the issue of any securities.

(2) In determining for the purposes of paragraph (1)(b) whether deposits are accepted only on particular occasions, regard is to be had to the frequency of those occasions and to any characteristics distinguishing them from each other.

[4146]

3 Investment business

(1) A person is not to be regarded as carrying on by way of business an activity to which [paragraph (2) applies], unless he carries on the business of engaging in one or more such activities.

(2) [This paragraph] applies to an activity of the kind specified by any of the following provisions of the Regulated Activities Order, namely—

(a) article 14 (dealing in investments as principal);
(b) article 21 (dealing in investments as agent);
(c) article 25 (arranging deals in investments), except in so far as that activity relates to an investment of the kind specified by article 86 of that Order (Lloyd's syndicate capacity and syndicate membership), or article 89 of that Order (rights and interests) so far as relevant to that article;
[(ca) article 25D (operating a multilateral trading facility);]
(d) article 37 (managing investments);
(e) article 40 (safeguarding and administering investments);
(f) article 45 (sending dematerialised instructions);
(g) article 51 (establishing etc a collective investment scheme);
(h) article 52 (establishing etc a … pension scheme);
(i) article 53 (advising on investments); and
[(j) article 64 (agreeing) so far as relevant to any of the articles mentioned in sub-paragraphs (a) to (i),

but does not apply to any insurance mediation activity].

(3) [Paragraph (1)] is without prejudice to article 4 of this Order.

[(4) A person is not to be regarded as carrying on by way of business any insurance mediation activity unless he takes up or pursues that activity for remuneration.

(5) In this article, "insurance mediation activity" means any activity of the kind specified by article 21, 25(1) or (2), 39A or 53 of the Regulated Activities Order, or, so far as relevant to any of those articles, article 64 of that Order, which is carried on in relation to a contract of insurance.]

[4147]

NOTES

Paras (1), (3): words in square brackets substituted by the Financial Services and Markets Act 2000 (Regulated Activities) (Amendment) (No 2) Order 2003, SI 2003/1476, art 18(1), (3)(a), (c), as from 31 October 2004 (in so far as relating to contracts of long-term care insurance), and as from 14 January 2005 (otherwise); for transitional provisions see arts 22–27 of that Order at **[4665]** et seq.

Para (2): words in first pair of square brackets and sub-para (j) (and the following words) substituted by SI 2003/1476, art 18(1), (3)(b), as from 31 October 2004 (in so far as relating to contracts of long-term care insurance), and as from 14 January 2005 (otherwise), for transitional provisions see arts 22–27 of that Order at **[4665]** et seq; sub-para (ca) inserted by the Financial Services and Markets Act 2000 (Regulated Activities) (Amendment No 3) Order 2006, SI 2006/3384, art 37, as from 1 November 2007 (for the full commencement details of SI 2006/3384, see the Note for that Order at **[4826A]**); word omitted from sub-para (h) revoked by the Financial Services and Markets Act 2000 (Regulated Activities) (Amendment) Order 2006, SI 2006/1969, art 9(1), (2), as from 6 April 2007.

Paras (4), (5): added by SI 2003/1476, art 18(1), (3)(d), as from 31 October 2004 (in so far as relating to contracts of long-term care insurance), and as from 14 January 2005 (otherwise); for transitional provisions see arts 22–27 of that Order at **[4665]** et seq.

[3A Arranging and advising on regulated mortgage contracts

A person is not to be regarded as carrying on by way of business an activity of the kind specified by—
(a) article 25A of the Regulated Activities Order (arranging regulated mortgage contracts);
(b) article 53A of that Order (advising on regulated mortgage contracts); or
(c) article 64 of that Order (agreeing), so far as relevant to any of the articles mentioned in sub-paragraphs (a) and (b),

unless he carries on the business of engaging in that activity.]

[4147A]

NOTES

Inserted by the Financial Services and Markets Act 2000 (Regulated Activities) (Amendment) (No 1) Order 2003, SI 2003/1475, art 25, as from 31 October 2004; for transitional provisions see arts 26–29 at **[4659]** et seq.

[3B Arranging and advising on regulated home reversion plans

A person is not to be regarded as carrying on by way of business an activity specified by—
(a) article 25B of the Regulated Activities Order (arranging regulated home reversion plans);

(b) article 53B of that Order (advising on regulated home reversion plans); or
(c) article 64 of that Order (agreeing), so far as relevant to either of the articles mentioned in sub-paragraphs (a) and (b),

unless he carries on the business of engaging in that activity.]

[4147B]

NOTES

Commencement: 6 April 2007.

Inserted, together with art 3C, by the Financial Services and Markets Act 2000 (Regulated Activities) (Amendment) (No 2) Order 2006, SI 2006/2383, art 29, as from 6 April 2007 (for the full commencement details of SI 2006/2383, see art 1 of that Order at **[4820]**).

[3C Arranging and advising on regulated home purchase plans

A person is not to be regarded as carrying on by way of business an activity specified by—
(a) article 25C of the Regulated Activities Order (arranging regulated home purchase plans);
(b) article 53C of that Order (advising on regulated home purchase plans); or
(c) article 64 of that Order (agreeing), so far as relevant to either of the articles mentioned in sub-paragraphs (a) and (b),

unless he carries on the business of engaging in that activity.]

[4147C]

NOTES

Commencement: 6 April 2007.

Inserted as noted to art 3C at **[4147B]**.

4 Managing investments: occupational pension schemes

(1) A person who carries on an activity of the kind specified by article 37 of the Regulated Activities Order (managing investments), where the assets in question are held for the purposes of an occupational pension scheme, is to be regarded as carrying on that activity by way of business, except where—
(a) he is a person to whom paragraph (2) applies; or
(b) all … day to day decisions in the carrying on of that activity (other than decisions falling within paragraph (6)), so far as relating to relevant assets, are taken on his behalf by—
(i) an authorised person who has permission to carry on activities of the kind specified by article 37 of the Regulated Activities Order;
(ii) a person who is an exempt person in relation to activities of that kind; or
(iii) an overseas person.

(2) This paragraph applies to—
(a) any trustee of a relevant scheme who is a beneficiary or potential beneficiary under the scheme; and
(b) any other trustee of a relevant scheme who takes no … day to day decisions relating to the management of any relevant assets.

(3) In this article—

["occupational pension scheme" has the meaning given by section 1 of the Pension Schemes Act 1993 but with paragraph (b) of the definition omitted;]

"relevant assets" means assets of the scheme in question which are securities or contractually based investments;

"relevant scheme" means any occupational pension scheme of a kind falling within paragraph (4) or (5).

(4) A scheme falls within this paragraph if—
(a) it is constituted under an irrevocable trust:
(b) it has no more than twelve relevant members;
(c) all relevant members, other than any relevant member who is unfit to act, or is incapable of acting, as trustee of the scheme, are trustees of it; and
(d) all … day to day decisions relating to the management of the assets of the scheme which are relevant assets are required to be taken by all, or a majority of, relevant

members who are trustees of the scheme or by a person of a kind falling within paragraph (1)(b)(i) or (ii) acting alone or jointly with all, or a majority of, such relevant members;

and for these purposes a person is a relevant member of a scheme if he is an employee or former employee by or in respect of whom contributions to the scheme are being or have been made and to or in respect of whom benefits are or may become payable under the scheme.

(5) A scheme falls within this paragraph if—

(a) it has no more than fifty members;

(b) the contributions made by or in respect of each member of the scheme are used in the acquisition of a contract of insurance on the life of that member or in the acquisition of a contract to pay an annuity on that life;

(c) the only decision of a kind described in paragraph (1)(b) which may be taken in relation to the scheme is the selection of such contracts; and

(d) each member is given the opportunity to select the contract which the contributions made by or in respect of him will be used to acquire.

(6) A decision falls within this paragraph if—

[(a) it is a decision by the trustees of an occupational pension scheme to buy, sell or subscribe for—

(i) units in a collective investment scheme;

(ii) shares or debentures (or warrants relating to such shares or debentures) issued by a body corporate having as its purpose the investment of its funds with the aim of spreading investment risk and giving its members the benefit of the results of the management of those funds by or on behalf of that body; or

(iii) rights under (or rights to or interests in) any contract of insurance;]

…

[(b) the decision is taken after advice has been obtained and considered from a person who falls within any of the cases in paragraph (7);]

(c), (d) …

[(7) The cases are where the person is—

(a) an authorised person who has permission to carry on activities of the kind specified by article 53 of the Regulated Activities Order in relation to the decision in question;

(b) an exempt person in relation to such activities;

(c) exempt from the general prohibition by virtue of section 327 of the Financial Services and Markets Act 2000; or

(d) an overseas person.]

[4148]

NOTES

Paras (1), (2), (4): words omitted revoked by the Financial Services and Markets Act 2000 (Carrying on Regulated Activities by Way of Business) (Amendment) Order 2005, SI 2005/922, art 2(1), (2), as from 6 April 2005.

Para (3): definition "occupational pension scheme" substituted by the Financial Services and Markets Act 2000 (Regulated Activities) (Amendment) Order 2006, SI 2006/1969, art 9(1), (3), as from 6 April 2007.

Para (6): sub-paras (a), (b) substituted, omitted words following sub-para (a) revoked, and sub-paras (c), (d) revoked, by SI 2005/922, art 2(1), (4)–(7), as from 6 April 2005.

Para (7): substituted by SI 2005/922, art 2(1), (8), as from 6 April 2005.

FINANCIAL SERVICES AND MARKETS ACT 2000 (EXEMPTION) ORDER 2001

(SI 2001/1201)

NOTES

Made: 26 March 2001.

Authority: Financial Services and Markets Act 2000, ss 38, 428(3).

Commencement: 1 December 2001 (being the date on which the Financial Services and Markets Act 2000, s 19 came into force); see art 1 at **[4149]**. Where any provision in this work (including any

inserted or substituted provision) came into force for all purposes on or before 1 July 2005, commencement information is not noted at provision level.

This Order is reproduced as amended by: the Tourist Boards (Scotland) Act 2006; the Financial Services and Markets Act 2000 (Exemption) (Amendment) Order 2001, SI 2001/3623; the Financial Services and Markets Act 2000 (Financial Promotion and Miscellaneous Amendments) Order 2002, SI 2002/1310; the Financial Services and Markets Act 2000 (Exemption) (Amendment) Order 2003, SI 2003/47; the Financial Services and Markets Act 2000 (Exemption) (Amendment) (No 2) Order 2003, SI 2003/1675; the Financial Services and Markets Act 2000 (Exemption) (Amendment) Order 2005, SI 2005/592; the Civil Partnership Act 2004 (Amendments to Subordinate Legislation) Order 2005, SI 2005/2114; the Wales Tourist Board (Transfer of Functions to the National Assembly for Wales and Abolition) Order 2005, SI 2005/3225; the Charities and Trustee Investment (Scotland) Act 2005 (Consequential Provisions and Modifications) Order 2006, SI 2006/242; the Financial Services and Markets Act 2000 (Regulated Activities) (Amendment) Order 2006, SI 2006/1969; the Financial Services and Markets Act 2000 (Regulated Activities) (Amendment) (No 2) Order 2006, SI 2006/2383; the Financial Services and Markets Act 2000 (Exemption) (Amendment) Order 2007, SI 2007/125; the Tourist Boards (Scotland) Act 2006 (Consequential Modifications) Order 2007, SI 2007/1103; the Financial Services and Markets Act 2000 (Exemption) (Amendment No 2) Order 2007, SI 2007/1821.

ARRANGEMENT OF ARTICLES

1 Citation and commencement

This Order may be cited as the Financial Services and Markets Act 2000 (Exemption) Order 2001 and comes into force on the day on which section 19 of the Act comes into force.

[4149]

NOTES

FSMA 2000, s 19 came into force on 1 December 2001 (see the Financial Services and Markets Act 2000 (Commencement No 7) Order 2001, SI 2001/3538).

2 Interpretation

In this Order—

"the Act" means the Financial Services and Markets Act 2000;

"charity"—

(a) in relation to Scotland, means a [body entered in the Scottish Charity Register]; and

(b) otherwise, has the meaning given by section 96(1) of the Charities Act 1993 or by section 35 of the Charities Act (Northern Ireland) 1964;

["credit institution" has the meaning given by the Regulated Activities Order;]

"deposit" has the meaning given by the Regulated Activities Order;

"industrial and provident society" has the meaning given by section 417(1) of the Act but does not include a credit union within the meaning of the Credit Unions Act 1979 or the Credit Unions (Northern Ireland) Order 1985;

["investment firm" has the meaning given by the Regulated Activities Order;]

"local authority" means—

(a) in England and Wales, a local authority within the meaning of the Local Government Act 1972, the Greater London Authority, the Common Council of the City of London or the Council of the Isles of Scilly;

(b) in Scotland, a local authority within the meaning of the Local Government (Scotland) Act 1973; and

(c) in Northern Ireland, a district council within the meaning of the Local Government Act (Northern Ireland) 1972;

["non-qualifying contract of insurance" means a contract of insurance (within the meaning of the Regulated Activities Order) which is not a qualifying contract of insurance (within the meaning of that Order);]

"the Regulated Activities Order" means the Financial Services and Markets Act 2000 (Regulated Activities) Order 2001.

[4150]

NOTES

Words in square brackets in definition "charity" substituted by the Charities and Trustee Investment (Scotland) Act 2005 (Consequential Provisions and Modifications) Order 2006, SI 2006/242, art 5, Schedule, Pt 2, para 11, as from 1 April 2006; definitions "credit institution" and "investment firm" inserted by the Financial Services and Markets Act 2000 (Exemption) (Amendment) Order 2007, SI 2007/125, art 3, as from 1 November 2007; definition "non-qualifying contract of insurance" inserted by the Financial Services and Markets Act 2000 (Exemption) (Amendment) (No 2) Order 2003, SI 2003/1675, art 2(1), (2), as from 14 January 2005.

3 Persons exempt in respect of any regulated activity other than insurance business

Each of the persons listed in Part I of the Schedule is exempt from the general prohibition in respect of any regulated activity other than an activity of the kind specified by article 10 of the Regulated Activities Order (effecting and carrying out contracts of insurance).

[4151]

4 Persons exempt in respect of accepting deposits

Subject to the limitations, if any, expressed in relation to him, each of the persons listed in Part II of the Schedule is exempt from the general prohibition in respect of any regulated activity of the kind specified by article 5 of the Regulated Activities Order (accepting deposits).

[4152]

5 Persons exempt in respect of particular regulated activities

(1) Subject to the limitation, if any, expressed in relation to him, each of the persons listed in Part III of the Schedule is exempt from the general prohibition in respect of any regulated activity of the kind specified by any of the following provisions of the Regulated Activities Order, or article 64 of that Order (agreeing to carry on specified kinds of activity) so far as relevant to any such activity—

(a) article 14 (dealing in investments as principal);
(b) article 21 (dealing in investments as agent);
(c) article 25 (arranging deals in investments);
[(ca) article 25D (operating a multilateral trading facility);]
(d) article 37 (managing investments);
[(da) article 39A (assisting in the administration and performance of a contract of insurance);]
(e) article 40 (safeguarding and administering investments);
(f) article 45 (sending dematerialised instructions);
(g) article 51 (establishing etc a collective investment scheme);
(h) article 52 (establishing etc a … pension scheme);
(i) article 53 (advising on investments).

(2) Subject to the limitation, if any, expressed in relation to him, each of the persons listed in Part IV of the Schedule is exempt from the general prohibition in respect of any regulated activity of the kind referred to in relation to him, or an activity of the kind specified by article 64 of the Regulated Activities Order so far as relevant to any such activity.

[4153]

NOTES

Para (1): sub-para (ca) inserted by the Financial Services and Markets Act 2000 (Exemption) (Amendment) Order 2007, SI 2007/125, art 4, as from 1 November 2007; sub-para (da) inserted by the Financial Services and Markets Act 2000 (Exemption) (Amendment) (No 2) Order 2003, SI 2003/1675, art 2(1), (3), as from 14 January 2005; word omitted from sub-para (h) revoked by the Financial Services and Markets Act 2000 (Regulated Activities) (Amendment) Order 2006, SI 2006/1969, art 10, as from 6 April 2007.

6 Transitional exemption for credit unions

A credit union, within the meaning of the Credit Unions Act 1979 … , is exempt from the general prohibition in respect of any regulated activity of the kind specified by article 5 of the Regulated Activities Order, but only until 1st July 2002.

[4154]

NOTES

Words omitted revoked by the Financial Services and Markets Act 2000 (Exemption) (Amendment) Order 2001, SI 2001/3623, arts 2, 3, as from 1 December 2001.

SCHEDULE

Articles 3 to 5

PART I
PERSONS EXEMPT IN RESPECT OF ANY REGULATED ACTIVITY OTHER THAN INSURANCE BUSINESS

1. The Bank of England.

2. The central bank of an EEA State other than the United Kingdom.

3. The European Central Bank.

4. The European Community.

5. The European Atomic Energy Community.

6. The European Coal and Steel Community.

7. The European Investment Bank.

8. The International Bank for Reconstruction and Development.

9. The International Finance Corporation.

10. The International Monetary Fund.

11. The African Development Bank.

12. The Asian Development Bank.

13. The Caribbean Development Bank.

14. The Inter-American Development Bank.

15. The European Bank for Reconstruction and Development.

[15A. Bank for International Settlements.]

[4155]

NOTES

Para 15A: added by the Financial Services and Markets Act 2000 (Exemption) (Amendment) Order 2003, SI 2003/47, art 2, as from 1 March 2003.

PART II
PERSONS EXEMPT IN RESPECT OF ACCEPTING DEPOSITS

16. A municipal bank, that is to say a company which was, immediately before the coming into force of this Order, exempted from the prohibition in section 3 of the Banking Act 1987 by virtue of section 4(1) of, and paragraph 4 of Schedule 2 to, that Act.

17.—(1) Keesler Federal Credit Union, in so far as it accepts deposits from members, or dependants of members, of a visiting force of the United States of America, or from members, or dependants of members, of a civilian component of such a force.

(2) In sub-paragraph (1), "member", "dependent" and "visiting force" have the meanings given by section 12 of the Visiting Forces Act 1952 and "member of a civilian component" has the meaning given by section 10 of that Act.

18. A body of persons certified as a school bank by the National Savings Bank or by an authorised person who has permission to accept deposits.

19. A local authority.

20.—(1) Any body which by virtue of any enactment has power to issue a precept to a local authority in England or Wales or a requisition to a local authority in Scotland, or to the expenses of which, by virtue of any enactment, a local authority in the United Kingdom is or can be required to contribute.

(2) In sub-paragraph (1), "enactment" includes an enactment comprised in, or in an instrument made under, an Act of the Scottish Parliament.

[21. The Council of Europe Development Bank.]

22. A charity, in so far as it accepts deposits—
(a) from another charity; or
(b) in respect of which no interest or premium is payable.

23. The National Children's Charities Fund in so far as—
(a) it accepts deposits in respect of which no interest or premium is payable; and
(b) the total value of the deposits made by any one person does not exceed £10,000.

24. An industrial and provident society, in so far as it accepts deposits in the form of withdrawable share capital.

[24A. A credit union, within the meaning of the Credit Unions (Northern Ireland) Order 1985.]

25.—(1) The Student Loans Company Limited, in so far as it accepts deposits from the Secretary of State or the Scottish Ministers in connection with, or for the purposes of, enabling eligible students to receive loans.

(2) In sub-paragraph (1), "eligible student" means—
(a) any person who is an eligible student pursuant to regulations made under Part II of the Teaching and Higher Education Act 1998;
(b) any person to whom, or in respect of whom, loans may be paid under section 73(f) of the Education (Scotland) Act 1980;
(c) any person who is an eligible student pursuant to regulations made under article 3 of the Education (Student Support) (Northern Ireland) Order 1998; or
(d) any person who is in receipt of or who is eligible to receive a loan of the kind mentioned in article 3(1) of the Teaching and Higher Education Act 1998 (Commencement No 2 and Transitional Provisions) Order 1998 or article 3(1) of the Education (Student Support) (Northern Ireland) Order 1998 (Commencement and Transitional Provisions) Order (Northern Ireland) 1998.

[4156]

NOTES

Para 21: substituted by the Financial Services and Markets Act 2000 (Financial Promotion and Miscellaneous Amendments) Order 2002, SI 2002/1310, art 4(2), as from 5 June 2002.

Para 24A: inserted by the Financial Services and Markets Act 2000 (Exemption) (Amendment) Order 2001, SI 2001/3623, arts 2, 4, as from 1 December 2001.

PART III
PERSONS EXEMPT IN RESPECT OF ANY REGULATED ACTIVITY MENTIONED IN ARTICLE 5(1)

26. The National Debt Commissioners.

[27. Partnerships UK.]

28. The International Development Association.

29. The English Tourist Board.

30. …

[31. VisitScotland.]

32. The Northern Ireland Tourist Board.

33. Scottish Enterprise.

[33A. Invest Northern Ireland.]

34. The Multilateral Investment Guarantee Agency.

[34A. The Board of the Pension Protection Fund.]

35. A person acting as an official receiver within the meaning of section 399 of the Insolvency Act 1986 or article 2 of the Insolvency (Northern Ireland) Order 1989.

36.—(1) A person who provides the trading facilities which constitute a regulated market, in so far as he carries on a regulated activity in connection with, or for the purposes of, the provision of those trading facilities.

(2) In sub-paragraph (1), "regulated market" means a market which—

- *(a) appears on the list drawn up by an EEA State other than the United Kingdom pursuant to Article 16 of the investment services directive; and*
- *(b) operates without any requirement that a person dealing on the market should have a physical presence in the EEA State from which the trading facilities are provided or on any trading floor that the market may have.*

37.—[(1) An Operator, in so far as he carries on—

- (a) any regulated activity for the purposes of the performance of his functions as an Operator under the Uncertificated Securities Regulations 1995; or
- (b) any other regulated activity for the purposes of operating a computer-based system and procedures which—
  - (i) enable title to investments to be evidenced and transferred without a written instrument; or
  - (ii) facilitate matters supplementary or incidental to those specified in sub-paragraph (i),

other than a regulated activity in respect of which a recognised clearing house is exempt from the general prohibition by virtue of section 285(3) of the Act.]

(2) In sub-paragraph (1), "Operator" means a person approved as such by the Treasury under the Uncertificated Securities Regulations 1995.

38. A person acting as a judicial factor.

39. A person acting as an insolvency practitioner within the meaning of section 388 of the Insolvency Act 1986 [or article 3 of the Insolvency (Northern Ireland) Order 1989].

[4157]

NOTES

Para 27: substituted by the Financial Services and Markets Act 2000 (Exemption) (Amendment) (No 2) Order 2003, SI 2003/1675, art 2(1), (4)(a), as from 13 July 2003.

Para 30: revoked by the Wales Tourist Board (Transfer of Functions to the National Assembly for Wales and Abolition) Order 2005, SI 2005/3225, art 6(2), Sch 2, Pt 2, para 4, as from 1 April 2006.

Para 31: substituted by the Tourist Boards (Scotland) Act 2006, s 4, Sch 2, Pt 2, para 10, as from 1 April 2007 (in relation to Scotland), and by the Tourist Boards (Scotland) Act 2006 (Consequential Modifications) Order 2007, SI 2007/1103, art 2, Schedule, Pt 2, para 6, as from 29 March 2007 (in relation to England and Wales).

Para 33A: inserted by the Financial Services and Markets Act 2000 (Exemption) (Amendment No 2) Order 2007, SI 2007/1821, art 2(1), (2), as from 20 July 2007.

Para 34A: inserted by the Financial Services and Markets Act 2000 (Exemption) (Amendment) Order 2005, SI 2005/592, art 2(1), as from 6 April 2005.

Para 36: revoked by the Financial Services and Markets Act 2000 (Exemption) (Amendment) Order 2007, SI 2007/125, art 5, as from 1 November 2007.
Para 37: sub-para (1) substituted by the Financial Services and Markets Act 2000 (Exemption) (Amendment) Order 2001, SI 2001/3623, arts 2, 5, as from 1 December 2001.
Para 39: words in square brackets added by SI 2001/3623, arts 2, 6, as from 1 December 2001.
Uncertificated Securities Regulations 1995 (SI 1995/3272): revoked and replaced by the Uncertificated Securities Regulations 2001, SI 2001/3755.

PART IV
PERSONS EXEMPT IN RESPECT OF PARTICULAR REGULATED ACTIVITIES

Enterprise schemes

40.—(1) Any body corporate which has as its principal object (or one of its principal objects)—

(a) the promotion or encouragement of industrial or commercial activity or enterprise in the United Kingdom or in any particular area of it; or

(b) the dissemination of information concerning persons engaged in such activity or enterprise or requiring capital to become so engaged;

is exempt from the general prohibition in respect of any regulated activity of the kind specified by article 25 of the Regulated Activities Order (arranging deals in investments) so long as it does not carry on that activity for, or with the prospect of, direct or indirect pecuniary gain.

(2) For the purposes of this paragraph, such sums as may reasonably be regarded as necessary to meet the costs of carrying on the activity mentioned in sub-paragraph (1) do not constitute a pecuniary gain.

[(3) This paragraph does not apply where an investment firm or credit institution—

(a) provides or performs investment services and activities on a professional basis, and

(b) in doing so, but for the operation of *this paragraph*, it would be treated as carrying on an activity of a kind specified by Part 2 of the Regulated Activities Order [in breach of the general prohibition].]

Employee share schemes in electricity industry shares

41.—(1) Each of the persons to whom this paragraph applies is exempt from the general prohibition in respect of any regulated activity of the kind specified by article 14, 21 or 25 of the Regulated Activities Order (dealing in investments as principal or agent or arranging deals in investments) which he carries on for the purpose of—

(a) enabling or facilitating transactions in electricity industry shares or debentures between or for the benefit of any qualifying person; or

(b) the holding of electricity industry shares or debentures by or for the benefit of any qualifying person.

(2) This paragraph applies to—

(a) The National Grid Holding plc;

(b) Electricity Association Limited;

(c) any body corporate in the same group as the person mentioned in sub-paragraph (a) or (b);

(d) any company listed in Schedule 1 to the Electricity Act 1989 (Nominated Companies) (England and Wales) Order 1990; and

(e) a person holding shares in or debentures of a body corporate as trustee in pursuance of arrangements made for either of the purposes mentioned in sub-paragraph (1) by the Secretary of State, by any of the bodies mentioned in sub-paragraphs (a) to (c) or by an electricity successor company or by some or all of them.

(3) In this paragraph—

(a) "electricity industry shares or debentures" means—

(i) any investment of the kind specified by article 76 or 77 of the Regulated Activities Order (shares or instruments creating or acknowledging indebtedness) in or of an electricity successor company;

(ii) any investment of the kind specified by article 79 or 80 of that Order (instruments giving entitlement to investments and certificates representing certain securities), so far as relevant to the investments mentioned in sub-paragraph (i); and

(iii) any investment of the kind specified by article 89 of that Order (rights to or interests in investments) so far as relevant to the investments mentioned in sub-paragraphs (i) and (ii);

(b) "qualifying person" means—

(i) the bona fide employees or former employees of The National Grid Holding plc, Electricity Association Limited or any other body corporate in the same group as either of them; and

(ii) the wives, husbands, widows, widowers[, civil partners, surviving civil partners,] or children (including, in Northern Ireland, adopted children) or step-children under the age of eighteen of such employees or former employees;

(c) references to an electricity successor company include any body corporate that is in the same group and "electricity successor company" means a body corporate which is a successor company for the purposes of Part II of the Electricity Act 1989;

(d) "former employees" of a person ("the employer") include any person who has never been employed by the employer so long as he occupied a position in relation to some other person of such a kind that it may reasonably be assumed that he would have been a former employee of the employer had the reorganisation of the electricity industry under Part II of the Electricity Act 1989 been affected before he ceased to occupy the relevant position.

Gas industry

42.—(1) Transco plc is exempt from the general prohibition in respect of any regulated activity of the kind specified by article 14, 21 *or 25* of the Regulated Activities Order (dealing in investments as principal or agent *or arranging deals in investments*) which it carries on—

(a) in its capacity as a gas transporter under the Transco Licence; and

(b) for the purposes of enabling or facilitating gas shippers to buy or sell an investment of the kind specified by article 84 or 85 of the Regulated Activities Order (futures or contracts for differences etc).

(2) ENMO Ltd is exempt from the general prohibition in respect of any regulated activity of the kind specified by article 14, 21 *or 25* of the Regulated Activities Order (dealing in investments as principal or agent *or arranging deals in investments*) which it carries on—

(a) in its capacity as the operator of the balancing market; and

(b) for the purpose of enabling or facilitating Transco plc and relevant gas shippers, for the purpose of participating in the balancing market, to buy or sell investments of the kind specified by article 84 or 85 of that Order (futures or contracts for differences etc).

(3) Transco plc and relevant gas shippers are exempt from the general prohibition in respect of any regulated activity of the kind specified by article 14 or 21 of the Regulated Activities Order (dealing in investments as principal or agent) in so far as that activity relates to an investment of the kind specified by article 84 or 85 of that Order (futures or contracts for differences etc) and is carried on for the purpose of participating in the balancing market.

(4) In this paragraph—

(a) "the balancing market" means the market to regulate the delivery and off-take of gas in Transco plc's pipeline system for the purpose of balancing the volume of gas in that system;

(b) "gas shipper" has the same meaning as in Part I of the Gas Act 1986;

(c) "relevant gas shippers" means gas shippers who have entered into a subscription agreement with ENMO Ltd for the purpose of participating in the balancing market;

(d) "Transco Licence" means the licence treated as granted to Transco plc as a gas transporter under section 7 of the Gas Act 1986;

(e) the reference to enabling or facilitating includes acting pursuant to rules governing the operation of the balancing market which apply in the event of one of the participants appearing to be unable, or likely to become unable, to meet his obligations in respect of one or more contracts entered into through the balancing market.

Trade unions and employers' associations

43.—(1) A trade union or employers' association is exempt from the general prohibition in respect of any regulated activity of the kind specified by article 10 of the Regulated Activities Order (effecting and carrying out contracts of insurance) which it carries on in order to provide provident benefits or strike benefits for its members.

(2) In sub-paragraph (1), "trade union" and "employers' association" have the meanings given by section 1 and section 122(1) of the Trade Union and Labour Relations (Consolidation) Act 1992 or, in Northern Ireland, the meanings given by article 3(1) and article 4(1) of the Industrial Relations (Northern Ireland) Order 1992.

Charities

44.—(1) A charity is exempt from the general prohibition in respect of any regulated activity of the kind specified by article 51 of the Regulated Activities Order (establishing etc a collective investment scheme) which it carries on in relation to a fund established under—
- (a) section 22A of the Charities Act 1960;
- (b) section 25 of the Charities Act 1993; or
- (c) section 25 of the Charities Act (Northern Ireland) 1964.

(2) A charity is exempt from the general prohibition in respect of any regulated activity of the kind specified by article 51 of the Regulated Activities Order (establishing etc a collective investment scheme) which it carries on in relation to a pooling scheme fund established under—
- (a) section 22 of the Charities Act 1960; or
- (b) section 24 of the Charities Act 1993.

(3) In sub-paragraph (2), "pooling scheme fund" means a fund established by a common investment scheme the trusts of which provide that property is not to be transferred to the fund except by or on behalf of a charity, the charity trustees (within the meaning of section 97(1) of the Charities Act 1993) of which are the trustees appointed to manage the fund.

Schemes established under the Trustee Investments Act 1961

45. A person acting in his capacity as manager or operator of a fund established under section 11 of the Trustee Investments Act 1961 is exempt from the general prohibition in respect of any regulated activity of the kind specified by article 51 of the Regulated Activities Order (establishing etc a collective investment scheme) which he carries on in relation to that fund.

Former members of Lloyd's

46. Any person who ceased to be an underwriting member (within the meaning of Lloyd's Act 1982) of Lloyd's before 24th December 1996 is exempt from the general prohibition in respect of any regulated activity of the kind specified by article 10(2) of the Regulated Activities Order (carrying out contracts of insurance) which relates to contracts of insurance that he has underwritten at Lloyd's.

Local authorities

[47. A local authority is exempt from the general prohibition in respect of any regulated activity of the kind specified by—
- (a) article 21, 25(1) or (2), 39A or 53 of the Regulated Activities Order (dealing in investments as agent, arranging deals in investments, assisting in the administration and performance of a contract of insurance or advising on investments) which relates to a non-qualifying contract of insurance; …
- (b) article 25A, 53A or 61 of that Order (arranging, advising on, entering into or administering a regulated mortgage contract)[;
- (c) article 25B, 53B or 63B of that Order (arranging, advising on, entering into or administering a regulated home reversion plan); or

(d) article 25C, 53C or 63F of that Order (arranging, advising on, entering into or administering a regulated home purchase plan)].]

Social housing

[48.—(1) A relevant housing body is exempt from the general prohibition in respect of any regulated activity of the kind specified by—

(a) article 21, 25(1) or (2), 39A or 53 of the Regulated Activities Order (dealing in investments as agent, arranging deals in investments, assisting in the administration and performance of a contract of insurance or advising on investments) which relates to a non-qualifying contract of insurance; …

(b) article 25A, 53A or 61 of that Order (arranging, advising on, entering into or administering a regulated mortgage contract)[;

(c) article 25B, 53B or 63B of that Order (arranging, advising on, entering into or administering a regulated home reversion plan); or

(d) article 25C, 53C or 63F of that Order (arranging, advising on, entering into or administering a regulated home purchase plan)].

(2) In this paragraph, "relevant housing body" means any of the following—

(a) a registered social landlord within the meaning of Part I of the Housing Act 1996;

(b) a registered social landlord within the meaning of the Housing (Scotland) Act 2001;

(c) the Housing Corporation;

(d) Scottish Homes;

(e) the body established under article 9 of the Housing (Northern Ireland) Order 1981 known as the Northern Ireland Housing Executive;

[(f) Communities Scotland]].

[Electricity industry

49.—(1) NGC is exempt from the general prohibition in respect of any regulated activity of the kind specified by article 14, 21, 25[, 25D] or 53 of the Regulated Activities Order (dealing in investments as principal or agent, arranging deals in investments or advising on investments) which it carries on in the course of—

(a) its participation in the Balancing and Settlement Arrangements as operator of the electricity transmission system in [Great Britain] under the Transmission Licence; or

(b) the acquisition by it of Balancing Services in accordance with the Electricity Act 1989 and the Transmission Licence.

(2) ELEXON Clear Limited is exempt from the general prohibition in respect of any regulated activity of the kind specified by article 14, 21 *or 25* of that Order which it carries on in the course of its participation in the Balancing and Settlement Arrangements as clearer for the purposes of (among other things) receiving from and paying to BSC Parties trading and reconciliation charges arising under the Balancing and Settlement Arrangements.

(3) Each BSC Party is exempt from the general prohibition in respect of any regulated activity of the kind specified by article 14, 21, 25[, 25D] or 53 of that Order which it carries on in the course of—

(a) its participation in the Balancing and Settlement Arrangements; or

(b) the provision by it (or, in the case of an activity of the kind specified by article 21 of that Order, its principal) of Balancing Services to NGC.

(4) ELEXON Limited is exempt from the general prohibition in respect of any regulated activity of the kind specified by article 25[, 25D] of that Order which it carries on in the course of its participation in the Balancing and Settlement Arrangements as administrator.

(5) Each BSC Agent and each Volume Notification Agent is exempt from the general prohibition in respect of any regulated activity of the kind specified by article 25[, 25D] of that Order which it carries on in that capacity.

(6) …

(7) In this paragraph—

"Ancillary Services" means services which generators and suppliers of electricity and those making transfers of electricity across an Interconnector are required (as a condition of their connection to the transmission system in [Great Britain]), or have agreed, to make available to NGC for the purpose of securing the stability of the electricity transmission or any distribution system in [Great Britain] or any system linked to it by an Interconnector;

"Balancing and Settlement Arrangements" means—

(a) the Balancing Mechanism; and

(b) arrangements—

(i) for the determination and allocation to BSC Parties of the quantities of electricity that have been delivered to and taken off the electricity transmission system and any distribution system in [Great Britain]; and

(ii) which set, and provide for the determination and financial settlement of, BSC Parties' obligations arising by reference to the quantities referred to in sub-paragraph (i), including the difference between such quantities (after taking account of accepted bids and offers in the Balancing Mechanism) and the quantities of electricity contracted for sale and purchase between BSC Parties;

"Balancing Mechanism" means the arrangements pursuant to which BSC Parties may make, and NGC may accept, offers or bids to increase or decrease the quantities of electricity to be delivered to or taken off the electricity transmission system or any distribution system in [Great Britain] at any time or during any period so as to assist NGC in operating and balancing the electricity transmission system, and arrangements for the settlement of financial obligations arising from the acceptance of such offers and bids;

"Balancing Services" means—

(a) offers and bids made in the Balancing Mechanism;

(b) Ancillary Services; and

(c) other services available to NGC which assist it in operating the electricity transmission system in accordance with the Electricity Act 1989 and the Transmission Licence;

"BSC Agents" means the persons for the time being engaged by or on behalf of ELEXON Limited for the purpose of providing services to all BSC Parties, NGC, ELEXON Limited and ELEXON Clear Limited in connection with the operation of the Balancing and Settlement Arrangements;

["BSC Framework Agreement" means the agreement of that title in the form approved by the Secretary of State for the purpose of conditions of the Transmission Licence and which is dated 14 August 2000; and "conditions" for the purposes of this definition means conditions determined by the Secretary of State under powers granted by section 137(1) of the Energy Act 2004. and incorporated into existing electricity transmission licences by a scheme made by the Secretary of State pursuant to section 138 of, and Schedule 17 to, that Act;]

"BSC Parties" means those persons (other than NGC, ELEXON Limited and ELEXON Clear Limited) who have signed or acceded to (in accordance with the terms of the BSC Framework Agreement), and not withdrawn from, the BSC Framework Agreement;

"Interconnector" means the electric lines and electrical plant [and meters] used [solely] for the transfer of electricity to or from the electricity transmission system … in [Great Britain] into or out of [Great Britain];

"NGC" means … National Grid Company plc;

…

"the Transmission Licence" means the licence to [participate in the transmission of] electricity in [Great Britain] granted[, or treated as granted,] to NGC under section 6(1)(b) of the Electricity Act 1989; and

"Volume Notification Agents" means the persons for the time being appointed and authorised under and in accordance with the Balancing and Settlement Arrangements on behalf of BSC Parties to notify to the BSC Agent designated for that purpose pursuant to the Balancing and Settlement Arrangements quantities of electricity contracted for the sale and purchase between those BSC Parties to be taken into account for the purposes of the Balancing and Settlement Arrangements.]

[Freight Forwarders and Storage Firms

50.—(1) A freight forwarder or storage firm is exempt from the general prohibition in respect of any regulated activity of the kind specified by article 21, 25, 39A or 53 of the Regulated Activities Order (dealing in investments as agent, arranging deals in investments, assisting in the administration and performance of a contract of insurance or advising on investments) in the circumstances referred to in paragraph 2.

(2) The circumstances are—

(a) where a freight forwarder ("F")—

(i) holds a policy of insurance which insures F in respect of loss of or damage to goods which F transports or of which F arranges the transportation, and

(ii) makes available to a customer rights under that policy to enable the customer to claim directly against the insurer in respect of loss or damage to those goods; or

(b) where a storage firm ("S")—

(i) holds a policy of insurance which insures S in respect of loss of or damage to goods which S stores or for which S arranges storage, and

(ii) makes available to a customer rights under that policy to enable the customer to claim directly against the insurer in respect of loss or damage to those goods.

(3) In this paragraph—

(a) "freight forwarder" means a person whose principal business is arranging or carrying out the transportation of goods;

(b) "storage firm" means a person whose principal business is storing goods or arranging storage for goods;

(c) "customer" means a person who is not an individual who uses the service of a freight forwarder or storage firm.

Policyholder Advocates

51.—(1) A person acting as a policyholder advocate is exempt from the general prohibition in respect of any regulated activity of the kind specified by article 25 or 53 of the Regulated Activities Order (arranging deals in investments or advising on investments) in so far as he carries on these activities in connection with, or for the purposes of, his role as policyholder advocate.

(2) In sub-paragraph (1), "policyholder advocate" means a person who is—

(a) appointed by an insurer ("I") to represent the interests of policyholders in negotiations with I about I's proposals to redefine the rights and interests in any surplus assets arising in I's with-profits fund; and

(b) approved or nominated by the Authority to carry out that role.

(3) In sub-paragraph (2), "with-profits fund" means a long-term insurance fund in which policyholders are eligible to participate in surplus assets of the fund.]

[4158]

NOTES

Para 40: sub-para (3) added by the Financial Services and Markets Act 2000 (Exemption) (Amendment) Order 2007, SI 2007/125, art 6(a), as from 1 November 2007; for the words in italics in sub-para (3)(b) there are substituted the words "sub-paragraph (1)", and the words in square brackets are added, by the Financial Services and Markets Act 2000 (Exemption) (Amendment No 2) Order 2007, SI 2007/1821, art 2(1), (3), as from 1 November 2007.

Para 41: words in square brackets in sub-para (3)(b)(ii) inserted by the Civil Partnership Act 2004 (Amendments to Subordinate Legislation) Order 2005, SI 2005/2114, art 2(16), Sch 16, Pt 1, para 4, as from 5 December 2005.

Para 42: for the words "or 25" in italics (in both places they occur) there are substituted the words ", 25 or 25D", and for the words "or arranging deals in investments" in italics (in both places they occur) there are substituted the words ", arranging deals in investments or operating a multilateral trading facility", by SI 2007/125, art 6(b), as from 1 November 2007.

Para 47: substituted by the Financial Services and Markets Act 2000 (Exemption) (Amendment) (No 2) Order 2003, SI 2003/1675, art 2(1), (4)(b), as from 31 October 2004 (in so far as providing for an exemption in relation to any mortgage activity), and as from 14 January 2005 (otherwise); word omitted from sub-para (a) revoked, and sub-paras (c), (d) inserted, by the Financial Services and Markets Act 2000 (Regulated Activities) (Amendment) (No 2) Order 2006, SI 2006/2383, art 30(a), as from 6 April 2007 (for the full commencement details of SI 2006/2383, see art 1 of that Order at **[4820]**).

Para 48: substituted by SI 2003/1675, art 2(1), (4)(c), as from 31 October 2004 (in so far as providing for an exemption in relation to any mortgage activity), and as from 14 January 2005 (otherwise); word omitted from sub-para (1)(a) revoked, and sub-paras (1)(c), (d) inserted, by SI 2006/2383, art 30(b), as from 6 April 2007 (for the full commencement details of SI 2006/2383, see art 1 of that Order at **[4820]**); sub-para (2)(f) added by the Financial Services and Markets Act 2000 (Exemption) (Amendment) Order 2005, SI 2005/592, art 2(2), as from 6 April 2005.

Para 49: added by the Financial Services and Markets Act 2000 (Exemption) (Amendment) Order 2001, SI 2001/3623, arts 2, 8, as from 1 December 2001; words ", operating a multilateral trading facility" in square brackets in sub-para (1), and the figure ", 25D" in square brackets in sub-paras (1), (3)–(5) inserted by SI 2007/125, art 6(c)(i), (iii)–(v), as from 1 November 2007; for the words "or 25" in italics in sub-para (2) there are substituted the words ", 25 or 25D" by SI 2007/125, art 6(c)(ii), as from 1 November 2007; other words in square brackets substituted or inserted, and words omitted revoked, by the Financial Services and Markets Act 2000 (Exemption) (Amendment) Order 2005, SI 2005/592, art 3, as from 1 April 2005.

Paras 50, 51: added by SI 2007/1821, art 2(1), (4), as from 20 July 2007.

Transfer of functions: by the Housing (Scotland) Act 2001, s 84, the functions of Scottish Homes are transferred to the Scottish Ministers.

Step-children, etc: as to the meaning of this, and related expressions, see the Civil Partnership Act 2004, s 246 (as applied to this Order by the Civil Partnership Act 2004 (Relationships Arising Through Civil Partnership) Order 2005, SI 2005/3137, art 3, Schedule).

FINANCIAL SERVICES AND MARKETS ACT 2000 (APPOINTED REPRESENTATIVES) REGULATIONS 2001

(SI 2001/1217)

NOTES

Made: 28 March 2001.

Authority: Financial Services and Markets Act 2000, ss 39(1), 417(1).

Commencement: 1 December 2001 (being the date on which the Financial Services and Markets Act 2000, s 19 came into force); see reg 1 at **[4159]**. Where any provision in this work (including any inserted or substituted provision) came into force for all purposes on or before 1 July 2005, commencement information is not noted at provision level.

These Regulations are reproduced as amended by: the Financial Services and Markets Act 2000 (Appointed Representatives) (Amendment) Regulations 2001, SI 2001/2508; the Financial Services and Markets Act 2000 (Regulated Activities) (Amendment) (No 1) Order 2003, SI 2003/1475; the Financial Services and Markets Act 2000 (Regulated Activities) (Amendment) (No 2) Order 2003, SI 2003/1476; the Financial Services and Markets Act 2000 (Appointed Representatives) (Amendment) Regulations 2004, SI 2004/453; the Financial Services and Markets Act 2000 (Regulated Activities) (Amendment) (No 2) Order 2004, SI 2004/2737; the Financial Services and Markets Act 2000 (Regulated Activities) (Amendment) (No 2) Order 2006, SI 2006/2383; the Financial Services and Markets Act 2000 (Appointed Representatives) (Amendment) Regulations 2006, SI 2006/3414; the Financial Services and Markets Act 2000 (Markets in Financial Instruments) (Amendment) Regulations 2007, SI 2007/763.

1 Citation, commencement and interpretation

(1) These Regulations may be cited as the Financial Services and Markets Act 2000 (Appointed Representatives) Regulations 2001, and come into force on the day on which section 19 of the Act comes into force.

(2) In these Regulations—

"buy", "sell", "security"[, "contract of insurance", "[qualifying contract of insurance]" and "relevant investment"] have the same meaning as in the Regulated Activities Order;

["contract of long-term care insurance" means a contract of insurance in respect of which the following conditions are met—

(a) the purpose (or one of the purposes) of the policy is to protect the policyholder against the risk of becoming unable to live independently without assistance in consequence of a deterioration of mental or physical health, injury, sickness or other infirmity;

(b) benefits under the contract are payable in respect of—

(i) services,

(ii) accommodation, or

(iii) goods,

which are (or which is) necessary or desirable due to a deterioration of mental or physical health, injury, sickness or other infirmity;

(c) the contract is expressed to be in effect until the death of the policyholder (except that the contract may give the policyholder the option to surrender the policy); and

(d) the benefits under the contract are capable of being paid throughout the life of the policyholder;]

["EEA credit institution" means a credit institution authorised under the banking consolidation directive which has its relevant office in an EEA State other than the United Kingdom;

"EEA investment firm" means an investment firm as defined in section 424A of the Act which has its relevant office in an EEA State other than the United Kingdom;]

["home purchaser" has the same meaning as in article 63F(3) of the Regulated Activities Order;]

"other counterparties" means persons other than the principal;

["plan provider" has the meaning given by paragraph (3) of article 63B of the Regulated Activities Order, read with paragraphs (7) and (8) of that article;]

"the principal", in relation to a contract, means the party who is an authorised person, and "the representative" means the other party;

"the Regulated Activities Order" means the Financial Services and Markets Act 2000 (Regulated Activities) Order 2001;

["regulated home purchase plan" has the same meaning as in article 63F(3) of the Regulated Activities Order;

"regulated home reversion plan" has the same meaning as in article 63B(3) of the Regulated Activities Order;]

["regulated mortgage contract", and "borrower" in relation to such a contract, have the same meaning as in article 61(3) of the Regulated Activities Order;]

["reversion seller" has the same meaning as in article 63B(3) of the Regulated Activities Order].

[4159]

NOTES

Para (2) is amended as follows:

In the first definitions (ie, the ones beginning with "buy"), words in first (outer) pair of square brackets substituted by the Financial Services and Markets Act 2000 (Regulated Activities) (Amendment) (No 2) Order 2003, SI 2003/1476, art 14(1), (2), as from 31 October 2004 (in so far as relating to contracts of long-term care insurance), and as from 14 January 2005 (otherwise), for transitional provisions see arts 22–27 of that Order at **[4665]** et seq; words in second (inner) pair of square brackets substituted by the Financial Services and Markets Act 2000 (Appointed Representatives) (Amendment) Regulations 2004, SI 2004/453, reg 2(1), (2), as from 25 April 2004.

Definition "contract of long-term care insurance" inserted by SI 2004/453, reg 2(1), (3), as from 31 October 2004.

Definitions "EEA credit institution" and "EEA investment firm" inserted by the Financial Services and Markets Act 2000 (Appointed Representatives) (Amendment) Regulations 2006, SI 2006/3414, regs 2, 3, as from 1 November 2007.

Definitions "home purchaser", "plan provider", "regulated home purchase plan", "regulated home reversion plan", and "reversion seller" inserted by the Financial Services and Markets Act 2000 (Regulated Activities) (Amendment) (No 2) Order 2006, SI 2006/2383, art 31(1), (2), as from 6 April 2007 (for the full commencement details of SI 2006/2383, see art 1 of that Order at **[4820]**).

Definition "regulated mortgage contract" inserted by the Financial Services and Markets Act 2000 (Regulated Activities) (Amendment) (No 1) Order 2003, SI 2003/1475, art 23(1), (2), as from 31 October 2004; for transitional provisions see arts 26–29 of that Order at **[4659]** et seq.

FSMA 2000, s 19 came into force on 1 December 2001 (see the Financial Services and Markets Act 2000 (Commencement No 7) Order 2001, SI 2001/3538).

2 Descriptions of business for which appointed representatives are exempt

[(1)] [Subject to paragraph (2),] any business which comprises—

[(aa) an activity of the kind specified by article 21 of the Regulated Activities Order (dealing in investments as agent), where the transaction relates to [a contract of insurance which is not a qualifying contract of insurance or a contract of long-term care insurance];]

(a) an activity of the kind specified by article 25 of [that Order] (arranging deals in investments), where the arrangements are for or with a view to transactions relating to securities or [relevant investments];

[(ab) an activity of the kind specified by article 25A of that Order (arranging regulated mortgage contracts);]

[(aba) an activity of the kind specified by article 25B of that Order (arranging regulated home reversion plans);

(abb) an activity of the kind specified by article 25C of that Order (arranging regulated home purchase plans);]

[(ac) an activity of the kind specified by article 39A of that Order (assisting in the administration and performance of a contract of insurance) … ;]

(b) an activity of the kind specified by article 40 of that Order (safeguarding and

PART IV STATUTORY INSTRUMENTS

administering investments), where the activity consists of arranging for one or more other persons to safeguard and administer assets;

[(ba) an activity of the kind specified by article 52B of that Order (providing basic advice on stakeholder products);]

(c) an activity of the kind specified by article 53 of that Order (advising on investments); …

[(ca) an activity of the kind specified by article 53A of that Order (advising on regulated mortgage contracts); …]

[(cb) an activity of the kind specified by article 53B of that Order (advising on regulated home reversion plans);

(cc) an activity of the kind specified by article 53C of that Order (advising on regulated home purchase plans); or]

(d) an activity of the kind specified by article 64 of that Order (agreeing to carry on activities), so far as relevant to an activity falling within [sub-paragraph (aa), (a), (ab), (ac), [(aba), (abb), (b), (c), (ca), (cb) or (cc)]];

is prescribed for the purposes of subsection (1)(a)(i) of section 39 of the Act (exemption of appointed representatives).

[(1A) In its application to a contract with a principal who is an EEA investment firm or an EEA credit institution, the list in paragraph (1) shall be treated as including in addition—

(a) the activity of placing financial instruments,

(b) the activity of providing advice to clients or potential clients in relation to the placing of financial instruments.

(1B) In paragraph (1A), "clients" and "financial instruments" have the meanings given in, respectively, paragraphs 1.10 and 1.17 of Article 4 of the markets in financial instruments directive.]

[(2) Paragraph (1) does not prescribe any business to the extent that it comprises the provision by an investment firm of a service specified in paragraph 1(a) of Section A of the Annex to the investment services directive (reception and transmission of orders), unless that activity is carried on solely for the account of another investment firm.

(3) In paragraph (2), "investment firm" means a person whose regular occupation or business is the provision of core investment services (that is to say, services listed in Section A of the Annex to the investment services directive) to third parties on a professional basis, other than a person to whom that directive does not apply by virtue of Article 2.2 of that directive.]

[4160]

NOTES

Para (1) is amended as follows:

Numbered as such, and words in first pair of square brackets inserted, by the Financial Services and Markets Act 2000 (Appointed Representatives) (Amendment) Regulations 2001, SI 2001/2508, reg 2(a), (b), as from 1 December 2001.

Sub-paras (aa), (ac) inserted, and words in square brackets in sub-para (a) substituted, by the Financial Services and Markets Act 2000 (Regulated Activities) (Amendment) (No 2) Order 2003, SI 2003/1476, art 14(1), (3)(a)–(c), as from 31 October 2004 (in so far as relating to contracts of long-term care insurance), and as from 14 January 2005 (otherwise); for transitional provisions see arts 22–27 of that Order at **[4665]** et seq.

Words in square brackets in sub-para (aa) substituted by the Financial Services and Markets Act 2000 (Appointed Representatives) (Amendment) Regulations 2004, SI 2004/453, reg 3(1), (2), as from 25 April 2004.

Sub-paras (ab), (ca) inserted, and word omitted from sub-para (c) revoked, by the Financial Services and Markets Act 2000 (Regulated Activities) (Amendment) (No 1) Order 2003, SI 2003/1475, art 23(1), (3)(a)–(c), as from 31 October 2004; for transitional provisions see arts 26–29 of that Order at **[4659]** et seq.

Sub-paras (aba), (abb), (cb), (cc) inserted, word omitted from sub-para (ca) revoked, and words in second (inner) pair of square brackets in sub-para (d) substituted, by the Financial Services and Markets Act 2000 (Regulated Activities) (Amendment) (No 2) Order 2006, SI 2006/2383, art 31(1), (3), as from 6 April 2007 (for the full commencement details of SI 2006/2383, see art 1 of that Order at **[4820]**).

Words omitted from sub-para (ac) revoked by SI 2004/453, reg 3(1), (3), as from 25 April 2004.

Sub-para (ba) inserted by the Financial Services and Markets Act 2000 (Regulated Activities) (Amendment) (No 2) Order 2004, SI 2004/2737, art 5(1), (2), as from 6 April 2005.

Words in first (outer) pair of square brackets in sub-para (d) substituted by a combination of SI 2003/1475, art 23(1), (3)(d), as from 31 October 2004 (for transitional provisions see arts 26–29 of that Order at **[4659]** et seq) and SI 2003/1476, art 14(1), (3)(d), as from 31 October 2004 (in so far as relating to contracts of long-term care insurance), and as from 14 January 2005 (otherwise) (for transitional provisions see arts 22–27 of that Order at **[4665]** et seq).

Paras (1A), (1B): inserted by the Financial Services and Markets Act 2000 (Appointed Representatives) (Amendment) Regulations 2006, SI 2006/3414, regs 2, 4(a), as from 1 November 2007.

Paras (2), (3): added by SI 2001/2508, reg 2(c), as from 1 December 2001; revoked by SI 2006/3414, regs 2, 4(b), as from 1 November 2007.

3 Requirements applying to contracts between authorised persons and appointed representatives

(1) *For the purposes of subsection (1)(a)(ii) of that section, it is a prescribed requirement that the contract between the principal and the representative* must (unless it prohibits the representative from representing other counterparties) contain a provision enabling the principal to—

(a) impose such a prohibition; or

(b) impose restrictions as to the other counterparties which the representative may represent, or as to the types of investment in relation to which the representative may represent other counterparties.

[(1A) This paragraph applies to a contract where the principal is an EEA investment firm or an EEA credit institution.]

(2) For the purposes of paragraph (1) a representative is to be treated as representing other counterparties where he—

[(aa) he enters into investment transactions as agent (in circumstances constituting the carrying on of an activity of the kind specified by article 21 of the Regulated Activities Order) for other counterparties;]

(a) makes arrangements (in circumstances constituting the carrying on of an activity of the kind specified by article 25 of [that Order]) for persons to enter (or with a view to persons entering) into investment transactions with other counterparties;

[(ab) he assists in the administration and performance of a contract of insurance (in circumstances constituting the carrying on of an activity of the kind specified by article 39A of that Order) for other counterparties;]

(b) arranges (in circumstances constituting the carrying on of an activity of the kind specified by article 40 of that Order) for other counterparties to safeguard and administer assets; or

(c) gives advice (in circumstances constituting the carrying on of an activity of the kind specified by article 53 of that Order) on the merits of entering into investment transactions with other counterparties;

where an "investment transaction" means a transaction to buy, sell, subscribe for or underwrite an investment which is a security or a [relevant investment].

[(3) A representative is also to be treated as representing other counterparties for the purposes of paragraph (1) where he—

(a) makes arrangements (in circumstances constituting the carrying on of an activity of the kind specified by article 25A of that Order)—

 (i) for persons to enter (or with a view to persons entering) as borrowers into regulated mortgage contracts with other counterparties, or

 (ii) for a person to vary a regulated mortgage contract entered into by a person as borrower after the coming into force of article 61 of that Order with other counterparties; or

(b) gives advice (in circumstances constituting the carrying on of an activity of the kind specified by article 53A of that Order) on the merits of—

 (i) persons entering as borrowers into regulated mortgage contracts with other counterparties, or

 (ii) persons varying regulated mortgage contracts entered into by them as borrower after the coming into force of article 61 of that Order with other counterparties.]

[(3A) A representative is also to be treated as representing other counterparties for the purposes of paragraph (1) where he—

(a) makes arrangements (in circumstances constituting the carrying on of an activity of the kind specified by article 25B of that Order)—

 (i) for a person to enter (or with a view to a person entering) as reversion seller or plan provider into a regulated home reversion plan with other counterparties, or

 (ii) for a person to vary a regulated home reversion plan entered into on or after 6th April 2007 by him as reversion seller or plan provider with other counterparties; or

(b) gives advice (in circumstances constituting the carrying on of an activity of the kind specified by article 53B of that Order) on the merits of—
  (i) a person entering as reversion seller or plan provider into a regulated home reversion plan with other counterparties, or
  (ii) a person varying a regulated home reversion plan entered into on or after 6th April 2007 by him as reversion seller or plan provider with other counterparties.

(3B) A representative is also to be treated as representing other counterparties for the purposes of paragraph (1) where he—

(a) makes arrangements (in circumstances constituting the carrying on of an activity of the kind specified by article 25C of that Order)—
  (i) for a person to enter (or with a view to a person entering) as home purchaser into a regulated home purchase plan with other counterparties, or
  (ii) for a person to vary a regulated home purchase plan entered into on or after 6th April 2007 by a person as home purchaser with other counterparties; or

(b) gives advice (in circumstances constituting the carrying on of an activity of the kind specified by article 53C of that Order) on the merits of—
  (i) a person entering as home purchaser into a regulated home purchase plan with other counterparties, or
  (ii) a person varying a regulated home purchase plan entered into on or after 6th April 2007 by him as home purchaser with other counterparties.]

[(4) Where the contract between the principal and the representative permits or requires the representative to carry on business which includes an activity—

(a) of the kind specified by article 21, 25, 39A or 53 of the Regulated Activities Order or an activity of the kind specified by article 64 of that Order, so far as relevant to any of those articles, and

(b) which relates to a contract of insurance,

paragraph (5) applies.

(5) Where this paragraph applies, it is also a prescribed requirement for the purposes of subsection (1)(a)(ii) of section 39 of the Act that the contract between the principal and the representative contain a provision providing that the representative is not permitted or required to carry on business, so far as it comprises an activity of the kind specified by paragraph (4), unless he is included in the record maintained by the Authority under section 347 of the Act by virtue of article 93 of the Regulated Activities Order (recorded insurance intermediaries).]

[(6) In the case of a representative to whom subsection (1A) of section 39 of the Act applies, it is a prescribed requirement for the purposes of subsection (1)(a)(ii) of that section, except where paragraph (1A) applies, that the contract between the principal and the representative must contain a provision that the representative is only permitted to provide the services and carry on the activities referred to in Article 4.1.25 of the markets in financial instruments directive while he is entered on the applicable register.]

[4161]

NOTES

Para (1): for the words in italics there are substituted the words "Except where paragraph (1A) applies to a contract between a principal and a representative, it is a prescribed requirement for the purposes of section 39(1)(a)(ii) of the Act that such a contract" by the Financial Services and Markets Act 2000 (Appointed Representatives) (Amendment) Regulations 2006, SI 2006/3414, regs 2, 5(a), as from 1 November 2007.

Paras (1A), (6): inserted and added respectively by SI 2006/3414, regs 2, 5(b), (c), as from 1 November 2007.

Para (2): sub-paras (aa), (ab) inserted, and words in square brackets in sub-para (a) and the final words in square brackets substituted, by the Financial Services and Markets Act 2000 (Regulated Activities) (Amendment) (No 2) Order 2003, SI 2003/1476, art 14(1), (4)(a), as from 31 October 2004 (in so far as relating to contracts of long-term care insurance), and as from 14 January 2005 (otherwise); for transitional provisions see arts 22–27 of that Order at **[4665]** et seq.

Para (3): added by the Financial Services and Markets Act 2000 (Regulated Activities) (Amendment) (No 1) Order 2003, SI 2003/1475, art 23(1), (4), as from 31 October 2004; for transitional provisions see arts 26–29 at **[4659]** et seq.

Paras (3A), (3B): inserted by the Financial Services and Markets Act 2000 (Regulated Activities) (Amendment) (No 2) Order 2006, SI 2006/2383, art 31(1), (4), as from 6 April 2007 (for the full commencement details of SI 2006/2383, see art 1 of that Order at **[4820]**).

Paras (4), (5): added by SI 2003/1476, art 14(1), (4)(b), as from 31 October 2004 (in so far as relating to contracts of long-term care insurance), and as from 14 January 2005 (otherwise); for transitional provisions see arts 22–27 of that Order at **[4665]** et seq.

[4 Transitional provision in relation to contracts

Regulation 3(6) does not apply in relation to a contract made on or before 31st October 2007.]

[4161A]

NOTES

Commencement: 1 November 2007.

Added by the Financial Services and Markets Act 2000 (Markets in Financial Instruments) (Amendment) Regulations 2007, SI 2007/763, reg 7, as from 1 November 2007.

FINANCIAL SERVICES AND MARKETS ACT 2000 (DESIGNATED PROFESSIONAL BODIES) ORDER 2001

(SI 2001/1226)

NOTES

Made: 27 March 2001.

Authority: Financial Services and Markets Act 2000, s 326.

Commencement: 28 March 2001; see art 1 at **[4162]**. Where any provision in this work (including any inserted or substituted provision) came into force for all purposes on or before 1 July 2005, commencement information is not noted at provision level.

This Order is reproduced as amended by: the Financial Services and Markets Act 2000 (Designated Professional Bodies) (Amendment) Order 2004, SI 2004/3352; the Financial Services and Markets Act 2000 (Designated Professional Bodies) (Amendment) Order 2006, SI 2006/58.

1 Citation, commencement and interpretation

(1) This Order may be cited as the Financial Services and Markets Act 2000 (Designated Professional Bodies) Order 2001.

(2) This Order comes into force on the day after the day on which it is made.

(3) In this Order, "the Act" means the Financial Services and Markets Act 2000.

[4162]

2 Designated professional bodies

The following bodies are designated under section 326(1) of the Act for the purposes of Part XX of the Act—

(a) the Law Society;
(b) the Law Society of Scotland;
(c) the Law Society of Northern Ireland;
(d) the Institute of Chartered Accountants in England and Wales;
(e) the Institute of Chartered Accountants of Scotland;
(f) the Institute of Chartered Accountants in Ireland;
(g) the Association of Chartered Certified Accountants;
(h) the Institute of Actuaries;
[(i) the Council for Licensed Conveyancers][;
(j) the Royal Institution of Chartered Surveyors].

[4163]

NOTES

Para (i) added by the Financial Services and Markets Act 2000 (Designated Professional Bodies) (Amendment) Order 2004, SI 2004/3352, art 2, as from 14 January 2005; para (j) added by the Financial Services and Markets Act 2000 (Designated Professional Bodies) (Amendment) Order 2006, SI 2006/58, art 2, as from 10 February 2006.

PART IV STATUTORY INSTRUMENTS

FINANCIAL SERVICES AND MARKETS ACT 2000 (PROFESSIONS) (NON-EXEMPT ACTIVITIES) ORDER 2001

(SI 2001/1227)

NOTES

Made: 27 March 2001.

Authority: Financial Services and Markets Act 2000, ss 327(6), 428(3).

Commencement: see art 1 at **[4164]**. Where any provision in this work (including any inserted or substituted provision) came into force for all purposes on or before 1 July 2005, commencement information is not noted at provision level.

This Order is reproduced as amended by: the Financial Services and Markets Act 2000 (Miscellaneous Provisions) Order 2001, SI 2001/3650; the Financial Services and Markets Act 2000 (Regulated Activities) (Amendment) Order 2002, SI 2002/682; the Financial Services and Markets Act 2000 (Commencement of Mortgage Regulation) (Amendment) Order 2002, SI 2002/1777; the Financial Services and Markets Act 2000 (Regulated Activities) (Amendment) (No 1) Order 2003, SI 2003/1475; the Financial Services and Markets Act 2000 (Regulated Activities) (Amendment) (No 2) Order 2003, SI 2003/1476; the Financial Services and Markets Act 2000 (Regulated Activities) (Amendment) (No 2) Order 2004, SI 2004/2737; the Financial Services and Markets Act 2000 (Regulated Activities) (Amendment) Order 2006, SI 2006/1969; the Financial Services and Markets Act 2000 (Regulated Activities) (Amendment) (No 2) Order 2006, SI 2006/2383.

1 Citation and commencement

(1) This Order may be cited as the Financial Services and Markets Act 2000 (Professions) (Non-Exempt Activities) Order 2001.

(2) Subject to paragraph (3), this Order comes into force on the day on which section 19 of the Act comes into force.

(3) This Order comes into force—

(a) for the purposes of article 4(g), on 1st January 2002; and

(b) for the purposes of [article 6A], [on such a day as the Treasury may specify].

[(4) Any day specified under paragraph 3(b) must be caused to be notified in the London, Edinburgh and Belfast Gazettes published not later than one week before that day.]

[4164]

NOTES

Para (3): words in first pair of square brackets substituted by the Financial Services and Markets Act 2000 (Miscellaneous Provisions) Order 2001, SI 2001/3650, art 3(a), as from 31 October 2004; words in second pair of square brackets substituted by the Financial Services and Markets Act 2000 (Commencement of Mortgage Regulation) (Amendment) Order 2002, SI 2002/1777, art 3(1), (2), as from 30 August 2002.

Para (4): added by SI 2002/1777, art 3(1), (3), as from 30 August 2002.

FSMA 2000, s 19 came into force on 1 December 2001 (see the Financial Services and Markets Act 2000 (Commencement No 7) Order 2001, SI 2001/3538).

On such a day as the Treasury may specify: 31 October 2004 (see the London Gazette, 14 July 2003).

2 Interpretation

(1) In this Order—

"the Act" means the Financial Services and Markets Act 2000;

["contract of insurance" has the meaning given by article 3(1) of the Regulated Activities Order;]

"contractually based investment" has the meaning given by article 3(1) of the Regulated Activities Order;

["home purchase provider" has the meaning given by article 63F(3) of the Regulated Activities Order;

"home purchaser" has the meaning given by article 63F(3) of the Regulated Activities Order;]

"occupational pension scheme" and "personal pension scheme" have the meaning given by section 1 of the Pension Schemes Act 1993;

["plan provider" has the meaning given by paragraph (3) of article 63B of the Regulated Activities Order, read with paragraphs (7) and (8) of that article;]

["record of insurance intermediaries" means the record maintained by the Authority under section 347 of the Act (the public record) by virtue of article 93 of the Regulated Activities Order (recorded insurance intermediaries);]

"the Regulated Activities Order" means the Financial Services and Markets Act 2000 (Regulated Activities) Order 2001;

["regulated home purchase plan" has the meaning given by article 63F(3) of the Regulated Activities Order;

"regulated home reversion plan" has the meaning given by article 63B(3) of the Regulated Activities Order;

"regulated mortgage contract" has the meaning given by article 61 of the Regulated Activities Order;]

["relevant investment" has the meaning given by article 3(1) of the Regulated Activities Order;]

["reversion seller" has the meaning given by article 63B(3) of the Regulated Activities Order;]

"security" has the meaning given by article 3(1) of the Regulated Activities Order;

"syndicate" has the meaning given by article 3(1) of the Regulated Activities Order.

(2) For the purposes of this Order, a person is a member of a personal pension scheme if he is a person to or in respect of whom benefits are or may become payable under the scheme. **[4165]**

NOTES

Para (1): definitions "contract of insurance" and "record of insurance intermediaries" inserted, and definition "relevant investment" substituted, by the Financial Services and Markets Act 2000 (Regulated Activities) (Amendment) (No 2) Order 2003, SI 2003/1476, art 16(1), (2), as from 31 October 2004 (in so far as relating to contracts of long-term care insurance), and as from 14 January 2005 (otherwise), for transitional provisions see arts 22–27 of that Order at **[4665]** et seq; definitions "home purchase provider", "home purchaser", "plan provider", "regulated home purchase plan", "regulated home reversion plan", "regulated mortgage contract", and "reversion seller" inserted by the Financial Services and Markets Act 2000 (Regulated Activities) (Amendment) (No 2) Order 2006, SI 2006/2383, art 32(1), (2), as from 6 April 2007 (for the full commencement details of SI 2006/2383, see art 1 of that Order at **[4820]**).

3 Activities to which exemption from the general prohibition does not apply

The activities in articles 4 to 8 are specified for the purposes of section 327(6) of the Act. **[4166]**

4 An activity of the kind specified by any of the following provisions of the Regulated Activities Order—

(a) article 5 (accepting deposits);

[(aa) article 9B (issuing electronic money);]

(b) article 10 (effecting and carrying out contracts of insurance);

(c) article 14 (dealing in investments as principal);

(d) article 51 (establishing etc a collective investment scheme);

(e) article 52 (establishing etc a … pension scheme);

[(ea) article 52B (providing basic advice on stakeholder products);]

(f) article 57 (managing the underwriting capacity of a Lloyd's syndicate);

(g) article 59 (funeral plan contracts);

(h) … **[4167]**

NOTES

Para (aa) inserted by the Financial Services and Markets Act 2000 (Regulated Activities) (Amendment) Order 2002, SI 2002/682, art 7(1), as from 27 April 2002.

Word omitted from para (e) revoked by the Financial Services and Markets Act 2000 (Regulated Activities) (Amendment) Order 2006, SI 2006/1969, art 11, as from 6 April 2007.

Para (ea) inserted by the Financial Services and Markets Act 2000 (Regulated Activities) (Amendment) (No 2) Order 2004, SI 2004/2737, art 5(3), (4), as from 6 April 2005.

Para (h) revoked by the Financial Services and Markets Act 2000 (Miscellaneous Provisions) Order 2001, SI 2001/3650, art 3(b), as 31 October 2004.

[4A An activity of the kind specified by article 21 or 25 of the Regulated Activities Order (dealing in investments as agent or arranging deals in investments) in so far as it—

(a) relates to a transaction for the sale or purchase of rights under a contract of insurance; and

(b) is carried on by a person who is not included in the record of insurance intermediaries.]

[4167A]

NOTES

Inserted by the Financial Services and Markets Act 2000 (Regulated Activities) (Amendment) (No 2) Order 2003, SI 2003/1476, art 16(1), (3), as from 31 October 2004 (in so far as relating to contracts of long-term care insurance), and as from 14 January 2005 (otherwise); for transitional provisions see arts 22–27 of that Order at **[4665]** et seq.

5—(1) An activity of the kind specified by article 37 of the Regulated Activities Order (managing investments) in so far as it consists of buying or subscribing for a [security or contractually based investment].

(2) Paragraph (1) does not apply—

(a) if all routine or day to day decisions, so far as relating to that activity, are taken by an authorised person with permission to carry on that activity or by a person who is an exempt person in relation to such an activity; or

(b) to an activity undertaken in accordance with the advice of an authorised person with permission to give advice in relation to such an activity or a person who is an exempt person in relation to the giving of such advice.

[4168]

NOTES

Para (1): words in square brackets substituted by the Financial Services and Markets Act 2000 (Regulated Activities) (Amendment) (No 2) Order 2003, SI 2003/1476, art 16(1), (4), as from 31 October 2004 (in so far as relating to contracts of long-term care insurance), and as from 14 January 2005 (otherwise); for transitional provisions see arts 22–27 of that Order at **[4665]** et seq.

[5A An activity of the kind specified by article 39A of the Regulated Activities Order (assisting in the administration and performance of a contract of insurance) if it is carried on by a person who is not included in the record of insurance intermediaries.]

[4168A]

NOTES

Inserted by the Financial Services and Markets Act 2000 (Regulated Activities) (Amendment) (No 2) Order 2003, SI 2003/1476, art 16(1), (5), as from 31 October 2004 (in so far as relating to contracts of long-term care insurance), and as from 14 January 2005 (otherwise); for transitional provisions see arts 22–27 of that Order at **[4665]** et seq.

6—(1) An activity of the kind specified by article 53 of the Regulated Activities Order (advising on investments) where the advice in question falls within [paragraph (2), (3) or (5)].

(2) Subject to paragraph (4), advice falls within this paragraph in so far as—

(a) it is given to an individual (or his agent) other than where the individual acts—

(i) in connection with the carrying on of a business of any kind by himself or by an undertaking of which he is, or would become as a result of the transaction to which the advice relates, a controller; or

(ii) in his capacity as a trustee of an occupational pension scheme;

(b) it consists of a recommendation to buy or subscribe for a particular [security or contractually based investment]; and

(c) the transaction to which the advice relates would be made—

(i) with a person acting in the course of carrying on the business of buying, selling, subscribing for or underwriting the [security or contractually based investment], whether as principal or agent;

(ii) on an investment exchange or any other market to which that investment is admitted for dealing; or

(iii) in response to an invitation to subscribe for [such an investment] which is, or is to be, admitted for dealing on an investment exchange or any other market.

(3) Subject to paragraph (4), advice falls within this paragraph in so far as it consists of a recommendation to a member of a personal pension scheme (or his agent) to dispose of any rights or interests which the member has in or under the scheme.

(4) Advice does not fall within paragraph (2) or (3) if it endorses a corresponding recommendation given to the individual (or, as the case may be, the member) by an authorised person with permission to give advice in relation to the proposed transaction or a person who is an exempt person in relation to the giving of such advice.

[(5) Advice falls within this paragraph in so far as—

(a) it relates to a transaction for the sale or purchase of rights under a contract of insurance; and

(b) it is given by a person who is not included in the record of insurance intermediaries.]

[4169]

NOTES

Paras (1), (2): words in square brackets substituted by the Financial Services and Markets Act 2000 (Regulated Activities) (Amendment) (No 2) Order 2003, SI 2003/1476, art 16(1), (6)(a), (b), as from 31 October 2004 (in so far as relating to contracts of long-term care insurance), and as from 14 January 2005 (otherwise); for transitional provisions see arts 22–27 of that Order at **[4665]** et seq.

Para (5): added by SI 2003/1476, art 16(1), (6)(c), as from 31 October 2004 (in so far as relating to contracts of long-term care insurance), and as from 14 January 2005 (otherwise); for transitional provisions see arts 22–27 of that Order at **[4665]** et seq.

[6A—(1) An activity of the kind specified by article 53A of the Regulated Activities Order (advising on regulated mortgage contracts) where the advice in question falls within paragraph (2).

(2) Subject to paragraph (3), advice falls within this paragraph in so far as—

(a) it consists of a recommendation, given to an individual, to enter as borrower into a regulated mortgage contract with a particular person; and

(b) in entering into a regulated mortgage contract that person would be carrying on an activity of the kind specified by article 61(1) of the Regulated Activities Order (regulated mortgage contracts).

(3) Advice does not fall within paragraph (2) if it endorses a corresponding recommendation given to the individual by an authorised person with permission to carry on an activity of the kind specified by article 53A of the Regulated Activities Order or a person who is an exempt person in relation to an activity of that kind.]

[4169A]

NOTES

Inserted by the Financial Services and Markets Act 2000 (Regulated Activities) (Amendment) (No 1) Order 2003, SI 2003/1475, art 24(1), (3), as from 31 October 2004; for transitional provisions see arts 26–29 at **[4659]** et seq.

[[6B]—(1) An activity of the kind specified by article 61(1) or (2) of the Regulated Activities Order (regulated mortgage contracts).

(2) Paragraph (1) does not apply to an activity carried on by a person in his capacity as a trustee or personal representative where the borrower under the regulated mortgage contract in question is a beneficiary under the trust, will or intestacy.]

[4170]

NOTES

Inserted (as art 6A) by the Financial Services and Markets Act 2000 (Miscellaneous Provisions) Order 2001, SI 2001/3650, art 3(c), as from 31 October 2004; renumbered as art 6B by the Financial Services and Markets Act 2000 (Regulated Activities) (Amendment) (No 1) Order 2003, SI 2003/1475, art 24(1), (2), as from 31 October 2004 (for transitional provisions see arts 26–29 at **[4659]** et seq).

[6C—(1) An activity of the kind specified by article 53B of the Regulated Activities Order (advising on regulated home reversion plans) where the advice in question falls within paragraph (2).

(2) Subject to paragraph (3), advice falls within this paragraph in so far as—

(a) it consists of a recommendation, given to an individual to enter as reversion seller or plan provider into a regulated home reversion plan with a particular person; and

(b) in entering into a regulated home reversion plan that person would be carrying on an activity of the kind specified by article 63B(1) of the Regulated Activities Order (regulated home reversion plans).

(3) Advice does not fall within paragraph (2) if it endorses a corresponding recommendation given to the individual by an authorised person with permission to carry on an activity of the kind specified by article 53B of the Regulated Activities Order or a person who is an exempt person in relation to an activity of that kind.]

[4170A]

NOTES

Commencement: 6 April 2007.

Inserted, together with arts 6D–6F, by the Financial Services and Markets Act 2000 (Regulated Activities) (Amendment) (No 2) Order 2006, SI 2006/2383, art 32(1), (3), as from 6 April 2007 (for the full commencement details of SI 2006/2383, see art 1 of that Order at **[4820]**).

[6D—(1) An activity of the kind specified by article 63B(1) or (2) of the Regulated Activities Order (regulated home reversion plans).

(2) Paragraph (1) does not apply to an activity carried on by a person in his capacity as a trustee or personal representative where the reversion seller under the regulated home reversion plan in question is a beneficiary under the trust, will or intestacy.]

[4170B]

NOTES

Commencement: 6 April 2007

Inserted as noted to art 6C at **[4170A]**.

[6E—(1) An activity of the kind specified by article 53C of the Regulated Activities Order (advising on regulated home purchase plans) where the advice in question falls within paragraph (2).

(2) Subject to paragraph (3), advice falls within this paragraph in so far as—

(a) it consists of a recommendation, given to an individual to enter as home purchaser into a regulated home purchase plan with a particular person; and

(b) in entering into a regulated home purchase plan that person would be carrying on an activity of the kind specified by article 63F(1) of the Regulated Activities Order (regulated home purchase plans).

(3) Advice does not fall within paragraph (2) if it endorses a corresponding recommendation given to the individual by an authorised person with permission to carry on an activity of the kind specified by article 53C of the Regulated Activities Order or a person who is an exempt person in relation to an activity of that kind.]

[4170C]

NOTES

Commencement: 6 April 2007.

Inserted as noted to art 6C at **[4170A]**.

[6F—(1) An activity of the kind specified by article 63F(1) or (2) of the Regulated Activities Order (regulated home purchase plans).

(2) Paragraph (1) does not apply to an activity carried on by a person in his capacity as a trustee or personal representative where the home purchaser under the regulated home purchase plan in question is a beneficiary under the trust, will or intestacy.]

[4170D]

NOTES

Commencement: 6 April 2007.

Inserted as noted to art 6C at **[4170A]**.

7—(1) Advising a person to become a member of a particular Lloyd's syndicate.

(2) Paragraph (1) does not apply to advice which endorses that of an authorised person with permission to give such advice or a person who is an exempt person in relation to the giving of such advice.

[4171]

8 Agreeing to carry on any of the activities mentioned in articles 4 to 7 other than the activities mentioned in article 4(a), [(aa),] (b), (d) and (e).

[4172]

NOTES

Reference to "(aa)" in square brackets inserted by the Financial Services and Markets Act 2000 (Regulated Activities) (Amendment) Order 2002, SI 2002/682, art 7(2), as from 27 April 2002, subject to transitional provisions in relation to persons issuing electronic money immediately before that date contained in art 9 at **[4637]**.

OPEN-ENDED INVESTMENT COMPANIES REGULATIONS 2001

(SI 2001/1228)

NOTES

These Regulations have been omitted from this Edition of the *Company Law Handbook* in order to create space for other legislation (ie, the Companies Act 2006 and the associated destination and derivation tables). They were printed in full in the 20th Edition of this work (at p 1656 et seq) and, as of 1 July 2007, they had not been amended since the publication of that Edition. These Regulations are, however, included in the CD version of this work (which may be ordered from the LexisNexis Butterworths Customer Services Department) and can be accessed in the online version of the *Company Law Handbook* which is updated fortnightly (at www.lexisnexis.com/uk/legal). They are also printed in full in the 8th Edition of *Butterworths Financial Services Law Handbook* (February 2007).

[4173]–[4263]

FINANCIAL SERVICES AND MARKETS ACT 2000 (FINANCIAL PROMOTION) ORDER 2001 (NOTE)

(SI 2001/1335)

NOTES

This Order was revoked and replaced by the Financial Services and Markets Act 2000 (Financial Promotion) Order 2005, SI 2005/1529 (at **[4717]**), as from 1 July 2005.

[4264]–[4350]

FINANCIAL SERVICES AND MARKETS ACT 2000 (SERVICE OF NOTICES) REGULATIONS 2001

(SI 2001/1420)

NOTES

Made: 10 April 2001.

Authority: Financial Services and Markets Act 2000, ss 414, 428(3).

Commencement: 18 June 2001 (being the date on which the Financial Services and Markets Act 2000, s 1 came into force); see reg 1 at **[4351]**. Where any provision in this work (including any inserted or substituted provision) came into force for all purposes on or before 1 July 2005, commencement information is not noted at provision level.

These Regulations are reproduced as amended by: the Enterprise Act 2002; the Financial Services and Markets Act 2000 (Service of Notices) (Amendment) Regulations 2005, SI 2005/274.

ARRANGEMENT OF REGULATIONS

1 Citation, commencement and interpretation

(1) These Regulations may be cited as the Financial Services and Markets Act 2000 (Service of Notices) Regulations 2001, and come into force on the day on which section 1 of the Act comes into force.

(2) In these Regulations—

"the Act" means the Financial Services and Markets Act 2000;

"appropriate person" means—

(a) an individual to whom a relevant document may be given, in accordance with regulation 3(1), in order to give that document to a person who is not an individual, or

(b) in the case of a relevant document given to an appointed representative, his principal;

"business day" means any day except Saturday, Sunday or a bank holiday, where "bank holiday" includes Christmas Day and Good Friday;

"document" means a notice, direction or document (as defined in section 417 of the Act) of any kind;

"host state regulator" has the meaning given in paragraph 11 of Schedule 3 to the Act;

"an investigating authority" means the Authority or the Secretary of State, as the case may be;

"investigator" means a person appointed by an investigating authority under section 97(2), 167, 168(3) or (5), 169(1)(b) or 284 of the Act, or under regulations made under section 262 of the Act, to carry out an investigation;

"nominee", in relation to any person to whom a document is to be given ("A"), means a person ("B") who is authorised for the time being to receive relevant documents on behalf of A, to whom relevant documents may be given—

(a) if A has notified the Authority in writing that B is so authorised, by any relevant authority, or

(b) if A has notified a relevant authority in writing that B is so authorised, by that relevant authority;

"ombudsman" has the meaning given in paragraph 1 of Schedule 17 to the Act;

"relevant authority" means—

(a) the Authority,

(b) the Secretary of State,

(c) the [Office of Fair Trading],

(d) an investigator,

(e) the scheme manager,

(f) the scheme operator, or

(g) an ombudsman;

"a relevant document" means—

(a) a document in relation to which a provision of or made under the Act (other than a provision of or made under Part IX or Part XXIV of the Act) requires a document of that kind to be given, or

(b) where a provision of or made under the Act (other than a provision of or made under Part IX or Part XXIV) authorises the imposition of a requirement, a document by which such a requirement is imposed.

(3) For the purposes of these Regulations, the scheme operator and ombudsmen are treated as the same relevant authority (with the effect, in particular, that a document given to one is to be treated as also given to the other).

(4) In these Regulations references to a requirement to give any document apply however the requirement is expressed (and so, in particular, include any requirement for a document to be served or sent).

(5) For the purposes of these Regulations, writing includes any means of electronic communication which may be processed to produce a legible text.

(6) These Regulations have effect subject to any contrary provision made by a relevant authority under the Act with respect to the service of documents.

[4351]

NOTES

Para (2): in definition "relevant authority" words in square brackets substituted by virtue of the Enterprise Act 2002, s 2(1), as from 1 April 2003 (see further the note below).

Substitution of references to the Director General of Fair Trading: the Enterprise Act 2002, s 2(1) provides that, as from the coming into force of that section (on 1 April 2003, see the Enterprise Act 2002 (Commencement No 2, Transitional and Transitory Provisions) Order 2003, SI 2003/766), the functions of the Director General of Fair Trading, his property, rights and liabilities are transferred to the Office of Fair Trading. Accordingly, (by virtue of s 2(2), (3) of the 2002 Act) the office of the Director is abolished, and any enactment, etc, which refers to the Director shall have effect, so far as necessary for the purposes of or in consequence of anything being transferred, as if any reference to the Director were a reference to the Office of Fair Trading. For transitional provisions in connection with the transfer, see s 276(1) of, and Sch 24, para 6 to, the 2002 Act.

FSMA 2000, s 1 came into force on 18 June 2001 (see the Financial Services and Markets Act 2000 (Commencement No 3) Order 2001, SI 2001/1820).

2 Methods of service

(1) This regulation has effect in relation to any relevant document given by a relevant authority to any person ("the recipient") other than a relevant authority.

(2) Any such document must be given by one of the following methods—

- (a) by delivering it to the recipient, the recipient's nominee or the appropriate person;
- (b) by leaving it at the proper address of the recipient, the recipient's nominee or the appropriate person, determined in accordance with regulation 4;
- (c) by posting it to that address; or
- (d) by transmitting it by fax or other means of electronic communication to the recipient, the recipient's nominee or the appropriate person, in accordance with regulation 5.

(3) For the purposes of this regulation, "posting" a relevant document means sending that document pre-paid by a postal service which seeks to deliver documents by post within the United Kingdom no later than the next working day in all or the majority of cases, and to deliver by post outside the United Kingdom within such a period as is reasonable in all the circumstances.

[4352]

3 Appropriate person to be served

(1) A relevant document which is required to be given by a relevant authority to a person (other than a relevant authority) who is not an individual may—

- (a) where that person is a body corporate (other than a limited liability partnership), be given to the secretary or the clerk of that body, or to any person holding a senior position in that body;
- (b) where that person is a limited liability partnership, be given to any designated member, within the meaning given in section 8 of the Limited Liability Partnerships Act 2000;
- (c) where that person is a partnership (other than a limited liability partnership), be given to any partner;
- (d) where that person is an unincorporated association other than a partnership, be given to any member of the governing body of the association.

(2) A relevant document which is required to be given to an appointed representative may be given to his principal.

(3) For the purposes of this regulation, persons holding a senior position in a body corporate include—

- (a) a director, the treasurer, secretary or chief executive, and

(b) a manager or other officer of that body who, in either case, has responsibility for the matter to which the relevant document relates.

[4353]

4 Proper address for service

(1) The proper address—

(a) in the case of any person who is required by any provision of or made under the Act to provide to the Authority an address of a place in the United Kingdom for the service of documents, is the address so provided, and

(b) in the case of a person to whom no such requirement applies and subject to paragraph (3), is any current address provided by that person as an address for service of relevant documents.

(2) In the case of any person who has not provided an address as mentioned in paragraph (1), the proper address is the last known address of that person (whether of his residence, or of a place where he carries on business or is employed), or any address under such of the following provisions as may be applicable—

(a) in the case of a body corporate (other than a limited liability partnership), its secretary or its clerk, the address of its registered or principal office in the United Kingdom;

(b) in the case of a limited liability partnership or any of its designated members, the address of its registered or principal office in the United Kingdom;

(c) in the case of a partnership (other than a limited liability partnership) or any of its partners, the address of its principal office in the United Kingdom;

(d) in the case of an unincorporated association other than a partnership, or its governing body, the address of its principal office in the United Kingdom;

(e) in the case of a member of a designated professional body, if the member does not have a place of business in the United Kingdom, the address of that body.

(3) Where the address mentioned in paragraph (1)(b) is situated in a country or territory other than the United Kingdom, a relevant authority may give a relevant document by leaving it at, or posting it to, any applicable address of a place in the United Kingdom falling within paragraph (2).

[4354]

5 Service by electronic means of communication

(1) A relevant authority may give a relevant document by fax only if the person to whom it is to be given has indicated in writing to that authority (and has not withdrawn the indication)—

(a) that he is willing to receive relevant documents by fax, and

(b) the fax number to which such documents should be sent.

(2) If a relevant authority gives a relevant document by fax it must, by the end of the business day following the day on which it did so, send a copy of that document to the person to whom the document is to be given by any method specified in regulation 2 other than fax.

(3) A relevant authority may give a relevant document by any other electronic means of communication only if the person to whom it is to be given—

(a) has indicated in writing to that authority (and has not withdrawn the indication) that he is willing to receive relevant documents by those means, and

(b) has provided, in writing to that authority for this purpose, an e-mail address, or other electronic identification such as an ISDN or other telephonic link number.

(4) A fax number, e-mail address or other electronic identification provided to the Authority for the purpose of accepting the service of relevant documents is sufficient indication, for any relevant authority, for the purposes of paragraph (1) or (3).

[4355]

6 Deemed service

(1) Subject to regulation 11, a relevant document which is given by a relevant authority to any person in accordance with these Regulations is to be treated as having been received on the day shown in the table below.

Method of giving	*Deemed day of receipt*
Leaving the document at the proper address	The business day after the day on which it is left at the proper address
Post to an address in the United Kingdom	The second business day after posting
Post to an address in any EEA State (other than the United Kingdom)	The fifth business day after posting
Fax	The business day after the day on which the document is transmitted
Other electronic means of communication	The business day after the day on which the document is transmitted

(2) Where a relevant document is given by fax, that document is to be treated as having been received on the deemed day of receipt of the fax, determined in accordance with paragraph (1), regardless of whether a relevant authority has sent a copy of that document in accordance with paragraph (2) of regulation 5.

[(3) Where—

(a) a notice given under section 53(4) (exercise of own-initiative power: procedure) of the Act states that a variation of an authorised person's Part IV permission takes effect immediately,

(b) a notice given under section 78(2) (discontinuance or suspension: procedure) of the Act states that a discontinuance or suspension of the listing of any securities takes effect immediately, or

(c) a notice given under section 259(3) (procedure on giving directions under section 257 and varying them on Authority's own initiative) of the Act, or under regulation 27 (procedure on giving directions under regulation 25 and varying them on Authority's own initiative) of the Open-Ended Investment Companies Regulations 2001 states that a direction to which it relates takes effect immediately,

that notice is to be treated as having been received at the time it is in fact received if that is earlier than the day on which paragraph (1) would otherwise require it to be treated as having been received.]

[4356]

NOTES

Para (3): added by the Financial Services and Markets Act 2000 (Service of Notices) (Amendment) Regulations 2005, SI 2005/274, reg 2, as from 6 April 2005.

7 Service on a relevant authority

(1) Subject to paragraphs (2) and (3) and regulations 8 and 10, a relevant document which is to be given to a relevant authority may be given by any method of serving or transmitting documents.

(2) Where a relevant document is given by delivering it to the relevant authority, it must be delivered—

(a) to the employee or other individual with responsibility for the matter to which the document relates, if the identity of that individual is known, or

(b) in any other case, to the published address of that authority.

(3) Where a relevant document is given to a relevant authority by leaving it at, or posting it to, the address of a relevant authority, it must be left at or posted to the published address of that authority.

(4) For the purposes of this regulation, "posting" a document means sending it by a pre-paid postal service.

[4357]

8 Electronic service on a relevant authority

(1) Where a relevant document which is to be given to a relevant authority is given by fax or other electronic means it must be sent to a fax number, e-mail address or other electronic identification—

(a) which has been notified to the sender by the relevant authority as the appropriate number, address or other electronic identification for the purpose of receiving relevant documents of the kind in question, or
(b) in all other cases, which has been published by the relevant authority for the purpose of receiving relevant documents.

(2) Where any provision of or made under the Act requires a person to give a relevant document to the Authority before the end of a specified period, that person may give that document by fax only if by the end of the business day following the day on which he did so, he sends a copy of that document to the Authority by any method other than fax.

[4358]

9 Day of service on a relevant authority

(1) No relevant document which is to be given to a relevant authority is to be treated as given until it is received by that authority in legible form, and for the purposes of any provision of or made under the Act which requires a relevant authority to take any action within a specified period beginning with the day on which a document was received by that authority, that day is the day on which the document is actually received in legible form.

(2) For the purposes of paragraph (1), where a relevant document is given by fax and a copy sent in accordance with paragraph (2) of regulation 8, that document is to be treated as given to the Authority on either the day on which the fax is actually received by the Authority or the day on which the copy is actually received by the Authority, whichever day is the earlier.

[4359]

10 Compliance with a requirement to serve a document on the Authority by a specified day

(1) For the purposes of any provision of or made under the Act which requires a person to give a document to the Authority before the end of a specified period, that person is to be regarded as having complied with that requirement (irrespective of the day on which the document is in fact received by the Authority if it is sent by post, fax or other electronic means) if he sends the document to the Authority in accordance with any applicable directions before the end of the specified period or, where no such directions apply, if he—
(a) delivers the document to an employee of the Authority with responsibility for the matter to which the document relates before the end of the specified period;
(b) leaves the document at the Authority's address before the end of the specified period, and obtains a time stamped receipt;
(c) posts the document to the Authority's address before the final day of the specified period;
(d) sends the document to the Authority by fax before the end of the specified period, provided that he has also sent or subsequently sends a copy of that document in accordance with paragraph (2) of regulation 8; or
(e) sends the document to the Authority by other electronic means of communication before the end of the specified period, and obtains electronic confirmation of receipt.

(2) For the purposes of this regulation—
(a) "posts" means—
(i) where the person who is required to give a document is located in the United Kingdom, sending that document pre-paid by a postal service which seeks to deliver documents by post within the United Kingdom no later than the next working day in all or the majority of cases, and
(ii) where the person who is required to give a document is located outside the United Kingdom, sending that document pre-paid by a postal service which seeks to deliver documents by post in the fastest time which is reasonable in the circumstances;
(b) "applicable direction" means any direction given by the Authority under the Act which specifies the manner in which the relevant document in question is to be given.

[4360]

11 Day of service on a host state regulator

No relevant document is to be treated as given by a relevant authority to a host state regulator until it is received by that regulator.

[4361]

FINANCIAL SERVICES AND MARKETS ACT 2000 (COMPENSATION SCHEME: ELECTING PARTICIPANTS) REGULATIONS 2001

(SI 2001/1783)

NOTES

Made: 9 May 2001.

Authority: Financial Services and Markets Act 2000, ss 213(10), 214(5), 224(4), 417(1), 428(3).

Commencement: 18 June 2001 (see reg 1 at **[4362]**). Where any provision in this work (including any inserted or substituted provision) came into force for all purposes on or before 1 July 2005, commencement information is not noted at provision level.

These Regulations are reproduced as amended by: the Financial Services and Markets Act 2000 (Regulated Activities) (Amendment) (No 2) Order 2003, SI 2003/1476; the Collective Investment Schemes (Miscellaneous Amendments) Regulations 2003, SI 2003/2066; the Capital Requirements Regulations 2006, SI 2006/3221.

Gibraltar: as to the application of these Regulations, with modifications, to Gibraltar, see the Financial Services and Markets Act 2000 (Gibraltar) Order 2001, SI 2001/3084 at **[4504]**.

1 Citation, commencement and interpretation

(1) These Regulations may be cited as the Financial Services and Markets Act 2000 (Compensation Scheme: Electing Participants) Regulations 2001 and come into force on 18th June 2001.

(2) In these Regulations—

"branch"—

(a) in relation to an investment firm, has the meaning given by Article 1.5 of the investor-compensation schemes directive;

(b) in relation to a credit institution, has the meaning given by Article 1.5 of the deposit-guarantee schemes directive;

[(c) in relation to a relevant management company, has the meaning given by Article 1.5 of the investor-compensation schemes directive (as applied by Article 5f.2 of the UCITS directive);]

"credit institution" has the meaning given by [Article 4(1)] of the banking consolidation directive;

"deposit-guarantee schemes directive" means Council and European Parliament Directive 94/19/EC on deposit-guarantee schemes;

"depositor" has the same meaning as in the deposit-guarantee schemes directive;

"Financial Services Compensation Scheme" means the compensation scheme established pursuant to Part XV of the Act;

"home State deposit-guarantee scheme" means—

(a) in relation to a credit institution which is exempted by the EEA State in which that institution has its head office from the obligation to belong to a deposit-guarantee scheme by virtue of belonging to a system which protects the credit institution as mentioned in Article 3 of the deposit-guarantee schemes directive, that system; and

(b) in all other cases, the deposit-guarantee scheme officially recognised by that EEA State for the purposes of Article 3.1 of the deposit-guarantee schemes directive;

"home State investor-compensation scheme" means—

(a) in relation to a credit institution which is exempted by the EEA State in which that institution has its head office from the obligation to belong to an investor-compensation scheme by virtue of Article 2.1 of the investor-compensation schemes directive (participation in a system that protects the credit institution), that system; and

(b) in all other cases, the investor-compensation scheme officially recognised by that EEA State for the purposes of Article 2.1 of the investor-compensation schemes directive;

["insurance intermediary" means an insurance intermediary (within the meaning of Article 2(5) of the insurance mediation directive) or a reinsurance intermediary (within the meaning of Article 2(6) of that Directive);]

"investment firm" has the meaning given by Article 1.1 of the investor-compensation schemes directive;

PART IV STATUTORY INSTRUMENTS

"investor" has the meaning given by Article 1.4 of the investor-compensation schemes directive;

"investor-compensation schemes directive" means the Council and European Parliament Directive 97/9/EC on investor-compensation schemes;

["relevant management company" means an EEA firm falling within paragraph 5(f) of Schedule 3 to the Act which—

(a) is authorised by its home state regulator to provide services of the kind specified by Article 5.3(a) of the UCITS directive (management of portfolios of investments); and

(b) is providing those services in the United Kingdom].

[4362]

NOTES

Para (2): para (c) of the definition "branch" inserted, and definition "relevant management company" added, by the Collective Investment Schemes (Miscellaneous Amendments) Regulations 2003, SI 2003/2066, reg 7(a), as from 13 February 2004; words in square brackets in definition "credit institution" substituted by the Capital Requirements Regulations 2006, SI 2006/3221, reg 29(4), Sch 6, para 7, as from 1 January 2007; definition "insurance intermediary" inserted by the Financial Services and Markets Act 2000 (Regulated Activities) (Amendment) (No 2) Order 2003, SI 2003/1476, art 15(1), (2), as from 31 October 2004 (in so far as relating to contracts of long-term care insurance), and as from 14 January 2005 (otherwise), for transitional provisions see arts 22–27 of that Order at **[4665]** et seq.

2 Persons not to be regarded as relevant persons

For the purposes of section 213(10) of the Act (certain persons not to be regarded as relevant persons unless they elect to participate), the following categories are prescribed—

(a) any investment firm; …

(b) any credit institution[; …

(c) any insurance intermediary][; and

(d) any relevant management company.]

[4363]

NOTES

Word omitted from para (a) revoked, and para (c) and the word immediately preceding it inserted, by the Financial Services and Markets Act 2000 (Regulated Activities) (Amendment) (No 2) Order 2003, SI 2003/1476, art 15(1), (3), as from 31 October 2004 (in so far as relating to contracts of long-term care insurance), and as from 14 January 2005 (otherwise) (for transitional provisions see arts 22–27 of that Order at **[4665]** et seq); word omitted from para (b) revoked, and para (d) and the word immediately preceding it inserted, by the Collective Investment Schemes (Miscellaneous Amendments) Regulations 2003, SI 2003/2066, reg 7(b), as from 13 February 2004.

3 Persons who may elect to participate

(1) For the purposes of section 214(5) of the Act (persons who may elect to participate), the following categories are prescribed—

(a) any investment firm [or relevant management company] which has established a branch in the United Kingdom in exercise of an EEA right and is a member of a home State investor-compensation scheme which meets the condition in paragraph (2); …

(b) any credit institution which has established a branch in the United Kingdom in exercise of an EEA right and is a member of a home State deposit-guarantee scheme which meets the condition in paragraph (3)[; and

(c) any insurance intermediary which is not an investment firm or a credit institution].

(2) The condition mentioned in paragraph (1)(a) is that the scope or level (including percentage) of the protection afforded to investors by the Financial Services Compensation Scheme exceeds that afforded by the home State investor-compensation scheme.

(3) The condition mentioned in paragraph (1)(b) is that the scope or level (including percentage) of the protection afforded to depositors by the Financial Services Compensation Scheme exceeds that afforded by the home State deposit-guarantee scheme.

[4364]

NOTES

Para (1): words in square brackets in sub-para (a) inserted by the Collective Investment Schemes (Miscellaneous Amendments) Regulations 2003, SI 2003/2066, reg 7(c), as from 13 February 2004; word omitted from sub-para (a) revoked, and sub-para (c) and the word immediately preceding it inserted, by the Financial Services and Markets Act 2000 (Regulated Activities) (Amendment) (No 2) Order 2003, SI 2003/1476, art 15(1), (4), as from 31 October 2004 (in so far as relating to contracts of long-term care insurance), and as from 14 January 2005 (otherwise) (for transitional provisions see arts 22–27 of that Order at **[4665]** et seq).

4 Persons in respect of whom inspection under section 224 does not apply

For the purposes of section 224(4) of the Act (power to inspect documents held by Official Receiver), the following categories are prescribed—

(a) any investment firm; …

(b) any credit institution[; …

(c) any insurance intermediary][; and

(d) any relevant management company.]

[4365]–[4367]

NOTES

Word omitted from para (a) revoked, and para (c) and the word immediately preceding it inserted, by the Financial Services and Markets Act 2000 (Regulated Activities) (Amendment) (No 2) Order 2003, SI 2003/1476, art 15(1), (5), as from 31 October 2004 (in so far as relating to contracts of long-term care insurance), and as from 14 January 2005 (otherwise) (for transitional provisions see arts 22–27 of that Order at **[4665]** et seq); word omitted from para (b) revoked, and para (d) and the word immediately preceding it inserted, by the Collective Investment Schemes (Miscellaneous Amendments) Regulations 2003, SI 2003/2066, reg 7(d), as from 13 February 2004.

FINANCIAL SERVICES AND MARKETS ACT 2000 (DISCLOSURE OF INFORMATION BY PRESCRIBED PERSONS) REGULATIONS 2001

(SI 2001/1857)

NOTES

Made: 10 May 2001.

Authority: Financial Services and Markets Act 2000, ss 353(1), 417(1).

Commencement: 18 June 2001 (see reg 1 at **[4368]**). Where any provision in this work (including any inserted or substituted provision) came into force for all purposes on or before 1 July 2005, commencement information is not noted at provision level.

These Regulations are reproduced as amended by: the Financial Services and Markets Act 2000 (Disclosure of Information by Prescribed Persons) (Amendment) Regulations 2005, SI 2005/272.

1 Citation and commencement

These Regulations may be cited as the Financial Services and Markets Act 2000 (Disclosure of Information by Prescribed Persons) Regulations 2001 and come into force on 18th June 2001.

[4368]

2 Interpretation

In these Regulations—

"the Act" means the Financial Services and Markets Act 2000;

"Schedule person" means a person referred to in the Schedule;

"scheme person" means the scheme manager, the scheme operator, or a member of the panel of ombudsmen appointed by the scheme operator pursuant to paragraph 4 of Schedule 17 to the Act.

[4369]

3 Permitted disclosure

(1) Subject to paragraph (2), Schedule persons and scheme persons are permitted to disclose information to which this regulation applies—

(a) for the purpose of enabling or assisting them to discharge their functions under the Act, or any rules or regulations made thereunder; or

PART IV STATUTORY INSTRUMENTS

(b) to the Authority, for the purpose of enabling or assisting the Authority to discharge any of its public functions.

(2) Schedule persons are permitted to disclose information in accordance with paragraph (1)(b) only if—

(a) the disclosure is made in good faith; and

(b) the person disclosing the information reasonably believes that the information is relevant to the discharge of a public function by the Authority.

(3) This regulation applies to the following kinds of information—

(a) information received by Schedule persons or scheme persons for the purposes of, or in the discharge of, any functions conferred on them by or under the Act;

(b) other information received by Schedule persons if the information is, or would have been relevant to the performance of those functions; or

(c) the opinions of Schedule persons or scheme persons in relation to information falling within sub-paragraph (a) or (b).

(4) This regulation does not apply to confidential information within the meaning of section 348(2) of the Act.

[4370]

SCHEDULE

Regulation 2

A Schedule person is a person who is performing or has performed any of the following functions—

(a) the verification of information in a manner required by the Authority pursuant to section 165(6)(a) of the Act;

(b) the authentication of a document in a manner required by the Authority pursuant to section 165(6)(b) of the Act;

(c) the making of a report under section 166 of the Act;

[(ca) the conduct of an investigation under section 113(2) of the Act;]

(d) the conduct of an investigation under section 167, 168(3) or (5) or 169(1)(b) of the Act;

(e) the conduct of an investigation under section 284 of the Act;

[(ea) the conduct of an investigation under section 376(10) of the Act;]

(f) the conduct of an investigation pursuant to regulations made under section 262 of the Act.

[4371]

NOTES

Paras (ca), (ea) inserted by the Financial Services and Markets Act 2000 (Disclosure of Information by Prescribed Persons) (Amendment) Regulations 2005, SI 2005/272, reg 2, as from 6 April 2005.

FINANCIAL SERVICES AND MARKETS ACT 2000 (DISCLOSURE OF CONFIDENTIAL INFORMATION) REGULATIONS 2001

(SI 2001/2188)

NOTES

Made: 15 June 2001.

Authority: Financial Services and Markets Act 2000, ss 349(1)(b), (2), (3), 417(1), 426, 427, 428(3).

Commencement: 18 June 2001 (see reg 1 at **[4372]**). Where any provision in this work (including any inserted or substituted provision) came into force for all purposes on or before 1 July 2005, commencement information is not noted at provision level.

These Regulations are reproduced as amended by: the Enterprise Act 2002; the Financial Services and Markets Act 2000 (Disclosure of Confidential Information) (Amendment) Regulations 2001, SI 2001/3437; the Financial Services and Markets Act 2000 (Disclosure of Confidential Information) (Amendment) (No 2) Regulations 2001, SI 2001/3624; the Electronic Commerce Directive (Financial Services and Markets) Regulations 2002, SI 2002/1775; the Financial Services and Markets Act 2000 (Disclosure of Confidential Information) (Amendment) Regulations 2003, SI 2003/693; the Financial Services and Markets Act 2000 (Disclosure of Confidential Information) (Amendment) Regulations 2003, SI 2003/1092 (revoked); the Insurance Mediation Directive (Miscellaneous Amendments) Regulations 2003, SI 2003/1473; the Collective Investment Schemes (Miscellaneous Amendments)

Regulations 2003, SI 2003/2066; the Financial Services and Markets Act 2000 (Disclosure of Confidential Information) (Amendment) (No 2) Regulations 2003, SI 2003/2174; the Financial Services and Markets Act 2000 (Disclosure of Confidential Information) (Amendment) (No 3) Regulations 2003, SI 2003/2817; the Financial Conglomerates and Other Financial Groups Regulations 2004, SI 2004/1862; the Life Assurance Consolidation Directive (Consequential Amendments) Regulations 2004, SI 2004/3379; the Financial Services and Markets Act 2000 (Disclosure of Confidential Information) (Amendment) Regulations 2005, SI 2005/3071; the Capital Requirements Regulations 2006, SI 2006/3221; the Financial Services and Markets Act 2000 (Disclosure of Confidential Information) (Amendment) Regulations 2006, SI 2006/3413.

ARRANGEMENT OF REGULATIONS

PART I
PRELIMINARY

1 Citation and Commencement

These Regulations may be cited as the Financial Services and Markets Act 2000 (Disclosure of Confidential Information) Regulations 2001 and come into force on 18th June 2001.

[4372]

2 Interpretation

In these Regulations—

"the Act" means the Financial Services and Markets Act 2000;

"Authority worker" means—

(a) a person who is or has been employed by the Authority; or

(b) an auditor or expert instructed by the Authority;

["conglomerates directive" means Directive 2002/87/EC of the European Parliament and of the Council of 16th December 2002 on the supplementary supervision of credit institutions, insurance undertakings and investment firms in a financial conglomerate and amending Council Directives 73/239/EEC, 79/267/EEC, 92/49/EEC, 92/96/EEC, 93/6/EEC, 93/22/EEC, and Directives 98/78/EC and 2000/12/EC of the European Parliament and of the Council;]

"criminal investigation" means an investigation of any crime, including an investigation of any alleged or suspected crime and an investigation of whether a crime has been committed;

"dependent territory" means the Channel Islands, the Isle of Man and any territory outside the British Islands for whose external relations the United Kingdom is responsible;

"dependent territory regulatory authority" means an overseas regulatory authority which exercises its functions in, and in relation to, a dependent territory;

"directive restrictions" means the restrictions imposed on the disclosure of information by *article 25 of the investment services directive*, [Section 2 of Chapter 1 of Title V of the banking consolidation directive], [Articles 16 and 17 of Directive 2002/83/EC of the European Parliament and of the Council of 5th November 2002 concerning life assurance as amended by the conglomerates directive], article 16 of the third non-life insurance directive, article 50 of the UCITS directive [... and article 9 of the insurance mediation directive];

"disciplinary proceedings authority" means a person responsible for initiating prescribed disciplinary proceedings or determining the outcome of such proceedings;

"EEA competent authority" means a competent authority of an EEA state other than the United Kingdom for the purposes of any of the single market directives, ... ;

"EEA regulatory authority" means an EEA competent authority or an overseas regulatory authority which exercises its functions in, and in relation to, an EEA State other than the United Kingdom;

"former regulated activities" means activities carried on before the coming into force of section 19 of the Act and which constitute—

(a) investment business within the meaning of the Financial Services Act 1986;

(b) deposit-taking business within the meaning of the Banking Act 1987;

(c) insurance business within the meaning of the Insurance Companies Act 1982; or

(d) insurance business within the meaning of the Friendly Societies Act 1992;

"former regulated person" means a person who, at any time before the coming into force of section 19 of the Act, was—

(a) authorised under section 3 or 4 of the Insurance Companies Act 1982;

(b) an authorised person within the meaning of the Financial Services Act 1986, or an appointed representative within the meaning of section 44 (appointed representatives) of that Act;

(c) an authorised institution within the meaning of the Banking Act 1987;

(d) a European institution within the meaning of the Banking Coordination (Second Council Directive) Regulations 1992;

(e) a European investment firm within the meaning of the Investment Services Regulations 1995;

(f) an EC company within the meaning of the Insurance Companies Act 1982 able to carry on direct insurance business through a branch in the United Kingdom, or provide insurance in the United Kingdom by virtue of paragraph 1 or 8 of Schedule 2F to that Act;

(g) a friendly society authorised or treated as authorised for the purposes of Part IV of the Friendly Societies Act 1992, or permitted by virtue of section 31(2) or (3) of that Act to carry on activities without authorisation under that Part; or

(h) a building society authorised or treated as authorised for the purposes of the Building Societies Act 1986;

.....

["markets in financial instruments directive information" means confidential information received by the Authority in the course of discharging its functions as an EEA competent authority under the markets in financial instruments directive;]

"non-EEA regulatory authority" means an overseas regulatory authority other than an EEA regulatory authority or a dependent territory regulatory authority;

"overseas regulatory authority" means—

(a) an authority in a country or territory outside the United Kingdom which exercises any function of a kind mentioned in section 195(4) of the Act; or

(b) an overseas investment exchange or overseas clearing house;

"prescribed disciplinary proceedings" means the disciplinary proceedings prescribed in Schedule 3;

"Secretary of State worker" means—

(a) a person who is or has been employed by the Secretary of State; or

(b) an auditor or expert instructed by the Secretary of State;

"single market directive information" means confidential information received by the Authority in the course of discharging its functions as the competent authority under any of the single market directives [(except for the markets in financial instruments directive)] [or the conglomerates directive];

[["the third non-life insurance directive"] has the meaning given to it by paragraph 3 of Schedule 3 to the Act;]

.....

.....

[4373]

NOTES

Definition "conglomerates directive", and words in second pair of square brackets in definition "single market directive information", inserted by the Financial Conglomerates and Other Financial Groups Regulations 2004, SI 2004/1862, reg 11, as from 10 August 2004.

In definition "directive restrictions" for the words in italics there are substituted the words "articles 54 and 58 of the markets in financial instruments directive" by the Financial Services and Markets Act 2000 (Disclosure of Confidential Information) (Amendment) Regulations 2006, SI 2006/3413, regs 2, 3(a)(i), as from 1 November 2007; words in first pair of square brackets substituted by the Capital Requirements Regulations 2006, SI 2006/3221, reg 29(4), Sch 6, para 8(1), (2), as from 1 January 2007; words in second pair of square brackets substituted by the Life Assurance Consolidation Directive (Consequential Amendments) Regulations 2004, SI 2004/3379, reg 19(1), (2)(a), as from 11 January 2005; words in third pair of square brackets substituted by the Insurance Mediation Directive (Miscellaneous Amendments) Regulations 2003, SI 2003/1473, reg 10, as from 14 January 2005; words omitted revoked by SI 2006/3413, regs 2, 3(a)(ii), as from 20 January 2007.

First words omitted from definition "EEA competent authority", and definitions "the UCITS directive" and "UCITS directive information", revoked by the Collective Investment Schemes (Miscellaneous Amendments) Regulations 2003, SI 2003/2066, reg 12(a), as from 13 February 2004.

Second words omitted from definition "EEA competent authority" revoked by the Financial Services and Markets Act 2000 (Disclosure of Confidential Information) (Amendment) Regulations 2006, SI 2006/3413, regs 2, 3(b), as from 20 January 2007.

Definition "listing particulars directive" revoked by SI 2006/3413, regs 2, 3(c), as from 20 January 2007.

Definition "markets in financial instruments directive information", and words in first pair of square brackets in definition "single market directive information", inserted by SI 2006/3413, regs 2, 3(d), (e), as from 1 November 2007.

The final definition in square brackets was originally inserted (as the definitions "the third life insurance directive" and "the third non-life insurance directive") by the Financial Services and Markets Act 2000 (Disclosure of Confidential Information) (Amendment) Regulations 2003, SI 2003/693, reg 3(a), as from 3 April 2003; words in square brackets subsequently substituted by SI 2004/3379, reg 19(1), (2)(b), as from 11 January 2005.

PART II
DISCLOSURE OF CONFIDENTIAL INFORMATION GENERALLY

3 Disclosure by and to the Authority, the Secretary of State and the Treasury etc

(1) A disclosure of confidential information is permitted when it is made to any person—

(a) by the Authority or an Authority worker for the purpose of enabling or assisting the person making the disclosure to discharge any public functions of the Authority or (if different) of the Authority worker;

(b) by the Secretary of State or a Secretary of State worker for the purpose of

enabling or assisting the person making the disclosure to discharge any public functions of the Secretary of State or (if different) of the Secretary of State worker;
(c) by the Treasury for the purpose of enabling or assisting the Treasury to discharge any of their public functions.

(2) A disclosure of confidential information is permitted when it is made by any primary recipient, or person obtaining the information directly or indirectly from a primary recipient, to the Authority, the Secretary of State or the Treasury for the purpose of enabling or assisting the Authority, the Secretary of State or the Treasury (as the case may be) to discharge any of its, his or their public functions.

(3) Paragraphs (1) and (2) do not permit disclosure in contravention of any of the directive restrictions.

[4374]

4 Disclosure for the purposes of criminal proceedings and investigations

A primary recipient of confidential information, or a person obtaining such information directly or indirectly from a primary recipient, is permitted to disclose such information to any person—
(a) for the purposes of any criminal investigation whatever which is being or may be carried out, whether in the United Kingdom or elsewhere;
(b) for the purposes of any criminal proceedings whatever which have been or may be initiated, whether in the United Kingdom or elsewhere; or
[(ba) for the purposes of any proceedings under Part 2, 3 or 4 of the Proceeds of Crime Act 2002 which have been, or may be initiated;]
(c) for the purpose of initiating or bringing to an end any such investigation or proceedings, or of facilitating a determination of whether it or they should be initiated or brought to an end.

[4375]

NOTES

Para (ba) inserted by the Financial Services and Markets Act 2000 (Disclosure of Confidential Information) (Amendment) (No 2) Regulations 2003, SI 2003/2174, regs 2, 4(a), as from 23 August 2003 (see further the note below).

Note that an identical para (ba) was originally inserted by the Financial Services and Markets Act 2000 (Disclosure of Confidential Information) (Amendment) Regulations 2003, SI 2003/1092, as from 2 May 2003. However, those Regulations were revoked by SI 2003/2174, reg 3, as from 23 August 2003 due to a number of drafting errors contained in those Regulations. The para (ba) as inserted by SI 2003/1092 did not contain any such drafting error so, in effect, has been in operation since 2 May 2003.

5 Disclosure for the purposes of certain other proceedings

(1) Subject to paragraphs (4) and (5), a primary recipient of confidential information, or a person obtaining such information directly or indirectly from a primary recipient, is permitted to disclose such information to—
(a) a person mentioned in paragraph (3) for the purpose of initiating proceedings to which this regulation applies, or of facilitating a determination of whether they should be initiated; or
(b) any person for the purposes of proceedings to which this regulation applies and which have been initiated, or for the purpose of bringing to an end such proceedings, or of facilitating a determination of whether they should be brought to an end.

(2) A person mentioned in paragraph (3) (or a person who is employed by the Authority or the Secretary of State) is permitted to disclose confidential information to any person for a purpose mentioned in paragraph (1)(a).

(3) The persons referred to in paragraphs (1)(a) and (2) are—
(a) the Authority;
(b) the Secretary of State; and
(c) the Department of Enterprise, Trade and Investment in Northern Ireland.

(4) This regulation does not permit the disclosure of information with a view to the institution of, or in connection with, proceedings of the kind referred to in paragraph (6)(e) to the extent that—

(a) the information relates to an authorised person, former authorised person or former regulated person ("A");
(b) the information also relates to another person ("B") who, to the knowledge of the primary recipient (or person obtaining confidential information directly or indirectly from him), is or has been involved in an attempt to rescue A, or A's business, from insolvency or impending insolvency; and
(c) B is not a director, controller or manager of A.

(5) This regulation does not permit disclosure in contravention of any of the directive restrictions.

(6) The proceedings to which this regulation applies are—
(a) civil proceedings arising under or by virtue of the Act, an enactment referred to in section 338 of the Act, the Banking Act 1979, the Friendly Societies Act 1974, the Insurance Companies Act 1982, the Financial Services Act 1986, the Building Societies Act 1986, the Banking Act 1987, the Friendly Societies Act 1992 or the Investment Services Regulations 1995;
(b) proceedings before the Tribunal;
(c) any other civil proceedings to which the Authority is, or is proposed to be, a party;
(d) proceedings under section 7 or 8 of the Company Directors Disqualification Act 1986 or article 10 or 11 of the Companies (Northern Ireland) Order 1989 in respect of a director or former director of an authorised person, former authorised person or former regulated person; or
(e) proceedings under Parts I to VI or IX to X of the Insolvency Act 1986, the Bankruptcy (Scotland) Act 1985 or Parts II to VII or IX or X of the Insolvency (Northern Ireland) Order 1989 in respect of an authorised person, former authorised person or former regulated person.

[4376]

6 Disclosure in pursuance of a Community obligation

A primary recipient of confidential information, or a person receiving such information directly or indirectly from a primary recipient, is permitted to disclose such information in pursuance of a Community obligation.

[4377]

7 Restrictions on use of confidential information

Where confidential information is disclosed under these Regulations to a person other than the Authority, the Secretary of State, the Treasury or the Bank of England, and the disclosure is made subject to any conditions as to the use to which the information may be put, the person to whom the information has been disclosed may not use the information in breach of any such condition, without the consent of the person who disclosed it to him.

[4378]

PART III
DISCLOSURE OF SINGLE MARKET DIRECTIVE INFORMATION …

8 Application of this Part

This Part applies to single market directive information …

[4379]

NOTES

Substituted by the Financial Services and Markets Act 2000 (Disclosure of Confidential Information) (Amendment) Regulations 2006, SI 2006/3413, regs 2, 4, as from 1 November 2007, as follows—

"8 Application of this Part

This Part applies to—
(a) single market directive information; and
(b) markets in financial instruments directive information, where that information has been received from—
(i) an overseas regulatory authority under a cooperation agreement referred to in article 63 of the markets in financial instruments directive; or
(ii) an EEA competent authority under article 58.1 of the markets in financial instruments directive.".

PART IV
STATUTORY INSTRUMENTS

Words omitted (including those from the heading preceding this regulation) revoked by the Collective Investment Schemes (Miscellaneous Amendments) Regulations 2003, SI 2003/2066, reg 12(b), (c), as from 13 February 2004.

9 Disclosure by the Authority or Authority workers to certain other persons

(1) Subject to paragraphs (2) *and (3)*, the Authority or an Authority worker is permitted to disclose information to which this Part applies to a person specified in the first column in Schedule 1 for the purpose of enabling or assisting that person to discharge any of the functions listed beside him in the second column in that Schedule.

(2) Paragraph (1) does not permit disclosure to a person specified in the first column in Part 3 of Schedule 1 unless the disclosure is provided for by a cooperation agreement of the kind referred to in—

- *(a) article 25.3 of the investment services directive;*
- (b) [article 46] of the banking consolidation directive;
- (c) [article 16.3 of the life assurance consolidation directive];
- (d) article 16.3 of the third non-life insurance directive, or
- (e) article 50.4 of the UCITS directive.

[(2A) The references in paragraph (2) to the provisions mentioned in sub-paragraphs (a), … (d) and (e) are to those provisions as replaced by Directive 2000/64/EC of the European Parliament and of the Council of 7 November 2000.]

(3) Paragraph (1) does not permit disclosure to a person specified in the first column in Part 4 of Schedule 1—

- (a) of information obtained from an EEA competent authority, unless that authority has given its express consent to the disclosure; or
- (b) of information obtained in the course of an on-the-spot verification of the kind referred to in—
  - *(i) article 24 of the investment services directive,*
  - (ii) [article 43] of the banking consolidation directive,
  - (iii) [article 11 of the life assurance consolidation directive], or
  - (iv) article 14 of the first non-life insurance directive,

unless the EEA competent authority of the state in which the on-the-spot verification was carried out has given its express consent to the disclosure.

[(3A) Paragraph (1) does not permit disclosure of markets in financial instruments information to a person specified in the first column of Schedule 1 other than a person listed in paragraph (3B) where that information—

- (a) was obtained from an EEA competent authority under article 58.1 of the markets in financial instruments directive ("the directive") or an overseas regulatory authority under a cooperation agreement referred to in article 63 of the directive, and
- (b) that authority indicated at the time of communication that such information must not be disclosed,

unless that authority has given its express consent to the disclosure.

(3B) The persons are—

- (a) the Bank of England,
- (b) the European Central Bank,
- (c) the central bank of any country or territory outside the United Kingdom, or
- (d) a body (other than a central bank) in a country or territory outside the United Kingdom having—
  - (i) functions as a monetary authority; or
  - (ii) responsibility for overseeing payment systems.]

[4380]

NOTES

Para (1): for the words in italics there are substituted the words ", (3) and (3A)" by the Financial Services and Markets Act 2000 (Disclosure of Confidential Information) (Amendment) Regulations 2006, SI 2006/3413, regs 2, 5(a), as from 1 November 2007.

Para (2): words in first pair of square brackets substituted by the Capital Requirements Regulations 2006, SI 2006/3221, reg 29(4), Sch 6, para 8(1), (3), as from 1 January 2007; words in second pair of square brackets substituted by the Life Assurance Consolidation Directive (Consequential

Amendments) Regulations 2004, SI 2004/3379, reg 19(1), (3)(a), as from 11 January 2005 (with regard to this amendment see further the notes below); sub-para (a) substituted by SI 2006/3413, regs 2, 5(b), as from 1 November 2007, as follows—

"(a) article 63 of the markets in financial instruments directive;".

Para (2A): inserted by the Financial Services and Markets Act 2000 (Disclosure of Confidential Information) (Amendment) Regulations 2003, SI 2003/693, reg 3(b), as from 3 April 2003; word omitted revoked by SI 2004/3379, reg 19(1), (3)(b), as from 11 January 2005.

Para (3): words in first pair of square brackets substituted by SI 2006/3221, reg 29(4), Sch 6, para 8(1), (3), (4), as from 1 January 2007; words in second pair of square brackets substituted by SI 2004/3379, reg 19(1), (3)(a), (c), as from 11 January 2005; sub-para (b)(i) revoked by SI 2006/3413, regs 2, 5(c), as from 1 November 2007.

Paras (3A), (3B): added by SI 2006/3413, regs 2, 5(d), as from 1 November 2007.

Note: with regard to the amendment made by SI 2004/3379, reg 19(1), (3)(a) to para (2) above, reg 19(3) actually provides as follows—

"(3) In regulation 9 (disclosure by the authority or authority of workers to certain other persons)—

(a) in paragraph 2(c), for "article 15.3 of the third life assurance directive" substitute "article 16.3 of the life assurance consolidation directive";".

The original words in para (2)(c) above were "article 15.3 of the third life *insurance* directive". However, the amendment has been incorporated as it is believed that this was a drafting error in the 2004 Regulations.

10 Disclosure by Schedule 1 person

A person specified in the first column in Schedule 1 is permitted to disclose information to which this Part applies for the purpose of enabling or assisting him to discharge any of the functions listed beside him in that Schedule.

[4381]

PART IV
DISCLOSURE OF CONFIDENTIAL INFORMATION NOT SUBJECT TO DIRECTIVE RESTRICTIONS

11 Application of this Part

This Part applies to confidential information other than—

(a) single market directive information;

(b), (c) …

[(d) markets in financial instruments directive information, where that information has been received from—

(i) an overseas regulatory authority under a cooperation agreement referred to in article 63 of the markets in financial instruments directive; or

(ii) an EEA competent under article 58.1 of the markets in financial instruments directive,

unless that authority has given its express consent for disclosure that is covered by this Part].

[4382]

NOTES

Para (b) revoked by the Collective Investment Schemes (Miscellaneous Amendments) Regulations 2003, SI 2003/2066, reg 12(d), as from 13 February 2004; para (c) revoked, and para (d) added, by the Financial Services and Markets Act 2000 (Disclosure of Confidential Information) (Amendment) Regulations 2006, SI 2006/3413, regs 2, 6, as from 1 April 2007 (in so far as relating to the revocation of para (c)), and as from 1 November 2007 (in so far as relating to the addition of para (d)).

12 Disclosure by and to a Schedule 1 or 2 person or disciplinary proceedings authority

(1) A primary recipient of information to which this Part applies, or a person obtaining such information directly or indirectly from a primary recipient, is permitted to disclose such information to—

(a) a person specified in the first column in Schedule 1 or 2 for the purpose of enabling or assisting that person to discharge any function listed beside him in the second column in Schedule 1 or 2; or

(b) a disciplinary proceedings authority for the purposes of any prescribed disciplinary proceedings which have been or may be initiated, or for the purpose of initiating or bringing to an end any such proceedings, or of facilitating a determination of whether they should be initiated or brought to an end.

(2) A person specified in the first column in Schedule 1 or 2 is permitted to disclose information to which this Part applies to any person for the purpose of enabling or assisting the person making the disclosure to discharge any function listed beside him in the second column in Schedule 1 or 2.

(3) A disciplinary proceedings authority is permitted to disclose information to which this Part applies to any person for any of the purposes mentioned in paragraph (1)(b).

[4383]

[12A The National Lottery Commission may disclose information to which this Part applies to the National Audit Office for the purpose of enabling or assisting the Comptroller and Auditor General to carry out an examination under Part II of the National Audit Act 1983 in relation to the Commission.]

[4384]

NOTES

Inserted by the Financial Services and Markets Act 2000 (Disclosure of Confidential Information) (Amendment) (No 2) Regulations 2001, SI 2001/3624, reg 2(1), (4), as from 1 December 2001.

[12B Electronic commerce

The Authority may disclose information to which this Part applies for the purpose of publishing that information in accordance with regulation 10(8) of the Electronic Commerce Directive (Financial Services and Markets) Regulations 2002.]

[4384A]

NOTES

Inserted by the Electronic Commerce Directive (Financial Services and Markets) Regulations 2002, SI 2002/1775, reg 16, as from 21 August 2002.

[12C A primary recipient of information to which this Part applies, or a person obtaining such information directly or indirectly from a primary recipient is permitted to disclose such information to any person for the purposes of any proceedings under the Proceeds of Crime Act 2002 which have been or may be initiated.]

[4384B]

NOTES

Inserted by the Financial Services and Markets Act 2000 (Disclosure of Confidential Information) (Amendment) (No 2) Regulations 2003, SI 2003/2174, regs 2, 4(c), as from 23 August 2003 (see further the note below).

Note that this Regulation was originally inserted as reg 12B by the Financial Services and Markets Act 2000 (Disclosure of Confidential Information) (Amendment) Regulations 2003, SI 2003/1092, as from 2 May 2003. However, those Regulations were revoked by SI 2003/2174, reg 3, as from 23 August 2003 due to a number of drafting errors contained in those Regulations (including the fact that this regulation should have been numbered as 12C as a reg 12B had previously been inserted).

PART V
TRANSITIONAL PROVISIONS

13 Interpretation

In this Part—

"pre-commencement information" means information which is subject to restrictions (with or without qualifications or exceptions) on disclosure by virtue of a pre-commencement provision;

"pre-commencement provision" means—

(a) any provision in—

(i) Schedule 2B to the Insurance Companies Act 1982;

(ii) Part VIII of the Financial Services Act 1986;

(iii) Part V of the Banking Act 1987; or

(iv) SRO rules;

which imposes restrictions on the disclosure of information, or creates exceptions or qualifications to such restrictions; or

(b) regulation 48 of the Investment Services Regulations 1995;

"recognised self-regulating organisation" means a body which immediately before the coming into force of section 348 of the Act was a recognised self-regulating organisation within the meaning of section 8(1) of the Financial Services Act 1986, or a recognised self-regulating organisation for friendly societies within the meaning of Schedule 11 to that Act;

"SRO rules" means the rules of a recognised self-regulating organisation;

"transitional information" means information which immediately before the coming into force of section 19 of the Act was subject to restrictions on disclosure by virtue of a pre-commencement provision.

[4385]

14 Disclosure of pre-commencement information

(1) Before the coming into force of section 19 of the Act, each pre-commencement provision is to be treated as permitting the disclosure of pre-commencement information—

(a) in accordance with regulation 3(1) as if it were confidential information;

(b) to the Authority, the Secretary of State or the Treasury for the purpose referred to in regulation 3(2);

(c) to any person for the purposes referred to in regulation 4; and

(d) to—

(i) a person mentioned in regulation 5(3) for the purpose referred to in regulation 5(1)(a); or

(ii) any person for the purposes referred to in regulation 5(1)(b),

but only if the proceedings in question are of the kind referred to in regulation 5(6)(a), (b) or (c).

(2) Paragraph (1) is not to be taken as—

(a) precluding disclosure of pre-commencement information where that is otherwise permitted under the pre-commencement provision in question; or

(b) permitting disclosure in contravention of any of the directive restrictions.

[4386]

15 Disclosure of transitional information

(1) After the coming into force of section 19 of the Act, sections 348, 349 and 352 of the Act apply in relation to transitional information in the same way as they apply in relation to confidential information within the meaning of section 348(2) of the Act.

(2) Paragraph (1) does not apply to transitional information which—

(a) has been made available to the public by virtue of being disclosed in any circumstances in which, or for any purposes for which, disclosure is not precluded by section 348 of the Act or a pre-commencement provision; or

(b) satisfies the criterion set out in section 348(4)(b) of the Act.

(3) For the purposes of sections 348 and 349 of the Act as they apply by virtue of paragraph (1)—

(a) a person who holds transitional information is to be treated as a primary recipient of the information if he—

(i) obtained it as mentioned in paragraph 1(2) or 5(1)(a) of Schedule 2B to the Insurance Companies Act 1982;

(ii) was a primary recipient of the information for the purposes of section 179 of the Financial Services Act 1986;

[(iia) obtained or received it as mentioned in subsection (5) of that section;]

(iii) received it as mentioned in section 82(1)(a) of the Banking Act 1987; or

(iv) received it as mentioned in regulation 48(1) of the Investment Services Regulations 1995;

(b) any other person who holds transitional information is to be treated as having obtained the information directly or indirectly from a primary recipient.

(4) Transitional information which is subject to directive restrictions imposed by the single market directives … is to be treated for the purposes of these Regulations as single market directive information …

PART IV
STATUTORY INSTRUMENTS

(5) Part IV of these Regulations does not apply to transitional information which is subject to directive restrictions imposed by [article 107.3] of the listing particulars directive.

[4387]

NOTES

Para (3): sub-para (a)(iia) inserted by the Financial Services and Markets Act 2000 (Disclosure of Confidential Information) (Amendment) (No 2) Regulations 2001, SI 2001/3624, reg 2(1), (5)(a), as from 1 December 2001.

Para (4): words omitted revoked by the Collective Investment Schemes (Miscellaneous Amendments) Regulations 2003, SI 2003/2066, reg 12(e), as from 13 February 2004.

Para (5): words in square brackets substituted by SI 2001/3624, reg 2(1), (5)(b), as from 1 December 2001.

16 Disclosure by recognised self-regulating organisations

If a recognised self-regulating organisation discloses any information to the Authority for the purpose of enabling or assisting the Authority to discharge functions corresponding to functions of the organisation, the disclosure is not to be taken as a contravention of any duty to which the organisation is subject.

[17 Investment services directive information: transitional provision

In these Regulations confidential information received by the Authority in the course of discharging its functions as an EEA competent authority under Council Directive 93/22/EEC of 10th May 1993 on investment services in the securities field shall be deemed to have been received by the Authority in the course of discharging its functions as an EEA competent authority under the markets in financial instruments directive.]

[4388A]

NOTES

Commencement: 1 November 2007

Inserted by the Financial Services and Markets Act 2000 (Disclosure of Confidential Information) (Amendment) Regulations 2006, SI 2006/3413, regs 2, 7, as from 1 November 2007.

SCHEDULES

SCHEDULE 1
DISCLOSURE OF CONFIDENTIAL INFORMATION WHETHER OR NOT SUBJECT TO DIRECTIVE RESTRICTIONS

Regulations 9, 10 and 12

PART 1

Person	*Functions*
The Bank of England, the European Central Bank or the central bank of any country or territory outside the United Kingdom	(a) Its functions as a monetary authority (b) Its functions in relation to overseeing payment systems
A body (other than a central bank) in a country or territory outside the United Kingdom having (a) functions as a monetary authority or (b) responsibility for overseeing payment systems	Its functions as such
A recognised investment exchange (other than an overseas investment exchange)	Its functions as such

Person	*Functions*
The body known as the Panel on Takeovers and Mergers	All of its functions
The Society of Lloyd's	Its regulatory functions
The [Office of Fair Trading]	(a) [Its] functions under the Act (b) [Its] functions under any other enactment in so far as they relate to the supervision of: (i) former authorised persons or persons who have carried on former regulated activities; or (ii) persons carrying on, or who have carried on, regulated activities[; or (iii) financial organisations within the meaning of article 30.5 of the banking consolidation directive]
The Competition Commission	(a) Its functions under the Act (b) Its functions under any other enactment in so far as they relate to the supervision of: (i) former authorised persons or persons who have carried on former regulated activities; or (ii) persons carrying on, or who have carried on, regulated activities[; or (iii) financial organisations within the meaning of article 30.5 of the banking consolidation directive]
An official receiver appointed under section 399 of the Insolvency Act 1986, or an official receiver for Northern Ireland appointed under article 355 of the Insolvency (Northern Ireland) Order 1989	His functions under enactments relating to insolvency, in so far as they relate to— (i) former authorised persons or persons who have carried on former regulated activities; or (ii) persons carrying on, or who have carried on, regulated activities
The scheme manager	Its functions under Part XV of the Act
A body responsible, in an EEA State other than the United Kingdom, for administering a deposit-guarantee scheme recognised in accordance with directive 94/19/EC, or an investor-compensation scheme recognised in accordance with Directive 97/9/EC	Its functions as such
A designated professional body within the meaning of Part XX of the Act	Its functions as such

PART IV STATUTORY INSTRUMENTS

Person	Functions
A body which was, immediately before the coming into force of section 19 of the Act, a recognised professional body within the meaning of the Financial Services Act 1986	Its functions as such under that Act or under the Act
A person appointed to make a report under section 166 of the Act	His functions as such
A person appointed to conduct an investigation under section 167 or section 168(3) or (5) of the Act	His functions as such
An auditor exercising functions conferred by or under the Act	Those functions
An auditor of an authorised person appointed under or as a result of an enactment (other than the Act)	His functions as such
An actuary exercising functions conferred by or under the Act	Those functions
A person appointed as an inspector under section 49 of the Industrial and Provident Societies Act 1965	His functions as such
A person appointed as an inspector under section 18 of the Credit Unions Act 1979	His functions as such
A person appointed to make a report under section 52(5)(d) of the Building Societies Act 1986	His functions as such
A person appointed as an investigator under section 55 of the Building Societies Act 1986 or as an inspector under section 56 of that Act	His functions as such
A person appointed to make a report under section 62(3)(d) of the Friendly Societies Act 1992	His functions as such
A person appointed as an investigator under section 65 of the Friendly Societies Act 1992 or as an inspector under 66 of that Act	His functions as such
A recognised supervisory body within the meaning of Part II of the Companies Act 1989 or Part III of the Companies (Northern Ireland) Order 1990	(a) Its functions as such a body under that Part
	(b) Its functions in relation to disciplinary proceedings against auditors
A qualifying body as defined by section 32 of the Companies Act 1989	Its functions as such
The Institute of Actuaries or the Faculty of Actuaries	[Their supervisory functions in relation to the exercise by an actuary of his professional duties, including the conduct of disciplinary proceedings and determining whether to institute or terminate such proceedings]
A recognised professional body within the meaning of section 391 of the Insolvency Act 1986 or article 350 of the Insolvency (Northern Ireland) Order 1989	(a) Its functions as such a body under that Act or that Order

Person	*Functions*
	(b) Its functions in relation to disciplinary proceedings against insolvency practitioners
The Department of Enterprise, Trade and Investment in Northern Ireland	(a) Its functions under Part V of the Companies (No 2) (Northern Ireland) Order 1990 (financial markets and insolvency) (b) Its functions under Part XII of the Insolvency (Northern Ireland) Order 1989 (c) Its functions under any other enactment in so far as they relate to the supervision of: (i) former authorised persons or persons who have carried on former regulated activities; or (ii) persons carrying on, or who have carried on, regulated activities
[The Pensions Regulator]	[Its functions as such] in so far as they relate to the supervision of: (i) former authorised persons or persons who have carried on former regulated activities; or (ii) persons carrying on, or who have carried on, regulated activities
The Charity Commissioners for England and Wales	Their functions under any enactment in so far as they relate to the supervision of: (i) former authorised persons or persons who have carried on former regulated activities; or (ii) persons carrying on, or who have carried on, regulated activities
The investigator appointed by the Authority in accordance with paragraph 7 of Schedule 1 to the Act	His functions as such
[A person appointed by the Treasury to hold an inquiry into matters relating to financial services (including an inquiry under section 15 of the Act), or an officer or member of staff of such an inquiry	His functions in carrying out the inquiry and reporting to the Treasury]
[An investment exchange which has its head office in an EEA State other than the United Kingdom, and which is recognised as an investment exchange under the law of that state	Its functions as a supervisor of financial markets]
[A person upon whom functions are conferred by or under Part 2, 3 or 4 of the Proceeds of Crime Act 2002	Those functions]
[A person authorised by the Secretary of State for the purposes of section 245B(1)(b) of the Companies Act 1985	His functions as such]

PART IV
STATUTORY INSTRUMENTS

Person	Functions
[Any body carrying on activities concerned with any of the matters set out in section 16(2) of the Companies (Audit, Investigations and Community Enterprise) Act 2004	Its functions as such]
[Any body carrying on activities concerned with any of the matters set out in section 14 of the Companies (Audit, Investigations and Community Enterprise) Act 2004	Its functions as such]
[The Financial Reporting Council and its operating bodies	Their supervisory functions in relation to the exercise by an actuary of his professional duties, the conduct of disciplinary proceedings and determining whether to institute or terminate such proceedings]

[4389]

NOTES

In entry relating to the Office of Fair Trading words "Office of Fair Trading" and "Its" in square brackets substituted by virtue of the Enterprise Act 2002, s 2(1), as from 1 April 2003 (see further the note "Substitution of references to the Director General of Fair Trading" at **[4351]**); sub-para (b)(iii) (and the word immediately preceding it) inserted by the Financial Services and Markets Act 2000 (Disclosure of Confidential Information) (Amendment) Regulations 2006, SI 2006/3413, regs 2, 8(1)(a), as from 20 January 2007.

In entry relating to the Competition Commission sub-para (b)(iii) (and the word immediately preceding it) inserted by SI 2006/3413, regs 2, 8(1)(b), as from 20 January 2007.

In entry relating to the Institute of Actuaries or the Faculty of Actuaries words in square brackets substituted by the Financial Services and Markets Act 2000 (Disclosure of Confidential Information) (Amendment) (No 3) Regulations 2003, SI 2003/2817, reg 2(a), as from 26 November 2003.

In entry relating to "The Pensions Regulator" (formerly "The Occupational Pensions Regulatory Authority") words in square brackets substituted by Financial Services and Markets Act 2000 (Disclosure of Confidential Information) (Amendment) Regulations 2005, SI 2005/3071, reg 2(1), (2), as from 25 November 2005.

First entry in square brackets added by the Financial Services and Markets Act 2000 (Disclosure of Confidential Information) (Amendment) Regulations 2001, SI 2001/3437, reg 2, as from 8 November 2001.

Second entry in square brackets added by the Financial Services and Markets Act 2000 (Disclosure of Confidential Information) (Amendment) (No 2) Regulations 2001, SI 2001/3624, reg 2(1), (6), as from 1 December 2001.

Third entry in square brackets inserted by the Financial Services and Markets Act 2000 (Disclosure of Confidential Information) (Amendment) (No 2) Regulations 2003, SI 2003/2174, regs 2, 4(b), as from 23 August 2003. Note that an identical entry was originally inserted by the Financial Services and Markets Act 2000 (Disclosure of Confidential Information) (Amendment) Regulations 2003, SI 2003/1092, as from 2 May 2003. However, those Regulations were revoked by SI 2003/2174, reg 3, as from 23 August 2003 due to a number of drafting errors contained in those Regulations. The entry as inserted by SI 2003/1092 did not contain any such drafting error so, in effect, has been in operation since 2 May 2003.

Fourth entry in square brackets inserted by SI 2003/2817, reg 2(b), as from 26 November 2003.

Final three entries in square brackets added by SI 2006/3413, regs 2, 8(2), as from 20 January 2007.

Charity Commissioners: as to the abolition of the office of Charity Commissioner for England and Wales, the establishment of the Charity Commission for England and Wales, and the transfer of the functions, rights, liabilities, etc from the Charity Commissioners to the Charity Commission, see the Charities Act 2006, s 6.

PART 2

Person	Functions
An EEA regulatory authority	(a) Its functions as an EEA competent authority

Person	*Functions*
	(b) Its functions corresponding to any of the functions specified in the second column of Part 1 of this Schedule

[4390]

PART 3

Person	*Functions*
A dependent territory regulatory authority	Its functions as such
A non-EEA regulatory authority	Its functions as such

[4391]

PART 4

Person	*Functions*
An inspector appointed under Part XIV of the Companies Act 1985	His functions as such
A person authorised to exercise powers under section 447 of the Companies Act 1985	His functions as such
A person authorised under section 84 of the Companies Act 1989 to exercise on behalf of the Secretary of State powers conferred by section 83 of that Act	His functions as such
The Department of Enterprise, Trade and Investment in Northern Ireland	(a) Its functions under Part XV of the Companies (Northern Ireland) Order 1986 (investigation of companies and their affairs; requisition of documents) (b) Its functions under Part III of the Companies (Northern Ireland) Order 1990 (eligibility for appointment as company auditor) (c) Its functions under the Companies (Northern Ireland) Order 1989 (disqualification of company directors)
An inspector appointed under Part XV of the Companies (Northern Ireland) Order 1986	His functions under that Part
A person appointed to exercise powers under article 440 of the Companies (Northern Ireland) Order 1986	His functions as such
A recognised clearing house (other than an overseas clearing house)	Its functions as a clearing house in so far as they are exercisable in relation to defaults or potential defaults by market participants
A person included on the list maintained by the Authority for the purposes of section 301 of the Act	His functions under settlement arrangements to which regulations made under that section relate

PART IV
STATUTORY INSTRUMENTS

Person	*Functions*
A person approved under the Uncertificated Securities Regulations 1995 as an operator of a relevant system (within the meaning of those Regulations)	His functions as such in so far as they are exercisable in relation to defaults or potential defaults by market participants
[A clearing house or other similar body which has its head office in an EEA State other than the United Kingdom, and which is recognised under the law of that state as a provider of clearing or settlement services	Its functions in relation to defaults or potential defaults by market participants]

[4392]

NOTES

Entry in square brackets added by the Financial Services and Markets Act 2000 (Disclosure of Confidential Information) (Amendment) (No 2) Regulations 2001, SI 2001/3624, reg 2(1), (7), as from 1 December 2001.

Uncertificated Securities Regulations 1995 (SI 1995/3272): revoked and replaced by the Uncertificated Securities Regulations 2001, SI 2001/3755.

SCHEDULE 2
DISCLOSURE OF CONFIDENTIAL INFORMATION NOT SUBJECT TO DIRECTIVE RESTRICTIONS

Regulation 12

Person	*Functions*
The Bank of England	All its public functions (so far as not mentioned in Schedule 1)
The International Monetary Fund	All its functions
The [Office of Fair Trading]	[Its] functions under any enactment (so far as not mentioned in Schedule 1)
The Competition Commission	Its functions under any enactment (so far as not mentioned in Schedule 1)
The Gas and Electricity Markets Authority	Its functions under any enactment
A local weights and measures authority in Great Britain	Its functions as such under any enactment
An EEA regulatory authority	Its functions as such (so far as not mentioned in Schedule 1)
The Department of Enterprise, Trade and Investment in Northern Ireland	(a) Its functions under Part V of the Companies (No 2) (Northern Ireland) Order 1990 (Financial Markets and Insolvency) (b) Its functions under Part XII of the Insolvency (Northern Ireland) Order 1989 (c) Its functions under any other enactment (so far as not mentioned in Schedule 1) (d) Its functions as a weights and measures authority for Northern Ireland
A recognised clearing house (other than an overseas clearing house)	Its functions as such (so far as not mentioned in Schedule 1)

Person	*Functions*
A person approved under the Uncertificated Securities Regulations 1995 as an operator of a relevant system (within the meaning of those regulations)	His functions as such (so far as not mentioned in Schedule 1)
The scheme operator	Its functions as such
The Chief Ombudsman appointed in accordance with paragraph 5 of Schedule 17 to the Act, and any other member of the panel of ombudsmen appointed in accordance with paragraph 4 of that Schedule	Their functions as such
An inspector appointed under section 284 of the Act	His functions as such
A person appointed in accordance with regulations made under section 262(1) of the Act to carry out an investigation in relation to an open-ended investment company	His functions as such
[The Pensions Regulator]	[Its functions as such] (so far as not mentioned in Schedule 1 to these Regulations)
The Charity Commissioners for England and Wales	Their functions under any enactment (so far as not mentioned in Schedule 1)
The Commissioners of Customs and Excise	Their functions under any enactment
The Postal Services Commission	Its functions under the Postal Services Act 2000
The Pensions Ombudsman	His functions under the Pension Schemes Act 1993 and the Pensions Act 1995
[The National Lottery Commission	All its public functions]
[A person upon whom functions are conferred by or under Part 2, 3 or 4 of the Proceeds of Crime Act 2002	Those functions]
[The Gambling Commission	Its functions as such]

[4393]

NOTES

In entry relating to the Office of Fair Trading words in square brackets substituted by virtue of the Enterprise Act 2002, s 2(1), as from 1 April 2003 (see further the note "Substitution of references to the Director General of Fair Trading" at **[4351]**).

In entry relating to "The Pensions Regulator" (formerly "The Occupational Pensions Regulatory Authority") words in square brackets substituted by Financial Services and Markets Act 2000 (Disclosure of Confidential Information) (Amendment) Regulations 2005, SI 2005/3071, reg 2(1), (3), as from 25 November 2005.

First entry in square brackets added by the Financial Services and Markets Act 2000 (Disclosure of Confidential Information) (Amendment) (No 2) Regulations 2001, SI 2001/3624, reg 2(1), (8), as from 1 December 2001.

Second entry in square brackets added by the Financial Services and Markets Act 2000 (Disclosure of Confidential Information) (Amendment) (No 2) Regulations 2003, SI 2003/2174, regs 2, 4(d), as from 23 August 2003. Note that an identical entry was originally inserted by the Financial Services and Markets Act 2000 (Disclosure of Confidential Information) (Amendment) Regulations 2003, SI 2003/1092, reg 3, as from 2 May 2003. However, those Regulations were revoked by SI 2003/2174, as from 23 August 2003 due to a number of drafting errors contained in those Regulations. The entry as inserted by SI 2003/1092 did not contain any such drafting error so, in effect, has been in operation since 2 May 2003.

Final entry in square brackets added by the Financial Services and Markets Act 2000 (Disclosure of Confidential Information) (Amendment) Regulations 2006, SI 2006/3413, regs 2, 9, as from 20 January 2007.

Commissioners of Customs and Excise: a reference to the Commissioners of Customs and Excise is now to be taken as a reference to the Commissioners for Her Majesty's Revenue and Customs; see the Commissioners for Revenue and Customs Act 2005, s 50(1), (7).

Charity Commissioners: as to the abolition of the office of Charity Commissioner for England and Wales, the establishment of the Charity Commission for England and Wales, and the transfer of the functions, rights, liabilities, etc from the Charity Commissioners to the Charity Commission, see the Charities Act 2006, s 6.

Uncertificated Securities Regulations 1995 (SI 1995/3272): revoked and replaced by the Uncertificated Securities Regulations 2001, SI 2001/3755.

SCHEDULE 3
PRESCRIBED DISCIPLINARY PROCEEDINGS

Regulation 2

The following disciplinary proceedings are prescribed for the purposes of section 349(5)(d) of the Act—

(a) disciplinary proceedings relating to the exercise by a barrister, solicitor, auditor, accountant, valuer or actuary of his professional duties;

(b) disciplinary proceedings relating to the discharge of his duties by an officer or servant of—

(i) the Crown;
(ii) the Authority;
(iii) the body known as the Panel on Takeovers and Mergers;
(iv) the Charity Commissioners for England and Wales;
(v) the [Office of Fair Trading];
(vi) the Competition Commission;
(vii) the Insolvency Practitioners Tribunal in relation to its functions under the Insolvency Act 1986;
(viii) the Occupational Pensions Board in relation to its functions under the Social Security Act 1973 and the Social Security Acts 1975 to 1986;
(ix) the organs of the Society of Lloyd's being organs constituted by or under Lloyd's Act 1982 in relation to their functions under Lloyd's Acts 1871–1982 and the byelaws made thereunder of the Society of Lloyd's;
(x) the National Lottery Commission in relation to their functions under the National Lottery etc Act 1993.

[4394]

NOTES

Words in square brackets substituted by virtue of the Enterprise Act 2002, s 2(1), as from 1 April 2003 (see further the note "Substitution of references to the Director General of Fair Trading" at **[4351]**).

Charity Commissioners: as to the abolition of the office of Charity Commissioner for England and Wales, the establishment of the Charity Commission for England and Wales, and the transfer of the functions, rights, liabilities, etc from the Charity Commissioners to the Charity Commission, see the Charities Act 2006, s 6.

FINANCIAL SERVICES AND MARKETS ACT 2000 (RIGHTS OF ACTION) REGULATIONS 2001

(SI 2001/2256)

NOTES

Made: 20 June 2001.

Authority: Financial Services and Markets Act 2000, ss 20(3), 71(2), (3), 150(3), (5), 202(2), 417(1), 428(3).

Commencement: 1 December 2001 (being the date on which the Financial Services and Markets Act 2000, s 19 came into force); see reg 1 at **[4395]**. Where any provision in this work (including any inserted or substituted provision) came into force for all purposes on or before 1 July 2005, commencement information is not noted at provision level.

These Regulations are reproduced as amended by: the Electronic Commerce Directive (Financial Services and Markets) Regulations 2002, SI 2002/1775; the Financial Services and Markets Act 2000 (Fourth Motor Insurance Directive) Regulations 2002, SI 2002/2706.

ARRANGEMENT OF REGULATIONS

1 Citation and commencement

These Regulations may be cited as the Financial Services and Markets Act 2000 (Rights of Action) Regulations 2001 and come into force on the day on which section 19 of the Act comes into force.

[4395]

NOTES

FSMA 2000, s 19 came into force on 1 December 2001 (see the Financial Services and Markets Act 2000 (Commencement No 7) Order 2001, SI 2001/3538).

2 Interpretation

In these Regulations—

"the Act" means the Financial Services and Markets Act 2000;

"government" means—

(a) the government of the United Kingdom;
(b) the Scottish Administration;
(c) the Executive Committee of the Northern Ireland Assembly;
(d) the National Assembly for Wales; or
(e) the government of any country or territory outside the United Kingdom;

"international organisation" means any international organisation the members of which include the United Kingdom or any other state;

"local authority", in relation to the United Kingdom, means—

(a) in England and Wales, a local authority within the meaning of the Local Government Act 1972, the Greater London Authority, the Common Council of the City of London or the Council of the Isles of Scilly;
(b) in Scotland, a local authority within the meaning of the Local Government (Scotland) Act 1973; and
(c) in Northern Ireland, a district council within the meaning of the Local Government Act (Northern Ireland) 1972;

"Part IV financial resources requirement" means a requirement imposed on an authorised person by the Authority under Part IV of the Act to have or maintain financial resources;

"Part XIII financial resources requirement" means a requirement imposed on an incoming firm (within the meaning of section 193(1) of the Act) by the Authority under Part XIII of the Act to have or maintain financial resources;

"the Regulated Activities Order" means the Financial Services and Markets Act 2000 (Regulated Activities) Order 2001.

[4396]

3 Private person

(1) In these Regulations, "private person" means—

(a) any individual, unless he suffers the loss in question in the course of carrying on—
  (i) any regulated activity; or
  (ii) any activity which would be a regulated activity apart from any exclusion made by [article 72 (overseas persons) or 72A (information society services) of the Regulated Activities Order]; and
(b) any person who is not an individual, unless he suffers the loss in question in the course of carrying on business of any kind;

but does not include a government, a local authority (in the United Kingdom or elsewhere) or an international organisation.

(2) For the purposes of paragraph (1)(a), an individual who suffers loss in the course of effecting or carrying out contracts of insurance (within the meaning of article 10 of the Regulated Activities Order) written at Lloyd's is not to be taken to suffer loss in the course of carrying on a regulated activity.

[4397]

PART IV
STATUTORY INSTRUMENTS

NOTES

Para (1): words in square brackets in sub-para (a)(ii) substituted by the Electronic Commerce Directive (Financial Services and Markets) Regulations 2002, SI 2002/1775, reg 18, as from 21 August 2002.

4 Authorised person acting otherwise than in accordance with permission

(1) A case where the conditions specified by paragraph (2) are satisfied is prescribed for the purposes of section 20(3) of the Act (and so in such a case the contravention of a requirement imposed by the Authority under the Act is actionable at the suit of a person who suffers loss as a result of that contravention).

(2) The conditions specified by this paragraph are that—

(a) the action would be brought at the suit of—

(i) a private person; or

(ii) a person acting in a fiduciary or representative capacity on behalf of a private person and any remedy would be exclusively for the benefit of that private person and could not be effected through an action brought otherwise than at the suit of the fiduciary or representative; and

(b) the contravention is not of a Part IV financial resources requirement.

[4398]

5 Prohibition orders and performance of a controlled function

(1) The definition of "private person" in regulation 3 is prescribed for the purposes of section 71(3) of the Act (and so the contravention of section 56(6) or 59(1) or (2) of the Act is actionable at the suit of a person who falls within that definition and who suffers loss as a result of that contravention).

(2) A case where the condition specified by paragraph (3) is satisfied is prescribed for the purposes of section 71(2) of the Act (and so in such a case the contravention of section 56(6) or 59(1) or (2) of the Act is actionable at the suit of a person who is not a private person).

(3) The condition specified by this paragraph is that the action would be brought at the suit of a person (who is not a private person) acting in a fiduciary or representative capacity on behalf of a private person and any remedy would be exclusively for the benefit of that private person and could not be effected through an action brought otherwise than at the suit of the fiduciary or representative.

[4399]

6 Authority rules

(1) The definition of "private person" in regulation 3 is prescribed for the purposes of section 150(5) of the Act (and so the contravention by an authorised person of a rule is actionable at the suit of a person who falls within that definition and who suffers loss as a result of that contravention).

(2) A case where any of the conditions specified by paragraph (3) is satisfied is prescribed for the purposes of section 150(3) of the Act (and so in such a case the contravention of a rule is actionable at the suit of a person who is not a private person).

(3) The conditions specified by this paragraph are that—

(a) the rule that has been contravened prohibits an authorised person from seeking to make provision excluding or restricting any duty or liability;

(b) the rule that has been contravened is directed at ensuring that transactions in any security or contractually based investment (within the meaning of the Regulated Activities Order) are not effected with the benefit of unpublished information that, if made public, would be likely to affect the price of that security or investment;

(c) the action would be brought at the suit of a person (who is not a private person) acting in a fiduciary or representative capacity on behalf of a private person and any remedy would be exclusively for the benefit of that private person and could not be effected through an action brought otherwise than at the suit of the fiduciary or representative;

[(d) the rule that has been contravened requires a relevant authorised person to respond to a claim for compensation within a specified time limit, or to pay interest in specified circumstances in respect of any such claim.]

[(4) In this regulation—

(a) "relevant authorised person" means an authorised person with a Part IV permission—
   (i) to effect or to carry out relevant contracts of insurance; or
   (ii) to manage the underwriting capacity of a Lloyd's syndicate as a managing agent, the members of which effect or carry out relevant contracts of insurance underwritten at Lloyd's;

where a "relevant contract of insurance" means a contract of insurance against damage arising out of or in connection with the use of motor vehicles on land (other than carrier's liability);

(b) "rule" has the meaning given by section 150(4) of the Act; and
(c) "specified" means specified in rules.]

[4400]

NOTES

Para (3): sub-para (d) added by the Financial Services and Markets Act 2000 (Fourth Motor Insurance Directive) Regulations 2002, SI 2002/2706, reg 3(a), as from 20 November 2002.

Para (4): added by SI 2002/2706, reg 3(b), as from 20 November 2002.

7 Incoming firms

(1) A case where the conditions specified by paragraph (2) are satisfied is prescribed for the purposes of section 202(2) of the Act (and so in such a case the contravention of a requirement imposed by the Authority under Part XIII of the Act is actionable at the suit of a person who suffers loss as a result of that contravention).

(2) The conditions specified by this paragraph are that—
(a) the action would be brought at the suit of—
   (i) a private person; or
   (ii) a person acting in a fiduciary or representative capacity on behalf of a private person and any remedy would be exclusively for the benefit of that private person and could not be effected through an action brought otherwise than at the suit of the fiduciary or representative; and
(b) the contravention is not of a Part XIII financial resources requirement.

[4401]

FINANCIAL SERVICES AND MARKETS ACT 2000 (MEANING OF "POLICY" AND "POLICYHOLDER") ORDER 2001

(SI 2001/2361)

NOTES

Made: 2 July 2001.

Authority: Financial Services and Markets Act 2000, ss 424(2), 428(3).

Commencement: 1 December 2001 (being the date on which the Financial Services and Markets Act 2000, s 19 came into force); see art 1 at **[4402]**. Where any provision in this work (including any inserted or substituted provision) came into force for all purposes on or before 1 July 2005, commencement information is not noted at provision level.

As of 1 July 2007, this Order had not been amended.

1 Citation, commencement and interpretation

(1) This Order may be cited as the Financial Services and Markets Act 2000 (Meaning of "Policy" and "Policyholder") Order 2001 and comes into force on the day on which section 19 of the Act comes into force.

(2) In this Order, "contract of insurance" has the meaning given by article 3 of the Financial Services and Markets Act 2000 (Regulated Activities) Order 2001.

[4402]

NOTES

FSMA 2000, s 19 came into force on 1 December 2001 (see the Financial Services and Markets Act 2000 (Commencement No 7) Order 2001, SI 2001/3538).

2 Meaning of "policy"

For the purposes of section 424(2) of the Act, "policy" means, as the context requires,
(a) a contract of insurance, including one under which an existing liability has already accrued, or
(b) any instrument evidencing such a contract.

[4403]

3 Meaning of "policyholder"

For the purposes of section 424(2) of the Act, "policyholder" means the person who for the time being is the legal holder of the policy, and includes any person to whom, under the policy, a sum is due, a periodic payment is payable or any other benefit is to be provided or to whom such a sum, payment or benefit is contingently due, payable or to be provided.

[4404]

FINANCIAL SERVICES AND MARKETS ACT 2000 (COLLECTIVE INVESTMENT SCHEMES CONSTITUTED IN OTHER EEA STATES) REGULATIONS 2001

(SI 2001/2383)

NOTES

Made: 4 July 2001.

Authority: Financial Services and Markets Act 2000, ss 264, 417(1).

Commencement: 1 December 2001 (being the date on which the Financial Services and Markets Act 2000, s 19 came into force); see reg 1 at **[4405]**. Where any provision in this work (including any inserted or substituted provision) came into force for all purposes on or before 1 July 2005, commencement information is not noted at provision level.

These Regulations are reproduced as amended by: the Collective Investment Schemes (Miscellaneous Amendments) Regulations 2003, SI 2003/2066.

1 These Regulations may be cited as the Financial Services and Markets Act 2000 (Collective Investment Schemes Constituted in Other EEA States) Regulations 2001 and come into force on the day on which section 19 of the Act comes into force.

[4405]

NOTES

FSMA 2000, s 19 came into force on 1 December 2001 (see the Financial Services and Markets Act 2000 (Commencement No 7) Order 2001, SI 2001/3538).

2 In these Regulations—

"the Act" means the Financial Services and Markets Act 2000;

. . . . .

[4406]

NOTES

Definition "the UCITS Directive" revoked by the Collective Investment Schemes (Miscellaneous Amendments) Regulations 2003, SI 2003/2066, reg 11(a), as from 13 February 2004.

3 The requirements prescribed for the purposes of section 264 of the Act are that a collective investment scheme is one which, in accordance with [the UCITS directive], is an undertaking for collective investment in transferable securities subject to [that directive] ("the undertaking").

[4407]

NOTES

Words in square brackets substituted by the Collective Investment Schemes (Miscellaneous Amendments) Regulations 2003, SI 2003/2066, reg 11(b), as from 13 February 2004.

4 The notice to be given to the Authority under section 264(1) of the Act must contain or be accompanied by—

(a) the undertaking's fund rules or instrument of incorporation;

[(b) its full and simplified prospectus (within the meaning of Section VI of the UCITS directive); and]

(c) where appropriate, its latest annual report and any subsequent half-yearly report.

[4408]

NOTES

Para (b): substituted by the Collective Investment Schemes (Miscellaneous Amendments) Regulations 2003, SI 2003/2066, reg 11(c), as from 13 February 2004.

FINANCIAL SERVICES AND MARKETS TRIBUNAL RULES 2001

(SI 2001/2476)

NOTES

Made: 9 July 2001.

Authority: Financial Services and Markets Act 2000, ss 132(3), 137(6), Sch 13, para 9.

Commencement: 3 September 2001 (being the date on which the Financial Services and Markets Act 2000, s 132(2) came into force); see r 1 at **[4409]**. Where any provision in this work (including any inserted or substituted provision) came into force for all purposes on or before 1 July 2005, commencement information is not noted at provision level.

As of 1 July 2007, these Rules had not been amended.

Transitional provisions: these Rules are modified by the Financial Services and Markets Act 2000 (Transitional Provisions) (Partly Completed Procedures) Order 2001, SI 2001/3592, arts 63, 80, 95, Schedule, in relation to appeals from determinations of the interim tribunal, rights of appeal against disciplinary measures, and rights of third parties to refer matters to the tribunal.

ARRANGEMENT OF RULES

PART I
INTRODUCTION

1 Citation and commencement

These Rules may be cited as the Financial Services and Markets Tribunal Rules 2001 and shall come into force on the day on which section 132(2) of the Act comes into force.

[4409]

NOTES

FSMA 2000, s 132(2) came into force on 3 September 2001 (see the Financial Services and Markets Act 2000 (Commencement No 5) Order 2001, SI 2001/2632).

2 Interpretation

(1) In these Rules, unless the context requires otherwise—

"the Act" means the Financial Services and Markets Act 2000;

"applicant" means a person who refers a case to the Tribunal and, if there is more than one such person, "applicant" means each such person;

"the Authority" means the Financial Services Authority;

"Authority notice" means the decision notice, supervisory notice or other notice relating to the referred action that was given to the applicant by the Authority;

"Chairman" means the person from time to time acting as chairman of the Tribunal in respect of a reference;

"direction" includes any direction, summons or order given or made by the Tribunal;

"documents" includes information recorded in any form and, in relation to information recorded otherwise than in legible form, references to its production include references to producing a copy of the information in legible form;

"file" means send to the Tribunal;

"further material" means documents which—

(a) were considered by the Authority in reaching or maintaining the decision to give an Authority notice; or

(b) were obtained by the Authority in connection with the matter to which that notice relates (whether they were obtained before or after giving the notice) but which were not considered by it in reaching or maintaining that decision,

but does not include documents on which the Authority relies in support of the referred action;

"party" means the applicant or the Authority (or, if there is more than one applicant, any of the applicants or the Authority) and "other party" shall be construed accordingly;

"protected item" has the meaning in section 413;

"reference" means a reference to the Tribunal under or by virtue of the Act or any other enactment (including an enactment comprised in subordinate legislation within the meaning of the Interpretation Act 1978);

"reference notice" means a notice filed under rule 4(1);

"referred action" means the act (or proposed act) on the part of the Authority that gave rise to the reference;

"register" means the register of references and decisions kept in connection with the Tribunal's functions and which is open to the inspection of any person without charge at all reasonable hours;

"reply" means a reply filed by the applicant under rule 6(1);

"representations" means written representations or (with the consent of the Tribunal, or at its request) oral representations;

"response document" means:

(a) in relation to the Authority, its statement of case;

(b) in relation to the applicant, his reply;

"the Secretary" means the person from time to time appointed as secretary to the Tribunal, being a member of staff appointed under paragraph 6(1) of Schedule 13;

"statement of case" means a statement filed by the Authority under rule 5(1);

"supplementary statement" means a statement that is supplementary to a response document and filed in accordance with a direction given under rule 10(1)(f); and

"the Tribunal" means the Financial Services and Markets Tribunal.

(2) Unless the context requires otherwise—

(a) a reference in these Rules to a rule by number alone means the rule so numbered in these Rules;

(b) a reference in these Rules to a section or Schedule by number alone means the section or Schedule so numbered in the Act;

(c) words and expressions defined in the Act have the same meaning in these Rules; and

(d) anything permitted or required by these Rules to be done by a party may be done by any representative of that party.

[4410]

3 Application of these Rules

These Rules apply to all references to the Tribunal.

[4411]

PART II
PRELIMINARY MATTERS

4 Reference notice

(1) A reference shall be made by way of a written notice ("the reference notice") signed by or on behalf of the applicant and filed by the applicant.

(2) In any case not covered by section 133(1)(a) (which provides that a reference must be made before the end of the period of 28 days beginning with the date on which a decision notice or supervisory notice is given), the period specified for the purposes of section 133(1)(b) (such other period as may be specified for making a reference) shall be the period of 28 days beginning with the date on which the Authority notice is given.

(3) The reference notice shall state—

(a) the name and address of the applicant;

(b) the name and address of the applicant's representative (if any);

(c) if no representative is named under sub-paragraph (b), the applicant's address for service in the United Kingdom (if different from the address notified under sub-paragraph (a));

(d) that the notice is a reference notice; and

(e) the issues concerning the Authority notice that the applicant wishes the Tribunal to consider.

(4) In sub-paragraph (3)(a), "address", where the applicant is a corporation, means the address of the applicant's registered or principal office.

(5) The applicant shall file with the reference notice a copy of any Authority notice to which the reference relates.

(6) The applicant may include with the reference notice an application for directions, such as a direction extending any time limit for making a reference, a direction under rule 10(1)(e) (suspension of Authority's action) or a direction under rule 10(1)(p) (that the register shall include no particulars about the reference).

(7) At the same time as he files the reference notice, the applicant shall send a copy of that notice (and of any application for directions in accordance with paragraph (6)) to the Authority.

(8) In all cases where an application for directions is made under paragraph (6) the Secretary shall refer the application for directions to the Tribunal for determination and he shall take no further action in relation to the reference notice until the application for directions has been determined.

(9) Subject to paragraph (8) and to any directions given by the Tribunal, upon receiving a reference notice the Secretary shall—

(a) enter particulars of the reference in the register; and

(b) inform the parties in writing of—

(i) the fact that the reference has been received;

(ii) the date when the Tribunal received the notice; and

(iii) the Tribunal's decision on any application made for directions (and include a copy of any direction given),

and the Secretary when sending the parties this information shall specify the date on which he is sending it.

[4412]

5 Authority's statement of case

(1) The Authority shall file a written statement ("a statement of case") in support of the referred action so that it is received by the Tribunal no later than 28 days after the day on which the Authority received the information sent by the Secretary in accordance with rule 4(9)(b).

(2) The statement of case shall—

(a) specify the statutory provisions providing for the referred action;

(b) specify the reasons for the referred action;

(c) set out all the matters and facts upon which the Authority relies to support the referred action; and

(d) specify the date on which the statement of case is filed.

(3) The statement of case shall be accompanied by a list of—

(a) the documents on which the Authority relies in support of the referred action; and

(b) the further material which in the opinion of the Authority might undermine the decision to take that action.

(4) At the same time as it files the statement of case, the Authority shall send to the applicant a copy of the statement of case and of the list referred to in paragraph (3).

[4413]

6 Applicant's reply

(1) The applicant shall file a written reply so that it is received by the Tribunal no later than 28 days after—

(a) the date on which the applicant received a copy of the statement of case; or

(b) if the Authority amends its statement of case, the date on which the applicant received a copy of the amended statement of case.

(2) The reply shall—

(a) state the grounds on which the applicant relies in the reference;

(b) identify all matters contained in the statement of case which are disputed by the applicant;

(c) state the applicant's reasons for disputing them; and

(d) specify the date on which it is filed.

(3) The reply shall be accompanied by a list of all the documents on which the applicant relies in support of his case.

(4) At the same time as he files the reply, the applicant shall send to the Authority a copy of the reply and of the list referred to in paragraph (3).

[4414]

7 Secondary disclosure by the Authority

(1) Following the filing of the applicant's reply, if there is any further material which might be reasonably expected to assist the applicant's case as disclosed by the applicant's

reply and which is not mentioned in the list provided in accordance with rule 5(3), the Authority shall file a list of such further material.

(2) Any list required to be filed by paragraph (1) shall be filed so that it is received no later than 14 days after the day on which the Authority received the applicant's reply.

(3) At the same time as it files any list required by paragraph (1) the Authority shall send a copy to the applicant.

[4415]

8 Exceptions to disclosure

(1) A list provided in accordance with rule 5(3) or 7(1) need not include any document that relates to a case involving a person other than the applicant which was taken into account by the Authority in the applicant's case only for the purposes of comparison with other cases.

(2) A list provided in accordance with rule 5(3), 6(3) or 7(1) need not include any document that is material the disclosure of which for the purposes of or in connection with any legal proceedings is prohibited by section 17 of the Regulation of Investigatory Powers Act 2000.

(3) A list provided in accordance with rule 5(3), 6(3) or 7(1) need not include any document in respect of which an application has been or is being made under paragraph (4).

(4) A party may apply to the Tribunal (without giving notice to the other party) for a direction authorising that party not to include in the list required by rule 5(3), 6(3) or 7(1) a document on the ground that disclosure of the document—

(a) would not be in the public interest; or

(b) would not be fair, having regard to—

(i) the likely significance of the document to the applicant in relation to the matter referred to the Tribunal; and

(ii) the potential prejudice to the commercial interests of a person other than the applicant which would be caused by disclosure of the document.

(5) For the purpose of deciding an application by a party under paragraph (4), the Tribunal may—

(a) require that the document be produced to the Tribunal together with a statement of the reasons why its inclusion in the list would—

(i) in the case of an application under paragraph (4)(a), not be in the public interest; or

(ii) in the case of an application under paragraph (4)(b), not be fair; and

(b) invite the other party to make representations.

(6) If the Tribunal refuses an application under paragraph (4) for a direction authorising a party not to include a document in a list, it shall direct that party—

(a) to revise the list so as to include the document; and

(b) to file a copy of that list as revised and send a copy to the other party.

(7) A party who has filed a list under rule 5(3), 6(3) or 7(1) shall, upon the request of the other party, provide that other party with a copy of any document specified in the list or make any such document available to that party for inspection or copying.

(8) Paragraph (7) does not apply to any document that is a protected item.

[4416]

9 Directions

(1) The Tribunal may at any time give directions to enable the parties to prepare for the hearing of the reference, to assist the Tribunal to determine the issues and generally to ensure the just, expeditious and economical determination of the reference.

(2) The Tribunal may give directions on the application of any party or of all the parties or of its own initiative and, where it gives a direction of its own initiative, it may (but need not) give prior notice to the parties of its intention to do so.

(3) Any application for directions shall include the reasons for making that application.

(4) Except where it is made during the pre-hearing review or during the hearing of the reference, an application for directions shall be filed and, unless the application is accompanied by the written consent of all the parties or an application without notice is permitted by these Rules, the party making the application shall at the same time send a copy to the other party.

(5) If any party objects to the directions applied for, the Tribunal shall consider the objection and, if it considers it necessary for the determination of the application, shall give the parties an opportunity to make representations.

(6) Directions may be given orally or in writing and, unless the Tribunal decides otherwise in any particular case, notice of any written direction (or refusal to give a direction) shall be given to the parties.

(7) Directions containing a requirement may specify a time limit for complying with the requirement and shall include a statement of the possible consequences of a party's failure to comply with the requirement.

(8) A person to whom a direction is given under these Rules may apply to the Tribunal showing good cause why it should be varied or set aside, but the Tribunal shall not grant such an application without first notifying any person who applied for the direction and giving that party an opportunity to make representations.

(9) The following paragraphs of this rule shall apply if the Chairman directs that it is appropriate to hold a pre-hearing review.

(10) The Secretary shall give the parties not less than 14 days' notice of the time and place of the pre-hearing review.

(11) At the pre-hearing review, which shall be held before the Chairman—

(a) the Chairman shall give all directions appearing necessary or desirable for securing the just, expeditious and economical conduct of the reference; and

(b) the Chairman shall endeavour to secure that the parties make all admissions and agreements as they ought reasonably to have made in relation to the proceedings.

(12) In this rule, "pre-hearing review" means a review of the reference that may be held at any time before the hearing of the reference.

[4417]

10 Particular types of direction

(1) Directions given by the Tribunal may—

(a) fix the time and place of the hearing of the reference and alter any time and place so fixed;

(b) provide for an oral hearing, upon such notice as the Tribunal may determine, in connection with any matter arising under the reference;

(c) adjourn any oral hearing;

(d) extend any time limit for making a reference under the Act or these Rules, or vary (whether by extending or shortening) any other time limit for anything to be done under these Rules;

(e) suspend the effect of an Authority notice (or prevent it taking effect) until the reference has been finally disposed of, or until any appeal against the Tribunal's determination of the reference has been finally disposed of, or both;

(f) permit or require any party to provide further information or supplementary statements or to amend a response document or a supplementary statement;

(g) require any party to file any document—

(i) that is in the custody or under the control of that party;

(ii) that the Tribunal considers is or may be relevant to the determination of the reference; and

(iii) that has neither been exempted from disclosure by direction given pursuant to rule 8(4) nor been made available pursuant to rule 8(7),

and may also require that any such document directed for filing as above shall be copied to the other party or else be made available to that other party for inspection and copying;

(h) require any party to provide a statement of relevant issues and facts, identifying those which are, and are not, agreed by the other party;

(j) require any party to file documents for any hearing under these Rules or to agree with the other party the documents to be filed;

(k) require any party to file—

(i) a list of the witnesses whom the party wishes to call to give evidence at the hearing of the reference; and

(ii) statements of the evidence which those witnesses intend to give, if called;

(l) make provision as to any expert witnesses to be called including the number of such witnesses and the evidence to be given by them;

(m) provide for the appointment of any expert under paragraph 7(4) of Schedule 13 and for that expert to send the parties copies of any report that he produces;
(n) provide for the manner in which any evidence may be given;
(o) provide for the use of languages in addition to English, including provision—
  (i) as to the venue of any hearing under these Rules so as to ensure the availability of simultaneous translation facilities; and
  (ii) for the translation of any document;
(p) require that the register shall include no particulars about the reference; and
(q) where two or more reference notices have been filed—
  (i) in respect of the same matter;
  (ii) in respect of separate interests in the same subject in dispute; or
  (iii) which involve the same issues,

provide that the references or any particular issue or matter raised in the references be consolidated or heard together.

(2) In the case of an application for a direction under paragraph (1)(d) extending any time limit, the Tribunal may direct that the time limit be extended (whether or not it has already expired) if it is satisfied that to do so would be in the interests of justice but, in the case of an application for a direction extending any time limit for making a reference, the Tribunal shall not determine the application without—
(a) considering whether the Authority notice was such as to notify the applicant properly and effectively of the referred action; and
(b) considering whether the existence of the right to make the reference and the time limit had been notified to the applicant, whether in the Authority notice or otherwise.

(3) A time limit extended under paragraph (2) may from time to time be further extended by directions of the Tribunal (whether or not that or any subsequent such time limit has already expired) made upon an application under paragraph (1)(d), but no such direction shall be given unless the Tribunal is satisfied that the further extension would be in the interests of justice.

(4) Where a party files a response document or list later than any time limit imposed by or extended under these Rules but without applying for a direction under paragraph (1)(d) extending the time limit, that party shall be treated as applying for such a direction but no such direction shall be given unless the Tribunal is satisfied that such an extension would be in the interests of justice.

(5) If a response document or list is not filed in accordance with the time limit imposed by (or extended under) these Rules, the Tribunal may of its own initiative direct that the document or list be filed by a specified date.

(6) Where an application for a direction is made under paragraph (1)(e), the Tribunal may give such a direction only if it is satisfied that to do so would not prejudice—
(a) the interests of any persons (whether consumers, investors or otherwise) intended to be protected by the Authority notice; or
(b) the smooth operation or integrity of any market intended to be protected by that notice.

(7) If the Tribunal gives a direction under paragraph (1)(f) to permit or require a party to provide a supplementary statement or to amend a response document or supplementary statement, the direction may require that party to file any such statement or amendment and send a copy to the other party.

(8) The Tribunal shall not give a direction under paragraph (1)(g) or (1)(j) in relation to the disclosure of any document to the extent that the Tribunal is satisfied that—
(a) it is a protected item or would be included in an exemption provided by rule 8(1) or (2); or
(b) it should not be disclosed on one of the grounds specified in rule 8(4),

and, for the purpose of determining whether such a direction should be given in respect of any such document, the Tribunal may—
  (i) require that the document be produced to the Tribunal;
  (ii) hear the application in the absence of any party; and
  (iii) invite any party to make representations.

(9) In the case of an application for a direction under paragraph (1)(p) that the register should include no particulars about the reference, the Tribunal may give such a direction if it is satisfied that this is necessary, having regard to—

(a) the interests of morals, public order, national security or the protection of the private lives of the parties; or

(b) any unfairness to the applicant or prejudice to the interests of consumers that might result from the register including particulars about the reference.

[4418]

11 Filing of subsequent notices in relation to the referred action

Where, after the filing of a reference notice, the Authority gives the applicant any notice under the Act in relation to the referred action, the Authority shall without delay file a copy of that notice.

[4419]

12 Summoning of witnesses

(1) The Tribunal may by summons require any person to—

(a) attend, at such time and place as is specified in the summons, to give evidence as a witness;

(b) file, within the time specified in the summons, any document in his custody or under his control which the Tribunal considers it necessary to examine; or

(c) both attend and file in accordance with sub-paragraphs (a) and (b) above.

(2) No person may be required under this rule to file a document to the extent that the Tribunal is satisfied that—

(a) it is a protected item or would be included in an exemption provided by rule 8(1) or (2); or

(b) it should not be disclosed on one of the grounds specified in rule 8(4),

and, for the purpose of satisfying itself in respect of any such document, the Tribunal may—

(i) require that the document be produced to the Tribunal;

(ii) conduct any hearing in the absence of any party; and

(iii) invite any party to make representations.

(3) A witness summons shall be sent so as to be received by the person to whom it is addressed not less than seven days before the time specified in the summons.

(4) Every summons under paragraph (1) shall contain a statement warning of the effect of paragraph 11(3) to (5) of Schedule 13 (penalty for refusal or failure to attend or give evidence).

(5) No person shall be required, in obedience to a summons under paragraph (1), to travel more than 16 kilometres from his place of residence unless the necessary expenses of his attendance are paid or tendered to him in advance, and when the summons is issued at the request of a party, those expenses shall be paid by that party.

(6) The Tribunal may, upon the application of the person to whom the witness summons is addressed, direct that the witness summons be set aside or varied.

[4420]

13 Preliminary hearing

(1) The Tribunal may direct that any question of fact or law which appears to be in issue in relation to the reference be determined at a preliminary hearing.

(2) If, in the opinion of the Tribunal, the determination of that question substantially disposes of the reference, the Tribunal may treat the preliminary hearing as the hearing of the reference and may make such order by way of disposing of the reference as it thinks fit.

(3) If the parties so agree in writing, the Tribunal may determine the question without an oral hearing, but, in any such case, the Tribunal may not at the same time dispose of the reference unless the parties have agreed in writing that it may do so.

[4421]

14 Withdrawal of reference and unopposed references

(1) The applicant may withdraw the reference—

(a) at any time before the hearing of the reference, without permission, by filing a notice to that effect; or

(b) at the hearing of the reference, with the Tribunal's permission,

and the Tribunal may determine any reference that is so withdrawn.

(2) The Authority may state that it does not oppose the reference or that it is withdrawing its opposition to it—

(a) at any time before the hearing of the reference, without permission, by filing a notice to that effect; or

(b) at the hearing of the reference, with the Tribunal's permission.

(3) In any case where—

(a) the Authority makes a statement within paragraph (2)(a);

(b) the Authority does not file a statement of case within the time limit imposed by rule 5(1) (or any such time limit as extended under rule 10(1)(d)); or

(c) the applicant does not file a reply within any time limit imposed by rule 6(1) (or any such time limit as extended under rule 10(1)(d)),

the Tribunal may (subject to its power to give a direction pursuant to rule 10(5)) determine the reference without an oral hearing in accordance with rule 16, but it shall not dismiss a reference without notifying the applicant that it is minded to do so and giving him an opportunity to make representations.

(4) When determining proceedings pursuant to paragraph (1) or (3), the Tribunal may make a costs order under rule 21.

[4422]

15 References by third parties

(1) In the case of any reference made by an applicant under section 393 (third party rights) these Rules apply subject to the modifications set out in this rule.

(2) The following definitions apply in place of the definitions of "Authority notice" and "referred action" given in rule 2(1)—

(a) if the reference was made under section 393(9) (reference to the Tribunal by a third party to whom a decision notice was copied), "Authority notice" means the decision notice which was copied to the applicant by the Authority;

(b) if the reference was made under section 393(11) (reference to the Tribunal by a third party who alleges that he was not given a copy of a decision notice), "Authority notice" means the decision notice which the applicant alleges was not copied to him; and

(c) in either case, "referred action" means the action set out in the Authority notice.

(3) If the reference was made under section 393(11), rule 4(5) (requirement on applicant to file a copy of the Authority notice) does not apply.

(4) The duties of the Authority to set out information under rule 5(2) (statement of case) or to list material under rule 5(3) or 7(1) (lists of documents and further material) apply only to information, documents or material which relate to the matters referred to the Tribunal in accordance with section 393(9) or (as the case may be) section 393(11).

[4423]

PART III
HEARINGS

16 Determination without oral hearing

(1) The Tribunal may determine a reference, or any particular issue, without an oral hearing if—

(a) the parties agree in writing;

(b) the issue concerns an application for directions; or

(c) rule 14(3) applies.

(2) Where a reference or an issue is determined in accordance with this rule, the Tribunal shall consider whether there are circumstances making it undesirable to make a public pronouncement of the whole or part of its decision and may in consequence take any steps, including any one or more of the steps specified in paragraph (3), but any such step shall be taken with a view to ensuring the minimum restriction on public pronouncement that is consistent with the need for the restriction.

(3) The steps referred to in paragraph (2) are—

(a) anonymising the decision;

(b) editing the text of the decision;

(c) declining to publish the whole or part of the decision.

(4) Before reaching a decision under paragraph (2), the Tribunal shall invite the parties to make representations on the matter.

[4424]

17 Hearings in public

(1) In this rule, "hearing" means any hearing under these Rules but does not include any determination under rule 16(1) or the hearing of any application made to the Tribunal without notice to the other party.

(2) Subject to the following paragraphs of this rule, all hearings shall be in public.

(3) The Tribunal may direct that all or part of a hearing shall be in private—
- (a) upon the application of all the parties; or
- (b) upon the application of any party, if the Tribunal is satisfied that a hearing in private is necessary, having regard to—
  - (i) the interests of morals, public order, national security or the protection of the private lives of the parties; or
  - (ii) any unfairness to the applicant or prejudice to the interests of consumers that might result from a hearing in public,

if, in either case, the Tribunal is satisfied that a hearing in private would not prejudice the interests of justice.

(4) Before determining an application under paragraph (3)(b), the Tribunal shall give the other party an opportunity to make representations.

(5) Before giving a direction under paragraph (3) that the entire hearing should be in private, the Tribunal shall consider whether only part of the hearing should be heard in private.

(6) The following persons shall be entitled to attend any hearing of the Tribunal whether or not it is in private—
- (a) the parties and their representatives;
- (b) the President or any member of the panel of chairmen or of the lay panel notwithstanding that they are not members of the Tribunal for the purpose of the reference to which the hearing relates;
- (c) the Secretary and any member of the Tribunal's staff appointed under paragraph 6 of Schedule 13; and
- (d) a member of the Council on Tribunals or the Scottish Committee of that Council.

(7) The Tribunal may permit any other person to attend a hearing which is held in private.

(8) The persons mentioned in paragraph (6)(b) and (d) shall be entitled to attend the deliberations of the Tribunal but shall take no part in those deliberations.

(9) The Tribunal may exclude from the whole or part of a hearing any person whose conduct, in the opinion of the Tribunal, has disrupted or is likely to disrupt the hearing.

(10) Subject to any direction under paragraph (11), the Secretary shall provide for the public inspection at the Tribunal's offices of a daily list of all hearings which are to be held together with information about the time and place fixed for the hearings.

(11) Where all or part of a hearing is held or is to be held in private, the Tribunal may direct that information about the whole or part of the proceedings before the Tribunal (including information that might help to identify any person) shall not be made public, and such a direction may provide for the information (if any) that is to be entered in the register or removed from it.

[4425]

18 Representation at hearings

(1) Subject to paragraph (2), the parties may appear at the hearing (with assistance from any person if desired), and may be represented by any person, whether or not that person is legally qualified.

(2) If in any particular case the Tribunal is satisfied that there are good and sufficient reasons for doing so, it may refuse to permit a person to assist or represent a party at the hearing.

(3) In this rule, "hearing" means any hearing under these Rules.

[4426]

19 Procedure at hearings

(1) Subject to the Act and these Rules, the Tribunal shall conduct all hearings under these Rules in such manner as it considers most suitable to the clarification of the issues before it and generally to the just, expeditious and economical determination of the proceedings.

(2) Subject to any directions by the Tribunal, the parties shall be entitled—
- (a) to give evidence (and, with the consent of the Tribunal, to bring expert evidence);
- (b) to call witnesses;
- (c) to question any witnesses; and
- (d) to address the Tribunal on the evidence, and generally on the subject matter of the reference.

(3) Evidence may be admitted by the Tribunal whether or not it would be admissible in a court of law and whether or not it was available to the Authority when taking the referred action.

(4) If a party fails to attend or be represented at any hearing of which it has been duly notified, the Tribunal may, if it is satisfied that there is no good and sufficient reason for the absence—
- (a) in the case of the hearing of the reference, hear and determine the reference in the party's absence; or
- (b) in the case of any other hearing, give any direction, determine any issue or adjourn the hearing.

[4427]

20 Decisions of Tribunal

(1) Subject to paragraph (2) and to rule 16(2), the Tribunal shall make arrangements for the public pronouncement of its decisions, whether by giving its decisions orally in open court or by publishing its decisions in writing.

(2) Where the whole or any part of any hearing under these Rules was in private, the Tribunal shall consider whether, having regard to—
- (a) the reason for the hearing or any part of it being in private; and
- (b) the outcome of the hearing,

it would be undesirable to make a public pronouncement of the whole or part of its decision and may in consequence take any steps, including one or more of the steps specified in paragraph (3), but any such step shall be taken with a view to ensuring the minimum restriction on public pronouncement that is consistent with the need for the restriction.

(3) The steps referred to in paragraph (2) are—
- (b) anonymising the decision;
- (b) editing the text of the decision;
- (c) declining to publish the whole or part of the decision.

(4) Before reaching a decision under paragraph (2), the Tribunal shall invite the parties to make representations on the matter.

(5) The Secretary shall as soon as may be practicable enter every decision (and the reasons for the decision) in the register, but this is subject to any steps taken under paragraph (2) or under rule 16(2) and to any direction given under rule 17(11).

(6) Every notification of a decision determining a reference which is sent to the parties shall be accompanied by a notification of any provision of the Act relating to appeals from the Tribunal and of the time within which and the place at which such appeal or application for permission to appeal may be made.

[4428]

21 Costs

(1) In this rule, "costs order" means an order under paragraph 13 of Schedule 13 (power of Tribunal to order payment of costs) that a party pay the whole or part of the costs or expenses incurred by another party, and "the paying party" and "the receiving party" mean, respectively, the parties against whom and in whose favour the Tribunal makes, or (as the case may be) considers making a costs order.

(2) The Tribunal shall not make a costs order without first giving the paying party an opportunity to make representations against the making of the order.

(3) Where the Tribunal makes a cost order it may order—
- (a) that an amount fixed by the Tribunal shall be paid to the receiving party by way of costs or (as the case may be) expenses; or
- (b) that the costs shall be assessed or (as the case may be) expenses shall be taxed on such basis as it shall specify—
  - (i) in England and Wales, by a costs official;
  - (ii) in Scotland, by the Auditor of the Court of Session;
  - (iii) in Northern Ireland, by the Taxing Master of the Supreme Court of Northern Ireland.

[4429]

NOTES

Supreme Court of Northern Ireland: the Supreme Court of Judicature of Northern Ireland is renamed the Court of Judicature of Northern Ireland; see the Constitutional Reform Act 2005, s 59(2) (as from a day to be appointed).

22 Review of Tribunal's decision

(1) If, on the application of a party or of its own initiative, the Tribunal is satisfied that—
- (a) its decision determining a reference was wrongly made as a result of an error on the part of the Tribunal staff; or
- (b) new evidence has become available since the conclusion of the hearing to which that decision relates, the existence of which could not have been reasonably known of or foreseen,

the Tribunal may review and, by certificate signed by the Chairman, set aside the relevant decision.

(2) An application for the purposes of paragraph (1) may either be made immediately following the decision at the hearing of the reference or shall be filed (stating the grounds in full) not later than 14 days after the date on which notification of the decision was sent to the parties.

(3) Where the Tribunal proposes to review its decision of its own initiative, it shall notify the parties of that proposal not later than 14 days after the date on which the decision was sent to the parties.

(4) The parties shall have an opportunity to make representations on any application or proposal for review under this rule and the review shall be determined either by the same members of the Tribunal who decided the case or by a differently constituted Tribunal appointed by the President.

(5) If, having reviewed the decision, the decision is set aside, the Tribunal shall substitute such decision as it thinks fit or order a re-hearing before either the same or a differently constituted Tribunal.

(6) The certificate of the Chairman as to the setting aside of the Tribunal's decision under this rule shall be sent to the Secretary who shall immediately make such correction as may be necessary in the register and shall send a copy of the entry so corrected to each party.

[4430]

PART IV
APPEALS FROM THE TRIBUNAL

23 Application for permission to appeal

(1) In this Part, "appeal" means appeal (or an appeal) under section 137(1) to the Court of Appeal or the Court of Session from a decision of the Tribunal disposing of a reference, and "appellant" means a party applying for permission to appeal.

(2) An application to the Tribunal for permission to appeal may be made—
- (a) orally at the hearing after the decision is announced by the Tribunal; or
- (b) by way of written application filed not later than 14 days after the decision is sent to the party making the application.

(3) When an application is made under paragraph (2)(b), it shall be signed by the appellant and shall—

(a) state the name and address of the appellant and any representative of the appellant;

(b) identify the decision of the Tribunal to which the application relates; and

(c) state the grounds on which the appellant intends to rely in the appeal.

(4) An application under this rule may include an application for a direction under rule 10(1)(e) (suspension of Authority's action).

[4431]

24 Decision as to permission to appeal

(1) An application to the Tribunal for permission to appeal may be decided by the Chairman, on consideration of the application.

(2) Unless the decision is made immediately following an oral application or the Chairman considers that special circumstances render a hearing desirable, the application for permission to appeal shall be decided without an oral hearing.

(3) The decision of the Tribunal on an application for permission to appeal, together with the reasons for its decision, shall be recorded in writing.

(4) Unless the decision is given immediately following an oral application, the Secretary shall notify the appellant and each of the other parties of the decision and the reasons for the decision.

(5) Where the Tribunal refuses the application, it shall issue a direction that the appellant, if he wishes to seek permission from the Court of Appeal or the Court of Session to appeal, must do so within 14 days of the Tribunal's refusal.

[4432]

25 Reference remitted for rehearing

(1) The following paragraphs of this rule apply where the Court of Appeal or the Court of Session remits a reference to the Tribunal under section 137(3)(a) for rehearing and determination ("rehearing").

(2) These Rules, so far as relevant, shall apply to the rehearing as they did to the original hearing of the reference.

(3) The Tribunal shall, within 28 days of the remittal, give directions in relation to the rehearing.

[4433]

PART V
GENERAL

26 Miscellaneous powers of Tribunal

(1) Any functions of the Secretary may be performed by an Assistant Secretary to the Tribunal or by some other member of the Tribunal staff authorised for the purpose by the Secretary.

(2) Subject to the provisions of the Act and these Rules, the Tribunal may regulate its own procedure.

(3) Without limiting any other powers conferred on it by the Act or by these Rules, the Tribunal may, if it thinks fit—

(a) order any response document, supplementary statement or written representation to be struck out at any stage of the proceedings on the ground that it is scandalous, frivolous or vexatious; or

(b) order any reference to be struck out for want of prosecution.

(4) Before making any order under paragraph (3), the Tribunal shall give notice to the party against whom it is proposed that the order should be made, giving it an opportunity to make representations against the making of the order.

[4434]

27 Failure to comply

(1) Where a party has, without reasonable excuse, failed to comply—

(a) with a direction given under these Rules; or
(b) with a provision of these Rules,

the Tribunal may take any one or more of the following steps in respect of that party—

(i) make a costs order under rule 21 against that party;
(ii) where that party is the applicant, dismiss the whole or part of the reference (or, if there is more than one applicant, that applicant's reference);
(iii) where that party is the Authority, strike out the whole or part of the statement of case and, where appropriate, direct that the Authority be debarred from contesting the reference altogether.

(2) The Tribunal shall not take any of these steps in respect of a party unless it has given that party notice giving it an opportunity to make representations against the taking of any such steps.

[4435]

28 Irregularities

(1) Any irregularity resulting from failure to comply with any provision of these Rules or of any direction of the Tribunal before the Tribunal has reached its decision shall not of itself render the proceedings void.

(2) Where any such irregularity comes to the attention of the Tribunal, the Tribunal may, and shall if it considers that any person may have been prejudiced by the irregularity, give such directions as it thinks just to cure or waive the irregularity.

(3) Clerical mistakes in any document recording a direction or decision of the Chairman or the Tribunal, or errors arising in such a document from an accidental slip or omission, may be corrected by a certificate signed by the Chairman.

[4436]

29 Power of Chairman to exercise powers of Tribunal

Any matter (other than the determination of a reference or the setting aside of a decision on a reference) required or authorised by these Rules to be done by the Tribunal may be done by the Chairman.

[4437]

30 Proof of documents

(1) Any document purporting to a document duly executed or issued by the Chairman or the Secretary on behalf of the Tribunal shall, unless proved to the contrary, be deemed to be a document so executed or issued.

(2) A document purporting to be certified by the Secretary to be a true copy of any entry of a decision in the register shall, unless proved to the contrary, be sufficient evidence of the entry and of the matters referred to in it.

[4438]

31 Sending notices

(1) This rule applies to any notice sent under these Rules, and in this rule—

"send" to a person includes deliver or give to, or serve on, that person;

"notice" includes any notice or other thing required or authorised by these Rules to be sent or delivered to, or served on, any person; and

"recipient" means a person to or on whom any notice is required or authorised to be sent for the purposes of these Rules.

(2) A notice may be sent—

(a) by a postal service which seeks to deliver documents or other things by post no later than the next working day in all or in the majority of cases;
(b) by fax or other means of electronic communication; or
(c) by personal delivery.

(3) A notice shall be sent—

(a) in the case of a notice directed to the Tribunal, to the Tribunal's office;
(b) in the case of a notice directed to the applicant—
 (i) to his representative; or
 (ii) (in any case where there is no representative) to the applicant,

at the appropriate address notified to the Tribunal in accordance with rule 4(3);

(c) in the case of a notice directed to the Authority, to the Authority's head office; or

(d) otherwise, to the recipient's registered office or last known address.

(4) Subject to paragraphs (5) and (6), a notice that is sent shall be deemed, unless the contrary is proved, to have been received—

(a) where it was sent by post, on the second day after it was sent; and

(b) in any other case, on the day it was sent.

(5) Where a notice is sent by post to the Tribunal, it shall be deemed to have been received on the day it was actually received by the Tribunal.

(6) No notice shall be deemed to have been received if it is not received in legible form (or, in the case of a document received in electronic form, if the recipient is not readily able to elicit the information in legible form).

(7) Where the time prescribed by these Rules for doing any act expires on a Saturday, Sunday, Christmas Day, Good Friday or bank holiday, the act shall be in time if done on the next following working day.

(8) Paragraph (9) applies where—

(a) a recipient cannot be found;

(b) a recipient has died and has no known personal representative;

(c) a recipient has no address for service in the United Kingdom; or

(d) for any other reason service on a recipient cannot be readily effected.

(9) Where this paragraph applies the Chairman may dispense with service on the recipient or may make an order for alternative service on such other person or in such other form (whether by advertisement in a newspaper or otherwise) as the Chairman may think fit.

(10) In this rule, "bank holiday" means a day that is specified in, or appointed under, the Banking and Financial Dealings Act 1971.

[4439]

FINANCIAL SERVICES AND MARKETS ACT 2000 (CONSULTATION WITH COMPETENT AUTHORITIES) REGULATIONS 2001

(SI 2001/2509)

NOTES

Made: 12 July 2001.

Authority: Financial Services and Markets Act 2000, ss 183(2), 188(2), 417(1), 428(3).

Commencement: 1 December 2001 (being the date on which the Financial Services and Markets Act 2000, s 19 came into force); see reg 1 at **[4440]**. Where any provision in this work (including any inserted or substituted provision) came into force for all purposes on or before 1 July 2005, commencement information is not noted at provision level.

These Regulations are reproduced as amended by: the Collective Investment Schemes (Miscellaneous Amendments) Regulations 2003, SI 2003/2066; the Financial Conglomerates and Other Financial Groups Regulations 2004, SI 2004/1862; the Capital Requirements Regulations 2006, SI 2006/3221; the Financial Services and Markets Act 2000 (Regulated Activities) (Amendment No 3) Order 2006, SI 2006/3384; the Financial Services and Markets Act 2000 (Markets in Financial Instruments) Regulations 2007, SI 2007/126.

1 These Regulations may be cited as the Financial Services and Markets Act 2000 (Consultation with Competent Authorities) Regulations 2001 and come into force on the day on which section 19 of the Act comes into force.

[4440]

NOTES

FSMA 2000, s 19 came into force on 1 December 2001 (see the Financial Services and Markets Act 2000 (Commencement No 7) Order 2001, SI 2001/3538).

2 In these Regulations—

"the Act" means the Financial Services and Markets Act 2000;

PART IV
STATUTORY INSTRUMENTS

["capital adequacy directive" means Council Directive 2006/49/EC of the European Parliament and of the Council of 14 June 2006 relating to the capital adequacy of investment firms and credit institutions;]

["EEA consolidated supervisor" means the competent authority responsible, under Articles 71 or 72 of the banking consolidation directive or under Articles 71 or 72 of the banking consolidation directive as applied by Articles 2(2) and 37(1) of the capital adequacy directive, for the exercise of supervision of—

(a) an EEA parent credit institution;

(b) an EEA parent investment firm; or

(c) credit institutions or investment firms controlled by an EEA parent financial holding company where the parent is authorised in a different EEA State to at least one of the subsidiary undertakings;]

"EEA credit institution" means an EEA firm falling within paragraph 5(b) of Schedule 3 to the Act;

["EEA insurance undertaking" means an EEA firm falling within paragraph 5(d) of Schedule 3 to the Act;]

"EEA investment firm" means an EEA firm falling within paragraph 5(a) of Schedule 3 to the Act;

["EEA management company" means an EEA firm falling within paragraph 5(f) of Schedule 3 to the Act;]

["EEA parent credit institution" means a parent credit institution in an EEA State which is not a subsidiary undertaking of another credit institution or investment firm authorised in any EEA State, or of a financial holding company set up in any EEA State;]

["EEA parent investment firm" means a parent investment firm in an EEA State which is not a subsidiary undertaking of another credit institution or investment firm authorised in any EEA State or of a financial holding company set up in any EEA State;]

["EEA parent financial holding company" means a parent financial holding company in an EEA State which is not a subsidiary undertaking of a credit institution or investment firm authorised in any EEA State or of another financial holding company set up in any EEA State;]

["financial holding company" has the meaning given by Article 4(19) of the banking consolidation directive;]

"investment firm", except in the term "EEA investment firm", has the meaning given by article 4(5) of the Regulated Activities Order;

"the Regulated Activities Order" means the Financial Services and Markets Act 2000 (Regulated Activities) Order 2001;

["relevant competent authority" means a competent authority which is not the EEA consolidated supervisor and which has authorised a subsidiary undertaking of an EEA parent credit institution, a subsidiary undertaking of an EEA parent investment firm or a subsidiary undertaking of an EEA parent financial holding company.]

"UK authorised person" has the meaning given by section 178(4) of the Act.

[4441]

NOTES

Definitions "capital adequacy directive", "EEA consolidated supervisor", "EEA parent credit institution", "EEA parent investment firm", "EEA parent financial holding company", "financial holding company", and "relevant competent authority" inserted by the Capital Requirements Regulations 2006, SI 2006/3221, regs 18, 19, as from 1 January 2007.

Definition "EEA insurance undertaking" inserted by the Financial Conglomerates and Other Financial Groups Regulations 2004, SI 2004/1862, reg 13(1), (2), as from 10 August 2004.

Definition "EEA management company" inserted by the Collective Investment Schemes (Miscellaneous Amendments) Regulations 2003, SI 2003/2066, reg 6(a), as from 13 February 2004.

Definition "investment firm" revoked by the Financial Services and Markets Act 2000 (Regulated Activities) (Amendment No 3) Order 2006, SI 2006/3384, art 38, as from 1 November 2007 (for the full commencement details of SI 2006/3384, see the Note for that Order at **[4826A]**).

3 Where [paragraph (1), (2), (3) or (4)] of regulation 5 applies, the requirement specified by regulation 6 is prescribed for the purposes of section 183(2) of the Act (and so must be complied with by the Authority before determining whether to approve of the change of control or to give a warning notice under section 183(3) or 185(3) of the Act).

[4442]

NOTES

Words in square brackets substituted by the Financial Conglomerates and Other Financial Groups Regulations 2004, SI 2004/1862, reg 13(1), (3), as from 10 August 2004.

4 Where—

(a) [paragraph (1), (2), (3) or (4)] of regulation 5 applies; and

(b) the Authority proposes to give a notice of objection under 187(1) of the Act;

the requirement specified by regulation 6 is prescribed for the purposes of section 188(2) of the Act (and so must be complied with by the Authority before it gives a warning notice under section 188(1) of the Act).

[4443]

NOTES

Words in square brackets substituted by the Financial Conglomerates and Other Financial Groups Regulations 2004, SI 2004/1862, reg 13(1), (4), as from 10 August 2004.

5—(1) This paragraph applies where—

(a) a person ("the acquirer") proposes to acquire or has acquired control, an additional kind of control or an increase in a relevant kind of control over a UK authorised person in circumstances falling within section 178(1) or (2) of the Act;

(b) that UK authorised person is an investment firm;

[(c) the acquirer is any of the following—

(i) an EEA investment firm;

(ii) an EEA credit institution;

(iii) an EEA insurance undertaking; or

(iv) the parent undertaking of an EEA firm of a kind specified by paragraph (i), (ii) or (iii);] and

(d) as a result of the acquisition or proposed acquisition, the acquirer is or would become a parent undertaking of the UK authorised person.

(2) This paragraph applies where—

(a) a person ("the acquirer") proposes to acquire or has acquired control, an additional kind of control or an increase in a relevant kind of control over a UK authorised person in circumstances falling within section 178(1) or (2) of the Act;

(b) that UK authorised person has permission to accept deposits (within the meaning of the Regulated Activities Order);

[(c) the acquirer is any of the following—

(i) an EEA investment firm;

(ii) an EEA credit institution;

(iii) an EEA insurance undertaking; or

(iv) the parent undertaking of an EEA firm of a kind specified by paragraph (i), (ii) or (iii);] and

(d) as a result of the acquisition or proposed acquisition, the acquirer is or would become a parent undertaking of the UK authorised person.

[(3) This paragraph applies where—

(a) a person ("the acquirer") proposes to acquire or has acquired control, an additional kind of control or an increase in a relevant kind of control over a UK authorised person in circumstances falling within section 178(1) or (2) of the Act;

(b) that UK authorised person has permission to operate a collective investment scheme;

[(c) the acquirer is any of the following—

(i) an EEA investment firm;

(ii) an EEA credit institution;

(iii) an EEA insurance undertaking;

(iv) an EEA management company; or

(v) the parent undertaking of an EEA firm of a kind specified by paragraph (i), (ii), (iii) or (iv);] and

(d) as a result of the acquisition or proposed acquisition, the acquirer is or would become a parent undertaking of the UK authorised person.]

[(4) This paragraph applies where—

(a) a person ("the acquirer") proposes to acquire or has acquired control, an

PART IV
STATUTORY INSTRUMENTS

additional kind of control or an increase in a relevant kind of control over a UK authorised person in circumstances falling within section 178(1) or (2) of the Act;

(b) that UK authorised person has permission to effect or carry on contracts of insurance (within the meaning of the Regulated Activities Order);

(c) the acquirer is any of the following—

(i) an EEA investment firm;

(ii) an EEA credit institution;

(iii) an EEA insurance undertaking; or

(iv) the parent undertaking of an EEA firm of a kind specified by paragraph (i), (ii) or (iii); and

(d) as a result of the acquisition or proposed acquisition, the acquirer is or would become a parent undertaking of the UK authorised person.]

[4444]

NOTES

Paras (1), (2): sub-para (c) substituted by the Financial Conglomerates and Other Financial Groups Regulations 2004, SI 2004/1862, reg 13(1), (5)(a), (b), as from 10 August 2004.

Para (3): added by the Collective Investment Schemes (Miscellaneous Amendments) Regulations 2003, SI 2003/2066, reg 6(d), as from 13 February 2004; sub-para (c) substituted by SI 2004/1862, reg 13(1), (5)(c), as from 10 August 2004.

Para (4): added by SI 2004/1862, reg 13(1), (5)(d), as from 10 August 2004.

[6 The requirement specified by this regulation is that the Authority must, as the case may be, consult the home state regulator of any EEA firm that is mentioned in paragraph (1)(c), (2)(c), (3)(c) or (4)(c) of regulation 5.]

[4445]

NOTES

Substituted by the Financial Conglomerates and Other Financial Groups Regulations 2004, SI 2004/1862, reg 13(1), (6), as from 10 August 2004.

[7—(1) Where paragraph (3) applies, the requirement specified by paragraph (5) is prescribed for the purposes of section 183(2) of the Act and so must be complied with by the Authority before it determines whether to approve the change of control or give a warning notice under section 183(3) or 185(3) of the Act.

(2) Where paragraph (4) applies, the requirement specified by paragraph (5) is prescribed for the purposes of section 188(2) of the Act and so must be complied with by the Authority before it gives a warning notice under section 188(1) of the Act.

(3) This paragraph applies where—

(a) a person ("the acquirer") proposes to acquire or has acquired control, an additional kind of control or an increase in a relevant kind of control over a UK authorised person in circumstances falling within section 178(1) or (2) of the Act;

(b) that UK authorised person has an EEA right to carry on an activity in an EEA State other than the United Kingdom which derives from any of—

(i) the insurance directives;

(ii) the banking consolidation directive;

(iii) the *investment services directive*; or

(iv) the UCITS directive; and

(c) that UK authorised person is a member of a financial conglomerate (within the meaning of article 2(14) of Directive 2002/87/EC of the European Parliament and of the Council of 16 December 2002 on the supplementary supervision of credit institutions, insurance undertakings and investment firms in a financial conglomerate and amending Council Directives 73/239/EEC, 79/267/EEC, 92/49/EEC, 93/6/EEC, 93/22/EEC and Directives 98/78/EC and 2000/12/EC of the European Parliament and of the Council).

(4) This paragraph applies where—

(a) a circumstance has arisen in respect of which the Authority may give a decision notice to a UK authorised person under section 187 of the Act;

(b) that UK authorised person has an EEA right to carry on activity in an EEA State other than the United Kingdom which derives from any of—

(i) the insurance directives;

(ii) the banking consolidation directive;

(iii) the *investment services directive*; or
(iv) the UCITS directive;

(c) that UK authorised person is a member of a financial conglomerate (within the meaning of article 2(14) of Directive 2002/87/EC of the European Parliament and of the Council of 16 December 2002 on the supplementary supervision of credit institutions, insurance undertakings and investment firms in a financial conglomerate and amending Council Directives 73/239/EEC, 79/267/EEC, 92/49/EEC, 93/6/EEC, 93/22/EEC and Directives 98/78/EC and 2000/12/EC of the European Parliament and of the Council).

(5) The requirement specified by this paragraph is that the Authority must, where it considers that the action it proposes to take—

(a) constitutes a major sanction or an exceptional measure; and
(b) is of importance for the supervisory tasks of the home state regulator of any EEA firm that is a member of a financial conglomerate and is—
  (i) an EEA investment firm;
  (ii) an EEA credit institution; or
  (iii) an EEA insurance undertaking,

consult that home state regulator.

(6) But paragraph (5) does not apply where the Authority—

(a) considers that there is an urgent need to act;
(b) considers that such consultation may jeopardise the effectiveness of any action to be taken by it; or
(c) has already consulted that home state regulator regarding that matter.

(7) Where paragraph (5) does not apply by virtue of paragraph (6)(a) or (b), the Authority must inform the home state regulator in question as soon as is reasonably practicable.]

[4445A]

NOTES

Added by the Financial Conglomerates and Other Financial Groups Regulations 2004, SI 2004/1862, reg 13(1), (7), as from 10 August 2004.

Paras (3), (4): for the words in italics there are substituted the words "markets in financial instruments directive" by the Financial Services and Markets Act 2000 (Markets in Financial Instruments) Regulations 2007, SI 2007/126, reg 3(6), Sch 6, Pt 2, para 16, as from 1 November 2007 (for the full commencement details of SI 2007/126, see reg 1 of those Regulations at **[7596]**).

[8—(1) Where paragraph (3) applies, the requirement specified by paragraph (5) is prescribed for the purposes of section 183(2) of the Act and so must be complied with by the Authority before it determines whether to approve the change of control or give a warning notice under section 183(3) or 185(3) of the Act.

(2) Where paragraph (4) applies, the requirement specified by paragraph (5) is prescribed for the purposes of section 188(2) of the Act and so must be complied with by the Authority before it gives a warning notice under section 188(1) of the Act.

(3) This paragraph applies where—

(a) a person ("the acquirer") proposes to acquire or has acquired control or an additional kind of control over a UK authorised person in circumstances falling within section 178(1) or (2) of the Act;
(b) that UK authorised person is, or is controlled by, an EEA parent credit institution or an EEA parent investment firm or is controlled by an EEA parent financial holding company which is subject to supervision on a consolidated basis in accordance with the banking consolidation directive or with the banking consolidation directive as applied by Articles 2(2) and 37(1) of the capital adequacy directive.

(4) This paragraph applies where—

(a) a circumstance has arisen in respect of which the Authority may give a decision notice to a UK authorised person under section 187 of the Act;
(b) that UK authorised person is, or is controlled by, an EEA parent credit institution or an EEA parent investment firm or is controlled by an EEA parent financial holding company which is subject to supervision on a consolidated basis in

accordance with the banking consolidation directive or with the banking consolidation directive as applied by Articles 2(2) and 37(1) of the capital adequacy directive.

(5) The requirement specified by this paragraph is that the Authority must consult—

(a) the EEA consolidated supervisor where it considers that the action it proposes to take constitutes a major sanction or an exceptional measure; and

(b) a relevant competent authority where it considers that the action it proposes to take constitutes a major sanction or an exceptional measure which is of importance for the supervisory tasks of that relevant competent authority.

(6) Paragraphs (1) and (2) of this regulation do not apply where the Authority considers that—

(a) there is an urgent need to act; or

(b) such consultation may jeopardise the effectiveness of the actions referred to in paragraph (5),

but in such a case the Authority must, without delay, inform the EEA consolidated supervisor and the relevant competent authorities referred to in paragraph (5)(b) of the action that it has taken.]

[4445B]

NOTES

Commencement: 1 January 2007.

Added by the Capital Requirements Regulations 2006, SI 2006/3221, regs 18, 20, as from 1 January 2007.

FINANCIAL SERVICES AND MARKETS ACT 2000 (GAMING CONTRACTS) ORDER 2001

(SI 2001/2510)

NOTES

Made: 12 July 2001.

Authority: Financial Services and Markets Act 2000, s 412(2), (6).

Commencement: 1 December 2001 (being the date on which the Financial Services and Markets Act 2000, s 19 came into force); see art 1 at **[4446]**. Where any provision in this work (including any inserted or substituted provision) came into force for all purposes on or before 1 July 2005, commencement information is not noted at provision level.

As of 1 July 2007, this Order had not been amended.

1 This Order may be cited as the Financial Services and Markets Act 2000 (Gaming Contracts) Order 2001 and comes into force on the day on which section 19 of the Act comes into force.

[4446]

NOTES

FSMA 2000, s 19 came into force on 1 December 2001 (see the Financial Services and Markets Act 2000 (Commencement No 7) Order 2001, SI 2001/3538).

2—(1) Any activity of the kind—

(a) specified by article 14 or 21 of the Financial Services and Markets Act 2000 (Regulated Activities) Order 2001 ("the Regulated Activities Order") (dealing in investments as principal or agent);

(b) specified by article 64 of that Order (agreeing to carry on specified kinds of activity), so far as relevant to either of those articles; or

(c) which would be so specified apart from any exclusion from any of those articles made by that Order;

is specified for the purposes of paragraph (b) of subsection (2) of section 412 of the Act (contracts not to be void or unenforceable because of the law relating to gaming).

(2) The class of investment consisting of securities and contractually based investments (within the meaning of the Regulated Activities Order) is specified for the purposes of paragraph (c) of subsection (2) of that section.

[4447]

FINANCIAL SERVICES AND MARKETS ACT 2000 (EEA PASSPORT RIGHTS) REGULATIONS 2001

(SI 2001/2511)

NOTES

Made: 12 July 2001.

Authority: Financial Services and Markets Act 2000, ss 417(1), 426–428, Sch 3, paras 13(1)(b)(iii), 14(1)(b), 17(a), (b), (c), 18, 22.

Commencement: 1 December 2001 (being the date on which the Financial Services and Markets Act 2000, s 19 came into force); see reg 1 at **[4448]**. Where any provision in this work (including any inserted or substituted provision) came into force for all purposes on or before 1 July 2005, commencement information is not noted at provision level.

These Regulations are reproduced as amended by: the Electronic Money (Miscellaneous Amendments) Regulations 2002, SI 2002/765; the Insurance Mediation Directive (Miscellaneous Amendments) Regulations 2003, SI 2003/1473; the Collective Investment Schemes (Miscellaneous Amendments) Regulations 2003, SI 2003/2066; the Financial Conglomerates and Other Financial Groups Regulations 2004, SI 2004/1862; the Capital Requirements Regulations 2006, SI 2006/3221; the Financial Services and Markets Act 2000 (EEA Passport Rights) (Amendment) Regulations 2006, SI 2006/3385; the Financial Services and Markets Act 2000 (Markets in Financial Instruments) (Amendment) Regulations 2007, SI 2007/763.

Gibraltar: as to the application of these Regulations, with modifications, to Gibraltar, see the Financial Services and Markets Act 2000 (Gibraltar) Order 2001, SI 2001/3084 at **[4504]**.

ARRANGEMENT OF REGULATIONS

PART I
GENERAL

1 Citation, commencement and interpretation

(1) These Regulations may be cited as the Financial Services and Markets Act 2000 (EEA Passport Rights) Regulations 2001, and come into force on the day on which section 19 of the Act comes into force.

(2) In these Regulations—

"the 2BCD Regulations" means the Banking Coordination (Second Council Directive) Regulations 1992;

"the Act" means the Financial Services and Markets Act 2000;

"authorised agent" means, in relation to an EEA firm or UK firm, an agent or employee of the firm who has authority to bind the firm in its relations with third parties, and to represent the firm in its relations with the Authority or the host state regulator (as the case may be) and with the courts in the United Kingdom or the EEA State concerned (as the case may be);

"claims representative", in relation to a UK firm and an EEA State, means a person who has been designated as the firm's representative in that EEA State, and has authority—

(a) to act on behalf of the firm and to represent, or to instruct others to represent, the firm in relation to any matters giving rise to claims made against policies issued by the firm, to the extent that they cover motor vehicles risks situated in the EEA State;

(b) to pay sums in settlement of such claims (but not to settle such claims); and

(c) to accept service on behalf of the firm of proceedings in respect of such claims;

"commencement" means the beginning of the day on which section 19 of the Act comes into force;

"contract of insurance", "contract of general insurance" and "contract of long-term insurance" have the same meaning as in the Regulated Activities Order;

"credit institution" means an EEA firm falling within paragraph 5(b) of Schedule 3;

["electronic money institution" means an electronic money institution as defined in Article 1 of directive 2000/46/EC of the European Parliament and of the Council of 18th September 2000 on the taking up, pursuit of and prudential supervision of the business of electronic money institutions;]

"EEA activities" means—

(a) in relation to an EEA firm, activities which the firm is seeking to carry on in the United Kingdom in exercise of an EEA right;

(b) in relation to a UK firm, activities which the firm is seeking to carry on in another EEA State in exercise of an EEA right;

"financial institution" means an EEA firm falling within paragraph 5(c) of Schedule 3;

"the Friendly Societies Act" means the Friendly Societies Act 1992;

"health insurance risks", in relation to an EEA State, means risks of a kind mentioned in paragraph 2 of Schedule 1 to the Regulated Activities Order (sickness), where—

(a) contracts of insurance covering those risks serve as a partial or complete alternative to the health cover provided by the statutory social security system in that EEA State; and
(b) the law of that EEA State requires such contracts to be operated on a technical basis similar to life assurance in accordance with all the conditions listed in the first sub-paragraph of Article 54(2) of the third non-life insurance directive;

"the Insurance Companies Act" means the Insurance Companies Act 1982;

"insurance firm" means an EEA firm falling within paragraph 5(d) of Schedule 3;

["insurance intermediary" means an EEA firm falling within paragraph 5(e) of Schedule 3;]

"investment firm" means an EEA firm falling within paragraph 5(a) of Schedule 3;

"the ISD Regulations" means the Investment Services Regulations 1995;

["management company" means an EEA firm falling within paragraph 5(f) of Schedule 3;]

"national bureau", in relation to an EEA State, means a professional organisation—
(a) which has been constituted in that EEA State in accordance with Recommendation No 5 adopted on 25th January 1949 by the Road Transport Sub-committee of the Inland Transport Committee of the United Nations Economic Commission for Europe; and
(b) which groups together undertakings which in that EEA State are authorised to conduct the business of motor vehicle liability insurance;

"national guarantee fund", in relation to an EEA State, means a body—
(a) which has been set up or authorised in that EEA State in accordance with Article 1(4) of Council Directive 84/5/EEC on the approximation of laws of the Member States relating to insurance against civil liability in respect of the use of motor vehicles; and
(b) which provides compensation for damage to property or personal injuries caused by unidentified vehicles or vehicles for which the insurance obligation provided for in Article 1(1) of that Directive has not been satisfied;

"the Regulated Activities Order" means the Financial Services and Markets Act 2000 (Regulated Activities) Order 2001;

"relevant motor vehicle risks" means risks of damage arising out of or in connection with the use of motor vehicles on land, including third party risks (but excluding carrier's liability);

"requisite details", in relation to a branch, means—
(a) particulars of the programme of operations carried on, or to be carried on, from the branch, including a description of the particular EEA activities to be carried on, and of the structural organisation of the branch;
(b) the address in the EEA State in which the branch is, or is to be, established from which information about the business may be obtained; and
(c) the names of the managers of the business;

"Schedule 3" means Schedule 3 to the Act;

["tied agent" has the meaning given in Article 4.1.25 of the markets in financial instruments directive;

"UK investment firm" means a UK firm—
(a) which is an investment firm [(within the meaning of section 424A of the Act)],
(b) whose EEA right derives from the markets in financial instruments directive].

[4448]

NOTES

Para (2) is amended as follows:

Definition "electronic money institution" inserted by the Electronic Money (Miscellaneous Amendments) Regulations 2002, SI 2002/765, art 10(1), (2), as from 27 April 2002.

Definition "insurance intermediary" inserted by the Insurance Mediation Directive (Miscellaneous Amendments) Regulations 2003, SI 2003/1473, reg 8(1), (2), as from 14 January 2005.

Definition "management company" inserted by the Collective Investment Schemes (Miscellaneous Amendments) Regulations 2003, SI 2003/2066, reg 2(3), as from 13 February 2004.

Definitions "tied agent" and "UK investment firm" inserted by the Financial Services and Markets Act 2000 (EEA Passport Rights) (Amendment) Regulations 2006, SI 2006/3385, regs 2, 3, as from 1 November 2007 (as to the commencement of SI 2006/3385, see further the final note below).

Words in square brackets in definition "UK investment firm" inserted by the Financial Services and Markets Act 2000 (Markets in Financial Instruments) (Amendment) Regulations 2007, SI 2007/763, reg 8, as from 1 November 2007.

FSMA 2000, s 19 came into force on 1 December 2001 (see the Financial Services and Markets Act 2000 (Commencement No 7) Order 2001, SI 2001/3538).

Note: SI 2006/3385, reg 1(2), (3) (commencement) provide as follows—

"(2) These Regulations come into force on 1st April 2007 for the purposes of—

(a) regulations 4 and 5;

(b) enabling the Authority to treat a notice referred to in regulation 4A(3)(a) or 5A(3)(a) of the principal Regulations (inserted by these Regulations) given on or after that date as effective for the purpose of regulation 4A(3) or 5A(3) (as the case may be);

(c) enabling the Authority, on receipt on or after that date of notice under regulation 11A(2)(a) or 12A(2)(a) of the principal Regulations (inserted by these Regulations), to inform the host state regulator of the proposed change in accordance with regulation 11A(3) or 12A(3) (as the case may be); and

(d) enabling the Authority to give notice under regulation 11A(3) or 12A(3) of the principal Regulations (inserted by these Regulations),

and for all other purposes on 1st November 2007.

(3) Nothing in paragraph (2) gives an investment firm or a UK investment firm an EEA right to carry on, before 1st November 2007, an activity—

(a) which is an ancillary service listed in Section B of Annex I to the markets in financial instruments directive but which is not a non-core service listed in Section C of the Annex to the investment services directive;

(b) in relation to an investment which is a financial instrument listed in Section C of Annex I to the markets in financial instruments directive but which is not an instrument listed in Section B of the Annex to the investment services directive; or

(c) referred to in paragraph 5 of Section A of Annex I to the markets in financial instruments directive unless the firm has an EEA right to carry on one or more core services listed in Section A of the Annex to the investment services directive.".

PART II
EXERCISE OF PASSPORT RIGHTS BY EEA FIRMS

Contents of consent notice and regulator's notice

2 Establishment of a branch: contents of consent notice

(1) The following information is prescribed for the purposes of paragraph 13(1)(b)(iii) of Schedule 3 (and is therefore to be included in a consent notice given to the Authority by a firm's home state regulator pursuant to paragraph 13(1)(a) of Schedule 3).

(2) In the case of an investment firm, the prescribed information is—

(a) a statement that the firm is an investment firm;

(b) the requisite details of the branch; ...

[(c) details of the accredited compensation scheme of which the firm is a member in accordance with Directive 97/9/EC of the European Parliament and of the Council of 3rd March 1997 on investor-compensation schemes; and

(d) a statement of whether the firm intends to use a tied agent established in the United Kingdom.]

[(2A) In the case of a management company, the prescribed information is—

(a) a statement that the firm is a management company;

(b) the requisite details of the branch; and

(c) details of any compensation scheme which is intended to protect the branch's investors.]

(3) In the case of a credit institution, the prescribed information is—

(a) a statement that the firm is a credit institution;

(b) the requisite details of the branch;

(c) the amount of the firm's own funds (as defined in Section 1 of Chapter 2 of Title V to the banking consolidation directive); and

(d) [except where the firm is an electronic money institution,] [the sum of the capital requirements under Article 75 of the banking consolidation directive].

(4) In the case of a financial institution, the prescribed information is—

(a) a statement that—

(i) the firm is a financial institution;

(ii) the firm is a subsidiary undertaking of a credit institution [(other than an electronic money institution)] which is authorised in the EEA State in question and which holds at least 90 per cent of the voting rights in the firm (and for the purpose of this paragraph any two or more credit institutions which are authorised in that EEA State and hold voting rights in the firm are to be treated as a single credit institution, and as being "parent undertakings" of the firm);

(iii) the firm carries on in that EEA State the EEA activities in question;

(iv) the memorandum and articles of association, or other constituent instrument, of the firm permit it to carry on those activities;

(v) the consolidated supervision of the firm's parent undertaking or, if more than one, any one of them effectively includes supervision of the firm;

(vi) the firm's parent undertaking has guaranteed or, if more than one, they have jointly and severally guaranteed, the firm's obligations, with the consent of the home state regulator;

(vii) the firm's business is being conducted in a prudent manner;

(b) the requisite details of the branch;

(c) the amount of the firm's own funds (as defined in Section 1 of Chapter 2 of Title V to the banking consolidation directive); and

[(d) the sum of the capital requirements under Article 75 of the banking consolidation directive of the firm's parent undertaking.]

(5) In the case of an insurance firm, the prescribed information is—

(a) a scheme of operations prepared in accordance with such requirements as may be imposed by the firm's home state regulator, setting out (amongst other things) the types of business to be carried on and the structural organisation of the branch;

(b) the name of the firm's authorised agent;

(c) the address in the United Kingdom from which information about the business may be obtained, and a statement that this is the address for service on the firm's authorised agent;

(d) in the case of a firm which intends to cover relevant motor vehicle risks, a declaration by the firm that it has become a member of the Motor Insurers' Bureau (being a company limited by guarantee and incorporated under the Companies Act 1929 on the 14th June 1946); and

(e) a statement by the firm's home state regulator attesting that the firm has the minimum margin of solvency calculated in accordance with such of the following as are appropriate—

(i) Articles 16 and 17 of the first non-life insurance directive [(as last amended by Directive 2002/87/EC of the European Parliament and of the Council)], and

(ii) Articles 18, 19 and 20 of the first life insurance directive.

[4449]

NOTES

Para (2): word omitted from sub-para (b) revoked, and sub-paras (c), (d) substituted (for the original sub-para (c), by the Financial Services and Markets Act 2000 (EEA Passport Rights) (Amendment) Regulations 2006, SI 2006/3385, regs 2, 4, as from 1 April 2007 (for the full commencement details of SI 2006/3385 see the final note to reg 1 *ante*).

Para (2A): inserted by the Collective Investment Schemes (Miscellaneous Amendments) Regulations 2003, SI 2003/2066, reg 3(2)(a), as from 13 February 2004.

Para (3): words in first pair of square brackets in sub-para (d) inserted by the Electronic Money (Miscellaneous Amendments) Regulations 2002, SI 2002/765, art 10(1), (2), as from 27 April 2002; words in second pair of square brackets in sub-para (d) substituted by the Capital Requirements Regulations 2006, SI 2006/3221, reg 29(4), Sch 6, para 9(1), (2), as from 1 January 2007.

Para (4): words in square brackets in sub-para (a) inserted by SI 2002/765, art 10(1), (2), as from 27 April 2002; sub-para (d) substituted by the Capital Requirements Regulations 2006, SI 2006/3221, reg 29(4), Sch 6, para 9(1), (3), as from 1 January 2007.

Para (5): words in square brackets in sub-para (e)(i) inserted by the Financial Conglomerates and Other Financial Groups Regulations 2004, SI 2004/1862, reg 14(4), as from 10 August 2004.

3 Provision of services: contents of regulator's notice

(1) The following information is prescribed for the purposes of paragraph 14(1)(b) of Schedule 3 (and is therefore to be included in a regulator's notice given to the Authority by a firm's home state regulator pursuant to that paragraph).

(2) [Subject to paragraph (2ZA), in] the case of an investment firm, the prescribed information is—

(a) a statement that the firm is an investment firm; …

(b) particulars of the programme of operations to be carried on in the United Kingdom, including a description of the particular EEA activities to be carried on[; and

(c) a statement of whether the firm intends to use a tied agent to provide services in the United Kingdom].

[(2ZA) In the case of an investment firm exercising the right under Article 31.5 of the markets in financial instruments directive, the prescribed information is—

(a) a statement that the firm is an investment firm; and

(b) a statement that the firm intends to exercise that right in the United Kingdom.]

[(2A) In the case of a management company, the prescribed information is—

(a) a statement that the firm is a management company;

(b) particulars of the programme of operations to be carried on in the United Kingdom including a description of the particular EEA activities to be carried on; and

(c) details of any compensation scheme which is intended to protect investors.]

(3) In the case of an insurance firm, the prescribed information is—

(a) a statement of the classes of business which the firm is authorised to carry on in accordance with Article 6 of the first non-life insurance directive or Article 6 of the first life insurance directive;

(b) the name and address of the firm;

(c) the nature of the risks or commitments which the firm proposes to cover in the United Kingdom;

(d) in the case of a firm which intends to cover relevant motor vehicle risks—

(i) the name and address of the claims representative; and

(ii) a declaration by the firm that it has become a member of the Motor Insurers' Bureau; and

(e) a statement by the firm's home state regulator attesting that the firm has the minimum margin of solvency calculated in accordance with such of the following as are appropriate—

(i) Articles 16 and 17 of the first non-life insurance directive [(as last amended by Directive 2002/87/EC of the European Parliament and of the Council)], and

(ii) Articles 18, 19 and 20 of the first life insurance directive.

[(4) In the case of an insurance intermediary, the prescribed information is that the firm intends to carry on insurance mediation or reinsurance mediation (in each case, within the meaning of the insurance mediation directive) by providing services in the United Kingdom.]

[4450]

NOTES

Para (2): words in first pair of square brackets substituted, word omitted revoked, and sub-para (c) (and the preceding word) added, by the Financial Services and Markets Act 2000 (EEA Passport Rights) (Amendment) Regulations 2006, SI 2006/3385, regs 2, 5(a), as from 1 April 2007 (for the full commencement details of SI 2006/3385 see the final note to reg 1 *ante*).

Para (2ZA): inserted by SI 2006/3385, regs 2, 5(b), as from 1 April 2007 (for the full commencement details of SI 2006/3385 see the final note to reg 1 *ante*).

Para (2A): inserted by the Collective Investment Schemes (Miscellaneous Amendments) Regulations 2003, SI 2003/2066, reg 3(2)(b), as from 13 February 2004.

Para (3): words in square brackets in sub-para (e)(i) inserted by the Financial Conglomerates and Other Financial Groups Regulations 2004, SI 2004/1862, reg 14(4), as from 10 August 2004.

Para (4): added by the Insurance Mediation Directive (Miscellaneous Amendments) Regulations 2003, SI 2003/1473, reg 8(1), (3), as from 14 January 2005.

Changes relating to EEA firms

4 *Investment firms*[, *management* companies], credit institutions and financial institutions: changes to branch details

(1) *An investment firm[,* management company], credit institution or financial institution which has established a branch in the United Kingdom in exercise of an EEA right must not make a change in the requisite details of the branch, unless the relevant requirements have been complied with.

(2) Where the relevant requirements have been complied with, the firm's permission is to be treated as varied accordingly.

(3) For the purposes of this regulation, the "relevant requirements" are those of paragraph (4) or (if the change is occasioned by circumstances beyond the firm's control) paragraph (5).

(4) The requirements of this paragraph are that—
(a) the firm has given a notice to the Authority and to its home state regulator stating the details of the proposed change;
(b) the Authority has received from the home state regulator a notice stating those details; and
(c) either the Authority has informed the firm that it may make the change, or the period of one month beginning with the day on which the firm gave the Authority the notice mentioned in sub-paragraph (a) has elapsed.

(5) The requirements of this paragraph are that the firm has as soon as practicable (whether before or after the change) given a notice to the Authority and to its home state regulator, stating the details of the change.

(6) The Authority must, as soon as practicable after receiving a notice from *an investment firm[,* management company], credit institution or financial institution under this regulation, inform the firm of any consequential changes in the applicable provisions (within the meaning of paragraph 13 of Schedule 3).

[4451]

NOTES

Regulation heading: words in square brackets inserted by the Collective Investment Schemes (Miscellaneous Amendments) Regulations 2003, SI 2003/2066, reg 3(2)(c), as from 13 February 2004; for the words in italics there is substituted the word "Management" by the Financial Services and Markets Act 2000 (EEA Passport Rights) (Amendment) Regulations 2006, SI 2006/3385, regs 2, 6(a), as from 1 November 2007 (for transitional provisions and details as to the commencement of SI 2006/3385, see the note below).

Para (1): words in square brackets inserted by SI 2003/2066, reg 3(2)(c), as from 13 February 2004; for the words in italics there is substituted the word "A" by SI 2006/3385, regs 2, 6(b), as from 1 November 2007 (for transitional provisions and details as to the commencement of SI 2006/3385, see the note below).

Para (6): words in square brackets inserted by SI 2003/2066, reg 3(2)(c), as from 13 February 2004; for the words in italics there is substituted the word "A" by SI 2006/3385, regs 2, 6(b), as from 1 November 2007 (for transitional provisions and details as to the commencement of SI 2006/3385, see the note below).

Note: as to the commencement of SI 2006/3385 see the final note to reg 1 *ante*. Note also that SI 2006/3385, reg 15 provides as follows—

"15 Transitional and saving provisions

(1) Where an investment firm has given notice to the Authority and to its home state regulator pursuant to regulation 4(4)(a) of the principal Regulations (of a change in the requisite details of its branch) on or before 31st October 2007, regulation 4 continues to apply in relation to that change as if it had not been amended by these Regulations, and regulation 4A of the principal Regulations (inserted by these Regulations) does not apply in relation to that change.

(2) Where an investment firm has given notice to the Authority and to its home state regulator pursuant to regulation 5(3)(a) of the principal Regulations or before 31st October 2007 (in relation to a change in the matters referred to in regulation 3(2)(b) of those Regulations), regulation 5 continues to apply in relation to that change as if it had not been amended by these Regulations, and regulation 5A of the principal Regulations (inserted by these Regulations) does not apply in relation to that change.

(3) Where on or before 31st October 2007—
(a) a UK investment firm has given notice to the Authority and to its host state regulator pursuant to regulation 11(2)(a) of the principal Regulations (of a change in the requisite details of the branch) on or before 31st October 2007, but
(b) the Authority has not performed its function under regulation 11(4) of those Regulations,

the Authority must inform the host state regulator of the change pursuant to regulation 11A(3) of the principal Regulations (inserted by these Regulations) instead of performing its function under regulation 11(4).

(4) Where the Authority has performed its function under regulation 11(4) of the principal Regulations (in relation to a change in the requisite details of a branch by a UK investment firm) on or before 31st October 2007, regulation 11 of the principal Regulations continues to apply in relation to that change as if it had not been amended by these Regulations, and regulation 11A of the principal Regulations (inserted by these Regulations) does not apply in relation to that change.

(5) Where a UK investment firm has given notice to the Authority and to its host state regulator pursuant to regulation 12(2)(a) of the principal Regulations (in relation to a change in its programme of operations or EEA activities) on or before 31st October 2007—

(a) regulation 12A of the principal Regulations (inserted by these Regulations) does not apply in relation to that change;

(b) the firm must not make the change to which the notice relates until the period of one month beginning with the day on which it gave the notice pursuant to regulation 12(2)(a) of the principal Regulations has elapsed; and

(c) the Authority must, as soon as reasonably practicable after receiving the notice, inform the host state regulator of the proposed change.

(6) In this regulation, "UK investment firm" means a UK firm (within the meaning of Schedule 3)—

(a) which is an investment firm (within the meaning of the investment services directive); and

(b) whose EEA right derives from that directive.".

[4A Investment firms: changes to branch details

(1) An investment firm which has established a branch in the United Kingdom in exercise of an EEA right must not—

(a) make a change in the requisite details of the branch,

(b) use, for the first time, any tied agent established in the United Kingdom, or

(c) cease to use tied agents established in the United Kingdom,

unless the requirements of paragraph (3) have been complied with.

(2) Where those requirements have been complied with, the firm's permission is to be treated as varied accordingly.

(3) The requirements are that—

(a) the firm has given a notice to its home state regulator stating the details of the proposed change, and

(b) the period of one month beginning with the day on which the firm gave the notice has elapsed.

(4) Paragraph (1) does not apply to a change occasioned by circumstances beyond the firm's control.]

[4451A]

NOTES

Commencement: 1 April 2007 (certain purposes); 1 November 2007 (otherwise) (for more information see below).

Inserted by the Financial Services and Markets Act 2000 (EEA Passport Rights) (Amendment) Regulations 2006, SI 2006/3385, regs 2, 7, as from 1 April 2007 (certain purposes), and as from 1 November 2007 (otherwise) (for the full commencement details of SI 2006/3385 see the final note to reg 1 *ante*, and for transitional provisions see the note to reg 4 at **[4451]**).

5 *Investment firms [and management* companies]: changes to services

(1) An investment firm which is providing services in the United Kingdom in exercise of an EEA right must not make a change in any of the matters referred to in regulation 3(2)(b), unless the relevant requirements have been complied with.

[(1A) A management company which is providing services in the United Kingdom in the exercise of an EEA right must not make a change in any of the matters referred to in regulation 3(2A)(b), unless the relevant requirements have been complied with.]

(2) Where the relevant requirements have been complied with, the firm's permission is to be treated as varied accordingly.

(3) For the purposes of this regulation, the "relevant requirements" are that—

(a) the firm has given a notice to the Authority and to its home state regulator stating the details of the proposed change; or

(b) if the change is occasioned by circumstances beyond the firm's control, it has as soon as practicable (whether before or after the change) given to the Authority and to its home state regulator a notice stating the details of the change.

(4) The Authority must, as soon as practicable after receiving a notice from an investment firm [or a management company] under this regulation, inform the firm of any consequential changes in the applicable provisions (within the meaning of paragraph 14 of Schedule 3).

[4452]

NOTES

Regulation heading: words in square brackets inserted by the Collective Investment Schemes (Miscellaneous Amendments) Regulations 2003, SI 2003/2066, reg 3(2)(d)(i), as from 13 February 2004; for the words in italics there is substituted the word "Management" by the Financial Services and Markets Act 2000 (EEA Passport Rights) (Amendment) Regulations 2006, SI 2006/3385, regs 2, 8(a), as from 1 November 2007 (for the full commencement details of SI 2006/3385 see the final note to reg 1 *ante*, and for transitional provisions see the note to reg 4 at **[4451]**).

Para (1): revoked by SI 2006/3385, regs 2, 8(b), as from 1 November 2007 (for the full commencement details of SI 2006/3385 see the final note to reg 1 *ante*, and for transitional provisions see the note to reg 4 at **[4451]**).

Para (1A): inserted by SI 2003/2066, reg 3(2)(d)(ii), as from 13 February 2004.

Para (4): words in square brackets inserted by SI 2003/2066, reg 3(2)(d)(iii), as from 13 February 2004.

[5A Investment firms: changes to services

(1) An investment firm which is providing services in the United Kingdom in exercise of an EEA right must not—

(a) make a change in any of the matters referred to in regulation 3(2)(b),
(b) use, for the first time, any tied agent to provide services in the United Kingdom, or
(c) cease to use tied agents to provide services in the United Kingdom,

unless the requirements of paragraph (3) have been complied with.

(2) Where those requirements have been complied with, the firm's permission is to be treated as varied accordingly.

(3) The requirements are that—

(a) the firm has given a notice to its home state regulator stating the details of the proposed change, and
(b) the period of one month beginning with the day on which the firm gave the notice has elapsed.

(4) Paragraph (1) does not apply to a change occasioned by circumstances beyond the firm's control.]

[4452A]

NOTES

Commencement: 1 April 2007 (certain purposes); 1 November 2007 (otherwise) (for more information see below).

Inserted by the Financial Services and Markets Act 2000 (EEA Passport Rights) (Amendment) Regulations 2006, SI 2006/3385, regs 2, 9, as from 1 April 2007 (certain purposes), and as from 1 November 2007 (otherwise) (for the full commencement details of SI 2006/3385 see the final note to reg 1 ante, and for transitional provisions see the note to reg 4 at **[4451]**).

6 Insurance firms: changes to branch details

(1) An insurance firm which has established a branch in the United Kingdom in exercise of an EEA right must not make a change in any of the details referred to in regulation 2(5)(a) to (c) with respect to the branch, unless the relevant requirements have been complied with.

(2) Where the relevant requirements have been complied with, the firm's permission is to be treated as varied accordingly.

(3) For the purposes of this regulation, the relevant requirements are those of paragraph (4) or (if the change is occasioned by circumstances beyond the firm's control) paragraph (5).

(4) The requirements of this paragraph are that—

(a) the firm has given a notice to the Authority and to its home state regulator stating the details of the proposed change;

(b) the Authority has received from the home state regulator a notice stating that it has approved the proposed change;
(c) the period of one month beginning with the day on which the firm gave the Authority the notice mentioned in sub-paragraph (a) has elapsed; and
(d) either—
(i) a further period of one month has elapsed; or
(ii) the Authority has informed the home state regulator of any consequential changes in the applicable provisions (within the meaning of paragraph 13 of Schedule 3).

(5) The requirements of this paragraph are that the firm has as soon as practicable (whether before or after the change) given a notice to the Authority and to its home state regulator, stating the details of the change.

(6) The Authority must, as soon as practicable—
(a) acknowledge receipt of the documents sent under paragraph (4) or (5); and
(b) in the case of a notice under paragraph (5), inform the firm's home state regulator of any consequential changes in the applicable provisions (within the meaning of paragraph 13 of Schedule 3).

[4453]

7 Insurance firms: changes to services

(1) An insurance firm which is providing services in the United Kingdom in exercise of an EEA right must not make a change in any of the matters referred to in regulation 3(3)(b), (c) or (d), unless the relevant requirements have been complied with.

(2) Where the relevant requirements have been complied with, the firm's permission is to be treated as varied accordingly.

(3) For the purposes of this regulation, the "relevant requirements" are those of paragraph (4) or (if the change is occasioned by circumstances beyond the firm's control) paragraph (5).

(4) The requirements of this paragraph are that—
(a) the firm has given a notice to its home state regulator stating the details of the proposed change; and
(b) the home state regulator has passed to the Authority the information contained in that notice.

(5) The requirements of this paragraph are that the firm has as soon as practicable (whether before or after the change) given to its home state regulator a notice stating the details of the change.

[4454]

Cancellation of qualification for authorisation

8 EEA firms ceasing to carry on regulated activities in the United Kingdom

Where an EEA firm which is qualified for authorisation under Schedule 3—
(a) has ceased, or is to cease to carry on regulated activities in the United Kingdom, and
(b) gives notice of that fact to the Authority,

the notice is to be treated as a request for cancellation of the firm's qualification for authorisation under Schedule 3 (and hence as a request under section 34(2) of the Act).

[4455]

9 Financial institutions giving up right to authorisation

(1) The Authority may, on an application by a financial institution which is qualified for authorisation under Schedule 3, direct that the firm's qualification for authorisation under Schedule 3 is cancelled from such date as may be specified in the direction.

(2) The Authority must not give such a direction unless—
(a) the firm has given notice to its home state regulator; and
(b) the Authority has agreed with the home state regulator that the direction should be given.

(3) The date specified in such a direction—

(a) must not be earlier than the date requested in the application; but

(b) subject to that, is to be such date as may be agreed between the Authority and the firm's home state regulator.

(4) The Authority must, as soon as practicable, send a copy of the direction to the firm and to the firm's home state regulator.

(5) A firm in respect of which such a direction has been given may (notwithstanding subsection (3) of section 40 of the Act) apply for permission under that section, to take effect not earlier than the date referred to in paragraph (1).

[4456]

Applications for approval under section 60 by EEA firms

10 Applications for approval under section 60 by EEA firms

In section 60 of the Act (applications for approval for persons to perform controlled functions), "the authorised person concerned" includes an EEA firm with respect to which the Authority has received a consent notice [or regulator's notice] under paragraph 13 of Schedule 3 or a regulator's notice under paragraph 14 of that Schedule, and which will be the authorised person concerned if it qualifies for authorisation under that Schedule.

[4457]

NOTES

Words in square brackets inserted by the Insurance Mediation Directive (Miscellaneous Amendments) Regulations 2003, SI 2003/1473, reg 8(1), (4), as from 14 January 2005.

PART III
EXERCISE OF PASSPORT RIGHTS BY UK FIRMS

Changes relating to UK firms

11 UK *investment firms*[, management companies], credit institutions and financial institutions: changes to branch details

(1) A UK firm which has exercised an EEA right, deriving from *the investment services directive[,* the UCITS directive] or the banking consolidation directive, to establish a branch must not make a change in the requisite details of the branch unless the requirements of paragraph (2) or (if the change is occasioned by circumstances beyond the firm's control) paragraph (3) have been complied with.

(2) The requirements of this paragraph are that—

(a) the firm has given a notice to the Authority and to the host state regulator stating the details of the proposed change;

(b) the Authority has given the host state regulator a notice under paragraph (5)(a); and

(c) either the host state regulator has informed the firm that it may make the change, or the period of one month beginning with the day on which the firm gave the host state regulator the notice mentioned in sub-paragraph (a) has elapsed.

(3) The requirements of this paragraph are that the firm has as soon as practicable (whether before or after the change) given a notice to the Authority and to the host state regulator, stating the details of the change.

(4) the Authority must, within the period of one month beginning with the day on which it received the notice referred to in paragraph (2)(a), either consent to the change or refuse to consent to the change.

(5) If the Authority consents to the change, it must—

(a) give a notice to the host state regulator informing it of the details of the proposed change; and

(b) inform the firm that if has given that notice, stating the date on which it did so.

(6) If the Authority refuses to consent to the change—

(a) the firm may refer the matter to the Tribunal; and

(b) the Authority must give notice to the firm of the refusal, stating the reasons for it, and giving an indication of the firm's right to refer the matter to the Tribunal, and the procedure on such a reference.

(7) The Authority may not refuse to consent to the change unless, having regard to the change and to the EEA activities which the firm is seeking to carry on, it doubts the adequacy of the administrative structure or the financial situation of the firm; and in reaching a determination as to the adequacy of the administrative structure, the Authority may have regard to the adequacy of management, systems and controls and the presence of relevant skills needed for the EEA activities to be carried on.

[4458]

NOTES

Regulation heading, para (1): words in square brackets inserted by the Collective Investment Schemes (Miscellaneous Amendments) Regulations 2003, SI 2003/2066, reg 4(2)(a), as from 13 February 2004; words in italics revoked by the Financial Services and Markets Act 2000 (EEA Passport Rights) (Amendment) Regulations 2006, SI 2006/3385, regs 2, 10, as from 1 November 2007 (for the full commencement details of SI 2006/3385 see the final note to reg 1 *ante*, and for transitional provisions see the note to reg 4 at **[4451]**).

[11A UK investment firms: changes to branch details

(1) A UK investment firm which has exercised an EEA right deriving from the markets in financial instruments directive to establish a branch must not—

(a) make a change in the requisite details of the branch,

(b) use, for the first time, any tied agent established in the EEA State in which the branch is established, or

(c) cease to use tied agents established in the EEA State in which the branch is established,

unless the requirements of paragraph (2) have been complied with.

(2) The requirements are that—

(a) the firm has given a notice to the Authority stating the details of the proposed change, and

(b) the period of one month beginning with the day on which the firm gave the notice has elapsed.

(3) The Authority must, as soon as reasonably practicable after receiving a notice under paragraph (2), inform the host state regulator of the proposed change.

(4) Paragraph (1) does not apply to a change occasioned by circumstances beyond the firm's control.]

[4458A]

NOTES

Commencement: 1 April 2007 (certain purposes); 1 November 2007 (otherwise) (for more information see below).

Inserted by the Financial Services and Markets Act 2000 (EEA Passport Rights) (Amendment) Regulations 2006, SI 2006/3385, regs 2, 11, as from 1 April 2007 (certain purposes), and as from 1 November 2007 (otherwise) (for the full commencement details of SI 2006/3385 see the final note to reg 1 *ante*, and for transitional provisions see the note to reg 4 at **[4451]**).

12 UK *investment firms* [*and* management companies]: changes to services

(1) A UK firm which is providing services in exercise of an EEA right, deriving from *the investment services directive [or* the UCITS directive], must not make a change in the programme of operations, or the EEA activities, to be carried on in exercise of that right, unless the relevant requirements have been complied with.

(2) For the purposes of this regulation, the "relevant requirements" are that—

(a) the firm has given a notice to the Authority and to the host state regulator stating the details of the proposed change; or

(b) if the change is occasioned by circumstances beyond the firm's control, it has as soon as practicable (whether before or after the change) given a notice to the Authority and to the host state regulator, stating the details of the change.

[4459]

NOTES

Regulation heading, para (1): words in square brackets inserted by the Collective Investment Schemes (Miscellaneous Amendments) Regulations 2003, SI 2003/2066, reg 4(2)(b), as from 13 February 2004; words in italics revoked by the Financial Services and Markets Act 2000 (EEA Passport Rights) (Amendment) Regulations 2006, SI 2006/3385, regs 2, 12, as from 1 November 2007 (for the full commencement details of SI 2006/3385 see the final note to reg 1 *ante*, and for transitional provisions see the note to reg 4 at **[4451]**).

[12A UK investment firms: changes to services

(1) A UK investment firm which is providing services in a particular EEA State in exercise of an EEA right deriving from the markets in financial instruments directive must not—

(a) make a change in the programme of operations, or the EEA activities, to be carried on in exercise of that right,

(b) use, for the first time, any tied agent to provide services in the territory of that State, or

(c) cease to use tied agents to provide services in the territory of that State,

unless the requirements of paragraph (2) have been complied with.

(2) The requirements are that—

(a) the firm has given a notice to the Authority stating the details of the proposed change, and

(b) the period of one month beginning with the day on which the firm gave the notice has elapsed.

(3) The Authority must, as soon as reasonably practicable after receiving a notice under paragraph (2), inform the host state regulator of the proposed change.

(4) Paragraph (1) does not apply to a change occasioned by circumstances beyond the firm's control.]

[4459A]

NOTES

Commencement: 1 April 2007 (certain purposes); 1 November 2007 (otherwise) (for more information see below).

Inserted by the Financial Services and Markets Act 2000 (EEA Passport Rights) (Amendment) Regulations 2006, SI 2006/3385, regs 2, 13, as from 1 April 2007 (certain purposes), and as from 1 November 2007 (otherwise) (for the full commencement details of SI 2006/3385 see the final note to reg 1 *ante*, and for transitional provisions see the note to reg 4 at **[4451]**).

13 UK insurance firms: changes to relevant EEA details of branches

(1) A UK firm which has exercised an EEA right, deriving from any of the insurance directives, to establish a branch must not make a change in the relevant EEA details (as defined in regulation 14), unless the requirements of paragraph (2) or (if the change is occasioned by circumstances beyond the firm's control) paragraph (3) have been complied with.

(2) The requirements of this paragraph are that—

(a) the firm has given a notice to the Authority and to the host state regulator stating the details of the proposed change;

(b) the Authority has given the host state regulator a notice under paragraph (5)(a);

(c) the period of one month beginning with the day on which the firm gave the Authority the notice mentioned in sub-paragraph (a) has elapsed; and

(d) either—

(i) a further period of one month has elapsed; or

(ii) the Authority has informed the firm of any consequential changes in the applicable provisions (within the meaning of paragraph 19 of Schedule 3) of which the Authority has been notified by the host state regulator.

(3) The requirements of this paragraph are that the firm has as soon as practicable (whether before or after the change) given a notice to the Authority and to the host state regulator, stating the details of the change.

(4) The Authority must, within one month of receiving the notice referred to in paragraph (2)(a), either consent to the change or refuse to consent to the change.

PART IV STATUTORY INSTRUMENTS

(5) If the Authority consents to the change, it must—
(a) give a notice to the host state regulator informing it of the details of the proposed change; and
(b) inform the firm that it has given that notice, stating the date on which it did so.

(6) If the Authority refuses to consent to the change—
(a) the firm may refer the matter to the Tribunal; and
(b) the Authority must give notice to the firm of the refusal, stating the reasons for it, and giving an indication of the firm's right to refer the matter to the Tribunal, and the procedure on such a reference.

(7) The Authority may not refuse to consent to the change unless, having regard to the change, the Authority has reason—
(a) to doubt the adequacy of the firm's administrative structure or financial situation, or
(b) to question the reputation, qualifications or experience of the directors or managers of the firm or the authorised agent,

in relation to the business conducted, or to be conducted, through the branch.

[4460]

14 Relevant EEA details for the purposes of regulation 13

(1) For the purposes of regulation 13, the relevant EEA details, with respect to a branch, are—
(a) the address of the branch;
(b) the name of the UK firm's authorised agent and, in the case of a member of Lloyd's, confirmation that the authorised agent has power to accept service of proceedings on behalf of Lloyd's;
(c) the classes or parts of classes of business carried on, or to be carried on, and the nature of the risks or commitments covered, or to be covered, in the EEA State concerned;
(d) details of the structural organisation of the branch;
(e) the guiding principles as to reinsurance of business carried on, or to be carried on, in the EEA State concerned, including the firm's maximum retention per risk or event after all reinsurance ceded;
(f) estimates of—
(i) the costs of installing administrative services and the organisation for securing business in the EEA State concerned;
(ii) the resources available to cover those costs; and
(iii) if contracts of a kind falling within paragraph 18 of Schedule 1 to the Regulated Activities Order (assistance) are, or are to be, effected or carried out, the resources available for providing assistance;
(g) for each of the first three years following the establishment of the branch—
(i) estimates of the firm's margin of solvency and the margin of solvency required, and the method of calculation;
(ii) if the firm carries on, or intends to carry on, business comprising the effecting or carrying out of contracts of long-term insurance, the details mentioned in paragraph (2) as respects the business carried on, or to be carried on, in the EEA State concerned; and
(iii) if the firm carries on, or intends to carry on, business comprising the effecting or carrying out of contracts of general insurance, the details mentioned in paragraph (3) as respects the business carried on, or to be carried on, in the EEA State concerned;
(h) if the insurer covers, or intends to cover, relevant motor vehicle risks, details of the firm's membership of the national bureau and the national guarantee fund in the EEA State concerned; and
(i) if the firm covers, or intends to cover, health insurance risks, the technical bases used, or to be used, for calculating premiums in respect of such risks.

(2) The details referred to in paragraph (l)(g)(ii) are—
(a) the following information, on both optimistic and pessimistic bases, for each type of contract or treaty—
(i) the number of contracts or treaties expected to be issued;
(ii) the total premium income, both gross and net of reinsurance ceded; and
(iii) the total sums assured or the total amounts payable each year by way of annuity;

(b) detailed estimates, on both optimistic and pessimistic bases, of income and expenditure in respect of direct business, reinsurance acceptances and reinsurance cessions; and
(c) estimates relating to the financial resources intended to cover underwriting liabilities.

(3) The details referred to in paragraph (1)(g)(iii) are—
(a) estimates relating to expenses of management (other than costs of installation), and in particular those relating to current expenses and commissions;
(b) estimates relating to premiums or contributions (both gross and net of all reinsurance ceded) and to claims (after all reinsurance recoveries); and
(c) estimates relating to the financial resources to cover underwriting liabilities.

[4461]

15 UK insurance firms: changes to relevant UK details of branches

(1) A UK firm which has exercised an EEA right, deriving from any of the insurance directives, to establish a branch must not make a change falling within paragraph (2) with respect to the branch, unless—
(a) the firm has given a notice to the Authority stating the details of the proposed change at least one month before the change is effected; or
(b) if the change is occasioned by circumstances beyond the firm's control, the firm has as soon as practicable (whether before or after the change) given a notice to the Authority stating the details of the change.

(2) A change falls within this paragraph if it is a change in any of the information which the UK firm was required to provide to the Authority by or under paragraph 19(2) of Schedule 3, other than a change in the relevant EEA details referred to in regulation 13.

[4462]

16 UK insurance firms: changes to services

(1) A UK firm which is providing services in exercise of an EEA right, deriving from any of the insurance directives, must not make a change in the relevant details (as defined in regulation 17), unless the relevant requirements have been complied with.

(2) For the purposes of this regulation, the "relevant requirements" are those of paragraph (3) or (if the change is occasioned by circumstances beyond the firm's control) paragraph (4).

(3) The requirements of this paragraph are that—
(a) the firm has given a notice to the Authority stating the details of the proposed change; and
(b) the Authority has given the host state regulator a notice under paragraph (6)(a).

(4) The requirements of this paragraph are that the firm has as soon as practicable (whether before or after the change) given a notice to the Authority stating the details of the change.

(5) The Authority must, within one month of receiving a notice under paragraph (3)(a), either consent to the change or refuse to consent to the change.

(6) If the Authority consents to the change, it must—
(a) give a notice to the host state regulator informing it of the details of the proposed change; and
(b) inform the firm that it has given that notice, stating the date on which it did so.

(7) If the Authority refuses to consent to the change—
(a) the firm may refer the matter to the Tribunal; and
(b) the Authority must give notice to the firm of the refusal, stating the reasons for it, and giving an indication of the firm's right to refer the matter to the Tribunal, and the procedure on such a reference.

[4463]

17 Relevant details for the purposes of regulation 16

The relevant details for the purposes of regulation 16 are—
(a) the EEA State in which the EEA activities are carried on, or are to be carried on;
(b) the nature of the risks or commitments covered, or to be covered, in the EEA State concerned;

(c) if the firm covers, or intends to cover, relevant motor vehicle risks—
  (i) the name and address of the claims representative; and
  (ii) details of the firm's membership of the national bureau and the national guarantee fund in the EEA State concerned; and

(d) if the insurer covers, or intends to cover, health insurance risks, the technical bases used, or to be used, for calculating premiums in respect of such risks.

[4464]

18 Offences relating to failure to notify changes

(1) If a UK firm which is not an authorised person contravenes the prohibition imposed by regulation 11(1), [11A(1),] 12(1), [12A(1),] 13(1), 15(1), or 16(1) it is guilty of an offence, punishable—

(a) on summary conviction, by a fine not exceeding the statutory maximum; or

(b) on conviction on indictment, by a fine.

(2) In proceedings for an offence under paragraph (1), it is a defence for the firm to show that it took all reasonable precautions and exercised all due diligence to avoid committing the offence.

[4465]

NOTES

Para (1): figures in square brackets inserted by the Financial Services and Markets Act 2000 (EEA Passport Rights) (Amendment) Regulations 2006, SI 2006/3385, regs 2, 14, as from 1 November 2007 (for the full commencement details of SI 2006/3385 see the final note to reg 1 *ante*).

UK firms: scope of outward passport

19 UK firms: scope of outward passport

Where—

(a) the activities identified in a notice of intention under paragraph 19 or 20 of Schedule 3 include (in accordance with paragraph 19(3) or 20(2) of that Schedule) any activity which is not a regulated activity, and

(b) that activity is one which the UK firm in question is able to carry on in the EEA State in question without contravening any provision of the law of the United Kingdom (or any part of the United Kingdom),

the UK firm is to be treated, for the purposes of the exercise of its EEA right, as being authorised to carry on that activity.

[4466]

PART IV
TRANSITIONAL PROVISIONS

20 Changes relating to EEA firms: procedures partly completed at commencement

(1) If before commencement—

(a) an EEA firm which was a European institution within the meaning of the 2BCD Regulations gave a notice under paragraph 4(1)(a) of Schedule 2 to those Regulations (changes to details of branch), and

(b) not all the other requirements set out in paragraph 4(1) of that Schedule were satisfied,

the notice is to be treated as given under regulation 4(4)(a), and the other requirements set out in regulation 4(4) treated as satisfied to the extent to which the corresponding requirements in paragraph 4(1) of that Schedule had been satisfied.

(2) If before commencement—

(a) an EEA firm which was a European investment firm within the meaning of the ISD Regulations gave a notice under paragraph 5(1)(a) of Schedule 3 to those Regulations (changes to details of branch), and

(b) not all the other requirements set out in paragraph 5(1) of that Schedule were satisfied, the notice is to be treated as given under regulation 4(4)(a), and the other requirements set out in regulation 4(4) treated as satisfied to the extent to which the corresponding requirements in paragraph 5(1) of that Schedule had been satisfied.

(3) In a case falling within paragraph (1) or (2), regulation 4(6) applies unless the Authority had, before commencement, complied with the duty in regulation 8(3) of the 2BCD Regulations or regulation 8(4) of the ISD Regulations.

(4) If before commencement—

(a) an EEA firm which was an EC company within the meaning of the Insurance Companies Act gave a notice under paragraph 2(2)(a) of Schedule 2F to that Act (changes to details of branch), and

(b) not all the other requirements set out in paragraph 2(2) of that Schedule were satisfied,

the notice is to be treated as given under regulation 6(4)(a), and the other requirements set out in regulation 6(4) treated as satisfied to the extent to which the corresponding requirements in paragraph 2(2) of that Schedule had been satisfied.

(5) In a case falling within paragraph (4), regulation 6(6) applies except to the extent that the duty in paragraph 2(4) of Schedule 2F to the Insurance Companies Act had been complied with before commencement.

(6) If before commencement—

(a) an EEA firm which was an EC company within the meaning of the Insurance Companies Act gave a notice under paragraph 9(2)(a) of Schedule 2F to that Act (changes relating to the provision of services), and

(b) the requirement in paragraph 9(2)(b) of that Schedule was not satisfied,

the notice is to be treated as given under regulation 7(4)(a).

[4467]

21 Changes relating to UK firms: procedures partly completed at commencement

(1) If before commencement a UK firm gave notice under paragraph 5(1)(a) of Schedule 6 to the 2BCD Regulations or paragraph 6(1)(a) of Schedule 6 to the ISD Regulations (changes to details of branch)—

(a) the notice is to be treated as given under regulation 11(2)(a), and

(b) any notice given under paragraph 5(1)(b) of Schedule 6 to the 2BCD Regulations or paragraph 6(1)(b) of Schedule 6 to the ISD Regulations is to be treated as given under regulation 11(2)(b),

unless paragraph (2) applies.

(2) This paragraph applies if, before commencement, either—

(a) all the requirements set out in paragraph 5(1) of Schedule 6 to the 2BCD Regulations or paragraph 6(1) of Schedule 6 to the ISD Regulations had been satisfied, or

(b) in response to the notice a notice of refusal was given to the firm under paragraph 6(5)(b) of Schedule 6 to the 2BCD Regulations or paragraph 7(5)(b) of Schedule 6 to the ISD Regulations, and the refusal was not at commencement capable of being reversed on an appeal, reference to a tribunal or a review as mentioned in paragraph 7(5) of Schedule 6 to the ISD Regulations.

(3) If before commencement a UK firm gave notice under paragraph 2(2)(a) of Schedule 2G to the Insurance Companies Act or Schedule 13B to the Friendly Societies Act (changes to details of branch)—

(a) the notice is to be treated as given to the Authority under regulation 13(2)(a), and

(b) the other requirements set out in regulation 13(2) are to be treated as satisfied to the extent to which the corresponding requirements in paragraph 2(2) of Schedule 2G to the Insurance Companies Act or of Schedule 13B to the Friendly Societies Act had been satisfied,

unless paragraph (4) applies.

(4) This paragraph applies if, before commencement, either—

(a) all the requirements set out in paragraph 2(2) of Schedule 2G to the Insurance Companies Act or of Schedule 13B to the Friendly Societies Act had been satisfied, or

(b) in response to the notice a notice of refusal was given to the firm under paragraph 2(5)(b) of that Schedule.

(5) If before commencement a UK firm gave notice under paragraph 6(2)(a) of Schedule 2G to the Insurance Companies Act or of Schedule 13B to the Friendly Societies Act (changes relating to the provision of services)—

(a) the notice is to be treated as given to the Authority under regulation 16(3)(a) and

(b) if a notice was sent under paragraph 6(2)(b) of Schedule 2G to the Insurance Companies Act or of Schedule 13B to the Friendly Societies Act, that notice is to be treated as given under regulation 16(3)(b),

unless, before commencement, the firm had been notified under paragraph 6(5)(a) or (b) of Schedule 2G to the Insurance Companies Act or of Schedule 13B to the Friendly Societies Act of the decision taken in response to the notice.

[4468]

FINANCIAL SERVICES AND MARKETS ACT 2000 (COMMUNICATIONS BY AUDITORS) REGULATIONS 2001

(SI 2001/2587)

NOTES

Made: 17 July 2001.

Authority: Financial Services and Markets Act 2000, ss 342(5), 343(5), 428(3).

Commencement: 1 December 2001 (being the date on which the Financial Services and Markets Act 2000, s 19 came into force); see reg 1 at **[4469]**. Where any provision in this work (including any inserted or substituted provision) came into force for all purposes on or before 1 July 2005, commencement information is not noted at provision level.

As of 1 July 2007, these Regulations had not been amended.

1 Citation, commencement and interpretation

(1) These Regulations may be cited as the Financial Services and Markets Act 2000 (Communications by Auditors) Regulations 2001 and come into force on the day on which section 19 of the Act (the general prohibition) comes into force.

(2) In these Regulations—

"the Act" means the Financial Services and Markets Act 2000;

"the person concerned" means—

(a) in relation to an auditor of an authorised person, that authorised person;

(b) in relation to an auditor of a person who has close links (within the meaning of section 343 of the Act) with an authorised person, that authorised person;

"relevant requirement" means—

(a) a requirement which is imposed by or under any provision of the Act other than Part VI (listing) and which relates to authorisation under the Act (whether by way of permission under Part IV of the Act or otherwise) or to the carrying on of any regulated activity; or

(b) a requirement which is imposed by or under any other Act and whose contravention constitutes an offence which the Authority has power to prosecute under the Act.

[4469]

NOTES

FSMA 2000, s 19 came into force on 1 December 2001 (see the Financial Services and Markets Act 2000 (Commencement No 7) Order 2001, SI 2001/3538).

2 Circumstances in which an auditor is to communicate

(1) An auditor to whom section 342 or 343 of the Act applies must communicate to the Authority information on, or his opinion on, matters mentioned in section 342(3)(a) or 343(3)(a) of the Act (matters of which he has, or had, become aware in his capacity as auditor of an authorised person or as auditor of a person who has close links with an authorised person) in the following circumstances.

(2) The circumstances are that—

(a) the auditor reasonably believes that, as regards the person concerned—

(i) there is or has been, or may be or may have been, a contravention of any relevant requirement that applies to the person concerned; and
(ii) that contravention may be of material significance to the Authority in determining whether to exercise, in relation to the person concerned, any functions conferred on the Authority by or under any provision of the Act other than Part VI;

(b) the auditor reasonably believes that the information on, or his opinion on, those matters may be of material significance to the Authority in determining whether the person concerned satisfies and will continue to satisfy the threshold conditions;

(c) the auditor reasonably believes that the person concerned is not, may not be or may cease to be a going concern;

(d) the auditor is precluded from stating in his report that the annual accounts or, where they are required to be made by any of the following provisions, other financial reports of the person concerned—
(i) have been properly prepared in accordance with the Companies Act 1985 or, where applicable, give a true and fair view of the matters referred to in section 235(2) of that Act;
(ii) have been prepared so as to conform with the requirements of Part VIII of the Building Societies Act 1986 and the regulations made under it or, where applicable, give a true and fair view of the matters referred to in subsection (4) or (7) of section 78 of that Act;
(iii) have been prepared so as to conform with the Friendly Societies Act 1992 and the regulations made under it or, where applicable, give a true and fair view of the matters referred to in section 73(5) of that Act;
(iv) have been prepared so as to conform with the requirements of the Friendly and Industrial and Provident Societies Act 1968 or, where applicable, give a true and fair view of the matters referred to in section 9(2) and (3) of that Act; or
(v) have been prepared so as to conform with the requirements of rules made under the Act where the auditor is, by rules made under section 340 of the Act, required to make such a statement;

as the case may be; or

(e) where applicable, the auditor is required to state in his report in relation to the person concerned any of the facts referred to in subsection (2), (3) or (4A) of section 237 of the Companies Act 1985.

[4470]

FINANCIAL SERVICES AND MARKETS ACT 2000 (INSOLVENCY) (DEFINITION OF "INSURER") ORDER 2001

(SI 2001/2634)

NOTES

This Order has been omitted from this Edition of the *Company Law Handbook* in order to create space for other legislation (ie, the Companies Act 2006 and the associated destination and derivation tables). It was printed in full in the 20th Edition of this work (at p 1764 et seq) and, as of 1 July 2007, it had not been amended since the publication of that Edition. This Order is, however, included in the CD version of this work (which may be ordered from the LexisNexis Butterworths Customer Services Department) and can be accessed in the online version of the *Company Law Handbook* which is updated fortnightly (at www.lexisnexis.com/uk/legal). It is also printed in full in the 8th Edition of *Butterworths Financial Services Law Handbook* (February 2007).

[4471]–[4472]

FINANCIAL SERVICES AND MARKETS ACT 2000 (CONTROLLERS) (EXEMPTION) ORDER 2001

(SI 2001/2638)

NOTES

Made: 19 July 2001.
Authority: Financial Services and Markets Act 2000, ss 192(a), 428(3).

Commencement: 1 December 2001 (being the date on which the Financial Services and Markets Act 2000, s 19 came into force). See art 1 at **[4473]**. Where any provision in this work (including any inserted or substituted provision) came into force for all purposes on or before 1 July 2005, commencement information is not noted at provision level.

As of 1 July 2007, this Order had not been amended.

1 Citation and commencement

This Order may be cited as the Financial Services and Markets Act 2000 (Controllers) (Exemption) Order 2001 and comes into force on the day on which section 19 of the Act comes into force.

[4473]

NOTES

FSMA 2000, s 19 came into force on 1 December 2001 (see the Financial Services and Markets Act 2000 (Commencement No 7) Order 2001, SI 2001/3538).

2 Friendly societies

(1) In any case where a person ("the acquirer")—

(a) proposes to take, in relation to a relevant friendly society, such a step as is mentioned in section 178(1) of the Act, or

(b) acquires control, an additional kind of control or an increase in a relevant kind of control (in each case, within the meaning of Part XII of the Act) over a relevant friendly society without himself taking any such step,

the acquirer is exempt from any obligation imposed by section 178 of the Act to notify the Authority of his proposal or acquisition.

(2) In any case where a controller of a relevant friendly society—

(a) proposes to take, in relation to that relevant friendly society, such a step as is mentioned in section 190(1) of the Act, or

(b) ceases to have or reduces a relevant kind of control (within the meaning of Part XII of the Act) over that relevant friendly society without himself taking any such step,

the controller is exempt from any obligation imposed by section 190 of the Act to notify the Authority.

(3) In this article, "relevant friendly society" means any UK authorised person (within the meaning of Part XII of the Act) who is a friendly society to which neither subsection (2) nor (3) of section 37 of the Friendly Societies Act 1992 applies.

[4474]

FINANCIAL SERVICES AND MARKETS ACT 2000 (OWN-INITIATIVE POWER) (OVERSEAS REGULATORS) REGULATIONS 2001

(SI 2001/2639)

NOTES

Made: 19 July 2001.

Authority: Financial Services and Markets Act 2000, ss 47(1), (3), 417(1), 428(3).

Commencement: 1 December 2001 (being the date on which the Financial Services and Markets Act 2000, s 19 came into force). See reg 1 at **[4475]**. Where any provision in this work (including any inserted or substituted provision) came into force for all purposes on or before 1 July 2005, commencement information is not noted at provision level.

As of 1 July 2007, these Regulations had not been amended.

1 Citation and commencement

These Regulations may be cited as the Financial Services and Markets Act 2000 Own-initiative Power) (Overseas Regulators) Regulations 2001 and come into force on the day on which section 19 of the Act comes into force.

[4475]

NOTES

FSMA 2000, s 19 came into force on 1 December 2001 (see the Financial Services and Markets Act 2000 (Commencement No 7) Order 2001, SI 2001/3538).

2 Overseas regulators

(1) The kind of regulator to which paragraph (2) applies is prescribed for the purposes of section 47(1)(b) of the Act.

(2) This paragraph applies to a regulator who exercises—

(a) a function corresponding to any function of the Authority under the Act;

(b) a function corresponding to any function exercised by the competent authority under Part VI of the Act (official listing);

(c) a function corresponding to any function exercised by the Secretary of State under the Companies Act 1985; or

(d) a function in connection with—

(i) the investigation of conduct of the kind prohibited by Part V of the Criminal Justice Act 1993 (insider dealing); or

(ii) the enforcement of rules (whether or not having the force of law) relating to such conduct.

[4476]

3 Duty to consider Community obligation

(1) The kinds of regulator to which paragraph (2) applies are prescribed for the purposes of section 47(3)(b) of the Act.

(2) This paragraph applies to—

(a) any host state regulator (within the meaning of Schedule 3 to the Act); and

(b) the supervisory authority in Switzerland (within the meaning of the Agreement between the European Economic Community and the Swiss Confederation on direct insurance other than life assurance, signed at Luxembourg on 10th October 1989 ("the Agreement")).

(3) The following kinds of provisions are prescribed for the purposes of section 47(3)(c) of the Act—

(a) in the case of a regulator to whom paragraph (2)(a) applies—

(i) any provision of Community legislation; and

(ii) any rule of law in force in an EEA State for purposes connected with the implementation of any such provision;

(b) in the case of a regulator to whom paragraph (2)(b) applies—

(i) any provision of the Agreement; and

(ii) any rule of law in force in Switzerland for purposes connected with the implementation of any such provision.

[4477]

FINANCIAL SERVICES AND MARKETS ACT 2000 (OFFICIAL LISTING OF SECURITIES) REGULATIONS 2001

(SI 2001/2956)

NOTES

Made: 22 August 2001.

Authority: Financial Services and Markets Act 2000, ss 75(3), 79(3), 103(1), 417(1), 428(3), Sch 10, para 9, Sch 11, paras 16(3), (4), 20(2).

Commencement: 1 December 2001 (being the date on which the Financial Services and Markets Act 2000, s 74(1) came into force); see reg 1 at **[4478]**. Where any provision in this work (including any inserted or substituted provision) came into force for all purposes on or before 1 July 2005, commencement information is not noted at provision level.

These Regulations are reproduced as amended by: the Financial Services and Markets Act 2000 (Official Listing of Securities) (Amendment) Regulations 2001, SI 2001/3439; the Prospectus Regulations 2005, SI 2005/1433.

ARRANGEMENT OF REGULATIONS

PART 1
GENERAL

PART 2
MISCELLANEOUS MATTERS PRESCRIBED FOR THE PURPOSES OF PART VI OF THE ACT

PART 3
PERSONS RESPONSIBLE FOR LISTING PARTICULARS, PROSPECTUSES AND NON-LISTING PROSPECTUSES

PART 1
GENERAL

1 Citation and commencement

These Regulations may be cited as the Financial Services and Markets Act 2000 (Official Listing of Securities) Regulations 2001 and come into force on the day on which section 74(1) comes into force.

[4478]

NOTES

FSMA 2000, s 74(1) came into force on 1 December 2001 (see the Financial Services and Markets Act 2000 (Commencement No 7) Order 2001, SI 2001/3538).

2 Interpretation

(1) In these Regulations—

"the Act" means the Financial Services and Markets Act 2000;

"competent authority" is to be construed in accordance with section 72;

"the Financial Promotion Order" means the Financial Services and Markets Act 2000 (Financial Promotion) Order 2001;

"issuer" has the same meaning as is given, for the purposes of section 103(1), in regulation 4 below;

"non-listing prospectus" has the meaning given in section 87(2); and

"the Regulated Activities Order" means the Financial Services and Markets Act 2000 (Regulated Activities) Order 2001.

(2) Any reference in these Regulations to a section or Schedule is, unless otherwise stated or unless the context otherwise requires, a reference to that section of or Schedule to the Act.

[4479]

PART 2
MISCELLANEOUS MATTERS PRESCRIBED FOR THE PURPOSES OF PART VI OF THE ACT

3 Bodies whose securities may not be listed

For the purposes of section 75(3) (which provides that no application for listing may be entertained in respect of securities issued by a body of a prescribed kind) there are prescribed the following kinds of body—

(a) [where the securities are securities within the meaning of the Regulated Activities

Order,] a private company within the meaning of section 1(3) of the Companies Act 1985 or article 12(3) of the Companies (Northern Ireland) Order 1986;

(b) an old public company within the meaning of section 1 of the Companies Consolidation (Consequential Provisions) Act 1985 or article 3 of the Companies Consolidation (Consequential Provisions) (Northern Ireland) Order 1986.

[4480]

NOTES

Words in square brackets in para (a) inserted by the Financial Services and Markets Act 2000 (Official Listing of Securities) (Amendment) Regulations 2001, SI 2001/3439, reg 2, as from 1 December 2001.

4 Meaning of "issuer"

(1) For the purposes of section 103(1), "issuer" has the meaning given in this regulation.

(2) In relation to certificates or other instruments falling within article 80 of the Regulated Activities Order (certificates representing certain securities), "issuer" means—

(a) …

(b) for all other purposes, the person who issued or is to issue the securities to which the certificates or instruments relate.

(3) In relation to any other securities, "issuer" means the person by whom the securities have been or are to be issued.

[4481]

NOTES

Para (2): sub-para (a) revoked by the Prospectus Regulations 2005, SI 2005/1433, reg 2(3), Sch 3, para 3, as from 1 July 2005.

5 Meaning of "approved exchange"

For the purposes of paragraph 9 of Schedule 10, "approved exchange" means a recognised investment exchange approved by the Treasury for the purposes of the Public Offers of Securities Regulations 1995 (either generally or in relation to dealings in securities).

[4482]

PART 3
PERSONS RESPONSIBLE FOR LISTING PARTICULARS, PROSPECTUSES AND NON-LISTING PROSPECTUSES

6 Responsibility for listing particulars

(1) Subject to the following provisions of this Part, for the purposes of Part VI of the Act the persons responsible for listing particulars (including supplementary listing particulars) are—

(a) the issuer of the securities to which the particulars relate;

(b) where the issuer is a body corporate, each person who is a director of that body at the time when the particulars are submitted to the competent authority;

(c) where the issuer is a body corporate, each person who has authorised himself to be named, and is named, in the particulars as a director or as having agreed to become a director of that body either immediately or at a future time;

(d) each person who accepts, and is stated in the particulars as accepting, responsibility for the particulars;

(e) each person not falling within any of the foregoing sub-paragraphs who has authorised the contents of the particulars.

(2) A person is not to be treated as responsible for any particulars by virtue of paragraph (1)(b) above if they are published without his knowledge or consent and on becoming aware of their publication he forthwith gives reasonable public notice that they were published without his knowledge or consent.

(3) When accepting responsibility for particulars under paragraph (1)(d) above or authorising their contents under paragraph (1)(e) above, a person may state that he does so only in relation to certain specified parts of the particulars, or only in certain specified respects, and in such a case he is responsible under paragraph (1)(d) or (e) above—

(a) only to the extent specified; and
(b) only if the material in question is included in (or substantially in) the form and context to which he has agreed.

(4) Nothing in this regulation is to be construed as making a person responsible for any particulars by reason of giving advice as to their contents in a professional capacity.

(5) Where by virtue of this regulation the issuer of any shares pays or is liable to pay compensation under section 90 for loss suffered in respect of shares for which a person has subscribed no account is to be taken of that liability or payment in determining any question as to the amount paid on subscription for those shares or as to the amount paid up or deemed to be paid up on them.

[4483]

7 Securities issued in connection with takeovers and mergers

(1) This regulation applies where—
(a) listing particulars relate to securities which are to be issued in connection with—
(i) an offer by the issuer (or by a wholly-owned subsidiary of the issuer) for securities issued by another person ("A");
(ii) an agreement for the acquisition by the issuer (or by a wholly-owned subsidiary of the issuer) of securities issued by another person ("A"); or
(iii) any arrangement whereby the whole of the undertaking of another person ("A") is to become the undertaking of the issuer (or of a wholly-owned subsidiary of the issuer, or of a body corporate which will become such a subsidiary by virtue of the arrangement); and
(b) each of the specified persons is responsible by virtue of regulation 6(1)(d) above for any part ("the relevant part") of the particulars relating to A or to the securities or undertaking to which the offer, agreement or arrangement relates.

(2) In paragraph (1)(b) above the "specified persons" are—
(a) A; and
(b) where A is a body corporate—
(i) each person who is a director of A at the time when the particulars are submitted to the competent authority; and
(ii) each other person who has authorised himself to be named, and is named, in the particulars as a director of A.

(3) Where this regulation applies, no person is to be treated as responsible for the relevant part of the particulars under regulation 6(1)(a), (b) or (c) above but without prejudice to his being responsible under regulation 6(1)(d).

(4) In this regulation—
(a) "listing particulars" includes supplementary listing particulars; and
(b) "wholly-owned subsidiary" is to be construed in accordance with section 736 of the Companies Act 1985 (and, in relation to an issuer which is not a body corporate, means a body corporate which would be a wholly-owned subsidiary of the issuer within the meaning of that section if the issuer were a body corporate).

[4484]

8 Successor companies under legislation relating to electricity

(1) Where—
(a) the same document contains listing particulars relating to the securities of—
(i) two or more successor companies within the meaning of Part II of the Electricity Act 1989, or
(ii) two or more successor companies within the meaning of Part III of the Electricity (Northern Ireland) Order 1992; and
(b) the responsibility of any person for any information included in the document ("the relevant information") is stated in the document to be confined to its inclusion as part of the particulars relating to the securities of any one of those companies,

that person is not to be treated as responsible, by virtue of regulation 6 above, for the relevant information in so far as it is stated in the document to form part of the particulars relating to the securities of any other of those companies.

(2) "Listing particulars" includes supplementary listing particulars.

[4485]

9 Specialist securities

(1) This regulation applies where listing particulars relate to securities of a kind specified by listing rules for the purposes of section 82(1)(c), other than securities which are to be issued in the circumstances mentioned in regulation 7(1)(a) above.

(2) No person is to be treated as responsible for the particulars under regulation 6(1)(a), (b) or (c) above but without prejudice to his being responsible under regulation 6(1)(d).

(3) "Listing particulars" includes supplementary listing particulars.

[4486]–[4489]

10–12 (*Revoked by the Prospectus Regulations 2005, SI 2005/1433, reg 2(3), Sch 3, para 3, as from 1 July 2005.*)

FINANCIAL SERVICES AND MARKETS ACT 2000 (OFFERS OF SECURITIES) ORDER 2001 (NOTE)

(SI 2001/2958)

NOTES

This Order was revoked by the Prospectus Regulations 2005, SI 2005/1433, reg 2(3), Sch 3, para 4, as from 1 July 2005.

[4490]–[4503]

FINANCIAL SERVICES AND MARKETS ACT 2000 (GIBRALTAR) ORDER 2001

(SI 2001/3084)

NOTES

Made: 11 September 2001.

Authority: Financial Services and Markets Act 2000, ss 409(1), 428(3).

Commencement: 5 October 2001 (for the purpose of making rules); 1 December 2001 (otherwise; being the date on which the Financial Services and Markets Act 2000, s 19 came into force); see art 1 at **[4504]**. Where any provision in this work (including any inserted or substituted provision) came into force for all purposes on or before 1 July 2005, commencement information is not noted at provision level.

This Order is reproduced as amended by: the Financial Services and Markets Act 2000 (Gibraltar) (Amendment) Order 2005, SI 2005/1; the Financial Services and Markets Act 2000 (Gibraltar) (Amendment) Order 2006, SI 2006/1805; the Capital Requirements Regulations 2006, SI 2006/3221.

1 Citation, commencement and interpretation

(1) This Order may be cited as the Financial Services and Markets Act 2000 (Gibraltar) Order 2001 and comes into force—

(a) for the purpose of making rules, on 5th October 2001;

(b) otherwise, on the day on which section 19 of the Act comes into force.

(2) In this Order—

"the Act" means the Financial Services and Markets Act 2000;

"Gibraltar-based firm" means a firm which has its head office in Gibraltar;

"the Passport Rights Regulations" means the Financial Services and Markets Act 2000 (EEA Passport Rights) Regulations 2001;

"Schedule 3" means Schedule 3 to the Act.

[4504]

NOTES

FSMA 2000, s 19 came into force on 1 December 2001 (see the Financial Services and Markets Act 2000 (Commencement No 7) Order 2001, SI 2001/3538).

2 Exercise of deemed passport rights by Gibraltar-based firms

(1) Schedule 3 applies in relation to a Gibraltar-based firm as follows.

[(1A) A Gibraltar-based firm falling within paragraph 5(a) of Schedule 3 is to be treated as having an entitlement, corresponding to its EEA right deriving from the investment services directive, to establish a branch or provide services in the United Kingdom.]

(2) A Gibraltar-based firm falling within paragraph 5(b) or (c) of Schedule 3 is to be treated as having an entitlement, corresponding to its EEA right deriving from the banking consolidation directive … , to establish a branch or provide services in the United Kingdom.

(3) A Gibraltar-based firm falling within paragraph 5(d) of Schedule 3 is to be treated as having an entitlement, corresponding to its EEA right deriving from any of the insurance directives, to establish a branch or provide services in the United Kingdom.

[(3A) A Gibraltar-based firm falling within paragraph 5(e) of Schedule 3 is to be treated as having an entitlement, corresponding to its EEA right deriving from the insurance mediation directive, to establish a branch or provide services in the United Kingdom.]

(4) For the purposes of paragraphs [(1A),] [(2), (3) and (3A)], references in paragraph [[5(a), (b)], (d) and (e)] of Schedule 3 to the home state regulator are to be treated as references to the competent authority (within the meaning of the relevant single market directive) in Gibraltar in relation to the Gibraltar-based firm concerned.

(5) In relation to such a Gibraltar-based firm as is mentioned in paragraph [(1A),] [(2), (3) or (3A)], references in Schedule 3, the Passport Rights Regulations and the Financial Services and Markets Act 2000 (Compensation Scheme: Electing Participants) Regulations 2001 to—

- (a) "an EEA State" are to be treated as references to Gibraltar;
- (b) "an EEA right" are to be treated as references to the entitlement mentioned in paragraph [(1A),] [(2), (3) or (3A)];
- (c) rights deriving from a single market directive are to be treated as references to that entitlement, so far as corresponding to those rights; and
- (d) "EEA activities" are to be treated as references to the activities which the firm is seeking to carry on in exercise of that entitlement.

(6) Paragraph 16 of Schedule 3 does not apply to Gibraltar-based firms.

(7) For the avoidance of doubt, a Gibraltar-based firm which is exercising, or has exercised, the entitlement mentioned in paragraph [(1A),] [(2), (3) or (3A)] is to be taken to be an "incoming firm" for the purposes of Part XIII of the Act (incoming firms: intervention by the Authority); but section 199(7) of the Act has effect, in relation to such a Gibraltar-based firm, as if the words "and the Commission" were omitted.

[4505]

NOTES

Para (1A): inserted by the Financial Services and Markets Act 2000 (Gibraltar) (Amendment) Order 2006, SI 2006/1805, art 2(1), (2), as from 31 July 2006.

Para (2): words omitted revoked by SI 2006/1805, art 2(1), (3), as from 31 July 2006.

Para (3A): inserted by the Financial Services and Markets Act 2000 (Gibraltar) (Amendment) Order 2005, SI 2005/1, art 2(1), (2), as from 14 January 2005.

Para (4): figure in first pair of square brackets inserted, and figure in third (inner) pair of square brackets substituted, by SI 2006/1805, art 2(1), (4), as from 31 July 2006; words in second (outer) pair of square brackets substituted by SI 2005/1, art 2(1), (3), as from 14 January 2005.

Para (5): figures in first and third pairs of square brackets inserted by SI 2006/1805, art 2(1), (5), as from 31 July 2006; words in second and fourth pairs of square brackets substituted by SI 2005/1, art 2(1), (4), as from 14 January 2005.

Para (7): figure in first pair of square brackets inserted by SI 2006/1805, art 2(1), (5), as from 31 July 2006; words in second pair of square brackets substituted by SI 2005/1, art 2(1), (4), as from 14 January 2005.

3 EEA firms satisfying conditions under Gibraltar law

(1) A relevant EEA firm which—

- (a) has satisfied Gibraltar establishment conditions (whether before or after commencement), and
- (b) has (whether before or after commencement) established a branch in the United Kingdom for the purpose of carrying on any relevant activity,

is to be treated as having satisfied the establishment conditions within the meaning of Part II of Schedule 3, and accordingly qualifies for authorisation under paragraph 12(1) of that Schedule.

(2) A relevant EEA firm which—

(a) has satisfied Gibraltar service conditions (whether before or after commencement), and

(b) is carrying on any relevant activity by providing services in the United Kingdom,

is to be treated as having satisfied the service conditions within the meaning of Part II of Schedule 3, and accordingly qualifies for authorisation under paragraph 12(2) of that Schedule.

(3) Where a relevant EEA firm has (whether before or after commencement) established a branch, or is providing services, in Gibraltar (but not in the United Kingdom) in exercise of an EEA right, regulations 4 to 7 of the Passport Rights Regulations apply to changes affecting that firm (so far as those changes relate to the establishment of a branch, or the provision of services, in the United Kingdom) as they apply to changes affecting a firm which has established a branch, or is providing services, in the United Kingdom in exercise of an EEA right.

(4) In relation to a firm falling within paragraph (1) or (2)—

(a) the references in paragraph 15 of Schedule 3 to a "permitted activity" are references to a relevant activity; and

(b) the reference in paragraph 15(2) of Schedule 3 to the consent notice, regulator's notice or notice of intention is a reference to whichever of the corresponding notices mentioned in paragraph (5)(d) is applicable.

(5) In this article—

(a) "commencement" means the beginning of the day on which section 19 of the Act comes into force;

(b) "Gibraltar establishment conditions" means conditions under the law of Gibraltar corresponding to those in paragraph 13(1) of Schedule 3; and

(c) "Gibraltar service conditions" means conditions under the law of Gibraltar corresponding to those in paragraph 14(1) of Schedule 3;

(d) "relevant activity" means an activity specified in the notice corresponding to—

(i) the consent notice (within the meaning of paragraph 13 of Schedule 3), or

(ii) the regulator's notice or the notice of intention (within the meaning of paragraph 14 of Schedule 3),

as the case may be, which was given to the relevant authority in Gibraltar pursuant to the Gibraltar establishment conditions or the Gibraltar service conditions;

(e) "relevant EEA firm" means an EEA firm other than a Gibraltar-based firm.

[4506]

4 Exercise by UK firms of deemed passport rights in Gibraltar

(1) Schedule 3 applies in relation to the establishment by a UK firm of a branch in Gibraltar, or the provision by a UK firm of services in Gibraltar, as follows.

(2) A UK firm is to be treated as having an entitlement, corresponding to its EEA right, to establish a branch or provide services in Gibraltar.

(3) In relation to a UK firm, references in Schedule 3, the Passport Rights Regulations and article 77 of the Financial Services and Markets Act 2000 (Transitional Provisions) (Authorised Persons etc) Order 2001 to—

(a) "an EEA State" are to be treated as including references to Gibraltar;

(b) "an EEA right" are to be treated as including references to the entitlement mentioned in paragraph (2);

(c) rights deriving from a single market directive are to be treated as including references to that entitlement, so far as corresponding to those rights; and

(d) "EEA activities" are to be treated as including references to the activities which the firm is seeking to carry on in exercise of that entitlement.

(4) In paragraph 24(1)(b) of Schedule 3, the reference to the right conferred by [Article 24] of the banking consolidation directive includes a reference to the entitlement mentioned in paragraph (2), so far as corresponding to that right.

[4507]

NOTES

Para (4): words in square brackets substituted by the Capital Requirements Regulations 2006, SI 2006/3221, reg 29(4), Sch 6, para 10, as from 1 January 2007.

FINANCIAL SERVICES AND MARKETS ACT 2000 (CONTROLLERS) (EXEMPTION) (NO 2) ORDER 2001

(SI 2001/3338)

NOTES

Made: 4 October 2001.

Authority: Financial Services and Markets Act 2000, ss 192(a), 428(3).

Commencement: 1 December 2001 (being the date on which the Financial Services and Markets Act 2000, s 19 came into force); see art 1 at **[4508]**. Where any provision in this work (including any inserted or substituted provision) came into force for all purposes on or before 1 July 2005, commencement information is not noted at provision level.

As of 1 July 2007, this Order had not been amended.

1 Citation, commencement and interpretation

(1) This Order may be cited as the Financial Services and Markets Act 2000 (Controllers) (Exemption) (No 2) Order 2001 and comes into force on the day on which section 19 of the Act comes into force.

(2) In this Order—

"the Act" means the Financial Services and Markets Act 2000;

"associate" has the meaning given by section 422(4) of the Act;

"authorised building society" means a building society (within the meaning of the Building Societies Act 1986) which is a UK authorised person for the purposes of Part XII of the Act;

"capital", in relation to an authorised building society, consists of the following—

(a) any shares of a class defined as deferred shares for the purposes of section 119 of the Building Societies Act 1986 which have been issued by that society; and

(b) the general reserves of that society.

[4508]

NOTES

FSMA 2000, s 19 came into force on 1 December 2001 (see the Financial Services and Markets Act 2000 (Commencement No 7) Order 2001, SI 2001/3538).

2 Acquiring and increasing control over an authorised building society

(1) In any case where a person ("the acquirer")—

(a) proposes to take a step which would result in his—

(i) acquiring control over an authorised building society in the case mentioned in paragraph (a) of subsection (2) of section 179 of the Act (holding of 10% or more of the shares), or

(ii) acquiring an additional kind of control over such a society of the kind mentioned in paragraph (a) of subsection (4) of that section (holding of shares), or

(b) without himself taking any such step, has acquired such control or such an additional kind of control over such a society,

the acquirer is exempt from any obligation imposed by section 178 of the Act to notify the Authority of his proposal or his acquisition unless paragraph (2) applies.

(2) This paragraph applies if the proposed step would result in the acquirer holding, or the acquirer holds, a holding of 10% or more of the capital of that authorised building society.

(3) In paragraph (2), "acquirer" means—

(a) the acquirer;

(b) any of the acquirer's associates; or

(c) the acquirer and any of his associates.

(4) In any case where a controller of an authorised building society—

(a) proposes to take a step which would result in his acquiring an increase of his control over that society in the circumstances mentioned in paragraph (a) of subsection (1) of section 180 of the Act (increase in percentage of shares), or

(b) without himself taking any such step, has acquired increased control over that society in those circumstances,

the controller is exempt from any obligation imposed by section 178 of the Act to notify the Authority of his proposal or his acquisition unless paragraph (5) applies.

(5) This paragraph applies if the proposed step would result in the controller increasing, or the controller has increased, his holding of the capital of that authorised building society by any of the steps mentioned in section 180(2) of the Act.

(6) In paragraph (5), "controller" means—

(a) the controller;

(b) any of the controller's associates; or

(c) the controller and any of his associates.

[4509]

3 Reducing control over an authorised building society

(1) In any case where a controller of an authorised building society—

(a) proposes to take a step which would result in his ceasing to have control of the kind mentioned in paragraph (a) of subsection (4) of section 179 of the Act (holding of shares) over that society, or

(b) without himself taking any such step, has ceased to have such control,

the controller is exempt from any obligation imposed by section 190 of the Act to notify the Authority of his proposal or that cessation unless paragraph (2) applies.

(2) This paragraph applies if the proposed step would result in the controller ceasing, or the controller has ceased, to hold 10% or more of the capital of that authorised building society.

(3) In any case where a controller of an authorised building society—

(a) proposes to take a step which would result in his reducing his control over that society in the circumstances mentioned in paragraph (a) of subsection (1) of section 181 of the Act (decrease in percentage of shares), or

(b) without himself taking any such step, has reduced his control in those circumstances,

the controller is exempt from any obligation imposed by section 190 of the Act to notify the Authority of his proposal or that reduction unless paragraph (4) applies.

(4) This paragraph applies if the proposed step would result in the controller reducing, or the controller has reduced, his holding of the capital of that authorised building society by any of the steps mentioned in section 181(2) of the Act.

(5) In paragraphs (2) and (4), "controller" means—

(a) the controller;

(b) any of the controller's associates; or

(c) the controller and any of his associates.

[4510]

FINANCIAL SERVICES AND MARKETS ACT 2000 (CONTROL OF BUSINESS TRANSFERS) (REQUIREMENTS ON APPLICANTS) REGULATIONS 2001

(SI 2001/3625)

NOTES

Made: 7 November 2001.

Authority: Financial Services and Markets Act 2000, ss 108, 417(1), 428(3), Sch 12, para 6(2).

Commencement: 1 December 2001 (see reg 1 at **[4511]**). Where any provision in this work (including any inserted or substituted provision) came into force for all purposes on or before 1 July 2005, commencement information is not noted at provision level.

These Regulations are reproduced as amended by: the Life Assurance Consolidation Directive (Consequential Amendments) Regulations 2004, SI 2004/3379.

1 Citation, commencement and interpretation

(1) These Regulations may be cited as the Financial Services and Markets Act 2000 (Control of Business Transfers) (Requirements on Applicants) Regulations 2001 and come into force on 1st December 2001.

(2) In these Regulations—

"the Act" means the Financial Services and Markets Act 2000;

"the parties" means the authorised person concerned and the transferee (within the meaning of section 105(2) or, as the case may be, section 106(2) of the Act);

"the report" means the scheme report mentioned in section 109(1) of the Act;

"State of the commitment" has the meaning given by paragraph 6(1) of Schedule 12 to the Act;

"State in which the risk is situated" has the meaning given by paragraph 6(3) of Schedule 12 to the Act;

"a summary of the report" means a summary of the report sufficient to indicate the opinion of the person making the report of the likely effects of the insurance business transfer scheme on the policyholders of the parties.

[4511]

2 Meaning of "commitment"

There is prescribed for the purposes of paragraph 6(2) of Schedule 12 to the Act any contract of insurance of a kind referred to in [Article 2 of the life assurance consolidation directive].

[4512]

NOTES

Words in square brackets substituted by the Life Assurance Consolidation Directive (Consequential Amendments) Regulations 2004, SI 2004/3379, reg 20, as from 11 January 2005.

3 Transfer of an insurance business

(1) An applicant under section 107 of the Act for an order sanctioning an insurance business transfer scheme ("the scheme") must comply with the following requirements.

(2) A notice stating that the application has been made must be—

(a) published—

(i) in the London, Edinburgh and Belfast Gazettes;

(ii) in two national newspapers in the United Kingdom; and

(iii) where, as regards any policy included in the proposed transfer, an EEA State other than the United Kingdom is the State of the commitment or the State in which the risk is situated, in two national newspapers in that EEA State; and

(b) sent to every policyholder of the parties.

(3) The notices mentioned in paragraph (2) must—

(a) be approved by the Authority prior to publication (or, as the case may be, being sent); and

(b) contain the address from which the documents mentioned in paragraph (4) may be obtained.

(4) A copy of the report and a statement setting out the terms of the scheme and containing a summary of the report must be given free of charge to any person who requests them.

(5) A copy of the application, the report and the statement mentioned in paragraph (4) must be given free of charge to the Authority.

(6) In the case of any such scheme as is mentioned in section 105(5) of the Act, copies of the documents listed in paragraph 6(1) of Schedule 15B to the Companies Act 1985 or in paragraph 6(1) of Schedule 15B to the Companies (Northern Ireland) Order 1986 (application

of provisions about compromises and arrangements to mergers and divisions of public companies) must be given to the Authority by the beginning of the period referred to in paragraph 3(e) of that Schedule.

[4513]

4—(1) Subject to paragraph (2), the court may not determine an application under section 107 for an order sanctioning an insurance business transfer scheme—

(a) where the applicant has failed to comply with the requirements in regulation 3(2), (3) or (6); and

(b) until a period of not less than twenty-one days has elapsed since the Authority was given the documents mentioned in regulation 3(5).

(2) The requirements in regulation 3(2)(a)(ii) and (iii) and (b) may be waived by the court in such circumstances and subject to such conditions as the court considers appropriate.

[4514]

5 Transfer of a banking business

(1) An applicant under section 107 of the Act for an order sanctioning a banking business transfer scheme ("the scheme") must comply with the following requirements.

(2) A notice stating that the application has been made must be published—

(a) in the London, Edinburgh and Belfast Gazettes; and

(b) in two national newspapers in the United Kingdom.

(3) The notice mentioned in paragraph (2) must—

(a) be approved by the Authority prior to its publication; and

(b) contain the address from which the statement mentioned in paragraph (4) may be obtained.

(4) A statement setting out the terms of the scheme must be given free of charge to any person who requests it.

(5) Copies of the application and the statement mentioned in paragraph (4) must be given free of charge to the Authority.

[4515]

6—(1) Subject to paragraph (2), the court may not determine an application under section 107 for an order sanctioning a banking business transfer scheme—

(a) where the applicant has failed to comply with the requirements in regulation 5(2) or (3); and

(b) until a period of not less than twenty-one days has elapsed since the Authority was given the documents mentioned in regulation 5(5).

(2) The requirement in regulation 5(2)(b) may be waived by the court in such circumstances and subject to such conditions as the court considers appropriate.

[4516]

FINANCIAL SERVICES AND MARKETS TRIBUNAL (LEGAL ASSISTANCE) REGULATIONS 2001

(SI 2001/3632)

NOTES

Made: 8 November 2001.

Authority: Financial Services and Markets Act 2000, ss 134, 135, 428(1), (3).

Commencement: 30 November 2001 (see reg 1 at **[4517]**). Where any provision in this work (including any inserted or substituted provision) came into force for all purposes on or before 1 July 2005, commencement information is not noted at provision level.

As of 1 July 2007, these Regulations had not been amended.

ARRANGEMENT OF REGULATIONS

PART I
GENERAL

PART IV
STATUTORY INSTRUMENTS

PART I
GENERAL

1 Citation and commencement

These Regulations may be cited as the Financial Services and Markets Tribunal (Legal Assistance) Regulations 2001 and shall come into force on 30th November 2001.

[4517]

2 Interpretation

In these Regulations—

"the Act" means the Financial Services and Markets Act 2000;

"advocate" means—

(a) a barrister, or a solicitor who has obtained a higher courts advocacy qualification in accordance with regulations and rules of conduct of the Law Society; or

(b) in relation to Scotland, a member of the Faculty of Advocates or a solicitor who holds rights of audience under section 25A of the Solicitors (Scotland) Act 1980;

"assisted person" means a person in receipt of legal assistance;

"the Authority" means the Financial Services Authority;

"decision notice" means a decision notice given by the Authority under section 127(1) of the Act;

"disposable income" and "disposable capital" mean, respectively, income and capital, calculated in accordance with regulations 16 to 34;

"legal assistance" means legal assistance in connection with proceedings which are before the Tribunal pursuant to a reference under section 127(4) of the Act and with regard to which a determination of the Tribunal disposing of the reference has not yet been made, and include advice, assistance and representation for the purpose of those proceedings;

"partner" except in the expression "partner in a business" means a person with whom the applicant lives as a couple, and includes a person with whom the applicant is not currently living but from whom he is not living separate and apart;

"representative" means a solicitor or an advocate; and

"the Tribunal" means the Financial Services and Markets Tribunal established under section 132 of the Act, and, for the purposes of these Regulations, includes—

(a) any member of the panel of chairmen of the Tribunal established under paragraph 3 of Schedule 13 to the Act acting alone; and

(b) any person acting on behalf of the Tribunal in accordance with regulation 43.

[4518]

3 Scope

(1) The Lord Chancellor shall fund such legal assistance as the Tribunal directs regarding a relevant reference.

(2) For the purposes of this regulation, a relevant reference is a reference which the Tribunal is to determine in relation to any individual who—

(a) has received a decision notice from the Authority;

(b) has referred the matter to the Tribunal under section 127(4) of the Act; and

(c) fulfils the criteria set out in regulation 8.

[4519]

4 Applications for legal assistance

(1) Any application shall be made in writing to the Tribunal.

(2) The application shall state—

(a) the name and address of the applicant;

(b) the name and address of the applicant's solicitor;

(c) the Tribunal reference number allocated to the case, if known;

(d) the reasons why the applicant considers it to be in the interests of justice for legal assistance to be granted; and

(e) details of the financial resources of the applicant and of any other person whose resources are to be treated as his resources under these Regulations.

[4520]

5 Provision of information

(1) The Tribunal may direct the applicant to provide any information it requires in order to decide whether to grant his application.

(2) The applicant shall provide the Tribunal with any information it requires under paragraph (1).

[4521]

6 Legal assistance order

(1) Where an application for legal assistance is granted, the Tribunal shall—

(a) issue a legal assistance order; and

(b) send a copy of the order to—

(i) the applicant;

(ii) the applicant's solicitor; and

(iii) the Authority.

(2) The legal assistance order shall include details of any contribution payable.

[4522]

7 Refusal of legal assistance

(1) Where an application for legal assistance is refused, the Tribunal shall send written reasons for the refusal to the applicant.

(2) An applicant whose application for legal assistance has been refused may make a renewed application in writing to the Tribunal.

(3) Any renewed application to the Tribunal under paragraph (2) shall specify any new or additional factors which the applicant wishes the Tribunal to take into account.

[4523]

PART II
ELIGIBILITY, ASSESSMENT AND CONTRIBUTIONS

8 Eligibility

The Tribunal shall grant legal assistance to an individual if it is satisfied that—

(a) it is in the interests of justice to do so; and

(b) his financial resources are such that he requires assistance in meeting the legal costs he would, but for these Regulations, be likely to incur in relation to the proceedings before the Tribunal.

[4524]

9 Interests of justice test

In deciding whether it is in the interests of justice for legal assistance to be granted, the Tribunal shall take all relevant factors into account, including—

(a) whether the individual would, if any matter arising in the proceedings before the Tribunal is decided against him, be likely to lose his livelihood or suffer serious damage to his reputation;

(b) whether the determination of any matter arising in the proceedings may involve consideration of a substantial question of law;

(c) whether the individual may be unable to understand the proceedings or to state his own case;

(d) whether the proceedings may involve the tracing, interviewing or expert cross-examination of witnesses on behalf of the individual; and

(e) whether it is in the interests of another person that the individual be represented.

[4525]

10 Financial eligibility

(1) Where a doubt arises as to whether the financial resources of an individual are such that he requires legal assistance, the doubt shall be resolved in his favour.

(2) The Tribunal shall determine the financial eligibility of the applicant and any contribution payable in accordance with these Regulations.

(3) The Tribunal may appoint an expert to prepare a report with regard to the financial resources of the applicant.

[4526]

11 Resources of other persons

(1) In calculating the disposable income and disposable capital of the applicant, the resources of his partner shall be treated as his resources.

(2) Where it appears to the Tribunal that—

(a) another person is, has been or is likely to be substantially maintaining the applicant; or

(b) any of the resources of another person have been or are likely to be made available to the applicant

the Tribunal may treat all or any part of the resources of that other person as the resources of the applicant.

(3) In this regulation and regulation 12 "person" includes a company, partnership, body of trustees and any body of persons, whether corporate or not corporate.

[4527]

12 Deprivation or conversion of resources

If it appears to the Tribunal that the applicant has, with intent to reduce the amount of his disposable income or disposable capital, whether for the purpose of making himself eligible to receive legal assistance, reducing his liability to pay a contribution, or otherwise—

(a) directly or indirectly deprived himself of any resources;

(b) transferred any resources to another person; or
(c) converted any part of his resources into resources which under these Regulations are to be wholly or partly disregarded

the resources which he has so deprived himself of, transferred or converted shall be treated as part of his resources or as not so converted as the case may be.

[4528]

13 Duty to report change in financial circumstances

The assisted person shall immediately inform the Tribunal of any change in his financial circumstances (or those of any other person whose resources are to be treated as his resources under these Regulations) of which he is, or should reasonably be aware, which has occurred since any assessment of his resources, and which might affect the terms on which he was assessed as eligible to receive legal assistance.

[4529]

14 Amendment of assessment due to error or receipt of new information

Where—

(a) it appears to the Tribunal that there has been an error in the assessment of a person's resources or contribution, or in any calculation or estimate upon which such assessment was based; or
(b) new information which is relevant to the assessment has come to light

the Tribunal may make an amended assessment, and may take such steps equitable to give effect to it in relation to any period during which legal assistance has already been provided.

[4530]

15 Further assessments

(1) Where it appears that the circumstances of the assisted person may have altered so that—

(a) his disposable income has increased by an amount greater than £750 or decreased by an amount greater than £300; or
(b) his disposable capital has increased by an amount greater than £750

the Tribunal shall, subject to paragraph (6), make a further assessment of the assisted person's resources and any contribution which he is required to pay under regulation 35, in accordance with these Regulations.

(2) Where a further assessment is made, the period of calculation for the purposes of disposable income shall be the period of 12 months following the date of the change of circumstances or such other period of 12 months as the Tribunal considers appropriate.

(3) Where a further assessment is made, the amount or value of every resource of a capital nature acquired since the date of the original application shall be ascertained as at the date of receipt of that resource.

(4) Any capital contribution which becomes payable as a result of a further assessment shall be payable in respect of the cost of the legal assistance, including costs already incurred.

(5) Where legal assistance is withdrawn as a result of a further assessment of capital, the Tribunal may require a contribution to be paid in respect of costs already incurred.

(6) The Tribunal may decide not to make a further assessment under paragraph (1) if it considers such a further assessment inappropriate, having regard in particular to the period during which legal assistance is likely to continue to be provided to the assisted person.

[4531]

16 Calculation of income

(1) The income of the individual from any source shall be taken to be the income which he may reasonable expect to receive (in cash or in kind) during the period of calculation.

(2) For the purpose of this regulation and regulation 32, the period of calculation shall be the 12 months starting on the date of the application for legal assistance or such other 12 month period as the Tribunal considers appropriate.

[4532]

17—(1) The income from a trade, business or gainful occupation other than an occupation at a wage or salary shall be deemed to be whichever of the following the Tribunal considers more appropriate and practicable—

(a) the profits which have accrued or will accrue to the individual in respect of the period of calculation; or

(b) the drawings of the individual.

(2) In calculating the profits under paragraph (1)(a)—

(a) the Tribunal may have regard to the profits of the last accounting period of such trade, business or gainful occupation for which accounts have been prepared; and

(b) there shall be deducted all sums necessarily expended to earn those profits, but no deduction shall be made in respect of the living expenses of the individual or any member of his family or household, except in so far as that person is wholly or mainly employed in that trade or business and such living expenses form part of his remuneration.

[4533]

18—(1) For the purposes of this regulation, "national insurance contributions" means contributions under Part I of the Social Security Contributions and Benefits Act 1992.

(2) In calculating the disposable income of the individual, any income tax and national insurance contributions paid or payable on that income in respect of the period of calculation shall be deducted.

[4534]

19—(1) For the purposes of this regulation, "the Schedule" means Schedule 2 to the Income Support (General) Regulations 1987.

(2) Subject to paragraph (3), in calculating the disposable income of the individual there shall be a deduction at or equivalent to the following rates (as they applied at the beginning of the period of calculation)—

(a) in respect of the maintenance of his partner, the difference between the income support allowance for a couple both aged not less than 18 (which is specified in column 2 of paragraph 1(3)(d) of the Schedule), and the allowance for a single person aged not less than 25 (which is specified in column 2 of paragraph 1(1)(e) of the Schedule); and

(b) in respect of the maintenance of any dependant child or dependant relative of his, where such persons are members of his household—

(i) in the case of a dependant child or a dependant relative aged 15 or under at the beginning of the period of calculation, the amount specified at (a) in column 2 in paragraph 2(1) of the Schedule; and

(ii) in the case of a dependant child or a dependant relative aged 16 or over at the beginning of the period of calculation, the amount specified at (b) in column 2 in paragraph 2(1) of the Schedule.

(3) The Tribunal may reduce any rate provided by virtue of paragraph (2)(b) by taking into account the income and other resources of the dependant child or dependant relative to such extent as appears to the Tribunal to be equitable.

(4) In ascertaining whether a child is a dependant child or whether a person is a dependant relative for the purpose of this regulation, regard shall be had to their income and other resources.

[4535]

20 Where the individual is making and, throughout such period as the Tribunal considers adequate, has regularly made payments for the maintenance of—

(a) a former partner;

(b) a child; or

(c) a relative

who is not a member of his household, in calculating the disposable income of the individual a reasonable amount shall be deducted in respect of such payments.

[4536]

21 In calculating the disposable income of the individual from any source, the Tribunal shall disregard such amount (if any) as it considers reasonable, having regard to the nature of the income or to any other circumstances.

[4537]

22 In calculating the disposable income of the individual, any sums (net of council tax benefit) payable by him in respect of the council tax to which he is liable by virtue of section 6 of the Local Government Finance Act 1992 shall be deducted.

[4538]

23 Where the income of the individual consists, wholly or partly, of a wage or salary from employment, in calculating his disposable income there shall be deducted—

(a) the reasonable expenses of travelling to and from his place of employment;
(b) the amount of any payments reasonably made for membership of a trade union or professional organisation;
(c) where it would be reasonable to do so, an amount to provide for the care of any dependant child living with the individual during the time that he is absent from home by reason of his employment; and
(d) the amount of any contribution paid, whether under a legal obligation or not, to an occupational pension scheme or a personal pension scheme within the meaning of section 1 of the Pension Schemes Act 1993.

[4539]

24—(1) Paragraphs (2) to (5) apply only if the individual is a householder.

(2) In calculating the disposable income of the individual, the net rent payable by him in respect of his main or only dwelling, or such part of it as is reasonable in the circumstances, shall be deducted.

(3) Where the individual lives in more than one dwelling, the Tribunal shall decide which is the main dwelling.

(4) For the purpose of this regulation, "net rent" includes—

(a) any annual rent payable;
(b) any annual instalment (whether of interest or capital) in respect of a mortgage debt or heritable security up to a maximum of an amount bearing the same proportion to the amount of the annual instalment as £100,000 bears to the debt secured; and
(c) a sum in respect of yearly outgoings borne by the householder including, in particular, any water and sewerage charges, and a reasonable allowance towards any necessary expenditure on repairs and insurance.

(5) In calculating the amount of net rent payable, there shall be deducted—

(a) any housing benefit paid under the Social Security Contributions and Benefits Act 1992;
(b) any proceeds of sub-letting any part of the premises; and
(c) an amount reasonably attributable to any person other than the individual, his partner or any dependant, who is accommodated in the premises otherwise than as a sub-tenant.

(6) If the individual is not a householder, a reasonable amount in respect of the cost of his living accommodation shall be deducted.

[4540]

25 Calculation of capital

Subject to the provisions of these Regulations, in calculating the disposable capital of the individual, the amount or value of every resource of a capital nature belonging to him on the date on which the application for legal assistance is made shall be included.

[4541]

26 In so far as any resource of a capital nature does not consist of money, its value shall be taken to be—

(a) the amount which that resource would realise if sold; or
(b) the value assessed in such other manner as appears to the Tribunal to be equitable.

[4542]

27 Where money is due to the individual, whether it is payable immediately or otherwise and whether payment is secured or not, its value shall be taken to be its present value.

[4543]

28 The value to the individual of any life insurance or endowment policy shall be taken to be the amount which he could readily borrow on the security of that policy.

[4544]

29 Other than in circumstances which are exceptional having regard in particular to the quantity or value of the items concerned, nothing shall be included in the disposable capital of the individual in respect of—

(a) the household furniture and effects of the main or only dwelling house occupied by him;

(b) articles of personal clothing; and

(c) the tools and equipment of his trade, unless they form part of the plant or equipment of a business to which the provisions of regulation 30 apply.

[4545]

30—(1) Where the individual is the sole owner of or partner in a business, the value of the business to him shall be taken to be the greater of—

(a) such sum, or his share of such sum, as could be withdrawn from the assets of his business without substantially impairing its profits or normal development; and

(b) such sum as the individual could borrow on the security of his interest in the business without substantially injuring its commercial credit.

(2) Where the individual stands in relation to a company in a position analogous to that of a sole owner or partner in a business, the Tribunal may, instead of ascertaining the value of his stocks, shares, bonds or debentures in that company, treat him as if he were a sole owner or partner in a business and calculate the amount of his capital in respect of that resource in accordance with paragraph (1).

(3) Where the individual owns solely, jointly or in common with other persons, any interest on the termination of a prior estate, whether

(a) legal or equitable;

(b) vested or contingent;

(c) in reversion or remainder; and

(d) whether in real or personal property or in a trust or other fund

the value of such interest shall be calculated in such manner as is both equitable and practicable.

(4) In Scotland, the value of any interest, whether vested or contingent, of the individual in the fee of any heritable or moveable property forming the whole or part of any trust or other estate, shall be calculated in such manner as is both equitable and practicable.

[4546]

31—(1) In calculating the disposable capital of the individual, the value of any interest in land shall be taken to be the amount for which that interest could be sold less the amount of any mortgage debt or heritable security, subject to the following—

(a) in calculating the value of his interests, the total amount to be deducted in respect of all mortgage debts or heritable securities shall not exceed £100,000;

(b) in making the deductions in sub-paragraph (a), any mortgage debt or heritable security in respect of the main or only dwelling shall be deducted last; and

(c) the first £100,000 of the value of his interest (if any) in the main or only dwelling in which he resides, after the application of sub-paragraphs (a) and (b), shall be disregarded.

(2) Where the individual resides in more than one dwelling, the Tribunal shall decide which is the main dwelling.

[4547]

32 Where under any statute, bond, covenant, guarantee or other instrument the individual is under a contingent liability to pay any sum or is liable to pay a sum not yet ascertained, the Tribunal shall disregard such amount as is reasonably likely to become payable within the period of calculation in regulation 16(2).

[4548]

33 In calculating the disposable capital of the individual, the Tribunal may disregard any capital resource where—

(a) the individual is restrained from dealing with that resource by order of a court;

(b) he has requested the court which made the order to release part or all of that resource for use in connection with the proceedings before the Tribunal; and

(c) that request has been refused.

[4549]

34 In calculating the disposable capital of the individual, the Tribunal may disregard such amount of capital (if any) as it considers reasonable, having regard to the nature of the capital or to any other circumstances.

[4550]

35 Contributions

(1) The assisted person shall make the following contributions—

(a) where his annual disposable income exceeds £3,110, monthly contributions of one thirty-sixth of the excess; and

(b) where his disposable capital exceeds £3,000, a contribution of the whole of the amount of the excess.

(2) All contributions shall be payable in such manner as the Tribunal directs.

(3) All contributions payable under paragraph (1)(a) shall be payable monthly throughout the period the legal assistance order is in force.

(4) All contributions payable under paragraph (1)(b) shall be payable upon assessment, or at such other time as the Tribunal directs.

(5) Where the contribution made by the assisted person exceeds the cost to the Tribunal of the legal assistance provided to him, the excess shall be refunded to the assisted person.

[4551]

36—(1) Where, on determining a reference, the Tribunal directs the Authority to—

(a) take no action against the assisted person;

(b) impose a penalty on the assisted person of a lesser amount than that stated in the decision notice; or

(c) instead of imposing a penalty on the assisted person, publish a statement to the effect that he has engaged in market abuse

the Tribunal may, at the hearing of the reference, order the refund of some or all of any contribution made by the assisted person.

(2) In making a decision under paragraph (1), the Tribunal shall have regard to all the circumstances of the case, including the conduct of the parties.

[4552]

PART III
ASSIGNMENT OF REPRESENTATIVE

37—(1) A legal assistance order may provide for legal assistance to be provided by a solicitor alone, or by a solicitor and one or more advocates.

(2) The Tribunal, in deciding what legal assistance to grant under paragraph (1), shall take all relevant factors into account, including—

(a) whether the case appears to involve substantial, novel or complex issues of law or fact;

(b) whether the case is exceptional compared with the generality of such cases; and

(c) the number and level of advocates instructed on behalf of the Authority.

[4553]

38 Where the Authority has issued a decision notice against more than one assisted person in the same case, the Tribunal may, unless it considers it not to be in the interests of justice to do so, assign the same solicitor and, if any, advocate, to each of those individuals.

[4554]

39 Amendment of legal assistance order

(1) An application may be made to the Tribunal to amend a legal assistance order, and any such application shall state the grounds on which it is made.

(2) The Tribunal may grant or refuse any application made under paragraph (1).

(3) The Tribunal may, before granting legal assistance for more than one advocate, require written advice from any advocate already assigned to the assisted person on the question of what legal assistance is required in the proceedings.

[4555]

40—(1) Where an application for legal assistance has been granted, an application may be made to the Tribunal to select a representative in place of a representative previously assigned and any such application shall state the grounds on which it is made.

(2) The Tribunal may grant or refuse any application made under paragraph (1).

[4556]

PART IV
WITHDRAWAL OF LEGAL ASSISTANCE

41—(1) The Tribunal may withdraw legal assistance where—

(a) the assisted person has requested that it do so;

(b) there has been a change of circumstances in relation to any of the factors which the Tribunal took into account in deciding that legal assistance should be granted;

(c) the assisted person has failed to provide any relevant information or evidence;

(d) the assisted person has made a false statement regarding his financial resources;

(e) the assisted person has failed to pay all or part of any contribution required by the Tribunal; or

(f) it appears to the Tribunal to be in the interests of justice to do so.

(2) Before the Tribunal withdraws legal assistance, it shall take into account any representations which are made within a reasonable time by or on behalf of the assisted person.

(3) Where legal assistance is withdrawn, the Tribunal shall provide written notification of the withdrawal and of the reason for it to the assisted person and his solicitor, who shall inform any assigned advocate.

(4) On any subsequent application by the assisted person for legal assistance in respect of the same proceedings, he shall declare the withdrawal of legal assistance and the reason for it.

[4557]

42 Duty to report abuse

Notwithstanding the relationship between or rights of a representative and client or any privilege arising out of any such relationship, where the representative for an assisted person knows or suspects that that person—

(a) has intentionally failed to comply with any provision of these Regulations concerning the information to be provided by him; or

(b) in providing such information has knowingly made a false statement or false representation

the representative shall immediately report the circumstances to the Tribunal.

[4558]

PART V
CONSTITUTION

43 Any act required or authorised by these Regulations to be done by the Tribunal may be done by a member of the panel of chairmen of the Tribunal acting alone or by a person authorised by the Tribunal to carry out that act.

[4559]

FINANCIAL SERVICES AND MARKETS TRIBUNAL (LEGAL ASSISTANCE SCHEME—COSTS) REGULATIONS 2001

(SI 2001/3633)

NOTES

Made: 8 November 2001.

Authority: Financial Services and Markets Act 2000, ss 134, 135, 428(1), (3).

Commencement: 30 November 2001 (see reg 1 at **[4560]**). Where any provision in this work (including any inserted or substituted provision) came into force for all purposes on or before 1 July 2005, commencement information is not noted at provision level.

As of 1 July 2007, these Regulations had not been amended.

ARRANGEMENT OF REGULATIONS

SCHEDULES

1 Citation, commencement and extent

(1) These Regulations may be cited as the Financial Services and Markets Tribunal (Legal Assistance Scheme—Costs) Regulations 2001 and shall come into force on 30th November 2001.

(2) These Regulations apply to the whole of the United Kingdom, except that—

(a) regulations 20, 21 and 23(5) do not apply in relation to a Tribunal reference in Scotland; and

(b) regulation 22 only applies in relation to a Tribunal reference in Scotland.

[4560]

2 Interpretation

In these Regulations—

"the Act" means the Financial Services and Markets Act 2000;

"advocate" means—

(a) a barrister, or a solicitor who has obtained a higher courts advocacy qualification in accordance with regulations and rules of conduct of the Law Society; or

(b) in relation to Scotland, a member of the Faculty of Advocates or a solicitor who holds rights of audience under section 25A of the Solicitors (Scotland) Act 1980;

"appropriate officer" means a costs officer of the Supreme Court Costs Office;

"assisted person" means a person in receipt of legal assistance;

"the Authority" means the Financial Services Authority;

"costs", in relation to Scotland, means expenses;

"legal assistance" means legal assistance in connection with proceedings which are before the Tribunal pursuant to a reference under section 127(4) of the Act and with regard to which a determination of the Tribunal disposing of the reference has not yet been made, and includes advice, assistance and representation for the purpose of those proceedings;

PART IV
STATUTORY INSTRUMENTS

"legal assistance order" means a document granting a right to legal assistance in respect of proceedings before the Tribunal;

"the main hearing" means the hearing at which a decision of the Tribunal disposing of the reference is made;

"representative" means a solicitor or an advocate;

"the Tribunal" means the Financial Services and Markets Tribunal established under section 132 of the Act, and includes any person authorised by it to act on its behalf in that regard.

[4561]

3 Determination of costs

(1) Costs in respect of work done under a legal assistance order shall be determined by the appropriate officer in accordance with these Regulations.

(2) In determining costs, the appropriate officer shall, subject to the provisions of these Regulations—

(a) take into account all the relevant circumstances of the case including the nature, importance, complexity or difficulty of the work and the time involved; and

(b) allow a reasonable amount in respect of all work actually and reasonably done.

[4562]

4 Authorisation of expenditure

(1) Where it appears to the solicitor necessary for the proper conduct of proceedings before the Tribunal for costs to be incurred under the legal assistance order by taking any of the following steps—

(a) obtaining a written report or opinion of one or more experts;

(b) employing a person to provide a written report or opinion (otherwise than as an expert); or

(c) performing an act which is either unusual in its nature or involves unusually large expenditure

he may apply to the Tribunal for prior authority to do so.

(2) Where the Tribunal authorises the taking of any step specified in paragraph (1), it shall also authorise the maximum to be paid in respect of that step.

[4563]

5 Authorisation of travelling and accommodation expenses

A representative assigned to an assisted person in any proceedings before the Tribunal may apply to the Tribunal for prior authority for the incurring of travelling and accommodation expenses in order to attend at any hearing in those proceedings.

[4564]

6 Interim payment of disbursements

(1) A solicitor may submit a claim to the appropriate officer for payment of a disbursement for which he has incurred liability in proceedings before the Tribunal in accordance with the provisions of this regulation.

(2) A claim for payment may be made where—

(a) a solicitor has obtained prior authority to incur expenditure of £100 or more under regulation 4 or 5; and

(b) he has incurred such a liability.

(3) Without prejudice to regulation 14(2), a claim under paragraph (1) shall not exceed the maximum fee authorised under the prior authority.

(4) A claim for payment under paragraph (1) may be made at any time before the solicitor submits a claim for costs under regulation 12(2).

(5) A claim under paragraph (1) shall be submitted to the appropriate officer in such form and manner as he may direct and shall be accompanied by the authority to incur expenditure and any invoices or other documents in support of the claim.

(6) The appropriate officer shall allow the disbursement subject to the limit in paragraph (3) if it appears to have been reasonably incurred in accordance with the prior authority.

(7) Where the appropriate officer allows the disbursement, he shall notify the solicitor and, where the disbursement includes the fees or charges of any person, that person, of the amount payable, and shall authorise payment to the solicitor accordingly.

(8) Regulations 19 to 22 (redetermination etc) shall not apply to a payment under this regulation.

[4565]

7 Interim disbursements and final determination of costs

(1) On a final determination of costs, regulations 12(2) and (3)(e) and 14 shall apply notwithstanding that a payment has been made under regulation 6.

(2) Where the amount found to be due under regulation 14 in respect of a disbursement is less than the amount paid under regulation 6 ("the interim disbursement"), the appropriate officer shall deduct the difference from the sum otherwise payable to the solicitor on the determination of costs, and where the amount due under regulation 14 exceeds the interim disbursement, the appropriate officer shall add the difference to the amount otherwise payable to the solicitor.

[4566]

8 Staged payments in long cases

(1) A representative may submit a claim to the appropriate officer for a staged payment of his fees in relation to proceedings before the Tribunal.

(2) Where a claim is submitted in accordance with the provisions of this regulation, a staged payment shall be allowed where the appropriate officer is satisfied—

- (a) that the claim relates to fees for a period of preparation of 100 hours or more, for which the representative will, subject to final determination of the costs payable, be entitled to be paid in accordance with these Regulations; and
- (b) that the period from the date of the legal assistance order to the conclusion of the proceedings before the Tribunal will be likely to exceed 12 months, having regard, amongst other matters, to the number of individuals against whom a decision notice has been issued in the same case, and the weight and complexity of the case.

(3) In this regulation, "preparation" means work done before the main hearing, including—

- (a) reading the papers in the case;
- (b) attendance at conferences;
- (c) contact with the Authority;
- (d) providing written or oral advice;
- (e) researching the law;
- (f) preparation for the examination of witnesses and of oral submissions for the main hearing;
- (g) preparation of written submissions, notices or other documents for use at the main hearing;
- (h) attendance at any hearing before the main hearing; and
- (i) all preparation within the meaning of regulation 13(1)(a) not falling within the preceding sub-paragraphs.

(4) The amount to be allowed for preparation falling within paragraph (3)(a) to (h) shall be computed by reference to the number of hours of preparation which it appears to the appropriate officer, without prejudice to the final determination of the costs payable, has been reasonably done, multiplied by the relevant hourly rate, namely—

- (a) in the case of an advocate who is a Queen's Counsel, the hourly rate for subsidiary fees for Queen's Counsel prescribed in Table 2 in Schedule 2;
- (b) in the case of any other advocate, the hourly rate for subsidiary fees for junior counsel prescribed in Table 1 in Schedule 2.

(5) The amount to be allowed for preparation falling within paragraph (3)(i) shall be computed by reference to the number of hours of preparation which it appears to the appropriate officer, without prejudice to the final determination of the costs payable, has been reasonably done, multiplied by the relevant hourly rate prescribed in Schedule 1, applicable to the class of work and the grade of fee-earner.

(6) A claim shall be submitted in such form and manner as the appropriate officer may direct, including such case plan as he may require for the purposes of paragraph (2)(a).

(7) A representative may claim further staged payments in accordance with this regulation in respect of further periods of preparation exceeding 100 hours which were not included in an earlier claim.

(8) Regulations 19 to 22 (redetermination etc) shall not apply to a payment under this regulation.

[4567]

9 Interim payments for attendance at hearing and refreshers

(1) A representative may submit a claim to the appropriate officer for an interim payment in respect of attendance at the Tribunal or refreshers where the main hearing lasts for a qualifying period.

(2) Where a claim is submitted in accordance with the provisions of this regulation, an interim payment shall, without prejudice to the final determination of the costs payable, be allowed—

(a) to a solicitor where he or a fee-earner representing him has attended at the hearing on each day of the qualifying period;

(b) to an advocate where he has undertaken advocacy on the first day of the main hearing or carried out preparation or advocacy on any other day.

(3) The qualifying period for the purposes of this regulation shall be 20 days (which need not be continuous), and a day shall qualify as part of that period if the hearing begins at any time on that day.

(4) The amount payable in respect of each day which qualifies as part of the qualifying period shall be—

(a) in the case of a solicitor—

(i) where the hearing begins before and ends after the luncheon adjournment, five times the hourly rate for a trainee or fee-earner of equivalent experience attending court where more than one representative is assigned as prescribed in Schedule 1;

(ii) where the hearing begins and ends before the luncheon adjournment, or begins after the luncheon adjournment, two and a half times the hourly rate referred to in (i) above;

(b) in the case of an advocate who is a Queen's Counsel, the maximum amount of the full day refresher fee for Queen's Counsel prescribed in Table 2 in Schedule 2;

(c) in the case of an advocate retained solely for the purpose of making a note of any hearing, one-half of the maximum amount of the full day refresher fee for junior counsel prescribed in Table 1 in Schedule 2;

(d) in the case of any other advocate, the maximum amount of the full day refresher fee for junior counsel prescribed in Table 1 in Schedule 2.

(5) A claim for an interim payment may be made in respect of a qualifying period and shall be submitted in such form and manner as the appropriate officer may direct.

(6) Further interim payments under this regulation may be claimed if the hearing lasts for further qualifying periods.

(7) A representative who has obtained prior approval under regulation 5 for the incurring of travelling or accommodation expenses may, at the same time as he submits a claim for an interim payment under this regulation, submit a claim for an interim payment of all such expenses incurred to date (less any expenses previously recovered by him by way of interim payment under this regulation).

(8) A claim under paragraph (7) shall be submitted in such form and manner as the appropriate officer may direct, and shall be supported by such evidence of the expense claimed as he may require.

(9) Regulations 19 to 22 (redetermination etc) shall not apply to a payment under this regulation.

[4568]

10 Hardship payments

(1) The appropriate officer may allow a hardship payment to a representative in the circumstances set out in paragraph (2), subject to the provisions of this regulation.

(2) Those circumstances are that the representative—

(a) represents the assisted person in proceedings before the Tribunal;
(b) applies for such payment, in such form and manner as the appropriate officer may direct, not less than six months after he was first instructed in those proceedings;
(c) is not, at the date of the application, entitled to any payment under regulation 8 (staged payments) or 9 (interim payments);
(d) is unlikely to receive final payment in respect of the proceedings, as determined under regulation 13 or 16, within the three months following the application for the hardship payment; and
(e) satisfies the appropriate officer that, by reason of the circumstance in sub-paragraph (d), he is likely to suffer financial hardship.

(3) Every application for a hardship payment shall be accompanied by such information and documents as the appropriate officer may require as evidence of—
(a) the work done by the representative in relation to the proceedings up to the date of the application; and
(b) the likelihood of financial hardship.

(4) The amount of any hardship payment shall be in the discretion of the appropriate officer, but shall not exceed such sum as would be reasonable remuneration for the work done by the representative in the proceedings up to the date of the application.

(5) No hardship payment shall be made if it appears to the appropriate officer that the sum which would be reasonable remuneration for the representative, or the sum required to relieve his financial hardship, is less than £5,000 (excluding any VAT).

(6) Any hardship payment shall be set off against the remuneration finally payable to the representative under regulation 13 or 16.

[4569]

11 Computation of final claim

(1) At the conclusion of a case in which one or more payments have been made to a representative under regulation 8, 9 or 10 he shall submit a claim under regulation 12 or 15 for the determination of his overall remuneration, whether or not such a claim will result in any payment additional to those already made.

(2) In the determination of the amount payable to a representative under regulation 13 or 16, the appropriate officer shall deduct the amount of any advance payment made under regulation 8, 9 or 10 in respect of the same case from the amount that would otherwise be payable; and, if the amount of the advance payment is greater than the amount that would otherwise be payable, the appropriate officer shall be entitled to recover the amount of the difference, either by way of repayment by the representative or by way of deduction from any other amount that may be due to him.

[4570]

12 Claims for costs by solicitors

(1) Subject to regulation 23, no claim by a solicitor for costs in respect of work done under a legal assistance order shall be considered unless he submits it within three months of the conclusion of the proceedings to which it relates.

(2) A claim for costs shall be submitted to the appropriate officer in such form and manner as he may direct and shall be accompanied by the legal assistance order and any receipts or other documents in support of any disbursement claimed.

(3) A claim shall—
(a) summarise the items of work in respect of which fees are claimed according to the classes of work specified in regulation 13(1);
(b) state, where appropriate, the dates on which the items of work were done, the time taken, the sums claimed and whether the work was done for more than one individual;
(c) specify, where appropriate, the fee-earner who undertook each of the items of work claimed;
(d) give particulars of any work done in relation to a rehearing; and
(e) specify any disbursements claimed, the circumstances in which they were incurred and the amounts claimed in respect of them.

(4) Where the solicitor claims that paragraph 3 of Schedule 1 (enhanced rates) should be applied in relation to an item of work, he shall give full particulars in support of his claim.

(5) The solicitor shall supply such further particulars, information and documents as the appropriate officer may require.

[4571]

13 Determination of solicitors' fees

(1) The appropriate officer may allow work done by fee-earners in the following classes—

(a) preparation, including taking instructions, advising, interviewing witnesses, ascertaining the Authority's case, preparing and perusing documents, dealing with letters and telephone calls which are not routine, preparing for advocacy, instructing an advocate and expert witnesses, conferences and consultations;
(b) advocacy;
(c) attending at court where an advocate is assigned, including conferences with the advocate at court;
(d) travelling and waiting; and
(e) dealing with routine letters written and routine telephone calls.

(2) The appropriate officer shall consider the claim, any further particulars, information or documents submitted by the solicitor under regulation 12 and any other relevant information and shall allow—

(a) such work as appears to him to have been reasonably done under the legal assistance order by a fee-earner, classifying such work according to the classes specified in paragraph (1) as he considers appropriate; and
(b) such time in each class of work allowed by him (other than routine letters written and routine telephone calls) as he considers reasonable.

(3) In respect of all cases where the solicitor acts as advocate before the Tribunal, the appropriate officer shall proceed in accordance with the provisions of regulation 16 as if the fee-earner who did the work had been an advocate.

(4) In respect of all other classes of work, the provisions of this regulation shall apply.

(5) Subject to paragraph (2), (3), (4) and (6), the appropriate officer shall allow fees for work allowed by him under this regulation in accordance with Schedule 1.

(6) The fees allowed in accordance with Schedule 1 shall be those appropriate to such of the following grades of fee-earner as the appropriate officer considers reasonable—

(a) senior solicitor;
(b) solicitor, legal executive or fee-earner of equivalent experience;
(c) trainee or fee-earner of equivalent experience.

[4572]

14 Determination of solicitors' disbursements

(1) Subject to the provisions of this regulation, the appropriate officer shall allow such disbursements claimed under regulation 12 as appear to him to have been reasonably incurred.

(2) No question as to the propriety of any step, or as to the amount of the payment within the maximum authorised, with regard to which prior authority has been given under regulation 4 or 5, shall be raised on any determination of costs unless the representative knew or should reasonably have known that the purpose for which it was given had become unnecessary.

(3) Payment may be allowed on a determination of costs in respect of any step with regard to which prior authority may be given, notwithstanding that no such authority was given or that the maximum authorised was exceeded.

[4573]

15 Claims for fees by an advocate

(1) Subject to regulation 23, no claim by an advocate for fees in respect of work done under a legal assistance order shall be considered unless he submits it within three months of the conclusion of the proceedings to which it relates.

(2) A claim for fees shall be submitted to the appropriate officer in such form and manner as he may direct.

(3) A claim shall—

(a) summarise the items of work in respect of which fees are claimed according to the classes of fee specified in regulation 16(2);

(b) state, where appropriate, the dates on which the items of work were done, the time taken, the sums claimed and whether the work was done for more than one individual; and

(c) give particulars of any work done in relation to a rehearing.

(4) Where an advocate claims that the provision for enhanced rates in regulation 16(3) should be applied in relation to an item of work, he shall give full particulars in support of his claim.

(5) The advocate shall supply such further particulars, information and documents as the appropriate officer may require.

[4574]

16 Determination of advocates' fees

(1) The appropriate officer shall consider the claim, any further particulars and information submitted by an advocate under regulation 15 and any other relevant information and shall allow such work as appears to him to have been reasonably done.

(2) The appropriate officer may allow any of the following classes of fee to an advocate in respect of work allowed by him under this regulation—

(a) a basic fee for preparation including preparation for any hearing before the main hearing and, where appropriate, the first day of the main hearing including, where they took place on that day, short conferences, consultations, applications and appearances, and any other preparation;

(b) a refresher fee for any day or part of a day during which a hearing continued, including, where they took place on that day, short conferences, consultations, applications and appearances, and any other preparation;

(c) subsidiary fees for—

(i) attendance at conferences and consultations not covered by (a) or (b) above;

(ii) written advices or other written work; and

(iii) attendance at hearings before the main hearing, applications and appearances not covered by (a) or (b) above.

(3) The appropriate officer shall allow such fees in respect of such work as he considers reasonable in such amounts as he may determine in accordance with Schedule 2, provided that where it appears to the appropriate officer, taking into account all the relevant circumstances of the case, that owing to the exceptional circumstances of the case the amount payable by way of fees in accordance with Schedule 2 would not provide reasonable remuneration for some or all of the work he has allowed, he may allow such amounts as appear to him to be reasonable remuneration for the relevant work.

[4575]

17 Payment of costs

(1) Having determined the costs payable to a representative in accordance with these Regulations, the appropriate officer shall notify the representative of the costs payable and authorise payment accordingly.

(2) Where the costs payable under paragraph (1) are varied as a result of any redetermination or appeal made or brought pursuant to these Regulations—

(a) where the costs are increased, the appropriate officer shall authorise payment of the increase;

(b) where the costs are decreased, the representative shall repay the amount of such decrease; and

(c) where the payment of any costs of the representative is ordered under regulation 20(14) or 21(8), the appropriate officer shall authorise payment.

[4576]

18 Recovery of overpayments

(1) This regulation applies where a representative is entitled to be paid a certain sum ("the amount due") by virtue of the provisions of these Regulations and, for whatever reason, he is paid an amount greater than that sum.

(2) Where the circumstances in paragraph (1) arise, the appropriate officer may—

(a) require immediate repayment of the amount in excess of the amount due ("the excess amount") and the representative shall on demand repay the excess amount to the appropriate officer; or

(b) deduct the excess amount from any other sum which is or becomes payable to the representative by virtue of the provisions of these Regulations.

(3) The appropriate officer may proceed under paragraph (2)(b) without first proceeding under paragraph (2)(a).

(4) Paragraph (2) shall apply notwithstanding that the representative to whom the excess amount was paid is exercising, or may exercise, a right under regulations 19 to 22.

[4577]

19 Redetermination of costs by appropriate officer

(1) Where a representative is dissatisfied with the costs determined in accordance with the provisions of these Regulations by the appropriate officer, he may apply to the appropriate officer to redetermine those costs.

(2) Subject to regulation 23, the application shall be made within 21 days of the receipt of notification of the costs payable under regulation 17.

(3) The application shall be made by giving notice to the appropriate officer in such form as he may direct specifying the matters in respect of which the application is made and the grounds of objection.

(4) The notice of application shall be accompanied by the particulars, information and documents supplied under regulation 12 or 15, as appropriate.

(5) The notice of application shall state whether the applicant wishes to appear or to be represented and, if the applicant so wishes, the appropriate officer shall notify the applicant of the time at which he is prepared to hear him or his representative.

(6) The applicant shall supply such further particulars, information and documents as the appropriate officer may require.

(7) The appropriate officer shall redetermine the costs, whether by way of increase or decrease in the amount previously determined, in the light of the objections made by the applicant or on his behalf, and shall notify the applicant of his decision.

(8) The applicant may request the appropriate officer to give reasons in writing for his decision and the appropriate officer shall comply with any such request.

(9) Subject to regulation 23, any request under paragraph (8) shall be made within 21 days of the receipt of notification of the decision.

[4578]

20 Appeals to a Costs Judge

(1) Where the appropriate officer has given his reasons for his decisions under regulation 19, a representative who is dissatisfied with that decision may appeal to a Costs Judge.

(2) Subject to regulation 23, an appeal shall be brought within 21 days of the receipt of the appropriate officer's reasons, by giving notice of appeal in writing to the Senior Costs Judge.

(3) The appellant shall send a copy of any notice given under paragraph (2) to the appropriate officer.

(4) The notice of appeal shall—

(a) be in such form as the Senior Costs Judge may direct;

(b) specify separately each item appealed against, showing (where appropriate) the amount claimed for the item, the amount determined and the grounds of the objection to the determination; and

(c) state whether the appellant wishes to appear or to be represented or whether he will accept a decision given in his absence.

(5) The notice of appeal shall be accompanied by—

(a) a copy of the written representations given under regulation 19(3);

(b) the appropriate officer's reasons for his decision given under regulation 19(8); and

(c) the particulars, information and documents supplied to the appropriate officer under regulation 19.

(6) The Senior Costs Judge may, and if so directed by the Lord Chancellor either generally or in a particular case shall, send to the Lord Chancellor a copy of the notice of appeal together with copies of such other documents as the Lord Chancellor may require.

(7) The Lord Chancellor may arrange for written or oral representations to be made on his behalf and, if he intends to do so, he shall inform the Senior Costs Judge and the appellant.

(8) Any written representations made on behalf of the Lord Chancellor under paragraph (7) shall be sent to the Senior Costs Judge and the appellant and, in the case of oral representations, the Senior Costs Judge and the appellant shall be informed of the grounds on which such representations will be made.

(9) The appellant shall be permitted a reasonable opportunity to make representations in reply.

(10) The Costs Judge shall inform the appellant (or his representative) and the Lord Chancellor, where representations have been or are to be made on his behalf, of the date of any hearing and, subject to the provisions of this regulation, may give directions as to the conduct of the appeal.

(11) The Costs Judge may consult the Tribunal or the appropriate officer and may require the appellant to provide any further information which he requires for the purpose of the appeal and, unless the Costs Judge otherwise directs, no further evidence shall be received on the hearing of the appeal and no ground of objection shall be valid which was not raised under regulation 19.

(12) The Costs Judge shall have the same powers as the appropriate officer under these Regulations and, in the exercise of such powers, may alter the redetermination of the appropriate officer in respect of any sum allowed, whether by increase or decrease as he thinks fit.

(13) The Costs Judge shall inform the appellant, the Lord Chancellor and the appropriate officer of his decision and the reasons for it in writing.

(14) Except where he confirms or decreases the sums redetermined under regulation 19, the Costs Judge may allow the appellant a sum in respect of part or all of any reasonable costs (including any fee payable in respect of an appeal) incurred by him in connection with the appeal.

[4579]

21 Appeals to the High Court

(1) A representative who is dissatisfied with the decision of the Costs Judge on an appeal under regulation 20 may apply to a Costs Judge to certify a point of principle of general importance.

(2) Subject to regulation 23, an application under paragraph (1) shall be made within 21 days of notification of the Costs Judge's decision under regulation 20(13).

(3) Where a Costs Judge certifies a point of principle of general importance, the representative may appeal to the High Court against the decision of the Costs Judge on an appeal under regulation 20, and the Lord Chancellor shall be a respondent to such an appeal.

(4) Subject to regulation 23, an appeal under paragraph (3) shall be brought within 21 days of receipt of the Costs Judge's certificate under paragraph (1).

(5) Where the Lord Chancellor is dissatisfied with the decision of the Costs Judge on an appeal under regulation 20, he may, if no appeal has been made by the representative under paragraph (3) appeal to the High Court against that decision, and the representative shall be a respondent to the appeal.

(6) Subject to regulation 23, an appeal under paragraph (5) shall be brought within 21 days of receipt of notification of the Costs Judge's decision under regulation 20(13).

(7) An appeal under paragraph (3) or (5) shall—

(a) be brought in the Queen's Bench Division of the High Court;

(b) follow the procedure set out in Part 8 of the Civil Procedure Rules 1998; and

(c) be heard and determined by a single judge, whose decision shall be final.

(8) The judge shall have the same powers as the appropriate officer and the Costs Judge under these Regulations and may reverse, affirm or amend the decision appealed against or make such other order as he thinks fit.

[4580]

22 Reference to the Auditor in Scottish cases

(1) Where the appropriate officer has given his reasons for his decisions under regulation 19, a representative who is dissatisfied with that decision may refer the matter for taxation by the auditor.

(2) The auditor shall give reasonable notice of the diet of taxation to the representative and the appropriate officer, and shall issue a report of the taxation.

(3) The appropriate officer and any other party to a reference to the auditor under paragraph (1) may make written representations to the Court of Session in relation to the auditor's report within 14 days of the issue of that report, and may be heard thereon, and rule 42.4 of the Act of Sederunt (Rules of the Court of Session 1994) 1994 shall apply to the determination of any such representations.

(4) In this regulation, "auditor" means the Auditor of the Court of Session.

[4581]

23 Time limits

(1) Subject to paragraph (2), the time limit within which any act is required or authorised to be done may, for good reason, be extended—

- (a) In the case of acts required or authorised to be done under regulations 20 to 22, by a Costs Judge, the High Court or the Court of Session, as the case may be; and
- (b) in the case of acts required or authorised to be done by a representative under any other regulation, by the appropriate officer.

(2) Where a representative without good reason has failed (or, if an extension were not granted, would fail) to comply with a time limit, the appropriate officer, a Costs Judge, the High Court, or the Court of Session, as the case may be—

- (a) may, in exceptional circumstances, extend the time limit; and
- (b) shall consider whether it is reasonable in the circumstances to reduce the costs.

(3) Costs shall not be reduced under paragraph (2)(b) unless the representative has been allowed a reasonable opportunity to show cause orally or in writing why they should not be reduced.

(4) A representative may appeal to a Costs Judge, or, in Scotland, to the Court of Session, against a decision made under this regulation by an appropriate officer.

(5) An appeal against a decision made under this regulation shall be brought within 21 days of receipt of the decision by giving notice in writing to the Senior Costs Judge specifying the grounds of appeal.

[4582]

SCHEDULES

SCHEDULE 1
SOLICITORS' FEES

FEES DETERMINED UNDER REGULATION 13

1. Subject to paragraph 2, the appropriate officer shall allow fees for work allowed by him under regulation 13 at the following prescribed rates—

Class of work	*Grade of fee-earner*	*Rate*
Preparation	Senior solicitor	£55.75 per hour
	Solicitor, legal executive or fee-earner of equivalent experience	£47.25 per hour

Class of work	*Grade of fee-earner*	*Rate*
	Trainee or fee-earner of equivalent experience	£34.00 per hour
Attendance at the Tribunal where more than one representative assigned	Senior solicitor	£42.25 per hour
	Solicitor, legal executive or fee-earner of equivalent experience	£34.00 per hour
	Trainee or fee-earner of equivalent experience	£20.50 per hour
Travelling and waiting	Senior solicitor, solicitor, legal executive or fee-earner of equivalent experience	£24.75 per hour
	Trainee or fee-earner of equivalent experience	£12.50 per hour
Routine letters written and routine telephone calls		£3.60 per item

2. In respect of any item of work, the appropriate officer may allow fees at less than the relevant prescribed rate specified in paragraph 1 where it appears to him reasonable to do so having regard to the competence and despatch with which the work was done.

3.—(1) Upon a determination in respect of any case the appropriate officer may allow fees at more than the relevant prescribed rate specified in paragraph 1, subject to the provisions of this paragraph, where it appears to him, taking into account all the relevant circumstances of the case, that—

(a) the work was done with exceptional competence, skill or expertise;
(b) the work was done with exceptional despatch; or
(c) the case involved exceptional circumstances or complexity.

(2) Where the appropriate officer considers that any item or class of work should be allowed at more than the prescribed rate, he shall apply to that item or class of work a percentage enhancement in accordance with the following provisions of this paragraph.

(3) In determining the percentage by which fees should be enhanced above the prescribed rate the appropriate officer should have regard to—

(a) the degree of responsibility accepted by the solicitor and his staff;
(b) the care, speed and economy with which the case was prepared; and
(c) the novelty, weight and complexity of the case.

(4) The percentage above the relevant prescribed rate by which fees for work may be enhanced shall not exceed 200 per cent.

[4583]

SCHEDULE 2
ADVOCATES' FEES

1. The appropriate officer shall allow such fee in respect of an item of work allowed under regulation 16(3), not exceeding the maximum amount specified in respect of that item of work, as appears to him to provide reasonable remuneration.

2. Where an hourly rate is specified in a Table in this Schedule in respect of an item of work allowed under regulation 16(3), the appropriate officer shall determine any fee for such work in accordance with that hourly rate, provided that the fee determined shall not be less than the minimum amount specified.

3. Where a refresher fee is claimed in respect of less than a full day, the appropriate officer shall allow such fee as appears to him reasonable having regard to the fee which would be allowable for a full day.

TABLE 1:
JUNIOR COUNSEL/SOLICITOR ADVOCATE

Basic fee	*Full day refresher*	*Subsidiary fees*		
		Attendance at consultations and conferences	Written work	Attendance at hearings before the main hearing
Maximum amount: £545.50	Maximum amount: £178.75	£33.50 per hour Minimum amount: £16.75	Maximum amount: £58.25	Maximum amount: £110

TABLE 2:
QUEEN'S COUNSEL

Basic fee	*Full day refresher*	*Subsidiary fees*		
		Attendance at consultations and conferences	Written work	Attendance at hearings before the main hearing
Maximum amount: £5,400.00	Maximum amount: £330.50	£62.50 per hour Minimum amount: £32.00	Maximum amount: £119.50	Maximum amount: £257.50

[4584]

INSURERS (WINDING UP) RULES 2001

(SI 2001/3635)

NOTES

These Rules have been omitted from this Edition of the *Company Law Handbook* in order to create space for other legislation (ie, the Companies Act 2006 and the associated destination and derivation tables). They were printed in full in the 20th Edition of this work (at p 1797 et seq) and, as of 1 July 2007, they had not been amended since the publication of that Edition. These Rules are, however, included in the CD version of this work (which may be ordered from the LexisNexis Butterworths Customer Services Department) and can be accessed in the online version of the *Company Law Handbook* which is updated fortnightly (at www.lexisnexis.com/uk/legal). They are also printed in full in the 8th Edition of *Butterworths Financial Services Law Handbook* (February 2007).

[4585]–[4619]

FINANCIAL SERVICES AND MARKETS ACT 2000 (MISLEADING STATEMENTS AND PRACTICES) ORDER 2001

(SI 2001/3645)

NOTES

Made: 9 November 2001.

Authority: Financial Services and Markets Act 2000, s 397(9), (10), (14).

Commencement: 1 December 2001 (all provisions except arts 3(b), (c), 4(b), (c)); 1 January 2002 (for the purposes of arts 3(b), 4(b)); 31 October 2004 (for the purposes of arts 3(c), 4(c)); see art 1 at **[4620]**).

Where any provision in this work (including any inserted or substituted provision) came into force for all purposes on or before 1 July 2005, commencement information is not noted at provision level.

This Order is reproduced as amended by: the Financial Services and Markets Act 2000 (Commencement of Mortgage Regulation) (Amendment) Order 2002, SI 2002/1777; the Financial Services and Markets Act 2000 (Misleading Statements and Practices) (Amendment) Order 2003, SI 2003/1474; the Financial Services and Markets Act 2000 (Regulated Activities) (Amendment) (No 2) Order 2003, SI 2003/1476.

1 Citation and commencement

(1) This order may be cited as the Financial Services and Markets Act 2000 (Misleading Statements and Practices) Order 2001.

(2) This Order comes into force—

(a) for the purposes of articles 3(b) and 4(b), on 1st January 2002;

(b) for the purposes of articles 3(c) and 4(c), [on such a day as the Treasury may specify];

(c) for all other purposes, on 1st December 2001.

[(3) Any day specified under paragraph (2)(b) must be caused to be notified in the London, Edinburgh and Belfast Gazettes published not later than one week before that day.]

[4620]

NOTES

Para (2): words in square brackets substituted by the Financial Services and Markets Act 2000 (Commencement of Mortgage Regulation) (Amendment) Order 2002, SI 2002/1777, art 6(1), (2), as from 30 August 2002.

Para (3): added by SI 2002/1777, art 6(1), (3), as from 30 August 2002.

On such a day as the Treasury may specify: 31 October 2004 (see the London Gazette, 14 July 2003).

2 Interpretation

In this Order—

"the Act" means the Financial Services and Markets Act 2000;

["contract of insurance" has the meaning given by article 3(1) of the Regulated Activities Order;]

"controlled activity" means an activity which falls within Part I of Schedule 1 to the Financial Promotion Order other than an activity which falls within—

(a) [paragraph 9, 10, 10A or 10B] of that Schedule, or

(b) paragraph 11 so far as relating to [paragraph 9, 10, 10A or 10B];

"controlled investment" means an investment which falls within Part II of Schedule 1 to the Financial Promotion Order other than an investment which falls within paragraph 25 or 26 of that Schedule;

"the Financial Promotion Order" means the Financial Services and Markets Act 2000 (Financial Promotion) Order 2001;

["Regulated Activities Order" means the Financial Services and Markets Act 2000 (Regulated Activities) Order 2001].

[4621]

NOTES

Para (1): definitions "contract of insurance" and "Regulated Activities Order" inserted by the Financial Services and Markets Act 2000 (Regulated Activities) (Amendment) (No 2) Order 2003, SI 2003/1476, art 17(1), (2), as from 31 October 2004 (in so far as relating to contracts of long-term care insurance), and as from 14 January 2005 (otherwise) (for transitional provisions see arts 22–27 of that Order at **[4665]** et seq); in definition "controlled activity" words in square brackets substituted by the Financial Services and Markets Act 2000 (Misleading Statements and Practices) (Amendment) Order 2003, SI 2003/1474, art 2(1), (2), as from 31 October 2004.

3 Specified kinds of activity

The following kinds of activity are specified for the purposes of section 397(9)(a) of the Act—

(a) a controlled activity;

(b) an activity which falls within paragraph 9 (providing funeral plan contracts) of Schedule 1 to the Financial Promotion Order, or agreeing to carry on such an activity;

(c) an activity which falls within paragraph 10 (providing qualifying credit) of that Schedule, or agreeing to carry on such an activity;

[(ca) an activity which falls within paragraph 10A (arranging qualifying credit) or 10B (advising on qualifying credit) of that Schedule, or agreeing to carry on any such activity;]

(d) an activity of the kind specified by article 45 (sending dematerialised instructions), 51 (establishing etc a collective investment scheme), 52 (establishing etc a stakeholder pension scheme) or 57 (managing the underwriting capacity of a Lloyd's syndicate) of [the Regulated Activities Order];

[(e) (so far as not already specified by paragraph (a)), an activity of the kind specified by—

(i) article 14 of the Regulated Activities Order (dealing in investments as principal),

(ii) article 21 of that Order (dealing in investments as agent),

(iii) article 25(1) or (2) of that Order (arranging deals in investments),

(iv) article 39A of that Order (assisting in the administration and performance of a contract of insurance),

(v) article 53 of that Order (advising on investments), or

(vi) so far as relevant to any of those articles, article 64 of that Order (agreeing), so far as it relates to a contract of insurance].

[4622]

NOTES

Para (ca) inserted by the Financial Services and Markets Act 2000 (Misleading Statements and Practices) (Amendment) Order 2003, SI 2003/1474, art 2(1), (3), as from 31 October 2004; words in square brackets in para (d) substituted, and para (e) added, by the Financial Services and Markets Act 2000 (Regulated Activities) (Amendment) (No 2) Order 2003, SI 2003/1476, art 17(1), (3), as from 31 October 2004 (in so far as relating to contracts of long-term care insurance), and as from 14 January 2005 (otherwise) (for transitional provisions see arts 22–27 of that Order at **[4665]** et seq).

4 Specified kinds of investment

The following kinds of investment are specified for the purposes of section 397(10) of the Act—

(a) a controlled investment;

(b) an investment which falls within paragraph 25 (funeral plan contracts) of Schedule 1 to the Financial Promotion Order;

(c) an investment which falls within paragraph 26 (agreements for qualifying credit) of that Schedule.

[4623]

FINANCIAL SERVICES AND MARKETS ACT 2000 (CONFIDENTIAL INFORMATION) (BANK OF ENGLAND) (CONSEQUENTIAL PROVISIONS) ORDER 2001

(SI 2001/3648)

NOTES

Made: 8 November 2001.

Authority: Financial Services and Markets Act 2000, ss 426, 427.

Commencement: 1 December 2001 (see art 1 at **[4624]**). Where any provision in this work (including any inserted or substituted provision) came into force for all purposes on or before 1 July 2005, commencement information is not noted at provision level.

This Order is reproduced as amended by: the Capital Requirements Regulations 2006, SI 2006/3221.

ARRANGEMENT OF ARTICLES

PART I
PRELIMINARY

PART II
INFORMATION SUPPLIED TO THE BANK BY AN OVERSEAS REGULATORY AUTHORITY

PART III
DISCLOSURE OF INFORMATION OBTAINED UNDER COMPANIES LEGISLATION

PART IV
TRANSITIONAL PROVISIONS

PART I
PRELIMINARY

1 Citation and commencement

This Order may be cited as the Financial Services and Markets Act 2000 (Confidential Information) (Bank of England) (Consequential Provisions) Order 2001 and comes into force on the 1st of December 2001.

[4624]

2 Interpretation

(1) In these Regulations—

"the 1998 Act" means the Bank of England Act 1998;

"the Act" means the Financial Services and Markets Act 2000;

"the Bank" means the Bank of England;

"commencement" means the beginning of the day on which section 19 of the Act comes into force;

"an EEA regulatory authority" means a competent authority of an EEA State other than the United Kingdom for the purposes of the banking consolidation directive;

"a non-EEA regulatory authority" means an authority in a country or territory outside the EEA which has regulatory functions in relation to the acceptance of deposits from the public;

"the Disclosure Regulations" means the Financial Services and Markets Act 2000 (Disclosure of Confidential Information) Regulations 2001;

"overseas regulatory authority" means an EEA regulatory authority or a non-EEA regulatory authority;

"relevant functions", in relation to the Bank, means—

(a) its functions as a monetary authority, and

(b) its functions in relation to overseeing payment systems.

(2) In this Order, references to the acceptance of deposits must be read with—

(a) section 22 of the Act;

(b) any relevant Order under that section; and

(c) Schedule 2 to the Act.

[4625]

PART II
INFORMATION SUPPLIED TO THE BANK BY AN OVERSEAS REGULATORY AUTHORITY

3 Information to which this Part applies

(1) This Part applies to information ("overseas regulatory information") which—

(a) is supplied to the Bank after commencement for the purposes of any relevant functions by an overseas regulatory authority; or

(b) is obtained after commencement for those purposes by the Bank, or by a person acting on its behalf, in another member State.

PART IV
STATUTORY INSTRUMENTS

(2) Subject to paragraphs (3) and (4) and article 4, sections 348, 349 and 352 of the Act apply in relation to overseas regulatory information in the same way as they apply in relation to confidential information within the meaning of section 348(2) of the Act.

(3) Overseas regulatory information is not subject to the restrictions on disclosure imposed by section 348(1) of the Act (as it applies by virtue of paragraph (2)) if it satisfies any of the criteria set out in section 348(4)(a) or (b) of the Act.

(4) For the purposes of this Part, section 348 of the Act and the Disclosure Regulations have effect as if the primary recipients mentioned in section 348(5) included the Bank.

[4626]

4 Information to be treated as single market directive information

(1) The Disclosure Regulations apply in relation to information of the kind mentioned in article 3(1)(a) which is supplied by an EEA regulatory authority as they apply in relation to single market directive information (within the meaning of those Regulations).

(2) The Disclosure Regulations apply in relation to information of the kind mentioned in article 3(1)(b) as they apply in relation to single market directive information which is obtained in the course of an on-the-spot verification of the kind referred to in [Article 43] of the banking consolidation directive.

(3) For the purposes of this Part, Part III of the Disclosure Regulations (disclosure of single market directive information) has effect as if references to the Authority included a reference to the Bank.

[4627]

NOTES

Para (2): words in square brackets substituted by the Capital Requirements Regulations 2006, SI 2006/3221, reg 29(4), Sch 6, para 11, as from 1 January 2007.

PART III
DISCLOSURE OF INFORMATION OBTAINED UNDER COMPANIES LEGISLATION

5 Information to which this Part applies

(1) This Part applies to information disclosed after commencement to the Bank—

(a) under subsection (1) of section 449 of the Companies Act 1985, or

(b) under paragraph (1) of Article 442 of the Companies (Northern Ireland) Order 1986,

in its capacity as a competent authority under section 449(3) of that Act or Article 442(3) of that Order (as the case may be) ("companies information").

(2) Subject to paragraphs (3) and (4), companies information may be disclosed in accordance with section 349 of the Act and the Disclosure Regulations as if—

(a) it were confidential information within the meaning of section 348(2) of the Act; and

(b) the Bank were a primary recipient of the information.

(3) The Bank may disclose companies information in accordance with Part IV of the Disclosure Regulations only with—

(a) in the case of information disclosed as mentioned in paragraph (1)(a), the consent of the Secretary of State, or

(b) in the case of information disclosed as mentioned in paragraph (1)(b), the consent of the Department of Enterprise, Trade and Investment in Northern Ireland.

(4) A person other than the Bank must not disclose such information under paragraph (2) except with the consent of—

(a) in the case of information disclosed as mentioned in paragraph (1)(a), the consent of the Secretary of State, or

(b) in the case of information disclosed as mentioned in paragraph (1)(b), the consent of the Department of Enterprise, Trade and Investment in Northern Ireland.

[4628]

PART IV
TRANSITIONAL PROVISIONS

6 Information supplied before commencement by an overseas regulatory authority

(1) This article applies to information which fell within section 86(1) of the Banking Act 1987 and immediately before commencement was subject to restrictions on disclosure by virtue of section 82 of that Act, as those sections had effect by virtue of paragraph 57 of Schedule 5 to the 1998 Act ("transitional overseas regulatory information").

(2) Subject to paragraphs (3) and (4), regulation 15 of the Disclosure Regulations (disclosure of transitional information) has effect in relation to transitional overseas regulatory information which the Bank holds after commencement as if the persons to be treated as a primary recipient by virtue of paragraph (3)(a) of that regulation included the Bank in relation to such information.

(3) Transitional overseas regulatory information which fell within section 86(1)(a) of the Banking Act 1987 and was supplied by an EEA regulatory authority is to be treated for the purposes of the Disclosure Regulations as single market directive information (within the meaning of those Regulations).

(4) Transitional overseas regulatory information which fell within section 86(1)(b) of the Banking Act 1987 is to be treated for the purposes of the Disclosure Regulations as single market directive information which is obtained in the course of an on-the-spot verification of the kind referred to in [Article 43] of the banking consolidation directive.

(5) For the purposes of this article, references in Part III of the Disclosure Regulations (disclosure of single market directive information) to the Authority are to be treated as including the Bank.

[4629]

NOTES

Para (4): words in square brackets substituted by the Capital Requirements Regulations 2006, SI 2006/3221, reg 29(4), Sch 6, para 11, as from 1 January 2007.

7 Companies information supplied before commencement

(1) This article applies to information ("transitional companies information")—

(a) disclosed before commencement to the Bank under section 449(1) of the Companies Act 1985, or under Article 442(1) of the Companies (Northern Ireland) Order 1986, in its capacity as a competent authority under section 449(3) of that Act or Article 442(3) of that Order (as the case may be); and

(b) which immediately before commencement was subject to any of the powers of disclosure conferred by subsection (2) or (3) of section 87 of the Banking Act 1987, as that section had effect by virtue of paragraph 59 of Schedule 5 to the 1998 Act.

(2) Subject to paragraphs (3) and (4), transitional companies information may be disclosed in accordance with section 349 of the Act and the Disclosure Regulations as if—

(a) it were confidential information within the meaning of section 348(2) of the Act; and

(b) the Bank were a primary recipient of the information.

(3) The Bank may disclose transitional companies information in accordance with Part IV of the Disclosure Regulations only with the consent of—

(a) in the case of information of the kind mentioned in paragraph (1)(a), the Secretary of State, or

(b) in the case of information of the kind mentioned in paragraph (1)(b), the Department of Enterprise, Trade and Investment in Northern Ireland.

(4) A person other than the Bank must not disclose such information under paragraph (2) except with the consent of—

(a) in the case of information disclosed as mentioned in paragraph (1)(a), the Secretary of State, or

(b) in the case of information disclosed as mentioned in paragraph (1)(b), the Department of Enterprise, Trade and Investment in Northern Ireland.

[4630]

8 Information supplied before commencement by the Building Societies Commission

(1) This article applies to information ("transitional building societies information")—

(a) disclosed before commencement by the Building Societies Commission to the Bank for the purpose of enabling or assisting the Bank to discharge its relevant functions; and

(b) which immediately before commencement was subject to the powers of disclosure conferred by section 87(3A) of the Banking Act 1987, as that section had effect by virtue of paragraph 59 of Schedule 5 to the 1998 Act.

(2) Transitional building societies information may be disclosed in accordance with section 349 of the Act and the Disclosure Regulations as if—

(a) it were confidential information within the meaning of section 348(2) of the Act; and

(b) the Bank were a primary recipient of the information.

[4631]

FINANCIAL SERVICES AND MARKETS ACT 2000 (SCOPE OF PERMISSION NOTICES) ORDER 2001

(SI 2001/3771)

NOTES

Made: 26 November 2001.

Authority: Financial Services and Markets Act 2000, ss 426–428.

Commencement: 1 December 2001 (see art 1 at **[4632]**). Where any provision in this work (including any inserted or substituted provision) came into force for all purposes on or before 1 July 2005, commencement information is not noted at provision level.

As of 1 July 2007, this Order had not been amended.

1 Citation, commencement and interpretation

(1) This Order may be cited as the Financial Services and Markets Act 2000 (Scope of Permission Notices) Order 2001 and comes into force on 1st December 2001.

(2) In this Order—

"the Act" means the Financial Services and Markets Act 2000;

"the Authorised Persons Order" means the Financial Services and Markets Act 2000 (Transitional Provisions) (Authorised Persons etc) Order 2001;

"commencement" means the beginning of 1st December 2001;

"the Regulated Activities Order" means the Financial Services and Markets Act 2000 (Regulated Activities) Order 2001.

[4632]

2 Revision of scope of permission notices

(1) This article applies where—

(a) the Authority has given, before commencement, a scope of permission notice under article 55 of the Authorised Persons Order;

(b) that notice falls within one of the cases specified in article 3;

(c) the recipient of the notice has, before commencement, notified the Authority in accordance with article 56(1)(a) of the Authorised Persons Order that he agrees with the matters stated in the notice;

(d) the Authority has, before commencement, given that recipient a notice ("the revision notice") revising the scope of permission notice in a permitted manner.

(2) If the recipient of the scope of permission notice does not, on or before 4 January 2002, notify the Authority that he objects to the revision notice, then article 57(1) of the Authorised Persons Order applies as if—

(a) the reference to the scope of permission notice in that article were to the scope of permission notice as revised by the revision notice; and

(b) the person has agreed to that notice as so revised.

(3) If the recipient of the scope of permission notice notifies the Authority on or before 4 January 2002 that he objects to the revision notice, then article 57(1) of the Authorised Persons Order applies as if the revision notice had not been sent.

[4633]

3 Cases in which scope of permission notices may be revised

The cases specified in this article are as follows—

CASE 1

Where—

(a) the recipient of the scope of permission notice was, at the time the notice was sent, an authorised person within the meaning of the Financial Services Act 1986;

(b) that person is to be treated, by virtue of Part II of the Authorised Persons Order, as having a Part IV permission to carry on a regulated activity of the kind specified by article 14 of the Regulated Activities Order (dealing in investments as principal) in so far as the activity consists of his entering into a transaction relating to contractually based investments;

(c) the person is not subject, by virtue of Part III of the Authorised Persons Order, to a requirement imposed under section 43 of the Act preventing him from carrying on the regulated activity in paragraph (b); and

(d) the scope of permission notice did not specify that the person had a Part IV permission to carry on the regulated activity in paragraph (b).

CASE 2

Where—

(a) the recipient of the scope of permission notice was, at the time the notice was sent, a member of the Personal Investment Authority Limited;

(b) the scope of permission notice specified that he had a Part IV permission to carry on a regulated activity of the kind specified by article 53 of the Regulated Activities Order (advising on investments) in relation to a particular specified kind of investment ("investment A");

(c) the person is to be treated, by virtue of Part II of the Authorised Persons Order, as having a Part IV permission to carry on that regulated activity also in relation to rights to or interests in (within the meaning of activity 89 of the Regulated Activities Order) investment A;

(d) the person is not subject, by virtue of Part III of the Authorised Persons Order, to a requirement imposed under section 43 of the Act preventing him from carrying on that regulated activity in relation to rights to or interests in investment A; and

(e) the scope of permission notice did not specify that he had a Part IV permission to carry on that regulated activity in relation to rights to or interests in investment A.

CASE 3

Where—

(a) the scope of permission notice specified that the recipient of the notice has a Part IV permission to carry on a regulated activity in relation to a particular specified kind of investment ("investment B"); and

(b) the scope of permission notice purported also to specify that he had permission to carry on that regulated activity in relation to rights to and interests in investments generally rather than only in relation to rights to or interests in investment B.

CASE 4

Where—

(a) the recipient of the scope of permission notice was, at the time the notice was sent, a member of either the Investment Management Regulatory Organisation Limited or the Personal Investment Authority Limited;

(b) the scope of permission notice specified that he had a Part IV permission to carry on a regulated activity of the kind specified by article 40 of the Regulated Activities Order (safeguarding and administering investments);

(c) the scope of permission notice also specified that he was subject to a requirement under section 43 of the Act that he should not hold or control client money; and

(d) the person is not subject, by virtue of Part III of the Authorised Persons Order, to that requirement.

CASE 5

Where—

(a) the recipient of the scope of permission notice was, at the time the notice was sent, a member of either the Investment Management Regulatory Organisation Limited or the Personal Investment Authority Limited;

(b) the scope of permission notice specified that he had a Part IV permission to carry on a regulated activity of the kind specified by either article 51 of the Regulated Activities Order (establishing etc a collective investment scheme) or article 52 of that Order (establishing etc a stakeholder pension scheme);

(c) the scope of permission notice purported to limit that permission to carrying on the activity in relation to a specified kind of investment; and

(d) the Part IV permission that the person is to be treated as having by virtue of Parts II and III of the Authorised Persons Order is not subject to that limitation.

CASE 6

Where—

(a) the recipient of the scope of permission notice was, at the time the notice was sent, a member of the Investment Management Regulatory Organisation Limited;

(b) the scope of permission notice specified that he had a Part IV permission to carry on a regulated activity of the kind specified by article 21 of the Regulated Activities Order (dealing in investments as agent) for the purpose of stock lending activities;

(c) the scope of permission notice purported further to limit his permission so that he could not carry on that activity in relation to investments of the kind specified by article 78 of the Regulated Activities Order (government and public securities); and

(d) the Part IV permission that the person is to be treated as having by virtue of Parts II and III of the Authorised Persons Order is not subject to that limitation.

[4634]

4 Permitted revisions

For the purposes of article 2(1)(d), a revision notice revises the scope of permission notice in a permitted manner if—

(a) in Case 1 in article 3, it results in the scope of permission notice specifying that the recipient has a Part IV permission to carry on the regulated activities described in paragraph (b) of that Case;

(b) in Case 2 in article 3, it results in the scope of permission notice specifying that the recipient has a Part IV permission to carry on the regulated activity described in paragraph (c) of that Case;

(c) in Case 3 in article 3, it results in the scope of permission notice specifying that his Part IV permission to carry on a particular regulated activity in relation to rights to or interests in investments is limited to rights to or interests in investment B (as defined in that Case);

(d) in Case 4 in article 3, it results either in the lifting of the requirement that the recipient should not control client money or in the lifting of the requirement that he should not hold or control client money;

(e) in Case 5 in article 3, it results in the removal of the limitation described in paragraph (c) of that Case;

(f) in Case 6 in article 3, it results in the removal of the limitation described in paragraph (c) of that Case;

(g) in any Case in article 3, it results in the scope of permission notice specifying that the recipient has a Part IV permission to carry on a regulated activity of the kind specified by article 64 of the Regulated Activities Order (agreeing to carry on specified kinds of activity) to the extent appropriate having regard to paragraphs (a) to (f) above.

[4635]

5 (*Substitutes the Financial Services and Markets Act 2000 (Miscellaneous Provisions) Order 2001, SI 2001/3650, arts 29(2), (3), 30(2), (3).*)

FINANCIAL SERVICES AND MARKETS ACT 2000 (REGULATED ACTIVITIES) (AMENDMENT) ORDER 2002

(SI 2002/682)

NOTES

Made: 14 March 2002.

Authority: Financial Services and Markets Act 2000, ss 22(1), (5), 428(3), Sch 2 para 25.

Commencement: 11 April 2002 (certain purposes); 27 April 2002 (otherwise); see art 1 at **[4636]**. Where any provision in this work (including any inserted or substituted provision) came into force for all purposes on or before 1 July 2005, commencement information is not noted at provision level.

This Order is reproduced as amended by: the Capital Requirements Regulations 2006, SI 2006/3221.

PART I
PRELIMINARY

1 Citation, commencement and interpretation

(1) This Order may be cited as the Financial Services and Markets Act 2000 (Regulated Activities) (Amendment) Order 2002.

(2) This Order comes into force—

(a) on 11th April 2002, for the purpose of making rules under articles 9G and 9H of the principal Order (as inserted by article 4 of this Order);

(b) on 27th April 2002, for all other purposes.

(3) In this Order—

(a) "the Act" means the Financial Services and Markets Act 2000;

(b) "the principal Order" means the Financial Services and Markets Act 2000 (Regulated Activities) Order 2001.

[4636]

PART II
ELECTRONIC MONEY

2–6 (*Amend the Financial Services and Markets Act 2000* (*Regulated Activities*) *Order 2001*, *SI 2001/544*, *arts 3*, *5*, *64 at* **[4003]**, **[4005]**, **[4075]**, *and insert arts 9A–9K*, *74A at* **[4010]**–**[4020]**, **[4086]**.)

Supplemental and transitional provisions

7, 8 (*Art 7 amends the Financial Services and Markets Act 2000* (*Professions*) (*Non-Exempt Activities*) *Order 2001*, *SI 2001/1227*, *arts 4*, *8 at* **[4167]**, **[4172]**; *art 8 amends the Financial Services and Markets Act 2000*, *Sch 6*, *para 1*(2) *at* **[2443]**.)

9 Transitional provisions for persons issuing electronic money at commencement

(1) Where, immediately before commencement, a credit institution with Part IV permission to accept deposits was carrying on by way of business in the United Kingdom the activity of issuing electronic money, the institution's permission is to be treated as including, for a period of six months beginning at commencement, permission to carry on an activity of the kind specified by article 9B of the principal Order.

(2) Where, immediately before commencement—

(a) an EEA firm of the kind mentioned in paragraph 5(b) or (c) of Schedule 3 to the Act qualified for authorisation under that Schedule, and

(b) the activities which were treated as permitted activities for the purposes of paragraph 13 or 14 of that Schedule as it applied to that firm included the issuing of electronic money,

the firm's permission under paragraph 15 of that Schedule is to be treated, at commencement, as including permission to carry on that activity.

PART IV STATUTORY INSTRUMENTS

(3) Where an existing issuer having his head office in the United Kingdom is, after commencement, granted a Part IV permission to carry on an activity of the kind specified by article 9B (and hence becomes a UK firm, within the meaning of Schedule 3 to the Act, in relation to that activity)—

(a) if, immediately before commencement, the existing issuer was carrying on the activity of issuing electronic money from a branch established in another EEA State, the conditions in paragraph 19(2) to (5) of that Schedule are to be treated as satisfied with respect to that branch;

(b) if, immediately before commencement, the existing issuer was carrying on the activity of issuing electronic money by providing services in another EEA State, the conditions in paragraph 20(1) of that Schedule are to be treated as satisfied with respect to the provision of those services in that EEA State.

(4) An existing issuer having his head office in an EEA State other than the United Kingdom who, after commencement, becomes authorised (within the meaning of [Article 4(2)] of the banking consolidation directive) by his home state regulator (and hence becomes an EEA firm)—

(a) is to be treated as having complied with the establishment conditions (within the meaning of paragraph 13 of Schedule 3 to the Act) where, immediately before commencement, he was carrying on the activity of issuing electronic money from a branch established in the United Kingdom;

(b) is to be treated as having complied with the service conditions (within the meaning of paragraph 14 of that Schedule) where, immediately before commencement, he was carrying on the activity of issuing electronic money by providing services in the United Kingdom.

(5) Where paragraph (4)(a) or (b) applies, the existing issuer is to be treated as having permission to carry on the activity mentioned in that paragraph through its United Kingdom branch or (as the case may be) by providing services in the United Kingdom.

(6) There is excluded from article 9B of the principal Order any activity carried on by an existing issuer before 27th October 2002, unless he has been granted a Part IV permission to carry on that activity, or has permission to carry on that activity as a result of paragraph (5).

(7) There is also excluded from article 9B of the principal Order any activity carried on by an existing issuer after the beginning of 27th October 2002, provided—

(a) he has made an application before 27th June 2002 under section 40 of the Act for permission to carry on that activity, and has not withdrawn it; and

(b) the application has not been finally determined.

(8) For the purposes of paragraph (7), an application is to be treated as finally determined—

(a) in a case where the Authority gives permission to carry on the activity and does not exercise its power under section 42(7)(a) or (b) or section 43(1) of the Act, on the date on which the permission takes effect;

(b) in a case where the Authority refuses permission, or gives permission but exercises its power under section 42(7)(a) or (b) or section 43 of the Act, at the time when the matter ceases to be open to review (within the meaning of section 391(8) of the Act).

(9) In this article—

(a) "commencement" means the beginning of 27th April 2002;

(b) "credit institution" means a credit institution as defined in [Article 4(1)(a)] of the banking consolidation directive;

(c) an "existing issuer" means a body corporate or partnership (other than one falling within paragraph (1) or (2)) which, immediately before commencement—

(i) has its head office in the United Kingdom, and is carrying on by way of business in the United Kingdom the activity of issuing electronic money; or

(ii) has its head office in an EEA State other than the United Kingdom, and is carrying on such an activity by way of business in the United Kingdom without contravening the law of that other EEA State;

(d) in paragraph (1) and in sub-paragraph (c) of this paragraph, the references to carrying on an activity in the United Kingdom are to be construed without reference to section 418 of the Act (carrying on regulated activities in the United Kingdom).

[4637]

NOTES

Paras (4), (9): words in square brackets substituted by the Capital Requirements Regulations 2006, SI 2006/3221, reg 29(4), Sch 6, para 13, as from 1 January 2007.

10 Anticipatory consultation on rules

If—

(a) before 11th April 2002 any steps were taken in relation to a draft of rules which the Authority proposes to make under article 9G(1) or 9H of the principal Order (as inserted by article 4 of this Order), and

(b) those steps, had they been taken after that day, would to any extent have satisfied the requirements of section 155 of the Act,

those requirements are to that extent to be taken to have been satisfied.

[4638]

11–13 (*Arts 11–13* (*Pt III*) *amend the Financial Services and Markets Act 2000* (*Regulated Activities*) *Order 2001, SI 2001/544, arts 4, 9, 45, 46, 49, 69 at* **[4004]**, **[4009]**, **[4056]**, **[4057]**, **[4060]**, **[4080]**.)

FINANCIAL SERVICES AND MARKETS ACT 2000 (ADMINISTRATION ORDERS RELATING TO INSURERS) ORDER 2002

(SI 2002/1242)

NOTES

This Order has been omitted from this Edition of the *Company Law Handbook* in order to create space for other legislation (ie, the Companies Act 2006 and the associated destination and derivation tables). It was printed in full in the 20th Edition of this work (at p 1823 et seq) and, as of 1 July 2007, it had not been amended since the publication of that Edition. This Order is, however, included in the CD version of this work (which may be ordered from the LexisNexis Butterworths Customer Services Department) and can be accessed in the online version of the *Company Law Handbook* which is updated fortnightly (at www.lexisnexis.com/uk/legal). It is also printed in full in the 8th Edition of *Butterworths Financial Services Law Handbook* (February 2007).

[4638A]–[4638E]

ELECTRONIC COMMERCE DIRECTIVE (FINANCIAL SERVICES AND MARKETS) REGULATIONS 2002

(SI 2002/1775)

NOTES

Made: 12 July 2002.

Authority: European Communities Act 1972, s 2(2); Financial Services and Markets Act 2000, ss 349(1), 414, 428(3).

Commencement: 18 July 2002 (for the purpose of enabling the Authority to make rules); 21 August 2002 (otherwise); see reg 1 at **[4639]**. Where any provision in this work (including any inserted or substituted provision) came into force for all purposes on or before 1 July 2005, commencement information is not noted at provision level.

These Regulations are reproduced as amended by: the Electronic Commerce Directive (Financial Services and Markets) (Amendment) Regulations 2002, SI 2002/2015; the Electronic Commerce Directive (Financial Services and Markets) (Amendment) Regulations 2004, SI 2004/3378; the Financial Services (EEA State) Regulations 2007, SI 2007/108.

ARRANGEMENT OF REGULATIONS

PART 1
GENERAL

PART 2
MODIFICATION OF FUNCTIONS OF THE FINANCIAL SERVICES AUTHORITY

PART 3
ARTICLE 3.4 OF THE ELECTRONIC COMMERCE DIRECTIVE

PART 4
ENFORCEMENT

PART 6
MISCELLANEOUS AND CONSEQUENTIAL PROVISIONS

PART 1
GENERAL

1 Citation and commencement

These Regulations may be cited as the Electronic Commerce Directive (Financial Services and Markets) Regulations 2002, and come into force—

(a) for the purpose of enabling the Authority to make rules, on 18th July 2002;

(b) otherwise, on 21st August 2002.

[4639]

2 Interpretation

(1) In these Regulations—

"the 2000 Act" means the Financial Services and Markets Act 2000;

"authorised incoming provider" means an incoming provider who is an authorised person within the meaning of the 2000 Act;

"the Authority" means the Financial Services Authority;

"commercial communication" means a communication, in any form, designed to promote, directly or indirectly, the goods, services or image of any person pursuing a commercial activity or exercising a regulated profession, other than a communication—

(a) consisting only of information allowing direct access to the activity of that person, including a geographic address, domain name or electronic mail address; or

(b) relating to the goods, services or image of that person provided that the communication has been prepared independently of the person making it (and for this purpose, a communication prepared without financial consideration is to be taken to have been prepared independently unless the contrary is shown);

"the Commission" means the Commission of the European Communities;

"consumer" means any individual who is acting for purposes other than those of his trade, business or profession;

"country of origin" in relation to an incoming electronic commerce activity means the EEA State in which is situated the establishment from which the information society service in question is provided;

"criminal conduct" means conduct which constitutes an offence in any part of the United Kingdom, or would constitute an offence in any part of the United Kingdom if it occurred there;

"direction" means a direction made, or proposed to be made, by the Authority under regulation 6;

"EEA regulator" means an authority in an EEA State other than the United Kingdom which exercises any function of a kind mentioned in section 195(4) of the 2000 Act;

["EEA State" has the meaning given by Schedule 1 to the Interpretation Act 1978;]

"electronic commerce directive" means Directive 2000/31/EC of the European Parliament and of the Council of 8 June 2000 on certain legal aspects of information society services, in particular electronic commerce, in the Internal Market (Directive on electronic commerce);

"financial instrument" includes an investment of a kind specified by any of articles 76 to 85 of the Regulated Activities Order;

"incoming electronic commerce activity" means an activity—

(a) which consists of the provision of an information society service from an establishment in an EEA State other than the United Kingdom to a person or persons in the United Kingdom, and

(b) which would, but for article 72A of the Regulated Activities Order (and irrespective of the effect of article 72 of that Order), be a regulated activity within the meaning of the 2000 Act;

"incoming provider" means a person carrying on an incoming electronic commerce activity;

"information society service" means an information society service within the meaning of Article 2(a) of the electronic commerce directive;

"investment" means an investment of a kind specified by any provision of Part III of the Regulated Activities Order;

"Regulated Activities Order" means the Financial Services and Markets Act 2000 (Regulated Activities) Order 2001;

"regulated profession" means any profession within the meaning of—

(a) Article 1(d) of Directive 89/48/EEC of the Council of the European Communities of 21 December 1988 on a general system for the recognition of higher-education diplomas awarded on completion of professional education and training of at least three years' duration, or

(b) Article 1(f) of Directive 92/51/EEC of the Council of the European Communities of 18 June 1992 on a second general system for the recognition of professional education and training to supplement Directive 89/48/EEC;

"relevant EEA regulator", in relation to a direction, means the EEA regulator in the country of origin of the incoming electronic commerce activity to which the direction does, or would if made, relate, and which is responsible in that country for the regulation of that activity;

"rule" means a rule made by the Authority under the 2000 Act;

"Tribunal" means the Financial Services and Markets Tribunal referred to in section 132 of the 2000 Act;

"UCITS Directive" means Directive 85/611/EEC of the Council of the European Communities of 20 December 1985 on the co-ordination of laws, regulations and administrative provisions relating to undertakings for collective investment in transferable securities;

"UCITS Directive scheme" means an undertaking for collective investment in transferable securities which is subject to the UCITS Directive, and has been authorised in accordance with Article 4 of that Directive;

"unauthorised incoming provider" means an incoming provider who is not an authorised person within the meaning of the 2000 Act.

(2) A reference in these Regulations to a requirement imposed by the Authority under these Regulations is a reference to—

(a) a requirement (including a requirement that a person no longer carry on an incoming electronic commerce activity) imposed by a direction; or

(b) a requirement imposed by a rule applicable to incoming providers in accordance with regulation 3(4).

(3) For the purposes of these Regulations—

(a) an establishment, in connection with an information society service, is the place at which the provider of the service (being a national of an EEA State or a company or firm as mentioned in Article 48 of the treaty establishing the European Community) effectively pursues an economic activity for an indefinite period;

(b) the presence or use in a particular place of equipment or other technical means of providing an information society service does not, of itself, constitute that place as an establishment of the kind mentioned in sub-paragraph (a);

(c) where it cannot be determined from which of a number of establishments a given information society service is provided, that service is to be regarded as provided from the establishment where the provider has the centre of his activities relating to the service;

(d) a communication by electronic mail is to be regarded as unsolicited, unless it is made in response to an express request from the recipient of the communication.

[4640]

NOTES

Para (1): definition "EEA State" substituted by the Financial Services (EEA State) Regulations 2007, SI 2007/108, reg 6, as from 13 February 2007.

PART 2
MODIFICATION OF FUNCTIONS OF THE FINANCIAL SERVICES AUTHORITY

3 Consumer contract requirements: modification of rule-making power

(1) The power to make rules conferred by section 138 of the 2000 Act is to be taken to include a power to make rules applying to unauthorised incoming providers.

(2) In consequence of paragraph (1)—

(a) any reference in sections 138(4), (5) and (7) to (9), 148, 150 and 156 of the 2000 Act to an authorised person includes a reference to an unauthorised incoming provider;

(b) any reference in those sections to a regulated activity includes a reference to an incoming electronic commerce activity.

(3) For the purpose of the exercise by the Authority of the power conferred by section 138 of the 2000 Act to make rules applying to incoming providers with respect to the carrying on by them of incoming electronic commerce activities, subsections (7) and (9) of that section have effect as if the reference to "person" where first occurring were a reference to an individual acting for purposes other than those of his trade, business or profession.

(4) Rules made by the Authority under section 138 of the 2000 Act do not apply to incoming providers with respect to the carrying on by them of incoming electronic commerce activities unless they—

(a) impose consumer contract requirements;

(b) apply with respect to communications that constitute an advertisement by the operator of a UCITS Directive scheme of units in that scheme; or

(c) relate to the permissibility of unsolicited commercial communications by electronic mail.

[(4A) Notwithstanding paragraph (4)(a), rules made by the Authority under section 138 of the 2000 Act which impose consumer contract requirements do not apply to an incoming provider with respect to the carrying on by him of an incoming electronic commerce activity which consists of the provision of an information society service from an establishment in an EEA State other than the United Kingdom, if the provisions by which that State has transposed the Financial Services Distance Marketing Directive, or the obligations in the domestic law of that State corresponding to those provided for in that Directive, as the case may be, apply to that activity.]

(5) A consumer contract rule may provide that conduct engaged in by a person to whom the rule applies, and which is in conformity with a provision corresponding to the rule made by a body or authority in an EEA State other than the United Kingdom, is to be treated as conduct in conformity with the rule.

(6) "Consumer contract requirement" means a requirement—

(a) that information of a kind referred to in regulation 4 be provided to a consumer before he enters into a contract for the provision of one or more information society services, or

(b) as to the manner in which such information is to be provided.

[(6A) "The Financial Services Distance Marketing Directive" means Directive 2002/65/EC of the European Parliament and the Council of 23 September 2002 concerning the distance marketing of consumer financial services and amending Council Directive 90/619/EEC and Directives 97/7/EC and 98/27/EC.]

(7) "Consumer contract rule" means a rule made by the Authority under section 138 of the 2000 Act which imposes a consumer contract requirement on incoming providers.

[4641]

NOTES

Paras (4A), (6A): inserted by the Electronic Commerce Directive (Financial Services and Markets) (Amendment) Regulations 2004, SI 2004/3378, reg 2, as from 11 January 2005.

4 Consumer contract requirements: information

The information which may be the subject of a consumer contract requirement is—

(a) the identity and description of the main business of the other party to the proposed contract ("the supplier"), the geographic address at which the supplier is established, and any other geographic address relevant to the consumer's relations with the supplier;

(b) if the supplier has a representative established in the consumer's country of residence with whom the consumer is to have dealings, the identity and geographic address of the representative, and any other geographic address relevant to the consumer's relations with the representative;

(c) if the consumer is to have dealings with any professional person in connection with the contract, the identity of that person, a statement of the capacity in which he is to act, and the geographic address relevant to the consumer's relations with him;

(d) if the supplier is registered on any public register in connection with the carrying on of his business (or such of his business as is relevant to the contract), the name of that register, and any registration number or other means of identifying the relevant entry on the register;

(e) if the carrying on of the supplier's business (or such of it as is relevant to the contract) is subject to a requirement that he be authorised by a person or body in order to carry it on, the name and geographic address of that person or body;

(f) a description of the main features of the service or services to which the contract relates;

(g) either—

(aa) the total price to be paid by the consumer under the contract, including all related fees, charges and expenses, and all taxes paid by or through the supplier (in so far as these are reflected in the total price); or

(bb) if the total price cannot be given, the basis for the calculation of the total price, in a form enabling the consumer to verify the total price when calculated by the supplier;

(h) where the service to be provided under the contract relates to one or more financial instruments—

(aa) if the instruments are subject to special risks relating to their specific features or operations to be executed in relation to them, notice of the existence of those risks,

(bb) if the price of the instruments is subject to fluctuation depending on market conditions outside the supplier's control, notice of that fact, and

(cc) notice that movements in the price of the instruments in the past are not necessarily an indicator of future performance;

(i) notice of the possibility that taxes or other costs may exist which are not imposed or paid by or through the supplier;

(j) the arrangements for payment under, and the performance of, the contract;

(k) any specific additional cost imposed by the supplier on the consumer in relation to the consumer's use of the means for concluding the contract or communicating with the supplier;

(l) the existence or absence of any legal right of the consumer to withdraw from the contract after it has been entered into, the conditions attached to the exercise of any such right, and the consequences for the consumer of not exercising it;

(m) where the contract relates to services to be performed on an indefinite or recurrent basis, the minimum duration of the contract;

(n) any rights of the consumer or the supplier to terminate the contract in accordance with one of its express terms, any contractual penalties which may apply in that event, and the procedure to be followed by the consumer in that event (including the address to which any notification of withdrawal from the contract should be sent);

(o) the state or states whose laws are taken by the supplier as a basis for the establishment of relations with the consumer before the contract is concluded;

(p) any express term in the contract relating to the law governing it, or to the jurisdiction of courts;

(q) the language or languages in which the supplier—

(aa) proposes to offer the terms of, and information concerning, the contract, and

(bb) undertakes (with the agreement of the consumer) to communicate with the consumer during the existence of the contract;

(r) whether any mechanism other than redress through a court (including guarantee funds and compensation schemes and arrangements) is available to the consumer in relation to matters arising in connection with the contract, and if so, the procedure to be followed by the consumer in order to gain access to it;

(s) any limitations, of which the supplier could reasonably be taken to be aware, of the period for which any information referred to in paragraphs (a) to (r) will be valid.

[4642]

5 Application of certain rules

Rules made by the Authority under section 140 or 141 of the 2000 Act do not apply to incoming providers to the extent that they specify an activity which is an incoming electronic commerce activity.

[4643]

PART 3

ARTICLE 3.4 OF THE ELECTRONIC COMMERCE DIRECTIVE

6 Direction by Authority

(1) If the policy conditions and the procedural conditions are met, the Authority may direct that an incoming provider may no longer carry on a specified incoming electronic commerce activity, or may only carry it on subject to specified requirements.

(2) A direction—

(a) must be in writing;

(b) has effect from—

(i) a specified date (which may be the date on which it is made); or

(ii) if no date is specified, the date on which the direction is no longer open to review;

(c) must include a statement to the effect that the person to whom it applies may refer the matter to the Tribunal;

(d) may have effect for a specified period, until the occurrence of a specified event, until specified conditions are met, or for an indefinite period.

(3) The requirements referred to in paragraph (1) may include the requirement that the person to whom the direction applies must comply with one or more rules (with such modifications (if any) as may be specified) with respect to the carrying on by him of an incoming electronic commerce activity.

(4) If a requirement of a kind mentioned in subsection (3) of section 48 of the 2000 Act is specified in a direction, the requirement has the same effect in relation to the person to whom the direction applies as it would have if it had been imposed on that person by the Authority acting under section 45 of that Act.

(5) Contravention of a specified requirement does not make a person guilty of an offence, or make any transaction void or unenforceable.

(6) Contravention of a specified requirement by an incoming provider is actionable at the suit of a person who suffers loss as a result of the contravention, subject to—

(a) the defences and other incidents applying to actions for breach of statutory duty; and

(b) the conditions mentioned in regulation 7(2) of the Financial Services and Markets Act 2000 (Rights of Action) Regulations 2001 ("the Rights of Action Regulations").

(7) For the purposes of paragraph (6)(b), the reference in regulation 7(2)(b) of the Rights of Action Regulations to a Part XIII financial resources requirement is to be taken to include a reference to a specified requirement to have or maintain financial resources.

(8) For the purposes of this regulation, a direction is no longer open to review if any of the conditions in section 391(8) (a) to (d) of the 2000 Act are satisfied.

(9) In this regulation, "specified" in relation to a direction means specified in the direction.

[4644]

7 Policy conditions

The policy conditions are that—

(a) the Authority considers—

(i) the making of the direction to be necessary for—

(aa) the prevention, investigation, detection or prosecution of criminal conduct;

(bb) the protection of consumers; or

(cc) other reasons of public policy relevant to the regulatory objectives set out in Part I of the 2000 Act; and

(ii) that the carrying on of the incoming electronic commerce activity by the person to whom the direction is to apply prejudices, or presents a serious and grave risk of prejudice to, any of the objectives referred to in sub-paragraph (i); and

(b) the direction appears to the Authority to be a proportionate means of achieving, or addressing the prejudice or risk of prejudice to, any of those objectives.

[4645]

8 Procedural conditions

The procedural conditions are that—

(a) the Authority has requested the relevant EEA regulator to take measures to remedy the situation giving rise to the request;

(b) the relevant EEA regulator—

(i) has not, within what appears to the Authority to be a reasonable time, taken such measures; or

(ii) has taken such measures, but the measures appear to the Authority to be inadequate in the circumstances;

(c) the Authority has notified the Commission and the relevant EEA regulator of its intention to make the direction; and

(d) the Authority has notified the person to whom the direction is to apply of its proposal to make the direction, and afforded that person the opportunity to make representations to the Authority in such manner, and within such period, as the Authority may determine.

[4646]

9 Urgent cases

(1) If the case appears to the Authority to be one of urgency, it may make a direction regardless of whether the procedural conditions are met.

(2) If the Authority makes a direction in reliance on paragraph (1), it must notify the Commission and the relevant EEA regulator as soon as possible that the direction has been made, and provide each of those bodies with a statement of its reasons for considering the case to be one of urgency.

[4647]

10 Directions made under regulation 6

(1) Subject to the following provisions of this regulation, the Authority may vary or revoke a direction by notice in writing to the person to whom the direction applies.

(2) The Authority may vary or revoke a direction under this regulation on its own initiative, or on the application of the person to whom the direction applies.

(3) If the Authority decides to refuse an application for the variation or revocation of a direction made under this regulation, it must notify the applicant in writing of its decision.

(4) The Authority must not vary a direction on its own initiative under this regulation unless it has afforded the person to whom the direction applies the opportunity to make representations to the Authority in such manner, and within such period, as the Authority may determine.

(5) Paragraph (4) does not apply if the case appears to the Authority to be one of urgency.

(6) A decision by the Authority to vary a direction has effect from—

(a) a date referred to in the notice given under paragraph (1) (which must not be earlier than the date on which the decision was made); or

(b) if no such date is referred to, the date on which the decision was made.

(7) If the case is one to which regulation 11(b) or (c) applies, a notice under paragraph (1) or (3) must include a statement to the effect that the person to whom the direction applies may refer the matter to the Tribunal.

(8) If the Authority makes a direction it may publish, in such manner as it considers appropriate, such information about the matter to which the direction relates as it considers appropriate in furtherance of any of the objectives referred to in regulation 7(a)(i).

(9) The Authority may not publish information under paragraph (8) if publication of it would, in the Authority's opinion, be unfair to the person to whom the direction applies or prejudicial to the interests of consumers.

[4648]

11 Referral to the Tribunal

If the Authority—

(a) makes a direction;

(b) varies a direction on its own initiative; or

(c) decides to refuse an application for the variation or revocation of a direction,

the person to whom the direction applies may refer the matter to the Tribunal.

[4649]

PART 4
ENFORCEMENT

12 Application of certain provisions of the 2000 Act

(1) For the purposes of sections 205 to 209 and 384 of the 2000 Act, a requirement imposed by the Authority under these Regulations upon an authorised incoming provider is to be treated as imposed on him by or under that Act.

(2) For the purposes of sections 380, 382 and 398 of, and paragraph 6 of Schedule 1 to, the 2000 Act, a requirement imposed by the Authority under these Regulations upon an incoming provider is to be treated as imposed on him by or under that Act.

(3) Any reference in sections 165 to 168 and 176 of the 2000 Act to an authorised person includes a reference to an unauthorised incoming provider.

(4) Any reference in sections 132 and 133 of the 2000 Act to that Act includes a reference to these Regulations.

(5) The reference in section 168(4)(c) of the 2000 Act to a rule made by the Authority includes a reference to a requirement imposed by the Authority under these Regulations.

[4650]

13 ((*Pt V*) *amends the Financial Services and Markets Act 2000, ss 417, 418 at* **[2414]**, **[2415]**.)

PART 6
MISCELLANEOUS AND CONSEQUENTIAL PROVISIONS

14 Disclosure of information

In any enactment that requires or permits the disclosure of information to or by the Authority, a reference (however expressed) to powers or functions conferred on the Authority by or under the 2000 Act includes, for the purposes of such disclosure, a reference to the Authority's functions under these Regulations.

[4651]

15 Notices

The Financial Services and Markets Act 2000 (Service of Notices) Regulations 2001 apply for the purposes of these Regulations as if any reference in those Regulations to "the Act" included a reference to these Regulations.

[4652]

16 (*Inserts the Financial Services and Markets Act 2000 (Disclosure of Confidential Information) Regulations 2001, SI 2001/2188, reg 12B, at* **[4384A]**.)

17 Functions of the Authority

For the purposes of the 2000 Act, a function conferred on the Authority by these Regulations is to be taken to be a function conferred on the Authority by or under that Act.

[4653]

18 (*Amends the Financial Services and Markets Act 2000 (Rights of Action) Regulations 2001, SI 2001/2256, reg 3 at* **[4397]**.)

[19 Exclusion of general regulations

(1) Regulation 4(1) of the general regulations does not affect any legal requirement imposed by or under the 2000 Act or these Regulations.

(2) Regulation 4(2) and (3) of the general regulations do not apply to the Authority or any enforcement authority in respect of its responsibility in relation to a requirement of the kind mentioned in paragraph (1).

(3) A rule that corresponds to a relevant regulation applies instead of that regulation.

(4) The reference in regulation 22(a) of the general regulations to regulation 6(1)(c) of those regulations is to be taken to include a reference to a provision in a rule that corresponds to regulation 6(1)(c) (and so applies in its stead by virtue of paragraph (3)).

(5) In this regulation—

"enforcement authority" has the same meaning as in the general regulations;

"general regulations" means the Electronic Commerce (EC Directive) Regulations 2002;

"relevant regulation" means regulation 6 to 9, 11 or 15 of the general regulations.]

[4654]

NOTES

Added by the Electronic Commerce Directive (Financial Services and Markets) (Amendment) Regulations 2002, SI 2002/2015, reg 2, as from 21 August 2002.

FINANCIAL SERVICES AND MARKETS ACT 2000 (COMMUNICATIONS BY ACTUARIES) REGULATIONS 2003

(SI 2003/1294)

NOTES

Made: 12 May 2003.
Authority: Financial Services and Markets Act 2000, ss 342(5), 343(5), 428(3).

Commencement: 1 September 2003 (see reg 1 at **[4655]**). Where any provision in this work (including any inserted or substituted provision) came into force for all purposes on or before 1 July 2005, commencement information is not noted at provision level.

As of 1 July 2007, these Regulations had not been amended.

---

1 Citation, commencement and interpretation

(1) These Regulations may be cited as the Financial Services and Markets Act 2000 (Communications by Actuaries) Regulations 2003 and come into force on 1st September 2003.

(2) In these Regulations—

"the Act" means the Financial Services and Markets Act 2000;

"contract of long-term insurance" has the same meaning as in the Financial Services and Markets Act 2000 (Regulated Activities) Order 2001;

"relevant requirement" means—

(a) a requirement which is imposed by or under any provision of the Act other than Part VI (official listing); or

(b) a requirement which is imposed by or under any other Act and whose contravention constitutes an offence which the Authority has power to prosecute under the Act.

[4655]

2 Circumstances in which an actuary is to communicate

(1) This regulation applies to any person who is, or has been, an actuary acting for an authorised person ("A") and who is or was—

(a) appointed under or as a result of rules made by the Authority under section 340 of the Act; or

(b) appointed under or as a result of any other statutory provision and subject to duties imposed by such rules.

(2) An actuary to whom this regulation applies must communicate to the Authority information on, or his opinion on, matters mentioned in section 342(3)(a) of the Act (matters of which he has, or had, become aware in his capacity as actuary acting for an authorised person) in the circumstances specified in paragraph (4).

(3) An actuary—

(a) to whom this regulation applies, and

(b) who is or has been an actuary acting for a person who has close links with A (within the meaning of section 343(8) of the Act),

must communicate to the Authority information on, or his opinion on, matters mentioned in section 343(3)(a) of the Act (information on a matter concerning A of which he has, or had, become aware in his capacity as actuary acting for the person who has close links with A) in the circumstances specified in paragraph (4).

(4) The circumstances are that the actuary reasonably believes that—

(a) as regards A—

(i) there is or has been, or may be or may have been, a contravention of any relevant requirement that applies to A; and

(ii) that contravention may be of material significance to the Authority in determining whether to exercise, in relation to A, any functions conferred on the Authority by or under any provision of the Act other than Part VI;

(b) the information on, or his opinion on, those matters may be of material significance to the Authority in determining whether A satisfies and will continue to satisfy the threshold conditions;

(c) where applicable, there is a significant risk that assets representing a fund or funds maintained by A in respect of contracts of long-term insurance effected or carried out by him are or may be, or may become, insufficient to meet his liabilities attributable to such contracts; or

(d) where applicable, there is a significant risk that A—

(i) did not,

(ii) does not or is unable to, or

(iii) will not, may not or may become unable to,

take into account in a reasonable and proportionate manner the interests of the policyholders of contracts of long-term insurance effected or carried out by him.

(5) In determining whether there is a significant risk of the kind specified by paragraph (4)(d), the actuary may take into account—

(a) the manner in which A exercises his discretion in relation to the operation of the fund or funds maintained by A in respect of contracts of long-term insurance effected or carried out by him, including the distribution and use of surplus assets;

(b) the methodology used to determine bonuses;

(c) the manner in which A takes into account the interests of different classes of policyholder;

(d) the application of fixed or discretionary charges or benefits payable under such contracts;

(e) representations made by A to policyholders or potential policyholders; and

(f) any obligation (however phrased) imposed on A under the Act to treat policyholders fairly.

[4656]

FINANCIAL SERVICES AND MARKETS ACT 2000 (REGULATED ACTIVITIES) (AMENDMENT) (NO 1) ORDER 2003

(SI 2003/1475)

NOTES

Made: 5 June 2003.

Authority: Financial Services and Markets Act 2000, ss 22(1), (5), 426, 427, 428(3), Sch 2, para 25.

Commencement: 1 January 2004 (arts 26–29); 31 October 2004 (otherwise); see art 1 at **[4657]**. Where any provision in this work (including any inserted or substituted provision) came into force for all purposes on or before 1 July 2005, commencement information is not noted at provision level.

As of 1 July 2007, this Order had not been amended.

PART 1
GENERAL

1 Citation and commencement

(1) This Order may be cited as the Financial Services and Markets Act 2000 (Regulated Activities) (Amendment) (No 1) Order 2003.

(2) Articles 26 to 29 come into force on 1st January 2004.

(3) Otherwise, this Order comes into force on 31st October 2004.

[4657]

2 Interpretation

In this Order, "the Regulated Activities Order" means the Financial Services and Markets Act 2000 (Regulated Activities) Order 2001.

[4658]

3–25 (*Arts 3–20* (*Pt 2*) *amend the Financial Services and Markets Act 2000* (*Regulated Activities*) *Order 2001, SI 2001/544 at* **[4001]** *et seq; arts 21, 22* (*Pt 3*) *amend the Consumer Credit Act 1974; arts 23–25* (*Pt 4*) *amend the Financial Services and Markets Act 2000* (*Carrying on Regulated Activities by Way of Business*) *Order 2001, SI 2001/1177 at* **[4145]** *et seq, the Financial Services and Markets Act 2000* (*Appointed Representatives*) *Regulations 2001, SI 2001/1217 at* **[4159]** *et seq, and the Financial Services and Markets Act 2000* (*Professions*) (*Non-Exempt Activities*) *Order 2001, SI 2001/1227 at* **[4164]** *et seq.*)

PART 5
TRANSITIONAL PROVISIONS

26 Interpretation

In this Part—

"the Act" means the Financial Services and Markets Act 2000;

"commencement" means the beginning of 31st October 2004;

"mortgage mediation activity" means any regulated activity of the kind specified by article 25A or 53A of the Regulated Activities Order (arranging or advising on regulated mortgage contracts), or article 64 of that Order, so far as relevant to any such activity.

[4659]

27 Applications for Part IV permission

(1) This article applies to any completed application for Part IV permission which is made before 30th April 2004 by a person who is not an authorised person, to the extent that the application relates to any mortgage mediation activity ("an early Part IV application").

(2) Section 52(1) of the Act (applications to be determined by the Authority within six months) does not apply to early Part IV applications.

(3) If the Authority has not determined an early Part IV application before the end of the period of six months beginning on the date on which it received the completed application, it must inform the applicant of the progress being made on the application (unless it has already done so).

(4) In any event, the Authority must determine all early Part IV applications before commencement.

[4660]

28 Applications for approval

(1) This article applies to any application made before 31st July 2004 under section 59 of the Act (approval of the performance of controlled functions) by a person who is not an authorised person for the Authority's approval of the performance by a person of any controlled function (within the meaning of section 59(3) of the Act), to the extent that that function relates to the carrying on of any mortgage mediation activity ("an early Part V application").

(2) Section 61(3) of the Act (applications to be determined by the Authority within three months) does not apply to early Part V applications.

(3) If the Authority has not determined an early Part V application before the end of the period of six months beginning on the date on which it received the application, it must inform the applicant of the progress being made on the application (unless it has already done so).

(4) In any event, the Authority must determine all early Part V applications before commencement.

[4661]

29 Modifications and waivers

(1) Before commencement, section 148 of the Act (modification or waiver of rules) has effect as if the references to "authorised person" (except in subsection (9)) included a reference to a person who has Part IV permission to carry on any mortgage mediation activity, albeit that that permission is not in force.

(2) To the extent that it relates to any mortgage mediation activity, any direction given by the Authority under section 148(2) of the Act as modified by paragraph (1) may not come into force before commencement.

[4662]

FINANCIAL SERVICES AND MARKETS ACT 2000 (REGULATED ACTIVITIES) (AMENDMENT) (NO 2) ORDER 2003

(SI 2003/1476)

NOTES

Made: 5 June 2003.

Authority: Financial Services and Markets Act 2000, ss 22(1), (5), 192(a), 426, 427, 428(3), Sch 2, para 25.

Commencement: 1 January 2004 (arts 22–27); 31 October 2004 (arts 1–21 in so far as they relate to contracts of long-term care insurance); 14 January 2005 (otherwise); see art 1 at **[4663]**. Where any provision in this work (including any inserted or substituted provision) came into force for all purposes on or before 1 July 2005, commencement information is not noted at provision level.

This Order is reproduced as amended by: the Financial Services and Markets Act 2000 (Regulated Activities) (Amendment) Order 2004, SI 2004/1610.

PART 1
GENERAL

1 Citation, commencement and interpretation

(1) This Order may be cited as the Financial Services and Markets Act 2000 (Regulated Activities) (Amendment) (No 2) Order 2003.

(2) Articles 22 to 27 of this Order come into force on 1st January 2004.

(3) The other provisions of this Order come into force—

(a) in so far as they relate to contracts of long-term care insurance, on 31st October 2004;

(b) for all other purposes, on 14th January 2005.

(4) In this Order—

"the Act" means the Financial Services and Markets Act 2000;

"contract of long-term care insurance" means a contract of insurance (within the meaning of the principal Order) in respect of which the following conditions are met—

(a) the purpose (or one of the purposes) of the policy is to protect the policyholder against the risk of becoming unable to live independently without assistance in consequence of a deterioration of mental or physical health, injury, sickness or other infirmity;

(b) benefits under the contract are payable in respect of—

(i) services,

(ii) accommodation, or

(iii) goods,

which are (or which is) necessary or desirable due to a deterioration of mental or physical health, injury, sickness or other infirmity;

(c) the contract is expressed to be in effect until the death of the policyholder (except that the contract may give the policyholder the option to surrender the policy); and

(d) the benefits under the contract are capable of being paid throughout the life of the policyholder;

"the principal Order" means the Financial Services and Markets Act 2000 (Regulated Activities) Order 2001.

[4663]

2–18 (*Arts 2–13* (*Pts 2, 3*) *amend the Financial Services and Markets Act 2000* (*Regulated Activities*) *Order 2001, SI 2001/544 at* **[4001]** *et seq; arts 14–18* (*Pt 4*) *amends the Financial Services and Markets Act 2000* (*Carrying on Regulated Activities by Way of Business*) *Order 2001, SI 2001/1177 at* **[4145]** *et seq, the Financial Services and Markets Act 2000* (*Appointed Representatives*) *Regulations 2001, SI 2001/1217 at* **[4159]** *et seq, the Financial Services and Markets Act 2000* (*Professions*) (*Non-Exempt Activities*) *Order 2001, SI 2001/1227 at* **[4164]** *et seq, the Financial Services and Markets Act 2000* (*Compensation Scheme: Electing Participants*) *Regulations 2001, SI 2001/1783 at* **[4362]** *et seq, and the Financial Services and Markets Act 2000* (*Misleading Statements and Practices*) *Order 2001, SI 2001/3645 at* **[4620]** *et seq.*)

PART 5
MISCELLANEOUS

19, 20 (*Art 19 amends the Financial Services and Markets Act 2000, Sch 6, para 2, at* **[2443]**; *art 20(1), (2) amend s 49(2) of that Act at* **[2049]**; *art 20(3) revoked by the Financial Services and Markets Act 2000 (Regulated Activities) (Amendment) Order 2004, SI 2004/1610, art 2, as from 15 July 2004.*)

21 Controllers of insurance intermediaries

(1) In any case where a person ("the acquirer")—

(a) proposes to take, in relation to a UK insurance intermediary ("A"), such a step as is mentioned in section 178(1) of the Act (obligation to notify the Authority of control over authorised persons), or

(b) acquires control, an additional kind of control or an increase in a relevant kind of control over a UK insurance intermediary without himself taking any such step,

the acquirer is exempt from any obligation imposed by section 178 of the Act to notify the Authority of his proposal or acquisition unless paragraph (2) applies.

(2) This paragraph applies—

(a) where the acquirer falls within paragraph (1)(a), if the acquirer does not currently, but would if he took the proposed step, fall within any of the cases in paragraph (3); or

(b) where the acquirer falls within paragraph (1)(b), if the acquirer did not immediately before acquiring control, but as a result of that acquisition does, fall within any of those cases.

(3) The cases are where the acquirer—

(a) holds 20% or more of the shares in A;

(b) is able to exercise significant influence over the management of A by virtue of his shareholding in A;

(c) holds 20% or more of the shares in a parent undertaking ("P") of A;

(d) is able to exercise significant influence over the management of P by virtue of his shareholding in P;

(e) is entitled to exercise, or control the exercise of, 20% or more of the voting power in A;

(f) is able to exercise significant influence over the management of A by virtue of his voting power in A;

(g) is entitled to exercise, or control the exercise of, 20% or more of the voting power in P; or

(h) is able to exercise a significant influence over the management of P by virtue of his voting power in P.

(4) In paragraph (3), "the acquirer" means—

(a) the acquirer;

(b) any of the acquirer's associates; or

(c) the acquirer and any of his associates.

(5) In any case where a controller of A—

(a) proposes to take, in relation to A, such a step as is mentioned in section 190(1) of the Act (obligation to notify the Authority of a reduction in control over an authorised person), or

(b) ceases to have, or reduces a relevant kind of, control over A without himself taking any such step,

the controller is exempt from any obligation imposed by subsection (1) or (2) of section 190 of the Act to notify the Authority unless paragraph (6) applies.

(6) This paragraph applies if—

(a) the percentage of shares held by the controller in A decreases (or would decrease) from 20% or more to less than 20%;

(b) the percentage of shares held by the controller in a parent undertaking ("P") of A decreases (or would decrease) from 20% or more to less than 20%;

(c) the percentage of voting power which the controller is entitled to exercise, or control the exercise of, in A decreases (or would decrease) from 20% or more to less than 20%; or

(d) the percentage of voting power which the controller is entitled to exercise, or control the exercise of, in P decreases (or would decrease) from 20% or more to less than 20%.

(7) In paragraph (6), "the controller" means—

(a) the controller;

(b) any of the controller's associates; or

(c) the controller and any of his associates.

(8) References in this article to acquiring control, or an additional kind of control, increasing control and reducing control are to be read with Part XII of the Act.

(9) In this article—

"associate", "shares" and "voting power" have the same meaning as in section 422 of the Act;

"UK insurance intermediary" means any UK authorised person (within the meaning of section 178(4) of the Act) who has Part IV permission to carry on any regulated activity of the kind specified by article 21, 25(1) or (2), 39A or 53 of the principal Order, or, so far as relevant to any of those articles, article 64 of that Order, which is carried on in relation to a contract of insurance, but who does not have Part IV permission to carry on any other regulated activity.

[4664]

PART 6
TRANSITIONAL PROVISIONS

22 Interpretation

In this Part—

"commencement" means the beginning of 14th January 2005;

"general insurance mediation activity" means any regulated activity of the kind specified by article 21, 25(1) or (2), 39A or 53 of the principal Order, or, so far as relevant to any of those articles, article 64 of that Order, which is carried on in relation to a contract of insurance which is not—

(a) a qualifying contract of insurance; or

(b) a contract of long-term care insurance;

"long-term care insurance mediation activity" means any regulated activity of the kind specified by article 21, 25(1) or (2), 39A or 53 of the principal Order, or, so far as relevant to any of those articles, article 64 of that Order, which is carried on in relation to a contract of insurance which is a contract of long-term care insurance.

[4665]

23 Applications for Part IV permission—general insurance mediation

(1) This article applies to any completed application for Part IV permission which is made before 14th July 2004 by a person who is not an authorised person, to the extent that the application relates to any general insurance mediation activity ("an early Part IV application").

(2) Section 52(1) of the Act (applications to be determined by the Authority within six months) does not apply to early Part IV applications.

(3) If the Authority has not determined an early Part IV application before the end of the period of six months beginning on the date on which it received the completed application, it must inform the applicant of the progress being made on the application (unless it has already done so).

(4) In any event, the Authority must determine all early Part IV applications before 14th January 2005.

[4666]

24 Application for approval—general insurance mediation

(1) This article applies to any application made before 14th October 2004 under section 59 of the Act (approval of the performance of controlled functions) by a person who is not an authorised person for the Authority's approval of the performance by a person of any

controlled function (within the meaning of section 59(3) of the Act), to the extent that that function relates to the carrying on of any general insurance mediation activity ("an early Part V application").

(2) Section 61(3) of the Act (applications to be determined by the Authority within three months) does not apply to early Part V applications.

(3) If the Authority has not determined an early Part V application before the end of the period of six months beginning on the date on which it received the application, it must inform the applicant of the progress being made on the application (unless it has already done so).

(4) In any event, the Authority must determine all early Part V applications before 14th January 2005.

[4667]

25 Applications for Part IV permission—long-term care insurance mediation

(1) This article applies to any completed application for Part IV permission which is made before 30th April 2004 by a person who is not an authorised person, to the extent that the application relates to any long-term care insurance mediation activity ("an early Part IV long-term care application").

(2) Section 52(1) of the Act (applications to be determined by the Authority within six months) does not apply to early Part IV long-term care applications.

(3) If the Authority has not determined an early Part IV long-term care application before the end of the period of six months beginning on the date on which it received the completed application, it must inform the applicant of the progress being made on the application (unless it has already done so).

(4) In any event, the Authority must determine all early Part IV long-term care applications before 31st October 2004.

[4668]

26 Application for approval—long-term care insurance mediation

(1) This article applies to any application made before 31st July 2004 under section 59 of the Act (approval of the performance of controlled functions) by a person who is not an authorised person for the Authority's approval of the performance by a person of any controlled function (within the meaning of section 59(3) of the Act), to the extent that that function relates to the carrying on of any long-term care insurance mediation activity ("an early Part V long-term care application").

(2) Section 61(3) of the Act (applications to be determined by the Authority within three months) does not apply to early Part V long-term care applications.

(3) If the Authority has not determined an early Part V long-term care application before the end of the period of six months beginning on the date on which it received the application, it must inform the applicant of the progress being made on the application (unless it has already done so).

(4) In any event, the Authority must determine all early Part V long-term care applications before 31st October 2004.

[4669]

27 Modifications and waivers

(1) Before commencement, section 148 of the Act (modification or waiver of rules) has effect as if the references to "authorised person" (except in subsection (9)) included a reference to a person who has Part IV permission to carry on any general insurance mediation activity or any long-term care insurance mediation activity, albeit that that permission is not in force.

(2) To the extent that it relates to any general insurance mediation activity, any direction given by the Authority under section 148(2) of the Act as modified by paragraph (1) may not come into force before commencement.

(3) To the extent that it relates to any long-term care insurance mediation activity, any such direction may not come into force before 31st October 2004.

[4670]

FINANCIAL SERVICES AND MARKETS ACT 2000 (TRANSITIONAL PROVISIONS) (COMPLAINTS RELATING TO GENERAL INSURANCE AND MORTGAGES) ORDER 2004

(SI 2004/454)

NOTES

Made: 25 February 2004.

Authority: Financial Services and Markets Act 2000, ss 426–428.

Commencement: 31 October 2004 (in so far as it relates to a complaint relating to an activity to which, immediately before that date, the MCAS Scheme applied); 14 January 2005 (otherwise). See art 1 at **[4671]**. Where any provision in this work (including any inserted or substituted provision) came into force for all purposes on or before 1 July 2005, commencement information is not noted at provision level.

This Order is reproduced as amended by: the Financial Services and Markets Act 2000 (Transitional Provisions) (Complaints Relating to General Insurance and Mortgages) (Amendment) Order 2004, SI 2004/1609.

ARRANGEMENT OF ARTICLES

1 Citation, commencement and interpretation

(1) This Order may be cited as the Financial Services and Markets Act 2000 (Transitional Provisions) (Complaints Relating to General Insurance and Mortgages) Order 2004.

(2) This Order comes into force—

(a) in so far as it relates to a complaint relating to an activity to which, immediately before 31st October 2004, the MCAS Scheme applied, on 31st October 2004;

(b) for all other purposes, on 14th January 2005.

(3) In this Order—

"the Act" means the Financial Services and Markets Act 2000;

"former scheme" means the GISC Facility or, as the case may be, the MCAS Scheme;

"GISC Facility" means the Dispute Resolution Facility established by the General Insurance Standards Council;

"MCAS Scheme" means the Mortgage Code Arbitration Scheme;

"new scheme" means the ombudsman scheme provided for by Part 16 of the Act [(the ombudsman scheme)];

"relevant commencement date" means—

(a) in relation to a complaint which relates to an activity to which, immediately before 14th January 2005, the GISC Facility applied, … 14th January 2005;

(b) in relation to a complaint which relates to an activity to which, immediately before 31st October 2004, the MCAS Scheme applied, … 31st October 2004.

[4671]

NOTES

Para (3): words in square brackets in definition "new scheme" substituted, and words omitted from definition "relevant commencement date" revoked, by the Financial Services and Markets Act 2000 (Transitional Provisions) (Complaints Relating to General Insurance and Mortgages) (Amendment) Order 2004, SI 2004/1609, art 2, as from 15 July 2004.

PART IV STATUTORY INSTRUMENTS

2 Complaints made after commencement about acts or omissions before commencement

(1) Subject to the provisions of this Order, the compulsory jurisdiction resulting from section 226 of the Act applies to a complaint referred to the new scheme [on or] after the relevant commencement date which relates to an act or omission occurring before that date if the conditions mentioned in paragraph (2) are satisfied (notwithstanding that the conditions in subsection (2)(b) and (c) of that section are not met).

(2) The conditions are that—

(a) the act or omission is that of a person ("R") who, at the time of that act or omission, was subject to a former scheme;

(b) R was an authorised person on or after the relevant commencement date;

(c) the act or omission occurred in the carrying on by R of an activity to which that former scheme applied; and

(d) the complainant is eligible and wishes to have the complaint dealt with under the new scheme.

(3) For the purposes of paragraph (2)(d), where the complainant is not eligible in accordance with the rules made under section 226(6) and (7) of the Act (power to specify in rules the classes of persons who are eligible complainants), an ombudsman may nonetheless, if he considers it appropriate, treat the complainant as eligible if he would have been entitled to refer an equivalent complaint to the former scheme in question immediately before the relevant commencement date.

(4) Where the former scheme in question is the GISC Facility, a complainant is not to be treated as eligible for the purposes of paragraph (2)(d) unless—

(a) he is an individual; and

(b) he is acting otherwise than solely for the purposes of his business.

(5) Where the former scheme in question is the MCAS Scheme, a complainant is not to be treated as eligible for the purposes of paragraph (2)(d) if—

(a) the complaint does not relate to a breach of the Mortgage Code;

(b) the complaint concerns physical injury, illness, nervous shock or their consequences; or

(c) the complainant is claiming a sum of money that exceeds £100,000.

(6) A complaint falling within paragraph (1) is referred to in this Order as a "relevant transitional complaint".

[4672]

NOTES

Para (1): words in square brackets inserted by the Financial Services and Markets Act 2000 (Transitional Provisions) (Complaints Relating to General Insurance and Mortgages) (Amendment) Order 2004, SI 2004/1609, art 3, as from 15 July 2004.

3 Procedure applying to relevant transitional complaints

In paragraph 13 of Schedule 17 to the Act (Authority's procedural rules)—

(a) the references to a complaint are to be taken to include a relevant transitional complaint; and

(b) the references to the ombudsman scheme are, in relation to a relevant transitional complaint, to be taken to mean the new scheme as it applies to such complaints by virtue of this Order; and

(c) in sub-paragraph (4), the reference to complaints which may be referred to the scheme is to be taken to include any complaint which may be referred to the scheme as a relevant transitional complaint.

[4673]

4 Scheme rules applying to relevant transitional complaints

(1) In paragraph 14 of Schedule 17 to the Act (the scheme operator's rules)—

(a) references to "complaints" are to be taken to include relevant transitional complaints;

(b) sub-paragraph (2)(a) (matters which are to be taken into account in making determinations) does not apply to a relevant transitional complaint.

(2) In deciding whether a relevant transitional complaint is to be dismissed without consideration of its merits as mentioned in paragraph 14(2)(b) of that Schedule, an ombudsman must take into account whether an equivalent complaint would have been so dismissed under the former scheme in question, as it had effect immediately before the relevant commencement date; and any scheme rules made under paragraph 14(2)(b) and (3) of that Schedule (rejection of a complaint without consideration of its merits) are to be construed accordingly.

[4674]

5 Determination of relevant transitional complaints

(1) Sections 228 to 232 of the Act apply in relation to a relevant transitional complaint as they apply in relation to a complaint of the kind mentioned in section 226(1) of the Act (compulsory jurisdiction), subject to paragraph (2).

(2) In determining, in relation to a relevant transitional complaint—

(a) what is fair and reasonable in all the circumstances of the case, for the purposes of section 228(2) of the Act, and

(b) what amount (if any) constitutes fair compensation for the purposes of section 229(2)(a) of the Act,

an ombudsman is to take into account what determination might have been expected to be made under the former scheme in question, and what amount (if any) might have been expected to be awarded or recommended by way of compensation under that scheme, in relation to an equivalent complaint dealt with under the former scheme immediately before the relevant commencement date.

[4675]

6 Funding and fees

(1) In section 234(1) of the Act (industry funding), the reference to the operation of the new scheme in relation to the compulsory jurisdiction is to be taken to include the operation of the scheme in relation to relevant transitional complaints.

(2) In paragraph 15 of Schedule 17 to the Act (fees), the references to a complaint are to be taken to include a relevant transitional complaint.

(3) Any fee which, by reason of paragraph (2), is owed to the scheme operator by a respondent who is not an authorised person, may be recovered as a debt due to the scheme operator.

[4676]

7 Exemption from liability in damages

In paragraph 10(1) of Schedule 17 to the Act (exemption from liability in damages), the reference to functions under the Act in relation to the compulsory jurisdiction is to be taken to include functions exercisable by virtue of this Order.

[4677]

8 Privilege

In paragraph 11 of Schedule 17 to the Act (privilege), the reference to a complaint which is subject to the compulsory jurisdiction is to be taken to include a relevant transitional complaint.

[4678]

9 Record-keeping and reporting requirements relating to relevant transitional complaints

The Authority may make rules applying to authorised persons with respect to the keeping of records and the making of reports in relation to relevant transitional complaints.

[4679]–[4680]

10 (*Revoked by the Financial Services and Markets Act 2000* (*Transitional Provisions*) (*Complaints Relating to General Insurance and Mortgages*) (*Amendment*) *Order 2004, SI 2004/1609, art 4, as from 15 July 2004.*)

11 Information

(1) Any information held by any person responsible for the operation of a former scheme ("the former holder") in connection with the operation of a former scheme may be disclosed by that person to the scheme operator or to an ombudsman ("the new holder").

(2) Any such disclosure is not to be treated as contravening any restriction on disclosure of the information (imposed by statute or otherwise) to which the former holder is subject.

(3) When information has been disclosed in accordance with this article, the new holder is to be treated as subject to any such restriction on disclosure as would have applied to the former holder (subject to any exceptions which would have so applied).

(4) But paragraph (3) does not prevent the application of section 31(4A) of the Data Protection Act 1998 to information which has been disclosed in accordance with this article.

(5) Sections 231 and 232 apply in relation to relevant transitional complaints as they apply in relation to complaints relating to acts or omissions occurring after commencement.

[4681]

[12 Application of rules etc in relation to relevant matters

(1) If the Authority proposes to make any rules or give guidance in relation to relevant matters, sections 155 and 157(3) of the Act do not apply to the proposed rules or guidance.

(2) When the scheme operator proposes to make any scheme rules in relation to relevant matters, sub-paragraphs (4) to (6) of paragraph 14 of Schedule 17 to the Act do not apply to the proposed rules.

(3) In this article, "relevant matters" means—
- (a) the effect of this Order;
- (b) the application of rules or guidance made or to be made before the relevant commencement date relating to relevant transitional complaints.]

[4682]

NOTES

Added by the Financial Services and Markets Act 2000 (Transitional Provisions) (Complaints Relating to General Insurance and Mortgages) (Amendment) Order 2004, SI 2004/1609, art 5, as from 15 July 2004.

FINANCIAL CONGLOMERATES AND OTHER FINANCIAL GROUPS REGULATIONS 2004

(SI 2004/1862)

NOTES

Made: 19 July 2004.

Authority: European Communities Act 1972, s 2(2); Financial Services and Markets Act 2000, ss 183(2), 188(2), 417(1), 428(3).

Commencement: 10 August 2004 (see reg 1 at **[4683]**). Where any provision in this work (including any inserted or substituted provision) came into force for all purposes on or before 1 July 2005, commencement information is not noted at provision level.

These Regulations are reproduced as amended by: the Capital Requirements Regulations 2006, SI 2006/3221; the Financial Services and Markets Act 2000 (Markets in Financial Instruments) Regulations 2007, SI 2007/126.

ARRANGEMENT OF REGULATIONS

PART 1
INTRODUCTION

PART 2
EXERCISE OF SUPPLEMENTARY SUPERVISION OF REGULATED ENTITIES IN A FINANCIAL CONGLOMERATE

PART 1
INTRODUCTION

1 Citation, commencement and interpretation

(1) These Regulations may be cited as the Financial Conglomerates and Other Financial Groups Regulations 2004 and come into force on 10th August 2004.

(2) In these Regulations—

"the Act" means the Financial Services and Markets Act 2000;

["the European Banking Committee" means the Committee established pursuant to a Commission Decision of 5 November 2003 establishing the European Banking Committee (No 2004/10/EC);]

"the capital adequacy directive" means [Directive 2006/49/EC of the European Parliament and of the Council of 14 June 2006] on the capital adequacy of investment firms and credit institutions;

"competent authority", except in the term "third-country competent authority" as defined in regulation 7(1), means any national authority of an EEA State which is empowered by law or regulation to supervise regulated entities, whether on an individual or group-wide basis;

"the conglomerates directive" means Directive 2002/87/EC of the European Parliament and of the Council of 16th December 2002 on the supplementary supervision of credit institutions, insurance undertakings and investment firms in a financial conglomerate and amending Council Directives 73/239/EEC, 79/267/EEC, 92/49/EEC, 92/96/EEC, 93/6/EEC, 93/22/EEC, and Directives 98/78/EC and 2000/12/EC of the European Parliament and of the Council;

"co-ordinator" means the competent authority which has been appointed, for the purposes of Article 10 of the conglomerates directive, as the competent authority which is responsible for the co-ordination and exercise of supplementary supervision of a financial conglomerate;

"directive requirement" means any procedural requirement (including a requirement to consult or obtain consent) imposed on a competent authority by—

(a) the conglomerates directive; or

(b) [Article 143] of the banking consolidation directive (as it is applied by that directive or by [Article 2 and 37(1)] of the capital adequacy directive);

"financial conglomerate", except in the term "third-country financial conglomerate" as defined in regulation 7(1), has the meaning given by Article 2(14) of the conglomerates directive;

"the Financial Conglomerates Committee" means the Committee established pursuant to Article 21 of the conglomerates directive;

"relevant competent authorities" means those competent authorities, within the meaning of Article 2(17) of the conglomerates directive, which are, or which have been appointed as, relevant competent authorities in relation to a financial conglomerate;

"regulated entity" means—

(a) a credit institution (within the meaning of the second sub-paragraph of [Article 4(1)] of the banking consolidation directive);

PART IV
STATUTORY INSTRUMENTS

(b) an insurance undertaking (within the meaning of Article 4 of Directive 2002/83/EC of the European Parliament and of the Council of 5th November 2002 concerning life assurance, Article 6 of the first non-life insurance directive or Article 1(b) of Directive 98/78/EC of the European Parliament and of the Council of 27th October 1998 on the supplementary supervision of insurance undertakings in an insurance group);

(c) a management company (within the meaning of Article 1a(2) of the UCITS directive) or an undertaking which is outside the EEA but which would require authorisation in accordance with Article 5 of the UCITS directive if it had its registered office in the EEA; or

(d) an investment firm (within the meaning of *Article 1(2) of the investment services directive*, [including the undertakings referred to in Article 3(1)(b)] of the capital adequacy directive); and

"supplementary supervision" means the supervision of a regulated entity to the extent and in the manner prescribed by the conglomerates directive.

(3) Save as is otherwise provided, any expression used in these Regulations which is defined for the purposes of the Act has the meaning given by the Act.

[4683]

NOTES

Para (2): definition "the European Banking Committee" substituted for original definition "the Banking Advisory Committee", and words in square brackets in definitions "the capital adequacy directive", "directive requirement", and "regulated entity", substituted, by the Capital Requirements Regulations 2006, SI 2006/3221, reg 29(3), Sch 5, para 1(1), (2), as from 1 January 2007; for the words in italics in definition "regulated entity" there are substituted the words "Article 4.1.1 of the markets in financial instruments directive" by the Financial Services and Markets Act 2000 (Markets in Financial Instruments) Regulations 2007, SI 2007/126, reg 3(6), Sch 6, Pt 2, para 19(1), (2), as from 1 November 2007 (for the full commencement details of SI 2007/126, see reg 1 of those Regulations at **[7596]**).

PART 2
EXERCISE OF SUPPLEMENTARY SUPERVISION OF REGULATED ENTITIES IN A FINANCIAL CONGLOMERATE

2 Notification of identification as a financial conglomerate and choice of co-ordinator

(1) Where the Authority has become the co-ordinator for a financial conglomerate, it must notify—

(a) the relevant member of that financial conglomerate;

(b) any competent authority which has given EEA authorisation to a regulated entity which is a member of that financial conglomerate;

(c) the competent authorities of the EEA State in which the parent undertaking of that financial conglomerate has its head office, unless that parent undertaking is a regulated entity; and

(d) the Commission,

that the group has been identified as a financial conglomerate for the purposes of Article 4 of the conglomerates directive and that the Authority is the co-ordinator for that financial conglomerate.

(2) Paragraph (3) applies if—

(a) the Authority is a relevant competent authority in relation to a financial conglomerate, and

(b) the Authority, in conjunction with the other relevant competent authorities, proposes to waive the criteria specified in Article 10(2) of the conglomerates directive (selection of the co-ordinator) and appoint a different competent authority as co-ordinator.

(3) Before the Authority, in conjunction with the other relevant competent authorities, waives the criteria specified in Article 10(2) of the conglomerates directive and appoints a different competent authority as co-ordinator, the Authority must, where there is a directive requirement to do so, give the financial conglomerate an opportunity to make representations.

(4) In this regulation, "the relevant member" of a financial conglomerate is—

(a) the parent undertaking at the head of the financial conglomerate; or

(b) where there is no parent undertaking at the head of the financial conglomerate, the regulated entity which—

(i) is in the most important financial sector (within the meaning given by Article 3(2) of the conglomerates directive); and

(ii) has the largest balance-sheet total in that sector.

[4684]

3 Exercise of functions under Part IV of the Act for the purposes of carrying on supplementary supervision

(1) This regulation applies if the Authority is considering varying the Part IV permission of any person ("A") where—

(a) A is a member of a financial conglomerate; and

(b) the Authority is acting in the course of carrying on supplementary supervision for the purposes of any provision (other than Article 11, 12, 16, 17 or 18(3)) of the conglomerates directive.

(2) Section 49(2) of the Act (obligation to consult home state regulators of connected persons) does not apply.

(3) Before varying the Part IV permission of A, the Authority must, where there is a directive requirement to do so—

(a) consult the relevant competent authorities in relation to the financial conglomerate of which A is a member;

(b) obtain the consent of those competent authorities; and

(c) consult the financial conglomerate of which A is a member.

[4685]

4 Exercise of functions under section 148 of the Act for the purposes of carrying on supplementary supervision

(1) Paragraph (2) applies if the Authority is considering exercising any of the powers conferred on it by section 148 of the Act (modification or waiver of rules) in the course of carrying on supplementary supervision of a financial conglomerate for the purposes of any provision (other than Article 11, 12, 16, 17 or 18(3)) of the conglomerates directive.

(2) Before the Authority exercises such a power in relation to an authorised person who is a member of a financial conglomerate, the Authority must, where there is a directive requirement to do so—

(a) consult the relevant competent authorities in relation to the financial conglomerate of which that person is a member;

(b) obtain the consent of those competent authorities; and

(c) consult the financial conglomerate of which that person is a member.

[4686]

5 Consultation in the case of major sanctions or exceptional measures

(1) Before the Authority—

(a) varies the Part IV permission of a member of a financial conglomerate ("D");

(b) publishes a statement under section 205 of the Act (public censure) that it considers that D has contravened a requirement imposed on him by or under the Act;

(c) imposes a penalty on D in respect of such a contravention under section 206 of the Act (financial penalties); or

(d) exercises any of its powers (other than its powers under section 381, 383 or 384(2)) under Part XXV of the Act (injunctions and restitution) in relation to D,

it must, if it considers that the action constitutes a major sanction or an exceptional measure and is of importance for the supervisory tasks of the competent authority of any regulated entity which is a member of the same financial conglomerate as D, consult that competent authority.

(2) But paragraph (1) does not apply—

(a) where the Authority considers that there is an urgent need to act;

(b) where the Authority considers that such consultation may jeopardise the effectiveness of the action mentioned in paragraph (1); or

(c) where regulation 3, 8(3) or (4), 9 or 10 applies.

(3) Where paragraph (1) does not apply by virtue of paragraph (2)(a) or (b), the Authority must, as soon as is reasonably practicable, inform the competent authority referred to in paragraph (1) of the action that it has taken.

[4687]

6 Authority functions and service of notifications

(1) Any function carried out by the Authority (whether in the capacity of a co-ordinator, a relevant competent authority or otherwise) for the purposes of the conglomerates directive (including a function conferred by these Regulations) is to be treated as a function conferred on the Authority by a provision of the Act.

(2) The Financial Services and Markets Act 2000 (Service of Notices) Regulations 2001 apply to any notifications given under regulation 2(1)(a) as they apply to any notice, direction or document of any kind given under the Act.

[4688]

PART 3
SUPPLEMENTARY SUPERVISION OF THIRD-COUNTRY FINANCIAL CONGLOMERATES AND THIRD-COUNTRY GROUPS

7 Supervision of third-country financial conglomerates and third-country groups—interpretation

(1) For the purposes of this Part—

"asset management company" means—
- (a) any EEA firm falling within paragraph 5(f) of Schedule 3 to the Act; or
- (b) any UK firm whose EEA right derives from the UCITS directive;

"credit institution" means—
- (a) any EEA firm falling within paragraph 5(b) of Schedule 3 to the Act; or
- (b) any UK firm whose EEA right derives from the banking consolidation directive;

"investment firm" means—
- (a) any EEA firm falling within paragraph 5(a) of Schedule 3 to the Act; or
- (b) any UK firm whose EEA right derives from the *investment services directive*;

"third-country competent authority" means the authority of a country or territory which is not an EEA State which is empowered by law or regulation to supervise (whether on an individual or group-wide basis) regulated entities;

"third-country financial conglomerate" means a group—
- (a) which, subject to Article 3 of the conglomerates directive, meets the conditions in Article 2(14) of that directive, and
- (b) in which the parent undertaking has its head office outside the EEA;

"third-country group" means a group of which the parent undertaking has its head office outside the EEA.

(2) For the purposes of this Part a regulated entity is in a third-country group if the parent undertaking of the group in which it is a member has its head office outside the EEA.

[4689]

NOTES

Para (1): for the words in italics in para (b) of the definition "investment firm" there are substituted the words "markets in financial instruments directive" by the Financial Services and Markets Act 2000 (Markets in Financial Instruments) Regulations 2007, SI 2007/126, reg 3(6), Sch 6, Pt 2, para 19(1), (3), as from 1 November 2007 (for the full commencement details of SI 2007/126, see reg 1 of those Regulations at **[7596]**).

8 Supervision of third-country financial conglomerates

(1) Where the Authority is, for the purposes of Article 18(1) of the conglomerates directive (parent undertakings outside the Community), verifying whether the regulated entities in a third-country financial conglomerate are subject to supervision, by a third-country competent authority, which is equivalent to that provided for by the provisions of the conglomerates directive, it must, where there is a directive requirement to do so, before completing this verification—

(a) consult the other relevant competent authorities in relation to that third-county financial conglomerate;
(b) consult the Financial Conglomerates Committee for the purposes of obtaining any applicable guidance prepared by that Committee in accordance with Article 21(5) of the conglomerates directive (guidance on whether third-country competent authorities are likely to achieve objectives of supplementary supervision); and
(c) take into account any such guidance.

(2) Paragraphs (3) and (4) apply if the Authority, for the purposes of Article 18(3) of the conglomerates directive (application of other methods for the purposes of ensuring appropriate supplementary supervision of the regulated entities in a third-country financial conglomerate), exercises its powers to—
(a) vary the Part IV permission of a regulated entity in a third-country financial conglomerate;
(b) disapply from, or apply in a modified form to, such a regulated entity the rules specified in subsection (1) of section 148 of the Act (modification or waiver of rules) in accordance with that section;
(c) impose conditions under section 185 of the Act (conditions attached to approval of change of control) on a person who is, or proposes to be, a controller of such a regulated entity; or
(d) give a notice under section 186 or 187 of the Act (notice of objection to acquisition of, or existing, control) to a person who is, or proposes to be, a controller of such a regulated entity.

(3) Where there is a directive requirement to do so, the Authority must before taking the action specified in paragraph (2)—
(a) where the Authority is the co-ordinator, consult the relevant competent authorities in relation to that third-country financial conglomerate; or
(b) where the Authority is not the co-ordinator, obtain the consent of the co-ordinator for that third-country financial conglomerate to take that action.

(4) If the Authority decides to take that action, it must, where there is a directive requirement to do so, notify—
(a) the competent authority of each regulated entity in that third-country financial conglomerate, and
(b) the Commission,
that it has done so.

[4690]

9 Supervision of third-country banking groups

(1) Where the Authority is, for the purposes of [Article 143] of the banking consolidation directive (third-country parent undertakings), verifying whether a credit institution in a third-country group is subject to supervision by a third-country competent authority which is equivalent to that governed by the principles laid down in [Articles 71, 72 and 73(1) and (3)] of that directive (supervision on a consolidated basis of credit institutions), it must, where there is a directive requirement to do so, before completing this verification—
(a) consult any competent authority which supervises a credit institution in that third-country group;
(b) consult [the European Banking Committee] for the purposes of obtaining any applicable guidance prepared by that Committee in accordance with [the first sub-paragraph of Article 143(2)] of that directive; and
(c) take into account any such guidance.

(2) Paragraphs (3) and (4) apply if the Authority exercises, for the purposes of [Article 143(3)] of the banking consolidation directive, its powers to—
(a) vary the Part IV permission of a credit institution in a third-country group;
(b) disapply from, or apply in modified form to, such a credit institution, the rules specified in subsection (1) of section 148 of the Act in accordance with that section;
(c) impose conditions under section 185 of the Act on a person who is, or proposes to be, a controller of such a credit institution; or
(d) give a notice under section 186 or 187 of the Act to a person who is, or proposes to be, a controller of such a credit institution.

(3) Where there is a directive requirement to do so, the Authority must before exercising its powers to take the action specified in paragraph (2)—

(a) where the Authority would be responsible for supervising that third-country group for the purposes of [Articles 125 or 126] of the banking consolidation directive (competent authorities responsible for exercising supervision on a consolidated basis) if alternative techniques were not applied, consult the competent authorities which are involved in the supervision of any of the credit institutions in that third-country group; and

(b) where the Authority would not be so responsible, obtain the consent of the competent authority which would be responsible for supervising that third-country group for the purposes of [Articles 125 or 126] of the banking consolidation directive if alternative techniques were not applied.

(4) If the Authority decides to take that action, it must, where there is a directive requirement to do so, notify—

(a) any competent authority which supervises a credit institution in that third-country group; and

(b) the Commission,

that it has done so.

(5) Where the Authority has, for the purposes of Article 30 of the conglomerates directive (asset management companies), included an asset management company in the scope of supervision of a credit institution in a third-country group, each reference in this regulation to a "credit institution" is to be treated as including a reference to that asset management company.

[4691]

NOTES

Paras (1)–(3): words in square brackets substituted by the Capital Requirements Regulations 2006, SI 2006/3221, reg 29(3), Sch 5, para 1(1), (3), as from 1 January 2007.

10 Supervision of third-country groups subject to the capital adequacy directive

(1) Paragraph (2) applies if—

[(a) the Authority is, for the purposes of Article 143 of the banking consolidation directive, as applied by Articles 2(1) and 37(1) of the capital adequacy directive (supervision) verifying whether a credit institution or an investment firm in a third-country group is subject to supervision by a third-country competent authority which is equivalent to that governed by the principles laid down in Articles 2(1) and 37(1) of the capital adequacy directive; or]

(b) the Authority is, for the purposes of [Article 143] of the banking consolidation directive, as applied by [Articles 2(2) and 37(1)] of the capital adequacy directive (groups containing investment firms but no credit institutions), verifying whether an investment firm in a third-country group is subject to supervision, by a third-country competent authority, which is equivalent to that governed by the principles laid down in [Articles 2(2) and 37(1)] of the capital adequacy directive.

(2) The Authority must, where there is a directive requirement to do so, before completing the verification referred to in paragraph (1)—

(a) consult any competent authority which supervises an investment firm or a credit institution (if any) in that third-country group;

(b) consult [the European Banking Committee] for the purposes of obtaining any applicable guidance prepared by that Committee in accordance with [Article 143(2)] of that directive; and

(c) take into account any such guidance.

(3) Paragraphs (4) and (5) apply if the Authority exercises, for the purposes of [Article 143(3)] of the banking consolidation directive as applied by [Articles 2 and 37(1)] of the capital adequacy directive, its powers to—

(a) vary the Part IV permission of an investment firm or credit institution in a third-country group;

(b) disapply from or apply in modified form to, such an investment firm or credit institution the rules specified in subsection (1) of section 148 of the Act in accordance with that section;

(c) impose conditions under section 185 of the Act on a person who is, or proposes to be, a controller of such an investment firm or credit institution; or

(d) give a notice under section 186 or 187 of the Act to a person who is, or proposes to be, a controller of such an investment firm or credit institution.

(4) Where there is a directive requirement to do so, the Authority must, before exercising its powers to take the action specified in paragraph (3)—

(a) where the Authority would be responsible for supervision of that third-country group for the purposes of [Articles 125 or 126] of the banking consolidation directive, as applied by [Articles 2 and 37(1)] of the capital adequacy directive, if alternative techniques were not applied, consult the competent authorities which are involved in the supervision of any of the investment firms or credit institutions (if any) in that third-country group; and

(b) where the Authority would not be so responsible, obtain the consent of the competent authority which would be responsible for supervision of that third-country group for the purposes of [Articles 125 or 126] of the banking consolidation directive, as applied by [Articles 2 and 37(1)] of the capital adequacy directive, if alternative techniques were not applied.

(5) If the Authority decides to take that action, it must, where there is a directive requirement to do so, notify—

(a) any competent authority which supervises an investment firm or a credit institution (if any) in that third-country group; and

(b) the Commission,

that it has done so.

(6) If the Authority has, for the purposes of Article 30 of the conglomerates directive, included an asset management company in the scope of supervision of—

(a) credit institutions and investment firms in a third-country group; or

(b) investment firms in a third-country group,

each reference in this regulation to an "investment firm" is to be treated as including a reference to that asset management company.

[4692]

NOTES

Paras (1)–(4): words in square brackets substituted by the Capital Requirements Regulations 2006, SI 2006/3221, reg 29(3), Sch 5, para 1(1), (4), as from 1 January 2007.

PART 4
PROVISIONS RELATING TO INFORMATION

11 (*Amends the Financial Services and Markets Act 2000 (Disclosure of Confidential Information) Regulations 2001, SI 2001/2188, reg 2 at* **[4373]**.)

12 Obtaining information—avoidance of duplication of reporting

(1) Paragraph (2) applies if the Authority is the co-ordinator in relation to any financial conglomerate.

(2) If the Authority requires any disclosed information in connection with its functions as the co-ordinator, it must so far as possible obtain that information by requesting the competent authority which holds that information to disclose it to the Authority.

(3) In this regulation, "disclosed information" means information which a regulated entity in a financial conglomerate has disclosed to its competent authority.

[4693]

PART 5
MISCELLANEOUS

13, 14 (*Reg 13 amends the Financial Services and Markets Act 2000 (Consultation with Competent Authorities) Regulations 2001, SI 2001/2509 at* **[4440]** *et seq; reg 14 amends the Building Societies Act 1986, s 119(2B), the Bank of England Act 1998, s 17, the Cash Ratio Deposits (Eligible Liabilities) Order 1998, SI 1998/1130, art 2, and the Financial Services and Markets Act 2000 (EEA Passport Rights) Regulations 2001, SI 2001/2511 at* **[4448]** *et seq*)

15 Extension of power to vary Part IV permissions

(1) Subject to paragraph (2), the Authority may exercise its own-initiative power (within the meaning of section 45 of the Act (variation etc on the Authority's own initiative)) in relation to an authorised person, if it appears to it that it is desirable to do so for the purpose of—

(a) carrying out supplementary supervision in accordance with the conglomerates directive;

(b) acting in accordance with any of [Articles 133, 134, 136, 138, 141, 142 or 143] of the banking consolidation directive (as they are applied by that directive or by [Article 2(1) or (2) and 37(1)] of the capital adequacy directive); or

(c) acting in accordance with Article 8(2) or Annex I.1.B of Directive 98/78/EC of the European Parliament and of the Council of 27 October 1998 on the supplementary supervision of insurance undertakings in an insurance group.

(2) The Authority may exercise its own-initiative power, for the purposes set out in paragraph (1), to vary a Part IV permission in any of the ways mentioned in section 44(1) of the Act (variation etc at request of authorised person); and this extends to including any provision in the permission as varied that could be included if a fresh permission were given in response to an application under section 40 of the Act (application for permission).

(3) The duty imposed by subsection (2) of section 41 of the Act (the threshold conditions) does not prevent the Authority from exercising its own-initiative power for the purposes set out in paragraph (1).

[4694]

NOTES

Para (1): words in square brackets in sub-para (b) substituted by the Capital Requirements Regulations 2006, SI 2006/3221, reg 29(3), Sch 5, para 1(1), (5), as from 1 January 2007.

FINANCIAL SERVICES AND MARKETS ACT 2000 (TRANSITIONAL PROVISIONS) (MORTGAGES) ORDER 2004 (NOTE)

(SI 2004/2615)

NOTES

This Order effectively became spent on 31 October 2005; see the note to FSMA 2000, s 427 at **[2424]**.

[4695]–[4700]

FINANCIAL SERVICES AND MARKETS ACT 2000 (STAKEHOLDER PRODUCTS) REGULATIONS 2004

(SI 2004/2738)

NOTES

Made: 16 November 2004.

Authority: Financial Services and Markets Act 2000, s 428; Financial Services and Markets Act 2000 (Regulated Activities) Order, SI 2001/544, art 52B(3).

Commencement: 6 April 2005 (see reg 1 at **[4701]**). Where any provision in this work (including any inserted or substituted provision) came into force for all purposes on or before 1 July 2005, commencement information is not noted at provision level.

These Regulations are reproduced as amended by: the Financial Services and Markets Act 2000 (Stakeholder Products) (Amendment) Regulations 2005, SI 2005/594.

ARRANGEMENT OF REGULATIONS

1 Citation and commencement

These Regulations may be cited as the Financial Services and Markets 2000 (Stakeholder Products) Regulations 2004 and come into force on 6th April 2005.

[4701]

2 Interpretation

(1) In these Regulations—

"the 2000 Act" means the Financial Services and Markets Act 2000;

"account-holder" means the holder of a deposit account;

"Bank of England base rate" means the rate announced from time to time by the Monetary Policy Committee of the Bank of England as the official dealing rate, being the rate at which the Bank of England is willing to enter into transactions for providing short-term liquidity in the money markets;

"the Conduct of Business Rules" means the Conduct of Business Rules made by the Financial Services Authority under section 153 of the 2000 Act;

"relevant contract of insurance" means a contract of insurance—

(a) which, or any part of which, is one or more of the following kinds—

(i) life and annuity,

(ii) linked long-term, and

(b) which is carried out by an insurer who has permission, as the case may be, under—

(i) Part 4 of the 2000 Act, or

(ii) paragraph 15 of Schedule 3 to the 2000 Act,

to effect or carry out contracts of insurance of that kind, and

(c) is not a with-profits policy and does not include rights in a with-profits fund;

"deposit account" means a deposit account with a deposit-taker and includes a share account with a building society within the meaning of the Building Societies Act 1986;

"deposit-taker" means—

(a) a person who has permission under Part 4 of the 2000 Act to accept deposits, or

(b) an EEA firm of the kind mentioned in paragraph 5(b) of Schedule 3 to the 2000 Act which has permission under paragraph 15 of that Schedule (as a result of qualifying for authorisation under paragraph 12 of that Schedule) to accept deposits;

"dilution levy" has the meaning given by the handbook made by the Financial Services Authority under section 153 of the 2000 Act;

"insurer" means—

(a) a person who has permission under Part 4 of the 2000 Act to effect or carry out contracts of insurance, or

(b) an EEA firm of the kind mentioned in paragraph 5(d) of Schedule 3 to that Act, which has permission under paragraph 15 of that Schedule (as a result of qualifying for authorisation under paragraph 12 of that Schedule) to effect or carry out contracts of insurance;

"investor" means a member of a collective investment scheme which complies with regulation 5 or an underlying fund which complies with regulation 6 as the case may be;

"investment property" means the scheme property of a collective investment scheme which complies with regulation 5 or an underlying fund which complies with regulation 6 as the case may be;

"investment scheme" means a collective investment scheme which complies with regulation 5 or a linked long-term contract which complies with regulation 6 as the case may be;

"land and buildings" means interests in any land or buildings which satisfy the conditions in rule 5A.8.5R of the Collective Investment Schemes Sourcebook made by the Financial Services Authority under section 153 of the 2000 Act;

"linked long-term contract" means a contract of long-term insurance as specified in paragraph 3 of Part 2 of Schedule 1 to the principal Order;

"manager" means the manager of a relevant collective investment scheme or the insurer of a relevant linked long-term contract as the case may be;

"the principal Order" means the Financial Services and Markets Act 2000 (Regulated Activities) Order 2001;

"relevant collective investment scheme" means an authorised unit trust scheme, an authorised open-ended investment company or a recognised scheme, as the case may be, as defined in section 237(3) of the 2000 Act;

"relevant investments" means—

(a) shares issued by a company wherever incorporated and officially listed on a recognised stock exchange;

(b) units in a relevant collective investment scheme where a substantial proportion of the scheme property is invested, directly or indirectly, in shares, as defined in paragraph (a) or land and buildings; and

(c) rights under a contract of insurance where a substantial proportion of the assets of the funds held in respect of that contract are invested, directly or indirectly, in shares as set out in sub-paragraph (a) or land and buildings;

"relevant linked long-term contract" means a linked long-term contract which meets the conditions and characteristics specified in regulation 6(1);

"units" means the rights or interests (however described) of the members of a relevant collective investment scheme.

(2) The definitions of "deposit-taker" and "insurer" in paragraph (1) must be read with—

(a) section 22 of the 2000 Act,

(b) any relevant order under that section, and

(c) Schedule 2 to that Act.

[4702]

3 Meaning of stakeholder product

These Regulations specify kinds of investment for the purposes of sub-paragraph (c) of the definition of "stakeholder product" in article 52B(3) of the principal Order and accordingly an investment of one of these kinds is a stakeholder product for the purposes of article 52B of that Order.

[4703]

4 Certain deposit accounts

A deposit account ("the account") is a stakeholder product if the following conditions are fulfilled—

(a) the minimum amount which an account-holder may deposit on a single occasion is £10, except where the deposit-taker permits a smaller payment;

(b) the deposit-taker permits [payment to the account by any of the following means, at the option of the account-holder]—

(i) cash;

(ii) cheque;

(iii) …

(iv) standing order;

(v) direct credit (other than standing order),

excluding payments by credit card or debit card or any combination including a payment by credit card or debit card;

(c) interest accrues on the account on a daily basis at a rate that is not less than the Bank of England base rate minus 1 per cent per annum ("the interest rate");

(d) when the Bank of England base rate increases, the interest rate must be raised within one month of the date of that increase;

(e) on the instructions of the account holder, any cash and interest held in the account is transferred or paid to the account holder within a period which may not exceed seven days ("withdrawal instructions"); and

(f) there is no limitation on the frequency with which an account holder may issue withdrawal instructions.

[4704]

NOTES

Words in square brackets in para (b) substituted, and para (b)(iii) revoked, by the Financial Services and Markets Act 2000 (Stakeholder Products) (Amendment) Regulations 2005, SI 2005/594, reg 2(1), (2), as from 6 April 2005.

5 Units in certain collective investment schemes

Units in a relevant collective investment scheme are a stakeholder product where that scheme has the characteristics, and complies with the conditions, set out in regulation 7.

[4705]

6 Rights under certain linked long-term contracts

(1) Rights under a linked long-term contract are a stakeholder product where the insurer ensures that the fund held in respect of that contract ("the underlying fund")—

(a) has the characteristics and complies with the conditions set out in regulation 7; and

(b) where the investment returns are smoothed, complies with the conditions set out in regulation 8.

(2) For the purposes of this regulation and regulations 8 and 9, investment returns are smoothed when the insurer offers the product on the basis that the amount in respect of the investment returns earned from time to time by the underlying funds to be attributed under the contract to the policyholder will be managed and attributed with a view to reducing the volatility of such returns over given periods, and "smoothing", "smoothed" and "unsmoothed" are to be construed accordingly.

[4706]

7 Characteristics and conditions applicable to certain stakeholder products

(1) The characteristics in relation to an investment scheme are—

(a) no more than 60 per cent in value of the investment property, calculated in accordance with paragraph (3), consists of relevant investments;

(b) the investment property should be selected and managed having regard to the need to achieve a balance between—

(i) the opportunity for the investor to benefit from growth in the value of investments generally; and

(ii) control of the risk of loss of value in the investment; and

(c) the manager has regard to—

(i) the need for diversification of the investment property, in so far as appropriate to the circumstances of the investment scheme; and

(ii) the suitability for the purposes of the scheme of any investment option proposed.

(2) The conditions with which the investment scheme must comply are—

(a) the minimum amount which an investor may contribute to the investment scheme on a single occasion is £20, except where the manager permits a smaller amount;

(b) the manager must permit [payment to the investment scheme by any of the following means, at the option of the investor]—

(i) cheque;

(ii) direct debit;

(iii) standing order;

(iv) direct credit (other than standing order),

and excluding payments by cash, credit card or debit card or any combination including a payment by cash, credit card or debit card;

(c) the value of an investor's rights in the investment scheme and the value of the investment property may be reduced in the circumstances and to the extent set out in regulation 9; and

(d) where the stakeholder product consists of—

(i) units in a relevant collective investment scheme, it must be a requirement of that scheme that the purchase and sale price of those units shall, at any given time, not differ from each other and that price must be made available to the public on a daily basis;

(ii) rights under a relevant linked long-term contract which are expressed as shares in funds, it must be a requirement of that contract that the purchase and sale price of those shares shall, at any given time, not differ from each other and that price must be made available to the public on a daily basis.

(3) For the purposes of the calculation set out in paragraph (1)(a), the following provisions apply—

(a) where any of the investment property is invested in units in a relevant collective investment scheme, only such of the assets of that scheme as are invested, directly or indirectly, in relevant investments shall be taken into account; and

(b) the calculation shall be taken as an average over a period of 3 months.

(4) When calculating the average over a period of 3 months for the purposes of paragraph (3)(b) ("the average"), where the manager has specified under paragraph (5) that the calculation is to be carried out weekly or monthly—

(a) where the average is to be calculated weekly, it is to be carried out on such day of the week ("the specified day") as has been so specified by the manager (except that, where that day is not a working day, the average is to be calculated on the next working day), and the average on each subsequent day prior to the next specified day is to be taken to be the average on the previous specified day; and

(b) where the average is to be calculated monthly, it is to be so calculated on such day in each month ("the specified day") as has been so specified by the manager (except that, where that date is not a working day, the average is to be calculated on the next working day), and the average on each subsequent day prior to the next specified date is to be taken to be the average on the previous specified date.

(5) For the purposes of paragraph (4)—

(a) the frequency, which must be daily, weekly or monthly, with which the average is to be calculated; and

(b) where the average is to be calculated using weekly or monthly figures, that day of the week or, as the case may be, the date in the month on which it is to take place,

must be specified in writing by the manager; and the specification may not be amended during the period of 12 months after the date on which it is made.

(6) Where, following the calculation under paragraph (4), the average value of the investment property comprises more than 60 per cent of relevant investments, the manager must take steps to bring that average value within the limit prescribed in regulation 7(1)(a) as soon as reasonably practicable and in any event within 3 months.

[4707]

NOTES

Para (2): words in square brackets in sub-para (b) substituted by the Financial Services and Markets Act 2000 (Stakeholder Products) (Amendment) Regulations 2005, SI 2005/594, reg 2(1), (3), as from 6 April 2005.

8 Additional conditions applicable to smoothed linked long-term contracts

The conditions under this paragraph are—

(a) the manager must make available, to each investor who is also a policyholder or to anyone else requesting it, the information necessary to enable a person making such a request properly to understand the essential elements of the insurer's commitment under the terms of the policy;

(b) the manager must make available, to each investor and anyone else requesting it, information on its policy on and charges for smoothing;

(c) no payment may be made or property attributed from the underlying fund to any person other than an investor, except for permitted reductions in the investor's rights and investment property in accordance with regulation 9;

(d) the manager must manage the underlying fund with the aim of attributing to each investor on the maturity or surrender of his rights under the linked long-term contract a value that falls within a target range which is notified to each investor before he enters into the linked long-term contract;

(e) except as provided for in paragraph (f), there is no guarantee of the value of an investor's rights under the linked long-term contract;

(f) the manager may guarantee that, on the death of an investor, the value of an investor's rights under the linked long-term contract are no more than 101 per cent of the total of the value of the units allocated to that contract.

[4708]

9 Permitted reductions in investor's rights and investment property

(1) The value of an investor's rights in an investment scheme may be reduced in the circumstances, and to the extent, set out in paragraphs (3) to (5).

(2) The value of the investment property may be reduced in the circumstances, and to the extent, set out in paragraph (9).

(3) To the extent that an investor's rights in an investment scheme are represented by a fund allocated to him to the exclusion of other investors, the value of those rights may be reduced by the making of deductions from that fund no greater than, at the choice of the manager—

- (a) the relevant percentage of its value for each day on which it is held; or
- (b) the proportion attributable to the investor's fund of the relevant percentage of the value of the investment property for each day on which the investor's fund is held for the purposes of the scheme.

(4) To the extent that an investor's rights in an investment scheme are represented by a share of funds held for the purposes of the scheme, the amount of that share not being determined by reference to a discretion exercisable by any person, the value of those rights may be reduced by the making of deductions from that share no greater than, at the choice of the manager—

- (a) the relevant percentage of its value for each day on which it is held; or
- (b) the proportion attributable to the investor's share of the relevant percentage of the value of the investment property for each day on which the investor's share is held for the purposes of the scheme.

(5) To the extent that an investor's rights are represented by rights under a linked long-term contract to which regulations 6(1)(b) and 8 apply, the value of those rights may be reduced by the making of deductions from those rights no greater than, at the choice of the manager—

- (a) the relevant percentage of the value of the investor's rights under the contract; or
- (b) the proportion attributable to the investor's rights of the relevant percentage of the value of the underlying fund for each day on which the investor has rights under the contract.

(6) When calculating the value of the rights of an investor for the purposes of paragraphs (3) to (5) above, where the manager has specified under paragraph (7) that such rights are to be valued weekly or monthly—

- (a) where such rights are to be valued weekly, they are to be valued on such day of the week ("the specified day") as has been so specified by the manager (except that, where that day is not a working day, the rights are to be valued on the next working day), and the value of the rights on each subsequent day prior to the next specified day is to be taken to be the value of the rights on the previous specified day; and
- (b) where the rights are to be valued monthly, they are to be valued on such date in each month ("the specified date") as has been so specified by the manager (except that, where that date is not a working day, the rights are to be valued on the next working day), and the value of the rights on each subsequent day prior to the next specified date is to be taken to be the value of the rights on the previous specified date.

(7) For the purposes of paragraph (6)—

- (a) the frequency, which must be daily, weekly or monthly, with which rights are to be valued; and
- (b) where valuation is to take place weekly or monthly, the day of the week or, as the case may be, the date in the month on which it is to take place,

must be specified in writing by the manager; and the specification may not be amended during the period of 12 months after the date on which it is made.

(8) For the purposes of paragraphs (3) to (5), "the relevant percentage" means—

- (a) during the period of 10 years beginning with the day on which the first contribution is made by the investor to the investment scheme or linked long-term contract (as the case may be), 3/730 per cent;
- (b) otherwise 1/365 per cent.

(9) The value of the investment property may be reduced—

- (a) where any stamp duty, stamp duty reserve tax, value added tax or other charge (including any dilution levy) are incurred by the manager directly or indirectly in or consequent upon the sale or purchase of investments held for the purposes of the investment scheme, by the amount of those charges;

(b) where any amount of tax is paid or anticipated to be payable in respect of income received or capital gains realised by the manager in respect of investments held for the purposes of the investment scheme, by the amount so deducted or anticipated;

(c) where any charges or expenses are incurred by the manager directly or indirectly in maintaining or repairing any land or building in which the investment property is invested or in connection with the collection of rent, service charge or other sum due under the terms of a lease from occupiers of any land or building in which the investment property is invested, by the amount of those charges or expenses;

(d) where any charges or expenses are incurred by the manager directly or indirectly in complying with an order of the court or any similar requirements imposed by law, by the amount of those charges or expenses;

(e) to the extent that the manager incurs any expenses in complying with a requirement—

(i) to arrange for the investor to receive a copy of the annual report and accounts issued to investors by any company, unit trust, open-ended investment company or other entity in which the investment scheme is invested directly or indirectly ("the relevant entities"), or

(ii) to arrange for the investor to attend, vote or receive any other information issued to investors by the relevant entities,

by the amount of such of those expenses; and

(f) in respect of a linked long-term contract referred to in regulation 6 which is subject to smoothing, by the amount of the charges or expenses incurred by the manager in providing funds to smooth investment returns but only when the provision of such funds is in accordance with the manager's stated policy on smoothing.

(10) Where the value of the investment property is reduced by reference to an amount of charges or expenses referred to in paragraph (9), then, for the purposes of calculating any reduction in the investor's rights under paragraphs (3), (4) or (5), the value of those rights is to be calculated after the deductions of any such amount.

(11) Where an investment scheme is brought to an end by a manager and the investor takes up a transfer facility to another investment scheme, the relevant percentage for the purposes of paragraphs (3) to (5) shall be the same as that which would have been applied under or in respect of the original investment scheme as if the original investment scheme were continuing, notwithstanding any rules of the new investment scheme.

[4709]

FINANCIAL SERVICES AND MARKETS ACT 2000 (TRANSITIONAL PROVISIONS) (GENERAL INSURANCE INTERMEDIARIES) ORDER 2004 (NOTE)

(SI 2004/3351)

NOTES

This Order effectively became spent on 14 January 2006; see the note to FSMA 2000, s 427 at **[2424]**.

[4710]–[4716]

FINANCIAL SERVICES AND MARKETS ACT 2000 (FINANCIAL PROMOTION) ORDER 2005

(SI 2005/1529)

NOTES

Made: 8 June 2005.

Authority: Financial Services and Markets Act 2000, ss 21(5), (6), (9), (10), 428(3), Sch 2, para 25.

Commencement: 1 July 2005 (see art 1 at **[4717]**). Where any provision in this work (including any inserted or substituted provision) came into force for all purposes on or before 1 July 2005, commencement information is not noted at provision level.

Note: this Order revokes and re-enacts, with certain amendments, the Financial Services and Markets Act 2000 (Financial Promotion) Order 2001, SI 2001/1335 (as amended).

This Order is reproduced as amended by: the Financial Services and Markets Act 2000 (Financial Promotion) (Amendment) Order 2005, SI 2005/3392; the Financial Services and Markets Act 2000 (Regulated Activities) (Amendment) Order 2006, SI 2006/1969; the Financial Services and Markets Act 2000 (Regulated Activities) (Amendment) (No 2) Order 2006, SI 2006/2383; the Financial Services and Markets Act 2000 (Regulated Activities) (Amendment No 3) Order 2006, SI 2006/3384; the Financial Services and Markets Act 2000 (Financial Promotion) (Amendment) Order 2007, SI 2007/1083; the Companies Act 2006 (Commencement No 2, Consequential Amendments, Transitional Provisions and Savings) Order 2007, SI 2007/1093.

ARRANGEMENT OF ARTICLES

PART I
CITATION, COMMENCEMENT AND INTERPRETATION

PART II
CONTROLLED ACTIVITIES AND CONTROLLED INVESTMENTS

PART III
EXEMPTIONS: INTERPRETATION AND APPLICATION

PART IV
EXEMPT COMMUNICATIONS: ALL CONTROLLED ACTIVITIES

PART V
EXEMPT COMMUNICATIONS: DEPOSITS AND INSURANCE

PART VI
EXEMPT COMMUNICATIONS: CERTAIN CONTROLLED ACTIVITIES

SCHEDULES

PART I
CITATION, COMMENCEMENT AND INTERPRETATION

1 Citation and commencement

This Order may be cited as the Financial Services and Markets Act 2000 (Financial Promotion) Order 2005 and comes into force on 1st July 2005.

[4717]

2 Interpretation: general

(1) In this Order, except where the context otherwise requires—

"the 1985 Act" means the Companies Act 1985;

"the 1986 Order" means the Companies (Northern Ireland) Order 1986;

"the Act" means the Financial Services and Markets Act 2000;

"close relative" in relation to a person means—

(a) his spouse [or civil partner];

(b) his children and step-children, his parents and step-parents, his brothers and sisters and his step-brothers and step-sisters; and

(c) the spouse [or civil partner] of any person within sub-paragraph (b);

"controlled activity" has the meaning given by article 4 and Schedule 1;

"controlled investment" has the meaning given by article 4 and Schedule 1;

"deposit" means a sum of money which is a deposit for the purposes of article 5 of the Regulated Activities Order;

"equity share capital" has the meaning given in the 1985 Act or in the 1986 Order;

"financial promotion restriction" has the meaning given by article 5;

"government" means the government of the United Kingdom, the Scottish Administration, the Executive Committee of the Northern Ireland Assembly, the National Assembly for Wales and any government of any country or territory outside the United Kingdom;

"instrument" includes any record whether or not in the form of a document;

"international organisation" means any body the members of which comprise—

(a) states including the United Kingdom or another EEA State; or

(b) bodies whose members comprise states including the United Kingdom or another EEA State;

"overseas communicator" has the meaning given by article 30;

"previously overseas customer" has the meaning given by article 31;

"publication" means—

(a) a newspaper, journal, magazine or other periodical publication;

(b) a web site or similar system for the electronic display of information;

(c) any programme forming part of a service consisting of the broadcast or transmission of television or radio programmes;

(d) any teletext service, that—is to say a service consisting of television transmissions consisting of a succession of visual displays (with or without accompanying sound) capable of being selected and held for separate viewing or other use;

"qualifying contract of insurance" has the meaning given in the Regulated Activities Order;

"qualifying credit" has the meaning given by paragraph 10 of Schedule 1;

"the Regulated Activities Order" means the Financial Services and Markets Act 2000 (Regulated Activities) Order 2001;

"relevant insurance activity" has the meaning given by article 21;

"relevant investment activities" has the meaning given by article 30;

"solicited real time communication" has the meaning given by article 8;

"units", in a collective investment scheme, has the meaning given by Part XVII of the Act;

"unsolicited real time communication" has the meaning given by article 8.

(2) References to a person engaging in investment activity are to be construed in accordance with subsection (8) of section 21 of the Act; and for these purposes, "controlled activity" and "controlled investment" in that subsection have the meaning given in this Order.

[4718]

NOTES

Para (1): words in square brackets in definition "close relative" inserted by the Financial Services and Markets Act 2000 (Financial Promotion) (Amendment) Order 2005, SI 2005/3392, art 2(1), (2), as from 21 December 2005.

"Close relative": as to the meaning of "step-children", and related expressions, see the Civil Partnership Act 2004, s 246 (as applied to this Order by the Civil Partnership Act 2004 (Relationships Arising Through Civil Partnership) Order 2005, SI 2005/3137, art 3, Schedule).

3 Interpretation: unlisted companies

(1) In this Order, an "unlisted company" means a body corporate the shares in which are not—

(a) listed or quoted on an investment exchange whether in the United Kingdom or elsewhere;

(b) shares in respect of which information is, with the agreement or approval of any officer of the company, published for the purpose of facilitating deals in the shares indicating prices at which persons have dealt or are willing to deal in them other than persons who, at the time the information is published, are existing members of a relevant class; or

(c) subject to a marketing arrangement which accords to the company the facilities referred to in section 163(2)(b) of the 1985 Act or article 173(2)(b) of the 1986 Order.

(2) For the purpose of paragraph (1)(b), a person is to be regarded as a member of a relevant class if he was, at the relevant time—

(a) an existing member or debenture holder of the company;

(b) an existing employee of the company;

(c) a close relative of such a member or employee; or

(d) a trustee (acting in his capacity as such) of a trust, the principal beneficiary of which is a person within any of sub-paragraphs (a), (b) and (c).

(3) In this Order references to shares in and debentures of an unlisted company are references to—

(a) in the case of a body corporate which is a company within the meaning of the 1985 Act, shares and debentures within the meaning of that Act;

(b) in the case of a body corporate which is a company within the meaning of the 1986 Order, shares and debentures within the meaning of that Order;

(c) in the case of any other body corporate, investments falling within paragraph 14 or 15 of Schedule 1 to this Order.

[4719]

PART II
CONTROLLED ACTIVITIES AND CONTROLLED INVESTMENTS

4 Definition of controlled activities and controlled investments

(1) For the purposes of section 21(9) of the Act, a controlled activity is an activity which falls within any of paragraphs 1 to 11 of Schedule 1.

(2) For the purposes of section 21(10) of the Act, a controlled investment is an investment which falls within any of paragraphs 12 to 27 of Schedule 1.

[4720]

PART III
EXEMPTIONS: INTERPRETATION AND APPLICATION

5 Interpretation: financial promotion restriction

In this Order, any reference to the financial promotion restriction is a reference to the restriction in section 21(1) of the Act.

[4721]

6 Interpretation: communications

In this Order—

(a) any reference to a communication is a reference to the communication, in the course of business, of an invitation or inducement to engage in investment activity;

(b) any reference to a communication being made to another person is a reference to a communication being addressed, whether orally or in legible form, to a particular person or persons (for example where it is contained in a telephone call or letter);

(c) any reference to a communication being directed at persons is a reference to a communication being addressed to persons generally (for example where it is contained in a television broadcast or web site);

(d) "communicate" includes causing a communication to be made or directed;

(e) a "recipient" of a communication is the person to whom the communication is made or, in the case of a non-real time communication which is directed at persons generally, any person who reads or hears the communication;

(f) "electronic commerce communication" means a communication, the making of which constitutes the provision of an information society service;

(g) "incoming electronic commerce communication" means an electronic commerce communication made from an establishment in an EEA State other than the United Kingdom;

(h) "outgoing electronic commerce communication" means an electronic commerce communication made from an establishment in the United Kingdom to a person in an EEA State other than the United Kingdom.

[4722]

7 Interpretation: real time communications

(1) In this Order, references to a real time communication are references to any communication made in the course of a personal visit, telephone conversation or other interactive dialogue.

(2) A non-real time communication is a communication not falling within paragraph (1).

(3) For the purposes of this Order, non-real time communications include communications made by letter or e-mail or contained in a publication.

(4) For the purposes of this Order, the factors in paragraph (5) are to be treated as indications that a communication is a non-real time communication.

(5) The factors are that—

(a) the communication is made to or directed at more than one recipient in identical terms (save for details of the recipient's identity);

(b) the communication is made or directed by way of a system which in the normal course constitutes or creates a record of the communication which is available to the recipient to refer to at a later time;

(c) the communication is made or directed by way of a system which in the normal course does not enable or require the recipient to respond immediately to it.

[4723]

8 Interpretation: solicited and unsolicited real time communications

(1) A real time communication is solicited where it is made in the course of a personal visit, telephone call or other interactive dialogue if that call, visit or dialogue—

(a) was initiated by the recipient of the communication; or

(b) takes place in response to an express request from the recipient of the communication.

(2) A real time communication is unsolicited where it is made otherwise than as described in paragraph (1).

(3) For the purposes of paragraph (1)—

(a) a person is not to be treated as expressly requesting a call, visit or dialogue—

(i) because he omits to indicate that he does not wish to receive any or any further visits or calls or to engage in any or any further dialogue;

(ii) because he agrees to standard terms that state that such visits, calls or dialogue will take place, unless he has signified clearly that, in addition to agreeing to the terms, he is willing for them to take place;

PART IV
STATUTORY INSTRUMENTS

(b) a communication is solicited only if it is clear from all the circumstances when the call, visit or dialogue is initiated or requested that during the course of the visit, call or dialogue communications will be made concerning the kind of controlled activities or investments to which the communications in fact made relate;

(c) it is immaterial whether the express request was made before or after this article comes into force.

(4) Where a real time communication is solicited by a recipient ("R"), it is treated as having also been solicited by any other person to whom it is made at the same time as it is made to R if that other recipient is—

(a) a close relative of R; or

(b) expected to engage in any investment activity jointly with R.

[4724]

8A Interpretation: outgoing electronic commerce communications

(1) For the purposes of the application of those articles to outgoing electronic commerce communications—

(a) any reference in article 48(7)(c), 50(1)(a) or (3)(e) or 52(3)(c) to an authorised person includes a reference to a person who is entitled, under the law of an EEA State other than the United Kingdom, to carry on regulated activities in that State;

(b) any reference in article 68(1) or 71 to rules or legislation includes a reference to provisions corresponding to those rules or legislation in the law of an EEA State other than the United Kingdom;

(c) any reference in article 49 to an amount in pounds sterling includes a reference to an equivalent amount in another currency.

(2) For the purposes of the application of article 49 to outgoing electronic commerce communications, any reference in section 264(2) or 737 of the 1985 Act (or the equivalent provisions in the 1986 Order) to a body corporate or company includes a reference to a body corporate or company registered under the law of an EEA State other than the United Kingdom.

(3) For the purposes of the application of article 3 in respect of outgoing electronic commerce communications—

(a) any reference in section 163(2)(b) of the 1985 Act (or the equivalent provision in the 1986 Order) to a company includes a reference to a company registered under the law of an EEA State other than the United Kingdom;

(b) any reference in that section to an investment exchange includes a reference to an investment exchange which is recognised as an investment exchange under the law of an EEA State other than the United Kingdom.

[4725]

9 Degree of prominence to be given to required indications

Where a communication must, if it is to fall within any provision of this Order, be accompanied by an indication of any matter, the indication must be presented to the recipient—

(a) in a way that can be easily understood; and

(b) in such manner as, depending on the means by which the communication is made or directed, is best calculated to bring the matter in question to the attention of the recipient and to allow him to consider it.

[4726]

10 Application to qualifying contracts of insurance

(1) Nothing in this Order exempts from the application of the financial promotion restriction a communication which invites or induces a person to enter into a qualifying contract of insurance with a person who is not—

(a) an authorised person;

(b) an exempt person who is exempt in relation to effecting or carrying out contracts of insurance of the class to which the communication relates;

(c) a company which has its head office in an EEA State other than the United Kingdom and which is entitled under the law of that State to carry on there insurance business of the class to which the communication relates;

(d) a company which has a branch or agency in an EEA State other than the United

Kingdom and is entitled under the law of that State to carry on there insurance business of the class to which the communication relates;

(e) a company authorised to carry on insurance business of the class to which the communication relates in any country or territory which is listed in Schedule 2.

(2) In this article, references to a class of insurance are references to the class of insurance contract described in Schedule 1 to the Regulated Activities Order into which the effecting or carrying out of the contract to which the communication relates would fall.

[4727]

11 Combination of different exemptions

(1) In respect of a communication relating to—

(a) a controlled activity falling within paragraph 2 of Schedule 1 carried on in relation to a qualifying contract of insurance; or

(b) a controlled activity falling within any of paragraphs 3 to 11 of Schedule 1,

a person may rely on the application of one or more of the exemptions in Parts IV and VI.

(2) In respect of a communication relating to—

(a) an activity falling within paragraph 1 of Schedule 1; or

(b) a relevant insurance activity,

a person may rely on one or more of the exemptions in Parts IV and V; and, where a communication relates to any such activity and also to an activity mentioned in paragraph (1)(a) or (b), a person may rely on one or more of the exemptions in Parts IV and V in respect of the former activity and on one or more of the exemptions in Parts V and VI in respect of the latter activity.

[4728]

PART IV
EXEMPT COMMUNICATIONS: ALL CONTROLLED ACTIVITIES

12 Communications to overseas recipients

(1) Subject to paragraphs (2) and (7), the financial promotion restriction does not apply to any communication—

(a) which is made (whether from inside or outside the United Kingdom) to a person who receives the communication outside the United Kingdom; or

(b) which is directed (whether from inside or outside the United Kingdom) only at persons outside the United Kingdom.

(2) Paragraph (1) does not apply to an unsolicited real time communication unless—

(a) it is made from a place outside the United Kingdom; and

(b) it is made for the purposes of a business which is carried on outside the United Kingdom and which is not carried on in the United Kingdom.

(3) For the purposes of paragraph (1)(b)—

(a) if the conditions set out in paragraph (4)(a), (b), (c) and (d) are met, a communication directed from a place inside the United Kingdom is to be regarded as directed only at persons outside the United Kingdom;

(b) if the conditions set out in paragraph (4)(c) and (d) are met, a communication directed from a place outside the United Kingdom is to be regarded as directed only at persons outside the United Kingdom;

(c) in any other case where one or more of the conditions in paragraph (4)(a) to (e) are met, that fact is to be taken into account in determining whether or not a communication is to be regarded as directed only at persons outside the United Kingdom (but a communication may still be regarded as directed only at persons outside the United Kingdom even if none of the conditions in paragraph (4) is met).

(4) The conditions are that—

(a) the communication is accompanied by an indication that it is directed only at persons outside the United Kingdom;

(b) the communication is accompanied by an indication that it must not be acted upon by persons in the United Kingdom;

(c) the communication is not referred to in, or directly accessible from, any other communication made to a person or directed at persons in the United Kingdom by the person directing the communication;

(d) there are in place proper systems and procedures to prevent recipients in the United Kingdom (other than those to whom the communication might otherwise lawfully have been made by the person directing it or a member of the same group) engaging in the investment activity to which the communication relates with the person directing the communication, a close relative of his or a member of the same group;

(e) the communication is included in—

(i) a web site, newspaper, journal, magazine or periodical publication which is principally accessed in or intended for a market outside the United Kingdom;

(ii) a radio or television broadcast or teletext service transmitted principally for reception outside the United Kingdom.

(5) For the purpose of paragraph (1)(b), a communication may be treated as directed only at persons outside the United Kingdom even if—

(a) it is also directed, for the purposes of article 19(1)(b), at investment professionals falling within article 19(5) (but disregarding paragraph (6) of that article for this purpose);

(b) it is also directed, for the purposes of article 49(1)(b), at high net worth persons to whom article 49 applies (but disregarding paragraph (2)(e) of that article for this purpose) and it relates to a controlled activity to which article 49 applies;

(c) it is a communication to which article 31 applies.

(6) Where a communication falls within paragraph (5)(a) or (b)—

(a) the condition in paragraph (4)(a) is to be construed as requiring an indication that the communication is directed only at persons outside the United Kingdom or persons having professional experience in matters relating to investments or high net worth persons (as the case may be);

(b) the condition in paragraph (4)(b) is to be construed as requiring an indication that the communication must not be acted upon by persons in the United Kingdom except by persons who have professional experience in matters relating to investments or who are not high net worth persons (as the case may be);

(c) the condition in paragraph (4)(c) will not apply where the other communication referred to in that paragraph is made to a person or directed at a person in the United Kingdom to whom paragraph (5) applies.

(7) Paragraph (1) does not apply to an outgoing electronic commerce communication.

[4729]

13 Communications from customers and potential customers

(1) The financial promotion restriction does not apply to any communication made by or on behalf of a person ("customer") to one other person ("supplier")—

(a) in order to obtain information about a controlled investment available from or a controlled service provided by the supplier; or

(b) in order that the customer can acquire a controlled investment from that supplier or be supplied with a controlled service by that supplier.

(2) For the purposes of paragraph (1), a controlled service is a service the provision of which constitutes engaging in a controlled activity by the supplier.

[4730]

14 Follow up non-real time communications and solicited real time communications

(1) Where a person makes or directs a communication ("the first communication") which is exempt from the financial promotion restriction because, in compliance with the requirements of another provision of this Order, it is accompanied by certain indications or contains certain information, then the financial promotion restriction does not apply to any subsequent communication which complies with the requirements of paragraph (2).

(2) The requirements of this paragraph are that the subsequent communication—

(a) is a non-real time communication or a solicited real time communication;

(b) is made by, or on behalf of, the same person who made the first communication;

(c) is made to a recipient of the first communication;

(d) relates to the same controlled activity and the same controlled investment as the first communication; and

(e) is made within 12 months of the recipient receiving the first communication.

(3) The provisions of this article only apply in the case of a person who makes or directs a communication on behalf of another where the first communication is made by that other person.

(4) Where a person makes or directs a communication on behalf of another person in reliance on the exemption contained in this article the person on whose behalf the communication was made or directed remains responsible for the content of that communication.

(5) A communication made or directed before this article comes into force is to be treated as a first communication falling within paragraph (1) if it would have fallen within that paragraph had it been made or directed after this article comes into force.

[4731]

15 Introductions

(1) If the requirements of paragraph (2) are met, the financial promotion restriction does not apply to any communication which is made with a view to or for the purposes of introducing the recipient to—

(a) an authorised person who carries on the controlled activity to which the communication relates; or

(b) an exempt person where the communication relates to a controlled activity which is also a regulated activity in relation to which he is an exempt person.

(2) The requirements of this paragraph are that—

(a) the maker of the communication ("A") is not a close relative of, nor a member of the same group as, the person to whom the introduction is, or is to be, made;

(b) A does not receive from any person other than the recipient any pecuniary reward or other advantage arising out of his making the introduction; and

(c) it is clear in all the circumstances that the recipient, in his capacity as an investor, is not seeking and has not sought advice from A as to the merits of the recipient engaging in investment activity (or, if the client has sought such advice, A has declined to give it, but has recommended that the recipient seek such advice from an authorised person).

[4732]

16 Exempt persons

(1) The financial promotion restriction does not apply to any communication which—

(a) is a non-real time communication or a solicited real time communication;

(b) is made or directed by an exempt person; and

(c) is for the purposes of that exempt person's business of carrying on a controlled activity which is also a regulated activity in relation to which he is an exempt person.

(2) The financial promotion restriction does not apply to any unsolicited real time communication made by a person ("AR") who is an appointed representative (within the meaning of section 39(2) of the Act) where—

(a) the communication is made by AR in carrying on the business—

(i) for which his principal ("P") has accepted responsibility for the purposes of section 39 of the Act; and

(ii) in relation to which AR is exempt from the general prohibition by virtue of that section; and

(b) the communication is one which, if it were made by P, would comply with any rules made by the Authority under section 145 of the Act (financial promotion rules) which are relevant to a communication of that kind.

[4733]

17 Generic promotions

The financial promotion restriction does not apply to any communication which—

(a) does not identify (directly or indirectly) a person who provides the controlled investment to which the communication relates; and

(b) does not identify (directly or indirectly) any person as a person who carries on a controlled activity in relation to that investment.

[4734]

17A Communications caused to be made or directed by unauthorised persons

(1) If a condition in paragraph (2) is met, the financial promotion restriction does not apply to a communication caused to be made or directed by an unauthorised person which is made or directed by an authorised person.

(2) The conditions in this paragraph are that—

(a) the authorised person prepared the content of the communication; or

(b) it is a real-time communication.

[4735]

18 Mere conduits

(1) Subject to paragraph (4), the financial promotion restriction does not apply to any communication which is made or directed by a person who acts as a mere conduit for it.

(2) A person acts as a mere conduit for a communication if—

(a) he communicates it in the course of an activity carried on by him, the principal purpose of which is transmitting or receiving material provided to him by others;

(b) the content of the communication is wholly devised by another person; and

(c) the nature of the service provided by him in relation to the communication is such that he does not select, modify or otherwise exercise control over its content prior to its transmission or receipt.

(3) For the purposes of paragraph (2)(c) a person does not select, modify or otherwise exercise control over the content of a communication merely by removing or having the power to remove material—

(a) which is, or is alleged to be, illegal, defamatory or in breach of copyright;

(b) in response to a request to a body which is empowered by or under any enactment to make such a request; or

(c) when otherwise required to do so by law.

(4) Nothing in paragraph (1) prevents the application of the financial promotion restriction in so far as it relates to the person who has caused the communication to be made or directed.

(5) This article does not apply to an electronic commerce communication.

[4736]

18A Electronic commerce communications: mere conduits, caching and hosting

The financial promotion restriction does not apply to an electronic commerce communication in circumstances where—

(a) the making of the communication constitutes the provision of an information society service of a kind falling within paragraph 1 of Article 12, 13 or 14 of the electronic commerce directive ("mere conduit", "caching" and "hosting"); and

(b) the conditions mentioned in the paragraph in question, to the extent that they are applicable at the time of, or prior to, the making of the communication, are or have been met at that time.

[4737]

19 Investment professionals

(1) The financial promotion restriction does not apply to any communication which—

(a) is made only to recipients whom the person making the communication believes on reasonable grounds to be investment professionals; or

(b) may reasonably be regarded as directed only at such recipients.

(2) For the purposes of paragraph (1)(b), if all the conditions set out in paragraph (4)(a) to (c) are met in relation to the communication, it is to be regarded as directed only at investment professionals.

(3) In any other case in which one or more of the conditions set out in paragraph (4)(a) to (c) are met, that fact is to be taken into account in determining whether the communication

is directed only at investment professionals (but a communication may still be regarded as so directed even if none of the conditions in paragraph (4) is met).

(4) The conditions are that—

(a) the communication is accompanied by an indication that it is directed at persons having professional experience in matters relating to investments and that any investment or investment activity to which it relates is available only to such persons or will be engaged in only with such persons;

(b) the communication is accompanied by an indication that persons who do not have professional experience in matters relating to investments should not rely on it;

(c) there are in place proper systems and procedures to prevent recipients other than investment professionals engaging in the investment activity to which the communication relates with the person directing the communication, a close relative of his or a member of the same group.

(5) "Investment professionals" means—

(a) an authorised person;

(b) an exempt person where the communication relates to a controlled activity which is a regulated activity in relation to which the person is exempt;

(c) any other person—

(i) whose ordinary activities involve him in carrying on the controlled activity to which the communication relates for the purpose of a business carried on by him; or

(ii) who it is reasonable to expect will carry on such activity for the purposes of a business carried on by him;

(d) a government, local authority (whether in the United Kingdom or elsewhere) or an international organisation;

(e) a person ("A") who is a director, officer or employee of a person ("B") falling within any of sub-paragraphs (a) to (d) where the communication is made to A in that capacity and where A's responsibilities when acting in that capacity involve him in the carrying on by B of controlled activities.

(6) For the purposes of paragraph (1), a communication may be treated as made only to or directed only at investment professionals even if it is also made to or directed at other persons to whom it may lawfully be communicated.

[4738]

20 Communications by journalists

(1) Subject to paragraph (2), the financial promotion restriction does not apply to any non-real time communication if—

(a) the content of the communication is devised by a person acting in the capacity of a journalist;

(b) the communication is contained in a qualifying publication; and

(c) in the case of a communication requiring disclosure, one of the conditions in paragraph (2) is met.

(2) The conditions in this paragraph are that—

(a) the communication is accompanied by an indication explaining the nature of the author's financial interest or that of a member of his family (as the case may be);

(b) the authors are subject to proper systems and procedures which prevent the publication of communications requiring disclosure without the explanation referred to in sub-paragraph (a); or

(c) the qualifying publication in which the communication appears falls within the remit of—

(i) the Code of Practice issued by the Press Complaints Commission;

(ii) the OFCOM Broadcasting Code; or

(iii) the Producers' Guidelines issued by the British Broadcasting Corporation.

(3) For the purposes of this article, a communication requires disclosure if—

(a) an author of the communication or a member of his family is likely to obtain a financial benefit or avoid a financial loss if people act in accordance with the invitation or inducement contained in the communication;

(b) the communication relates to a controlled investment of a kind falling within paragraph (4); and

(c) the communication identifies directly a person who issues or provides the controlled investment to which the communication relates.

(4) A controlled investment falls within this paragraph if it is—

(a) an investment falling within paragraph 14 of Schedule 1 (shares or stock in share capital);

(b) an investment falling within paragraph 21 of that Schedule (options) to acquire or dispose of an investment falling within sub-paragraph (a);

(c) an investment falling within paragraph 22 of that Schedule (futures) being rights under a contract for the sale of an investment falling within sub-paragraph (a); or

(d) an investment falling within paragraph 23 of that Schedule (contracts for differences etc) being rights under a contract relating to, or to fluctuations in, the value or price of an investment falling within sub-paragraph (a).

(5) For the purposes of this article—

(a) the authors of the communication are the person who devises the content of the communication and the person who is responsible for deciding to include the communication in the qualifying publication;

(b) a "qualifying publication" is a publication or service of the kind mentioned in paragraph (1) or (2) of article 54 of the Regulated Activities Order and which is of the nature described in that article, and for the purposes of this article, a certificate given under paragraph (3) of article 54 of that Order and not revoked is conclusive evidence of the matters certified;

(c) the members of a person's family are his spouse [or civil partner] and any children of his under the age of 18 years.

[4739]

NOTES

Para (5): words in square brackets in sub-para (c) inserted by the Financial Services and Markets Act 2000 (Financial Promotion) (Amendment) Order 2005, SI 2005/3392, art 2(1), (3), as from 21 December 2005.

20A Promotion broadcast by company director etc

(1) The financial promotion restriction does not apply to a communication which is communicated as part of a qualifying service by a person ("D") who is a director or employee of an undertaking ("U") where—

(a) the communication invites or induces the recipient to acquire—

(i) a controlled investment of the kind falling within article 20(4) which is issued by U (or by an undertaking in the same group as U); or

(ii) a controlled investment issued or provided by an authorised person in the same group as U;

(b) the communication—

(i) comprises words which are spoken by D and not broadcast, transmitted or displayed in writing; or

(ii) is displayed in writing only because it forms part of an interactive dialogue to which D is a party and in the course of which D is expected to respond immediately to questions put by a recipient of the communication;

(c) the communication is not part of an organised marketing campaign; and

(d) the communication is accompanied by an indication that D is a director or employee (as the case may be) of U.

(2) For the purposes of this article, a "qualifying service" is a service—

(a) which is broadcast or transmitted in the form of television or radio programmes; or

(b) displayed on a web site (or similar system for the electronic display of information) comprising regularly updated news and information,

provided that the principal purpose of the service, taken as a whole and including any advertisements and other promotional material contained in it, is neither of the purposes described in article 54(1)(a) or (b) of the Regulated Activities Order.

(3) For the purposes of paragraph (2), a certificate given under article 54(3) of the Regulated Activities Order and not revoked is conclusive evidence of the matters certified.

[4740]

20B Incoming electronic commerce communications

(1) The financial promotion restriction does not apply to an incoming electronic commerce communication.

(2) Paragraph (1) does not apply to—

(a) a communication which constitutes an advertisement by the operator of a UCITS directive scheme of units in that scheme;

(b) a communication consisting of an invitation or inducement to enter into a contract of insurance, where—

(i) the communication is made by an undertaking which has received official authorisation in accordance with Article 4 of the life assurance consolidation directive or the first non-life insurance directive, and

(ii) the insurance falls within the scope of any of the insurance directives; or

(c) an unsolicited communication made by electronic mail.

(3) In this article, "UCITS directive scheme" means an undertaking for collective investment in transferable securities which is subject to Directive 85/611/EEC of the Council of the European Communities of 20 December 1985 on the co-ordination of laws, regulations and administrative provisions relating to undertakings for collective investment in transferable securities, and has been authorised in accordance with Article 4 of that Directive.

(4) For the purposes of this article, a communication by electronic mail is to be regarded as unsolicited, unless it is made in response to an express request from the recipient of the communication.

[4741]

PART V
EXEMPT COMMUNICATIONS: DEPOSITS AND INSURANCE

21 Interpretation: relevant insurance activity

In this Part, a "relevant insurance activity" means a controlled activity falling within paragraph 2 of Schedule 1 carried on in relation to an investment falling within paragraph 13 of that Schedule where that investment is not a qualifying contract of insurance.

[4742]

22 Deposits: non-real time communications

(1) If the requirements of paragraph (2) are met, the financial promotion restriction does not apply to any non-real time communication which relates to a controlled activity falling within paragraph 1 of Schedule 1.

(2) The requirements of this paragraph are that the communication is accompanied by an indication—

(a) of the full name of the person with whom the investment which is the subject of the communication is to be made ("deposit-taker");

(b) of the country or territory in which a deposit-taker that is a body corporate is incorporated (described as such);

(c) if different, of the country or territory in which the deposit-taker's principal place of business is situated (described as such);

(d) whether or not the deposit-taker is regulated in respect of his deposit-taking business;

(e) if the deposit-taker is so regulated, of the name of the regulator in the deposit-taker's principal place of business, or if there is more than one such regulator, the prudential regulator;

(f) whether any transaction to which the communication relates would, if entered into by the recipient and the deposit-taker, fall within the jurisdiction of any dispute resolution scheme or deposit guarantee scheme and if so, identifying each such scheme;

(g) the necessary capital information.

(3) In this article—

"full name", in relation to a person, means the name under which that person carries on business and, if different, that person's corporate name;

"liabilities" includes provisions where such provisions have not been deducted from the value of the assets;

"necessary capital information" means—

(a) in relation to a deposit-taker which is a body corporate, either the amount of its paid up capital and reserves, described as such, or a statement that the amount of its paid up capital and reserves exceeds a particular amount (stating it);

PART IV
STATUTORY INSTRUMENTS

(b) in relation to a deposit-taker which is not a body corporate, either the amount of the total assets less liabilities (described as such) or a statement that the amount of its total assets exceeds a particular amount (stating it) and that its total liabilities do not exceed a particular amount (stating it).

[4743]

23 Deposits: real time communications

The financial promotion restriction does not apply to any real time communication (whether solicited or unsolicited) which relates to an activity falling within paragraph 1 of Schedule 1.

[4744]

24 Relevant insurance activity: non-real time communications

(1) If the requirements of paragraph (2) are met, the financial promotion restriction does not apply to any non-real time communication which relates to a relevant insurance activity.

(2) The requirements of this paragraph are that the communication is accompanied by an indication—

(a) of the full name of the person with whom the investment which is the subject of the communication is to be made ("the insurer");

(b) of the country or territory in which the insurer is incorporated (described as such);

(c) if different, of the country or territory in which the insurer's principal place of business is situated (described as such);

(d) whether or not the insurer is regulated in respect of its insurance business;

(e) if the insurer is so regulated, of the name of the regulator of the insurer in its principal place of business or, if there is more than one such regulator, the name of the prudential regulator;

(f) whether any transaction to which the communication relates would, if entered into by the recipient and the insurer, fall within the jurisdiction of any dispute resolution scheme or compensation scheme and if so, identifying each such scheme.

(3) In this article "full name", in relation to a person, means the name under which that person carries on business and, if different, that person's corporate name.

[4745]

25 Relevant insurance activity: non-real time communications: reinsurance and large risks

(1) The financial promotion restriction does not apply to any non-real time communication which relates to a relevant insurance activity and concerns only—

(a) a contract of reinsurance; or

(b) a contract that covers large risks.

(2) "Large risks" means—

(a) risks falling within paragraph 4 (railway rolling stock), 5 (aircraft), 6 (ships), 7 (goods in transit), 11 (aircraft liability) or 12 (liability of ships) of Schedule 1 to the Regulated Activities Order;

(b) risks falling within paragraph 14 (credit) or 15 (suretyship) of that Schedule provided that the risks relate to a business carried on by the recipient;

(c) risks falling within paragraph 3 (land vehicles), 8 (fire and natural forces), 9 (damage to property), 10 (motor vehicle liability), 13 (general liability) or 16 (miscellaneous financial loss) of that Schedule provided that the risks relate to a business carried on by the recipient and that the condition specified in paragraph (3) is met in relation to that business.

(3) The condition specified in this paragraph is that at least two of the three following criteria were exceeded in the most recent financial year for which information is available prior to the making of the communication—

(a) the balance sheet total of the business (within the meaning of section 247(5) of the 1985 Act or article 255(5) of the 1986 Order) was 6.2 million euros;

(b) the net turnover (within the meaning given to "turnover" by section 262(1) of the 1985 Act or article 270(1) of the 1986 Order) was 12.8 million euros;

(c) the number of employees (within the meaning given by section 247(6) of the 1985 Act or article 255(6) of the 1986 Order) was 250;

and for a financial year which is a company's financial year but not in fact a year, the net turnover of the recipient shall be proportionately adjusted.

(4) For the purposes of paragraph (3), where the recipient is a member of a group for which consolidated accounts (within the meaning of the Seventh Company Law Directive) are drawn up, the question whether the condition met in that paragraph is met is to be determined by reference to those accounts.

[4746]

26 Relevant insurance activity: real time communication

The financial promotion restriction does not apply to any real time communication (whether solicited or unsolicited) which relates to a relevant insurance activity.

[4747]

PART VI
EXEMPT COMMUNICATIONS: CERTAIN CONTROLLED ACTIVITIES

27 Application of exemptions in this Part

Except where otherwise stated, the exemptions in this Part apply to communications which relate to—

(a) a controlled activity falling within paragraph 2 of Schedule 1 carried on in relation to a qualifying contract of insurance;

(b) controlled activities falling within any of paragraphs 3 to 11 of Schedule 1.

[4748]

28 One off non-real time communications and solicited real time communications

(1) The financial promotion restriction does not apply to a one off communication which is either a non-real time communication or a solicited real time communication.

(2) If all the conditions set out in paragraph (3) are met in relation to a communication it is to be regarded as a one off communication. In any other case in which one or more of those conditions are met, that fact is to be taken into account in determining whether the communication is a one off communication (but a communication may still be regarded as a one off communication even if none of the conditions in paragraph (3) is met).

(3) The conditions are that—

(a) the communication is made only to one recipient or only to one group of recipients in the expectation that they would engage in any investment activity jointly;

(b) the identity of the product or service to which the communication relates has been determined having regard to the particular circumstances of the recipient;

(c) the communication is not part of an organised marketing campaign.

[4749]

28A One off unsolicited real time communications

(1) The financial promotion restriction does not apply to an unsolicited real time communication if the conditions in paragraph (2) are met.

(2) The conditions in this paragraph are that—

(a) the communication is a one off communication;

(b) the communicator believes on reasonable grounds that the recipient understands the risks associated with engaging in the investment activity to which the communication relates;

(c) at the time that the communication is made, the communicator believes on reasonable grounds that the recipient would expect to be contacted by him in relation to the investment activity to which the communication relates.

(3) Paragraphs (2) and (3) of article 28 apply in determining whether a communication is a one off communication for the purposes of this article as they apply for the purposes of article 28.

[4750]

28B Real time communications: introductions …

(1) If the requirements of paragraph (2) are met, the financial promotion restriction does not apply to any real time communication which—

(a) relates to a controlled activity falling within [paragraph 10, 10A, 10B, 10C, 10D, 10E, 10F, 10G or 10H] of Schedule 1; and

(b) is made for the purpose of, or with a view to, introducing the recipient to a person ("N") who is—

(i) an authorised person who carries on the controlled activity to which the communication relates,

(ii) an appointed representative, where the controlled activity to which the communication relates is also a regulated activity in respect of which he is exempt from the general prohibition, or

(iii) an overseas person who carries on the controlled activity to which the communication relates.

(2) The requirements of this paragraph are that the maker of the communication ("M")—

(a) does not receive any money, other than money payable to M on his own account, paid by the recipient for or in connection with any transaction which the recipient enters into with or through N as a result of the introduction; and

(b) before making the introduction, discloses to the recipient such of the information mentioned in paragraph (3) as applies to M.

(3) That information is—

(a) that M is a member of the same group as N;

(b) details of any payment which M will receive from N, by way of fee or commission, for introducing the recipient to N;

(c) an indication of any other reward or advantage received or to be received by M that arises out of his making introductions to N.

(4) In this article, "overseas person" means a person who carries on controlled activities which fall within paragraph 10, 10A or 10B of Schedule 1, but who does not carry on any such activity, or offer to do so, from a permanent place of business maintained by him in the United Kingdom.

[4751]

NOTES

Article heading: words omitted revoked by the Financial Services and Markets Act 2000 (Regulated Activities) (Amendment) (No 2) Order 2006, SI 2006/2383, art 35(1), (2), as from 6 April 2007 (for the full commencement details of SI 2006/2383, see art 1 of that Order at **[4820]**).

Para (1): words in square brackets substituted by SI 2006/2383, art 35(1), (3), as from 6 April 2007 (for the full commencement details of SI 2006/2383, see art 1 of that Order at **[4820]**).

29 Communications required or authorised by enactments

(1) Subject to paragraph (2), the financial promotion restriction does not apply to any communication which is required or authorised by or under any enactment other than the Act.

(2) This article does not apply to a communication which relates to a controlled activity falling within paragraph 10, 10A or 10B of Schedule 1 or within paragraph 11 in so far as it relates to that activity.

[4752]

30 Overseas communicators: solicited real time communications

(1) The financial promotion restriction does not apply to any solicited real time communication which is made by an overseas communicator from outside the United Kingdom in the course of or for the purposes of his carrying on the business of engaging in relevant investment activities outside the United Kingdom.

(2) In this article—

"overseas communicator" means a person who carries on relevant investment activities outside the United Kingdom but who does not carry on any such activity from a permanent place of business maintained by him in the United Kingdom;

"relevant investment activities" means controlled activities which fall within paragraphs 3 to 7 or 10 to 10B of Schedule 1 or, so far as relevant to any of those paragraphs, paragraph 11 of that Schedule.

[4753]

31 Overseas communicators: non-real time communications to previously overseas customers

(1) The financial promotion restriction does not apply to any non-real time communication which is communicated by an overseas communicator from outside the United Kingdom to a previously overseas customer of his.

(2) In this article a "previously overseas customer" means a person with whom the overseas communicator has done business within the period of twelve months ending with the day on which the communication was received ("the earlier business") and where—

- (a) at the time that the earlier business was done, the customer was neither resident in the United Kingdom nor had a place of business there; or
- (b) at the time the earlier business was done, the overseas communicator had on a former occasion done business with the customer, being business of the same description as the business to which the communication relates, and on that former occasion the customer was neither resident in the United Kingdom nor had a place of business there.

(3) For the purposes of this article, an overseas communicator has done business with a customer if, in the course of carrying on his relevant investment activities outside the United Kingdom, he has—

- (a) effected a transaction, or arranged for a transaction to be effected, with the customer;
- (b) provided, outside the United Kingdom; a service to the customer as described in paragraph 6 of Schedule 1 (whether or not that paragraph was in force at the time the business was done); or
- (c) given, outside the United Kingdom, any advice to the customer as described in paragraph 7 of that Schedule (whether or not that paragraph was in force at the time the business was done).

[4754]

32 Overseas communicators: unsolicited real time communications to previously overseas customers

(1) If the requirements of paragraphs (2) and (3) are met, the financial promotion restriction does not apply to an unsolicited real time communication which is made by an overseas communicator from outside the United Kingdom to a previously overseas customer of his.

(2) The requirements of this paragraph are that the terms on which previous transactions and services had been effected or provided by the overseas communicator to the previously overseas customer were such that the customer would reasonably expect, at the time that the unsolicited real time communication is made, to be contacted by the overseas communicator in relation to the investment activity to which the communication relates.

(3) The requirements of this paragraph are that the previously overseas customer has been informed by the overseas communicator on an earlier occasion—

- (a) that the protections conferred by or under the Act will not apply to any unsolicited real time communication which is made by the overseas communicator and which relates to that investment activity;
- (b) that the protections conferred by or under the Act may not apply to any investment activity that may be engaged in as a result of the communication; and
- (c) whether any transaction between them resulting from the communication would fall within the jurisdiction of any dispute resolution scheme or compensation scheme or, if there is no such scheme, of that fact.

[4755]

33 Overseas communicators: unsolicited real time communications to knowledgeable customers

(1) If the requirements of paragraphs (2), (3) and (4) are met, the financial promotion restriction does not apply to an unsolicited real time communication which is made by an overseas communicator from outside the United Kingdom in the course of his carrying on relevant investment activities outside the United Kingdom.

(2) The requirements of this paragraph are that the overseas communicator believes on reasonable grounds that the recipient is sufficiently knowledgeable to understand the risks associated with engaging in the investment activity to which the communication relates.

(3) The requirements of this paragraph are that, in relation to any particular investment activity, the recipient has been informed by the overseas communicator on an earlier occasion—

(a) that the protections conferred by or under the Act will not apply to any unsolicited real time communication which is made by him and which relates to that activity;
(b) that the protections conferred by or under the Act may not apply to any investment activity that may be engaged in as a result of the communication; and
(c) whether any transaction between them resulting from the communication would fall within the jurisdiction of any dispute resolution scheme or compensation scheme or, if there is no such scheme, of that fact.

(4) The requirements of this paragraph are that the recipient, after being given a proper opportunity to consider the information given to him in accordance with paragraph (3), has clearly signified that he understands the warnings referred to in paragraph (3)(a) and (b) and that he accepts that he will not benefit from the protections referred to.

[4756]

34 Governments, central banks etc

The financial promotion restriction does not apply to any communication which—

(a) is a non-real time communication or a solicited real time communication;
(b) is communicated by and relates only to controlled investments issued, or to be issued, by—
  (i) any government;
  (ii) any local authority (in the United Kingdom or elsewhere);
  (iii) any international organisation;
  (iv) the Bank of England;
  (v) the European Central Bank;
  (vi) the central bank of any country or territory outside the United Kingdom.

[4757]

35 Industrial and provident societies

The financial promotion restriction does not apply to any communication which—

(a) is a non-real time communication or a solicited real time communication;
(b) is communicated by an industrial and provident society; and
(c) relates only to an investment falling within paragraph 15 of Schedule 1 issued, or to be issued, by the society in question.

[4758]

36 Nationals of EEA States other than United Kingdom

The financial promotion restriction does not apply to any communication which—

(a) is a non-real time communication or a solicited real time communication;
(b) is communicated by a national of an EEA State other than the United Kingdom in the course of any controlled activity lawfully carried on by him in that State; and
(c) conforms with any rules made by the Authority under section 145 of the Act (financial promotion rules) which are relevant to a communication of that kind.

[4759]

37 Financial markets

(1) The financial promotion restriction does not apply to any communication—

(a) which is a non-real time communication or a solicited real time communication;
(b) which is communicated by a relevant market; and
(c) to which paragraph (2) or (3) applies.

(2) This paragraph applies to a communication if—

(a) it relates only to facilities provided by the market; and
(b) it does not identify (directly or indirectly)—
  (i) any particular investment issued, or to be issued, by or available from an identified person as one that may be traded or dealt in on the market; or
  (ii) any particular person as a person through whom transactions on the market may be effected.

(3) This paragraph applies to a communication if—

(a) it relates only to a particular investment falling within paragraph 21, 22 or 23 of Schedule 1; and

(b) it identifies the investment as one that may be traded or dealt in on the market.

(4) "Relevant market" means a market which—

(a) meets the criteria specified in Part I of Schedule 3; or

(b) is specified in, or is established under the rules of an exchange specified in, Part II, III or IV of that Schedule.

[4760]

38 Persons in the business of placing promotional material

The financial promotion restriction does not apply to any communication which is made to a person whose business it is to place, or arrange for the placing of, promotional material provided that it is communicated so that he can place or arrange for placing it.

[4761]

39 Joint enterprises

(1) The financial promotion restriction does not apply to any communication which is made or directed by a participator in a joint enterprise to or at another participator in the same joint enterprise in connection with, or for the purposes of, that enterprise.

(2) "Joint enterprise" means an enterprise into which two or more persons ("the participators") enter for commercial purposes related to a business or businesses (other than the business of engaging in a controlled activity) carried on by them; and, where a participator is a member of a group, each other member of the group is also to be regarded as a participator in the enterprise.

(3) "Participator" includes potential participator.

[4762]

40 Participants in certain recognised collective investment schemes

The financial promotion restriction does not apply to any non-real time communication or solicited real time communication which is made—

(a) by a person who is the operator of a scheme recognised under section 270 or 272 of the Act; and

(b) to persons in the United Kingdom who are participants in any such recognised scheme operated by the person making the communication,

and which relates only to such recognised schemes as are operated by that person or to units in such schemes.

[4763]

41 Bearer instruments: promotions required or permitted by market rules

(1) The financial promotion restriction does not apply to any communication which—

(a) is a non-real time communication or a solicited real time communication;

(b) is communicated by a body corporate ("A") that is not an open-ended investment company;

(c) is made to or may reasonably be regarded as directed at persons entitled to bearer instruments issued by A, a parent undertaking of A or a subsidiary undertaking of A; and

(d) is required or permitted by the rules of a relevant market to be communicated to holders of instruments of a class which consists of or includes the bearer instruments in question.

(2) "Bearer instrument" means any of the following investments title to which is capable of being transferred by delivery—

(a) any investment falling within paragraph 14 or 15 of Schedule 1;

(b) any investment falling within paragraph 17 or 18 of that Schedule which confers rights in respect of an investment falling within paragraph 14 or 15.

(3) For the purposes of this article, a bearer instrument falling within paragraph 17 or 18 of Schedule 1 is treated as issued by the person ("P") who issued the investment in respect of which the bearer instrument confers rights if it is issued by—

(a) an undertaking in the same group as P; or

(b) a person acting on behalf of, or pursuant to arrangements made with, P.

(4) "Relevant market", in relation to instruments of any particular class, means any market on which instruments of that class can be traded or dealt in and which—

(a) meets the criteria specified in Part I of Schedule 3; or

(b) is specified in, or established under the rules of an exchange specified in, Part II or III of that Schedule.

[4764]

42 Bearer instruments: promotions to existing holders

(1) The financial promotion restriction does not apply to any communication which—

(a) is a non-real time communication or a solicited real time communication;

(b) is communicated by a body corporate ("A") that is not an open-ended investment company;

(c) is made to or may reasonably be regarded as directed at persons entitled to bearer instruments issued by A, a parent undertaking of A or a subsidiary undertaking of A;

(d) relates only to instruments of a class which consists of or includes either the bearer instruments to which the communication relates or instruments in respect of which those bearer instruments confer rights; and

(e) is capable of being accepted or acted on only by persons who are entitled to instruments (whether or not bearer instruments) issued by A, a parent undertaking of A or a subsidiary undertaking of A.

(2) "Bearer instruments" has the meaning given by article 41.

(3) For the purposes of this article, an instrument falling within paragraph 17 or 18 of Schedule 1 is treated as issued by the person ("P") who issued the investment in respect of which the bearer instrument confers rights if it is issued by—

(a) an undertaking in the same group as P; or

(b) a person acting on behalf of, or pursuant to arrangements made with, P.

[4765]

43 Members and creditors of certain bodies corporate

(1) The financial promotion restriction does not apply to any non-real time communication or solicited real time communication which is communicated—

(a) by, or on behalf of, a body corporate ("A") that is not an open-ended investment company; and

(b) to persons whom the person making or directing the communication believes on reasonable grounds to be persons to whom paragraph (2) applies,

and which relates only to a relevant investment which is issued or to be issued by A, or by an undertaking ("U") in the same group as A that is not an open-ended investment company.

(2) This paragraph applies to—

(a) a creditor or member of A or of U;

(b) a person who is entitled to a relevant investment which is issued, or to be issued, by A or by U;

(c) a person who is entitled, whether conditionally or unconditionally, to become a member of A or of U but who has not yet done so;

(d) a person who is entitled, whether conditionally or unconditionally, to have transferred to him title to a relevant investment which is issued by A or by U but has not yet acquired title to the investment.

(3) "Relevant investment" means—

(a) an investment falling within paragraph 14 or 15 of Schedule 1;

(b) an investment falling within paragraph 17 or 18 of that Schedule so far as relating to any investments within sub-paragraph (a).

(4) For the purposes of this article, an investment falling within paragraph 17 or 18 of Schedule 1 is treated as issued by the person ("P") who issued the investment in respect of which the instrument confers rights if it is issued by—

(a) an undertaking in the same group as P; or

(b) a person acting on behalf of, or pursuant to arrangements made with, P.

[4766]

44 Members and creditors of open-ended investment companies

(1) The financial promotion restriction does not apply to any communication which—

(a) is a non-real time communication or a solicited real time communication;
(b) is communicated by, or on behalf of, a body corporate ("A") that is an open-ended investment company;
(c) is communicated to persons whom the person making or directing the communication believes on reasonable grounds to be persons to whom paragraph (2) applies; and
(d) relates only to an investment falling within paragraph 15, 17 or 19 of Schedule 1 which is issued, or to be issued, by A.

(2) This paragraph applies to—
(a) a creditor or member of A;
(b) a person who is entitled to an investment falling within paragraph 15, 17 or 19 of Schedule 1 which is issued, or to be issued, by A;
(c) a person who is entitled, whether conditionally or unconditionally, to become a member of A but who has not yet done so;
(d) a person who is entitled, whether conditionally or unconditionally, to have transferred to him title to an investment falling within paragraph 15, 17 or 19 of Schedule 1 which is issued by A but has not yet acquired title to the investment.

(3) For the purposes of this article, an investment falling within paragraph 17 of Schedule 1 is treated as issued by the person ("P") who issued the investment in respect of which the instrument confers rights if it is issued by—
(a) an undertaking in the same group as P; or
(b) a person acting on behalf of, or pursuant to arrangements made with, P.

[4767]

45 Group companies

The financial promotion restriction does not apply to any communication made by one body corporate in a group to another body corporate in the same group.

[4768]

46 Qualifying credit to bodies corporate

The financial promotion restriction does not apply to any communication which relates to a controlled activity falling within paragraph 10, 10A or 10B of Schedule 1 (or within paragraph 11 so far as it relates to that activity) if the communication is—
(a) made to or directed at bodies corporate only; or
(b) accompanied by an indication that the qualifying credit to which it relates is only available to bodies corporate.

[4769]

47 Persons in the business of disseminating information

(1) The financial promotion restriction does not apply to any communication which is made only to recipients whom the person making the communication believes on reasonable grounds to be persons to whom paragraph (2) applies.

(2) This paragraph applies to—
(a) a person who receives the communication in the course of a business which involves the dissemination through a publication of information concerning controlled activities;
(b) a person whilst acting in the capacity of director, officer or employee of a person falling within sub-paragraph (a) being a person whose responsibilities when acting in that capacity involve him in the business referred to in that sub-paragraph;
(c) any person to whom the communication may otherwise lawfully be made.

[4770]

48 Certified high net worth individuals

(1) If the requirements of paragraphs (4) and (7) are met, the financial promotion restriction does not apply to any communication which—
(a) is a non-real time communication or a solicited real time communication;
(b) is made to an individual whom the person making the communication believes on reasonable grounds to be a certified high net worth individual, and
(c) relates only to one or more investments falling within paragraph (8).

(2) "Certified high net worth individual" means an individual who has signed, within the period of twelve months ending with the day on which the communication is made, a statement complying with Part I of Schedule 5.

(3) The validity of a statement signed for the purposes of paragraph (2) is not affected by a defect in the form or wording of the statement, provided that the defect does not alter the statement's meaning and that the words shown in bold type in Part I of Schedule 5 are so shown in the statement.

(4) The requirements of this paragraph are that either the communication is accompanied by the giving of a warning in accordance with paragraphs (5) and (6) or where, because of the nature of the communication, this is not reasonably practicable,—

(a) a warning in accordance with paragraph (5) is given to the recipient orally at the beginning of the communication together with an indication that he will receive the warning in legible form and that, before receipt of that warning, he should consider carefully any decision to engage in investment activity to which the communication relates; and

(b) a warning in accordance with paragraphs (5) and (6) (d) to (h) is sent to the recipient of the communication within two business days of the day on which the communication is made.

(5) The warning must be in the following terms—

"The content of this promotion has not been approved by an authorised person within the meaning of the Financial Services and Markets Act 2000. Reliance on this promotion for the purpose of engaging in any investment activity may expose an individual to a significant risk of losing all of the property or other assets invested.".

But where a warning is sent pursuant to paragraph (4)(b), for the words "this promotion" in both places where they occur there must be substituted wording which clearly identifies the promotion which is the subject of the warning.

(6) The warning must—

(a) be given at the beginning of the communication;

(b) precede any other written or pictorial matter;

(c) be in a font size consistent with the text forming the remainder of the communication;

(d) be indelible;

(e) be legible;

(f) be printed in black, bold type;

(g) be surrounded by a black border which does not interfere with the text of the warning; and

(h) not be hidden, obscured or interrupted by any other written or pictorial matter.

(7) The requirements of this paragraph are that the communication is accompanied by an indication—

(a) that it is exempt from the general restriction (in section 21 of the Act) on the communication of invitations or inducements to engage in investment activity on the ground that it is made to a certified high net worth individual;

(b) of the requirements that must be met for an individual to qualify as a certified high net worth individual; and

(c) that any individual who is in any doubt about the investment to which the communication relates should consult an authorised person specialising in advising on investments of the kind in question.

(8) An investment falls within this paragraph if—

(a) it is an investment falling within paragraph 14 of Schedule 1 being stock or shares in an unlisted company;

(b) it is an investment falling within paragraph 15 of Schedule 1 being an investment acknowledging the indebtedness of an unlisted company;

(c) it is an investment falling within paragraph 17 or 18 of Schedule 1 conferring entitlement or rights with respect to investments falling within sub-paragraph (a) or (b);

(d) it comprises units in a collective investment scheme being a scheme which invests wholly or predominantly in investments falling within sub-paragraph (a) or (b);

(e) it is an investment falling within paragraph 21 of Schedule 1 being an option to acquire or dispose of an investment falling within sub-paragraph (a), (b) or (c);

(f) it is an investment falling within paragraph 22 of Schedule 1 being rights under a contract for the sale of an investment falling within sub-paragraph (a), (b) or (c);

(g) it is an investment falling within paragraph 23 of Schedule 1 being a contract relating to, or to fluctuations in value or price of, an investment falling within sub-paragraph (a), (b) or (c),

provided in each case that it is an investment under the terms of which the investor cannot incur a liability or obligation to pay or contribute more than he commits by way of investment.

(9) "Business day" means any day except a Saturday, a Sunday, Christmas Day, Good Friday or a day which is a bank holiday under the Banking and Financial Dealings Act 1971 in any part of the United Kingdom.

[4771]

49 High net worth companies, unincorporated associations etc

(1) The financial promotion restriction does not apply to any communication which—

(a) is made only to recipients whom the person making the communication believes on reasonable grounds to be persons to whom paragraph (2) applies; or

(b) may reasonably be regarded as directed only at persons to whom paragraph (2) applies.

(2) This paragraph applies to—

(a) any body corporate which has, or which is a member of the same group as an undertaking which has, a called-up share capital or net assets of not less than—

(i) if the body corporate has more than 20 members or is a subsidiary undertaking of an undertaking which has more than 20 members, £500,000;

(ii) otherwise, £5 million;

(b) any unincorporated association or partnership which has net assets of not less than £5 million;

(c) the trustee of a high value trust;

(d) any person ("A") whilst acting in the capacity of director, officer or employee of a person ("B") falling within any of sub-paragraphs (a) to (c) where A's responsibilities, when acting in that capacity, involve him in B's engaging in investment activity;

(e) any person to whom the communication may otherwise lawfully be made.

(3) For the purposes of paragraph (1)(b)—

(a) if all the conditions set out in paragraph (4)(a) to (c) are met, the communication is to be regarded as directed at persons to whom paragraph (2) applies;

(b) in any other case in which one or more of those conditions are met, that fact is to be taken into account in determining whether the communication is directed at persons to whom paragraph (2) applies (but a communication may still be regarded as so directed even if none of the conditions in paragraph (4) is met).

(4) The conditions are that—

(a) the communication includes an indication of the description of persons to whom it is directed and an indication of the fact that the controlled investment or controlled activity to which it relates is available only to such persons;

(b) the communication includes an indication that persons of any other description should not act upon it;

(c) there are in place proper systems and procedures to prevent recipients other than persons to whom paragraph (2) applies engaging in the investment activity to which the communication relates with the person directing the communication, a close relative of his or a member of the same group.

(5) "Called-up share capital" has the meaning given in the 1985 Act or in the 1986 Order.

(6) "High value trust" means a trust where the aggregate value of the cash and investments which form part of the trust's assets (before deducting the amount of its liabilities)—

(a) is £10 million or more; or

(b) has been £10 million or more at anytime during the year immediately preceding the date on which the communication in question was first made or directed.

(7) "Net assets" has the meaning given by section 264 of the 1985 Act or the equivalent provision of the 1986 Order.

[4772]

PART IV STATUTORY INSTRUMENTS

50 Sophisticated investors

(1) "Certified sophisticated investor", in relation to any description of investment, means a person—

(a) who has a current certificate in writing or other legible form signed by an authorised person to the effect that he is sufficiently knowledgeable to understand the risks associated with that description of investment; and

(b) who has signed, within the period of twelve months ending with the day on which the communication is made, a statement in the following terms:

"I make this statement so that I am able to receive promotions which are exempt from the restrictions on financial promotion in the Financial Services and Markets Act 2000. The exemption relates to certified sophisticated investors and I declare that I qualify as such in relation to investments of the following kind [list them]. I accept that the contents of promotions and other material that I receive may not have been approved by an authorised person and that their content may not therefore be subject to controls which would apply if the promotion were made or approved by an authorised person. I am aware that it is open to me to seek advice from someone who specialises in advising on this kind of investment.".

(1A) The validity of a statement signed in accordance with paragraph (1)(b) is not affected by a defect in the wording of the statement, provided that the defect does not alter the statement's meaning.

(2) If the requirements of paragraph (3) are met, the financial promotion restriction does not apply to any communication which—

(a) is made to a certified sophisticated investor;

(b) does not invite or induce the recipient to engage in investment activity with the person who has signed the certificate referred to in paragraph (1)(a); and

(c) relates only to a description of investment in respect of which that investor is certified.

(3) The requirements of this paragraph are that the communication is accompanied by an indication—

(a) that it is exempt from the general restriction (in section 21 of the Act) on the communication of invitations or inducements to engage in investment activity on the ground that it is made to a certified sophisticated investor;

(b) of the requirements that must be met for a person to qualify as a certified sophisticated investor;

(c) that the content of the communication has not been approved by an authorised person and that such approval is, unless this exemption or any other exemption applies, required by section 21 of the Act;

(d) that reliance on the communication for the purpose of engaging in any investment activity may expose the individual to a significant risk of losing all of the property invested or of incurring additional liability;

(e) that any person who is in any doubt about the investment to which the communication relates should consult an authorised person specialising in advising on investments of the kind in question.

(4) For the purposes of paragraph (1)(a), a certificate is current if it is signed and dated not more than three years before the date on which the communication is made.

[4773]

50A Self-certified sophisticated investors

(1) "Self-certified sophisticated investor" means an individual who has signed within the period of twelve months ending with the day on which the communication is made, a statement complying with Part II of Schedule 5.

(2) The validity of a statement signed for the purposes of paragraph (1) is not affected by a defect in the form or wording of the statement, provided that the defect does not alter the statement's meaning and that the words shown in bold type in Part II of Schedule 5 are so shown in the statement.

(3) If the requirements of paragraphs (4) and (7) are met, the financial promotion restriction does not apply to any communication which—

(a) is made to an individual whom the person making the communication believes on reasonable grounds to be a self-certified sophisticated investor; and

(b) relates only to one or more investments falling within paragraph (8).

(4) The requirements of this paragraph are that either the communication is accompanied by the giving of a warning in accordance with paragraphs (5) and (6) or where, because of the nature of the communication this is not reasonably practicable—

(a) a warning in accordance with paragraph (5) is given to the recipient orally at the beginning of the communication together with an indication that he will receive the warning in legible form and that, before receipt of that warning, he should consider carefully any decision to engage in investment activity to which the communication relates; and

(b) a warning in accordance with paragraphs (5) and (6) (d) to (h) is sent to the recipient of the communication within two business days of the day on which the communication is made.

(5) The warning must be in the following terms—

"The content of this promotion has not been approved by an authorised person within the meaning of the Financial Services and Markets Act 2000. Reliance on this promotion for the purpose of engaging in any investment activity may expose an individual to a significant risk of losing all of the property or other assets invested.".

But where a warning is sent pursuant to paragraph (4)(b), for the words "this promotion" in both places where they occur there must be substituted wording which clearly identifies the promotion which is the subject of the warning.

(6) The warning must—

(a) be given at the beginning of the communication;

(b) precede any other written or pictorial matter;

(c) be in a font size consistent with the text forming the remainder of the communication;

(d) be indelible;

(e) be legible;

(f) be printed in black, bold type;

(g) be surrounded by a black border which does not interfere with the text of the warning; and

(h) not be hidden, obscured or interrupted by any other written or pictorial matter.

(7) The requirements of this paragraph are that the communication is accompanied by an indication—

(a) that it is exempt from the general restriction (in section 21 of the Act) on the communication of invitations or inducements to engage in investment activity on the ground that it is made to a self-certified sophisticated investor;

(b) of the requirements that must be met for an individual to qualify as a self-certified sophisticated investor;

(c) that any individual who is in any doubt about the investment to which the communication relates should consult an authorised person specialising in advising on investments of the kind in question.

(8) An investment falls within this paragraph if—

(a) it is an investment falling within paragraph 14 of Schedule 1 being stock or shares in an unlisted company;

(b) it is an investment falling within paragraph 15 of Schedule l being an investment acknowledging the indebtedness of an unlisted company;

(c) it is an investment falling within paragraph 17 or 18 of Schedule 1 conferring entitlement or rights with respect to investments falling within sub-paragraph (a) or (b);

(d) it comprises units in a collective investment scheme being a scheme which invests wholly or predominantly in investments falling within sub-paragraph (a) or (b);

(e) it is an investment falling within paragraph 21 of Schedule 1 being an option to acquire or dispose of an investment falling within sub-paragraph (a), (b) or (c);

(f) it is an investment falling within paragraph 22 of Schedule 1 being rights under a contract for the sale of an investment falling within sub-paragraph (a), (b) or (c);

(g) it is an investment falling within paragraph 23 of Schedule 1 being a contract relating to, or to fluctuations in value or price of, an investment falling within sub-paragraph (a), (b) or (c),

provided in each case that it is an investment under the terms of which the investor cannot incur a liability or obligation to pay or contribute more than he commits by way of investment.

(9) "Business day" means any day except a Saturday, a Sunday, Christmas Day, Good Friday or a day which is a bank holiday under the Banking and Financial Dealings Act 1971 in any part of the United Kingdom.

[4774]

51 Associations of high net worth or sophisticated investors

The financial promotion restriction does not apply to any non-real time communication or solicited real time communication which—

(a) is made to an association, or to a member of an association, the membership of which the person making the communication believes on reasonable grounds comprises wholly or predominantly persons who are—

(i) certified or self-certified high net worth individuals within the meaning of article 48;

(ii) high net worth persons falling within article 49(2)(a) to (d);

(iii) certified or self-certified sophisticated investors within the meaning of article 50 or 50A; and

(b) relates only to an investment under the terms of which a person cannot incur a liability or obligation to pay or contribute more than he commits by way of investment.

[4775]

52 Common interest group of a company

(1) "Common interest group", in relation to a company, means an identified group of persons who at the time the communication is made might reasonably be regarded as having an existing and common interest with each other and that company in—

(a) the affairs of the company; and

(b) what is done with the proceeds arising from any investment to which the communication relates.

(2) If the requirements of paragraphs (3) and either (4) or (5) are met, the financial promotion restriction does not apply to any communication which—

(a) is a non-real time communication or a solicited real time communication;

(b) is made only to persons who are members of a common interest group of a company, or may reasonably be regarded as directed only at such persons; and

(c) relates to investments falling within paragraph 14 or 15 of Schedule 1 which are issued, or to be issued, by that company.

(3) The requirements of this paragraph are that the communication is accompanied by an indication—

(a) that the directors of the company (or its promoters named in the communication) have taken all reasonable care to ensure that every statement of fact or opinion included in the communication is true and not misleading given the form and context in which it appears;

(b) that the directors of the company (or its promoters named in the communication) have not limited their liability with respect to the communication; and

(c) that any person who is in any doubt about the investment to which the communication relates should consult an authorised person specialising in advising on investments of the kind in question.

(4) The requirements of this paragraph are that the communication is accompanied by an indication—

(a) that the directors of the company (or its promoters named in the communication) have taken all reasonable care to ensure that any person belonging to the common interest group (and his professional advisers) can have access, at all reasonable times, to all the information that he or they would reasonably require, and reasonably expect to find, for the purpose of making an informed assessment of the assets and liabilities, financial position, profits and losses and prospects of the company and of the rights attaching to the investments in question; and

(b) describing the means by which such information can be accessed.

(5) The requirements of this paragraph are that the communication is accompanied by an indication that any person considering subscribing for the investments in question should regard any subscription as made primarily to assist the furtherance of the company's objectives (other than any purely financial objectives) and only secondarily, if at all, as an investment.

(6) For the purposes of paragraph (2)(b)—

(a) if all the conditions set out in paragraph (7) are met, the communication is to be regarded as directed at persons who are members of the common interest group;

(b) in any other case in which one or more of those conditions are met, that fact shall be taken into account in determining whether the communication is directed at persons who are members of the common interest group (but a communication may still be regarded as directed only at such persons even if none of the conditions in paragraph (7) is met).

(7) The conditions are that—

(a) the communication is accompanied by an indication that it is directed at persons who are members of the common interest group and that any investment or activity to which it relates is available only to such persons;

(b) the communication is accompanied by an indication that it must not be acted upon by persons who are not members of the common interest group;

(c) there are in place proper systems and procedures to prevent recipients other than members of the common interest group engaging in the investment activity to which the communication relates with the person directing the communication, a close relative of his or a member of the same group.

(8) Persons are not to be regarded as having an interest of the kind described in paragraph (1) if the only reason why they would be so regarded is that—

(a) they will have such an interest if they become members or creditors of the company;

(b) they all carry on a particular trade or profession; or

(c) they are persons with whom the company has an existing business relationship, whether by being its clients, customers, contractors, suppliers or otherwise.

[4776]

53 Settlors, trustees and personal representatives

The financial promotion restriction does not apply to any communication which is made between—

(a) a person when acting as a settlor or grantor of a trust, a trustee or a personal representative; and

(b) a trustee of the trust, a fellow trustee or a fellow personal representative (as the case may be),

if the communication is made for the purposes of the trust or estate.

[4777]

54 Beneficiaries of trust, will or intestacy

The financial promotion restriction does not apply to any communication which is made—

(a) between a person when acting as a settlor or grantor of a trust, trustee or personal representative and a beneficiary under the trust, will or intestacy; or

(b) between a beneficiary under a trust, will or intestacy and another beneficiary under the same trust, will or intestacy,

if the communication relates to the management or distribution of that trust fund or estate.

[4778]

55 Communications by members of professions

(1) The financial promotion restriction does not apply to a real time communication (whether solicited or unsolicited) which—

(a) is made by a person ("P") who carries on a regulated activity to which the general prohibition does not apply by virtue of section 327 of the Act; and

(b) is made to a recipient who has, prior to the communication being made, engaged P to provide professional services,

where the controlled activity to which the communication relates is an excluded activity which would be undertaken by P for the purposes of, and incidental to, the provision by him of professional services to or at the request of the recipient.

(2) "Professional services" has the meaning given in section 327 of the Act.

(3) An "excluded activity" is an activity to which the general prohibition would apply but for the application of—

(a) section 327 of the Act; or
(b) article 67 of the Regulated Activities Order.

[4779]

55A Non-real time communication by members of professions

(1) The financial promotion restriction does not apply to a non-real time communication which is—
(a) made by a person ("P") who carries on Part XX activities; and
(b) limited to what is required or permitted by paragraphs (2) and (3).

(2) The communication must be in the following terms—

"This [firm/company] is not authorised under the Financial Services and Markets Act 2000 but we are able in certain circumstances to offer a limited range of investment services to clients because we are members of [relevant designated professional body]. We can provide these investment services if they are an incidental part of the professional services we have been engaged to provide."

(3) The communication may in addition set out the Part XX activities which P is able to offer to his clients, provided it is clear that these are the investment services to which the statement in paragraph (2) relates.

(4) The validity of a communication made in accordance with paragraph (2) is not affected by a defect in the wording of it provided that the defect does not alter the communication's meaning.

(5) "Part XX activities" means the regulated activities to which the general prohibition does not apply when they are carried on by P by virtue of section 327 of the Act.

[4780]

56 Remedy following report by Parliamentary Commissioner for Administration

The financial promotion restriction does not apply to any communication made or directed by a person for the purpose of enabling any injustice, stated by the Parliamentary Commissioner for Administration in a report under section 10 of the Parliamentary Commissioner Act 1967 to have occurred, to be remedied with respect to the recipient.

[4781]

57 Persons placing promotional material in particular publications

The financial promotion restriction does not apply to any communication received by a person who receives the publication in which the communication is contained because he has himself placed an advertisement in that publication.

[4782]

58 Acquisition of interest in premises run by management companies

(1) "Management company" means a company established for the purpose of—
(a) managing the common parts or fabric of premises used for residential or business purposes; or
(b) supplying services to such premises.

(2) The financial promotion restriction does not apply to any non-real time communication or solicited real time communication if it relates to an investment falling within paragraph 14 of Schedule 1 which—
(a) is issued, or to be issued, by a management company; and
(b) is to be acquired by any person in connection with the acquisition of an interest in the premises in question.

[4783]

59 Annual accounts and directors' report

(1) If the requirements in paragraphs (2) to (5) are met, the financial promotion restriction does not apply to any communication by a body corporate (other than an open-ended investment company) which—
(a) consists of, or is accompanied by, the whole or any part of the annual accounts of a body corporate (other than an open-ended investment company); or
(b) is accompanied by any report which is prepared and approved by the directors of such a body corporate under—

(i) sections 234 and 234A of the 1985 Act;
(ii) the corresponding Northern Ireland enactment; or
(iii) the law of an EEA State other than the United Kingdom which corresponds to the provisions mentioned in paragraph (i) or (ii).

(2) The requirements of this paragraph are that the communication—
(a) does not contain any invitation to persons to underwrite, subscribe for, or otherwise acquire or dispose of, a controlled investment; and
(b) does not advise persons to engage in any of the activities within sub-paragraph (a).

(3) The requirements of this paragraph are that the communication does not contain any invitation to persons to—
(a) effect any transaction with the body corporate (or with any named person) in the course of that body's (or person's) carrying on of any activity falling within any of paragraphs 3 to 11 of Schedule 1; or
(b) make use of any services provided by that body corporate (or by any named person) in the course of carrying on such activity.

(4) The requirements of this paragraph are that the communication does not contain any inducement relating to an investment other than one issued, or to be issued, by the body corporate (or another body corporate in the same group) which falls within—
(a) paragraph 14 or 15 of Schedule 1; or
(b) paragraph 17 or 18 of that Schedule, so far as relating to any investments within sub-paragraph (a).

(5) The requirements of this paragraph are that the communication does not contain any reference to—
(a) the price at which investments issued by the body corporate have in the past been bought or sold; or
(b) the yield on such investments,

unless it is also accompanied by an indication that past performance cannot be relied on as a guide to future performance.

(6) For the purposes of paragraph (5)(b), a reference, in relation to an investment, to earnings, dividend or nominal rate of interest payable shall not be taken to be a reference to the yield on the investment.

(7) "Annual accounts" means—
(a) accounts produced by virtue of Part VII of the 1985 Act (or of that Part as applied by virtue of any other enactment);
(b) accounts produced by virtue of the corresponding Northern Ireland enactment (or of that enactment as applied by virtue of any other enactment);
(c) a summary financial statement prepared under section 251 of the 1985 Act;
(d) accounts delivered to the registrar under Chapter II of Part XXIII of the 1985 Act;
(e) accounts which are produced or published by virtue of the law of an EEA State other than the United Kingdom and which correspond to accounts within any of sub-paragraphs (a) to (d).

[4784]

60 Participation in employee share schemes

(1) The financial promotion restriction does not apply to any communication by a person ("C"), a member of the same group as C or a relevant trustee where the communication is for the purposes of an employee share scheme and relates to any of the following investments issued, or to be issued, by C—
(a) investments falling within paragraph 14 or 15 of Schedule 1;
(b) investments falling within paragraph 17 or 18 so far as relating to any investments within sub-paragraph (a); or
(c) investments falling within paragraph 21 or 27 so far as relating to any investments within sub-paragraph (a) or (b).

(2) "Employee share scheme", in relation to any investments issued by C, means arrangements made or to be made by C or by a person in the same group as C to enable or facilitate—
(a) transactions in the investments specified in paragraphs (1)(a) or (b) between or for the benefit of—
(i) the bona fide employees or former employees of C or of another member of the same group as C;

(ii) the wives, husbands, widows, widowers[, civil partners, surviving civil partners] or children or step-children under the age of eighteen of such employees or former employees; or

(b) the holding of those investments by, or for the benefit of, such persons.

(3) "Relevant trustee" means a person who, in pursuance of an actual or proposed employee share scheme, holds as trustee or will hold as trustee investments issued by C.

[4785]

NOTES

Para (2): words in square brackets in sub-para (a)(ii) inserted by the Financial Services and Markets Act 2000 (Financial Promotion) (Amendment) Order 2005, SI 2005/3392, art 2(1), (4), as from 21 December 2005.

Step-children, etc: as to the meaning of this, and related expressions, see the Civil Partnership Act 2004, s 246 (as applied to this Order by the Civil Partnership Act 2004 (Relationships Arising Through Civil Partnership) Order 2005, SI 2005/3137, art 3, Schedule).

61 Sale of goods and supply of services

(1) In this article—

"supplier" means a person whose main business is to sell goods or supply services and not to carry on controlled activities falling within any of paragraphs 3 to 7 of Schedule 1 and, where the supplier is a member of a group, also means any other member of that group;

"customer" means a person, other than an individual, to whom a supplier sells goods or supplies services, or agrees to do so, and, where the customer is a member of a group, also means any other member of that group;

"a related sale or supply" means a sale of goods or supply of services to the customer otherwise than by the supplier, but for or in connection with the same purpose as the sale or supply mentioned above.

(2) The financial promotion restriction does not apply to any non-real time communication or any solicited real time communication made by a supplier to a customer of his for the purposes of, or in connection with, the sale of goods or supply of services or a related sale or supply.

(3) But the exemption in paragraph (2) does not apply if the communication relates to—

(a) a qualifying contract of insurance or units in a collective investment scheme; or

(b) investments falling within paragraph 27 of Schedule 1 so far as relating to investments within paragraph (a).

[4786]

62 Sale of body corporate

(1) The financial promotion restriction does not apply to any communication by, or on behalf of, a body corporate, a partnership, a single individual or a group of connected individuals which relates to a transaction falling within paragraph (2).

(2) A transaction falls within this paragraph if—

(a) it is one to acquire or dispose of shares in a body corporate other than an open-ended investment company, or is entered into for the purposes of such an acquisition or disposal; and

(b) either—

(i) the conditions set out in paragraph (3) are met; or

(ii) those conditions are not met, but the object of the transaction may nevertheless reasonably be regarded as being the acquisition of day to day control of the affairs of the body corporate.

(3) The conditions mentioned in paragraph (2)(b) are that—

(a) the shares consist of or include 50 per cent or more of the voting shares in the body corporate; or

(b) the shares, together with any already held by the person acquiring them, consist of or include at least that percentage of such shares; and

(c) in either case, the acquisition or disposal is, or is to be, between parties each of whom is a body corporate, a partnership, a single individual or a group of connected individuals.

(4) "A group of connected individuals" means—

(a) in relation to a party disposing of shares in a body corporate, a single group of persons each of whom is—
  (i) a director or manager of the body corporate;
  (ii) a close relative of any such director or manager; or
  (iii) a person acting as trustee for, or nominee of, any person falling within paragraph (i) or (ii); and

(b) in relation to a party acquiring shares in a body corporate, a single group of persons each of whom is—
  (i) a person who is or is to be a director or manager of the body corporate;
  (ii) a close relative of any such person; or
  (iii) a person acting as trustee for or nominee of any person falling within paragraph (i) or (ii).

(5) "Voting shares" in relation to a body corporate, means shares carrying voting rights attributable to share capital which are exercisable in all circumstances at any general meeting of that body corporate.

[4787]

63 Takeovers of relevant unlisted companies: interpretation

(1) In this article and in articles 64, 65 and 66, a "relevant unlisted company", in relation to a takeover offer, means a company which is an unlisted company at the time that the offer is made and which has been an unlisted company throughout the period of ten years immediately preceding the date of the offer.

(2) In this article and in articles 64, 65 and 66, references to a takeover offer for a relevant unlisted company are references to an offer which meets the requirements of Part I of Schedule 4 and which is an offer—

(a) for all the shares in, or all the shares comprised in the equity or non-equity share capital of, a relevant unlisted company (other than any shares already held by or on behalf of the person making the offer); or

(b) for all the debentures of such a company (other than debentures already held by or on behalf of the person making the offer).

(3) Shares in or debentures of an unlisted company are to be regarded as being held by or on behalf of the person making the offer if the person who holds them, or on whose behalf they are held, has agreed that an offer should not be made in respect of them.

[4788]

64 Takeovers of relevant unlisted companies

(1) If the requirements of paragraphs (2) and (3) are met, the financial promotion restriction does not apply to any communication which is communicated in connection with a takeover offer for a relevant unlisted company.

(2) The requirements of this paragraph are that the communication is accompanied by the material listed in Part II of Schedule 4.

(3) The requirements of this paragraph are that the material listed in Part III of Schedule 4 is available at a place in the United Kingdom at all times during normal office hours for inspection free of charge.

[4789]

65 Takeovers of relevant unlisted companies: warrants etc

The financial promotion restriction does not apply to any communication which—

(a) is communicated at the same time as, or after, a takeover offer for a relevant unlisted company is made; and

(b) relates to investments falling within paragraph 17 or 18 of Schedule 1 so far as relating to the shares in or debentures of the unlisted company which are the subject of the offer.

[4790]

66 Takeovers of relevant unlisted companies: application forms

The financial promotion restriction does not apply to any communication made in connection with a takeover offer for a relevant unlisted company which is a form of application for—

(a) shares in or debentures of the unlisted company; or

(b) investments falling within paragraphs 17 or 18 of Schedule 1 so far as relating to the shares in or debentures of the company which are the subject of the offer.

[4791]

67 Promotions required or permitted by market rules

(1) The financial promotion restriction does not apply to any communication which—

(a) is a non-real time communication or a solicited real time communication;

(b) relates to an investment which falls within any of paragraphs 14 to 18 of Schedule 1 and which is permitted to be traded or dealt in on a relevant market; and

(c) is required or permitted to be communicated by—

(i) the rules of the relevant market;

(ii) a body which regulates the market; or

(iii) a body which regulates offers or issues of investments to be traded on such a market.

(2) "Relevant market" means a market which—

(a) meets the criteria specified in Part I of Schedule 3; or

(b) is specified in, or established under the rules of an exchange specified in, Part II or III of that Schedule.

[4792]

68 Promotions in connection with admission to certain EEA markets

(1) The financial promotion restriction does not apply to any communication—

(a) which is a non-real time communication or a solicited real time communication;

(b) which a relevant EEA market requires to be communicated before an investment can be admitted to trading on that market;

(c) which, if it were included in a prospectus issued in accordance with prospectus rules made under Part VI of the Act, would be required to be communicated by those rules; and

(d) which is not accompanied by any information other than information which is required or permitted to be published by the rules of that market.

(2) In this article "relevant EEA market" means any market on which investments can be traded or dealt in and which—

(a) meets the criteria specified in Part I of Schedule 3; or

(b) is specified in, or established under the rules of an exchange specified in, Part II of that Schedule.

[4793]

69 Promotions of securities already admitted to certain markets

(1) In this article—

"relevant investment" means any investment falling within—

(a) paragraph 14 or 15 of Schedule 1; or

(b) paragraph 17 or 18 of that Schedule so far as relating to any investment mentioned in sub-paragraph (a);

"relevant market" means any market on which investments can be traded and which—

(a) meets the criteria specified in Part I of Schedule 3; or

(b) is specified in, or established under, the rules of an exchange specified in, Part II or III of that Schedule.

(2) If the requirements of paragraph (3) are met, the financial promotion restriction does not apply to any communication which—

(a) is a non-real time communication or a solicited real time communication;

(b) is communicated by a body corporate ("A"), other than an open-ended investment company; and

(c) relates only to relevant investments issued, or to be issued, by A or by another body corporate in the same group,

if relevant investments issued by A or by any such body corporate are permitted to be traded on a relevant market.

(3) The requirements of this paragraph are that the communication—

(a) is not, and is not accompanied by, an invitation to engage in investment activity;

(b) is not, and is not accompanied by, an inducement relating to an investment other than one issued, or to be issued, by A (or another body corporate in the same group);
(c) is not, and is not accompanied by, an inducement relating to a relevant investment which refers to—
 (i) the price at which relevant investments have been bought or sold in the past, or
 (ii) the yield on such investments,

unless the inducement also contains an indication that past performance cannot be relied on as a guide to future performance.

(4) For the purposes of this article, an investment falling within paragraph 17 or 18 of Schedule 1 is treated as issued by the person ("P") who issued the investment in respect of which the investment confers rights if it is issued by—
(a) an undertaking in the same group as P; or
(b) a person acting on behalf of, or pursuant to, arrangements made with P.

(5) For the purposes of paragraph (3)(a), "engaging in investment activity" has the meaning given in section 21(8) of the Act; and for the purposes of paragraph (3)(c)(ii), a reference, in relation to an investment, to earnings, dividend or nominal rate of interest payable shall not be taken to be a reference to the yield on the investment.

[4794]

70 Promotions included in listing particulars etc

(1) The financial promotion restriction does not apply to any non-real time communication which is included in—
(a) listing particulars;
(b) supplementary listing particulars;
(c) a prospectus or supplementary prospectus approved in accordance with prospectus rules made under Part VI of the Act; or
(d) any other document required or permitted to be published by listing rules or prospectus rules under Part VI of the Act (except an advertisement within the meaning of the prospectus directive).

(2) In this article "listing particulars", "listing rules", "the prospectus directive" and "prospectus rules" have the meaning given by Part VI of the Act.

[4795]

71 Material relating to prospectus for public offer of unlisted securities

(1) The financial promotion restriction does not apply to any non-real time communication relating to a prospectus or supplementary prospectus where the only reason for considering it to be an invitation or inducement is that it does one or more of the following—
(a) it states the name and address of the person by whom the transferable securities to which the prospectus or supplementary prospectus relates are to be offered;
(b) it gives other details for contacting that person;
(c) it states the nature and the nominal value of the transferable securities to which the prospectus or supplementary prospectus relates, the number offered and the price at which they are offered;
(d) it states that a prospectus or supplementary prospectus is or will be available (and, if it is not yet available, when it is expected to be);
(e) it gives instructions for obtaining a copy of the prospectus or supplementary prospectus.

(2) In this article—
(a) "transferable securities" has the same meaning as in section 102A(3) of the Act;
(b) references to a prospectus or supplementary prospectus are references to a prospectus or supplementary prospectus which is published in accordance with prospectus rules made under Part VI of the Act.

[4796]

72 Pension products offered by employers

(1) If the requirements of paragraph (2) are met, the financial promotion restriction does not apply to any communication which is made by an employer to an employee in relation to a group personal pension scheme or a stakeholder pension scheme.

(2) The requirements of this paragraph are that—

(a) the employer will make a contribution to the group personal pension scheme or stakeholder pension scheme to which the communication relates in the event of the employee becoming a member of the scheme and the communication contains a statement informing the employee of this;

(b) the employer has not received, and will not receive, any direct financial benefit from the scheme;

(c) the employer notifies the employee in writing prior to the employee becoming a member of the scheme of the amount of the contribution that the employer will make to the scheme in respect of that employee; and

(d) in the case of a non-real time communication, the communication contains, or is accompanied by, a statement informing the employee of his right to seek advice from an authorised person or an appointed representative.

(3) For the purposes of paragraph (2)(b) "direct financial benefit" includes—

(a) any commission paid to the employer by the provider of the scheme; and

(b) any reduction in the amount of the premium payable by the employer in respect of any insurance policy issued to the employer by the provider of the scheme.

(4) In this article—

"group personal pension scheme" means arrangements administered on a group basis under a personal pension scheme and which are available to employees of the same employer or of employers within a group;

["personal pension scheme" means a scheme or arrangement which is not an occupational pension scheme or a stakeholder pension scheme and which is comprised in one or more instruments or agreements, having or capable of having effect so as to provide benefits to or in respect of people—

(a) on retirement,

(b) on having reached a particular age, or

(c) on termination of service in an employment.]

"stakeholder pension scheme" has the meaning given by section 1 of the Welfare Reform and Pensions Act 1999.

[4797]

NOTES

Para (4): definition "personal pension scheme" substituted by the Financial Services and Markets Act 2000 (Regulated Activities) (Amendment) Order 2006, SI 2006/1969, art 12(1), (2), as from 6 April 2007.

Commissioners of Inland Revenue: a reference to the Commissioners of Inland Revenue is now to be taken as a reference to the Commissioners for Her Majesty's Revenue and Customs; see the Commissioners for Revenue and Customs Act 2005, s 50(1), (7).

73 Advice centres

(1) If the requirements of paragraph (2) are met, the financial promotion restriction does not apply to any communication which is made by a person in the course of carrying out his duties as an adviser for, or employee of, an advice centre.

(2) The requirements of this paragraph are that the communication relates to—

(a) qualifying credit;

(b) rights under, or rights to or interests in rights under, qualifying contracts of insurance; …

(c) a child trust fund[;

(d) a regulated home reversion plan; or

(e) a regulated home purchase plan].

(3) In this article—

"adequate professional indemnity insurance", in relation to an advice centre, means insurance providing cover that is adequate having regard to—

(a) the claims record of the centre;

(b) the financial resources of the centre; and

(c) the right of clients of the centre to be compensated for loss arising from the negligent provision of financial advice;

"advice centre" means a body which—

(a) gives advice which is free and in respect of which the centre does not receive any fee, commission or other reward;

(b) provides debt advice as its principal financial services activity; and

(c) in the case of a body which is not part of a local authority, holds adequate professional indemnity insurance or a guarantee providing comparable cover;

"child trust fund" has the meaning given by section 1(2) of the Child Trust Funds Act 2004;

"local authority" has the meaning given in article 2 of the Financial Services and Markets Act 2000 (Exemption) Order 2001.

[4798]

NOTES

Para (2): word omitted from sub-para (b) revoked, and sub-paras (d), (e) inserted, by the Financial Services and Markets Act 2000 (Regulated Activities) (Amendment) (No 2) Order 2006, SI 2006/2383, art 35(1), (4), as from 6 April 2007 (for the full commencement details of SI 2006/2383, see art 1 of that Order at **[4820]**).

74 Revocation

The Orders specified in the first column of Schedule 6 are revoked to the extent specified in the third column of that Schedule.

[4799]

SCHEDULES

SCHEDULE 1

Article 4

PART I
CONTROLLED ACTIVITIES

1 Accepting deposits

Accepting deposits is a controlled activity if—

(a) money received by way of deposit is lent to others; or

(b) any other activity of the person accepting the deposit is financed wholly, or to a material extent, out of the capital of or interest on money received by way of deposit,

and the person accepting the deposit holds himself out as accepting deposits on a day to day basis.

2 Effecting or carrying out contracts of insurance

(1) Effecting a contract of insurance as principal is a controlled activity.

(2) Carrying out a contract of insurance as principal is a controlled activity.

(3) There is excluded from sub-paragraph (1) or (2) the effecting or carrying out of a contract of insurance of the kind described in article 12 of the Regulated Activities Order by a person who does not otherwise carry on an activity falling within those sub-paragraphs.

3 Dealing in securities and contractually based investments

(1) Buying, selling, subscribing for or underwriting securities or contractually based investments (other than investments of the kind specified by paragraph 25, or paragraph 27 so far as relevant to that paragraph) as principal or agent is a controlled activity.

(2) A person does not carry on the activity in sub-paragraph (1) by accepting an instrument creating or acknowledging indebtedness in respect of any loan, credit, guarantee or other similar financial accommodation or assurance which he has made, granted or provided.

(3) The reference in sub-paragraph (2) to a person accepting an instrument includes a reference to a person becoming a party to an instrument otherwise than as a debtor or a surety.

4 Arranging deals in investments

(1) Making arrangements for another person (whether as principal or agent) to buy, sell, subscribe for or underwrite a particular investment which is—

(a) a security;

(b) a contractually based investment; or

(c) an investment of the kind specified by paragraph 24, or paragraph 27 so far as relevant to that paragraph,

is a controlled activity.

(2) Making arrangements with a view to a person who participates in the arrangements buying, selling, subscribing for or underwriting investments falling within sub-paragraph (1)(a), (b) or (c) (whether as principal or agent) is a controlled activity.

(3) A person does not carry on an activity falling within paragraph (2) merely by providing means by which one party to a transaction (or potential transaction) is able to communicate with other such parties.

[4A Operating a multilateral trading facility

Operating a multilateral trading facility on which MiFID instruments are traded is a controlled activity.]

5 Managing investments

Managing assets belonging to another person, in circumstances involving the exercise of discretion, is a controlled activity if—

(a) the assets consist of or include any investment which is a security or a contractually based investment; or

(b) the arrangements for their management are such that the assets may consist of or include such investments, and either the assets have at any time since 29th April 1988 done so, or the arrangements have at any time (whether before or after that date) been held out as arrangements under which the assets would do so.

6 Safeguarding and administering investments

(1) The activity consisting of both—

(a) the safeguarding of assets belonging to another; and

(b) the administration of those assets,

or arranging for one or more other persons to carry on that activity, is a controlled activity if either the condition in paragraph (a) or (b) of sub-paragraph (2) is met.

(2) The condition is that—

(a) the assets consist of or include any investment which is a security or a contractually based investment; or

(b) the arrangements for their safeguarding and administration are such that the assets may consist of or include investments of the kind mentioned in sub-paragraph (a) and either the assets have at any time since 1st June 1997 done so, or the arrangements have at any time (whether before or after that date) been held out as ones under which such investments would be safeguarded and administered.

(3) For the purposes of this article—

(a) it is immaterial that title to the assets safeguarded and administered is held in uncertificated form;

(b) it is immaterial that the assets safeguarded and administered may be transferred to another person, subject to a commitment by the person safeguarding and administering them, or arranging for their safeguarding and administration, that they will be replaced by equivalent assets at some future date or when so requested by the person to whom they belong.

(4) For the purposes of this article, the following activities do not constitute the administration of assets—

(a) providing information as to the number of units or the value of any assets safeguarded;

(b) converting currency;

(c) receiving documents relating to an investment solely for the purpose of onward transmission to, from or at the direction of the person to whom the investment belongs.

7 Advising on investments

Advising a person is a controlled activity if the advice is—

(a) given to the person in his capacity as an investor or potential investor, or in his capacity as agent for an investor or a potential investor; and

(b) advice on the merits of his doing any of the following (whether as principal or agent)—
   (i) buying, selling, subscribing for or underwriting a particular investment which is a security or a contractually based investment; or
   (ii) exercising any right conferred by such an investment to buy, sell, subscribe for or underwrite such an investment.

8 Advising on syndicate participation at Lloyd's

Advising a person to become, or continue or cease to be, a member of a particular Lloyd's syndicate is a controlled activity.

9 Providing funeral plan contracts

(1) Entering as provider into a qualifying funeral plan contract is a controlled activity.

(2) A "qualifying funeral plan contract" is a contract under which—
   (a) a person ("the customer") makes one or more payments to another person ("the provider");
   (b) the provider undertakes to provide, or to secure that another person provides, a funeral in the United Kingdom for the customer (or some other person who is living at the date when the contract is entered into) on his death; and
   (c) the provider is a person who carries on the regulated activity specified in article 59 of the Regulated Activities Order.

10 Providing qualifying credit

(1) Providing qualifying credit is a controlled activity.

(2) "Qualifying credit" is a credit provided pursuant to an agreement under which—
   (a) the lender is a person who carries on the regulated activity specified in article 61 of the Regulated Activities Order; and
   (b) the obligation of the borrower to repay is secured (in whole or in part) on land.

(3) "Credit" includes a cash loan and any other form of financial accommodation.

10A Arranging qualifying credit etc

Making arrangements—
   (a) for another person to enter as borrower into an agreement for the provision of qualifying credit; or
   (b) for a borrower under a regulated mortgage contract, within the meaning of article 61(3) of the Regulated Activities Order, entered into after the coming into force of that article, to vary the terms of that contract in such a way as to vary his obligations under that contract,

is a controlled activity.

10B Advising on qualifying credit etc

(1) Advising a person is a controlled activity if the advice is—
   (a) given to the person in his capacity as a borrower or potential borrower; and
   (b) advice on the merits of his doing any of the following—
      (i) entering into an agreement for the provision of qualifying credit, or
      (ii) varying the terms of a regulated mortgage contract entered into by him after the coming into force of article 61 of the Regulated Activities Order in such a way as to vary his obligations under that contract.

(2) In this paragraph, "borrower" and "regulated mortgage contract" have the meaning given by article 61(3) of the Regulated Activities Order.

[10C Providing a regulated home reversion plan

Entering into a regulated home reversion plan as plan provider is a controlled activity.

10D Arranging a regulated home reversion plan

Making arrangements—
   (a) for another person to enter as reversion seller or plan provider into a regulated home reversion plan; or
   (b) for a reversion seller or a plan provider under a regulated home reversion plan,

entered into on or after 6th April 2007 by him, to vary the terms of that plan in such a way as to vary his obligations under that plan,

is a controlled activity.

10E Advising on a regulated home reversion plan

Advising a person is a controlled activity if the advice is—

(a) given to the person in his capacity as reversion seller, potential reversion seller, plan provider or potential plan provider; and

(b) advice on the merits of his doing either of the following—

(i) entering into a regulated home reversion plan, or

(ii) varying the terms of a regulated home reversion plan, entered into on or after 6th April 2007 by him, in such a way as to vary his obligations under that plan.

10F Providing a regulated home purchase plan

Entering into a regulated home purchase plan as home purchase provider is a controlled activity.

10G Arranging a regulated home purchase plan

Making arrangements—

(a) for another person to enter as home purchaser into a regulated home purchase plan; or

(b) for a home purchaser under a regulated home purchase plan, entered into on or after 6th April 2007 by him, to vary the terms of that plan in such a way as to vary his obligations under that plan,

is a controlled activity.

10H Advising on a regulated home purchase plan

Advising a person is a controlled activity if the advice is—

(a) given to the person in his capacity as home purchaser or potential home purchaser; and

(b) advice on the merits of his doing either of the following—

(i) entering into a regulated home purchase plan, or

(ii) varying the terms of a regulated home purchase plan, entered into on or after 6th April 2007 by him, in such a way as to vary his obligations under that plan.]

11 Agreeing to carry on specified kinds of activity

Agreeing to carry on any controlled activity falling within any of paragraphs 3 to 10B [(other than paragraph 4A)] above is a controlled activity.

[4800]

NOTES

Para 4A: inserted by the Financial Services and Markets Act 2000 (Regulated Activities) (Amendment No 3) Order 2006, SI 2006/3384, art 40(1), (2)(a), as from 1 November 2007 (for the full commencement details of SI 2006/3384, see the Note for that Order at **[4826A]**).

Paras 10C–10H: inserted by the Financial Services and Markets Act 2000 (Regulated Activities) (Amendment) (No 2) Order 2006, SI 2006/2383, art 35(1), (5), as from 6 April 2007 (for the full commencement details of SI 2006/2383, see art 1 of that Order at **[4820]**).

Para 11: words in square brackets inserted by SI 2006/3384, art 40(1), (2)(b), as from 1 November 2007 (for the full commencement details of SI 2006/3384, see the Note for that Order at **[4826A]**).

PART II
CONTROLLED INVESTMENTS

12. A deposit.

13. Rights under a contract of insurance.

14.—(1) Shares or stock in the share capital of—

(a) any body corporate (wherever incorporated);
(b) any unincorporated body constituted under the law of a country or territory outside the United Kingdom.

(2) Sub-paragraph (1) includes—
(a) any shares of a class defined as deferred shares for the purposes of section 119 of the Building Societies Act 1986;
(b) any transferable shares in a body incorporated under the law of, or any part of, the United Kingdom relating to industrial and provident societies or credit unions or in a body constituted under the law of another EEA State for purposes equivalent to those of such a body.

(3) But subject to sub-paragraph (2) there are excluded from sub-paragraph (1) shares or stock in the share capital of—
(a) an open-ended investment company;
(b) a building society incorporated under the law of, or any part of, the United Kingdom;
(c) any body incorporated under the law of, or any part of, the United Kingdom relating to industrial and provident societies or credit unions;
(d) any body constituted under the law of an EEA State for purposes equivalent to those of a body falling within paragraph (b) or (c).

15 Instruments creating or acknowledging indebtedness

(1) Subject to sub-paragraph (2), such of the following as do not fall within paragraph 16—
(a) debentures;
(b) debenture stock;
(c) loan stock;
(d) bonds;
(e) certificates of deposit;
(f) any other instrument creating or acknowledging a present or future indebtedness.

(2) If and to the extent that they would otherwise fall within sub-paragraph (1), there are excluded from that sub-paragraph—
(a) any instrument acknowledging or creating indebtedness for, or for money borrowed to defray, the consideration payable under a contract for the supply of goods or services;
(b) a cheque or other bill of exchange, a banker's draft or a letter of credit (but not a bill of exchange accepted by a banker);
(c) a banknote, a statement showing a balance on a current, deposit or saving account, a lease or other disposition of property, a heritable security; and
(d) a contract of insurance.

(3) An instrument excluded from sub-paragraph (1) of paragraph 16 by paragraph 16(2)(b) is not thereby to be taken to fall within sub-paragraph (1) of this paragraph.

16 Government and public securities

(1) Subject to sub-paragraph (2), loan stock, bonds and other instruments—
(a) creating or acknowledging indebtedness; and
(b) issued by or on behalf of a government, local authority (whether in the United Kingdom or elsewhere) or international organisation.

(2) There are excluded from sub-paragraph (1)—
(a) so far as applicable, the instruments mentioned in paragraph 15(2)(a) to (d);
(b) any instrument creating or acknowledging indebtedness in respect of—
(i) money received by the Director of Savings as deposits or otherwise in connection with the business of the National Savings Bank;
(ii) money raised under the National Loans Act 1968 under the auspices of the Director of Savings or treated as so raised by virtue of section 11(3) of the National Debt Act 1972.

17 Instruments giving entitlements to investments

(1) Warrants and other instruments entitling the holder to subscribe for any investment falling within paragraph 14, 15 or 16.

(2) It is immaterial whether the investment to which the entitlement relates is in existence or identifiable.

(3) An investment falling within this paragraph shall not be regarded as falling within paragraph 21, 22 or 23.

18 Certificates representing certain securities

(1) Subject to sub-paragraph (2), certificates or other instruments which confer contractual or property rights (other than rights consisting of an investment of the kind specified by paragraph 21)—

(a) in respect of any investment of the kind specified by any of paragraphs 14 to 17 being an investment held by a person other than the person on whom the rights are conferred by the certificate or instrument; and

(b) the transfer of which may be effected without the consent of that person.

(2) There is excluded from sub-paragraph (1) any instrument which confers rights in respect of two or more investments issued by different persons, or in respect of two or more different investments of the kind specified by paragraph 16 and issued by the same person.

19 Units in a collective investment scheme

Units in a collective investment scheme.

[20 Rights under a pension scheme

(1) Rights under a stakeholder pension scheme.

(2) Rights under a personal pension scheme.

(3) "Stakeholder pension scheme" and "personal pension scheme" have the meanings given by article 72(4).]

21 Options

[(1)] Options to acquire or dispose of—

(a) a security or contractually based investment (other than one of a kind specified in this paragraph);

(b) currency of the United Kingdom or of any other country or territory;

(c) palladium, platinum, gold or silver; *or*

(d) an option to acquire or dispose of an investment falling within this paragraph by virtue of sub-paragraph (a), (b) or (c)[;

(e) subject to sub-paragraph (4), an option to acquire or dispose of an option to which paragraph 5, 6, 7 or 10 of Section C of Annex I to the markets in financial instruments directive applies].

[(2) Subject to sub-paragraph (4), options—

(a) to which sub-paragraph (1) does not apply;

(b) which relate to commodities;

(c) which may be settled physically; and

(d) either—

(i) to which paragraph 5 or 6 of Section C of Annex I to the markets in financial instruments directive applies, or

(ii) which in accordance with Article 38 of the Commission Regulation are to be considered as having the characteristics of other derivative financial instruments and not being for commercial purposes, and to which paragraph 7 of Section C of Annex I to the markets in financial instruments directive applies.

(3) Subject to sub-paragraph (4), options—

(a) to which sub-paragraph (1) does not apply;

(b) which may be settled physically; and

(c) to which paragraph 10 of Section C of Annex I to the markets in financial instruments directive (read with the Commission Regulation) applies.

(4) Sub-paragraphs (1)(e), (2) and (3) only apply to options in relation to which—

(a) an investment firm or credit institution is providing or performing investment services and activities on a professional basis,

(b) a management company is providing, in accordance with Article 5(3) of the UCITS directive, the investment service specified in paragraph 4 or 5 of Section

A, or the ancillary service specified in paragraph 1 of Section B, of Annex I to the markets in financial instruments directive, or

(c) a market operator is providing the investment service specified in paragraph 8 of Section A of Annex I to the markets in financial instruments directive.

(5) Expressions used in sub-paragraphs (1)(e), (2) and (3) and in the markets in financial instruments directive have the same meaning as in that directive.]

22 Futures

(1) Subject to sub-paragraph (2), rights under a contract for the sale of a commodity or property of any other description under which delivery is to be made at a future date and at a price agreed on when the contract is made.

[(1A) Subject to sub-paragraph (1D), futures—

(a) to which sub-paragraph (1) does not apply;

(b) which relate to commodities;

(c) which may be settled physically; and

(d) to which paragraph 5 or 6 of Section C of Annex I to the markets in financial instruments directive applies.

(1B) Subject to sub-paragraph (1D), futures and forwards—

(a) to which sub-paragraph (1) does not apply;

(b) which relate to commodities;

(c) which may be settled physically;

(d) which in accordance with Article 38 of the Commission Regulation are to be considered as having the characteristics of other derivative financial instruments and not being for commercial purposes; and

(e) to which paragraph 7 of Section C of Annex I to the markets in financial instruments directive applies.

(1C) Subject to sub-paragraph (1D), futures—

(a) to which sub-paragraph (1) does not apply;

(b) which may be settled physically; and

(c) to which paragraph 10 of Section C of Annex I to the markets in financial instruments directive (read with the Commission Regulation) applies.

(1D) Sub-paragraphs (1A), (1B) and (1C) only apply to futures or forwards in relation to which—

(a) an investment firm or credit institution is providing or performing investment services and activities on a professional basis,

(b) a management company is providing, in accordance with Article 5(3) of the UCITS directive, the investment service specified in paragraph 4 or 5 of Section A, or the ancillary service specified in paragraph 1 of Section B, of Annex I to the markets in financial instruments directive, or

(c) a market operator is providing the investment service specified in paragraph 8 of Section A of Annex I to the markets in financial instruments directive.

(1E) Expressions used in sub-paragraphs (1A) to (1C) and in the markets in financial instruments directive have the same meaning as in that directive.]

(2) There are excluded from sub-paragraph (1) rights under any contract which is made for commercial and not investment purposes.

(3) For the purposes of sub-paragraph (2), in considering whether a contract is to be regarded as made for investment purposes or for commercial purposes, the indicators set out in article 84 of the Regulated Activities Order shall be applied in the same way as they are applied for the purposes of that article.

23 Contracts for differences etc

(1) Subject to sub-paragraph (2), rights under—

(a) a contract for differences; or

(b) any other contract the purpose or pretended purpose of which is to secure a profit or avoid a loss by reference to fluctuations in—

(i) the value or price of property of any description;

(ii) an index or other factor designated for that purpose in the contract.

(2) There are excluded from sub-paragraph (1)—

(a) rights under a contract if the parties intend that the profit is to be secured or the loss is to be avoided by one or more of the parties taking delivery of any property to which the contract relates;

(b) rights under a contract under which money is received by way of deposit on terms that any interest or other return to be paid on the sum deposited will be calculated by reference to fluctuations in an index or other factor;

(c) rights under any contract under which—

(i) money is received by the Director of Savings as deposits or otherwise in connection with the business of the National Savings Bank; or

(ii) money is raised under the National Loans Act 1968 under the auspices of the Director of Savings or treated as so raised by virtue of section 11(3) of the National Debt Act 1972;

(d) rights under a qualifying contract of insurance.

[(3) Subject to sub-paragraph (4), derivative instruments for the transfer of credit risk—

(a) to which neither paragraph 21 nor sub-paragraph (1) applies; and

(b) to which paragraph 8 of Section C of Annex I to the markets in financial instruments directive applies.

(4) Sub-paragraph (3) only applies to derivatives in relation to which—

(a) an investment firm or credit institution is providing or performing investment services and activities on a professional basis,

(b) a management company is providing, in accordance with Article 5(3) of the UCITS directive, the investment service specified in paragraph 4 or 5 of Section A, or the ancillary service specified in paragraph 1 of Section B, of Annex I to the markets in financial instruments directive, or

(c) a market operator is providing the investment service specified in paragraph 8 of Section A of Annex I to the markets in financial instruments directive.

(5) "Derivative instruments for the transfer of credit risk" has the same meaning as in the markets in financial instruments directive.]

24 Lloyd's syndicate capacity and syndicate membership

(1) The underwriting capacity of a Lloyd's syndicate.

(2) A person's membership (or prospective membership) of a Lloyd's syndicate.

25 Funeral plan contracts

Rights under a qualifying funeral plan contract.

26 Agreements for qualifying credit

Rights under an agreement for qualifying credit.

[26A Regulated home reversion plans

Rights under a regulated home reversion plan.

26B Regulated home purchase plans

Rights under a regulated home purchase plan.]

27 Rights to or interests in investments

(1) Subject to sub-paragraphs (2) and (3), any right to or interest in anything which is specified by any other provision of this Part of this Schedule (other than [paragraph 26, 26A or 26B]).

(2) Sub-paragraph (1) does not apply to interests under the trusts of an occupational pension scheme.

(2A) Sub-paragraph (1) does not apply to any right or interest acquired as a result of entering into a funeral plan contract (and for this purpose a "funeral plan contract" is a contract of a kind described in paragraph 9(2)(a) and (b)).

(3) Sub-paragraph (1) does not apply to anything which falls within any other provision of this Part of this Schedule.

28 Interpretation

In this Schedule—

"buying" includes acquiring for valuable consideration;

["Commission Regulation" means Commission Regulation 1287/2006 of 10 August 2006;]

"contract of insurance" has the meaning given in the Regulated Activities Order;

"contractually based investment" means—

(a) rights under a qualifying contract of insurance;

(b) any investment of the kind specified by any of paragraphs 21, 22, 23 and 25;

(c) any investment of the kind specified by paragraph 27 so far as relevant to an investment falling within (a) or (b);

["credit institution" has the meaning given in the Regulated Activities Order;]

["home purchase provider" and "home purchaser" have the meanings given in article 63F(3) of the Regulated Activities Order;]

["investment firm" has the meaning given in the Regulated Activities Order;]

["investment services and activities" has the meaning given in the Regulated Activities Order;]

["management company" has the meaning given in the Regulated Activities Order;]

["market operator" has the meaning given in the Regulated Activities Order;]

["MiFID instrument" has the meaning given in article 25D(2) of the Regulated Activities Order;]

["multilateral trading facility" has the meaning given in the Regulated Activities Order;]

["occupational pension scheme" has the meaning given by section 1 of the Pension Schemes Act 1993 but with paragraph (b) of the definition omitted;]

["plan provider" has the meaning given by paragraph (3) of article 63B of the Regulated Activities Order, read with paragraphs (7) and (8) of that article;]

"property" includes currency of the United Kingdom or any other country or territory;

"qualifying funeral plan contract" has the meaning given by paragraph 9;

["regulated home purchase plan" has the meaning given in article 63F(3) of the Regulated Activities Order;

"regulated home reversion plan" and "reversion seller" have the meanings given in article 63B(3) of the Regulated Activities Order;]

"security" means a controlled investment falling within any of paragraphs 14 to 20 or, so far as relevant to any such investment, paragraph 27;

"selling", in relation to any investment, includes disposing of the investment for valuable consideration, and for these purposes "disposing" includes—

(a) in the case of an investment consisting of rights under a contract—

(i) surrendering, assigning or converting those rights; or

(ii) assuming the corresponding liabilities under the contract;

(b) in the case of an investment consisting of rights under other arrangements, assuming the corresponding liabilities under the arrangements; and

(c) in the case of any other investment, issuing or creating the investment or granting the rights or interests of which it consists;

"syndicate" has the meaning given in the Regulated Activities Order.

[4801]

NOTES

Para 20: substituted by the Financial Services and Markets Act 2000 (Regulated Activities) (Amendment) Order 2006, SI 2006/1969, art 12(1), (3), as from 6 April 2007.

Para 21: sub-para (1) numbered as such, word in italics in sub-para (1)(c) revoked, and sub-paras (1)(e), (2)–(5) inserted, by the Financial Services and Markets Act 2000 (Regulated Activities) (Amendment No 3) Order 2006, SI 2006/3384, art 40(1), (3), as from 1 November 2007 (for the full commencement details of SI 2006/3384, see the Note for that Order at **[4826A]**).

Para 22: sub-paras (1A)–(1E) inserted by SI 2006/3384, art 40(1), (4), as from 1 November 2007 (for the full commencement details of SI 2006/3384, see the Note for that Order at **[4826A]**).

Para 23: sub-paras (3)–(5) added by SI 2006/3384, art 40(1), (5), as from 1 November 2007 (for the full commencement details of SI 2006/3384, see the Note for that Order at **[4826A]**).

Paras 26A, 26B: inserted by the Financial Services and Markets Act 2000 (Regulated Activities) (Amendment) (No 2) Order 2006, SI 2006/2383, art 35(1), (6)(a), as from 6 April 2007 (for the full commencement details of SI 2006/2383, see art 1 of that Order at **[4820]**).

Para 27: words in square brackets substituted by SI 2006/2383, art 35(1), (6)(b), as from 6 April 2007 (for the full commencement details of SI 2006/2383, see art 1 of that Order at **[4820]**).

Para 28 is amended as follows:

Definitions "Commission Regulation", "credit institution", "investment firm", "investment services and activities", "management company", "market operator", "MiFID instrument", and "multilateral trading facility" inserted by SI 2006/3384, art 40(1), (6), as from 1 November 2007 (for the full commencement details of SI 2006/3384, see the Note for that Order at **[4826A]**).

Definitions "home purchase provider", "home purchaser", "plan provider", "regulated home purchase plan", "regulated home reversion plan", and "reversion seller" inserted by SI 2006/2383, art 35(1), (6)(c), as from 6 April 2007 (for the full commencement details of SI 2006/2383, see art 1 of that Order at **[4820]**).

Definition "occupational pension scheme" substituted by SI 2006/1969, art 12(1), (4), as from 6 April 2007.

SCHEDULE 2
COUNTRIES AND TERRITORIES

Article 10

1. The Bailiwick of Guernsey.

2. The Isle of Man.

3. The Commonwealth of Pennsylvania.

4. The State of Iowa.

5. The Bailiwick of Jersey.

[4802]

SCHEDULE 3
MARKETS AND EXCHANGES

Articles 37, 41, 67, 68 and 69

PART I
CRITERIA FOR RELEVANT EEA MARKETS

The criteria are—

(a) the head office of the market must be situated in an EEA State; and

(b) the market must be subject to requirements in the EEA State in which its head office is situated as to—

(i) the manner in which it operates;

(ii) the means by which access may be had to the facilities it provides;

(iii) the conditions to be satisfied before an investment may be traded or dealt in by means of its facilities;

(iv) the reporting and publication of transactions effected by means of its facilities.

[4803]

[PART II
CERTAIN INVESTMENT EXCHANGES OPERATING RELEVANT EEA MARKETS

Aktietorget I Norden (Sweden).

Amsterdam Options Exchange (Netherlands).

Athens Stock Exchange (Greece).

Athens Derivative Exchange (Greece).

Barcelona Stock Exchange (Spain).

Bavarian Stock Exchange (Germany).

Belgian Secondary Market for Treasury Certificates (Belgium).

Berlin-Bremen Stock Exchange (Germany).

Bilbao Stock Exchange (Spain).

Böag Borsen AG (Germany).

Bratislava Stock Exchange (Slovakia).

Bucharest Stock Exchange (Romania).

Budapest Stock Exchange (Hungary).

Bulgaria Stock Exchange (Bulgaria).

Copenhagen Stock Exchange (Denmark).

Cyprus Stock Exchange (Cyprus).

Danish Authorised Market Place (Denmark).

Dusseldorf Stock Market (Germany).

EDX (UK).

Eurex Deutschland (Germany).

Euronext Amsterdam (Netherlands).

Euronext Brussels (Belgium).

Euronext Lisbon (Portugal).

Euronext Paris (France).

Frankfurt Stock Exchange (Germany).

Helsinki Stock Exchange and Securities and Derivatives Exchange (Finland).

Irish Stock Exchange (Ireland).

Italian and Foreign Government Bonds Market (Italy).

Italian Stock Exchange (Italy).

Ljubliana Stock Exchange (Slovenia).

London International Financial Futures and Options Exchange (UK).

London Stock Exchange (UK).

Luxembourg Stock Exchange (Luxembourg).

Madrid Stock Exchange (Spain)

Malta Stock Exchange (Malta).

Market for Public Debt (Spain).

MEFF Renta Variable Futures Options Exchange (Spain).

MEFF Renta Fija Equity Futures Exchange (Spain).

MTS Italy (Italy).

MTS Poland (Poland).

MTS Portugal (Portugal).

National Stock Exchange of Lithuania (Lithuania).

Nordic Growth Market (Sweden).

PLUS (UK).

Prague Stock Exchange (Czech Republic).

Riga Stock Exchange (Latvia).

ShareMark (UK).

Stockholm Stock Exchange (Sweden).

Stuttgart Stock Exchange (Germany).

Tallinn Stock Exchange (Estonia).

Valencia Stock Exchange (Spain).

Vienna Stock Exchange (Austria).

Virt-x (UK).

Warsaw Stock Exchange (Poland).]

[4804]

NOTES

Commencement: 20 April 2007.

Substituted by the Financial Services and Markets Act 2000 (Financial Promotion) (Amendment) Order 2007, SI 2007/1083, art 2, as from 20 April 2007.

PART III
CERTAIN NON-EEA INVESTMENT EXCHANGES OPERATING RELEVANT MARKETS

America Stock Exchange.

Australian Stock Exchange.

Basler Effektenbourse.

Boston Stock Exchange.

Bourse de Geneve.

Buenos Aires Stock Exchange.

Canadian Venture Exchange.

Chicago Board Options Exchange.

Chicago Stock Exchange.

Effektenborsenverein Zurich.

Fukuoka Stock Exchange.

Hiroshima Stock Exchange.

Iceland Stock Exchange.

Johannesburg Stock Exchange.

Korean Stock Exchange.

Kuala Lumpur Stock Exchange.

Kyoto Stock Exchange.

Midwest Stock Exchange.

Montreal Stock Exchange.

Nagoya Stock Exchange.

NASDAQ.

National Stock Exchange.

New York Stock Exchange.

New Zealand Stock Exchange Limited.

Niigita Stock Exchange.

Osaka Stock Exchange.

Oslo Stock Exchange.

Pacific Stock Exchange.

Philadelphia Stock Exchange.

Sapporo Stock Exchange.

Singapore Stock Exchange.

Stock Exchange of Hong Kong Limited.

Stock Exchange of Thailand.

Tokyo Stock Exchange.

Toronto Stock Exchange.

[4805]

PART IV
OTHER RELEVANT MARKETS

American Commodity Exchange.

Australian Financial Futures Market.

Chicago Board of Trade.

Chicago Mercantile Exchange.

Chicago Rice and Cotton Exchange.

Commodity Exchange Inc.

Eurex US.

Eurex Zurich.

International Securities Market Association.

International Petroleum Exchange.

Kansas City Board of Trade.

London Metal Exchange.

Minneapolis Grain Exchange.

New York Board of Trade.

New York Futures Exchange.

New York Mercantile Exchange.

New Zealand Futures Exchange.

Pacific Commodity Exchange.

Philadelphia Board of Trade.

Singapore International Monetary Exchange.

Sydney Futures Exchange.

Toronto Futures Exchange.

[4806]

SCHEDULE 4
TAKEOVERS OF RELEVANT UNLISTED COMPANIES

Articles 63 and 64

PART I
REQUIREMENTS RELATING TO THE OFFER

1. The terms of the offer must be recommended by all the directors of the company other than any director who is—
   (a) the person by whom, or on whose behalf, an offer is made ("offeror"); or
   (b) a director of the offeror.

2.—(1) This paragraph applies to an offer for debentures or for non-equity share capital.

(2) Where, at the date of the offer, shares carrying 50 per cent or less of the voting rights attributable to the equity share capital are held by or on behalf of the offeror, the offer must include or be accompanied by an offer made by the offeror for the rest of the shares comprised in the equity share capital.

3.—(1) This paragraph applies to an offer for shares comprised in the equity share capital.

PART IV
STATUTORY INSTRUMENTS

(2) Where, at the date of the offer, shares which carry 50 per cent or less of the categories of voting rights described in sub-paragraph (3) are held by or on behalf of the offeror, it must be a condition of the offer that sufficient shares will be acquired or agreed to be acquired by the offeror pursuant to or during the offer so as to result in shares carrying more than 50 per cent of one or both categories of relevant voting rights being held by him or on his behalf.

(3) The categories of voting rights mentioned in sub-paragraph (2) are—
(a) voting rights exercisable in general meetings of the company;
(b) voting rights attributable to the equity share capital.

4.—(1) Subject to sub-paragraph (2), the offer must be open for acceptance by every recipient for the period of at least 21 days beginning with the day after the day on which the invitation or inducement in question was first communicated to recipients of the offer.

(2) Sub-paragraph (1) does not apply if the offer is totally withdrawn and all persons are released from any obligation incurred under it.

5. The acquisition of the shares or debentures to which the offer relates must not be conditional upon the recipients approving, or consenting, to any payment or other benefit being made or given to any director or former director of the company in connection with, or as compensation or consideration for—
(a) his ceasing to be a director;
(b) his ceasing to hold any office held in conjunction with any directorship; or
(c) in the case of a former director, his ceasing to hold any office which he held in conjunction with his former directorship and which he continued to hold after ceasing to be a director.

6. The consideration for the shares or debentures must be—
(a) cash; or
(b) in the case of an offeror which is a body corporate other than an open-ended investment company, either cash or shares in, or debentures of, the body corporate or any combination of such cash, shares or debentures.

[4807]

PART II
ACCOMPANYING MATERIAL

7. An indication of the identity of the offeror and, if the offer is being made on behalf of another person, the identity of that person.

8. An indication of the fact that the terms of the offer are recommended by all directors of the company other than (if that is the case) any director who is the offeror or a director of the offeror.

9. An indication to the effect that any person who is in any doubt about the invitation or inducement should consult a person authorised under the Act.

10. An indication that, except insofar as the offer may be totally withdrawn and all persons released from any obligation incurred under it, the offer is open for acceptance by every recipient for the period of at least 21 days beginning with the day after the day on which the invitation or inducement in question was first communicated to recipients of the offer.

11. An indication of the date on which the invitation or inducement was first communicated to the recipients of the offer.

12. An indication that the acquisition of the shares or debentures to which the offer relates is not conditional upon the recipients approving, or consenting, to any payment or other benefit being made or given to any director or former director of the company in connection with, or as compensation or consideration for—
(a) his ceasing to be a director;
(b) his ceasing to hold any office held in conjunction with any directorship; or

(c) in the case of a former director, his ceasing to hold any office which he held in conjunction with his former directorship and which he continued to hold after ceasing to be a director.

13. An indication of the place where additional material listed in Part III may be inspected.

14. The audited accounts of the company in respect of the latest accounting reference period for which the period for laying and delivering accounts under the 1985 Act or the 1986 Order has passed or, if accounts in respect of a later accounting reference period have been delivered under the relevant legislation, as shown in those accounts and not the earlier accounts.

15. Advice to the directors of the company on the financial implications of the offer which is given by a competent person who is independent of and who has no substantial financial interest in the company or the offeror, being advice which gives the opinion of that person in relation to the offer.

16. An indication by the directors of the company, acting as a board, of the following matters—

(a) whether or not there has been any material change in the financial position or prospects of the company since the end of the latest accounting reference period in respect of which audited accounts have been delivered to the relevant registrar of companies under the relevant legislation;

(b) if there has been any such change, the particulars of it;

(c) any interests, in percentage terms, which any of them have in the shares in or debentures of the company and which are required to be entered in the register kept by the company under section 325 of the 1985 Act or article 333 of the 1986 Order;

(d) any interests, in percentage terms, which any of them have in the shares in or debentures of any offeror which is a body corporate and which, if the director were a director of the offeror, would—

(i) in the case of a company within the meaning of the 1985 Act or the 1986 Order, be required to be entered in the register kept by the offeror under section 325 of the 1985 Act or article 333 of the 1986 Order; and

(ii) in any other case, be required to be so entered if the offeror were such a company.

17. An indication of any material interest which any director has in any contract entered into by the offeror and in any contract entered into by any member of any group of which the offeror is a member.

18. An indication as to whether or not each director intends to accept the offer in respect of his own beneficial holdings in the company.

19. In the case of an offeror which is a body corporate and the shares in or debentures of which are to be the consideration or any part of the consideration for the offer, an indication by the directors of the offeror that the information concerning the offeror and those shares or debentures contained in the document is correct.

20. If the offeror is making the offer on behalf of another person—

(a) an indication by the offeror as to whether or not he has taken any steps to ascertain whether that person will be in a position to implement the offer;

(b) if he has taken any such steps, an indication by him as to what those steps are; and

(c) the offeror's opinion as to whether that person will be in a position to implement the offer.

21. An indication that each of the following—

(a) each of the directors of the company;

(b) the offeror; and

(c) if the offeror is a body corporate, each of the directors of the offeror;

is responsible for the information required by Part I and this Part of this Schedule insofar as it relates to themselves or their respective bodies corporate and that, to the best of their knowledge and belief (having taken all reasonable care to ensure that such is the case) the information is in accordance with the facts and that no material fact has been omitted.

22. The particulars of—
- (a) all shares in or debentures of the company; and
- (b) all investments falling within paragraph 17, 19 or 21 of Schedule 1 so far as relating to shares in or debentures of the company;

which are held by or on behalf of the offeror or each offeror, if there is more than one, or if none are so held an appropriate negative statement.

23. An indication as to whether or not the offer is conditional upon acceptance in respect of a minimum number of shares or debentures being received and, if the offer is so conditional, what the minimum number is.

24. Where the offer is conditional upon acceptances, an indication of the date which is the latest date on which it can become unconditional.

25. If the offer is, or has become, unconditional an indication of the fact that it will remain open until further notice and that at least 14 days' notice will be given before it is closed.

26. An indication as to whether or not, if circumstances arise in which an offeror is able compulsorily to acquire shares of any dissenting minority under [Chapter 3 of Part 28 of the Companies Act 2006 (c 46)], that offeror intends to so acquire those shares.

27. If shares or debentures are to be acquired for cash, an indication of the period within which the payment will be made.

28.—(1) Subject to sub-paragraph (2), if the consideration or any part of the consideration for the shares or debentures to be acquired is shares in or debentures of an offeror—
- (a) an indication of the nature and particulars of the offeror's business, its financial and trading prospects and its place of incorporation;
- (b) the following information, in respect of any offeror which is a body corporate and in respect of the company, for the period of five years immediately preceding the date on which the invitation or inducement in question was first communicated to recipients of the offer—
  - (i) turnover,
  - (ii) profit on ordinary activities before and after tax,
  - (iii) extraordinary items,
  - (iv) profits and loss, and
  - (v) the rate per cent of any dividends paid, adjusted as appropriate to take account of relevant changes over the period and the total amount absorbed thereby.

(2) In the case of a body corporate—
- (a) which was incorporated during the period of five years immediately preceding the date on which the invitation or inducement in question was first communicated to recipients of the offer; or
- (b) which has, at any time during that period, been exempt from the provisions of Part VII of the 1985 Act relating to the audit of accounts by virtue of section 249A or 249AA of that Act or been exempt from the provisions of Part VIII of the 1986 Order relating to the audit of accounts by virtue of article 257A or 257AA of that Order;

the information described in sub-paragraph (1) with respect to that body corporate need be included only in relation to the period since its incorporation or since it last ceased to be exempt from those provisions of Part VII of the 1985 Act or Part VIII of the 1986 Order as the case may be.

29. Particulars of the first dividend in which any such shares or debentures will participate and of the rights attaching to them (including in the case of debentures, rights as to interest) and of any restrictions on their transfer.

30. An indication of the effect of the acceptance on the capital and income position of the holder of the shares in or debentures of the company.

31. Particulars of all material contracts (not being contracts which were entered into in the ordinary course of business) which were entered into by each of the company and the offeror during the period of two years immediately preceding the date on which the invitation or inducement in question was first communicated to recipients of the offer.

32. Particulars of the terms on which shares in or debentures of the company acquired in pursuance of the offer will be transferred and any restrictions on their transfer.

33. An indication as to whether or not it is proposed, in connection with the offer, that any payment or other benefit be made or given to any director or former director of the company in connection with, or as compensation or consideration for—

(a) his ceasing to be a director;
(b) his ceasing to hold any office held in conjunction with any directorship; or
(c) in the case of a former director, his ceasing to hold any office which he held in conjunction with his former directorship and which he continued to hold after ceasing to be a director;

and, if such payments or benefits are proposed, details of each one.

34. An indication as to whether or not there exists any agreement or arrangement between—

(a) the offeror or any person with whom the offeror has an agreement of the kind described in section 204 of the 1985 Act or article 216 of the 1986 Order; and
(b) any director or shareholder of the company or any person who has been such a director or shareholder;

at any time during the period of twelve months immediately preceding the date on which the invitation or inducement in question was first communicated to recipients of the offer, being an agreement or arrangement which is connected with or dependent on the offer and, if there is any such agreement or arrangement, particulars of it.

35. An indication whether or not the offeror has reason to believe that there has been any material change in the financial position or prospects of the company since the end of the accounting reference period to which the accounts referred to in paragraph 14 relate, and if the offeror has reason to believe that there has been such a change, the particulars of it.

36. An indication as to whether or not there is any agreement or arrangement whereby any shares or debentures acquired by the offeror in pursuance of the offer will or may be transferred to any other person, together with the names of the parties to any such agreement or arrangement and particulars of all shares and debentures in the company held by such persons.

37. Particulars of any dealings—

(a) in the shares in or debentures of the company; and
(b) if the offeror is a body corporate, in the shares in or debentures of the offeror;

which took place during the period of twelve months immediately preceding the date on which the invitation or inducement in question was first communicated to recipients of the offer and which were entered into by every person who was a director of either the company or the offeror during that period; and, if there have been no such dealings, an indication to that effect.

38. In a case in which the offeror is a body corporate which is required to deliver accounts under the 1985 Act or the 1986 Order, particulars of the assets and liabilities as shown in its audited accounts in respect of the latest accounting reference period for which the period for laying and delivering accounts under the relevant legislation has passed or, if accounts in respect of a later accounting reference period have been delivered under the relevant legislation, as shown in those accounts and not the earlier accounts.

39. Where valuations of assets are given in connection with the offer, the basis on which the valuation was made and the names and addresses of the persons who valued them and particulars of any relevant qualifications.

40. If any profit forecast is given in connection with the offer, an indication of the assumptions on which the forecast is based.

[4808]

NOTES

Para 26: words in square brackets substituted by the Companies Act 2006 (Commencement No 2, Consequential Amendments, Transitional Provisions and Savings) Order 2007, SI 2007/1093, art 6(1), Sch 3, para 10, as from 6 April 2007.

PART III
ADDITIONAL MATERIAL AVAILABLE FOR INSPECTION

41. The memorandum and articles of association of the company.

42. If the offeror is a body corporate, the memorandum and articles of association of the offeror or, if there is no such memorandum and articles, any instrument constituting or defining the constitution of the offeror and, in either case, if the relevant document is not written in English, a certified translation in English.

43. In the case of a company that does not fall within paragraph 45—
- (a) the audited accounts of the company in respect of the last two accounting reference periods for which the laying and delivering of accounts under the 1985 Act or the 1986 Order has passed; and
- (b) if accounts have been delivered to the relevant registrar of companies, in respect of a later accounting reference period, a copy of those accounts.

44. In the case of an offeror which is required to deliver accounts to the registrar of companies and which does not fall within paragraph 45—
- (a) the audited accounts of the offeror in respect of the last two accounting reference periods for which the laying and delivering of accounts under the 1985 Act or the 1986 Order has passed; and
- (b) if accounts have been delivered to the relevant registrar of companies in respect of a later accounting reference period, a copy of those accounts.

45. In the case of a company or an offeror—
- (a) which was incorporated during the period of three years immediately preceding the date on which the invitation or inducement in question was first communicated to recipients of the offer; or
- (b) which has, at any time during that period, been exempt from the provisions of Part VII of the 1985 Act relating to the audit of accounts by virtue of section 249A or 249AA of that Act or been exempt from the provisions of Part VIII of the 1986 Order relating to the audit of accounts by virtue of article 257A or 257AA of that Order;

the information described in whichever is relevant of paragraph 43 or 44 with respect to that body corporate need be included only in relation to the period since its incorporation or since it last ceased to be exempt from those provisions of Part VII of the 1985 Act or Part VIII of the 1986 Order, as the case may be.

46. All existing contracts of service entered into for a period of more than one year between the company and any of its directors and, if the offeror is a body corporate, between the offeror and any of its directors.

47. Any report, letter, valuation or other document any part of which is exhibited or referred to in the information required to be made available by Part II and this Part of this Schedule.

48. If the offer document contains any statement purporting to have been made by an expert, that expert's written consent to the inclusion of that statement.

49. All material contracts (if any) of the company and of the offeror (not, in either case, being contracts which were entered into in the ordinary course of business) which were entered into during the period of two years immediately preceding the date on which the invitation or inducement in question was first communicated to recipients of the offer.

[4809]

SCHEDULE 5
STATEMENTS FOR CERTIFIED HIGH NET WORTH INDIVIDUALS AND SELF-CERTIFIED SOPHISTICATED INVESTORS

Articles 48 and 50A

PART I
STATEMENT FOR CERTIFIED HIGH NET WORTH INDIVIDUALS

1. The statement to be signed for the purposes of article 48(2) (definition of high net worth individual) must be in the following form and contain the following content—

"STATEMENT FOR CERTIFIED HIGH NET WORTH INDIVIDUAL

I declare that I am a certified high net worth individual for the purposes of the Financial Services and Markets Act 2000 (Financial Promotion) Order 2005.

I understand that this means:

(a) I can receive financial promotions that may not have been approved by a person authorised by the Financial Services Authority;

(b) the content of such financial promotions may not conform to rules issued by the Financial Services Authority;

(c) by signing this statement I may lose significant rights;

(d) I may have no right to complain to either of the following—

(i) the Financial Services Authority; or

(ii) the Financial Ombudsman Scheme;

(e) I may have no right to seek compensation from the Financial Services Compensation Scheme.

I am a certified high net worth individual because **at least one of the following applies—**

(a) I had, during the financial year immediately preceding the date below, an annual income to the value of £100,000 or more;

(b) I held, throughout the financial year immediately preceding the date below, net assets to the value of £250,000 or more. Net assets for these purposes do not include—

(i) the property which is my primary residence or any loan secured on that residence;

(ii) any rights of mine under a qualifying contract of insurance within the meaning of the Financial Services and Markets Act 2000 (Regulated Activities) Order 2001; or

(iii) any benefits (in the form of pensions or otherwise) which are payable on the termination of my service or on my death or retirement and to which I am (or my dependants are), or may be, entitled.

I accept that I can lose my property and other assets from making investment decisions based on financial promotions.

I am aware that it is open to me to seek advice from someone who specialises in advising on investments.

Signature...

Date...".

[4810]

PART II
STATEMENT FOR SELF-CERTIFIED SOPHISTICATED INVESTORS

2. The statement to be signed for the purposes of article 50A(1) (definition of self-certified sophisticated investor) must be in the following form and contain the following content—

"STATEMENT FOR SELF-CERTIFIED SOPHISTICATED INVESTOR

I declare that I am a self-certified sophisticated investor for the purposes of the Financial Services and Markets Act (Financial Promotion) Order 2005.

PART IV STATUTORY INSTRUMENTS

I understand that this means:

(a) I can receive financial promotions that may not have been approved by a person authorised by the Financial Services Authority;

(b) the content of such financial promotions may not conform to rules issued by the Financial Services Authority;

(c) **by signing this statement I may lose significant rights;**

(d) I may have no right to complain to either of the following—

(i) the Financial Services Authority; or

(ii) the Financial Ombudsman Scheme;

(e) I may have no right to seek compensation from the Financial Services Compensation Scheme.

I am a self-certified sophisticated investor because **at least one of the following applies—**

(a) I am a member of a network or syndicate of business angels and have been so for at least the last six months prior to the date below;

(b) I have made more than one investment in an unlisted company in the two years prior to the date below;

(c) I am working, or have worked in the two years prior to the date below, in a professional capacity in the private equity sector, or in the provision of finance for small and medium enterprises;

(d) I am currently, or have been in the two years prior to the date below, a director of a company with an annual turnover of at least £1 million.

I accept that I can lose my property and other assets from making investment decisions based on financial promotions.

I am aware that it is open to me to seek advice from someone who specialises in advising on investments.

Signature...

Date...".

[4811]

SCHEDULE 6
REVOCATION

Article 74

Order	*Reference*	*Extent of revocation*
The Financial Services and Markets Act 2000 (Financial Promotion) Order 2001	SI 2001/1335	The whole Order
The Financial Services and Markets Act 2000 (Financial Promotion) (Amendment) Order 2001	SI 2001/2633	The whole Order
The Financial Services and Markets Act 2000 (Miscellaneous Provisions) Order 2001	SI 2001/3650	Article 4 and 5
The Financial Services and Markets Act 2000 (Financial Promotion) (Amendment No 2) Order 2001	SI 2001/3800	The whole Order
The Financial Services and Markets Act 2000 (Financial Promotion and Miscellaneous Amendments) Order 2002	SI 2002/1310	Article 2
The Financial Services and Markets Act 2000 (Commencement of Mortgage Regulation) (Amendment) Order 2002	SI 2002/1777	Article 4
The Financial Services and Markets Act 2000 (Financial Promotion) (Amendment) (Electronic Communications Directive) Order 2002	SI 2002/2157	The whole Order

Order	*Reference*	*Extent of revocation*
The Financial Services and Markets Act 2000 (Financial Promotion) (Amendment) Order 2003	SI 2003/1676	The whole Order
The Financial Services and Markets Act 2000 (Financial Promotion and Promotion of Collective Investment Schemes) (Miscellaneous Amendments) Order 2005	SI 2005/270	Article 2 and Schedule 1

[4812]

FINANCIAL SERVICES AND MARKETS ACT 2000 (REGULATED ACTIVITIES) (AMENDMENT) ORDER 2006

(SI 2006/1969)

NOTES

Made: 28 June 2006.

Authority: Financial Services and Markets Act 2000, ss 22(1), (5), 426, 427, 428(3), Sch 2, para 25.

Commencement: 1 October 2006 (arts 1, 2, 4, for the purposes of enabling applications to be made for Part IV permission or for a variation of Part IV permission in relation to the regulated activity specified by art 52(b) of the Regulated Activities Order 2001 as amended by this Order or in relation to an investment specified by art 82(2) of the 2001 Order as amended by this Order); 6 April 2007 (otherwise). See art 1 at **[4813]**.

As of 1 July 2007, this Order had not been amended.

ARRANGEMENT OF ARTICLES

1 Citation, commencement and interpretation

(1) This Order may be cited as the Financial Services and Markets Act 2000 (Regulated Activities) (Amendment) Order 2006.

(2) Articles 1, 2 and 4 of this Order come in to force—

(a) for the purposes of enabling applications to be made for Part IV permission or for a variation of Part IV permission in relation to the regulated activity specified by article 52(b) of the Principal Order as amended by this Order or in relation to an investment specified by article 82(2) of the Principal Order as amended by this Order on 1st October 2006;

(b) and for all other purposes on 6th April 2007.

(3) All other articles of this Order come into force on 6th April 2007.

(4) In this Order—

"the Principal Order" means the Financial Services and Markets Act 2000 (Regulated Activities) Order 2001;

"the Act" means the Financial Services and Markets Act 2000;

"commencement" means 6th April 2007.

[4813]

PART IV STATUTORY INSTRUMENTS

NOTES

Commencement: 1 October 2006 (for certain purposes); 6 April 2007 (otherwise) (see para (2) above).

2 (*Amends the Financial Services and Markets Act 2000* (*Regulated Activities*) *Order 2001, SI 2001/544 at* **[4001]** *et seq.*)

3 Transitional provisions

(1) Paragraph (2) applies to a person ("A") who immediately before commencement had Part IV permission to carry on an activity of the kind specified by article 52 of the Principal Order.

(2) On commencement A is to be treated as also having Part IV permission to carry on the activity of establishing, operating or winding up a personal pension scheme.

(3) Paragraph (4) applies to a person ("B") who immediately before commencement had Part IV permission to carry on an activity of the kind specified by article—

- (a) 14 (dealing in investments as principal),
- (b) 21 (dealing in investments as agent),
- (c) 25 (arranging deals in investments),
- (d) 37 (managing investments),
- (e) 40 (safeguarding and administering investments),
- (f) 45 (sending dematerialised instructions),
- (g) 53 (advising on investments), or
- (h) in so far as relevant to any activity specified in this paragraph or by article 52 of the Principal Order, 64 (agreeing to carry on specified kinds of activity),

of the Principal Order in relation to rights under a stakeholder pension scheme ("a relevant permission").

(4) On commencement B is to be treated as also having Part IV permission to carry on, in relation to rights under a personal pension scheme, any of the activities of a kind mentioned in paragraph (3) for which he had a relevant permission immediately before commencement.

(5) No person shall be treated as having his Part IV permission extended in accordance with this article if on or before 23rd March 2007 he gave written notice to the Authority that he did not wish to have his permission extended.

[4814]

NOTES

Commencement: 6 April 2007.

4 Interim permission

(1) This article applies where—

- (a) a person has submitted an application for Part IV permission or a variation of Part IV permission ("the applicant"), to the extent that the application relates to—
  - (i) a regulated activity specified by article 52(b) of the Principal Order (as amended by this Order),
  - (ii) an investment specified by article 82(2) of the Principal Order (as amended by this Order);
- (b) on or before 1st October 2006, the applicant had been carrying on an activity that following commencement will be—
  - (i) a regulated activity of establishing, operating or winding up a personal pension scheme; or
  - (ii) an activity of a kind specified by article—
    - (aa) 14 (dealing in investments as principal),
    - (bb) 21 (dealing in investments as agent),
    - (cc) 25 (arranging deals in investments),
    - (dd) 37 (managing investments),
    - (ee) 40 (safeguarding and administering investments),
    - (ff) 45 (sending dematerialised instructions),
    - (gg) 53 (advising on investments), or
    - (hh) in so far as relevant to any activity specified in this sub-paragraph, 64 (agreeing to carry on specified kinds of activity),

of the Principal Order in relation to rights under a personal pension scheme;
(c) the Authority received the application on or before 23rd March 2007; and
(d) the application had not been finally decided before commencement.

(2) The applicant is to be treated as having at commencement the permission to which the application relates.

(3) A permission which an applicant is to be treated as having is referred to in this Order as an "interim permission".

(4) Without prejudice to the exercise by the Authority of its powers under Part 4 of the Act an interim permission lapses when the application has been finally decided.

(5) In this article "finally decided" means—
(a) subject to paragraph (6), when the application is withdrawn;
(b) when the Authority grants permission under section 42 of the Act (giving permission) to carry on the activity in question;
(c) where the Authority has refused an application and the matter is not referred to the Tribunal, when the time for referring the matter to the Tribunal has expired;
(d) where the Authority has refused an application and the matter is referred to the Tribunal when—
(i) if the reference is determined by the Tribunal (including a determination following remission back to the Tribunal for rehearing in accordance with subsection (3)(a) of section 137 of the Act (appeal on a point of law)), the time for bringing an appeal has expired, or
(ii) on an appeal from a determination by the Tribunal on a point of law, the Court itself determines the application in accordance with section 137 of the Act.

(6) An applicant who is treated as having interim permission may not withdraw the application without first obtaining the consent of the Authority.

(7) Where—
(a) the Authority exercises its power under section 45 (variation etc on the Authority's own initiative) in relation to an authorised person who holds an interim permission; and
(b) as a result of the variation there are no longer any regulated activities for which the authorised person has permission,

the Authority must, once it is satisfied that it is no longer necessary to keep the interim permission in force, cancel it.

[4815]

NOTES

Commencement: 1 October 2006 (for certain purposes); 6 April 2007 (otherwise) (see art 1(2) at **[4813]**).

5 Interim approval

(1) This article applies where—
(a) an applicant (within the meaning of article 4(1)) has submitted, before commencement, an application to the Authority under section 60 of the Act (applications for approval); and
(b) the application has not been finally decided.

(2) The person in respect of whom the application is made is to be treated as having at commencement the Authority's approval for the purposes of section 59 of the Act (approval for particular arrangements) in relation to the functions to which the application relates.

(3) An approval which an applicant is to be treated as having is referred to in this Order as an "interim approval".

(4) Without prejudice to the exercise by the Authority of its powers under Part 4 of the Act an interim approval lapses when the application has been finally decided.

(5) In this article, "finally decided" means—
(a) when the application is withdrawn;
(b) when the Authority grants the application for approval under section 62 of the Act (applications for approval: procedure and right to refer to Tribunal);

(c) where the Authority has refused an application and the matter is not referred to the Tribunal, when the time for referring the matter to the Tribunal has expired;

(d) where the Authority has refused an application and the matter is referred to the Tribunal, when—

(i) if the reference is determined by the Tribunal (including a determination following remission back to the Tribunal for rehearing in accordance with subsection (3)(a) of section 137 of the Act), the time for bringing an appeal has expired, or

(ii) on an appeal from a determination by the Tribunal on a point of law, the Court itself determines the application in accordance with section 137 of the Act.

[4816]

NOTES

Commencement: 6 April 2007.

6 Application of the Authority's rules etc to persons with interim permission or interim approval

(1) The Authority may direct in writing that any relevant provision which would otherwise apply to a person by virtue of his interim permission or interim approval is not to apply, or is to apply to him as modified in the way specified in the direction.

(2) Where the Authority makes a rule, gives guidance or issues a statement or code which applies only to persons with an interim permission or an interim approval (or only to a class of such persons), sections 65 (statements and codes: procedure) and 155 (consultation) and subsection (3) of section 157 (guidance) of the Act do not apply to that rule, guidance, statement or code.

(3) For the purposes of paragraph (1), a "relevant provision" is any provision made as a result of the exercise by the Authority of any of its legislative functions mentioned in paragraph 1(2) of Schedule 1 to the Act (the Financial Services Authority).

[4817]

NOTES

Commencement: 6 April 2007.

7 Application of the Act etc

The Schedule modifies the application of the Act and the Principal Order in relation to persons with an interim permission or an interim approval.

[4818]

NOTES

Commencement: 6 April 2007.

8–12 (*Art 8 amends the Financial Services and Markets Act 2000* (*Collective Investment Schemes*) *Order 2001, SI 2001/1062, art 2 at* **[4142]**; *art 9 amends the Financial Services and Markets Act 2000* (*Carrying on Regulated Activities by Way of Business*) *Order 2001, SI 2001/1177, arts 3, 4 at* **[4147]**, **[4148]**; *art 10 amends the Financial Services and Markets Act 2000* (*Exemption*) *Order 2001, SI 2001/1201, art 5 at* **[4153]**; *art 11 amends the Financial Services and Markets Act 2000* (*Professions*) (*Non-Exempt Activities*) *Order 2001, SI 2001/1227, art 4 at* **[4167]**; *art 12 amends the Financial Services and Markets Act 2000* (*Financial Promotion*) *Order 2005, SI 2005/1529, art 72, Sch 1, Pt II at* **[4797]**, **[4801]**.)

SCHEDULE
APPLICATION OF THE ACT AND THE PRINCIPAL ORDER TO PERSONS WITH AN INTERIM PERMISSION OR AN INTERIM APPROVAL

Article 7

1. Paragraphs 2 and 3 apply to every person with interim permission.

2. For the purposes of section 20 (authorised persons acting without permission), a person's interim permission is treated as having been given to him under Part 4 of the Act.

3. A person's interim permission is to be disregarded for the purposes of—

(a) subsection (2) of section 38 (exemption orders),

(b) subsection (2) of section 40 (application for permission),

(c) subject to paragraph 7, section 42 (giving permission),

(d) section 43 (imposition of requirements), and

(e) subsections (1), (4) and (5) of section 44 (variation etc at request of authorised person).

4. Paragraphs 5(1), 6 to 9, 11, 12 and 13 apply to a person who falls within subsection (1) of section 31 (authorised persons) only by virtue of having an interim permission.

5.—(1) A person with interim permission is to be treated after commencement as an authorised person for the purposes of the Act (and any provision made under the Act), unless otherwise expressly provided for by this Schedule.

(2) A person with an interim approval is to be treated after commencement as an approved person for the purposes of the Act (and any provision made under the Act), unless otherwise expressly provided for by this Schedule.

6. For the purposes of subsection (1) of section 21 (restrictions on financial promotion) a person with an interim permission is not to be treated as an authorised person for the purposes of communicating or approving the content of a communication except where the communication invites or induces a person to enter into (or offer to enter into) an agreement the making or the performance of which constitutes a controlled activity which corresponds to a regulated activity which is covered by his interim permission.

7. A person with an interim permission may still be an appointed representative within the meaning of subsection (2) of section 39 (exemption of appointed representatives) (and hence may be treated as exempt from the general prohibition as a result of section 39(1) for the purposes of subsection (3)(a) of section 42 (giving permission)).

8. Subsection (3)(a) of section 213 (the compensation scheme) does not apply to a person who is a relevant person (within the meaning of that section) only by virtue of his having interim permission.

9. Subsection (1)(a) of section 347 (the record of authorised persons etc) is disapplied in relation to persons with interim permission.

10. Section 347(1)(h) is disapplied in relation to persons with interim approval.

11. In article 22 of the Principal Order (deals with or through authorised persons), with the exception of the first reference, the references to an "authorised person" do not include a person with interim permission.

12. In article 29 of the Principal Order (arranging deals with or through authorised persons), with the exception of the first reference, the references to an "authorised person" do not include a person with interim permission.

13. For the purposes of paragraphs (1)(a), (2)(a), (3) and (4)(a) of article 72 of the Principal Order (overseas persons), a person with an interim permission is not to be treated as an authorised person.

[4819]

NOTES

Commencement: 6 April 2007.

FINANCIAL SERVICES AND MARKETS ACT 2000 (REGULATED ACTIVITIES) (AMENDMENT) (NO 2) ORDER 2006

(SI 2006/2383)

NOTES

Made: 12 September 2006.

Authority: Financial Services and Markets Act 2000, ss 22(1), (5), 426, 427, 428(3), Sch 2, para 25.

Commencement: 6 November 2006 (for the purposes of enabling applications to be made for (i) a Pt IV permission, or a variation of a Pt IV permission, in relation to activities of the kind specified by arts 25B, 25C, 53B, 53C, 63B or 63F or, so far as relevant to any such activity, art 64 of the Regulated Activities Order 2001, or (ii) the Authority's approval under FSMA 2000, s 59 in relation to any of those activities); 6 April 2007 (otherwise). See art 1 at **[4820]**.

As of 1 July 2007, this Order had not been amended.

PART 1
GENERAL

1 Citation and commencement

(1) This Order may be cited as the Financial Services and Markets Act 2000 (Regulated Activities) (Amendment) (No 2) Order 2006.

(2) This Order comes into force—

(a) for the purposes of enabling applications to be made for—

(i) a Part IV permission, or a variation of a Part IV permission, in relation to activities of the kind specified by article 25B, 25C, 53B, 53C, 63B or 63F or, so far as relevant to any such activity, article 64 of the Financial Services and Markets Act 2000 (Regulated Activities) Order 2001; or

(ii) the Authority's approval under section 59 of the Financial Services and Markets Act 2000 in relation to any of those activities,

on 6th November 2006; and

(b) for all other purposes, on 6th April 2007.

[4820]

NOTES

Commencement: 6 November 2006 (certain purposes); 6 April 2007 (otherwise) (see para (2) above).

2–24 (*Arts 2–24* (*Pt 2*) *amend the Financial Services and Markets Act 2000* (*Regulated Activities*) *Order 2001, SI 2001/544, arts 3, 26, 27, 28A, 29, 29A, 33, 33A, 36, 54, 54A, 55, 61, 66, 67, 72, 72F, 89, and insert arts 25B, 25C, 53B, 53C, 63B–63I, 88A, 88B* (*see the 2001 Order at* **[4001]** *et seq*); *arts 25–28* (*Pt 3*) *amend the Consumer Credit Act 1974 and the Law of Property* (*Miscellaneous Provisions*) *Act 1989* (*outside the scope of this work*), *and amend the Companies Act 1985, s 262 at* **[266]**, *and the Financial Services and Markets Act 2000, s 49 at* **[2049]**; *arts 29–35* (*Pt 4*) *add the Financial Services and Markets Act 2000* (*Carrying on Regulated Activities by Way of Business*) *Order 2001, SI 2001/1177, arts 3B, 3C at* **[4147B]**, **[4147C]**, *amend the Financial Services and Markets Act 2000* (*Exemption*) *Order 2001, SI 2001/1201, Schedule, Pt IV at* **[4158]**, *the Financial Services and Markets Act 2000* (*Appointed Representatives*) *Regulations 2001, SI 2001/1217, regs 1–3 at* **[4159]**–**[4161]**, *the Financial Services and Markets Act 2000* (*Professions*) (*Non-Exempt Activities*) *Order 2001, SI 2001/1227, art 2 at* **[4165]**, *and insert arts 6C–6F of that Order at* **[4170A]**–**[4170D]**, *amend the Financial Services and Markets Act 2000* (*Financial Promotion*) *Order 2005, SI 2005/1529, arts 28B, 73, Sch 1, Pts I, II at* **[4751]**, **[4798]**, **[4800]**, **[4801]**, *and amend the Money Laundering Regulations 2003, SI 2003/3075, and the Consumer Credit* (*Advertisement*) *Regulations 2004, SI 2004/1484* (*outside the scope of this work.*)

PART 5
TRANSITIONAL PROVISIONS

36 Interpretation

In this Part—

"the Act" means the Financial Services and Markets Act 2000;

"commencement" means the beginning of 6th April 2007;

"the Regulated Activities Order" means the Financial Services and Markets Act 2000 (Regulated Activities) Order 2001.

[4821]

NOTES

Commencement: 6 November 2006 (certain purposes); 6 April 2007 (otherwise) (see art 1 at **[4820]**).

37 Interim permission

(1) This article applies where—

(a) a person ("the applicant") has submitted to the Authority an application for Part IV permission or a variation of a Part IV permission, to the extent that the application relates to an activity of the kind specified by any of the following articles of the Regulated Activities Order (as amended by this Order)—

(i) article 25B (arranging regulated home reversion plans);

(ii) article 25C (arranging regulated home purchase plans);

(iii) article 53B (advising on regulated home reversion plans);

(iv) article 53C (advising on regulated home purchase plans);

(v) article 63B (entering into and administering regulated home reversion plans);

(vi) article 63F (entering into and administering regulated home purchase plans); or

(vii) article 64 (agreeing to carry on specified kinds of activity), so far as relevant to any of the above activities;

(b) the applicant had carried on such activity before 6th November 2006;

(c) the Authority received the application on or before 23rd March 2007; and

(d) the application has not been finally decided before commencement.

(2) The applicant is to be treated as having on commencement the permission to which the application relates.

(3) A permission which an applicant is to be treated as having is referred to in this Part as an "interim permission".

(4) Without prejudice to the exercise by the Authority of its powers under Part 4 of the Act, an interim permission lapses—

(a) where the application relates to an activity of the kind specified by article 63B or 63F of the Regulated Activities Order or article 64 of that Order, so far as relevant to any such activity, when the application has been finally decided;

(b) where the application relates to an activity of the kind specified by article 25B, 25C, 53B or 53C of the Regulated Activities Order or article 64 of that Order, so far as relevant to any such activity—

(i) when the application has been finally decided; or

(ii) at the beginning of 6th April 2008,

whichever is the earlier.

(5) In this article, "finally decided" means—

(a) subject to paragraph (6), when the application is withdrawn;

(b) when the Authority grants permission under section 42 of the Act (giving permission) to carry on the activity in question;

(c) when the Authority varies a permission under section 44 of the Act (variation etc at request of authorised person) to add the activity in question;

(d) where the Authority has refused an application and the matter is not referred to the Tribunal, when the time for referring the matter to the Tribunal has expired;

(e) where the Authority has refused an application and the matter is referred to the Tribunal, when—

(i) if the reference is determined by the Tribunal (including a determination

PART IV
STATUTORY INSTRUMENTS

following remission back to the Tribunal for rehearing in accordance with section 137(3)(a) of the Act (appeal on a point of law)), the time for bringing an appeal has expired; or

(ii) on an appeal from a determination by the Tribunal on a point of law, the Court itself determines the application in accordance with section 137 of the Act.

(6) An applicant who is treated as having an interim permission may not withdraw the application without first obtaining the consent of the Authority.

(7) Where—

(a) the Authority exercises its powers under section 45 (variation etc on the Authority's own initiative) in relation to an authorised person who holds an interim permission; and

(b) as a result of the variation there are no longer any regulated activities for which the authorised person has permission,

the Authority must, once it is satisfied that it is no longer necessary to keep the interim permission in force, cancel it.

[4822]

NOTES

Commencement: 6 November 2006 (certain purposes); 6 April 2007 (otherwise) (see art 1 at **[4820]**).

38 Interim approval

(1) This article applies where—

(a) the applicant (within the meaning of article 37(1)(a)) has submitted to the Authority an application made under section 60 of the Act (applications for approval); and

(b) the application has not been finally decided before commencement.

(2) The person in respect of whom the application is made is to be treated as having on commencement the approval of the Authority for the purposes of section 59 of the Act (approval for particular arrangements) in relation to the functions to which the application relates.

(3) An approval which a person is to be treated as having is referred to in this Part as an "interim approval".

(4) Without prejudice to the exercise by the Authority of its powers under Part 5 of the Act, an interim approval lapses—

(a) where the application relates to an activity of the kind specified by article 63B or 63F of the Regulated Activities Order or article 64 of that Order, so far as relevant to any such activity, when the application has been finally decided;

(b) where the application relates to an activity of the kind specified by article 25B, 25C, 53B or 53C of the Regulated Activities Order or article 64 of that Order, so far as relevant to any such activity—

(i) when the application has been finally decided; or

(ii) at the beginning of 6th April 2008,

whichever is the earlier.

(5) In this article, "finally decided" means—

(a) when the application is withdrawn;

(b) when the Authority grants the application for approval under section 62 of the Act (applications for approval: procedure and right to refer to Tribunal);

(c) where the Authority has refused an application and the matter is not referred to the Tribunal, when the time for referring the matter to the Tribunal has expired;

(d) where the Authority has refused an application and the matter is referred to the Tribunal, when—

(i) if the reference is determined by the Tribunal (including a determination following remission back to the Tribunal for rehearing in accordance with section 137(3)(a) of the Act), the time for bringing an appeal has expired; or

(ii) on an appeal from a determination by the Tribunal on a point of law, the Court itself determines the application in accordance with section 137 of the Act.

[4823]

NOTES

Commencement: 6 November 2006 (certain purposes); 6 April 2007 (otherwise) (see art 1 at **[4820]**).

39 Application of the Authority's rules etc to persons with an interim permission or an interim approval

(1) The Authority may direct in writing that any relevant provision which would otherwise apply to a person by virtue of his interim permission or interim approval is not to apply or is to apply to him as modified in the way specified in the direction.

(2) Where the Authority makes a rule, gives guidance or issues a statement or code which applies only to persons with an interim permission or an interim approval (or only to a class of such persons), sections 65 (statements and codes: procedure), 155 (consultation) and 157(3) (guidance) of the Act do not apply to that rule, guidance, statement or code.

(3) For the purposes of paragraph (1) a "relevant provision" is any provision made as a result of the exercise by the Authority of any of its legislative functions mentioned in paragraph 1(2) of Schedule 1 to the Act (the Financial Services Authority).

[4824]

NOTES

Commencement: 6 November 2006 (certain purposes); 6 April 2007 (otherwise) (see art 1 at **[4820]**).

40 Application of the Act etc

The Schedule modifies the application of the Act and the Regulated Activities Order in relation to persons with an interim permission or an interim approval.

[4825]

NOTES

Commencement: 6 November 2006 (certain purposes); 6 April 2007 (otherwise) (see art 1 at **[4820]**).

SCHEDULE

APPLICATION OF THE ACT AND THE REGULATED ACTIVITIES ORDER TO PERSONS WITH AN INTERIM PERMISSION OR AN INTERIM APPROVAL

Article 40

1. Paragraphs 2 and 3 apply to every person with an interim permission.

2. For the purposes of section 20 (authorised persons acting without permission), a person's interim permission is treated as having been given to him under Part 4 of the Act.

3. A person's interim permission is to be disregarded for the purposes of—
   (a) section 38(2) (exemption orders);
   (b) section 40(2) (application for permission);
   (c) subject to paragraph 7, section 42 (giving permission);
   (d) section 43 (imposition of requirements); and
   (e) section 44(1), (4) and (5) (variation etc at request of authorised person).

4. Paragraphs 5(1) and 6 to 10 apply to a person who falls within section 31(1) (authorised persons) by virtue only of having an interim permission.

5.—(1) A person with an interim permission is to be treated on or after commencement as an authorised person for the purposes of the Act (and any provision made under the Act), unless otherwise expressly provided for by this Schedule.

(2) A person with an interim approval is to be treated on or after commencement as an approved person for the purposes of the Act (and any provision made under the Act).

6. For the purposes of section 21(2) (restrictions on financial promotion), a person with an interim permission is not to be treated as an authorised person for the purposes of communicating or approving the content of a communication except where the communication invites or induces a person to enter into (or offer to enter into) an agreement

the making or performance of which constitutes a controlled activity which corresponds to a regulated activity which is covered by his interim permission.

7. A person with an interim permission may still be an appointed representative within the meaning of section 39(2) (exemption of appointed representatives) (and hence may be treated as exempt from the general prohibition as a result of section 39(1) for the purposes of section 42(3)(a) (giving permission)).

8. Subsection (3)(a) of section 213 (the compensation scheme) does not apply to—
- (a) a person who is a relevant person, within the meaning of that section, by virtue only of having an interim permission; or
- (b) an appointed representative of such person.

9. In article 29 of the Regulated Activities Order (arranging deals with or through authorised persons), with the exception of the first reference, the references to an "authorised person" do not include a person with an interim permission.

10. In sub-paragraph (a) of both paragraphs (2) and (3) of article 29A of the Regulated Activities Order (arrangements made in the course of administration by authorised person), the references to an "authorised person" do not include a person with an interim permission.
[4826]

NOTES

Commencement: 6 November 2006 (certain purposes); 6 April 2007 (otherwise) (see art 1 at **[4820]**).

FINANCIAL SERVICES AND MARKETS ACT 2000 (REGULATED ACTIVITIES) (AMENDMENT NO 3) ORDER 2006 (NOTE)

(SI 2006/3384)

NOTES

This Order was made on 18 December 2006 under FSMA 2000, ss 22(1), (5), 428(3), Sch 2, para 25. It amends the Financial Services and Markets Act 2000 (Regulated Activities) Order 2001, SI 2001/544 at **[4001]** et seq. It also contains consequential amendments to the Fair Trading Act 1973, the Companies Act 1989, the Terrorism Act 2000, the Consumer Protection (Cancellation of Contracts Concluded away from Business Premises) Regulations 1987, the Companies (No 2) (Northern Ireland) Order 1990, the Financial Services and Markets Act 2000 (Collective Investment Schemes Order) 2001, the Financial Services and Markets Act 2000 (Carrying on Regulated Activities by Way of Business) Order 2001, the Financial Services and Markets Act 2000 (Consultation with Competent Authorities) Regulations 2001, the Money Laundering Regulations 2003, and the Financial Services and Markets Act 2000 (Financial Promotion) Order 2005. In so far as relevant to this work, these amendments have been incorporated at the appropriate place. Article 1 of this Order provides that this Order comes into force (a) on 1 April 2007 for the purposes of enabling applications to be made for (i) a Part IV permission, (ii) a variation of a Part IV permission, (iii) the Authority's approval under FSMA 2000, s 59, in relation to an activity of the kind specified by art 25D of the Regulated Activities Order, or in relation to an investment of the kind specified by arts 83, 84 or 85 of that Order; and (b) for all other purposes, on 1st November 2007.

[4826A]

FINANCIAL SERVICES AND MARKETS ACT 2000 (OMBUDSMAN SCHEME) (CONSUMER CREDIT ETC) ORDER 2007

(SI 2007/383)

NOTES

Made: 7 February 2007.
Authority: Financial Services and Markets Act 2000, s 226A(2)(e).
Commencement: 8 March 2007 (certain purposes); to be appointed (otherwise). See art 1 at **[4827]**.
As of 1 July 2007, this Order had not been amended.

1 Citation and commencement

This Order may be cited as the Financial Services and Markets Act 2000 (Ombudsman Scheme) (Consumer Credit Jurisdiction) Order 2007 and shall come into force—

(a) for the purposes of article 2(a) to (f) and (i) on 8th March 2007; and

(b) for all other purposes on the day sections 24 and 25 of the Consumer Credit Act 2006 come fully into force.

[4827]

NOTES

Commencement: 8 March 2007.

2 Types of Business

The Secretary of State specifies the following types of business for the purposes of section 226A(2)(e) of the Financial Services and Markets Act 2000—

(a) a consumer credit business;

(b) a consumer hire business;

(c) a business so far as it comprises or relates to credit brokerage;

(d) a business so far as it comprises or relates to debt-adjusting;

(e) a business so far as it comprises or relates to debt-counselling;

(f) a business so far as it comprises or relates to debt-collecting;

(g) a business so far as it comprises or relates to debt administration;

(h) a business so far as it comprises or relates to the provision of credit information services;

(i) a business so far as it comprises or relates to the operation of a credit reference agency.

[4828]–[6000]

NOTES

Commencement: 8 March 2007 (paras (a)–(f), (i)); to be appointed (paras (g), (h)).

B. OTHER STATUTORY INSTRUMENTS

COMPANY AND BUSINESS NAMES REGULATIONS 1981

(SI 1981/1685)

NOTES

Made: 24 November 1981.

Authority: CA 1981, ss 31, 32; these regulations now have effect as if made under CA 1985, s 29, and the Business Names Act 1985, ss 3, 6.

Commencement: 26 February 1982 (see reg 1 at **[6001]**). Where any provision in this work (including any inserted or substituted provision) came into force for all purposes on or before 1 July 2005, commencement information is not noted at provision level.

These Regulations are reproduced as amended by: the Company and Business Names (Amendment) Regulations 1982, SI 1982/1653; the Company and Business Names (Amendment) Regulations 1992, SI 1992/1196; the Company and Business Names (Amendment) Regulations 1995, SI 1995/3022; the Scotland Act 1998 (Consequential Modifications) (No 2) Order 1999, SI 1999/1820; the Companies and Business Names (Amendment) Regulations 2001, SI 2001/259; the Transfer of Functions (Miscellaneous) Order 2001, SI 2001/3500; the Secretaries of State for Education and Skills and for Work and Pensions Order 2002, SI 2002/1397; the Health Act 1999 (Consequential Amendments) (Nursing and Midwifery) Order 2004, SI 2004/1771; the Company and Business Names (Amendment) Regulations 2007, SI 2007/1947.

Limited liability partnerships: by the Limited Liability Partnerships Regulations 2001, SI 2001/1090, reg 10, Sch 6, Pt III, these Regulations apply, with modifications, to limited liability partnerships (see **[7000]**).

1 These Regulations may be cited as the Company and Business Names Regulations 1981 and shall come into operation on 26th February 1982.

[6001]

2 In these Regulations, unless the context otherwise requires, "the Act" means the Companies Act 1981.

[6002]

NOTES

Companies Act 1981: repealed and replaced by CA 1985.

3 The words and expressions stated in column (1) of the Schedule hereto [together with the plural and the possessive forms of those words and expressions] are hereby specified as words and expressions for the registration of which as or as part of a company's corporate name the approval of the Secretary of State is required by section 22(2)(b) of the Act or for the use of which as or as part of a business name his approval is required by section 28(2)(b) of the Act.

[6003]

NOTES

Words in square brackets inserted by the Company and Business Names (Amendment) Regulations 1992, SI 1992/1196, reg 2(1), (2), as from 12 June 1992.

Sections 22(2)(b), 28(2)(b) of the Act: see now CA 1985, s 26(2)(b), the Business Names Act 1985, s 2(1)(b), respectively.

4 Subject to Regulation 5, each Government department or other body stated in column (2) of the Schedule hereto is hereby specified as the relevant body for the purposes of section 31(2) and (3) of the Act in relation to the word or expression [and the plural and the possessive forms of that word or expression] opposite to it in column (1).

[6004]

NOTES

Words in square brackets inserted by the Company and Business Names (Amendment) Regulations 1992, SI 1992/1196, reg 2(1), (3), as from 12 June 1992.

Section 31(2), (3) of the Act: see now CA 1985, s 29(2), (3) and the Business Names Act 1985, s 3(2).

5 Where two Government departments or other bodies are specified in the alternative in Column (2) of the Schedule hereto the second alternative is to be treated as specified,

(a) in the case of the corporate name of a company,

(i) if the company has not yet been registered and its principal or only place of business in Great Britain is to be in Scotland or, if it will have no place of business in Great Britain, its proposed registered office is in Scotland, and

(ii) if the company is already registered and its principal or only place of business in Great Britain is in Scotland or, if it has no place of business in Great Britain, its registered office is in Scotland, and

(b) in the case of a business name, if the principal or only place of the business carried on or to be carried on in Great Britain is or is to be in Scotland,

and the first alternative is to be treated as specified in any other case.

[6005]

SCHEDULE
SPECIFICATION OF WORDS, EXPRESSIONS AND RELEVANT BODIES

Regulations 3–5

Column (1) *Word or expression*	*Column (2)* *Relevant body*
Abortion	Department of Health (formerly of Health and Social Security)
Apothecary	[Worshipful Society of Apothecaries of London] or Pharmaceutical Society of Great Britain
Association	
Assurance	
Assurer	
Authority	
Benevolent	
Board	
. . .	
British	
. . .	
[Chamber (or Chambers) of Business (or their Welsh equivalents, Siambr Fusnes; Siambrau Busnes)	
Chamber (or Chambers) of Commerce (or their Welsh equivalents, Siambr Fasnach; Siambrau Masnach)	
Chamber (or Chambers) of Commerce and Industry (or their Welsh equivalents, Siambr Masnach a Diwydiant; Siambrau Masnach a Diwydiant)	
Chamber (or Chambers) of Commerce, Training and Enterprise (or their Welsh equivalents, Siambr Masnach, Hyfforddiant a Menter; Siambrau Masnach, Hyfforddiant a Menter)	

PART IV STATUTORY INSTRUMENTS

Column (1) *Word or expression*	*Column (2)* *Relevant body*
Chamber (or Chambers) of Enterprise (or their Welsh equivalents, Siambr Fenter; Siambrau Menter)	
Chamber (or Chambers) of Industry (or their Welsh equivalents, Siambr Ddiwydiant; Siambrau Diwydiant)	
Chamber (or Chambers) of Trade (or their Welsh equivalents, Siambr Fasnach; Siambrau Masnach)	
Chamber (or Chambers) of Trade and Industry (or their Welsh equivalents, Siambr Masnach a Diwydiant; Siambrau Masnach a Diwydiant)	
Chamber (or Chambers) of Training (or their Welsh equivalents, Siambr Hyfforddiant; Siambrau Hyfforddiant)	
Chamber (or Chambers) of Training and Enterprise (or their Welsh equivalents, Siambr Hyfforddiant a Menter; Siambrau Hyfforddiant a Menter)]	
Chamber of Industry	
Chamber of Trade	
Charitable	Charity Commission or [the Scottish Ministers]
Charity	Charity Commission or [the Scottish Ministers]
Charter	
Chartered	
[Chemist	
Chemistry]	
Contact Lens	General Optical Council
Co-operative	
Council	
Dental	General Dental Council
Dentistry	General Dental Council
District Nurse	[Nursing and Midwifery Council]
Duke	Home Office or [the Scottish Ministers]
England	
English	
European	
Federation	

Column (1) *Word or expression*	*Column (2)* *Relevant body*
Friendly Society	
Foundation	
Fund	
Giro	
[Government]	
Great Britain	
Group	
Health Centre	Department of Health (formerly of Health and Social Security)
Health Service	Department of Health (formerly of Health and Social Security)
Health Visitor	[Nursing and Midwifery Council]
Her Majesty	Home Office or [the Scottish Ministers]
His Majesty	Home Office or [the Scottish Ministers]
Holding	
Industrial and Provident Society	
Institute	
Institution	
Insurance	
Insurer	
International	
Ireland	
Irish	
King	Home Office or [the Scottish Ministers]
Midwife	[Nursing and Midwifery Council]
Midwifery	[Nursing and Midwifery Council]
National	
Nurse	[Nursing and Midwifery Council]
Nursing	[Nursing and Midwifery Council]
. . .	
Patent	
Patentee	
Police	Home Office or [the Scottish Ministers]
[Polytechnic]	[Department for Education and Skills]
Post Office	
Pregnancy Termination	Department of Health (formerly of Health and Social Security)
Prince	Home Office or [the Scottish Ministers]
Princess	Home Office or [the Scottish Ministers]
Queen	Home Office or [the Scottish Ministers]
Reassurance	
Reassurer	
Register	

PART IV
STATUTORY INSTRUMENTS

Column (1) *Word or expression*	*Column (2)* *Relevant body*
Registered	
Reinsurance	
Reinsurer	
Royal	Home Office or [the Scottish Ministers]
Royale	Home Office or [the Scottish Ministers]
Royalty	Home Office or [the Scottish Ministers]
Scotland	
Scottish	
Sheffield	
Society	
Special School	[Department for Education and Skills]
Stock Exchange	
Trade Union	
Trust	
United Kingdom	
[University]	[The Privy Council]
Wales	
Welsh	
Windsor	Home Office or [the Scottish Ministers]

[Note: The reference in Column (2) to the Home Office shall be treated as a reference to the Lord Chancellor's Department in relation to the following entries in Column (1)—

(a) Duke,
(b) Her Majesty,
(c) His Majesty,
(d) King,
(e) Prince,
(f) Princess,
(g) Queen,
(h) Royal,
(i) Royale,
(j) Royalty, and
(k) Windsor.]

[6006]

NOTES

In entry "Apothecary" words in square brackets substituted by the Company and Business Names (Amendment) Regulations 1982, SI 1982/1653, reg 2(a), as from 1 January 1983.

Entries "Breed", "Breeder", "Breeding" and "Nursing Home" revoked by the Company and Business Names (Amendment) Regulations 1995, SI 1995/3022, reg 3(b), as from 1 January 1996.

Entry "Building Society" revoked by the Company and Business Names (Amendment) Regulations 1992, SI 1992/1196, reg 2(1), (4), as from 12 June 1992.

Entries from "Chamber (or Chambers) of Business" to "Chamber (or Chambers) of Training and Enterprise" substituted, for entries "Chamber of Commerce", "Chamber of Industry", "Chamber of Commerce, Training and Enterprise" (originally inserted by SI 1995/3022, reg 3(a)) and "Chamber of Trade" by the Companies and Business Names (Amendment) Regulations 2001, SI 2001/259, reg 3, as from 10 May 2001.

Entries "Chemist", "Chemistry", "Polytechnic" and "University" inserted by SI 1982/1653, reg 2(b), (c), as from 1 January 1983.

Entry "Government" inserted by the Company and Business Names (Amendment) Regulations 2007, SI 2007/1947, reg 2, as from 10 July 2007; for savings see the note below.

Words "Nursing and Midwifery Council" in square brackets in Column 2 opposite entries for "District Nurse", "Health Visitor", "Midwife", "Midwifery", "Nurse", and "Nursing" substituted by the Health Act 1999 (Consequential Amendments) (Nursing and Midwifery) Order 2004, SI 2004/1771, art 3, Schedule, Pt 2, para 52, as from 1 August 2004.

In column (2) words "Department for Education and Skills" in square brackets in each place they appear substituted by the Secretaries of State for Education and Skills and for Work and Pensions Order 2002, SI 2002/1397, art 12, Schedule, Pt II, para 17, as from 27 June 2002.

In entry "University" words in square brackets substituted by SI 1992/1196, reg 2(1), (5).

Note in final pair of square brackets added by the Transfer of Functions (Miscellaneous) Order 2001, SI 2001/3500, art 8, Sch 2, Pt II, para 14, as from 26 November 2001.

In column (2), the words "the Scottish Ministers" in square brackets in each place they appear substituted by the Scotland Act 1998 (Consequential Modifications) (No 2) Order 1999, SI 1999/1820, art 4, Sch 2, Pt II, para 139, as from 1 July 1999.

Savings: the Company and Business Names (Amendment) Regulations 2007, SI 2007/1947, reg 3 provides as follows—

"Business names

(1) Section 2(1)(b) of the Act does not apply to the carrying on of a business under a name which includes the word "Government" by a person—

(a) to whom the business is transferred on or after the date on which these Regulations came into force; and

(b) who carries on the business under the name which was its lawful business name immediately before that transfer,

during the period of 12 months beginning with the date of the transfer.

(2) Section 2(1)(b) of the Act does not apply to the carrying on of a business under a name which includes the word "Government" by a person who—

(a) carried on that business immediately before the date on which these Regulations came into force; and

(b) continues to carry it on under the name which immediately before that date was its lawful business name.".

COMPANIES (INSPECTORS' REPORTS) (FEES) REGULATIONS 1981 (NOTE)

(SI 1981/1686)

NOTES

See Appendix 3 (Fees Instruments) at **[A3]**.

[6007]–[6021]

COMPANIES (UNREGISTERED COMPANIES) REGULATIONS 1985

(SI 1985/680)

NOTES

Made: 29 April 1985.

Authority: CA 1985, s 718, Sch 22.

Commencement: 1 July 1985 (see reg 1 at **[6022]**). Where any provision in this work (including any inserted or substituted provision) came into force for all purposes on or before 1 July 2005, commencement information is not noted at provision level.

These Regulations are reproduced as amended by: the Companies (Unregistered Companies) (Amendment) Regulations 1990, SI 1990/438; the Companies (Unregistered Companies) (Amendment No 2) Regulations 1990, SI 1990/1394; the Companies (Unregistered Companies) (Amendment No 3) Regulations 1990, SI 1990/2571; the Companies (Unregistered Companies) (Amendment) Regulations 2001, SI 2001/86.

1 These Regulations may be cited as the Companies (Unregistered Companies) Regulations 1985 and shall come into operation on 1st July 1985.

[6022]

2 In these Regulations—

"the Act" means the Companies Act 1985;

PART IV
STATUTORY INSTRUMENTS

"instrument constituting or regulating the company" means any Act of Parliament, royal charter, letters patent, deed of settlement, contract of co-partnery, or other instrument constituting or regulating the company; and

"unregistered company" means any body corporate, incorporated in and having a principal place of business in Great Britain, other than a body corporate mentioned in section 718(2) of the Act.

[6023]

3 (*Revokes the Companies (Unregistered Companies) (Completion of Stock Exchange Bargains) Regulations 1980, SI 1980/926, and the Companies (Unregistered Companies) Regulations 1984, SI 1984/682.*)

4 Subject to Regulation 5 below, the provisions of the Act specified in the Schedule to these Regulations shall apply to any unregistered company.

[6024]

5 For the purposes of the application to any unregistered company of the provisions which apply to it by virtue of Regulation 4 above—

(a) that company shall be deemed to be—

(i) a company registered in England and Wales if its principal office on 5th January 1976 or, in the case of a company incorporated after that date, immediately after its incorporation was situated in England or Wales; or

(ii) a company registered in Scotland if its principal office on 5th January 1976 or, in the case of a company incorporated after that date, immediately after its incorporation was situated in Scotland;

and "registrar of companies" shall be construed accordingly;

(b) references to the registered office of a company shall be construed as references to the principal office of the company in England, Wales or Scotland, as the case may be;

(c) references to a public company shall be construed as references to an unregistered company which has power under the instrument constituting or regulating it to offer its shares or debentures to the public, and references to a private company shall be construed as references to an unregistered company which does not have power so to offer its shares or debentures;

(d) in relation to expenses and commissions incurred before 1st January 1985, Schedule 4 to the Act shall have effect, for the purposes of accounts of the company for any financial year beginning before 1st January 1990, as though paragraphs 3(2)(a) and (b) were omitted; and

(e) the said provisions shall be subject to the modifications and extensions set out in Regulation 6 below.

[6025]

6 The modifications and extensions referred to in Regulation 5(e) above are the following—

(a) for references to the memorandum or articles of association of a company there shall be substituted references to any instrument constituting or regulating the company;

(b) section 18 of the Act shall have effect as if—

(i) for the words "by any statutory provision, whether contained in an Act of Parliament or in an instrument made under an Act, a printed copy of the Act or instrument" there were substituted the words "a printed copy of the instrument effecting the alteration" and for the words "that provision comes into force" there were substituted the words "that instrument comes into effect"; and

(ii) in the case of a company incorporated on or after 5th January 1976, it required a printed copy of any instrument constituting or regulating the company to be forwarded to the registrar of companies not later than fifteen days after the date of the incorporation of the company and recorded by him, notwithstanding that such instrument has not been the subject of any alteration;

(c) [sections 35 and 35B] of the Act shall have effect as though [they] were expressed to be without prejudice to any rule of law which gives to a person dealing with a company incorporated by letters patent or by royal charter any greater protection in relation to the capacity of such a company than that afforded by [those sections];

(d) in sections [36 to 36B] 40 and 186, for the references to the common seal of the company there shall be substituted references to the common or other authorised seal of the company;

(e) section 185(4) shall have effect as if for the words "subsection (1)" there were substituted "any provision of any instrument constituting or regulating the company";

(f) in section 351(1) of the Act for paragraphs (a) to (d) there shall be substituted the following—

"(a) whether the company has its principal office in England, Wales or Scotland, as the case may be, and the number which has been allocated to the company by the registrar of companies;

(b) the address of its principal office; and

(c) the manner in which it was incorporated and, if it is a limited company, that fact";

(g) notice of the receipt by the registrar of companies of

(i) any instrument constituting or regulating the company; and

(ii) any notice of the situation of the company's principal office

shall be included in the matters which the registrar is required to cause to be published in the Gazette by virtue of section 711 of the Act;

(h) Schedule 4 to the Act shall have effect as if—

(i) item K, II in balance sheet format 1 and liability item A, II in balance sheet format 2;

(ii) paragraph 51(2);

(iii) Part V; and

(iv) …

were omitted;

[(hh) Schedule 5 to the Act shall have effect as if paragraphs 10 and 29 were omitted.]

(i) Schedule 9 to the Act shall have effect as if [paragraph 13(4) was] omitted.

[6026]

NOTES

Para (c): words in square brackets substituted by the Companies (Unregistered Companies) (Amendment No 3) Regulations 1990, SI 1990/2571, reg 2(a), as from 4 February 1991.

Para (d): words in square brackets inserted by the Companies (Unregistered Companies) (Amendment No 2) Regulations 1990, SI 1990/1394, reg 2(a), as from 31 July 1990.

Para (h): sub-para (iv) revoked by the Companies (Unregistered Companies) (Amendment) Regulations 1990, SI 1990/438, reg 2(a), as from 1 April 1990.

Para (hh): inserted by SI 1990/438, reg 2(a), as from 1 April 1990.

Para (i): words in square brackets substituted by SI 1990/438, reg 2(b), as from 1 April 1990.

SCHEDULE
PROVISIONS OF THE ACT APPLIED TO UNREGISTERED COMPANIES BY REGULATION 4

Regulation 4

Provisions of the Act applied	*Subject matter*
In Part I—	
—section 18	Statutory and other amendments of memorandum and articles to be registered.
—[sections 35 to 35B	Company's capacity; power of directors to bind it.]
—[sections 36 to 36C	Company contracts and execution of documents by companies.]
—section 40	Official seal for share certificates etc.
—section 42	Events affecting a company's status to be officially notified.
In Part III, Chapter I (with Schedule 3)	Prospectus and requirements in connection with it.

PART IV STATUTORY INSTRUMENTS

Provisions of the Act applied	*Subject matter*
In Part IV, sections 82, 86 and 87............	Allotments
In Part V	
—section 185(4)..	Exemption from duty to prepare certificates where shares etc, issued to stock exchange nominee.
—section 186..	Certificate as evidence of title.
Part VII [(except sections 252 and 253)]..	}
—Schedules 4 to 6	}
—Schedule 7 (except [paragraphs 2 to 2B, 7 and 8]	}
—Schedule 8	} Accounts and Audit
—Schedule 9 (except sub-paragraphs (a) to (d) of paragraph 2, sub-paragraphs (c), (d) and (e) of paragraph 3 and sub-paragraph (1)(c) of paragraph 10), and [Schedules 10 and 10A]	}
In Part IX—	
—section 287..	Accounts and Audit
In Part X—	
—[section 322A	Invalidity of certain transactions involving directors, etc.]
—sections 343 to 347	Register to be kept of certain transactions not disclosed in accounts; other related matters.
[Part XA	Control of political donations by companies]
In Part XI—	
—sections 351(1), (2) and (5)(a).............	Particulars of company to be given in correspondence.
—sections 363 (with Schedule 15) to 365	Annual return.
—[sections 384 to 394A (except sections 385A, 386 and 393)]..................	Appointment, … etc, of auditors.
In Part XXIV—	
—section 711..	Public notice by registrar of companies with respect to certain documents.
In Part XXV—	
—section 720..	Companies to publish periodical statement.

[6027]

NOTES

Words in first pair of square brackets substituted, and words in sixth pair of square brackets inserted, by the Companies (Unregistered Companies) (Amendment No 3) Regulations 1990, SI 1990/2571, reg 2(b), (c), as from 4 February 1991; words in second pair of square brackets substituted by the Companies (Unregistered Companies) (Amendment No 2) Regulations 1990, SI 1990/1394, as from 31 July 1990; entry relating to Part XA inserted by the Companies (Unregistered Companies) (Amendment) Regulations 2001, SI 2001/86, reg 2, as from 16 February 2001; other words in square brackets substituted, and words omitted revoked, by the Companies (Unregistered Companies) (Amendment) Regulations 1990, SI 1990/438, reg 2(c), (d), as from 1 April 1990.

COMPANIES (REGISTERS AND OTHER RECORDS) REGULATIONS 1985

(SI 1985/724)

NOTES

Made: 8 May 1985.
Authority: CA 1985, s 723(4).
Commencement: 1 July 1985 (see reg 1 at **[6028]**). Where any provision in this work (including any inserted or substituted provision) came into force for all purposes on or before 1 July 2005, commencement information is not noted at provision level.

These Regulations are reproduced as amended by: the Uncertificated Securities Regulations 2001, SI 2001/3755.

Limited liability partnerships: by the Limited Liability Partnerships Regulations 2001, SI 2001/1090, reg 10, Sch 6, Pt I, these Regulations apply, with modifications, to limited liability partnerships (see **[6998]**).

ARRANGEMENT OF REGULATIONS

SCHEDULES

1 Citation, commencement, revocation and interpretation

(1) These Regulations may be cited as the Companies (Registers and other Records) Regulations 1985 and shall come into operation on 1st July 1985.

(2) In these Regulations, unless the context otherwise requires—

"the Act" means the Companies Act 1985;

"the place for inspection" means, in relation to a register, or a register of holders of debentures of a company, which is kept by recording the matters in question otherwise than in a legible form, the place where the duty to allow inspection of the register is for the time being performed in accordance with these Regulations;

"register" means a register or other record as is mentioned in section 722(1) of the Act [or regulation 20 of the 2001 Regulations];

"the register of directors' interests" means the register required to be kept under section 325(1) of the Act.

["the 2001 Regulations" means the Uncertificated Securities Regulations 2001; and expressions defined in the 2001 Regulations shall have the same meaning in these Regulations.]

(3) Any reference in these Regulations to the duty to allow inspection of a register, or of the register of holders of debentures, is a reference to the duty provided for in section 723(3) of the Act to allow inspection of, or to furnish, a reproduction of the recording of the register, or of the relevant part of the recording in a legible form.

(4) Any reference in these Regulations to the register of interests in voting shares shall be construed as including a reference to the separate part of that register referred to in section 213(1) of the Act.

(5) …

[6028]

NOTES

Para (2): in definition "register" words in square brackets added, and definition "the 2001 Regulations" added, by the Uncertificated Securities Regulations 2001, SI 2001/3755, reg 51, Sch 7, Pt 2, para 17(a), as from 26 November 2001.

Para (5): revokes the Companies (Registers and other Records) Regulations 1979, SI 1979/53.

2 Requirements with respect to registers kept otherwise than in a legible form

(1) This Regulation applies with respect to any register specified in Schedule 1 to these Regulations which is kept by a company by recording the matters in question otherwise than in a legible form.

(2) The company shall perform the duty to allow inspection of any register to which this Regulation applies at a place specified in the said Schedule 1 in relation to that register.

(3) In the case of any register to which this Regulation applies, the company shall not be required—

(a) to keep the register in any place where it is required to be kept under the Act,

(b) to give any notice to the registrar of companies required to be given under the Act of the place where the register is kept, or of any change in that place, or

(c) to include in its annual return any statement required to be given under the Act of the address of the place where the register is kept.

(4) Where provision is made in the Act with respect to default in complying with any requirement of that Act regarding the place where a register specified in Schedule 1 to these Regulations is to be kept, that provision shall have effect in relation to any such register to which this Regulation applies as if there were substituted for the reference therein to such default, a reference to default in complying with the requirements of paragraph (2) above.

[(5) This Regulation applies with respect to an issuer of members and a record of uncertificated shares which is kept by a company by recording the matters in question otherwise than in legible form—

(a) as it applies to a register of members under the Act which is kept in like fashion; and

(b) as if references to the Act were references to the 2001 Regulations.

(6) This Regulation applies with respect to an index kept by virtue of paragraph 7 of Schedule 4 to the 2001 Regulations which is kept by a company by recording the matters in question otherwise than in legible form—

(a) as it applies to an index of a register of members under the Act which is kept in like fashion; and

(b) as if references to the Act were references to the 2001 Regulations.]

[6029]

NOTES

Paras (5), (6): added by the Uncertificated Securities Regulations 2001, SI 2001/3755, reg 51, Sch 7, Pt 2, para 17(b), as from 26 November 2001.

3 Notification of place for inspection of registers

(1) Subject to the provisions of paragraph (3) below, where a company keeps any register specified in paragraph (2) below by recording the matters in question otherwise than in a legible form, the company shall send to the registrar of companies notice, in the form indicated in Part I of Schedule 2 to these Regulations, of the place for inspection of that register and of any change in that place.

(2) The registers referred to in paragraph (1) above are

(a) the register of members,

(b) an overseas branch register, and

(c) the register of directors' interests.

(3) The company shall not be obliged to give notice under paragraph (1) above—

(a) where the company changes from keeping a register in a legible form to keeping it otherwise than in a legible form and the place for inspection of the register immediately following the change is the same as the place where the register was kept in a legible form immediately prior to the change, or

(b) in the case of a register specified in paragraph 2(a) or (c) above, where since the register first came into existence—

(i) it has been kept by recording the matters in question otherwise than in a legible form, and

(ii) the place for inspection has been the registered office of the company.

(4) Where the register of members of a company is kept by recording the matters in question otherwise than in a legible form and the place for inspection of that register is elsewhere than at the registered office, the company shall include in its annual return a statement of the address of the place for inspection of that register.

(5) Subsection (4) of section 353 of the Act shall apply with respect to any default in complying with paragraph (1) above as it applies in relation to a default in complying with subsection (2) of that section; and subsection (7) of section 363 of the Act shall apply with respect to any failure to comply with paragraph (4) above as it applies in relation to a failure to comply with that section.

[(6) In the case of a company which is a participating issuer, references in this regulation to the register of members shall be taken to be a reference to the company's issuer register of members and record of uncertificated shares.]

[6030]

NOTES

Para (6): added by the Uncertificated Securities Regulations 2001, SI 2001/3755, reg 51, Sch 7, Pt 2, para 17(c), as from 26 November 2001.

4 Requirements with respect to a register of debenture holders kept otherwise than in a legible form

(1) This Regulation applies to any register of holders of debentures of a company which is kept by a company by recording the matters in question otherwise than in a legible form.

(2) A company registered in England and Wales shall not perform the duty to allow inspection of a register to which this Regulation applies in Scotland and a company registered in Scotland shall not perform such duty in England and Wales.

(3) A company shall not perform the duty to allow inspection of a register to which this Regulation applies in England and Wales, in the case of a company registered in England and Wales, or in Scotland, in the case of a company registered in Scotland, elsewhere than at—

(a) the registered office of the company,

(b) any other office of the company at which the work of ensuring that the register is duly made up is done, or

(c) if the company arranges with some other person for the carrying out of the work referred to in (b) above to be undertaken on behalf of the company by that other person, the office of that other person at which the work is done.

(4) The requirements of section 190 of the Act (provisions as to registers of debenture holders) and sections 363 and 364 of and Schedule 15 to that Act (annual returns) shall not apply to a register to which this Regulation applies insofar as they relate to any of the following matters—

(a) the place where the register is permitted to be kept,

(b) the giving of notice to the registrar of companies of the place where the register is kept, or of any change in that place, and

(c) the inclusion in the annual return of a statement of the address of the place where the register is kept.

[6031]

5 Notification of the place for inspection of registers of debenture holders

(1) Subject to paragraph (2) below, where the place for inspection of a register to which Regulation 4 above applies is in England and Wales or Scotland, the company shall send to the registrar of companies, notice in the form indicated in Part II of Schedule 2 to these Regulations of the place for inspection of that register and of any change in that place.

(2) The company shall not be obliged to give notice under paragraph (1) above—

(a) where a company changes from keeping the register in a legible form to keeping it otherwise than in a legible form and the place for inspection of the register immediately following the change is the same as the place where the register was kept in a legible form immediately prior to the change, or

(b) where since the register first came into existence—

(i) it has been kept by recording the matters in question otherwise than in a legible form, and

(ii) the place for inspection has been the registered office of the company.

(3) Where the place for inspection of a register to which Regulation 4 above applies is situated in England and Wales, in the case of a company registered in England and Wales, or in Scotland, in the case of a company registered in Scotland, elsewhere than at the registered office of the company, the company shall include in its annual return a statement of the address of that place.

(4) Subsection (7) of section 363 of the Act shall apply with respect to any failure to comply with paragraph (3) above as it applies in relation to a failure to comply with that section.

[6032]

6 Other provisions relating to registers kept otherwise than in a legible form

(1) Where a register or a register of holders of debentures is kept by recording the matters in question otherwise than in a legible form, any reference to such register in any provision of the Act [or the 2001 Regulations] relating to the place where a duplicate of such register, another register or duplicate of another register is required to be kept, shall be construed as a reference to the place for inspection of the first mentioned register.

(2) Where the place for inspection of the register of members is the office of some person other than the company and by reason of any default of that person the company fails to comply with—

(a) the provisions of Regulation 2 above relating to the duty to allow inspection of the index of the register of members, or

(b) the provisions of Regulation 3 above relating to the register of members, section 357 of the Act (consequences of failure to comply with requirements as to register owing to agent's default) shall apply with respect to such failure as it applies in relation to a failure to comply with the provisions specified in that section by reason of any default of the person other than the company, at whose office the register of members is kept.

[(2A) In the case of a company which is a participating issuer, paragraph (2) shall apply as if—

(a) references to the register of members were references to the company's issuer register of members and record of uncertificated shares; and

(b) the reference to the index of the register of members were a reference to an index kept by virtue of paragraph 7 of Schedule 4 to the 2001 Regulations.]

(3) Where an overseas branch register is kept by a company by recording the matters in question otherwise than in a legible form, paragraphs 2(2) and 3(1) of Schedule 14 to the Act shall have effect as if, for the references to the country or territory where that register is kept, there were substituted references to the country or territory where the place for inspection of the register is situated.

(4) Where the register of directors' interests is kept by a company by recording the matters in question otherwise than in a legible form, paragraph 29 of Schedule 13 to the Act shall have effect as if, for the reference to that register, there were substituted a reference to a reproduction of the recording of that register in a legible form.

(5) Where the accounting records of a company are kept otherwise than in a legible form and the place for inspection of such records is outside Great Britain, section 222(2) of the Act shall have effect as if, for the references to the accounting records being kept at a place outside Great Britain, there were substituted references to the place for inspection of such records being at a place outside Great Britain.

[6033]

NOTES

Para (1): words in square brackets inserted by the Uncertificated Securities Regulations 2001, SI 2001/3755, reg 51, Sch 7, Pt 2, para 17(d)(i), as from 26 November 2001.

Para (2A): inserted by SI 2001/3755, reg 51, Sch 7, Pt 2, para 17(d)(ii), as from 26 November 2001.

SCHEDULES

SCHEDULE 1
PLACES FOR PERFORMANCE OF DUTY TO ALLOW INSPECTION OF REGISTERS KEPT OTHERWISE THAN IN A LEGIBLE FORM

Regulation 2

Statutory Provision	*Register*	*Place*
COMPANIES ACT 1985		
Section 211(8)	Register and any associated index of interests in voting shares	(a) Where the register of directors' interests is kept otherwise than in a legible form, the place for inspection of that register. (b) Where the register of directors' interests is kept in a legible form, the place where it is so kept.
Section 222(1)	Accounting records	The registered office of the company or such other place as the directors of the company think fit.
Section 288(1)	Register of directors and secretaries	The registered office of the company.
Section 353(1)	Register of members	The registered office of the company provided that— (a) if the work of ensuring that the requirements of the Act with regard to entries in the register are complied with is done at another office of the company, the place for inspection may be that other office and (b) if the company arranges with some other person for the carrying out of the work referred to in (a) above to be undertaken on behalf of the company by that other person, the place for inspection may be the office of that other person at which the work is done; so however that the place for inspection shall not, in the case of a company registered in England and Wales, be at a place outside England and Wales and, in the case of a company registered in Scotland, be at a place outside Scotland.
Section 354(3)	Index of the register of members	(a) Where the register of members is kept otherwise than in a legible form, the place for inspection of that register. (b) Where the register of members is kept in a legible form, the place where it is so kept.
Section 362(1)	Overseas branch register	Any place where, but for these Regulations, the register would be permitted to be kept under section 362(1) of the Act.
Sections 407(1) and 422(1)	Register of charges	The registered office of the company.

PART IV
STATUTORY INSTRUMENTS

Statutory Provision	*Register*	*Place*
Schedule 13, paragraph 25	Register of directors' interests	(a) Where the register of members is kept otherwise than in a legible form— (i) if the place for inspection of that register is the registered office of the company, that office, and (ii) if not, the place for inspection of that register or the registered office of the company. (b) Where the register of members is kept in a legible form— (i) if that register is kept at the registered office of the company, that office, and (ii) if that register is not so kept, the place where that register is kept or the registered office of the company.
Schedule 13, paragraph 28	Index of the register of directors' interests	(a) Where the register of directors' interests is kept otherwise than in a legible form, the place for inspection of that register. (b) Where the register of directors' interests is kept in a legible form, the place where it is so kept.
Schedule 14, paragraph 4(1)	Duplicate of overseas branch register	(a) Where the register of members is kept otherwise than in a legible form, the place for inspection of that register. (b) Where the register of members is kept in a legible form, the place where it is so kept.

[6034]

(*Sch 2 contains forms; see Appendix 4 at* **[A4]**.)

COMPANIES (DISCLOSURE OF DIRECTORS' INTERESTS) (EXCEPTIONS) REGULATIONS 1985 (NOTE)

(SI 1985/802)

NOTES

These Regulations were made on the 21 May 1985 under CA 1985, s 324(3). They lapsed on 6 April 2007 following the repeal of s 324 by the Companies Act 2006, ss 1177, 1295, Sch 16.

[6035]–[6036A]

COMPANIES (TABLES A TO F) REGULATIONS 1985

(SI 1985/805)

NOTES

Made: 22 May 1985.
Authority: CA 1985, ss 3, 8.

Commencement: 1 July 1985. Where any provision in this work (including any inserted or substituted provision) came into force for all purposes on or before 1 July 2005, commencement information is not noted at provision level.

These Regulations are reproduced as amended by: as to amendments to Table A, see Appendix 2 at **[A2]**. None of the other provisions of these Regulations had been amended as of 1 July 2007.

1 These Regulations may be cited as the Companies (Tables A to F) Regulations 1985 and shall come into operation on 1st July 1985.

[6037]

2 The regulations in Table A and the forms in Tables B, C, D, E and F in the Schedule to these Regulations shall be the regulations and forms of memorandum and articles of association for the purposes of sections 3 and 8 of the Companies Act 1985.

[6038]

3 (*Revokes the Companies (Alteration of Table A etc) Regulations 1984, SI 1984/717.*)

SCHEDULE

(*Table A reproduced at* **[A2]**.)

TABLE B

A PRIVATE COMPANY LIMITED BY SHARES

MEMORANDUM OF ASSOCIATION

1. The company's name is "The South Wales Motor Transport Company cyfyngedig".

2. The company's registered office is to be situated in Wales.

3. The company's objects are the carriage of passengers and goods in motor vehicles between such places as the company may from time to time determine and the doing of all such other things as are incidental or conducive to the attainment of that object.

4. The liability of the members is limited.

5. The company's share capital is £50,000 divided into 50,000 shares of £1 each.

We, the subscribers to this memorandum of association, wish to be formed into a company pursuant to this memorandum; and we agree to take the number of shares shown opposite our respective names.

Names and Addresses of Subscribers	Number of shares taken by each Subscriber
1. Thomas Jones, 138 Mountfield Street, Tredegar.	1
2. Mary Evans, 19 Merthyr Road, Aberystwyth.	1
Total shares taken	2

Dated 19

Witness to the above signatures,

Anne Brown, "Woodlands", Fieldside Road, Bryn Mawr.

[6039]

TABLE C

A COMPANY LIMITED BY GUARANTEE AND NOT HAVING A SHARE CAPITAL

MEMORANDUM OF ASSOCIATION

1. The company's name is "The Dundee School Association Limited".

2. The company's registered office is to be situated in Scotland.

3. The company's objects are the carrying on of a school for boys and girls in Dundee and the doing of all such other things as are incidental or conducive to the attainment of that object.

4. The liability of the members is limited.

5. Every member of the company undertakes to contribute such amount as may be required (not exceeding £100) to the company's assets if it should be wound up while he is a member or within one year after he ceases to be a member, for payment of the company's debts and liabilities contracted before he ceases to be a member, and of the costs, charges and expenses of winding up, and for the adjustment of the rights of the contributories among themselves.

We, the subscribers to this memorandum of association, wish to be formed into a company pursuant to this memorandum.

Names and Addresses of Subscribers.

1. Kenneth Brodie, 14 Bute Street, Dundee.

2. Ian Davis, 2 Burns Avenue, Dundee.

Dated .... 19..... .

Witness to the above signatures.

Anne Brown, 149 Princes Street, Edinburgh.

ARTICLES OF ASSOCIATION

Preliminary

1. Regulations 2 to 35 inclusive, 54, 55, 57, 59, 102 to 108 inclusive, 110, 114, 116 and 117 of Table A, shall not apply to the company but the articles hereinafter contained and, subject to the modifications hereinafter expressed, the remaining regulations of Table A shall constitute the articles of association of the company.

Interpretation

2. In regulation 1 of Table A, the definition of "the holder" shall be omitted.

Members

3. The subscribers to the memorandum of association of the company and such other persons as are admitted to membership in accordance with the articles shall be members of the company. No person shall be admitted a member of the company unless he is approved by the directors. Every person who wishes to become a member shall deliver to the company an application for membership in such form as the directors require executed by him.

4. A member may at any time withdraw from the company by giving at least seven clear days' notice to the company. Membership shall not be transferable and shall cease on death.

Notice of General Meetings

5. In regulation 38 of Table A—

   (a) in paragraph (b) the words "of the total voting rights at the meeting of all the members" shall be substituted for "in nominal value of the shares giving that right" and

   (b) the words "The notice shall be given to all the members and to the directors and auditors" shall be substituted for the last sentence.

Proceedings at General Meetings

6. The words "and at any separate meeting of the holders of any class of shares in the company" shall be omitted from regulation 44 of Table A.

7. Paragraph (d) of regulation 46 of Table A shall be omitted.

Votes of Members

8. On a show of hands every member present in person shall have one vote. On a poll every member present in person or by proxy shall have one vote.

Directors' Expenses

9. The words "of any class of shares or" shall be omitted from regulation 83 of Table A.

Proceedings of Directors

10. In paragraph (c) of regulation 94 of Table A the word "debentures" shall be substituted for the words "shares, debentures or other securities" in both places where they occur.

Minutes

11. The words "of the holders of any class of shares in the company" shall be omitted from regulation 100 of Table A.

Notices

12. The second sentence of regulation 112 of Table A shall be omitted.

13. The words "or of the holders of any class of shares in the company" shall be omitted from regulation 113 of Table A.

[6040]

TABLE D

PART I
A PUBLIC COMPANY LIMITED BY GUARANTEE AND HAVING A SHARE CAPITAL

MEMORANDUM OF ASSOCIATION

1. The company's name is "Gwestai Glyndwr, cwmni cyfyngedig cyhoeddus".

2. The company is to be a public company.

3. The company's registered office is to be situated in Wales.

4. The company's objects are facilitating travelling in Wales by providing hotels and conveyances by sea and by land for the accommodation of travellers and the doing of all such other things as are incidental or conducive to the attainment of those objects.

5. The liability of the members is limited.

6. Every member of the company undertakes to contribute such amount as may be required (not exceeding £100) to the company's assets if it should be wound up while he is a member or within one year after he ceases to be a member, for payment of the company's debts and liabilities contracted before he ceases to be a member, and of the costs, charges and expenses of winding up, and for the adjustment of the rights of the contributories among themselves.

7. The company's share capital is £50,000 divided into 50,000 shares of £1 each.

We, the subscribers to this memorandum of association, wish to be formed into a company pursuant to this memorandum; and we agree to take the number of shares shown opposite our respective names.

Names and Addresses of Subscribers	Number of shares taken by each Subscriber
1. Thomas Jones, 138 Mountfield Street, Tredegar.	1
2. Mary Evans, 19 Merthyr Road, Aberystwyth.	1
Total shares taken	2

Dated 19

Witness to the above signatures,

Anne Brown, "Woodlands", Fieldside Road, Bryn Mawr.

PART II
A PRIVATE COMPANY LIMITED BY GUARANTEE AND HAVING A SHARE CAPITAL

MEMORANDUM OF ASSOCIATION

1. The company's name is "The Highland Hotel Company Limited".

2. The company's registered office is to be situated in Scotland.

3. The company's objects are facilitating travelling in the Highlands of Scotland by providing hotels and conveyances by sea and by land for the accommodation of travellers and the doing of all such other things as are incidental or conducive to the attainment of those objects.

4. The liability of the members is limited.

5. Every member of the company undertakes to contribute such amount as may be required (not exceeding £100) to the company's assets if it should be wound up while he is a member or within one year after he ceases to be a member, for payment of the company's debts and liabilities contracted before he ceases to be a member, and of the costs, charges and expenses of winding up, and for the adjustment of the rights of the contributories among themselves.

6. The company's share capital is £50,000 divided into 50,000 shares of £1 each.

We, the subscribers to this memorandum of association, wish to be formed into a company pursuant to this memorandum; and we agree to take the number of shares shown opposite our respective names.

Names and Addresses of Subscribers	Number of shares taken by each Subscriber
Kenneth Brodie, 14 Bute Street, Dundee.	1
Ian Davis, 2 Burns Avenue, Dundee.	1
Total shares taken	2

Dated 19

Witness to the above signatures,

Anne Brown, 149 Princes Street, Edinburgh.

PART III
A COMPANY (PUBLIC OR PRIVATE) LIMITED BY GUARANTEE AND HAVING A SHARE CAPITAL

ARTICLES OF ASSOCIATION

The regulations of Table A shall constitute the articles of association of the company.

[6041]

TABLE E

AN UNLIMITED COMPANY HAVING A SHARE CAPITAL

MEMORANDUM OF ASSOCIATION

1. The company's name is "The Woodford Engineering Company".

2. The company's registered office is to be situated in England and Wales.

3. The company's objects are the working of certain patented inventions relating to the application of microchip technology to the improvement of food processing, and the doing of all such other things as are incidental or conducive to the attainment of that object.

We, the subscribers to this memorandum of association, wish to be formed into a company pursuant to this memorandum; and we agree to take the number of shares shown opposite our respective names.

Names and Addresses of Subscribers	Number of shares taken by each Subscriber
1. Brian Smith, 24 Nibley Road, Wotton-under-Edge, Gloucestershire.	3
2. William Green, 278 High Street, Chipping Sodbury, Avon.	5
Total shares taken	8

Dated 19

Witness to the above signatures,

Anne Brown, 108 Park Way, Bristol 8.

ARTICLES OF ASSOCIATION

1. Regulations 3, 32, 34 and 35 of Table A shall not apply to the company, but the articles hereinafter contained and, subject to the modification hereinafter expressed, the remaining regulations of Table A shall constitute the articles of association of the company.

2. The words "at least seven clear days' notice" shall be substituted for the words "at least fourteen clear days' notice" in regulation 38 of Table A.

3. The share capital of the company is £20,000 divided into 20,000 shares of £1 each.

4. The company may by special resolution—
   (a) increase the share capital by such sum to be divided into shares of such amount as the resolution may prescribe;
   (b) consolidate and divide all or any of its share capital into shares of a larger amount than its existing shares;
   (c) subdivide its shares, or any of them, into shares of a smaller amount than its existing shares;
   (d) cancel any shares which at the date of the passing of the resolution have not been taken or agreed to be taken by any person;

(e) reduce its share capital and any share premium account in any way.

[6042]

TABLE F

A PUBLIC COMPANY LIMITED BY SHARES

MEMORANDUM OF ASSOCIATION

1. The company's name is "Western Electronics Public Limited Company".

2. The company is to be a public company.

3. The company's registered office is to be situated in England and Wales.

4. The company's objects are the manufacture and development of such descriptions of electronic equipment, instruments and appliances as the company may from time to time determine, and the doing of all such other things as are incidental or conducive to the attainment of that object.

5. The liability of the members is limited.

6. The company's share capital is £5,000,000 divided into 5,000,000 shares of £1 each.

We, the subscribers of this memorandum of association, wish to be formed into a company pursuant to this memorandum; and we agree to take the number of shares shown opposite our respective names.

Names and Addresses of Subscribers	Number of shares taken by each Subscriber
1. James White, 12 Broadmead, Birmingham.	1
2. Patrick Smith, 145A Huntley House, London Wall, London EC2.	1
Total shares taken	2

Dated 19

Witness to the above signatures,

Anne Brown, 13 Hute Street, London WC2.

[6043]

COMPANIES (FORMS) REGULATIONS 1985 (NOTE)

(SI 1985/854)

NOTES

See Appendix 4 at **[A4]**.

[6043A]

INSOLVENCY PRACTITIONERS TRIBUNAL (CONDUCT OF INVESTIGATIONS) RULES 1986

(SI 1986/952)

NOTES

Made: 5 June 1986.

Authority: Insolvency Act 1985, Sch 1, para 4(4); these rules now have effect as if made under the Insolvency Act 1986, Sch 7, para 4(4).

Commencement: 1 July 1986 (see r 1 at **[6044]**). Where any provision in this work (including any inserted or substituted provision) came into force for all purposes on or before 1 July 2005, commencement information is not noted at provision level.

As of 1 July 2007, these Rules had not been amended.

Limited liability partnerships: by the Limited Liability Partnerships Regulations 2001, SI 2001/1090, reg 10, Sch 6, Pt II, these Rules apply, with modifications, to limited liability partnerships (see **[6999]**).

ARRANGEMENT OF RULES

1 Citation, commencement and interpretation

(1) These Rules may be cited as the Insolvency Practitioners Tribunal (Conduct of Investigations) Rules 1986 and shall come into force on 1st July 1986.

(2) In these Rules—

(a) references to "the Act" are references to the Insolvency Act 1985;

(b) "the applicant" means an applicant for authorisation under section 5 of the Act or, where it is proposed to withdraw an authorisation granted under that section, the holder of the authorisation;

(c) "Treasury Solicitor" means the Solicitor for the affairs of Her Majesty's Treasury as provided in the Treasury Solicitor Act 1876; and

(d) "a Scottish case" means any case where at the time of the reference of the case to the Tribunal the applicant is either habitually resident in or has his principal place of business in Scotland.

[6044]

NOTES

Insolvency Act 1985: mostly repealed by a combination of the Insolvency Act 1986 and the Company Directors Disqualification Act 1986.

Section 5 of the Act: see now the Insolvency Act 1986, s 393.

2 Reference to the tribunal

(1) On referring a case to the tribunal under section 8(2) of the Act the relevant authority shall—

(a) send to the tribunal a copy of the written notice served by it on the applicant in pursuance of section 6(2) of the Act, together with a copy of the notification by the applicant that he wishes the case to be referred to the tribunal, and

(b) give notice to the applicant of the date on which the case has been referred by it to the tribunal and of the address to which any statement notice or other document required by these Rules to be given or sent to the tribunal is to be given or sent.

(2) Within 21 days of referring the case to the tribunal the relevant authority shall send to the tribunal such further information and copies of such other documents and records as it considers would be of assistance to the tribunal, and shall, at the same time, send to the applicant such further information and copies of such other documents and records; or, if there is no such information or copies, the relevant authority shall within the said period notify the tribunal and the applicant to that effect.

[6045]

NOTES

Sections 8(2), 6(2) of the Act: see now the Insolvency Act 1986, ss 396(3), 394(2).

3 Statement of the applicant

(1) Within 21 days after the relevant authority has sent to the applicant the material mentioned in Rule 2(2) or, as the case may be, after it has sent to him the notification mentioned in that Rule, the applicant shall send to the tribunal a statement of his grounds for requiring the case to be investigated by the tribunal specifying—

(a) which matters of fact (if any) contained in the written notice served on him under section 6(2) of the Act he disputes,

(b) any other matters which he considers should be drawn to the attention of the tribunal, and

(c) the names and addresses of any witnesses whose evidence he wishes the tribunal to hear.

(2) The applicant shall, on sending the statement referred to in paragraph (1) of this Rule to the tribunal, send a copy to the relevant authority.

[6046]

NOTES

Section 6(2) of the Act: see now the Insolvency Act 1986, s 394(2).

4 Appointment of solicitors and counsel to the tribunal

At any time after the case has been referred to it the tribunal may appoint the Treasury Solicitor and Counsel, or, in Scottish cases, may request the Treasury Solicitor to appoint a solicitor and may appoint Counsel, to exercise the functions of—

(a) assisting the tribunal in seeking and presenting evidence in accordance with the requirements of the tribunal; and

(b) representing the public interest in relation to the matters before the tribunal.

[6047]

5 Investigation by the tribunal

After the receipt of the statement referred to in Rule 3 or, if no such statement is received, after the expiry of the period referred to in that Rule the tribunal shall investigate the case and make a report by carrying out such inquiries as it thinks appropriate for that purpose into and concerning the information, documents, records and matters placed before it under the provisions of Rules 2 and 3 above; and in carrying out such inquiries the requirements set out in the following Rules shall apply.

[6048]

6 Methods of inquiry by the tribunal

(1) As soon as practicable after the tribunal has considered the subject matter of the investigation it shall notify the relevant authority and the applicant of the manner in which it proposes to conduct its inquiries and in particular whether oral evidence is to be taken.

(2) The tribunal shall give the relevant authority and the applicant a reasonable opportunity of making representations on the manner in which it proposes to conduct its inquiries and such representations may be made orally or in writing at the option of the relevant authority or the applicant as the case may be.

(3) After considering any representations that may be made under paragraph (2) above the tribunal shall notify the relevant authority and the applicant whether and, if so, in what respects, it has decided to alter the manner in which it proposes to carry out its inquiries.

(4) If at any subsequent stage in the investigation the tribunal proposes to make any material change in the manner in which its inquiries are to be carried out it shall notify the relevant authority and the applicant and the provisions of paragraphs (2) and (3) above shall apply accordingly.

[6049]

7 Taking of evidence

When in the carrying out of its inquiries the tribunal—

(a) wishes to examine a witness orally—

(i) it shall give notice to the applicant and the relevant authority of the time and place at which the examination will be held, and

(ii) the applicant and the relevant authority shall be entitled to be present at the examination by the tribunal of any witness and to put such additional questions to him as may appear to the tribunal to be relevant to the subject matter of the investigation; or

(b) takes into consideration documentary evidence or evidence in the form of computer or other non documentary records not placed before the tribunal under the provisions of Rules 2 and 3 above, the tribunal shall give the applicant and the relevant authority an opportunity of inspecting that evidence and taking copies or an appropriate record thereof.

[6050]

8 Final representations

After the tribunal has completed the taking of such evidence as it considers necessary for the purpose of the investigation it shall give the applicant and the relevant authority a reasonable opportunity of making representations on the evidence and on the subject matter of the investigation generally. Such representations may be made orally or in writing at the option of the applicant or, as the case may be, of the relevant authority.

[6051]

9 Representation at a hearing

At the hearing of oral representations or the taking of oral evidence—

(a) the applicant may be represented by Counsel or solicitor, or by any other person allowed by the tribunal to appear on his behalf; and

(b) the relevant authority may be represented by Counsel or solicitor or by any officer of the relevant authority.

[6052]

10 Service of written representations

Where the relevant authority or the applicant makes any written representations to the tribunal in the course of its investigation the relevant authority or, as the case may be, the applicant shall send a copy of such representations to the other.

[6053]

11 Hearings in public or in private

(1) The tribunal shall conduct its investigation in private and, save to the extent that these Rules provide for the hearing of oral representations or for the taking of oral evidence and the applicant requests that any such hearing be in public, no person other than those specified in Rule 9 above or having the leave of the tribunal shall be entitled to be present at any such hearing.

(2) Nothing in this Rule shall prevent a member of the Council on Tribunals or of its Scottish Committee from attending in his capacity as such a member any such hearing.

[6054]

12 Notices

Any notice or other document required by these Rules to be given or sent may be given or sent by first class post.

[6055]

13 Time limits

The tribunal may in any investigation permit the relevant authority or the applicant to send any document or perform any act after the time prescribed in the Rules for so sending or performing and such permission may be granted after any such time has expired.

[6056]

14 Powers of chairman

Anything required or authorised to be done by the tribunal in the course of an investigation may be done by the chairman except—

(a) the settling of the manner in which the tribunal is to conduct its investigation,
(b) the hearing or consideration of any representations made by the relevant authority or the applicant, and
(c) the taking of evidence, whether orally or in the form of documents or non-documentary records.

[6057]

15 Period within which report to be made

(1) The tribunal shall make its report on the case to the relevant authority no later than four months after the date on which the case is referred to it under section 8(2) of the Act unless the relevant authority, on the application of the tribunal, permits the report to be made within such further period as the relevant authority may notify in writing to the tribunal.

(2) The relevant authority may only permit the report to be made within the further period referred to in paragraph (1) above where it appears to that authority that, through exceptional circumstances, the tribunal will be unable to make its report within the period of four months referred to in paragraph (1) above.

[6058]

NOTES

Section 8(2) of the Act: see now the Insolvency Act 1986, s 396(2).

16 Scottish Cases

Any hearing or oral representations under Rule 6(2) or 8 or any examination of a witness under Rule 7(a) in a Scottish case shall be made or held in Scotland unless the applicant consents to any such hearing or examination taking place elsewhere.

[6059]

INSOLVENCY RULES 1986

(SI 1986/1925)

NOTES

Made: 10 November 1986.

Authority: Insolvency Act 1986, ss 411, 412.

Commencement: These rules, as originally made, came into force on 29 December 1986; see r 0.1. The rules as amended by the Insolvency (Amendment) Rules 1987, SI 1987/1919 apply to proceedings on and after 11 January 1988 whenever those proceedings were commenced, the rules as amended by SI 1989/397 apply to proceedings on or after 3 April 1989 whenever those proceedings were commenced, the rules as amended by SI 1991/495 apply to proceedings on or after 2 April 1991 whenever those proceedings were commenced, the rules as amended by SI 1993/602 apply to proceedings on or after 5 April 1993 whenever those proceedings were commenced, and the rules as amended by SI 1995/586 apply to winding up proceedings commenced after 1 April 1995 and bankruptcy proceedings commenced after that date. Where any provision in this work (including any inserted or substituted provision) came into force for all purposes on or before 1 July 2005, commencement information is not noted at provision level.

These Rules are reproduced as amended by: the Insolvency (Amendment) Rules 1987, SI 1987/1919; the Insolvency (Amendment) Rules 1989, SI 1989/397; the Insolvency (Amendment) Rules 1991, SI 1991/495; the Insolvency (Amendment) Rules 1993, SI 1993/602; the Insolvency (Amendment) Rules 1995, SI 1995/586; the Bank of England Act 1998 (Consequential Amendments of Subordinate Legislation) Order 1998, SI 1998/1129; the Insolvency (Amendment) (No 2) Rules 1999, SI 1999/1022; the Insolvency (Amendment) Rules 2001, SI 2001/763; the Financial Services and Markets Act 2000 (Consequential Amendments and Repeals) Order 2002, SI 2001/3649; the Insolvency (Amendment) Rules 2002, SI 2002/1307; the Insolvency (Amendment) (No 2) Rules 2002, SI 2002/2712; the Insolvency (Amendment) Rules 2003, SI 2003/1730; the Insolvency (Amendment) Rules 2004, SI 2004/584; the Insolvency (Amendment) Rules 2005, SI 2005/527; the Insolvency (Amendment) Rules 2006, SI 2006/1272; the Mental Capacity Act 2005 (Transitional and Consequential Provisions) Order 2007, SI 2007/1898.

ARRANGEMENT OF RULES

THE FIRST GROUP OF PARTS
COMPANY INSOLVENCY; COMPANIES WINDING UP

INTRODUCTORY PROVISIONS

PART 1
COMPANY VOLUNTARY ARRANGEMENTS

CHAPTER 1
PRELIMINARY

CHAPTER 2
PROPOSAL BY DIRECTORS

CHAPTER 3
PROPOSAL BY ADMINISTRATOR OR LIQUIDATOR (HIMSELF THE NOMINEE)

CHAPTER 4
PROPOSAL BY ADMINISTRATOR OR LIQUIDATOR (ANOTHER INSOLVENCY PRACTITIONER THE NOMINEE)

CHAPTER 5
PROCEEDINGS ON A PROPOSAL MADE BY THE DIRECTORS, OR BY THE ADMINISTRATOR, OR BY THE LIQUIDATOR

Section A: Meetings of Company's Creditors and Members

Section B: Voting Rights and Majorities

Section C: Implementation of the Arrangement

CHAPTER 7
EC REGULATION—CONVERSION OF VOLUNTARY ARRANGEMENT INTO WINDING UP

CHAPTER 8
EC REGULATION—MEMBER STATE LIQUIDATOR

CHAPTER 9
OBTAINING A MORATORIUM
PROCEEDINGS DURING A MORATORIUM
NOMINEES
CONSIDERATION OF PROPOSALS WHERE MORATORIUM OBTAINED

Section A: Obtaining a Moratorium

Section B: Proceedings During a Moratorium

Section C: Nominees

Section D: Consideration of Proposals Where Moratorium Obtained

PART 2
ADMINISTRATION PROCEDURE

CHAPTER 1
PRELIMINARY

CHAPTER 2
APPOINTMENT OF ADMINISTRATOR BY COURT

CHAPTER 3
APPOINTMENT OF ADMINISTRATOR BY HOLDER OF FLOATING CHARGE

CHAPTER 4
APPOINTMENT OF ADMINISTRATOR BY COMPANY OR DIRECTORS

CHAPTER 5
PROCESS OF ADMINISTRATION

CHAPTER 6
MEETINGS AND REPORTS

Section A: Creditors' Meetings

Section B: Company Meetings

CHAPTER 7
THE CREDITORS' COMMITTEE

CHAPTER 8
DISPOSAL OF CHARGED PROPERTY

CHAPTER 9
EXPENSES OF THE ADMINISTRATION

CHAPTER 10
DISTRIBUTIONS TO CREDITORS

Section A: Application of Chapter and General

Section B: Machinery of Proving a Debt

Section C: Quantification of Claims

CHAPTER 11
THE ADMINISTRATOR

CHAPTER 12
ENDING ADMINISTRATION

CHAPTER 13
REPLACING ADMINISTRATOR

CHAPTER 14
EC REGULATION—CONVERSION OF ADMINISTRATION INTO WINDING UP

CHAPTER 15
EC REGULATION—MEMBER STATE LIQUIDATOR

PART 3
ADMINISTRATIVE RECEIVERSHIP

CHAPTER 1
APPOINTMENT OF ADMINISTRATIVE RECEIVER

CHAPTER 2
STATEMENT OF AFFAIRS AND REPORT TO CREDITORS

CHAPTER 3
CREDITORS' MEETING

CHAPTER 4
THE CREDITORS' COMMITTEE

CHAPTER 5
THE ADMINISTRATIVE RECEIVER (MISCELLANEOUS)

CHAPTER 6
VAT BAD DEBT RELIEF

CHAPTER 7
SECTION 176A: THE PRESCRIBED PART

PART 4
COMPANIES WINDING UP

CHAPTER 1
THE SCHEME OF THIS PART OF THE RULES

CHAPTER 2
THE STATUTORY DEMAND

(No CVL Application)

CHAPTER 3
PETITION TO WINDING-UP ORDER

(No CVL Application)
(No Application to Petition by Contributories)

CHAPTER 4
PETITION BY CONTRIBUTORIES

(No CVL Application)

CHAPTER 5
PROVISIONAL LIQUIDATOR

(No CVL Application)

CHAPTER 6
STATEMENT OF AFFAIRS AND OTHER INFORMATION

CHAPTER 7
INFORMATION TO CREDITORS AND CONTRIBUTORIES

CHAPTER 8
MEETINGS OF CREDITORS AND CONTRIBUTORIES

Section A: Rules of General Application

CHAPTER 13
THE LIQUIDATION COMMITTEE WHERE WINDING UP FOLLOWS IMMEDIATELY ON ADMINISTRATION

(*No CVL Application*)

CHAPTER 14
COLLECTION AND DISTRIBUTION OF COMPANY'S ASSETS BY LIQUIDATOR

CHAPTER 15
DISCLAIMER

CHAPTER 16
SETTLEMENT OF LIST OF CONTRIBUTORIES

(*No CVL Application*)

CHAPTER 17
CALLS

(*No CVL Application*)

CHAPTER 18
SPECIAL MANAGER

CHAPTER 19
PUBLIC EXAMINATION OF COMPANY OFFICERS AND OTHERS

CHAPTER 20
ORDER OF PAYMENT OF COSTS, ETC, OUT OF ASSETS

CHAPTER 21
MISCELLANEOUS RULES

Section A: Return of Capital
(No CVL Application)

Section B: Conclusion of Winding Up

Section C: Dissolution After Winding Up

CHAPTER 22
LEAVE TO ACT AS DIRECTOR, ETC, OF COMPANY WITH PROHIBITED NAME
(SECTION 216 OF THE ACT)

CHAPTER 23
EC REGULATION—MEMBER STATE LIQUIDATOR

THE THIRD GROUP OF PARTS

PART 7
COURT PROCEDURE AND PRACTICE

CHAPTER 1
APPLICATIONS

PART 12
MISCELLANEOUS AND GENERAL

PART 13
INTERPRETATION AND APPLICATION

SCHEDULES

NOTES

Application of these Rules to LLPs:

Limited liability partnerships: by the Limited Liability Partnerships Regulations 2001, SI 2001/1090, reg 10, Sch 6, Pt II, these Rules apply, with modifications, to limited liability partnerships (see **[6999]**).

Other applications and miscellaneous:

As to the application of these rules to Insurers, see the Insurers (Winding Up) Rules 2001 SI 2001/3635 and the Insurers (Reorganisation and Winding Up) Regulations 2004, SI 2004/353; as to their application to EEA credit institutions, see the Credit Institutions (Reorganisation and Winding up) Regulations 2004, SI 2004/1045; as to their application to railway administration proceedings, see the Railway Administration Order Rules 2001, SI 2001/3352. Note that the Energy Administration Rules 2005, SI 2005/2483 are based upon the provisions of these Rules but are a stand alone set of rules applicable only to energy administration proceedings.

Modification: these Rules, except rr 4.12, 4.215, 7.53, 7.54, 7.57, 9.4, are modified by the Solicitors' Incorporated Practices Order 1991, SI 1991/2684, so that any reference to a solicitor or solicitors shall be construed as including a reference to a recognised body, meaning a body corporate recognised by the Council of the Law Society under the Administration of Justice Act 1985, s 9, and related expressions are to be construed accordingly.

Official receiver: as to the contracting out of certain functions of the Official receiver conferred by or under these rules, see the Contracting Out (Functions of the Official Receiver) Order 1995, SI 1995/1386 at **[6844]**.

INTRODUCTORY PROVISIONS

0.1 Citation and commencement

These Rules may be cited as the Insolvency Rules 1986 and shall come into force on 29th December 1986.

[6060]

[0.2 Construction and interpretation

(1) In these Rules—

"the Act" means the Insolvency Act 1986 (any reference to a numbered section being to a section of that Act);

"the Companies Act" means the Companies Act 1985;

"CPR" means the Civil Procedure Rules 1998 and "CPR" followed by a Part or rule by number means the Part or rule with that number in those Rules;

"RSC" followed by an Order by number means the Order with that number set out in Schedule 1 to the CPR; and

"the Rules" means the Insolvency Rules 1986.

(2) References in the Rules to *ex parte* hearings shall be construed as references to hearings without notice being served on any other party; references to applications made *ex parte* as references to applications made without notice being served on any other party and other references which include the expression "*ex parte*" shall be similarly construed.

(3) Subject to paragraphs (1) and (2), Part 13 of the Rules has effect for their interpretation and application.]

[6061]

NOTES

Substituted by the Insolvency (Amendment) (No 2) Rules 1999, SI 1999/1022, r 3, Schedule, para 1, as from 26 April 1999.

0.3 Extent

(1) Parts 1, 2 and 4 of the Rules, and Parts 7 to 13 as they relate to company insolvency, apply in relation to companies which the courts in England and Wales have jurisdiction to wind up.

[(2) Rule 3.1 applies to all receivers to whom Part III of the Act applies, Rule 3.39 and 3.40 apply to all receivers who are not administrative receivers, and the remainder of Part 3 of the Rules applies to administrative receivers appointed otherwise than under section 51 (Scottish Receivership).]

(3) Parts 5 and 6 of the Rules, and Parts 7 to 13 as they relate to individual insolvency, extend to England and Wales only.

[6062]

NOTES

Para (2): substituted by the Insolvency (Amendment) Rules 2003, SI 2003/1730, r 3, as from 15 September 2003.

THE FIRST GROUP OF PARTS
COMPANY INSOLVENCY; COMPANIES WINDING UP

PART 1
COMPANY VOLUNTARY ARRANGEMENTS

CHAPTER 1
PRELIMINARY

1.1 Scope of this Part; interpretation

(1) The Rules in this Part apply where, pursuant to Part I of the Act, it is intended to make, and there is made, a proposal to a company and its creditors for a voluntary arrangement, that is to say, a composition in satisfaction of its debts or a scheme of arrangement of its affairs.

(2) In this Part—

[(a) Chapter 2 applies where the proposal for the voluntary arrangement is made by the directors of the company and

(i) the company is neither in liquidation nor is [the company in administration]; and

(ii) no steps have been taken to obtain a moratorium under Schedule A1 to the Act in connection with the proposal;]

(b) Chapter 3 applies where the company is in liquidation or [the company is in administration], and the proposal is made by the liquidator or (as the case may be) the administrator, he in either case being the nominee for the purposes of the proposal;

[(c) Chapter 4 applies in the same case as Chapter 3, but where the nominee is not the liquidator or administrator;

(d) Chapter 5 applies in all the three cases mentioned in sub-paragraphs (a) to (c) above;

(e) Chapters 7 and 8 apply to all voluntary arrangements with or without a moratorium; and

(f) Chapter 9 applies where the proposal is made by the directors of an eligible company with a view to obtaining a moratorium.]

(3) In Chapters 3, 4 and 5, the liquidator or the administrator is referred to as "the responsible insolvency practitioner".

[(4) In this Part, a reference to an "eligible company" is to a company that is eligible for a moratorium in accordance with paragraph 2 of Schedule A1 to the Act.]

[6063]

NOTES

Para (2): sub-para (a) substituted, and sub-paras (c)–(f) substituted for original sub-paras (c), (d), by the Insolvency (Amendment) (No 2) Rules 2002, SI 2002/2712, r 3(1), Schedule, Pt 1, para 1, as from 1 January 2003 (subject to transitional provisions as noted below); words in square brackets in sub-paras (a), (b) substituted by the Insolvency (Amendment) Rules 2003, SI 2003/1730, r 4, Sch 1, Pt 1, para 1, as from 15 September 2003 (for transitional provisions and savings see the note preceding r 2.1 at **[6097]**).

Para (4): added by SI 2002/2712, r 3(1), Schedule, Pt 1, para 1(c), as from 1 January 2003, subject to transitional provisions as noted below.

Transitional provisions: SI 2002/2712, r 3(2) provides as follows (note that by virtue of r 1 "the commencement date" is 1 January 2003)—

"(2) The amendments to Part 1 of the principal Rules set out in Part 1 of the Schedule to these Rules do not apply in relation to a voluntary arrangement under Part I of the Act where—

(a) a proposal is made by the directors of a company and before the commencement date the intended nominee has endorsed a copy of the written notice of the proposal under Rule 1.4(3);

(b) a proposal is made by the liquidator or the administrator (acting as the nominee) and before the commencement date the liquidator or administrator (as the case may be) has sent out a notice summoning the meetings under section 3 of the Act as required by Rule 1.11; or

(c) a proposal is made by the liquidator or the administrator of a company (not acting as the nominee) and before the commencement date the intended nominee has endorsed a copy of the written notice of the proposal under Rule 1.12(2);

and Part 1 of the principal Rules without the amendments made in Part 1 of the Schedule to these Rules shall continue to apply in such cases.".

CHAPTER 2
PROPOSAL BY DIRECTORS

1.2 Preparation of proposal

The directors shall prepare for the intended nominee a proposal on which (with or without amendments to be made under Rule 1.3 below) to make his report to the court under section 2.

[6064]

1.3 Contents of proposal

(1) The directors' proposal shall provide a short explanation why, in their opinion, a voluntary arrangement under Part I of the Act is desirable, and give reasons why the company's creditors may be expected to concur with such an arrangement.

(2) The following matters shall be stated, or otherwise dealt with, in the directors' proposal—

(a) the following matters, so far as within the directors' immediate knowledge—
   (i) the company's assets, with an estimate of their respective values,
   (ii) the extent (if any) to which the assets are charged in favour of creditors,
   (iii) the extent (if any) to which particular assets are to be excluded from the voluntary arrangement;

(b) particulars of any property, other than assets of the company itself, which is proposed to be included in the arrangement, the source of such property and the terms on which it is to be made available for inclusion;

(c) the nature and amount of the company's liabilities (so far as within the directors' immediate knowledge), the manner in which they are proposed to be met, modified, postponed or otherwise dealt with by means of the arrangement, and (in particular)—
   (i) how it is proposed to deal with preferential creditors (defined in section 4(7)) and creditors who are, or claim to be, secured,
   (ii) how persons connected with the company (being creditors) are proposed to be treated under the arrangement, and
   (iii) where there are, to the directors' knowledge, any circumstances giving rise to the possibility, in the event that the company should go into liquidation, of claims under—
   section 238 (transactions at an undervalue),
   section 239 (preferences),
   section 244 (extortionate credit transactions), or
   section 245 (floating charges invalid);

   and, where any such circumstances are present, whether, and if so how, it is proposed under the voluntary arrangement to make provision for wholly or partly indemnifying the company in respect of such claims;

[(ca) an estimate (to the best of the directors' knowledge and belief and subject to paragraph (4)) of—
   (i) the value of the prescribed part, should the company go into liquidation if the proposal for the voluntary arrangement is not accepted, whether or not section 176A is to be disapplied; and
   (ii) the value of the company's net property on the date that the estimate is made;]

(d) whether any, and if so what, guarantees have been given of the company's debts by other persons, specifying which (if any) of the guarantors are persons connected with the company;

(e) the proposed duration of the voluntary arrangement;

(f) the proposed dates of distributions to creditors, with estimates of their amounts;

[(fa) How it is proposed to deal with the claim of any person who is bound by the arrangement by virtue of section 5(2)(b)(ii);]

(g) the amount proposed to be paid to the nominee (as such) by way of remuneration and expenses;

(h) the manner in which it is proposed that the supervisor of the arrangement should be remunerated, and his expenses defrayed;

(j) whether, for the purposes of the arrangement, any guarantees are to be offered by directors, or other persons, and whether (if so) any security is to be given or sought;

(k) the manner in which funds held for the purposes of the arrangement are to be banked, invested or otherwise dealt with pending distribution to creditors;

(l) the manner in which funds held for the purpose of payment to creditors, and not so paid on the termination of the arrangement, are to be dealt with;
(m) the manner in which the business of the company is proposed to be conducted during the course of the arrangement;
(n) details of any further credit facilities which it is intended to arrange for the company, and how the debts so arising are to be paid;
(o) the functions which are to be undertaken by the supervisor of the arrangement; …
[(p) the name, address and qualification of the person proposed as supervisor of the voluntary arrangement, and confirmation that he is either qualified to act as an insolvency practitioner in relation to the company or is an authorised person in relation to the company; and]
[(q) whether the EC Regulation will apply and, if so, whether the proceedings will be main proceedings, secondary proceedings or territorial proceedings].

(3) With the agreement in writing of the nominee, the directors' proposal may be amended at any time up to delivery of the former's report to the court under section 2(2).

[(4) Nothing in paragraph (2)(ca) is to be taken as requiring the estimate referred to in that paragraph to include any information, the disclosure of which could seriously prejudice the commercial interests of the company. If such information is excluded from the calculation the estimate shall be accompanied by a statement to that effect.]

[6065]

NOTES

Para (2): sub-para (ca) inserted by the Insolvency (Amendment) Rules 2003, SI 2003/1730, r 4, Sch 1, Pt 1, para 2(1), as from 15 September 2003 (for transitional provisions and savings see the note preceding r 2.1 at **[6097]**); sub-para (fa) inserted, and sub-para (p) substituted, by the Insolvency (Amendment) (No 2) Rules 2002, SI 2002/2712, r 3(1), Schedule, Pt 1, para 2, as from 1 January 2003 (subject to transitional provisions as noted to r 1.1 at **[6063]**); word omitted from sub-para (o) revoked, and sub-para (q) added, by the Insolvency (Amendment) Rules 2002, SI 2002/1307, rr 3, 4(2), as from 31 May 2002, with savings in relation to anything done under, or for the purposes of, this provision before that date.

Para (4): added by SI 2003/1730, r 4, Sch 1, Pt 1, para 2(2), as from 15 September 2003 (for transitional provisions and savings see the note preceding r 2.1 at **[6097]**).

EC Regulation: ie, Council Regulation 1346/2000/EC on insolvency proceedings at **[9290]**.

1.4 Notice to intended nominee

(1) The directors shall give to the intended nominee written notice of their proposal.

(2) The notice, accompanied by a copy of the proposal, shall be delivered either to the nominee himself, or to a person authorised to take delivery of documents on his behalf.

(3) If the intended nominee agrees to act, he shall cause a copy of the notice to be endorsed to the effect that it has been received by him on a specified date; and the period of 28 days referred to in section 2(2) then runs from that date.

(4) The copy of the notice so endorsed shall be returned by the nominee forthwith to the directors at an address specified by them in the notice for that purpose.

[6066]

1.5 Statement of affairs

(1) The directors shall, within 7 days after their proposal is delivered to the nominee, or within such longer time as he may allow, deliver to him a statement of the company's affairs.

(2) The statement shall comprise the following particulars (supplementing or amplifying, so far as is necessary for clarifying the state of the company's affairs, those already given in the directors' proposal)—
(a) a list of the company's assets, divided into such categories as are appropriate for easy identification, with estimated values assigned to each category;
(b) in the case of any property on which a claim against the company is wholly or partly secured, particulars of the claim and its amount, and of how and when the security was created;
(c) the names and addresses of the company's preferential creditors (defined in section 4(7)), with the amounts of their respective claims;
(d) the names and addresses of the company's unsecured creditors, with the amounts of their respective claims;

(e) particulars of any debts owed by or to the company to or by persons connected with it;

(f) the names and addresses of the company's members, with details of their respective shareholdings;

(g) such other particulars (if any) as the nominee may in writing require to be furnished for the purposes of making his report to the court on the directors' proposal.

(3) The statement of affairs shall be made up to a date not earlier than 2 weeks before the date of the notice to the nominee under Rule 1.4.

However, the nominee may allow an extension of that period to the nearest practicable date (not earlier than 2 months before the date of the notice under Rule 1.4); and if he does so, he shall give his reasons in his report to the court on the directors' proposal.

(4) The statement shall be certified as correct, to the best of their knowledge and belief, by two or more directors of the company, or by the company secretary and at least one director (other than the secretary himself).

[6067]

1.6 Additional disclosure for assistance of nominee

(1) If it appears to the nominee that he cannot properly prepare his report on the basis of information in the directors' proposal and statement of affairs, he may call on the directors to provide him with—

(a) further and better particulars as to the circumstances in which, and the reasons why, the company is insolvent or (as the case may be) threatened with insolvency;

(b) particulars of any previous proposals which have been made in respect of the company under Part I of the Act;

(c) any further information with respect to the company's affairs which the nominee thinks necessary for the purposes of his report.

(2) The nominee may call on the directors to inform him, with respect to any person who is, or at any time in the 2 years preceding the notice under Rule 1.4 has been, a director or officer of the company, whether and in what circumstances (in those 2 years or previously) that person—

(a) has been concerned in the affairs of any other company (whether or not incorporated in England and Wales) which has become insolvent, or

(b) has himself been adjudged bankrupt or entered into an arrangement with his creditors.

(3) For the purpose of enabling the nominee to consider their proposal and prepare his report on it, the directors must give him access to the company's accounts and records.

[6068]

1.7 Nominee's report on the proposal

(1) With his report to the court under section 2 the nominee shall deliver—

(a) a copy of the directors' proposal (with amendments, if any, authorised under Rule 1.3(3)); and

(b) a copy or summary of the company's statement of affairs.

(2) If the nominee makes known his opinion [that the directors' proposal has a reasonable prospect of being approved and implemented and] that meetings of the company and its creditors should be summoned under section 3, his report shall have annexed to it his comments on the proposal.

If his opinion is otherwise, he shall give his reasons for that opinion.

(3) The court shall cause the nominee's report to be endorsed with the date on which it is filed in court. Any director, member or creditor of the company is entitled, at all reasonable times on any business day, to inspect the file.

(4) The nominee shall send a copy of his report, and of his comments (if any), to the company.

[6069]

NOTES

Para (2): words in square brackets inserted by the Insolvency (Amendment) (No 2) Rules 2002, SI 2002/2712, r 3(1), Schedule, Pt 1, para 3, as from 1 January 2003, subject to transitional provisions as noted to r 1.1 at **[6063]**.

[1.8 Replacement of nominee

(1) Where a person other than the nominee intends to apply to the court under section 2(4) for the nominee to be replaced, (except in any case where the nominee has died) he shall give to the nominee at least 7 days' notice of his application.

(2) Where the nominee intends to apply to the court under section 2(4) of the Act to be replaced, he shall give at least 7 days' notice of his application to the person intending to make the proposal.

(3) No appointment of a replacement nominee shall be made by the court unless there is filed in court a statement by the replacement nominee—

(a) indicating his consent to act, and

(b) that he is qualified to act as an insolvency practitioner in relation to the company or is an authorised person in relation to the company.]

[6070]

NOTES

Substituted by the Insolvency (Amendment) (No 2) Rules 2002, SI 2002/2712, r 3(1), Schedule, Pt 1, para 4, as from 1 January 2003, subject to transitional provisions as noted to r 1.1 at **[6063]**.

See Form 1.8 in Appendix 4 at **[A4]**.

1.9 Summoning of meetings under s 3

(1) If in his report the nominee states that in his opinion meetings of the company and its creditors should be summoned to consider the directors' proposal, the date on which the meetings are to be held shall be not less than 14, nor more than 28, days from that on which the nominee's report is filed in court under Rule 1.7.

(2) Notices calling the meetings shall be sent by the nominee, at least 14 days before the day fixed for them to be held—

(a) in the case of the creditors' meeting, to all the creditors specified in the statement of affairs, and any other creditors of the company of whom he is otherwise aware; and

(b) in the case of the meeting of members of the company, to all persons who are, to the best of the nominee's belief, members of it.

(3) Each notice sent under this Rule shall specify the court to which the nominee's report under section 2 has been delivered and shall state the effect of Rule 1.19(1), (3) and (4) (requisite majorities (creditors)); and with each notice there shall be sent—

(a) a copy of the directors' proposal;

(b) a copy of the statement of affairs or, if the nominee thinks fit, a summary of it (the summary to include a list of creditors and the amount of their debts); and

(c) the nominee's comments on the proposal.

[6071]

CHAPTER 3

PROPOSAL BY ADMINISTRATOR OR LIQUIDATOR (HIMSELF THE NOMINEE)

1.10 Preparation of proposal

(1) The responsible insolvency practitioner's proposal shall specify—

(a) all such matters as under Rule 1.3 [(subject to paragraph (3) below)] in Chapter 2 the directors of the company would be required to include in a proposal by them[, with the addition, where the company is [in administration], of the names and addresses of the company's preferential creditors (defined in section 4(7)), with the amounts of their respective claims], and

(b) such other matters (if any) as the insolvency practitioner considers appropriate for ensuring that members and creditors of the company are enabled to reach an informed decision on the proposal.

(2) Where the company is being wound up by the court, the insolvency practitioner shall give notice of the proposal to the official receiver.

[(3) The administrator or liquidator shall include, in place of the estimate required by Rule 1.3(2)(ca), a statement which contains—

(a) to the best of the administrator or liquidator's knowledge and belief—

(i) an estimate of the value of the prescribed part (whether or not he proposes to make an application to court under section 176A(5) or section 176A(3) applies), and

(ii) an estimate of the value of the company's net property, and

(b) whether, and, if so, why, the administrator or liquidator proposes to make an application to court under section 176A(5).

(4) Nothing in this Rule is to be taken as requiring any such estimate to include any information, the disclosure of which could seriously prejudice the commercial interests of the company. If such information is excluded from the calculation the estimate shall be accompanied by a statement to that effect.]

[6072]

NOTES

Para (1): words in first pair of square brackets inserted, and words in third (inner) pair of square brackets substituted, by the Insolvency (Amendment) Rules 2003, SI 2003/1730, r 4, Sch 1, Pt 1, para 3(a), as from 15 September 2003 (for transitional provisions and savings see the note preceding r 2.1 at **[6097]**); words in second pair of square brackets inserted by the Insolvency (Amendment) Rules 1987, SI 1987/1919, r 3(1), Schedule, Pt 1, para 3, as from 11 January 1988.

Paras (3), (4): added by SI 2003/1730, r 4, Sch 1, Pt 1, para 3(b), as from 15 September 2003 (for transitional provisions and savings see the note preceding r 2.1 at **[6097]**).

1.11 Summoning of meetings under s 3

(1) The responsible insolvency practitioner shall fix a venue for the creditors' meeting and the company meeting, and give at least 14 days' notice of the meetings—

(a) in the case of the creditors' meeting, to all the creditors specified in the company's statement of affairs, and to any other creditors of whom the insolvency practitioner is aware; and

(b) in the case of the company meeting, to all persons who are, to the best of his belief, members of the company.

(2) Each notice sent out under this Rule shall state the effect of Rule 1.19(1), (3) and (4) (requisite majorities (creditors)); and with it there shall be sent—

(a) a copy of the responsible insolvency practitioner's proposal, and

(b) a copy of the statement of affairs or, if he thinks fit, a summary of it (the summary to include a list of creditors and the amounts of their debts).

[6073]

CHAPTER 4
PROPOSAL BY ADMINISTRATOR OR LIQUIDATOR (ANOTHER INSOLVENCY PRACTITIONER THE NOMINEE)

1.12 Preparation of proposal and notice to nominee

(1) The responsible insolvency practitioner shall give notice to the intended nominee, and prepare his proposal for a voluntary arrangement, in the same manner as is required of the directors, in the case of a proposal by them, under Chapter 2.

(2) Rule 1.2 applies to the responsible insolvency practitioner as it applies to the directors; and Rule 1.4 applies as regards the action to be taken by the nominee.

(3) The content of the proposal shall be as required by Rule 1.3 [(and, where relevant, Rule 1.10)], reading references to the directors as referring to the responsible insolvency practitioner.

(4) Rule 1.6 applies in respect of the information to be furnished to the nominee, reading references to the directors as referring to the responsible insolvency practitioner.

(5) With the proposal the responsible insolvency practitioner shall provide a copy of the company's statement of affairs.

(6) Where the company is being wound up by the court, the responsible insolvency practitioner shall send a copy of the proposal to the official receiver, accompanied by the name and address of the insolvency practitioner [or authorised person] who has agreed to act as nominee.

(7) Rules 1.7 to 1.9 apply as regards a proposal under this Chapter as they apply to a proposal under Chapter 2.

[6074]

NOTES

Para (3): words in square brackets inserted by the Insolvency (Amendment) Rules 1987, SI 1987/1919, r 3(1), Schedule, Pt 1, para 4, as from 11 January 1988.

Para (6): words in square brackets added by the Insolvency (Amendment) (No 2) Rules 2002, SI 2002/2712, r 3(1), Schedule, Pt 1, para 5, as from 1 January 2003, subject to transitional provisions as noted to r 1.1 at **[6063]**.

CHAPTER 5
PROCEEDINGS ON A PROPOSAL MADE BY THE DIRECTORS, OR BY THE ADMINISTRATOR, OR BY THE LIQUIDATOR

SECTION A: MEETINGS OF COMPANY'S CREDITORS AND MEMBERS

[1.13 Summoning of meetings

(1) Subject as follows, in fixing the venue for the creditors' meeting and the company meeting, the person summoning the meeting ("the convener") shall have regard primarily to the convenience of the creditors.

(2) Meetings shall in each case be summoned for commencement between 10.00 and 16.00 hours on a business day.

(3) The meetings may be held on the same day or on different days. If held on the same day, the meetings shall be held in the same place, but in either case the creditors' meeting shall be fixed for a time in advance of the company meeting.

(4) Where the meetings are not held on the same day, they shall be held within 7 days of each other.

(5) With every notice summoning either meeting there shall be sent out forms of proxy.]

[6075]

NOTES

Substituted by the Insolvency (Amendment) Rules 2003, SI 2003/1730, r 4, Sch 1, Pt 1, para 4, as from 15 September 2003 (for transitional provisions and savings see the note preceding r 2.1 at **[6097]**).

Para (5): see Form 8.1 in Appendix 4 at **[A4]**.

1.14 The chairman at meetings

(1) Subject as follows, at both the creditors' meeting and the company meeting, and at any combined meeting, the convener shall be chairman.

(2) If for any reason he is unable to attend, he may nominate another person to act as chairman in his place; but a person so nominated must be … —

[(a) a person qualified to act as an insolvency practitioner in relation to the company;

(b) an authorised person in relation to the company; or

(c) an employee of the convenor or his firm who is experienced in insolvency matters.]

[6076]

NOTES

Para (2): word omitted revoked, and sub-paras (a)–(c) substituted for original paras (a), (b), by the Insolvency (Amendment) (No 2) Rules 2002, SI 2002/2712, r 3(1), Schedule, Pt 1, para 7, as from 1 January 2003, subject to transitional provisions as noted to r 1.1 at **[6063]**.

1.15 The chairman as proxy-holder

The chairman shall not by virtue of any proxy held by him vote to increase or reduce the amount of the remuneration or expenses of the nominee or the supervisor of the proposed arrangement, unless the proxy specifically directs him to vote in that way.

[6077]

1.16 Attendance by company officers

(1) At least 14 days' notice to attend the meetings shall be given by the convener—

(a) to all directors of the company, and
(b) to any persons in whose case the convener thinks that their presence is required as being officers of the company, or as having been directors or officers of it at any time in the 2 years immediately preceding the date of the notice.

(2) The chairman may, if he thinks fit, exclude any present or former director or officer from attendance at a meeting, either completely or for any part of it; and this applies whether or not a notice under this Rule has been sent to the person excluded.

[6078]

SECTION B: VOTING RIGHTS AND MAJORITIES

[1.17 Entitlement to vote (creditors)

(1) Subject as follows, every creditor who has notice of the creditors' meeting is entitled to vote at the meeting or any adjournment of it.

(2) Votes are calculated according to the amount of the creditor's debt as at the date of the meeting or, where the company is being wound up or is [in administration], the date of its going into liquidation or (as the case may be) [when the company entered administration].

(3) A creditor may vote in respect of a debt for an unliquidated amount or any debt whose value is not ascertained and for the purposes of voting (but not otherwise) his debt shall be valued at £1 unless the chairman agrees to put a higher value on it.]

[6079]

NOTES

Substituted, together with r 1.17A for original r 1.17, by the Insolvency (Amendment) (No 2) Rules 2002, SI 2002/2712, r 3(1), Schedule, Pt 1, para 8, as from 1 January 2003, subject to transitional provisions as noted to r 1.1 at **[6063]**.

Para (2): words in square brackets substituted by the Insolvency (Amendment) Rules 2003, SI 2003/1730, r 4, Sch 1, Pt 1, para 5, as from 15 September 2003 (for transitional provisions and savings see the note preceding r 2.1 at **[6097]**).

[1.17A Procedure for admission of creditors' claims for voting purposes

(1) Subject as follows, at any creditors' meeting the chairman shall ascertain the entitlement of persons wishing to vote and shall admit or reject their claims accordingly.

(2) The chairman may admit or reject a claim in whole or in part.

(3) The chairman's decision on any matter under this Rule or under paragraph (3) of Rule 1.17 is subject to appeal to the court by any creditor or member of the company.

(4) If the chairman is in doubt whether a claim should be admitted or rejected, he shall mark it as objected to and allow votes to be cast in respect of it, subject to such votes being subsequently declared invalid if the objection to the claim is sustained.

(5) If on an appeal the chairman's decision is reversed or varied, or votes are declared invalid, the court may order another meeting to be summoned, or make such order as it thinks just.

The court's power to make an order under this paragraph is exercisable only if it considers that the circumstances giving rise to the appeal give rise to unfair prejudice or material irregularity.

(6) An application to the court by way of appeal against the chairman's decision shall not be made after the end of the period of 28 days beginning with the first day on which the report required by section 4(6) has been made to the court.

(7) The chairman is not personally liable for any costs incurred by any person in respect of an appeal under this Rule.]

[6079A]

NOTES

Substituted as noted to r 1.17 at **[6079]**.

1.18 Voting rights (members)

(1) Subject as follows, members of the company at their meeting vote according to the rights attaching to their shares respectively in accordance with the articles.

(2) …

(3) References in this Rule to a person's shares include any other interest which he may have as a member of the company.

[6080]

NOTES

Para (2): revoked by the Insolvency (Amendment) (No 2) Rules 2002, SI 2002/2712, r 3(1), Schedule, Pt 1, para 9, as from 1 January 2003, subject to transitional provisions as noted to r 1.1 at **[6063]**.

1.19 Requisite majorities (creditors)

(1) Subject as follows, at the creditors' meeting for any resolution to pass approving any proposal or modification there must be a majority in excess of three-quarters in value of the creditors present in person or by proxy and voting on the resolution.

(2) The same applies in respect of any other resolution proposed at the meeting, but substituting one-half for three-quarters.

(3) In the following cases there is to be left out of account a creditor's vote in respect of any claim or part of a claim—

(a) where written notice of the claim was not given, either at the meeting or before it, to the chairman or convenor of the meeting;

(b) where the claim or part is secured;

(c) where the claim is in respect of a debt wholly or partly on, or secured by, a current bill of exchange or promissory note, unless the creditor is willing—

(i) to treat the liability to him on the bill or note of every person who is liable on it antecedently to the company, and against whom a bankruptcy order has not been made (or in the case of a company, which has not gone into liquidation), as a security in his hands, and

(ii) to estimate the value of the security and (for the purpose of entitlement to vote, but not of any distribution under the arrangement) to deduct it from his claim.

(4) Any resolution is invalid if those voting against it include more than half in value of the creditors, counting in these latter only those—

(a) to whom notice of the meeting was sent;

(b) whose votes are not be left out of account under paragraph (3); and

(c) who are not, to the best of the chairman's belief, persons connected with the company.

(5) It is for the chairman of the meeting to decide whether under this Rule—

(a) a vote is to be left out of account in accordance with paragraph (3), or

(b) a person is a connected person for the purposes of paragraph (4)(c);

and in relation to the second of these two cases the chairman is entitled to rely on the information provided by the company's statement of affairs or otherwise in accordance with this Part of the Rules.

(6) If the chairman uses a proxy contrary to Rule 1.15, his vote with that proxy does not count towards any majority under this Rule.

[(7) The chairman's decision on any matter under this Rule is subject to appeal to the court by any creditor or member and paragraphs (5) to (7) of Rule 1.17A apply as regards such an appeal.]

[6081]

NOTES

Para (7): substituted by the Insolvency (Amendment) (No 2) Rules 2002, SI 2002/2712, r 3(1), Schedule, Pt 1, para 10, as from 1 January 2003, subject to transitional provisions as noted to r 1.1 at **[6063]**.

1.20 Requisite majorities (members)

(1) Subject as follows, and to any express provision made in the articles, at a company meeting any resolution is to be regarded as passed if voted for by more than one-half [in value] of the members present in person or by proxy and voting on the resolution.

[The value of members is determined by reference to the number of votes conferred on each member by the company's articles.]

(2) …

(3) If the chairman uses a proxy contrary to Rule 1.15, his vote with that proxy does not count towards any majority under this Rule.

[6082]

NOTES

Para (1): words in square brackets inserted by the Insolvency (Amendment) Rules 1987, SI 1987/1919, r 3(1), Schedule, Pt 1, para 5, as from 11 January 1988.

Para (2): revoked by the Insolvency (Amendment) (No 2) Rules 2002, SI 2002/2712, r 3(1), Schedule, Pt 1, para 11, as from 1 January 2003, subject to transitional provisions as noted to r 1.1 at **[6063]**.

[1.21—(1) If the chairman thinks fit, the creditors' meeting and the company meeting may be held together.

(2) The chairman may, and shall if it is so resolved at the meeting in question, adjourn that meeting for not more than 14 days.

(3) If there are subsequently further adjournments, the final adjournment shall not be to a day later than 14 days after the date on which the meeting in question was originally held.

(4) In the case of a proposal by the directors, if the meetings are adjourned under paragraph (2), notice of the fact shall be given by the nominee forthwith to the court.

(5) If following the final adjournment of the creditors' meeting the proposal (with or without modifications) has not been approved by the creditors, it is deemed rejected.]

[6083]

NOTES

Substituted by the Insolvency (Amendment) (No 2) Rules 2002, SI 2002/2712, r 3(1), Schedule, Pt 1, para 12, as from 1 January 2003, subject to transitional provisions as noted to r 1.1 at **[6063]**.

Note: the substitution of this rule by SI 2002/2712 did not provide for a new rule name. Prior to its substitution this rule was named "Proceedings to obtain agreement on the proposal".

SECTION C: IMPLEMENTATION OF THE ARRANGEMENT

1.22 Resolutions to follow approval

[(1) If the voluntary arrangement is approved (with or without modifications) by the creditors' meeting, a resolution may be taken by the creditors, where two or more supervisors are appointed, on the question whether acts to be done in connection with the arrangement may be done by any one or more of them, or must be done by all of them.]

(2) …

(3) If at either meeting a resolution is moved for the appointment of some person other than the nominee to be supervisor of the arrangement, there must be produced to the chairman, at or before the meeting—

- (a) that person's written consent to act (unless he is present and then and there signifies his consent), and
- (b) his written confirmation that he is qualified to act as an insolvency practitioner in relation to the company [or is an authorised person in relation to the company].

[6084]

NOTES

Para (1): substituted by the Insolvency (Amendment) (No 2) Rules 2002, SI 2002/2712, r 3(1), Schedule, Pt 1, para 13(a), as from 1 January 2003, subject to transitional provisions as noted to r 1.1 at **[6063]**.

Para (2): revoked by SI 2002/2712, r 3(1), Schedule, Pt 1, para 13(b), as from 1 January 2003, subject to transitional provisions as noted to r 1.1 at **[6063]**.

Para (3): words in square brackets added by SI 2002/2712, r 3(1), Schedule, Pt 1, para 13(c), as from 1 January 2003, subject to transitional provisions as noted to r 1.1 at **[6063]**.

[1.22A Notice of order made under section 4A(6)

(1) This Rule applies where the court makes an order under section 4A(6).

(2) The member of the company who applied for the order shall serve sealed copies of it on—

(a) the supervisor of the voluntary arrangement; and
(b) the directors of the company.

(3) Service on the directors may be effected by service of a single copy on the company at its registered office.

(4) The directors or (as the case may be) the supervisor shall forthwith after receiving a copy of the court's order, give notice of it to all persons who were sent notice of the creditors' or company meetings or who, not having been sent such notice, are affected by the order.

(5) The person on whose application the order of the court was made shall, within 7 days of the order, deliver an office copy to the registrar of companies.]

[6084A]

NOTES

Inserted by the Insolvency (Amendment) (No 2) Rules 2002, SI 2002/2712, r 3(1), Schedule, Pt 1, para 14, as from 1 January 2003, subject to transitional provisions as noted to r 1.1 at **[6063]**.

1.23 Hand-over of property etc to supervisor

(1) [Where the decision approving the voluntary arrangement has effect under section 4A—]

(a) the directors, or
(b) where the company is in liquidation or is [in administration], and a person other than the responsible insolvency practitioner is appointed as supervisor of the voluntary arrangement, the insolvency practitioner,

shall forthwith do all that is required for putting the supervisor into possession of the assets included in the arrangement.

(2) Where the company is in liquidation or is [in administration], the supervisor shall on taking possession of the assets discharge any balance due to the insolvency practitioner by way of remuneration or on account of—

(a) fees, costs, charges and expenses properly incurred and payable under the Act or the Rules, and
(b) any advances made in respect of the company, together with interest on such advances at the rate specified in section 17 of the Judgments Act 1838 at the date on which the company went into liquidation or (as the case may be) [entered administration].

(3) Alternatively, the supervisor must, before taking possession, give the responsible insolvency practitioner a written undertaking to discharge any such balance out of the first realisation of assets.

(4) The insolvency practitioner has a charge on the assets included in the voluntary arrangement in respect of any sums due as above until they have been discharged, subject only to the deduction from realisations by the supervisor of the proper costs and expenses of such realisations.

(5) The supervisor shall from time to time out of the realisation of assets discharge all guarantees properly given by the responsible insolvency practitioner for the benefit of the company, and shall pay all the insolvency practitioner's expenses.

(6) References in this Rule to the responsible insolvency practitioner include, where a company is being wound up by the court, the official receiver, whether or not in his capacity as liquidator; and any sums due to the official receiver take priority over those due to a liquidator.

[6085]

NOTES

Para (1): words in first pair of square brackets substituted by the Insolvency (Amendment) (No 2) Rules 2002, SI 2002/2712, r 3(1), Schedule, Pt 1, para 15, as from 1 January 2003, subject to transitional provisions as noted to r 1.1 at **[6063]**; words in second pair of square brackets substituted by the Insolvency (Amendment) Rules 2003, SI 2003/1730, r 4, Sch 1, Pt 1, para 6(a), as from 15 September 2003 (for transitional provisions and savings see the note preceding r 2.1 at **[6097]**).

Para (2): words in square brackets substituted by SI 2003/1730, r 4, Sch 1, Pt 1, para 6(b), as from 15 September 2003 (for transitional provisions and savings see the note preceding r 2.1 at **[6097]**).

1.24 Report of meetings

(1) A report of the meetings shall be prepared by the person who was chairman of them.

(2) The report shall—

[(a) state whether the proposal for a voluntary arrangement was approved by the creditors of the company alone or by both the creditors and members of the company and in either case whether such approval was with any modifications;]

(b) set out the resolutions which were taken at each meeting, and the decision on each one;

(c) list the creditors and members of the company (with their respective values) who were present or represented at the meetings, and how they voted on each resolution; …

[(ca) state whether, in the opinion of the supervisor, (i) the EC Regulation applies to the voluntary arrangement and (ii) if so, whether the proceedings are main proceedings, secondary proceedings or territorial proceedings; and]

(d) include such further information (if any) as the chairman thinks it appropriate to make known to the court.

(3) A copy of the chairman's report shall, within 4 days of the meetings being held, be filed in court; and the court shall cause that copy to be endorsed with the date of filing.

(4) In respect of each of the meetings, the persons to whom notice of its result is to be sent by the chairman under section 4(6) are all those who were sent notice of the meeting under this Part of the Rules.

The notice shall be sent immediately after a copy of the chairman's report is filed in court under paragraph (3).

(5) [If the decision approving the voluntary arrangement has effect under section 4A] (whether or not in the form proposed), the supervisor shall forthwith send a copy of the chairman's report to the registrar of companies.

[6086]

NOTES

Para (2): sub-para (a) substituted by the Insolvency (Amendment) (No 2) Rules 2002, SI 2002/2712, r 3(1), Schedule, Pt 1, para 16(a), as from 1 January 2003, subject to transitional provisions as noted to r 1.1 at **[6063]**; word omitted from sub-para (c) revoked, and sub-para (ca) inserted, by the Insolvency (Amendment) Rules 2002, SI 2002/1307, rr 3, 4(3), as from 31 May 2002, with savings in relation to anything done under, or for the purposes of, this provision before that date.

Para (5): words in square brackets substituted by SI 2002/2712, r 3(1), Schedule, Pt 1, para 16(b), as from 1 January 2003, subject to transitional provisions as noted to r 1.1 at **[6063]**.

EC Regulation: ie, Council Regulation 1346/2000/EC on insolvency proceedings at **[9290]**.

Para (5): see Form 1.1 in Appendix 4 at **[A4]**.

1.25 Revocation or suspension of the arrangement

(1) This Rule applies where the court makes an order of revocation or suspension under section 6.

(2) The person who applied for the order shall serve sealed copies of it—

(a) on the supervisor of the voluntary arrangement, and

(b) on the directors of the company or the administrator or liquidator (according to who made the proposal for the arrangement).

Service on the directors may be effected by service of a single copy of the order on the company at its registered office.

(3) If the order includes a direction by the court under section 6(4)(b) for any further meetings to be summoned, notice shall also be given (by the person who applied for the order) to whoever is, in accordance with the direction, required to summon the meetings.

(4) The directors or (as the case may be) the administrator or liquidator shall—

(a) forthwith after receiving a copy of the court's order, give notice of it to all persons who were sent notice of the creditors' and company meetings or who, not having been sent that notice, appear to be affected by the order;

(b) within 7 days of their receiving a copy of the order (or within such longer period as the court may allow), give notice to the court whether it is intended to make a revised proposal to the company and its creditors, or to invite re-consideration of the original proposal.

(5) The person on whose application the order of revocation or suspension was made shall, within 7 days after the making of the order, deliver a copy of the order to the registrar of companies.

[6087]

NOTES

Para (5): see Form 1.2 in Appendix 4 at **[A4]**.

1.26 Supervisor's accounts and reports

(1) Where the voluntary arrangement authorises or requires the supervisor—

(a) to carry on the business of the company or trade on its behalf or in its name, or

(b) to realise assets of the company, or

(c) otherwise to administer or dispose of any of its funds,

he shall keep accounts and records of his acts and dealings in and in connection with the arrangement, including in particular records of all receipts and payments of money.

(2) The supervisor shall, not less often than once in every 12 months beginning with the date of his appointment, prepare an abstract of such receipts and payments, and send copies of it, accompanied by his comments on the progress and efficacy of the arrangement, to—

(a) the court,

(b) the registrar of companies,

(c) the company,

(d) all those of the company's creditors who are bound by the arrangement,

(e) subject to paragraph (5) below, the members of the company who are so bound, and

(f) if the company is not in liquidation, the company's auditors for the time being.

If in any period of 12 months he has made no payments and had no receipts, he shall at the end of that period send a statement to that effect to all those specified in sub-paragraphs (a) to (f) above.

(3) An abstract provided under paragraph (2) shall relate to a period beginning with the date of the supervisor's appointment or (as the case may be) the day following the end of the last period for which an abstract was prepared under this Rule; and copies of the abstract shall be sent out, as required by paragraph (2), within the 2 months following the end of the period to which the abstract relates.

(4) If the supervisor is not authorised as mentioned in paragraph (1), he shall, not less often than once in every 12 months beginning with the date of his appointment, send to all those specified in paragraph (2)(a) to (f) a report on the progress and efficacy of the voluntary arrangement.

(5) The court may, on application by the supervisor—

(a) dispense with the sending under this Rule of abstracts or reports to members of the company, either altogether or on the basis that the availability of the abstract or report to members is to be advertised by the supervisor in a specified manner;

(b) vary the dates on which the obligation to send abstracts or reports arises.

[6088]

NOTES

Para (2): see Form 1.3 in Appendix 4 at **[A4]**.

1.27 Production of accounts and records to Secretary of State

(1) The Secretary of State may at any time during the course of the voluntary arrangement or after its completion [or termination] require the supervisor to produce for inspection—

(a) his records and accounts in respect of the arrangement, and

(b) copies of abstracts and reports prepared in compliance with Rule 1.26.

(2) The Secretary of State may require production either at the premises of the supervisor or elsewhere; and it is the duty of the supervisor to comply with any requirement imposed on him under this Rule.

(3) The Secretary of State may cause any accounts and records produced to him under this Rule to be audited; and the supervisor shall give to the Secretary of State such further information and assistance as he needs for the purposes of his audit.

[6089]

NOTES

Para (1): words in square brackets added by the Insolvency (Amendment) (No 2) Rules 2002, SI 2002/2712, r 3(1), Schedule, Pt 1, para 17, as from 1 January 2003, subject to transitional provisions as noted to r 1.1 at **[6063]**.

1.28 Fees, costs, charges and expenses

(1) The fees, costs, charges and expenses that may be incurred for any of the purposes of the voluntary arrangement are—

(a) any disbursements made by the nominee prior to the [decision approving the arrangement taking effect under section 4A], and any remuneration for his services as such agreed between himself and the company (or, as the case may be, the administrator or liquidator);

(b) any fees, costs, charges or expenses which—

  (i) are sanctioned by the terms of the arrangement, or

  (ii) would be payable, or correspond to those which would be payable, in an administration or winding up.

[6090]

NOTES

Para (1): words in square brackets in sub-para (a) substituted by the Insolvency (Amendment) (No 2) Rules 2002, SI 2002/2712, r 3(1), Schedule, Pt 1, para 18, as from 1 January 2003, subject to transitional provisions as noted to r 1.1 at **[6063]**.

[1.29 Completion or termination of the arrangement

(1) Not more than 28 days after the final completion or termination of the voluntary arrangement, the supervisor shall send to creditors and members of the company who are bound by it a notice that the voluntary arrangement has been fully implemented or (as the case may be) has terminated.

(2) With the notice there shall be sent to each creditor and member a copy of a report by the supervisor summarising all receipts and payments made by him in pursuance of the arrangement, and explaining in relation to implementation of the arrangement any departure from the proposals as they originally took effect, or (in the case of termination of the arrangement) explaining the reasons why the arrangement has terminated.

(3) The supervisor shall, within the 28 days mentioned above, send to the registrar of companies and to the court a copy of the notice to creditors and members under paragraph (1), together with a copy of the report under paragraph (2), and the supervisor shall not vacate office until after such copies have been sent.]

[(4) In the report under paragraph (2), the supervisor shall include a statement as to the amount paid, if any, to unsecured creditors by virtue of the application of section 176A (prescribed part).]

[6091]–[6092]

NOTES

Substituted by the Insolvency (Amendment) (No 2) Rules 2002, SI 2002/2712, r 3(1), Schedule, Pt 1, para 19, as from 1 January 2003, subject to transitional provisions as noted to r 1.1 at **[6063]**.

Para (4): added by the Insolvency (Amendment) Rules 2003, SI 2003/1730, r 4, Sch 1, Pt 1, para 7, as from 15 September 2003 (for transitional provisions and savings see the note preceding r 2.1 at **[6097]**).

Para (3): see Form 1.4 in Appendix 4 at **[A4]**.

1.30 (*(Chap 6) revoked by the Insolvency (Amendment) (No 2) Rules 2002, SI 2002/2712, r 3(1), Schedule, Pt 1, para 20, as from 1 January 2003, subject to transitional provisions as noted to r 1.1 at* **[6063]**.)

[CHAPTER 7
EC REGULATION—CONVERSION OF VOLUNTARY ARRANGEMENT INTO WINDING UP

1.31 Application for conversion into winding up

(1) Where a member State liquidator proposes to apply to the court for the conversion under Article 37 of the EC Regulation (conversion of earlier proceedings) of a voluntary arrangement into a winding up, an affidavit complying with Rule 1.32 must be prepared and sworn, and filed in court in support of the application.

(2) An application under this Rule shall be by originating application.

(3) The application and the affidavit required under this Rule shall be served upon—
(a) the company; and
(b) the supervisor.]

[6093]

NOTES

Inserted, together with preceding heading and rr 1.32–1.34 (Chaps 7, 8), by the Insolvency (Amendment) Rules 2002, SI 2002/1307, rr 3, 4(4), as from 31 May 2002.

EC Regulation: ie, Council Regulation 1346/2000/EC on insolvency proceedings at **[9290]**.

[1.32 Contents of affidavit

(1) The affidavit shall state—
(a) that main proceedings have been opened in relation to the company in a member State other than the United Kingdom;
(b) the deponent's belief that the conversion of the voluntary arrangement into a winding up would prove to be in the interests of the creditors in the main proceedings;
(c) the deponent's opinion as to whether the company ought to enter voluntary winding up or be wound up by the court; and
(d) all other matters that, in the opinion of the member State liquidator, would assist the court—
(i) in deciding whether to make such an order, and
(ii) if the court were to do so, in considering the need for any consequential provision that would be necessary or desirable.

(2) An affidavit under this Rule shall be sworn by, or on behalf of, the member State liquidator.]

[6094]

NOTES

Inserted as noted to r 1.31 at **[6093]**.

[1.33 Power of court

(1) On hearing the application for conversion into winding up the court may make such order as it thinks fit.

(2) If the court makes an order for conversion into winding up the order may contain all such consequential provisions as the court deems necessary or desirable.

(3) Without prejudice to the generality of paragraph (1), an order under that paragraph may provide that the company be wound up as if a resolution for voluntary winding up under section 84 were passed on the day on which the order is made.

(4) Where the court makes an order for conversion into winding up under paragraph (1), any expenses properly incurred as expenses of the administration of the voluntary arrangement in question shall be a first charge on the company's assets.]

[6095]

NOTES

Inserted as noted to r 1.31 at **[6093]**.

[CHAPTER 8
EC REGULATION—MEMBER STATE LIQUIDATOR

1.34 Interpretation of creditor and notice to member State liquidator

(1) This Rule applies where a member State liquidator has been appointed in relation to the company.

(2) Where the supervisor is obliged to give notice to, or provide a copy of a document (including an order of court) to, the court, the registrar of companies or the official receiver, the supervisor shall give notice or provide copies, as appropriate, to the member State liquidator.

(3) Paragraph (2) is without prejudice to the generality of the obligations imposed by Article 31 of the EC Regulation (duty to cooperate and communicate information).]

[6096]

NOTES

Inserted as noted to r 1.31 at **[6093]**.

EC Regulation: ie, Council Regulation 1346/2000/EC on insolvency proceedings at **[9290]**.

[CHAPTER 9
OBTAINING A MORATORIUM
PROCEEDINGS DURING A MORATORIUM
NOMINEES
CONSIDERATION OF PROPOSALS WHERE MORATORIUM OBTAINED

SECTION A: OBTAINING A MORATORIUM

1.35 Preparation of proposal by directors and submission to nominee

(1) The document containing the proposal referred to in paragraph 6(1)(a) of Schedule A1 to the Act shall—

(a) be prepared by the directors;

(b) comply with the requirements of paragraphs (1) and (2) of Rule 1.3 (save that the reference to preferential creditors shall be to preferential creditors within the meaning of paragraph 31(8) of Schedule A1 to the Act); and

(c) state the address to which notice of the consent of the nominee to act and the documents referred to in Rule 1.38 shall be sent.

(2) With the agreement in writing of the nominee, the directors may amend the proposal at any time before submission to them by the nominee of the statement required by paragraph 6(2) of Schedule A1 to the Act.]

[6096A]

NOTES

Chapter 9 (rr 1.35–1.54) inserted by the Insolvency (Amendment) (No 2) Rules 2002, SI 2002/2712, r 3(1), Schedule, Pt 1, para 21, as from 1 January 2003, subject to transitional provisions as noted to r 1.1 at **[6063]**.

[1.36 Delivery of documents to the intended nominee etc

(1) The documents required to be delivered to the nominee pursuant to paragraph 6(1) of Schedule A1 to the Act shall be delivered to the nominee himself or to a person authorised to take delivery of documents on his behalf.

(2) On receipt of the documents, the nominee shall forthwith issue an acknowledgement of receipt of the documents to the directors which shall indicate the date on which the documents were received.]

[6096B]

NOTES

Inserted as noted to r 1.35 at **[6096A]**.

[1.37 Statement of affairs

(1) The statement of the company's affairs required to be delivered to the nominee pursuant to paragraph 6(1)(b) of Schedule A1 to the Act shall be delivered to the nominee no

later than 7 days after the delivery to him of the document setting out the terms of the proposed voluntary arrangement or such longer time as he may allow.

(2) The statement of affairs shall comprise the same particulars as required by Rule 1.5(2) (supplementing or amplifying, so far as is necessary for clarifying the state of the company's affairs, those already given in the directors' proposal).

(3) The statement of affairs shall be made up to a date not earlier than 2 weeks before the date of the delivery of the document containing the proposal for the voluntary arrangement to the nominee under Rule 1.36(1).

However, the nominee may allow an extension of that period to the nearest practicable date (not earlier than 2 months before the date of delivery of the documents referred to in Rule 1.36(1)) and if he does so, he shall give a statement of his reasons in writing to the directors.

(4) The statement of affairs shall be certified as correct, to the best of their knowledge and belief, by two or more directors of the company, or by the company secretary and at least one director (other than the secretary himself).]

[6096C]

NOTES

Inserted as noted to r 1.35 at **[6096A]**.
See Form 1.6 in Appendix 4 at **[A4]**.

[1.38 The nominee's statement

(1) The nominee shall submit to the directors the statement required by paragraph 6(2) of Schedule A1 to the Act within 28 days of the submission to him of the document setting out the terms of the proposed voluntary arrangement.

(2) The statement shall have annexed to it—

(a) the nominee's comments on the proposal, unless the statement contains an opinion in the negative on any of the matters referred to in paragraph 6(2)(a) and (b) of Schedule A1 to the Act, in which case he shall instead give his reasons for that opinion, and

(b) where he is willing to act in relation to the proposed arrangement, a statement of his consent to act.]

[6096D]

NOTES

Inserted as noted to r 1.35 at **[6096A]**.
See Forms 1.5, 1.8 in Appendix 4 at **[A4]**.

[1.39 Documents submitted to the court to obtain moratorium

(1) Where pursuant to paragraph 7 of Schedule A1 to the Act the directors file the document and statements referred to in that paragraph in court, those documents shall be delivered together with 4 copies of a schedule listing them within 3 working days of the date of the submission to them of the nominee's statement under paragraph 6(2) of Schedule A1 to the Act.

(2) When the directors file the document and statements referred to in paragraph (1), they shall also file—

(a) a copy of any statement of reasons made by the nominee pursuant to Rule 1.37(3); and

(b) a copy of the nominee's comments on the proposal submitted to them pursuant to Rule 1.38(2).

(3) The copies of the schedule shall be endorsed by the court with the date on which the documents were filed in court and 3 copies of the schedule sealed by the court shall be returned by the court to the person who filed the documents in court.

(4) The statement of affairs required to be filed under paragraph 7(1)(b) of Schedule A1 to the Act shall comprise the same particulars as required by Rule 1.5(2).]

[6096E]

NOTES
Inserted as noted to r 1.35 at **[6096A]**.
See Forms 1.5 to 1.9 in Appendix 4 at **[A4]**.

[1.40 Notice and advertisement of beginning of a moratorium

(1) After receiving the copies of the schedule endorsed by the court under Rule 1.39(3), the directors shall forthwith serve 2 of them on the nominee and one on the company.

(2) Forthwith after receiving the copies of the schedule pursuant to paragraph (1) the nominee shall advertise the coming into force of the moratorium once in the Gazette, and once in such newspaper as he thinks most appropriate for ensuring that its coming into force comes to the notice of the company's creditors.

(3) The nominee shall forthwith notify the registrar of companies, the company and any petitioning creditor of the company of whose claim he is aware of the coming into force of the moratorium and such notification shall specify the date on which the moratorium came into force.

(4) The nominee shall give notice of the coming into force of the moratorium specifying the date on which it came into force to—

(a) any [enforcement officer] or other officer who, to his knowledge, is charged with an execution or other legal process against the company or its property; and

(b) any person who, to his knowledge, has distrained against the company or its property.]

[6096F]

NOTES
Inserted as noted to r 1.35 at **[6096A]**.
Para (4): words in square brackets substituted by the Insolvency (Amendment) Rules 2005, SI 2005/527, r 4, as from 1 April 2005.
See Forms 1.10, 1.11 in Appendix 4 at **[A4]**.

[1.41 Notice of extension of moratorium

(1) The nominee shall forthwith notify the registrar of companies and the court of a decision taking effect pursuant to paragraph 36 of Schedule A1 to the Act to extend or further extend the moratorium and such notice shall specify the new expiry date of the moratorium.

(2) Where an order is made by the court extending or further extending or renewing or continuing a moratorium, the nominee shall forthwith after receiving a copy of the same give notice to the registrar of companies and with the notice shall send an office copy of the order.]

[6096G]

NOTES
Inserted as noted to r 1.35 at **[6096A]**.
See Forms 1.12, 1.13 in Appendix 4 at **[A4]**.

[1.42 Notice and advertisement of end of moratorium

(1) After the moratorium comes to an end, the nominee shall forthwith advertise its coming to an end once in the Gazette, and once in such newspaper as he thinks most appropriate for ensuring that its coming to an end comes to the notice of the company's creditors, and such notice shall specify the date on which the moratorium came to an end.

(2) The nominee shall forthwith give notice of the ending of the moratorium to the registrar of companies, the court, the company and any creditor of the company of whose claim he is aware and such notice shall specify the date on which the moratorium came to an end.]

[6096H]

NOTES
Inserted as noted to r 1.35 at **[6096A]**.
See Forms 1.10, 1.14, 1.15 in Appendix 4 at **[A4]**.

[SECTION B: PROCEEDINGS DURING A MORATORIUM

1.43 Disposal of charged property etc during a moratorium

(1) This Rule applies in any case where the company makes an application to the court under paragraph 20 of Schedule A1 to the Act for leave to dispose of property of the company which is subject to a security, or goods in possession of the company under an agreement to which that paragraph relates.

(2) The court shall fix a venue for the hearing of the application and the company shall forthwith give notice of the venue to the person who is the holder of the security or, as the case may be, the owner under the agreement.

(3) If an order is made, the company shall forthwith give notice of it to that person or owner.

(4) The court shall send 2 sealed copies of the order to the company, who shall send one of them to that person or owner.]

[6096I]

NOTES

Inserted as noted to r 1.35 at **[6096A]**.

[SECTION C: NOMINEES

1.44 Withdrawal of nominee's consent to act

Where the nominee withdraws his consent to act he shall, pursuant to paragraph 25(5) of Schedule A1 to the Act, forthwith give notice of his withdrawal and the reason for withdrawing his consent to act to—

(a) the registrar of companies;
(b) the court;
(c) the company; and
(d) any creditor of the company of whose claim he is aware.]

[6096J]

NOTES

Inserted as noted to r 1.35 at **[6096A]**.
See Forms 1.16, 1.17 in Appendix 4 at **[A4]**.

[1.45 Replacement of nominee by the court

(1) Where the directors intend to make an application to the court under paragraph 28 of Schedule A1 to the Act for the nominee to be replaced, they shall give to the nominee at least 7 days' notice of their application.

(2) Where the nominee intends to make an application to the court under that paragraph to be replaced, he shall give to the directors at least 7 days' notice of his application.

(3) No appointment of a replacement nominee shall be made by the court unless there is filed in court a statement by the replacement nominee indicating his consent to act.]

[6096K]

NOTES

Inserted as noted to r 1.35 at **[6096A]**.
See Form 1.8 in Appendix 4 at **[A4]**.

[1.46 Notification of appointment of a replacement nominee

Where a person is appointed as a replacement nominee, he shall forthwith give notice of his appointment to—

(a) the registrar of companies;
(b) the court (in any case where he was not appointed by the court); and
(c) the person whom he has replaced as nominee.]

[6096L]

NOTES

Inserted as noted to r 1.35 at **[6096A]**.
See Forms 1.18, 1.19 in Appendix 4 at **[A4]**.

[1.47 Applications to court under paragraphs 26 or 27 of Schedule A1 to the Act

Where any person intends to make an application to the court pursuant to paragraph 26 or 27 of Schedule A1 to the Act, he shall give to the nominee at least 7 days' notice of his application.]

[6096M]

NOTES

Inserted as noted to r 1.35 at **[6096A]**.

[SECTION D: CONSIDERATION OF PROPOSALS WHERE MORATORIUM OBTAINED

1.48 Summoning of meetings; procedure at meetings etc

(1) Where the nominee summons meetings of creditors and the company pursuant to paragraph 29(1) of Schedule A1 to the Act, each of those meetings shall be summoned for a date that is not more than 28 days from the date on which the moratorium came into force.

(2) Notices calling the creditors' meetings shall be sent by the nominee to all creditors specified in the statement of affairs and any other creditors of the company of whose address he is aware at least 14 days before the day fixed for the meeting.

(3) Notices calling the company meeting shall be sent by the nominee to all persons who are, to the best of the nominee's belief, members of the company at least 14 days before the day fixed for the meeting.

(4) Each notice sent under this Rule shall specify the court in which the documents relating to the obtaining of the moratorium were filed and state the effect of paragraphs (1), (3) and (4) of Rule 1.52 (requisite majorities (creditors)) and with each notice there shall be sent—

(a) a copy of the directors' proposal;
(b) a copy of the statement of the company's affairs or, if the nominee thinks fit, a summary of it (the summary to include a list of creditors and the amount of their debts); and
(c) the nominee's comments on the proposal.

(5) The provisions of Rules 1.13 to 1.16 shall apply.]

[6096N]

NOTES

Inserted as noted to r 1.35 at **[6096A]**.

[1.49 Entitlement to vote (creditors)

(1) Subject as follows, every creditor who has notice of the creditors' meeting is entitled to vote at the meeting or any adjournment of it.

(2) Votes are calculated according to the amount of the creditor's debt as at the beginning of the moratorium, after deducting any amounts paid in respect of that debt after that date.

(3) A creditor may vote in respect of a debt for an unliquidated amount or any debt whose value is not ascertained and for the purposes of voting (but not otherwise) his debt shall be valued at £1 unless the chairman agrees to put a higher value on it.]

[6096O]

NOTES

Inserted as noted to r 1.35 at **[6096A]**.

[1.50 Procedure for admission of creditors' claims for voting purposes

(1) Subject as follows, at any creditors' meeting the chairman shall ascertain the entitlement of persons wishing to vote and shall admit or reject their claims accordingly.

PART IV
STATUTORY INSTRUMENTS

(2) The chairman may admit or reject a claim in whole or in part.

(3) The chairman's decision on any matter under this Rule or under paragraph (3) of Rule 1.49 is subject to appeal to the court by any creditor or member of the company.

(4) If the chairman is in doubt whether a claim should be admitted or rejected, he shall mark it as objected to and allow votes to be cast in respect of it, subject to such votes being subsequently declared invalid if the objection to the claim is sustained.

(5) If on an appeal the chairman's decision is reversed or varied, or votes are declared invalid, the court may order another meeting to be summoned, or make such order as it thinks just.

The court's power to make an order under this paragraph is exercisable only if it considers that the circumstances giving rise to the appeal are such as give rise to unfair prejudice or material irregularity.

(6) An application to the court by way of appeal against the chairman's decision shall not be made after the end of the period of 28 days beginning with the first day on which the report required by paragraph 30(3) of Schedule A1 to the Act has been made to the court.

(7) The chairman is not personally liable for any costs incurred by any person in respect of an appeal under this Rule.]

[6096P]

NOTES

Inserted as noted to r 1.35 at **[6096A]**.

[1.51 Voting rights (members)

Rule 1.18 shall apply.]

[6096Q]

NOTES

Inserted as noted to r 1.35 at **[6096A]**.

[1.52 Requisite majorities (creditors)

(1) Subject as follows, at the creditors' meeting for any resolution to pass approving any proposal or modification there must be a majority in excess of three-quarters in value of the creditors present in person or by proxy and voting on the resolution.

(2) The same applies in respect of any other resolution proposed at the meeting, but substituting one-half for three-quarters.

(3) At a meeting of the creditors for any resolution to pass extending (or further extending) a moratorium, or to bring a moratorium to an end before the end of the period of any extension, there must be a majority in excess of three quarters in value of the creditors present in person or by proxy and voting on the resolution. For this purpose paragraph (4)(b) below shall not apply and a secured creditor is entitled to vote in respect of the amount of his claim without deducting the value of his security.

(4) In the following cases there is to be left out of account a creditor's vote in respect of any claim or part of a claim—

- (a) where written notice of the claim was not given, either at the meeting or before it, to the chairman or convenor of the meeting;
- (b) where the claim or part is secured;
- (c) where the claim is in respect of a debt wholly or partly on, or secured by, a current bill of exchange or promissory note, unless the creditor is willing—
  - (i) to treat the liability to him on the bill or note of every person who is liable on it antecedently to the company, and against whom a bankruptcy order has not been made (or, in the case of a company, which has not gone into liquidation), as a security in his hands, and
  - (ii) to estimate the value of the security and (for the purpose of entitlement to vote, but not of any distribution under the arrangement) to deduct it from his claim.

(5) Any resolution is invalid if those voting against it include more than half in value of the creditors, counting in these latter only those—

(a) who have notice of the meeting;
(b) whose votes are not to be left out of account under paragraph (4); and
(c) who are not, to the best of the chairman's belief, persons connected with the company.

(6) It is for the chairman of the meeting to decide whether under this Rule—
(a) a vote is to be left out of account in accordance with paragraph [(4)], or
(b) a person is a connected person for the purposes of paragraph (5)(c);

and in relation to the second of these two cases the chairman is entitled to rely on the information provided by the statement of the company's affairs or otherwise in accordance with this Part of the Rules.

(7) If the chairman uses a proxy contrary to Rule 1.15 as it applies by virtue of Rule [1.48(5)], his vote with that proxy does not count towards any majority under this Rule.

(8) The chairman's decision on any matter under this Rule is subject to appeal to the court by any creditor or member and paragraphs (5) to (7) of Rule 1.50 apply as regards such an appeal.]

[6096R]

NOTES

Inserted as noted to r 1.35 at **[6096A]**.

Paras (6), (7): figures in square brackets substituted by the Insolvency (Amendment) Rules 2003, SI 2003/1730, r 4, Sch 1, Pt 1, para 8, as from 15 September 2003 (for transitional provisions and savings see the note preceding r 2.1 at **[6097]**).

[1.53 Requisite majorities (members) and proceedings to obtain agreement on the proposal

(1) Rule 1.20 shall apply.

(2) If the chairman thinks fit, the creditors' meeting and the company meeting may be held together.

(3) The chairman may, and shall if it is so resolved at the meeting in question, adjourn that meeting, but any adjournment shall not be to a day which is more than 14 days after the date on which the moratorium (including any extension) ends.

(4) If the meetings are adjourned under paragraph (3), notice of the fact shall be given by the nominee forthwith to the court.

(5) If following the final adjournment of the creditors' meeting the proposal (with or without modifications) has not been approved by the creditors, it is deemed rejected.]

[6096S]

NOTES

Inserted as noted to r 1.35 at **[6096A]**.

[1.54 Implementation of the arrangement

(1) Where a decision approving the arrangement has effect under paragraph 36 of Schedule A1 to the Act, the directors shall forthwith do all that is required for putting the supervisor into possession of the assets included in the arrangement.

(2) Subject to paragraph (3), Rules 1.22, 1.22A and 1.24 to 1.29 apply.

(3) The provisions referred to in paragraph (2) are modified as follows—
(a) in paragraph (1) of Rule 1.22A the reference to section 4A(6) is to be read as a reference to paragraph 36(5) of Schedule A1 to the Act;
(b) in paragraph (4) of Rule 1.24 the reference to section 4(6) is to be read as a reference to paragraph 30(3) of Schedule A1 to the Act;
(c) in paragraph (5) of Rule 1.24 the reference to section 4A is to be read as a reference to paragraph 36 of Schedule A1 to the Act;
(d) in paragraph (1) of Rule 1.25 the reference to section 6 is to be read as a reference to paragraph 38 of Schedule A1 to the Act and the references in paragraphs (2) and (4) to the administrator or liquidator shall be ignored;
(e) in paragraph (3) of Rule 1.25 the reference to section 6(4)(b) is to be read as a reference to paragraph 38 (4)(b) of Schedule A1 to the Act; and

(f) in sub-paragraph (a) of paragraph (1) of Rule 1.28 the reference to section 4A is to be read as a reference to paragraph 36 of Schedule A1 to the Act.]

[6096T]

NOTES

Inserted as noted to r 1.35 at **[6096A]**.

[PART 2
ADMINISTRATION PROCEDURE

NOTES

Substitution of Pt 2: the original Pt 2 (rr 2.1–2.62) was substituted by a new Pt 2 (rr 2.1–2.133) by the Insolvency (Amendment) Rules 2003, SI 2003/1730, r 5(1), Sch 1, Pt 2, para 9, as from 15 September 2003, subject to transitional provisions and savings as noted below.

Transitional provisions: the Insolvency (Amendment) Rules 2003, SI 2003/1730, r 5 provides as follows (note that by virtue of r 2(3), the "first commencement date" is 15 September 2003)—

"5 Amendments to Part 2 of the principal Rules

(1) Subject to paragraphs (2), (3) and (4), for Part 2 of the principal Rules there are substituted the provisions set out in Part 2 of Schedule 1 to these Rules.

(2) The provisions of Part 2 of Schedule 1 to these Rules shall not apply and Part 2 of the principal Rules as it stood before the coming into force of these Rules shall continue to apply, where a petition for an administration order has been presented to the court before the first commencement date.

(3) The former Rules shall continue to apply (with or without modification made by or under any enactment) where a provision made by or under any enactment preserves the continuing operation (with or without modification) after the first commencement date of old Part II of the Act and in such a case the provisions of Part 2 of Schedule 1 to these Rules shall not apply.

(4) In paragraph (3) "the former Rules" means the Insolvency Rules 1986 without the amendments made by these Rules and "old Part II" means Part II of the Act without the amendments made by the Enterprise Act 2002.".

CHAPTER 1
PRELIMINARY

2.1 Introductory and interpretation

(1) In this Part—

(a) Chapter 2 applies in relation to the appointment of an administrator by the court;
(b) Chapter 3 applies in relation to the appointment of an administrator by the holder of a qualifying floating charge under paragraph 14;
(c) Chapter 4 applies in relation to the appointment of an administrator by the company or the directors under paragraph 22;
(d) The following Chapters apply in all the cases mentioned in sub-paragraphs (a)–(c) above:

— Chapter 5: Process of administration;
— Chapter 6: Meetings and reports;
— Chapter 7: The creditors' committee;
— Chapter 8: Disposal of charged property;
— Chapter 9: Expenses of the administration;
— Chapter 10: Distributions to creditors;
— Chapter 11: The administrator;
— Chapter 12: Ending administration;
— Chapter 13: Replacing administrator;
— Chapter 14: EC Regulation—conversion of administration into winding up;
— Chapter 15: EC Regulation—member State liquidator.

(2) In this Part of these Rules a reference to a numbered paragraph shall, unless otherwise stated, be to the paragraph so numbered in Schedule B1 to the Act.]

[6097]

NOTES

Substituted, subject to transitional provisions, as noted above.
EC Regulation: ie, Council Regulation 1346/2000/EC on insolvency proceedings at **[9290]**.

[CHAPTER 2
APPOINTMENT OF ADMINISTRATOR BY COURT

2.2 Affidavit in support of administration application

(1) Where it is proposed to apply to the court for an administration order to be made in relation to a company, the administration application shall be in Form 2.1B and an affidavit complying with Rule 2.4 must be prepared and sworn, with a view to its being filed with the court in support of the application.

(2) If the administration application is to be made by the company or by the directors, the affidavit shall be made by one of the directors, or the secretary of the company, stating himself to make it on behalf of the company or, as the case may be, on behalf of the directors.

(3) If the application is to be made by creditors, the affidavit shall be made by a person acting under the authority of them all, whether or not himself one of their number. In any case there must be stated in the affidavit the nature of his authority and the means of his knowledge of the matters to which the affidavit relates.

(4) If the application is to be made by the supervisor of a voluntary arrangement under Part I of the Act, it is to be treated as if it were an application by the company.]

[6098]

NOTES

Substituted, subject to transitional provisions; see the note preceding r 2.1 at **[6097]**.
Forms: see Appendix 4 at **[A4]**.

[2.3 Form of application

(1) If made by the company or by the directors, the application shall state the name of the company and its address for service, which (in the absence of special reasons to the contrary) is that of the company's registered office.

(2) If the application is made by the directors, it shall state that it is so made under paragraph 12(1)(b); but from and after making it is to be treated for all purposes as the application of the company.

(3) If made by a single creditor, the application shall state his name and address for service.

(4) If the application is made by two or more creditors, it shall state that it is so made (naming them); but from and after making it is to be treated for all purposes as the application of only one of them, named in the application as applying on behalf of himself and other creditors. An address for service for that one shall be specified.

(5) There shall be attached to the application a written statement which shall be in Form 2.2B by each of the persons proposed to be administrator stating—

(a) that he consents to accept appointment;

(b) details of any prior professional relationship(s) that he has had with the company to which he is to be appointed as administrator; and

(c) his opinion that it is reasonably likely that the purpose of administration will be achieved.]

[6099]

NOTES

Substituted, subject to transitional provisions; see the note preceding r 2.1 at **[6097]**.
Forms: see Appendix 4 at **[A4]**.

[2.4 Contents of application and affidavit in support

(1) The administration application shall contain a statement of the applicant's belief that the company is, or is likely to become, unable to pay its debts, except where the applicant is the holder of a qualifying floating charge and is making the application in reliance on paragraph 35.

(2) There shall be attached to the application an affidavit in support which shall contain—

(a) a statement of the company's financial position, specifying (to the best of the applicant's knowledge and belief) the company's assets and liabilities, including contingent and prospective liabilities;
(b) details of any security known or believed to be held by creditors of the company, and whether in any case the security is such as to confer power on the holder to appoint an administrative receiver or to appoint an administrator under paragraph 14. If an administrative receiver has been appointed, that fact shall be stated;
(c) details of any insolvency proceedings in relation to the company including any petition that has been presented for the winding up of the company so far as within the immediate knowledge of the applicant;
(d) where it is intended to appoint a number of persons as administrators, details of the matters set out in paragraph 100(2) regarding the exercise of the function of the administrators; and
(e) any other matters which, in the opinion of those intending to make the application for an administration order, will assist the court in deciding whether to make such an order, so far as lying within the knowledge or belief of the applicant.

(3) Where the application is made by the holder of a qualifying floating charge in reliance on paragraph 35, he shall give sufficient details in the affidavit in support to satisfy the court that he is entitled to appoint an administrator under paragraph 14.

(4) The affidavit shall state whether, in the opinion of the person making the application, (i) the EC Regulation will apply and (ii) if so, whether the proceedings will be main proceedings or territorial proceedings.]

[6100]

NOTES

Substituted, subject to transitional provisions; see the note preceding r 2.1 at **[6097]**.
EC Regulation: ie, Council Regulation 1346/2000/EC on insolvency proceedings at **[9290]**.

[2.5 Filing of application

(1) The application (and all supporting documents) shall be filed with the court, with a sufficient number of copies for service and use as provided by Rule 2.6.

(2) Each of the copies filed shall have applied to it the seal of the court and be issued to the applicant; and on each copy there shall be endorsed the date and time of filing.

(3) The court shall fix a venue for the hearing of the application and this also shall be endorsed on each copy of the application issued under paragraph (2).

(4) After the application is filed, it is the duty of the applicant to notify the court in writing of the existence of any insolvency proceedings, and any insolvency proceedings under the EC Regulation, in relation to the company, as soon as he becomes aware of them.]

[6101]

NOTES

Substituted, subject to transitional provisions; see the note preceding r 2.1 at **[6097]**.
EC Regulation: ie, Council Regulation 1346/2000/EC on insolvency proceedings at **[9290]**.

[2.6 Service of application

(1) In the following paragraphs of this Rule, references to the application are to a copy of the application issued by the court under Rule 2.5(2) together with the affidavit in support of it and the documents attached to the application.

(2) Notification for the purposes of paragraph 12(2) shall be by way of service in accordance with Rule 2.8, verified in accordance with Rule 2.9.

(3) The application shall be served in addition to those persons referred to in paragraph 12(2)—
(a) if an administrative receiver has been appointed, on him;
(b) if there is pending a petition for the winding-up of the company, on the petitioner (and also on the provisional liquidator, if any);
(c) if a member State liquidator has been appointed in main proceedings in relation to the company, on him;

(d) on the person proposed as administrator;
(e) on the company, if the application is made by anyone other than the company;
(f) if a supervisor of a voluntary arrangement under Part I of the Act has been appointed, on him.]

[6102]

NOTES

Substituted, subject to transitional provisions; see the note preceding r 2.1 at **[6097]**.

[2.7 Notice to [officers charged with execution of writs or other process], etc

The applicant shall as soon as reasonably practicable after filing the application give notice of its being made to—

(a) any [enforcement officer] or other officer who to his knowledge is charged with an execution or other legal process against the company or its property; and
(b) any person who to his knowledge has distrained against the company or its property.]

[6103]

NOTES

Substituted, subject to transitional provisions; see the note preceding r 2.1 at **[6097]**.
Words in square brackets substituted by the Insolvency (Amendment) Rules 2005, SI 2005/527, r 5, as from 1 April 2005.

[2.8 Manner in which service to be effected

(1) Service of the application in accordance with Rule 2.6 shall be effected by the applicant, or his solicitor, or by a person instructed by him or his solicitor, not less than 5 days before the date fixed for the hearing.

(2) Service shall be effected as follows—

(a) on the company (subject to paragraph (3) below), by delivering the documents to its registered office;
(b) on any other person (subject to paragraph (4) below), by delivering the documents to his proper address;
(c) in either case, in such other manner as the court may direct.

(3) If delivery to a company's registered office is not practicable, service may be effected by delivery to its last known principal place of business in England and Wales.

(4) Subject to paragraph (5), for the purposes of paragraph (2)(b) above, a person's proper address is any which he has previously notified as his address for service; but if he has not notified any such address, service may be effected by delivery to his usual or last known address.

(5) In the case of a person who—

(a) is an authorised deposit-taker or former authorised deposit-taker;
(b)
  (i) has appointed, or is or may be entitled to appoint, an administrative receiver of the company, or
  (ii) is, or may be, entitled to appoint an administrator of the company under paragraph 14; and
(c) has not notified an address for service,

the proper address is the address of an office of that person where, to the knowledge of the applicant, the company maintains a bank account or, where no such office is known to the applicant, the registered office of that person, or, if there is no such office, his usual or last known address.

(6) Delivery of documents to any place or address may be made by leaving them there, or sending them by first class post.]

[6104]

NOTES

Substituted, subject to transitional provisions; see the note preceding r 2.1 at **[6097]**.

[2.9 Proof of service

(1) Service of the application shall be verified by an affidavit of service in Form 2.3B, specifying the date on which, and the manner in which, service was effected.

(2) The affidavit of service, with a sealed copy of the application exhibited to it, shall be filed with the court as soon as reasonably practicable after service, and in any event not less than 1 day before the hearing of the application.]

[6105]

NOTES

Substituted, subject to transitional provisions; see the note preceding r 2.1 at **[6097]**.
Forms: see Appendix 4 at **[A4]**.

[2.10 Application to appoint specified person as administrator by holder of qualifying floating charge

(1) Where the holder of a qualifying floating charge applies to the court under paragraph 36(1)(b), he shall produce to the court—

(a) the written consent of all holders of any prior qualifying floating charge;

(b) a written statement in the Form 2.2B made by the specified person proposed by him as administrator; and

(c) sufficient evidence to satisfy the court that he is entitled to appoint an administrator under paragraph 14.

(2) If an administration order is made appointing the specified person, the costs of the person who made the administration application and the applicant under paragraph 36(1)(b) shall, unless the court otherwise orders, be paid as an expense of the administration.]

[6106]

NOTES

Substituted, subject to transitional provisions; see the note preceding r 2.1 at **[6097]**.

[2.11 Application where company in liquidation

(1) Where an administration application is made under paragraph 37 or paragraph 38, the affidavit in support of the administration application shall contain—

(a) full details of the existing insolvency proceedings, the name and address of the liquidator, the date he was appointed and by whom;

(b) the reasons why it has subsequently been considered appropriate that an administration application should be made;

(c) all other matters that would, in the opinion of the applicant, assist the court in considering the need to make provisions in respect of matters arising in connection with the liquidation; and

(d) the details required in Rules 2.4(2) and (4).

(2) Where the application is made by the holder of a qualifying floating charge he shall set out sufficient evidence in the affidavit to satisfy the court that he is entitled to appoint an administrator under paragraph 14.]

[6107]

NOTES

Substituted, subject to transitional provisions; see the note preceding r 2.1 at **[6097]**.

[2.12 The hearing

(1) At the hearing of the administration application, any of the following may appear or be represented—

(a) the applicant;

(b) the company;

(c) one or more of the directors;

(d) if an administrative receiver has been appointed, that person;

(e) any person who has presented a petition for the winding-up of the company;

(f) the person proposed for appointment as administrator;

(g) if a member State liquidator has been appointed in main proceedings in relation to the company, that person;
(h) any person that is the holder of a qualifying floating charge;
(j) any supervisor of a voluntary arrangement under Part I of the Act;
(k) with the permission of the court, any other person who appears to have an interest justifying his appearance.

(2) If the court makes an administration order, it shall be in Form 2.4B.

(3) If the court makes an administration order, the costs of the applicant, and of any person whose costs are allowed by the court, are payable as an expense of the administration.]

[6108]

NOTES

Substituted, subject to transitional provisions; see the note preceding r 2.1 at **[6097]**.
Forms: see Appendix 4 at **[A4]**.

[2.13 Where the court makes an administration order in relation to a company upon an application under paragraph 37 or 38, the court shall include in the order—

(a) in the case of a liquidator appointed in a voluntary winding-up, his removal from office;
(b) details concerning the release of the liquidator;
(c) provision for payment of the expenses of the liquidation;
(d) provisions regarding any indemnity given to the liquidator;
(e) provisions regarding the handling or realisation of any of the company's assets in the hands of or under the control of the liquidator;
(f) such provision as the court thinks fit with respect to matters arising in connection with the liquidation; and
(g) such other provisions as the court shall think fit.]

[6109]

NOTES

Substituted, subject to transitional provisions; see the note preceding r 2.1 at **[6097]**.

[2.14 Notice of administration order

(1) If the court makes an administration order, it shall as soon as reasonably practicable send two sealed copies of the order to the person who made the application.

(2) The applicant shall send a sealed copy of the order as soon as reasonably practicable to the person appointed as administrator.

(3) If the court makes an order under paragraph 13(1)(d) or any other order under paragraph 13(1)(f), it shall give directions as to the persons to whom, and how, notice of that order is to be given.]

[6110]

NOTES

Substituted, subject to transitional provisions; see the note preceding r 2.1 at **[6097]**.

[CHAPTER 3
APPOINTMENT OF ADMINISTRATOR BY HOLDER OF FLOATING CHARGE

2.15 Notice of intention to appoint

(1) The prescribed form for the notice of intention to appoint for the purposes of paragraph 44(2) is Form 2.5B.

(2) For the purposes of paragraph 44(2), a copy of Form 2.5B shall be filed with the court at the same time as it is sent in accordance with paragraph 15(1) to the holder of any prior qualifying floating charge.

(3) The provisions of Rule 2.8(2) to 2.8(6) shall apply to the sending of a notice under this Rule as they apply to the manner in which service of an administration application is effected under that Rule.]

[6111]

NOTES

Substituted, subject to transitional provisions; see the note preceding r 2.1 at **[6097]**.
Forms: see Appendix 4 at **[A4]**.

[2.16 Notice of appointment

(1) The notice of appointment for the purposes of an appointment under paragraph 14 shall be in Form 2.6B.

(2) The copies of the notice filed with the court, shall be accompanied by—

(a) the administrator's written statement in Form 2.2B; and

(b) either—

(i) evidence that the person making the appointment has given such notice as may be required by paragraph 15(1)(a); or

(ii) copies of the written consent of all those required to give consent in accordance with paragraph 15(1)(b); and

(c) a statement of those matters provided for in paragraph 100(2), if applicable.

(3) The statutory declaration on Form 2.6B shall be made not more than 5 business days before the form is filed with the court.

(4) Written consent may be given by the holder of a prior qualifying floating charge where a notice of intention to appoint an administrator has been given and filed with the court in accordance with Rule 2.15 above, by completing the section provided on Form 2.5B and returning to the appointor a copy of the form.

(5) Where the holder of a prior qualifying floating charge does not choose to complete the section provided on Form 2.5B to indicate his consent, or no such form has been sent to him, his written consent shall include—

(a) details of the name, address of registered office and registered number of the company in respect of which the appointment is proposed to be made;

(b) details of the charge held by him including the date it was registered and, where applicable, any financial limit and any deeds of priority;

(c) his name and address;

(d) the name and address of the holder of the qualifying floating charge who is proposing to make the appointment;

(e) the date that notice of intention to appoint was given;

(f) the name of the proposed administrator;

(g) a statement of consent to the proposed appointment,

and it shall be signed and dated.

(6) This Rule and the following Rule are subject to Rule 2.19, the provisions of which apply when an appointment is to be made out of court business hours.]

[6112]

NOTES

Substituted, subject to transitional provisions; see the note preceding r 2.1 at **[6097]**.
Forms: see Appendix 4 at **[A4]**.

[2.17—(1) Three copies of the notice of appointment shall be filed with the court and shall have applied to them the seal of the court and be endorsed with the date and time of filing.

(2) The court shall issue two of the sealed copies of the notice of appointment to the person making the appointment, who shall as soon as reasonably practicable send one of the sealed copies to the administrator.]

[6113]

NOTES

Substituted, subject to transitional provisions; see the note preceding r 2.1 at **[6097]**.

[2.18 Where, after receiving notice that an administration application has been made, the holder of a qualifying floating charge appoints an administrator in reliance on paragraph 14, he shall as soon as reasonably practicable send a copy of the notice of appointment to the person making the administration application and to the court in which the application has been made.]

[6114]

NOTES

Substituted, subject to transitional provisions; see the note preceding r 2.1 at **[6097]**.

[2.19 Appointment taking place out of court business hours

(1) The holder of a qualifying floating charge may file a notice of appointment with the court, notwithstanding that the court is not open for public business. When the court is closed (and only when it is closed) a notice of appointment may be filed with the court by faxing that form in accordance with paragraph (3). The notice of appointment shall be in Form 2.7B.

(2) The filing of a notice in accordance with this Rule shall have the same effect for all purposes as a notice of appointment filed in accordance with Rule 2.16 with the court specified in the notice as having jurisdiction in the case.

(3) The notice shall be faxed to a designated telephone number which shall be provided by the Court Service for that purpose. The Secretary of State shall publish the telephone number of the relevant fax machine on The Insolvency Service website and on request to The Insolvency Service, make it available in writing.

(4) The appointor shall ensure that a fax transmission report detailing the time and date of the fax transmission and containing a copy of the first page (in part or in full) of the document faxed is created by the fax machine that is used to fax the form.

(5) The appointment shall take effect from the date and time of that fax transmission. The appointor shall notify the administrator, as soon as reasonably practicable, that the notice has been filed.

(6) The copy of the faxed notice of appointment received by the Court Service fax machine shall be forwarded as soon as reasonably practicable to the court specified in the notice as the court having jurisdiction in the case, to be placed on the relevant court file.

(7) The appointor shall take three copies of the notice of appointment that was faxed to the designated telephone number, together with the transmission report showing the date and time that the form was faxed to the designated telephone number and all the necessary supporting documents listed on Form 2.7B, to the court on the next day that the court is open for business.

(8) The appointor shall attach to the notice a statement providing full reasons for the out of hours filing of the notice of appointment, including why it would have been damaging to the company and its creditors not to have so acted.

(9) The copies of the notice shall be sealed by the court and shall be endorsed with the date and time when, according to the appointor's fax transmission report, the notice was faxed and the date when the notice and accompanying documents were delivered to the court.

(10) The administrator's appointment shall cease to have effect if the requirements of paragraph (7) are not completed within the time period indicated in that paragraph.

(11) Where any question arises in respect of the date and time that the notice of appointment was filed with the court it shall be a presumption capable of rebuttal that the date and time shown on the appointor's fax transmission report is the date and time at which the notice was so filed.

(12) The court shall issue two of the sealed copies of the notice of appointment to the person making the appointment, who shall, as soon as reasonably practicable, send one of the copies to the administrator.]

[6115]

NOTES

Substituted, subject to transitional provisions; see the note preceding r 2.1 at **[6097]**.
Forms: see Appendix 4 at **[A4]**.

[CHAPTER 4
APPOINTMENT OF ADMINISTRATOR BY COMPANY OR DIRECTORS

2.20 Notice of intention to appoint

(1) The notice of intention to appoint an administrator for the purposes of paragraph 26 shall be in Form 2.8B.

(2) A copy of the notice of intention to appoint must, in addition to the persons specified in paragraph 26, be given to—

(a) any [enforcement officer] who, to the knowledge of the person giving the notice, is charged with execution or other legal process against the company;
(b) any person who, to the knowledge of the person giving the notice, has distrained against the company or its property;
(c) any supervisor of a voluntary arrangement under Part I of the Act; and
(d) the company, if the company is not intending to make the appointment.

(3) The provisions of Rule 2.8(2) to 2.8(6) shall apply to the sending or giving of a notice under this Rule as they apply to the manner in which service of an administration application is effected under that Rule.]

[6116]

NOTES

Substituted, subject to transitional provisions; see the note preceding r 2.1 at **[6097]**.
Para (2): words in square brackets substituted by the Insolvency (Amendment) Rules 2005, SI 2005/527, r 6, as from 1 April 2005.
Forms: see Appendix 4 at **[A4]**.

[2.21 The statutory declaration on Form 2.8B shall be made not more than 5 business days before the notice is filed with the court.]

[6117]

NOTES

Substituted, subject to transitional provisions; see the note preceding r 2.1 at **[6097]**.

[2.22 The notice of intention to appoint shall be accompanied by either a copy of the resolution of the company to appoint an administrator (where the company intends to make the appointment) or a record of the decision of the directors (where the directors intend to make the appointment).]

[6118]

NOTES

Substituted, subject to transitional provisions; see the note preceding r 2.1 at **[6097]**.

[2.23 Notice of appointment

(1) The notice of appointment for the purposes of an appointment under paragraph 22 shall be in Form 2.9B or Form 2.10B, as appropriate.

(2) The copies of the notice filed with the court shall be accompanied by—

(a) the administrator's written statement in Form 2.2B;
(b) the written consent of all those persons to whom notice was given in accordance with paragraph 26(1) unless the period of notice set out in paragraph 26(1) has expired; and
(c) a statement of the matters provided for in paragraph 100(2), where applicable.]

[6119]

NOTES

Substituted, subject to transitional provisions; see the note preceding r 2.1 at **[6097]**.
Forms: see Appendix 4 at **[A4]**.

[2.24 The statutory declaration on Form 2.9B or Form 2.10B shall be made not more than 5 business days before the notice is filed with the court.]

[6120]

NOTES

Substituted, subject to transitional provisions; see the note preceding r 2.1 at **[6097]**.

[2.25 Where a notice of intention to appoint an administrator has not been given, the notice of appointment shall be accompanied by the documents specified in Rule 2.22 above.]

[6121]

NOTES

Substituted, subject to transitional provisions; see the note preceding r 2.1 at **[6097]**.

[2.26—(1) Three copies of the notice of appointment shall be filed with the court and shall have applied to them the seal of the court and be endorsed with the date and time of filing.

(2) The court shall issue two of the sealed copies of the notice of appointment to the person making the appointment who shall as soon as reasonably practicable send one of the sealed copies to the administrator.]

[6122]

NOTES

Substituted, subject to transitional provisions; see the note preceding r 2.1 at **[6097]**.

[CHAPTER 5
PROCESS OF ADMINISTRATION

2.27 Notification and advertisement of administrator's appointment

(1) The administrator shall advertise his appointment once in the Gazette, and once in such newspaper as he thinks most appropriate for ensuring that the appointment comes to the notice of the company's creditors. The advertisement shall be in Form 2.11B.

(2) The administrator shall, as soon as reasonably practicable after the date specified in paragraph 46(6), give notice of his appointment—

(a) if a receiver or an administrative receiver has been appointed, to him;

(b) if there is pending a petition for the winding up of the company, to the petitioner (and also to the provisional liquidator, if any);

(c) to any [enforcement officer] who, to the administrator's knowledge, is charged with execution or other legal process against the company;

(d) to any person who, to the administrator's knowledge, has distrained against the company or its property; and

(e) any supervisor of a voluntary arrangement under Part I of the Act.

(3) Where, under a provision of Schedule B1 to the Act or these Rules, the administrator is required to send a notice of his appointment to any person he shall do so in Form 2.12B.]

[6123]

NOTES

Substituted, subject to transitional provisions; see the note preceding r 2.1 at **[6097]**.

Para (2): words in square brackets substituted by the Insolvency (Amendment) Rules 2005, SI 2005/527, r 7, as from 1 April 2005.

Forms: see Appendix 4 at **[A4]**.

[2.28 Notice requiring statement of affairs

(1) In this Chapter "relevant person" shall have the meaning given to it in paragraph 47(3).

(2) The administrator shall send notice in Form 2.13B to each relevant person whom he determines appropriate requiring him to prepare and submit a statement of the company's affairs.

(3) The notice shall inform each of the relevant persons—

(a) of the names and addresses of all others (if any) to whom the same notice has been sent;

(b) of the time within which the statement must be delivered;
(c) of the effect of paragraph 48(4) (penalty for non-compliance); and
(d) of the application to him, and to each other relevant person, of section 235 (duty to provide information, and to attend on the administrator, if required).

(4) The administrator shall furnish each relevant person to whom he has sent notice in Form 2.13B with the forms required for the preparation of the statement of affairs.]

[6124]

NOTES

Substituted, subject to transitional provisions; see the note preceding r 2.1 at **[6097]**.
Forms: see Appendix 4 at **[A4]**.

[2.29 Verification and filing

(1) The statement of the company's affairs shall be in Form 2.14B, contain all the particulars required by that form and be verified by a statement of truth by the relevant person.

(2) The administrator may require any relevant person to submit a statement of concurrence in Form 2.15B stating that he concurs in the statement of affairs. Where the administrator does so, he shall inform the person making the statement of affairs of that fact.

(3) The statement of affairs shall be delivered by the relevant person making the statement of truth, together with a copy, to the administrator. The relevant person shall also deliver a copy of the statement of affairs to all those persons whom the administrator has required to make a statement of concurrence.

(4) A person required to submit a statement of concurrence shall do so before the end of the period of 5 business days (or such other period as the administrator may agree) beginning with the day on which the statement of affairs being concurred with is received by him.

(5) A statement of concurrence may be qualified in respect of matters dealt with in the statement of affairs, where the maker of the statement of concurrence is not in agreement with the relevant person, or he considers the statement of affairs to be erroneous or misleading, or he is without the direct knowledge necessary for concurring with it.

(6) Every statement of concurrence shall be verified by a statement of truth and be delivered to the administrator by the person who makes it, together with a copy of it.

(7) Subject to Rule 2.30 below, the administrator shall as soon as reasonably practicable send to the registrar of companies and file with the court a Form 2.16B together with a copy of the statement of affairs and any statement of concurrence.]

[6125]

NOTES

Substituted, subject to transitional provisions; see the note preceding r 2.1 at **[6097]**.
Forms: see Appendix 4 at **[A4]**.

[2.30 Limited disclosure

(1) Where the administrator thinks that it would prejudice the conduct of the administration for the whole or part of the statement of the company's affairs to be disclosed, he may apply to the court for an order of limited disclosure in respect of the statement, or any specified part of it.

(2) The court may, on such application, order that the statement or, as the case may be, the specified part of it, shall not be filed with the registrar of companies.

(3) The administrator shall as soon as reasonably practicable send to the registrar of companies a Form 2.16B together with a copy of the order and the statement of affairs (to the extent provided by the order) and any statement of concurrence.

(4) If a creditor seeks disclosure of a statement of affairs or a specified part of it in relation to which an order has been made under this Rule, he may apply to the court for an order that the administrator disclose it or a specified part of it. The application shall be supported by written evidence in the form of an affidavit.

(5) The applicant shall give the administrator notice of his application at least 3 days before the hearing.

(6) The court may make any order for disclosure subject to any conditions as to confidentiality, duration, the scope of the order in the event of any change of circumstances, or other matters as it sees fit.

(7) If there is a material change in circumstances rendering the limit on disclosure or any part of it unnecessary, the administrator shall, as soon as reasonably practicable after the change, apply to the court for the order or any part of it to be rescinded.

(8) The administrator shall, as soon as reasonably practicable after the making of an order under paragraph (7) above, file with the registrar of companies Form 2.16B together with a copy of the statement of affairs to the extent provided by the order.

(9) When the statement of affairs is filed in accordance with paragraph (8), the administrator shall, where he has sent a statement of proposals under paragraph 49, provide the creditors with a copy of the statement of affairs as filed, or a summary thereof.

(10) The provisions of Part 31 of the CPR shall not apply to an application under this Rule.]

[6126]

NOTES

Substituted, subject to transitional provisions; see the note preceding r 2.1 at **[6097]**.

[2.31 Release from duty to submit statement of affairs; extension of time

(1) The power of the administrator under paragraph 48(2) to give a release from the obligation imposed by paragraph 47(1), or to grant an extension of time, may be exercised at the administrator's own discretion, or at the request of any relevant person.

(2) A relevant person may, if he requests a release or extension of time and it is refused by the administrator, apply to the court for it.

(3) The court may, if it thinks that no sufficient cause is shown for the application, dismiss it without a hearing but it shall not do so without giving the relevant person at least 7 days' notice, upon receipt of which the relevant person may request the court to list the application for a without notice hearing. If the application is not dismissed the court shall fix a venue for it to be heard, and give notice to the relevant person accordingly.

(4) The relevant person shall, at least 14 days before the hearing, send to the administrator a notice stating the venue and accompanied by a copy of the application and of any evidence which he (the relevant person) intends to adduce in support of it.

(5) The administrator may appear and be heard on the application and, whether or not he appears, he may file a written report of any matters which he considers ought to be drawn to the court's attention.

If such a report is filed, a copy of it shall be sent by the administrator to the relevant person, not later than 5 days before the hearing.

(6) Sealed copies of any order made on the application shall be sent by the court to the relevant person and the administrator.

(7) On any application under this Rule the relevant person's costs shall be paid in any event by him and, unless the court otherwise orders, no allowance towards them shall be made out of the assets.]

[6127]

NOTES

Substituted, subject to transitional provisions; see the note preceding r 2.1 at **[6097]**.

[2.32 Expenses of statement of affairs

(1) A relevant person making the statement of the company's affairs or statement of concurrence shall be allowed, and paid by the administrator out of his receipts, any expenses incurred by the relevant person in so doing which the administrator considers reasonable.

(2) Any decision by the administrator under this Rule is subject to appeal to the court.

(3) Nothing in this Rule relieves a relevant person from any obligation with respect to the preparation, verification and submission of the statement of affairs, or to the provision of information to the administrator.]

[6128]

NOTES

Substituted, subject to transitional provisions; see the note preceding r 2.1 at **[6097]**.

[2.33 Administrator's proposals

(1) The administrator shall, under paragraph 49, make a statement which he shall send to the registrar of companies attached to Form 2.17B.

(2) The statement shall include, in addition to those matters set out in paragraph 49—

(a) details of the court where the proceedings are and the relevant court reference number;

(b) the full name, registered address, registered number and any other trading names of the company;

(c) details relating to his appointment as administrator, including the date of appointment and the person making the application or appointment and, where there are joint administrators, details of the matters set out in paragraph 100(2);

(d) the names of the directors and secretary of the company and details of any shareholdings in the company they may have;

(e) an account of the circumstances giving rise to the appointment of the administrator;

(f) if a statement of the company's affairs has been submitted, a copy or summary of it, with the administrator's comments, if any;

(g) if an order limiting the disclosure of the statement of affairs (under Rule 2.30) has been made, a statement of that fact, as well as—

(i) details of who provided the statement of affairs;

(ii) the date of the order of limited disclosure; and

(iii) the details or a summary of the details that are not subject to that order;

(h) if a full statement of affairs is not provided, the names, addresses and debts of the creditors including details of any security held;

(j) if no statement of affairs has been submitted, details of the financial position of the company at the latest practicable date (which must, unless the court otherwise orders, be a date not earlier than that on which the company entered administration), a list of the company's creditors including their names, addresses and details of their debts, including any security held, and an explanation as to why there is no statement of affairs;

(k) the basis upon which it is proposed that the administrator's remuneration should be fixed under Rule 2.106;

(l) (except where the administrator proposes a voluntary arrangement in relation to the company and subject to paragraph (3))—

(i) to the best of the administrator's knowledge and belief—

(aa) an estimate of the value of the prescribed part (whether or not he proposes to make an application to court under section 176A(5) or section 176A(3) applies); and

(bb) an estimate of the value of the company's net property; and

(ii) whether, and, if so, why, the administrator proposes to make an application to court under section 176A(5);

(m) how it is envisaged the purpose of the administration will be achieved and how it is proposed that the administration shall end. If a creditors' voluntary liquidation is proposed, details of the proposed liquidator must be provided, and a statement that, in accordance with paragraph 83(7) and Rule 2.117(3), creditors may nominate a different person as the proposed liquidator, provided that the nomination is made after the receipt of the proposals and before the proposals are approved;

(n) where the administrator has decided not to call a meeting of creditors, his reasons;

(o) the manner in which the affairs and business of the company—

(i) have, since the date of the administrator's appointment, been managed and financed, including, where any assets have been disposed of, the reasons for such disposals and the terms upon which such disposals were made; and

(ii) will, if the administrator's proposals are approved, continue to be managed and financed;

(p) whether—
  (i) the EC Regulation applies; and
  (ii) if so, whether the proceedings are main proceedings or territorial proceedings; and

(q) such other information (if any) as the administrator thinks necessary to enable creditors to decide whether or not to vote for the adoption of the proposals.

(3) Nothing in paragraph (2)(l) is to be taken as requiring any such estimate to include any information, the disclosure of which could seriously prejudice the commercial interests of the company. If such information is excluded from the calculation the estimate shall be accompanied by a statement to that effect.

(4) Where the court orders, upon an application by the administrator under paragraph 107, an extension of the period of time in paragraph 49(5), the administrator shall notify in Form 2.18B all the persons set out in paragraph 49(4) as soon as reasonably practicable after the making of the order.

(5) Where the administrator has made a statement under paragraph 52(1) and has not called an initial meeting of creditors, the proposals sent out under this Rule and paragraph 49 will (if no meeting has been requisitioned under paragraph 52(2) within the period set out in Rule 2.37(1)) be deemed to have been approved by the creditors.

(6) Where the administrator intends to apply to the court (or file a notice under paragraph 80(2)) for the administration to cease at a time before he has sent a statement of his proposals to creditors in accordance with paragraph 49, he shall, at least 10 days before he makes such an application (or files such a notice), send to all creditors of the company (so far as he is aware of their addresses) a report containing the information required by paragraphs (2)(a)–(p) of this Rule.

(7) Where the administrator wishes to publish a notice under paragraph 49(6) he shall publish the notice once in such newspaper as he thinks most appropriate for ensuring that the notice comes to the attention of the company's members. The notice shall—

(a) state the full name of the company;
(b) state the full name and address of the administrator;
(c) give details of the administrator's appointment; and
(d) specify an address to which members can write for a copy of the statement of proposals.

(8) This notice must be published as soon as reasonably practicable after the administrator sends his statement of proposals to the company's creditors but no later than 8 weeks (or such other period as may be agreed by the creditors or as the court may order) from the date that the company entered administration.]

[6129]

NOTES

Substituted, subject to transitional provisions; see the note preceding r 2.1 at **[6097]**.
EC Regulation: ie, Council Regulation 1346/2000/EC on insolvency proceedings at **[9290]**.
Forms: see Appendix 4 at **[A4]**.

[CHAPTER 6
MEETINGS AND REPORTS

SECTION A: CREDITORS' MEETINGS

2.34 Meetings to consider administrator's proposals

(1) Notice of an initial creditors' meeting shall (unless the court otherwise directs) be given by notice in the newspaper in which the administrator's appointment was advertised and, if he considers it appropriate to do so, in such other newspaper as he thinks most appropriate for ensuring that the notice comes to the attention of the company's creditors.

(2) Notice in Form 2.19B to attend the meeting shall be sent out at the same time to any directors or officers of the company (including persons who have been directors or officers in the past) whose presence at the meeting is, in the administrator's opinion, required.

(3) Where the court orders an extension to the period set out in paragraph 51(2)(b) the administrator shall send a notice in Form 2.18B to each person to whom he is required to send notice by paragraph 49(4).

(4) If at the meeting there is not the requisite majority for approval of the administrator's proposals (with modifications, if any), the chairman may, and shall if a resolution is passed to that effect, adjourn the meeting for not more than 14 days and may only adjourn once (subject to any direction by the court).]

[6130]

NOTES

Substituted, subject to transitional provisions; see the note preceding r 2.1 at **[6097]**.
Forms: see Appendix 4 at **[A4]**.

[2.35 Creditors' meetings generally

(1) This Rule applies to creditors' meetings summoned by the administrator under—

- (a) paragraph 51 (initial creditors' meeting);
- (b) paragraph 52(2) (at the request of the creditors);
- (c) paragraph 54(2) (to consider revision to the administrator's proposals);
- (d) paragraph 56(1) (further creditors' meetings); and
- (e) paragraph 62 (general power to summon meetings of creditors).

(2) Notice of any of the meetings set out in paragraph (1) above shall be in Form 2.20B.

(3) In fixing the venue for the meeting, the administrator shall have regard to the convenience of creditors and the meeting shall be summoned for commencement between 10.00 and 16.00 hours on a business day, unless the court otherwise directs.

(4) Subject to paragraphs (6) and (7) below, at least 14 days' notice of the meeting shall be given to all creditors who are known to the administrator and had claims against the company at the date when the company entered administration unless that creditor has subsequently been paid in full; and the notice shall—

- (a) specify the purpose of the meeting;
- (b) contain a statement of the effect of Rule 2.38 (entitlement to vote); and
- (c) contain the forms of proxy.

(5) If within 30 minutes from the time fixed for commencement of the meeting there is no person present to act as chairman, the meeting stands adjourned to the same time and place in the following week or, if that is not a business day, to the business day immediately following.

(6) The meeting may be adjourned once, if the chairman thinks fit, but not for more than 14 days from the date on which it was fixed to commence, subject to the direction of the court.

(7) If a meeting is adjourned the administrator shall as soon as reasonably practicable notify the creditors of the venue of the adjourned meeting.]

[6131]

NOTES

Substituted, subject to transitional provisions; see the note preceding r 2.1 at **[6097]**.
Forms: see Appendix 4 at **[A4]**.

[2.36 The chairman at meetings

(1) At any meeting of creditors summoned by the administrator, either he shall be chairman, or a person nominated by him in writing to act in his place.

(2) A person so nominated must be either—

- (a) one who is qualified to act as an insolvency practitioner in relation to the company; or
- (b) an employee of the administrator or his firm who is experienced in insolvency matters.]

[6132]

NOTES

Substituted, subject to transitional provisions; see the note preceding r 2.1 at **[6097]**.

[2.37 Meeting requisitioned by creditors

(1) The request for a creditors' meeting under paragraph 52(2) or 56(1) shall be in Form 2.21B. A request for an initial creditors' meeting shall be made within 12 days of the date on which the administrator's statement of proposals is sent out. A request under paragraph 52(2) or 56(1) shall include—

(a) a list of the creditors concurring with the request, showing the amounts of their respective debts in the administration;

(b) from each creditor concurring, written confirmation of his concurrence; and

(c) a statement of the purpose of the proposed meeting,

but sub-paragraph (a) does not apply if the requisitioning creditor's debt is alone sufficient without the concurrence of other creditors.

(2) A meeting requested under paragraph 52(2) or 56(1) shall be held within 28 days of the administrator's receipt of the notice requesting the meeting.

(3) The expenses of summoning and holding a meeting at the request of a creditor shall be paid by that person, who shall deposit with the administrator security for their payment.

(4) The sum to be deposited shall be such as the administrator may determine, and he shall not act without the deposit having been made.

(5) The meeting may resolve that the expenses of summoning and holding it are to be payable out of the assets of the company as an expense of the administration.

(6) To the extent that any deposit made under this Rule is not required for the payment of expenses of summoning and holding the meeting, it shall be repaid to the person who made it.]

[6133]

NOTES

Substituted, subject to transitional provisions; see the note preceding r 2.1 at **[6097]**.
Forms: see Appendix 4 at **[A4]**.

[2.38 Entitlement to vote

(1) Subject as follows, at a meeting of creditors in administration proceedings a person is entitled to vote only if—

(a) he has given to the administrator, not later than 12.00 hours on the business day before the day fixed for the meeting, details in writing of the debt which—

(i) he claims to be due to him from the company; or

(ii) in relation to a member State liquidator, is claimed to be due to creditors in proceedings in relation to which he holds office;

(b) the claim has been duly admitted under the following provisions of this Rule; and

(c) there has been lodged with the administrator any proxy which he intends to be used on his behalf,

and details of the debt must include any calculation for the purposes of Rules 2.40 to 2.42.

(2) The chairman of the meeting may allow a creditor to vote, notwithstanding that he has failed to comply with paragraph (1)(a), if satisfied that the failure was due to circumstances beyond the creditor's control.

(3) The chairman of the meeting may call for any document or other evidence to be produced to him, where he thinks it necessary for the purpose of substantiating the whole or any part of the claim.

(4) Votes are calculated according to the amount of a creditor's claim as at the date on which the company entered administration, less any payments that have been made to him after that date in respect of his claim and any adjustment by way of set-off in accordance with Rule 2.85 as if that Rule were applied on the date that the votes are counted.

(5) A creditor shall not vote in respect of a debt for an unliquidated amount, or any debt whose value is not ascertained, except where the chairman agrees to put upon the debt an estimated minimum value for the purpose of entitlement to vote and admits the claim for that purpose.

(6) No vote shall be cast by virtue of a claim more than once on any resolution put to the meeting.

(7) Where—
(a) a creditor is entitled to vote under this Rule;
(b) has lodged his claim in one or more sets of other proceedings; and
(c) votes (either in person or by proxy) on a resolution put to the meeting; and
(d) the member State liquidator casts a vote in respect of the same claim,

only the creditor's vote shall be counted.

(8) Where—
(a) a creditor has lodged his claim in more than one set of other proceedings; and
(b) more than one member State liquidator seeks to vote by virtue of that claim,

the entitlement to vote by virtue of that claim is exercisable by the member State liquidator in main proceedings, whether or not the creditor has lodged his claim in the main proceedings.

(9) For the purposes of paragraph (6), the claim of a creditor and of any member State liquidator in relation to the same debt are a single claim.

(10) For the purposes of paragraphs (7) and (8), "other proceedings" means main proceedings, secondary proceedings or territorial proceedings in another member State.]

[6134]

NOTES

Substituted, subject to transitional provisions; see the note preceding r 2.1 at **[6097]**.

[2.39 Admission and rejection of claims

(1) At any creditors' meeting the chairman has power to admit or reject a creditor's claim for the purpose of his entitlement to vote; and the power is exercisable with respect to the whole or any part of the claim.

(2) The chairman's decision under this Rule, or in respect of any matter arising under Rule 2.38, is subject to appeal to the court by any creditor.

(3) If the chairman is in doubt whether a claim should be admitted or rejected, he shall mark it as objected to and allow the creditor to vote, subject to his vote being subsequently declared invalid if the objection to the claim is sustained.

(4) If on an appeal the chairman's decision is reversed or varied, or a creditor's vote is declared invalid, the court may order that another meeting be summoned, or make such other order as it thinks fit.

(5) In the case of the meeting summoned under paragraph 51 to consider the administrator's proposals, an application to the court by way of appeal under this Rule against a decision of the chairman shall not be made later than 14 days after the delivery of the administrator's report in accordance with paragraph 53(2).

(6) Neither the administrator nor any person nominated by him to be chairman is personally liable for costs incurred by any person in respect of an appeal to the court under this Rule, unless the court makes an order to that effect.]

[6135]

NOTES

Substituted, subject to transitional provisions; see the note preceding r 2.1 at **[6097]**.

[2.40 Secured creditors

(1) At a meeting of creditors a secured creditor is entitled to vote only in respect of the balance (if any) of his debt after deducting the value of his security as estimated by him.

(2) However, in a case where the administrator has made a statement under paragraph 52(1)(b) and an initial creditors' meeting has been requisitioned under paragraph 52(2) then a secured creditor is entitled to vote in respect of the full value of his debt without any deduction of the value of his security.]

[6136]

NOTES

Substituted, subject to transitional provisions; see the note preceding r 2.1 at **[6097]**.

[2.41 Holders of negotiable instruments

A creditor shall not vote in respect of a debt on, or secured by, a current bill of exchange or promissory note, unless he is willing—

(a) to treat the liability to him on the bill or note of every person who is liable on it antecedently to the company, and against whom a bankruptcy order has not been made (or, in the case of a company, which has not gone into liquidation), as a security in his hands; and

(b) to estimate the value of the security and, for the purpose of his entitlement to vote, to deduct it from his claim.]

[6137]

NOTES

Substituted, subject to transitional provisions; see the note preceding r 2.1 at **[6097]**.

[2.42 Hire-purchase, conditional sale and chattel leasing agreements

(1) Subject as follows, an owner of goods under a hire-purchase or chattel leasing agreement, or a seller of goods under a conditional sale agreement, is entitled to vote in respect of the amount of the debt due and payable to him by the company on the date that the company entered administration.

(2) In calculating the amount of any debt for this purpose, no account shall be taken of any amount attributable to the exercise of any right under the relevant agreement, so far as the right has become exercisable solely by virtue of the making of an administration application, a notice of intention to appoint an administrator or any matter arising as a consequence, or of the company entering administration.]

[6138]

NOTES

Substituted, subject to transitional provisions; see the note preceding r 2.1 at **[6097]**.

[2.43 Resolutions

(1) Subject to paragraph (2), at a creditors' meeting in administration proceedings, a resolution is passed when a majority (in value) of those present and voting, in person or by proxy, have voted in favour of it.

(2) Any resolution is invalid if those voting against it include more than half in value of the creditors to whom notice of the meeting was sent and who are not, to the best of the chairman's belief, persons connected with the company.]

[6139]

NOTES

Substituted, subject to transitional provisions; see the note preceding r 2.1 at **[6097]**.

[2.44 Minutes

(1) The chairman of the meeting shall cause minutes of its proceedings to be entered in the company's minute book.

(2) The minutes shall include a list of the names and addresses of creditors who attended (personally or by proxy) and, if a creditors' committee has been established, the names and addresses of those elected to be members of the committee.]

[6140]

NOTES

Substituted, subject to transitional provisions; see the note preceding r 2.1 at **[6097]**.

[2.45 Revision of the administrator's proposals

(1) The administrator shall, under paragraph 54, make a statement setting out the proposed revisions to his proposals which he shall attach to Form 2.22B and send to all those to whom he is required to send a copy of his revised proposals.

(2) The statement of revised proposals shall include—

(a) details of the court where the proceedings are and the relevant court reference number;

(b) the full name, registered address, registered number and any other trading names of the company;

(c) details relating to his appointment as administrator, including the date of appointment and the person making the administration application or appointment;

(d) the names of the directors and secretary of the company and details of any shareholdings in the company they may have;

(e) a summary of the initial proposals and the reason(s) for proposing a revision;

(f) details of the proposed revision including details of the administrator's assessment of the likely impact of the proposed revision upon creditors generally or upon each class of creditors (as the case may be);

(g) where a proposed revision relates to the ending of the administration by a creditors' voluntary liquidation and the nomination of a person to be the proposed liquidator of the company, a statement that, in accordance with paragraph 83(7) and Rule 2.117(3), creditors may nominate a different person as the proposed liquidator, provided that the nomination is made after the receipt of the revised proposals and before those revised proposals are approved; and

(h) any other information that the administrator thinks necessary to enable creditors to decide whether or not to vote for the proposed revisions.

(3) Subject to paragraph 54(3), within 5 days of sending out the statement in paragraph (1) above, the administrator shall send a copy of the statement to every member of the company.

(4) When the administrator is acting under paragraph 54(3), the notice shall be published once in such newspaper as he thinks most appropriate for ensuring that the notice comes to the attention of the company's members. The notice shall—

(a) state the full name of the company;

(b) state the name and address of the administrator;

(c) specify an address to which members can write for a copy of the statement; and

(d) be published as soon as reasonably practicable after the administrator sends the statement to creditors.]

[6141]

NOTES

Substituted, subject to transitional provisions; see the note preceding r 2.1 at **[6097]**.
Forms: see Appendix 4 at **[A4]**.

[2.46 Notice to creditors

As soon as reasonably practicable after the conclusion of a meeting of creditors to consider the administrator's proposals or revised proposals, the administrator shall—

(a) send notice in Form 2.23B of the result of the meeting (including details of any modifications to the proposals that were approved) to every creditor who received notice of the meeting and any other person who received a copy of the original proposals; and

(b) file with the court, and send to the registrar of companies, and any creditors who did not receive notice of the meeting (of whose claim he has become subsequently aware), a copy of Form 2.23B, attaching a copy of the proposals considered at the meeting.]

[6142]

NOTES

Substituted, subject to transitional provisions; see the note preceding r 2.1 at **[6097]**.
Forms: see Appendix 4 at **[A4]**.

[2.47 Reports to creditors

(1) "Progress report" means a report which includes—

(a) details of the court where the proceedings are and the relevant court reference number;

(b) full details of the company's name, address of registered office and registered number;

(c) full details of the administrator's name and address, date of appointment and name and address of appointor, including any changes in office-holder, and, in the case of joint administrators, their functions as set out in the statement made for the purposes of paragraph 100(2);
(d) details of any extensions to the initial period of appointment;
(e) details of progress during the period of the report, including a receipts and payments account (as detailed in paragraph (2) below);
(f) details of any assets that remain to be realised; and
(g) any other relevant information for the creditors.

(2) A receipts and payments account shall state what assets of the company have been realised, for what value, and what payments have been made to creditors or others. The account is to be in the form of an abstract showing receipts and payments during the period of the report and where the administrator has ceased to act, the receipts and payments account shall include a statement as to the amount paid to unsecured creditors by virtue of the application of section 176A (prescribed part).

(3) The progress report shall cover—
(a) the period of 6 months commencing on the date that the company entered administration, and every subsequent period of 6 months; and
(b) when the administrator ceases to act, any period from the date of the previous report, if any, and from the date that the company entered administration if there is no previous report, until the time that the administrator ceases to act.

(4) The administrator shall send a copy of the progress report, attached to Form 2.24B, within 1 month of the end of the period covered by the report, to—
(a) the creditors;
(b) the court; and
(c) the registrar of companies.

(5) The court may, on the administrator's application, extend the period of 1 month mentioned in paragraph (4) above, or make such other order in respect of the content of the report as it thinks fit.

(6) If the administrator makes default in complying with this Rule, he is liable to a fine and, for continued contravention, to a daily default fine.]

[6143]

NOTES
Substituted, subject to transitional provisions; see the note preceding r 2.1 at **[6097]**.
Forms: see Appendix 4 at **[A4]**.

[2.48 Correspondence instead of creditors' meetings

(1) The administrator may seek to obtain the passing of a resolution by the creditors by sending a notice in Form 2.25B to every creditor who is entitled to be notified of a creditors' meeting under Rule 2.35(4).

(2) In order to be counted, votes must be received by the administrator by 12.00 hours on the closing date specified on Form 2.25B and must be accompanied by the statement in writing on entitlement to vote required by Rule 2.38.

(3) If any votes are received without the statement as to entitlement, or the administrator decides that the creditor is not entitled to vote according to Rules 2.38 and 2.39, then that creditor's votes shall be disregarded.

(4) The closing date shall be set at the discretion of the administrator. In any event it must not be set less than 14 days from the date of issue of the Form 2.25B.

(5) For any business to be transacted the administrator must receive at least 1 valid Form 2.25B by the closing date specified by him.

(6) If no valid Form 2.25B is received by the closing date specified then the administrator shall call a meeting of the creditors in accordance with Rule 2.35.

(7) Any single creditor, or a group of creditors, of the company whose debt(s) amount to at least 10% of the total debts of the company may, within 5 business days from the date of the administrator sending out a resolution or proposals, require him to summon a meeting of

creditors to consider the matters raised therein in accordance with Rule 2.37. Any meeting called under this Rule shall be conducted in accordance with Rule 2.35.

(8) If the administrator's proposals or revised proposals are rejected by the creditors pursuant to this Rule, the administrator may call a meeting of creditors.

(9) A reference in these Rules to anything done, or required to be done, at, or in connection with, or in consequence of, a creditors' meeting includes a reference to anything done in the course of correspondence in accordance with this Rule.]

[6144]

NOTES

Substituted, subject to transitional provisions; see the note preceding r 2.1 at **[6097]**.
Forms: see Appendix 4 at **[A4]**.

[SECTION B: COMPANY MEETINGS

2.49 Venue and conduct of company meeting

(1) Where the administrator summons a meeting of members of the company, he shall fix a venue for it having regard to their convenience.

(2) The chairman of the meeting shall be the administrator or a person nominated by him in writing to act in his place.

(3) A person so nominated must be either—

(a) one who is qualified to act as an insolvency practitioner in relation to the company; or

(b) an employee of the administrator or his firm who is experienced in insolvency matters.

(4) If within 30 minutes from the time fixed for commencement of the meeting there is no person present to act as chairman, the meeting stands adjourned to the same time and place in the following week or, if that is not a business day, to the business day immediately following.

(5) Subject as above, the meeting shall be summoned and conducted as if it were a general meeting of the company summoned under the company's articles of association, and in accordance with the applicable provisions of the Companies Act.

(6) Paragraph (5) does not apply where the laws of a member State and not the laws of England and Wales apply in relation to the conduct of the meeting. The meeting shall be summoned and conducted in accordance with the constitution of the company and the laws of the member State referred to in this paragraph shall apply to the conduct of the meeting.

(7) The chairman of the meeting shall cause minutes of its proceedings to be entered in the company's minute book.]

[6145]

NOTES

Substituted, subject to transitional provisions; see the note preceding r 2.1 at **[6097]**.

[CHAPTER 7
THE CREDITORS' COMMITTEE

2.50 Constitution of committee

(1) Where it is resolved by a creditors' meeting to establish a creditors' committee for the purposes of the administration, the committee shall consist of at least 3 and not more than 5 creditors of the company elected at the meeting.

(2) Any creditor of the company is eligible to be a member of the committee, so long as his claim has not been rejected for the purpose of his entitlement to vote.

(3) A body corporate may be a member of the committee, but it cannot act as such otherwise than by a representative appointed under Rule 2.55 below.]

[6146]

NOTES

Substituted, subject to transitional provisions; see the note preceding r 2.1 at **[6097]**.

[2.51 Formalities of establishment

(1) The creditors' committee does not come into being, and accordingly cannot act, until the administrator has issued a certificate in Form 2.26B of its due constitution.

(2) No person may act as a member of the committee unless and until he has agreed to do so and, unless the relevant proxy or authorisation contains a statement to the contrary, such agreement may be given by his proxy-holder or representative under section 375 of the Companies Act present at the meeting establishing the committee.

(3) The administrator's certificate of the committee's due constitution shall not be issued unless and until at least 3 of the persons who are to be members of the committee have agreed to act and shall be issued as soon as reasonably practicable thereafter.

(4) As and when the others (if any) agree to act, the administrator shall issue an amended certificate in Form 2.26B.

(5) The certificate, and any amended certificate, shall be filed with the court and a copy sent to the registrar of companies by the administrator, as soon as reasonably practicable.

(6) If after the first establishment of the committee there is any change in its membership, the administrator shall as soon as reasonably practicable report the change to the court and the registrar of companies in Form 2.27B.]

[6147]

NOTES

Substituted, subject to transitional provisions; see the note preceding r 2.1 at **[6097]**.
Forms: see Appendix 4 at **[A4]**.

[2.52 Functions and meetings of the committee

(1) The creditors' committee shall assist the administrator in discharging his functions, and act in relation to him in such manner as may be agreed from time to time.

(2) Subject as follows, meetings of the committee shall be held when and where determined by the administrator.

(3) The administrator shall call a first meeting of the committee not later than 6 weeks after its first establishment, and thereafter he shall call a meeting—

(a) if so requested by a member of the committee or his representative (the meeting then to be held within 14 days of the request being received by the administrator); and

(b) for a specified date, if the committee has previously resolved that a meeting be held on that date.

(4) The administrator shall give 7 days' written notice of the venue of any meeting to every member of the committee (or his representative designated for that purpose), unless in any case the requirement of notice has been waived by or on behalf of any member. Waiver may be signified either at or before the meeting.]

[6148]

NOTES

Substituted, subject to transitional provisions; see the note preceding r 2.1 at **[6097]**.

[2.53 The chairman at meetings

(1) Subject to Rule 2.62(3), the chairman at any meeting of the creditors' committee shall be the administrator or a person nominated by him in writing to act.

(2) A person so nominated must be either—

(a) one who is qualified to act as an insolvency practitioner in relation to the company; or

(b) an employee of the administrator or his firm who is experienced in insolvency matters.]

[6149]

NOTES

Substituted, subject to transitional provisions; see the note preceding r 2.1 at **[6097]**.

[2.54 Quorum

A meeting of the committee is duly constituted if due notice of it has been given to all the members, and at least 2 members are present or represented.]

[6150]

NOTES

Substituted, subject to transitional provisions; see the note preceding r 2.1 at **[6097]**.

[2.55 Committee-members' representatives

(1) A member of the committee may, in relation to the business of the committee, be represented by another person duly authorised by him for that purpose.

(2) A person acting as a committee-member's representative must hold a letter of authority entitling him so to act (either generally or specially) and signed by or on behalf of the committee-member, and for this purpose any proxy or any authorisation under section 375 of the Companies Act in relation to any meeting of creditors of the company shall, unless it contains a statement to the contrary, be treated as a letter of authority to act generally signed by or on behalf of the committee-member.

(3) The chairman at any meeting of the committee may call on a person claiming to act as a committee-member's representative to produce his letter of authority, and may exclude him if it appears that his authority is deficient.

(4) No member may be represented by a body corporate, a person who is an undischarged bankrupt, [or] a disqualified director or a person who is subject to a [bankruptcy restrictions order, bankruptcy restrictions undertaking or interim bankruptcy restrictions order].

(5) No person shall on the same committee, act at one and the same time as representative of more than one committee-member.

(6) Where a member's representative signs any document on the member's behalf, the fact that he so signs must be stated below his signature.]

[6151]

NOTES

Substituted, subject to transitional provisions; see the note preceding r 2.1 at **[6097]**.

Para (4): word in first pair of square brackets inserted, and words in second pair of square brackets substituted, by the Insolvency (Amendment) Rules 2004, SI 2004/584, r 4, as from 1 April 2004.

[2.56 Resignation

A member of the committee may resign by notice in writing delivered to the administrator.]

[6152]

NOTES

Substituted, subject to transitional provisions; see the note preceding r 2.1 at **[6097]**.

[2.57 Termination of membership

(1) Membership of the creditors' committee is automatically terminated if the member—

(a) becomes bankrupt … ; or

(b) at 3 consecutive meetings of the committee is neither present nor represented (unless at the third of those meetings it is resolved that this Rule is not to apply in his case); or

(c) ceases to be, or is found never to have been, a creditor.

(2) However, if the cause of termination is the member's bankruptcy, his trustee in bankruptcy replaces him as a member of the committee.]

[6153]

NOTES

Substituted, subject to transitional provisions; see the note preceding r 2.1 at **[6097]**.

Para (1): words omitted revoked by the Insolvency (Amendment) Rules 2004, SI 2004/584, r 5, as from 1 April 2004.

[2.58 Removal

A member of the committee may be removed by resolution at a meeting of creditors' at least 14 days' notice having been given of the intention to move that resolution.]

[6154]

NOTES

Substituted, subject to transitional provisions; see the note preceding r 2.1 at **[6097]**.

[2.59 Vacancies

(1) The following applies if there is a vacancy in the membership of the creditors' committee.

(2) The vacancy need not be filled if the administrator and a majority of the remaining members of the committee so agree, provided that the total number of members does not fall below the minimum required under Rule 2.50(1).

(3) The administrator may appoint any creditor (being qualified under the Rules to be a member of the committee) to fill the vacancy, if a majority of the other members of the committee agree to the appointment, and the creditor concerned consents to act.]

[6155]

NOTES

Substituted, subject to transitional provisions; see the note preceding r 2.1 at **[6097]**.

[2.60 Procedure at meetings

(1) At any meeting of the creditors' committee, each member of it (whether present himself, or by his representative) has one vote; and a resolution is passed when a majority of the members present or represented have voted in favour of it.

(2) Every resolution passed shall be recorded in writing, either separately or as part of the minutes of the meeting.

(3) A record of each resolution shall be signed by the chairman and placed in the company's minute book.]

[6156]

NOTES

Substituted, subject to transitional provisions; see the note preceding r 2.1 at **[6097]**.

[2.61 Resolutions of creditors' committee by post

(1) In accordance with this Rule, the administrator may seek to obtain the agreement of members of the creditors' committee to a resolution by sending to every member (or his representative designated for the purpose) a copy of the proposed resolution.

(2) Where the administrator makes use of the procedure allowed by this Rule, he shall send out to members of the committee or their representatives (as the case may be) a copy of any proposed resolution on which a decision is sought, which shall be set out in such a way that agreement with or dissent from each separate resolution may be indicated by the recipient on the copy so sent.

(3) Any member of the committee may, within 7 business days from the date of the administrator sending out a resolution, require him to summon a meeting of the committee to consider matters raised by the resolution.

(4) In the absence of such a request, the resolution is deemed to have been passed by the committee if and when the administrator is notified in writing by a majority of the members that they concur with it.

(5) A copy of every resolution passed under this Rule, and a note that the committee's concurrence was obtained, shall be placed in the company's minute book.]

[6157]

NOTES

Substituted, subject to transitional provisions; see the note preceding r 2.1 at **[6097]**.

[2.62 Information from administrator

(1) Where the committee resolves to require the attendance of the administrator under paragraph 57(3)(a), the notice to him shall be in writing signed by the majority of the members of the committee for the time being. A member's representative may sign for him.

(2) The meeting at which the administrator's attendance is required shall be fixed by the committee for a business day, and shall be held at such time and place as he determines.

(3) Where the administrator so attends, the members of the committee may elect any one of their number to be chairman of the meeting, in place of the administrator or a nominee of his.]

[6157A]

NOTES

Substituted, subject to transitional provisions; see the note preceding r 2.1 at **[6097]**.

[2.63 Expenses of members

(1) Subject as follows, the administrator shall, out of the assets of the company, defray any reasonable travelling expenses directly incurred by members of the creditors' committee or their representatives in relation to their attendance at the committee's meetings, or otherwise on the committee's business, as an expense of the administration.

(2) Paragraph (1) does not apply to any meeting of the committee held within 6 weeks of a previous meeting, unless the meeting in question is summoned at the instance of the administrator.]

[6157B]

NOTES

Substituted, subject to transitional provisions; see the note preceding r 2.1 at **[6097]**.

[2.64 Members' dealing with the company

(1) Membership of the committee does not prevent a person from dealing with the company while the company is in administration, provided that any transactions in the course of such dealings are in good faith and for value.

(2) The court may, on the application of any person interested, set aside any transaction which appears to it to be contrary to the requirements of this Rule, and may give such consequential directions as it thinks fit for compensating the company for any loss which it may have incurred in consequence of the transaction.]

[6157C]

NOTES

Substituted, subject to transitional provisions; see the note preceding r 2.1 at **[6097]**.

[2.65 Formal defects

The acts of the creditors' committee established for any administration are valid notwithstanding any defect in the appointment, election or qualifications of any member of the committee or any committee-member's representative or in the formalities of its establishment.]

[6157D]

NOTES

Substituted, subject to transitional provisions; see the note preceding r 2.1 at **[6097]**.

[CHAPTER 8 DISPOSAL OF CHARGED PROPERTY

2.66—(1) The following applies where the administrator applies to the court under paragraphs 71 or 72 for authority to dispose of property of the company which is subject to a security (other than a floating charge), or goods in the possession of the company under a hire purchase agreement.

(2) The court shall fix a venue for the hearing of the application, and the administrator shall as soon as reasonably practicable give notice of the venue to the person who is the holder of the security or, as the case may be, the owner under the agreement.

(3) If an order is made under paragraphs 71 or 72 the court shall send two sealed copies to the administrator.

(4) The administrator shall send one of them to that person who is the holder of the security or owner under the agreement.

(5) The administrator shall send a Form 2.28B to the registrar of companies with a copy of the sealed order.]

[6157E]

NOTES

Substituted, subject to transitional provisions; see the note preceding r 2.1 at **[6097]**.
Forms: see Appendix 4 at **[A4]**.

[CHAPTER 9 EXPENSES OF THE ADMINISTRATION

2.67—(1) The expenses of the administration are payable in the following order of priority—

(a) expenses properly incurred by the administrator in performing his functions in the administration of the company;

(b) the cost of any security provided by the administrator in accordance with the Act or the Rules;

(c) where an administration order was made, the costs of the applicant and any person appearing on the hearing of the application and where the administrator was appointed otherwise than by order of the court, any costs and expenses of the appointor in connection with the making of the appointment and the costs and expenses incurred by any other person in giving notice of intention to appoint an administrator;

(d) any amount payable to a person employed or authorised, under Chapter 5 of this Part of the Rules, to assist in the preparation of a statement of affairs or statement of concurrence;

(e) any allowance made, by order of the court, towards costs on an application for release from the obligation to submit a statement of affairs or statement of concurrence;

(f) any necessary disbursements by the administrator in the course of the administration (including any expenses incurred by members of the creditors' committee or their representatives and allowed for by the administrator under Rule 2.63, but not including any payment of corporation tax in circumstances referred to in sub-paragraph (j) below);

(g) the remuneration or emoluments of any person who has been employed by the administrator to perform any services for the company, as required or authorised under the Act or the Rules;

(h) the remuneration of the administrator agreed under Chapter 11 of this Part of the Rules;

(j) the amount of any corporation tax on chargeable gains accruing on the realisation of any asset of the company (without regard to whether the realisation is effected by the administrator, a secured creditor, or a receiver or manager appointed to deal with a security).

(2) The priorities laid down by paragraph (1) of this Rule are subject to the power of the court to make orders under paragraph (3) of this Rule where the assets are insufficient to satisfy the liabilities.

PART IV STATUTORY INSTRUMENTS

(3) The court may, in the event of the assets being insufficient to satisfy the liabilities, make an order as to the payment out of the assets of the expenses incurred in the administration in such order of priority as the court thinks just.

[(4) For the purposes of paragraph 99(3), the former administrator's remuneration and expenses shall comprise all those items set out in paragraph (1) of this Rule.]]

[6157F]

NOTES

Substituted, subject to transitional provisions; see the note preceding r 2.1 at **[6097]**.

Para (4): added by the Insolvency (Amendment) Rules 2005, SI 2005/527, r 8, as from 1 April 2005, subject to transitional provisions as noted below.

Transitional provisions: the Insolvency (Amendment) Rules 2005, SI 2005/527, r 3(1) provides as follows (note that by virtue of r 1(2) of those Rules "the commencement date" is 1 April 2005)—

"(1) The provisions of Rules 8 to 17, 23 to 27, 43 and 44 of these Rules shall not apply, and the provisions of the principal Rules shall continue to apply without the amendments made by those Rules, in any case where a company has entered administration or gone into liquidation, or a bankruptcy order has been made, before the commencement date.".

[CHAPTER 10
DISTRIBUTIONS TO CREDITORS

SECTION A: APPLICATION OF CHAPTER AND GENERAL

2.68—(1) This Chapter applies where the administrator makes, or proposes to make, a distribution to any class of creditors. Where the distribution is to a particular class of creditors, references in this Chapter to creditors shall, in so far as the context requires, be a reference to that class of creditors only.

(2) The administrator shall give notice to the creditors of his intention to declare and distribute a dividend in accordance with Rule 2.95.

(3) Where it is intended that the distribution is to be a sole or final dividend, the administrator shall, after the date specified in the notice referred to in paragraph (2)—

(a) defray any outstanding expenses of a liquidation (including any of the items mentioned in Rule 4.218) or provisional liquidation that immediately preceded the administration;

(b) defray any items payable in accordance with the provisions of paragraph 99;

(c) defray any amounts (including any debts or liabilities and his own remuneration and expenses) which would, if the administrator were to cease to be the administrator of the company, be payable out of the property of which he had custody or control in accordance with the provisions of paragraph 99; and

(d) declare and distribute that dividend without regard to the claim of any person in respect of a debt not already proved.

(4) The court may, on the application of any person, postpone the date specified in the notice.]

[6157G]

NOTES

Substituted, subject to transitional provisions; see the note preceding r 2.1 at **[6097]**.

[2.69 Debts of insolvent company to rank equally

Debts other than preferential debts rank equally between themselves in the administration and, after the preferential debts, shall be paid in full unless the assets are insufficient for meeting them, in which case they abate in equal proportions between themselves.]

[6157H]

NOTES

Substituted, subject to transitional provisions; see the note preceding r 2.1 at **[6097]**.

[2.70 Supplementary provisions as to dividend

(1) In the calculation and distribution of a dividend the administrator shall make provision for—

(a) any debts which appear to him to be due to persons who, by reason of the distance of their place of residence, may not have had sufficient time to tender and establish their proofs;

(b) any debts which are the subject of claims which have not yet been determined; and

(c) disputed proofs and claims.

(2) A creditor who has not proved his debt before the declaration of any dividend is not entitled to disturb, by reason that he has not participated in it, the distribution of that dividend or any other dividend declared before his debt was proved, but—

(a) when he has proved that debt he is entitled to be paid, out of any money for the time being available for the payment of any further dividend, any dividend or dividends which he has failed to receive; and

(b) any dividends payable under sub-paragraph (a) shall be paid before the money is applied to the payment of any such further dividend.

(3) No action lies against the administrator for a dividend; but if he refuses to pay a dividend the court may, if it thinks fit, order him to pay it and also to pay, out of his own money—

(a) interest on the dividend, at the rate for the time being specified in section 17 of the Judgments Act 1838, from the time when it was withheld; and

(b) the costs of the proceedings in which the order to pay is made.]

[6157I]

NOTES

Substituted, subject to transitional provisions; see the note preceding r 2.1 at **[6097]**.

[2.71 Division of unsold assets

The administrator may, with the permission of the creditors' committee, or if there is no creditors' committee, the creditors, divide in its existing form amongst the company's creditors, according to its estimated value, any property which from its peculiar nature or other special circumstances cannot be readily or advantageously sold.]

[6157J]

NOTES

Substituted, subject to transitional provisions; see the note preceding r 2.1 at **[6097]**.

[SECTION B: MACHINERY OF PROVING A DEBT

2.72 Proving a debt

(1) A person claiming to be a creditor of the company and wishing to recover his debt in whole or in part must (subject to any order of the court to the contrary) submit his claim in writing to the administrator.

(2) A creditor who claims is referred to as "proving" for his debt and a document by which he seeks to establish his claim is his "proof".

(3) Subject to the next paragraph, a proof must—

(a) be made out by, or under the direction of, the creditor and signed by him or a person authorised in that behalf; and

(b) state the following matters—

(i) the creditor's name and address;

(ii) the total amount of his claim as at the date on which the company entered administration, less any payments that have been made to him after that date in respect of his claim and any adjustment by way of set-off in accordance with Rule 2.85;

(iii) whether or not the claim includes outstanding uncapitalised interest;

(iv) whether or not the claim includes value added tax;

(v) whether the whole or any part of the debt falls within any, and if so, which categories of preferential debts under section 386;

(vi) particulars of how and when the debt was incurred by the company;

(vii) particulars of any security held, the date on which it was given and the value which the creditor puts on it;

(viii) details of any reservation of title in respect of goods to which the debt refers; and

(ix) the name, address and authority of the person signing the proof (if other than the creditor himself).

(4) There shall be specified in the proof details of any documents by reference to which the debt can be substantiated; but (subject as follows) it is not essential that such document be attached to the proof or submitted with it.

(5) The administrator may call for any document or other evidence to be produced to him, where he thinks it necessary for the purpose of substantiating the whole or any part of the claim made in the proof.]

[6157K]

NOTES

Substituted, subject to transitional provisions; see the note preceding r 2.1 at **[6097]**.

[2.73 Claim established by affidavit

(1) The administrator may, if he thinks it necessary, require a claim of debt to be verified by means of an affidavit in Form 2.29B.

(2) An affidavit may be required notwithstanding that a proof of debt has already been lodged.]

[6157L]

NOTES

Substituted, subject to transitional provisions; see the note preceding r 2.1 at **[6097]**.
Forms: see Appendix 4 at **[A4]**.

[2.74 Costs of proving

Unless the court otherwise orders—

(a) every creditor bears the cost of proving his own debt, including costs incurred in providing documents or evidence under Rule 2.72(5); and

(b) costs incurred by the administrator in estimating the quantum of a debt under Rule 2.81 are payable out of the assets as an expense of the administration.]

[6157M]

NOTES

Substituted, subject to transitional provisions; see the note preceding r 2.1 at **[6097]**.

[2.75 Administrator to allow inspection of proofs

The administrator shall, so long as proofs lodged with him are in his hands, allow them to be inspected, at all reasonable times on any business day, by any of the following persons—

(a) any creditor who has submitted a proof of debt (unless his proof has been wholly rejected for purposes of dividend or otherwise);

(b) any contributory of the company; and

(c) any person acting on behalf of either of the above.]

[6157N]

NOTES

Substituted, subject to transitional provisions; see the note preceding r 2.1 at **[6097]**.

[2.76 New administrator appointed

(1) If a new administrator is appointed in place of another, the former administrator shall transmit to him all proofs which he has received, together with an itemised list of them.

(2) The new administrator shall sign the list by way of receipt for the proofs, and return it to his predecessor.]

[6157O]

NOTES

Substituted, subject to transitional provisions; see the note preceding r 2.1 at **[6097]**.

[2.77 Admission and rejection of proofs for dividend

(1) A proof may be admitted for dividend either for the whole amount claimed by the creditor, or for part of that amount.

(2) If the administrator rejects a proof in whole or in part, he shall prepare a written statement of his reasons for doing so, and send it as soon as reasonably practicable to the creditor.]

[6157P]

NOTES

Substituted, subject to transitional provisions; see the note preceding r 2.1 at **[6097]**.

[2.78 Appeal against decision on proof

(1) If a creditor is dissatisfied with the administrator's decision with respect to his proof (including any decision on the question of preference), he may apply to the court for the decision to be reversed or varied. The application must be made within 21 days of his receiving the statement sent under Rule 2.77(2).

(2) Any other creditor may, if dissatisfied with the administrator's decision admitting or rejecting the whole or any part of a proof, make such an application within 21 days of becoming aware of the administrator's decision.

(3) Where application is made to the court under this Rule, the court shall fix a venue for the application to be heard, notice of which shall be sent by the applicant to the creditor who lodged the proof in question (if it is not himself) and the administrator.

(4) The administrator shall, on receipt of the notice, file with the court the relevant proof, together (if appropriate) with a copy of the statement sent under Rule 2.77(2).

(5) After the application has been heard and determined, the proof shall, unless it has been wholly disallowed, be returned by the court to the administrator.

(6) The administrator is not personally liable for costs incurred by any person in respect of an application under this Rule unless the court otherwise orders.]

[6157Q]

NOTES

Substituted, subject to transitional provisions; see the note preceding r 2.1 at **[6097]**.

[2.79 Withdrawal or variation of proof

A creditor's proof may at any time, by agreement between himself and the administrator, be withdrawn or varied as to the amount claimed.]

[6157R]

NOTES

Substituted, subject to transitional provisions; see the note preceding r 2.1 at **[6097]**.

[2.80 Expunging of proof by the court

(1) The court may expunge a proof or reduce the amount claimed—

(a) on the administrator's application, where he thinks that the proof has been improperly admitted, or ought to be reduced; or

(b) on the application of a creditor, if the administrator declines to interfere in the matter.

(2) Where application is made to the court under this Rule, the court shall fix a venue for the application to be heard, notice of which shall be sent by the applicant—

(a) in the case of an application by the administrator, to the creditor who made the proof; and

(b) in the case of an application by a creditor, to the administrator and to the creditor who made the proof (if not himself).]

[6157S]

NOTES

Substituted, subject to transitional provisions; see the note preceding r 2.1 at **[6097]**.

[SECTION C: QUANTIFICATION OF CLAIMS

2.81 Estimate of quantum

(1) The administrator shall estimate the value of any debt which, by reason of its being subject to any contingency or for any other reason, does not bear a certain value; and he may revise any estimate previously made, if he thinks fit by reference to any change of circumstances or to information becoming available to him. He shall inform the creditor as to his estimate and any revision of it.

(2) Where the value of a debt is estimated under this Rule, the amount provable in the administration in the case of that debt is that of the estimate for the time being.]

[6157T]

NOTES

Substituted, subject to transitional provisions; see the note preceding r 2.1 at **[6097]**.

[2.82 Negotiable instruments, etc

Unless the administrator allows, a proof in respect of money owed on a bill of exchange, promissory note, cheque or other negotiable instrument or security cannot be admitted unless there is produced the instrument or security itself or a copy of it, certified by the creditor or his authorised representative to be a true copy.]

[6157U]

NOTES

Substituted, subject to transitional provisions; see the note preceding r 2.1 at **[6097]**.

[2.83 Secured creditors

(1) If a secured creditor realises his security, he may prove for the balance of his debt, after deducting the amount realised.

(2) If a secured creditor voluntarily surrenders his security for the general benefit of creditors, he may prove for his whole debt, as if it were unsecured.]

[6157V]

NOTES

Substituted, subject to transitional provisions; see the note preceding r 2.1 at **[6097]**.

[2.84 Discounts

There shall in every case be deducted from the claim all trade and other discounts which would have been available to the company but for its administration except any discount for immediate, early or cash settlement.]

[6157W]

NOTES

Substituted, subject to transitional provisions; see the note preceding r 2.1 at **[6097]**.

[2.85 Mutual credits and set-off

(1) This Rule applies where the administrator, being authorised to make the distribution in question, has, pursuant to Rule 2.95 given notice that he proposes to make it.

(2) In this Rule "mutual dealings" means mutual credits, mutual debts or other mutual dealings between the company and any creditor of the company proving or claiming to prove for a debt in the administration but does not include any of the following—

(a) any debt arising out of an obligation incurred after the company entered administration;

(b) any debt arising out of an obligation incurred at a time when the creditor had notice that—

(i) an application for an administration order was pending; or

(ii) any person had given notice of intention to appoint an administrator;

(c) any debt arising out of an obligation where—

(i) the administration was immediately preceded by a winding up; and

(ii) at the time the obligation was incurred the creditor had notice that a meeting of creditors had been summoned under section 98 or a petition for the winding up of the company was pending;

(d) any debt arising out of an obligation incurred during a winding up which immediately preceded the administration; or

(e) any debt which has been acquired by a creditor by assignment or otherwise, pursuant to an agreement between the creditor and any other party where that agreement was entered into—

(i) after the company entered administration;

(ii) at a time when the creditor had notice that an application for an administration order was pending;

(iii) at a time when the creditor had notice that any person had given notice of intention to appoint an administrator;

(iv) where the administration was immediately preceded by a winding up, at a time when the creditor had notice that a meeting of creditors had been summoned under section 98 or that a winding up petition was pending; or

(v) during a winding up which immediately preceded the administration.

(3) An account shall be taken as at the date of the notice referred to in paragraph (1) of what is due from each party to the other in respect of the mutual dealings and the sums due from one party shall be set off against the sums due from the other.

(4) A sum shall be regarded as being due to or from the company for the purposes of paragraph (3) whether—

(a) it is payable at present or in the future;

(b) the obligation by virtue of which it is payable is certain or contingent; or

(c) its amount is fixed or liquidated, or is capable of being ascertained by fixed rules or as a matter of opinion.

(5) Rule 2.81 shall apply for the purposes of this Rule to any obligation to or from the company which, by reason of its being subject to any contingency or for any other reason, does not bear a certain value;

(6) Rules 2.86 to 2.88 shall apply for the purposes of this Rule in relation to any sums due to the company which—

(a) are payable in a currency other than sterling;

(b) are of a periodical nature; or

(c) bear interest.

(7) Rule 2.105 shall apply for the purposes of this Rule to any sum due to or from the company which is payable in the future.

(8) Only the balance (if any) of the account owed to the creditor is provable in the administration. Alternatively the balance (if any) owed to the company shall be paid to the administrator as part of the assets except where all or part of the balance results from a contingent or prospective debt owed by the creditor and in such a case the balance (or that part of it which results from the contingent or prospective debt) shall be paid if and when that debt becomes due and payable.

(9) In this Rule "obligation" means an obligation however arising, whether by virtue of an agreement, rule of law or otherwise.]

[6157X]

NOTES

Substituted, subject to transitional provisions; see the note preceding r 2.1 at **[6097]**.

This rule was further substituted by the Insolvency (Amendment) Rules 2005, SI 2005/527, r 9, as from 1 April 2005, subject to transitional provisions as noted to r 2.67 at **[6157F]**.

[2.86 Debt in foreign currency

(1) For the purpose of proving a debt incurred or payable in a currency other than sterling, the amount of the debt shall be converted into sterling at the official exchange rate prevailing on the date when the company entered administration [or, if the administration was immediately preceded by a winding up, on the date that the company went into liquidation].

(2) "The official exchange rate" is the middle exchange rate on the London Foreign Exchange Market at the close of business, as published for the date in question. In the absence of any such published rate, it is such rate as the court determines.]

[6157Y]

NOTES

Substituted, subject to transitional provisions; see the note preceding r 2.1 at **[6097]**.

Para (1): words in square brackets added by the Insolvency (Amendment) Rules 2005, SI 2005/527, r 10, as from 1 April 2005, subject to transitional provisions as noted to r 2.67 at **[6157F]**.

[2.87 Payments of a periodical nature

(1) In the case of rent and other payments of a periodical nature, the creditor may prove for any amounts due and unpaid up to the date when the company entered administration [or, if the administration was immediately preceded by a winding up, up to the date that the company went into liquidation].

(2) Where at that date any payment was accruing due, the creditor may prove for so much as would have fallen due at that date, if accruing from day to day.]

[6157Z]

NOTES

Substituted, subject to transitional provisions; see the note preceding r 2.1 at **[6097]**.

Para (1): words in square brackets added by the Insolvency (Amendment) Rules 2005, SI 2005/527, r 11, as from 1 April 2005, subject to transitional provisions as noted to r 2.67 at **[6157F]**.

[2.88 Interest

(1) Where a debt proved in the administration bears interest, that interest is provable as part of the debt except in so far as it is payable in respect of any period after the company entered administration [or, if the administration was immediately preceded by a winding up, any period after the date that the company went into liquidation].

(2) In the following circumstances the creditor's claim may include interest on the debt for periods before the company entered administration, although not previously reserved or agreed.

(3) If the debt is due by virtue of a written instrument, and payable at a certain time, interest may be claimed for the period from that time to the date when the company entered administration.

(4) If the debt is due otherwise, interest may only be claimed if, before that date, a demand for payment of the debt was made in writing by or on behalf of the creditor, and notice given that interest would be payable from the date of the demand to the date of payment.

(5) Interest under paragraph (4) may only be claimed for the period from the date of the demand to that of the company's entering administration and for all the purposes of the Act and the Rules shall be chargeable at a rate not exceeding that mentioned in paragraph (6).

(6) The rate of interest to be claimed under paragraphs (3) and (4) is the rate specified in section 17 of the Judgments Act 1838 on the date when the company entered administration.

(7) … any surplus remaining after payment of the debts proved shall, before being applied for any purpose, be applied in paying interest on those debts in respect of the periods during which they have been outstanding since the company entered administration.

(8) All interest payable under paragraph (7) ranks equally whether or not the debts on which it is payable rank equally.

(9) The rate of interest payable under paragraph (7) is whichever is the greater of the rate specified under paragraph (6) or the rate applicable to the debt apart from the administration.]

[6158]

NOTES

Substituted, subject to transitional provisions; see the note preceding r 2.1 at **[6097]**.

Para (1): words in square brackets added by the Insolvency (Amendment) Rules 2005, SI 2005/527, r 12(a), as from 1 April 2005, subject to transitional provisions as noted to r 2.67 at **[6157F]**.

Para (7): words omitted revoked by SI 2005/527, r 12(b), as from 1 April 2005, subject to transitional provisions as noted to r 2.67 at **[6157F]**.

[2.89 Debt payable at future time

A creditor may prove for a debt of which payment was not yet due on the date when the company entered administration, [or, if the administration was immediately preceded by a winding up, up to the date that the company went into liquidation] subject to Rule 2.105 (adjustment of dividend where payment made before time).]

[6158A]

NOTES

Substituted, subject to transitional provisions; see the note preceding r 2.1 at **[6097]**.

Words in square brackets inserted by the Insolvency (Amendment) Rules 2005, SI 2005/527, r 13, as from 1 April 2005, subject to transitional provisions as noted to r 2.67 at **[6157F]**.

[2.90 Value of security

(1) A secured creditor may, with the agreement of the administrator or the leave of the court, at any time alter the value which he has, in his proof of debt, put upon his security.

(2) However, if a secured creditor—

(a) being the applicant for an administration order or the appointor of the administrator, has in the application or the notice of appointment put a value on his security; or

(b) has voted in respect of the unsecured balance of his debt,

he may re-value his security only with permission of the court.]

[6158B]

NOTES

Substituted, subject to transitional provisions; see the note preceding r 2.1 at **[6097]**.

[2.91 Surrender for non-disclosure

(1) If a secured creditor omits to disclose his security in his proof of debt, he shall surrender his security for the general benefit of creditors, unless the court, on application by him, relieves him from the effect of this Rule on the ground that the omission was inadvertent or the result of honest mistake.

(2) If the court grants that relief, it may require or allow the creditor's proof of debt to be amended, on such terms as may be just.

(3) Nothing in this Rule or the following two Rules may affect the rights in rem of creditors or third parties protected under Article 5 of the EC Regulation (third parties' rights in rem).]

[6158C]

NOTES

Substituted, subject to transitional provisions; see the note preceding r 2.1 at **[6097]**.

EC Regulation: ie, Council Regulation 1346/2000/EC on insolvency proceedings at **[9290]**.

[2.92 Redemption by administrator

(1) The administrator may at any time give notice to a creditor whose debt is secured that he proposes, at the expiration of 28 days from the date of the notice, to redeem the security at the value put upon it in the creditor's proof.

(2) The creditor then has 21 days (or such longer period as the administrator may allow) in which, if he so wishes, to exercise his right to revalue his security (with the permission of the court, where Rule 2.90(2) applies).

If the creditor re-values his security, the administrator may only redeem at the new value.

(3) If the administrator redeems the security, the cost of transferring it is payable out of the assets.

(4) A secured creditor may at any time, by a notice in writing, call on the administrator to elect whether he will or will not exercise his power to redeem the security at the value then placed on it; and the administrator then has 3 months in which to exercise the power or determine not to exercise it.]

[6158D]

NOTES

Substituted, subject to transitional provisions; see the note preceding r 2.1 at **[6097]**.

[2.93 Test of security's value

(1) Subject as follows, the administrator, if he is dissatisfied with the value which a secured creditor puts on his security (whether in his proof or by way of re-valuation under Rule 2.90), may require any property comprised in the security to be offered for sale.

(2) The terms of sale shall be such as may be agreed, or as the court may direct; and if the sale is by auction, the administrator on behalf of the company, and the creditor on his own behalf, may appear and bid.]

[6158E]

NOTES

Substituted, subject to transitional provisions; see the note preceding r 2.1 at **[6097]**.

[2.94 Realisation of security by creditor

If a creditor who has valued his security subsequently realises it (whether or not at the instance of the administrator)—

(a) the net amount realised shall be substituted for the value previously put by the creditor on the security; and

(b) that amount shall be treated in all respects as an amended valuation made by him.]

[6158F]

NOTES

Substituted, subject to transitional provisions; see the note preceding r 2.1 at **[6097]**.

[2.95 Notice of proposed distribution

(1) Where an administrator is proposing to make a distribution to creditors he shall give 28 days' notice of that fact.

(2) The notice given pursuant to paragraph (1) shall—

(a) be sent to—

(i) all creditors whose addresses are known to the administrator; and

(ii) where a member State liquidator has been appointed in relation to the company, to the member State liquidator;

(b) state whether the distribution is to preferential creditors or preferential creditors and unsecured creditors; and

(c) where the administrator proposes to make a distribution to unsecured creditors, state the value of the prescribed part, except where the court has made an order under section 176A(5).

(3) Subject to paragraph (5), the administrator shall not declare a dividend unless he has by public advertisement invited creditors to prove their debts.

(4) A notice pursuant to paragraphs (1) or (3) shall—

(a) state that it is the intention of the administrator to make a distribution to creditors within the period of 2 months from the last date for proving;

(b) specify whether the proposed dividend is interim or final;

(c) specify a date up to which proofs may be lodged being a date which—

(i) is the same date for all creditors; and

(ii) is not less than 21 days from that of the notice.

(5) A notice pursuant to paragraph (1) where a dividend is to be declared for preferential creditors, need only be given to those creditors in whose case he has reason to believe that their debts are preferential and public advertisement of the intended dividend need only be given if the administrator thinks fit.]

[6158G]

NOTES

Substituted, subject to transitional provisions; see the note preceding r 2.1 at **[6097]**.

[2.96 Admission or rejection of proofs

(1) Unless he has already dealt with them, within 7 days of the last date for proving, the administrator shall—

(a) admit or reject proofs submitted to him; or

(b) make such provision in respect of them as he thinks fit.

(2) The administrator is not obliged to deal with proofs lodged after the last date for proving, but he may do so, if he thinks fit.

(3) In the declaration of a dividend no payment shall be made more than once by virtue of the same debt.

(4) Subject to Rule 2.104, where—

(a) a creditor has proved; and

(b) a member State liquidator has proved in relation to the same debt,

payment shall only be made to the creditor.]

[6158H]

NOTES

Substituted, subject to transitional provisions; see the note preceding r 2.1 at **[6097]**.

[2.97 Declaration of dividend

(1) Subject to paragraph (2), within the 2 month period referred to in Rule 2.95(4)(a) the administrator shall proceed to declare the dividend to one or more classes of creditor of which he gave notice.

(2) Except with the permission of the court, the administrator shall not declare a dividend so long as there is pending any application to the court to reverse or vary a decision of his on a proof, or to expunge a proof or to reduce the amount claimed.]

[6158I]

NOTES

Substituted, subject to transitional provisions; see the note preceding r 2.1 at **[6097]**.

[2.98 Notice of declaration of a dividend

(1) Where the administrator declares a dividend he shall give notice of that fact to all creditors who have proved their debts and, where a member State liquidator has been appointed in relation to the company, to the member State liquidator.

(2) The notice shall include the following particulars relating to the administration—

(a) amounts raised from the sale of assets, indicating (so far as practicable) amounts raised by the sale of particular assets;

(b) payments made by the administrator when acting as such;

(c) where the administrator proposed to make a distribution to unsecured creditors, the value of the prescribed part, except where the court has made an order under section 176A(5);

(d) provision (if any) made for unsettled claims, and funds (if any) retained for particular purposes;

(e) the total amount of dividend and the rate of dividend;

(f) how he proposes to distribute the dividend; and

(g) whether, and if so when, any further dividend is expected to be declared.]

[6158J]

NOTES

Substituted, subject to transitional provisions; see the note preceding r 2.1 at **[6097]**.

[2.99 Payments of dividends and related matters

(1) The dividend may be distributed simultaneously with the notice declaring it.

(2) Payment of dividend may be made by post, or arrangements may be made with any creditor for it to be paid to him in another way, or held for his collection.

(3) Where a dividend is paid on a bill of exchange or other negotiable instrument, the amount of the dividend shall be endorsed on the instrument, or on a certified copy of it, if required to be produced by the holder for that purpose.]

[6158K]

NOTES

Substituted, subject to transitional provisions; see the note preceding r 2.1 at **[6097]**.

[2.100 Notice of no dividend, or no further dividend

If the administrator gives notice to creditors that he is unable to declare any dividend or (as the case may be) any further dividend, the notice shall contain a statement to the effect either—

(a) that no funds have been realised; or
(b) that the funds realised have already been distributed or used or allocated for defraying the expenses of administration.]

[6158L]

NOTES

Substituted, subject to transitional provisions; see the note preceding r 2.1 at **[6097]**.

[2.101 Proof altered after payment of dividend

(1) If after payment of dividend the amount claimed by a creditor in his proof is increased, the creditor is not entitled to disturb the distribution of the dividend; but he is entitled to be paid, out of any money for the time being available for the payment of any further dividend, any dividend or dividends which he has failed to receive.

(2) Any dividend or dividends payable under paragraph (1) shall be paid before the money there referred to is applied to the payment of any such further dividend.

(3) If, after a creditor's proof has been admitted, the proof is withdrawn or expunged, or the amount is reduced, the creditor is liable to repay to the administrator any amount overpaid by way of dividend.]

[6158M]

NOTES

Substituted, subject to transitional provisions; see the note preceding r 2.1 at **[6097]**.

[2.102 Secured creditors

(1) The following applies where a creditor re-values his security at a time when a dividend has been declared.

(2) If the revaluation results in a reduction of his unsecured claim ranking for dividend, the creditor shall forthwith repay to the administrator, for the credit of the administration, any amount received by him as dividend in excess of that to which he would be entitled having regard to the revaluation of the security.

(3) If the revaluation results in an increase of his unsecured claim, the creditor is entitled to receive from the administrator, out of any money for the time being available for the payment of a further dividend, before any such further dividend is paid, any dividend or dividends which he has failed to receive, having regard to the revaluation of the security.

However, the creditor is not entitled to disturb any dividend declared (whether or not distributed) before the date of the revaluation.]

[6158N]

NOTES

Substituted, subject to transitional provisions; see the note preceding r 2.1 at **[6097]**.

[2.103 Disqualification from dividend

If a creditor contravenes any provision of the Act or the Rules relating to the valuation of securities, the court may, on the application of the administrator, order that the creditor be wholly or partly disqualified from participation in any dividend.]

[6158O]

NOTES

Substituted, subject to transitional provisions; see the note preceding r 2.1 at **[6097]**.

[2.104 Assignment of right to dividend

(1) If a person entitled to a dividend gives notice to the administrator that he wishes the dividend to be paid to another person, or that he has assigned his entitlement to another person, the administrator shall pay the dividend to that other accordingly.

(2) A notice given under this Rule must specify the name and address of the person to whom payment is to be made.]

[6158P]

NOTES

Substituted, subject to transitional provisions; see the note preceding r 2.1 at **[6097]**.

[2.105 Debt payable at future time

(1) Where a creditor has proved for a debt of which payment is not due at the date of the declaration of dividend, he is entitled to dividend equally with other creditors, but subject as follows.

[(2) For the purpose of dividend (and no other purpose) the amount of the creditor's admitted proof (or, if a distribution has previously been made to him, the amount remaining outstanding in respect of his admitted proof) shall be reduced by applying the following formula—

$$X / 1.05^n$$

where—

(a) "X" is the value of the admitted proof; and

(b) "n" is the period beginning with the relevant date and ending with the date on which the payment of the creditor's debt would otherwise be due expressed in years and months in a decimalised form.

(3) In paragraph (2) "relevant date" means—

(a) in the case of an administration which was not immediately preceded by a winding up, the date that the company entered administration;

(b) in the case of an administration which was immediately preceded by a winding up, the date that the company went into liquidation.]]

[6158Q]

NOTES

Substituted, subject to transitional provisions; see the note preceding r 2.1 at **[6097]**.

Paras (2), (3) substituted (for the original para (2)), and the original para (3) was revoked, by the Insolvency (Amendment) Rules 2005, SI 2005/527, r 15, as from 1 April 2005, subject to transitional provisions as noted to r 2.67 at **[6157F]**.

[CHAPTER 11
THE ADMINISTRATOR

2.106 Fixing of remuneration

(1) The administrator is entitled to receive remuneration for his services as such.

(2) The remuneration shall be fixed either—

(a) as a percentage of the value of the property with which he has to deal; or
(b) by reference to the time properly given by the insolvency practitioner (as administrator) and his staff in attending to matters arising in the administration.

(3) It is for the creditors' committee (if there is one) to determine whether the remuneration is to be fixed under paragraph (2)(a) or (b) and, if under paragraph (2)(a), to determine any percentage to be applied as there mentioned.

(4) In arriving at that determination, the committee shall have regard to the following matters—
(a) the complexity (or otherwise) of the case;
(b) any respects in which, in connection with the company's affairs, there falls on the administrator any responsibility of an exceptional kind or degree;
(c) the effectiveness with which the administrator appears to be carrying out, or to have carried out, his duties as such; and
(d) the value and nature of the property with which he has to deal.

(5) If there is no creditors' committee, or the committee does not make the requisite determination, the administrator's remuneration may be fixed (in accordance with paragraph (2)) by a resolution of a meeting of creditors; and paragraph (4) applies to them as it does to the creditors' committee.

[(5A) In a case where the administrator has made a statement under paragraph 52(1)(b), if there is no creditors' committee, or the committee does not make the requisite determination, the administrator's remuneration may be fixed (in accordance with paragraph (2)) by the approval of—
(a) each secured creditor of the company: or
(b) if the administrator has made or intends to make a distribution to preferential creditors—
(i) each secured creditor of the company; and
(ii) preferential creditors whose debts amount to more than 50% of the preferential debts of the company, disregarding debts of any creditor who does not respond to an invitation to give or withhold approval;

and paragraph (4) applies to them as it does to the creditors' committee.]

(6) If not fixed as above, the administrator's remuneration shall, on his application, be fixed by the court.

(7) Where there are joint administrators, it is for them to agree between themselves as to how the remuneration payable should be apportioned. Any dispute arising between them may be referred—
(a) to the court, for settlement by order; or
(b) to the creditors' committee or a meeting of creditors, for settlement by resolution.

(8) If the administrator is a solicitor and employs his own firm, or any partner in it, to act on behalf of the company, profit costs shall not be paid unless this is authorised by the creditors' committee, the creditors or the court.

(9) ...]

[6158R]

NOTES

Substituted, subject to transitional provisions; see the note preceding r 2.1 at **[6097]**.

Para (5A): inserted by the Insolvency (Amendment) Rules 2005, SI 2005/527, r 15(1), as from 1 April 2005, subject to transitional provisions as noted to r 2.67 at **[6157F]**.

Para (9): revoked by SI 2005/527, r 15(2), as from 1 April 2005, subject to transitional provisions as noted to r 2.67 at **[6157F]**.

[2.107 Recourse to meeting of creditors

[(1)] If the administrator's remuneration has been fixed by the creditors' committee, and he considers the rate or amount to be insufficient, he may request that it be increased by resolution of the creditors.

[(2) In a case where the administrator has made a statement under paragraph 52(1)(b), if the administrator's remuneration has been fixed by the creditors' committee, and he considers the rate or amount to be insufficient, he may request that it be increased by the approval of—
(a) each secured creditor of the company: or

(b) if the administrator has made or intends to make a distribution to preferential creditors—
  (i) each secured creditor of the company; and
  (ii) preferential creditors whose debts amount to more than 50% of the preferential debts of the company, disregarding debts of any creditor who does not respond to an invitation to give or withhold approval.]]

[6158S]

NOTES

Substituted, subject to transitional provisions; see the note preceding r 2.1 at **[6097]**.

Para (1) numbered as such, and para (2) added, by the Insolvency (Amendment) Rules 2005, SI 2005/527, r 16, as from 1 April 2005, subject to transitional provisions as noted to r 2.67 at **[6157F]**.

[2.108 Recourse to the court

(1) If the administrator considers that the remuneration fixed for him by the creditors' committee, or by resolution of the creditors, is insufficient, he may apply to the court for an order increasing its amount or rate.

[(1A) In a case where the administrator has made a statement under paragraph 52(1)(b), if the administrator considers that the remuneration fixed by the approval of the creditors in accordance with Rule 2.107(2) is insufficient, he may apply to the court for an order increasing its amount or rate.]

(2) The administrator shall give at least 14 days' notice of his application to the members of the creditors' committee; and the committee may nominate one or more members to appear, or be represented, and to be heard on the application.

(3) If there is no creditors' committee, the administrator's notice of his application shall be sent to such one or more of the company's creditors as the court may direct, which creditors may nominate one or more of their number to appear or be represented.

(4) The court may, if it appears to be a proper case, order the costs of the administrator's application, including the costs of any member of the creditors' committee appearing or being represented on it, or any creditor so appearing or being represented, to be paid as an expense of the administration.]

[6158T]

NOTES

Substituted, subject to transitional provisions; see the note preceding r 2.1 at **[6097]**.

Para (1A): inserted by the Insolvency (Amendment) Rules 2005, SI 2005/527, r 17, as from 1 April 2005, subject to transitional provisions as noted to r 2.67 at **[6157F]**.

[2.109 Creditors' claim that remuneration is excessive

(1) Any creditor of the company may, with the concurrence of at least 25 per cent in value of the creditors (including himself), apply to the court for an order that the administrator's remuneration be reduced, on the grounds that it is, in all the circumstances, excessive.

(2) The court may, if it thinks that no sufficient cause is shown for a reduction, dismiss it without a hearing but it shall not do so without giving the applicant at least 7 days' notice, upon receipt of which the applicant may require the court to list the application for a without notice hearing. If the application is not dismissed, the court shall fix a venue for it to be heard, and give notice to the applicant accordingly.

(3) The applicant shall, at least 14 days before the hearing, send to the administrator a notice stating the venue and accompanied by a copy of the application, and of any evidence which the applicant intends to adduce in support of it.

(4) If the court considers the application to be well-founded, it shall make an order fixing the remuneration at a reduced amount or rate.

(5) Unless the court orders otherwise, the costs of the application shall be paid by the applicant, and are not payable as an expense of the administration.]

[6158U]

NOTES

Substituted, subject to transitional provisions; see the note preceding r 2.1 at **[6097]**.

[CHAPTER 12
ENDING ADMINISTRATION

2.110 Final progress reports

(1) In this Chapter reference to a progress report is to a report in the form specified in Rule 2.47.

(2) The final progress report means a progress report which includes a summary of—
- (a) the administrator's proposals;
- (b) any major amendments to, or deviations from, those proposals;
- (c) the steps taken during the administration; and
- (d) the outcome.]

[6158V]

NOTES

Substituted, subject to transitional provisions; see the note preceding r 2.1 at **[6097]**.

[2.111 Notice of automatic end of administration

(1) Where the appointment of an administrator has ceased to have effect, and the administrator is not required by any other Rule to give notice of that fact, he shall, as soon as reasonably practicable, and in any event within 5 business days of the date when the appointment has ceased, file a notice of automatic end of administration in Form 2.30B with the court. The notice shall be accompanied by a final progress report.

(2) A copy of the notice and accompanying document shall be sent as soon as reasonably practicable to the registrar of companies, and to all persons who received a copy of the administrator's proposals.

(3) If the administrator makes default in complying with this Rule, he is liable to a fine and, for continued contravention, to a daily default fine.]

[6158W]

NOTES

Substituted, subject to transitional provisions; see the note preceding r 2.1 at **[6097]**.
Forms: see Appendix 4 at **[A4]**.

[2.112 Applications for extension of administration

(1) An application to court for an extension of administration shall be accompanied by a progress report for the period since the last progress report (if any) or the date the company entered administration.

(2) When the administrator requests an extension of the period of the administration by consent of creditors, his request shall be accompanied by a progress report for the period since the last progress report (if any) or the date the company entered administration.

(3) The administrator shall use the notice of extension of period of administration in Form 2.31B in all circumstances where he is required to give such notice.]

[6158X]

NOTES

Substituted, subject to transitional provisions; see the note preceding r 2.1 at **[6097]**.
Forms: see Appendix 4 at **[A4]**.

[2.113 Notice of end of administration

(1) Where an administrator who was appointed under paragraph 14 or 22 gives notice that the purpose of administration has been sufficiently achieved he shall use Form 2.32B. The notice shall be accompanied by a final progress report.

(2) The administrator shall send a copy of the notice to the registrar of companies.

(3) Two copies of the notice shall be filed with the court and shall contain a statement that a copy of the notice has been sent to the registrar of companies. The court shall endorse each copy with the date and time of filing. The appointment shall cease to have effect from that date and time.

(4) The court shall give a sealed copy of the notice to the administrator.

(5) The administrator shall, as soon as reasonably practicable, and within 5 business days, send a copy of the notice of end of administration (and the accompanying report) to every creditor of the company of whose claim and address he is aware, to all those persons who were notified of his appointment and to the company.

(6) The administrator shall be taken to have complied with the requirements of paragraph 80(5) if, within 5 business days of filing the notice of end of administration with the court, he publishes once in the same newspaper as he published his notice of appointment, and in the Gazette, a notice undertaking to provide a copy of the notice of end of administration to any creditor of the company.

(7) The notice must—

(a) state the full name of the company;

(b) state the name and address of the administrator;

(c) state the date that the administration ended; and

(d) specify an address to which the creditors can write for a copy of the notice of end of administration.]

[6158Y]

NOTES

Substituted, subject to transitional provisions; see the note preceding r 2.1 at **[6097]**.

Forms: see Appendix 4 at **[A4]**.

[2.114 Application to court by administrator

(1) An application to court under paragraph 79 for an order ending an administration shall have attached to it a progress report for the period since the last progress report (if any) or the date the company entered administration and a statement indicating what the administrator thinks should be the next steps for the company (if applicable).

(2) Where the administrator applies to the court because the creditors' meeting has required him to, he shall also attach a statement to the application in which he shall indicate (giving reasons) whether or not he agrees with the creditors' requirement to him to make the application.

(3) When the administrator applies other than at the request of a creditors' meeting, he shall—

(a) give notice in writing to the applicant for the administration order under which he was appointed, or the person by whom he was appointed and the creditors of his intention to apply to court at least 7 days before the date that he intends to makes his application; and

(b) attach to his application to court a statement that he has notified the creditors, and copies of any response from creditors to that notification.

(4) Where the administrator applies to court under paragraph 79 in conjunction with a petition under section 124 for an order to wind up the company, he shall, in addition to the requirements of paragraph (3), notify the creditors whether he intends to seek appointment as liquidator.]

[6158Z]

NOTES

Substituted, subject to transitional provisions; see the note preceding r 2.1 at **[6097]**.

[2.115 Application to court by creditor

(1) Where a creditor applies to the court to end the administration a copy of the application shall be served on the administrator and the person who either made the application for the administration order or made the appointment. Where the appointment was

made under paragraph 14, a copy of the application shall be served on the holder of the floating charge by virtue of which the appointment was made.

(2) Service shall be effected not less than 5 business days before the date fixed for the hearing. The administrator, applicant or appointor, or holder of the floating charge by virtue of which the appointment was made may appear at the hearing of the application.

(3) Where the court makes an order to end the administration, the court shall send a copy of the order to the administrator.]

[6159]

NOTES

Substituted, subject to transitional provisions; see the note preceding r 2.1 at **[6097]**.

[2.116 Notification by administrator of court order

Where the court makes an order to end the administration, the administrator shall notify the registrar of companies in Form 2.33B, attaching a copy of the court order and a copy of his final progress report.]

[6159A]

NOTES

Substituted, subject to transitional provisions; see the note preceding r 2.1 at **[6097]**.
Forms: see Appendix 4 at **[A4]**.

[2.117 Moving from administration to creditors' voluntary liquidation

(1) Where for the purposes of paragraph 83(3) the administrator sends a notice of moving from administration to creditors' voluntary liquidation to the registrar of companies, he shall do so in Form 2.34B and shall attach to that notice a final progress report which must include details of the assets to be dealt with in the liquidation.

(2) As soon as reasonably practicable the administrator shall send a copy of the notice and attached document to all those who received notice of the administrator's appointment.

(3) For the purposes of paragraph 83(7) a person shall be nominated as liquidator in accordance with the provisions of Rule 2.33(2)(m) or Rule 2.45(2)(g) and his appointment takes effect by the creditors' approval, with or without modification, of the administrator's proposals or revised proposals.]

[6159B]

NOTES

Substituted, subject to transitional provisions; see the note preceding r 2.1 at **[6097]**.
Forms: see Appendix 4 at **[A4]**.

[2.118 Moving from administration to dissolution

(1) Where, for the purposes of paragraph 84(1), the administrator sends a notice of moving from administration to dissolution to the registrar of companies, he shall do so in Form 2.35B and shall attach to that notice a final progress report.

(2) As soon as reasonably practicable a copy of the notice and the attached document shall be sent to all those who received notice of the administrator's appointment.

(3) Where a court makes an order under paragraph 84(7) it shall, where the applicant is not the administrator, give a copy of the order to the administrator.

(4) The administrator shall use Form 2.36B to notify the registrar of companies in accordance with paragraph 84(8) of any order made by the court under paragraph 84(7).]

[6159C]

NOTES

Substituted, subject to transitional provisions; see the note preceding r 2.1 at **[6097]**.
Forms: see Appendix 4 at **[A4]**.

[CHAPTER 13
REPLACING ADMINISTRATOR

2.119 Grounds for resignation

(1) The administrator may give notice of his resignation on grounds of ill health or because—

(a) he intends ceasing to be in practice as an insolvency practitioner; or

(b) there is some conflict of interest, or change of personal circumstances, which precludes or makes impracticable the further discharge by him of the duties of administrator.

(2) The administrator may, with the permission of the court, give notice of his resignation on grounds other than those specified in paragraph (1).]

[6159D]

NOTES

Substituted, subject to transitional provisions; see the note preceding r 2.1 at **[6097]**.

[2.120 Notice of intention to resign

(1) The administrator shall in all cases give at least 7 days' notice in Form 2.37B of his intention to resign, or to apply for the court's permission to do so, to the following persons—

(a) if there is a continuing administrator of the company, to him; and

(b) if there is a creditors' committee to it; but

(c) if there is no such administrator and no creditors' committee, to the company and its creditors.

(2) Where the administrator gives notice under paragraph (1), he shall also give notice to a member State liquidator, if such a person has been appointed in relation to the company.

(3) Where the administrator was appointed by the holder of a qualifying floating charge under paragraph 14, the notice of intention to resign shall also be sent to all holders of prior qualifying floating charges, and to the person who appointed the administrator. A copy of the notice shall also be sent to the holder of the floating charge by virtue of which the appointment was made.

(4) Where the administrator was appointed by the company or the directors of the company under paragraph 22, a copy of the notice of intention to resign shall also be sent to the appointor and all holders of a qualifying floating charge.]

[6159E]

NOTES

Substituted, subject to transitional provisions; see the note preceding r 2.1 at **[6097]**.
Forms: see Appendix 4 at **[A4]**.

[2.121 Notice of resignation

(1) The notice of resignation shall be in Form 2.38B.

(2) Where the administrator was appointed under an administration order, the notice shall be filed with the court, and a copy sent to the registrar of companies. A copy of the notice of resignation shall be sent not more than 5 business days after it has been filed with the court to all those to whom notice of intention to resign was sent.

(3) Where the administrator was appointed by the holder of a qualifying floating charge under paragraph 14, a copy of the notice of resignation shall be filed with the court and sent to the registrar of companies, and anyone else who received a copy of the notice of intention to resign, within 5 business days of the notice of resignation being sent to the holder of the floating charge by virtue of which the appointment was made.

(4) Where the administrator was appointed by the company or the directors under paragraph 22, a copy of the notice of resignation shall be filed with the court and sent to the registrar of companies and to anyone else who received notice of intention to resign within 5 business days of the notice of resignation being sent to either the company or the directors that made the appointment.]

[6159F]

NOTES

Substituted, subject to transitional provisions; see the note preceding r 2.1 at **[6097]**.
Forms: see Appendix 4 at **[A4]**.

[2.122 Application to court to remove administrator from office

(1) Any application under paragraph 88 shall state the grounds on which it is requested that the administrator should be removed from office.

(2) Service of the notice of the application shall be effected on the administrator, the person who made the application for the administration order or the person who appointed the administrator, the creditors' committee (if any), the joint administrator (if any), and where there is neither a creditors' committee or joint administrator, to the company and all the creditors, including any floating charge holders not less than 5 business days before the date fixed for the application to be heard. Where the appointment was made under paragraph 14, the notice shall be served on the holder of the floating charge by virtue of which the appointment was made.

(3) Where a court makes an order removing the administrator it shall give a copy of the order to the applicant who as soon as reasonably practicable shall send a copy to the administrator.

(4) The applicant shall also within 5 business days of the order being made send a copy of the order to all those to whom notice of the application was sent.

(5) A copy of the order shall also be sent to the registrar of companies in Form 2.39B within the same time period.]

[6159G]

NOTES

Substituted, subject to transitional provisions; see the note preceding r 2.1 at **[6097]**.
Forms: see Appendix 4 at **[A4]**.

[2.123 Notice of vacation of office when administrator ceases to be qualified to act

Where the administrator who has ceased to be qualified to act as an insolvency practitioner in relation to the company gives notice in accordance with paragraph 89, he shall also give notice to the registrar of companies in Form 2.39B.]

[6159H]

NOTES

Substituted, subject to transitional provisions; see the note preceding r 2.1 at **[6097]**.

[2.124 Administrator deceased

(1) Subject as follows, where the administrator has died, it is the duty of his personal representatives to give notice of the fact to the court, specifying the date of the death. This does not apply if notice has been given under either paragraph (2) or (3) of this Rule.

(2) If the deceased administrator was a partner in a firm, notice may be given by a partner in the firm who is qualified to act as an insolvency practitioner, or is a member of any body recognised by the Secretary of State for the authorisation of insolvency practitioners.

(3) Notice of the death may be given by any person producing to the court the relevant death certificate or a copy of it.

(4) Where a person gives notice to the court under this Rule, he shall also give notice to the registrar of companies in Form 2.39B.]

[6159I]

NOTES

Substituted, subject to transitional provisions; see the note preceding r 2.1 at **[6097]**.

[2.125 Application to replace

(1) Where an application is made to court under paragraphs 91(1) or 95 to appoint a replacement administrator, the application shall be accompanied by a written statement in Form 2.2B by the person proposed to be the replacement administrator.

(2) Where the original administrator was appointed under an administration order, a copy of the application shall be served, in addition to those persons listed in paragraph 12(2) and Rule 2.6(3), on the person who made the application for the administration order.

(3) Where the application to court is made under paragraph 95, the application shall be accompanied by an affidavit setting out the applicant's belief as to the matters set out in that paragraph.

(4) Rule 2.8 shall apply to the service of an application under paragraphs 91(1) and 95 as it applies to service in accordance with Rule 2.6.

(5) Rules 2.9, 2.10, 2.12 and 2.14(1) and (2) apply to an application under paragraphs 91(1) and 95.]

[6159J]

NOTES

Substituted, subject to transitional provisions; see the note preceding r 2.1 at **[6097]**.

[2.126 Notification and advertisement of appointment of replacement administrator

Where a replacement administrator is appointed, the same provisions apply in respect of giving notice of, and advertising, the replacement appointment as in the case of the appointment (subject to Rule 2.128), and all statements, consents etc as are required shall also be required in the case of the appointment of a replacement. All forms and notices shall clearly identify that the appointment is of a replacement administrator.]

[6159K]

NOTES

Substituted, subject to transitional provisions; see the note preceding r 2.1 at **[6097]**.

[2.127 Notification and advertisement of appointment of joint administrator

Where, after an initial appointment has been made, an additional person or persons are to be appointed as joint administrator the same Rules shall apply in respect of giving notice of and advertising the appointment as in the case of the initial appointment, subject to Rule 2.128.]

[6159L]

NOTES

Substituted, subject to transitional provisions; see the note preceding r 2.1 at **[6097]**.

[2.128 The replacement or additional administrator shall send notice of the appointment in Form 2.40B to the registrar of companies.]

[6159M]

NOTES

Substituted, subject to transitional provisions; see the note preceding r 2.1 at **[6097]**.
Forms: see Appendix 4 at **[A4]**.

[2.129 Administrator's duties on vacating office

(1) Where the administrator ceases to be in office as such, in consequence of removal, resignation or cesser of qualification as an insolvency practitioner, he is under obligation as soon as reasonably practicable to deliver up to the person succeeding him as administrator the assets (after deduction of any expenses properly incurred and distributions made by him) and further to deliver up to that person—

(a) the records of the administration, including correspondence, proofs and other related papers appertaining to the administration while it was within his responsibility; and

(b) the company's books, papers and other records.

(2) If the administrator makes default in complying with this Rule, he is liable to a fine and, for continued contravention, to a daily default fine.]

[6159N]

NOTES

Substituted, subject to transitional provisions; see the note preceding r 2.1 at **[6097]**.

[CHAPTER 14
EC REGULATION: CONVERSION OF ADMINISTRATION INTO WINDING UP

2.130 Application for conversion into winding up

(1) Where a member State liquidator proposes to apply to the court for the conversion under Article 37 of the EC Regulation (conversion of earlier proceedings) of an administration into a winding up, an affidavit complying with Rule 2.131 must be prepared and sworn, and filed with the court in support of the application.

(2) An application under this Rule shall be by originating application.

(3) The application and the affidavit required under this Rule shall be served upon—
- (a) the company; and
- (b) the administrator.]

[6159O]

NOTES

Substituted, subject to transitional provisions; see the note preceding r 2.1 at **[6097]**.
EC Regulation: ie, Council Regulation 1346/2000/EC on insolvency proceedings at **[9290]**.

[2.131 Contents of affidavit

(1) The affidavit shall state—
- (a) that main proceedings have been opened in relation to the company in a member State other than the United Kingdom;
- (b) the deponent's belief that the conversion of the administration into a winding up would prove to be in the interests of the creditors in the main proceedings;
- (c) the deponent's opinion as to whether the company ought to enter voluntary winding up or be wound up by the court; and
- (d) all other matters that, in the opinion of the member State liquidator, would assist the court—
  - (i) in deciding whether to make such an order; and
  - (ii) if the court were to do so, in considering the need for any consequential provision that would be necessary or desirable.

(2) An affidavit under this rule shall be sworn by, or on behalf of, the member State liquidator.]

[6159P]

NOTES

Substituted, subject to transitional provisions; see the note preceding r 2.1 at **[6097]**.

[2.132 Power of court

(1) On hearing the application for conversion into winding up the court may make such order as it thinks fit.

(2) If the court makes an order for conversion into winding up the order may contain all such consequential provisions as the court deems necessary or desirable.

(3) Without prejudice to the generality of paragraph (1), an order under that paragraph may provide that the company be wound up as if a resolution for voluntary winding up under section 84 were passed on the day on which the order is made.]

[6159Q]

NOTES

Substituted, subject to transitional provisions; see the note preceding r 2.1 at **[6097]**.

[CHAPTER 15
EC REGULATION: MEMBER STATE LIQUIDATOR

2.133 Interpretation of creditor and notice to member State liquidator

(1) This Rule applies where a member State liquidator has been appointed in relation to the company.

(2) For the purposes of the Rules referred to in paragraph (3) the member State liquidator is deemed to be a creditor.

(3) The Rules referred to in paragraph (2) are Rules 2.34 (notice of creditors' meeting), 2.35(4) (creditors' meeting), 2.37 (requisitioning of creditors' meeting), 2.38 (entitlement to vote), 2.39 (admission and rejection of claims), 2.40 (secured creditors), 2.41 (holders of negotiable instruments), 2.42 (hire-purchase, conditional sale and chattel leasing agreements), 2.46 (notice to creditors), 2.47 (reports to creditors), 2.48 (correspondence instead of creditors' meeting), 2.50(2) (creditors' committee), 2.57(1)(b) and (c) (termination of membership of creditors' committee), 2.59(3) (vacancies in creditors' committee), 2.108(3) (administrator's remuneration—recourse to court) and 2.109 (challenge to administrator's remuneration).

(4) Paragraphs (2) and (3) are without prejudice to the generality of the right to participate referred to in paragraph 3 of Article 32 of the EC Regulation (exercise of creditor's rights).

(5) Where the administrator is obliged to give notice to, or provide a copy of a document (including an order of court) to, the court, the registrar of companies or the official receiver, the administrator shall give notice or provide copies, as the case may be, to the member State liquidator.

(6) Paragraph (5) is without prejudice to the generality of the obligations imposed by Article 31 of the EC Regulation (duty to co-operate and communicate information).]

[6160]

NOTES

Substituted, subject to transitional provisions; see the note preceding r 2.1 at **[6097]**.
EC Regulation: ie, Council Regulation 1346/2000/EC on insolvency proceedings at **[9290]**.

PART 3
ADMINISTRATIVE RECEIVERSHIP

CHAPTER 1
APPOINTMENT OF ADMINISTRATIVE RECEIVER

[3.1 Acceptance and confirmation of acceptance of appointment

(1) Where two or more persons are appointed as joint receivers or managers of a company's property under powers contained in an instrument, the acceptance of such an appointment shall be made by each of them in accordance with section 33 as if that person were a sole appointee, but the joint appointment takes effect only when all such persons have so accepted and is then deemed to have been made at the time at which the instrument of appointment was received by or on behalf of all such persons.

(2) Subject to the next paragraph, where a person is appointed as the sole or joint receiver of a company's property under powers contained in an instrument, the appointee shall, if he accepts the appointment, within 7 days confirm his acceptance in writing to the person appointing him.

(3) Paragraph (2) does not apply where an appointment is accepted in writing.

(4) Any acceptance or confirmation of acceptance of appointment as a receiver or manager of a company's property, whether under the Act or the Rules, may be given by any person (including, in the case of a joint appointment, any joint appointee) duly authorised for that purpose on behalf of the receiver or manager.

(5) In confirming acceptance the appointee or person authorised for that purpose shall state—

(a) the time and date of receipt of the instrument of appointment, and
(b) the time and date of acceptance.]

[6161]

NOTES

Substituted by the Insolvency (Amendment) Rules 1987, SI 1987/1919, r 3(1), Schedule, Pt 1, para 23, as from 11 January 1988.

Para (3): see Form 3.1 in Appendix 4 at **[A4]**.

3.2 Notice and advertisement of appointment

(1) This Rule relates to the notice which a person is required by section 46(1) to send and publish, when appointed as administrative receiver.

(2) The following matters shall be stated in the [notices sent to the company and the creditors]—

(a) the registered name of the company, as at the date of the appointment, and its registered number;

(b) any other name with which the company has been registered in the 12 months preceding that date;

(c) any name under which the company has traded at any time in those 12 months, if substantially different from its then registered name;

(d) the name and address of the administrative receiver, and the date of his appointment;

(e) the name of the person by whom the appointment was made;

(f) the date of the instrument conferring the power under which the appointment was made, and a brief description of the instrument;

(g) a brief description of the assets of the company (if any) in respect of which the person appointed is not made the receiver.

(3) The administrative receiver shall cause notice of his appointment to be advertised once in the Gazette, and once in such newspaper as he thinks most appropriate for ensuring that it comes to the notice of the company's creditors.

(4) The advertisement shall state all the matters specified in sub-paragraphs (a) to (e) of paragraph (2) above.

[6162]

NOTES

Para (2): words in square brackets substituted by the Insolvency (Amendment) Rules 1987, SI 1987/1919, r 3(1), Schedule, Pt 1, para 24, as from 11 January 1988.

Para (3): see Form 3.1A in Appendix 4 at **[A4]**.

CHAPTER 2
STATEMENT OF AFFAIRS AND REPORT TO CREDITORS

3.3 Notice requiring statement of affairs

(1) [Where] the administrative receiver determines to require a statement of the company's affairs to be made out and submitted to him in accordance with section 47, he shall send notice to each of the persons whom he considers should be made responsible under that section, requiring them to prepare and submit the statement.

(2) The persons to whom the notice is sent are referred to in this Chapter as "the deponents".

(3) The notice shall inform each of the deponents—

(a) of the names and addresses of all others (if any) to whom the same notice has been sent;

(b) of the time within which the statement must be delivered;

(c) of the effect of section 47(6) (penalty for non-compliance); and

(d) of the application to him, and to each of the other deponents, of section 235 (duty to provide information, and to attend on the administrative receiver if required).

(4) The administrative receiver shall, on request, furnish each deponent with [the forms required for the preparation of the statement of affairs].

[6163]

NOTES

Paras (1), (4): words in square brackets substituted by the Insolvency (Amendment) Rules 1987, SI 1987/1919, r 3(1), Schedule, Pt 1, para 25(1), (2), as from 11 January 1988.

Para (1): see Form 3.1B in Appendix 4 at **[A4]**.

3.4 Verification and filing

(1) The statement of affairs shall be in Form 3.2, shall contain all the particulars required by that form and shall be verified by affidavit by the deponents (using the same form).

(2) The administrative receiver may require any of the persons mentioned in section 47(3) to submit an affidavit of concurrence, stating that he concurs in the statement of affairs.

(3) An affidavit of concurrence may be qualified in respect of matters dealt with in the statement of affairs, where the maker of the affidavit is not in agreement with the deponents, or he considers the statement to be erroneous or misleading, or he is without the direct knowledge necessary for concurring with it.

(4) The statement of affairs shall be delivered to the receiver by the deponent making the affidavit of verification (or by one of them, if more than one), together with a copy of the verified statement.

(5) Every affidavit of concurrence shall be delivered by the person who makes it, together with a copy.

(6) The administrative receiver shall retain the verified copy of the statement and the affidavits of concurrence (if any) as part of the records of the receivership.

[6164]

NOTES

Form 3.2: see Appendix 4 at **[A4]**.

3.5 Limited disclosure

(1) Where the administrative receiver thinks that it would prejudice the conduct of the receivership for the whole or part of the statement of affairs to be disclosed, he may apply to the court for an order of limited disclosure in respect of the statement or a specified part of it.

(2) The court may on the application order that the statement, or, as the case may be, the specified part of it, be not open to inspection otherwise than with leave of the court.

(3) The court's order may include directions as to the delivery of documents to the registrar of companies and the disclosure of relevant information to other persons.

[6165]

3.6 Release from duty to submit statement of affairs; extension of time

(1) The power of the administrative receiver under section 47(5) to give a release from the obligation imposed by that section, or to grant an extension of time, may be exercised at the receiver's own discretion, or at the request of any deponent.

(2) A deponent may, if he requests a release or extension of time and it is refused by the receiver, apply to the court for it.

(3) The court may, if it thinks that no sufficient cause is shown for the application, dismiss it; but it shall not do so unless the applicant has had an opportunity to attend the court for an *ex parte* hearing, of which he has been given at least 7 days' notice.

If the application is not dismissed under this paragraph, the court shall fix a venue for it to be heard, and give notice to the deponent accordingly.

(4) The deponent shall, at least 14 days before the hearing, send to the receiver a notice stating the venue and accompanied by a copy of the application, and of any evidence which he (the deponent) intends to adduce in support of it.

(5) The receiver may appear and he heard on the application; and, whether or not he appears, he may file a written report of any matters which he considers ought to be drawn to the court's attention.

If such a report is filed, a copy of it shall be sent by the receiver to the deponent, not later than 5 days before the hearing.

(6) Sealed copies of any order made on the application shall be sent by the court to the deponent and the receiver.

(7) On any application under this Rule the applicant's costs shall be paid in any event by him and, unless the court otherwise orders, no allowance towards them shall be made out of the assets under the administrative receiver's control.

[6166]

3.7 Expenses of statement of affairs

(1) A deponent making the statement of affairs and affidavit shall be allowed, and paid by the administrative receiver out of his receipts, any expenses incurred by the deponent is so doing which the receiver thinks reasonable.

(2) Any decision by the receiver under this Rule is subject to appeal to the court.

(3) Nothing in this Rule relieves a deponent from any obligation with respect to the preparation, verification and submission of the statement of affairs, or to the provision of information to the receiver.

[6167]

3.8 Report to creditors

(1) If under section 48(2) the administrative receiver determines not to send a copy of his report to creditors, but to publish notice under paragraph (b) of that subsection, the notice shall be published in the newspaper in which the receiver's appointment was advertised.

(2) If he proposes to apply to the court to dispense with the holding of the meeting of unsecured creditors (otherwise required by section 48(2)), he shall in his report to creditors or (as the case may be) in the notice published as above, state the venue fixed by the court for the hearing of the application.

(3) Subject to any order of the court under Rule 3.5, the copy of the receiver's report which under section 48(1) is to be sent to the registrar of companies shall have attached to it a copy of any statement of affairs under section 47, and copies of any affidavits of concurrence.

(4) If the statement of affairs or affidavits of concurrence, if any, have not been submitted to the receiver by the time he sends a copy of his report to the registrar of companies, he shall send a copy of the statement and any affidavits of concurrence as soon thereafter as he receives them.

[(5) The receiver's report under section 48(1) shall state, to the best of his knowledge and belief—

- (a) an estimate of the value of the prescribed part (whether or not he proposes to make an application under section 176A(5) or whether section 176A(3) applies); and
- (b) an estimate of the value of the company's net property.

(6) Nothing in this Rule is to be taken as requiring any such estimate to include any information, the disclosure of which could seriously prejudice the commercial interests of the company.

If such information is excluded from the calculation the estimate shall be accompanied by a statement to that effect.

(7) The report shall also state whether, and if so why, the receiver proposes to make an application to court under section 176A(5).]

[6168]

NOTES

Paras (5)–(7): added by the Insolvency (Amendment) Rules 2003, SI 2003/1730, r 6, Sch 1, Pt 3, para 10, as from 15 September 2003 (for transitional provisions and savings see the note preceding r 2.1 at **[6097]**).

Para (4): see Form 3.3 in Appendix 4 at **[A4]**.

CHAPTER 3
CREDITORS' MEETING

3.9 Procedure for summoning meeting under s 48(2)

(1) In fixing the venue for a meeting of creditors summoned under section 48(2), the administrative receiver shall have regard to the convenience of the persons who are invited to attend.

(2) The meeting shall be summoned for commencement between 10.00 and 16.00 hours on a business day, unless the court otherwise directs.

(3) At least 14 days' notice of the venue shall be given to all creditors of the company who are identified in the statement of affairs, or are known to the receiver and had claims against the company at the date of his appointment.

(4) With the notice summoning the meeting there shall be sent out forms of proxy.

(5) The notice shall include a statement to the effect that creditors whose claims are wholly secured are not entitled to attend or be represented at the meeting.

(6) Notice of the venue shall also be published in the newspaper in which the receiver's appointment was advertised.

(7) The notice to creditors and the newspaper advertisement shall contain a statement of the effect of Rule 3.11(1) below (voting rights).

[6169]

NOTES

Para (4): see Form 8.3 in Appendix 4 at **[A4]**.

3.10 The chairman at the meeting

(1) The chairman at the creditors' meeting shall be the receiver, or a person nominated by him in writing to act in his place.

(2) A person so nominated must be either—

(a) one who is qualified to act as an insolvency practitioner in relation to the company, or

(b) an employee of the receiver or his firm who is experienced in insolvency matters.

[6170]

3.11 Voting rights

(1) Subject as follows, at the creditors' meeting a person is entitled to vote only if—

(a) he has given to the receiver, not later than 12.00 hours on the business day before the day fixed for the meeting, details in writing of the debt that he claims to be due to him from the company, and the claim has been duly admitted under the following provisions of this Rule, and

(b) there has been lodged with the administrative receiver any proxy which the creditor intends to be used on his behalf.

(2) The chairman of the meeting may allow a creditor to vote, notwithstanding that he has failed to comply with paragraph (1)(a), if satisfied that the failure was due to circumstances beyond the creditor's control.

(3) The receiver or (if other) the chairman of the meeting may call for any document or other evidence to be produced to him where he thinks it necessary for the purpose of substantiating the whole or any part of the claim.

(4) Votes are calculated according to the amount of a creditor's debt as at the date of the appointment of the receiver, after deducting any amounts paid in respect of that debt after that date.

(5) A creditor shall not vote in respect of a debt for an unliquidated amount, or any debt whose value is not ascertained, except where the chairman agrees to put upon the debt an estimated minimum value for the purpose of entitlement to vote and admits the claim for that purpose.

(6) A secured creditor is entitled to vote only in respect of the balance (if any) of his debt after deducting the value of his security as estimated by him.

(7) A creditor shall not vote in respect of a debt on, or secured by, a current bill of exchange or promissory note, unless he is willing—

(a) to treat the liability to him on the bill or note of every person who is liable on it antecedently to the company, and against whom a bankruptcy order had not been made (or, in the case of a company, which has not gone into liquidation), as a security in his hands, and

(b) to estimate the value of the security and, for the purpose of his entitlement to vote, to deduct it from his claim.

[6171]

3.12 Admission and rejection of claim

(1) At the creditors' meeting the chairman has power to admit or reject a creditor's claim for the purpose of his entitlement to vote; and the power is exercisable with respect to the whole or any part of the claim.

(2) The chairman's decision under this Rule, or in respect of any matter arising under Rule 3.11, is subject to appeal to the court by any creditor.

(3) If the chairman is in doubt whether a claim should be admitted or rejected, he shall mark it as objected to and allow the creditor to vote, subject to his vote being subsequently declared invalid if the objection to the claim is sustained.

(4) If on an appeal the chairman's decision is reversed or varied, or a creditor's vote is declared invalid, the court may order that another meeting be summoned, or make such other order as it thinks just.

(5) Neither the receiver nor any person nominated by him to be chairman is personally liable for costs incurred by any person in respect of an appeal to the court under this Rule, unless the court makes an order to that effect.

[6172]

3.13 (*Revoked by the Insolvency* (*Amendment*) *Rules 1987, SI 1987/1919, r 3(1), Schedule, Pt 1, para 26, as from 11 January 1988.*)

3.14 Adjournment

(1) The creditors' meeting shall not be adjourned, even if no quorum is present, unless the chairman decides that it is desirable; and in that case he shall adjourn it to such date, time and place as he thinks fit.

(2) Rule 3.9(1) and (2) applies, with necessary modifications, to any adjourned meeting.

(3) If there is no quorum, and the meeting is not adjourned, it is deemed to have been duly summoned and held.

[6173]

3.15 Resolutions and minutes

(1) At the creditors' meeting, a resolution is passed when a majority (in value) of those present and voting in person or by proxy have voted in favour of it.

(2) The chairman of the meeting shall cause a record to be made of the proceedings, and kept as part of the records of the receivership.

(3) The record shall include a list of the creditors who attended (personally or by proxy) and, if a creditors' committee has been established, the names and addresses of those elected to be members of the committee.

[6174]

CHAPTER 4
THE CREDITORS' COMMITTEE

3.16 Constitution of committee

(1) Where it is resolved by the creditors' meeting to establish a creditors' committee, the committee shall consist of at least 3 and not more than 5 creditors of the company elected at the meeting.

(2) Any creditor of the company is eligible to be a member of the committee, so long as his claim has not been rejected for the purpose of his entitlement to vote.

(3) A body corporate may be a member of the committee, but it cannot act as such otherwise than by a representative appointed under Rule 3.21 below.

[6175]

3.17 Formalities of establishment

(1) The creditors' committee does not come into being, and accordingly cannot act, until the administrative receiver has issued a certificate of its due constitution.

[(2) No person may act as a member of the committee unless and until he has agreed to do so and, unless the relevant proxy or authorisation contains a statement to the contrary, such agreement may be given by his proxy-holder or representative under section 375 of the Companies Act present at the meeting establishing the committee.

(2A) The receiver's certificate of the committee's due constitution shall not issue unless and until at least 3 of the persons who are to be members of the committee have agreed to act.]

(3) As and when the others (if any) agree to act, the receiver shall issue an amended certificate.

(4) The certificate, and any amended certificate, shall be sent by the receiver to the registrar of companies.

(5) If, after the first establishment of the committee, there is any change in its membership, the receiver shall report the change to the registrar of companies.

[6176]

NOTES

Paras (2), (2A): substituted, for original para (2), by the Insolvency (Amendment) Rules 1987, SI 1987/1919, r 3(1), Schedule, Pt 1, para 27, as from 11 January 1988.

Paras (4), (5): see Forms 3.4, 3.5 in Appendix 4 at **[A4]**.

3.18 Functions and meetings of the committee

(1) The creditors' committee shall assist the administrative receiver in discharging his functions, and act in relation to him in such manner as may be agreed from time to time.

(2) Subject as follows, meetings of the committee shall be held when and where determined by the receiver.

(3) The receiver shall call a first meeting of the committee not later than 3 months after its establishment; and thereafter he shall call a meeting—

(a) if requested by a member of the committee or his representative (the meeting then to be held within 21 days of the request being received by the receiver), and

(b) for a specified date, if the committee has previously resolved that a meeting be held on that date.

(4) The receiver shall give 7 days' written notice of the venue of any meeting to every member (or his representative designated for that purpose), unless in any case the requirement of notice has been waived by or on behalf of any member.

Waiver may be signified either at or before the meeting.

[6177]

3.19 The chairman at meetings

(1) Subject to Rule 3.28(3), the chairman at any meeting of the creditors' committee shall be the administrative receiver, or a person nominated by him in writing to act.

(2) A person so nominated must be either—

(a) one who is qualified to act as an insolvency practitioner in relation to the company, or

(b) an employee of the receiver or his firm who is experienced in insolvency matters.

[6178]

3.20 Quorum

A meeting of the committee is duly constituted if due notice has been given to all the members, and at least 2 members are present or represented.

[6179]

3.21 Committee-members' representatives

(1) A member of the committee may, in relation to the business of the committee, be represented by another person duly authorised by him for that purpose.

(2) A person acting as a committee-member's representative must hold a letter of authority entitling him so to act (either generally or specially) and signed by or on behalf of the committee-member[, and for this purpose any proxy or any authorisation under section 375 of the Companies Act in relation to any meeting of creditors of the company shall, unless it contains a statement to the contrary, be treated as a letter of authority to act generally signed by or on behalf of the committee-member].

(3) The chairman at any meeting of the committee may call on a person claiming to act as a committee-member's representative to produce his letter of authority, and may exclude him if it appears that his authority is deficient.

(4) No member may be represented by a body corporate, or by a person who is an undischarged bankrupt, [or a disqualified director,] or is subject to a [bankruptcy restrictions order, bankruptcy restrictions undertaking or interim bankruptcy restrictions order].

(5) No person shall—

(a) on the same committee, act at one and the same time as representative of more than one committee-member, or

(b) act both as a member of the committee and as representative of another member.

(6) Where a member's representative signs any document on the member's behalf, the fact that he so signs must be stated below his signature.

[6180]

NOTES

Para (2): words in square brackets added by the Insolvency (Amendment) Rules 1987, SI 1987/1919, r 3(1), Schedule, Pt 1, para 28, as from 11 January 1988.

Para (4): words in first pair of square brackets inserted, and words in second pair of square brackets substituted, by the Insolvency (Amendment) Rules 2004, SI 2004/584, r 6, as from 1 April 2004.

3.22 Resignation

A member of the committee may resign by notice in writing delivered to the administrative receiver.

[6181]

3.23 Termination of membership

(1) Membership of the creditors' committee is automatically terminated if the member—

(a) becomes bankrupt …, or

(b) at 3 consecutive meetings of the committee is neither present nor represented (unless at the third of those meetings it is resolved that this Rule is not to apply in his case), or

(c) ceases to be, or is found never to have been, a creditor.

(2) However, if the cause of termination is the member's bankruptcy, his trustee in bankruptcy replaces him as a member of the committee.

[6182]

NOTES

Para (1): words omitted revoked by the Insolvency (Amendment) Rules 2004, SI 2004/584, r 7, as from 1 April 2004.

3.24 Removal

A member of the committee may be removed by resolution at a meeting of creditors, at least 14 days' notice having been given of the intention to move that resolution.

[6183]

3.25 Vacancies

(1) The following applies if there is a vacancy in the membership of the creditors' committee.

(2) The vacancy need not be filled if the administrative receiver and a majority of the remaining members of the committee so agree, provided that the total number of members does not fall below the minimum required under Rule 3.16.

(3) The receiver may appoint any creditor (being qualified under the Rules to be a member of the committee) to fill the vacancy, if a majority of the other members of the committee agree to the appointment and the creditor concerned consents to act.

[6184]

3.26 Procedure at meetings

(1) At any meeting of the committee, each member of it (whether present himself or by his representative) has one vote; and a resolution is passed when a majority of the members present or represented have voted in favour of it.

(2) Every resolution passed shall be recorded in writing, either separately or as part of the minutes of the meeting.

(3) A record of each resolution shall be signed by the chairman and kept as part of the records of the receivership.

[6185]

3.27 Resolutions by post

(1) In accordance with this Rule, the administrative receiver may seek to obtain the agreement of members of the creditors' committee to a resolution by sending to every member (or his representative designated for the purpose) a copy of the proposed resolution.

(2) Where the receiver makes use of the procedure allowed by this Rule, he shall send out to members of the committee or their representatives (as the case may be) [a copy of any proposed resolution on which a decision is sought, which shall be set out in such a way that agreement with or dissent from each separate resolution may be indicated by the recipient on the copy so sent].

(3) Any member of the committee may, within 7 business days from the date of the receiver sending out a resolution, require him to summon a meeting of the committee to consider the matters raised by the resolution.

(4) In the absence of such a request, the resolution is deemed to have been passed by the committee if and when the receiver is notified in writing by a majority of the members that they concur with it.

(5) A copy of every resolution passed under this Rule, and a note that the committee's concurrence was obtained, shall be kept with the records of the receivership.

[6186]

NOTES

Para (2): words in square brackets substituted by the Insolvency (Amendment) Rules 1987, SI 1987/1919, r 3(1), Schedule, Pt 1, para 29, as from 11 January 1988.

3.28 Information from receiver

(1) Where the committee resolves to require the attendance of the administrative receiver under section 49(2), the notice to him shall be in writing signed by the majority of the members of the committee for the time being. A member's representative may sign for him.

(2) The meeting at which the receiver's attendance is required shall be fixed by the committee for a business day, and shall be held at such time and place as he determines.

(3) Where the receiver so attends, the members of the committee may elect any one of their number to be chairman of the meeting, in place of the receiver or any nominee of his.

[6187]

3.29 Expenses of members

(1) Subject as follows, the administrative receiver shall out of the assets of the company defray any reasonable travelling expenses directly incurred by members of the creditors' committee or their representatives in relation to their attendance at the committee's meetings, or otherwise on the committee's business, as an expense of the receivership.

(2) Paragraph (1) does not apply to any meeting of the committee held within 3 months of a previous meeting, unless the meeting in question is summoned at the instance of the administrative receiver.

[6188]

3.30 Members' dealings with the company

(1) Membership of the committee does not prevent a person from dealing with the company while the receiver is acting, provided that any transactions in the course of such dealings are entered into in good faith and for value.

(2) The court may, on the application of any person interested, set aside a transaction which appears to it to be contrary to the requirements of this Rule, and may give such consequential directions as it thinks fit for compensating the company for any loss which it may have incurred in consequence of the transaction.

[6189]

[3.30A Formal defects

The acts of the creditors' committee established for any administrative receivership are valid notwithstanding any defect in the appointment, election or qualifications of any member of the committee or any committee-member's representative or in the formalities of its establishment.]

[6190]

NOTES

Inserted by the Insolvency (Amendment) Rules 1987, SI 1987/1919, r 3(1), Schedule, Pt 1, para 30, as from 11 January 1988.

CHAPTER 5
THE ADMINISTRATIVE RECEIVER (MISCELLANEOUS)

3.31 Disposal of charged property

(1) The following applies where the administrative receiver applies to the court under section 43(1) for authority to dispose of property of the company which is subject to a security.

(2) The court shall fix a venue for the hearing of the application, and the receiver shall forthwith give notice of the venue to the person who is the holder of the security.

(3) If an order is made under section 43(1), the receiver shall forthwith give notice of it to that person.

(4) The court shall send 2 sealed copies of the order to the receiver, who shall send one of them to that person.

[6191]

3.32 Abstract of receipts and payments

(1) The administrative receiver shall—

- (a) within 2 months after the end of 12 months from the date of his appointment, and of every subsequent period of 12 months, and
- (b) within 2 months after he ceases to act as administrative receiver,

send to the registrar of companies, to the company and to the person by whom he was appointed, and to each member of the creditors' committee (if there is one), the requisite accounts of his receipts and payments as receiver.

(2) The court may, on the receiver's application, extend the period of 2 months referred to in paragraph (1).

(3) The accounts are to be in the form of an abstract showing—

- (a) receipts and payments during the relevant period of 12 months, or
- (b) where the receiver has ceased to act, receipts and payments during the period from the end of the last 12-month period to the time when he so ceased (alternatively, if there has been no previous abstract, receipts and payments in the period since his appointment as administrative receiver).

(4) This Rule is without prejudice to the receiver's duty to render proper accounts required otherwise than as above.

(5) If the administrative receiver makes default in complying with this Rule, he is liable to a fine and, for continued contravention, to a daily default fine.

[6192]

NOTES

Para (1): see Form 3.6 in Appendix 4 at **[A4]**.

3.33 Resignation

(1) Subject as follows, before resigning his office the administrative receiver shall give at least 7 days' notice of his intention to do so to—

(a) the person by whom he was appointed, …
(b) the company or, if it is then in liquidation, its liquidator [, and
(c) in any case, to the members of the creditors' committee (if any)].

(2) A notice given under this Rule shall specify the date on which the receiver intends his resignation to take effect.

(3) No notice is necessary if the receiver resigns in consequence of the making of an administration order.

[6193]

NOTES

Para (1): word omitted from sub-para (a) revoked, and sub-para (c) and the word immediately preceding it added, by SI 1987/1919, r 3(1), Schedule, Pt 1, para 31, as from 11 January 1988.

3.34 Receiver deceased

If the administrative receiver dies, the person by whom he was appointed shall, forthwith on his becoming aware of the death, give notice of it to—

(a) the registrar of companies, …
(b) the company or, if it is in liquidation, the liquidator[, and
(c) in any case, to the members of the creditors' committee (if any)].

[6194]

NOTES

Word omitted from sub-para (a) revoked, and sub-para (c) and the word immediately preceding it added, by the Insolvency (Amendment) Rules 1987, SI 1987/1919, r 3(1), Schedule, Pt 1, para 32, as from 11 January 1988.

See Form 3.7 in Appendix 4 at **[A4]**.

3.35 Vacation of office

(1) The administrative receiver, on vacating office on completion of the receivership, or in consequence of his ceasing to be qualified as an insolvency practitioner, shall forthwith give notice of his doing so—

[(a) to the company or, if it is in liquidation, the liquidator, and]
(b) … to the members of the creditors' committee (if any).

(2) Where the receiver's office is vacated, the notice to the registrar of companies which is required by section 45(4) may be given by means of an indorsement on the notice required by section 405(2) of the Companies Act (notice for the purposes of the register of charges).

[6195]

NOTES

Para (1): sub-para (a) substituted, and words omitted from sub-para (b) revoked, by the Insolvency (Amendment) Rules 1987, SI 1987/1919, r 3(1), Schedule, Pt 1, para 33, as from 11 January 1988.

CHAPTER 6
VAT BAD DEBT RELIEF

3.36 Issue of certificate of insolvency

(1) In accordance with this Rule, it is the duty of the administrative receiver to issue a certificate in the terms of paragraph (b) of section 22(3) of the Value Added Tax Act 1983

(which specifies the circumstances in which a company is deemed insolvent for the purposes of that section) forthwith upon his forming the opinion described in that paragraph.

(2) There shall in the certificate be specified—

(a) the name of the company and its registered number;
(b) the name of the administrative receiver and the date of his appointment; and
(c) the date on which the certificate is issued.

(3) The certificate shall be intituled "CERTIFICATE OF INSOLVENCY FOR THE PURPOSES OF SECTION 22(3)(b) OF THE VALUE ADDED TAX ACT 1983".

[6196]

NOTES

Value Added Tax Act 1983, s 22: repealed by the Finance Act 1990, s 132, Sch 19, Pt III, and replaced by s 11 thereof (itself repealed, subject to transitional provisions, by the Value Added Tax Act 1994, s 100(1), (2), Sch 13, Sch 15.)

3.37 Notice to creditors

(1) Notice of the issue of the certificate shall be given by the administrative receiver within 3 months of his appointment or within 2 months of issuing the certificate, whichever is the later, to all of the company's unsecured creditors of whose address he is then aware and who have, to his knowledge, made supplies to the company, with a charge to value added tax, at any time before his appointment.

(2) Thereafter, he shall give the notice to any such creditor of whose address and supplies to the company he becomes aware.

(3) He is not under obligation to provide any creditor with a copy of the certificate.

[6197]

3.38 Preservation of certificate with company's records

(1) The certificate shall be retained with the company's accounting records, and section 222 of the Companies Act (where and for how long records are to be kept) shall apply to the certificate as it applies to those records.

(2) It is the duty of the administrative receiver, on vacating office, to bring this Rule to the attention of the directors or (as the case may be) any successor of his as receiver.

[6198]

[CHAPTER 7
SECTION 176A: THE PRESCRIBED PART

3.39 Report to creditors

(1) This Rule applies where—

(a) a receiver (other than an administrative receiver) is appointed by the court or otherwise under a charge which as created was a floating charge; and
(b) section 176A applies.

(2) Within 3 months (or such longer period as the court may allow) of the date of his appointment the receiver shall send to creditors, details of whose names and addresses are available to him, notice of his appointment and a report which will include the following matters—

(a) to the best of the receiver's knowledge and belief—
  (i) an estimate of the value of the prescribed part (whether or not he proposes to make an application to the court under section 176A(5) or section 176A(3) applies); and
  (ii) an estimate of the value of company's net property;
(b) whether, and if so, why, he proposes to make an application to court under section 176A(5); and
(c) whether he proposes to present a petition for the winding up of the company.

(3) Nothing in this Rule is to be taken as requiring any such estimate to include any information, the disclosure of which could seriously prejudice the commercial interests of the company. If such information is excluded from the calculation the estimate shall be accompanied by a statement to that effect.

(4) Where the receiver thinks that it is impracticable to send the report required under paragraph (2) or where full details of the unsecured creditors of the company are not available to him, he may, instead of sending a report as required by this Rule, publish a notice to the same effect in such newspaper as he thinks most appropriate for ensuring that it comes to the notice of the company's unsecured creditors.]

[6198A]

NOTES

Chapter 7 (rr 3.39, 3.40) added by the Insolvency (Amendment) Rules 2003, SI 2003/1730, r 6, Sch 1, Pt 3, para 11, as from 15 September 2003 (for transitional provisions and savings see the note preceding r 2.1 at **[6097]**).

[3.40 Receiver to deal with prescribed part

Where Rule 3.39 applies—

(a) the receiver may present a petition for the winding up of the company if the ground of the petition is that in section 122(1)(f);

(b) where a liquidator or administrator has been appointed to the company, the receiver shall deliver up the sums representing the prescribed part to him;

(c) in any other case, the receiver shall apply to the court for directions as to the manner in which he is to discharge his duty under section 176A(2)(a) and shall act in accordance with such directions as are given by the court.]

[6198B]

NOTES

Added as noted to r 3.39 at **[6198A]**.

PART 4
COMPANIES WINDING UP

CHAPTER 1
THE SCHEME OF THIS PART OF THE RULES

4.1 Voluntary winding up; winding up by the court

[(1) In a member's voluntary winding up, the Rules in this Part do not apply, except as follows—

(a) Rule 4.3 applies in the same way as it applies in a creditor's voluntary winding up;

(b) Rule 4.72 (additional provisions concerning meetings in relation to [the Financial Services Authority] and [the scheme manager]) applies in the winding up of [authorised deposit-takers or former authorised deposit-takers], whether members' or creditors' voluntary or by the court;

(c) Chapters 9 (proof of debts in a liquidation), 10 (secured creditors), 15 (disclaimer) and 18 (special manager) apply wherever, and in the same way as, they apply in a creditors' voluntary winding up;

(d) Section F of Chapter 11 (the liquidation) applies only in a members' voluntary winding up, and not otherwise;

(e) Section G of that Chapter (court's power to set aside certain transactions; rule against solicitation) applies in any winding up, whether members' or creditors' voluntary or by the court;

(f) Rule 4, 182A applies only in a members' voluntary winding up, and not otherwise; and

(g) Rule 4.223-CVL (liquidator's statements) applies in the same way as it applies in a creditors' voluntary winding up.]

(2) Subject as follows, the Rules in this Part apply both in a creditors' voluntary winding up and in a winding up by the court; and for this purpose a winding up is treated as a creditors' voluntary [winding up] if, and from the time when, the liquidator forms the opinion that the company will be unable to pay its debts in full, and determines accordingly to summon a creditors' meeting under section 95.

(3) The following Chapters, or Sections of Chapters, of this Part do not apply in a creditors' voluntary winding up—

Chapter 2—The statutory demand;

Chapter 3—Petition to winding-up order;
Chapter 4—Petition by contributories;
Chapter 5—Provisional liquidator;
[Chapter 11 (Section F)—The Liquidator in a members' voluntary winding up;]
Chapter 13—The liquidation committee where winding up follows immediately on administration;
Chapter 16—Settlement of list of contributories;
Chapter 17—Calls;
Chapter 19—Public examination of company officers and others; and
Chapter 21 (Section A)—Return of capital.
[Chapter 21 (Section C)—Dissolution after winding up

(4) Where at the head of any Rule, or at the end of any paragraph of a Rule, there appear the words "(NO CVL APPLICATION)", this signifies that the Rule or, as the case may be, the paragraph does not apply in a creditors' voluntary winding up.

However, this does not affect the court's power to make orders under section 112 (exercise in relation to voluntary winding up of powers available in winding up by the court).

(5) Where to any Rule or paragraph there is given a number incorporating the letters "CVL", that signifies that the Rule or (as the case may be) the paragraph applies in a creditors' voluntary winding up, and not in a winding up by the court.

[(6) In a voluntary winding up which is commenced by the registration of a notice under paragraph 83(3) of Schedule B1 to the Act, the following provisions of this Part shall not apply—

Rules 4.34, 4.38, 4.49, 4.51, 4.53, 4.62, 4.101, 4.103, 4.106, 4.152, 4.153, 4.206–4.210.]

[6199]

NOTES

Para (1): substituted by the Insolvency (Amendment) Rules 1987, SI 1987/1919, r 3(1), Schedule, Pt 1, para 34(1), as from 11 January 1988; words in first pair of square brackets in sub-para (b) substituted by the Bank of England Act 1998 (Consequential Amendments of Subordinate Legislation) Order 1998, SI 1998/1129, art 2, Sch 1, para 4(1), (2), as from 1 June 1998; words in second and third pairs of square brackets in sub-para (b) substituted by the Financial Services and Markets Act 2000 (Consequential Amendments and Repeals) Order 2001, SI 2001/3649, arts 377(1), (3), 378(1), as from 1 December 2001.

Paras (2), (3): words in square brackets inserted by SI 1987/1919, r 3(1), Schedule, Pt 1, para 34(2), (3), as from 11 January 1988.

Para (6): added by the Insolvency (Amendment) Rules 2003, SI 2003/1730, r 7, Sch 1, Pt 4, para 12, as from 15 September 2003 (for transitional provisions and savings see the note preceding r 2.1 at **[6097]**).

4.2 Winding up by the court: the various forms of petition [(NO CVL APPLICATION)]

(1) Insofar as the Rules in this Part apply to winding up by the court, they apply (subject as follows) whether the petition for winding up is presented under any of the several paragraphs of section 122(1), namely—

paragraph (a)—company special resolution for winding up by the court;
paragraph (b)—public company without certificate under section 117 of the Companies Act;
paragraph (c)—old public company;
paragraph (d)—company not commencing business after formation, or suspending business;
paragraph (e)—number of company's members reduced below 2;
paragraph (f)—company unable to pay its debts;
[paragraph (fa)—end of moratorium without approval of voluntary arrangement;]
paragraph (g)—court's power under the "just and equitable" rule,

or under any enactment enabling the presentation of a winding-up petition.

(2) Except as provided by the following two paragraphs or by any particular Rule, the Rules apply whether the petition for winding up is presented by the company, the directors, one or more creditors, one or more contributories, the Secretary of State, the official receiver, or any person entitled under any enactment to present such a petition.

(3) Chapter 2 (statutory demand) has no application except in relation to an unpaid creditor of the company satisfying section 123(1)(a) (the first of the two cases specified, in

relation to England and Wales, of the company being deemed unable to pay its debts within section 122(1)(f)) or section 222(1) (the equivalent provision in relation to unregistered companies).

(4) Chapter 3 (petition to winding-up order) has no application to a petition for winding up presented by one or more contributories; and in relation to a petition so presented Chapter 4 has effect.

[6200]

NOTES

Rule heading: words in square brackets added by the Insolvency (Amendment) Rules 1987, SI 1987/1919, r 3(1), Schedule, Pt 1, para 35, as from 11 January 1988.

Para (1): words in square brackets inserted by the Insolvency (Amendment) (No 2) Rules 2002, SI 2002/2712, r 4(1), Schedule, Part 2, para 22, as from 1 January 2003, subject to transitional provisions as noted below.

Transitional provisions: SI 2002/2712, r 4(2) provides as follows (note that by virtue of r 1, "the commencement date" is 1 January 2003)—

"(2) The amendments to Part 4 of the principal Rules set out in Part 2 of the Schedule do not apply in relation to—

(a) a winding up by the court where the petition on which the winding-up order was made was presented prior to the commencement date; or

(b) a voluntary winding up where the resolution for winding up was passed prior to the commencement date;

and Part 4 of the principal Rules without the amendments made in Part 2 of the Schedule to these Rules shall continue to apply in such cases.".

4.3 Time-limits

Where by any provision of the Act or the Rules about winding up, the time for doing anything is limited, the court may extend the time, either before or after it has expired, on such terms, if any, as it thinks fit.

[6201]

CHAPTER 2
THE STATUTORY DEMAND

(NO CVL APPLICATION)

4.4 Preliminary

(1) This Chapter does not apply where a petition for the winding up of a company is presented under section 124 on or after the date on which the Rules come into force and the petition is based on failure to comply with a written demand served on the company before that date.

(2) A written demand served by a creditor on a company under section 123(1)(a) (registered companies) or 222(1)(a) (unregistered companies) is known in winding-up proceedings as "the statutory demand".

(3) The statutory demand must be dated, and be signed either by the creditor himself or by a person stating himself to be authorised to make the demand on the creditor's behalf.

[6202]

4.5 Form and content of statutory demand

(1) The statutory demand must state the amount of the debt and the consideration for it (or, if there is no consideration, the way in which it arises).

(2) If the amount claimed in the demand includes—

(a) any charge by way of interest not previously notified to the company as included in its liability, or

(b) any other charge accruing from time to time,

the amount or rate of the charge must be separately identified, and the grounds on which payment of it is claimed must be stated.

In either case the amount claimed must be limited to that which has accrued due at the date of the demand.

[6203]

NOTES

Para (1): see Form 4.1 in Appendix 4 at **[A4]**.

4.6 Information to be given in statutory demand

(1) The statutory demand must include an explanation to the company of the following matters—

- (a) the purpose of the demand, and the fact that, if the demand is not complied with, proceedings may be instituted for the winding up of the company;
- (b) the time within which it must be complied with, if that consequence is to be avoided; and
- (c) the methods of compliance which are open to the company.

(2) Information must be provided for the company as to how an officer or representative of it may enter into communication with one or more named individuals, with a view to securing or compounding for the debt to the creditor's satisfaction.

In the case of any individual so named in the demand, his address and telephone number (if any) must be given.

[6204]

CHAPTER 3
PETITION TO WINDING-UP ORDER

(NO CVL APPLICATION)

(*No Application to Petition by Contributories*)

4.7 Presentation and filing of petition

(1) The petition, verified by affidavit in accordance with Rule 4.12 below, shall be filed in court.

[(2) No petition shall be filed unless there is produced on presentation of the petition a receipt for the deposit payable or paragraph (2A) applies.

(2A) This paragraph applies in any case where the Secretary of State has given written notice to the court that the petitioner has made suitable alternative arrangements for the payment of the deposit to the official receiver and such notice has not been revoked in relation to the petitioner in accordance with paragraph (2B).

(2B) A notice of the kind referred to in paragraph (2A) may be revoked in relation to the petitioner in whose favour it is given by a further notice in writing to the court stating that the earlier notice is revoked in relation to the petitioner.]

(3) If the petitioner is other than the company itself, there shall be delivered with the petition—

- (a) one copy for service on the company, and
- (b) one copy to be exhibited to the affidavit verifying service.

(4) There shall in any case be delivered with the petition—

- (a) if the company is in course of being wound up voluntarily, and a liquidator has been appointed, one copy of the petition to be sent to him;
- (b) [if the company is in administration], one copy […] to be sent to the administrator;
- (c) if an administrative receiver has been appointed in relation to the company, one copy to be sent to him;
- (d) if there is in force for the company a voluntary arrangement under Part I of the Act, one copy for the supervisor of the arrangement; …
- [(da) if a member State liquidator has been appointed in main proceedings in relation to the company, one copy to be sent to him; and]
- (e) if the company is [an authorised deposit-taker or a former authorised deposit-taker], and the petitioner is not the [Financial Services Authority], one copy to be sent to the [Authority].

(5) Each of the copies delivered shall have applied to it the seal of the court, and shall be issued to the petitioner.

(6) The court shall fix a venue for the hearing of the petition; and this shall be endorsed on any copy issued to the petitioner under paragraph (5).

[(7) Where a petition is filed at the instance of a company's administrator the petition shall—

(a) be expressed to be the petition of the company by its administrator,

(b) state the name of the administrator, [the court case number and the date that the company entered administration], and

[(c) where applicable, contain an application under paragraph 79 of Schedule B1, requesting that the appointment of the administrator shall cease to have effect.]

[(8) Any petition filed in relation to a company in respect of which there is in force a voluntary arrangement under Part I of the Act or which is in administration shall be presented to the court to which the nominee's report under section 2 was submitted or the court having jurisdiction for the administration.]

(9) Any petition such as is mentioned in paragraph (7) above or presented by the supervisor of a voluntary arrangement under Part I of the Act in force for the company shall be treated as if it were a petition filed by contributories, and Chapter 4 in this Part of the Rules shall apply accordingly.

(10) Where a petition contains a request for the appointment of a person as liquidator in accordance with section 140 (appointment of former administrator or supervisor as liquidator) the person whose appointment is sought shall, not less than 2 days before the return day for the petition, file in court a report including particulars of—

(a) a date on which he notified creditors of the company, either in writing or at a meeting of creditors, of the intention to seek his appointment as liquidator, such date to be at least 10 days before the day on which the report under this paragraph is filed, and

(b) details of any response from creditors to that notification, including any objections to his appointment.]

[6205]

NOTES

Paras (2), (2A), (2B): substituted, for original para (2), by the Insolvency (Amendment) Rules 2004, SI 2004/584, r 8(a), as from 1 April 2004.

Para (4): words in first pair of square brackets in sub-para (b) substituted by the Insolvency (Amendment) Rules 2003, SI 2003/1730, r 7, Sch 1, Pt 4, para 13(a), as from 15 September 2003 (for transitional provisions and savings see the note preceding r 2.1 at **[6097]**); words omitted from sub-para (b) originally inserted by SI 2003/1730, r 7, Sch 1, Pt 4, para 13(a), as from 15 September 2003, and revoked by SI 2004/584, r 8(b), as from 1 April 2004; word omitted from sub-para (d) revoked, and sub-para (da) inserted, by the Insolvency (Amendment) Rules 2002, SI 2002/1307, rr 3, 6(1), as from 31 May 2002, with savings in relation to anything done under, or for the purposes of, this provision before that date; words in first pair of square brackets in sub-para (e) substituted by the Financial Services and Markets Act 2000 (Consequential Amendments and Repeals) Order 2001, SI 2001/3649, art 377(1), (4), as from 1 December 2001; words in second and third pairs of square brackets in sub-para (e) substituted by the Bank of England Act 1998 (Consequential Amendments of Subordinate Legislation) Order 1998, SI 1998/1129, art 2, Sch 1, para 4(1), (3), as from 1 June 1998.

Para (7): added, together with paras (8)–(10), by the Insolvency (Amendment) Rules 1987, SI 1987/1919, r 3(1), Schedule, Pt 1, para 36(2), as from 11 January 1988; words in square brackets in sub-para (b) substituted by SI 2003/1730, r 7, Sch 1, Pt 4, para 13(b), as from 15 September 2003 (for transitional provisions and savings see the note preceding r 2.1 at **[6097]**); para (c) substituted by the Insolvency (Amendment) Rules 2005, SI 2005/527, r 18, as from 1 April 2005.

Para (8): added as noted above; substituted by SI 2003/1730, r 7, Sch 1, Pt 4, para 13(d), as from 15 September 2003 (for transitional provisions and savings see the note preceding r 2.1 at **[6097]**).

Paras (9), (10): added as noted above.

Para (1): see Form 4.2 in Appendix 4 at **[A4]**.

4.8 Service of petition

(1) The following paragraphs apply as regards service of the petition on the company (where the petitioner is other than the company itself); and references to the petition are to a copy of the petition bearing the seal of the court in which it is presented.

(2) Subject as follows, the petition shall be served at the company's registered office, that is to say—

(a) the place which is specified, in the company's statement delivered under section 10 of the Companies Act as the intended situation of its registered office on incorporation, or

(b) if notice has been given by the company to the registrar of companies under section 287 of that Act (change of registered office), the place specified in that notice or, as the case may be, in the last such notice.

(3) Service of the petition at the registered office may be effected in any of the following ways—

(a) it may be handed to a person who there and then acknowledges himself to be, or to the best of the server's knowledge, information and belief is, a director or other officer, or employee, of the company; or

(b) it may be handed to a person who there and then acknowledges himself to be authorised to accept service of documents on the company's behalf; or

(c) in the absence of any such person as is mentioned in sub-paragraph (a) or (b), it may be deposited at or about the registered office in such a way that it is likely to come to the notice of a person attending at the office.

[(4) If for any reason service at the registered office is not practicable, or the company has no registered office or is an unregistered company, the petition may be served on the company by leaving it at the company's last known principal place of business in such a way that it is likely to come to the attention of a person attending there, or by delivering it to the secretary or some director, manager or principal officer of the company, wherever that person may be found.]

(5) In the case of an oversea company, service may be effected in any manner provided for by section 695 of the Companies Act.

(6) If for any reason it is impracticable to effect service as provided by paragraphs (2) to (5), the petition may be served in such other manner as the court may [approve or] direct.

(7) Application for leave of the court under paragraph (6) may be made *ex parte*, on affidavit stating what steps have been taken to comply with paragraphs (2) to (5), and the reasons why it is impracticable to effect service as there provided.

[6206]

NOTES

Para (4): substituted by the Insolvency (Amendment) Rules 1987, SI 1987/1919, r 3(1), Schedule, Pt 1, para 37(1), as from 11 January 1988.

Para (6): words in square brackets inserted by SI 1987/1919, r 3(1), Schedule, Pt 1, para 37(2), as from 11 January 1988.

4.9 Proof of service

(1) Service of the petition shall be proved by affidavit, specifying the manner of service.

(2) The affidavit shall have exhibited to it—

(a) a sealed copy of the petition, and

(b) if substituted service has been ordered, a sealed copy of the order;

and it shall be filed in court immediately after service.

[6207]

NOTES

Para (1): see Forms 4.4, 4.5 in Appendix 4 at **[A4]**.

4.10 Other persons to receive copies of petition

(1) If to the petitioner's knowledge the company is in course of being wound up voluntarily, a copy of the petition shall be sent by him to the liquidator.

(2) If to the petitioner's knowledge an administrative receiver has been appointed in relation to the company, or [the company is in administration], a copy of the petition shall be sent by him to the receiver or, as the case may be, the administrator.

(3) If to the petitioner's knowledge there is in force for the company a voluntary arrangement under Part I of the Act, a copy of the petition shall be sent by him to the supervisor of the voluntary arrangement.

[(3A) If to the petitioner's knowledge, there is a member State liquidator appointed in main proceedings in relation to the company, a copy of the petition shall be sent by him to that person.

This does not apply if the petitioner referred to in this paragraph is a member State liquidator.]

(4) If the company is [an authorised institution or former authorised institution within the meaning of the Banking Act 1987], a copy of the petition shall be sent by the petitioner to the [Financial Services Authority].

This does not apply if the petitioner is the [Financial Services Authority] itself.

(5) A copy of the petition which is required by this Rule to be sent shall be despatched on the next business day after the day on which the petition is served on the company.

[6208]

NOTES

Para (2): words in square brackets substituted by the Insolvency (Amendment) Rules 2003, SI 2003/1730, r 7, Sch 1, Pt 4, para 14, as from 15 September 2003 (for transitional provisions and savings see the note preceding r 2.1 at **[6097]**).

Para (3A): inserted by the Insolvency (Amendment) Rules 2002, SI 2002/1307, rr 3, 6(2), as from 31 May 2002, with savings in relation to anything done under, or for the purposes of, this provision before that date.

Para (4): words in first pair of square brackets substituted by the Insolvency (Amendment) Rules 1987, SI 1987/1919, r 3(1), Schedule, Pt 1, para 38, as from 11 January 1988; words in second and third pairs of square brackets substituted by the Bank of England Act 1998 (Consequential Amendments of Subordinate Legislation) Order 1998, SI 1998/1129, art 2, Sch 1, para 4(1), (4), as from 1 June 1998.

Banking Act 1987: repealed by the Financial Services and Markets Act 2000 (Consequential Amendments and Repeals) Order 2001, SI 2001/3649, art 3(1)(d), as from 1 December 2001.

4.11 Advertisement of petition

(1) Unless the court otherwise directs, the petition shall be advertised once in the Gazette.

(2) The advertisement must be made to appear—

(a) if the petitioner is the company itself, not less than 7 business days before the day appointed for the hearing, and

(b) otherwise, not less than 7 business days after service of the petition on the company, nor less than 7 business days before the day so appointed.

(3) The court may, if compliance with paragraph (2) is not reasonably practicable, direct that advertisement of the petition be made to appear in a specified … newspaper, instead of in the Gazette.

(4) The advertisement of the petition must state—

(a) the name [and registered number] of the company and the address of its registered office, or—

(i) in the case of an unregistered company, the address of its principal place of business;

(ii) in the case of an oversea company, the address at which service of the petition was effected;

(b) the name and address of the petitioner;

(c) where the petitioner is the company itself, the address of its registered office or, in the case of an unregistered company, of its principal place of business;

(d) the date on which the petition was presented;

(e) the venue fixed for the hearing of the petition;

(f) the name and address of the petitioner's solicitor (if any); and

(g) that any person intending to appear at the hearing (whether to support or oppose the petition) must give notice of his intention in accordance with Rule 4.16.

(5) If the petition is not duly advertised in accordance with this Rule, the court may dismiss it.

[6209]

NOTES

Para (3): words omitted revoked by the Insolvency (Amendment) Rules 1991, SI 1991/495, r 3, Schedule, para 1, as from 2 April 1991.

Para (4): words in square brackets inserted by the Insolvency (Amendment) Rules 2005, SI 2005/527, r 19, as from 1 April 2005.

Para (1): see Form 4.6 in Appendix 4 at **[A4]**.

4.12 Verification of petition

(1) The petition shall be verified by an affidavit that the statements in the petition are true, or are true to the best of the deponent's knowledge, information and belief.

(2) If the petition is in respect of debts due to different creditors, the debts to each creditor must be separately verified.

(3) The petition shall be exhibited to the affidavit verifying it.

(4) The affidavit shall be made—

(a) by the petitioner (or if there are two or more petitioners, any one of them), or

(b) by some person such as a director, company secretary or similar company officer, or a solicitor, who has been concerned in the matters giving rise to the presentation of the petition, or

(c) by some responsible person who is duly authorised to make the affidavit and has the requisite knowledge of those matters.

(5) Where the deponent is not the petitioner himself, or one of the petitioners, he must in the affidavit identify himself and state—

(a) the capacity in which, and the authority by which, he makes it, and

(b) the means of his knowledge of the matters sworn to in the affidavit.

(6) The affidavit is prima facie evidence of the statements in the petition to which it relates.

(7) An affidavit verifying more than one petition shall include in its title the names of the companies to which it relates and shall set out, in respect of each company, the statements relied on by the petitioner; and a clear and legible photocopy of the affidavit shall be filed with each petition which it verifies.

[(8) The affidavit shall state whether, in the opinion of the person making the application, (i) the EC Regulation will apply and (ii) if so, whether the proceedings will be main proceedings or territorial proceedings.]

[6210]

NOTES

Para (8): added by the Insolvency (Amendment) Rules 2005, SI 2005/527, r 20, as from 1 April 2005.
EC Regulation: ie, Council Regulation 1346/2000/EC on insolvency proceedings at **[9290]**.
Para (1): see Form 4.2 in Appendix 4 at **[A4]**.

4.13 Persons entitled to copy of petition

Every director, contributory or creditor of the company is entitled to be furnished by the solicitor for the petitioner (or by the petitioner himself, if acting in person) with a copy of the petition within 2 days after requiring it, on payment of the appropriate fee.

[6211]

4.14 Certificate of compliance

(1) The petitioner or his solicitor shall, at least 5 days before the hearing of the petition, file in court a certificate of compliance with the Rules relating to service and advertisement.

(2) The certificate shall show—

(a) the date of presentation of the petition,

(b) the date fixed for the hearing, and

(c) the date or dates on which the petition was served and advertised in compliance with the Rules.

A copy of the advertisement of the petition shall be filed in court with the certificate.

(3) Non-compliance with this Rule is a ground on which the court may, if it thinks fit, dismiss the petition.

[6212]

NOTES

Para (1): see Form 4.7 in Appendix 4 at **[A4]**.

4.15 Leave for petitioner to withdraw

If at least 5 days before the hearing the petitioner, on an *ex parte* application, satisfies the court that—

(a) the petition has not been advertised, and

(b) no notices (whether in support or in opposition) have been received by him with reference to the petition, and

(c) the company consents to an order being made under this Rule,

the court may order that the petitioner has leave to withdraw the petition on such terms as to costs as the parties may agree.

[6213]

NOTES

See Form 4.8 in Appendix 4 at **[A4]**.

4.16 Notice of appearance

(1) Every person who intends to appear on the hearing of the petition shall give to the petitioner notice of his intention in accordance with this Rule.

(2) The notice shall specify—

(a) the name and address of the person giving it, and any telephone number and reference which may be required for communication with him or with any other person (to be also specified in the notice) authorised to speak or act on his behalf;

(b) whether his intention is to support or oppose the petition; and

(c) the amount and nature of his debt.

(3) The notice shall be sent to the petitioner at the address shown for him in the court records, or in the advertisement of the petition required by Rule 4.11; or it may be sent to his solicitor.

(4) The notice shall be sent so as to reach the addressee not later than 16.00 hours on the business day before that which is appointed for the hearing (or, where the hearing has been adjourned, for the adjourned hearing).

(5) A person failing to comply with this Rule may appear on the hearing of the petition only with the leave of the court.

[6214]

NOTES

Para (1): see Form 4.9 in Appendix 4 at **[A4]**.

4.17 List of appearances

(1) The petitioner shall prepare for the court a list of the persons (if any) who have given notice under Rule 4.16, specifying their names and addresses and (if known to him) their respective solicitors.

(2) Against the name of each creditor in the list it shall be stated whether his intention is to support the petition, or to oppose it.

(3) On the day appointed for the hearing of the petition, a copy of the list shall be handed to the court before the commencement of the hearing.

(4) If any leave is given under Rule 4.16(5), the petitioner shall add to the list the same particulars in respect of the person to whom leave has been given.

[6215]

NOTES

Para (1): see Form 4.10 in Appendix 4 at **[A4]**.

4.18 Affidavit in opposition

(1) If the company intends to oppose the petition, its affidavit in opposition shall be filed in court not less than 7 days before the date fixed for the hearing.

(2) A copy of the affidavit shall be sent by the company to the petitioner, forthwith after filing.

[6216]

4.19 Substitution of creditor or contributory for petitioner

(1) This Rule applies where a person petitions and is subsequently found not entitled to do so, or where the petitioner—

(a) fails to advertise his petition within the time prescribed by the Rules or such extended time as the court may allow, or

(b) consents to withdraw his petition, or to allow it to be dismissed, consents to an adjournment, or fails to appear in support of his petition when it is called on in court on the day originally fixed for the hearing, or on a day to which it is adjourned, or

(c) appears, but does not apply for an order in the terms of the prayer of his petition.

(2) The court may, on such terms as it thinks just, substitute as petitioner any creditor or contributory who in its opinion would have a right to present a petition, and who is desirous of prosecuting it.

[(2A) Where a member State liquidator has been appointed in main proceedings in relation to the company, without prejudice to paragraph (2), the court may, on such terms as it thinks just, substitute the member State liquidator as petitioner, where he is desirous of prosecuting the petition.]

(3) An order of the court under this Rule may, where a petitioner fails to advertise his petition within the time prescribed by these Rules, or consents to withdraw his petition, be made at any time.

[6217]

NOTES

Para (2A): inserted by the Insolvency (Amendment) Rules 2002, SI 2002/1307, rr 3, 6(3), as from 31 May 2002, with savings in relation to anything done under, or for the purposes of, this provision before that date.

4.20 Notice and settling of winding-up order

(1) When a winding-up order has been made, the court shall forthwith give notice of the fact to the official receiver.

(2) The petitioner and every other person who has appeared on the hearing of the petition shall, not later than the business day following that on which the order is made, leave at the court all the documents required for enabling the order to be completed forthwith.

(3) It is not necessary for the court to appoint a venue for any person to attend to settle the order, unless in any particular case the special circumstances make an appointment necessary.

[6218]

NOTES

Para (1): see Forms 4.11, 4.12, 4.13 in Appendix 4 at **[A4]**.

4.21 Transmission and advertisement of order

(1) When the winding-up order has been made, 3 copies of it, sealed with the seal of the court, shall be sent forthwith by the court to the official receiver.

(2) The official receiver shall cause a sealed copy of the order to be served on the company by prepaid letter addressed to it at its registered office (if any) or, if there is no registered office, at its principal or last known principal place of business.

Alternatively, the order may be served on such other person or persons, or in such other manner, as the court directs.

(3) The official receiver shall forward to the registrar of companies the copy of the order which by section 130(1) is directed to be so forwarded by the company.

(4) The official receiver shall forthwith—

(a) cause the order to be gazetted, and

(b) advertise the order in such … newspaper as the official receiver may select.

[6219]

NOTES

Para (4): word omitted from sub-para (b) revoked by the Insolvency (Amendment) Rules 1991, SI 1991/495, r 3, Schedule, para 2, as from 2 April 1991.

[4.21A Expenses of voluntary arrangement

Where a winding-up order is made and there is at the time of the presentation of the petition in force for the company a voluntary arrangement under Part I of the Act, any expenses properly incurred as expenses of the administration of the arrangement in question shall be a first charge on the company's assets.

[6220]

NOTES

Inserted by the Insolvency (Amendment) Rules 1987, SI 1987/1919, r 3(1), Schedule, Pt 1, para 39, as from 11 January 1988.

CHAPTER 4
PETITION BY CONTRIBUTORIES

(NO CVL APPLICATION)

4.22 Presentation and service of petition

(1) The petition shall specify the grounds on which it is presented … , and shall be filed in court with one copy for service under this Rule.

[(1A) No petition shall be filed unless there is produced with it the receipt for the deposit payable on presentation.]

(2) The court shall fix a hearing for a day ("the return day") on which, unless the court otherwise directs, the petitioner and the company shall attend before the registrar in chambers for directions to be given in relation to the procedure on the petition.

(3) On fixing the return day, the court shall return to the petitioner a sealed copy of the petition for service, endorsed with the return day and time of hearing.

(4) The petitioner shall, at least 14 days before the return day, serve a sealed copy of the petition on the company.

[(5) Where a member State liquidator has been appointed in main proceedings in relation to the company, the petitioner shall send a copy of the petition to him.]

[6221]

NOTES

Para (1): words omitted revoked by the Insolvency (Amendment) Rules 1987, SI 1987/1919, r 3(1), Schedule, Pt 1, para 40(1), as from 11 January 1988.

Para (1A): inserted by SI 1987/1919, r 3(1), Schedule, Pt 1, para 40(2), as from 11 January 1988.

Para (5): added by the Insolvency (Amendment) Rules 2002, SI 2002/1307, rr 3, 6(4), as from 31 May 2002, with savings in relation to anything done under, or for the purposes of, this provision before that date.

See Form 4.14 in Appendix 4 at **[A4]**.

4.23 Return of petition

(1) On the return day, or at any time after it, the court shall give such directions as it thinks appropriate with respect to the following matters—

- (a) service of the petition, whether in connection with the venue for a further hearing, or for any other purpose;
- (b) whether particulars of claim and defence are to be delivered, and generally as to the procedure on the petition;
- (c) whether, and if so by what means, the petition is to be advertised;
- (d) the manner in which any evidence is to be adduced at any hearing before the judge and in particular (but without prejudice to the generality of the above) as to—

(i) the taking of evidence wholly or in part by affidavit or orally;
(ii) the cross-examination of any deponents to affidavits;
(iii) the matters to be dealt with in evidence;

(e) any other matter affecting the procedure on the petition or in connection with the hearing and disposal of the petition.

(2) In giving directions under paragraph (1)(a), the court shall have regard to whether any of the persons specified in Rule 4.10 should be served with a copy of the petition.

[6222]

4.24 Application of Rules in Chapter 3

The following Rules in Chapter 3 apply, with the necessary modifications—

Rule 4.16 (notice of appearance);
Rule 4.17 (list of appearances);
Rule 4.20 (notice and settling of winding-up order); …
Rule 4.21 (transmission and advertisement of order)[; and
Rule 4.21A (expenses of voluntary arrangement)].

[6223]

NOTES

Words omitted revoked, and words in square brackets added, by the Insolvency (Amendment) Rules 1987, SI 1987/1919, r 3(1), Schedule, Pt 1, para 41, as from 11 January 1988.

CHAPTER 5
PROVISIONAL LIQUIDATOR

(NO CVL APPLICATION)

4.25 Appointment of provisional liquidator

[(1) An application to the court for the appointment of a provisional liquidator under section 135 may be made by—

(a) the petitioner;
(b) a creditor of the company;
(c) a contributory;
(d) the company;
(e) the Secretary of State;
(f) a temporary administrator;
(g) a member State liquidator appointed in main proceedings; or
(h) any person who under any enactment would be entitled to present a petition for the winding up of the company.]

(2) The application must be supported by an affidavit stating—

(a) the grounds on which it is proposed that a provisional liquidator should be appointed;
(b) if some person other than the official receiver is proposed to be appointed, that the person has consented to act and, to the best of the applicant's belief, is qualified to act as an insolvency practitioner in relation to the company;
(c) whether or not the official receiver has been informed of the application and, if so, has been furnished with a copy of it;
(d) whether to the applicant's knowledge—
    (i) there has been proposed or is in force for the company a voluntary arrangement under Part I of the Act, or
    (ii) an administrator or administrative receiver is acting in relation to the company, or
    (iii) a liquidator has been appointed for its voluntary winding up; and
(e) the applicant's estimate of the value of the assets in respect of which the provisional liquidator is to be appointed.

(3) The applicant shall send copies of the application and of the affidavit in support to the official receiver, who may attend the hearing and make any representations which he thinks appropriate.

If for any reason it is not practicable to comply with this paragraph, the official receiver must be informed of the application in sufficient time for him to be able to attend.

(4) The court may on the application, if satisfied that sufficient grounds are shown for the appointment, make it on such terms as it thinks fit.

[6224]

NOTES

Para (1): substituted by the Insolvency (Amendment) Rules 2002, SI 2002/1307, rr 3, 6(5), as from 31 May 2002, with savings in relation to anything done under, or for the purposes of, this provision before that date.

[4.25A Notice of appointment

(1) Where a provisional liquidator has been appointed the court shall forthwith give notice of the fact to the official receiver.

(2) A copy of that notice shall at the same time be sent by the court to the provisional liquidator where he is not the official receiver.]

[6225]

NOTES

Inserted by the Insolvency (Amendment) Rules 1987, SI 1987/1919, r 3(1), Schedule, Pt 1, para 42, as from 11 January 1988.

Para (1): see Form 4.14A in Appendix 4 at **[A4]**.

4.26 Order of appointment

(1) The order appointing the provisional liquidator shall specify the functions to be carried out by him in relation to the company's affairs.

(2) The court shall, forthwith after the order is made, send sealed copies of the order as follows—

(a) if the official receiver is appointed, [three] copies to him;

(b) if a person other than the official receiver is appointed—

(i) [three] copies of that person, and

(ii) one copy to the official receiver;

(c) if there is an administrative receiver acting in relation to the company, one copy to him.

[(3) Of the three copies of the order sent to the official receiver under paragraph (2)(a), or to another person under paragraph (2)(b)(i)—

(i) one shall in each case be sent by the recipient to the company, or if a liquidator has been appointed for the company's voluntary winding-up, to him; and

(ii) one shall be sent with Form 4.15A to the registrar of companies.]

[6226]

NOTES

Para (2): words in square brackets substituted by the Insolvency (Amendment) Rules 2005, SI 2005/527, r 21(a), as from 1 April 2005.

Para (3): substituted by SI 2005/527, r 21(b), as from 1 April 2005.

Para (1): see Form 4.15 in Appendix 4 at **[A4]**.

4.27 Deposit

(1) Before an order appointing the official receiver as provisional liquidator is issued, the applicant for it shall deposit with him, or otherwise secure to his satisfaction, such sum as the court directs to cover the official receiver's remuneration and expenses.

(2) If the sum deposited or secured subsequently proves to be insufficient, the court may, on application by the official receiver, order that an additional sum be deposited or secured. If the order is not complied with within 2 days after service of it on the person to whom it is directed, the court may discharge the order appointing the provisional liquidator.

(3) If a winding-up order is made after a provisional liquidator has been appointed, any money deposited under this Rule shall (unless it is required by reason of insufficiency of assets for payment of remuneration and expenses of the provisional liquidator) be repaid to the person depositing it (or as that person may direct) out of the assets, in the prescribed order of priority.

[6227]

4.28 Security

(1) The following applies where an insolvency practitioner is appointed to be provisional liquidator under section 135.

(2) The cost of providing the security required under the Act shall be paid in the first instance by the provisional liquidator; but—

(a) if a winding-up order is not made, the person so appointed is entitled to be reimbursed out of the property of the company, and the court may make an order on the company accordingly, and

(b) if a winding-up order is made, he is entitled to be reimbursed out of the assets in the prescribed order of priority.

[6228]

4.29 Failure to give or keep up security

(1) If the provisional liquidator fails to give or keep up his security, the court may remove him, and make such order as it thinks fit as to costs.

(2) If an order is made under this Rule removing the provisional liquidator, or discharging the order appointing him, the court shall give directions as to whether any, and if so what, steps should be taken for the appointment of another person in his place.

[6229]

4.30 Remuneration

(1) The remuneration of the provisional liquidator (other than the official receiver) shall be fixed by the court from time to time on his application.

(2) In fixing his remuneration, the court shall take into account—

(a) the time properly given by him (as provisional liquidator) and his staff in attending to the company's affairs;

(b) the complexity (or otherwise) of the case;

(c) any respects in which, in connection with the company's affairs, there falls on the provisional liquidator any responsibility of an exceptional kind or degree;

(d) the effectiveness with which the provisional liquidator appears to be carrying out, or to have carried out, his duties; and

(e) the value and nature of the property with which he has to deal.

(3) [Without prejudice to any order the court may make as to costs, the provisional liquidator's remuneration (whether the official receiver or another) shall be paid to him, and the amount of any expenses incurred by him (including the remuneration and expenses of any special manager appointed under section 177) reimbursed—

(a) if a winding-up order is not made, out of the property of the company], and

(b) if a winding-up order is made, out of the assets, in the prescribed order of priority,

or, in either case (the relevant funds being insufficient), out of the deposit under Rule 4.27.

[(3A) Unless the court otherwise directs, in a case falling within paragraph (3)(a) above the provisional liquidator may retain out of the company's property such sums or property as are or may be required for meeting his remuneration and expenses.]

(4) Where a person other than the official receiver has been appointed provisional liquidator, and the official receiver has taken any steps for the purpose of obtaining a statement of affairs or has performed any other duty under the Rules, he shall pay the official receiver such sum (if any) as the court may direct.

[6230]

NOTES

Para (3): words in square brackets substituted by the Insolvency (Amendment) Rules 1987, SI 1987/1919, r 3(1), Schedule, Pt 1, para 43(1), as from 11 January 1988.

Para (3A): inserted by SI 1987/1919, r 3(1), Schedule, Pt 1, para 43(2), as from 11 January 1988.

4.31 Termination of appointment

(1) The appointment of the provisional liquidator may be terminated by the court on his application, or on that of any of the persons specified in Rule 4.25(1).

(2) If the provisional liquidator's appointment terminates, in consequence of the dismissal of the winding-up petition or otherwise, the court may give such directions as it thinks fit with respect to the accounts of his administration or any other matters which it thinks appropriate.

(3) …

[6231]

NOTES

Para (3): revoked by the Insolvency (Amendment) Rules 1987, SI 1987/1919, r 3(1), Schedule, Pt 1, para 44, as from 11 January 1988.

CHAPTER 6
STATEMENT OF AFFAIRS AND OTHER INFORMATION

4.32 Notice requiring statement of affairs (NO CVL APPLICATION)

(1) The following applies where the official receiver determines to require a statement of the company's affairs to be made out and submitted to him in accordance with section 131.

(2) He shall send notice to each of the persons whom he considers should be made responsible under that section, requiring them to prepare and submit the statement.

(3) The persons to whom that notice is sent are referred to in this Chapter as "the deponents".

(4) The notice shall inform each of the deponents—

(a) of the names and addresses of all others (if any) to whom the same notice has been sent;

(b) of the time within which the statement must be delivered;

(c) of the effect of section 131(7) (penalty for non-compliance); and

(d) of the application to him, and to each of the other deponents, of section 235 (duty to provide information, and to attend on the official receiver if required).

(5) The official receiver shall, on request, furnish a deponent with instructions for the preparation of the statement and with the forms required for that purpose.

[6232]

NOTES

Para (1): see Form 4.16 in Appendix 4 at **[A4]**.

4.33 Verification and filing (NO CVL APPLICATION)

(1) The statement of affairs shall be in Form 4.17, shall contain all the particulars required by that form and shall be verified by affidavit by the deponents (using the same form).

(2) The official receiver may require any of the persons mentioned in section 131(3) to submit an affidavit of concurrence, stating that he concurs in the statement of affairs.

(3) An affidavit of concurrence made under paragraph (2) may be qualified in respect of matters dealt with in the statement of affairs, where the maker of the affidavit is not in agreement with the deponents, or he considers the statement to be erroneous or misleading, or he is without the direct knowledge necessary for concurring in the statement.

(4) The statement of affairs shall be delivered to the official receiver by the deponent making the affidavit of verification (or by one of them, if more than one), together with a copy of the verified statement.

(5) Every affidavit of concurrence shall be delivered to the official receiver by the person who makes it, together with a copy.

(6) The official receiver shall file the verified copy of the statement and the affidavits of concurrence (if any) in court.

(7) The affidavit may be sworn before an official receiver or a deputy official receiver, or before an officer of the Department or the court duly authorised in that behalf.

[6233]

NOTES

Para (1): as to Form 4.17, see Appendix 4 at **[A4]**.

4.34–CVL Statement of affairs

(1) This Rule applies with respect to the statement of affairs made out by the liquidator under section 95(3) or (as the case may be) by the directors under section 99(1).

(2) Where it is made out by the liquidator, the statement of affairs shall be delivered by him to the registrar of companies within 7 days after the creditors' meeting summoned under section 95(2).

[(3) Where it is made out by the directors under section 99(1) the statement of affairs shall be delivered by them to the liquidator in office following the creditors' meeting summoned under section 98 forthwith after that meeting has been held; and he shall, within 7 days, deliver it to the registrar of companies.

(4) A statement of affairs under section 99(1) may be made up to a date not more than 14 days before that on which the resolution for voluntary winding up is passed by the company.]

[6234]

NOTES

Paras (3), (4): substituted, for original para (3), by the Insolvency (Amendment) Rules 1987, SI 1987/1919, r 3(1), Schedule, Pt 1, para 45, as from 11 January 1988.

See Forms 4.18, 4.19, 4.20 in Appendix 4 at **[A4]**.

[4.34A–CVL Copy Statement of affairs

Where a liquidator is nominated by the company at a general meeting held on a day prior to that on which the creditors' meeting summoned under section 98 is held, the directors shall forthwith after his nomination or the making of the statement of affairs, whichever is the later, deliver to him a copy of the statement of affairs.]

[6235]

NOTES

Inserted by the Insolvency (Amendment) Rules 1987, SI 1987/1919, r 3(1), Schedule, Pt 1, para 46, as from 11 January 1988.

4.35 Limited disclosure (NO CVL APPLICATION)

(1) Where the official receiver thinks that it would prejudice the conduct of the liquidation for the whole or part of the statement of affairs to be disclosed, he may apply to the court for an order of limited disclosure in respect of the statement, or any specified part of it.

(2) The court may on the application order that the statement or, as the case may be, the specified part of it be not filed, or that it is to be filed separately and not be open to inspection otherwise than with leave of the court.

[6236]

4.36 Release from duty to submit statement of affairs; extension of time (NO CVL APPLICATION)

(1) The power of the official receiver under section 131(5) to give a release from the obligation imposed by that section, or to grant an extension of time, may be exercised at the official receiver's own discretion, or at the request of any deponent.

(2) A deponent may, if he requests a release or extension of time and it is refused by the official receiver, apply to the court for it.

(3) The court may, if it thinks that no sufficient cause is shown for the application, dismiss it; but it shall not do so unless the applicant has had an opportunity to attend the court for an *ex parte* hearing, of which he has been given at least 7 days' notice.

If the application is not dismissed under this paragraph, the court shall fix a venue for it to be heard, and give notice to the deponent accordingly.

(4) The deponent shall, at least 14 days before the hearing, send to the official receiver a notice stating the venue and accompanied by a copy of the application, and of any evidence which he (the deponent) intends to adduce in support of it.

(5) The official receiver may appear and be heard on the application; and, whether or not he appears, he may file a written report of any matters which he considers ought to be drawn to the court's attention.

If such a report is filed, a copy of it shall be sent by the official receiver to the deponent, not later than 5 days before the hearing.

(6) Sealed copies of any order made on the application shall be sent by the court to the deponent and the official receiver.

(7) On any application under this Rule the applicant's costs shall be paid in any event by him and, unless the court otherwise orders, no allowance towards them shall be made out of the assets.

[6237]

4.37 Expenses of statement of affairs (NO CVL APPLICATION)

(1) If any deponent cannot himself prepare a proper statement of affairs, the official receiver may, at the expense of the assets, employ some person or persons to assist in the preparation of the statement.

(2) At the request of any deponent, made on the grounds that he cannot himself prepare a proper statement, the official receiver may authorise an allowance, payable out of the assets, towards expenses to be incurred by the deponent in employing some person or persons to assist him in preparing it.

(3) Any such request by the deponent shall be accompanied by an estimate of the expenses involved; and the official receiver shall only authorise the employment of a named person or a named firm, being in either case approved by him.

(4) An authorisation given by the official receiver under this Rule shall be subject to such conditions (if any) as he thinks fit to impose with respect to the manner in which any person may obtain access to relevant books and papers.

(5) Nothing in this Rule relieves a deponent from any obligation with respect to the preparation, verification and submission of the statement of affairs, or to the provision of information to the official receiver or the liquidator.

(6) Any payment out of the assets under this Rule shall be made in the prescribed order of priority.

(7) Paragraphs (2) to (6) of this Rule may be applied, on application to the official receiver by any deponent, in relation to the making of an affidavit of concurrence.

[6238]

4.38–CVL Expenses of statements of affairs

(1) Payment may be made out of the company's assets, either before or after the commencement of the winding up, of any reasonable and necessary expenses of preparing the statement of affairs under section 99.

Any such payment is an expense of the liquidation.

(2) Where such a payment is made before the commencement of the winding up, the director presiding at the creditors' meeting held under section 98 shall inform the meeting of the amount of the payment and the identity of the person to whom it was made.

(3) The liquidator appointed under section 100 may make such a payment (subject to the next paragraph); but if there is a liquidation committee, he must give the committee at least 7 days' notice of his intention to make it.

(4) Such a payment shall not be made by the liquidator to himself, or to any associate of his, otherwise than with the approval of the liquidation committee, the creditors, or the court.

(5) This Rule is without prejudice to the powers of the court under Rule 4.219 (voluntary winding up superseded by winding up by the court).

[6239]

4.39 Submission of accounts (NO CVL APPLICATION)

(1) Any of the persons specified in section 235(3) shall, at the request of the official receiver, furnish him with accounts of the company of such nature, as at such date, and for such period, as he may specify.

(2) The period specified may begin from a date up to 3 years preceding the date of the presentation of the winding-up petition, or from an earlier date to which audited accounts of the company were last prepared.

(3) The court may, on the official receiver's application, require accounts for any earlier period.

(4) Rule 4.37 applies (with the necessary modifications) in relation to accounts to be furnished under this Rule as it applies in relation to the statement of affairs.

(5) The accounts shall, if the official receiver so requires, be verified by affidavit and (whether or not so verified) delivered to him within 21 days of the request under paragraph (1), or such longer period as he may allow.

(6) Two copies of the accounts and (where required) the affidavit shall be delivered to the official receiver by whoever is required to furnish them; and the official receiver shall file one copy in court (with the affidavit, if any).

[6240]

4.40–CVL Submission of accounts

(1) Any of the persons specified in section 235(3) shall, at the request of the liquidator, furnish him with accounts of the company of such nature, as at such date, and for such period, as he may specify.

(2) The specified period for the accounts may begin from a date up to 3 years preceding the date of the resolution for winding up, or from an earlier date to which audited accounts of the company were last prepared.

(3) The accounts shall, if the liquidator so requires, be verified by affidavit and (whether or not so verified) delivered to him, with the affidavit if required, within 21 days from the request under paragraph (1), or such longer period as he may allow.

[6241]

4.41–CVL Expenses of preparing accounts

(1) Where a person is required under Rule 4.40–CVL to furnish accounts, the liquidator may, with the sanction of the liquidation committee (if there is one) and at the expense of the assets, employ some person or persons to assist in the preparation of the accounts.

(2) At the request of the person subject to the requirement, the liquidator may, with that sanction, authorise an allowance, payable out of the assets, towards expenses to be incurred by that person in employing others to assist him in preparing the accounts.

(3) Any such request shall be accompanied by an estimate of the expenses involved; and the liquidator shall only authorise the employment of a named person or a named firm, being in either case approved by him.

[6242]

4.42 Further disclosure (NO CVL APPLICATION)

(1) The official receiver may at any time require the deponents, or any one or more of them, to submit (in writing) further information amplifying, modifying or explaining any matter contained in the statement of affairs, or in accounts submitted in pursuance of the Act or the Rules.

(2) The information shall, if the official receiver so directs, be verified by affidavit, and (whether or not so verified) delivered to him within 21 days of the requirement under paragraph (1), or such longer period as he may allow.

(3) Two copies of the documents containing the information and (where verification is directed) the affidavit shall be delivered by the deponent to the official receiver, who shall file one copy in court (with the affidavit, if any).

[6243]

CHAPTER 7
INFORMATION TO CREDITORS AND CONTRIBUTORIES

4.43 Reports by official receiver (NO CVL APPLICATION)

[(1)] The official receiver shall, at least once after the making of the winding-up order, send a report to creditors and contributories with respect to the proceedings in the winding up, and the state of the company's affairs.

[(1A) The official receiver shall also include in the report under paragraph (1)—

(a) to the best of his knowledge and belief—

(i) an estimate of the value of the prescribed part (whether or not he proposes to make an application to the court under section 176A(5) or section 176A(3) applies);

(ii) an estimate of the value of the company's net property; and

(b) whether, and if so, why, he proposes to make an application to court under section 176A(5).

(1B) Nothing in this Rule is to be taken as requiring any such estimate to include any information, the disclosure of which could seriously prejudice the commercial interests of the company. If such information is excluded from the calculation the estimate shall be accompanied by a statement to that effect.]

[(2) The official receiver shall file in court a copy of any report sent under this Chapter.]

[6244]

NOTES

Para (1) numbered as such, and para (2) added, by the Insolvency (Amendment) Rules 1987, SI 1987/1919, r 3(1), Schedule, Pt 1, para 47, as from 11 January 1988.

Paras (1A), (1B): inserted by the Insolvency (Amendment) Rules 2003, SI 2003/1730, r 7, Sch 1, Pt 4, para 15, as from 15 September 2003 (for transitional provisions and savings see the note preceding r 2.1 at **[6097]**).

4.44 Meaning of "creditors"

Any reference in this Chapter to creditors is to creditors of the company who are known to the official receiver or (as the case may be) the liquidator or, where a statement of the company's affairs has been submitted, are identified in the statement.

[6245]

4.45 Report where statement of affairs lodged (NO CVL APPLICATION)

(1) Where a statement of affairs has been submitted and filed in court, the official receiver shall send out to creditors and contributories a report containing a summary of the statement [(if he thinks fit, as amplified, modified or explained by virtue of Rule 4.42)] and such observations (if any) as he thinks fit to make with respect to it, or to the affairs of the company in general.

(2) The official receiver need not comply with paragraph (1) if he has previously reported to creditors and contributories with respect to the company's affairs (so far as known to him) and he is of opinion that there are no additional matters which ought to be brought to their attention.

[6246]

NOTES

Para (1): words in square brackets inserted by the Insolvency (Amendment) Rules 1987, SI 1987/1919, r 3(1), Schedule, Pt 1, para 48, as from 11 January 1988.

4.46 Statement of affairs dispensed with (NO CVL APPLICATION)

(1) This Rule applies where, in the company's case, release from the obligation to submit a statement of affairs has been granted by the official receiver or the court.

(2) As soon as may be after the release has been granted, the official receiver shall send to creditors and contributories a report containing a summary of the company's affairs (so far as within his knowledge), and his observations (if any) with respect to it, or to the affairs of the company in general.

(3) The official receiver need not comply with paragraph (2) if he has previously reported to creditors and contributories with respect to the company's affairs (so far as known to him) and he is of opinion that there are no additional matters which ought to be brought to their attention.

[6247]

4.47 General rule as to reporting (NO CVL APPLICATION)

(1) The court may, on the official receiver's application, relieve him of any duty imposed on him by this Chapter, or authorise him to carry out the duty in a way other than there required.

(2) In considering whether to act under this Rule, the court shall have regard to the cost of carrying out the duty, to the amount of the assets available, and to the extent of the interest of creditors or contributories, or any particular class of them.

[6248]

4.48 Winding up stayed (NO CVL APPLICATION)

(1) If proceedings in the winding up are stayed by order of the court, any duty of the official receiver to send reports under the preceding Rules in this Chapter ceases.

(2) Where the court grants a stay, it may include in its order such requirements on the company as it thinks fit with a view to bringing the stay to the notice of creditors and contributories.

[6249]

4.49–CVL Information to creditors and contributories

[(1)] The liquidator shall, within 28 days of a meeting held under section 95 or 98, send to creditors and contributories of the company—

(a) a copy or summary of the statement of affairs, and

(b) a report of the proceedings at the meeting.

[(2) The report under paragraph (1) shall also include—

(a) to the best of the liquidator's knowledge and belief—

(i) an estimate of the value of the prescribed part (whether or not he proposes to make an application to court under section 176A(5) or section 176A(3) applies); and

(ii) an estimate of the value of the company's net property; and

(b) whether, and if so, why, the liquidator proposes to make an application to court under section 176A(5).

(3) Nothing in this Rule is to be taken as requiring any such estimate to include any information, the disclosure of which could seriously prejudice the commercial interests of the company. If such information is excluded from the calculation the estimate shall be accompanied by a statement to that effect.]

[6250]

NOTES

Para (1) numbered as such, and paras (2), (3) added, by the Insolvency (Amendment) Rules 2003, SI 2003/1730, r 7, Sch 1, Pt 4, para 16, as from 15 September 2003 (for transitional provisions and savings see the note preceding r 2.1 at **[6097]**).

[4.49A Further information where liquidation follows administration

Where under section 140 the court appoints as the company's liquidator a person who was formerly its administrator [or a person is appointed as liquidator upon the registration of a notice under paragraph 83(3) of Schedule B1 to the Act] and that person becomes aware of creditors not formerly known to him in his capacity as administrator, he shall send to those creditors a copy of any statement or report sent by him to creditors under [Rule 2.33], so noted as to indicate that it is being sent under this Rule.]

[6251]

NOTES

Inserted by the Insolvency (Amendment) Rules 1987, SI 1987/1919, r 3(1), Schedule, Pt 1, para 49, as from 11 January 1988.

Words in first pair of square brackets inserted, and words in second pair of square brackets substituted, by the Insolvency (Amendment) Rules 2003, SI 2003/1730, r 7, Sch 1, Pt 4, para 17, as from 15 September 2003 (for transitional provisions and savings see the note preceding r 2.1 at **[6097]**).

CHAPTER 8
MEETINGS OF CREDITORS AND CONTRIBUTORIES

SECTION A: RULES OF GENERAL APPLICATION

4.50 First meetings (NO CVL APPLICATION)

(1) If under section 136(5) the official receiver decides to summon meetings of the company's creditors and contributories for the purpose of nominating a person to be liquidator in place of himself, he shall fix a venue for each meeting, in neither case more than 4 months from the date of the winding-up order.

(2) When for each meeting a venue has been fixed, notice of the meetings shall be given to the court and—

(a) in the case of the creditors' meeting, to every creditor who is known to the official receiver or is identified in the company's statement of affairs; and

(b) in the case of the contributories' meeting, to every person appearing (by the company's books or otherwise) to be a contributory of the company.

(3) Notice to the court shall be given forthwith, and the other notices shall be given at least 21 days before the date fixed for each meeting respectively.

(4) The notice to creditors shall specify a time and date, not more than 4 days before the date fixed for the meeting, by which they must lodge proofs and (if applicable) proxies, in order to be entitled to vote at the meeting; and the same applies in respect of contributories and their proxies.

(5) Notice of the meetings shall also be given by public advertisement.

(6) Where the official receiver receives a request by creditors under section 136(5)(c) for meetings of creditors and contributories to be summoned, and it appears to him that the request is properly made in accordance with the Act, he shall—

(a) withdraw any notices previously given by him under section 136(5)(b) (that he has decided not to summon such meetings),

(b) fix the venue of each meeting for not more than 3 months from his receipt of the creditors' request, and

(c) act in accordance with paragraphs (2) to (5) above, as if he had decided under section 136 to summon the meetings.

(7) Meetings summoned by the official receiver under this Rule are known respectively as "the first meeting of creditors" and "the first meeting of contributories", and jointly as "the first meetings in the liquidation".

(8) Where the company is a [an authorised deposit-taker or a former authorised deposit-taker], additional notices are required by Rule 4.72.

[6252]

NOTES

Para (8): words in square brackets substituted by the Financial Services and Markets Act 2000 (Consequential Amendments and Repeals) Order 2001, SI 2001/3649, art 377(1), (5), as from 1 December 2001.

Para (6): see Form 4.21 in Appendix 4 at **[A4]**.

4.51–CVL First meeting of creditors

(1) This Rule applies in the case of a meeting of creditors summoned by the liquidator under section 95 (where, in what starts as a members' voluntary winding up, he forms the opinion that the company will be unable to pay its debts) or a meeting under section 98 (first meeting of creditors in a creditors' voluntary winding up).

(2) The notice summoning the meeting shall [state the name of the company and the registered number of the company, and] specify a venue for the meeting and the time (not earlier than 12.00 hours on the business day before the day fixed for the meeting) by which, and the place at which, creditors must lodge [any proxies necessary to entitle them to vote at the meeting].

(3) Where the company is [an authorised deposit-taker or a former authorised deposit-taker], additional notices are required by Rule 4.72.

[6253]

NOTES

Para (2): words in first pair of square brackets inserted by the Insolvency (Amendment) Rules 2005, SI 2005/527, r 22, as from 1 April 2005; words in second pair of square brackets substituted by the Insolvency (Amendment) Rules 1987, SI 1987/1919, r 3(1), Schedule, Pt 1, para 51(1), as from 11 January 1988.

Para (3): words in square brackets substituted by the Financial Services and Markets Act 2000 (Consequential Amendments and Repeals) Order 2001, SI 2001/3649, art 377(1), (6), as from 1 December 2001.

4.52 Business at first meetings in the liquidation (NO CVL APPLICATION)

(1) At the first meeting of creditors, no resolutions shall be taken other than the following—

(a) a resolution to appoint a named insolvency practitioner to be liquidator, or two or more insolvency practitioners as joint liquidators;
(b) a resolution to establish a liquidation committee;
(c) (unless it has been resolved to establish a liquidation committee) a resolution specifying the terms on which the liquidator is to be remunerated, or to defer consideration of that matter;
(d) (if, and only if, two or more persons are appointed to act jointly as liquidator) a resolution specifying whether acts are to be done by both or all of them, or by only one;
(e) (where the meeting has been requisitioned under section 136), a resolution authorising payment out of the assets, as an expense of the liquidation, of the cost of summoning and holding the meeting and any meeting of contributories so requisitioned and held;
(f) a resolution to adjourn the meeting for not more than 3 weeks;
(g) any other resolution which the chairman thinks it right to allow for special reasons.

(2) The same applies as regards the first meeting of contributories, but that meeting shall not pass any resolution to the effect of paragraph (1)(c) or (e).

(3) At neither meeting shall any resolution be proposed which has for its object the appointment of the official receiver as liquidator.

[6254]

4.53–CVL Business at meeting under s 95 or 98

Rule 4.52(1), except sub-paragraph (e), applies to a creditors' meeting under section 95 or 98.

[6255]

[4.53A–CVL Effect of adjournment of company meeting

Where a company meeting at which a resolution for voluntary winding up is to be proposed is adjourned, any resolution passed at a meeting under section 98 held before the holding of the adjourned company meeting only has effect on and from the passing by the company of a resolution for winding up.]

[6256]

NOTES

Inserted, together with r 4.53B CVL, by the Insolvency (Amendment) Rules 1987, SI 1987/1919, r 3(1), Schedule, Pt 1, para 52, as from 11 January 1988.

[4.53B–CVL Report by director, etc

(1) At any meeting held under section 98 where the statement of affairs laid before the meeting does not state the company's affairs as at the date of the meeting, the directors of the company shall cause to be made to the meeting, either by the director presiding at the meeting or by another person with knowledge of the relevant matters, a report (written or oral) on any material transactions relating to the company occurring between the date of the making of the statement of affairs and that of the meeting.

(2) Any such report shall be recorded in the minutes of the meeting kept under Rule 4.71.]

[6257]

NOTES

Inserted as noted to r 4.53A CVL at **[6256]**.

4.54 General power to call meetings

(1) The official receiver or the liquidator may at any time summon and conduct meetings of creditors or of contributories for the purpose of ascertaining their wishes in all matters relating to the liquidation; and in relation to any meeting summoned under the Act or the Rules, the person summoning it is referred to as "the convener".

(2) When (in either case) a venue for the meeting has been fixed, notice of it shall be given by the convener—

(a) in the case of a creditors' meeting, to every creditor who is known to him or is identified in the company's statement of affairs; and

(b) in the case of a meeting of contributories, to every person appearing (by the company's books or otherwise) to be a contributory of the company.

(3) Notice of the meeting shall be given at least 21 days before the date fixed for it, and shall specify the purpose of the meeting.

(4) The notice shall specify a time and date, not more than 4 days before the date fixed for the meeting, by which, and the place at which, creditors must lodge proofs and proxies, in order to be entitled to vote at the meeting; and the same applies in respect of contributories and their proxies.

(NO CVL APPLICATION)

(5–CVL) The notice shall specify a time and date, not more than 4 days before that fixed for the meeting, by which, and the place at which, creditors (if not individuals attending in person) must lodge proxies, in order to be entitled to vote at the meeting.

(6) Additional notice of the meeting may be given by public advertisement if the convener thinks fit, and shall be so given if the court orders.

[6258]

NOTES

Para (2): see Forms 4.22, 4.23 in Appendix 4 at **[A4]**.

4.55 The chairman at meetings (NO CVL APPLICATION)

(1) This Rule applies both to a meeting of creditors and to a meeting of contributories.

(2) Where the convener of the meeting is the official receiver, he, or a person nominated by him, shall be chairman.

A nomination under this paragraph shall be in writing, unless the nominee is another official receiver or a deputy official receiver.

(3) Where the convener is other than the official receiver, the chairman shall be he, or a person nominated in writing by him.

A person nominated under this paragraph must be either—

(a) one who is qualified to act as an insolvency practitioner in relation to the company, or

(b) an employee of the liquidator or his firm who is experienced in insolvency matters.

[6259]

4.56–CVL The chairman at meetings

(1) This Rule applies both to a meeting of creditors (except a meeting under [section 95 or 98]) and to a meeting of contributories.

(2) The liquidator, or a person nominated by him in writing to act, shall be chairman of the meeting.

A person nominated under this paragraph must be either—

(a) one who is qualified to act as an insolvency practitioner in relation to the company, or

(b) an employee of the liquidator or his firm who is experienced in insolvency matters.

[6260]

NOTES

Para (1): words in square brackets substituted by the Insolvency (Amendment) Rules 1987, SI 1987/1919, r 3(1), Schedule, Pt 1, para 53, as from 11 January 1988.

4.57 Requisitioned meetings

(1) Any request by creditors to the liquidator (whether or not the official receiver) for a meeting of creditors or contributories or meetings of both, to be summoned shall be accompanied by—

(a) a list of the creditors concurring with the request and the amount of their respective claims in the winding up;

(b) from each creditor concurring, written confirmation of his concurrence; and

(c) a statement of the purpose of the proposed meeting.

Sub-paragraphs (a) and (b) do not apply if the requisitioning creditor's debt is alone sufficient, without the concurrence of other creditors.

(2) The liquidator shall, if he considers the request to be properly made in accordance with the Act, fix a venue for the meeting, not more than 35 days from his receipt of the request.

(3) The liquidator shall give 21 days' notice of the meeting, and the venue for it, to creditors.

(4) Paragraphs (1) to (3) above apply to the requisitioning by contributories of contributories' meetings, with the following modifications—

(a) for the reference in paragraph (1)(a) to the creditors' respective claims substitute the contributories' respective values (being the amounts for which they may vote at any meeting); and

(b) the persons to be given notice under paragraph (3) are those appearing (by the company's books or otherwise) to be contributories of the company.

(NO CVL APPLICATION)

[6261]

NOTES

Paras (1), (4): see Forms 4.21, 4.24 in Appendix 4 at **[A4]**.

4.58 Attendance at meetings of company's personnel

(1) This Rule applies to meetings of creditors and to meetings of contributories.

(2) Whenever a meeting is summoned, the convener shall give at least 21 days' notice to such of the company's personnel as he thinks should be told of, or be present at, the meeting.

"The company's personnel" means the persons referred to in paragraphs (a) to (d) of section 235(3) (present and past officers, employees, etc).

(3) If the meeting is adjourned, the chairman of the meeting shall, unless for any reason he thinks it unnecessary or impracticable, give notice of the adjournment to such (if any) of the company's personnel as he considers appropriate, being persons who were not themselves present at the meeting.

(4) The convener may, if he thinks fit, give notice to any one or more of the company's personnel that he is, or they are, required to be present at the meeting, or to be in attendance.

(5) In the case of any meeting, any one or more of the company's personnel, and any other persons, may be admitted, but—

(a) they must have given reasonable notice of their wish to be present, and

(b) it is a matter for the chairman's discretion whether they are to be admitted or not, and his decision is final as to what (if any) intervention may be made by any of them.

(6) If it is desired to put questions to any one of the company's personnel who is not present, the chairman may adjourn the meeting with a view to obtaining his attendance.

(7) Where one of the company's personnel is present at a meeting, only such questions may be put to him as the chairman may in his discretion allow.

[6262]

4.59 Notice of meetings by advertisement only

(1) In the case of any meeting of creditors or contributories to be held under the Act or the Rules, the court may order that notice of the meeting be given by public advertisement, and not by individual notice to the persons concerned.

(2) In considering whether to act under this Rule, the court shall have regard to the cost of public advertisement, to the amount of the assets available, and to the extent of the interest of creditors or of contributories, or any particular class of either of them.

[6263]

4.60 Venue

(1) In fixing the venue for a meeting of creditors or contributories, the convener shall have regard to the convenience of the persons (other than whoever is to be chairman) who are invited to attend.

(2) Meetings shall in all cases be summoned for commencement between the hours of 10.00 and 16.00 hours on a business day, unless the court otherwise directs.

(3) With every notice summoning a meeting of creditors or contributories there shall be sent out forms of proxy.

[6264]

NOTES

Para (3): see Forms 8.4, 8.5 in Appendix 4 at **[A4]**.

4.61 Expenses of summoning meetings

(1) Subject as follows, the expenses of summoning and holding a meeting of creditors or contributories at the instance of any person other than the official receiver or the liquidator shall be paid by that person, who shall deposit with the liquidator security for their payment.

(2) The sum to be deposited shall be such as the official receiver or liquidator (as the case may be) determines to be appropriate; and neither shall act without the deposit having been made.

(3) Where a meeting of creditors is so summoned, it may vote that the expenses of summoning and holding it, and of summoning and holding any meeting of contributories requisitioned at the same time, shall be payable out of the assets, as an expense of the liquidation.

(4) Where a meeting of contributories is summoned on the requisition of contributories, it may vote that the expenses of summoning and holding it shall be payable out of the assets, but subject to the right of creditors to be paid in full, with interest.

(5) To the extent that any deposit made under this Rule is not required for the payment of expenses of summoning and holding a meeting, it shall be repaid to the person who made it.

[6265]

4.62–CVL Expenses of meeting under s 98

(1) Payment may be made out of the company's assets, either before or after the commencement of the winding up, of any reasonable and necessary expenses incurred in connection with the summoning, advertisement and holding of a creditors' meeting under section 98.

Any such payment is an expense of the liquidation.

(2) Where such payments are made before the commencement of the winding up, the director presiding at the creditors' meeting shall inform the meeting of their amount and the identity of the persons to whom they were made.

(3) The liquidator appointed under section 100 may make such a payment (subject to the next paragraph); but if there is a liquidation committee, he must give the committee at least 7 days' notice of his intention to make the payment.

(4) Such a payment shall not be made by the liquidator to himself, or to any associate of his, otherwise than with the approval of the liquidation committee, the creditors, or the court.

(5) This Rule is without prejudice to the powers of the court under Rule 4.219 (voluntary winding up superseded by winding up by the court).

[6266]

4.63 Resolutions

(1) [Subject as follows] at a meeting of creditors or contributories, a resolution is passed when a majority (in value) of those present and voting, in person or by proxy, have voted in favour of the resolution.

The value of contributories is determined by reference to the number of votes conferred on each contributory by the company's articles.

(2) In the case of resolution for the appointment of a liquidator—

(a) [subject to paragraph (2A)] if on any vote there are two nominees for appointment, the person who obtains the most support is appointed;

(b) if there are three or more nominees, and one of them has a clear majority over both or all the others together, that one is appointed; and

(c) in any other case, the chairman of the meeting shall continue to take votes (disregarding at each vote any nominee who has withdrawn and, if no nominee has withdrawn, the nominee who obtained the least support last time), until a clear majority is obtained for any one nominee.

[(2A) In a winding up by the court the support referred to in paragraph (2)(a) must represent a majority in value of all those present (in person or by proxy) at the meeting and entitled to vote. (NO CVL APPLICATION)].

(3) The chairman may at any time put to the meeting a resolution for the joint appointment of any two or more nominees.

(4) Where a resolution is proposed which affects a person in respect of his remuneration or conduct as liquidator, or as proposed or former liquidator, the vote of that person, and of any partner or employee of his, shall not be reckoned in the majority required for passing the resolution.

This paragraph applies with respect to a vote given by a person [(whether personally or on his behalf by a proxy-holder)] either as creditor or contributory or as [proxy-holder] for a creditor or a contributory (but subject to Rule 8.6 in Part 8 of the Rules).

[6267]

NOTES

Paras (1), (2): words in square brackets inserted by the Insolvency (Amendment) Rules 1987, SI 1987/1919, r 3(1), Schedule, Pt 1, para 54(1), (2), as from 11 January 1988.

Para (2A): inserted by SI 1987/1919, r 3(1), Schedule, Pt 1, para 54(3), as from 11 January 1988.

Para (4): words in first pair of brackets inserted, and words in second pair of square brackets substituted, by SI 1987/1919, r 3(1), Schedule, Pt 1, para 54(4), as from 11 January 1988.

4.64 Chairman of meeting as proxy-holder

Where the chairman at a meeting of creditors or contributories holds a proxy which requires him to vote for a particular resolution, and no other person proposes that resolution—

(a) he shall himself propose it, unless he considers that there is good reason for not doing so, and

(b) if he does not propose it, he shall forthwith after the meeting notify his principal of the reason why not.

[6268]

4.65 Suspension and adjournment

(1) This Rule applies to meetings of creditors and to meetings of contributories.

(2) Once only in the course of any meeting, the chairman may, in his discretion and without an adjournment, declare the meeting suspended for any period up to one hour.

(3) The chairman at any meeting may in his discretion, and shall if the meeting so resolves, adjourn it to such time and place as seems to him to be appropriate in the circumstances.

This is subject to Rule 4.113(3) [or, as the case may be, 4.114-CVL(3)] in case where the liquidator or his nominee is chairman, and a resolution has been proposed for the liquidator's removal.

(4) If within a period of 30 minutes from the time appointed for the commencement of a meeting a quorum is not present, then [the chairman may, at his discretion, adjourn the meeting to such time and place as he may appoint].

(5) An adjournment under this Rule shall not be for a period of more than 21 days; and Rule 4.60(1) and (2) applies.

(6) If there is no person present to act as chairman, some other person present (being entitled to vote) may make the appointment under paragraph (4), with the agreement of others present (being persons so entitled).

Failing agreement, the adjournment shall be to the same time and place in the next following week or, if that is not a business day, to the business day immediately following.

(7) Where a meeting is adjourned under this Rule, proofs and proxies may be used if lodged at any time up to midday on the business day immediately before the adjourned meeting.

[6269]

NOTES

Para (3): words in square brackets inserted by the Insolvency (Amendment) Rules 1987, SI 1987/1919, r 3(1), Schedule, Pt 1, para 55(1), as from 11 January 1988.

Para (4): words in square brackets substituted by SI 1987/1919, r 3(1), Schedule, Pt 1, para 55(2), as from 11 January 1988.

4.66 *(Revoked by the Insolvency (Amendment) Rules 1987, SI 1987/1919, r 3(1), Schedule, Pt 1, para 56, as from 11 January 1988.)*

4.67 Entitlement to vote (creditors)

(1) Subject as follows in this Rule and the next, at a meeting of creditors a person is entitled to vote as a creditor only if—

- (a) there has been duly lodged (in a winding up by the court by the time and date stated in the notice of the meeting) a proof of the debt—
  - [(i) claimed to be due to him from the company, or
  - (ii) in relation to a member State liquidator, is claimed to be due to creditors in proceedings in relation to which he holds office], and the claim has been admitted under Rule 4.70 for the purpose of entitlement to vote, and
- (b) there has been lodged, by the time and date stated in the notice of the meeting, any proxy requisite for that entitlement.

(2) The court may, in exceptional circumstances, by order declare the creditors, or any class of them, entitled to vote at creditors' meetings, without being required to prove their debts.

Where a creditor is so entitled, the court may, on the application of the liquidator, make such consequential orders as it thinks fit (as for example an order treating a creditor as having proved his debt for the purpose of permitting payment of dividend).

(3) A creditor shall not vote in respect of a debt for an unliquidated amount, or any debt whose value is not ascertained, except where the chairman agrees to put upon the debt an estimated minimum value for the purpose of entitlement to vote and admits his proof for that purpose.

(4) A secured creditor is entitled to vote only in respect of the balance (if any) of his debt after deducting the value of his security as estimated by him.

(5) A creditor shall not vote in respect of a debt on, or secured by, a current bill of exchange or promissory note, unless he is willing—

- (a) to treat the liability to him on the bill or note of every person who is liable on it antecedently to the company, and against whom a bankruptcy order has not been made (or, in the case of a company, which has not gone into liquidation), as a security in his hands, and
- (b) to estimate the value of the security and (for the purpose of entitlement to vote, but not for dividend) to deduct it from his proof.

[(6) No vote shall be cast by virtue of a debt more than once on any resolution put to the meeting.

(7) Where—

(a) a creditor is entitled to vote under this Rule and Rule 4.70 (admission of proof),
(b) has lodged his claim in one or more sets of other proceedings, and
(c) votes (either in person or by proxy) on a resolution put to the meeting, only the creditor's vote shall be counted.

(8) Where—

(a) a creditor has lodged his claim in more than one set of other proceedings, and
(b) more than one member State liquidator seeks to vote by virtue of that claim,

the entitlement to vote by virtue of that claim is exercisable by the member State liquidator in main proceedings, whether or not the creditor has lodged his claim in the main proceedings.

(9) For the purposes of paragraphs (7) and (8), "other proceedings" means main proceedings, secondary proceedings or territorial proceedings in another member State.]

[6270]

NOTES

Para (1): words in square brackets substituted by the Insolvency (Amendment) Rules 2002, SI 2002/1307, rr 3, 6(6)(a), as from 31 May 2002, with savings in relation to anything done under, or for the purposes of, this provision before that date.

Paras (6)–(9): added by SI 2002/1307, rr 3, 6(6)(b), as from 31 May 2002, with savings in relation to anything done under, or for the purposes of, this provision before that date.

4.68–CVL Chairman's discretion to allow vote

At a creditors' meeting, the chairman may allow a creditor to vote, notwithstanding that he has failed to comply with Rule 4.67(1)(a), if satisfied that the failure was due to circumstances beyond the creditor's control.

[6271]

4.69 Entitlement to vote (contributories)

At a meeting of contributories, voting rights are as at a general meeting of the company, subject to any provision in the articles affecting entitlement to vote, either generally or at a time when the company is in liquidation.

[6272]

4.70 Admission and rejection of proof (creditors' meeting)

(1) At any creditors' meeting the chairman has power to admit or reject a creditor's proof for the purpose of his entitlement to vote; and the power is exercisable with respect to the whole or any part of the proof.

(2) The chairman's decision under this Rule, or in respect of any matter arising under Rule 4.67, is subject to appeal to the court by any creditor or contributory.

(3) If the chairman is in doubt whether a proof should be admitted or rejected, he shall mark it as objected to and allow the creditor to vote, subject to his vote being subsequently declared invalid if the objection to the proof is sustained.

(4) If on an appeal the chairman's decision is reversed or varied, or a creditor's vote is declared invalid, the court may order that another meeting be summoned, or make such other order as it thinks just.

(5) Neither the official receiver, nor any person nominated by him to be chairman, is personally liable for costs incurred by any person in respect of an application under this Rule; and the chairman (if other than the official receiver or a person so nominated) is not so liable unless the court makes an order to that effect.

(NO CVL APPLICATION)

(6–CVL) The liquidator or his nominee as chairman is not personally liable for costs incurred by any person in respect of an application under this Rule, unless the court makes an order to that effect.

[6273]

4.71 Record of proceedings

(1) At any meeting, the chairman shall cause minutes of the proceedings to be kept. The minutes shall be signed by him, and retained as part of the records of the liquidation.

(2) The chairman shall also cause to be made up and kept a list of all the creditors or, as the case may be, contributories who attended the meeting.

(3) The minutes of the meeting shall include a record of every resolution passed.

(4) It is the chairman's duty to see top it that particulars of all such resolutions, certified by him, are filed in court not more than 21 days after the date of the meeting.

(NO CVL APPLICATION)

[6274]

SECTION B: WINDING UP OF RECOGNISED BANKS, ETC

4.72 Additional provisions as regards certain meetings

(1) This Rule applies where a company goes, or proposes to go, into liquidation and it is [an authorised deposit-taker or a former authorised deposit-taker].

(2) Notice of any meeting of the company at which it is intended to propose a resolution for its winding up shall be given by the directors to the [Financial Services Authority] and [to the scheme manager established under section 212(1) of the Financial Services and Markets Act 2000].

(3) Notice to the [Authority] and [the scheme manager] shall be the same as given to members of the company.

(4) Where a creditors' meeting is summoned by the liquidator under section 95 or, in a creditors' voluntary winding up, is summoned under section 98, the same notice of the meeting must be given to the [Authority] and [the scheme manager] as is given to creditors under Rule 4.51–CVL.

(5) Where the company is being wound up by the court, notice of the first meetings of creditors and contributories shall be given to the [Authority] and [the scheme manager] by the official receiver.

(6) Where in the winding up (whether voluntary or by the court) a meeting of creditors or contributories or of the company is summoned for the purpose of—

- (a) receiving the liquidator's resignation, or
- (b) removing the liquidator, or
- (c) appointing a new liquidator,

the person summoning the meeting and giving notice of it shall also give notice to the [Authority] and [the scheme manager].

(7) [The scheme manager] is entitled to be represented at any meeting of which it is required by this Rule to be given notice; and Schedule 1 to the Rules has effect with respect to the voting rights of [the scheme manager] at such a meeting.

[6275]

NOTES

Words "Financial Services Authority" and "Authority" in square brackets substituted by the Bank of England Act 1998 (Consequential Amendments of Subordinate Legislation) Order 1998, SI 1998/1129, art 2, Sch 1, para 4(1), (5), as from 1 June 1998; other words in square brackets substituted by the Financial Services and Markets Act 2000 (Consequential Amendments and Repeals) Order 2001, SI 2001/3649, arts 377(1), (7), 378(2), as from 1 December 2001.

CHAPTER 9
PROOF OF DEBTS IN A LIQUIDATION

SECTION A: PROCEDURE FOR PROVING

4.73 Meaning of "prove"

(1) Where a company is being wound up by the court, a person claiming to be a creditor of the company and wishing to recover his debt in whole or in part must (subject to any order of the court under Rule 4.67(2)) submit his claim in writing to the liquidator. (NO CVL APPLICATION)

(2–CVL) In a voluntary winding up (whether members' or creditors') the liquidator may require a person claiming to be a creditor of the company and wishing to recover his debt in whole or in part, to submit the claim in writing to him.

(3) A creditor who claims (whether or not in writing) is referred to as "proving" for his debt; and a document by which he seeks to establish his claim is his "proof".

(4) Subject to the next paragraph, a proof must be in the form known as "proof of debt" (whether the form prescribed by the Rules, or a substantially similar form), which shall be made out by or under the directions of the creditor, and signed by him or a person authorised in that behalf. (NO CVL APPLICATION)

(5) Where a debt is due to a Minister of the Crown or a Government Department, the proof need not be in that form, provided that there are shown all such particulars of the debt as are required in the form used by other creditors, and as are relevant in the circumstances. (NO CVL APPLICATION)

(6–CVL) The creditor's proof may be in any form.

(7) In certain circumstances, specified below in this Chapter, the proof must be in the form of an affidavit.

[(8) Where a winding up is immediately preceded by an administration, a creditor proving in the administration shall be deemed to have proved in the winding up.]

[6276]

NOTES

Para (8): added by the Insolvency (Amendment) Rules 2003, SI 2003/1730, r 7, Sch 1, Pt 4, para 18, as from 15 September 2003 (for transitional provisions and savings see the note preceding r 2.1 at **[6097]**).

Para (4): see Form 4.25 in Appendix 4 at **[A4]**.

[4.74 Supply of Forms (NO CVL APPLICATION)

A form of proof shall be sent to any creditor of the company by the liquidator where the creditor so requests.]

[6277]

NOTES

Substituted by the Insolvency (Amendment) Rules 2004, SI 2004/584, r 9, as from 1 April 2004.

4.75 Contents of proof (NO CVL APPLICATION)

[(1) Subject to Rule 4.73(5), the following matters shall be stated in a creditor's proof of debt—

(a) the creditor's name and address, and, if a company, its company registration number;
(b) the total amount of his claim (including any Value Added Tax) as at the date on which the company went into liquidation;
(c) whether or not that amount includes outstanding uncapitalised interest;
(d) particulars of how and when the debt was incurred by the company;
(e) particulars of any security held, the date when it was given and the value which the creditor puts upon it;
(f) details of any reservation of title in respect of goods to which the debt refers; and
(g) the name, and address and authority of the person signing the proof (if other than the creditor himself).]

(2) There shall be specified in the proof any documents by reference to which the debt can be substantiated; but (subject as follows) it is not essential that such documents be attached to the proof or submitted with it.

(3) The liquidator, or the chairman or convener of any meeting, may call for any document or other evidence to be produced to him, where he thinks it necessary for the purpose of substantiating the whole or any part of the claim made in the proof.

[6278]

NOTES

Para (1): substituted by the Insolvency (Amendment) Rules 2004, SI 2004/584, r 10, as from 1 April 2004.

Social Security Pensions Act 1975, Sch 3: repealed by the Pension Schemes Act 1993, s 188(1), Sch 5, Pt I, and replaced by Sch 4 to that Act.

4.76–CVL Particulars of creditor's claim

The liquidator, or the convener or chairman of any meeting, may, if he thinks it necessary for the purpose of clarifying or substantiating the whole or any part of a creditor's claim made in his proof, call for details of any matter specified in paragraphs (a) to (h) of Rule 4.75(1), or for the production to him of such documentary or other evidence as he may require.

[6279]

4.77 Claim established by affidavit

(1) The liquidator may, if he thinks it necessary, require a claim of debt to be verified by means of an affidavit, for which purpose there shall be used the form known as "affidavit of debt", or a substantially similar form.

(2) An affidavit may be required notwithstanding that a proof of debt has already been lodged.

(3) The affidavit may be sworn before an official receiver or deputy official receiver, or before an officer of the Department or of the court duly authorised in that behalf. (NO CVL APPLICATION)

[6280]

NOTES

Para (1): see Form 4.26 in Appendix 4 at **[A4]**.

4.78 Cost of proving

(1) Subject as follows, every creditor bears the cost of proving his own debt, including such as may be incurred in providing documents or evidence under Rule 4.75(3) or 4.76–CVL.

(2) Costs incurred by the liquidator in estimating the quantum of a debt under Rule 4.86 (debts not bearing a certain value) are payable out of the assets, as an expense of the liquidation.

(3) Paragraphs (1) and (2) apply unless the court otherwise orders.

[6281]

4.79 Liquidator to allow inspection of proofs

The liquidator shall, so long as proofs lodged with him are in his hands, allow them to be inspected, at all reasonable times on any business day, by any of the following persons—

(a) any creditor who has submitted his proof of debt (unless his proof has been wholly rejected for purposes of dividend or otherwise);

(b) any contributory of the company;

(c) any person acting on behalf of either of the above.

[6282]

4.80 Transmission of proofs to liquidator (NO CVL APPLICATION)

(1) Where a liquidator is appointed, the official receiver shall forthwith transmit to him all the proofs which he has so far received, together with an itemised list of them.

(2) The liquidator shall sign the list by way of receipt for the proofs, and return it to the official receiver.

(3) From then on, all proofs of debt shall be sent to the liquidator, and retained by him.

[6283]

4.81 New liquidator appointed

(1) If a new liquidator is appointed in place of another, the former liquidator shall transmit to him all proofs which he has received, together with an itemised list of them.

(2) The new liquidator shall sign the list by way of receipt for the proofs, and return it to his predecessor.

[6284]

4.82 Admission and rejection of proofs for dividend

(1) A proof may be admitted for dividend either for the whole amount claimed by the creditor, or for part of that amount.

(2) If the liquidator rejects a proof in whole or in part, he shall prepare a written statement of his reasons for doing so, and send it forthwith to the creditor.

[6285]

4.83 Appeal against decision on proof

(1) If a creditor is dissatisfied with the liquidator's decision with respect to his proof (including any decision on the question of preference), he may apply to the court for the decision to be reversed or varied.

The application must be made within 21 days of his receiving the statement sent under Rule 4.82(2).

(2) A contributory or any other creditor may, if dissatisfied with the liquidator's decision admitting or rejecting the whole or any part of a proof, make such an application within 21 days of becoming aware of the liquidator's decision.

(3) Where an application is made to the court under this Rule, the court shall fix a venue for the application to be heard, notice of which shall be sent by the applicant to the creditor who lodged the proof in question (if it is not himself) and to the liquidator.

(4) The liquidator shall, on receipt of the notice, file in court the relevant proof, together (if appropriate) with a copy of the statement sent under Rule 4.82(2).

(5) After the application has been heard and determined, the proof shall, unless it has been wholly disallowed, be returned by the court to the liquidator.

(6) The official receiver is not personally liable for costs incurred by any person in respect of an application under this Rule; and the liquidator (if other than the official receiver) is not so liable unless the court makes an order to that effect.

[6286]

4.84 Withdrawal or variation of proof

A creditor's proof may at any time, by agreement between himself and the liquidator, be withdrawn or varied as to the amount claimed.

[6287]

4.85 Expunging of proof by the court

(1) The court may expunge a proof or reduce the amount claimed—
- (a) on the liquidator's application, where he thinks that the proof has been improperly admitted, or ought to be reduced; or
- (b) on the application of a creditor, if the liquidator declines to interfere in the matter.

(2) Where application is made to the court under this Rule, the court shall fix a venue for the application to be heard, notice of which shall be sent by the applicant—
- (a) in the case of an application by the liquidator, to the creditor who made the proof, and
- (b) in the case of an application by a creditor, to the liquidator and to the creditor who made the proof (if not himself).

[6288]

SECTION B: QUANTIFICATION OF CLAIM

4.86 Estimate of quantum

(1) The liquidator shall estimate the value of any debt which, by reason of its being subject to any contingency or for any other reason, does not bear a certain value; and he may revise any estimate previously made, if he thinks fit by reference to any change of circumstances or to information becoming available to him.

He shall inform the creditor as to his estimate and any revision of it.

(2) Where the value of a debt is estimated under this Rule, or by the court under section 168(3) or (5), the amount provable in the winding up in the case of that debt is that of the estimate for the time being.

[6289]

4.87 Negotiable instruments, etc

Unless the liquidator allows, a proof in respect of money owed on a bill of exchange, promissory note, cheque or other negotiable instrument or security cannot be admitted unless there is produced the instrument or security itself or a copy of it, certified by the creditor or his authorised representative to be a true copy.

[6290]

4.88 Secured creditors

(1) If a secured creditor realises his security, he may prove for the balance of his debt, after deducting the amount realised.

(2) If a secured creditor voluntarily surrenders his security for the general benefit of creditors, he may prove for his whole debt, as if it were unsecured.

[6291]

4.89 Discounts

There shall in every case be deducted from the claim all trade and other discounts which would have been available to the company but for its liquidation, except any discount for immediate, early or cash settlement.

[6292]

[4.90 Mutual credits and set-off

(1) This Rule applies where, before the company goes into liquidation there have been mutual credits, mutual debts or other mutual dealings between the company and any creditor of the company proving or claiming to prove for a debt in the liquidation.

(2) The reference in paragraph (1) to mutual credits, mutual debts or other mutual dealings does not include—

- (a) any debt arising out of an obligation incurred at a time when the creditor had notice that—
  - (i) a meeting of creditors had been summoned under section 98; or
  - (ii) a petition for the winding up of the company was pending;
- (b) any debt arising out of an obligation where—
  - (i) the liquidation was immediately preceded by an administration; and
  - (ii) at the time the obligation was incurred the creditor had notice that an application for an administration order was pending or a person had given notice of intention to appoint an administrator;
- (c) any debt arising out of an obligation incurred during an administration which immediately preceded the liquidation; or
- (d) any debt which has been acquired by a creditor by assignment or otherwise, pursuant to an agreement between the creditor and any other party where that agreement was entered into—
  - (i) after the company went into liquidation;
  - (ii) at a time when the creditor had notice that a meeting of creditors had been summoned under section 98;
  - (iii) at a time when the creditor had notice that a winding up petition was pending;
  - (iv) where the liquidation was immediately preceded by an administration, at a time when the creditor had notice that an application for an administration order was pending or a person had given notice of intention to appoint an administrator; or
  - (v) during an administration which immediately preceded the liquidation.

(3) An account shall be taken of what is due from each party to the other in respect of the mutual dealings, and the sums due from one party shall be set off against the sums due from the other.

(4) A sum shall be regarded as being due to or from the company for the purposes of paragraph (3) whether—

- (a) it is payable at present or in the future;
- (b) the obligation by virtue of which it is payable is certain or contingent; or
- (c) its amount is fixed or liquidated, or is capable of being ascertained by fixed rules or as a matter of opinion.

(5) Rule 4.86 shall also apply for the purposes of this Rule to any obligation to or from the company which, by reason of its being subject to any contingency or for any other reason, does not bear a certain value.

(6) Rules 4.91 to 4.93 shall apply for the purposes of this Rule in relation to any sums due to the company which—

(a) are payable in a currency other than sterling;

(b) are of a periodical nature; or

(c) bear interest.

(7) Rule 11.13 shall apply for the purposes of this Rule to any sum due to or from the company which is payable in the future.

(8) Only the balance (if any) of the account owed to the creditor is provable in the liquidation. Alternatively the balance (if any) owed to the company shall be paid to the liquidator as part of the assets except where all or part of the balance results from a contingent or prospective debt owed by the creditor and in such a case the balance (or that part of it which results from the contingent or prospective debt) shall be paid if and when that debt becomes due and payable.

(9) In this Rule "obligation" means an obligation however arising, whether by virtue of an agreement, rule of law or otherwise.]

[6293]

NOTES

Substituted by the Insolvency (Amendment) Rules 2005, SI 2005/527, r 23, as from 1 April 2005, subject to transitional provisions as noted to r 2.67 at **[6157F]**.

4.91 Debt in foreign currency

(1) For the purpose of proving a debt incurred or payable in a currency other than sterling, the amount of the debt shall be converted into sterling at the official exchange rate prevailing on the date when the company went into liquidation [or, if the liquidation was immediately preceded by an administration, on the date that the company entered administration].

(2) "The official exchange rate" is the [middle exchange rate on the London Foreign Exchange Market at the close of business], as published for the date in question. In the absence of any such published rate, it is such rate as the court determines.

[6294]

NOTES

Para (1): words in square brackets added by the Insolvency (Amendment) Rules 2005, SI 2005/527, r 24, as from 1 April 2005, subject to transitional provisions as noted to r 2.67 at **[6157F]**.

Para (2): words in square brackets substituted by the Insolvency (Amendment) Rules 2003, SI 2003/1730, r 7, Sch 1, Pt 4, para 20, as from 15 September 2003 (for transitional provisions and savings see the note preceding r 2.1 at **[6097]**).

4.92 Payments of a periodical nature

(1) In the case of rent and other payments of a periodical nature, the creditor may prove for any amounts due and unpaid up to the date when the company went into liquidation [or, if the liquidation was immediately preceded by an administration, up to the date that the company entered administration].

(2) Where at that date any payment was accruing due, the creditor may prove for so much as would have fallen due at that date, if accruing from day to day.

[6295]

NOTES

Para (1): words in square brackets added by the Insolvency (Amendment) Rules 2005, SI 2005/527, r 25, as from 1 April 2005, subject to transitional provisions as noted to r 2.67 at **[6157F]**.

4.93 Interest

(1) Where a debt proved in the liquidation bears interest, that interest is provable as part of the debt except in so far as it is payable in respect of any period after the company went

into liquidation [or, if the liquidation was immediately preceded by an administration, any period after the date that the company entered administration].

(2) In the following circumstances the creditor's claim may include interest on the debt for periods before the company went into liquidation, although not previously reserved or agreed.

(3) If the debt is due by virtue of a written instrument, and payable at a certain time, interest may be claimed for the period from that time to the date when the company went into liquidation.

(4) If the debt is due otherwise, interest may only be claimed if, before that date, a demand for payment of the debt was made in writing by or on behalf of the creditor, and notice given that interest would be payable from the date of the demand to the date of payment.

(5) Interest under paragraph (4) may only be claimed for the period from the date of the demand to that of the company's going into liquidation [and for all the purposes of the Act and the Rules shall be chargeable at a rate not exceeding that mentioned in paragraph (6)].

[(6) The rate of interest to be claimed under paragraphs (3) and (4) is the rate specified in section 17 of the Judgments Act 1838 on the date when the company went into liquidation.]

[6296]

NOTES

Para (1): words in square brackets added by the Insolvency (Amendment) Rules 2005, SI 2005/527, r 26, as from 1 April 2005, subject to transitional provisions as noted to r 2.67 at **[6157F]**.

Para (5): words in square brackets added by the Insolvency (Amendment) Rules 1987, SI 1987/1919, r 3(1), Schedule, Pt 1, para 59(1), as from 11 January 1988.

Para (6): added by SI 1987/1919, r 3(1), Schedule, Pt 1, para 59(2), as from 11 January 1988.

4.94 Debt payable at future time

A creditor may prove for a debt of which payment was not yet due on the date when the company went into liquidation, [or, if the liquidation was immediately preceded by an administration, on the date that the company entered administration] but subject to Rule 11.13 in Part 11 of the Rules (adjustment of dividend where payment made before time).

[6297]

NOTES

Words in square brackets added by the Insolvency (Amendment) Rules 2005, SI 2005/527, r 27, as from 1 April 2005, subject to transitional provisions as noted to r 2.67 at **[6157F]**.

CHAPTER 10
SECURED CREDITORS

4.95 Value of security

(1) A secured creditor may, with the agreement of the liquidator or the leave of the court, at any time alter the value which he has, in his proof of debt, put upon his security.

(2) However, if a secured creditor—

(a) being the petitioner, has in the petition put a value on his security, or

(b) has voted in respect of the unsecured balance of his debt,

he may re-value his security only with leave of the court. (NO CVL APPLICATION)

[6298]

4.96 Surrender for non-disclosure

(1) If a secured creditor omits to disclose his security in his proof of debt, he shall surrender his security for the general benefit of creditors, unless the court, on application by him, relieves him for the effect of this Rule on the ground that the omission was inadvertent or the result of honest mistake.

(2) If the court grants that relief, it may require or allow the creditor's proof of debt to be amended, on such terms as may be just.

[(3) Nothing in this Rule or the following two Rules may affect the rights in rem of creditors or third parties protected under Article 5 of the EC Regulation (third parties' rights in rem).]

[6299]

NOTES

Para (3): added by the Insolvency (Amendment) Rules 2002, SI 2002/1307, rr 3, 6(8), as from 31 May 2002, with savings in relation to anything done under, or for the purposes of, this provision before that date.

EC Regulation: ie, Council Regulation 1346/2000/EC on insolvency proceedings at **[9290]**.

4.97 Redemption by liquidator

(1) The liquidator may at any time give notice to a creditor whose debt is secured that he proposes, at the expiration of 28 days from the date of the notice, to redeem the security at the value put upon it in the creditor's proof.

(2) The creditor then has 21 days (or such longer period as the liquidator may allow) in which, if he so wishes, to exercise his right to re-value his security (with the leave of the court, when Rule 4.95(2) applies).

If the creditor re-values his security, the liquidator may only redeem at the new value.

(3) If the liquidator redeems the security, the cost of transferring it is payable out of the assets.

(4) A secured creditor may at any time, by a notice in writing, call on the liquidator to elect whether he will or will not exercise his power to redeem the security at the value then placed on it; and the liquidator then has 6 months in which to exercise the power or determine not to exercise it.

[6300]

4.98 Test of security's value

(1) Subject as follows, the liquidator, if he is dissatisfied with the value which a secured creditor puts on his security (whether in his proof or by way of re-valuation under Rule 4.97), may require any property comprised in the security to be offered for sale.

(2) The terms of sale shall be such as may be agreed, or as the court may direct; and if the sale is by auction, the liquidator on behalf of the company, and the creditor on his own behalf, may appear and bid.

[6301]

4.99 Realisation of security by creditor

If a creditor who has valued his security subsequently realises it (whether or not at the instance of the liquidator)—

(a) the net amount realised shall be substituted for the value previously put by the creditor on the security, and

(b) that amount shall be treated in all respects as an amended valuation made by him.

[6302]

CHAPTER 11
THE LIQUIDATOR

SECTION A: APPOINTMENT AND ASSOCIATED FORMALITIES

4.100 Appointment by creditors or contributories (NO CVL APPLICATION)

(1) This Rule applies where a person is appointed as liquidator either by a meeting of creditors or by a meeting of contributories.

(2) The chairman of the meeting shall certify the appointment, but not unless and until the person appointed has provided him with a written statement to the effect that he is an insolvency practitioner, duly qualified under the Act to be the liquidator, and that he consents so to act.

[(3) The liquidator's appointment, is effective from the date on which the appointment is certified, that date to be endorsed on the certificate.

(4) The chairman of the meeting (if not himself the official receiver) shall send the certificate to the official receiver.

(5) The official receiver shall in any case send the certificate to the liquidator and file a copy of it in court.]

[6303]

NOTES

Paras (3)–(5): substituted by the Insolvency (Amendment) Rules 1987, SI 1987/1919, r 3(1), Schedule, Pt 1, para 60, as from 11 January 1988.

See Forms 4.27, 4.28 in Appendix 4 at **[A4]**.

4.101–CVL Appointment by creditors or by the company

(1) This Rule applies where a person is appointed as liquidator either by a meeting of creditors or by a meeting of the company.

(2) Subject as follows, the chairman of the meeting shall certify the appointment, but not unless and until the person appointed has provided him with a written statement to the effect that he is an insolvency practitioner, duly qualified under the Act to be the liquidator, and that he consents so to act; the liquidator's appointment [takes effect upon the passing of the resolution for that appointment].

(3) The chairman shall send the certificate forthwith to the liquidator, who shall keep it as part of the records of the liquidation.

(4) Paragraphs (2) and (3) need not be complied with in the case of a liquidator appointed by a company meeting and replaced by another liquidator appointed on the same day by a creditors' meeting.

[6304]

NOTES

Para (2): words in square brackets substituted by the Insolvency (Amendment) Rules 1987, SI 1987/1919, r 3(1), Schedule, Pt 1, para 61, as from 11 January 1988.

[4.101A–CVL Power to fill vacancy in office of liquidator

Where a vacancy in the office of liquidator occurs in the manner mentioned in section 104 a meeting of creditors to fill the vacancy may be convened by any creditor or, if there were more liquidators than one, by the continuing liquidators.]

[6305]

NOTES

Inserted by the Insolvency (Amendment) Rules 1987, SI 1987/1919, r 3(1), Schedule, Pt 1, para 62, as from 11 January 1988.

4.102 Appointment by the court (NO CVL APPLICATION)

(1) This Rule applies where the liquidator is appointed by the court under section 139(4) (different persons nominated by creditors and contributories) or section 140 (liquidation following administration or voluntary arrangement).

(2) The court's order shall not issue unless and until the person appointed has filed in court a statement to the effect that he is an insolvency practitioner, duly qualified under the Act to be the liquidator, and that he consents so to act.

(3) Thereafter, the court shall send 2 copies of the order to the official receiver. One of the copies shall be sealed, and this shall be sent to the person appointed as liquidator.

(4) The liquidator's appointment takes effect from the date of the order.

(5) The liquidator shall, within 28 days of his appointment, give notice of it to all creditors and contributories of the company of whom he is aware in that period. Alternatively, if the court allows, he may advertise his appointment in accordance with the court's directions.

(6) In his notice or advertisement under this Rule the liquidator shall—

(a) state whether he proposes to summon meetings of creditors and contributories for the purpose of establishing a liquidation committee, or proposes to summon only a meeting of creditors for that purpose, and

(b) if he does not propose to summon any such meeting, set out the powers of the creditors under the Act to require him to summon one.

[6306]

NOTES

Para (1): see Forms 4.29, 4.30 in Appendix 4 at **[A4]**.

4.103–CVL Appointment by the court

(1) This Rule applies where the liquidator is appointed by the court under section 100(3) or 108.

(2) The court's order shall not issue unless and until the person appointed has filed in court a statement to the effect that he is an insolvency practitioner, duly qualified under the Act to be the liquidator, and that he consents so to act.

(3) Thereafter, the court shall send a sealed copy of the order to the liquidator, whose appointment takes effect from the date of the order.

(4) Not later than 28 days from his appointment, the liquidator shall give notice of it to all creditors of the company of whom he is aware in that period. Alternatively, if the court allows, he may advertise his appointment in accordance with the court's directions.

[6307]

NOTES

See Forms 4.29, 4.30 in Appendix 4 at **[A4]**.

4.104 Appointment by Secretary of State (NO CVL APPLICATION)

(1) This Rule applies where the official receiver applies to the Secretary of State to appoint a liquidator in place of himself, or refers to the Secretary of State the need for an appointment.

(2) If the Secretary of State makes an appointment, he shall send two copies of the certificate of appointment to the official receiver, who shall transmit one such copy to the person appointed, and file the other in court.

(3) The certificate shall specify the date from which the liquidator's appointment is to be effective.

[6308]

4.105 Authentication of liquidator's appointment

A copy of the certificate of the liquidator's appointment or (as the case may be) a sealed copy of the court's order [or a copy of the notice registered in accordance with paragraph 83(3) of Schedule B1 to the Act], may in any proceedings be adduced as proof that the person appointed is duly authorised to exercise the powers and perform the duties of liquidator in the company's winding up.

[6309]

NOTES

Words in square brackets inserted by the Insolvency (Amendment) Rules 2003, SI 2003/1730, r 7, Sch 1, Pt 4, para 21, as from 15 September 2003 (for transitional provisions and savings see the note preceding r 2.1 at **[6097]**).

4.106 Appointment to be advertised and registered

(1) Subject as follows, where the liquidator is appointed by a creditors' or contributories' meeting, or by a meeting of the company, he shall, on receiving his certificate of appointment, give notice of his appointment in such newspaper as he thinks most appropriate for ensuring that it comes to the notice of the company's creditors and contributories.

(2–CVL) Paragraph (1) need not be complied with in the case of a liquidator appointed by a company meeting and replaced by another liquidator appointed on the same day by a creditors' meeting.

(3) The expense of giving notice under this rule shall be borne in the first instance by the liquidator; but he is entitled to be reimbursed out of the assets, as an expense of the liquidation.

The same applies also in the case of the notice or advertisement required where the appointment is made by the court or the Secretary of State.

(4) In the case of a winding up by the court, the liquidator shall also forthwith notify his appointment to the registrar of companies.

This applies however the liquidator is appointed. [(NO CVL APPLICATION)]

[6310]

NOTES

Para (4): words in square brackets added by the Insolvency (Amendment) Rules 1987, SI 1987/1919, r 3(1), Schedule, Pt 1, para 63, as from 11 January 1988.

Para (4): see Form 4.31 in Appendix 4 at **[A4]**.

4.107 Hand-over of assets to liquidator (NO CVL APPLICATION)

(1) This Rule applies only where the liquidator is appointed in succession to the official receiver acting as liquidator.

(2) When the liquidator's appointment takes effect, the official receiver shall forthwith do all that is required for putting him into possession of the assets.

(3) On taking possession of the assets, the liquidator shall discharge any balance due to the official receiver on account of—

- (a) expenses properly incurred by him and payable under the Act or the Rules, and
- (b) any advances made by him in respect of the assets, together with interest on such advances at the rate specified in section 17 of the Judgments Act 1838 at the date of the winding-up order.

(4) Alternatively, the liquidator may (before taking office) give to the official receiver a written undertaking to discharge any such balance out of the first realisation of assets.

(5) The official receiver has a charge on the assets in respect of any sums due to him under paragraph (3). But, where the liquidator has realised assets with a view to making those payments, the official receiver's charge does not extend in respect of sums deductible by the liquidator from the proceeds of realisation, as being expenses properly incurred therein.

(6) The liquidator shall from time to time out of the realisation of assets discharge all guarantees properly given by the official receiver for the benefit of the estate, and shall pay all the official receiver's expenses.

(7) The official receiver shall give to the liquidator all such information relating to the affairs of the company and the course of the winding up as he (the official receiver) considers to be reasonably required for the effective discharge by the liquidator of his duties as such.

(8) The liquidator shall also be furnished with a copy of any report made by the official receiver under Chapter 7 of this Part of the Rules.

[6311]

SECTION B: RESIGNATION AND REMOVAL; VACATION OF OFFICE

4.108 Creditors' meeting to receive liquidator's resignation

(1) Before resigning his office, the liquidator must call a meeting of creditors for the purpose of receiving his resignation. The notice summoning the meeting shall indicate that this is the purpose, or one of the purposes, of it, and shall draw the attention of creditors to Rule 4.121 or, as the case may be, Rule 4.122–CVL with respect to the liquidator's release.

(2) A copy of the notice shall at the same time also be sent to the official receiver. (NO CVL APPLICATION)

(3) The notice to creditors under paragraph (1) must be accompanied by an account of the liquidator's administration of the winding up, including—

- (a) a summary of his receipts and payments, and
- (b) a statement by him that he has reconciled his account with that which is held by the Secretary of State in respect of the winding up.

(4) Subject as follows, the liquidator may only proceed under this Rule on grounds of ill health or because—

(a) he intends ceasing to be in practice as an insolvency practitioner, or

(b) there is some conflict of interest or change of personal circumstances which precludes or makes impracticable the further discharge by him of the duties of liquidator.

(5) Where two or more persons are acting as liquidator jointly, any one of them may proceed under this Rule (without prejudice to the continuation in office of the other or others) on the ground that, in his opinion and that of the other or others, it is no longer expedient that there should continue to be the present number of joint liquidators.

[(6) If there is no quorum present at the meeting summoned to receive the liquidator's resignation, the meeting is deemed to have been held, a resolution is deemed to have been passed that the liquidator's resignation be accepted and the creditors are deemed not to have resolved against the liquidator having his release.

(7) Where paragraph (6) applies any reference in the Rules to a resolution that the liquidator's resignation be accepted is replaced by a reference to the making of a written statement, signed by the person who, had there been a quorum present, would have been chairman of the meeting, that no quorum was present and that the liquidator may resign.]

[6312]

NOTES

Paras (6), (7): added by the Insolvency (Amendment) Rules 1987, SI 1987/1919, r 3(1), Schedule, Pt 1, para 64, as from 11 January 1988.

See Form 4.22 in Appendix 4 at **[A4]**.

4.109 Action following acceptance of resignation (NO CVL APPLICATION)

(1) This Rule applies where a meeting is summoned to receive the liquidator's resignation.

(2) If the chairman of the meeting is other than the official receiver, and there is passed at the meeting any of the following resolutions—

(a) that the liquidator's resignation be accepted,

(b) that a new liquidator be appointed,

(c) that the resigning liquidator be not given his release,

the chairman shall, within 3 days, send to the official receiver a copy of the resolution.

If it has been resolved to accept the liquidator's resignation, the chairman shall send to the official receiver a certificate to that effect.

(3) If the creditors have resolved to appoint a new liquidator, the certificate of his appointment shall also be sent to the official receiver within that time; and Rule 4.100 shall be complied with in respect of it.

(4) If the liquidator's resignation is accepted, the notice of it required by section 172(6) shall be given by him forthwith after the meeting; and he shall send a copy of the notice to the official receiver.

The notice shall be accompanied by a copy of the account sent to creditors under Rule 4.108(3).

(5) The official receiver shall file a copy of the notice in court.

(6) The liquidator's resignation is effective as from the date on which the official receiver files the copy notice in court, that date to be endorsed on the copy notice.

[6313]

NOTES

Para (4): see Form 4.32 in Appendix 4 at **[A4]**.

4.110–CVL Action following acceptance of resignation

(1) This Rule applies where a meeting is summoned to receive the liquidator's resignation.

(2) If his resignation is accepted, the notice of it required by section 171(5) shall be given by him forthwith after the meeting.

(3) Where a new liquidator is appointed in place of the one who has resigned, the certificate of his appointment shall be delivered forthwith by the chairman of the meeting to the new liquidator.

[6314]

NOTES

Para (2): see Form 4.33 in Appendix 4 at **[A4]**.

4.111 Leave to resign granted by the court

(1) If at a creditors' meeting summoned to accept the liquidator's resignation it is resolved that it be not accepted, the court may, on the liquidator's application, make an order giving him leave to resign.

(2) The court's order may include such provision as it thinks fit with respect to matters arising in connection with the resignation, and shall determine the date from which the liquidator's release is effective.

(3) The court shall send two sealed copies of the order to the liquidator, who shall send one of the copies forthwith to the official receiver. (NO CVL APPLICATION)

(4–CVL) The court shall send two sealed copies of the order to the liquidator, who shall forthwith send one of them to the registrar of companies.

(5) On sending notice of his resignation to the court, the liquidator shall send a copy of it to the official receiver. (NO CVL APPLICATION)

[6315]

NOTES

Paras (1), (4), (5): see Forms 4.34, 4.35, 4.36 in Appendix 4 at **[A4]**.

4.112 Advertisement of resignation

Where a new liquidator is appointed in place of one who has resigned, the former shall, in giving notice of his appointment, state that his predecessor has resigned and (if it be the case) that he has been given his release.

[6316]

4.113 Meeting of creditors to remove liquidator (NO CVL APPLICATION)

(1) Where a meeting of creditors is summoned for the purpose of removing the liquidator, the notice summoning it shall indicate that this is the purpose, or one of the purposes, of the meeting; and the notice shall draw the attention of creditors to section 174(4) with respect to the liquidator's release.

(2) A copy of the notice shall at the same time also be sent to the official receiver.

(3) At the meeting, a person other than the liquidator or his nominee may be elected to act as chairman; but if the liquidator or his nominee is chairman and a resolution has been proposed for the liquidator's removal, the chairman shall not adjourn the meeting without the consent of at least one-half (in value) of the creditors present (in person or by proxy) and entitled to vote.

(4) Where the chairman of the meeting is other than the official receiver, and there is passed at the meeting any of the following resolutions—

(a) that the liquidator be removed,

(b) that a new liquidator be appointed,

(c) that the removed liquidator be not given his release,

the chairman shall, within 3 days, send to the official receiver a copy of the resolution.

If it has been resolved to remove the liquidator, the chairman shall send to the official receiver a certificate to that effect.

(5) If the creditors have resolved to appoint a new liquidator, the certificate of his appointment shall also be sent to the official receiver within that time; and Rule 4.100 above shall be complied with in respect of it.

[6317]

NOTES

Paras (1), (4): see Form 4.22, 4.37 in Appendix 4 at **[A4]**.

4.114–CVL Meeting of creditors to remove liquidator

(1) A meeting held under section 171(2)(b) for the removal of the liquidator shall be summoned by him if requested by 25 per cent in value of the company's creditors, excluding those who are connected with it.

(2) The notice summoning the meeting shall indicate that the removal of the liquidator is the purpose, or one of the purposes, of the meeting; and the notice shall draw the attention of creditors to section 173(2) with respect to the liquidator's release.

(3) At the meeting, a person other than the liquidator or his nominee may be elected to act as chairman; but if the liquidator or his nominee is chairman and a resolution has been proposed for the liquidator's removal, the chairman shall not adjourn the meeting without the consent of at least one-half (in value) of the creditors present (in person or by proxy) and entitled to vote.

[6318]

NOTES

Para (2): see Form 4.22 in Appendix 4 at **[A4]**.

4.115 Court's power to regulate meetings under Rules 4.113, 4.114—CVL

Where a meeting under Rule 4.113 or 4.114–CVL is to be held, or is proposed to be summoned, the court may, on the application of any creditor, give directions as to the mode of summoning it, the sending out and return of forms of proxy, the conduct of the meeting, and any other matter which appears to the court to require regulation or control under this Rule.

[6319]

4.116 Procedure on removal (NO CVL APPLICATION)

(1) Where the creditors have resolved that the liquidator be removed, the official receiver shall file in court the certificate of removal.

(2) The resolution is effective as from the date on which the official receiver files the certificate of removal in court, and that date shall be endorsed on the certificate.

(3) A copy of the certificate, so endorsed, shall be sent by the official receiver to the liquidator who has been removed and, if a new liquidator has been appointed, to him.

(4) The official receiver shall not file the certificate in court unless and until the Secretary of State has certified to him that the removed liquidator has reconciled his account with that held by the Secretary of State in respect of the winding up.

[6320]

4.117–CVL Procedure on removal

Where the creditors have resolved that the liquidator be removed, the chairman of the creditors' meeting shall forthwith—

(a) if at the meeting another liquidator was not appointed, send the certificate of the liquidator's removal to the registrar of companies, and

(b) otherwise, deliver the certificate to the new liquidator, who shall send it to the registrar.

[6321]

NOTES

See Form 4.38 in Appendix 4 at **[A4]**.

4.118 Advertisement of removal

Where a new liquidator is appointed in place of one removed, the former shall, in giving notice of his appointment, state that his predecessor has been removed and (if it be the case) that he has been given his release.

[6322]

4.119 Removal of liquidator by the court (NO CVL APPLICATION)

(1) This Rule applies where application is made to the court for the removal of the liquidator, or for an order directing the liquidator to summon a meeting of creditors for the purpose of removing him.

(2) The court may, if it thinks that no sufficient cause is shown for the application, dismiss it; but it shall not do so unless the applicant has had an opportunity to attend the court for an *ex parte* hearing, of which he has been given at least 7 days' notice.

If the application is not dismissed under this paragraph, the court shall fix a venue for it to be heard.

(3) The court may require the applicant to make a deposit or give security for the costs to be incurred by the liquidator on the application.

(4) The applicant shall, at least 14 days before the hearing, send to the liquidator and the official receiver a notice stating the venue and accompanied by a copy of the application, and of any evidence which he intends to adduce in support of it.

(5) Subject to any contrary order of the court, the costs of the application are not payable out of the assets.

(6) Where the court removes the liquidator—

(a) it shall send copies of the order of removal to him and to the official receiver;

(b) the order may include such provision as the court thinks fit with respect to matters arising in connection with the removal; and

(c) if the court appoints a new liquidator, Rule 4.102 applies.

[6323]

NOTES

Para (1): see Form 4.39 in Appendix 4 at **[A4]**.

4.120–CVL Removal of liquidator by the court

(1) This Rule applies where the application is made to the court for the removal of the liquidator, or for an order directing the liquidator to summon a creditors' meeting for the purpose of removing him.

(2) The court may, if it thinks that no sufficient cause is shown for the application, dismiss it; but it shall not do so unless the applicant has had an opportunity to attend the court for an *ex parte* hearing, of which he has been given at least 7 days' notice.

If the application is not dismissed under this paragraph, the court shall fix a venue for it to be heard.

(3) The court may require the applicant to make a deposit or give security for the costs to be incurred by the liquidator on the application.

(4) The applicant shall, at least 14 days before the hearing, send to the liquidator a notice stating the venue and accompanied by a copy of the application, and of any evidence which he intends to adduce in support of it.

(5) Subject to any contrary order of the court, the costs of the application are not payable out of the assets.

(6) Where the court removes the liquidator—

(a) it shall send 2 copies of the order of removal to him, one to be sent by him forthwith to the registrar of companies, with notice of his ceasing to act;

(b) the order may include such provision as the court thinks fit with respect to matters arising in connection with the removal; and

(c) if the court appoints a new liquidator, Rule 4.103–CVL applies.

[6324]

NOTES

Paras (1), (6)(a): see Form 4.39, 4.40 in Appendix 4 at **[A4]**.

4.121 Release of resigning or removed liquidator (NO CVL APPLICATION)

(1) Where the liquidator's resignation is accepted by a meeting of creditors which has not resolved against his release, he has his release from when his resignation is effective under Rule 4.109.

(2) Where the liquidator is removed by a meeting of creditors which has not resolved against his release, the fact of his release shall be stated in the certificate of removal.

(3) Where—

(a) the liquidator resigns, and the creditors' meeting called to receive his resignation has resolved against his release, or

(b) he is removed by a creditors' meeting which has so resolved, or is removed by the court,

he must apply to the Secretary of State for his release.

(4) When the Secretary of State gives the release, he shall certify it accordingly, and send the certificate to the official receiver, to be filed in court.

(5) A copy of the certificate shall be sent by the Secretary of State to the former liquidator, whose release is effective from the date of the certificate.

[6325]

NOTES

Para (3): see Form 4.41 in Appendix 4 at **[A4]**.

4.122–CVL Release of resigning or removed liquidator

(1) Where the liquidator's resignation is accepted by a meeting of creditors which has not resolved against his release, he has his release from when he gives notice of his resignation to the registrar of companies.

(2) Where the liquidator is removed by a creditors' meeting which has not resolved against his release, the fact of his release shall be stated in the certificate of removal.

(3) Where—

(a) the liquidator resigns, and the creditors' meeting called to receive his resignation has resolved against his release, or

(b) he is removed by a creditors' meeting which has so resolved, or is removed by the court,

he must apply to the Secretary of State for his release.

(4) When the Secretary of State gives the release, he shall certify it accordingly, and send the certificate to the registrar of companies.

(5) A copy of the certificate shall be sent by the Secretary of State to the former liquidator, whose release is effective from the date of the certificate.

[6326]

NOTES

Paras (1), (3): see Forms 4.40, 4.41 in Appendix 4 at **[A4]**.

4.123 Removal of liquidator by Secretary of State (NO CVL APPLICATION)

(1) If the Secretary of State decides to remove the liquidator, he shall before doing so notify the liquidator and the official receiver of his decision and the grounds of it, and specify a period within which the liquidator may make representations against implementation of the decision.

(2) If the Secretary of State directs the removal of the liquidator, he shall forthwith—

(a) file notice of his decision in court, and

(b) send notice to the liquidator and the official receiver.

(3) If the liquidator is removed by direction of the Secretary of State—

(a) Rule 4.121 applies as regards the liquidator obtaining his release, as if he had been removed by the court, and

(b) the court may make any such order in his case as it would have power to make if he had been so removed.

[6327]

SECTION C: RELEASE ON COMPLETION OF ADMINISTRATION

4.124 Release of official receiver (NO CVL APPLICATION)

(1) The official receiver shall, before giving notice to the Secretary of State under section 174(3) (that the winding up is for practical purposes complete), send out notice of his intention to do so to all creditors [of which he is aware].

(2) The notice shall in each case be accompanied by a summary of the official receiver's receipts and payments as liquidator.

[(2A) The summary of receipts and payments referred to in paragraph (2) shall also include a statement as to the amount paid to unsecured creditors by virtue of the application of section 176A (prescribed part).]

(3) The Secretary of State, when he has determined the date from which the official receiver is to have his release, shall give notice to the court that he has done so. The notice shall be accompanied by the summary referred to in paragraph (2).

[6328]

NOTES

Para (1): words in square brackets substituted by the Insolvency (Amendment) Rules 2004, SI 2004/584, r 11, as from 1 April 2004.

Para (2A): inserted by the Insolvency (Amendment) Rules 2003, SI 2003/1730, r 7, Sch 1, Pt 4, para 22, as from 15 September 2003 (for transitional provisions and savings see the note preceding r 2.1 at **[6097]**).

4.125 Final meeting (NO CVL APPLICATION)

(1) Where the liquidator is other than the official receiver, he shall give at least 28 days' notice of the final meeting of creditors to be held under section 146. The notice shall be sent to all creditors [of which he is aware]; and the liquidator shall cause it to be gazetted at least one month before the meeting is to be held.

(2) The liquidator's report laid before the meeting under that section shall contain an account of the liquidator's administration of the winding up, including—

(a) a summary of his receipts and payments, and

(b) a statement by him that he has reconciled his account with that which is held by the Secretary of State in respect of the winding up.

[(2A) The liquidator's report shall also contain a statement as to the amount paid to unsecured creditors by virtue of the application of section 176A (prescribed part).]

(3) At the final meeting, the creditors may question the liquidator with respect to any matter contained in his report, and may resolve against him having his release.

(4) The liquidator shall give notice to the court that the final meeting has been held; and the notice shall state whether or not he has been given his release, and be accompanied by a copy of the report laid before the final meeting. A copy of the notice shall be sent by the liquidator to the [Secretary of State].

(5) If there is no quorum present at the final meeting, the liquidator shall report to the court that a final meeting was summoned in accordance with the Rules, but there was no quorum present; and the final meeting is then deemed to have been held, and the creditors not to have resolved against the liquidator having his release.

(6) If the creditors at the final meeting have not so resolved, the liquidator is released when the notice under paragraph (4) is filed in court. If they have so resolved, the liquidator must obtain his release from the Secretary of State and Rule 4.121 applies accordingly.

[6329]

NOTES

Para (1): words in square brackets substituted by the Insolvency (Amendment) Rules 2004, SI 2004/584, r 12, as from 1 April 2004.

Para (2A): inserted by the Insolvency (Amendment) Rules 2003, SI 2003/1730, r 7, Sch 1, Pt 4, para 23, as from 15 September 2003 (for transitional provisions and savings see the note preceding r 2.1 at **[6097]**).

Para (4): words in square brackets substituted the Insolvency (Amendment) Rules 2005, SI 2005/527, r 28, as from 1 April 2005.

Paras (1), (4): see Forms 4.22, 4.42 in Appendix 4 at **[A4]**.

[4.125A Rule as to reporting

(1) The court may, on the liquidator or official receiver's application, relieve him of any duty imposed on him by Rule 4.124 or 4.125, or authorise him to carry out the duty in a way other than there required.

(2) In considering whether to act under this Rule, the court shall have regard to the cost of carrying out the duty, to the amount of the assets available, and to the extent of the interest of creditors or contributories, or any particular class of them.]

[6329A]

NOTES

Inserted by the Insolvency (Amendment) Rules 2004, SI 2004/584, r 13, as from 1 April 2004.

4.126–CVL Final meeting

(1) The liquidator shall give at least 28 days' notice of the final meeting of creditors to be held under section 106. The notice shall be sent to all creditors who have proved their debts.

(2) At the final meeting, the creditors may question the liquidator with respect to any matter contained in the account required under the section [or paragraph (4) of this Rule], and may resolve against the liquidator having his release.

(3) Where the creditors have so resolved, he must obtain his release from the Secretary of State; and Rule 4.122–CVL applies accordingly.

[(4) The account of the winding up required under section 106 shall also include a statement as to the amount paid to unsecured creditors by virtue of the application of section 176A (prescribed part).]

[6330]

NOTES

Para (2): words in square brackets inserted by the Insolvency (Amendment) Rules 2003, SI 2003/1730, r 7, Sch 1, Pt 4, para 24(a), as from 15 September 2003 (for transitional provisions and savings see the note preceding r 2.1 at **[6097]**).

Para (4): added by SI 2003/1730, r 7, Sch 1, Pt 4, para 24(b), as from 15 September 2003 (for transitional provisions and savings see the note preceding r 2.1 at **[6097]**).

Para (1): see Form 4.22 in Appendix 4 at **[A4]**.

SECTION D: REMUNERATION

4.127 Fixing of remuneration

(1) The liquidator is entitled to receive remuneration for his services as such.

(2) The remuneration shall be fixed either—

(a) as a percentage of the value of the assets which are realised or distributed, or of the one value and the other in combination, or

(b) by reference to the time properly given by the insolvency practitioner (as liquidator) and his staff in attending to matters arising in the winding up.

(3) Where the liquidator is other than the official receiver, it is for the liquidation committee (if there is one) to determine whether the remuneration is to be fixed under paragraph (2)(a) or (b) and, if under paragraph (2)(a), to determine any percentage to be applied as there mentioned.

(4) In arriving at that determination, the committee shall have regard to the following matters—

(a) the complexity (or otherwise) of the case,

(b) any respects in which, in connection with the winding up, there falls on the insolvency practitioner (as liquidator) any responsibility of an exceptional kind or degree,

(c) the effectiveness with which the insolvency practitioner appears to be carrying out, or to have carried out, his duties as liquidator, and

(d) the value and nature of the assets with which the liquidator has to deal.

(5) If there is no liquidation committee, or the committee does not make the requisite determination, the liquidator's remuneration may be fixed (in accordance with paragraph (2)) by a resolution of a meeting of creditors; and paragraph (4) applies to them as it does to the liquidation committee.

[(6) Where the liquidator is not the official receiver and his remuneration is not fixed as above, the liquidator shall be entitled to remuneration fixed in accordance with the provisions of Rule 4.127A.]

[6331]

NOTES

Para (6): substituted by the Insolvency (Amendment) Rules 2004, SI 2004/584, r 14, as from 1 April 2004, subject to transitional provisions as noted below.

Transitional provisions: the Insolvency (Amendment) Rules 2004, SI 2004/584, r 3 provides as follows (note that by virtue of r 1(2) of those Rules "the commencement date" is 1 April 2004)—

"3 Transitional provisions

(1) This Rule applies in any case where before the commencement date—

(a) a winding-up order is made or a resolution for the winding up of the company is passed and the liquidator is entitled to remuneration by virtue of Rule 4.127(6), Rule 4.128(1) or Rule 4.148A(4); or

(b) a bankruptcy order is made and the trustee is entitled to remuneration by virtue of Rule 6.138(6) or Rule 6.139(1).

(2) In a case to which this Rule applies the liquidator or, as the case may be, the trustee shall continue to be entitled to remuneration on the basis that—

(a) the amendments made to the principal Rules by these Rules do not apply; and

(b) the amendments made to the Insolvency Regulations 1994 by the Insolvency (Amendment) Regulations 2004 had not been made.".

[4.127A Liquidator's entitlement to remuneration where it is not fixed under Rule 4.127

(1) This Rule applies where the liquidator is not the official receiver and his remuneration is not fixed in accordance with Rule 4.127.

(2) The liquidator shall be entitled by way of remuneration for his services as such, to such sum as is arrived at by—

(a) first applying the realisation scale set out in Schedule 6 to the monies received by him from the realisation of the assets of the company (including any Value Added Tax thereon but after deducting any sums paid to secured creditors in respect of their securities and any sums spent out of money received in carrying on the business of the company); and

(b) then by adding to the sum arrived at under sub-paragraph (a) such sum as is arrived at by applying the distribution scale set out in Schedule 6 to the value of assets distributed to creditors of the company (including payments made in respect of preferential debts) and to contributories.]

[6331A]

NOTES

Inserted, together with r 4.127B, by the Insolvency (Amendment) Rules 2004, SI 2004/584, r 15, as from 1 April 2004.

[4.127B Liquidator's remuneration where he realises assets on behalf of chargeholder

(1) This Rule applies where the liquidator is not the official receiver and realises assets on behalf of a secured creditor.

(2) Where the assets realised for a secured creditor are subject to a charge which when created was a mortgage or a fixed charge, the liquidator shall be entitled to such sum by way of remuneration as is arrived at by applying the realisation scale set out in Schedule 6 to the monies received by him in respect of the assets realised (including any sums received in respect of Value Added Tax thereon but after deducting any sums spent out of money received in carrying on the business of the company).

(3) Where the assets realised for a secured creditor are subject to a charge which when created was a floating charge, the liquidator shall be entitled to such sum by way of remuneration as is arrived at by—

(a) first applying the realisation scale set out in Schedule 6 to monies received by him from the realisation of those assets (including any Value Added Tax thereon but ignoring any sums received which are spent in carrying on the business of the company); and

(b) then by adding to the sum arrived at under sub-paragraph (a) such sum as is arrived at by applying the distribution scale set out in Schedule 6 to the value of the assets distributed to the holder of the charge [and payments made in respect of preferential debts].]

[6331B]

NOTES

Inserted as noted to r 4.127A at **[6331A]**.

Para (3): words in square brackets added by the Insolvency (Amendment) Rules 2005, SI 2005/527, r 29, as from 1 April 2005, subject to transitional provisions as noted below.

Transitional provisions: the Insolvency (Amendment) Rules 2005, SI 2005/527, r 3(2) provides as follows (note that by virtue of r 1(2) of those Rules "the commencement date" is 1 April 2005)—

"(2) The provisions of Rules 29, 30, 32 and 39 to these Rules shall apply in any case where, on or after 1st April 2004, a winding-up order has been made or a resolution for the winding up of a company has been passed or a bankruptcy order has been made, before the commencement date.".

4.128 Other matters affecting remuneration

(1) …

(2) Where there are joint liquidators, it is for them to agree between themselves as to how the remuneration payable should be apportioned. Any dispute arising between them may be referred—

(a) to the court, for settlement by order, or

(b) to the liquidation committee or a meeting of creditors, for settlement by resolution.

(3) If the liquidator is a solicitor and employs his own firm, or any partner in it, to act on behalf of the company, profit costs shall not be paid unless this is authorised by the liquidation committee, the creditors or the court.

[6332]

NOTES

Para (1): revoked by the Insolvency (Amendment) Rules 2004, SI 2004/584, r 16, as from 1 April 2004, subject to transitional provisions as noted to r 4.127 at **[6331]**.

4.129 Recourse of liquidator to meeting of creditors

If the liquidator's remuneration has been fixed by the liquidation committee, and he considers the rate or amount to be insufficient, he may request that it be increased by resolution of the creditors.

[6333]

4.130 Recourse to the court

(1) If the liquidator considers that the remuneration fixed for him by the liquidation committee, or by resolution of the creditors, or as under Rule 4.127(6), is insufficient, he may apply to the court for an order increasing its amount or rate.

(2) The liquidator shall give at least 14 days' notice of his application to the members of the liquidation committee; and the committee may nominate one or more members to appear or be represented, and to be heard, on the application.

(3) If there is no liquidation committee, the liquidator's notice of his application shall be sent to such one or more of the company's creditors as the court may direct, which creditors may nominate one or more of their number to appear or be represented.

(4) The court may, if it appears to be a proper case, order the costs of the liquidator's application, including the costs of any member of the liquidation committee appearing [or being represented] on it, or any creditor so appearing [or being represented], to be paid out of the assets.

[6334]

NOTES

Para (4): words in square brackets inserted by the Insolvency (Amendment) Rules 1987, SI 1987/1919, r 3(1), Schedule, Pt 1, para 65, as from 11 January 1988.

4.131 Creditors' claim that remuneration is excessive

(1) Any creditor of the company may, with the concurrence of at least 25 per cent in value of the creditors (including himself), apply to the court for an order that the liquidator's remuneration be reduced, on the grounds that it is, in all the circumstances, excessive.

(2) The court may, if it thinks that no sufficient cause is shown for a reduction, dismiss the application; but it shall not do so unless the applicant has had an opportunity to attend the court for an *ex parte* hearing, of which he has been given at least 7 days' notice.

If the application is not dismissed under this paragraph, the court shall fix a venue for it to be heard, and give notice to the applicant accordingly.

(3) The applicant shall, at least 14 days before the hearing, send to the liquidator a notice stating the venue and accompanied by a copy of the application, and of any evidence which the applicant intends to adduce in support of it.

(4) If the court considers the application to be well-founded, it shall make an order fixing the remuneration at a reduced amount or rate.

(5) Unless the court orders otherwise, the costs of the application shall be paid by the applicant, and are not payable out of the assets.

[6335]

SECTION E: SUPPLEMENTARY PROVISIONS

4.132 Liquidator deceased (NO CVL APPLICATION)

(1) Subject as follows, where the liquidator (other than the official receiver) has died, it is the duty of his personal representatives to give notice of the fact to the official receiver, specifying the date of the death.

This does not apply if notice has been given under any of the following paragraphs of this Rule.

(2) If the deceased liquidator was a partner in a firm, notice may be given to the official receiver by a partner in the firm who is qualified to act as an insolvency practitioner, or is a member of any body recognised by the Secretary of State for the authorisation of insolvency practitioners.

(3) Notice of the death may be given by any person producing to the official receiver the relevant death certificate or a copy of it.

(4) The official receiver shall give notice to the court, for the purpose of fixing the date of the deceased liquidator's release.

[6336]

4.133–CVL Liquidator deceased

(1) Subject as follows, where the liquidator has died, it is the duty of his personal representatives to give notice of the fact, and of the date of death, to the registrar of companies and to the liquidation committee (if any) or a member of that committee.

(2) In the alternative, notice of the death may be given—

(a) if the deceased liquidator was a partner in a firm, by a partner qualified to act as an insolvency practitioner or who is a member of any body approved by the Secretary of State for the authorisation of insolvency practitioners, or

(b) by any person, if he delivers with the notice a copy of the relevant death certificate.

[6337]

NOTES

Para (1): see Form 4.44 in Appendix 4 at **[A4]**.

4.134 Loss of qualification as insolvency practitioner (NO CVL APPLICATION)

(1) This Rule applies where the liquidator vacates office on ceasing to be qualified to act as an insolvency practitioner in relation to the company.

(2) He shall forthwith give notice of his doing so to the official receiver, who shall give notice to the Secretary of State.

The official receiver shall file in court a copy of his notice under this paragraph.

(3) Rule 4.121 applies as regards the liquidator obtaining his release, as if he had been removed by the court.

[6338]

NOTES

Para (2): see Form 4.45 in Appendix 4 at **[A4]**.

4.135–CVL Loss of qualification as insolvency practitioner

(1) This Rule applies where the liquidator vacates office on ceasing to be qualified to act as an insolvency practitioner in relation to the company.

(2) He shall forthwith give notice of his doing so to the registrar of companies and the Secretary of State.

(3) Rule 4.122–CVL applies as regards the liquidator obtaining his release, as if he had been removed by the court.

[6339]

NOTES

Para (2): see Forms 4.45, 4.46 in Appendix 4 at **[A4]**.

4.136–CVL Vacation of office on making of winding-up order

Where the liquidator vacates office in consequence of the court making a winding-up order against the company, Rule 4.122-CVL applies as regards his obtaining his release, as if he had been removed by the court.

[6340]

[4.137 Notice to official receiver of intention to vacate office (NO CVL APPLICATION)

(1) Where the liquidator intends to vacate office, whether by resignation or otherwise, he shall give notice of his intention to the official receiver together with notice of any creditors' meeting to be held in respect of his vacation of office, including any meeting to receive his resignation.

(2) The notice to the official receiver must be given at least 21 days before any such creditors' meeting.

(3) Where there remains any property of the company which has not been realised, applied, distributed or otherwise fully dealt with in the winding up, the liquidator shall include in his notice to the official receiver details of the nature of that property, its value (or the fact that it has no value), its location, any action taken by the liquidator to deal with that property or any reason for his not dealing with it, and the current position in relation to it.]

[6341]

NOTES

Substituted by the Insolvency (Amendment) Rules 1987, SI 1987/1919, r 3(1), Schedule, Pt 1, para 66, as from 11 January 1988.

4.138 Liquidator's duties on vacating office

(1) Where the liquidator ceases to be in office as such, in consequence of removal, resignation or cesser of qualification as an insolvency practitioner, he is under obligation forthwith to deliver up to the person succeeding him as liquidator the assets (after deduction of any expenses properly incurred, and distributions made, by him) and further to deliver up to that person—

(a) the records of the liquidation, including correspondence, proofs and other related papers appertaining to the administration while it was within his responsibility, and

(b) the company's books, papers and other records.

(2) …

[(3) Where the liquidator vacates office under section 172(8) (final meeting of creditors), he shall deliver up to the official receiver the company's books, papers and other records which have not already been disposed of in accordance with general regulations in the course of the liquidation. (NO CVL APPLICATION)]

[6342]

NOTES

Para (2): revoked by the Insolvency (Amendment) Rules 2004, SI 2004/584, r 17, as from 1 April 2004.

Para (3): added by the Insolvency (Amendment) Rules 1987, SI 1987/1919, r 3(1), Schedule, Pt 1, para 67, as from 11 January 1988.

SECTION F: THE LIQUIDATOR IN A MEMBERS' VOLUNTARY WINDING UP

4.139 Appointment by the company

(1) This Rule applies where the liquidator is appointed by a meeting of the company.

(2) Subject as follows, the chairman of the meeting shall certify the appointment, but not unless and until the person appointed has provided him with a written statement to the effect that he is an insolvency practitioner, duly qualified under the Act to be the liquidator, and that he consents so to act.

(3) The chairman shall send the certificate forthwith to the liquidator, who shall keep it as part of the records of the liquidation.

(4) Not later than 28 days from his appointment, the liquidator shall give notice of it to all creditors of the company of whom he is aware in that period.

[6343]

NOTES

Para (2): see Forms 4.27, 4.28 in Appendix 4 at **[A4]**.

4.140 Appointment by the court

(1) This Rule applies where the liquidator is appointed by the court under section 108.

(2) The court's order shall not issue unless and until the person appointed has filed in court a statement to the effect that he is an insolvency practitioner, duly qualified under the Act to be the liquidator, and that he consents so to act.

(3) Thereafter, the court shall send a sealed copy of the order to the liquidator, whose appointment takes effect from the date of the order.

(4) Not later than 28 days from his appointment, the liquidator shall give notice of it to all creditors of the company of whom he is aware in that period.

[6344]

NOTES

Para (2): see Forms 4.29, 4.30 in Appendix 4 at **[A4]**.

4.141 Authentication of liquidator's appointment

A copy of the certificate of the liquidator's appointment or (as the case may be) a sealed copy of the court's order appointing him may in any proceedings be adduced as proof that the person appointed is duly authorised to exercise the powers and perform the duties of liquidator in the company's winding up.

[6345]

4.142 Company meeting to receive liquidator's resignation

(1) Before resigning his office, the liquidator must call a meeting of the company for the purpose of receiving his resignation. The notice summoning the meeting shall indicate that this is the purpose, or one of the purposes, of it.

(2) The notice under paragraph (1) must be accompanied by an account of the liquidator's administration of the winding up, including—

(a) a summary of his receipts and payments, and

(b) a statement by him that he has reconciled his account with that which is held by the Secretary of State in respect of the winding up.

(3) Subject as follows, the liquidator may only proceed under this Rule on grounds of ill health or because—

(a) he intends ceasing to be in practice as an insolvency practitioner, or

(b) there is some conflict of interest or change of personal circumstances which precludes or makes impracticable the further discharge by him of the duties of liquidator.

(4) Where two or more persons are acting as liquidator jointly, any one of them may proceed under this Rule (without prejudice to the continuation in office of the other or others) on the ground that, in his opinion or that of the other or others, it is no longer expedient that there should continue to be the present number of joint liquidators.

[(4A) If there is no quorum present at the meeting summoned to receive the liquidator's resignation, the meeting is deemed to have been held.]

(5) The notice of the liquidator's resignation required by section 171(5) shall be given by him forthwith after the meeting.

(6) Where a new liquidator is appointed in place of one who has resigned, the former shall, in giving notice of his appointment, state that his predecessor has resigned.

[6346]

NOTES

Para (4A): inserted by the Insolvency (Amendment) Rules 1987, SI 1987/1919, r 3(1), Schedule, Pt 1, para 68, as from 11 January 1988.

See Form 4.33 in Appendix 4 at **[A4]**.

4.143 Removal of liquidator by the court

(1) This Rule applies where application is made to the court for the removal of the liquidator, or for an order directing the liquidator to summon a company meeting for the purpose of removing him.

(2) The court may, if it thinks that no sufficient cause is shown for the application, dismiss it; but it shall not do so unless the applicant has had an opportunity to attend the court for an *ex parte* hearing, of which he has been given at least 7 days' notice.

If the application is not dismissed under this paragraph, the court shall fix a venue for it to be heard.

(3) The court may require the applicant to make a deposit or give security for the costs to be incurred by the liquidator on the application.

(4) The applicant shall, at least 14 days before the hearing, send to the liquidator a notice stating the venue and accompanied by a copy of the application, and of any evidence which he intends to adduce in support of it.

Subject to any contrary order of the court, the costs of the application are not payable out of the assets.

(5) Where the court removes the liquidator—

(a) it shall send 2 copies of the order of removal to him, one to be sent by him forthwith to the registrar of companies, with notice of his ceasing to act;

(b) the order may include such provision as the court thinks fit with respect to matters arising in connection with the removal; and

(c) if the court appoints a new liquidator, Rule 4.140 applies.

[6347]

NOTES

Para (5): see Forms 4.39, 4.40 in Appendix 4 at **[A4]**.

4.144 Release of resigning or removed liquidator

(1) Where the liquidator resigns, he has his release from the date on which he gives notice of his resignation to the registrar of companies.

(2) Where the liquidator is removed by a meeting of the company, he shall forthwith give notice to the registrar of companies of his ceasing to act.

(3) Where the liquidator is removed by the court, he must apply to the Secretary of State for his release.

(4) When the Secretary of State gives the release, he shall certify it accordingly, and send the certificate to the registrar of companies.

(5) A copy of the certificate shall be sent by the Secretary of State to the former liquidator, whose release is effective from the date of the certificate.

[6348]

NOTES

See Forms 4.40, 4.41 in Appendix 4 at **[A4]**.

4.145 Liquidator deceased

(1) Subject as follows, where the liquidator has died, it is the duty of his personal representatives to give notice of the fact, and of the date of death, to the company's directors, or any one of them, and to the registrar of companies.

(2) In the alternative, notice of the death may be given—

(a) if the deceased liquidator was a partner in a firm, by a partner qualified to act as an insolvency practitioner or who is a member of any body approved by the Secretary of State for the authorisation of insolvency practitioners, or

(b) by any person, if he delivers with the notice a copy of the relevant death certificate.

[6349]

NOTES

Para (1): see Form 4.44 in Appendix 4 at **[A4]**.

4.146 Loss of qualification as insolvency practitioner

(1) This Rules applies where the liquidator vacates office on ceasing to be qualified to act as an insolvency practitioner in relation to the company.

(2) He shall forthwith give notice of his doing so to the registrar of companies and the Secretary of State.

(3) Rule 4.144 applies as regards the liquidator obtaining his release, as if he had been removed by the court.

[6350]

NOTES

Para (2): see Forms 4.45, 4.46 in Appendix 4 at **[A4]**.

4.147 Vacation of office on making of winding-up order

Where the liquidator vacates office in consequence of the court making a winding-up order against the company, Rule 4.144 applies as regards his obtaining his release, as if he had been removed by the court.

[6351]

4.148 Liquidator's duties on vacating office

Where the liquidator ceases to be in office as such, in consequence of removal, resignation or cesser of qualification as an insolvency practitioner, he is under obligation forthwith to deliver up to the person succeeding him as liquidator the assets (after deduction of any expenses properly incurred, and distributions made, by him) and further to deliver up to that person—

(a) the records of the liquidation, including correspondence, proofs and other related papers appertaining to the administration while it was within his responsibility, and

(b) the company's books, papers and other records.

[6352]

[4.148A Remuneration of liquidator in members' voluntary winding up

(1) The liquidator is entitled to receive remuneration for his services as such.

(2) The remuneration shall be fixed either—

(a) as a percentage of the value of the assets which are realised or distributed, or of the one value and the other in combination, or

(b) by reference to the time properly given by the insolvency practitioner (as liquidator) and his staff in attending to matters arising in the winding up;

and the company in general meeting shall determine whether the remuneration is to be fixed under sub-paragraph (a) or (b) and, if under sub-paragraph (a), the percentage to be applied as there mentioned.

(3) In arriving at that determination the company in general meeting shall have regard to the matters set out in paragraph (4) of Rule 4.127.

[(4) Where the liquidator's remuneration is not fixed as above, the liquidator shall be entitled to remuneration calculated in accordance with the provisions of Rule 4.148B.]

(5) Rule 4.128 [and Rule 4.127B] shall apply in relation to the remuneration of the liquidator in respect of the matters there mentioned and for this purpose references in that Rule to "the liquidation committee" and "a meeting of creditors" shall be read as references to the company in general meeting.

(6) If the liquidator considers that the remuneration fixed for him by the company in general meeting, or as under paragraph (4), is insufficient, he may apply to the court for an order increasing its amount or rate.

(7) The liquidator shall give at least 14 days' notice of an application under paragraph (6) to the company's contributories, or such one or more of them as the court may direct, and the contributories may nominate any one or more of their number to appear or be represented.

(8) The court may, if it appears to be a proper case, order the costs of the liquidator's application, including the costs of any contributory appearing or being represented on it, to be paid out of the assets.]

[6353]

NOTES

Inserted by the Insolvency (Amendment) Rules 1987, SI 1987/1919, r 3(1), Schedule, Pt 1, para 69, as from 11 January 1988.

Para (4): substituted by the Insolvency (Amendment) Rules 2004, SI 2004/584, r 18, as from 1 April 2004, subject to transitional provisions as noted to r 4.127 at **[6331]**.

Para (5): words in square brackets inserted by the Insolvency (Amendment) Rules 2005, SI 2005/527, r 30, as from 1 April 2005, subject to transitional provisions as noted to r 4.127B at **[6331B]**.

[4.148B Liquidator's remuneration in members' voluntary liquidation where it is not fixed under Rule 4.148A

(1) This Rule applies where the liquidator's remuneration is not fixed in accordance with Rule 4.148A.

(2) The liquidator shall be entitled by way of remuneration for his services as such, to such sum as is arrived at by—

(a) first applying the realisation scale set out in Schedule 6 to the monies received by him from the realisation of the assets of the company (including any Value Added Tax thereon but after deducting any sums paid to secured creditors in respect of their securities and any sums spent out of money received in carrying on the business of the company); and

(b) then by adding to the sum arrived at under sub-paragraph (a) such sum as is arrived at by applying the distribution scale set out in Schedule 6 to the value of assets distributed to creditors of the company (including payments made in respect of preferential debts) and to contributories.]

[6353A]

NOTES

Inserted by the Insolvency (Amendment) Rules 2004, SI 2004/584, r 19, as from 1 April 2004.

SECTION G: RULES APPLYING IN EVERY WINDING UP, WHETHER VOLUNTARY OR BY THE COURT

4.149 Power of court to set aside certain transactions

(1) If in the administration of the estate the liquidator enters into any transaction with a person who is an associate of his, the court may, on the application of any person interested, set the transaction aside and order the liquidator to compensate the company for any loss suffered in consequence of it.

(2) This does not apply if either—

(a) the transaction was entered into with the prior consent of the court, or

(b) it is shown to the court's satisfaction that the transaction was for value, and that it was entered into by the liquidator without knowing, or having any reason to suppose, that the person concerned was an associate.

(3) Nothing in this Rule is to be taken as prejudicing the operation of any rule of law or equity with respect to a liquidator's dealings with trust property, or the fiduciary obligations of any person.

[6354]

4.150 Rule against solicitation

(1) Where the court is satisfied that any improper solicitation has been used by or on behalf of the liquidator in obtaining proxies or procuring his appointment, it may order that no remuneration out of the assets be allowed to any person by whom, or on whose behalf, the solicitation was exercised.

(2) An order of the court under this Rule overrides any resolution of the liquidation committee or the creditors, or any other provision of the Rules relating to the liquidator's remuneration.

[6355]

CHAPTER 12
THE LIQUIDATION COMMITTEE

4.151 Preliminary (NO CVL APPLICATION)

For the purposes of this Chapter—

(a) an "insolvent winding up" is where the company is being wound up on grounds which include inability to pay its debts, and

(b) a "solvent winding up" is where the company is being wound up on grounds which do not include that one.

[6356]

4.152 Membership of committee

(1) Subject to Rule 4.154 below, the liquidation committee shall consist as follows—

(a) in any case of at least 3, and not more than 5, creditors of the company, elected by the meeting of creditors held under section 141 of the Act, and

(b) also, in the case of a solvent winding up, where the contributories' meeting held under that section so decides, of up to 3 contributories, elected by that meeting.

(NO CVL APPLICATION)

(2–CVL) The committee must have at least 3 members before it can be established.

(3) Any creditor of the company (other than one whose debt is fully secured) is eligible to be a member of the committee, so long as—

(a) he has lodged a proof of his debt, and

(b) his proof has neither been wholly disallowed for voting purposes, nor wholly rejected for purposes of distribution or dividend.

(4) No person can be a member as both a creditor and a contributory.

(5) A body corporate may be a member of the committee, but it cannot act as such otherwise than by a representative appointed under Rule 4.159.

(6) Members of the committee elected or appointed to represent the creditors are called "creditor members"; and those elected or appointed to represent the contributories are called "contributory members".

PART IV
STATUTORY INSTRUMENTS

[(7) The following categories of person are to be regarded as additional creditor members—

(a) a representative of the Financial Services Authority who exercises the right under section 371(4)(b) of the Financial Services and Markets Act 2000 to be a member of the committee;

(b) a representative of the scheme manager who exercises the right under section 215(4) of that Act to be a member of the committee.]

[6357]

NOTES

Para (7): substituted by the Financial Services and Markets Act 2000 (Consequential Amendments and Repeals) Order 2001, SI 2001/3649, art 379, as from 1 December 2001.

4.153 Formalities of establishment

(1) The liquidation committee does not come into being, and accordingly cannot act, until the liquidator has issued a certificate of its due constitution.

(2) If the chairman of the meeting which resolves to establish the committee is not the liquidator, he shall forthwith give notice of the resolution to the liquidator (or, as the case may be, the person appointed as liquidator by that same meeting), and inform him of the names and addresses of the persons elected to be members of the committee.

[(3) No person may act as a member of the committee unless and until he has agreed to do so and, unless the relevant proxy or authorisation contains a statement to the contrary, such agreement may be given by his proxy-holder or representative under section 375 of the Companies Act present at the meeting establishing the committee.

(3A) The liquidator's certificate of the committee's due constitution shall not issue before the minimum number of persons (in accordance with Rule 4.152) who are to be members of the committee have agreed to act.]

(4) As and when the others (if any) agree to act, the liquidator shall issue an amended certificate.

(5) The certificate, and any amended certificate, shall be filed in court by the liquidator.

(NO CVL APPLICATION)

(6–CVL) The certificate, and any amended certificate, shall be sent by the liquidator to the registrar of companies.

(7) If after the first establishment of the committee there is any change in its membership, the liquidator shall report the change to the court. (NO CVL APPLICATION)

(8–CVL) If after the first establishment of the committee there is any change in its membership, the liquidator shall report the change to the registrar of companies.

[6358]

NOTES

Paras (3), (3A): substituted, for original para (3), by the Insolvency (Amendment) Rules 1987, SI 1987/1919, r 3(1), Schedule, Pt 1, para 71, as from 11 January 1988.

Para (1): see Form 4.47 in Appendix 4 at **[A4]**.

Para (6): see Forms 4.47, 4.48 in Appendix 4 at **[A4]**.

Para (7): see Form 4.49 in Appendix 4 at **[A4]**.

Para (8): see Forms 4.48, 4.49 in Appendix 4 at **[A4]**.

4.154 Committee established by contributories (NO CVL APPLICATION)

(1) The following applies where the creditors' meeting under section 141 does not decide that a liquidation committee should be established, or decides that a committee should not be established.

(2) The meeting of contributories under that section may appoint one of their number to make application to the court for an order to the liquidator that a further creditors' meeting be summoned for the purpose of establishing a liquidation committee; and—

(a) the court may, if it thinks that there are special circumstances to justify it, make that order, and

(b) the creditors' meeting summoned by the liquidator in compliance with the order is deemed to have been summoned under section 141.

(3) If the creditors' meeting so summoned does not establish a liquidation committee, a meeting of contributories may do so.

(4) The committee shall then consist of at least 3, and not more than 5, contributories elected by that meeting; and Rule 4.153 applies [substituting for the reference in paragraph (3A) of that Rule to Rule 4.152 a reference to this paragraph].

[6359]

NOTES

Para (4): words in square brackets substituted by the Insolvency (Amendment) Rules 1987, SI 1987/1919, r 3(1), Schedule, Pt 1, para 72, as from 11 January 1988.

4.155 Obligations of liquidator to committee

(1) Subject as follows, it is the duty of the liquidator to report to the members of the liquidation committee all such matters as appear to him to be, or as they have indicated to him as being, of concern to them with respect to the winding up.

(2) In the case of matters so indicated to him by the committee, the liquidator need not comply with any request for information where it appears to him that—

(a) the request is frivolous or unreasonable, or
(b) the cost of complying would be excessive, having regard to the relative importance of the information, or
(c) there are not sufficient assets to enable him to comply.

(3) Where the committee has come into being more than 28 days after the appointment of the liquidator, he shall report to them, in summary form, what actions he has taken since his appointment, and shall answer all such questions as they may put to him regarding his conduct of the winding up hitherto.

(4) A person who becomes a member of the committee at any time after its first establishment is not entitled to require a report to him by the liquidator, otherwise than in summary form, of any matters previously arising.

(5) Nothing in this Rule disentitles the committee, or any member of it, from having access to the liquidator's records of the liquidation, or from seeking an explanation of any matter within the committee's responsibility.

[6360]

4.156 Meetings of the committee

(1) Subject as follows, meetings of the liquidation committee shall be held when and where determined by the liquidator.

(2) The liquidator shall call a first meeting of the committee to take place within 3 months of his appointment or of the committee's establishment (whichever is the later); and thereafter he shall call a meeting—

(a) if so requested by a creditor member of the committee or his representative (the meeting then to be held within 21 days of the request being received by the liquidator), and
(b) for a specified date, if the committee has previously resolved that a meeting be held on that date.

(3) The liquidator shall give 7 days' written notice of the venue of a meeting to every member of the committee (or his representative, if designated for that purpose), unless in any case the requirement of the notice has been waived by or on behalf of any member.

Waiver may be signified either at or before the meeting.

[6361]

4.157 The chairman at meetings

(1) The chairman at any meetings of the liquidation committee shall be the liquidator, or a person nominated by him to act.

(2) A person so nominated must be either—

(a) one who is qualified to act as an insolvency practitioner in relation to the company, or

(b) an employee of the liquidator or his firm who is experienced in insolvency matters.

[6362]

4.158 Quorum

(1) A meeting of the committee is duly constituted if due notice of it has been given to all the members, and at least 2 creditor members are present or represented.

(NO CVL APPLICATION)

(2–CVL) A meeting of the committee is duly constituted if due notice of it has been given to all the members, and at least 2 members are present or represented.

[6363]

4.159 Committee-members' representatives

(1) A member of the liquidation committee may, in relation to the business of the committee, be represented by another person duly authorised by him for that purpose.

(2) A person acting as a committee-member's representative must hold a letter of authority entitling him so to act (either generally or specially) and signed by or on behalf of the committee-member[, and for this purpose any proxy or any authorisation under section 375 of the Companies Act in relation to any meeting of creditors (or, as the case may be, members or contributories) of the company shall, unless it contains a statement to the contrary, be treated as such a letter of authority to act generally signed by or on behalf of the committee-member].

(3) The chairman at any meeting of the committee may call on a person claiming to act as a committee-member's representative to produce his letter of authority, and may exclude him if it appears that his authority is deficient.

(4) No member may be represented by a body corporate, or by a person who is an undischarged bankrupt [or a disqualified director,] or is subject to a [bankruptcy restrictions order, bankruptcy restrictions undertaking or an interim bankruptcy restrictions order].

(5) No person shall—

(a) on the same committee, act at one and the same time as representative of more than one committee-member, or

(b) act both as a member of the committee and as representative of another member.

(6) Where a member's representative signs any document on the member's behalf, the fact that he so signs must be stated below his signature.

[6364]

NOTES

Para (2): words in square brackets added by the Insolvency (Amendment) Rules 1987, SI 1987/1919, r 3(1), Schedule, Pt 1, para 73, as from 11 January 1988.

Para (4): words in first pair of square brackets inserted, and words in second pair of square brackets substituted, by the Insolvency (Amendment) Rules 2004, SI 2004/584, r 20, as from 1 April 2004.

4.160 Resignation

A member of the liquidation committee may resign by notice in writing delivered to the liquidator.

[6365]

4.161 Termination of membership

(1) A person's membership of the liquidation committee is automatically terminated if—

(a) he becomes bankrupt … , or

(b) at 3 consecutive meetings of the committee he is neither present nor represented (unless at the third of those meetings it is resolved that this Rule is not to apply in his case).

(2) However, if the cause of termination is the member's bankruptcy, his trustee in bankruptcy replaces him as a member of the committee.

(3) The membership of a creditor member is also automatically terminated if he ceases to be, or is found never to have been, a creditor.

[6366]

NOTES

Para (1): words omitted revoked by the Insolvency (Amendment) Rules 2004, SI 2004/584, r 21, as from 1 April 2004.

4.162 Removal

(1) A creditor member of the committee may be removed by resolution at a meeting of creditors; and a contributory member may be removed by a resolution of a meeting of contributories.

(2) In either case, 14 days' notice must be given of the intention to move the resolution.

[6367]

4.163 Vacancy (creditor members)

(1) The following applies if there is a vacancy among the creditor members of the committee.

(2) The vacancy need not be filled if the liquidator and a majority of the remaining creditor members so agree, provided that the total number of members does not fall below the minimum required by Rule 4.152.

(3) The liquidator may appoint any creditor (being qualified under the Rules to be a member of the committee) to fill the vacancy, if a majority of the other creditor members agree to the appointment, and the creditor concerned consents to act.

(4) Alternatively, a meeting of creditors may resolve that a creditor be appointed (with his consent) to fill the vacancy. In this case, at least 14 days' notice must have been given of the resolution to make such an appointment (whether or not of a person named in the notice).

(5) Where the vacancy is filled by an appointment made by a creditors' meeting at which the liquidator is not present, the chairman of the meeting shall report to the liquidator the appointment which has been made.

[6368]

4.164 Vacancy (contributory members)

(1) The following applies if there is a vacancy among the contributory members of the committee.

(2) The vacancy need not be filled if the liquidator and a majority of the remaining contributory members so agree, provided that, in the case of a committee of contributory members only, the total number of members does not fall below the minimum required by Rule 4.154(4) or, as the case may be, 4.171(5).

(3) The liquidator may appoint any contributory member (being qualified under the Rules to be a member of the committee) to fill the vacancy, if a majority of the other contributory members agree to the appointment, and the contributory concerned consents to act.

(4) Alternatively, a meeting of contributories may resolve that a contributory be appointed (with his consent) to fill the vacancy. In this case, at least 14 days' notice must have been given of the resolution to make such an appointment (whether or not of a person named in the notice).

(5–CVL) Where the contributories make an appointment under paragraph (4), the creditor members of the committee may, if they think fit, resolve that the person appointed ought not to be a member of the committee; and—

- (a) that person is not then, unless the court otherwise directs, qualified to act as a member of the committee, and
- (b) on any application to the court for a direction under this paragraph the court may, if it thinks fit, appoint another person (being a contributory) to fill the vacancy on the committee.

(6) Where the vacancy is filled by an appointment made by a contributories' meeting at which the liquidator is not present, the chairman of the meeting shall report to the liquidator the appointment which has been made.

[6369]

4.165 Voting rights and resolutions (NO CVL APPLICATION)

(1) At any meeting of the committee, each member of it (whether present himself, or by his representative) has one vote; and a resolution is passed when a majority of the creditor members present or represented have voted in favour of it.

(2) Subject to the next paragraph, the votes of contributory members do not count towards the number required for passing a resolution, but the way in which they vote on any resolution shall be recorded.

(3) Paragraph (2) does not apply where, by virtue of Rule 4.154 or 4.171, the only members of the committee are contributories. In that case the committee is to be treated for voting purposes as if all its members were creditors.

(4) Every resolution passed shall be recorded in writing, either separately or as part of the minutes of the meeting. The record shall be signed by the chairman and kept with the records of the liquidation.

[6370]

4.166–CVL Voting rights and resolutions

(1) At any meeting of the committee, each member of it (whether present himself, or by his representative) has one vote; and a resolution is passed when a majority of the members present or represented have voted in favour of it.

(2) Every resolution passed shall be recorded in writing, either separately or as part of the minutes of the meeting. The record shall be signed by the chairman and kept with the records of the liquidation.

[6371]

4.167 Resolutions by post

(1) In accordance with this Rule, the liquidator may seek to obtain the agreement of members of the liquidation committee to a resolution by sending to every member (or his representative designated for the purpose) a copy of the proposed resolution.

(2) Where the liquidator makes use of the procedure allowed by this Rule, he shall send out to members of the committee or their representatives (as the case may be) a statement incorporating [a copy of any proposed resolution on which a decision is sought, which shall be set out in such a way that agreement with or dissent from each separate resolution may be indicated by the recipient on the copy so sent].

(3) Any creditor member of the committee may, within 7 business days from the date of the liquidator sending out a resolution, require him to summon a meeting of the committee to consider the matters raised by the resolution. (NO CVL APPLICATION)

(4–CVL) Any member of the committee may, within 7 business days from the date of the liquidator sending out a resolution, require him to summon a meeting of the committee to consider the matters raised by the resolution.

(5) In the absence of such a request, the resolution is deemed to have been passed by the committee if and when the liquidator is notified in writing by a majority of the creditor members that they concur with it. (NO CVL APPLICATION)

(6–CVL) In the absence of such a request, the resolution is deemed to have been passed by the committee if and when the liquidator is notified in writing by a majority of the members that they concur with it.

(7) A copy of every resolution passed under this Rule, and a note that the committee's concurrence was obtained, shall be kept with the records of the liquidation.

[6372]

NOTES

Para (2): words in square brackets substituted by the Insolvency (Amendment) Rules 1987, SI 1987/1919, r 3(1), Schedule, Pt 1, para 74, as from 11 January 1988.

4.168 Liquidator's reports

(1) The liquidator shall, as and when directed by the liquidation committee (but not more often than once in any period of 2 months), send a written report to every member of the

committee setting out the position generally as regards the progress of the winding up and matters arising in connection with it, to which he (the liquidator) considers the committee's attention should be drawn.

(2) In the absence of such directions by the committee, the liquidator shall send such a report not less often than once in every period of 6 months.

(3) The obligations of the liquidator under this Rule are without prejudice to those imposed by Rule 4.155.

[6373]

4.169 Expenses of members, etc

The liquidator shall defray out of the assets, in the prescribed order of priority, any reasonable travelling expenses directly incurred by members of the liquidation committee or their representatives in respect of their attendance at the committee's meetings, or otherwise on the committee's business.

[6374]

4.170 Dealings by committee-members and others

(1) This Rule applies to—
- (a) any member of the liquidation committee,
- (b) any committee-member's representative,
- (c) any person who is an associate of a member of the committee or a committee-member's representative, and
- (d) any person who has been a member of the committee at any time in the last 12 months.

(2) Subject as follows, a person to whom this Rule applies shall not enter into any transaction whereby he—
- (a) receives out of the company's assets any payment for services given or goods supplied in connection with the administration, or
- (b) obtains any profit from the administration, or
- (c) acquires any asset forming part of the estate.

(3) Such a transaction may be entered into by a person to whom this Rule applies—
- (a) with the prior leave of the court, or
- (b) if he does so as a matter of urgency, or by way of performance of a contract in force before the date on which the company went into liquidation, and obtains the court's leave for the transaction, having applied for it without undue delay, or
- (c) with the prior sanction of the liquidation committee, where it is satisfied (after full disclosure of the circumstances) that the person will be giving full value in the transaction.

(4) Where in the committee a resolution is proposed that sanction be accorded for a transaction to be entered into which, without that sanction or the leave of the court, would be in contravention of this Rule, no member of the committee, and no representative of a member, shall vote if he is to participate directly or indirectly in the transaction.

(5) The court may, on the application of any person interested—
- (a) set aside a transaction on the ground that it has been entered into in contravention of this Rule, and
- (b) make with respect to it such other order as it thinks fit, including (subject to the following paragraph) an order requiring a person to whom this Rule applies to account for any profit obtained from the transaction and compensate the estate for any resultant loss.

(6) In the case of a person to whom this Rule applies as an associate of a member of the committee or of a committee-member's representative, the court shall not make any order under paragraph (5), if satisfied that he entered into the relevant transaction without having any reason to suppose that in doing so he would contravene this Rule.

(7) The costs of an application to the court for leave under this Rule are not payable out of the assets, unless the court so orders.

[6375]

4.171 Composition of committee when creditors paid in full

(1) This Rule applies if the liquidator issues a certificate that the creditors have been paid in full, with interest in accordance with section 189.

(2) The liquidator shall forthwith file the certificate in court. (NO CVL APPLICATION)

(3–CVL) The liquidator shall forthwith send a copy of the certificate to the registrar of companies.

(4) The creditor members of the liquidation committee cease to be members of the committee.

(5) The committee continues in being unless and until abolished by decision of a meeting of contributories, and (subject to the next paragraph) so long as it consists of at least 3 contributory members.

(6) The committee does not cease to exist on account of the number of contributory members falling below 3, unless and until 28 days have elapsed since the issue of the liquidator's certificate under paragraph (1).

But at any time when the committee consists of less than 3 contributory members, it is suspended and cannot act.

(7) Contributories may be co-opted by the liquidator, or appointed by a contributories' meeting, to be members of the committee; but the maximum number of members is 5.

(8) The foregoing Rules in this Chapter continue to apply to the liquidation committee (with any necessary modifications) as if all the members of the committee were creditor members.

[6376]

NOTES

Paras (2), (3): see Form 4.50, 4.51 in Appendix 4 at **[A4]**.

4.172 Committee's functions vested in Secretary of State (**NO CVL APPLICATION**)

(1) At any time when the functions of the liquidation committee are vested in the Secretary of State under section 141(4) or (5), requirements of the Act or the Rules about notices to be given, or reports to be made, to the committee by the liquidator do not apply, otherwise than as enabling the committee to require a report as to any matter.

(2) Where the committee's functions are so vested under section 141(5), they may be exercised by the official receiver.

[6377]

[4.172A Formal defects

The acts of the liquidation committee established for any winding up are valid notwithstanding any defect in the appointment, election or qualifications of any member of the committee or any committee-member's representative or in the formalities of its establishment.]

[6378]

NOTES

Inserted by the Insolvency (Amendment) Rules 1987, SI 1987/1919, r 3(1), Schedule, Pt 1, para 75, as from 11 January 1988.

CHAPTER 13
THE LIQUIDATION COMMITTEE WHERE WINDING UP FOLLOWS IMMEDIATELY ON ADMINISTRATION

(NO CVL APPLICATION)

4.173 Preliminary

(1) The rules in this Chapter apply where—

(a) the winding-up order has been made [by the court upon an application under paragraph 79 of Schedule B1 to the Act], and

(b) the court makes an order under section 140(1) of the Act appointing as liquidator the person who was previously the administrator.

(2) In this Chapter, "insolvent winding up", "solvent winding up", "creditor member" and "contributory member" mean the same as in Chapter 12.

[6379]

NOTES

Para (1): words in square brackets substituted by the Insolvency (Amendment) Rules 2003, SI 2003/1730, r 7, Sch 1, Pt 4, para 25, as from 15 September 2003 (for transitional provisions and savings see the note preceding r 2.1 at **[6097]**).

4.174 Continuation of creditors' committee

(1) If under [paragraph 57 of Schedule B1 to the Act] a creditors' committee has been established for the purposes of the administration, then (subject as follows in this Chapter) that committee continues in being as the liquidation committee for the purposes of the winding up, and—

(a) it is deemed to be a committee established as such under section 141, and

(b) no action shall be taken under subsections (1) to (3) of that section to establish any other.

(2) This Rule does not apply if, at the time when the court's order under section 140(1) is made, the committee under [paragraph 57 of Schedule B1 to the Act] consists of less than 3 members; and a creditor who was, immediately before that date, a member of it, ceases to be a member on the making of the order if his debt is fully secured.

[6380]

NOTES

Paras (1), (2): words in square brackets substituted by the Insolvency (Amendment) Rules 2003, SI 2003/1730, r 7, Sch 1, Pt 4, para 26, as from 15 September 2003 (for transitional provisions and savings see the note preceding r 2.1 at **[6097]**).

4.175 Membership of committee

(1) Subject as follows, the liquidation committee shall consist of at least 3, and not more than 5, creditors of the company, elected by the creditors' meeting held under [paragraph 57 of Schedule B1 to the Act] or (in order to make up numbers or fill vacancies) by a creditors' meeting summoned by the liquidator after the company goes into liquidation.

(2) In the case of a solvent winding up, the liquidator shall, on not less than 21 days' notice, summon a meeting of contributories, in order to elect (if it so wishes) contributory members of the liquidation committee, up to 3 in number.

[6381]

NOTES

Para (1): words in square brackets substituted by the Insolvency (Amendment) Rules 2003, SI 2003/1730, r 7, Sch 1, Pt 4, para 27, as from 15 September 2003 (for transitional provisions and savings see the note preceding r 2.1 at **[6097]**).

4.176 Liquidator's certificate

(1) The liquidator shall issue a certificate of the liquidation committee's continuance, specifying the persons who are, or are to be, members of it.

(2) It shall be stated in the certificate whether or not the liquidator has summoned a meeting of contributories under Rule 4.175(2), and whether (if so) the meeting has elected contributories to be members of the committee.

(3) Pending the issue of the liquidator's certificate, the committee is suspended and cannot act.

(4) No person may act, or continue to act, as a member of the committee unless and until he has agreed to do so; and the liquidator's certificate shall not issue until at least the minimum number of persons required under Rule 4.175 to form a committee have signified their agreement.

(5) As and when the others signify their agreement, the liquidator shall issue an amended certificate.

(6) The liquidator's certificate (or, as the case may be, the amended certificate) shall be filed by him in court.

(7) If subsequently there is any change in the committee's membership, the liquidator shall report the change to the court.

[6382]

NOTES

Paras (1), (5) and (7): see Forms 4.52 and 4.49 in Appendix 4 at **[A4]**.

4.177 Obligations of liquidator to committee

(1) As soon as may be after the issue of the liquidator's certificate under Rule 4.176, the liquidator shall report to the liquidation committee what actions he has taken since the date on which the company went into liquidation.

(2) A person who becomes a member of the committee after that date is not entitled to require a report to him by the liquidator, otherwise than in a summary form, of any matters previously arising.

(3) Nothing in this rule disentitles the committee, or any member of it, from having access to the records of the liquidation (whether relating to the period when he was administrator, or to any subsequent period), or from seeking an explanation of any matter within the committee's responsibility.

[6383]

4.178 Application of Chapter 12

Except as provided above in this Chapter, Rules 4.155 to [4.172A] in Chapter 12 apply to the liquidation committee following the issue of the liquidator's certificate under Rule 4.176, as if it had been established under section 141.

[6384]

NOTES

Figure in square brackets substituted by the Insolvency (Amendment) Rules 1987, SI 1987/1919, r 3(1), Schedule, Pt 1, para 76, as from 11 January 1988.

CHAPTER 14
COLLECTION AND DISTRIBUTION OF COMPANY'S ASSETS BY LIQUIDATOR

4.179 General duties of liquidator (NO CVL APPLICATION)

(1) The duties imposed on the court by the Act with regard to the collection of the company's assets and their application in discharge of its liabilities are discharged by the liquidator as an officer of the court subject to its control.

(2) In the discharge of his duties the liquidator, for the purposes of acquiring and retaining possession of the company's property, has the same powers as a receiver appointed by the High Court, and the court may on his application enforce such acquisition or retention accordingly.

[6385]

4.180 Manner of distributing assets

(1) Whenever the liquidator has sufficient funds in hand for the purpose he shall, subject to the retention of such sums as may be necessary for the expenses of the winding up, declare and distribute dividends among the creditors in respect of the debts which they have respectively proved.

(2) The liquidator shall give notice of his intention to declare and distribute a dividend.

(3) Where the liquidator has declared a dividend, he shall give notice of it to the creditors, stating how the dividend is proposed to be distributed. The notice shall contain such particulars with respect to the company, and to its assets and affairs, as will enable the creditors to comprehend the calculation of the amount of the dividend and the manner of its distribution.

[6386]

4.181 Debts of insolvent company to rank equally (NO CVL APPLICATION)

[(1)] Debts other than preferential debts rank equally between themselves in the winding up, and, after the preferential debts, shall be paid in full unless the assets are insufficient for meeting them, in which case they abate in equal proportions between themselves.

[(2) Paragraph (1) applies whether or not the company is unable to pay its debts.]

[6387]

NOTES

Para (1) numbered as such, and para (2) added, by the Insolvency (Amendment) Rules 1987, SI 1987/1919, r 3(1), Schedule, Pt 1, para 77, as from 11 January 1988.

4.182 Supplementary provisions as to dividend

(1) In the calculation and distribution of a dividend the liquidator shall make provision—

(a) for any debts which appear to him to be due to persons who, by reason of the distance of their place of residence, may not have had sufficient time to tender and establish their proofs,

(b) for any debts which are the subject of claims which have not yet been determined, and

(c) for disputed proofs and claims.

(2) A creditor who has not proved his debt before the declaration of any dividend is not entitled to disturb, by reason that he has not participated in it, the distribution of that dividend or any other dividend declared before his debt was proved, but—

(a) when he has proved that debt he is entitled to be paid, out of any money for the time being available for the payment of any further dividend, any dividend or dividends which he has failed to receive, and

(b) any dividend or dividends payable under sub-paragraph (a) shall be paid before that money is applied to the payment of any such further dividend.

(3) No action lies against the liquidator for a dividend; but if he refuses to pay a dividend the court may, if it thinks fit, order him to pay it and also to pay, out of his own money—

(a) interest on the dividend, at the rate for the time being specified in section 17 of the Judgments Act 1838, from the time when it was withheld, and

(b) the costs of the proceedings in which the order to pay is made.

[6388]

[4.182A Distribution in members' voluntary winding up (NO CVL APPLICATION)

(1) In a member's voluntary winding up the liquidator may give notice in such newspaper as he considers most appropriate for the purpose of drawing the matter to the attention of the company's creditors that he intends to make a distribution to creditors.

(2) The notice shall specify a date ("the last date for proving") up to which proofs may be lodged. The date shall be the same for all creditors and not less than 21 days from that of the notice.

(3) The liquidator is not obliged to deal with proofs lodged after the last date for proving; but he may do so, if he thinks fit.

(4) A creditor who has not proved his debt before the last date for proving or after that date increases the claim in his proof is not entitled to disturb, by reason that he has not participated in it, either at all or, as the case may be, to the extent that his increased claim would allow, that distribution or any other distribution made before his debt was proved or his claim increased; but when he has proved his debt or, as the case may be, increased his claim, he is entitled to be paid, out of any money for the time being available for the payment of any further distribution, any distribution or distributions which he has failed to receive.

(5) Where the distribution proposed to be made is to be the only or the final distribution in that winding up, the liquidator may, subject to paragraph (6), make that distribution without regard to the claim of any person in respect of a debt not already proved.

(6) Where the distribution proposed to be made is one specified in paragraph (5), the notice given under paragraph (1) shall state the effect of paragraph (5).]

[6389]

NOTES

Inserted by the Insolvency (Amendment) Rules 1987, SI 1987/1919, r 3(1), Schedule, Pt 1, para 78, as from 11 January 1988.

4.183 Division of unsold assets

Without prejudice to provisions of the Act about disclaimer, the liquidator may, with the permission of the liquidation committee, divide in its existing form amongst the company's creditors, according to its estimated value, any property which from its peculiar nature or other special circumstances cannot be readily or advantageously sold.

[6390]

4.184 General powers of liquidator

(1) Any permission given by the liquidation committee [(or if there is no such committee, a meeting of the company's creditors)] or the court under [section 165(2) or] section 167(1)(a), or under the Rules, shall not be a general permission but shall relate to a particular proposed exercise of the liquidator's power in question; and a person dealing with the liquidator in good faith and for value is not concerned to enquire whether any such permission has been given.

(2) Where the liquidator has done anything without that permission, the court or the liquidation committee may, for the purpose of enabling him to meet his expenses out of the assets, ratify what he has done; but neither shall do so unless it is satisfied that the liquidator has acted in a case of urgency and has sought ratification without undue delay.

[6391]

NOTES

Para (1): words in square brackets inserted by the Insolvency (Amendment) Rules 2005, SI 2005/527, r 31, as from 1 April 2005.

4.185 Enforced delivery up of company's property (NO CVL APPLICATION)

(1) The powers conferred on the court by section 234 (enforced delivery of company property) are exercisable by the liquidator or, where a provisional liquidator has been appointed, by him.

(2) Any person on whom a requirement under section 234(2) is imposed by the liquidator or provisional liquidator shall, without avoidable delay, comply with it.

[6392]

4.186 Final distribution

(1) When the liquidator has realised all the company's assets or so much of them as can, in his opinion, be realised without needlessly protracting the liquidation, he shall give notice, under Part 11 of the Rules, either—

(a) of his intention to declare a final dividend, or
(b) that no dividend, or further dividend, will be declared.

(2) The notice shall contain all such particulars as are required by Part 11 of the rules and shall require claims against the assets to be established by a date specified in the notice.

(3) After that date, the liquidator shall—

(a) defray any outstanding expenses of the winding up out of the assets, and
(b) if he intends to declare a final dividend, declare and distribute that dividend without regard to the claim of any person in respect of a debt not already proved.

(4) The court may, on the application of any person, postpone the date specified in the notice.

[6393]

CHAPTER 15
DISCLAIMER

4.187 Liquidator's notice of disclaimer

(1) Where the liquidator disclaims property under section 178, the notice of disclaimer shall contain such particulars of the property disclaimed as enable it to be easily identified.

(2) The notice shall be signed by the liquidator and filed in court, with a copy. The court shall secure that both the notice and the copy are sealed and endorsed with the date of filing.

(3) The copy notice, so sealed and endorsed, shall be returned by the court to the liquidator as follows—

(a) if the notice has been delivered at the offices of the court by the liquidator in person, it shall be handed to him,

(b) if it has been delivered by some person acting on the liquidator's behalf, it shall be handed to that person, for immediate transmission to the liquidator, and

(c) otherwise, it shall be sent to the liquidator by first class post.

The court shall cause to be endorsed on the original notice, or otherwise recorded on the file, the manner in which the copy notice was returned to the liquidator.

(4) For the purposes of section 178, the date of the prescribed notice is that which is endorsed on it, and on the copy, in accordance with this Rule.

[6394]

NOTES

Para (1): see Form 4.53 in Appendix 4 at **[A4]**.

4.188 Communication of disclaimer to persons interested

(1) Within 7 days after the day on which the copy of the notice of disclaimer is returned to him under Rule 4.187, the liquidator shall send or give copies of the notice (showing the date endorsed as required by that Rule) to the persons mentioned in paragraphs (2) to (4) below.

(2) Where the property disclaimed is of a leasehold nature, he shall send or give a copy to every person who (to his knowledge) claims under the company as underlessee or mortgagee.

(3) He shall in any case send or give a copy of the notice to every person who (to his knowledge)—

(a) claims an interest in the disclaimed property, or

(b) is under any liability in respect of the property, not being a liability discharged by the disclaimer.

(4) If the disclaimer is of an unprofitable contract, he shall send or give copies of the notice to all such persons as, to his knowledge, are parties to the contract or have interests under it.

(5) If subsequently it comes to the liquidator's knowledge, in the case of any person, that he has such an interest in the disclaimed property as would have entitled him to receive a copy of the notice of disclaimer in pursuance of paragraphs (2) to (4), the liquidator shall then forthwith send or give to that person a copy of the notice.

But compliance with this paragraph is not required if—

(a) the liquidator is satisfied that the person has already been made aware of the disclaimer and its date, or

(b) the court, on the liquidator's application, orders that compliance is not required in that particular case.

[6395]

NOTES

Para (1): see Form 4.53 in Appendix 4 at **[A4]**.

4.189 Additional notices

The liquidator disclaiming property may, without prejudice to his obligations under sections 178 to 180 and Rules 4.187 and 4.188, at any time give notice of the disclaimer to any persons who in his opinion ought, in the public interest or otherwise, to be informed of it.

[6396]

NOTES

See Form 4.53 in Appendix 4 at **[A4]**.

4.190 Duty to keep court informed

The liquidator shall notify the court from time to time as to the persons to whom he has sent or given copies of the notice of disclaimer under the two preceding Rules, giving their names and addresses, and the nature of their respective interests.

[6397]

4.191 Application by interested party under s 178(5)

Where, in the case of any property, application is made to the liquidator by an interested party under section 178(5) (request for decision whether the property is to be disclaimed or not), the application—

(a) shall be delivered to the liquidator personally or by registered post, and
(b) shall be made in the form known as "notice to elect", or a substantially similar form.

[6398]

NOTES

See Form 4.54 in Appendix 4 at **[A4]**.

4.192 Interest in property to be declared on request

(1) If, in the case of property which the liquidator has the right to disclaim, it appears to him that there is some person who claims, or may claim, to have an interest in the property, he may give notice to that person calling on him to declare within 14 days whether he claims any such interest and, if so, the nature and extent of it.

(2) Failing compliance with the notice, the liquidator is entitled to assume that the person concerned has no such interest in the property as will prevent or impede its disclaimer.

[6399]

NOTES

Para (1): see Form 4.55 in Appendix 4 at **[A4]**.

4.193 Disclaimer presumed valid and effective

Any disclaimer of property by the liquidator is presumed valid and effective, unless it is proved that he has been in breach of his duty with respect to the giving of notice of disclaimer, or otherwise under sections 178 to 180, or under this Chapter of the Rules.

[6400]

4.194 Application for exercise of court's powers under s 181

(1) This Rule applies with respect to an application by any person under section 181 for an order of the court to vest or deliver disclaimed property.

(2) The application must be made within 3 months of the applicant becoming aware of the disclaimer, or of his receiving a copy of the liquidator's notice of disclaimer sent under Rule 4.188, whichever is the earlier.

(3) The applicant shall with his application file in court an affidavit—

(a) stating whether he applies under paragraph (a) of section 181(2) (claim of interest in the property) or under paragraph (b) (liability not discharged);
(b) specifying the date on which he received a copy of the liquidator's notice of disclaimer, or otherwise became aware of the disclaimer; and
(c) specifying the grounds of his application and the order which he desires the court to make under section 181.

(4) The court shall fix a venue for the hearing of the application; and the applicant shall, not later than 7 days before the date fixed, give to the liquidator notice of the venue, accompanied by copies of the application and the affidavit under paragraph (3).

(5) On the hearing of the application, the court may give directions as to other persons (if any) who should be sent or given notice of the application and the grounds on which it is made.

(6) Sealed copies of any order made on the application shall be sent by the court to the applicant and the liquidator.

(7) In a case where the property disclaimed is of a leasehold nature, and section 179 applies to suspend the effect of the disclaimer, there shall be included in the court's order a direction giving effect to the disclaimer.

This paragraph does not apply if, at the time when the order is issued, other applications under section 181 are pending in respect of the same property.

[6401]

CHAPTER 16
SETTLEMENT OF LIST OF CONTRIBUTORIES

(NO CVL APPLICATION)

4.195 Preliminary

The duties of the court with regard to the settling of the list of contributories are, by virtue of the Rules, delegated to the liquidator.

[6402]

4.196 Duty of liquidator to settle list

(1) Subject as follows, the liquidator shall, as soon as may be after his appointment, exercise the court's power to settle a list of the company's contributories for the purposes of section 148 and, with the court's approval, rectify the register of members.

(2) The liquidator's duties under this Rule are performed by him as an officer of the court subject to the court's control.

[6403]

4.197 Form of list

(1) The list shall identify—

(a) the several classes of the company's shares (if more than one), and

(b) the several classes of contributories, distinguishing between those who are contributories in their own right and those who are so as representatives of, or liable for the debts of, others.

(2) In the case of each contributory there shall in the list be stated—

(a) his address,

(b) the number and class of shares, or the extent of any other interest to be attributed to him, and

(c) if the shares are not fully paid up, the amounts which have been called up and paid in respect of them (and the equivalent, if any, where his interest is other than shares).

[6404]

4.198 Procedure for settling list

(1) Having settled the list, the liquidator shall forthwith give notice, to every person included in the list, that he has done so.

(2) The notice given to each person shall state—

(a) in what character, and for what number of shares or what interest, he is included in the list,

(b) what amounts have been called up and paid up in respect of the shares or interest, and

(c) that in relation to any shares or interest not fully paid up, his inclusion in the list may result in the unpaid capital being called.

(3) The notice shall inform any person to whom it is given that, if he objects to any entry in, or omission from, the list, he should so inform the liquidator in writing within 21 days from the date of the notice.

(4) On receipt of any such objection, the liquidator shall within 14 days give notice to the objector either—

(a) that he has amended the list (specifying the amendment), or

(b) that he considers the objection to be not well-founded and declines to amend the list.

The notice shall in either case inform the objector of the effect of Rule 4.199.

[6405]

4.199 Application to court for variation of the list

(1) If a person objects to any entry in, or exclusion from, the list of contributories as settled by the liquidator and, notwithstanding notice by the liquidator declining to amend the list, maintains his objection, he may apply to the court for an order removing the entry to which he objects or (as the case may be) otherwise amending the list.

(2) The application must be made within 21 days of the service on the applicant of the liquidator's notice under Rule 4.198(4).

[6406]

4.200 Variation of, or addition to, the list

The liquidator may from time to time vary or add to the list of contributories as previously settled by him, but subject in all respects to the preceding Rules in this Chapter.

[6407]

4.201 Costs not to fall on official receiver

The official receiver is not personally liable for any costs incurred by a person in respect of an application to set aside or vary his act or decision in settling the list of contributories, or varying or adding to the list; and the liquidator (if other than the official receiver) is not so liable unless the court makes an order to that effect.

[6408]

CHAPTER 17
CALLS

(NO CVL APPLICATION)

4.202 Calls by liquidator

Subject as follows, the powers conferred by the Act with respect to the making of calls on contributories are exercisable by the liquidator as an officer of the court subject to the court's control.

[6409]

4.203 Control by liquidation committee

(1) Where the liquidator proposes to make a call, and there is a liquidation committee, he may summon a meeting of the committee for the purpose of obtaining its sanction.

(2) At least 7 days' notice of the meeting shall be given by the liquidator to each member of the committee.

(3) The notice shall contain a statement of the proposed amount of the call, and the purpose for which it is intended to be made.

[6410]

4.204 Application to court for leave to make a call

(1) For the purpose of obtaining the leave of the court for the making of a call on any contributories of the company, the liquidator shall apply *ex parte*, supporting his application by affidavit.

(2) There shall in the application be stated the amount of the proposed call, and the contributories on whom it is to be made.

(3) The court may direct that notice of the order be given to the contributories concerned, or to other contributories, or may direct that the notice be publicly advertised.

[6411]

NOTES

Paras (1), (2): see Forms 4.56, 4.57 in Appendix 4 at **[A4]**.

4.205 Making and enforcement of the call

(1) Notice of the call shall be given to each of the contributories concerned, and shall specify—

(a) the amount or balance due from him in respect of it, and

(b) whether the call is made with the sanction of the court or the liquidation committee.

(2) Payment of the amount due from any contributory may be enforced by order of the court.

[6412]

NOTES

Paras (1), (2): see Forms 4.58, 4.59 in Appendix 4 at **[A4]**.

CHAPTER 18
SPECIAL MANAGER

4.206 Appointment and remuneration

(1) An application made by the liquidator under section 177 for the appointment of a person to be special manager shall be supported by a report setting out the reasons for the application.

The report shall include the applicant's estimate of the value of the assets in respect of which the special manager is to be appointed.

(2) This Chapter applies also with respect to an application by the provisional liquidator, where one has been appointed, and references to the liquidator are to be read accordingly as including the provisional liquidator. (NO CVL APPLICATION)

(3) The court's order appointing the special manager shall specify the duration of his appointment, which may be for a period of time, or until the occurrence of a specified event. Alternatively, the order may specify that the duration of the appointment is to be subject to a further order of the court.

(4) The appointment of a special manager may be renewed by order of the court.

(5) The special manager's remuneration shall be fixed from time to time by the court.

(6) The acts of the special manager are valid notwithstanding any defect in his appointment or qualifications.

[6413]

NOTES

Para (3): see Form 4.60 in Appendix 4 at **[A4]**.

4.207 Security

(1) The appointment of the special manager does not take effect until the person appointed has given (or, being allowed by the court to do so, undertaken to give) security to the person who applies for him to be appointed.

(2) It is not necessary that security shall be given for each separate company liquidation; but it may be given either specially for a particular liquidation, or generally for any liquidation in relation to which the special manager may be employed as such.

(3) The amount of the security shall be not less than the value of the assets in respect of which he is appointed, as estimated by the applicant in his report under Rule 4.206.

(4) When the special manager has given security to the person applying for his appointment, that person shall file in court a certificate as to the adequacy of the security.

(5) The cost of providing the security shall be paid in the first instance by the special manager; but—

(a) where a winding-up order is not made, he is entitled to be reimbursed out of the property of the company, and the court may make an order on the company accordingly, and

(b) where a winding-up order is made, he is entitled to be reimbursed out of the assets in the prescribed order of priority.

(NO CVL APPLICATION)

(6–CVL) The cost of providing the security shall be paid in the first instance by the special manager; but he is entitled to be reimbursed out of the assets, in the prescribed order of priority.

[6414]

4.208 Failure to give or keep up security

(1) If the special manager fails to give the required security within the time stated for that purpose by the order appointing him, or any extension of that time that may be allowed, the liquidator shall report the failure to the court, which may thereupon discharge the order appointing the special manager.

(2) If the special manager fails to keep up his security, the liquidator shall report his failure to the court, which may thereupon remove the special manager, and make such order as it thinks fit as to costs.

(3) If an order is made under this Rule removing the special manager, or discharging the order appointing him, the court shall give directions as to whether any, and if so what, steps should be taken for the appointment of another special manager in his place.

[6415]

4.209 Accounting

(1) The special manager shall produce accounts, containing details of his receipts and payments, for the approval of the liquidator.

(2) The accounts shall be in respect of 3–month periods for the duration of the special manager's appointment (or for a lesser period, if his appointment terminates less than 3 months from its date, or from the date to which the last accounts were made up).

(3) When the accounts have been approved, the special manager's receipts and payments shall be added to those of the liquidator.

[6416]

4.210 Termination of appointment

(1) The special manager's appointment terminates if the winding-up petition is dismissed or if, a provisional liquidator having been appointed, the latter is discharged without a winding-up order having been made. (NO CVL APPLICATION)

(2) If the liquidator is of opinion that the employment of the special manager is no longer necessary or profitable for the company, he shall apply to the court for directions, and the court may order the special manager's appointment to be terminated.

(3) The liquidator shall make the same application if a resolution of the creditors is passed, requesting that the appointment be terminated.

[6417]

CHAPTER 19
PUBLIC EXAMINATION OF COMPANY OFFICERS AND OTHERS

4.211 Order for public examination

(1) If the official receiver applies to the court under section 133 for the public examination of any person, a copy of the court's order shall, forthwith after its making, be served on that person.

(2) Where the application relates to a person falling within section 133(1)(c) (promoters, past managers, etc), it shall be accompanied by a report by the official receiver indicating—

(a) the grounds on which the person is supposed to fall within that paragraph, and

(b) whether, in the official receiver's opinion, it is likely that service of the order on the person can be effected by post at a known address.

(3) If in his report the official receiver gives it as his opinion that, in a case to which paragraph (2) applies, there is no reasonable certainty that service by post will be effective, the court may direct that the order be served by some means other than, or in addition to, post.

(4) In a case to which paragraphs (2) and (3) apply, the court shall rescind the order if satisfied by the person to whom it is directed that he does not fall within section 133(1)(c).

[6418]

NOTES

Para (1): see Form 4.61 in Appendix 4 at **[A4]**.

4.212 Notice of hearing

(1) The court's order shall appoint a venue for the examination of the person to whom it is directed ("the examinee"), and direct his attendance thereat.

(2) The official receiver shall give at least 14 days' notice of the hearing—

(a) if a liquidator has been nominated or appointed, to him;

(b) if a special manager has been appointed, to him; and

(c) subject to any contrary direction of the court, to every creditor and contributory of the company who is known to the official receiver or is identified in the company's statement of affairs.

(3) The official receiver may, if he thinks fit, cause notice of the order to be given, by advertisement in one or more newspapers, at least 14 days before the date fixed for the hearing; but, unless the court otherwise directs, there shall be no such advertisement before at least 7 days have elapsed since the examinee was served with the order.

[6419]

4.213 Order on request by creditors or contributories

(1) A request to the official receiver by creditors or contributories under section 133(2) shall be made in writing and be accompanied by—

(a) a list of the creditors concurring with the request and the amounts of their respective claims in the liquidation or (as the case may be) of the contributories so concurring, with their respective values, and

(b) from each creditor or contributory concurring, written confirmation of his concurrence.

This paragraph does not apply if the requisitioning creditor's debt or, as the case may be, requisitioning contributory's shareholding is alone sufficient, without the concurrence of others.

(2) The request must specify the name of the proposed examinee, the relationship which he has, or has had, to the company and the reasons why his examination is requested.

(3) Before an application to the court is made on the request, the requisitionists shall deposit with the official receiver such sum as the latter may determine to be appropriate by way of security for the expenses of the hearing of a public examination, if ordered.

(4) Subject as follows, the official receiver shall, within 28 days of receiving the request, make the application to the court required by section 133(2).

(5) If the official receiver is of opinion that the request is an unreasonable one in the circumstances, he may apply to the court for an order relieving him from the obligation to make the application otherwise required by that subsection.

(6) If the court so orders, and the application for the order was made *ex parte*, notice of the order shall be given forthwith by the official receiver to the requisitionists. If the application for an order is dismissed, the official receiver's application under section 133(2) shall be made forthwith on conclusion of the hearing of the application first mentioned.

[6420]

NOTES

Para (1): see Forms 4.62, 4.63 in Appendix 4 at **[A4]**.

4.214 Witness unfit for examination

(1) Where the examinee [is a person who lacks capacity within the meaning of the Mental Capacity Act 2005 (c 9) or] is suffering from any *mental disorder or* physical affliction or disability rendering him unfit to undergo or attend for public examination, the

court may, on application in that behalf, either stay the order for his public examination or direct that it shall be conducted in such manner and at such place as it thinks fit.

(2) Application under this Rule shall be made—

(a) by a person who has been appointed by a court in the United Kingdom or elsewhere to manage the affairs of, or to represent, the examinee, or

(b) by a relative or friend of the examinee whom the court considers to be a proper person to make the application, or

(c) by the official receiver.

(3) Where the application is made by a person other than the official receiver, then—

(a) it shall, unless the examinee is a *patient within the meaning of the Mental Health Act 1983*, be supported by the affidavit of a registered medical practitioner as to the examinee's mental and physical condition;

(b) at least 7 days' notice of the application shall be given to the official receiver and the liquidator (if other than the official receiver); and

(c) before any order is made on the application, the applicant shall deposit with the official receiver such sum as the latter certifies to be necessary for the additional expenses of any examination that may be ordered on the application.

An order made on the application may provide that the expenses of the examination are to be payable, as to a specified proportion, out of the deposit under sub-paragraph (c), instead of out of the assets.

(4) Where the application is made by the official receiver it may be made *ex parte*, and may be supported by evidence in the form of a report by the official receiver to the court.

[6421]

NOTES

Para (1): words in square brackets inserted, and words in italics revoked, by the Mental Capacity Act 2005 (Transitional and Consequential Provisions) Order 2007, SI 2007/1898, at 6, Sch 1, para 12(1), (2)(a), as from 1 October 2007.

Para (3): for the words in italics there are substituted the words "person who lacks capacity within the meaning of the Mental Capacity Act 2005" by SI 2007/1898, at 6, Sch 1, para 12(1), (2)(b), as from 1 October 2007.

Para (1): see Form 4.64 in Appendix 4 at **[A4]**.

4.215 Procedure at hearing

(1) The examinee shall at the hearing be examined on oath; and he shall answer all such questions as the court may put, or allow to be put, to him.

(2) Any of the persons allowed by section 133(4) to question the examinee may, with the approval of the court (made known either at the hearing or in advance of it), appear by solicitor or counsel; or he may in writing authorise another person to question the examinee on his behalf.

(3) The examinee may at his own expense employ a solicitor with or without counsel, who may put to him such questions as the court may allow for the purpose of enabling him to explain or qualify any answers given by him, and may make representations on his behalf.

(4) There shall be made in writing such record of the examination as the court thinks proper. The record shall be read over either to or by the examinee, signed by him, and verified by affidavit at a venue fixed by the court.

(5) The written record may, in any proceedings (whether under the Act or otherwise) be used as evidence against the examinee of any statement made by him in the course of his public examination.

(6) If criminal proceedings have been instituted against the examinee, and the court is of opinion that the continuance of the hearing would be calculated to prejudice a fair trial of those proceedings, the hearing may be adjourned.

[6422]

NOTES

Para (4): see Form 4.65 in Appendix 4 at **[A4]**.

4.216 Adjournment

(1) The public examination may be adjourned by the court from time to time, either to a fixed date or generally.

(2) Where the examination has been adjourned generally, the court may at any time on the application of the official receiver or of the examinee—

(a) fix a venue for the resumption of the examination, and

(b) give directions as to the manner in which, and the time within which, notice of the resumed public examination is to be given to persons entitled to take part in it.

(3) Where application under paragraph (2) is made by the examinee, the court may grant it on terms that the expenses of giving the notices required by that paragraph shall be paid by him and that, before a venue for the resumed public examination is fixed, he shall deposit with the official receiver such sum as the latter considers necessary to cover those expenses.

[6423]

NOTES

Paras (1), (2): see Forms 4.66, 4.67 in Appendix 4 at **[A4]**.

4.217 Expenses of examination

(1) Where a public examination of the examinee has been ordered by the court on a creditors' or contributories' requisition under Rule 4.213, the court may order that the expenses of the examination are to be paid, as to a specified proportion, out of the deposit under Rule 4.213(3), instead of out of the assets.

(2) In no case do the costs and expenses of a public examination fall on the official receiver personally.

[6424]

CHAPTER 20
ORDER OF PAYMENT OF COSTS, ETC, OUT OF ASSETS

4.218 General rule as to priority

(1) The expenses of the liquidation are payable out of the assets in the following order of priority—

[(a) expenses or costs which—

(i) are properly chargeable or incurred by the official receiver or the liquidator in preserving, realising or getting in any of the assets of the company or otherwise relating to the conduct of any legal proceedings which he has power to bring or defend whether in his own name or the name of the company;

(ii) relate to the employment of a shorthand writer, if appointed by an order of the court made at the instance of the official receiver in connection with an examination; or

(iii) are incurred in holding an examination under Rule 4.214 (examinee unfit) where the application for it was made by the official receiver:]

(b) any other expenses incurred or disbursements made by the official receiver or under his authority, including those incurred or made in carrying on the business of the company;

[(c) the fees payable under any order made under section 414 [or section 415A], including those payable to the official receiver (other than the fee referred to in sub-paragraph (d)(i) below), and any remuneration payable to him under general regulations;

(d)

(i) the fee payable under any order made under section 414 for the performance by the official receiver of his general duties as official receiver;

(ii) any repayable deposit lodged under any such order as security for the fee mentioned in sub-paragraph (i);]

(e) the cost of any security provided by a provisional liquidator, liquidator or special manager in accordance with the Act or the Rules;

(f) the remuneration of the provisional liquidator (if any);

PART IV STATUTORY INSTRUMENTS

(g) any deposit lodged on an application for the appointment of a provisional liquidator;
(h) the costs of the petitioner, and of any person appearing on the petition whose costs are allowed by the court;
(j) the remuneration of the special manager (if any);
(k) any amount payable to a person employed or authorised, under Chapter 6 of this Part of the Rules, to assist in the preparation of a statement of affairs or of accounts;
(l) any allowance made, by order of the court, towards costs on an application for release from the obligation to submit a statement of affairs, or for an extension of time for submitting such a statement;
[(la) the costs of employing a shorthand writer in any case other than one appointed by an order of the court at the instance of the official receiver in connection with an examination;]
(m) any necessary disbursements by the liquidator in the course of his administration (including any expenses incurred by members of the liquidation committee or their representatives and allowed by the liquidator under Rule 4.169, but not including any payment of [corporation] tax in circumstances referred to in sub-paragraph (p) below);
(n) the remuneration or emoluments of any person who has been employed by the liquidator to perform any services for the company, as required or authorised by or under the Act or the Rules;
(o) the remuneration of the liquidator, up to any amount not exceeding that which is payable [under Schedule 6];
(p) the amount of any corporation] tax on chargeable gains accruing on the realisation of any asset of the company (without regard to whether the realisation is effected by the liquidator, a secured creditor, or a receiver or manager appointed to deal with a security);
(q) the balance, after payment of any sums due under sub-paragraph (o) above, of any remuneration due to the liquidator[;
(r) any other expenses properly chargeable by the liquidator in carrying out his functions in the liquidation].

(2), (3) …

[6425]

NOTES

Para (1): sub-para (a) substituted, and sub-paras (la), (r) inserted, by the Insolvency (Amendment) (No 2) Rules 2002, SI 2002/2712, r 4(1), Schedule, Part 2, para 23, as from 1 January 2003, subject to transitional provisions as noted to r 4.2 at **[6200]**; sub-paras (c), (d) substituted by the Insolvency (Amendment) Rules 1995, SI 1995/586, r 3(1), Schedule, para 1, as from 1 April 1995; words in square brackets in sub-para (c) inserted by the Insolvency (Amendment) Rules 2004, SI 2004/584, r 22, as from 1 April 2004; words in square brackets in sub-paras (m), (p) substituted by the Insolvency (Amendment) Rules 1987, SI 1987/1919, r 3(1), Schedule, Pt 1, para 79, as from 11 January 1988; words in square brackets in sub-para (o) substituted by the Insolvency (Amendment) Rules 2005, SI 2005/527, r 32, as from 1 April 2005, subject to transitional provisions as noted to r 4.127B at **[6331B]**.

Paras (2), (3): revoked by SI 2002/2712, r 4(1), Schedule, Part 2, para 23(d), as from 1 January 2003, subject to transitional provisions as noted to r 4.2 at **[6200]**.

4.219 Winding up commencing as voluntary

In a winding up by the court which follows immediately on a voluntary winding up (whether members' voluntary or creditors' voluntary), such remuneration of the voluntary liquidator and costs and expenses of the voluntary liquidation as the court may allow are to rank in priority with the expenses specified in Rule 4.218(1)(a).

[6426]

4.220 Saving for powers of the court

(1) In a winding up by the court, the priorities laid down by Rules 4.218 and 4.219 are subject to the power of the court to make orders under section 156, where the assets are insufficient to satisfy the liabilities.

(2) Nothing in those Rules applies to or affects the power of any court, in proceedings by or against the company, to order costs to be paid by the company, or the liquidator; nor do they affect the rights of any person to whom such costs are ordered to be paid.

[6427]

CHAPTER 21
MISCELLANEOUS RULES

SECTION A: RETURN OF CAPITAL
(NO CVL APPLICATION)

4.221 Application to court for order authorising return

(1) This Rule applies where the liquidator intends to apply to the court for an order authorising a return of capital.

(2) The application shall be accompanied by a list of the persons to whom the return is to be made.

(3) The list shall include the same details of those persons as appears in the settled list of contributories, with any necessary alterations to take account of matters after settlement of the list, and the amount to be paid to each person.

(4) Where the court makes an order authorising the return, it shall send a sealed copy of the order to the liquidator.

[6428]

4.222 Procedure for return

(1) The liquidator shall inform each person to whom a return is made of the rate of return per share, and whether it is expected that any further return will be made.

(2) Any payments made by the liquidator by way of the return may be sent by post, unless for any reason another method of making the payment has been agreed with the payee.

[6429]

SECTION B: CONCLUSION OF WINDING UP

4.223–CVL Statements to registrar of companies under s 192

[(1) Subject to paragraphs (3) and (3A), the statement which section 192 requires the liquidator to send to the registrar of companies, if the winding up is not concluded within one year from its commencement, shall be sent not more than 30 days after the expiration of that year, and thereafter 6-monthly until the winding up is concluded.]

(2) For this purpose the winding up is concluded at the date of the dissolution of the company, except that if at that date any assets or funds of the company remain unclaimed or undistributed in the hands or under the control of the liquidator or any former liquidator, the winding up is not concluded until those assets or funds have either been distributed or paid into the Insolvency Services Account.

(3) Subject as above, the liquidator's final statement shall be sent forthwith after the conclusion of the winding up.

[(3A) No statement shall be required to be delivered under this Rule where the return of the final meeting in respect of the company under sections 94 or 106 is delivered before the date at which the statement is to be delivered and that return shows that no assets or funds of the company remain unclaimed or undistributed in the hands or under the control of the liquidator or any former liquidator; but where this paragraph applies, the liquidator shall deliver a copy of that return to the Secretary of State.]

(4) …

[6430]

NOTES

Para (1): substituted by the Insolvency (Amendment) Rules 1987, SI 1987/1919, r 3(1), Schedule, Pt 1, para 80(1), as from 11 January 1988.

Para (3A): inserted by SI 1987/1919, r 3(1), Schedule, Pt 1, para 80(2), as from 11 January 1988.

Para (4): revoked by the Insolvency (Amendment) Rules 2005, SI 2005/527, r 33, as from 1 April 2005.

Para (1): see Form 4.68 in Appendix 4 at **[A4]**.

SECTION C: DISSOLUTION AFTER WINDING UP

4.224 Secretary of State's directions under ss 203, 205

(1) Where the Secretary of State gives a direction under—

(a) section 203 (where official receiver applies to registrar of companies for a company's early dissolution), or
(b) section 205 (application by interested person for postponement of dissolution),

he shall send two copies of the direction to the applicant for it.

(2) Of those copies one shall be sent by the applicant to the registrar of companies, to comply with section 203(5) or, as the case may be, 205(6).

[6431]

4.225 Procedure following appeal under s 203(4) or 205(4)

Following an appeal under section 203(4) or 205(4) (against a decision of the Secretary of State under the applicable section) the court shall send two sealed copies of its order to the person in whose favour the appeal was determined; and that party shall send one of the copies to the registrar of companies to comply with section 203(5) or, as the case may be, 205(6).

[6432]

NOTES

See Form 4.69 in Appendix 4 at **[A4]**.

CHAPTER 22
LEAVE TO ACT AS DIRECTOR, ETC, OF COMPANY WITH PROHIBITED NAME (SECTION 216 OF THE ACT)

4.226 Preliminary

The Rules in this Chapter—

(a) relate to the leave required under section 216 (restriction on re-use of name of company in insolvent liquidation) for a person to act as mentioned in section 216(3) in relation to a company with a prohibited name, …
(b) prescribe the cases excepted from that provision, that is to say, those in which a person to whom the section applies may so act without that leave[, and
(c) apply to all windings up to which section 216 applies, whether or not the winding up commenced before the coming into force of the Rules].

[6433]

NOTES

Word omitted revoked, and words in square brackets added, by the Insolvency (Amendment) Rules 1987, SI 1987/1919, r 3(1), Schedule, Pt 1, para 81, as from 11 January 1988.

4.227 Application for leave under s 216(3)

When considering an application for leave under section 216, the court may call on the liquidator, or any former liquidator, of the liquidating company for a report of the circumstances in which that company became insolvent, and the extent (if any) of the applicant's apparent responsibility for its doing so.

[6434]

4.228 First excepted case

(1) Where a company ("the successor company") acquires the whole, or substantially the whole, of the business of an insolvent company, under arrangements made by an insolvency practitioner acting as its liquidator, administrator or administrative receiver, or as supervisor of a voluntary arrangement under Part I of the Act, the successor company may for the purposes of section 216 give notice under this Rule to the insolvent company's creditors.

(2) To be effective, the notice must be given within 28 days from the completion of the arrangements, to all creditors of the insolvent company of whose addresses the successor company is aware in that period; and it must specify—

(a) the name and registered number of the insolvent company and the circumstances in which its business has been acquired by the successor company.
(b) the name which the successor company has assumed, or proposes to assume for the purpose of carrying on the business, if that name is or will be a prohibited name under section 216, and
(c) any change of name which it has made, or proposes to make, for that purpose under section 28 of the Companies Act.

(3) The notice may name a person to whom section 216 may apply as having been a director or shadow director of the insolvent company, and give particulars as to the nature and duration of that directorship, with a view to his being a director of the successor company or being otherwise associated with its management.

(4) If the successor company has effectively given notice under this Rule to the insolvent company's creditors, a person who is so named in the notice may act in relation to the successor company in any of the ways mentioned in section 216(3), notwithstanding that he has not the leave of the court under that section.

[6435]

[4.229 Second excepted case

(1) Where a person to whom section 216 applies as having been a director or shadow director of the liquidating company applies for leave of the court under that section not later than 7 days from the date on which the company went into liquidation, he may, during the period specified in paragraph (2) below, act in any of the ways mentioned in section 216(3), notwithstanding that he has not the leave of the court under that section.

(2) The period referred to in paragraph (1) begins with the day on which the company goes into liquidation and ends either on the day falling six weeks after that date or on the day on which the court disposes of the application for leave under section 216, whichever of those days occurs first.]

[6436]

NOTES

Substituted by the Insolvency (Amendment) Rules 1987, SI 1987/1919, r 3(1), Schedule, Pt 1, para 82, as from 11 January 1988.

4.230 Third excepted case

The court's leave under section 216(3) is not required where the company there referred to, though known by a prohibited name within the meaning of the section—

(a) has been known by that name for the whole of the period of 12 months ending with the day before the liquidating company went into liquidation, and

(b) has not at any time in those 12 months been dormant within the meaning of section 252(5) of the Companies Act.

[6437]

NOTES

Dormant within the meaning of section 252(5) of the Companies Act; dormant company is now defined in CA 1985, s 249AA.

[CHAPTER 23
EC REGULATION—MEMBER STATE LIQUIDATOR

4.231 Interpretation of creditor and notice to member State liquidator

(1) This Rule applies where a member State liquidator has been appointed in relation to the company.

(2) For the purposes of the Rules referred to in paragraph (3) the member State liquidator is deemed to be a creditor.

(3) The Rules referred to in paragraph (2) are Rules 4.43(1) (official receiver's report), 4.45(1) (report on statement of affairs), 4.46(2) (report where no statement of affairs), 4.47(2) (general rule on reporting), 4.48(2) (winding up stayed), 4.49 (information to creditors), 4.50(2) (notice of meetings), 4.51(2) (notice of creditors' meeting—CVL), 4.54 (power to call meetings), 4.57(1) (requisitioned meetings), 4.57(3), 4.67 (entitlement to vote (creditors)), 4.68 (chairman's discretion to allow vote—CVL), 4.70 (admission and rejection of proof (creditors' meeting)), 4.73 (meaning of "prove"), 4.74 (supply of forms), 4.75 (contents of proof), 4.76 (particulars of creditor's claim), 4.77 (claim established by affidavit), 4.78 (cost of proving), 4.79 (inspection of proofs), 4.82 (admission and rejection of proofs for dividend), 4.83(1) (appeal against decision in relation to proof), 4.83(2), 4.84 (withdrawal or variation of proof), 4.85(1) (expunging of proof), 4.86 (estimate of quantum), 4.87 (negotiable instruments, etc), 4.88 (secured creditors), 4.89 (discounts), 4.90 (mutual credit and set-off),

PART IV
STATUTORY INSTRUMENTS

4.91 (debt in foreign currency), 4.92 (payment of a periodical nature), 4.93 (interest), 4.94 (debt payable at future time), 4.101A (power to fill vacancy in office of liquidator), 4.102(5) (appointment by court), 4.103(4) (appointment by court), 4.113(1) (meeting of creditors to remove liquidator), 4.114(1) (meeting of creditors to remove liquidator), 4.115 (regulation of meetings), 4.124(1) (release of official receiver), 4.125(1) (final meeting), [4.125A(2) (rule on reporting),] 4.126(1) (final meeting), 4.131(1) (challenge to liquidator's remuneration), 4.152(1) (liquidation committee), 4.152(3) (eligibility for liquidation committee), 4.163(3) (vacancy on liquidation committee), 4.175(1) (liquidation committee), 4.180 (notice of dividend) and 4.212(2) (notice of public examination hearing).

(4) Paragraphs (2) and (3) are without prejudice to the generality of the right to participate referred to in paragraph 3 of Article 32 of the EC Regulation (exercise of creditor's rights).

(5) Where the liquidator is obliged to give notice to, or provide a copy of a document (including an order of court) to, the court, the registrar of companies or the official receiver, the liquidator shall give notice or provide copies, as the case may be, to the member State liquidator.

(6) Paragraph (5) is without prejudice to the generality of the obligations imposed by Article 31 of the EC Regulation (duty to cooperate and communicate information).]

[6438]

NOTES

Added, together with preceding heading, by the Insolvency (Amendment) Rules 2002, SI 2002/1307, rr 3, 6(9), as from 31 May 2002.

Para (3): words in square brackets inserted by the Insolvency (Amendment) Rules 2004, SI 2004/584, r 23, as from 1 April 2004.

EC Regulation: ie, Council Regulation 1346/2000/EC on insolvency proceedings at **[9290]**.

(Pts 5, 6, 6A outside the scope of this work.)

THE THIRD GROUP OF PARTS

PART 7
COURT PROCEDURE AND PRACTICE

CHAPTER 1
APPLICATIONS

7.1 Preliminary

This Chapter applies to any application made to the court under the Act or Rules except … —

(a) [an application for] an administration order under Part II,

(b) [a petition for] a winding-up order under Part IV, or

(c) [a petition for] a bankruptcy order under Part IX

of the Act.

[6439]

NOTES

Words omitted revoked, and words in square brackets inserted, by the Insolvency (Amendment) Rules 2003, SI 2003/1730, r 11, Sch 1, Pt 8, para 54, as from 15 September 2003 (for transitional provisions and savings see the note preceding r 2.1 at **[6097]**).

See Form 7.1 in Appendix 4 at **[A4]**.

7.2 Interpretation

(1) In this Chapter, except in so far as the context otherwise requires—

"originating application" means an application to the court which is not an application in pending proceedings before the court; and

"ordinary application" means any other application to the court.

(2) Every application shall be in the form appropriate to the application concerned.

[6440]

NOTES

See Forms 7.1, 7.2 in Appendix 4 at **[A4]**.

7.3 Form and contents of application

(1) Each application shall be in writing and shall state—

(a) the names of the parties;

(b) the nature of the relief or order applied for or the directions sought from the court;

(c) the names and addresses of the persons (if any) on whom it is intended to serve the application or that no person is intended to be served;

(d) where the Act or Rules require that notice of the application is to be given to specified persons, the names and addresses of all those persons (so far as known to the applicant); and

(e) the applicant's address for service.

(2) An originating application shall set out the grounds on which the applicant claims to be entitled to the relief or order sought.

(3) The application must be signed by the applicant if he is acting in person or, when he is not so acting, by or on behalf of his solicitor.

[6441]

[7.3A Application under section 176A(5) to disapply section 176A

(1) An application under section 176A(5) shall be accompanied by an affidavit prepared and sworn by the liquidator, administrator or receiver.

(2) The affidavit shall state—

(a) the type of insolvency proceedings in which the application arises;

(b) a summary of the financial position of the company;

(c) the information substantiating the applicant's view that the cost of making a distribution to unsecured creditors would be disproportionate to the benefits; and

(d) whether any other insolvency practitioner is acting in relation to the company and if so his address.]

[6441A]

NOTES

Inserted by the Insolvency (Amendment) Rules 2003, SI 2003/1730, r 11, Sch 1, Pt 8, para 55, as from 15 September 2003 (for transitional provisions and savings see the note preceding r 2.1 at **[6097]**).

7.4 Filing and service of application

(1) The application shall be filed in court, accompanied by one copy and a number of additional copies equal to the number of persons who are to be served with the application.

(2) Subject as follows in this Rule and the next, or unless the Rule under which the application is brought provides otherwise, or the court otherwise orders, upon the presentation of the documents mentioned in paragraph (1) above, the court shall fix a venue for the application to be heard.

(3) Unless the court otherwise directs, the applicant shall serve a sealed copy of the application, endorsed with the venue for the hearing, on the respondent named in the application (or on each respondent if more than one).

(4) The court may give any of the following directions—

(a) that the application be served upon persons other than those specified by the relevant provision of the Act or Rules;

(b) that the giving of notice to any person may be dispensed with;

(c) that notice be given in some way other than that specified in paragraph (3).

(5) Unless the provision of the Act or Rules under which the application is made provides otherwise, and subject to the next paragraph, the application must be served at least 14 days before the date fixed for the hearing.

(6) Where the case is one of urgency, the court may (without prejudice to its general power to extend or abridge time limits)—

(a) hear the application immediately, either with or without notice to, or the attendance of, other parties, or

(b) authorise a shorter period of service than that provided for by paragraph (5);

and any such application may be heard on terms providing for the filing or service of documents, or the carrying out of other formalities, as the court thinks fit.

[6442]

[7.4A Notice of application under section 176A(5)

An application under section 176A(5) may be made without the application being served upon or notice being given to any other party, save that notice of the application shall be given to any other insolvency practitioner who acts as such in relation to the company including any member State liquidator.]

[6442A]

NOTES

Inserted by the Insolvency (Amendment) Rules 2003, SI 2003/1730, r 11, Sch 1, Pt 8, para 56, as from 15 September 2003 (for transitional provisions and savings see the note preceding r 2.1 at **[6097]**).

7.5 Other hearings ex parte

(1) Where the relevant provisions of the Act or Rules do not require service of the application on, or notice of it to be given to, any person, the court may hear the application *ex parte*.

(2) Where the application is properly made *ex parte*, the court may hear it forthwith, without fixing a venue as required by Rule 7.4(2).

(3) Alternatively, the court may fix a venue for the application to be heard, in which case Rule 7.4 applies (so far as relevant).

[6443]

7.6 Hearing of application

(1) Unless allowed or authorised to be made otherwise, every application before the registrar shall, and every application before the judge may, be heard in chambers.

(2) Unless either—

(a) the judge has given a general or special direction to the contrary, or

(b) it is not within the registrar's power to make the order required.

the jurisdiction of the court to hear and determine the application may be exercised by the registrar, and the application shall be made to the registrar in the first instance.

(3) Where the application is made to the registrar he may refer to the judge any matter which he thinks should properly be decided by the judge, and the judge may either dispose of the matter or refer it back to the registrar with such directions as he thinks fit.

(4) Nothing in the Rule precludes an application being made directly to the judge in a proper case.

[6444]

7.7 Use of affidavit evidence

(1) In any proceedings evidence may be given by affidavit unless by any provision of the Rules it is otherwise provided or the court otherwise directs; but the court may, on the application of any party, order the attendance for cross-examination of the person making the affidavit.

(2) Where, after such an order has been made, the person in question does not attend, his affidavit shall not be used in evidence without the leave of the court.

[6445]

7.8 Filing and service of affidavits

(1) Unless the provision of the Act or Rules under which the application is made provides otherwise, or the court otherwise allows—

(a) if the applicant intends to rely at the first hearing on affidavit evidence, he shall file the affidavit or affidavits (if more than one) in court and serve a copy or copies on the respondent, not less than 14 days before the date fixed for the hearing, and

(b) where a respondent to an application intends to oppose it and to rely for that purpose on affidavit evidence, he shall file the affidavit or affidavits (if more than one) in court and serve a copy or copies on the applicant, not less than 7 days before the date fixed for the hearing.

(2) Any affidavit may be sworn by the applicant or by the respondent or by some other person possessing direct knowledge of the subject matter of the application.

[6446]

7.9 Use of reports

(1) A report may be filed in court instead of an affidavit—

(a) in any case, by the official receiver (whether or not he is acting in any capacity mentioned in sub-paragraph (b)), or a deputy official receiver, or

(b) unless the application involves other parties or the court otherwise orders, by—

(i) an administrator, a liquidator or a trustee in bankruptcy,

(ii) a provisional liquidator or an interim receiver,

(iii) a special manager, or

(iv) an insolvency practitioner appointed under section 273(2).

(2) In any case where a report is filed instead of an affidavit, the report shall be treated for the purposes of Rule 7.8(1) and any hearing before the court as if it were an affidavit.

(3) Any report filed by the official receiver in accordance with the Act or the Rules is prima facie evidence of any matter contained in it.

[6447]

7.10 Adjournment of hearing; directions

(1) The court may adjourn the hearing of an application on such terms (if any) as it thinks fit.

(2) The court may at any time give such directions as it thinks fit as to—

(a) service or notice of the application on or to any person, whether in connection with the venue of a resumed hearing or for any other purpose;

(b) whether particulars of claim and defence are to be delivered and generally as to the procedure on the application;

(c) the manner in which any evidence is to be adduced at a resumed hearing and in particular (but without prejudice to the generality of this sub-paragraph) as to—

(i) the taking of evidence wholly or in part by affidavit or orally;

(ii) the cross-examination either before the judge or registrar on the hearing in court or in chambers, of any deponents to affidavits;

(iii) any report to be given by the official receiver or any person mentioned in Rule 7.9(1)(b);

(d) the matters to be dealt with in evidence.

[6448]

CHAPTER 2
TRANSFER OF PROCEEDINGS BETWEEN COURTS

7.11 General power of transfer

(1) Where winding-up or bankruptcy proceedings are pending in the High Court, the court may order them to be transferred to a specified county court.

(2) Where winding-up or bankruptcy proceedings are pending in a county court, the court may order them to be transferred either to the High Court or to another county court.

(3) In any case where proceedings are transferred to a county court, the transfer must be to a court which has jurisdiction to wind up companies or, as the case may be, jurisdiction in bankruptcy.

(4) Where winding-up or bankruptcy proceedings are pending in a county court, a judge of the High Court may order them to be transferred to that Court.

(5) A transfer of proceedings under this Rule may be ordered—

(a) by the court of its own motion, or

(b) on the application of the official receiver, or
(c) on the application of a person appearing to the court to have an interest in the proceedings.

(6) A transfer of proceedings under this Rule may be ordered notwithstanding that the proceedings commenced before the coming into force of the Rules.

[6449]

7.12 Proceedings commenced in wrong court

Where winding-up or bankruptcy proceedings are commenced in a court which is, in relation to those proceedings, the wrong court, that court may—
(a) order the transfer of the proceedings to the court in which they ought to have been commenced;
(b) order that the proceedings be continued in the court in which they have been commenced; or
(c) order the proceedings to be struck out.

[6450]

7.13 Applications for transfer

(1) An application by the official receiver for proceedings to be transferred shall be made with a report by him—
(a) setting out the reasons for the transfer, and
(b) including a statement either that the petitioner consents to the transfer, or that he has been given at least 14 days' notice of the official receiver's application.

(2) If the court is satisfied from the official receiver's report that the proceedings can be conducted more conveniently in another court, the proceedings shall be transferred to that court.

(3) Where an application for the transfer of proceedings is made otherwise than by the official receiver, at least 14 days' notice of the application shall be given by the applicant—
(a) to the official receiver attached to the court in which the proceedings are pending, and
(b) to the official receiver attached to the court to which it is proposed that they should be transferred.

[6451]

7.14 Procedure following order for transfer

(1) Subject as follows, the court making an order under Rule 7.11 shall forthwith send to the transferee court a sealed copy of the order, and the file of the proceedings.

(2) On receipt of these, the transferee court shall forthwith send notice of the transfer to the official receivers attached to that court and the transferor court respectively.

(3) Paragraph (1) does not apply where the order is made by the High Court under Rule 7.11(4). In that case—
(a) the High Court shall send sealed copies of the order to the county court from which the proceedings are to be transferred, and to the official receivers attached to that court and the High Court respectively, and
(b) that county court shall send the file of the proceedings to the High Court.

(4) Following compliance with this Rule, if the official receiver attached to the court to which the proceedings are ordered to be transferred is not already, by virtue of directions given by the Secretary of State under section 399(6)(a), the official receiver in relation to those proceedings, he becomes, in relation to those proceedings, the official receiver in place of the official receiver attached to the other court concerned.

[6452]

7.15 Consequential transfer of other proceedings

(1) This Rule applies where—
(a) an order for the winding up of a company, or a bankruptcy order in the case of an individual, has been made by the High Court, or
(b) in either such case, a provisional liquidator or (as the case may be) an interim receiver has been appointed, or

(c) winding-up or bankruptcy proceedings have been transferred to that Court from a county court.

(2) A judge of any Division of the High Court may, of his own motion, order the transfer to that Division of any such proceedings as are mentioned below and are pending against the company or individual concerned ("the insolvent") either in another Division of the High Court or in a court in England and Wales other than the High Court.

(3) Proceedings which may be so transferred are those brought by or against the insolvent for the purpose of enforcing a claim against the insolvent estate, or brought by a person other than the insolvent for the purpose of enforcing any such claim (including in either case proceedings of any description by a debenture-holder or mortgagee).

(4) Where proceedings are transferred under this Rule, the registrar may (subject to general or special directions of the judge) dispose of any matter arising in the proceedings which would, but for the transfer, have been disposed of in chambers or, in the case of proceedings transferred from a county court, by the registrar of that court.

[6453]

CHAPTER 3
SHORTHAND WRITERS

7.16 Nomination and appointment of shorthand writers

(1) In the High Court the judge and, in a county court, the registrar may in writing nominate one or more persons to be official shorthand writers to the court.

(2) The court may, at any time in the course of insolvency proceedings, appoint a shorthand writer to take down the evidence of a person examined under section 133, 236, 290 or 366.

(3) Where the official receiver applies to the court for an order appointing a shorthand writer, he shall name the person he proposes for appointment; and that appointment shall be made, unless the court otherwise orders.

[6454]

NOTES

Paras (1), (2): see Forms 7.3, 7.4 in Appendix 4 at **[A4]**.

7.17 Remuneration

(1) The remuneration of a shorthand writer appointed in insolvency proceedings shall be paid by the party at whose instance the appointment was made, or out of the insolvent estate, or otherwise, as the court may direct.

[(2) Any question arising as to the rates of remuneration payable under this Rule shall be determined by the court in its discretion.]

[6455]

NOTES

Para (2): substituted by the Insolvency (Amendment) Rules 1993, SI 1993/602, r 3, Schedule, para 1, as from 5 April 1993.

7.18 Cost of shorthand note

Where in insolvency proceedings the court appoints a shorthand writer on the application of the official receiver, in order that a written record may be taken of the evidence of a person to be examined, the cost of the written record is deemed an expense of the official receiver in the proceedings.

[6456]

CHAPTER 4
ENFORCEMENT PROCEDURES

7.19 Enforcement of court orders

(1) In any insolvency proceedings, orders of the court may be enforced in the same manner as a judgment to the same effect.

(2) Where an order in insolvency proceedings is made, or any process is issued, by a county court ("the primary court"), the order or process may be enforced, executed and dealt with by any other county court ("the secondary court"), as if it had been made or issued for the enforcement of a judgment or order to the same effect made by the secondary court.

This applies whether or not the secondary court has jurisdiction to take insolvency proceedings.

[6457]

7.20 Orders enforcing compliance with the Rules

(1) The court may, on application by the competent person, make such orders as it thinks necessary for the enforcement of obligations falling on any person in accordance with—

- (a) [paragraph 47 of Schedule B1 to the Act or section] 47 or 131 (duty to submit statement of affairs in administration, administrative receivership or winding up),
- (b) section 143(2) (liquidator to furnish information, books, papers, etc), or
- (c) section 235 (duty of various persons to co-operate with office-holder).

(2) The competent person for this purpose is—

- (a) under [paragraph 47 of Schedule B1 to the Act], the administrator,
- (b) under section 47, the administrative receiver,
- (c) under section 131 or 143(2), the official receiver, and
- (d) under section 235, the official receiver, the administrator, the administrative receiver, the liquidator or the provisional liquidator, as the case may be.

(3) An order of the court under this Rule may provide that all costs of and incidental to the application for it shall be borne by the person against whom the order is made.

[6458]

NOTES

Paras (1), (2): words in square brackets substituted by the Insolvency (Amendment) Rules 2003, SI 2003/1730, r 11, Sch 1, Pt 8, para 57, as from 15 September 2003 (for transitional provisions and savings see the note preceding r 2.1 at **[6097]**).

7.21 Warrants (general provisions)

(1) A warrant issued by the court under any provision of the Act shall be addressed to such officer of the High Court or of a county court (whether or not having jurisdiction in insolvency proceedings) as the warrant specifies, or to any constable.

(2) The persons referred to in sections 134(2), 236(5), 364(1), 365(3) and 366(3) (court's powers of enforcement) as the prescribed officer of the court are—

- (a) in the case of the High Court, the tipstaff and his assistants of the court, and
- (b) in the case of a county court, the registrar and the bailiffs.

(3) In this Chapter references to property include books, papers and records.

[6459]

7.22 Warrants under ss 134, 364

When a person is arrested under a warrant issued by the court under section 134 (officer of company failing to attend for public examination), or section 364 (arrest of debtor or bankrupt)—

- (a) the officer apprehending him shall give him into the custody of the governor of the prison named in the warrant, who shall keep him in custody until such time as the court otherwise orders and shall produce him before the court as it may from time to time direct; and
- (b) any property in the arrested person's possession which may be seized shall be—
  - (i) lodged with, or otherwise dealt with as instructed by, whoever is specified in the warrant as authorised to receive it, or
  - (ii) kept by the officer seizing it pending the receipt of written orders from the court as to its disposal,

as may be directed by the court in the warrant.

[6460]

NOTES

See Forms 7.6, 7.7 in Appendix 4 at **[A4]**.

7.23 Warrants under ss 236, 366

(1) When a person is arrested under a warrant issued under section 236 (inquiry into insolvent company's dealings) or 366 (the equivalent in bankruptcy), the officer arresting him shall forthwith bring him before the court issuing the warrant in order that he may be examined.

(2) If he cannot immediately be brought up for examination, the officer shall deliver him into the custody of the governor of the prison named in the warrant, who shall keep him in custody and produce him before the court as it may from time to time direct.

(3) After arresting the person named in the warrant, the officer shall forthwith report to the court the arrest or delivery into custody (as the case may be) and apply to the court to fix a venue for the person's examination.

(4) The court shall appoint the earliest practicable time for the examination, and shall—
- (a) direct the governor of the prison to produce the person for examination at the time and place appointed, and
- (b) forthwith give notice of the venue to the person who applied for the warrant.

(5) Any property in the arrested person's possession which may be seized shall be—
- (a) lodged with, or otherwise dealt with as instructed by, whoever is specified in the warrant as authorised to receive it, or
- (b) kept by the officer seizing it pending the receipt of written orders from the court as to its disposal,

as may be directed by the court.

[6461]

NOTES

See Forms 7.8 and 7.9 in Appendix 4 at **[A4]**.

7.24 Execution of warrants outside court's district

(1) This Rule applies where a warrant for a person's arrest has been issued in insolvency proceedings by a county court ("the primary court") and is addressed to another county court ("the secondary court") for execution in its district.

(2) The secondary court may send the warrant to the registrar of any other county court (whether or not having jurisdiction to take insolvency proceedings) in whose district the person to be arrested is or is believed to be, with a notice to the effect that the warrant is transmitted to that court under this Rule for execution in its district at the request of the primary court.

(3) The court receiving a warrant transmitted by the secondary court under this Rule shall apply its seal to the warrant, and secure that all such steps are taken for its execution as would be appropriate in the case of a warrant issued by itself.

[6462]

NOTES

Para (1): see Form 7.10 in Appendix 4 at **[A4]**.

7.25 Warrants under s 365

(1) A warrant issued under section 365(3) (search of premises not belonging to the bankrupt) shall authorise any person executing it to seize any property of the bankrupt found as a result of the execution of the warrant.

(2) Any property seized under a warrant issued under section 365(2) or (3) shall be—
- (a) lodged with, or otherwise dealt with as instructed by, whoever is specified in the warrant as authorised to receive it, or
- (b) kept by the officer seizing it pending the receipt of written orders from the court as to its disposal,

as may be directed by the warrant.

[6463]

NOTES

Para (2): see Forms 7.12, 7.13 in Appendix 4 at **[A4]**.

CHAPTER 5
COURT RECORDS AND RETURNS

7.26 Title of proceedings

(1) Every proceeding under Parts I to VII of the Act shall, with any necessary additions, be intituled "IN THE MATTER OF .... (naming the company to which the proceedings relate) AND IN THE MATTER OF THE INSOLVENCY ACT 1986".

(2) Every proceeding under Parts IX to XI of the Act shall be intituled "IN BANKRUPTCY".

[6464]

7.27 Court records

The court shall keep records of all insolvency proceedings, and shall cause to be entered in the records the taking of any step in the proceedings, and such decisions of the court in relation thereto, as the court thinks fit.

[6465]

7.28 Inspection of records

(1) Subject as follows, the court's records of insolvency proceedings shall be open to inspection by any person.

(2) If in the case of a person applying to inspect the records the registrar is not satisfied as to the propriety of the purpose for which inspection is required, he may refuse to allow it. The person may then apply forthwith and *ex parte* to the judge, who may refuse the inspection, or allow it on such terms as he thinks fit.

(3) The judge's decision under paragraph (2) is final.

[6466]

7.29 Returns to Secretary of State

(1) The court shall from time to time send to the Secretary of State the following particulars relating to winding-up and bankruptcy proceedings—

(a) the full title of the proceedings, including the number assigned to each case;

(b) where a winding-up or bankruptcy order has been made, the date of the order.

(2) The Secretary of State may, on the request of any person, furnish him with particulars sent by the court under this Rule.

[6467]

7.30 File of court proceedings

(1) In respect of all insolvency proceedings, the court shall open and maintain a file for each case; and (subject to directions of the registrar) all documents relating to such proceedings shall be placed on the relevant file.

(2) No proceedings shall be filed in the Central Office of the High Court.

[6468]

7.31 Right to inspect the file

(1) In the case of any insolvency proceedings, the following have the right, at all reasonable times, to inspect the court's file of the proceedings—

(a) the person who, in relation to those proceedings, is the responsible insolvency practitioner;

(b) any duly authorised officer of the Department; and

(c) any person stating himself in writing to be a creditor of the company to which, or the individual to whom, the proceedings relate.

(2) The same right of inspection is exercisable—

(a) in proceedings under Parts I to VII of the Act, by every person who is, or at any time has been, a director or officer of the company to which the proceedings relate, or who is a member of the company or a contributory in its winding up;

(b) in proceedings with respect to a voluntary arrangement proposed by a debtor under Part VIII of the Act, by the debtor;

(c) in bankruptcy proceedings, by—
  (i) the bankrupt,
  (ii) any person against whom, or by whom, a bankruptcy petition has been presented, and
  (iii) any person who has been served, in accordance with Chapter 1 of Part 6 of the Rules, with a statutory demand.

(3) The right of inspection conferred as above on any person may be exercised on his behalf by a person properly authorised by him.

(4) Any person may, by special leave of the court, inspect the file.

(5) The right of inspection conferred by this Rule is not exercisable in the case of documents, or parts of documents, as to which the court directs (either generally or specially) that they are not to be made open to inspection without the court's leave.

An application for a direction of the court under this paragraph may be made by the official receiver, by the person who in relation to any proceedings is the responsible insolvency practitioner, or by any party appearing to the court to have an interest.

(6) If, for the purpose of powers conferred by the Act or the Rules, the Secretary of State, the Department or the official receiver requires to inspect the file of any insolvency proceedings, and requests the transmission of the file, the court shall comply with the request (unless the file is for the time being in use for the court's own purposes).

(7) Paragraphs (2) and (3) of Rule 7.28 apply in respect of the court's file of any proceedings as they apply in respect of court records.

[6469]

7.32 Filing of Gazette notices and advertisements

(1) In any court in which insolvency proceedings are pending, an officer of the court shall file a copy of every issue of the Gazette which contains an advertisement relating to those proceedings.

(2) Where there appears in a newspaper an advertisement relating to insolvency proceedings pending in any court, the person inserting the advertisement shall file a copy of it in that court.

The copy of the advertisement shall be accompanied by, or have endorsed on it, such particulars as are necessary to identify the proceedings and the date of the advertisement's appearance.

(3) An officer of any court in which insolvency proceedings are pending shall from time to time file a memorandum giving the dates of, and other particulars relating to, any notice published in the Gazette, and any newspaper advertisements, which relate to proceedings so pending.

The officer's memorandum is prima facie evidence that any notice or advertisement mentioned in it was duly inserted in the issue of the newspaper or the Gazette which is specified in the memorandum.

[6470]

[CHAPTER 6
COSTS AND DETAILED ASSESSMENT

7.33 Application of the CPR

Subject to provision to inconsistent effect made as follows in this Chapter, CPR Part 43 (scope of costs rules and definitions), Part 44 (general rules about costs), Part 45 (fixed costs), Part 47 (procedure for detailed assessment of costs and default provisions) and Part 48 (costs special cases) shall apply to insolvency proceedings with any necessary modifications.]

[6471]

NOTES

Chapter 6 (rr 7.33–7.42) substituted by the Insolvency (Amendment) (No 2) Rules 1999, SI 1999/1022, r 3, Schedule, para 3, as from 26 April 1999.

[7.34 Requirement to assess costs by the detailed procedure

(1) Subject as follows, where the costs, charges or expenses of any person are payable out of the insolvent estate, the amount of those costs, charges or expenses shall be decided by

detailed assessment unless agreed between the responsible insolvency practitioner and the person entitled to payment, and in the absence of such agreement the responsible insolvency practitioner may serve notice in writing requiring that person to commence detailed assessment proceedings in accordance with CPR Part 47 (procedure for detailed assessment of costs and default provisions) in the court to which the insolvency proceedings are allocated or, where in relation to a company there is no such court, that in relation to any court having jurisdiction to wind up the company.

(2) If a liquidation or creditors' committee established in insolvency proceedings (except administrative receivership) resolves that the amount of any such costs, charges or expenses should be decided by detailed assessment, the insolvency practitioner shall require detailed assessment in accordance with CPR Part 47.

(3) Where the amount of the costs, charges or expenses of any person employed by an insolvency practitioner in insolvency proceedings are required to be decided by detailed assessment or fixed by order of the court this does not preclude the insolvency practitioner from making payments on account to such person on the basis of an undertaking by that person to repay immediately any money which may, when detailed assessment is made, prove to have been overpaid, with interest at the rate specified in section 17 of the Judgments Act 1838 on the date payment was made and for the period from the date of payment to that of repayment.

(4) In any proceedings before the court, including proceedings on a petition, the court may order costs to be decided by detailed assessment.

(5) Unless otherwise directed or authorised, the costs of a trustee in bankruptcy or a liquidator are to be allowed on the standard basis for which provision is made in CPR rule 44.4 (basis of assessment) and rule 44.5 (factors to be taken into account in deciding the amount of costs).

(6) This Rule applies additionally (with any necessary modifications) to winding-up and bankruptcy proceedings commenced before the coming into force of the Rules.]

[6472]

NOTES

Substituted as noted to r 7.33 at **[6471]**.

[7.35 Procedure where detailed assessment required

(1) Before making a detailed assessment of the costs of any person employed in insolvency proceedings by a responsible insolvency practitioner, the costs officer shall require a certificate of employment, which shall be endorsed on the bill and signed by the insolvency practitioner.

(2) The certificate shall include—

(a) the name and address of the person employed,

(b) details of the functions to be carried out under the employment, and

(c) a note of any special terms of remuneration which have been agreed.

(3) Every person whose costs in insolvency proceedings are required to be decided by detailed assessment shall, on being required in writing to do so by the insolvency practitioner, commence detailed assessment proceedings in accordance with CPR Part 47 (procedure for detailed assessment of costs and default provisions).

(4) If that person does not commence detailed assessment proceedings within 3 months of the requirement under paragraph (3), or within such further time as the court, on application, may permit, the insolvency practitioner may deal with the insolvent estate without regard to any claim by that person, whose claim is forfeited by such failure to commence proceedings.

(5) Where in any such case such a claim lies additionally against an insolvency practitioner in his personal capacity, that claim is also forfeited by such failure to commence proceedings.

(6) Where costs have been incurred in insolvency proceedings in the High Court and those proceedings are subsequently transferred to a county court, all costs of those

proceedings directed by the court or otherwise required to be assessed may nevertheless, on the application of the person who incurred the costs, be ordered to be decided by detailed assessment in the High Court.]

[6473]

NOTES

Substituted as noted to r 7.33 at **[6471]**.

[7.36 Costs of [officers charged with execution of writs or other process]

(1) Where [an enforcement officer, or other officer, charged with execution of the writ or other process]—

(a) is required under section 184(2) or 346(2) to deliver up goods or money, or

(b) has under section 184(3) or 346(3) deducted costs from the proceeds of an execution or money paid to him,

the responsible insolvency practitioner may require in writing that the amount of [the enforcement officer's or other officer's] bill of costs be decided by detailed assessment.'

(2) Where such a requirement is made, Rule 7.35(4) applies.

(3) Where, in the case of a deduction under paragraph (1)(b), any amount deducted is disallowed at the conclusion of the detailed assessment proceedings, the [enforcement officer] shall forthwith pay a sum equal to that disallowed to the insolvency practitioner for the benefit of the insolvent estate.]

[6474]

NOTES

Substituted as noted to r 7.33 at **[6471]**.

Words in square brackets substituted the Insolvency (Amendment) Rules 2005, SI 2005/527, r 42, as from 1 April 2005.

[7.37 Petitions presented by insolvents

(1) In any case where a petition is presented by a company or individual ("the insolvent") against himself, any solicitor acting for the insolvent shall in his bill of costs give credit for any sum or security received from the insolvent as a deposit on account of the costs and expenses to be incurred in respect of the filing and prosecution of the petition; and the deposit shall be noted by the costs officer on the final costs certificate.

(2) Paragraph (3) applies where a petition is presented by a person other than the insolvent to whom the petition relates and before it is heard the insolvent presents a petition for the same order, and that order is made.

(3) Unless the court considers that the insolvent estate has benefited by the insolvent's conduct, or that there are otherwise special circumstances justifying the allowance of costs, no costs shall be allowed to the insolvent or his solicitor out of the insolvent estate.]

[6475]

NOTES

Substituted as noted to r 7.33 at **[6471]**.

[7.38 Costs paid otherwise than out of the insolvent estate

Where the amount of costs is decided by detailed assessment under an order of the court directing that those costs are to be paid otherwise than out of the insolvent estate, the costs officer shall note on the final costs certificate by whom, or the manner in which, the costs are to be paid.]

[6476]

NOTES

Substituted as noted to r 7.33 at **[6471]**.

[7.39 Award of costs against official receiver or responsible insolvency practitioner

Without prejudice to any provision of the Act or Rules by virtue of which the official receiver is not in any event to be liable for costs and expenses, where the official receiver or a responsible insolvency practitioner is made a party to any proceedings on the application of another party to the proceedings, he shall not be personally liable for costs unless the court otherwise directs.]

[6477]

NOTES

Substituted as noted to r 7.33 at **[6471]**.

[7.40 Applications for costs

(1) This Rule applies where a party to, or person affected by, any proceedings in an insolvency—

(a) applies to the court for an order allowing his costs, or part of them, incidental to the proceedings, and

(b) that application is not made at the time of the proceedings.

(2) The person concerned shall serve a sealed copy of his application on the responsible insolvency practitioner, and, in winding up by the court or bankruptcy, on the official receiver.

(3) The insolvency practitioner and, where appropriate, the official receiver may appear on the application.

(4) No costs of or incidental to the application shall be allowed to the applicant unless the court is satisfied that the application could not have been made at the time of the proceedings.]

[6478]

NOTES

Substituted as noted to r 7.33 at **[6471]**.

[7.41 Costs and expenses of witnesses

(1) Except as directed by the court, no allowance as a witness in any examination or other proceedings before the court shall be made to the bankrupt or an officer of the insolvent company to which the proceedings relate.

(2) A person presenting any petition in insolvency proceedings shall not be regarded as a witness on the hearing of the petition, but the costs officer may allow his expenses of travelling and subsistence.]

[6479]

NOTES

Substituted as noted to r 7.33 at **[6471]**.

[7.42 Final costs certificate

(1) A final costs certificate of the costs officer is final and conclusive as to all matters which have not been objected to in the manner provided for under the rules of the court.

(2) Where it is proved to the satisfaction of a costs officer that a final costs certificate has been lost or destroyed, he may issue a duplicate.]

[6480]

NOTES

Substituted as noted to r 7.33 at **[6471]**.

CHAPTER 7
PERSONS INCAPABLE OF MANAGING THEIR AFFAIRS

NOTES

Chapter heading: for the words "Persons Incapable of Managing their Affairs" there are substituted the words "Persons who Lack Capacity to Manage their Affairs" by the Mental Capacity Act 2005 (Transitional and Consequential Provisions) Order 2007, SI 2007/1898, art 6, Sch 1, para 12(1), (4), as from 1 October 2007.

7.43 Introductory

(1) The Rules in this Chapter apply where in insolvency proceedings it appears to the court that a person affected by the proceedings is one who *is incapable of managing and administering his property and affairs* either—

(a) by reason of *mental disorder within the meaning of the Mental Health Act 1983*, or

(b) due to physical affliction or disability.

(2) The person concerned is referred to as "the incapacitated person".

[6481]

NOTES

Para (1): for the first words in italics there are substituted the words "lacks capacity within the meaning of the Mental Capacity Act 2005 to manage and administer his property and affairs", and for the second words in italics there are substituted the words "lacking capacity within the meaning of the Mental Capacity Act 2005", by the Mental Capacity Act 2005 (Transitional and Consequential Provisions) Order 2007, SI 2007/1898, art 6, Sch 1, para 12(1), (5), as from 1 October 2007.

7.44 Appointment of another person to act

(1) The court may appoint such person as it thinks fit to appear for, represent or act for the incapacitated person.

(2) The appointment may be made either generally or for the purpose of any particular application or proceeding, or for the exercise of particular rights or powers which the incapacitated person might have exercised but for his incapacity.

(3) The court may make the appointment either of its own motion or on application by—

(a) a person who has been appointed by a court in the United Kingdom or elsewhere to manage the affairs of, or to represent, the incapacitated person, or

(b) any relative or friend of the incapacitated person who appears to the court to be a proper person to make the application, or

(c) the official receiver, or

(d) the person who, in relation to the proceedings, is the responsible insolvency practitioner.

(4) Application under paragraph (3) may be made *ex parte*; but the court may require such notice of the application as it thinks necessary to be given to the person alleged to be incapacitated, or any other person, and may adjourn the hearing of the application to enable the notice to be given.

[6482]

NOTES

Para (1): see Form 7.19 in Appendix 4 at **[A4]**.

7.45 Affidavit in support of application

(1) Except where made by the official receiver, an application under Rule 7.44(3) shall be supported by an affidavit of a registered medical practitioner as to the mental or physical condition of the incapacitated person.

(2) In the excepted case, a report made by the official receiver is sufficient.

[6483]

7.46 Service of notices following appointment

Any notice served on, or sent to, a person appointed under Rule 7.44 has the same effect as if it had been served on, or given to, the incapacitated person.

[6484]

CHAPTER 8
APPEALS IN INSOLVENCY PROCEEDINGS

7.47 Appeals and reviews of court orders (winding up)

(1) Every court having jurisdiction under the Act to wind up companies may review, rescind or vary any order made by it in the exercise of that jurisdiction.

(2) An appeal from a decision made in the exercise of that jurisdiction by a county court or by a registrar of the High Court lies to a single judge of the High Court; and an appeal from a decision of that judge on such an appeal lies, with the leave of that judge or the Court of Appeal, to the Court of Appeal.

(3) A county court is not, in the exercise of its jurisdiction to wind up companies, subject to be restrained by the order of any other court, and no appeal lies from its decision in the exercise of that jurisdiction except as provided by this Rule.

(4) Any application for the rescission of a winding-up order shall be made within 7 days after the date on which the order was made.

[6485]

7.48 Appeals in bankruptcy

(1) In bankruptcy proceedings, an appeal lies at the instance of the Secretary of State from any order of the court made on an application for the rescission or annulment of a bankruptcy order, or for a bankrupt's discharge.

(2) In the case of an order made by a county court or by a registrar of the High Court, the appeal lies to a single judge of the High Court; and an appeal from a decision of that judge on such an appeal lies, with the leave of that judge or the Court of Appeal, to the Court of Appeal.

[6486]

[7.49 Procedure on appeal

(1) Subject as follows, the procedure and practice of the Supreme Court relating to appeals to the Court of Appeal apply to appeals in insolvency proceedings.

(2) In relation to any appeal to a single judge of the High Court under section 375(2) (individual insolvency) or Rule 7.47(2) above (company insolvency), any reference in the CPR to the Court of Appeal is replaced by a reference to that judge and any reference to the registrar of civil appeals is replaced by a reference to the registrar of the High Court who deals with insolvency proceedings of the kind involved.

(3) In insolvency proceedings, the procedure under RSC Order 59 (appeals to the Court of Appeal) is by ordinary application and not by application notice.]

[6487]

NOTES

Substituted by the Insolvency (Amendment) (No 2) Rules 1999, SI 1999/1022, r 3, Schedule, para 4, as from 26 April 1999.

RSC Order 59: revoked by the Civil Procedure (Amendment) Rules 2000, SI 2000/221. For general rules with regard to appeals, see now the Civil Procedure Rules 1998, SI 1998/3132, Pt 52.

7.50 Appeal against decision of Secretary of State or official receiver

[(1)] An appeal under the Act or the Rules against a decision of the Secretary of State or the official receiver shall be brought within 28 days of the notification of the decision.

[(2) In respect of a decision under Rule 6.214A(5)(b), an appeal shall be brought within 14 days of the notification of the decision.]

[6488]

NOTES

Para (1) numbered as such, and para (2) added, by the Insolvency (Amendment) Rules 2003, SI 2003/1730, r 11, Sch 1, Pt 8, para 58, as from 1 April 2004 (for transitional provisions and savings see the note preceding r 2.1 at **[6097]**).

CHAPTER 9
GENERAL

[7.51 Principal court rules and practice to apply

(1) The CPR, the practice and procedure of the High Court and of the county court (including any practice direction) apply to insolvency proceedings in the High Court and county court as the case may be, in either case with any necessary modifications, except so far as inconsistent with the Rules.

(2) All insolvency proceedings shall be allocated to the multi-track for which CPR Part 29 (the multi-track) makes provision, accordingly those provisions of the CPR which provide for allocation questionnaires and track allocation will not apply.]

[6489]

NOTES

Substituted by the Insolvency (Amendment) (No 2) Rules 1999, SI 1999/1022, r 3, Schedule, para 5, as from 26 April 1999.

7.52 Right of audience

(1) Official receivers and deputy official receivers have right of audience in insolvency proceedings, whether in the High Court or a county court.

(2) Subject as above, rights of audience in insolvency proceedings are the same as obtained before the coming into force of the Rules.

[6490]

7.53 Right of attendance (company insolvency)

(1) Subject as follows, in company insolvency proceedings any person stating himself in writing, in records kept by the court for that purpose, to be a creditor or member of the company or, where the company is being wound up, a contributory, is entitled, at his own cost, to attend in court or in chambers at any stage of the proceedings.

(2) Attendance may be by the person himself, or his solicitor.

(3) A person so entitled may request the court in writing to give him notice of any step in the proceedings; and, subject to his paying the costs involved and keeping the court informed as to his address, the court shall comply with the request.

(4) If the court is satisfied that the exercise by a person of his rights under this Rule has given rise to costs for the insolvent estate which would not otherwise have been incurred and ought not, in the circumstances, to fall on that estate, it may direct that the costs be paid by the person concerned, to an amount specified.

The person's rights under this Rule are in abeyance so long as those costs are not paid.

(5) The court may appoint one or more persons to represent the creditors, the members or the contributories of an insolvent company, or any class of them, to have the rights conferred by this Rule, instead of the rights being exercisable by any or all of them individually.

If two or more persons are appointed under this paragraph to represent the same interest, they must (if at all) instruct the same solicitor.

[6491]

7.54 Insolvency practitioner's solicitor

Where in any proceedings the attendance of the responsible insolvency practitioner's solicitor is required, whether in court or in chambers, the insolvency practitioner himself need not attend, unless directed by the court.

[6492]

7.55 Formal defects

No insolvency proceedings shall be invalidated by any formal defect or by any irregularity, unless the court before which objection is made considers that substantial injustice has been caused by the defect or irregularity, and that the injustice cannot be remedied by any order of the court.

[6493]

7.56 Restriction on concurrent proceedings and remedies

Where in insolvency proceedings the court makes an order staying any action, execution or other legal process against the property of a company, or against the property or person of an individual debtor or bankrupt, service of the order may be effected by sending a sealed copy of the order to whatever is the address for service of the plaintiff or other party having the carriage of the proceedings to be stayed.

[6494]

[7.57 Affidavits

(1) Subject to the following paragraphs of this Rule the practice and procedure of the High Court with regard to affidavits, their form and contents and the procedure governing their use are to apply to all insolvency proceedings.

(2) Where, in insolvency proceedings, an affidavit is made by the official receiver or the responsible insolvency practitioner, the deponent shall state the capacity in which he makes it, the position which he holds, and the address at which he works.

(3) A creditor's affidavit of debt may be sworn before his own solicitor.

(4) The official receiver, any deputy official receiver, or any officer of the court duly authorised in that behalf, may take affidavits and declarations.

(5) Subject to paragraph (6), where the Rules provide for the use of an affidavit, a witness statement verified by a statement of truth may be used as an alternative.

(6) Paragraph (5) does not apply to Rules … , 3.4, 4.33, 6.60 (statement of affairs), 4.42, 6.66, 6.72 (further disclosure), 4.39, 4.40, 6.65, 6.70 (accounts), 4.73, 4.77, 6.96, 6.99 (claims) and 9.3, 9.4 (examinations).

(7) Where paragraph (5) applies any form prescribed by Rule 12.7 of these Rules shall be modified as necessary.]

[6495]

NOTES

Substituted by the Insolvency (Amendment) (No 2) Rules 1999, SI 1999/1022, r 3, Schedule, para 6, as from 26 April 1999.

Para (6): figure omitted revoked by the Insolvency (Amendment) Rules 2003, SI 2003/1730, r 11, Sch 1, Pt 8, para 59, as from 15 September 2003 (for transitional provisions and savings see the note preceding r 2.1 at **[6097]**).

7.58 Security in court

(1) Where security has to be given to the court (otherwise than in relation to costs), it may be given by guarantee, bond or the payment of money into court.

(2) A person proposing to give a bond as security shall give notice to the party in whose favour the security is required, and to the court, naming those who are to be sureties to the bond.

(3) The court shall forthwith give notice to both the parties concerned of a venue for the execution of the bond and the making of any objection to the sureties.

(4) The sureties shall make an affidavit of their sufficiency (unless dispensed with by the party in whose favour the security is required) and shall, if required by the court, attend the court to be cross-examined.

[6496]

[7.59 Payment into court

The CPR relating to payment into and out of court of money lodged in court as security for costs apply to money lodged in court under the Rules.]

[6497]

NOTES

Substituted by the Insolvency (Amendment) (No 2) Rules 1999, SI 1999/1022, r 3, Schedule, para 7, as from 26 April 1999.

[7.60 Further Information and Disclosure

(1) Any party to insolvency proceedings may apply to the court for an order—

(a) that any other party

(i) clarify any matter which is in dispute in the proceedings, or

(ii) give additional information in relation to any such matter;

in accordance with CPR Part 18 (further information); or

(b) to obtain disclosure from any other party in accordance with CPR Part 31 (disclosure and inspection of documents).

(2) An application under this Rule may be made without notice being served on any other party.]

[6498]

NOTES

Substituted by the Insolvency (Amendment) (No 2) Rules 1999, SI 1999/1022, r 3, Schedule, para 8, as from 26 April 1999.

7.61 Office copies of documents

(1) Any person who has under the Rules the right to inspect the court file of insolvency proceedings may require the court to provide him with an office copy of any document from the file.

(2) A person's rights under this Rule may be exercised on his behalf by his solicitor.

(3) An office copy provided by the court under this Rule shall be in such form as the registrar thinks appropriate, and shall bear the court's seal.

[6499]

[CHAPTER 10
EC REGULATION—CREDITORS' VOLUNTARY WINDING UP—CONFIRMATION BY THE COURT

7.62 Application for confirmation

(1) Where a company has passed a resolution for voluntary winding up, and no declaration under section 89 has been made, the liquidator may apply to court for an order confirming the creditors' voluntary winding up for the purposes of the EC Regulation.

(2) The application shall be in writing and verified by affidavit by the liquidator (using [FORM 7.20] the same form) and shall state—

- (a) the name of the applicant,
- (b) the name of the company and its registered number,
- (c) the date on which the resolution for voluntary winding up was passed,
- (d) that the application is accompanied by all of the documents required under paragraph (3) which are true copies of the documents required, and
- (e) that the EC Regulation will apply to the company and whether the proceedings will be main proceedings, territorial proceedings or secondary proceedings.

(3) The liquidator shall file in court two copies of the application, together with one copy of the following—

- (a) a copy of the resolution for voluntary winding up referred to by section 84(3),
- (b) evidence of his appointment as liquidator of the company, and
- (c) a copy of the statement of affairs required under section 99.

(4) It shall not be necessary to serve the application on, or give notice of it to, any person.

(5) On an application under this Rule the court may confirm the creditors' voluntary winding up.

(6) If the court confirms the creditor's voluntary winding up—

- (a) it may do so without a hearing,
- (b) it shall affix its seal to the application.

(7) A member of the court staff may deal with an application under this Rule.]

[(8) This Rule shall also apply where a company has moved to a voluntary liquidation in accordance with paragraph 83 of Schedule B1 to the Act.]

[6500]

NOTES

Inserted, together with preceding heading and rr 7.63, 7.64 (Chaps 10, 11) by the Insolvency (Amendment) Rules 2002, SI 2002/1307, rr 3, 9(1), as from 31 May 2002.

Para (8): added by the Insolvency (Amendment) Rules 2003, SI 2003/1730, r 11, Sch 1, Pt 8, para 60, as from 15 September 2003 (for transitional provisions and savings see the note preceding r 2.1 at **[6097]**).

EC Regulation: ie, Council Regulation 1346/2000/EC on insolvency proceedings at **[9290]**.

[7.63 Notice to member State liquidator and creditors in member States

Where the court has confirmed the creditors' voluntary winding up, the liquidator shall forthwith give notice—

(a) if there is a member State liquidator in relation to the company, to the member State liquidator;

(b) in accordance with Article 40 of the EC Regulation (duty to inform creditors).]

[6501]

NOTES

Inserted as noted to r 7.62 at **[6500]**.

EC Regulation: ie, Council Regulation 1346/2000/EC on insolvency proceedings at **[9290]**.

[CHAPTER 11
EC REGULATION—MEMBER STATE LIQUIDATOR

7.64 Interpretation of creditor

(1) This Rule applies where a member State liquidator has been appointed in relation to a person subject to insolvency proceedings.

(2) For the purposes of the Rules referred to in paragraph (3) a member State liquidator appointed in main proceedings is deemed to be a creditor.

(3) The Rules referred to in paragraph (2) are Rules 7.31(1) (right to inspect court file) and 7.53(1) (right of attendance).

(4) Paragraphs (2) and (3) are without prejudice to the generality of the right to participate referred to in paragraph 3 of Article 32 of the EC Regulation (exercise of creditor's rights).]

[6502]

NOTES

Inserted as noted to r 7.62 at **[6500]**.

EC Regulation: ie, Council Regulation 1346/2000/EC on insolvency proceedings at **[9290]**.

PART 8
PROXIES AND COMPANY REPRESENTATION

8.1 Definition of "proxy"

(1) For the purposes of the Rules, a proxy is an authority given by a person ("the principal") to another person ("the proxy-holder") to attend a meeting and speak and vote as his representative.

(2) Proxies are for use at creditors', company or contributories' meetings [summoned or called] under the Act or the Rules.

(3) Only one proxy may be given by a person for any one meeting at which he desires to be represented; and it may only be given to one person, being an individual aged 18 or over. But the principal may specify one or more other such individuals to be proxy-holder in the alternative, in the order in which they are named in the proxy.

(4) Without prejudice to the generality of paragraph (3), a proxy for a particular meeting may be given to whoever is to be the chairman of the meeting; and for a meeting held as part of the proceedings in a winding up by the court, or in a bankruptcy, it may be given to the official receiver.

[(5) A person given a proxy under paragraph (4) cannot decline to be the proxy-holder in relation to that proxy.

(6) A proxy requires the holder to give the principal's vote on matters arising for determination at the meeting, or to abstain, or to propose, in the principal's name, a resolution to be voted on by the meeting, either as directed or in accordance with the holder's own discretion.]

[6503]

NOTES

Para (2): words in square brackets inserted by the Insolvency (Amendment) Rules 1987, SI 1987/1919, r 3(1), Schedule, Pt 1, para 134(1), as from 11 January 1988.

Paras (5), (6): substituted, for original para (5), by SI 1987/1919, r 3(1), Schedule, Pt 1, para 134(2), as from 11 January 1988.
See Forms 8.1–8.5 in Appendix 4 at **[A4]**.

8.2 Issue and use of forms

(1) When notice is given of a meeting to be held in insolvency proceedings, and forms of proxy are sent out with the notice, no form so sent out shall have inserted in it the name or description of any person.

(2) No form of proxy shall be used at any meeting except that which is sent out with the notice summoning the meeting, or a substantially similar form.

(3) A form of proxy shall be signed by the principal, or by some person authorised by him (either generally or with reference to a particular meeting). If the form is signed by a person other than the principal, the nature of the person's authority shall be stated.

[6504]

8.3 Use of proxies at meetings

(1) A proxy given for a particular meeting may be used at any adjournment of that meeting.

(2) Where the official receiver holds proxies for use at any meeting, his deputy, or any other official receiver, may act as proxy-holder in his place.

Alternatively, the official receiver may in writing authorise another officer of the Department to act for him at the meeting and use the proxies as if that other officer were himself proxy-holder.

(3) Where the responsible insolvency practitioner holds proxies to be used by him as chairman of a meeting, and some other person acts as chairman, the other person may use the insolvency practitioner's proxies as if he were himself proxy-holder.

[(4) Where a proxy directs a proxy-holder to vote for or against a resolution for the nomination or appointment of a person as the responsible insolvency practitioner, the proxy-holder may, unless the proxy states otherwise, vote for or against (as he thinks fit) any resolution for the nomination or appointment of that person jointly with another or others.

(5) A proxy-holder may propose any resolution which, if proposed by another, would be a resolution in favour of which by virtue of the proxy he would be entitled to vote.

(6) Where a proxy gives specific directions as to voting, this does not, unless the proxy states otherwise, preclude the proxy-holder from voting at his discretion on resolutions put to the meeting which are not dealt with in the proxy.]

[6505]

NOTES

Paras (4)–(6): added by the Insolvency (Amendment) Rules 1987, SI 1987/1919, r 3(1), Schedule, Pt 1, para 135, as from 11 January 1988.

8.4 Retention of proxies

(1) Subject as follows, proxies used for voting at any meeting shall be retained by the chairman of the meeting.

(2) The chairman shall deliver the proxies, forthwith after the meeting, to the responsible insolvency practitioner (where that is someone other than himself).

[6506]

8.5 Right of inspection

(1) The responsible insolvency practitioner shall, so long as proxies lodged with him are in his hands, allow them to be inspected, at all reasonable times on any business day, by—

- (a) the creditors, in the case of proxies used at a meeting of creditors, and
- (b) a company's members or contributories, in the case of proxies used at a meeting of the company or of its contributories.

(2) The reference in paragraph (1) to creditors is—

(a) in the case of a company in liquidation or of an individual's bankruptcy, those creditors who have proved their debts, and

(b) in any other case, persons who have submitted in writing a claim to be creditors of the company or individual concerned;

but in neither case does it include a person whose proof or claim has been wholly rejected for purposes of voting, dividend or otherwise.

(3) the right of inspection given by this Rule is also exercisable—

(a) in the case of an insolvent company, by its directors, and

(b) in the case of an insolvent individual, by him.

(4) Any person attending a meeting in insolvency proceedings is entitled, immediately before or in the course of the meeting, to inspect proxies and associated documents [(including proofs) sent or given, in accordance with directions contained in any notice convening the meeting, to the chairman of that meeting or to any other person by a creditor, member or contributory for the purpose of that meeting.]

[6507]

NOTES

Para (4): words in square brackets substituted by the Insolvency (Amendment) Rules 1987, SI 1987/1919, r 3(1), Schedule, Pt 1, para 136, as from 11 January 1988.

8.6 Proxy-holder with financial interest

(1) A proxy-holder shall not vote in favour of any resolution which would directly or indirectly place him, or any associate of his, in a position to receive any remuneration out of the insolvent estate, unless the proxy specifically directs him to vote in that way.

[(1A) Where a proxy-holder has signed the proxy as being authorised to do so by his principal and the proxy specifically directs him to vote in the way mentioned in paragraph (1), he shall nevertheless not vote in that way unless he produces to the chairman of the meeting written authorisation from his principal sufficient to show that the proxy-holder was entitled so to sign the proxy.]

(2) This Rule applies also to any person acting as chairman of a meeting and using proxies in that capacity [under Rule 8.3]; and in its application to him, the proxy-holder is deemed an associate of his.

[6508]

NOTES

Para (1A): inserted by the Insolvency (Amendment) Rules 1987, SI 1987/1919, r 3(1), Schedule, Pt 1, para 137(1), as from 11 January 1988.

Para (2): words in square brackets inserted by SI 1987/1919, r 3(1), Schedule, Pt 1, para 137(2), as from 11 January 1988.

8.7 Company representation

(1) Where a person is authorised under section 375 of the Companies Act to represent a corporation at a meeting of creditors or of the company or its contributories, he shall produce to the chairman of the meeting a copy of the resolution from which he derives his authority.

(2) The copy resolution must be under the seal of the corporation, or certified by the secretary or a director of the corporation to be a true copy.

[(3) Nothing in this Rule requires the authority of a person to sign a proxy on behalf of a principal which is a corporation to be in the form of a resolution of that corporation.]

[6509]

NOTES

Para (3): added by the Insolvency (Amendment) Rules 1987, SI 1987/1919, r 3(1), Schedule, Pt 1, para 138, as from 11 January 1988.

[8.8 Interpretation of creditor

(1) This Rule applies where a member State liquidator has been appointed in relation to a person subject to insolvency proceedings.

(2) For the purposes of rule 8.5(1) (right of inspection of proxies) a member State liquidator appointed in main proceedings is deemed to be a creditor.

(3) Paragraph (2) is without prejudice to the generality of the right to participate referred to in paragraph 3 of Article 32 of the EC Regulation (exercise of creditor's rights).]

[6510]

NOTES

Inserted by the Insolvency (Amendment) Rules 2002, SI 2002/1307, rr 3, 9(2), as from 31 May 2002.

EC Regulation: ie, Council Regulation 1346/2000/EC on insolvency proceedings at **[9290]**.

PART 9
EXAMINATION OF PERSONS CONCERNED IN COMPANY AND INDIVIDUAL INSOLVENCY

9.1 Preliminary

(1) The Rules in this Part relate to applications to the court for an order under—

(a) section 236 (inquiry into company's dealings when it is, or is alleged to be, insolvent), or

(b) section 366 (inquiry in bankruptcy, with respect to the bankrupt's dealings).

(2) The following definitions apply—

(a) the person in respect of whom an order is applied for is "the respondent";

(b) "the applicable section" is section 236 or section 366, according to whether the affairs of a company or those of a bankrupt or (where the application under section 366 is made by virtue of section 368) a debtor are in question;

(c) the company or, as the case may be, the bankrupt or debtor concerned is "the insolvent".

[6511]

NOTES

See Form 9.1 in Appendix 4 at **[A4]**.

9.2 Form and contents of application

(1) The application shall be in writing, and be accompanied by a brief statement of the grounds on which it is made.

(2) The respondent must be sufficiently identified in the application.

(3) It shall be stated whether the application is for the respondent—

(a) to be ordered to appear before the court, or

[(b) to be ordered to clarify any matter which is in dispute in the proceedings or to give additional information in relation to any such matter and if so CPR Part 18 (further information) shall apply to any such order, or]

(c) to submit affidavits (if so, particulars to be given of the matters to which he is required to swear), or

(d) to produce books, papers or other records (if so, the items in question to be specified),

or for any two or more of those purposes.

(4) The application may be made *ex parte*.

[6512]

NOTES

Para (3): sub-para (b) substituted by the Insolvency (Amendment) (No 2) Rules 1999, SI 1999/1022, r 3, Schedule, para 9, as from 26 April 1999.

9.3 Order for examination, etc

(1) The court may, whatever the purpose of the application, make any order which it has power to make under the applicable section.

(2) The court, if it orders the respondent to appear before it, shall specify a venue for his appearance, which shall be not less than 14 days from the date of the order.

(3) If he is ordered to submit affidavits, the order shall specify—

(a) the matters which are to be dealt with in his affidavits, and

(b) the time within which they are to be submitted to the court.

(4) If the order is to produce books, papers or other records, the time and manner of compliance shall be specified.

(5) The order must be served forthwith on the respondent; and it must be served personally, unless the court otherwise orders.

[6513]

9.4 Procedure for examination

(1) At any examination of the respondent, the applicant may attend in person, or be represented by a solicitor with or without counsel, and may put such questions to the respondent as the court may allow.

(2) Any other person who could have applied for an order under the applicable section in respect of the insolvent's affairs may, with the leave of the court and if the applicant does not object, attend the examination and put questions to the respondent (but only through the applicant).

[(3) If the respondent is ordered to clarify any matter or to give additional information, the court shall direct him as to the questions which he is required to answer, and as to whether his answers (if any) are to be made on affidavit.]

(4) Where application has been made under the applicable section on information provided by a creditor of the insolvent, that creditor may, with the leave of the court and if the applicant does not object, attend the examination and put questions to the respondent (but only through the applicant).

(5) The respondent may at his own expense employ a solicitor with or without counsel, who may put to him such questions as the court may allow for the purpose of enabling him to explain or qualify any answers given by him, and may make representations on his behalf.

(6) There shall be made in writing such record of the examination as the court thinks proper. The record shall be read over either to or by the respondent and signed by him at a venue fixed by the court.

(7) The written record may, in any proceedings (whether under the Act or otherwise) be used as evidence against the respondent of any statement made by him in the course of his examination.

[6514]

NOTES

Para (3): substituted by the Insolvency (Amendment) (No 2) Rules 1999, SI 1999/1022, r 3, Schedule, para 10, as from 26 April 1999.

9.5 Record of examination

(1) Unless the court otherwise directs, the written record of the respondent's examination, and any answer given by him to interrogatories, and any affidavits submitted by him in compliance with an order of the court under the applicable section, shall not be filed in court.

(2) The written record, answers and affidavits shall not be open to inspection, without an order of the court, by any person other than—

(a) the applicant for an order under the applicable section, or

(b) any person who could have applied for such an order in respect of the affairs of the same insolvent.

(3) Paragraph (2) applies also to so much of the court file as shows the grounds of the application for an order under the applicable section and to any copy of proposed interrogatories.

(4) The court may from time to time give directions as to the custody and inspection of any documents to which this Rule applies, and as to the furnishing of copies of, or extracts from, such documents.

[6515]

9.6 Costs of proceedings under ss 236, 366

(1) Where the court has ordered an examination of any person under the applicable section, and it appears to it that the examination was made necessary because information had been unjustifiably refused by the respondent, it may order that the costs of the examination be paid by him.

(2) Where the court makes an order against a person under—

(a) section 237(1) or 367(1) (to deliver up property in his possession which belongs to the insolvent), or

(b) section 237(2) or 367(2) (to pay any amount in discharge of a debt due to the insolvent),

the costs of the application for the order may be ordered by the court to be paid by the respondent.

(3) Subject to paragraphs (1) and (2) above, the applicant's costs shall, unless the court otherwise orders, be paid out of the insolvent estate.

(4) A person summoned to attend for examination under this Chapter shall be tendered a reasonable sum in respect of travelling expenses incurred in connection with his attendance. Other costs falling on him are at the court's discretion.

(5) Where the examination is on the application of the official receiver otherwise than in the capacity of liquidator or trustee, no order shall be made for the payment of costs by him.

[6516]

PART 10
OFFICIAL RECEIVERS

10.1 Appointment of official receivers

Judicial notice shall be taken of the appointment under sections 399 to 401 of official receivers and deputy official receivers.

[6517]

10.2 Persons entitled to act on official receiver's behalf

(1) In the absence of the official receiver authorised to act in a particular case, an officer authorised in writing for the purpose by the Secretary of State, or by the official receiver himself, may, with the leave of the court, act on the official receiver's behalf and in his place—

(a) in any examination under section 133, 236, 290 or 366, and

(b) in respect of any application to the court.

(2) In case of emergency, where there is no official receiver capable of acting, anything to be done by, to or before the official receiver may be done by, to or before the registrar of the court.

[6518]

10.3 Application for directions

The official receiver may apply to the court for directions in relation to any matter arising in insolvency proceedings.

[6519]

10.4 Official receiver's expenses

(1) Any expenses incurred by the official receiver (in whatever capacity he may be acting) in connection with proceedings taken against him in insolvency proceedings are to be treated as expenses of the insolvency proceedings.

"Expenses" includes damages.

(2) In respect of any sums due to him under paragraph (1), the official receiver has a charge on the insolvent estate.

[6520]

PART 11
DECLARATION AND PAYMENT OF DIVIDEND (WINDING UP AND BANKRUPTCY)

11.1 Preliminary

(1) The Rules in this Part relate to the declaration and payment of dividends in companies winding up and in bankruptcy.

(2) The following definitions apply—

(a) "the insolvent" means the company in liquidation or, as the case may be, the bankrupt; and

(b) "creditors" means those creditors of the insolvent of whom the responsible insolvency practitioner is aware, or who are identified in the insolvent's statement of affairs.

[(3) For the purposes of this Part, a member State liquidator appointed in relation to an insolvent is deemed to be a creditor.]

[6521]

NOTES

Para (3): added by the Insolvency (Amendment) Rules 2002, SI 2002/1307, rr 3, 10(1), as from 31 May 2002, with savings in relation to anything done under, or for the purposes of, this provision before that date.

11.2 Notice of intended dividend

(1) Before declaring a dividend, the responsible insolvency practitioner shall give notice of his intention to do so—

[(a) to all creditors whose addresses are known to him and who have not proved their debts, and

(b) where a member State liquidator has been appointed in relation to the insolvent, to that person.]

[(1A) Before declaring a first dividend, the responsible insolvency practitioner, shall, unless he has previously by public advertisement invited creditors to prove their debts, give notice of the intended dividend by public advertisement.]

(2) [Any notice under paragraph (1) and any notice of a first dividend under paragraph (1A)] shall specify a date ("the last date for proving") up to which proofs may be lodged. The date shall be the same for all creditors, and not less than 21 days from that of the notice.

(3) The insolvency practitioner shall in the notice state his intention to declare a dividend (specified as interim or final, as the case may be) within the period of 4 months from the last date for proving.

[6522]

NOTES

Para (1): words in square brackets substituted by the Insolvency (Amendment) Rules 2002, SI 2002/1307, rr 3, 10(2), as from 31 May 2002, with savings in relation to anything done under, or for the purposes of, this provision before that date.

Para (1A): inserted by the Insolvency (Amendment) Rules 1987, SI 1987/1919, r 3(1), Schedule, Pt 1, para 139(2), as from 11 January 1988.

Para (2): words in square brackets substituted by SI 1987/1919, r 3(1), Schedule, Pt 1, para 139(3), as from 11 January 1988.

11.3 Final admission/rejection of proofs

(1) The responsible insolvency practitioner, shall within 7 days from the last date of proving, deal with every creditor's proof (in so far as not already dealt with) by admitting or rejecting it in whole or in part, or by making such provision as he thinks fit in respect of it.

(2) The insolvency practitioner is not obliged to deal with proofs lodged after the last date for proving; but he may do so, if he thinks fit.

[(3) In the declaration of a dividend no payment shall be made more than once by virtue of the same debt.

(4) Subject to Rule 11.11, where—

(a) a creditor has proved, and

(b) a member State liquidator has proved in relation to the same debt,

payment shall only be made to the creditor.]

[6523]

NOTES

Paras (3), (4): added by the Insolvency (Amendment) Rules 2002, SI 2002/1307, rr 3, 10(3), as from 31 May 2002, with savings in relation to anything done under, or for the purposes of, this provision before that date.

11.4 Postponement or cancellation of dividend

If in the period of 4 months referred to in Rule 11.2(3)—

(a) the responsible insolvency practitioner has rejected a proof in whole or in part and application is made to the court for his decision to be reversed or varied, or

(b) application is made to the court for the insolvency practitioner's decision on a proof to be reversed or varied, or for a proof to be expunged, or for a reduction of the amount claimed.

the insolvency practitioner may postpone or cancel the dividend.

[6524]

11.5 Decision to declare dividend

(1) If the responsible insolvency practitioner has not, in the 4-month period referred to in Rule 11.2(3), had cause to postpone or cancel the dividend, he shall within that period proceed to declare the dividend of which he gave notice under that Rule.

(2) Except with the leave of the court, the insolvency practitioner shall not declare the dividend so long as there is pending any application to the court to reverse or vary a decision of his on a proof, or to expunge a proof or to reduce the amount claimed.

If the court gives leave under this paragraph, the insolvency practitioner shall make such provision in respect of the proof in question as the court directs.

[6525]

11.6 Notice of declaration

(1) The responsible insolvency practitioner shall give notice of the dividend to—

[(a) all creditors who have proved their debts, and

(b) where a member State liquidator has been appointed in relation to the insolvent, to that person.]

(2) the notice shall include the following particulars relating to the insolvency and the administration of the insolvent estate—

(a) amounts realised from the sale of assets, indicating (so far as practicable) amounts raised by the sale of particular assets;

(b) payments made by the insolvency practitioner in the administration of the insolvent estate;

(c) provision (if any) made for the unsettled claims, and funds (if any) retained for particular purposes;

(d) the total amount to be distributed, and the rate of dividend;

(e) whether, and if so when, any further dividend is expected to be declared.

(3) The dividend may be distributed simultaneously with the notice declaring it.

(4) Payment of dividend may be made by post, or arrangements may be made with any creditor for it to be paid to him in another way, or held for his collection.

(5) Where a dividend is paid on a bill of exchange or other negotiable instrument, the amount of the dividend shall be endorsed on the instrument, or on a certified copy of it, if required to be produced by the holder for that purpose.

[6526]

NOTES

Para (1): sub-paras (a), (b) substituted by the Insolvency (Amendment) Rules 2002, SI 2002/1307, rr 3, 10(4), as from 31 May 2002, with savings in relation to anything done under, or for the purposes of, this provision before that date.

11.7 Notice of no, or no further, dividend

If the responsible insolvency practitioner gives notice to creditors that he is unable to declare any dividend or (as the case may be) any further dividend, the notice shall contain statement to the effect either—

(a) that no funds have been realised, or

(b) that the funds realised have already been distributed or used or allocated for defraying the expenses of administration.

[6527]

11.8 Proof altered after payment of dividend

(1) If after payment of dividend the amount claimed by a creditor in his proof is increased, the creditor is not entitled to disturb the distribution of the dividend; but he is entitled to be paid, out of any money for the time being available for the payment of any further dividend, any dividend or dividends which he has failed to receive.

(2) Any dividend or dividends payable under paragraph (1) shall be paid before the money there referred to is applied to the payment of any such further dividend.

(3) If, after a creditor's proof has been admitted, the proof is withdrawn or expunged, or the amount of it is reduced, the creditor is liable to repay to the responsible insolvency practitioner, for the credit of the insolvent estate, any amount overpaid by way of dividend.

[6528]

11.9 Secured creditors

(1) The following applies where a creditor re-values his security at a time when a dividend has been declared.

(2) If the revaluation results in a reduction of his unsecured claim ranking for dividend, the creditor shall forthwith repay to the responsible insolvency practitioner, for the credit of the insolvent estate, any amount received by him as dividend in excess of that to which he would be entitled having regard to the revaluation of the security.

(3) If the revaluation results in an increase of his unsecured claim, the creditor is entitled to receive from the insolvency practitioner, out of any money for the time being available for the payment of a further dividend, before any such further dividend is paid, any dividend or dividends which he has failed to receive, having regard to the revaluation of the security.

However, the creditor is not entitled to disturb any dividend declared (whether or not distributed) before the date of the revaluation.

[6529]

11.10 Disqualification from dividend

If a creditor contravenes any provision of the Act or the Rules relating to the valuation of securities, the court may, on the application of the responsible insolvency practitioner, order that the creditor be wholly or partly disqualified from participation in any dividend.

[6530]

11.11 Assignment of right to dividend

(1) If a person entitled to a dividend gives notice to the responsible insolvency practitioner that he wishes the dividend to be paid to another person, or that he has assigned his entitlement to another person, the insolvency practitioner shall pay the dividend to that other accordingly.

(2) A notice given under this Rule must specify the name and address of the person to whom payment is to be made.

[6531]

11.12 Preferential creditors

(1) Subject as follows, the Rules in this Part apply with respect to any distribution made in the insolvency to preferential creditors, with such adaptations as are appropriate considering that such creditors are of a limited class.

(2) The notice by the responsible insolvency practitioner under Rule 11.2, where a dividend is to be declared for preferential creditors, need only be given to those creditors in

whose case he has reason to believe that their debts are preferential [and public advertisement of the intended dividend need only be given if the insolvency practitioner thinks fit].

[6532]

NOTES

Para (2): words in square brackets added by the Insolvency (Amendment) Rules 1987, SI 1987/1919, r 3(1), Schedule, Pt 1, para 140, as from 11 January 1988.

11.13 Debt payable at future time

(1) Where a creditor has proved for a debt of which payment is not due at the date of the declaration of dividend, he is entitled to dividend equally with other creditors, but subject as follows.

[(2) For the purpose of dividend (and no other purpose) the amount of the creditor's admitted proof (or, if a distribution has previously been made to him, the amount remaining outstanding in respect of his admitted proof) shall be reduced by applying the following formula—

$$X / 1.05^{n}$$

where—

(a) "X" is the value of the admitted proof; and

(b) "n" is the period beginning with the relevant date and ending with the date on which the payment of the creditor's debt would otherwise be due expressed in years and months in a decimalised form.

(3) In paragraph (2) "relevant date" means—

(a) in the case of a winding up which was not immediately preceded by an administration, the date that the company went into liquidation;

(b) in the case of a winding up which was immediately preceded by an administration, the date that the company entered administration; and

(c) in the case of a bankruptcy, the date of the bankruptcy order.]

[6533]

NOTES

Paras (2), (3) substituted (for the original para (2)), and the original para (3) was revoked, by the Insolvency (Amendment) Rules 2005, SI 2005/527, r 43, as from 1 April 2005, subject to transitional provisions as noted to r 2.67 at **[6157F]**.

PART 12
MISCELLANEOUS AND GENERAL

12.1 Power of Secretary of State to regulate certain matters

(1) Pursuant to paragraph 27 of Schedule 8 to the Act, and paragraph 30 of Schedule 9 to the Act, the Secretary of State may[, subject to the Act and the Rules, make regulations with respect to any matter provided for in the Rules as relates to the carrying out of the functions of a liquidator, provisional liquidator, administrator or administrative receiver of a company, an interim receiver appointed under section 286, of the official receiver while acting as receiver or manager under section 287 or of a trustee of a bankrupt's estate, including, without prejudice to the generality of the foregoing provision] with respect to the following matters arising in companies winding up and individual bankruptcy—

(a) the preparation and keeping by liquidators, trustees, provisional liquidators, interim receivers and the official receiver, of books, accounts and other records, and their production to such persons as may be authorised or required to inspect them;

(b) the auditing of liquidators' and trustees' accounts;

(c) the manner in which liquidators and trustees are to act in relation to the insolvent company's or bankrupt's books, papers and other records, and the manner of their disposal by the responsible insolvency practitioner or others;

(d) the supply—

(i) in company insolvency, by the liquidator to creditors and members of the company, contributories in its winding up and the liquidation committee, and

(ii) in individual insolvency, by the trustee to creditors and the creditors' committee,

of copies of documents relating to the insolvency and the affairs of the insolvent company or individual (on payment, in such cases as may be specified by the regulations, of the specified fee);

(e) the manner in which insolvent estates are to be distributed by liquidators and trustees, including provision with respect to unclaimed funds and dividends;

(f) the manner in which moneys coming into the hands of a liquidator or trustee in the course of his administration are to be handled and … invested, and the payment of interest on sums which, in pursuance of regulations made by virtue of this sub-paragraph, have been paid into the Insolvency Services Account;

(g) the amount (or the manner of determining the amount) to be paid to the official receiver by way of remuneration when acting as provisional liquidator, liquidator, interim receiver or trustee.

(2) Any reference in paragraph (1) to a trustee includes a reference to the official receiver when acting as receiver and manager under section 287.

(3) Regulations made pursuant to paragraph (1) may—

(a) confer a discretion on the court;

(b) make non-compliance with any of the regulations a criminal offence;

(c) make different provision for different cases, including different provision for different areas[; and

(d) contain such incidental, supplemental and transitional provisions as may appear to the Secretary of State necessary or expedient].

[6534]

NOTES

Para (1): words in square brackets substituted by the Insolvency (Amendment) Rules 1987, SI 1987/1919, r 3(1), Schedule, Pt 1, para 142(1), as from 11 January 1988; words omitted from sub-para (f) revoked by the Insolvency (Amendment) Rules 2001, SI 2001/763, r 2, as from 2 April 2001.

Para (3): sub-para (d) added by SI 1987/1919, r 3(1), Schedule, Pt 1, para 142(2), as from 11 January 1988.

Regulations: the Insolvency Regulations 1994, SI 1994/2507 at **[6794]**.

12.2 Costs, expenses, etc

[(1)] All fees, costs, charges and other expenses incurred in the course of winding up[, administration] or bankruptcy proceedings are to be regarded as expenses of the winding up [or the administration] or, as the case may be, of the bankruptcy.

[(2) The costs associated with the prescribed part shall be paid out of the prescribed part.]

[6535]

NOTES

Para (1) numbered as such, words in square brackets in that paragraph inserted, and para (2) added, by the Insolvency (Amendment) Rules 2003, SI 2003/1730, r 12, Sch 1, Pt 9, para 61, as from 15 September 2003 (for transitional provisions and savings see the note preceding r 2.1 at **[6097]**).

12.3 Provable debts

(1) Subject as follows, [in administration, winding up and bankruptcy], all claims by creditors are provable as debts against the company or, as the case may be, the bankrupt, whether they are present or future, certain or contingent, ascertained or sounding only in damages.

(2) The following are not provable—

(a) in bankruptcy, any fine imposed for an offence, and any obligation [(other than an obligation to pay a lump sum or to pay costs)] arising under an order made in family … proceedings [or [any obligation arising] under a maintenance assessment made under the Child Support Act 1991];

(b) in [administration,] winding up or bankruptcy, any obligation arising under a confiscation order made under section 1 of the Drug Trafficking Offences Act 1986 [or section 1 of the Criminal Justice (Scotland) Act 1987] [or section 71 of the Criminal Justice Act 1988] [or under Parts 2, 3 or 4 of the Proceeds of Crime Act 2002].

"Fine", ... and "family proceedings" have the meanings given by section 281(8) of the Act (which applies the Magistrates' Courts Act 1980 and the Matrimonial and Family Proceedings Act 1984).

[(2A) The following are not provable except at a time when all other claims of creditors in the insolvency proceedings (other than any of a kind mentioned in this paragraph) have been paid in full with interest under section 189(2)[, Rule 2.88] or, as the case may be, section 328(4)—

[(a) in [an administration,] a winding up or a bankruptcy, any claim arising by virtue of section 382(1)(a) of the Financial Services and Markets Act 2000, not being a claim also arising by virtue of section 382(1)(b) of that Act;]

(c) in [an administration or] a winding up, any claim which by virtue of the Act or any other enactment is a claim the payment of which in a bankruptcy[, an administration] or a winding up is to be postponed.]

(3) Nothing in this Rule prejudices any enactment or rule of law under which a particular kind of debt is not provable, whether on grounds of public policy or otherwise.

[6536]

NOTES

Para (1): words in square brackets substituted by the Insolvency (Amendment) Rules 2003, SI 2003/1730, r 12, Sch 1, Pt 9, para 62(a), as from 15 September 2003 (for transitional provisions and savings see the note preceding r 2.1 at **[6097]**).

Para (2): words in first pair and third (inner) pair of square brackets in sub-para (a) inserted by the Insolvency (Amendment) Rules 2005, SI 2005/527, r 44, as from 1 April 2005; words in second (outer) pair of square brackets in sub-para (a) added, and words omitted from that sub-paragraph revoked, by the Insolvency (Amendment) Rules 1993, SI 1993/602, r 3, Schedule, para 2, as from 5 April 1993; words in first and final pairs of square brackets in sub-para (b) inserted by SI 2003/1730, r 12, Sch 1, Pt 9, para 62(b), as from 15 September 2003 (for transitional provisions and savings see the note preceding r 2.1 at **[6097]**); words in second pair of square brackets in sub-para (b) added by the Insolvency (Amendment) Rules 1987, SI 1987/1919, r 3(1), Schedule, Pt 1, para 143(1), as from 11 January 1988, and words in third pair of square brackets in that sub-paragraph added by the Insolvency (Amendment) Rules 1989, SI 1989/397, r 3(1), Schedule, para 2, as from 3 April 1989; final words omitted revoked by SI 1993/602, r 3, Schedule, para 3, as from 5 April 1993.

Para (2A): inserted by SI 1987/1919, r 3(1), Schedule, Pt 1, para 143(2), as from 11 January 1988; sub-para (a) substituted, for original sub-paras (a), (b), by the Financial Services and Markets Act 2000 (Consequential Amendments and Repeals) Order 2001, SI 2001/3649, art 380, as from 1 December 2001; words in first pair of square brackets and words in square brackets in sub-paras (a), (c) inserted by SI 2003/1730, r 12, Sch 1, Pt 9, para 62(c)–(e), as from 15 September 2003 (for transitional provisions and savings see the note preceding r 2.1 at **[6097]**).

Confiscation orders: the Drug Trafficking Offences Act 1986, s 1, the Criminal Justice (Scotland) Act 1987, s 1, and the Criminal Justice Act 1988, s 71 are repealed; as to the making of confiscation orders, see now the Proceeds of Crime Act 2002, ss 6, 92, 156.

12.4 Notices

(1) All notices required or authorised by or under the Act or the Rules to be given must be in writing, unless it is otherwise provided, or the court allows the notice to be given in some other way.

(2) Where in any proceedings a notice is required to be sent or given by the official receiver or by the responsible insolvency practitioner, the sending or giving of it may be proved by means of a certificate—

(a) in the case of the official receiver, by him or a member of his staff, and

(b) in the case of the insolvency practitioner, by him, or his solicitor, or a partner or an employee of either of them,

that the notice was duly posted.

(3) In the case of a notice to be sent or given by a person other than the official receiver or insolvency practitioner, the sending or giving of it may be proved by means of a certificate by that person that he posted the notice, or instructed another person (naming him) to do so.

(4) A certificate under this Rule may be endorsed on a copy or specimen of the notice to which it relates.

[6537]

[12.4A Quorum at meeting of creditors or contributories

(1) Any meeting of creditors or contributories in insolvency proceedings is competent to act if a quorum is present.

(2) Subject to the next paragraph, a quorum is—
(a) in the case of a creditors' meeting, at least one creditor entitled to vote;
(b) in the case of a meeting of contributories, at least 2 contributories so entitled, or all the contributories, if their number does not exceed 2.

(3) For the purposes of this Rule, the reference to the creditor or contributories necessary to constitute a quorum is to those persons present or represented by proxy by any person (including the chairman) and in the case of any proceedings under Parts I–VII of the Act includes persons duly represented under section 375 of the Companies Act.

(4) Where at any meeting of creditors or contributories—
(a) the provisions of this Rule as to a quorum being present are satisfied by the attendance of—
(i) the chairman alone, or
(ii) one other person in addition to the chairman, and
(b) the chairman is aware, by virtue of proofs and proxies received or otherwise, that one or more additional persons would, if attending, be entitled to vote,

the meeting shall not commence until at least the expiry of 15 minutes after the time appointed for its commencement.]

[6538]

NOTES

Inserted by the Insolvency (Amendment) Rules 1987, SI 1987/1919, r 3(1), Schedule, Pt 1, para 144, as from 11 January 1988.

12.5 Evidence of proceedings at meetings

(1) A minute of proceedings at a meeting (held under the Act or the Rules) of a person's creditors, or of the members of a company, or of the contributories in a company's liquidation, signed by a person describing himself as, or appearing to be, the chairman of that meeting is admissible in insolvency proceedings without further proof.

(2) The minute is prima facie evidence that—
(a) the meeting was duly convened and held,
(b) all resolutions passed at the meeting were duly passed, and
(c) all proceedings at the meeting duly took place.

[6539]

12.6 Documents issuing from Secretary of State

(1) Any document purporting to be, or to contain, any order, directions or certificate issued by the Secretary of State shall be received in evidence and deemed to be or (as the case may be) contain that order or certificate, or those directions, without further proof, unless the contrary is shown.

(2) Paragraph (1) applies whether the document is signed by the Secretary of State himself or an officer on his behalf.

(3) Without prejudice to the foregoing, a certificate signed by the Secretary of State or an officer on his behalf and confirming—
(a) the making of any order,
(b) the issuing of any document, or
(c) the exercise of any discretion, power or obligation arising or imposed under the Act or the Rules,

is conclusive evidence of the matters dealt with in the certificate.

[6540]

12.7 Forms for use in insolvency proceedings

(1) The forms contained in Schedule 4 to the Rules shall be used in and in connection with, insolvency proceedings, whether in the High Court or a county court.

(2) The forms shall be used with such variations, if any, as the circumstances may require.

[(3) Where any form contained in Schedule 4 is substantially the same as one used for a corresponding purpose under either—
(a) the law and practice obtaining before the coming into force of the Rules; or

(b) if the form was first required to be used after the coming into force of the Rules, the law and practice obtaining before the making of the requirement,

whichever shall be appropriate in any case, the latter may continue to be used (with the necessary modifications) until 1 March 1988.]

[6541]

NOTES

Para (3): substituted by the Insolvency (Amendment) Rules 1987, SI 1987/1919, r 3(1), Schedule, Pt 1, para 145, as from 11 January 1988.

12.8 Insolvency practitioner's security

(1) Wherever under the Rules any person has to appoint, or certify the appointment of, an insolvency practitioner to any office, he is under a duty to satisfy himself that the person appointed or to be appointed has security for the proper performance of his functions.

(2) It is the duty—

(a) of the creditors' committee in companies administration, administrative receivership and bankruptcy,

(b) of the liquidation committee in companies winding up, and

(c) of any committee of creditors established for the purposes of a voluntary arrangement under Part I or VIII of the Act,

to review from time to time the adequacy of the responsible insolvency practitioner's security.

(3) In any insolvency proceedings the cost of the responsible insolvency practitioner's security shall be defrayed as an expense of the proceedings.

[6542]

[12.9 Time-Limits

(1) The provisions of CPR rule 2.8 (time) apply, as regards computation of time, to anything required or authorised to be done by the Rules.

(2) The provisions of CPR rule 3.1(2)(a) (the court's general powers of management) apply so as to enable the court to extend or shorten the time for compliance with anything required or authorised to be done by the Rules.]

[6543]

NOTES

Substituted by the Insolvency (Amendment) (No 2) Rules 1999, SI 1999/1022, r 3, Schedule, para 11, as from 26 April 1999.

12.10 Service by post

(1) For a document to be properly served by post, it must be contained in an envelope addressed to the person on whom service is to be effected, and pre-paid for either first or second class post.

[(1A) A document to be served by post may be sent to the last known address of the person to be served.]

(2) Where first class post is used, the document is treated as served on the second business day after the date of posting, unless the contrary is shown.

(3) Where second class post is used, the document is treated as served on the fourth business day after the date of posting, unless the contrary is shown.

(4) The date of posting is presumed, unless the contrary is shown, to be the date shown in the post-mark on the envelope in which the document is contained.

[6544]

NOTES

Para (1A): inserted by the Insolvency (Amendment) Rules 1987, SI 1987/1919, r 3(1), Schedule, Pt 1, para 146, as from 11 January 1988.

[12.11 General provisions as to service

Subject to Rule 12.10 [and Rule 12.12], CPR Part 6 (service of documents) applies as regards any matter relating to the service of documents and the giving of notice in insolvency proceedings.]

[6545]

NOTES

Substituted by the Insolvency (Amendment) (No 2) Rules 1999, SI 1999/1022, r 3, Schedule, para 12, as from 26 April 1999.

Words in square brackets inserted by the Insolvency (Amendment) Rules 2005, SI 2005/527, r 45, as from 1 April 2005.

12.12 Service outside the jurisdiction

[(1) [CPR Part 6, paragraphs 6.17 to 6.35] (service of process, etc, out of the jurisdiction) [do] not apply in insolvency proceedings.]

(2) A bankruptcy petition may, with the leave of the court, be served outside England and Wales in such manner as the court may direct.

(3) Where for the purposes of insolvency proceedings any process or order of the court, or other document, is required to be served on a person who is not in England and Wales, the court may order service to be effected within such time, on such person, at such place and in such manner as it thinks fit, and may also require such proof of service as it thinks fit.

(4) An application under this Rule shall be supported by an affidavit stating—
- (a) the grounds on which the application is made, and
- (b) in what place or country the person to be served is, or probably may be found.

[(5) Leave of the court is not required to serve anything referred to in this Rule on a member State liquidator.]

[6546]

NOTES

Para (1): substituted by the Insolvency (Amendment) (No 2) Rules 1999, SI 1999/1022, r 3, Schedule, para 13, as from 26 April 1999; words in square brackets substituted by the Insolvency (Amendment) Rules 2005, SI 2005/527, r 46, as from 1 April 2005.

Para (5): added by the Insolvency (Amendment) Rules 2002, SI 2002/1307, rr 3, 10(5), as from 31 May 2002, with savings in relation to anything done under, or for the purposes of, this provision before that date.

12.13 Confidentiality of documents

(1) Where in insolvency proceedings the responsible insolvency practitioner considers, in the case of a document forming part of the records of the insolvency, that—
- (a) it should be treated as confidential, or
- (b) it is of such a nature that its disclosure would be calculated to be injurious to the interests of the insolvent's creditors or, in the case of a company's insolvency, its members or the contributories in its winding up,

he may decline to allow it to be inspected by a person who would otherwise be entitled to inspect it.

(2) The persons to whom the insolvency practitioner may under this Rule refuse inspection include the members of a liquidation committee or a creditors' committee.

(3) Where under this Rule the insolvency practitioner determines to refuse inspection of a document, the person wishing to inspect it may apply to the court for that determination to be overruled; and the court may either overrule it altogether, or sustain it subject to such conditions (if any) as it thinks fit to impose.

[(4) Nothing in this Rule entitles the insolvency practitioner to decline to allow the inspection of any proof or proxy.]

[6547]

NOTES

Para (4): added by the Insolvency (Amendment) Rules 1987, SI 1987/1919, r 3(1), Schedule, Pt 1, para 148, as from 11 January 1988.

12.14 Notices sent simultaneously to the same person

Where under the Act or the Rules a document of any description is to be sent to a person (whether or not as a member of a class of persons to whom that same document is to be sent), it may be sent as an accompaniment to any other document or information which the person is to receive, with or without modification or adaptation of the form applicable to that document.

[6548]

12.15 Right to copy documents

Where the [Act or the] Rules confer a right for any person to inspect documents, the right includes that of taking copies of those documents, on payment—

(a) in the case of documents on the court's file of proceedings, of the fee chargeable under any order made under [section 92 of the Courts Act 2003], and

(b) otherwise, of the appropriate fee.

[6549]

NOTES

Words in first pair of square brackets inserted by the Insolvency (Amendment) Rules 1987, SI 1987/1919, r 3(1), Schedule, Pt 1, para 149, as from 11 January 1988; words in second pair of square brackets substituted by the Insolvency (Amendment) Rules 2005, SI 2005/527, r 47, as from 1 April 2005.

[12.15A Charge for copy documents

Where the responsible insolvency practitioner or the official receiver is requested by a creditor, member, contributory or member of a liquidation or creditors' committee to supply copies of any documents he is entitled to require the payment of the appropriate fee in respect of the supply of the documents.]

[6550]

NOTES

Inserted by the Insolvency (Amendment) Rules 1987, SI 1987/1919, r 3(1), Schedule, Pt 1, para 150, as from 11 January 1988.

12.16 Non-receipt of notice of meeting

Where in accordance with the Act or the Rules a meeting of creditors or other persons is summoned by notice, the meeting is presumed to have been duly summoned and held, notwithstanding that not all those to whom the notice is to be given have received it.

[6551]

12.17 Right to have list of creditors

(1) This Rule applies in any of the following proceedings—

(a) proceedings under Part II of the Act (company administration),

(b) a creditors' voluntary winding up, or a winding up by the court, and

(c) proceedings in bankruptcy.

(2) In any such proceedings a creditor who under the Rules has the right to inspect documents on the court file also has the right to require the responsible insolvency practitioner to furnish him with a list of the insolvent's creditors and the amounts of their respective debts.

This does not apply if a statement of the insolvent's affairs has been filed in court or, in the case of a creditors' voluntary winding up, been delivered to the registrar of companies.

[(2A) For the purpose of this Rule a member State liquidator appointed in main proceedings in relation to a person is deemed to be a creditor.]

(3) The insolvency practitioner, on being required by any person to furnish the list, shall send it to him, but is entitled to charge the appropriate fee for doing so.

[6552]

NOTES

Para (2A): inserted by the Insolvency (Amendment) Rules 2002, SI 2002/1307, rr 3, 10(6), as from 31 May 2002, with savings in relation to anything done under, or for the purposes of, this provision before that date.

12.18 False claim of status as creditor, etc

(1) Where the Rules provide for creditors, members of a company or contributories in a company's winding up a right to inspect any documents, whether on the court's file or in the hands of a responsible insolvency practitioner or other person, it is an offence for a person, with the intention of obtaining a sight of documents which he has not under the Rules any right to inspect, falsely to claim a status which would entitle him to inspect them.

(2) A person guilty of an offence under this Rule is liable to imprisonment or a fine, or both.

[6553]

12.19 Execution overtaken by judgment debtor's insolvency

(1) This Rule applies where execution has been taken out against property of a judgment debtor, and notice is given to the [enforcement officer] or other officer charged with the execution—

(a) under section 184(1) (that a winding-up order has been made against the debtor, or that a provisional liquidator has been appointed, or that a resolution for voluntary winding up has been passed); or

(b) under section 184(4) (that a winding-up petition has been presented or a winding-up order made, or that a meeting has been called at which there is to be proposed a resolution for voluntary winding up, or that such a resolution has been passed); or

(c) under section 346(2) (that the judgment debtor has been adjudged bankrupt); or

(d) under section 346(3)(b) (that a bankruptcy petition has been presented in respect of him).

(2) Subject as follows, the notice shall be in writing and be delivered by hand, at, or sent by recorded delivery to, the office of the [enforcement officer] or (as the case may be) of the officer charged with the execution.

(3) Where the execution is in a county court, and the officer in charge of it is the registrar of that court, then if—

(a) there is filed in that court in respect of the judgment debtor a winding-up or bankruptcy petition, or

(b) there is made by that court in respect of him a winding-up order or an order appointing a provisional liquidator, or a bankruptcy order or an order appointing an interim receiver,

section 184 or (as the case may be) 346 is deemed satisfied as regards the requirement of a notice to be served on, or given to, the officer in charge of the execution.

[6554]

NOTES

Paras (1), (2): words in square brackets substituted by the Insolvency (Amendment) Rules 2005, SI 2005/527, r 48, as from 1 April 2005.

Registrar of that court; now district judge, see the Courts and Legal Services Act 1990, s 74(1)(a).

12.20 The Gazette

(1) A copy of the Gazette containing any notice required by the Act or the Rules to be gazetted is evidence of any facts stated in the notice.

(2) In the case of an order of the court notice of which is required by the Act or the Rules to be gazetted, a copy of the Gazette containing the notice may in any proceedings be produced as conclusive evidence that the order was made on the date specified in the notice.

(3) Where an order of the court which is gazetted has been varied, and where any matter has been erroneously or inaccurately gazetted, the person whose responsibility it was to procure the requisite entry in the Gazette shall forthwith cause the variation of the order to be gazetted or, as the case may be, a further entry to be made in the Gazette for the purpose of correcting the error or inaccuracy.

[6555]

12.21 Punishment of offences

(1) Schedule 5 to the Rules has effect with respect to the way in which contraventions of the Rules are punishable on conviction.

(2) In relation to an offence under a provision of the Rules specified in the first column of the Schedule (the general nature of the offence being described in the second column), the third column shows whether the offence is punishable on conviction on indictment, or on summary conviction, or either in the one way or the other.

(3) The fourth column shows, in relation to an offence, the maximum punishment by way of fine or imprisonment which may be imposed on a person convicted of the offence in the way specified in relation to it in the third column (that is to say, on indictment or summarily), a reference to a period of years or months being to a term of imprisonment of that duration.

(4) The fifth column shows (in relation to an offence for which there is an entry in that column) that a person convicted of the offence after continued contravention is liable to a daily default fine; that is to say, he is liable on a second or subsequent conviction of the offence to the fine specified in that column for each day on which the contravention is continued (instead of the penalty specified for the offence in the fourth column of the Schedule).

(5) Section 431 (summary proceedings), as it applies to England and Wales, has effect in relation to offences under the Rules as to offences under the Act.

[6556]

[12.22 Notice of order under section 176A(5)

(1) Where the court makes an order under section 176A(5), it shall as soon as reasonably practicable send two sealed copies of the order to the applicant and a sealed copy to any other insolvency practitioner who holds office in relation to the company.

(2) Where the court has made an order under section 176A(5), the liquidator, administrator or receiver, as the case may be, shall, as soon as reasonably practicable, send a sealed copy of the order to the company.

(3) Where the court has made an order under section 176A(5), the liquidator, administrator or receiver, as the case may be, shall as soon as reasonably practicable, give notice to each creditor of whose claim and address he is aware.

(4) Paragraph (3) shall not apply where the court directs otherwise.

(5) The court may direct that the requirement in paragraph (3) is complied with by the liquidator, administrator or receiver, as the case may be, publishing a notice in such newspaper as he thinks most appropriate for ensuring that it comes to the notice of the company's unsecured creditors stating that the court has made an order disapplying the requirement to set aside the prescribed part.

(6) The liquidator, administrator or receiver shall send a copy of the order to the registrar of companies as soon as reasonably practicable after the making of the order.]

[6556A]

NOTES

Inserted by the Insolvency (Amendment) Rules 2003, SI 2003/1730, r 12, Sch 1, Pt 9, para 63, as from 15 September 2003 (for transitional provisions and savings see the note preceding r 2.1 at **[6097]**).

Para (6): see Form 12.1 in Appendix 4 at **[A4]**.

PART 13
INTERPRETATION AND APPLICATION

13.1 Introductory

This Part of the Rules has effect for their interpretation and application; and any definition given in this Part applies except, and in so far as, the context otherwise requires.

[6557]

13.2 "The court"; "the registrar"

(1) Anything to be done under or by virtue of the Act or the Rules by, to or before the court may be done by, to or before a judge or the registrar.

(2) The registrar may authorise any act of a formal or administrative character which is not by statute his responsibility to be carried out by the chief clerk or any other officer of the court acting on his behalf, in accordance with directions given by the Lord Chancellor.

(3) In individual insolvency proceedings, "the registrar" means a Registrar in Bankruptcy of the High Court, or the registrar or deputy registrar of a county court.

(4) In company insolvency proceedings in the High Court, "the registrar" means—

- (a) subject to the following paragraph, a Registrar in Bankruptcy of the High Court;
- (b) where the proceedings are in the District Registry of Birmingham, Bristol, Cardiff, Leeds, Liverpool, Manchester, Newcastle-upon-Tyne or Preston, the District Registrar.

(5) In company insolvency proceedings in a county court, "the registrar" means the officer of the court whose duty it is to exercise the functions which in the High Court are exercised by a registrar.

[6558]

NOTES

Registrar or deputy registrar of a county court: now district judge or deputy district judge; see the Courts and Legal Services Act 1990, s 74(1).

13.3 "Give notice", etc

(1) A reference in the Rules to giving notice, or to delivering, sending or serving any document, means that the notice or document may be sent by post, unless under a particular Rule personal service is expressly required.

(2) Any form of post may be used, unless under a particular Rule a specified form is expressly required.

(3) Personal service of a document is permissible in all cases.

(4) Notice of the venue fixed for an application may be given by service of the sealed copy of the application under Rule 7.4(3).

[6559]

13.4 Notice, etc to solicitors

Where under the Act or the Rules a notice or other document is required or authorised to be given to a person, it may, if he has indicated that his solicitor is authorised to accept service on his behalf, be given instead to the solicitor.

[6560]

13.5 Notice to joint liquidators, joint trustees, etc

Where two or more persons are acting jointly as the responsible insolvency practitioner in any proceedings, delivery of a document to one of them is to be treated as delivery to them all.

[6561]

13.6 "Venue"

References to the "venue" for any proceeding or attendance before the court, or for a meeting, are to the time, date and place for the proceeding, attendance or meeting.

[6562]

13.7 "Insolvency proceedings"

"Insolvency proceedings" means any proceedings under the Act or the Rules.

[6563]

13.8 "Insolvent estate"

References to "the insolvent estate" are—

- (a) in relation to a company insolvency, the company's assets, and
- (b) in relation to an individual insolvency, the bankrupt's estate or (as the case may be) the debtor's property.

[6564]

13.9 "Responsible insolvency practitioner", etc

(1) In relation to any insolvency proceedings, "the responsible insolvency practitioner" means—

(a) the person acting in a company insolvency, as supervisor of a voluntary arrangement under Part I of the Act, or as administrator, administrative receiver, liquidator or provisional liquidator;

(b) the person acting in an individual insolvency, as the supervisor of a voluntary arrangement under Part VIII of the Act, or as trustee or interim receiver;

(c) the official receiver acting as receiver and manager of a bankrupt's estate.

(2) Any reference to the liquidator, provisional liquidator, trustee or interim receiver includes the official receiver when acting in the relevant capacity.

[(3) A reference to an "authorised person" is a reference to a person who is authorised pursuant to section 389A of the Act to act as nominee or supervisor of a voluntary arrangement proposed or approved under Part I or Part VIII of the Act.]

[6565]

NOTES

Para (3): added by the Insolvency (Amendment) (No 2) Rules 2002, SI 2002/2712, r 7, as from 1 January 2003.

13.10 "Petitioner"

In winding up and bankruptcy, references to "the petitioner" or "the petitioning creditor" include any person who has been substituted as such, or been given carriage of the petition.

[6566]

13.11 "The appropriate fee"

"The appropriate fee" means—

(a) in Rule 6.192(2) (pay or under income payments order entitled to clerical etc costs) [or Rule 6.193C(4) (payor under income payments agreement entitled to clerical etc costs)], 50 pence; and

(b) in other cases, 15 pence per A4 or A5 page, and 30 pence per A3 page.

[6567]

NOTES

Words in square brackets inserted by the Insolvency (Amendment) Rules 2003, SI 2003/1730, r 13, Sch 1, Pt 10, para 64, as from 1 April 2004 (for transitional provisions and savings see the note preceding r 2.1 at **[6097]**).

[13.12 "Debt", "liability" (winding up)

(1) "Debt", in relation to the winding up of a company, means (subject to the next paragraph) any of the following—

(a) any debt or liability to which the company is subject at the date on which it goes into liquidation;

(b) any debt or liability to which the company may become subject after that date by reason of any obligation incurred before that date; and

(c) any interest provable as mentioned in Rule 4.93(1).

(2) For the purposes of any provision of the Act or the Rules about winding up, any liability in tort is a debt provable in the winding up, if either—

(a) the cause of action has accrued at the date on which the company goes into liquidation; or

(b) all the elements necessary to establish the cause of action exist at that date except for actionable damage.

(3) For the purposes of references in any provision of the Act or the Rules about winding up to a debt or liability, it is immaterial whether the debt or liability is present or future, whether it is certain or contingent, or whether its amount is fixed or liquidated, or is capable of being ascertained by fixed rules or as a matter of opinion; and references in any such provision to owing a debt are to be read accordingly.

(4) In any provision of the Act or the Rules about winding up, except in so far as the context otherwise requires, "liability" means (subject to paragraph (3) above) a liability to pay money or money's worth, including any liability under an enactment, any liability for breach of trust, any liability in contract, tort or bailment, and any liability arising out of an obligation to make restitution.

(5) This Rule shall apply where a company is in administration and shall be read as if references to winding-up were a reference to administration.]

[6568]

NOTES

Commencement: 1 June 2006.

Substituted by the Insolvency (Amendment) Rules 2006, SI 2006/1272, r 4, as from 1 June 2006, subject to transitional provisions as noted below.

Transitional provisions: SI 2006/1272, r 3 provides for the following transitional provisions in relation to the substitution of this rule (note that by virtue of r 1(2), the "commencement date" is 1 June 2006)—

"3 Transitional provisions

The amendment to the principal Rules made by Rule 4 of these Rules shall apply in respect of a company which—

(a) on or after the commencement date enters administration except where—
  (i) it enters administration by virtue of an administration order under paragraph 10 of Schedule B1 to the Act on an application made before the commencement date;
  (ii) the administration is immediately preceded by a voluntary liquidation in respect of which the resolution to wind up was passed before the commencement date; or
  (iii) the administration is immediately preceded by a liquidation on the making of a winding-up order on a petition which was presented before the commencement date;

(b) goes into liquidation upon the passing, on or after the commencement date, of a resolution to wind up;

(c) goes into voluntary liquidation under paragraph 83 of Schedule B1 except where the preceding administration—
  (i) commenced before the commencement date; or
  (ii) is an administration which commenced by virtue of an administration order under paragraph 10 of Schedule B1 on an application which was made before the commencement date;

(d) goes into liquidation on the making of a winding-up order on a petition presented on or after the commencement date except where the liquidation is immediately preceded by—
  (i) an administration under paragraph 10 of Schedule B1 to the Act where the administration order was made on an application made before the commencement date;
  (ii) an administration in respect of which the appointment of an administrator under paragraphs 14 or 22 of Schedule B1 took effect before the commencement date; or
  (iii) a voluntary liquidation in respect of which the resolution to wind up was passed before the commencement date.".

[13.12A Authorised deposit-taker and former authorised deposit-taker"

(1) "Authorised deposit-taker" means a person with permission under Part 4 of the Financial Services and Markets Act 2000 to accept deposits.

(2) "Former authorised deposit-taker" means a person who—

(a) is not an authorised deposit-taker,

(b) was formerly an authorised institution under the Banking Act 1987, or a recognised bank or a licensed institution under the Banking Act 1979, and

(c) continues to have liability in respect of any deposit for which it had a liability at a time when it was an authorised institution, recognised bank or licensed institution.

(3) Paragraphs (1) and (2) must be read with—

(a) section 22 of the Financial Services and Markets Act 2000;

(b) any relevant order under that section; and

(c) Schedule 2 to that Act.]

[6569]

NOTES

Inserted by the Financial Services and Markets Act 2000 (Consequential Amendments and Repeals) Order 2001, SI 2001/3649, art 381, as from 1 December 2001.

Banking Act 1987: repealed by the Financial Services and Markets Act 2000 (Consequential Amendments and Repeals) Order 2001, SI 2001/3649, art 3(1)(d), as from 1 December 2001.

13.13 Expressions used generally

(1) "Business day" means any day other than a Saturday, a Sunday, Christmas Day, Good Friday or a day which is a bank holiday in any part of Great Britain under or by virtue of the

Banking and Financial Dealings Act 1971 except in Rules 1.7, 4.10, 4.11, 4.16, 4.20, 5.10 and 6.23 where "business day" shall include any day which is a bank holiday in Scotland but not in England and Wales.]

(2) "The Department" means the Department of Trade and Industry.

(3) "File in court" [and file with the court] means deliver to the court for filing.

(4) "The Gazette" means the London Gazette.

(5) "General regulations" means regulations made by the Secretary of State under Rule 12.1.

[(6) "Practice direction" means a direction as to the practice and procedure of any court within the scope of the CPR.

(7) "Prescribed order of priority" means the order of priority of payments laid down by Chapter 20 of Part 4 of the Rules, or Chapter 23 of Part 6.]

[(8) "Centre of main interests" has the same meaning as in the EC Regulation.

(9) "Establishment" has the meaning given by Article 2(h) of the EC Regulation.

(10) "Main proceedings" means proceedings opened in accordance with Article 3(1) of the EC Regulation and falling within the definition of insolvency proceedings in Article 2(a) of the EC Regulation and

(a) in relation to England and Wales and Scotland set out in Annex A to the EC Regulation under the heading "United Kingdom", and

(b) in relation to another member State, set out in Annex A to the EC Regulation under the heading relating to that member State.

(11) "Member State liquidator" means a person falling within the definition of liquidator in Article 2(b) of the EC Regulation appointed in proceedings to which it applies in a member State other than the United Kingdom.

(12) "Secondary proceedings" means proceedings opened in accordance with Articles 3(2) and 3(3) of the EC Regulation and falling within the definition of winding-up proceedings in Article 2(c) of the EC Regulation, and

(a) in relation to England and Wales and Scotland, set out in Annex B to the EC Regulation under the heading "United Kingdom", and

(b) in relation to another member State, set out in Annex B to the EC Regulation under the heading relating to that member State.

(13) "Temporary administrator" means a temporary administrator referred to by Article 38 of the EC Regulation.

(14) "Territorial proceedings" means proceedings opened in accordance with Articles 3(2) and 3(4) of the EC Regulation and falling within the definition of insolvency proceedings in Article 2(a) of the EC Regulation, and

(a) in relation to England and Wales and Scotland, set out in Annex A to the EC Regulation under the heading "United Kingdom", and

(b) in relation to another member State, set out in Annex A to the EC Regulation under the heading relating to that member State.]

[(15) "Prescribed part" has the same meaning as it does in section 176A(2)(a).]

[6570]

NOTES

Para (1): substituted by the Insolvency (Amendment) (No 2) Rules 1999, SI 1999/1022, r 3, Schedule, para 14(a), as from 26 April 1999.

Para (3): words in square brackets inserted by the Insolvency (Amendment) Rules 2003, SI 2003/1730, r 13, Sch 1, Pt 10, para 66(a), as from 15 September 2003 (for transitional provisions and savings see the note preceding r 2.1 at **[6097]**).

Paras (6), (7): substituted, for original para (6), by SI 1999/1022, r 3, Schedule, para 14(b), as from 26 April 1999.

Paras (8)–(14): added by the Insolvency (Amendment) Rules 2002, SI 2002/1307, rr 3, 10(7), as from 31 May 2002, with savings in relation to anything done under, or for the purposes of, this provision before that date.

Para (15): added by SI 2003/1730, r 13, Sch 1, Pt 10, para 66(b), as from 15 September 2003 (for transitional provisions and savings see the note preceding r 2.1 at **[6097]**).

EC Regulation: ie, Council Regulation 1346/2000/EC on insolvency proceedings at **[9290]**.

13.14 Application

(1) Subject to paragraph (2) of this Rule, and save where otherwise expressly provided, the Rules apply—

(a) to … receivers appointed on or after the day on which the Rules come into force,
(b) to bankruptcy proceedings where the bankruptcy petition is presented on or after the day on which the Rules come into force, and
(c) to all other insolvency proceedings commenced on or after that day.

(2) The Rules also apply to winding-up and bankruptcy proceedings commenced before that day to which provisions of the Act are applied by Schedule 11 to the Act, to the extent necessary to give effect to those provisions.

[6571]

NOTES

Para (1): word omitted from sub-para (a) revoked by the Insolvency (Amendment) Rules 1987, SI 1987/1919, r 3(1), Schedule, Pt 1, para 152, as from 11 January 1988.

SCHEDULES

SCHEDULE 1
[SCHEME MANAGER'S] VOTING RIGHTS

Rule 4.72(7)

1. This Schedule applies as does rule 4.72.

2. In relation to any meeting at which the [scheme manager] is under Rule 4.72 entitled to be represented, the [scheme manager] may submit in the liquidation, instead of a proof, a written statement of voting rights ("the statement").

3. The statement shall contain details of—

(a) the names of creditors of the company in respect of whom an obligation of the [scheme manager] has arisen or may reasonably be expected to arise as a result of the liquidation or proposed liquidation;
(b) the amount of the obligation so arising; and
(c) the total amount of all such obligations specified in the statement.

4. The [scheme manager's] statement shall, for the purpose of voting at a meeting (but for no other purpose), be treated in all respects as if it were a proof.

5. Any voting rights which a creditor might otherwise exercise at a meeting in respect of a claim against the company are reduced by a sum equal to the amount of that claim in relation to which the [scheme manager], by virtue of its having submitted a statement, is entitled to exercise voting rights at that meeting.

6. The [scheme manager] may from time to time submit a further statement, and, if it does so, that statement supersedes any statement previously submitted.

[6572]

NOTES

Words in square brackets (including those in the Schedule heading) substituted by the Financial Services and Markets Act 2000 (Consequential Amendments and Repeals) Order 2001, SI 2001/3649, art 378*3), as from 1 December 2001

(*Sch 2 outside the scope of this work; Sch 3 revoked by the Insolvency (Amendment) Rules 1993, SI 1993/602, r 3, Schedule, para 4, as from 5 April 1993; Sch 4 contains forms (as to which see Appendix 4 at* **[A4]**.)

SCHEDULE 5
PUNISHMENT OF OFFENCES UNDER THE RULES

Rule 12.21

Note: In the fourth and fifth columns of this Schedule, "the statutory maximum" means the prescribed sum under section 32 of the Magistrates' Courts Act 1980 (c 43).

Rule creating offence.	General nature of offence.	Mode of prosecution.	Punishment.	Daily default fine (where applicable).
…	…	…	…	
In Part 2, [Rule 2.47(6)].	Administrator failing to send notification as to progress of administration.	Summary.	One-fifth of the statutory maximum.	One-fiftieth of the statutory maximum.
[Rule 2.111(3).	Administrator failing to send notification as to progress of administration.	Summary.	One-fifth of the statutory maximum.]	One-fiftieth of the statutory maximum.]
[Rule 2.129(2)	Administrator failing to file a notice of automatic end of administration.	Summary.	One-fifth of the statutory maximum.]	One-fiftieth of the statutory maximum.]
In Part 3, Rule 3.32(5).	Administrative receiver failing to send notification as to progress of receivership.	Summary.	One-fifth of the statutory maximum.	One-fiftieth of the statutory maximum.
…	…	…	…	
In Part 12, Rule 12.18.	False representation of status for purpose of inspecting documents.	1. On indictment.	2 years or a fine, or both.	
		2. Summary.	6 months or the statutory maximum, or both.	

[6573]

NOTES

Entries omitted revoked by the Insolvency (Amendment) (No 2) Rules 2002, SI 2002/2712, r 9, as from 1 January 2003.

Words in square brackets in entry relating to rule 2.47(6) substituted, and entries relating to rules 2.111(3), 2.129(2) inserted, by the Insolvency (Amendment) Rules 2003, SI 2003/1730, r 15, as from 15 September 2003 (for transitional provisions and savings see the note preceding r 2.1 at **[6097]**).

Statutory maximum: by the Magistrates' Courts Act 1980, s 32(9), as amended, the statutory maximum is currently £5,000.

[SCHEDULE 6
DETERMINATION OF INSOLVENCY OFFICE HOLDER'S REMUNERATION
Rules 4.127A, 4.127B , 4.148B and 6.138A

As regards the determination of the remuneration of trustees and liquidators the realisation and distribution scales are as set out in the table below—

The realisation scale		
(i)	on the first £5000 or fraction thereof	20%
(ii)	on the next £5000 or fraction thereof	15%
(iii)	on the next £90000 or fraction thereof	10%
(iv)	on all further sums realised	5%

The distribution scale		
(i)	on the first £5000 or fraction thereof	10%
(ii)	on the next £5000 or fraction thereof	7.5%
(iii)	on the next £90000 or fraction thereof	5%
(iv)	on all further sums distributed	2.5%.]

[6573A]

NOTES

Inserted by the Insolvency (Amendment) Rules 2004, SI 2004/584, r 47, as from 1 April 2004.

COMPANIES (UNFAIR PREJUDICE APPLICATIONS) PROCEEDINGS RULES 1986

(SI 1986/2000)

NOTES

Made: 21 November 1986.
Authority: Insolvency Act 1986, s 411.
Commencement: 29 December 1986 (see r 1 at **[6574]**). Where any provision in this work (including any inserted or substituted provision) came into force for all purposes on or before 1 July 2005, commencement information is not noted at provision level.
As of 1 July 2007, these Rules had not been amended.

ARRANGEMENT OF RULES

1 Citation, commencement and interpretation

(1) These Rules may be cited as the Companies (Unfair Prejudice Applications) Proceedings Rules 1986 and shall come into force on 29th December 1986.

(2) In these Rules "the Act" means the Companies Act 1985.

[6574]

2 Preliminary

(1) These Rules apply in relation to petitions presented to the court on or after 29th December 1986 under Part XVII of the Act (protection of company's members against unfair prejudice) by a member of a company under section 459(1), by a person treated as a member under section 459(2) or by the Secretary of State under section 460.

(2) Except so far as inconsistent with the Act and these Rules, the Rules of the Supreme Court and the practice of the High Court apply to proceedings under Part XVII of the Act in the High Court, and the Rules and practice of the County Court apply to such proceedings in a county court, with any necessary modifications.

[6575]

3 Presentation of petition

(1) The petition shall be in the form set out in the Schedule to these Rules, with such variations, if any, as the circumstances may require.

(2) The petition shall specify the grounds on which it is presented and the nature of the relief which is sought by the petitioner, and shall be delivered to the court for filing with sufficient copies for service under Rule 4.

(3) The court shall fix a hearing for a day ("the return day") on which, unless the court otherwise directs, the petitioner and any respondent (including the company) shall attend before the registrar in chambers for directions to be given in relation to the procedure on the petition.

(4) On fixing the return day, the court shall return to the petitioner sealed copies of the petition for service, each endorsed with the return day and the time of hearing.

[6576]

4 Service of petition

(1) The petitioner shall, at least 14 days before the return day, serve a sealed copy of the petition on the company.

(2) In the case of a petition based upon section 459 of the Act, the petitioner shall also, at least 14 days before the return day, served a sealed copy of the petition on every respondent named in the petition.

[6577]

5 Return of petition

On the return day, or at any time after it, the court shall give such directions as it thinks appropriate with respect to the following matters—

(a) service of the petition on any person, whether in connection with the time, date and place of a further hearing, or for any other purpose;

(b) whether particulars of claim and defence are to be delivered, and generally as to the procedure on the petition;

(c) whether, and if so by what means, the petition is to be advertised;

(d) the manner in which any evidence is to be adduced at any hearing before the judge and in particular (but without prejudice to the generality of the above) as to—

  (i) the taking of evidence wholly or in part by affidavit or orally;

  (ii) the cross-examination of any deponents to affidavits;

  (iii) the matters to be dealt with in evidence;

(e) any other matter affecting the procedure on the petition or in connection with the hearing and disposal of the petition.

[6578]

6 Settlement and advertisement of the order

(1) When an order has been made by the court under Part XVII of the Act, the petitioner and every other person who has appeared on the hearing of the petition shall, not later than the business day following that on which the order is made, leave at the court all the documents required for enabling the order to be completed forthwith.

(2) It is not necessary for the court to appoint a time, date and place for any person to attend to settle the order, unless in any particular case the special circumstances make an appointment necessary.

(3) If the court considers that the order should be advertised, it shall give directions as to the manner and time of advertisement.

[6579]

SCHEDULE
PETITION ON GROUND THAT MEMBERS UNFAIRLY PREJUDICED

Rule 3

(a) Insert title of court	To (a)
(b) Insert full name(s) and address(es) of petitioner	The petition of (b)
(c) Insert full name of company (d) Insert date	1. (c) (hereinafter called "the company" was incorporated on (d) under the Companies Act(s) 19
(e) Insert address of registered office	2. The registered office of the company is at (e)
	3. The nominal capital of the company is £ divided into shares of £ each. The amount of the capital paid up or credited as paid up is £
	The petitioner(s) is/are the holders of shares of £ each.
(f) Delete as applicable	Such shares at the date of this petition (f) [are registered in the name(s) of the petitioner(s)] [have been transferred or transmitted to the petitioner(s) by operation of law].
	4. The principal objects for which the company was established are as follows:
	and other objects stated in the memorandum of association of the company.
(g) Set out the grounds on which the petition is presented	5. (g)
	In these circumstances your petitioner submits that the affairs of the company are being conducted in a manner which is unfairly prejudicial to the interests of (f) [some part of the members including your petitioner)] [your petitioner] or
	(f) [The act or omission] [the proposed act or omission] referred to in part 5 above (f) [is] [would be] unfairly prejudicial to the interests of (f) [some part of the members (including your petitioner)] [your petitioner].
(h) Here set out the nature of relief sought	The petitioner therefore prays as follows (h)
	or
	that such other order may be made as the court thinks fit.
	Note
	It is intended to serve this petition on:

	Endorsement This petition having been presented to the court on let all parties attend before the Registrar in Chambers on: Date.......... Time.......... Place.......... for directions to be given The Solicitor(s) for the petitioner is/are: Name.......... Address.......... .... Tel. No.......... Reference..........
(j) Delete if London Agents not instructed	(j) Whose London Agents are: Name.......... Address.......... .... Tel. No.......... Reference..........

[6580]

INSOLVENCY FEES ORDER 1986 (NOTE)

(SI 1986/2030)

NOTES

See Appendix 3 (Fees Instruments) at **[A3]**.

[6580A]

COMPANIES (FORMS) (AMENDMENT) REGULATIONS 1987

(SI 1987/752)

NOTES

Made: 6 April 1987.

Authority: CA 1985, ss 6(1)(b)(i), 54(4), 88(2)(a), (3), 122(1), 123(2), 128(1), (3), (4), 129(1), (2), (3), 157(3), 169(1), 176(3)(a), 190(5), 224(2), 225(1), (2), 266(1), (3), 287(2), 288(2), 318(4), 325(5), 353(2), 362(3), 386(2), 400(2), 403(1), 416(1), 419(1), 428(2), 429(2), (3), (4), 430A(3), 744, Sch 13, para 27, Sch 14, para 1(1); Companies Consolidation (Consequential Provisions) Act 1985, s 4(1); Insolvency Act 1986, s 109; FSA 1986, s 172. It should be noted that CA 1985, ss 224(2), 225(1), (2), 287 have been substituted by new ss 224(2), 225(1), (2), 287 thereof; s 386(2) of the 1985 Act has been replaced by a new s 391(2) thereof; ss 400, 403, 416, 419 of the 1985 Act are replaced by certain provisions of new ss 395–420 thereof (inserted by CA 1989, ss 93–104), as from a day to be appointed. FSA 1986 is repealed.

Commencement: 30 April 1987 (see reg 1 at **[6581]**). Where any provision in this work (including any inserted or substituted provision) came into force for all purposes on or before 1 July 2005, commencement information is not noted at provision level.

These Regulations are reproduced as amended by: the Companies Act 2006 (Commencement No 2, Consequential Amendments, Transitional Provisions and Savings) Order 2007, SI 2007/1093.

1 These Regulations may be cited as the Companies (Forms) (Amendment) Regulations 1987 and shall come into force on 30th April 1987.

[6581]

2 In these Regulations "the 1985 Regulations" means the Companies (Forms) Regulations 1985.

[6581A]

3 (*Reg 3 revokes the Companies (Forms) Regulations 1985, SI 1985/854, reg 9.*)

4—(1) For the purposes of [sections 980(1) and 984(3) of the Companies Act 2006], a notice to a holder of shares in the company shall be given to him, in the form prescribed by regulation 5(2), either personally or by sending it to him by post.

(2) Where such a notice cannot be given personally or by post because the holder of the shares is the holder of a share warrant to bearer, the notice shall be given—

(a) in a case where the articles of association or the regulations of the company provide that notice to such holders of shares may be given by advertisement, by advertisement in the manner so provided, and

(b) in any other case, by advertisement in the Gazette.

(3) Where in accordance with paragraph (1) a notice is sent to a holder of shares by post it shall be sent to him—

(a) at his address in the United Kingdom registered in the books of the company;

(b) if no such address is registered, to the address (if any) in the United Kingdom given by him to the company for the giving of notices to him; or

(c) if no address in the United Kingdom is registered or has been so notified, to his address outside the United Kingdom registered in the books of the company.

(4) Where in accordance with paragraph (1) a notice is sent to a holder of shares by post—

(a) if it is sent to an address in the United Kingdom, it shall be sent by recorded delivery; and

(b) if it is sent to an address outside the United Kingdom it shall be sent by airmail, if that form of post is available.

[(5) "the Gazette" has the meaning in section 1173 of the Companies Act 2006.]

[6582]

NOTES

Para (1): words in square brackets substituted by the Companies Act 2006 (Commencement No 2, Consequential Amendments, Transitional Provisions and Savings) Order 2007, SI 2007/1093, art 6(1), Sch 3, para 4(1), (2), as from 6 April 2007.

Para (5): added by SI 2007/1093, art 6(1), Sch 3, para 4(1), (3), as from 6 April 2007.

5–7 (*Regs 5, 6 introduce Sch 2 to these Regulations (prescribed forms) and amend the Companies (Forms) Regulations 1985, SI 1985/854, Sch 3 (forms); reg 7 contained transitional provisions and was revoked by a combination of SI 1990/572, reg 4 and SI 2007/1093, art 7, Sch 5 (as from 6 April 2007).*)

(*Sch 1 lists the enabling powers under which these regulations were made; Schs 2, 3, in so far as unrevoked, set out forms which relate to the CA 1985 (as to which see Appendix 4 at* **[A4]**).)

INSOLVENT COMPANIES (DISQUALIFICATION OF UNFIT DIRECTORS) PROCEEDINGS RULES 1987

(SI 1987/2023)

NOTES

Made: 25 November 1987.

Authority: Insolvency Act 1986, s 411; Company Directors Disqualification Act 1986, s 21.

Commencement: 11 January 1988 (see r 1 at **[6583]**). Where any provision in this work (including any inserted or substituted provision) came into force for all purposes on or before 1 July 2005, commencement information is not noted at provision level.

These Rules are reproduced as amended by: the Insolvent Companies (Disqualification of Unfit Directors) Proceedings (Amendment) Rules 1999, SI 1999/1023; the Insolvent Companies (Disqualification of Unfit Directors) Proceedings (Amendment) Rules 2001, SI 2001/765; the Insolvent Companies (Disqualification of Unfit Directors) Proceedings (Amendment) Rules 2003, SI 2003/1367.

Limited liability partnerships: by the Limited Liability Partnerships Regulations 2001, SI 2001/1090, reg 10, Sch 6, Pt III, these Rules apply, with modifications, to limited liability partnerships (see **[7000]**).

ARRANGEMENT OF RULES

1 Citation, commencement and interpretation

(1) These Rules may be cited as the Insolvent Companies (Disqualification of Unfit Directors) Proceedings Rules 1987 and shall come into force on 11th January 1988.

[(2) In these Rules—

(a) "the Companies Act" means the Companies Act 1985,

(b) "the Company Directors Disqualification Act" means the Company Directors Disqualification Act 1986,

(c) "CPR" followed by a Part or rule by number means that Part or rule with that number in the Civil Procedure Rules 1998,

(d) "practice direction" means a direction as to the practice and procedure of any court within the scope of the Civil Procedure Rules,

(e) "registrar" has the same meaning as in paragraphs (4) and (5) of rule 13.2 of the Insolvency Rules 1986, and

(f) "file in court" means deliver to the court for filing.]

(3) These Rules apply with respect to an application for a disqualification order against any person ("the [defendant]"), where made—

(a) by the Secretary of State or the official receiver under section 7(1) of the Company Directors Disqualification Act (on the grounds of the person's unfitness to be concerned in the management of a company), or

(b) by the Secretary of State under section 8 of that Act (alleged expedient in the public interest, following report of inspectors under section 437 of the Companies Act, or information or documents obtained under section 447 or 448 of that Act), [or

(c) by the Office of Fair Trading or (as the case may be) a specified regulator under section 9A of that Act (breach of competition law by undertaking and unfitness to be concerned in the management of a company),]

on or after the date on which these Rules come into force.

[6583]

NOTES

Para (2): substituted by the Insolvent Companies (Disqualification of Unfit Directors) Proceedings (Amendment) Rules 1999, SI 1999/1023, r 3, Schedule, para 2, as from 26 April 1999.

PART IV STATUTORY INSTRUMENTS

Para (3): word in first pair of square brackets substituted by SI 1999/1023, r 3, Schedule, para 1, as from 26 April 1999; sub-para (c) and the word immediately proceeding it inserted by the Insolvent Companies (Disqualification of Unfit Directors) Proceedings (Amendment) Rules 2003, SI 2003/1367, r 3, Schedule, para 1, as from 20 June 2003.

[2 Form and conduct of applications

(1) The Civil Procedure Rules 1998, and any relevant practice direction, apply in respect of any application to which these Rules apply, except where these Rules make provision to inconsistent effect.

(2) An application shall be made by claim form as provided by the relevant practice direction and the claimant must use the CPR Part 8 (alternative procedure for claims) procedure.

(3) CPR rule 8.1(3) (power of the court to order the claim to continue as if the claimant had not used the Part 8 procedure), CPR rule 8.2 (contents of the claim form) and CPR rule 8.7 (Part 20 claims) do not apply.

(4) Rule 7.47 (appeals and reviews of court orders) and rule 7.49 (procedure on appeal) of the Insolvency Rules 1986 apply.]

[6584]

NOTES

Substituted by the Insolvent Companies (Disqualification of Unfit Directors) Proceedings (Amendment) Rules 1999, SI 1999/1023, r 3, Schedule, para 3, as from 26 April 1999.

3 The case against the [defendant]

(1) There shall, at the time when the [claim form] is issued, be filed in court evidence in support of the application for a disqualification order; and copies of the evidence shall be served with the [claim form] on the [defendant].

(2) The evidence shall be by one or more affidavits, except where the [claimant] is the official receiver, in which case it may be in the form of a written report (with or without affidavits by other persons) which shall be treated as if it had been verified by affidavit by him and shall be prima facie evidence of any matter contained in it.

(3) There shall in the affidavit or affidavits or (as the case may be) the official receiver's report be included a statement of the matters by reference to which the [defendant] is alleged to be unfit to be concerned in the management of a company.

[6585]

NOTES

Words in square brackets substituted by the Insolvent Companies (Disqualification of Unfit Directors) Proceedings (Amendment) Rules 1999, SI 1999/1023, r 3, Schedule, para 1, as from 26 April 1999.

4 Endorsement on [claim form]

There shall on the [claim form] be endorsed information to the [defendant] as follows—

(a) that the application is made in accordance with these Rules;

(b) that, in accordance with the relevant enactments, the court has power to impose disqualifications as follows—

  (i) where the application is under section 7 of the Company Directors Disqualification Act, for a period of not less than 2, and up to 15, years; and

  (ii) where the application is [under section 8 or 9A of that Act], for a period of up to 15 years;

(c) that the application for a disqualification order may, in accordance with these Rules, be heard and determined summarily, without further or other notice to the [defendant], and that, if it is so heard and determined, the court may impose disqualification for a period of up to 5 years;

(d) that if at the hearing of the application the court, on the evidence then before it, is minded to impose, in the [defendant]'s case, disqualification for any period longer than 5 years, it will not make a disqualification order on that occasion but will adjourn the application to be heard (with further evidence, if any) at a later date to be notified; and

(e) that any evidence which the [defendant] wishes to be taken into consideration by the court must be filed in court in accordance with the time limits imposed under Rule 6 (the provisions of which shall be set out on the [claim form]).

[6586]

NOTES

Words in square brackets in sub-para (b)(ii) substituted by the Insolvent Companies (Disqualification of Unfit Directors) Proceedings (Amendment) Rules 2003, SI 2003/1367, r 3, Schedule, para 2, as from 20 June 2003; other words in square brackets substituted by the Insolvent Companies (Disqualification of Unfit Directors) Proceedings (Amendment) Rules 1999, SI 1999/1023, r 3, Schedule, para 1, as from 26 April 1999.

5 Service and acknowledgement

(1) The [claim form] shall be served on the [defendant] by sending it by first class post to his last known address; and the date of service shall, unless the contrary is shown, be deemed to be the 7th day next following that on which the [claim form] was posted.

(2) Where any process or order of the court or other document is required under proceedings subject to these Rules to be served on any person who is not in England and Wales, the court may order service on him of that process or order or other document to be effected within such time and in such manner as it thinks fit, and may also require such proof of service as it thinks fit.

[(3) The claim form served on the defendant shall be accompanied by an acknowledgment of service as provided for by practice direction and CPR rule 8.3(2) (dealing with the contents of an acknowledgment of service) does not apply.]

(4) The … acknowledgement of service shall state that the [defendant] should indicate—

(a) whether he contests the application on the grounds that, in the case of any particular company—

(i) he was not a director or shadow director of the company at a time when conduct of his, or of other persons, in relation to that company is in question, or

(ii) his conduct as director or shadow director of that company was not as alleged in support of the application for a disqualification order,

(b) whether, in the case of any conduct of his, he disputes the allegation that such conduct makes him unfit to be concerned in the management of a company, and

(c) whether he, while not resisting the application for a disqualification order, intends to adduce mitigating factors with a view to justifying only a short period of disqualification.

[6587]

NOTES

Para (1): words in square brackets substituted by the Insolvent Companies (Disqualification of Unfit Directors) Proceedings (Amendment) Rules 1999, SI 1999/1023, r 3, Schedule, para 1, as from 26 April 1999.

Para (3): substituted by SI 1999/1023, r 3, Schedule, para 4(1), as from 26 April 1999.

Para (4): words omitted revoked, and word in square brackets substituted, by SI 1999/1023, r 3, Schedule, paras 1, 4(2), as from 26 April 1999.

6 Evidence

(1) The [defendant] shall, within 28 days from the date of service of the [claim form], file in court any affidavit evidence in opposition to the application he wishes the court to take into consideration and shall forthwith serve upon the [claimant] a copy of such evidence.

(2) The [claimant] shall, within 14 days from receiving the copy of the [defendant]'s evidence, file in court any further evidence in reply he wishes the court to take into consideration and shall forthwith serve a copy of that evidence upon the [defendant].

[(3) CPR rules 8.5 (filing and serving written evidence) and 8.6(1) (requirements where written evidence is to be relied on) do not apply.]

[6588]

NOTES

Paras (1), (2): words in square brackets substituted by the Insolvent Companies (Disqualification of Unfit Directors) Proceedings (Amendment) Rules 1999, SI 1999/1023, r 3, Schedule, para 1, as from 26 April 1999.

Para (3): added by SI 1999/1023, r 3, Schedule, para 5, as from 26 April 1999.

7 The hearing of the application

[(1) When the claim form is issued, the court will fix a date for the first hearing of the claim which shall not be less than 8 weeks from the date of issue of the claim form.]

(2) The hearing shall in the first instance be before the registrar in open court.

(3) The registrar shall either determine the case on the date fixed or adjourn it.

(4) The registrar shall adjourn the case for further consideration if—

(a) he forms the provisional opinion that a disqualification order ought to be made, and that a period of disqualification longer than 5 years is appropriate, or

(b) he is of opinion that questions of law or fact arise which are not suitable for summary determination.

(5) If the registrar adjourns the case for further consideration he shall—

(a) direct whether the case is to be heard by a registrar or, if he thinks it appropriate, by the judge, for determination by him;

(b) state the reasons for the adjournment; and

(c) give directions as to the following matters—

(i) the manner in which and the time within which notice of the adjournment and the reasons for it are to be given to the [defendant],

(ii) the filing in court and the service of further evidence (if any) by the parties,

(iii) such other matters as the registrar thinks necessary or expedient with a view to an expeditious disposal of the application, and

(iv) the time and place of the adjourned hearing.

(6) Where a case is adjourned other than to the judge, it may be heard by the registrar who originally dealt with the case or by another registrar.

[6589]

NOTES

Para (1): substituted by the Insolvent Companies (Disqualification of Unfit Directors) Proceedings (Amendment) Rules 1999, SI 1999/1023, r 3, Schedule, para 6, as from 26 April 1999.

Para (5): word in square brackets in sub-para (c) substituted by SI 1999/1023, r 3, Schedule, para 1, as from 26 April 1999.

8 Making and setting aside of disqualification order

(1) The court may make a disqualification order against the [defendant], whether or not the latter appears, and whether or not he has completed and returned the acknowledgement of service of the [claim form], or filed evidence in accordance with Rule 6.

(2) Any disqualification order made in the absence of the [defendant] may be set aside or varied by the court on such terms as it thinks just.

[6590]

NOTES

Words in square brackets substituted by the Insolvent Companies (Disqualification of Unfit Directors) Proceedings (Amendment) Rules 1999, SI 1999/1023, r 3, Schedule, para 1, as from 26 April 1999.

9 (*Revoked by the Insolvent Companies* (*Disqualification of Unfit Directors*) *Proceedings* (*Amendment*) *Rules 2001, SI 2001/765, as from 2 April 2001.*)

10 Right of audience

Official receivers and deputy official receivers have right of audience in any proceedings to which these Rules apply, whether the application is made by the Secretary of State or by the official receiver at his direction, and whether made in the High Court or a county court.

[6591]

11 Revocation and saving

(1) …

(2) Notwithstanding paragraph (1) the former Rules shall continue to apply and have effect in relation to any application described in paragraph 3(a) or (b) of Rule 1 of these Rules made before the date on which these Rules come into force.

[6592]

NOTES

Para (1): revokes the Insolvent Companies (Disqualification of Unfit Directors) Proceedings Rules 1986, SI 1986/612.

DEPARTMENT OF TRADE AND INDUSTRY (FEES) ORDER 1988

(SI 1988/93)

NOTES

Made: 21 January 1988.

Authority: Finance (No 2) Act 1987, s 102.

Commencement: 22 January 1988 (see art 1 at **[6593]**). Where any provision in this work (including any inserted or substituted provision) came into force for all purposes on or before 1 July 2005, commencement information is not noted at provision level.

This Order is reproduced as amended by: the Wireless Telegraphy Act 1998; the Department of Trade and Industry (Fees) (Amendment) Order 1995, SI 1995/1294; the Financial Services and Markets Act 2000 (Consequential Amendments and Repeals) Order 2001, SI 2001/3649.

1 Citation and commencement

This Order may be cited as the Department of Trade and Industry (Fees) Order 1988, and shall come into force on the day after the day on which it is made.

[6593]

2 Interpretation

In this Order—

(a) "the Act" means the Finance (No 2) Act 1987;

.....

"the 1985 Act" means the Companies Act 1985;
"the 1986 Act" means the Insolvency Act 1986;

.....

(b) any reference to any provision of the 1985 Act includes any corresponding provision of any enactment repealed and re-enacted, with or without modification, by the 1985 Act.

[6594]

NOTES

Definitions omitted outside the scope of this work.

3—(1) In relation to the power of the Secretary of State under section 708 of the 1985 Act by regulations made by statutory instrument to require the payment to the registrar of companies of such fees as may be specified in the regulations in respect of—

(a) the performance by the registrar of such functions under the 1985 Act or the 1986 Act as may be so specified, including the receipt by him of any notice or other document which under either of those Acts is required to be given, delivered, sent or forwarded to him,

(b) the inspection of documents or other material kept by him under either of those Acts,

the functions specified for the purpose of section 102(3) of the Act shall be those specified in Part I of Schedule 1 hereto.

PART IV
STATUTORY INSTRUMENTS

(2) In relation to the power of the Secretary of State specified in paragraph (1) above, the matters specified for the purposes of section 102(4) of the Act shall be those specified in Part I of Schedule 2 hereto.

[6595]

4—(1) In relation to the power of the Secretary of State to fix fees under sections 53(5), 54(4) and 71(2) of the 1986 Act, the functions specified for the purposes of section 102(3) of the Act shall be those specified in Part I of Schedule 1 hereto.

(2) In relation to the power of the Secretary of State specified in paragraph (1) above, the matters specified for the purposes of section 102(4) of the Act shall be those specified in Part I of Schedule 2 hereto.

[6596]

5–8 (*Arts 5–7 outside the scope of this work; art 8 revoked by the Wireless Telegraphy Act 1998, s 7, Sch 2, Pt II.*)

9—(1) In relation to the power of the Lord Chancellor to fix fees under section 133(1) of the Bankruptcy Act 1914, section 663(4) of the 1985 Act and sections 414 and 415 of the 1986 Act and in relation to the power of the Secretary of State to fix fees under sections 4 and 10 of the Insolvency Act 1985 and sections 392, 414 and 419 of the 1986 Act, the functions specified for the purposes of section 102(3) of the Act shall be those specified in Part VI of Schedule 1 hereto.

(2) In relation to the power of the Lord Chancellor specified in paragraph (1) above and in relation to the power of the Secretary of State specified in that paragraph, the matters specified for the purposes of section 102(4) of the Act shall be those specified in Part I of Schedule 2 hereto.

[6597]

[10] (*Added by the Department of Trade and Industry (Fees) (Amendment) Order 1995, SI 1995/1294, art 2(b), as from 11 May 1995; revoked by the Financial Services and Markets Act 2000 (Consequential Amendments and Repeals) Order 2001, SI 2001/3649, art 388(1), (3), as from 1 December 2001.*)

SCHEDULES

SCHEDULE 1

PART I

1. Functions of the Secretary of State and the registrar of companies by virtue of the 1985 Act.

2. Functions of the registrar of companies by virtue of the 1986 Act.

3. Functions of inspectors appointed under Part XIV of the 1985 Act and of officers authorised under section 447 of that Act.

4. Functions of the Secretary of State in relation to anything done by the European Communities or any of their institutions with respect to company law, and the maintenance of relations with authorities and other persons both within the United Kingdom and abroad in respect of matters relating to company law.

5. Any other functions of the Secretary of State and the registrar of companies in relation to companies, including, without prejudice to the generality of the foregoing:—
   - (a) prosecution of offences under the 1985 Act and the taking of action with a view to ensuring compliance with any obligation arising under the 1985 Act;
   - (b) investigation of complaints relating to the conduct of the affairs of companies and consideration of requests for advice on questions of company law;
   - (c) review of the functioning of company law and consideration and development of proposals for legislation relating to companies;
   - (d) consideration, including in international fora, of accounting standards and auditing practices in relation to accounts of companies;

(e) the conduct of civil proceedings in relation to any of the functions specified in this part of this Schedule.

[6598]

(Pts II–V in so far as still in force, outside the scope of this work.)

PART VI

16. Functions of official receivers as provisional liquidators, interim receivers of a debtor's property, receivers and managers of a bankrupt's estate, liquidators, trustees in bankruptcy and in their capacity as official receivers, under the Companies Act 1948, the 1985 Act, the Bankruptcy Acts 1914 and 1926, the Powers of Criminal Courts Act 1973, the Insolvency Act 1976, the Insolvency Act 1985, the 1986 Act and the Company Directors Disqualification Act 1986 and subordinate legislation made under those enactments.

17. Functions of the Secretary of State, the Board of Trade and the Insolvency Practitioners Tribunal under Part V of the Companies Act 1948, Parts IX and XX of the 1985 Act, the Deeds of Arrangement Act 1914, the Bankruptcy Acts 1914 and 1926, the Insolvency Services (Accounting and Investment) Act 1970, the Insolvency Act 1976, the Insolvency Act 1985, the 1986 Act and the Company Directors Disqualification Act 1986 and subordinate legislation made under those enactments.

18. Functions of official receivers, the Secretary of State and the Board of Trade in relation to the investigation and prosecution or fraud or other malpractice in respect of the affairs of bankrupts and bodies in liquidation.

19. Functions of the Secretary of State in relation to the supervision of the operation of all the insolvency and related procedures set out in the Insolvency Act 1986, the Bankruptcy (Scotland) Act 1985, the other enactments set out in paragraphs 16 and 17 above and the Bankruptcy (Scotland) Act 1913, including the development and implementation of proposals for the modification or improvement of those procedures by primary or subordinate legislation and the consideration of and contribution to proposals for other United Kingdom legislation having an impact on those procedures.

20. Functions of the Secretary of State in relation to anything done by the European Communities or any of their institutions, or any international instruments, in relation to insolvency and the maintenance of relations with authorities and other persons both within the United Kingdom and abroad in respect of insolvency matters.

[6599]

(Pt VII added by the Department of Trade and Industry (Fees) (Amendment) Order 1995, SI 1995/1294, art 2(c), as from 11 May 1995, and revoked by the Financial Services and Markets Act 2000 (Consequential Amendments and Repeals) Order 2001, SI 2001/3649, art 388(1), (4), as from 1 December 2001.)

SCHEDULE 2

PART I

1. All costs incurred by the Secretary of State, the registrar of companies, the Comptroller-General of Patents, Designs and Trade Marks, official receivers, the Board of Trade and the Insolvency Practitioners Tribunal which are directly attributable to the functions specified in Schedule 1 above.

2. That proportion of the costs, not falling within paragraph 1 above, incurred by, or on behalf of, any of the persons specified in paragraph 1 above, in relation to staff, equipment, premises, facilities and matters connected, whether directly or indirectly, therewith, being the proportion which falls to be attributed to any of the functions specified in Schedule 1 above.

3. A return on the resources employed in carrying out any of the functions specified in Schedule 1 above.

4. The allocation of a sum in respect of matters which would otherwise be covered by insurance, the allocation of a sum in respect of superannuation payments and provision for bad debts, in relation to any of the functions specified in Schedule 1 above.

5. The recovery of any past deficits incurred in relation to any of the functions specified in Schedule 1 above.

6. Amounts recovered in relation to any of the functions specified in Schedule 1 above other than from such fees as are referred to in this Order.

7. The allocation, over a period of years, of an initial or exceptional cost in relation to any of the functions specified in Schedule 1 above.

[6600]

PART II

8. In respect of any function of any of the persons specified in paragraph 1 above consisting of the payment or remittance of any sum or amount, both the sum or amount in question and the cost incurred in effecting the payment or remittance.

[6601]

EUROPEAN ECONOMIC INTEREST GROUPING REGULATIONS 1989

(SI 1989/638)

NOTES

Made: 10 April 1989.

Authority: European Communities Act 1972, s 2.

Commencement: 1 July 1989 (see reg 1 at **[6602]**). Where any provision in this work (including any inserted or substituted provision) came into force for all purposes on or before 1 July 2005, commencement information is not noted at provision level.

These Regulations are reproduced as amended by: the Deregulation and Contracting Out Act 1994; the Constitutional Reform Act 2005.

Registrar of Companies: as to the contracting out of certain functions of the registrar of companies conferred by or under these regulations, see the Contracting Out (Functions in relation to the Registration of Companies) Order 1995, SI 1995/1013, arts 3, 4, Sch 1, paras 7, 8, Sch 2, para 3 at **[6838]**, **[6839]**, **[6841]**, **[6842]**.

ARRANGEMENT OF REGULATIONS

PART I
GENERAL

PART II
PROVISIONS RELATING TO ARTICLES 1–38 OF THE EC REGULATION

PART III
REGISTRATION ETC (ARTICLE 39 OF THE EC REGULATION)

PART IV
SUPPLEMENTAL PROVISIONS

SCHEDULES

PART I
GENERAL

1 Citation, commencement and extent

These Regulations, which extend to Great Britain, may be cited as the European Economic Interest Grouping Regulations 1989 and shall come into force on 1st July 1989.

[6602]

2 Interpretation

(1) In these Regulations—

"the 1985 Act" means the Companies Act 1985;

"the contract" means the contract for the formation of an EEIG;

"the EC Regulation" means Council Regulation (EEC) No 2137/85 set out in Schedule 1 to these Regulations;

"EEIG" means a European Economic Interest Grouping being a grouping formed in pursuance of article 1 of the EC Regulation;

"officer", in relation to an EEIG, includes a manager, or any other person provided for in the contract as an organ of the EEIG; and

"the registrar" has the meaning given by regulations 9(1) and 12(1) below;

and other expressions used in these Regulations and defined by section 744 of the 1985 Act or in relation to insolvency and winding up by the Insolvency Act 1986 have the meanings assigned to them by those provisions as if any reference to a company in any such definition were a reference to an EEIG.

(2) A Form referred to in these Regulations by "EEIG" followed by a number means the Form so numbered in Schedule 2 to these Regulations.

(3) In these Regulations, "certified translation" means a translation certified to be a correct translation—

(a) if the translation was made in the United Kingdom, by

(i) a notary public in any part of the United Kingdom;

(ii) a solicitor (if the translation was made in Scotland), a solicitor of the Supreme Court of Judicature of England and Wales (if it was made in England or Wales), or a *solicitor of the Supreme Court of Judicature of Northern Ireland* (if it was made in Northern Ireland); or

(iii) a person certified by a person mentioned above to be known to him to be competent to translate the document into English; or

(b) if the translation was made outside the United Kingdom, by—

(i) a notary public;

(ii) a person authorised in the place where the translation was made to administer an oath;

(iii) any of the British officials mentioned in section 6 of the Commissioners for Oaths Act 1889;

(iv) a person certified by a person mentioned in sub-paragraph (i), (ii) or (iii) of this paragraph to be known to him to be competent to translate the document into English.

[6603]

NOTES

Para (3): for the words in italics there are substituted the words "solicitor of the Court of Judicature of Northern Ireland" by the Constitutional Reform Act 2005, s 59, Sch 11, Pt 2, para 5, as from a day to be appointed.

Supreme Court of England and Wales: the Supreme Court of England and Wales is renamed the Senior Courts of England and Wales; see the Constitutional Reform Act 2005, s 59(1) (as from a day to be appointed).

PART II
PROVISIONS RELATING TO ARTICLES 1–38 OF THE EC REGULATION

3 Legal personality (Article 1(3) of the EC Regulation)

From the date of registration of an EEIG in Great Britain mentioned in a certificate given under regulation 9(5) below the EEIG shall, subject to regulation 11 below, be a body corporate by the name contained in the contract.

[6604]

4 Transfer of official address (Article 14 of the EC Regulation)

(1) Notice of any proposal to transfer the official address of an EEIG registered in Great Britain to any other place shall, where such transfer would result in a change in the law applicable to the contract under article 2 of the EC Regulation, be filed at the registry where the EEIG was registered by delivery of a notice in Form EEIG 4 in pursuance of regulation 13(1) below.

(2) Where the registrar, being the competent authority within the meaning of article 14(4) of the EC Regulation, receives a notice under paragraph (1) above and within the period of two months beginning with its publication in the Gazette under regulation 15(1) below opposes that transfer on the grounds of public interest, that transfer shall not take effect.

[6605]

NOTES

Form EEIG 4: see Appendix 4 at **[A4]**.

5 Managers (Article 19(2) of the EC Regulation)

(1) A manager of an EEIG registered in Great Britain may be a legal person other than a natural person, on condition that it designates one or more natural persons to represent it and notice of particulars of each such person is sent to the registrar in Form EEIG 3 as though he were a manager.

(2) Any natural person designated under paragraph (1) above shall be subject to the same liabilities as if he himself were a manager.

(3) There shall be delivered to the registrar in accordance with the provisions of regulation 13(1) below notice of appointment of any manager and the following particulars with respect to each manager—

(a)
 (i) his present Christian name and surname;
 (ii) any former Christian name or surname;
 (iii) his usual residential address;
 (iv) his nationality;
 (v) his business occupation (if any); and
 (vi) the date of his birth; and

(b) in the case of a legal person other than a natural person, its name and registered or principal office.

(4) Section 289(2) of the 1985 Act applies as regards the meaning of "Christian name", "surname" and "former Christian name or surname".

[6606]

NOTES

Form EEIG 3: see Appendix 4 at **[A4]**.

6 Cessation of membership (Article 28(1) of the EC Regulation)

For the purposes of national law on liquidation, winding up, insolvency or cessation of payments, a member of an EEIG registered under these Regulations shall cease to be a member if—

(a) in the case of an individual—

(i) a bankruptcy order has been made against him in England and Wales; or

(ii) sequestration of his estate has been awarded by the court in Scotland under the Bankruptcy (Scotland) Act 1985;

(b) in the case of a partnership—

(i) a winding up order has been made against the partnership in England and Wales;

(ii) a bankruptcy order has been made against its members in England and Wales on a bankruptcy petition presented under article 13(1) of the Insolvent Partnerships Order 1986; or

(iii) sequestration of the estate of the partnership has been awarded by the court in Scotland under the Bankruptcy (Scotland) Act 1985;

(c) in the case of a company, the company goes into liquidation in Great Britain; or

(d) in the case of any legal person or partnership, it is otherwise wound up or otherwise ceases to exist after the conclusion of winding up or insolvency.

[6607]

7 Competent authority (Articles 32(1) and (3) and 38 of the EC Regulation)

(1) The Secretary of State shall be the competent authority for the purposes of making an application to the court under article 32(1) of the EC Regulation (winding up of EEIG in certain circumstances).

(2) The court may, on an application by the Secretary of State, order the winding up of an EEIG which has its official address in Great Britain, if the EEIG acts contrary to the public interest and it is expedient in the public interest that the EEIG should be wound up and the court is of the opinion that it is just and equitable for it to be so.

(3) The court, on an application by the Secretary of State, shall be the competent authority for the purposes of prohibiting under article 38 of the EC Regulation any activity carried on in Great Britain by an EEIG where such an activity is in contravention of the public interest there.

[6608]

8 Winding up and conclusion of liquidation (Articles 35 and 36 of the EC Regulation)

(1) Where an EEIG is wound up as an unregistered company under Part V of the Insolvency Act 1986, the provisions of Part V shall apply in relation to the EEIG as if any reference in that Act and the 1985 Act to a director or past director of a company included a reference to a manager of the EEIG and any other person who has or has had control or management of the EEIG's business and with the modification that in section 221(1) after the words "all the provisions" there shall be added the words "of Council Regulation (EEC) No 2137/85 and".

(2) At the end of the period of three months beginning with the day of receipt by the registrar of a notice of the conclusion of the liquidation of an EEIG, the EEIG shall be dissolved.

[6609]

PART III
REGISTRATION ETC (ARTICLE 39 OF THE EC REGULATION)

9 Registration of EEIG whose official address is in Great Britain

(1) The registrar for the purposes of registration of an EEIG in Great Britain where its official address is in Great Britain shall be the registrar within the meaning of the 1985 Act and the contract shall be delivered—

(a) to the registrar or other officer performing under that Act the duty of registration of companies in England and Wales, if the contract states that the official address of the EEIG is to be situated in England and Wales, or that it is to be situated in Wales; and

(b) to the registrar or other officer performing under that Act the duty of registration of companies in Scotland, if the contract states that the official address of the EEIG is to be situated in Scotland.

(2) With the contract there shall be delivered a registration form in Form EEIG 1 containing a statement of the names and the particulars set out in article 5 of the EC Regulation.

(3) The registrar shall not register an EEIG under this regulation unless he is satisfied that all the requirements of these Regulations and of the EC Regulation in respect of registration and of matters precedent and incidental to it have been complied with but he may accept a declaration in Form EEIG 1 as sufficient evidence of compliance.

(4) Subject to paragraph (3) above, the registrar shall retain the contract, and any certified translation, delivered to him under this regulation and register the EEIG.

(5) On the registration of an EEIG the registrar shall give a certificate that the EEIG has been registered stating the date of registration.

(6) The certificate may be signed by the registrar, or authenticated by his official seal.

(7) A certificate of registration given in respect of an EEIG under this regulation is conclusive evidence that the requirements of these Regulations and of the EC Regulation in respect of registration and of matters precedent and incidental to it have been complied with, and that the EEIG is an organisation authorised to be registered, and is duly registered, under these Regulations.

(8) Where an EEIG is to be registered with the contract written in any language other than English, the contract to be delivered under paragraph (1) above may be in the other language provided that it is accompanied by a certified translation into English.

(9) Where an EEIG has published a proposal to transfer its official address to a place in Great Britain under article 14(1) of the EC Regulation, the registrar responsible for the registration of the EEIG with the new official address shall, where the transfer of the official address has not been opposed under paragraph (4) of that article, register the EEIG with its new official address on receipt of a registration form in Form EEIG 1 containing—

(a) evidence of the publication of the transfer proposal; and

(b) a statement that no competent authority has opposed the transfer under article 14(4) of the EC Regulation.

(10) Any communication or notice may be addressed to an EEIG where its official address is in Great Britain at its official address stated on Form EEIG 1 or in the case of any change in the situation of that address at any new official address stated on Form EEIG 4.

[6610]

NOTES

Forms: see Appendix 4 at **[A4]**.

10 Prohibition on registration of certain names

(1) An EEIG shall not be registered in Great Britain under regulation 9 above by a name which includes any of the following words or expressions, or abbreviations thereof, that is to say, "limited", "unlimited" or "public limited company" or their Welsh equivalents.

(2) In determining for the purposes of section 26(1)(c) of the 1985 Act (as applied by regulation 18 of, and Schedule 4 to, these Regulations) whether one name is the same as another, there are to be disregarded the words "European Economic Interest Grouping" or the initials "EEIG" or their authorised equivalents in official languages of the Economic Community, other than English, the authorised equivalents being set out in Schedule 3 to these Regulations.

[6611]

11 Change of name

(1) Regulation 10(2) above applies in determining under section 28(2) of the 1985 Act as applied by regulation 18 of, and Schedule 4 to, these Regulations whether a name is the same as or too like another.

(2) Where an EEIG changes its name the registrar shall (subject to the provisions of section 26 of the 1985 Act which apply by virtue of regulation 18 of, and Schedule 4 to, these Regulations and regulation 10 above) enter the new name on the register in place of the former name, and shall issue a certificate of registration altered to meet the circumstances of the case.

(3) A change of name has effect from the date on which the altered certificate is issued.

[6612]

12 Registration of establishment of EEIG whose official address is outside the United Kingdom

(1) The registrar for the purposes of registration under this regulation of an EEIG establishment situated in Great Britain where the EEIG's official address is outside the United Kingdom shall be the registrar within the meaning of the 1985 Act.

(2) For the purposes of registration under paragraph (1) above there shall be delivered, within one month of the establishment becoming so situated at any place in Great Britain, to the registrar at the registration office in England and Wales or Scotland, according to where the establishment is situated, a certified copy of the contract together with—

(a) a certified translation into English of the contract and other documents and particulars to be filed with it under article 10 of the EC Regulation if the contract and other documents and particulars, or any part thereof, are not in English; and

(b) a registration form in Form EEIG 2 containing a statement of the names and particulars set out in articles 5 and 10 of the EC Regulation.

(3) Paragraph (2) above shall not apply where an establishment is already registered in Great Britain under paragraph (1) above.

(4) The registrar shall not register an EEIG establishment under this regulation unless he is satisfied that all the requirements of these Regulations and of the EC Regulation in respect of registration and of matters precedent and incidental to it have been complied with but he may accept a declaration in Form EEIG 2 as sufficient evidence of compliance.

(5) Subject to paragraph (4) above, the registrar shall retain the copy of the contract, and any certified translation, delivered to him under paragraph (2) above and register the EEIG establishment.

(6) Any communication or notice may be addressed to an EEIG where its official address is outside the United Kingdom at any of its establishments in Great Britain.

(7) Regulation 10 above shall apply to an EEIG establishment to be registered under this regulation as it applies to an EEIG to be registered under regulation 9.

(8) If an EEIG fails to comply with any provision of paragraph (2) above, the EEIG, and any officer of it who intentionally authorises or permits the default, is guilty of an offence and liable on summary conviction to a fine not exceeding level 3 on the standard scale and if the failure to comply with any such provision continues after conviction, the EEIG and any such officer shall be guilty of a further offence of failure to comply with that provision and shall be liable to be proceeded against and punished accordingly.

[6613]

NOTES

Forms: see Appendix 4 at **[A4]**.

13 Filing of documents

(1) The documents and particulars referred to in paragraphs (a) to (j) of article 7 of the EC Regulation and required to be filed under that article in Great Britain shall be filed within 15 days (or, in the case of an EEIG whose official address is outside the United Kingdom, 30 days) of the event to which the document in question relates by delivery to the registrar for registration of a notice, together with a certified translation into English of any documents and particulars, or any part thereof, which are not in English—

(a) in the case of paragraph (d) where the official address of the EEIG is in Great Britain, in Form EEIG 3 of the names of the managers and the particulars referred to in regulation 5(3) above, of particulars of whether they may act alone or must act jointly and of the termination of any manager's appointment;

(b) in the case of paragraphs (a), (c) and (e) to (j), and in the case of paragraph (d) where the official address of the EEIG is outside the United Kingdom, in Form EEIG 4 of the documents and particulars referred to in that Form; and

(c) in the case of paragraph (b), in Form EEIG 5 of the setting up or closure of an establishment of an EEIG in Great Britain, except where regulation 12(1) above applies.

(2) The registrar shall retain the documents and particulars and any certified translation delivered to him under this regulation.

(3) If an EEIG fails to comply with any provision of paragraph (1) above, the EEIG, and any officer of it who intentionally authorises or permits the default, is guilty of an offence and liable on summary conviction to a fine not exceeding level 3 on the standard scale and if the failure to comply with any such provision continues after conviction, the EEIG and any such officer shall be guilty of a further offence of failure to comply with that provision and shall be liable to be proceeded against and punished accordingly.

[6614]

NOTES

Forms: see Appendix 4 at **[A4]**.

14 Inspection of documents

Any person may—

(a) inspect any document or particulars kept by the registrar under these Regulations or a copy thereof; and

(b) require the registrar to deliver or send by post to him a copy or extract of any such document or particulars or any part thereof.

[6615]

15 Publication of documents in the Gazette and Official Journal of the Communities

(1) The registrar shall cause to be published in the Gazette—

(a) the documents and particulars issued or received by him under these Regulations and referred to in article 8(a) and (b) of the EC Regulation; and

(b) in the case of those documents and particulars referred to in article 7(b) to (j) of the EC Regulation a notice (stating in the notice the name of the EEIG, the description of the documents or particulars and the date of receipt).

(2) The registrar shall forward to the Office for Official Publications of the European Communities the information referred to in article 11 of the EC Regulation within one month of the publication of the relevant documents and particulars in the Gazette under paragraph (1) above.

[6616]

16 EEIG identification

(1) If an EEIG fails to comply with article 25 of the EC Regulation it is guilty of an offence and liable on summary conviction to a fine not exceeding level 3 on the standard scale.

(2) If an officer of an EEIG or a person on its behalf issues or authorises the issue of any letter, order form or similar document not complying with the requirements of article 25 of the EC Regulation, he is guilty of an offence and liable on summary conviction to a fine not exceeding level 3 on the standard scale.

[6617]

PART IV
SUPPLEMENTAL PROVISIONS

17 Application of the Business Names Act 1985

The Business Names Act 1985 shall apply in relation to an EEIG which carries on business in Great Britain as if the EEIG were a company formed and registered under the 1985 Act.

[6618]

18 Application of the Companies Act 1985

The provisions of the 1985 Act specified in Schedule 4 to these Regulations shall apply to EEIGs, and their establishments, registered or in the process of being registered under these Regulations, as if they were companies formed and registered or in the process of being registered under the 1985 Act and as if in those provisions any reference to the Companies Act included a reference to these Regulations and any reference to a registered office included a reference to an official address, but subject to any limitations mentioned in relation to those provisions in that Schedule and to the omission of any reference to a daily default fine.

[6619]

19 Application of Insolvency Act 1986

(1) Part III of the Insolvency Act 1986 shall apply to EEIGs, and their establishments, registered under these Regulations, as if they were companies registered under the 1985 Act.

(2) Section 120 of the Insolvency Act 1986 shall apply to an EEIG, and its establishments, registered under these Regulations in Scotland, as if it were a company registered in Scotland the paid-up or credited as paid-up share capital of which did not exceed £120,000 and as if in that section any reference to the Company's registered office were a reference to the official address of the EEIG.

[6620]

20 Application of the Company Directors Disqualification Act 1986

Where an EEIG is wound up as an unregistered company under Part V of the Insolvency Act 1986, the provisions of sections 1, 2, 4 to 11, 12(2), 15 to 17, 20 and 22 of, and Schedule 1 to, the Company Directors Disqualification Act 1986 shall apply in relation to the EEIG as if any reference to a director or past director of a company included a reference to a manager of the EEIG and any other person who has or has had control or management of the EEIG's business and the EEIG were a company as defined by section 22(2)(b) of that Act.

[6621]

21 Penalties

Nothing in these Regulations shall create any new criminal offence punishable to a greater extent than is permitted under paragraph 1(1)(d) of Schedule 2 to the European Communities Act 1972.

[6622]

SCHEDULES

(Sch 1 reproduces the text of Council Regulation (EEC) No 2137/85 (as to which, see **[9001]**); *Sch 2 contains forms (as to which, see Appendix 4 at* **[A4]**).)

SCHEDULE 3
AUTHORISED EQUIVALENTS IN OTHER COMMUNITY OFFICIAL LANGUAGES OF "EUROPEAN ECONOMIC INTEREST GROUPING" AND "EEIG"

Regulation 10(2)

DANISH:	Europaeiske Økonomiske Firmagruppe (EØFG)
DUTCH:	Europese Economische Samenwerkingsverbanden (EESV)
FRENCH:	Groupement Européen d'intérêt économique (GEIE)
GERMAN:	Europäische Wirtschaftliche Interessenvereinigung (EWIV)

GREEK:	Ευρωπαικος ομιλος οικονομικου σκοπου (ΕΟΟΣ) (written phonetically in letters of the Latin alphabet as "Evropaikos omilos economicou skopou (EOOS)")
IRISH:	Grupail Eorpach um Leas Eacnamaioch (GELE)
ITALIAN:	Gruppo Europeo di Interesse Economico (GEIE)
PORTUGUESE:	Agrupamento Europeu de Interesse Econômico (AEIE)
SPANISH:	Agrupación Europea de Interés Económico (AEIE)

[6623]

SCHEDULE 4
PROVISIONS OF COMPANIES ACT 1985 APPLYING TO EEIGS AND THEIR ESTABLISHMENTS

Regulation 18

1. section 26(1)(c) to (e), (2) and (3).

2. section 28(2) to (5) and (7) so far as it relates to a direction given under subsection (2).

3. section 29(1)(a).

4. Part XII for the purpose of the creation and registration of charges to which it applies.

5. section 432(1) and (2).

6. section 434 so far as it refers to inspectors appointed under section 432 as applied by regulation 18 above and this Schedule.

7. section 436 so far as it refers to inspectors appointed under section 432, and to section 434, as applied by regulation 18 above and this Schedule.

8. sections 437 to 439.

9. section 441 so far as it applies to inspectors appointed under section 432 as applied by regulation 18 above and this Schedule.

10. section 447, as if paragraph (1)(d) referred to any EEIG which is carrying on business in Great Britain or has at any time carried on business there, whether or not any such EEIG is a body corporate.

11. sections 448 to 452.

12. section 458.

13. Part XVIII relating to floating charges and receivers (Scotland).

14. section 694 as if it referred to—
    (a) the registered name of an EEIG whose establishment is registered or is in the process of being registered under regulation 12 above with the necessary modifications;
    (b) regulation 10 above as applied by regulation 12(7) in addition to section 26;
    (c) in subsection (4)(a), a statement in Form EEIG 6; and
    (d) in subsection (4)(b), a statement in Form EEIG 7.

15. section 697(2) as if it referred to an EEIG whose establishment is registered or is in the process of being registered under regulation 12 above.

16. [section 704(5), (7) and (8)].

17. section 705(2).

18. sections 706, 707 and 710(1) to (3) and (5) as if they referred to documents and particulars delivered to or furnished by the registrar under these Regulations.

19. section 714(1) as if it referred to EEIGs or their establishments registered under these Regulations or in Northern Ireland.

20. section 718(2) as if it included a reference to an EEIG registered in Great Britain under these Regulations.

21. section 725.

22. section 730 and Schedule 24 so far as they refer to offences under sections applied by regulation 18 above and this Schedule.

23. section 731.

24. sections 732 and 733 so far as they refer to sections 447 to 451 as applied by regulation 18 above and this Schedule.

[6624]

NOTES

Para 16: words in square brackets substituted by the Deregulation and Contracting Out Act 1994, s 76, Sch 16, para 15.

COMPANIES ACT 1989 (COMMENCEMENT NO 3, TRANSITIONAL PROVISIONS AND TRANSFER OF FUNCTIONS UNDER THE FINANCIAL SERVICES ACT 1986) ORDER 1990

(SI 1990/354)

NOTES

Made: 26 February 1990.
Authority: CA 1989, s 215(2), (3).
As of 1 July 2007, this Order had not been amended.

1 Citation and interpretation

This Order may be cited as the Companies Act 1989 (Commencement No 3, Transitional Provisions and Transfer of Functions under the Financial Services Act 1986) Order 1990.

[6625]

2 In this Order:—

"SIB" means the body known as The Securities and Investments Board;
"the 1986 Act" means the Financial Services Act 1986; and
"the 1989 Act" means the Companies Act 1989.

[6626]

3 (*Brings into force certain provisions of CA 1989 subject to transitional provisions in art 6.*)

4 Transfer of functions

(1) All those functions of the Secretary of State which are specified in paragraphs (2) and (3) of this article shall be transferred to SIB on 15th March 1990, in the case of those functions specified in paragraph (2), without limitation and, in the case of those functions specified in paragraph (3), subject to the limitations specified in the said paragraph (3).

(2) The functions specified in this paragraph are—

(a) all functions under section 63A of the 1986 Act;
(b) all functions under section 128A of the 1986 Act.

(3) The functions specified in this paragraph are—

(a) all functions under section 47A of the 1986 Act except that the function of taking disciplinary action under that section is transferred only to the extent that the functions under the provisions referred to in section 47A(4) have been transferred to SIB;

(b) all functions under section 63C of the 1986 Act insofar as those functions relate to—

(i) statements of principles; and

(ii) rules and regulations the function of making of which has been transferred to SIB;

(c) all functions under section 128B(1) to (4) of the 1986 Act to the extent that such functions relate to functions of the Secretary of State under the 1986 Act which have been transferred to SIB;

(d) all functions under section 128C of the 1986 Act except that—

(i) the function of taking disciplinary action under that section is transferred only to the extent that the functions under the provisions referred to in section 128C(2) have been transferred to SIB; and

(ii) the function of prescribing functions under section 128C(3)(c) is not transferred.

(4) The references in paragraphs (2) and (3) of this article to the 1986 Act are to the 1986 Act as amended by those provisions of the 1989 Act brought into force by this Order.

(5) Where any amendment made by Part I of Schedule 23 to the 1989 Act to the provisions contained in Chapters III to XI of Part I of the 1986 Act or to section 206 of the 1986 Act confers a new function on the Secretary of State or alters a function already conferred on him by the 1986 Act the new function or the function as altered, as the case may be, is hereby transferred to SIB.

(6) Sections 204(2) and (3) of the 1989 Act shall have effect as if the references to the Secretary of State therein were to SIB and in relation to a recognised self-regulating organisation for friendly societies or transferee body the references to the Secretary of State in the said sections 204(2) and (3) (which by virtue of section 204(7) of the 1989 Act are to be construed as references to the Registrar (within the meaning of Schedule 11 to the 1986 Act)) shall have effect as if they were references to SIB.

[6627]

5—(1) All the functions of the Registrar (within the meaning of Schedule 11 to the 1986 Act) under paragraphs 13A, 22B and 22D of Schedule 11 to the 1986 Act (as amended by those provisions of the 1989 Act brought into force by this Order) are hereby transferred to SIB.

(2) Where any amendment made by Part II of Schedule 23 to the 1989 Act to the provisions contained in paragraphs 2 to 25 and 38 of Schedule 11 to the 1986 Act confers a new function on the Registrar (within the meaning of Schedule 11 to the 1986 Act) or alters a function already conferred on him by the 1986 Act the new function or the function as altered, as the case may be, is hereby transferred to SIB.

[6628]

6 Transitional provisions and savings

(1) For a transitional period as mentioned in subsection (3) of section 203 of the 1989 Act beginning on 15th March 1990, a self-regulating organisation or professional body may elect whether to comply with the new requirement having effect by virtue of subsection (1) or (2) of that section or with the requirement which it replaces ("the equivalence test").

(2) For the transitional period referred to above:—

(a) statements of principle, rules, regulations and codes of practice to which (in the case of a self-regulating organisation) its members or (in the case of a professional body) persons certified by it are subject under Chapter V of Part I of the 1986 Act (as amended by those provisions of the 1989 Act brought into force by this Order) shall be taken into account for the purposes of the equivalence test, so that—

(i) in the case of a self-regulating organisation the requirement is for the rules of the organisation governing the carrying on of investment business of any kind by its members, together with any relevant statements of principle, rules, regulations or codes of practice as mentioned above, to afford investors protection at least equivalent to that afforded in respect of investment business of that kind by the statements of principle, rules, regulations and codes of practice for the time being in force under Chapter V of Part I of the 1986 Act (as amended by those provisions of the 1989 Act brought into force by this Order);

(ii) in the case of a professional body the requirement is for the rules regulating the carrying on of investment business of any kind by persons certified by it, together with any relevant statements of principle, rules, regulations or codes of practice as mentioned above, to afford to investors protection at least equivalent to that afforded in respect of investment business of that kind by the statements of principle, rules, regulations and codes of practice for the time being in force under Chapter V of Part I of the 1986 Act (as amended by those provisions of the 1989 Act brought into force by this Order);

(b) the amendments made to section 13 of the 1986 Act by paragraph 1 of Schedule 23 to the 1989 Act and the omission of paragraph 7 of Schedule 11 to the 1986 Act by paragraph 29 of Schedule 23 to the 1989 Act shall not have effect in any case where the equivalence test applies.

(3) Any election under this article shall be notified in writing to SIB which shall send a copy of the notice to the Secretary of State and, where the election is made by a self-regulating organisation for friendly societies, to the Registrar (within the meaning of Schedule 11 to the 1986 Act); the Secretary of State shall send a copy of any notice received by him to Director General of Fair Trading.

(4) The amendments made to section 55 of the 1986 Act by paragraph 6 of Schedule 23 to the 1989 Act and to paragraph 19 of Schedule 11 to the 1986 Act by paragraph 34 of the said Schedule 23 and the related repeals under Schedule 24 to the 1989 Act shall not affect the validity or application of any regulations which have been made under the said section 55 or the said paragraph 19.

[6628A]

INSOLVENCY PRACTITIONERS REGULATIONS 1990 (NOTE)

(SI 1990/439)

NOTES

These Regulations were revoked and replaced by the Insolvency Practitioners Regulations 2005, SI 2005/524 at **[7369]** et seq, as from 1 April 2005. For transitional provisions and savings see reg 4 of the 2005 Regulations at **[7372]**.

[6629]–[6654]

OVERSEA COMPANIES (ACCOUNTS) (MODIFICATIONS AND EXEMPTIONS) ORDER 1990

(SI 1990/440)

NOTES

Made: 5 March 1990.

Authority: CA 1985, s 700(2), (3).

Commencement: 1 April 1990 (see art 1 at **[6655]**). Where any provision in this work (including any inserted or substituted provision) came into force for all purposes on or before 1 July 2005, commencement information is not noted at provision level.

As of 1 July 2007, this Order had not been amended.

1—(1) This Order may be cited as the Oversea Companies (Accounts) (Modifications and Exemptions) Order 1990 and shall come into force on 1st April 1990.

(2) In this Order—

"the 1989 Act" means the Companies Act 1989;

"the 1985 Act" means the Companies Act 1985 as amended by the 1989 Act; and

"the unamended 1985 Act" means the provisions of the 1985 Act prior to their amendment by the 1989 Act.

(3) . . .

[6655]

NOTES

Para (3): revokes the Oversea Companies (Accounts) (Modifications and Exemptions) Order 1982, SI 1982/676.

2—(1) The requirements referred to in section 700(1) of the 1985 Act shall, for the purposes of their application to oversea companies, be modified as follows—

(a) subject to the following provisions of this article, Part VII of the 1985 Act shall apply as if it had not been amended by the 1989 Act and as if any provisions of the 1985 Act necessary for the interpretation of that Part had not been amended or repealed by the 1989 Act;

(b) sections 228 and 230 of the unamended 1985 Act shall not apply in relation to such companies but sections 258 and 259 of the unamended 1985 Act shall apply as if such companies were special category companies within the meaning of section 257(1) of that Act and in particular shall (subject to the provisions of those sections) require the balance sheet, profit and loss account and group accounts of such companies to comply with the requirements of Schedule 9 to the unamended 1985 Act so far as applicable; and

(c) sections 245 and 247 to 253 of, and Schedule 8 and paragraph 29 of Schedule 9 to, the unamended 1985 Act shall not apply to such companies.

(2) Oversea companies shall be exempt from such requirements of the unamended 1985 Act referred to in section 700(1) of the 1985 Act as are specified in the Schedule to this Order.

(3) Oversea companies which would be exempt under section 700(3) of the unamended 1985 Act from compliance with that section (independent company with unlimited liability) shall be exempt from the requirements referred to in section 700(1) of the 1985 Act.

[6656]

SCHEDULE
REQUIREMENTS OF THE UNAMENDED 1985 ACT FROM WHICH OVERSEA COMPANIES ARE EXEMPT

Article 2(2)

1. Sections 231 and 260 and Schedule 5, except for the disclosure in the accounts of oversea companies, or in a document annexed thereto, of the information required to be given in paragraphs 22 and 28 to 34 of the said Schedule 5 and section 260(2) so far as it relates to those paragraphs.

2. Sections 232 to 234 and Schedule 6.

3. Sections 235 and 261 and Schedules 7 and 10.

4. Sections 236, 238(3), so far as that subsection requires the auditors' report to be attached to the balance sheet, and 262.

5. Section 257(3).

6. Paragraphs 13(17), 14(1)(c), 17 and 18(3) of Schedule 9.

[6657]–[6668]

COMPANY AUDITORS (RECOGNITION ORDERS) (APPLICATION FEES) REGULATIONS 1990 (NOTE)

(SI 1990/1206)

NOTES

See Appendix 3 (Fees Instruments) at **[A3]**.

[6669]

MERGER (FEES) REGULATIONS 1990 (NOTE)

(SI 1990/1660)

NOTES

See Appendix 3 (Fees Instruments) at **[A3]**.

[6670]

COMPANIES (REVISION OF DEFECTIVE ACCOUNTS AND REPORT) REGULATIONS 1990

(SI 1990/2570)

NOTES

Made: 17 December 1990.

Authority: CA 1985, s 245(3)–(5).

Commencement: 7 January 1991 (see reg 1 at **[6671]**). Where any provision in this work (including any inserted or substituted provision) came into force for all purposes on or before 1 July 2005, commencement information is not noted at provision level.

These Regulations are reproduced as amended by: the Companies (Summary Financial Statement) Regulations 1992, SI 1992/3075 (revoked); the Companies Act 1985 (Audit Exemption) Regulations 1994, SI 1994/1935; the Companies (Summary Financial Statement) Regulations 1995, SI 1995/2092; the Companies (Revision of Defective Accounts and Report) (Amendment) Regulations 1996, SI 1996/315; the Companies (Revision of Defective Accounts and Report) (Amendment) Regulations 2005, SI 2005/2282; the Companies Act 1985 (Operating and Financial Review) (Repeal) Regulations 2005, SI 2005/3442.

Limited liability partnerships: by the Limited Liability Partnerships Regulations 2001, SI 2001/1090, reg 10, Sch 6, Pt I, these Regulations apply, with modifications, to limited liability partnerships (see **[6998]**).

ARRANGEMENT OF REGULATIONS

1 Citation and commencement

These Regulations may be cited as the Companies (Revision of Defective Accounts and Report) Regulations 1990 and shall come into force on 7th January 1991.

[6671]

2 Interpretation

In these Regulations—

"the Act" means the Companies Act 1985;

"date of the original annual accounts" means the date on which the original annual accounts were approved by the board of directors under section 233 of the Act;

["date of the original directors' remuneration report" means the date on which the original directors' remuneration report was approved by the board of directors under section 234C of the Act;]

PART IV STATUTORY INSTRUMENTS

"date of the original directors' report" means the date on which the original directors' report was approved by the board of directors under section 234A of the Act;

[......]

"date of revision" means the date on which revised accounts are approved by the board of directors under Regulation 4 below or (as the case may be) a revised [directors' report [or directors' remuneration report]] is approved by them under [Regulation 5 or 5A] below;

"original", in relation to annual accounts or a directors' report [or directors' remuneration report], means the annual accounts or (as the case may be) directors' report [or directors' remuneration report] which are the subject of revision by, respectively, revised accounts or a [revised report ...] and, in relation to abbreviated accounts (within the meaning of Regulation 13(1) below) or a summary financial statement, means abbreviated accounts or a summary financial statement based on the original annual accounts or directors' report [or directors' remuneration report]

"revised accounts" mean revised annual accounts of a company prepared by the directors under section 245 of the Act, either through revision by replacement or revision by supplementary note; in the latter case the revised accounts comprise the original annual accounts together with the supplementary note;

"revised report" means a revised directors' report [or directors' remuneration report] prepared by the directors under section 245 of the Act, either through revision by replacement or revision by supplementary note; in the latter case the revised report comprises the original directors' report [or directors' remuneration report] together with the supplementary note;

[......]

"revision by replacement" means revision by the preparation of a replacement set of accounts[, directors' report [or directors' remuneration report]] in substitution for the original annual accounts[, directors' report [or directors' remuneration report]]; and

"revision by supplementary note" means revision by the preparation of a note indicating corrections to be made to the original annual accounts[, directors' report [or directors' remuneration report]].

[6672]

NOTES

Definition "date of the original directors' remuneration report" inserted by the Companies (Revision of Defective Accounts and Report) (Amendment) Regulations 2005, SI 2005/2282, regs 2, 3(1), (2), as from 1 October 2005.

Definitions "date of the original operating and financial review" and "revised review" inserted by SI 2005/2282, regs 2, 3(1), (2), as from 1 October 2005, and revoked by the Companies Act 1985 (Operating and Financial Review) (Repeal) Regulations 2005, SI 2005/3442, reg 2(2)(b), Sch 2, para 1(1), (2)(a), as from 12 January 2006.

Words in first (outer) pair of square brackets in definition "date of revision" substituted by SI 2005/2282, regs 2, 3(1), (3), as from 1 October 2005; words in second (inner) pair of square brackets and third pair of square brackets substituted by SI 2005/3442, reg 2(2)(b), Sch 2, para 1(1), (2)(b), as from 12 January 2006.

Words in first, second and fourth pairs of square brackets in definition "original" substituted, and words omitted revoked, by SI 2005/3442, reg 2(2)(b), Sch 2, para 1(1), (2)(c), as from 12 January 2006; words in third pair of square brackets inserted by SI 2005/2282, regs 2, 3(1), (4), as from 1 October 2005.

Words in square brackets in definition "revised report" inserted by SI 2005/2282, regs 2, 3(1), (5), as from 1 October 2005.

In definition "revision by replacement" words in first and third (outer) pairs of square brackets substituted by SI 2005/2282, regs 2, 3(1), (6), as from 1 October 2005; words in second and fourth (inner) pairs of square brackets substituted by SI 2005/3442, reg 2(2)(b), Sch 2, para 1(1), (2)(d), as from 12 January 2006.

In definition "revision by supplementary note" words in first (outer) pair of square brackets substituted by SI 2005/2282, regs 2, 3(1), (6), as from 1 October 2005; words in second (inner) pair of square brackets substituted by SI 2005/3442, reg 2(2)(b), Sch 2, para 1(1), (2)(d), as from 12 January 2006.

3 [Content of revised accounts [or revised report]]

(1) Subject to Regulation 16(1), the provisions of the Act [(and, where applicable, Article 4 of the IAS Regulation)] as to the matters to be included in the annual accounts of a company shall apply to revised accounts as if the revised accounts were prepared and approved by the directors as at the date of the original annual accounts.

[(2) In particular—

(a) in the case of Companies Act accounts, sections 226A(2) and 227A(2) of the Act, and

(b) in the case of IAS accounts, international accounting standards,

shall apply so as to require a true and fair view to be shown in the revised accounts of the matters therein referred to viewed as at the date of the original annual accounts.]

(3) [In the case of Companies Act accounts,] paragraph 12(b) of Schedule 4 to the Act shall apply to revised accounts as if the reference therein to the date on which the accounts were signed was to the date of the original annual accounts.

(4) The provisions of the Act as to the matters to be included in a directors' report [or directors' remuneration report] apply to a [revised report …] as if the [revised report …] was prepared and approved by the directors of the company as at the date of the original directors' report [or directors' remuneration report].

[6673]

NOTES

Regulation heading: words in first (outer) pair of square brackets substituted by the Companies (Revision of Defective Accounts and Report) (Amendment) Regulations 2005, SI 2005/2282, regs 2, 4(1), (2), as from 1 October 2005; words in second (inner) pair of square brackets substituted by the Companies Act 1985 (Operating and Financial Review) (Repeal) Regulations 2005, SI 2005/3442, reg 2(2)(b), Sch 2, para 1(1), (3)(a), as from 12 January 2006.

Paras (1), (3): words in square brackets inserted by SI 2005/2282, regs 2, 4(1), (3), (5), as from 1 October 2005.

Para (2): substituted by SI 2005/2282, regs 2, 4(1), (4), as from 1 October 2005.

Para (4): words in first and fourth pairs of square brackets substituted, and words omitted revoked, by SI 2005/3442, reg 2(2)(b), Sch 2, para 1(1), (3)(b), as from 12 January 2006; words in second and third pairs of square brackets substituted by SI 2005/2282, regs 2, 4(1), (6), as from 1 October 2005.

4 [Approval and signature of revised accounts or a revised directors' report]

(1) Section 233 of the Act (approval and signing of accounts) shall apply to revised accounts, save that in the case of a revision by supplementary note, it shall apply as if it required a signature on the supplementary note instead of on the company's balance sheet.

(2) Where copies of the original annual accounts have been sent out to members under section 238(1) of the Act, laid before the company in general meeting under section 241(1) of the Act or delivered to the registrar under section 242(1) of the Act, the directors shall before approving the revised accounts under section 233 of the Act, cause statements as to the following matters to be made in a prominent position in the revised accounts (in the case of a revision by supplementary note, in that note)—

(a) in the case of revision by replacement—
   (i) that the revised accounts replace the original annual accounts for the financial year (specifying it);
   (ii) that they are now the statutory accounts of the company for that financial year;
   (iii) that they have been prepared as at the date of the original annual accounts and not as at the date of revision and accordingly do not deal with events between those dates;
   (iv) the respects in which the original annual accounts did not comply with the requirements of the Act; and
   (v) any significant amendments made consequential upon the remedying of those defects;

(b) in the case of revision by a supplementary note—
   (i) that the note revises in certain respects the original annual accounts of the company and is to be treated as forming part of those accounts; and
   (ii) that the annual accounts have been revised as at the date of the original annual accounts and not as at the date of revision and accordingly do not deal with events between those dates,

and shall, when approving the revised accounts, cause the date on which the approval is given to be stated in them (in the case of revision by supplementary note, in that note); section 233(5) of the Act shall apply with respect to a failure to comply with this paragraph as if the requirements of this paragraph were requirements of the Act.

[6674]

NOTES

Regulation heading: words in square brackets substituted by the Companies (Revision of Defective Accounts and Report) (Amendment) Regulations 2005, SI 2005/2282, regs 2, 5(1), (2), as from 1 October 2005.

5—(1) Section 234A of the Act (approval and signing of directors' report) shall apply to a [revised directors' report], save that in the case of revision by supplementary note, it shall apply as if it required the signature to be on the supplementary note.

(2) Where the original directors' report has been sent out to members under section 238(1) of the Act, laid before the company in general meeting under section 241(1) of the Act or delivered to the registrar under section 242(1) of the Act, the directors shall, before approving the revised report under section 234A of the Act, cause statements as to the following matters to be made in a prominent position in the revised report (in the case of a revision by supplementary note, in that note)—

(a) in the case of a revision by replacement—

(i) that the revised report replaces the original report for the financial year (specifying it);

(ii) that it has been prepared as at the date of the original directors' report and not as at the date of revision and accordingly does not deal with any events between those dates;

(iii) the respects in which the original directors' report did not comply with the requirements of the Act; and

(iv) any significant amendments made consequential upon the remedying of those defects;

(b) in the case of revision by a supplementary note—

(i) that the note revises in certain respects the original directors' report of the company and is to be treated as forming part of that report; and

(ii) that the directors' report has been revised as at the date of the original directors' report and not as at the date of the revision and accordingly does not deal with events between those dates,

and shall, when approving the revised report, cause the date on which the approval is given to be stated in them (in the case of a revision by supplementary note, in that note); section 234(5) of the Act shall apply with respect to a failure to comply with this paragraph as if the requirements of this paragraph were requirements of Part VII of the Act.

[6675]

NOTES

Para (1): words in square brackets substituted by the Companies (Revision of Defective Accounts and Report) (Amendment) Regulations 2005, SI 2005/2282, regs 2, 5(1), (3), as from 1 October 2005.

[5A Approval and signature of revised directors' remuneration report

(1) Section 234C of the Act (approval and signing of directors' remuneration report) shall apply to a revised directors' remuneration report, save that in the case of revision by supplementary note, it shall apply as if it required the signature to be on the supplementary note.

(2) Where copies of the original directors' remuneration report have been sent out to members under section 238(1) of the Act, laid before the company in general meeting under section 241(1) of the Act or delivered to the registrar under section 242(1) of the Act, the directors shall, before approving the revised report under section 234C of the Act, cause statements as to the following matters to be made in a prominent position in the revised report (in the case of a revision by supplementary note, in that note)—

(a) in the case of a revision by replacement—

(i) that the revised report replaces the original report for the financial year (specifying it);

(ii) that it has been prepared as at the date of the original directors' remuneration report and not as at the date of revision and accordingly does not deal with any events between those dates;

(iii) the respects in which the original directors' remuneration report did not comply with the requirements of the Act; and

(iv) any significant amendments made consequential upon the remedying of those defects;

(b) in the case of revision by a supplementary note—

(i) that the note revises in certain respects the original directors' remuneration report of the company and is to be treated as forming part of that report; and

(ii) that the directors' remuneration report has been revised as at the date of the original directors' remuneration report and not as at the date of the revision and accordingly does not deal with events between those dates,

and shall, when approving the revised report, cause the date on which the approval is given to be stated in it (in the case of a revision by supplementary note, in that note); section 234B(3) shall apply with respect to a failure to comply with this paragraph as if the requirements of this paragraph were requirements of Part 7 of the Act.]

[6675A]

NOTES

Commencement: 1 October 2005.

Inserted by the Companies (Revision of Defective Accounts and Report) (Amendment) Regulations 2005, SI 2005/2282, regs 2, 6, as from 1 October 2005.

5B (*Inserted by the Companies (Revision of Defective Accounts and Report) (Amendment) Regulations 2005, SI 2005/2282, regs 2, 6, as from 1 October 2005; revoked by the Companies Act 1985 (Operating and Financial Review) (Repeal) Regulations 2005, SI 2005/3442, reg 2(2)(b), Sch 2, para 1(1), (4), as from 12 January 2006.*)

6 Auditors' report […] on revised accounts and revised report

(1) Subject to the next paragraph, [a company's current auditors shall make a report or (as the case may be) further report under section 235 of the Act] to the company's members under this Regulation on any revised accounts prepared under section 245 of the Act and—

(a) section 237 (duties of auditors) shall apply *mutatis mutandis*; and

(b) section 235(1) shall not apply with respect to the revised accounts.

(2) Where the auditors' report on the original annual accounts was not made by the company's current auditors, the directors of the company may resolve that the report required by paragraph (1) is to be made by the person or persons who made that report, provided that that person or those persons agree to do so and he or they would be qualified for appointment as auditor of the company.

(3) Subject to Regulation 16(1), an auditors' report under this Regulation shall state whether in the auditors' opinion the revised accounts have been properly prepared in accordance with the provisions of the Act [(and, where applicable, Article 4 of the IAS Regulation)] as they have effect under these Regulations, and in particular whether a true and fair view, seen as at the date the original annual accounts were approved, is given by the revised accounts with respect to the matters set out in section 235(2)(a) to (c) of the Act.

The report shall also state whether in the auditors' opinion the original annual accounts failed to comply with the requirements of the Act [(and, where applicable, Article 4 of the IAS Regulation)] in the respects identified by the directors (in the case of revision by replacement) in the statement required by Regulation 4(2)(a)(iv) or (in the case of revision by supplementary note) in the supplementary note.

(4) The auditors shall also [state] whether the information contained in the directors' report […] for the financial year for which the annual accounts are prepared (which is, if the report […] has been revised under these Regulations, that revised report […]) is consistent with those accounts; …

(5) Section 236 of the Act (signature of auditors' report) shall apply to an auditors' report under this Regulation as it applies to an auditors' report under section 235(1) *mutatis mutandis*.

(6) An auditors' report under this regulation shall, upon being signed under section 236 as so applied, be, as from the date of signature, the auditors' report on the annual accounts of the company in place of the report on the original annual accounts.

[6676]

NOTES

Regulation heading: words in square brackets originally inserted by the Companies (Revision of Defective Accounts and Report) (Amendment) Regulations 2005, SI 2005/2282, regs 2, 7(1), (2), as from

PART IV
STATUTORY INSTRUMENTS

1 October 2005, and revoked by the Companies Act 1985 (Operating and Financial Review) (Repeal) Regulations 2005, SI 2005/3442, reg 2(2)(b), Sch 2, para 1(1), (5)(a), as from 12 January 2006.

Para (1): words in square brackets substituted by the Companies (Revision of Defective Accounts and Report) (Amendment) Regulations 1996, SI 1996/315, regs 1–3, as from 1 April 1996.

Para (3): words in square brackets inserted by the Companies (Revision of Defective Accounts and Report) (Amendment) Regulations 2005, SI 2005/2282, regs 2, 7(1), (3), as from 1 October 2005.

Para (4): word in first pair of square brackets substituted, and final words omitted revoked, by SI 2005/2282, regs 2, 7(1), (4)(a), (e), as from 1 October 2005; other words in square brackets originally inserted by SI 2005/2282, regs 2, 7(1), (4)(b)–(d), as from 1 October 2005, and revoked by SI 2005/3442, reg 2(2)(b), Sch 2, para 1(1), (5)(b), as from 12 January 2006.

[6A—(1) Subject to the next paragraph, where a company's reporting accountant has, prior to the preparation of the revised accounts, made a report for the purposes of section 249A(2) of the Act on the original annual accounts, he shall make a further report to the company's members under this Regulation on any revised accounts prepared under section 245 of the Act and section 249C of the Act shall apply mutatis mutandis.

(2) The directors of the company may resolve that the further report is to be made by a person who was not the original reporting accountant, but is qualified to act as the reporting accountant of the company.

(3) Subsections (2) to (4) of section 236 of the Act shall apply to a report under this Regulation as they apply, by virtue of section 249E(2)(a) of the Act, to a report made for the purposes of section 249A(2) of the Act.

(4) A report under this Regulation shall, upon being signed by the reporting accountant, be, as from the date of the signature, the report on the annual accounts of the company for the purposes of section 249A(2) of the Act in place of the report on the original annual accounts.]

[6677]

NOTES

Inserted, together with reg 6B, by the Companies Act 1985 (Audit Exemption) Regulations 1994, SI 1994/1935, reg 5, Sch 2, para 2, as from 11 August 1994, in relation to annual accounts of a company which are approved by the board of directors on or after 11 August 1994 (and not in relation to any annual accounts the period for laying and delivering of which expired before that date).

[6B—(1) Where as a result of the revisions to the accounts a company which, in respect of the original accounts, was exempt from audit by virtue of subsection (1) of section 249A of the Act, becomes a company which is eligible for exemption from audit only by virtue of subsection (2) of that section, it shall cause a report to be prepared in accordance with section 249C of the Act in respect of the revised accounts.

(2) Where as a result of the revisions to the accounts, the company is no longer entitled to exemption from audit under section 249A(1) or (2) of the Act, the company shall cause an auditors' report on the revised accounts to be prepared.

(3) The report made in accordance with section 249C of the Act or auditors' report shall be delivered to the registrar within 28 days after the date of revision of the revised accounts.

(4) Subsections (2) to (5) of section 242 of the Act shall apply with respect to a failure to comply with the requirements of this Regulation as they apply with respect to a failure to comply with the requirements of subsection (1) of that section but as if—

(a) the references in subsections (2) and (4) of that section to "the period allowed for laying and delivering accounts and reports" were references to the period of 28 days referred to in paragraph (3); and

(b) the references in subsection (5) to "the documents in question" and "this Part" were, respectively, a reference to the documents referred to in paragraph (3) and to the provisions of Part VII of the Act as applied by these Regulations.]

[6678]

NOTES

Inserted as noted to reg 6A at **[6677]**.

7 Auditors' report [...] on revised report alone

(1) Subject to the next paragraph, [a company's current auditors shall make a report or (as the case may be) further report under section 235 of the Act] to the company's members

under this Regulation on any revised report […] prepared under section 245 of the Act if the relevant annual accounts have not been revised at the same time.

(2) Where the auditors' report on the annual accounts for the financial year covered by the revised report […] was not made by the company's current auditors, the directors of the company may resolve that the report required by paragraph (1) is to be made by the person or persons who made that report, provided that that person or those persons agree to do so and he or they would be qualified for appointment as auditor of the company.

[(3) Where a revised directors' report is prepared under section 245, the auditors' report shall state whether in their opinion the information given in that revised report is consistent with the annual accounts for the relevant year (specifying it).

(3A) …

(3B) Where a revised directors' remuneration report is prepared under section 245, the auditors' report shall state whether in their opinion any auditable part of that revised report has been properly prepared ("auditable part" being a part containing information required by Part 3 of Schedule 7A to the Act).]

(4) Section 236 of the Act (signature of auditors' report) shall apply to an auditors' report under this Regulation as it applies to an auditors' report under section 235(1) *mutatis mutandis*.

[6679]

NOTES

Regulation heading: words in square brackets originally inserted by the Companies (Revision of Defective Accounts and Report) (Amendment) Regulations 2005, SI 2005/2282, regs 2, 8(1), (2), as from 1 October 2005, and revoked by the Companies Act 1985 (Operating and Financial Review) (Repeal) Regulations 2005, SI 2005/3442, reg 2(2)(b), Sch 2, para 1(1), (6)(a), as from 12 January 2006.

Para (1): words in first pair of square brackets substituted by the Companies (Revision of Defective Accounts and Report) (Amendment) Regulations 1996, SI 1996/315, regs 1–3, as from 1 April 1996; words in second pair of square brackets originally inserted by SI 2005/2282, regs 2, 8(1), (3), as from 1 October 2005, and revoked by SI 2005/3442, reg 2(2)(b), Sch 2, para 1(1), (6)(b), as from 12 January 2006.

Para (2): words in square brackets originally inserted by the Companies (Revision of Defective Accounts and Report) (Amendment) Regulations 2005, SI 2005/2282, regs 2, 8(1), (3), as from 1 October 2005, and revoked by SI 2005/3442, reg 2(2)(b), Sch 2, para 1(1), (6)(b), as from 12 January 2006.

Paras (3), (3B): substituted, together with para (3A) for original para (3), by SI 2005/2282, regs 2, 8(1), (4), as from 1 October 2005.

Para (3A): substituted as noted above; revoked by SI 2005/3442, reg 2(2)(b), Sch 2, para 1(1), (6)(c), as from 12 January 2006.

8 Effect of revision

(1) Upon the directors approving revised accounts under Regulation 4, the provisions of the Act shall have effect as if the revised accounts were, as from the date of their approval, the annual accounts of the company in place of the original annual accounts.

(2) In particular, the revised accounts shall thereupon be the company's annual accounts for the relevant financial year for the purposes of—

(a) sections 239 (right to demand copies of accounts and reports) and 240(5) (requirements in connection with publication of accounts) of the Act; and

(b) sections 238 (persons entitled to receive copies of accounts and reports), 241 (accounts and reports to be laid before company in general meeting) and 242 (accounts and reports to be delivered to the registrar) if the requirements of those sections have not been complied with prior to the date of revision.

[6680]

9—(1) Subject to the following provisions of these Regulations, upon the directors approving a [revised report] under [[Regulation 5 or 5A] (as the case may be)] the provisions of the Act shall have effect as if the [revised report] was, as from the date of its approval, the directors' report [[or directors' remuneration report] (as the case may be)] in place of the original directors' report [[or directors' remuneration report] (as the case may be)].

(2) In particular, the revised report […] shall thereupon be the directors' report [or directors' remuneration report] for the relevant financial year for the purposes of—

(a) section 239 (right to demand copies of accounts and reports); and

PART IV STATUTORY INSTRUMENTS

(b) sections 238 (persons entitled to receive copies of accounts and reports), 241 (accounts and reports to be laid before company in general meeting) and 242 (accounts and reports to be delivered to the registrar) if the requirements of those sections have not been complied with prior to the date of revision.

[6681]

NOTES

Para (1): words in first pair, third (inner) pair, fourth pair, sixth (inner) pair, and eighth (inner) pair of square brackets substituted by the Companies Act 1985 (Operating and Financial Review) (Repeal) Regulations 2005, SI 2005/3442, reg 2(2)(b), Sch 2, para 1(1), (7)(a), as from 12 January 2006; words in second (outer) pair, fifth (outer) pair and seventh (outer) pair of square brackets inserted by the Companies (Revision of Defective Accounts and Report) (Amendment) Regulations 2005, SI 2005/2282, regs 2, 9(1), (2), as from 1 October 2005.

Para (2): words in first pair of square brackets inserted by SI 2005/2282, regs 2, 9(1), (3), as from 1 October 2005, and revoked by SI 2005/3442, reg 2(2)(b), Sch 2, para 1(1), (7)(b)(i), as from 12 January 2006; words in second pair of square brackets substituted by SI 2005/3442, reg 2(2)(b), Sch 2, para 1(1), (7)(b)(ii), as from 12 January 2006.

10 Publication of revised accounts [and reports]

(1) This Regulation has effect where the directors have prepared revised accounts or a [revised report] under section 245 of the Act and copies of the original annual accounts [or report] have been sent to any person under section 238 of the Act.

(2) The directors shall send to any such person—

(a) in the case of a revision by replacement, a copy of the revised accounts, or (as the case may be) the revised report […], together with a copy of the auditors' report on those accounts, or (as the case may be) on that report […]; or

(b) in the case of revision by supplementary note, a copy of that note together with a copy of the auditors' report on the revised accounts, or (as the case may be) on the revised report […],

not more than 28 days after the date of revision.

(3) The directors shall also[, not more than 28 days after the revision,] send a copy of the revised accounts or (as the case may be) the revised report […], together with a copy of the auditors' report on those accounts or (as the case may be) on that report […], to any person who is not a person entitled to receive a copy under the last paragraph but who is, as at the date of revision—

(a) a member of the company;

(b) a holder of the company's debentures; or

(c) a person who is entitled to receive notice of general meetings,

unless … the company would be entitled at that date to send to that person a summary financial statement under section 251 of the Act. Section 238(2) and (3) of the Act shall apply to this paragraph as they have effect with respect to section 238(1).

(4) Section 238(5) shall apply to a default in complying with this Regulation as if the provisions of this Regulation were provisions of section 238 and as if the reference therein to "the company and every officer of it who is in default" was a reference to each of the directors who approved the revised accounts under Regulation 4 above or revised report […] under [[Regulation 5 or 5A] (as the case may be)] above.

(5) Where, prior to the date of revision of the original annual accounts, the company had completed sending out copies of those accounts under section 238, references in the Act to the day on which accounts are sent out under section 238 shall be construed as referring to the day on which the original accounts were sent out (applying section 238(6) as necessary) notwithstanding that those accounts have been revised; where the company had not completed, prior to the date of revision, the sending out of copies of those accounts under that section, such references shall be to the day, or the last day, on which the revised accounts are sent out.

[6682]

NOTES

Regulation heading, para (1): words in square brackets substituted by the Companies Act 1985 (Operating and Financial Review) (Repeal) Regulations 2005, SI 2005/3442, reg 2(2)(b), Sch 2, para 1(1), (8)(a), (b), as from 12 January 2006.

Para (2): words in square brackets inserted by SI 2005/2282, regs 2, 10(1), (4), as from 1 October 2005, and revoked by SI 2005/3442, reg 2(2)(b), Sch 2, para 1(1), (8)(c), as from 12 January 2006.

Para (3): words in first pair of square brackets inserted by the Companies (Revision of Defective Accounts and Report) (Amendment) Regulations 1996, SI 1996/315, regs 1, 2, 5, as from 1 April 1996; other words in square brackets inserted by SI 2005/2282, regs 2, 10(1), (4), as from 1 October 2005, and revoked by SI 2005/3442, reg 2(2)(b), Sch 2, para 1(1), (8)(c), as from 12 January 2006; final words omitted revoked by the Companies (Summary Financial Statement) Regulations 1992, SI 1992/3075, reg 10(1), (2), as from 1 January 1993.

Para (4): words in first pair of square brackets inserted by SI 2005/2282, regs 2, 10(1), (5), as from 1 October 2005, and revoked by SI 2005/3442, reg 2(2)(b), Sch 2, para 1(1), (8)(d)(i), as from 12 January 2006; words in second (outer) pair of square brackets inserted by SI 2005/2282, regs 2, 10(1), (5), as from 1 October 2005; words in third (inner) pair of square brackets substituted by SI 2005/3442, reg 2(2)(b), Sch 2, para 1(1), (8)(d)(ii), as from 12 January 2006.

11 Laying of revised accounts or a revised report […]

(1) This Regulation has effect where the directors have prepared revised accounts or a [revised report] under section 245 of the Act and copies of the original annual accounts [or report] have been laid before a general meeting under section 241 of the Act.

(2) A copy of the revised accounts or (as the case may be) the revised report […], together with a copy of the auditors' report on those accounts, or (as the case may be) on that report […], shall be laid before the next general meeting of the company held after the date of revision at which any annual accounts for a financial year are laid, unless the revised accounts, or (as the case may be) the revised report […], have already been laid before an earlier general meeting.

(3) Section 241(2) to (4) shall apply with respect to a failure to comply with the requirements of this Regulation as they have effect with respect to a failure to comply with the requirements of section 241(1) but as if—

- (a) the reference in section 241(2) to "the period allowed for laying and delivering accounts and reports" was a reference to the period between the date of revision of the revised accounts or (as the case may be) the revised report […] and the date of the next general meeting of the company held after the date of revision at which any annual accounts for a financial year are laid; references in section 241(2) and (3) to "that period" shall be construed accordingly; and
- (b) the references in section 241(4) to "the documents in question" and "this Part" were, respectively, a reference to the documents referred to in the last paragraph and the provisions of Part VII of the 1985 Act as applied by these Regulations.

[6683]

NOTES

Regulation heading: words in square brackets inserted by the Companies (Revision of Defective Accounts and Report) (Amendment) Regulations 2005, SI 2005/2282, regs 2, 11(1), (2), as from 1 October 2005, and revoked by the Companies Act 1985 (Operating and Financial Review) (Repeal) Regulations 2005, SI 2005/3442, reg 2(2)(b), Sch 2, para 1(1), (9)(a), as from 12 January 2006.

Para (1): words in square brackets substituted by SI 2005/3442, reg 2(2)(b), Sch 2, para 1(1), (9)(b), as from 12 January 2006.

Paras (2), (3): words in square brackets inserted by SI 2005/2282, regs 2, 11(1), (4), (5), as from 1 October 2005, and revoked by SI 2005/3442, reg 2(2)(b), Sch 2, para 1(1), (9)(c), as from 12 January 2006.

12 Delivery of revised accounts or a revised report […]

(1) This Regulation has effect where the directors have prepared revised accounts or a [revised report] under section 245 of the Act and a copy of the original annual accounts [or report] has been delivered to the registrar under section 242 of the Act.

(2) The directors of the company shall, within 28 days of the date of revision, deliver to the registrar—

- (a) in the case of a revision by replacement, a copy of the revised accounts or (as the case may be) the revised report […], together with a copy of the auditors' report on those accounts or (as the case may be) on that report […]; or
- (b) in the case of a revision by supplementary note, a copy of that note, together with a copy of the auditors' report on the revised accounts or (as the case may be) on the revised report […].

(3) Section 242(2) to (5) shall apply with respect to a failure to comply with the requirements of this Regulation as they apply with respect to a failure to comply with the requirements of section 242(1) but as if—

(a) the references in section 242(2) and (4) to "the period allowed for laying and delivering accounts and reports" was a reference to the period of 28 days referred to in the last paragraph; the reference in section 242(2) to "that period" shall be construed accordingly; and

(b) the references in section 242(5) to "the documents in question" and "this Part" were, respectively, a reference to the documents referred to in the last paragraph and the provisions of Part VII of the 1985 Act as applied by these Regulations.

[6684]

NOTES

Regulation heading: words in square brackets inserted by the Companies (Revision of Defective Accounts and Report) (Amendment) Regulations 2005, SI 2005/2282, regs 2, 12(1), (2), as from 1 October 2005, and revoked by the Companies Act 1985 (Operating and Financial Review) (Repeal) Regulations 2005, SI 2005/3442, reg 2(2)(b), Sch 2, para 1(1), (10)(a), as from 12 January 2006.

Para (1): words in square brackets substituted by SI 2005/3442, reg 2(2)(b), Sch 2, para 1(1), (10)(b), as from 12 January 2006.

Para (2): words in square brackets inserted by SI 2005/2282, regs 2, 12(1), (4), as from 1 October 2005, and revoked by SI 2005/3442, reg 2(2)(b), Sch 2, para 1(1), (10)(a), as from 12 January 2006.

13 Small and medium sized companies

(1) This Regulation has effect (subject to Regulation 16(2)) where the directors have prepared revised accounts under section 245 of the Act and the company has, prior to the date of revision, delivered to the registrar accounts which take advantage of the exemptions for a small or medium-sized company conferred by [sections 246 and 246A] of the Act (referred to in these Regulations as "abbreviated accounts").

(2) Where the abbreviated accounts so delivered to the registrar would, if they had been prepared by reference to the revised accounts, not comply with the provisions of the Act (whether because the company would not have qualified as a small or (as the case may be) medium-sized company in the light of the revised accounts or because the accounts have been revised in a manner which affects the content of the abbreviated accounts), the directors of the company shall cause the company either—

(a) to deliver to the registrar a copy of the revised accounts, together with a copy of the directors' report and the auditors' report on the revised accounts; or

(b) (if on the basis of the revised accounts they would be entitled under the Act to do so) to prepare further accounts under section 246 [or 246A (as the case may be) in accordance with the provisions of those sections and (in the case of small companies) of Schedule 8A to the Act] and deliver them to the registrar together with a statement as to the effect of the revisions made.

(3) Where the abbreviated accounts would, if they had been prepared by reference to the revised accounts, comply with the requirements of the Act, the directors of the company shall cause the company to deliver to the registrar—

(a) a note stating that the annual accounts of the company for the relevant financial year (specifying it) have been revised in a respect which has no bearing on the abbreviated accounts delivered for that year; together with

(b) a copy of the auditors' report on the revised accounts.

(4) Revised abbreviated accounts or a note under this Regulation shall be delivered to the registrar within 28 days after the date of revision of the revised accounts.

(5) Section 242(2) to (5) shall apply with respect to a failure to comply with the requirements of this Regulation as they apply with respect to a failure to comply with the requirements of section 242(1) but as if—

(a) the references in section 242(2) and (4) to "the period allowed for laying and delivering accounts and reports" was a reference to the period of 28 days referred to in the last paragraph; the reference in section 242(2) to "that period" shall be construed accordingly; and

(b) the references in section 242(5) to "the documents in question" and "this Part" were, respectively, a reference to the documents referred to in paragraphs (2)(a) or (b) or (as the case may be) (3)(a) and (b) and to the provisions of Part VII of the 1985 Act as applied by these Regulations.

[6685]

NOTES

Paras (1), (2): words in square brackets substituted by the Companies (Revision of Defective Accounts and Report) (Amendment) Regulations 2005, SI 2005/2282, regs 2, 13, as from 1 October 2005.

[13A—(1) This Regulation has effect (subject to Regulation 16(2)) where the directors have delivered to the registrar abbreviated accounts which do not comply with the provisions of the Act for reasons other than those specified in Regulation 13(2) above.

(2) The directors of the company shall cause the company—

(a) to prepare further abbreviated accounts under section 246 [or 246A (as the case may be) in accordance with the provisions of those sections and (in the case of small companies) of Schedule 8A to the Act], and

(b) to deliver those accounts to the registrar within 28 days after the date of revision together with a statement as to the effect of the revisions made.

(3) Section 242(2) to (5) shall apply with respect to a failure to comply with the requirements of this Regulation as they apply with respect to a failure to comply with the requirements of section 242(1) but as if–

(a) the references in section 242(2) and (4) to "the period allowed for laying and delivering accounts and reports" was a reference to the period of 28 days referred to in the last paragraph; the reference in section 242(2) to "that period" shall be construed accordingly, and

(b) the references in section 242(5) to "the documents in question" were a reference to the documents referred to in paragraph (2)(a) and to the provisions of Part VII of the 1985 Act as applied by these Regulations.".]

[6686]

NOTES

Inserted by the Companies (Revision of Defective Accounts and Report) (Amendment) Regulations 1996, SI 1996/315, regs 1, 2, 6, as from 1 April 1996.

Para (2): words in square brackets substituted by the Companies (Revision of Defective Accounts and Report) (Amendment) Regulations 2005, SI 2005/2282, regs 2, 14, as from 1 October 2005.

14 Summary financial statements

[(1) This Regulation has effect (subject to Regulation 16(3)) where a summary financial statement has been sent to any person under section 251 of the Act.]

(2) [Where the summary financial statement does not comply with section 251 or the Companies (Summary Financial Statement) Regulations 1995, or if it had been prepared by reference to revised accounts or a revised report … would not have complied with those requirements, the directors of the company shall, subject to paragraphs (3A) and (3B) below,] cause the company to prepare a further summary financial statement under section 251 and to send that statement to—

(a) any person who received a copy of the original summary financial statement; and

(b) any person to whom the company would be entitled, as at the date the revised summary financial statement is prepared, to send a summary financial statement for the current financial year;

and section 251(1) to (4) and (7) shall apply *mutatis mutandis* to a summary financial statement hereunder.

(3) A summary financial statement prepared under the last paragraph shall contain a short statement of the revisions made and their effect.

[(3A) The directors of the company may, instead of causing the company to prepare a further summary financial statement under paragraph (2) above, cause the company to prepare and send to the persons mentioned in that paragraph a supplementary note indicating the corrections to the original summary financial statement, and section 251(1) to (2E) and (7) shall apply mutatis mutandis to such a supplementary note.

(3B) A supplementary note prepared under the last paragraph shall contain a statement that it revises the original summary financial statement in certain respects and is to be treated as forming part of that statement.]

(4) Where the summary financial statement would, if it had been prepared by reference to the revised accounts or revised report […], comply with the requirements of section 251

and [the Companies (Summary Financial Statement) Regulations 1995], the directors of the company shall cause the company to send to the persons referred to in paragraph (2) above a note stating that the annual accounts of the company for the relevant financial year (specifying it) or (as the case may be) the directors' report [or directors' remuneration report] for that year have or has been revised in a respect which has no bearing on the summary financial statement for that year.

If the auditors' report under Regulation 6 or 7 above on the revised accounts or revised report […] is qualified, a copy of that report shall be attached to the note sent out under this paragraph.

(5) A summary financial statement revised, or a note prepared, under this Regulation shall be sent to the persons referred to in paragraph (2) above within 28 days after the date of revision of the revised accounts or revised report […].

(6) Section 251(6) of the Act shall apply with respect to a failure to comply with the requirements of this Regulation as if the provisions of this Regulation were provisions of section 251 and as if the reference therein to "the company and every officer of it who is in default" was a reference to each of the directors of the company who approved the revised accounts under Regulation 4 above[, the revised directors' report under Regulation 5 above [or the revised directors' remuneration report under Regulation 5A above]] under Regulation 5 above.

[6687]

NOTES

Para (1): substituted by the Companies (Revision of Defective Accounts and Report) (Amendment) Regulations 2005, SI 2005/2282, regs 2, 15(1), (2), as from 1 October 2005.

Para (2): words in square brackets substituted by SI 2005/2282, regs 2, 15(1), (3), (7), as from 1 October 2005; words omitted revoked by the Companies Act 1985 (Operating and Financial Review) (Repeal) Regulations 2005, SI 2005/3442, reg 2(2)(b), Sch 2, para 1(1), (11)(a), as from 12 January 2006.

Paras (3A), (3B): inserted by SI 2005/2282, regs 2, 15(1), (4), as from 1 October 2005.

Para (4): words in first and fourth pairs of square brackets inserted by SI 2005/2282, regs 2, 15(1), (5), as from 1 October 2005, and revoked by SI 2005/3442, reg 2(2)(b), Sch 2, para 1(1), (11)(b)(i), as from 12 January 2006; words in second pair of square brackets substituted by the Companies (Summary Financial Statement) Regulations 1995, SI 1995/2092, reg 12(1), (2), as from 1 September 1995; words in third pair of square brackets substituted by SI 2005/3442, reg 2(2)(b), Sch 2, para 1(1), (11)(b)(ii), as from 12 January 2006.

Para (5): words in square brackets inserted by SI 2005/2282, regs 2, 15(1), (6), as from 1 October 2005, and revoked by SI 2005/3442, reg 2(2)(b), Sch 2, para 1(1), (11)(c), as from 12 January 2006.

Para (6): words in first (outer) pair of square brackets substituted by SI 2005/2282, regs 2, 15(1), (7), as from 1 October 2005; words in second (inner) pair of square brackets substituted by SI 2005/3442, reg 2(2)(b), Sch 2, para 1(1), (11)(d), as from 12 January 2006.

[14A Companies exempt from audit by virtue of section 249A of Companies Act 1985

(1) Where a company is exempt by virtue of section 249A(1) of the Act from the provisions of Part VII of the Act relating to the audit of accounts, these Regulations shall have effect as if any reference to an auditors' report, or to the making of such a report, were omitted.

(2) Where a company is exempt by virtue of section 249A(2) of the Act from the provisions of Part VII of the Act relating to the audit of accounts, regulations 10 to 13 shall have effect as if—

(a) references to the auditors' report on any accounts were references to the report made for the purposes of section 249A(2) in respect of those accounts, and

(b) references to the auditors' report on a revised directors' report were omitted.]

[6688]

NOTES

Inserted by the Companies Act 1985 (Audit Exemption) Regulations 1994, SI 1994/1935, reg 5, Sch 2, para 3, as from 11 August 1994, in relation to annual accounts of a company which are approved by the board of directors on or after 11 August 1994 (and not in relation to any annual accounts the period for laying and delivering of which expired before that date).

15 Dormant companies

Where a company [is exempt under section 249AA of the Act] from the requirements of Part VII of the Act relating to the audit of accounts, these Regulations shall apply as if they omitted any reference to an auditors' report, or to the making of such a report.

[6689]

NOTES

Words in square brackets substituted by the Companies (Revision of Defective Accounts and Report) (Amendment) Regulations 2005, SI 2005/2282, regs 2, 16, as from 1 October 2005.

16 Modifications of Act

(1) Where the provisions of the Act as to the matters to be included in the annual accounts of a company or (as the case may be) in a directors' report [or directors' remuneration report] have been amended after the date of the original annual accounts or (as the case may be) directors' report [or directors' remuneration report] but prior to the date of revision, references in Regulations 3 and 6(3) above to the provisions of the Act shall be construed as references to the provisions of the Act as in force at the date of the original annual accounts or (as the case may be) directors' report [or directors' remuneration report].

(2) Where the provisions of section 246 [or 246A] of, and [Schedule 8A] to, the Act as to the matters to be included in abbreviated accounts (within the meaning of Regulation 13(1) above) have been amended after the date of delivery of the original abbreviated accounts but prior to the date of revision of the revised accounts or report, references in Regulation 13 [or 13A] to the provisions of the Act or to any particular provision thereof shall be construed as references to the provisions of the Act, or to the particular provision, as in force at the date of the delivery of the original abbreviated accounts.

(3) Where the provisions of section 251 of the Act, or of [the Companies (Summary Financial Statement) Regulations 1995], as to the matters to be included in a summary financial statement have been amended after the date of the sending out of the original summary financial statement but prior to the date of revision of the revised [accounts, report …], references in Regulation 14 to section 251 or to those Regulations shall be construed as references to that section or those Regulations as in force at the date of the sending out of the original summary financial statements.

[…]

[6690]

NOTES

Para (1): words in square brackets substituted by the Companies Act 1985 (Operating and Financial Review) (Repeal) Regulations 2005, SI 2005/3442, reg 2(2)(b), Sch 2, para 1(1), (12)(a), as from 12 January 2006.

Para (2): words in first pair of square brackets inserted, and words in second pair of square brackets substituted, by the Companies (Revision of Defective Accounts and Report) (Amendment) Regulations 2005, SI 2005/2282, regs 2, 17(1), (3), as from 1 October 2005; words in third pair of square brackets inserted by the Companies (Revision of Defective Accounts and Report) (Amendment) Regulations 1996, SI 1996/315, regs 1, 2, 7, as from 1 April 1996.

Para (3): words in first pair of square brackets substituted by the Companies (Summary Financial Statement) Regulations 1995, SI 1995/2092, reg 12, as from 1 September 1995; words in second pair of square brackets substituted by SI 2005/2282, regs 2, 17(1), (4), as from 1 October 2005, and words omitted therefrom revoked by SI 2005/3442, reg 2(2)(b), Sch 2, para 1(1), (12)(b), as from 12 January 2006; final words omitted originally added by SI 1995/2092, reg 12, as from 1 September 1995, and revoked by SI 2005/2282, regs 2, 17(1), (4), as from 1 October 2005.

FINANCIAL MARKETS AND INSOLVENCY REGULATIONS 1991

(SI 1991/880)

NOTES

Made: 27 March 1991.

Authority: CA 1989, ss 155(4), (5), 158(4), (5), 160(5), 173(4), (5), 174(2)–(4), 185, 186, 187(3).

Commencement: 25 April 1991 (see reg 1 at **[6691]**). Where any provision in this work (including any inserted or substituted provision) came into force for all purposes on or before 1 July 2005, commencement information is not noted at provision level.

These Regulations are reproduced as amended by: the Financial Markets and Insolvency (Amendment) Regulations 1992, SI 1992/716; the Financial Markets and Insolvency (CGO Service) Regulations 1999, SI 1999/1209; the Financial Services and Markets Act 2000 (Consequential Amendments and Repeals) Order 2001, SI 2001/3649; the Enterprise Act 2002 (Insolvency) Order 2003, SI 2003/2096.

ARRANGEMENT OF REGULATIONS

PART I
GENERAL

1 Citation and commencement

These Regulations may be cited as the Financial Markets and Insolvency Regulations 1991 and shall come into force on 25th April 1991.

[6691]

2 Interpretation: general

(1) In these Regulations "the Act" means the Companies Act 1989.

(2) A reference in any of these Regulations to a numbered regulation shall be construed as a reference to the regulation bearing that number in these Regulations.

(3) A reference in any of these Regulations to a numbered paragraph shall, unless the reference is to a paragraph of a specified regulation, be construed as a reference to the paragraph bearing that number in the regulation in which the reference is made.

[6692]

3–6 ((*Pts II–IV*) *amend CA 1989, ss 155, 159, 160, 162 at* **[828]**, **[831]**, **[832]**, **[834]**.)

PART V
MARKET CHARGES

7 Interpretation of Part V

In this Part of these Regulations, unless the context otherwise requires—

"the Bank" means the Bank of England;

"business day" has the same meaning as in section 167(3) of the Act;

.....

"CGO" means the Central Gilts Office of the Bank;

"CGO Service" means the computer-based system established by the Bank and The Stock Exchange to facilitate the transfer of specified securities;

"CGO Service charge" means a charge of the kind described in section 173(1)(c) of the Act;

"CGO Service member" means a person who is entitled by contract with [CRESTCo Limited (which is now responsible for operating the CGO Service)] to use the CGO Service;

"former CGO Service member" means a person whose entitlement … to use the CGO Service has been terminated or suspended;

"market charge" means a charge which is a market charge for the purposes of Part VII of the Act;

"settlement bank" means a person who has agreed under a contract with [CRESTCo Limited (which is now responsible for operating the CGO Service)] to make payments of the kind mentioned in section 173(1)(c) of the Act;

"specified securities" has the meaning given in section 173(3) of the Act;

"Talisman" means The Stock Exchange settlement system known as Talisman;

"Talisman charge" means a charge granted in favour of The Stock Exchange over property credited to an account within Talisman maintained in the name of the chargor in respect of certain property beneficially owned by the chargor; and

"transfer" when used in relation to specified securities has the meaning given in section 173(3) of the Act.

[6693]

NOTES

Definition "CGO" revoked, words in square brackets in definitions "CGO Service member" and "settlement bank" substituted, and words omitted from definition "former CGO Service member" revoked, by the Financial Markets and Insolvency (CGO Service) Regulations 1999, SI 1999/1209, reg 3(1), as from 24 May 1999.

8 Charges on land or any interest in land not to be treated as market charges

(1) No charge, whether fixed or floating, shall be treated as a market charge to the extent that it is a charge on land or any interest in land.

(2) For the purposes of paragraph (1), a charge on a debenture forming part of an issue or series shall not be treated as a charge on land or any interest in land by reason of the fact that the debenture is secured by a charge on land or any interest in land.

[6694]

9 (*Amends CA 1989, s 173 at* **[843]**.)

10 Extent to which charge granted in favour of recognised investment exchange to be treated as market charge

(1) A charge granted in favour of a recognised investment exchange other than The Stock Exchange shall be treated as a market charge only to the extent that—

(a) it is a charge over property provided as margin in respect of market contracts entered into by the exchange for the purposes of or in connection with the provision of clearing services;

(b) in the case of a recognised UK investment exchange, it secures the obligation to pay to the exchange the net sum referred to in paragraph 9(2)(a) of Schedule 21 of the Act as it applies by virtue of paragraph 1(4) of that Schedule; and

(c) in the case of a recognised overseas investment exchange, it secures the obligation to reimburse the cost (other than fees and other incidental expenses) incurred by the exchange in settling unsettled market contracts in respect of which the charged property is provided as margin.

PART IV STATUTORY INSTRUMENTS

(2) A charge granted in favour of The Stock Exchange shall be treated as a market charge only to the extent that—

(a) it is a charge of the kind described in paragraph (1); or

(b) it is a Talisman charge and secures an obligation of either or both of the kinds mentioned in paragraph (3).

(3) The obligations mentioned in this paragraph are—

(a) the obligation of the chargor to reimburse The Stock Exchange for payments (including stamp duty and taxes but excluding Stock Exchange fees and incidental expenses arising from the operation by The Stock Exchange of settlement arrangements) made by The Stock Exchange in settling, through Talisman, market contracts entered into by the chargor; and

(b) the obligation of the chargor to reimburse The Stock Exchange the amount of any payment it has made pursuant to a short term certificate.

(4) In paragraph (3), "short term certificate" means an instrument issued by The Stock Exchange undertaking to procure the transfer of property of a value and description specified in the instrument to or to the order of the person to whom the instrument is issued or his endorsee or to a person acting on behalf of either of them and also undertaking to make appropriate payments in cash, in the event that the obligation to procure the transfer of property cannot be discharged in whole or in part.

[6695]

11 Extent to which charge granted in favour of recognised clearing house to be treated as market charge

A charge granted in favour of a recognised clearing house shall be treated as a market charge only to the extent that—

(a) it is a charge over property provided as margin in respect of market contracts entered into by the clearing house;

(b) in the case of a recognised UK clearing house, it secures the obligation to pay to the clearing house the net sum referred to in paragraph 9(2)(a) of Schedule 21 to the Act; and

(c) in the case of a recognised overseas clearing house, it secures the obligation to reimburse the cost (other than fees or other incidental expenses) incurred by the clearing house in settling unsettled market contracts in respect of which the charged property is provided as margin.

[6696]

12 Circumstances in which CGO Service charge to be treated as market charge

A CGO Service charge shall be treated as a market charge only if—

(a) it is granted to a settlement bank by a person for the purpose of securing debts or liabilities of the kind mentioned in section 173(1)(c) of the Act incurred by that person through his use of the CGO Service as a CGO Service member; and

(b) it contains provisions which refer expressly to the [CGO Service].

[6697]

NOTES

Words in square brackets substituted by the Financial Markets and Insolvency (CGO Service) Regulations 1999, SI 1999/1209, reg 3(2), as from 24 May 1999.

13 Extent to which CGO Service charge to be treated as market charge

A CGO Service charge shall be treated as a market charge only to the extent that—

(a) it is a charge over any one or more of the following—

(i) specified securities held within the CGO Service to the account of a CGO Service member or a former CGO Service member;

(ii) specified securities which were held as mentioned in sub-paragraph (i) above immediately prior to their being removed from the CGO Service consequent upon the person in question becoming a former CGO Service member;

(iii) sums receivable by a CGO Service member or former CGO Service member representing interest accrued on specified securities held within the CGO Service to his account or which were so held immediately prior to their being removed from the CGO Service consequent upon his becoming a former CGO Service member;

(iv) sums receivable by a CGO Service member or former CGO Service member in respect of the redemption or conversion of specified securities which were held within the CGO Service to his account at the time that the relevant securities were redeemed or converted or which were so held immediately prior to their being removed from the CGO Service consequent upon his becoming a former CGO Service member; and

(v) sums receivable by a CGO Service member or former CGO Service member in respect of the transfer by him of specified securities through the medium of the CGO Service; and

(b) it secures the obligation of a CGO Service member or former CGO Service member to reimburse a settlement bank for the amount due from him to the settlement bank as a result of the settlement bank having discharged or become obliged to discharge payment obligations in respect of transfers or allotments of specified securities made to him through the medium of the CGO Service.

[6698]

14 [Limitation on disapplication of moratorium on certain legal processes under Schedule B1 to the Insolvency Act 1986 (administration) in relation to CGO Service charges]

(1) In this regulation "qualifying period" means the period beginning with the fifth business day before the day on which [an application] for the making of an administration order in relation to the relevant CGO Service member or former CGO Service member is presented and ending with the second business day after the day on which an administration order is made in relation to the relevant CGO Service member or former CGO Service member pursuant to the petition.

[(1A) A reference in paragraph (1) to an application for an administration order shall be treated as including a reference to—

(a) appointing an administrator under paragraph 14 or 22 of Schedule B1 to the Insolvency Act 1986, or

(b) filing with the court a notice of intention to appoint an administrator under either of those paragraphs,

and a reference to "an administration order" shall include the appointment of an administrator under paragraph 14 or 22 of Schedule B1 to the Insolvency Act 1986.]

(2) [The disapplication of paragraph 43(2) of Schedule B1 to the Insolvency Act 1986 (including that provisions as applied by paragraph 44 of that Schedule)] by section 175(1)(a) of the Act shall be limited in respect of a CGO Service charge so that it has effect only to the extent necessary to enable there to be realised, whether through the sale of specified securities or otherwise, a sum equal to whichever is less of the following—

(a) the total amount of payment obligations discharged by the settlement bank in respect of transfers and allotments of specified securities made during the qualifying period to the relevant CGO Service member or former CGO Service member through the medium of the CGO Service less the total amount of payment obligations discharged to the settlement bank in respect of transfers of specified securities made during the qualifying period by the relevant CGO Service member or former CGO Service member through the medium of the CGO Service; and

(b) the amount (if any) described in regulation 13(b) due to the settlement bank from the relevant CGO Service member or former CGO Service member.

[6699]

NOTES

Regulation heading: substituted by the Enterprise Act 2002 (Insolvency) Order 2003, SI 2003/2096, arts 5, 6, Schedule, Pt 2, paras 47, 48(a), as from 15 September 2003, except in relation to any case where a petition for an administration order was presented before that date.

Paras (1), (2): words in square brackets substituted by SI 2003/2096, arts 5, 6, Schedule, Pt 2, paras 47, 48(b), (d), as from 15 September 2003, except in relation to any case where a petition for an administration order was presented before that date. Note, it is assumed that the words "the petition" at the end of para (1) should have been similarly substituted, but the Queen's Printer's copy of SI 2003/2096 made no such provision.

Para (1A): inserted by SI 2003/2096, arts 5, 6, Schedule, Pt 2, paras 47, 48(c), as from 15 September 2003, except in relation to any case where a petition for an administration order was presented before that date.

15 Ability of administrator or receiver to recover assets in case of property subject to CGO Service charge or Talisman charge

(1) [The disapplication—

(a) by section 175(1)(b) of the Act, of paragraphs 70, 71 and 72 of Schedule B1 to the Insolvency Act 1986, and

(b) by section 175(3) of the Act, of sections 43 and 61 of the 1986 Act,

shall cease to have effect] in respect of a charge which is either a CGO Service charge or a Talisman charge after the end of the second business day after the day on which an administration order is made or, as the case may be, an administrative receiver or a receiver is appointed, in relation to the grantor of the charge, in relation to property subject to it which—

(a) in the case of a CGO Service charge, is not, on the basis of a valuation in accordance with paragraph (2), required for the realisation of whichever is the less of the sum referred to in regulation 14(2)(a) and the amount referred to in regulation 14(2)(b) due to the settlement bank at the close of business on the second business day referred to above; and

(b) in the case of a Talisman charge is not, on the basis of a valuation in accordance with paragraph (2), required to enable The Stock Exchange to reimburse itself for any payment it has made of the kind referred to in regulation 10(3).

[(1A) A reference in paragraph (1) to "an administration order" shall include the appointment of an administrator under paragraph 14 or 22 of Schedule B1 to the Insolvency Act 1986.]

(2) For the purposes of paragraph (1) the value of property shall, except in a case falling within paragraph (3), be such as may be agreed between whichever is relevant of the administrator, administrative receiver or receiver on the one hand and the settlement bank or The Stock Exchange on the other.

(3) For the purposes of paragraph (1), the value of any investment for which a price for the second business day referred to above is quoted in the Daily Official List of The Stock Exchange shall—

(a) in a case in which two prices are so quoted, be an amount equal to the average of those two prices, adjusted where appropriate to take account of any accrued interest; and

(b) in a case in which one price is so quoted, be an amount equal to that price, adjusted where appropriate to take account of any accrued interest.

[6700]

NOTES

Para (1): words in square brackets substituted by the Enterprise Act 2002 (Insolvency) Order 2003, SI 2003/2096, arts 5, 6, Schedule, Pt 2, paras 47, 49(a), as from 15 September 2003, except in relation to any case where a petition for an administration order was presented before that date.

Para (1A): inserted by SI 2003/2096, arts 5, 6, Schedule, Pt 2, paras 47, 49(b), as from 15 September 2003, except in relation to any case where a petition for an administration order was presented before that date.

PART VI
CONSTRUCTION OF REFERENCES TO PARTIES TO MARKET CONTRACTS

16 Circumstances in which member or designated non-member dealing as principal to be treated as acting in different capacities

(1) In this regulation "relevant transaction" means—

(a) a market contract effected as principal by a member or designated non-member of a recognised investment exchange or a member of a recognised clearing house being a market contract—

[(i) which is a relevant investment; and]

(ii) in relation to which money received by the member or designated non-member is client money for the purposes of [the Financial Services (Client Money) Regulations 1991] or would be client money for the purposes of those regulations were it not money which, in accordance with those regulations, may be regarded as immediately due and payable to the member or designated non-member for his own account; and

(b) a market contract which would be regarded as a relevant transaction by virtue of sub-paragraph (a) above were it not for the fact that no money is received by the member or designated non-member in relation to the contract

(2) For the purposes of subsection (1) of section 187 of the Act (construction of references to parties to market contracts) a member or designated non-member of a recognised investment exchange or a member of a recognised clearing house shall be treated as effecting relevant transactions in a different capacity from other market contracts he has effected as principal.

[(3) In paragraph (1)(a)(i) "relevant investment" means an investment of one of the following kinds—

(a) options;

(b) futures;

(c) contracts for differences;

(d) rights to or interests in an investment of a kind mentioned in sub-paragraphs (a) to (c).

(4) Paragraph (3) must be read with—

(a) section 22 of the Financial Services and Markets Act 2000;

(b) any relevant order under that section; and

(c) Schedule 2 to that Act.]

[6701]

NOTES

Para (1): sub-para (a)(i) substituted by the Financial Services and Markets Act 2000 (Consequential Amendments and Repeals) Order 2001, SI 2001/3649, art 415(1), (2), as from 1 December 2001; words in square brackets in sub-para (a)(ii) substituted by the Financial Markets and Insolvency (Amendment) Regulations 1992, SI 1992/716, as from 1 May 1992.

Paras (3), (4): added by SI 2001/3649, art 415(1), (3), as from 1 December 2001.

17 ((*Pt VII*) *Amends CA 1989, Sch 21.*)

PART VIII
LEGAL PROCEEDINGS

18 (*Amends CA 1989, s 175 at* **[845]**.)

19 Court having jurisdiction in respect of proceedings under Part VII of Act

(1) For the purposes of sections 161, 163, 164, 175(5) and 182 of the Act (various legal proceedings under Part VII of Act) "the court" shall be the court which has last heard an application in the proceedings under the Insolvency Act 1986 or the Bankruptcy (Scotland) Act 1985 in which the relevant office-holder is acting or, as the case may be, any court having jurisdiction to hear applications in those proceedings.

(2) For the purposes of subsection (2) [and (2A)] of section 175 of the Act (administration orders etc), "the court" shall be the court which has made the administration order or, as the case may be, to which the [application] for an administration order has been presented [or the notice of intention to appoint has been filed].

(3) The rules regulating the practice and procedure of the court in relation to applications to the court in England and Wales under sections 161, 163, 164, 175 and 182 of the Act shall be the rules applying in relation to applications to that court under the Insolvency Act 1986.

[6702]

NOTES

Para (2): words in first and third pairs of square brackets inserted, and word in second pair of square brackets substituted, by the Enterprise Act 2002 (Insolvency) Order 2003, SI 2003/2096, arts 5, 6, Schedule, Pt 2, paras 47, 50, as from 15 September 2003, except in relation to any case where a petition for an administration order was presented before that date.

COMPANIES (FEES) REGULATIONS 1991 (NOTE)

(SI 1991/1206)

NOTES

See Appendix 3 (Fees Instruments) at **[A3]**.

[6702A]

COMPANIES ACT 1989 (REGISTER OF AUDITORS AND INFORMATION ABOUT AUDIT FIRMS) REGULATIONS 1991

(SI 1991/1566)

NOTES

Made: 7 July 1991.

Authority: CA 1989, ss 35, 36.

Commencement: 1 October 1991 (see reg 1 at **[6703]**). Where any provision in this work (including any inserted or substituted provision) came into force for all purposes on or before 1 July 2005, commencement information is not noted at provision level.

As of 1 July 2007, these Regulations had not been amended.

Note that the original Queen's Printer's copy of these Regulations contain two regulations numbered "2".

ARRANGEMENT OF REGULATIONS

1 Citation, commencement and interpretation

These Regulations may be cited as the Companies Act 1989 (Register of Auditors and Information about Audit Firms) Regulations 1991 and shall come into force on 1st October 1991.

[6703]

2 In these Regulations, unless the context otherwise requires—

"the Act" means the Companies Act 1989;

"business day" means any day which is not Saturday, Sunday, Christmas Day, Good Friday or a bank holiday within the meaning of the Banking and Financial Dealings Act 1971; and

"the register" means the register to be kept by virtue of regulation 2 below.

[6704]

NOTES

Note that the original Queen's Printer's copy of these Regulations contain two regulations numbered "2".

2 Recognised supervisory bodies to keep register of auditors

(1) The recognised supervisory bodies, or, if there is only one recognised supervisory body, that recognised supervisory body, shall keep a register of—

(a) the individuals and firms eligible for appointment as company auditor, and

(b) the individuals holding an appropriate qualification who are responsible for company audit work on behalf of such firms.

(2) Each person's entry in the register shall give—

(a) his name and address; and

(b) in the case of a person eligible as mentioned in paragraph (1)(a) of this regulation, the name of the relevant supervisory body.

(3) The responsibilities of each supervisory body, or, if there is only one supervisory body, of that supervisory body, in connection with the obligation imposed by paragraph (1) of this regulation shall be determined in accordance with regulation 3 of these Regulations.

[6705]

NOTES

Note that the original Queen's Printer's copy of these Regulations contain two regulations numbered "2".

3 Obligations of recognised supervisory bodies with respect to maintenance of register

(1) Where there is more than one recognised supervisory body, each recognised supervisory body shall co-operate with each other recognised supervisory body for the purpose of ensuring that each enter information on the register.

(2) Each recognised supervisory body, or if there is only one recognised supervisory body, that supervisory body, shall take reasonable care to ensure that, at all times—

(a) the register accurately states the individuals and firms eligible for appointment as company auditor under its rules and the individuals holding an appropriate qualification who are responsible for company audit work on behalf of such firms;

(b) the names and addresses shown on the register relating to persons falling within (a) above are correct; and

(c) its name appears on the register by virtue of regulation 2(2)(b) above only if the person in question is eligible for appointment as company auditor under its rules.

(3) To the extent that paragraph (2) of this regulation imposes a duty on a recognised supervisory body to take reasonable care to ensure that the register is amended to reflect changes in the information specified in that paragraph, the recognised supervisory body in question shall be regarded as having discharged that duty if it ensures that the register is appropriately amended within the period of 10 business days beginning with the day on which it becomes aware of the relevant change.

[6706]

4 Information about firms to be available to the public

A recognised supervisory body shall, in accordance with these Regulations, keep and make available to the public the following information in relation to each firm eligible under its rules for appointment as company auditor—

(a) where the firm is a body corporate, the name and address of each person who is a director of the body or holds any shares in it; and

(b) where the firm is a partnership, the name and address of each partner,

indicating which of the persons mentioned in sub-paragraphs (a) and (b) above is responsible for company audit work on behalf of the firm.

[6707]

5 Place of keeping and inspection of register

(1) The register shall be kept at the principal office in the United Kingdom of one of the recognised supervisory bodies, or, if there is only one recognised supervisory body, at the principal office in the United Kingdom of that body.

(2) The recognised supervisory body at whose principal office the register is kept shall ensure that it is open to inspection by any person during a period of at least two hours between the hours of 9am and 5pm in any business day.

(3) The recognised supervisory bodies, or if there is only one recognised supervisory body, that recognised supervisory body, shall ensure that the register may be inspected in each of the following ways—

(a) alphabetically; and

(b) by reference to recognised supervisory bodies.

(4) The recognised supervisory bodies, or, if there is only one recognised supervisory body, that recognised supervisory body, may charge a fee for inspection of the register or any part of it not exceeding £2.50 for each hour, or part of an hour, that is spent in conducting an inspection.

[6708]

6 Inspection of information kept under regulation 4

(1) Subject to paragraph (3), a recognised supervisory body shall ensure that the information it is required to keep and make available to the public by virtue of regulation 4 of these Regulations is open to inspection by any person during a period of at least two hours between the hours of 9am and 5pm in every business day at its principal office in the United Kingdom.

(2) A recognised supervisory body shall ensure that the information may be inspected in each of the following ways—

(a) alphabetically; and

(b) by reference to firm.

(3) A recognised supervisory body may charge a fee for inspection of the information or any part of it not exceeding £2.50 for each hour, or part of an hour, spent by a person in conducting an inspection.

[6709]

7 Copies of entries on register

(1) Subject to paragraph (2), the recognised supervisory bodies, or, if there is only one recognised supervisory body, that recognised supervisory body, shall ensure that any person may obtain a copy of any entry in the register, being a copy which is certified to be a true copy of the relevant entry by or on behalf of a recognised supervisory body.

(2) The recognised supervisory bodies, or, if there is only one recognised supervisory body, that recognised supervisory body, may charge a person a fee not exceeding 5p for a copy of an entry in the register.

(3) The recognised supervisory bodies, or, if there is only one recognised supervisory body, that recognised supervisory body, shall ensure that it is possible for a person to require copies of entries by each of the means mentioned in regulation 5(3) of these Regulations.

[6710]

8 Copies of information kept under regulation 4

(1) Subject to paragraph (2), a recognised supervisory body shall ensure that any person may obtain a copy of the whole or any part of the information which it is required to keep by virtue of regulation 4 of these Regulations certified by the body to be a true copy of the relevant information.

(2) A recognised supervisory body may charge a person a fee not exceeding 5p for a copy of the information it keeps relating to any director of or shareholder in a firm which is a body corporate or any partner in a firm which is a partnership.

(3) A recognised supervisory body shall ensure that it is possible for a person to require copies of information by each of the means mentioned in regulation 6(2) of the Regulations.

[6711]

COMPANIES ACT 1989 (ELIGIBILITY FOR APPOINTMENT AS COMPANY AUDITOR) (CONSEQUENTIAL AMENDMENTS) REGULATIONS 1991

(SI 1991/1997)

NOTES

Made: 3 September 1991.
Authority: CA 1989, s 50.

Commencement: 1 October 1991 (see reg 1 at **[6712]**). Where any provision in this work (including any inserted or substituted provision) came into force for all purposes on or before 1 July 2005, commencement information is not noted at provision level.

As of 1 July 2007, these Regulations (as reproduced here) had not been amended.

1 Citation, commencement and interpretation

(1) These Regulations may be cited as the Companies Act 1989 (Eligibility for Appointment as Company Auditor) (Consequential Amendments) Regulations 1991 and shall come into force on 1st October 1991.

(2) In these Regulations, "the Act" means the Companies Act 1989.

[6712]

2 Consequential amendments

The enactments mentioned in the Schedule to these Regulations shall have effect with the amendments specified therein.

[6713]

3 Where a partnership constituted under the law of England and Wales or under the law of any other country or territory in which a partnership is not a legal person is appointed under any enactment as amended by these Regulations, the provisions of section 26 of the Act apply to the appointment in the same way as they apply to the appointment as company auditor of such a partnership.

[6714]

4 Transitional provision

None of the amendments specified in the Schedule to these Regulations shall have the effect that a person is required to resign from or otherwise surrender an appointment, or that the appointment of a person must be terminated, before the date on which the person's appointment would, apart from these Regulations, have expired.

[6715]

(*Schedule* (*Amendments to Enactments*) *in so far as relevant, the amendments have been incorporated at the appropriate place.*)

COMPANIES (INSPECTION AND COPYING OF REGISTERS, INDICES AND DOCUMENTS) REGULATIONS 1991

(SI 1991/1998)

NOTES

Made: 2 September 1991.

Authority: CA 1985, ss 191(1)–(3), 219(2), 288(3), 325(5), 356(1), (3), 383(3), 723A, Sch 13, Pt IV, paras 25, 26(1).

Commencement: 1 November 1991 (see reg 1 at **[6716]**). Where any provision in this work (including any inserted or substituted provision) came into force for all purposes on or before 1 July 2005, commencement information is not noted at provision level.

As of 1 July 2007, these Regulations had not been amended.

Limited liability partnerships: by the Limited Liability Partnerships Regulations 2001, SI 2001/1090, reg 10, Sch 6, Pt I, these Regulations apply, with modifications, to limited liability partnerships (see **[6998]**).

ARRANGEMENT OF REGULATIONS

SCHEDULES

1 Citation and commencement

These Regulations may be cited as the Companies (Inspection and Copying of Registers, Indices and Documents) Regulations 1991 and shall come into force on 1st November 1991.

[6716]

2 Interpretation

In these Regulations—

"the Act" means the Companies Act 1985;

"business day" means, in relation to a company subject to any provision of these Regulations, any day except a Saturday or Sunday, Christmas Day, Good Friday and any other day which is a bank holiday in the part of Great Britain where that company is registered (or in the case of a company that is a body corporate to which section 723A of the Act is applied by section 718 thereof, the part of Great Britain where its principal office was situated on 5th January 1976 or if it was incorporated after that date, the part of Great Britain where its principal office was situated immediately after incorporation); and

"company" includes a body corporate to which section 723A of the Act is applied by any enactment.

[6717]

3 Inspection

(1) This Regulation applies to an obligation to make a register, index or document available for inspection imposed on a company by sections 169(5) (contract for purchase by company of its own shares), 175(6) (statutory declaration and auditors' report relating to payment out of capital), 191(1) (register of debenture holders), 219(1) (register of interests in shares &c), 288(3) (register of directors and secretaries), 318(7) (directors' service contracts), 356(1) (register and index of members) and 383(1) (minute books) of the Act, as well as to section 325 of, and paragraph 25 of Part IV of Schedule 13 to, the Act (register of directors' interests).

(2) The company shall—

(a) make the register, index or document available for such inspection for not less than two hours during the period between 9am and 5pm on each business day; and

(b) permit a person inspecting the register, index or document to copy any information made available for inspection by means of the taking of notes or the transcription of the information.

(3) Paragraph (2)(b) shall not be construed as obliging a company to provide any facilities additional to those provided for the purposes of facilitating inspection.

[6718]

4 Registers of members and debenture holders: presentation and extraction of entries

(1) This Regulation applies to a company's register of members maintained under section 352 of the Act, to an index of the names of the company's members maintained under section 354 thereof and to a register of debenture holders maintained under section 190 thereof.

(2) A company is not obliged—

(a) by virtue of section 356(1) of the Act to present for inspection its register of members or an index of members' names; or

(b) by virtue of section 191(1) of the Act to present for inspection a register of debenture holders maintained by it,

in a manner which groups together entries by reference to whether a member or (as the case may be) a debenture holder has given an address in a particular geographical location, is of a particular nationality, has a holding of a certain size, is a natural person or not or is of a particular gender.

(3) Nor is a company obliged—

(a) by virtue of section 356(3) of the Act, in providing a copy of a part of its register of members; or

(b) by virtue of section 191(2) of the Act, in providing a copy of a part of a register of debenture holders, to extract entries from the register by reference to whether a member or (as the case may be) a debenture holder has given an address in a particular geographical location, is of a particular nationality, has a holding of a certain size, is a natural person or not or is of a particular gender.

[6719]

5 Fees

Schedule 2 to these Regulations prescribes the fees payable for the purposes of the provisions of the Act listed therein.

[6720]

SCHEDULES

(*Sch 1 lists the enabling powers for these Regulations.*)

SCHEDULE 2

Regulation 5

1. Fees in respect of inspections of registers by non-members

The fee prescribed for the purposes of the following provisions of the Act—

(a) section 191(1) (Fee for inspection of register of debenture holders);
(b) section 288(3) (Fee for inspection of register of directors and secretaries);
(c) section 325(5) and paragraph 25 of Part IV of Schedule 13 (Fee for inspection of register of directors' interests in shares or debentures); and
(d) section 356(1) (Fee for inspection of register of members and index);

is £2.50 for each hour or part thereof during which the right of inspection is exercised.

2. Fees for provision of copies and entries in registers and copies of reports

The fee prescribed for the purposes of the following provisions of the Act—

(a) section 191(2) (Fee for copies of entries in the register of debentures);
(b) section 219(2) (Fees for copies of entries in the register of interests in shares or copies of reports or part of reports made pursuant to section 215(7));
(c) section 325(5) and paragraph 26(1) of Part IV of Schedule 13 (Fee for copies of entries in the register of directors' interests in shares or debentures); and
(d) section 356(3) (Fee for copies of entries in the register of members); is—
    (i) for the first 100 entries, or part thereof copied, … £2.50;
    (ii) for the next 1000 entries, or part thereof copied, … £20.00; and
    (iii) for every subsequent 1000 entries, or part thereof copied … £15.00.

3. Fees for copies of other documents

The fee prescribed for the purposes of the following provisions of the Act—

(a) section 191(3) (Fee for copies of trust deeds); and
(b) section 383(3) (Fee for copies of minutes)

is 10 pence per hundred words, or part thereof, copied.

[6721]

COMPANIES ACT 1985 (DISCLOSURE OF REMUNERATION FOR NON-AUDIT WORK) REGULATIONS 1991 (NOTE)

(SI 1991/2128)

NOTES

Disapplication (revocation) of these Regulations: the Companies (Disclosure of Auditor Remuneration) Regulations 2005, SI 2005/2417, reg 1 (at **[7444]**) provides that these Regulations shall not apply to the accounts of a company for any financial year beginning on or after 1 October 2005. The 2005 Regulations apply to the accounts of a company for any financial year beginning on or after that date.

[6722]–[6728]

TRANSFER OF FUNCTIONS (FINANCIAL SERVICES) ORDER 1992

(SI 1992/1315)

NOTES

Made: 4 June 1992.

Authority: Ministers of the Crown Act 1975, ss 1, 2; European Communities Act 1972, s 2(2).

Commencement: 7 June 1992 (see art 1 at **[6729]**). Where any provision in this work (including any inserted or substituted provision) came into force for all purposes on or before 1 July 2005, commencement information is not noted at provision level.

This Order is reproduced as amended by: the European Communities (Designation) (No 4) Order 2002, SI 2002/2840 which revokes the designation of the Treasury in respect of measures relating to open-ended collective investment schemes which have as their purpose investment in transferable securities, with the aim of spreading investment risk of funds raised from the public; see further art 9 at **[6737]**.

ARRANGEMENT OF ARTICLES

SCHEDULES

1 Citation and commencement

(1) This Order may be cited as the Transfer of Functions (Financial Services) Order 1992.

(2) This Order shall come into force on 7th June 1992.

[6729]

2 Transfer of functions from the Secretary of State to the Treasury

(1) Subject to the following provisions of this Order, the functions of the Secretary of State under—

(a) the Company Securities (Insider Dealing) Act 1985,

(b) the Financial Services Act 1986,

(c) Parts VII (financial markets and insolvency) and IX (transfer of securities) of the Companies Act 1989, and

(d) the Uncertificated Securities Regulations 1992,

are hereby transferred to the Treasury.

(2) The functions of the Secretary of State under the following provisions of the Companies Act 1989 are also hereby transferred to the Treasury—

(a) section 203(3), so far as it concerns the making of an order specifying when the transitional period referred to in that section is to end;

(b) section 206(2) (power to make a delegation order on bringing into force any provision of Part VIII of the Act which amends the Financial Services Act 1986); and

(c) section 215(2), (3) and (4) so far as it relates to the bringing into force of—

(i) any provision of Part VII; or

(ii) any provision of Part VIII of the Act which amends the Financial Services Act 1986.

(3) Subject to the following provisions of this Order, in so far as the Secretary of State retains any functions under Part III of the Companies Act 1985 and the Prevention of Fraud (Investments) Act 1958 (which enactments have been repealed with savings) those functions are also hereby transferred to the Treasury.

(4) In relation to the enactments referred to in paragraph (3) above, references in this Order to the Secretary of State or to the Secretary of State for Trade and Industry include references to the Board of Trade.

[6730]

3 Functions retained by the Secretary of State

The functions of the Secretary of State mentioned in Schedule 1 to this Order are not transferred to the Treasury.

[6731]

4 Functions to be exercisable jointly by the Secretary of State and the Treasury

The functions of the Secretary of State mentioned in Schedule 2 to this Order shall be exercisable by the Secretary of State jointly with the Treasury.

[6732]

5 Functions to be exercisable by the Secretary of State and the Treasury concurrently

The functions of the Secretary of State mentioned in Schedule 3 to this Order shall be exercisable by the Secretary of State and the Treasury concurrently.

[6733]

6 Functions transferred to designated agency

(1) Nothing in this Order affects the exercise (including any exercise concurrently with the Secretary of State) of any function which, before the coming into force of this Order, has been transferred from the Secretary of State to a designated agency by an order (in this Article referred to as a "delegation order") under section 114 of the Financial Services Act 1986 or section 168(2) or section 206(2) of the Companies Act 1989.

(2) Where, before the coming into force of this Order, any function has been so transferred, the powers under section 115 of the Financial Services Act 1986 or section 168(3) of the Companies Act 1989 to make an order resuming that function shall be construed as powers of the Treasury to make an order assuming that function; and references in those sections to the resumption of functions shall be construed accordingly.

(3) The transfer to the Treasury by virtue of this Order of the power to make a delegation order does not affect the operation of any enactment under which such an order may be subject to a reservation that the function which is transferred is to be exercisable concurrently by the Secretary of State.

[6734]

7 Barlow Clowes ex gratia payments scheme

(1) The functions of the Secretary of State for Trade and Industry with respect to the Barlow Clowes ex gratia payments scheme are hereby transferred to the Treasury.

(2) In this Order "the Barlow Clowes ex gratia payments scheme" means the scheme announced in a statement made in the House of Commons on 19th December 1989 by the Secretary of State for Trade and Industry.

[6735]

8 Transfers of property, rights and liabilities

There are hereby transferred—

(a) to the Solicitor for the affairs of Her Majesty's Treasury any property, rights and liabilities to which, immediately before the coming into force of this Order, the Secretary of State for Trade and Industry is entitled or subject in connection with the Barlow Clowes ex gratia payments scheme; and

(b) to the Treasury all other property, rights and liabilities to which, immediately before the coming into force of this Order, the Secretary of State for Trade and Industry is entitled or subject in connection with any functions transferred by this Order.

[6736]

9 Designation for purposes of European Communities Act 1972

For the purposes of section 2(2) of the European Communities Act 1972, the Treasury is hereby designated (in place of the Secretary of State) in relation to—

(a) matters relating to listing of securities on a stock exchange and information concerning listed securities,

(*b*) *measures relating to open-ended collective investment schemes which have as their purpose investment in transferable securities, with the aim of spreading investment risk of funds raised from the public, and*

(c) measures relating to prospectuses on offers of transferable securities to the public,

and in relation to anything supplemental or incidental to those matters or measures.

[6737]

NOTES

The European Communities (Designation) (No 4) Order 2002, SI 2002/2840 provides that, as from 23 December 2002, the designation of the Treasury in relation to the matters specified in para (b) above is revoked. The 2002 Order provides that, inter alia, the Treasury is designated in relation to matters relating to collective investment in transferable securities and other liquid assets.

10 Supplementary

(1) The enactments mentioned in Schedule 4 to this Order shall be amended in accordance with that Schedule.

(2) Subject to paragraph (1) above, in any enactment or instrument passed or made before the coming into force of this Order, any reference to the Secretary of State shall be construed, so far as necessary in consequence of any transfers effected by this Order as if it were a reference to the Treasury, to the Secretary of State and the Treasury acting jointly, to the Secretary of State or the Treasury or, as the case may be, to the Solicitor for the affairs of Her Majesty's Treasury.

(3) In this Order "instrument" includes (without prejudice to the generality of that expression) regulations, rules, orders, contracts, memoranda and articles of association and other documents.

(4) Any legal proceedings to which the Secretary of State for Trade and Industry or his Department is a party at the coming into force of this Order may—

(a) if they relate to any property, rights and liabilities transferred by Article 8(a) above, be continued by or against the Treasury and the Solicitor for the affairs of Her Majesty's Treasury;

(b) if they relate to any other transfer effected by this Order, be continued by or against the Treasury.

(5) This Order shall not affect the validity of anything done (or having effect as if done) by or in relation to the Secretary of State for Trade and Industry before the coming into force of this Order, and (subject to paragraph (4) above) anything which at that date is in process of being done by or in relation to him may, if it relates to any function or any property, rights and liabilities transferred by this Order, be continued by or in relation to the Treasury.

(6) Anything done (or having effect as if done) by the Secretary of State for Trade and Industry for the purpose of or in connection with anything transferred by this Order which immediately before the coming into force of this Order is in force shall have effect, so far as required for continuing its effect on and after that date, as if done by the Treasury.

[6738]

SCHEDULES

SCHEDULE 1
FUNCTIONS RETAINED BY THE SECRETARY OF STATE

Article 3

The Prevention of Fraud (Investments) Act 1958

1. The function under section 14(8) (consent to prosecutions).

The Companies Act 1985

2. The functions under sections 65(3)(b) and 77(5)(a) (prescribing manner in which translation to be certified as correct translation).

The Company Securities (Insider Dealing) Act 1985

3. The function under section 8 (punishment of contraventions).

The Financial Services Act 1986

4. The functions under section 6 (injunctions and restitution orders).

5. The function of taking disciplinary action under section 47A (in respect of failure to comply with statements of principle) in so far as the action consists of a function specified in this Schedule.

6. The function of giving a direction under section 59 (employment of prohibited persons) and associated functions, where the direction would have the effect of prohibiting the employment of an individual in connection with investment business carried on in connection with or for the purpose of insurance business at Lloyd's, being employment by any person who is an exempted person as respects such business.

7. The functions under section 60 (public statements as to a person's misconduct) and 61(1) (injunctions) in any case in which those functions are exercisable by virtue of a contravention of a direction of any kind described in paragraph 6 above.

8. The functions under section 61(1)—

(a) with respect to a person who is an exempted person by virtue of section 42 in any case in which the contravention or proposed contravention arises or is likely to arise in the course of investment business as respects which the person is exempt; or

(b) exercisable by virtue of section 61(1)(a)(ii) or (iii) (injunctions relating to contraventions of sections 47, 56, 57 or 59 or of requirements imposed under section 58(3)).

9. The functions under section 61(3) in relation to a contravention of a provision referred to in section 61(1)(a)(ii) or (iii) by a person who neither is, nor has ever been, an authorised person or appointed representative.

10. The functions under section 61 in relation to a contravention or proposed contravention of section 130.

11. The functions under sections 72 and 73 (winding up orders).

12. The functions under section 94 (investigations).

13. The functions under sections 97 to 101 (references to Tribunal) in so far as they arise out of a notice or a copy of a notice which, by virtue of any other paragraph of this Schedule, falls, after the coming into force of this Order, to be served by the Secretary of State.

14. The functions under section 105 (investigation powers).

15. The functions under section 106 (exercise of investigative powers by officer etc).

16. The functions under section 128B (relevance of information given and action taken by other regulatory authorities) and subsections (1), (4) and (5) of section 128C (enforcement in support of overseas regulatory authority) in so far as they relate to any other function specified in this Schedule.

17. The function under subsection (3)(c) of section 128C.

18. The functions under subsections (3) and (4) of section 130 (restriction on promotion of contracts of insurance).

19. The functions under section 138 (insurance brokers).

20. The functions under subsection (3) of section 148 (exemptions from disclosure) but without prejudice to the existing concurrent power of the Treasury under that subsection.

21. The functions under subsection (3) of section 165 (exemptions from disclosure) but without prejudice to the existing concurrent power of the Treasury under that subsection.

22. The functions under sections 177 and 178 (investigations into insider dealing and penalties for failure to co-operate).

23. In so far as they relate to insurance business which is not also investment business, the functions under—

(a) section 183 (reciprocal facilities for financial business),
(b) section 184 (investment and insurance business), or
(c) section 186 (variation and revocation of notices).

24. The functions under section 199 (powers of entry).

25. The functions under section 201 (prosecutions).

26. The following functions under Schedule 10 (regulated insurance companies)—

(a) the function under sub-paragraph (2) of paragraph 3 (certification as to requirement in sub-paragraph (1));
(b) the function under paragraph 4(6) of determining (before a delegation order is made transferring functions of making rules and regulations in relation to a regulated insurance company) whether the rules and regulations will take proper account of Part II of the Insurance Companies Act 1982 or, as the case may be, of the provisions for corresponding purposes in the law of the member State in which the company is established;
(c) functions under paragraph 6 (procedure on exercise of powers of intervention);
(d) functions under paragraph 10 (consultation with designated agency).

The Uncertificated Securities Regulations 1992

27. The functions under regulations 26(2) (inspection of registers) and 110 (investigations). **[6739]**

NOTES

Prevention of Fraud (Investments) Act 1958: repealed by FSA 1986.

Company Securities (Insider Dealing) Act 1985: repealed by the Criminal Justice Act 1993; see now Pt V of the 1993 Act at **[877]** et seq.

Financial Services Act 1986: repealed by the Financial Services and Markets Act 2000 (Consequential Amendments and Repeals) Order 2001, SI 2001/3649; see now the Financial Services and Markets Act 2000 at **[2001]** et seq.

Uncertificated Securities Regulations 1992, SI 1992/225: revoked by Uncertificated Securities Regulations 1995, SI 1995/3272 (also revoked); see now the Uncertificated Securities Regulations 2001, SI 2001/3755 at **[7001]** et seq.

SCHEDULE 2
FUNCTIONS EXERCISABLE JOINTLY BY THE SECRETARY OF STATE AND THE TREASURY

Article 4

The Financial Services Act 1986

1. The function of revoking a recognition order in respect of a recognised self-regulating organisation whose members include or may include regulated insurance companies on the ground that—

(a) the requirement specified in paragraph 3(1) of Schedule 10 is not satisfied; or

(b) the organisation has contravened sub-paragraph (3) or (4) of paragraph 6 of that Schedule as applied by sub-paragraph (5) of paragraph 6.

2. The function of giving a direction under subsection (1) of section 33, where the function—
(a) falls within paragraph (a) of that subsection, and
(b) is made in respect of a regulated insurance company.

3. The function of taking disciplinary action under section 47A (in respect of failure to comply with statements of principle) in so far as the action consists of a function specified in this Schedule.

4. In so far as they relate to investment business which is also insurance business, the functions under—
(a) section 183 (reciprocal facilities for financial business),
(b) section 184 (investment and insurance business),
(c) sections 28, 29, 33, 34, 60, 61 and 97 to 101 in relation to a contravention of a partial restriction notice under section 184(4), or
(d) section 186 (variation and revocation of notices).

5. The functions under section 128B (relevance of information given and action taken by other regulatory authorities) and subsections (1), (4) and (5) of section 128C (enforcement in support of overseas regulatory authority) in so far as they relate to any other function specified in this Schedule.

6. In Schedule 10 (regulated insurance companies) the functions under paragraph 8(2) to (5) in so far as they relate to a direction of a description mentioned in paragraph 2 above.

The Companies Act 1989

7.—(1) Subject to sub-paragraphs (2) and (3) below, functions under the following provisions of Part VII, namely, sections 158(4) and (5), 160(5), 170 to 174, 176, 181, 185 and 186.

(2) The reference in sub-paragraph (1) above to the functions under section 170 does not include a reference to the function under subsection (1) of that section of approving an overseas investment exchange.

(3) The reference in sub-paragraph (1) above to functions under section 186 is a reference only to so much of the functions under that section as relates to any function under the other enactments specified in sub-paragraph (1) above.

[6740]

NOTES

Financial Services Act 1986: repealed and replaced as noted at **[6739]**.

SCHEDULE 3
FUNCTIONS EXERCISABLE CONCURRENTLY BY THE SECRETARY OF STATE AND THE TREASURY

Article 5

1. The functions under section 180 and 181 of the Financial Services Act 1986 (restrictions on disclosure).

2. In Schedule 9 to that Act (designated agency status etc), the function under paragraph 13 (communication of information).

3. In section 82 of the Companies Act 1989 (request for assistance by overseas regulatory authority), the function under subsection (3) of being satisfied as to whether assistance requested by an overseas regulatory authority is for the purpose of its regulatory functions.

[6741]

NOTES

Financial Services Act 1986: repealed and replaced as noted at **[6739]**.

(*Sch 4 (Modification of enactments) the amendments made by this Schedule have been incorporated in this work.*)

COMPANIES (SINGLE MEMBER PRIVATE LIMITED COMPANIES) REGULATIONS 1992

(SI 1992/1699)

NOTES

Made: 14 July 1992.

Authority: European Communities Act 1972, s 2(2).

Commencement: 15 July 1992 (see reg 1 at **[6742]**). Where any provision in this work (including any inserted or substituted provision) came into force for all purposes on or before 1 July 2005, commencement information is not noted at provision level.

As of 1 July 2007, these Regulations had not been amended.

1 Citation and commencement

These Regulations may be cited as the Companies (Single Member Private Limited Companies) Regulations 1992 and shall come into force on the day after the day on which they were made.

[6742]

2 Single member private companies limited by shares or by guarantee

(1) Notwithstanding any enactment or rule of law to the contrary, a private company limited by shares or by guarantee within the meaning of section 1 of the Companies Act 1985 may be formed by one person (in so far as permitted by that section as amended by these Regulations) and may have one member; and accordingly—

(a) any enactment or rule of law which applies in relation to a private company limited by shares or by guarantee shall, in the absence of any express provision to the contrary, apply with such modification as may be necessary in relation to such a company which is formed by one person or which has only one person as a member as it does in relation to such a company which is formed by two or more persons or which has two or more persons as members; and

(b) without prejudice to the generality of the foregoing, the Companies Act 1985 and the Insolvency Act 1986 shall have effect with the amendments specified in the Schedule to these Regulations.

(2) In this regulation "enactment" shall include an enactment comprised in subordinate legislation and "subordinate legislation" shall have the same meaning as in section 21(1) of the Interpretation Act 1978.

[6743]

3 Transitional provision

A person who, before the coming into force of these Regulations, is liable by virtue of section 24 of the Companies Act 1985 for the payment of the debts of a private company limited by shares or by guarantee, shall not be so liable for the payment of the company's debts contracted on or after the day on which these Regulations come into force.

[6744]

(*Schedule amends CA 1985, ss 1, 24, 680, 741, Sch 24 at* **[1]**, **[25]**, **[522]**, **[689]**, *inserts CA 1985, ss 322B, 352A, 370A, 382B at* **[322]**, **[364]**, **[385]**, **[403]**, *and amends the Insolvency Act 1986, s 122 at* **[3278]**.)

OVERSEA COMPANIES AND CREDIT AND FINANCIAL INSTITUTIONS (BRANCH DISCLOSURE) REGULATIONS 1992

(SI 1992/3179)

NOTES

Made: 13 December 1992.

Authority: European Communities Act 1972, s 2(2).

Commencement: 1 January 1993 (see reg 1 at **[6744A]**). Where any provision in this work (including any inserted or substituted provision) came into force for all purposes on or before 1 July 2005, commencement information is not noted at provision level.
As of 1 July 2007, these Regulations had not been amended.

1 Citation etc

(1) These Regulations may be cited as the Oversea Companies and Credit and Financial Institutions (Branch Disclosure) Regulations 1992.

(2) In these Regulations, "the principal Act" means the Companies Act 1985 and "the 1989 Act" means the Companies Act 1989.

(3) These Regulations shall come into force on 1st January 1993.

(4) These Regulations extend to England and Wales and Scotland.

[6744A]

2–5 *(Reg 2 (implementation of the Bank Branches Directive) inserts the CA 1985, ss 699A, 699B (at* **[547]**, **[549]***) and introduces Sch 1 to these Regulations; reg 3 (implementation of the Eleventh Company Law Directive) inserts CA 1985, s 705A (at* **[574]***) and introduces Sch 2 to these Regulations; regs 4 and 5 introduce Schs 3 and 4 to these Regulations (consequential amendments and transitional provisions).)*

SCHEDULES

(Sch 1 inserts CA 1985, Sch 21C at **[683]** *et seq; Sch 2 contains amendments to CA 1985, Pt XXIII at* **[533]** *et seq; Sch 3 contains consequential amendments to CA 1985, CA 1989 and other legislation and, in so far as relevant to this work and still in force, they have been incorporated at the appropriate place.)*

SCHEDULE 4
TRANSITIONAL PROVISIONS

Regulation 5

Branch registration

1.—(1) This paragraph applies to any limited company incorporated outside the United Kingdom and Gibraltar which, immediately after 31st December 1992, has a branch in England and Wales which it had there immediately before 1st January 1993.

(2) A company to which this paragraph applies shall be treated for the purposes of paragraph 1(1) of Schedule 21A to the principal Act as having opened on 1st January 1993 any branch which it has in England and Wales immediately after 31st December 1992 and had there immediately before 1st January 1993.

(3) Where a company to which this paragraph applies was a registered oversea company in relation to England and Wales immediately before 1st January 1993, paragraph 1(1) of Schedule 21A to the principal Act shall have effect, in its application by virtue of sub-paragraph (2) above, with the substitution for "one month" of "six months".

(4) For the purposes of sub-paragraph (3) above, a company is a registered oversea company in relation to England and Wales if it has duly delivered documents to the registrar for England and Wales under section 691 of the principal Act and has not subsequently given notice to him under section 696(4) of that Act that it has ceased to have an established place of business there.

(5) Subject to sub-paragraph (6), sections 691 and 692 of the principal Act shall, in relation to England and Wales, continue to apply to a company to which this paragraph applies (notwithstanding section 690B of that Act) until such time as it has—

(a) complied with paragraph 1 of Schedule 21A to the principal Act in respect of a branch in England and Wales, or
(b) ceased to have a branch there.

(6) Sections 691 and 692 of the principal Act shall not however apply to any company to which this paragraph applies, if the company had no place of business in England and Wales immediately prior to 1st December 1992.

PART IV STATUTORY INSTRUMENTS

(7) This paragraph shall also apply with the substitution for references to England and Wales of references to Scotland.

(8) For the purposes of this paragraph "branch" has the same meaning as in section 698(2) of the principal Act and whether a branch is in England and Wales or Scotland is to be determined in accordance with that section.

2.—(1) This paragraph applies to any limited company incorporated outside the United Kingdom and Gibraltar which—

(a) has an established place of business in England and Wales both immediately before 1st January 1993 and immediately after 31st December 1992, and

(b) does not have a branch there immediately after 31st December 1992.

(2) Where, immediately after 31st December 1992, a company to which this paragraph applies has a branch elsewhere in the United Kingdom, sections 691 and 692 of the principal Act shall, in relation to England and Wales, continue to apply to the company (notwithstanding section 690B of that Act) until such time as it gives the registrar for England and Wales notice of the fact that it is a company to which section 690A applies.

(3) In sub-paragraph (2) above, "registrar" has the same meaning as in the principal Act.

(4) This paragraph shall also apply with the substitution for references to England and Wales of references to Scotland.

(5) For the purposes of this paragraph "branch" has the same meaning as in section 698(2) of the principal Act and whether a branch is in England and Wales or Scotland or Northern Ireland is to be determined in accordance with that section.

3.—(1) Where—

(a) a company to which paragraph 1 above applies delivers a return under paragraph 1(1) of Schedule 21A to the principal Act in respect of a branch in England and Wales or Scotland,

(b) the return is the first which the company has delivered under that provision in respect of a branch in that part of Great Britain,

(c) immediately before delivering the return, the company was a registered oversea company in relation to that part of Great Britain, and

(d) the company states in the return that the particulars have previously been delivered in respect of a place of business of the company in that part, giving the company's registered number,

the documents previously registered under section 691(1)(a) of that Act shall be treated as registered under paragraph 1 of Schedule 21A to that Act in respect of the branch to which the return relates.

(2) For the purposes of this paragraph, a company is a registered oversea company in relation to England and Wales or Scotland if—

(a) it has duly delivered documents to the registrar for that part of Great Britain under section 691 of the principal Act,

(b) it has duly complied with any obligation to make a return to that registrar under section 692(1)(a) of that Act, and

(c) it has not subsequently given notice to that registrar under section 696(4) of that Act that it has ceased to have an established place of business in that part.

(3) For the purposes of this paragraph "branch" has the same meaning as in section 698(2) of the principal Act.

Delivery of accounts and reports: institutions and companies previously subject to section 700

4.—(1) This paragraph applies to any company which—

(a) immediately after 31st December 1992, is an institution to which Part I of Schedule 21C to the principal Act applies, and

(b) immediately before 1st January 1993, was a company to which section 700 of that Act applies.

(2) Notwithstanding section 699B of the principal Act, sections 700 to 703 of that Act shall continue to apply in relation to any financial year of a company to which this paragraph applies beginning before 1st January 1993.

(3) Schedule 21C to the principal Act shall only have effect to require a company to which this paragraph applies to deliver accounting documents for registration if they have been prepared with reference to a period ending after the end of the last financial year of the company in relation to which sections 700 to 703 of that Act apply.

(4) In this paragraph, "financial year" has the same meaning as in section 700 of the principal Act.

5.—(1) This paragraph applies to any company which—

(a) immediately after 31st December 1992, is an institution to which Part II of Schedule 21C to the principal Act applies, and

(b) immediately before 1st January 1993, was a company to which section 700 of that Act applies.

(2) Paragraphs 10 and 12(1) of Schedule 21C to the principal Act shall have effect, in relation to any company to which this paragraph applies, with the insertion after "each financial year of the institution "of" ending after 31st December 1992".

(3) Any date which, immediately before 1st January 1993, is established for the purposes of sections 224 and 225 of the principal Act, as applied by section 701 of that Act, as the accounting reference date of a company to which this paragraph applies shall, immediately after 31st December 1992, be treated as established as the accounting reference date of the company for the purposes of those sections, as applied by paragraph 11 of Schedule 21C to that Act.

(4) In their application to a company to which this paragraph applies, paragraphs 11(a) and 13(2) of Schedule 21C to the principal Act shall have effect with the substitution for "becoming an institution to which this Part of this Schedule applies" of "establishing a place of business in Great Britain".

6.—(1) This paragraph applies to any company which—

(a) immediately after 31st December 1992, is a company to which Part I of Schedule 21D to the principal Act applies, and

(b) immediately before 1st January 1993, was a company to which Chapter II of Part XXIII of that Act applies.

(2) Notwithstanding section 699B of the principal Act, sections 700 to 703 of that Act shall continue to apply in relation to any financial year of a company to which this paragraph applies beginning before 1st January 1993.

(3) Schedule 21D to the principal Act shall only have effect to require a company to which this paragraph applies to deliver accounting documents for registration if they have been prepared with reference to a period ending after the end of the last financial year of the company in relation to which sections 700 to 703 of that Act apply.

(4) In this paragraph, "financial year" has the same meaning as in section 700 of the principal Act.

7.—(1) This paragraph applies to any company which—

(a) immediately after 31st December 1992, is a company to which Part II of Schedule 21D to the principal Act applies, and

(b) immediately before 1st January 1993, was a company to which section 700 of that Act applies.

(2) Paragraphs 8 and 10(1) of Schedule 21D to the principal Act shall have effect, in relation to a company to which this paragraph applies, with the insertion after "each financial year of the company" of "ending after 31st December 1992".

(3) Any date which, immediately before 1st January 1993, is established for the purposes of sections 224 and 225 of the principal Act, as applied by section 701 of that Act, as the accounting reference date of a company to which this paragraph applies shall, immediately after 31st December 1992, be treated as established as the accounting reference date of the company for the purposes of those sections, as applied by paragraph 9 of Schedule 21D to that Act.

(4) In its application to a company to which this paragraph applies, paragraphs 9(a) and 12(2) of Schedule 21D to the principal Act shall have effect with the substitution for "becoming a company to which this Part of this Schedule applies" of "establishing a place of business in Great Britain".

Delivery of accounts and reports: other institutions and companies

8.—(1) This paragraph applies to an institution to which Part I of Schedule 21C applies and to a company to which Part I of Schedule 21D applies, other than a company to which paragraphs 4 to 7 apply.

(2) Paragraph 1(2) of Schedule 21A and the provisions of Schedules 21C and 21D to the principal Act shall only have effect to require a company to which this paragraph applies to deliver accounting documents for registration if they have been prepared with reference to a period commencing on or after 1st January 1993.

References to enactments and continuance of law

9.—(1) Any reference in any enactment (including any subordinate legislation within the meaning of section 21 of the Interpretation Act 1978) to any provision in Part XXIII of the principal Act as unamended by these Regulations shall be construed as including a reference to the corresponding provision inserted by these Regulations with respect to companies to which section 690A and 699A or (as the case may be) section 699AA of that Act applies, unless the context otherwise requires.

(2) This provision made by this paragraph is without prejudice to the operation of the Interpretation Act 1978 or to any amendments effected by Schedule 3 to these Regulations.

[6744B]

DISCLOSURE OF INTERESTS IN SHARES (AMENDMENT) REGULATIONS 1993 (NOTE)

(SI 1993/1819)

NOTES

These Regulations were made under CA 1985, s 210A and came into force on 18 September 1993. They amended certain provisions in Pt VI of the 1985 Act (at **[184]** et seq) all of which were repealed, subject to savings, by CA 2006, as from 20 January 2007. They also made consequential amendments and revocations. Reg 11 of these Regulations provided for transitional provisions and imposed an obligation of disclosure in relation to interests which become notifiable as a result of the coming into force of these Regulations. These Regulations are now effectively spent.

[6745]–[6746]

PARTNERSHIPS AND UNLIMITED COMPANIES (ACCOUNTS) REGULATIONS 1993

(SI 1993/1820)

NOTES

Made: 20 July 1993.

Authority: European Communities Act 1972, s 2(2); CA 1985, s 257.

Commencement: 21 July 1993 (see reg 1 at **[6747]**). Where any provision in this work (including any inserted or substituted provision) came into force for all purposes on or before 1 July 2005, commencement information is not noted at provision level.

These Regulations are reproduced as amended by: the Partnerships and Unlimited Companies (Accounts) (Amendment) Regulations 2005, SI 2005/1987.

ARRANGEMENT OF REGULATIONS

1 Citation, commencement and extent

(1) These Regulations may be cited as the Partnerships and Unlimited Companies (Accounts) Regulations 1993.

(2) These Regulations shall come into force on the day after the day on which they are made.

(3) These Regulations do not extend to Northern Ireland.

[6747]

2 Interpretation

(1) In these Regulations, unless the context otherwise requires—

"the 1985 Act" means the Companies Act 1985;

"the accounts", in relation to a qualifying partnership, means the annual accounts, the annual report and the auditors' report required by regulation 4 below;

"dealt with on a consolidated basis" means dealt with by the method of full consolidation, the method of proportional consolidation or the equity method of accounting;

"financial year", in relation to a qualifying partnership, means any period of not more than 18 months in respect of which a profit and loss account of the partnership is required to be made up by or in accordance with its constitution or, failing any such requirement, each period of 12 months beginning with 1st April;

"the Fourth Directive" means the Fourth Council Directive (78/660/EEC) of 25th July 1978 on the annual accounts of certain types of companies, as amended;

"general partner" has the same meaning as in the Limited Partnerships Act 1907;

"limited company" means a company limited by shares or limited by guarantee;

"limited partnership" means a partnership formed in accordance with the Limited Partnerships Act 1907;

"qualifying company" has the meaning given by regulation 9 below;

"qualifying partnership" has the meaning given by regulation 3 below;

"the Seventh Directive" means the Seventh Council Directive (83/349/EEC) of 13th June 1983 on consolidated accounts, as amended;

and other expressions shall have the meanings ascribed to them by the 1985 Act.

(2) Any reference in these Regulations to the members of a qualifying partnership shall be construed, in relation to a limited partnership, as a reference to its general partner or partners.

[6748]–[6749]

3 Qualifying partnerships

(1) A partnership which is governed by the laws of any part of Great Britain is a qualifying partnership for the purposes of these Regulations if each of its members is—

(a) a limited company, or

(b) an unlimited company, or a Scottish firm, each of whose members is a limited company.

(2) Where the members of a qualifying partnership include—

(a) an unlimited company, or a Scottish firm, each of whose members is a limited company, or

(b) a member of another partnership each of whose members is—

(i) a limited company, or

(ii) an unlimited company, or a Scottish firm, each of whose members is a limited company,

any references in regulations 4 to 8 below to the members of the qualifying partnership includes a reference to the members of that company, firm or other partnership.

(3) The requirements of regulations 4 to 8 below shall apply without regard to any change in the members of a qualifying partnership which does not result in it ceasing to be such a partnership.

(4) Any reference in paragraph (1) or (2) above to a limited company, an unlimited company, a Scottish firm or another partnership includes a reference to any comparable undertaking incorporated in or formed under the law of any country or territory outside Great Britain.

[6750]

4 Preparation of accounts of qualifying partnerships

(1) Subject to regulation 7 below, the persons who are members of a qualifying partnership at the end of any financial year of the partnership shall, in respect of that year—

(a) prepare the like annual accounts and annual report, and

(b) cause to be prepared such an auditors' report,

as would be required under Part VII of the 1985 Act (accounts and audit) if the partnership were a company formed and registered under that Act.

(2) The accounts required by this regulation—

(a) shall be prepared within a period of 10 months beginning immediately after the end of the financial year, and

(b) shall state that they are prepared under this regulation.

(3) The Schedule to these Regulations (which makes certain modifications and adaptations for the purposes of this regulation) shall have effect.

[6751]

5 Delivery of accounts of qualifying partnerships to registrar etc

(1) Subject to regulation 7 below, each limited company which is a member of a qualifying partnership at the end of any financial year of the partnership shall append to the copy of its annual accounts which is next delivered to the registrar in accordance with section 242 of the 1985 Act a copy of the accounts of the partnership prepared for that year under regulation 4 above.

(2) Subject to regulation 7 below, a limited company which is a member of a qualifying partnership shall supply to any person upon request—

(a) the name of each member which is to deliver, or has delivered, a copy of the latest accounts of the partnership to the registrar under paragraph (1) above, and

(b) the name of each member incorporated in a member State other than the United Kingdom which is to publish, or has published, the latest accounts of the partnership in accordance with the provisions of the Fourth or Seventh Directive.

[6752]

6 Publication of accounts of qualifying partnerships at head office

(1) Subject to paragraph (2) and regulation 7 below, this regulation applies where a qualifying partnership's head office is in Great Britain and each of its members is—

(a) an undertaking comparable to a limited company which is incorporated in a country or territory outside the United Kingdom, or

(b) an undertaking comparable to an unlimited company or partnership—

(i) which is incorporated in or formed under the law of such a country or territory, and

(ii) each of whose members is such an undertaking as is mentioned in paragraph (a) above.

(2) Paragraph (1) above does not apply where any member of a qualifying partnership is—

(a) an undertaking comparable to a limited company which is incorporated in a member State other than the United Kingdom, or

(b) an undertaking comparable to an unlimited company or partnership—

(i) which is incorporated in or formed under the law of such a State, and

(ii) each of whose members is such an undertaking as is mentioned in paragraph (a) above,

and (in either case) the latest accounts of the qualifying partnership have been or are to be appended to the accounts of any member of the partnership and published under the law of that State and in accordance with the provisions of the Fourth or Seventh Directive.

(3) The members of the qualifying partnership—

(a) shall make the latest accounts of the partnership available for inspection by any person, without charge and during business hours, at the head office of the partnership, and

(b) if any document comprised in those accounts is in a language other than English, shall annex to that document a translation of it into English, certified in accordance with regulation 5 of the Companies (Forms) (Amendment) Regulations 1990 to be a correct translation.

(4) A member of the qualifying partnership shall supply to any person upon request—

(a) a copy of the accounts required by paragraph (3)(a) above to be made available for inspection, and

(b) a copy of any translation required by paragraph (3)(b) above to be annexed to any document comprised in those accounts,

at a price not exceeding the administrative cost of making the copy.

[6753]

7 Exemption from regulations 4 to 6 where accounts consolidated

(1) The members of a qualifying partnership are exempt from the requirements of regulations 4 to 6 above if the partnership is dealt with on a consolidated basis in group accounts prepared by—

(a) a member of the partnership which is established under the law of a member State, or

(b) a parent undertaking of such a member which is so established,

and (in either case) the conditions mentioned in paragraph (2) below are complied with.

(2) The conditions are—

(a) that the group accounts are prepared and audited under the law of the member State concerned in accordance with the provisions of the Seventh Directive [or of international accounting standards], and

(b) the notes to those accounts disclose that advantage has been taken of the exemption conferred by this regulation.

(3) Where advantage is taken of the exemption conferred by this regulation, any member of the qualifying partnership which is a limited company must disclose on request the name of at least one member or parent undertaking in whose group accounts the partnership has been or is to be dealt with on a consolidated basis.

[6754]

NOTES

Sub-s (2): words in square brackets inserted by the Partnerships and Unlimited Companies (Accounts) (Amendment) Regulations 2005, SI 2005/1987, reg 2, as from 1 October 2005, in relation to financial years which begin on or after 1 January 2005 and which end on or after 1 October 2005.

8 Penalties for non-compliance with regulations 4 to 6

(1) If, in respect of a financial year of a qualifying partnership, the requirements of paragraph (1) of regulation 4 above are not complied with within the period referred to in paragraph (2) of that regulation, every person who was a member of the partnership or a director of such a member at the end of that year is guilty of an offence and liable on summary conviction to a fine not exceeding level 5 on the standard scale.

(2) If the accounts of a qualifying partnership—

(a) a copy of which is delivered to the registrar under regulation 5 above, or

(b) which are made available for inspection under regulation 6 above,

do not comply with the requirements of regulation 4(1) above, every person who, at the time when the copy was so delivered or (as the case may be) the accounts were first made available for inspection, was a member of the partnership or a director of such a member is guilty of an offence and liable on summary conviction to a fine not exceeding level 5 on the standard scale.

(3) If a member of a qualifying partnership fails to comply with regulation 5, 6 or 7(3) above, that member and any director of that member is guilty of an offence and liable on summary conviction to a fine not exceeding level 5 on the standard scale.

(4) It is a defence for a person charged with an offence under this regulation to show that he took all reasonable steps for securing that the requirements in question would be complied with.

(5) The following provisions of the 1985 Act, namely—

(a) section 731 (summary proceedings),

(b) section 733 (offences by bodies corporate), and

(c) section 734 (criminal proceedings against unincorporated bodies),

shall apply to an offence under this regulation.

[6755]

9 Qualifying companies

(1) An unlimited company incorporated in Great Britain is a qualifying company for the purposes of these Regulations if each of its members is—

(a) a limited company, or

(b) another unlimited company, or a Scottish firm, each of whose members is a limited company.

(2) Any reference in paragraph (1) above to a limited company, another unlimited company or a Scottish firm includes a reference to any comparable undertaking incorporated in or formed under the law of any country or territory outside Great Britain.

[6756]

10, 11 (*Reg 10 amends CA 1985, s 254(3) at* **[255]**; *reg 11 amends CA 1985, s 231 at* **[217]**, *and inserts Sch 5, Pt I, para 9A, and Sch 5, Pt II, para 28A to the 1985 Act at* **[644]**, **[645]**.)

12 Transitional provisions

(1) The members of a qualifying partnership need not prepare accounts in accordance with regulation 4 above for a financial year commencing before 23rd December 1994.

(2) Where advantage is taken of the exemption conferred by paragraph (1) above, regulations 5 and 6 shall not apply, and the amendments to the 1985 Act effected by regulation 11 above shall be treated as not having been made.

[6757]

SCHEDULE

MODIFICATIONS AND ADAPTATIONS FOR PURPOSES OF REGULATION 4

Regulation 4

1.—(1) Accounts prepared under regulation 4 of these Regulations shall comply with the requirements of Part VII of the 1985 Act as to the content of accounts subject to the following, namely—

(a) the provisions of section 259(2) and (3) of that Act (meaning of "undertaking" and related expressions),

(b) the omission of the provisions mentioned in paragraph 2(1) below, and

(c) any necessary modifications to take account of the fact that partnerships are unincorporated.

(2) For the purposes of the provisions of Part VII of the 1985 Act as applied to accounts so prepared, these Regulations shall be regarded as part of the requirements of that Act.

2.—(1) The provisions referred to in paragraph 1(1)(b) above are—

(a) in Part I of Schedule 4 to the 1985 Act, paragraph 3(6) and, in paragraph 3(2), the words from "adopted" to the end;

(b) in Part II of that Schedule, paragraph 20;

(c) in Part III of that Schedule, paragraphs 36A, 41, 43, 44, 45, …51(2), 53 and 54;

(d) in Schedule 4A to that Act, paragraphs [13(3) and (5)], 14 and 15;

(e) in Schedule 5 to that Act, [paragraphs 4 and 12];

(f) in Schedule 6 to that Act, [paragraphs 2], 8 and 9; and

(g) Schedule 7 to that Act except paragraph 6.

(2) Sub-paragraph (1) above shall not be construed as affecting the requirement to give a true and fair view under [sections 226A and 227A] of the 1985 Act.

3. Part II of the Companies Act 1989 (eligibility for appointment as auditors) shall apply to auditors appointed for the purposes of regulation 4 of these Regulations as if qualifying

partnerships were companies formed and registered under the 1985 Act, subject to any necessary modifications to take account of the fact that partnerships are unincorporated.

[6758]

NOTES

Para 2: figure omitted from sub-para (1)(c) revoked, and words in square brackets substituted, by the Partnerships and Unlimited Companies (Accounts) (Amendment) Regulations 2005, SI 2005/1987, reg 3, as from 1 October 2005, in relation to financial years which begin on or after 1 January 2005 and which end on or after 1 October 2005.

COMPANIES ACT 1989 (RECOGNISED SUPERVISORY BODIES) (PERIODICAL FEES) REGULATIONS 1993 (NOTE)

(SI 1993/1881)

NOTES

See Appendix 3 (Fees Instruments) at **[A3]**.

[6759]–[6763]

COMPANIES ACT 1985 (INSURANCE COMPANIES ACCOUNTS) REGULATIONS 1993

(SI 1993/3246)

NOTES

Made: 18 December 1993.

Authority: CA 1985, s 257.

Commencement: 19 December 1993 (see reg 1 at **[6764]**). Where any provision in this work (including any inserted or substituted provision) came into force for all purposes on or before 1 July 2005, commencement information is not noted at provision level.

These Regulations are reproduced as amended by: the Life Assurance Consolidation Directive (Consequential Amendments) Regulations 2004, SI 2004/3379.

1 Citation and interpretation

(1) These Regulations may be cited as the Companies Act 1985 (Insurance Companies Accounts) Regulations 1993 and shall come into force on the day after the day on which they are made.

(2) In these Regulations "the 1985 Act" means the Companies Act 1985.

[6764]

2–5 (*Reg 2 amends CA 1985, s 255 at* **[256]**; *reg 3 amends CA 1985, s 255A at* **[257]**; *regs 4, 5(1) introduce Schs 1, 2 to these regulations; reg 5(2) amends the Companies Act 1989 (Commencement No 4 and Transitional and Saving Provisions) Order 1990, SI 1990/355, Sch 2.*)

6 Exempted companies

(1) A company to which paragraph (2) below applies may, with respect to any financial year, prepare such annual accounts as it would have been required to prepare had the modifications to the 1985 Act effected by these Regulations not been made.

(2) This paragraph applies to—

(a) any company which is excluded from the scope of Council Directive 73/239/EEC by Article 3 of that Directive, and

(b) any company referred to in [Article 3(2) to (6) of Directive 2002/83/EC of the European Parliament and of the Council of 5th November 2002 concerning life assurance].

(3) The modifications effected by regulations 2 to 5 above shall, where a company prepares accounts under paragraph (1) of this Regulation, be treated (as regards that company) as not having been made.

[6765]

NOTES

Para (2): words in square brackets in sub-para (b) substituted by the Life Assurance Consolidation Directive (Consequential Amendments) Regulations 2004, SI 2004/3379, reg 9, as from 11 January 2005.

7 Transitional provisions

(1) A company (including any body corporate to which Part VII of the 1985 Act is applied by any enactment) may, with respect to a financial year of the company commencing before 23rd December 1994, prepare such annual accounts as it would have been required to prepare had the modifications to the 1985 Act effected by these Regulations not been made.

(2) The modifications effected by regulations 2 to 5 above shall, where a company prepares accounts under paragraph (1) of this Regulation, be treated (as regards that company) as not having been made.

[6766]

(Sch 1 substitutes CA 1985, Sch 9A at **[664]** *et seq; Sch 2 makes consequential amendments, the effects of which have been incorporated at the appropriate place.)*

INSIDER DEALING (SECURITIES AND REGULATED MARKETS) ORDER 1994

(SI 1994/187)

NOTES

Made: 1 February 1994.

Authority: Criminal Justice Act 1993, ss 54(1), 60(1), 62(1), 64(3).

Commencement: 1 March 1994 (see art 1 at **[6767]**). Where any provision in this work (including any inserted or substituted provision) came into force for all purposes on or before 1 July 2005, commencement information is not noted at provision level.

This Order is reproduced as amended by: the Insider Dealing (Securities and Regulated Markets) (Amendment) Order 1996, SI 1996/1561; the Insider Dealing (Securities and Regulated Markets) (Amendment) Order 2000, SI 2000/1923; the Insider Dealing (Securities and Regulated Markets) (Amendment) Order 2002, SI 2002/1874.

ARRANGEMENT OF ARTICLES

1 Title, commencement and interpretation

This Order may be cited as the Insider Dealing (Securities and Regulated Markets) Order 1994 and shall come into force on the twenty eighth day after the day on which it is made.

[6767]

2 In this Order a "State within the European Economic Area" means a State which is a member of the European Communities and the Republics of Austria, Finland and Iceland, the Kingdoms of Norway and Sweden and the Principality of Liechtenstein.

[6768]

3 Securities

Articles 4 to 8 set out conditions for the purposes of section 54(1) of the Criminal Justice Act 1993 (securities to which Part V of the Act of 1993 applies).

[6769]

4 The following condition applies in relation to any security which falls within any paragraph of Schedule 2 to the Act of 1993, that is, that it is officially listed in a State within the European Economic Area or that it is admitted to dealing on, or has its price quoted on or under the rules of, a regulated market.

[6770]

5 The following alternative condition applies in relation to a warrant, that is, that the right under it is a right to subscribe for any share or debt security of the same class as a share or debt security which satisfies the condition in article 4.

[6771]

6 The following alternative condition applies in relation to a depositary receipt, that is, that the rights under it are in respect of any share or debt security which satisfies the condition in article 4.

[6772]

7 The following alternative conditions apply in relation to an option or a future, that is, that the option or rights under the future are in respect of—

(a) any share or debt security which satisfies the condition in article 4, or

(b) any depositary receipt which satisfies the condition in article 4 or article 6.

[6773]

8 The following alternative condition applies in relation to a contract for differences, that is, that the purpose or pretended purpose of the contract is to secure a profit or avoid a loss by reference to fluctuations in—

(a) the price of any shares or debt securities which satisfy the condition in article 4, or

(b) an index of the price of such shares or debt securities.

[6774]

9 Regulated markets

The following markets are regulated markets for the purposes of Part V of the Act of 1993—

[(a)] any market which is established under the rules of an investment exchange specified in the Schedule to this Order

(b) the market known as OFEX …]

[6775]

NOTES

Para (a) lettered as such and para (b) added by the Insider Dealing (Securities and Regulated Markets) (Amendment) Order 2000, SI 2000/1923, art 2(1), (2), as from 20 July 2000; words omitted from para (b) revoked by the Insider Dealing (Securities and Regulated Markets) (Amendment) Order 2002, SI 2002/1874, art 2(1), (2), as from 19 July 2002.

10 United Kingdom regulated markets

The regulated markets which are regulated in the United Kingdom for the purposes of Part V of the Act of 1993 are any market which is established under the rules of—

[(a) the London Stock Exchange Limited;]

(b) LIFFE Administration & Management; …

(c) OMLX, the London Securities and Derivatives Exchange Limited […

(d) [virt-x Exchange Limited].]

[(e) [the exchange known as COREDEALMTS]; together with the market known as OFEX …]

[6776]

NOTES

Para (a) substituted, word omitted from para (b) revoked, and para (d) and the word immediately preceding it added, by the Insider Dealing (Securities and Regulated Markets) (Amendment) Order 1996, SI 1996/1561, art 3, as from 1 July 1996; word omitted from para (c) revoked, and para (e) added, by the Insider Dealing (Securities and Regulated Markets) (Amendment) Order 2000, SI 2000/1923, art 2(1), (3), as from 20 July 2000; words in square brackets in paras (d), (e) substituted, and words omitted from para (e) revoked, by the Insider Dealing (Securities and Regulated Markets) (Amendment) Order 2002, SI 2002/1874, art 2(1), (3) as from 19 July 2002.

SCHEDULE
REGULATED MARKETS

Article 9

Any market which is established under the rules of one of the following investment exchanges:

Amsterdam Stock Exchange.

Antwerp Stock Exchange.

Athens Stock Exchange.

Barcelona Stock Exchange.

Bavarian Stock Exchange.

Berlin Stock Exchange.

Bilbao Stock Exchange.

Bologna Stock Exchange.

…

Bremen Stock Exchange.

Brussels Stock Exchange.

Copenhagen Stock Exchange.

[The exchange known as COREDEALMTS.]

Dusseldorf Stock Exchange.

[The exchange known as EASDAQ.]

Florence Stock Exchange.

Frankfurt Stock Exchange.

Genoa Stock Exchange.

…

Hamburg Stock Exchange.

Hanover Stock Exchange.

Helsinki Stock Exchange.

[Iceland Stock Exchange.

The Irish Stock Exchange Limited.]

…

…

Lisbon Stock Exchange.

LIFFE Administration & Management.

[The London Stock Exchange Limited.]

Luxembourg Stock Exchange.

Lyon Stock Exchange.

Madrid Stock Exchange.

…

Milan Stock Exchange.

…

…

Naples Stock Exchange.

The exchange known as NASDAQ.

[The exchange known as the Nouveau Marché.]

OMLX, the London Securities and Derivatives Exchange Limited.

Oporto Stock Exchange.

Oslo Stock Exchange.

Palermo Stock Exchange.

Paris Stock Exchange.

Rome Stock Exchange.

…

Stockholm Stock Exchange.

Stuttgart Stock Exchange.

[The exchange known as SWX Swiss Exchange.]

[…]

Trieste Stock Exchange.

Turin Stock Exchange.

Valencia Stock Exchange.

Venice Stock Exchange.

Vienna Stock Exchange.

[virt-x Exchange Limited.]

[6777]

NOTES

First to seventh entries omitted revoked, entries "Iceland Stock Exchange" and "The Irish Stock Exchange Limited" substituted, and entries "The London Stock Exchange Limited" and "The exchange known as the Nouveau Marché inserted, by the Insider Dealing (Securities and Regulated Markets) (Amendment) Order 1996, SI 1996/1561, art 4, as from 1 July 1996; entry "The exchange known as COREDEALMTS" originally inserted by the Insider Dealing (Securities and Regulated Markets) (Amendment) Order 2000, SI 2000/1923, art 2(1), (4)(a), as from 20 July 2000, and substituted by the Insider Dealing (Securities and Regulated Markets) (Amendment) Order 2002, SI 2002/1874, art 2(1), (4)(a) as from 19 July 2002; entry "The exchange known as EASDAQ" inserted, and eighth entry omitted revoked, by SI 2000/1923, art 2(1), (4)(b), (c), as from 20 July 2000; entries "The exchange known as SWX Swiss Exchange" and "virt-x Exchange Limited" inserted by SI 2002/1874, art 2(1), (4)(b), (d) as from 19 July 2002; final entry omitted originally inserted by SI 1996/1561, art 4, as from 1 July 1996, and revoked by SI 2002/1874, art 2(1), (4)(c) as from 19 July 2002.

TRADED SECURITIES (DISCLOSURE) REGULATIONS 1994 (NOTE)

(SI 1994/188)

NOTES

These Regulations were revoked by the Financial Services and Markets Act 2000 (Market Abuse) Regulations 2005, SI 2005/381, reg 9, as from 1 July 2005.

[6778]–[6782]

COMPANIES ACT 1985 (BANK ACCOUNTS) REGULATIONS 1994 (NOTE)

(SI 1994/233)

NOTES

These Regulations were made under CA 1985, s 257 and came into force on 11 February 1994 (for certain purposes) and 28 February 1994 (otherwise). They amend Pt VII of the 1985 Act (at **[207]** et seq) and make other consequential amendments to the 1985 Act. Reg 7 of these Regulations provides for transitional provisions as noted to the amended provisions of the 1985 Act *ante*. That regulation provides that the directors of a company (including a body corporate, or unincorporated body of persons, to which

Part VII of the 1985 Act is applied by virtue of any enactment, including any subordinate legislation within the meaning of the Interpretation Act 1978, s 21), may prepare annual accounts under Part VII of the 1985 Act for a financial year of the company commencing on a date prior to 23 December 1992 as if the amendments effected by reg 4 of these Regulations (to s 262A and Sch 9, Part I, para 82) had not been made. Reg 8 also provided for transitional provisions in connection with the amendment to s 343 of the 1985 Act, but that regulation became spent on the repeal of that section by the Companies Act 2006 on 6 April 2007.

[6783]–[6786]

FOREIGN COMPANIES (EXECUTION OF DOCUMENTS) REGULATIONS 1994

(SI 1994/950)

NOTES

Made: 24 March 1994.

Authority: CA 1989, s 130(6).

Commencement: 16 May 1994 (see reg 1 at **[6787]**). Where any provision in this work (including any inserted or substituted provision) came into force for all purposes on or before 1 July 2005, commencement information is not noted at provision level.

These Regulations are reproduced as amended by: the Foreign Companies (Execution of Documents) (Amendment) Regulations 1995, SI 1995/1729.

1 Citation and commencement

These Regulations may be cited as the Foreign Companies (Execution of Documents) Regulations 1994 and shall come into force on 16th May 1994.

[6787]

2 Application of sections 36 to 36C Companies Act 1985

[Sections 36, 36A, 36B and 36C] of the Companies Act 1985 shall apply to companies incorporated outside Great Britain with the adaptations and modifications set out in [regulations 3 to 5 below.]

[6788]

NOTES

Words in square brackets substituted by the Foreign Companies (Execution of Documents) (Amendment) Regulations 1995, SI 1995/1729, reg 3, as from 1 August 1995.

3 References in the said sections [36, 36A, 36B and 36C] to a company shall be construed as references to a company incorporated outside Great Britain.

[6789]

NOTES

Words in square brackets substituted by the Foreign Companies (Execution of Documents) (Amendment) Regulations 1995, SI 1995/1729, reg 4, as from 1 August 1995.

4 Adaptation of section 36

(1) Section 36 shall apply as if—

(a) after the words "common seal," in paragraph (a) there were inserted "or in any manner permitted by the laws of the territory in which the company is incorporated for the execution of documents by such a company,", and

(b) for paragraph (b) there were substituted—

"(b) on behalf of a company, by any person who, in accordance with the laws of the territory in which the company is incorporated, is acting under the authority (express or implied) of that company;".

[6790]

5 Adaptation of section 36A

Section 36A shall apply as if—

(a) at the end of subsection (2) there were inserted—

", or if it is executed in any manner permitted by the laws of the territory in which the company is incorporated for the execution of documents by such a company.",

(b) for subsection (4) there were substituted—

"(4) A document which—

(a) is signed by a person or persons who, in accordance with the laws of the territory in which the company is incorporated, is or are acting under the authority (express or implied) of that company, and

(b) is expressed (in whatever form of words) to be executed by the company,

has the same effect in relation to that company as it would have in relation to a company incorporated in England and Wales if executed under the common seal of a company so incorporated.", and

(c) in subsection (6) for the words from "a director" to "directors of the company" there were substituted "a person or persons who, in accordance with the laws of the territory in which the company is incorporated, is or are acting under the authority (express or implied) of that company".

[6791]

6 (*Revoked by the Foreign Companies* (*Execution of Documents*) (*Amendment*) *Regulations 1995, SI 1995/1729, reg 5.*)

COMPANIES ACT 1985 (AUDIT EXEMPTION) REGULATIONS 1994 (NOTE)

(SI 1994/1935)

NOTES

These Regulations were made under CA 1985, ss 245(3)–(5), 257 and came into force on 11 August 1994. They amend Pt VII of the 1985 Act (at **[207]** et seq), make other consequential amendments to the 1985 Act, and amend the Companies (Revision of Defective Accounts and Report) Regulations 1990, SI 1990/2570 at **[6671]** et seq. Reg 6 of these Regulations provides that they shall apply to any annual accounts of a company which are approved by the board of directors on or after 11 August 1994, and that they do not apply to any annual accounts the period for laying and delivering of which expired before that date.

[6792]–[6793]

INSOLVENCY REGULATIONS 1994

(SI 1994/2507)

NOTES

Made: 26 September 1994.

Authority: Insolvency Rules 1986, SI 1986/1925, r 12.1; Insolvency Act 1986, ss 411, 412, Sch 8, para 27, Sch 9, para 30.

Commencement: 24 October 1994 (see reg 1 at **[6794]**). Where any provision in this work (including any inserted or substituted provision) came into force for all purposes on or before 1 July 2005, commencement information is not noted at provision level.

These Regulations are reproduced as amended by: the Insolvency (Amendment) Regulations 2000, SI 2000/485; the Insolvency (Amendment) Regulations 2001, SI 2001/762; the Financial Services and Markets Act 2000 (Consequential Amendments and Repeals) Order 2001, SI 2001/3649; the Insolvency (Amendment) Regulations 2004, SI 2004/472; the Insolvency (Amendment) Regulations 2005, SI 2005/512.

Limited liability partnerships: by the Limited Liability Partnerships Regulations 2001, SI 2001/1090, reg 10, Sch 6, Pt II, these Regulations (and the amending Insolvency (Amendment) Regulations 2000, SI 2000/485) apply, with modifications, to limited liability partnerships (see **[6999]**).

ARRANGEMENT OF REGULATIONS

PART 1
GENERAL

PART 1A
ADMINISTRATION

PART 2
WINDING UP

PAYMENT INTO AND OUT OF THE INSOLVENCY SERVICES ACCOUNT

DIVIDENDS TO CREDITORS AND RETURNS OF CAPITAL TO CONTRIBUTORIES OF A COMPANY

INVESTMENT OR OTHERWISE HANDLING OF FUNDS IN WINDING UP OF COMPANIES AND PAYMENT OF INTEREST

RECORDS TO BE MAINTAINED BY LIQUIDATORS AND THE PROVISION OF INFORMATION

PART 3
BANKRUPTCY

PAYMENTS INTO AND OUT OF THE INSOLVENCY SERVICES ACCOUNT

DIVIDENDS TO CREDITORS

RECORDS TO BE MAINTAINED BY TRUSTEES AND THE PROVISION OF INFORMATION

PART 1
GENERAL

1 Citation and commencement

These Regulations may be cited as the Insolvency Regulations 1994 and shall come into force on 24th October 1994.

[6794]

2 Revocations

Subject to regulation 37 below, the Regulations listed in Schedule 1 to these Regulations are hereby revoked.

[6795]

3 Interpretation and application

(1) In these Regulations, except where the context otherwise requires—

["bank" means—

(a) a person who has permission under Part 4 of the Financial Services and Markets Act 2000 to accept deposits, or

(b) an EEA firm of the kind mentioned in paragraph 5(b) of Schedule 3 to that Act, which has permission under paragraph 15 of that Schedule (as a result of qualifying for authorisation under paragraph 12(1) of that Schedule) to accept deposits;]

"bankrupt" means the bankrupt or his estate;

"company" means the company which is being wound up;

"creditors' committee" means any committee established under section 301;

["electronic transfer" means transmission by any electronic means;]

"liquidation committee" means, in the case of a winding up by the court, any committee established under section 141 and, in the case of a creditors' voluntary winding up, any committee established under section 101;

"liquidator" includes, in the case of a company being wound up by the court, the official receiver when so acting;

"local bank" means any bank in, or in the neighbourhood of, the insolvency district, or the district in respect of which the court has winding-up jurisdiction, in which the proceedings are taken, or in the locality in which any business of the company or, as the case may be, the bankrupt is carried on;

"local bank account" means, in the case of a winding up by the court, a current account opened with a local bank under regulation 6(2) below and, in the case of a bankruptcy, a current account opened with a local bank under regulation 21(1) below;

"payment instrument" means a cheque or payable order;

"the Rules" means the Insolvency Rules 1986; and

"trustee", subject to regulation 19(2) below, means trustee of a bankrupt's estate including the official receiver when so acting;

and other expressions used in these Regulations and defined by the Rules have the meanings which they bear in the Rules.

(2) A Rule referred to in these Regulations by number means the Rule so numbered in the Rules.

(3) Any application to be made to the Secretary of State or to the Department or anything required to be sent to the Secretary of State or to the Department under these Regulations shall be addressed to the Department of Trade and Industry, The Insolvency Service, PO Box 3690, Birmingham B2 4UY.

(4) Where a regulation makes provision for the use of a form obtainable from the Department, the Department may provide different forms for different cases arising under that regulation.

(5) Subject to regulation 37 below, these Regulations [(except for regulations 3A and 36A)] apply—

(a) to winding-up proceedings commenced on or after 29th December 1986; and

(b) to bankruptcy proceedings where the bankruptcy petition is or was presented on or after that day.

[(6) Regulation 3A applies in any case where a company entered into administration on or after 15th September 2003 other than a case where the company entered into administration by virtue of a petition presented before that date.

(7) Regulation 36A applies in any case where an insolvency practitioner is appointed on or after 1st April 2005.]

[6796]

NOTES

Para (1): definition "bank" substituted by the Financial Services and Markets Act 2000 (Consequential Amendments and Repeals) Order 2001, SI 2001/3649, art 471, as from 1 December 2001; definition "electronic transfer" inserted by the Insolvency (Amendment) Regulations 2000, SI 2000/485, reg 3, Schedule, para 1, as from 31 March 2000.

Para (5): words in square brackets inserted by the Insolvency (Amendment) Regulations 2005, SI 2005/512, regs 4, 5(1), (2), as from 1 April 2005.

Paras (6), (7): added by SI 2005/512, regs 4, 5(1), (3), as from 1 April 2005.

[PART 1A
ADMINISTRATION

3A Disposal of company's records and provision of information to the Secretary of State

(1) The person who was the last administrator of a company which has been dissolved may, at any time after the expiration of a period of one year from the date of dissolution, destroy or otherwise dispose of the books, papers and other records of the company.

(2) An administrator or former administrator shall within 14 days of a request by the Secretary of State give the Secretary of State particulars of any money in his hands or under his control representing unclaimed or undistributed assets of the company or dividends or other sums due to any person as a member or former member of the company.]

[6796A]

NOTES

Inserted, together with the preceding heading, by the Insolvency (Amendment) Regulations 2005, SI 2005/512, regs 4, 6, as from 1 April 2005.

PART 2
WINDING UP

4 Introductory

This Part of these Regulations relates to—

(a) voluntary winding up and
(b) winding up by the court

of companies which the courts in England and Wales have jurisdiction to wind up.

[6797]

PAYMENT INTO AND OUT OF THE INSOLVENCY SERVICES ACCOUNT

5 Payments into the Insolvency Services Account

(1) In the case of a winding up by the court, subject to regulation 6 below, the liquidator shall pay all money received by him in the course of carrying out his functions as such without any deduction into the Insolvency Services Account kept by the Secretary of State with the Bank of England to the credit of the company once every 14 days or forthwith if £5,000 or more has been received.

[(2) In the case of a voluntary winding up, the liquidator may make payments into the Insolvency Services Account to the credit of the company.]

[(3) Every payment of money into the Insolvency Services Account under this regulation shall be—

(a) made through the Bank Giro system; or
(b) sent direct to the Bank of England, Threadneedle Street, London EC2R 8AH by cheque drawn in favour of the "Insolvency Services Account" and crossed "A/c payee only" "Bank of England"; or
(c) made by electronic transfer,

and the liquidator shall on request be given by the Department a receipt for the money so paid.]

(4) Every payment of money [made under sub-paragraph (a) or (b) of paragraph (3) above] shall be accompanied by a form obtainable from the Department for that purpose or by a form that is substantially similar.

[Every payment of money made under sub-paragraph (c) of paragraph (3) above shall specify the name of the liquidator making the payment and the name of the company to whose credit such payment is made.]

(5) Where in a voluntary winding up a liquidator pays any unclaimed dividend into the Insolvency Services Account, he shall at the same time give notice to the Secretary of State, on a form obtainable from the Department or on one that is substantially similar, of the name and address of the person to whom the dividend is payable and the amount of the dividend.

[6798]

NOTES

Para (2): substituted by the Insolvency (Amendment) Regulations 2004, SI 2004/472, reg 2, Schedule, para 1, as from 1 April 2004.

Para (3): substituted by the Insolvency (Amendment) Regulations 2000, SI 2000/485, reg 3, Schedule, para 2, as from 31 March 2000.

Para (4): words in first pair of square brackets substituted, and words in second pair of square brackets added, by SI 2000/485, reg 3, Schedule, para 3, as from 31 March 2000.

6 Local bank account and handling of funds not belonging to the company

(1) This regulation does not apply in the case of a voluntary winding up.

(2) Where the liquidator intends to exercise his power to carry on the business of the company, he may apply to the Secretary of State for authorisation to open a local bank account, and the Secretary of State may authorise him to make his payments into and out of a specified bank, subject to a limit, instead of into and out of the Insolvency Services Account if satisfied that an administrative advantage will be derived from having such an account.

(3) Money received by the liquidator relating to the purpose for which the account was opened may be paid into the local bank account to the credit of the company to which the account relates.

(4) Where the liquidator opens a local bank account pursuant to an authorisation granted under paragraph (2) above, he shall open and maintain the account in the name of the company.

(5) Where money which is not an asset of the company is provided to the liquidator for a specific purpose, it shall be clearly identifiable in a separate account.

(6) The liquidator shall keep proper records, including documentary evidence of all money paid into and out of every local bank account opened and maintained under this regulation.

(7) The liquidator shall pay without deduction any surplus over any limit imposed by an authorisation granted under paragraph (2) above into the Insolvency Services Account in accordance with regulation 5 above as that regulation applies in the case of a winding up by the court.

(8) As soon as the liquidator ceases to carry on the business of the company or vacates office or an authorisation given in pursuance of an application under paragraph (2) above is withdrawn, he shall close the account and pay any balance into the Insolvency Services Account in accordance with regulation 5 above as that regulation applies in the case of a winding up by the court.

[6799]

7 Payment of disbursements etc out of the Insolvency Services Account

[(A1) Paragraphs (1) to (3) of this regulation are subject to paragraph (3A).]

(1) In the case of a winding up by the court, on application to the Department, the liquidator shall be repaid all necessary disbursements made by him, and expenses properly incurred by him, in the course of his administration to the date of his vacation of office out of any money standing to the credit of the company in the Insolvency Services Account.

(2) In the case of a winding up by the court, the liquidator shall on application to the Department obtain payment instruments to the order of the payee for sums which become payable on account of the company for delivery by the liquidator to the persons to whom the payments are to be made.

(3) In the case of a voluntary winding up, where the liquidator requires to make payments out of any money standing to the credit of the company in the Insolvency Services Account in respect of the expenses of the winding up, he shall apply to the Secretary of State who may either authorise payment to the liquidator of the sum required by him, or may direct payment instruments to be issued to the liquidator for delivery by him to the persons to whom the payments are to be made.

[(3A) In respect of an application made by the liquidator under paragraphs (1) to (3) above, the Secretary of State, if requested to do so by the liquidator, may, at his discretion,

(a) make the payment which is the subject of the application to the liquidator by electronic transfer; or

(b) as an alternative to the issue of payment instruments, make payment by electronic transfer to the persons to whom the liquidator would otherwise deliver payment instruments.]

(4) Any application under this regulation shall be made by the liquidator on a form obtainable from the Department for the purpose or on a form that is substantially similar.

(5) In the case of a winding up by the court, on the liquidator vacating office, he shall be repaid by any succeeding liquidator out of any funds available for the purpose any necessary disbursements made by him and any expenses properly incurred by him but not repaid before he vacates office.

[6800]

NOTES

Paras (A1), (3A): inserted by the Insolvency (Amendment) Regulations 2000, SI 2000/485, reg 3, Schedule, paras 4, 5, as from 31 March 2000.

DIVIDENDS TO CREDITORS AND RETURNS OF CAPITAL TO CONTRIBUTORIES OF A COMPANY

8 Payment

[(A1) Paragraphs (1) to (3) of this regulation are subject to paragraph (3A).]

(1) In the case of a winding up by the court, the liquidator shall pay every dividend by payment instruments which shall be prepared by the Department on the application of the liquidator and transmitted to him for distribution amongst the creditors.

(2) In the case of a winding up by the court, the liquidator shall pay every return of capital to contributories by payment instruments which shall be prepared by the Department on application.

(3) In the case of a voluntary winding up, where the liquidator requires to make payments out of any money standing to the credit of the company in the Insolvency Services Account by way of distribution, he shall apply in writing to the Secretary of State who may either authorise payment to the liquidator of the sum required by him, or may direct payment instruments to be issued to the liquidator for delivery by him to the persons to whom the payments are to be made.

[(3A) In respect of an application made by the liquidator under paragraphs (1) to (3) above, the Secretary of State, if requested to do so by the liquidator, may, at his discretion,

(a) as an alternative to the issue of payment instruments, make payment by electronic transfer to the persons to whom the liquidator would otherwise deliver payment instruments; or

(b) make the payment which is the subject of the application to the liquidator by electronic transfer.]

(4) Any application under this regulation for a payment instrument [or payment by electronic transfer] shall be made by the liquidator on a form obtainable from the Department for the purpose or on a form which is substantially similar.

(5) In the case of a winding up by the court, the liquidator shall enter the total amount of every dividend and of every return to contributories that he desires to pay under this regulation in the records to be kept under regulation 10 below in one sum.

(6) On the liquidator vacating office, he shall send to the Department any valid unclaimed or undelivered payment instruments for dividends or returns to contributories after endorsing them with the word "cancelled".

[6801]

NOTES

Paras (A1), (3A): inserted by the Insolvency (Amendment) Regulations 2000, SI 2000/485, reg 3, Schedule, paras 6, 7, as from 31 March 2000.

Para (4): words in square brackets inserted by SI 2000/485, reg 3, Schedule, para 8, as from 31 March 2000.

INVESTMENT OR OTHERWISE HANDLING OF FUNDS IN WINDING UP OF COMPANIES AND PAYMENT OF INTEREST

9—(1) When the cash balance standing to the credit of the company in the account in respect of that company kept by the Secretary of State is in excess of the amount which, in the opinion of the liquidator, is required for the immediate purposes of the winding up and should be invested, he may request the Secretary of State to invest the amount not so required in Government securities, to be placed to the credit of that account for the company's benefit.

(2) When any of the money so invested is, in the opinion of the liquidator, required for the immediate purposes of the winding up, he may request the Secretary of State to raise such sum as may be required by the sale of such of those securities as may be necessary.

(3) In cases where investments have been made at the request of the liquidator in pursuance of paragraph (1) above and additional sums to the amounts so invested, including money received under paragraph (7) below, are paid into the Insolvency Services Account to the credit of the company, a request shall be made to the Secretary of State by the liquidator if it is desired that these additional sums should be invested.

(4) Any request relating to the investment in, or sale of, as the case may be, Treasury Bills made under paragraphs (1), (2) or (3) above shall be made on a form obtainable from the Department or on one that is substantially similar and any request relating to the purchase or sale, as the case may be, of any other type of Government security made under the provisions of those paragraphs shall be made in writing.

(5) Any request made under paragraphs (1), (2) or (3) above shall be sufficient authority to the Secretary of State for the investment or sale as the case may be.

[(6) Subject to paragraphs (6A) and (6B), at any time after 1st April 2004 whenever there are any monies standing to the credit of the company in the Insolvency Services Account the company shall be entitled to interest on those monies at the rate of 4.25 per cent per annum.

PART IV STATUTORY INSTRUMENTS

(6A) Interest shall cease to accrue pursuant to paragraph (6) from the date of receipt by the Secretary of State of a notice in writing from the liquidator that in the opinion of the liquidator it is necessary or expedient in order to facilitate the conclusion of the winding up that interest should cease to accrue but interest shall start to accrue again pursuant to paragraph (6) where the liquidator gives a further notice in writing to the Secretary of State requesting that interest should start to accrue again.

(6B) The Secretary of State may by notice published in the London Gazette vary the rate of interest prescribed by paragraph (6) and such variation shall have effect from the day after the date of publication of the notice in the London Gazette or such later date as may be specified in the notice.]

(7) All money received in respect of investments and interest earned under this regulation shall be paid into the Insolvency Services Account to the credit of the company.

(8) In addition to the application of paragraphs (1) to (7) above, in a voluntary winding up—

(a) any money invested or deposited at interest by the liquidator shall be deemed to be money under his control, and when such money forms part of the balance of funds in his hands or under his control relating to the company required to be paid into the Insolvency Services Account under regulation 5 above, the liquidator shall realise the investment or withdraw the deposit and shall pay the proceeds into that Account: Provided that where the money is invested in Government securities, such securities may, with the permission of the Secretary of State, be transferred to the control of the Secretary of State instead of being forthwith realised and the proceeds paid into the Insolvency Services Account; and

(b) where any of the money represented by securities transferred to the control of the Secretary of State pursuant to sub-paragraph (a) above is, in the opinion of the liquidator, required for the immediate purposes of the winding up he may request the Secretary of State to raise such sums as may be required by the sale of such of those securities as may be necessary and such request shall be sufficient authority to the Secretary of State for the sale and the Secretary of State shall pay the proceeds of the realisation into the Insolvency Services Account in accordance with paragraph (7) above and deal with them in the same way as other money paid into that Account may be dealt with.

[6802]

NOTES

Paras (6), (6A), (6B): substituted, for original para (6), by the Insolvency (Amendment) Regulations 2004, SI 2004/472, reg 2, Schedule, para 2, as from 1 April 2004, subject to transitional provisions providing that where a notice that interest should cease is given pursuant to para (6)(a) as it stood immediately before that date, it shall be treated as having been given for the purposes of para (6A) above.

Treasury bills: a reference to a Treasury bill in this regulation includes a reference to uncertificated units of eligible Treasury bills; see the Uncertificated Securities (Amendment) (Eligible Debt Securities) Regulations 2003, SI 2003/1633, reg 15, Sch 2, para 2(h).

The current rate of interest for the purpose of para (6) above is 6.75%; see the London Gazette, 17 May 2007.

RECORDS TO BE MAINTAINED BY LIQUIDATORS AND THE PROVISION OF INFORMATION

10 Financial records

(1) This regulation does not apply in the case of a members' voluntary winding up.

(2) The liquidator shall prepare and keep—

(a) separate financial records in respect of each company; and

(b) such other financial records as are required to explain the receipts and payments entered in the records described in sub-paragraph (a) above or regulation 12(2) below, including an explanation of the source of any receipts and the destination of any payments;

and shall, subject to regulation 12(2) below as to trading accounts, from day to day enter in those records all the receipts and payments (including, in the case of a voluntary winding up, those relating to the Insolvency Services Account) made by him.

(3) In the case of a winding up by the court, the liquidator shall obtain and keep bank statements relating to any local bank account in the name of the company.

(4) The liquidator shall submit financial records to the liquidation committee when required for inspection.

(5) In the case of a winding up by the court, if the liquidation committee is not satisfied with the contents of the financial records submitted under paragraph (4) above it may so inform the Secretary of State, giving the reasons for its dissatisfaction, and the Secretary of State may take such action as he thinks fit.

[6803]

11 Provision of information by liquidator

(1) In the case of a winding up by the court, the liquidator shall, within 14 days of the receipt of a request for a statement of his receipts and payments as liquidator from any creditor, contributory or director of the company, supply free of charge to the person making the request, a statement of his receipts and payments as liquidator during the period of one year ending on the most recent anniversary of his becoming liquidator which preceded the request.

(2) In the case of a voluntary winding up, the liquidator shall, on request from any creditor, contributory or director of the company for a copy of a statement for any period, including future periods, sent to the registrar of companies under section 192, send such copy free of charge to the person making the request and the copy of the statement shall be sent within 14 days of the liquidator sending the statement to the registrar or the receipt of the request whichever is the later.

[6804]

12 Liquidator carrying on business

(1) This regulation does not apply in the case of a members' voluntary winding up.

(2) Where the liquidator carries on any business of the company, he shall—

(a) keep a separate and distinct account of the trading, including, where appropriate, in the case of a winding up by the court, particulars of all local bank account transactions; and

(b) incorporate in the financial records required to be kept under regulation 10 above the total weekly amounts of the receipts and payments made by him in relation to the account kept under sub-paragraph (a) above.

[6805]

13 Retention and delivery of records

(1) All records kept by the liquidator under regulations 10 and 12(2) and any such records received by him from a predecessor in that office shall be retained by him for a period of 6 years following—

(a) his vacation of office, or

(b) in the case of the official receiver, his release as liquidator under section 174,

unless he delivers them to another liquidator who succeeds him in office.

(2) Where the liquidator is succeeded in office by another liquidator, the records referred to in paragraph (1) above shall be delivered to that successor forthwith, unless, in the case of a winding up by the court, the winding up is for practical purposes complete and the successor is the official receiver, in which case the records are only to be delivered to the official receiver if the latter so requests.

[6806]

14 Provision of accounts by liquidator and audit of accounts

(1) The liquidator shall, if required by the Secretary of State at any time, send to the Secretary of State an account in relation to the company of the liquidator's receipts and payments covering such period as the Secretary of State may direct and such account shall, if so required by the Secretary of State, be certified by the liquidator.

(2) Where the liquidator in a winding up by the court vacates office prior to the holding of the final general meeting of creditors under section 146, he shall within 14 days of vacating office send to the Secretary of State an account of his receipts and payments as liquidator for any period not covered by an account previously so sent by him or if no such account has been sent, an account of his receipts and payments in respect of the whole period of his office.

(3) In the case of a winding up by the court, where—

(a) a final general meeting of creditors has been held pursuant to section 146, or

(b) a final general meeting is deemed to have been held by virtue of Rule 4.125(5),

the liquidator shall send to the Secretary of State, in case (a), within 14 days of the holding of the final general meeting of creditors and, in case (b), within 14 days of his report to the court pursuant to Rule 4.125(5), an account of his receipts and payments as liquidator which are not covered by any previous account so sent by him, or if no such account has been sent an account of his receipts and payments in respect of the whole period of his office.

(4) In the case of a winding up by the court, where a statement of affairs has been submitted under the Act, any account sent under this regulation shall be accompanied by a summary of that statement of affairs and shall show the amount of any assets realised and explain the reasons for any non-realisation of any assets not realised.

(5) In the case of a winding up by the court, where a statement of affairs has not been submitted under the Act, any account sent under this regulation shall be accompanied by a summary of all known assets and their estimated values and shall show the amounts actually realised and explain the reasons for any non-realisation of any assets not realised.

(6) Any account sent to the Secretary of State shall, if he so requires, be audited, but whether or not the Secretary of State requires the account to be audited, the liquidator shall send to the Secretary of State on demand any documents (including vouchers and bank statements) and any information relating to the account.

[6807]

15 Production and inspection of records

(1) The liquidator shall produce on demand to the Secretary of State, and allow him to inspect, any accounts, books and other records kept by him (including any passed to him by a predecessor in office), and this duty to produce and allow inspection shall extend—

(a) to producing and allowing inspection at the premises of the liquidator; and

(b) to producing and allowing inspection of any financial records of the kind described in regulation 10(2)(b) above prepared by the liquidator (or any predecessor in office of his) before 24th October 1994 and kept by the liquidator;

and any such demand may—

(i) require the liquidator to produce any such accounts, books or other records to the Secretary of State, and allow him to inspect them—

(a) at the same time as any account is sent to the Secretary of State under regulation 14 above; or

(b) at any time after such account is sent to the Secretary of State;

whether or not the Secretary of State requires the account to be audited; or

(ii) where it is made for the purpose of ascertaining whether the provisions of these Regulations relating to the handling of money received by the liquidator in the course of carrying out his functions have been or are likely to be complied with, be made at any time, whether or not an account has been sent or should have been sent to the Secretary of State under regulation 14 above and whether or not the Secretary of State has required any account to be audited.

(2) The liquidator shall allow the Secretary of State on demand to remove and take copies of any accounts, books and other records kept by the liquidator (including any passed to him by a predecessor in office), whether or not they are kept at the premises of the liquidator.

[6808]

16 Disposal of company's books, papers and other records

(1) The liquidator in a winding up by the court, on the authorisation of the official receiver, during his tenure of office or on vacating office, or the official receiver while acting as liquidator, may at any time sell, destroy or otherwise dispose of the books, papers and other records of the company.

(2) In the case of a voluntary winding up, the person who was the last liquidator of a company which has been dissolved may, at any time after the expiration of a period of one year from the date of dissolution, destroy or otherwise dispose of the books, papers and other records of the company.

[6809]

17 Voluntary liquidator to provide information to Secretary of State

(1) In the case of a voluntary winding up, a liquidator or former liquidator, whether the winding up has been concluded under Rule 4.223 or not, shall, within 14 days of a request by the Secretary of State, give the Secretary of State particulars of any money in his hands or under his control representing unclaimed or undistributed assets of the company or dividends or other sums due to any person as a member or former member of the company and such other particulars as the Secretary of State may require for the purpose of ascertaining or getting in any money payable into the Insolvency Services Account.

(2) The particulars referred to in paragraph (1) above shall, if the Secretary of State so requires, be certified by the liquidator, or former liquidator, as the case may be.

[6810]

18 Payment of unclaimed or undistributed assets, dividends or other money on dissolution of company

In the case of a company which has been dissolved, notwithstanding anything in these Regulations, any money in the hands of any or any former liquidator at the date of dissolution of the company or his earlier vacation of office, representing unclaimed or undistributed assets of the company or dividends or held by the company in trust in respect of dividends or other sums due to any person as a member or former member of the company, shall forthwith be paid by him into the Insolvency Services Account.

[6811]

PART 3
BANKRUPTCY

19 Introductory

(1) This Part of these Regulations relates to bankruptcy and extends to England and Wales only.

(2) In addition to the application of the provisions of this Part to the official receiver when acting as trustee, the provisions of this Part (other than regulations 30 and 31) shall also apply to him when acting as receiver or manager under section 287 and the term "trustee" shall be construed accordingly.

[6812]

PAYMENTS INTO AND OUT OF THE INSOLVENCY SERVICES ACCOUNT

20 Payments into the Insolvency Services Account

(1) Subject to regulation 21 below, the trustee shall pay all money received by him in the course of carrying out his functions as such without any deduction into the Insolvency Services Account kept by the Secretary of State with the Bank of England to the credit of the bankrupt once every 14 days or forthwith if £5,000 or more has been received.

[(2) Every payment of money into the Insolvency Services Account under this regulation shall be—

- (a) made through the Bank Giro system; or
- (b) sent direct to the Bank of England, Threadneedle Street, London EC2R 8AH by cheque drawn in favour of the "Insolvency Services Account" and crossed "A/c payee only" "Bank of England"; or
- (c) made by electronic transfer,

and the trustee shall on request be given by the Department a receipt for the money so paid.]

(3) Every payment of money [made under sub-paragraph (a) or (b) of paragraph (2) above] shall be accompanied by a form obtainable from the Department for that purpose or by a form that is substantially similar.

[Every payment of money made under sub-paragraph (c) of paragraph (2) above shall specify the name of the trustee making the payment and the name of the bankrupt to whose credit such payment is made.]

[6813]

NOTES

Para (2): substituted by the Insolvency (Amendment) Regulations 2000, SI 2000/485, reg 3, Schedule, para 9, as from 31 March 2000.

PART IV STATUTORY INSTRUMENTS

Para (3): words in first pair of square brackets substituted, and words in second pair of square brackets added, by SI 2000/485, reg 3, Schedule, para 10, as from 31 March 2000.

21 Local bank account and handling of funds not forming part of the bankrupt's estate

(1) Where the trustee intends to exercise his power to carry on the business of the bankrupt, he may apply to the Secretary of State for authorisation to open a local bank account, and the Secretary of State may authorise him to make his payments into and out of a specified bank, subject to a limit, instead of into and out of the Insolvency Services Account if satisfied that an administrative advantage will be derived from having such an account.

(2) Money received by the trustee relating to the purpose for which the account was opened may be paid into the local bank account to the credit of the bankrupt to whom the account relates.

(3) Where the trustee opens a local bank account pursuant to an authorisation granted under paragraph (1) above he shall open and maintain the account in the name of the bankrupt.

(4) Where money which does not form part of the bankrupt's estate is provided to the trustee for a specific purpose it shall be clearly identifiable in a separate account.

(5) The trustee shall keep proper records, including documentary evidence of all money paid into and out of every local bank account opened and maintained under this regulation.

(6) The trustee shall pay without deduction any surplus over any limit imposed by an authorisation granted under paragraph (1) above into the Insolvency Services Account in accordance with regulation 20(1) above.

(7) As soon as the trustee ceases to carry on the business of the bankrupt or vacates office or an authorisation given in pursuance of an application under paragraph (1) above is withdrawn, he shall close the account and pay any balance into the Insolvency Services Account in accordance with regulation 20(1) above.

[6814]

22 Payment of disbursements etc out of the Insolvency Services Account

[(A1) Paragraphs (1) and (2) of this regulation are subject to paragraph (2A).]

(1) On application to the Department, the trustee shall be repaid all necessary disbursements made by him, and expenses properly incurred by him, in the course of his administration to the date of his vacation of office out of any money standing to the credit of the bankrupt in the Insolvency Services Account.

(2) The trustee shall on application to the Department obtain payment instruments to the order of the payee for sums which become payable on account of the bankrupt for delivery by the trustee to the persons to whom the payments are to be made.

[(2A) In respect of an application made by the trustee under paragraph (1) or (2) above, the Secretary of State, if requested to do so by the trustee, may, at his discretion,

(a) make the payment which is the subject of the application to the trustee by electronic transfer; or

(b) as an alternative to the issue of payment instruments, make payment by electronic transfer to the persons to whom the trustee would otherwise deliver payment instruments.]

(3) Any application under this regulation shall be made on a form obtainable from the Department or on one that is substantially similar.

(4) On the trustee vacating office, he shall be repaid by any succeeding trustee out of any funds available for the purpose any necessary disbursements made by him and any expenses properly incurred by him but not repaid before he vacates office.

[6815]

NOTES

Paras (A1), (2A): inserted by the Insolvency (Amendment) Regulations 2000, SI 2000/485, reg 3, Schedule, paras 11, 12, as from 31 March 2000.

DIVIDENDS TO CREDITORS

23 Payment

(1) [Subject to paragraph (1A),] the trustee shall pay every dividend by payment instruments which shall be prepared by the Department on the application of the trustee and transmitted to him for distribution amongst the creditors.

[(1A) In respect of an application made by the trustee under paragraph (1) above, the Secretary of State, if requested to do so by the trustee, may, at his discretion, as an alternative to the issue of payment instruments, make payment by electronic transfer to the persons to whom the trustee would otherwise deliver payment instruments.]

(2) Any application under this regulation for a payment instrument [or payment by electronic transfer] shall be made by the trustee on a form obtainable from the Department for the purpose or on a form which is substantially similar.

(3) The trustee shall enter the total amount of every dividend that he desires to pay under this regulation in the records to be kept under regulation 24 below in one sum.

(4) On the trustee vacating office, he shall send to the Department any valid unclaimed or undelivered payment instruments for dividends after endorsing them with the word "cancelled".

[6816]

NOTES

Paras (1), (2): words in square brackets inserted by the Insolvency (Amendment) Regulations 2000, SI 2000/485, reg 3, Schedule, paras 13, 15, as from 31 March 2000.

Para (1A): inserted by SI 2000/485, reg 3, Schedule, para 14, as from 31 March 2000.

[23A Investment or otherwise handling of funds in bankruptcy and payment of interest

(1) When the cash balance standing to the credit of the bankrupt in the account in respect of that bankrupt kept by the Secretary of State is in excess of the amount which, in the opinion of the trustee, is required for the immediate purposes of the bankruptcy and should be invested, he may request the Secretary of State to invest the amount not so required in Government securities, to be placed to the credit of that account for the benefit of the bankrupt.

(2) When any of the money so invested is, in the opinion of the trustee, required for the immediate purposes of the bankruptcy, he may request the Secretary of State to raise such sum as may be required by the sale of such of those securities as may be necessary.

(3) In cases where investments have been made at the request of the trustee in pursuance of paragraph (1) above and additional sums to the amounts so invested, including money received under paragraph (7) below, are paid into the Insolvency Services Account to the credit of the bankrupt, a request shall be made to the Secretary of State by the trustee if it is desired that these additional funds should be invested.

(4) Any request relating to the investment in, or sale of, as the case may be, Treasury Bills under paragraphs (1), (2) or (3) above shall be made on a form obtainable from the Department or on one that is substantially similar and any request relating to the purchase or sale, as the case may be, of any other type of Government security made under the provisions of those paragraphs shall be made in writing.

(5) Any request made under paragraphs (1), (2) or (3) above shall be sufficient authority to the Secretary of State for the investment or sale as the case may be.

[(6) Subject to paragraphs (6A) and (6B), at any time after 1st April 2004 whenever there are any monies standing to the credit of the estate of the bankrupt in the Insolvency Services Account the estate shall be entitled to interest on those monies at the rate of 4.25 per cent per annum.

(6A) Interest shall cease to accrue pursuant to paragraph (6) from the date of receipt by the Secretary of State of a notice in writing from the trustee that in the opinion of the trustee it is necessary or expedient in order to facilitate the conclusion of the bankruptcy that interest should cease to accrue but interest shall start to accrue again pursuant to paragraph (6) where the trustee gives a further notice in writing to the Secretary of State requesting that interest should start to accrue again.

(6B) The Secretary of State may by notice published in the London Gazette vary the rate of interest prescribed by paragraph (6) and such variation shall have effect from the day after the date of publication of the notice in the London Gazette or such later date as may be specified in the notice.]

(7) All money received in respect of investments and interest earned under this regulation shall be paid into the Insolvency Services Account to the credit of the bankrupt.]

[6817]

NOTES

Inserted by the Insolvency (Amendment) Regulations 2001, SI 2001/762, reg 3, Schedule, as from 2 April 2001.

Paras (6), (6A), (6B): substituted, for original para (6), by the Insolvency (Amendment) Regulations 2004, SI 2004/472, reg 2, Schedule, para 3, as from 1 April 2004, subject to transitional provisions which provide that where a notice that interest should cease is given pursuant to para (6)(a) as it stood immediately before that date, it shall be treated as having been given for the purposes of para (6A) above.

Treasury bills: a reference to a Treasury bill in this regulation includes a reference to uncertificated units of eligible Treasury bills; see the Uncertificated Securities (Amendment) (Eligible Debt Securities) Regulations 2003, SI 2003/1633, reg 15, Sch 2, para 2(h).

The current rate of interest for the purpose of para (6) above is 6.75%; see the London Gazette, 17 May 2007.

RECORDS TO BE MAINTAINED BY TRUSTEES AND THE PROVISION OF INFORMATION

24 Financial records

(1) The trustee shall prepare and keep—

- (a) separate financial records in respect of each bankrupt; and
- (b) such other financial records as are required to explain the receipts and payments entered in the records described in sub-paragraph (a) above or regulation 26 below, including an explanation of the source of any receipts and the destination of any payments;

and shall, subject to regulation 26 below as to trading accounts, from day to day enter in those records all the receipts and payments made by him.

(2) The trustee shall obtain and keep bank statements relating to any local bank account in the name of the bankrupt.

(3) The trustee shall submit financial records to the creditors' committee when required for inspection.

(4) If the creditors' committee is not satisfied with the contents of the financial records submitted under paragraph (3) above it may so inform the Secretary of State, giving the reasons for its dissatisfaction and the Secretary of State may take such action as he thinks fit.

[6818]

25 Provision of information by trustee

The trustee shall, within 14 days of the receipt of a request from any creditor or the bankrupt for a statement of his receipts and payments as trustee, supply free of charge to the person making the request, a statement of his receipts and payments as trustee during the period of one year ending on the most recent anniversary of his becoming trustee which preceded the request.

[6819]

26 Trustee carrying on business

Subject to paragraph (2) below, where the trustee carries on any business of the bankrupt, he shall—

- (a) keep a separate and distinct account of the trading, including, where appropriate, particulars of all local bank account transactions; and
- (b) incorporate in the financial records required to be kept under regulation 24 above the total weekly amounts of the receipts and payments made by him in relation to the account kept under paragraph (a) above.

[6820]

27 Retention and delivery of records

(1) All records kept by the trustee under regulations 24 and 26 and any such records received by him from a predecessor in that office shall be retained by him for a period of 6 years following—

(a) his vacation of office, or

(b) in the case of the official receiver, his release as trustee under section 299,

unless he delivers them to another trustee who succeeds him in office.

(2) Where the trustee is succeeded in office by another trustee, the records referred to in paragraph (1) above shall be delivered to that successor forthwith, unless the bankruptcy is for practical purposes complete and the successor is the official receiver, in which case the records are only to be delivered to the official receiver if the latter so requests.

[6821]

28 Provision of accounts by trustee and audit of accounts

(1) The trustee shall, if required by the Secretary of State at any time, send to the Secretary of State an account of his receipts and payments as trustee of the bankrupt covering such period as the Secretary of State may direct and such account shall, if so required by the Secretary of State, be certified by the trustee.

(2) Where the trustee vacates office prior to the holding of the final general meeting of creditors under section 331, he shall within 14 days of vacating office send to the Secretary of State an account of his receipts and payments as trustee for any period not covered by an account previously so sent by him, or if no such account has been sent, an account of his receipts and payments in respect of the whole period of his office.

(3) Where—

(a) a final general meeting of creditors has been held pursuant to section 331, or

(b) a final general meeting is deemed to have been held by virtue of Rule 6.137(5),

the trustee shall send to the Secretary of State, in case (a), within 14 days of the holding of the final general meeting of creditors and, in case (b), within 14 days of his report to the court pursuant to Rule 6.137(5), an account of his receipts and payments as trustee which are not covered by any previous account so sent by him, or if no such account has been sent, an account of his receipts and payments in respect of the whole period of his office.

(4) Where a statement of affairs has been submitted under the Act, any account sent under this regulation shall be accompanied by a summary of that statement of affairs and shall show the amount of any assets realised and explain the reasons for any non-realisation of any assets not realised.

(5) Where a statement of affairs has not been submitted under the Act, any account sent under this regulation shall be accompanied by a summary of all known assets and their estimated values and shall show the amounts actually realised and explain the reasons for any non-realisation of any assets not realised.

(6) Any account sent to the Secretary of State shall, if he so requires, be audited, but whether or not the Secretary of State requires the account to be audited, the trustee shall send to the Secretary of State on demand any documents (including vouchers and bank statements) and any information relating to the account.

[6822]

29 Production and inspection of records

(1) The trustee shall produce on demand to the Secretary of State, and allow him to inspect, any accounts, books and other records kept by him (including any passed to him by a predecessor in office), and this duty to produce and allow inspection shall extend—

(a) to producing and allowing inspection at the premises of the trustee; and

(b) to producing and allowing inspection of any financial records of the kind described in regulation 24(1)(b) above prepared by the trustee before 24th October 1994 and kept by him;

and any such demand may—

(i) require the trustee to produce any such accounts, books or other records to the Secretary of State, and allow him to inspect them—

(a) at the same time as any account is sent to the Secretary of State under regulation 28 above; or

(b) at any time after such account is sent to the Secretary of State;

whether or not the Secretary of State requires the account to be audited; or

(ii) where it is made for the purpose of ascertaining whether the provisions of these Regulations relating to the handling of money received by the trustee in the course of carrying out his functions have been or are likely to be complied with, be made at any time, whether or not an account has been sent or should have been sent to the Secretary of State under regulation 28 above and whether or not the Secretary of State has required any account to be audited.

(2) The trustee shall allow the Secretary of State on demand to remove and take copies of any accounts, books and other records kept by the trustee (including any passed to him by a predecessor in office), whether or not they are kept at the premises of the trustee.

[6823]

30 Disposal of bankrupt's books, papers and other records

The trustee, on the authorisation of the official receiver, during his tenure of office or on vacating office, or the official receiver while acting as trustee, may at any time sell, destroy or otherwise dispose of the books, papers and other records of the bankrupt.

[6824]

31 Payment of unclaimed or undistributed assets, dividends or other money

Notwithstanding anything in these Regulations, any money—

(a) in the hands of the trustee at the date of his vacation of office, or

(b) which comes into the hands of any former trustee at any time after his vacation of office,

representing, in either case, unclaimed or undistributed assets of the bankrupt or dividends, shall forthwith be paid by him into the Insolvency Services Account.

[6825]

PART 4
CLAIMING MONEY PAID INTO THE INSOLVENCY SERVICES ACCOUNT

32—(1) Any person claiming to be entitled to any money paid into the Insolvency Services Account may apply to the Secretary of State for payment and shall provide such evidence of his claim as the Secretary of State may require.

(2) Any person dissatisfied with the decision of the Secretary of State in respect of his claim made under this regulation may appeal to the court.

[6826]–[6828]

PART 5
REMUNERATION OF OFFICIAL RECEIVER

33, 34 (*Revoked by the Insolvency (Amendment) Regulations 2004, SI 2004/472, reg 2, Schedule, para 4, as from 1 April 2004.*)

[35 Official receiver's general remuneration while acting as interim receiver, provisional liquidator, liquidator or trustee

(1) The official receiver shall be entitled to remuneration calculated in accordance with the applicable hourly rates set out in paragraph (2) for services provided by him (or any of his officers) in relation to—

(a) a distribution made by him when acting as liquidator or trustee to creditors (including preferential or secured creditors or both such classes of creditor);

(b) the realisation of assets on behalf of the holder of a fixed or floating charge or both types of those charges;

(c) the supervision of a special manager;

(d) the performance by him of any functions where he acts as provisional liquidator; or

(e) the performance by him of any functions where he acts as an interim receiver.

(2) The applicable hourly rates referred to in paragraph (1) are—

(a) in relation to the official receiver of the London insolvency district, those set out in Table 2 in Schedule 2; and

(b) in relation to any other official receiver, those set out in Table 3 in Schedule 2.]

[6829]–[6830]

NOTES

Substituted by the Insolvency (Amendment) Regulations 2005, SI 2005/512, regs 4, 7, as from 1 April 2005, subject to transitional provisions as noted below.

Transitional provisions: the Insolvency (Amendment) Regulations 2005, SI 2005/512, reg 3 provides as follows—

"3 Transitional provisions

The substitution of regulation 35 by regulation 7 of these Regulations only applies in relation to services provided by the official receiver (or any of his officers) in relation to—

(a) a company in respect of which a winding-up order is made on or after the commencement date;

(b) a bankruptcy where the bankruptcy order is made on or after the commencement date; or

(c) his appointment as an interim receiver or provisional liquidator where he is appointed on or after the commencement date.".

36 (*Revoked by the Insolvency (Amendment) Regulations 2004, SI 2004/472, reg 2, Schedule, para 4, as from 1 April 2004.*)

[PART 5A
INFORMATION ABOUT TIME SPENT ON A CASE TO BE PROVIDED BY INSOLVENCY PRACTITIONER TO CREDITORS ETC

36A—(1) Subject as set out in this regulation, in respect of any case in which he acts, an insolvency practitioner shall on request in writing made by any person mentioned in paragraph (2), supply free of charge to that person a statement of the kind described in paragraph (3).

(2) The persons referred to in paragraph (1) are—

(a) any creditor in the case;

(b) where the case relates to a company, any director or contributory of that company; and

(c) where the case relates to an individual, that individual.

(3) The statement referred to in paragraph (1) shall comprise in relation to the period beginning with the date of the insolvency practitioner's appointment and ending with the relevant date the following details—

(a) the total number of hours spent on the case by the insolvency practitioner and any staff assigned to the case during that period;

(b) for each grade of individual so engaged, the average hourly rate at which any work carried out by individuals in that grade is charged; and

(c) the number of hours spent by each grade of staff during that period.

(4) In relation to paragraph (3) the "relevant date" means the date next before the date of the making of the request on which the insolvency practitioner has completed any period in office which is a multiple of six months or, where the insolvency practitioner has vacated office, the date that he vacated office.

(5) Where an insolvency practitioner has vacated office, an obligation to provide information under this regulation shall only arise in relation to a request that is made within 2 years of the date he vacates office.

(6) Any statement required to be provided to any person under this regulation shall be supplied within 28 days of the date of the receipt of the request by the insolvency practitioner.

(7) In this regulation the expression "insolvency practitioner" shall be construed in accordance with section 388 of the Insolvency Act 1986.]

[6830A]

NOTES

Inserted, together with the preceding heading, by the Insolvency (Amendment) Regulations 2005, SI 2005/512, regs 4, 8, as from 1 April 2005.

PART 6
TRANSITIONAL AND SAVING PROVISIONS

37 The Regulations shall have effect subject to the transitional and saving provisions set out in Schedule 3 to these Regulations.

[6831]

SCHEDULES

(Sch 1 revokes the Insolvency Regulations 1986, SI 1986/1994, and the amending SI 1987/1959, SI 1988/1739, and SI 1991/380.)

SCHEDULE 2

Regulations 33 to 36

...

[TABLE 2—LONDON RATES

Grade according to the Insolvency Service grading structure/Status of Official	*Total hourly rate £*
D2/Official Receiver	65
C2/Deputy or Assistant Official Receiver	55
C1/Senior Examiner	50
B3/Examiner	40
B2/Administrator	40
B1/Examiner	35
B1/Administrator	40
A2/Administrator	35
A1/Administrator	30]

[TABLE 3—PROVINCIAL RATES

Grade according to the Insolvency Service grading structure /Status of Official	*Total hourly rate £*
D2/Official Receiver	60
C2/Deputy or Assistant Official Receiver	50
C1/Senior Examiner	45
B3/Examiner	40
B2/Administrator	37
B1/Examiner	33
B1/Administrator	36
A2/Administrator	31
A1/Administrator	27]

[6832]

NOTES

Table 1: revoked by the Insolvency (Amendment) Regulations 2004, SI 2004/472, reg 2, Schedule, para 6, as from 1 April 2004.

Tables 2, 3: substituted by SI 2004/472, reg 2, Schedule, para 7, as from 1 April 2004.

SCHEDULE 3

Regulation 37

1 Interpretation

In this Schedule the expression "the former Regulations" means the Insolvency Regulations 1986 as amended by the Insolvency (Amendment) Regulations 1987, the Insolvency (Amendment) Regulations 1988 and the Insolvency (Amendment) Regulations 1991.

2 Requests pursuant to regulation 13(1) of the former Regulations

Any request made pursuant to regulation 13(1) of the former Regulations which has not been complied with prior to 24th October 1994 shall be treated, in the case of a company that is being wound up by the court, as a request made pursuant to regulation 11(1) of these Regulations and, in the case of a bankruptcy, as a request made pursuant to regulation 25 of these Regulations and in each case the request shall be treated as if it had been made on 24th October 1994.

3 Things done under the provisions of the former Regulations

So far as anything done under, or for the purposes of, any provision of the former Regulations could have been done under, or for the purposes of, the corresponding provision of these Regulations, it is not invalidated by the revocation of that provision but has effect as if done under, or for the purposes of, the corresponding provision.

4 Time periods

Where any period of time specified in a provision of the former Regulations is current immediately before 24th October 1994, these Regulations have effect as if the corresponding provision of these Regulations had been in force when the period began to run; and (without prejudice to the foregoing) any period of time so specified and current is deemed for the purposes of these Regulations—

(a) to run from the date or event from which it was running immediately before 24th October 1994, and

(b) to expire whenever it would have expired if these Regulations had not been made;

and any rights, obligations, requirements, powers or duties dependent on the beginning, duration or end of such period as above-mentioned shall be under these Regulations as they were or would have been under the former Regulations.

5 References to other provisions

Where in any provision of these Regulations there is reference to another provision of these Regulations, and the first-mentioned provision operates, or is capable of operating, in relation to things done or omitted, or events occurring or not occurring, in the past (including in particular past acts of compliance with the former Regulations), the reference to that other provision is to be read as including a reference to the corresponding provision of the former Regulations.

6 Provisions of Schedule to be without prejudice to the operation of sections 16 and 17 of the Interpretation Act 1978

The provisions of this Schedule are to be without prejudice to the operation of sections 16 and 17 of the Interpretation Act 1978 (saving from, and effect of, repeals) as they are applied by section 23 of that Act.

7 Meaning of "corresponding provision"

(1) A provision in the former Regulations, except regulation 13(1) of those Regulations, is to be regarded as the corresponding provision of a provision in these Regulations notwithstanding any modifications made to the provision as it appears in these Regulations.

(2) Without prejudice to the generality of the term "corresponding provision" the following table shall, subject to sub-paragraph (3) below, have effect in the interpretation of that expression with a provision of these Regulations listed in the left hand column being regarded as the corresponding provision of a provision of the former Regulations listed opposite it in the right hand column and that latter provision being regarded as the corresponding provision of the first-mentioned provision—

TABLE

Provision in these Regulations	*Provision in the former Regulations*
5(1), 5(3), 5(4)	4
5(2), 5(3), 5(4)	24
6	6
7(1), 7(2), 7(4), 7(5)	5
7(3), 7(4)	25
8(1), 8(2), 8(4), 8(5), 8(6)	15
8(3), 8(4)	25
9	18, 34
10	9, 27
11(2)	31
12	10, 28
13	10A, 28A
15	12A, 30A
16(1)	14
16(2)	32
17	35
18	16, 33
20	4
21	6
22	5
23	15
24	9
26	10
27	10A
29	12A
30	14
31	16A
32	17, 33
33, Table 1 in Schedule 2	19
35, Tables 2 and 3 in Schedule 2	20
36, Table 1 in Schedule 2	22

(3) Where a provision of the former Regulations is expressed in the Table in sub-paragraph (2) above to be the corresponding provision of a provision in these Regulations and the provision in the former Regulations was capable of applying to other proceedings in addition to those to which the provision in these Regulations is capable of applying, the provision in the former Regulations shall be construed as the corresponding provision of the provision in these Regulations only to the extent that they are both capable of applying to the same type of proceedings.

[6833]–[6835]

CONTRACTING OUT (FUNCTIONS IN RELATION TO THE REGISTRATION OF COMPANIES) ORDER 1995

(SI 1995/1013)

NOTES

Made: 4 April 1995.

Authority: Deregulation and Contracting Out Act 1994, s 69.

Commencement: 5 April 1995 (in part); 1 July 1995 (otherwise); see art 1(2), (3) at **[6836]**. Where any provision in this work (including any inserted or substituted provision) came into force for all purposes on or before 1 July 2005, commencement information is not noted at provision level.

This Order is reproduced as amended by: the Financial Services and Markets Act 2000 (Consequential Amendments and Repeals) Order 2001, SI 2001/3649.

ARRANGEMENT OF ARTICLES

SCHEDULES

1 Citation and Commencement

(1) This Order may be cited as the Contracting Out (Functions in relation to the Registration of Companies) Order 1995.

(2) Save as provided in paragraph (3) below, this Order shall come into force on the day after the day on which it is made.

(3) This Order shall come into force in relation to any functions conferred by or under sections 652A to F of the Companies Act 1985 (striking off register of non-trading private companies) immediately after those sections come into force.

[6836]

2 Interpretation

(1) In this Order—

"the Act" means the Companies Act 1985;

"the Regulations" mean the European Economic Interest Grouping Regulations 1989; and

"EEIG" means a European Economic Interest Grouping as defined in regulation 2(1) of the Regulations.

(2) Any expression used in the Act, if used in this Order, bears the same meaning as it bears in the Act unless the context otherwise requires.

[6837]

3 Contracting out of functions of the registrar in relation to England and Wales

Any function of the registrar of companies for England and Wales which is listed in Schedule 1 to this Order may be exercised by, or by employees of, such person (if any) as may be authorised in that behalf by the registrar of companies for England and Wales.

[6838]

4 Contracting out of functions of the registrar in relation to Scotland

(1) Subject to paragraph (2) below, any function of the registrar of companies for Scotland which is conferred by or under any enactment may be exercised by, or by employees of, such person (if any) as may be authorised in that behalf by the registrar of companies for Scotland.

PART IV
STATUTORY INSTRUMENTS

(2) Paragraph (1) above does not apply to the functions listed in Schedule 2 to this Order.
[6839]

5 Contracting out of functions of the Secretary of State

Any function of the Secretary of State which is listed in Schedule 3 to this Order may be exercised by, or by employees of, such person (if any) as may be authorised in that behalf by the Secretary of State.

[6840]

SCHEDULES

SCHEDULE 1
FUNCTIONS OF THE REGISTRAR OF COMPANIES FOR ENGLAND AND WALES ENABLED TO BE CONTRACTED OUT

Article 3

1. Any function of receiving any return, account or other document required to be filed with, delivered or sent, or notice of any matter required to be given, to the registrar which is conferred by or under any enactment.

2. Any functions in relation to—
   (a) the incorporation of companies and the change of name of companies by or under Chapters I and II of Part I of the Act (company formation; company names);
   (b) the re-registration and change of status of companies by or under Part II (re-registration as a means of altering a company's status) and sections 138 (registration of order and minute of reduction), 139 and 147 of the Act (re-registration of public companies on reduction of capital).

3. Functions conferred by or under any of the following provisions of the Act—
   (a) sections 705 and 705A (companies' registered numbers and registration of branches of oversea companies) except insofar as they relate respectively to the determination of the form of companies' registered numbers and branches' registered numbers;
   (b) section 706 (delivery to the registrar of documents in legible form) except insofar as they relate to specification of requirements for the purpose of enabling the copying of documents delivered to the registrar;
   (c) section 707 (delivery to the registrar of documents other than in legible form) except insofar as they relate to the approval of the non-legible form in which information may be conveyed to the registrar;
   (d) section 709 (inspection etc of records kept by the registrar) except insofar as they relate to the determination of the means of facilitating the exercise of the right of persons to inspect records kept by the registrar, or the form in which copies of the information contained in those records may be made available;
   (e) section 710 (certificate of incorporation); and
   (f) section 710A (provision and authentication by registrar of documents in non-legible form) except insofar as they relate to the approval of the means of communication to the registrar of information in non-legible form.

4. Functions conferred by or under section 13 of the Newspaper Libel and Registration Act 1881 (registrar to enter returns on register).

5. Functions conferred by or under section 16 of the Limited Partnerships Act 1907 (inspection of statements registered).

6. …

7. Functions conferred by or under regulation 14 of the Regulations (inspection of documents).

8. Functions conferred by or under any provision of the Act listed in paragraphs 2 and 3 above to the extent specified in those paragraphs where any such provision is applied to EEIGs by regulation 18 of the Regulations (application of the Companies Act 1985).

[6841]

NOTES

Para 6: revoked by the Financial Services and Markets Act 2000 (Consequential Amendments and Repeals) Order 2001, SI 2001/3649, art 490, as from 1 December 2001.

SCHEDULE 2
FUNCTIONS OF REGISTRAR OF COMPANIES FOR SCOTLAND EXCLUDED FROM CONTRACTING OUT

Article 4

1. Functions conferred by or under any of the following provisions of the Act—
   (a) section 242 (accounts and reports to be delivered to the registrar) so far as they relate to the making of an application to the court;
   (b) sections 705 and 705A so far as they relate respectively to the determination of the form of companies' registered numbers and branches' registered numbers;
   (c) section 706 so far as they relate to the specification of requirements for the purpose of enabling the copying of documents delivered to the registrar;
   (d) section 707 so far as they relate to the approval of the non-legible form in which information may be conveyed to the registrar;
   (e) section 707A (the keeping of company records by the registrar) so far as they relate to the determination of the form in which the information contained in documents delivered to the registrar may be recorded and kept;
   (f) section 708(5) (fees payable to the registrar);
   (g) section 709 so far as they relate to the determination of the means of facilitating the exercise of the right of persons to inspect records kept by the registrar, or of the form in which copies of the information contained in these records may be made available;
   (h) section 710A so far as they relate to the approval of the means of communication by the registrar of information in non-legible form; and
   (i) section 713 (enforcement of company's duty to make returns) so far as they relate to the making of an application to the court.

2. Functions conferred by or under any of the following provisions of the Insolvency Act 1986—
   (a) section 69 (enforcement of receiver's duty to make returns etc); and
   (b) section 170 (enforcement of liquidator's duty to make returns etc).

3. Functions conferred by or under regulation 4(2) of the Regulations (transfer of official address).

4. Functions conferred by or under any provision of the Act or the Insolvency Act 1986 listed in paragraphs 1 and 2(a) above to the extent specified in these paragraphs where any such provision is applied to EEIGs by regulation 18 or 19 of the Regulations.

[6842]

SCHEDULE 3
FUNCTIONS OF THE SECRETARY OF STATE ENABLED TO BE CONTRACTED OUT

Article 5

1. Functions conferred by or under any of the following provisions of the Act—
   (a) section 26(2) (prohibition on registration of certain names except with the approval of the Secretary of State);
   (b) section 244(5) (extension by Secretary of State of the period allowed for laying and delivering accounts and reports); and
   (c) section 702(5) (extension by Secretary of State of period for delivering accounts and reports of an oversea company).

2. Functions conferred by or under section 2 of the Business Names Act 1985 (prohibition of use of certain business names).

3. Functions conferred by or under section 2 of the Business Names Act 1985 as applied to EEIGs by regulation 17 of the Regulations (application of Business Names Act 1985).

[6843]

CONTRACTING OUT (FUNCTIONS OF THE OFFICIAL RECEIVER) ORDER 1995

(SI 1995/1386)

NOTES

Made: 29 May 1995.

Authority: Deregulation and Contracting Out Act 1994, s 69.

Commencement: 30 May 1995 (see art 1 at **[6844]**). Where any provision in this work (including any inserted or substituted provision) came into force for all purposes on or before 1 July 2005, commencement information is not noted at provision level.

As of 1 July 2007, this Order had not been amended.

Limited liability partnerships: by the Limited Liability Partnerships Regulations 2001, SI 2001/1090, reg 10, Sch 6, Pt III, this Order applies, with modifications, to limited liability partnerships (see **[7000]**).

1 Citation and commencement

(1) This Order may be cited as the Contracting Out (Functions of the Official Receiver) Order 1995.

(2) This Order shall come into force on the day after the day on which it is made.

[6844]

2 Interpretation

(1) In this Order—

"the 1986 Act" means the Insolvency Act 1986;

"the insolvency legislation" means the Insolvency Act 1986, the Companies Act 1985, the Company Directors Disqualification Act 1986, any subordinate legislation made under any of those Acts and any regulations made under rule 12.1 of the Rules;

"the Rules" means the Insolvency Rules 1986; and

"right of audience" has the meaning given to it by section 119(1) of the Courts and Legal Services Act 1990.

(2) Any expression used in this Order other than one referred to in paragraph (1) above shall bear the same meaning as it bears in the 1986 Act.

(3) In this Order a rule referred to by number means the rule so numbered in the Rules and, except where otherwise expressly provided, a section referred to by number means the section so numbered in the 1986 Act.

[6845]

3 Contracting out of functions

(1) Subject to paragraph (2) below, any function of the official receiver which is conferred by or under the insolvency legislation, except one which is listed in the Schedule to this Order, may be exercised by, or by employees of, such person (if any) as may be authorised in that behalf by the official receiver.

(2) A function to which paragraph (1) above applies, and which involves the exercise of a right of audience in relation to any proceedings before a court, may only be exercised subject to the fulfilment of the condition specified in paragraph (3) below.

(3) Such right of audience as is mentioned in paragraph (2) shall not be exercised by any person other than a person who has a right of audience in relation to the proceedings in question by virtue of the provisions of Part II of the Courts and Legal Services Act 1990.

[6846]

SCHEDULE

Article 3

1. The functions of the official receiver as—
   (a) a receiver appointed pursuant to section 32 (power for court to appoint official receiver);
   (b) a provisional liquidator appointed pursuant to section 135 (appointment and powers of provisional liquidator); or

(c) an interim receiver appointed pursuant to section 286 (power to appoint interim receiver).

2. The receipt of any deposit which relates to a bankruptcy or winding-up petition.

3. The chairing—
   (a) by virtue of rule 4.55 of the first meeting of creditors (as defined by rule 4.50(7)) or the first meeting of contributories (as defined by rule 4.50(7)) in a winding up by the court; or
   (b) by virtue of rule 6.82 of the first meeting of creditors (as defined in rule 6.79(7)) in a bankruptcy.

4. The making of an application to the Secretary of State—
   (a) under section 137(1) for the appointment of another person as liquidator in the place of the official receiver; or
   (b) under section 296(1) for the appointment of a person as trustee instead of the official receiver.

5. The taking of a decision—
   (a) pursuant to section 137(2), whether or not to refer to the Secretary of State the need for an appointment of a liquidator in any case where at meetings held in pursuance of a decision under section 136(5)(a) no person is chosen to be liquidator;
   (b) pursuant to section 295(1), whether or not to refer to the Secretary of State the need for an appointment of a trustee in any case where at a meeting summoned under section 293 or 294 no appointment of a person as trustee is made.

6. The making of a reference to the Secretary of State under section 300(4) of the need for an appointment of a trustee by the Secretary of State in the circumstances referred to in that sub-section.

7. The making of a reference to the court or the Secretary of State, as the case may be, under section 300(5) of the need to fill any vacancy in the circumstances referred to in that sub-section.

8. The functions of the official receiver—
   (a) exercisable under rule 4.172(2) (functions of liquidation committee exercisable by official receiver) or rule 6.166(2) (functions of creditors' committee exercisable by official receiver); or
   (b) in relation to the hearing of an application made under—
      (i) section 280 (discharge by order of the court);
      (ii) rule 4.36(2) (application to court for a release or extension of time in respect of statement of affairs in a winding up by the court); or
      (iii) rule 6.62(2) (application to court by bankrupt for a release or extension of time in respect of statement of affairs).

9. The bringing or the conduct of proceedings under the Company Directors Disqualification Act 1986.

10. The giving of notice to the Secretary of State pursuant to section 174(3) (release of official receiver in winding up by the court) or section 299(2) (release of official receiver as trustee).

11. Consideration—
   (a) pursuant to rule 4.57(2) as to whether a request by creditors for a meeting of creditors or contributories or meetings of both, or
   (b) pursuant to rule 4.57(2) as it applies by virtue of rule 4.57(4) as to whether a request by contributories for a meeting of contributories, or
   (c) pursuant to rule 6.83(2) as to whether a request by creditors for a meeting of creditors,

has been properly made in accordance with the 1986 Act.

12. The making or conduct of any application to the court—

(a) to commit a bankrupt for contempt of court for failure to comply with an obligation imposed on him by—
  (i) section 288 (statement of affairs);
  (ii) section 291 (duties of bankrupt in relation to official receiver);
  (iii) section 312 (obligation to surrender control to trustee);
  (iv) section 333 (duties of bankrupt in relation to trustee); or
  (v) section 363 (general control of court); or
(b) pursuant to section 279(3) (suspension of discharge on application by official receiver).

13. The making or conduct of any application to the court to commit for contempt of court—
(a) a person who has failed to attend his public examination under section 133 (public examination of officers, etc); or
(b) a bankrupt who has failed to attend his public examination under section 290 (public examination of bankrupt).

14. The making of a report to the court pursuant to—
(a) section 132(1) (investigation by official receiver);
(b) section 289(1) (investigatory duties of official receiver);
(c) section 289(2) (report to the court on application by bankrupt for discharge from bankruptcy);
(d) rule 4.36(5) (report to court, etc on application by officers of company, etc for release from duty to submit statement of affairs or for extension of time);
(e) rule 6.62(5) (report to court, etc on application by bankrupt for release from duty to submit statement of affairs or for extension of time); or
(f) rule 6.215(2) (report in support of application for suspension of discharge).

15. The making or conduct of an application to the court for a public examination under section 133(1) or section 290(1) and the making or conduct of any application in relation to any public examination.

16. The making or conduct of an application to the court to relieve the official receiver from an obligation to make an application for a public examination requested pursuant to section 133(2) or required pursuant to section 290(2).

17. The taking part in a public examination or the questioning of a person pursuant to section 133(4)(a) or the taking part in a public examination or the questioning of a bankrupt pursuant to section 290(4)(a).

18. The making or conduct of an application to the court—
(a) pursuant to section 134(2) for the issue of a warrant for the arrest of a person and for the seizure of any books, papers, records, money or goods in that person's possession; or
(b) pursuant to section 364, for the issue of a warrant for the arrest of a debtor, an undischarged bankrupt or a discharged bankrupt, and for the seizure of any books, papers, records, money or goods in the debtor's or the bankrupt's possession, as the case may be.

19. The making or conduct of an application to the court pursuant to section 158 for the arrest of a contributory and for the seizure of his books, papers and movable personal property.

20. The making or conduct of an application to the court for the transfer of winding-up or bankruptcy proceedings from one court to another.

21. The taking of affidavits and declarations pursuant to rule 7.57(5) (taking of affidavits and declarations).

22. Any function of the official receiver in relation to the hearing of—
(a) an application by a bankrupt for leave to act as a director of, or directly or indirectly to take part in or be concerned in the promotion, formation or management of, a company; or
(b) an application by a director in respect of whom a disqualification order made under the Company Directors Disqualification Act 1986 is in force, for leave—

(a) to be a director of a company,
(b) to be a liquidator or administrator of a company,
(c) to be a receiver or manager of a company's property, or
(d) to be concerned or to take part in the promotion, formation or management of a company in any way, whether directly or indirectly.

23. The making of a report to the Secretary of State pursuant to section 7(3) of the Company Directors Disqualification Act 1986.

24. Any function corresponding to one referred to in paragraphs 1 to 23 above which is exercisable by the official receiver by virtue of the application (with or without modifications) of any provision of the insolvency legislation to insolvent partnerships or unregistered companies.

25. The presentation of a winding-up petition pursuant to section 124(5) (application by official receiver for winding up of company being wound up voluntarily).

[6847]

PUBLIC OFFERS OF SECURITIES REGULATIONS 1995 (NOTE)

(SI 1995/1537)

NOTES

These Regulations were revoked by the Prospectus Regulations 2005, SI 2005/1433, reg 2(3), Sch 3, para 2, as from 1 July 2005.

[6848]–[6881]

COMPANIES (SUMMARY FINANCIAL STATEMENT) REGULATIONS 1995

(SI 1995/2092)

NOTES

Made: 4 August 1995.

Authority: CA 1985, ss 245(3), (4), 251(1)–(3).

Commencement: 1 September 1995 (see reg 1 at **[6882]**). Where any provision in this work (including any inserted or substituted provision) came into force for all purposes on or before 1 July 2005, commencement information is not noted at provision level.

These Regulations are reproduced as amended by: the Companies Act 1985 (Electronic Communications) Order 2000, SI 2000/3373; the Companies (Summary Financial Statement) Amendment Regulations 2002, SI 2002/1780; the Companies (Summary Financial Statement) (Amendment) Regulations 2005, SI 2005/2281; the Companies Act 1985 (Operating and Financial Review) (Repeal) Regulations 2005, SI 2005/3442; the Companies (EEA State) Regulations 2007, SI 2007/732.

ARRANGEMENT OF REGULATIONS

PART I
GENERAL

PART II
CONDITIONS FOR SENDING OUT SUMMARY FINANCIAL STATEMENT

PART I
GENERAL

1 Citation and commencement

These Regulations may be cited as the Companies (Summary Financial Statement) Regulations 1995 and shall come into force on 1st September 1995.

[6882]

2 Interpretation

[(1)] In these Regulations, unless otherwise stated—

["address" means the same as in section 262(1) of the Companies Act 1985;]

"the 1985 Act" means the Companies Act 1985;

"banking company" means a company the directors of which prepare accounts for a financial year in accordance with the special provisions of Part VII of the 1985 Act relating to banking companies;

["communication" means the same as in the Electronic Communications Act 2000;]

["EEA State" has the meaning given by Schedule 1 to the Interpretation Act 1978;]

["electronic communication" means the same as in the Electronic Communications Act 2000;]

"entitled persons" means the same as in section 251 of the 1985 Act;

"full accounts and reports" means a company's annual accounts, the directors' report[, the directors' remuneration report (if any)][…] and the auditors' report on those accounts required to be sent to entitled persons under section 238(1) of the 1985 Act and "full" in relation to any balance sheet, profit and loss account, [group accounts, directors' report [or directors' remuneration report]] means any such document comprised in the full accounts and reports;

"insurance company" means a company the directors of which prepare accounts for a financial year in accordance with the special provisions of Part VII of the 1985 Act relating to insurance companies;

.....

[(2) References in these Regulations to sending an entitled person copies of the full accounts and reports include sending such copies in accordance with section 238(4A) and (4B), and references to sending an entitled person a summary financial statement include sending such a statement in accordance with section 251(2A) and (2B).]

[6883]

NOTES

Para (1) is amended as follows:

Numbered as such, and definitions "address", "communication" and "electronic communication" inserted, by the Companies Act 1985 (Electronic Communications) Order 2000, SI 2000/3373, art 32(2), Sch 2, paras 1, 2(1), as from 22 December 2000.

Definition "EEA State" substituted by the Companies (EEA State) Regulations 2007, SI 2007/732, reg 5, as from 9 March 2007.

Words in first pair of square brackets in definition "full accounts and reports" inserted, and words in third (outer) pair of square brackets substituted, by the Companies (Summary Financial Statement) Amendment Regulations 2002, SI 2002/1780, reg 2, as from 1 August 2002, with effect as respects companies' financial years ending on or after 31 December 2002; words in second pair of square brackets inserted by the Companies (Summary Financial Statement) (Amendment) Regulations 2005, SI 2005/2281, reg 2(1), (2), as from 1 October 2005, and revoked by the Companies Act 1985 (Operating and Financial Review) (Repeal) Regulations 2005, SI 2005/3442, reg 2(2)(b), Sch 2, para 2(1), (2)(a), as from 12 January 2006; words in fourth (inner) pair of square brackets substituted by SI 2005/3442, reg 2(2)(b), Sch 2, para 2(1), (2)(b), as from 12 January 2006.

Definition "listed public company" revoked by SI 2005/2281, reg 2(1), (3), as from 1 October 2005.

Para (2): added by SI 2000/3373, art 32(2), Sch 2, paras 1, 2(2), as from 22 December 2000.

PART II
CONDITIONS FOR SENDING OUT SUMMARY FINANCIAL STATEMENT

3 Cases in which sending of summary financial statement prohibited

(1) A ... company may not send a summary financial statement to an entitled person instead of copies of its full accounts and reports, in any case where it is prohibited from doing so by any relevant provision (within the meaning of paragraph (2) below)—

(a) in its memorandum or articles of association, or

(b) where the entitled person is a holder of the company's debentures, in any instrument constituting or otherwise governing any of the company's debentures of which that person is a holder.

[(1A) A company may not send a summary financial statement to an entitled person instead of copies of its full accounts and reports in respect of any financial year for which no auditors' report has been made under section 235 of the 1985 Act.]

(2) For the purposes of paragraph (1) above, any provision (however expressed) which requires copies of the full accounts and reports to be sent to entitled persons, or which forbids the sending of summary financial statements under section 251 of the 1985 Act, is a relevant provision.

[6884]

NOTES

Para (1): words omitted revoked by the Companies (Summary Financial Statement) (Amendment) Regulations 2005, SI 2005/2281, reg 3(1), (2), as from 1 October 2005.

Para (1A): inserted by SI 2005/2281, reg 3(1), (3), as from 1 October 2005.

4 Ascertainment of entitled person's wishes

(1) A ... company may not send a summary financial statement to an entitled person in place of copies of its full accounts and reports, unless the company has ascertained that the entitled person does not wish to receive copies of those documents.

(2) Whether or not an entitled person wishes to receive copies of the full accounts and reports for a financial year is to be ascertained—

(a) from any relevant notification ... he has given to the company (either as an entitled person or as a person to whom paragraph (5) of this regulation applies) as to whether he wishes to receive copies of the full accounts and reports or as to whether he wishes, instead of copies of those documents, to receive summary financial statements; or

(b) failing any such express notification, from any failure to respond to an opportunity given to the entitled person (including for this purpose a person to whom paragraph (5) of this regulation applies) to elect to receive copies of the full accounts and reports either in response to a notice sent by the company under regulation 5 below, or as part of a relevant consultation of his wishes by the company under regulation 6 below.

(3) For the purposes of paragraph (2)(a) above [and subject to paragraph (3A) below], a notification is a relevant notification with respect to a financial year if it relates to that year

PART IV STATUTORY INSTRUMENTS

(whether or not it has been given at the invitation of the company) and if it is received by the company not later than 28 days before the first date on which copies of the full accounts and reports are sent out to entitled persons in compliance with section 238(1) of the 1985 Act with respect to the financial year.

[(3A) If a relevant notification is not in writing, it must be contained in an electronic communication transmitted to the company at an address specified by or on behalf of the company for that purpose.]

(4) A company may not send a summary financial statement to an entitled person in relation to any financial year in place of copies of the full accounts and reports unless—

(a) the period allowed for laying and delivering full accounts and reports under section 244 of the 1985 Act for that year has not expired, and

(b) the summary financial statement has been approved by the board of directors and the original statement signed on behalf of the board by a director of the company.

(5) This paragraph applies to a person who is entitled, whether conditionally or unconditionally, to become an entitled person in relation to the company, but who has not yet become such an entitled person.

[6885]

NOTES

Para (1): words omitted revoked by the Companies (Summary Financial Statement) (Amendment) Regulations 2005, SI 2005/2281, reg 4, as from 1 October 2005, subject to transitional provisions as noted below.

Para (2): words omitted revoked by the Companies Act 1985 (Electronic Communications) Order 2000, SI 2000/3373, art 32(2), Sch 2, paras 1, 3(a), as from 22 December 2000.

Para (3): words in square brackets inserted by SI 2000/3373, art 32(2), Sch 2, paras 1, 3(b), as from 22 December 2000.

Para (3A): inserted by SI 2000/3373, art 32(2), Sch 2, paras 1, 3(c), as from 22 December 2000.

Transitional provisions: the Companies (Summary Financial Statement) (Amendment) Regulations 2005, SI 2005/2281, reg 16, which provides as follows—

"16 Transitional provision

(1) Where a company (whether or not a listed public company) has, before 1st October 2005, ascertained in accordance with regulation 4 of the unamended 1995 Regulations that an entitled person does not wish to receive copies of the full accounts and reports, it may send a summary financial statement to such an entitled person in place of the full accounts and reports.

(2) In paragraph (1)—

(a) "unamended 1995 Regulations" means the 1995 Regulations without the amendments contained in these Regulations, and disregarding any references to the company being a listed public company, and

(b) "full accounts and reports" is construed in accordance with regulation 2 of the unamended 1995 Regulations.".

5 Consultation by notice

(1) A … company may give a notice to an entitled person (including for this purpose a person to whom regulation 4(5) above applies), by sending it by post or giving it in any other manner [in which the company may send notices of meetings pursuant to the 1985 Act or its] articles, which shall—

(a) state that for the future, so long as he is an entitled person, he will be sent a summary financial statement for each financial year instead of a copy of the company's full accounts and reports, unless he notifies the company [either in writing or by sending the notification in an electronic communication to an address specified for that purpose] that he wishes to receive full accounts and reports,

(b) state that the summary financial statement for a financial year will contain a summary of the company's or group's profit and loss account, balance sheet and[, in the case of a quoted company, directors' remuneration report for that year, and may contain additional information derived from the directors' report …],

[(bb) …]

(c) state that the … card or form accompanying the notice in accordance with paragraph (2) below must be returned by a date specified in the notice, being a date at least 21 days after service of the notice and not less than 28 days before the first date on which copies of the full accounts and reports for the next financial year for which the entitled person is entitled to receive them are sent out to entitled persons in compliance with section 238(1) of the 1985 Act,

(d) include a statement in a prominent position to the effect that a summary financial statement will not contain sufficient information to allow as full an understanding of the results and state of affairs of the company or group as would be provided by the full annual accounts and reports and that members and debenture holders requiring more detailed information have the right to obtain, free of charge, a copy of the company's last full accounts and reports, and

[(e) state that the summary financial statement will contain a statement by the company's auditors as to whether—

(i) the summary financial statement is consistent with the company's annual accounts and, in the case of a quoted company, directors' remuneration report, and where information derived from the directors' report … is included in the statement, with that report …

(ii) the summary financial statement complies with the requirements of section 251 of the 1985 Act and of these Regulations, and

(iii) the auditors' report on the company's annual accounts was qualified or unqualified.]

(2) Subject to paragraph (3) below, the notice shall be accompanied by a [card or form (in respect of which, in the case of a card or form sent by post, any postage necessary for its return to the company has been, or will be, paid by the company)], which is so worded as to enable an entitled person (including a person to whom regulation 4(5) above applies), by marking a box and returning the card or form [either by post or in an electronic communication sent to a specified address], to notify the company that he wishes to receive full accounts and reports for the next financial year for which he is entitled to receive them as an entitled person and for all future financial years thereafter.

(3) The company need not pay the postage in respect of the return of the … card or form in the following circumstances—

(a) if the address of a member to which notices are sent in accordance with the company's articles is not within an EEA State,

(b) if the address of a debenture holder to which notices are sent in accordance with the terms of any instrument constituting or otherwise governing the debentures of which he is a holder is not within an EEA State, or

(c) if the address of a person to whom regulation 4(5) above applies to which notices are sent, in accordance with the contractual provisions whereunder he has a right (conditionally or unconditionally) to become an entitled person, is not within an EEA State.

[6886]

NOTES

Para (1) is amended as follows:

First words omitted revoked by the Companies (Summary Financial Statement) (Amendment) Regulations 2005, SI 2005/2281, reg 5(1), (2)(a), as from 1 October 2005.

Words in first pair of square brackets, and words in square brackets in sub-para (a), substituted by the Companies Act 1985 (Electronic Communications) Order 2000, SI 2000/3373, art 32(2), Sch 2, paras 1, 4(1), (2)(a), (b), as from 22 December 2000.

Words in square brackets in sub-para (b) substituted by SI 2005/2281, reg 5(1), (2)(b), as from 1 October 2005; words omitted therefrom revoked by the Companies Act 1985 (Operating and Financial Review) (Repeal) Regulations 2005, SI 2005/3442, reg 2(2)(b), Sch 2, para 2(1), (3)(a), as from 12 January 2006.

Sub-para (bb) inserted by SI 2005/2281, reg 5(1), (2)(c), as from 1 October 2005, and revoked by SI 2005/3442, reg 2(2)(b), Sch 2, para 2(1), (3)(b), as from 12 January 2006.

Word omitted from sub-para (c) revoked by SI 2000/3373, art 32(2), Sch 2, paras 1, 4(1), (2)(c), as from 22 December 2000.

Sub-para (e) substituted by SI 2005/2281, reg 5(1), (2)(d), as from 1 October 2005; words omitted revoked by SI 2005/3442, reg 2(2)(b), Sch 2, para 2(1), (3)(c), as from 12 January 2006.

Para (2): words in first pair of square brackets substituted, and words in second pair of square brackets inserted, by SI 2000/3373, art 32(2), Sch 2, paras 1, 4(1), (3), as from 22 December 2000.

Para (3): word omitted revoked by SI 2000/3373, art 32(2), Sch 2, paras 1, 4(1), (4), as from 22 December 2000.

---

6 Relevant consultation

(1) A … company may conduct a relevant consultation to ascertain the wishes of an entitled person.

(2) For the purposes of this regulation, a relevant consultation of the wishes of an entitled person is a notice given to the entitled person (including for this purpose a person to whom regulation 4(5) above applies), by sending it by post or giving it in any other manner [in which the company may send notices of meetings pursuant to the 1985 Act or its] articles, which—

(a) states that for the future, so long as he is an entitled person, he will be sent a summary financial statement instead of the full accounts and reports of the company, unless he notifies the company [either in writing or by sending the notification in an electronic communication to an address specified for that purpose] that he wishes to continue to receive full accounts and reports;

(b) accompanies a copy of the full accounts and reports;

(c) accompanies a copy of a summary financial statement, prepared in accordance with section 251 of the 1985 Act and these Regulations, with respect to the financial year covered by those full accounts and reports and which is identified in the notice as an example of the document which the entitled person will receive for the future, so long as he is an entitled person, unless he notifies the company to the contrary; and

(d) subject to paragraph (3) below, is accompanied by a … card or form, in respect of which[, in the case of a card or form sent by post,] any postage necessary for its return to the company has been, or will be, paid by the company, which is so worded as to enable an entitled person (including a person to whom regulation 4(5) above applies), by marking a box and returning the card or form [either by post or in an electronic communication sent to a specified address], to notify the company that he wishes to receive full accounts and reports for the next financial year for which he is entitled to receive them as an entitled person and for all future financial years thereafter.

(3) Regulation 5(3) above applies in respect of the payment of postage for the return of the printed card or form referred to in paragraph (2)(d) of this regulation.

[6887]

NOTES

Para (1): words omitted revoked by the Companies (Summary Financial Statement) (Amendment) Regulations 2005, SI 2005/2281, reg 6, as from 1 October 2005.

Para (2): words in square brackets substituted or inserted, and word omitted from sub-para (d) revoked, by the Companies Act 1985 (Electronic Communications) Order 2000, SI 2000/3373, art 32(2), Sch 2, paras 1, 5, as from 22 December 2000.

PART III
FORM AND CONTENT OF SUMMARY FINANCIAL STATEMENT

7 Provisions applying to all companies and groups

(1) Every summary financial statement issued by a … company in place of the full accounts and reports must comply with this regulation.

(2) The summary financial statement must state the name of the person who signed it on behalf of the board.

(3) The summary financial statement of a company which is not required to prepare group accounts under Part VII of the 1985 Act must include a statement in a prominent position to the effect that the summary financial statement does not contain sufficient information to allow as full an understanding of the results and state of affairs of the company[, and of its policies and arrangements concerning directors' remuneration,] as would be provided by the full annual accounts and reports, and that members and debenture holders requiring more detailed information have the right to obtain, free of charge, a copy of the company's last full accounts and reports.

(4) The summary financial statement of a company which is required to prepare group accounts under Part VII of the 1985 Act must include a statement in a prominent position to the effect that the summary financial statement does not contain sufficient information to allow as full an understanding of the results of the group and state of affairs of the company or of the group[, and of their policies and arrangements concerning directors' remuneration,] as would be provided by the full annual accounts and reports, and that members and debenture holders requiring more detailed information have the right to obtain, free of charge, a copy of the company's last full accounts and reports.

(5) The summary financial statement must contain a clear, conspicuous statement—

(a) of how members and debenture holders can obtain, free of charge, a copy of the company's last full accounts and reports, and

(b) of how members and debenture holders may elect … to receive full accounts and reports in place of summary financial statements for all future financial years.

[6888]

NOTES

Para (1): words omitted revoked by the Companies (Summary Financial Statement) (Amendment) Regulations 2005, SI 2005/2281, reg 7, as from 1 October 2005.

Paras (3), (4): words in square brackets inserted by the Companies (Summary Financial Statement) Amendment Regulations 2002, SI 2002/1780, reg 3, as from 1 August 2002, with effect as respects companies' financial years ending on or after 31 December 2002.

Para (5): words omitted revoked by the Companies Act 1985 (Electronic Communications) Order 2000, SI 2000/3373, art 32(2), Sch 2, paras 1, 6, as from 22 December 2000.

8 Companies and groups other than banking and insurance companies and groups

(1) [Subject to regulation 10A,] the summary financial statement of a … company (other than a banking or insurance company) the directors of which are not required to prepare group accounts under Part VII of the 1985 Act, shall be in the form, and contain the information, required by Schedule 1 to these Regulations, so far as applicable to such a company.

(2) [Subject to regulation 10A,] the summary financial statement of a … company (other than the parent company of a banking or insurance group) the directors of which are required to prepare group accounts under Part VII of the 1985 Act, shall be in the form, and contain the information, required by Schedule 1 to these Regulations, so far as applicable to such a company.

[6889]

NOTES

Paras (1), (2): words in square brackets inserted, and words omitted revoked, by the Companies (Summary Financial Statement) (Amendment) Regulations 2005, SI 2005/2281, reg 8, as from 1 October 2005.

9 Banking companies and groups

(1) [Subject to regulation 10A,] the summary financial statement of a … company which is in relation to the financial year in question a banking company the directors of which are not required to prepare group accounts under Part VII of the 1985 Act, shall be in the form, and contain the information, required by Schedule 2 to these Regulations, so far as applicable to such a company.

(2) [Subject to regulation 10A,] the summary financial statement of a … company which is the parent company of a banking group shall be in the form, and contain the information, required by Schedule 2 to these Regulations, so far as applicable to such a company.

[6890]

NOTES

Paras (1), (2): words in square brackets inserted, and words omitted revoked, by the Companies (Summary Financial Statement) (Amendment) Regulations 2005, SI 2005/2281, reg 9, as from 1 October 2005.

10 Insurance companies and groups

(1) [Subject to regulation 10A,] the summary financial statement of a … company which is in relation to the financial year in question an insurance company the directors of which are not required to prepare group accounts under Part VII of the 1985 Act, shall be in the form, and contain the information, required by Schedule 3 to these Regulations, so far as applicable to such a company.

(2) [Subject to regulation 10A,] the summary financial statement of a … company which is the parent company of an insurance group shall be in the form, and contain the information, required by Schedule 3 to these Regulations, so far as applicable to such a company.

[6891]

NOTES

Paras (1), (2): words in square brackets inserted, and words omitted revoked, by the Companies (Summary Financial Statement) (Amendment) Regulations 2005, SI 2005/2281, reg 10, as from 1 October 2005.

[10A The summary financial statement of a company that is required to prepare group accounts and prepares IAS group accounts or, in the case of a company that is not required to prepare group accounts, prepares IAS individual accounts, must be in the form and contain the information required by Schedule 3A to these Regulations, so far as applicable to such a company.]

[6891A]

NOTES

Commencement: 1 October 2005.

Inserted by the Companies (Summary Financial Statement) (Amendment) Regulations 2005, SI 2005/2281, reg 11, as from 1 October 2005.

PART IV
TRANSITIONALS ETC

11 Revocation, transitionals and saving

(1), (2) ...

(3) Paragraph (4) below has effect in relation to the ascertainment of the wishes of an entitled person for the purposes of section 251(2) of the 1985 Act.

(4) So far as anything done under or for the purposes of any provision of the Companies (Summary Financial Statement) Regulations 1992 could have been done under or for the purposes of the corresponding provision of these Regulations, it is not invalidated by the revocation of that provision but has effect as if done under or for the purposes of the corresponding provision.

[6892]

NOTES

Para (1): revokes the Companies (Summary Financial Statement) Regulations 1992, SI 1992/3075.

Para (2): revoked by the Companies (Summary Financial Statement) (Amendment) Regulations 2005, SI 2005/2281, reg 17(a), as from 1 October 2005.

12 (*Amends the Companies* (*Revision of Defective Accounts and Report*) *Regulations*, *SI 1990/2570*, *regs 14*(2), (4), *16*(3) *at* **[6687]**, **[6690]**).

SCHEDULES

SCHEDULE 1
FORM AND CONTENT OF SUMMARY FINANCIAL STATEMENT OF COMPANIES AND GROUPS OTHER THAN BANKING OR INSURANCE COMPANIES AND GROUPS

Regulation 8

Form of summary financial statement

1.—(1) The summary financial statement shall contain the information prescribed by the following paragraphs of this Schedule, in such order and under such headings as the directors consider appropriate, together with any other information necessary to ensure that the summary financial statement is consistent with the full accounts and reports for the financial year in question.

(2) Nothing in this Schedule shall be construed as prohibiting the inclusion in the summary financial statement of any additional information derived from [the company's annual accounts, the directors' remuneration report (if any) [...] and the directors' report].

...

2. ...

[Summary of paragraph 1(1) of Schedule 6 to the 1985 Act and of the directors' remuneration report

2A. The summary financial statement shall contain the whole of, or a summary of—
(a) that portion of the notes to the accounts for the year in question which set out the information required by paragraph 1(1) of Part I of Schedule 6 to the 1985 Act (Aggregate amount of directors' emoluments etc); and
(b) to the extent that the company is required to produce a directors' remuneration report, those portions of the directors' remuneration report for the year in question which set out the matters required by paragraphs 3 (Statement of company's policy on directors' remuneration) and 4 (Performance graph) of Schedule 7A to the 1985 Act.]

Summary profit and loss account: companies not required to prepare group accounts

3.—(1) The summary financial statement shall contain, in the case of a company the directors of which are not required to prepare group accounts for the financial year, a summary profit and loss account showing, in so far as they may be derived from the full profit and loss account, the items, or combinations of items, listed in sub-paragraph (3) below, in the order set out in that sub-paragraph.

(2) The items or combinations of items listed in sub-paragraph (3) below may appear under such headings as the directors consider appropriate.

(3) The items, or combinations of items, referred to in sub-paragraph (1) above are—
(a) turnover—
— format 1, item 1
— format 2, item 1
— format 3, item B1
— format 4, item B1;
(b) income from shares in group undertakings and participating interests: the combination of the following two items—
— format 1, items 7 and 8
— format 2, items 9 and 10
— format 3, items B3 and B4
— format 4, items B5 and B6;
(c) other interest receivable and similar income and interest payable and similar charges: the net figure resulting from the combination of the following two items—
— format 1, items 10 and 12
— format 2, items 12 and 14
— format 3, items B6 and A5
— format 4, items B8 and A7;
(d) the profit or loss on ordinary activities before taxation;
(e) tax on profit or loss on ordinary activities—
— format 1, item 13
— format 2, item 15
— format 3, item A6
— format 4, item A8;
(f) profit or loss on ordinary activities after tax—
— format 1, item 14
— format 2, item 16
— format 3, item A7 or B7
— format 4, item A9 or B9;
(g) extraordinary income and charges after tax: the net figure resulting from the combination of the following items—
— format 1, items 17 and 18
— format 2, items 19 and 20
— format 3, items A8, A9 and B8
— format 4, items A10, A11 and B10;
(h) profit or loss for the financial year—

— format 1, item 20
— format 2, item 22
— format 3, item A11 or B9
— format 4, item A13 or B11; and

(i) …

(4) …

[Dividends

3A. The summary financial statement shall also contain the information concerning recognised and proposed dividends included in the full accounts and reports.]

Summary profit and loss account: companies required to prepare group accounts

4.—(1) The summary financial statement shall contain, in the case of a company the directors of which are required to prepare group accounts for the financial year, a summary consolidated profit and loss account showing the items or combinations of items required by paragraph 3 above, in the order required by that paragraph and under such headings as the directors consider appropriate, but with the modifications specified in sub-paragraph (2) below[, and shall also contain the information required by paragraph 3A above].

(2) The modifications referred to in sub-paragraph (1) above are as follows—

(a) in place of the information required by paragraph 3(3)(b), there shall be shown, under such heading as the directors consider appropriate, the item "Income from interests in associated undertakings" required to be shown in the Schedule 4 formats by paragraph 21(3) of Schedule 4A to the 1985 Act;

(b) between the information required by paragraph 3(3)(f) and that required by paragraph 3(3)(g) there shall in addition be shown, under such heading as the directors consider appropriate, the item "Minority interests" required to be shown in the Schedule 4 formats by paragraph 17(3) of Schedule 4A to the 1985 Act: and

(c) the figure required by paragraph 3(3)(g) shall be shown after the deduction or the addition (as the case may be) of the item "Minority interests" required to be shown in the Schedule 4 formats by paragraph 17(4) of Schedule 4A to the 1985 Act.

Summary balance sheet: companies not required to prepare group accounts

5.—(1) The summary financial statement shall contain, in the case of a company the directors of which are not required to prepare group accounts for the financial year, a summary balance sheet.

(2) Subject to sub-paragraphs (3) and (4) below, the summary balance sheet shall show, in so far as it can be derived from the full balance sheet and under such heading as the directors consider appropriate, a single amount for each of the headings to which letters are assigned in the balance sheet format which has been used for the full balance sheet (where necessary by the combination of the items to which Roman and Arabic numbers are assigned under those headings) in the order set out in the full balance sheet.

(3) Where an alternative position is permitted for any item in the balance sheet format used, the summary balance sheet shall use the position used by the full balance sheet.

(4) Where the full balance sheet used is format 2 in Schedule 4 to the 1985 Act, then in the case of heading C under "Liabilities", two figures must be shown, one figure for amounts falling due within one year and one for amounts falling due after one year.

Summary balance sheet: companies required to prepare group accounts

6. The summary financial statement shall contain, in the case of a company the directors of which are required to prepare group accounts for the financial year, a summary consolidated balance sheet which shall show the items required by paragraph 5 above, in the order required by that paragraph and under such headings as the directors consider appropriate, but with the addition of the item "Minority interests" required by paragraph 17(2) of Schedule 4A to the 1985 Act, to be inserted as required by that paragraph.

Corresponding amounts

7. In respect of every item shown in the summary profit and loss account or summary consolidated profit and loss account (as the case may be), or in the summary balance sheet or summary consolidated balance sheet (as the case may be) the corresponding amount shall be shown for the immediately preceding financial year; for this purpose "the corresponding amount" is the amount shown in the summary financial statement for that year or which would have been so shown had such a statement been prepared for that year, [taking account of any adjustments to corresponding amounts made in the full accounts and reports].

[6893]

NOTES

Para 1: words in first (outer) pair of square brackets in sub-para (2) substituted by the Companies (Summary Financial Statement) Amendment Regulations 2002, SI 2002/1780, reg 4, as from 1 August 2002, with effect as respects companies' financial years ending on or after 31 December 2002; words in second (inner) pair of square brackets inserted by the Companies (Summary Financial Statement) (Amendment) Regulations 2005, SI 2005/2281, reg 12(1), (2), as from 1 October 2005, and revoked by the Companies Act 1985 (Operating and Financial Review) (Repeal) Regulations 2005, SI 2005/3442, reg 2(2)(b), Sch 2, para 2(1), (4), as from 12 January 2006.

Para 2: revoked by SI 2005/2281, reg 12(1), (3), as from 1 October 2005.

Para 2A: inserted by SI 2002/1780, reg 5(1), as from 1 August 2002, with effect as respects companies' financial years ending on or after 31 December 2002.

Para 3: sub-para (3)(i) revoked by SI 2005/2281, reg 12(1), (4), as from 1 October 2005; sub-para (4) revoked by SI 2002/1780, reg 5(2), as from 1 August 2002, with effect as respects companies' financial years ending on or after 31 December 2002.

Para 3A: inserted by SI 2005/2281, reg 12(1), (5), as from 1 October 2005.

Para 4: words in square brackets in sub-para (1) inserted by SI 2005/2281, reg 12(1), (6), as from 1 October 2005.

Para 7: words in square brackets substituted by SI 2005/2281, reg 12(1), (7), as from 1 October 2005.

SCHEDULE 2
FORM AND CONTENT OF SUMMARY FINANCIAL STATEMENT OF BANKING COMPANIES AND GROUPS

Regulation 9

Form of summary financial statement

1.—(1) The summary financial statement shall contain the information prescribed by the following paragraphs of this Schedule, in such order and under such headings as the directors consider appropriate, together with any other information necessary to ensure that the summary financial statement is consistent with the full accounts and reports for the financial year in question.

(2) Nothing in this Schedule shall be construed as prohibiting the inclusion in the summary financial statement of any additional information derived from the company's annual accounts[, the directors' remuneration report (if any) …] and the directors' report.

…

2. …

[Summary of paragraph 1(1) of Schedule 6 to the 1985 Act and of the directors' remuneration report

2A. The summary financial statement shall contain the whole of, or a summary of—

(a) that portion of the notes to the accounts for the year in question which set out the information required by paragraph 1(1) of Part I of Schedule 6 to the 1985 Act (Aggregate amount of directors' emoluments etc); and

(b) to the extent that the company is required to produce a directors' remuneration report, those portions of the directors' remuneration report for the year in question which set out the matters required by paragraphs 3 (Statement of company's policy on directors' remuneration) and 4 (Performance graph) of Schedule 7A to the 1985 Act.]

Summary profit and loss account: companies not required to prepare group accounts

3.—(1) The summary financial statement shall contain, in the case of a company the directors of which are not required to prepare group accounts for the financial year, a summary profit and loss account showing, in so far as they may be derived from the full profit and loss account, the items, or combinations of items, listed in sub-paragraph (3) below, in the order set out in that sub-paragraph.

(2) The items or combinations of items listed in sub-paragraph (3) below may appear under such headings as the directors consider appropriate.

(3) The items, or combinations of items, referred to in sub-paragraph (1) above are—

(a) interest receivable and payable: the net figure resulting from the combination of the following two items—
— format 1, items 1 and 2
— format 2, items A1 and B1;

(b) dividend income, fees and commissions receivable and payable, dealing profits or losses and other operating income: the net figure resulting from the combination of the following items—
— format 1, items 3, 4, 5, 6 and 7
— format 2, items A2, A3, B2, B3, B4 and B7;

(c) administrative expenses, depreciation and amortisation, other operating charges, amounts written off, and adjustments to amounts written off, fixed asset investments: the net figure resulting from the combination of the following items—
— format 1, items 8, 9, 10, 13 and 14
— format 2, items A4, A5, A6, A8 and B6;

(d) provisions and adjustments to provisions: the net figure resulting from the combination of the following two items—
— format 1, items 11 and 12
— format 2, items A7 and B5;

(e) profit or loss on ordinary activities before tax—
— format 1, item 15
— format 2, item A9 or B8;

(f) tax on profit or loss on ordinary activities—
— format 1, item 16
— format 2, item A10;

(g) profit or loss on ordinary activities after tax—
— format 1, item 17
— format 2, item A11 or B9;

(h) extraordinary profit or loss after tax—
— format 1, item 22
— the net figure resulting from the combination of format 2, items A14 and B11;

(i) other taxes not shown under the preceding items—
— format 1, item 23
— format 2, item A15;

(j) profit or loss for the financial year—
— format 1, item 24
— format 2, item A16 or B12; and

(k) …

(4) …

[Dividends

3A. The summary financial statement shall also contain the information concerning recognised and proposed dividends included in the full accounts and reports.]

Summary profit and loss account: companies required to prepare group accounts

4.—(1) The summary financial statement shall contain, in the case of a company the directors of which are required to prepare group accounts for the financial year, a summary consolidated profit and loss account showing the items, or combinations of items, required by paragraph 3 above, in the order required by that paragraph and under such headings as the directors consider appropriate, but with the modifications specified in sub-paragraph (2) below[, and shall also contain the information required by paragraph 3A above].

(2) The modifications referred to in sub-paragraph (1) above are as follows—

(a) between the information required by paragraph 3(3)(d) and that required by paragraph 3(3)(e) there shall in addition be shown, under such heading as the directors consider appropriate, the item "Income from associated undertakings" required to be shown in the Schedule 9 formats by paragraph 3(7)(ii) of Part II of Schedule 9 to the 1985 Act;

(b) between the information required by paragraph 3(3)(g) and that required by paragraph 3(3)(h) there shall in addition be shown, under such heading as the directors consider appropriate, the item "Minority interests" required to be shown in the Schedule 9 formats by paragraph 17(3) of Schedule 4A to the 1985 Act as adapted by paragraph 3(3) of Part II of Schedule 9 to that Act; and

(c) the figures required by paragraph 3(3)(h) and (i) shall each be shown after the deduction or the addition (as the case may be) of the item "Minority interests" required to be shown in the Schedule 9 formats by paragraph 17(4) of Schedule 4A to the 1985 Act as adapted by paragraph 3(4) of Part II of Schedule 9 to that Act.

Summary balance sheet: companies not required to prepare group accounts

5.—(1) The summary financial statement shall contain, in the case of a company the directors of which are not required to prepare group accounts for the financial year, a summary balance sheet which shall show, in so far as they may be derived from the full balance sheet, the items, or combinations of items, set out in sub-paragraph (2) below, in the order set out in that sub-paragraph and under such headings as the directors consider appropriate.

(2) The items, or combinations of items, referred to in sub-paragraph (1) above are as follows—

(a) cash and balances at central [or post office] banks, treasury bills and other eligible bills—
— the aggregate of items 1 and 2 under the heading "ASSETS";

(b) loans and advances to banks—
— item 3 under the heading "ASSETS";

(c) loans and advances to customers—
— item 4 under the heading "ASSETS";

(d) debt securities [and other fixed income securities], equity shares [and other variable-yield securities], participating interests and shares in group undertakings—
— the aggregate of items 5, 6, 7 and 8 under the heading "ASSETS";

(e) intangible and tangible fixed assets—
— the aggregate of items 9 and 10 under the heading "ASSETS";

(f) called up capital not paid, own shares, other assets, prepayments and accrued income—
— the aggregate of items 11 (or 14), 12, 13 and 15 under the heading "ASSETS";

(g) total assets under the heading "ASSETS";

(h) deposits by banks—
— item 1 under the heading "LIABILITIES";

(i) customer accounts—
— item 2 under the heading "LIABILITIES";

(j) debt securities in issue—
— item 3 under the heading "LIABILITIES";

(k) other liabilities, accruals and deferred income and provisions for liabilities and charges—
— the aggregate of items 4, 5 and 6 under the heading "LIABILITIES";

(l) subordinated liabilities—
— item 7 under the heading "LIABILITIES";

(m) called up share capital, share premium account, reserves, revaluation reserve and profit and loss account—
— the aggregate of items 8, 9, 10, 11 and 12 under the heading "LIABILITIES";

(n) total liabilities under the heading "LIABILITIES";

(o) contingent liabilities—

PART IV
STATUTORY INSTRUMENTS

— item 1 under the heading "MEMORANDUM ITEMS"; and

(p) commitments—

— item 2 under the heading "MEMORANDUM ITEMS".

Summary balance sheet: companies required to prepare group accounts

6.—(1) The summary financial statement shall contain, in the case of a company the directors of which are required to prepare group accounts for the financial year, a summary consolidated balance sheet showing the items required by paragraph 5 above, in the order required by that paragraph and under such headings as the directors consider appropriate, but with the addition specified in sub-paragraph (2) below.

(2) Between the items required by paragraph 5(2)(l) and (m) or after the item required by paragraph 5(2)(m) (whichever is the position adopted for the full accounts), there shall in addition be shown under an appropriate heading the item "Minority interests" required to be shown in the Schedule 9 format by paragraph 17(2) of Schedule 4A to the 1985 Act, as adapted by paragraph 3(2) of Part II of Schedule 9 to the 1985 Act.

Corresponding amounts

7. In respect of every item shown in the summary profit and loss account or summary consolidated profit and loss account (as the case may be), or in the summary balance sheet or summary consolidated balance sheet (as the case may be) the corresponding amount shall be shown for the immediately preceding financial year; for this purpose "the corresponding amount" is the amount shown in the summary financial statement for that year or which would have been so shown had such a statement been prepared for that year, [taking account of any adjustments to corresponding amounts made in the full accounts and reports].

[6894]

NOTES

Para 1: words in square brackets in sub-para (2) inserted by the Companies (Summary Financial Statement) (Amendment) Regulations 2005, SI 2005/2281, reg 13(1), (2), as from 1 October 2005; words omitted revoked by the Companies Act 1985 (Operating and Financial Review) (Repeal) Regulations 2005, SI 2005/3442, reg 2(2)(b), Sch 2, para 2(1), (5), as from 12 January 2006.

Para 2: revoked by SI 2005/2281, reg 13(1), (3), as from 1 October 2005.

Para 2A: inserted by the Companies (Summary Financial Statement) Amendment Regulations 2002, SI 2002/1780, reg 6(1), as from 1 August 2002, with effect as respects companies' financial years ending on or after 31 December 2002.

Para 3: sub-para (3)(k) revoked by SI 2005/2281, reg 13(1), (4), as from 1 October 2005; sub-para (4) revoked by SI 2002/1780, reg 6(2), as from 1 August 2002, with effect as respects companies' financial years ending on or after 31 December 2002.

Para 3A: inserted by SI 2005/2281, reg 13(1), (5), as from 1 October 2005.

Para 4: words in square brackets inserted by SI 2005/2281, reg 13(1), (6), as from 1 October 2005.

Para 7: words in square brackets substituted by SI 2005/2281, reg 13(1), (7), as from 1 October 2005.

Treasury bills: a reference to a Treasury bill in this Schedule includes a reference to uncertificated units of eligible Treasury bills; see the Uncertificated Securities (Amendment) (Eligible Debt Securities) Regulations 2003, SI 2003/1633, reg 15, Sch 2, para 2(i).

SCHEDULE 3
FORM AND CONTENT OF SUMMARY FINANCIAL STATEMENT OF INSURANCE COMPANIES AND GROUPS

Regulation 10

...

1. ...

Form of summary financial statement

2.—(1) The summary financial statement shall contain the information prescribed by the following paragraphs of this Schedule, in such order and under such headings as the directors consider appropriate, together with any other information necessary to ensure that the summary financial statement is consistent with the full accounts and reports for the financial year in question.

(2) Nothing in this Schedule shall be construed as prohibiting the inclusion in the summary financial statement of any additional information derived from the company's annual accounts[, the directors' remuneration report (if any) …] and the directors' report.

…

3. …

[Summary of paragraph 1(1) of Schedule 6 to the 1985 Act and of the directors' remuneration report

3A. The summary financial statement shall contain the whole of, or a summary of—
- (a) that portion of the notes to the accounts for the year in question which set out the information required by paragraph 1(1) of Part I of Schedule 6 to the 1985 Act (Aggregate amount of directors' emoluments etc); and
- (b) to the extent that the company is required to produce a directors' remuneration report, those portions of the directors' remuneration report for the year in question which set out the matters required by paragraphs 3 (Statement of company's policy on directors' remuneration) and 4 (Performance graph) of Schedule 7A to the 1985 Act.]

Summary profit and loss account: companies not required to prepare group accounts

4.—(1) The summary financial statement shall contain, in the case of a company the directors of which are not required to prepare group accounts for the financial year, a summary profit and loss account showing, in so far as they may be derived from the full profit and loss account, the items, or combinations of items, listed in sub-paragraph (3) below, in the order set out in that sub-paragraph.

(2) The items or combinations of items listed in sub-paragraph (3) below may appear under such headings as the directors consider appropriate.

(3) The items, or combinations of items, referred to in sub-paragraph (1) above are—
- (a) gross premiums written–general business—
  - — item I 1(a);
- (b) gross premiums written–long term business—
  - — item II 1(a);
- (c) balance on the technical account for general business—
  - — item I 10;
- (d) balance on the technical account for long term business—
  - — item II 13;
- (e) other income and charges: the net figure resulting from the combination of the following items—
  - — item III 3
  - — item III 3a
  - — item III 4
  - — item III 5
  - — item III 5a
  - — item III 6
  - — item III 7
  - — item III 8;
- (f) the profit or loss on ordinary activities before tax—
  - — item III 8a;
- (g) tax on profit or loss on ordinary activities—
  - — item III 9;
- (h) profit or loss on ordinary activities after tax—
  - — item III 10;
- (i) extraordinary profit or loss after tax—
  - — the net figure resulting from the combination of items III 13 and 14;
- (j) other taxes—

PART IV
STATUTORY INSTRUMENTS

— item III 15;

(k) profit or loss for the financial year—

— item III 16; and

(l) …

(4) …

[Dividends

4A The summary financial statement shall also contain the information concerning recognised and proposed dividends included in the full accounts and reports.]

Summary profit and loss account: companies required to prepare group accounts

5.—(1) The summary financial statement shall contain, in the case of a company the directors of which are required to prepare group accounts for the financial year, a summary consolidated profit and loss account showing the items, or combinations of items, required by paragraph 4 above, in the order required by that paragraph and under such headings as the directors consider appropriate, but with the modifications specified in sub-paragraph (2) below[, and shall also contain the information required by paragraph 4A above].

(2) The modifications referred to in sub-paragraph (1) above are as follows—

(a) between the information required by paragraph 4(3)(e) and that required by paragraph 4(3)(f) there shall in addition be shown, under such heading as the directors consider appropriate, the item "Income from associated undertakings" required to be shown in the Schedule 9A formats by paragraph 21(3)(b) of Schedule 4A to the 1985 Act, as adapted by paragraph 1(8) of Part II of Schedule 9A to that Act;

(b) between the information required by paragraph 4(3)(h) and that required by paragraph 4(3)(i) there shall in addition be shown, under such heading as the directors consider appropriate, the item "Minority interests" required to be shown in the Schedule 9A formats by paragraph 17(3) of Schedule 4A to the 1985 Act as adapted by paragraph 1(6)(c) of Part II of Schedule 9A to that Act; and

(c) the figures required by paragraph 4(3)(i) and (j) shall each be shown after the deduction or the addition (as the case may be) of the item "Minority interests" required to be shown in the Schedule 9A formats by paragraph 17(4) of Schedule 4A to the 1985 Act as adapted by paragraph 1(6)(d) of Part II of Schedule 9A to that Act.

Summary balance sheet: companies not required to prepare group accounts

6.—(1) The summary financial statement shall contain, in the case of a company the directors of which are not required to prepare group accounts for the financial year, a summary balance sheet which shall show, in so far as they may be derived from the full balance sheet, the items, or combinations of items, set out in sub-paragraph (2) below in the order of that sub-paragraph and under such headings as the directors consider appropriate.

(2) The items, or combinations of items, referred to in sub-paragraph (1) above are—

(a) investments—

— the aggregate of items C and D under the heading "ASSETS";

(b) reinsurers' share of technical provisions—

— item Da under the heading "ASSETS";

(c) other assets—

— the aggregate of items A or E(IV), B, E(I) to (III), F and G under the heading "ASSETS";

(d) total assets under the heading "ASSETS";

(e) capital and reserves—

— item A under the heading "LIABILITIES";

(f) subordinated liabilities—

— item B under the heading "LIABILITIES";

(g) fund for future appropriations—

— item Ba under the heading "LIABILITIES";

(h) gross technical provisions—

— the aggregate of items C.1(a), C.2(a), C.3(a), C.4(a), C.5, C.6(a) and D(a) under the heading "LIABILITIES";

(i) technical provisions–reinsurance amounts—
— the aggregate of items C.1(b), C.2(b), C.3(b), C.4(b), C.6(b) and D(b) under the heading "LIABILITIES";

(j) other liabilities—
— the aggregate of items E, F, G and H under the heading "LIABILITIES"; and

(k) total liabilities under the heading "LIABILITIES".

Summary balance sheet: companies required to prepare group accounts

7.—(1) The summary financial statement shall contain, in the case of a company the directors of which are required to prepare group accounts for the financial year, a summary consolidated balance sheet which shall show the items required by paragraph 6 above, in the order required by that paragraph and under such headings as the directors consider appropriate, but with the addition of the item specified in sub-paragraph (2) below.

(2) Between the items required by paragraph 6(2)(d) and (e) above, there shall in addition be shown under an appropriate heading the item "Minority interests" required to be shown in the Schedule 9A format by paragraph 17(2) of Schedule 4A to the 1985 Act, as adapted by paragraph 1(6)(b) of Part II of Schedule 9A to the 1985 Act.

Corresponding amounts

8. In respect of every item shown in the summary profit and loss account or summary consolidated profit and loss account (as the case may be) or in the summary balance sheet or summary consolidated balance sheet (as the case may be) the corresponding amount shall be shown for the immediately preceding financial year; for this purpose "the corresponding amount" is the amount shown in the summary financial statement for that year or which would have been so shown had such a statement been prepared for that year, [taking account of any adjustments to corresponding amounts made in the full accounts and reports].

...

9–12. ...

[6895]

NOTES

Paras 1, 3 ,9–12: revoked by the Companies (Summary Financial Statement) (Amendment) Regulations 2005, SI 2005/2281, regs 14(1), (3), 17(b), as from 1 October 2005.

Para 2: words in square brackets in sub-para (2) inserted by SI 2005/2281, reg 14(1), (2), as from 1 October 2005; words omitted revoked by the Companies Act 1985 (Operating and Financial Review) (Repeal) Regulations 2005, SI 2005/3442, reg 2(2)(b), Sch 2, para 2(1), (6), as from 12 January 2006.

Para 3A: inserted by the Companies (Summary Financial Statement) Amendment Regulations 2002, SI 2002/1780, reg 7(1), as from 1 August 2002, with effect as respects companies' financial years ending on or after 31 December 2002.

Para 4: sub-para (3)(l) revoked by SI 2005/2281, reg 14(1), (4), as from 1 October 2005; sub-para (4) revoked by SI 2002/1780, reg 7(2), as from 1 August 2002, with effect as respects companies' financial years ending on or after 31 December 2002.

Para 4A: inserted by SI 2005/2281, reg 14(1), (5), as from 1 October 2005.

Para 5: words in square brackets inserted by SI 2005/2281, reg 14(1), (6), as from 1 October 2005.

Para 8: words in square brackets substituted by SI 2005/2281, reg 14(1), (7), as from 1 October 2005.

[SCHEDULE 3A
FORM AND CONTENT OF SUMMARY FINANCIAL STATEMENT OF COMPANIES AND GROUPS PREPARING ACCOUNTS IN ACCORDANCE WITH INTERNATIONAL ACCOUNTING STANDARDS

Regulation 10A

Form of summary financial statement

1.—(1) The summary financial statement shall contain the information prescribed by the following paragraphs of this Schedule in such order, and under such headings, as the directors consider appropriate.

(2) The summary financial statement shall contain any other information necessary to ensure that the statement is consistent with the full accounts and reports for the year in question.

(3) Nothing in this Schedule shall be construed as prohibiting the inclusion in the summary financial statement of any additional information derived from the company's annual accounts, directors' report, directors' remuneration report (if any) or operating and financial review (if any).

Summary of paragraph 1(1) of Schedule 6 to the 1985 Act and of the directors' remuneration report

2. The summary financial statement shall contain the whole of, or a summary of—
   (a) that portion of the notes to the accounts for the year in question which set out the information required by paragraph 1(1) of Part I of Schedule 6 to the 1985 Act (aggregate amount of directors' emoluments etc); and
   (b) to the extent that the company is required to produce a directors' remuneration report, those portions of the directors' remuneration report for the year in question which set out the matters required by paragraphs 3 (statement of company's policy on directors' remuneration) and 4 (performance graph) of Schedule 7A to the 1985 Act.

Summary profit loss and account: companies not required to prepare group accounts

3.—(1) The summary financial statement shall contain, in the case of a company the directors of which are not required to prepare group accounts for the financial year, a summary profit and loss account showing either—
   (a) each of the headings and sub-totals included in the full profit and loss account in accordance with international accounting standards, or
   (b) where the directors consider it appropriate, a combination of such headings and sub-totals where they are of a similar nature.

(2) The summary financial statement shall also contain the information concerning recognised and proposed dividends included in the full accounts and reports.

(3) In this paragraph, and in paragraphs 4 to 6 below, the expressions "headings and "subtotals" have the same meaning as in international accounting standard 1 on the presentation of financial statements.

Summary profit and loss account: companies required to prepare group accounts

4.—(1) The summary financial statement shall contain, in the case of a company the directors of which are required to prepare group accounts for the financial year, a summary consolidated profit and loss account showing either—
   (a) each of the headings and sub-totals included in the full consolidated profit and loss account in accordance with international accounting standards, or
   (b) where the directors consider it appropriate, a combination of such headings and sub-totals where they are of a similar nature.

(2) The summary financial statement shall also contain the information concerning recognised and proposed dividends included in the full accounts and reports.

Summary balance sheet: companies not required to prepare group accounts

5. The summary financial statement shall contain, in the case of a company the directors of which are not required to prepare group accounts for the financial year, a summary balance sheet showing either—
   (a) each of the headings and sub-totals included in the full balance sheet in accordance with international accounting standards, or
   (b) where the directors consider it appropriate, a combination of such headings and sub-totals where they are of a similar nature.

Summary balance sheet: companies required to prepare group accounts

6. The summary financial statement shall contain, in the case of a company the directors of which are required to prepare group accounts for the financial year, a summary consolidated balance sheet showing either—

(a) each of the headings and sub-totals included in the full consolidated balance sheet in accordance with international accounting standards, or

(b) where the directors consider it appropriate, a combination of such headings and sub-totals where they are of a similar nature.

Corresponding amounts

7.—(1) In respect of every item shown in the summary profit and loss account or summary consolidated profit and loss account (as the case may be), or in the summary balance sheet or summary consolidated balance sheet (as the case may be),the corresponding amount must be shown for the immediately preceding financial year.

(2) For the purposes of sub-paragraph (1), "the corresponding amount" is the amount shown in the summary financial statement for that year or which would have been so shown had such a statement been prepared for that year, taking account of any adjustments to corresponding amounts made in the full accounts and reports.]

[6895A]

NOTES

Commencement: 1 October 2005.

Added by the Companies (Summary Financial Statement) (Amendment) Regulations 2005, SI 2005/2281, reg 15, Schedule, as from 1 October 2005.

COMPANY AND BUSINESS NAMES (AMENDMENT) REGULATIONS 1995

(SI 1995/3022)

NOTES

Made: 23 November 1995.

Authority: CA 1985, s 29; Business Names Act 1985, ss 3, 6.

Commencement: 1 January 1996 (see reg 1 at **[6896]**). Where any provision in this work (including any inserted or substituted provision) came into force for all purposes on or before 1 July 2005, commencement information is not noted at provision level.

As of 1 July 2007, these Regulations had not been amended.

1 These Regulations may be cited as the Company and Business Names (Amendment) Regulations 1995 and shall come into force on 1st January 1996.

[6896]

2 In these Regulations—

"the 1981 Regulations" means the Company and Business Names Regulations 1981;

"the Act" means the Business Names Act 1985.

[6897]

3 (*Amends the Company and Business Names Regulations 1981, SI 1981/1685, Schedule at* **[6006]**.)

4—(1) Sections 2 and 3 of the Act shall not prohibit a person from carrying on any business under a name which includes any word or expression specified for the purposes of those sections by virtue of the amendment made by regulation 3(a) above to the 1981 Regulations, if—

(a) he carried on that business immediately before 1st January 1996; and

(b) he continues to carry it on under the name which immediately before that day was its lawful business name.

(2) Nor shall sections 2 and 3 of the Act prohibit a person to whom a business has been transferred on or after 1st January 1996 from carrying on that business during the period of twelve months beginning with the date of transfer so long as he continues to carry it on under the name which was its lawful business name immediately before the date of transfer.

[6898]

COMPANIES ACT 1985 (MISCELLANEOUS ACCOUNTING AMENDMENTS) REGULATIONS 1996 (NOTE)

(SI 1996/189)

NOTES

These Regulations were made under CA 1985, s 257 and came into force on 2 February 1996 (for certain purposes) and 1 April 1996 (otherwise). They amend various provisions in Part VII of the 1985 Act (at **[207]** et seq). Reg 16 of these Regulations provides for transitional provisions as noted to the amended provisions of the 1985 Act *ante*. In particular, reg 16(2) provides that a company may, with respect to a financial year of the company ending on or before 24 March 1996, prepare and deliver to the registrar of companies such annual accounts and annual report as it would have been required to prepare and deliver had the amendments to the 1985 Act effected by these Regulations not been made.

[6899]–[6900]

CO-OPERATION OF INSOLVENCY COURTS (DESIGNATION OF RELEVANT COUNTRIES) ORDER 1996 (NOTE)

(SI 1996/253)

NOTES

This Order was made on 8 February 1996 under the powers conferred by the Insolvency Act 1986, s 426(11) and came into force on 1 March 1996. It designates Malaysia and the Republic of South Africa as relevant countries for the purposes of the said 426.

[6901]–[6907]

FINANCIAL MARKETS AND INSOLVENCY REGULATIONS 1996

(SI 1996/1469)

NOTES

Made: 5 June 1996.

Authority: CA 1989, ss 185, 186.

Commencement: 15 July 1996 (see reg 1 at **[6908]**). Where any provision in this work (including any inserted or substituted provision) came into force for all purposes on or before 1 July 2005, commencement information is not noted at provision level.

These Regulations are reproduced as amended by: the Uncertificated Securities Regulations 2001, SI 2001/3755; the Enterprise Act 2002 (Insolvency) Order 2003, SI 2003/2096; the Enterprise Act 2002 (Insolvency) Order 2004, SI 2004/2312.

ARRANGEMENT OF REGULATIONS

PART I
GENERAL

1 Citation and commencement

These Regulations may be cited as the Financial Markets and Insolvency Regulations 1996 and shall come into force on 15th July 1996.

[6908]

2 Interpretation

(1) In these Regulations—

"the Act" means the Companies Act 1989;

"business day" means any day which is not a Saturday or Sunday, Christmas Day, Good Friday or a bank holiday in any part of the United Kingdom under the Banking and Financial Dealings Act 1971;

"issue", in relation to an uncertificated unit of a security, means to confer on a person title to a new unit;

"register of securities"—

(a) in relation to shares, means a register of members; and

(b) in relation to units of a security other than shares, means [a register, whether maintained by virtue of the Uncertificated Securities Regulations 2001 or otherwise], of persons holding the units;

. . . .

"relevant nominee" means a system-member who is a subsidiary undertaking of the Operator designated by him as such in accordance with such rules and practices as are mentioned in [paragraph 25(f) of Schedule 1 to the Uncertificated Securities Regulations 2001];

"settlement bank" means a person who has contracted with an Operator to make payments in connection with transfers, by means of a relevant system, of title to uncertificated units of a security and of interests of system-beneficiaries in relation to such units;

"system-beneficiary" means a person on whose behalf a system-member or former system-member holds or held uncertificated units of a security;

"system-charge" means a charge of a kind to which regulation 3(2) applies;

"system-member" means a person who is permitted by an Operator to transfer by means of a relevant system title to uncertificated units of a security held by him; and "former system-member" means a person whose participation in the relevant system is terminated or suspended;

"transfer", in relation to title to uncertificated units of a security, means [the registration of a transfer of title to those units in the relevant Operator register of securities;] and in relation to an interest of a system-beneficiary in relation to uncertificated units of a security, means the transfer of the interest to another system-beneficiary by means of a relevant system; and

other expressions used in these Regulations which are also used in [the Uncertificated Securities Regulations 2001] have the same meanings as in those Regulations.

(2) For the purposes of these Regulations, a person holds a unit of a security if—

(a) in the case of an uncertificated unit, he is entered on a register of securities in relation to the unit in accordance with [regulation 20, 21 or 22 of the Uncertificated Securities Regulations 2001]; and

(b) in the case of a certificated unit, he has title to the unit.

(3) A reference in any of these Regulations to a numbered regulation shall be construed as a reference to the regulation bearing that number in these Regulations.

(4) A reference in any of these Regulations to a numbered paragraph shall, unless the reference is to a paragraph of a specified regulation, be construed as a reference to the paragraph bearing that number in the regulation in which the reference is made.

[6909]

NOTES

Para (1): words in square brackets substituted, and definition "the 1995 Regulations" revoked, by the Uncertificated Securities Regulations 2001, SI 2001/3755, reg 51, Sch 7, Pt 2, para 20(a), as from 26 November 2001.

Para (2): words in square brackets substituted by SI 2001/3755, reg 51, Sch 7, Pt 2, para 20(b), as from 26 November 2001.

PART II
SYSTEM-CHARGES

3 Application of Part VII of the Act in relation to system-charges

(1) Subject to the provisions of these Regulations, Part VII of the Act shall apply in relation to—

(a) a charge to which paragraph (2) applies ("a system-charge") and any action taken to enforce such a charge; and

(b) any property subject to a system-charge,

in the same way as it applies in relation to a market charge, any action taken to enforce a market charge and any property subject to a market charge.

(2) This paragraph applies in relation to a charge granted in favour of a settlement bank for the purpose of securing debts or liabilities arising in connection with any of the following—

(a) a transfer of uncertificated units of a security to a system-member by means of a relevant system whether the system-member is acting for himself or on behalf of a system-beneficiary;

(b) a transfer, by one system-beneficiary to another and by means of a relevant system, of his interests in relation to uncertificated units of a security held by a relevant nominee where the relevant nominee will continue to hold the units;

(c) an agreement to make a transfer of the kind specified in paragraph (a);

(d) an agreement to make a transfer of the kind specified in paragraph (b); and

(e) an issue of uncertificated units of a security to a system-member by means of a relevant system whether the system-member is acting for himself or on behalf of a system-beneficiary.

(3) In its application, by virtue of these Regulations, in relation to a system-charge, section 173(2) of the Act shall have effect as if the references to "purposes specified" and "specified purposes" were references to any one or more of the purposes specified in paragraph (2).

[6910]

4 Circumstances in which Part VII applies in relation to system-charge

(1) Part VII of the Act shall apply in relation to a system-charge granted by a system-member and in relation to property subject to such a charge only if—

(a) it is granted to a settlement bank by a system-member for the purpose of securing debts or liabilities arising in connection with any of the transactions specified in regulation 3(2), being debts or liabilities incurred by that system-member or by a system-beneficiary on whose behalf he holds uncertificated units of a security; and

(b) it contains provisions which refer expressly to the relevant system in relation to which the grantor is a system-member.

(2) Part VII of the Act shall apply in relation to a system-charge granted by a system-beneficiary and in relation to property subject to such a charge only if—

(a) it is granted to a settlement bank by a system-beneficiary for the purpose of securing debts or liabilities arising in connection with any of the transactions specified in regulation 3(2), incurred by that system-beneficiary or by a system-member who holds uncertificated units of a security on his behalf; and

(b) it contains provisions which refer expressly to the relevant system in relation to which the system-member who holds the uncertificated units of a security in relation to which the system-beneficiary has the interest is a system-member.

[6911]

5 Extent to which Part VII applies to a system-charge

Part VII of the Act shall apply in relation to a system-charge only to the extent that—

(a) it is a charge over any one or more of the following—

(i) uncertificated units of a security held by a system-member or a former system-member;

(ii) interests of a kind specified in [regulation 31(2)(b) or 31(4)(b) of the Uncertificated Securities Regulations 2001] in uncertificated units of a security in favour of a system member or a former system-member;

(iii) interests of a system-beneficiary in relation to uncertificated units of a security;

(iv) units of a security which are no longer in uncertificated form because the person holding the units has become a former system-member;

(v) sums or other benefits receivable by a system-member or former system-member by reason of his holding uncertificated units of a security, or units which are no longer in uncertificated form because the person holding the units has become a former system-member;

(vi) sums or other benefits receivable by a system-beneficiary by reason of his having an interest in relation to uncertificated units of a security or in relation to units which are no longer in uncertificated form because the person holding the units has become a former system-member;

(vii) sums or other benefits receivable by a system-member or former system-member by way of repayment, bonus, preference, redemption, conversion or accruing or offered in respect of uncertificated units of a security, or units which are no longer in uncertificated form because the person holding the units has become a former system-member;

(viii) sums or other benefits receivable by a system-beneficiary by way of repayment, bonus, preference, redemption, conversion or accruing or offered in respect of uncertificated units of a security in relation to which he has an interest or in respect of units in relation to which the system-beneficiary has an interest and which are no longer in uncertificated form because the person holding the units has become a former system-member;

(ix) sums or other benefits receivable by a system-member or former system-member in respect of the transfer of uncertificated units of a security by or to him by means of a relevant system;

(x) sums or other benefits receivable by a system-member or former system-member in respect of an agreement to transfer uncertificated units of a security by or to him by means of a relevant system;

(xi) sums or other benefits receivable by a system-beneficiary in respect of the transfer of the interest of a system-beneficiary in relation to uncertificated units of a security by or to him by means of a relevant system or in respect of the transfer of uncertificated units of a security by or to a system-member acting on his behalf by means of a relevant system;

(xii) sums or other benefits receivable by a system-beneficiary in respect of an agreement to transfer the interest of a system-beneficiary in relation to uncertificated units of a security by or to him by means of a relevant system, or in respect of an agreement to transfer uncertificated units of a security by or to a system-member acting on his behalf by means of a relevant system; and

(b) it secures—

(i) the obligation of a system-member or former system-member to reimburse a settlement bank, being an obligation which arises in connection with any of the transactions specified in regulation 3(2) and whether the obligation was incurred by the system-member when acting for himself or when acting on behalf of a system-beneficiary; or

(ii) the obligation of a system-beneficiary to reimburse a settlement bank, being an obligation which arises in connection with any of the transactions specified in regulation 3(2) and whether the obligation was incurred by the system-beneficiary when acting for himself or by reason of a system-member acting on his behalf.

[6912]

PART IV
STATUTORY INSTRUMENTS

NOTES

Words in square brackets in sub-para (a)(ii) substituted by the Uncertificated Securities Regulations 2001, SI 2001/3755, reg 51, Sch 7, Pt 2, para 20(c), as from 26 November 2001.

6 [Limitation on disapplication of moratorium on certain legal processes under Schedule B1 to the Insolvency Act 1986 (administration) in relation to system-charges]

(1) This regulation applies where an administration order is made in relation to a system-member or former system-member.

[(1A) A reference in paragraph (1) to "an administration order" shall include the appointment of an administrator under paragraph 14 or 22 of Schedule B1 to the Insolvency Act 1986].

(2) [The disapplication of paragraph 43(2) of Schedule B1 to the Insolvency Act 1986 (including that provision as applied by paragraph 44 of that Schedule)] by section 175(1)(a) of the Act shall have effect, in relation to a system-charge granted by a system-member or former system-member, only to the extent necessary to enable there to be realised, whether through the sale of uncertificated units of a security or otherwise, the lesser of the two sums specified in paragraphs (3) and (4).

(3) The first sum of the two sums referred to in paragraph (2) is the net sum of—

(a) all payment obligations discharged by the settlement bank in connection with—

(i) transfers of uncertificated units of a security by means of a relevant system made during the qualifying period to or by the relevant system-member or former system-member, whether acting for himself or on behalf of a system-beneficiary;

(ii) agreements made during the qualifying period to transfer uncertificated units of a security by means of a relevant system to or from the relevant system-member or former system-member, whether acting for himself or on behalf of a system-beneficiary; and

(iii) issues of uncertificated units of a security by means of a relevant system made during the qualifying period to the relevant system-member or former system-member, whether acting for himself or on behalf of a system-beneficiary; less

(b) all payment obligations discharged to the settlement bank in connection with transactions of any kind described in paragraph (3)(a)(i) and (ii).

(4) The second of the two sums referred to in paragraph (2) is the sum (if any) due to the settlement bank from the relevant system-member or former system-member by reason of an obligation of the kind described in regulation 5(b)(i).

(5) In this regulation and regulation 7, "qualifying period" means the period—

(a) beginning with the fifth business day before the day on which [an application] for the making of the administration order was presented; and

(b) ending with the second business day after the day on which the administration order is made.

[(5A) A reference in paragraph (5) to an application for an administration order shall be treated as including a reference to—

(a) appointing an administrator under [paragraph 14] or 22 of Schedule B1 to the Insolvency Act 1986, or

(b) filing with the court a notice of intention to appoint an administrator under either of those paragraphs,

and a reference to "an administration order" shall include the appointment of an administrator under paragraph 14 or 22 of Schedule B1 to the Insolvency Act 1986.]

[6913]

NOTES

Regulation heading: substituted by the Enterprise Act 2002 (Insolvency) Order 2003, SI 2003/2096, arts 5, 6, Schedule, Pt 2, paras 61, 62(a), as from 15 September 2003, except in relation to any case where a petition for an administration order was presented before that date.

Para (1A): inserted by SI 2003/2096, arts 5, 6, Schedule, Pt 2, paras 61, 62(b), as from 15 September 2003, except in relation to any case where a petition for an administration order was presented before that date.

Paras (2), (5): words in square brackets substituted by SI 2003/2096, arts 5, 6, Schedule, Pt 2, paras 61, 62(c), (d), as from 15 September 2003, except in relation to any case where a petition for an administration order was presented before that date.

Para (5A): added by SI 2003/2096, arts 5, 6, Schedule, Pt 2, paras 61, 62(e), as from 15 September 2003, except in relation to any case where a petition for an administration order was presented before that date; words in square brackets substituted by the Enterprise Act 2002 (Insolvency) Order 2004, SI 2004/2312, art 3, as from 15 October 2004.

7 [Limitation on disapplication of moratorium on certain legal processes under Schedule B1 to the Insolvency Act 1986 (administration) in relation to system-charges granted by a system-beneficiary]

(1) This regulation applies where an administration order is made in relation to a system-beneficiary.

[(1A) A reference in paragraph (1) to "an administration order" shall include the appointment of an administrator under paragraph 14 or 22 of Schedule B1 to the Insolvency Act 1986].

(2) [The disapplication of paragraph 43(2) of Schedule B1 to the Insolvency Act 1986 (including that provision as applied by paragraph 44 of that Schedule)] by section 175(1)(a) of the Act shall have effect, in relation to a system-charge granted by a system-beneficiary, only to the extent necessary to enable there to be realised, whether through the sale of interests of a system-beneficiary in relation to uncertificated units of a security or otherwise, the lesser of the two sums specified in paragraphs (3) and (4).

(3) The first of the two sums referred to in paragraph (2) is the net sum of—

(a) all payment obligations discharged by the settlement bank in connection with—

(i) transfers, to or by the relevant system-beneficiary by means of a relevant system made during the qualifying period, of interests of the system-beneficiary in relation to uncertificated units of a security held by a relevant nominee, where the relevant nominee has continued to hold the units;

(ii) agreements made during the qualifying period to transfer, to or from the relevant system-beneficiary by means of a relevant system, interests of the system-beneficiary in relation to uncertificated units of a security held by a relevant nominee, where the relevant nominee will continue to hold the units;

(iii) transfers, during the qualifying period and by means of a relevant system, of uncertificated units of a security, being transfers made to or by a system-member acting on behalf of the relevant system-beneficiary;

(iv) agreements made during the qualifying period to transfer uncertificated units of a security by means of a relevant system to or from a system-member acting on behalf of the relevant system-beneficiary; and

(v) issues of uncertificated units of a security made during the qualifying period and by means of a relevant system, being issues to a system-member acting on behalf of the relevant system-beneficiary; less

(b) all payment obligations discharged to the settlement bank in connection with transactions of any kind described in paragraph (3)(a)(i) to (iv).

(4) The second of the two sums referred to in paragraph (2) is the sum (if any) due to the settlement bank from the relevant system-beneficiary by reason of an obligation of the kind described in regulation 5(b)(ii).

[6914]

NOTES

Regulation heading: substituted by the Enterprise Act 2002 (Insolvency) Order 2003, SI 2003/2096, arts 5, 6, Schedule, Pt 2, paras 61, 63(a), as from 15 September 2003, except in relation to any case where a petition for an administration order was presented before that date.

Para (1A): inserted by SI 2003/2096, arts 5, 6, Schedule, Pt 2, paras 61, 63(b), as from 15 September 2003, except in relation to any case where a petition for an administration order was presented before that date.

Para (2): words in square brackets substituted by SI 2003/2096, arts 5, 6, Schedule, Pt 2, paras 61, 63(c), as from 15 September 2003, except in relation to any case where a petition for an administration order was presented before that date.

8 Ability of administrator or receiver to recover assets in case of property subject to system-charge

(1) This regulation applies where an administration order is made or an administrator or an administrative receiver or a receiver is appointed, in relation to a system-member, former system-member or system-beneficiary.

[(1A) A reference in paragraph (1) to "an administration order" shall include the appointment of an administrator under paragraph 14 or 22 of Schedule B1 to the Insolvency Act 1986.]

(2) [The disapplication—

(a) by section 175(1)(b) of the Act, of paragraphs 70, 71 and 72 of Schedule B1 to the Insolvency Act 1986, and

(b) by section 175(3) of the Act, of sections 43 and 61 of the 1986 Act,

shall cease to have effect] after the end of the relevant day in respect of any property which is subject to a system-charge granted by the system-member, former system-member or system-beneficiary if on the basis of a valuation in accordance with paragraph (3), the charge is not required for the realisation of the sum specified in paragraph (4) or (5).

(3) For the purposes of paragraph (2), the value of property shall, except in a case falling within paragraph (6), be such as may be agreed between the administrator, administrative receiver or receiver on the one hand and the settlement bank on the other.

(4) Where the system-charge has been granted by a system-member or former system-member, the sum referred to in paragraph (2) is whichever is the lesser of—

(a) the sum referred to in regulation 6(3);

(b) the sum referred to in regulation 6(4) due to the settlement bank at the close of business on the relevant day.

(5) Where the system-charge has been granted by a system-beneficiary, the sum referred to in paragraph (2) is whichever is the lesser of—

(a) the sum referred to in regulation 7(3);

(b) the sum referred to in regulation 7(4) due to the settlement bank at the close of business on the relevant day.

(6) For the purposes of paragraph (2), the value of any property for which a price for the relevant day is quoted in the Daily Official List of The London Stock Exchange Limited shall—

(a) in a case in which two prices are so quoted, be an amount equal to the average of those two prices, adjusted where appropriate to take account of any accrued dividend or interest; and

(b) in a case in which one price is so quoted, be an amount equal to that price, adjusted where appropriate to take account of any accrued dividend or interest.

(7) In this regulation "the relevant day" means the second business day after the day on which the [company enters administration], or the administrative receiver or receiver is appointed.

[6915]

NOTES

Para (1A): inserted by the Enterprise Act 2002 (Insolvency) Order 2003, SI 2003/2096, arts 5, 6, Schedule, Pt 2, paras 61, 64(a), as from 15 September 2003, except in relation to any case where a petition for an administration order was presented before that date.

Paras (2), (7): words in square brackets substituted by SI 2003/2096, arts 5, 6, Schedule, Pt 2, paras 61, 64(b), (c), as from 15 September 2003, except in relation to any case where a petition for an administration order was presented before that date.

9 ((*Pt III*) *spent; amended CA 1989, s 156* (*repealed*).)

INSOLVENT COMPANIES (REPORTS ON CONDUCT OF DIRECTORS) RULES 1996

(SI 1996/1909)

NOTES

Made: 22 July 1996.

Authority: Insolvency Act 1986, s 411; Company Directors Disqualification Act 1986, s 21(2).

Commencement: 30 September 1996 (see r 1 at **[6916]**). Where any provision in this work (including any inserted or substituted provision) came into force for all purposes on or before 1 July 2005, commencement information is not noted at provision level.

These Rules (as set out here) are reproduced as amended by: the Enterprise Act 2002 (Insolvency) Order 2003, SI 2003/2096.

Limited liability partnerships: by the Limited Liability Partnerships Regulations 2001, SI 2001/1090, reg 10, Sch 6, Pt III, these Rules apply, with modifications, to limited liability partnerships (see **[7000]**).

ARRANGEMENT OF RULES

1 Citation, commencement and interpretation

(1) These Rules may be cited as the Insolvent Companies (Reports on Conduct of Directors) Rules 1996.

(2) These Rules shall come into force on 30th September 1996.

(3) In these Rules—

"the Act" means the Company Directors Disqualification Act 1986;

"the former Rules" means the Insolvent Companies (Reports on Conduct of Directors) No 2 Rules 1986; and

"the commencement date" means 30th September 1996.

[6916]

2 Revocation

Subject to rule 7 below, the former Rules are hereby revoked.

[6916A]

3 Reports required under section 7(3) of the Act

(1) This rule applies to any report made to the Secretary of State under section 7(3) of the Act by:—

(a) the liquidator of a company which the courts in England and Wales have jurisdiction to wind up which passes a resolution for voluntary winding up on or after the commencement date;

(b) an administrative receiver of a company appointed otherwise than under section 51 of the Insolvency Act 1986 (power to appoint receiver under the law of Scotland) on or after the commencement date; or

(c) the administrator of a company which the courts in England and Wales have jurisdiction to wind up [which enters administration] on or after the commencement date.

(2) Such a report shall be made in the Form D1 set out in the Schedule hereto, or in a form which is substantially similar, and in the manner and to the extent required by the Form D1.

[6917]

NOTES

Para (1): words in square brackets substituted by the Enterprise Act 2002 (Insolvency) Order 2003, SI 2003/2096, arts 5, 6, Schedule, Pt 2, paras 68, 69, as from 15 September 2003, except in relation to any case where a petition for an administration order was presented before that date.

4 Return by office-holder

(1) This rule applies where it appears to a liquidator of a company as mentioned in rule 3(1)(a), to an administrative receiver as mentioned in rule 3(1)(b), or to an administrator as mentioned in rule 3(1)(c) (each of whom is referred to hereinafter as "an office-holder") that the company has at any time become insolvent within the meaning of section 6(2) of the Act.

(2) Subject as follows there may be furnished to the Secretary of State by an office-holder at any time during the period of 6 months from the relevant date (defined in paragraph (4) below) a return with respect to every person who:—

(a) was, on the relevant date, a director or shadow director of the company, or

(b) had been a director or shadow director of the company at any time in the 3 years immediately preceding that date.

(3) The return shall be made in the Form D2 set out in the Schedule hereto, or in a form which is substantially similar, and in the manner and to the extent required by the Form D2.

(4) For the purposes of this rule, "the relevant date" means:—

(a) in the case of a company in creditors' voluntary winding up (there having been no declaration of solvency by the directors under section 89 of the Insolvency Act 1986), the date of the passing of the resolution for voluntary winding up,

(b) in the case of a company in members' voluntary winding up, the date on which the liquidator forms the opinion that, at the time when the company went into liquidation, its assets were insufficient for the payment of its debts and other liabilities and the expenses of winding up,

(c) in the case of the administrative receiver, the date of his appointment,

(d) in the case of the administrator, the date [that the company enters administration],

and for the purposes of sub-paragraph (c) above the only appointment of an administrative receiver to be taken into account in determining the relevant date shall be that appointment which is not that of a successor in office to an administrative receiver who has vacated office either by death or pursuant to section 45 of the Insolvency Act 1986.

(5) Subject to paragraph (6) below, it shall be the duty of an office-holder to furnish a return complying with the provisions of paragraphs (3) and (4) of this rule to the Secretary of State:—

(a) where he is in office in relation to the company on the day one week before the expiry of the period of 6 months from the relevant date, not later than the expiry of such period;

(b) where he vacates office (otherwise than by death) before the day one week before the expiry of the period of 6 months from the relevant date, within 14 days after his vacation of office except where he has furnished such a return on or prior to the day one week before the expiry of such period.

(6) A return need not be provided under this rule by an office-holder if he has, whilst holding that office in relation to the company, since the relevant date, made a report under rule 3 with respect to all persons falling within paragraph (2) of this rule and (apart from this paragraph) required to be the subject of a return.

(7) If an office-holder without reasonable excuse fails to comply with the duty imposed by paragraph (5) of this rule, he is guilty of an offence and—

(a) on summary conviction of the offence, is liable to a fine not exceeding level 3 on the standard scale, and

(b) after continued contravention, is liable to a daily default fine; that is to say, he is liable on a second or subsequent summary conviction of the offence to a fine of one-tenth of level 3 on the standard scale for each day on which the contravention is continued (instead of the penalty specified in sub-paragraph (a)).

(8) Section 431 of the Insolvency Act 1986 (summary proceedings), as it applies to England and Wales, has effect in relation to an offence under this rule as to offences under Parts I to VII of that Act.

[6918]

NOTES

Para (4): words in square brackets substituted by the Enterprise Act 2002 (Insolvency) Order 2003, SI 2003/2096, arts 5, 6, Schedule, Pt 2, paras 68, 70, as from 15 September 2003, except in relation to any case where a petition for an administration order was presented before that date.

5 Forms

The forms referred to in rule 3(2) and rule 4(3) shall be used with such variations, if any, as the circumstances may require.

[6919]

6 Enforcement of section 7(4)

(1) This rule applies where under section 7(4) of the Act (power to call on liquidators, former liquidators and others to provide information) the Secretary of State or the official receiver requires or has required a person:—

(a) to furnish him with information with respect to a person's conduct as director or shadow director of a company, and

(b) to produce and permit inspection of relevant books, papers and other records.

(2) On the application of the Secretary of State or (as the case may be) the official receiver, the court may make an order directing compliance within such period as may be specified.

(3) The court's order may provide that all costs of and incidental to the application shall be borne by the person to whom the order is directed.

[6920]

7 Transitional and saving provisions

(1) Subject to paragraph (2) below, rules 3 and 4 of the former Rules shall continue to apply as if the former Rules had not been revoked when any of the events mentioned in sub-paragraphs (a), (b) or (c) of rule 3(1) of the former Rules (passing of resolution for voluntary winding up, appointment of administrative receiver, making of administration order) occurred on or after 29th December 1986 but before the commencement date.

(2) Until 31st December 1996—

(a) the forms contained in the Schedule to the former Rules which were required to be used for the purpose of complying with those Rules, or

(b) the Form D1 or D2 as set out in the Schedule to these Rules, as appropriate, or a form which is substantially similar thereto, with such variations, if any, as the circumstances may require,

may be used for the purpose of complying with rules 3 and 4 of the former Rules as applied by paragraph (1) above; but after that date the forms mentioned in sub-paragraph (b) of this paragraph shall be used for that purpose.

(3) When a period referred to in rule 5(2) of the former Rules is current immediately before the commencement date, these Rules have effect as if rule 6(2) of these Rules had been in force when the period began and the period is deemed to expire whenever it would have expired if these Rules had not been made and any right, obligation or power dependent on the beginning, duration or end of such period shall be under rule 6(2) of these Rules as it was or would have been under the said rule 5(2).

(4) The provisions of this rule are to be without prejudice to the operation of section 16 of the Interpretation Act 1978 (saving from repeals) as it is applied by section 23 of that Act.

[6921]

(Schedule sets out Forms D1, D2; see Appendix 4 at **[A4]**.)

INSOLVENT COMPANIES (REPORTS ON CONDUCT OF DIRECTORS) (SCOTLAND) RULES 1996

(SI 1996/1910)

NOTES

Authority: Insolvency Act 1986, s 411; Company Directors Disqualification Act 1986, s 21(2).
Made: 22 July 1996.
Commencement: 30 September 1996 (see r 1 at **[6922]**). Where any provision in this work (including any inserted or substituted provision) came into force for all purposes on or before 1 July 2005, commencement information is not noted at provision level.

As of 1 July 2007, these Rules (as reproduced here) had not been amended.
Limited liability partnerships: by the Limited Liability Partnerships Regulations 2001, SI 2001/1090, reg 10, Sch 6, Pt III, these Rules apply, with modifications, to limited liability partnerships (see **[7000]**).

ARRANGEMENT OF RULES

1 Citation, commencement and interpretation

(1) These Rules may be cited as the Insolvent Companies (Reports on Conduct of Directors) (Scotland) Rules 1996.

(2) These Rules shall come into force on 30th September 1996.

(3) In these Rules—

"the Act" means the Company Directors Disqualification Act 1986;

"the former Rules" means the Insolvent Companies (Reports on Conduct of Directors) (No 2) (Scotland) Rules 1986;

"the commencement date" means 30th September 1996; and

"a company" means a company which the courts in Scotland have jurisdiction to wind up.

[6922]

2 Revocation

Subject to rule 7 below, the former Rules are hereby revoked.

[6923]

3 Reports required under section 7(3) of the Act

(1) This rule applies to any report made to the Secretary of State under section 7(3) of the Act by—

(a) the liquidator of a company which is being wound up by an order of the court made on or after the commencement date;

(b) the liquidator of a company which passes a resolution for voluntary winding up on or after that date;

(c) a receiver of a company appointed under section 51 of the Insolvency Act 1986 (power to appoint receiver under the law of Scotland) on or after that date, who is an administrative receiver; or

(d) the administrator of a company in relation to which the court makes an administration order on or after that date.

(2) Such a report shall be made in the Form D1 (Scot) set out in the Schedule hereto, or in a form which is substantially similar, and in the manner and to the extent required by the Form D1 (Scot).

[6924]

4 Return by office-holder

(1) This rule applies where it appears to a liquidator of a company as mentioned in rule 3(1)(a) or (b), to an administrative receiver as mentioned in rule 3(1)(c), or to an administrator as mentioned in rule 3(1)(d) (each of whom is referred to hereinafter as "an office-holder") that the company has at any time become insolvent within the meaning of section 6(2) of the Act.

(2) Subject as follows there may be furnished to the Secretary of State by an office-holder at any time during the period of 6 months from the relevant date (defined in paragraph (4) below) a return with respect to every person who:—

(a) was, on the relevant date, a director or shadow director of the company, or

(b) had been a director or shadow director of the company at any time in the 3 years immediately preceding that date.

(3) The return shall be made in the Form D2 (Scot) set out in the Schedule hereto, or in a form which is substantially similar, and in the manner and to the extent required by the Form D2 (Scot).

(4) For the purposes of this rule, 'the relevant date' means—

(a) in the case of a company in liquidation (except in the case mentioned in paragraph (4)(b) below), the date on which the company goes into liquidation within the meaning of section 247(2) of the Insolvency Act 1986,

(b) In the case of a company in members' voluntary winding up, the date on which the liquidator forms the opinion that, at the time when the company went into liquidation, its assets were insufficient for the payment of its debts and other liabilities and the expenses of winding up,

(c) in the case of the administrative receiver, the date of his appointment,

(d) in the case of the administrator, the date of the administration order made in relation to the company,

and for the purposes of sub-paragraph (c) above the only appointment of an administrative receiver to be taken into account in determining the relevant date shall be that appointment which is not that of a successor in office to an administrative receiver who has vacated office either by death or pursuant to section 62 of the Insolvency Act 1986.

(5) Subject to paragraph (6) below, it shall be the duty of an office-holder to furnish a return complying with the provisions of paragraphs (3) and (4) of this rule to the Secretary of State—

(a) where he is in office in relation to the company on the day one week before the expiry of the period of 6 months from the relevant date, not later than the expiry of such period;

(b) where he vacates office (otherwise than by death) before the day one week before the expiry of the period of 6 months from the relevant date, within 14 days after his vacation of office except where he has furnished such a return on or prior to the day one week before the expiry of such period.

(6) A return need not be provided under this rule by an office-holder if he has, whilst holding that office in relation to the company, since the relevant date, made a report under rule 3 with respect to all persons falling within paragraph (2) of this rule and (apart from this paragraph) required to be the subject of a return.

(7) If an office-holder without reasonable excuse fails to comply with the duty imposed by paragraph (5) of this rule, he is guilty of an offence and—

(a) on summary conviction of the offence, is liable to a fine not exceeding level 3 on the standard scale, and

(b) after continued contravention, is liable to a daily default fine; that is to say, he is liable on a second or subsequent summary conviction of the offence to a fine of one-tenth of level 3 on the standard scale for each day on which the contravention is continued (instead of the penalty specified in sub-paragraph (a)).

(8) Section 431 of the Insolvency Act 1986 (summary proceedings), as it applies to Scotland, has effect in relation to an offence under this rule as to offences under Parts I to VII of that Act.

[6925]

5 Forms

The forms referred to in rule 3(2) and rule 4(3) shall be used with such variations, if any, as the circumstances may require.

[6926]

6 Enforcement of section 7(4)

(1) This rule applies where under section 7(4) of the Act (power to call on liquidators, former liquidators and others to provide information) the Secretary of State requires or has required a person:—

(a) to furnish him with information with respect to a person's conduct as director or shadow director of a company, and

(b) to produce and permit inspection of relevant books, papers and other records.

(2) On the application of the Secretary of State, the court may make an order directing compliance within such period as may be specified.

(3) The court's order may provide that all expenses of and incidental to the application shall be borne by the person to whom the order is directed.

[6927]

7 Transitional and saving provisions

(1) Subject to paragraph (2) below, rules 2 and 3 of the former Rules shall continue to apply as if the former Rules had not been revoked when any of the events mentioned in sub-paragraphs (a), (b), (c) or (d) of rule 2(1) of the former Rules (order of the court for winding up, passing of resolution for voluntary winding up, appointment of administrative receiver, making of administration order) occurred on or after 29th December 1986 but before the commencement date.

(2) Until 31st December 1996—

(a) the forms contained in the Schedule to the former Rules which were required to be used for the purpose of complying with those Rules, or

(b) the Form D1 (Scot) or D2 (Scot) as set out in the Schedule to these Rules, as appropriate, or a form which is substantially similar thereto, with such variations, if any, as the circumstances may require,

may be used for the purpose of complying with rules 2 and 3 of the former Rules as applied by paragraph (1) above; but after that date the forms mentioned in sub-paragraph (b) of this paragraph shall be used for that purpose.

(3) When a period referred to in rule 4(2) of the former Rules is current immediately before the commencement date, these Rules have effect as if rule 6(2) of these Rules had been in force when the period began and the period is deemed to expire whenever it would have expired if these Rules had not been made and any right, obligation or power dependent on the beginning, duration or end of such period shall be under rule 6(2) of these Rules as it was or would have been under the said rule 4(2).

(4) The provisions of this rule are to be without prejudice to the operation of section 16 of the Interpretation Act 1978 (saving from repeals) as it is applied by section 23 of that Act.

[6928]

(*Schedule sets out Forms D1* (*Scot*), *D2* (*Scot*) *and is not reproduced.*)

COMPANIES ACT 1985 (ACCOUNTS OF SMALL AND MEDIUM-SIZED COMPANIES AND MINOR ACCOUNTING AMENDMENTS) REGULATIONS 1997 (NOTE)

(SI 1997/220)

NOTES

These Regulations were made under CA 1985, s 257 and came into force on 1 March 1997. They amend Pt VII of the 1985 Act (at **[207]** et seq) and make other consequential amendments to the 1985 Act. Reg 1(4) of these Regulations provides for transitional provisions as noted to the amended sections of the 1985 Act *ante*. That paragraph provides that a company may, with respect to a financial year of the company ending on or before 24 March 1997, prepare and deliver to the registrar of companies such annual accounts and directors' and auditors' reports as it would have been required to prepare and deliver had the amendments to the 1985 Act effected by these Regulations not been made.

[6929]–[6943]

TRANSFER OF FUNCTIONS (INSURANCE) ORDER 1997 (NOTE)

(SI 1997/2781)

NOTES

This Order was made on the 26 November 1997 under the powers conferred by the Ministers of the Crown Act 1975, s 1, and the European Communities Act 1972, s 2(2) and came into force on 5 January 1998. It transfers a number of functions previously exercisable by the Secretary of State to the Treasury, so as to make them exercisable by the Treasury alone or by the Secretary of State and the Treasury concurrently. The main functions transferred are functions under the Policyholders Protection Acts 1975 and 1997 (repealed), the Insurance Brokers (Registration) Act 1977 (repealed), the Insurance Companies Act 1982 (repealed), the Financial Services Act 1986 (repealed), and the Reinsurance (Acts of Terrorism) Act 1993. The statutory powers are transferred by virtue of art 2, which is subject to arts 3 and 4. Article 3 sets out the functions which are retained by the Secretary of State which relate to his powers to prescribe fees for inspecting certain documents deposited with or served on the registrar of companies. Article 4 sets out the functions which are exercisable by the Secretary of State and the Treasury concurrently. These functions are connected, essentially, with enforcement (including investigations and prosecutions) and the winding-up of insurance companies. Article 5 transfers to the Treasury the property, rights and liabilities to which the Secretary of State is entitled or subject in connection with the functions transferred by art 2. Article 6 designates the Treasury as the appropriate authority to make regulations implementing certain EC Directives in the area of insurance in place of the Secretary of State.

[6944]–[6945]

FINANCIAL MARKETS AND INSOLVENCY (SETTLEMENT FINALITY) REGULATIONS 1999

(SI 1999/2979)

NOTES

Made: 2 November 1999.

Authority: European Communities Act 1972, s 2(2).

Commencement: 11 December 1999 (see reg 1 at **[6946]**). Where any provision in this work (including any inserted or substituted provision) came into force for all purposes on or before 1 July 2005, commencement information is not noted at provision level.

These Regulations are reproduced as amended by: the Banking Consolidation Directive (Consequential Amendments) Regulations 2000, SI 2000/2952; the Civil Jurisdiction and Judgments Order 2001, SI 2001/3929; the Electronic Money (Miscellaneous Amendments) Regulations 2002, SI 2002/765; the Financial Services and Markets Act 2000 (Consequential Amendments) Order 2002, SI 2002/1555; the Enterprise Act 2002 (Insolvency) Order 2003, SI 2003/2096; the Financial Markets and Insolvency (Settlement Finality) (Amendment) Regulations 2006, SI 2006/50; the Capital Requirements Regulations 2006, SI 2006/3221; the Financial Services (EEA State) Regulations 2007, SI 2007/108; the Financial Services and Markets Act 2000 (Markets in Financial Instruments) Regulations 2007, SI 2007/126; the Financial Markets and Insolvency (Settlement Finality) (Amendment) Regulations 2007, SI 2007/832; the Civil Jurisdiction and Judgments Regulations 2007, SI 2007/1655.

ARRANGEMENT OF REGULATIONS

PART I
GENERAL

PART II
DESIGNATED SYSTEMS

PART III
TRANSFER ORDERS EFFECTED THROUGH A DESIGNATED SYSTEM AND COLLATERAL SECURITY

PART IV
STATUTORY INSTRUMENTS

PART I GENERAL

1 Citation, commencement and extent

(1) These Regulations may be cited as the Financial Markets and Insolvency (Settlement Finality) Regulations 1999 and shall come into force on 11th December 1999.

(2) …

[6946]

NOTES

Para (2): revoked by the Financial Markets and Insolvency (Settlement Finality) (Amendment) Regulations 2006, SI 2006/50, reg 2(1), (2), as from 2 February 2006. Note that para (2) previously provided that these Regulations do not extend to Northern Ireland.

2 Interpretation

(1) In these Regulations—

["the 2000 Act" means the Financial Services and Markets Act 2000;]

"central bank" means a central bank of an EEA State or the European Central Bank;

"central counterparty" means a body corporate or unincorporated association interposed between the institutions in a designated system and which acts as the exclusive counterparty of those institutions with regard to transfer orders;

"charge" means any form of security, including a mortgage and, in Scotland, a heritable security;

"clearing house" means a body corporate or unincorporated association which is responsible for the calculation of the net positions of institutions and any central counterparty or settlement agent in a designated system;

"collateral security" means any realisable assets provided under a charge or a repurchase or similar agreement, or otherwise (including money provided under a charge)—

(a) for the purpose of securing rights and obligations potentially arising in connection with a designated system ("collateral security in connection with participation in a designated system"); or

(b) to a central bank for the purpose of securing rights and obligations in connection with its operations in carrying out its functions as a central bank ("collateral security in connection with the functions of a central bank");

"collateral security charge" means, where collateral security consists of realisable assets (including money) provided under a charge, that charge;

["credit institution" means a credit institution as defined in Article 4(1)(a) of Directive 2006/48/EC of the European Parliament and of the Council of 14 June 2006 relating to the taking up and pursuit of the business of credit institutions, including the bodies set out in the list in Article 2;]

"creditors' voluntary winding-up resolution" means a resolution for voluntary winding up (within the meaning of the Insolvency Act 1986 [or the Insolvency (Northern Ireland) Order 1989]) where the winding up is a creditors' winding up (within the meaning of that Act[or that Order]);

"default arrangements" means the arrangements put in place by a designated system to limit systemic and other types of risk which arise in the event of a participant appearing to be unable, or likely to become unable, to meet its obligations in respect of a transfer order, including, for example, any default rules within the meaning of Part VII [or Part V] or any other arrangements for—

(a) netting,
(b) the closing out of open positions, or
(c) the application or transfer of collateral security;

"defaulter" means a person in respect of whom action has been taken by a designated system under its default arrangements;

"designated system" means a system which is declared by a designation order for the time being in force to be a designated system for the purposes of these Regulations;

"designating authority" means—

(a) in the case of a system—
    (i) which is, or the operator of which is, a recognised investment exchange or a recognised clearing house for the purposes of [the 2000 Act],
    (ii) which is, or the operator of which is, a listed person within the meaning of the Financial Markets and Insolvency (Money Market) Regulations 1995, or
    (iii) through which securities transfer orders are effected (whether or not payment transfer orders are also effected through that system),

the Financial Services Authority;

(b) in any other case, the Bank of England;

"designation order" has the meaning given by regulation 4;

["EEA State" has the meaning given by Schedule 1 to the Interpretation Act 1978;]

"guidance", in relation to a designated system, means guidance issued or any recommendation made by it which is intended to have continuing effect and is issued in writing or other legible form to all or any class of its participants or users or persons seeking to participate in the system or to use its facilities and which would, if it were a rule, come within the definition of a rule;

"indirect participant" means a credit institution for which payment transfer orders are capable of being effected through a designated system pursuant to its contractual relationship with an institution;

"institution" means—

(a) a credit institution;
(b) an investment firm as defined in *point 2 of Article 1 of Council Directive 93/22/EEC excluding the bodies set out in the list in Article* 2(2)(*a*) *to* (*k*);
(c) a public authority or publicly guaranteed undertaking;
(d) any undertaking whose head office is outside the European Community and whose functions correspond to those of a credit institution or investment firm as defined in (a) and (b) above; or
(e) any undertaking which is treated by the designating authority as an institution in accordance with regulation 8(1),

which participates in a designated system and which is responsible for discharging the financial obligations arising from transfer orders which are effected through the system;

"netting" means the conversion into one net claim or obligation of different claims or obligations between participants resulting from the issue and receipt of transfer orders between them, whether on a bilateral or multilateral basis and whether through the interposition of a clearing house, central counterparty or settlement agent or otherwise;

["Part V" means Part V of the Companies (No 2) (Northern Ireland) Order 1990;]

"Part VII" means Part VII of the Companies Act 1989;

"participant" means—

(a) an institution,
(b) a body corporate or unincorporated association which carries out any combination of the functions of a central counterparty, a settlement agent or a clearing house, with respect to a system, or
(c) an indirect participant which is treated as a participant, or is a member of a class of indirect participants which are treated as participants, in accordance with regulation 9;

"protected trust deed" and "trust deed" shall be construed in accordance with section 73(1) of the Bankruptcy (Scotland) Act 1985 (interpretation);

"relevant office-holder" means—

(a) the official receiver;
(b) any person acting in relation to a company as its liquidator, provisional liquidator, or administrator;

(c) any person acting in relation to an individual (or, in Scotland, any debtor within the meaning of the Bankruptcy (Scotland) Act 1985) as his trustee in bankruptcy or interim receiver of his property or as permanent or interim trustee in the sequestration of his estate or as his trustee under a protected trust deed; or

(d) any person acting as administrator of an insolvent estate of a deceased person;

and in sub-paragraph (b), "company" means any company, society, association, partnership or other body which may be wound up under the Insolvency Act 1986 [or the Insolvency (Northern Ireland) Order 1989];

"rules", in relation to a designated system, means rules or conditions governing the system with respect to the matters dealt with in these Regulations;

"securities" means (except for the purposes of the definition of "charge") any instruments referred to in section *B of the Annex to Council Directive 93/22/EEC*;

"settlement account" means an account at a central bank, a settlement agent or a central counterparty used to hold funds or securities (or both) and to settle transactions between participants in a designated system;

"settlement agent" means a body corporate or unincorporated association providing settlement accounts to the institutions and any central counterparty in a designated system for the settlement of transfer orders within the system and, as the case may be, for extending credit to such institutions and any such central counterparty for settlement purposes;

"the Settlement Finality Directive" means Directive 98/26/EC of the European Parliament and of the Council of 19th May 1998 on settlement finality in payment and securities settlement systems;

"transfer order" means—

(a) an instruction by a participant to place at the disposal of a recipient an amount of money by means of a book entry on the accounts of a credit institution, a central bank or a settlement agent, or an instruction which results in the assumption or discharge of a payment obligation as defined by the rules of a designated system ("a payment transfer order"); or

(b) an instruction by a participant to transfer the title to, or interest in, securities by means of a book entry on a register, or otherwise ("a securities transfer order");

"winding up" means—

(a) winding up by the court, or

(b) creditors' voluntary winding up,

within the meaning of the Insolvency Act 1986 [or the Insolvency (Northern Ireland) Order 1989] (but does not include members' voluntary winding up within the meaning of that Act [or that Order]).

(2) In these Regulations—

(a) references to the law of insolvency include references to every provision made by or under the Insolvency Act 1986[, the Insolvency (Northern Ireland) Order 1989] or the Bankruptcy (Scotland) Act 1985; and in relation to a building society references to insolvency law or to any provision of the Insolvency Act 1986 [or the Insolvency (Northern Ireland) Order 1989] are to that law or provision as modified by the Building Societies Act 1986;

(b) in relation to Scotland, references to—

(i) sequestration include references to the administration by a judicial factor of the insolvent estate of a deceased person,

(ii) an interim or permanent trustee include references to a judicial factor on the insolvent estate of a deceased person, and

(iii) "set off" include compensation.

(3) Subject to paragraph (1), expressions used in these Regulations which are also used in the Settlement Finality Directive have the same meaning in these Regulations as they have in the Settlement Finality Directive.

(4) References in these Regulations to things done, or required to be done, by or in relation to a designated system shall, in the case of a designated system which is neither a body corporate nor an unincorporated association, be treated as references to things done, or required to be done, by or in relation to the operator of that system.

[6947]

NOTES

Para (1) is amended as follows:

Definition "the 2000 Act" substituted (for original definition "the 1986 Act"), and words in square brackets in definition "designating authority" substituted, by the Financial Services and Markets Act 2000 (Consequential Amendments) Order 2002, SI 2002/1555, art 39(1), (2), as from 3 July 2002.

Definition "credit institution" substituted by the Capital Requirements Regulations 2006, SI 2006/3221, reg 29(4), Sch 6, para 3, as from 1 January 2007.

Words in square brackets in definitions "creditors' voluntary winding up resolution", "default arrangements", "relevant office-holder", and "winding up" inserted, and definition "Part V" inserted, by the Financial Markets and Insolvency (Settlement Finality) (Amendment) Regulations 2006, SI 2006/50, reg 2(1), (3), as from 2 February 2006.

Definition "EEA State" substituted by the Financial Services (EEA State) Regulations 2007, SI 2007/108, reg 5, as from 13 February 2007.

For the words in italics in the definition "institution" there are substituted the words "Article 4.1.1 of Directive 2004/39/EC of the European Parliament and of the Council of 21 April 2004 on markets in financial instruments, other than a person to whom Article 2 applies" by the Financial Services and Markets Act 2000 (Markets in Financial Instruments) Regulations 2007, SI 2007/126, reg 3(6), Sch 6, Pt 2, para 14(a), as from 1 November 2007 (for the full commencement details of SI 2007/126, see reg 1 of those Regulations at **[7596]**).

For the words in italics in the definition "securities" there are substituted the words "C of Annex I to Directive 2004/39/EC of the European Parliament and of the Council of 21 April 2004 on markets in financial instruments" by SI 2007/126, reg 3(6), Sch 6, Pt 2, para 14(b), as from 1 November 2007 (for the full commencement details of SI 2007/126, see reg 1 of those Regulations at **[7596]**).

Para (2): words in square brackets inserted by SI 2006/50, reg 2(1), (4), as from 2 February 2006.

PART II
DESIGNATED SYSTEMS

3 Application for designation

(1) Any body corporate or unincorporated association may apply to the designating authority for an order declaring it, or any system of which it is the operator, to be a designated system for the purposes of these Regulations.

(2) Any such application—
- (a) shall be made in such manner as the designating authority may direct; and
- (b) shall be accompanied by such information as the designating authority may reasonably require for the purpose of determining the application.

(3) At any time after receiving an application and before determining it, the designating authority may require the applicant to furnish additional information.

(4) The directions and requirements given or imposed under paragraphs (2) and (3) may differ as between different applications.

(5) Any information to be furnished to the designating authority under this regulation shall be in such form or verified in such manner as it may specify.

(6) Every application shall be accompanied by copies of the rules of the system to which the application relates and any guidance relating to that system.

[6948]

4 Grant and refusal of designation

(1) Where—
- (a) an application has been duly made under regulation 3;
- (b) the applicant has paid any fee charged by virtue of regulation 5(1); and
- (c) the designating authority is satisfied that the requirements of the Schedule are satisfied with respect to the system to which the application relates;

the designating authority may make an order (a "designation order") declaring the system to be a designated system for the purposes of these Regulations.

(2) In determining whether to make a designation order, the designating authority shall have regard to systemic risks.

(3) Where an application has been made to the Financial Services Authority under regulation 3 in relation to a system through which both securities transfer orders and payment transfer orders are effected, the Authority shall consult the Bank of England before deciding whether to make a designation order.

(4) A designation order shall state the date on which it takes effect.

(5) Where the designating authority refuses an application for a designation order it shall give the applicant a written notice to that effect stating the reasons for the refusal.

[6949]

5 Fees

(1) The designating authority may charge a fee to an applicant for a designation order.

(2) The designating authority may charge a designated system a periodical fee.

(3) Fees chargeable by the designating authority under this regulation shall not exceed an amount which reasonably represents the amount of costs incurred or likely to be incurred—

- (a) in the case of a fee charged to an applicant for a designation order, in determining whether the designation order should be made; and
- (b) in the case of a periodical fee, in satisfying itself that the designated system continues to meet the requirements of the Schedule and is complying with any obligations to which it is subject by virtue of these Regulations.

[6950]

6 Certain bodies deemed to satisfy requirements for designation

(1) Subject to paragraph (2), an investment exchange or clearing house declared by an order for the time being in force to be a recognised investment exchange or recognised clearing house for the purposes of [the 2000 Act], whether that order was made before or is made after the coming into force of these Regulations, shall be deemed to satisfy the requirements in paragraphs 2 and 3 of the Schedule.

(2) Paragraph (1) does not apply to overseas investment exchanges or overseas clearing houses within the meaning of the 1986 Act.

[6951]

NOTES

Para (1): words in square brackets substituted by the Financial Services and Markets Act 2000 (Consequential Amendments) Order 2002, SI 2002/1555, art 39(1), (3), as from 3 July 2002.

7 Revocation of designation

(1) A designation order may be revoked by a further order made by the designating authority if at any time it appears to the designating authority—

- (a) that any requirement of the Schedule is not satisfied in the case of the system to which the designation order relates; or
- (b) that the system has failed to comply with any obligation to which it is subject by virtue of these Regulations.

(2) [Subsections (1) to (7) of section 298 of the 2000 Act] shall apply in relation to the revocation of a designation order under paragraph (1) as they apply in relation to the revocation of a recognition order *under* [section 297(2) of that Act]; and in those subsections as they so apply—

- [(a) any reference to a recognised body shall be taken to be a reference to a designated system;
- (b) any reference to members of a recognised body shall be taken to be a reference to participants in a designated system;
- (c) references to the Authority shall, in cases where the Bank of England is the designating authority, be taken to be a reference to the Bank of England; and
- (d) subsection (4)(a) shall have effect as if for "two months" there were substituted "three months".]

[(3) An order revoking a designation order—

- (a) shall state the date on which it takes effect, being no earlier than three months after the day on which the revocation order is made; and
- (b) may contain such transitional provisions as the designating authority thinks necessary or expedient.

(4) A designation order may be revoked at the request or with the consent of the designated system, and any such revocation shall not be subject to the restriction imposed by paragraph (3)(a), or to the requirements imposed by subsections (1) to (6) of section 298 of the 2000 Act.]

[6952]

NOTES

Para (2): words in square brackets substituted by the Financial Services and Markets Act 2000 (Consequential Amendments) Order 2002, SI 2002/1555, art 39(1), (4), as from 3 July 2002. Note that art 39(4)(b) of the 2002 Order actually provides—

"for "*under* subsection (1) of that section" substitute "section 297(2) of that Act"";

It is believed that this is an error and that the word "under" (in italics) should not be removed from para (2).

Paras (3), (4): added by SI 2002/1555, art 39(1), (5), as from 3 July 2002.

8 Undertakings treated as institutions

(1) A designating authority may treat as an institution any undertaking which participates in a designated system and which is responsible for discharging financial obligations arising from transfer orders effected through that system, provided that—

(a) the designating authority considers such treatment to be required on grounds of systemic risk, and

(b) the designated system is one in which at least three institutions (other than any undertaking treated as an institution by virtue of this paragraph) participate and through which securities transfer orders are effected.

(2) Where a designating authority decides to treat an undertaking as an institution in accordance with paragraph (1), it shall give written notice of that decision to the designated system in which the undertaking is to be treated as a participant.

[6953]

9 Indirect participants treated as participants

(1) A designating authority may treat—

(a) an indirect participant as a participant in a designated system, or

(b) a class of indirect participants as participants in a designated system,

where it considers this to be required on grounds of systemic risk, and shall give written notice of any decision to that effect to the designated system.

[6954]

10 Provision of information by designated systems

(1) A designated system shall, on being declared to be a designated system, provide to the designating authority in writing a list of its participants and shall give written notice to the designating authority of any amendment to the list within seven days of such amendment.

(2) The designating authority may, in writing, require a designated system to furnish to it such other information relating to that designated system as it reasonably requires for the exercise of its functions under these Regulations, within such time, in such form, at such intervals and verified in such manner as the designating authority may specify.

(3) When a designated system amends, revokes or adds to its rules or its guidance, it shall within fourteen days give written notice to the designating authority of the amendment, revocation or addition.

(4) A designated system shall give the designating authority at least fourteen days' written notice of any proposal to amend, revoke or add to its default arrangements.

(5) Nothing in this regulation shall require a designated system to give any notice or furnish any information to the Financial Services Authority which it has given or furnished to the Authority pursuant to any requirement imposed by or under [section 293 of the 2000 Act] (notification requirements) or any other enactment.

[6955]

NOTES

Para (5): words in square brackets substituted by the Financial Services and Markets Act 2000 (Consequential Amendments) Order 2002, SI 2002/1555, art 39(1), (6), as from 3 July 2002.

11 Exemption from liability in damages

(1) Neither the designating authority nor any person who is, or is acting as, a member, officer or member of staff of the designating authority shall be liable in damages for anything done or omitted in the discharge, or purported discharge, of the designating authority's functions under these Regulations.

(2) Paragraph (1) does not apply—

(a) if the act or omission is shown to have been in bad faith; or

(b) so as to prevent an award of damages made in respect of an act or omission on the ground that the act or omission was unlawful as a result of section 6(1) of the Human Rights Act 1998 (acts of public authorities).

[6956]

12 Publication of information and advice

A designating authority may publish information or give advice, or arrange for the publication of information or the giving of advice, in such form and manner as it considers appropriate with respect to any matter dealt with in these Regulations.

[6957]

PART III
TRANSFER ORDERS EFFECTED THROUGH A DESIGNATED SYSTEM AND COLLATERAL SECURITY

13 Modifications of the law of insolvency

(1) The general law of insolvency has effect in relation to—

(a) transfer orders effected through a designated system and action taken under the rules of a designated system with respect to such orders; and

(b) collateral security,

subject to the provisions of this Part.

(2) Those provisions apply in relation to—

(a) insolvency proceedings in respect of a participant in a designated system; and

(b) insolvency proceedings in respect of a provider of collateral security in connection with the functions of a central bank, in so far as the proceedings affect the rights of the central bank to the collateral security;

but not in relation to any other insolvency proceedings, notwithstanding that rights or liabilities arising from transfer orders or collateral security fall to be dealt with in the proceedings.

(3) Subject to regulation 21, nothing in this Part shall have the effect of disapplying Part VII [or Part V].

[6958]

NOTES

Para (3): words in square brackets added by the Financial Markets and Insolvency (Settlement Finality) (Amendment) Regulations 2006, SI 2006/50, reg 2(1), (5), as from 2 February 2006.

14 Proceedings of designated system take precedence over insolvency proceedings

(1) None of the following shall be regarded as to any extent invalid at law on the ground of inconsistency with the law relating to the distribution of the assets of a person on bankruptcy, winding up, sequestration or under a protected trust deed, or in the administration of an insolvent estate—

(a) a transfer order;

(b) the default arrangements of a designated system;

(c) the rules of a designated system as to the settlement of transfer orders not dealt with under its default arrangements;

(d) a contract for the purpose of realising collateral security in connection with participation in a designated system otherwise than pursuant to its default arrangements; or

(e) a contract for the purpose of realising collateral security in connection with the functions of a central bank.

(2) The powers of a relevant office-holder in his capacity as such, and the powers of the court under the Insolvency Act 1986[, the Insolvency (Northern Ireland) Order 1989] or the Bankruptcy (Scotland) Act 1985, shall not be exercised in such a way as to prevent or interfere with—

(a) the settlement in accordance with the rules of a designated system of a transfer order not dealt with under its default arrangements;

(b) any action taken under its default arrangements;
(c) any action taken to realise collateral security in connection with participation in a designated system otherwise than pursuant to its default arrangements; or
(d) any action taken to realise collateral security in connection with the functions of a central bank.

This does not prevent the court from afterwards making any such order or decree as is mentioned in regulation 17(1) or (2).

(3) Nothing in the following provisions of this Part shall be construed as affecting the generality of the above provisions.

(4) A debt or other liability arising out of a transfer order which is the subject of action taken under default arrangements may not be proved in a winding up or bankruptcy, or in Scotland claimed in a winding up, sequestration or under a protected trust deed, until the completion of the action taken under default arrangements.

A debt or other liability which by virtue of this paragraph may not be proved or claimed shall not be taken into account for the purposes of any set-off until the completion of the action taken under default arrangements.

(5) Paragraph (1) has the effect that the following provisions (which relate to preferential debts and the payment of expenses etc) apply subject to paragraph (6), namely—
(a) in the case of collateral security provided by a company (within the meaning of section 735 of the Companies Act 1985 [or Article 3 of the Companies (Northern Ireland) Order 1986])—
(i) section 175 of the Insolvency Act 1986 [or Article 149 of the Insolvency (Northern Ireland) Order 1989], and
(ii) where the company is [in administration], [section 40 (or, in Scotland, section 59 and 60(1)(e)) of the Insolvency Act 1986, paragraph 99(3) of Schedule B1 to that Act] [or paragraph 100(3) of Schedule B1 to, and Article 50 of, the Insolvency (Northern Ireland) Order 1989], and section 196 of the Companies Act 1985 [or Article 205 of the Companies (Northern Ireland) Order 1986]; and
(b) in the case of collateral security provided by an individual, section 328(1) and (2) of the Insolvency Act 1986[or, in Northern Ireland, Article 300(1) and (2) of the Insolvency (Northern Ireland) Order 1989] or, in Scotland, in the case of collateral security provided by an individual or a partnership, section 51 of the Bankruptcy (Scotland) Act 1985 and any like provision or rule of law affecting a protected trust deed.

(6) The claim of a participant or central bank to collateral security shall be paid in priority to—
(a) the expenses of the winding up mentioned in sections 115 and 156 of the Insolvency Act 1986 [or Articles 100 and 134 of the Insolvency (Northern Ireland) Order 1989], the expenses of the bankruptcy within the meaning of that Act [or that Order] or, as the case may be, the remuneration and expenses of the administrator mentioned in [paragraph 99(3) of Schedule B1 to that Act] [or in paragraph 100(3) to Schedule B1 to that Order], and
(b) the preferential debts of the company or the individual (as the case may be) within the meaning given by section 386 of that Act [or Article 346 of that Order],

unless the terms on which the collateral security was provided expressly provide that such expenses, remuneration or preferential debts are to have priority.

(7) As respects Scotland—
(a) the reference in paragraph (6)(a) to the expenses of bankruptcy shall be taken to be a reference to the matters mentioned in paragraphs (a) to (d) of section 51(1) of the Bankruptcy (Scotland) Act 1985, or any like provision or rule of law affecting a protected trust deed; and
(b) the reference in paragraph (6)(b) to the preferential debts of the individual shall be taken to be a reference to the preferred debts of the debtor within the meaning of the Bankruptcy (Scotland) Act 1985, or any like definition applying with respect to a protected trust deed by virtue of any provision or rule of law affecting it.

[6959]

NOTES

Para (2): words in square brackets inserted by the Financial Markets and Insolvency (Settlement Finality) (Amendment) Regulations 2006, SI 2006/50, reg 2(1), (6)(a), as from 2 February 2006.

Para (5): words in first, second, sixth and seventh pairs of square brackets inserted by SI 2006/50, reg 2(1), (6)(b), (c), (e), as from 2 February 2006; words in fifth pair of square brackets originally inserted by SI 2006/50, reg 2(1), (6)(d), as from 2 February 2006, and substituted by the Financial Markets and Insolvency (Settlement Finality) (Amendment) Regulations 2007, SI 2007/832, reg 2(1), (2), as from 6 April 2007; other words in square brackets substituted by the Enterprise Act 2002 (Insolvency) Order 2003, SI 2003/2096, arts 5, 6, Schedule, Pt 2, paras 74, 75, as from 15 September 2003, except in relation to any case where a petition for an administration order was presented before that date.

Para (6): words in first, second, and fifth pairs of square brackets inserted by SI 2006/50, reg 2(1), (6)(f), (g), as from 2 February 2006; words in fourth pair of square brackets originally inserted by SI 2006/50, reg 2(1), (6)(f), as from 2 February 2006, and substituted by SI 2007/832, reg 2(1), (3), as from 6 April 2007; other words in square brackets substituted by SI 2003/2096, arts 5, 6, Schedule, Pt 2, paras 74, 75, as from 15 September 2003, except in relation to any case where a petition for an administration order was presented before that date.

15 Net sum payable on completion of action taken under default arrangements

(1) The following provisions apply with respect to any sum which is owed on completion of action taken under default arrangements by or to a defaulter but do not apply to any sum which (or to the extent that it) arises from a transfer order which is also a market contract within the meaning of Part VII [or Part V], in which case sections 162 and 163 of the Companies Act 1989 [or Articles 85 and 86 of the Companies (No 2) (Northern Ireland) Order 1990] apply subject to the modification made by regulation 21.

(2) If, in England and Wales [or Northern Ireland], a bankruptcy or winding-up order has been made or a creditors' voluntary winding-up resolution has been passed, the debt—

(a) is provable in the bankruptcy or winding up or, as the case may be, is payable to the relevant office-holder; and

(b) shall be taken into account, where appropriate, under section 323 of the Insolvency Act 1986 [or Article 296 of the Insolvency (Northern Ireland) Order 1989] (mutual dealings and set-off) or the corresponding provision applicable in the case of winding up;

in the same way as a debt due before the commencement of bankruptcy, the date on which the body corporate goes into liquidation (within the meaning of section 247 of the Insolvency Act 1986 [or Article 6 of the Insolvency (Northern Ireland) Order 1989]) or, in the case of a partnership, the date of the winding-up order.

(3) If, in Scotland, an award of sequestration or a winding-up order has been made, or a creditors' voluntary winding-up resolution has been passed, or a trust deed has been granted and it has become a protected trust deed, the debt—

(a) may be claimed in the sequestration or winding up or under the protected trust deed or, as the case may be, is payable to the relevant office-holder; and

(b) shall be taken into account for the purposes of any rule of law relating to set-off applicable in sequestration, winding up or in respect of a protected trust deed;

in the same way as a debt due before the date of sequestration (within the meaning of section 73(1) of the Bankruptcy (Scotland) Act 1985) or the commencement of the winding up (within the meaning of section 129 of the Insolvency Act 1986) or the grant of the trust deed.

[6960]

NOTES

Paras (1), (2): words in square brackets inserted by the Financial Markets and Insolvency (Settlement Finality) (Amendment) Regulations 2006, SI 2006/50, reg 2(1), (7), as from 2 February 2006.

16 Disclaimer of property, rescission of contracts, &c

(1) Sections 178, 186, 315 and 345 of the Insolvency Act 1986 [or Articles 152, 157, 288 and 318 of the Insolvency (Northern Ireland) Order 1989] (power to disclaim onerous property and court's power to order rescission of contracts, &c) do not apply in relation to—

(a) a transfer order; or

(b) a contract for the purpose of realising collateral security.

In the application of this paragraph in Scotland, the reference to sections 178, 315 and 345 shall be construed as a reference to any rule of law having the like effect as those sections.

(2) In Scotland, a permanent trustee on the sequestrated estate of a defaulter or a liquidator or a trustee under a protected trust deed granted by a defaulter is bound by any transfer order given by that defaulter and by any such contract as is mentioned in

paragraph (1)(b) notwithstanding section 42 of the Bankruptcy (Scotland) Act 1985 or any rule of law having the like effect applying in liquidations or any like provision or rule of law affecting the protected trust deed.

(3) Sections 127 and 284 of the Insolvency Act 1986 [or Articles 107 and 257 of the Insolvency (Northern Ireland) Order 1989] (avoidance of property dispositions effected after commencement of winding up or presentation of bankruptcy petition), section 32(8) of the Bankruptcy (Scotland) Act 1985 (effect of dealing with debtor relating to estate vested in permanent trustee) and any like provision or rule of law affecting a protected trust deed, do not apply to—

(a) a transfer order, or any disposition of property in pursuance of such an order;

(b) the provision of collateral security;

(c) a contract for the purpose of realising collateral security or any disposition of property in pursuance of such a contract; or

(d) any disposition of property in accordance with the rules of a designated system as to the application of collateral security.

[6961]

NOTES

Paras (1), (3): words in square brackets inserted by the Financial Markets and Insolvency (Settlement Finality) (Amendment) Regulations 2006, SI 2006/50, reg 2(1), (8), as from 2 February 2006.

17 Adjustment of prior transactions

(1) No order shall be made in relation to a transaction to which this regulation applies under—

(a) section 238 or 339 of the Insolvency Act 1986 [or Article 202 or 312 of the Insolvency (Northern Ireland) Order 1989] (transactions at an undervalue);

(b) section 239 or 340 of that Act [or Article 203 or 313 of that Order] (preferences); or

(c) section 423 of that Act [or Article 367 of that Order] (transactions defrauding creditors).

(2) As respects Scotland, no decree shall be granted in relation to any such transaction—

(a) under section 34 or 36 of the Bankruptcy (Scotland) Act 1985 or section 242 or 243 of the Insolvency Act 1986 (gratuitous alienations and unfair preferences); or

(b) at common law on grounds of gratuitous alienations or fraudulent preferences.

(3) This regulation applies to—

(a) a transfer order, or any disposition of property in pursuance of such an order;

(b) the provision of collateral security;

(c) a contract for the purpose of realising collateral security or any disposition of property in pursuance of such a contract; or

(d) any disposition of property in accordance with the rules of a designated system as to the application of collateral security.

[6962]

NOTES

Para (1): words in square brackets inserted by the Financial Markets and Insolvency (Settlement Finality) (Amendment) Regulations 2006, SI 2006/50, reg 2(1), (9), as from 2 February 2006. Note that the Queen's Printer's copy of the 2006 Regulations actually provides that the words "or Article 203 or 313 of that Order" are to be inserted after the words "section 239 or 340 of that Act" in para (2)(b) of this regulation. It is assumed that this is a drafting error.

Collateral security charges

18 Modifications of the law of insolvency

The general law of insolvency has effect in relation to a collateral security charge and the action taken to enforce such a charge, subject to the provisions of regulation 19.

[6963]

19 Administration orders, &c

(1) The following provisions of [Schedule B1 to] the Insolvency Act 1986 (which relate to administration orders and administrators) do not apply in relation to a collateral security charge—

[(a) paragraph 43(2) including that provision as applied by paragraph 44; and
(b) paragraphs 70, 71 and 72 of that Schedule,]

and [paragraph 41(2) of that Schedule] (receiver to vacate office when so required by administrator) does not apply to a receiver appointed under such a charge.

[(1A) The following provisions of [Schedule B1 to] the Insolvency (Northern Ireland) Order 1989 (which relate to administration orders and administrators) do not apply in relation to a collateral security charge—

[(a) paragraph 44(2), including that provision as applied by paragraph 45 (restrictions on enforcement of security where company in administration or where administration application has been made); and
(b) paragraphs 71, 72 and 73 (charged and hire purchase property);]

and [paragraph 42(2)] (receiver to vacate office when so required by administrator) does not apply to a receiver appointed under such a charge.]

(2) However, where a collateral security charge falls to be enforced after an administration order has been made or a petition for an administration order has been presented, and there exists another charge over some or all of the same property ranking in priority to or *pari passu* with the collateral security charge, on the application of any person interested, the court may order that there shall be taken after enforcement of the collateral security charge such steps as the court may direct for the purpose of ensuring that the chargee under the other charge is not prejudiced by the enforcement of the collateral security charge.

[(2A) A reference in paragraph (2) to "an administration order" shall include the appointment of an administrator under paragraph 14 or 22 of Schedule B1 to the Insolvency Act 1986 [or under paragraph 15 or 23 of Schedule B1 to the Insolvency (Northern Ireland) Order 1989].]

(3) Sections 127 and 284 of the Insolvency Act 1986 [or Articles 107 and 257 of the Insolvency (Northern Ireland) Order 1989] (avoidance of property dispositions effected after commencement of winding up or presentation of bankruptcy petition), section 32(8) of the Bankruptcy (Scotland) Act 1985 (effect of dealing with debtor relating to estate vested in permanent trustee) and any like provision or rule of law affecting a protected trust deed, do not apply to a disposition of property as a result of which the property becomes subject to a collateral security charge or any transactions pursuant to which that disposition is made. **[6964]**

NOTES

Para (1): words in first pair of square brackets inserted, words in third pair of square brackets substituted, and sub-paras (a), (b) substituted, by the Enterprise Act 2002 (Insolvency) Order 2003, SI 2003/2096, arts 5, 6, Schedule, Pt 2, paras 74, 76(a), as from 15 September 2003, except in relation to any case where a petition for an administration order was presented before that date.

Para (1A): inserted by the Financial Markets and Insolvency (Settlement Finality) (Amendment) Regulations 2006, SI 2006/50, reg 2(1), (10)(a), as from 2 February 2006; words in square brackets substituted by the Financial Markets and Insolvency (Settlement Finality) (Amendment) Regulations 2007, SI 2007/832, reg 2(1), (4), as from 6 April 2007.

Para (2A): inserted by SI 2003/2096, arts 5, 6, Schedule, Pt 2, paras 74, 76(b), as from 15 September 2003, except in relation to any case where a petition for an administration order was presented before that date; words in square brackets inserted by SI 2007/832, reg 2(1), (5), as from 6 April 2007.

Para (3): words in square brackets inserted by SI 2006/50, reg 2(1), (10)(b), as from 2 February 2006.

General

20 Transfer order entered into designated system following insolvency

(1) This Part does not apply in relation to any transfer order given by a participant which is entered into a designated system after—

(a) a court has made an order of a type referred to in regulation 22 in respect of that participant, or
(b) that participant has passed a creditors' voluntary winding-up resolution, or
(c) a trust deed granted by that participant has become a protected trust deed,

unless the conditions mentioned in paragraph (2) are satisfied.

(2) The conditions referred to in paragraph (1) are that—

(a) the transfer order is carried out on the same day that the event specified in paragraph (1)(a), (b) or (c) occurs, and

(b) the settlement agent, the central counterparty or the clearing house can show that it did not have notice of that event at the time of settlement of the transfer order.

(3) For the purposes of paragraph (2)(b), the relevant settlement agent, central counterparty or clearing house shall be taken to have notice of an event specified in paragraph (1)(a), (b) or (c) if it deliberately failed to make enquiries as to that matter in circumstances in which a reasonable and honest person would have done so.

[6965]

21 Disapplication of certain provisions of Part VII [and Part V]

(1) The provisions of the Companies Act 1989 [or the Companies (No 2) (Northern Ireland) Order 1990] mentioned in paragraph (2) do not apply in relation to—

(a) a market contract which is also a transfer order effected through a designated system; or

(b) a market charge which is also a collateral security charge.

(2) The provisions referred to in paragraph (1) are as follows—

(a) section 163(4) to (6) [and Article 86(3) to (5)] (net sum payable on completion of default proceedings);

(b) section 164(4) to (6) [and Article 87(3) to (5)] (disclaimer of property, rescission of contracts, &c); and

(c) section 175(5) and (6) [and Article 97(5) and (6)] (administration orders, &c).

[6966]

NOTES

Words in square brackets inserted by the Financial Markets and Insolvency (Settlement Finality) (Amendment) Regulations 2006, SI 2006/50, reg 2(1), (11), as from 2 February 2006.

22 Notification of insolvency order or passing of resolution for creditors' voluntary winding up

(1) Upon the making of an order for bankruptcy, sequestration, administration or winding up in respect of a participant in a designated system, the court shall forthwith notify both the system and the designating authority that such an order has been made.

(2) Following receipt of—

(a) such notification from the court, or

(b) notification from a participant of the passing of a creditors' voluntary winding-up resolution or of a trust deed becoming a protected trust deed, pursuant to paragraph 5(4) of the Schedule,

the designating authority shall forthwith inform the Treasury of the notification.

[6967]

23 Applicable law relating to securities held as collateral security

Where—

(a) securities (including rights in securities) are provided as collateral security to a participant or a central bank (including any nominee, agent or third party acting on behalf of the participant or the central bank), and

(b) a register, account or centralised deposit system located in an EEA State legally records the entitlement of that person to the collateral security,

the rights of that person as a holder of collateral security in relation to those securities shall be governed by the law of the EEA State or, where appropriate, the law of the part of the EEA State, where the register, account, or centralised deposit system is located.

[6968]

24 Applicable law where insolvency proceedings are brought

Where insolvency proceedings are brought in any jurisdiction against a person who participates, or has participated, in a system designated for the purposes of the Settlement Finality Directive, any question relating to the rights and obligations arising from, or in connection with, that participation and falling to be determined by a court in England and Wales[, the High Court in Northern Ireland] or in Scotland shall (subject to regulation 23) be determined in accordance with the law governing that system.

[6969]

NOTES

Words in square brackets inserted by the Financial Markets and Insolvency (Settlement Finality) (Amendment) Regulations 2006, SI 2006/50, reg 2(1), (12), as from 2 February 2006.

25 Insolvency proceedings in other jurisdictions

(1) The references to insolvency law in section 426 of the Insolvency Act 1986 (co-operation between courts exercising jurisdiction in relation to insolvency) include, in relation to a part of the United Kingdom, this Part and, in relation to a relevant country or territory within the meaning of that section, so much of the law of that country or territory as corresponds to this Part.

(2) A court shall not, in pursuance of that section or any other enactment or rule of law, recognise or give effect to—

(a) any order of a court exercising jurisdiction in relation to insolvency law in a country or territory outside the United Kingdom, or

(b) any act of a person appointed in such a country or territory to discharge any functions under insolvency law,

in so far as the making of the order or the doing of the act would be prohibited in the case of a court in England and Wales or Scotland[, the High Court in Northern Ireland] or a relevant office-holder by this Part.

(3) Paragraph (2) does not affect the recognition or enforcement of a judgment required to be recognised or enforced under or by virtue of the Civil Jurisdiction and Judgments Act 1982 [or Council Regulation (EC) No 44/2001 of 22nd December 2000 on jurisdiction and the recognition and enforcement of judgments in civil and commercial matters][, as amended from time to time and as applied by the Agreement made on 19th October 2005 between the European Community and the Kingdom of Denmark on jurisdiction and the recognition and enforcement of judgments in civil and commercial matters].

[6970]

NOTES

Para (2): words in square brackets inserted by the Financial Markets and Insolvency (Settlement Finality) (Amendment) Regulations 2006, SI 2006/50, reg 2(1), (13), as from 2 February 2006.

Para (3): words in first pair of square brackets added by the Civil Jurisdiction and Judgments Order 2001, SI 2001/3929, art 5, Sch 3, para 27, as from 1 March 2002; words in second pair of square brackets added by the Civil Jurisdiction and Judgments Regulations 2007, SI 2007/1655, reg 5, Schedule, Pt 2, para 32, as from 1 July 2007.

26 Systems designated in other EEA States … and Gibraltar

(1) Where an equivalent overseas order or equivalent overseas security is subject to the insolvency law of England and Wales or Scotland [or Northern Ireland], this Part shall apply—

(a) in relation to the equivalent overseas order as it applies in relation to a transfer order; and

(b) in relation to the equivalent overseas security as it applies in relation to collateral security in connection with a designated system.

(2) In paragraph (1)—

(a) "equivalent overseas order" means an order having the like effect as a transfer order which is effected through a system designated for the purposes of the Settlement Finality Directive in another EEA State … or Gibraltar; and

(b) "equivalent overseas security" means any realisable assets provided under a charge or a repurchase or similar agreement, or otherwise (including money provided under a charge) for the purpose of securing rights and obligations potentially arising in connection with such a system.

[6971]

NOTES

Words omitted revoked, and words in square brackets inserted, by the Financial Markets and Insolvency (Settlement Finality) (Amendment) Regulations 2006, SI 2006/50, reg 2(1), (14), as from 2 February 2006.

SCHEDULE
REQUIREMENTS FOR DESIGNATION OF SYSTEM

Regulation 4(1)

1 Establishment, participation and governing law

(1) The head office of at least one of the participants in the system must be in … [the United Kingdom] and the law of England and Wales[, Northern Ireland] or Scotland must be the governing law of the system.

(2) There must be not less than three institutions participating in the system, unless otherwise determined by the designating authority in any case where—
- (a) there are two institutions participating in a system; and
- (b) the designating authority considers that designation is required on the grounds of systemic risk.

(3) The system must be a system through which transfer orders are effected.

(4) Where orders relating to financial instruments other than securities are effected through the system—
- (a) the system must primarily be a system through which securities transfer orders are effected; and
- (b) the designating authority must consider that designation is required on grounds of systemic risk.

2 Arrangements and resources

The system must have adequate arrangements and resources for the effective monitoring and enforcement of compliance with its rules or, as respects monitoring, arrangements providing for that function to be performed on its behalf (and without affecting its responsibility) by another body or person who is able and willing to perform it.

3 Financial resources

The system must have financial resources sufficient for the proper performance of its functions as a system.

4 Co-operation with other authorities

The system must be able and willing to co-operate, by the sharing of information and otherwise, with—
- (a) the Financial Services Authority,
- (b) the Bank of England,
- (c) any relevant office-holder, and
- (d) any authority, body or person having responsibility for any matter arising out of, or connected with, the default of a participant.

5 Specific provision in the rules

(1) The rules of the system must—
- (a) specify the point at which a transfer order takes effect as having been entered into the system,
- (b) specify the point after which a transfer order may not be revoked by a participant or any other party, and
- (c) prohibit the revocation by a participant or any other party of a transfer order from the point specified in accordance with paragraph (b).

(2) The rules of the system must require each institution which participates in the system to provide upon payment of a reasonable charge the information mentioned in sub-paragraph (3) to any person who requests it, save where the request is frivolous or vexatious. The rules must require the information to be provided within fourteen days of the request being made.

(3) The information referred to in sub-paragraph (2) is as follows—

(a) details of the systems which are designated for the purposes of the Settlement Finality Directive in which the institution participates, and

(b) information about the main rules governing the functioning of those systems.

(4) The rules of the system must require each participant upon—

(a) the passing of a creditors' voluntary winding up resolution, or

(b) a trust deed granted by him becoming a protected trust deed,

to notify forthwith both the system and the designating authority that such a resolution has been passed, or, as the case may be, that such a trust deed has become a protected trust deed.

6 Default arrangements

The system must have default arrangements which are appropriate for that system in all the circumstances.

[6972]–[6973]

NOTES

Para 1: words omitted revoked, and words in square brackets inserted, by the Financial Markets and Insolvency (Settlement Finality) (Amendment) Regulations 2006, SI 2006/50, reg 2(1), (15), as from 2 February 2006.

LIMITED LIABILITY PARTNERSHIPS (SCOTLAND) REGULATIONS 2001

(SSI 2001/128)

NOTES

Made: 28 March 2001.

Authority: Limited Liability Partnerships Act 2000, ss 14(1), (2), 15, 16, 17(1), (3).

Commencement: 6 April 2001 (see reg 1 at **[6974]**). Where any provision in this work (including any inserted or substituted provision) came into force for all purposes on or before 1 July 2005, commencement information is not noted at provision level.

As of 1 July 2007, these Regulations had not been amended.

ARRANGEMENT OF REGULATIONS

PART I
CITATION, COMMENCEMENT EXTENT AND INTERPRETATION

1 Citation, commencement and extent

(1) These Regulations may be cited as the Limited Liability Partnerships (Scotland) Regulations 2001 and shall come into force on 6th April 2001.

(2) These Regulations extend to Scotland only.

[6974]

2 Interpretation

In these Regulations—

"the 1985 Act" means the Companies Act 1985;

"the 1986 Act" means the Insolvency Act 1986;

"limited liability partnership agreement", in relation to a limited liability partnership, means any agreement, express or implied, made between the members of the limited liability partnership or between the limited liability partnership and the members of the limited liability partnership which determines the mutual rights and duties of the members, and their rights and duties in relation to the limited liability partnership;

"the principal Act" means the Limited Liability Partnerships Act 2000; and

"shadow member", in relation to a limited liability partnership, means a person in accordance with whose directions or instructions the members of the limited liability partnership are accustomed to act (but so that a person is not deemed a shadow member by reason only that the members of the limited liability partnership act on advice given by that person in a professional capacity).

[6975]

PART II
COMPANIES ACT

3 Application of the 1985 Act to limited liability partnerships

The provisions of the 1985 Act specified in the first column of Schedule 1 to these Regulations shall apply to limited liability partnerships, with the following modifications—

(a) references to a company shall include references to a limited liability partnership;

(b) references to the Companies Acts shall include references to the principal Act and any regulations made thereunder;

(c) references to the 1986 Act shall include references to that Act as it applies to limited liability partnerships by virtue of Part III of these Regulations;

(d) references in a provision of the 1985 Act to other provisions of that Act shall include references to those other provisions as they apply to limited liability partnerships by virtue of these Regulations; and

(e) the modifications, if any, specified in the second column of Schedule 1 of the provision specified opposite them in the first column.

[6976]

PART III
WINDING UP AND INSOLVENCY

4 Application of the 1986 Act to limited liability partnerships

(1) Subject to paragraph (2), the provisions of the 1986 Act listed in Schedule 2 shall apply in relation to limited liability partnerships as they apply in relation to companies.

(2) The provisions of the 1986 Act referred to in paragraph (1) shall so apply, with the following modifications—

(a) references to a company shall include references to a limited liability partnership;

(b) references to a director or to an officer of a company shall include references to a member of a limited liability partnership;

(c) references to a shadow director shall include references to a shadow member;

(d) references to the 1985 Act, the Company Directors Disqualification Act 1986, the Companies Act 1989 or to any provisions of those Acts or to any provisions of the

PART IV STATUTORY INSTRUMENTS

1986 Act shall include references to those Acts or provisions as they apply to limited liability partnerships by virtue of the principal Act or these Regulations; and

(e) the modifications set out in Schedule 3 to these Regulations.

[6977]

PART IV
MISCELLANEOUS

5 General and consequential amendments

The enactments referred to in Schedule 4 shall have effect subject to the amendments specified in that Schedule.

[6978]

6 Application of subordinate legislation

(1) The Insolvency (Scotland) Rules 1986 shall apply to limited liability partnerships with such modifications as the context requires for the purpose of giving effect to the provisions of the Insolvency Act 1986 which are applied by these Regulations.

(2) In the case of any conflict between any provision of the subordinate legislation applied by paragraph (1) and any provision of these Regulations, the latter shall prevail.

[6979]

SCHEDULES

SCHEDULE 1
MODIFICATIONS TO PROVISIONS OF THE 1985 ACT

Regulation 3

Formalities of Carrying on Business	
36B (execution of documents by companies)	
Floating charges and Receivers (Scotland)	
462 (power of incorporated company to create floating charge)	In subsection (1), for the words "an incorporated company (whether a company within the meaning of this Act or not)," substitute "a limited liability partnership", and the words "(including uncalled capital)" are omitted.
463 (effect of floating charge on winding up)	
466 (alteration of floating charges) Subsections (1), (2), (3) and (6)	
486 (interpretation for Part XVIII generally)	For the definition of "company" substitute ""company" means a limited liability partnership;"
487 (extent of Part XVIII)	

[6980]

SCHEDULE 2
PROVISIONS OF THE 1986 ACT

Regulation 4(1)

The relevant provisions of the 1986 Act are as follows:

Sections 50 to 52;

Section 53(1) and (2), to the extent that those subsections do not relate to the requirement for a copy of the instrument and notice being delivered to the registrar of companies;

Section 53(4), (6) and (7);

Section 54(1), (2), (3) (to the extent that that subsection does not relate to the requirement for a copy of the interlocutor to be delivered to the registrar of companies), and subsections (5), (6) and (7);

Sections 55 to 58;

Section 60, other than subsection (1);

Section 61, including subsections (6) and (7) to the extent that those subsections do not relate to anything to be done or which may be sent to the registrar of companies;

Section 62, including subsection (5) to the extent that that subsection does not relate to anything to be done or which may be sent to the registrar of companies;

Sections 63 to 66;

Section 67, including subsections (1) and (8) to the extent that those subsections do not relate to anything to be sent to the registrar of companies;

Section 68;

Section 69, including subsections (1) and (2) to the extent that those subsections do not relate to anything to be done or which may be done by the registrar of companies;

Sections 70 and 71;

Subsection 84(3) to the extent that it does not concern the copy of the resolution being forwarded to the registrar of companies within 15 days;

Sections 91 to 93;

Section 94, including subsections (3) and (4) to the extent that those subsections do not relate to the liquidator being required to send to the registrar of companies a copy of the account and a return of the final meeting;

Section 95;

Section 97;

Sections 100 to 102;

Sections 104 to 105;

Section 106, including subsections (3), (4) and (5) to the extent that those subsections do not relate to the liquidator being required to send to the registrar of companies a copy of the account of winding up and a return of the final meeting/quorum;

Sections 109 to 111;

Section 112, including subsection (3) to the extent that that subsection does not relate to the liquidator being required to send to the registrar of companies a copy of the order made by the court;

Sections 113 to 115;

Sections 126 to 128;

Section 130(1) to the extent that that subsection does not relate to a copy of the order being forwarded by the court to the registrar of companies;

Section 131;

Sections 133 to 135;

Sections 138 to 140;

Sections 142 to 146;

Section 147, including subsection (3) to the extent that that subsection does not relate to a copy of the order being forwarded by the company to the registrar of companies;

Section 162 to the extent that the section concerns the matters set out in Section C 2 of Schedule 5 to the Scotland Act 1998 as being exceptions to the reservation of insolvency;

Sections 163 to 167;

Section 169;

Section 170, including subsection (2) to the extent that that subsection does not relate to an application being made by the registrar to make good the default;

Section 171;

Section 172, including subsection (8) to the extent that that subsection does not relate to the liquidator being required to give notice to the registrar of companies;

Sections 173 and 174;

Section 177;

Sections 185 to 189;

Sections 191 to 194;

Section 196;

Section 199;

Section 200;

Sections 206 to 215;

Section 218 subsections (1), (2),(4) and (6);

Sections 231 to 232 to the extent that the sections apply to administrative receivers, liquidators and provisional liquidators;

Section 233 to the extent that that section applies in the case of the appointment of an administrative receiver, of a voluntary arrangement taking effect, of a company going into liquidation or where a provisional liquidator is appointed;

Section 234 to the extent that that section applies to situations other than those where an administration order applies;

Section 235 to the extent that that section applies to situations other than those where an administration order applies;

Sections 236 to 237 to the extent that those sections apply to situations other than administration orders and winding up;

Sections 242 to 243;

Section 244 to the extent that that section applies in circumstances other than a company which is subject to an administration order;

Section 245;

Section 251;

Section 416(1) and (4) to the extent that those subsections apply to section 206(1)(a) and (b) in connection with the offence provision relating to the winding up of a limited liability partnership;

Section 430;

Section 436;

Schedule 2;

Schedule 3;

Schedule 4;

Schedule 8 to the extent that that Schedule does not apply to voluntary arrangements or administrations within the meaning of Parts I and II of the 1986 Act;

Schedule 10 to the extent that it refers to any of the sections referred to above.

[6980A]

SCHEDULE 3
MODIFICATIONS TO PROVISIONS OF THE 1986 ACT

Regulation 4(2)

Provisions	**Modifications**
Section 84 (circumstances in which company may be wound up voluntarily)	
Subsection (3)	For subsection (3) substitute the following—
	"(3) Within 15 days after a limited liability partnership has determined that it be wound up there shall be forwarded to the registrar of companies either a printed copy or a copy in some other form approved by the registrar of the determination."
	After subsection (3) insert a new subsection—
Subsection (4)	"(4) If a limited liability partnership fails to comply with this regulation the limited liability partnership and every designated member of it who is in default is liable on summary conviction to a fine not exceeding level 3 on the standard scale."
Section 91 (appointment of liquidator)	
Subsection (1)	Delete "in general meeting".
Subsection (2)	For subsection (2) substitute the following—
	"(2) On the appointment of a liquidator the powers of the members of the limited liability partnership shall cease except to the extent that a meeting of the members of the limited liability partnership summoned for the purpose or the liquidator sanctions their continuance."
	After subsection (2) insert—
	"(3) Subsections (3) and (4) of section 92 shall apply for the purposes of this section as they apply for the purposes of that section."
Section 92 (power to fill vacancy in office of liquidator)	
Subsection (1)	For "the company in general meeting" substitute "a meeting of the members of the limited liability partnership summoned for the purpose".
Subsection (2)	For "a general meeting" substitute "a meeting of the members of the limited liability partnership".
Subsection (3)	In subsection (3), for "articles" substitute "limited liability partnership agreement".
new subsection (4)	Add a new subsection (4) as follows—
	"(4) The quorum required for a meeting of the members of the limited liability partnership shall be any quorum required by the limited liability partnership agreement for meetings of the members of the limited liability partnership and if no requirement for a quorum has been agreed upon the quorum shall be 2 members."
Section 93 (general company meeting at each year's end)	
subsection (1)	For "a general meeting of the company" substitute "a meeting of the members of the limited liability partnership".
new subsection (4)	Add a new subsection (4) as follows—
	"(4) Subsections (3) and (4) of section 92 shall apply for the purposes of this section as they apply for the purposes of that section."

Provisions	Modifications
Section 94 (final meeting prior to dissolution)	
subsection (1)	For "a general meeting of the company" substitute "a meeting of the members of the limited liability partnership".
new subsection (5A)	Add a new subsection (5A) as follows— "(5A) Subsections (3) and (4) of section 92 shall apply for the purposes of this section as they apply for the purposes of that section."
subsection (6)	For "a general meeting of the company" substitute "a meeting of the members of the limited liability partnership".
Section 95 (effect of company's insolvency)	
subsection (1)	For "directors'" substitute "designated members'".
subsection (7)	For subsection (7) substitute the following— "(7) In this section 'the relevant period' means the period of 6 months immediately preceding the date on which the limited liability partnership determined that it be wound up voluntarily."
Section 100 (appointment of liquidator)	
subsection (1)	For "The creditors and the company at their respective meetings mentioned in section 98" substitute "The creditors at their meeting mentioned in section 98 and the limited liability partnership".
subsection (3)	Delete "director,".
Section 101(appointment of liquidation committee)	
subsection (2)	For subsection (2) substitute the following— "(2) If such a committee is appointed, the limited liability partnership may, when it determines that it be wound up voluntarily or at any time thereafter, appoint such number of persons as they think fit to act as members of the committee, not exceeding 5."
Section 105 (meetings of company and creditors at each year's end)	
subsection (1)	For "a general meeting of the company" substitute "a meeting of the members of the limited liability partnership".
new subsection (5)	Add a new subsection (5) as follows— "(5) Subsections (3) and (4) of section 92 shall apply for the purposes of this section as they apply for the purposes of that section."
Section 106 (final meeting prior to dissolution)	
subsection (1)	For "a general meeting of the company" substitute "a meeting of the members of the limited liability partnership".
new subsection (5A)	After subsection (5) insert a new subsection (5A) as follows— "(5A) Subsections (3) and (4) of section 92 shall apply for the purposes of this section as they apply for the purposes of that section."
subsection (6)	For "a general meeting of the company" substitute "a meeting of the members of the limited liability partnership".

Provisions	**Modifications**
Sections 110 (acceptance of shares, etc, as consideration for sale of company property)	
	For the existing section substitute the following:
	"(1) This section applies, in the case of a limited liability partnership proposed to be, or being, wound up voluntarily, where the whole or part of the limited liability partnership's business or property is proposed to be transferred or sold to another company whether or not it is a company within the meaning of the Companies Act ("the transferee company") or to a limited liability partnership ("the transferee limited liability partnership").
	(2) With the requisite sanction, the liquidator of the limited liability partnership being, or proposed to be, wound up ("the transferor limited liability partnership") may receive, in compensation or part compensation for the transfer or sale, shares, policies or other like interests in the transferee company or the transferee limited liability partnership for distribution among the members of the transferor limited liability partnership.
	(3) The sanction required under subsection (2) is—
	(a) in the case of a members' voluntary winding up, that of a determination of the limited liability partnership at a meeting of the members of the limited liability partnership conferring either a general authority on the liquidator or an authority in respect of any particular arrangement, (subsections (3) and (4) of section 92 to apply for this purpose as they apply for the purposes of that section), and
	(b) in the case of a creditor's voluntary winding up, that of either court or the liquidation committee.
	(4) Alternatively to subsection (2), the liquidator may (with the sanction) enter into any other arrangement whereby the members of the transferor limited liability partnership may, in lieu of receiving cash, shares, policies or other like interests (or in addition thereto), participate in the profits, or receive any other benefit from the transferee company or the transferee limited liability partnership.
	(5) A sale or arrangement in pursuance of this section is binding on members of the transferor limited liability partnership.
	(6) A determination by the limited liability partnership is not invalid for the purposes of this section by reason that it is made before or concurrently with a determination by the limited liability partnership that it be wound up voluntarily or for appointing liquidators; but, if an order is made within a year for winding up the limited liability partnership by the court, the determination by the limited liability partnership is not valid unless sanctioned by the court."
Section 111 (dissent from arrangement under section 110)	
subsections (1)–(3)	For subsections (1)–(3) substitute the following—

PART IV
STATUTORY INSTRUMENTS

Provisions	Modifications
	"(1) This section applies in the case of a voluntary winding up where, for the purposes of section 110(2) or (4), a determination of the limited liability partnership has provided the sanction requisite for the liquidator under that section. (2) If a member of the transferor limited liability partnership who did not vote in favour of providing the sanction required for the liquidator under section 110 expresses his dissent from it in writing addressed to the liquidator and left at the registered office of the limited liability partnership within 7 days after the date on which that sanction was given, he may require the liquidator either to abstain from carrying the arrangement so sanctioned into effect or to purchase his interest at a price to be determined by agreement or arbitration under this section. (3) If the liquidator elects to purchase the member's interest, the purchase money must be paid before the limited liability partnership is dissolved and be raised by the liquidator in such manner as may be determined by the limited liability partnership."
subsection (4)	Omit subsection (4).
Section 126 (power to stay or restrain proceedings against company)	
subsection (2)	Delete subsection (2).
Section 127 (avoidance of property dispositions, etc)	
	For "any transfer of shares" substitute "any transfer by a member of the limited liability partnership of his interest in the property of the limited liability partnership".
Section 165 (voluntary winding up)	
subsection (2)	In paragraph (a) for "an extraordinary resolution of the company" substitute "a determination by a meeting of the members of the limited liability partnership".
subsection (4)	For paragraph (c) substitute the following— "(c) summon meetings of the members of the limited liability partnership for the purpose of obtaining their sanction or for any other purpose he may think fit."
new subsection (4A)	Insert a new subsection (4A) as follows— "(4A) Subsections (3) and (4) of section 92 shall apply for the purposes of this section as they apply for the purposes of that section."
Section 166 (creditors' voluntary winding up)	
subsection (5)	In paragraph (b) for "directors" substitute "designated members".
Section 171 (removal, etc (voluntary winding up))	
subsection (2)	For paragraph (a) substitute the following— "(a) in the case of a members' voluntary winding up, by a meeting of the members of the limited liability partnership summoned specially for that purpose, or".
subsection (6)	In paragraph (a) for "final meeting of the company" substitute "final meeting of the members of the limited liability partnership" and in paragraph (b) for "final meetings of the company" substitute "final meetings of the members of the limited liability partnership".

Provisions	**Modifications**
new subsection (7)	Insert a new subsection (7) as follows— "(7) Subsections (3) and (4) of section 92 apply for the purposes of this section as they apply for the purposes of that section ."
Section 173 (release (voluntary winding up))	
subsection (2)	In paragraph (a) for "a general meeting of the company" substitute "a meeting of the members of the limited liability partnership".
Section 187 (power to make over assets to employees)	
	Delete section 187
Section 194 (resolutions passed at adjourned meetings)	
	After "contributories" insert "or of the members of a limited liability partnership".
Section 206 (fraud, etc in anticipation of winding up)	
subsection (1)	For "passes a resolution for voluntary winding up" substitute "makes a determination that it be wound up voluntarily".
Section 207 (transactions in fraud of creditors)	
subsection (1)	For "passes a resolution for voluntary winding up" substitute "makes a determination that it be wound up voluntarily".
Section 210 (material omissions from statement relating to company's affairs)	
subsection (2)	For "passed a resolution for voluntary winding up" substitute "made a determination that it be wound up voluntarily".
Section 214 (wrongful trading)	
subsection (2)	Delete from "but the court shall not" to the end of the subsection.
After section 214	Insert the following new section 214A "214A Adjustment of withdrawals (1) This section has effect in relation to a person who is or has been a member of a limited liability partnership where, in the course of the winding up of that limited liability partnership, it appears that subsection (2) of this section applies in relation to that person. (2) This subsection applies in relation to a person if— (a) within the period of two years ending with the commencement of the winding up, he was a member of the limited liability partnership who withdrew property of the limited liability partnership, whether in the form of a share of profits, salary, repayment of or payment of interest on a loan to the limited liability partnership or any other withdrawal of property, and (b) it is proved by the liquidator to the satisfaction of the court that at the time of the withdrawal he knew or had reasonable grounds for believing that the limited liability partnership— (i) was at the time of the withdrawal unable to pay its debts within the meaning of section 123 of the Act, or

Provisions	Modifications
	(ii) would become so unable to pay its debts after the assets of the limited liability partnership had been depleted by that withdrawal taken together with all other withdrawals (if any) made by any members contemporaneously with that withdrawal or in contemplation when that withdrawal was made.
	(3) Where this section has effect in relation to any person the court, on the application of the liquidator, may declare that that person is to be liable to make such contribution (if any) to the limited liability partnership's assets as the court thinks proper.
	(4) The court shall not make a declaration in relation to any person the amount of which exceeds the aggregate of the amounts or values of all the withdrawals referred to in subsection (2) made by that person within the period of 2 years referred to in that subsection.
	(5) The court shall not make a declaration under this section with respect to any person unless that person knew or ought to have concluded that after each withdrawal referred to in subsection (2) there was no reasonable prospect that the limited liability partnership would avoid going into insolvent liquidation.
	(6) For the purposes of subsection (5) the facts which a member ought to know or ascertain, the conclusions which he ought to reach and the steps which he ought to have taken are those which would be known or ascertained, or reached or taken, by a reasonably diligent person having both:
	(a) the general knowledge, skill and experience that may reasonably be expected of a person carrying out the same functions as are carried out by that member in relation to the limited liability partnership, and
	(b) the general knowledge, skill and experience that that member has.
	(7) For the purposes of this section a limited liability partnership goes into insolvent liquidation if it goes into liquidation at a time when its assets are insufficient for the payment of its debts and other liabilities and the expenses of the winding up.
	(8) In this section "member" includes a shadow member.
	(9) This section is without prejudice to section 214."
Section 215 (proceedings under ss 213, 214)	
subsection (1)	Omit the word "or" between the words "213" and "214" and insert after "214" "or 214A".
subsection (2)	For "either section" substitute "any of those sections".
subsection (4)	For "either section" substitute "any of those sections".
subsection (5)	For "Sections 213 and 214" substitute "Sections 213, 214 or 214A".
Section 218 (prosecution of delinquent officers and members of company)	
subsection (1)	For "officer, or any member, of the company" substitute "member of the limited liability partnership"

Provisions	**Modifications**
subsections (4) and (6)	For "officer of the company, or any member of it," substitute "officer or member of the limited liability partnership".
Section 233 (supplies of gas, water, electricity etc)	
subsection (1)	For paragraph (c) substitute the following— "(c) a voluntary arrangement under Part I has taken effect in accordance with section 5".
subsection (4)	For paragraph (c) substitute the following— "(c) the date on which the voluntary arrangement took effect in accordance with section 5".
Section 251 (expressions used generally)	
	Delete the word "and" appearing after the definition of "the rules" and insert the word "and" after the definition of "shadow director". After the definition of "shadow director" insert the following— ""shadow member", in relation to a limited liability partnership, means a person in accordance with whose directions or instructions the members of the limited liability partnership are accustomed to act (but so that a person is not deemed a shadow member by reason only that the members of the limited liability partnership act on advice given by him in a professional capacity);"
Section 416 (monetary limits (companies winding up))	
subsection (1)	In subsection (1), omit the words "section 117(2) (amount of company's share capital determining whether county court has jurisdiction to wind it up);" and the words "section 120(3) (the equivalent as respects sheriff court jurisdiction in Scotland);".
Section 436 (expressions used generally)	
	The following expressions and definitions shall be added to the section— "designated member" has the same meaning as it has in the Limited Liability Partnerships Act 2000; "limited liability partnership" means a limited liability partnership formed and registered under the Limited Liability Partnership Act 2000; "limited liability partnership agreement", in relation to a limited liability partnership, means any agreement, express or implied, made between the members of the limited liability partnership or between the limited liability partnership and the members of the limited liability partnership which determines the mutual rights and duties of the members, and their rights and duties in relation to the limited liability partnership.
Schedule 2	
Paragraph 17	For paragraph 17 substitute the following— "**17.** Power to enforce any rights the limited liability partnership has against the members under the terms of the limited liability partnership agreement"
Schedule 10	

Provisions	Modifications
Section 93(3)	In the entry relating to section 93(3) for "general meeting of the company" substitute "meeting of members of the limited liability partnership".
Section 105(3)	In the entry relating to section 105(3) for "company general meeting" substitute "meeting of the members of the limited liability partnership".
Section 106(6)	In the entry relating to section 106(6) for "company" substitute "the members of the limited liability partnership"

[6980B]

SCHEDULE 4

GENERAL AND CONSEQUENTIAL AMENDMENTS IN OTHER LEGISLATION

Regulation 5

1–5. …

Culpable officer provision

6.—(1) A culpable officer provision applies in the case of a limited liability partnership as if the reference in the provision to a director (or a person purporting to act as a director) were a reference to a member (or a person purporting to act as a member) of the limited liability partnership.

(2) A culpable officer provision is a devolved provision in any Act or subordinate legislation (within the meaning of the Interpretation Act 1978 or the Scotland Act 1998 (Transitory and Transitional Provisions) (Publication and Interpretation etc of Acts of the Scottish Parliament) Order 1999) to the effect that where—

(a) a body corporate is guilty of a particular offence, and

(b) the offence is proved to have been committed with the consent or connivance of, or to be attributable to the neglect on the part of, (among others) a director of the body corporate,

he (as well as the body corporate) is guilty of the offence.

(3) In this paragraph "devolved provision" means any provision that would be within devolved competence for the purposes of section 101 of the Scotland Act 1998.

[6981]

NOTES

Paras 1–5: amend the Insolvency Act 1986, ss 110 at **[3266]**, the Criminal Procedure (Scotland) Act 1995, ss 70, 141, 143, and the Requirements of Writing (Scotland) Act 1995, s 7, Schs 1, 2.

LIMITED LIABILITY PARTNERSHIPS (FORMS) REGULATIONS 2001 (NOTE)

(SI 2001/927)

NOTES

See Appendix 4 at **[A4]**.

[6981ZA]

COMPANIES (DISQUALIFICATION ORDERS) REGULATIONS 2001

(SI 2001/967)

NOTES

Made: 13 March 2001.

Authority: Company Directors Disqualification Act 1986, s 18.

Commencement: 6 April 2001 (see reg 1 at **[6981A]**). Where any provision in this work (including any inserted or substituted provision) came into force for all purposes on or before 1 July 2005, commencement information is not noted at provision level.

These Regulations (as set out here) are reproduced as amended by: the Companies (Disqualification Orders) (Amendment) Regulations 2004, SI 2004/1940.

Limited liability partnerships: these Regulations apply, with modifications, to limited liability partnerships; see the Limited Liability Partnerships Regulations 2001, SI 2001/1090, reg 10, Sch 6, Pt III (at **[7000]**), and the Interpretation Act 1978, ss 17(2)(a), 23(1), (2).

ARRANGEMENT OF REGULATIONS

1 Citation and commencement

These Regulations may be cited as the Companies (Disqualification Orders) Regulations 2001 and shall come into force on 6th April 2001.

[6981A]

2 Definitions

In these Regulations:

"the Act" means the Company Directors Disqualification Act 1986;

"disqualification order" means an order of the court under any of sections 2 to 6, 8, and 10 of the Act;

"disqualification undertaking" means an undertaking accepted by the Secretary of State under section 7 or 8 of the Act;

"grant of leave" means a grant by the court of leave under section 17 of the Act to any person in relation to a disqualification order or a disqualification undertaking.

[6981B]

3 (*Revokes the Companies (Disqualification Orders) Regulations 1986, SI 1986/2067.*)

4 Transitional provisions

Other than regulation 9, these regulations apply in relation to:

(a) a disqualification order made after the coming into force of these Regulations; and

(b)

(i) a grant of leave made after the coming into force of these Regulations; or

(ii) any action taken by a court after the coming into force of these Regulations in consequence of which a disqualification order or a disqualification undertaking is varied or ceases to be in force,

whether the disqualification order or disqualification undertaking to which, as the case may be, the grant of leave or the action relates was made by the court or accepted by the Secretary of State before or after the coming into force of these Regulations.

[6981C]

5 Regulation 9 applies to particulars of orders made and leave granted under Part II of the Companies (Northern Ireland) Order 1989 received by the Secretary of State after the coming into force of these Regulations other than particulars of orders made and leave granted under that Order which relate to disqualification orders made by the courts of Northern Ireland before 2 April 2001.

[6981D]

PART IV STATUTORY INSTRUMENTS

6 Particulars to be furnished by officers of the court

(1) The following officers of the court shall furnish to the Secretary of State the particulars specified in Regulation 7(a) to (c) below in the form and manner there specified:

(a) where a disqualification order is made by the Crown Court, the Court Manager;

(b) where a disqualification order or grant of leave is made by the High Court, the Court Manager;

(c) where a disqualification order or grant of leave is made by a County Court, the Court Manager;

(d) where a disqualification order is made by a Magistrates' Court, the Chief Executive to the Justices;

(e) where a disqualification order is made by the High Court of Justiciary, the Deputy Principal Clerk of Justiciary;

(f) where a disqualification order or grant of leave is made by a Sheriff Court, the Sheriff Clerk;

(g) where a disqualification order or grant of leave is made by the Court of Session, the Deputy Principal Clerk of Session;

(h) where a disqualification order or grant of leave is made by the Court of Appeal, the Court Manager; and

(i) where a disqualification order or grant of leave is made by the House of Lords, the Judicial Clerk.

(2) Where a disqualification order has been made by any of the courts mentioned in paragraph (1) above or a disqualification undertaking has been accepted by the Secretary of State, and subsequently any action is taken by a court in consequence of which, as the case may be, that order or that undertaking is varied or ceases to be in force, the officer specified in paragraph (1) above of the court which takes such action shall furnish to the Secretary of State the particulars specified in Regulation 7(d) below in the form and manner there specified.

[6981E]

7 The form in which the particulars are to be furnished is:

(a) that set out in Schedule 1 to these Regulations with such variations as circumstances require when the person against whom the disqualification order is made is an individual, and the particulars contained therein are the particulars specified for that purpose;

(b) that set out in Schedule 2 to these Regulations with such variations as circumstances require when the person against whom the disqualification order is made is a body corporate, and the particulars contained therein are the particulars specified for that purpose;

(c) that set out in Schedule 3 to these Regulations with such variations as circumstances require when a grant of leave is made by the court, and the particulars contained therein are the particulars specified for that purpose;

(d) that set out in Schedule 4 to these Regulations with such variations as circumstances require when any action is taken by a court in consequence of which a disqualification order or a disqualification undertaking is varied or ceases to be in force, and the particulars contained therein are the particulars specified for that purpose.

[6981F]

8 The time within which the officer specified in regulation 6(1) is to furnish the Secretary of State with the said particulars shall be a period of fourteen days beginning with the day on which the disqualification order or grant of leave is made, or any action is taken by a court in consequence of which the disqualification order or disqualification undertaking is varied or ceases to be in force, as the case may be.

[6981G]

9 Extension of certain of the provisions of section 18 of the Act to orders made and leave granted in Northern Ireland

(1) Section 18(2) of the Act is hereby extended to the particulars furnished to the Secretary of State of orders made and leave granted under Part II of the Companies (Northern Ireland) Order 1989.

[(1A) Section 18(2A) is hereby extended to the particulars of disqualification undertakings accepted under and orders made and leave granted in relation to disqualification undertakings under the Company Directors Disqualification (Northern Ireland) Order 2002.]

(2) Section 18(3) of the Act is hereby extended to all entries in the register and particulars relating to them furnished to the Secretary of State in respect of orders made under Part II of the Companies (Northern Ireland) Order 1989 [or disqualification undertakings accepted under the Company Directors Disqualification (Northern Ireland) Order 2002].

[6981H]

NOTES

Para (1A): inserted by the Companies (Disqualification Orders) (Amendment) Regulations 2004, SI 2004/1940, reg 3(a), as from 1 September 2004, in relation to (a) particulars of undertakings accepted under the Company Directors Disqualification (Northern Ireland) Order 2002 on or after that date, and (b) orders made and leave granted under the 2002 Order relating to undertakings to which (a) above applies.

Para (2): words in square brackets inserted by SI 2004/1940, reg 3(b), as from 1 September 2004 (subject as noted above).

(*Schs 1–4* (*Forms*); *see Appendix 4 at* **[A4]**.)

LIMITED LIABILITY PARTNERSHIPS (FEES) (NO 2) REGULATIONS 2001 (NOTE)

(SI 2001/969)

NOTES

See Appendix 3 (Fees Instruments) at **[A3]**.

[6981I]

LIMITED LIABILITY PARTNERSHIPS REGULATIONS 2001

(SI 2001/1090)

NOTES

Made: 19 March 2001.

Authority: Limited Liability Partnerships Act 2000, ss 14–17.

Commencement: 6 April 2001 (see reg 1 at **[6982]**). Where any provision in this work (including any inserted or substituted provision) came into force for all purposes on or before 1 July 2005, commencement information is not noted at provision level.

These Regulations are reproduced as amended by: the Financial Services and Markets Act 2000 (Consequential Amendments) Order 2004, SI 2004/355; the Limited Liability Partnerships (Amendment) Regulations 2005, SI 2005/1989; the Companies Act 1985 (Investment Companies and Accounting and Audit Amendments) Regulations 2005, SI 2005/2280; the Civil Partnership Act 2004 (Amendments to Subordinate Legislation) Order 2005, SI 2005/2114; the Companies Act 1985 (Operating and Financial Review) (Repeal) Regulations 2005, SI 2005/3442; the Companies Act 1985 (Small Companies' Accounts and Audit) Regulations 2006, SI 2006/2782. See also the draft Limited Liability Partnerships (Amendment) Regulations 2007 in Appendix 10 at **[A10]**.

Note: the commencement by the Companies Act 2006 (Commencement No 1, Transitional Provisions and Savings) Order 2006 (SI 2006/3428) and the Companies Act 2006 (Commencement No 2, Consequential Amendments, Transitional Provisions and Savings) Order 2007 (SI 2007/1093) of certain amendments made by the Companies Act 2006 to the Companies Act 1985, does not affect the operation of the 1985 Act as applied by these Regulations; see art 8 of the 2006 Order (at **[7581]**) and art 11 of the 2007 Order (at **[7624]**). See also the draft Companies Act 2006 (Commencement No 3, Consequential Amendments, Transitional Provisions and Savings) Order 2007 in Appendix 12 at **[A12]**. Article 12(2) of that draft SI provides for similar savings to those noted above.

ARRANGEMENT OF REGULATIONS

PART I
CITATION, COMMENCEMENT AND INTERPRETATION

PART I
CITATION, COMMENCEMENT AND INTERPRETATION

1 Citation and commencement

These Regulations may be cited as the Limited Liability Partnerships Regulations 2001 and shall come into force on 6th April 2001.

[6982]

2 Interpretation

In these Regulations—

"the 1985 Act" means the Companies Act 1985;

"the 1986 Act" means the Insolvency Act 1986;

"the 2000 Act" means the Financial Services and Markets Act 2000;

"devolved", in relation to the provisions of the 1986 Act, means the provisions of the 1986 Act which are listed in Schedule 4 and, in their application to Scotland, concern wholly or partly, matters which are set out in Section C 2 of Schedule 5 to the Scotland Act 1998 as being exceptions to the reservations made in that Act in the field of insolvency;

"limited liability partnership agreement", in relation to a limited liability partnership, means any agreement express or implied between the members of the limited liability partnership or between the limited liability partnership and the members of the limited liability partnership which determines the mutual rights and duties of the members, and their rights and duties in relation to the limited liability partnership;

"the principal Act" means the Limited Liability Partnerships Act 2000; and

"shadow member", in relation to limited liability partnerships, means a person in accordance with whose directions or instructions the members of the limited liability partnership are accustomed to act (but so that a person is not deemed a shadow member by reason only that the members of the limited partnership act on advice given by him in a professional capacity).

[6983]

PART II
ACCOUNTS AND AUDIT

3 Application of the accounts and audit provisions of the 1985 Act to limited liability partnerships

(1) Subject to paragraph (2), the provisions of Part VII of the 1985 Act (Accounts and Audit) shall apply to limited liability partnerships.

(2) The enactments referred to in paragraph (1) shall apply to limited liability partnerships, except where the context otherwise requires, with the following modifications—

(a) references to a company shall include references to a limited liability partnership;

(b) references to a director or to an officer of a company shall include references to a member of a limited liability partnership;

(c) references to other provisions of the 1985 Act and to provisions of the Insolvency Act 1986 shall include references to those provisions as they apply to limited liability partnerships in accordance with Parts III and IV of these Regulations;

(d) the modifications set out in Schedule 1 to these Regulations; and

(e) such further modifications as the context requires for the purpose of giving effect to those provisions as applied by this Part of these Regulations.

[6984]

PART III
COMPANIES ACT 1985 AND COMPANY DIRECTORS DISQUALIFICATION ACT 1986

4 Application of the remainder of the provisions of the 1985 Act and of the provisions of the Company Directors Disqualification Act 1986 to limited liability partnerships

(1) The provisions of the 1985 Act specified in the first column of Part I of Schedule 2 to these Regulations shall apply to limited liability partnerships, except where the context otherwise requires, with the following modifications—

(a) references to a company shall include references to a limited liability partnership;

(b) references to the Companies Acts shall include references to the principal Act and regulations made thereunder;

(c) references to the Insolvency Act 1986 shall include references to that Act as it applies to limited liability partnerships by virtue of Part IV of these Regulations;

(d) references in a provision of the 1985 Act to other provisions of that Act shall include references to those other provisions as they apply to limited liability partnerships by virtue of these Regulations;

(e) references to the memorandum of association of a company shall include references to the incorporation document of a limited liability partnership;

(f) references to a shadow director shall include references to a shadow member;

(g) references to a director of a company or to an officer of a company shall include references to a member of a limited liability partnership;

(h) the modifications, if any, specified in the second column of Part I of Schedule 2 opposite the provision specified in the first column; and

(i) such further modifications as the context requires for the purpose of giving effect to that legislation as applied by these Regulations.

(2) The provisions of the Company Director Disqualification Act 1986 shall apply to limited liability partnerships, except where the context otherwise requires, with the following modifications—

(a) references to a company shall include references to a limited liability partnership;

(b) references to the Companies Acts shall include references to the principal Act and regulations made thereunder and references to the companies legislation shall include references to the principal Act, regulations made thereunder and to any enactment applied by regulations to limited liability partnerships;

(d) references to the Insolvency Act 1986 shall include references to that Act as it applies to limited liability partnerships by virtue of Part IV of these Regulations;

(e) references to the memorandum of association of a company shall include references to the incorporation document of a limited liability partnership;

(f) references to a shadow director shall include references to a shadow member;

(g) references to a director of a company or to an officer of a company shall include references to a member of a limited liability partnership;

(h) the modifications, if any, specified in the second column of Part II of Schedule 2 opposite the provision specified in the first column; and

(i) such further modifications as the context requires for the purpose of giving effect to that legislation as applied by these Regulations.

[6985]

PART IV
WINDING UP AND INSOLVENCY

5 Application of the 1986 Act to limited liability partnerships

(1) Subject to paragraphs (2) and (3), the following provisions of the 1986 Act, shall apply to limited liability partnerships—

(a) Parts I, II, III, IV, VI and VII of the First Group of Parts (company insolvency; companies winding up),

(b) the Third Group of Parts (miscellaneous matters bearing on both company and individual insolvency; general interpretation; final provisions).

(2) The provisions of the 1986 Act referred to in paragraph (1) shall apply to limited liability partnerships, except where the context otherwise requires, with the following modifications—

(a) references to a company shall include references to a limited liability partnership;

(b) references to a director or to an officer of a company shall include references to a member of a limited liability partnership;

(c) references to a shadow director shall include references to a shadow member;

(d) references to the 1985 Act, the Company Directors Disqualification Act 1986, the Companies Act 1989 or to any provisions of those Acts or to any provisions of the 1986 Act shall include references to those Acts or provisions as they apply to limited liability partnerships by virtue of the principal Act;

(e) references to the memorandum of association of a company and to the articles of association of a company shall include references to the limited liability partnership agreement of a limited liability partnership;

(f) the modifications set out in Schedule 3 to these Regulations; and

(g) such further modifications as the context requires for the purpose of giving effect to that legislation as applied by these Regulations.

(3) In the application of this regulation to Scotland, the provisions of the 1986 Act referred to in paragraph (1) shall not include the provisions listed in Schedule 4 to the extent specified in that Schedule.

[6986]

PART V
FINANCIAL SERVICES AND MARKETS

6 Application of provisions contained in Parts XV and XXIV of the 2000 Act to limited liability partnerships

(1) Subject to paragraph (2), sections 215(3),(4) and (6), 356, 359(1) to (4), 361 to 365, 367, 370 and 371 of the 2000 Act shall apply to limited liability partnerships.

(2) The provisions of the 2000 Act referred to in paragraph (1) shall apply to limited liability partnerships, except where the context otherwise requires, with the following modifications—

(a) references to a company shall include references to a limited liability partnership;
(b) references to body shall include references to a limited liability partnership; and
(c) references to the 1985 Act, the 1986 Act or to any of the provisions of those Acts shall include references to those Acts or provisions as they apply to limited liability partnerships by virtue of the principal Act.

[6987]

PART VI
DEFAULT PROVISION

7 Default provision for limited liability partnerships

The mutual rights and duties of the members and the mutual rights and duties of the limited liability partnership and the members shall be determined, subject to the provisions of the general law and to the terms of any limited liability partnership agreement, by the following rules:

(1) All the members of a limited liability partnership are entitled to share equally in the capital and profits of the limited liability partnership.

(2) The limited liability partnership must indemnify each member in respect of payments made and personal liabilities incurred by him—
(a) in the ordinary and proper conduct of the business of the limited liability partnership; or
(b) in or about anything necessarily done for the preservation of the business or property of the limited liability partnership.

(3) Every member may take part in the management of the limited liability partnership.

(4) No member shall be entitled to remuneration for acting in the business or management of the limited liability partnership.

(5) No person may be introduced as a member or voluntarily assign an interest in a limited liability partnership without the consent of all existing members.

(6) Any difference arising as to ordinary matters connected with the business of the limited liability partnership may be decided by a majority of the members, but no change may be made in the nature of the business of the limited liability partnership without the consent of all the members.

(7) The books and records of the limited liability partnership are to be made available for inspection at the registered office of the limited liability partnership or at such other place as the members think fit and every member of the limited liability partnership may when he thinks fit have access to and inspect and copy any of them.

(8) Each member shall render true accounts and full information of all things affecting the limited liability partnership to any member or his legal representatives.

(9) If a member, without the consent of the limited liability partnership, carries on any business of the same nature as and competing with the limited liability partnership, he must account for and pay over to the limited liability partnership all profits made by him in that business.

(10) Every member must account to the limited liability partnership for any benefit derived by him without the consent of the limited liability partnership from any transaction concerning the limited liability partnership, or from any use by him of the property of the limited liability partnership, name or business connection.

[6988]

8 Expulsion

No majority of the members can expel any member unless a power to do so has been conferred by express agreement between the members.

[6989]

PART VII
MISCELLANEOUS

9 General and consequential amendments

(1) Subject to paragraph (2), the enactments mentioned in Schedule 5 shall have effect subject to the amendments specified in that Schedule.

(2) In the application of this regulation to Scotland—

(a) paragraph 15 of Schedule 5 which amends section 110 of the 1986 Act shall not extend to Scotland; and

(b) paragraph 22 of Schedule 5 which applies to limited liability partnerships the culpable officer provisions in existing primary legislation shall not extend to Scotland insofar as it relates to matters which have not been reserved by Schedule 5 to the Scotland Act 1998.

[6990]

10 Application of subordinate legislation

(1) The subordinate legislation specified in Schedule 6 shall apply as from time to time in force to limited liability partnerships and—

(a) in the case of the subordinate legislation listed in Part I of that Schedule with such modifications as the context requires for the purpose of giving effect to the provisions of the Companies Act 1985 which are applied by these Regulations;

(b) in the case of the subordinate legislation listed in Part II of that Schedule with such modifications as the context requires for the purpose of giving effect to the provisions of the Insolvency Act 1986 which are applied by these Regulations; and

(c) in the case of the subordinate legislation listed in Part III of that Schedule with such modifications as the context requires for the purpose of giving effect to the provisions of the Business Names Act 1985 and the Company Directors Disqualification Act 1986 which are applied by these Regulations.

(2) In the case of any conflict between any provision of the subordinate legislation applied by paragraph (1) and any provision of these Regulations, the latter shall prevail.

[6991]

SCHEDULES

SCHEDULE 1
MODIFICATIONS TO PROVISIONS OF PART VII OF THE 1985 ACT APPLIED BY THESE REGULATIONS

Regulation 3

Provision of Part VII	**Modification**
Section 222 (Where and for how long accounting records to be kept)	
subsection (5)	In paragraph (a), omit the words "in the case of a private company," and the word "and".
	Omit paragraph (b).
Section 224 (accounting reference periods and accounting reference date)	
subsections (2) and (3)	Omit subsections (2) and (3).
subsection (3A)	Omit the words "incorporated on or after 1st April 1996".
Section 225 (alteration of accounting reference date)	
subsection (5)	For the words "laying and delivering accounts and reports" substitute "delivering the accounts and the auditors' report".

Provision of Part VII	**Modification**
[Section 226 (duty to prepare individual accounts).	Omit subsection (3).
Section 227 (duty to prepare group accounts)	Omit subsection (4).]
Section 228 (exemption for parent companies included in accounts of larger group)	Omit subsection (4).
[Section 228A (exemption for parent companies included in non-EEA group accounts)	Omit subsection (4).]
Section 231 (disclosure required in notes to accounts: related undertakings)	
subsection (3)	Omit the words from "This subsection" to the end.
Section 232 (disclosure in notes to accounts: emoluments etc of directors and others)	Omit section 232, save that Schedule 6 shall apply for the purpose of paragraph 56A of Schedule 4, as inserted by this Schedule.
Section 233 (approval and signing of accounts)	
subsection (1)	For subsection (1) substitute— "(1) A limited liability partnership's annual accounts shall be approved by the members, and shall be signed on behalf of all the members by a designated member.".
subsection (3)	Omit the words from "laid before" to "otherwise", and for the words "the board" substitute "the members of the limited liability partnership".
subsection (4)	For the words "the board by a director of the company" substitute "the members by a designated member".
subsection (6)	In paragraph (a), omit the words "laid before the company, or otherwise".
[Sections 234 to 234ZZB (duty to prepare directors' report)	Omit sections 234 to 234ZZB.
Section 234ZA (statement as to disclosure of information to auditors)	Omit section 234ZA.
Section 234A (approval and signing of directors' report)	Omit section 234A.
…	…
Sections 234B (duty to prepare directors' remuneration report) and 234C (approval and signing of directors' remuneration report)	Omit sections 234B and 234C]
Section 235 (auditors' report)	
subsection (1)	For subsection (1) substitute— "(1) The limited liability partnership's annual accounts shall be submitted to its auditors, who shall make a report on them to the members of the limited liability partnership.".
[subsections (3) to (5)]	Omit [subsections (3) to (5)].
Section 236 (signature of auditors' report)	
subsection (2)	For subsection (2) substitute— "(2) Every copy of the auditors' report which is circulated, published or issued shall state the names of the auditors.".
subsection (4)	In paragraph (a) omit the words "laid before the company, or otherwise".
Section 237 (duties of auditors)	

Provision of Part VII	Modification
subsection (4)	Omit subsection (4).
Section 238 (persons entitled to receive copies of accounts and report)	
subsection (1)	For subsection (1) substitute— "(1) A copy of the limited liability partnership's annual accounts, together with a copy of the auditors' report on those accounts, shall be sent to every member of the limited liability partnership and to every holder of the limited liability partnership's debentures, within one month of their being signed in accordance with section 233(1) and in any event not later than 10 months after the end of the relevant accounting reference period."
[subsection (1A)	Omit subsection (1A)(b) to (d).]
subsection (2)	(a) In paragraph (a), omit the words from "who is" to "meetings and", and (b) in paragraph (b) and (c), omit the words "shares or" in both places where they occur.
subsections (3) and (4)	Omit subsections (3) and (4).
subsection (4A)	Omit the words ", of the directors' report".
subsections (4C) to (4E)	Omit subsections (4C) to (4E).
Section 239 (right to demand copies of accounts and report)	
[subsection (1)	(a) Omit paragraphs (b), … and (c), and (b) in paragraph (d), omit the words from "and that directors' report" to the end.]
subsection (2B)	Omit subsection (2B).
Section 240 (requirements in connection with publication of accounts)	
subsection (1)	Omit the words from "or, as the case may be," to the end.
subsection (3)	(a) In paragraph (c) omit the words from "and, if no such report has been made", to "any financial year", [(b) omit paragraph (e), and] (c) omit the words "or any report made for the purposes of section 249A(2)".
Section 241 (accounts and report to be laid before general meeting)	Omit section 241.
[Section 241A (members' approval of directors' remuneration report)	Omit section 241A.]
Section 242 (accounts and report to be delivered to registrar)	
[subsection (1)	(a) For the words "The directors of a company" substitute "The designated members of a limited liability partnership", (b) omit paragraphs (b), … and (c), (c) in paragraph (d), omit from "and that directors' report" to the end, and (d) for "the directors must annex" substitute "the designated members must annex".]

Provision of Part VII	**Modification**
subsection (2)	(a) For the words "laying and delivering accounts and reports", substitute "delivering the accounts and the auditors' report", and (b) for the word "director" substitute the words "designated member".
subsection (3)	For the words "the directors" in each place where they occur substitute the words "the designated members".
subsection (4)	For the words "laying and delivering accounts and reports", substitute "delivering the accounts and the auditors' report".
Section 242A (civil penalty for failure to deliver accounts)	
subsection (1)	(a) For the words "laying and delivering accounts and reports" substitute "delivering the accounts and the auditors' report", and (b) for the words "the directors" substitute "the designated members".
subsection (2)	(a) For the words "laying and delivering accounts and reports" substitute "delivering the accounts and the auditors' report", (b) omit the words ", and whether the company is a public or private company,", (c) omit the heading "*Public company*" and all entries under it, and (d) for the heading "*Private company*" substitute "*Amount of penalty*".
Section 242B (delivery and publications of accounts in euros)	
subsection (2)	For the words "the directors of a company" substitute "the designated members of a limited liability partnership".
…	…
Section 244 (period allowed for delivering accounts and report)	
subsection (1)	For subsection (1), substitute the following— "(1) The period allowed for delivering the accounts and the auditors' report is 10 months after the end of the relevant accounting reference period. This is subject to the following provisions of this section."
subsection (2)	In paragraph (a), omit the words "or 7 months, as the case may be,".
…	…
subsection (4)	For the words "laying and delivering accounts" substitute "delivering the accounts and the auditors' report".
[Section 245 (voluntary revision of accounts)	
subsection (1)	For subsection (1) substitute— "(1) If it appears to the members of a limited liability partnership that any annual accounts did not comply with the requirements of this Act, they may prepare revised accounts.".

Provision of Part VII	Modification
subsection (2)	[(a) Omit the words "or report" in both places where they occur, and]
	(b) omit the words "laid before the company in general meeting or".
subsection (3)	Omit the words from "or a revised summary financial statement" to the end.
subsection (4)	[(a) In paragraph (a), omit the words ", statement or report",
	(b) in paragraph (b), omit the words "or reporting accountant" and the words ", statement or report", and
	(c) in paragraph (c)—
	(i) for "where the previous accounts or report" substitute "where the previous accounts",]
	(ii) omit sub-paragraph (ii), and
	(iii) omit the words from ", or where a summary financial statement" to the end.]
[Section 245A (Secretary of State's notice in respect of annual accounts)	
subsection (1)	(a) For paragraphs (a) and (b) substitute—
	"a copy of a limited liability partnership's annual accounts has been delivered to the registrar,", and
	[(b) omit the words "or report".]
subsection (2)	[Omit the words "or report" and the words "or a revised report".]
subsection (3)	[Omit the words "or report" in both places where they occur.]
subsection (4)	[Omit the words "and revised directors' reports" and the words "or reports" in both places where they occur.]]
[Section 245B (application in respect of defective accounts, reports and reviews)	
subsection (1)	[Omit the words ", or a directors' report does not comply," and the words "or a revised report".]
subsection (3)	Omit paragraph (b).
subsection (3A)	Omit subsection (3A).
subsection (4)	[Omit the words "or report" in each place where they occur and the words "or a revised report".]
subsection (5)	[Omit the words "or report" in both places where they occur.]
subsection (7)	[Omit the words "and revised directors' reports" and the words "or reports" in both places where they occur.]]
[Section 245C (other persons authorised to apply to court)	
subsection (1)	[Omit the words "and directors' reports" in both places where they occur.]]
Section 246 (special provisions for small companies)	
subsection (3)	Omit paragraph (a), and paragraph (b)(ii), (iii) and (iv).
subsection (4)	Omit subsection (4).

Provision of Part VII	**Modification**
subsection (5)	(a) For the words "the directors of the company" substitute "the designated members of the limited liability partnership", and (b) omit paragraph (b).
subsection (6)	Omit paragraphs (b) and (c).
subsection (8)	Omit paragraph (b) and the words ", in the report" and ", 234A".
Section 246A (special provisions for medium-sized companies)	
[subsection (2A)	Omit subsection (2A).]
subsection (3)	(a) For the words "The company" substitute "The designated members", and (b) for paragraph (a), substitute the following— "(a) which includes a profit and loss account in which the following items listed in the profit and loss account formats set out in Part I of Schedule 4 are combined as one item under the heading "gross profit or loss"— Items 1 to 3 and 6 in Format 1 Items 1 to 5 in Format 2.".
Section 247 (qualification of company as small or medium sized)	
subsection (5)	In paragraph (a), for the words "items A to D" substitute "items B to D".
[Section 247A (cases in which special provisions do not apply)	
[subsection (1B)	Omit paragraphs (a) and (c), and the words "an authorised insurance company, a banking company," in paragraph (b).
Subsection (1C)	Omit paragraphs (a) and (c). In paragraph (b), after "it" insert "is a person (other than a banking limited liability partnership) who".]]
Section 247B (special auditors' report)	
subsection (1)	(a) In paragraph (a), for the words "the directors of a company" substitute "the designated members of a limited liability partnership", and (b) in paragraph (b) omit the words "or (2)".
Section 249A (exemptions from audit)	
subsection (2)	Omit subsection (2).
subsection (3A)	Omit subsection (3A).
subsection (4)	Omit subsection (4).
subsection (6)	Omit the words "or gross income".
subsection (6A)	Omit the words "or (2)".
subsection (7)	Omit the words from ", and 'gross income'" to the end.
Section 249AA (dormant companies)	
subsection (1)	For the words section 249B(2) to (5) substitute "section 249B (4) and (5)".
subsection (2)	[In paragraph (a), omit "(1B)(a) or (1C)(a)"].
[subsection (3)	For subsection (3) substitute the following—

Provision of Part VII	Modification
	"(3) Subsection (1) does not apply if at any time in the financial year in question the limited liability partnership was an e-money issuer, an ISD investment firm or a UCITS management company."]
subsection (5)	In paragraph (b), omit the words "(6) or".
subsection (6)	Omit subsection (6).
subsection (7)	In paragraph (a), for the words "section 28 (change of name)" substitute "paragraph 5 of the Schedule to the Limited Liability Partnerships Act 2000".
	Omit paragraph (b).
Section 249B (cases where audit exemption not available)	
subsection (1)	[(a) omit the words "or (2)" and paragraphs (a) and (bb), and
	[in paragraph (b), omit the words "an authorised insurance company, a banking company,".].]
subsection (1C)	For paragraph (b), substitute "that the group's aggregate turnover in that year (calculated in accordance with section 249) is not more than £1 million net (or £1.2 million gross),".
subsections (2) and (3)	Omit subsections (2) and (3).
subsection (4)	(a) Omit the words "or (2)" in both places where they occur, and (b) omit paragraph (b).
Sections 249C (the report required for the purposes of section 249A(2)) and 249D (the reporting accountant)	Omit sections 249C and 249D.
Section 249E (effect of exemption from audit)	
subsection (1)	(a) In paragraph (b) omit the words from "or laid" to the end, and
	(b) omit paragraph (c).
subsection (2)	Omit subsection (2).
Section 251 (provision of summary financial statement by listed public companies)	Omit section 251.
Sections 252 and 253 (private company election to dispense with laying of accounts and reports)	Omit section 252 and 253.
Section 254 (exemption for unlimited companies from requirement to deliver accounts and reports)	Omit section 254.
Section 255 (special provisions for banking and insurance companies)	Omit section 255.
Section 255A (special provisions for banking and insurance groups)	Omit section 255A.
Section 255B (modification of disclosure requirements in relation to banking company or group)	Omit section 255B.
Section 255D (power to apply provisions to banking partnerships)	Omit section 255D.
[…	…]
Section 257 (power of Secretary of State to alter accounting requirements)	Omit section 257.
Section 260 (participating interests)	

Provision of Part VII	**Modification**
subsection (6)	For the words from ", Schedule 8A," to "Schedule 9A" substitute the words "and Schedule 8A".
Section 262 (minor definitions)	
subsection (1)	(a) Omit the definitions of "annual report", ["credit institution" and "quoted company"], and (b) insert the following [definitions] at the appropriate place— [""banking limited liability partnership" means a limited liability partnership which has permission under Part 4 of the Financial Services and Markets Act 2000 to accept deposits (but does not include such a partnership which has permission to accept deposits only for the purpose of carrying on another regulated activity in accordance with that permission);"] ""limited liability partnership" means a limited liability partnership formed and registered under the Limited Liability Partnerships Act 2000;".
subsection (2)	Omit subsection (2).
[subsection (3)	Insert the following subsection after subsection (3)— "(3A) The definition of banking limited liability partnership in subsection (1) must be read with— (a) section 22 of the Financial Services and Markets Act 2000, (b) any relevant order under that section, and (c) Schedule 2 to that Act.".]
Section 262A (index of defined expressions)	In the index of defined expressions— (a) the entries relating to "annual report" "credit institution" ["quoted company"] and "reporting accountant", and all entries relating to sections 255 and 255A and to Schedules 9 and 9A, shall be omitted, and (b) the following [entries] shall be inserted at the appropriate place— [""banking limited liability partnership" section 262"] ""limited liability partnership" section 262".
Schedule 4 (form and content of company accounts)	
Paragraph 1	In sub-paragraph (1)(b), for the words "any one of" substitute "either of".
Paragraph 3	In sub-paragraph (2)(b), omit the words "shares or".
	…
Balance Sheet Format 1	Omit the following items and the notes on the balance sheet formats which relate to them— (a) item A (called up share capital not paid), (b) item B.III.7 (own shares), (c) item C.II.5 (called up share capital not paid), and (d) item C.III.2 (own shares).

PART IV STATUTORY INSTRUMENTS

Provision of Part VII	Modification
	For item K (capital and reserves) substitute— "K. Loans and other debts due to members (*12*) L. Members' other interests I Members' capital II Revaluation reserve III Other reserves."
Balance Sheet Format 2	Omit the following items and the notes on the balance sheet format which relate to them— (a) Assets item A (called up share capital not paid), (b) Assets item B.III.7 (own shares), (c) Assets item C.II.5 (called up share capital not paid), and (d) Assets item C.III.2 (own shares).
	For Liabilities item A (capital and reserves) substitute— "A. Loans and other debts due to members (*12*) AA. Members' other interests I Members' capital II Revaluation reserve III Other reserves."
Notes on the balance sheet formats	
Note (12)	Substitute the following as Note (*12*)— "(*12*) *Loans and other debts due to members* (Format 1, item K and Format 2, item A) The following amounts shall be shown separately under this item— (a) the aggregate amount of money advanced to the limited liability partnership by the members by way of loan, (b) the aggregate amount of money owed to members by the limited liability partnership in respect of profits, (c) any other amounts."
Profit and Loss Account Formats	In Format 1, for item 20 (profit or loss for the financial year) substitute "20. Profit or loss for the financial year before members' remuneration and profit shares" In Format 2, for item 22 (profit or loss for the financial year) substitute "22. Profit or loss for the financial year before members' remuneration and profit shares" Omit Profit and Loss Account Formats 3 and 4 and the notes on the profit and loss account formats which relate to them.
Notes on the profit and loss account Formats	
Note (*15*) (income from other fixed asset investments: other interest receivable and similar income)	At the end of Note (*15*) insert the words "Interest receivable from members shall not be included under this item."
Note (*16*) (interest payable and similar charges)	At the end of Note (*16*) insert "Interest payable to members shall not be included under this item."

Provision of Part VII	Modification
Accounting principles and rules	
Paragraph 12	In sub-paragraph (b) omit the words "on behalf of the board of directors".
Paragraph 34	Omit sub-paragraph (3), (3A) and (3B).
Notes to the accounts	
[Paragraph 35A	Omit paragraphs (b), (c) and (d).]
Paragraph 37	For the words "38 to 51" substitute the words "41 to 51(1)".
Insertion of new paragraph after paragraph 37	Insert the following new paragraph after paragraph 37— *"Loans and other debts due to members* 37A. The following information shall be given— (a) the aggregate amounts of loans and other debts due to members as at the date of the beginning of the financial year, (b) the aggregate amounts contributed by members during the financial year, (c) the aggregate amounts transferred to or from the profit and loss account during that year, (d) the aggregate amounts withdrawn by members or applied on behalf of members during that year, (e) the aggregate amount of loans and other debts due to members as at the balance sheet date, and (f) the aggregate amount of loans and other debts due to members that fall due after one year.".
Paragraphs 38 to 40	Omit paragraphs 38 to 40.
Paragraphs 49 and 51(2)	Omit paragraphs 49 and 51(2).
Paragraph 56	Insert the following paragraph after paragraph 56— *"Particulars of members* 56A(1) Particulars shall be given of the average number of members of the limited liability partnership in the financial year, which number shall be determined by dividing the relevant annual number by the number of months in the financial year. (2) The relevant annual number shall be determined by ascertaining for each month in the financial year the number of members of the limited liability partnership for all or part of that month, and adding together all the monthly numbers. (3) Where the amount of the profit of the limited liability partnership for the financial year before members' remuneration and profit shares exceeds £200,000, there shall be disclosed the amount of profit (including remuneration) which is attributable to the member with the largest entitlement to profit (including remuneration). For the purpose of determining the amount to be disclosed, "remuneration" includes any emoluments specified in paragraph 1(1)(a), (c) or (d) of Schedule 6 to this Act which are paid by or receivable from— (i) the limited liability partnership; and

Provision of Part VII	Modification
	(ii) the limited liability partnership's subsidiary undertakings; and
	(iii) any other person.".
Paragraph 58	Omit sub-paragraph (3)(c).
Special provisions where the company is an investment company	
Paragraphs 71 to 73	Omit paragraphs 71 to 73.
Schedule 4A (form and content of group accounts)	
Paragraph 1	Omit sub-paragraph (3).
Paragraph 10	Omit sub-paragraph (1)(a) to (c).
	Omit sub-paragraph (2).
Paragraph 11	For sub-paragraph (1), substitute—
	"(1) Where a limited liability partnership adopts the merger method of accounting, it must comply with this paragraph, and with generally accepted accounting principles or practice."
	Omit sub-paragraphs (5) to (7).
Paragraph 17	(a) In sub-paragraph (2)(a), for the words "item K" substitute "item L",
	(b) in sub-paragraph (2)(b), for the words "item A" substitute "item AA", and
	(c) In sub-paragraphs (3) and (4), omit paragraphs (c) and (d).
Paragraph 21	In sub-paragraph (3), omit paragraphs (c) and (d).
Schedule 5 (disclosure of information: related undertakings)	
Paragraph 6	Omit paragraph 6.
Paragraph 9A	Omit paragraph 9A.
Paragraph 20	Omit paragraph 20.
Paragraph 28A	Omit paragraph 28A.
Schedule 8 (form and content of accounts prepared by small companies)	
Paragraph 1	In sub-paragraph (1)(b), for the words "any one of" substitute "either of".
Paragraph 3	In sub-paragraph (2)(b), omit the words "shares or".
	…
Balance Sheet Format 1	Omit item A (called up share capital not paid) and note (*1*) on the balance sheet format.
	For item K (capital and reserves) substitute—
	"K. Loans and other debts due to members (*9*)
	L. Members' other interests
	I Members' capital
	II Revaluation reserve
	III Other reserves".
Balance Sheet Format 2	Omit Assets item A (called up share capital not paid) and note (1) on the balance sheet format.
	For Liabilities item A (capital and reserves) substitute—

Provision of Part VII	**Modification**
	"A. Loans and other debts due to members (*9*) AA. Members' other interests I Members' capital II Revaluation reserve III Other reserves".
Notes on the balance sheet formats	
Note (*4*) (Others: Other investments)	Omit Note (*4*).
Note (*9*)	Substitute the following as Note (*9*)— "(*9*) *Loans and other debts due to members* (Format 1, item K and Format 2, item A) The following amounts shall be shown separately under this item— (a) the aggregate amount of money advanced to the limited liability partnership by the members by way of loan, (b) the aggregate amount of money owed to members by the limited liability partnership in respect of profits, (c) any other amounts.".
Profit and Loss Account Formats	In Format 1, for item 20 (profit or loss for the financial year) substitute "20. Profit or loss for the financial year before members' remuneration and profit shares" In Format 2, for item 22 (profit or loss for the financial year) substitute "22. Profit or loss for the financial year before members' remuneration and profit shares" Omit Profit and Loss Account Formats 3 and 4 and the notes on the profit and loss account formats which relate to them.
Notes on the profit and loss account formats	
Note (*12*) (income from other fixed asset investments: other interest receivable and similar income)	At the end of Note (*12*) insert the words "Interest receivable from members shall not be included under this item."
Note (*13*) (interest payable and similar charges)	At the end of Note (*13*) insert "Interest payable to members shall not be included under this item.".
Accounting principles and rules	
Paragraph 12	In sub-paragraph (b), omit the words "on behalf of the board of directors".
Paragraph 34	Omit sub-paragraphs (3), (4) and (5).
Notes to the accounts	
[Paragraph 35A	Omit paragraphs (b), (c) and (d).]
Paragraph 37	For the words "Paragraphs 38 to 47" substitute "Paragraphs 40 to 47".
Insertion of new paragraph after paragraph 37	Insert the following new paragraph after paragraph 37— *"Loans and other debts due to members* 37A. The following information shall be given— (a) the aggregate amount of loans and other debts due to members as at the date of the beginning of the financial year,

Provision of Part VII	Modification
	(b) the aggregate amounts contributed by members during the financial year, (c) the aggregate amounts transferred to or from the profit and loss account during that year, (d) the aggregate amounts withdrawn by members or applied on behalf of members during that year, (e) the aggregate amount of loans and other debts due to members as at the balance sheet date, and (f) the aggregate amount of loans and other debts due to members that fall due after one year.".
Paragraphs 38 and 39	Omit paragraphs 38 and 39.
Paragraph 45	Omit paragraph 45.
Paragraph 51	Omit sub-paragraph (3)(c).
Schedule 8A (form and content of abbreviated accounts of small companies delivered to registrar)	
Balance Sheet Format 1	Omit item A (called up share capital not paid). For item K (capital and reserves) substitute— "K. Loans and other debts due to members L. Members' other interests I Members' capital II Revaluation reserve III Other reserves".
Balance Sheet Format 2	Omit Assets item A (called up share capital not paid). For Liabilities item A (capital and reserves) substitute— "A. Loans and other debts due to members AA. Members' other interests I Members' capital II Revaluation reserve III Other reserves".
Notes to the accounts	
Paragraphs 5 and 6	Omit paragraphs 5 and 6.
Paragraph 9	Omit sub-paragraph (3)(c).

[6992]

NOTES

Entries relating to ss 226, 227 inserted by the Limited Liability Partnerships (Amendment) Regulations 2005, SI 2005/1989, reg 2, Sch 1, paras 1, 2, as from 1 October 2005, in relation to financial years which begin on or after 1 January 2005 and which end on or after 1 October 2005.

Entry relating to Section 228A inserted by SI 2005/1989, reg 2, Sch 1, paras 1, 3, as from 1 October 2005, in relation to financial years which begin on or after 1 January 2005 and which end on or after 1 October 2005.

Entries relating to ss 234–234ZZB, 234ZA, 234A, 234AA, 234AB, 234B, 234C substituted (for original entries relating to ss 234, 234A) by SI 2005/1989, reg 2, Sch 1, paras 1, 4, as from 1 October 2005, in relation to financial years which begin on or after 1 January 2005 and which end on or after 1 October 2005.

Entries relating to ss 234AA, 234AB revoked by the Companies Act 1985 (Operating and Financial Review) (Repeal) Regulations 2005, SI 2005/3442, reg 2(2)(b), Sch 2, para 3(1), (2), as from 12 January 2006.

In entry relating to s 235 words in square brackets substituted by SI 2005/1989, reg 2, Sch 1, paras 1, 5, as from 1 October 2005, in relation to financial years which begin on or after 1 January 2005 and which end on or after 1 October 2005.

Entry relating to Section 238(1A) inserted by SI 2005/1989, reg 2, Sch 1, paras 1, 6, as from 1 October 2005, in relation to financial years which begin on or after 1 January 2005 and which end on or after 1 October 2005.

Entry relating to s 239(1) substituted by SI 2005/1989, reg 2, Sch 1, paras 1, 7, as from 1 October 2005, in relation to financial years which begin on or after 1 January 2005 and which end on or after 1 October 2005.

Word omitted from entry relating to s 239(1) revoked by SI 2005/3442, reg 2(2)(b), Sch 2, para 3(1), (3), as from 12 January 2006.

In entry relating to s 240(3), para (b) substituted by SI 2005/1989, reg 2, Sch 1, paras 1, 8, as from 1 October 2005, in relation to financial years which begin on or after 1 January 2005 and which end on or after 1 October 2005.

Entry relating to Section 241A inserted by SI 2005/1989, reg 2, Sch 1, paras 1, 9, as from 1 October 2005, in relation to financial years which begin on or after 1 January 2005 and which end on or after 1 October 2005.

Entry relating to 242(1) substituted by SI 2005/1989, reg 2, Sch 1, paras 1, 10, as from 1 October 2005, in relation to financial years which begin on or after 1 January 2005 and which end on or after 1 October 2005.

Word omitted from entry relating to s 242(1) revoked by SI 2005/3442, reg 2(2)(b), Sch 2, para 3(1), (3), as from 12 January 2006.

Entry relating to s 243 revoked by SI 2005/1989, reg 2, Sch 1, paras 1, 11, as from 1 October 2005, in relation to financial years which begin on or after 1 January 2005 and which end on or after 1 October 2005.

Entry relating to s 244(3) revoked by SI 2005/1989, reg 2, Sch 1, paras 1, 12, as from 1 October 2005, in relation to financial years which begin on or after 1 January 2005 and which end on or after 1 October 2005.

Entry relating to s 245 substituted by SI 2005/1989, reg 2, Sch 1, paras 1, 13, as from 1 October 2005, in relation to financial years which begin on or after 1 January 2005 and which end on or after 1 October 2005.

Words in square brackets in entry relating to s 245 substituted by SI 2005/3442, reg 2(2)(b), Sch 2, para 3(1), (4), as from 12 January 2006.

Entries relating to ss 245A, 245B substituted by SI 2005/1989, reg 2, Sch 1, paras 1, 14, 15, as from 1 October 2005, in relation to financial years which begin on or after 1 January 2005 and which end on or after 1 October 2005.

Words in square brackets in entries relating to ss 245A, 245B substituted by SI 2005/3442, reg 2(2)(b), Sch 2, para 3(1), (5), (6), as from 12 January 2006.

Entry relating to Section 245C inserted by SI 2005/1989, reg 2, Sch 1, paras 1, 16, as from 1 October 2005, in relation to financial years which begin on or after 1 January 2005 and which end on or after 1 October 2005.

Words in square brackets in entry relating to s 245C(1) substituted by SI 2005/3442, reg 2(2)(b), Sch 2, para 3(1), (5), (7), as from 12 January 2006.

Entry relating to Section 246A(2A) inserted by SI 2005/1989, reg 2, Sch 1, paras 1, 17, as from 1 October 2005, in relation to financial years which begin on or after 1 January 2005 and which end on or after 1 October 2005.

Entry relating to s 247A substituted by SI 2005/1989, reg 2, Sch 1, paras 1, 18, as from 1 October 2005, in relation to financial years which begin on or after 1 January 2005 and which end on or after 1 October 2005; words in square brackets substituted by the Companies Act 1985 (Small Companies' Accounts and Audit) Regulations 2006, SI 2006/2782, reg 7(1), (2), as from 8 November 2006, in relation to annual accounts and reports in respect of financial years ending on or after 31 December 2006.

In entry relating to s 249AA words in square brackets in entry relating to subsection (2) substituted, and whole of entry relating to subsection (3) substituted, by SI 2006/2782, reg 6(1), (3), as from 8 November 2006, in relation to annual accounts and reports in respect of financial years ending on or after 31 December 2006.

In entry relating to s 249B words in first (outer) pair of square brackets substituted by SI 2004/355, art 8(1), (4), as from 4 March 2004; words in second (inner) pair of square brackets substituted by SI 2006/2782, reg 6(1), (4), as from 8 November 2006, in relation to annual accounts and reports in respect of financial years ending on or after 31 December 2006.

Entry relating to Section 256A inserted by SI 2005/1989, reg 2, Sch 1, paras 1, 19, as from 1 October 2005, in relation to financial years which begin on or after 1 January 2005 and which end on or after 1 October 2005; revoked by SI 2005/3442, reg 2(2)(b), Sch 2, para 3(1), (2), as from 12 January 2006.

In entry relating to s 262 words ""credit institution" and "quoted company"" in square brackets substituted by SI 2005/1989, reg 2, Sch 1, paras 1, 20, as from 1 October 2005, in relation to financial years which begin on or after 1 January 2005 and which end on or after 1 October 2005; other words in square brackets substituted or inserted by SI 2004/355, art 8(1), (5), as from 4 March 2004.

In entry relating to s 262A(1) words ""quoted company"" in square brackets inserted by SI 2005/1989, reg 2, Sch 1, paras 1, 21, as from 1 October 2005, in relation to financial years which begin on or after 1 January 2005 and which end on or after 1 October 2005; other words in square brackets substituted or inserted by SI 2004/355, art 8(1), (6), as from 4 March 2004.

In entry relating to Sch 4, para 3 words omitted revoked by SI 2005/1989, reg 2, Sch 1, paras 1, 22, as from 1 October 2005, in relation to financial years which begin on or after 1 January 2005 and which end on or after 1 October 2005.

Entry relating to Schedule 4, para 35A inserted by SI 2005/1989, reg 2, Sch 1, paras 1, 23, as from 1 October 2005, in relation to financial years which begin on or after 1 January 2005 and which end on or after 1 October 2005.

In entry relating to Sch 8, para 3 words omitted revoked by SI 2005/1989, reg 2, Sch 1, paras 1, 24, as from 1 October 2005, in relation to financial years which begin on or after 1 January 2005 and which end on or after 1 October 2005.

Entry relating to Schedule 8, para 35A inserted by SI 2005/1989, reg 2, Sch 1, paras 1, 25, as from 1 October 2005, in relation to financial years which begin on or after 1 January 2005 and which end on or after 1 October 2005.

SCHEDULE 2

PART I
MODIFICATIONS TO PROVISIONS OF THE 1985 ACT APPLIED TO LIMITED LIABILITY PARTNERSHIPS

Regulation 4

Provisions	Modification
	Formalities of Carrying on Business
24 (minimum membership for carrying on business)	In the first paragraph omit the words ", other than a private company limited by shares or by guarantee,".
36 (company contracts England and Wales)	
36A (execution of documents England and Wales)	In subsection (4) for "a director and the secretary of a company, or by two directors of a company," substitute "two members of a limited liability partnership".
	In subsection (6) for "a director and the secretary of a company, or by two directors of the company" substitute "two members of a limited liability partnership".
36C (pre-incorporation contracts, deeds and obligations)	
37 (bills of exchange and promissory notes)	
38 (execution of deeds abroad)	
39 (power of company to have official seal for use abroad)	In subsection (1), omit the words "whose objects require or comprise the transaction of business in foreign countries may, if authorised by its articles" and before the word "have" insert the word "may".
41 (authentication of documents)	For "director, secretary or other authorised officer" substitute "member".
42 (events affecting a company's status)	
subsection (1)	In subsection (1), for "other persons" substitute "persons other than members of the limited liability partnership".
subsection (1)(b)	In subsection (1)(b) omit the words "or articles".
subsection (1)(c)	Omit subsection (1)(c).
	Miscellaneous provisions about shares and debentures
183 (transfer and registration)	
subsection (1)	Subsection (1), omit the words "shares in or". For the words "company's articles" substitute "limited liability partnership agreement.".
subsection (2)	Subsection (2), omit the words "shareholder or" together with the words "shares in or".
subsection (3)	Omit subsection (3).
subsection (4)	Omit subsection (4).
subsection (5)	Omit the words "shares or".

Provisions	**Modification**
184 (certification of transfers)	
subsection (1)	Subsection (1), omit the words "shares in or" together with the words "shares or".
185 (duty of company as to issue of certificates)	
subsection (1)	Subsection (1), omit the words "shares," in each of the four places that it occurs.
subsection (3)	Omit subsection (3).
subsection (4)	Omit the words "shares or" together with the words "shares,".
	Debentures
190 (register of debenture holders)	
191 (right to inspect register)	
subsection (1)	In subsection (1), paragraph (a), for the words "or any holder of shares in the company" substitute "or any member of the limited liability partnership".
subsection (2)	In subsection (2), delete "or holder of shares".
subsection (6)	In subsection (6), delete the words "in the articles or".
192 (liability of trustees of debentures)	
193 (perpetual debentures)	
194 (power to re-issue redeemed debentures)	
subsection (1)(a)	In subsection (1)(a), omit the words "in the articles or".
subsection (1)(b)	In subsection (1)(b), for "passing a resolution" substitute "making a determination".
195 (contract to subscribe for debentures)	
196 (payment of debts out of assets subject to floating charge (England and Wales))	
	Officers and registered office
287 (registered office)	For section 287 there shall be substituted— "(1) The change of registered office takes effect upon the notice of change of registered office (delivered to the registrar in accordance with paragraph 10 of the Schedule to the Limited Liability Partnerships Act 2000), being registered by the registrar, but until the end of the period of 14 days beginning with the date on which it is registered a person may validly serve any document on the limited liability partnership at its previous registered office. (2) Where a limited liability partnership unavoidably ceases to perform at its registered office any duty to keep at its registered office any register, index or other document or to mention the address of its registered office in any document in circumstances in which it was not practicable to give prior notice to the registrar of a change in the situation of the registered office, but— (a) resumes performance of that duty at other premises as soon as practicable, and (b) gives notice accordingly to the registrar of a change in the situation of its registered office within 14 days of doing so it shall not be treated as having failed to comply with that duty".

Provisions	Modification
288 (register of directors and secretaries)	For section 288 there shall be substituted— "Where a person becomes a member or designated member of a limited liability partnership the notice to be delivered to the registrar under section 9(1)(a) of the Limited Liability Partnerships Act 2000 shall contain the following particulars with respect to that person— (1) name, which (a) in the case of an individual means his forename and surname (or, in the case of a peer or other person usually known by a title, his title instead of or in addition to either or both his forename and surname), and (b) if a corporation or a Scottish firm, its corporate or firm name; and (2) address, which— (a) in the case of an individual means his usual residential address; and (b) if a corporation or a Scottish firm, its registered or principal office; and (3) in the case of an individual, the date of his birth."
Company Identification	
348 (company name to appear outside place of business)	
349 (company's name to appear in its correspondence)	
350 (company seal)	
351 (particulars in correspondence etc)	In subsection (1) for paragraph (c) substitute the words "in the case of a limited liability partnership, whose name ends with the abbreviation "llp", "LLP", "pac" or "PAC", the fact that it is a limited liability partnership or a partneriaeth atebolrwydd cyfyngedig." Also in subsection (1) delete paragraph (d) and delete subsection (2).
Annual Return	
363 (duty to deliver annual returns)	Section 363 of the 1985 Act shall apply to a limited liability partnership being modified so as to read as follows— "(1) Every limited liability partnership shall deliver to the registrar successive annual returns each of which is made up to a date not later than the date which is from time to time the "return date" of the limited liability partnership, that is— (a) the anniversary of the incorporation of the limited liability partnership, or (b) if the last return delivered by the limited liability partnership in accordance with this section was made up to a different date, the anniversary of that date. (2) Each return shall— (a) be in a form approved by the registrar,

Provisions	Modification
	(b) contain the information required by section 364, and
	(c) be signed by a designated member of the limited liability partnership.
	(3) If a limited liability partnership fails to deliver an annual return in accordance with this section before the end of the period of 28 days after the return date, the limited liability partnership is guilty of an offence and liable on summary conviction to a fine not exceeding level 5 on the standard scale. The contravention continues until such time as an annual return made up to that return date and complying with the requirements of subsection (2) (except as to date of delivery) is delivered by the limited liability partnership to the registrar.
	(4) Where a limited liability partnership is guilty of an offence under subsection (3) every designated member of the limited liability partnership is similarly liable unless he shows that he took all reasonable steps to avoid the commission of or the continuance of the offence."
364 (contents of annual return: general)	For section 364 substitute the following—
	"Every annual return shall state the date to which it is made up and shall contain the following information—
	(a) the address of the registered office of the limited liability partnership,
	(b) the names and usual residential addresses of the members of the limited liability partnership and, if some only of them are designated members, which of them are designated members, and
	(c) if any register of debenture holders (or a duplicate of any such register or a part of it) is not kept at the registered office of the limited liability partnership, the address of the place where it is kept."
	Auditors
384 (duty to appoint auditors)	
subsection (2)	In subsection (2), for the words from "(appointment at general meeting at which accounts are laid)" to the end substitute the words "(appointment of auditors)".
subsection (3)	In subsection (3), omit the words from "or 385A(2)" to the end.
subsection (4)	For subsection (4) substitute the following subsection—
	"(4) A person is eligible for appointment by a limited liability partnership as auditor only if, were the limited liability partnership a company, he would be eligible under Part II of the Companies Act 1989 for appointment as a "company auditor"."
subsection (5)	Insert a new subsection (5)—

Provisions	Modification
	"(5) Part II of the Companies Act 1989 shall apply in respect of auditors of limited liability partnerships as if the limited liability partnerships were companies formed and registered under this Act, and references in Part II to an officer of a company shall include reference to a member of a limited liability partnership."
385 (appointment at general meeting at which accounts laid)	
title to the section	In the title to the section for the existing wording substitute "Appointment of auditors".
subsection (1)	Omit subsection (1).
subsection (2)	For subsection (2) substitute— "(2) The designated members of a limited liability partnership shall appoint the auditors for the first financial year in respect of which auditors are appointed before the end of that financial year and thereafter before the expiration of not more than two months following the approval of the accounts for the preceding financial year in accordance with section 233.".
subsection (3)	For subsection (3) substitute— "(3) The auditor of a limited liability partnership shall hold office until not later than the expiration of two months following the approval in accordance with section 233 of the accounts for the financial year in respect of which the auditor was appointed."
subsection (4)	For subsection (4) substitute— "(4) If the designated members fail to exercise their powers under subsection (2), the powers may be exercised by the members of the limited liability partnership in a meeting convened for the purpose".
387 (appointment by Secretary of State in default of appointment by company)	
subsection (1)	In subsection (1), omit the words "re-appointed or deemed to be re-appointed".
subsection (2)	In subsection (2), for the word "officer" substitute the words "designated member".
388 (filling of casual vacancies)	
subsection (1)	In subsection (1), for "directors, or the company in general meeting," substitute "designated members".
subsection (3)	Omit subsection (3).
subsection (4)	Omit subsection (4).
388A (certain companies exempt from obligation to appoint auditors)	
subsection (3)	For subsection (3) substitute— "(3) The designated members may appoint auditors and the auditors so appointed shall hold office until the expiration of two months following the approval in accordance with section 233 of the accounts for the financial year in respect of which the auditor was appointed."
subsection (4)	Omit subsection (4).

Provisions	Modification
subsection (5)	For subsection (5) substitute— "(5) If the designated members fail to exercise their powers under subsection (3), the powers may be exercised by the members of the limited liability partnership in a meeting convened for the purpose."
389A (rights to information)	
390 (right to attend company meetings)	
subsection (1)	In paragraph (a), (b) and (c) of subsection (1) omit the word "general" in each place where it occurs. At the end of paragraph (a) add the words "and where any part of the business of the meeting concerns them as auditors." At the end of paragraph (b) add the words "where any part of the business of the meeting concerns them as auditors."
subsection (1A)	Omit subsection (1A).
subsection (2)	Omit subsection (2).
390A (remuneration of auditors)	
subsection (1)	For subsection (1) substitute— "The remuneration of auditors appointed by the limited liability partnership shall be fixed by the designated members or in such manner as the members of the limited liability partnership may determine".
subsection (2)	In subsection (2), omit the words "directors or the", in both places where they occur, and omit the words "as the case may be".
390B (remuneration of auditors or their associates for non-audit work)	
391 (removal of auditors)	
subsection (1)	In subsection (1), for the words "A company may by ordinary resolution" substitute "The designated members of a limited liability partnership may" and for the words "between it and" substitute "with".
subsection (2)	(a) In subsection (2), for the words "a resolution removing an auditor is passed at a general meeting of a company, the company" substitute the words "the designated members of the limited liability partnership have made a determination to remove an auditor, the designated members". (b) For the words "every officer of it who is in default" substitute "every designated member of it who is in default".
subsection (4)	In subsection (4), omit the word "general".
391A (rights of auditors who are removed or not re-appointed)	
subsection (1)	For subsection (1) substitute— "The designated members shall give seven days' prior written notice to (a) any auditor whom it is proposed to remove before the expiration of his term of office; or

PART IV STATUTORY INSTRUMENTS

Provisions	Modification
	(b) a retiring auditor where it is proposed to appoint as auditor a person other than the retiring auditor."
subsection (2)	Omit subsection (2).
subsection (3)	In subsection (3), for the words "intended resolution" substitute the word "proposal" and omit the words "of the company".
subsection (4)	Omit the words "(unless the representations are received by it too late for it to do so)".
	Omit subsection (4)(a).
	In subsection (4)(b), for the words "of the company to whom notice in writing of the meeting is or has been sent." Substitute "within twenty one days of receipt.".
subsection (5)	For subsection (5) substitute—
	"If a copy of the representations is not sent out as required by subsection (4), then unless subsection (6) applies, the limited liability partnership and any designated member in default commits an offence. A person guilty of an offence under this section is liable on summary conviction to a fine not exceeding level 3 on the standard scale."
subsection (6)	In subsection (6), the words "and the representations need not be read at the meeting" shall be omitted.
392 (resignation of auditors)	
subsection (3)	In the second paragraph of subsection (3) for "and every officer of it who is in default" substitute "and every designated member of it who is in default".
392A (rights of resigning auditors)	
subsection (2)	In subsection (2), for "directors" substitute "designated members" and for "an extraordinary general meeting of the company" substitute "a meeting of the members of the limited liability partnership".
subsection (3)	In subsection (3), omit ", or" from paragraph (a) and omit paragraph (b).
subsection (5)	In subsection (5), for "directors" substitute "designated members" and for "director" substitute "designated member".
subsection (8)	In subsection (8), omit the word "general" and the phrase "(a) or (b)".
394 (statement by person ceasing to hold office as auditor)	
394A (offences of failing to comply with section 394)	

Registration of charges

The following references are to sections of the 1985 Act which were replaced by section 92 of the Companies Act 1989. They will apply to limited liability partnerships until the said section 92 is commenced.

395 (certain charges void if not registered)	
396 (charges which have to be registered)	In subsection (1) delete paragraphs (b) and (g).

Provisions	**Modification**
397 (formalities of registration (debentures))	In subsection (1), paragraph (b) for the word "resolutions" substitute "determinations of the limited liability partnership".
398 (verification of charge on property outside United Kingdom)	
399 (company's duty to register charges it creates)	
400 (charges existing on property acquired)	
401 (register of charges to be kept by registrar of companies)	
402 (endorsement of certificate on debentures)	
403 (entries of satisfaction and release)	In subsection (1A), after "of the company" insert "or designated member, administrator or administrative receiver of the limited liability partnership".
404 (rectification of register of charges)	In subsection (1), omit the words "or shareholders".
405 (registration of enforcement of security)	
406 (companies to keep copies of instruments creating charges)	
407 (company's register of charges)	In subsection (1), for "limited company" substitute "company (including limited liability partnership)".
408 (right to inspect instruments which create charges etc)	In subsection (1) delete "in general meeting".
410 (charges void unless registered)	In subsection (4) delete paragraph (b) and sub-paragraph (ii) of paragraph (c). In subsection (5) for "an incorporated company" substitute "a limited liability partnership".
411 (charges on property outside the United Kingdom)	
412 (negotiable instrument to secure book debts)	
413 (charges associated with debentures)	In subsection (2)(b), for the word "resolutions" substitute "determinations of the limited liability partnership".
414 (charge by way of ex facie absolute disposition, etc)	
415 (company's duty to register charges created by it)	
416 (duty to register charges existing on property acquired)	
417 (register of charges to be kept by registrar of companies)	
418 (certificate of registration to be issued)	
419 (entries of satisfaction and relief)	In subsection (1A), after the words "of the company" insert "or a designated member, liquidator, receiver or administrative receiver of the limited liability partnership".
420 (rectification of the register)	Omit the words "or shareholders".
421 (copies of instruments creating charges to be kept by the company)	
422 (company's register of charges)	

Provisions	**Modification**
423 (right to inspect copies of instruments, and the company's register)	In subsection (1) delete "in general meeting".
Arrangements and Reconstructions	
425 (power of company to compromise with creditors and members)	
subsection (3)	Omit the words "and a copy of every such order shall be annexed to every copy of the company's memorandum issued after the order has been made or, in the case of a company not having a memorandum, of every copy so issued of the instrument constituting the company or defining its constitution." For the semi-colon after the word "registration" substitute a full stop.
subsection (6)	Omit subsection (6).
426 (information as to compromise to be circulated)	
subsection (2)	Omit the words "as directors or".
427 (provisions for facilitating company reconstruction or amalgamation)	
subsection (3)	In paragraph (b) for the words "policies or other like interests" substitute "policies, other like interests or, in the case of a limited liability partnership, property or interests in the limited liability partnership".
subsection (6)	For the words ""company" includes only accompany as defined in section 735(1)" substitute ""company" includes only a company as defined in section 735(1) or a limited liability partnership".
Investigation of companies and their affairs: Requisition of documents	
431 (investigation of a company on its own application or that of its members)	For subsection (2) substitute the following— "(2) The appointment may be made on the application of the limited liability partnership or on the application of not less than one-fifth in number of those who appear from notifications made to the registrar of companies to be currently members of the limited liability partnership."
432 (other company investigations)	
subsection (4)	For the words "but to whom shares in the company have been transferred or transmitted by operation of law" substitute "but to whom a member's share in the limited liability partnership has been transferred or transmitted by operation of law."
433 (inspectors' powers during investigation)	
434 (production of documents and evidence to inspectors)	
436 (obstruction of inspectors treated as contempt of court)	
437 (inspectors' reports)	
438 (power to bring civil proceedings on company's behalf)	
439 (expenses of investigating a company's affairs)	
subsection (5)	Omit paragraph (b) together with the word "or" at the end of paragraph (a).

Provisions	**Modification**
441 (inspectors' report to be evidence)	
447 (Secretary of State's power to require production of documents)	
448 (entry and search of premises)	
449 (provision for security of information obtained)	
450 (punishment for destroying, mutilating etc company documents)	[Omit subsection (1A).]
451 (punishment for furnishing false information)	
451A (disclosure of information by Secretary of State or inspector)	In subsection (1), for the words "sections 434 to 446" substitute "sections 434 to 441". Omit subsection (5).
452 (privileged information)	In subsection (1), for the words "sections 431 to 446" substitute "sections 431 to 441". In subsection (1A), for the words "sections 434, 443 or 446" substitute "section 434".
Fraudulent Trading	
458 (punishment for fraudulent trading)	
Protection of company's members against unfair prejudice	
459 (order on application of company member)	At the beginning of subsection (1), insert the words "Subject to subsection (1A),". After subsection (1) insert as subsection (1A)— "The members of a limited liability partnership may by unanimous agreement exclude the right contained in subsection 459(1) for such period as shall be agreed. The agreement referred to in this subsection shall be recorded in writing." Omit subsections (2) and (3).
460 (order on application of Secretary of State)	… Omit subsection (2).
461 (provisions as to orders and petitions under this Part)	In subsection (2)(d) for the words "the shares of any members of the company by other members or by the company itself and, in the case of a purchase by the company itself, the reduction of the company's capital accordingly" substitute the words "the shares of any members in the limited liability partnership by other members or by the limited liability partnership itself.". In subsection (3) for the words "memorandum or articles" substitute the words "limited liability partnership agreement". For the existing words of subsection (4) substitute the words "Any alteration in the limited liability partnership agreement made by virtue of an order under this Part is of the same effect as if duly agreed by the members of the limited liability partnership and the provisions of this Act apply to the limited liability partnership agreement as so altered accordingly.". Omit subsection (5).
Floating charges and Receivers (Scotland)	
464 (ranking of floating charges)	In subsection (1), for the words "section 462" substitute "the law of Scotland".

Provisions	**Modification**
466 (alteration of floating charges)	Omit subsections (1), (2), (3) and (6).
486 (interpretation for Part XVIII generally)	For the current definition of “company” substitute ““company” means a limited liability partnership;”
	Omit the definition of “Register of Sasines”.
487 (extent of Part XVIII)	
Matters arising subsequent to winding up	
651 (power of court to declare dissolution of company void)	
652 (registrar may strike defunct company off the register)	In subsection (6) paragraph (a) omit the word “director”.
652A (registrar may strike private company off the register on application)	In this section the references to “a private company” shall include a reference to “a limited liability partnership”.
subsection (1)	In subsection (1) the following shall be substituted for the existing wording—
	“On application by two or more designated members of a limited liability partnership, the registrar of companies may strike the limited liability partnership’s name off the register”.
	Omit subsection 2(a) and in subsection 2(b) after the word “be” insert the word “made”.
	In subsection (6), omit the word “director”.
652B (duties in connection with making an application under section 652A)	In paragraph (a) of subsection (5) for “no meetings are” substitute “no meeting is”.
	In paragraph (b) of subsection (5) for “meetings summoned under that section fail” substitute “the meeting summoned under that section fails”.
	In paragraph (c) of subsection (5) for “meetings” substitute “a meeting”.
	In paragraph (d) of subsection (5) for “at previous meetings” substitute “at a previous meeting”.
652C (directors’ duties following application under section 652A)	In subsection (2), for the words “is a director of the company” substitute “is a designated member of the limited liability partnership”.
	In subsection (2) omit paragraph (d).
	In subsection (5) for the words “is a director of the company” substitute “is a designated member of the limited liability partnership”.
	In subsection (6), omit paragraph (d).
652D (sections 652B and 652C: supplementary provisions)	
652E (sections 652B and 652C: enforcement)	
652F (other offences connected with section 652A)	
653 (objection to striking off by person aggrieved)	
654 (property of dissolved company to be bona vacantia)	
655 (effect on section 654 of company’s revival after dissolution)	
656 (crown disclaimer of property vesting as bona vacantia)	

Provisions	**Modification**
657 (effect of crown disclaimer under section 656)	
658 (liability for rentcharge on company's land after dissolution)	
Oversea Limited Liability Partnerships	
693 (obligation to state name and other particulars)	For the wording of subsection (1) there shall be substituted the following words— "Every oversea limited liability partnership shall— (a) in every prospectus inviting subscriptions for its debentures in Great Britain, state the country in which the limited liability partnership is incorporated, (b) conspicuously exhibit on every place where it carries on business in Great Britain the name of the limited liability partnership and the country in which it is incorporated, (c) cause the name of the limited liability partnership and the country in which it is incorporated to be stated in legible characters in all bill heads, letter paper, and in all notices and other official publications and communications of the limited liability partnership." For subsection (2) there shall be substituted the following words "For the purposes of this section "oversea limited liability partnership" means a body incorporated or otherwise established outside Great Britain whose name under its law of incorporation or establishment includes the words "limited liability partnership."". Subsections (3) and (4) shall be omitted.
The Registrar of Companies: His functions and offices	
704 (registration offices)	
705 (companies' registered numbers)	Omit subsection (5).
706 (delivery to the registrar of documents in legible form)	In subsection (2)(a), omit the words from "and, if the document is delivered" to the end of that paragraph.
707A (the keeping of company records by the registrar)	Omit subsection (4).
707B (delivery to the registrar using electronic communications)	In subsection (3), omit the "or" at the end of paragraph (a) and omit paragraph (b).
708 (fees payable to the registrar)	
709 (inspection of records kept by the registrar)	
710 (certificate of incorporation)	
710A (provision and authentication by registrar of documents in non-legible form)	
710B (documents relating to Welsh companies)	In subsection (7), omit the words "272(5) and 273(7) and paragraph 7(3) of Part II of Schedule 9".
711 (public notice by registrar of receipt and issue of certain documents)	In subsection (1) delete "or articles" in paragraph (b) and delete paragraphs (d) to (j), (l), (m) and (s) to (z).
713 (enforcement of company's duty to make returns)	In subsection (1), in the penultimate line for "any officer" substitute "any designated member".

Provisions	Modification
	In subsections (2) and (3) for "officers" substitute "designated members".
714 (registrar's index of company and corporate names)	
715A (interpretation)	
Miscellaneous and supplementary provisions	
721 (production and inspection of books where offence suspected)	In subsection (2)(b), for the words "the secretary of the company or such other" substitute "such".
722 (form of company registers, etc)	
723 (use of computers for company records)	Omit subsection (2).
723A (obligations of company as to inspections of registers, & etc)	
725 (service of documents)	In subsection (2), for the words "other head officer" substitute "a designated member".
726 (costs and expenses in actions by certain limited companies)	References to a "limited company" shall include references to a "limited liability partnership".
727 (power of court to grant relief in certain cases)	In subsection (1) delete the words "an officer of a company or" and "officer or". In subsection (2), delete the words "officer or".
728 (enforcement of High Court orders)	
729 (annual report by Secretary of State)	
730 (punishment of offences)	
731 (summary proceedings)	
732 (prosecution by public authorities)	Delete the references to sections 210, 324, 329 and 455. Omit subsection (2) paragraphs (a) and (c). In subsection (2)(b), for the words "either one of those two persons" substitute "either the Secretary of State, the Director of Public Prosecutions". Omit subsection (3).
733 (offences by bodies corporate)	
subsection (1)	In subsection (1), delete the references to section 210 and 216(3).
subsection (2)	In subsection (2), omit the word "secretary".
subsection (3)	Omit subsection (3).
734 (criminal proceedings against unincorporated bodies)	
Interpretation	
735A (relationship of this Act to the Insolvency Act)	In subsection (1), delete all the references to provisions of the 1985 Act other than the references to sections 425(6)(a), 460(2) and 728.
736 ("subsidiary", "holding company", and "wholly-owned subsidiary")	
subsection (1)	For subsection (1) there shall be substituted the following words— "(1) Subject to subsection (1A), a company is a subsidiary of a limited liability partnership, its "holding company", if that limited liability partnership— (a) holds a majority of the voting rights in it, or

Provisions	**Modification**
	(b) is a member of it and has the right to appoint or remove a majority of its board of directors, or (c) is a member of it and controls alone, pursuant to an agreement with other shareholders or members, a majority of the voting rights in it, or if it is a subsidiary of a company or limited liability partnership which is itself a subsidiary of that other company."
subsection (1A)	Insert as subsection (1A)— "(1A) A limited liability partnership is a subsidiary of a company or a subsidiary of another limited liability partnership, (such company or limited liability partnership being referred to in this section as its "holding company") if that company or limited liability partnership— (a) holds a majority of the voting rights in it; (b) is a member of it and has the right to appoint or remove a majority of other members; or (c) is a member of it and controls, alone or pursuant to an agreement with other members, a majority of voting rights in it, or if it is a subsidiary of a company or limited liability partnership which is itself a subsidiary of that holding company".
subsection (2)	For subsection (2) substitute "A company or a limited liability partnership is a "wholly-owned subsidiary" of another company or limited liability partnership if it has no members except that other and that other's wholly-owned subsidiaries or persons acting on behalf of that other or its wholly owned subsidiaries."
736A (provisions supplementing section 736)	After subsection (1) insert a new subsection (1A) in the following form— "(1A) In section 736(1A)(a) and (c) the references to the voting rights in a limited liability partnership are to the rights conferred on members in respect of their interest in the limited liability partnership to vote on those matters which are to be decided upon by a vote of the members of the limited liability partnership." After subsection (2) insert the new subsection (2A) in the following form— "(2A) In section 736(1A)(b) the reference to the right to appoint or remove a majority of the members of the limited liability partnership is to the right to appoint or remove members holding a majority of the voting rights referred to in subsection (1A) and for this purpose— (a) a person shall be treated as having the right to appoint a member if (i) a person's appointment as member results directly from his appointment as a director or member of the holding company, or

PART IV
STATUTORY INSTRUMENTS

Provisions	Modification
	(ii) the member of the limited liability partnership is the company or limited liability partnership which is the holding company; and
	(b) a right to appoint or remove which is exercisable only with the consent or concurrence of another person shall be left out of account."
	In subsection (7) after the words "Rights attached to shares" insert the words "or to a member's interest in a limited liability partnership".
	In subsection (8) after the words "held by a company", in both places where they occur, insert "or a limited liability partnership".
	In subsection (9) after the words "in the interest of company" insert "or a limited liability partnership" and after the words "that company" in both places where they occur insert "or limited liability partnership".
	In subsection (10) after the words "a company" insert the words "or a limited liability partnership" and after the words "by the company" insert the words "or the limited liability partnership".
	In subsection (12) for the existing words substitute "In this section "company" includes a body corporate other than a limited liability partnership."
739 ("non-cash asset")	
740 ("body corporate" and "corporation")	
741 ("director" and "shadow director")	Omit subsection (3).
742 (expressions used in connection with accounts)	
743A (meaning of "office copy" in Scotland)	
744 (expressions used generally in this Act)	Delete the definitions of expressions not used in provisions which apply to limited liability partnerships and insert the following definitions— ""limited liability partnership" has the meaning given it in section 1(2) of the Limited Liability Partnerships Act 2000". ""shadow member" has the same meaning as it has in the Limited Liability Partnerships Regulations 2001".
744A (index of defined expressions)	Delete the references to expressions not used in provisions which apply to limited liability partnerships including, in particular, the following expressions— Allotment (and related expressions) Section 738 Annual general meeting Section 366 Authorised minimum Section 118 Called up share capital Section 737(1) Capital redemption reserve

Provisions	Modification
	Section 170(1)
	Elective resolution
	Section 379A
	Employees' share scheme
	Section 743
	Existing company
	Section 735(1)
	Extraordinary general meeting
	Section 368
	Extraordinary resolution
	Section 378(1)
	The former Companies Acts
	Section 735(1)
	The Joint Stock Companies Acts
	Section 735(3)
	Overseas branch register
	Section 362
	Paid up (and related expressions)
	Section 738
	Registered office (of a company)
	Section 287
	Resolution for reducing share capital
	Section 135(3)
	Share premium account
	Section 130(1)
	Share warrant
	Section 188
	Special notice (in relation to a resolution)
	Section 379
	Special resolution
	Section 378(2)
	Uncalled share capital
	Section 737(2)
	Undistributable reserves
	Section 264(3)
	Unlimited company
	Section 1(2)
	Unregistered company
	Section 718
SCHEDULE 24 (PUNISHMENT OF OFFENCES UNDER THIS ACT)	Delete the references to those sections which are not applied to limited liability partnerships including, in particular, the following sections—
	Section 6(3) company failing to deliver to the registrar notice or other document, following alteration of its objects;
	Section 18(3) company failing to register change in memorandum or articles;

PART IV STATUTORY INSTRUMENTS

Provisions	Modification
	Section 19(2) company failing to send to one of its members a copy of the memorandum or articles, when so required by the member;
	Section 20(2) where company's memorandum altered, company issuing copy of the memorandum without the alteration;
	Section 28(5) company failing to change name on direction of Secretary of State;
	Section 31(5) company altering its memorandum or articles, so ceasing to be exempt from having "limited" after its name;
	Section 31(6) company failing to change name, on Secretary of State's direction, so as to have "limited" (or Welsh equivalent) at the end;
	Section 32(4) company failing to comply with the Secretary of State's direction to change its name, on grounds that the name is misleading;
	Section 33 trading under misleading name (use of "public limited company" or Welsh equivalent when not so entitled); purporting to be a private company;
	Section 34 trading or carrying on business with improper use of "limited" or "cyfyngedig";
	Section 54(10) public company failing to give notice, or copy of court order, to registrar, concerning application to reregister as private company;
	Section 80(9) directors exercising company's power of allotment without the authority required by section 80(1);
	Section 81(2) private company offering shares to the public, or allotting shares with a view to their being so offered;
	Section 82(5) allotting shares or debentures before third day after issue of prospectus;
	Section 86(6) company failing to keep money in separate bank account, where received in pursuance of prospectus stating that stock exchange listing is to be applied for;
	Section 87(4) offeror of shares for sale failing to keep proceeds in separate bank account;
	Section 88(5) officer of company failing to deliver return of allotments, etc to the registrar;
	Section 95(6) knowingly or recklessly authorising or permitting misleading, false or deceptive material in statement by directors under section 95(5);
	Section 97(4) company failing to deliver to registrar the prescribed form disclosing amount or rate of share commission;
	Section 110(2) making misleading, false or deceptive statement in connection with valuation under section 103 or 104;
	Section 111(3) officer of company failing to deliver copy of asset valuation report to registrar;

Provisions	Modification
	Section 111(4) company failing to deliver to registrar copy of resolution under Section 104(4), with respect to transfer of an asset as consideration for allotment;
	Section 114 contravention of any of the provisions of sections 99 to 104, 106;
	Section 117(7) company doing business or exercising borrowing powers contrary to section 117;
	Section 122(2) company failing to give notice to registrar of reorganisation of share capital;
	Section 123(4) company failing to give notice to registrar of increase of share capital;
	Section 127(5) company failing to forward to registrar copy of court order, when application made to cancel resolution varying shareholders' rights;
	Section 128(5) company failing to send to registrar statement or notice required by section 128 (particulars of shares carrying special rights);
	Section 129(4) company failing to deliver to registrar statement or notice required by section 129 (registration of newly created class rights);
	Section 141 officer of company concealing name of creditor entitled to object to reduction of capital, or wilfully misrepresenting the nature or amount of debt or claim, etc;
	Section 142(2) director authorising or permitting non-compliance with section 142 (requirement to convene company meeting to consider serious loss of capital);
	Section 143(2) company acquiring its own shares in breach of section 143;
	Section 149(2) company failing to cancel its own shares acquired by itself, as required by section 146(2); or failing to apply for reregistration as private company as so required in the case there mentioned;
	Section 151(3) company giving financial assistance towards acquisition of its own shares;
	Section 156(6) company failing to register statutory declaration under section 155;
	Section 156(7) director making statutory declaration under section 155, without having reasonable grounds for opinion expressed in it;
	Section 169(6) default by company's officer in delivering to registrar the return required by section 169 (disclosure by company of purchase of its own shares);
	Section 169(7) company failing to keep copy of contract, etc, at registered office; refusal of inspection to person demanding it;

Provisions	Modification
	Section 173(6) director making statutory declaration under section 173 without having reasonable grounds for the opinion expressed in the declaration;
	Section 175(7) refusal of inspection of statutory declaration and auditor's report under section 173, etc;
	Section 176(4) company failing to give notice to registrar of application to court under section 176, or to register court order;
	Section 183(6) company failing to send notice of refusal to register a transfer of shares or debentures;
	Section 185(5) company default in compliance with section 185(1) (certificates to be made ready following allotment or transfer of shares, etc);
	Section 189(1) offences of fraud and forgery in connection with share warrants in Scotland;
	Section 189(2) unauthorised making of, or using or possessing apparatus for making share warrants in Scotland;
	Section 210(3) failure to discharge obligation of disclosure under Part VI; other forms of non-compliance with that Part;
	Section 211(10) company failing to keep register of interests disclosed under Part IV; other contraventions of section 211;
	Section 214(5) company failing to exercise powers under section 212, when so required by the members;
	Section 215(8) company default in compliance with section 215 (company report of investigation of shareholdings on members' requisition);
	Section 216(3) failure to comply with company notice under section 212;
	Making false statement in response etc;
	Section 217(7) company failing to notify a person that he has been named as a shareholder; on removal of name from register, failing to alter associated index;
	Section 218(3) improper removal of entry from register of interests disclosed;
	company failing to restore entry improperly removed;
	Section 219(3) refusal of inspection of register or report under Part VI; failure to send copy when required;
	Section 232(4) default by director or officer of a company in giving notice of matters relating to himself for purposes of Schedule 6 Part I;
	Section 234(5) non-compliance with Part VII as to directors' report and its content;
	directors individually liable;
	Section 234A(4) laying, circulating or delivering directors' report without required signature;

Provisions	Modification
	Section 241(2) failure to lay accounts and reports before the company in general meeting before the end of the period allowed for doing this;
	Section 251(6) failure to comply with requirements in relation to summary financial statements;
	Section 288(4) default in complying with section 288 (keeping register of directors and secretaries, refusal of inspection);
	Section 291(5) acting as director of a company without having the requisite share qualification;
	Section 294(3) director failing to give notice of his attaining retirement age;
	acting as director under appointment invalid due to his attaining it;
	Section 305(3) company default in complying with section 305 (directors' name to appear on company correspondence, etc);
	Section 306(4) failure to state that liability of proposed director or manager is unlimited; failure to give notice of that fact to person accepting office;
	Section 314(3) director failing to comply with section 314;
	Section 317(7) director failing to disclose interest in contract;
	Section 318(8) company in default in complying with section 318(1) or (5);
	Section 322B(4) terms of unwritten contract between sole member of a private company limited by shares or by guarantee and the company not set out in a written memorandum or recorded in minutes of a directors' meeting;
	Section 323(2) director dealing in options to buy or sell company's listed shares or debentures;
	Section 324(7) director failing to notify interest in company's shares; making false statement in purported notification;
	Section 326(2), (3), (4) and (5) various defaults in connection with company register of directors' interests;
	Section 328(6) director failing to notify company that members of his family etc have or have exercised options to buy shares or debentures; making false statement in purported notification;
	Section 329(3) company failing to notify investment exchange of acquisition of its securities by a director;
	Section 342(1) director or relevant company authorising or permitting company to enter into transaction or arrangement, knowing or suspecting it to contravene section 330;
	Section 342(2) relevant company entering into transaction or arrangement for a director in contravention of section 330;

Provisions	Modification
	Section 342(3) procuring a relevant company to enter into transaction or arrangement known to be contrary to section 330;
	Section 343(8) company failing to maintain register of transactions etc made with and for directors and not disclosed in company accounts; failing to make register available at registered office or at company meeting;
	Section 352(5) company default in complying with section 352 (requirement to keep register of members and their particulars);
	Section 352A(3) company default in complying with section 352A (statement that company has only one member);
	Section 353(4) company failing to send notice to registrar as to place where register of members is kept;
	Section 354(4) company failing to keep index of members;
	Section 356(5) refusal of inspection of members' register; failure to send copy on requisition;
	Section 364(4) company without share capital failing to complete and register annual return in due time;
	Section 366(4) company default in holding annual general meeting;
	Section 367(3) company default in complying with Secretary of State's direction to hold a company meeting;
	Section 367(5) company failing to register resolution that meeting held under section 367 is to be its annual general meeting;
	Section 372(4) failure to give notice, to member entitled to vote at company meeting, that he may do so by proxy;
	Section 372(6) officer of company authorising or permitting issue of irregular invitations to appoint proxies;
	Section 376(7) officer of company in default as to circulation of members' resolutions for company meeting;
	Section 380(5) company failing to comply with section 380 (copies of certain resolutions etc to be sent to registrar of companies);
	Section 380(6) company failing to include copy of resolution to which section 380 applies in articles; failing to forward copy to member on request;
	Section 381B(2) director or secretary of company failing to notify auditors of proposed written resolution;
	Section 382(5) company failing to keep minutes of proceedings at company and board meetings, etc;
	Section 382B(2) failure of sole member to provide the company with a written record of a decision;

Provisions	**Modification**
	Section 383(4) refusal of inspection of minutes of general meeting; failure to send copy of minutes on member's request;
	Section 389(10) person acting as a company auditor knowing himself to be disqualified: failing to give notice vacating office when he becomes disqualified;
	Section 429(6) offeror failing to send copy of notice or making statutory declaration knowing it to be false etc;
	Section 430A(6) offeror failing to give rights to minority shareholder;
	Section 444(3) failing to give Secretary of State, when required to do so, information about interests in shares etc; giving false information;
	Section 455(1) exercising a right to dispose of, or vote in respect of, shares which are subject to restrictions under Part XV; failing to give notice in respect of shares so subject; entering into agreement void under section 454(2), (3);
	Section 455(2) issuing shares in contravention of restrictions under Part XV;
	Section 461(5) failure to register office copy of court order under Part XVII altering, or giving leave to alter, company's memorandum;
	Section 697(1) oversea company failing to comply with any of sections 691 to 693 or 696;
	Section 697(2) oversea company contravening section 694(6) (carrying on business under its corporate name after Secretary of State's direction);
	Section 697(3) oversea company failing to comply with section 695A or Schedule 21A;
	Section 703(1) oversea company failing to comply with requirements as to accounts and reports;
	Section 703D(5) oversea company failing to deliver particulars of charge to registrar;
	Section 703R(1) company failing to register winding up or commencement of insolvency proceedings etc;
	Section 703R(2) liquidator failing to register appointment, termination of winding up or striking off of company;
	Section 720(4) insurance company etc failing to send twice yearly statement in form of Schedule 23;
	Schedule 14, Pt II, paragraph 1(3) company failing to give notice of location of overseas branch register, etc;
	Schedule 14, Pt II, paragraph 4(2) company failing to transmit to its registered office in Great Britain copies of entries in overseas branch register or to keep duplicate of overseas branch register;
	Schedule 21C, Pt I, paragraph 7 credit or financial institution failing to deliver accounting documents;

Provisions	Modification
	Schedule 21C, Pt II, paragraph 15 credit or financial institution failing to deliver accounts and reports; Schedule 21D, Pt I, paragraph 5 company failing to deliver accounting documents; Schedule 21D, Pt I, Paragraph 13 company failing to deliver accounts and reports.

[6993]

NOTES

Words in square brackets in entry relating to the Companies Act 1985, s 450 substituted, and words omitted from entry relating to s 460 revoked, by the Financial Services and Markets Act 2000 (Consequential Amendments) Order 2004, SI 2004/355, art 9, as from 4 March 2004.

PART II
MODIFICATIONS TO THE COMPANY DIRECTORS DISQUALIFICATION ACT 1986

Part II of Schedule I	After paragraph 8 insert— "8A The extent of the member's and shadow members' responsibility for events leading to a member or shadow member, whether himself or some other member or shadow member, being declared by the court to be liable to make a contribution to the assets of the limited liability partnership under section 214A of the Insolvency Act 1986."

[6994]

SCHEDULE 3
MODIFICATIONS TO THE 1986 ACT

Regulation 5

Provisions	Modifications
Section 1 (those who may propose an arrangement)	
subsection (1)	For "The directors of a company" substitute "A limited liability partnership" and delete "to the company and".
subsection (3)	At the end add "but where a proposal is so made it must also be made to the limited liability partnership".
[Section 1A (moratorium)	
subsection (1)	For "the directors of an eligible company intend" substitute "an eligible limited liability partnership intends". For "they" substitute "it".]

The following modifications to sections 2 to 7 apply where a proposal under section 1 has been made by the limited liability partnership.

Section 2 (procedure where the nominee is not the liquidator or administrator)

Provisions	**Modifications**
[subsection (1)	[For "the directors do" substitute "the limited liability partnership does".
subsection (2)	In paragraph [(aa)] for "meetings of the company and of it creditors" substitute "a meeting of the creditors of the limited liability partnership";
	In paragraph (b) for the first "meetings" substitute "a meeting" and for the second "meetings" substitute "meeting".
subsection (3)	For "the person intending to make the proposal" substitute "the designated members of the limited liability partnership".
subsection (4)	[In paragraph (a)] for "the person intending to make the proposal" substitute "the designated members of the limited liability partnership". [In paragraph (b) for "that person" substitute "those designated members".]
Section 3 (summoning of meetings)	
subsection (1)	For "such meetings as are mentioned in section 2(2)" substitute "a meeting of creditors" and for "those meetings" substitute "that meeting".
subsection (2)	Delete subsection (2).
Section 4 (decisions of meetings)	
subsection (1)	For "meetings" substitute "meeting".
subsection (5)	For "each of the meetings" substitute "the meeting".
new subsection (5A)	Insert a new subsection (5A) as follows— "(5A) If modifications to the proposal are proposed at the meeting the chairman of the meeting shall, before the conclusion of the meeting, ascertain from the limited liability partnership whether or not it accepts the proposed modifications; and if at that conclusion the limited liability partnership has failed to respond to a proposed modification it shall be presumed not to have agreed to it."
subsection (6)	For "either" substitute "the"; after "the result of the meeting", in the first place where it occurs, insert "(including, where modifications to the proposal were proposed at the meeting, the response to those proposed modifications made by the limited liability partnership)"; and at the end add "and to the limited liability partnership".
[Section 4A (approval of arrangement)	
subsection (2)	Omit "—(a)".
	For "both meetings" substitute "the meeting".
	Omit the words from ", or" to "that section".
subsection (3)	Omit.
subsection (4)	Omit.
subsection (5)	Omit.
subsection (6)	Omit.]
Section 5 (effect of approval)	

Provisions	Modifications
…	…
subsection (4)	For "each of the reports" substitute "the report".
Section 6 (challenge of decisions)	
subsection (1)	For … "either of the meetings" substitute "the meeting".
subsection (2)	For "either of the meetings" substitute "the meeting" and after paragraph [(aa)] add a new paragraph [(ab) as follows— "(ab)] any member of the limited liability partnership; and". Omit the word "and" at the end of paragraph (b) and omit paragraph (c).
subsection (3)	For "each of the reports" substitute "the report".
subsection (4)	For subsection (4) substitute the following— "(4) Where on such an application the court is satisfied as to either of the grounds mentioned in subsection (1), it may do one or both of the following, namely— (a) revoke or suspend [any decision approving the voluntary arrangement which has effect under section 4A]; (b) give a direction to any person for the summoning of a further meeting to consider any revised proposal the limited liability partnership may make or, in a case falling within subsection (1)(b), a further meeting to consider the original proposal.".
subsection (5)	For … "meetings" substitute "a meeting", for … and for "person who made the original proposal" substitute "limited liability partnership".
[Section 6A (false representations, etc)	
subsection (1)	Omit "members or".]
Section 7 (implementation of proposal)	
…	…
[subsection (2)	In paragraph (a) omit "one or both of" and for "meetings" substitute "meeting".]

The following modifications to sections 2 and 3 apply where a proposal under section 1 has been made, where [the limited liability partnership is in administration], by the administrator or, where the limited liability partnership is being wound up, by the liquidator.

Provisions	Modifications
Section 2 (procedure where the nominee is not the liquidator or administrator)	
subsection (2)	In paragraph (a) for "meetings of the company" substitute "meetings of the members of the limited liability partnership".
Section 3 (summoning of meetings)	
subsection (2)	For "meetings of the company" substitute "a meeting of the members of the limited liability partnership".
…	…
…	…

Provisions	**Modifications**
…	…
…	…
…	…
…	…
Section 73 (alternative modes of winding up)	
subsection (1)	Delete ", within the meaning given to that expression by section 735 of the Companies Act,".
Section 74 (liability as contributories of present and past members)	For section 74 there shall be substituted the following— "74. When a limited liability partnership is wound up every present and past member of the limited liability partnership who has agreed with the other members or with the limited liability partnership that he will, in circumstances which have arisen, be liable to contribute to the assets of the limited liability partnership in the event that the limited liability partnership goes into liquidation is liable, to the extent that he has so agreed, to contribute to its assets to any amount sufficient for payment of its debts and liabilities, and the expenses of the winding up, and for the adjustment of the rights of the contributories among themselves. However, a past member shall only be liable if the obligation arising from such agreement survived his ceasing to be a member of the limited liability partnership."
Section 75 to 78	Delete sections 75 to 78.
Section 79 (meaning of "contributory")	
subsection (1)	In subsection (1) for "every person" substitute "(a) every present member of the limited liability partnership and (b) every past member of the limited liability partnership".
subsection (2)	After "section 214 (wrongful trading)" insert "or 214A (adjustment of withdrawals)".
subsection (3)	Delete subsection (3).
Section 83 (companies registered under Companies Act, Part XXII, Chapter II)	Delete section 83.
Section 84 (circumstances in which company may be wound up voluntarily)	
subsection (1)	For subsection (1) substitute the following— "(1) A limited liability partnership may be wound up voluntarily when it determines that it is to be wound up voluntarily."
subsection (2)	Omit subsection (2).
[subsection (2A)	For "company passes a resolution for voluntary winding up" substitute "limited liability partnership determines that it is to be wound up voluntarily" and for "resolution" where it appears for the second time substitute "determination".

PART IV STATUTORY INSTRUMENTS

Provisions	Modifications
subsection (2B)	For "resolution for voluntary winding up may be passed only" substitute "determination to wind up voluntarily may only be made" and in sub-paragraph (b), for "passing of the resolution" substitute "making of the determination".]
subsection (3)	For subsection (3) substitute the following— "(3) Within 15 days after a limited liability partnership has determined that it be wound up there shall be forwarded to the registrar of companies either a printed copy or else a copy in some other form approved by the registrar of the determination."
subsection [(5)]	After subsection [(4)] insert a new subsection [(5)]— "[(5)] If a limited liability partnership fails to comply with this regulation the limited liability partnership and every designated member of it who is in default is liable on summary conviction to a fine not exceeding level 3 on the standard scale."
Section 85 (notice of resolution to wind up)	
subsection (1)	For subsection (1) substitute the following— "(1) When a limited liability partnership has determined that it shall be wound up voluntarily, it shall within 14 days after the making of the determination give notice of the determination by advertisement in the Gazette."
Section 86 (commencement of winding up)	Substitute the following new section— "86. A voluntary winding up is deemed to commence at the time when the limited liability partnership determines that it be wound up voluntarily.".
Section 87 (effect on business and status of company)	
subsection (2)	In subsection (2), for "articles" substitute "limited liability partnership agreement".
Section 88 (avoidance of share transfers, etc after winding-up resolution)	For "shares" substitute "the interest of any member in the property of the limited liability partnership".
Section 89 (statutory declaration of solvency)	For "director(s)" wherever it appears in section 89 substitute "designated member(s)";
subsection (2)	For paragraph (a) substitute the following— "(a) it is made within the 5 weeks immediately preceding the date when the limited liability partnership determined that it be wound up voluntarily or on that date but before the making of the determination, and".
subsection (3)	For "the resolution for winding up is passed" substitute "the limited liability partnership determined that it be wound up voluntarily".

Provisions	**Modifications**
subsection (5)	For "in pursuance of a resolution passed" substitute "voluntarily".
Section 90 (distinction between "members" and "creditors" voluntary winding up)	For "directors'" substitute "designated members'".
Section 91 (appointment of liquidator)	
subsection (1)	Delete "in general meeting".
subsection (2)	For the existing wording substitute— "(2) On the appointment of a liquidator the powers of the members of the limited liability partnership shall cease except to the extent that a meeting of the members of the limited liability partnership summoned for the purpose or the liquidator sanctions their continuance." After subsection (2) insert— "(3) Subsections (3) and (4) of section 92 shall apply for the purposes of this section as they apply for the purposes of that section."
Section 92 (power to fill vacancy in office of liquidator)	
subsection (1)	For "the company in general meeting" substitute "a meeting of the members of the limited liability partnership summoned for the purpose".
subsection (2)	For "a general meeting" substitute "a meeting of the members of the limited liability partnership".
subsection (3)	In subsection (3), for "articles" substitute "limited liability partnership agreement".
new subsection (4)	Add a new subsection (4) as follows— "(4) The quorum required for a meeting of the members of the limited liability partnership shall be any quorum required by the limited liability partnership agreement for meetings of the members of the limited liability partnership and if no requirement for a quorum has been agreed upon the quorum shall be 2 members."
Section 93 (general company meeting at each year's end)	
subsection (1)	For "a general meeting of the company" substitute "a meeting of the members of the limited liability partnership".
new subsection (4)	Add a new subsection (4) as follows— "(4) subsections (3) and (4) of section 92 shall apply for the purposes of this section as they apply for the purposes of that section."
Section 94 (final meeting prior to dissolution)	
subsection (1)	For "a general meeting of the company" substitute "a meeting of the members of the limited liability partnership".
new subsection (5A)	Add a new subsection (5A) as follows

PART IV
STATUTORY INSTRUMENTS

Provisions	Modifications
	"(5A) Subsections (3) and (4) of section 92 shall apply for the purposes of this section as they apply for the purposes of that section."
subsection (6)	For "a general meeting of the company" substitute "a meeting of the members of the limited liability partnership".
Section 95 (effect of company's insolvency)	
subsection (1)	For "directors'" substitute "designated members'".
subsection (7)	For subsection (7) substitute the following— "(7) In this section "the relevant period" means the period of 6 months immediately preceding the date on which the limited liability partnership determined that it be wound up voluntarily."
Section 96 (conversion to creditors' voluntary winding up)	
paragraph (a)	For "directors'" substitute "designated members'".
paragraph (b)	Substitute a new paragraph (b) as follows— "(b) the creditors' meeting was the meeting mentioned in section 98 in the next Chapter;".
Section 98 (meeting of creditors)	
subsection (1)	For paragraph (a) substitute the following— "(a) cause a meeting of its creditors to be summoned for a day not later than the 14th day after the day on which the limited liability partnership determines that it be wound up voluntarily;".
subsection (5)	For "were sent the notices summoning the company meeting at which it was resolved that the company be wound up voluntarily" substitute "the limited liability partnership determined that it be wound up voluntarily".
Section 99 (directors to lay statement of affairs before creditors)	
subsection (1)	For "the directors of the company" substitute "the designated members" and for "the director so appointed" substitute "the designated member so appointed".
subsection (2)	For "directors" substitute "designated members".
subsection (3)	For "directors" substitute "designated members" and for "director" substitute "designated member".
Section 100 (appointment of liquidator)	
subsection (1)	For "The creditors and the company at their respective meetings mentioned in section 98" substitute "The creditors at their meeting mentioned in section 98 and the limited liability partnership".
subsection (3)	Delete "director,".
Section 101 (appointment of liquidation committee)	
subsection (2)	For subsection (2) substitute the following—

Provisions	Modifications
	"(2) If such a committee is appointed, the limited liability partnership may, when it determines that it be wound up voluntarily or at any time thereafter, appoint such number of persons as they think fit to act as members of the committee, not exceeding 5."
Section 105 (meetings of company and creditors at each year's end)	
subsection (1)	For "a general meeting of the company" substitute "a meeting of the members of the limited liability partnership".
new subsection (5)	Add a new subsection (5) as follows— "(5) Subsections (3) and (4) of section 92 shall apply for the purposes of this section as they apply for the purposes of that section."
Section 106 (final meeting prior to dissolution)	
subsection (1)	For "a general meeting of the company" substitute "a meeting of the members of the limited liability partnership".
new subsection (5A)	After subsection (5) insert a new subsection (5A) as follows— "(5A) Subsections (3) and (4) of section 92 shall apply for the purposes of this section as they apply for the purposes of that section."
subsection (6)	For "a general meeting of the company" substitute "a meeting of the members of the limited liability partnership".
Section 110 (acceptance of shares, etc, as consideration for sale of company property)	For the existing section substitute the following— "(1) This section applies, in the case of a limited liability partnership proposed to be, or being, wound up voluntarily, where the whole or part of the limited liability partnership's business or property is proposed to be transferred or sold to another company whether or not it is a company within the meaning of the Companies Act ("the transferee company") or to a limited liability partnership ("the transferee limited liability partnership"). (2) With the requisite sanction, the liquidator of the limited liability partnership being, or proposed to be, wound up ("the transferor limited liability partnership") may receive, in compensation or part compensation for the transfer or sale, shares, policies or other like interests in the transferee company or the transferee limited liability partnership for distribution among the members of the transferor limited liability partnership. (3) The sanction required under subsection (2) is—

PART IV STATUTORY INSTRUMENTS

Provisions	**Modifications**
	(a) in the case of a members' voluntary winding up, that of a determination of the limited liability partnership at a meeting of the members of the limited liability partnership conferring either a general authority on the liquidator or an authority in respect of any particular arrangement, (subsections (3) and (4) of section 92 to apply for this purpose as they apply for the purposes of that section), and (b) in the case of a creditor's voluntary winding up, that of either court or the liquidation committee. (4) Alternatively to subsection (2), the liquidator may (with the sanction) enter into any other arrangement whereby the members of the transferor limited liability partnership may, in lieu of receiving cash, shares, policies or other like interests (or in addition thereto), participate in the profits, or receive any other benefit from the transferee company or the transferee limited liability partnership. (5) A sale or arrangement in pursuance of this section is binding on members of the transferor limited liability partnership. (6) A determination by the limited liability partnership is not invalid for the purposes of this section by reason that it is made before or concurrently with a determination by the limited liability partnership that it be wound up voluntarily or for appointing liquidators; but, if an order is made within a year for winding up the limited liability partnership by the court, the determination by the limited liability partnership is not valid unless sanctioned by the court."
Section 111 (dissent from arrangement under section 110)	
subsections (1)–(3)	For subsections (1)–(3) substitute the following— "(1) This section applies in the case of a voluntary winding up where, for the purposes of section 110(2) or (4), a determination of the limited liability partnership has provided the sanction requisite for the liquidator under that section. (2) If a member of the transferor limited liability partnership who did not vote in favour of providing the sanction required for the liquidator under section 110 expresses his dissent from it in writing addressed to the liquidator and left at the registered office of the limited liability partnership within 7 days after the date on which that sanction was given, he may require the liquidator either to abstain from carrying the arrangement so sanctioned into effect or to purchase his interest at a price to be determined by agreement or arbitration under this section.

Provisions	**Modifications**
	(3) If the liquidator elects to purchase the member's interest, the purchase money must be paid before the limited liability partnership is dissolved and be raised by the liquidator in such manner as may be determined by the limited liability partnership."
subsection (4)	Omit subsection (4).
Section 117 (high court and county court jurisdiction)	
subsection (2)	Delete "Where the amount of a company's share capital paid up or credited as paid up does not exceed £120,000, then (subject to this section)".
subsection (3)	Delete subsection (3).
Section 120 (court of session and sheriff court jurisdiction)	
subsection (3)	Delete "Where the amount of a company's share capital paid up or credited as paid up does not exceed £120,000,".
subsection (5)	Delete subsection (5).
Section 122 (circumstances in which company may be wound up by the court)	
subsection (1)	For subsection (1) substitute the following— "(1) A limited liability partnership may be wound up by the court if— (a) the limited liability partnership has determined that the limited liability partnership be wound up by the court, (b) the limited liability partnership does not commence its business within a year from its incorporation or suspends its business for a whole year, (c) the number of members is reduced below two, (d) the limited liability partnership is unable to pay its debts … [(da) at the time at which a moratorium for the limited liability partnership under section 1A comes to an end, no voluntary arrangement approved under Part I has effect in relation to the limited liability partnership,] (e) the court is of the opinion that it is just and equitable that the limited liability partnership should be wound up."
Section 124 (application for winding up)	
subsections (2), (3) and (4)(a)	Delete these subsections.
[subsection (3A)	For "122(1)(fa)" substitute "122(1)(da)".]
Section 124A (petition for winding-up on grounds of public interest)	
subsection (1)	[Omit paragraphs (b) and (bb).]
Section 126 (power to stay or restrain proceedings against company)	
subsection (2)	Delete subsection (2).
Section 127 (avoidance of property dispositions, etc)	

PART IV
STATUTORY INSTRUMENTS

Provisions	Modifications
[subsection (1)]	For "any transfer of shares" substitute "any transfer by a member of the limited liability partnership of his interest in the property of the limited liability partnership".
Section 129 (commencement of winding up by the court)	
subsection (1)	For "a resolution has been passed by the company" substitute "a determination has been made" and for "at the time of the passing of the resolution" substitute "at the time of that determination".
Section 130 (consequences of winding-up order)	
subsection (3)	Delete subsection (3).
Section 148 (settlement of list of contributories and application of assets)	
subsection (1)	Delete ", with power to rectify the register of members in all cases where rectification is required in pursuance of the Companies Act or this Act,".
Section 149 (debts due from contributory to company)	
subsection (1)	Delete "the Companies Act or".
subsection (2)	Delete subsection (2).
subsection (3)	Delete ", whether limited or unlimited,".
Section 160 (delegation of powers to liquidator (England and Wales))	
subsection (1)	In subsection (1)(b) delete "and the rectifying of the register of members".
subsection (2)	For subsection (2) substitute the following— "(2) But the liquidator shall not make any call without the special leave of the court or the sanction of the liquidation committee."
Section 165 (voluntary winding up)	
subsection (2)	In paragraph (a) for "an extraordinary resolution of the company" substitute "a determination by a meeting of the members of the limited liability partnership".
subsection (4)	For paragraph (c) substitute the following— "(c) summon meetings of the members of the limited liability partnership for the purpose of obtaining their sanction or for any other purpose he may think fit."
new subsection (4A)	Insert a new subsection (4A) as follows— "(4A) Subsections (3) and (4) of section 92 shall apply for the purposes of this section as they apply for the purposes of that section."
Section 166 (creditors' voluntary winding up)	
subsection (5)	In paragraph (b) for "directors" substitute "designated members".
Section 171 (removal, etc (voluntary winding up))	
subsection (2)	For paragraph (a) substitute the following—

Provisions	**Modifications**
	"(a) in the case of a members' voluntary winding up, by a meeting of the members of the limited liability partnership summoned specially for that purpose, or".
subsection (6)	In paragraph (a) for "final meeting of the company" substitute "final meeting of the members of the limited liability partnership" and in paragraph (b) for "final meetings of the company" substitute "final meetings of the members of the limited liability partnership".
new subsection (7)	Insert a new subsection (7) as follows—
	"(7) Subsections (3) and (4) of section 92 are to apply for the purposes of this section as they apply for the purposes of that section."
Section 173 (release (voluntary winding up))	
subsection (2)	In paragraph (a) for "a general meeting of the company" substitute "a meeting of the members of the limited liability partnership".
Section 183 (effect of execution or attachment (England and Wales))	
subsection (2)	Delete paragraph (a).
Section 184 (duties of sheriff (England and Wales))	
subsection (1)	For "a resolution for voluntary winding up has been passed" substitute "the limited liability partnership has determined that it be wound up voluntarily".
subsection (4)	Delete "or of a meeting having been called at which there is to be proposed a resolution for voluntary winding up," and "or a resolution is passed (as the case may be)".
Section 187 (power to make over assets to employees)	Delete section 187.
Section 194 (resolutions passed at adjourned meetings)	After "contributories" insert "or of the members of a limited liability partnership".
Section 195 (meetings to ascertain wishes of creditors or contributories)	
subsection (3)	Delete "the Companies Act or".
Section 206 (fraud, etc in anticipation of winding up)	
subsection (1)	For "passes a resolution for voluntary winding up" substitute "makes a determination that it be wound up voluntarily".
Section 207 (transactions in fraud of creditors)	
subsection (1)	For "passes a resolution for voluntary winding up" substitute "makes a determination that it be wound up voluntarily".
Section 210 (material omissions from statement relating to company's affairs)	
subsection (2)	For "passed a resolution for voluntary winding up" substitute "made a determination that it be wound up voluntarily".

Provisions	Modifications
Section 214 (wrongful trading)	
subsection (2)	Delete from "but the court shall not" to the end of the subsection.
After section 214	Insert the following new section 214A— **"214A Adjustment of withdrawals** (1) This section has effect in relation to a person who is or has been a member of a limited liability partnership where, in the course of the winding up of that limited liability partnership, it appears that subsection (2) of this section applies in relation to that person. (2) This subsection applies in relation to a person if— (a) within the period of two years ending with the commencement of the winding up, he was a member of the limited liability partnership who withdrew property of the limited liability partnership, whether in the form of a share of profits, salary, repayment of or payment of interest on a loan to the limited liability partnership or any other withdrawal of property, and (b) it is proved by the liquidator to the satisfaction of the court that at the time of the withdrawal he knew or had reasonable ground for believing that the limited liability partnership— (i) was at the time of the withdrawal unable to pay its debts within the meaning of section 123, or (ii) would become so unable to pay its debts after the assets of the limited liability partnership had been depleted by that withdrawal taken together with all other withdrawals (if any) made by any members contemporaneously with that withdrawal or in contemplation when that withdrawal was made. (3) Where this section has effect in relation to any person the court, on the application of the liquidator, may declare that that person is to be liable to make such contribution (if any) to the limited liability partnership's assets as the court thinks proper. (4) The court shall not make a declaration in relation to any person the amount of which exceeds the aggregate of the amounts or values of all the withdrawals referred to in subsection (2) made by that person within the period of two years referred to in that subsection.

Provisions	**Modifications**
	(5) The court shall not make a declaration under this section with respect to any person unless that person knew or ought to have concluded that after each withdrawal referred to in subsection (2) there was no reasonable prospect that the limited liability partnership would avoid going into insolvent liquidation.
	(6) For the purposes of subsection (5) the facts which a member ought to know or ascertain and the conclusions which he ought to reach are those which would be known, ascertained, or reached by a reasonably diligent person having both:
	(a) the general knowledge, skill and experience that may reasonably be expected of a person carrying out the same functions as are carried out by that member in relation to the limited liability partnership, and
	(b) the general knowledge, skill and experience that that member has.
	(7) For the purposes of this section a limited liability partnership goes into insolvent liquidation if it goes into liquidation at a time when its assets are insufficient for the payment of its debts and other liabilities and the expenses of the winding up.
	(8) In this section "member" includes a shadow member.
	(9) This section is without prejudice to section 214."
Section 215 (proceedings under ss 213, 214)	
subsection (1)	Omit the word "or" between the words "213" and "214" and insert after "214" "or 214A".
subsection (2)	For "either section" substitute "any of those sections".
subsection (4)	For "either section" substitute "any of those sections".
subsection (5)	For "Sections 213 and 214" substitute "Sections 213, 214 or 214A".
Section 218 (prosecution of delinquent officers and members of company)	
subsection (1)	For "officer, or any member, of the company" substitute "member of the limited liability partnership".
subsections (3), (4) and (6)	For "officer of the company, or any member of it," substitute "officer or member of the limited liability partnership".
…	…
Section 247 ("insolvency" and "go into liquidation")	
subsection (2)	For "passes a resolution for voluntary winding up" substitute "makes a determination that it be wound up voluntarily" and for "passing such a resolution" substitute "making such a determination".

PART IV
STATUTORY INSTRUMENTS

Provisions	**Modifications**
[subsection (3)	For "resolution for voluntary winding up" substitute "determination to wind up voluntarily".]
Section 249 ("connected with a company")	For the existing words substitute— "For the purposes of any provision in this Group of Parts, a person is connected with a company (including a limited liability partnership) if— (a) he is a director or shadow director of a company or an associate of such a director or shadow director (including a member or a shadow member of a limited liability partnership or an associate of such a member or shadow member); or (b) he is an associate of the company or of the limited liability partnership."
Section 250 ("member" of a company)	Delete section 250.
Section 251 (expressions used generally)	Delete the word "and" appearing after the definition of "the rules" and insert the word "and" after the definition of "shadow director". After the definition of "shadow director" insert the following— ""shadow member", in relation to a limited liability partnership, means a person in accordance with whose directions or instructions the members of the limited liability partnership are accustomed to act (but so that a person is not deemed a shadow member by reason only that the members of the limited liability partnership act on advice given by him in a professional capacity);".
Section 386 (categories of preferential debts)	
subsection (1)	In subsection (1), omit the words "or an individual".
subsection (2)	In subsection (2), omit the words "or the individual".
Section 387 ("the relevant date")	
subsection (3)	[In paragraph (ab) for "passed a resolution for voluntary winding up" substitute "made a determination that it be wound up voluntarily".] In paragraph (c) for "passing of the resolution for the winding up of the company" substitute "making of the determination by the limited liability partnership that it be wound up voluntarily".
subsection (5)	Omit subsection (5).
subsection (6)	Omit subsection (6).
Section 388 (meaning of "act as insolvency practitioner")	
subsection (2)	Omit subsection (2).
subsection (3)	Omit subsection (3).

Provisions	**Modifications**
subsection (4)	Delete ""company" means a company within the meaning given by section 735(1) of the Companies Act or a company which may be wound up under Part V of this Act (unregistered companies);" and delete ""interim trustee" and "permanent trustee" mean the same as the Bankruptcy (Scotland) Act 1985".
Section 389 (acting without qualification an offence)	
subsection (1)	Omit the words "or an individual".
[Section 389A (authorisation of nominees and supervisors)	
subsection (1)	Omit "or Part VIII".]
Section 402 (official petitioner)	Delete section 402.
Section 412 (individual insolvency rules (England and Wales))	Delete section 412.
Section 415 (Fees orders (individual insolvency proceedings in England and Wales))	Delete section 415.
Section 416 (monetary limits (companies winding up))	
subsection (1)	In subsection (1), omit the words "section 117(2) (amount of company's share capital determining whether county court has jurisdiction to wind it up);" and the words "section 120(3) (the equivalent as respects sheriff court jurisdiction in Scotland);".
subsection (3)	In subsection (3), omit the words "117(2), 120(3) or".
Section 418 (monetary limits (bankruptcy))	Delete section 418.
Section 420 (insolvent partnerships)	Delete section 420.
Section 421 (insolvent estates of deceased persons)	Delete section 421.
Section 422 (recognised banks, etc)	Delete section 422.
[Section 426A (disqualification from Parliament (England and Wales))	Omit.
Section 426B (devolution)	Omit.
Section 426C (irrelevance of privilege)	Omit.]
Section 427 (parliamentary disqualification)	Delete section 427.
Section 429 (disabilities on revocation or administration order against an individual)	Delete section 429.
Section 432 (offences by bodies corporate)	
subsection (2)	Delete "secretary or".
Section 435 (meaning of "associate")	
new subsection (3A)	Insert a new subsection (3A) as follows—

PART IV
STATUTORY INSTRUMENTS

Provisions	Modifications
	"(3A) A member of a limited liability partnership is an associate of that limited liability partnership and of every other member of that limited liability partnership and of the husband or wife [or civil partner] or relative of every other member of that limited liability partnership.".
subsection (11)	For subsection (11) there shall be substituted— "(11) In this section "company" includes any body corporate (whether incorporated in Great Britain or elsewhere); and references to directors and other officers of a company and to voting power at any general meeting of a company have effect with any necessary modifications.".
Section 436 (expressions used generally)	The following expressions and definitions shall be added to the section— ""designated member" has the same meaning as it has in the Limited Liability Partnerships Act 2000; "limited liability partnership" means a limited liability partnership formed and registered under the Limited Liability Partnerships Act 2000; "limited liability partnership agreement", in relation to a limited liability partnership, means any agreement, express or implied, made between the members of the limited liability partnership or between the limited liability partnership and the members of the limited liability partnership which determines the mutual rights and duties of the members, and their rights and duties in relation to the limited liability partnership.".
Section 437 (transitional provisions, and savings)	Delete section 437.
Section 440 (extent (Scotland))	
subsection (2)	In subsection (2), omit paragraph (b).
Section 441 (extent (Northern Ireland))	Delete section 441.
Section 442 (extent (other territories))	Delete section 442.
[**Schedule A1**	
Paragraph 6	
sub-paragraph (1)	For "directors of a company wish" substitute "limited liability partnership wishes". For "they" substitute "the designated members of the limited liability partnership".
sub-paragraph (2)	For "directors" substitute "the designated members of the limited liability partnership". In sub-paragraph (c), for "meetings of the company and" substitute "a meeting of".
Paragraph 7	

Provisions	**Modifications**
sub-paragraph (1)	For "directors of a company" substitute "designated members of the limited liability partnership". In sub-paragraph (e)(iii), for "meetings of the company and" substitute "a meeting of".
Paragraph 8	
sub-paragraph (2)	For "meetings" substitute "meeting". For "are" substitute "is". Omit the words in parenthesis.
sub-paragraph (3)	For "either of those meetings" substitute "the meeting". For "those meetings were" substitute "that meeting was". Omit the words in parenthesis.
sub-paragraph (4)	For "either" substitute "the".
sub-paragraph (6)(c)	For "one or both of the meetings" substitute "the meeting".
Paragraph 9	
sub-paragraph (1)	For "directors" substitute "designated members of the limited liability partnership".
sub-paragraph (2)	For "directors" substitute "designated members of the limited liability partnership".
Paragraph 12	
sub-paragraph (1)(b)	Omit.
sub-paragraph (1)(c)	For "resolution may be passed" substitute "determination that it may be wound up may be made".
sub-paragraph (2)	For "transfer of shares" substitute "any transfer by a member of the limited liability partnership of his interest in the property of the limited liability partnership".
Paragraph 20	
sub-paragraph (8)	For "directors" substitute "designated members of the limited liability partnership".
sub-paragraph (9)	For "directors" substitute "designated members of the limited liability partnership".
Paragraph 24	
sub-paragraph (2)	For "directors" substitute "designated members of the limited liability partnership".
Paragraph 25	
sub-paragraph (2)(c)	For "directors" substitute "designated members of the limited liability partnership".
Paragraph 26	
sub-paragraph (1)	Omit ", director".
Paragraph 29	
sub-paragraph (1)	For "meetings of the company and its creditors" substitute "a meeting of the creditors of the limited liability partnership".
Paragraph 30	
sub-paragraph (1)	For "meetings" substitute "meeting".
new sub-paragraph (2A)	Insert new sub-paragraph (2A) as follows—

PART IV
STATUTORY INSTRUMENTS

Provisions	Modifications
	"(2A) If modifications to the proposal are proposed at the meeting the chairman of the meeting shall, before the conclusion of the meeting, ascertain from the limited liability partnership whether or not it accepts the proposed modifications; and if at that conclusion the limited liability partnership has failed to respond to a proposed modification it shall be presumed not to have agreed to it.".
sub-paragraph (3)	For "either" substitute "the".
	After "the result of the meeting" in the first place where it occurs insert "(including, where modifications to the proposal were proposed at the meeting, the response to those proposed modifications made by the limited liability partnership)".
	At the end add "and to the limited liability partnership".
Paragraph 31	
sub-paragraph (1)	For "meetings" substitute "meeting".
sub-paragraph (7)	For "directors of the company" substitute "designated members of the limited liability partnership".
	For "meetings (or either of them)" substitute "meeting".
	For "directors" substitute "limited liability partnership".
	For "those meetings" substitute "that meeting".
Paragraph 32	
sub-paragraph (2)	For sub-paragraphs (a) and (b) substitute "with the day on which the meeting summoned under paragraph 29 is first held.".
Paragraph 36	
sub-paragraph (2)	For sub-paragraph (2) substitute—
	"(2) The decision has effect if, in accordance with the rules, it has been taken by the creditors' meeting summoned under paragraph 29.".
sub-paragraph (3)	Omit.
sub-paragraph (4)	Omit.
sub-paragraph (5)	Omit.
Paragraph 37	
sub-paragraph (5)	For "each of the reports of the meetings" substitute "the report of the meeting".
Paragraph 38	
sub-paragraph (1)(a)	For "one or both of the meetings" substitute "the meeting".
sub-paragraph (1)(b)	For "either of those meetings" substitute "the meeting".
sub-paragraph (2)(a)	For "either of the meetings" substitute "the meeting".
	After sub-paragraph (2)(a) insert new (aa) as follows—

Provisions	**Modifications**
	"(aa) any member of the limited liability partnership;".
sub-paragraph (2)(b)	Omit "creditors'".
sub-paragraph (3)(a)	For "each of the reports" substitute "the report".
sub-paragraph (3)(b)	Omit "creditors'".
sub-paragraph (4)(a)(ii)	Omit "in question".
sub-paragraph (4)(b)(i)	For "further meetings" substitute "a further meeting" and for "directors" substitute "limited liability partnership".
sub-paragraph (4)(b)(ii)	Omit "company or (as the case may be) creditors'".
sub-paragraph (5)	For "directors do" substitute "limited liability partnerships does".
Paragraph 39	
sub-paragraph (1)	For "one or both of the meetings" substitute "the meeting".
Schedule B1	
Paragraph 2	
sub-paragraph (c)	For "company or its directors" substitute "limited liability partnership".
Paragraph 8	
sub-paragraph (1)(a)	For "resolution for voluntary winding up" substitute "determination to wind up voluntarily".
Paragraph 9	Omit.
Paragraph 12	
sub-paragraph (1)(b)	Omit.
Paragraph 22	For sub-paragraph (1) substitute— "(1) A limited liability partnership may appoint an administrator.". Omit sub-paragraph (2).
Paragraph 23	
sub-paragraph (1)(b)	Omit "or its directors".
Paragraph 42	
sub-paragraph (2)	For "resolution may be passed for the winding up of" substitute "determination to wind up voluntarily may be made by".
Paragraph 61	For paragraph 61 substitute—" "61. The administrator has power to prevent any person from taking part in the management of the business of the limited liability partnership and to appoint any person to be a manager of that business.".
Paragraph 62	At the end add the following— "Subsections (3) and (4) of section 92 shall apply for the purposes of this paragraph as they apply for the purposes of that section.".
Paragraph 83	

Provisions	Modifications
sub-paragraph (6)(b)	For "resolution for voluntary winding up" substitute "determination to wind up voluntarily".
sub-paragraph (8)(b)	For "passing of the resolution for voluntary winding up" substitute "determination to wind up voluntarily".
sub-paragraph (8)(e)	For "passing of the resolution for voluntary winding up" substitute "determination to wind up voluntarily".
Paragraph 87	
sub-paragraph (2)(b)	Insert at the end "or".
sub-paragraph (2)(c)	Omit ", or".
sub-paragraph (2)(d)	Omit the words from "(d)" to "company".
Paragraph 89	
sub-paragraph (2)(b)	Insert at the end "or".
sub-paragraph (2)(c)	Omit ", or".
sub-paragraph (2)(d)	Omit the words from "(d)" to "company".
Paragraph 91	
sub-paragraph (1)(c)	Omit.
Paragraph 94	Omit.
Paragraph 95	For "to 94" substitute "and 93".
Paragraph 97	
sub-paragraph (1)(a)	Omit "or directors".
Paragraph 103	
sub-paragraph (5)	Omit.
Paragraph 105	Omit.]
Schedule 1	
Paragraph 19	For paragraph 19 substitute the following— "19. Power to enforce any rights the limited liability partnership has against the members under the terms of the limited liability partnership agreement."
Schedule 10	
[Section 6A(1)	In the entry relating to section 6A omit "members' or".]
Section 85(2)	In the entry relating to section 85(2) for "resolution for voluntary winding up" substitute "making of determination for voluntary winding up".
Section 89(4)	In the entry relating to section 89(4) for "Director" substitute "Designated member".
Section 93(3)	In the entry relating to section 93(3) for "general meeting of the company" substitute "meeting of members of the limited liability partnership".
Section 99(3)	In the entries relating to section 99(3) for "director" and "directors" where they appear substitute "designated member" or "designated members" as appropriate.

Provisions	**Modifications**
Section 105(3)	In the entry relating to section 105(3) for "company general meeting" substitute "meeting of the members of the limited liability partnership".
Section 106(6)	In the entry relating to section 106(6) for "final meeting of the company" substitute "final meeting of the members of the limited liability partnership".
Sections 353(1) to 362	Delete the entries relating to sections 353(1) to 362 inclusive.
Section 429(5)	Delete the entry relating to section 429(5).
[Schedule A1, paragraph 9(2)	For "Directors" substitute "Designated Members".
Schedule A1, paragraph 20(9)	For "Directors" substitute "Designated Members".
Schedule B1, paragraph 27(4)	Omit "or directors".
Schedule B1, paragraph 29(7)	Omit "or directors".
Schedule B1, paragraph 32	Omit "or directors".]

[6995]

NOTES

Entries relating to ss 1A, 4A, 6A, 389A, 426A–426C inserted by the Limited Liability Partnerships (Amendment) Regulations 2005, SI 2005/1989, reg 3, Sch 2, paras 1, 2, 3(b), (e), 12, 13, as from 1 October 2005, except in relation to a case where a petition for an administration order has been presented before that date.

In the entry relating to s 2, words in first, third and fourth pairs of square brackets inserted, and "(aa)" substituted, by SI 2005/1989, reg 3, Sch 2, paras 1, 3(a), as from 1 October 2005, except in relation to a case where a petition for an administration order has been presented before that date.

Entry relating to s 5(1) revoked by SI 2005/1989, reg 3, Sch 2, paras 1, 3(c), as from 1 October 2005, except in relation to a case where a petition for an administration order has been presented before that date.

Words omitted from entry relating to s 6 revoked, and words in square brackets substituted, by SI 2005/1989, reg 3, Sch 2, paras 1, 3(d), as from 1 October 2005, except in relation to a case where a petition for an administration order has been presented before that date.

Entry relating to s 7(1) revoked, and entry relating to s 7(2) inserted, by SI 2005/1989, reg 3, Sch 2, paras 1, 3(f), as from 1 October 2005, except in relation to a case where a petition for an administration order has been presented before that date.

In the paragraph following the entry for s 7, words in square brackets substituted by SI 2005/1989, reg 3, Sch 2, paras 1, 3(g), as from 1 October 2005, except in relation to a case where a petition for an administration order has been presented before that date.

Entries relating to ss 8, 9, 10, 11, 13, 14 revoked by SI 2005/1989, reg 3, Sch 2, paras 1, 4, as from 1 October 2005, except in relation to a case where a petition for an administration order has been presented before that date.

Entries relating to s 84(2A), (2B) inserted, and in the entry relating to s 84(5) figures in square brackets substituted, by SI 2005/1989, reg 3, Sch 2, paras 1, 5, as from 1 October 2005, except in relation to a case where a petition for an administration order has been presented before that date.

Words in square brackets in entries relating to ss 122, 124, 127, 247, 387 inserted by SI 2005/1989, reg 3, Sch 2, paras 1, 6–8, 10, 11, as from 1 October 2005, except in relation to a case where a petition for an administration order has been presented before that date.

In entry relating to s 124A, words in square brackets substituted by the Financial Services and Markets Act 2000 (Consequential Amendments) Order 2004, SI 2004/355, art 10(1), (3), as from 4 March 2004.

Entry relating to s 233 revoked by SI 2005/1989, reg 3, Sch 2, paras 1, 9, as from 1 October 2005, except in relation to a case where a petition for an administration order has been presented before that date.

In entry relating to s 435, words in square brackets inserted by the Civil Partnership Act 2004 (Amendments to Subordinate Legislation) Order 2005, SI 2005/2114, art 2(18), Sch 18, Pt 1, para 3, as from 5 December 2005.

Entries relating to Sch A1 and Sch B1 inserted by SI 2005/1989, reg 3, Sch 2, paras 1, 14, as from 1 October 2005, except in relation to a case where a petition for an administration order has been presented before that date.

Words in square brackets in entry relating to Sch 10 inserted by SI 2005/1989, reg 3, Sch 2, paras 1, 15, as from 1 October 2005, except in relation to a case where a petition for an administration order has been presented before that date.

SCHEDULE 4

Regulation 5(3)

The provisions listed in this Schedule are not applied to Scotland to the extent specified below—

Sections 50 to 52;
Section 53(1) and (2), to the extent that those subsections do not relate to the requirement for a copy of the instrument and notice being forwarded to the registrar of companies;
Section 53(4) (6) and (7);
Section 54(1), (2), (3) (to the extent that that subsection does not relate to the requirement for a copy of the interlocutor to be sent to the registrar of companies), and subsections (5), (6) and (7);
Sections 55 to 58;
Section 60, other than subsection (1);
Section 61, including subsections (6) and (7) to the extent that those subsections do not relate to anything to be done or which may be done to or by the registrar of companies;
Section 62, including subsection (5) to the extent that that subsection does not relate to anything to be done or which may be done to or by the registrar of companies;
Sections 63 to 66;
Section 67, including subsections (1) and (8) to the extent that those subsections do not relate to anything to be done or which may be done to the registrar of companies;
Section 68;
Section 69, including subsections (1) and (2) to the extent that those subsections do not relate to anything to be done or which may be done by the registrar of companies;
Sections 70 and 71;
Subsection 84(3), to the extent that it does not concern the copy of the resolution being forwarded to the registrar of companies within 15 days;
Sections 91 to 93;
Section 94, including subsections (3) and (4) to the extent that those subsections do not relate to the liquidator being required to send to the registrar of companies a copy of the account and a return of the final meeting;
Section 95;
Section 97;
Sections 100 to 102;
Sections 104 to 105;
Section 106, including subsections (3), (4) and (5) to the extent that those subsections do not relate to the liquidator being required to send to the registrar of companies a copy of the account of winding up and a return of the final meeting/quorum;
Sections 109 to 111;
Section 112, including subsection (3) to the extent that that subsection does not relate to the liquidator being required to send to the registrar a copy of the order made by the court;
Sections 113 to 115;
Sections 126 to 128;
Section 130(1) to the extent that that subsection does not relate to a copy of the order being forwarded by the court to the registrar;
Section 131;
Sections 133 to 135;
Sections 138 to 140;
Sections 142 to 146;
Section 147, including subsection (3) to the extent that that subsection does not relate to a copy of the order being forwarded by the company to the registrar;
Section 162 to the extent that that section concerns the matters set out in Section C.2 of Schedule 5 to the Scotland Act 1998 as being exceptions to the insolvency reservation;
Sections 163 to 167;
Section 169;
Section 170, including subsection (2) to the extent that that subsection does not relate to an application being made by the registrar to make good the default;
Section 171;
Section 172, including subsection (8) to the extent that that subsection does not relate to the liquidator being required to give notice to the registrar;
Sections 173 and 174;
Section 177;
Sections 185 to 189;

Sections 191 to 194;
Section 196 to the extent that that section applies to the specified devolved functions of Part IV of the Insolvency Act 1986;
Section 199;
Section 200 to the extent that it applies to the specified devolved functions of Part IV of the First Group of Parts of the 1986 Act;
Sections 206 to 215;
Section 218 subsections (1), (2), (4) and (6);
Section 231 to 232 to the extent that the sections apply to administrative receivers, liquidators and provisional liquidators;
Section 233, to the extent that that section applies in the case of the appointment of an administrative receiver, of a voluntary arrangement taking effect, of a company going into liquidation or where a provisional liquidator is appointed;
Section 234 to the extent that that section applies to situations other than those where an administration order applies;
Section 235 to the extent that that section applies to situations other than those where an administration order applies;
Sections 236 to 237 to the extent that those sections apply to situations other than administration orders and winding up;
Sections 242 to 243;
Section 244 to the extent that that section applies in circumstances other than a company which is subject to an administration order;
Section 245;
Section 251, to the extent that that section contains definitions which apply only to devolved matters;
Section 416(1) and (4), to the extent that those subsections apply to section 206(1)(a) and (b) in connection with the offence provision relating to the winding up of a limited liability partnership;
Schedule 2;
Schedule 3;
Schedule 4;
Schedule 8, to the extent that that Schedule does not apply to voluntary arrangements or administrations within the meaning of Parts I and II of the 1986 Act.

In addition, Schedule 10, which concerns punishment of offences under the Insolvency Act 1986, lists various sections of the Insolvency Act 1986 which create an offence. The following sections, which are listed in Schedule 10, are devolved in their application to Scotland:

Section 51(4);
Section 51(5);
Sections 53(2) to 62(5) to the extent that those subsections relate to matters other than delivery to the registrar of companies;
Section 64(2);
Section 65(4);
Section 66(6);
Section 67(8) to the extent that that subsection relates to matters other than delivery to the registrar of companies;
Section 93(3);
Section 94(4) to the extent that that subsection relates to matters other than delivery to the registrar of companies;
Section 94(6);
Section 95(8);
Section 105(3);
Section 106(4) to the extent that that subsection relates to matters other than delivery to the registrar of companies;
Section 106(6);
Section 109(2);
Section 114(4);
Section 131(7);
Section 164;
Section 166(7);
Section 188(2);
Section 192(2);
Sections 206 to 211; and
Section 235(5) to the extent that it relates to matters other than administration orders.

[6996]

SCHEDULE 5
GENERAL AND CONSEQUENTIAL AMENDMENTS IN OTHER LEGISLATION

Regulation 9

1.–21. …

Culpable officer provisions

22.—(1) A culpable officer provision applies in the case of a limited liability partnership as if the reference in the provision to a director (or a person purporting to act as a director) were a reference to a member (or a person purporting to act as a member) of the limited liability partnership.

(2) A culpable officer provision is a provision in any Act or subordinate legislation (within the meaning of the Interpretation Act 1978) to the effect that where—

(a) a body corporate is guilty of a particular offence, and

(b) the offence is proved to have been committed with the consent or connivance of, or to be attributable to the neglect on the part of, (among others) a director of the body corporate,

he (as well as the body corporate) is guilty of the offence.

[6997]

NOTES

Paras 1–21: amend the Bills of Sale Act (1878) Amendment Act 1882, s 17; insert the Third Parties (Rights Against Insurers) Act 1930, s 3A; amend the Corporate Bodies' Contracts Act 1960, s 2, the Criminal Justice Act 1967, s 9, the Solicitors Act 1974, s 87, the Sex Discrimination Act 1975, s 11, the Race Relations Act 1976, s 10, the Betting and Gaming Duties Act 1981, s 32, the Companies Act 1985, s 26 at **[27]**, the Business Names Act 1985, ss 1, 4 at **[691]**, **[694]**, the Administration of Justice Act 1985, ss 9, 39, Sch 2, the Insolvency Act 1986, s 110 at **[3266]**, the Building Societies Act 1986, Sch 21, the Courts and Legal Services Act 1990, s 19, the Employment Rights Act 1996, ss 166, 183, the Contracts (Rights of Third Parties) Act 1999, s 6, and the Financial Services and Markets Act 2000, ss 177, 221 and 232 at **[2177]**, **[2221]**, **[2232]**.

SCHEDULE 6
APPLICATION OF SUBORDINATE LEGISLATION

Regulation 10

PART I
REGULATIONS MADE UNDER THE 1985 ACT

1. The Companies (Revision of Defective Accounts and Report) Regulations 1990

2. The Companies (Defective Accounts) (Authorised Person) Order 1991

3. The Accounting Standards (Prescribed Body) Regulations 1990

4. The Companies (Inspection and Copying of Registers, Indices and Documents) Regulations 1991

5. The Companies (Registers and other Records) Regulations 1985

6. Companies Act 1985 (Disclosure of Remuneration for Non-Audit Work) Regulations 1991.

[6998]

NOTES

Companies (Defective Accounts) (Authorised Person) Order 1991, SI 1991/13: revoked and replaced by the Companies (Defective Accounts) (Authorised Person) Order 2005, SI 2005/699.

Accounting Standards (Prescribed Body) Regulations 1990, SI 1990/1667: revoked and replaced by the Accounting Standards (Prescribed Body) Regulations 2005, SI 2005/697.

Companies Act 1985 (Disclosure of Remuneration for Non-Audit Work) Regulations 1991, SI 1991/2128: these Regulations are disapplied in relation to the accounts of a company for any financial year beginning on or after 1 October 2005; see the Companies (Disclosure of Auditor Remuneration) Regulations 2005, SI 2005/2417.

PART II
REGULATIONS MADE UNDER THE 1986 ACT

1. Insolvency Practitioners Regulations 1990

2. The Insolvency Practitioners (Recognised Professional Bodies) Order 1986

3. The Insolvency Rules 1986 and the Insolvency (Scotland) Rules 1986 (except in so far as they relate to the exceptions to the reserved matters specified in section C 2 of Part II of Schedule 5 to the Scotland Act 1998)

4. The Insolvency Fees Order 1986

5. The Co-operation of Insolvency Courts (Designation of Relevant Countries and Territories) Order 1986

6. The Co-operation of Insolvency Courts (Designation of Relevant Countries and Territories) Order 1996

7. The Co-operation of Insolvency Courts (Designation of Relevant Country) Order 1998

8. Insolvency Proceedings (Monetary Limits) Order 1986

9. Insolvency Practitioners Tribunal (Conduct of Investigations) Rules 1986

10. Insolvency Regulations 1994

11. Insolvency (Amendment) Regulations 2000.

[6999]

NOTES

Insolvency Practitioners Regulations 1990, SI 1990/439: revoked and replaced by the Insolvency Practitioners Regulations 2005, SI 2005/524.

Insolvency Fees Order 1986, SI 1986/2030: revoked and replaced by the Insolvency Proceedings (Fees) Order 2004, SI 2004/593.

Co-operation of Insolvency Courts (Designation of Relevant Countries and Territories) Order 1996: it is assumed that this refers to the Co-operation of Insolvency Courts (Designation of Relevant Countries) Order 1996, SI 1996/253.

PART III
REGULATIONS MADE UNDER OTHER LEGISLATION

1. Company and Business Names Regulations 1981

2. The Companies (Disqualification Orders) Regulations 1986

3. The Insolvent Companies (Disqualification of Unfit Directors) Proceedings Rules 1987

4. The Contracting Out (Functions of the Official Receiver) Order 1995

5. The Uncertificated Securities Regulations 1995

6. The Insolvent Companies (Reports on Conduct of Directors) Rules 1996

7. The Insolvent Companies (Reports on Conduct of Directors) (Scotland) Rules 1996.

[7000]

NOTES

Companies (Disqualification Orders) Regulations 1986, SI 1986/2067: revoked and replaced by the Companies (Disqualification Orders) Regulations 2001, SI 2001/967.

Uncertificated Securities Regulations 1995, SI 1995/3272: revoked and replaced by the Uncertificated Securities Regulations 2001, SI 2001/3755.

UNCERTIFICATED SECURITIES REGULATIONS 2001

(SI 2001/3755)

NOTES

Made: 23 November 2001.

Authority: Companies Act 1989, s 207.

Commencement: 26 November 2001 (see reg 1 at **[7001]**). Where any provision in this work (including any inserted or substituted provision) came into force for all purposes on or before 1 July 2005, commencement information is not noted at provision level.

These Regulations are reproduced as amended by: the Enterprise Act 2002 (Consequential and Supplemental Provisions) Order 2003, SI 2003/1398; the Uncertificated Securities (Amendment) (Eligible Debt Securities) Regulations 2003, SI 2003/1633; the Enterprise Act 2002 and Media Mergers (Consequential Amendments) Order 2003, SI 2003/3180; the Government Stock (Consequential and Transitional Provision) (No 2) Order 2004, SI 2004/1662; the Local Authorities (Capital Finance) (Further Consequential and Saving Provisions) Order 2004, SI 2004/2044; the Capital Requirements Regulations 2006, SI 2006/3221; the Uncertificated Securities (Amendment) Regulations 2007, SI 2007/124; the Companies Act 2006 (Commencement No 2, Consequential Amendments, Transitional Provisions and Savings) Order 2007, SI 2007/1093. See also the prospective amendments made to these Regulations by the draft Companies Act 2006 (Commencement No 3, Consequential Amendments, Transitional Provisions and Savings) Order 2007 (see **[A12]**).

Limited liability partnerships: these Regulations apply, with modifications, to limited liability partnerships; see the Limited Liability Partnerships Regulations 2001, SI 2001/1090, reg 10, Sch 6, Pt III (at **[7000]**), and the Interpretation Act 1978, ss 17(2)(a), 23(1), (2).

ARRANGEMENT OF REGULATIONS

PART 1
CITATION, COMMENCEMENT AND INTERPRETATION

PART 2
THE OPERATOR

Approval and compliance

Supervision

Miscellaneous

PART 3
PARTICIPATING SECURITIES

Participation by issuers

Keeping of registers and records

PART 1
CITATION, COMMENCEMENT, AND INTERPRETATION

1 Citation and commencement

These Regulations may be cited as the Uncertificated Securities Regulations 2001 and shall come into force on 26th November 2001.

[7001]

2 Purposes and basic definition

(1) These Regulations enable title to units of a security to be evidenced otherwise than by a certificate and transferred otherwise than by a written instrument, and make provision for

PART IV STATUTORY INSTRUMENTS

certain supplementary and incidental matters; and in these Regulations "relevant system" means a computer-based system, and procedures, which enable title to units of a security to be evidenced and transferred without a written instrument, and which facilitate supplementary and incidental matters.

(2) Where a title to a unit of a security is evidenced otherwise than by a certificate by virtue of these Regulations, the transfer of title to such a unit of a security shall be subject to these Regulations.

[7002]

3 Interpretation

(1) In these Regulations—

["the 1877 Act" means the Treasury Bills Act 1877;

"the 1950 Act" means the Exchequer and Financial Provisions Act (Northern Ireland) 1950;]

"the 1985 Act" means the Companies Act 1985;

"the 1986 Act" means the Financial Services Act 1986;

[.....]

"the 2000 Act" means the Financial Services and Markets Act 2000;

"the 1986 Order" means the Companies (Northern Ireland) Order 1986;

.....

["the 1968 Regulations" means the Treasury Bills Regulations 1968;]

"the 1974 Regulations" means the Local Authority (Stocks and Bonds) Regulations 1974;

.....

[.....]

"the 1995 Regulations" means the Uncertificated Securities Regulations 1995;

["the 2003 Regulations" means the Uncertificated Securities (Amendment) (Eligible Debt Securities) Regulations 2003;]

["the 2004 Regulations" means the Government Stock Regulations 2004;]

"the Authority" means the Financial Services Authority referred to in section 1 of the 2000 Act;

"certificate" means any certificate, instrument or other document of, or evidencing, title to units of a security;

"company" means a company within the meaning of section 735(1) of the 1985 Act;

"dematerialised instruction" means an instruction sent or received by means of a relevant system;

[.....]

"designated agency" has the meaning given by regulation 11(1);

["eligible debt security" means—

(a) a security that satisfies the following conditions—

(i) the security is constituted by an order, promise, engagement or acknowledgement to pay on demand, or at a determinable future time, a sum in money to, or to the order of, the holder of one or more units of the security; and

(ii) the current terms of issue of the security provide that its units may only be held in uncertificated form and title to them may only be transferred by means of a relevant system;

(b) an eligible Northern Ireland Treasury Bill; or

(c) an eligible Treasury bill;

"eligible Northern Ireland Treasury Bill" means a security—

(a) constituted by a Northern Ireland Treasury Bill issued in accordance with the 1950 Act as modified by Part 2 of Schedule 1 to the 2003 Regulations; and

(b) whose current terms of issue provide that its units may only be held in uncertificated form and title to them may only be transferred by means of a relevant system;

"eligible Treasury bill" means a security—

(a) constituted by a Treasury bill issued in accordance with the 1877 Act and the 1968 Regulations as modified by Part 1 of Schedule 1 to the 2003 Regulations; and

(b) whose current terms of issue provide that its units may only be held in uncertificated form and title to them may only be transferred by means of a relevant system;]

"enactment" includes an enactment comprised in any subordinate legislation within the meaning of the Interpretation Act 1978, and an enactment comprised in, or in an instrument made under, an Act of the Scottish Parliament;

["general local authority security" means a local authority security that is not an eligible debt security;

"general public sector security" means a public sector security that is not an eligible debt security;

"general UK Government security" means a UK Government security that is not an eligible debt security;]

"generate", in relation to an Operator-instruction, means to initiate the procedures by which the Operator-instruction comes to be sent;

"guidance", in relation to an Operator, means guidance issued by him which is intended to have continuing effect and is issued in writing or other legible form, which if it were a rule, would come within the definition of a rule;

"instruction" includes any instruction, election, acceptance or any other message of any kind;

"interest in a security" means any legal or equitable interest or right in relation to a security, including—

(a) an absolute or contingent right to acquire a security created, allotted or issued or to be created, allotted or issued; and

(b) the interests or rights of a person for whom a security is held on trust or by a custodian or depositary;

"issue", in relation to a new unit of a security, means to confer title to a new unit on a person;

"issuer-instruction" means a properly authenticated dematerialised instruction attributable to a participating issuer;

"issuer register of members" has the meaning given by regulation 20(1)(a);

"issuer register of securities"—

(a) in relation to shares, means an issuer register of members; and

[(b) in relation to units of securities other than—

(i) shares,

(ii) securities in respect of which regulation 22(3) applies, or

(iii) wholly dematerialised securities,

means a register of persons holding the units, maintained by or on behalf of the issuer or, in the case of general public sector securities, by or on behalf of the person specified in regulation 21(3);]

["local authority"—

(a) in relation to a security referred to in paragraph (a)(i) of the definition of "local authority security", has the same meaning as in the 1974 Regulations;

[(b) in relation to a security referred to in paragraph (b) of the definition of "local authority security", has the same meaning as in section 23 of the Local Government Act 2003 ("local authority");]

["local authority security" means a security which is either—

(a) a security other than an eligible debt security which, when held in certificated form is—

(i) transferable in accordance with regulation 7(1) of the 1974 Regulations and title to which must be registered in accordance with regulation 5 of those Regulations; or

(ii) ...

(b) an eligible debt security issued by a local authority;]

"officer", in relation to an Operator or a participating issuer, includes—

(a) where the Operator or the participating issuer is a company, such persons as are mentioned in section 744 of the 1985 Act;

(b) where the Operator or the participating issuer is a partnership, a partner; or in the event that no partner is situated in the United Kingdom, a person in the United Kingdom who is acting on behalf of a partner; and

(c) where the Operator or the participating issuer is neither a company nor a partnership, any member of its governing body; or in the event that no member of its governing body is situated in the United Kingdom, a person in the United Kingdom who is acting on behalf of any member of its governing body;

"Operator" means a person approved by the Treasury under these Regulations as Operator of a relevant system (and in Schedule 1 includes a person who has applied to the Treasury under regulation 4 for their approval of him as an Operator);

"Operator-instruction" means a properly authenticated dematerialised instruction attributable to an Operator;

"Operator register of corporate securities" has the meaning given by regulation 22(2)(a)(i);

["Operator register of eligible debt securities" has the meaning given by regulation 22(3A)(a);

"Operator register of general public sector securities" has the meaning given by regulation 21(1)(a);]

"Operator register of members" has the meaning given by regulation 20(1)(b);

.....

"Operator register of securities"—

(a) in relation to shares, means an Operator register of members;

(b) in relation to units of a security other than shares, means an Operator register of corporate securities, an Operator register of [general public sector securities, an Operator register of eligible debt securities or, as the case may be, a register maintained by an Operator in accordance with regulation 22(3)(a)];

"Operator's conversion rules" means the rules made and practices instituted by the Operator in order to comply with paragraph 18 of Schedule 1;

"Operator-system" means those facilities and procedures which are part of the relevant system, which are maintained and operated by or for an Operator, by which he generates Operator-instructions and receives dematerialised instructions from system-participants and by which persons change the form in which units of a participating security are held;

"participating issuer" means (subject to paragraph (3)) a person who has issued a security which is a participating security;

"participating security" means a security title to units of which is permitted by an Operator to be transferred by means of a relevant system;

"public sector securities" means UK Government securities and local authority securities;

["record of uncertificated general public sector securities" has the meaning given by regulation 21(2)(a);]

"record of securities" means any of a record of uncertificated corporate securities, a record of uncertificated shares and a record of uncertificated [general public sector securities];

"record of uncertificated corporate securities" has the meaning given by regulation 22(2)(b)(ii);

"record of uncertificated shares" has the meaning given by regulation 20(6)(a);

"register of members" means either or both of an issuer register of members and an Operator register of members;

"register of securities" means either or both of an issuer register of securities and an Operator register of securities;

"relevant system" has the meaning given by regulation 2(1); and "relevant system" includes an Operator-system;

"rules", in relation to an Operator, means rules made or conditions imposed by him with respect to the provision of the relevant system;

"securities" means shares, stock, debentures, debenture stock, loan stock, bonds, units of a collective investment scheme within the meaning of section 235 of the 2000 Act, rights under a depositary receipt within the meaning of paragraph 4 of Schedule 2 to the Criminal Justice Act 1993, and other securities of any description, and interests in a security;

"settlement", [except in paragraph 28 of Schedule 1,] in relation to a transfer of uncertificated units of a security between two system-members by means of a relevant system, means the delivery of those units to the transferee and, where appropriate, the creation of any associated obligation to make payments, in accordance with the rules and practices of the Operator; and "settle" shall be construed accordingly;

"settlement bank", in relation to a relevant system, means a person who has contracted to make payments in connection with transfers of title to uncertificated units of a security by means of that system;

"share" means share (or stock) in the share capital of a company;

"system-member", in relation to a relevant system, means a person who is permitted by an Operator to transfer by means of that system title to uncertificated units of a security held by him, and shall include, where relevant, two or more persons who are jointly so permitted;

"system-member instruction" means a properly authenticated dematerialised instruction attributable to a system-member;

"system-participant", in relation to a relevant system, means a person who is permitted by an Operator to send and receive properly authenticated dematerialised instructions; and "sponsoring system-participant" means a system-participant who is permitted by an Operator to send properly authenticated dematerialised instructions attributable to another person and to receive properly authenticated dematerialised instructions on another person's behalf;

"system-user", in relation to a relevant system, means a person who as regards that system is a participating issuer, a system-member, system-participant or settlement bank;

"UK Government security" means a security issued by Her Majesty's Government in the United Kingdom or by a Northern Ireland department;

"uncertificated", in relation to a unit of a security, means (subject to Regulation 42(11)(a)) that title to the unit is recorded on the relevant Operator register of securities, and may, by virtue of these Regulations, be transferred by means of a relevant system; and "certificated", in relation to a unit of a security, means that the unit is not an uncertificated unit;

"unit", in relation to a security, means the smallest possible transferable unit of the security (for example a single share);

"wholly dematerialised security" means—

(a) a strip, in relation to any stock or bond, within the meaning of section 47(1B) of the Finance Act 1942; or

(b) a participating security whose terms of issue (or, in the case of shares, where its terms of issue or the articles of association of the company in question) provide that its units may only be held in uncertificated form and title to them may only be transferred by means of a relevant system;

and other expressions have the meanings given to them by the 1985 Act.

(2) For the purposes of these Regulations—

(a) a dematerialised instruction is properly authenticated if it complies with the specifications referred to in paragraph 5(3) of Schedule 1; or if it was given, and not withdrawn, before these Regulations came into force and was properly authenticated within the meaning of regulation 3(2)(a) of the 1995 Regulations;

(b) a dematerialised instruction is attributable to a person if it is expressed to have been sent by that person, or if it is expressed to have been sent on behalf of that person, in accordance with the rules and specifications referred to in paragraph 5(4) of Schedule 1; and a dematerialised instruction may be attributable to more than one person.

(3) In respect of a participating security which is a [general] public sector security, references in these Regulations to the participating issuer shall, other than in Regulation 41, be taken to be references—

(a) in the case of a local authority security—

(i) to the relevant local authority; or

(ii) if the local authority has appointed another person to act as registrar for the purpose of the 1974 Regulations in respect of that security, to the person so appointed […

(iii) …]; and

(b) in the case of any other [general] public sector security, to [the Registrar of Government Stock].

[(4) In respect of a security which is an eligible debt security, references in these regulations to the issuer or the participating issuer of that security (or units of that security) shall be taken to be references to—

(a) a person ("P") who undertakes as principal to perform the payment obligation constituted by the security in accordance with its current terms of issue; and

(b) any other person who undertakes as principal to perform that obligation in accordance with those terms in the event that P fails to do so.

(5) For the purposes of paragraph (4)(b), a person who undertakes to perform an obligation under a contract of guarantee or other contract of suretyship is not to be regarded as undertaking to perform it as principal.

(6) For the purposes of paragraph (a) of the definition of "eligible debt security" in paragraph (1), a sum of money—

(a) is to be regarded as payable at a determinable future time if it is payable—

(i) at a future time fixed by or in accordance with the current terms of issue of the security; or

(ii) at the expiry of a fixed period after the occurrence of a specified event which is certain to happen, though the time of happening may be uncertain; and

(b) is not to be regarded as payable at a determinable future time if it is payable on a contingency.]

[7003]

NOTES

Para (1) is amended as follows:

Definitions "the 1877 Act", "the 1950 Act", "the 1968 Regulations", "the 2003 Regulations", "eligible debt security", "eligible Northern Ireland Treasury Bill", "eligible Treasury bill", "general local authority security", "general public sector security", "general UK Government security", "local authority", "Operator register of eligible debt securities" and "Operator register of general public sector securities" inserted, words omitted from definition "the 1974 Regulations", and the definition "Operator register of public sector securities" revoked, words in square brackets in definitions "issuer register of securities", "Operator register of securities" and "record of securities" substituted, and definition "record of uncertificated general public sector securities" substituted (for original definition "record of uncertificated public sector securities"), by the Uncertificated Securities (Amendment) (Eligible Debt Securities) Regulations 2003, SI 2003/1633, reg 3, as from 24 June 2003.

Definitions "the 1989 Act", "the 1990 Regulations" and "dematerialised loan instrument" inserted by SI 2003/1633, reg 3, as from 24 June 2003, and revoked by the Local Authorities (Capital Finance) (Further Consequential and Saving Provisions) Order 2004, SI 2004/2044, art 6(1)(a), as from 1 October 2004.

Definition "the 1965 Regulations" revoked, and definition "the 2004 Regulations" inserted, by the Government Stock (Consequential and Transitional Provision) (No 2) Order 2004, SI 2004/1662, art 2, Schedule, Pt 3, para 29(1), (2)(a), as from 1 July 2004.

In definition "local authority" para (b) substituted by SI 2004/2044, art 6(1)(b), as from 1 October 2004.

Definition "local authority security" substituted by SI 2003/1633, reg 3, as from 24 June 2003; para (a)(ii) revoked by SI 2004/2044, art 6(1)(c), as from 1 October 2004.

Words in square brackets in definition "settlement" inserted by the Uncertificated Securities (Amendment) Regulations 2007, SI 2007/124, reg 2, as from 1 November 2007.

Para (3): the word "general" in square brackets in both places it occurs inserted by SI 2003/1633, reg 4(1)(a), as from 24 June 2003; para (a)(iii) and the word immediately preceding it originally inserted by SI 2003/1633, reg 4(1)(b), as from 24 June 2003, and revoked by SI 2004/2044, art 6(1)(d), as from 1 October 2004; words in final pair of square brackets substituted by SI 2004/1662, art 2, Schedule, Pt 3, para 29(1), (2)(b), as from 1 July 2004.

Paras (4)–(6): added by SI 2003/1633, reg 4(2), as from 24 June 2003.

Note: in the original Queen's Printer's copy of these Regulations there were two definitions of "record of securities" in para (1) above. It is believed that the second one (ie, the one that followed the definition "register of members") should be the definition "*register* of securities". The above text has been changed accordingly, but no correction slip has been issued to confirm this.

Financial Services Act 1986: repealed by the Financial Services and Markets Act 2000 (Consequential Amendments and Repeals) Order 2001, SI 2001/3649, art 3(1)(c), as from 1 December 2001.

Uncertificated Securities Regulations 1995, SI 1995/3272: revoked by these Regulations.

PART 2
THE OPERATOR

Approval and compliance

4 Applications for approval

(1) Any person may apply to the Treasury for their approval of him as Operator of a relevant system.

(2) The application shall be made in such manner as the Treasury may direct and shall be accompanied by—

(a) a copy of the rules and any guidance to be issued by the applicant; and

(b) such other information as the Treasury may reasonably require for the purpose of determining the application.

(3) At any time after receiving an application and before determining it, the Treasury may require the applicant to provide such further information as they reasonably consider necessary to enable them to determine the application.

(4) Information which the Treasury require under this regulation shall, if they so require, be provided in such form, or verified in such manner, as they may direct.

(5) Different directions may be given, or requirements imposed, by the Treasury with respect to different applications.

[7004]

5 Grant and refusal of approval

(1) If, on an application made under regulation 4, it appears to the Treasury that the requirements of Schedule 1 (which imposes requirements which must appear to the Treasury to be satisfied with respect to an Operator, his rules and practices and the relevant system) are satisfied with respect to the application, they may—

(a) subject to the payment of any fee charged by virtue of regulation 6(1); and

(b) subject to the provisions of Schedule 2,

approve the applicant as Operator of a relevant system.

(2) In considering an application, the Treasury may have regard to any information which they consider is relevant to the application.

(3) An approval under this regulation shall be by instrument in writing and shall state the date on which it is to take effect.

(4) Schedule 3 shall have effect in relation to a decision to refuse an application made under regulation 4 as if references to an Operator were to the applicant.

(5) Provided that it had not been withdrawn before these Regulations came into force, an approval granted to a person under regulation 5 of the 1995 Regulations shall be treated as having been granted under this regulation.

[7005]

6 Fees charged by the Treasury

(1) The Treasury may charge a fee to a person seeking approval as Operator of a relevant system.

(2) The Treasury may charge an Operator a periodical fee.

(3) Any fee chargeable by the Treasury under this regulation shall not exceed an amount which reasonably represents the amount of costs incurred—

(a) in the case of a fee charged to a person seeking approval, in determining whether to grant approval; and

(b) in the case of a periodical fee, in satisfying themselves that the Operator, his rules and practices and the relevant system continue to meet the requirements of Schedule 1 and that the Operator is complying with any obligations imposed on him by or under these Regulations.

(4) For the purposes of paragraph (3), the costs incurred by the Treasury shall be determined on the basis that they include such proportion of the following matters as are properly attributable to the performance of the relevant function—

(a) expenditure on staff, equipment, premises, facilities, research and development;

(b) the allocation, over a period of years, whether before or after the coming into force of these Regulations, of any initial expenditure incurred wholly and exclusively to perform the function or to prepare for its performance;

(c) any notional interest incurred on any capital expended on or in connection with the performance of the function or in preparing for its performance and, in a case in which any function is exercisable by the designated agency, any actual interest payable on any sums borrowed which have been so expended; and

(d) any other matter which, in accordance with generally accepted accounting principles, may properly be taken account of in ascertaining the costs properly attributable to the performance of the function.

(5) For the purposes of paragraph (4)(c)—

(a) "notional interest" means any interest which that person might reasonably have been expected to have been liable to pay had the sums expended been borrowed at arm's length; and

(b) "actual interest" means the actual interest paid on sums borrowed in a transaction at arm's length and, where a sum has been borrowed otherwise than in such a transaction, means whichever is the lesser of the interest actually paid and the interest that might reasonably have been expected to be paid had the transaction been at arm's length.

(6) Any fee received by the Treasury under this regulation shall be paid into the Consolidated Fund.

(7) Any fee received by the designated agency under this regulation may be retained by it.

[7006]

Supervision

7 Withdrawal of approval

(1) The Treasury may withdraw an Operator's approval at the request, or with the consent, of the Operator.

(2) If it appears to the Treasury that—

(a) any requirement of Schedule 1 is not satisfied in relation to an Operator; or

(b) an Operator is failing or has failed to comply with any obligation imposed on him by or under these Regulations,

they may withdraw approval from that Operator by written instrument even though the Operator does not wish his approval to be withdrawn.

(3) Schedule 3 shall have effect as regards the procedure to be followed before withdrawing an Operator's approval under paragraph (2).

(4) An instrument withdrawing an Operator's approval shall state the date on which it is to take effect.

(5) In the case of an instrument withdrawing an Operator's approval under paragraph (2), the date stated shall not be earlier than the end of the period of three months beginning with the day on which the instrument is executed.

(6) An instrument withdrawing an Operator's approval may contain such transitional provisions as the Treasury think necessary or expedient.

[7007]

8 Compliance orders and directions

(1) This regulation applies if it appears to the Treasury that—

(a) any requirement of Schedule 1 is not satisfied, or is likely not to be satisfied, in relation to an Operator; or

(b) an Operator has failed to comply with any obligation imposed on him by or under these Regulations.

(2) The Treasury may—

(a) make an application to the court; or

(b) subject to paragraph (4), direct the Operator to take specified steps for the purpose of securing—

(i) that the relevant requirement of Schedule 1 is satisfied in relation to the Operator; or

(ii) the Operator's compliance with any obligation of the kind in question.

(3) If on any application by the Treasury under paragraph (2)(a) the court is satisfied that the relevant requirement of Schedule 1 is not satisfied or is likely not to be satisfied, or, as the case may be, that the Operator has failed to comply with the obligation in question, it may order the Operator to take such steps as the court directs for securing that the requirement is satisfied or that the obligation is complied with.

(4) Schedule 3 shall have effect as regards the procedure to be followed before giving a direction under paragraph (2)(b).

(5) A direction under paragraph (2)(b) is enforceable, on the application of the Treasury, by an injunction or, in Scotland, by an order for specific performance under section 45 of the Court of Session Act 1988.

(6) The jurisdiction conferred by paragraph (3) shall be exercisable by the High Court and the Court of Session.

(7) The fact that a rule made or condition imposed by an Operator has been altered in response to a direction given by the Treasury under paragraph (2)(b) or an order of the court under paragraph (3) does not prevent it from being subsequently altered or revoked by the Operator.

[7008]

9 Injunctions and restitution orders

(1) If on the application of the Treasury the court is satisfied—

(a) that there is a reasonable likelihood that any person will contravene a relevant rule; or

(b) that any person has contravened a relevant rule, and that there is a reasonable likelihood that the contravention will continue or be repeated,

the court may make an order restraining (or in Scotland an interdict prohibiting) the contravention.

(2) If on the application of the Treasury the court is satisfied—

(a) that any person has contravened a relevant rule; and

(b) that there are steps which could be taken for remedying the contravention,

the court may make an order requiring that person and any other person who appears to the court to have been knowingly concerned in the contravention to take such steps as the court may direct to remedy it.

(3) No application shall be made by the Treasury under paragraph (1) or (2) in respect of a relevant rule unless it appears to them that the Operator of the relevant system is unable or unwilling to take appropriate steps to restrain the contravention or to require the person concerned to take such steps as are mentioned in paragraph (2)(b).

(4) If on the application of the Treasury the court is satisfied that any person may have—

(a) contravened a relevant rule; or

(b) been knowingly concerned in the contravention of a relevant rule,

the court may make an order restraining (or in Scotland an interdict prohibiting) him from disposing of, or otherwise dealing with, any assets of his which it is satisfied he is reasonably likely to dispose of or otherwise deal with.

(5) The court may, on the application of the Treasury, make an order under paragraph (6) if it is satisfied that a person has contravened a relevant rule, or been knowingly concerned in the contravention of such a rule, and—

(a) that profits have accrued to him as a result of the contravention; or

(b) that one or more persons have suffered loss or been otherwise adversely affected as a result of the contravention.

(6) The court may order the person concerned to pay to the Treasury such sum as appears to the court to be just having regard—

(a) in a case within subparagraph (a) of paragraph (5), to the profits appearing to the court to have accrued;

(b) in a case within subparagraph (b) of that paragraph, to the extent of the loss or other adverse effect; or

(c) in a case within both of those subparagraphs, to the profits appearing to the court to have accrued and to the extent of the loss or other adverse effect.

(7) Subsections (3) to (5) and (8) of section 382 of the 2000 Act shall apply in relation to an application of the Treasury under paragraph (5) as they have effect in relation to an application of the Authority under subsection (1) of that section; and in those subsections as they so apply—

(a) the references to subsections (1) and (2) shall be taken to be references to paragraphs (5) and (6) respectively;

(b) the references to paragraphs (a) and (b) of subsection (1) shall be taken to be references to subparagraphs (a) and (b) respectively of paragraph (5).

(8) The jurisdiction conferred by this Regulation shall be exercisable by the High Court and the Court of Session.

(9) Nothing in this regulation affects the right of any person other than the Treasury to bring proceedings in respect of matters to which this regulation applies.

(10) In this regulation, "relevant rule" means any provision of the rules of an Operator to which the person in question is subject and which regulate the carrying on by that person of business of any of the following kinds—

(a) dealing in investments as principal;
(b) dealing in investments as agent;
(c) arranging deals in investments;
(d) managing investments;
(e) safeguarding and administering investments;
(f) sending dematerialised instructions;
(g) establishing etc a collective investment scheme;
(h) advising on investments; or
(i) agreeing to carry on any of the activities mentioned in paragraphs (a) to (h).

(11) In paragraph (2), references to remedying a contravention include references to mitigating its effect.

(12) Paragraph (10) shall be read with—
(a) section 22 of the 2000 Act;
(b) any relevant order under that section; and
(c) Schedule 2 to that Act.

[7009]

10 Provision of information by Operators

(1) The Treasury may, in writing, require an Operator to give them such information as they may specify.

(2) The Treasury may also, in writing, require an Operator to give them, at such times or in respect of such periods as they may specify, such information relating to that Operator as they may specify.

(3) Any information required to be given under this regulation shall be only such as the Treasury may reasonably require for the exercise of their functions under these Regulations.

(4) The Treasury may require information to be given by a specified time, in a specified form and to be verified in a specified manner.

(5) If an Operator—
(a) alters or revokes any of his rules or guidance; or
(b) makes new rules or issues new guidance,

he shall give written notice to the Treasury without delay.

[7010]

11 Delegation of Treasury functions

(1) Subject to paragraphs (2) and (5), the Treasury may by instrument in writing delegate all or any of the functions conferred by this Part of these Regulations to the Authority; and references in these Regulations to the "designated agency" are references to the Authority so far as such functions are so delegated.

(2) The functions conferred on the Treasury by regulation 12 may not be delegated.

(3) The designated agency shall send to the Treasury a copy of any guidance issued by virtue of these Regulations and any requirements imposed by it on an Operator by virtue of regulation 10, and give them written notice of any amendment or revocation of, or addition to, any such guidance or requirements.

(4) The designated agency shall—
(a) send to the Treasury a copy of any guidance issued by it which is intended to have continuing effect and is issued in writing or other legible form; and
(b) give them written notice of any amendment or revocation of, or addition to, guidance issued by it,

but notice need not be given of the revocation of guidance other than is mentioned in subparagraph (a) or of any amendment or addition which does not result in or consist of such guidance as is there mentioned.

(5) The Treasury shall not delegate any function to the Authority unless they are satisfied that—
(a) any guidance issued by it in the exercise of its functions under these Regulations;
(b) any requirements imposed by it on an Operator by virtue of regulation 10;
(c) any guidance proposed to be issued by it in the exercise of its functions under these Regulations; and

(d) any requirements it proposes to impose on an Operator by virtue of regulation 10,

do not have, and are not intended or likely to have, to any significant extent the effect of restricting, distorting or preventing competition, or if they have or are intended or likely to have that effect to any significant extent, that the effect is not greater than is necessary for the protection of investors.

(6) The powers conferred by paragraph (7) shall be exercisable by the Treasury if at any time it appears to them that—

(a) any guidance issued by the designated agency in the exercise of its functions under these Regulations;

(b) any requirements imposed by the designated agency on an Operator by virtue of regulation 10; or

(c) any practices of the designated agency followed in the exercise of its functions under these Regulations,

have, or are intended or likely to have, to any significant extent the effect of restricting, distorting or preventing competition and that the effect is greater than is necessary for the protection of investors.

(7) The powers exercisable under this paragraph are—

(a) to resume all or any of the functions delegated to the designated agency by the written instrument referred to in paragraph (1); or

(b) to direct the designated agency to take specified steps for the purpose of securing that the guidance, requirements or practices in question do not have the effect mentioned in paragraph (6).

(8) The Treasury may by written instrument—

(a) at the request or with the consent of the designated agency; or

(b) if at any time it appears to them that the designated agency is unable or unwilling to discharge all or any of the functions delegated to it,

resume all or any of the functions delegated to the designated agency under paragraph (1).

(9) Neither the designated agency nor any person who is, or is acting as, a member, officer or member of staff of the designated agency shall be liable in damages for anything done or omitted in the discharge or purported discharge of functions delegated under paragraph (1) unless the act or omission is shown to have been in bad faith.

(10) In this regulation—

(a) any reference to guidance issued to an Operator by the designated agency is a reference to any guidance issued or any recommendation made by the designated agency in writing, or other legible form, which is intended to have continuing effect, and is issued or made to an Operator; and

(b) references to the practices of the designated agency are references to the practices of the designated agency in its capacity as such.

(11) If under paragraph (1) the Treasury delegate to the designated agency the Treasury's function of making applications to the court under regulation 9(5), the reference to the Treasury in regulation 9(6) shall, unless the Treasury otherwise provide in the instrument by which that function is delegated, be taken as a reference to the designated agency.

[7011]

12 International obligations

(1) If it appears to the Treasury that any action proposed to be taken by an Operator or the designated agency would be incompatible with Community obligations or any other international obligations of the United Kingdom they may direct the Operator or the designated agency, as the case may be, not to take that action.

(2) If it appears to the Treasury that any action which an Operator or the designated agency has power to take is required for the purpose of implementing any such obligations, they may direct the Operator or the designated agency, as the case may be, to take that action.

(3) A direction under this regulation—

(a) may include such supplemental or incidental requirements as the Treasury consider necessary or expedient; and

(b) is enforceable, on an application made by the Treasury, by injunction or, in Scotland, by an order for specific performance under section 45 of the Court of Session Act 1988.

[7012]

13 Prevention of restrictive practices

Schedule 2 (prevention of restrictive practices) shall have effect.

[7013]

PART 3
PARTICIPATING SECURITIES

Participation by issuers

14 Participation in respect of shares

Where—

(a) an Operator permits title to shares of a class in relation to which regulation 15 applies, or in relation to which a directors' resolution passed in accordance with regulation 16 is effective, to be transferred by means of a relevant system; and

(b) the company in question permits the holding of shares of that class in uncertificated form and the transfer of title to any such shares by means of a relevant system,

title to shares of that class which are recorded on an Operator register of members may be transferred by means of that relevant system.

[7014]

15 This regulation applies to a class of shares if the company's articles of association are in all respects consistent with—

(a) the holding of shares of that class in uncertificated form;

(b) the transfer of title to shares of that class by means of a relevant system; and

(c) these Regulations.

[7015]

16—(1) This regulation applies to a class of shares if a company's articles of association in any respect are inconsistent with—

(a) the holding of shares of that class in uncertificated form;

(b) the transfer of title to shares of that class by means of a relevant system; or

(c) any provision of these Regulations.

(2) A company may resolve, subject to paragraph (6)(a), by resolution of its directors (in this Part referred to as a "director's resolution") that title to shares of a class issued or to be issued by it may be transferred by means of a relevant system.

(3) Upon a directors' resolution becoming effective in accordance with its terms, and for as long as it is in force, the articles of association in relation to the class of shares which were the subject of the directors' resolution shall not apply to any uncertificated shares of that class to the extent that they are inconsistent with—

(a) the holding of shares of that class in uncertificated form;

(b) the transfer of title to shares of that class by means of a relevant system; or

(c) any provision of these Regulations.

(4) Unless a company has given notice to every member of the company in accordance with its articles of association of its intention to pass a directors' resolution before the passing of such a resolution, it shall give such notice within 60 days of the passing of the resolution.

(5) Notice given by the company before the coming into force of these Regulations of its intention to pass a directors' resolution which, if it had been given after the coming into force of these Regulations would have satisfied the requirements of paragraph (4), shall be taken to satisfy the requirements of that paragraph.

(6) In respect of a class of shares, the members of a company may by ordinary resolution—

(a) if a directors' resolution has not been passed, resolve that the directors of the company shall not pass a directors' resolution;

(b) if a directors' resolution has been passed but not yet come into effect in accordance with its terms, resolve that it shall not come into effect;

(c) if a directors' resolution has been passed and is effective in accordance with its terms but the class of shares has not yet been permitted by the Operator to be a participating security, resolve that the directors' resolution shall cease to have effect; or

(d) if a directors' resolution has been passed and is effective in accordance with its terms and the class of shares has been permitted by the Operator to be a participating security, resolve that the directors shall take the necessary steps to ensure that title to shares of the class that was the subject of the directors' resolution shall cease to be transferable by means of a relevant system and that the directors' resolution shall cease to have effect,

and the directors shall be bound by the terms of any such ordinary resolution.

(7) Such sanctions as apply to a company and its officers in the event of a default in complying with section 376 of the 1985 Act shall apply to a participating issuer and his officers in the event of a default in complying with paragraph (4).

(8) A company shall not permit the holding of shares in such a class as is referred to in paragraph (1) in uncertificated form, or the transfer of title to shares in such a class by means of a relevant system, unless in relation to that class of shares a directors' resolution is effective.

(9) This regulation shall not be taken to exclude the right of the members of a company to amend the articles of association of the company, in accordance with the articles, to allow the holding of any class of its shares in uncertificated form and the transfer of title to shares in such a class by means of a relevant system.

[7016]

17—(1) A class of shares in relation to which, immediately before the coming into force of these Regulations—

(a) regulation 15 of the 1995 Regulations applied; or

(b) a directors' resolution passed in accordance with regulation 16 of the 1995 Regulations was effective,

shall be taken to be a class of shares in relation to which regulation 15 of these Regulations applies or, as the case may be, a directors' resolution passed in accordance with regulation 16 is effective.

(2) On the coming into force of these Regulations a company's articles of association in relation to any such class of shares, and the terms of issue of any such class of shares, shall cease to apply to the extent that they are inconsistent with any provision of these Regulations.

[7017]

18 Interpretation of regulations 15, 16 and 17

For the purposes of regulations 15, 16 and 17 any shares with respect to which share warrants to bearer are issued under section 188 of the 1985 Act shall be regarded as forming a separate class of shares.

[7018]

19 Participation in respect of securities other than shares

(1) Subject to paragraph (2), where—

(a) an Operator permits title to a security other than a share to be transferred by means of a relevant system; and

(b) the issuer permits the holding of units of that security in uncertificated form and the transfer of title to units of that security by means of a relevant system,

title to units of that security which are recorded on an Operator register of securities may be transferred by means of that relevant system.

(2) In relation to any security other than a share, if the law under which it is constituted is not the law of England and Wales, Northern Ireland or Scotland, or if the current terms of its issue are in any respect inconsistent with—

(a) the holding of title to units of that security in uncertificated form;

(b) the transfer of title to units of that security by means of a relevant system; or

(c) subject to paragraph (3), these Regulations,

[an issuer of that security] shall not permit the holding of units of that security in uncertificated form, or the transfer of title to units of that security by means of a relevant system.

(3) On the coming into force of these Regulations the current terms of issue of a relevant participating security shall cease to apply to the extent that they are inconsistent with any provision of these Regulations.

(4) For the purposes of this regulation—

(a) a relevant participating security is a participating security (other than a share) the terms of issue of which, immediately before the coming into force of these Regulations, were in all respects consistent with the 1995 Regulations; and

(b) the terms of issue of a security shall be taken to include the terms prescribed by the issuer on which units of the security are held and title to them is transferred.

[7019]

NOTES

Para (2): words in square brackets substituted by the Uncertificated Securities (Amendment) (Eligible Debt Securities) Regulations 2003, SI 2003/1633, regs 2, 5, as from 24 June 2004.

Keeping of registers and records

20 Entries on registers and records in respect of shares

(1) In respect of every company which is a participating issuer, there shall be—

(a) a register maintained by the participating issuer, and such a register is referred to in these Regulations as an "issuer register of members"; and

(b) a register maintained by the Operator, and such a register is referred to in these Regulations as an "Operator register of members".

(2) A participating issuer which is a company shall keep and enter up the issuer register of members in accordance with paragraph 2 of Schedule 4.

(3) In respect of every company which is a participating issuer, the Operator shall keep and enter up the Operator register of members in accordance with paragraph 4 of Schedule 4.

(4) References in any enactment or instrument to a company's register of members shall, unless the context otherwise requires, be construed in relation to a company which is a participating issuer as referring to the company's issuer register of members and Operator register of members.

(5) Paragraph (4) does not apply in relation to a company's issuer register of members to the extent that any of the particulars entered in that register in accordance with paragraph 2(1) of Schedule 4 are inconsistent with the company's Operator register of members.

(6) A participating issuer which is a company shall—

(a) maintain a record of the entries made in its Operator register of members; and such a record is referred to in these Regulations as a "record of uncertificated shares"; and

(b) keep and enter up that record in accordance with paragraph 5 of Schedule 4.

(7) Such sanctions as apply to a company and its officers in the event of a default in complying with section 352 of the 1985 Act shall apply to—

(a) a company which is a participating issuer and its officers in the event of a default in complying with paragraph (1)(a) or (6)(a), or

(b) an Operator and his officers in the event of a default in complying with paragraph (1)(b).

[7020]

21 Entries on registers and records in respect of [general] public sector securities

(1) In respect of every participating security which is a [general] public sector security the Operator shall—

(a) maintain a register, and such a register is referred to in these Regulations as an "Operator register of [general] public sector securities"; and

(b) keep and enter up the Operator register of [general] public sector securities in accordance with paragraph 12 of Schedule 4.

(2) The person specified in paragraph (3) shall—

(a) maintain a record of the entries made in an Operator register of [general] public sector securities; and such a record is referred to in these Regulations as a "record of uncertificated [general] public sector securities"; and

(b) keep and enter up that record in accordance with paragraph 13 of Schedule 4.

(3) The person referred to in paragraph (2) is [the Registrar of Government Stock], except where the security to which an Operator register of [general] public sector securities relates is a [general] local authority security, in which case it is—

(a) the relevant local authority; or

(b) if the local authority has appointed another person to act as registrar for the purpose of the 1974 Regulations in respect of that security, the person so appointed […

(c) …].

(4) Such sanctions as apply to a company and its officers in the event of a default in complying with section 352 of the 1985 Act shall apply to an Operator and his officers in the event of a default in complying with paragraph (1)(a).

(5) Such sanctions as apply to the registrar, within the meaning of the 1974 Regulations, in the event of a default in complying with regulation 5 of those Regulations shall apply to a participating issuer and his officers in the event of a default in complying with paragraph (2)(a) in respect of a local authority security [falling within paragraph (a)(i) of the definition of "local authority security" in regulation 3(1)].

[(6) …]

[7021]

NOTES

Regulation heading, paras (1), (2), (5): words in square brackets inserted by the Uncertificated Securities (Amendment) (Eligible Debt Securities) Regulations 2003, SI 2003/1633, regs 6(1), (2), 8(2), as from 24 June 2003.

Para (3): words in first pair of square brackets substituted by the Government Stock (Consequential and Transitional Provision) (No 2) Order 2004, SI 2004/1662, art 2, Schedule, Pt 3, para 29(1), (3), as from 1 July 2004; the word "general" in square brackets in both places it occurs inserted by the Uncertificated Securities (Amendment) (Eligible Debt Securities) Regulations 2003, SI 2003/1633, regs 6(2), 8(1)(a), (2), as from 24 June 2003; para (c) and the word immediately preceding it originally inserted by SI 2003/1633, art 8(1)(b), as from 24 June 2003, and revoked by the Local Authorities (Capital Finance) (Further Consequential and Saving Provisions) Order 2004, SI 2004/2044, art 6(2)(a), as from 1 October 2004.

Para (6): added by SI 2003/1633, reg 8(3), as from 24 June 2003, and revoked by SI 2004/2044, art 6(2)(b), as from 1 October 2004.

22 Entries on registers and records in respect of other securities

(1) Paragraph (2) applies where a participating issuer is required by or under an enactment or instrument to maintain in the United Kingdom a register of persons holding securities (other than shares[, general public sector securities or eligible debt securities]) issued by him.

(2) Where this paragraph applies, then in so far as the register in question relates to any class of security which is a participating security—

(a) the Operator shall—

(i) maintain a register, and such a register is referred to in these Regulations as an "Operator register of corporate securities"; and

(ii) keep and enter up the Operator register of corporate securities in accordance with paragraph 14 of Schedule 4;

(b) the participating issuer—

(i) shall not maintain the register to the extent that it relates to securities held in uncertificated form;

(ii) shall maintain a record of the entries made in any Operator register of corporate securities, and such a record is referred to in these Regulations as a "record of uncertificated corporate securities"; and

(iii) shall keep and enter up that record in accordance with paragraph 15 of Schedule 4.

(3) Where a participating issuer is not required by or under an enactment or instrument to maintain in the United Kingdom in respect of a participating security [(other than an eligible debt security)] issued by him a register of persons holding units of that participating security, the Operator shall—

(a) maintain a register in respect of that participating security; and

(b) record in that register—

(i) the names and addresses of the persons holding units of that security in uncertificated form, and

(ii) how many units of that security each such person holds in that form.

[(3A) In respect of every participating security which is an eligible debt security, the Operator shall—

(a) maintain a register, and such a register is referred to in these Regulations as an "Operator register of eligible debt securities"; and

(b) record in that register—

(i) the names and addresses of the persons holding units of that security; and

(ii) how many units of that security each such person holds.]

(4) Such sanctions as apply to a company and its officers in the event of a default in complying with section 352 of the 1985 Act shall apply to an Operator and his officers in the event of a default in complying with paragraph [(2)(a)(i), (3) or (3A)].

(5) Such sanctions as apply in the event of a default in complying with the requirement to maintain a register imposed by the relevant enactment or instrument referred to in paragraph (1) shall apply to a participating issuer and his officers in the event of a default in complying with paragraph (2)(b)(ii).

[7022]

NOTES

Paras (1), (4): words in square brackets substituted by the Uncertificated Securities (Amendment) (Eligible Debt Securities) Regulations 2003, SI 2003/1633, regs 6(3), 9(3), as from 24 June 2003.

Para (3): words in square brackets inserted by SI 2003/1633, reg 9(1), as from 24 June 2003.

Para (3A): inserted by SI 2003/1633, reg 9(2), as from 24 June 2003.

23 General provisions concerning keeping registers and records

(1) The obligations of an Operator to maintain and to keep and enter up any register of securities, imposed by these Regulations—

(a) shall not give rise to any form of duty or liability on the Operator, except such as is expressly provided for in these Regulations or as arises from fraud or other wilful default, or negligence, on the part of the Operator;

(b) shall not give rise to any form of duty or liability on a participating issuer, other than where the Operator acts on the instructions of that participating issuer, in the absence of fraud or other wilful default, or negligence, on the part of that participating issuer; and

(c) shall not give rise to any form of duty or liability enforceable by civil proceedings for breach of statutory duty.

(2) Without prejudice to paragraph (1) or to any lesser period of limitation and to any rule as to the prescription of rights, liability incurred by a participating issuer or by an Operator arising—

(a) from the making or deletion of an entry in a register of securities or record of securities pursuant to these Regulations; or

(b) from a failure to make or delete any such entry,

shall not be enforceable more than 20 years after the date on which the entry was made or deleted or, in the case of a failure, the failure first occurred.

(3) No notice of any trust, expressed, implied or constructive, shall be entered on an Operator register of securities, or a part of such a register, or be receivable by an Operator.

(4) Schedule 4 (which provides for the keeping of registers and records of participating securities, and which excludes, or applies with appropriate modifications, certain provisions of the 1985 Act) shall have effect.

[7023]

24 Effect of entries on registers

(1) Subject to regulation 29 and to paragraphs (2) and (3) below, a register of members is prima facie evidence, and in Scotland sufficient evidence unless the contrary is shown, of any matters which are by these Regulations directed or authorised to be inserted in it.

(2) Paragraph (1) does not apply to a company's issuer register of members to the extent that any of the particulars entered in that register in accordance with paragraph 2(1) of Schedule 4 are inconsistent with the company's Operator register of members.

(3) The entry of a person's name and address in a company's issuer register of members shall not be treated as showing that person to be a member of the company unless—

(a) the issuer register of members also shows him as holding shares in the company in certificated form;

(b) the Operator register of members shows him as holding shares in the company in uncertificated form; or

(c) he is deemed to be a member of the company by regulation 32(6)(b).

(4) Section 361 of the 1985 Act shall not apply with respect to a company which is a participating issuer.

(5) Subject to regulation 29, an Operator register of [general] public sector securities is prima facie evidence, and in Scotland sufficient evidence unless the contrary is shown, of any matters which are by these Regulations directed or authorised to be inserted in it.

(6) Subject to regulation 29, an entry on an Operator register of corporate securities which records a person as holding units of a security in uncertificated form shall be evidence of such title to the units as would be evidenced if the entry on that register—

(a) were an entry on the part maintained by the participating issuer of such register as is mentioned in regulation 22(1); and

(b) where appropriate, related to units of that security held in certificated form.

(7) Subject to regulation 29, an entry on a register maintained by virtue of regulation 22(3)(a) shall (where the units are capable of being held in certificated form) be prima facie evidence, and in Scotland sufficient evidence unless the contrary is shown, that the person to whom the entry relates has such title to the units of the security which he is recorded as holding in uncertificated form as he would have if he held the units in certificated form.

[(8) Subject to regulation 29, an entry on an Operator register of eligible debt securities shall be prima facie evidence, and in Scotland sufficient evidence unless the contrary is shown, of any matters which are by these Regulations directed or authorised to be inserted in it.]

[7024]

NOTES

Para (5): word in square brackets inserted by the Uncertificated Securities (Amendment) (Eligible Debt Securities) Regulations 2003, SI 2003/1633, reg 6(4), as from 24 June 2003.

Para (8): added by SI 2003/1633, reg 10, as from 24 June 2003.

25 Rectification of registers of securities

(1) Unless the circumstances described in paragraph (2) apply, a participating issuer shall not rectify an issuer register of securities if such rectification would also require the rectification of an Operator register of securities.

(2) The circumstances referred to in paragraph (1) are that the rectification of an issuer register of securities is effected—

(a) with the consent of the Operator; or

(b) by order of a court in the United Kingdom.

(3) A participating issuer who rectifies an issuer register of securities in order to give effect to an order of a court in the United Kingdom shall immediately give the Operator written notification of the change to the entry, if any rectification of the Operator register of securities may also be required (unless the change to the issuer register is made in response to an Operator-instruction).

(4) An Operator who rectifies an Operator register of securities shall immediately—

(a) generate an Operator-instruction to inform the relevant participating issuer of the change to the entry (unless the change is made in response to an issuer-instruction); and

(b) generate an Operator-instruction to inform the system-members concerned of the change to the entry.

[7025]

26 Closing registers

Notwithstanding section 358 of the 1985 Act or any other enactment, a participating issuer shall not close a register of securities relating to a participating security without the consent of the Operator.

[7026]

27 Registration by an Operator of transfers of securities

(1) Except where relevant units of a security are transferred by means of a relevant system to a person who is to hold them thereafter in certificated form (and subject to paragraphs (2) and (4))—

(a) upon settlement of a transfer of uncertificated units of a security in accordance with his rules;

(b) following receipt of an issuer-instruction notifying him that the circumstances specified in regulation 33(2)(b) have arisen in respect of a transfer of units of a participating security; or

(c) following receipt of an issuer-instruction given under Regulation 42(8)(b),

an Operator shall register on the relevant Operator register of securities the transfer of title to those units of that security.

(2) An Operator shall refuse to register a transfer of title to units of a participating security in accordance with a system-member instruction or an issuer-instruction (as the case may be) if he has actual notice that the transfer is—

(a) prohibited by order of a court in the United Kingdom;

(b) prohibited or avoided by or under an enactment;

(c) a transfer to a deceased person; or

(d) where the participating issuer is constituted under the law of Scotland, prohibited by or under an arrestment.

(3) Notwithstanding that an Operator has received, in respect of a transfer of title to units of a participating security, actual notice of the kind referred to in paragraph (2), the Operator may register that transfer of title on the relevant Operator register of securities if at the time that he received the actual notice it was not practicable for him to halt the process of registration.

(4) Without prejudice to his rules, an Operator may refuse to register a transfer of title to units of a participating security in accordance with a system-member instruction or an issuer-instruction (as the case may be) if the instruction requires a transfer of units—

(a) to an entity which is not a natural or legal person;

(b) to a minor (which, in relation to a participating issuer constituted under the law of Scotland, shall mean a person under 16 years of age);

(c) to be held jointly in the names of more persons than is permitted under the terms of the issue of the security; or

(d) where, in relation to the system-member instruction or the issuer-instruction (as the case may be), the Operator has actual notice of any of the matters specified in regulation 35(5)(a)(i) to (iii).

(5) An Operator shall not register a transfer of title to uncertificated units of a security on an Operator register of securities otherwise than in accordance with paragraph (1) unless he is required to do so by order of a court in the United Kingdom or by or under an enactment.

(6) Paragraph (5) shall not be taken to prevent an Operator from entering on an Operator register of securities a person who is a system-member to whom title to uncertificated units of a security has been transmitted by operation of law.

(7) [Subject to paragraph (7A), immediately upon]—

(a) the registration by an Operator of the transfer of title to units of a participating security in accordance with—

(i) paragraph (1);

(ii) an order of a court in the United Kingdom; or

(iii) a requirement arising by or under an enactment; or

(b) the making or deletion by an Operator of an entry on an Operator register of securities—

(i) following the transmission of title to uncertificated units of a security by operation of law; or

(ii) upon the transfer of uncertificated units of a security to a person who is to hold them thereafter in certificated form, the Operator shall generate an Operator-instruction to inform the relevant participating issuer of the registration, or of the making or deletion of the entry (as the case may be); and where appropriate the participating issuer shall register the transfer or transmission of title to those units on an issuer register of securities in accordance with regulation 28.

[(7A) Paragraph (7) does not apply in relation to units of an eligible debt security.]

(8) Subsection (5) of section 183 of the 1985 Act shall apply in relation to a refusal by an Operator to register a transfer of securities in any of the circumstances specified in paragraphs (2) and (4), as it applies in relation to a refusal by a company to register a transfer of shares or debentures; and in that subsection as it so applies—

(a) the reference to the date on which the transfer was lodged with the company shall be taken to be a reference to the date on which the relevant system-member instruction or issuer-instruction (as the case may be) was received by the Operator; and

(b) the reference to a notice of the refusal shall be taken to be a reference to an Operator-instruction, or written notification from the Operator, informing the relevant system-member or participating issuer (as the case may be) of the refusal.

(9) Such sanctions as apply to a company and its officers in the event of a default in complying with subsection (5) of section 183 of the 1985 Act shall apply to an Operator and his officers in the event of a default in complying with that subsection as applied by paragraph (8).

[7027]

NOTES

Para (7): words in square brackets substituted by the Uncertificated Securities (Amendment) (Eligible Debt Securities) Regulations 2003, SI 2003/1633, reg 11(a), as from 24 June 2003.

Para (7A): added by SI 2003/1633, reg 11(b), as from 24 June 2003.

28 Registration by a participating issuer of transfers of securities upon conversion into certificated form

(1) Paragraphs (2) to (5) apply where relevant units of a security are transferred by means of a relevant system to a person who is to hold them thereafter in certificated form.

(2) Subject to paragraphs (3) and (4), a participating issuer shall (where appropriate) register a transfer of title to relevant units of a security on an issuer register of securities in accordance with an Operator-instruction.

(3) A participating issuer shall refuse to register a transfer of title to relevant units of a security in accordance with an Operator-instruction if he has actual notice that the transfer is—

(a) prohibited by order of a court in the United Kingdom;

(b) prohibited or avoided by or under an enactment;

(c) a transfer to a deceased person; or

(d) where the participating issuer is constituted under the law of Scotland, prohibited by or under an arrestment.

(4) A participating issuer may refuse to register a transfer of title to relevant units of a security in accordance with an Operator-instruction if the instruction requires a transfer of units—

(a) to an entity which is not a natural or legal person;

(b) to a minor (which, in relation to a participating issuer constituted under the law of Scotland, shall mean a person under 16 years of age);

(c) to be held jointly in the names of more persons than is permitted under the terms of the issue of the security; or

(d) where, in relation to the Operator-instruction, the participating issuer has actual notice from the Operator of any of the matters specified in regulation 35(5)(a)(i) to (iii).

(5) A participating issuer shall notify the Operator by issuer-instruction whether he has registered a transfer in response to an Operator-instruction to do so.

(6) A participating issuer shall not register a transfer of title to relevant units of a security on an issuer register of securities unless he is required to do so—

(a) by an Operator-instruction;

(b) by an order of a court in the United Kingdom; or

(c) by or under an enactment.

(7) A unit of a security is a relevant unit for the purposes of this regulation if, immediately before the transfer in question, it was held by the transferor in uncertificated form.

(8) Subsection (5) of section 183 of the 1985 Act shall apply in relation to a refusal by a participating issuer to register under paragraph (2) a transfer of securities in any of the circumstances specified in paragraphs (3) and (4), as it applies in relation to a refusal by a company to register a transfer of shares or debentures; and in that subsection as it so applies the reference to the date on which the transfer was lodged with the company shall be taken to be a reference to the date on which the Operator-instruction was received by the participating issuer.

(9) Such sanctions as apply to a company and its officers in the event of a default in complying with subsection (5) of section 183 of the 1985 Act shall apply to a participating issuer and his officers in the event of a default in complying with that subsection as applied by paragraph (8).

[7028]

29 Registration to be in accordance with regulations 27 and 28

Any purported registration of a transfer of title to an uncertificated unit of a security other than in accordance with regulation 27 or 28 shall be of no effect.

[7029]

30 Registration of linked transfers

(1) Paragraph (2) applies where an Operator receives two or more system-member instructions requesting him to register two or more transfers of title to uncertificated units of a security, and it appears to the Operator—

(a) either—

(i) that there are fewer units of the security registered on an Operator register of securities in the name of a person identified in any of the system-member instructions as a transferor than the number of units to be transferred from him under those system-member instructions; or

(ii) that it has not been established in accordance with paragraph 21(1)(c) of Schedule 1, in relation to any of the transfers taken without regard to the other transfers, that a settlement bank has agreed to make a payment; and

(b) that registration of all of the transfers would result in each of the persons identified in the system-member instructions as a transferor having title to a number of uncertificated units of a security equal to or greater than nil; and

(c) that the combined effect of all the transfers taken together would result in paragraph 21(1)(c) of Schedule 1 being satisfied.

(2) Where this paragraph applies, the Operator may either—

(a) register the combined effect of all the transfers taken together; or

(b) register all the transfers simultaneously,

unless one or more of those transfers may not be registered by virtue of the fact that the Operator has actual notice of any of the circumstances specified in regulation 27(2), or is to be refused registration by virtue of regulation 27(4).

(3) Notwithstanding that an Operator has received, in respect of two or more such system-member instructions as are referred to in paragraph (1), actual notice of the kind referred to in paragraph (2), the Operator may register all the transfers in question or their combined effect if at the time that he received the actual notice it was not practicable for him to halt the process of registration.

[7030]

31 Position of a transferee prior to entry on an issuer register of securities

(1) Paragraph (2) applies when an Operator deletes an entry on an Operator register of securities in consequence of which—

(a) the Operator must generate an Operator-instruction in accordance with regulation 27(7); and

(b) by virtue of that instruction a participating issuer must register, on an issuer register of securities, a transfer of title to units of a participating security constituted under the law of England and Wales or Northern Ireland.

(2) Where this paragraph applies—

(a) subject to—

(i) subparagraph (b); and

(ii) any enactment or rule of law,

the transferor shall, notwithstanding the deletion of the entry in the Operator register of securities, retain title to the requisite number of units of the relevant participating security until the transferee is entered on the relevant issuer register of securities as the holder thereof; and

(b) the transferee shall acquire an equitable interest in the requisite number of units of that security.

(3) Paragraph (4) applies when an Operator deletes an entry on an Operator register of securities in consequence of which—

(a) the Operator must generate an Operator-instruction in accordance with regulation 27(7); and

(b) by virtue of that instruction a participating issuer must register, on an issuer register of securities, a transfer of title to units of a participating security constituted under the law of Scotland.

(4) Where this paragraph applies—

(a) subject to—

(i) subparagraph (b); and

(ii) any enactment or rule of law,

the transferor shall, notwithstanding the deletion of the entry in the Operator register of securities, retain title to the requisite number of units of the relevant participating security until the transferee is entered on the relevant issuer register of securities as the holder thereof; and

(b) the transferor shall hold the requisite number of units of that security on trust for the benefit of the transferee.

(5) The requisite number for the purposes of this regulation is the number of units which are to be specified in the Operator-instruction which the Operator must generate in accordance with regulation 27(7).

(6) This regulation has effect notwithstanding that the units to which the deletion of the entry in the Operator register of securities relates, or in which an interest arises by virtue of paragraph (2)(b) or (4)(b), or any of them, may be unascertained.

(7) In Scotland—

(a) this regulation has effect notwithstanding that the requirements relating to the creation of a trust under any enactment or rule of law have not been complied with; and

(b) as from the time the trust referred to in paragraph (4)(b) arises, any holder, or any holder thereafter, of a floating charge over any part of the property of the transferor shall be deemed to have received notice of the trust's existence and of the property to which it relates.

(8) Subject to paragraphs (6) and (7), this regulation shall not be construed as conferring a proprietary interest (whether of the kind referred to in paragraph (2)(b) or (4)(b), or of any other kind) in units of a security if the conferring of such an interest at the time specified in these Regulations would otherwise be void by or under any enactment or rule of law.

(9) In this regulation—

(a) "the transferee" means the person to be identified in the Operator-instruction as the transferee; and

(b) "the transferor" means the person to be identified in the Operator-instruction as the transferor.

[7031]

Conversions and New Issues

32 Conversion of securities into certificated form

(1) Except as provided in regulation 42, a unit of a participating security shall not be converted from uncertificated form into certificated form unless an Operator generates an Operator-instruction to notify the relevant participating issuer that a conversion event has occurred; and in this regulation such an Operator-instruction is referred to as a "rematerialisation notice".

(2) A conversion event occurs—

(a) where such a conversion is permitted by the Operator's conversion rules; or

(b) following receipt by an Operator of a system-member instruction requiring the conversion into certificated form of uncertificated units of a participating security registered in the name of the system-member; or

(c) following receipt by an Operator of written notification from a participating issuer which is a company requiring the conversion into certificated form of uncertificated units of a participating security, issued by that participating issuer and registered in the name of a system-member, and which contains a statement that the conversion is required to enable the participating issuer to deal with the units in question in accordance with provisions in that participating issuer's memorandum or articles or in the terms of issue of the units in question.

(3) An Operator—

(a) may generate a rematerialisation notice following a conversion event occurring in the circumstances specified in paragraph (2)(a);

(b) shall generate a rematerialisation notice following a conversion event occurring in the circumstances specified in paragraph (2)(b) unless the participation in the relevant system, by the system-member in whose name the uncertificated units in question are registered, has been suspended pursuant to the Operator's rules; and

(c) shall generate a rematerialisation notice following a conversion event occurring in the circumstances specified in paragraph (2)(c).

(4) On the generation of a rematerialisation notice, the Operator shall delete any entry in an Operator register of securities which shows the relevant system-member as the holder of the unit or units specified in the rematerialisation notice.

(5) On receipt of a rematerialisation notice, the participating issuer to whom the rematerialisation notice is addressed shall, where relevant, enter the name of the system-member on an issuer register of securities as the holder of the unit or units specified in the rematerialisation notice.

(6) During any period between the deletion of any entry in an Operator register of securities required to be made by paragraph (4) and the making of the entry in an issuer register of securities required to be made by paragraph (5)—

(a) the relevant system-member shall retain title to the units of the security specified in the rematerialisation notice notwithstanding the deletion of any entry in the Operator register of securities; and

(b) where those units are shares, the relevant system-member shall be deemed to continue to be a member of the company.

(7) Following—

(a) the making of an entry in an issuer register of securities in accordance with paragraph (5); or

(b) registration of a transfer of title to units of a security in accordance with regulation 28,

the relevant participating issuer shall, where the terms of issue of the security in question provide for a certificate to be issued, issue a certificate in respect of the units of the security to the relevant person.

(8) Subsection (1)(b) of section 185 of the 1985 Act shall apply in relation to the issue of a certificate by a participating issuer pursuant to paragraph (7) as it applies in relation to the completion and having ready for delivery by a company of share certificates, debentures or certificates of debenture stock; and in that subsection as it so applies the reference to the date on which a transfer is lodged with the company shall be a reference to the date on which the participating issuer receives the relevant rematerialisation notice in accordance with this regulation, or the relevant Operator-instruction in accordance with regulation 27(7).

(9) Such sanctions as apply to a company and its officers in the event of a default in complying with subsection (5) of section 183 of the 1985 Act shall apply—

(a) to an Operator and his officers in the event of a default in complying with paragraph (4); and

(b) to a participating issuer and his officers in the event of a default in complying with paragraph (5).

(10) Such sanctions as apply to a company and its officers in the event of a default in complying with subsection (1) of section 185 of the 1985 Act shall apply to a participating

issuer and his officers in the event of a default in complying with paragraph (7) in accordance with the requirements laid down in paragraph (8).

[7032]

33 Conversion of securities into uncertificated form

(1) A unit of a participating security shall not be converted from certificated form into uncertificated form unless the participating issuer notifies the Operator by means of an issuer-instruction that any of the circumstances specified in paragraph (2) have arisen; and in this regulation such an issuer-instruction is referred to as a "dematerialisation notice".

(2) The circumstances referred to in paragraph (1) are—

(a) where the unit of the participating security is held by a system-member, that the participating issuer has received—

(i) a request in writing from the system-member in the form required by the Operator's conversion rules that the unit be converted from certificated form to uncertificated form; and

(ii) subject to paragraph (4), the certificate relating to that unit; or

(b) where the unit of the participating security is to be registered on an Operator register of securities in the name of a system-member following a transfer of the unit to him, that the participating issuer—

(i) subject to paragraph (3), has received (by means of the Operator-system unless the Operator's conversion rules permit otherwise) a proper instrument of transfer in favour of the system-member relating to the unit to be transferred;

(ii) subject to paragraph (4), has received (by means of the Operator-system unless the Operator's conversion rules permit otherwise) the certificate relating to that unit; and

(iii) may accept by virtue of the Operator's conversion rules that the system-member to whom the unit is to be transferred wishes to hold it in uncertificated form.

(3) The requirement in paragraph (2)(b)(i) that the participating issuer shall have received an instrument of transfer relating to the unit of the participating security shall not apply in a case where for a transfer of a unit of that security no instrument of transfer is required.

(4) The requirements in paragraphs (2)(a)(ii) and (2)(b)(ii) that the participating issuer shall have received a certificate relating to the unit of the participating security shall not apply in a case where the system-member or transferor (as the case may be) does not have a certificate in respect of the unit to be converted into uncertificated form because no certificate has yet been issued to him or is due to be issued to him in accordance with the terms of issue of the relevant participating security.

(5) Subject to paragraphs (3) and (4), a participating issuer shall not give a dematerialisation notice except in the circumstances specified in paragraph (2).

(6) Upon giving a dematerialisation notice, a participating issuer shall delete any entry in any issuer register of securities which evidences title to the unit or units of the participating security in question.

(7) Following receipt of a dematerialisation notice, an Operator shall enter the name of the relevant system-member on an Operator register of securities as the holder of the relevant unit or units of the participating security in question, provided that this obligation shall be subject to regulation 27 if the notice was given in the circumstances specified in paragraph (2)(b).

(8) When a dematerialisation notice is given, the relevant system-member, or the transferor of the unit or units of the security in question, as the case may be, shall (without prejudice to any equitable interest which the transferee may have acquired in the unit or units in question)—

(a) retain title to the units of the security specified in the dematerialisation notice notwithstanding the deletion of any entry in any issuer register of securities required to be made by paragraph (6); and

(b) where those units are shares, be deemed to continue to be a member of the company.

(9) Where a dematerialisation notice is given in the circumstances specified in paragraph (2)(b), such title shall be retained, and (where appropriate) such membership shall

be deemed to continue, until the time at which the Operator enters the name of the relevant system-member on an Operator register of securities in accordance with paragraph (7).

(10) Within 2 months of receiving a dematerialisation notice, an Operator shall generate an Operator-instruction informing the participating issuer whether an entry has been made in an Operator register of securities in response to the dematerialisation notice.

(11) Such sanctions as apply to a company and its officers in the event of a default in complying with subsection (5) of section 183 of the 1985 Act shall apply—

(a) to a participating issuer and his officers in the event of a default in complying with paragraph (6); and

(b) to an Operator and his officers in the event of a default in complying with paragraph (7) or (10).

[7033]

34 New issues in uncertificated form

(1) For the purposes of an issue of units of a participating security, a participating issuer may require the Operator to enter the name of a person in an Operator register of securities as the holder of new units of that security in uncertificated form if, and only if, that person is a system-member; and provided that compliance with any such requirement shall be subject to the rules of the Operator.

(2) For the purposes of calculating the number of new units to which a system-member is entitled a participating issuer may treat a system-member's holdings of certificated and uncertificated units of a security as if they were separate holdings.

(3) A requirement made by a participating issuer under paragraph (1) may be made by means of an issuer-instruction and shall specify the names of the persons to be entered in the Operator register of securities as the holders of new uncertificated units of the security, and the number of such units to be issued to each of those persons.

(4) An Operator who receives a requirement made by a participating issuer under paragraph (1) shall notify the participating issuer, by Operator-instruction or in writing, if he has not entered the name of any one or more of the persons in question in the Operator register of securities as the holder of new units of the security.

[7034]

PART 4
DEMATERIALISED INSTRUCTIONS ETC

35 Properly authenticated dematerialised instructions, etc

(1) This regulation has effect for the purpose of determining the rights and obligations of persons to whom properly authenticated dematerialised instructions are attributable and of persons to whom properly authenticated dematerialised instructions are addressed, when such instructions relate to an uncertificated unit of a security, or relate to a right, benefit or privilege attaching to or arising from such a unit, or relate to the details of a holder of such a unit.

(2) Where a properly authenticated dematerialised instruction is expressed to have been sent on behalf of a person by a sponsoring system-participant or the Operator—

(a) the person on whose behalf the instruction is expressed to have been sent shall not be able to deny to the addressee—

(i) that the properly authenticated dematerialised instruction was sent with his authority; or

(ii) that the information contained in the properly authenticated dematerialised instruction is correct; and

(b) the sponsoring system-participant or the Operator (as the case may be) shall not be able to deny to the addressee—

(i) that he has authority to send the properly authenticated dematerialised instruction; or

(ii) that he has sent the properly authenticated dematerialised instruction.

(3) Where a properly authenticated dematerialised instruction is expressed to have been sent by a person, and the properly authenticated dematerialised instruction is not expressed to have been sent on behalf of another person, the person shall not be able to deny to the addressee—

(a) that the information contained in the properly authenticated dematerialised instruction is correct; or

(b) that he has sent the properly authenticated dematerialised instruction.

(4) An addressee who receives (whether directly, or by means of the facilities of a sponsoring system-participant acting on his behalf) a properly authenticated dematerialised instruction may, subject to paragraph (5), accept that at the time at which the properly authenticated dematerialised instruction was sent or at any time thereafter—

(a) the information contained in the instruction was correct;

(b) the system-participant or the Operator (as the case may be) identified in the instruction as having sent the instruction sent the instruction; and

(c) the instruction, where relevant, was sent with the authority of the person on whose behalf it is expressed to have been sent.

(5) Subject to paragraph (6), an addressee may not accept any of the matters specified in paragraph (4) if at the time he received the properly authenticated dematerialised instruction or at any time thereafter—

(a) he was a person other than a participating issuer or a sponsoring system-participant receiving properly authenticated dematerialised instructions on behalf of a participating issuer, and he had actual notice—

(i) that any information contained in it was incorrect;

(ii) that the system-participant or the Operator (as the case may be) expressed to have sent the instruction did not send the instruction; or

(iii) where relevant, that the person on whose behalf it was expressed to have been sent had not given to the Operator or the sponsoring system-participant (as the case may be), identified in the properly authenticated dematerialised instruction as having sent it, his authority to send the properly authenticated dematerialised instruction on his behalf; or

(b) he was a participating issuer, or a sponsoring system-participant receiving properly authenticated dematerialised instructions on behalf of a participating issuer, and—

(i) he had actual notice from the Operator of any of the matters specified in subparagraph (a)(i) to (iii); or

(ii) if the instruction was an Operator-instruction requiring the registration of a transfer of title, he had actual notice of any of the circumstances specified in regulation 28(3); or

(c) he was an Operator and the instruction related to a transfer of units of a security which was in excess of any limit imposed by virtue of paragraph 15 of Schedule 1; or

(d) he was an Operator and he had actual notice of any of the circumstances specified in regulation 27(2) in a case where the instruction was—

(i) a system-member instruction requesting him to settle a transfer in accordance with his rules; or

(ii) an issuer-instruction given in the circumstances specified in regulation 33(2)(b) requesting him to register a transfer of title.

(6) Notwithstanding that an addressee has received, in respect of a properly authenticated dematerialised instruction, actual notice of the kind referred to in paragraph (5), the addressee may accept the matters specified in paragraph (4) if at the time that he received the actual notice it was not practicable for him to halt the processing of the instruction.

(7) Subject to paragraph (8), this regulation has effect without prejudice to the liability of any person for causing or permitting a dematerialised instruction—

(a) to be sent without authority; or

(b) to contain information which is incorrect; or

(c) to be expressed to have been sent by a person who did not send it.

(8) Subject to paragraph (9), a person who is permitted by this regulation to accept any matter shall not be liable in damages or otherwise to any person by reason of his having relied on the matter that he was permitted to accept.

(9) The provisions of paragraph (8) do not affect—

(a) any liability of the Operator to pay compensation under regulation 36; or

(b) any liability of a participating issuer under regulation 46 arising by reason of a default in complying with, or contravention of, regulation 28(6).

(10) For the purposes of this regulation—

(a) a properly authenticated dematerialised instruction is expressed to have been sent by a person or on behalf of a person if it is attributable to that person; and

(b) an addressee is the person to whom a properly authenticated dematerialised instruction indicates it is addressed in accordance with the rules and specifications referred to in paragraph 5(5) of Schedule 1.

(11) Nothing in this regulation shall be taken, in respect of any authority, to modify or derogate from the protections to a donee or third person given by or under any enactment or to prohibit a donee or third person so protected from accepting any of the matters specified in paragraph (4).

(12) Paragraphs (2) to (4), (5)(a), (6) to (9) and (11) of this regulation shall apply in relation to a written notification given under regulation 25(3) or 32(2)(c) as if—

(a) each reference to a properly authenticated dematerialised instruction were to such a notification which has been authenticated by the Operator in accordance with rules made and practices instituted by the Operator in order to comply with paragraph 25(g) of Schedule 1;

(b) each reference to information contained in the properly authenticated dematerialised instruction being correct (or incorrect) included, in the case of written notification given under subparagraph (c) of regulation 32(2), a reference to any statement of the sort referred to in that subparagraph being true (or untrue, as the case may be);

(c) each reference to an addressee were a reference to the Operator; and

(d) the reference in paragraph (6) to the processing of the instruction were to acting on the written notification.

[7035]

36 Liability for forged dematerialised instructions, induced amendments to Operator registers of securities, and induced Operator-instructions

(1) For the purpose of this regulation—

(a) a dematerialised instruction is a forged dematerialised instruction if—

(i) it was not sent from the computers of a system-participant or the computers comprising an Operator-system; or

(ii) it was not sent from the computers of the system-participant or the computers comprising an Operator-system (as the case may be) from which it is expressed to have been sent;

(b) an act is a causative act if, not being a dematerialised instruction and not being an act which causes a dematerialised instruction to be sent from the computer of a system-participant, it unlawfully causes the Operator—

(i) to make, delete or amend an entry on an Operator register of securities; or

(ii) to send an Operator-instruction to a participating issuer;

(c) an entry on, deletion from, or amendment to an Operator register of securities is an induced amendment if it is an entry on, deletion from, or amendment to an Operator register of securities which results from a causative act or a forged dematerialised instruction; and

(d) an Operator-instruction is an induced Operator-instruction if it is an Operator-instruction to a participating issuer which results from a causative act or a forged dematerialised instruction.

(2) If, as a result of a forged dematerialised instruction (not being one which results in an induced amendment to an Operator register of securities or an induced Operator-instruction), an induced amendment to an Operator register of securities, or an induced Operator-instruction, any one or more of the following events occurs—

(a) the name of any person remains on, is entered on, or is removed or omitted from, a register of securities;

(b) the number of units of a security in relation to which the name of any person is entered on a register of securities is increased, reduced, or remains unaltered;

(c) the description of any units of a security in relation to which the name of any person is entered on a register of securities is changed or remains unaltered,

and that person suffers loss as a result, he may apply to the court for an order that the Operator compensate him for his loss.

(3) It is immaterial for the purposes of subparagraphs (a) to (c) of paragraph (2) whether the event is permanent or temporary.

(4) The court shall not make an order under paragraph (2)—

(a) if the Operator identifies a person as being responsible (whether alone or with others) for the forged dematerialised instruction (not being one which results in an induced amendment to an Operator register of securities or an induced Operator-instruction) or the causative act or forged dematerialised instruction resulting in the induced amendment to the Operator register of securities or the induced Operator-instruction (as the case may be) notwithstanding that it is impossible (for whatever reason) for the applicant to obtain satisfactory compensation from that person; or

(b) if the Operator shows that a participating issuer would be liable under regulation 46 to compensate the applicant for the loss in respect of which the application is made, by reason of the participating issuer's default in complying with, or contravention of, regulation 28(6).

(5) Subject to paragraphs (6) and (7), the court may award to an applicant compensation for—

(a) each forged dematerialised instruction (not being one which results in an induced amendment to an Operator register of securities or an induced Operator-instruction);

(b) each induced amendment to an Operator register of securities; and

(c) each induced Operator-instruction,

resulting in an event mentioned in subparagraph (a), (b) or (c) of paragraph (2).

(6) The court shall not under paragraph (5) award to an applicant—

(a) more than £50,000 for each such forged dematerialised instruction, induced amendment to an Operator register of securities, or induced Operator-instruction;

(b) compensation for both an induced amendment to an Operator register of securities and an induced Operator-instruction if that induced amendment and that induced Operator-instruction resulted from the same causative act or the same forged dematerialised instruction.

(7) In respect of liability arising under this regulation the court shall—

(a) in awarding compensation only order the Operator to pay such amount of compensation as it appears to it to be just and equitable in all the circumstances having regard to the loss sustained by the applicant as a result of the forged dematerialised instruction, induced amendment to the Operator register of securities, or induced Operator-instruction;

(b) in ascertaining the loss, apply the same rules concerning the duty of a person to mitigate his loss as apply to damages recoverable under the common law of England and Wales, Northern Ireland, or Scotland, (as the case may be); and

(c) where it finds that the loss was to any extent caused or contributed to by any act or omission of the applicant, reduce the amount of the award by such proportion as it thinks just and equitable having regard to that finding.

(8) An application to the court for an order under paragraph (2) shall not prejudice any right of the Operator to recover from a third party any sum that he may be ordered to pay.

(9) An event mentioned in subparagraph (a), (b) or (c) of paragraph (2) shall not give rise to any liability on the Operator other than such as is expressly provided for in this regulation, except such as may arise from fraud or other wilful default, or negligence, on the part of the Operator.

(10) Subject to paragraph (9), this regulation does not affect—

(a) any right which any person may have other than under this regulation (not being a right against the Operator); or

(b) any liability which any person other than the Operator may incur other than under this regulation.

(11) Where an application is made under paragraph (2), and the Operator receives from the applicant a request for information or documents relating to—

(a) a forged dematerialised instruction;

(b) an induced amendment to an Operator register of securities; or

(c) an induced Operator-instruction,

in respect of which the application is made, the Operator shall, in so far as he is able, and in so far as the request is reasonable, within one month give the applicant the information and documents.

(12) The applicant shall, in so far as he is able, within one month give the Operator such information or documents as the Operator reasonably requests in connection with an application under paragraph (2) with respect to—

(a) steps taken by the applicant to prevent the giving of any forged dematerialised instruction (whether of the kind referred to in paragraph (2) or of any other kind); and

(b) steps taken by the applicant to mitigate the loss suffered by him,

provided that the applicant need not give information or documents pursuant to this paragraph until the Operator has complied with any request made by virtue of paragraph (11).

(13) Neither the Operator nor the applicant shall be required to disclose any information by virtue of, respectively, paragraph (11) or (12) which would be privileged in the course of civil proceedings, or, in Scotland, which they would be entitled to refuse to disclose—

(a) on grounds of confidentiality as between client and professional legal adviser in proceedings in the Court of Session; or

(b) on grounds of confidentiality of communications made in connection with, or in contemplation of, such proceedings and for the purposes of those proceedings.

(14) The jurisdiction conferred by this regulation shall be exercisable, in the case of a participating security constituted under the law of England and Wales, or Northern Ireland, by the High Court; and in the case of a participating security constituted under the law of Scotland by the Court of Session.

[7036]

PART 5
MISCELLANEOUS AND SUPPLEMENTAL

Miscellaneous

37 Construction of references to transfers etc

References in any enactment or rule of law to a proper instrument of transfer or to a transfer with respect to securities, or any expression having like meaning, shall be taken to include a reference to an Operator-instruction to a participating issuer to register a transfer of title on the relevant issuer register of securities in accordance with the Operator-instruction.

[7037]

38 Certain formalities and requirements not to apply

(1) Any requirements in an enactment or rule of law which apply in respect of the transfer of securities otherwise than by means of a relevant system shall not prevent—

(a) an Operator from registering a transfer of title to uncertificated units of a security upon settlement of a transfer of such units in accordance with his rules; or

(b) an Operator-instruction from requiring a participating issuer to register a transfer of title to uncertificated units of a security.

(2) Subject to regulation 32(7), notwithstanding any enactment, instrument or rule of law, a participating issuer shall not issue a certificate in relation to any uncertificated units of a participating security.

(3) A document issued by or on behalf of a participating issuer purportedly evidencing title to an uncertificated unit of a participating security shall not be evidence of title to the unit of the security; and in particular—

(a) section 186 of the 1985 Act shall not apply to any document issued with respect to uncertificated shares; and

(b) [regulation 9(3) of the 2004 Regulations] and regulation 6(3) of the 1974 Regulations shall not apply to any document issued with respect to uncertificated units of a public sector security.

(4) Any requirement in or under any enactment to endorse any statement or information on a certificate evidencing title to a unit of a security—

(a) shall not prohibit the conversion into, or issue of, units of the security in uncertificated form; and

(b) in relation to uncertificated units of the security, shall be taken to be a requirement for the relevant participating issuer to provide the holder of the units with the statement or information on request by him.

(5) Sections 53(1)(c) and 136 of the Law of Property Act 1925 (which impose requirements for certain dispositions and assignments to be in writing) shall not apply (if they would otherwise do so) to—

(a) any transfer of title to uncertificated units of a security by means of a relevant system; and

(b) any disposition or assignment of an interest in uncertificated units of a security title to which is held by a relevant nominee.

(6) In paragraph (5) "relevant nominee" means a subsidiary undertaking of an Operator designated by him as a relevant nominee in accordance with such rules and practices as are mentioned in paragraph 25(f) of Schedule 1.

(7) Subsection (4) of section 183 of the 1985 Act shall not apply in relation to the transfer of uncertificated units of a security by means of a relevant system.

[7038]

NOTES

Para (3): words in square brackets substituted by the Government Stock (Consequential and Transitional Provision) (No 2) Order 2004, SI 2004/1662, art 2, Schedule, Pt 3, para 29(1), (4), as from 1 July 2004.

39 Fees charged by Operators

(1) Subject to paragraph (2), nothing in these Regulations prevents an Operator from charging a fee for carrying out any function under Part 3 of these Regulations.

(2) An Operator may not charge a fee to a participating issuer for maintaining or keeping and entering up an Operator register of securities.

[7039]

40 Trusts, trustees and personal representatives etc

(1) Unless expressly prohibited from transferring units of a security by means of any computer-based system, a trustee or personal representative shall not be chargeable with a breach of trust or, as the case may be, with default in administering the estate by reason only of the fact that—

(a) for the purpose of acquiring units of a security which he has the power to acquire in connection with the trust or estate, he has paid for the units under arrangements which provide for them to be transferred to him from a system-member but not to be so transferred until after the payment of the price;

(b) for the purpose of disposing of units of a security which he has power to dispose of in connection with the trust or estate, he has transferred the units to a system-member under arrangements which provide that the price is not to be paid to him until after the transfer is made; or

(c) for the purpose of holding units of a security belonging to the trust or estate in uncertificated form and for transferring title to them by means of a relevant system, he has become a system-member.

(2) Notwithstanding section 192 of the 1985 Act, a trustee of a trust deed for securing an issue of debentures shall not be chargeable with a breach of trust by reason only of the fact that he has assented to an amendment of the trust deed only for the purposes of—

(a) allowing the holding of debentures in uncertificated form;

(b) allowing the exercise of rights attaching to the debentures by means of a relevant system; or

(c) allowing the transfer of title to the debentures by means of a relevant system, provided that he has given or caused to be given notice of the amendment in accordance with the trust deed not less than 30 days prior to its becoming effective to all persons registered as holding the debentures on a date not more than 21 days before the dispatch of the notice.

(3) Without prejudice to regulation 23(3) or section 360 of the 1985 Act, the Operator shall not be bound by or compelled to recognise any express, implied or constructive trust or other interest in respect of uncertificated units of a security, even if he has actual or constructive notice of the said trust or interest.

(4) Paragraph (3) shall not prevent, in the case of a participating issuer constituted under the law of Scotland, an Operator giving notice of a trust to the participating issuer on behalf of a system-member.

[7040]

41 Notices of meetings etc

(1) For the purposes of determining which persons are entitled to attend or vote at a meeting, and how many votes such persons may cast, the participating issuer may specify in the notice of the meeting a time, not more than 48 hours before the time fixed for the meeting, by which a person must be entered on the relevant register of securities in order to have the right to attend or vote at the meeting.

(2) Changes to entries on the relevant register of securities after the time specified by virtue of paragraph (1) shall be disregarded in determining the rights of any person to attend or vote at the meeting, notwithstanding any provisions in any enactment, articles of association or other instrument to the contrary.

(3) For the purposes of—

(a) serving notices of meetings, whether under section 370(2) of the 1985 Act, any other enactment, a provision in the articles of association or any other instrument; or

(b) sending copies of the documents required to be sent to any person by section 238 of the 1985 Act,

a participating issuer may determine that persons entitled to receive such notices, or copies of such documents (as the case may be), are those persons entered on the relevant register of securities at the close of business on a day determined by him.

(4) The day determined by a participating issuer under paragraph (3) may not be more than 21 days before the day that the notices of the meeting, or the copies of the documents as the case may be, are sent.

(5) This regulation is without prejudice to the protection afforded—

(a) by paragraph 5(3) of Schedule 4, to a participating issuer which is a company; and

(b) by paragraph 13(4) or 15(3) of Schedule 4, to a participating issuer.

[7041]

42 Notices to minority shareholders

(1) Paragraphs (2) to (4) shall apply in relation to any uncertificated units of a security (other than a wholly dematerialised security) to which a notice given under [section 979 of the Companies Act 2006] relates, in place of the provisions of [section 981(7)] of that Act.

(2) Immediately on receipt of a copy sent under [section 981(6)(a) of the Companies Act 2006] of a notice given under [section 979] relating to uncertificated units of a participating security (whether or not it also relates to certificated units of the security), a company which is a participating issuer shall—

(a) by issuer-instruction—

(i) inform the Operator that the copy notice has been received, and

(ii) identify the holding of uncertificated units of the participating security to which the notice relates; and

(b) enter the name of the relevant system-member on an issuer register of securities as the holder of those uncertificated units.

(3) On receipt of an issuer-instruction under paragraph (2)(a), the Operator shall delete any entry in an Operator register of securities which shows the relevant system-member as the holder of the uncertificated units of the participating security to which the notice relates.

(4) On registration on an issuer register of securities (in accordance with paragraph (2)(b)) of the relevant system-member as the holder of the uncertificated units of the participating security to which the notice relates, the participating issuer—

(a) shall be under the same obligation to enter the offeror on that register as the holder of those units, in place of the relevant system-member, as it would be if it had received an Operator-instruction under regulation 28(2) requiring it to register a transfer of title to those units in that manner; and regulation 28(9) shall have effect accordingly; and

(b) where the terms of issue of the security in question provide for a certificate to be issued, shall issue to the offeror a certificate in respect of those units.

(5) Subsection (1)(b) of section 185 of the 1985 Act shall apply in relation to the issue of a certificate by a participating issuer pursuant to paragraph (4)(b) as it applies in relation to the completion and having ready for delivery by a company of share certificates, debentures or certificates of debenture stock; and in that subsection as it so applies the reference to the

date on which a transfer is lodged with the company shall be a reference to the date on which the participating issuer receives the copy notice sent under [section 981(6)(a) of the Companies Act 2006].

(6) Such sanctions as apply to a company and its officers in the event of a default in complying with subsection (1) of section 185 of the 1985 Act shall apply to a participating issuer and his officers in the event of a default in complying with paragraph (4)(b) in accordance with the requirements laid down in paragraph (5).

(7) Paragraphs (8) to (11) shall apply in relation to any units of a wholly dematerialised security to which a notice given under [section 979 of the Companies Act 2006] relates, in place of the provisions of [section 981(7)] of that Act.

(8) Immediately on receipt of a copy sent under [section 981(6)(a) of the Companies Act 2006] of a notice given under [section 979] relating to units of a wholly dematerialised security, a company which is a participating issuer shall—

(a) by issuer-instruction—
   (i) inform the Operator that the copy notice has been received; and
   (ii) identify the holding of units of the wholly dematerialised security to which the notice relates; and

(b) by a further issuer-instruction, inform the Operator of the name of the transferee.

(9) On receipt of an issuer-instruction under paragraph (8)(a), the Operator shall delete any entry in an Operator register of securities which shows the relevant system-member as the holder of the units to which the notice relates.

(10) On receipt of an issuer-instruction under paragraph (8)(b), the Operator shall enter the transferee on the relevant Operator register of securities as the holder of the units to which the notice relates, in place of the relevant system-member.

(11) Where an Operator deletes an entry in an Operator register of securities pursuant to paragraph (9)—

(a) the units of the wholly dematerialised security to which the notice relates shall notwithstanding that deletion, continue to be regarded as uncertificated units for the purposes of these Regulations until the Operator enters the transferee on the relevant Operator register of securities as the holder of those units;

(b) subject to—
   (i) subparagraph (c) or (d), as the case may be; and
   (ii) any enactment or rule of law,

the relevant system-member shall, notwithstanding that deletion, retain title to the units of the wholly dematerialised security to which the notice relates until the transferee is entered on the relevant Operator register of securities pursuant to paragraph (10);

(c) in the case of a security constituted under the law of England and Wales or Northern Ireland, the transferee shall acquire an equitable interest in the units of the wholly dematerialised security to which the notice relates;

(d) in the case of a security constituted under the law of Scotland, the relevant system-member shall hold the units of the wholly dematerialised security to which the notice relates on trust for the benefit of the transferee.

(12) Such sanctions as apply to a company and its officers in the event of a default in complying with subsection (5) of section 183 of the 1985 Act shall apply—

(a) to a participating issuer and his officers in the event of a default in complying with paragraph (2)(b) or (8); and

(b) to an Operator and his officers in the event of a default in complying with paragraph (3), (9) or (10).

(13) For the purposes of this regulation—

(a) "offeror" has the meaning [in section 991(1) of the Companies Act 2006;]

(b) "relevant system-member" means the system-member identified in the copy notice sent under [section 981(6)(a) of the Companies Act 2006] as the holder of the uncertificated units, or as the case may be the units of the wholly dematerialised security, to which the notice relates; and

(c) "transferee" means the offeror or, if the offeror is not a system-member, the system-member in whose name the units of the wholly dematerialised security to which the notice given under [section 979 of the Companies Act 2006] relates are to be registered on the Operator register of securities.

(14) The reference in [section 987(8) of the Companies Act 2006 to section 981(7)] shall be taken to include a reference to the provisions of paragraphs (4), (8) and (9).

[7042]

NOTES

Paras (1), (2), (5), (7), (8), (13), (14): words in square brackets substituted by the Companies Act 2006 (Commencement No 2, Consequential Amendments, Transitional Provisions and Savings) Order 2007, SI 2007/1093, art 6(1), Sch 3, para 9, as from 6 April 2007.

43 Irrevocable powers of attorney

(1) This regulation applies where the terms of an offer for all or any uncertificated units of a participating security provide that a person accepting the offer creates an irrevocable power of attorney in favour of the offeror, or a person nominated by the offeror, in the terms set out in the offer.

(2) An acceptance communicated by properly authenticated dematerialised instruction in respect of uncertificated units of a security shall constitute a grant of an irrevocable power of attorney by the system-member accepting the offer in favour of the offeror, or person nominated by the offeror, in the terms set out in the offer.

(3) Where the contract constituted by such offer and acceptance as are referred to in paragraphs (1) and (2) respectively is governed by the law of England and Wales, section 4 of the Powers of Attorney Act 1971 shall apply to a power of attorney constituted in accordance with this regulation.

(4) A declaration in writing by the offeror stating the terms of a power of attorney and that it has been granted by virtue of this regulation and stating the name and address of the grantor shall be prima facie evidence, and in Scotland sufficient evidence unless the contrary is shown, of the grant; and any requirement in any enactment, rule of law, or instrument to produce a copy of the power of attorney, or such a copy certified in a particular manner, shall be satisfied by the production of the declaration or a copy of the declaration certified in that manner.

(5) In the application of this regulation to an offer, acceptance or contract governed by the law of Scotland, any reference to an irrevocable power of attorney shall mean and include reference to an irrevocable mandate, however expressed.

[7043]

44 Actual notice

For the purpose of determining under these Regulations whether a person has actual notice of a fact, matter or thing that person shall not under any circumstances be taken to be concerned to establish whether or not it exists or has occurred.

[7044]

45 Participating securities issued in uncertificated form

Nothing in these Regulations shall require—

(a) a participating issuer or its officers to maintain a register which records how many units of a wholly dematerialised security are held in certificated form; or

(b) an Operator or participating issuer, or their officers, to take any action to change a unit of a wholly dematerialised security from uncertificated form to certificated form or vice versa.

[7045]

Defaults and Contraventions

46 Breaches of statutory duty

(1) A default in complying with, or a contravention of, regulation 16(8), 19(2), 25(1), 26, 28(5) or (6), 32(5), 33(5), or 42(2) or (8) shall be actionable at the suit of a person who suffers loss as a result of the default or contravention, or who is otherwise adversely affected by it, subject to the defences and other incidents applying to actions for breach of statutory duty.

(2) Paragraph (1) shall not affect the liability which any person may incur, nor affect any right which any person may have, apart from paragraph (1).

[7046]

47 Liability of officers for contraventions

(1) In regulation 16(7), 20(7), 21(5), 22(5), 28(9), 32(9) or (10), 33(11) or 42(6) or (12) an officer of a participating issuer shall be in default in complying with, or in contravention of, the provision mentioned in that regulation if, and only if, he knowingly and wilfully authorised or permitted the default or contravention.

(2) In regulation 20(7), 21(4), 22(4), 27(9), 32(9), 33(11) or 42(12) an officer of an Operator shall be in default in complying with, or in contravention of, the provision mentioned in that regulation if, and only if, he knowingly and wilfully authorised or permitted the default or contravention.

[7047]

48 Exemption from liability

Regulations 21(5), 28(9), 32(9) and (10), and 33(11) shall not apply to any of the following or its officers—

(a) the Crown;
(b) any person acting on behalf of the Crown;
[(c) the Bank of England;
(d) the Registrar of Government Stock;
(e) any previous Registrar of Government Stock; or
(f) in respect of a security which immediately before it became a participating security was transferable by exempt transfer within the meaning of the Stock Transfer Act 1982, a participating issuer].

[7048]

NOTES

Paras (c)–(f) substituted, for original paras (c), (d), by the Government Stock (Consequential and Transitional Provision) (No 2) Order 2004, SI 2004/1662, art 2, Schedule, Pt 3, para 29(1), (5), as from 1 July 2004.

Northern Ireland

49 Application to Northern Ireland

(1) In their application to Northern Ireland, these Regulations shall have effect with the following modifications.

(2) In regulation 38(5)—

(a) for the reference to section 53(1)(c) of the Law of Property Act 1925 there shall be substituted a reference to section 6 of the Statute of Frauds (Ireland) 1695; and
(b) for the reference to section 136 of the Law of Property Act 1925 there shall be substituted a reference to section 87 of the Judicature (Northern Ireland) Act 1978.

(3) In regulation 43(3) for the reference to section 4 of the Powers of Attorney Act 1971 there shall be substituted a reference to section 3 of the Powers of Attorney Act (Northern Ireland) 1971.

(4) In Schedule 4—

(a) for references to the registrar of companies there shall be substituted references to the registrar of companies appointed under Article 653 of the 1986 Order;
(b) for references to an overseas branch register there shall be substituted references to an external branch register within the meaning of Article 370 of the 1986 Order;
(c) in paragraph 6(1), for the words from "in the case of a company registered in England and Wales" to the end there shall be substituted "elsewhere than in Northern Ireland";
(d) in paragraphs 9 and 15(5), for the words from "and references to the 1985 Act" to the end there shall be substituted "and references to the 1986 Order in the Companies (Inspection and Copying of Registers, Indices and Documents) Regulations (Northern Ireland) 1993 shall be construed accordingly";
(e) in paragraph 16(2), for subparagraphs (a) and (b) there shall be substituted "in Northern Ireland"; and
(f) in paragraph 18(a), for the reference to the Companies Acts there shall be substituted a reference to the Companies Orders within the meaning of Article 2(3) of the 1986 Order.

(5) For references to provisions of the 1985 Act there shall be substituted references to the equivalent provisions of the 1986 Order and, in particular, for the references to the 1985 Act listed in column 1 of Schedule 5, in the provisions of these Regulations listed in column 2 of that Schedule, there shall be substituted the references to the 1986 Order listed in column 3 of that Schedule.

[7049]

Transitory Provisions, Amendments and Revocations

50 Transitory provisions

Schedule 6 (transitory provisions) shall have effect.

[7050]

51 Minor and consequential amendments

Schedule 7 (minor and consequential amendments) shall have effect.

[7051]

52 *(Revokes the Government Stock Regulations 1965, SI 1965/1420, regs 4(3), (4), 4A, 4B, 6(5), 17(7), 18(5), 19(2), 20(2), Sch 1, the Local Authority (Stocks and Bonds) Regulations 1974, SI 1974/519, reg 6(6), 6A, 7(1)(b), (4), (5), 8(2), (3), 9(4), 10(3), 16(4), 21(3), Sch 2, the Uncertificated Securities Regulations 1995, SI 1995/3272, the Open-Ended Investment Companies Regulations 2001, SI 2001/1228, reg 47(1), Sch 3, paras 2(2), 5(1)(c), 6(3)(d), Sch 4, para 3, Sch 7, para 12.)*

SCHEDULES

SCHEDULE 1
REQUIREMENTS FOR APPROVAL OF A PERSON AS OPERATOR

Regulation 5(1)

Arrangements and resources

1. An Operator must have adequate arrangements and resources for the effective monitoring and enforcement of compliance with his rules or, as respects monitoring, arrangements providing for that function to be performed on his behalf (and without affecting his responsibility) by another body or person who is able and willing to perform it.

Financial resources

2. An Operator must have financial resources sufficient for the proper performance of his functions as an Operator.

Promotion and maintenance of standards

3. An Operator must be able and willing to promote and maintain high standards of integrity and fair dealing in the operation of the relevant system and to cooperate, by the sharing of information or otherwise, with the Treasury and any other authority, body or person having responsibility for the supervision or regulation of investment business or other financial services.

Operation of the relevant system

4.—(1) Except in the circumstances referred to in subparagraph (2), where an Operator causes or permits a part of the relevant system which is not the Operator-system to be operated by another person (other than as his agent) the Operator—

(a) shall monitor compliance by the person and that part with the requirements of this Schedule; and

(b) shall have arrangements to ensure that the person provides him with such information and such assistance as he may require in order to meet his obligations under these Regulations.

(2) Where a part of the relevant system which is not the Operator-system comprises procedures which enable dematerialised instructions to be authenticated in accordance with paragraph 5(3)(b), the Operator shall have arrangements to ensure that he is provided with such information and such assistance as he may require in order to keep under review his agreement to the specifications by which those dematerialised instructions may be authenticated.

System security

5.—(1) A relevant system must be so constructed and operate in such a way that it satisfies the requirements of subparagraphs (2) to (6).

(2) The relevant system must minimise the possibility of unauthorised access to, or modification of, any program or data held in any computer forming part of the Operator-system.

(3) Each dematerialised instruction must be authenticated—

(a) in accordance with the specifications of the Operator, and those specifications shall provide that each dematerialised instruction—

(i) is identifiable as being from the computers of the Operator or of a particular system-participant; and

(ii) is designed to minimise fraud and forgery; or

(b) if it is sent to the Operator by, or by the Operator to, a depositary, a clearing house or an exchange, in accordance with specifications of that depositary, clearing house or exchange to which the Operator has agreed and which provide that each dematerialised instruction—

(i) is identifiable as being from the computers of the Operator or of the depositary, clearing house or exchange which sent it; and

(ii) is designed to minimise fraud and forgery.

(4) Each dematerialised instruction must, in accordance with any relevant rules of the Operator and with the specifications of the Operator or the specifications referred to in subparagraph (3)(b) (as the case may be), express by whom it has been sent and, where relevant, on whose behalf it has been sent.

(5) Each dematerialised instruction must, in accordance with any relevant rules of the Operator and with the specifications of the Operator or the specifications referred to in subparagraph (3)(b) (as the case may be), indicate—

(a) where it is sent to a system-participant or the Operator, that it is addressed to that system-participant or the Operator;

(b) where it is sent to a person who is using the facilities of a sponsoring system-participant to receive dematerialised instructions, that it is addressed to that person and the sponsoring system-participant; and

(c) where it is sent to the Operator in order for him to send an Operator-instruction to a system-participant, that it is addressed to the Operator, to the system-participant and, if the system-participant is acting as a sponsoring system-participant, to the relevant person on whose behalf the sponsoring system-participant receives dematerialised instructions; and

(6) The relevant system must minimise the possibility for a system-participant to send a dematerialised instruction on behalf of a person from whom he has no authority.

(7) For the purposes of this paragraph—

"clearing house" means a body or association—

(a) which is a recognised clearing house within section 285(1)(b) of the 2000 Act;

(b) which is authorised under that Act to provide clearing services in the United Kingdom; or

(c) which provides services outside the United Kingdom which are similar in nature to those provided by any such body or association, and which is regulated or supervised in the provision of those services by a regulatory body or agency of government;

"depositary" means a body or association carrying on business outside the United Kingdom with whom an Operator has made arrangements—

(a) to enable system-members to hold (whether directly or indirectly) and transfer title to securities (other than participating securities) by means of facilities provided by that body or association; or

(b) to enable that body or association to permit persons to whom it provides services in the course of its business to hold (whether directly or indirectly) and transfer title to participating securities by means of the Operator's relevant system; and

"exchange" means a body or association—

(a) which is a recognised investment exchange within section 285(1)(a) of the 2000 Act;

(b) which is authorised under that Act to provide a facility for the matching and execution of transactions in securities in the United Kingdom; or

(c) which provides services outside the United Kingdom which are similar in nature to those provided by any such body or association, and which is regulated or supervised in the provision of those services by a regulatory body or agency of government.

System capabilities

6. A relevant system must ensure that the Operator-system can send and respond to properly authenticated dematerialised instructions in sufficient volume and speed.

7. Before an Operator registers a transfer of title to uncertificated units of a security, a relevant system must be able to establish—

(a) that the transferor has title to such number of units of the security as is in aggregate at least equal to the number to be transferred; or

(b) that the transfer is one of two or more transfers which may be registered in accordance with regulation 30(2).

8. Before an Operator-instruction to a participating issuer to register a transfer of title to uncertificated units of a security is generated, a relevant system must be able to establish that the transferor has title to such number of units of the security as is in aggregate at least equal to the number to be transferred.

9. A relevant system must enable an Operator to comply with his obligations to keep all necessary Operator registers of securities in accordance with these Regulations.

10. A relevant system must maintain adequate records of all dematerialised instructions.

11. A relevant system must—

(a) enable each system-member to obtain a copy of any records relating to him as are maintained by the relevant system in order to comply with paragraph 7(a), 8 or 10; and

(b) be able to make correcting entries in such records as are maintained in order to comply with paragraph 7(a) or 8 which are inaccurate.

12. A relevant system must be able to permit each participating issuer to inspect the entries from time to time appearing in an Operator register of securities [(other than an Operator register of eligible debt securities)] relating to any participating security issued by him.

13. A relevant system must be able to establish, where there is a transfer of uncertificated units of a security to a system-member for value, that a settlement bank has agreed to make payment in respect of the transfer, whether alone or taken together with another transfer for value.

14. A relevant system must ensure that the Operator-system is able to generate Operator-instructions—

(a) requiring participating issuers to amend the appropriate issuer registers of securities kept by them;

(b) informing participating issuers in a way which enables them to amend the appropriate records of securities kept by them; and

(c) informing settlement banks of their payment obligations.

15. A relevant system must—

(a) enable a system-member—

(i) to grant authority to a sponsoring system-participant to send properly authenticated dematerialised instructions on his behalf; and

(ii) to limit such authority by reference to the net value of the units of the securities to be transferred in any one day; and

(b) prevent the transfer of units in excess of that limit.

16. For the purposes of paragraph 15(a)(ii), once authority is granted pursuant to a system charge (within the meaning of regulation 3 of the Financial Markets and Insolvency Regulations 1996) a limit of such authority shall not be imposed or changed without the consent of the donee of that authority.

17. Nothing in paragraph 15 or 16 shall be taken, in respect of an authority, to modify or derogate from the protections given by or under any enactment to a donee of the authority or a third person.

18. A relevant system must enable system-members—

(a) to change the form in which they hold units of a participating security; and

(b) where appropriate, to require participating issuers to issue certificates relating to units of a participating security held or to be held by them.

19. Paragraph 18 shall not apply to any wholly dematerialised security.

Operating procedures

20. A relevant system must comprise procedures which provide that it responds only to properly authenticated dematerialised instructions which are attributable to a system-user or an Operator.

21.—(1) Subject to subparagraphs (2) to (5), a relevant system must comprise procedures which provide that an Operator only registers a transfer of title to uncertificated units of a security or generates an Operator-instruction requiring a participating issuer to register such a transfer, and only generates an Operator-instruction informing a settlement bank of its payment obligations in respect of such a transfer, if—

(a) it has—

(i) received a system-member instruction which is attributable to the transferor; or

(ii) been required to do so by a court in the United Kingdom or by or under an enactment;

(b) it has—

(i) established that the transferor has title to such number of units as is in aggregate at least equal to the number to be transferred; or

(ii) established that the transfer is one of two or more transfers which may be registered in accordance with regulation 30(2);

(c) in the case of a transfer to a system-member for value, it has established that a settlement bank has agreed to make payment in respect of the transfer, whether alone or taken together with another transfer for value; and

(d) the transfer is not in excess of any limit which by virtue of paragraph 15(a)(ii) the transferor has set on an authority given by him to a sponsoring system-participant.

(2) Subparagraph (1)(a) shall not prevent the registration by an Operator of a transfer of title to uncertificated units of a security, or the generation of an Operator-instruction, in accordance with procedures agreed between the Operator and the transferor to enable the transfer by means of a relevant system of uncertificated units of a security provided that such transfer is for the purpose of, or relates to, facilitating the provision of financial credit or financial liquidity to the transferor by a settlement bank, the Bank of England, the European Central Bank, any other central bank, or any other body having functions as a monetary authority.

(3) A relevant system must comprise procedures which provide that—

(a) the Operator may amend an Operator register of securities; and

(b) an Operator-instruction requiring a participating issuer to register a transfer of uncertificated units of a security, or informing a settlement bank of its payment obligations in respect of such a transfer, may be generated,

if necessary to correct an error and if in accordance with the rules made and practices instituted by the Operator in order to comply with this Schedule.

(4) A relevant system must comprise procedures which provide that—

(a) the Operator may amend an Operator register of securities; and

(b) an Operator-instruction requiring a participating issuer to register a transfer of units of a wholly dematerialised security, or informing a settlement bank of its payment obligations in respect of such a transfer, may be generated,

if necessary to effect a transfer of such units, on the termination of participation in the relevant system by the system-member by whom those units are held and if in accordance with the rules made and practices instituted by the Operator in order to comply with this Schedule, to a person nominated under the Operator's rules.

(5) Subparagraph (1)(a) shall not prevent the registration by an Operator of a transfer of title to uncertificated units of a security, or the generation of an Operator-instruction, in order to give effect to the procedures referred to in subparagraph (3) or (4).

22.—(1) Subject to subparagraph (2), a relevant system must comprise procedures which provide that an Operator-instruction to a participating issuer relating to a right, privilege or benefit attaching to or arising from an uncertificated unit of a security, is generated only if it has—

(a) received a properly authenticated dematerialised instruction attributable to the system-member having the right, privilege or benefit requiring the Operator to generate an Operator-instruction to the participating issuer; or

(b) been required to do so by a court in the United Kingdom or by or under an enactment.

(2) A relevant system must comprise procedures which provide that an Operator-instruction to a participating issuer relating to a right, privilege or benefit attaching to or arising from an uncertificated unit of a security, may be generated if necessary to correct an error and if in accordance with the rules made and practices instituted by an Operator in order to comply with this Schedule.

23. A relevant system must comprise procedures which ensure that, where participating issuers keep records of securities, those records are regularly reconciled with the relevant Operator registers of securities.

24. A relevant system must comprise procedures which—

(a) enable system-users to notify the Operator of an error in or relating to a dematerialised instruction; and

(b) ensure that, where the Operator becomes aware of an error in or relating to a dematerialised instruction, he takes appropriate corrective action.

Rules and Practices

25. An Operator's rules and practices—

(a) must bind system-members and participating issuers—

(i) so as to ensure the efficient processing of transfers of title to uncertificated units of a security in response to Operator-instructions; and

(ii) as to the action to be taken where transfer of title in response to a system-member instruction or an Operator-instruction cannot be effected;

(b) must make provision as to the manner in which a system-member or the relevant participating issuer may change the form in which that system-member holds units of a participating security (other than a wholly dematerialised security);

(c) must make provision for a participating issuer to cease to participate in respect of a participating security so as—

(i) to minimise so far as practicable any disruption to system-members in respect of their ability to transfer the relevant security; and

(ii) to provide the participating issuer with any relevant information held by the Operator relating to the uncertificated units of the relevant security held by system-members;

(d) must make provision for the orderly termination of participation by system-members and system-participants whose participation is disruptive to other system-members or system-participants or to participating issuers;

(e) must make provision—

(i) as to which of the Operator's records are to constitute an Operator register of securities in relation to a participating security, or a participating security of a particular kind; and

(ii) as to the times at which, and the manner in which, a participating issuer may inspect an Operator register of securities [(other than an Operator register of eligible debt securities)] in accordance with paragraph 12;

(f) if they make provision for the designation of a subsidiary undertaking as a relevant nominee, must require that the relevant nominee maintain adequate records of—

(i) the names of the persons who have an interest in the securities it holds; and

(ii) the nature and extent of their interests; and

(g) must make provision for the authentication by the Operator of any written notification given under regulation 25(3) or 32(2)(c).

26. An Operator's rules and practices must require—

(a) that each system-participant is able to send and receive properly authenticated dematerialised instructions;

(b) that each system-member has arrangements—

(i) for properly authenticated dematerialised instructions attributable to him to be sent;

(ii) for properly authenticated dematerialised instructions to be received by or for him; and

(iii) with a settlement bank for payments to be made, where appropriate, for units of a security transferred by means of the relevant system; and

(c) that each participating issuer is able to respond with sufficient speed to Operator-instructions.

27. An Operator must have rules which require system-users and former system-users to provide him with such information in their possession as he may require in order to meet his obligations under these Regulations.

[Access to central counterparty, clearing and settlement facilities

28.—(1) The Operator must make transparent and non-discriminatory rules, based on objective criteria, governing access to his settlement facilities.

(2) The rules under sub-paragraph (1) must enable an investment firm or a credit institution authorised by the competent authority of another EEA State (including a branch established in the United Kingdom of such a firm or institution) to have access to those facilities on the same terms as a UK firm for the purposes of finalising or arranging the finalisation of transactions in financial instruments.

(3) The Operator may refuse access to those facilities on legitimate commercial grounds.

(4) In this paragraph—

"banking consolidation directive" means Directive 2006/48/EC of the European Parliament and of the Council of 14th June 2006 relating to the taking up and pursuit of the business of credit institutions;

"branch" in relation to an investment firm has the meaning given in Article 4.1.26 of the markets in financial instruments directive and in relation to a credit institution has the meaning given in Article 4.3 of the banking consolidation directive;

"competent authority", in relation to an investment firm or credit institution, means the competent authority in relation to that firm or institution for the purposes of the markets in financial instruments directive;

"credit institution" means—

(a) a credit institution authorised under the banking consolidation directive, or

(b) an institution which would satisfy the requirements for authorisation as a credit institution under that directive if it had its registered office (or if it does not have a registered office, its head office) in an EEA State;

"EEA State" has the meaning given by paragraph 8 of Schedule 3 to the 2000 Act;

"financial instrument" has the meaning given by Article 4.1.17 of the markets in financial instruments directive;

"investment firm" has the meaning given by section 424A of the 2000 Act;

"markets in financial instruments directive" means Directive 2004/39/EC of the European Parliament and of the Council of 21st April 2004 on markets in financial instruments;

"regulated activity" has the meaning given by section 22 of the 2000 Act;

"settlement" has the same meaning as in the markets in financial instruments directive;

"UK firm" means an investment firm or credit institution which has a permission given by the Authority under Part 4 of the 2000 Act (or having effect as if so given) to carry on one or more regulated activities.]

[7052]

NOTES

Paras 12, 25: words in square brackets inserted by the Uncertificated Securities (Amendment) (Eligible Debt Securities) Regulations 2003, SI 2003/1633, reg 12, as from 24 June 2003.

Para 28: added by the Uncertificated Securities (Amendment) Regulations 2007, SI 2007/124, reg 3, as from 1 November 2007.

SCHEDULE 2
PREVENTION OF RESTRICTIVE PRACTICES

Regulation 13

Examination of rules and practices

1.—(1) The Treasury shall not approve a person as Operator of a relevant system unless they are satisfied that the rules and any guidance of which copies are furnished with the application for approval—

(a) do not have, and are not intended or likely to have, to any significant extent the effect of restricting, distorting or preventing competition; or

(b) if they have or are intended to have that effect to any significant extent, that the effect is not greater than is necessary for the protection of investors, or for compliance with [Directive 2006/48/EC of the European Parliament and of the Council of 14 June 2006 relating to the taking up and pursuit of the business of credit institutions].

(2) Subject to subparagraph (5), the powers conferred by subparagraph (3) shall be exercisable by the Treasury if at any time it appears to them that—

(a) any rules made or guidance issued by an Operator;

(b) any practices of an Operator in his capacity as such; or

(c) any practices of a system-user,

have, or are intended or likely to have, to a significant extent the effect of restricting, distorting or preventing competition and that the effect is greater than is necessary for the protection of investors or for compliance with Directive 2000/12/EC of the European Parliament and of the Council.

(3) the powers exercisable under this paragraph are—

(a) to withdraw approval from the Operator;

(b) to direct the Operator to take specified steps for the purpose of securing that the rules, guidance or practices in question do not have the effect mentioned in subparagraph (2); or

(c) to make alterations in the rules of the Operator for that purpose.

(4) The practices referred to in subparagraph (2)(c) are practices in relation to business in respect of which system-users are subject to the rules of the Operator and which are required or contemplated by his rules or guidance or otherwise attributable to his conduct in his capacity as Operator.

(5) The provisions of Schedule 3 shall apply as regards the procedure to be followed before—

(a) refusing to approve a person as Operator of a relevant system pursuant to subparagraph (1); or

(b) exercising any of the powers conferred by subparagraph (3).

Modification of paragraph 1 where delegation order is made

2.—(1) This paragraph applies instead of paragraph 1 where the function of approving a person as Operator has been delegated to the designated agency by virtue of regulation 11.

(2) The designated agency—

(a) shall send to the Treasury a copy of the rules and any guidance copies of which accompany the application for approval together with any other information supplied with or in connection with the application; and

(b) shall not grant the approval without the leave of the Treasury,

and the Treasury shall not give leave in any case in which they would (apart from the delegation of functions to the designated agency) have been precluded by paragraph 1(1) from granting approval.

(3) The designated agency shall send to the Treasury a copy of any notice received by it from an Operator under regulation 10(5).

(4) If at any time it appears to the Treasury that there are circumstances such that (apart from the delegation of functions to the designated agency) they would have been able to exercise any of the powers conferred by paragraph 1(3) they may, notwithstanding the delegation of functions to the designated agency but subject to paragraph 1(5)—

(a) themselves exercise the power conferred by paragraph 1(3)(a); or

(b) direct the designated agency to exercise the power conferred by paragraph 1(3)(b) or (c) in such manner as they may specify.

(5) The provisions of Schedule 3 shall apply as regards the procedure to be followed before the Treasury exercise their power to refuse leave under subparagraph (2), or their power to give a direction under subparagraph (4), in respect of an Operator.

Reports by the [Office of Fair Trading]

3.—(1) The Treasury shall before deciding—

(a) whether to refuse to approve a person as Operator of a relevant system pursuant to paragraph 1(1); or

(b) whether to refuse for the granting of an approval pursuant to paragraph 2(2),

send to the [Office of Fair Trading (in this Schedule referred to as "the OFT")] a copy of the rules and of any guidance which the Treasury are required to consider in making that decision together with such other information as the Treasury consider will assist in discharging [its] functions under subparagraph (2).

(2) The [OFT] shall report to the Treasury whether, in [its] opinion, the rules and guidance copies of which are sent to [it] under subparagraph (1) have, or are intended or likely to have, to any significant extent the effect of restricting, distorting or preventing competition and, if so, what that effect is likely to be; and in making any decision as is mentioned in subparagraph (1) the Treasury shall have regard to the [OFT's] report.

(3) The Treasury shall send to the [OFT] copies of any notice received by them under regulation 10(5) or paragraph 2(3) together with such other information as the Treasury consider will assist the [OFT] in discharging [its] functions under subparagraphs (4) and (5).

(4) The [OFT] shall keep under review—

(a) the rules, guidance and practices mentioned in paragraph 1(2); and

(b) the matters specified in the notices of which copies are sent to [it] under subparagraph (3),

and if at any time [it] is of the opinion that any such rules or guidance taken together with any such matters, have, or are intended or likely to have, to any significant extent the effect mentioned in subparagraph (2), [it] shall report [its] opinion to the Treasury stating what in [its] opinion that effect is or is likely to be.

(5) The [OFT] may report to the Treasury [its] opinion that any such matter as is mentioned in subparagraph (4)(b) does not in [its] opinion have, and is not intended or likely to have, to any significant extent the effect mentioned in subparagraph (2).

(6) The [OFT] may from time to time consider whether any such practices as are mentioned in paragraph 1(2) have, or are intended or likely to have, to any significant extent the effect mentioned in subparagraph (2) and, if so, what that effect is or is likely to be; and if [it] is of that opinion [it] shall make a report to the Treasury stating [its] opinion and what the effect is or is likely to be.

(7) The Treasury shall not exercise their powers under paragraph 1(3) or 2(4) except after receiving a report from the [OFT] under subparagraph (4) or (6).

(8) The [OFT] may, if [it] thinks fit, publish any report made by [it] under this paragraph but shall exclude from a published report, so far as practicable, any matter which relates to the affairs of a particular person (other than the person seeking approval as an Operator) the publication of which would or might in [its] opinion seriously and prejudicially affect the interests of that person.

Investigations by the [Office of Fair Trading]

4.—(1) For the purpose of investigating any matter with a view to [its] consideration under paragraph 3 the [OFT] may by a notice in writing—

(a) require any person to produce, at any time and place specified in the notice, to the [OFT] or to any person appointed by [it] for the purpose, any documents which are specified or described in the notice and which are documents in his custody or under his control and relating to any matter relevant to the investigation; or

(b) require any person carrying on business to furnish to the [OFT] such information as may be specified or described in the notice, and specify the time within which, and the manner and form in which, any such information is to be furnished.

(2) A person shall not under this paragraph be required to produce any document or disclose any information which he would be entitled to refuse to produce or disclose on grounds of legal professional privilege in proceedings in the High Court or on grounds of confidentiality as between client and professional legal adviser proceedings in the Court of Session.

(3) ...

[Enforcement

4A.—(1) The court may, on an application by the OFT, enquire into whether any person ("the defaulter") has refused or otherwise failed, without reasonable excuse, to comply with a notice under paragraph 4(1).

(2) An application under sub-paragraph (1) shall include details of the possible failure which the OFT considers has occurred.

(3) In enquiring into a case under sub-paragraph (1), the court shall hear any witness who may be produced against or on behalf of the defaulter and any statement which may be offered in defence.

(4) Sub-paragraphs (5) and (6) apply where the court is satisfied, after hearing any witnesses and statements as mentioned in sub-paragraph (3), that the defaulter has refused or otherwise failed, without reasonable excuse, to comply with a notice under paragraph 4(1).

(5) The court may punish the defaulter as it would have been able to punish him had he been guilty of contempt of court.

(6) Where the defaulter is a body corporate or is a partnership constituted under the law of Scotland, the court may punish any director, officer or (as the case may be) partner of the defaulter as it would have been able to punish that director, officer or partner had he been guilty of contempt of court.

(7) In this paragraph "the court"—

(a) in relation to England and Wales or Northern Ireland, means the High Court, and

(b) in relation to Scotland, means the Court of Session.

4B.—(1) A person commits an offence if he intentionally alters, suppresses or destroys a document which he has been required to produce by a notice under paragraph 4(1).

(2) A person who commits an offence under sub-paragraph (1) shall be liable—

(a) on summary conviction, to a fine not exceeding the statutory maximum;

(b) on conviction on indictment, to imprisonment for a term not exceeding two years or to a fine or to both.]

...

5. ...

Exemptions from the Competition Act 1998

6.—(1) The Chapter I prohibition does not apply to—

(a) an agreement for the constitution of an Operator; or

(b) an agreement for the constitution of a person who has applied for approval as an Operator in accordance with these Regulations and whose application has not yet been determined,

to the extent to which the agreement relates to rules made or guidance issued by the Operator.

(2) The Chapter I prohibition does not apply to a decision made by an Operator to the extent to which the decision relates to any of the rules made or guidance issued by that Operator or to the Operator's specified practices.

(3) The Chapter I prohibition does not apply to the specified practices of—

(a) an Operator; or

(b) a person who is subject to the rules of an Operator.

(4) The Chapter I prohibition does not apply to any agreement the parties to which consist of or include—

(a) an Operator; or

(b) a person who is subject to the rules of an Operator,

to the extent to which the agreement consists of provisions the inclusion of which is required or contemplated by these Regulations or by any rules made or guidance issued by the Operator or by the Operator's specified practices.

(5) In this paragraph—

"the Chapter I prohibition" means the prohibition imposed by section 2(1) of the Competition Act 1998; and

"specified practices" means—

(a) any practices of an Operator in its capacity as such; or

(b) any practices of persons who are members of, or otherwise subject to rules made by, an Operator and which are practices—

(i) in relation to business in respect of which the persons in question are subject to the rules of the Operator where those practices are required or contemplated by the rules of the Operator or by guidance issued by the Operator; or

(ii) otherwise attributable to the conduct of the Operator as such;

and expressions used in this paragraph which are also used in Part I of the Competition Act 1998 are to be interpreted in same way as for the purposes of that Part of that Act.

Supplementary provisions

7.—(1) Any direction given under this Schedule shall, on the application of the person by whom it was given, be enforceable by injunction or, in Scotland, by an order for specific performance under section 45 of the Court of Session Act 1988.

(2) The fact that any rules made by an Operator have been altered by or pursuant to a direction given by the Treasury under this Schedule shall not preclude their subsequent alteration or revocation by the Operator.

(3) In determining under this Schedule whether any guidance has, or is likely to have, any particular effect the Treasury and the [OFT] may assume that the persons to whom it is addressed will act in conformity with it.

[7053]

NOTES

Para 1: words in square brackets substituted by the Capital Requirements Regulations 2006, SI 2006/3221, reg 29(4), Sch 6, para 12, as from 1 January 2007.

Para 3: all words in square brackets (with the exception of the penultimate word in square brackets in sub-para (8)) substituted by the Enterprise Act 2002 (Consequential and Supplemental Provisions) Order 2003, SI 2003/1398, art 2, Schedule, para 43(1), (2)(a), as from 20 June 2003; penultimate word in square brackets in sub-para (8) substituted by the Enterprise Act 2002 and Media Mergers (Consequential Amendments) Order 2003, SI 2003/3180, art 2, Schedule, para 9, as from 29 December 2003.

Para 4: words in square brackets substituted, and sub-para (3) revoked, by SI 2003/1398, art 2, Schedule, para 43(1), (2)(b), as from 20 June 2003.

Paras 4A, 4B: inserted by SI 2003/1398, art 2, Schedule, para 43(1), (2)(c), as from 20 June 2003.

Para 5: revoked by SI 2003/1398, art 2, Schedule, para 43(1), (2)(d), as from 20 June 2003.

Para 7: reference to "OFT" in square brackets substituted by virtue of the Enterprise Act 2002, s 2(1), as from 1 April 2003.

Office of Fair Trading: see the note "Substitution of references to the Director General of Fair Trading" at **[4351]**.

SCHEDULE 3
PROCEDURE FOR REFUSAL OR WITHDRAWAL OF APPROVAL AS AN OPERATOR, OR FOR GIVING DIRECTIONS, ETC

Regulations 5(4), 7(3) and 8(4)

1. Before—
   (a) refusing an application for approval as an Operator made under regulation 4 (whether or not pursuant to paragraph 1(1) of Schedule 2);
   (b) withdrawing an Operator's approval under regulation 7(2);
   (c) giving a direction under regulation 8;
   (d) exercising any power conferred by paragraph 1(3) of Schedule 2;
   (e) exercising the power to refuse leave under paragraph 2(2) of Schedule 2; or
   (f) giving a direction under paragraph 2(4) of Schedule 2, the Treasury shall—
      (i) give written notice of their intention to do so to the Operator;
      (ii) take such steps as they consider reasonably practicable to bring the notice to the attention of system-users; and
      (iii) publish the notice in such manner as they think appropriate for bringing it to the attention of other persons who are, in their opinion, likely to be affected.

2. A notice under paragraph 1 shall—
   (a) state why the Treasury intend to refuse the application, withdraw the approval, give the direction, or exercise the power in question; and
   (b) draw attention to the right to make representations conferred by paragraph 3.

3. Before the end of the period for making representations—
   (a) the Operator,
   (b) any system-user, and
   (c) any other person who is likely to be affected by the proposed withdrawal or direction, may make representations to the Treasury.

4. The period for making representations is—
   (a) two months beginning—
      (i) with the date on which the notice under paragraph 1 is served on the Operator; or
      (ii) if later, with the date on which that notice is published; or
   (b) such longer period as the Treasury may allow in the particular case.

5. In deciding whether to refuse the application, withdraw the approval, give the direction, or exercise the power in question, the Treasury shall have regard to any representations made in accordance with paragraph 3.

6. When the Treasury have decided whether to refuse the application, withdraw the approval, give the direction, or exercise the power in question they shall, if they have decided to refuse the application, withdraw the Operator's approval under regulation 7(2), give a direction under regulation 8 or exercise a power conferred by paragraph 1(3) of Schedule 2—
   (a) give the Operator written notice of their decision; and
   (b) take such steps as they consider reasonably practicable for bringing their decision to the attention of system-users and of any other persons who are, in the Treasury's opinion, likely to be affected.

7. If the Treasury consider it essential to do so, they may withdraw an Operator's approval under regulation 7(2) or give a direction under regulation 8—
   (a) without following the procedure set out in this Schedule; or
   (b) if the Treasury have begun to follow that procedure, regardless of whether the period for making representations has expired.

8. If the Treasury have, in relation to a particular matter, followed the procedure set out in paragraphs 1 to 5, they need not follow it again if, in relation to that matter, they decide to take action other than that specified in their notice under paragraph 1.

[7054]

SCHEDULE 4
KEEPING OF REGISTERS AND RECORDS OF PARTICIPATING SECURITIES

Regulation 23(4)

Interpretation

1. In this Schedule—

"uncertificated shares" means shares title to which may be transferred by means of a relevant system; and

"certificated shares" means shares which are not uncertificated shares; and "uncertificated stock" means stock title to which may be transferred by means of a relevant system; and "certificated stock" means stock which is not uncertificated stock.

Registers of members

2.—(1) Every participating issuer which is a company shall enter in its issuer register of members—

(a) the names and addresses of the members;
(b) the date on which each person was registered as a member; and
(c) the date at which any person ceased to be a member.

(2) With the names and addresses of the members there shall be entered a statement—

(a) of the certificated shares held by each member, distinguishing each share by its number (so long as the share has a number) and, where the company has more than one class of issued shares, by its class; and
(b) of the amount paid or agreed to be considered as paid on the certificated shares of each member.

(3) Where the company has converted any of its shares into stock and given notice of the conversion to the registrar of companies, the issuer register of members shall show the amount and class of the certificated stock held by each member, instead of the amount of shares and the particulars relating to shares specified in subparagraph (2).

(4) Subject to subparagraph (5), section 352 of the 1985 Act shall not apply to a company which is a participating issuer, other than as respects any overseas branch register.

(5) Section 352(5) of the 1985 Act shall apply to a participating issuer which is a company which makes default in complying with this paragraph and every officer of it who is in default as if such a default were a default in complying with section 352 of the Act.

(6) An entry relating to a former member of the company may be removed from the issuer register of members after the expiration of 20 years beginning with the day on which he ceased to be a member.

(7) For the purposes of this paragraph references to an issuer register of members shall not be taken to include an overseas branch register.

3. Section 352A of the 1985 Act shall apply to a participating issuer which is a private company limited by shares as if references therein to the company's register of members were references to its issuer register of members.

4.—(1) In relation to every participating issuer which is a company, an Operator of a relevant system shall, in respect of any class of shares which is a participating security for the purposes of that system, enter on an Operator register of members—

(a) the names and addresses of the members who hold uncertificated shares in the company;
(b) with those names and addresses a statement of the uncertificated shares held by each member and, where the company has more than one class of issued uncertificated shares, distinguishing each share by its class; and
(c) where the company has converted any of its shares into stock and given notice of the conversion to the registrar of companies, the Operator register of members shall show the amount and class of uncertificated stock held by each member, instead of the amount of shares and the particulars relating to shares specified in subparagraph (b).

PART IV STATUTORY INSTRUMENTS

(2) An entry relating to a member of a company who has ceased to hold any uncertificated shares in the company may be removed from the Operator register of members after the expiration of 20 years beginning with the day on which he ceased to hold any such shares.

(3) For the purposes of this paragraph references to an Operator register of members shall not be taken to include an overseas branch register.

(4) Members of a company who hold shares in uncertificated form may not be entered as holders of those shares on an overseas branch register.

Records of uncertificated shares

5.—(1) Every participating issuer which is a company shall enter in its record of uncertificated shares—

(a) the same particulars, so far as practicable, as are required by paragraph 4(1) to be entered in the Operator register of members; and

(b) a statement of the amount paid or agreed to be considered as paid on the uncertificated shares of each member.

(2) A company to which this paragraph applies shall, unless it is impracticable to do so by virtue of circumstances beyond its control, ensure that the record of uncertificated shares is regularly reconciled with the Operator register of members.

(3) Provided that it has complied with subparagraph (2), a company shall not be liable in respect of any act or thing done or omitted to be done by or on behalf of the company in reliance upon the assumption that the particulars entered in any record of uncertificated shares which the company is required to keep by these Regulations accord with the particulars entered in its Operator register of members.

(4) Section 352(5) of the 1985 Act shall apply to a participating issuer which is a company which makes default in complying with this paragraph and every officer of it who is in default as if such a default were a default in complying with section 352 of that Act.

Location of issuer register of members and records of uncertificated shares, and ancillary matters

6.—(1) Subject to subparagraph (2), a company's issuer register of members and its record of uncertificated shares shall be kept at its registered office, except that—

(a) if the work of making up the issuer register of members or the record of uncertificated shares is done at another office of the company, they may be kept there; and

(b) if the company arranges with some other person for the making up of the issuer register of members or the record of uncertificated shares to be undertaken on its behalf by that other, they may be kept at the office of the other at which the work is done;

but the issuer register of members must not be kept, in the case of a company registered in England and Wales, at any place elsewhere than in England and Wales or, in the case of a company registered in Scotland, at any place elsewhere than in Scotland.

(2) A company's issuer register of members and its record of uncertificated shares shall at all times be kept at the same place.

(3) Subject as follows, every participating issuer which is a company shall send notice in the prescribed form to the registrar of companies of the place where its issuer register of members and its record of uncertificated shares are kept, and of any change in that place, provided that any notice sent by such a company in accordance with section 353(2) of the 1985 Act, and which has effect on the coming into force of these Regulations, shall be treated as being a notice sent in compliance with this subparagraph.

(4) The notice need not be sent if the issuer register of members and the record of uncertificated shares have at all times since they came into existence been kept at the company's registered office.

(5) Subject to subparagraph (6), sections 353 and 357 of the 1985 Act shall not apply to a company which is a participating issuer.

(6) Section 353(4) of the 1985 Act shall apply to a participating issuer which is a company which makes default in complying with subparagraph (2) at any time, or makes default for 14 days in complying with subparagraph (3), and every officer of it who is in default as if such a default were a default in complying with section 353(2) of that Act.

7.—(1) Every participating issuer which is a company having more than 50 members shall, unless the particulars required by paragraph 2(1) to be entered in the issuer register of members are kept in such a form as to constitute in themselves an index, keep an index of the names of the members of the company and shall, within 14 days after the date on which any alteration is made in the issuer register of members or the Operator register of members, make any necessary alteration in the index.

(2) The index shall in respect of each member contain a sufficient indication to enable the account of that member in the issuer register of members and, in the case of a member who holds uncertificated shares in the company, in the record of uncertificated shares, to be readily found.

(3) The index shall be at all times kept at the same place as the issuer register of members and the record of uncertificated shares.

(4) Subject to subparagraph (5), section 354 of the 1985 Act shall not apply to a company which is a participating issuer.

(5) Section 354(4) of the 1985 Act shall apply to a participating issuer which is a company which makes default in complying with this paragraph and every officer of it who is in default as if such a default were a default in complying with section 354 of that Act.

8. Section 355 of the 1985 Act shall apply to a company which is a participating issuer as if references in that section to the company's register of members were references instead to its issuer register of members.

9. Section 356 of, and paragraph 25 of Schedule 13 to, the 1985 Act shall apply to a company which is a participating issuer as if—

(a) references in those provisions to the company's register of members were references to its issuer register of members and its record of uncertificated shares; and

(b) references in section 356 to the company's index of members were references to the index required to be kept by paragraph 7,

and references to the 1985 Act in the Companies (Inspection and Copying of Registers, Indices and Documents) Regulations 1991 shall be construed accordingly.

10. Where under paragraph 6(1)(b), a company's issuer register of members and record of uncertificated shares is kept at the office of some person other than the company, and by reason of any default of his the company fails to comply with—

paragraph 6(2) (record of uncertificated shares to be kept with issuer register of members);

paragraph 6(3) (notice to registrar);

paragraph 7(3) (index to be kept with issuer register of members and record of uncertificated shares); or

section 356 of the 1985 Act (inspection),

or with any requirement of the 1985 Act as to the production of the register of members or any part thereof, that other person is liable to the same penalties as if he were an officer of the company who was in default, and the power of the court under section 356(6) of the 1985 Act extends to the making of orders against that other and his officers and servants.

11. Where, under section 359 of the 1985 Act, the court orders rectification of the register of members of a company which is a participating issuer, it shall not order the payment of any damages under subsection (2) of that section to the extent that such rectification relates to the company's Operator register of members and does not arise from an act or omission of the Operator on the instructions of that company or from fraud or other wilful default, or negligence, on the part of that company.

Registers of [general] public sector securities

12.—(1) Where an Operator of a relevant system is required to maintain an Operator register of [general] public sector securities that register shall comprise the following particulars which the Operator shall enter on it, namely—

(a) the names and address of the persons holding units of the relevant participating security in uncertificated form; and

(b) how many units of that security each such person holds in that form.

[(2) The following provisions of the 2004 Regulations shall not apply in respect of units of general UK Government securities held in uncertificated form—

regulations 7 to 9;
regulations 12 to 14;
regulations 16 to 24;
regulation 28; and
regulations 30 to 31.]

(3) The following provisions of the 1974 Regulations shall not apply in respect of units of [general] local authority securities held in uncertificated form—

regulations 5 and 6;
regulations 8 to 14;
regulation 16; and
regulation 21.

Records of uncertificated [general] public sector securities

13.—(1) The participating issuer shall enter in a record of uncertificated [general] public sector securities the same particulars, so far as is practicable, as are required by paragraph 12(1) to be entered in the relevant Operator register of [general] public sector securities.

(2) In respect of every participating security which is a [general] UK Government security, the record of uncertificated [general] public sector securities shall be kept [by the Registrar of Government Stock].

(3) The participating issuer shall, unless it is impracticable to do so by virtue of circumstances beyond his control, ensure that the record of uncertificated [general] public sector securities is regularly reconciled with the Operator register of [general] public sector securities.

(4) Provided that he has complied with subparagraph (3), a participating issuer shall not be liable in respect of any act or thing done or omitted to be done by him or on his behalf in reliance upon the assumption that the particulars entered in any record of uncertificated [general] public sector securities which he is required to keep by these Regulations accord with particulars entered in the Operator register of [general] public sector securities to which the record relates.

(5) The provisions of the Bankers' Books Evidence Act 1879 shall apply for the purpose of proving any entry in the record of uncertificated [general] public sector securities as if the participating issuer were a bank and a banker within the meaning of that Act, and as if such entry in the record, or, where the information recorded therein is not in readable form and is later transcribed into readable form, the transcribed version of such entry, were an entry in a banker's book.

Registers of corporate securities

14.—(1) Where an Operator of a relevant system is required to maintain an Operator register of corporate securities, that register shall comprise the following particulars which the Operator shall enter on it, namely—

(a) the names and addresses of the persons holding units of the relevant participating security in uncertificated form; and

(b) how many units of that security each such person holds in that form.

(2) Sections 190 and 191 of the 1985 Act shall not apply to any part of an Operator register of corporate securities.

Records of uncertificated corporate securities

15.—(1) A participating issuer shall enter in a record of uncertificated corporate securities the same particulars, so far as practicable, as are required by paragraph 14(1) to be entered in the relevant Operator register of corporate securities.

(2) A participating issuer to which this paragraph applies shall, unless it is impracticable to do so by virtue of circumstances beyond its control, ensure that the record of uncertificated corporate securities is regularly reconciled with the Operator register of corporate securities.

(3) Provided that it has complied with subparagraph (2), a participating issuer shall not be liable in respect of any act or thing done or omitted to be done by it or on its behalf in reliance upon the assumption that the particulars entered in any record of uncertificated corporate securities which the participating issuer is required to keep by these Regulations accord with particulars entered in any Operator register of corporate securities relating to it.

(4) In the case of a participating issuer which is a company, the record of uncertificated corporate securities shall be kept at the same place as the part of any register of debenture holders maintained by the company would be required to be kept.

(5) Section 191(1), (2), (4) and (5) of the 1985 Act shall apply in relation to a record of uncertificated corporate securities maintained by a participating issuer which is a company, so far as that record relates to debentures, as it applies or would apply to any register of debenture holders maintained by the company; and references to the 1985 Act in the Companies (Inspection and Copying of Registers, Indices and Documents) Regulations 1991 shall be construed accordingly.

(6) Any provision of an enactment or instrument which requires a register of persons holding securities (other than shares or public sector securities) to be open to inspection shall also apply to the record of uncertificated corporate securities relating to any units of those securities which are participating securities.

Miscellaneous

16.—(1) Every register which an Operator is required to maintain by virtue of these Regulations shall be kept in the United Kingdom.

(2) Provided that it is kept in the United Kingdom, any such register [(other than an Operator register of eligible debt securities)] which relates to securities issued by a company shall be deemed to be kept—

(a) in the case of a company registered in England and Wales, in England and Wales; or

(b) in the case of a company registered in Scotland, in Scotland.

17.—(1) An entry in a register of securities or in a record of securities relating to a person who no longer holds the securities which are the subject of the entry may be removed from the register or the record (as the case may be) after the expiration of 20 years beginning with the day on which the person ceased to hold any of those securities.

(2) Subparagraph (1) does not apply in respect of an entry in a register of members.

18. Sections 722 and 723(1) and (2) of the 1985 Act shall apply—

(a) to any register, record or index required to be kept by any person in accordance with these Regulations as they apply to any register, record or index required by the Companies Acts to be kept by a company; and

(b) to an Operator and its officers as they apply to a company and its officers.

19.—(1) Such sanctions as apply to a company and its officers in the event of a default in complying with section 352 of the 1985 Act shall apply to an Operator and his officers in the event of a default in complying with paragraph 4, 12 or 14.

(2) Such sanctions as apply to the registrar, within the meaning of the 1974 Regulations, in the event of a default in complying with regulation 5 of those Regulations shall apply to a participating issuer and his officers in the event of a default in complying with paragraph 13 in respect of a local authority security [falling within paragraph (a)(i) of the definition of "local authority security" in regulation 3(1)].

[(2A) …]

(3) Such sanctions as apply in the event of a default in complying with the requirement to maintain a register imposed by the relevant enactment or instrument referred to in Regulation 22(1) shall apply to—

(a) a participating issuer other than a company; and

(b) a participating issuer which is a company, in relation to so much of the record of uncertificated corporate securities as does not relate to debentures,

and his officers in the event of a default in complying with paragraph 15.

(4) Subparagraphs (2) and (3) shall not apply to any of the following or its officers—

(a) the Crown;

(b) any person acting on behalf of the Crown;

[(c) the Bank of England;

(d) the Registrar of Government Stock;

(e) any previous Registrar of Government Stock; or

(f) in respect of a security which immediately before it became a participating security was transferable by exempt transfer within the meaning of the Stock Transfer Act 1982, a participating issuer].

20. An officer of a participating issuer shall be in default in complying with, or in contravention of paragraph 2, 5, 6, 7, 13 or 15, or section 722(2) of the 1985 Act as applied by paragraph 18, if, and only if, he knowingly and wilfully authorised or permitted the default or contravention.

21. An officer of an Operator shall be in default in complying with, or in contravention of, the provisions referred to in paragraph 19(1) of this Schedule, or of section 722(2) of the 1985 Act as applied by paragraph 18, if, and only if, he knowingly and wilfully authorised or permitted the default or contravention.

[7055]–[7056]

NOTES

Para 12: word "general" in square brackets in every place it occurs substituted by the Uncertificated Securities (Amendment) (Eligible Debt Securities) Regulations 2003, SI 2003/1633, regs 6(5)(a), (b), 7, 8(4)(a), as from 24 June 2003; sub-para (2) substituted by the Government Stock (Consequential and Transitional Provision) (No 2) Order 2004, SI 2004/1662, art 2, Schedule, Pt 3, para 29(1), (6)(a), as from 1 July 2004.

Para 13: word "general" in square brackets in every place it occurs substituted by SI 2003/1633, regs 6(5)(c), (d), 7, as from 24 June 2003; final words in square brackets in sub-para (2) substituted by SI 2004/1662, art 2, Schedule, Pt 3, para 29(1), (6)(b), as from 1 July 2004.

Para 16: words in square brackets inserted by SI 2003/1633, reg 13, as from 24 June 2003.

Para 19: words in square brackets in sub-para (2) and the whole of sub-para (2A) inserted by SI 2003/1633, reg 8(4)(b), (c), as from 24 June 2003; sub-para (2A) revoked by the Local Authorities (Capital Finance) (Further Consequential and Saving Provisions) Order 2004, SI 2004/2044, art 6(3), as from 1 October 2004; sub-para (4)(c)–(f) substituted, for original sub-para (4)(c), (d), by SI 2004/1662, art 2, Schedule, Pt 3, para 29(1), (6)(c), as from 1 July 2004.

(*Sch 5 (Adaptations in Respect of Northern Ireland) outside the scope of this work.*)

SCHEDULE 6
TRANSITORY PROVISIONS

Regulation 50

1. Prior to the day on which section 19 of the 2000 Act comes into force, each provision of these Regulations specified in this Schedule shall have effect modified as provided in this Schedule.

2. The definition of "securities" in Regulation 3(1) shall be modified by the substitution of the words "the 1986 Act" for the words "section 235 of the 2000 Act".

3. Regulation 5 shall be modified by the substitution for paragraph (4) of—

"(4) Where the Treasury refuse an application for approval they shall give the applicant a written notice to that effect stating the reasons for the refusal.".

4. Regulation 7 shall be modified by—

(a) the insertion in paragraph (2) of the words "subject to paragraph (3)" after the words "they may"; and

(b) the substitution for paragraphs (3) to (6) of—

"(3) Subsections (2) to (7) and (9) of section 11 of the 1986 Act shall apply in relation to the withdrawal by the Treasury of approval from an Operator under paragraph (2) as they apply in relation to the revocation by the Secretary of State of a recognition order under subsection (1) of that section; and in those subsections as they so apply—

(a) any reference to a recognised organisation shall be taken to be a reference to an Operator;

(b) any reference to members of a recognised organisation shall be taken to be a reference to system-users;

(c) any reference to the Secretary of State shall be taken to be a reference to the Treasury;

(d) any reference to an order other than a recognition order shall be taken to be a reference to a written instrument; and

(e) the reference in subsection (6) to the interests of investors shall be taken to be a reference to the interests of system-users."

5. Regulation 8 shall be modified by—

(a) the substitution for paragraph (4) of—

"(4) Before giving a direction under paragraph (2)(b) the Treasury shall—

(a) if the circumstances permit, consult the Operator and afford him an opportunity to make representations; and

(b) so far as is practicable to estimate it, have regard to the cost to the Operator of complying with any term of any direction and to the costs to other persons resulting from the Operator's compliance."; and

(b) the omission of paragraphs (5) and (7).

6. In Regulation 9—

(a) paragraph (7) shall be modified by the substitution of the words "Subsections (6) and (7) of section 61 of the 1986 Act" for the words "Subsections (3) to (5) and (8) of section 382 of the 2000 Act";

(b) paragraphs (10) to (12) shall be modified by the substitution of the words "investment business within the meaning of the 1986 Act" for the words from "business of any of the following kinds" in paragraph (10) to the end of paragraph (12).

7. Regulation 11(1) shall be modified to read—

"(1) If it appears to the Treasury that there is a body corporate—

(a) to which functions have been transferred under section 114 of the 1986 Act; and

(b) which is able and willing to discharge all or any of the functions conferred by this Part of these Regulations,

they may, subject to paragraphs (2) and (5), by instrument in writing delegate all or any of those functions to that body; and a body to which functions are so delegated is referred to in these Regulations as a "designated agency".".

8. In paragraph 5(7) of Schedule 1—

(a) paragraph (a) of the definition of "clearing house" shall be modified by the substitution of the words "for the purposes of the 1986 Act" for the words "within section 285(1)(b) of the 2000 Act"; and

(b) paragraph (a) of the definition of "exchange" shall be modified by the substitution of the words "for the purposes of the 1986 Act" for the words "within section 285(1)(a) of the 2000 Act".

9. Schedule 2 shall be modified by—

(a) the substitution for subparagraph (5) in paragraph 1 of—

"(5) Subsections (2) to (5), (7) and (9) of section 11 of the 1986 Act shall apply in relation to the withdrawal of approval under subparagraph (3) as they apply in relation to the revocation by the Secretary of State of a recognition order under subsection (1) of that section; and in those subsections as they so apply—

(a) any reference to a recognised organisation shall be taken to be a reference to an Operator;

(b) any reference to members of a recognised organisation shall be taken to be a reference to system-users;

(c) any reference to the Secretary of State shall be taken to be a reference to the Treasury; and

(d) any reference to an order other than a recognition order shall be taken to be a reference to a written instrument.";

(b) the omission from paragraph 2 of subparagraph (5); and

(c) the insertion after paragraph 7 of a new paragraph reading—

"8.—(1) Before the Treasury exercise a power under paragraph 1(3)(b) or (c), or their power to refuse leave under paragraph 2(2), or their power to give a direction under paragraph 2(4), in respect of an Operator, they shall—

(a) give written notice of their intention to do so to the Operator and take such steps (whether by publication or otherwise) as they think appropriate for bringing the notice to the attention of any other person who in their opinion is likely to be affected by the exercise of the power; and

(b) have regard to any representation made within such time as they consider reasonable by the Operator or by any such other person.

(2) A notice under subparagraph (1) shall give particulars of the manner in which the Treasury propose to exercise the power in question and state the reasons for which they propose to act; and the statement of reasons may include matters contained in any report received by them under paragraph 3.".

[7057]

(Sch 7 (minor and consequential amendments to statutes and secondary legislation); in so far as these are relevant to this work, they have been incorporated at the appropriate place.)

COMPANIES (COMPETENT AUTHORITY) (FEES) REGULATIONS 2002 (NOTE)

(SI 2002/502)

NOTES

See Appendix 3 (Fees Instruments) at **[A3]**.

[7057A]

LIMITED LIABILITY PARTNERSHIPS (COMPETENT AUTHORITY) (FEES) REGULATIONS 2002 (NOTE)

(SI 2002/503)

NOTES

See Appendix 3 (Fees Instruments) at **[A3]**.

[7057B]

LIMITED LIABILITY PARTNERSHIPS (FORMS) REGULATIONS 2002 (NOTE)

(SI 2002/690)

NOTES

See Appendix 4 at **[A4]**.

[7057C]

COMPANIES (PARTICULARS OF USUAL RESIDENTIAL ADDRESS) (CONFIDENTIALITY ORDERS) REGULATIONS 2002

(SI 2002/912)

NOTES

Made: 31 March 2002.

Authority: Companies Act 1985, ss 723B–723E.

Commencement: 2 April 2002 (see reg 1 at **[7058]**). Where any provision in this work (including any inserted or substituted provision) came into force for all purposes on or before 1 July 2005, commencement information is not noted at provision level.

These Regulations are reproduced as amended by: the Enterprise Act 2002.

ARRANGEMENT OF REGULATIONS

1 Citation, commencement and interpretation

(1) These Regulations may be cited as the Companies (Particulars of Usual Residential Address) (Confidentiality Orders) Regulations 2002.

(2) These Regulations shall come into force on 2nd April 2002.

(3) In these Regulations—

"the 1985 Act" means the Companies Act 1985;

"the LLP Regulations" mean the Limited Liability Partnerships (Particulars of Usual Residential Address) (Confidentiality Orders) Regulations 2002;

"beneficiary of an order" means an individual in relation to whom a confidentiality order is in force;

"company" means a relevant company within the meaning of section 723D of the 1985 Act and a company incorporated outside Great Britain proposing to establish a place of business, or open a branch in Great Britain, which would require that company to deliver for registration the information specified in section 691 of the 1985 Act, or Schedule 21A, as the case may be;

"competent authority" means any authority specified in Schedule 1 to these Regulations;

PART IV STATUTORY INSTRUMENTS

"police force" means a police force within the meaning of section 101(1) of the Police Act 1996 or section 50 of the Police (Scotland) Act 1967;

"service address" means the address specified pursuant to regulation 2(2)(b) in an application made under section 723B(1) of the 1985 Act or, if another address has been substituted under regulation 7, the address most recently substituted under that regulation; and

"working day" means any day other than a Saturday, a Sunday, Christmas Day, Good Friday or a day which is a bank holiday in any part of England or Wales under or by virtue of the Banking and Financial Dealings Act 1971.

[7058]

PART I

2 Applications for confidentiality orders under section 723B of the 1985 Act

(1) An application for a confidentiality order shall be made to the Secretary of State.

(2) An application for a confidentiality order shall:

(a) be in such form and contain such information and be accompanied by such evidence as the Secretary of State may from time to time direct;

(b) specify each company of which the applicant is or proposes to become a director, secretary or permanent representative and shall specify an address complying with regulation 9;

(3) The Secretary of State may from time to time direct different information or evidence be provided for different cases or categories of application.

(4) The Secretary of State may require any information or evidence delivered by an applicant to be verified in such manner as she may direct.

(5) The Secretary of State may require any application to be supported by a statement by any company to which the application relates that that company wishes a confidentiality order to be made in respect of the applicant together with the statement of the reasons for that wish.

(6) At any time after receiving an application and before determining it, the Secretary of State may require that any applicant deliver additional information or evidence including the delivery by a company of a statement complying with paragraph (5).

(7) Subject to paragraph (8) each application shall be accompanied by a fee of £100, and the Secretary of State may reject any application without considering it unless it is accompanied by such fee.

(8) No fee shall be payable where an application is made by an applicant—

(a) who at the same time has made an application for a confidentiality order under the LLP Regulations, and where a fee has been paid in respect of that application; or

(b) in respect of whom, at the time of the application, a confidentiality order made under the LLP Regulations is in force.

(9) An applicant may withdraw his application, by notice delivered to the Secretary of State, at any time before the Secretary of State makes a decision on the application, and the Secretary of State may retain the fee paid in respect of that application.

[7059]

3 Referral of questions for the purposes of the determination of an application

(1) The Secretary of State may, in respect of any application or category of applications, refer to a relevant body any question relating to an assessment, in the case of such application or category of applications, of the nature and extent of any risk of violence or intimidation considered by the applicant as likely to be created in relation to the applicant, or any person living with him, by virtue of the availability for inspection by members of the public of particulars of his usual residential address.

(2) The Secretary of State may also refer to a relevant body any question as to the nature or extent of any risk of violence or intimidation likely to be created in relation to any applicant or category of applicants or persons living with them as a result of their involvement in the activities of a particular company or category of companies or of a particular sector of commerce or industry.

(3) The Secretary of State may accept any answer to a question referred in accordance with paragraph (1) or (2) as providing sufficient evidence of the nature and extent of any risk relevant to an applicant or any person living with him for the purposes of any determination under section 723B(3) or (4) of the 1985 Act.

(4) In this regulation, "relevant body" means any police force and any other person whom the Secretary of State considers may be able to assist in answering a question referred to that person under paragraph (1) or (2).

[7060]

4 Notification of the outcome of an application

The Secretary of State shall send the applicant at his usual residential address, as stated in his application, notice of her decision under section 723B(3) or (4) of the 1985 Act and such notice shall be sent within five working days of the decision being made.

[7061]

5 Appeals

(1) An applicant who has received notice under regulation 4 that his application for a confidentiality order has been unsuccessful may appeal to the High Court or the Court of Session on the grounds that the decision—

(a) is unlawful;

(b) is irrational or unreasonable; or

(c) has been made on the basis of a procedural impropriety or otherwise contravenes the rules of natural justice.

(2) No appeal under this regulation may be brought unless the leave of the court has been obtained.

(3) An applicant must bring an appeal within 21 days of the sending of the notice under regulation 4 or, with the court's permission, after the end of such period, but only if the court is satisfied:

(a) where permission is sought before the end of that period, that there is good reason for the applicant being unable to bring the appeal in time; or

(b) where permission is sought after that time, that there was a good reason for the applicant's failure to bring the appeal in time and for any delay in applying for permission.

(4) The court determining an appeal may—

(a) dismiss the appeal; or

(b) quash the decision,

and where the court quashes a decision it may refer the matter to the Secretary of State with a direction to reconsider it and to make a determination in accordance with the findings of the court.

[7062]

PART II

6 Service addresses

Where an application for a confidentiality order is made by a director, secretary or permanent representative, that individual shall notify to each of the companies specified in the application the service address specified in the application pursuant to regulation 2(2)(b).

[7063]

7 If a beneficiary of an order wishes to substitute another address, complying with regulation 9, for an address specified by him under regulation 2(2)(b) or previously notified by him under this regulation, he shall do so by notifying every company of which he is a director, secretary or permanent representative of the address to be substituted.

[7064]

8 Where the beneficiary of an order—

(a) becomes a director, secretary or permanent representative of a company; or

(b) is to be named in a statement delivered under section 10(2) of the 1985 Act as a director or secretary of a company to be formed under the 1985 Act; or

(c) is a director, secretary or permanent representative of a company at the time when it establishes a place of business in Great Britain requiring registration of information under section 691 of the 1985 Act or opens a branch in Great Britain requiring registration of information under Schedule 21A to the 1985 Act, or proposes to establish such a place of business or open such a branch

that beneficiary shall, in a case falling within (a) or (c) above notify to the company the service address, and in a case falling within (b) above notify the service address to be included in the statement as provided in Schedule 1 to the 1985 Act.

[7065]

9—(1) Where an applicant for a confidentiality order or a beneficiary of an order holds, or proposes to hold, office as a director, secretary or permanent representative of more than one company the service address specified by that applicant or beneficiary in relation to each such company must be the same, and that address shall have effect for all offices held, or proposed to be held, by that applicant or beneficiary.

(2) A service address must be at a place at which service of documents may be effected by physical delivery other than a PO or a DX Box Number and where that delivery is capable of being recorded by the obtaining of an acknowledgement of delivery by any person.

(3) A service address must be situated within a state within the European Economic Area, and "a state within the European Economic Area" means a state which is a member of the European Communities and the Republic of Iceland, the Kingdom of Norway and the Principality of Liechtenstein.

[7066]

PART III

10 Duration and renewal of a confidentiality order

(1) Subject to paragraphs (2), (3), and (4) a confidentiality order shall remain in force for the period of five years from the date on which it is made unless revoked earlier under regulation 11.

(2) Where the beneficiary of a confidentiality order ("the existing order") delivers an application under section 723B(1) of the 1985 Act for a further confidentiality order ("the new order") before the expiry of the existing order ("the expiry date") and the Secretary of State decides before the expiry date to make a new order under section 723B(3) of the 1985 Act, the new order shall come into force on the expiry of the existing order.

(3) Where the beneficiary of an existing order delivers an application under section 723B(1) of the 1985 Act for a new order before the expiry date and the Secretary of State has not made a decision under section 723B(3) or (4) of the 1985 Act before that date, the existing order shall continue in force until—

(a) the Secretary of State makes a decision under section 723B(3) of the 1985 Act and the new order is made; or

(b) the application is dismissed under section 723B(4) of the 1985 Act.

(4) Where a confidentiality order is made in relation to an application in respect of which no fee has been paid pursuant to paragraph (8) of regulation 2 that order shall remain in force for a period equal to the period for which the confidentiality order referred to in paragraph (8) of regulation 2, made under the LLP Regulations, is to remain in force.

[7067]

11 Revocation of a confidentiality order

(1) The Secretary of State may revoke a confidentiality order at any time if she is satisfied that—

(a) the beneficiary of the order, or any other person, in purported compliance with any provision of these Regulations, has furnished the Secretary of State with false, misleading or inaccurate information; or

(b) the registrar has not received, within the period of 28 days beginning with the date on which the beneficiary of the order was sent notice under regulation 4 of the Secretary of State's decision, in relation to each company of which that beneficiary is a director, secretary or permanent representative, the information in respect of the service address required to be delivered to the registrar under sections 288, 692 or Schedule 21A of the 1985 Act, as the case may be, by virtue of the making of the order; or

(c) the registrar has not received within the period of 28 days from—
   (i) any change or alteration among, or to, the directors, the secretary or permanent representatives by virtue of the appointment of a beneficiary of any order; or
   (ii) any change in the particulars of the usual residential address or the service address of the beneficiary of an order, in relation to each company of which that beneficiary is a director, secretary or permanent representative,

the information required to be delivered to the registrar under sections 288, 692 or Schedule 21A of the 1985 Act, as the case may be, of any such change or alteration, whether that change or alteration occurred before or after the making of the confidentiality order; or

(d) any statement delivered to the registrar under section 10(2) of the 1985 Act naming an individual in respect of whom a confidentiality order under section 723B of that Act has been made did not contain the service address of the beneficiary or was not accompanied by a statement under section 10(2A) containing the usual residential address of the beneficiary; or

(e) any return required to be delivered to the registrar under section 691(1)(b)(i) of, or paragraph 1(1) of Schedule 21A to, the 1985 Act does not contain the service address of the beneficiary or any return required to be delivered to the registrar under sub-section (5) of section 691 of, or paragraph 9 of Schedule 21A to, the 1985 Act is not so delivered; or

(f) any address purporting to be the service address of a beneficiary of an order which has been notified to the registrar under any provision of the 1985 Act which does not comply with all the requirements of regulation 9.

(2) Where a beneficiary of an order is also the beneficiary of a confidentiality order made under the LLP Regulations which is revoked under those Regulations, the order made under section 723B of the 1985 Act is also revoked.

(3) If the Secretary of State proposes to revoke an order under this regulation, other than one revoked under paragraph (2), she shall send the beneficiary of the order notice.

(4) The notice must—

(a) state the grounds on which it is proposed to revoke the order;

(b) inform the beneficiary that he may, within the period of 21 days beginning with the date of the notice, deliver representations to the Secretary of State; and

(c) state that if representations are not received by the Secretary of State within that period, the order will be revoked at the expiry of that period.

(5) If the beneficiary delivers representations as to why the order should not be revoked within the period specified in paragraph (4), the Secretary of State shall have regard to the representations in determining whether to revoke the order, and shall send the beneficiary notice of her decision, and such notice shall be sent within five working days of the decision being made.

(6) Any communication by the Secretary of State in respect of the revocation or proposed revocation of a confidentiality order shall be sent to the beneficiary at his usual residential address.

[7068]

12 Notification of cessation of a confidentiality order

On a confidentiality order ceasing to have effect, for whatever reason, the beneficiary of that order shall notify every relevant company within the meaning of section 723D(1)(a) of the 1985 Act of which he is a director or secretary, of that order ceasing to have effect within five days of its so ceasing to have effect.

[7069]

PART IV

13 Access to confidential records

(1) Subject to paragraph (2) a competent authority is entitled to inspect, and take copies of, confidential records.

(2) The circumstances in which a competent authority may inspect, and take copies of, confidential records are that the registrar has made a determination, in respect of that

competent authority, as to the manner in which that competent authority and its officers, servants and representatives may inspect, and take copies of, confidential records.

(3) The registrar may from time to time vary or revoke any determination with the consent of the competent authority in respect of whom it has been made.

[7070]

NOTES

Fees: see Appendix 3 (Fees Instruments) at **[A3]**.

14 Disclosure of relevant information

(1) Subject to regulation 13 the disclosure of relevant information by any person is prohibited in the following circumstances—

(a) where the information disclosed was delivered to the registrar, after the making of a confidentiality order in relation to the beneficiary of an order to whom the information relates, in the course of the performance of the duties of the registrar under the 1985 Act in respect of that information and the information was obtained by the person disclosing it from the registrar;

(b) where the information disclosed was provided to a company, of which the beneficiary of the order to which the information relates was a director, secretary or permanent representative, after the making of that order, for the purpose of enabling the company to comply with sections 288, 289, 290, 691, 692 and Schedule 21A of the 1985 Act, as the case may be, and the information was obtained by the person disclosing it from the company.

(2) Paragraph (1) does not prohibit the disclosure of relevant information by a competent authority which is made for the purpose of facilitating the carrying out of a public function and "public function" includes—

(a) any function conferred by or in accordance with any provision contained in any enactment or subordinate legislation;

(b) any function conferred by or in accordance with any provision contained in the Community Treaties or any Community instrument;

(c) any similar function conferred on persons by or under provisions having effect as part of the law of a country or territory outside the United Kingdom;

(d) any function exercisable in relation to the investigation of any criminal offence or for the purposes of any criminal proceedings,

and disclosure for the purpose of facilitating the carrying out of a public function includes disclosure in relation to, and for the purpose of, any proceedings whether civil, criminal or disciplinary in which the competent authority engages while carrying out its public functions.

(3) Paragraph (1) does not prohibit the disclosure of relevant information where the disclosure—

(a) facilitates the creation and maintenance of confidential records, the protected part of the register of a company, any return by an oversea company of information which is to form part of confidential records and the provision of facilities for the inspection and copying of confidential records; or

(b) is by the registrar, or any person performing functions on his behalf, of any relevant information obtained in the circumstances described in sub-paragraph (1)(a), included in any document delivered to the registrar under any provision of the 1985 Act where that document is prescribed in respect of the delivery to the registrar of any information which is not relevant information and that document is made available for inspection and copying as if that were required by section 709(1) of the 1985 Act; or

(c) is by any person of any relevant information obtained by that person from any document as is referred to in sub-paragraph (b).

(4) Paragraph (1) does not prohibit the disclosure by any person of relevant information obtained in the course of the performance of their duties or functions, where that disclosure occurred notwithstanding the exercise by that person of the due care and diligence in maintaining the confidentiality, required by the 1985 Act and these Regulations, of that information, that could reasonably be expected of a person performing those duties and functions.

(5) In this regulation—

"enactment" includes—

(a) an Act of the Scottish Parliament;
(b) Northern Ireland legislation;

"subordinate legislation" has the meaning given in the Interpretation Act 1978 and also includes an instrument made under an Act of the Scottish Parliament or under Northern Ireland legislation.

[7071]

PART V

15 Form and delivery of notices etc

(1) Any notice—

(a) by the Secretary of State under regulation 4, 11(3) or 11(5); or

(b) to the Secretary of State under regulation 2(9);

and any representations made to the Secretary of State under regulation 11 shall be in legible form.

(2) Where any notice is required to be sent by the Secretary of State to the usual residential address of any person, that notice is validly sent if sent to the address of that person, shown in the records of the registrar available for inspection or copying under section 709 of the 1985 Act or the confidential records as the case may be when the notice is sent.

[7072]

16 Amendments of enactments

The enactments mentioned in Schedule 2 to these Regulations shall have effect with the amendments specified being amendments supplemental to, and consequential upon, the making of these Regulations.

[7073]

17 Offences and penalties

(1) Any person who, in an application under section 723B of the 1985 Act, makes a statement which he knows to be false in a material particular, or recklessly makes a statement, which is false in a material particular, shall be guilty of an offence.

(2) Any person who discloses information in contravention of regulation 14 shall be guilty of an offence.

(3) A person guilty of an offence under paragraph (1) or (2) shall be liable—

(a) on conviction on indictment, to imprisonment for a term not exceeding two years or to a fine or to both; and

(b) on summary conviction, to imprisonment not exceeding six months, or to a fine not exceeding the statutory maximum or to both.

[7074]

SCHEDULES

SCHEDULE 1
COMPETENT AUTHORITIES

Regulation 1

the Secretary of State;

the registrar and the registrar of companies for Northern Ireland;

an inspector appointed under Part XIV of the Companies Act 1985 or regulation 30 of the Open-Ended Investment Companies Regulations 2001;

any person authorised to exercise powers under section 447 of the Companies Act 1985, or section 84 of the Companies Act 1989;

any person exercising functions conferred by Part VI of the Financial Services and Markets Act 2000 or the competent authority under that Part;

a person appointed to make a report under section 166 of the Financial Services and Markets Act 2000;

a person appointed to conduct an investigation under section 167 or 168(3) or (5) of the Financial Services and Markets Act 2000;

an inspector appointed under section 284 of the Financial Services and Markets Act 2000;

the Department of Enterprise, Trade and Investment in Northern Ireland;

the Scottish Executive;

the Scotland Office;

the National Assembly for Wales;

the Wales Office (Office of the Secretary of State for Wales);

the Treasury;

the Commissioners of HM Customs and Excise;

the Commissioners of Inland Revenue;

the Bank of England;

the Director of Public Prosecutions and the Director of Public Prosecutions in Northern Ireland;

the Serious Fraud Office;

the Secret Intelligence Service;

the Security Service;

the Financial Services Authority;

the Competition Commission;

the Occupational Pensions Regulatory Authority;

the Panel on Takeovers and Mergers;

the Chief Registrar of Friendly Societies and the Registrar for Credit Unions and Industrial and Provident Societies for Northern Ireland;

the [Office of Fair Trading];

the Office of the Information Commissioner;

the Friendly Societies Commission;

a local weights and measures authority;

the Charity Commission;

an official receiver appointed under section 399 of the Insolvency Act 1986;

a person acting as an insolvency practitioner within the meaning of section 388 of the Insolvency Act 1986;

an inspector appointed under Part XV of the Companies (Northern Ireland) Order 1986 or Regulation 22 of the Open-Ended Investment Companies (Companies with Variable Capital) Regulations (Northern Ireland) 1997;

any person authorized to exercise powers under Article 440 of the Companies (Northern Ireland) Order 1986;

the Official Receiver for Northern Ireland;

a police force;

any procurator fiscal;

an overseas regulatory authority within the meaning of section 82 of the Companies Act 1989.

[7075]

NOTES

Words in square brackets substituted by virtue of the Enterprise Act 2002, s 2(1), as from 1 April 2003.

Office of fair Trading: see the note "Substitution of references to the Director General of Fair Trading" at **[4351]**.

Commissioners of Inland Revenue; Commissioners of Customs and Excise: references to the Commissioners of Inland Revenue and the Commissioners of Customs and Excise are now to be taken as a reference to the Commissioners for Her Majesty's Revenue and Customs; see the Commissioners for Revenue and Customs Act 2005, s 50(1), (7).

(*Sch 2 amends CA 1985, ss 10, 288, 289, 290, 691, 692, Schs 1, 21A at* **[12]**, **[293]**, **[295]**, **[296]**, **[535]**, **[536]**, **[634]**, **[681]**.)

LIMITED LIABILITY PARTNERSHIPS (NO 2) REGULATIONS 2002

(SI 2002/913)

NOTES

Made: 31 March 2002.

Authority: Limited Liability Partnerships Act 2000, ss 15–17.

Commencement: 2 April 2002 (see reg 1 at **[7076]**). Where any provision in this work (including any inserted or substituted provision) came into force for all purposes on or before 1 July 2005, commencement information is not noted at provision level.

As of 1 July 2007, these Regulations had not been amended.

1 Citation and commencement

(1) These Regulations may be cited as the Limited Liability Partnerships (No 2) Regulations 2002.

(2) These Regulations shall come into force on 2nd April 2002.

[7076]

2 Interpretation

(1) In these Regulations—

"the 1985 Act" means the Companies Act 1985;

"the principal Act" means the Limited Liability Partnerships Act 2000; and

"the principal Regulations" means the Limited Liability Partnerships Regulations 2001.

(2) In these Regulations, unless the contrary intention appears, expressions which are also used in the principal Act or the principal Regulations shall have the same meanings as in that Act or in those Regulations.

[7077]

3 Application of Sections 723B–723F of the 1985 Act to limited liability partnerships

Sections 723B–723F of the 1985 Act shall apply to limited liability partnerships with the modifications set out in the Schedule.

[7078]

NOTES

Note: the commencement by the Companies Act 2006 (Commencement No 1, Transitional Provisions and Savings) Order 2006, SI 2006/3428 of the repeal of s 723C(1)(a) of the 1985 Act by the Companies Act 2006, does not affect the operation of that section as applied by these Regulations; see the Companies Act 2006 (Commencement No 2, Consequential Amendments, Transitional Provisions and Savings) Order 2007, SI 2007/1093, art 11 at **[7624]**.

SCHEDULE
MODIFICATIONS TO PROVISIONS OF SECTIONS 723B–723F OF THE 1985 ACT IN THEIR APPLICATION TO LIMITED LIABILITY PARTNERSHIPS

Regulation 3

Provision of Part VII	**Modification**
Section 723B (confidentiality orders)	In subsection (2)(a), for "a director, secretary or permanent representative of a relevant company" substitute "a member or designated member of a relevant limited liability partnership".

Provision of Part VII	Modification
	In subsection (5), for "company" substitute "limited liability partnership" and for "a director, secretary or permanent representative" substitute "a member or a designated member".
Section 723C (effect of confidentiality orders)	For subsection (1)(b), substitute "section 364 shall have effect in relation to each affected limited liability partnership of which the individual is a member or designated member as if the reference in subsection (b) of that section to the individual's usual residential address were a reference to the address for the time being specified by the individual in relation to that limited liability partnership under section 723B(5) or subsection (7) below.".
	Omit subsection (6).
	In subsection (7)(a), for "company of which he becomes a director, secretary or permanent representative" substitute "limited liability partnership of which he becomes a member or a designated member".
	In subsection (8), for "A company is an affected company" substitute "A limited liability partnership is an affected limited liability partnership".
Section 723D (construction of sections 723B and 723C)	In subsection (1), for ""relevant company"" substitute ""relevant limited liability partnership"".
	In subsection (1)(a) for "a company formed and registered under this Act or an existing company" substitute "a limited liability partnership formed and registered under the Limited Liability Partnerships Act 2000"; and delete the words "or (b) an oversea company".
	Omit subsection (2).
	In subsection (4), omit ""director" and "secretary", in relation to an oversea company, have the same meanings as in Chapter 1 of Part 23 of this Act;".
	In subsection (7), for "company" in the first place where it occurs substitute "limited liability partnership" and for "company or a company to which section 690A applies" substitute "limited liability partnership".
Section 723F (Regulations under sections 723B to 723E)	Omit the words "In section 288 (register of directors and secretaries), after subsection (6) there shall be inserted—
	"(7) Subsections (3) and (5) are subject to section 723B."

[7079]

NOTES

See also the note to reg 3 at **[7078]**.

LIMITED LIABILITY PARTNERSHIPS (PARTICULARS OF USUAL RESIDENTIAL ADDRESS) (CONFIDENTIALITY ORDERS) REGULATIONS 2002

(SI 2002/915)

NOTES

Made: 31 March 2002.

Authority: Companies Act 1985, ss 723B–723F.

Commencement: 2 April 2002 (see reg 1 at **[7080]**). Where any provision in this work (including any inserted or substituted provision) came into force for all purposes on or before 1 July 2005, commencement information is not noted at provision level.

These Regulations are reproduced as amended by: the Enterprise Act 2002.

ARRANGEMENT OF REGULATIONS

1 Citation, commencement and interpretation

(1) These Regulations may be cited as the Limited Liability Partnerships (Particulars of Usual Residential Address) (Confidentiality Orders) Regulations 2002.

(2) These Regulations shall come into force on 2nd April 2002.

(3) In these Regulations—

"the 1985 Act" means the Companies Act 1985 as applied to limited liability partnerships by the Limited Liability Partnerships Regulations 2001 and by the Limited Liability Partnerships (No 2) Regulations 2002;

"the 2000 Act" means the Limited Liability Partnerships Act 2000;

"beneficiary of an order" means an individual in relation to whom a confidentiality order is in force;

"Companies (Particulars of Usual Residential Address) Regulations" means the Companies (Particulars of Usual Residential Address) (Confidentiality Orders) Regulations 2002;

"competent authority" means any authority specified in Schedule 1 to these Regulations;

"police force" means a police force within the meaning of section 101(1) of the Police Act 1996 or section 50 of the Police (Scotland) Act 1967;

PART IV
STATUTORY INSTRUMENTS

"member" includes "designated member";

"principal Regulations" means the Limited Liability Partnerships Regulations 2001;

"service address" means the address specified pursuant to regulation 2(2)(b) in an application made under section 723B(1) of the 1985 Act or, if another address has been substituted under regulation 7, the address most recently substituted under that regulation; and

"working day" means any day other than a Saturday, a Sunday, Christmas Day, Good Friday or a day which is a bank holiday in any part of England or Wales under or by virtue of the Banking and Financial Dealings Act 1971.

(4) In these Regulations unless the contrary intention appears, expressions which are also used in the 2000 Act or in the principal Regulations shall have the same meanings as in that Act or in those Regulations.

[7080]

PART I

2 Applications for confidentiality orders under section 723B of the 1985 Act

(1) An application for a confidentiality order shall be made to the Secretary of State.

(2) An application for a confidentiality order shall—

(a) be in such form and contain such information and be accompanied by such evidence as the Secretary of State may from time to time direct;

(b) specify each limited liability partnership of which the applicant is or proposes to become a member and shall specify an address complying with regulation 9.

(3) The Secretary of State may from time to time direct different information or evidence be provided for different cases or categories of application.

(4) The Secretary of State may require any information or evidence delivered by an applicant to be verified in such manner as she may direct.

(5) The Secretary of State may require any application to be supported by a statement by any limited liability partnership to which the application relates that the limited liability partnership wishes a confidentiality order to be made in respect of the applicant together with the statement of the reasons for that wish.

(6) At any time after receiving an application and before determining it, the Secretary of State may require that any applicant deliver additional information or evidence including the delivery by a limited liability partnership of a statement complying with paragraph (5).

(7) Subject to paragraph (8) each application shall be accompanied by a fee of £100, and the Secretary of State may reject any application without considering it unless it is accompanied by such fee.

(8) No fee shall be payable where an application is made by an applicant—

(a) who at the same time has made an application for a confidentiality order under the Companies (Particulars of Usual Residence Address) Regulations, and where a fee has been paid in respect of that application; or

(b) in respect of whom, at the time of the application, a confidentiality order made under the Companies (Particulars of Usual Residential Address) Regulations is in force.

(9) An applicant may withdraw his application, by notice delivered to the Secretary of State, at any time before the Secretary of State makes a decision on the application, and the Secretary of State may retain the fee paid in respect of that application.

[7081]

3 Referral of questions for the purposes of the determination of an application

(1) The Secretary of State may, in respect of any application or category of applications, refer to a relevant body any question relating to an assessment, in the case of such application or category of applications, of the nature and extent of any risk of violence or intimidation considered by the applicant as likely to be created in relation to the applicant, or any person living with him, by virtue of the availability for inspection by members of the public of particulars of his usual residential address.

(2) The Secretary of State may also refer to a relevant body any question as to the nature or extent of any risk of violence or intimidation likely to be created in relation to any applicant or category of applicants or persons living with them as a result of their involvement in the activities of a particular limited liability partnership or category of limited liability partnerships, of a particular sector of commerce or industry or of a particular type of business activity.

(3) The Secretary of State may accept any answer to a question referred in accordance with paragraph (1) or (2) as providing sufficient evidence of the nature and extent of any risk relevant to an applicant or any person living with him for the purposes of any determination under section 723B(3) or (4) of the 1985 Act.

(4) In this regulation, "relevant body" means any police force and any other person whom the Secretary of State considers may be able to assist in answering a question referred to that person under paragraph (1) or (2).

[7082]

4 Notification of the outcome of an application

The Secretary of State shall send the applicant at his usual residential address, as stated in his application, notice of her decision under section 723B(3) or (4) of the 1985 Act and such notice shall be sent within five working days of the decision being made.

[7083]

5 Appeals

(1) An applicant who has received notice under regulation 4 that his application for a confidentiality order has been unsuccessful may appeal to the High Court or the Court of Session on the grounds that the decision—

(a) is unlawful;

(b) is irrational or unreasonable; or

(c) has been made on the basis of procedural impropriety or otherwise contravenes the rules of natural justice.

(2) No appeal under this regulation may be brought unless the leave of the court has been obtained.

(3) An applicant must bring an appeal within 21 days of the sending of the notice under regulation 4 or, with the court's permission, after the end of such period, but only if the court is satisfied—

(a) where permission is sought before the end of that period, that there is good reason for the applicant being unable to bring the appeal in time; or

(b) where permission is sought after that time, that there was a good reason for the applicant's failure to bring the appeal in time and for any delay in applying for permission.

(4) The court determining an appeal may—

(a) dismiss the appeal; or

(b) quash the decision,

and where the court quashes a decision it may refer the matter to the Secretary of State with a direction to reconsider it and to make a determination in accordance with the findings of the court.

[7084]

PART II

6 Service addresses

Where an application for a confidentiality order is made by a member, that individual shall notify to each of the limited liability partnerships specified in the application the service address specified in the application pursuant to regulation 2(2)(b).

[7085]

7 If a beneficiary of an order wishes to substitute another address, complying with regulation 9, for an address specified by him under regulation 2(2)(b) or previously notified by him under this regulation, he shall do so by notifying every limited liability partnership of which he is a member of the address to be substituted.

[7086]

8 Where the beneficiary of an order—

(a) becomes a member of a limited liability partnership; or

(b) is to be named in an incorporation document delivered under sections 2 and 3 of the 2000 Act as a member of a limited liability partnership to be formed under the 2000 Act,

that beneficiary shall, in a case falling within (a) above notify to the limited liability partnership the service address, and in a case falling within (b) above notify the service address to be included in the statement as provided in section 2(2A) of the 2000 Act.

[7087]

9—(1) Where an applicant for a confidentiality order or a beneficiary of an order is, or proposes to become, a member of more than one limited liability partnership the service address specified by that applicant or beneficiary in relation to each such limited liability partnership must be the same, and that address shall have effect in all cases where the applicant is or proposes to become a member of a limited liability partnership.

(2) A service address must be at a place at which service of documents may be effected by physical delivery other than a PO or a DX Box Number and where that delivery is capable of being recorded by the obtaining of an acknowledgement of delivery by any person.

(3) A service address must be situated within a state within the European Economic Area, and "a state within the European Economic Area" means a state which is a member of the European Communities and the Republic of Iceland, the Kingdom of Norway and the Principality of Liechtenstein.

[7088]

PART III

10 Duration and renewal of a confidentiality order

(1) Subject to paragraphs (2), (3) and (4) a confidentiality order shall remain in force for the period of five years from the date on which it is made unless revoked earlier under regulation 11.

(2) Where the beneficiary of a confidentiality order ("the existing order") delivers an application under section 723B(1) of the 1985 Act for a further confidentiality order ("the new order") before the expiry of the existing order ("the expiry date") and the Secretary of State decides before the expiry date to make a new order under section 723B(3) of the 1985 Act, the new order shall come into force on the expiry of the existing order.

(3) Where the beneficiary of an existing order delivers an application under section 723B(1) of the 1985 Act for a new order before the expiry date and the Secretary of State has not made a decision under section 723B(3) or (4) of the 1985 Act before that date, the existing order shall continue in force until—

(a) the Secretary of State makes a decision under section 723B(3) of the 1985 Act and the new order is made; or

(b) the application is dismissed under section 723B(4) of the 1985 Act.

(4) Where a confidentiality order is made in relation to an application in respect of which no fee has been paid pursuant to paragraph (8) of regulation 2 that order shall remain in force for a period equal to the period for which the confidentiality order referred to in paragraph (8) of regulation 2, made under the Companies (Particulars of Usual Residential Address) Regulations, is to remain in force.

[7089]

11 Revocation of a confidentiality order

(1) The Secretary of State may revoke a confidentiality order at any time if she is satisfied that—

(a) the beneficiary of the order, or any other person, in purported compliance with any provision of these Regulations, has furnished the Secretary of State with false, misleading or inaccurate information; or

(b) the registrar has not received, within the period of 28 days beginning with the date on which the beneficiary of the order was sent notice under regulation 4 of the Secretary of State's decision, in relation to each limited liability partnership of which that beneficiary is a member, the information in respect of the service address required to be delivered to the registrar under section 9 of the 2000 Act, by virtue of the making of the order; or

(c) the registrar has not received, within the period of 28 days from—

(i) any change or alteration among, or to, the members by virtue of the appointment of a beneficiary of an order; or

(ii) any change in the particulars of the usual residential address or the service address of the beneficiary of an order, in relation to each limited liability partnership of which that beneficiary is a member,

the information required to be delivered to the registrar under section 9 of the 2000 Act or sections 288 or 288A of the 1985 Act, of any such change or alteration, whether that change or alteration occurred before or after the making of the confidentiality order; or

(d) any statement delivered to the registrar under sections 2 and 3 of the 2000 Act naming as a member an individual in respect of whom a confidentiality order under the 1985 Act has been made did not contain the service address of the beneficiary or was not accompanied by a statement under the 2000 Act containing the usual residential address of the beneficiary; or

(e) any address purporting to be the service address of a beneficiary of an order which has been notified to the registrar under any provision of the 1985 Act or of the 2000 Act which does not comply with all the requirements of regulation 9.

(2) Where a beneficiary is also the beneficiary of a confidentiality order made under the Companies (Particulars of Usual Residential Address) Regulations which is revoked, any confidentiality order made in respect of that beneficiary as a member of a limited liability partnership is also revoked.

(3) If the Secretary of State proposes to revoke an order under this regulation, other than one revoked under paragraph (2), she shall send the beneficiary of the order notice.

(4) The notice must—

(a) state the grounds on which it is proposed to revoke the order;

(b) inform the beneficiary that he may, within a period of 21 days beginning with the date of the notice, deliver representations to the Secretary of State; and

(c) state that if representations are not received by the Secretary of State within that period, the order will be revoked at the expiry of that period.

(5) If the beneficiary delivers representations as to why the order should not be revoked within the period specified in paragraph (4), the Secretary of State shall have regard to the representations in determining whether to revoke the order, and shall send the beneficiary notice of her decision, and such notice shall be sent within five working days of the decision being made.

(6) Any communication by the Secretary of State in respect of the revocation or proposed revocation of a confidentiality order shall be sent to the beneficiary at his usual residential address.

[7090]

12 Notification of cessation of a confidentiality order

On a confidentiality order ceasing to have effect, for whatever reason, the beneficiary of that order shall notify every relevant limited liability partnership within the meaning of section 723D(1)(a) of the 1985 Act of which he is a member, of that order ceasing to have effect within five days of its so ceasing to have effect.

[7091]

PART IV

13 Access to confidential records

(1) Subject to paragraph (2), a competent authority is entitled to inspect, and take copies of, confidential records.

(2) The circumstances in which a competent authority may inspect, and take copies of, confidential records are that the registrar has made a determination, in respect of that

competent authority, as to the manner in which that competent authority and its officers, servants and representatives may inspect, and take copies of, confidential records.

(3) The registrar may from time to time vary or revoke any determination with the consent of the competent authority in respect of whom it has been made.

[7092]

NOTES

Fees: see Appendix 3 (Fees Instruments) at **[A3]**.

14 Disclosure of relevant information

(1) Subject to regulation 13 the disclosure of relevant information by any person is prohibited in the following circumstances—

(a) where the information disclosed was delivered to the registrar, after the making of a confidentiality order in relation to the beneficiary of an order to whom the information relates, in the course the performance of the duties of the registrar under the 1985 Act or the 2000 Act in respect of that information and the information was obtained by the person disclosing it from the registrar;

(b) where the information disclosed was provided to a limited liability partnership, of which the beneficiary of the order to which the information relates was a member, after the making of that order, for the purpose of enabling the limited liability partnership to comply with the requirements of the 2000 Act and of the 1985 Act, as the case may be, and the information was obtained by the person disclosing it from the limited liability partnership.

(2) Paragraph (1) does not prohibit the disclosure of relevant information by a competent authority which is made for the purpose of facilitating the carrying out of a public function and "public function" includes—

(a) any function conferred by or in accordance with any provision contained in any enactment or subordinate legislation;

(b) any function conferred by or in accordance with any provision contained in the Community Treaties or any Community instrument;

(c) any similar function conferred on persons by or under provisions having effect as part of the law of a country or territory outside the United Kingdom;

(d) any function exercisable in relation to the investigation of any criminal offence or for the purposes of any criminal proceedings,

and disclosure for the purpose of facilitating the carrying out of a public function includes disclosure in relation to, and for the purpose of, any proceedings whether civil, criminal or disciplinary in which the competent authority engages while carrying out its public functions.

(3) Paragraph (1) does not prohibit the disclosure of relevant information where the disclosure—

(a) facilitates the creation and maintenance of confidential records of a limited liability partnership, and the provision of facilities for the inspection and copying of confidential records; or

(b) is by the registrar, or any person performing functions on his behalf, of any relevant information obtained in the circumstances described in sub-paragraph (1)(a), included in any document delivered to the registrar under any provision of the 1985 Act or of the 2000 Act where that document is prescribed or approved by the registrar in respect of the delivery to the registrar of any information which is not relevant information and that document is made available for inspection and copying as if that were required by section 709(1) of the 1985 Act; or

(c) is by any person of any relevant information obtain by that person from any document as is referred to in sub-paragraph (b).

(4) Paragraph (1) does not prohibit the disclosure by any person of relevant information obtained in the course of the performance of their duties or functions, where that disclosure occurred notwithstanding the exercise by that person of the due care and diligence in maintaining the confidentiality, required by the 1985 Act and these Regulations, of that information, that could reasonably by expected of a person performing those duties and functions.

(5) In this regulation—

"enactment" includes—

(a) an Act of the Scottish Parliament;
(b) Northern Ireland legislation;

"subordinate legislation" has the meaning given in the Interpretation Act 1978 and also includes an instrument made under an Act of the Scottish Parliament or under Northern Ireland legislation.

[7093]

PART V

15 Form and delivery of notices etc

(1) Any notice—

(a) by the Secretary of State under regulation 4, 11(3) or 11(5); or

(b) to the Secretary of State under regulation 2(9);

and any representations made to the Secretary of State under regulation 11 shall be legible form.

(2) Where any notice is required to be sent by the Secretary of State to the usual residential address of any person, that notice is validly sent if sent to the address of that person, shown in the records of the registrar available for inspection or copying under section 709 of the 1985 Act or the confidential records as the case may be when the notice is sent.

[7094]

16 Amendments of enactments

The enactments mentioned in Schedule 2 to these Regulations shall have effect with the amendments specified being amendments supplemental to, and consequential upon, the making of these Regulations.

[7095]

17 Offence and penalties

(1) Any person who, in an application under 723B of the 1985 Act, makes a statement which he knows to be false in a material particular, or recklessly makes a statement which is false in a material particular, shall be guilty of an offence.

(2) Any person who discloses information in contravention of regulation 14 shall be guilty of an offence.

(3) A person guilty of an offence under paragraph (1) or (2) shall be liable—

(a) on conviction on indictment, to imprisonment for a term not exceeding two years or to a fine or to both; and

(b) on summary conviction, to imprisonment not exceeding six months, or to a fine not exceeding the statutory maximum or to both.

[7096]

SCHEDULES

SCHEDULE 1
COMPETENT AUTHORITIES

Regulation 1

the Secretary of State;

the registrar and the registrar of companies for Northern Ireland;

an inspector appointed under Part XIV of the Companies Act 1985 or regulation 30 of the Open-Ended Investment Companies Regulations 2001;

any person authorised to exercise powers under section 447 of the Companies Act 1985 or section 84 of the Companies Act 1989;

any person exercising functions conferred by Part VI of the Financial Services and Markets Act 2000 or the competent authority under that Part;

a person appointed to make a report under section 166 of the Financial Services and Markets Act 2000;

a person appointed to conduct an investigation under section 167 or 168(3) or (5) of the Financial Services and Markets Act 2000;

an inspector appointed under section 284 of the Financial Services and Markets Act 2000;

the Department of Enterprise, Trade and Investment in Northern Ireland;

the Scottish Executive;

the Scotland Office;

the National Assembly for Wales;

the Wales Office (Office of the Secretary of State for Wales);

the Treasury;

the Commissioners of HM Customs and Excise;

the Commissioners of Inland Revenue;

the Bank of England;

the Director of Public Prosecutions and the Director of Public Prosecutions in Northern Ireland;

the Serious Fraud Office;

the Secret Intelligence Service;

the Security Service;

the Financial Services Authority;

the Competition Commission;

the Occupational Pensions Regulatory Authority;

the Panel on Takeovers and Mergers;

the Chief Registrar of Friendly Societies and the Registrar for Credit Unions and Industrial and Provident Societies for Northern Ireland;

the [Office of Fair Trading];

the Office of the Information Commissioner;

the Friendly Societies Commission;

a local weights and measures authority;

the Charity Commission;

an official receiver appointed under section 399 of the Insolvency Act 1986;

a person acting as an insolvency practitioner within the meaning of section 388 of the Insolvency Act 1986;

an inspector appointed under Part XV of the Companies (Northern Ireland) Order 1986 or Regulation 22 of the Open-Ended Investment Companies (Companies with Variable Capital) Regulations (Northern Ireland) 1997;

any person authorised to exercise powers under Article 440 of the Companies (Northern Ireland) Order 1986;

the Official Receiver for Northern Ireland;

a police force;

any procurator fiscal;

an overseas regulatory authority within the meaning of section 82 of the Companies Act 1989.

[7097]–[7147]

NOTES

Words in square brackets substituted by virtue of the Enterprise Act 2002, s 2(1), as from 1 April 2003.

Office of fair Trading: see the note "Substitution of references to the Director General of Fair Trading" at **[4351]**.

Commissioners of Inland Revenue; Commissioners of Customs and Excise: references to the Commissioners of Inland Revenue and the Commissioners of Customs and Excise are now to be taken as a reference to the Commissioners for Her Majesty's Revenue and Customs; see the Commissioners for Revenue and Customs Act 2005, s 50(1), (7).

(*Sch 2 inserts the Limited Liability Partnerships Act 2000, ss 2(2A), (2B), 9(3A), (3B) at* **[3501]**, **[3508]**, *and CA 1985 s 288A at* **[294]**.)

ENTERPRISE ACT 2002 (MERGER PRENOTIFICATION) REGULATIONS 2003

(SI 2003/1369)

NOTES

Made: 23 May 2003.

Authority: Enterprise Act 2002, ss 101,124(2).

Commencement: 20 June 2003 (see reg 1 at **[7148]**). Where any provision in this work (including any inserted or substituted provision) came into force for all purposes on or before 1 July 2005, commencement information is not noted at provision level.

As of 1 July 2007, these Regulations had not been amended.

ARRANGEMENT OF REGULATIONS

1 Citation and commencement

This Order may be cited as the Enterprise Act 2002 (Merger Prenotification) Regulations 2003 and shall come into force on 20th June 2003.

[7148]

2 Interpretation

(1) In these Regulations

"the Act" means the Enterprise Act 2002; and

"working day" means any day which is not—

(a) Saturday, Sunday, Good Friday or Christmas Day; or

(b) a bank holiday in England and Wales.

(2) A reference in these Regulations to a person who does anything on behalf of a person who is authorised to give a merger notice or who has given such notice shall be construed as limited to a reference to a person who does so having been authorised so to act in accordance with regulation 14 of these Regulations.

[7149]

3 Person authorised to give a merger notice

A merger notice may be given under section 96(1) of the Act by any person carrying on an enterprise to which the notified arrangements relate.

[7150]

4 Time limit for disclosure of material information

The time specified for the purpose of section 100(1)(c) of the Act (the time before the end of the period for considering a merger notice within which material information must be disclosed) is five working days.

[7151]

5 Time at which a merger notice is to be treated as received

A merger notice given under section 96(1) of the Act shall be treated as having been received by the OFT—

(a) subject to paragraph (b), on the day on which it is in fact received by the OFT;

(b) where it is received by the OFT on any day which is not a working day or after 5.00 pm on any working day, on the next working day,

and section 7 of the Interpretation Act 1978 shall not apply.

[7152]

6 Rejection of a merger notice

A rejection of a merger notice under section 99(5) of the Act shall be given in writing and such a notice shall be treated as having been rejected at the time when the rejection is sent to the person who gave the merger notice or a person acting on his behalf.

[7153]

7 Withdrawal of a merger notice

A merger notice may be withdrawn by or on behalf of the person who gave the notice by a notice in writing sent to the OFT.

[7154]

8 Provision of information to the OFT

(1) Any information which—

(a) is, or ought to be, known to the person who gave the merger notice or any connected person, and

(b) is material to the notified arrangements,

or any information requested by the OFT under section 99(2) of the Act, shall be provided or disclosed in writing.

(2) Subject to paragraph (3), any information provided or disclosed to the OFT under this regulation shall be treated as having been so provided or disclosed on the day on which it is in fact received by the OFT.

(3) Where information provided or disclosed to the OFT under this regulation is received by the OFT on any day which is not a working day or after 5.00 pm on any working day, it shall be treated as having been provided or disclosed to the OFT on the next working day.

(4) Section 7 of the Interpretation Act 1978 shall not apply to the provision or disclosure of any information under this regulation.

(5) Any information requested by the OFT under section 99(2) of the Act shall be treated as provided to the satisfaction of the OFT, for the purposes of section 97(6) of the Act, on the day on which the OFT informs the person who gave the merger notice, or a person acting on his behalf, of the fact that it is satisfied as to the provision of the information requested by it.

[7155]

9 Extension of period for consideration of a merger notice for failure to provide information requested under section 99(2)

In the circumstances in which section 97(6) of the Act applies, the OFT shall inform the person who gave the merger notice, or a person acting on his behalf—

(a) of the fact that it is satisfied as to the provision of the information requested by it or (as the case may be) of its decision to cancel the extension; and

(b) of the time at which it is to be treated as so satisfied or (as the case may be) of the time at which the cancellation is to be treated as having effect.

[7156]

10 Extension of period for consideration of a merger notice to seek undertakings

In the circumstances in which section 97(8) of the Act applies, the OFT shall inform the person who gave the merger notice, or a person acting on his behalf—

(a) of any decision by it to cancel the extension; and

(b) of the time at which such a cancellation is to be treated as having effect.

[7157]

11 Time at which notices relating to undertakings are to be treated as received

A notice given to the OFT under section 97(8)(b) of the Act shall be treated as having been received by it—

(a) subject to paragraph (b), on the day on which it is in fact received by the OFT;

(b) where it is received by the OFT on any day which is not a working day or after 5.00 pm on any working day, on the next working day,

and section 7 of the Interpretation Act 1978 shall not apply.

[7158]

12 Time at which section 97(7), (11) or (13) notices are to be treated as received

A notice given to the person who gave the merger notice, or a person acting on his behalf, under section 97(7), (11) or (13) of the Act shall be treated as having been received by that person—

(a) subject to paragraph (b), on the day on which it is in fact received by that person;

(b) where it is received by that person on any day which is not a working day or after 5.00 pm on any working day, on the next working day,

and section 7 of the Interpretation Act 1978 shall not apply.

[7159]

13 Time at which fees are to be treated as paid

(1) Subject to paragraphs (2) and (3), any fee payable in accordance with a merger notice shall be treated as having been paid on the day on which a valid cheque or other instrument for the correct amount is received by the OFT.

(2) Where a cheque or other instrument received as payment for a fee referred to in paragraph (1) is dishonoured on presentation, the fee shall, subject to paragraph (3), nevertheless be treated as having been paid on the day on which that cheque or other instrument is received if the condition specified in paragraph (4) is subsequently satisfied.

(3) Where a cheque or other instrument in respect of a fee referred to in paragraph (1) is received by the OFT on any day which is not a working day or after 5.00 pm on any working day, it shall be treated as having been received on the next working day.

(4) The condition referred to in paragraph (2) is that, within the period of 20 working days beginning with the first day after the merger notice is, in accordance with regulation 5 of these Regulations, treated as having been received by the OFT, the correct amount of the fee has been properly paid by a valid cheque or other instrument.

(5) Section 7 of the Interpretation Act 1978 shall not apply to the giving or sending of a cheque or other instrument in respect of a fee referred to in paragraph (1).

[7160]

14 Circumstances in which a person is or is not to be treated as acting on behalf of the giver of a merger notice

(1) A person shall be treated as acting on behalf of a person who is authorised to give a merger notice or who has given such a notice only if the person on whose behalf he is to be treated as acting has authorised him so to act in accordance with paragraph (2).

(2) An authorisation to act on behalf of another person for the purposes of paragraph (1) shall be given to the OFT in writing and an authorisation to act on behalf of a company shall be signed by a director or other officer of that company.

(3) A person who has given an authorisation in accordance with paragraph (1) may revoke it by a notice in writing given to the OFT and, where that person is a company, the notice shall be signed by a director or other officer of that company.

[7161]

ENTERPRISE ACT 2002 (MERGER FEES AND DETERMINATION OF TURNOVER) ORDER 2003

(SI 2003/1370)

NOTES

Made: 23 May 2003.

Authority: Enterprise Act 2002, ss 28, 121, 124(2).

Commencement: 20 June 2003 (see art 1 at **[7162]**). Where any provision in this work (including any inserted or substituted provision) came into force for all purposes on or before 1 July 2005, commencement information is not noted at provision level.

Only Pts 1 and 3 of this Order are reproduced here. For Pt 2 (Merger fees), see Appendix 3 (Fees Instruments) at **[A3]**. Pts 1, 3 are reproduced as amended by the Enterprise Act 2002 (Merger Fees and Determination of Turnover) (Amendment) Order 2004, SI 2004/3204 and the Capital Requirements Regulations 2006, SI 2006/3221.

PART 1
GENERAL

1 Citation and commencement

This Order may be cited as the Enterprise Act 2002 (Merger Fees and Determination of Turnover) Order 2003 and shall come into force on 20th June 2003.

[7162]

2 Interpretation

In this Order—

(a) "the Act" means the Enterprise Act 2002;

(b) "applicable turnover" means the turnover of an enterprise in the preceding business year, or in a case to which article 11(4) applies, in the period referred to in that article, determined in accordance with the Schedule to this Order; and where a business year or a period under article 11(4) does not equal 12 months the applicable turnover shall be the amount which bears the same proportion to the applicable turnover during that business year as 12 months does to that period;

(c) "business year" means a period of more than six months in respect of which an enterprise or, if applicable, the business of which it forms part, prepares or is required to prepare accounts; …

(d) "merger reference" means a reference by the OFT to the Commission under section 22 or 33 of the Act [or section 32 of the Water Industry Act 1991] or a reference by the Secretary of State to the Commission under [section 45 of the Act;]

[(e) "water enterprise" means an enterprise carried on by a water undertaker or sewerage undertaker.]

[7163]–[7171]

NOTES

Word omitted revoked, words in second pair of square brackets in para (d) substituted, and para (e) and words in first pair of square brackets in para (d) inserted, by the Enterprise Act 2002 (Merger Fees and Determination of Turnover) (Amendment) Order 2004, SI 2004/3204, art 2(1), (2), as from 29 December 2004.

3–10 (*For arts 3–10 (Pt 2: merger fees) see Appendix 3 (Fees Instruments) at* **[A3]**).

PART 3
DETERMINATION OF TURNOVER

11 Determination of turnover in the United Kingdom of an enterprise

(1) This article shall apply for the purposes referred to in section 28(2) of the Act and [article 5(3)].

(2) The turnover in the United Kingdom of an enterprise shall be, subject to paragraph (3), the applicable turnover for the business year preceding—

(a) where the question whether a relevant merger situation has been created is being determined, the date when the enterprises concerned ceased to be distinct enterprises or such earlier date as the decision-making authority considers appropriate;

(b) where the question whether it is or may be the case that arrangements are in progress or in contemplation which, if carried into effect, will result in the creation of a relevant merger situation is being determined, the date when the decision in relation to a possible reference has been or is to be made, or such earlier date as the decision-making authority considers appropriate.

(3) Where an acquisition or divestment or other transaction or event has occurred since the end of the preceding business year which the decision-making authority considers may have a significant impact on the turnover of the enterprise, that acquisition or divestment or other transaction or event may be taken into account if the decision-making authority considers it appropriate to do so.

(4) Where in the application of this article there is any period in respect of which there is no preceding business year then the applicable turnover shall be the turnover for that period.

[7172]

NOTES

Para (1): words in square brackets substituted the Enterprise Act 2002 (Merger Fees and Determination of Turnover) (Amendment) Order 2004, SI 2004/3204, art 2(1), (8), as from 29 December 2004.

SCHEDULE
APPLICABLE TURNOVER

Article 2

Interpretation

1. In this Schedule:

"aid" means aid within the meaning of Article 87 of the EC Treaty;

"branch" means a place of business in the United Kingdom which forms a legally dependent part of a credit institution or financial institution and which conducts directly all or some of the operations inherent in the business of the undertaking and any number of branches set up in the United Kingdom shall for the purposes of this Order be regarded as a single branch;

"credit institution" means a credit institution for the purposes of [Article 4(1) of Directive 2006/48/EC of the European Parliament and of the Council of 14 June 2006] relating to the taking up and pursuit of the business of credit institutions;

"financial institution" means a financial institution for the purposes of Article 1 of Directive 2000/12/EC of the European Parliament and of the Council of 20 March 2000 relating to the taking up and pursuit of the business of credit institutions;

"insurance undertaking" means an insurance undertaking carrying on the business of direct insurance of a class set out in the Annex to Council Directive (EEC) 73/239 the First Council Directive on the co-ordination of laws, regulations and administrative provisions relating to the taking-up and pursuit of the business of direct insurance other than life assurance or in Article 2 of Directive 2002/83/EC of the European Parliament and of the Council of 5th November 2002 concerning life assurance; and

terms used in this Schedule in respect of the determination of the applicable turnover of credit institutions, financial institutions and insurance undertakings shall (except where the contrary intention appears) have the same meaning as in the relevant Directive.

2. Save in paragraphs 4 to 9, the provisions of this Schedule shall be interpreted in accordance with accounting principles and practices that are generally accepted in the United Kingdom.

General

3. The applicable turnover of an enterprise, other than an enterprise which is a credit institution, financial institution or insurance undertaking shall be limited to the amounts derived from the sale of products and the provision of services falling within the ordinary activities of the enterprise to businesses or consumers in the United Kingdom after deduction of sales rebates, value added tax and other taxes directly related to turnover.

4. Subject to paragraphs 8 and 9, where an enterprise consists of two or more enterprises which are under common ownership or control the applicable turnover shall be calculated by adding together the respective applicable turnover of each of the enterprises under common ownership or control.

5. For the purposes of paragraphs 4 and 7 to 9, enterprises shall in particular be treated as being under common control if they are—

(a) enterprises of interconnected bodies corporate;

(b) enterprises carried on by two or more bodies corporate of which one and the same person or group of persons has control; or

(c) an enterprise carried on by a body corporate and an enterprise carried on by a person or group of persons having control of that body corporate.

6. A person or group of persons able, directly or indirectly, to control or materially influence the policy of a body corporate, or the policy of any person in carrying on an enterprise but without having a controlling interest in that body corporate or in that enterprise, may, for the purposes of paragraph 4, be treated by the decision-making authority as having control of it.

7. Section 127 of the Act shall apply to the determination of whether enterprises are under common control for the purposes of paragraphs 5 and 6 as it applies, for the purposes specified in section 127, to section 26 of the Act.

8. Subject to paragraph 9, applicable turnover shall not include amounts derived from the sale of products or the provision of services between enterprises under common ownership or control.

9. Where, as a result of the merger situation, one or more enterprises ceases or will cease to be under common ownership or control with the enterprise being taken over, the decision-making authority may treat amounts derived from the sale of products or the provision of services between the enterprise being taken over and any enterprises ceasing to be under common ownership or control with that enterprise as applicable turnover and if such sale of products or provision of services has not resulted in any turnover or the decision-making authority considers that the turnover attributed to them does not reflect open market value, the decision-making authority may attribute such value to them as it considers appropriate and include them in the calculation of applicable turnover.

10. Where an enterprise has applicable turnover part of which is attributable to a credit institution, financial institution or insurance undertaking, that part or those parts of the applicable turnover shall be calculated in accordance with paragraphs 3, 11 and 12.

Credit institutions and financial institutions

11. The applicable turnover of an enterprise which is a credit institution or financial institution shall be limited to the sum of the following income as defined in Council Directive (EEC) 86/635 received by the branch or division of that institution established in the United Kingdom after deduction of value added tax and other taxes directly related to those items:

(a) interest income and similar income;

(b) income from securities:
- income from shares and other variable yield securities;
- income from participating interests;
- income from shares in affiliated undertakings;

(c) commissions receivable;

(d) net profit on financial operations;

(e) other operating income.

Insurance undertakings

12. The applicable turnover of an enterprise which is an insurance undertaking shall be limited to the value of gross premiums received from residents of the United Kingdom which shall comprise all amounts received and receivable in respect of insurance contracts issued by or on behalf of the undertaking, including outgoing reinsurance premiums, and after deduction of taxes and parafiscal contributions or levies charged by reference to the amounts of individual premiums or the total volume of premiums.

Aid granted to businesses

13. Any aid granted by a public body to a business which relates to one of the ordinary activities of the business shall be included in the calculation of turnover if the business is itself the recipient of the aid and if the aid is directly linked to the sale of products or the provision of services by the business and is therefore reflected in the price.

[7173]

NOTES

Para 1: words in square brackets in definition "credit institution" substituted by the Capital Requirements Regulations 2006, SI 2006/3221, reg 29(4), Sch 6, para 14, as from 1 January 2007.

ENTERPRISE ACT 2002 (PROTECTION OF LEGITIMATE INTERESTS) ORDER 2003

(SI 2003/1592)

NOTES

Made: 17 June 2003.

Authority: Enterprise Act 2002, ss 68, 124(2), (4).

Commencement: 20 June 2003 (see art 1 at **[7174]**). Where any provision in this work (including any inserted or substituted provision) came into force for all purposes on or before 1 July 2005, commencement information is not noted at provision level.

This Order is reproduced as amended by: the Enterprise Act 2002 and Media Mergers (Consequential Amendments) Order 2003, SI 2003/3180.

ARRANGEMENT OF ARTICLES

SCHEDULES

1 Citation, commencement and interpretation

(1) This Order may be cited as the Enterprise Act 2002 (Protection of Legitimate Interests) Order 2003 and shall come into force on 20th June 2003.

(2) In this Order—

"the Act" means the Enterprise Act 2002;

"a European intervention notice" means a notice given by the Secretary of State to the OFT pursuant to section 67 of the Act;

["media public interest consideration" means any consideration which, at the time of the giving of the European intervention notice concerned, is specified in section 58(2A) to (2C) of the Act, or in the opinion of the Secretary of State, is concerned with broadcasting or newspapers and ought to be specified in section 58 of the Act.]

PART IV
STATUTORY INSTRUMENTS

"public interest consideration" means a consideration which, at the time of the giving of the European intervention notice concerned, is specified in section 58 of the Act, or is not so specified but, in the opinion of the Secretary of State, ought to be so specified.

[7174]

NOTES

Para (2): definition "media public interest consideration" inserted by the Enterprise Act 2002 and Media Mergers (Consequential Amendments) Order 2003, SI 2003/3180, art 2, Schedule, para 10(1), (2), as from 29 December 2003.

2 Determination of a relevant merger situation

For the purposes of deciding whether a relevant merger situation has been created or whether arrangements are in progress or in contemplation which, if carried into effect, will result in the creation of a relevant merger situation, for the purposes of section 68(2)(a) of the Act and this Order, sections 23 to 32 of the Act (read together with section 34 of the Act and any Order made pursuant to that section) shall apply, but subject to the modifications mentioned in Schedule 1.

[7175]

3 European intervention notices under section 67 of the Act

(1) A European intervention notice shall come into force when it is given and shall cease to be in force when the matter to which it relates is finally determined in accordance with paragraphs (2) and (3).

(2) A matter to which a European intervention notice relates is finally determined if—

(a) the time within which the OFT [or (if relevant) OFCOM] is to report to the Secretary of State under article 4 [or (as the case may be) 4A] has expired and no such report has been made;

(b) the Secretary of State decides to accept an undertaking or group of undertakings under paragraph 3 of Schedule 2 instead of making a reference under article 5;

(c) the Secretary of State otherwise decides not to make a reference under article 5;

(d) the Commission cancels such a reference under article 7(1) or article 11(1);

(e) the time within which the Commission is to prepare a report under article 8 and give it to the Secretary of State has expired and no such report has been prepared and given to the Secretary of State;

(f) the time within which the Secretary of State is to make and publish a decision under article 12(2) has expired and no such decision has been made and published;

(g) the Secretary of State decides under paragraph (2) of article 12 otherwise than as mentioned in paragraph (6) of that article;

(h) the Secretary of State decides under paragraph (2) of article 12 as mentioned in paragraph (6) of that article but decides neither to accept an undertaking under paragraph 9 of Schedule 2 nor to make an order under paragraph 11 of that Schedule; or

(i) the Secretary of State decides under paragraph (2) of article 12 as mentioned in paragraph (6) of that article and accepts an undertaking under paragraph 9 of Schedule 2 or makes an order under paragraph 11 of that Schedule.

(3) The time when a matter to which a European intervention notice relates is finally determined is—

(a) in a case falling within paragraph (2)(a), (e) or (f), the expiry of the time concerned;

(b) in a case falling within paragraph (2)(b), the acceptance of the undertaking or group of undertakings concerned;

(c) in a case falling within paragraph (2)(c), (d) or (g), the making of the decision concerned;

(d) in a case falling within paragraph (2)(h), the making of the decision neither to accept an undertaking under paragraph 9 of Schedule 2 nor to make an order under paragraph 11 of that Schedule; and

(e) in a case falling within paragraph (2)(i), the acceptance of the undertakings concerned or (as the case may be) the making of the order concerned.

[7176]

NOTES

Para (2): words in square brackets in sub-para (a) inserted by the Enterprise Act 2002 and Media Mergers (Consequential Amendments) Order 2003, SI 2003/3180, art 2, Schedule, para 10(1), (3), as from 29 December 2003.

4 Initial investigation and report by OFT

(1) Paragraph (2) applies where the Secretary of State has given a European intervention notice in relation to a relevant merger situation under section 67 of the Act.

(2) The OFT shall, within such period as the Secretary of State may require, give a report to the Secretary of State in relation to the case.

(3) The report shall contain—

(a) advice from the OFT on the considerations relevant to the making of a reference under section 22 or 33 of the Act which are also relevant to the Secretary of State's decision as to whether to make a reference under article 5; and

(b) a summary of any representations about the case which have been received by the OFT and which relate to any public interest consideration mentioned in the European intervention notice concerned [(other than a media public interest consideration)] and which is or may be relevant to the Secretary of State's decision as to whether to make a reference under article 5.

(4) The report shall include a decision as to whether the OFT believes that it is, or may be, the case that a European relevant merger situation has been created or (as the case may be) arrangements are in progress or in contemplation which, if carried into effect, will result in the creation of a European relevant merger situation.

[(4A) The report may, in particular, contain a summary of any representations about the case which have been received by the OFT and which relate to any media public interest consideration mentioned in the European intervention notice concerned and which is or may be relevant to the Secretary of State's decision as to whether to make a reference under article 5.]

(5) The report may, in particular, include advice and recommendations on any public interest consideration mentioned in the European intervention notice concerned and which is or may be relevant to the Secretary of State's decision as to whether to make a reference under article 5.

(6) The OFT shall carry out such investigations as it considers appropriate for the purpose of producing a report under this article. **[7177]**

NOTES

Para (3): words in square brackets in sub-para (b) inserted by the Enterprise Act 2002 and Media Mergers (Consequential Amendments) Order 2003, SI 2003/3180, art 2, Schedule, para 10(1), (4)(a), as from 29 December 2003.

Para (4A): inserted by SI 2003/3180, art 2, Schedule, para 10(1), (4)(b), as from 29 December 2003.

[4A Additional investigation and report by OFCOM: media mergers

(1) Paragraph (2) applies where—

(a) the Secretary of State has given a European intervention notice in relation to a relevant merger situation under section 67 of the Act; and

(b) the European intervention notice mentions any media public interest consideration.

(2) OFCOM shall, within such period as the Secretary of State may require, give a report to the Secretary of State on the effect of the consideration or considerations concerned on the case.

(3) The report shall contain—

(a) advice and recommendations on any media public interest consideration mentioned in the European intervention notice concerned and which is or may be relevant to the Secretary of State's decision as to whether to make a reference under article 5; and

(b) a summary of any representations about the case which have been received by OFCOM and which relate to any such consideration.

(4) OFCOM shall carry out such investigations as they consider appropriate for the purposes of producing a report under this article.]

[7177A]

NOTES

Inserted by the Enterprise Act 2002 and Media Mergers (Consequential Amendments) Order 2003, SI 2003/3180, art 2, Schedule, para 10(1), (5), as from 29 December 2003.

5 Power of Secretary of State to refer the matter

(1) Paragraphs (2) and (3) apply where the Secretary of State—

(a) has given a European intervention notice in relation to a relevant merger situation; and

(b) has received a report of the OFT under article 4[, and any report of OFCOM which is required by virtue of article 4A,] in relation to the matter.

(2) The Secretary of State may make a reference to the Commission if she believes that it is or may be the case that—

(a) a European relevant merger situation has been created;

(b) one or more than one public interest consideration mentioned in the European intervention notice is relevant to a consideration of the European relevant merger situation concerned; and

(c) taking account only of the relevant public interest consideration or considerations concerned, the creation of that situation operates or may be expected to operate against the public interest.

(3) The Secretary of State may make a reference to the Commission if she believes that it is or may be the case that—

(a) arrangements are in progress or in contemplation which, if carried into effect, will result in the creation of a European relevant merger situation;

(b) one or more than one public interest consideration mentioned in the European intervention notice is relevant to a consideration of the European relevant merger situation concerned; and

(c) taking account only of the relevant public interest consideration or considerations concerned, the creation of that situation operates or may be expected to operate against the public interest.

(4) No reference shall be made under this article if the making of the reference is prevented by … paragraph 4 of Schedule 2.

(5) The Secretary of State, in deciding whether to make a reference under this article, shall accept the decision of the OFT included in its report under article 4 by virtue of paragraph (4) of that article.

(6) Where the decision to make a reference under article 5 is made at any time on or after the end of the period of 24 weeks beginning with the giving of the European intervention notice concerned, the Secretary of State shall, in deciding whether to make such a reference, disregard any public interest consideration which is mentioned in the European intervention notice but which has not been finalised before the end of that period.

(7) The Secretary of State may, if she believes that there is a realistic prospect of the public interest consideration mentioned in paragraph (6) being finalised within the period of 24 weeks beginning with the giving of the European intervention notice concerned, delay deciding whether to make the reference concerned until the public interest consideration is finalised or, if earlier, the period expires.

(8) A reference under this article shall, in particular, specify—

(a) the paragraph of this article under which it is made;

(b) the date on which it is made; and

(c) the public interest consideration or considerations mentioned in the European intervention notice concerned which the Secretary of State is not under a duty to disregard by virtue of paragraph (6) and which she believes are or may be relevant to a consideration of the relevant merger situation concerned.

[7178]

NOTES

Para (1): words in square brackets in sub-para (b) inserted by the Enterprise Act 2002 and Media Mergers (Consequential Amendments) Order 2003, SI 2003/3180, art 2, Schedule, para 10(1), (6)(a), as from 29 December 2003.

Para (4): words omitted revoked by SI 2003/3180, art 2, Schedule, para 10(1), (6)(b), as from 29 December 2003.

6 Questions to be decided on references under article 5

(1) The Commission shall, on a reference under article 5(2), decide whether a European relevant merger situation has been created.

(2) The Commission shall, on a reference under article 5(3), decide whether arrangements are in progress or in contemplation which, if carried into effect, will result in the creation of a European relevant merger situation.

(3) If the Commission decides that a European relevant merger situation has been created, or that arrangements are in progress or in contemplation which, if carried into effect, will result in the creation of a European relevant merger situation, it shall, on a reference under article 5, decide whether, taking account only of the admissible public interest consideration or considerations concerned, the creation of that situation operates or may be expected to operate against the public interest.

(4) The Commission shall, if it has decided on a reference under article 5 that the creation of a European relevant merger situation operates or may be expected to operate against the public interest, decide the following additional questions—

- (a) whether action should be taken by the Secretary of State under article 12 for the purpose of remedying, mitigating or preventing any of the effects adverse to the public interest which have resulted from, or may be expected to result from, the creation of the European relevant merger situation concerned;
- (b) whether the Commission should recommend the taking of other action by the Secretary of State or action by persons other than itself and the Secretary of State for the purpose of remedying, mitigating or preventing any of the effects adverse to the public interest which have resulted from, or may be expected to result from, the creation of the European relevant merger situation concerned; and
- (c) in either case, if action should be taken, what action should be taken and what is to be remedied, mitigated or prevented.

(5) In this article "admissible public interest consideration" means any public interest consideration which is specified in the reference under article 5 and which the Commission is not under a duty to disregard.

[7179]

7 Cancellation or variation of references under article 5

(1) The Commission shall cancel a reference under article 5(3) if it considers that the proposal to make arrangements of the kind mentioned in the reference has been abandoned.

(2) In relation to the question whether a European relevant merger situation has been created or the question whether a European relevant merger situation will be created, a reference under article 5 may be framed so as to require the Commission to exclude from consideration—

- (a) subsection (1) of section 23 of the Act;
- (b) subsection (2) of that section; or
- (c) one of those subsections if the Commission finds that the other is satisfied.

(3) In relation to the question whether any such result as is mentioned in section 23(2)(b) of the Act has arisen or the question whether any such result will arise, a reference under article 5 may be framed so as to require the Commission to confine its investigation to the supply of goods or services in a part of the United Kingdom specified in the reference.

(4) The Commission may, if it considers that doing so is justified by the facts (including events occurring on or after the making of the reference concerned), treat a reference made under paragraph (2) or (3) of article 5 as if it had been made under paragraph (3) or (as the case may be) (2) of that article; and, in such cases, references in this Order to references under those enactments shall, so far as may be necessary, be construed accordingly.

(5) Where by virtue of paragraph (4), the Commission treats a reference made under paragraph (2) or (3) of article 5 as if it had been made under paragraph (3) or (as the case may be) (2) of that article, paragraphs 1, 2, 7 and 8 of Schedule 2, in particular, apply as if the reference had been made under paragraph (3) or (as the case may be) (2) of that article instead of under paragraph (2) or (3) of that article.

(6) Paragraph (7) applies in relation to any undertaking accepted under paragraph 1 of Schedule 2, or any order made under paragraph 2 of that Schedule, which is in force immediately before the Commission, by virtue of paragraph (4), treats a reference made under paragraph (2) or (3) of article 5 as if it had been made under paragraph (3) or (as the case may be) (2) of that article.

(7) The undertaking or order shall, so far as applicable, continue in force as if it were—

(a) in the case of an undertaking or order which relates to a reference under paragraph (2) of article 5, accepted or made in relation to a reference made under paragraph (3) of that article; and

(b) in the case of an undertaking or order which relates to a reference made under paragraph (3) of that article, accepted or made in relation to a reference made under paragraph (2) of that article;

and the undertaking or order concerned may be varied, superseded, released or revoked accordingly.

(8) The Secretary of State may at any time vary a reference under article 5.

(9) The Secretary of State shall consult the Commission before varying any such reference.

(10) Paragraph (9) shall not apply if the Commission has requested the variation concerned.

(11) No variation by the Secretary of State under this article shall be capable of altering the public interest consideration or considerations specified in the reference or the period permitted by virtue of article 8 within which the report of the Commission under that article is to be prepared and given to the Secretary of State.

[7180]

8 Investigations and reports on references under article 5

(1) The Commission shall prepare a report on a reference under article 5 and give it to the Secretary of State within the period permitted by article 9.

(2) The report shall, in particular, contain—

(a) the decisions of the Commission on the questions which it is required to answer by virtue of article 6;

(b) its reasons for its decisions; and

(c) such information as the Commission considers appropriate for facilitating a proper understanding of those questions and of its reasons for its decisions.

[(2A) Where the report relates to a reference under article 5 which has been made after a report of OFCOM under article 4A, the Commission shall give a copy of its report (whether or not published) to OFCOM.]

(3) The Commission shall carry out such investigations as it considers appropriate for the purpose of producing a report under this article.

[7181]

NOTES

Para (2A): inserted by the Enterprise Act 2002 and Media Mergers (Consequential Amendments) Order 2003, SI 2003/3180, art 2, Schedule, para 10(1), (7), as from 29 December 2003.

9 Time-limits and investigations and reports by Commission

(1) The Commission shall prepare its report under article 8 and give it to the Secretary of State under that article within the period of 24 weeks beginning with the date of the reference concerned.

(2) The Commission may extend, by no more than 8 weeks, the period within which a report under article 8 is to be prepared and given to the Secretary of State if it considers that there are special reasons why the report cannot be prepared and given to the Secretary of State within that period.

(3) The Commission may extend the period within which a report under article 8 is prepared and given to the Secretary of State if it considers that a relevant person has failed (whether with or without a reasonable excuse) to comply with any requirement of a notice under section 109 of the Act.

(4) In paragraph (3) "relevant person" means—
- (a) any person carrying on any of the enterprises concerned;
- (b) any person who (whether alone or as a member of a group) owns or has control of any such person; or
- (c) any officer, employee or agent of any person mentioned in sub-paragraph (a) or (b).

(5) For the purposes of paragraph (4) a person or group of persons able, directly or indirectly, to control or materially to influence the policy of a body of persons corporate or unincorporate, but without having a controlling interest in that body of persons, may be treated as having control of it.

(6) An extension under paragraph (2) or (3) shall come into force when published in accordance with article 14.

(7) An extension under paragraph (3) shall continue in force until—
- (a) the person concerned provides the information or documents to the satisfaction of the Commission or (as the case may be) appears as a witness in accordance with the requirements of the Commission; or
- (b) the Commission publishes its decision to cancel the extension.

[7182]

10 Article 9: supplementary

(1) A period extended under paragraph (2) of article 9 may also be extended under paragraph (3) of that article and a period extended under paragraph (3) of that article may also be extended under paragraph (2) of that article.

(2) No more than one extension is possible under article 9(2).

(3) Where a period within which a report under article 8 is prepared and given to the Secretary of State is extended or further extended under article 9(2) or (3), the period as extended or (as the case may be) further extended, shall, subject to paragraphs (4) and (5), be calculated by taking the period being extended and adding to it the period of the extension (whether or not those periods overlap in time).

(4) Paragraph (5) applies where—
- (a) the period within which the report under article 8 is to be prepared and given to the Secretary of State is further extended;
- (b) the further extension and at least one previous extension is made under article 9(3); and
- (c) the same days or fractions of days are included in or comprise the further extension and are included in or comprise at least one such previous extension.

(5) In calculating the period of the further extension, any days or fractions of days of the kind mentioned in paragraph (4)(c) shall be disregarded.

(6) Any Regulations made pursuant to section 52(12) of the Act shall apply for the purposes of article 9(7).

[7183]

11 Restrictions on action where public interest considerations not finalised

(1) The Commission shall cancel a reference under article 5 if—
- (a) the European intervention notice concerned mentions a public interest consideration which was not finalised on the giving of that notice or public interest considerations which, at the time, were not finalised;
- (b) no other public interest consideration is mentioned in the notice;
- (c) at least 24 weeks has elapsed since the giving of the notice; and
- (d) the public interest consideration mentioned in the notice has not been finalised within that period of 24 weeks or (as the case may be) none of the public interest considerations mentioned in the notice has been finalised within that period of 24 weeks.

(2) Where a reference to the Commission under article 5 specifies a public interest consideration which has not been finalised before the making of the reference, the Commission shall not give its report to the Secretary of State under article 8 in relation to that reference unless—

(a) the period of 24 weeks beginning with the giving of the European intervention notice has expired; or

(b) the public interest consideration has been finalised.

(3) The Commission shall, in reporting on any of the questions mentioned in article 6(3) and (4), disregard any public interest consideration which was not finalised on the giving of the European intervention notice and has not been finalised within the period of 24 weeks beginning with the giving of the notice concerned.

(4) Paragraphs (1) to (3) are without prejudice to the power of the Commission to carry out investigations in relation to any public interest consideration to which it might be able to have regard in its report.

[7184]

12 Decision and enforcement by Secretary of State

(1) Paragraph (2) applies where the Secretary of State has received a report of the Commission under article 8 in relation to a European relevant merger situation.

(2) The Secretary of State shall, in connection with a reference under article 5(2) or (3), decide the questions which the Commission is required to decide by virtue of article 6(1) to (3).

(3) The Secretary of State shall publish her decision under paragraph (2) within a period of 30 days beginning with the receipt of the report of the Commission under article 8.

(4) In making her decisions under paragraph (2), the Secretary of State shall disregard any public interest consideration not specified in the reference under article 5 and any public interest consideration disregarded by the Commission for the purposes of its report.

(5) In making her decisions under paragraph (2), the Secretary of State shall accept the decisions of the report of the Commission under article 8 as to whether a European relevant merger situation has been created or whether arrangements are in progress or in contemplation which, if carried into effect, will result in the creation of a European relevant merger situation.

(6) Paragraph (7) applies where the Secretary of State has decided under paragraph (2) that—

(a) a European relevant merger situation has been created or arrangements are in progress or in contemplation which, if carried into effect, will result in the creation of a European relevant merger situation;

(b) at least one public interest consideration which is mentioned in the European intervention notice concerned is relevant to a consideration of the European relevant merger situation concerned; and

(c) taking account only of the relevant public interest consideration or considerations concerned, the creation of that situation operates or may be expected to operate against the public interest;

and has so decided, and published her decision, within the period required by paragraph (3).

(7) The Secretary of State may take such action under paragraph 9 or 11 of Schedule 2 as she considers reasonable and practicable to remedy, mitigate or prevent any of the effects adverse to the public interest which have resulted from, or may be expected to result from, the creation of the European relevant merger situation concerned.

(8) In making a decision under paragraph (7), the Secretary of State shall, in particular, have regard to the report of the Commission under article 8.

(9) In determining for the purpose of paragraph (3) the period of 30 days no account shall be taken of—

(a) Saturday, Sunday, Good Friday and Christmas Day; and

(b) any day which is a bank holiday in England and Wales.

[7185]

13 Enforcement action in European intervention notice cases

(1) Schedule 2 (which provides for enforcement action in European intervention notice cases) shall have effect.

(2) The OFT may advise the Secretary of State in relation to the taking by her of enforcement action under Schedule 2.

[7186]

14 Publicity requirements

(1) The Commission shall publish—

(a) any cancellation made by it under article 7(1) of a reference under article 5;

(b) any extension by it under article 9 of the period within which a report under article 8 is to be prepared and published;

(c) any decision made by it under article 9(7)(b) to cancel such an extension; and

(d) any decision made by it under article 7(4) to treat a reference made under paragraph (2) or (3) of article 5 as if it had been made under paragraph (3) or (as the case may be) (2) of that article.

(2) The Secretary of State shall publish—

(a) any European intervention notice given by her;

(b) any report of the OFT under article 4 which has been received by her;

[(ba) any report of OFCOM under article 4A which has been received by her;]

(c) any reference made by her under article 5 or any decision made by her not to make a reference;

(d) any variation by her under article 7 of a reference under article 5;

(e) any report of the Commission under article 8 which has been received by her;

(f) any decision made by her neither to accept an undertaking under paragraph 9 of Schedule 2 nor to make an order under paragraph 11 of that Schedule;

(g) any enforcement undertaking accepted by her under paragraph 1 of Schedule 2;

(h) any variation or release of such an undertaking;

(i) any decision made by her as mentioned in paragraph 6(6)(b) of Schedule 2; and

(j) any decision to dispense with the requirements of Schedule 10 of the Act.

(3) Where any person is under a duty by virtue of paragraphs (1) or (2) to publish the result of any action taken by that person or any decision made by that person, the person concerned shall, subject to paragraph (4), also publish that person's reasons for the action concerned or (as the case may be) the decision concerned.

(4) Such reasons need not, if it is not reasonably practicable to do so, be published at the same time as the result of the action concerned or (as the case may be) as the decision concerned.

(5) The Secretary of State shall publish her reasons for any decision made by her under article 12(2).

(6) Such reasons may be published after the publication of the decision concerned if it is not reasonably practicable to publish them at the same time as the publication of the decision.

(7) The Secretary of State shall publish—

(a) the report of the OFT under article 4[, and any report of OFCOM under article 4A,] in relation to a matter no later than publication of her decision as to whether to make a reference under article 5 in relation to that matter; and

(b) the report of the Commission under article 8 in relation to a matter no later than publication of her decision under article 12(2) in relation to that matter.

(8) Where the Secretary of State has decided under article 12(7) to accept an undertaking under paragraph 9 of Schedule 2 or to make an order under paragraph 11 of that Schedule, she shall (after the acceptance of the undertaking or (as the case may be) the making of the order) lay details of her decision and her reasons for it, and the Commission's report under article 8, before each House of Parliament.

[7187]

NOTES

Paras (2), (7): words in square brackets inserted by SI 2003/3180, art 2, Schedule, para 10(1), (8), as from 29 December 2003.

15 Other provisions of the Act applicable to this Order

The other provisions of the Act mentioned in Schedule 3 shall apply for the purposes of this Order with the modifications mentioned in that Schedule.

[7188]

16 (*Introduces Sch 4* (*consequential amendments*).)

SCHEDULES

SCHEDULE 1
MODIFICATIONS TO SECTIONS 23 TO 32 OF THE ACT

Article 2

Sections 23 to 32 of the Act shall apply as if—

(a) references in those sections to "the decision-making authority" were references to the OFT, the Commission or (as the case may be) the Secretary of State;

(b) in section 23(1) and (2) the words "For the purposes of this Part," were omitted;

(c) in section 23(9) the words "For the purposes of this Chapter," were omitted;

(d) for section 23(9)(a) there were substituted—

"(a) in relation to the giving of a European intervention notice, the time when the notice is given;

(aa) in relation to the making of a report by the OFT under article 4 of the Enterprise Act 2002 (Protection of Legitimate Interests) Order 2003, the time of the making of the report;

(ab) in the case of a reference which is treated as having been made under article 5(2) of the Enterprise Act 2002 (Protection of Legitimate Interests) Order 2003 by virtue of article 7(4) of that Order, such time as the Commission may determine; and";

(e) the references to the OFT in section 24(2)(a) and (b) included references to the Secretary of State;

(f) the references to the OFT in sections 25(1) to (3), (6) and (8) and 31 included references to the Secretary of State;

(g) the references to the OFT in section 25(4) and (5) were references to the Secretary of State;

(h) the reference in section 25(4) to section 73 were a reference to paragraph 3 of Schedule 2 to this Order;

(i) after section 25(5) of the Act there were inserted—

"(5A) The Secretary of State may by notice to the persons carrying on the enterprises which have or may be ceased to be distinct enterprises extend the four month period mentioned in section 24(1)(a) or (2)(b) if, by virtue of article 5(7) of the Enterprise Act 2002 (Protection of Legitimate Interests) Order 2003 or paragraph 3(5) of Schedule 2 to that Order, he decides to delay a decision as to whether to make a reference under article 5 of that Order.

(5B) An extension under subsection (5A) shall be for the period of the delay.";

(j) in section 25(10)(b) after word "(4)" there were inserted ", (5A)";

(k) the reference in section 25(12) to one extension were a reference to one extension by the OFT and one extension by the Secretary of State;

(l) the powers to extend time-limits under section 25 and the power to request information under section 31(1) were not exercisable by the OFT or the Secretary of State before the giving of a European intervention notice;

(m) in section 26(1) the words "For the purposes of this Part" were omitted;

(n) in section 28(2) the words from "For the purposes" to "121(4)(c)(ii))" were omitted;

(o) in subsection (1) of section 31 for the words "section 22" there were substituted "article 5(2) of the Enterprise Act 2002 (Protection of Legitimate Interests) Order 2003" and, in the application of that subsection to the OFT, for the word "deciding" there were substituted "enabling the Secretary of State to decide";

(p) in the case of the giving of European intervention notices, the references in sections 23 to 29 to the making of a reference or a reference were, so far as necessary, references to the giving of a European intervention notice or a European intervention notice; and

(q) the references to the OFT in section 32(2)(a) to (c) and (3) were construed in accordance with the above modifications.

[7189]

SCHEDULE 2
ENFORCEMENT ACTION IN EUROPEAN INTERVENTION NOTICE CASES

Article 13

Pre-emptive undertakings and orders

1.—(1) Sub-paragraph (2) applies where a European intervention notice is in force.

(2) The Secretary of State may, for the purposes of preventing pre-emptive action, accept from such of the parties concerned as she considers appropriate undertakings to take such action as she considers appropriate.

(3) An undertaking under this paragraph—

(a) shall come into force when accepted;
(b) may be varied or superseded by another undertaking; and
(c) may be released by the Secretary of State.

(4) An undertaking which is in force under this paragraph in relation to a reference or possible reference under article 5 shall cease to be in force if an order under paragraph 2 or an undertaking under paragraph 3 comes into force in relation to that reference.

(5) An undertaking under this paragraph shall, if it has not previously ceased to be in force, cease to be in force when the European intervention notice concerned ceases to be in force.

(6) No undertaking shall be accepted by the Secretary of State under this paragraph before the making of a reference under article 5 unless the undertaking relates to a European relevant merger situation which has been, or may have been, created.

(7) The Secretary of State shall, as soon as reasonably practicable, consider any representations received by her in relation to varying or releasing an undertaking under this paragraph.

(8) In this paragraph and paragraph 2 "pre-emptive action" means action which might prejudice the reference or possible reference concerned under article 5 or impede the taking of any action under this Order which may be justified by the Secretary of State's decisions on the reference.

2.—(1) Sub-paragraph (2) applies where a European intervention notice is in force.

(2) The Secretary of State may by order, for the purpose of preventing pre-emptive action—

(a) prohibit or restrict the doing of things which the Secretary of State considers would constitute pre-emptive action;
(b) impose on any person concerned obligations as to the carrying on of any activities or the safeguarding of any assets;
(c) provide for the carrying on of any activities or the safeguarding of any assets either by the appointment of a person to conduct or supervise the conduct of any activities (on such terms and with such powers as may be specified or described in the order) or in any other manner;
(d) do anything which may be done by virtue of paragraph 19 of Schedule 8 to the Act.

(3) An order under this paragraph—

(a) shall come into force at such time as is determined by or under the order; and
(b) may be varied or revoked by another order.

(4) An order which is in force under this paragraph in relation to a reference or possible reference under article 5 shall cease to be in force if an undertaking under paragraph 1 or 3 comes into force in relation to that reference.

(5) An order under this paragraph shall, if it has not previously ceased to be in force, cease to be in force when the European intervention notice concerned ceases to be in force.

(6) No order shall be made by the Secretary of State under this paragraph before the making of a reference under article 5 unless the order relates to a European relevant merger situation which has been, or may have been, created.

(7) The Secretary of State shall, as soon as reasonably practicable, consider any representations received by her in relation to varying or revoking an order under this paragraph.

Undertakings in lieu of reference under article 5

3.—(1) Sub-paragraph (2) applies if the Secretary of State has power to make a reference to the Commission under article 5 and otherwise intends to make such a reference.

(2) The Secretary of State may, instead of making such a reference and for the purpose of remedying, mitigating or preventing any of the effects adverse to the public interest which have or may have resulted, or which may be expected to result, from the creation of the European relevant merger situation concerned accept from such of the parties concerned as she considers appropriate undertakings to take such action as she considers appropriate.

(3) In proceeding under sub-paragraph (2), the Secretary of State shall, in particular, accept the decisions of the OFT included in its report under article 4 so far as they relate to the matters mentioned in paragraphs (3)(a) and (4) of that article.

(4) No undertaking shall be accepted by the Secretary of State under this paragraph in connection with a possible reference under article 5 if a public interest consideration mentioned in the European intervention notice concerned has not been finalised and the period of 24 weeks beginning with the giving of that notice has not expired.

(5) The Secretary of State may delay making a decision as to whether to accept any such undertaking (and any related decision as to whether to make a reference under article 5) if she considers that there is a realistic prospect of the public interest consideration being finalised within the period of 24 weeks beginning with the giving of the European intervention notice concerned.

(6) A delay under sub-paragraph (5) shall not extend beyond—
- (a) the time when the public interest consideration is finalised; or
- (b) if earlier, the expiry of the period of 24 weeks mentioned in that sub-paragraph.

(7) An undertaking under this paragraph—
- (a) shall come into force when accepted;
- (b) may be varied or superseded by another undertaking; or
- (c) may be released by the Secretary of State.

(8) An undertaking under this paragraph which is in force in relation to a European relevant merger situation shall cease to be in force if an order comes into force under paragraph 5 or 6 in relation to that undertaking.

(9) The Secretary of State shall, as soon as reasonably practicable, consider any representations received by her in relation to varying or releasing an undertaking under this paragraph.

4.—(1) The Secretary of State shall not make a reference under article 5 in relation to the creation of a European relevant merger situation if—
- (a) the Secretary of State has accepted an undertaking or group of undertakings under paragraph 3; and
- (b) the European relevant merger situation is the situation by reference to which the undertaking or group of undertakings was accepted.

(2) Sub-paragraph (1) does not prevent the making of a reference if material facts about relevant arrangements or transactions, or relevant proposed arrangements or transactions, were not notified (whether in writing or otherwise) to the Secretary of State or the OFT or made public before any undertaking concerned was accepted.

(3) For the purposes of sub-paragraph (2) arrangements or transactions, or proposed arrangements or transactions, are relevant if they are the ones in consequence of which the enterprises concerned ceased or may have ceased, or may cease, to be distinct enterprises.

(4) In sub-paragraph (2) "made public" means so publicised as to be generally known or readily ascertainable.

5.—(1) Sub-paragraph (2) applies where the Secretary of State considers that—
- (a) an undertaking accepted by her under paragraph 3 has not been, is not being or will not be fulfilled; or
- (b) in relation to an undertaking accepted by her under that paragraph, information which was false or misleading in a material respect was given to her or the OFT by the person giving the undertaking before she decided to accept the undertaking.

(2) The Secretary of State may, for any of the purposes mentioned in paragraph 3(2), make an order under this paragraph.

(3) Sub-paragraph (3) of paragraph 3 shall apply for the purposes of sub-paragraph (2) above as it applies for the purposes of sub-paragraph (2) of that paragraph.

(4) An order under this paragraph may contain—
- (a) anything permitted by Schedule 8 to the Act; and
- (b) such supplementary, consequential or incidental provision as the Secretary of State considers appropriate.

(5) An order under this paragraph—
- (a) shall come into force at such time as is determined by or under the order; and
- (b) may contain provision which is different from the provision contained in the undertaking concerned.

(6) No order shall be varied or revoked under this paragraph unless the OFT advises that such a variation or revocation is appropriate by reason of a change of circumstances.

6.—(1) Sub-paragraph (2) applies where—
- (a) the Secretary of State has the power to make an order under paragraph 5 in relation to a particular undertaking and intends to make such an order; or
- (b) the Secretary of State has the power to make an order under paragraph 10 in relation to a particular undertaking and intends to make such an order.

(2) The Secretary of State may, for the purpose of preventing any action which might prejudice the making of that order, make an order under this paragraph.

(3) No order shall be made under sub-paragraph (2) unless the Secretary of State has reasonable grounds for suspecting that it is or may be the case that action which might prejudice the making of the order under paragraph 5 or (as the case may be) 10 is in progress or in contemplation.

(4) An order under sub-paragraph (2) may—
- (a) prohibit or restrict the doing of things which the Secretary of State considers would prejudice the making of the order under paragraph 5 or 10;
- (b) impose on any person concerned obligations as to the carrying on of any activities or the safeguarding of any assets;
- (c) provide for the carrying on of any activities or the safeguarding of any assets either by the appointment of a person to conduct or supervise the conduct of any activities (on such terms and with such powers as may be specified or described in the order) or in any other manner;
- (d) do anything which may be done by virtue of paragraph 19 of Schedule 8 to the Act.

(5) An order under this paragraph shall come into force at such time as is determined by or under the order.

(6) An order under this paragraph shall, if it has not previously ceased to be in force, cease to be in force on—
- (a) the coming into force of an order under paragraph 5 or (as the case may be) 10 in relation to the undertaking concerned; or
- (b) the making of the decision not to proceed with such an order.

(7) The Secretary of State shall, as soon as reasonably practicable, consider any representations received by her in relation to varying or revoking an order under this paragraph.

Statutory restrictions following reference under article 5

7.—(1) Sub-paragraphs (2) and (3) apply where—
- (a) a reference has been made under article 5 but not finally determined; and
- (b) no undertakings under paragraph 1 are in force in relation to the European relevant merger situation concerned and no orders under paragraph 2 are in force in relation to that situation.

(2) No relevant person shall, without the consent of the Secretary of State—
- (a) complete any outstanding matters in connection with any arrangements which have resulted in the enterprises concerned ceasing to be distinct enterprises;
- (b) make any further arrangements in consequence of that result (other than arrangements which reverse that result); or
- (c) transfer the ownership or control of any enterprises to which the reference relates.

PART IV
STATUTORY INSTRUMENTS

(3) No relevant person shall, without the consent of the Secretary of State, assist in any of the activities mentioned in paragraphs (a) to (c) of sub-paragraph (2).

(4) The prohibitions in sub-paragraphs (2) and (3) do not apply in relation to anything which the person concerned is required to do by virtue of any enactment.

(5) The consent of the Secretary of State under sub-paragraph (2) or (3)—
- (a) may be general or specific;
- (b) may be revoked by the Secretary of State; and
- (c) shall be published in such manner as the Secretary of State considers appropriate for bringing it to the attention of any person entitled to the benefit of it.

(6) Paragraph (c) of sub-paragraph (5) shall not apply if the Secretary of State considers that publication is not necessary for the purposes mentioned in that paragraph.

(7) Sub-paragraphs (2) and (3) shall apply to a person's conduct outside the United Kingdom if (and only if) he is—
- (a) a United Kingdom national;
- (b) a body incorporated under the law of the United Kingdom or of any part of the United Kingdom; or
- (c) a person carrying on business in the United Kingdom.

(8) For the purpose of this paragraph a reference under article 5 is finally determined if—
- (a) the time within which the Commission is to prepare a report under article 8 in relation to the reference and give it to the Secretary of State has expired and no such report has been so prepared and given;
- (b) the Commission decides to cancel the reference under article 11(1);
- (c) the time within which the Secretary of State is to make and publish a decision under article 12(2) has expired and no such decision has been made and published;
- (d) the Secretary of State decides under paragraph (2) of article 12 otherwise than as mentioned in paragraph (6) of that article;
- (e) the Secretary of State decides under paragraph (2) of article 12 as mentioned in paragraph (6) of that article but decides neither to accept an undertaking under paragraph 9 of this Schedule nor to make an order under paragraph 11 of this Schedule; or
- (f) the Secretary of State decides under paragraph (2) of article 12 as mentioned in paragraph (6) of that article and accepts an undertaking under paragraph 9 of this Schedule or makes an order under paragraph 11 of this Schedule.

(9) For the purposes of this paragraph the time when a reference under article 5 is finally determined is—
- (a) in a case falling within sub-paragraph (8)(a) or (c), the expiry of the time concerned;
- (b) in a case falling within sub-paragraph (8)(b) or (d), the making of the decision concerned;
- (c) in a case falling within sub-paragraph (8)(e), the making of the decision neither to accept an undertaking under paragraph 9 of this Schedule nor to make an order under paragraph 11 of this Schedule; and
- (d) in a case falling within sub-paragraph (8)(f), the acceptance of the undertaking concerned or (as the case may be) the making of the order concerned.

(10) In this paragraph "relevant person" means—
- (a) any person who carries on any enterprise to which the reference relates or who has control of any such enterprise;
- (b) any subsidiary of any person falling within paragraph (a); or
- (c) any person associated with any person falling within paragraph (a) or any subsidiary of any person so associated.

8.—(1) Sub-paragraph (2) applies where—
- (a) a reference has been made under article 5, and
- (b) no undertakings under paragraph 1 are in force in relation to the European relevant merger situation concerned and no orders under paragraph 2 are in force in relation to that situation.

(2) No relevant person shall, without the consent of the Secretary of State, directly or indirectly acquire during the relevant period an interest in shares in a company if any enterprise to which the reference relates is carried on by or under the control of that company.

(3) The consent of the Secretary of State under sub-paragraph (2)—

(a) may be general or specific;
(b) may be revoked by the Secretary of State; and
(c) shall be published in such manner as the Secretary of State considers appropriate for bringing it to the attention of any person entitled to the benefit of it.

(4) Paragraph (c) of sub-paragraph (3) shall not apply if the Secretary of State considers that publication is not necessary for the purpose mentioned in that paragraph.

(5) Sub-paragraph (2) shall apply to a person's conduct outside the United Kingdom if (and only if) he is—
(a) a United Kingdom national;
(b) a body incorporated under the law of the United Kingdom or of any part of the United Kingdom; or
(c) a person carrying on business in the United Kingdom.

(6) In this paragraph—
"company" includes any body corporate;
"relevant period" means the period beginning with the publication of the decision of the Secretary of State to make the reference concerned and ending when the reference is finally determined;
"relevant person" means—
(a) any person who carries on any enterprise to which the reference relates or who has control of any such enterprise;
(b) any subsidiary of any person falling within paragraph (a); or
(c) any person associated with any person falling within paragraph (a) or any subsidiary of any person so associated; and
"share" means share in the capital of a company, and includes stock.

(7) For the purposes of the definition of "relevant period" in sub-paragraph (6), a reference under article 5 is finally determined if—
(a) the Commission cancels the reference under article 7(1) or article 11(1);
(b) the time within which the Commission is to prepare a report under article 8 in relation to the reference and give it to the Secretary of State has expired and no such report has been so prepared and given;
(c) the time within which the Secretary of State is to make and publish a decision under article 12(2) has expired and no such decision has been made and published;
(d) the Secretary of State decides under paragraph (2) of article 12 otherwise than as mentioned in paragraph (6) of that article;
(e) the Secretary of State decides under paragraph (2) of article 12 as mentioned in paragraph (6) of that article but decides neither to accept an undertaking under paragraph 9 of this Schedule nor to make an order under paragraph 11 of this Schedule; or
(f) the Secretary of State decides under paragraph (2) of article 12 as mentioned in paragraph (6) of that article and accepts an undertaking under paragraph 9 of this Schedule or makes an order under paragraph 11 of this Schedule.

(8) For the purposes of the definition of "relevant period" in sub-paragraph (6) above, the time when a reference under article 5 is finally determined is—
(a) in a case falling within sub-paragraph (7)(a) or (d), the making of the decision concerned;
(b) in a case falling within sub-paragraph (7)(b) or (c), the expiry of the time concerned;
(c) in a case falling within sub-paragraph (7)(e), the making of the decision neither to accept an undertaking under paragraph 9 of this Schedule nor to make an order under paragraph 11 of this Schedule; and
(d) in a case falling within sub-paragraph (7)(f) the acceptance of the undertaking concerned or (as the case may be) the making of the order concerned.

(9) Section 79 of the Act shall apply for the purposes of paragraph 7 and this paragraph in relation to a reference under article 5 as it applies for the purposes of sections 77 and 78 in relation to a reference under section 22 or 33 of the Act.

(10) In its application by virtue of sub-paragraph (9) section 79 shall have effect as if—
(a) subsections (1) and (2) were omitted; and
(b) for the reference in subsection (4) to the OFT there were substituted a reference to the Secretary of State.

Final undertakings and orders

9.—(1) The Secretary of State may, in accordance with article 12(6) to (8) accept, from such persons as she considers appropriate, undertakings to take action specified or described in the undertakings.

(2) An undertaking under this paragraph—

(a) shall come into force when accepted;

(b) may be varied or superseded by another undertaking; and

(c) may be released by the Secretary of State.

(3) An undertaking which is in force under this paragraph in relation to a reference under article 5 shall cease to be in force if an order under paragraph 6(1)(b) or 10 comes into force in relation to the subject-matter of the undertaking.

(4) No undertaking shall be accepted under this paragraph in relation to a reference under article 5 if an order has been made under—

(a) paragraph 6(1)(b) or 10 in relation to the subject-matter of the undertaking; or

(b) paragraph 11 in relation to that reference.

(5) The Secretary of State shall, as soon as reasonably practicable, consider any representations received by her in relation to varying or releasing an undertaking under this paragraph.

10.—(1) Sub-paragraph (2) applies where the Secretary of State considers that—

(a) an undertaking accepted by her under paragraph 9 has not been, is not being or will not be fulfilled; or

(b) in relation to an undertaking accepted by her under that paragraph, information which was false or misleading in a material respect was given to her or the OFT by the person giving the undertaking before she decided to accept the undertaking.

(2) The Secretary of State may, for any purpose mentioned in article 12(7), make an order under this paragraph.

(3) Paragraph (8) of article 12 shall apply for the purpose of sub-paragraph (2) above as it applies for the purposes of article 12(7).

(4) An order under this paragraph may contain—

(a) anything permitted by Schedule 8 to the Act; and

(b) such supplementary, consequential or incidental provision as the Secretary of State considers appropriate.

(5) An order under this paragraph—

(a) shall come into force at such time as is determined by or under the order; and

(b) may contain provision which is different from the provision contained in the undertaking concerned.

(6) No order shall be varied or revoked under this paragraph unless the OFT advises that such a variation or revocation is appropriate by reason of a change of circumstances.

11.—(1) The Secretary of State may, in accordance with article 12(7), make an order under this paragraph.

(2) An order under this paragraph may contain—

(a) anything permitted by Schedule 8 to the Act; and

(b) such supplementary, consequential or incidental provision as the Secretary of State considers appropriate.

(3) An order under this paragraph shall come into force at such time as is determined by or under the order.

(4) No order shall be made under this paragraph in relation to a reference under article 5 if an undertaking has been accepted under paragraph 9 in relation to that reference.

(5) No order shall be varied or revoked under this paragraph unless the OFT advises that such a variation or revocation is appropriate by reason of a change of circumstances.

[7190]

SCHEDULE 3
OTHER PROVISIONS OF THE ACT APPLICABLE TO THE ORDER

Article 15

1.—(1) The following sections of Part 3 of the Act shall apply, with the modifications mentioned in sub-paragraphs (2) to (27) below, for the purposes of this Order—

(a) section 69 (newspaper mergers);
(b) section 86 (enforcement orders: general provisions);
(c) section 87 (delegated power of directions);
(d) section 88 (contents of certain enforcement orders);
(e) section 89 (subject-matter of undertakings);
(f) section 91 (register of undertakings and orders);
(g) section 92 (duty of OFT to monitor undertakings and orders);
(h) section 93 (further role of OFT in relation to undertakings and orders);
(i) section 94 (rights to enforce undertakings and orders);
(j) section 95 (rights to enforce statutory restrictions);
(k) section 103 (duty of expedition in relation to references);
(l) section 104 (certain duties of relevant authorities to consult);
[(la) section 104A (public consultation in relation to media mergers);]
(m) section 105 (general information duties of OFT and Commission);
[(ma) section 106B (general advisory functions of OFCOM);]
(n) section 108 (defamation);
(o) section 109 (attendance of witnesses and production of documents etc);
(p) section 110 (enforcement of powers under section 109: general);
(q) section 111 (penalties);
(r) section 112 (penalties: main procedural requirements);
(s) section 113 (payments and interest by instalments);
(t) section 114 (appeals in relation to penalties);
(u) section 115 (recovery of penalties);
(v) section 116 (statement of policy);
(w) section 117 (false or misleading information);
(x) section 118 (excisions from reports);
(y) section 119 (minority reports of Commission);
[(ya) section 119A (other general functions of OFCOM);]
(z) section 120 (review of decisions under Part 3);
(aa) section 124 (orders and regulations under Part 3);
(bb) section 125 (offences by bodies corporate);
(cc) section 126 (service of documents);
(dd) section 127 (associated persons);
(ee) section 128 (supply of services and market for services etc); and
(ff) section 129 (other interpretation provisions).

(2) Section 69 shall apply as if in subsection (1) for the words "section 22, 33, 45 or 62" there were substituted "article 5 of the Enterprise Act 2002 (Protection of Legitimate Interests) Order 2003".

(3) Section 86 shall apply as if—
(a) subsection (5) were omitted; and
(b) in subsection (6)—
(i) the words from "section 72" to "under", where it appears for the second time, were omitted; and
(ii) for the words "Schedule 7" there were substituted "Schedule 2 to the Enterprise Act 2002 (Protection of Legitimate Interests) Order 2003".

(4) Section 88 shall apply as if in subsection (1)—
(a) the words from "section 75" to "under" were omitted; and
(b) for the words "Schedule 7" there were substituted "Schedule 2 to the Enterprise Act 2002 (Protection of Legitimate Interests) Order 2003".

(5) Section 89 shall apply as if in subsection (2)—
(a) the words from "section 71" to "under", where it appears for the second time, were omitted; and
(b) for the words "Schedule 7" there were substituted "Schedule 2 to the Enterprise Act 2002 (Protection of Legitimate Interests) Order 2003".

(6) Section 91 shall apply as if—
(a) in subsections (1), (3)(a) and (b) for the words "this Part" there were substituted "the Enterprise Act 2002 (Protection of Legitimate Interests) Order 2003";
(b) in subsection (3)(d)—
(i) the words from "by the Commission" to "78(2) or" were omitted; and
(ii) for the words "Schedule 7" there were substituted "Schedule 2 to the Enterprise Act 2002 (Protection of Legitimate Interests) Order 2003"; and
(c) in subsection (5)—
(i) the words "Commission and the" were omitted; and

PART IV
STATUTORY INSTRUMENTS

(ii) for the words "them" in all three places where they appear there were substituted "him".

(7) Section 92 shall apply as if—

(a) in subsections (1)(b), (3)(f) and (4)(f)—

(i) the words from "in sections 77(2)" to "78(2) and" were omitted; and

(ii) for the words "Schedule 7" there were substituted "Schedule 2 to the Enterprise Act 2002 (Protection of Legitimate Interests) Order 2003";

(b) in subsection (3) the words "the Commission or (as the case may be)", in all places where they appear, were omitted;

(c) in subsection (3)(a) the words "it or (as the case may be)" were omitted;

(d) in subsection (3)(e) for the word "to" there were substituted "and";

(e) in subsection (3)(f) the words "(4) and" were omitted;

(f) subsections (4)(a) to (d) were omitted; and

(g) in subsection (5) for the words "this Part" in both places where they appear there were substituted "the Enterprise Act 2002 (Protection of Legitimate Interests) Order 2003".

(8) Section 93 shall apply as if—

(a) subsection (1)(a) were omitted;

(b) in subsections (1)(b), (2) and (4) for the words "Schedule 7" there were substituted "Schedule 2 to the Enterprise Act 2002 (Protection of Legitimate Interests) Order 2003";

(c) in subsection (2) the words "Commission or (as the case may be) the" were omitted; and

(d) in subsections (2) and (4) the words "section 80 or 82 or (as the case may be)" were omitted.

(9) Section 94 shall apply as if—

(a) subsection (7) were omitted;

(b) in subsection (8) for the words "Schedule 7" there were substituted "Schedule 2 to the Enterprise Act 2002 (Protection of Legitimate Interests) Order 2003";

(c) in subsection (9) for the words "to (8)" there were substituted "and (8)".

(10) Section 95 shall apply as if—

(a) in subsections (1), (3) and (6)—

(i) the words from "section 77(2)" to "78(2) or" were omitted; and

(ii) for the words "Schedule 7" there were substituted "Schedule 2 to the Enterprise Act 2002 (Protection of Legitimate Interests) Order 2003";

(b) subsection (4) were omitted;

(c) in subsection (5) for the words "Schedule 7" there were substituted "Schedule 2 to the Enterprise Act 2002 (Protection of Legitimate Interests) Order 2003"; and

(d) in subsection (6) for the words "Subsections (4) and" there were substituted "Subsection".

(11) Section 103 shall apply as if—

(a) subsection (1) were omitted; and

(b) in subsection (2) for the words "section 45 or 62" there were substituted "article 5 of the Enterprise Act 2002 (Protection of Legitimate Interests) Order 2003".

(12) Section 104 shall apply as if—

(a) in subsection (5) for the words "this Part" there were substituted "the Enterprise Act 2002 (Protection of Legitimate Interests) Order 2003";

(b) in subsection (6) the words "the OFT," where they appear for the first time were omitted;

(c) paragraph (a) in the definition of "relevant decision" in subsection (6) were omitted;

(d) in paragraph (b) in the definition of "relevant decision" in subsection (6), for the words from "section 35(1)" to "63" there were substituted "article 6 of the Enterprise Act 2002 (Protection of Legitimate Interests) Order 2003";

(e) in paragraph (c)(i) in the definition of "relevant decision" in subsection (6), for the words "section 45 or 62" there were substituted "article 5 of the Enterprise Act 2002 (Protection of Legitimate Interests Order) 2003"; and

(f) in paragraph (c)(ii) in the definition of "relevant decision" in subsection (6), for the words "section 49 or (as the case may be) 64" there were substituted "article 7 of the Enterprise Act 2002 (Protection of Legitimate Interests) Order 2003".

[(12A) Section 104A shall apply as if—

(a) for the words in subsection (1) there were substituted—

"(1) Subsection (2) applies where the Commission is preparing a report under article 5 of the Enterprise Act 2002 (Protection of Legitimate Interests) Order 2003 which specifies a media public interest consideration."; and

(b) in subsection (2) the words "or special merger situation" were omitted.]

(13) Section 105 shall apply as if—

(a) in subsection (1)—

(i) for the words from "so as to enable" to "44 or 61" there were substituted "so as to make a report under article 4 of the Enterprise Act 2002 (Protection of Legitimate Interests) Order 2003"; and

(ii) for the words from "relevant merger situation" to the end of that subsection there were substituted "European relevant merger situation concerned";

[(ab) in subsection (1A) for the words "section 44A or 61A" there were substituted "article 4A of the Enterprise Act 2002 (Protection of Legitimate Interests) Order 2003".]

(b) subsection (2) were omitted; and

(c) in subsections (3)(a) and (3)(b), (4), (5)(a) and (5)(b) and (6) for the words "this Part" there were substituted "the Enterprise Act 2002 (Protection of Legitimate Interests) Order 2003".

[(13A) Section 106B shall apply as if—

(a) for the words in subsection (1) there were substituted—

"(1) OFCOM may, in connection with any case on which they are required to give a report by virtue of article 4A of the Enterprise Act 2002 (Protection of Legitimate Interests) Order 2003, give such advice as they consider appropriate to the Secretary of State in relation to—

(a) any report made by the Commission under article 8 of the Enterprise Act 2002 (Protection of Legitimate Interests) Order 2003; and

(b) the taking by the Secretary of State of enforcement action under Schedule 2 to the Enterprise Act 2002 (Protection of Legitimate Interests) Order 2003";

(b) in subsection (2) for the words "section 44A or 61A" there were substituted "article 4A of the Enterprise Act 2002 (Protection of Legitimate Interests) Order 2003"; and

(c) in subsection (3) for the words "section 50 or 65" there were substituted "article 8 of the Enterprise Act 2002 (Protection of Legitimate Interests) Order 2003".]

(14) Section 108 shall apply as if for the words "this Part" there were substituted "the Enterprise Act 2002 (Protection of Legitimate Interests) Order 2003".

(15) Section 109 shall apply as if in subsections (1), (2), (3), (5) and (6) for the words "this Part" there were substituted "the Enterprise Act 2002 (Protection of Legitimate Interests) Order 2003".

(16) Section 110 shall apply as if in subsections (2) and (9) for the words from "section 39(4)" to "65(3))" there were substituted "article 9(3) of the Enterprise Act 2002 (Protection of Legitimate Interests) Order 2003".

(17) Section 111 shall apply as if in subsection (5)(b)(ii) for the words from "published", where it appears for the first time, to "(or given)", where it appears for the second time, there were substituted "given under article 8 of the Enterprise Act 2002 (Protection of Legitimate Interests) Order 2003, or, if no such report is given within the period permitted for that purpose by that Order, the latest day on which the report may be given".

(18) Section 117 shall apply as if in subsections (1)(a) and (2) for the words "this Part" there were substituted "the Enterprise Act 2002 (Protection of Legitimate Interests) Order 2003".

(19) Section 118 shall apply as if—

(a) in subsection (1)(a) for the words "section 44 or 61" there were substituted "article 4 of the Enterprise Act 2002 (Protection of Legitimate Interests) Order 2003";

(b) in subsection (1)(b) for the words "section 50 or 65" there were substituted "article 8 of the Enterprise Act 2002 (Protection of Legitimate Interests) Order 2003"; and

(c) in subsection (5) for the words "sections 38(4) and 107(11)" there were substituted "article 14(8) of the Enterprise Act 2002 (Protection of Legitimate Interests) Order 2003".

(20) Section 119 shall apply as if in subsection (1) for the words "this Part", in both places where they appear, there were substituted "the Enterprise Act 2002 (Protection of Legitimate Interests) Order 2003".

[(20A) Section 119A shall apply as if in subsections (1) and (4) for the words "this Part" there were substituted "the Enterprise Act 2002 (Protection of Legitimate Interests) Order 2003".]

(21) Section 120 shall apply as if—

(a) in subsections (1) and (2)(b) for the words "this Part" there were substituted "the Enterprise Act 2002 (Protection of Legitimate Interests) Order 2003"; and

(b) in subsection (1) for the words "relevant merger situation or a special merger situation" there were substituted "European relevant merger situation".

(22) Section 124 shall apply as if—

(a) in subsections (1) and (2) for the words "this Part" there were substituted "the Enterprise Act 2002 (Protection of Legitimate Interests) Order 2003";

(b) subsections (3) and (4) and (6) to (10) were omitted; and

(c) for subsection (5) there were substituted—

"(5) An order made by the Secretary of State under section 28, 111(4) or (6) or 114(3)(b) or (4)(b) as applied by the Enterprise Act 2002 (Protection of Legitimate Interests) Order 2003, or under Schedule 2 to that Order shall be subject to annulment in pursuance of a resolution of either House of Parliament.".

(23) Section 125 shall apply as if in subsections (1) and (3) for the words "this Part" there were substituted "the Enterprise Act 2002 (Protection of Legitimate Interests) Order 2003".

(24) Section 126 shall apply as if in subsections (1), (4) and (6) for the words "this Part" there were substituted "the Enterprise Act 2002 (Protection of Legitimate Interests) Order 2003".

(25) Section 127 shall apply as if in subsection (3) for the words "section 22, 33, 45 or 62" there were substituted "article 5 of the Enterprise Act 2002 (Protection of Legitimate Interests) Order 2003".

(26) Section 128 shall apply as if in subsection (1) for the words "this Part" where they appear on both occasions there were substituted "the Enterprise Act 2002 (Protection of Legitimate Interests) Order 2003".

(27) Section 129 shall apply as if in subsections (1) to (4) for the words "this Part" where they appear on all occasions there were substituted "the Enterprise Act 2002 (Protection of Legitimate Interests) Order 2003".

2.—(1) The following Schedules of the Act shall apply, with the modifications mentioned in sub-paragraphs (2) and (3) below, for the purposes of this Order—

(a) Schedule 8 (provision that may be contained in certain enforcement orders); and

(b) Schedule 10 (procedural requirements for certain enforcement undertakings and orders).

(2) Schedule 8 shall apply as if—

(a) in paragraph 1 for the words "this Part and Part 4" there were substituted "the Enterprise Act 2002 (Protection of Legitimate Interests) Order 2003";

(b) in paragraph 14—

(i) the words "an order under section 75, 83, 84, 160 or 161, or" were omitted; and

(ii) for the words "Schedule 7" there were substituted "Schedule 2 to the Enterprise Act 2002 (Protection of Legitimate Interests) Order 2003"; …

[(ba) in paragraph 20A(1)(a) for the words "intervention notice" there were substituted "European intervention notice" and in paragraph 20A(1)(a)(ii) for the words "relevant merger situation" there were substituted "European relevant merger situation"; and]

(c) in paragraph 24 for paragraphs (a) to (c) there were substituted "the Secretary of State".

(3) Schedule 10 shall apply as if—

(a) in paragraphs 1(a) and 6(a)—

(i) the words "section 73 or 82 or" were omitted; and

(ii) for the words "Schedule 7" there were substituted "Schedule 2 to the Enterprise Act 2002 (Protection of Legitimate Interests) Order 2003";

(b) in paragraphs 1(b) and 6(b)—

(i) the words "section 75, 83 or 84 or" were omitted; and

(ii) for the words "Schedule 7" there were substituted "Schedule 2 to the Enterprise Act 2002 (Protection of Legitimate Interests) Order 2003"; and

(c) in paragraph 2(1) the words "the OFT, the Commission or (as the case may be)" were omitted.

3. Section 243(1) of the Act (overseas disclosures) shall not apply to information which comes to a public authority in connection with an investigation under this Order.

[7191]

NOTES

Para 1: sub-paras (1)(la), (ma), (ya), (12A), (13)(ab), (13A), (20A) inserted by the Enterprise Act 2002 and Media Mergers (Consequential Amendments) Order 2003, SI 2003/3180, art 2, Schedule, para 10(1), (9)–(15), as from 29 December 2003.

Para 2: sub-para (2)(ba) inserted, and word immediately preceding it revoked, by SI 2003/3180, art 2, Schedule, para 10(1), (16), as from 29 December 2003.

(Schedule 4 (Consequential Amendments) contains amendments to enactments that are outside the scope of this work.)

INSOLVENCY ACT 1986 (PRESCRIBED PART) ORDER 2003

(SI 2003/2097)

NOTES

Made: 8 August 2003.

Authority: Insolvency Act 1986, s 176A.

Commencement: 15 September 2003 (see art 1 at **[7192]**). Where any provision in this work (including any inserted or substituted provision) came into force for all purposes on or before 1 July 2005, commencement information is not noted at provision level.

As of 1 July 2007, this Order had not been amended.

1 Citation, Commencement and Interpretation

(1) This Order may be cited as the Insolvency Act 1986 (Prescribed Part) Order 2003 and shall come into force on 15th September 2003.

(2) In this order "the 1986 Act" means the Insolvency Act 1986.

[7192]

2 Minimum value of the company's net property

For the purposes of section 176A(3)(a) of the 1986 Act the minimum value of the company's net property is £10,000.

[7193]

3 Calculation of prescribed part

(1) The prescribed part of the company's net property to be made available for the satisfaction of unsecured debts of the company pursuant to section 176A of the 1986 Act shall be calculated as follows—

(a) where the company's net property does not exceed £10,000 in value, 50% of that property;

(b) subject to paragraph (2), where the company's net property exceeds £10,000 in value the sum of—

(i) 50% of the first £10,000 in value; and

(ii) 20% of that part of the company's net property which exceeds £10,000 in value.

(2) The value of the prescribed part of the company's net property to be made available for the satisfaction of unsecured debts of the company pursuant to section 176A shall not exceed £600,000.

[7194]

INSOLVENCY PRACTITIONERS AND INSOLVENCY SERVICES ACCOUNT (FEES) ORDER 2003 (NOTE)

(SI 2003/3363)

NOTES

See Appendix 3 (Fees Instruments) at **[A3]**.

[7195]–[7200]

INSURERS (REORGANISATION AND WINDING UP) REGULATIONS 2004

(SI 2004/353)

NOTES

These Regulations have been omitted from this Edition of the *Company Law Handbook* in order to create space for other legislation (ie, the Companies Act 2006 and the associated destination and derivation tables). They were printed in full in the 20th Edition of this work (at p 2517 et seq) and, since 1 July 2006, they have been amended by the Financial Services (EEA State) Regulations 2007, SI 2007/108, the Financial Services and Markets Act 2000 (Markets in Financial Instruments) Regulations 2007, SI 2007/126, and the Insurers (Reorganisation and Winding Up) (Amendment) Regulations 2007, SI 2007/851. These Regulations are, however, included in the CD version of this work (which may be ordered from the LexisNexis Butterworths Customer Services Department) and can be accessed in the online version of the *Company Law Handbook* which is updated fortnightly (at www.lexisnexis.com/uk/legal). They are also printed in full in the 8th Edition of *Butterworths Financial Services Law Handbook* (February 2007).

[7200A]–[7200ZY]

INSOLVENCY PROCEEDINGS (FEES) ORDER 2004 (NOTE)

(SI 2004/593)

NOTES

See Appendix 3 (Fees Instruments) at **[A3]**.

[7201]–[7210]

CREDIT INSTITUTIONS (REORGANISATION AND WINDING UP) REGULATIONS 2004

(SI 2004/1045)

NOTES

These Regulations have been omitted from this Edition of the *Company Law Handbook* in order to create space for other legislation (ie, the Companies Act 2006 and the associated destination and derivation tables). They were printed in full in the 20th Edition of this work (at p 2546 et seq) and, since 1 July 2006, they have been amended by the Capital Requirements Regulations 2006, SI 2006/3221, the Financial Services (EEA State) Regulations 2007, SI 2007/108, the Financial Services and Markets Act 2000 (Markets in Financial Instruments) Regulations 2007, SI 2007/126, and the Credit Institutions (Reorganisation and Winding Up) (Amendment) Regulations 2007, SI 2007/830. These Regulations are, however, included in the CD version of this work (which may be ordered from the LexisNexis Butterworths Customer Services Department) and can be accessed in the online version of the *Company*

Law Handbook which is updated fortnightly (at www.lexisnexis.com/uk/legal). They are also printed in full in the 8th Edition of *Butterworths Financial Services Law Handbook* (February 2007).

[7211]–[7248]

EUROPEAN PUBLIC LIMITED-LIABILITY COMPANY REGULATIONS 2004

(SI 2004/2326)

NOTES

Made: 6 September 2004.

Authority: European Communities Act 1972, s 2(2).

Commencement: 8 October 2004 (see reg 1 at **[7249]**). Where any provision in this work (including any inserted or substituted provision) came into force for all purposes on or before 1 July 2005, commencement information is not noted at provision level.

As of 1 July 2007, these Regulations had not been amended.

ARRANGEMENT OF REGULATIONS

PART 1
GENERAL

PART 2
REGISTRATION OF SES AND THE REGISTRAR ETC

PART 3
EMPLOYEE INVOLVEMENT

CHAPTER 1
INTERPRETATION OF PART 3

CHAPTER 2
PARTICIPATING COMPANIES AND THE SPECIAL NEGOTIATING BODY

CHAPTER 3
ELECTION OR APPOINTMENT OF UK MEMBERS OF THE SPECIAL NEGOTIATING BODY

CHAPTER 4
NEGOTIATION OF THE EMPLOYEE INVOLVEMENT AGREEMENT

CHAPTER 5
STANDARD RULES ON EMPLOYEE INVOLVEMENT

CHAPTER 6
COMPLIANCE AND ENFORCEMENT

CHAPTER 7
CONFIDENTIAL INFORMATION

CHAPTER 8
PROTECTION FOR MEMBERS OF SPECIAL NEGOTIATING BODY, ETC

CHAPTER 9
MISCELLANEOUS

PART 4
EXERCISE OF MEMBER STATES OPTIONS UNDER THE EC REGULATION

PART 1
GENERAL

1 Citation, commencement and extent

(1) These Regulations may be cited as the European Public Limited-Liability Company Regulations 2004.

(2) These Regulations come into force on 8th October 2004.

(3) These Regulations extend to Great Britain.

[7249]

PART IV
STATUTORY INSTRUMENTS

NOTES

Note that despite para (3) above, the enactments in force in Great Britain relating to SEs extend to Northern Ireland; see the Companies Act 2006, s 1285(1) at **[S1285]**.

2 EC Directive and EC Regulation

In these Regulations—

"the EC Directive" means Council Directive 2001/86/EC of 8 October 2001 supplementing the Statute for a European Company with regard to the involvement of employees;

"the EC Regulation" means Council Regulation 2157/2001/EC of 8 October 2001 on the Statute for a European Company;

and references to numbered Articles are, unless otherwise specified, references to Articles in the EC Regulation.

[7250]

3 Interpretation

(1) In these Regulations—

the "1985 Act" mean the Companies Act 1985;

the "1996 Act" means the Employment Rights Act 1996;

"SE" means a European Public Limited-Liability Company (or Societas Europaea) within the meaning of the EC Regulation and, except as provided in these Regulations, means an SE which is to be, or is, registered in Great Britain.

(2) Except as otherwise provided in these Regulations, words and expressions listed in the index of defined expressions in section 744A of the 1985 Act have the same meaning as they have in that Act.

(3) Except as otherwise provided in these Regulations, words and expressions which are used in the EC Regulation or the EC Directive have the same meaning as they have in that Regulation or Directive.

(4) Where a word or expression is both listed in the index of defined expressions referred to in paragraph (2) and used in the EC Regulation or the EC Directive, it has the meaning it has in that Regulation or Directive except as otherwise provided in these Regulations.

[7251]

PART 2
REGISTRATION OF SES AND THE REGISTRAR ETC

4 The registrar

The registrar has the functions conferred by this Part in relation to the registration, or the deletion of the registration, of an SE.

[7252]

5 Registration of an SE formed by merger in accordance with Article 2(1)

Where it is proposed to register an SE formed by merger in accordance with Article 2(1) there shall be delivered to the registrar a registration form in Form SE5, and, if applicable, Form SE(SR) set out in Schedule 1 together with the documents specified in respect of each Form.

[7253]

6 Registration of the formation of a holding SE in accordance with Article 2(2)

Where it is proposed to register a holding SE formed in accordance with Article 2(2) there shall be delivered to the registrar a registration form in Form SE6, and, if applicable, Form SE(SR), set out in Schedule 1 together with the documents specified in respect of each Form.

[7254]

7 Registration of the formation of a subsidiary SE in accordance with Article 2(3)

Where it is proposed to register a subsidiary SE formed in accordance with Article 2(3) there shall be delivered to the registrar a registration form in Form SE7, and, if applicable, Form SE(SR), set out in Schedule 1 together with the documents specified in respect of each Form.

[7255]

8 Registration of an SE by the transformation of a public company in accordance with Article 2(4)

Where it is proposed to register an SE by the transformation of a public company in accordance with Article 2(4) there shall be delivered to the registrar a registration form in Form SE8, and, if applicable, Form SE(SR) set out in Schedule 1 together with the documents specified in respect of each Form.

[7256]

9 Registration of an SE formed as the subsidiary of an SE in accordance with Article 3(2)

(1) Where it is proposed to register an SE formed as the subsidiary of an SE in accordance with Article 3(2) there shall be delivered to the registrar a registration form in Form SE9(1), and, if applicable, Form SE(SR), set out in Schedule 1 together with the documents specified in respect of each Form.

(2) The reference to an SE, a subsidiary of which is to be registered under this regulation, includes a reference to an SE whose registered office is in another Member State.

[7257]

10 Registration of an SE on the transfer of its registered office to Great Britain in accordance with Article 8

Where it is proposed to transfer to Great Britain the registered office of an SE whose registered office is situated in another Member State there shall be delivered to the registrar a registration form in respect of that SE in Form SE10, and, if applicable, Form SE(SR), set out in Schedule 1 together with the documents specified in respect of each Form.

[7258]

11 Certificate of the competent authority under Article 8(8)

Where it is proposed to transfer the registered office of an SE from Great Britain to another Member State there shall be delivered to the Secretary of State for the purposes of applying for the issue of a certificate under Article 8(8), a transfer form in Form SE11 set out in Schedule 1 together with the documents specified in that Form.

[7259]

12 Registration of an SE

The registrar shall register an SE formed or transformed under the provisions of Articles 2 and 3 or an SE whose registered office is transferred to Great Britain under Article 8 where she is satisfied that all the requirements of these Regulations and the EC Regulation in respect of such formation, transformation or transfer of an SE, as the case may be, have been complied with in respect of that SE.

[7260]

13 Documents sent to the registrar

(1) The registrar shall retain any document delivered to her under any provision of these Regulations or the EC Regulation and such documents shall be treated as records kept by the registrar for the purposes of the 1985 Act in respect of the SE or the company to which they relate.

(2) For the purposes of this regulation documents delivered to the Secretary of State under regulation 11 shall be treated as documents delivered to the registrar on the deletion of the registration of the SE making the application under the regulation and the provisions of regulation 14 will apply accordingly.

[7261]

14 Application of the 1985 Act to the registration of SEs

The provisions of the 1985 Act specified in Schedule 2 to these Regulations shall apply in respect of

- (a) the registration or the deletion of registration of SEs under these Regulations and the EC Regulation;
- (b) the functions of the registrar in respect of such registrations or deletions.

Those provisions shall apply under this regulation subject to any limitations or qualifications specified in relation to each such provision in that Schedule.

[7262]

15 False statements in documents sent to the registrar or the Secretary of State

Any person who makes a false statement:

(a) in any registration form sent to the registrar under regulations 5 to 10 and regulation 85,

(b) in any transfer form sent to the Secretary of State under regulation 11,

(c) in any document, specified in such a form, or

(d) in any other document required to be sent to the registrar under these Regulations,

which he knows to be false or does not believe to be true is liable, on conviction on indictment to imprisonment not exceeding two years, or to a fine, or to both, and on summary conviction to imprisonment not exceeding three months, or to a fine not exceeding the statutory maximum or to both.

[7263]

PART 3
EMPLOYEE INVOLVEMENT

CHAPTER 1
INTERPRETATION OF PART 3

16 Interpretation of Part 3

(1) In this Part—

"absolute majority vote" means a vote passed by a majority of the total membership of the special negotiating body where the members voting with that majority represent the majority of the employees of the participating companies and their concerned subsidiaries and establishments employed in the Member States;

"Appeal Tribunal" means the Employment Appeal Tribunal;

"CAC" means the Central Arbitration Committee;

"dismissed" and "dismissal", in relation to an employee, shall be construed in accordance with Part 10 of the 1996 Act;

"EEA state" means a Member State, Norway, Iceland and Lichtenstein;

"employee" means an individual who has entered into or works under a contract of employment and includes, where the employment has ceased, an individual who worked under a contract of employment;

"employee involvement agreement" means an agreement reached between the special negotiating body and the competent organs of the participating companies governing the arrangements for the involvement of employees within the SE;

"employees' representatives" means—

(a) if the employees are of a description in respect of which an independent trade union is recognised by their employer for the purpose of collective bargaining, representatives of the trade union who normally take part as negotiators in the collective bargaining process, and

(b) any other employees of their employer who are elected or appointed as employee representatives to positions in which they are expected to receive, on behalf of the employees, information—

(i) which is relevant to the terms and conditions of employment of the employees, or

(ii) about the activities of the undertaking which may significantly affect the interests of the employees,

but excluding representatives who are expected to receive information relevant only to a specific aspect of the terms and conditions or interests of the employees, such as health and safety or collective redundancies;

"information and consultation representative" has the meaning given to it in regulation 27(5);

"participation" means the influence of the representative body and the employees' representatives in the SE or a participating company by way of the right to—

(a) elect or appoint some of the members of the SE's or the participating company's supervisory or administrative organ; or

(b) recommend and/or oppose the appointment of some or all of the members of the SE's or the participating company's supervisory or administrative organ;

"representative body" means the persons elected or appointed under the employee involvement agreement or under the standard rules on employee involvement;

"SE established by merger" means an SE established in accordance with Article 2(1);

"SE established by formation of a holding company or subsidiary company" means an SE established in accordance with Article 2(2) or 2(3), as the case may be;

"SE established by transformation" means an SE established in accordance with Article 2(4);

"standard rules on employee involvement" means the rules in Schedule 3;

"two thirds majority vote" means a vote passed by a majority of at least two thirds of the total membership of the special negotiating body where the members voting with that majority—

(a) represent at least two thirds of the employees of the participating companies and their concerned subsidiaries and establishments employed in the Member States; and

(b) include members representing employees employed in at least two Member States;

"UK employee" means an employee employed to work in the United Kingdom; and

"UK members of the special negotiating body" means members of the special negotiating body elected or appointed by UK employees.

(2) In this Part, the following terms have the meaning given by Article 2 of the EC Directive—

"participating companies"
"subsidiary"
"special negotiating body"
"involvement of employees"
"information"
"consultation"

and references to a "concerned subsidiary" or a "concerned establishment" shall be construed in accordance with the definition of "concerned subsidiary or establishment" in the EC Directive.

[7264]

CHAPTER 2
PARTICIPATING COMPANIES AND THE SPECIAL NEGOTIATING BODY

17 Circumstances in which certain provisions of Part 3 apply

(1) Subject to paragraphs (2) and (3), this Part shall apply where—

(a) a participating company intends to establish an SE whose registered office is to be in Great Britain; or

(b) an SE has its registered office in Great Britain.

(2) Where there are UK employees, Chapter 2 (election or appointment of members of special negotiating body and representation of employees) shall apply, regardless of where the registered office is to be situated, in relation to the election or appointment of UK members of the special negotiating body unless the majority of those employees is employed to work in Northern Ireland.

(3) Chapters 6 to 9 shall apply, regardless of where the registered office of the SE is, or is intended to be situated, where—

(a) a participating company, its concerned subsidiaries or establishments;

(b) a subsidiary of an SE;

(c) an establishment of an SE; or

(d) an employee or an employees' representative,

is registered or situated, as the case may be, in Great Britain.

[7265]

18 Duty on participating company to provide information

(1) When the competent organ of a participating company decides to form an SE, that organ shall, as soon as possible after—

(a) publishing the draft terms of merger,

(b) creating a holding company, or
(c) agreeing a plan to form a subsidiary or to transform into an SE,

provide information to the employees' representatives of the participating company, its concerned subsidiaries and establishments or, if no such representatives exist, the employees themselves.

(2) The information referred to in paragraph (1) must include, as a minimum, information—

(a) identifying the participating companies, concerned subsidiaries and establishments,
(b) giving the number of employees employed by each participating company and concerned subsidiary and at each concerned establishment, and
(c) giving the number of employees employed to work in each EEA State.

(3) When a special negotiating body has been formed in accordance with regulation 20, the competent organs of each participating company must provide that body with such information as is necessary to keep it informed of the plan and progress of establishing the SE up to the time the SE has been registered.

[7266]

19 Complaint of failure to provide information

(1) An employees' representative or, where there is no such representative for an employee, the employee may present a complaint to the CAC that—

(a) the competent organ of a participating company has failed to provide the information referred to in regulation 18; or
(b) the information provided by the competent organ of a participating company for the purpose of complying with regulation 18 is false or incomplete in a material particular.

(2) Where the CAC finds the complaint well-founded it shall make an order requiring the competent organ to disclose information to the complainant which order shall specify—

(a) the information in respect of which the CAC finds that the complaint is well-founded and which is to be disclosed to the complainant; and
(b) a date (not being less than one week from the date of the order) by which the competent organ must disclose the information specified in the order.

[7267]

20 Function of the special negotiating body

The special negotiating body and the competent organs of the participating companies shall have the task of reaching an employee involvement agreement.

[7268]

21 Composition of the special negotiating body

(1) The competent organs of the participating companies shall make arrangements for the establishment of a special negotiating body which shall be constituted in accordance with paragraphs (2) to (7) below.

(2) In each EEA state in which employees of a participating company or concerned subsidiary are employed to work, those employees shall be given an entitlement to elect or appoint one member of the special negotiating body for each 10% or fraction thereof which those employees represent of the total workforce. These members shall be the 'ordinary members'.

(3) If, in the case of an SE to be established by merger, following an election or appointment under paragraph (2), the members elected or appointed to the special negotiating body do not include at least one eligible member in respect of each relevant company the employees of any relevant company in respect of which there is no eligible member shall be given an entitlement, subject to paragraph (4), to elect or appoint an additional member to the special negotiating body.

(4) The number of additional members which the employees are entitled to elect or appoint under paragraph (3) shall not exceed 20% of the number of ordinary members elected or appointed under paragraph (2) and if the number of additional members under paragraph (3) would exceed that percentage the employees who are entitled to appoint or elect the additional members shall be:

(a) if one additional member is to be appointed or elected, those employed by the company not represented under paragraph (3) having the highest number of employees; and

(b) if more than one additional member is to be appointed or elected, those employed by the companies in each EEA state that are not represented under paragraph (3) having the highest number of employees in descending order, starting with the company with the highest number, followed by those employed by the companies in each EEA state that are not so represented having the second highest number of employees in descending order, starting with the company (among those companies) with the highest number.

(5) The competent organs of the participating companies shall, as soon as reasonably practicable and in any event no later than one month after the establishment of the special negotiating body, inform their employees and those of their concerned subsidiaries of the identity of the members of the special negotiating body.

(6) If, following the appointment or election of members to the special negotiating body in accordance with this regulation,

(a) changes to the participating companies, concerned subsidiaries or concerned establishments result in the number of ordinary or additional members which employees would be entitled to elect or appoint under this regulation either increasing or decreasing, the original appointment or election of members of the special negotiating body shall cease to have effect and those employees shall be entitled to elect or appoint the new number of members in accordance with the provisions of these Regulations; and

(b) a member of the special negotiating body is no longer willing or able to continue serving as such a member, the employees whom he represents shall be entitled to elect or appoint a new member in his place.

(7) In this regulation—

(a) "eligible member" means a person who is—

(i) in the case of a relevant company registered in a EEA state whose legislation allows representatives of trade unions who are not employees to be elected to the special negotiating body, an employee of the relevant company or a trade union representative; and

(ii) in the case of a relevant company not registered in such a EEA state, an employee of the relevant company.

(b) "relevant company" means a participating company which has employees in the EEA state in which it is registered and which it is proposed will cease to exist on or following the registration of the SE; and

(c) "the total workforce" means the total number of employees employed by all participating companies and concerned subsidiaries throughout all EEA states.

[7269]

22 Complaint about establishment of special negotiating body

(1) An application may be presented to the CAC for a declaration that the special negotiating body has not been established at all or has not been established properly in accordance with regulation 21.

(2) An application may be presented under this regulation by—

(a) a person elected or appointed to be a member of the special negotiating body;

(b) an employees' representative or, where no such representative exists in respect of a participating company or concerned subsidiary, an employee of that participating company or concerned subsidiary; or

(c) the competent organ of a participating company or concerned subsidiary.

(3) The CAC shall only consider an application made under paragraph (1) if it is made within a period of one month from the date or, if more than one, the last date on which the participating companies complied or should have complied with the obligation to inform their employees under regulation 21(5).

(4) Where the CAC finds the application well-founded it shall make a declaration that the special negotiating body has not been established at all or has not been established properly and the competent organs of the participating companies continue to be under the obligation in regulation 21(1).

[7270]

CHAPTER 3
ELECTION OR APPOINTMENT OF UK MEMBERS OF THE SPECIAL NEGOTIATING BODY

23 Ballot arrangements

(1) Subject to regulation 24, the UK members of the special negotiating body shall be elected by balloting the UK employees.

(2) The management of the participating companies that employ UK employees ("the management") must arrange for the holding of a ballot or ballots of those employees in accordance with the requirements of paragraph (3).

(3) The requirements referred to in paragraph (2) are—

(a) in relation to the election of ordinary members under regulation 21(2), that—

(i) if the number of members which UK employees are entitled to elect to the special negotiating body is equal to the number of participating companies which have UK employees, there shall be separate ballots of the UK employees in each participating company;

(ii) if the number of members which the UK employees are entitled to elect to the special negotiating body is greater than the number of participating companies which have UK employees, there shall be separate ballots of the UK employees in each participating company and the management shall ensure, as far as practicable, that at least one member representing each such participating company is elected to the special negotiating body and that the number of members representing each company is proportionate to the number of employees in that company;

(iii) if the number of members which the UK employees are entitled to elect to the special negotiating body is smaller than the number of participating companies which have employees in the UK,—

(aa) the number of ballots held shall be equivalent to the number of members to be elected;

(bb) a separate ballot shall be held in respect of each of the participating companies with the higher or highest number of employees; and

(cc) it shall be ensured that any employees of a participating company in respect of which a ballot does not have to be held are entitled to vote in a ballot held in respect of one of the other participating companies; and

(iv) if there are any UK employees employed by a concerned subsidiary or establishment of non-UK participating companies, the management shall ensure that those employees are entitled to vote in a ballot held pursuant to this regulation.

(b) that in relation to the ballot of additional members under regulation 21(3) the management shall hold a separate ballot in respect of each participating company entitled to elect an additional member.

(c) that in a ballot in respect of a particular participating company, all UK employees employed by that participating company or by its concerned subsidiaries or at its concerned establishments are entitled to vote;

(d) that in a ballot in respect of a particular participating company, any person who is immediately before the latest time at which a person may become a candidate—

(i) a UK employee employed by that participating company, by any of its concerned subsidiaries or at any of its concerned establishments; or

(ii) if the management of that participating company so permits, a representative of a trade union who is not an employee of that participating company or any of its concerned subsidiaries, is entitled to stand as a candidate for election as a member of the special negotiating body in that ballot.

(e) that the management must, in accordance with paragraph (7), appoint an independent ballot supervisor to supervise the conduct of the ballot of UK employees but may instead, where there is to be more than one ballot, appoint more than one independent ballot supervisor in accordance with that paragraph, each of whom is to supervise such of the separate ballots as the management may determine, provided that each separate ballot is supervised by a supervisor;

(f) that after the management has formulated proposals as to the arrangements for the ballot of UK employees and before it has published the final arrangements under sub-paragraph (g) it must, so far as reasonably practicable, consult with the UK employees' representatives on the proposed arrangements for the ballot of UK employees; and

(g) that the management must publish the final arrangements for the ballot of UK employees in such manner as to bring them to the attention of, so far as reasonably practicable, all UK employees and the UK employees' representatives.

(4) Any UK employee or UK employees' representative who believes that the arrangements for the ballot of the UK employees do not comply with the requirements of paragraph (3) may, within a period of 21 days beginning on the date on which the management published the final arrangements under sub-paragraph (g), present a complaint to the CAC.

(5) Where the CAC finds the complaint well-founded it shall make a declaration to that effect and may make an order requiring the management to modify the arrangements it has made for the ballot of UK employees or to satisfy the requirements in sub-paragraph (f) or (g) of paragraph (3).

(6) An order under paragraph (5) shall specify the modifications to the arrangements which the management is required to make and the requirements it must satisfy.

(7) A person is an independent ballot supervisor for the purposes of paragraph (3)(e) if the management reasonably believes that he will carry out any functions conferred on him in relation to the ballot competently and has no reasonable grounds for believing that his independence in relation to the ballot might reasonably be called into question.

[7271]

24 Conduct of the ballot

(1) The management must—

(a) ensure that a ballot supervisor appointed under regulation 23(3)(e) carries out his functions under this regulation and that there is no interference with his carrying out of those functions from the management; and

(b) comply with all reasonable requests made by a ballot supervisor for the purposes of, or in connection with, the carrying out of those functions.

(2) A ballot supervisor's appointment shall require that he—

(a) supervises the conduct of the ballot, or the separate ballots he is being appointed to supervise, in accordance with the arrangements for the ballot of UK employees published by the management under regulation 23(3)(g) or, where appropriate, in accordance with the arrangements as required to be modified by an order made as a result of a complaint presented under regulation 23(4);

(b) does not conduct the ballot or any of the separate ballots before the UK management has satisfied the requirement specified in regulation 23(3)(g) and—

(i) where no complaint has been presented under regulation 23(4), before the expiry of a period of 21 days beginning on the date on which the management published its arrangements under regulation 23(3)(g); or

(ii) where a complaint has been presented under regulation 23(4), before the complaint has been determined and, where appropriate, the arrangements have been modified as required by an order made as a result of that complaint;

(c) conducts the ballot, or each separate ballot so as to secure that—

(i) so far as reasonably practicable, those entitled to vote are given the opportunity to vote;

(ii) so far as reasonably practicable, those entitled to stand as candidates are given the opportunity to stand;

(iii) so far as reasonably practicable, those voting are able to do so in secret, and

(iv) the votes given in the ballot are fairly and accurately counted.

(3) As soon as reasonably practicable after the holding of the ballot, the ballot supervisor must publish the results of the ballot in such manner as to make them available to the management and, so far as reasonably practicable, the UK employees entitled to vote in the ballot and the persons who stood as candidates.

(4) A ballot supervisor shall publish a report ("an ineffective ballot report") where he considers (whether on the basis of representations made to him by another person or otherwise) that—

(a) any of the requirements referred to in paragraph (2) was not satisfied with the result that the outcome of the ballot would have been different; or

(b) there was an interference with the carrying out of his functions or a failure by management to comply with all reasonable requests made by him with the result that he was unable to form a proper judgement as to whether each of the requirements referred to in paragraph (2) was satisfied in the ballot.

(5) Where a ballot supervisor publishes an ineffective ballot report the report must be published within a period of one month commencing on the date on which the ballot supervisor publishes the results of the ballot under paragraph (3).

(6) A ballot supervisor shall publish an ineffective ballot report in such manner as to make it available to the management and, so far as reasonably practicable, the UK employees entitled to vote in the ballot and the persons who stood as candidates in the ballot.

(7) Where a ballot supervisor publishes an ineffective ballot report then—

(a) if there has been a single ballot or an ineffective ballot report has been published in respect of every separate ballot, the outcome of the ballot or ballots shall have no effect and the UK management shall again be under the obligation in regulation 23(2).

(b) If there have been separate ballots and sub-paragraph (a) does not apply—

(i) the management shall arrange for the separate ballot or ballots in respect of which an ineffective ballot report was published to be re-held in accordance with regulation 23 and this regulation; and

(ii) no such ballot shall have effect until it has been re-held and no ineffective ballot report has been published in respect of it.

(8) All costs relating to the holding of a ballot, including payments made to a ballot supervisor for supervising the conduct of the ballot, shall be borne by the management (whether or not an ineffective ballot report has been published).

[7272]

25 Appointment of UK members by a consultative committee

(1) This regulation applies where—

(a) regulation 23(3)(a)(i) or (ii) or (b) would require a ballot to be held; and

(b) there exists in the participating company in respect of which a ballot would be held under regulation 23, a consultative committee.

(2)

(a) Where this regulation applies, the election provided for in regulation 23 shall not take place but the consultative committee shall be entitled to appoint the UK member or members of the special negotiating body who would otherwise be elected pursuant to regulation 22 provided that the consultative committee's appointment complied with sub-paragraph (b).

(b) The consultative committee is entitled to appoint as a member of the special negotiating body:

(i) one of their number; or

(ii) if the management of the participating company in respect of which the consultative committee exists so permits, a trade union representative who is not an employee of that company.

(3) In this regulation, "a consultative committee" means a body of persons—

(a) whose normal functions include or comprise the carrying out of an information and consultation function;

(b) which is able to carry out its information and consultation function without interference from the management of the participating company;

(c) which, in carrying out its information and consultation function, represents all the employees of the participating company; and

(d) which consists wholly of persons who are employees of the participating company or its concerned subsidiaries.

(4) In paragraph (3) "information and consultation function" means the function of—

(a) receiving, on behalf of all the employees of the participating company, information which may significantly affect the interests of the employees of that company, but excluding information which is relevant only to a specific aspect of the interests of the employees, such as health and safety or collective redundancies; and

(b) being consulted by the management of the participating company on the information referred to in sub-paragraph (a) above.

(5) The consultative committee must publish the names of the persons whom it has appointed to be members of the special negotiating body in such a manner as to bring them to the attention of the management of the participating company and, so far as reasonably practicable, the employees and the employees' representatives of that company and its concerned subsidiaries.

(6) Where the management of the participating company, an employee or an employees' representative believes that—

(a) the consultative committee does not satisfy the requirements in paragraph (3) above; or

(b) any of the persons appointed by the consultative committee is not entitled to be appointed,

it, or as the case may be, he may, within a period of 21 days beginning on the date on which the consultative committee published under paragraph (5) the names of the persons appointed, present a complaint to the CAC.

(7) Where the CAC finds the complaint well-founded it shall make a declaration to that effect.

(8) Where the CAC has made a declaration under paragraph (7)—

(a) no appointment made by the consultative committee shall have effect; and

(b) the members of the special negotiating body shall be elected by a ballot of the employees in accordance with regulation 23.

(9) Where the consultative committee appoints any person to be a member of the special negotiating body, that appointment shall have effect—

(a) where no complaint has been presented under paragraph (6), after the expiry of a period of 21 days beginning on the date on which the consultative committee published under paragraph (5) the names of the persons nominated; or

(b) where a complaint has been presented under paragraph (6), as from the day on which the complaint has been determined without a declaration under paragraph (7) being made.

[7273]

26 Representation of employees

(1) Subject to paragraphs (2) and (3) below, a member elected in a ballot in accordance with regulation 21(2), shall be treated as representing the employees for the time being of the participating company and of any concerned subsidiary or establishment whose employees were entitled to vote in the ballot in which he was elected.

(2) If an additional member is elected in accordance with regulation 21(3) and (4), he, and not any member elected in accordance with regulation 21(2), shall be treated as representing the employees for the time being of the participating company and of any concerned subsidiary or establishment whose employees were entitled to vote in the ballot in which he was elected.

(3) When a member of the special negotiating body is appointed by a consultative committee in accordance with regulation 25, the employees whom the consultative committee represents and the employees of any concerned subsidiary shall be treated as being represented by the member so appointed.

[7274]

CHAPTER 4
NEGOTIATION OF THE EMPLOYEE INVOLVEMENT AGREEMENT

27 Negotiations to reach an employee involvement agreement

(1) In this regulation and in regulation 28 the competent organs of the participating companies and the special negotiating body are referred to as "the parties".

(2) The parties are under a duty to negotiate in a spirit of cooperation with a view to reaching an employee involvement agreement.

(3) The duty referred to in paragraph (2) commences one month after the date or, if more than one, the last date on which the members of the special negotiating body were elected or appointed and applies—

(a) for the period of six months starting with the day on which the duty commenced or, where an employee involvement agreement is successfully negotiated within that period, until the completion of the negotiations;

PART IV STATUTORY INSTRUMENTS

(b) where the parties agree before the end of that six month period that it is to be extended, for the period of twelve months starting with the day on which the duty commenced or, where an employee involvement agreement is successfully negotiated within the twelve month period, until the completion of the negotiations.

[7275]

28 The employee involvement agreement

(1) The employee involvement agreement must be in writing.

(2) Without prejudice to the autonomy of the parties and subject to paragraph (4), the employee involvement agreement shall specify:

(a) the scope of the agreement;
(b) the composition, number of members and allocation of seats on the representative body;
(c) the functions and the procedure for the information and consultation of the representative body;
(d) the frequency of meetings of the representative body;
(e) the financial and material resources to be allocated to the representative body;
(f) if, during negotiations, the parties decide to establish one or more information and consultation procedures instead of a representative body, the arrangements for implementing those procedures;
(g) if, during negotiations, the parties decide to establish arrangements for participation, the substance of those arrangements including (if applicable) the number of members in the SE's administrative or supervisory body which the employees will be entitled to elect, appoint, recommend or oppose, the procedures as to how these members may be elected, appointed, recommended or opposed by the employees, and their rights; and
(h) the date of entry into force of the agreement and its duration, the circumstances, if any in which the agreement is required to be re-negotiated and the procedure for its re-negotiation.

(3) The employee involvement agreement shall not be subject to the standard rules on employee involvement, unless it contains a provision to the contrary.

(4) In relation to an SE to be established by way of transformation, the employee involvement agreement shall provide for the elements of employee involvement at all levels to be at least as favourable as those which exist in the company to be transformed into an SE.

(5) If the parties decide, in accordance with paragraph (2)(f), to establish one or more information and consultation procedures instead of a representative body and if those procedures include a provision for representatives to be elected or appointed to act in relation to information and consultation, those representatives shall be "information and consultation representatives".

[7276]

29 Decisions of the special negotiating body

(1) Each member of the special negotiating body shall have one vote.

(2) Subject to paragraph (3) and regulation 30, the special negotiating body shall take decisions by an absolute majority vote.

(3) In the following circumstances any decision which would result in a reduction of participation rights must be taken by a two thirds majority vote:

(a) where an SE is to be established by merger and at least 25% of the employees employed to work in the EEA states by the participating companies which are due to merge have participation rights; and
(b) where an SE is to be established by formation of a holding company or of a subsidiary company and at least 50% of the total number of employees employed to work in the EEA states by the participating companies have participation rights, and

in this paragraph, reduction of participation rights means that the body representative of the employees has participation rights in relation to a smaller proportion of members of the supervisory or administrative organs of the SE than the employees' representatives had in the participating company which gave participation rights in relation to the highest proportion of such members in that company.

(4) The special negotiating body must publish the details of any decision taken under this regulation or under regulation 30 in such a manner as to bring the decision, so far as reasonably practicable, to the attention of the employees whom they represent and such publication shall take place as soon as reasonably practicable and, in any event no later than 14 days after the decision has been taken.

(5) For the purpose of negotiations, the special negotiating body may be assisted by experts of its choice.

(6) The participating company or companies shall pay for any reasonable expenses of the functioning of the special negotiating body and any reasonable expenses relating to the negotiations that are necessary to enable the special negotiating body to carry out its functions in an appropriate manner; but where the special negotiating body is assisted by more than one expert the participating company is not required to pay such expenses in respect of more than one of them.

[7277]

30 Decision not to open or to terminate negotiations

(1) Subject to paragraph (2), the special negotiating body may decide, by a two thirds majority vote, not to open negotiations with the competent organs of the participating companies or to terminate any such negotiations.

(2) The special negotiating body cannot take the decision referred to in paragraph (1) in relation to an SE to be established by transformation if any employees of the company to be transformed have participation rights.

(3) Any decision made under paragraph (1) shall have the following effects—

(a) the duty in regulation 27(2) to negotiate with a view to reaching an employee involvement agreement shall cease as from the date of the decision;

(b) any rules relating to the information and consultation of employees in a EEA state in which employees of the SE are employed shall apply to the employees of the SE in that EEA state; and

(c) the special negotiating body shall be reconvened only if a valid request in accordance with paragraph (4) is made by employees or employees' representatives.

(4) To amount to a valid request, the request referred to in paragraph (3)(c) must—

(a) be in writing;

(b) be made by at least 10% of the employees of, or by employees' representatives representing at least 10% of the total number of employees employed by—

(i) the participating companies and its concerned subsidiaries, or

(ii) where the SE has been registered, the SE and it subsidiaries; and

(c) be made no earlier than two years after the decision made under paragraph (1) was or should have been published in accordance with regulation 29(4) unless the special negotiating body and the competent organs of every participating company or, where the SE has been registered, the SE agree to the special negotiating body being reconvened earlier.

[7278]

31 Complaint about decisions of special negotiating body

(1) If a member of the special negotiating body, an employees' representative, or where there is no such representative in respect of an employee, that employee believes that the special negotiating body has taken a decision referred to in regulation 29 or 30 and—

(a) that the decision was not taken by the majority required by regulation 29 or 30, as the case may be; or

(b) the special negotiating body failed to publish the decision in accordance with regulation 29(4),

he may present a complaint to the CAC within 21 days of the date the special negotiating body did or should have published their decision in accordance with regulation 29(4).

(2) Where the CAC finds the complaint well-founded it shall make a declaration that the decision was not taken properly and that it shall have no effect.

[7279]

CHAPTER 5
STANDARD RULES ON EMPLOYEE INVOLVEMENT

32 Standard rules on employee involvement

(1) Without prejudice to paragraph (3), where this regulation applies, the competent organ of the SE and its subsidiaries and establishments shall make arrangements for the involvement of employees of the SE and its subsidiaries and establishments in accordance with the standard rules on employee involvement.

(2) This regulation applies in the following circumstances:

(a) where the parties agree that the standard rules on employee involvement shall apply; or

(b) where the period specified in regulation 27(3)(a) or, where applicable, (b) has expired without the parties reaching an employee involvement agreement and—

(i) the competent organs of each of the participating companies agree that the standard rules on employee involvement shall apply and so continue with the registration of the SE; and

(ii) the special negotiating body has not taken any decision under regulation 30(1) either not to open or to terminate the negotiations referred to in that regulation.

(3) The standard rules set out in Part 3 of Schedule 3 to these Regulations (standard rules on participation) only apply in the following circumstances—

(a) in the case of an SE established by merger if, before registration of the SE, one or more forms of participation existed in at least one of the participating companies and either—

(i) that participation applied to at least 25% of the total number of employees of the participating companies employed in the EEA states, or

(ii) that participation applied to less than 25% of the total number of employees of the participating companies employed in the EEA states but the special negotiating body has decided that the standard rules of participation will apply to the employees of the SE; or

(b) in the case of an SE established by formation of a holding company or subsidiary company if, before registration of the SE, one or more forms of employee participation existed in at least one of the participating companies and either:

(i) that participation applied to at least 50% of the total number of employees of the participating companies employed in the EEA states; or

(ii) that participation applied to less than 50% of the total number of employees of the participating companies employed in the EEA states but the special negotiating body has decided that the standard rules of participation will apply to the employees of the SE.

(4) Where the standard rules on participation apply and more than one form of employee participation exist in the participating companies, the special negotiating body shall decide which of the existing forms of participation shall exist in the SE and shall inform the competent organs of the participating companies accordingly.

[7280]

CHAPTER 6
COMPLIANCE AND ENFORCEMENT

33 Disputes about operation of an employee involvement agreement or the standard rules on employee involvement

(1) Where—

(a) an employee involvement agreement has been agreed; or

(b) the standard rules on employee involvement apply,

a complaint may be presented to the CAC by a relevant applicant who considers that the competent organ of a participating company or of the SE has failed to comply with the terms of the employee involvement agreement or, as the case may be, one or more of the standard information and consultation provisions.

(2) A complaint brought under paragraph (1) must be brought within a period of 3 months commencing with the date of the alleged failure or where the failure takes place over a period, the last day of that period.

(3) In this regulation—

"failure" means an act or omission;
"relevant applicant" means—
(a) in a case where a representative body has been appointed or elected, a member of that body; or
(b) in a case where no representative body has been elected or appointed, an information and consultation representative or an employee of the SE.

(4) Where the CAC finds the complaint well-founded it shall make a declaration to that effect and may make an order requiring the SE to take such steps as are necessary to comply with the terms of the employee involvement agreement or, as the case may be, the standard rules on employee involvement.

(5) An order made under paragraph (4) shall specify—
(a) the steps which the SE is required to take;
(b) the date of the failure; and
(c) the period within which the order must be complied with.

(6) If the CAC makes a declaration under paragraph (4), the relevant applicant may, within the period of three months beginning with the day on which the decision is made, make an application to the Appeal Tribunal for a penalty notice to be issued.

(7) Where such an application is made, the Appeal Tribunal shall issue a written penalty notice to the SE requiring it to pay a penalty to the Secretary of State in respect of the failure unless satisfied, on hearing representations from the SE, that the failure resulted from a reason beyond the its control or that he has some other reasonable excuse for its failure.

(8) Regulation 33 shall apply in respect of a penalty notice issued under this regulation.

(9) No order of the CAC under this regulation shall have the effect of suspending or altering the effect of any act done or of any agreement made by the participating company of the SE.

[7281]

34 Penalties

(1) A penalty notice issued under regulation 33 shall specify—
(a) the amount of the penalty which is payable;
(b) the date before which the penalty must be paid; and
(c) the failure and period to which the penalty relates.

(2) No penalty set by the Appeal Tribunal under this regulation may exceed £75,000.

(3) When setting the amount of the penalty, the Appeal Tribunal shall take into account—
(a) the gravity of the failure;
(b) the period of time over which the failure occurred;
(c) the reason for the failure;
(d) the number of employees affected by the failure; and
(e) the number of employees employed by the undertaking.

(4) The date specified under paragraph (1)(b) above must not be earlier than the end of the period within which an appeal against a decision or order made by the CAC under regulation 33 may be made.

(5) If the specified date in a penalty notice has passed and—
(a) the period during which an appeal may be made has expired without an appeal having been made; or
(b) such an appeal has been made and determined,

the Secretary of State may recover from the SE, as a civil debt due to him, any amount payable under the penalty notice which remains outstanding.

(6) The making of an appeal suspends the effect of the penalty notice.

(7) Any sums received by the Secretary of State under regulation 33 or this regulation shall be paid into the Consolidated Fund.

[7282]

35 Misuse of procedures

(1) If an employees' representative or where there is no such representative in relation to an employee, the employee, believes that a participating company or an SE is misusing or intending to misuse the SE or the powers in these Regulations for the purpose of—

(a) depriving the employees of that participating company or of any of its concerned subsidiaries or, as the case may be, of the SE or of its subsidiaries of their rights to employee involvement; or

(b) withholding rights from any of the people referred to in sub-paragraph (a),

he may make present a complaint to the CAC

(2) Where a complaint is made to the CAC under paragraph (1) before registration or within a period of 12 months of the date of the registration of the SE, the CAC shall uphold the complaint unless the respondent proves that it did not misuse or intend to misuse the SE or the powers in these Regulations for either of the purposes set out in sub-paragraphs (a) or (b) of paragraph (1).

(3) If the CAC finds the complaint to be well founded—

(a) it shall make a declaration to that effect and may make an order requiring the participating company or of the SE, as the case may be, to take such action as is specified in the order to ensure that the employees referred to in paragraph (1)(a) are not deprived of their rights to employee involvement or that such rights are not withheld from them; and

(b) the provisions in regulations 33(6) to (9) and 34 shall apply to the complaint.

[7283]

36 Exclusivity of remedy

The remedy for infringement of the rights conferred by these Regulations is by way of complaint to the CAC in accordance with Chapters 1 to 5 of this Part and not otherwise.

[7284]

CHAPTER 7
CONFIDENTIAL INFORMATION

37 Breach of statutory duty

(1) Where an SE, a subsidiary of an SE, a participating company or any concerned subsidiary entrusts a person, pursuant to the provisions of this Part of these Regulations, with any information or document on terms requiring it to be held in confidence, the person shall not disclose that information or document except in accordance with the terms on which it was disclosed to him.

(2) In this regulation a person referred to in paragraph (1) to whom information or a document is entrusted is referred to as a "recipient".

(3) The obligation to comply with paragraph (1) is a duty owed to the company that disclosed the information to the person and a breach of the duty is actionable accordingly (subject to the defences and other incidents applying to actions for breach of statutory duty).

(4) Paragraph (3) does not affect any legal liability which any person may incur by disclosing the information, or any right which any person may have in relation to such disclosure otherwise than under this Regulation.

(5) No action shall lie under paragraph (3) where the recipient reasonably believed the disclosure to be a "protected disclosure" within the meaning given to that expression by section 43A of the 1996 Act.

(6) A recipient to whom a company has entrusted any information or document on terms requiring it to be held in confidence may apply to the CAC for a declaration as to whether it was reasonable for the company to require the recipient to hold the information or document in confidence.

(7) If the CAC considers that the disclosure of the information or the document by the recipient would not, or would not be likely to, harm the legitimate interests of the undertaking, it shall make a declaration that it was not reasonable for the competent organ to require the recipient to hold the information or document in confidence.

(8) If a declaration is made under paragraph (7), the information or document shall not at any time thereafter be regarded as having been entrusted to the recipient who made the application under paragraph (6), or to any other recipient, on terms requiring it to be held in confidence.

[7285]

38 Withholding of information by the competent organ

(1) Neither an SE registered in Great Britain nor a participating company registered in Great Britain is required to disclose any information or document to a person for the purposes of this Part of these Regulations where the nature of the information or document is such that, according to objective criteria, the disclosure of the information or document would seriously harm the functioning of, or would be prejudicial to the SE or any subsidiary or establishment of the SE or, as the case may be, to the participating company or any subsidiary or establishment of the participating company.

(2) Where there is a dispute between the SE or participating company and—

(a) where a representative body has been appointed or elected, a member of that body; or

(b) where no representative body has been elected or appointed, an information and consultation representative or an employee,

as to whether the nature of the information or document which the SE or the participating company has failed to provide is such as is described in paragraph (1), the SE or participating company or a person referred to in sub-paragraph (a) or (b) may apply to the CAC for a declaration as to whether the information or document is of such a nature.

(3) If the CAC makes a declaration that the disclosure of the information or document in question would not, according to objective criteria, be seriously harmful or prejudicial as mentioned in paragraph (1), the CAC shall order the competent organ to disclose the information or document.

(4) An order under paragraph (3) shall specify—

(a) the information or document to be disclosed;

(b) the person or persons to whom the information or document is to be disclosed;

(c) any terms on which the information or document is to be disclosed; and

(d) the date before which the information or document is to be disclosed.

[7286]

CHAPTER 8
PROTECTION FOR MEMBERS OF SPECIAL NEGOTIATING BODY, ETC

39 Right to time off for members of special negotiating body, etc

(1) An employee who is—

(a) a member of a special negotiating body;

(b) a member of a representative body;

(c) an information and consultation representative;

(d) an employee member on a supervisory or administrative organ; or

(e) a candidate in an election in which any person elected will, on being elected, be such a member or a representative,

is entitled to be permitted by his employer to take reasonable time off during the employee's working hours in order to perform his functions as such a member, representative or candidate.

(2) For the purpose of this regulation the working hours of an employee shall be taken to be any time when, in accordance with his contract of employment, the employee is required to be at work.

[7287]

40 Right to remuneration for time off under regulation 39

(1) An employee who is permitted to take time off under regulation 39 is entitled to be paid remuneration by his employer for the time taken off at the appropriate hourly rate.

(2) Chapter II of Part XIV of the 1996 Act (a week's pay) shall apply in relation to this regulation as it applies in relation to section 62 of the 1996 Act.

(3) The appropriate hourly rate, in relation to an employee, is the amount of one week's pay divided by the number of normal working hours in a week for that employee when employed under the contract of employment in force on the day when the time is taken.

(4) But where the number of normal working hours differs from week to week or over a longer period, the amount of one week's pay shall be divided instead by—

(a) the average number of normal working hours calculated by dividing by twelve the total number of the employee's normal working hours during the period of twelve weeks ending with the last complete week before the day on which the time off is taken; or

(b) where the employee has not been employed for a sufficient period to enable the calculation to be made under sub-paragraph (a), a number which fairly represents the number of normal working hours in a week having regard to such of the considerations specified in paragraph (5) as are appropriate in the circumstances.

(5) The considerations referred to in paragraph (4)(b) are—

(a) the average number of normal working hours in a week which the employee could expect in accordance with the terms of his contract; and

(b) the average number of normal working hours of other employees engaged in relevant comparable employment with the same employer.

(6) A right to any amount under paragraph (1) does not affect any right of an employee in relation to remuneration under his contract of employment.

(7) Any contractual remuneration paid to an employee in respect of a period of time off under regulation 39 goes towards discharging any liability of the employer to pay remuneration under paragraph (1) in respect of that period, and conversely, any payment of remuneration under paragraph (1) in respect of a period goes towards discharging any liability of the employer to pay contractual remuneration in respect of that period.

[7288]

41 Right to time off: complaints to tribunals

(1) An employee may present a complaint to an employment tribunal that his employer—

(a) has unreasonably refused to permit him to take time off as required under regulation 39; or

(b) has failed to pay the whole or any part of any amount to which the employee is entitled under regulation 40.

(2) A tribunal shall not consider a complaint under this regulation unless it is presented—

(a) before the end of the period of three months beginning with the day on which the time off was taken or on which it is alleged the time off should have been permitted; or

(b) within such further period as the tribunal considers reasonable in a case where it is satisfied that it was not reasonably practicable for the complaint to be presented before the end of that period of three months.

(3) Where a tribunal finds a complaint under this regulation well-founded, the tribunal shall make a declaration to that effect.

(4) If the complaint is that the employer has unreasonably refused to permit the employee to take time off, the tribunal shall also order the employer to pay to the employee an amount equal to the remuneration to which he would have been entitled under regulation 40 if the employer had not refused.

(5) If the complaint is that the employer has failed to pay the employee the whole or part of any amount to which he is entitled under regulation 40, the tribunal shall also order him to pay to the employee the amount which it finds is due to him.

[7289]

42 Unfair dismissal

(1) An employee who is dismissed and to whom paragraph (2) or (5) applies shall be regarded, if the reason (or, if more than one, the principal reason) for the dismissal is a reason specified in, respectively, paragraph (3) or (6), as unfairly dismissed for the purposes of Part 10 of the 1996 Act.

(2) This paragraph applies to an employee who is—

(a) a member of a special negotiating body;

(b) a member of a representative body;

(c) an information and consultation representative;

(d) an employee member in a supervisory or administrative organ; or

(e) a candidate in an election in which any person elected will, on being elected, be such a member or a representative.

(3) The reason is that—
- (a) the employee performed or proposed to perform any functions or activities as such a member, representative or candidate; or
- (b) the employee or a person acting on his behalf made or proposed to make a request to exercise an entitlement conferred on the employee by regulation 39 or 40.

(4) Paragraph (1) does not apply in the circumstances set out in paragraph (3)(a) where the reason (or principal reason) for the dismissal is that in the performance, or purported performance, of the employee's functions or activities he has disclosed any information or document in breach of the duty in regulation 37, unless the employee reasonably believed the disclosure to be a 'protected disclosure' within the meaning given to that expression by section 43A of the 1996 Act.

(5) This paragraph applies to any employee whether or not he is an employee to whom paragraph (2) applies.

(6) The reasons are that the employee—
- (a) took, or proposed to take, any proceedings before an employment tribunal to enforce any right conferred on him by these Regulations;
- (b) exercised, or proposed to exercise, any entitlement to apply or complain to the CAC or the Appeal Tribunal conferred by these Regulations or to exercise the right to appeal in connection with any rights conferred by these Regulations;
- (c) acted with a view to securing that a special negotiating body, a representative body or an information and consultation procedure did or did not come into existence;
- (d) indicated that he did or did not support the coming into existence of a special negotiating body, a representative body or an information and consultation procedure;
- (e) stood as a candidate in an election in which any person elected would, on being elected, be a member of a special negotiating body, a representative body, an employee member on a supervisory or administrative organ or be an information and consultation representative;
- (f) influenced or sought to influence by lawful means the way in which votes were to be cast by other employees in a ballot arranged under these Regulations;
- (g) voted in such a ballot;
- (h) expressed doubts, whether to a ballot supervisor or otherwise, as to whether such a ballot had been properly conducted; or
- (i) proposed to do, failed to do, or proposed to decline to do, any of the things mentioned in sub-paragraphs (d) to (h).

(7) It is immaterial for the purposes of paragraph (6)(a)—
- (a) whether or not the employee has the right or entitlement; or
- (b) whether or not the right has been infringed,

but for that sub-paragraph to apply, the claim to the right and, if applicable, the claim that it has been infringed must be made in good faith.

[7290]

43 (*Amends the Employment Rights Act 1996, ss 105, 108 and 109* (*repealed*).)

44 Detriment

(1) An employee to whom paragraph (2) or (5) applies has the right not to be subjected to any detriment by any act, or deliberate failure to act, by his employer, done on a ground specified in, respectively, paragraph (3) or (6).

(2) This paragraph applies to an employee who is—
- (a) a member of a special negotiating body;
- (b) a member of a representative body;
- (c) an information and consultation representative;
- (d) an employee member on a supervisory or administrative organ; or
- (e) a candidate in an election in which any person elected will, on being elected, be such a member or a representative.

(3) The ground is that—
- (a) the employee performed or proposed to perform any functions or activities as such a member, representative or candidate; or
- (b) the employee or person acting on his behalf made or proposed to make a request to exercise an entitlement conferred on the employee by regulation 39 or 40.

(4) Paragraph (1) does not apply in the circumstances set out in paragraph (3)(a) where the ground for the subjection to detriment is that in the performance, or purported performance, of the employee's functions or activities he has disclosed any information or document in breach of the duty in regulation 37, unless the employee reasonably believed the disclosure to be a "protected disclosure" within the meaning given to that expression by section 43A of the 1996 Act.

(5) This paragraph applies to any employee, whether or not he is an employee to whom paragraph (2) applies.

(6) The grounds are that the employee—

(a) took, or proposed to take, any proceedings before an employment tribunal to enforce any right conferred on him by these Regulations;

(b) exercised, or proposed to exercise, any entitlement to apply or complain to the CAC or the Appeal Tribunal conferred by these Regulations or to exercise the right to appeal in connection with any rights conferred by these Regulations;

(c) acted with a view to securing that a special negotiating body, a representative body or an information and consultation procedure did or did not come into existence;

(d) indicated that he did or did not support the coming into existence of a special negotiating body, a representative body or an information and consultation procedure;

(e) stood as a candidate in an election in which any person elected would, on being elected, be a member of a special negotiating body, a representative body, an employee member on a supervisory or administrative organ or be an information and consultation representative;

(f) influenced or sought to influence by lawful means the way in which votes were to be cast by other employees in a ballot arranged under these Regulations;

(g) voted in such a ballot;

(h) expressed doubts, whether to a ballot supervisor or otherwise, as to whether such a ballot had been properly conducted; or

(i) proposed to do, failed to do, or proposed to decline to do, any of the things mentioned in sub-paragraphs (d) to (h).

(7) It is immaterial for the purposes of paragraph (6)(a)—

(a) whether or not the employee has the right or entitlement; or

(b) whether or not the right has been infringed,

but for that sub-paragraph to apply, the claim to the right and, if applicable, the claim that has been infringed must be made in good faith.

(8) This regulation does not apply where the detriment in question amounts to dismissal.

[7291]

45 Detriment: enforcement and subsidiary provisions

(1) An employee may present a complaint to an employment tribunal that he has been subjected to a detriment in contravention of regulation 44.

(2) The provisions of sections 48(2) to (4) of the 1996 Act (complaints to employment tribunals and remedies) shall apply in relation to a complaint under this regulation as they apply in relation to a complaint under section 48 of that Act but taking references in those provisions to the employer as references to the employer within the meaning of regulation 44(1) above.

(3) The provisions of section 49(1) to (5) of the 1996 Act shall apply in relation to a complaint under this regulation.

[7292]

46 (*Amends the Employment Tribunals Act 1996, s 18.*)

CHAPTER 9
MISCELLANEOUS

47 CAC proceedings

(1) Where under these Regulations a person presents a complaint or makes an application to the CAC the complaint or application must be in writing and in such form as the CAC may require.

(2) In its consideration of a complaint or application under these Regulations, the CAC shall make such enquiries as it sees fit and give any person whom it considers has a proper interest in the complaint or application an opportunity to be heard.

(3) Where the participating company, concerned subsidiary or establishment or the SE has its registered office in England and Wales—

(a) a declaration made by the CAC under these Regulations may be relied on as if it were a declaration or order made by the High Court in England and Wales; and

(b) an order made by the CAC under these Regulations may be enforced in the same way as an order of the High Court in England and Wales.

(4) Where a participating company or concerned subsidiary or an SE has its registered office in Scotland—

(a) a declaration or order made by the CAC under these Regulations may be relied on as if it were a declaration or order made by the Court of Session; and

(b) an order made by the CAC under these Regulations may be enforced in the same way as an order of the Court of Session.

(5) A declaration or order made by the CAC under these Regulations must be in writing and state the reasons for the CAC's findings.

(6) An appeal lies to the Appeal Tribunal on any question of law arising from any declaration or order of, or arising in any proceedings before, the CAC under these Regulations.

[7293]

48 Appeal Tribunal: location of certain proceedings under these Regulations

(1) Any proceedings before the Appeal Tribunal under these Regulations, other than appeals under paragraph (o) of section 21(1) of the Employment Tribunals Act 1996 (appeals from employment tribunals on questions of law), shall—

(a) where the registered office of the participating company, concerned subsidiary or the SE is situated in England and Wales, be held in England and Wales; and

(b) where the registered office of the participating company, concerned subsidiary or the SE is situated in Scotland, be held in Scotland.

(2) …

[7294]

NOTES

Para (2): amends the Employment Tribunals Act 1996, s 20.

49 (*Amends the Employment Tribunals Act 1996, s 21.*)

50 ACAS

(1) If on receipt of an application or complaint under these Regulations the CAC is of the opinion that it is reasonably likely to be settled by conciliation, it shall refer the application or complaint to the Advisory, Conciliation and Arbitration Service ("ACAS") and shall notify the applicant or complainant and any persons whom it considers have a proper interest in the application or complaint accordingly, whereupon ACAS shall seek to promote a settlement of the matter.

(2) If an application or complaint so referred is not settled or withdrawn and ACAS is of the opinion that further attempts at conciliation are unlikely to result in a settlement, it shall inform the CAC of its opinion.

(3) If the application or complaint is not referred to ACAS or if it is so referred, on ACAS informing the CAC of its opinion that further attempts at conciliation are unlikely to result in a settlement, the CAC shall proceed to hear and determine the application or complaint.

[7295]

51 Restrictions on contracting out: general

(1) Any provision in any agreement (whether an employee's contract or not) is void in so far as it purports—

(a) to exclude or limit the operation of any provision of this Part of these Regulations other than a provision of Chapter 8 of this Part; or

(b) to preclude a person from bringing any proceedings before the CAC, under any provision of this Part of these Regulations other than a provision of that Chapter.

(2) Paragraph (1) does not apply to any agreement to refrain from continuing any proceedings referred to in sub-paragraph (b) of that paragraph made after the proceedings have been instituted.

[7296]

52 Restrictions on contracting out: Chapter 8 of this Part

(1) Any provision in any agreement (whether an employee's contract or not) is void in so far as it purports—

(a) to exclude or limit the operation of any provision of Chapter 8 of this Part of these Regulations; or

(b) to preclude a person from bringing any proceedings before an employment tribunal under that Chapter.

(2) Paragraph (1) does not apply to any agreement to refrain from instituting or continuing proceedings before an employment tribunal where a conciliation officer has taken action under section 18 of the Employment Tribunals Act 1996 (conciliation).

(3) Paragraph (1) does not apply to any agreement to refrain from instituting or continuing before an employment tribunal proceedings within section 18(1)(k) of the Employment Tribunals Act 1996 (proceedings under these Regulations where conciliation is available) if the conditions regulating compromise agreements under these Regulations are satisfied in relation to the agreement.

(4) For the purposes of paragraph (3) the conditions regulating compromise agreements are that—

(a) the agreement must be in writing;

(b) the agreement must relate to the particular proceedings;

(c) the employee must have received advice from a relevant independent adviser as to the terms and effect of the proposed agreement and, in particular, its effect on his ability to pursue his rights before an employment tribunal;

(d) there must be in force, when the adviser gives the advice, a contract of insurance, or an indemnity provided for members of a profession or professional body, covering the risk of a claim by the employee in respect of loss arising in consequence of the advice;

(e) the agreement must identify the adviser; and

(f) the agreement must state that the conditions in sub-paragraphs (a) to (e) are satisfied.

(5) A person is a relevant independent adviser for the purposes of paragraph (4)(c)—

(a) if he is a qualified lawyer;

(b) if he is an officer, official, employee or member of an independent trade union who has been certified in writing by the trade union as competent to give advice and authorised to do so on behalf of the trade union; or

(c) if he works at an advice centre (whether as an employee or as a volunteer) and has been certified in writing by the centre as competent to give advice and authorised to do so on behalf of the centre.

(6) But a person is not a relevant independent adviser for the purposes of paragraph (4)(c) in relation to the employee—

(a) if he is, is employed by or is acting in the matter for the employer or an associated employer;

(b) in the case of a person within paragraph (5)(b) or (c), if the trade union or advice centre is the employer or an associated employer; or

(c) in the case of a person within paragraph (5)(c), if the employee makes a payment for the advice received by him.

(7) In paragraph (5)(a), a "qualified lawyer" means—

(a) as respects England and Wales, a barrister (whether in practice as such or employed to give legal advice), a solicitor who holds a practicing certificate, or a person other than a barrister or solicitor who is an authorised advocate or authorised litigator (within the meaning of the Courts and Legal Services Act 1990); and

(b) as respects Scotland, an advocate (whether in practice as such or employed to give legal advice) or a solicitor who holds a practising certificate.

(8) For the purposes of paragraph (6) any two employers shall be treated as associated if—

(a) one is a company of which the other (directly or indirectly) has control; or

(b) both are companies of which a third person (directly or indirectly) has control;

and "associated employer" shall be construed accordingly.

[7297]

53 (*Inserts the Transnational Information and Consultation of Employees Regulations 1999, SI 1999/3323, reg 46A.*)

54 Existing employee involvement rights

(1) Subject to paragraph (2), nothing in these Regulations shall affect involvement rights of employees of an SE, its subsidiaries or establishments provided for by law or practice in the EEA state in which they were employed immediately prior to the registration of the SE.

(2) Paragraph (1) does not apply to rights to participation.

[7298]

PART 4
EXERCISE OF MEMBER STATES OPTIONS UNDER THE EC REGULATION

55 Participation in the formation of an SE by a company formed under the law of a Member State whose head office is not in the Community (Article 2(5))

A company, formed under the law of a Member State, the head office of which is not in the Community, may participate in the formation of an SE where the company's registered office is in that Member State and it has a real and continuous link with a Member State's economy.

[7299]

56 Additional forms of publication of transfer proposal (Article 8(2))

(1) The SE shall notify in writing its shareholders, and every creditor of whose claim and address it is aware, of the right to examine the transfer proposal and the report drawn up under Article 8(3), at its registered office and, on request, to obtain copies of those documents free of charge, not later than one month before the general meeting called to decide on the transfer.

(2) Every invoice, order for goods or business letter, which, at any time between the date on which the transfer proposal and report become available for inspection at the registered office of the SE and the deletion of its registration on transfer, is issued by or on behalf of the SE, shall contain a statement that the SE is proposing to transfer its registered office to another Member State under Article 8 and identifying that Member State.

(3) If default is made in complying with paragraphs (1) or (2) above the SE is liable on summary conviction to a fine not exceeding level 3 on the standard scale.

[7300]

57 Extension of protection given by Article 8(7) to liabilities incurred prior to transfer (Article 8(7))

The first sub-paragraph of Article 8(7) shall apply to liabilities that arise (or may arise) prior to the transfer.

[7301]

58 Power of the competent authorities of a Member State to oppose a transfer on public interest grounds (Article 8(14))

If a transfer of a registered office of an SE would result in a change in the law applicable to the SE, the competent authorities may, within the two month period referred to within Article 8(6), oppose the transfer, on public interest grounds.

[7302]

59 Power of the management or administrative organ of an SE to amend statutes where in conflict with employee involvement arrangements (Article 12(4))

Where there is a conflict between the arrangements for employee involvement and the existing statutes the management or administrative organ of the SE may amend the statutes to the extent necessary to resolve the conflict without any further decision from the general shareholders meeting.

[7303]

60 Power of the competent authorities of a Member State to oppose the participation of a merging company governed by its law on public interest grounds (Article 19)

A company of a type specified in relation to the United Kingdom in Annex 1 to the EC Regulation may not take part in the formation of an SE, whether or not it is to be registered in Great Britain, by merger if any of the competent authorities oppose it before the issue of the certificate referred to in Article 25(2) on public interest grounds.

[7304]

61 Minimum number of members of the management organ (Article 39(4))

The minimum number of the members of the management organ of an SE is two.

[7305]

62 Minimum number of members of the supervisory organ (Article 40(3))

The minimum number of the members of the supervisory organ of an SE is two.

[7306]

63 Members of the supervisory organ to be entitled to require the management organ to provide certain information (Article 41(3))

Each member of the supervisory organ is entitled to require the management organ to provide to that member information of a kind which the supervisory organ needs to exercise supervision in accordance with Article 40(1).

[7307]

64 Minimum number of members of an administrative organ (Article 43(2))

The minimum number of the members of the administrative organ of an SE is two.

[7308]

65 Timing of the first general meeting of an SE (Article 54(1))

The first general meeting of an SE may be held at any time in the 18 months following an SE's incorporation.

[7309]

66 Proportion of shareholders of an SE who may require one or more additional items to be put on the agenda of any general meeting (Article 56)

The proportion of the shareholders of an SE who may require one or more additional items put on the agenda of any general meeting is to be the holders of at least 5% of the SE's subscribed capital.

[7310]

67 SEs subject to law on public limited liability companies as regard the expression of their capital (Article 67(1))

An SE shall be subject to the provisions of the enactments and rules of law applying to a public company as regards the expression of its capital.

[7311]

PART 5
PROVISIONS REQUIRED BY THE EC REGULATION

68 Publication of terms of transfer, formation and conversion (Articles 8(2), 32(3) and 37(5))

(1) Where a transfer proposal is drawn up under Article 8(2)—

(a) a copy of the proposal shall be delivered to the registrar together with Form SE68(1)(a), and

(b) the registrar shall cause notice of the receipt of the copy of the proposal to be published in the Gazette.

(2) Where draft terms for the formation of a holding SE, whether or not its registered office is to be in Great Britain, are drawn up under Article 32(2)—

(a) a copy of the draft terms shall be delivered to the registrar together with Form SE68(2)(a), and
(b) the registrar shall cause notice of the receipt of the copy of the draft terms to be published in the Gazette.

(3) Where draft terms for the conversion of a public limited-liability company into an SE are drawn up under Article 37(4)—
(a) a copy of the draft terms shall be delivered to the registrar together with Form SE68(3)(a), and
(b) the registrar shall cause notice of the receipt of the copy of the draft terms to be published in the Gazette.

(4) The Forms referred to in paragraphs (1) to (3) are those set out in Schedule 1.

[7312]

69 Publication of completion of merger (**Article 28**)

Where an SE is formed by merger, whether its registered office is in Great Britain or not, and a public company has taken part in that procedure, the registrar shall cause to be published in the Gazette notice that the merger has been completed.

[7313]

70 Publication of fulfilment of conditions for the formation of a holding SE (**Article 33(3)**)

(1) Where, in respect of a company of a type specified in relation to the United Kingdom in Annex II to the EC Regulation, the conditions for the formation of a holding SE, whether or not it is to be registered in Great Britain, are fulfilled, the company shall deliver to the registrar within 14 days of such fulfilment notice of that event in the Form SE70(1) set out in Schedule 1 and the registrar shall cause to be published in the Gazette notice that these conditions have been fulfilled.

(2) If default is made in complying with paragraph (1), the company is liable on summary conviction to a fine not exceeding level 3 on the standard scale.

[7314]

71 Publication of other documents or information (**Articles 8(12), 15(2), 59(3) and 65**)

(1) Where, under the Articles of the EC Regulation listed in paragraph (2), the occurrence of an event is required to be publicised, the registrar shall cause to be published in the Gazette notice of receipt of the particulars of that event described in those Articles.

(2) The Articles referred to in paragraph (1) above are:
Article 59(3)
Article 65.

(3) Where, under the Articles listed in paragraph (4), the registration of an SE, whether on formation under Title II of the EC Regulation, or on the transfer of the registered office of an SE under Article 8 or the deletion of a registration under that Article is required to be publicised, the registrar shall cause to be published in the Gazette notice of that registration or the deletion of that registration and of the receipt of the documents and particulars related to that registration or deletion required to be delivered to the registrar by the EC Regulation or these Regulations.

(4) The Articles referred to in paragraph (3) are:
Article 8(12)
Article 15(2).

[7315]

72 Protection of creditors and others on a transfer (**Article 8(7)**)

(1) Where an SE proposes to transfer its registered office to another Member State under Article 8 the SE shall satisfy the Secretary of State that the interests of creditors and holders of other rights in respect of the SE (including those of public bodies) have been adequately protected in respect of any liabilities arising (or that may arise) prior to the transfer by the making of a statement of solvency in the terms set out in paragraphs (4) and (5).

(2) The statement of solvency must be made by all the members of the administrative organ in the case of an SE within the one-tier system and by all the members of the management organ in the case of an SE within the two-tier system.

(3) In the case of an SE within the two-tier system the statement of solvency may not be made unless authorised by the supervisory organ.

(4) The statement shall state that the members of the administrative or management organ, as the case may be, have formed the opinion—

(a) as regards its financial situation immediately following the date on which the transfer is proposed to be made, that there will be no grounds on which the SE could then be found to be unable to pay its debts, and

(b) as regards its prospects for the year immediately following that date, that, having regard to their intentions with respect to the management of the SE's business during that year and to the amount and character of the financial resources which will in their view be available to the SE during that year, the SE will be able to carry on business as a going concern (and will accordingly be able to pay its debts as they fall due throughout that year).

(5) In forming their opinion for the purposes of paragraph (4)(a), the members of the administrative or the management organ, as the case may be, shall take into account the same liabilities (including prospective and contingent liabilities) as would be relevant under section 122 of the Insolvency Act 1986 (winding up by the court) to the question whether a company is unable to pay its debts.

(6) The statement required by this regulation shall be in the Form SE72(6) set out in Schedule 1.

(7) A member of an administrative or management organ who makes a statement under this regulation without having reasonable grounds for the opinion expressed in the statement is liable, on conviction on indictment, to imprisonment not exceeding two years, or to a fine, or to both, and on summary conviction to imprisonment not exceeding three months, or to a fine not exceeding the statutory maximum, or to both.

[7316]

73 Power of Secretary of State where an SE no longer complies with the requirements of Article 7

(1) If it appears that an SE no longer complies with the requirements laid down in Article 7, the Secretary of State may direct the SE to regularise its position in accordance with Article 64(1)(a) or (b) within such period as may be specified in the direction.

(2) A direction under paragraph (1) is enforceable by the Secretary of State—

(a) in the case of an SE whose registered office is in England and Wales, by an application to the High Court for an injunction; or

(b) in the case of an SE whose registered office is in Scotland, by an application to the Court of Session for an order under section 45 of the Court of Session Act 1988.

(3), (4) ...

[7317]

NOTES

Sub-s (3): inserts the Insolvency Act 1986, s 124B at **[3281A]**.

Sub-s (4): amends the Insolvency Act 1986, s 124, Sch A1, Pt III, Sch B1 at **[3280]**, **[3466]**, **[3469A]**.

74 Review of decisions of a competent authority (Articles 8(14) and 19)

(1) Where any competent authority or competent authorities oppose—

(a) the transfer of the registered office of an SE under Article 8(14); or

(b) the taking part by a company of the type specified in relation to the United Kingdom in Annex 1 to the EC Regulation in the formation of an SE by merger under Article 19 whether or not its registered office is to be in Great Britain,

the provisions of paragraphs (2) to (5) shall apply.

(2) An SE, the transfer of whose registered office is opposed by a competent authority or authorities under Article 8(14) or a company whose taking part in the formation of an SE by merger, whether or not its registered office is to be in Great Britain, is opposed by a competent authority or competent authorities under Article 19, may appeal to the relevant court on the grounds that the opposition:

(a) is unlawful; or

(b) is irrational or unreasonable; or

(c) has been made on the basis of a procedural impropriety or otherwise contravenes the rules of natural justice.

(3) For the purposes of this regulation the "relevant court" is in the case of—

(a) an SE, or a company, whose registered office is in England or Wales, the High Court; and

(b) an SE, or a company, whose registered office is in Scotland, the Court of Session.

(4) An appeal may only be brought under this regulation with the permission of the court.

(5) The court determining an appeal may—

(a) dismiss the appeal; or

(b) quash the opposition, and where the court quashes an opposition it may refer the matter to the opposing competent authority or authorities with a direction to reconsider it and to make a determination in accordance with the findings of the court.

[7318]

PART 6
PROVISIONS RELATING TO THE EFFECTIVE APPLICATION OF THE EC REGULATION

75 Competent authorities

The competent authorities designated under Article 68(2) are—

(a) in respect of Articles 8, 54, 55 and 64, the Secretary of State;

(b) in respect of Article 25, the High Court in relation to a public company whose registered office is in England and Wales, and, in relation to a public company whose registered office is in Scotland, the Court of Session; and

(c) in respect of Article 26, the High Court in relation to an SE where the registered office is proposed to be in England and Wales, and, in relation to an SE where the registered office is proposed to be in Scotland, the Court of Session.

[7319]

76 Enforcement of obligation to amend Statutes in conflict with Arrangements for Employee Involvement

(1) If it appears to the Secretary of State that—

(a) the statutes of an SE are in conflict with the arrangements for employee involvement determined in accordance with Part 3 of these Regulations; and

(b) the statutes have not, to the necessary extent, been amended she may direct the SE to amend the statutes to that extent within such period as she may specify in the direction.

(2) A direction under this regulation is enforceable on the application of the Secretary of State—

(a) in respect of an SE with its registered office in England and Wales, to the High Court by injunction; and

(b) in respect of an SE with its registered office in Scotland, to the Court of Session by an order under section 45 of the Court of Session Act 1988.

[7320]

77 Records of an SE transferred under Article 8(11) or a public company ceasing to exist under Article 29(1) and (2)

(1) Where—

(a) the registration of an SE is deleted under Article 8(11) pursuant to a transfer of its registered office to another Member State; or

(b) a public company ceases to exist under Article 29(1)(c) or (2)(c), the records of that SE or public company, as the case may be, kept by the registrar shall continue to be kept by her for a period of twenty years following such a deletion or cessation of existence.

(2) Where the registration of an SE is deleted, the Form, and the documents accompanying it, delivered to the Secretary of State under regulation 11, together with a copy

PART IV
STATUTORY INSTRUMENTS

of the certificate issued under Article 8(8) shall be deemed to be documents to be retained by the registrar under regulation 13 and the provisions of these Regulations apply accordingly.

[7321]

78 Application of enactments to members of supervisory, management and administrative organs

(1) This regulation applies to enactments relating to public companies to the extent that they are required, by the EC Regulation, in the manner described in paragraph 2, to be applied in relation to SEs.

(2) Enactments are required to be applied for the purposes of paragraph (1) where—

(a) any provision of the EC Regulation, other than Article 9, requires the application of any enactment relating to public companies to determine any question or matter; or

(b) in the case of any matter not regulated by the EC Regulation or, where matters are partly regulated by it, of those aspects not covered by it, Article 9 requires the application of any enactment relating to public companies.

(3) Subject to paragraphs (4), (5) and (6) references to "directors" or "board of directors" in any enactment to which this regulation applies shall have effect as if they were references—

(a) in a one-tier system, to the members of the administrative organ; and

(b) in a two-tier system, to the members of the supervisory and management organs.

(4) Any enactment so applied in relation to a two-tier system shall be applied separately in respect of the members of the supervisory organ and the members of the management organ in relation to the functions of the organ, and in respect of the acts and omissions of the members of those organs.

(5) Where, in a two-tier system, any function relates to the management of the SE and, by virtue of Articles 39(1) or 40(1), is a function that cannot be carried out by the supervisory organ, nothing in paragraph (3) has the effect of permitting or requiring the members of the supervisory organ to carry out any such functions.

(6) Where, by virtue of any provision in the EC Regulation or in the statutes, any transaction or function carried out by the management organ in a two-tier system requires the authorisation of the supervisory organ, nothing in paragraph (3) affects, or removes, the requirement for such authorisation.

[7322]

79 Register of members of supervisory organ

(1) Every SE which has adopted the form of a two-tier system in its statutes shall keep at its registered office a register of the members of its supervisory organ ("the members"); and the register shall, with respect to the particulars to be contained in it of those persons, comply with the paragraphs below.

(2) The SE shall, within the period of 14 days from the occurrence of—

(a) any change among the members, or

(b) any change in the particulars contained in the register,

send to the registrar a notification in the Form SE79A, SE79B or SE79C, as may be appropriate, and, if applicable, Form SE(SR) or Form SE(SR) change, set out in Schedule 1, of the change and of the date on which it occurred; and a notification of a person having become a member shall contain a consent, signed by that person, to act in the relevant capacity.

(3) The register shall be open to the inspection of any shareholder of the SE without charge and of any other person on payment of a fee of £2.50 for each hour or part of an hour during which the right of inspection is exercised.

(4) If an inspection required under this section is refused, or if default is made in complying with paragraph (1) or (2), the SE is liable on summary conviction to a fine not exceeding level 5 on the standard scale.

(5) In the case of a refusal of inspection of the register, the court may by order compel an immediate inspection of it.

(6) Where a confidentiality order, made under section 723B of the 1985 Act, or under that section to the extent that that enactment is applied by any provision of the EC Regulation,

is in force in respect of a member, subsections (3) and (5) of that section shall not apply in relation to that part of the register of the SE as contains particulars of the usual residential address of that individual.

(7) For purposes of this and the next regulation, where, to the extent that the application of section 741(2) of the 1985 Act under any provision of the EC Regulation requires it, a shadow director of an SE, by virtue of the members of the supervisory organ acting in accordance with his directions or instructions, is deemed a member of that organ.

(8) Where an SE is required to keep a register of members of the supervisory organ by this regulation, the application of regulation 78 to that SE shall not require that particulars of members of the supervisory organ to be kept on any register required be kept under section 288 of the 1985 Act.

[7323]

80 Particulars of members to be registered under regulation 79

(1) Subject to the provisions of this regulation, the register kept by an SE under regulation 79 shall contain the following particulars with respect to each member—

(a) in the case of an individual—

(i) his present name,

(ii) any former name,

(iii) his usual residential address,

(iv) his nationality,

(v) his business occupation (if any),

(vi) particulars of any other directorships held by him or which have been held by him, and

(vii) the date of his birth;

(b) in the case of a corporation or Scottish firm, its corporate or firm name and registered or principal office.

(2) Where a confidentiality order made under section 723B of the 1985 Act or under that section to the extent that is applicable by any provision of the EC Regulation is in force in respect of a member, the register shall contain, in addition to the particulars specified in paragraph (1)(a), such address as is for the time being notified by the member to the company under regulations made under sections 723B to 723F of the 1985 Act.

(3) In paragraph (1)(a)—

(a) "name" means a person's Christian name (or other forenames) and surname, except that in the case of a peer, or an individual usually known by a title, the title may be stated instead of his Christian name (or other forename) and surname, or in addition to either or both of them; and

(b) the reference to a former name does not include—

(i) in the case of a peer, or an individual normally known by a British title, the name by which he was known previous to the adoption of or succession to the title, or

(ii) in the case of any person, a former name which was changed or disused before he attained the age of 18 years or which has been changed or disused for 20 years or more, or

(iii) in the case of a married woman, the name by which she was known previous to the marriage.

(4) It is not necessary for the register to contain on any day particulars of a directorship of a company—

(a) which has not been held by a director at any time during the 5 years preceding that day,

(b) which is held by a director in a company which—

(i) is dormant or grouped with the SE keeping the register, and

(ii) if he also held that directorship for any period during those 5 years, was for the whole of that period either dormant or so grouped,

(c) which was held by a member for any period during those 5 years in a company which for the whole of that period was either dormant or grouped with the SE keeping the register.

(5) For purposes of paragraph (4), "company" has the meaning given it in section 735(1) of the 1985 Act and includes any body corporate incorporated in Great Britain; and—

(a) section 249AA(3) of the 1985 Act applies as regards whether and when a company is or has been dormant,

(b) section 249AA(3) of the 1985 Act, to the extent that enactment is applied by any provision of the EC Regulation, applies as regards whether and when an SE is or has been dormant, and

(c) a company or SE is to be regarded as being, or having been, grouped with another at any time if at that time it is or was a company or SE of which the other is or was a wholly-owned subsidiary, or if it is or was a wholly-owned subsidiary of the other or of another company or SE of which that other is or was a wholly-owned subsidiary.

[7324]

81 The SE as a body corporate

(1) Where—

(a) any enactment is applied in the manner described in regulation 78(2); or

(b) any enactment applies to an SE otherwise than in the manner described in regulation 78(2)

and those enactments are expressed to apply to, or in respect of, a body corporate, an SE, whether or not registered in Great Britain, shall be treated for the purposes of the application of those enactments as if it were a body corporate.

(2) Nothing in this regulation has the effect of constituting an SE as a body corporate incorporated in, or formed under the law of, Great Britain.

[7325]

82 Notification of Amendments to Statutes and Insolvency Events (Articles 59(3) and 65)

(1) Where, under Articles 59(3) and 65, publication by the registrar in the Gazette of the events described in those Articles is required by regulation 71(1)—

(a) in the case of Article 59(3), the amendments to the statutes shall be delivered to the registrar by the SE accompanied by Form SE82(1)(a) in Schedule 1 within 14 days of the adoption of those amendments; and

(b) in the case of Article 65, notice of the relevant event set out in Form SE82(1)(b) in Schedule 1 shall be delivered to the registrar by the SE within 14 days of the occurrence of the event.

(2) If default is made in complying with paragraph (1)(a) or (b) the SE is liable on summary conviction to a fine not exceeding level 3 on the standard scale.

[7326]

83 Accounting Reference Period and Financial Year of Transferring SE

(1) Where an SE transfers its registered office to Great Britain under Article 8—

(a) its first accounting reference period, for the purposes of section 224 of the 1985 Act, is the period of twelve months beginning with its last balance sheet date before the registration of the transfer and the date on which that period ends is its accounting reference date for those purposes; and

(b) its first financial year for the purposes of section 223 of the 1985 Act begins with the first day of its first accounting reference period and ends with the last day of that period or such other date, not more than seven days before or after the end of that period as the SE may determine.

(2) For purposes of this regulation "the last balance sheet date" is the date as at which the balance sheet of the transferring SE was required to be drawn up under the provisions of the law of the Member State in which it had its registered office, where the balance sheet was the last one required to be drawn up before the registration of the transfer in Great Britain.

(3) Where the transferring SE has not been required to draw up a balance sheet under the provisions of the law of the Member State where it had its registered office, or, if different, of the Member State where it was first registered, before the registration of the transfer in Great Britain, its accounting reference date for the purposes of section 224 of the 1985 Act is the last day of the month in which the anniversary of its registration on formation falls and its first accounting reference period is the period beginning with its date of registration on formation and ending with its accounting reference date; and paragraph (1)(b) above applies in respect of its first financial year accordingly.

[7327]

84 Penalties for Breach of Article 11 (use of SE in name)

Where:

(a) an SE fails to comply with Article 11(1); or

(b) any person fails to comply with Article 11(2)

the SE or that person is liable on summary conviction to a fine not exceeding level 3 on the standard scale.

[7328]

PART 7
PROVISIONS RELATING TO THE CONVERSION OF AN SE TO A PUBLIC COMPANY IN ACCORDANCE WITH ARTICLE 66 OF THE EC REGULATION

85 Registration of a public company by the conversion of an SE

Where it is proposed to convert an SE to a public company in accordance with Article 66 there shall be delivered to the registrar a registration form in Form SE85 set out in Schedule 1 together with the documents specified in that Form; and, for the purposes of registering the SE, (in this Part referred to as the "converting SE"), as a public company under the provisions of the 1985 Act, the provisions of that Act shall have effect with the modifications set out in paragraph 1 of Schedule 4 to these Regulations and subject to the provisions of this Part.

[7329]

86 Publication of draft terms of conversion

Where under Article 66(4) draft terms of conversion are required to be publicised there shall be delivered to the registrar a copy of such draft terms accompanied by Form SE86 set out in Schedule 1 and the registrar shall cause to be published in the Gazette notice of the receipt by her of the copy of the draft terms.

[7330]

87 Registration under the 1985 Act

(1) On and after the day on which Form SE85 is delivered to the registrar section 12(2) of the 1985 Act (duty of the registrar) shall apply in relation to the memorandum and articles of association of the converting SE delivered with Form SE85 as if—

(a) they have been delivered under section 10 of the 1985 Act (documents to be delivered to the registrar), and

(b) the requirements of that Act in respect of registration and of matters precedent and incidental to it had been complied with.

(2) The registrar shall carry out her duty under section 12 of the 1985 Act to register the memorandum and articles of the converting SE.

(3) On registration of the memorandum and articles of association of the converting SE the registrar shall give a certificate—

(a) that the converting SE is incorporated and retains the legal personality it had when an SE;

(b) that its memorandum and articles of association are registered under the 1985 Act; and

(c) that it is a public company limited by shares.

(4) The certificate is conclusive evidence—

(a) that the requirements of the 1985 Act in respect of registration and of matters precedent and incidental to it have been complied with, and

(b) that on and after the registration the converting SE is a public company limited by shares.

[7331]

88 Effect of registration

(1) In its application to a converting SE on or after registration the 1985 Act shall have effect with the modifications set out in paragraphs 2 to 10 of Schedule 4 to these Regulations.

(2) On and after registration a converting SE shall be known by the name contained in its memorandum (subject to section 28 of the 1985 Act).

(3) The persons named in Form SE85 shall be deemed to have been appointed as the first directors or secretaries of a converting SE on registration.

[7332]

89 Records of a converting SE

The records of a converting SE, when the converting SE has been registered as a public company limited by shares under the provisions of this Part, relating to any period before its registration as a public company shall be treated for the purposes of the 1985 Act as if they were records of that public company.

[7333]

SCHEDULES

(*Sch 1 contains forms* (*as to which, see Appendix 4 at* **[A4]**).)

SCHEDULE 2
PROVISIONS OF THE 1985 ACT APPLYING TO THE REGISTRATION OF SES

Regulation 14

1. Section 704(5), (7) and (8) (registrar).

2. Section 705 (registered numbers) applies in relation to SEs as it applies in relation to companies, as if it referred to the allocation of a number to an SE.

3. Sections 706, 707A and 707B (documents delivered to the registrar etc) apply to documents delivered to the registrar under these Regulations as they apply to documents etc delivered to the registrar under the 1985 Act.

4. Section 713 (enforcement of duty to make returns) applies to a default in complying with any provision of these Regulations requiring the delivery of documents, or the giving of notice, to the registrar as it applies to a default in complying with a provision of the 1985 Act.

[7334]

SCHEDULE 3
STANDARD RULES ON EMPLOYEE INVOLVEMENT

Regulation 32

PART 1
COMPOSITION OF THE REPRESENTATIVE BODY

1.—(1) The management of the SE shall arrange for the establishment of a representative body in accordance with the following provisions-

(a) the representative body shall be composed of employees of the SE and its subsidiaries and establishments;

(b) the representative body shall be composed of one member for each 10% of fraction thereof of employees of the SE, its subsidiaries and establishments employed for the time being in each Member State;

(c) the members of the representative body shall be elected or appointed by the members of the special negotiating body; and

(d) the election or appointment shall be carried out by whatever method the special negotiating body decides.

2. Where its size so warrants, the representative body shall elect a select committee from among its members comprising at most three members.

3. The representative body shall adopt rules of procedure.

4. The representative body shall inform the competent organ of the SE of the composition of the representative body and any changes in its composition.

5.—(1) Four years after its establishment, the representative body shall decide whether to open negotiations with the competent organ of the SE to reach an employee involvement agreement or whether the standard rules in Part 2 and, where applicable, Part 3 of this Schedule shall continue to apply.

(2) Where a decision is taken under sub-paragraph (1) to open negotiations, regulations 27 to 29 and 31 shall apply to the representative body as they apply to the special negotiating body.

[7335]

PART 2
STANDARD RULES FOR INFORMATION AND CONSULTATION

6.—(1) The competence of the representative body shall be limited to questions which concern the SE itself and any of its subsidiaries or establishments in another Member State or which exceed the powers of the decision-making organ in a single Member State.

(2) For the purpose of informing and consulting under sub-paragraph (1) the competent organ of the SE shall:

(a) prepare and provide to the representative body regular reports on the progress of the business of the SE and the SE's prospects;

(b) provide the representative body with the agenda for meetings of the administrative or, where appropriate, the management or supervisory organs and copies of all documents submitted to the general meeting of its shareholders.

(c) inform the representative body when there are exceptional circumstances affecting the employees' interests to a considerable extent, particularly in the event of relocations, transfers, the closure of establishments or undertakings or collective redundancies.

(3)

(a) The competent organ shall, if the representative body so desires, meet with that body, without prejudice to sub-paragraph (b) below, at least once a year to discuss the reports referred to in sub-paragraph (2)(a). The meetings shall relate in particular to the structure, economic and financial situation, the probable development of business and of production and sales, the situation and probable trend of employment, investments and substantial changes concerning organisation, introduction of new working methods or production processes, transfers of production, mergers, cut-backs or closures of undertakings, establishments or important parts thereof and collective redundancies;

(b) in the circumstances set out in sub-paragraph (2)(c), the representative body may decide, for reasons of urgency, to allow the select committee to meet the competent organ and it shall have the right to meet a more appropriate level of management within the SE rather than the competent organ itself;

(c) in the event of the competent organ not acting in accordance with the opinion expressed by the representative body, the two bodies shall meet again to seek an agreement, if the representative body so wishes.

(4) In the circumstances set out in (3)(b) above, if the select committee attends the meeting, any other members of the representative body who represent employees who are directly concerned by the measures being discussed also have the right to participate in the meeting.

(5) Before any meeting referred to in paragraph (3), the members of the representative body or the select committee, as the case may be shall be entitled to meet without the representatives of the competent organ being present.

(6) Without prejudice to regulations 37 and 38, the members of the representative body shall inform the employees' representatives or, if no such representatives exist, the employees of the SE and its subsidiaries and establishments, of the content and outcome of the information and consultation procedures.

(7) The representative body and the select committee may be assisted by experts of its choice.

(8) The costs of the representative body shall be borne by the SE which shall provide the members of that body with financial and material resources needed to enable them to perform their duties in an appropriate manner, including (unless agreed otherwise) the cost of organising meetings, providing interpretation facilities and accommodation and travelling expenses. However, where the representative body or the select committee is assisted by more than one expert the SE is not required to pay the expenses of more than one of them.

[7336]

PART 3
STANDARD RULES FOR PARTICIPATION

7.—(1) In the case of an SE established by transformation, if the rules of a Member State relating to employee participation in the administrative or supervisory body applied before registration, all aspects of employee participation shall continue to apply to the SE. Sub-paragraph (2) shall apply *mutatis mutandis* to that end.

(2) In the case where an SE is established other than by transformation and where the employees or their representatives of at least one of the participating companies had participation rights, the representative body shall have the right to elect, appoint, recommend or oppose the appointment of a number of members of the administrative or supervisory body of the SE, such number shall be equal to the highest proportion in force in the participating companies concerned before the registration of the SE.

(3)

(a) Subject to sub-paragraph (b), the representative body shall, taking into account the proportion of employees of the SE employed in each Member State, decide on the allocation of seats within the administrative or supervisory body.

(b) In making the decision set out in sub-paragraph (a), if the employees of one or more Member State is not covered by the proportional criterion set out in (a), the representative body shall appoint a member from one of those Member States including one from the Member State in which the SE is registered, if appropriate.

(c) Every member of the administrative body or, where appropriate, the supervisory body of the SE who has been elected, appointed or recommended by the representative body or the employees shall be a full member with the same rights and obligations as the members representing shareholders, including the right to vote.

[7337]

SCHEDULE 4
MODIFICATIONS OF THE 1985 ACT AND THE INSOLVENCY ACT 1986
Regulations 85 and 88

Modifications applying before registration

1.—(1) The converting SE's memorandum and articles of association shall not have names subscribed on it.

(2) Section 2(5)(b) and (c), (6) and (6A) of the 1985 Act (memorandum of association: subscribers) shall not apply.

(3) In section 7 of the 1985 Act (articles of association) the following shall not apply—

(a) the requirement in subsection (1) for signature by the subscribers to the memorandum,

(b) subsection (3)(c), and

(c) subsection (3A).

(4) Section 10 of the 1985 Act (documents to be sent to the registrar) shall not apply.

Modifications applying on or after registration

2. A reference to a company's incorporation shall be construed as a reference to the registration of a converting SE's memorandum and articles of association.

3. A reference to documents delivered under the 1985 Act shall be taken to include a reference to documents delivered under regulation 85.

4.—(1) A reference to a company's certificate of incorporation shall be construed as a reference to the certificate given under regulation 87(3).

(2) A requirement for the registrar of companies to issue a certificate of incorporation to a company shall—

(a) be construed as a requirement to issue a certificate of registration similar to the certificate under regulation 87(3), and

(b) apply with such other modifications as the registrar considers necessary in consequence of paragraph (a).

5. In section 735 of the 1985 Act (definition of company), and in other legislation relating to companies, any reference to a company formed and registered under that Act shall have effect as if the reference to formation were omitted.

Effect of registration

6. Section 13 of the 1985 Act (effect of registration) shall not apply.

7. Section 22(1) of the 1985 Act (definition of "member") shall not apply.

Use of "limited"

8. In section 34 of the 1985 Act (penalty for improper use of "limited") the reference to incorporation with limited liability shall be construed as a reference to registration as a company with limited liability.

Certificate as to share capital

9. The following provisions shall not apply—
   (a) section 117 of the 1985 Act (public company share capital requirements), and
   (b) section 122(1)(b) of the Insolvency Act 1986 (winding up by the court: lack of certificate under section 117 of 1985 Act).

Fees

10. In any regulations made under section 708 of the 1985 Act a reference to a certificate of incorporation shall be construed as including a reference to—
   (a) a certificate under regulation 87(3), and
   (b) a certificate issued in accordance with paragraph 4(2).

Accounting Reference Date

11. No modification made under this Schedule shall affect the determination of the accounting reference date of a converting SE by the application of section 224(3A) of the 1985 Act, by virtue of Article 61 of the EC Regulation, or of regulation 83 prior to the registration of the converting SE under regulation 87.

[7338]

EUROPEAN PUBLIC LIMITED-LIABILITY COMPANY (FEES) REGULATIONS 2004 (NOTE)

(SI 2004/2407)

NOTES

See Appendix 3 (Fees Instruments) at **[A3]**.

[7338A]

LIMITED LIABILITY PARTNERSHIPS (FEES) REGULATIONS 2004 (NOTE)

(SI 2004/2620)

NOTES

See Appendix 3 (Fees Instruments) at **[A3]**.

[7338B]

PART IV STATUTORY INSTRUMENTS

COMPANIES (FEES) REGULATIONS 2004 (NOTE)

(SI 2004/2621)

NOTES

See Appendix 3 (Fees Instruments) at **[A3]**.

[7338C]

EUROPEAN ECONOMIC INTEREST GROUPING (FEES) REGULATIONS 2004 (NOTE)

(SI 2004/2643)

NOTES

See Appendix 3 (Fees Instruments) at **[A3]**.

[7338D]

COMPANIES (AUDIT, INVESTIGATIONS AND COMMUNITY ENTERPRISE) ACT 2004 (COMMENCEMENT) AND COMPANIES ACT 1989 (COMMENCEMENT NO 18) ORDER 2004

(SI 2004/3322)

NOTES

Made: 9 December 2004.

Authority: CA 1989, s 215(2); Companies (Audit, Investigations and Community Enterprise) Act 2004, s 65.

As of 1 July 2007, this Order had not been amended.

ARRANGEMENT OF ARTICLES

1 Citation and interpretation

(1) This Order may be cited as the Companies (Audit, Investigations and Community Enterprise) Act 2004 (Commencement) and Companies Act 1989 (Commencement No 18) Order 2004.

(2) In this Order—
"the 1985 Act" means the Companies Act 1985; and
"the 2004 Act" means the Companies (Audit, Investigations and Community Enterprise) Act 2004.

(3) References in articles 3 to 11 to sections are references to those sections of the 1985 Act; and the references in article 3 to Schedule 4A and in article 7 to Schedule 24 are references to those Schedules to that Act.

(4) References in this Order to old sections of the 1985 Act are references to the sections in question as they had effect before their amendment by the 2004 Act; and references to new sections of that Act are references to the sections in question as inserted by the 2004 Act.

[7339]

2 Commencement

(1) Section 46 of and Schedule 13 to the Companies Act 1989 and the provisions of the 2004 Act set out in Schedule 1 hereto shall come into force on 1st January 2005.

(2) The provisions of the 2004 Act set out in Schedule 2 hereto shall, subject to articles 4 to 13 below, come into force on 6th April 2005.

(3) The provisions of the 2004 Act set out in Schedule 3 hereto shall come into force on 1st July 2005.

(4) The provisions of the 2004 Act set out in Schedule 4 hereto shall, subject to article 3 below, come into force on 1st October 2005.

[7340]

3 Transitional provision for section 7 of the 2004 Act

New section 390B, and the repeal of old section 390A(3) and of words in paragraph 1(1) of Schedule 4A relating thereto, shall have no effect in relation to the accounts of a company for a financial year beginning before 1st October 2005.

[7341]

4 Transitional provision for section 9 of the 2004 Act

New sections 234(2A) and 234ZA shall not apply in relation to any report of the directors of a company prepared under section 234 concerning a financial year beginning before 1st April 2005 or ending before 6th April 2005.

[7342]

5 Transitional provision for section 19 of the 2004 Act

New section 309A shall have no effect in relation to provisions made before 29th October 2004 which are not void under old section 310.

[7343]

6 Authorisations under old section 447 of the 1985 Act effective immediately before 6th April 2005

An authorisation under old section 447(3) which was effective immediately before 6th April 2005 shall have effect on and after 6th April 2005 as though it were an authorisation under new section 447(3).

[7344]

7 Outstanding requirements under old section 447 of the 1985 Act

(1) An outstanding requirement imposed under old section 447 shall be treated, on and after 6th April 2005, as a requirement imposed under new section 447, whether or not the requirement could have been imposed under new section 447.

(2) But old section 447(6) and (7) shall apply, and section 453C shall not apply, in relation to a failure to comply with such an outstanding requirement.

(3) The following shall continue to have effect for the purposes of paragraph (2):

(a) the references to section 447 in sections 732, 733 and 734; and

(b) the entry in Schedule 24 relating to old section 447(6).

(4) Where a person provides information on or after 6th April 2005 in purported compliance with an outstanding requirement and in doing so commits an offence under section 451, the court, on summary conviction of that person for that offence, may not impose a term of imprisonment greater than six months.

(5) For the purposes of this article, an outstanding requirement is a requirement imposed under old section 447, either in directions given by the Secretary of State or by a person authorised by the Secretary of State, which—

(a) was imposed before 6th April 2005;
(b) was required to be complied with on or after that date; and
(c) had not been complied with before that date.

[7345]

8 Power to take copies of or extracts from documents produced under old section 447 of the 1985 Act before 6th April 2005

The powers in new section 447(7) are exercisable on and after 6th April 2005 in relation to any document produced before that date in pursuance of old section 447.

[7346]

9 Use in evidence of statements made in compliance with requirements under section 447 of the 1985 Act

(1) Subsections (8) to (8B) of old section 447 continue to have effect on and after 6th April 2005 in relation to any statement made before that date as if the reference in subsection (8B)(a) to section 451 were a reference to old or new section 451.

(2) In its application to any statement made on or after 6th April 2005 by a person in compliance with an outstanding requirement imposed under old section 447 or a requirement imposed under new section 447, section 447A has effect as if the relevant offences in section 447A(3) included the offences under old sections 451 and 447(6).

[7347]

10 Security of information obtained under old section 447 of the 1985 Act

New section 449 applies, and old section 449 does not apply, to information to which old section 449(1) applied immediately before 6th April 2005.

[7348]

11 Power to enter and remain on premises: persons authorised under old section 447 of the 1985 Act

For the purposes of sections 453A and 453B, and for the purposes of section 453C as it relates to section 453A, an investigator includes a person authorised for the purposes of old section 447 whose authorisation was effective immediately before 6th April 2005.

[7349]

12 Use of information obtained under the 1985 Act for the purposes of proceedings under section 8 of the Company Directors Disqualification Act 1986

The references to sections 447 and 448 of the 1985 Act in section 8(1A)(b)(i) of the Company Directors Disqualification Act 1986 are references to either the old or the new sections.

[7350]

13 Use of information obtained under Part 14 of the 1985 Act for the purposes of proceedings under section 124A of the Insolvency Act 1986

The reference to information obtained under Part 14 of the 1985 Act in section 124A(1)(a) of the Insolvency Act 1986, insofar as it is a reference to information obtained under section 447 or 448 of the 1985 Act, is a reference to information obtained either the old or the new section.

[7351]–[7355]

(*Sch 1 brings the following provisions of the 2004 Act into force on 1 January 2005: ss 3–5, 10, 13, 14, 16–18, 25 (in respect of the provisions of Sch 2 mentioned below), 27, 64 (in respect of the provisions of Sch 8 mentioned below), Sch 2, paras 1, 3, 4, Sch 3, and Sch 8 (in respect of the entries relating to the 1985 Act, ss 245C(6), 256(3), CA 1989, s 48(3), the Companies (Northern Ireland) Order 1990, the Competition Act 1998, the Competition*

Act 1998 (Competition Commission) Transitional, Consequential and Supplemental Provisions Order 1999, and the Enterprise Act 2002); Sch 2 brings the following provisions of the 2004 Act into force on 6 April 2005: ss 1, 2, 6, 8, 9, 11, 12, 15, 19–24, 25 (in respect of the provisions of Sch 2 mentioned below), 64 (in respect of the provisions of Sch 8 mentioned below), Sch 1, Sch 2, paras 2, 5–24, 25 (except in respect of paras 40 and 45 of new Sch 15D to the 1985 Act), 26–28, 30, 31, and Sch 8 (in respect of the entries relating to the 1985 Act, ss 310, 734(1), Sch 24, IA 1986, IA 1986, CA 1989, ss 63, 65, 67, 69, 120, the Friendly Societies Act 1992, the Pensions Act 1995, the Bank of England Act 1998, and the Youth Justice and Criminal Evidence Act 1999); Sch 3 brings the following provisions of the 2004 Act into force on 1 July 2005: ss 25 (so far as not already in force), 26, 28–63, 64 (in respect of the provisions of Sch 8 mentioned below), Sch 2 (so far as not already in force), Schs 4–7, and Sch 8 (in respect of the entry relating to the 1985 Act, s 27(4)); Sch 4 brings the following provisions of the 2004 Act into force on 1 October 2005: ss 7, 64 (so far as not already in force), Sch 8 (so far as not already in force).)

FINANCIAL SERVICES AND MARKETS ACT 2000 (MARKET ABUSE) REGULATIONS 2005 (NOTE)

(SI 2005/381)

NOTES

Made: 23 February 2005.

Authority: European Communities Act 1972, s 2(2).

Commencement: 17 March 2005 (regs 2, 3 8, Sch 1, paras 2, 3, 6, 11); 1 July 2005 (otherwise).

These Regulations implement, in part, European Parliament and Council Directive 2003/6/EC on insider dealing and market manipulation (at **[9437]**) and the following measures which were made under Article 17 of that Directive—

- Commission Regulation (EC) No 2273/2003 implementing Directive 2003/6/EC of the European Parliament and of the Council as regards exemptions for buy-back programmes and stabilisation of financial instruments (at **[9520]**);
- Commission Directive 2003/124/EC implementing Directive 2003/6 of the European Parliament and of the Council as regards the definition and public disclosure of inside information and the definition of market manipulation (at **[9498]**); and
- Commission Directive 2004/72/EC implementing Directive 2003/6 of the European Parliament and of the Council as regards accepted market practices, the definition of inside information in relation to derivatives on commodities, the drawing up of lists of insiders, the notification of managers' transactions and the notification of suspicious transactions (at **[9691]**).

Reg 1 of these Regulations provides for citation and commencement.

Reg 2 provides for interpretation.

Reg 3 amends the Criminal Justice Act 1993, Sch 1, para 5(1) at **[892]**.

Reg 4 introduces Sch 1 to these Regulations (amendments of FSMA 2000, Part VI).

Reg 5 introduces Sch 2 to these Regulations (amendments of FSMA 2000, Part VIII).

Reg 6 amends FSMA 2000, s 150 at **[2150]**.

Reg 7 amends FSMA 2000, s 395 at **[2393]**.

Reg 8 amends FSMA 2000, s 397 at **[2395]**.

Reg 9 revokes the Traded Securities (Disclosure) Regulations 1994, SI 1994/188.

Reg 10 amends the Financial Services and Markets Act 2000 (Prescribed Markets and Qualifying Investments) Order 2001, SI 2001/996 at **[4106]**.

Reg 11 amends the Financial Services and Markets Act 2000 (Recognition Requirements for Investment Exchanges and Clearing Houses) Regulations 2001, SI 2001/995.

Sch 1 amends FSMA 2000, Pt VI (Official listing) at **[2071]** et seq.

Sch 2 amends FSMA 2000, Pt VIII (Penalties for market abuse) at **[2118]** et seq.

As of 1 July 2007, these Regulations had not been amended.

[7355A]

INVESTMENT RECOMMENDATION (MEDIA) REGULATIONS 2005

(SI 2005/382)

NOTES

Made: 23 February 2005.

Authority: European Communities Act 1972, s 2(2).

PART IV
STATUTORY INSTRUMENTS

Commencement: 1 July 2005 (see reg 1 at **[7356]**). Where any provision in this work (including any inserted or substituted provision) came into force for all purposes on or before 1 July 2005, commencement information is not noted at provision level.

These Regulations are reproduced as amended by: the Financial Services (EEA State) Regulations 2007, SI 2007/108; the Financial Services and Markets Act 2000 (Markets in Financial Instruments) Regulations 2007, SI 2007/126.

ARRANGEMENT OF REGULATIONS

PART 1
CITATION, INTERPRETATION AND APPLICATION

1 Citation and commencement

These Regulations may be cited as the Investment Recommendation (Media) Regulations 2005 and come into force on 1st July 2005.

[7356]

2 Interpretation

In these Regulations—

["EEA State" has the meaning given by Schedule 1 to the Interpretation Act 1978;]

"financial instrument" means any of the instruments listed in Article 1(3) of Directive 2003/6/EC of the European Parliament and the Council of 28 January 2003 on insider dealing and market manipulation that are admitted to trading on a regulated market (as defined in article *1(13) of Council Directive 93/22/EEC on investment services in the securities field*) in an EEA State or for which a request for admission to trading on such a market has been made;

"investment recommendation" means information that directly recommends the buying, selling, subscribing for or the underwriting of a financial instrument or the exercise of any right conferred by such instrument to buy, sell, subscribe for or underwrite it; and

"media" means—

(a) a newspaper, journal, magazine or other periodical publication;

(b) a service consisting of the broadcast or transmission of television or radio programmes; or

(c) a service (including the internet) comprising regularly updated news or information;

but excluding any such publication or service the principal purpose of which (taken as a whole and including any advertisements or other promotional material contained in it) is a purpose mentioned in article 54(1)(a) or (b) of the Financial Services and Markets Act 2000 (Regulated Activities) Order 2001.

[7357]

NOTES

Definition "EEA State" substituted by the Financial Services (EEA State) Regulations 2007, SI 2007/108, reg 11, as from 13 February 2007.

For the words in italics in the definition "financial instrument" there are substituted the words "4.1.14 of Directive 2004/39/EC of the European Parliament and of the Council of 21 April 2004 on markets in financial instruments" by the Financial Services and Markets Act 2000 (Markets in Financial Instruments) Regulations 2007, SI 2007/126, reg 3(6), Sch 6, Pt 2, para 20, as from 1 November 2007 (for the full commencement details of SI 2007/126, see reg 1 of those Regulations at **[7596]**).

3 Application of Regulations

(1) These Regulations apply in respect of the production and the dissemination of an investment recommendation which the producer of that recommendation intends to be, or to become, publicly available in or through the media.

(2) Subject to paragraphs (3) and (4), any person whose business or profession is in the media and who, in the conduct of that business, or in the exercise of that profession, either—

(a) produces an investment recommendation, or

(b) disseminates an investment recommendation produced by a third party,

must do so in accordance with Parts 2 and 3; and references to a "person producing an investment recommendation" and to a "person disseminating an investment recommendation produced by a third party" are references respectively to such persons.

(3) These Regulations do not apply to—

(a) a person (being an authorised person within section 31 of the Financial Services and Markets Act 2000) ("the Act") producing an investment recommendation where such production by him is regulated pursuant to section 22 of the Act; and

(b) a person (being an authorised person within section 31 of the Act) disseminating an investment recommendation produced by a third party where such dissemination is regulated pursuant to section 22 of the Act.

(4) Parts 2 and 3 do not apply to the production and dissemination of an investment recommendation where—

(a) the media in or through which the recommendation appears is subject either to a self-regulatory code or to an appropriate system or procedure with respect to the presentation of investment recommendations and to the disclosure of financial interests and conflicts of interest, and

(b) the publication, programme or regularly updated news or information service in or through which the recommendation appears includes a clear and prominent reference to the relevant code, system or procedure.

(5) In paragraph (4)(a), a "self-regulatory code" means the Code of Practice issued by the Press Complaints Commission, the Producers' Guidelines issued by the British Broadcasting Corporation and any code published by the Office of Communications pursuant to section 324 of the Communications Act 2003.

[7358]

PART 2
PRODUCTION OF INVESTMENT RECOMMENDATIONS

4 Disclosure of identity of producers

A person producing an investment recommendation must disclose clearly and prominently in that recommendation his identity, in particular, the name and job title of the individual who prepared it and the name of the legal person responsible for its production.

[7359]

5 Fair presentation

Reasonable care must be taken by a person producing an investment recommendation to ensure that in that recommendation—

(a) facts are clearly distinguished from interpretations, estimates, opinions and other types of non-factual information;

(b) all the documents, figures, names and other records used are reliable and if there is any doubt as to their reliability that this is clearly indicated; and

(c) all projections, forecasts and price targets are clearly labelled as such and that any material assumptions made in producing or using them are indicated.

[7360]

6 Disclosure of interests etc

(1) Subject to paragraph (6), a person producing an investment recommendation must disclose, in the recommendation itself, all relationships and circumstances that may reasonably be expected to impair the objectivity of that recommendation, in particular, where he has—

(a) a significant financial interest in one or more of the financial instruments which are the subject of the investment recommendation, or

(b) a significant conflict of interest with respect to an issuer of a financial instrument to which the investment recommendation (directly or indirectly) relates.

(2) For the purposes of paragraph (1)(a), a "significant" financial interest includes—

(a) in relation to a legal person, a holding exceeding 5% of the total issued share capital in the issuer of the shares in question, and

(b) in relation to a natural person, a holding exceeding £3000 of the total issued share capital in the issuer of the shares in question.

(3) Where the person producing the investment recommendation is a legal person—

(a) the significant financial interests and the significant conflicts of interest that it must disclose under paragraph (1) include any such interests or interest that it (or any connected legal person) has that are—

(i) accessible, or reasonably expected to be accessible, to the persons involved in the preparation of the recommendation, or

(ii) that are known to persons who, although not involved in the preparation of the recommendation, had, or could reasonably be expected to have, access to the recommendation prior to its being disseminated to customers or to the public; and

(b) the requirement of disclosure of significant financial interests and of significant conflicts of interest under paragraph (1) applies also to any person who (whether under a contract of employment or otherwise) works for the person producing the investment recommendation and who was directly involved in preparing that recommendation.

(4) The reference in paragraph (3)(a) to a legal person being "connected" to the person ("A") producing the investment recommendation, means—

(a) a parent undertaking of A;

(b) a subsidiary undertaking of A;

(c) a subsidiary undertaking of the parent undertaking of A;

(d) a parent undertaking of a subsidiary undertaking of A; or

(e) an undertaking in which A or an undertaking mentioned in sub-paragraph (a), (b), (c) or (d) has a participating interest.

(5) In paragraph (4)—

"parent undertaking" in sub-paragraphs (a), (c) and (d) has the same meaning as in Part 7 of the Companies Act 1985 (or Part 8 of the Companies (Northern Ireland) Order 1986); and includes an individual who would be a parent undertaking for the purposes of those provisions if he were an undertaking (and "subsidiary undertaking" is to be read accordingly).

"subsidiary undertaking" in sub-paragraphs (b), (c) and (d) has the same meaning as in Part 7 of the Companies Act 1985 (or Part 8 of the Companies (Northern Ireland) Order 1986); and includes, in relation to a body incorporated in or formed under the law of any EEA State other than the United Kingdom, an undertaking which is a subsidiary undertaking within the meaning of any rule of law in that State for the purposes of the Seventh Company Law Directive (and "parent undertaking" is to be read accordingly); and

"participating interest" in sub-paragraph (e) has the same meaning as in Part 7 of the Companies Act 1985 (or Part 8 of the Companies (Northern Ireland) Order 1986); and includes an interest held by an individual which would be a participating interest for the purposes of these provisions if he were taken to be an undertaking.

(6) A person producing an investment recommendation may, if he considers that the disclosure required under paragraph (1) would be disproportionate in relation to the length of that recommendation, comply with the requirements of that paragraph—

(a) by including in the recommendation itself a clear and prominent reference to the place where the disclosure can be directly and easily accessed by the public (such as an appropriate internet site of his from which a direct internet link can be made to such disclosures), or

(b) where he produces two or more recommendations which appear together, by including in one of the recommendations a single clear and prominent reference to the place where the disclosures required for all the recommendations can be directly and easily accessed by the public.

[7361]

7 Non-written investment recommendations

(1) A person producing a non-written investment recommendation may comply with the requirements of regulations 4 to 6 to disclose information or indicate certain matters—

(a) by including in the recommendation itself a clear and prominent reference to the place where the information and matters that would otherwise have to be disclosed or indicated in it can be directly and easily accessed by the public (such as at an appropriate internet site to which a direct internet link can be made to those matters or to that information), or

(b) where he produces two or more recommendations which appear together, by including in one of the recommendations a single clear and prominent reference to the place where the information and matters required to be disclosed or indicated for all the recommendations can be directly and easily accessed by the public.

(2) A "non-written investment recommendation" is an investment recommendation that is—

(a) broadcast or transmitted in the form of a television or radio programme, or

(b) displayed on a web site (or similar system for the electronic display of information).

[7362]

PART 3
DISSEMINATION OF INVESTMENT RECOMMENDATIONS PRODUCED BY THIRD PARTIES

8 Disclosure of identity of persons disseminating investment recommendations

If a person having no authority from the person who produced an investment recommendation to do so nevertheless on his own behalf disseminates that recommendation, he must indicate his own identity clearly and prominently in the recommendation or ensure that it is otherwise clearly and prominently indicated to the persons to whom that recommendation is being disseminated.

[7363]

9 Dissemination of altered investment recommendations

(1) A person disseminating an investment recommendation produced by a third party who makes a change to the direction of the recommendation (such as the change of a recommendation to "buy" into one to "hold" or to "sell" (or vice versa)), must comply with regulations 4 to 6.

(2) A person disseminating an investment recommendation produced by a third party who does not make a change to the direction of the recommendation but who makes some other substantial alteration, must ensure that the details of that alteration are clearly indicated.

(3) Where the dissemination referred to in paragraph (2) is by a legal person (either itself or through a natural person) that legal person must have a formal written policy so that those receiving the information are directed to where they can have access to—

(a) the identity of the person who produced that recommendation,

(b) the investment recommendation itself, and

(c) any disclosures of the financial interests and conflicts of interest of the person who produced the recommendation which have been made pursuant to regulation 6(1) or in accordance with any rules made by the Financial Services Authority.

[7364]

10 Dissemination of summaries of investment recommendations

Where an investment recommendation produced by a third party is summarised and the summary is then disseminated, the summary must—

(a) be clear and not misleading,

(b) mention the document in which the investment recommendation appears, and

(c) indicate where any disclosures as to the financial interests and conflicts of interest of the person who produced the investment recommendation which have been disclosed pursuant to regulation 6(1) or in accordance with any rules made by the Financial Services Authority, can be directly and clearly accessed by the public.

[7365]

11 News reporting on investment recommendations

Where no change is made to the essence of an investment recommendation produced by a third party or where a summary is made of an investment recommendation produced by a third party, the requirements respectively of regulations 9 and 10 need not be complied with as respects news reporting on that recommendation or summary in or through the media.

[7366]

PART 4
TERRITORIAL SCOPE AND ACTIONS FOR DAMAGES

12 Territorial scope

These Regulations apply to any act or course of conduct of—

(a) a person producing an investment recommendation, if his act is done, or his course of conduct is engaged in, in the United Kingdom, regardless of whether that recommendation is then disseminated in or from the United Kingdom or in or from another EEA State;

(b) a person disseminating an investment recommendation produced by a third party, if his act is done, or his course of conduct is engaged in, in or from—

(i) his registered office (or if he does not have a registered office his head office), or

(ii) another establishment maintained by him,

in the United Kingdom, regardless of whether any person to whom that recommendation is disseminated is in the United Kingdom or in another EEA State.

[7367]

13 Actions for damages

(1) A contravention of a provision in Part 2 or 3 is actionable at the suit of a private person who suffers loss as a result of the contravention, subject to the defences and other incidents applying to actions for breach of statutory duty.

(2) A "private person" is a person who is a private person within regulation 3(1) of the Financial Services and Markets Act 2000 (Rights of Action) Regulations 2001.

[7368]

INSOLVENCY PRACTITIONERS REGULATIONS 2005

(SI 2005/524)

NOTES

Made: 8 March 2005.

Authority: IA 1986, ss 390, 392, 393, 419.

Commencement: 1 April 2005 (see reg 1 at **[7369]**). Where any provision in this work (including any inserted or substituted provision) came into force for all purposes on or before 1 July 2005, commencement information is not noted at provision level.

As of 1 July 2007, these Regulations had not been amended.

ARRANGEMENT OF REGULATIONS

PART 1
INTRODUCTORY

PART 2
AUTHORISATION OF INSOLVENCY PRACTITIONERS BY COMPETENT AUTHORITIES

PART 3
THE REQUIREMENTS FOR SECURITY AND CAUTION FOR THE PROPER PERFORMANCE OF THE FUNCTIONS OF AN INSOLVENCY PRACTITIONER ETC

PART 4
RECORDS TO BE MAINTAINED BY INSOLVENCY PRACTITIONERS—INSPECTION OF RECORDS

SCHEDULES

PART 1
INTRODUCTORY

1 Citation and commencement.

These Regulations may be cited as the Insolvency Practitioners Regulations 2005 and shall come into force on 1st April 2005.

[7369]

2 Interpretation: general

(1) In these Regulations—

"the Act" means the Insolvency Act 1986;

"commencement date" means the date on which these Regulations come into force;

"initial capacity" shall be construed in accordance with regulation 3;

"insolvency practitioner" means a person who is authorised to act as an insolvency practitioner by virtue of—

(a) membership of a body recognised pursuant to section 391 of the Act; or

(b) an authorisation granted pursuant to section 393 of the Act;

"insolvent" means a person in respect of whom an insolvency practitioner is acting;

"interim trustee", "permanent trustee" and "trust deed for creditors" have the same meanings as in the Bankruptcy (Scotland) Act 1985;

PART IV
STATUTORY INSTRUMENTS

"subsequent capacity" shall be construed in accordance with regulation 3.

(2) In these Regulations a reference to the date of release or discharge of an insolvency practitioner includes—

(a) where the insolvency practitioner acts as nominee in relation to proposals for a voluntary arrangement under Part I or VIII of the Act, whichever is the earlier of the date on which—

(i) the proposals are rejected by creditors;

(ii) he is replaced as nominee by another insolvency practitioner; or

(iii) the arrangement takes effect without his becoming supervisor in relation to it; and

(b) where an insolvency practitioner acts as supervisor of a voluntary arrangement, whichever is the earlier of the date on which—

(i) the arrangement is completed or terminated; or

(ii) the insolvency practitioner otherwise ceases to act as supervisor in relation to the arrangement.

[7370]

3 Interpretation—meaning of initial and subsequent capacity

(1) In these Regulations an insolvency practitioner holds office in relation to an insolvent in a "subsequent capacity" where he holds office in relation to that insolvent in one of the capacities referred to in paragraph (3) and immediately prior to his holding office in that capacity, he held office in relation to that insolvent in another of the capacities referred to in that paragraph.

(2) The first office held by the insolvency practitioner in the circumstances referred to in paragraph (1) is referred to in these Regulations as the "initial capacity".

(3) The capacities referred to in paragraph (1) are, nominee in relation to proposals for a voluntary arrangement under Part I of the Act, supervisor of a voluntary arrangement under Part I of the Act, administrator, provisional liquidator, liquidator, nominee in relation to proposals for a voluntary arrangement under Part VIII of the Act, supervisor of a voluntary arrangement under Part VIII of the Act, trustee, interim trustee and permanent trustee.

[7371]

4 Revocations and transitional and saving provisions

(1) Subject to paragraphs (2), (3) and (4), the Regulations listed in Schedule 1 are revoked.

(2) Parts I and II of the Insolvency Practitioners Regulations 1990 shall continue to apply in relation to an application for authorisation under section 393 of the Act to act as an insolvency practitioner made to the Secretary of State before the commencement date and accordingly nothing in these Regulations shall apply to such an application.

(3) Parts I, III and IV of the Insolvency Practitioners Regulations 1990 shall continue to apply in relation to any case in respect of which an insolvency practitioner is appointed—

(a) before the commencement date; or

(b) in a subsequent capacity and he was appointed in an initial capacity in that case before the commencement date.

(4) Only regulations 16 and 17 of these Regulations shall apply in relation to the cases mentioned in paragraph (3).

[7372]

PART 2
AUTHORISATION OF INSOLVENCY PRACTITIONERS BY COMPETENT AUTHORITIES

5 Interpretation of Part

In this Part—

"advisory work experience" means experience obtained in providing advice to the office-holder in insolvency proceedings or anyone who is a party to, or whose interests are affected by, those proceedings;

"application" means an application made by an individual to the competent authority for authorisation under section 393 of the Act to act as an insolvency practitioner and "applicant" shall be construed accordingly;

"authorisation" means an authorisation to act as an insolvency practitioner granted under section 393 of the Act;

"continuing professional development" has the meaning given to it by regulation 8(3);

"higher insolvency work experience" means engagement in work in relation to insolvency proceedings where the work involves the management or supervision of the conduct of those proceedings on behalf of the office-holder acting in relation to them;

"insolvency legislation" means the provisions of, or any provision made under, the Act, the Bankruptcy (Scotland) Act 1985 or the Deeds of Arrangement Act 1914 and any other enactment past or present applying to Great Britain (or any part of it) that relates to the insolvency of any person;

"insolvency practice" means the carrying on of the business of acting as an insolvency practitioner or in a corresponding capacity under the law of any country or territory outside Great Britain, and for this purpose acting as an insolvency practitioner shall include acting as a judicial factor on the bankrupt estate of a deceased person;

"insolvency proceedings" means any proceedings in which an office-holder acts under any provision of insolvency legislation or the corresponding provision of the law of any country or territory outside Great Britain;

"insolvency work experience" means engagement in work related to the administration of insolvency proceedings—

(a) as the office-holder in those proceedings;

(b) in the employment of a firm or body whose members or employees act as insolvency practitioners; or

(c) in the course of employment in the Insolvency Service of the Department of Trade and Industry.

"office-holder" means a person who acts as an insolvency practitioner or a judicial factor on the bankrupt estate of a deceased person or in a corresponding capacity under the law of any country or territory outside Great Britain and includes the official receiver acting as liquidator, provisional liquidator, trustee, interim receiver or nominee or supervisor of a voluntary arrangement; and

"regulatory work experience" means experience of work relating to the regulation of insolvency practitioners for or on behalf of a competent authority or a body recognised pursuant to section 391 of the Act or experience of work in connection with any function of the Secretary of State under that section.

[7373]

6 Matters for determining whether an applicant for an authorisation is a fit and proper person

The matters to be taken into account by a competent authority in deciding whether an individual is a fit and proper person to act as an insolvency practitioner for the purpose of section 393(2)(a) or 393(4)(a) shall include:—

(a) whether the applicant has been convicted of any offence involving fraud or other dishonesty or violence;

(b) whether the applicant has contravened any provision in any enactment contained in insolvency legislation;

(c) whether the applicant has engaged in any practices in the course of carrying on any trade, profession or vocation or in the course of the discharge of any functions relating to any office or employment appearing to be deceitful or oppressive or otherwise unfair or improper, whether unlawful or not, or which otherwise cast doubt upon his probity or competence for discharging the duties of an insolvency practitioner;

(d) whether in respect of any insolvency practice carried on by the applicant at the date of or at any time prior to the making of the application, there were established adequate systems of control of the practice and adequate records relating to the practice, including accounting records, and whether such systems of control and records have been or were maintained on an adequate basis;

(e) whether the insolvency practice of the applicant is, has been or, where the applicant is not yet carrying on such a practice, will be, carried on with the independence, integrity and the professional skills appropriate to the range and scale of the practice and the proper performance of the duties of an insolvency practitioner and in accordance with generally accepted professional standards, practices and principles;

(f) whether the applicant, in any case where he has acted as an insolvency practitioner, has failed to disclose fully to such persons as might reasonably be expected to be affected thereby circumstances where there is or appears to be a conflict of interest between his so acting and any interest of his own, whether personal, financial or otherwise, without having received such consent as might be appropriate to his acting or continuing to act despite the existence of such circumstances.

[7374]

7 Requirements as to education and training—applicants who have never previously been authorised to act as insolvency practitioners

(1) The requirements as to education, training and practical experience prescribed for the purposes of section 393(2)(b) of the Act in relation to an applicant who has never previously been authorised to act as an insolvency practitioner (whether by virtue of membership of a body recognised under section 391 of the Act or by virtue of an authorisation granted by a competent authority under section 393 of the Act) shall be as set out in this regulation.

(2) An applicant must at the date of the making of his application have passed the Joint Insolvency Examination set by the Joint Insolvency Examination Board or have acquired in, or been awarded in, a country or territory outside Great Britain professional or vocational qualifications which indicate that the applicant has the knowledge and competence that is attested by a pass in that examination.

(3) An applicant must either—

(a) have held office as an office-holder in not less than 30 cases during the period of 10 years immediately preceding the date on which he made his application for authorisation; or

(b) have acquired not less than 7000 hours of insolvency work experience of which no less than 1400 hours must have been acquired within the period of two years immediately prior to the date of the making of his application and show that he satisfies one of the three requirements set out in paragraph (4).

(4) The three requirements referred to in paragraph (3)(b) are—

(a) the applicant has become an office-holder in at least 5 cases within the period of 5 years immediately prior to the date of the making of his application;

(b) the applicant has acquired 1,000 hours or more of higher insolvency work experience or experience as an office-holder within the period referred to in sub-paragraph (a); and

(c) the applicant can show that within the period referred to in sub-paragraph (a) he has achieved one of the following combinations of positions as an office-holder and hours acquired of higher insolvency work experience—

(i) 4 cases and 200 hours;

(ii) 3 cases and 400 hours;

(iii) 2 cases and 600 hours; or

(iv) 1 case and 800 hours.

(5) Where in order to satisfy all or any of the requirements set out in paragraphs (3) and (4) an applicant relies on appointment as an office-holder or the acquisition of insolvency work experience or higher insolvency work experience in relation to cases under the laws of a country or territory outside the United Kingdom, he shall demonstrate that he has no less than 1,400 hours of insolvency work experience in cases under the law of any part of the United Kingdom acquired within the period of two years immediately prior to the date of the making of his application.

(6) In ascertaining whether an applicant meets all or any of the requirements of paragraphs (3) and (4)—

(a) no account shall be taken of any case where—

(i) he was appointed to the office of receiver (or to a corresponding office under the law of a country or territory outside Great Britain) by or on behalf of a creditor who at the time of the appointment was an associate of the applicant; or

(ii) in a members' voluntary winding up or in a corresponding procedure under the laws of a country or territory outside Great Britain he was appointed liquidator at a general meeting where his associates were entitled to exercise or control the exercise of one third or more of the voting power at that general meeting;

(b) where the applicant has been an office-holder in relation to—

(i) two or more companies which were associates at the time of appointment; or

(ii) two or more individuals who were carrying on business in partnership with each other at the time of appointment,

he shall be treated as having held office in only one case in respect of all offices held in relation to the companies which were associates or in respect of all offices held in relation to the individuals who were in partnership, as the case may be.

(7) An applicant must have a good command of the English language.

[7375]

8 Requirements relating to education and training etc—applicants previously authorised to act as insolvency practitioners

(1) The requirements prescribed for the purposes of section 393(2)(b) of the Act in relation to an applicant who has at any time been authorised to act as an insolvency practitioner (whether by virtue of membership of a body recognised under section 391 of the Act or an authorisation granted by a competent authority under section 393 of the Act) shall be as set out in this regulation.

(2) The applicant must—

(a) satisfy the requirements set out in regulation 7(3) to (5) or have acquired within the period of three years preceding the date of the making of his application 500 hours of any combination of the following types of experience—

(i) experience as an office-holder;

(ii) higher insolvency work experience;

(iii) regulatory work experience; or

(iv) advisory work experience; and

(b) subject to paragraph (4), have completed at least 108 hours of continuing professional development in the period of three years ending on the day before the date of the making of his application of which—

(i) a minimum of 12 hours must be completed in each of those years; and

(ii) 54 hours must fall into the categories in paragraphs (3)(b)(i) to (v).

(3) "Continuing professional development" means any activities which—

(a) relate to insolvency law or practice or the management of the practice of an insolvency practitioner; and

(b) fall into any of the following categories—

(i) the production of written material for publication;

(ii) attendance at courses, seminars or conferences;

(iii) the viewing of any recording of a course, seminar or conference;

(iv) the giving of lectures or the presentation of papers at courses, seminars or conferences;

(v) the completion of on-line tests; and

(vi) the reading of books or periodical publications (including any on-line publication).

(4) The requirement in paragraph (2)(b) shall only apply in relation to any application made on or after the third anniversary of the commencement date.

(5) For the purposes of paragraph (3)(b)(i), "publication" includes making material available to a body recognised in pursuance of section 391 of the Act or any association or body representing the interests of those who act as insolvency practitioners.

[7376]

9 Records of continuing professional development activities

(1) Every holder of an authorisation granted by the Secretary of State shall maintain a record of each continuing professional development activity undertaken by him for a period of six years from the date on which the activity was completed.

(2) The record shall contain details of—

(a) which of the categories in regulation 8(3)(b) the activity comes within;

(b) the date that the activity was undertaken;

(c) the duration of the activity; and

(d) the topics covered by the activity.

(3) Where the continuing professional development comprises—

(a) attendance at a course, seminar or conference; or

(b) the giving of a lecture or presentation of a paper at a course, seminar or conference,

the holder of the authorisation shall keep with the record evidence from the organiser of the course, seminar or conference of the attendance of the holder at the course, seminar or conference.

(4) The Secretary of State may, on the giving of reasonable notice, inspect and take copies of any records or evidence maintained pursuant to this regulation.

[7377]

10 Maximum period of authorisation

For the purposes of section 393(3) of the Act, the maximum period that an authorisation may continue in force shall be three years.

[7378]

11 Returns by insolvency practitioners authorised by the Secretary of State

(1) Every holder of an authorisation granted by the Secretary of State shall make a return to the Secretary of State in respect of each period of 12 months ending on 31st December during the whole or any part of which he held an authorisation granted by the Secretary of State containing the following information—

(a) the number of cases in respect of whom the holder of the authorisation has acted as an insolvency practitioner during the period;

(b) in respect of each case where the holder of the authorisation has acted as an insolvency practitioner—

(i) the name of the person in respect of whom the insolvency practitioner is acting,

(ii) the date of the appointment of the holder of the authorisation,

(iii) the type of proceedings involved, and

(iv) the number of hours worked in relation to the case by the holder of the authorisation and any person assigned to assist him in the case; and

(c) the following details of any continuing professional development undertaken activity during the period by the holder of the authorisation—

(i) the nature of the activity;

(ii) the date that the activity was undertaken;

(iii) the duration of the activity; and

(iv) the topics covered by the activity.

(2) Every return required to be submitted pursuant to this regulation shall be submitted within one month of the end of the period to which it relates.

(3) The Secretary of State may at any time request the holder of an authorisation to provide any information relating to any matters of the kind referred to in paragraph (1) and any such request shall be complied with by the holder of the authorisation within one month of its receipt or such longer period as the Secretary of State may allow.

[7379]

PART 3
THE REQUIREMENTS FOR SECURITY AND CAUTION FOR THE PROPER PERFORMANCE OF THE FUNCTIONS OF AN INSOLVENCY PRACTITIONER ETC

12—(1) Schedule 2 shall have effect in respect of the requirements prescribed for the purposes of section 390(3)(b) in relation to security or caution for the proper performance of the functions of an insolvency practitioner and for related matters.

(2) Where two or more persons are appointed jointly to act as insolvency practitioners in relation to any person, the provisions of this regulation shall apply to each of them individually.

[7380]

PART 4
RECORDS TO BE MAINTAINED BY INSOLVENCY PRACTITIONERS—INSPECTION OF RECORDS

13 Records to be maintained by insolvency practitioners

(1) In respect of each case in which he acts, an insolvency practitioner shall maintain records containing at least the information specified in Schedule 3 to these Regulations as is applicable to the case.

(2) Where at any time the records referred to in paragraph (1) do not contain all the information referred to in Schedule 3 as is applicable to the case, the insolvency practitioner shall forthwith make such changes to the records as are necessary to ensure that the records contains all such information.

(3) References in Schedule 3 to "the Accountant in Bankruptcy" shall be construed in accordance with section 1 of the Bankruptcy (Scotland) Act 1985.

(4) Each record maintained pursuant to paragraph (1) shall be capable of being produced by the insolvency practitioner separately from any other record.

(5) Any records created in relation to a case pursuant to this regulation shall be preserved by the insolvency practitioner until whichever is the later of—

(a) the sixth anniversary of the date of the grant to the insolvency practitioner of his release or discharge in that case; or

(b) the sixth anniversary of the date on which any security or caution maintained in that case expires or otherwise ceases to have effect.

[7381]

14 Notification of whereabouts of records

The insolvency practitioner shall notify the persons referred to in regulation 15(1)(a) and 15(1)(b) of the place where the records required to be maintained under this Part are so maintained and the place (if different) where they may be inspected pursuant to regulation 15.

[7382]

15 Inspection of records

(1) Any records maintained by an insolvency practitioner pursuant to this Part shall on the giving of reasonable notice be made available by him for inspection by—

(a) any professional body recognised under section 391 of the Act of which he is a member and the rules of membership of which entitle him to act as an insolvency practitioner;

(b) any competent authority by whom the insolvency practitioner is authorised to act pursuant to section 393 of the Act; and

(c) the Secretary of State.

(2) Any person who is entitled to inspect any record pursuant to paragraph (1) shall also be entitled to take a copy of those records.

[7383]

16 Inspection of practice records

(1) This regulation applies to any relevant records which are held by—

(a) the holder of an authorisation to act as an insolvency practitioner granted by the Secretary of State pursuant to section 393 of the Act;

(b) his employer or former employer; or

(c) any firm or other body of which he is or was a member or partner.

(2) In this regulation "relevant records" mean any records which relate to any case where the holder of the authorisation mentioned in paragraph (1) has acted as an insolvency practitioner and which—

(a) record receipts and payments made in relation to, or in connection with, that case;

(b) record time spent on that case by the holder of the authorisation or any person assigned to assist the holder;

(c) relate to any business carried on in the case by or at the direction of the holder of the authorisation; or

(d) otherwise relate to the management of that case.

(3) The Secretary of State may, on the giving of reasonable notice to their holder, inspect and take copies of any records to which this regulation applies.

[7384]

17 Inspection of records in administration and administrative receiverships

On the giving of reasonable notice to the insolvency practitioner, the Secretary of State shall be entitled to inspect and take copies of any records in the possession or control of that insolvency practitioner which—

(a) were required to be created by or under any provision of the Act (or any provision made under the Act); and

(b) relate to an administration or an administrative receivership.

[7385]–[7386]

SCHEDULES

(*Sch 1 revokes the Insolvency Practitioners Regulations 1990, SI 1990/439, and the amending SI 1993/221, SI 2002/2710, SI 2002/2748, and SI 2004/373.*)

SCHEDULE 2
REQUIREMENTS FOR SECURITY OR CAUTION AND RELATED MATTERS

Regulation 12

PART 1
INTERPRETATION

1 Interpretation

In this Schedule—

"cover schedule" means the schedule referred to in paragraph 3(2)(c);

"the insolvent" means the individual or company in relation to which an insolvency practitioner is acting;

"general penalty sum" shall be construed in accordance with paragraph 3(2)(b);

"insolvent's assets" means all assets comprised in the insolvent's estate together with any monies provided by a third party for the payment of the insolvent's debts or the costs and expenses of administering the insolvent's estate;

"specific penalty sum" shall be construed in accordance with paragraph 3(2)(a).

[7387]

PART 2
REQUIREMENTS RELATING TO SECURITY AND CAUTION

2 Requirements in respect of security or caution

The requirements in respect of security or caution for the proper performance of the duties of insolvency practitioners prescribed for the purposes of section 390(3)(b) shall be as set out in this Part.

3 Requirement for Bonding—Terms of the Bond

(1) Where an insolvency practitioner is appointed to act in respect of an insolvent there shall be in force a bond in a form approved by the Secretary of State which—

(a) contains provision whereby a surety or cautioner undertakes to be jointly and severally liable for losses in relation to the insolvent caused by—

(i) the fraud or dishonesty of the insolvency practitioner whether acting alone or in collusion with one or more persons; or

(ii) the fraud or dishonesty of any person committed with the connivance of the insolvency practitioner and

(b) otherwise conforms to the requirements of this Part.

(2) The terms of the bond shall provide—

(a) for the payment, in respect of each case where the insolvency practitioner acts, of claims in respect of liabilities for losses of the kind mentioned in sub-paragraph (1) up to an aggregate maximum sum in respect of that case ("the specific penalty sum") calculated in accordance with the provisions of this Schedule;

(b) in the event that any amounts payable under (a) are insufficient to meet all claims arising out of any case, for a further sum of £250,000 ("the general penalty sum") out of which any such claims are to be met;

(c) for a schedule containing the name of the insolvent and the value of the insolvent's assets to be submitted to the surety or cautioner within such period as may be specified in the bond;

(d) that where at any time before the insolvency practitioner obtains his release or discharge in respect of his acting in relation to an insolvent, he forms the opinion that the value of that insolvent's assets is greater than the current specific penalty sum, a revised specific penalty sum shall be applicable on the submission within such time as may be specified in the bond of a cover schedule containing a revised value of the insolvent's assets;

(e) for the payment of losses of the kind mentioned in sub-paragraph (1), whether they arise during the period in which the insolvency practitioner holds office in the capacity in which he was initially appointed or a subsequent period where he holds office in a subsequent capacity;

(3) The terms of the bond may provide—

(a) that total claims in respect of the acts of the insolvency practitioner under all bonds relating to him are to be limited to a maximum aggregate sum (which shall not be less than £25,000,000); and

(b) for a time limit within which claims must be made.

4. Subject to paragraphs 5, 6 and 7, the amount of the specific penalty in respect of a case in which the insolvency practitioner acts, shall equal at least the value of the insolvent's assets as estimated by the insolvency practitioner as at the date of his appointment but ignoring the value of any assets—

(a) charged to a third party to the extent of any amount which would be payable to that third party; or

(b) held on trust by the insolvent to the extent that any beneficial interest in those assets does not belong to the insolvent.

5. In a case where an insolvency practitioner acts as a nominee or supervisor of a voluntary arrangement under Part I or Part VIII of the Act, the amount of the specific penalty shall be equal to at least the value of those assets subject to the terms of the arrangement (whether or not those assets are in his possession) including, where under the terms of the arrangement the debtor or a third party is to make payments, the aggregate of any payments to be made.

6. Where the value of the insolvent's assets is less than £5,000, the specific penalty sum shall be £5,000.

7. Where the value of the insolvent's assets is more than £5,000,000 the specific penalty sum shall be £5,000,000.

8. In estimating the value of an insolvent's assets, unless he has reason to doubt their accuracy, the insolvency practitioner may rely upon—

(a) any statement of affairs produced in relation to that insolvent pursuant to any provision of the Act; and

(b) in the case of a sequestration—

(i) the debtor's list of assets and liabilities under section 19 of the Bankruptcy (Scotland) Act 1985;

(ii) the preliminary statement under that Act; or

(iii) the final statement of the debtor's affairs by the interim trustee under section 23 of the Bankruptcy (Scotland) Act 1985.

[7388]

PART 3
RECORDS RELATING TO BONDING AND CONNECTED MATTERS

9 Record of specific penalty sums to be maintained by insolvency practitioner

(1) An insolvency practitioner shall maintain a record of all specific penalty sums that are applicable in relation to any case where he is acting and such record shall contain the name of each person to whom the specific penalty sum relates and the amount of each penalty sum that is in force.

(2) Any record maintained by an insolvency practitioner pursuant to this paragraph shall, on the giving of reasonable notice, be made available for inspection by—

(a) any professional body recognised under section 391 of the Act of which he is or was a member and the rules of membership of which entitle or entitled him to act as an insolvency practitioner;

(b) any competent authority by whom the insolvency practitioner is or was authorised to act pursuant to section 393 of the Act; and

(c) the Secretary of State.

10 Retention of bond by recognised professional body or competent authority

The bond referred to in paragraph 3 shall be sent by the insolvency practitioner to—

(a) any professional body recognised under section 391 of the Act of which he is a member and the rules of membership of which entitle him to act as an insolvency practitioner; or

(b) any competent authority by whom the insolvency practitioner is authorised to act pursuant to section 393 of the Act.

11 Inspection and retention requirements relating to cover schedule—England and Wales

(1) This regulation applies to an insolvency practitioner appointed in insolvency proceedings under the Act to act—

(a) in relation to a company which the courts in England and Wales have jurisdiction to wind up; or

(b) in respect of an individual.

(2) The insolvency practitioner shall retain a copy of the cover schedule submitted by him in respect of his acting in relation to the company or, as the case may be, individual until the second anniversary of the date on which he is granted his release or discharge in relation to that company or, as the case may be, that individual.

(3) The copy of a schedule kept by an insolvency practitioner in pursuance of sub-paragraph (2) shall be produced by him on demand for inspection by—

(a) any creditor of the person to whom the schedule relates;

(b) where the schedule relates to an insolvent who is an individual, that individual;

(c) where the schedule relates to an insolvent which is a company, any contributory or director or other officer of the company; and

(d) the Secretary of State.

12 Inspection and retention requirements relating to the cover schedule—Scotland

(1) Where an insolvency practitioner is appointed to act in relation to a company which the courts in Scotland have jurisdiction to wind up, he shall retain in the sederunt book kept under rule 7.33 of the Insolvency (Scotland) Rules 1986, the principal copy of any cover schedule containing entries in relation to his so acting.

(2) Where an insolvency practitioner is appointed to act as interim trustee or permanent trustee or as a trustee under a trust deed for creditors, he shall retain in the sederunt book kept for those proceedings, the principal copy of any cover schedule containing entries in relation to his so acting.

13 Requirements to submit cover schedule to authorising body

(1) Every insolvency practitioner shall submit to his authorising body not later than 20 days after the end of each month during which he holds office in a case—

(a) the information submitted to a surety or cautioner in any cover schedule related to that month;

(b) where no cover schedule is submitted in relation to the month, a statement either that there are no relevant particulars to be supplied or, as the case may be, that it is not practicable to supply particulars in relation to any appointments taken in that month; and

(c) a statement identifying any case in respect of which he has been granted his release or discharge.

(2) In this regulation "authorising body" means in relation to an insolvency practitioner—

(a) any professional body recognised under section 391 of the Act of which he is a member and the rules of membership of which entitle him to act as an insolvency practitioner; or
(b) any competent authority by whom he is authorised to act as an insolvency practitioner pursuant to section 393 of the Act.

[7389]

SCHEDULE 3
RECORDS TO BE MAINTAINED—MINIMUM REQUIREMENTS

Regulation 13

Details of the insolvency practitioner acting in the case

1. The name of the insolvency practitioner acting in the case.

2. The identifying number or reference issued to the insolvency practitioner by a competent authority or any body recognised under section 391 of the Act.

3. The principal business address of the insolvency practitioner.

4. The name of—
(a) any body by virtue of whose rules the insolvency practitioner is entitled to practice; or
(b) any competent authority by whom the insolvency practitioner is authorised.

Details of the insolvent

5. The name of the person in respect of whom the insolvency practitioner is acting.

6. The type of the insolvency proceedings.

Progress of administration

7. As regards the progress of the administration of the case the following details if applicable—
(a) the date of commencement of the proceedings;
(b) the date of appointment of the insolvency practitioner;
(c) the date on which the appointment was notified to—
(i) the Registrar of Companies; or
(ii) the Accountant in Bankruptcy.

Bonding arrangements in the case

8. As regards the arrangements for security or caution in the case—
(a) the date of submission of the cover schedule which has the details of the specific penalty sum applicable in the case;
(b) the amount of the specific penalty sum;
(c) the name of the surety or cautioner;
(d) the date of submission to surety or cautioner of a cover schedule with any increase in the amount of the specific penalty sum;
(e) the amount of any revised specific penalty sum; and
(f) the date of submission to the surety or cautioner of details of termination of the office held by the insolvency practitioner.

Matters relating to remuneration

9. As regards the remuneration of the insolvency practitioner—
(a) the basis on which the remuneration of the insolvency practitioner is to be calculated; and
(b) the date and content of any resolution of creditors in relation to the remuneration of the insolvency practitioner.

PART IV
STATUTORY INSTRUMENTS

Meetings (other than any final meeting of creditors)

10. The dates of—
   (a) the meeting of members;
   (b) the date of first meeting of creditors—
      (i) to consider an administrator's proposals;
      (ii) to consider an administrative receiver's report;
      (iii) in liquidation or bankruptcy;
      (iv) to consider a voluntary arrangement proposal; or
      (v) according to a trust deed for creditors;
   (c) the date of the statutory meeting in sequestration; and
   (d) the dates and purposes of any subsequent meetings.

Disqualification of Directors

11. As regards the insolvency practitioner's duties under section 7 of the Company Directors Disqualification Act 1986 to report the conduct of directors—
   (a) the date a return under section 7 is due;
   (b) the date a return is submitted to the Secretary of State;
   (c) the date a conduct report is submitted to the Secretary of State; and
   (d) the date on which any further reports are submitted to the Secretary of State.

Vacation of office etc

12. The following details regarding the completion of the case—
   (a) the date of the final notice to, or meeting of, creditors;
   (b) the date that the insolvency practitioner vacates office; and
   (c) the date of release or discharge of the insolvency practitioner (or if there is no final meeting of creditors, the date of the final return of receipts and payments to the Secretary of State).

Distributions to creditors etc

13. As regards distributions—
   (a) in relation to each payment to preferential or preferred creditors—
      (i) the name of the person to whom the payment was made;
      (ii) the date of the payment;
      (iii) the amount of the payment;
   (b) in relation to each payment to unsecured creditors—
      (i) the name of the person to whom the payment was made;
      (ii) the date of the payment;
      (iii) the amount of the payment; and
   (c) in relation to each return of capital—
      (i) the name of the person to whom the return of capital was made;
      (ii) the date of the payment; and
      (iii) the amount of capital returned or the value of any assets returned.

Statutory Returns

14. As regards any returns or accounts to be made to the Secretary of State, the Registrar of Companies or the Accountant in Bankruptcy—
   (a) as regards each interim return or abstract of receipts and payments;
      (i) the date the return or abstract is due;
      (ii) the date on which the return is filed; and
   (b) as regards any final return or abstract of receipts and payments—
      (i) the date that the return or abstract is due; and
      (ii) the date on which the return is filed.

Time recording

15. Records of the amount of time spent on the case by the insolvency practitioner and any persons assigned to assist in the administration of the case.

[7390]

COMPANIES ACT 1985 (POWER TO ENTER AND REMAIN ON PREMISES: PROCEDURAL) REGULATIONS 2005

(SI 2005/684)

NOTES

Made: 9 March 2005.

Authority: CA 1985, s 453B(4), (7).

Commencement: 6 April 2005 (see reg 1 at **[7391]**). Where any provision in this work (including any inserted or substituted provision) came into force for all purposes on or before 1 July 2005, commencement information is not noted at provision level.

As of 1 July 2007, these Regulations had not been amended.

Application to limited liability partnerships: see the draft Limited Liability Partnerships (Amendment) Regulations 2007 in Appendix 10 at **[A10]**. Those draft Regulations amend the Limited Liability Partnerships Regulations 2001, SI 2001/1090, Sch 6, Pt I at **[6998]** by adding an entry for these Regulations.

1 Citation, commencement and interpretation

(1) These Regulations may be cited as the Companies Act 1985 (Power to Enter and Remain on Premises: Procedural) Regulations 2005 and shall come into force on 6 April 2005.

(2) In these Regulations "the 1985 Act" means the Companies Act 1985.

(3) References in regulations 2 and 3 to sections are references to those sections of the 1985 Act.

[7391]

2 Prescribed contents of the written statement given under section 453B(4) or sent under section 453B(5)

The written statement which section 453B(4) requires the inspector or investigator to give to an appropriate recipient (or which section 453B(5), where it applies, requires him to send to the company) must contain the following information—

(a) a statement that the inspector or investigator has been appointed or (as the case may be) authorised by the Secretary of State to carry out an investigation and a reference to the enactment under which that appointment or authorisation was made;

(b) a statement that the inspector or investigator has been authorised by the Secretary of State under section 453A to exercise the powers in that section;

(c) a description of the conditions which are required by section 453A(1) to be satisfied before an inspector or investigator can act under section 453A(2);

(d) a description of the powers in sub-section 453A(2);

(e) a statement that the inspector or investigator must, at the time he seeks to enter premises under section 453A, produce evidence of his identity and evidence of his appointment or authorisation (as the case may be);

(f) a statement that any person accompanying the inspector or investigator when the inspector or investigator seeks to enter the premises must, at that time, produce evidence of his identity;

(g) a statement that entry to premises under section 453A may be refused to an inspector, investigator or other person who fails to produce the evidence referred to (in the case of an inspector or investigator) in paragraph (e) or (in the case of any other person) in paragraph (f);

(h) a statement that the company, occupier and the persons present on the premises may be required by the inspector or investigator, while he is on the premises, to comply with any powers the inspector or investigator may have by virtue of his appointment or authorisation (as the case may be) to require documents or information;

PART IV
STATUTORY INSTRUMENTS

(i) a statement that the inspector or investigator is not permitted to use any force in exercising his powers under section 453A and is not permitted during the course of his visit to search the premises or to seize any document or other thing on the premises;

(j) a description of the effect of section 453C as it relates to a requirement imposed by an inspector or investigator under section 453A;

(k) a statement that it is an offence under section 453A(5) intentionally to obstruct an inspector, investigator or other person lawfully acting under section 453A;

(l) a description of the inspector's or investigator's obligations under section 453B(6) and (7) to prepare a written record of the visit and to give a copy of the record, when requested, to the company and any other occupier of the premises; and

(m) information about how any person entitled under section 453B(6) to receive a copy of that record can request it.

[7392]

3 Prescribed contents of the written record prepared under section 453B(6)

The written record which section 453B(6) requires an inspector or investigator to prepare must contain the following information—

(a) the name by which the company in relation to which the powers under section 453A were exercised was registered at the time of the authorisation under section 453A(1)(a);

(b) the company's registered number at that time;

(c) the postal address of the premises visited;

(d) the name of the inspector or investigator who visited the premises and the name of any person accompanying him;

(e) the date and time when the inspector or investigator entered the premises and the duration of his visit;

(f) the name (if known by the inspector or investigator) of the person to whom the inspector or investigator and any person accompanying him produced evidence of their identity under section 453B(3);

(g) the name (if known by the inspector or investigator) of the person to whom the inspector or investigator produced evidence of his appointment or authorisation (as the case may be) as required by section 453B(3);

(h) if the inspector or investigator does not know the name of the person to whom he produced evidence of his identity and appointment or authorisation as required by section 453B(3), an account of how he produced that evidence under that section;

(i) if the inspector or investigator does not know the name of the person to whom any person accompanying the inspector or investigator produced evidence of his identity under section 453B(3), an account of how that evidence was produced under that section;

(j) the name (if known by the inspector or investigator) of the person who admitted the inspector or investigator to the premises or, if the inspector or investigator does not know that person's name, an account of how he was admitted to the premises;

(k) the name (if known by the inspector or investigator) of every appropriate recipient to whom the inspector or investigator, while on the premises, gave a written statement of powers, rights and obligations as required by section 453B(4);

(l) if the inspector or investigator does not know the name of a person referred to in paragraph (k), an account of how the written statement was given to that person;

(m) the name (if known by the inspector or investigator) of any person physically present on the premises (to the inspector's or investigator's knowledge) at any time during the inspector's or investigator's visit (other than another inspector or investigator, a person accompanying the inspector or investigator or a person referred to in paragraph (k)) and with whom the inspector or investigator communicated in relation to the inspector's or investigator's presence on the premises;

(n) a record of any apparent failure by any person during the course of the inspector's or investigator's visit to the premises to comply with any requirement imposed by the inspector or investigator under Part 14 of the 1985 Act; and

(o) a record of any conduct by any person during the course of the inspector's or investigator's visit to the premises which the inspector or investigator believes amounted to the intentional obstruction of him, or anyone accompanying him, in the lawful exercise of the power to enter and remain on the premises under section 453A.

[7393]

REPORTING STANDARDS (SPECIFIED BODY) ORDER 2005

(SI 2005/692)

NOTES

Made: 11 March 2005.

Authority: CA 1985, s 257(4A)(a), (4B).

Commencement: 6 April 2005 (see art 1 at **[7393A]**). Where any provision in this work (including any inserted or substituted provision) came into force for all purposes on or before 1 July 2005, commencement information is not noted at provision level.

As of 1 July 2007, this Order had not been amended.

1 Citation and Commencement

This Order may be cited as the Reporting Standards (Specified Body) Order 2005 and shall come into force on 6th April 2005.

[7393A]

2 Specified Body

The body known as the Accounting Standards Board established under the articles of association of The Accounting Standards Board Limited is hereby specified for the purposes of the issuing of standards under regulations made under section 257(4A) of the Companies Act 1985

[7393B]

ACCOUNTING STANDARDS (PRESCRIBED BODY) REGULATIONS 2005

(SI 2005/697)

NOTES

Made: 11 March 2005.

Authority: CA 1985, s 256(1), (4).

Commencement: 6 April 2005 (see reg 1 at **[7393C]**). Where any provision in this work (including any inserted or substituted provision) came into force for all purposes on or before 1 July 2005, commencement information is not noted at provision level.

As of 1 July 2007, these Regulations had not been amended.

Limited liability partnerships: these Regulations apply, with modifications, to limited liability partnerships; see the Limited Liability Partnerships Regulations 2001, SI 2001/1090, reg 10, Sch 6, Pt I (at **[6998]**), and the Interpretation Act 1978, ss 17(2)(a), 23(1), (2).

1 Citation and Commencement

These Regulations may be cited as the Accounting Standards (Prescribed Body) Regulations 2005 and shall come into force on 6th April 2005.

[7393C]

2 Prescribed Body

The body known as the Accounting Standards Board established under the articles of association of The Accounting Standards Board Limited is hereby prescribed for the purposes of section 256(1) of the Companies Act 1985.

[7393D]

3 Revocation

The Accounting Standards (Prescribed Body) Regulations 1990 are hereby revoked.

[7393E]

4 Transitional Provision

Statements of standard accounting practice which have been issued and not withdrawn by The Accounting Standards Board Limited for the purposes of section 256(1) of the Companies

Act 1985 immediately before 6th April 2005 shall be treated on and after that date as statements of standard accounting practice issued by the Accounting Standards Board for the purposes of that section.

[7393F]

COMPANIES (DEFECTIVE ACCOUNTS) (AUTHORISED PERSON) ORDER 2005

(SI 2005/699)

NOTES

Made: 11 March 2005.

Authority: CA 1985, s 245C(1), (4A), (5).

Commencement: 6 April 2005 (see art 1 at **[7393G]**). Where any provision in this work (including any inserted or substituted provision) came into force for all purposes on or before 1 July 2005, commencement information is not noted at provision level.

As of 1 July 2007, this Order had not been amended.

Limited liability partnerships: this Order applies, with modifications, to limited liability partnerships; see the Limited Liability Partnerships Regulations 2001, SI 2001/1090, reg 10, Sch 6, Pt I (at **[6998]**), and the Interpretation Act 1978, ss 17(2)(a), 23(1), (2).

1 Citation, commencement and interpretation

This Order may be cited as the Companies (Defective Accounts) (Authorised Person) Order 2005 and shall come into force on 6th April 2005.

[7393G]

2 In this Order—

(a) "the Act" means the Companies Act 1985;

(b) "the authorised person" means the body known as the Financial Reporting Review Panel established under the articles of association of The Financial Reporting Review Panel Limited.

[7393H]

3 Authorisation

The authorised person is hereby authorised for the purposes of section 245B of the Act.

[7393I]

4 The authorised person shall have satisfactory arrangements for recording decisions made in the exercise of the functions it exercises by virtue of its authorisation and for the safekeeping of those records which ought to be preserved.

[7393J]

5 Revocation

The Companies (Defective Accounts) (Authorised Person) Order 1991 is hereby revoked.

[7393K]

6 Transitional Provision

Any proceedings by The Financial Reporting Review Panel Limited under section 245B of the Act which are pending immediately before 6th April 2005 are to continue as proceedings by the authorised person.

[7393L]

SUPERVISION OF ACCOUNTS AND REPORTS (PRESCRIBED BODY) ORDER 2005

(SI 2005/715)

NOTES

Made: 15 March 2005.

Authority: Companies (Audit, Investigations and Community Enterprise) Act 2004, s 14(1), (5), (8).

Commencement: 6 April 2005 (see art 1 at **[7394]**). Where any provision in this work (including any inserted or substituted provision) came into force for all purposes on or before 1 July 2005, commencement information is not noted at provision level.

As of 1 July 2007, this Order had not been amended.

1 Citation, commencement and interpretation

This Order may be cited as the Supervision of Accounts and Reports (Prescribed Body) Order 2005 and shall come into force on 6th April 2005.

[7394]

2 In this Order—

(a) "listing" has the meaning given in section 74(5) of the Financial Services and Markets Act 2000;

(b) "the prescribed body" means the body known as the Financial Reporting Review Panel established under the articles of association of The Financial Reporting Review Panel Limited;

[7395]

3 Appointment

The prescribed body is hereby appointed to exercise the functions mentioned in section 14(2) of the Companies (Audit, Investigations and Community Enterprise) Act 2004 in respect of any issuer of listed securities which is:

(a) a body corporate incorporated or otherwise formed under the law of, or of a part of, the United Kingdom; or

(b) a body corporate incorporated or otherwise formed under the law of a place outside the United Kingdom where:

(i) any of the listed securities which that body corporate issues are in the form of shares comprised in the issued share capital of the body corporate, or securities convertible into such shares, with the exception of:

(aa) shares in any part of the issued share capital of the body corporate which, neither in relation to dividends nor in relation to capital, carry any right to participate beyond a specified amount in a distribution; or

(bb) securities convertible into such shares; and

(ii) the listing of the shares or other securities referred to in sub-paragraph (i) is a primary listing under listing rules.

[7396]

4 The prescribed body shall have satisfactory arrangements for recording decisions made in the exercise of the functions it exercises by virtue of its appointment and for the safeguarding of those records which ought to be preserved.

[7397]

PROSPECTUS REGULATIONS 2005 (NOTE)

(SI 2005/1433)

NOTES

Made: 26 May 2005.

Authority: European Communities Act 1972, s 2(2).

Commencement: 1 July 2005.

These Regulations implement Directive 2003/71/EC of the European Parliament and of the Council of 4th November 2003 on the prospectus to be published when securities are offered to the public or admitted to trading on a regulated market ("the prospectus directive") at **[9460]**. They substitute FSMA 2000, ss 84–87 with new ss 84–87, 87A–87R (at **[2084]**–**[2087R]**) and replace Sch 11 to that Act with a new Sch 11A (Transferable Securities at **[2450A]** et seq). These Regulations also revoke the Public Offers of Securities Regulations 1995 (SI 1995/1537) and the Financial Services and Markets Act 2000 (Offers of Securities) Order 2001 (SI 2001/2958), and make minor and consequential amendments to CA 1989, the Companies (Audit, Investigations and Community Enterprise) Act 2004, and the Financial Services and Markets Act 2000 (Official Listing of Securities) Regulations 2001 (SI 2001/2956). All amendments have been incorporated at the appropriate place in this Handbook.

As of 1 July 2007, these Regulations had not been amended.

[7398]

COMMUNITY INTEREST COMPANY REGULATIONS 2005

(SI 2005/1788)

NOTES

Made: 30 June 2005.

Authority: Companies (Audit, Investigations and Community Enterprise) Act 2004, ss 30(1)–(4), (7), 31, 32(3), (4), (6), 34(3), 35(4)–(6), 36(2), 37(7), 47(12), (13), 57(1), (2), 58, 59(1), 62(2), (3), Sch 4, para 4.

Commencement: 1 July 2005 (see reg 1 at **[7399]**). Where any provision in this work (including any inserted or substituted provision) came into force for all purposes on or before 1 July 2005, commencement information is not noted at provision level.

These Regulations are reproduced as amended by: the Charities and Trustee Investment (Scotland) Act 2005 (Consequential Provisions and Modifications) Order 2006, SI 2006/242; the Companies Act 2006 (Commencement No 2, Consequential Amendments, Transitional Provisions and Savings) Order 2007, SI 2007/1093.

ARRANGEMENT OF REGULATIONS

PART 7
COMMUNITY INTEREST COMPANY REPORT

PART 8
MANAGERS

PART 9
THE REGISTRAR OF COMPANIES

PART 11
THE APPEAL OFFICER

SCHEDULES

PART 1
CITATION, COMMENCEMENT AND INTERPRETATION

1 Citation and commencement

These Regulations may be cited as the Community Interest Company Regulations 2005 and shall come into force on 1 July 2005.

[7399]

2 Interpretation

In these Regulations—

"the 1985 Act" means the Companies Act 1985;

["the 1986 Order" means the Companies (Northern Ireland) Order 1986;]

"the 2004 Act" means the Companies (Audit, Investigations and Community Enterprise) Act 2004;

"aggregate dividend cap" means a cap set under regulation 22 for the purposes of determining maximum aggregate dividends;

"appellant" means, in respect of an appeal to the Appeal Officer, the person bringing the appeal;

"applicable share dividend cap" has the meaning given in regulation 18(2) and (3);

"applicable interest cap" has the meaning given in regulation 21(3);

"asset-locked body" means—

(a) a community interest company, [or a charity]; or

PART IV
STATUTORY INSTRUMENTS

(b) a body established outside [the United Kingdom] that is equivalent to [either of those];

"community interest statement" means a statement in a form approved by the Regulator which—

(a) contains a declaration that the company will carry on its activities for the benefit of the community or a section of the community; and

(b) indicates how it is proposed that the company's activities will benefit the community (or a section of the community);

"distributable profits" means, in relation to a company, its accumulated, realised profits, so far as not previously utilised by distribution or capitalisation, less its accumulated, realised losses, so far as not previously written off in a reduction or reorganisation of capital duly made, and is to be interpreted in accordance with the provisions of section 263(3) of the 1985 Act [or Article 271(3) of the 1986 Order] relating to the meaning of a company's profits available for distribution;

"election" means any election to public office held in [the United Kingdom] or elsewhere;

"employee" means a person who has entered into or works under (or, where the employment has ceased, worked under)—

(a) a contract of service or apprenticeship; or

(b) a contract for services under which it is agreed that a specified individual is to perform services,

whether express or implied, and (if it is express) whether oral or in writing;

"employer" means the person by whom an employee is (or, where the employment has ceased, was) employed;

"exempt dividend" has the meaning given in regulation 17(3);

"governmental authority" includes—

(a) any national, regional or local government in [the United Kingdom] or elsewhere, including any organ or agency of any such government;

(b) the European Community, or any of its institutions or agencies; and

(c) any organisation which is able to make rules or adopt decisions which are legally binding on any governmental authority falling within sub-paragraph (a) or (b);

"interest cap" means a cap set under regulation 22 for the purpose of determining the maximum rate of interest payable under regulation 21;

"manager" means a person appointed by order under section 47(1) of the 2004 Act;

"maximum aggregate dividend" has the meaning given to it in regulation 19;

"maximum dividend per share" has the meaning given to it in regulation 18(1);

"paid up value" means, in respect of any share in a company, the sum of—

(a) so much of the share's nominal value as has been paid up; and

(b) any premium on that share paid to the company;

"performance-related rate" means any rate which is linked to the company's profits or turnover or to any item in the balance sheet of the company;

"political party" includes any person standing, or proposing to stand, as a candidate at any election, and any person holding public office following his election to that office;

"political campaigning organisation" means any person carrying on, or proposing to carry on activities—

(a) to promote, or oppose, changes in any law applicable in [the United Kingdom] or elsewhere, or any policy of a governmental or public authority (unless such activities are incidental to other activities carried on by that person); or

(b) which could reasonably be regarded as intended to affect public support for a political party, or to influence voters in relation to any election or referendum (unless such activities are incidental to other activities carried on by that person);

"public authority" includes—

(a) a court or tribunal; and

(b) any person certain of whose functions are functions of a public nature;

"referendum" includes any national or regional referendum or other poll held in pursuance of any provision made by or under the law of any state on one or more questions or propositions specified in or in accordance with any such provision;

"relevant company" means a community interest company which is a company limited by shares or a company limited by guarantee with a share capital;

"share dividend cap" means a cap set under regulation 22 for the purpose of determining maximum dividends per share;

"subsidiary" has the meaning given to it in section 736 of the 1985 Act [or Article 4 of the 1986 Order]; and

"unused dividend capacity" has the meaning given to it in regulation 20(2).

[7400]

NOTES

Definition "the 1986 Order" inserted, words in square brackets in definitions "asset-locked body", "election", "governmental authority", and "political campaigning organisation" substituted, and words in square brackets in definitions "distributable profits" and "subsidiary" inserted, by the Companies Act 2006 (Commencement No 2, Consequential Amendments, Transitional Provisions and Savings) Order 2007, SI 2007/1093, art 6(2), Sch 4, Pt 2, para 27, as from 6 April 2007.

PART 2
THE COMMUNITY INTEREST TEST AND EXCLUDED COMPANIES

3 Political activities not to be treated as being carried on for the benefit of the community

(1) For the purposes of the community interest test the following activities are to be treated as not being activities which a reasonable person might consider are activities carried on for the benefit of the community:

- (a) the promotion of, or the opposition to, changes in—
  - (i) any law applicable in [the United Kingdom] or elsewhere; or
  - (ii) the policy adopted by any governmental or public authority in relation to any matter;
- (b) the promotion of, or the opposition (including the promotion of changes) to, the policy which any governmental or public authority proposes to adopt in relation to any matter; and
- (c) activities which can reasonably be regarded as intended or likely to—
  - (i) provide or affect support (whether financial or otherwise) for a political party or political campaigning organisation; or
  - (ii) influence voters in relation to any election or referendum.

(2) But activities of the descriptions prescribed in paragraph (1) are to be treated as being activities which a reasonable person might consider are activities carried on for the benefit of the community if—

- (a) they can reasonably be regarded as incidental to other activities, which a reasonable person might consider are being carried on for the benefit the community; and
- (b) those other activities cannot reasonably be regarded as incidental to activities of any of the descriptions prescribed in paragraph (1).

[7401]

NOTES

Para (1): words in square brackets substituted by the Companies Act 2006 (Commencement No 2, Consequential Amendments, Transitional Provisions and Savings) Order 2007, SI 2007/1093, art 6(2), Sch 4, Pt 2, para 28, as from 6 April 2007.

4 Other activities not to be treated as being carried on for the benefit of the community

For the purposes of the community interest test, an activity is to be treated as not being an activity which a reasonable person might consider is an activity carried on for the benefit of the community if, or to the extent that, a reasonable person might consider that that activity benefits only the members of a particular body or the employees of a particular employer.

[7402]

5 Section of the community

For the purposes of the community interest test, any group of individuals may constitute a section of the community if—

- (a) they share a readily identifiable characteristic; and
- (b) other members of the community of which that group forms part do not share that characteristic.

[7403]

PART IV STATUTORY INSTRUMENTS

6 Excluded companies

For the purposes of section 35(6) of the 2004 Act, the following are excluded companies:

(a) a company which is (or when formed would be) a political party;

(b) a company which is (or when formed would be) a political campaigning organisation; or

(c) a company which is (or when formed would be) a subsidiary of a political party or of a political campaigning organisation.

[7404]

PART 3

REQUIREMENTS CONCERNING THE MEMORANDUM AND ARTICLES

7 Company without share capital

A community interest company which is a company limited by guarantee without a share capital must include in its memorandum or articles the provisions prescribed by Schedule 1.

[7405]

NOTES

Saving for provisions relating to community interest companies: the Companies Act 2006 (Commencement No 2, Consequential Amendments, Transitional Provisions and Savings) Order 2007, SI 2007/1093, Sch 6, para 4 (at **[7629]**) provides as follows—

"4 Saving for provisions relating to community interest companies

A community interest company in relation to which regulations 7 to 9 of the 2005 Regulations (matters to be included in memorandum and articles) were complied with immediately before the coming into force of this Order need not alter its memorandum or articles to take account of any amendment made by this Order.".

8 Company with share capital

A community interest company which is a company limited by shares or a company limited by guarantee with a share capital must include in its memorandum or articles either—

(a) the provisions prescribed by Schedule 2; or

(b) the provisions prescribed by Schedule 3.

[7406]

NOTES

Saving for provisions relating to community interest companies: see the note to reg 7 at **[7405]**.

9 Alternative provisions

(1) For paragraph 1(4)(a) of the provisions prescribed by Schedule 1, 2 or 3 a community interest company may substitute—

""charitable body" means [a charity or an equivalent body established outside the United Kingdom;]"

(2) If a community interest company makes the substitution permitted by paragraph (1), it must also for every reference to "asset-locked body" in paragraph 1(2) of the provisions prescribed by Schedule 1, 2 or 3 substitute a reference to "charitable body".

[7407]

NOTES

Para (1): words in square brackets substituted by the Companies Act 2006 (Commencement No 2, Consequential Amendments, Transitional Provisions and Savings) Order 2007, SI 2007/1093, art 6(2), Sch 4, Pt 2, para 29, as from 6 April 2007.

Saving for provisions relating to community interest companies: see the note to reg 7 at **[7405]**. Note that the substituted words in sub-s (1) previously read as follows "a charity, Scottish charity or a body established outside Great Britain that is equivalent to any of those persons".

10 Declaration of dividends

A relevant company must not include in its memorandum or articles any provision which purports to permit a dividend to be declared otherwise than by an ordinary or special resolution of its members.

[7408]

PART 4
PRESCRIBED DOCUMENTS

11 Prescribed formation documents

(1) For the purposes of section 36 of the 2004 Act, the prescribed formation documents are—

(a) a community interest statement signed by each person who is to be a first director of the company; and

(b) a declaration that the company, when formed, will not be an excluded company.

(2) The declaration referred to in paragraph (1)(b) must be in a form approved by the Regulator and must be made by each person who is to be a first director of the company.

[7409]

12 Prescribed conversion documents

(1) For the purposes of section 37 of the 2004 Act, the prescribed conversion documents are—

(a) a community interest statement signed by each person who is a director of the company;

(b) a declaration that the company is not an excluded company; and

[(c) either—

(i) a declaration that the company is not a charity, or

(ii) in the case of a company that is an English charity, a declaration that the Charity Commissioners have given the company the written consent required by section 39 of the 2004 Act].

(2) The declarations referred to in sub-paragraphs (b) and (c) of paragraph (1) must be in a form approved by the Regulator and must be made by each person who is a director of the company.

[7410]

NOTES

Para (1): sub-para (c) substituted by the Companies Act 2006 (Commencement No 2, Consequential Amendments, Transitional Provisions and Savings) Order 2007, SI 2007/1093, art 6(2), Sch 4, Pt 2, para 30, as from 6 April 2007.

Charity Commissioners: as to the abolition of the office of Charity Commissioner for England and Wales, the establishment of the Charity Commission for England and Wales, and the transfer of the functions, rights, liabilities, etc from the Charity Commissioners to the Charity Commission, see the Charities Act 2006, s 6.

PART 5
ALTERATION OF OBJECTS

13 Requirement for Regulator's approval

An alteration of the memorandum of a community interest company with respect to the statement of the company's objects does not have effect except in so far as it is approved by the Regulator.

[7411]

14 Documents to be delivered to registrar of companies

(1) If a copy of a special resolution under section 4(1) of the 1985 [or Article 15(1) of the 1986 Order] Act is delivered to the registrar of companies pursuant to section 380 of the 1985 Act [or Article 388 of the 1986 Order] (registration of resolutions), the company must also deliver—

(a) a community interest statement; and

(b) a statement, in a form approved by the Regulator, of the steps that have been taken to bring the proposed alteration to the notice of persons affected by the company's activities.

(2) The community interest statement and the statement under paragraph (1)(b) must be signed by each person who is a director of the company.

[7412]

NOTES

Para (1): words in square brackets inserted by the Companies Act 2006 (Commencement No 2, Consequential Amendments, Transitional Provisions and Savings) Order 2007, SI 2007/1093, art 6(2), Sch 4, Pt 2, para 31, as from 6 April 2007.

15 Decisions etc

(1) On receiving the copies of the special resolution under section 4(1) of the 1985 Act [or Article 15(1) of the 1986 Order], the community interest statement delivered under regulation 14(1)(a) and the statement delivered under regulation 14(1)(b), the registrar of companies must—

(a) forward a copy of each of the documents to the Regulator; and

(b) retain the documents pending the Regulator's decision.

(2) The Regulator must decide whether to approve the proposed alteration of the memorandum of the community interest company with respect to the statement of the company's objects.

(3) The Regulator may approve the proposed alteration if he considers that—

(a) the statement of the company's objects as altered by the special resolution will comply with the requirements imposed by and by virtue of section 32 of the 2004 Act;

(b) the company will satisfy the community interest test; and

(c) the company has taken reasonable steps to bring the proposed alteration to the notice of persons affected by its activities.

(4) In considering whether the company will satisfy the community interest test, the Regulator shall have regard to—

(a) the statement of the company's objects as altered by the special resolution;

(b) the community interest statement; and

(c) any other relevant considerations.

(5) The Regulator must give notice of the decision to the registrar (but the registrar is not required to record it).

(6) The registrar shall not—

(a) record the special resolution delivered pursuant to section 380 of the 1985 Act [or Article 388 of the 1986 Order];

(b) register any copy of the altered memorandum delivered pursuant to section 6 of the 1985 Act [or Article 17 of the 1986 Order]; or

(c) cause notice of that alteration to be published pursuant to [section 1077 of the Companies Act 2006] (public notice by registrar of receipt of documents),

unless and until the Regulator has given notice of a decision to approve the proposed alteration.

(7) If the Regulator gives notice of a decision to approve the proposed alteration, the registrar shall also—

(a) record the community interest statement; and

(b) record the statement delivered under regulation 14(1)(b).

(8) If the Regulator decides not to approve the proposed alteration of the memorandum of the community interest company with respect to the statement of the company's objects, the company may appeal to the Appeal Officer against the decision.

[7413]

NOTES

Para (1): words in square brackets inserted by the Companies Act 2006 (Commencement No 2, Consequential Amendments, Transitional Provisions and Savings) Order 2007, SI 2007/1093, art 6(2), Sch 4, Pt 2, para 32(a), as from 6 April 2007.

Para (6): words in square brackets in sub-paras (a), (b) inserted, and words in square brackets in sub-para (c) substituted, by SI 2007/1093, art 6(2), Sch 4, Pt 2, para 32(b)–(d), as from 6 April 2007.

16 Exemptions

Regulations 13 to 15 do not apply where a community interest company is to cease being a community interest company by becoming a charity or … and the special resolution to alter the memorandum of the company with respect to the statement of its objects is forwarded to the registrar of companies in accordance with section 54 of the 2004 Act.

[7414]

NOTES

Words omitted revoked by the Companies Act 2006 (Commencement No 2, Consequential Amendments, Transitional Provisions and Savings) Order 2007, SI 2007/1093, art 6(2), Sch 4, Pt 2, para 33, as from 6 April 2007.

PART 6
RESTRICTIONS ON DISTRIBUTIONS AND INTEREST

17 Declaration of dividends

(1) A relevant company may declare a dividend to its members only—

(a) to the extent that its memorandum and articles permit it to do so;

(b) if an ordinary or special resolution of the company's members has approved the declaration of the dividend; and

(c) if the declaration of the dividend does not cause—

(i) the total amount of dividend declared on any of the company's shares for the financial year for which it is declared to exceed the maximum dividend per share for that financial year; or

(ii) the total amount of all the dividends declared on shares in the relevant company for the financial year for which it is declared to exceed the maximum aggregate dividend for that financial year.

(2) Paragraph (1)(c) does not apply to a dividend if, or to the extent that, it is an exempt dividend.

(3) A dividend declared on a share in a relevant company is an exempt dividend if one of the conditions specified in paragraph (4) and one of the conditions specified in paragraph (5) is satisfied in respect of it.

(4) The conditions specified in this paragraph are—

(a) that the dividend is declared on a share which is held by an asset-locked body (but this condition is not satisfied in respect of a share which the directors recommending the dividend are aware is being held on trust for a person who is not an asset-locked body);

(b) that the dividend is declared on a share which is held on behalf of an asset-locked body (or is believed by the directors recommending the dividend to be so held).

(5) The conditions specified in this paragraph are—

(a) that the Regulator has consented to the declaration of the dividend;

(b) that the asset-locked body by or on behalf of which the share on which the dividend is declared is held (or on behalf of which the directors declaring the dividend believe that it is held) is named in the memorandum or articles of the company as a possible recipient of the assets of the company.

(6) If a relevant company has made the substitutions prescribed in regulation 9(2), references to "asset-locked body" in this article shall have effect as if there were substituted for them references to "charitable body", with the meaning prescribed in regulation 9(1).

[7415]

18 Maximum dividend per share

(1) The maximum dividend per share for a financial year is the dividend which a relevant company declares on a share when the total amount of dividend declared on that share for that year (when expressed as a percentage of the paid up value of the share) equals that share's applicable share dividend cap.

(2) The applicable share dividend cap of a share in a relevant company is the share dividend cap which had effect in relation to that share at the time that the share was issued or the company became a community interest company, whichever is the later.

(3) Where the expression of the applicable dividend cap includes reference to a rate or figure determined by any person other than the company, the Regulator or the Secretary of State [(in Northern Ireland, the Department of Enterprise, Trade and Investment for Northern

Ireland)], the maximum dividend per share for any financial year shall be calculated by reference to that rate or figure as it had effect at the beginning of the first day of that financial year.

[7416]

NOTES

Para (3): words in square brackets inserted by the Companies Act 2006 (Commencement No 2, Consequential Amendments, Transitional Provisions and Savings) Order 2007, SI 2007/1093, art 6(2), Sch 4, Pt 2, para 34, as from 6 April 2007.

19 Maximum aggregate dividend

The maximum aggregate dividend for a financial year of a relevant company is declared when the total amount of all dividends declared on its shares for that year, less the amount of any exempt dividends, equals (when expressed as a percentage of the relevant company's distributable profits) the aggregate dividend cap which had effect in relation to that company on the first day of the financial year in respect of which the dividends are declared.

[7417]

20 Carrying forward of unused dividend capacity from previous financial years

(1) Notwithstanding regulation 17(1)(c)(i), but subject to regulation 17(1)(c)(ii), the total amount of dividends declared on a share in a relevant company for a financial year may, subject to the company's articles, include the whole or any part of the share's unused dividend capacity.

(2) For the purposes of this regulation, a share's unused dividend capacity is A minus B where—

A is the aggregate of any sums by which, for any of the four financial years immediately preceding the financial year for which a dividend is to be declared under this regulation, the total amount of dividend declared and paid on the share for that financial year was less than the maximum dividend per share for that financial year; and

B is any part of A which has already been distributed by way of a dividend declared and paid for a previous financial year.

[7418]

21 The interest cap

(1) This regulation applies to debentures issued by, and debts of, a community interest company in respect of which—

(a) a performance-related rate of interest is payable; and

(b) the agreement to pay interest at a performance-related rate was entered into by the company on or after the date on which it became a community interest company.

(2) In connection with debentures and debts of the kind specified in paragraph (1), a community interest company shall not be liable to pay, and shall not pay, interest at a higher rate than the applicable interest cap.

(3) The applicable interest cap is the interest cap which had effect at the time that the agreement to pay interest at a performance-related rate was made.

(4) Where the expression of the interest cap includes reference to a rate or figure determined by any person other than the company, the Regulator or the Secretary of State [(in Northern Ireland, the Department of Enterprise, Trade and Investment for Northern Ireland)], the interest payable on any debt or debenture to which the interest cap applies shall be calculated by reference to that rate or figure as it had effect at the beginning of the first day of the financial year in which the interest became due.

(5) Nothing in paragraph (2) shall be taken as releasing a community interest company from liability to pay, or as preventing a community interest company from paying—

(a) interest which accrued before the company became a community interest company; or

(b) arrears of interest which if it had been paid at the time it became due would not have breached paragraph (2).

[7419]

NOTES

Para (4): words in square brackets inserted by the Companies Act 2006 (Commencement No 2, Consequential Amendments, Transitional Provisions and Savings) Order 2007, SI 2007/1093, art 6(2), Sch 4, Pt 2, para 35, as from 6 April 2007.

22 Initial level and subsequent variation of dividend caps and interest cap

(1) Subject to paragraph (3)—

(a) the share dividend cap shall be that percentage of the paid up value of a share in a relevant company which is 5 percentage points higher than the Bank of England's base lending rate;

(b) the aggregate dividend cap shall be 35 per cent of a relevant company's distributable profits; and

(c) the interest cap shall be that percentage of the average amount of a community interest company's debt, or the sum outstanding under a debenture issued by it, during the 12 month period immediately preceding the date on which the interest on that debt or debenture becomes due (determined in accordance with Schedule 4) which is 4 percentage points higher than the Bank of England's base lending rate.

(2) For the purposes of paragraph (1), the Bank of England's base lending rate is the base lending rate most recently set by the Monetary Policy Committee of the Bank of England in connection with its responsibilities under Part II of the Bank of England Act 1998.

(3) The Regulator may from time to time, with the approval of the Secretary of State, set a new share dividend cap, aggregate dividend cap, or interest cap.

(4) A new cap set under paragraph (3)—

(a) shall not take effect from a date less than three months after it is published; and

(b) subject to paragraphs (5) to (7), may result in a change to both the level of any cap and the way in which it is expressed.

(5) The share dividend cap must be expressed as a percentage of the paid up value of the shares to which it applies.

(6) The aggregate dividend cap must be expressed as a percentage of distributable profits.

(7) The interest cap must be expressed as a percentage of the average amount of a debt, or the sum outstanding under a debenture, during the 12 month period immediately preceding the date on which the interest on that debt or debenture becomes due (determined in accordance with Schedule 4).

(8) The Secretary of State may from time to time require the Regulator to review any cap set under this regulation.

[7420]

23 Distribution of assets on a winding up

(1) This regulation applies where—

(a) a community interest company is wound up under the Insolvency Act 1986 [or the Insolvency (Northern Ireland) Order 1989]; and

(b) some property of the company (the "residual assets") remains after satisfaction of the company's liabilities.

(2) Subject to paragraph (3), the residual assets shall be distributed to those members of the community interest company (if any) who are entitled to share in any distribution of assets on the winding up of the company according to their rights and interests in the company.

(3) No member shall receive under paragraph (2) an amount which exceeds the paid up value of the shares which he holds in the company.

(4) If any residual assets remain after any distribution to members under paragraph (2) (the "remaining residual assets"), they shall be distributed in accordance with paragraphs (5) and (6).

(5) If the memorandum or articles of the company specify an asset-locked body to which any remaining residual assets of the company should be distributed, then, unless either of the

conditions specified in sub-paragraphs (b) and (c) of paragraph (6) is satisfied, the remaining residual assets shall be distributed to that asset-locked body in such proportions or amounts as the Regulator shall direct.

(6) If—

(a) the memorandum and articles of the company do not specify an asset-locked body to which any remaining residual assets of the company should be distributed;

(b) the Regulator is aware that the asset-locked body to which the memorandum or articles of the company specify that the remaining residual assets of the company should be distributed is itself in the process of being wound up; or

(c) the Regulator—

(i) has received representations from a member or director of the company stating, with reasons, that the asset-locked body to which the memorandum or articles of the company specify that the remaining residual assets of the company should be distributed is not an appropriate recipient of the company's remaining residual assets; and

(ii) has agreed with those representations,

then the remaining residual assets shall be distributed to such asset-locked bodies, and in such proportions or amounts, as the Regulator shall direct.

(7) In considering any direction to be made under this regulation, the Regulator must—

(a) consult the directors and members of the company, to the extent that he considers it practicable and appropriate to do so; and

(b) have regard to the desirability of distributing assets in accordance with any relevant provisions of the company's memorandum and articles.

(8) The Regulator must give notice of any direction under this regulation to the company and the liquidator.

(9) This regulation has effect notwithstanding anything in the Insolvency Act 1986 [or the Insolvency (Northern Ireland) Order 1989].

(10) This regulation has effect subject to the provisions of the Housing Act 1996 and the Housing (Scotland) Act 2001.

(11) Any member or director of the company may appeal to the Appeal Officer against a direction of the Regulator made under this regulation.

[7421]

NOTES

Paras (1), (9): words in square brackets inserted by the Companies Act 2006 (Commencement No 2, Consequential Amendments, Transitional Provisions and Savings) Order 2007, SI 2007/1093, art 6(2), Sch 4, Pt 2, para 36, as from 6 April 2007.

24 Redemption and purchase of shares

A relevant company may not distribute assets to its members by way of the redemption or purchase of the company's own shares, unless the amount to be paid by the company in respect of any such share does not exceed the paid up value of the share.

[7422]

25 Reduction of share capital

A relevant company may not distribute assets to its members by way of a reduction of the company's share capital unless—

(a) the reduction is made by extinguishing or reducing the liability of any of the members on any of the company's shares in respect of share capital not paid up; or

(b) the amount to be paid by the company to members in paying off paid up share capital does not exceed the paid up value of their respective shares.

[7423]

PART 7
COMMUNITY INTEREST COMPANY REPORT

26 General

(1) Every community interest company report shall contain—

(a) a fair and accurate description of the manner in which the company's activities during the financial year have benefited the community;

(b) a description of the steps, if any, which the company has taken during the financial year to consult persons affected by the company's activities, and the outcome of any such consultation; and

(c) the information specified in paragraphs 1 to 14 of Part 1 of Schedule 6 to the 1985 Act [or paragraphs 1 to 14 of Part 1 of Schedule 6 to the 1986 Order] (chairman's and directors' emoluments, pensions and compensation for loss of office) save that the information specified in paragraphs 2 to 14 shall be given only in the case of a company which is not a quoted company.

(2) If, during a financial year, a community interest company has transferred any of its assets other than for full consideration—

(a) to any asset-locked body (other than by way of an exempt dividend); or

(b) for the benefit of the community other than by way of transfer to an asset-locked body,

its community interest report for that financial year shall specify the amount, or contain a fair estimate of the value, of such transfer.

(3) If—

(a) a community interest company has provided the information required by paragraph (1)(c) in its copy of the annual accounts for the year delivered to the registrar of companies under section 242(1) of the 1985 Act [or Article 250(1) of the 1986 Order]; and

(b) its community interest company report contains a statement that details of the remuneration of the directors of the company during the financial year may be found in the notes to the annual accounts of the company,

the community interest company report need not contain the information required by paragraph (1)(c).

[7424]

NOTES

Paras (1), (3): words in square brackets inserted by the Companies Act 2006 (Commencement No 2, Consequential Amendments, Transitional Provisions and Savings) Order 2007, SI 2007/1093, art 6(2), Sch 4, Pt 2, para 37, as from 6 April 2007.

27 Information about dividends

(1) This regulation applies to the community interest company report of any community interest company—

(a) which has declared, or whose directors propose to declare, a dividend for the financial year to which the report relates; or

(b) which has declared a dividend for any of the four financial years immediately preceding that financial year.

(2) The report must state—

(a) the amount of any dividend declared, or proposed to be declared, by the company on each of its shares for the financial year to which the report relates; and

(b) for each of the four financial years immediately preceding the financial year to which the report relates (in so far as the company was formed and trading during that period)—

(i) the amount of any dividend declared and paid on each of the company's shares; and

(ii) the maximum dividend per share in respect of each of the company's shares.

(3) The report must also explain how the declaration or proposed declaration of any dividend declared, or proposed to be declared, by the company in respect of the financial year to which the report relates complies, or will comply, with regulations 17 to 20.

(4) The explanation provided under paragraph (3) must include details of—

(a) in the case of an exempt dividend, why it is an exempt dividend;

(b) in the case of any other dividend—

(i) the applicable share dividend cap and the maximum dividend per share for each share on which the dividend has been, or is to be, declared;

(ii) the amount of any unused dividend capacity distributed or to be distributed as part of the dividend declared, or proposed to be declared; and

(iii) the maximum aggregate dividend,

and how each of these has been determined.

[7425]

28 Information about debts or debentures on which a performance-related rate is payable

(1) Where a community interest company has at any time during the financial year a debt outstanding, or a debenture in issue, to which regulation 21 applies, its community interest company report must state—

(a) the rate of interest payable on that debt or debenture as calculated over a 12 month period ending with the most recent date on which interest became payable in respect of that debt or debenture during the financial year; and

(b) the applicable interest cap applying to that debt or debenture,

and how each of these has been determined.

(2) Where the company has at any time during the financial year a debt outstanding, or a debenture in issue, to which regulation 21 does not apply, but on which a performance-related rate is payable, its community interest company report must state—

(a) the rate of interest payable on that debt or debenture as calculated over a 12 month period ending with the most recent date on which interest became payable in respect of that debt or debenture during the financial year; and

(b) why regulation 21 does not apply to that debt or debenture.

[7426]

29 Application of [provisions relating to the directors' report]

(1) The following provisions … shall apply to the community interest company report as they apply to the directors' report:

[section 234A of the 1985 Act or Article 242A of the 1986 Order] (approval and signing of directors' report);

[section 238 of the 1985 Act or Article 246 of the 1986 Order] (persons entitled to receive copies of accounts and reports);

[section 239 of the 1985 Act or Article 247 of the 1986 Order] (right to demand copies of accounts and reports);

[section 241 of the 1985 Act or Article 249 of the 1986 Order] (accounts and reports to be laid before company in general meeting);

[section 244 of the 1985 Act or Article 252 of the 1986 Order] (period allowed for laying and delivering accounts and reports);

[section 245(1) and (2) of the 1985 Act or Article 253(1) and (2) of the 1986 Order] (voluntary revision of accounts or directors' report); and

[section 252(1), (2) and (4) of the 1985 Act or Article 260(1), (2) and (4) of the 1986 Order] (election to dispense with laying of accounts and reports before general meeting).

[7427]

NOTES

Words in square brackets substituted, and words omitted revoked, by the Companies Act 2006 (Commencement No 2, Consequential Amendments, Transitional Provisions and Savings) Order 2007, SI 2007/1093, art 6(2), Sch 4, Pt 2, para 38, as from 6 April 2007.

PART 8
MANAGERS

30 Remuneration

(1) The Regulator is authorised to determine the amount of a manager's remuneration.

(2) The remuneration of a manager shall be payable out of the income of the community interest company in respect of which the manager was appointed.

(3) The Regulator is authorised to disallow any amount of remuneration of a manager if—

(a) the time specified in the notice referred to in regulation 32(2) has expired; and
(b) the Regulator—
  (i) has considered such representations, if any, as are duly made in response to such a notice; and
  (ii) is satisfied that the manager has failed in such manner as is set out in sub-paragraph (a)(i) or (ii) of regulation 32(1) and specified in such a notice.

[7428]

31 Security

The Regulator is authorised to require the manager to give security to him for the due discharge of the manager's functions within such time and in such form as the Regulator may specify.

[7429]

32 Failure and removal

(1) Where—
(a) it appears to the Regulator that a manager has failed—
  (i) to give security within such time or in such form as the Regulator has specified; or
  (ii) satisfactorily to discharge any function imposed on the manager by or by virtue of the order by which the manager was appointed or by regulation 33; and
(b) the Regulator wishes to consider exercising his powers under regulation 30(3) or paragraph (3) of this regulation,

the Regulator shall give the manager, whether in person or by post, a written notice complying with paragraph (2).

(2) A notice given to a manager under paragraph (1) shall inform the manager of—
(a) any failure under paragraph (1)(a) in respect of which the notice is issued;
(b) the Regulator's power under regulation 30(3) to authorise the disallowance of any amount of remuneration if satisfied as to any such failure;
(c) the Regulator's power under paragraph (3) to remove the manager if satisfied as to any such failure; and
(d) the manager's right to make representations to the Regulator in respect of any such alleged failure within such reasonable time as is specified in the notice.

(3) The Regulator may remove a manager (whether or not he also exercises the power conferred by regulation 30(3)) if—
(a) the time specified in the notice referred to in paragraph (2) has expired; and
(b) the Regulator—
  (i) has considered such representations, if any, as are duly made in response to such a notice; and
  (ii) is satisfied that the manager has failed in such manner as is set out in paragraph (1)(a)(i) or (ii) and specified in such notice.

[7430]

33 Reports

The manager must make such reports to the Regulator as the Regulator may from time to time require on such matters and in such form as the Regulator specifies.

[7431]

PART 9
THE REGISTRAR OF COMPANIES

34 Modifications and amendments

(1) The registrar of companies shall not cause to be published in the Gazette notice pursuant to [section 1077 of the Companies Act 2006] of the receipt of documents under sections 37 or 54 of the 2004 Act unless the registrar records those documents pursuant to sections 38(6) or 55(6) of the 2004 Act.

(2), (3) …

(4) For the purposes of Part 24 of the 1985 Act, these Regulations shall be regarded as provisions of Part 2 of the 2004 Act.

[7432]

NOTES

Para (1): words in square brackets substituted by the Companies Act 2006 (Commencement No 2, Consequential Amendments, Transitional Provisions and Savings) Order 2007, SI 2007/1093, art 6(2), Sch 4, Pt 2, para 39(a), as from 6 April 2007.

Para (2): amends CA 1985, ss 715A at **[587]**.

Para (3): revoked by SI 2007/1093, art 6(2), Sch 4, Pt 2, para 39(b), as from 6 April 2007.

35 Documents

(1) The registrar of companies shall, on receiving any notice under section 109(1) of the Insolvency Act 1986 [or Article 95 of the Insolvency (Northern Ireland) Order 1989] (notice by liquidator of his appointment) in relation to a community interest company, provide a copy of that notice to the Regulator.

(2) The registrar of companies shall, on receiving any copy of a winding-up order forwarded under section 130(1) of the Insolvency Act 1986 [or Article 110 of the Insolvency (Northern Ireland) Order 1989] (consequences of a winding-up order) in relation to a community interest company, provide the Regulator with a copy of that winding-up order.

[7433]

NOTES

Words in square brackets inserted by the Companies Act 2006 (Commencement No 2, Consequential Amendments, Transitional Provisions and Savings) Order 2007, SI 2007/1093, art 6(2), Sch 4, Pt 2, para 40, as from 6 April 2007.

36 (*Pt 10 (reg 36: Fees payable by a community interest company); see Appendix 3 at* **[A3]**.)

PART 11
THE APPEAL OFFICER

37 Time limits

(1) Unless paragraph (2) applies, an appeal to the Appeal Officer must be made by sending a notice of appeal to the Regulator so that it is received within two months of the date upon which the appellant was given reasons for the disputed order or decision in accordance with section 61(5) of the 2004 Act.

(2) When an appeal is brought against a direction of the Regulator made under regulation 23, it must be made by sending a notice of appeal to the Regulator so that it is received within three weeks of the date upon which notice of the disputed direction was given to the community interest company in accordance with regulation 23(8).

(3) On receiving the notice of appeal, the Regulator must—

- (a) send an acknowledgement of its receipt to the appellant together with a copy of any statement made under paragraph (4); and
- (b) forward the notice of appeal to the Appeal Officer endorsed with the date of receipt.

(4) Where paragraph (2) applies, the Regulator must forward with the notice of appeal a statement—

- (a) of the date upon which notice of the disputed direction or decision was given to the community interest company in accordance with regulation 23(8); or
- (b) that no such notice was given.

[7434]

38 Notice of appeal

(1) The notice of appeal must state—

- (a) the name and address of the appellant; and
- (b) an address for service in [the United Kingdom].

(2) Unless regulation 37(2) applies, the notice of appeal must—

(a) specify as precisely as the appellant is able the date or dates on which the appellant was given reasons by the Regulator for the disputed order or decision; or

(b) include a statement that no such reasons were given.

(3) The notice of appeal must contain—

(a) a statement of the grounds for the appeal;

(b) details of the disputed order, decision or direction;

(c) a succinct presentation of the arguments supporting each of the grounds of appeal; and

(d) a schedule listing all the documents annexed to the notice of appeal.

(4) There shall be annexed to the notice of appeal—

(a) in the case of a disputed order or decision, a copy of any reasons given by the Regulator under section 61(5) of the 2004 Act; and

(b) as far as practicable a copy of every document on which the appellant relies.

(5) The notice of appeal must be signed and dated by the appellant, or on his behalf by his duly authorised officer or his legal representative.

[7435]

NOTES

Para (1): words in square brackets substituted by the Companies Act 2006 (Commencement No 2, Consequential Amendments, Transitional Provisions and Savings) Order 2007, SI 2007/1093, art 6(2), Sch 4, Pt 2, para 41, as from 6 April 2007.

---

39 Appeal procedure etc

(1) The Regulator may make a written response to the notice of appeal.

(2) Any such written response must be sent to the Appeal Officer so that it is received by him within two weeks of the date on which the Regulator received the notice of appeal or such further time as the Appeal Officer may allow.

(3) The Appeal Officer must send a copy of the written response to the appellant.

(4) The Appeal Officer may give the appellant and the Regulator the opportunity to make further written or oral representations.

(5) The Appeal Officer may specify the time and manner in which such further representations are to be made.

(6) The Appeal Officer may—

(a) make enquiries of any person;

(b) receive representations from any person;

(c) hold any meeting or hearing; and

(d) subject to these Regulations, follow such practice and procedure,

as he thinks fit, having regard to the just, expeditious and economical conduct of the appeal.

(7) The Appeal Officer may specify the time and place at which any meeting or hearing is to be held.

[7436]

40 Determination of appeal

In determining an appeal, the Appeal Officer shall have regard to all matters that appear to him to be relevant.

[7437]

41 Dismissal of appeal

(1) The Appeal Officer may dismiss an appeal at any stage if he considers that—

(a) the notice of appeal discloses no valid ground of appeal;

(b) the notice of appeal fails to comply with the requirements of regulation 38; or

(c) the appellant is not entitled to bring the appeal.

(2) The Appeal Officer must dismiss an appeal if he considers that the appeal was not brought within the time limits imposed by regulation 37 unless he is satisfied that the circumstances are exceptional.

(3) The Appeal Officer may dismiss an appeal at any stage at the request of the appellant.

[7438]

42 Reasons

(1) The Appeal Officer must give reasons for a decision to—

(a) dismiss an appeal;

(b) allow an appeal; or

(c) remit a case to the Regulator.

(2) The reasons must be given to the Regulator and to the person bringing the appeal.

(3) The Appeal Officer must make such arrangements for the publication of the decisions listed in paragraph (1) and his reasons for them as he considers appropriate.

[7439]

SCHEDULES

SCHEDULE 1
PROVISIONS PRESCRIBED FOR THE MEMORANDUM OR ARTICLES OF A COMMUNITY INTEREST COMPANY LIMITED BY GUARANTEE WITHOUT A SHARE CAPITAL

Regulation 7

1.—(1) The company shall not transfer any of its assets other than for full consideration.

(2) Provided the conditions in sub-paragraph (3) are satisfied, sub-paragraph (1) shall not apply to—

(a) the transfer of assets to any specified asset-locked body, or (with the consent of the Regulator) to any other asset-locked body; and

(b) the transfer of assets made for the benefit of the community other than by way of a transfer of assets to an asset-locked body.

(3) The conditions are that the transfer of assets must comply with any restrictions on the transfer of assets for less than full consideration which may be set out elsewhere in the memorandum or articles of the company.

(4) In this paragraph—

(a) "asset-locked body" means—

(i) a community interest company, [or a charity]; or

(ii) a body established outside the United Kingdom that is equivalent to [either of those];

(b) "community" is to be construed in accordance with section 35(5) of the Companies (Audit, Investigations and Community Enterprise) Act 2004;

(c) …

(d) "the Regulator" means the Regulator of Community Interest Companies;

[(e) …]

(f) "specified" means specified in the memorandum or articles of association of the company for the purposes of this paragraph; and

(g) "transfer" includes every description of disposition, payment, release or distribution, and the creation or extinction of an estate or interest in, or a right over, any property.

2.—(1) The subscribers to the memorandum are the first members of the company.

(2) Such other persons as are admitted to membership in accordance with the articles shall be members of the company.

(3) No person shall be admitted a member of the company unless he is approved by the directors.

(4) Every person who wishes to become a member shall deliver to the company an application for membership in such form (and containing such information) as the directors require and executed by him.

(5) Membership is not transferable to anyone else.

(6) Membership is terminated if:

(a) the member dies or ceases to exist; or

(b) otherwise in accordance with the articles.

3.—(1) A person who is not a member of the company shall not have any right to vote at a general meeting of the company; but this is without prejudice to any right to vote on a resolution affecting the rights attached to a class of the company's debentures.

(2) No powers to appoint directors of the company may be given to persons who are not members of the company which immediately after their exercise could result in the majority of the directors of the company having been appointed by persons who are not members of the company.

(3) No powers to remove directors of the company may be given to persons who are not members of the company which immediately after their exercise could result in either—

(a) the majority of the remaining directors of the company having been appointed by persons who are not members of the company; or

(b) the number of directors removed during the current financial year of the company by persons who are not members of the company exceeding the number of the remaining directors of the company.

(4) However, sub-paragraphs (2) and (3) shall not prevent a director from appointing, or subsequently removing, an alternate director, if permitted to do so by the articles.

(5) In this paragraph, "financial year" has the meaning given in [section 223 of the 1985 Act or Article 231 of the 1986 Order].

4.—(1) Questions arising at a meeting of directors shall be decided by a majority of votes; in case of an equality of votes, the chairman shall have a second or casting vote.

(2) A director who is also an alternate director shall be entitled in the absence of his appointer to a separate vote on behalf of his appointer in addition to his own vote.

(3) Except as provided by sub-paragraphs (1) and (2) in all proceedings of directors each director must not have more than one vote.

[7440]

NOTES

Para 1: words in square brackets in sub-para (4)(a) substituted, and sub-paras (4)(c), (e) revoked, by the Companies Act 2006 (Commencement No 2, Consequential Amendments, Transitional Provisions and Savings) Order 2007, SI 2007/1093, art 6(2), Sch 4, Pt 2, para 42(a)–(c), as from 6 April 2007 (sub-para (4)(e) was previously substituted by the Charities and Trustee Investment (Scotland) Act 2005 (Consequential Provisions and Modifications) Order 2006, SI 2006/242, art 5, Schedule, Pt 2, para 12, as from 1 April 2006).

Para 3: words in square brackets in sub-para (5) substituted by SI 2007/1093, art 6(2), Sch 4, Pt 2, para 42(d), as from 6 April 2007.

SCHEDULE 2
PROVISIONS PRESCRIBED FOR THE MEMORANDUM OR ARTICLES OF A COMMUNITY INTEREST COMPANY LIMITED BY SHARES, OR LIMITED BY GUARANTEE WITH A SHARE CAPITAL

Regulation 8(a)

1.—(1) The company shall not transfer any of its assets other than for full consideration.

(2) Provided the conditions in sub-paragraph (3) are satisfied, sub-paragraph (1) shall not apply to—

(a) the transfer of assets to any specified asset-locked body, or (with the consent of the Regulator) to any other asset-locked body; and

(b) the transfer of assets made for the benefit of the community other than by way of a transfer of assets to an asset-locked body.

(3) The conditions are that the transfer of assets must comply with any restrictions on the transfer of assets for less than full consideration which may be set out elsewhere in the memorandum or articles of the company.

(4) In this paragraph—

(a) "asset-locked body" means—

(i) a community interest company, [or a charity]; or

(ii) a body established outside [the United Kingdom] that is equivalent to [either of those];

(b) "community" is to be construed in accordance with section 35(5) of the Companies (Audit, Investigations and Community Enterprise) Act 2004;

(c) …

(d) "the Regulator" means the Regulator of Community Interest Companies;

[(e) …]

(f) "specified" means specified in the memorandum or articles of association of the company for the purposes of this paragraph; and

(g) "transfer" includes every description of disposition, payment, release or distribution, and the creation or extinction of an estate or interest in, or a right over, any property.

2.—(1) The directors may refuse to register the transfer of a share to a person of whom they do not approve.

(2) They may also refuse to register the transfer unless it is lodged at the registered office of the company or at such other place as the directors may appoint and is accompanied by such evidence as the directors may reasonably require to show the right of the transferor to make the transfer, and by such other information as they may reasonably require.

(3) If the directors refuse to register such a transfer, they shall within two months after the date on which the transfer was lodged with the company send to the transferee notice of the refusal.

(4) The provisions of this paragraph apply in addition to any restrictions on the transfer of a share which may be set out elsewhere in the memorandum or articles of the company.

3.—(1) A person who is not a member of the company shall not have any right to vote at a general meeting of the company; but this is without prejudice to any right to vote on a resolution affecting the rights attached to a class of the company's debentures.

(2) No powers to appoint directors of the company may be given to persons who are not members of the company which immediately after their exercise could result in the majority of the directors of the company having been appointed by persons who are not members of the company.

(3) No powers to remove directors of the company may be given to persons who are not members of the company which immediately after their exercise could result in either—

(a) the majority of the remaining directors of the company having been appointed by persons who are not members of the company; or

(b) the number of directors removed during the current financial year of the company by persons who are not members of the company exceeding the number of the remaining directors of the company.

(4) However, sub-paragraphs (2) and (3) shall not prevent a director from appointing, or subsequently removing, an alternate director, if permitted to do so by the articles.

(5) In this paragraph, "financial year" has the meaning given in [section 223 of the 1985 Act or Article 231 of the 1986 Order].

4.—(1) Questions arising at a meeting of directors shall be decided by a majority of votes; in case of an equality of votes, the chairman shall have a second or casting vote.

(2) A director who is also an alternate director shall be entitled in the absence of his appointer to a separate vote on behalf of his appointer in addition to his own vote.

(3) Except as provided by sub-paragraphs (1) and (2) in all proceedings of directors each director must not have more than one vote.

[7441]

NOTES

Para 1: words in square brackets in sub-para (4)(a) substituted, and sub-paras (4)(c), (e) revoked, by the Companies Act 2006 (Commencement No 2, Consequential Amendments, Transitional Provisions and Savings) Order 2007, SI 2007/1093, art 6(2), Sch 4, Pt 2, para 43(a)–(c), as from 6 April 2007 (sub-para (4)(e) was previously substituted by the Charities and Trustee Investment (Scotland) Act 2005 (Consequential Provisions and Modifications) Order 2006, SI 2006/242, art 5, Schedule, Pt 2, para 12, as from 1 April 2006).

Para 3: words in square brackets in sub-para (5) substituted by SI 2007/1093, art 6(2), Sch 4, Pt 2, para 43(d), as from 6 April 2007.

SCHEDULE 3
ALTERNATIVE PROVISIONS PRESCRIBED FOR THE MEMORANDUM OR ARTICLES OF A COMMUNITY INTEREST COMPANY LIMITED BY SHARES, OR LIMITED BY GUARANTEE WITH A SHARE CAPITAL

Regulation 8(b)

1.—(1) The company shall not transfer any of its assets other than for full consideration.

(2) Provided the conditions in sub-paragraph (3) are satisfied, sub-paragraph (1) shall not apply to—

(a) the transfer of assets to any specified asset-locked body, or (with the consent of the Regulator) to any other asset-locked body;
(b) the transfer of assets made for the benefit of the community other than by way of a transfer of assets to an asset-locked body;
(c) the payment of dividends in respect of shares in the company;
(d) the distribution of assets on a winding up;
(e) payments on the redemption or purchase of the company's own shares;
(f) payments on the reduction of share capital; and
(g) the extinguishing or reduction of the liability of members in respect of share capital not paid up on the reduction of share capital.

(3) The conditions are that the transfer of assets—

(a) must comply with any restrictions on the transfer of assets for less than full consideration which may be set out elsewhere in the memorandum or articles of the company; and
(b) must not exceed any limits imposed by, or by virtue of, Part 2 of the Companies (Audit, Investigations and Community Enterprise) Act 2004.

(4) In this paragraph—

(a) "asset-locked body" means—
  (i) a community interest company, [or a charity]; or
  (ii) a body established outside [the United Kingdom] that is equivalent to [either of those];
(b) "community" is to be construed in accordance with section 35(5) of the Companies (Audit, Investigations and Community Enterprise) Act 2004;
(c) ...
(d) "the Regulator" means the Regulator of Community Interest Companies;
[(e) ...]
(f) "specified" means specified in the memorandum or articles of association of the company for the purposes of this paragraph; and
(g) "transfer" includes every description of disposition, payment, release or distribution, and the creation or extinction of an estate or interest in, or a right over, any property.

2.—(1) The directors may refuse to register the transfer of a share to a person of whom they do not approve.

(2) They may also refuse to register the transfer unless it is lodged at the registered office of the company or at such other place as the directors may appoint and is accompanied by such evidence as the directors may reasonably require to show the right of the transferor to make the transfer, and by such other information as they may reasonably require.

(3) If the directors refuse to register such a transfer, they shall within two months after the date on which the transfer was lodged with the company send to the transferee notice of the refusal.

(4) The provisions of this paragraph apply in addition to any restrictions on the transfer of a share which may be set out elsewhere in the memorandum or articles of the company.

3.—(1) A person who is not a member of the company shall not have any right to vote at a general meeting of the company; but this is without prejudice to any right to vote on a resolution affecting the rights attached to a class of the company's debentures.

(2) No powers to appoint directors of the company may be given to persons who are not members of the company which immediately after their exercise could result in the majority of the directors of the company having been appointed by persons who are not members of the company.

(3) No powers to remove directors of the company may be given to persons who are not members of the company which immediately after their exercise could result in either—

(a) the majority of the remaining directors of the company having been appointed by persons who are not members of the company; or

(b) the number of directors removed during the current financial year of the company by persons who are not members of the company exceeding the number of the remaining directors of the company.

(4) However, sub-paragraphs (2) and (3) shall not prevent a director from appointing, or subsequently removing, an alternate director, if permitted to do so by the articles.

(5) In this paragraph "financial year" has the meaning given in [section 223 of the 1985 Act or Article 231 of the 1986 Order].

4.—(1) Questions arising at a meeting of directors shall be decided by a majority of votes; in case of an equality of votes, the chairman shall have a second or casting vote.

(2) A director who is also an alternate director shall be entitled in the absence of his appointer to a separate vote on behalf of his appointer in addition to his own vote.

(3) Except as provided by sub-paragraphs (1) and (2) in all proceedings of directors each director must not have more than one vote.

[7442]

NOTES

Para 1: words in square brackets in sub-para (4)(a) substituted, and sub-paras (4)(c), (e) revoked, by the Companies Act 2006 (Commencement No 2, Consequential Amendments, Transitional Provisions and Savings) Order 2007, SI 2007/1093, art 6(2), Sch 4, Pt 2, para 44(a)–(c), as from 6 April 2007 (sub-para (4)(e) was previously substituted by the Charities and Trustee Investment (Scotland) Act 2005 (Consequential Provisions and Modifications) Order 2006, SI 2006/242, art 5, Schedule, Pt 2, para 12, as from 1 April 2006).

Para 3: words in square brackets in sub-para (5) substituted by SI 2007/1093, art 6(2), Sch 4, Pt 2, para 44(d), as from 6 April 2007.

SCHEDULE 4
CALCULATION OF THE AVERAGE DEBT OR SUM OUTSTANDING UNDER A DEBENTURE DURING A 12 MONTH PERIOD

Regulation 22(7)

1.—(1) The average amount of a debt or sum outstanding under a debenture during any 12 month period is the amount which satisfies the calculation set out in sub-paragraph (2).

(2) The calculation referred to in sub-paragraph (1) is A divided by B where:

A is the aggregate of the amount of the debt or the sum outstanding under the debenture as at the end of each day during the 12 month period; and

B is the number of days during that 12 month period.

(3) For the purposes of A in sub-paragraph (2) there shall be excluded any sums which represent interest which has accrued on that debt or debenture within that 12 month period.

(4) For the purposes of A in sub-paragraph (2) where the debt or debenture did not exist at the end of any day during the 12 month period, the amount of the debt or the sum outstanding under the debenture as at the end of that day shall be treated as being zero for the purposes of the calculation in A.

2. Where the amount of the debt or the sum outstanding under the debenture is not known as at the end of any particular date, the directors of the community interest company may, for the purposes of the calculation referred to in paragraph 1, substitute for the debt or the sum outstanding under the debenture such amount or sum as they estimate to be the amount of the debt or the sum outstanding under the debenture as at the end of that particular date.

[7443]

(*Sch 5 (Fees Payable to the Registrar of Companies); see Appendix 3 at* **[A3]**.)

COMPANIES ACT 1989 (DELEGATION) ORDER 2005

(SI 2005/2337)

NOTES

Made: 22 August 2005.

Authority: Companies Act 1989, ss 46(1), (2), 46A(4), Sch 13, para 11(3)(a), (d), (e).

Commencement: 5 September 2005.
As of 1 July 2007, this Order had not been amended.

ARRANGEMENT OF ARTICLES

1 Citation and commencement

This Order may be cited as the Companies Act 1989 (Delegation) Order 2005 and shall come into force on the fourteenth day after the day on which it is made.

[7444]

NOTES

Commencement: 5 September 2005.

2 Interpretation

In this Order—

(1) "the Act" means the Companies Act 1989;

(2) "designated body" means the body known as the Professional Oversight Board for Accountancy established under the articles of association of The Professional Oversight Board for Accountancy Limited; and

(3) "start date" means the date on which this Order comes into force.

[7445]

NOTES

Commencement: 5 September 2005.
Note that as from 5 May 2006 the Professional Oversight Board for Accountancy changed its name to the Professional Oversight Board.

3 Transfer of functions

(1) Except as provided in paragraph (2) and subject to the exception in section 46(2)(b) of the Act and the reservations in section 46(3) of the Act, all the functions of the Secretary of State under Part 2 of the Act (eligibility for appointment as company auditor) are hereby transferred to the designated body.

(2) The functions of the Secretary of State under section 50 of the Act (power to make consequential amendments) and under section 51 of the Act (power to make provision in consequence of changes affecting accountancy bodies) are not transferred by this Order.

[7446]

NOTES

Commencement: 5 September 2005.

4 Requirements concerning exercise of functions

(1) Subject to paragraph (2), before making any regulations by virtue of the functions transferred to it by this Order the designated body shall:

(a) publish the proposed regulations in such manner as appears to the body to be best calculated to bring them to the attention of persons who may be affected by the proposed regulations;

(b) publish at the same time a statement that representations in respect of the proposals may be made to the body within a specified period which shall not be less than 12 weeks following the date of publication of the proposed regulations; and

(c) have regard to any representations duly made in accordance with the statement before making the regulations.

(2) Paragraph (1) does not apply in any case in which the body considers that the delay involved in complying with that paragraph would be prejudicial to the public interest.

[7447]

NOTES

Commencement: 5 September 2005.

5 The designated body shall have satisfactory arrangements for recording decisions made in the exercise of the functions transferred by this Order and for the safekeeping of those records which ought to be preserved.

[7448]

NOTES

Commencement: 5 September 2005.

6 The designated body shall forthwith send to the Secretary of State a copy of any notification made, or any information given, by a recognised supervisory body to the designated body pursuant to a requirement under section 37 of the Act (matters to be notified to the Secretary of State).

[7449]

NOTES

Commencement: 5 September 2005.

7 Transitional and supplementary provisions

Any legal proceedings by the Secretary of State brought in or in connection with the exercise of any of the functions transferred by this Order which are in existence immediately prior to the start date are to continue as proceedings by the designated body.

[7450]

NOTES

Commencement: 5 September 2005.

8 Any requirement made by the Secretary of State under section 37 of the Act where any notice or information which is required to be given to the Secretary of State in accordance with that section has not been given before the start date shall be treated on and after the start date as a requirement made by the designated body.

[7451]

NOTES

Commencement: 5 September 2005.

9 Any application made to the Secretary of State before the start date in accordance with paragraph 1 of Schedule 11 or paragraph 1 of Schedule 12 to the Act in respect of which the Secretary of State has neither made nor has refused to make a recognition order shall be treated on and after the start date as an application made to the designated body.

[7452]

NOTES

Commencement: 5 September 2005.

10 Section 43(1), (2) and (4) of the Act shall have effect as if the references to the Secretary of State included a reference to the designated body.

[7453]

NOTES

Commencement: 5 September 2005.

COMPANIES (DISCLOSURE OF AUDITOR REMUNERATION) REGULATIONS 2005

(SI 2005/2417)

NOTES

Made: 25 August 2005.
Authority: Companies Act 1985, s 390B.
Commencement: 1 October 2005.
As of 1 July 2007, these Regulations had not been amended.
Limited liability partnerships: this Order applies, with modifications, to limited liability partnerships; see the Limited Liability Partnerships Regulations 2001, SI 2001/1090, reg 10, Sch 6, Pt I (at **[6998]**), and the Interpretation Act 1978, ss 17(2)(a), 23(1), (2).

ARRANGEMENT OF REGULATIONS

SCHEDULES

1 Citation, commencement and transitional provision

(1) These Regulations may be cited as the Companies (Disclosure of Auditor Remuneration) Regulations 2005 and shall come into force on 1st October 2005.

(2) These Regulations shall not apply to the accounts of a company for any financial year beginning before 1st October 2005; and the Companies Act 1985 (Disclosure of Remuneration for Non-Audit Work) Regulations 1991 shall not apply to the accounts of a company for any financial year beginning on or after that date.

[7454]

NOTES

Commencement: 1 October 2005.

2 Interpretation

(1) In these Regulations—

"the 1985 Act" means the Companies Act 1985;

"associated pension scheme" means, in relation to a company, a scheme for the provision of benefits for or in respect of directors or employees (or former directors or employees) of the company or any subsidiary of the company where—

(a) the benefits consist of or include any pension, lump sum, gratuity or other like benefit given or to be given on retirement or on death or in anticipation of retirement or, in connection with past service, after retirement or death, and

(b) either—

(i) a majority of the trustees are appointed by (or by a person acting on behalf of) the company or a subsidiary of the company, or

(ii) the company, or a subsidiary of the company, exercises a dominant influence over the appointment of the auditor (if any) of the scheme;

"director" has the meaning given in section 53(1) of the Companies Act 1989;

"parent" and "subsidiary" mean respectively a parent undertaking and a subsidiary undertaking as defined in section 258 of the 1985 Act which is a body corporate; and a "parent company" and a "subsidiary company" are respectively a parent and a subsidiary which is a company;

"remuneration" includes payments in respect of expenses and benefits in kind.

PART IV
STATUTORY INSTRUMENTS

(2) For the purposes of these Regulations—

(a) a company is small or medium-sized in relation to a financial year if it qualifies as small or medium-sized in relation to that year by virtue of section 247 of the 1985 Act and is entitled to the exemptions mentioned in section 246 or 246A (as the case may be) of that Act in its accounts for that year;

(b) references to an associate of a company are references to—

(i) any subsidiary of that company, other than a subsidiary in respect of which severe long-term restrictions substantially hinder the exercise of the rights of the company over the assets or management of the subsidiary; and

(ii) any scheme which is an associated pension scheme in relation to that company.

(c) a person is to be regarded as an associate of a company's auditors if he is a person specified as such by Schedule 1 to these Regulations.

[7455]

NOTES

Commencement: 1 October 2005.

3 Disclosure of remuneration: small and medium-sized companies

(1) In the notes to the annual accounts of a small or medium-sized company, there shall be disclosed the amount of any remuneration receivable by the company's auditors for the auditing of the accounts.

(2) Where remuneration includes benefits in kind, its nature and estimated money-value shall also be disclosed in the notes.

(3) Where more than one person has been appointed as a company's auditor during the period to which the accounts relate, separate disclosure is required in respect of remuneration of each such person.

[7456]

NOTES

Commencement: 1 October 2005.

4 Disclosure of remuneration: other companies

(1) In the notes to the annual accounts of a company which is not a small or medium-sized company, there shall be disclosed the amount of—

(a) any remuneration receivable by the company's auditors for the auditing of the accounts and

(b) subject to regulation 5(2), any remuneration receivable by—

(i) the company's auditors or

(ii) any person who was, at any time during the period to which the accounts relate, an associate of the company's auditors

for the supply of other services to the company or its associates.

(2) Where remuneration includes benefits in kind, its nature and estimated money-value shall also be disclosed in the notes.

(3) Separate disclosure is required in respect of the auditing of the accounts in question and of each type of service specified in Schedule 2, but not in respect of each service falling within a type of service.

(4) Separate disclosure is required in respect of services supplied to the company and its subsidiaries on the one hand and to associated pension schemes on the other.

(5) Where more than one person has been appointed as a company's auditor during the period to which the accounts relate, separate disclosure is required in respect of the remuneration of each such person and his associates.

[7457]

NOTES

Commencement: 1 October 2005.

5 Group accounts

(1) Group accounts shall comply with regulation 4(1)(b) as if the undertakings included in the consolidation were a single company, except where the group qualifies as small or medium-sized under section 249 of the 1985 Act and is not an ineligible group under section 248(2) of that Act.

(2) The notes to the individual accounts of—

(a) a parent company which is required to prepare and does prepare group accounts in accordance with the 1985 Act; and

(b) a subsidiary company where its parent is required to prepare and does prepare group accounts in accordance with the 1985 Act and the company is included in the consolidation,

need not disclose the information required by regulation 4(1)(b) if the group accounts are required to comply with paragraph (1) of this regulation and the individual accounts state that the group accounts are so required.

[7458]

NOTES

Commencement: 1 October 2005.

6 Duty of auditors to supply information

The auditors of a company shall supply the directors of the company with such information as is necessary to enable the disclosure required by regulation 4(1)(b) or 5(1) to be made.

[7459]

NOTES

Commencement: 1 October 2005.

7 Failure to make the required disclosure

Sections 233(5) and 245 to 245C of the 1985 Act shall apply in relation to a failure to make the disclosure required by regulations 3 and 4 as they apply in relation to a failure to comply with a requirement of the 1985 Act.

[7460]

NOTES

Commencement: 1 October 2005.

SCHEDULES

SCHEDULE 1
ASSOCIATES OF A COMPANY'S AUDITORS

Regulation 2(2)(c)

1. Each of the following shall be regarded as an associate of a company's auditors—

(a) any person controlled by the company's auditors or by any associate of the company's auditors (whether alone or through two or more persons acting together to secure or exercise control), but only if that control does not arise solely by virtue of the company's auditors or any associate of the company's auditors acting—

(i) as an insolvency practitioner in relation to any person,

(ii) in the capacity of a receiver, or a receiver or manager, of the property of a company or other body corporate, or

(iii) as a judicial factor on the estate of any person;

(b) any person who, or group of persons acting together which, has control of the company's auditors;

(c) any person using a trading name which is the same as or similar to a trading name used by the company's auditors, but only if the company's auditors use that trading name with the intention of creating the impression of a connection between them and that other person

(d) any person who is party to an arrangement with the company's auditors, with or without any other person, under which costs, profits, quality control, business strategy or significant professional resources are shared.

2. Where a company's auditors are a partnership, each of the following shall also be regarded as an associate of theirs—

(a) any other partnership which has a partner in common with the company's auditors;
(b) any partner in the company's auditors;
(c) any body corporate which is in the same group as a body corporate which is a partner in the company's auditors or in a partnership which has a partner in common with the company's auditors;
(d) any body corporate of which a partner in the company's auditors is a director.

3. Where a company's auditors are a body corporate (other than one which is also a partnership as defined in paragraph 4(c) below), each of the following shall also be regarded as an associate of theirs—

(a) any other body corporate which has a director in common with the company's auditors;
(b) any director of the company's auditors;
(c) any body corporate which is in the same group as a body corporate which is a director of, or has a director in common with, the company's auditors;
(d) any partnership in which a director of the company's auditors is a partner;
(e) any body corporate which is in the same group as the company's auditors;
(f) any partnership in which any such body corporate which is in the same group as the company's auditors is a partner.

4. For the purposes of this Schedule—

(a) "acting as an insolvency practitioner" shall be construed in accordance with section 388 of the Insolvency Act 1986;
(b) "partner" includes a member of a limited liability partnership;
(c) "partnership" includes a limited liability partnership and a partnership constituted under the law of a country or a territory outside Great Britain;
(d) a reference to "a receiver, or a receiver or manager, of the property of a company or other body corporate" includes a receiver, or (as the case may be) a receiver or manager, of part only of that property;
(e) a person able, directly or indirectly, to control or materially to influence the operating and financial policy of another person shall be treated as having control of that other person; and
(f) a body corporate is in the same group as another body corporate if it is a parent or subsidiary of that body corporate, or a subsidiary of a parent of that body corporate.

[7461]

NOTES

Commencement: 1 October 2005.

SCHEDULE 2
TYPES OF SERVICE IN RESPECT OF WHICH DISCLOSURE IS TO BE MADE

Regulation 4(3)

(Where a service could fall within more than one type, it shall be treated as falling within the first-mentioned.)

1. The auditing of accounts of associates of the company pursuant to legislation (including that of countries and territories outside Great Britain).

2. Other services supplied pursuant to such legislation.

3. Other services relating to taxation.

4. Services relating to information technology.

5. Internal audit services.

6. Valuation and actuarial services.

7. Services relating to litigation.

8. Services relating to recruitment and remuneration.

9. Services relating to corporate finance transactions entered into or proposed to be entered into by or on behalf of the company or any of its associates.

10. All other services.

[7462]

NOTES

Commencement: 1 October 2005.

TRANSFER OF UNDERTAKINGS (PROTECTION OF EMPLOYMENT) REGULATIONS 2006 (NOTE)

(SI 2006/246)

NOTES

These Regulations have been omitted from this Edition of the *Company Law Handbook* in order to create space for other legislation (ie, the Companies Act 2006 and the associated destination and derivation tables). They were printed in full in the 20th Edition of this work (at p 2668 et seq) and, as of 1 July 2007, they had not been amended since the publication of that Edition. These Regulations are, however, included in the CD version of this work (which may be ordered from the LexisNexis Butterworths Customer Services Department) and can be accessed in the online version of the *Company Law Handbook* which is updated fortnightly (at www.lexisnexis.com/uk/legal).

[7463]–[7482]

CROSS-BORDER INSOLVENCY REGULATIONS 2006 (NOTE)

(SI 2006/1030)

NOTES

These Regulations have been omitted from this Edition of the *Company Law Handbook* in order to create space for other legislation (ie, the Companies Act 2006 and the associated destination and derivation tables). They were printed in full in the 20th Edition of this work (at p 2681 et seq) and, as of 1 July 2007, they had not been amended since the publication of that Edition. These Regulations are, however, included in the CD version of this work (which may be ordered from the LexisNexis Butterworths Customer Services Department) and can be accessed in the online version of the *Company Law Handbook* which is updated fortnightly (at www.lexisnexis.com/uk/legal).

[7483]–[7508]

TAKEOVERS DIRECTIVE (INTERIM IMPLEMENTATION) REGULATIONS 2006

(SI 2006/1183)

NOTES

Made: 25 April 2006.
Authority: European Communities Act 1972, s 2(2).
Commencement: 20 May 2006 (see reg 1 at **[7509]**).
These Regulations are reproduced as amended by: the Companies (EEA State) Regulations 2007, SI 2007/732. See also the note below.

Revocation of these Regulations: these Regulations are revoked by the Companies Act 2006 (Commencement No 2, Consequential Amendments, Transitional Provisions and Savings) Order 2007, SI 2007/1093, art 7, Sch 5, as from 6 April 2007, subject to savings in Sch 6, paras 2, 3 to that Order (at **[7629]**) as follows—

"Savings for provisions relating to takeovers

2. The revocation of the Interim Regulations by article 7 does not affect the operation of Part 5 of those Regulations (squeeze-out and sell-out) in relation to a takeover offer where the date of the offer is before 6th April 2007.

3. The revocation of the Interim Regulations by article 7, and the coming into force of section 949 of the Companies Act 2006 (offence of disclosure in contravention of section 948), and in particular of section 949(2)(b), by virtue of article 2, does not affect the continued operation of regulation 8(2)(b) of the Interim Regulations in respect of offences committed prior to 6th April 2007.".

See also the Companies Act 2006, Part 28 (Takeovers etc) at **[S942]** et seq. The Takeovers Directive (Directive 2004/25/EC of the European Parliament and of the Council of 21 April 2004 on Takeover Bids) had to be implemented by 20 May 2006 and, as the Companies Act 2006 had not completed Parliamentary passage by that date, this was achieved by means of these Regulations. Part 28 was brought into force on 6 April 2007 (the same date as the revocation of these Regulations).

ARRANGEMENT OF REGULATIONS

PART 1
GENERAL

PART 2
THE TAKEOVER PANEL

CHAPTER 1
THE PANEL AND ITS RULES

CHAPTER 2
INFORMATION

CHAPTER 3
CO-OPERATION

CHAPTER 4
CONTRAVENTION OF RULES ETC

CHAPTER 5
MISCELLANEOUS AND SUPPLEMENTARY

PART 3
IMPEDIMENTS TO TAKEOVERS

CHAPTER 1
INTERPRETATION

CHAPTER 2
OPTING IN AND OPTING OUT

CHAPTER 3
CONSEQUENCES OF OPTING IN

CHAPTER 4
SUPPLEMENTARY

PART 4
DIRECTORS' REPORT ETC

PART 5
SQUEEZE-OUT AND SELL-OUT

SCHEDULES

PART 1
GENERAL

1 Citation and Commencement

These Regulations may be cited as the Takeovers Directive (Interim Implementation) Regulations 2006 and shall come into force on 20th May 2006.

[7509]

NOTES

Commencement: 20 May 2006.
Revoked, subject to savings, as noted at the beginning of these Regulations.

2 Interpretation

(*1*) *In these Regulations—*

"Code" means the City Code on Takeovers and Mergers and the Rules of Procedure of the Panel's Hearings Committee as they stand immediately before the day these Regulations are made and are expressed to have effect on 20th May 2006;

["EEA State" has the meaning given by Schedule 1 to the Interpretation Act 1978;]

"Panel" means the Panel on Takeovers and Mergers;

"regulated market" has the meaning given by Article 1(13) of Directive 93/22/EEC on investment services in the securities field;

"takeover bid" has the same meaning as in the Takeovers Directive;

"Takeovers Directive" means Directive 2004/25/EC of the European Parliament and of the Council on Takeover Bids;

PART IV
STATUTORY INSTRUMENTS

"voting rights" means rights to vote at general meetings of the company in question, including rights that arise only in certain circumstances;

"voting shares" means shares carrying voting rights.

(2) *In these Regulations "rules" means rules in the Code insofar as necessary to implement Articles 3.1, 4.2, 5, 6.1 to 6.3, 7 to 9 and 13 of the Takeovers Directive or arising out of or related to obligations in those Articles, including rules which—*

(*a*) *confer on the Panel the power to—*

(*i*) *give a direction to a person to secure compliance with a rule; or*

(*ii*) *order a person to pay compensation if he is in breach of a rule; or*

(*iii*) *impose sanctions on a person who has acted in breach of a rule or failed to comply with a direction;*

(*b*) *make provision for a decision of the Panel to be reviewed by a committee of the Panel and for a decision of that committee to be appealed to an independent tribunal;*

(*c*) *make provision for fees or charges to be payable to the Panel for the purpose of meeting its expenses;*

(*d*) *make provision subject to exceptions or exemptions;*

(*e*) *authorise the Panel to dispense with or modify the application of rules in particular cases and by reference to any circumstances;*

(*f*) *provide for the Panel to make rulings on the interpretation, application or effect of rules;*

(*g*) *provide for rulings in sub-paragraph (f) to have binding effect.*

(*3*) *For the purposes of regulations 8 and 24—*

(*a*) *"officer" includes director, manager or secretary;*

(*b*) *an officer is "in default" if he authorises or permits, participates in, or fails to take all reasonable steps to prevent, a contravention.*

(*4*) *Except as provided in paragraph (5), in these Regulations "court", in relation to a company, means—*

(*a*) *in Great Britain, the court having jurisdiction to wind up the company; and*

(*b*) *in Northern Ireland, the High Court.*

(*5*) *For the purposes of regulations 11, 17 and 22 "court" means the High Court or, in Scotland, the Court of Session.*

[7510]

NOTES

Commencement: 20 May 2006.

Revoked, subject to savings, as noted at the beginning of these Regulations.

Para (1): definition "EEA State" substituted by the Companies (EEA State) Regulations 2007, SI 2007/732, reg 7, as from 9 March 2007.

PART 2
THE TAKEOVER PANEL

CHAPTER 1
THE PANEL AND ITS RULES

3 The rules

The rules shall have effect.

[7511]

NOTES

Commencement: 20 May 2006.

Revoked, subject to savings, as noted at the beginning of these Regulations.

4 The Panel

(*1*) *For the purposes of these Regulations, a reference to the functions of the Panel is a reference to functions provided for in this Part.*

(2) *The Panel shall supervise takeover bids for the purposes of the rules.*

(3) The Panel may do anything that it considers necessary or expedient for the purposes of, or in connection with, its functions.

(4) The Panel may make arrangements for any of its functions to be discharged by—
(a) a committee or sub-committee of the Panel; or
(b) an officer or member of staff of the Panel, or a person acting as such.

[7512]

NOTES
Commencement: 20 May 2006.
Revoked, subject to savings, as noted at the beginning of these Regulations.

5 Publication of the Code

(1) The Code must be made available to the public, with or without payment, in whatever way the Panel thinks appropriate.

(2) A person is not to be taken to have contravened a rule if he shows that at the time of the alleged contravention the Code had not been made available as required by paragraph (1).

(3) The production of a document purporting to be a printed copy of the Code endorsed with a certificate signed by an officer of the Panel authorised by it for that purpose and stating—
(a) that it is a true copy of the Code, and
(b) that on a specified date the Code was made available to the public as required by paragraph (1),

is evidence (or in Scotland sufficient evidence) of the facts contained in the certificate.

(4) A certificate purporting to be signed as mentioned in paragraph (3) is to be treated as having been properly signed unless the contrary is shown.

(5) A person who wishes in any legal proceedings to rely on the Code may require the Panel to endorse a copy of the Code with a certificate of the kind mentioned in paragraph (3).

[7513]

NOTES
Commencement: 20 May 2006.
Revoked, subject to savings, as noted at the beginning of these Regulations.

CHAPTER 2
INFORMATION

6 Power to require documents and information

(1) The Panel may by notice in writing require a person—
(a) to produce any documents that are specified or described in the notice;
(b) to provide, in the form and manner specified in the notice, such information as may be specified or described in the notice.

(2) A requirement under paragraph (1) must be complied with—
(a) at a place specified in the notice; and
(b) before the end of such reasonable period as may be so specified.

(3) This regulation applies only to documents and information reasonably required in connection with the exercise by the Panel of its functions.

(4) The Panel may require—
(a) any document produced to be authenticated, or
(b) any information provided (whether in a document or otherwise) to be verified,

in such manner as it may reasonably require.

(5) The Panel may authorise a person to exercise any of its powers under this regulation.

(6) A person exercising a power by virtue of paragraph (5) must, if required to do so, produce evidence of his authority to exercise the power.

(7) The production of a document in pursuance of this regulation does not affect any lien that a person has on the document.

(8) The Panel may take copies of or extracts from a document produced in pursuance of this regulation.

(9) A reference in this regulation to the production of a document includes a reference to the production of—

- *(a) a hard copy of information recorded otherwise than in hard copy form; or*
- *(b) information in a form from which a hard copy can be readily obtained.*

(10) A person is not required by this regulation to disclose documents or information in respect of which a claim to legal professional privilege (in Scotland, to confidentiality of communications) could be maintained in legal proceedings.

[7514]

NOTES

Commencement: 20 May 2006.
Revoked, subject to savings, as noted at the beginning of these Regulations.

7 Restrictions on disclosure

(1) This regulation applies to information (in whatever form)—

- *(a) relating to the private affairs of an individual, or*
- *(b) relating to any particular business,*

that is provided to the Panel in connection with the exercise of its functions.

(2) No such information may, during the lifetime of the individual or so long as the business continues to be carried on, be disclosed without the consent of that individual or (as the case may be) the person for the time being carrying on that business.

(3) Paragraph (2) does not apply to any disclosure of information that—

- *(a) is made for the purpose of facilitating the carrying out by the Panel of any of its functions;*
- *(b) is made to a person specified in Part 1 of Schedule 1;*
- *(c) is of a description specified in Part 2 of that Schedule; or*
- *(d) is made in accordance with Part 3 of that Schedule.*

(4) Paragraph (2) does not apply to—

- *(a) the disclosure by an authority within paragraph (5) of information disclosed to it by the Panel in reliance on paragraph (3);*
- *(b) the disclosure of such information by anyone who has obtained it directly or indirectly from an authority within paragraph (5).*

(5) The authorities within this paragraph are—

- *(a) the Financial Services Authority;*
- *(b) an authority designated as a supervisory authority for the purposes of Article 4.1 of the Takeovers Directive;*
- *(c) any other person or body that exercises functions of a public nature, under legislation in an EEA State other than the United Kingdom, that are similar to the Panel's functions or those of the Financial Services Authority.*

(6) This regulation does not prohibit the disclosure of information if the information is or has been available to the public from any other source.

(7) Nothing in this regulation authorises the making of a disclosure in contravention of the Data Protection Act 1998.

[7515]

NOTES

Commencement: 20 May 2006.
Revoked, subject to savings, as noted at the beginning of these Regulations.

8 Offence of disclosure in contravention of regulation 7

(1) A person who discloses information in contravention of regulation 7 is guilty of an offence, unless—

- *(a) he did not know, and had no reason to suspect, that the information had been provided as mentioned in regulation 7(1); or* (*b*) *he took all reasonable steps and exercised all due diligence to avoid the commission of the offence.*

(2) *A person guilty of an offence under this regulation is liable—*

(*a*) *on conviction on indictment, to imprisonment for a term not exceeding two years or a fine (or both);*

(*b*) *on summary conviction, to imprisonment for a term not exceeding three months, or to a fine not exceeding the statutory maximum (or both).*

(3) *Where a company or other body corporate commits an offence under this regulation, an offence is also committed by every officer of the company or other body corporate who is in default.*

(4) *Proceedings for an offence under this regulation are not to be brought—*

(*a*) *in England and Wales except by or with the consent of the Secretary of State or the Director of Public Prosecutions;*

(*b*) *in Northern Ireland except by or with the consent of the Department of Enterprise, Trade and Investment or the Director of Public Prosecutions for Northern Ireland.*

[7516]

NOTES

Commencement: 20 May 2006.
Revoked, subject to savings, as noted at the beginning of these Regulations.

CHAPTER 3
CO-OPERATION

9 Duty of co-operation

(*1*) *The Panel must take such steps as it considers appropriate to co-operate with—*

(*a*) *the Financial Services Authority;*

(*b*) *an authority designated as a supervisory authority for the purposes of Article 4.1 of the Takeovers Directive;*

(*c*) *any other person or body that exercises functions of a public nature, under legislation in any country or territory outside the United Kingdom, that appear to the Panel to be similar to its own functions or those of the Financial Services Authority.*

(2) *The Financial Services Authority must take such steps as it considers appropriate to co-operate with—*

(*a*) *the Panel;*

(*b*) *an authority designated as a supervisory authority for the purposes of Article 4.1 of the Takeovers Directive;*

(*c*) *any other person or body that exercises functions of a public nature, under legislation in any country or territory outside the United Kingdom, that appear to the Financial Services Authority to be similar to those of the Panel.*

(*3*) *Co-operation may include the sharing of information that the Panel or the Financial Services Authority, as the case may be, is not prevented from disclosing.*

[7517]

NOTES

Commencement: 20 May 2006.
Revoked, subject to savings, as noted at the beginning of these Regulations.

CHAPTER 4
CONTRAVENTION OF RULES ETC

10 Failure to comply with rules about bid documentation

(*1*) *This regulation applies where there is a takeover bid to which the offer document rules apply.*

(2) *Where an offer document published in respect of the bid does not comply with offer document rules, an offence is committed by—*

(*a*) *the person making the bid; and*

PART IV
STATUTORY INSTRUMENTS

(*b*) *where the person making the bid is a body of persons, any director, officer or member of that body who caused the document to be published.*

(3) A person commits an offence under paragraph (2) only if—

(*a*) *he knew that the offer document did not comply, or was reckless as to whether it complied; and*

(*b*) *he failed to take all reasonable steps to secure that it did comply.*

(4) Where a response document published in respect of the bid does not comply with response document rules, an offence is committed by any director or other officer of the company for which the bid is made, who—

(*a*) *knew that the response document did not comply, or was reckless as to whether it complied; and*

(*b*) *failed to take all reasonable steps to secure that it did comply.*

(5) Where an offence is committed under subsection (2)(b) or (4) by a company or other body corporate ("the relevant body")—

(*a*) *subsection (2)(b) has effect as if the reference to a director, officer or member of the person making the bid included a reference to a director, officer or member of the relevant body;*

(*b*) *subsection (4) has effect as if the reference to a director or other officer of the company referred to in subsection (1) included a reference to the director, officer or member of the relevant body.*

(6) A person guilty of an offence under this regulation is liable—

(*a*) *on conviction on indictment, to a fine;*

(*b*) *on summary conviction, to a fine not exceeding the statutory maximum.*

(7) Proceedings for an offence under this regulation are not to be brought—

(*a*) *in England and Wales except by or with the consent of the Secretary of State or the Director of Public Prosecutions;*

(*b*) *in Northern Ireland except by or with the consent of the Department of Enterprise, Trade and Investment or the Director of Public Prosecutions for Northern Ireland.*

(8) Nothing in this regulation affects any power of the Panel in relation to the enforcement of its rules.

[7518]

NOTES

Commencement: 20 May 2006.
Revoked, subject to savings, as noted at the beginning of these Regulations.

11 Enforcement by the court

(1) If, on the application of the Panel, the court is satisfied—

(*a*) *that there is a reasonable likelihood that a person will contravene a rule-based requirement, or*

(*b*) *that a person has contravened a rule-based requirement or a disclosure requirement,*

the court may make any order it thinks fit to secure compliance with the requirement.

(2) Except as provided by paragraph (1), no person—

(*a*) *has a right to seek an injunction, or*

(*b*) *in Scotland, has title or interest to seek an interdict or an order for specific performance,*

to prevent a person from contravening (or continuing to contravene) a rule-based requirement or a disclosure requirement.

[7519]

NOTES

Commencement: 20 May 2006.
Revoked, subject to savings, as noted at the beginning of these Regulations.

12 No action for breach of statutory duty etc

(1) Contravention of a rule-based requirement or a disclosure requirement does not give rise to any right of action for breach of statutory duty.

(2) Contravention of a rule-based requirement does not make any transaction void or unenforceable or affect the validity of any other thing.

[7520]

NOTES

Commencement: 20 May 2006.
Revoked, subject to savings, as noted at the beginning of these Regulations.

13 Interpretation of Chapter 4

In this Chapter—

"contravene" includes fail to comply;

"contravention" includes failure to comply;

"disclosure requirement" means a requirement imposed under regulation 6;

"offer document" means a document required to be published by Rules 30.1 and 32.1 of the Code;

"offer document rules" means rules set out in Rules 24 and 27 of the Code to the extent that they are referred to in section 10(e) of the Introduction to the Code;

"officer" includes director, manager or secretary;

"response document" means a document required to be published by Rules 30.2 and 32.6(a) of the Code;

"response document rules" means rules set out in Rules 25 and 27 of the Code to the extent that they are referred to in section 10(e) of the Introduction to the Code;

"rule-based requirement" means a requirement imposed by or under rules.

[7521]

NOTES

Commencement: 20 May 2006.
Revoked, subject to savings, as noted at the beginning of these Regulations.

CHAPTER 5
MISCELLANEOUS AND SUPPLEMENTARY

14 Recovery of fees or charges

A fee or charge payable by any person by virtue of the rules is a debt due from that person to the Panel, and is recoverable accordingly.

[7522]

NOTES

Commencement: 20 May 2006.
Revoked, subject to savings, as noted at the beginning of these Regulations.

15 Panel as party to proceedings

In the exercise of its functions the Panel is capable (despite being an unincorporated body) of—

(*a*) *bringing proceedings under this Part in its own name;*
(*b*) *bringing or defending any other proceedings in its own name.*

[7523]

NOTES

Commencement: 20 May 2006.
Revoked, subject to savings, as noted at the beginning of these Regulations.

16 Exemption from liability in damages

(1) Neither the Panel, nor any person within paragraph (2), is to be liable in damages for anything done (or omitted to be done) in, or in connection with, the discharge or purported discharge of the Panel's functions.

(2) A person is within this paragraph if—

(*a*) *he is (or is acting as) a member, officer or member of staff of the Panel; or*

(b) *he is a person authorised under regulation 6(5).*

(3) *Paragraph (1) does not apply—*

(a) *if the act or omission is shown to have been in bad faith; or*

(b) *so as to prevent an award of damages in respect of the act or omission on the ground that it was unlawful as a result of section 6(1) of the Human Rights Act 1998 (acts of public authorities incompatible with Convention rights).*

[7524]

NOTES

Commencement: 20 May 2006.
Revoked, subject to savings, as noted at the beginning of these Regulations.

17 Privilege against self-incrimination

(1) *A statement made by a person in response to—*

(a) *a requirement under regulation 6(1), or*

(b) *an order made by the court under regulation 11 to secure compliance with such a requirement,*

may not be used against him in criminal proceedings in which he is charged with an offence to which this paragraph applies.

(2) *Paragraph (1) applies to any offence other than an offence under one of the following provisions (which concern false statements made otherwise than on oath)—*

(a) *section 5 of the Perjury Act 1911;*

(b) *section 44(2) of the Criminal Law (Consolidation) (Scotland) Act 1995;*

(c) *Article 10 of the Perjury (Northern Ireland) Order 1979.*

[7525]

NOTES

Commencement: 20 May 2006.
Revoked, subject to savings, as noted at the beginning of these Regulations.

18 Amendments and modifications to Financial Services and Markets Act 2000

(1) *Section 348 of the Financial Services and Markets Act 2000 does not apply to—*

(a) *the disclosure by an authority to which paragraph (2) applies of confidential information disclosed to it by the Financial Services Authority in reliance on subsection (1) of that section;*

(b) *the disclosure of such information by a person obtaining it directly or indirectly from an authority to which paragraph (2) applies.*

"Confidential information" has the meaning given by section 348(2) of that Act.

(2) *This paragraph applies to—*

(a) *the Panel;*

(b) *an authority designated as a supervisory authority for the purposes of Article 4.1 of the Takeovers Directive;*

(c) *any other person or body that exercises functions of a public nature, under legislation in an EEA State other than the United Kingdom, that are similar to the Financial Services Authority's functions or those of the Panel.*

(3)–(5) …

[7526]

NOTES

Commencement: 20 May 2006.
Revoked, subject to savings, as noted at the beginning of these Regulations.
Paras (3)–(5): amend the Financial Services and Markets Act 2000, ss 143, 349 at **[2143]**, **[2347]**.

PART 3
IMPEDIMENTS TO TAKEOVERS

CHAPTER 1
INTERPRETATION

19 Interpretation of Part

(1) In this Part—

"company" means—

(a) a company within the meaning of section 735 of the Companies Act 1985;

(b) an unregistered company within the meaning of section 718 of that Act;

(c) a company within the meaning of Article 3 of the Companies (Northern Ireland) Order 1986; or

(d) an unregistered company within the meaning of Article 667 of that Order;

"daily default fine" has the meaning in section 730(4) of the Companies Act 1985 (or in the case of Northern Ireland, Article 678(4) of the Companies (Northern Ireland) Order 1986;

"offeror" has the same meaning as in the Takeovers Directive;

"offer period", in relation to a takeover bid, means the time allowed for acceptance of the bid by—

(a) rules in the Code giving effect to Article 7(1) of the Takeovers Directive; or

(b) where the rules giving effect to that Article which apply to the bid are those of an EEA State other than the United Kingdom, those rules;

"opted-in company" means a company in relation to which—

(a) an opting-in resolution has effect; and

(b) the conditions in regulation 20(2) and (4) continue to be met;

"opting-in resolution" has the meaning given by regulation 20(1);

"opting-out resolution" has the meaning given by regulation 20(5);

"registrar" has the meaning in section 744 of the Companies Act 1985 (or in the case of Northern Ireland in Article 653(2) of the Companies (Northern Ireland) Order 1986).

(2) For the purposes of this Part—

(a) securities of a company are treated as shares in the company if they are convertible into or entitle the holder to subscribe for such shares;

(b) debentures issued by a company are treated as shares in the company if they carry voting rights.

[7527]

NOTES

Commencement: 20 May 2006.

Revoked, subject to savings, as noted at the beginning of these Regulations.

CHAPTER 2
OPTING IN AND OPTING OUT

20 Opting in and opting out

(1) A company may by special resolution (an "opting-in resolution") opt in for the purposes of this Part if the following three conditions are met in relation to the company.

(2) The first condition is that the company has voting shares admitted to trading on a regulated market.

(3) The second condition is that—

(a) the company's articles of association—

(i) do not contain any such restrictions as are mentioned in Article 11 of the Takeovers Directive; or

(ii) if they do contain any such restrictions, provide for the restrictions not to apply at a time when, or in circumstances in which, they would be disapplied by that Article; and

(b) those articles do not contain any other provision which would be incompatible with that Article.

(4) The third condition is that—

(a) no shares conferring special rights in the company are held by—

(i) *a minister,*
(ii) *a nominee of, or any other person acting on behalf of, a minister, or*
(iii) *a company directly or indirectly controlled by a minister, and*
(b) *no such rights are exercisable by or on behalf of a minister under any enactment.*

(5) *A company may revoke an opting-in resolution by a further special resolution (an "opting-out resolution").*

(6) *For the purposes of paragraph (3), a reference in Article 11 of the Takeovers Directive to Article 7(1) or 9 of that Directive is to be read as referring to rules in the Code giving effect to the relevant Article.*

(7) *In paragraph (4) "minister" means—*
(a) *the holder of an office in Her Majesty's Government in the United Kingdom,*
(b) *the Scottish Ministers,*
(c) *a Minister within the meaning given by section 7(3) of the Northern Ireland Act 1998,*

and for the purposes of that paragraph "minister" also includes the Treasury, the Board of Trade, the Defence Council and the National Assembly for Wales.

[7528]

NOTES

Commencement: 20 May 2006.
Revoked, subject to savings, as noted at the beginning of these Regulations.

21 Further provisions about opting-in and opting-out resolutions

(1) *An opting-in resolution or an opting-out resolution must specify the date from which it is to have effect (the "effective date").*

(2) *The effective date of an opting-in resolution may not be earlier than the date on which the resolution is passed.*

(3) *The second and third conditions in regulation 20 must be met at the time when an opting-in resolution is passed, but the first one does not need to be met until the effective date.*

(4) *An opting-in resolution passed before the time when voting shares of the company are admitted to trading on a regulated market complies with the requirement in paragraph (1) if, instead of specifying a particular date, it provides for the resolution to have effect from that time.*

(5) *The effective date of an opting-out resolution may not be earlier than the first anniversary of the date on which a copy of the opting-in resolution was forwarded to the registrar.*

(6) *Where a company has passed an opting-in resolution, any alteration of its articles of association that would prevent the second condition in regulation 20 from being met is of no effect until the effective date of an opting-out resolution passed by the company.*

[7529]

NOTES

Commencement: 20 May 2006.
Revoked, subject to savings, as noted at the beginning of these Regulations.

CHAPTER 3
CONSEQUENCES OF OPTING IN

22 Effect on contractual restrictions

(1) *The following provisions have effect where a takeover bid is made for an opted-in company.*

(2) *An agreement to which this regulation applies is invalid in so far as it places any restriction—*
(a) *on the transfer to the offeror, or at his direction to another person, of shares in the company during the offer period;*
(b) *on the transfer to any person of shares in the company at a time during the offer period when the offeror holds shares amounting to not less than 75% in value of all the voting shares in the company;*

(*c*) *on rights to vote at a general meeting of the company that decides whether to take any action which might result in the frustration of the bid;*

(*d*) *on rights to vote at a general meeting of the company that—*

(*i*) *is the first such meeting to be held after the end of the offer period; and*

(*ii*) *is held at a time when the offeror holds shares amounting to not less than 75% in value of all the voting shares in the company.*

(*3*) *This regulation applies to an agreement—*

(*a*) *entered into between a person holding shares in the company and another such person on or after 21st April 2004, or*

(*b*) *entered into at any time between such a person and the company,*

and it applies to such an agreement even if the law applicable to the agreement (apart from this paragraph) is not the law of a part of the United Kingdom.

(*4*) *The reference in paragraph (2)(c) to rights to vote at a general meeting of the company that decides whether to take any action which might result in the frustration of the bid includes a reference to rights to vote on a written resolution concerned with that question.*

(*5*) *For the purposes of paragraph (2)(c), action which might result in the frustration of a bid is any action of that kind specified by rules in the Code giving effect to Article 9 of the Takeovers Directive.*

(*6*) *If a person suffers loss as a result of any act or omission that would (but for this regulation) be a breach of an agreement to which this regulation applies, he is entitled to compensation, of such amount as the court considers just and equitable, from any person who would (but for this paragraph) be liable to him for committing or inducing the breach.*

(*7*) *A reference in this regulation to voting shares in the company does not include—*

(*a*) *debentures; or*

(*b*) *shares carrying rights to vote that, under the company's articles of association, arise only where specified pecuniary advantages are not provided.*

In sub-paragraph (b) "rights to vote" means rights to vote at general meetings of the company.

[7530]

NOTES

Commencement: 20 May 2006.

Revoked, subject to savings, as noted at the beginning of these Regulations.

23 Power of offeror to require general meeting to be called

(*1*) *Where a takeover bid is made for an opted-in company, section 368 of the Companies Act 1985 (extraordinary general meeting on members' requisition) and section 378 of that Act (extraordinary and special resolutions) have effect as follows.*

(*2*) *Section 368 has effect as if a member's requisition included a requisition of a person who—*

(*a*) *is the offeror in relation to the takeover bid; and*

(*b*) *holds at the date of the deposit of the requisition shares amounting to not less than 75% in value of all the voting shares in the company.*

(*3*) *In relation to a general meeting of the company that—*

(*a*) *is the first such meeting to be held after the end of the offer period, and*

(*b*) *is held at a time when the offeror holds shares amounting to not less than 75% in value of all the voting shares in the company,*

section 378(2) (meaning of "special resolution") has effect as if "14 days' notice" were substituted for "21 days' notice".

(*4*) *A reference in this regulation to voting shares in the company does not include—*

(*a*) *debentures; or*

(*b*) *shares carrying rights to vote that, under the company's articles of association, arise only where specified pecuniary advantages are not provided.*

In sub-paragraph (b) "rights to vote" means rights to vote at general meetings of the company.

(5) In its application to Northern Ireland, references in this regulation to sections 368 and 378 of the Companies Act 1985 are to be read, respectively, as references to Articles 376 and 386 of the Companies (Northern Ireland) Order 1986.

[7531]

NOTES

Commencement: 20 May 2006.
Revoked, subject to savings, as noted at the beginning of these Regulations.

CHAPTER 4
SUPPLEMENTARY

24 Communication of decisions

(1) A company that has passed an opting-in resolution or an opting-out resolution must notify—

(a) the Panel; and

(b) where the company—

(i) has voting shares admitted to trading on a regulated market in an EEA State other than the United Kingdom, or

(ii) has requested such admission,

the authority designated by that State as the supervisory authority for the purposes of Article 4.1 of the Takeovers Directive.

(2) Notification must be given within 15 days after the resolution is passed and, if any admission or request such as is mentioned in paragraph (1)(b) occurs at a later time, within 15 days after that time.

(3) If a company fails to comply with this regulation, an offence is committed by—

(a) the company; and

(b) every officer of it who is in default.

(4) A person guilty of an offence under this regulation is liable on summary conviction to a fine not exceeding level 3 on the standard scale and, for continued contravention, to a daily default fine not exceeding £100.

[7532]

NOTES

Commencement: 20 May 2006.
Revoked, subject to savings, as noted at the beginning of these Regulations.

PART 4
DIRECTORS' REPORT ETC

25 Matters to be dealt with in directors' report

(1) In this Part "directors' report" means the report prepared under section 234 of the Companies Act 1985(or in the case of Northern Ireland, Article 242 of the Companies (Northern Ireland) Order 1986).

(2) This Part applies to a directors' report for a financial year beginning on or after 20th May 2006, if the company had securities carrying voting rights admitted to trading on a regulated market at the end of that year.

[7533]

NOTES

Commencement: 20 May 2006.
Revoked, subject to savings, as noted at the beginning of these Regulations.

***26**—(1) In addition to the matters required by section 234ZZA of the Companies Act 1985 (or in the case of Northern Ireland, Article 242ZZA of the Companies (Northern Ireland) Order 1986) to be contained in the directors' report, that report shall contain detailed information, by reference to the end of that year, on the following matters—*

(a) the structure of the company's capital, including in particular—

(i) *the rights and obligations attaching to the shares or, as the case may be, to each class of shares in the company; and*

(ii) *where there are two or more such classes, the percentage of the total share capital represented by each class;*

(*b*) *any restrictions on the transfer of securities in the company, including in particular—*

(i) *limitations on the holding of securities; and*

(ii) *requirements to obtain the approval of the company, or of other holders of securities in the company, for a transfer of securities;*

(*c*) *in the case of each person with a significant direct or indirect holding of securities in the company, such details as are known to the company of—*

(i) *the identity of the person;*

(ii) *the size of the holding; and*

(iii) *the nature of the holding;*

(*d*) *in the case of each person who holds securities carrying special rights with regard to control of the company—*

(i) *the identity of the person; and*

(ii) *the nature of the rights;*

(*e*) *where—*

(i) *the company has an employees' share scheme, and*

(ii) *shares to which the scheme relates have rights with regard to control of the company that are not exercisable directly by the employees,*

how those rights are exercisable;

(*f*) *any restrictions on voting rights, including in particular—*

(i) *limitations on voting rights of holders of a given percentage or number of votes;*

(ii) *deadlines for exercising voting rights; and*

(iii) *arrangements by which, with the company's co-operation, financial rights carried by securities are held by a person other than the holder of the securities;*

(*g*) *any agreements between holders of securities that are known to the company and may result in restrictions on the transfer of securities or on voting rights;*

(*h*) *any rules that the company has about—*

(i) *appointment and replacement of directors; or*

(ii) *amendment of the company's articles of association;*

(*i*) *the powers of the company's directors, including in particular any powers in relation to the issuing or buying back by the company of its shares;*

(*j*) *any significant agreements to which the company is a party that take effect, alter or terminate upon a change of control of the company following a takeover bid, and the effects of any such agreements;*

(*k*) *any agreements between the company and its directors or employees providing for compensation for loss of office or employment (whether through resignation, purported redundancy or otherwise) that occurs because of a takeover bid.*

(2) *For the purposes of paragraph (1)(a) a company's capital includes any securities in the company that are not admitted to trading on a regulated market.*

(3) *For the purposes of paragraph (1)(c) a person has an indirect holding of securities if—*

(*a*) *they are held on his behalf; or*

(*b*) *he is able to secure that rights carried by the securities are exercised in accordance with his wishes.*

(4) *Paragraph (1)(j) does not apply to an agreement if—*

(*a*) *disclosure of the agreement would be seriously prejudicial to the company; and*

(*b*) *the company is not under any other obligation to disclose it.*

(5) *The directors' report shall also contain any necessary explanatory material with regard to information that is required to be included in the report by paragraph (1).*

(6) *In this regulation "securities" means shares or debentures.*

[7534]

NOTES

Commencement: 20 May 2006.

Revoked, subject to savings, as noted at the beginning of these Regulations.

27 Summary financial statement

If, in accordance with section 251 of the Companies Act 1985 (or as the case may be Article 259 of the Companies (Northern Ireland) Order 1986), a company sends to an entitled person a summary financial statement instead of a copy of its directors' report the company shall—

(*a*) *include in the statement the explanatory material required to be included in the directors' report by regulation 26(5); or*

(*b*) *send that material to the entitled person at the same time as it sends the statement.*

For the purposes of paragraph (b), section 251(2A) to (2E) (or as the case may be Article 259(2A) to (2E)) applies in relation to the material referred to in that paragraph as it applies in relation to a summary financial statement.

[7535]

NOTES

Commencement: 20 May 2006.
Revoked, subject to savings, as noted at the beginning of these Regulations.

28 Expressions in the Companies Act 1985

Except as otherwise provided expressions that are defined for the purposes of Part 7 of the Companies Act 1985 (or in the case of Northern Ireland, Part 8 of the Companies (Northern Ireland) Order 1986) have the same meaning in this Part.

[7536]

NOTES

Commencement: 20 May 2006.
Revoked, subject to savings, as noted at the beginning of these Regulations.

PART 5
SQUEEZE-OUT AND SELL-OUT

29 Takeover offers

This Part applies to any takeover offer where the date of the offer as defined in paragraph 11 of Schedule 2 is on or after 20 May 2006.

[7537]

NOTES

Commencement: 20 May 2006.
Revoked, subject to savings, as noted at the beginning of these Regulations.

30 *Where a takeover offer is made for a company that has securities carrying voting rights admitted to trading on a regulated market, Part 13A of the Companies Act 1985 (or in the case of Northern Ireland, Part 14A of the Companies (Northern Ireland) Order 1986) shall not apply and Schedule 2 to these Regulations shall apply.*

[7538]

NOTES

Commencement: 20 May 2006.
Revoked, subject to savings, as noted at the beginning of these Regulations.

31 *In this Part "company" means—*

(*a*) *a company within the meaning of section 735 of the Companies Act 1985;*

(*b*) *an unregistered company within the meaning of section 718 of that Act;*

(*c*) *a company within the meaning of Article 3 of the Companies (Northern Ireland) Order 1986; or*

(*d*) *an unregistered company within the meaning of Article 667 of that Order.*

[7539]

NOTES

Commencement: 20 May 2006.

Revoked, subject to savings, as noted at the beginning of these Regulations.

32 Except as otherwise provided expressions that are defined for the purposes of Part 13A of the Companies Act 1985 (or in the case of Northern Ireland, Part 14A of the Companies (Northern Ireland) Order 1986) have the same meaning in this Part.

[7540]

NOTES

Commencement: 20 May 2006.

Revoked, subject to savings, as noted at the beginning of these Regulations.

SCHEDULES

SCHEDULE 1
SPECIFIED PERSONS, DESCRIPTIONS OF DISCLOSURES ETC FOR THE PURPOSES OF REGULATION 7

Regulation 7

PART 1
SPECIFIED PERSONS

1. The Secretary of State.

2. The Department of Enterprise, Trade and Investment for Northern Ireland.

3. The Treasury.

4. The Bank of England.

5. The Financial Services Authority.

6. The Commissioners for Her Majesty's Revenue and Customs.

7. The Lord Advocate.

8. The Director of Public Prosecutions.

9. The Director of Public Prosecutions for Northern Ireland.

10. A constable.

11. A procurator fiscal.

12. The Scottish Ministers.

[7541]

NOTES

Commencement: 20 May 2006.

Revoked, subject to savings, as noted at the beginning of these Regulations.

PART 2
SPECIFIED DESCRIPTIONS OF DISCLOSURES

13. A disclosure for the purpose of enabling or assisting a person authorised under section 245C of the Companies Act 1985 (persons authorised to apply to court) to exercise his functions.

PART IV
STATUTORY INSTRUMENTS

14. A disclosure for the purpose of enabling or assisting an inspector appointed under Part 14 of the Companies Act 1985 (investigation of companies and their affairs, etc) to exercise his functions.

15. A disclosure for the purpose of enabling or assisting a person authorised under section 447 of the Companies Act 1985 (power to require production of documents) or section 84 of the Companies Act 1989 (exercise of powers by officer etc) to exercise his functions.

16. A disclosure for the purpose of enabling or assisting a person appointed under section 167 of the Financial Services and Markets Act 2000 (general investigations) to conduct an investigation to exercise his functions.

17. A disclosure for the purpose of enabling or assisting a person appointed under section 168 of the Financial Services and Markets Act 2000 (investigations in particular cases) to conduct an investigation to exercise his functions.

18. A disclosure for the purpose of enabling or assisting a person appointed under section 169(1)(b) of the Financial Services and Markets Act 2000 (investigation in support of overseas regulator) to conduct an investigation to exercise his functions.

19. A disclosure for the purpose of enabling or assisting the body corporate responsible for administering the scheme referred to in section 225 of the Financial Services and Markets Act 2000 (the ombudsman scheme) to exercise its functions.

20. A disclosure for the purpose of enabling or assisting a person appointed under paragraph 4 (the panel of ombudsmen) or 5 (the Chief Ombudsman) of Schedule 17 to the Financial Services and Markets Act 2000 to exercise his functions.

21. A disclosure for the purpose of enabling or assisting a person appointed under regulations made under section 262(1) and (2)(k) of the Financial Services and Markets Act 2000 (investigations into open-ended investment companies) to conduct an investigation to exercise his functions.

22. A disclosure for the purpose of enabling or assisting a person appointed under section 284 of the Financial Services and Markets Act 2000 (investigations into affairs of certain collective investment schemes) to conduct an investigation to exercise his functions.

23. A disclosure for the purpose of enabling or assisting the investigator appointed under paragraph 7 of Schedule 1 to the Financial Services and Markets Act 2000 (arrangements for investigation of complaints) to exercise his functions.

24. A disclosure for the purpose of enabling or assisting a person appointed by the Treasury to hold an inquiry into matters relating to financial services (including an inquiry under section 15 of the Financial Services and Markets Act 2000) to exercise his functions.

25. A disclosure for the purpose of enabling or assisting the Secretary of State or the Treasury to exercise any of their functions under any of the following—

- *(a) the Companies Acts;*
- *(b) Part 5 of the Criminal Justice Act 1993 (insider dealing);*
- *(c) the Insolvency Act 1986;*
- *(d) the Company Directors Disqualification Act 1986;*
- *(e) Part 2 of the Companies Act 1989 (eligibility for appointment as company auditor);*
- *(f) Part 3 (investigations and powers to obtain information) or 7 (financial markets and insolvency) of the Companies Act 1989;*
- *(g) the Financial Services and Markets Act 2000.*

26. A disclosure for the purpose of enabling or assisting the Scottish Ministers to exercise their functions under the enactments relating to insolvency.

27. A disclosure for the purpose of enabling or assisting the Department of Enterprise, Trade and Investment for Northern Ireland to exercise any powers conferred on it by the enactments relating to companies or insolvency.

28. A disclosure for the purpose of enabling or assisting a person appointed or authorised by the Department of Enterprise, Trade and Investment for Northern Ireland under the enactments relating to companies or insolvency to exercise his functions.

29. A disclosure for the purpose of enabling or assisting the Pensions Regulator to exercise the functions conferred on it by or by virtue of any of the following—

(*a*) *the Pension Schemes Act 1993;*
(*b*) *the Pensions Act 1995;*
(*c*) *the Welfare Reform and Pensions Act 1999;*
(*d*) *the Pensions Act 2004;*
(*e*) *any enactment in force in Northern Ireland corresponding to any of those enactments.*

30. A disclosure for the purpose of enabling or assisting the Board of the Pension Protection Fund to exercise the functions conferred on it by or by virtue of Part 2 of the Pensions Act 2004 or any enactment in force in Northern Ireland corresponding to that Part.

31. A disclosure for the purpose of enabling or assisting—

(*a*) *the Bank of England,*
(*b*) *the European Central Bank, or*
(*c*) *the central bank of any country or territory outside the United Kingdom,*

to exercise its functions.

32. A disclosure for the purpose of enabling or assisting the Commissioners for Her Majesty's Revenue and Customs to exercise their functions.

33. A disclosure for the purpose of enabling or assisting organs of the Society of Lloyd's (being organs constituted by or under the Lloyd's Act 1982) to exercise their functions under or by virtue of the Lloyd's Acts 1871 to 1982.

34. A disclosure for the purpose of enabling or assisting the Office of Fair Trading to exercise its functions under any of the following—

(*a*) *the Fair Trading Act 1973;*
(*b*) *the Consumer Credit Act 1974;*
(*c*) *the Estate Agents Act 1979;*
(*d*) *the Competition Act 1980;*
(*e*) *the Competition Act 1998;*
(*f*) *the Financial Services and Markets Act 2000;*
(*g*) *the Enterprise Act 2002;*
(*h*) *the Control of Misleading Advertisements Regulations 1988;*
(*i*) *the Unfair Terms in Consumer Contracts Regulations 1999.*

35. A disclosure for the purpose of enabling or assisting the Competition Commission to exercise its functions under any of the following—

(*a*) *the Fair Trading Act 1973;*
(*b*) *the Competition Act 1980;*
(*c*) *the Competition Act 1998;*
(*d*) *the Enterprise Act 2002.*

36. A disclosure with a view to the institution of, or otherwise for the purposes of, proceedings before the Competition Appeal Tribunal.

37. A disclosure for the purpose of enabling or assisting an enforcer under Part 8 of the Enterprise Act 2002 (enforcement of consumer legislation) to exercise its functions under that Part.

38. A disclosure for the purpose of enabling or assisting the Charity Commissioners (or in the case of Northern Ireland, the Department for Social Development) to exercise their functions.

39. A disclosure for the purpose of enabling or assisting the Attorney General to exercise his functions in connection with charities.

40. A disclosure for the purpose of enabling or assisting the National Lottery Commission to exercise its functions under sections 5 to 10 (licensing) and 15 (power of Secretary of State to require information) of the National Lottery etc Act 1993.

41. A disclosure by the National Lottery Commission to the National Audit Office for the purpose of enabling or assisting the Comptroller and Auditor General to carry out an examination under Part 2 of the National Audit Act 1983 into the economy, effectiveness and efficiency with which the National Lottery Commission has used its resources in discharging its functions under sections 5 to 10 of the National Lottery etc Act 1993.

42. A disclosure for the purpose of enabling or assisting a qualifying body under the Unfair Terms in Consumer Contracts Regulations 1999 to exercise its functions under those Regulations.

43. A disclosure for the purpose of enabling or assisting an enforcement authority under the Consumer Protection (Distance Selling) Regulations 2000 to exercise its functions under those Regulations.

44. A disclosure for the purpose of enabling or assisting an enforcement authority under the Financial Services (Distance Marketing) Regulations 2004 to exercise its functions under those Regulations.

45. A disclosure for the purpose of enabling or assisting a local weights and measures authority in England and Wales to exercise its functions under section 230(2) of the Enterprise Act 2002 (notice of intention to prosecute, etc).

46. A disclosure for the purpose of enabling or assisting the Financial Services Authority to exercise its functions under any of the following—

- *(a) the legislation relating to friendly societies or to industrial and provident societies;*
- *(b) the Building Societies Act 1986;*
- *(c) Part 7 of the Companies Act 1989 (financial markets and insolvency);*
- *(d) the Financial Services and Markets Act 2000.*

47. A disclosure for the purpose of enabling or assisting the competent authority for the purposes of Part 6 of the Financial Services and Markets Act 2000 (official listing) to exercise its functions under that Part.

48. A disclosure for the purpose of enabling or assisting a body corporate established in accordance with section 212(1) of the Financial Services and Markets Act 2000 (compensation scheme manager) to exercise its functions.

49. A disclosure for the purpose of enabling or assisting a recognised investment exchange or a recognised clearing house to exercise its functions as such.

"Recognised investment exchange" and "recognised clearing house" have the same meaning as in section 285 of the Financial Services and Markets Act 2000.

50. A disclosure for the purpose of enabling or assisting a person approved under the Uncertificated Securities Regulations 2001 as an operator of a relevant system (within the meaning of those Regulations) to exercise his functions.

51. A disclosure for the purpose of enabling or assisting a body designated under section 326(1) of the Financial Services and Markets Act 2000 (designated professional bodies) to exercise its functions in its capacity as a body designated under that section.

52. A disclosure with a view to the institution of, or otherwise for the purposes of, civil proceedings arising under or by virtue of the Financial Services and Markets Act 2000.

53. A disclosure for the purpose of enabling or assisting a body designated by order under section 46 of the Companies Act 1989 (delegation of functions of Secretary of State) to exercise its functions under Part 2 of that Act (eligibility for appointment as company auditor).

54. A disclosure for the purpose of enabling or assisting a recognised supervisory or qualifying body, within the meaning of Part 2 of the Companies Act 1989.

55. A disclosure for the purpose of enabling or assisting an official receiver (including the Accountant in Bankruptcy in Scotland and the Official Assignee in Northern Ireland) to exercise his functions under the enactments relating to insolvency.

56. A disclosure for the purpose of enabling or assisting the Insolvency Practitioners Tribunal to exercise its functions under the Insolvency Act 1986.

57. A disclosure for the purpose of enabling or assisting a body that is for the time being a recognised professional body for the purposes of section 391 of the Insolvency Act 1986 (recognised professional bodies) to exercise its functions as such.

58. A disclosure for the purpose of enabling or assisting an overseas regulatory authority to exercise its regulatory functions.

"Overseas regulatory authority" and "regulatory functions" have the same meaning as in section 82 of the Companies Act 1989.

59. A disclosure for the purpose of enabling or assisting the Regulator of Community Interest Companies to exercise functions under the Companies (Audit, Investigations and Community Enterprise) Act 2004.

60. A disclosure with a view to the institution of, or otherwise for the purposes of, criminal proceedings.

61. A disclosure for the purpose of enabling or assisting a person authorised by the Secretary of State under Part 2, 3 or 4 of the Proceeds of Crime Act 2002 to exercise his functions.

62. A disclosure with a view to the institution of, or otherwise for the purposes of, proceedings on an application under section 6, 7 or 8 of the Company Directors Disqualification Act 1986 (disqualification for unfitness).

63. A disclosure with a view to the institution of, or otherwise for the purposes of, proceedings before the Financial Services and Markets Tribunal.

64. A disclosure for the purposes of proceedings before the Financial Services Tribunal by virtue of the Financial Services and Markets Act 2000 (Transitional Provisions) (Partly Completed Procedures) Order 2001.

65. A disclosure for the purposes of proceedings before the Pensions Regulator Tribunal.

66. A disclosure for the purpose of enabling or assisting a body appointed under section 14 of the Companies (Audit, Investigations and Community Enterprise) Act 2004 (supervision of periodic accounts and reports of issuers of listed securities) to exercise functions mentioned in subsection (2) of that section.

67. A disclosure with a view to the institution of, or otherwise for the purposes of, disciplinary proceedings relating to the performance by a solicitor, barrister, advocate, foreign lawyer, auditor, accountant, valuer or actuary of his professional duties.

"Foreign lawyer" has the meaning given by section 89(9) of the Courts and Legal Services Act 1990.

68. A disclosure with a view to the institution of, or otherwise for the purposes of, disciplinary proceedings relating to the performance by a public servant of his duties.

"Public servant" means an officer or employee of the Crown.

69. A disclosure for the purpose of the provision of a summary or collection of information framed in such a way as not to enable the identity of any person to whom the information relates to be ascertained.

70. A disclosure in pursuance of any Community obligation.

[7542]

NOTES

Commencement: 20 May 2006.

Revoked, subject to savings, as noted at the beginning of these Regulations.

Charity Commissioners: as to the abolition of the office of Charity Commissioner for England and Wales, the establishment of the Charity Commission for England and Wales, and the transfer of the functions, rights, liabilities, etc from the Charity Commissioners to the Charity Commission, see the Charities Act 2006, s 6.

PART 3
OVERSEAS REGULATORY BODIES

71. A disclosure is made in accordance with this Part of this Schedule if—

(a) it is made to a person or body within paragraph 72; and

(b) it is made for the purpose of enabling or assisting that person or body to exercise the functions mentioned in that paragraph.

72. The persons or bodies that are within this paragraph are those exercising functions of a public nature, under legislation in any country or territory outside the United Kingdom, that appear to the Panel to be similar to its own functions or those of the Financial Services Authority.

73. In determining whether to disclose information to a person or body in accordance with this Part of this Schedule, the Panel must have regard to the following considerations—

(a) whether the use that the person or body is likely to make of the information is sufficiently important to justify making the disclosure;

(b) whether the person or body has adequate arrangements to prevent the information from being used or further disclosed otherwise than for the purposes of carrying out the functions mentioned in paragraph 72 or any other purposes substantially similar to those for which information disclosed to the Panel could be used or further disclosed.

[7543]

NOTES

Commencement: 20 May 2006.

Revoked, subject to savings, as noted at the beginning of these Regulations.

SCHEDULE 2
SQUEEZE-OUT AND SELL-OUT

Regulation 30

1 Meaning of takeover offer

(1) In this Schedule "a takeover offer" means an offer to acquire all the shares, or all the shares of any class or classes, in a company (other than shares which at the date of the offer are already held by the offeror), being an offer on terms which are the same in relation to all the shares to which the offer relates or, where those shares include shares of different classes, in relation to all the shares of each class.

(2) In sub-paragraph (1) "shares" means shares (other than relevant treasury shares) which have been allotted on the date of the offer, but a takeover offer may include among the shares to which it relates—

(a) all or any shares that are allotted after the date of the offer but before a specified date;

(b) all or any relevant treasury shares that cease to be held as treasury shares before a specified date;

(c) all or any other relevant treasury shares.

(3) In this paragraph—

"relevant treasury shares" means shares which—

(a) are held by the company as treasury shares on the date of the offer; or

(*b*) *become shares held by the company as treasury shares after that date but before a specified date;*

"specified date" means a date specified in or determined in accordance with the terms of the offer.

(*4*) *The terms offered in relation to any shares shall for the purposes of this paragraph be treated as being the same in relation to all the shares or, as the case may be, all the shares of a class to which the offer relates notwithstanding—*

(*a*) *any difference permitted by sub-paragraph* (*5*)*; or*

(*b*) *any variation permitted by sub-paragraph* (*6*).

(*5*) *A difference is permitted by this sub-paragraph where—*

(*a*) *shares carry an entitlement to a particular dividend which other shares of the same class, by reason of being allotted later, do not carry; and*

(*b*) *the difference is the value of consideration offered for the shares allotted earlier as against that offered for those allotted later, and merely reflects the difference in entitlement to the dividend.*

(*6*) *A variation is permitted by this sub-paragraph where—*

(*a*) *the law of a country or territory outside the United Kingdom precludes an offer of consideration in the form or any of the forms specified in the terms in question or precludes it except after compliance by the offeror with conditions with which he is unable to comply or which he regards as unduly onerous; and*

(*b*) *the variation is such that the persons to whom an offer of consideration in that form is precluded are able to receive consideration otherwise than in that form but of substantially equivalent value.*

(*7*) *Where there are holders of shares in a company to whom an offer to acquire shares in the company is not communicated, that does not prevent the offer from being a takeover offer for the purposes of this Schedule if—*

(*a*) *those shareholders have no registered address in the United Kingdom;*

(*b*) *the offer was not communicated to those shareholders in order not to contravene the law of a country or territory outside the United Kingdom; and*

(*c*) *either—*

(*i*) *the offer is published in the Gazette; or*

(*ii*) *the offer can be inspected, or a copy of it obtained, at a place in an EEA State or on a website, and a notice is published in the Gazette specifying the address of that place or website.*

(*8*) *Where an offer is made to acquire shares in a company and there are persons for whom, by reason of the law of a country or territory outside the United Kingdom, it is impossible to accept the offer, or more difficult to do so, that does not prevent the offer from being a takeover offer for the purposes of this Schedule.*

(*9*) *It is not to be inferred—*

(*a*) *that an offer which is not communicated to every holder of shares in the company cannot be a takeover offer for the purposes of this Schedule unless the requirements of sub-paragraphs* (*7*)(*a*) *to* (*c*) *are met; or*

(*b*) *that an offer which is impossible, or more difficult, for certain persons to accept cannot be a takeover offer for those purposes unless the reason for the impossibility or difficulty is the one mentioned in sub-paragraph* (*8*).

(*10*) *The reference in sub-paragraph* (*1*) *to shares already held by the offeror includes a reference to shares which he has contracted to acquire* (*whether unconditionally or subject to conditions being met*) *but that shall not be construed as including shares which are the subject of a contract binding the holder to accept the offer when it is made, being a contract entered into by the holder either for no consideration and under seal or for no consideration other than a promise by the offeror to make the offer.*

(*11*) *In the application of sub-paragraph* (*10*) *to Scotland, the words "and under seal" shall be omitted.*

(*12*) *Where the terms of an offer make provision for their revision and for acceptances on the previous terms to be treated as acceptances on the revised terms, the revision shall not be regarded for the purposes of this Schedule as the making of a fresh offer and references in paragraph 11*(*1*) *to the offer shall accordingly be construed as references to the original offer.*

2 Right of offeror to buy out minority shareholders

(*1*) *Sub-paragraph* (*2*) *applies in a case where a takeover offer does not relate to shares of different classes.*

(2) If the offeror has, by virtue of acceptances of the offer, acquired or unconditionally contracted to acquire—

(a) not less than nine-tenths in value of the shares to which the offer relates, and

(b) in a case where the shares to which the offer relates are voting shares, not less than nine-tenths of the voting rights carried by those shares,

he may give notice to the holder of any shares to which the offer relates which the offeror has not acquired or unconditionally contracted to acquire that he desires to acquire those shares.

(3) Sub-paragraph (4) applies in a case where a takeover offer relates to shares of different classes.

(4) If the offeror has, by virtue of acceptances of the offer, acquired or unconditionally contracted to acquire—

(a) not less than nine-tenths in value of the shares of any class to which the offer relates, and

(b) in a case where the shares of that class are voting shares, not less than nine-tenths of the voting rights carried by those shares,

he may give notice to the holder of any shares of that class to which the offer relates which the offeror has not acquired or unconditionally contracted to acquire that he desires to acquire those shares.

(5) No notice shall be given under sub-paragraph (2) or (4) after the end of the period of three months beginning with the day after the last day on which the offer can be accepted.

(6) Sub-paragraph (7) applies where—

(a) the requirements for the giving of a notice under sub-paragraph (2) or (4) are satisfied; and

(b) there are shares in the company which the offeror has contracted to acquire subject to conditions being met, and in relation to which the contract has not become unconditional.

(7) The offeror's entitlement to give a notice under sub-paragraph (2) or (4) shall be determined as if—

(a) the shares to which the offer relates included shares falling within sub-paragraph (6)(b); and

(b) in relation to shares falling within that paragraph, the words "by virtue of acceptances of the offer" in sub-paragraph (2) or (4) were omitted.

(8) Any notice under this paragraph shall be given in the manner prescribed by regulation 4 of the Companies (Forms) Regulations 1985 ("the 1985 Regulations") for a notice given for the purposes of section 429(4) of the Companies Act 1985 (or in the case of Northern Ireland by regulation 4 of the Companies (Forms) Regulations (Northern Ireland) 1986 ("the 1986 Regulations") for a notice given for the purposes of Article 422(4) of the Companies (Northern Ireland) Order 1986); and when the offeror gives the first notice in relation to an offer he shall send a copy of it to the company together with a statutory declaration by him in the form prescribed by regulation 5(2) of the 1985 Regulations (or in the case of Northern Ireland by regulation 5(2) of the 1986 Regulations), stating that the conditions for the giving of the notice are satisfied.

(9) Where the offeror is a company (whether or not a company within the meaning of the Companies Act 1985 or, in the case of Northern Ireland, the Companies (Northern Ireland) Order 1986) the statutory declaration shall be signed by a director.

(10) Any person who fails to send a copy of a notice or a statutory declaration as required by sub-paragraph (8) or makes such a declaration for the purposes of that sub-paragraph knowing it to be false or without having reasonable grounds for believing it to be true commits an offence.

(11) A person who commits an offence under sub-paragraph (10), but would have committed an offence under section 429(6) of the Companies Act 1985 (or as the case may be, Article 422(6) of the Companies (Northern Ireland) Order 1986) had that section (or Article) not been disapplied by regulation 30, is liable on conviction to the penalties in that section (or Article).

(12) In all other cases a person who commits an offence under sub-paragraph (10) is liable—

(a) on conviction on indictment, to imprisonment for a term not exceeding two years or a fine or both;

(*b*) *on summary conviction, to imprisonment for a term not exceeding three months or to a fine not exceeding the statutory maximum or both;*

(*c*) *for continued contravention, to a daily default fine not exceeding £100.*

(13) If any person is charged with an offence for failing to send a copy of a notice as required by sub-paragraph (8) it is a defence for him to prove that he took reasonable steps for securing compliance with that sub-paragraph.

(14) Sub-paragraph (15) applies where a takeover offer is made and, during the period beginning with the date of the offer and ending when the offer can no longer be accepted, the offeror acquires or unconditionally contracts to acquire any of the shares to which the offer relates but otherwise than by virtue of acceptances of the offer.

(15) If—

(*a*) *the value of the consideration for which the shares are acquired or contracted to be acquired ("the acquisition consideration") does not at that time exceed the value of the consideration specified in the terms of the offer; or*

(*b*) *those terms are subsequently revised so that when the revision is announced the value of the acquisition consideration, at the time mentioned in paragraph (a), no longer exceeds the value of the consideration specified in those terms,*

the offeror shall be treated for the purposes of this paragraph as having acquired or contracted to acquire those shares by virtue of acceptances of the offer; but in any other case those shares shall be treated as excluded from those to which the offer relates.

3 Effect of notice under paragraph 2

(1) The following provisions shall, subject to paragraph 6, have effect where a notice is given in respect of any shares under paragraph 2.

(2) The offeror shall be entitled and bound to acquire those shares on the terms of the offer.

(3) Where the terms of an offer are such as to give the holder of any shares a choice of consideration the notice shall give particulars of the choice and state—

(*a*) *that the holder of the shares may within six weeks from the date of the notice indicate his choice by a written communication sent to the offeror at an address specified in the notice, and*

(*b*) *which consideration specified in the offer is to be taken as applying in default of his indicating a choice as aforesaid,*

and the terms of the offer mentioned in sub-paragraph (2) shall be determined accordingly.

(4) Sub-paragraph (3) applies whether or not any time-limit or other conditions applicable to the choice under the terms of the offer can still be complied with.

(5) If the consideration offered to or (as the case may be) chosen by the holder of the shares—

(*a*) *is not cash and the offeror is no longer able to provide it, or*

(*b*) *was to have been provided by a third party who is no longer bound or able to provide it,*

the consideration shall be taken to consist of an amount of cash payable by the offeror which at the date of the notice is equivalent to the consideration offered or (as the case may be) chosen.

(6) At the end of six weeks from the date of the notice the offeror shall forthwith—

(*a*) *send a copy of the notice to the company; and*

(*b*) *pay or transfer to the company the consideration for the shares to which the notice relates.*

(7) If the shares to which the notice relates are registered the copy of the notice sent to the company under sub-paragraph (6)(a) shall be accompanied by an instrument of transfer executed on behalf of the shareholder by a person appointed by the offeror; and on receipt of that instrument the company shall register the offeror as the holder of those shares.

(8) If the shares to which the notice relates are transferable by the delivery of warrants or other instruments the copy of the notice sent to the company under sub-paragraph (6)(a) shall be accompanied by a statement to that effect; and the company shall on receipt of the statement issue the offeror with warrants or other instruments in respect of the shares and those already in issue in respect of the shares shall become void.

(9) *Where the consideration referred to in paragraph (b) of sub-paragraph (6) consists of shares or securities to be allotted by the offeror the reference in that paragraph to the transfer of the consideration shall be construed as a reference to the allotment of the shares or securities to the company.*

(10) *Any sum received by a company under paragraph (b) of sub-paragraph (6) and any other consideration received under that paragraph shall be held by the company on trust for the person entitled to the shares in respect of which the sum or other consideration was received.*

(11) *Any sum received by a company under paragraph (b) of sub-paragraph (6), and any dividend or other sum accruing from any other consideration received by a company under that paragraph, shall be paid into a separate bank account, being an account the balance on which bears interest at an appropriate rate and can be withdrawn by such notice (if any) as is appropriate.*

(12) *Where after reasonable enquiry made at such intervals as are reasonable the person entitled to any consideration held on trust by virtue of sub-paragraph (10) cannot be found and twelve years have elapsed since the consideration was received or the company is wound up the consideration (together with any interest, dividend or other benefit that has accrued from it) shall be paid into court.*

(13) *In relation to a company registered in Scotland, sub-paragraphs (14) and (15) shall apply in place of sub-paragraph (12).*

(14) *Where after reasonable enquiry made at such intervals as are reasonable the person entitled to any consideration held on trust by virtue of sub-paragraph (10) cannot be found and twelve years have elapsed since the consideration was received or the company is wound up—*

- (a) *the trust shall terminate;*
- (b) *the company or, as the case may be, the liquidator shall sell any consideration other than cash and any benefit other than cash that has accrued from the consideration; and*
- (c) *a sum representing—*
  - (i) *the consideration so far as it is cash,*
  - (ii) *the proceeds of any sale under paragraph (b), and*
  - (iii) *any interest, dividend or other benefit that has accrued from the consideration,*

shall be deposited in the name of the Accountant of Court in a bank account such as is referred to in sub-paragraph (11) and the receipt for the deposit shall be transmitted to the Accountant of Court.

(15) *Section 58 of the Bankruptcy (Scotland) Act 1985 (so far as consistent with the Companies Act 1985) shall apply with any necessary modifications to sums deposited under sub-paragraph (14) as that sub-paragraph applies to sums deposited under section 57(1)(a) of the Bankruptcy (Scotland) Act 1985.*

(16) *The expenses of any such enquiry as is mentioned in sub-paragraph (12) or (14) may be defrayed out of the money or other property held on trust for the person or persons to whom the enquiry relates.*

4 Right of minority shareholder to be bought out by offeror

(1) *Sub-paragraphs (2) and (3) apply in a case where a takeover offer relates to all the shares in a company.*

For this purpose a takeover offer relates to all the shares in a company if it is an offer to acquire all the shares in the company within the meaning of paragraph 1.

(2) *The holder of any voting shares to which the offer relates who has not accepted the offer may require the offeror to acquire those shares if, at any time before the end of the period within which the offer can be accepted—*

- (a) *the offeror has by virtue of acceptances of the offer acquired or unconditionally contracted to acquire some (but not all) of the shares to which the offer relates; and*
- (b) *those shares, with or without any other shares in the company which he has acquired or contracted to acquire (whether unconditionally or subject to conditions being met)—*
  - (i) *amount to not less than nine-tenths in value of all the voting shares in the company (or would do so but for paragraph 10(1)); and*

(ii) carry not less than nine-tenths of the voting rights in the company (or would do so but for paragraph 10(1)).

(3) The holder of any non-voting shares to which the offer relates who has not accepted the offer may require the offeror to acquire those shares if, at any time before the end of the period within which the offer can be accepted—

(a) the offeror has by virtue of acceptances of the offer acquired or unconditionally contracted to acquire some (but not all) of the shares to which the offer relates; and

(b) those shares, with or without any other shares in the company which he has acquired or contracted to acquire (whether unconditionally or subject to conditions being met), amount to not less than nine-tenths in value of all the shares in the company (or would do so but for paragraph 10(1)).

(4) If a takeover offer relates to shares of any class or classes and at any time before the end of the period within which the offer can be accepted—

(a) the offeror has by virtue of acceptances of the offer acquired or unconditionally contracted to acquire some (but not all) of the shares of any class to which the offer relates, and

(b) those shares, with or without any other shares of that class which he has acquired or contracted to acquire (whether unconditionally or subject to conditions being met)—

(i) amount to not less than nine-tenths in value of all the shares of that class, and

(ii) in a case where the shares of that class are voting shares, carry not less than nine-tenths of the voting rights carried by the shares of that class,

the holder of any shares of that class to which the offer relates who has not accepted the offer may require the offeror to acquire those shares.

(5) For the purposes of sub-paragraphs (2), (3) and (4), in calculating nine-tenths of the value of all the shares in the company, or all the shares of any class or classes of shares of the company, any shares held by the company as treasury shares shall be treated as having been acquired by the offeror.

(6) Rights conferred on the holder of shares by sub-paragraph (2), (3) or (4) are exercisable by a written communication addressed to the offeror.

(7) Rights conferred on the holder of shares by sub-paragraph (2), (3) or (4) are not exercisable after the end of the period of three months from—

(a) the end of the period within which the offer can be accepted; or

(b) if later, the date of the notice that must be given under sub-paragraph (8).

(8) Within one month of the time specified in sub-paragraph (2), (3) or (4), as the case may be, the offeror shall give any shareholder who has not accepted the offer notice in the manner prescribed by regulation 4 of the Companies (Forms) Regulations 1985 for the purposes of section 430A(3) of the Companies Act 1985, (or in the case of Northern Ireland by regulation 4 of the Companies (Forms) Regulations (Northern Ireland) 1986 for the purposes of Article 423A(3) of the Companies (Northern Ireland) Order 1986), of—

(a) the rights that are exercisable by the shareholder under that sub-paragraph, and

(b) the period within which the rights are exercisable,

and if the notice is given before the end of the period within which the offer can be accepted, it shall state that the offer is still open for acceptance.

(9) Sub-paragraph (10) applies where—

(a) a shareholder exercises rights conferred on him by sub-paragraph (2), (3) or (4);

(b) at the time when he does so, there are shares in the company which the offeror has contracted to acquire subject to conditions being met, and in relation to which the contract has not become unconditional; and

(c) the requirement imposed by paragraph (b) of sub-paragraph (2), (3) or (4) (as the case may be) would not be satisfied if those shares were not taken into account.

(10) The shareholder shall be treated for the purposes of paragraph 5 as not having exercised his rights under this paragraph unless the requirement imposed by paragraph (b) of sub-paragraph (2), (3) or (4) (as the case may be) would be satisfied if—

(a) the reference in paragraph (b) of that sub-paragraph to other shares in the company which the offeror has contracted to acquire unconditionally or subject to conditions being met were a reference to such shares which he has unconditionally contracted to acquire; and

(*b*) *the reference in that sub-paragraph to the period within which the offer can be accepted were a reference to the period referred to in sub-paragraph (7).*

(11) Sub-paragraph (8) does not apply if the offeror has given the shareholder a notice in respect of the shares in question under paragraph 2.

(12) If the offeror fails to comply with sub-paragraph (8) he and, if the offeror is a company, every officer of the company who is in default or to whose neglect the failure is attributable, commits an offence.

(13) A person who commits an offence under sub-paragraph (12), but would have committed an offence under section 430A(6) of the Companies Act 1985 (or as the case may be, Article 423A(6) of the Companies (Northern Ireland) Order 1986) had that section (or Article) not been disapplied by regulation 30, is liable on conviction to the penalties in that section (or Article).

(14) In all other cases a person who commits an offence under sub-paragraph (12) is liable—

(*a*) *on conviction on indictment, to a fine;*
(*b*) *on summary conviction, to a fine not exceeding the statutory maximum;*
(*c*) *for continued contravention, to a daily default fine not exceeding £100.*

(15) If an offeror other than a company is charged with an offence for failing to comply with sub-paragraph (8) it is a defence for him to prove that he took all reasonable steps for securing compliance with that sub-paragraph.

5 Effect of requirement under paragraph 4

(1) The following provisions shall, subject to paragraph 6, have effect where a shareholder exercises his rights in respect of any shares under paragraph 4.

(2) The offeror shall be entitled and bound to acquire those shares on the terms of the offer or on such other terms as may be agreed.

(3) Where the terms of an offer are such as to give the holder of shares a choice of consideration the holder of the shares may indicate his choice when requiring the offeror to acquire them and the notice given to the holder under paragraph 4(8)—

(*a*) *shall give particulars of the choice and of the rights conferred by this sub-paragraph, and*
(*b*) *may state which consideration specified in the offer is to be taken as applying in default of his indicating a choice,*

and the terms of the offer mentioned in sub-paragraph (2) shall be determined accordingly.

(4) Sub-paragraph (3) applies whether or not any time-limit or other conditions applicable to the choice under the terms of the offer can still be complied with.

(5) If the consideration offered to or (as the case may be) chosen by the holder of the shares—

(*a*) *is not cash and the offeror is no longer able to provide it, or*
(*b*) *was to have been provided by a third party who is no longer bound or able to provide it,*

the consideration shall be taken to consist of an amount of cash payable by the offeror which at the date when the holder of the shares requires the offeror to acquire them is equivalent to the consideration offered or (as the case may be) chosen.

6 Applications to the court

(1) Where a notice is given under paragraph 2 to the holder of any shares the court may, on an application made by him within six weeks from the date on which the notice was given—

(*a*) *order that the offeror shall not be entitled and bound to acquire the shares; or*
(*b*) *specify terms of acquisition different from those of the offer.*

(2) If an application to the court under sub-paragraph (1) is pending at the end of the period mentioned in sub-paragraph (6) of paragraph 3 that sub-paragraph shall not have effect until the application has been disposed of.

(3) Where the holder of any shares exercises his rights under paragraph 4 the court may, on an application made by him or the offeror, order that the terms on which the offeror is entitled and bound to acquire the shares shall be such as the court thinks fit.

(4) On an application under sub-paragraph (1) or (3)—

(a) the court shall not require consideration of a higher value than that specified in the terms of the offer ("the offer value") to be given for the shares to which the application relates unless the holder of the shares shows that the offer value would be unfair;

(b) the court shall not require consideration of a lower value than the offer value to be given for the shares.

(5) No order for costs or expenses shall be made against a shareholder making an application under sub-paragraph (1) or (3) unless the court considers—

(a) that the application was unnecessary, improper or vexatious; or

(b) that there has been unreasonable delay in making the application or unreasonable conduct on his part in conducting the proceedings on the application.

(6) Where a takeover offer has not been accepted to the extent necessary for entitling the offeror to give notices under sub-paragraph (2) or (4) of paragraph 2 the court may, on the application of the offeror, make an order authorising him to give notices under that sub-paragraph if satisfied—

(a) that the offeror has after reasonable enquiry been unable to trace one or more of the persons holding shares to which the offer relates,

(b) that the requirements of that sub-paragraph would have been met if the person, or all the persons, mentioned in paragraph (a) had accepted the offer, and

(c) that the consideration offered is fair and reasonable,

but the court shall not make an order under this sub-paragraph unless it considers that it is just and equitable to do so having regard, in particular, to the number of shareholders who have been traced but who have not accepted the offer.

7 Joint offers

(1) A takeover offer may be made by two or more persons jointly and in that event this Schedule has effect with the following modifications.

(2) The conditions for the exercise of the rights conferred by paragraph 2 shall be satisfied by the joint offerors acquiring or unconditionally contracting to acquire the necessary shares jointly (as respects acquisitions by virtue of acceptances of the offer) and either jointly or separately (in other cases).

(3) The conditions for the exercise of the rights conferred by paragraph 4 shall be satisfied—

(a) as respects acquisitions by virtue of acceptances of the offer, by the joint offerors acquiring or unconditionally contracting to acquire the necessary shares jointly;

(b) in other cases, by the joint offerors acquiring or contracting (whether conditionally or subject to conditions being met) to acquire the necessary shares either jointly or separately.

(4) Subject to the following provisions, the rights and obligations of the offeror under paragraphs 2 to 5 shall be respectively joint rights and joint and several obligations of the joint offerors.

(5) It shall be a sufficient compliance with any provision of paragraphs 2 to 6 requiring or authorising a notice or other document to be given or sent by or to the joint offerors that it is given or sent by or to any of them; but the statutory declaration required by paragraph 2(8) shall be made by all of them and, in the case of a joint offeror being a company, signed by a director of that company.

(6) In paragraphs 1, 3(9) and 8 references to the offeror shall be construed as references to the joint offerors or any of them.

(7) In paragraph 3(7) and (8) references to the offeror shall be construed as references to the joint offerors or such of them as they may determine.

(8) In paragraphs 3(5)(a) and 5(5)(a) references to the offeror being no longer able to provide the relevant consideration shall be construed as references to none of the joint offerors being able to do so.

(9) In paragraph 6 references to the offeror shall be construed as references to the joint offerors except that any application under sub-paragraph (3) or (6) may be made by any of them and the reference in sub-paragraph (6)(a) to the offeror having been unable to trace one or more of the persons holding shares shall be construed as a reference to none of the offerors having been able to do so.

8 Associates

(1) The requirement in paragraph 1(1) that a takeover offer must extend to all the shares, or all the shares of any class or classes, in a company shall be regarded as satisfied notwithstanding that the offer does not extend to shares which associates of the offeror hold or have contracted to acquire; but, subject to sub-paragraph (3), shares which any such associate holds or has contracted to acquire, whether at the date of the offer or subsequently, shall be disregarded for the purposes of any reference in this Schedule to the shares to which a takeover offer relates.

(2) In sub-paragraph (1) "contracted" means contracted unconditionally or subject to conditions being met.

(3) Where during the period mentioned in paragraph 2(14) any associate of the offeror acquires or unconditionally contracts to acquire any of the shares to which the offer relates, then, if the condition specified in paragraph 2(15)(a) or (b) is satisfied as respects those shares they shall be treated for the purposes of that paragraph as shares to which the offer relates.

(4) A reference in paragraph 2(6) or paragraph 4(2)(b), (3)(b), (4)(b), (9) or (10) to shares which the offeror has acquired or contracted to acquire shall include a reference to shares which any associate of his has acquired or contracted to acquire.

(5) In this paragraph "associate", in relation to an offeror, means—

- *(a) a nominee of the offeror;*
- *(b) a holding company, subsidiary or fellow subsidiary of the offeror or a nominee of such a holding company, subsidiary or fellow subsidiary;*
- *(c) a body corporate in which the offeror is substantially interested; or*
- *(d) any person who is, or is a nominee of, a party to an agreement with the offeror for the acquisition of, or of an interest in, the shares which are the subject of the takeover offer, being an agreement which includes provisions imposing obligations or restrictions such as are mentioned in section 204(2)(a) of the Companies Act 1985 or as the case may be Article 212(2)(a) of the Companies (Northern Ireland) Order 1986.*

(6) For the purposes of sub-paragraph (5)(b) a company is a fellow subsidiary of another body corporate if both are subsidiaries of the same body corporate but neither is a subsidiary of the other.

(7) For the purposes of sub-paragraph (5)(c) an offeror has a substantial interest in a body corporate if—

- *(a) that body or its directors are accustomed to act in accordance with his directions or instructions; or*
- *(b) he is entitled to exercise or control the exercise of one-third or more of the voting power at general meetings of that body.*

(8) Subsections (5) and (6) of section 204 of the Companies Act 1985 or as the case may be paragraphs (5) and (6) of Article 212 of the Companies (Northern Ireland) Order 1986 shall apply to sub-paragraph (5)(d) above as they apply to that section and Article and subsections (3) and (4) of section 203 of the Companies Act 1985 or as the case may be paragraphs (3) and (4) of Article 211 of the Companies (Northern Ireland) Order 1986 shall apply for the purposes of sub-paragraph (7) above as they apply for the purposes of subsection (2)(b) of that section and paragraph (2)(b) of that Article.

(9) Where the offeror is an individual his associates shall also include his spouse or civil partner and any minor child or step-child of his.

9 Convertible securities

(1) For the purposes of this Schedule securities of a company shall be treated as shares in the company if they are convertible into or entitle the holder to subscribe for such shares; and references to the holder of shares or a shareholder shall be construed accordingly.

(2) Sub-paragraph (1) shall not be construed as requiring any securities to be treated—

- *(a) as shares of the same class as those into which they are convertible or for which the holder is entitled to subscribe; or*
- *(b) as shares of the same class as other securities by reason only that the shares into which they are convertible or for which the holder is entitled to subscribe are of the same class.*

10 Debentures carrying voting rights

(1) For the purposes of this Schedule debentures issued by a company to which sub-paragraph (2) applies shall be treated as shares in the company if they carry voting rights.

(2) This sub-paragraph applies to a company that has voting shares, or debentures carrying voting rights, which are admitted to trading on a regulated market.

(3) In this Schedule, in relation to debentures treated as shares by virtue of sub-paragraph (1)—

(a) references to the holder of shares or a shareholder shall be construed accordingly;

(b) references to shares being allotted shall be construed as references to debentures being issued.

11 Interpretation

(1) In this Schedule—

"the company" means the company whose shares are the subject of the offer;

"date of the offer" means—

(a) the date of publication; or

(b) where any notices of the offer are given before the date of publication, the date when notices of the offer (or the first such notices) are given;

"non-voting shares" means shares that are not voting shares;

"the offeror" means, subject to paragraph 7, the person making a takeover offer.

(2) For the purposes of this Schedule a person contracts unconditionally to acquire shares if his entitlement under the contract to acquire them is not (or is no longer) subject to conditions or if all conditions to which it was subject have been met.

A reference to a contract becoming unconditional is to be construed accordingly.

[7544]

NOTES

Commencement: 20 May 2006.
Revoked, subject to savings, as noted at the beginning of these Regulations.

CAPITAL REQUIREMENTS REGULATIONS 2006

(SI 2006/3221)

NOTES

Made: 4 December 2006.
Authority: European Communities Act 1972, s 2(2).
Commencement: 1 January 2007 (see reg 1 at **[7545]**).
As of 1 July 2007, these Regulations had not been amended.

ARRANGEMENT OF REGULATIONS

PART 1
INTRODUCTION

PART 2
APPLICATIONS FOR PERMISSIONS

PART 1
INTRODUCTION

1 Citation, commencement and interpretation

(1) These Regulations may be cited as the Capital Requirements Regulations 2006 and come into force on 1st January 2007.

(2) In these Regulations—

"the Act" means the Financial Services and Markets Act 2000;

"application" unless the context otherwise requires means an application—
- (a) for a permission;
- (b) to vary or revoke a permission; or
- (c) to vary or revoke the terms and conditions to which a permission is subject;

"banking consolidation directive" means Council Directive 2006/48/EC of the European Parliament and of the Council of 14 June 2006 relating to the taking up and pursuit of the business of credit institutions;

"capital adequacy directive" means Council Directive 2006/49/EC of the European Parliament and of the Council of 14 June 2006 relating to the capital adequacy of investment firms and credit institutions;

"decision" means a decision made by the EEA consolidated supervisor in relation to an application or a proposal;

"EEA consolidated supervisor" means the competent authority responsible, under the banking consolidation directive or under the banking consolidation directive as applied by Articles 2(2) and 37(1) of the capital adequacy directive, for the exercise of supervision on a consolidated basis of—
- (a) an EEA parent credit institution;
- (b) an EEA parent investment firm; or
- (c) credit institutions or investment firms controlled by an EEA parent financial holding company where the parent is authorised in a different EEA State to at least one of the subsidiaries;

"EEA parent credit institution" means a parent credit institution in an EEA State which is not a subsidiary of another credit institution or investment firm authorised in any EEA State, or of a financial holding company set up in any EEA State;

"EEA parent investment firm" means a parent investment firm in an EEA State which is not a subsidiary of another credit institution or investment firm authorised in any EEA State or of a financial holding company set up in any EEA State;

"EEA parent financial holding company" means a parent financial holding company in an EEA State which is not a subsidiary of another credit institution or investment firm authorised in any EEA State or of another financial holding company set up in any EEA State;

"joint decision" means a decision, made jointly by all relevant competent authorities and the EEA consolidated supervisor, in relation to an application or a proposal;

"national consolidated supervisor" means the competent authority responsible, under the banking consolidation directive or under the banking consolidation directive as applied by Articles 2(2) and 37(1) of the capital adequacy directive, for the exercise of supervision on a consolidated basis of—

(a) a parent credit institution in an EEA State;

(b) a parent investment firm in an EEA State; or

(c) credit institutions or investment firms controlled by a parent financial holding company in an EEA State;

"parent credit institution in an EEA State" means a credit institution which has a credit institution, an investment firm or a financial institution as a subsidiary or which holds a participation in such an institution, and which is not itself a subsidiary of another credit institution or investment firm authorised in the same EEA State, or of a financial holding company set up in the same EEA State;

"parent investment firm in an EEA State" means an investment firm which has a credit institution, an investment firm or a financial institution as a subsidiary or which holds a participation in such an institution, and which is not itself a subsidiary of another credit institution or investment firm authorised in the same EEA State or of a financial holding company set up in the same EEA State;

"parent financial holding company in an EEA State" means a financial holding company which is not itself a subsidiary of a credit institution or investment firm authorised in the same EEA State, or of another financial holding company set up in the same EEA State;

"permission" means a permission referred to in Article 84(1) or 87(9) of the banking consolidation directive, an approval referred to in Article 105 or Annex III, Part 6 of the banking consolidation directive or recognition referred to in Annex V of the capital adequacy directive;

"proposal" means a proposal made by the EEA consolidated supervisor to vary or revoke a permission or vary or revoke the terms or conditions to which it is subject;

"relevant competent authority" means a competent authority which is not the EEA consolidated supervisor and which has authorised a subsidiary of an EEA parent credit institution, a subsidiary of an EEA parent investment firm or a subsidiary of an EEA parent financial holding company.

(3) Save as provided by paragraph (2)—

(a) any expression used in these Regulations which is used in the banking consolidation directive or the capital adequacy directive shall have the meaning given by those directives; and

(b) any other expression used in these Regulations which is defined for the purposes of the Act has the meaning given by the Act.

[7545]

NOTES

Commencement: 1 January 2007.

PART 2
APPLICATIONS FOR PERMISSIONS

2 Application for permission

(1) This regulation applies where the Authority is the EEA consolidated supervisor.

(2) An application may be made to the Authority—

(a) by an EEA parent credit institution and its subsidiaries;

(b) by an EEA parent investment firm and its subsidiaries; or

(c) jointly by the subsidiaries of an EEA parent financial holding company.

(3) An application must be made in such manner as the Authority may direct.

[7546]

NOTES

Commencement: 1 January 2007.

3 Applications to the Authority as EEA consolidated supervisor

(1) This regulation applies where the Authority is the EEA consolidated supervisor and has received an application.

(2) The Authority must—

- (a) forward the complete application to the relevant competent authorities without delay;
- (b) work together, in full consultation with the relevant competent authorities, and do everything in its power to reach a joint decision within six months from the date on which it received the complete application; and
- (c) provide the applicants with a document containing the fully reasoned joint decision, if any.

(3) If a joint decision is not made by the Authority and the relevant competent authorities within the period specified in paragraph (2)(b), the Authority must—

- (a) make its own decision on the application, taking account of the views and reservations of the relevant competent authorities expressed during that period; and
- (b) provide the applicant and the relevant competent authorities with a document containing the fully reasoned decision.

[7547]

NOTES

Commencement: 1 January 2007.

4 Applications forwarded to the Authority as a relevant competent authority

(1) This regulation applies where the Authority is a relevant competent authority and has been forwarded a complete application by the EEA consolidated supervisor.

(2) The Authority must work together, in full consultation with the EEA consolidated supervisor and the other relevant competent authorities, and do everything in its power to reach a joint decision within six months from the date on which the EEA consolidated supervisor received the complete application.

[7548]

NOTES

Commencement: 1 January 2007.

5 Proposals to vary or revoke a decision or joint decision

(1) This regulation applies where the Authority is the EEA consolidated supervisor and intends to make a proposal.

(2) The Authority must give written notice to those persons to whom the permission, which is the subject of the intended proposal, applies.

(3) The notice must—

- (a) give details of the intended proposal; and
- (b) inform the persons to whom the permission applies that they may make representations to the Authority within such period as may be specified in the notice.

(4) If after the period specified in the notice has expired the Authority makes the proposal, it must—

- (a) send the proposal and forward any representations received during that period to the relevant competent authorities;
- (b) work together, in full consultation with the relevant competent authorities, taking account of such representations and do everything in its power to reach a joint decision within six months from the date on which the proposal was made; and

(c) provide the persons to whom the permission applies with a document containing the fully reasoned joint decision, if any.

(5) If a joint decision is not made by the Authority and the relevant competent authorities within the period specified in paragraph (4)(b), the Authority must—

(a) make its own decision on the proposal, taking account of the views and reservations of the relevant competent authorities expressed during that period and of any representations made by the persons to whom the permission applies;

(b) provide the persons to whom the permission applies and the relevant competent authorities with a document containing the fully reasoned decision.

[7549]

NOTES

Commencement: 1 January 2007.

6 Where the Authority is a relevant competent authority and receives a proposal from the EEA consolidated supervisor, it must work together, in full consultation with the EEA consolidated supervisor and the other relevant competent authorities, and do everything in its power to reach a joint decision within six months from the date on which the proposal was made.

[7550]

NOTES

Commencement: 1 January 2007.

7 Recognition and application of a decision or joint decision

The Authority must recognise a decision or a joint decision as determinative and apply it in respect of any authorised person to whom the banking consolidation directive or the capital adequacy directive applies.

[7551]

NOTES

Commencement: 1 January 2007.

8 Exercise of functions under section 148 of the Act for the purpose of applying a decision or a joint decision

(1) The Authority may exercise the powers conferred by section 148 of the Act (modification or waiver of rules) if it appears desirable to do so for the purpose of applying a decision or a joint decision.

(2) In such a case the requirements contained in—

(a) subsections (2) and (9)(b) of section 148 for the Authority's powers to be exercisable only on the application or with the consent of an authorised person; and

(b) section 148(4),

shall not apply.

[7552]

NOTES

Commencement: 1 January 2007.

9—(1) Where the Authority proposes to exercise the powers conferred by section 148 of the Act in relation to an authorised person for the purpose of applying a decision or a joint decision, other than on the application or with the consent of that person, it must give him written notice and have regard to any representations received within such period as is specified in the notice.

(2) The notice must—

(a) give details of any proposed direction or variation of a direction;

(b) give details of any proposed conditions;

(c) inform the person that, within such period as may be specified in the notice, he may make representations to the Authority;
(d) inform the person when the proposed direction, variation or condition takes effect.

[7553]

NOTES

Commencement: 1 January 2007.

PART 3
EXERCISE OF SUPERVISION

10 The Authority's duties as an EEA consolidated supervisor

Regulations 11 and 12 apply where the Authority is the EEA consolidated supervisor.

[7554]

NOTES

Commencement: 1 January 2007.

11—(1) The Authority must take such steps, in going concern and emergency situations, as it considers appropriate—

(a) to co-ordinate the gathering and dissemination of relevant or essential information; and
(b) in co-operation with the relevant competent authorities, to plan and co-ordinate supervisory activities.

(2) The Authority must provide a relevant competent authority with all information which the Authority considers to be essential for the exercise of the relevant competent authority's supervisory tasks.

(3) For the purposes of this regulation, information shall be regarded as essential if it could materially influence the assessment of the financial soundness of a credit institution, financial institution or investment firm in another EEA State. In particular essential information shall include:

(a) the group structure of all major credit institutions or investment firms in a group;
(b) the relevant competent authorities of the credit institutions or investment firms in a group;
(c) procedures for the collection and verification of information from credit institutions or investment firms in a group;
(d) adverse developments in credit institutions or investment firms or in other entities of a group, which could seriously affect other credit institutions or investment firms of that group;
(e) major sanctions and exceptional measures taken by the EEA consolidated supervisor or any of the relevant competent authorities under the banking consolidation directive or under the banking consolidation directive as applied by Articles 2(2) and 37(1) of the capital adequacy directive.

[7555]

NOTES

Commencement: 1 January 2007.

12—(1) On request, the Authority must provide a relevant competent authority with all the information which the Authority considers to be relevant for the exercise of the relevant competent authority's supervisory tasks.

(2) In determining the extent of relevant information, the Authority must have regard to the importance of the subsidiary within the financial system of the EEA State in which it is authorised.

[7556]

NOTES

Commencement: 1 January 2007.

13 The Authority's duties as EEA consolidated supervisor or national consolidated supervisor

Regulations 14, 15 and 16 apply where the Authority is either the EEA consolidated supervisor or the national consolidated supervisor.

[7557]

NOTES

Commencement: 1 January 2007.

14—(1) Where an emergency situation arises within a banking group which potentially jeopardises the stability of the financial system in any EEA State where an entity of a group has been authorised, the Authority must notify as soon as practicable—

(a) the central bank and other bodies with a similar function in their capacity as monetary authorities; and

(b) the department of the central government administration responsible for legislation on the supervision of credit institutions, financial institutions, investment services and insurance companies;

of the EEA State in which the entity has been authorised.

(2) The Authority, in notifying any body under paragraph (1), may share any information which it is not prevented from disclosing.

[7558]

NOTES

Commencement: 1 January 2007.

15 The Authority must, so far as necessary to facilitate and establish effective supervision and wherever possible, have written co-ordination and co-operation agreements in place with other competent authorities.

[7559]

NOTES

Commencement: 1 January 2007.

16—(1) Where the Authority is considering, in relation to a credit institution, an investment firm or a financial institution, whether to take action against that person which it considers will impose a major sanction or exceptional measure it must, before making a decision, consult the EEA consolidated supervisor, and where its decision would be of importance to a competent authority's supervisory tasks, that authority.

(2) Paragraph (1) does not apply where the Authority considers that—

(a) there is an urgent need to act; or

(b) such consultation may jeopardise the effectiveness of the decision referred to in paragraph (1).

(3) Where paragraph (1) does not apply by virtue of paragraph (2), the Authority must, without delay, inform the EEA consolidated supervisor and the other competent authorities referred to in paragraph (1) of the action that it has taken.

(4) In this regulation, the Authority may impose a major sanction or exceptional measure by—

(i) varying a Part IV permission;

(ii) exercising any of the powers conferred on it by section 148 of the Act;

(iii) publishing a statement under section 205 of the Act (public censure);

(iv) imposing a penalty in respect of a contravention under section 206 of the Act (financial penalties);

(v) exercising any of its powers (other than its powers under section 381, 383 or 384(2)) under Part XXV of the Act (injunctions and restitution).

[7560]

NOTES

Commencement: 1 January 2007.

17 Disclosed information

(1) Where the Authority is the EEA consolidated supervisor or a national consolidated supervisor and it needs information which has already been given to another competent authority, it must, wherever possible, obtain that information by requesting that the other competent authority which holds the information disclose it to the Authority.

(2) Where the Authority is the competent authority which has authorised a subsidiary of an EEA parent credit institution or a subsidiary of an EEA parent investment firm, and it needs information regarding the implementation of approaches and methodologies set out in the banking consolidation directive or the capital adequacy directive which may already be available to the EEA consolidated supervisor, it must, wherever possible, obtain that information by requesting that the EEA consolidated supervisor discloses the information to the Authority.

[7561]

NOTES

Commencement: 1 January 2007.

18–20 (*Amends the Financial Services and Markets Act 2000 (Consultation with Competent Authorities) Regulations 2001, SI 2001/2509, reg 2 at* **[4441]***, and inserts reg 8 at* **[4445B]**.)

PART 4

CREDIT INSTITUTIONS AND EXTERNAL CREDIT ASSESSMENT INSTITUTIONS

21 Interpretation

In this Part—

"assessment methodology" means a methodology for assigning credit assessments;

"ECAI" means an external credit assessment institution;

"exposure risk-weighting purposes" means the purposes of determining the risk weight of an exposure in accordance with Article 80 of the banking consolidation directive;

"securitisation risk-weighting purposes" means the purposes of determining the risk weight of a securitisation position in accordance with Article 96 of the banking consolidation directive.

[7562]

NOTES

Commencement: 1 January 2007.

22 Recognition for exposure risk-weighting purposes

(1) The Authority must recognise an ECAI as eligible for exposure risk-weighting purposes only if the Authority is satisfied, taking into account the requirements set out in Schedule 1, that—

(a) the ECAI's assessment methodology complies with the requirements of objectivity, independence, ongoing review and transparency; and

(b) the ECAI's credit assessments meet the requirements of credibility and transparency.

(2) The Authority may recognise an ECAI as eligible for exposure risk-weighting purposes without carrying out its own evaluation process if the ECAI has been recognised as eligible for those purposes by a competent authority of another EEA State.

(3) Where the Authority recognises an ECAI as eligible for exposure risk-weighting purposes, it must determine, taking into account the requirements set out in Schedule 2, with which of the credit quality steps set out in Part 1 of Annex VI of the banking consolidation directive the relevant credit assessments of the ECAI are to be associated.

(4) The Authority's determinations must be objective and consistent.

(5) The Authority may recognise, without carrying out its own determination process, a determination of the kind mentioned in paragraph (3) which has been made by a competent authority of another EEA State.

[7563]

NOTES

Commencement: 1 January 2007.

23 Recognition for securitisation risk-weighting purposes

(1) The Authority must recognise an ECAI as eligible for securitisation risk-weighting purposes only if the Authority is satisfied—

(a) taking into account the requirements set out in Schedule 1, that—

(i) the ECAI's assessment methodology complies with the requirements of objectivity, independence, ongoing review and transparency; and

(ii) the ECAI's credit assessments meet the requirements of credibility and transparency; and

(b) that the ECAI has a demonstrated ability in the area of securitisation.

(2) A demonstrated ability in the area of securitisation may be evidenced by a strong market acceptance.

(3) The Authority may recognise an ECAI as eligible for securitisation risk-weighting purposes without carrying out its own evaluation process if the ECAI has been recognised as eligible for those purposes by a competent authority of another Member State.

(4) Where the Authority recognises an ECAI as eligible for securitisation risk-weighting purposes, it must determine with which of the credit quality steps set out in Part 4 of Annex IX of the banking consolidation directive the relevant credit assessments of the ECAI are to be associated.

(5) The Authority's determinations must be objective and consistent.

(6) The Authority must, when making its determination—

(a) differentiate between the relative degrees of risk expressed by each assessment; and

(b) consider—

(i) quantitative factors (such as default rates and loss rates); and

(ii) qualitative factors (such as the range of transactions assessed by the ECAI and the meaning of the credit assessment).

(7) The Authority must seek to ensure that securitisation positions to which the same risk weight is applied on the basis of credit assessments of eligible ECAIs are subject to equivalent degrees of credit risk and, for this purpose the Authority may modify its determination as to the credit quality step with which a credit assessment is to be associated.

(8) The Authority may recognise, without carrying out its own determination process, a determination of the kind mentioned in paragraph (4) which has been made by a competent authority of another EEA State.

[7564]

NOTES

Commencement: 1 January 2007.

24 Publishing recognition process and list of ECAIs

The Authority must make publicly available—

(a) an explanation of its recognition process, and

(b) a list of eligible ECAIs.

[7565]

NOTES

Commencement: 1 January 2007.

25 Revoking recognition

The Authority may revoke the recognition of an ECAI—

(a) where the ECAI is recognised in accordance with paragraph (1) of regulation 22 or, as the case may be, paragraph (1) of regulation 23, if the Authority considers that the requirements of the applicable paragraph are no longer met; and

(b) where an ECAI is recognised in accordance with paragraph (2) of regulation 22 or, as the case may be, paragraph (3) of regulation 23, if the condition in the applicable paragraph is no longer met.

[7566]

NOTES

Commencement: 1 January 2007.

PART 5
MISCELLANEOUS

26 Restriction on disclosure

(1) This regulation applies where—

(a) a credit institution or investment firm does not meet a requirement of the banking consolidation directive, and

(b) by adopting a relevant measure, the Authority requires the credit institution or investment firm to take the necessary action or steps at an early stage to address the situation.

(2) A measure is relevant if its adoption—

(a) obliges the credit institution or investment firm to hold own funds in excess of the minimum level laid down in Article 75 of the banking consolidation directive;

(b) reinforces the arrangements, processes, mechanisms and strategies implemented to comply with Articles 22 and 123 of the banking consolidation directive;

(c) requires the credit institution or investment firm to apply a specific provisioning policy or treatment of assets in terms of own funds requirements;

(d) restricts or limits the business, operations or network of the credit institution or investment firm; or

(e) requires the reduction of the risk inherent in the credit institution's or investment firm's activities, products and systems.

(3) In such circumstances, sections 348, 349 and 352 of the Act apply to information about the adoption of the relevant measure—

(a) in the same way as they apply in relation to confidential information within the meaning of section 348(2) of the Act (subject to paragraph (4) of that section), and

(b) as if the Authority were a recipient of such information.

[7567]

NOTES

Commencement: 1 January 2007.

27 Functions of the Authority

Any function conferred by Part 2, 3 or 4 of these Regulations on the Authority (whether in the capacity of an EEA consolidated supervisor, a national consolidated supervisor, a relevant competent authority or otherwise) is to be treated as a function conferred on the Authority by a provision of the Act.

[7568]

NOTES

Commencement: 1 January 2007.

28 Service of notices

The Financial Services and Markets Act 2000 (Service of Notices) Regulations 2001 applies to any document given under regulation 3, 5 or 9 as they apply to any notice, direction or document of any kind under the Act.

[7569]

NOTES

Commencement: 1 January 2007.

29 Consequential amendments to primary and secondary legislation

(1) Schedule 3 (which amends the Act in consequence of the adoption of the banking consolidation directive) has effect.

(2) Schedule 4 (which amends other primary legislation in consequence of the adoption of the banking consolidation directive) has effect.

(3) Schedule 5 (which amends the Financial Conglomerates and other Financial Groups Regulations 2004 in consequence of the adoption of the banking consolidation directive and the capital adequacy directive) has effect.

(4) Schedule 6 (which amends other secondary legislation in consequence of the adoption of the banking consolidation directive and the capital adequacy directive) has effect.
[7570]

NOTES

Commencement: 1 January 2007.

SCHEDULES

SCHEDULE 1
RECOGNITION OF ECAIS

Regulations 22 and 23

PART 1
METHODOLOGY

Objectivity

1. The Authority must verify that an ECAI's assessment methodology is rigorous, systematic, continuous and subject to validation based on historical experience.

Independence

2. The Authority must verify that an ECAI's assessment methodology is free from external political influences or constraints, and from economic pressures that may influence a credit assessment.

3. The Authority must assess the independence of an ECAI's assessment methodology according to factors such as the following—
   (a) ownership and organisation structure of the ECAI;
   (b) financial resources of the ECAI;
   (c) staffing and expertise of the ECAI;
   (d) corporate governance of the ECAI.

Ongoing review

4. The Authority must verify that an ECAI's credit assessments—
   (a) are subject to ongoing review, taking place after all significant events and at least annually; and
   (b) are responsive to changes in the financial conditions.

5. The Authority must verify that the assessment methodology for each market segment is established according to standards such as the following—
   (a) that backtesting has been established for at least one year;
   (b) that the Authority monitors the regularity of the review process by the ECAI;
   (c) that the Authority is able to receive from the ECAI information as to the extent of the ECAI's contacts with the senior management of the entities which it rates.

6. The Authority must take such steps as it considers necessary to ensure that it is promptly informed by an ECAI of any material changes in the methodology that the ECAI uses for assigning credit assessments.

PART IV
STATUTORY INSTRUMENTS

Transparency and disclosure

7. The Authority must take such steps as it considers necessary to ensure that the principles of the methodology employed by an ECAI for the formulation of its credit assessments are publicly available so as to enable all potential users to decide whether they are derived in a reasonable way.

[7571]

NOTES

Commencement: 1 January 2007.

PART 2
CREDIT ASSESSMENTS

Credibility and market acceptance

8. The Authority must verify that the individual credit assessments of each ECAI are recognised in the market as credible and reliable by the users of such credit assessments.

9. The Authority must assess credibility according to factors such as the following—
  (a) market share of the ECAI;
  (b) revenues generated by the ECAI;
  (c) financial resources of the ECAI;
  (d) whether there is any pricing on the basis of the rating;
  (e) whether at least two credit institutions use the individual credit assessments of the ECAI for—
    (i) bond issuing, or
    (ii) assessing credit risks.

Transparency and Disclosure

10. The Authority must verify that individual credit assessments are—
  (a) accessible on equivalent terms to all credit institutions and investment firms having a legitimate interest in those individual credit assessments, and
  (b) available to non-domestic parties on equivalent terms as to domestic credit institutions and investment firms having a legitimate interest in those individual credit assessments.

[7572]

NOTES

Commencement: 1 January 2007.

SCHEDULE 2
MAPPING

Regulation 22

1.—(1) In order to differentiate between the relative degrees of risk expressed by each credit assessment, the Authority must consider quantitative factors such as the long-term default rate associated with all items assigned the same credit assessment.

(2) For recently established ECAIs and for those that have compiled only a short record of default data, the Authority must ask the ECAI what it believes to be the long-term default rate associated with all items assigned the same credit assessment.

2. In order to differentiate between the relative degrees of risk expressed by each credit assessment, the Authority must consider qualitative factors such as—
  (a) the pool of issuers that the ECAI covers;
  (b) the range of credit assessments that the ECAI assigns;
  (c) each credit assessment meaning;
  (d) the ECAI's definition of default.

3. The Authority must compare default rates experienced for each credit assessment of an ECAI and compare them with a benchmark built on the basis of default rates experienced by other ECAIs on a population of issuers which the Authority believes to present an equivalent level of credit risk.

4. Where the Authority believes that the default rates experienced for the credit assessment of an ECAI are materially and systematically higher than the benchmark, the Authority must assign a higher credit quality step in the credit quality assessment scale to the ECAI's credit assessment.

5. Where the Authority has increased the associated risk weight for a credit assessment of an ECAI, if the ECAI demonstrates that the default rates experienced for its credit assessment are no longer materially and systematically higher than the benchmark, the Authority may decide to restore the original credit quality step in the credit quality assessment scale for the ECAI's credit assessment.

[7573]–[9000]

NOTES

Commencement: 1 January 2007.

(Sch 3 amends the Financial Services and Markets Act 2000, s 405, Sch 3, Pts I, III Sch 11A, Pt 2 at **[2403]**, **[2438]**, **[2440]**, **[2450B]**; *Sch 4 amends the Companies Act 1985, ss 209, 262, 699 at* **[194]**, **[266]**, **[547]**, *and also amends the Consumer Credit Act 1974, the Building Societies Act 1986, the Bank of England Act 1998, the Criminal Justice Act 1993, the Terrorism Act 2000, and the Proceeds of Crime Act 2002 (outside the scope of this work); Sch 5 amends the Financial Conglomerates and Other Financial Groups Regulations 2004, SI 2004/1862, regs 1, 9, 10, 15 at* **[4863]**, **[4691]**, **[4692]**, **[4694]**; *Sch 6 (Consequential Amendments to Other Secondary Legislation) amends the Financial Markets and Insolvency (Settlement Finality) Regulations 1999, SI 1999/2979, reg 2 at* **[6947]**, *the Financial Services and Markets Act 2000 (Regulated Activities) Order 2001, SI 2001/544, art 9C, Sch 3 at* **[4012]**, **[4105]**, *the Financial Services and Markets Act 2000 (Compensation Scheme: Electing Participants) Regulations 2001, SI 2001/1783, reg 1 at* **[4362]**, *the Financial Services and Markets Act 2000 (Disclosure of Confidential Information) Regulations 2001, SI 2001/2188, regs 2, 9 at* **[4373]**, **[4380]**, *the Financial Services and Markets Act 2000 (EEA Passport Rights) Regulations 2001, SI 2001/2511, reg 2 at* **[4449]**, *the Financial Services and Markets Act 2000 (Gibraltar) Order 2001, SI 2001/3084, art 4 at* **[4507]**, *the Financial Services and Markets Act 2000 (Confidential Information) (Bank of England) (Consequential Provisions) Order 2001, SI 2001/3648, arts 4, 6 at* **[4627]**, **[4629]**, *the Uncertificated Securities Regulations 2001, SI 2001/3755, Sch 2 at* **[7503]**, *the Financial Services and Markets Act 2000 (Regulated Activities) (Amendment) Order 2002, SI 2002/682, art 9 at* **[4637]**, *the Enterprise Act 2002 (Merger Fees and Determination of Turnover) Order 2003, SI 2003/1370, Schedule at* **[7173]**, *the Credit Institutions (Reorganisation and Winding Up) Regulations 2004, SI 2004/1035, regs 2, 5, and contains various other amendments that are outside the scope of this work.)*

COMPANIES ACT 2006 (COMMENCEMENT NO 1, TRANSITIONAL PROVISIONS AND SAVINGS) ORDER 2006

(SI 2006/3428)

NOTES

Made: 20 December 2006.

Authority: Companies Act 2006, s 1296(1), (2), 1300(2).

Commencement: see art 1 at **[7575]**.

As of 1 July 2007, this Order had not been amended. However, see art 10 of the draft Companies Act 2006 (Commencement No 3, Consequential Amendments, Transitional Provisions and Savings) Order 2007 in Appendix 12 at **[A12]**. Article 10(1) of that draft SI provides for the revocation of Sch 1, paras 12(2), 16, as from 1 October 2007.

ARRANGEMENT OF ARTICLES

SCHEDULES

1 Citation, interpretation and coming into force

(1) This Order may be cited as the Companies Act 2006 (Commencement No 1, Transitional Provisions and Savings) Order 2006.

(2) In this Order—

"the 1985 Act" means the Companies Act 1985; and

"the 1986 Order" means the Companies (Northern Ireland) Order 1986.

(3) Articles 1, 2, 5, 6, 7(a) and 8 and Schedules 1 and 2 and Part 1 of Schedule 5 come into force on 1st January 2007.

(4) Articles 3 and 7(b) and Schedule 3 and Part 2 of Schedule 5 come into force on 20th January 2007.

(5) Articles 4 and 7(c) and Schedule 4 and Part 3 of Schedule 5 come into force on 6th April 2007.

[7574]

NOTES

Commencement: 1 January 2007.

2 Provisions coming into force on 1st January 2007

(1) The following provisions of the Companies Act 2006 come into force on 1st January 2007—

(a) section 1068(5) (registrar's duty to accept delivery by electronic means of documents subject to Directive disclosure requirements);
(b) section 1077 (public notice of receipt of certain documents);
(c) section 1078 (documents subject to Directive disclosure requirements);
(d) section 1079 (effect of failure to give public notice);
(e) section 1080 (the register);
(f) sections 1085 to 1092 (inspection etc of the register);
(g) sections 1102 to 1107 (language requirements: translation); and
(h) section 1111 (registrar's requirements as to certification or verification).

(2) The following provisions of the Companies Act 2006 come into force on 1st January 2007 so far as necessary for the purposes of the provisions mentioned in paragraph (1)—

(a) section 2 (the Companies Acts);
(b) section 1068(1) to (4), (6) and (7) (registrar's requirements as to form, authentication and manner of delivery);
(c) section 1114 (application of provisions about documents and delivery);
(d) section 1117 (registrar's rules);
(e) section 1120 (application of provisions to overseas companies);

(f) section 1168 (hard copy and electronic form and related expressions);
(g) in section 1173 (minor definitions: general), the definitions of "Gazette" and "working day"; and
(h) section 1284 (extension of Companies Acts to Northern Ireland).

[7575]

NOTES

Commencement: 1 January 2007.

3 Provisions coming into force on 20th January 2007

(1) The following provisions of the Companies Act 2006 come into force on 20th January 2007—

(a) sections 308 (manner in which notice to be given) and 309 (publication of notice of meeting on website);
(b) section 333 (sending documents relating to meetings etc in electronic form);
(c) section 463 (liability for false or misleading statements in reports);
(d) sections 791 to 810, 811(1) to (3), 813 and 815 to 828 (information about interests in a company's shares); and
(e) sections 1143 to 1148 and Schedules 4 and 5 (the company communications provisions).

(2) The following provisions of the Companies Act 2006 come into force on 20th January 2007 so far as necessary for the purposes of the provisions mentioned in paragraph (1)—

(a) section 2 (the Companies Acts);
(b) sections 1121, 1122, 1125 to 1131 and 1133 (provisions relating to offences);
(c) section 1168 (hard copy and electronic form and related expressions);
(d) in section 1173 (minor definitions: general), the definition of "working day"; and
(e) section 1284 (extension of Companies Acts to Northern Ireland).

(3) The provisions of the Companies Act 2006, so far as not brought into force by section 1300(1) of that Act or article 2 or the preceding provisions of this article, come into force on 20th January 2007 for the purpose of enabling the exercise of powers to make orders or regulations by statutory instrument.

[7576]

NOTES

Commencement: 20 January 2007.

4 Provisions coming into force on 6th April 2007

(1) The following provisions of the Companies Act 2006 come into force on 6th April 2007—

(a) section 1063 (fees payable to registrar), so far as not in force by virtue of article 3(3);
(b) section 1176 (power of Secretary of State to bring civil proceedings on company's behalf);
(c) section 1177 (repeal of certain provisions about company directors);
(d) section 1178 (repeal of requirement that certain companies publish periodical statement);
(e) section 1179 (repeal of requirement that Secretary of State prepare annual report); and
(f) section 1281 (disclosure of information under the Enterprise Act 2002).

(2) Section 1295 of, and Schedule 16 to, the Companies Act 2006 (repeals) come into force on 6th April 2007 so far as relating to the repeal of—

(a) the provisions of the 1986 Order corresponding to the provisions of the 1985 Act repealed by the provisions mentioned in paragraph (1)(b) to (e);
(b) section 41 of the 1985 Act and Article 51 of the 1986 Order (authentication of documents on behalf of company); and
(c) sections 293 and 294 of the 1985 Act and Articles 301 and 302 of the 1986 Order (age limits for directors).

(3) The following provisions of the Companies Act 2006 come into force on 6th April 2007 so far as necessary for the purposes of the provisions mentioned in paragraphs (1) and (2)—

(a) section 1060 (the registrar of companies);
(b) section 1061 (the registrar's functions); and
(c) section 1284 (extension of Companies Acts to Northern Ireland).

(4) The coming into force of section 1063 by virtue of paragraph (1)(a) does not extend to Northern Ireland.

[7577]

NOTES

Commencement: 6 April 2007.

5 Transitional adaptations of provisions brought into force

The provisions brought into force by articles 2, 3 and 4 have effect subject to any transitional adaptations specified in Schedule 1.

[7578]

NOTES

Commencement: 1 January 2007.

6 Interpretation of provisions brought into force

Where an expression in a provision brought into force by this Order (or in an adaptation made by this Order of such a provision)—

(a) is defined in the 1985 Act or the 1986 Order ("the old definition"); and
(b) is defined in the Companies Act 2006 by another provision that is not yet in force for the purposes of the provision brought into force ("the new definition"),

the expression has, for the purposes of the provision brought into force (or the adaptation), the meaning given by the old definition until the new definition is brought into force for the purposes of that provision.

[7579]

NOTES

Commencement: 1 January 2007.

7 Consequential repeals

Section 1295 of, and Schedule 16 to, the Companies Act 2006 (repeals) come into force—

(a) on 1st January 2007 so far as relating to the repeal of the provisions specified in Schedule 2;
(b) on 20th January 2007 so far as relating to the repeal of the provisions specified in Schedule 3; and
(c) on 6th April 2007 so far as relating to the repeal of the provisions specified in Schedule 4.

[7580]

NOTES

Commencement: 1 January 2007 (para (a)); 20 January 2007 (para (b)); 6 April 2007 (para (c)).

8 Transitional provisions and savings

(1) Schedule 5 contains transitional provisions and savings relating to the provisions (and repeals) brought into force by this Order.

(2) Nothing in this Order affects the application of any provision of the 1985 Act or the 1986 Order as applied by the Limited Liability Partnerships Regulations 2001 or the Limited Liability Partnerships Regulations (Northern Ireland) 2004 to limited liability partnerships.

[7581]

NOTES

Commencement: 1 January 2007.

SCHEDULES

SCHEDULE 1
TRANSITIONAL ADAPTATIONS OF PROVISIONS BROUGHT INTO FORCE
Article 5

The Companies Acts

1.—(1) Section 2 (the Companies Acts) has effect with the following adaptation.

(2) For subsection (1)(c) substitute—

"(c) the provisions of the Companies Acts as defined in section 744 of the Companies Act 1985, and the Companies Orders as defined in Article 2(3) of the Companies (Northern Ireland) Order 1986, that remain in force.".

Information about interests in a company's shares

2.—(1) Section 813 (register of interests disclosed: refusal of inspection or default in providing copy) has effect with the following adaptation.

(2) In subsection (1) omit ", otherwise than in accordance with an order of the court,".

3.—(1) Section 826 (information about interests in a company's shares protected from wider disclosure) has effect with the following adaptation.

(2) In subsection (1) for "regulations under section 409(3)" substitute "section 231(3) of the Companies Act 1985 or Article 239(3) of the Companies (Northern Ireland) Order 1986".

Documents delivered to registrar of companies

4.—(1) Section 1077 (public notice of receipt of certain documents) has effect with the following adaptation.

(2) Omit subsection (1)(b).

5.—(1) Section 1078 (documents subject to Directive disclosure requirements) has effect with the following adaptations.

(2) In subsection (2) (documents relating to any company)—

(a) under the heading "*Constitutional documents*"—

(i) in item 2 for "Any amendment of the company's articles" substitute "Any amendment of the company's memorandum or articles";

(ii) for item 3 substitute—

"3. After any amendment of the company's memorandum or articles, the text of the document as amended.";

(iii) omit item 4;

(b) under the heading "*Accounts, reports and returns*", in item 1 for "441" substitute "242 of the Companies Act 1985 or Article 250 of the Companies (Northern Ireland) Order 1986".

(3) In subsection (3) (documents relating to public company)—

(a) under the heading "*Share capital*"—

(i) in item 2 omit "and the statement of capital accompanying it";

(ii) in item 3 for "section 570 or 571" substitute "section 95(1), (2) or (3) of the Companies Act 1985 or Article 105(1), (2) or (3) of the Companies (Northern Ireland) Order 1986";

(iii) in item 4 for "section 593 or 599" substitute "section 103 or 104 of the Companies Act 1985 or Article 113 or 114 of the Companies (Northern Ireland) Order 1986";

(iv) omit items 5 and 6;

(v) for item 7 substitute—

"7. Statement or notice delivered under section 128 of the Companies Act 1985 or Article 138 of the Companies (Northern Ireland) Order 1986 (registration of particulars of special rights).";

(vi) omit item 8;

(vii) in item 9 for "section 689" substitute "section 122 of the Companies Act 1985 or Article 132 of the Companies (Northern Ireland) Order 1986" and omit "and the statement of capital accompanying it";

(viii) omit item 10;

(ix) for item 11 substitute—

"11. Any statutory declaration or statement delivered under section 117 of the Companies Act 1985 or Article 127 of the Companies (Northern Ireland) Order 1986 (public company share capital requirements).";

(b) under the heading "*Mergers and divisions*"—

(i) in item 1 for "section 906 or 921" substitute "paragraph 2(1) of Schedule 15B to the Companies Act 1985 or paragraph 2(1) of Schedule 15B to the Companies (Northern Ireland) Order 1986";

(ii) in item 2 for "section 899 or 900 in respect of a compromise or arrangement to which Part 27 (mergers and divisions of public companies) applies" substitute "section 425(2) or 427 of that Act in respect of a compromise or arrangement to which section 427A of that Act applies or under Article 418(2) or 420 of that Order in respect of a compromise or arrangement to which Article 420A of that Order applies".

(4) Omit subsection (4).

(5) For subsections (5) and (6) (power to make provision for documents relating to overseas company) substitute—

"(5) In the case of a company incorporated outside the United Kingdom or a credit or financial institution to which section 699A of the Companies Act 1985 or Article 648A of the Companies (Northern Ireland) Order 1986 applies—

1. Any return delivered under paragraph 1, 7 or 8 of Schedule 21A to that Act or paragraph 1, 7 or 8 of Schedule 20A to that Order (branch registration).
2. Any document delivered under paragraph 1 or 8 of Schedule 21A to that Act or under paragraph 1 or 8 of Schedule 20A to that Order.
3. Any notice under section 695A(3) of that Act or Article 645A of that Order of the closure of a branch.
4. Any document delivered under Schedule 21C to that Act or Schedule 20C to that Order (accounts and reports of foreign credit and financial institutions).
5. Any document delivered under Schedule 21D to that Act or Schedule 20D to that Order (accounts and reports of companies subject to branch registration, other than credit and financial institutions).
6. Any return delivered under section 703P of that Act or Article 652O of that Order (particulars on winding up).".

6.—(1) Section 1079 (effect of failure to give public notice) has effect with the following adaptations.

(2) In subsection (2)(a) and subsection (4)(a) for "amendment of the company's articles" substitute "amendment of the company's memorandum or articles".

7.—(1) Section 1080 (the register) has effect with the following adaptation.

(2) In subsection (1)(c), for "section 869(5) or 885(4)" substitute "section 401(2) or 418 of the Companies Act 1985 or Article 409(3) of the Companies (Northern Ireland) Order 1986".

8.—(1) Section 1085 (inspection of the register) has effect with the following adaptation.

(2) In subsection (2) for "section 1083(1)" substitute "section 707A(2) of the Companies Act 1985 or Article 656A(2) of the Companies (Northern Ireland) Order 1986".

9.—(1) Section 1087 (material not available for public inspection) has effect with the following adaptations.

(2) In subsection (1)(a) for "views expressed pursuant to section 56" substitute "a statement that a request has been made pursuant to section 29(2) of the Companies Act 1985 or Article 39(2) of the Companies (Northern Ireland) Order 1986 or any response to such a request".

(3) For subsection (1)(b) substitute—

"(b) at any time when an order made under section 723B of the Companies Act 1985 is in force in relation to an individual, so much of any record kept by the registrar as contains information which is recorded as particulars of the individual's residential address that were contained in a document delivered to the registrar after the order came into force;".

(4) Omit subsection (1)(c) to (g).

(5) In subsection (1)(h)(i), for "section 860" substitute "section 395 of the Companies Act 1985 or Article 402 of the Companies (Northern Ireland) Order 1986".

(6) In subsection (1)(h)(ii), for "section 878" substitute "section 410 of the Companies Act 1985".

10.—(1) Section 1103 (documents to be drawn up and delivered in English) has effect with the following adaptation.

(2) After subsection (2) insert—

"(3) This section does not affect the operation of the following provisions (under which documents may be delivered in a language other than English if a certified translation is delivered)—

(a) section 228(2)(f) or 228A(2)(g) of the Companies Act 1985 or Article 236(2)(f) of the Companies (Northern Ireland) Order 1986 (conditions for exemption from duty to prepare group accounts: delivery of certain accounts and reports);
(b) section 242(1) of that Act or Article 250(1) of that Order (main requirements as to accounts and reports);
(c) section 272(5) of that Act or Article 280(5) of that Order (interim accounts prepared for a proposed distribution by a public company);
(d) section 273(7) of that Act or Article 281(7) of that Order (initial accounts prepared for a proposed distribution by a public company);
(e) paragraph 7(3) of Part 2 of Schedule 9 to that Act or paragraph 7(3) of Part 2 of Schedule 9 to that Order (information as to undertaking in which shares held as a result of financial assistance operation).".

11.—(1) Section 1104 (documents relating to Welsh companies) has effect with the following adaptations.

(2) For subsection (5) substitute—

"(5) None of the following provisions (which require certified translations into English of documents delivered to the registrar in another language) applies to a document relating to a Welsh company that is drawn up and delivered in Welsh—

(a) section 228(2)(f) and section 228A(2)(g) of the Companies Act 1985;
(b) section 242(1) of that Act;
(c) section 272(5) of that Act;
(d) section 273(7) of that Act;
(e) paragraph 7(3) of Part 2 of Schedule 9 to that Act;
(f) section 1105 of this Act.".

(3) After that subsection insert—

"(6) In this section, "a Welsh company" means a company whose memorandum states that its registered office is to be situated in Wales.".

12.—(1) Section 1105 (documents that may be drawn up and delivered in other languages) has effect with the following adaptations.

(2) *In subsection (2)(a) for "Chapter 3 of Part 3" substitute "section 380 of the Companies Act 1985 or Article 388 of the Companies (Northern Ireland) Order 1986".*

(3) In subsection (2)(b) for "section 400(2)(e) or section 401(2)(f)" substitute "section 228(2)(e) or section 228A(2)(f) of the Companies Act 1985 or Article 236(2)(e) of the Companies (Northern Ireland) Order 1986".

(4) In subsection (2)(c) for "Part 25" substitute "Part 12 of the Companies Act 1985 or Part 13 of the Companies (Northern Ireland) Order 1986".

13.—(1) Section 1120 (application of Part 35 to overseas companies) has effect with the following adaptations.

(2) For "an overseas company" substitute "an oversea company (as defined in section 744 of the Companies Act 1985) or a Part 23 company (as defined in Article 640 of the Companies (Northern Ireland) Order 1986)".

(3) For "a company as defined in section 1" substitute "a company as defined in section 735(1) of that Act or Article 3(1) of that Order".

The company communications provisions

14.—(1) Section 1143 (the company communications provisions) has effect with the following adaptation.

(2) In subsection (3), after "Part 35" insert "and, to the extent that they remain in force, Part 24 of the Companies Act 1985 and Part 24 of the Companies (Northern Ireland) Order 1986".

Extension of Companies Acts to Northern Ireland

15.—(1) Section 1284 (extension of Companies Acts to Northern Ireland) has effect with the following adaptations.

(2) In subsection (1) for "The Companies Acts as defined by this Act (see section 2)" substitute "The company law provisions of this Act that are for the time being in force".

(3) For subsection (2) substitute—

"(2) The corresponding provisions of the Companies (Northern Ireland) Order 1986 shall cease to have effect accordingly.".

Communications by a company

16.—(1) Schedule 5 (communications by a company) has effect with the following adaptation.

(2) *In paragraph 10(5), for "Chapter 3 of Part 3" substitute "section 380 of the Companies Act 1985 or Article 388 of the Companies (Northern Ireland) Order 1986".*

[7582]

NOTES

Commencement: 1 January 2007.

Paras 12(2), 16: revoked by the draft Companies Act 2006 (Commencement No 3, Consequential Amendments, Transitional Provisions and Savings) Order 2007, art 11(a), as from 1 October 2007 (see **[A12]**).

SCHEDULE 2
REPEALS BROUGHT INTO FORCE ON 1ST JANUARY 2007

Article 7(a)

PART 1
GREAT BRITAIN

Short title and chapter	Extent of repeal brought into force
Companies Act 1985 (c 6)	Section 29(4).
	Section 42.
	In sections 228(2)(f) and 228A(2)(g), the words from "subject to" to "without a translation)".
	In sections 242(1), 272(5) and 273(7), the words from "then, subject to" to "without a translation)".
	Section 707A(1).
	Section 709.
	Section 710B.

	Section 711.
	Section 723C(1)(a).
	In paragraph 7(3) of Part 2 of Schedule 9, the words from "then, subject to" to "without a translation)".
Insolvency Act 1986 (c 45)	In Schedule 13, in Part 1, the entry relating to section 711(2) of the Companies Act 1985.
Welsh Language Act 1993 (c 38)	Section 30.

[7583]–[7584]

NOTES

Commencement: 1 January 2007.

(Sch 2, Pt 2 (Northern Ireland) contains various repeals of provisions in the Companies (Northern Ireland) Order 1986, SI 1986/1032, the Insolvency (Northern Ireland) Order 1989, SI 1989/2405, and the Companies (Northern Ireland) Order 1990, SI 1990/593 (outside the scope of this work).)

SCHEDULE 3
REPEALS BROUGHT INTO FORCE ON 20TH JANUARY 2007

Article 7(b)

PART 1
GREAT BRITAIN

Short title and chapter	Extent of repeal brought into force
Companies Act 1985 (c 6)	Sections 198 to 220.
	Section 238(4A) to (4E).
	Section 239(2A) and (2B).
	Section 251(2A) to (2E).
	Section 253(2A).
	In section 262(1), the definition of "address".
	In section 262A, the entry for "address".
	Section 366A(3A) and (5A).
	Section 369(4A) to (4G).
	Section 372(2A), (2B) and (6A).
	Section 379A(2B) to (2F) and (5A).
Companies Act 1989 (c 40)	Section 134.
	Section 143(5).
	In Schedule 10, paragraphs 3, 6 and 14.
Criminal Justice and Police Act 2001 (c 16)	Section 45(4).
Civil Partnership Act 2004 (c 33)	In Schedule 27, paragraph 99.

[7585]–[7586]

NOTES

Commencement: 20 January 2007.

PART IV STATUTORY INSTRUMENTS

(Sch 3, Pt 2 (Northern Ireland) contains various repeals of provisions in the Companies (Northern Ireland) Order 1986, SI 1986/1032, the Insolvency (Northern Ireland) Order 1989, SI 1990/593, and the Companies (No 2) (Northern Ireland) Order 1990, SI 1990/1504 (outside the scope of this work).)

SCHEDULE 4
REPEALS BROUGHT INTO FORCE ON 6TH APRIL 2007

Article 7(c)

PART 1
GREAT BRITAIN

Short title and chapter	**Extent of repeal brought into force**
Limited Partnerships Act 1907 (c 24)	In section 16(1)—
	(a) the words ", and there shall be paid for such inspection such fees as may be appointed by the Board of Trade, not exceeding 5p for each inspection"; and
	(b) the words from "and there shall be paid for each certificate" to the end.
	In section 17(1)—
	(a) the words "(but as to fees with the concurrence of the Treasury)"; and
	(b) paragraph (a).
Companies Act 1985 (c 6)	Section 311.
	Sections 323 to 329.
	Sections 343 and 344.
	Section 438.
	Section 439—
	(a) in subsection (2), the words ", or is ordered to pay the whole or any part of the costs of proceedings brought under section 438,";
	(b) subsections (3) and (7); and
	(c) in subsection (8), the words "; and any such liability imposed by subsection (2) is (subject as mentioned above) a liability also to indemnify all persons against liability under subsection (3)".
	Section 453(1A)(b).
	Section 708(5).
	Section 720.
	Section 729.
	Parts 2 to 4 of Schedule 13.
	Schedule 23.
Companies Act 1989 (c 40)	Section 58.
	Section 143(10).
	In Schedule 17, paragraph 4.
Age of Legal Capacity (Scotland) Act 1991 (c 50)	In Schedule 1, paragraph 39.
Civil Partnership Act 2004 (c 33)	In Schedule 27, paragraphs 100 and 101.

[7587]–[7588]

NOTES

Commencement: 6 April 2007.

(*Sch 4, Pt 2* (*Northern Ireland*) *contains various repeals of provisions in the Companies* (*Northern Ireland*) *Order 1986, SI 1986/1032, the Companies* (*Northern Ireland*) *Order 1990, SI 1990/593, and the Companies* (*No 2*) (*Northern Ireland*) *Order 1990, SI 1990/1504* (*outside the scope of this work*).)

SCHEDULE 5
TRANSITIONAL PROVISIONS AND SAVINGS

Article 8(1)

PART 1
PROVISIONS COMING INTO FORCE ON 1ST JANUARY 2007

1 Savings for certain provisions relating to Welsh companies

(1) Regulations 4 and 5 of the Companies (Welsh Language Forms and Documents) Regulations 1994 continue to have effect notwithstanding the repeal of section 710B of the 1985 Act.

(2) Regulation 4 (documents excepted from requirement to file certified translation into English) has effect as if made under section 1104(2) of the Companies Act 2006.

(3) As so continued in force, that regulation has effect with the following adaptations—

(a) in paragraph (1) for "section 710B(3)(a)" substitute "section 1104(2)(a) of the Companies Act 2006"; and

(b) in paragraph (3) for "such a company as is mentioned in section 710B(1)(b)" substitute "a Welsh company as defined in section 1104(6) of the Companies Act 2006".

(4) Regulation 5 (requirements as to person by whom a translation of a document into English is to be certified as correct) has effect as if the requirements imposed by it were requirements imposed by the registrar under section 1111 of the Companies Act 2006 by means of rules under section 1117 of that Act.

(5) As so continued in force, that regulation has effect with the following adaptations—

(a) in the opening words for "section 710B(8)" substitute "section 1107 of the Companies Act 2006"; and

(b) in paragraph (a)(iv) for "section 710(4)" substitute "section 1104(3) of the Companies Act 2006".

[7589]

NOTES

Commencement: 1 January 2007.

PART 2
PROVISIONS COMING INTO FORCE ON 20TH JANUARY 2007

2 Information about interests in a company's shares

(1) The repeal of sections 198 to 210 and 220 of the 1985 Act or Articles 206 to 218 and 228 of the 1986 Order (obligation to disclose acquisitions and disposals of interests in shares) does not affect any obligation to which a person became subject under section 198 of that Act or Article 206 of that Order before 20th January 2007.

(2) The repeal of sections 212 to 220 of the 1985 Act or Articles 220 to 228 of the 1986 Order (power of public company to require disclosure of interests in shares) does not affect the operation of those provisions in relation to a notice issued by a company under section 212 of the 1985 Act or Article 220 of the 1986 Order before 20th January 2007.

(3) On and after 20th January 2007 any separate part of a register kept by a company under section 213 of the 1985 Act or Article 221 of the 1986 Order (register of interests

disclosed in response to requirement by company) shall continue to be kept by the company and shall be treated as a register kept under and for the purposes of section 808 of the Companies Act 2006.

(4) Until regulations under section 1136 of the Companies Act 2006 (regulations about where certain company records are to be kept available for inspection) are made specifying a place for the purposes of section 809(1)(b) of that Act—

(a) the register kept under section 808 of that Act (register of interests disclosed) may be kept by a company at any place where its register of members is kept; and

(b) no notice need be given to the registrar of companies under section 809(2) of that Act.

3 False or misleading statements in reports

Section 463 of the Companies Act 2006 (liability for false or misleading statements in reports) does not apply to a directors' report, directors' remuneration report or summary financial statement first sent to members and others under section 238 or 251 of the 1985 Act, or Article 246 or 259 of the 1986 Order, before 20th January 2007.

4 Existing agreements to communication by electronic means

(1) This paragraph applies where an address has been notified by a person to a company for the purposes of—

(a) section 238(4A) or 239(2A) of the 1985 Act or Article 246(4A) or 247(2A) of the 1986 Order (sending or supply of accounts and reports by means of electronic communications);

(b) section 251(2A) of the 1985 Act or Article 259(2A) of the 1986 Order (sending of summary financial statement by means of electronic communications); or

(c) section 369(4A) or 379A(2B) of the 1985 Act or Article 377(5) or 387A(2B) of the 1986 Order (notice of meeting given by means of electronic communications).

(2) Any such notification that is in force immediately before 20th January 2007 shall have effect on and after that date, in relation to the matters to which it relates, as an agreement under paragraph 6(a) of Schedule 5 to the Companies Act 2006 (agreement to accept documents or information in electronic form) and as an address specified under paragraph 7(1) of Schedule 5 to that Act (address for communications in electronic form).

5.—(1) This paragraph applies where an agreement between a person and a company has been entered into for the purposes of—

(a) section 238(4B) of the 1985 Act or Article 246(4B) of the 1986 Order (sending or supply of copies of accounts and reports by means of website);

(b) section 251(2B) of the 1985 Act or Article 259(2B) of the 1986 Order (sending of summary financial statement by means of website); or

(c) section 369(4B) or 379A(2C) of the 1985 Act or Article 377(6) or 387A(2C) of the 1986 Order (notice of meeting given by means of website).

(2) Any such agreement that is in force immediately before 20th January 2007 shall have effect on and after that date, in relation to the matters to which it relates, as an agreement under paragraph 9(a) of Schedule 5 to the Companies Act 2006 (agreement to accept documents or information by means of a website).

[7590]

NOTES

Commencement: 20 January 2007.

PART 3
PROVISIONS COMING INTO FORCE ON 6TH APRIL 2007

6 Saving for existing provisions relating to fees

(1) The coming into force of section 1063 of the Companies Act 2006 (fees payable to the registrar) does not affect the continued operation of any other provision under which the payment of fees to the registrar of companies may be required until—

(a) the coming into force of the repeal of the other provision; or

(b) the exercise of the power in section 1063 in a manner inconsistent with its continued operation.

(2) Notwithstanding the coming into force of the repeals in section 16 of the Limited Partnerships Act 1907 and the repeal of section 17(a) of that Act, the fees appointed under the said section 16 and having effect immediately before 6th April 2007 shall continue to be payable, and the rules in force under the said section 17(a) immediately before 6th April 2007 shall continue to have effect.

(3) The repeal of section 708(5) of the 1985 Act shall not prevent the registrar from continuing to charge fees thereunder of which notice had before the repeal been given to those to whom the services in question have been, are being or are to be provided (including notice by publication of a list of fees in respect of services provided to any person who seeks their provision).

7 Saving for certain acts done by a person as director

The repeal of section 293(3) of the 1985 Act or Article 301(3) of the 1986 Order (age limit for directors: validity of acts done before it is discovered appointment has terminated) does not affect the validity of acts done by a person acting as director to whom that section or Article applied.

8 Saving for civil proceedings brought by Department of Enterprise, Trade and Investment

The repeal of Article 431 of the 1986 Order (power of Department of Enterprise, Trade and Investment to bring civil proceedings on company's behalf) does not affect proceedings brought under that Article before 6th April 2007.

[7591]

NOTES

Commencement: 6 April 2007.

COMPANIES (REGISTRAR, LANGUAGES AND TRADING DISCLOSURES) REGULATIONS 2006

(SI 2006/3429)

NOTES

Made: 20 December 2006.

Authority: European Communities Act 1972, s 2(2); Companies Act 2006, ss 1091(4), 1105(2)(d), 1106(2).

Commencement: 1 January 2007 (see reg 1 at **[7592]**).

As of 1 July 2007, this Order had not been amended.

1 Citation, commencement and interpretation

(1) These Regulations may be cited as the Companies (Registrar, Languages and Trading Disclosures) Regulations 2006 and shall come into force on 1st January 2007.

(2) In these Regulations—

"the 1985 Act" means the Companies Act 1985,

"the 1986 Order" means the Companies (Northern Ireland) Order 1986, and

"the 2006 Act" means the Companies Act 2006.

[7592]

NOTES

Commencement: 1 January 2007.

2 Certification of electronic copies by registrar

(1) Where—

- (a) a person requires a copy of material on the register under section 1086 of the 2006 Act,
- (b) that person expressly requests that the copy be certified as a true copy, and
- (c) the registrar provides the copy in electronic form,

the registrar's certificate that the copy is an accurate record of the contents of the original document must be provided in accordance with the following provisions.

(2) The certificate must be authenticated by means of an electronic signature that—
(a) is uniquely linked to the registrar,
(b) indicates that the registrar has caused it to be applied,
(c) is created using means that the registrar can maintain under his sole control, and
(d) is linked—
(i) to the certificate, and
(ii) to the copy provided under section 1086 of the 2006 Act
in such a manner that any subsequent change of the data comprised in either is detectable.

(3) For the purposes of this regulation, an "electronic signature" means data in electronic form which are attached to or logically associated with other electronic data and which serve as a method of authentication.

[7593]

NOTES

Commencement: 1 January 2007.

3 (*Amends the Companies Act 1985, ss 54, 425, 427 at* **[60]**, **[453]**, **[455]**, *the Insolvency Act 1986, s 201 at* **[3358]**, *and the Companies (Forms) Regulations 1985, SI 1985/854, Sch 3 (and contains other amendments to the Companies (Northern Ireland) Order 1986, the Insolvency (Northern Ireland) Order 1989, and the Companies (Forms) Regulations (Northern Ireland) 1986).*)

4 Language requirements: contracts relating to allotments of shares

Section 1105 of the 2006 Act (documents that may be drawn up and delivered in languages other than English) applies to contracts required to be delivered to the registrar under section 88(2)(b)(i) of the 1985 Act or article 98(2)(b)(i) of the 1986 Order.

[7594]

NOTES

Commencement: 1 January 2007.

5 Voluntary filing of translations

The facility described in section 1106 of the 2006 Act (voluntary filing of translations) is available in relation to—
(a) all the official languages of the European Union, and
(b) all documents subject to the Directive disclosure requirements.

[7595]

NOTES

Commencement: 1 January 2007.

6, 7 (*Reg 6 introduces Schs 1 and 2 to these Regulations (amendments to the Companies Act 1985 and the Companies (Northern Ireland) Order 1986); reg 7 amends the Insolvency Act 1986, s 188 at* **[3345]**, *and the Insolvency (Northern Ireland) Order 1989.*)

(*Sch 1 amends the Companies Act 1985, ss 349, 351, 705, Sch 24 at* **[360]**, **[362]**, **[573]**, **[689]**; *Sch 2 amends the Companies (Northern Ireland) Order 1986.*)

FINANCIAL SERVICES AND MARKETS ACT 2000 (MARKETS IN FINANCIAL INSTRUMENTS) REGULATIONS 2007

(SI 2007/126)

NOTES

Made: 24 January 2007.
Authority: European Communities Act 1972, s 2(2).

Commencement: 1 April 2007 (certain purposes); 1 November 2007 (otherwise) (see reg 1(2)).

These Regulations are reproduced as amended by: the Financial Services and Markets Act 2000 (Markets in Financial Instruments) (Amendment) Regulations 2007, SI 2007/763.

ARRANGEMENT OF REGULATIONS

PART 1
GENERAL

PART 2
PART IV PERMISSION: INVESTMENT FIRMS

PART 3
TRANSITIONAL AND SAVING PROVISIONS

SCHEDULES:

PART 1
GENERAL

1 Citation and commencement

(1) These Regulations may be cited as the Financial Services and Markets Act 2000 (Markets in Financial Instruments) Regulations 2007.

(2) These Regulations come into force on 1st April 2007 for the purposes of—

(a) enabling the Authority to receive a notice under subsection (1)(b) of section 312A of the Act (inserted by these Regulations) in preparation for the making of arrangements as mentioned in that section by an EEA market operator on or after 1st November 2007;

(b) enabling a recognised investment exchange to give notice under subsection (2) of section 312C of the Act (inserted by these Regulations), and enabling the Authority to send a copy of the notice to the host state regulator as required by subsection (3) of that section;

(c) enabling applications to be made for approval under section 412A of the Act (inserted by these Regulations);

(d) enabling the Authority to give a direction as to the manner in which an application under section 412A is to be made and as to the content of the application and information to accompany it, and enabling the Authority to require the applicant to provide further information in accordance with section 412A(3);

(e) enabling the Authority, on receipt on or after that date of a consent notice under paragraph 13(1)(a) of Schedule 3 in relation to a EEA firm exercising an EEA right deriving from the markets in financial instruments directive, to prepare for the firm's supervision in accordance with paragraph 13(2)(a) of that Schedule;

(f) enabling the Authority, on receipt of a regulator's notice under paragraph 14 of Schedule 3 or a notice referred to in paragraph 14(1)(ba) of that Schedule (inserted by these Regulations) in relation to a EEA firm exercising an EEA right deriving from the markets in financial instruments directive, to prepare for the firm's supervision in accordance with paragraph 14(2)(a) of that Schedule;

(g) enabling—

(i) a UK firm to give a notice of intention under paragraph 19 of Schedule 3 (as amended by these Regulations) in exercise of an EEA right deriving from the markets in financial instruments directive,

(ii) the Authority to give a consent notice referred to in paragraph 19(4) of that Schedule to the host state regulator or a notice referred to in paragraph 19(8), (11) or (12) of that Schedule in relation to the exercise of that EEA right, and

(iii) the firm to make a reference to the Tribunal in accordance with paragraph 19(12)(b) of that Schedule in relation to the exercise of that EEA right;

(h) enabling—

(i) a UK firm to give a notice of intention under paragraph 20 of Schedule 3 (as amended by these Regulations) in exercise of an EEA right deriving from the markets in financial instruments directive,

(ii) the Authority to send a copy of such a notice to the host state regulator under paragraph 20(3) of that Schedule and notify the UK firm under paragraph 20(4) of that Schedule that it has done so,

and for all other purposes on 1st November 2007.

(3) For the purposes of paragraph (2)(e) to (h)—

"EEA right" has the meaning given in paragraph 7 of Schedule 3;

an "EEA right deriving from the markets in financial instruments directive" means an EEA right to carry on an activity—

(a) which is an investment service or activity listed in Section A of Annex I to the markets in financial instruments directive;

(b) which is an ancillary service listed in Section B of Annex I to the markets in financial instruments directive; or

(c) in relation to an investment which is a financial instrument listed in Section C of Annex I to the markets in financial instruments directive;

"Schedule 3" means Schedule 3 to the Act.

(4) Nothing in paragraph (2)(e) to (h) gives an EEA firm or a UK firm an EEA right to carry on, before 1st November 2007, an activity—

(a) which is an ancillary service listed in Section B of Annex I to the markets in financial instruments directive but which is not a non-core service listed in Section C of the Annex to the investment services directive;

(b) in relation to an investment which is a financial instrument listed in Section C of Annex I to the markets in financial instruments directive but which is not an instrument listed in Section B of the Annex to the investment services directive; or

(c) referred to in paragraph 5 of Section A of Annex I to the markets in financial instruments directive unless the firm has an EEA right to carry on one or more core services listed in Section A of the Annex to the investment services directive.

[7596]

NOTES

Commencement: 1 April 2007 (certain purposes); 1 November 2007 (otherwise) (see reg 1(2)).

2 Interpretation

In these Regulations—

"the Act" means the Financial Services and Markets Act 2000;

"authorised person" has the meaning given in section 31(2) of the Act;

"the Authority" means the Financial Services Authority;

"investment services directive" means Council Directive 93/22/EEC of 10 May 1993 on investment services in the securities field;

"markets in financial instruments directive" means Directive 2004/39/EC of the European Parliament and of the Council of 21 April 2004 on markets in financial instruments;

"Part IV permission" has the meaning given in section 40(4) of the Act;

["regulated activity" has the meaning given in section 22 of the Act;]

"Schedule 3" means Schedule 3 to the Act;

[7597]

NOTES

Commencement: 1 April 2007 (certain purposes); 1 November 2007 (otherwise) (see reg 1(2)).

Definition "regulated activity" inserted by the Financial Services and Markets Act 2000 (Markets in Financial Instruments) (Amendment) Regulations 2007, SI 2007/763, reg 2(1), as from 1 November 2007.

3 Amendments of primary and secondary legislation

(1) Schedule 1, which contains amendments of Part 13 of the Act (incoming firms: intervention by authority), has effect.

(2) Schedule 2, which contains amendments of Part 18 of the Act (recognised investment exchanges and clearing houses), has effect.

(3) Schedule 3, which inserts Part 18A of the Act, has effect.

(4) Schedule 4, which contains amendments of Schedule 3 to the Act (EEA passport rights), has effect.

(5) Schedule 5, which contains other amendments of the Act, has effect.

(6) Schedule 6, which contains consequential amendments of other enactments, has effect.

[7598]

NOTES

Commencement: 1 April 2007 (certain purposes); 1 November 2007 (otherwise) (see reg 1(2)).

PART 2
PART IV PERMISSION: INVESTMENT FIRMS

4 [General restriction on giving Part IV permission]

(1) The Authority must not give a Part IV permission to an applicant who is an investment firm unless it is satisfied that the applicant complies with—

(a) the provisions contained in or made under the Act implementing Chapter I of Title II of the markets in financial instruments directive; and

(b) any directly applicable Community regulation made under that Chapter.

(2) Paragraph (1) also applies if an authorised person becomes an investment firm by virtue of a variation of his Part IV permission.

(3) "Investment firm" has the meaning given in section 424A of the Act.

[7599]

NOTES

Commencement: 1 April 2007 (certain purposes); 1 November 2007 (otherwise) (see reg 1(2)).

Regulation heading: inserted by the Financial Services and Markets Act 2000 (Markets in Financial Instruments) (Amendment) Regulations 2007, SI 2007/763, reg 2(2)(a), as from 1 November 2007.

[4A Applications to be an exempt investment firm

(1) A person may apply in accordance with section 40 of the Act for a Part IV permission to carry on regulated activities as an exempt investment firm.

(2) An authorised person may become entitled to carry on regulated activities as an exempt investment firm only by applying for a variation of his Part IV permission in accordance with section 44 of the Act.

(3) For the purposes of this regulation, and regulations 4B and 4C, "exempt investment firm" means an authorised person who—

(a) is an investment firm within the meaning given in Article 4.1.1 of the markets in financial instruments directive, and

(b) has a Part IV permission,

but to whom Title II of the markets in financial instruments directive does not apply.

(4) A person may only apply for a Part IV permission as mentioned in paragraph (1), and an authorised person may only apply for a variation of his Part IV permission as mentioned in paragraph (2), if the person or authorised person has his relevant office in the United Kingdom.

(5) In paragraph (4) "relevant office" means—

(a) in relation to a body corporate, its registered office or, if it has no registered office, its head office, and

(b) in relation to a person or authorised person other than a body corporate, the person's head office.]

[7599A]

NOTES

Commencement: 1 November 2007.

Inserted, together with regs 4B, 4C, by the Financial Services and Markets Act 2000 (Markets in Financial Instruments) (Amendment) Regulations 2007, SI 2007/763, reg 2(2)(b), as from 1 November 2007.

[4B Limitation on exempt investment firms

An exempt investment firm has no entitlement—

(a) to establish a branch by making use of the procedures in paragraph 19 of Schedule 3, or

(b) to provide any service by making use of the procedures in paragraph 20 of Schedule 3,

in a case where the entitlement of the firm to do so would, but for this regulation, derive from the markets in financial instruments directive.]

[7599B]

NOTES

Commencement: 1 November 2007.

Inserted as noted to reg 4A at **[7599A]**.

[4C Requirements to be applied to exempt investment firms

(1) If the Authority—

(a) gives to a person who has applied as mentioned in regulation 4A(1) a Part IV permission to carry on regulated activities as an exempt investment firm, or

(b) varies the Part IV permission of an authorised person who has applied as mentioned in regulation 4A(2) for a variation to permit him to carry on regulated activities as an exempt investment firm,

the requirements specified in paragraph (3) ("the specified requirements") shall be treated as being included in the permission by the Authority under section 43 of the Act.

(2) Notwithstanding paragraph (1)—

(a) the inclusion of the specified requirements in the Part IV permission does not—

(i) amount, for the purpose of section 52(6) of the Act, to a proposal to exercise the power of the Authority under section 43(1) of the Act,

(ii) amount, for the purpose of section 52(9) of the Act, to a decision to exercise the power of the Authority under section 43(1) of the Act, or

(iii) entitle the person to refer a matter under section 55(1) of the Act;

(b) the specified requirements shall not expire until the person ceases to be an exempt investment firm and, accordingly, section 43(5) shall not be treated as requiring the Authority to specify a period at the end of which they expire; and

(c) no application under section 44 of the Act to vary the permission by cancelling or varying any of the specified requirements may be made by the person unless he informs the Authority when making the application that he wishes to cease to be an exempt investment firm.

(3) The requirements are that the person—
- (a) does not hold clients' funds or securities and does not, for that reason, at any time, place himself in debt with his clients;
- (b) does not provide any investment service other than—
  - (i) the reception and transmission of orders in transferable securities and units in collective investment undertakings, and
  - (ii) the provision of investment advice in relation to the financial instruments mentioned in paragraph (i);
- (c) in the course of providing the investment services mentioned in sub-paragraph (b), transmits orders only to—
  - (i) investment firms authorised in accordance with the markets in financial instruments directive,
  - (ii) credit institutions authorised in accordance with the banking consolidation directive,
  - (iii) branches of investment firms or of credit institutions which are authorised in a third country and which are subject to and comply with prudential rules considered by the Authority to be at least as stringent as those laid down in the markets in financial instruments directive, the banking consolidation directive or Directive 2006/49/EC of the European Parliament and of the Council of 14 June 2006 on the capital adequacy of investment firms and credit institutions,
  - (iv) collective investment undertakings authorised under the law of a Member State to market units to the public and to the managers of such undertakings,
  - (v) investment companies with fixed capital, as defined in Article 15(4) of Second Council Directive 77/91/EEC of 13 December 1976 on the coordination of safeguards required of public companies in respect of their formation and the maintenance and alteration of their capital, the securities of which are listed or dealt in on a regulated market in a Member State.

(4) In paragraph (3)—
- (a) terms and expressions defined in Article 4 of the markets in financial instruments directive and used in the paragraph have the meanings given in that Article;
- (b) "the banking consolidation directive" means Directive 2006/48/EC of the European Parliament and of the Council of 14 June 2006 relating to the taking up and pursuit of the business of credit institutions;
- (c) other terms and expressions used both in the paragraph and in Article 3 of or Annex 1 to the markets in financial instruments directive have the same meanings in the paragraph as in that Article or Annex; and
- (d) "Member State", in sub-paragraph (c)(iv), includes an EEA State that is not a Member State.]

[7599C]

NOTES

Commencement: 1 November 2007.
Inserted as noted to reg 4A at **[7599A]**.

PART 3
TRANSITIONAL AND SAVING PROVISIONS

5 Transitional and saving provisions: market operators

(1) Section 312A(2) of the Act applies to arrangements made on or before 31st October 2007, in the United Kingdom, by an EEA market operator to facilitate access to, or use of, a regulated market or multilateral trading facility operated by it as it applies to arrangements under section 312A(1).

(2) Section 312C(2) and (4) of the Act does not apply in relation to arrangements made by a recognised investment exchange on or before 31st October 2007 in the territory of another EEA State to facilitate access to, or use of, a regulated market or multilateral trading facility operated by it by persons established in that State.

[7600]

NOTES

Commencement: 1 April 2007 (certain purposes); 1 November 2007 (otherwise) (see reg 1(2)).

6 Transitional and saving provisions: EEA firms

(1) Where the Authority has received a consent notice of the sort referred to in paragraph 13(1)(a) of Schedule 3 from the home state regulator of an EEA investment firm on or before 31st October 2007, paragraph 13 of Schedule 3 applies as if it had not been amended by paragraph 8 of Schedule 4 to these Regulations.

(2) In this regulation, "EEA investment firm" means an EEA firm falling within paragraph 5(a) of Schedule 3 (before its amendment by these Regulations).

[7601]

NOTES

Commencement: 1 April 2007 (certain purposes); 1 November 2007 (otherwise) (see reg 1(2)).

7 Transitional provisions: UK investment firms exercising passport rights under the investment services directive

(1) Where—

(a) a UK investment firm on or before 31st October 2007 has given—

(i) notice of intention under paragraph 19(2) or 20(1) of Schedule 3 in relation to an investment service specified in the first column in table 1 in Schedule 7 to these Regulations, or

(ii) notice of change under regulation 11(3) or 12(2)(a) of the EEA Passport Rights Regulations in relation to an investment service specified in the first column in table 1 in Schedule 7 to these Regulations, or

(b) the Authority on or before 31st October 2007 has given—

(i) a consent notice under paragraph 19(4) of Schedule 3 or a notice referred to in paragraph 20(3) of Schedule 3 in relation to an investment service specified in the first column in table 1 in Schedule 7 to these Regulations, or

(ii) a notice referred to in regulation 11(5) of the EEA Passport Rights Regulations in relation to an investment service specified in the first column in table 1 in Schedule 7 to these Regulations,

it is on 1st November 2007 to be treated as having given that notice in relation to the investment service or activity specified in the second column of table 1 opposite that investment service.

(2) Where—

(a) a UK investment firm on or before 31st October 2007 has given—

(i) notice of intention under paragraph 19(2) or 20(1) of Schedule 3 in relation to a non-core service specified in the first column in table 2 in Schedule 7 to these Regulations, or

(ii) notice of change under regulation 11(3) or 12(2)(a) of the EEA Passport Rights Regulations in relation to a non-core service specified in the first column in table 2 in Schedule 7 to these Regulations, or

(b) the Authority on or before 31st October 2007 has given—

(i) a consent notice under paragraph 19(4) of Schedule 3 or a notice referred to in paragraph 20(3) of Schedule 3 in relation to a non-core service specified in the first column in table 2 in Schedule 7 to these Regulations, or

(ii) a notice referred to in regulation 11(5) of the EEA Passport Rights Regulations in relation to a non-core service specified in the first column in table 2 in Schedule 7 to these Regulations,

it is on 1st November 2007 to be treated as having given that notice in relation to the ancillary service specified in the second column of table 2 opposite that non-core service.

(3) Where—

(a) a UK investment firm on or before 31st October 2007 has given—

(i) notice of intention under paragraph 19(2) or 20(1) of Schedule 3 in relation to the non-core service specified in paragraph 6 of Section C of the Annex to the investment services directive (investment advice concerning one or more of the instruments listed in Section B), or

(ii) notice of change under regulation 11(3) or 12(2)(a) of the EEA Passport Rights Regulations in relation to the non-core service specified in paragraph 6 of Section C of the Annex to the investment services directive, or

(b) the Authority on or before 31st October 2007 has given—

(i) a consent notice under paragraph 19(4) of Schedule 3 or a notice referred to in paragraph 20(3) of Schedule 3 in relation to the non-core service specified in paragraph 6 of Section C of the Annex to the investment services directive, or

(ii) a notice referred to in regulation 11(5) of the EEA Passport Rights Regulations in relation to the non-core service specified in paragraph 6 of Section C of the Annex to the investment services directive,

it is on 1st November 2007 to be treated as having given that notice in relation to the investment service specified in paragraph 5 of Section A of Annex I to the markets in financial instruments directive (investment advice) and the ancillary service specified in paragraph 5 of Section B of the Annex to that directive (investment research and financial analysis).

(4) Where—

(a) a UK investment firm on or before 31st October 2007 has given—

(i) notice of intention under 19(2) or 20(1) of Schedule 3 in relation to an instrument specified in the first column in table 3 in Schedule 7 to these Regulations, or

(ii) notice of change under regulation 11(3) or 12(2)(a) of the EEA Passport Rights Regulations in relation to an instrument specified in the first column in table 3 in Schedule 7 to these Regulations, or

(b) the Authority on or before 31st October 2007 has given—

(i) a consent notice under paragraph 19(4) of Schedule 3 or a notice referred to in paragraph 20(3) of Schedule 3 in relation to an instrument specified in the first column in table 3 in Schedule 7 to these Regulations, or

(ii) a notice referred to in regulation 11(5) of the EEA Passport Rights Regulations in relation to an instrument specified in the first column in table 3 in Schedule 7 to these Regulations,

it is on 1st November 2007 to be treated as having given that notice in relation to the financial instrument specified in the second column of table 3 opposite that instrument.

(5) Nothing in this regulation gives a UK investment firm the right to carry on a regulated activity (or an activity which, if it were regarded as carried on in the United Kingdom, would be a regulated activity) which it would require Part IV permission to carry on but for which it does not have Part IV permission.

[7602]

NOTES

Commencement: 1 April 2007 (certain purposes); 1 November 2007 (otherwise) (see reg 1(2)).

8 Additional saving provision: UK investment firms

Where the Authority has given a consent notice under paragraph 19(4) of Schedule 3 in relation to a UK investment firm on or before 31st October 2007, paragraph 19(6) of that Schedule applies as if it had not been amended by paragraph 10(c) of Schedule 4 to these Regulations, and paragraph 19(7B) (inserted by paragraph 10(d) of Schedule 4 to these Regulations) does not apply.

[7603]

NOTES

Commencement: 1 April 2007 (certain purposes); 1 November 2007 (otherwise) (see reg 1(2)).

9 Transitional provision: appointed representatives and tied agents

(1) A person—

(a) to whom section 39(1A) or 39A(1) of the Act (both inserted by these Regulations) applies,

(b) whose name appeared in the record maintained by the Authority under section 347(1)(i) of the Act immediately before 1st November 2007, is deemed, with effect from 1st November 2007, to be included in the record maintained by the Authority under section 347(1)(ha) of the Act (inserted by paragraph 12 of Schedule 5 to these Regulations).

(2) Paragraph (1) does not prevent the Authority from removing an entry from the record in accordance with section 347(3).

[7604]

NOTES

Commencement: 1 April 2007 (certain purposes); 1 November 2007 (otherwise) (see reg 1(2)).

[9A Transitional provision: exempt investment firms

(1) Except where paragraph (3) applies, an authorised person who immediately before 1st November 2007—

(a) is an investment firm within the meaning given in Article 4.1.1 of the markets in financial instruments directive,

(b) has his relevant office in the United Kingdom, and

(c) fulfils all the requirements set out in regulation 4C(3),

becomes an exempt investment firm with effect from that day as if he had applied as mentioned in regulation 4A(2) for a variation of his Part IV permission to permit him to carry on regulated activities as an exempt investment firm and the Authority had so varied the permission on that day.

(2) In paragraph (1) "relevant office" has the meaning given in regulation 4A(5).

(3) This paragraph applies—

(a) to an authorised person having a Part IV permission that, immediately before 1st November 2007—

(i) includes no requirement having the effect of prohibiting the person from holding clients' funds, or

(ii) permits the person, in connection with the carrying on of regulated activities comprising any investment services and activities (excluding activities to which, by virtue of Article 2, the markets in financial instruments directive does not apply), to carry on the activity consisting of both the safeguarding of assets belonging to another and the administration of those assets; and

(b) to an authorised person who, before 1st November 2007, gives the Authority notice, in such form as the Authority may direct, that he does not wish to become an exempt investment firm.

(4) In paragraph (3)—

(a) "clients' funds", in sub-paragraph (a)(i), has the same meaning as in Article 3 of the markets in financial instruments directive, and

(b) sub-paragraph (a)(ii) is to be construed in accordance with section 22 of the Act, any relevant order made under that section and Schedule 2 to the Act.

(5) The variation of a person's Part IV permission effected by paragraph (1) does not amount to the grant of an application for variation of a Part IV permission for the purpose of section 52(4) of the Act or to the determination of an application under Part IV for the purpose of section 55(1) of the Act.]

[7604A]

NOTES

Commencement: 1 April 2007 (certain purposes); 1 November 2007 (otherwise) (see further the note below).

Inserted by the Financial Services and Markets Act 2000 (Markets in Financial Instruments) (Amendment) Regulations 2007, SI 2007/763, reg 3, as from 1 April 2007 (certain purposes), and as from 1 November 2007 (otherwise) (see further the note below).

Note: reg 1(2) of the Financial Services and Markets Act 2000 (Markets in Financial Instruments) (Amendment) Regulations 2007, SI 2007/763 provides as follows—

"(2) These Regulations come into force—

(a) on 1st April 2007—

(i) for the purposes of enabling notices to be given in accordance with regulation 9A(3)(b) of the principal regulations (inserted by regulation 3) and enabling the Authority to give directions in accordance with that regulation as to the form of such notices,

(ii) for the purposes of enabling notice to be given under regulation 9B(2), 9C(2) or 9D(2) of the principal regulations (inserted by regulation 4),

(iii) for the purposes of regulation 9; and

(b) for all other purposes, on 1st November 2007.".

[9B Transitional provision: operators of alternative trading systems

(1) Any person who immediately before 1st November 2007—

(a) had a Part IV permission to carry on an activity of the kind specified by article 14, 21 or 25 of the principal Order in relation to an investment of a particular kind; and

(b) operated an alternative trading system (within the meaning of the Alternative Trading Systems Instrument 2003 (2003/45) made by the Authority under the Act on 19th June 2003),

is, subject to regulation 9C, from 1st November 2007 to be treated as having a Part IV permission to carry on the kind of activity specified by article 25D of the principal Order (inserted by the 2006 Order) in relation to an investment of the same kind which is a financial instrument.

(2) Where the person concerned gave written notice to the Authority on or before 1st October 2007 to that effect, paragraph (1) shall not apply to him.]

[7604B]

NOTES

Commencement: 1 April 2007 (certain purposes); 1 November 2007 (otherwise) (see further the note to reg 9A at **[7604A]**).

Inserted, together with regs 9C, 9D, by the Financial Services and Markets Act 2000 (Markets in Financial Instruments) (Amendment) Regulations 2007, SI 2007/763, reg 4, as from 1 April 2007 (certain purposes), and as from 1 November 2007 (otherwise) (see further the note to reg 9A at **[7604A]**).

[9C Transitional provision for investment firms and credit institutions in relation to options, futures and contracts for differences

(1) Any person who immediately before 1st November 2007—

(a) was an investment firm or a credit institution (in each case within the meaning of the principal Order as amended by the 2006 Order); and

(b) had a Part IV permission to carry on an activity of the kind specified by article 14, 21, 25, 37 or 53 of the principal Order in relation to an investment specified in the first column in the table in Schedule 8,

is from 1st November 2007 also to be treated as having a Part IV permission to carry on that kind of activity in relation to an investment specified in the second column of the table opposite that investment (in so far as he does not already have such permission).

(2) Where the person concerned gave written notice to the Authority on or before 1st October 2007 to that effect, paragraph (1) shall not apply to him.]

[7604C]

NOTES

Commencement: 1 April 2007 (certain purposes); 1 November 2007 (otherwise) (see further the note to reg 9A at **[7604A]**).

Inserted as noted to reg 9B at **[7604B]**.

[9D Transitional provision for management companies in relation to options, futures and contracts for differences

(1) Any person who immediately before 1st November 2007—

(a) was a management company (within the meaning of the principal Order as amended by the 2006 Order);

(b) was providing, in accordance with Article 5.3 of Council Directive 85/611/EEC of 20 December 1985 on the coordination of laws, regulations and administrative provisions relating to undertakings for collective investment in transferable securities, the investment service specified in paragraph 4 or 5 of Section A, or the ancillary service specified in paragraph 1 of Section B, of Annex I to the markets in financial instruments directive; and

(c) had a Part IV permission to carry on an activity of the kind specified by article 14,

21, 25, 37, 40 or 53 of the principal Order in relation to an investment specified in the first column in the table in Schedule 8,

is from 1st November 2007 also to be treated as having a Part IV permission to carry on that kind of activity in relation to an investment specified in the second column of the table opposite that investment (in so far as he does not already have such permission).

(2) Where the person concerned gave written notice to the Authority on or before 1st October 2007 to that effect, paragraph (1) shall not apply to him.]

[7604D]

NOTES

Commencement: 1 April 2007 (certain purposes); 1 November 2007 (otherwise) (see further the note to reg 9A at **[7604A]**).

Inserted as noted to reg 9B at **[7604B]**.

10 Interpretation of Part 3

In this Part—

["the principal Order" means the Financial Services and Markets Act 2000 (Regulated Activities) Order 2001;

"the 2006 Order" means the Financial Services and Markets Act 2000 (Regulated Activities) (Amendment No 3) Order 2006;]

"ancillary service" has the meaning given in Article 4.1.3 of the markets in financial instruments directive;

"EEA Passport Rights Regulations" means the Financial Services and Markets Act 2000 (EEA Passport Rights) Regulations 2001;

"EEA State" has the meaning given in paragraph 8 of Schedule 3;

"EEA market operator" has the meaning given in section 312D of the Act (inserted by these Regulations);

"financial instrument" has the meaning given in Article 4.1.17 of the markets in financial instruments directive;

"home state regulator" the meaning given in paragraph 9 of Schedule 3;

"instrument" (except in the expression "financial instrument") means any of the instruments listed in Section B of the Annex to the investment services directive;

"investment service" (except in the expression "investment services and activities") has the meaning given in Article 1.1 of the investment services directive;

"investment services and activities" has the meaning given in Article 4.1.2 of the markets in financial instruments directive;

"multilateral trading facility" has the meaning given in Article 4.1.15 of the markets in financial instruments directive;

"non-core service" means any of the services listed in Section C of the Annex to the investment services directive;

"recognised investment exchange" has the meaning given in section 285 of the Act;

"regulated activity" has the meaning given in section 22 of the Act;

"regulated market" has the meaning given in Article 4.1.14 of the markets in financial instruments directive;

"Schedule 3" means Schedule 3 to the Act;

"UK investment firm" means a UK firm (within the meaning of paragraph 10 of Schedule 3)—

(a) which is an investment firm (within the meaning of the investment services directive); and

(b) whose EEA right derives from that directive.

[7605]

NOTES

Commencement: 1 April 2007 (certain purposes); 1 November 2007 (otherwise) (see reg 1(2)).

Definitions "the principal Order" and "the 2006 Order" inserted, and definitions "regulated activity" and "Schedule 3" revoked, by the Financial Services and Markets Act 2000 (Markets in Financial Instruments) (Amendment) Regulations 2007, SI 2007/763, regs 2(3), 5, as from 1 November 2007.

SCHEDULES

(*Sch 1 inserts the Financial Services and Markets Act 2000, ss 194A, 195A at* **[2194A]**, **[2195A]**, *and amends s 199 of that Act at* **[2199]**; *Sch 2 amends ss 286, 287, 290, 296–298,*

302, 303, 306, 307, 313 of the 2000 Act, and inserts ss 292A, 293A, 301A–301G, 312A–312D (all in Part XVIII of the 2000 Act at **[2283]** *et seq); Sch 3 inserts Part XVIIIA of the 2000 Act (ss 313A–313D) at* **[2311A]** *et seq; Sch 4 amends Sch 3 to the 2000 Act at* **[2438]** *et seq; Sch 5 (Other Amendments of the Act) contains various other amendments to the 2000 Act; Sch 6 (Consequential Amendments of other Enactments) amends the Companies Act 1985, ss 23, 162, 162E, 226, 227, 228, 228A at* **[24]**, **[148]**, **[148E]**, **[212]**, **[213]**, **[214]**, **[214A]**, *the Financial Markets and Insolvency (Settlement Finality) Regulations 1999, SI 1999/2979, reg 2 at* **[6947]**, *the Financial Services and Markets Act 2000 (Prescribed Markets and Qualifying Investments) Order 2001, SI 2001/996, art 3 at* **[4108]**, *the Financial Services and Markets Act 2000 (Consultation with Competent Authorities) Regulations 2001, SI 2001/2509, reg 7 at* **[4445A]**, *the Financial Conglomerates and Other Financial Groups Regulations 2004, SI 2004/1862, regs 1, 7 at* **[4683]**, **[4689]**, *and the Investment Recommendation (Media) Regulations 2005, SI 2005/382, reg 2 at* **[7357]**, *and contains various other amendments that are outside the scope of this work.)*

SCHEDULE 7
EXERCISE OF PASSPORT RIGHTS UNDER THE INVESTMENT SERVICES DIRECTIVE

Regulation 7

Table 1

Investment service in Section A of the Annex to the investment services directive	*Corresponding investment service or activity in Section A of Annex I to the markets in financial instruments directive*
1(a) (reception and transmission, on behalf of investors, of orders in relation to one or more of the instruments listed in Section B)	1 (reception and transmission of orders in relation to one or more financial instruments)
1(b) (execution of such orders other than for own account)	2 (execution of orders on behalf of clients)
2 (dealing in any of the instruments listed in Section B for own account)	3 (dealing on own account)
3 (managing portfolios of investments in accordance with mandates given by investors on a discriminatory, client-by-client basis where such portfolios include one or more of the instruments listed in Section B)	4 (portfolio management)
4 (underwriting in respect of issues of any of the instruments listed in Section B and/or the placing of such issues)	6 (underwriting of financial instruments and/or placing of financial instruments on a firm commitment basis) and 7 (placing of financial instruments without a firm commitment basis)

Table 2

Non-core service in Section C of the Annex to the investment services directive	*Corresponding ancillary service in Section B of Annex I to the markets in financial instruments directive*
1 (safekeeping and administration in relation to one or more of the instruments listed in Section B)	1 (safekeeping and administration of financial instruments for the account of clients, including custodianship and related services such as cash/collateral management)
2 (safe custody services)	1

Non-core service in Section C of the Annex to the investment services directive	*Corresponding ancillary service in Section B of Annex I to the markets in financial instruments directive*
3 (granting credits or loans to an investor to allow him to carry out a transaction in one or more of the instruments listed in Section B, where the firm granting the credit or loan is involved in the transaction)	2 (granting credits or loans to an investor to allow him to carry out a transaction in one or more financial instruments, where the firm granting the credit or loan is involved in the transaction)
4 (advice to undertakings on capital structure, industrial strategy and related matters and advice and service relating to mergers and the purchase of undertakings)	3 (advice to undertakings on capital structure, industrial strategy and related matters and advice and services relating to mergers and the purchase of undertakings)
5 (services related to underwriting)	6 (services related to underwriting)
7 (foreign-exchange services where these are connected with the provision of investment services)	4 (foreign exchange services where these are connected to the provision of investment services)

Table 3

Instrument in Section B of the Annex to the investment services directive	*Corresponding financial instrument in Section C of Annex I to the markets in financial instruments directive*
1(a) (transferable securities)	1 (transferable securities)
1(b) (units in collective investment undertakings)	3 (units in collective investment undertakings)
2 (money-market instruments)	2 (money-market instruments)
3 (financial-futures contracts, including equivalent cash-settled instruments)	4 (options, futures, swaps, forward rate agreements and any other derivative contracts relating to securities, currencies, interest rates or yields, or other derivative instruments, financial indices or financial measures which may be settled physically or in cash)
4 (forward interest-rate agreements)	4
5 (interest-rate, currency and equity swaps)	4
6 (options to acquire or dispose of any instruments falling within this section of the Annex, including equivalent cash-settled instruments. This category includes in particular options on currency and on interest rates)	4

[7606]

NOTES

Commencement: 1 April 2007 (certain purposes); 1 November 2007 (otherwise) (see reg 1(2)).

[SCHEDULE 8
TRANSITIONAL PROVISION FOR PART IV PERMISSIONS

Regulations 9C and 9D

Table

Investment in relation to which the person has Part IV permission immediately before 1st November 2007	*Additional investments to which the person's Part IV permission is extended from 1st November 2007*
Option (excluding commodity options and options on a commodity future) within the meaning of the General Provisions and Glossary Instrument 2001 (2001/7) made by the Authority under the Act on 21st June 2001("the 2001 Instrument") as amended by the Handbook Administration (No 3) Instrument 2006 (2006/21) made by the Authority under the Act on 22nd June 2006 and the CRD (Consequential Amendments) Instrument 2006 (2006/53) made by the Authority under the Act on 23rd November 2006	Those options within the meaning of the 2001 Instrument as last amended by the Glossary (MIFID) Instrument 2007 (2007/1) made by the Authority under the Act on 25th January 2007 ("the 2007 Instrument") which are options falling within paragraph 10 of Section C of Annex I to the markets in financial instruments directive ("Section C")
Commodity option within the meaning of the 2001 Instrument[1]	Those commodity options within the meaning of the 2001 Instrument as last amended by the 2007 Instrument which are options falling within paragraphs 4, 5, 6 and 7 of Section C
Option on a commodity future within the meaning of the 2001 Instrument	Those options on a commodity future within the meaning of the 2001 Instrument as last amended by the 2007 Instrument which are options falling within paragraphs 4, 5, 6 and 7 of Section C
Future (excluding commodity futures and rolling spot forex contracts[2]) within the meaning of the 2001 Instrument	Those futures[3] (excluding commodity futures and rolling spot forex contracts) which are futures falling within paragraph 10 of Section C
Commodity future within the meaning of the 2001 Instrument	Those commodity futures within the meaning of the 2001 Instrument as last amended by the 2007 Instrument which are futures falling within paragraphs 5, 6 and 7 of Section C
Contract for differences (excluding spread bets[4] and rolling spot forex contracts) within the meaning of the 2001 Instrument	Those contracts for differences (excluding spread bets and rolling spot forex contracts) within the meaning of the 2001 Instrument as last amended by the 2007 Instrument which are derivative instruments for the transfer of credit risk falling within paragraph 8 of Section C".

[1] "Commodity" is amended by the CRD (Consequential Amendments) Instrument 2006 and the Handbook Administration (No 4) Instrument 2006 (2006/64) made by the Authority under the Act on 21st December 2006.

[2] "Rolling spot forex contract" is defined in the 2001 Instrument.

[3] The definition of "future" in the 2001 Instrument is from 1st November 2007 affected by the amendment made to article 84 of the Financial Services and Markets Act 2000 (Regulated Activities) Order 2001 (SI 2001/544) by article 27 of the Financial Services and Markets Act 2000 (Regulated Activities) (Amendment No 3) Order 2006 (SI 2006/3384).

[4] "Spread bet" is defined in the 2001 Instrument.]

[7606A]

NOTES

Commencement: 1 November 2007.

Added by the Financial Services and Markets Act 2000 (Markets in Financial Instruments) (Amendment) Regulations 2007, SI 2007/763, reg 6, as from 1 November 2007.

COMPANIES ACTS (UNREGISTERED COMPANIES) REGULATIONS 2007

(SI 2007/318)

NOTES

Made: 7 February 2007.
Authority: Companies Act 2006, s 1043.
Commencement: 6 April 2007.
As of 1 July 2007 these Regulations had not been amended.

ARRANGEMENT OF REGULATIONS

1 Citation and commencement

(1) These Regulations may be cited as the Companies Acts (Unregistered Companies) Regulations 2007.

(2) These Regulations come into force on 6th April 2007.

[7607]

NOTES

Commencement: 6 April 2007.

2 Meaning of "unregistered company"

In these Regulations an "unregistered company" means a body to which section 1043 of the Companies Act 2006 applies.

[7608]

NOTES

Commencement: 6 April 2007.

3 Application of provisions of the Companies Acts

The provisions of the Companies Acts listed in the Schedule to these Regulations apply to an unregistered company as to a company within the meaning of section 735(1) of the Companies Act 1985 or Article 3(1) of the Companies (Northern Ireland) Order 1986, subject to any limitation, adaptation or modification specified in the Schedule.

[7609]

NOTES

Commencement: 6 April 2007.

4 References to a company's registered office or the place where it is registered

In the application of any provision of the Companies Acts to an unregistered company by virtue of these Regulations—

(a) any reference to a company's registered office shall be read as a reference to the company's principal office in the United Kingdom,

(b) any reference to the part of the United Kingdom in which the company is registered shall be read as a reference to the part of the United Kingdom in which that office is situated, and

(c) any reference to the registrar of companies shall be read accordingly.

[7610]

NOTES

Commencement: 6 April 2007.

5 General adaptation of defined expressions etc

(1) In the application of any provision of the Companies Acts to an unregistered company by virtue of these Regulations, an expression defined, or otherwise having a particular meaning or effect, in relation to a company within the meaning of section 735(1) of the Companies Act 1985 or Article 3(1) of the Companies (Northern Ireland) Order 1986 has effect with any adaptations necessary to ensure a corresponding meaning or effect in relation to an unregistered company.

(2) This is without prejudice to any specific adaptation provided for in these Regulations.

[7611]

NOTES

Commencement: 6 April 2007.

6 Saving

Nothing in these Regulations affects the application of any provision to an unregistered company otherwise than by virtue of these Regulations.

[7612]

NOTES

Commencement: 6 April 2007.

SCHEDULE
PROVISIONS OF THE COMPANIES ACTS APPLYING TO UNREGISTERED COMPANIES

Regulation 3

Provisions applied (Companies Act 2006 (c 46))	**Limitations, adaptations or modifications**
In Part 28 (takeovers etc)—	
Chapter 2 (impediments to takeovers)	
Chapter 3 ("squeeze-out" and "sell-out")	The provisions of this Chapter so far as relating to the offeree company apply to an unregistered company only if it has voting shares admitted to trading on a regulated market.
In Part 17 (a company's share capital)—	
section 546 (issued and allotted share capital)	So far as necessary for the purposes of other provisions applied by these Regulations.
section 558 (when shares are allotted)	So far as necessary for the purposes of other provisions applied by these Regulations.
In Part 36 (offences)—	
section 1122 (liability of company as officer in default)	So far as relating to offences under provisions applied by these Regulations.

PART IV STATUTORY INSTRUMENTS

Provisions applied (Companies Act 2006 (c **46**))	Limitations, adaptations or modifications
section 1132 (production and inspection of documents where offence suspected)	So far as relating to offences under provisions applied by these Regulations.
In Part 37 (supplementary provisions)—	
sections 1134, 1135 and 1138 (company records)	So far as necessary for the purposes of provisions applied by these Regulations.
section 1139(1) and (4) (service of documents on company)	So far as necessary for the purposes of provisions applied by these Regulations.
section 1140 (service of documents on directors, secretaries and others)	So far as necessary for the purposes of provisions applied by these Regulations.
In Part 38 (companies: interpretation)—	
section 1173 (minor definitions: general), the definition of "Gazette"	So far as necessary for the purposes of provisions applied by these Regulations.
Parts 46 and 47 (general supplementary provisions and final provisions)	So far as necessary for the purposes of provisions applied by these Regulations.

[7613]

NOTES

Commencement: 6 April 2007.

COMPANIES ACT 2006 (COMMENCEMENT NO 2, CONSEQUENTIAL AMENDMENTS, TRANSITIONAL PROVISIONS AND SAVINGS) ORDER 2007

(SI 2007/1093)

NOTES

Made: 29 March 2007.

Authority: Companies Act 2006, ss 1292(1), 1294(1), 1296(1), (2), 1300(2).

Commencement: 6 April 2007 (see art 1 at **[7614]**).

As of 1 July 2007, this Order had not been amended. However, see art 10 of the draft Companies Act 2006 (Commencement No 3, Consequential Amendments, Transitional Provisions and Savings) Order 2007 in Appendix 12 at **[A12]**. Article 10(2) of that draft SI provides for the revocation of Sch 1, para 4, as from 1 October 2007.

ARRANGEMENT OF ARTICLES

SCHEDULES

1 Citation, interpretation and coming into force

(1) This Order may be cited as the Companies Act 2006 (Commencement No 2, Consequential Amendments, Transitional Provisions and Savings) Order 2007.

(2) In this Order—

"the 1985 Act" means the Companies Act 1985;

"the 1986 Order" means the Companies (Northern Ireland) Order 1986;

"the 2004 Act" means the Companies (Audit, Investigations and Community Enterprise) Act 2004;

"the 2005 Order" means the Companies (Audit, Investigations and Community Enterprise) (Northern Ireland) Order 2005;

"the 2005 Regulations" means the Community Interest Company Regulations 2005; and

"the Interim Regulations" means the Takeovers Directive (Interim Implementation) Regulations 2006.

(3) This Order comes into force on 6th April 2007.

[7614]

NOTES

Commencement: 6 April 2007.

2 Provisions coming into force on 6th April 2007

(1) The following provisions of the Companies Act 2006 come into force on 6th April 2007—

(a) section 2 (the Companies Acts);
(b) sections 942 to 992 and Schedule 2 (takeovers etc);
(c) section 1043 (unregistered companies);
(d) section 1170 (meaning of "EEA State" and related expressions); and
(e) section 1284(1) (extension of Companies Acts to Northern Ireland) so far as it relates to—
  (i) the provisions mentioned in sub-paragraphs (a), (b) and (c) above, and
  (ii) Part 2 of the 2004 Act (community interest companies).

(2) The following provisions of the Companies Act 2006 come into force on 6th April 2007 so far as necessary for the purposes of the provisions mentioned in paragraph (1)—

(a) section 546 (issued and allotted share capital);
(b) section 558 (when shares are allotted);
(c) sections 1121 to 1123 and 1125 to 1133 (provisions relating to offences);
(d) sections 1134, 1135 and 1138 (company records);
(e) section 1139 (service of documents on a company);
(f) section 1140 (service of documents on directors, secretaries and others);
(g) section 1168 (hard copy and electronic form and related expressions); and
(h) in section 1173 (minor definitions: general), the definitions of "body corporate", "the Gazette" and "regulated market".

[7615]

NOTES

Commencement: 6 April 2007.

3 Transitional adaptations of provisions brought into force

The provisions brought into force by article 2 have effect subject to any transitional adaptations specified in Schedule 1.

[7616]

NOTES

Commencement: 6 April 2007.

4 Interpretation of provisions brought into force

Where an expression in a provision brought into force by this Order (or in an adaptation made by this Order of such a provision)—

(a) is defined in the 1985 Act or the 1986 Order ("the old definition"); and

(b) is defined in the Companies Act 2006 by another provision that is not yet in force for the purposes of the provision brought into force ("the new definition"),

the expression has, for the purposes of the provision brought into force (or the adaptation), the meaning given by the old definition until the new definition is brought into force for the purposes of that provision.

[7617]

NOTES

Commencement: 6 April 2007.

5 Repeals

Sections 1284(2) and 1295 of, and Schedule 16 to, the Companies Act 2006 (repeals) come into force on 6th April 2007 so far as relating to the repeals specified in Schedule 2 to this Order.

[7618]

NOTES

Commencement: 6 April 2007.

6 Consequential amendments

(1) The amendments in Schedule 3 have effect in consequence of provision made by Part 28 of the Companies Act 2006 (takeovers etc).

(2) The amendments in Schedule 4 have effect in consequence of the extension to Northern Ireland of Part 2 of the 2004 Act (community interest companies) and the revocation of Part 3 of the 2005 Order (which made corresponding provision for Northern Ireland).

(3) In Schedule 4—

(a) Part 1 amends the 2004 Act,

(b) Part 2 amends the 2005 Regulations, and

(c) Part 3 makes amendments of other enactments.

[7619]

NOTES

Commencement: 6 April 2007.

7 Consequential repeals and revocations

The repeals and revocations in Schedule 5 have effect in consequence of provision made by Part 28 of the Companies Act 2006 (takeovers etc).

[7620]

NOTES

Commencement: 6 April 2007.

8 Transitional provisions and savings

Schedule 6 contains savings relating to the provisions (and repeals) brought into force by this Order.

[7621]

NOTES

Commencement: 6 April 2007.

9—(1) Section 992 of the Companies Act 2006 (matters to be dealt with in directors' report) applies to the 1986 Order with the following modifications.

(2) In subsection (1) for "Part 7 of the Companies Act 1985 (c 6)" substitute "Part 8 of the Companies (Northern Ireland) Order 1986".

(3) In subsection (3)—

(a) for "section 234ZZA" substitute "Article 242ZZA";
(b) for "subsection (4)" substitute "paragraph (4)".

(4) In subsection (4) for "subsection" substitute "paragraph".

(5) In subsection (5)—
(a) for "section 251" substitute "Article 259",
(b) for "subsection" substitute "paragraph",
(c) for "section 234ZZA(5)" substitute "Article 242ZZA(5)",
(d) for "paragraph" substitute "subparagraph",
(e) for "subsections (2A) to (2E)" substitute "paragraphs (2A) to (2E)".

[7622]

NOTES

Commencement: 6 April 2007.

10 Section 1297 of the Companies Act 2006 (continuity of the law) has effect as if, for the purpose of section 1297(1), the Interim Regulations were an enactment repealed and re-enacted by that Act.

[7623]

NOTES

Commencement: 6 April 2007.

11—(1) Nothing in this Order affects the application of any provision of the 1985 Act or the 1986 Order as applied by the Limited Liability Partnerships Regulations 2001 or the Limited Liability Partnerships Regulations (Northern Ireland) 2004 to limited liability partnerships.

(2) The repeal of section 723C(1)(a) of the 1985 Act by section 1295 of and Schedule 16 to the Companies Act 2006, brought into force by article 7(a) of the Companies Act 2006 (Commencement No 1, Transitional Provisions and Savings) Order 2006, does not apply to the application of the said section 723C(1)(a) to limited liability partnerships by the Limited Liability Partnerships (No 2) Regulations 2002.

[7624]

NOTES

Commencement: 6 April 2007.

SCHEDULES

SCHEDULE 1
TRANSITIONAL ADAPTATIONS OF PROVISIONS BROUGHT INTO FORCE

Article 3

The Companies Acts

1.—(1) Section 2 (the Companies Acts) has effect with the following adaptation.

(2) For subsection (1)(c) substitute—

"(c) the provisions of the Companies Acts as defined in section 744 of the Companies Act 1985, and the Companies Orders as defined in Article 2(3) of the Companies (Northern Ireland) Order 1986, that remain in force.".

Takeovers etc

2.—(1) Section 943 (power of Takeover Panel to make rules) has effect with the following adaptation.

(2) For subsection (6) substitute—

"(6) Section 735(1) of the Companies Act 1985 and Article 2(3) of the Companies (Northern Ireland) Order 1986 (meaning of "company") do not apply for the purposes of this section.".

PART IV STATUTORY INSTRUMENTS

3.—(1) Section 953 (failure to comply with rules about bid documentation) has effect with the following adaptation.

(2) For subsection (8) substitute—

"(8) Section 735(1) of the Companies Act 1985 and Article 2(3) of the Companies (Northern Ireland) Order 1986 (meaning of "company") do not apply for the purposes of this section.".

4.—(1) Section 968 (consequences of opting-in in relation to contractual restrictions on voting rights) has effect with the following adaptation.

(2) In subsection (4), at the end add "A "written resolution" means a resolution in writing agreed to in accordance with sections 381A to 381C of the Companies Act 1985, or Articles 389A to 389C of the Companies (Northern Ireland) Order 1986, or in accordance with the company's articles.".

Service of documents on a company

5.—(1) Section 1139 has effect with the following adaptation.

(2) In subsection (1) for "under this Act" substitute "under the Companies Act 1985 or the Companies (Northern Ireland) Order 1986".

[7625]

NOTES

Commencement: 6 April 2007.

Para 4: revoked by the draft Companies Act 2006 (Commencement No 3, Consequential Amendments, Transitional Provisions and Savings) Order 2007, art 11(b), as from 1 October 2007 (see **[A12]**).

SCHEDULE 2
REPEALS BROUGHT INTO FORCE

Article 5

PART 1
GREAT BRITAIN

Short title and chapter	*Extent of repeal brought into force*
Companies Act 1985 (c 6)	Sections 428 to 430F. In section 744, the definition of "EEA State". Paragraphs 2, 2A and 2B of Schedule 7.

[7626]–[7627]

NOTES

Commencement: 6 April 2007.

(Sch 2, Pt 2 (Northern Ireland) contains various repeals in the Companies (Northern Ireland) Order 1986, SI 1986/1032, and the Companies (Audit, Investigations and Community Enterprise) (Northern Ireland) Order 2005, SI 2005/1967 (outside the scope of this work).)

(Sch 3 (Amendments in Consequence of Provision made in Part 28 of the Companies Act 2006 (Takeovers etc)) amends CA 1985, s 162D at **[148D]**, *the Income Tax (Earnings and Pensions) Act 2003, the Companies (Forms) (Amendment) Regulations 1987, SI 1987/752 at* **[6581]** *et seq, the Financial Services and Markets Act 2000 (Regulated Activities) Order 2001, SI 2001/544 at* **[4001]** *et seq, the Uncertificated Securities Regulations 2001, SI 2001/3755 at* **[7001]** *et seq, the Financial Services and Markets Act 2000 (Financial Promotion) Order 2005, SI 2005/1529 at* **[4717]** *et seq, and contains various amendments to Northern*

Ireland legislation that is outside the scope of this work; Sch 4 (Consequential Amendments) amends the Companies (Audit, Investigations and Community Enterprise) Act 2004 at **[894]** *et seq, the Community Interest Company Regulations 2005, SI 2005/1788 at* **[7399]** *et seq, and contains various amendments to Northern Ireland legislation that is outside the scope of this work*

SCHEDULE 5
CONSEQUENTIAL REPEALS AND REVOCATIONS

Article 7

Short title and chapter	*Extent of repeal or revocation*
Financial Services and Markets Act 2000 (c 8)	Section 349(8).
Companies (Forms) (Amendment) Regulations 1987 (SI 1987/752)	In regulation 5(4), the words "except to the extent specified in regulation 7 below". Regulation 7(2) and (3).
Companies (Acquisition of Own Shares) (Treasury Shares) No 2 Regulations 2003 (SI 2003/3031)	Regulations 5 to 7.
Companies (Acquisition of Own Shares) (Treasury Shares) Regulations (Northern Ireland) 2004 (SR No 275)	In the Schedule, paragraphs 27 and 28.
Takeovers Directive (Interim Implementation) Regulations 2006 (SI 2006/1183)	The whole Regulations.

[7628]

NOTES

Commencement: 6 April 2007.

SCHEDULE 6
SAVINGS

Article 8

Savings for provisions relating to takeovers

1. The repeal of sections 428 to 430F of the 1985 Act and of Articles 421 to 423F of the 1986 Order (takeover offers) by article 5 does not affect the operation of those provisions in relation to a takeover offer where the date of the offer is before 6th April 2007.

The "date of the offer" for this purpose is the same as for the purposes of section 428(1) of the 1985 Act or Article 421(1) of the 1986 Order.

2. The revocation of the Interim Regulations by article 7 does not affect the operation of Part 5 of those Regulations (squeeze-out and sell-out) in relation to a takeover offer where the date of the offer is before 6th April 2007.

3. The revocation of the Interim Regulations by article 7, and the coming into force of section 949 of the Companies Act 2006 (offence of disclosure in contravention of section 948), and in particular of section 949(2)(b), by virtue of article 2, does not affect the continued operation of regulation 8(2)(b) of the Interim Regulations in respect of offences committed prior to 6th April 2007.

Saving for provisions relating to community interest companies

4. A community interest company in relation to which regulations 7 to 9 of the 2005 Regulations (matters to be included in memorandum and articles) were complied with

immediately before the coming into force of this Order need not alter its memorandum or articles to take account of any amendment made by this Order.

Saving for provision relating to directors' report

5. The repeal by article 5 of paragraphs 2, 2A and 2B of Schedule 7 to the 1985 Act and of paragraphs 2, 2A and 2B of Schedule 7 to the 1986 Order (directors' interests) does not affect the operation of these provisions in relation to any directors' report referred to in section 234 of the 1985 Act or Article 242 of the 1986 Order that is approved before 6th April 2007.

[7629]–[9000]

NOTES

Commencement: 6 April 2007.

PART V
EC LEGISLATION

COUNCIL REGULATION

of 25 July 1985

on the European Economic Interest Grouping (EEIG)

(2137/85/EEC)

NOTES

Date of publication in OJ: OJ L199, 31.7.85, p 1. Notes are as in the original OJ version.

THE COUNCIL OF THE EUROPEAN COMMUNITIES,

Having regard to the Treaty establishing the European Economic Community, and in particular Article 235 thereof,

Having regard to the proposal from the Commission,[1]

Having regard to the opinion of the European Parliament,[2]

Having regard to the opinion of the Economic and Social Committee,[3]

Whereas a harmonious development of economic activities and a continuous and balanced expansion throughout the Community depend on the establishment and smooth functioning of a common market offering conditions analogous to those of a national market; whereas to bring about this single market and to increase its unity a legal framework which facilitates the adaptation of their activities to the economic conditions of the Community should be created for natural persons, companies, firms and other legal bodies in particular; whereas to that end it is necessary that those natural persons, companies, firms and other legal bodies should be able to co-operate effectively across frontiers;

Whereas co-operation of this nature can encounter legal, fiscal or psychological difficulties; whereas the creation of an appropriate Community legal instrument in the form of a European Economic Interest Grouping would contribute to the achievement of the above-mentioned objectives and therefore proves necessary;

Whereas the Treaty does not provide the necessary powers for the creation of such a legal instrument;

Whereas a grouping's ability to adapt to economic conditions must be guaranteed by the considerable freedom for its members in their contractual relations and the internal organisation of the grouping;

Whereas a grouping differs from a firm or company principally in its purpose, which is only to facilitate or develop the economic activities of its members to enable them to improve their own results; whereas, by reason of that ancillary nature, a grouping's activities must be related to the economic activities of its members but not replace them so that, to that extent, for example, a grouping may not itself, with regard to third parties, practise a profession, the concept of economic activities being interpreted in the widest sense;

Whereas access to grouping form must be made as widely available as possible to natural persons, companies, firms and other legal bodies, in keeping with the aims of this Regulation; whereas this Regulation shall not, however, prejudice the application at national level of legal rules and/or ethical codes concerning the conditions for the pursuit of business and professional activities;

Whereas this Regulation does not itself confer on any person the right to participate in a grouping, even where the conditions it lays down are fulfilled;

Whereas the power provided by this Regulation to prohibit or restrict participation in a grouping on grounds of public interest is without prejudice to the laws of Member States which govern the pursuit of activities and which may provide further prohibitions or restrictions or otherwise control or supervise participation in a grouping by any natural person, company, firm or other legal body or any class of them;

Whereas, to enable a grouping to achieve its purpose, it should be endowed with legal capacity and provision should be made for it to be represented vis-à-vis third parties by an organ legally separate from its membership;

Whereas the protection of third parties requires widespread publicity; whereas the members of a grouping have unlimited joint and several liability for the grouping's debts and other liabilities, including those relating to tax or social security, without, however, that principle's affecting the freedom to exclude or restrict the liability of one or more of its members in respect of a particular debt or other liability by means of a specific contract between the grouping and a third party;

Whereas matters relating to the status or capacity of natural persons and to the capacity of legal persons are governed by national law;

Whereas the grounds for winding up which are peculiar to the grouping should be specific while referring to national law for its liquidation and the conclusion thereof;

Whereas groupings are subject to national laws relating to insolvency and cessation of payments; whereas such laws may provide other grounds for the winding up of groupings;

Whereas this Regulation provides that the profits or losses resulting from the activities of a grouping shall be taxable only in the hands of its members; whereas it is understood that otherwise national tax laws apply, particularly as regards the apportionment of profits, tax procedures and any obligations imposed by national tax law;

Whereas in matters not covered by this Regulation the laws of the Member States and Community law are applicable, for example with regard to—

- — social and labour laws,
- — competition law,
- — intellectual property law;

Whereas the activities of groupings are subject to the provisions of Member States' laws on the pursuit and supervision of activities; whereas in the event of abuse or circumvention of the laws of a Member State by a grouping or its members that Member State may impose appropriate sanctions;

Whereas the Member States are free to apply or to adopt any laws, regulations or administrative measures which do not conflict with the scope or objectives of this Regulation;

Whereas this Regulation must enter into force immediately in its entirety; whereas the implementation of some provisions must nevertheless be deferred in order to allow the Member States first to set up the necessary machinery for the registration of groupings in their territories and the disclosure of certain matters relating to groupings; whereas, with effect from the date of implementation of this Regulation, groupings set up may operate without territorial restrictions,

[9001]

NOTES

[1] OJ C14, 15.2.74, p 30; OJ C103, 28.4.78, p 4.
[2] OJ C163, 11.7.77, p 17.
[3] OJ C108, 15.5.75, p 46.

HAS ADOPTED THIS REGULATION—

Article 1

1. European Economic Interest Groupings shall be formed upon the terms, in the manner and with the effects laid down in this Regulation.

Accordingly, parties intending to form a grouping must conclude a contract and have the registration provided for in Article 6 carried out.

2. A grouping so formed shall, from the date of its registration as provided for in Article 6, have the capacity, in its own name, to have rights and obligations of all kinds, to make contracts or accomplish other legal acts, and to sue and be sued.

3. The Member States shall determine whether or not groupings registered at their registries, pursuant to Article 6, have legal personality.

[9002]

Article 2

1. Subject to the provisions of this Regulation, the law applicable, on the one hand, to the contract for the formation of a grouping, except as regards matters relating to the status or capacity of natural persons and to the capacity of legal persons and, on the other hand, to the internal organisation of a grouping shall be the internal law of the State in which the official address is situated, as laid down in the contract for the formation of the grouping.

2. Where a State comprises several territorial units, each of which has its own rules of law applicable to the matters referred to in paragraph 1, each territorial unit shall be considered as a State for the purposes of identifying the law applicable under this Article.

[9003]

Article 3

1. The purpose of a grouping shall be to facilitate or develop the economic activities of its members and to improve or increase the results of those activities; its purpose is not to make profits for itself.

Its activity shall be related to the economic activities of its members and must not be more than ancillary to those activities.

2. Consequently, a grouping may not—

(a) exercise, directly or indirectly, a power of management or supervision over its members' own activities or over the activities of another undertaking, in particular in the fields of personnel, finance and investment;

(b) directly or indirectly, on any basis whatsoever, hold shares of any kind in a member undertaking; the holding of shares in another undertaking shall be possible only in so far as it is necessary for the achievement of the grouping's objects and if it is done on its members' behalf;

(c) employ more than 500 persons;

(d) be used by a company to make a loan to a director of a company, or any person connected with him, when the making of such loans is restricted or controlled under the Member States' laws governing companies. Nor must a grouping be used for the transfer of any property between a company and a director, or any person connected with him, except to the extent allowed by the Member States' laws governing companies. For the purposes of this provision the making of a loan includes entering into any transaction or arrangement of similar effect, and property includes moveable and immoveable property;

(e) be a member of another European Economic Interest Grouping.

[9004]

Article 4

1. Only the following may be members of a grouping—

(a) companies or firms within the meaning of the second paragraph of Article 58 of the Treaty and other legal bodies governed by public or private law, which have been formed in accordance with the law of a Member State and which have their registered or statutory office and central administration in the Community; where, under the law of a Member State, a company, firm or other legal body is not obliged to have a registered or statutory office, it shall be sufficient for such a company, firm or other legal body to have its central administration in the Community;

(b) natural persons who carry on any industrial, commercial, craft or agricultural activity or who provide professional or other services in the Community.

2. A grouping must comprise at least—

(a) two companies, firms or other legal bodies, within the meaning of paragraph 1, which have their central administrations in different Member States, or

(b) two natural persons, within the meaning of paragraph 1, who carry on their principal activities in different Member States, or

(c) a company, firm or other legal body within the meaning of paragraph 1 and a natural person, of which the first has its central administration in one Member State and the second carries on his principal activity in another Member State.

3. A Member State may provide that groupings registered at its registries in accordance with Article 6 may have no more than 20 members. For this purpose, that Member State may provide that, in accordance with its laws, each member of a legal body formed under its laws, other than a registered company, shall be treated as a separate member of a grouping.

4. Any Member State may, on grounds of that State's public interest, prohibit or restrict participation in groupings by certain classes of natural persons, companies, firms, or other legal bodies.

[9005]

Article 5

A contract for the formation of a grouping shall include at least—

(a) the name of the grouping preceded or followed either by the words "European Economic Interest Grouping" or by the initials "EEIG", unless those words or initials already form part of the name;

(b) the official address of the grouping;

(c) the objects for which the grouping is formed;

(d) the name, business name, legal form, permanent address or registered office, and the number and place of registration, if any, of each member of the grouping;

(e) the duration of the grouping, except where this is indefinite.

[9006]

Article 6

A grouping shall be registered in the State in which it has its official address, at the registry designated pursuant to Article 39(1).

[9007]

Article 7

A contract for the formation of a grouping shall be filed at the registry referred to in Article 6.

The following documents and particulars must also be filed at that registry;

(a) any amendment to the contract for the formation of a grouping, including any change in the composition of a grouping;

(b) notice of the setting up or closure of any establishment of the grouping;

(c) any judicial decision establishing or declaring the nullity of a grouping, in accordance with Article 15;

(d) notice of the appointment of the manager or managers of a grouping, their names and any other identification particulars required by the law of the Member State in which the register is kept, notification that they may act alone or must act jointly, and the termination of any manager's appointment;

(e) notice of a member's assignment of his participation in a grouping or a proportion thereof, in accordance with Article 22(1);

(f) any decision by members ordering or establishing the winding up of a grouping, in accordance with Article 31, or any judicial decision ordering such winding up, in accordance with Articles 31 or 32;

(g) notice of the appointment of the liquidator or liquidators of a grouping, as referred to in Article 35, their names and any other identification particulars required by the law of the Member State in which the register is kept, and the termination of any liquidator's appointment;

(h) notice of the conclusion of a grouping's liquidation, as referred to in Article 35(2);

(i) any proposal to transfer the official address, as referred to in Article 14(1);

(j) any clause exempting a new member from the payment of debts and other liabilities which originated prior to his admission, in accordance with Article 26(2).

[9008]

Article 8

The following must be published, as laid down in Article 39, in the gazette referred to in paragraph 1 of that Article—

(a) the particulars which must be included in the contract for the formation of a grouping pursuant to Article 5, and any amendments thereto;

(b) the number, date and place of registration as well as notice of the termination of that registration;

(c) the documents and particulars referred to in Article 7(b) to (j).

The particulars referred to in (a) and (b) must be published in full. The documents and particulars referred to in (c) may be published either in full or in extract form or by means of a reference to their filing at the registry, in accordance with the national legislation applicable.

[9009]

Article 9

1. The documents and particulars which must be published pursuant to this Regulation may be relied on by a grouping as against third parties under the conditions laid down by the national law applicable pursuant to Article 3(5) and (7) of Council Directive 68/151/EEC of 9 March 1968 on co-ordination of safeguards which, for the protection of the interests of members and others, are required by Member States of companies within the meaning of the second paragraph of Article 58 of the Treaty, with a view to making such safeguards equivalent throughout the Community.

2. If activities have been carried on on behalf of a grouping before its registration in accordance with Article 6 and if the grouping does not, after its registration, assume the

obligations arising out of such activities, the natural persons, companies, firms or other legal bodies which carried on those activities shall bear unlimited joint and several liability for them.

[9010]

Article 10

Any grouping establishment situated in a Member State other than that in which the official address is situated shall be registered in that State. For the purpose of such registration, a grouping shall file, at the appropriate registry in that Member State, copies of the documents which must be filed at the registry of the Member State in which the official address is situated, together, if necessary, with a translation which conforms with the practice of the registry where the establishment is registered.

[9011]

Article 11

Notice that a grouping has been formed or that the liquidation of a grouping has been concluded stating the number, date and place of registration and the date, place and title of publication, shall be given in the *Official Journal of the European Communities* after it has been published in the gazette referred to in Article 39(1).

[9012]

Article 12

The official address referred to in the contract for the formation of a grouping must be situated in the Community.

The official address must be fixed either—

(a) where the grouping has its central administration, or

(b) where one of the members of the grouping has its central administration or, in the case of a natural person, his principal activity, provided that the grouping carries on an activity there.

[9013]

Article 13

The official address of a grouping may be transferred within the Community.

When such a transfer does not result in a change in the law applicable pursuant to Article 2, the decision to transfer shall be taken in accordance with the conditions laid down in the contract for the formation of the grouping.

[9014]

Article 14

1. When the transfer of the official address results in a change in the law applicable pursuant to Article 2, a transfer proposal must be drawn up, filed and published in accordance with the conditions laid down in Articles 7 and 8.

No decision to transfer may be taken for two months after publication of the proposal. Any such decision must be taken by the members of the grouping unanimously. The transfer shall take effect on the date on which the grouping is registered, in accordance with Article 6, at the registry for the new official address. That registration may not be effected until evidence has been produced that the proposal to transfer the official address has been published.

2. The termination of a grouping's registration at the registry for its old official address may not be effected until evidence has been produced that the grouping has been registered at the registry for its new official address.

3. Upon publication of a grouping's new registration the new official address may be relied on as against third parties in accordance with the conditions referred to in Article 9(1); however, as long as the termination of the grouping's registration at the registry for the old official address has not been published, third parties may continue to rely on the old official address unless the grouping proves that such third parties were aware of the new official address.

4. The laws of a Member State may provide that, as regards groupings registered under Article 6 in that Member State, the transfer of an official address which would result in a

change of the law applicable shall not take effect if, within the two-month period referred to in paragraph 1, a competent authority in that Member State opposes it. Such opposition may be based only on grounds of public interest. Review by a judicial authority must be possible.

[9015]

Article 15

1. Where the law applicable to a grouping by virtue of Article 2 provides for the nullity of that grouping, such nullity must be established or declared by judicial decision. However, the court to which the matter is referred must, where it is possible for the affairs of the grouping to be put in order, allow time to permit that to be done.

2. The nullity of a grouping shall entail its liquidation in accordance with the conditions laid down in Article 35.

3. A decision establishing or declaring the nullity of a grouping may be relied on as against third parties in accordance with the conditions laid down in Article 9(1).

Such a decision shall not of itself affect the validity of liabilities, owed by or to a grouping, which originated before it could be relied on as against third parties in accordance with the conditions laid down in the previous subparagraph.

[9016]

Article 16

1. The organs of a grouping shall be the members acting collectively and the manager or managers.

A contract for the formation of a grouping may provide for other organs; if it does it shall determine their powers.

2. The members of a grouping, acting as a body, may take any decision for the purpose of achieving the objects of the grouping.

[9017]

Article 17

1. Each member shall have one vote. The contract for the formation of a grouping may, however, give more than one vote to certain members, provided that no one member holds a majority of the votes.

2. A unanimous decision by the members shall be required to—

(a) alter the objects of a grouping;

(b) alter the number of votes allotted to each member;

(c) alter the conditions for the taking of decisions;

(d) extend the duration of a grouping beyond any period fixed in the contract for the formation of the grouping;

(e) alter the contribution by every member or by some members to the grouping's financing;

(f) alter any other obligation of a member, unless otherwise provided by the contract for the formation of the grouping;

(g) make any alteration to the contract for the formation of the grouping not covered by this paragraph, unless otherwise provided by that contract.

3. Except where this Regulation provides that decisions must be taken unanimously, the contract for the formation of a grouping may prescribe the conditions for a quorum and for a majority, in accordance with which the decisions, or some of them, shall be taken. Unless otherwise provided for by the contract, decisions shall be taken unanimously.

4. On the initiative of a manager or at the request of a member, the manager or managers must arrange for the members to be consulted so that the latter can take a decision.

[9018]

Article 18

Each member shall be entitled to obtain information from the manager or managers concerning the grouping's business and to inspect the grouping's books and business records.

[9019]

Article 19

1. A grouping shall be managed by one or more natural persons appointed in the contract for the formation of the grouping or by decision of the members.

No person may be a manager of a grouping if—

— by virtue of the law applicable to him, or
— by virtue of the internal law of the State in which the grouping has its official address, or
— following a judicial or administrative decision made or recognised in a Member State

he may not belong to the administrative or management body of a company, may not manage an undertaking or may not act as manager of a European Economic Interest Grouping.

2. A Member State may, in the case of groupings registered at their registries pursuant to Article 6, provide that legal persons may be managers on condition that such legal persons designate one or more natural persons, whose particulars shall be the subject of the filing provisions of Article 7(d) to represent them.

If a Member State exercises this option, it must provide that the representative or representatives shall be liable as if they were themselves managers of the groupings concerned.

The restrictions imposed in paragraph 1 shall also apply to those representatives.

3. The contract for the formation of a grouping or, failing that, a unanimous decision by the members shall determine the conditions for the appointment and removal of the manager or managers and shall lay down their powers.

[9020]

Article 20

1. Only the manager or, where there are two or more, each of the managers shall represent a grouping in respect of dealings with third parties.

Each of the managers shall bind the grouping as regards third parties when he acts on behalf of the grouping, even where his acts do not fall within the objects of the grouping, unless the grouping proves that the third party knew or could not, under the circumstances, have been unaware that the act fell outside the objects of the grouping; publication of the particulars referred to in Article 5(c) shall not of itself be proof thereof.

No limitation on the powers of the manager or managers, whether deriving from the contract for the formation of the grouping or from a decision by the members, may be relied on as against third parties even if it is published.

2. The contract for the formation of the grouping may provide that the grouping shall be validly bound only by two or more managers acting jointly. Such a clause may be relied on as against third parties in accordance with the conditions referred to in Article 9(1) only if it is published in accordance with Article 8.

[9021]

Article 21

1. The profits resulting from a grouping's activities shall be deemed to be the profits of the members and shall be apportioned among them in the proportions laid down in the contract for the formation of the grouping or, in the absence of any such provision, in equal shares.

2. The members of a grouping shall contribute to the payment of the amount by which expenditure exceeds income in the proportions laid down in the contract for the formation of the grouping or, in the absence of any such provision, in equal shares.

[9022]

Article 22

1. Any member of a grouping may assign his participation in the grouping, or a proportion thereof, either to another member or to a third party; the assignment shall not take effect without the unanimous authorisation of the other members.

2. A member of a grouping may use his participation in the grouping as security only after the other members have given their unanimous authorisation, unless otherwise laid down

in the contract for the formation of the grouping. The holder of the security may not at any time become a member of the grouping by virtue of that security.

[9023]

Article 23

No grouping may invite investment by the public.

[9024]

Article 24

1. The members of a grouping shall have unlimited joint and several liability for its debts and other liabilities of whatever nature. National law shall determine the consequences of such liability.

2. Creditors may not proceed against a member for payment in respect of debts and other liabilities, in accordance with the conditions laid down in paragraph 1, before the liquidation of a grouping is concluded, unless they have first requested the grouping to pay and payment has not been made within an appropriate period.

[9025]

Article 25

Letters, order forms and similar documents must indicate legibly—

(a) the name of the grouping preceded or followed either by the words "European Economic Interest Grouping" or by the initials "EEIG", unless those words or initials already occur in the name;
(b) the location of the registry referred to in Article 6, in which the grouping is registered, together with the number of the grouping's entry at the registry;
(c) the grouping's official address;
(d) where applicable, that the managers must act jointly;
(e) where applicable, that the grouping is in liquidation, pursuant to Article 15, 31, 32 or 36.

Every establishment of a grouping, when registered in accordance with Article 10, must give the above particulars, together with those relating to its own registration, on the documents referred to in the first paragraph of this Article uttered by it.

[9026]

Article 26

1. A decision to admit new members shall be taken unanimously by the members of the grouping.

2. Every new member shall be liable, in accordance with the conditions laid down in Article 24, for the grouping's debts and other liabilities, including those arising out of the grouping's activities before his admission.

He may, however, be exempted by a clause in the contract for the formation of the grouping or in the instrument of admission from the payment of debts and other liabilities which originated before his admission. Such a clause may be relied on as against third parties, under the conditions referred to in Article 9(1), only if it is published in accordance with Article 8.

[9027]

Article 27

1. A member of a grouping may withdraw in accordance with the conditions laid down in the contract for the formation of a grouping or, in the absence of such conditions, with the unanimous agreement of the other members.

Any member of a grouping may, in addition, withdraw on just and proper grounds.

2. Any member of a grouping may be expelled for the reasons listed in the contract for the formation of the grouping and, in any case, if he seriously fails in his obligations or if he causes or threatens to cause serious disruption in the operation of the grouping.

Such expulsion may occur only by the decision of a court to which joint application has been made by a majority of the other members, unless otherwise provided by the contract for the formation of a grouping.

[9028]

Article 28

1. A member of a grouping shall cease to belong to it on death or when he no longer complies with the conditions laid down in Article 4(1).

In addition, a Member State may provide, for the purposes of its liquidation, winding up, insolvency or cessation of payments laws, that a member shall cease to be a member of any grouping at the moment determined by those laws.

2. In the event of the death of a natural person who is a member of a grouping, no person may become a member in his place except under the conditions laid down in the contract for the formation of the grouping or, failing that, with the unanimous agreement of the remaining members.

[9029]

Article 29

As soon as a member ceases to belong to a grouping, the manager or managers must inform the other members of that fact; they must also take the steps required as listed in Articles 7 and 8. In addition, any person concerned may take those steps.

[9030]

Article 30

Except where the contract for the formation of a grouping provides otherwise and without prejudice to the rights acquired by a person under Articles 22(1) or 28(2), a grouping shall continue to exist for the remaining members after a member has ceased to belong to it, in accordance with the conditions laid down in the contract for the formation of the grouping or determined by unanimous decision of the members in question.

[9031]

Article 31

1. A grouping may be wound up by a decision of its members ordering its winding up. Such a decision shall be taken unanimously, unless otherwise laid down in the contract for the formation of the grouping.

2. A grouping must be wound up by a decision of its members—

(a) noting the expiry of the period fixed in the contract for the formation of the grouping or the existence of any other cause for winding up provided for in the contract, or

(b) noting the accomplishment of the grouping's purpose or the impossibility of pursuing it further.

Where, three months after one of the situations referred to in the first subparagraph has occurred, a members' decision establishing the winding up of the grouping has not been taken, any member may petition the court to order winding up.

3. A grouping must also be wound up by a decision of its members or of the remaining member when the conditions laid down in Article 4(2) are no longer fulfilled.

4. After a grouping has been wound up by decision of its members, the manager or managers must take the steps required as listed in Articles 7 and 8. In addition, any person concerned may take those steps.

[9032]

Article 32

1. On application by any person concerned or by a competent authority, in the event of the infringement of Articles 3, 12 or 31(3), the court must order a grouping to be wound up, unless its affairs can be and are put in order before the court has delivered a substantive ruling.

2. On application by a member, the court may order a grouping to be wound up on just and proper grounds.

3. A Member State may provide that the court may, on application by a competent authority, order the winding up of a grouping which has its official address in the State to which that authority belongs, wherever the grouping acts in contravention of that State's public interest, if the law of that State provides for such a possibility in respect of registered companies or other legal bodies subject to it.

[9033]

Article 33

When a member ceases to belong to a grouping for any reason other than the assignment of his rights in accordance with the conditions laid down in Article 22(1), the value of his rights and obligations shall be determined taking into account the assets and liabilities of the grouping as they stand when he ceases to belong to it.

The value of the rights and obligations of a departing member may not be fixed in advance.

[9034]

Article 34

Without prejudice to Article 37(1), any member who ceases to belong to a grouping shall remain answerable, in accordance with the conditions laid down in Article 24, for the debts and other liabilities arising out of the grouping's activities before he ceased to be a member.

[9035]

Article 35

1. The winding up of a grouping shall entail its liquidation.

2. The liquidation of a grouping and the conclusion of its liquidation shall be governed by national law.

3. A grouping shall retain its capacity, within the meaning of Article 1(2), until its liquidation is concluded.

4. The liquidator or liquidators shall take the steps required as listed in Articles 7 and 8.

[9036]

Article 36

Groupings shall be subject to national laws governing insolvency and cessation of payments. The commencement of proceedings against a grouping on grounds of its insolvency or cessation of payments shall not by itself cause the commencement of such proceedings against its members.

[9037]

Article 37

1. A period of limitation of five years after the publication, pursuant to Article 8, of notice of a member's ceasing to belong to a grouping shall be substituted for any longer period which may be laid down by the relevant national law for actions against that member in connection with debts and other liabilities arising out of the grouping's activities before he ceased to be a member.

2. A period of limitation of five years after the publication, pursuant to Article 8, of notice of the conclusion of the liquidation of a grouping shall be substituted for any longer period which may be laid down by the relevant national law for actions against a member of the grouping in connection with debts and other liabilities arising out of the grouping's activities.

[9038]

Article 38

Where a grouping carries on any activity in a Member State in contravention of that State's public interest, a competent authority of that State may prohibit that activity. Review of that competent authority's decision by a judicial authority shall be possible.

[9039]

Article 39

1. The Member States shall designate the registry or registries responsible for effecting the registration referred to in Articles 6 and 10 and shall lay down the rules governing registration. They shall prescribe the conditions under which the documents referred to in Articles 7 and 10 shall be filed. They shall ensure that the documents and particulars referred to in Article 8 are published in the appropriate official gazette of the Member State in which the grouping has its official address, and may prescribe the manner of publication of the documents and particulars referred to in Article 8(c).

The Member States shall also ensure that anyone may, at the appropriate registry pursuant to Article 6 or, where appropriate, Article 10, inspect the documents referred to in Article 7 and obtain, even by post, full or partial copies thereof.

The Member States may provide for the payment of fees in connection with the operations referred to in the preceding subparagraphs; those fees may not, however, exceed the administrative cost thereof.

2. The Member States shall ensure that the information to be published in the *Official Journal of the European Communities* pursuant to Article 11 is forwarded to the Office for Official Publications of the European Communities within one month of its publication in the official gazette referred to in paragraph 1.

3. The Member States shall provide for appropriate penalties in the event of failure to comply with the provisions of Articles 7, 8 and 10 on disclosure and in the event of failure to comply with Article 25.

[9040]

Article 40

The profits or losses resulting from the activities of a grouping shall be taxable only in the hands of its members.

[9041]

Article 41

1. The Member States shall take the measures required by virtue of Article 39 before 1 July 1989. They shall immediately communicate them to the Commission.

2. For information purposes, the Member States shall inform the Commission of the classes of natural persons, companies, firms and other legal bodies which they prohibit from participating in groupings pursuant to Article 4(4). The Commission shall inform the other Member States.

[9042]

Article 42

1. Upon the adoption of this Regulation, a Contact Committee shall be set up under the auspices of the Commission. Its function shall be—

(a) to facilitate, without prejudice to Articles 169 and 170 of the Treaty, application of this Regulation through regular consultation dealing in particular with practical problems arising in connection with its application;

(b) to advise the Commission, if necessary, on additions or amendments to this Regulation.

2. The Contact Committee shall be composed of representatives of the Member States and representatives of the Commission. The chairman shall be a representative of the Commission. The Commission shall provide the secretariat.

3. The Contact Committee shall be convened by its chairman either on his own initiative or at the request of one of its members.

[9043]

Article 43

This Regulation shall enter into force on the third day following its publication in the *Official Journal of the European Communities*.

It shall apply from 1 July 1989, with the exception of Articles 39, 41 and 42 which shall apply as from the entry into force of the Regulation.

This Regulation shall be binding in its entirety and directly applicable in all Member States.

[9044]–[9045]

Done at Brussels, 25 July 1985.

COUNCIL DIRECTIVE

of 17 April 1989

coordinating the requirements for the drawing-up, scrutiny and distribution of the prospectus to be published when transferable securities are offered to the public (**Note**)

(89/298/EEC)

NOTES

Date of publication in OJ: OJ L124, 5.5.89, p 8.

This Directive was repealed and replaced by European Parliament and Council Directive 2003/71/EC on the prospectus to be published when securities are offered to the public or admitted to trading and amending Directive 2001/34/EC (at **[9460]**). The 2003 Directive entered into force on 31 December 2003 (the date of its publication in the OJ) and has a transposition date of 1 July 2005 (see Art 29 at **[9489]**).

[9046]–[9143]

COUNCIL DIRECTIVE

of 10 May 1993

on investment services in the securities field (**Note**)

(93/22/EEC)

NOTES

Date of publication in OJ: OJ L141, 11.6.93, p 27. The text of this Directive incorporates the corrigenda published in OJ L194, 3.8.93, p 27, and OJ L170, 13.7.93, p 32. Notes are as in the original OJ version.

This Directive is repealed by European Parliament and Council Directive 2004/39/EC, Art 69 (at **[9682]**), as from 1 November 2007; for transitional provisions see Art 71. Note that 2004/39/EC has a transposition date of 31 January 2007 and must be applied from 1 November 2007 (see Art 70 at **[9683]**, as amended by European Parliament and Council Directive 2006/31/EC).

This Directive has been omitted from this Edition of the *Company Law Handbook* in order to create space for other legislation (ie, the Companies Act 2006 and the associated destination and derivation tables). It was printed in full in the 20th Edition of this work (at p 2764 et seq) and, as of 1 July 2007, it had not been amended since the publication of that Edition. This Directive is, however, currently included in the CD version of this work (which may be ordered from the LexisNexis Butterworths Customer Services Department) and can be accessed in the online version of the *Company Law Handbook* which is updated fortnightly (at www.lexisnexis.com/uk/legal). It was also printed in full in the 8th Edition of *Butterworths Financial Services Law Handbook* (February 2007).

[9144]–[9179]

DIRECTIVE OF THE EUROPEAN PARLIAMENT AND OF THE COUNCIL

of 3 March 1997

on investor-compensation schemes (**Note**)

(97/9/EC)

NOTES

Date of publication in OJ: OJ L84, 26.3.97, p 22.

This Directive has been omitted from this Edition of the *Company Law Handbook* in order to create space for other legislation (ie, the Companies Act 2006 and the associated destination and derivation tables). It was printed in full in the 20th Edition of this work (at p 2791 et seq) and, as of 1 July 2007, it had not been amended since the publication of that Edition. This Directive is, however, currently included in the CD version of this work (which may be ordered from the LexisNexis Butterworths Customer

Services Department) and can be accessed in the online version of the *Company Law Handbook* which is updated fortnightly (at www.lexisnexis.com/uk/legal). It was also printed in full in the 8th Edition of *Butterworths Financial Services Law Handbook* (February 2007).

[9180]–[9197]

COUNCIL REGULATION

of 17 June 1997

on certain provisions relating to the introduction of the euro

(1103/97/EC)

NOTES

Date of publication in OJ: OJ L162, 19.6.1997, p 1. Notes are as in the original OJ version.

THE COUNCIL OF THE EUROPEAN UNION,

Having regard to the Treaty establishing the European Community, and in particular Article 235 thereof,

Having regard to the proposal of the Commission,[1]

Having regard to the opinion of the European Parliament,[2]

Having regard to the opinion of the European Monetary Institute,[3]

(1) Whereas, at its meeting held in Madrid on 15 and 16 December 1995, the European Council confirmed that the third stage of Economic and Monetary Union will start on 1 January 1999 as laid down in Article 109j(4) of the Treaty; whereas the Member States which will adopt the euro as the single currency in accordance with the Treaty will be defined for the purposes of this Regulation as the "participating Member States";

(2) Whereas, at the meeting of the European Council in Madrid, the decision was taken that the term "ECU" used by the Treaty to refer to the European currency unit is a generic term; whereas the Governments of the fifteen Member States have achieved the common agreement that this decision is the agreed and definitive interpretation of the relevant Treaty provisions; whereas the name given to the European currency shall be the "euro"; whereas the euro as the currency of the participating Member States will be divided into one hundred sub-units with the name "cent"; whereas the European Council furthermore considered that the name of the single currency must be the same in all the official languages of the European Union, taking into account the existence of different alphabets;

(3) Whereas a Regulation on the introduction of the euro will be adopted by the Council on the basis of the third sentence of Article 109l(4) of the Treaty as soon as the participating Member States are known in order to define the legal framework of the euro; whereas the Council, when acting at the starting date of the third stage in accordance with the first sentence of Article 109l(4) of the Treaty, shall adopt the irrevocably fixed conversion rates;

(4) Whereas it is necessary, in the course of the operation of the common market and for the changeover to the single currency, to provide legal certainty for citizens and firms in all Member States on certain provisions relating to the introduction of the euro well before the entry into the third stage; whereas this legal certainty at an early stage will allow preparations by citizens and firms to proceed under good conditions;

(5) Whereas the third sentence of Article 109l(4) of the Treaty, which allows the Council, acting with the unanimity of participating Member States, to take other measures necessary for the rapid introduction of the single currency is available as a legal basis only when it has been confirmed, in accordance with Article 109j(4) of the Treaty, which Member States fulfil the necessary conditions for the adoption of a single currency; whereas it is therefore necessary to have recourse to Article 235 of the Treaty as a legal basis for those provisions where there is an urgent need for legal certainty; whereas therefore this Regulation and the aforesaid Regulation on the introduction of the euro will together provide the legal framework for the euro, the principles of which legal framework were agreed by the European Council in Madrid; whereas the introduction of the euro concerns day-to-day operations of the whole population in participating Member States; whereas measures other than those in this Regulation and in the Regulation which will be adopted under the third sentence of Article 109l(4) of the Treaty should be examined to ensure a balanced changeover, in particular for consumers;

(6) Whereas the ECU as referred to in Article 109g of the Treaty and as defined in Council Regulation (EC) No 3320/94 of 22 December 1994 on the consolidation of the existing Community legislation on the definition of the ECU following the entry into force of the Treaty on European Union[4] will cease to be defined as a basket of component currencies on 1 January 1999 and the euro will become a currency in its own right; whereas the decision of the Council regarding the adoption of the conversion rates shall not in itself modify the external value of the ECU; whereas this means that one ECU in its composition as a basket of component currencies will become one euro; whereas Regulation (EC) No 3320/94 therefore becomes obsolete and should be repealed; whereas for references in legal instruments to the ECU, parties shall be presumed to have agreed to refer to the ECU as referred to in Article 109g of the Treaty and as defined in the aforesaid Regulation; whereas such presumption should be rebuttable taking into account the intentions of the parties;

(7) Whereas it is a generally accepted principle of law that the continuity of contracts and other legal instruments is not affected by the introduction of a new currency; whereas the principle of freedom of contract has to be respected; whereas the principle of continuity should be compatible with anything which parties might have agreed with reference to the introduction of the euro; whereas, in order to reinforce legal certainty and clarity, it is appropriate explicitly to confirm that the principle of continuity of contracts and other legal instruments shall apply between the former national currencies and the euro and between the ECU as referred to in Article 109g of the Treaty and as defined in Regulation (EC) No 3320/94 and the euro; whereas this implies, in particular, that in the case of fixed interest rate instruments the introduction of the euro does not alter the nominal interest rate payable by the debtor; whereas the provisions on continuity can fulfil their objective to provide legal certainty and transparency to economic agents, in particular for consumers, only if they enter into force as soon as possible;

(8) Whereas the introduction of the euro constitutes a change in the monetary law of each participating Member State; whereas the recognition of the monetary law of a State is a universally accepted principle; whereas the explicit confirmation of the principle of continuity should lead to the recognition of continuity of contracts and other legal instruments in the jurisdictions of third countries;

(9) Whereas the term "contract used for the definition of legal instruments is meant to include all types of contracts, irrespective of the way in which they are concluded;

(10) Whereas the Council, when acting in accordance with the first sentence of Article 109l(4) of the Treaty, shall define the conversion rates of the euro in terms of each of the national currencies of the participating Member States; whereas these conversion rates should be used for any conversion between the euro and the national currency units or between the national currency units; whereas for any conversion between national currency units, a fixed algorithm should define the result; whereas the use of inverse rates for conversion would imply rounding of rates and could result in significant inaccuracies, notably if large amounts are involved;

(11) Whereas the introduction of the euro requires the rounding of monetary amounts; whereas an early indication of rules for rounding is necessary in the course of the operation of the common market and to allow a timely preparation and a smooth transition to Economic and Monetary Union; whereas these rules do not affect any rounding practice, convention or national provisions providing a higher degree of accuracy for intermediate computations;

(12) Whereas, in order to achieve a high degree of accuracy in conversion operations, the conversion rates should be defined with six significant figures; whereas a rate with six significant figures means a rate which, counted from the left and starting by the first non-zero figure, has six figures,

[9198]

NOTES

1 OJ C369, 7.12.96, p 8.
2 OJ C380, 16.12.96, p 49.
3 Opinion delivered on 29 November 1996.
4 OJ L350, 31.12.94, p 27.

HAS ADOPTED THIS REGULATION—

Article 1

For the purpose of this Regulation—

— "legal instruments" shall mean legislative and statutory provisions, acts of administration, judicial decisions, contracts, unilateral legal acts, payment instruments other than banknotes and coins, and other instruments with legal effect,

— "participating Member States" shall mean those Member States which adopt the single currency in accordance with the Treaty,

— "conversion rates" shall mean the irrevocably fixed conversion rates which the Council adopts in accordance with the first sentence of Article 109l(4) of the Treaty [or in accordance with paragraph 5 of that Article],

— "national currency units" shall mean the units of the currencies of participating Member States, as those units are defined on the day before the start of the third stage of Economic and Monetary Union [or, as the case may be, on the day before the euro is substituted for the currency of a member state which adopts the euro at a later date],

— "euro unit" shall mean the unit of the single currency as defined in the Regulation on the introduction of the euro which will enter into force at the starting date of the third stage of Economic and Monetary Union.

[9199]

NOTES

Words in square brackets inserted by Council Regulation 2595/2000/EC, Art 1, as from 1 January 2001.

Article 2

1. Every reference in a legal instrument to the ECU, as referred to in Article 109g of the Treaty and as defined in Regulation (EC) No 3320/94, shall be replaced by a reference to the euro at a rate of one euro to one ECU. References in a legal instrument to the ECU without such a definition shall be presumed, such presumption being rebuttable taking into account the intentions of the parties, to be references to the ECU as referred to in Article 109g of the Treaty and as defined in Regulation (EC) No 3320/94.

2. (*Repeals Regulation 3320/94/EC.*)

3. This Article shall apply as from 1 January 1999 in accordance with the decision pursuant to Article 109j(4) of the Treaty.

[9200]

Article 3

The introduction of the euro shall not have the effect of altering any term of a legal instrument or of discharging or excusing performance under any legal instrument, nor give a party the right unilaterally to alter or terminate such an instrument. This provision is subject to anything which parties may have agreed.

[9201]

Article 4

1. The conversion rates shall be adopted as one euro expressed in terms of each of the national currencies of the participating Member States. They shall be adopted with six significant figures.

2. The conversion rates shall not be rounded or truncated when making conversions.

3. The conversion rates shall be used for conversions either way between the euro unit and the national currency units. Inverse rates derived from the conversion rates shall not be used.

4. Monetary amounts to be converted from one national currency unit into another shall first be converted into a monetary amount expressed in the euro unit, which amount may be rounded to not less than three decimals and shall then be converted into the other national currency unit. No alternative method of calculation may be used unless it produces the same results.

[9202]

Article 5

Monetary amounts to be paid or accounted for when a rounding takes place after a conversion into the euro unit pursuant to Article 4 shall be rounded up or down to the nearest cent.

Monetary amounts to be paid or accounted for which are converted into a national currency unit shall be rounded up or down to the nearest sub-unit or in the absence of a sub-unit to the nearest unit, or according to national law or practice to a multiple or fraction of the sub-unit or unit of the national currency unit. If the application of the conversion rate gives a result which is exactly half-way, the sum shall be rounded up.

[9203]

Article 6

This Regulation shall enter into force on the day following that of its publication in the *Official Journal of the European Communities*.

This Regulation shall be binding in its entirety and directly applicable in all Member States.

[9204]–[9230]

Done at Luxembourg, 17 June 1997.

COUNCIL REGULATION

of 3 May 1998

on the introduction of the euro

(974/98/EC)

NOTES

Date of publication in OJ: OJ L139, 11.5.98, p 1. Notes are as in the original OJ version.

THE COUNCIL OF THE EUROPEAN UNION,

Having regard to the Treaty establishing the European Community, and in particular Article 109l(4), third sentence thereof,

Having regard to the proposal from the Commission,[1]

Having regard to the opinion of the European Monetary Institute,[2]

Having regard to the opinion of the European Parliament,[3]

(1) Whereas this Regulation defines monetary law provisions of the Member States which have adopted the euro; whereas provisions on continuity of contracts, the replacement of references to the ecu in legal instruments by references to the euro and rounding have already been laid down in Council Regulation (EC) No 1103/97 of 17 June 1997 on certain provisions relating to the introduction of the euro;[4] whereas the introduction of the euro concerns day-to-day operations of the whole population in participating Member States; whereas measures other than those in this Regulation and in Regulation (EC) No 1103/97 should be examined to ensure a balanced changeover, in particular for consumers;

(2) Whereas, at the meeting of the European Council in Madrid on 15 and 16 December 1995, the decision was taken that the term "ecu" used by the Treaty to refer to the European currency unit is a generic term; whereas the Governments of the 15 Member States have reached the common agreement that this decision is the agreed and definitive interpretation of the relevant Treaty provisions; whereas the name given to the European currency shall be the "euro"; whereas the euro as the currency of the participating Member States shall be divided into one hundred sub-units with the name "cent"; whereas the definition of the name "cent" does not prevent the use of variants of this term in common usage in the Member States; whereas the European Council furthermore considered that the name of the single currency must be the same in all the official languages of the European Union, taking into account the existence of different alphabets;

(3) Whereas the Council when acting in accordance with the third sentence of Article 109l(4) of the Treaty shall take the measures necessary for the rapid introduction of the euro other than the adoption of the conversion rates;

(4) Whereas whenever under Article 109k(2) of the Treaty a Member State becomes a participating Member State, the Council shall according to Article 109l(5) of the Treaty take the other measures necessary for the rapid introduction of the euro as the single currency of this Member State;

(5) Whereas according to the first sentence of Article 109l(4) of the Treaty the Council shall at the starting date of the third stage adopt the conversion rates at which the currencies of

the participating Member States shall be irrevocably fixed and at which irrevocably fixed rate the euro shall be substituted for these currencies;

(6) Whereas given the absence of exchange rate risk either between the euro unit and the national currency units or between these national currency units, legislative provisions should be interpreted accordingly;

(7) Whereas the term "contract" used for the definition of legal instruments is meant to include all types of contracts, irrespective of the way in which they are concluded;

(8) Whereas in order to prepare a smooth changeover to the euro a transitional period is needed between the substitution of the euro for the currencies of the participating Member States and the introduction of euro banknotes and coins; whereas during this period the national currency units will be defined as sub-divisions of the euro; whereas thereby a legal equivalence is established between the euro unit and the national currency units;

(9) Whereas in accordance with Article 109g of the Treaty and with Regulation (EC) No 1103/97, the euro will replace the ECU as from 1 January 1999 as the unit of account of the institutions of the European Communities; whereas the euro should also be the unit of account of the European Central Bank (ECB) and of the central banks of the participating Member States; whereas, in line with the Madrid conclusions, monetary policy operations will be carried out in the euro unit by the European System of Central Banks (ESCB); whereas this does not prevent national central banks from keeping accounts in their national currency unit during the transitional period, in particular for their staff and for public administrations;

(10) Whereas each participating Member State may allow the full use of the euro unit in its territory during the transitional period;

(11) Whereas during the transitional period contracts, national laws and other legal instruments can be drawn up validly in the euro unit or in the national currency unit; whereas during this period, nothing in this Regulation should affect the validity of any reference to a national currency unit in any legal instrument;

(12) Whereas, unless agreed otherwise, economic agents have to respect the denomination of a legal instrument in the performance of all acts to be carried out under that instrument;

(13) Whereas the euro unit and the national currency units are units of the same currency; whereas it should be ensured that payments inside a participating Member State by crediting an account can be made either in the euro unit or the respective national currency unit; whereas the provisions on payments by crediting an account should also apply to those cross-border payments, which are denominated in the euro unit or the national currency unit of the account of the creditor; whereas it is necessary to ensure the smooth functioning of payment systems by laying down provisions dealing with the crediting of accounts by payment instruments credited through those systems; whereas the provisions on payments by crediting an account should not imply that financial intermediaries are obliged to make available either other payment facilities or products denominated in any particular unit of the euro; whereas the provisions on payments by crediting an account do not prohibit financial intermediaries from coordinating the introduction of payment facilities denominated in the euro unit which rely on a common technical infrastructure during the transitional period;

(14) Whereas in accordance with the conclusions reached by the European Council at its meeting held in Madrid, new tradeable public debt will be issued in the euro unit by the participating Member States as from 1 January 1999; whereas it is desirable to allow issuers of debt to redenominate outstanding debt in the euro unit; whereas the provisions on redenomination should be such that they can also be applied in the jurisdictions of third countries; whereas issuers should be enabled to redenominate outstanding debt if the debt is denominated in a national currency unit of a Member State which has redenominated part or all of the outstanding debt of its general government; whereas these provisions do not address the introduction of additional measures to amend the terms of outstanding debt to alter, among other things, the nominal amount of outstanding debt, these being matters subject to relevant national law; whereas it is desirable to allow Member States to take appropriate measures for changing the unit of account of the operating procedures of organised markets;

(15) Whereas further action at the Community level may also be necessary to clarify the effect of the introduction of the euro on the application of existing provisions of Community law, in particular concerning netting, set-off and techniques of similar effect;

(16) Whereas any obligation to use the euro unit can only be imposed on the basis of Community legislation; whereas in transactions with the public sector participating Member States may allow the use of the euro unit; whereas in accordance with the reference scenario decided by the European Council at its meeting held in Madrid, the Community legislation laying down the time frame for the generalisation of the use of the euro unit might leave some freedom to individual Member States;

(17) Whereas in accordance with Article 105a of the Treaty the Council may adopt measures to harmonise the denominations and technical specifications of all coins;

(18) Whereas banknotes and coins need adequate protection against counterfeiting;

(19) Whereas banknotes and coins denominated in the national currency units lose their status of legal tender at the latest six months after the end of the transitional period; whereas limitations on payments in notes and coins, established by Member States for public reasons, are not incompatible with the status of legal tender of euro banknotes and coins, provided that other lawful means for the settlement of monetary debts are available;

(20) Whereas as from the end of the transitional period references in legal instruments existing at the end of the transitional period will have to be read as references to the euro unit according to the respective conversion rates; whereas a physical redenomination of existing legal instruments is therefore not necessary to achieve this result; whereas the rounding rules defined in Regulation (EC) No 1103/97 shall also apply to the conversions to be made at the end of the transitional period or after the transitional period; whereas for reasons of clarity it may be desirable that the physical redenomination will take place as soon as appropriate;

(21) Whereas paragraph 2 of Protocol 11 on certain provisions relating to the United Kingdom of Great Britain and Northern Ireland stipulates that, *inter alia*, paragraph 5 of that Protocol shall have effect if the United Kingdom notifies the Council that it does not intend to move to the third stage; whereas the United Kingdom gave notice to the Council on 30 October 1997 that it does not intend to move to the third stage; whereas paragraph 5 stipulates that, *inter alia*, Article 109l(4) of the Treaty shall not apply to the United Kingdom;

(22) Whereas Denmark, referring to paragraph 1 of Protocol 12 on certain provisions relating to Denmark has notified, in the context of the Edinburgh decision of 12 December 1992, that it will not participate in the third stage; whereas, therefore, in accordance with paragraph 2 of the said Protocol, all Articles and provisions of the Treaty and the Statute of the ESCB referring to a derogation shall be applicable to Denmark;

(23) Whereas, in accordance with Article 109l(4) of the Treaty, the single currency will be introduced only in the Member States without a derogation;

(24) Whereas this Regulation, therefore, shall be applicable pursuant to Article 189 of the Treaty, subject to Protocols 11 and 12 and Article 109k(1),

[9231]

NOTES

1 OJ C369, 7.12.96, p 10.
2 OJ C205, 5.7.97, p 18.
3 OJ C380, 16.12.96, p 50.
4 OJ L162, 19.6.97, p 1.

HAS ADOPTED THIS REGULATION—

PART I
DEFINITIONS

[Article 1

For the purpose of this Regulation:

(a) "participating Member States" shall mean the Member States listed in the table in the Annex;

(b) "legal instruments" shall mean legislative and statutory provisions, acts of administration, judicial decisions, contracts, unilateral legal acts, payment instruments other than banknotes and coins, and other instruments with legal effect;

(c) "conversion rate" shall mean the irrevocably fixed conversion rate adopted for the currency of each participating Member State by the Council in accordance with the first sentence of Article 123(4) of the Treaty or with paragraph 5 of that Article;

(d) "euro adoption date" shall mean either the date on which the respective Member State enters the third stage under Article 121(3) of the Treaty or the date on which the abrogation of the respective Member State's derogation under Article 122(2) of the Treaty enters into force, as the case may be;

(e) "cash changeover date" shall mean the date on which euro banknotes and coins acquire the status of legal tender in a given participating Member State;

(f) "euro unit" shall mean the currency unit as referred to in the second sentence of Article 2;

(g) "national currency units" shall mean the units of the currency of a participating Member State, as those units are defined on the day before the adoption of the euro in that Member State;

(h) "transitional period" shall mean a period of three years at the most beginning at 00.00 hours on the euro adoption date and ending at 00.00 hours on the cash changeover date;

(i) "phasing-out period" shall mean a period of one year at the most beginning on the euro adoption date, which can only apply to Member States where the euro adoption date and the cash changeover date fall on the same day;

(j) "redenominate" shall mean changing the unit in which the amount of outstanding debt is stated from a national currency unit to the euro unit, but which does not have through the act of redenomination the effect of altering any other term of the debt, this being a matter subject to relevant national law;

(k) "credit institutions" shall mean credit institutions as defined in Article 1(1) of Directive 2000/12/EC of the European Parliament and of the Council of 20 March 2000 relating to the taking up and pursuit of the business of credit institutions.[1] For the purpose of this Regulation, the institutions listed in Article 2(3) of that Directive with the exception of post office giro institutions shall not be considered as credit institutions.]

[9232]

NOTES

Substituted by Council Regulation 2169/2005/EC, Art 1, as from 18 January 2006.

[1] OJ L126, 26.5.2000, p 1. Directive as last amended by Directive 2005/1/EC of the European Parliament and of the Council (OJ L79, 24.3.2005, p 9).

[Article 1a

The euro adoption date, the cash changeover date, and the phasing-out period, if applicable, for each participating Member State shall be as set out in the Annex.]

[9232A]

NOTES

Inserted by Council Regulation 2169/2005/EC, Art 2, as from 18 January 2006.

PART II
SUBSTITUTION OF THE EURO FOR THE CURRENCIES OF THE PARTICIPATING MEMBER STATES

[Article 2

With effect from the respective euro adoption dates, the currency of the participating Member States shall be the euro. The currency unit shall be one euro. One euro shall be divided into one hundred cents.]

[9233]

NOTES

Substituted by Council Regulation 2169/2005/EC, Art 3, as from 18 January 2006.

Article 3

The euro shall be substituted for the currency of each participating Member State at the conversion rate.

[9234]

Article 4

The euro shall be the unit of account of the European Central Bank (ECB) and of the central banks of the participating Member States.

[9235]

PART III
TRANSITIONAL PROVISIONS

Article 5

Articles 6, 7, 8 and 9 shall apply during the transitional period.

[9236]

Article 6

1. The euro shall also be divided into the national currency units according to the conversion rates. Any subdivision thereof shall be maintained. Subject to the provisions of this Regulation the monetary law of the participating Member States shall continue to apply.

2. Where in a legal instrument reference is made to a national currency unit, this reference shall be as valid as if reference were made to the euro unit according to the conversion rates.

[9237]

Article 7

The substitution of the euro for the currency of each participating Member State shall not in itself have the effect of altering the denomination of legal instruments in existence on the date of substitution.

[9238]

Article 8

1. Acts to be performed under legal instruments stipulating the use of or denominated in a national currency unit shall be performed in that national currency unit. Acts to be performed under legal instruments stipulating the use of or denominated in the euro unit shall be performed in that unit.

2. The provisions of paragraph 1 are subject to anything which parties may have agreed.

3. Notwithstanding the provisions of paragraph 1, any amount denominated either in the euro unit or in the national currency unit of a given participating Member State and payable within that Member State by crediting an account of the creditor, can be paid by the debtor either in the euro unit or in that national currency unit. The amount shall be credited to the account of the creditor in the denomination of his account, with any conversion being effected at the conversion rates.

4. Notwithstanding the provisions of paragraph 1, each participating Member State may take measures which may be necessary in order to—

— redenominate in the euro unit outstanding debt issued by that Member State's general government, as defined in the European system of integrated accounts, denominated in its national currency unit and issued under its own law. If a Member State has taken such a measure, issuers may redenominate in the euro unit debt denominated in that Member State's national currency unit unless redenomination is expressly excluded by the terms of the contract; this provision shall apply to debt issued by the general government of a Member State as well as to bonds and other forms of securitised debt negotiable in the capital markets, and to money market instruments, issued by other debtors,

— enable the change of the unit of account of their operating procedures from a national currency unit to the euro unit by—

  (a) markets for the regular exchange, clearing and settlement of any instrument listed in section B of the Annex to Council Directive 93/22/EEC of 10 May 1993 on investment services in the securities field[1] and of commodities; and

  (b) systems for the regular exchange, clearing and settlement of payments.

5. Provisions other than those of paragraph 4 imposing the use of the euro unit may only be adopted by the participating Member States in accordance with any time-frame laid down by Community legislation.

6. National legal provisions of participating Member States which permit or impose netting, set-off or techniques with similar effects shall apply to monetary obligations, irrespective of their currency denomination, if that denomination is in the euro unit or in a national currency unit, with any conversion being effected at the conversion rates.

[9239]

NOTES

[1] OJ L141, 11.6.93, p 27. Directive as amended by Directive 95/26/EC of the European Parliament and of the Council (OJ L168, 18.7.95, p 7).

[Article 9

Banknotes and coins denominated in a national currency unit shall retain their status as legal tender within their territorial limits as from the day before the euro adoption date in the participating Member State concerned.]

[9240]

NOTES

Substituted by Council Regulation 2169/2005/EC, Art 4, as from 18 January 2006.

[Article 9a

The following shall apply in a Member State with a "phasing-out" period. In legal instruments created during the phasing-out period and to be performed in that Member State, reference may continue to be made to the national currency unit. These references shall be read as references to the euro unit according to the respective conversion rates. Without prejudice to Article 15, the acts performed under these legal instruments shall be performed only in the euro unit. The rounding rules laid down in Regulation (EC) No 1103/97 shall apply.

The Member State concerned shall limit the application of the first subparagraph to certain types of legal instrument, or to legal instruments adopted in certain fields.

The Member State concerned may shorten the period.]

[9240A]

NOTES

Inserted by Council Regulation 2169/2005/EC, Art 5, as from 18 January 2006.

PART IV
EURO BANKNOTES AND COINS

[Article 10

With effect from the respective cash changeover dates, the ECB and the central banks of the participating Member States shall put into circulation banknotes denominated in euro in the participating Member States.

Without prejudice to Article 15, these banknotes denominated in euro shall be the only banknotes which have the status of legal tender in participating Member States.]

[9241]

NOTES

Substituted by Council Regulation 2169/2005/EC, Art 6, as from 18 January 2006.

[Article 11

With effect from the respective cash changeover date, the participating Member States shall issue coins denominated in euro or in cent and complying with the denominations and technical specifications which the Council may lay down in accordance with the second sentence of Article 106(2) of the Treaty. Without prejudice to Article 15 and to the provisions of any agreement under Article 111(3) of the Treaty concerning monetary matters, those coins shall be the only coins which have the status of legal tender in participating Member States. Except for the issuing authority and for those persons specifically designated by the national legislation of the issuing Member State, no party shall be obliged to accept more than 50 coins in any single payment.]

[9242]

NOTES

Substituted by Council Regulation 2169/2005/EC, Art 6, as from 18 January 2006.

Article 12

Participating Member States shall ensure adequate sanctions against counterfeiting and falsification of euro banknotes and coins.

[9243]

PART V
FINAL PROVISIONS

[Article 13

Articles 10, 11, 14, 15 and 16 shall apply with effect from the respective cash changeover date in each participating Member State.]

[9244]

NOTES

Substituted by Council Regulation 2169/2005/EC, Art 7, as from 18 January 2006.

[Article 14

Where, in legal instruments existing on the day before the cash changeover date, reference is made to the national currency units, these references shall be read as references to the euro unit according to the respective conversion rates. The rounding rules laid down in Regulation (EC) No 1103/97 shall apply.]

[9245]

NOTES

Substituted by Council Regulation 2169/2005/EC, Art 7, as from 18 January 2006.

Article 15

1. Banknotes and coins denominated in a national currency unit as referred to in Article 6(1) shall remain legal tender within their territorial limits until six months [from the respective cash changeover date] at the latest; this period may be shortened by national law.

2. Each participating Member State may, for a period of up to six months [from the respective cash changeover date], lay down rules for the use of the banknotes and coins denominated in its national currency unit as referred to in Article 6(1) and take any measures necessary to facilitate their withdrawal.

[3. During the period referred to in paragraph 1, credit institutions in participating Member States adopting the euro after 1 January 2002 shall exchange their customers' banknotes and coins denominated in the national currency unit of that Member State for banknotes and coins in euro, free of charge, up to a ceiling which may be set by national law. Credit institutions may require that notice be given if the amount to be exchanged exceeds a ceiling set by national law or, in the absence of such provisions, by themselves and corresponding to a household amount.

The credit institutions referred to in the first subparagraph shall exchange banknotes and coins denominated in the national currency unit of that Member State of persons other than their customers, free of charge up to a ceiling set by national law or, in the absence of such provisions, by themselves.

National law may limit the obligation under the preceding two subparagraphs to specific types of credit institutions. National law may also extend this obligation upon other persons.]

[9246]

NOTES

Words in square brackets in paras 1, 2 substituted, and para 3 added, by Council Regulation 2169/2005/EC, Art 8, as from 18 January 2006.

Article 16

In accordance with the laws or practices of participating Member States, the respective issuers of banknotes and coins shall continue to accept, against euro at the conversion rate, the banknotes and coins previously issued by them.

[9247]

PART VI
ENTRY INTO FORCE

Article 17

This Regulation shall enter into force on 1 January 1999.

This Regulation shall be binding in its entirety and directly applicable in all Member States, in accordance with the Treaty, subject to Protocols 11 and 12 and Article 109k(1).

[9248]

Done at Brussels, 3 May 1998.

ANNEX

Member State	Euro adoption date	Cash changeover date	Member State with a "phasing-out" period
Belgium	1 January 1999	1 January 2002	n/a
Germany	1 January 1999	1 January 2002	n/a
Greece	1 January 2001	1 January 2002	n/a
Spain	1 January 1999	1 January 2002	n/a
France	1 January 1999	1 January 2002	n/a
Ireland	1 January 1999	1 January 2002	n/a
Italy	1 January 1999	1 January 2002	n/a
Luxembourg	1 January 1999	1 January 2002	n/a
Netherlands	1 January 1999	1 January 2002	n/a
Austria	1 January 1999	1 January 2002	n/a
Portugal	1 January 1999	1 January 2002	n/a
[Slovenia	1 January 2007	1 January 2007	No]
Finland	1 January 1999	1 January 2002	n/a]

[9248A]

NOTES

Added by Council Regulation 2169/2005/EC, Art 9, as from 18 January 2006.

Entry relating to Slovenia inserted by Council Regulation 1647/2006/EC, Art 1, Annex, as from 1 January 2007.

DIRECTIVE OF THE EUROPEAN PARLIAMENT AND OF THE COUNCIL

of 20 March 2000

relating to the taking up and pursuit of the business of credit institutions (Note)

(2000/12/EC)

NOTES

Date of publication in OJ: OJ L126, 26.5.2000, p 1.

Due to the large number of amendments made to this Directive it has been recast. It is repealed and replaced by European Parliament and Council Directive 2006/48/EC at **[9823]** et seq (see, in particular, recital (1) of Directive 2006/48/EC which provides that it also contains new amendments). As to the repeal of this Directive, see Art 158 of the 2006 Directive at **[9881]**, and as to the entry into force of 2006/48/EC (on 20 July 2006), see Art 159 at **[9882]**.

[9249]–[9289]

COUNCIL REGULATION

of 29 May 2000

on insolvency proceedings

(1346/2000/EC)

NOTES

Date of publication in OJ: OJ L160, 30.06.2000, p 1. Notes are as in the original OJ version.

THE COUNCIL OF THE EUROPEAN UNION,

Having regard to the Treaty establishing the European Community, and in particular Articles 61(c) and 67(1) thereof,

Having regard to the initiative of the Federal Republic of Germany and the Republic of Finland,

Having regard to the opinion of the European Parliament,[1]

Having regard to the opinion of the Economic and Social Committee,[2]

Whereas:

(1) The European Union has set out the aim of establishing an area of freedom, security and justice.

(2) The proper functioning of the internal market requires that cross-border insolvency proceedings should operate efficiently and effectively and this Regulation needs to be adopted in order to achieve this objective which comes within the scope of judicial cooperation in civil matters within the meaning of Article 65 of the Treaty.

(3) The activities of undertakings have more and more cross-border effects and are therefore increasingly being regulated by Community law. While the insolvency of such undertakings also affects the proper functioning of the internal market, there is a need for a Community act requiring coordination of the measures to be taken regarding an insolvent debtor's assets.

(4) It is necessary for the proper functioning of the internal market to avoid incentives for the parties to transfer assets or judicial proceedings from one Member State to another, seeking to obtain a more favourable legal position (forum shopping).

(5) These objectives cannot be achieved to a sufficient degree at national level and action at Community level is therefore justified.

(6) In accordance with the principle of proportionality this Regulation should be confined to provisions governing jurisdiction for opening insolvency proceedings and judgments which are delivered directly on the basis of the insolvency proceedings and are closely connected with such proceedings. In addition, this Regulation should contain provisions regarding the recognition of those judgments and the applicable law which also satisfy that principle.

(7) Insolvency proceedings relating to the winding-up of insolvent companies or other legal persons, judicial arrangements, compositions and analogous proceedings are excluded from the scope of the 1968 Brussels Convention on Jurisdiction and the Enforcement of Judgments in Civil and Commercial Matters,[3] as amended by the Conventions on Accession to this Convention.[4]

(8) In order to achieve the aim of improving the efficiency and effectiveness of insolvency proceedings having cross-border effects, it is necessary, and appropriate, that the provisions on jurisdiction, recognition and applicable law in this area should be contained in a Community law measure which is binding and directly applicable in Member States.

(9) This Regulation should apply to insolvency proceedings, whether the debtor is a natural person or a legal person, a trader or an individual. The insolvency proceedings to which this Regulation applies are listed in the Annexes. Insolvency proceedings concerning insurance undertakings, credit institutions, investment undertakings holding funds or securities for third parties and collective investment undertakings should be excluded from the scope of this Regulation. Such undertakings should not be covered by this Regulation since they are subject to special arrangements and, to some extent, the national supervisory authorities have extremely wide-ranging powers of intervention.

(10) Insolvency proceedings do not necessarily involve the intervention of a judicial authority; the expression "court" in this Regulation should be given a broad meaning and include a person or body empowered by national law to open insolvency proceedings. In order for this Regulation to apply, proceedings (comprising acts and formalities set down in law) should not only have to comply with the provisions of this Regulation, but they should also be officially recognised and legally effective in the Member State in which the insolvency proceedings are opened and should be collective insolvency proceedings which entail the partial or total divestment of the debtor and the appointment of a liquidator.

(11) This Regulation acknowledges the fact that as a result of widely differing substantive laws it is not practical to introduce insolvency proceedings with universal scope in the entire Community. The application without exception of the law of the State of opening of proceedings would, against this background, frequently lead to difficulties. This applies, for example, to the widely differing laws on security interests to be found in the Community. Furthermore, the preferential rights enjoyed by some creditors in the insolvency proceedings are, in some cases, completely different. This Regulation should take account of this in two different ways. On the one hand, provision should be made for special rules on applicable law in the case of particularly significant rights and legal relationships (e g rights in rem and contracts of employment). On the other hand, national proceedings covering only assets situated in the State of opening should also be allowed alongside main insolvency proceedings with universal scope.

(12) This Regulation enables the main insolvency proceedings to be opened in the Member State where the debtor has the centre of his main interests. These proceedings have universal scope and aim at encompassing all the debtor's assets. To protect the diversity of interests, this Regulation permits secondary proceedings to be opened to run in parallel with the main proceedings. Secondary proceedings may be opened in the Member State where the debtor has an establishment. The effects of secondary proceedings are limited to the assets located in that State. Mandatory rules of coordination with the main proceedings satisfy the need for unity in the Community.

(13) The "centre of main interests" should correspond to the place where the debtor conducts the administration of his interests on a regular basis and is therefore ascertainable by third parties.

(14) This Regulation applies only to proceedings where the centre of the debtor's main interests is located in the Community.

(15) The rules of jurisdiction set out in this Regulation establish only international jurisdiction, that is to say, they designate the Member State the courts of which may open insolvency proceedings. Territorial jurisdiction within that Member State must be established by the national law of the Member State concerned.

(16) The court having jurisdiction to open the main insolvency proceedings should be enabled to order provisional and protective measures from the time of the request to open proceedings. Preservation measures both prior to and after the commencement of the insolvency proceedings are very important to guarantee the effectiveness of the insolvency proceedings. In that connection this Regulation should afford different possibilities. On the one hand, the court competent for the main insolvency proceedings should be able also to order provisional protective measures covering assets situated in the territory of other Member States. On the other hand, a liquidator temporarily appointed prior to the opening of the main insolvency proceedings should be able, in the Member States in which an establishment belonging to the debtor is to be found, to apply for the preservation measures which are possible under the law of those States.

(17) Prior to the opening of the main insolvency proceedings, the right to request the opening of insolvency proceedings in the Member State where the debtor has an establishment should be limited to local creditors and creditors of the local establishment or to cases where main proceedings cannot be opened under the law of the Member State where the debtor has the centre of his main interest. The reason for this restriction is that cases where territorial insolvency proceedings are requested before the main insolvency proceedings are intended to be limited to what is absolutely necessary. If the main insolvency proceedings are opened, the territorial proceedings become secondary.

(18) Following the opening of the main insolvency proceedings, the right to request the opening of insolvency proceedings in a Member State where the debtor has an establishment is not restricted by this Regulation. The liquidator in the main proceedings or any other person empowered under the national law of that Member State may request the opening of secondary insolvency proceedings.

(19) Secondary insolvency proceedings may serve different purposes, besides the protection of local interests. Cases may arise where the estate of the debtor is too complex to administer as a unit or where differences in the legal systems concerned are so great that difficulties may arise from the extension of effects deriving from the law of the State of the

opening to the other States where the assets are located. For this reason the liquidator in the main proceedings may request the opening of secondary proceedings when the efficient administration of the estate so requires.

(20) Main insolvency proceedings and secondary proceedings can, however, contribute to the effective realisation of the total assets only if all the concurrent proceedings pending are coordinated. The main condition here is that the various liquidators must cooperate closely, in particular by exchanging a sufficient amount of information. In order to ensure the dominant role of the main insolvency proceedings, the liquidator in such proceedings should be given several possibilities for intervening in secondary insolvency proceedings which are pending at the same time. For example, he should be able to propose a restructuring plan or composition or apply for realisation of the assets in the secondary insolvency proceedings to be suspended.

(21) Every creditor, who has his habitual residence, domicile or registered office in the Community, should have the right to lodge his claims in each of the insolvency proceedings pending in the Community relating to the debtor's assets. This should also apply to tax authorities and social insurance institutions. However, in order to ensure equal treatment of creditors, the distribution of proceeds must be coordinated. Every creditor should be able to keep what he has received in the course of insolvency proceedings but should be entitled only to participate in the distribution of total assets in other proceedings if creditors with the same standing have obtained the same proportion of their claims.

(22) This Regulation should provide for immediate recognition of judgments concerning the opening, conduct and closure of insolvency proceedings which come within its scope and of judgments handed down in direct connection with such insolvency proceedings. Automatic recognition should therefore mean that the effects attributed to the proceedings by the law of the State in which the proceedings were opened extend to all other Member States. Recognition of judgments delivered by the courts of the Member States should be based on the principle of mutual trust. To that end, grounds for non-recognition should be reduced to the minimum necessary. This is also the basis on which any dispute should be resolved where the courts of two Member States both claim competence to open the main insolvency proceedings. The decision of the first court to open proceedings should be recognised in the other Member States without those Member States having the power to scrutinise the court's decision.

(23) This Regulation should set out, for the matters covered by it, uniform rules on conflict of laws which replace, within their scope of application, national rules of private international law. Unless otherwise stated, the law of the Member State of the opening of the proceedings should be applicable (lex concursus). This rule on conflict of laws should be valid both for the main proceedings and for local proceedings; the lex concursus determines all the effects of the insolvency proceedings, both procedural and substantive, on the persons and legal relations concerned. It governs all the conditions for the opening, conduct and closure of the insolvency proceedings.

(24) Automatic recognition of insolvency proceedings to which the law of the opening State normally applies may interfere with the rules under which transactions are carried out in other Member States. To protect legitimate expectations and the certainty of transactions in Member States other than that in which proceedings are opened, provisions should be made for a number of exceptions to the general rule.

(25) There is a particular need for a special reference diverging from the law of the opening State in the case of rights in rem, since these are of considerable importance for the granting of credit. The basis, validity and extent of such a right in rem should therefore normally be determined according to the lex situs and not be affected by the opening of insolvency proceedings. The proprietor of the right in rem should therefore be able to continue to assert his right to segregation or separate settlement of the collateral security. Where assets are subject to rights in rem under the lex situs in one Member State but the main proceedings are being carried out in another Member State, the liquidator in the main proceedings should be able to request the opening of secondary proceedings in the jurisdiction where the rights in rem arise if the debtor has an establishment there. If a secondary proceeding is not opened, the surplus on sale of the asset covered by rights in rem must be paid to the liquidator in the main proceedings.

(26) If a set-off is not permitted under the law of the opening State, a creditor should nevertheless be entitled to the set-off if it is possible under the law applicable to the claim of the insolvent debtor. In this way, set-off will acquire a kind of guarantee function based on legal provisions on which the creditor concerned can rely at the time when the claim arises.

(27) There is also a need for special protection in the case of payment systems and financial markets. This applies for example to the position-closing agreements and netting agreements to be found in such systems as well as to the sale of securities and to the guarantees provided for such transactions as governed in particular by Directive 98/26/EC of the European Parliament and of the Council of 19 May 1998 on settlement finality in payment

and securities settlement systems.[5] For such transactions, the only law which is material should thus be that applicable to the system or market concerned. This provision is intended to prevent the possibility of mechanisms for the payment and settlement of transactions provided for in the payment and set-off systems or on the regulated financial markets of the Member States being altered in the case of insolvency of a business partner. Directive 98/26/EC contains special provisions which should take precedence over the general rules in this Regulation.

(28) In order to protect employees and jobs, the effects of insolvency proceedings on the continuation or termination of employment and on the rights and obligations of all parties to such employment must be determined by the law applicable to the agreement in accordance with the general rules on conflict of law. Any other insolvency-law questions, such as whether the employees' claims are protected by preferential rights and what status such preferential rights may have, should be determined by the law of the opening State.

(29) For business considerations, the main content of the decision opening the proceedings should be published in the other Member States at the request of the liquidator. If there is an establishment in the Member State concerned, there may be a requirement that publication is compulsory. In neither case, however, should publication be a prior condition for recognition of the foreign proceedings.

(30) It may be the case that some of the persons concerned are not in fact aware that proceedings have been opened and act in good faith in a way that conflicts with the new situation. In order to protect such persons who make a payment to the debtor because they are unaware that foreign proceedings have been opened when they should in fact have made the payment to the foreign liquidator, it should be provided that such a payment is to have a debt-discharging effect.

(31) This Regulation should include Annexes relating to the organisation of insolvency proceedings. As these Annexes relate exclusively to the legislation of Member States, there are specific and substantiated reasons for the Council to reserve the right to amend these Annexes in order to take account of any amendments to the domestic law of the Member States.

(32) The United Kingdom and Ireland, in accordance with Article 3 of the Protocol on the position of the United Kingdom and Ireland annexed to the Treaty on European Union and the Treaty establishing the European Community, have given notice of their wish to take part in the adoption and application of this Regulation.

(33) Denmark, in accordance with Articles 1 and 2 of the Protocol on the position of Denmark annexed to the Treaty on European Union and the Treaty establishing the European Community, is not participating in the adoption of this Regulation, and is therefore not bound by it nor subject to its application,

[9290]

NOTES

1 Opinion delivered on 2 March 2000 (not yet published in the Official Journal).
2 Opinion delivered on 26 January 2000 (not yet published in the Official Journal).
3 OJ L299, 31.12.1972, p 32.
4 OJ L204, 2.8.1975, p 28; OJ L304, 30.10.1978, p 1; OJ L388, 31.12.1982, p 1; OJ L285, 3.10.1989, p 1; OJ C15, 15.1.1997, p 1.
5 OJ L166, 11.6.1998, p 45.

HAS ADOPTED THIS REGULATION—

CHAPTER I
GENERAL PROVISIONS

Article 1

Scope

1. This Regulation shall apply to collective insolvency proceedings which entail the partial or total divestment of a debtor and the appointment of a liquidator.

2. This Regulation shall not apply to insolvency proceedings concerning insurance undertakings, credit institutions, investment undertakings which provide services involving the holding of funds or securities for third parties, or to collective investment undertakings.

[9290A]

Article 2

Definitions

For the purposes of this Regulation—

(a) "insolvency proceedings" shall mean the collective proceedings referred to in Article 1(1). These proceedings are listed in Annex A;

(b) "liquidator" shall mean any person or body whose function is to administer or liquidate assets of which the debtor has been divested or to supervise the administration of his affairs. Those persons and bodies are listed in Annex C;

(c) "winding-up proceedings" shall mean insolvency proceedings within the meaning of point (a) involving realising the assets of the debtor, including where the proceedings have been closed by a composition or other measure terminating the insolvency, or closed by reason of the insufficiency of the assets. Those proceedings are listed in Annex B;

(d) "court" shall mean the judicial body or any other competent body of a Member State empowered to open insolvency proceedings or to take decisions in the course of such proceedings;

(e) "judgment" in relation to the opening of insolvency proceedings or the appointment of a liquidator shall include the decision of any court empowered to open such proceedings or to appoint a liquidator;

(f) "the time of the opening of proceedings" shall mean the time at which the judgment opening proceedings becomes effective, whether it is a final judgment or not;

(g) "the Member State in which assets are situated" shall mean, in the case of:

— tangible property, the Member State within the territory of which the property is situated,

— property and rights ownership of or entitlement to which must be entered in a public register, the Member State under the authority of which the register is kept,

— claims, the Member State within the territory of which the third party required to meet them has the centre of his main interests, as determined in Article 3(1);

(h) "establishment" shall mean any place of operations where the debtor carries out a non-transitory economic activity with human means and goods.

[9290B]

Article 3

International jurisdiction

1. The courts of the Member State within the territory of which the centre of a debtor's main interests is situated shall have jurisdiction to open insolvency proceedings. In the case of a company or legal person, the place of the registered office shall be presumed to be the centre of its main interests in the absence of proof to the contrary.

2. Where the centre of a debtor's main interests is situated within the territory of a Member State, the courts of another Member State shall have jurisdiction to open insolvency proceedings against that debtor only if he possesses an establishment within the territory of that other Member State. The effects of those proceedings shall be restricted to the assets of the debtor situated in the territory of the latter Member State.

3. Where insolvency proceedings have been opened under paragraph 1, any proceedings opened subsequently under paragraph 2 shall be secondary proceedings. These latter proceedings must be winding-up proceedings.

4. Territorial insolvency proceedings referred to in paragraph 2 may be opened prior to the opening of main insolvency proceedings in accordance with paragraph 1 only:

(a) where insolvency proceedings under paragraph 1 cannot be opened because of the conditions laid down by the law of the Member State within the territory of which the centre of the debtor's main interests is situated; or

(b) where the opening of territorial insolvency proceedings is requested by a creditor who has his domicile, habitual residence or registered office in the Member State within the territory of which the establishment is situated, or whose claim arises from the operation of that establishment.

[9290C]

Article 4

Law applicable

1. Save as otherwise provided in this Regulation, the law applicable to insolvency proceedings and their effects shall be that of the Member State within the territory of which such proceedings are opened, hereafter referred to as the "State of the opening of proceedings".

2. The law of the State of the opening of proceedings shall determine the conditions for the opening of those proceedings, their conduct and their closure. It shall determine in particular:

(a) against which debtors insolvency proceedings may be brought on account of their capacity;

(b) the assets which form part of the estate and the treatment of assets acquired by or devolving on the debtor after the opening of the insolvency proceedings;

(c) the respective powers of the debtor and the liquidator;

(d) the conditions under which set-offs may be invoked;

(e) the effects of insolvency proceedings on current contracts to which the debtor is party;

(f) the effects of the insolvency proceedings on proceedings brought by individual creditors, with the exception of lawsuits pending;

(g) the claims which are to be lodged against the debtor's estate and the treatment of claims arising after the opening of insolvency proceedings;

(h) the rules governing the lodging, verification and admission of claims;

(i) the rules governing the distribution of proceeds from the realisation of assets, the ranking of claims and the rights of creditors who have obtained partial satisfaction after the opening of insolvency proceedings by virtue of a right in rem or through a set-off;

(j) the conditions for and the effects of closure of insolvency proceedings, in particular by composition;

(k) creditors' rights after the closure of insolvency proceedings;

(l) who is to bear the costs and expenses incurred in the insolvency proceedings;

(m) the rules relating to the voidness, voidability or unenforceability of legal acts detrimental to all the creditors.

[9290D]

Article 5

Third parties' rights in rem

1. The opening of insolvency proceedings shall not affect the rights in rem of creditors or third parties in respect of tangible or intangible, moveable or immoveable assets—both specific assets and collections of indefinite assets as a whole which change from time to time—belonging to the debtor which are situated within the territory of another Member State at the time of the opening of proceedings.

2. The rights referred to in paragraph 1 shall in particular mean:

(a) the right to dispose of assets or have them disposed of and to obtain satisfaction from the proceeds of or income from those assets, in particular by virtue of a lien or a mortgage;

(b) the exclusive right to have a claim met, in particular a right guaranteed by a lien in respect of the claim or by assignment of the claim by way of a guarantee;

(c) the right to demand the assets from, and/or to require restitution by, anyone having possession or use of them contrary to the wishes of the party so entitled;

(d) a right in rem to the beneficial use of assets.

3. The right, recorded in a public register and enforceable against third parties, under which a right in rem within the meaning of paragraph 1 may be obtained, shall be considered a right in rem.

4. Paragraph 1 shall not preclude actions for voidness, voidability or unenforceability as referred to in Article 4(2)(m).

[9290E]

Article 6

Set-off

1. The opening of insolvency proceedings shall not affect the right of creditors to demand the set-off of their claims against the claims of the debtor, where such a set-off is permitted by the law applicable to the insolvent debtor's claim.

2. Paragraph 1 shall not preclude actions for voidness, voidability or unenforceability as referred to in Article 4(2)(m).

[9290F]

Article 7

Reservation of title

1. The opening of insolvency proceedings against the purchaser of an asset shall not affect the seller's rights based on a reservation of title where at the time of the opening of proceedings the asset is situated within the territory of a Member State other than the State of opening of proceedings.

2. The opening of insolvency proceedings against the seller of an asset, after delivery of the asset, shall not constitute grounds for rescinding or terminating the sale and shall not prevent the purchaser from acquiring title where at the time of the opening of proceedings the asset sold is situated within the territory of a Member State other than the State of the opening of proceedings.

3. Paragraphs 1 and 2 shall not preclude actions for voidness, voidability or unenforceability as referred to in Article 4(2)(m).

[9290G]

Article 8

Contracts relating to immoveable property

The effects of insolvency proceedings on a contract conferring the right to acquire or make use of immoveable property shall be governed solely by the law of the Member State within the territory of which the immoveable property is situated.

[9290H]

Article 9

Payment systems and financial markets

1. Without prejudice to Article 5, the effects of insolvency proceedings on the rights and obligations of the parties to a payment or settlement system or to a financial market shall be governed solely by the law of the Member State applicable to that system or market.

2. Paragraph 1 shall not preclude any action for voidness, voidability or unenforceability which may be taken to set aside payments or transactions under the law applicable to the relevant payment system or financial market.

[9290I]

Article 10

Contracts of employment

The effects of insolvency proceedings on employment contracts and relationships shall be governed solely by the law of the Member State applicable to the contract of employment.

[9290J]

Article 11

Effects on rights subject to registration

The effects of insolvency proceedings on the rights of the debtor in immoveable property, a ship or an aircraft subject to registration in a public register shall be determined by the law of the Member State under the authority of which the register is kept.

[9290K]

Article 12

Community patents and trade marks

For the purposes of this Regulation, a Community patent, a Community trade mark or any other similar right established by Community law may be included only in the proceedings referred to in Article 3(1).

[9290L]

Article 13

Detrimental acts

Article 4(2)(m) shall not apply where the person who benefited from an act detrimental to all the creditors provides proof that:

— the said act is subject to the law of a Member State other than that of the State of the opening of proceedings, and

— that law does not allow any means of challenging that act in the relevant case.

[9290M]

Article 14

Protection of third-party purchasers

Where, by an act concluded after the opening of insolvency proceedings, the debtor disposes, for consideration, of:

— an immoveable asset, or

— a ship or an aircraft subject to registration in a public register, or

— securities whose existence presupposes registration in a register laid down by law,

the validity of that act shall be governed by the law of the State within the territory of which the immoveable asset is situated or under the authority of which the register is kept.

[9290N]

Article 15

Effects of insolvency proceedings on lawsuits pending

The effects of insolvency proceedings on a lawsuit pending concerning an asset or a right of which the debtor has been divested shall be governed solely by the law of the Member State in which that lawsuit is pending.

[9290O]

CHAPTER II
RECOGNITION OF INSOLVENCY PROCEEDINGS

Article 16

Principle

1. Any judgment opening insolvency proceedings handed down by a court of a Member State which has jurisdiction pursuant to Article 3 shall be recognised in all the other Member States from the time that it becomes effective in the State of the opening of proceedings.

This rule shall also apply where, on account of his capacity, insolvency proceedings cannot be brought against the debtor in other Member States.

2. Recognition of the proceedings referred to in Article 3(1) shall not preclude the opening of the proceedings referred to in Article 3(2) by a court in another Member State. The latter proceedings shall be secondary insolvency proceedings within the meaning of Chapter III.

[9290P]

Article 17

Effects of recognition

1. The judgment opening the proceedings referred to in Article 3(1) shall, with no further formalities, produce the same effects in any other Member State as under this law of the State

of the opening of proceedings, unless this Regulation provides otherwise and as long as no proceedings referred to in Article 3(2) are opened in that other Member State.

2. The effects of the proceedings referred to in Article 3(2) may not be challenged in other Member States. Any restriction of the creditors' rights, in particular a stay or discharge, shall produce effects vis-à-vis assets situated within the territory of another Member State only in the case of those creditors who have given their consent.

[9290Q]

Article 18

Powers of the liquidator

1. The liquidator appointed by a court which has jurisdiction pursuant to Article 3(1) may exercise all the powers conferred on him by the law of the State of the opening of proceedings in another Member State, as long as no other insolvency proceedings have been opened there nor any preservation measure to the contrary has been taken there further to a request for the opening of insolvency proceedings in that State. He may in particular remove the debtor's assets from the territory of the Member State in which they are situated, subject to Articles 5 and 7.

2. The liquidator appointed by a court which has jurisdiction pursuant to Article 3(2) may in any other Member State claim through the courts or out of court that moveable property was removed from the territory of the State of the opening of proceedings to the territory of that other Member State after the opening of the insolvency proceedings. He may also bring any action to set aside which is in the interests of the creditors.

3. In exercising his powers, the liquidator shall comply with the law of the Member State within the territory of which he intends to take action, in particular with regard to procedures for the realisation of assets. Those powers may not include coercive measures or the right to rule on legal proceedings or disputes.

[9290R]

Article 19

Proof of the liquidator's appointment

The liquidator's appointment shall be evidenced by a certified copy of the original decision appointing him or by any other certificate issued by the court which has jurisdiction.

A translation into the official language or one of the official languages of the Member State within the territory of which he intends to act may be required. No legalisation or other similar formality shall be required.

[9290S]

Article 20

Return and imputation

1. A creditor who, after the opening of the proceedings referred to in Article 3(1) obtains by any means, in particular through enforcement, total or partial satisfaction of his claim on the assets belonging to the debtor situated within the territory of another Member State, shall return what he has obtained to the liquidator, subject to Articles 5 and 7.

2. In order to ensure equal treatment of creditors a creditor who has, in the course of insolvency proceedings, obtained a dividend on his claim shall share in distributions made in other proceedings only where creditors of the same ranking or category have, in those other proceedings, obtained an equivalent dividend.

[9290T]

Article 21

Publication

1. The liquidator may request that notice of the judgment opening insolvency proceedings and, where appropriate, the decision appointing him, be published in any other Member State in accordance with the publication procedures provided for in that State. Such publication shall also specify the liquidator appointed and whether the jurisdiction rule applied is that pursuant to Article 3(1) or Article 3(2).

2. However, any Member State within the territory of which the debtor has an establishment may require mandatory publication. In such cases, the liquidator or any authority empowered to that effect in the Member State where the proceedings referred to in Article 3(1) are opened shall take all necessary measures to ensure such publication.

[9290U]

Article 22

Registration in a public register

1. The liquidator may request that the judgment opening the proceedings referred to in Article 3(1) be registered in the land register, the trade register and any other public register kept in the other Member States.

2. However, any Member State may require mandatory registration. In such cases, the liquidator or any authority empowered to that effect in the Member State where the proceedings referred to in Article 3(1) have been opened shall take all necessary measures to ensure such registration.

[9290V]

Article 23

Costs

The costs of the publication and registration provided for in Articles 21 and 22 shall be regarded as costs and expenses incurred in the proceedings.

[9290W]

Article 24

Honouring of an obligation to a debtor

1. Where an obligation has been honoured in a Member State for the benefit of a debtor who is subject to insolvency proceedings opened in another Member State, when it should have been honoured for the benefit of the liquidator in those proceedings, the person honouring the obligation shall be deemed to have discharged it if he was unaware of the opening of proceedings.

2. Where such an obligation is honoured before the publication provided for in Article 21 has been effected, the person honouring the obligation shall be presumed, in the absence of proof to the contrary, to have been unaware of the opening of insolvency proceedings; where the obligation is honoured after such publication has been effected, the person honouring the obligation shall be presumed, in the absence of proof to the contrary, to have been aware of the opening of proceedings.

[9290X]

Article 25

Recognition and enforceability of other judgments

1. Judgments handed down by a court whose judgment concerning the opening of proceedings is recognised in accordance with Article 16 and which concern the course and closure of insolvency proceedings, and compositions approved by that court shall also be recognised with no further formalities. Such judgments shall be enforced in accordance with Articles 31 to 51, with the exception of Article 34(2), of the Brussels Convention on Jurisdiction and the Enforcement of Judgments in Civil and Commercial Matters, as amended by the Conventions of Accession to this Convention.

The first subparagraph shall also apply to judgments deriving directly from the insolvency proceedings and which are closely linked with them, even if they were handed down by another court.

The first subparagraph shall also apply to judgments relating to preservation measures taken after the request for the opening of insolvency proceedings.

2. The recognition and enforcement of judgments other than those referred to in paragraph 1 shall be governed by the Convention referred to in paragraph 1, provided that that Convention is applicable.

3. The Member States shall not be obliged to recognise or enforce a judgment referred to in paragraph 1 which might result in a limitation of personal freedom or postal secrecy.

[9290Y]

Article 26[1]

Public policy

Any Member State may refuse to recognise insolvency proceedings opened in another Member State or to enforce a judgment handed down in the context of such proceedings where the effects of such recognition or enforcement would be manifestly contrary to that State's public policy, in particular its fundamental principles or the constitutional rights and liberties of the individual.

[9290Z]

NOTES

[1] Note the Declaration by Portugal concerning the application of Articles 26 and 37 (OJ C183, 30.6.2000, p 1).

CHAPTER III
SECONDARY INSOLVENCY PROCEEDINGS

Article 27

Opening of proceedings

The opening of the proceedings referred to in Article 3(1) by a court of a Member State and which is recognised in another Member State (main proceedings) shall permit the opening in that other Member State, a court of which has jurisdiction pursuant to Article 3(2), of secondary insolvency proceedings without the debtor's insolvency being examined in that other State. These latter proceedings must be among the proceedings listed in Annex B. Their effects shall be restricted to the assets of the debtor situated within the territory of that other Member State.

[9290ZA]

Article 28

Applicable law

Save as otherwise provided in this Regulation, the law applicable to secondary proceedings shall be that of the Member State within the territory of which the secondary proceedings are opened.

[9290ZB]

Article 29

Right to request the opening of proceedings

The opening of secondary proceedings may be requested by:

(a) the liquidator in the main proceedings;

(b) any other person or authority empowered to request the opening of insolvency proceedings under the law of the Member State within the territory of which the opening of secondary proceedings is requested.

[9290ZC]

Article 30

Advance payment of costs and expenses

Where the law of the Member State in which the opening of secondary proceedings is requested requires that the debtor's assets be sufficient to cover in whole or in part the costs and expenses of the proceedings, the court may, when it receives such a request, require the applicant to make an advance payment of costs or to provide appropriate security.

[9290ZD]

Article 31

Duty to cooperate and communicate information

1. Subject to the rules restricting the communication of information, the liquidator in the main proceedings and the liquidators in the secondary proceedings shall be duty bound to

communicate information to each other. They shall immediately communicate any information which may be relevant to the other proceedings, in particular the progress made in lodging and verifying claims and all measures aimed at terminating the proceedings.

2. Subject to the rules applicable to each of the proceedings, the liquidator in the main proceedings and the liquidators in the secondary proceedings shall be duty bound to cooperate with each other.

3. The liquidator in the secondary proceedings shall give the liquidator in the main proceedings an early opportunity of submitting proposals on the liquidation or use of the assets in the secondary proceedings.

[9290ZE]

Article 32

Exercise of creditors' rights

1. Any creditor may lodge his claim in the main proceedings and in any secondary proceedings.

2. The liquidators in the main and any secondary proceedings shall lodge in other proceedings claims which have already been lodged in the proceedings for which they were appointed, provided that the interests of creditors in the latter proceedings are served thereby, subject to the right of creditors to oppose that or to withdraw the lodgement of their claims where the law applicable so provides.

3. The liquidator in the main or secondary proceedings shall be empowered to participate in other proceedings on the same basis as a creditor, in particular by attending creditors' meetings.

[9290ZF]

Article 33

Stay of liquidation

1. The court, which opened the secondary proceedings, shall stay the process of liquidation in whole or in part on receipt of a request from the liquidator in the main proceedings, provided that in that event it may require the liquidator in the main proceedings to take any suitable measure to guarantee the interests of the creditors in the secondary proceedings and of individual classes of creditors. Such a request from the liquidator may be rejected only if it is manifestly of no interest to the creditors in the main proceedings. Such a stay of the process of liquidation may be ordered for up to three months. It may be continued or renewed for similar periods.

2. The court referred to in paragraph 1 shall terminate the stay of the process of liquidation:

- — at the request of the liquidator in the main proceedings,
- — of its own motion, at the request of a creditor or at the request of the liquidator in the secondary proceedings if that measure no longer appears justified, in particular, by the interests of creditors in the main proceedings or in the secondary proceedings.

[9290ZG]

Article 34

Measures ending secondary insolvency proceedings

1. Where the law applicable to secondary proceedings allows for such proceedings to be closed without liquidation by a rescue plan, a composition or a comparable measure, the liquidator in the main proceedings shall be empowered to propose such a measure himself.

Closure of the secondary proceedings by a measure referred to in the first subparagraph shall not become final without the consent of the liquidator in the main proceedings; failing his agreement, however, it may become final if the financial interests of the creditors in the main proceedings are not affected by the measure proposed.

2. Any restriction of creditors' rights arising from a measure referred to in paragraph 1 which is proposed in secondary proceedings, such as a stay of payment or discharge of debt, may not have effect in respect of the debtor's assets not covered by those proceedings without the consent of all the creditors having an interest.

3. During a stay of the process of liquidation ordered pursuant to Article 33, only the liquidator in the main proceedings or the debtor, with the former's consent, may propose measures laid down in paragraph 1 of this Article in the secondary proceedings; no other proposal for such a measure shall be put to the vote or approved.

[9290ZH]

Article 35

Assets remaining in the secondary proceedings

If by the liquidation of assets in the secondary proceedings it is possible to meet all claims allowed under those proceedings, the liquidator appointed in those proceedings shall immediately transfer any assets remaining to the liquidator in the main proceedings.

[9290ZI]

Article 36

Subsequent opening of the main proceedings

Where the proceedings referred to in Article 3(1) are opened following the opening of the proceedings referred to in Article 3(2) in another Member State, Articles 31 to 35 shall apply to those opened first, in so far as the progress of those proceedings so permits.

[9290ZJ]

Article 37[1]

Conversion of earlier proceedings

The liquidator in the main proceedings may request that proceedings listed in Annex A previously opened in another Member State be converted into winding-up proceedings if this proves to be in the interests of the creditors in the main proceedings.

The court with jurisdiction under Article 3(2) shall order conversion into one of the proceedings listed in Annex B.

[9290ZK]

NOTES

[1] Note the Declaration by Portugal concerning the application of Articles 26 and 37 (OJ C183, 30.6.2000, p 1).

Article 38

Preservation measures

Where the court of a Member State which has jurisdiction pursuant to Article 3(1) appoints a temporary administrator in order to ensure the preservation of the debtor's assets, that temporary administrator shall be empowered to request any measures to secure and preserve any of the debtor's assets situated in another Member State, provided for under the law of that State, for the period between the request for the opening of insolvency proceedings and the judgment opening the proceedings.

[9290ZL]

CHAPTER IV
PROVISION OF INFORMATION FOR CREDITORS AND LODGEMENT OF THEIR CLAIMS

Article 39

Right to lodge claims

Any creditor who has his habitual residence, domicile or registered office in a Member State other than the State of the opening of proceedings, including the tax authorities and social security authorities of Member States, shall have the right to lodge claims in the insolvency proceedings in writing.

[9290ZM]

Article 40

Duty to inform creditors

1. As soon as insolvency proceedings are opened in a Member State, the court of that State having jurisdiction or the liquidator appointed by it shall immediately inform known creditors who have their habitual residences, domiciles or registered offices in the other Member States.

2. That information, provided by an individual notice, shall in particular include time limits, the penalties laid down in regard to those time limits, the body or authority empowered to accept the lodgement of claims and the other measures laid down. Such notice shall also indicate whether creditors whose claims are preferential or secured in rem need lodge their claims.

[9290ZN]

Article 41

Content of the lodgement of a claim

A creditor shall send copies of supporting documents, if any, and shall indicate the nature of the claim, the date on which it arose and its amount, as well as whether he alleges preference, security in rem or a reservation of title in respect of the claim and what assets are covered by the guarantee he is invoking.

[9290ZO]

Article 42

Languages

1. The information provided for in Article 40 shall be provided in the official language or one of the official languages of the State of the opening of proceedings. For that purpose a form shall be used bearing the heading "Invitation to lodge a claim. Time limits to be observed" in all the official languages of the institutions of the European Union.

2. Any creditor who has his habitual residence, domicile or registered office in a Member State other than the State of the opening of proceedings may lodge his claim in the official language or one of the official languages of that other State. In that event, however, the lodgement of his claim shall bear the heading "Lodgement of claim" in the official language or one of the official languages of the State of the opening of proceedings. In addition, he may be required to provide a translation into the official language or one of the official languages of the State of the opening of proceedings.

[9290ZP]

CHAPTER V
TRANSITIONAL AND FINAL PROVISIONS

Article 43

Applicability in time

The provisions of this Regulation shall apply only to insolvency proceedings opened after its entry into force. Acts done by a debtor before the entry into force of this Regulation shall continue to be governed by the law which was applicable to them at the time they were done.

[9290ZQ]

Article 44

Relationship to Conventions

1. After its entry into force, this Regulation replaces, in respect of the matters referred to therein, in the relations between Member States, the Conventions concluded between two or more Member States, in particular:

(a) the Convention between Belgium and France on Jurisdiction and the Validity and Enforcement of Judgments, Arbitration Awards and Authentic Instruments, signed at Paris on 8 July 1899;

(b) the Convention between Belgium and Austria on Bankruptcy, Winding-up,

Arrangements, Compositions and Suspension of Payments (with Additional Protocol of 13 June 1973), signed at Brussels on 16 July 1969;

(c) the Convention between Belgium and the Netherlands on Territorial Jurisdiction, Bankruptcy and the Validity and Enforcement of Judgments, Arbitration Awards and Authentic Instruments, signed at Brussels on 28 March 1925;

(d) the Treaty between Germany and Austria on Bankruptcy, Winding-up, Arrangements and Compositions, signed at Vienna on 25 May 1979;

(e) the Convention between France and Austria on Jurisdiction, Recognition and Enforcement of Judgments on Bankruptcy, signed at Vienna on 27 February 1979;

(f) the Convention between France and Italy on the Enforcement of Judgments in Civil and Commercial Matters, signed at Rome on 3 June 1930;

(g) the Convention between Italy and Austria on Bankruptcy, Winding-up, Arrangements and Compositions, signed at Rome on 12 July 1977;

(h) the Convention between the Kingdom of the Netherlands and the Federal Republic of Germany on the Mutual Recognition and Enforcement of Judgments and other Enforceable Instruments in Civil and Commercial Matters, signed at The Hague on 30 August 1962;

(i) the Convention between the United Kingdom and the Kingdom of Belgium providing for the Reciprocal Enforcement of Judgments in Civil and Commercial Matters, with Protocol, signed at Brussels on 2 May 1934;

(j) the Convention between Denmark, Finland, Norway, Sweden and Iceland on Bankruptcy, signed at Copenhagen on 7 November 1933;

(k) the European Convention on Certain International Aspects of Bankruptcy, signed at Istanbul on 5 June 1990;

[(l) the Convention between the Federative People's Republic of Yugoslavia and the Kingdom of Greece on the Mutual Recognition and Enforcement of Judgments, signed at Athens on 18 June 1959;

(m) the Agreement between the Federative People's Republic of Yugoslavia and the Republic of Austria on the Mutual Recognition and Enforcement of Arbitral Awards and Arbitral Settlements in Commercial Matters, signed at Belgrade on 18 March 1960;

(n) the Convention between the Federative People's Republic of Yugoslavia and the Republic of Italy on Mutual Judicial Cooperation in Civil and Administrative Matters, signed at Rome on 3 December 1960;

(o) the Agreement between the Socialist Federative Republic of Yugoslavia and the Kingdom of Belgium on Judicial Cooperation in Civil and Commercial Matters, signed at Belgrade on 24 September 1971;

(p) the Convention between the Governments of Yugoslavia and France on the Recognition and Enforcement of Judgments in Civil and Commercial Matters, signed at Paris on 18 May 1971;

(q) the Agreement between the Czechoslovak Socialist Republic and the Hellenic Republic on Legal Aid in Civil and Criminal Matters, signed at Athens on 22 October 1980, still in force between the Czech Republic and Greece;

(r) the Agreement between the Czechoslovak Socialist Republic and the Republic of Cyprus on Legal Aid in Civil and Criminal Matters, signed at Nicosia on 23 April 1982, still in force between the Czech Republic and Cyprus;

(s) the Treaty between the Government of the Czechoslovak Socialist Republic and the Government of the Republic of France on Legal Aid and the Recognition and Enforcement of Judgments in Civil, Family and Commercial Matters, signed at Paris on 10 May 1984, still in force between the Czech Republic and France;

(t) the Treaty between the Czechoslovak Socialist Republic and the Italian Republic on Legal Aid in Civil and Criminal Matters, signed at Prague on 6 December 1985, still in force between the Czech Republic and Italy;

(u) the Agreement between the Republic of Latvia, the Republic of Estonia and the Republic of Lithuania on Legal Assistance and Legal Relationships, signed at Tallinn on 11 November 1992;

(v) the Agreement between Estonia and Poland on Granting Legal Aid and Legal Relations on Civil, Labour and Criminal Matters, signed at Tallinn on 27 November 1998;

(w) the Agreement between the Republic of Lithuania and the Republic of Poland on Legal Assistance and Legal Relations in Civil, Family, Labour and Criminal Matters, signed in Warsaw on 26 January 1993;]

[(x) the Convention between Socialist Republic of Romania and the Hellenic Republic on legal assistance in civil and criminal matters and its Protocol, signed at Bucharest on 19 October 1972;

(y) the Convention between Socialist Republic of Romania and the French Republic on legal assistance in civil and commercial matters, signed at Paris on 5 November 1974;

(z) the Agreement between the People's Republic of Bulgaria and the Hellenic Republic on Legal Assistance in Civil and Criminal Matters, signed at Athens on 10 April 1976;

(aa) the Agreement between the People's Republic of Bulgaria and the Republic of Cyprus on Legal Assistance in Civil and Criminal Matters, signed at Nicosia on 29 April 1983;

(ab) the Agreement between the Government of the People's Republic of Bulgaria and the Government of the French Republic on Mutual Legal Assistance in Civil Matters, signed at Sofia on 18 January 1989;

(ac) the Treaty between Romania and the Czech Republic on judicial assistance in civil matters, signed at Bucharest on 11 July 1994;

(ad) the Treaty between Romania and Poland on legal assistance and legal relations in civil cases, signed at Bucharest on 15 May 1999.]

2. The Conventions referred to in paragraph 1 shall continue to have effect with regard to proceedings opened before the entry into force of this Regulation.

3. This Regulation shall not apply:

(a) in any Member State, to the extent that it is irreconcilable with the obligations arising in relation to bankruptcy from a convention concluded by that State with one or more third countries before the entry into force of this Regulation;

(b) in the United Kingdom of Great Britain and Northern Ireland, to the extent that is irreconcilable with the obligations arising in relation to bankruptcy and the winding-up of insolvent companies from any arrangements with the Commonwealth existing at the time this Regulation enters into force.

[9290ZR]

NOTES

Para 1: sub-paras (l)–(w) added by AA5, as from 1 May 2004; sub-paras (x)–(ad) added by Council Regulation 1791/2006/EC, Art 1, Annex, as from 1 January 2007.

Article 45

Amendment of the Annexes

The Council, acting by qualified majority on the initiative of one of its members or on a proposal from the Commission, may amend the Annexes.

[9290ZS]

Article 46

Reports

No later than 1 June 2012, and every five years thereafter, the Commission shall present to the European Parliament, the Council and the Economic and Social Committee a report on the application of this Regulation. The report shall be accompanied if need be by a proposal for adaptation of this Regulation.

[9290ZT]

Article 47

Entry into force

This Regulation shall enter into force on 31 May 2002.

This Regulation shall be binding in its entirety and directly applicable in the Member States in accordance with the Treaty establishing the European Community.

Done at Brussels, 29 May 2000.

[9290ZU]

[ANNEX A
INSOLVENCY PROCEEDINGS REFERRED TO IN ARTICLE 2(A)

BELGIË/BELGIQUE

— Het faillissement/La faillite

— Het gerechtelijk akkoord/Le concordat judiciaire

— De collectieve schuldenregeling/Le règlement collectif de dettes

— De vrijwillige vereffening/La liquidation volontaire

— De gerechtelijke vereffening/La liquidation judiciaire

— De voorlopige ontneming van beheer, bepaald in artikel 8 van de faillissementswet/Le dessaisissement provisoire, visé à l'article 8 de la loi sur les faillites

БЪЛГАРИЯ

— Производство по несъстоятелност

ČESKÁ REPUBLIKA

— Konkurs

— Reorganizace

— Oddlužení

DEUTSCHLAND

— Das Konkursverfahren

— Das gerichtliche Vergleichsverfahren

— Das Gesamtvollstreckungsverfahren

— Das Insolvenzverfahren

EESTI

— Pankrotimenetlus

ΕΛΛΑΣ

— Η πτώχευση

— Η ειδική εκκαυάριση

— Η προσωρινή διαχείριση εταιρείας. Η διοίκηση και διαχείριση των πιστωτών

— Η υπαγωγή επιχείρησης υπό επίτροπο με σκοπό τη σύναψη συμβιβασμού με τους πιστωτές

ESPAÑA

— Concurso

FRANCE

— Sauvegarde

— Redressement judiciaire

— Liquidation judiciaire

IRELAND

— Compulsory winding-up by the court

— Bankruptcy

— The administration in bankruptcy of the estate of persons dying insolvent

— Winding-up in bankruptcy of partnerships

— Creditors' voluntary winding-up (with confirmation of a court)

— Arrangements under the control of the court which involve the vesting of all or part of the property of the debtor in the Official Assignee for realisation and distribution

— Company examinership

ITALIA

— Fallimento

— Concordato preventivo

— Liquidazione coatta amministrativa

— Amministrazione straordinaria

ΚΥΠΡΟΣ

— Υποχρεωτική εκκαθάριση από το Δικαστήριο

— Εκούσια εκκαθάριση από πιστωτές κατόπιν Δικαστικού Διατάγματος

— Εκούσια εκκαθάριση από μέλη

— Εκκαθάριση με την εποπτεία του Δικαστηρίου

— Πτώχευση κατόπιν Δικαστικού Διατάγματος

— Διαχείριση της περιουσίας προσώπων που απεβίωσαν αφερέγγυα

LATVIJA

— Bankrots

— Izlīgums

— Sanācija

LIETUVA

— įmonės restruktūrizavimo byla

— įmonės bankroto byla

— įmonės bankroto procesas ne teismo tvarka

LUXEMBOURG

— Faillite

— Gestion contrôlée

— Concordat préventif de faillite (par abandon d'actif)

— Régime spécial de liquidation du notariat

MAGYARORSZÁG

— Csődeljárás

— Felszámolási eljárás

MALTA

— Xoljiment

— Amministrazzjoni

— Stralċvolontarju mill-membri jew mill-kredituri

— Stralċmill-Qorti

— Falliment f'każ ta' negozjant

NEDERLAND

— Het faillissement

— De surséance van betaling

— De schuldsaneringsregeling natuurlijke personen

ÖSTERREICH

— Das Konkursverfahren

— Das Ausgleichsverfahren

POLSKA

— Postępowanie upadłościowe

— Postępowanie układowe

— Upadłość obejmująca likwidację

— Upadłość z możliwością zawarcia układu

PORTUGAL

— O processo de insolvência

— O processo de falência

— Os processos especiais de recuperação de empresa, ou seja:
— A concordata
— A reconstituição empresarial
— A reestruturação financeira
— A gestão controlada

ROMÂNIA

— procedura insolvenţei

— reorganizarea judiciară

— procedura falimentului

SLOVENIJA

— Stečajni postopek

— Skrajšani stečajni postopek

— Postopek prisilne poravnave

— Prisilna poravnava v stečaju

SLOVENSKO

— Konkurzné konanie

— Reštrukturalizačné konanie

SUOMI/FINLAND

— Konkurssi/konkurs

— Yrityssaneeraus/företagssanering

SVERIGE

— Konkurs

— Företagsrekonstruktion

UNITED KINGDOM

— Winding-up by or subject to the supervision of the court

— Creditors' voluntary winding-up (with confirmation by the court)

— Administration, including appointments made by filing prescribed documents with the court

— Voluntary arrangements under insolvency legislation

— Bankruptcy or sequestration]

[9290ZV]

NOTES

Substituted by Council Regulation 681/2007EC, Art 1(1), Annex I, as from 21 June 2007. Note, however, that the designation in this Annex for the Czech Republic applies from 1 January 2008.

[ANNEX B

WINDING-UP PROCEEDINGS REFERRED TO IN ARTICLE 2(C)

BELGIË/BELGIQUE

— Het faillissement/La faillite

— De vrijwillige vereffening/La liquidation volontaire

— De gerechtelijke vereffening/La liquidation judiciaire

БЪЛГАРИЯ

— Производство по несъстоятелност

ČESKÁ REPUBLIKA

— Konkurs

DEUTSCHLAND

— Das Konkursverfahren

— Das Gesamtvollstreckungsverfahren

— Das Insolvenzverfahren

EESTI

— Pankrotimenetlus

ΕΛΛΑΣ

— Η πτώχευση

— Η ειδική εκκαθάριση

ESPAÑA

— Concurso

FRANCE

— Liquidation judiciaire

IRELAND

— Compulsory winding-up

— Bankruptcy

— The administration in bankruptcy of the estate of persons dying insolvent

— Winding-up in bankruptcy of partnerships

— Creditors' voluntary winding-up (with confirmation of a court)

— Arrangements under the control of the court which involve the vesting of all or part of the property of the debtor in the Official Assignee for realisation and distribution

ITALIA

— Fallimento

— Concordato preventivo con cessione dei beni

— Liquidazione coatta amministrativa

— Amministrazione straordinaria con programma di cessione dei complessi aziendali

— Amministrazione straordinaria con programma di ristrutturazione di cui sia parte integrante un concordato con cessione dei beni

ΚΥΠΡΟΣ

— Υποχρεωτική εκκαθάριση από το Δικαστήριο

— Εκκαθάριση με την εποπτεία του Δικαστηρίου

— Εκούσια εκκαθάριση από πιστωτές (με την επικύρωση του Δικαστηρίου)

— Πτώχευση

— Διαχείριση της περιουσίας προσώπων που απεβίωσαν αφερέγγυα

LATVIJA

— Bankrots

LIETUVA

— įmonės bankroto byla

— įmonės bankroto procesas ne teismo tvarka

LUXEMBOURG

— Faillite

— Régime spécial de liquidation du notariat

MAGYARORSZÁG

— Felszámolási eljárás

MALTA

— Stralċvolontarju

— Stralċmill-Qorti

— Falliment inkluż il-ħruġ ta' mandat ta' qbid mil-Kuratur f'każ ta' negozjant fallut

NEDERLAND

— Het faillissement

— De schuldsaneringsregeling natuurlijke personen

ÖSTERREICH

— Das Konkursverfahren

POLSKA

— Postępowanie upadłościowe

— Upadłość obejmująca likwidację

PORTUGAL

— O processo de insolvência

— O processo de falência

ROMÂNIA

— procedura falimentului

SLOVENIJA

— Stečajni postopek

— Skrajšani stečajni postopek

SLOVENSKO

— Konkurzné konanie

SUOMI/FINLAND

— Konkurssi/konkurs

SVERIGE

— Konkurs

UNITED KINGDOM

— Winding-up by or subject to the supervision of the court

— Winding-up through administration, including appointments made by filing prescribed documents with the court

— Creditors' voluntary winding-up (with confirmation by the court)

— Bankruptcy or sequestration]

[9290ZW]

NOTES

Substituted by Council Regulation 681/2007EC, Art 1(2), Annex II, as from 21 June 2007. Note, however, that the designation in this Annex for the Czech Republic applies from 1 January 2008.

[ANNEX C
LIQUIDATORS REFERRED TO IN ARTICLE 2(B)

BELGIË/BELGIQUE

— De curator/Le curateur

— De commissaris inzake opschorting/Le commissaire au sursis

— De schuldbemiddelaar/Le médiateur de dettes

— De vereffenaar/Le liquidateur

— De voorlopige bewindvoerder/L'administrateur provisoire

БЪЛГАРИЯ

— Назначен предварително временен синдик

— Временен синдик

— (Постоянен) синдик

— Служебен синдик

ČESKÁ REPUBLIKA

— Insolvenční správce

— Předběžný insolvenční správce

— Oddělený insolvenční správce

— Zvláštní insolvenční správce

— Zástupce insolvenčního správce

DEUTSCHLAND

— Konkursverwalter

— Vergleichsverwalter

— Sachwalter (nach der Vergleichsordnung)

— Verwalter

— Insolvenzverwalter

— Sachwalter (nach der Insolvenzordnung)

— Treuhänder

— Vorläufiger Insolvenzverwalter

EESTI

— Pankrotihaldur

— Ajutine pankrotihaldur

— Usaldusisik

ΕΛΛΑΣ

— Ο σύνδικος

— Ο προσωρινός διαχειριστής. Η διοικούσα επιτροπή των πιστωτών

— Ο ειδικός εκκαυαριστής

— Ο επίτροπος

ESPAÑA

— Administradores concursales

FRANCE

— Mandataire judiciaire

— Liquidateur

— Administrateur judiciaire

— Commissaire à l'exécution de plan

IRELAND

— Liquidator

— Official Assignee

— Trustee in bankruptcy

— Provisional liquidator

— Examiner

ITALIA

— Curatore

— Commissario giudiziale

— Commissario straordinario

— Commissario liquidatore

— Liquidatore giudiziale

ΚΥΠΡΟΣ

— Εκκαθαριστής και Προσωρινός Εκκαθαριστής

— Επίσημος Παραλήπτης

— Διαχειριστής της Πτώχευσης

— Εξεταστής

LATVIJA

— Maksātnespējas procesa administrators

LIETUVA

— Bankrutuojančių įmonių administratorius

— Restruktūrizuojamų įmonių administratorius

LUXEMBOURG

— Le curateur

— Le commissaire

— Le liquidateur

— Le conseil de gérance de la section d'assainissement du notariat

MAGYARORSZÁG

— Vagyonfelügyelő

— Felszámoló

MALTA

— Amministratur Provviżorju

— Riċevitur Uffiċjali

— Stralċjarju

— Manager Speċjali

— Kuraturi f'każ ta' proċeduri ta' falliment

NEDERLAND

— De curator in het faillissement

— De bewindvoerder in de surséance van betaling

— De bewindvoerder in de schuldsaneringsregeling natuurlijke personen

ÖSTERREICH

— Masseverwalter

— Ausgleichsverwalter

— Sachwalter

— Treuhänder

— Besondere Verwalter

— Konkursgericht

POLSKA

— Syndyk

— Nadzorca sądowy

— Zarządca

PORTUGAL

— Administrador da insolvência

— Gestor judicial

— Liquidatário judicial

— Comissão de credores

ROMÂNIA

— practician în insolvenţă

— Administrator judiciar

— Lichidator

SLOVENIJA

— Upravitelj prisilne poravnave

— Stečajni upravitelj

— Sodišče, pristojno za postopek prisilne poravnave

— Sodišče, pristojno za stečajni postopek

SLOVENSKO

— Predbežný správca

— Správca

SUOMI/FINLAND

— Pesänhoitaja/boförvaltare

— Selvittäjä/utredare

SVERIGE

— Förvaltare

— Rekonstruktör

UNITED KINGDOM

— Liquidator

— Supervisor of a voluntary arrangement

— Administrator
— Official receiver
— Trustee
— Provisional liquidator
— Judicial factor]

[9290ZX]

NOTES

Substituted by Council Regulation 681/2007EC, Art 1(3), Annex III, as from 21 June 2007. Note, however, that the designation in this Annex for the Czech Republic applies from 1 January 2008.

DIRECTIVE OF THE EUROPEAN PARLIAMENT AND OF THE COUNCIL

of 28 May 2001

on the admission of securities to official stock exchange listing and on information to be published on those securities

(2001/34/EC)

NOTES

Date of publication in OJ: OJ L184, 6.7.2001, p 1. Notes are as in the original OJ version.

THE EUROPEAN PARLIAMENT AND THE COUNCIL OF THE EUROPEAN UNION,

Having regard to the Treaty establishing the European Economic Community, and in particular Articles 44 and 95 thereof,

Having regard to the proposal from the Commission,

Having regard to the Opinion of the Economic and Social Committee,[1]

Acting in accordance with the procedure laid down in Article 251 of the Treaty,[2]

Whereas—

(1) Council Directive 79/279/EEC of 5 March 1979 coordinating the conditions for the admission of securities to official stock exchange listing,[3] Council Directive 80/390/EEC of 17 March 1980 coordinating the requirements for the drawing up, scrutiny and distribution of the listing particulars to be published for the admission of securities to official stock exchange listing,[4] Council Directive 82/121/EEC of 15 February 1982 on information to be published on a regular basis by companies the shares of which have been admitted to official stock-exchange listing[5] and Council Directive 88/627/EEC of 12 December 1988 on the information to be published when a major holding in a listed company is acquired or disposed of[6] have been substantially amended several times. In the interests of clarity and rationality, the said Directives should therefore be codified by grouping them together in a single text.

(2) The coordination of the conditions for the admission of securities to official listing on stock exchanges situated or operating in the Member States is likely to provide equivalent protection for investors at Community level, because of the more uniform guarantees offered to investors in the various Member States, it will facilitate both the admission to official stock exchange listing, in each such State, of securities from other Member States and the listing of any given security on a number of stock exchanges in the Community; it will accordingly make for greater interpenetration of national securities markets by removing those obstacles that may prudently be removed and therefore contribute to the prospect of establishing a European capital market.

(3) Such coordination must therefore apply to securities, independently of the legal status of their issuers, and must therefore also apply to securities issued by non-member States or their regional or local authorities or international public bodies; this Directive therefore covers entities not covered by the second paragraph of Article 48 of the Treaty.

(4) There should be the possibility of a right to apply to the courts against decisions by the competent national authorities in respect of the application of this Directive, concerning the admission of securities to official listing, although such right to apply must not be allowed to restrict the discretion of these authorities.

(5) Initially, this coordination of the conditions for admission of securities to official listing should be sufficiently flexible to enable account to be taken of present differences in the structures of securities markets in the Member States and to enable the Member States to take account of any specific situations with which they may be confronted.

(6) For this reason, coordination should first be limited to the establishment of minimum conditions for the admission of securities to official listing on stock exchanges situated or operating in the Member States, without however giving issuers any right to listing.

(7) This partial coordination of the conditions for admission to official listing constitutes a first step towards subsequent closer alignment of the rules of Member States in this field.

(8) The market in which undertakings operate has been enlarged to embrace the whole Community and this enlargement involves a corresponding increase in their financial requirements and extension of the capital markets on which they must call to satisfy them; admission to official listing on stock exchanges of Member States of securities issued by undertakings constitutes an important means of access to these capital markets; furthermore exchange restrictions on the purchase of securities traded on the stock exchanges of another Member State have been eliminated as part of the liberalisation of capital movements.

(9) Safeguards for the protection of the interests of actual and potential investors are required in most Member States of undertakings offering their securities to the public, either at the time of their offer or of their admission to official stock exchange listing; such safeguards require the provision of information which is sufficient and as objective as possible concerning the financial circumstances of the issuer and particulars of the securities for which admission to official listing is requested; the form under which this information is required usually consists of the publication of listing particulars.

(10) The safeguards required differ from Member State to Member State, both as regards the contents and the layout of the listing particulars and the efficacy, methods and timing of the check on the information given therein; the effect of these differences is not only to make it more difficult for undertakings to obtain admission of securities to official listing on stock exchanges of several Member States but also to hinder the acquisition by investors residing in one Member State of securities listed on stock exchanges of other Member States and thus to inhibit the financing of the undertakings and investment throughout the Community.

(11) These differences should be eliminated by coordinating the rules and regulations without necessarily making them completely uniform, in order to achieve an adequate degree of equivalence in the safeguards required in each Member State to ensure the provision of information which is sufficient and as objective as possible for actual or potential security holders.

(12) Such coordination must apply to securities independently of the legal status of the issuing undertaking; this Directive applies to entities to which no reference is made in the second paragraph of Article 48 of the Treaty.

(13) Mutual recognition of listing particulars to be published for the admission of securities to official listing represents an important step forward in the creation of the Community's internal market.

(14) In this connection, it is necessary to specify which authorities are competent to check and approve listing particulars to be published for the admission of securities to official listing in the event of simultaneous applications for admission to official listing in two or more Member States.

(15) Article 21 of Council Directive 89/298/EEC of 17 April 1989 coordinating the requirements for the drawing-up, scrutiny and distribution of the prospectus to be published when transferable securities are offered to the public[7] provides that where public offers are made simultaneously or within short intervals of one another in two or more Member States, a public-offer prospectus drawn up and approved in accordance with Article 7, 8 or 12 of that Directive must be recognised as a public-offer prospectus in the other Member States concerned on the basis of mutual recognition.

(16) It is also desirable to provide the recognition of a public-offer prospectus as listing particulars where admission to official stock-exchange listing is requested within a short period of the public offer.

(17) The mutual recognition of a public-offer prospectus and admission to official listings does not in itself confer a right to admissions.

(18) It is advisable to provide for the extension, by means of agreements to be concluded by the Community with non-member countries, of the recognition of listing particulars for admission to official listings from those countries on a reciprocal basis.

(19) It seems appropriate to provide for the possibility for the Member State in which admission to official listing is sought in certain cases to grant partial or complete exemption from the obligation to publish listing particulars for admission to official listings to issuers the securities of which have already been admitted to official stock-exchange listing in another Member State.

(20) Companies which have already been listed in the Community for some time and are of high quality and international standing are the most likely candidates for cross-border listing. Those companies are generally well known in most Member States: information concerning them is widely circulated and available.

(21) The aim of this Directive is to ensure that sufficient information is provided for investors; therefore, when such a company seeks to have its securities admitted to listing in a host Member State, investors operating on the market in that country may be sufficiently protected by receiving only simplified information rather than full listing particulars.

(22) Member States may find it useful to establish non-discriminatory minimum quantitative criteria, such as the current equity market capitalisation, which issuers must fulfil to be eligible to benefit from the possibilities for exemption provided for in this Directive; given the increasing integration of securities markets, it should equally be open to the competent authorities to give smaller companies similar treatment.

(23) Furthermore, many stock exchanges have second-tier markets in order to deal in shares of companies not admitted to official listing; in some cases the second-tier markets are regulated and supervised by authorities recognised by public bodies that impose on companies disclosure requirements equivalent in substance to those imposed on officially listed companies; therefore, the principle underlying Article 23 of this Directive could also be applied when such companies seek to have their securities admitted to official listing.

(24) In order to protect investors the documents intended to be made available to the public must first be sent to the competent authorities in the Member State in which admission to official listing is sought; it is for that Member State to decide whether those documents should be scrutinised by its competent authorities and to determine, if necessary, the nature and the manner in which that scrutiny should be carried out.

(25) In the case of securities admitted to official stock-exchange listing, the protection of investors requires that the latter be supplied with appropriate regular information throughout the entire period during which the securities are listed; coordination of requirements for this regular information has similar objectives to those envisaged for the listing particulars, namely to improve such protection and to make it more equivalent, to facilitate the listing of these securities on more than one stock exchange in the Community, and in so doing to contribute towards the establishment of a genuine Community capital market by permitting a fuller inter-penetration of securities markets.

(26) Under this Directive, listed companies must as soon as possible make available to investors their annual accounts and report giving information on the company for the whole of the financial year; whereas the Fourth Council Directive 78/660/EEC[8] has coordinated the laws, regulations and administrative provisions of the Member States concerning the annual accounts of certain types of companies.

(27) Companies should also, at least once during each financial year, make available to investors reports on their activities; this Directive can, consequently, be confined to coordinating the content and distribution of a single report covering the first six months of the financial year.

(28) However, in the case of ordinary debentures, because of the rights they confer on their holders, the protection of investors by means of the publication of a half-yearly report is not essential; by virtue of this Directive, convertible or exchangeable debentures and debentures with warrants may be admitted to official listing only if the related shares are already listed on the same stock exchange or on another regulated, regularly operating, recognised open market or are so admitted simultaneously; the Member States may derogate from this principle only if their competent authorities are satisfied that holders have at their disposal all the information necessary to form an opinion concerning the value of the shares to which these debentures relate; consequently, regular information needs to be coordinated only for companies whose shares are admitted to official stock-exchange listing.

(29) The half-yearly report must enable investors to make an informed appraisal of the general development of the company's activities during the period covered by the report; however, this report need contain only the essential details on the financial position and general progress of the business of the company in question.

(30) So as to ensure the effective protection of investors and the proper operation of stock exchanges, the rules relating to regular information to be published by companies, the shares of which are admitted to official stock-exchange listing within the Community, should apply not only to companies from Member States, but also to companies from non-member countries.

(31) A policy of adequate information of investors in the field of transferable securities is likely to improve investor protection, to increase investors' confidence in securities markets and thus to ensure that securities markets function correctly.

(32) By making such protection more equivalent, coordination of that policy at Community level is likely to make for greater inter-penetration of the Member States' transferable securities markets and therefore help to establish a true European capital market.

(33) To that end investors should be informed of major holdings and of changes in those holdings in Community companies the shares of which are officially listed on stock exchanges situated or operating within the Community.

(34) Coordinated rules should be laid down concerning the detailed content and the procedure for applying that requirement.

(35) Companies, the shares of which are officially listed on a Community stock exchange, can inform the public of changes in major holdings only if they have been informed of such changes by the holders of those holdings.

(36) Most Member States do not subject holders to such a requirement and where such a requirement exists there are appreciable differences in the procedures for applying it; coordinated rules should therefore be adopted at Community level in this field.

(37) This Directive should not affect the obligations of the Member States concerning the deadlines for transposition set out in Annex II, Part B,

[9291]

NOTES

1 OJ C116, 20.4.2001, p 69.
2 Opinion of the European Parliament of 14 March 2001 (not yet published in the Official Journal) and Council Decision of 7 May 2001.
3 OJ L66, 16.3.1979, p 21. Directive as last amended by Directive 88/627/EEC (OJ L348, 17.12.1988, p 62).
4 OJ L100, 17.4.1980, p 1. Directive as last amended by European Parliament and Council Directive 94/18/EC (OJ L135, 31.5.1994, p 1).
5 OJ L48, 20.2.1982, p 26.
6 OJ L348, 17.12.1988, p 62.
7 OJ L124, 5.5.1989, p 8.
8 OJ L222, 14.8.1978, p 11. Directive as last amended by Directive 1999/60/EC (OJ L162, 26.6.1999, p 65).

HAVE ADOPTED THIS DIRECTIVE—

TITLE I
DEFINITIONS AND SCOPE OF APPLICATION

CHAPTER I
DEFINITIONS

Article 1

For the purposes of this Directive—

(a) "issuers" shall mean companies and other legal persons and any undertaking whose securities are the subject of an application for admission to official listing on a stock exchange;

(b) "collective investment undertakings other than the closed-end type" shall mean unit trusts and investment companies—

(i) the object of which is the collective investment of capital provided by the public, and which operate on the principle of risk spreading, and

(ii) the units of which are, at the holders' request, repurchased or redeemed, directly or indirectly, out of the assets of these undertakings. Action taken by such undertakings to ensure that the stock exchange value of its units does not significantly vary from their net asset value shall be regarded as equivalent to such repurchase or redemption;

(c) for the purposes of this Directive "investment companies other than those of the closed-end type" shall mean investment companies—

(i) the object of which is the collective investment of capital provided by the public, and which operate on the principle of risk spreading, and

(ii) the shares of which are, at the holders' request, repurchased or redeemed, directly or indirectly, out of those companies' assets. Action taken by such companies to ensure that the stock exchange value operating of their shares does not significantly vary from their net asset value shall be regarded as equivalent to such repurchase or redemption;

(d) "credit institution" shall mean an undertaking whose business is to receive deposits or other repayable funds from the public and to grant credits for its own account;
(e) "units of a collective investment undertaking" shall mean securities issued by a collective investment undertaking as representing the rights of participants in the assets of such undertaking;
(f) "participating interest" shall mean rights in the capital of other undertakings, whether or not represented by certificates, which, by creating a durable link with those undertakings, are intended to contribute to the activities of the undertaking which holds these rights;
(g), (h) …

[9292]

NOTES

Points (g), (h) repealed by European Parliament and Council Directive 2004/109/EC, Art 32(1), as from 20 January 2007.

CHAPTER II
SCOPE OF APPLICATION

Article 2

1. Articles 5 to 19, 42 to 69, and 78 to 84 shall apply to securities which are admitted to official listing or are the subject of an application for admission to official listing on a stock exchange situated or operating within a Member State.

2. Member States may decide not to apply the provisions mentioned in paragraph 1 to—
(a) units issued by collective investment undertakings other than the closed-end type,
(b) securities issued by a Member State or its regional or local authorities.

[9293]–[9295]

Articles 3, 4

(*Article 3 repealed by European Parliament and Council Directive 2003/71/EC, Art 27(2), as from 1 July 2005; Article 4 repealed by European Parliament and Council Directive 2004/109/EC, Art 32(2), as from 20 January 2007.*)

TITLE II
GENERAL PROVISIONS CONCERNING THE OFFICIAL LISTING OF SECURITIES

CHAPTER I
GENERAL CONDITIONS FOR ADMISSION

Article 5

Member States shall ensure—
(a) securities may not be admitted to official listing on any stock exchange situated or operating within their territory unless the conditions laid down by this Directive are satisfied, and
(b) that issuers of securities admitted to such official listing, to regardless of the date on which this admission takes place, are subject to the obligations provided for by this Directive.

[9296]

Article 6

1. The admission of securities to official listing shall be subject to the conditions set out in Articles 42 to 51, or 52 to 63, relating to shares and debt securities respectively.

2. …

3. Certificates representing shares may be admitted to official listing only if the issuer of the shares represented fulfils the conditions set out in Articles 42 to 44 and the obligations set out in Articles 64 to 69 and if the certificates fulfil the conditions set out in Articles 45 to 50.

[9297]

NOTES

Para 2: repealed by European Parliament and Council Directive 2004/109/EC, Art 32(3), as from 20 January 2007.

Article 7

Member States may not make the admission to official listing of securities issued by companies or other legal persons which are nationals of another Member State subject to the condition that the securities must already have been admitted to official listing on a stock exchange situated or operating in one of the Member States.

[9298]

CHAPTER II
MORE STRINGENT OR ADDITIONAL CONDITIONS AND OBLIGATIONS

Article 8

1. Subject to the prohibitions provided for in Article 7 and in Articles 42 to 63, the Member States may make the admission of securities to official listing subject to more stringent conditions than those set out in Articles 42 to 63 or to additional conditions, provided that these more stringent and additional conditions apply generally for all issuers or for individual classes of issuer and that they have been published before application for admission of such securities is made.

[2. Member States may make the issuers of securities admitted to official listing subject to additional obligations, provided that those additional obligations apply generally for all issuers or for individual classes of issuers.]

3. Member States may, under the same conditions as those laid down in Article 9, authorise derogations from the additional or more stringent conditions and obligations referred to in paragraphs 1 and 2 hereof.

4. Member States may, in accordance with the applicable national rules require issuers of securities admitted to official listing to inform the public on a regular basis of their financial position and the general course of their business.

[9299]

NOTES

Para 2: substituted by European Parliament and Council Directive 2004/109/EC, Art 32(4), as from 20 January 2007.

CHAPTER III
DEROGATIONS

Article 9

Any derogations from the conditions for the admission of securities to official listing which may be authorised in accordance with Articles 42 to 63 must apply generally for all issuers where the circumstances justifying them are similar.

[9300]

Article 10

Member States may decide not to apply the conditions set out in Articles 52 to 63 and the obligations set out in Article 81(1) and (3) in respect of applications for admission to official listing of debt securities issued by companies and other legal persons which are nationals of a Member State and which are set up by, governed by or managed pursuant to a special law where repayments and interest payments in respect of those securities are guaranteed by a Member State or one of its federal states.

[9301]

CHAPTER IV
POWERS OF THE NATIONAL COMPETENT AUTHORITIES
SECTION 1
DECISION OF ADMISSION

Article 11

1. The competent authorities referred to in Article 105 shall decide on the admission of securities to official listing on a stock exchange situated or operating within their territories.

2. Without prejudice to the other powers conferred upon them, the competent authorities may reject an application for the admission of a security to official listing if, in their opinion, the issuer's situation is such that admission would be detrimental to investors' interests.

[9302]

Article 12

By way of derogation from Article 8, Member States may, solely in the interests of protecting the investors, give the competent authorities power to make the admission of a security to official listing subject to any special condition which the competent authorities consider appropriate and of which they have explicitly informed the applicant.

[9303]

Article 13

1. Where applications are to be made simultaneously or within short intervals of one another for admission of the same securities to official listing on stock exchanges situated or operating in more than one Member State, or where an application for admission is made in respect of a security already listed on a stock exchange in another Member State, the competent authorities shall communicate with each other and make such arrangements as may be necessary to expedite the procedure and simplify as far as possible the formalities and any additional conditions required for admission of the security concerned.

2. In order to facilitate the work of the competent authorities, any application for the admission of a security to official listing on a stock exchange situated or operating in a Member State must state whether a similar application is being or has been made in another Member State, or will be made in the near future.

[9304]

Article 14

The competent authorities may refuse to admit to official listing a security already officially listed in another Member State where the issuer fails to comply with the obligations resulting from admission in that Member State.

[9305]

Article 15

Where an application for admission to official listing relates to certificates representing shares, the application shall be considered only if the competent authorities are of the opinion that the issuer of the certificates is offering adequate safeguards for the protection of investors.

[9306]

SECTION 2
INFORMATION REQUESTED BY THE COMPETENT AUTHORITIES

Article 16

1. An issuer whose securities are admitted to official listing shall provide the competent authorities with all the information which the latter consider appropriate in order to protect investors or ensure the smooth operation of the market.

2. Where protection of investors or the smooth operation of the market so requires, an issuer may be required by the competent authorities to publish such information in such a form and within such time limits as they consider appropriate. Should the issuer fail to comply with such requirement, the competent authorities may themselves publish such information after having heard the issuer.

[9307]

SECTION 3
ACTION AGAINST AN ISSUER FAILING TO COMPLY WITH THE OBLIGATIONS RESULTING FROM ADMISSION

Article 17

Without prejudice to any other action or penalties which they may contemplate in the event of failure on the part of the issuer to comply with the obligations resulting from admission to official listing, the competent authorities may make public the fact that an issuer is failing to comply with those obligations.

[9308]

SECTION 4
SUSPENSION AND DISCONTINUANCE

Article 18

1. The competent authorities may decide to suspend the listing of a security where the smooth operation of the market is, or may be, temporarily jeopardised or where protection of investors so requires.

2. The competent authorities may decide that the listing of the security be discontinued where they are satisfied that, owing to special circumstances, normal regular dealings in a security are no longer possible.

[9309]

SECTION 5
RIGHT TO APPLY TO THE COURTS IN CASE OF REFUSAL OF ADMISSION OR DISCONTINUANCE

Article 19

1. Member States shall ensure decisions of the competent authorities refusing the admission of a security to official listing or discontinuing such a listing shall be subject to the right to apply to the courts.

2. An applicant shall be notified of a decision regarding his application for admission to official listing within six months of receipt of the application or, should the competent authority require any further information within that period, within six months of the applicant's supplying such information.

3. Failure to give a decision within the time limit specified in paragraph 2 shall be deemed a rejection of the application. Such rejection shall give rise to the right to apply to the courts provided for in paragraph 1.

[9310]–[9332]

TITLE III
PARTICULAR CONDITIONS RELATING TO OFFICIAL LISTINGS OF SECURITIES

Articles 20–41

(Articles 20–41 (Chapter I) repealed by European Parliament and Council Directive 2003/71/EC, Art 27(1), as from 1 July 2005.)

CHAPTER II
SPECIFIC CONDITIONS FOR THE ADMISSION OF SHARES

SECTION 1
CONDITIONS RELATING TO COMPANIES FOR THE SHARES OF WHICH ADMISSION TO OFFICIAL LISTING IS SOUGHT

Article 42

The legal position of the company must be in conformity with the laws and Regulations to which it is subject, as regards both its formation and its operation under its statutes.

[9333]

Article 43

1. The foreseeable market capitalisation of the shares for which admission to official listing is sought or, if this cannot be assessed, the company's capital and reserves, including profit or loss, from the last financial year, must be at least one million euro.

2. Member States may provide for admission to official listing, even when this condition is not fulfilled, provided that the competent authorities are satisfied that there will be an adequate market for the shares concerned.

3. A higher foreseeable market capitalisation or higher capital and reserves may be required by a Member State for admission to official listing only if another regulated, regularly operating, recognised open market exists in that State and the requirements for it are equal to or less than those referred to in paragraph 1.

4. The condition set out in paragraph 1 shall not be applicable for the admission to official listing of a further block of shares of the same class as those already admitted.

5. The equivalent in national currency of one million euro shall initially be the equivalent in national currency of one million European units of account that were applicable on 5 March 1979.

6. If, as a result of adjustment of the equivalent of the euro in national currency, the market capitalisation expressed in national currency remains for a period of one year at least 10% more or less than the value of one million euro the Member state must, within the 12 months following the expiry of that period, adjust its laws, regulations or administrative provisions to comply with paragraph 1.

[9334]

Article 44

A company must have published or filed its annual accounts in accordance with national law for the three financial years preceding the application for official listing. By way of exception, the competent authorities may derogate from this condition where such derogation is desirable in the interests of the company or of investors and where the competent authorities are satisfied that investors have the necessary information available to be able to arrive at an informed judgement on the company and the shares for which admission to official listing is sought.

[9335]

SECTION 2
CONDITIONS RELATING TO THE SHARES FOR WHICH ADMISSION IS SOUGHT

Article 45

The legal position of the shares must be in conformity with the laws and regulations to which they are subject.

[9336]

Article 46

1. The shares must be freely negotiable.

2. The competent authorities may treat shares which are not fully paid up as freely negotiable, if arrangements have been made to ensure that the negotiability of such shares is not restricted and that dealing is made open and proper by providing the public with all appropriate information.

3. The competent authorities may, in the case of the admission to official listing of shares which may be acquired only subject to approval, derogate from paragraph 1 only if the use of the approval clause does not disturb the market.

[9337]

Article 47

Where public issue precedes admission to official listing, the first listing may be made only after the end of the period during which subscription applications may be submitted.

[9338]

Article 48

1. A sufficient number of shares must be distributed to the public in one or more Member States not later than the time of admission.

2. The condition set out in paragraph 1 shall not apply where shares are to be distributed to the public through the stock exchange. In that event, admission to official listing may be granted only if the competent authorities are satisfied that a sufficient number of shares will be distributed through the stock exchange within a short period.

3. Where admission to official listing is sought for a further block of shares of the same class, the competent authorities may assess whether a sufficient number of shares has been distributed to the public in relation to all the shares issued and not only in relation to this further block.

4. By way of derogation from paragraph 1, if the shares are admitted to official listing in one or more non-member countries, the competent authorities may provide for their admission to official listing if a sufficient number of shares is distributed to the public in the non-Member State or States where they are listed.

5. A sufficient number of shares shall be deemed to have been distributed either when the shares in respect of which application for admission has been made are in the hands of the public to the extent of a least 25% of the subscribed capital represented by the class of shares concerned or when, in view of the large number of shares of the same class and the extent of their distribution to the public, the market will operate properly with a lower percentage.

[9339]

Article 49

1. The application for admission to official listing must cover all the shares of the same class already issued.

2. Member States may provide that this condition shall not apply to applications for admission not covering all the shares of the same class already issued where the shares of that class for which admission is not sought belong to blocks serving to maintain control of the company or are not negotiable for a certain time under agreements, provided that the public is informed of such situations and that there is no danger of such situations prejudicing the interests of the holders of the shares for which admission to official listing is sought.

[9340]

Article 50

1. For the admission to official listing of shares issued by companies which are nationals of another Member State and which shares have a physical form it is necessary and sufficient that their physical form comply with the standards laid down in that other Member State. Where the physical form does not conform to the standards in force in the Member State in which admission to official listing is applied for, the competent authorities of that state shall make that fact known to the public.

2. The physical form of shares issued by companies which are nationals of a non-member country must afford sufficient safeguard for the protection of the investors.

[9341]

Article 51

If the shares issued by a company which is a national of a non-member country are not listed in either the country of origin or in the country in which the major proportion of the shares is held, they may not be admitted to official listing unless the competent authorities are satisfied that the absence of a listing the in the country of origin or in the country in which the major proportion is held is not due to the need to protect investors.

[9342]

CHAPTER III
PARTICULAR CONDITIONS RELATING TO THE ADMISSION TO OFFICIAL LISTING OF DEBT SECURITIES ISSUED BY AN UNDERTAKING

SECTION 1
CONDITIONS RELATING TO UNDERTAKINGS FOR THE DEBT SECURITIES OF WHICH ADMISSION TO OFFICIAL LISTING IS SOUGHT

Article 52

The legal position of the undertaking must be in conformity with the laws and regulations to which it is subject, as regards both its formation and its operation under its statutes.

[9343]

SECTION 2
CONDITIONS RELATING TO THE DEBT SECURITIES FOR WHICH ADMISSION TO OFFICIAL LISTING IS SOUGHT

Article 53

The legal position of the debt securities must be in conformity with the laws and regulations to which they are subject.

[9344]

Article 54

1. The debt securities must be freely negotiable.

2. The competent authorities may treat debt securities which are not fully paid up as freely negotiable if arrangements have been made to ensure that the negotiability of these debt securities is not restricted and that dealing is made open and proper by providing the public with all appropriate information.

[9345]

Article 55

Where public issue precedes admission to official listing, the first listing may be made only after the end of the period during which subscription applications may be submitted. This provision shall not apply in the case of tap issues of debt securities when the closing date for subscription is not fixed.

[9346]

Article 56

The application for admission to official listing must cover all debt securities ranking *pari passu.*

[9347]

Article 57

1. For the admission to official listing of debt securities issued by undertakings which are nationals of another Member State and which debt securities have a physical form, it is necessary and sufficient that their physical form comply with the standards laid down in that other Member State. Where the physical form does not conform to the standards in force in the Member State in which admission to official listing is applied for, the competent authorities of that State shall make that fact known to the public.

2. The physical form of debt securities issued in a single Member State must conform to the standards in force in that State.

3. The physical form of debt securities issued by undertakings which are nationals of a non-member country must afford sufficient safeguard for the protection of the investors.

[9348]

SECTION 3
OTHER CONDITIONS

Article 58

1. The amount of the loan may not be less than EUR 200,000. This provision shall not be applicable in the case of tap issues where the amount of the loan is not fixed.

2. Member States may provide for admission to official listing even when this condition is not fulfilled, where the competent authorities are satisfied that there will be a sufficient market for the debt securities concerned.

3. The equivalent in national currency of EUR 200,000 shall initially be the equivalent in national currency of 200,000 units of account that were applicable on 5 March 1979.

4. If as a result of adjustment of the equivalent of the euro in national currency the minimum amount of the loan expressed in national currency remains, for a period of one year, at least 10% less than the value of EUR 200,000 the Member State must, within the 12 months following the expiry of that period, amend its laws, regulations and administrative provisions to comply with paragraph 1.

[9349]

Article 59

1. Convertible or exchangeable debentures and debentures with warrants may be admitted to official listing only if the related shares are already listed on the same stock exchange or on another regulated, regularly operating, recognised open market or are so admitted simultaneously.

2. Member States may, by way of derogation from paragraph 1, provide for the admission to official listing of convertible or exchangeable debentures or debentures with warrants, if the competent authorities are satisfied that holders have at their disposal all the information necessary to form an opinion concerning the value of the shares to which these debt securities relate.

[9350]

CHAPTER IV
PARTICULAR CONDITIONS RELATING TO THE ADMISSION TO OFFICIAL LISTING OF DEBT SECURITIES ISSUED BY A STATE, ITS REGIONAL OR LOCAL AUTHORITIES OR A PUBLIC INTERNATIONAL BODY

Article 60

The debt securities must be freely negotiable.

[9351]

Article 61

Where public issue precedes admission to official listing, the first listing may be made only after the end of the period during which subscription applications may be submitted. This provision shall not apply where the closing date for subscription is not fixed.

[9352]

Article 62

The application for admission to official listing must cover all the securities ranking *pari passu*.

[9353]

Article 63

1. For the admission to official listing of debt securities which are issued by a Member State or its regional or local authorities in a physical form, it is necessary and sufficient that such physical form comply with the standards in force in that Member State. Where the physical form does not comply with the standards in force in the Member State where admission to official listing is applied for, the competent authorities of that state shall bring this situation to the attention of the public.

2. The physical form of debt securities issued by non-member countries or their regional or local authorities or by public international bodies must afford sufficient safeguard for the protection of the investors.

[9354]

TITLE IV
OBLIGATIONS RELATING TO SECURITIES ADMITTED TO OFFICIAL LISTING

CHAPTER I
OBLIGATIONS OF COMPANIES WHOSE SHARES ARE ADMITTED TO OFFICIAL LISTING

SECTION 1
LISTING OF NEWLY ISSUED SHARES OF THE SAME CLASS

Article 64

Without prejudice to Article 49(2), in the case of a new public issue of shares of the same class as those already officially listed, the company shall be required, where the new shares are not automatically admitted, to apply for their admission to the same listing, either not more than a year after their issue or when they become freely negotiable.

[9355]–[9395]

Articles 65–104

(*Articles 65–97 (Title IV, Chapter I, Sections 2–8, and Chapters II, III) repealed by European Parliament and Council Directive 2004/109/EC, Art 32(5), as from 20 January 2007; Articles 98–104 (Title V) repealed by European Parliament and Council Directive 2003/71/EC, Art 27(2), as from 1 July 2005, and European Parliament and Council Directive 2004/109/EC, Art 32(6), as from 20 January 2007.*)

TITLE VI
COMPETENT AUTHORITIES AND COOPERATION BETWEEN MEMBER STATES

Article 105

1. Member States shall ensure that this Directive is applied and shall appoint one or more competent authorities for the purposes of the Directive. They shall notify the Commission thereof, giving details of any division of powers among them.

2. Member States shall ensure that the competent authorities have the powers necessary for them to carry out their task.

3. This Directive shall not affect the competent authorities' liability, which shall continue to be governed solely by national law.

[9396]

Article 106

The competent authorities shall cooperate whenever necessary for the purpose of carrying out their duties and shall exchange any information useful for that purpose.

[9397]

Article 107

1. Member States shall provide that all persons employed or formerly employed by the competent authorities shall be bound by professional secrecy. This means that any confidential information received in the course of their duties may not be divulged to any person or authority except by virtue of provisions laid down by law.

2. Paragraph 1 shall not, however, preclude the competent authorities of the various Member States from exchanging information as provided for in this Directive. Information thus exchanged shall be covered by the obligation of professional secrecy to which the persons employed or formerly employed by the competent authorities receiving the information are subject.

3. …

[9398]–[9399]

NOTES

Para 3: repealed by a combination of European Parliament and Council Directive 2003/71/EC, Art 27(2), as from 1 July 2005, and European Parliament and Council Directive 2004/109/EC, Art 32(7), as from 20 January 2007.

TITLE VII
CONTACT COMMITTEE

CHAPTER I
COMPOSITION, WORKING AND TASKS OF THE COMMITTEE

Article 108

(*Repealed by European Parliament and Council Directive 2005/1/EC, Art 10(1), as from 13 April 2005.*)

CHAPTER II
ADAPTATION OF THE AMOUNT OF EQUITY MARKET CAPITALISATION

[Article 109

1. For the purpose of adjusting, in the light of the requirements of the economic situation, the minimum amount of the foreseeable market capitalisation laid down in Article 43(1), the Commission shall submit to the European Securities Committee instituted by Commission Decision 2001/528/EC of 6 June 2001[1] a draft of the measures to be taken.

2. Where reference is made to this paragraph, Articles 5 and 7 of Council Decision 1999/468/EC of 28 June 1999 laying down the procedures for the exercise of implementing powers conferred on the Commission[2] shall apply, having regard to Article 8 thereof.

The period laid down in Article 5(6) of Decision 1999/468/EC shall be set at three months.

3. The Committee shall adopt its rules of procedure.]

[9400]

NOTES

Substituted by European Parliament and Council Directive 2005/1/EC, Art 10(2), as from 13 April 2005.

[1] OJ L191, 13.7.2001, p 45. Decision as amended by Decision 2004/8/EC (OJ L3, 7.1.2004, p 33).

[2] OJ L184, 17.7.1999, p 23.

TITLE VIII
FINAL PROVISIONS

Article 110

The Member States shall communicate to the Commission the texts of the main laws, regulations and administrative provisions which they adopt in the field covered by this Directive.

[9401]

Article 111

1. Directives 79/279/EEC, 80/390/EEC, 82/121/EEC and 88/627/EEC, as amended by the acts listed in Annex II Part A, are hereby repealed without prejudice to the obligations of the Member States concerning the time-limits for transposition set out in Annex II Part B.

2. References to the repealed Directives shall be construed as references to this Directive and should be read in accordance with the correlation table shown in Annex III.

[9402]

Article 112

This Directive shall enter into force the twentieth day following that of its publication in the *Official Journal of the European Communities*.

[9403]

Article 113

This Directive is addressed to the Member States.

[9404]–[9405]

Done at Brussels, 28 May 2001.

(*Annex I repealed by European Parliament and Council Directive 2003/71/EC, Art 27(4), as from 1 July 2005.*)

ANNEX II

PART A
REPEALED DIRECTIVES AND THEIR SUCCESSIVE AMENDMENTS
(REFERRED TO IN ARTICLE 111)

Council Directive 79/279/EEC	(OJ L66, 16.3.1979, p 21)
Council Directive 82/148/EEC	(OJ L62, 5.3.1982, p 22)
Council Directive 88/627/EEC	(OJ L348, 17.12.1988, p 62)
Council Directive 80/390/EEC	(OJ L100, 17.4.1980, p 1)
Council Directive 82/148/EEC	(OJ L62, 5.3.1982, p 22)
Council Directive 87/345/EEC	(OJ L185, 4.7.1987, p 81)
Council Directive 90/211/EEC	(OJ L112, 3.5.1990, p 24)
European Parliament and Council Directive 94/18/EC	(OJ L135, 31.5.1994, p 1)
Council Directive 82/121/EEC	(OJ L48, 20.2.1982, p 26)
Council Directive 88/627/EEC	(OJ L348, 17.12.1988, p 62)

[9406]

PART B
TIME-LIMITS FOR TRANSPOSITION INTO NATIONAL LAW
(REFERRED TO IN ARTICLE 111)

Directive	*Time-limit for transposition*
79/279/EEC	8 March 1981[1, 2]
80/390/EEC	19 September 1982[2]
82/121/EEC; 82/148/EEC	30 June 1983[3]
87/345/EEC	1 January 1990 1 January 1991 for Spain 1 January 1992 for Portugal
88/627/EEC	1 January 1991
90/211/EEC; 94/18/EC	17 April 1991

[9407]

NOTES

[1] 8.3.1982 for the Member States which introduce simultaneously Directives 79/279/EEC and 80/390/EEC.

[2] 30.6.1983 for the Member States which introduce simultaneously Directives 79/279/EEC, 80/390/EEC and 82/121/EEC.

[3] Time-limit for application: 30.6.1986.

(*Annex III* (*Correlation Table*) *not reproduced.*)

COUNCIL REGULATION

of 8 October 2001

on the Statute for a European company (SE)

(2157/2001/EC)

NOTES

Date of publication in OJ: OJ L294, 10.11.2001, p 1. Notes are as in the original OJ version.

THE COUNCIL OF THE EUROPEAN UNION,

Having regard to the Treaty establishing the European Community, and in particular Article 308 thereof,

Having regard to the proposal from the Commission,[1]

Having regard to the opinion of the European Parliament,[2]

Having regard to the opinion of the Economic and Social Committee,[3]

Whereas:

(1) The completion of the internal market and the improvement it brings about in the economic and social situation throughout the Community mean not only that barriers to trade must be removed, but also that the structures of production must be adapted to the Community dimension. For that purpose it is essential that companies the business of which is not limited to satisfying purely local needs should be able to plan and carry out the reorganisation of their business on a Community scale.

(2) Such reorganisation presupposes that existing companies from different Member States are given the option of combining their potential by means of mergers. Such operations can be carried out only with due regard to the rules of competition laid down in the Treaty.

(3) Restructuring and cooperation operations involving companies from different Member States give rise to legal and psychological difficulties and tax problems. The approximation of Member States' company law by means of Directives based on Article 44 of the Treaty can overcome some of those difficulties. Such approximation does not, however, release companies governed by different legal systems from the obligation to choose a form of company governed by a particular national law.

(4) The legal framework within which business must be carried on in the Community is still based largely on national laws and therefore no longer corresponds to the economic framework within which it must develop if the objectives set out in Article 18 of the Treaty are to be achieved. That situation forms a considerable obstacle to the creation of groups of companies from different Member States.

(5) Member States are obliged to ensure that the provisions applicable to European companies under this Regulation do not result either in discrimination arising out of unjustified different treatment of European companies compared with public limited-liability companies or in disproportionate restrictions on the formation of a European company or on the transfer of its registered office.

(6) It is essential to ensure as far as possible that the economic unit and the legal unit of business in the Community coincide. For that purpose, provision should be made for the creation, side by side with companies governed by a particular national law, of companies formed and carrying on business under the law created by a Community Regulation directly applicable in all Member States.

(7) The provisions of such a Regulation will permit the creation and management of companies with a European dimension, free from the obstacles arising from the disparity and the limited territorial application of national company law.

(8) The Statute for a European public limited-liability company (hereafter referred to as "SE") is among the measures to be adopted by the Council before 1992 listed in the Commission's White Paper on completing the internal market, approved by the European Council that met in Milan in June 1985. The European Council that met in Brussels in 1987 expressed the wish to see such a Statute created swiftly.

(9) Since the Commission's submission in 1970 of a proposal for a Regulation on the Statute for a European public limited-liability company, amended in 1975, work on the approximation of national company law has made substantial progress, so that on those points where the functioning of an SE does not need uniform Community rules reference may be made to the law governing public limited-liability companies in the Member State where it has its registered office.

(10) Without prejudice to any economic needs that may arise in the future, if the essential objective of legal rules governing SEs is to be attained, it must be possible at least to create such a company as a means both of enabling companies from different Member States to merge or to create a holding company and of enabling companies and other legal persons carrying on economic activities and governed by the laws of different Member States to form joint subsidiaries.

(11) In the same context it should be possible for a public limited-liability company with a registered office and head office within the Community to transform itself into an SE without going into liquidation, provided it has a subsidiary in a Member State other than that of its registered office.

(12) National provisions applying to public limited-liability companies that offer their securities to the public and to securities transactions should also apply where an SE is formed by means of an offer of securities to the public and to SEs wishing to utilise such financial instruments.

(13) The SE itself must take the form of a company with share capital, that being the form most suited, in terms of both financing and management, to the needs of a company carrying on business on a European scale. In order to ensure that such companies are of reasonable size, a minimum amount of capital should be set so that they have sufficient assets without making it difficult for small and medium-sized undertakings to form SEs.

(14) An SE must be efficiently managed and properly supervised. It must be borne in mind that there are at present in the Community two different systems for the administration of public limited-liability companies. Although an SE should be allowed to choose between the two systems, the respective responsibilities of those responsible for management and those responsible for supervision should be clearly defined.

(15) Under the rules and general principles of private international law, where one undertaking controls another governed by a different legal system, its ensuing rights and obligations as regards the protection of minority shareholders and third parties are governed by the law governing the controlled undertaking, without prejudice to the obligations imposed on the controlling undertaking by its own law, for example the requirement to prepare consolidated accounts.

(16) Without prejudice to the consequences of any subsequent coordination of the laws of the Member States, specific rules for SEs are not at present required in this field. The rules and general principles of private international law should therefore be applied both where an SE exercises control and where it is the controlled company.

(17) The rule thus applicable where an SE is controlled by another undertaking should be specified, and for this purpose reference should be made to the law governing public limited-liability companies in the Member State in which the SE has its registered office.

(18) Each Member State must be required to apply the sanctions applicable to public limited-liability companies governed by its law in respect of infringements of this Regulation.

(19) The rules on the involvement of employees in the European company are laid down in Directive 2001/86/EC,[4] and those provisions thus form an indissociable complement to this Regulation and must be applied concomitantly.

(20) This Regulation does not cover other areas of law such as taxation, competition, intellectual property or insolvency. The provisions of the Member States' law and of Community law are therefore applicable in the above areas and in other areas not covered by this Regulation.

(21) Directive 2001/86/EC is designed to ensure that employees have a right of involvement in issues and decisions affecting the life of their SE. Other social and labour legislation questions, in particular the right of employees to information and consultation as regulated in the Member States, are governed by the national provisions applicable, under the same conditions, to public limited-liability companies.

(22) The entry into force of this Regulation must be deferred so that each Member State may incorporate into its national law the provisions of Directive 2001/86/EC and set up in advance the necessary machinery for the formation and operation of SEs with registered offices within its territory, so that the Regulation and the Directive may be applied concomitantly.

(23) A company the head office of which is not in the Community should be allowed to participate in the formation of an SE provided that company is formed under the law of a Member State, has its registered office in that Member State and has a real and continuous link with a Member State's economy according to the principles established in the 1962 General Programme for the abolition of restrictions on freedom of establishment. Such a link exists in particular if a company has an establishment in that Member State and conducts operations therefrom.

(24) The SE should be enabled to transfer its registered office to another Member State. Adequate protection of the interests of minority shareholders who oppose the transfer, of

creditors and of holders of other rights should be proportionate. Such transfer should not affect the rights originating before the transfer.

(25) This Regulation is without prejudice to any provision which may be inserted in the 1968 Brussels Convention or in any text adopted by Member States or by the Council to replace such Convention, relating to the rules of jurisdiction applicable in the case of transfer of the registered offices of a public limited-liability company from one Member State to another.

(26) Activities by financial institutions are regulated by specific directives and the national law implementing those directives and additional national rules regulating those activities apply in full to an SE.

(27) In view of the specific Community character of an SE, the "real seat" arrangement adopted by this Regulation in respect of SEs is without prejudice to Member States' laws and does not pre-empt any choices to be made for other Community texts on company law.

(28) The Treaty does not provide, for the adoption of this Regulation, powers of action other than those of Article 308 thereof.

(29) Since the objectives of the intended action, as outlined above, cannot be adequately attained by the Member States in as much as a European public limited-liability company is being established at European level and can therefore, because of the scale and impact of such company, be better attained at Community level, the Community may take measures in accordance with the principle of subsidiarity enshrined in Article 5 of the Treaty. In accordance with the principle of proportionality as set out in the said Article, this Regulation does not go beyond what is necessary to attain these objectives,

[9407AA]

NOTES

[1] OJ C263, 16.10.1989, p 41 and OJ C176, 8.7.1991, p 1.
[2] Opinion of 4 September 2001 (not yet published in the Official Journal).
[3] OJ C124, 21.5.1990, p 34.
[4] See p 22 of this Official Journal.

HAS ADOPTED THIS REGULATION:

TITLE I
GENERAL PROVISIONS

Article 1

1. A company may be set up within the territory of the Community in the form of a European public limited-liability company (Societas Europaea or SE) on the conditions and in the manner laid down in this Regulation.

2. The capital of an SE shall be divided into shares. No shareholder shall be liable for more than the amount he has subscribed.

3. An SE shall have legal personality.

4. Employee involvement in an SE shall be governed by the provisions of Directive 2001/86/EC.

[9407AB]

Article 2

1. Public limited-liability companies such as referred to in Annex I, formed under the law of a Member State, with registered offices and head offices within the Community may form an SE by means of a merger provided that at least two of them are governed by the law of different Member States.

2. Public and private limited-liability companies such as referred to in Annex II, formed under the law of a Member State, with registered offices and head offices within the Community may promote the formation of a holding SE provided that each of at least two of them:

(a) is governed by the law of a different Member State, or
(b) has for at least two years had a subsidiary company governed by the law of another Member State or a branch situated in another Member State.

3. Companies and firms within the meaning of the second paragraph of Article 48 of the Treaty and other legal bodies governed by public or private law, formed under the law of a

Member State, with registered offices and head offices within the Community may form a subsidiary SE by subscribing for its shares, provided that each of at least two of them:

(a) is governed by the law of a different Member State, or

(b) has for at least two years had a subsidiary company governed by the law of another Member State or a branch situated in another Member State.

4. A public limited-liability company, formed under the law of a Member State, which has its registered office and head office within the Community may be transformed into an SE if for at least two years it has had a subsidiary company governed by the law of another Member State.

5. A Member State may provide that a company the head office of which is not in the Community may participate in the formation of an SE provided that company is formed under the law of a Member State, has its registered office in that Member State and has a real and continuous link with a Member State's economy.

[9407AC]

Article 3

1. For the purposes of Article 2(1), (2) and (3), an SE shall be regarded as a public limited-liability company governed by the law of the Member State in which it has its registered office.

2. An SE may itself set up one or more subsidiaries in the form of SEs. The provisions of the law of the Member State in which a subsidiary SE has its registered office that require a public limited-liability company to have more than one shareholder shall not apply in the case of the subsidiary SE. The provisions of national law implementing the twelfth Council Company Law Directive (89/667/EEC) of 21 December 1989 on single-member private limited-liability companies[1] shall apply to SEs mutatis mutandis.

[9407AD]

NOTES

[1] OJ L395, 30.12.1989, p 40. Directive as last amended by the 1994 Act of Accession.

Article 4

1. The capital of an SE shall be expressed in euro.

2. The subscribed capital shall not be less than EUR 120,000.

3. The laws of a Member State requiring a greater subscribed capital for companies carrying on certain types of activity shall apply to SEs with registered offices in that Member State.

[9407AE]

Article 5

Subject to Article 4(1) and (2), the capital of an SE, its maintenance and changes thereto, together with its shares, bonds and other similar securities shall be governed by the provisions which would apply to a public limited-liability company with a registered office in the Member State in which the SE is registered.

[9407AF]

Article 6

For the purposes of this Regulation, "the statutes of the SE" shall mean both the instrument of incorporation and, where they are the subject of a separate document, the statutes of the SE.

[9407AG]

Article 7

The registered office of an SE shall be located within the Community, in the same Member State as its head office. A Member State may in addition impose on SEs registered in its territory the obligation of locating their head office and their registered office in the same place.

[9407AH]

Article 8

1. The registered office of an SE may be transferred to another Member State in accordance with paragraphs 2 to 13. Such a transfer shall not result in the winding up of the SE or in the creation of a new legal person.

2. The management or administrative organ shall draw up a transfer proposal and publicise it in accordance with Article 13, without prejudice to any additional forms of publication provided for by the Member State of the registered office. That proposal shall state the current name, registered office and number of the SE and shall cover:

(a) the proposed registered office of the SE;
(b) the proposed statutes of the SE including, where appropriate, its new name;
(c) any implication the transfer may have on employees' involvement;
(d) the proposed transfer timetable;
(e) any rights provided for the protection of shareholders and/or creditors.

3. The management or administrative organ shall draw up a report explaining and justifying the legal and economic aspects of the transfer and explaining the implications of the transfer for shareholders, creditors and employees.

4. An SE's shareholders and creditors shall be entitled, at least one month before the general meeting called upon to decide on the transfer, to examine at the SE's registered office the transfer proposal and the report drawn up pursuant to paragraph 3 and, on request, to obtain copies of those documents free of charge.

5. A Member State may, in the case of SEs registered within its territory, adopt provisions designed to ensure appropriate protection for minority shareholders who oppose a transfer.

6. No decision to transfer may be taken for two months after publication of the proposal. Such a decision shall be taken as laid down in Article 59.

7. Before the competent authority issues the certificate mentioned in paragraph 8, the SE shall satisfy it that, in respect of any liabilities arising prior to the publication of the transfer proposal, the interests of creditors and holders of other rights in respect of the SE (including those of public bodies) have been adequately protected in accordance with requirements laid down by the Member State where the SE has its registered office prior to the transfer.

A Member State may extend the application of the first subparagraph to liabilities that arise (or may arise) prior to the transfer.

The first and second subparagraphs shall be without prejudice to the application to SEs of the national legislation of Member States concerning the satisfaction or securing of payments to public bodies.

8. In the Member State in which an SE has its registered office the court, notary or other competent authority shall issue a certificate attesting to the completion of the acts and formalities to be accomplished before the transfer.

9. The new registration may not be effected until the certificate referred to in paragraph 8 has been submitted, and evidence produced that the formalities required for registration in the country of the new registered office have been completed.

10. The transfer of an SE's registered office and the consequent amendment of its statutes shall take effect on the date on which the SE is registered, in accordance with Article 12, in the register for its new registered office.

11. When the SE's new registration has been effected, the registry for its new registration shall notify the registry for its old registration. Deletion of the old registration shall be effected on receipt of that notification, but not before.

12. The new registration and the deletion of the old registration shall be publicised in the Member States concerned in accordance with Article 13.

13. On publication of an SE's new registration, the new registered office may be relied on as against third parties. However, as long as the deletion of the SE's registration from the register for its previous registered office has not been publicised, third parties may continue to rely on the previous registered office unless the SE proves that such third parties were aware of the new registered office.

14. The laws of a Member State may provide that, as regards SEs registered in that Member State, the transfer of a registered office which would result in a change of the law

applicable shall not take effect if any of that Member State's competent authorities opposes it within the two-month period referred to in paragraph 6. Such opposition may be based only on grounds of public interest.

Where an SE is supervised by a national financial supervisory authority according to Community directives the right to oppose the change of registered office applies to this authority as well.

Review by a judicial authority shall be possible.

15. An SE may not transfer its registered office if proceedings for winding up, liquidation, insolvency or suspension of payments or other similar proceedings have been brought against it.

16. An SE which has transferred its registered office to another Member State shall be considered, in respect of any cause of action arising prior to the transfer as determined in paragraph 10, as having its registered office in the Member States where the SE was registered prior to the transfer, even if the SE is sued after the transfer.

[9407AI]

Article 9

1. An SE shall be governed:
   (a) by this Regulation,
   (b) where expressly authorised by this Regulation, by the provisions of its statutes or
   (c) in the case of matters not regulated by this Regulation or, where matters are partly regulated by it, of those aspects not covered by it, by:
      (i) the provisions of laws adopted by Member States in implementation of Community measures relating specifically to SEs;
      (ii) the provisions of Member States' laws which would apply to a public limited-liability company formed in accordance with the law of the Member State in which the SE has its registered office;
      (iii) the provisions of its statutes, in the same way as for a public limited-liability company formed in accordance with the law of the Member State in which the SE has its registered office.

2. The provisions of laws adopted by Member States specifically for the SE must be in accordance with Directives applicable to public limited-liability companies referred to in Annex I.

3. If the nature of the business carried out by an SE is regulated by specific provisions of national laws, those laws shall apply in full to the SE.

[9407AJ]

Article 10

Subject to this Regulation, an SE shall be treated in every Member State as if it were a public limited-liability company formed in accordance with the law of the Member State in which it has its registered office.

[9407AK]

Article 11

1. The name of an SE shall be preceded or followed by the abbreviation SE.

2. Only SEs may include the abbreviation SE in their name.

3. Nevertheless, companies, firms and other legal entities registered in a Member State before the date of entry into force of this Regulation in the names of which the abbreviation SE appears shall not be required to alter their names.

[9407AL]

Article 12

1. Every SE shall be registered in the Member State in which it has its registered office in a register designated by the law of that Member State in accordance with Article 3 of the first Council Directive (68/151/EEC) of 9 March 1968 on coordination of safeguards which, for the protection of the interests of members and others, are required by Member States of

companies within the meaning of the second paragraph of Article 58 of the Treaty, with a view to making such safeguards equivalent throughout the Community.[1]

2. An SE may not be registered unless an agreement on arrangements for employee involvement pursuant to Article 4 of Directive 2001/86/EC has been concluded, or a decision pursuant to Article 3(6) of the Directive has been taken, or the period for negotiations pursuant to Article 5 of the Directive has expired without an agreement having been concluded.

3. In order for an SE to be registered in a Member State which has made use of the option referred to in Article 7(3) of Directive 2001/86/EC, either an agreement pursuant to Article 4 of the Directive must have been concluded on the arrangements for employee involvement, including participation, or none of the participating companies must have been governed by participation rules prior to the registration of the SE.

4. The statutes of the SE must not conflict at any time with the arrangements for employee involvement which have been so determined. Where new such arrangements determined pursuant to the Directive conflict with the existing statutes, the statutes shall to the extent necessary be amended.

In this case, a Member State may provide that the management organ or the administrative organ of the SE shall be entitled to proceed to amend the statutes without any further decision from the general shareholders meeting.

[9407AM]

NOTES

[1] OJ L65, 14.3.1968, p 8. Directive as last amended by the 1994 Act of Accession.

Article 13

Publication of the documents and particulars concerning an SE which must be publicised under this Regulation shall be effected in the manner laid down in the laws of the Member State in which the SE has its registered office in accordance with Directive 68/151/EEC.

[9407AN]

Article 14

1. Notice of an SE's registration and of the deletion of such a registration shall be published for information purposes in the Official Journal of the European Communities after publication in accordance with Article 13. That notice shall state the name, number, date and place of registration of the SE, the date and place of publication and the title of publication, the registered office of the SE and its sector of activity.

2. Where the registered office of an SE is transferred in accordance with Article 8, notice shall be published giving the information provided for in paragraph 1, together with that relating to the new registration.

3. The particulars referred to in paragraph 1 shall be forwarded to the Office for Official Publications of the European Communities within one month of the publication referred to in Article 13.

[9407AO]

TITLE II
FORMATION

SECTION 1
GENERAL

Article 15

1. Subject to this Regulation, the formation of an SE shall be governed by the law applicable to public limited-liability companies in the Member State in which the SE establishes its registered office.

2. The registration of an SE shall be publicised in accordance with Article 13.

[9407AP]

Article 16

1. An SE shall acquire legal personality on the date on which it is registered in the register referred to in Article 12.

2. If acts have been performed in an SE's name before its registration in accordance with Article 12 and the SE does not assume the obligations arising out of such acts after its registration, the natural persons, companies, firms or other legal entities which performed those acts shall be jointly and severally liable therefor, without limit, in the absence of agreement to the contrary.

[9407AQ]

SECTION 2
FORMATION BY MERGER

Article 17

1. An SE may be formed by means of a merger in accordance with Article 2(1).

2. Such a merger may be carried out in accordance with:
   (a) the procedure for merger by acquisition laid down in Article 3(1) of the third Council Directive (78/855/EEC) of 9 October 1978 based on Article 54(3)(g) of the Treaty concerning mergers of public limited-liability companies[1] or
   (b) the procedure for merger by the formation of a new company laid down in Article 4(1) of the said Directive.

In the case of a merger by acquisition, the acquiring company shall take the form of an SE when the merger takes place. In the case of a merger by the formation of a new company, the SE shall be the newly formed company.

[9407AR]

NOTES

[1] OJ L295, 20.10.1978, p 36. Directive as last amended by the 1994 Act of Accession.

Article 18

For matters not covered by this section or, where a matter is partly covered by it, for aspects not covered by it, each company involved in the formation of an SE by merger shall be governed by the provisions of the law of the Member State to which it is subject that apply to mergers of public limited-liability companies in accordance with Directive 78/855/EEC.

[9407AS]

Article 19

The laws of a Member State may provide that a company governed by the law of that Member State may not take part in the formation of an SE by merger if any of that Member State's competent authorities opposes it before the issue of the certificate referred to in Article 25(2).

Such opposition may be based only on grounds of public interest. Review by a judicial authority shall be possible.

[9407AT]

Article 20

1. The management or administrative organs of merging companies shall draw up draft terms of merger. The draft terms of merger shall include the following particulars:
   (a) the name and registered office of each of the merging companies together with those proposed for the SE;
   (b) the share-exchange ratio and the amount of any compensation;
   (c) the terms for the allotment of shares in the SE;
   (d) the date from which the holding of shares in the SE will entitle the holders to share in profits and any special conditions affecting that entitlement;
   (e) the date from which the transactions of the merging companies will be treated for accounting purposes as being those of the SE;
   (f) the rights conferred by the SE on the holders of shares to which special rights are attached and on the holders of securities other than shares, or the measures proposed concerning them;

(g) any special advantage granted to the experts who examine the draft terms of merger or to members of the administrative, management, supervisory or controlling organs of the merging companies;

(h) the statutes of the SE;

(i) information on the procedures by which arrangements for employee involvement are determined pursuant to Directive 2001/86/EC.

2. The merging companies may include further items in the draft terms of merger.

[9407AU]

Article 21

For each of the merging companies and subject to the additional requirements imposed by the Member State to which the company concerned is subject, the following particulars shall be published in the national gazette of that Member State:

(a) the type, name and registered office of every merging company;

(b) the register in which the documents referred to in Article 3(2) of Directive 68/151/EEC are filed in respect of each merging company, and the number of the entry in that register;

(c) an indication of the arrangements made in accordance with Article 24 for the exercise of the rights of the creditors of the company in question and the address at which complete information on those arrangements may be obtained free of charge;

(d) an indication of the arrangements made in accordance with Article 24 for the exercise of the rights of minority shareholders of the company in question and the address at which complete information on those arrangements may be obtained free of charge;

(e) the name and registered office proposed for the SE.

[9407AV]

Article 22

As an alternative to experts operating on behalf of each of the merging companies, one or more independent experts as defined in Article 10 of Directive 78/855/EEC, appointed for those purposes at the joint request of the companies by a judicial or administrative authority in the Member State of one of the merging companies or of the proposed SE, may examine the draft terms of merger and draw up a single report to all the shareholders.

The experts shall have the right to request from each of the merging companies any information they consider necessary to enable them to complete their function.

[9407AW]

Article 23

1. The general meeting of each of the merging companies shall approve the draft terms of merger.

2. Employee involvement in the SE shall be decided pursuant to Directive 2001/86/EC. The general meetings of each of the merging companies may reserve the right to make registration of the SE conditional upon its express ratification of the arrangements so decided.

[9407AX]

Article 24

1. The law of the Member State governing each merging company shall apply as in the case of a merger of public limited-liability companies, taking into account the cross-border nature of the merger, with regard to the protection of the interests of:

(a) creditors of the merging companies;

(b) holders of bonds of the merging companies;

(c) holders of securities, other than shares, which carry special rights in the merging companies.

2. A Member State may, in the case of the merging companies governed by its law, adopt provisions designed to ensure appropriate protection for minority shareholders who have opposed the merger.

[9407AY]

Article 25

1. The legality of a merger shall be scrutinised, as regards the part of the procedure concerning each merging company, in accordance with the law on mergers of public limited-liability companies of the Member State to which the merging company is subject.

2. In each Member State concerned the court, notary or other competent authority shall issue a certificate conclusively attesting to the completion of the pre-merger acts and formalities.

3. If the law of a Member State to which a merging company is subject provides for a procedure to scrutinise and amend the share-exchange ratio, or a procedure to compensate minority shareholders, without preventing the registration of the merger, such procedures shall only apply if the other merging companies situated in Member States which do not provide for such procedure explicitly accept, when approving the draft terms of the merger in accordance with Article 23(1), the possibility for the shareholders of that merging company to have recourse to such procedure. In such cases, the court, notary or other competent authorities may issue the certificate referred to in paragraph 2 even if such a procedure has been commenced. The certificate must, however, indicate that the procedure is pending. The decision in the procedure shall be binding on the acquiring company and all its shareholders.

[9407AZ]

Article 26

1. The legality of a merger shall be scrutinised, as regards the part of the procedure concerning the completion of the merger and the formation of the SE, by the court, notary or other authority competent in the Member State of the proposed registered office of the SE to scrutinise that aspect of the legality of mergers of public limited-liability companies.

2. To that end each merging company shall submit to the competent authority the certificate referred to in Article 25(2) within six months of its issue together with a copy of the draft terms of merger approved by that company.

3. The authority referred to in paragraph 1 shall in particular ensure that the merging companies have approved draft terms of merger in the same terms and that arrangements for employee involvement have been determined pursuant to Directive 2001/86/EC.

4. That authority shall also satisfy itself that the SE has been formed in accordance with the requirements of the law of the Member State in which it has its registered office in accordance with Article 15.

[9407BA]

Article 27

1. A merger and the simultaneous formation of an SE shall take effect on the date on which the SE is registered in accordance with Article 12.

2. The SE may not be registered until the formalities provided for in Articles 25 and 26 have been completed.

[9407BB]

Article 28

For each of the merging companies the completion of the merger shall be publicised as laid down by the law of each Member State in accordance with Article 3 of Directive 68/151/EEC.

[9407BC]

Article 29

1. A merger carried out as laid down in Article 17(2)(a) shall have the following consequences ipso jure and simultaneously:

(a) all the assets and liabilities of each company being acquired are transferred to the acquiring company;

(b) the shareholders of the company being acquired become shareholders of the acquiring company;

(c) the company being acquired ceases to exist;

(d) the acquiring company adopts the form of an SE.

2. A merger carried out as laid down in Article 17(2)(b) shall have the following consequences ipso jure and simultaneously:

(a) all the assets and liabilities of the merging companies are transferred to the SE;
(b) the shareholders of the merging companies become shareholders of the SE;
(c) the merging companies cease to exist.

3. Where, in the case of a merger of public limited-liability companies, the law of a Member State requires the completion of any special formalities before the transfer of certain assets, rights and obligations by the merging companies becomes effective against third parties, those formalities shall apply and shall be carried out either by the merging companies or by the SE following its registration.

4. The rights and obligations of the participating companies on terms and conditions of employment arising from national law, practice and individual employment contracts or employment relationships and existing at the date of the registration shall, by reason of such registration be transferred to the SE upon its registration.

[9407BD]

Article 30

A merger as provided for in Article 2(1) may not be declared null and void once the SE has been registered.

The absence of scrutiny of the legality of the merger pursuant to Articles 25 and 26 may be included among the grounds for the winding-up of the SE.

[9407BE]

Article 31

1. Where a merger within the meaning of Article 17(2)(a) is carried out by a company which holds all the shares and other securities conferring the right to vote at general meetings of another company, neither Article 20(1)(b), (c) and (d), Article 29(1)(b) nor Article 22 shall apply. National law governing each merging company and mergers of public limited-liability companies in accordance with Article 24 of Directive 78/855/EEC shall nevertheless apply.

2. Where a merger by acquisition is carried out by a company which holds 90% or more but not all of the shares and other securities conferring the right to vote at general meetings of another company, reports by the management or administrative body, reports by an independent expert or experts and the documents necessary for scrutiny shall be required only to the extent that the national law governing either the acquiring company or the company being acquired so requires.

Member States may, however, provide that this paragraph may apply where a company holds shares conferring 90% or more but not all of the voting rights.

[9407BF]

SECTION 3
FORMATION OF A HOLDING SE

Article 32

1. A holding SE may be formed in accordance with Article 2(2).

A company promoting the formation of a holding SE in accordance with Article 2(2) shall continue to exist.

2. The management or administrative organs of the companies which promote such an operation shall draw up, in the same terms, draft terms for the formation of the holding SE. The draft terms shall include a report explaining and justifying the legal and economic aspects of the formation and indicating the implications for the shareholders and for the employees of the adoption of the form of a holding SE. The draft terms shall also set out the particulars provided for in Article 20(1)(a), (b), (c), (f), (g), (h) and (i) and shall fix the minimum proportion of the shares in each of the companies promoting the operation which the shareholders must contribute to the formation of the holding SE. That proportion shall be shares conferring more than 50% of the permanent voting rights.

3. For each of the companies promoting the operation, the draft terms for the formation of the holding SE shall be publicised in the manner laid down in each Member State's national law in accordance with Article 3 of Directive 68/151/EEC at least one month before the date of the general meeting called to decide thereon.

4. One or more experts independent of the companies promoting the operation, appointed or approved by a judicial or administrative authority in the Member State to which

each company is subject in accordance with national provisions adopted in implementation of Directive 78/855/EEC, shall examine the draft terms of formation drawn up in accordance with paragraph 2 and draw up a written report for the shareholders of each company. By agreement between the companies promoting the operation, a single written report may be drawn up for the shareholders of all the companies by one or more independent experts, appointed or approved by a judicial or administrative authority in the Member State to which one of the companies promoting the operation or the proposed SE is subject in accordance with national provisions adopted in implementation of Directive 78/855/EEC.

5. The report shall indicate any particular difficulties of valuation and state whether the proposed share-exchange ratio is fair and reasonable, indicating the methods used to arrive at it and whether such methods are adequate in the case in question.

6. The general meeting of each company promoting the operation shall approve the draft terms of formation of the holding SE.

Employee involvement in the holding SE shall be decided pursuant to Directive 2001/86/EC. The general meetings of each company promoting the operation may reserve the right to make registration of the holding SE conditional upon its express ratification of the arrangements so decided.

7. These provisions shall apply mutatis mutandis to private limited-liability companies.

[9407BG]

Article 33

1. The shareholders of the companies promoting such an operation shall have a period of three months in which to inform the promoting companies whether they intend to contribute their shares to the formation of the holding SE. That period shall begin on the date upon which the terms for the formation of the holding SE have been finally determined in accordance with Article 32.

2. The holding SE shall be formed only if, within the period referred to in paragraph 1, the shareholders of the companies promoting the operation have assigned the minimum proportion of shares in each company in accordance with the draft terms of formation and if all the other conditions are fulfilled.

3. If the conditions for the formation of the holding SE are all fulfilled in accordance with paragraph 2, that fact shall, in respect of each of the promoting companies, be publicised in the manner laid down in the national law governing each of those companies adopted in implementation of Article 3 of Directive 68/151/EEC.

Shareholders of the companies promoting the operation who have not indicated whether they intend to make their shares available to the promoting companies for the purpose of forming the holding SE within the period referred to in paragraph 1 shall have a further month in which to do so.

4. Shareholders who have contributed their securities to the formation of the SE shall receive shares in the holding SE.

5. The holding SE may not be registered until it is shown that the formalities referred to in Article 32 have been completed and that the conditions referred to in paragraph 2 have been fulfilled.

[9407BH]

Article 34

A Member State may, in the case of companies promoting such an operation, adopt provisions designed to ensure protection for minority shareholders who oppose the operation, creditors and employees.

[9407BI]

SECTION 4
FORMATION OF A SUBSIDIARY SE

Article 35

An SE may be formed in accordance with Article 2(3).

[9407BJ]

Article 36

Companies, firms and other legal entities participating in such an operation shall be subject to the provisions governing their participation in the formation of a subsidiary in the form of a public limited-liability company under national law.

[9407BK]

SECTION 5
CONVERSION OF AN EXISTING PUBLIC LIMITED-LIABILITY COMPANY INTO AN SE

Article 37

1. An SE may be formed in accordance with Article 2(4).

2. Without prejudice to Article 12 the conversion of a public limited-liability company into an SE shall not result in the winding up of the company or in the creation of a new legal person.

3. The registered office may not be transferred from one Member State to another pursuant to Article 8 at the same time as the conversion is effected.

4. The management or administrative organ of the company in question shall draw up draft terms of conversion and a report explaining and justifying the legal and economic aspects of the conversion and indicating the implications for the shareholders and for the employees of the adoption of the form of an SE.

5. The draft terms of conversion shall be publicised in the manner laid down in each Member State's law in accordance with Article 3 of Directive 68/151/EEC at least one month before the general meeting called upon to decide thereon.

6. Before the general meeting referred to in paragraph 7 one or more independent experts appointed or approved, in accordance with the national provisions adopted in implementation of Article 10 of Directive 78/855/EEC, by a judicial or administrative authority in the Member State to which the company being converted into an SE is subject shall certify in compliance with Directive 77/91/EEC[1] mutatis mutandis that the company has net assets at least equivalent to its capital plus those reserves which must not be distributed under the law or the Statutes.

7. The general meeting of the company in question shall approve the draft terms of conversion together with the statutes of the SE. The decision of the general meeting shall be passed as laid down in the provisions of national law adopted in implementation of Article 7 of Directive 78/855/EEC.

8. Member States may condition a conversion to a favourable vote of a qualified majority or unanimity in the organ of the company to be converted within which employee participation is organised.

9. The rights and obligations of the company to be converted on terms and conditions of employment arising from national law, practice and individual employment contracts or employment relationships and existing at the date of the registration shall, by reason of such registration be transferred to the SE.

[9407BL]

NOTES

1 Second Council Directive 77/91/EEC of 13 December 1976 on coordination of safeguards which, for the protection of the interests of members and others, are required by Member States of companies within the meaning of the second paragraph of Article 58 of the Treaty, in respect of the formation of public limited liability companies and the maintenance and alteration of their capital, with a view to making such safeguards equivalent (OJ L26, 31.1.1977, p 1). Directive as last amended by the 1994 Act of Accession.

TITLE III
STRUCTURE OF THE SE

Article 38

Under the conditions laid down by this Regulation an SE shall comprise:

(a) a general meeting of shareholders and
(b) either a supervisory organ and a management organ (two-tier system) or an administrative organ (one-tier system) depending on the form adopted in the statutes.

[9407BM]

SECTION 1
TWO-TIER SYSTEM

Article 39

1. The management organ shall be responsible for managing the SE. A Member State may provide that a managing director or managing directors shall be responsible for the current management under the same conditions as for public limited-liability companies that have registered offices within that Member State's territory.

2. The member or members of the management organ shall be appointed and removed by the supervisory organ.

A Member State may, however, require or permit the statutes to provide that the member or members of the management organ shall be appointed and removed by the general meeting under the same conditions as for public limited-liability companies that have registered offices within its territory.

3. No person may at the same time be a member of both the management organ and the supervisory organ of the same SE. The supervisory organ may, however, nominate one of its members to act as a member of the management organ in the event of a vacancy. During such a period the functions of the person concerned as a member of the supervisory organ shall be suspended. A Member State may impose a time limit on such a period.

4. The number of members of the management organ or the rules for determining it shall be laid down in the SE's statutes. A Member State may, however, fix a minimum and/or a maximum number.

5. Where no provision is made for a two-tier system in relation to public limited-liability companies with registered offices within its territory, a Member State may adopt the appropriate measures in relation to SEs.

[9407BN]

Article 40

1. The supervisory organ shall supervise the work of the management organ. It may not itself exercise the power to manage the SE.

2. The members of the supervisory organ shall be appointed by the general meeting. The members of the first supervisory organ may, however, be appointed by the statutes. This shall apply without prejudice to Article 47(4) or to any employee participation arrangements determined pursuant to Directive 2001/86/EC.

3. The number of members of the supervisory organ or the rules for determining it shall be laid down in the statutes. A Member State may, however, stipulate the number of members of the supervisory organ for SEs registered within its territory or a minimum and/or a maximum number.

[9407BO]

Article 41

1. The management organ shall report to the supervisory organ at least once every three months on the progress and foreseeable development of the SE's business.

2. In addition to the regular information referred to in paragraph 1, the management organ shall promptly pass the supervisory organ any information on events likely to have an appreciable effect on the SE.

3. The supervisory organ may require the management organ to provide information of any kind which it needs to exercise supervision in accordance with Article 40(1). A Member State may provide that each member of the supervisory organ also be entitled to this facility.

4. The supervisory organ may undertake or arrange for any investigations necessary for the performance of its duties.

5. Each member of the supervisory organ shall be entitled to examine all information submitted to it.

[9407BP]

Article 42

The supervisory organ shall elect a chairman from among its members. If half of the members are appointed by employees, only a member appointed by the general meeting of shareholders may be elected chairman.

[9407BQ]

SECTION 2
THE ONE-TIER SYSTEM

Article 43

1. The administrative organ shall manage the SE. A Member State may provide that a managing director or managing directors shall be responsible for the day-to-day management under the same conditions as for public limited-liability companies that have registered offices within that Member State's territory.

2. The number of members of the administrative organ or the rules for determining it shall be laid down in the SE's statutes. A Member State may, however, set a minimum and, where necessary, a maximum number of members.

The administrative organ shall, however, consist of at least three members where employee participation is regulated in accordance with Directive 2001/86/EC.

3. The member or members of the administrative organ shall be appointed by the general meeting. The members of the first administrative organ may, however, be appointed by the statutes. This shall apply without prejudice to Article 47(4) or to any employee participation arrangements determined pursuant to Directive 2001/86/EC.

4. Where no provision is made for a one-tier system in relation to public limited-liability companies with registered offices within its territory, a Member State may adopt the appropriate measures in relation to SEs.

[9407BR]

Article 44

1. The administrative organ shall meet at least once every three months at intervals laid down by the statutes to discuss the progress and foreseeable development of the SE's business.

2. Each member of the administrative organ shall be entitled to examine all information submitted to it.

[9407BS]

Article 45

The administrative organ shall elect a chairman from among its members. If half of the members are appointed by employees, only a member appointed by the general meeting of shareholders may be elected chairman.

[9407BT]

SECTION 3
RULES COMMON TO THE ONE-TIER AND TWO-TIER SYSTEMS

Article 46

1. Members of company organs shall be appointed for a period laid down in the statutes not exceeding six years.

2. Subject to any restrictions laid down in the statutes, members may be reappointed once or more than once for the period determined in accordance with paragraph 1.

[9407BU]

Article 47

1. An SE's statutes may permit a company or other legal entity to be a member of one of its organs, provided that the law applicable to public limited-liability companies in the Member State in which the SE's registered office is situated does not provide otherwise.

That company or other legal entity shall designate a natural person to exercise its functions on the organ in question.

2. No person may be a member of any SE organ or a representative of a member within the meaning of paragraph 1 who:

(a) is disqualified, under the law of the Member State in which the SE's registered office is situated, from serving on the corresponding organ of a public limited-liability company governed by the law of that Member State, or

(b) is disqualified from serving on the corresponding organ of a public limited-liability company governed by the law of a Member State owing to a judicial or administrative decision delivered in a Member State.

3. An SE's statutes may, in accordance with the law applicable to public limited-liability companies in the Member State in which the SE's registered office is situated, lay down special conditions of eligibility for members representing the shareholders.

4. This Regulation shall not affect national law permitting a minority of shareholders or other persons or authorities to appoint some of the members of a company organ.

[9407BV]

Article 48

1. An SE's statutes shall list the categories of transactions which require authorisation of the management organ by the supervisory organ in the two-tier system or an express decision by the administrative organ in the one-tier system.

A Member State may, however, provide that in the two-tier system the supervisory organ may itself make certain categories of transactions subject to authorisation.

2. A Member State may determine the categories of transactions which must at least be indicated in the statutes of SEs registered within its territory.

[9407BW]

Article 49

The members of an SE's organs shall be under a duty, even after they have ceased to hold office, not to divulge any information which they have concerning the SE the disclosure of which might be prejudicial to the company's interests, except where such disclosure is required or permitted under national law provisions applicable to public limited-liability companies or is in the public interest.

[9407BX]

Article 50

1. Unless otherwise provided by this Regulation or the statutes, the internal rules relating to quorums and decision-taking in SE organs shall be as follows:

(a) quorum: at least half of the members must be present or represented;

(b) decision-taking: a majority of the members present or represented.

2. Where there is no relevant provision in the statutes, the chairman of each organ shall have a casting vote in the event of a tie. There shall be no provision to the contrary in the statutes, however, where half of the supervisory organ consists of employees' representatives.

3. Where employee participation is provided for in accordance with Directive 2001/86/EC, a Member State may provide that the supervisory organ's quorum and decision-making shall, by way of derogation from the provisions referred to in paragraphs 1 and 2, be subject to the rules applicable, under the same conditions, to public limited-liability companies governed by the law of the Member State concerned.

[9407BY]

Article 51

Members of an SE's management, supervisory and administrative organs shall be liable, in accordance with the provisions applicable to public limited-liability companies in the Member State in which the SE's registered office is situated, for loss or damage sustained by the SE following any breach on their part of the legal, statutory or other obligations inherent in their duties.

[9407BZ]

SECTION 4
GENERAL MEETING

Article 52

The general meeting shall decide on matters for which it is given sole responsibility by:

(a) this Regulation or

(b) the legislation of the Member State in which the SE's registered office is situated adopted in implementation of Directive 2001/86/EC.

Furthermore, the general meeting shall decide on matters for which responsibility is given to the general meeting of a public limited-liability company governed by the law of the Member State in which the SE's registered office is situated, either by the law of that Member State or by the SE's statutes in accordance with that law.

[9407CA]

Article 53

Without prejudice to the rules laid down in this section, the organisation and conduct of general meetings together with voting procedures shall be governed by the law applicable to public limited-liability companies in the Member State in which the SE's registered office is situated.

[9407CB]

Article 54

1. An SE shall hold a general meeting at least once each calendar year, within six months of the end of its financial year, unless the law of the Member State in which the SE's registered office is situated applicable to public limited-liability companies carrying on the same type of activity as the SE provides for more frequent meetings. A Member State may, however, provide that the first general meeting may be held at any time in the 18 months following an SE's incorporation.

2. General meetings may be convened at any time by the management organ, the administrative organ, the supervisory organ or any other organ or competent authority in accordance with the national law applicable to public limited-liability companies in the Member State in which the SE's registered office is situated.

[9407CC]

Article 55

1. One or more shareholders who together hold at least 10% of an SE's subscribed capital may request the SE to convene a general meeting and draw up the agenda therefor; the SE's statutes or national legislation may provide for a smaller proportion under the same conditions as those applicable to public limited-liability companies.

2. The request that a general meeting be convened shall state the items to be put on the agenda.

3. If, following a request made under paragraph 1, a general meeting is not held in due time and, in any event, within two months, the competent judicial or administrative authority within the jurisdiction of which the SE's registered office is situated may order that a general meeting be convened within a given period or authorise either the shareholders who have requested it or their representatives to convene a general meeting. This shall be without prejudice to any national provisions which allow the shareholders themselves to convene general meetings.

[9407CD]

Article 56

One or more shareholders who together hold at least 10% of an SE's subscribed capital may request that one or more additional items be put on the agenda of any general meeting. The procedures and time limits applicable to such requests shall be laid down by the national law of the Member State in which the SE's registered office is situated or, failing that, by the SE's statutes. The above proportion may be reduced by the statutes or by the law of the Member State in which the SE's registered office is situated under the same conditions as are applicable to public limited-liability companies.

[9407CE]

Article 57

Save where this Regulation or, failing that, the law applicable to public limited-liability companies in the Member State in which an SE's registered office is situated requires a larger majority, the general meeting's decisions shall be taken by a majority of the votes validly cast.

[9407CF]

Article 58

The votes cast shall not include votes attaching to shares in respect of which the shareholder has not taken part in the vote or has abstained or has returned a blank or spoilt ballot paper.

[9407CG]

Article 59

1. Amendment of an SE's statutes shall require a decision by the general meeting taken by a majority which may not be less than two thirds of the votes cast, unless the law applicable to public limited-liability companies in the Member State in which an SE's registered office is situated requires or permits a larger majority.

2. A Member State may, however, provide that where at least half of an SE's subscribed capital is represented, a simple majority of the votes referred to in paragraph 1 shall suffice.

3. Amendments to an SE's statutes shall be publicised in accordance with Article 13.

[9407CH]

Article 60

1. Where an SE has two or more classes of shares, every decision by the general meeting shall be subject to a separate vote by each class of shareholders whose class rights are affected thereby.

2. Where a decision by the general meeting requires the majority of votes specified in Article 59(1) or (2), that majority shall also be required for the separate vote by each class of shareholders whose class rights are affected by the decision.

[9407CI]

TITLE IV
ANNUAL ACCOUNTS AND CONSOLIDATED ACCOUNTS

Article 61

Subject to Article 62 an SE shall be governed by the rules applicable to public limited-liability companies under the law of the Member State in which its registered office is situated as regards the preparation of its annual and, where appropriate, consolidated accounts including the accompanying annual report and the auditing and publication of those accounts.

[9407CJ]

Article 62

1. An SE which is a credit or financial institution shall be governed by the rules laid down in the national law of the Member State in which its registered office is situated in implementation of Directive 2000/12/EC of the European Parliament and of the Council of 20 March 2000 relating to the taking up and pursuit of the business of credit institutions[1] as regards the preparation of its annual and, where appropriate, consolidated accounts, including the accompanying annual report and the auditing and publication of those accounts.

2. An SE which is an insurance undertaking shall be governed by the rules laid down in the national law of the Member State in which its registered office is situated in implementation of Council Directive 91/674/EEC of 19 December 1991 on the annual accounts and consolidated accounts of insurance undertakings[2] as regards the preparation of its annual and, where appropriate, consolidated accounts including the accompanying annual report and the auditing and publication of those accounts.

[9407CK]

NOTES

1 OJ L126, 26.5.2000, p 1.
2 OJ L374, 31.12.1991, p 7.

TITLE V
WINDING UP, LIQUIDATION, INSOLVENCY AND CESSATION OF PAYMENTS

Article 63

As regards winding up, liquidation, insolvency, cessation of payments and similar procedures, an SE shall be governed by the legal provisions which would apply to a public limited-liability company formed in accordance with the law of the Member State in which its registered office is situated, including provisions relating to decision-making by the general meeting.

[9407CL]

Article 64

1. When an SE no longer complies with the requirement laid down in Article 7, the Member State in which the SE's registered office is situated shall take appropriate measures to oblige the SE to regularise its position within a specified period either:

(a) by re-establishing its head office in the Member State in which its registered office is situated or

(b) by transferring the registered office by means of the procedure laid down in Article 8.

2. The Member State in which the SE's registered office is situated shall put in place the measures necessary to ensure that an SE which fails to regularise its position in accordance with paragraph 1 is liquidated.

3. The Member State in which the SE's registered office is situated shall set up a judicial remedy with regard to any established infringement of Article 7. That remedy shall have a suspensory effect on the procedures laid down in paragraphs 1 and 2.

4. Where it is established on the initiative of either the authorities or any interested party that an SE has its head office within the territory of a Member State in breach of Article 7, the authorities of that Member State shall immediately inform the Member State in which the SE's registered office is situated.

[9407CM]

Article 65

Without prejudice to provisions of national law requiring additional publication, the initiation and termination of winding up, liquidation, insolvency or cessation of payment procedures and any decision to continue operating shall be publicised in accordance with Article 13.

[9407CN]

Article 66

1. An SE may be converted into a public limited-liability company governed by the law of the Member State in which its registered office is situated. No decision on conversion may be taken before two years have elapsed since its registration or before the first two sets of annual accounts have been approved.

2. The conversion of an SE into a public limited-liability company shall not result in the winding up of the company or in the creation of a new legal person.

3. The management or administrative organ of the SE shall draw up draft terms of conversion and a report explaining and justifying the legal and economic aspects of the conversion and indicating the implications of the adoption of the public limited-liability company for the shareholders and for the employees.

4. The draft terms of conversion shall be publicised in the manner laid down in each Member State's law in accordance with Article 3 of Directive 68/151/EEC at least one month before the general meeting called to decide thereon.

5. Before the general meeting referred to in paragraph 6, one or more independent experts appointed or approved, in accordance with the national provisions adopted in implementation of Article 10 of Directive 78/855/EEC, by a judicial or administrative

authority in the Member State to which the SE being converted into a public limited-liability company is subject shall certify that the company has assets at least equivalent to its capital.

6. The general meeting of the SE shall approve the draft terms of conversion together with the statutes of the public limited-liability company. The decision of the general meeting shall be passed as laid down in the provisions of national law adopted in implementation of Article 7 of Directive 78/855/EEC.

[9407CO]

TITLE VI
ADDITIONAL AND TRANSITIONAL PROVISIONS

Article 67

1. If and so long as the third phase of economic and monetary union (EMU) does not apply to it each Member State may make SEs with registered offices within its territory subject to the same provisions as apply to public limited-liability companies covered by its legislation as regards the expression of their capital. An SE may, in any case, express its capital in euro as well. In that event the national currency/euro conversion rate shall be that for the last day of the month preceding that of the formation of the SE.

2. If and so long as the third phase of EMU does not apply to the Member State in which an SE has its registered office, the SE may, however, prepare and publish its annual and, where appropriate, consolidated accounts in euro. The Member State may require that the SE's annual and, where appropriate, consolidated accounts be prepared and published in the national currency under the same conditions as those laid down for public limited-liability companies governed by the law of that Member State. This shall not prejudge the additional possibility for an SE of publishing its annual and, where appropriate, consolidated accounts in euro in accordance with Council Directive 90/604/EEC of 8 November 1990 amending Directive 78/60/EEC on annual accounts and Directive 83/349/EEC on consolidated accounts as concerns the exemptions for small and medium-sized companies and the publication of accounts in ecu.[1]

[9407CP]

NOTES

[1] OJ L317, 16.11.1990, p 57.

TITLE VII
FINAL PROVISIONS

Article 68

1. The Member States shall make such provision as is appropriate to ensure the effective application of this Regulation.

2. Each Member State shall designate the competent authorities within the meaning of Articles 8, 25, 26, 54, 55 and 64. It shall inform the Commission and the other Member States accordingly.

[9407CQ]

Article 69

Five years at the latest after the entry into force of this Regulation, the Commission shall forward to the Council and the European Parliament a report on the application of the Regulation and proposals for amendments, where appropriate. The report shall, in particular, analyse the appropriateness of:

(a) allowing the location of an SE's head office and registered office in different Member States;

(b) broadening the concept of merger in Article 17(2) in order to admit also other types of merger than those defined in Articles 3(1) and 4(1) of Directive 78/855/EEC;

(c) revising the jurisdiction clause in Article 8(16) in the light of any provision which may have been inserted in the 1968 Brussels Convention or in any text adopted by Member States or by the Council to replace such Convention;

(d) allowing provisions in the statutes of an SE adopted by a Member State in execution of authorisations given to the Member States by this Regulation or laws adopted to ensure the effective application of this Regulation in respect to the SE which deviate from or are complementary to these laws, even when such provisions would not be authorised in the statutes of a public limited-liability company having its registered office in the Member State.

[9407CR]

Article 70

This Regulation shall enter into force on 8 October 2004.

This Regulation shall be binding in its entirety and directly applicable in all Member States.

[9407CS]

Done at Luxembourg, 8 October 2001.

ANNEX I

PUBLIC LIMITED-LIABILITY COMPANIES REFERRED TO IN ARTICLE 2(1)

BELGIUM:

la société anonyme/de naamloze vennootschap

[BULGARIA:

акционерно дружество"

[CZECH REPUBLIC:

akciová společnost]

DENMARK:

aktieselskaber

GERMANY:

die Aktiengesellschaft

[ESTONIA:

aktsiaselts]

GREECE:

ανώνυμη εταιρία

SPAIN:

la sociedad anónima

FRANCE:

la société anonyme

IRELAND:

public companies limited by shares

public companies limited by guarantee having a share capital

ITALY:

società per azioni

[CYPRUS:

Δημόσια Εταιρεία περιορισμένης ευθύνης με μετοχές, Δημόσια Εταιρεία περιορισμένης ευθύνης με εγγύηση

LATVIA:

akciju sabiedrība

LITHUANIA:

akcinės bendrovės]

LUXEMBOURG:

la société anonyme

[HUNGARY:

részvénytársaság

MALTA:

kumpaniji pubbliċi / public limited liability companies]

NETHERLANDS:

de naamloze vennootschap

AUSTRIA:

die Aktiengesellschaft

[POLAND:

spółka akcyjna]

PORTUGAL:

a sociedade anónima de responsabilidade limitada

[ROMANIA:

societate pe acţiuni]

[SLOVENIA:

delniška družba

SLOVAKIA:

akciová spoločnos]

FINLAND:

julkinen osakeyhtiö/publikt aktiebolag

SWEDEN:

publikt aktiebolag

UNITED KINGDOM:

public companies limited by shares

public companies limited by guarantee having a share capital

[9407CT]

NOTES

Entries relating to Bulgaria and Romania inserted by Council Regulation 1791/2006/EC, Art 1, Annex, as from 1 January 2007; other entries in square brackets inserted by Council Regulation 885/2004/EC, Annex, as from 1 May 2004.

ANNEX II
PUBLIC AND PRIVATE LIMITED-LIABILITY COMPANIES REFERRED TO IN ARTICLE 2(2)

BELGIUM:

la société anonyme/de naamloze vennootschap,

la société privée à responsabilité limitée/besloten vennootschap met beperkte aansprakelijkheid

[BULGARIA:

акционерно дружество, дружество с ограничена отговорност]

[CZECH REPUBLIC:

akciová společnost,

společnost s ručením omezeným]

DENMARK:

aktieselskaber,

anpartselskaber

GERMANY:

die Aktiengesellschaft,

die Gesellschaft mit beschränkter Haftung

[ESTONIA:

aktsiaselts ja osaühing]

GREECE:

ανώνυμη εταιρία

εταιρία περιορισμένης ευθύνης

SPAIN:

la sociedad anónima,

la sociedad de responsabilidad limitada

FRANCE:

la société anonyme,

la société à responsabilité limitée

IRELAND:

public companies limited by shares,

public companies limited by guarantee having a share capital,

private companies limited by shares,

private companies limited by guarantee having a share capital

ITALY:

società per azioni,

società a responsabilità limitata

[CYPRUS:

Δημόσια εταιρεία περιορισμένης ευθύνης με μετοχές,

δημόσια Εταιρεία περιορισμένης ευθύνης με εγγύηση,

ιδιωτική εταιρεία

LATVIA:

akciju sabiedrība,

un sabiedrība ar ierobežotu atbildību

LITHUANIA:

akcinės bendrovės,

uždarosios akcinės bendrovės]

LUXEMBOURG:

la société anonyme,

la société à responsabilité limitée

[HUNGARY:

részvénytársaság,

korlátolt felelõsségû társaság

MALTA:

kumpaniji pubbliċi / public limited liability companies

kumpaniji privati / private limited liability companies]

NETHERLANDS:

de naamloze vennootschap,

de besloten vennootschap met beperkte aansprakelijkheid

AUSTRIA:

die Aktiengesellschaft,

die Gesellschaft mit beschränkter Haftung

[POLAND:

spółka akcyjna,

spółka z ograniczoną odpowiedzialnością]

PORTUGAL:

a sociedade anónima de responsabilidade limitada,

a sociedade por quotas de responsabilidade limitada

[ROMANIA:

societate pe acţiuni, societate cu rãspundere limitatã]

[SLOVENIA:

delniška družba,

družba z omejeno odgovornostjo

SLOVAKIA:

akciová spoločnos',

spoločnosts ručením obmedzeným]

FINLAND:

osakeyhtiö

aktiebolag

SWEDEN:

aktiebolag

UNITED KINGDOM:

public companies limited by shares,

public companies limited by guarantee having a share capital,

private companies limited by shares,

private companies limited by guarantee having a share capital

[9407CU]

NOTES

Entries relating to Bulgaria and Romania inserted by Council Regulation 1791/2006/EC, Art 1, Annex, as from 1 January 2007; other entries in square brackets inserted by Council Regulation 885/2004/EC, Annex, as from 1 May 2004.

EUROPEAN PARLIAMENT AND COUNCIL REGULATION

of 19 July 2002

on the application of international accounting standards

(1606/2002/EC)

NOTES

Date of publication in OJ: OJ L243, 11.9.2002, p 1. Notes are as in the original OJ version.

THE EUROPEAN PARLIAMENT AND THE COUNCIL OF THE EUROPEAN UNION,

Having regard to the Treaty establishing the European Community, and in particular Article 95(1) thereof,

Having regard to the proposal from the Commission,[1]

Having regard to the opinion of the Economic and Social Committee,[2]

Acting in accordance with the procedure laid down in Article 251 of the Treat,[3]

Whereas:

(1) The Lisbon European Council of 23 and 24 March 2000 emphasised the need to accelerate completion of the internal market for financial services, set the deadline of 2005 to implement the Commission's Financial Services Action Plan and urged that steps be taken to enhance the comparability of financial statements prepared by publicly traded companies.

(2) In order to contribute to a better functioning of the internal market, publicly traded companies must be required to apply a single set of high quality international accounting standards for the preparation of their consolidated financial statements. Furthermore, it is important that the financial reporting standards applied by Community companies participating in financial markets are accepted internationally and are truly global standards. This implies an increasing convergence of accounting standards currently used internationally with the ultimate objective of achieving a single set of global accounting standards.

(3) Council Directive 78/660/EEC of 25 July 1978 on the annual accounts of certain types of companies,[4] Council Directive 83/349/EEC of 13 June 1983 on consolidated accounts,[5] Council Directive 86/635/EEC of 8 December 1986 on the annual accounts and consolidated accounts of banks and other financial institutions[6] and Council Directive 91/674/EEC of 19 December 1991 on the annual accounts and consolidated accounts of insurance companies[7] are also addressed to publicly traded Community companies. The reporting requirements set out in these Directives cannot ensure the high level of transparency and comparability of financial reporting from all publicly traded Community companies which is a necessary condition for building an integrated capital market which operates effectively, smoothly and efficiently. It is therefore necessary to supplement the legal framework applicable to publicly traded companies.

(4) This Regulation aims at contributing to the efficient and cost-effective functioning of the capital market. The protection of investors and the maintenance of confidence in the financial markets is also an important aspect of the completion of the internal market in this area. This Regulation reinforces the freedom of movement of capital in the internal market and helps to enable Community companies to compete on an equal footing for financial resources available in the Community capital markets, as well as in world capital markets.

(5) It is important for the competitiveness of Community capital markets to achieve convergence of the standards used in Europe for preparing financial statements, with international accounting standards that can be used globally, for cross-border transactions or listing anywhere in the world.

(6) On 13 June 2000, the Commission published its Communication on "EU Financial Reporting Strategy: the way forward" in which it was proposed that all publicly traded Community companies prepare their consolidated financial statements in accordance with one single set of accounting standards, namely International Accounting Standards (IAS), at the latest by 2005.

(7) International Accounting Standards (IASs) are developed by the International Accounting Standards Committee (IASC), whose purpose is to develop a single set of global accounting standards. Further to the restructuring of the IASC, the new Board on 1 April 2001, as one of its first decisions, renamed the IASC as the International Accounting Standards Board (IASB) and, as far as future international accounting standards are concerned, renamed IAS as International Financial Reporting Standards (IFRS). These standards should, wherever possible and provided that they ensure a high degree of

transparency and comparability for financial reporting in the Community, be made obligatory for use by all publicly traded Community companies.

(8) The measures necessary for the implementation of this Regulation should be adopted in accordance with Council Decision 1999/468/EC of 28 June 1999 laying down the procedures for the exercise of implementing powers conferred on the Commission[8] and with due regard to the declaration made by the Commission in the European Parliament on 5 February 2002 concerning the implementation of financial services legislation.

(9) To adopt an international accounting standard for application in the Community, it is necessary firstly that it meets the basic requirement of the aforementioned Council Directives, that is to say that its application results in a true and fair view of the financial position and performance of an enterprise – this principle being considered in the light of the said Council Directives without implying a strict conformity with each and every provision of those Directives; secondly that, in accordance with the conclusions of the Council of 17 July 2000, it is conducive to the European public good and lastly that it meets basic criteria as to the quality of information required for financial statements to be useful to users.

(10) An accounting technical committee should provide support and expertise to the Commission in the assessment of international accounting standards.

(11) The endorsement mechanism should act expeditiously on proposed international accounting standards and also be a means to deliberate, reflect and exchange information on international accounting standards among the main parties concerned, in particular national accounting standard setters, supervisors in the fields of securities, banking and insurance, central banks including the ECB, the accounting profession and users and preparers of accounts. The mechanism should be a means to foster common understanding of adopted international accounting standards in the Community.

(12) In accordance with the principle of proportionality, the measures provided for in this Regulation, in requiring that a single set of international accounting standards be applied to publicly traded companies, are necessary to achieve the objective of contributing to the efficient and cost-effective functioning of Community capital markets and thereby to the completion of the internal market.

(13) In accordance with the same principle, it is necessary, as regards annual accounts, to leave to Member States the option to permit or require publicly traded companies to prepare them in conformity with international accounting standards adopted in accordance with the procedure laid down in this Regulation. Member States may decide as well to extend this permission or this requirement to other companies as regards the preparation of their consolidated accounts and/or their annual accounts.

(14) In order to facilitate an exchange of views and to allow Member States to coordinate their positions, the Commission should periodically inform the accounting regulatory committee about active projects, discussion papers, point outlines and exposure drafts issued by the IASB and about the consequential technical work of the accounting technical committee. It is also important that the accounting regulatory committee is informed at an early stage if the Commission intends not to propose to adopt an international accounting standard.

(15) In its deliberations on and in elaborating positions to be taken on documents and papers issued by the IASB in the process of developing international accounting standards (IFRS and SIC-IFRIC), the Commission should take into account the importance of avoiding competitive disadvantages for European companies operating in the global marketplace, and, to the maximum possible extent, the views expressed by the delegations in the Accounting Regulatory Committee. The Commission will be represented in constituent bodies of the IASB.

(16) A proper and rigorous enforcement regime is key to underpinning investors' confidence in financial markets. Member States, by virtue of Article 10 of the Treaty, are required to take appropriate measures to ensure compliance with international accounting standards. The Commission intends to liaise with Member States, notably through the Committee of European Securities Regulators (CESR), to develop a common approach to enforcement.

(17) Further, it is necessary to allow Member States to defer the application of certain provisions until 2007 for those companies publicly traded both in the Community and on a regulated third-country market which are already applying another set of internationally accepted standards as the primary basis for their consolidated accounts as well as for companies which have only publicly traded debt securities. It is nonetheless crucial that by 2007 at the latest a single set of global international accounting standards, the IAS, apply to all Community companies publicly traded on a Community regulated market.

(18) In order to allow Member States and companies to carry out the necessary adaptations to make the application of international accounting standards possible, it is necessary to apply certain provisions only in 2005. Appropriate provisions should be put in

place for the first-time application of IAS by companies as a result of the entry into force of the present regulation. Such provisions should be drawn up at international level in order to ensure international recognition of the solutions adopted,

[9407CV]

NOTES

[1] OJ C154E, 29.5.2001, p 285.
[2] OJ C260, 17.9.2001, p 86.
[3] Opinion of the European Parliament of 12 March 2002 (not yet published in the Official Journal) and Decision of the Council of 7 June 2002.
[4] OJ L222, 14.8.1978, p 11. Directive as last amended by European Parliament and Council Directive 2001/65/EC (OJ L283, 27.10.2001, p 28).
[5] OJ L193, 18.7.1983, p 1. Directive as last amended by European Parliament and Council Directive 2001/65/EC.
[6] OJ L372, 31.12.1986, p 1. Directive as last amended by European Parliament and Council Directive 2001/65/EC.
[7] OJ L374, 31.12.1991, p 7.
[8] OJ L184, 17.7.1999, p 23.

HAVE ADOPTED THIS REGULATION:

Article 1

Aim

This Regulation has as its objective the adoption and use of international accounting standards in the Community with a view to harmonising the financial information presented by the companies referred to in Article 4 in order to ensure a high degree of transparency and comparability of financial statements and hence an efficient functioning of the Community capital market and of the Internal Market.

[9407CW]

Article 2

Definitions

For the purpose of this Regulation, "international accounting standards" shall mean International Accounting Standards (IAS), International Financial Reporting Standards (IFRS) and related Interpretations (SIC-IFRIC interpretations), subsequent amendments to those standards and related interpretations, future standards and related interpretations issued or adopted by the International Accounting Standards Board (IASB).

[9407CX]

Article 3

Adoption and use of international accounting standards

1. In accordance with the procedure laid down in Article 6(2), the Commission shall decide on the applicability within the Community of international accounting standards.

2. The international accounting standards can only be adopted if:

— they are not contrary to the principle set out in Article 2(3) of Directive 78/660/EEC and in Article 16(3) of Directive 83/349/EEC and are conducive to the European public good and,

— they meet the criteria of understandability, relevance, reliability and comparability required of the financial information needed for making economic decisions and assessing the stewardship of management.

3. At the latest by 31 December 2002, the Commission shall, in accordance with the procedure laid down in Article 6(2), decide on the applicability within the Community of the international accounting standards in existence upon entry into force of this Regulation.

4. Adopted international accounting standards shall be published in full in each of the official languages of the Community, as a Commission Regulation, in the Official Journal of the European Communities.

[9407CY]

Article 4

Consolidated accounts of publicly traded companies

For each financial year starting on or after 1 January 2005, companies governed by the law of a Member State shall prepare their consolidated accounts in conformity with the international accounting standards adopted in accordance with the procedure laid down in Article 6(2) if, at their balance sheet date, their securities are admitted to trading on a regulated market of any Member State within the meaning of Article 1(13) of Council Directive 93/22/EEC of 10 May 1993 on investment services in the securities field.[1]

[9407CZ]

NOTES

[1] OJ L141, 11.6.1993, p 27. Directive as last amended by European Parliament and Council Directive 2000/64/EC (OJ L290, 17.11.2000, p 27).

Article 5

Options in respect of annual accounts and of non publicly-traded companies

Member States may permit or require:

(a) the companies referred to in Article 4 to prepare their annual accounts,

(b) companies other than those referred to in Article 4 to prepare their consolidated accounts and/or their annual accounts,

in conformity with the international accounting standards adopted in accordance with the procedure laid down in Article 6(2).

[9407DA]

Article 6

Committee procedure

1. The Commission shall be assisted by an accounting regulatory committee hereinafter referred to as "the Committee".

2. Where reference is made to this paragraph, Articles 5 and 7 of Decision 1999/468/EC shall apply, having regard to the provisions of Article 8 thereof.

The period laid down in Article 5(6) of Decision 1999/468/EC shall be set at three months.

3. The Committee shall adopt its rules of procedure.

[9407DB]

Article 7

Reporting and coordination

1. The Commission shall liaise on a regular basis with the Committee about the status of active IASB projects and any related documents issued by the IASB in order to coordinate positions and to facilitate discussions concerning the adoption of standards that might result from these projects and documents.

2. The Commission shall duly report to the Committee in a timely manner if it intends not to propose the adoption of a standard.

[9407DC]

Article 8

Notification

Where Member States take measures by virtue of Article 5, they shall immediately communicate these to the Commission and to other Member States.

[9407DD]

Article 9

Transitional provisions

By way of derogation from Article 4, Member States may provide that the requirements of Article 4 shall only apply for each financial year starting on or after January 2007 to those companies:

(a) whose debt securities only are admitted on a regulated market of any Member State within the meaning of Article 1(13) of Directive 93/22/EEC; or

(b) whose securities are admitted to public trading in a non-member State and which, for that purpose, have been using internationally accepted standards since a financial year that started prior to the publication of this Regulation in the *Official Journal of the European Communities*.

[9407DE]

Article 10

Information and review

The Commission shall review the operation of this Regulation and report thereon to the European Parliament and to the Council by 1 July 2007 at the latest.

[9407DF]

Article 11

Entry into force

This Regulation shall enter into force on the third day following that of its publication in the *Official Journal of the European Communities*.

This Regulation shall be binding in its entirety and directly applicable in all Member States.

[9407DG]

Done at Brussels, 19 July 2002.

DIRECTIVE OF THE EUROPEAN PARLIAMENT AND OF THE COUNCIL

of 16 December 2002

on the supplementary supervision of credit institutions, insurance undertakings and investment firms in a financial conglomerate and amending Council Directives 73/239/EEC, 79/267/EEC, 92/49/EEC, 92/96/EEC, 93/6/EEC and 93/22/EEC, and Directives 98/78/EC and 2000/12/EC of the European Parliament and of the Council (Note)

(2002/87/EC)

NOTES

Date of publication in OJ: OJ 35, 11.02.2003, p 1.

This Directive has been omitted from this Edition of the *Company Law Handbook* in order to create space for other legislation (ie, the Companies Act 2006 and the associated destination and derivation tables). It was printed in full in the 20th Edition of this work (at p 2888 et seq) and, as of 1 July 2007, it had not been amended since the publication of that Edition. This Directive is, however, currently included in the CD version of this work (which may be ordered from the LexisNexis Butterworths Customer Services Department) and can be accessed in the online version of the *Company Law Handbook* which is updated fortnightly (at www.lexisnexis.com/uk/legal). It was also printed in full in the 8th Edition of *Butterworths Financial Services Law Handbook* (February 2007).

[9408]–[9436]

DIRECTIVE OF THE EUROPEAN PARLIAMENT AND OF THE COUNCIL

of 28 January 2003

on insider dealing and market manipulation (market abuse)

(2003/6/EC)

NOTES

Date of publication in OJ: OJ L096, 12.4.2003, p 16. Notes are as in the original OJ version.

THE EUROPEAN PARLIAMENT AND THE COUNCIL OF THE EUROPEAN UNION,

Having regard to the Treaty establishing the European Community, and in particular Article 95 thereof,

Having regard to the proposal from the Commission,[1]

Having regard to the opinion of the European Economic and Social Committee,[2]

Having regard to the opinion of the European Central Bank,[3]

Acting in accordance with the procedure laid down in Article 251,[4]

Whereas:

(1) A genuine Single Market for financial services is crucial for economic growth and job creation in the Community.

(2) An integrated and efficient financial market requires market integrity. The smooth functioning of securities markets and public confidence in markets are prerequisites for economic growth and wealth. Market abuse harms the integrity of financial markets and public confidence in securities and derivatives.

(3) The Commission Communication of 11 May 1999 entitled "Implementing the framework for financial markets: action plan" identifies a series of actions that are needed in order to complete the single market for financial services. The Lisbon European Council of April 2000 called for the implementation of that action plan by 2005. The action plan stresses the need to draw up a Directive against market manipulation.

(4) At its meeting on 17 July 2000, the Council set up the Committee of Wise Men on the Regulation of European Securities Markets. In its final report, the Committee of Wise Men proposed the introduction of new legislative techniques based on a four-level approach, namely framework principles, implementing measures, cooperation and enforcement. Level 1, the Directive, should confine itself to broad general "framework" principles while Level 2 should contain technical implementing measures to be adopted by the Commission with the assistance of a committee.

(5) The Resolution adopted by the Stockholm European Council of March 2001 endorsed the final report of the Committee of Wise Men and the proposed four-level approach to make the regulatory process for Community securities legislation more efficient and transparent.

(6) The Resolution of the European Parliament of 5 February 2002 on the implementation of financial services legislation also endorsed the Committee of Wise Men's report, on the basis of the solemn declaration made before Parliament the same day by the Commission and the letter of 2 October 2001 addressed by the Internal Market Commissioner to the chairman of Parliament's Committee on Economic and Monetary Affairs with regard to the safeguards for the European Parliament's role in this process.

(7) The measures necessary for the implementation of this Directive should be adopted in accordance with Council Decision 1999/468/EC of 28 June 1999 laying down the procedures for the exercise of implementing powers conferred on the Commission.[5]

(8) According to the Stockholm European Council, Level 2 implementing measures should be used more frequently, to ensure that technical provisions can be kept up to date with market and supervisory developments, and deadlines should be set for all stages of Level 2 work.

(9) The European Parliament should be given a period of three months from the first transmission of draft implementing measures to allow it to examine them and to give its opinion. However, in urgent and duly justified cases, this period may be shortened. If, within that period, a resolution is passed by the European Parliament, the Commission should re-examine the draft measures.

(10) New financial and technical developments enhance the incentives, means and opportunities for market abuse: through new products, new technologies, increasing cross-border activities and the Internet.

(11) The existing Community legal framework to protect market integrity is incomplete. Legal requirements vary from one Member State to another, leaving economic actors often uncertain over concepts, definitions and enforcement. In some Member States there is no legislation addressing the issues of price manipulation and the dissemination of misleading information.

(12) Market abuse consists of insider dealing and market manipulation. The objective of legislation against insider dealing is the same as that of legislation against market manipulation: to ensure the integrity of Community financial markets and to enhance investor confidence in those markets. It is therefore advisable to adopt combined rules to combat both insider dealing and market manipulation. A single Directive will ensure throughout the Community the same framework for allocation of responsibilities, enforcement and cooperation.

(13) Given the changes in financial markets and in Community legislation since the adoption of Council Directive 89/592/EEC of 13 November 1989 coordinating regulations on insider dealing,[6] that Directive should now be replaced, to ensure consistency with legislation

against market manipulation. A new Directive is also needed to avoid loopholes in Community legislation which could be used for wrongful conduct and which would undermine public confidence and therefore prejudice the smooth functioning of the markets.

(14) This Directive meets the concerns expressed by the Member States following the terrorist attacks on 11 September 2001 as regards the fight against financing terrorist activities.

(15) Insider dealing and market manipulation prevent full and proper market transparency, which is a prerequisite for trading for all economic actors in integrated financial markets.

(16) Inside information is any information of a precise nature which has not been made public, relating, directly or indirectly, to one or more issuers of financial instruments or to one or more financial instruments. Information which could have a significant effect on the evolution and forming of the prices of a regulated market as such could be considered as information which indirectly relates to one or more issuers of financial instruments or to one or more related derivative financial instruments.

(17) As regards insider dealing, account should be taken of cases where inside information originates not from a profession or function but from criminal activities, the preparation or execution of which could have a significant effect on the prices of one or more financial instruments or on price formation in the regulated market as such.

(18) Use of inside information can consist in the acquisition or disposal of financial instruments by a person who knows, or ought to have known, that the information possessed is inside information. In this respect, the competent authorities should consider what a normal and reasonable person would know or should have known in the circumstances. Moreover, the mere fact that market-makers, bodies authorised to act as counterparties, or persons authorised to execute orders on behalf of third parties with inside information confine themselves, in the first two cases, to pursuing their legitimate business of buying or selling financial instruments or, in the last case, to carrying out an order dutifully, should not in itself be deemed to constitute use of such inside information.

(19) Member States should tackle the practice known as "front running", including "front running" in commodity derivatives, where it constitutes market abuse under the definitions contained in this Directive.

(20) A person who enters into transactions or issues orders to trade which are constitutive of market manipulation may be able to establish that his reasons for entering into such transactions or issuing orders to trade were legitimate and that the transactions and orders to trade were in conformity with accepted practice on the regulated market concerned. A sanction could still be imposed if the competent authority established that there was another, illegitimate, reason behind these transactions or orders to trade.

(21) The competent authority may issue guidance on matters covered by this Directive, eg definition of inside information in relation to derivatives on commodities or implementation of the definition of accepted market practices relating to the definition of market manipulation. This guidance should be in conformity with the provisions of the Directive and the implementing measures adopted in accordance with the comitology procedure.

(22) Member States should be able to choose the most appropriate way to regulate persons producing or disseminating research concerning financial instruments or issuers of financial instruments or persons producing or disseminating other information recommending or suggesting investment strategy, including appropriate mechanisms for self-regulation, which should be notified to the Commission.

(23) Posting of inside information by issuers on their internet sites should be in accordance with the rules on transfer of personal data to third countries as laid down in Directive 95/46/EC of the European Parliament and of the Council of 24 October 1995 on the protection of individuals with regard to the processing of personal data and on the movement of such data.[7]

(24) Prompt and fair disclosure of information to the public enhances market integrity, whereas selective disclosure by issuers can lead to a loss of investor confidence in the integrity of financial markets. Professional economic actors should contribute to market integrity by various means. Such measures could include, for instance, the creation of "grey lists", the application of "window trading" to sensitive categories of personnel, the application of internal codes of conduct and the establishment of "Chinese walls". Such preventive measures may contribute to combating market abuse only if they are enforced with determination and are dutifully controlled. Adequate enforcement control would imply for instance the designation of compliance officers within the bodies concerned and periodic checks conducted by independent auditors.

(25) Modern communication methods make it possible for financial market professionals and private investors to have more equal access to financial information, but also increase the risk of the spread of false or misleading information.

(26) Greater transparency of transactions conducted by persons discharging managerial responsibilities within issuers and, where applicable, persons closely associated with them, constitutes a preventive measure against market abuse. The publication of those transactions on at least an individual basis can also be a highly valuable source of information to investors.

(27) Market operators should contribute to the prevention of market abuse and adopt structural provisions aimed at preventing and detecting market manipulation practices. Such provisions may include requirements concerning transparency of transactions concluded, total disclosure of price-regularisation agreements, a fair system of order pairing, introduction of an effective atypical-order detection scheme, sufficiently robust financial instrument reference price-fixing schemes and clarity of rules on the suspension of transactions.

(28) This Directive should be interpreted, and implemented by Member States, in a manner consistent with the requirements for effective regulation in order to protect the interests of holders of transferable securities carrying voting rights in a company (or which may carry such rights as a consequence of the exercise of rights or conversion) when the company is subject to a public take-over bid or other proposed change of control. In particular, this Directive does not in any way prevent a Member State from putting or having in place such measures as it sees fit for these purposes.

(29) Having access to inside information relating to another company and using it in the context of a public take-over bid for the purpose of gaining control of that company or proposing a merger with that company should not in itself be deemed to constitute insider dealing.

(30) Since the acquisition or disposal of financial instruments necessarily involves a prior decision to acquire or dispose taken by the person who undertakes one or other of these operations, the carrying out of this acquisition or disposal should not be deemed in itself to constitute the use of inside information.

(31) Research and estimates developed from publicly available data should not be regarded as inside information and, therefore, any transaction carried out on the basis of such research or estimates should not be deemed in itself to constitute insider dealing within the meaning of this Directive.

(32) Member States and the European System of Central Banks, national central banks or any other officially designated body, or any person acting on their behalf, should not be restricted in carrying out monetary, exchange-rate or public debt management policy.

(33) Stabilisation of financial instruments or trading in own shares in buy-back programmes can be legitimate, in certain circumstances, for economic reasons and should not, therefore, in themselves be regarded as market abuse. Common standards should be developed to provide practical guidance.

(34) The widening scope of financial markets, the rapid change and the range of new products and developments require a wide application of this Directive to financial instruments and techniques involved, in order to guarantee the integrity of Community financial markets.

(35) Establishing a level playing field in Community financial markets requires wide geographical application of the provisions covered by this Directive. As regards derivative instruments not admitted to trading but falling within the scope of this Directive, each Member State should be competent to sanction actions carried out on its territory or abroad which concern underlying financial instruments admitted to trading on a regulated market situated or operating within its territory or for which a request for admission to trading on such a regulated market has been made. Each Member State should also be competent to sanction actions carried out on its territory which concern underlying financial instruments admitted to trading on a regulated market in a Member State or for which a request for admission to trading on such a market has been made.

(36) A variety of competent authorities in Member States, having different responsibilities, may create confusion among economic actors. A single competent authority should be designated in each Member State to assume at least final responsibility for supervising compliance with the provisions adopted pursuant to this Directive, as well as international collaboration. Such an authority should be of an administrative nature guaranteeing its independence of economic actors and avoiding conflicts of interest. In accordance with national law, Member States should ensure appropriate financing of the competent authority. That authority should have adequate arrangements for consultation concerning possible changes in national legislation such as a consultative committee composed of representatives of issuers, financial services providers and consumers, so as to be fully informed of their views and concerns.

(37) A common minimum set of effective tools and powers for the competent authority of each Member State will guarantee supervisory effectiveness. Market undertakings and all economic actors should also contribute at their level to market integrity. In this sense, the designation of a single competent authority for market abuse does not exclude collaboration links or delegation under the responsibility of the competent authority, between that authority and market undertakings with a view to guaranteeing efficient supervision of compliance with the provisions adopted pursuant to this Directive.

(38) In order to ensure that a Community framework against market abuse is sufficient, any infringement of the prohibitions or requirements laid down pursuant to this Directive will have to be promptly detected and sanctioned. To this end, sanctions should be sufficiently dissuasive and proportionate to the gravity of the infringement and to the gains realised and should be consistently applied.

(39) Member States should remain alert, in determining the administrative measures and sanctions, to the need to ensure a degree of uniformity of regulation from one Member State to another.

(40) Increasing cross-border activities require improved cooperation and a comprehensive set of provisions for the exchange of information between national competent authorities. The organisation of supervision and of investigatory powers in each Member State should not hinder cooperation between the competent national authorities.

(41) Since the objective of the proposed action, namely to prevent market abuse in the form of insider dealing and market manipulation, cannot be sufficiently achieved by the Member States and can therefore, by reason of the scale and effects of the measures, be better achieved at Community level, the Community may adopt measures, in accordance with the principle of subsidiarity as set out in Article 5 of the Treaty. In accordance with the principle of proportionality, as set out in that Article, this Directive does not go beyond what is necessary in order to achieve that objective.

(42) Technical guidance and implementing measures for the rules laid down in this Directive may from time to time be necessary to take account of new developments on financial markets. The Commission should accordingly be empowered to adopt implementing measures, provided that these do not modify the essential elements of this Directive and the Commission acts according to the principles set out in this Directive, after consulting the European Securities Committee established by Commission Decision 2001/528/EC.[8]

(43) In exercising its implementing powers in accordance with this Directive, the Commission should respect the following principles:

— the need to ensure confidence in financial markets among investors by promoting high standards of transparency in financial markets,
— the need to provide investors with a wide range of competing investments and a level of disclosure and protection tailored to their circumstances,
— the need to ensure that independent regulatory authorities enforce the rules consistently, especially as regards the fight against economic crime,
— the need for high levels of transparency and consultation with all market participants and with the European Parliament and the Council,
— the need to encourage innovation in financial markets if they are to be dynamic and efficient,
— the need to ensure market integrity by close and reactive monitoring of financial innovation,
— the importance of reducing the cost of, and increasing access to, capital,
— the balance of costs and benefits to market participants on a long-term basis (including small and medium-sized businesses and small investors) in any implementing measures,
— the need to foster the international competitiveness of EU financial markets without prejudice to a much-needed extension of international cooperation,
— the need to achieve a level playing field for all market participants by establishing EU-wide regulations every time it is appropriate,
— the need to respect differences in national markets where these do not unduly impinge on the coherence of the single market,
— the need to ensure coherence with other Community legislation in this area, as imbalances in information and a lack of transparency may jeopardise the operation of the markets and above all harm consumers and small investors.

(44) This Directive respects the fundamental rights and observes the principles recognised in particular by the Charter of Fundamental Rights of the European Union and in particular by Article 11 thereof and Article 10 of the European Convention on Human Rights. In this regard, this Directive does not in any way prevent Member States from applying their constitutional rules relating to freedom of the press and freedom of expression in the media,

NOTES

1 OJ C240E, 28.8.2001, p 265.
2 OJ C80, 3.4.2002, p 61.
3 OJ C24, 26.1.2002, p 8.
4 Opinion of the European Parliament of 14 March 2002 (not yet published in the Official Journal), Council Common Position of 19 July 2002 (OJ C228E, 25.9.2002, p 19) and Decision of the European Parliament of 24 October 2002 (not yet published in the Official Journal).
5 OJ L184, 17.7.1999, p 23.
6 OJ L334, 18.11.1989, p 30.
7 OJ L281, 23.11.1995, p 31.
8 OJ L191, 13.7.2001, p 45.

HAVE ADOPTED THIS DIRECTIVE:

Article 1

For the purposes of this Directive:

1. "Inside information" shall mean information of a precise nature which has not been made public, relating, directly or indirectly, to one or more issuers of financial instruments or to one or more financial instruments and which, if it were made public, would be likely to have a significant effect on the prices of those financial instruments or on the price of related derivative financial instruments.

In relation to derivatives on commodities, "inside information" shall mean information of a precise nature which has not been made public, relating, directly or indirectly, to one or more such derivatives and which users of markets on which such derivatives are traded would expect to receive in accordance with accepted market practices on those markets.

For persons charged with the execution of orders concerning financial instruments, "inside information" shall also mean information conveyed by a client and related to the client's pending orders, which is of a precise nature, which relates directly or indirectly to one or more issuers of financial instruments or to one or more financial instruments, and which, if it were made public, would be likely to have a significant effect on the prices of those financial instruments or on the price of related derivative financial instruments.

2. "Market manipulation" shall mean:

(a) transactions or orders to trade:
- which give, or are likely to give, false or misleading signals as to the supply of, demand for or price of financial instruments, or
- which secure, by a person, or persons acting in collaboration, the price of one or several financial instruments at an abnormal or artificial level,

unless the person who entered into the transactions or issued the orders to trade establishes that his reasons for so doing are legitimate and that these transactions or orders to trade conform to accepted market practices on the regulated market concerned;

(b) transactions or orders to trade which employ fictitious devices or any other form of deception or contrivance;

(c) dissemination of information through the media, including the Internet, or by any other means, which gives, or is likely to give, false or misleading signals as to financial instruments, including the dissemination of rumours and false or misleading news, where the person who made the dissemination knew, or ought to have known, that the information was false or misleading. In respect of journalists when they act in their professional capacity such dissemination of information is to be assessed, without prejudice to Article 11, taking into account the rules governing their profession, unless those persons derive, directly or indirectly, an advantage or profits from the dissemination of the information in question.

In particular, the following instances are derived from the core definition given in points (a), (b) and (c) above:

- conduct by a person, or persons acting in collaboration, to secure a dominant position over the supply of or demand for a financial instrument which has the effect of fixing, directly or indirectly, purchase or sale prices or creating other unfair trading conditions,
- the buying or selling of financial instruments at the close of the market with the effect of misleading investors acting on the basis of closing prices,
- taking advantage of occasional or regular access to the traditional or electronic media by voicing an opinion about a financial instrument (or indirectly about its issuer) while having previously taken positions on that financial instrument and

profiting subsequently from the impact of the opinions voiced on the price of that instrument, without having simultaneously disclosed that conflict of interest to the public in a proper and effective way.

The definitions of market manipulation shall be adapted so as to ensure that new patterns of activity that in practice constitute market manipulation can be included.

3. "Financial instrument" shall mean:

- transferable securities as defined in Council Directive 93/22/EEC of 10 May 1993 on investment services in the securities field,[1]
- units in collective investment undertakings,
- money-market instruments,
- financial-futures contracts, including equivalent cash-settled instruments,
- forward interest-rate agreements,
- interest-rate, currency and equity swaps,
- options to acquire or dispose of any instrument falling into these categories, including equivalent cash-settled instruments. This category includes in particular options on currency and on interest rates,
- derivatives on commodities,
- any other instrument admitted to trading on a regulated market in a Member State or for which a request for admission to trading on such a market has been made.

4. "Regulated market" shall mean a market as defined by Article 1(13) of Directive 93/22/EEC.

5. "Accepted market practices" shall mean practices that are reasonably expected in one or more financial markets and are accepted by the competent authority in accordance with guidelines adopted by the Commission in accordance with the procedure laid down in Article 17(2).

6. "Person" shall mean any natural or legal person.

7. "Competent authority" shall mean the competent authority designated in accordance with Article 11.

In order to take account of developments on financial markets and to ensure uniform application of this Directive in the Community, the Commission, acting in accordance with the procedure laid down in Article 17(2), shall adopt implementing measures concerning points 1, 2 and 3 of this Article.

[9438]

NOTES

[1] OJ L141, 11.6.1993, p 27. Directive as last amended by European Parliament and Council Directive 2000/64/EC (OJ L290, 17.11.2000, p. 27).

Article 2

1. Member States shall prohibit any person referred to in the second subparagraph who possesses inside information from using that information by acquiring or disposing of, or by trying to acquire or dispose of, for his own account or for the account of a third party, either directly or indirectly, financial instruments to which that information relates.

The first subparagraph shall apply to any person who possesses that information:

(a) by virtue of his membership of the administrative, management or supervisory bodies of the issuer; or

(b) by virtue of his holding in the capital of the issuer; or

(c) by virtue of his having access to the information through the exercise of his employment, profession or duties; or

(d) by virtue of his criminal activities.

2. Where the person referred to in paragraph 1 is a legal person, the prohibition laid down in that paragraph shall also apply to the natural persons who take part in the decision to carry out the transaction for the account of the legal person concerned.

3. This Article shall not apply to transactions conducted in the discharge of an obligation that has become due to acquire or dispose of financial instruments where that obligation results from an agreement concluded before the person concerned possessed inside information.

[9439]

Article 3

Member States shall prohibit any person subject to the prohibition laid down in Article 2 from:

(a) disclosing inside information to any other person unless such disclosure is made in the normal course of the exercise of his employment, profession or duties;

(b) recommending or inducing another person, on the basis of inside information, to acquire or dispose of financial instruments to which that information relates.

[9440]

Article 4

Member States shall ensure that Articles 2 and 3 also apply to any person, other than the persons referred to in those Articles, who possesses inside information while that person knows, or ought to have known, that it is inside information.

[9441]

Article 5

Member States shall prohibit any person from engaging in market manipulation.

[9442]

Article 6

1. Member States shall ensure that issuers of financial instruments inform the public as soon as possible of inside information which directly concerns the said issuers.

Without prejudice to any measures taken to comply with the provisions of the first subparagraph, Member States shall ensure that issuers, for an appropriate period, post on their Internet sites all inside information that they are required to disclose publicly.

2. An issuer may under his own responsibility delay the public disclosure of inside information, as referred to in paragraph 1, such as not to prejudice his legitimate interests provided that such omission would not be likely to mislead the public and provided that the issuer is able to ensure the confidentiality of that information. Member States may require that an issuer shall without delay inform the competent authority of the decision to delay the public disclosure of inside information.

3. Member States shall require that, whenever an issuer, or a person acting on his behalf or for his account, discloses any inside information to any third party in the normal exercise of his employment, profession or duties, as referred to in Article 3(a), he must make complete and effective public disclosure of that information, simultaneously in the case of an intentional disclosure and promptly in the case of a non-intentional disclosure.

The provisions of the first subparagraph shall not apply if the person receiving the information owes a duty of confidentiality, regardless of whether such duty is based on a law, on regulations, on articles of association or on a contract.

Member States shall require that issuers, or persons acting on their behalf or for their account, draw up a list of those persons working for them, under a contract of employment or otherwise, who have access to inside information. Issuers and persons acting on their behalf or for their account shall regularly update this list and transmit it to the competent authority whenever the latter requests it.

4. Persons discharging managerial responsibilities within an issuer of financial instruments and, where applicable, persons closely associated with them, shall, at least, notify to the competent authority the existence of transactions conducted on their own account relating to shares of the said issuer, or to derivatives or other financial instruments linked to them. Member States shall ensure that public access to information concerning such transactions, on at least an individual basis, is readily available as soon as possible.

5. Member States shall ensure that there is appropriate regulation in place to ensure that persons who produce or disseminate research concerning financial instruments or issuers of financial instruments and persons who produce or disseminate other information recommending or suggesting investment strategy, intended for distribution channels or for the public, take reasonable care to ensure that such information is fairly presented and disclose their interests or indicate conflicts of interest concerning the financial instruments to which that information relates. Details of such regulation shall be notified to the Commission.

6. Member States shall ensure that market operators adopt structural provisions aimed at preventing and detecting market manipulation practices.

7. With a view to ensuring compliance with paragraphs 1 to 5, the competent authority may take all necessary measures to ensure that the public is correctly informed.

8. Public institutions disseminating statistics liable to have a significant effect on financial markets shall disseminate them in a fair and transparent way.

9. Member States shall require that any person professionally arranging transactions in financial instruments who reasonably suspects that a transaction might constitute insider dealing or market manipulation shall notify the competent authority without delay.

10. In order to take account of technical developments on financial markets and to ensure uniform application of this Directive, the Commission shall adopt, in accordance with the procedure referred to in Article 17(2), implementing measures concerning:

— the technical modalities for appropriate public disclosure of inside information as referred to in paragraphs 1 and 3,
— the technical modalities for delaying the public disclosure of inside information as referred to in paragraph 2,
— the technical modalities designed to favour a common approach in the implementation of the second sentence of paragraph 2,
— the conditions under which issuers, or entities acting on their behalf, are to draw up a list of those persons working for them and having access to inside information, as referred to in paragraph 3, together with the conditions under which such lists are to be updated,
— the categories of persons who are subject to a duty of disclosure as referred to in paragraph 4 and the characteristics of a transaction, including its size, which trigger that duty, and the technical arrangements for disclosure to the competent authority,
— technical arrangements, for the various categories of person referred to in paragraph 5, for fair presentation of research and other information recommending investment strategy and for disclosure of particular interests or conflicts of interest as referred to in paragraph 5. Such arrangements shall take into account the rules, including self-regulation, governing the profession of journalist,
— technical arrangements governing notification to the competent authority by the persons referred to in paragraph 9.

[9443]

Article 7

This Directive shall not apply to transactions carried out in pursuit of monetary, exchange-rate or public debt-management policy by a Member State, by the European System of Central Banks, by a national central bank or by any other officially designated body, or by any person acting on their behalf. Member States may extend this exemption to their federated States or similar local authorities in respect of the management of their public debt.

[9444]

Article 8

The prohibitions provided for in this Directive shall not apply to trading in own shares in "buy-back" programmes or to the stabilisation of a financial instrument provided such trading is carried out in accordance with implementing measures adopted in accordance with the procedure laid down in Article 17(2).

[9445]

Article 9

This Directive shall apply to any financial instrument admitted to trading on a regulated market in at least one Member State, or for which a request for admission to trading on such a market has been made, irrespective of whether or not the transaction itself actually takes place on that market.

Articles 2, 3 and 4 shall also apply to any financial instrument not admitted to trading on a regulated market in a Member State, but whose value depends on a financial instrument as referred to in paragraph 1.

Article 6(1) to (3) shall not apply to issuers who have not requested or approved admission of their financial instruments to trading on a regulated market in a Member State.

[9446]

Article 10

Each Member State shall apply the prohibitions and requirements provided for in this Directive to:

(a) actions carried out on its territory or abroad concerning financial instruments that are admitted to trading on a regulated market situated or operating within its territory or for which a request for admission to trading on such market has been made;

(b) actions carried out on its territory concerning financial instruments that are admitted to trading on a regulated market in a Member State or for which a request for admission to trading on such market has been made.

[9447]

Article 11

Without prejudice to the competences of the judicial authorities, each Member State shall designate a single administrative authority competent to ensure that the provisions adopted pursuant to this Directive are applied.

Member States shall establish effective consultative arrangements and procedures with market participants concerning possible changes in national legislation. These arrangements may include consultative committees within each competent authority, the membership of which should reflect as far as possible the diversity of market participants, be they issuers, providers of financial services or consumers.

[9448]

Article 12

1. The competent authority shall be given all supervisory and investigatory powers that are necessary for the exercise of its functions. It shall exercise such powers:

(a) directly; or

(b) in collaboration with other authorities or with the market undertakings; or

(c) under its responsibility by delegation to such authorities or to the market undertakings; or

(d) by application to the competent judicial authorities.

2. Without prejudice to Article 6(7), the powers referred to in paragraph 1 of this Article shall be exercised in conformity with national law and shall include at least the right to:

(a) have access to any document in any form whatsoever, and to receive a copy of it;

(b) demand information from any person, including those who are successively involved in the transmission of orders or conduct of the operations concerned, as well as their principals, and if necessary, to summon and hear any such person;

(c) carry out on-site inspections;

(d) require existing telephone and existing data traffic records;

(e) require the cessation of any practice that is contrary to the provisions adopted in the implementation of this Directive;

(f) suspend trading of the financial instruments concerned;

(g) request the freezing and/or sequestration of assets;

(h) request temporary prohibition of professional activity.

3. This Article shall be without prejudice to national legal provisions on professional secrecy.

[9449]

Article 13

The obligation of professional secrecy shall apply to all persons who work or who have worked for the competent authority or for any authority or market undertaking to whom the competent authority has delegated its powers, including auditors and experts instructed by the competent authority. Information covered by professional secrecy may not be disclosed to any other person or authority except by virtue of provisions laid down by law.

[9450]

Article 14

1. Without prejudice to the right of Member States to impose criminal sanctions, Member States shall ensure, in conformity with their national law, that the appropriate administrative measures can be taken or administrative sanctions be imposed against the

persons responsible where the provisions adopted in the implementation of this Directive have not been complied with. Member States shall ensure that these measures are effective, proportionate and dissuasive.

2. In accordance with the procedure laid down in Article 17(2), the Commission shall, for information, draw up a list of the administrative measures and sanctions referred to in paragraph 1.

3. Member States shall determine the sanctions to be applied for failure to cooperate in an investigation covered by Article 12.

4. Member States shall provide that the competent authority may disclose to the public every measure or sanction that will be imposed for infringement of the provisions adopted in the implementation of this Directive, unless such disclosure would seriously jeopardise the financial markets or cause disproportionate damage to the parties involved.

[9451]

Article 15

Member States shall ensure that an appeal may be brought before a court against the decisions taken by the competent authority.

[9452]

Article 16

1. Competent authorities shall cooperate with each other whenever necessary for the purpose of carrying out their duties, making use of their powers whether set out in this Directive or in national law. Competent authorities shall render assistance to competent authorities of other Member States. In particular, they shall exchange information and cooperate in investigation activities.

2. Competent authorities shall, on request, immediately supply any information required for the purpose referred to in paragraph 1. Where necessary, the competent authorities receiving any such request shall immediately take the necessary measures in order to gather the required information. If the requested competent authority is not able to supply the required information immediately, it shall notify the requesting competent authority of the reasons. Information thus supplied shall be covered by the obligation of professional secrecy to which the persons employed or formerly employed by the competent authorities receiving the information are subject.

The competent authorities may refuse to act on a request for information where:

— communication might adversely affect the sovereignty, security or public policy of the Member State addressed,
— judicial proceedings have already been initiated in respect of the same actions and against the same persons before the authorities of the Member State addressed, or
— where a final judgment has already been delivered in relation to such persons for the same actions in the Member State addressed.

In any such case, they shall notify the requesting competent authority accordingly, providing as detailed information as possible on those proceedings or the judgment.

Without prejudice to Article 226 of the Treaty, a competent authority whose request for information is not acted upon within a reasonable time or whose request for information is rejected may bring that non-compliance to the attention of the Committee of European Securities Regulators, where discussion will take place in order to reach a rapid and effective solution.

Without prejudice to the obligations to which they are subject in judicial proceedings under criminal law, the competent authorities which receive information pursuant to paragraph 1 may use it only for the exercise of their functions within the scope of this Directive and in the context of administrative or judicial proceedings specifically related to the exercise of those functions. However, where the competent authority communicating information consents thereto, the authority receiving the information may use it for other purposes or forward it to other States' competent authorities.

3. Where a competent authority is convinced that acts contrary to the provisions of this Directive are being, or have been, carried out on the territory of another Member State or that acts are affecting financial instruments traded on a regulated market situated in another Member State, it shall give notice of that fact in as specific a manner as possible to the competent authority of the other Member State. The competent authority of the other Member

State shall take appropriate action. It shall inform the notifying competent authority of the outcome and, so far as possible, of significant interim developments. This paragraph shall not prejudice the competences of the competent authority that has forwarded the information. The competent authorities of the various Member States that are competent for the purposes of Article 10 shall consult each other on the proposed follow-up to their action.

4. A competent authority of one Member State may request that an investigation be carried out by the competent authority of another Member State, on the latter's territory.

It may further request that members of its own personnel be allowed to accompany the personnel of the competent authority of that other Member State during the course of the investigation.

The investigation shall, however, be subject throughout to the overall control of the Member State on whose territory it is conducted.

The competent authorities may refuse to act on a request for an investigation to be conducted as provided for in the first subparagraph, or on a request for its personnel to be accompanied by personnel of the competent authority of another Member State as provided for in the second subparagraph, where such an investigation might adversely affect the sovereignty, security or public policy of the State addressed, or where judicial proceedings have already been initiated in respect of the same actions and against the same persons before the authorities of the State addressed or where a final judgment has already been delivered in relation to such persons for the same actions in the State addressed. In such case, they shall notify the requesting competent authority accordingly, providing information, as detailed as possible, on those proceedings or judgment.

Without prejudice to the provisions of Article 226 of the Treaty, a competent authority whose application to open an inquiry or whose request for authorisation for its officials to accompany those of the other Member State's competent authority is not acted upon within a reasonable time or is rejected may bring that non-compliance to the attention of the Committee of European Securities Regulators, where discussion will take place in order to reach a rapid and effective solution.

5. In accordance with the procedure laid down in Article 17(2), the Commission shall adopt implementing measures on the procedures for exchange of information and cross-border inspections as referred to in this Article.

[9453]

Article 17

1. The Commission shall be assisted by the European Securities Committee instituted by Decision 2001/528/EC (hereinafter referred to as the "Committee").

2. Where reference is made to this paragraph, Articles 5 and 7 of Decision 1999/468/EC shall apply, having regard to the provisions of Article 8 thereof, provided that the implementing measures adopted according to this procedure do not modify the essential provisions of this Directive.

The period laid down in Article 5(6) of Decision 1999/468/EC shall be set at three months.

3. The Committee shall adopt its rules of procedure.

4. Without prejudice to the implementing measures already adopted, on the expiry of a four-year period following the entry into force of this Directive, the application of its provisions requiring the adoption of technical rules and decisions in accordance with paragraph 2 shall be suspended. On a proposal from the Commission, the European Parliament and the Council may renew the provisions concerned in accordance with the procedure laid down in Article 251 of the Treaty and, to that end, they shall review them prior to the expiry of the period referred to above.

[9454]

Article 18

Member States shall bring into force the laws, regulations and administrative provisions necessary to comply with this Directive not later than 12 October 2004. They shall forthwith inform the Commission thereof.

When Member States adopt those measures, they shall contain a reference to this Directive or be accompanied by such a reference on the occasion of their official publication. Member States shall determine how such reference is to be made.

[9455]

Article 19

Article 11 shall not prejudge the possibility for a Member State to make separate legal and administrative arrangements for overseas European territories for whose external relations that Member State is responsible.

[9456]

Article 20

Directive 89/592/EEC and Article 68(1) and Article 81(1) of Directive 2001/34/EC of the European Parliament and of the Council of 28 May 2001 on the admission of securities to official stock exchange listing and on information to be published on those securities[1] shall be repealed with effect from the date of entry into force of this Directive.

[9457]

NOTES

[1] OJ L184, 6.7.2001, p 1.

Article 21

This Directive shall enter into force on the day of its publication in the *Official Journal of the European Union*.

[9458]

Article 22

This Directive is addressed to the Member States.

[9459]

Done at Brussels, 28 January 2003.

COMMISSION REGULATION

of 29 September 2003

adopting certain international accounting standards in accordance with Regulation (EC) No 1606/2002 of the European Parliament and of the Council

(Text with EEA relevance)

(1725/2003/EC)

NOTES

Date of publication in OJ: OJ L261, 13.10.2003, p 1. Notes are as in the original OJ version.

THE COMMISSION OF THE EUROPEAN COMMUNITIES,

Having regard to the Treaty establishing the European Community.

Having regard to Regulation (EC) No 1606/2002 of the European Parliament and of the Council of 19 July 2002 on the application of international accounting standards,[1] and in particular Article 3(3) thereof,

Whereas:

(1) Regulation (EC) No 1606/2002 requires that for each financial year starting on or after 1 January 2005, publicly traded companies governed by the law of a Member State shall under certain conditions prepare their consolidated accounts in conformity with international accounting standards as defined in Article 2 of that Regulation.

(2) The Commission, having considered the advice provided by the Accounting Technical Committee, has concluded that the international accounting standards in existence on 14 September 2002 meet the criteria for adoption set out in Article 3 of Regulation (EC) No 1606/2002.

(3) The Commission has also considered the current improvements projects that propose to amend many existing standards. International accounting standards resulting from the finalisation of these proposals will be considered for adoption once those standards are final. The existence of these proposed amendments to existing standards does not impact upon the

Commission's decision to endorse the existing standards, except in the cases of IAS 32 Financial instruments: disclosure and presentation, IAS 39 Financial instruments: recognition and measurement and a small number of interpretations related to these standards, SIC 5 Classification of financial instruments — Contingent settlement provisions, SIC 16 Share capital — reacquired own equity instruments (treasury shares) and SIC 17 Equity — Costs of an equity transaction.

(4) The existence of high quality standards dealing with financial instruments, including derivatives, is important to the Community capital market. However, in the cases of IAS 32 and IAS 39, amendments currently being considered may be so considerable that it is appropriate not to adopt these standards at this time. As soon as the current improvement project is complete and revised standards issued, the Commission will consider, as a matter of priority, the adoption of the revised standards further to Regulation (EC) No 1606/2002.

(5) Accordingly, all international accounting standards in existence on 14 September 2002 except IAS 32, IAS 39 and the related interpretations should be adopted.

(6) The measures provided for in this Regulation are in accordance with the opinion of the Accounting Regulatory Committee.

[9459A]

NOTES

[1] OJ L243, 11.9.2002, p 1.

HAS ADOPTED THIS REGULATION,

Article 1

The international accounting standards set out in the Annex are adopted.

[9459B]

Article 2

This Regulation shall enter into force on the third day following its publication in the Official Journal of the European Union.

This Regulation shall be binding in its entirety and directly applicable in all Member States.

[9459C]

Done at Brussels, 29 September 2003.

ANNEX

(*The Annex sets out the international accounting standards introduced by Article 1. The Annex is hundreds of pages long and because of its size it has been omitted. The full text of the Annex is available on the Europa website at http://europa.eu/. Note that a consolidated version* (*incorporating all amendments up to 12 September 2006*) *is at: http://eur-lex.europa.eu/LexUriServ/site/en/consleg/2003/R/02003R1725–20060912-en.pdf and that it has been further amended by Commission Regulation 610/2007/EC and Commission Regulation 611/2007/EC* (*as from 5 June 2007 in both cases*).

DIRECTIVE OF THE EUROPEAN PARLIAMENT AND OF THE COUNCIL

of 4 November 2003

on the prospectus to be published when securities are offered to the public or admitted to trading and amending Directive 2001/34/EC

(2003/71/EC)

(Text with EEA relevance)

NOTES

Date of publication in OJ: OJ L345, 31.12.2003, p 64. Notes are as in the original OJ version.

THE EUROPEAN PARLIAMENT AND THE COUNCIL OF THE EUROPEAN UNION,

Having regard to the Treaty establishing the European Community, and in particular Articles 44 and 95 thereof,

Having regard to the proposal from the Commission,[1]

Having regard to the opinion of the European Economic and Social Committee,[2]

Having regard to the opinion of the European Central Bank,[3]

Acting in accordance with the procedure laid down in Article 251 of the Treaty,[4]

Whereas:

(1) Council Directives 80/390/EEC of 17 March 1980 coordinating the requirements for the drawing up, scrutiny and distribution of the listing particulars to be published for the admission of securities to official stock exchange listing[5] and 89/298/EEC of 17 April 1989 coordinating the requirements for the drawing up, scrutiny and distribution of the prospectus to be published when transferable securities are offered to the public[6] were adopted several years ago introducing a partial and complex mutual recognition mechanism which is unable to achieve the objective of the single passport provided for by this Directive. Those directives should be upgraded, updated and grouped together into a single text.

(2) Meanwhile, Directive 80/390/EEC was integrated into Directive 2001/34/EC of the European Parliament and of the Council of 28 May 2001 on the admission of securities to official stock exchange listing and on information to be published on those securities,[7] which codifies several directives in the field of listed securities.

(3) For reasons of consistency, however, it is appropriate to regroup the provisions of Directive 2001/34/EC which stem from Directive 80/390/EEC together with Directive 89/298/EEC and to amend Directive 2001/34/EC accordingly.

(4) This Directive constitutes an instrument essential to the achievement of the internal market as set out in timetable form in the Commission communications 'Risk capital action plan' and 'Implementing the framework for financial market: Action Plan' facilitating the widest possible access to investment capital on a Community-wide basis, including for small and medium-sized enterprises (SMEs) and start-ups, by granting a single passport to the issuer.

(5) On 17 July 2000, the Council set up the Committee of Wise Men on the regulation of European securities markets. In its initial report of 9 November 2000 the Committee stresses the lack of an agreed definition of public offer of securities, with the result that the same operation is regarded as a private placement in some Member States and not in others; the current system discourages firms from raising capital on a Community-wide basis and therefore from having real access to a large, liquid and integrated financial market.

(6) In its final report of 15 February 2001 the Committee of Wise Men proposed the introduction of new legislative techniques based on a four-level approach, namely framework principles, implementing measures, cooperation and enforcement. Level 1, the directive, should confine itself to broad, general 'framework' principles, while Level 2 should contain technical implementing measures to be adopted by the Commission with the assistance of a committee.

(7) The Stockholm European Council of 23 and 24 March 2001 endorsed the final report of the Committee of Wise Men and the proposed four-level approach to make the regulatory process for Community securities legislation more efficient and transparent.

(8) The resolution of the European Parliament of 5 February 2002 on the implementation of financial services legislation also endorsed the Committee of Wise Men's final report, on the basis of the solemn declaration made before Parliament the same day by the Commission and the letter of 2 October 2001 addressed by the Internal Market Commissioner to the chairman of Parliament's Committee on Economic and Monetary Affairs with regard to the safeguards for the European Parliament's role in this process.

(9) According to the Stockholm European Council, Level 2 implementing measures should be used more frequently to ensure that technical provisions can be kept up to date with market and supervisory developments and deadlines should be set for all stages of Level 2.

(10) The aim of this Directive and its implementing measures is to ensure investor protection and market efficiency, in accordance with high regulatory standards adopted in the relevant international fora.

(11) Non-equity securities issued by a Member State or by one of a Member State's regional or local authorities, by public international bodies of which one or more Member States are members, by the European Central Bank or by the central banks of the Member States are not covered by this Directive and thus remain unaffected by this Directive; the abovementioned issuers of such securities may, however, if they so choose, draw up a prospectus in accordance with this Directive.

(12) Full coverage of equity and non-equity securities offered to the public or admitted to trading on regulated markets as defined by Council Directive 93/22/EEC of 10 May 1993 on investment services in the securities field,[8] and not only securities which have been admitted

to the official lists of stock exchanges, is also needed to ensure investor protection. The wide definition of securities in this Directive, which includes warrants and covered warrants and certificates, is only valid for this Directive and consequently in no way affects the various definitions of financial instruments used in national legislation for other purposes, such as taxation. Some of the securities defined in this Directive entitle the holder to acquire transferable securities or to receive a cash amount through a cash settlement determined by reference to other instruments, notably transferable securities, currencies, interest rates or yields, commodities or other indices or measures. Depositary receipts and convertible notes, e g securities convertible at the option of the investor, fall within the definition of non-equity securities set out in this Directive.

(13) Issuance of securities having a similar type and/or class in the case of non-equity securities issued on the basis of an offering programme, including warrants and certificates in any form, as well as the case of securities issued in a continuous or repeated manner, should be understood as covering not only identical securities but also securities that belong in general terms to one category. These securities may include different products, such as debt securities, certificates and warrants, or the same product under the same programme, and may have different features notably in terms of seniority, types of underlying, or the basis on which to determine the redemption amount or coupon payment.

(14) The grant to the issuer of a single passport, valid throughout the Community, and the application of the country of origin principle require the identification of the home Member State as the one best placed to regulate the issuer for the purposes of this Directive.

(15) The disclosure requirements of the present Directive do not prevent a Member State or a competent authority or an exchange through its rule book to impose other particular requirements in the context of admission to trading of securities on a regulated market (notably regarding corporate governance). Such requirements may not directly or indirectly restrict the drawing up, the content and the dissemination of a prospectus approved by a competent authority.

(16) One of the objectives of this Directive is to protect investors. It is therefore appropriate to take account of the different requirements for protection of the various categories of investors and their level of expertise. Disclosure provided by the prospectus is not required for offers limited to qualified investors. In contrast, any resale to the public or public trading through admission to trading on a regulated market requires the publication of a prospectus.

(17) Issuers, offerors or persons asking for the admission to trading on a regulated market of securities which are exempted from the obligation to publish a prospectus will benefit from the single passport if they comply with this Directive.

(18) The provision of full information concerning securities and issuers of those securities promotes, together with rules on the conduct of business, the protection of investors. Moreover, such information provides an effective means of increasing confidence in securities and thus of contributing to the proper functioning and development of securities markets. The appropriate way to make this information available is to publish a prospectus.

(19) Investment in securities, like any other form of investment, involves risk. Safeguards for the protection of the interests of actual and potential investors are required in all Member States in order to enable them to make an informed assessment of such risks and thus to take investment decisions in full knowledge of the facts.

(20) Such information, which needs to be sufficient and as objective as possible as regards the financial circumstances of the issuer and the rights attaching to the securities, should be provided in an easily analysable and comprehensible form. Harmonisation of the information contained in the prospectus should provide equivalent investor protection at Community level.

(21) Information is a key factor in investor protection; a summary conveying the essential characteristics of, and risks associated with, the issuer, any guarantor and the securities should be included in the prospectus. To ensure easy access to this information, the summary should be written in non-technical language and normally should not exceed 2,500 words in the language in which the prospectus was originally drawn up.

(22) Best practices have been adopted at international level in order to allow cross-border offers of equities to be made using a single set of disclosure standards established by the International Organisation of Securities Commissions (IOSCO); the IOSCO disclosure standards[9] will upgrade information available for the markets and investors and at the same time will simplify the procedure for Community issuers wishing to raise capital in third countries. The Directive also calls for tailored disclosure standards to be adopted for other types of securities and issuers.

(23) Fast-track procedures for issuers admitted to trading on a regulated market and frequently raising capital on these markets require the introduction at Community level of a

new format of prospectuses for offering programmes or mortgage bonds and a new registration document system. Issuers may choose not to use those formats and therefore to draft the prospectus as a single document.

(24) The content of a base prospectus should, in particular, take into account the need for flexibility in relation to the information to be provided about the securities.

(25) Omission of sensitive information to be included in a prospectus should be allowed through a derogation granted by the competent authority in certain circumstances in order to avoid detrimental situations for an issuer.

(26) A clear time limit should be set for the validity of a prospectus in order to avoid outdated information.

(27) Investors should be protected by ensuring publication of reliable information. The issuers whose securities are admitted to trading on a regulated market are subject to an ongoing disclosure obligation but are not required to publish updated information regularly. Further to this obligation, issuers should, at least annually, list all relevant information published or made available to the public over the preceding 12 months, including information provided to the various reporting requirements laid down in other Community legislation. This should make it possible to ensure the publication of consistent and easily understandable information on a regular basis. To avoid excessive burdens for certain issuers, issuers of non-equity securities with high minimum denomination should not be required to meet this obligation.

(28) It is necessary for the annual information to be provided by issuers whose securities are admitted to trading on a regulated market to be appropriately monitored by Member States in accordance with their obligations under the provisions of Community and national law concerning the regulation of securities, issuers of securities and securities markets.

(29) The opportunity of allowing issuers to incorporate by reference documents containing the information to be disclosed in a prospectus—provided that the documents incorporated by reference have been previously filed with or accepted by the competent authority—should facilitate the procedure of drawing up a prospectus and lower the costs for the issuers without endangering investor protection.

(30) Differences regarding the efficiency, methods and timing of the checking of the information given in a prospectus not only make it more difficult for undertakings to raise capital or to obtain admission to trading on a regulated market in more than one Member State but also hinder the acquisition by investors established in one Member State of securities offered by an issuer established in another Member State or admitted to trading in another Member State. These differences should be eliminated by harmonising the rules and regulations in order to achieve an adequate degree of equivalence of the safeguards required in each Member State to ensure the provision of information which is sufficient and as objective as possible for actual or potential securities holders.

(31) To facilitate circulation of the various documents making up the prospectus, the use of electronic communication facilities such as the Internet should be encouraged. The prospectus should always be delivered in paper form, free of charge to investors on request.

(32) The prospectus should be filed with the relevant competent authority and be made available to the public by the issuer, the offeror or the person asking for admission to trading on a regulated market, subject to European Union provisions relating to data protection.

(33) It is also necessary, in order to avoid loopholes in Community legislation which would undermine public confidence and therefore prejudice the proper functioning of financial markets, to harmonise advertisements.

(34) Any new matter liable to influence the assessment of the investment, arising after the publication of the prospectus but before the closing of the offer or the start of trading on a regulated market, should be properly evaluated by investors and therefore requires the approval and dissemination of a supplement to the prospectus.

(35) The obligation for an issuer to translate the full prospectus into all the relevant official languages discourages cross-border offers or multiple trading. To facilitate cross-border offers, where the prospectus is drawn up in a language that is customary in the sphere of international finance, the host or home Member State should only be entitled to require a summary in its official language(s).

(36) The competent authority of the host Member State should be entitled to receive a certificate from the competent authority of the home Member State which states that the prospectus has been drawn up in accordance with this Directive. In order to ensure that the purposes of this Directive will be fully achieved, it is also necessary to include within its scope securities issued by issuers governed by the laws of third countries.

(37) A variety of competent authorities in Member States, having different responsibilities, may create unnecessary costs and overlapping of responsibilities without providing any additional benefit. In each Member State one single competent authority should be designated to approve prospectuses and to assume responsibility for supervising

compliance with this Directive. Under strict conditions, a Member State should be allowed to designate more than one competent authority, but only one will assume the duties for international cooperation. Such an authority or authorities should be established as an administrative authority and in such a form that their independence from economic actors is guaranteed and conflicts of interest are avoided. The designation of a competent authority for prospectus approval should not exclude cooperation between that authority and other entities, with a view to guaranteeing efficient scrutiny and approval of prospectuses in the interest of issuers, investors, markets participants and markets alike. Any delegation of tasks relating to the obligations provided for in this Directive and in its implementing measures should be reviewed, in accordance with Article 31, five years after the date of entry into force of this Directive and should, except for publication on the Internet of approved prospectuses, and the filing of prospectuses as mentioned in Article 14, end eight years after the entry into force of this Directive.

(38) A common minimum set of powers for the competent authorities will guarantee the effectiveness of their supervision. The flow of information to the markets required by Directive 2001/34/EC should be ensured and action against breaches should be taken by competent authorities.

(39) For the purposes of carrying out their duties, cooperation between competent authorities of the Member States is required.

(40) Technical guidance and implementing measures for the rules laid down in this Directive may from time to time be necessary to take into account developments on financial markets. The Commission should accordingly be empowered to adopt implementing measures, provided that these do not modify the essential elements of this Directive and provided that the Commission acts in accordance with the principles set out in this Directive, after consulting the European Securities Committee established by Commission Decision 2001/528/EC.[10]

(41) In exercising its implementing powers in accordance with this Directive, the Commission should respect the following principles:

— the need to ensure confidence in financial markets among small investors and small and medium-sized enterprises (SMEs) by promoting high standards of transparency in financial markets,
— the need to provide investors with a wide range of competing investment opportunities and a level of disclosure and protection tailored to their circumstances,
— the need to ensure that independent regulatory authorities enforce the rules consistently, especially as regards the fight against white-collar crime,
— the need for a high level of transparency and consultation with all market participants and with the European Parliament and the Council,
— the need to encourage innovation in financial markets if they are to be dynamic and efficient,
— the need to ensure systemic stability of the financial system by close and reactive monitoring of financial innovation,
— the importance of reducing the cost of, and increasing access to, capital,
— the need to balance, on a long-term basis, the costs and benefits to market participants (including SMEs and small investors) of any implementing measures,
— the need to foster the international competitiveness of the Community's financial markets without prejudice to a much-needed extension of international cooperation,
— the need to achieve a level playing field for all market participants by establishing Community legislation every time it is appropriate,
— the need to respect differences in national financial markets where these do not unduly impinge on the coherence of the single market,
— the need to ensure coherence with other Community legislation in this area, as imbalances in information and a lack of transparency may jeopardise the operation of the markets and above all harm consumers and small investors.

(42) The European Parliament should be given a period of three months from the first transmission of draft implementing measures to allow it to examine them and to give its opinion. However, in urgent and duly justified cases, this period may be shortened. If, within that period, a resolution is passed by the European Parliament, the Commission should re-examine the draft measures.

(43) Member States should lay down a system of sanctions for breaches of the national provisions adopted pursuant to this Directive and should take all the measures necessary to ensure that these sanctions are applied. The sanctions thus provided for should be effective, proportional and dissuasive.

(44) Provision should be made for the right of judicial review of decisions taken by Member States' competent authorities in respect of the application of this Directive.

(45) In accordance with the principle of proportionality, it is necessary and appropriate for the achievement of the basic objective of ensuring the completion of a single securities market to lay down rules on a single passport for issuers. This Directive does not go beyond what is necessary in order to achieve the objectives pursued in accordance with the third paragraph of Article 5 of the Treaty.

(46) The assessment made by the Commission of the application of this Directive should focus in particular on the process of approval of prospectuses by the competent authorities of the Member States, and more generally on the application of the home-country principle, and whether or not problems of investor protection and market efficiency might result from this application; the Commission should also examine the functioning of Article 10.

(47) For future developments of this Directive, consideration should be given to the matter of deciding which approval mechanism should be adopted to enhance further the uniform application of Community legislation on prospectuses, including the possible establishment of a European Securities Unit.

(48) This Directive respects the fundamental rights and observes the principles recognised in particular by the Charter of Fundamental Rights of the European Union.

(49) The measures necessary for the implementation of this Directive should be adopted in accordance with Council Decision 1999/468/EC of 28 June 1999 laying down the procedures for the exercise of implementing powers conferred on the Commission,[11]

[9460]

NOTES

1 OJ C240E, 28.8.2001, p 272 and OJ C20E, 28.1.2003, p 122.
2 OJ C80, 3.4.2002, p 52.
3 OJ C344, 6.12.2001, p 4.
4 Opinion of the European Parliament of 14 March 2002 (OJ C47E, 27.2.2003, p 417), Council Common Position of 24 March 2003 (OJ C125E, 27.5.2003, p 21) and Position of the European Parliament of 2 July 2003 (not yet published in the Official Journal). Decision of the Council of 15 July 2003.
5 OJ L100, 17.4.1980, p 1. Directive as last amended by Directive of the European Parliament and of the Council 94/18/EC (OJ L135, 31.5.1994, p 1).
6 OJ L124, 5.5.1989, p 8.
7 OJ L184, 6.7.2001, p 1.
8 OJ L141, 11.6.1993, p 27. Directive as last amended by Directive 2000/64/EC of the European Parliament and of the Council (OJ L290, 17.11.2000, p 27).
9 International disclosure standards for cross-border offering and initial listings by foreign issuers, Part I, International Organisation of Securities Commissions, September 1998.
10 OJ L191, 13.7.2001, p 45.
11 OJ L184, 17.7.1999, p 23.

HAVE ADOPTED THIS DIRECTIVE:

CHAPTER I
GENERAL PROVISIONS

Article 1

Purpose and scope

1. The purpose of this Directive is to harmonise requirements for the drawing up, approval and distribution of the prospectus to be published when securities are offered to the public or admitted to trading on a regulated market situated or operating within a Member State.

2. This Directive shall not apply to:
- (a) units issued by collective investment undertakings other than the closed-end type;
- (b) non-equity securities issued by a Member State or by one of a Member State's regional or local authorities, by public international bodies of which one or more Member States are members, by the European Central Bank or by the central banks of the Member States;
- (c) shares in the capital of central banks of the Member States;
- (d) securities unconditionally and irrevocably guaranteed by a Member State or by one of a Member State's regional or local authorities;
- (e) securities issued by associations with legal status or non-profit-making bodies,

recognised by a Member State, with a view to their obtaining the means necessary to achieve their non-profit-making objectives;

(f) non-equity securities issued in a continuous or repeated manner by credit institutions provided that these securities:
   (i) are not subordinated, convertible or exchangeable;
   (ii) do not give a right to subscribe to or acquire other types of securities and that they are not linked to a derivative instrument;
   (iii) materialise reception of repayable deposits;
   (iv) are covered by a deposit guarantee scheme under Directive 94/19/EC of the European Parliament and of the Council on deposit-guarantee schemes;[1]

(g) non-fungible shares of capital whose main purpose is to provide the holder with a right to occupy an apartment, or other form of immovable property or a part thereof and where the shares cannot be sold on without this right being given up;

(h) securities included in an offer where the total consideration of the offer is less than EUR 2,500,000, which limit shall be calculated over a period of 12 months;

(i) 'bostadsobligationer' issued repeatedly by credit institutions in Sweden whose main purpose is to grant mortgage loans, provided that
   (i) the 'bostadsobligationer' issued are of the same series;
   (ii) the 'bostadsobligationer' are issued on tap during a specified issuing period;
   (iii) the terms and conditions of the 'bostadsobligationer' are not changed during the issuing period;
   (iv) the sums deriving from the issue of the said 'bostadsobligationer', in accordance with the articles of association of the issuer, are placed in assets which provide sufficient coverage for the liability deriving from securities;

(j) non-equity securities issued in a continuous or repeated manner by credit institutions where the total consideration of the offer is less than EUR 50,000,000, which limit shall be calculated over a period of 12 months, provided that these securities:
   (i) are not subordinated, convertible or exchangeable;
   (ii) do not give a right to subscribe to or acquire other types of securities and that they are not linked to a derivative instrument.

3. Notwithstanding paragraph 2(b), (d), (h), (i) and (j), an issuer, an offeror or a person asking for admission to trading on a regulated market shall be entitled to draw up a prospectus in accordance with this Directive when securities are offered to the public or admitted to trading.

[9461]

NOTES

[1] OJ L135, 31.5.1994, p 5.

Article 2

Definitions

1. For the purposes of this Directive, the following definitions shall apply:

(a) 'securities' means transferable securities as defined by Article 1(4) of Directive 93/22/EEC with the exception of money market instruments as defined by Article 1(5) of Directive 93/22/EEC, having a maturity of less than 12 months. For these instruments national legislation may be applicable;

(b) 'equity securities' means shares and other transferable securities equivalent to shares in companies, as well as any other type of transferable securities giving the right to acquire any of the aforementioned securities as a consequence of their being converted or the rights conferred by them being exercised, provided that securities of the latter type are issued by the issuer of the underlying shares or by an entity belonging to the group of the said issuer;

(c) 'non-equity securities' means all securities that are not equity securities;

(d) 'offer of securities to the public' means a communication to persons in any form and by any means, presenting sufficient information on the terms of the offer and the securities to be offered, so as to enable an investor to decide to purchase or subscribe to these securities. This definition shall also be applicable to the placing of securities through financial intermediaries;

(e) 'qualified investors' means:

(i) legal entities which are authorised or regulated to operate in the financial markets, including: credit institutions, investment firms, other authorised or regulated financial institutions, insurance companies, collective investment schemes and their management companies, pension funds and their management companies, commodity dealers, as well as entities not so authorised or regulated whose corporate purpose is solely to invest in securities;

(ii) national and regional governments, central banks, international and supranational institutions such as the International Monetary Fund, the European Central Bank, the European Investment Bank and other similar international organisations;

(iii) other legal entities which do not meet two of the three criteria set out in paragraph (f);

(iv) certain natural persons: subject to mutual recognition, a Member State may choose to authorise natural persons who are resident in the Member State and who expressly ask to be considered as qualified investors if these persons meet at least two of the criteria set out in paragraph 2;

(v) certain SMEs: subject to mutual recognition, a Member State may choose to authorise SMEs which have their registered office in that Member State and who expressly ask to be considered as qualified investors;

(f) 'small and medium-sized enterprises' means companies, which, according to their last annual or consolidated accounts, meet at least two of the following three criteria: an average number of employees during the financial year of less than 250, a total balance sheet not exceeding EUR 43,000,000 and an annual net turnover not exceeding EUR 50,000,000;

(g) 'credit institution' means an undertaking as defined by Article 1(1)(a) of Directive 2000/12/EC of the European Parliament and of the Council of 20 March 2000 relating to the taking up and pursuit of the business of credit institutions;[1]

(h) 'issuer' means a legal entity which issues or proposes to issue securities;

(i) 'person making an offer' (or 'offeror') means a legal entity or individual which offers securities to the public;

(j) 'regulated market' means a market as defined by Article 1(13) of Directive 93/22/EEC;

(k) 'offering programme' means a plan which would permit the issuance of non-equity securities, including warrants in any form, having a similar type and/or class, in a continuous or repeated manner during a specified issuing period;

(l) 'securities issued in a continuous or repeated manner' means issues on tap or at least two separate issues of securities of a similar type and/or class over a period of 12 months;

(m) 'home Member State' means:

(i) for all Community issuers of securities which are not mentioned in (ii), the Member State where the issuer has its registered office;

(ii) for any issues of non-equity securities whose denomination per unit amounts to at least EUR 1,000, and for any issues of non-equity securities giving the right to acquire any transferable securities or to receive a cash amount, as a consequence of their being converted or the rights conferred by them being exercised, provided that the issuer of the non-equity securities is not the issuer of the underlying securities or an entity belonging to the group of the latter issuer, the Member State where the issuer has its registered office, or where the securities were or are to be admitted to trading on a regulated market or where the securities are offered to the public, at the choice of the issuer, the offeror or the person asking for admission, as the case may be. The same regime shall be applicable to non-equity securities in a currency other than euro, provided that the value of such minimum denomination is nearly equivalent to EUR 1,000;

(iii) for all issuers of securities incorporated in a third country, which are not mentioned in (ii), the Member State where the securities are intended to be offered to the public for the first time after the date of entry into force of this Directive or where the first application for admission to trading on a regulated market is made, at the choice of the issuer, the offeror or the person asking for admission, as the case may be, subject to a subsequent election by issuers incorporated in a third country if the home Member State was not determined by their choice;

(n) 'host Member State' means the State where an offer to the public is made or admission to trading is sought, when different from the home Member State;

(o) 'collective investment undertaking other than the closed-end type' means unit trusts and investment companies:
   (i) the object of which is the collective investment of capital provided by the public, and which operate on the principle of risk-spreading;
   (ii) the units of which are, at the holder's request, repurchased or redeemed, directly or indirectly, out of the assets of these undertakings;

(p) 'units of a collective investment undertaking' mean securities issued by a collective investment undertaking as representing the rights of the participants in such an undertaking over its assets;

(q) 'approval' means the positive act at the outcome of the scrutiny of the completeness of the prospectus by the home Member State's competent authority including the consistency of the information given and its comprehensibility;

(r) 'base prospectus' means a prospectus containing all relevant information as specified in Articles 5, 7 and 16 in case there is a supplement, concerning the issuer and the securities to be offered to the public or admitted to trading, and, at the choice of the issuer, the final terms of the offering.

2. For the purposes of paragraph 1(e)(iv) the criteria are as follows:

(a) the investor has carried out transactions of a significant size on securities markets at an average frequency of, at least, 10 per quarter over the previous four quarters;

(b) the size of the investor's securities portfolio exceeds EUR 0.5 million;

(c) the investor works or has worked for at least one year in the financial sector in a professional position which requires knowledge of securities investment.

3. For the purposes of paragraphs 1(e)(iv) and (v) the following shall apply:

Each competent authority shall ensure that appropriate mechanisms are in place for a register of natural persons and SMEs considered as qualified investors, taking into account the need to ensure an adequate level of data protection. The register shall be available to all issuers. Each natural person or SME wishing to be considered as a qualified investor shall register and each registered investor may decide to opt out at any moment.

4. In order to take account of technical developments on financial markets and to ensure uniform application of this Directive, the Commission shall, in accordance with the procedure set out in Article 24(2), adopt implementing measures concerning the definitions referred to in paragraph 1, including adjustment of the figures used for the definition of SMEs, taking into account Community legislation and recommendations as well as economic developments and disclosure measures relating to the registration of individual qualified investors.

[9462]

NOTES

[1] OJ L126, 26.5.2000, p 1. Directive as last amended by Directive 2000/28/EC (OJ L275, 27.10.2000, p 37).

Article 3

Obligation to publish a prospectus

1. Member States shall not allow any offer of securities to be made to the public within their territories without prior publication of a prospectus.

2. The obligation to publish a prospectus shall not apply to the following types of offer:

(a) an offer of securities addressed solely to qualified investors; and/or

(b) an offer of securities addressed to fewer than 100 natural or legal persons per Member State, other than qualified investors; and/or

(c) an offer of securities addressed to investors who acquire securities for a total consideration of at least EUR 50,000 per investor, for each separate offer; and/or

(d) an offer of securities whose denomination per unit amounts to at least EUR 50,000; and/or

(e) an offer of securities with a total consideration of less than EUR 100,000, which limit shall be calculated over a period of 12 months.

However, any subsequent resale of securities which were previously the subject of one or more of the types of offer mentioned in this paragraph shall be regarded as a separate offer and the definition set out in Article 2(1)(d) shall apply for the purpose of deciding whether that resale is an offer of securities to the public. The placement of securities through financial intermediaries shall be subject to publication of a prospectus if none of the conditions (a) to (e) are met for the final placement.

3. Member States shall ensure that any admission of securities to trading on a regulated market situated or operating within their territories is subject to the publication of a prospectus.

[9463]

Article 4

Exemptions from the obligation to publish a prospectus

1. The obligation to publish a prospectus shall not apply to offers of securities to the public of the following types of securities:

(a) shares issued in substitution for shares of the same class already issued, if the issuing of such new shares does not involve any increase in the issued capital;

(b) securities offered in connection with a takeover by means of an exchange offer, provided that a document is available containing information which is regarded by the competent authority as being equivalent to that of the prospectus, taking into account the requirements of Community legislation;

(c) securities offered, allotted or to be allotted in connection with a merger, provided that a document is available containing information which is regarded by the competent authority as being equivalent to that of the prospectus, taking into account the requirements of Community legislation;

(d) shares offered, allotted or to be allotted free of charge to existing shareholders, and dividends paid out in the form of shares of the same class as the shares in respect of which such dividends are paid, provided that a document is made available containing information on the number and nature of the shares and the reasons for and details of the offer;

(e) securities offered, allotted or to be allotted to existing or former directors or employees by their employer which has securities already admitted to trading on a regulated market or by an affiliated undertaking, provided that a document is made available containing information on the number and nature of the securities and the reasons for and details of the offer.

2. The obligation to publish a prospectus shall not apply to the admission to trading on a regulated market of the following types of securities:

(a) shares representing, over a period of 12 months, less than 10 per cent of the number of shares of the same class already admitted to trading on the same regulated market;

(b) shares issued in substitution for shares of the same class already admitted to trading on the same regulated market, if the issuing of such shares does not involve any increase in the issued capital;

(c) securities offered in connection with a takeover by means of an exchange offer, provided that a document is available containing information which is regarded by the competent authority as being equivalent to that of the prospectus, taking into account the requirements of Community legislation;

(d) securities offered, allotted or to be allotted in connection with a merger, provided that a document is available containing information which is regarded by the competent authority as being equivalent to that of the prospectus, taking into account the requirements of Community legislation;

(e) shares offered, allotted or to be allotted free of charge to existing shareholders, and dividends paid out in the form of shares of the same class as the shares in respect of which such dividends are paid, provided that the said shares are of the same class as the shares already admitted to trading on the same regulated market and that a document is made available containing information on the number and nature of the shares and the reasons for and details of the offer;

(f) securities offered, allotted or to be allotted to existing or former directors or employees by their employer or an affiliated undertaking, provided that the said securities are of the same class as the securities already admitted to trading on the same regulated market and that a document is made available containing information on the number and nature of the securities and the reasons for and detail of the offer;

(g) shares resulting from the conversion or exchange of other securities or from the exercise of the rights conferred by other securities, provided that the said shares are of the same class as the shares already admitted to trading on the same regulated market;

(h) securities already admitted to trading on another regulated market, on the following conditions:
   (i) that these securities, or securities of the same class, have been admitted to trading on that other regulated market for more than 18 months;
   (ii) that, for securities first admitted to trading on a regulated market after the date of entry into force of this Directive, the admission to trading on that other regulated market was associated with an approved prospectus made available to the public in conformity with Article 14;
   (iii) that, except where (ii) applies, for securities first admitted to listing after 30 June 1983, listing particulars were approved in accordance with the requirements of Directive 80/390/EEC or Directive 2001/34/EC;
   (iv) that the ongoing obligations for trading on that other regulated market have been fulfilled;
   (v) that the person seeking the admission of a security to trading on a regulated market under this exemption makes a summary document available to the public in a language accepted by the competent authority of the Member State of the regulated market where admission is sought;
   (vi) that the summary document referred to in (v) is made available to the public in the Member State of the regulated market where admission to trading is sought in the manner set out in Article 14(2); and
   (vii) that the contents of the summary document shall comply with Article 5(2). Furthermore the document shall state where the most recent prospectus can be obtained and where the financial information published by the issuer pursuant to his ongoing disclosure obligations is available.

3. In order to take account of technical developments on financial markets and to ensure uniform application of this Directive, the Commission shall, in accordance with the procedure referred to in Article 24(2), adopt implementing measures concerning paragraphs 1(b), 1(c), 2(c) and 2(d), notably in relation to the meaning of equivalence.

[9464]

CHAPTER II
DRAWING UP OF THE PROSPECTUS

Article 5

The prospectus

1. Without prejudice to Article 8(2), the prospectus shall contain all information which, according to the particular nature of the issuer and of the securities offered to the public or admitted to trading on a regulated market, is necessary to enable investors to make an informed assessment of the assets and liabilities, financial position, profit and losses, and prospects of the issuer and of any guarantor, and of the rights attaching to such securities. This information shall be presented in an easily analysable and comprehensible form.

2. The prospectus shall contain information concerning the issuer and the securities to be offered to the public or to be admitted to trading on a regulated market. It shall also include a summary. The summary shall, in a brief manner and in non-technical language, convey the essential characteristics and risks associated with the issuer, any guarantor and the securities, in the language in which the prospectus was originally drawn up. The summary shall also contain a warning that:

(a) it should be read as an introduction to the prospectus;

(b) any decision to invest in the securities should be based on consideration of the prospectus as a whole by the investor;

(c) where a claim relating to the information contained in a prospectus is brought before a court, the plaintiff investor might, under the national legislation of the Member States, have to bear the costs of translating the prospectus before the legal proceedings are initiated; and

(d) civil liability attaches to those persons who have tabled the summary including any translation thereof, and applied for its notification, but only if the summary is misleading, inaccurate or inconsistent when read together with the other parts of the prospectus.

Where the prospectus relates to the admission to trading on a regulated market of non-equity securities having a denomination of at least EUR 50,000, there shall be no requirement to provide a summary except when requested by a Member State as provided for in Article 19(4).

3. Subject to paragraph 4, the issuer, offeror or person asking for the admission to trading on a regulated market may draw up the prospectus as a single document or separate documents. A prospectus composed of separate documents shall divide the required information into a registration document, a securities note and a summary note. The registration document shall contain the information relating to the issuer. The securities note shall contain the information concerning the securities offered to the public or to be admitted to trading on a regulated market.

4. For the following types of securities, the prospectus can, at the choice of the issuer, offeror or person asking for the admission to trading on a regulated market consist of a base prospectus containing all relevant information concerning the issuer and the securities offered to the public or to be admitted to trading on a regulated market:

(a) non-equity securities, including warrants in any form, issued under an offering programme;

(b) non-equity securities issued in a continuous or repeated manner by credit institutions,

  (i) where the sums deriving from the issue of the said securities, under national legislation, are placed in assets which provide sufficient coverage for the liability deriving from securities until their maturity date;

  (ii) where, in the event of the insolvency of the related credit institution, the said sums are intended, as a priority, to repay the capital and interest falling due, without prejudice to the provisions of Directive 2001/24/EC of the European Parliament and of the Council of 4 April 2001 on the reorganisation and winding up of credit institutions.[1]

The information given in the base prospectus shall be supplemented, if necessary, in accordance with Article 16, with updated information on the issuer and on the securities to be offered to the public or to be admitted to trading on a regulated market.

If the final terms of the offer are not included in either the base prospectus or a supplement, the final terms shall be provided to investors and filed with the competent authority when each public offer is made as soon as practicable and if possible in advance of the beginning of the offer. The provisions of Article 8(1)(a) shall be applicable in any such case.

5. In order to take account of technical developments on financial markets and to ensure uniform application of this Directive, the Commission shall, in accordance with the procedure referred to in Article 24(2), adopt implementing measures concerning the format of the prospectus or base prospectus and supplements.

[9465]

NOTES

[1] OJ L125, 5.5.2001, p 15.

Article 6

Responsibility attaching to the prospectus

1. Member States shall ensure that responsibility for the information given in a prospectus attaches at least to the issuer or its administrative, management or supervisory bodies, the offeror, the person asking for the admission to trading on a regulated market or the guarantor, as the case may be. The persons responsible shall be clearly identified in the prospectus by their names and functions or, in the case of legal persons, their names and registered offices, as well as declarations by them that, to the best of their knowledge, the information contained in the prospectus is in accordance with the facts and that the prospectus makes no omission likely to affect its import.

2. Member States shall ensure that their laws, regulation and administrative provisions on civil liability apply to those persons responsible for the information given in a prospectus.

However, Member States shall ensure that no civil liability shall attach to any person solely on the basis of the summary, including any translation thereof, unless it is misleading, inaccurate or inconsistent when read together with the other parts of the prospectus.

[9466]

Article 7

Minimum information

1. Detailed implementing measures regarding the specific information which must be included in a prospectus, avoiding duplication of information when a prospectus is composed of separate documents, shall be adopted by the Commission in accordance with the procedure referred to in Article 24(2). The first set of implementing measures shall be adopted by 1 July 2004.

2. In particular, for the elaboration of the various models of prospectuses, account shall be taken of the following:

(a) the various types of information needed by investors relating to equity securities as compared with non-equity securities; a consistent approach shall be taken with regard to information required in a prospectus for securities which have a similar economic rationale, notably derivative securities;

(b) the various types and characteristics of offers and admissions to trading on a regulated market of non-equity securities. The information required in a prospectus shall be appropriate from the point of view of the investors concerned for non-equity securities having a denomination per unit of at least EUR 50,000;

(c) the format used and the information required in prospectuses relating to non-equity securities, including warrants in any form, issued under an offering programme;

(d) the format used and the information required in prospectuses relating to non-equity securities, in so far as these securities are not subordinated, convertible, exchangeable, subject to subscription or acquisition rights or linked to derivative instruments, issued in a continuous or repeated manner by entities authorised or regulated to operate in the financial markets within the European Economic Area;

(e) the various activities and size of the issuer, in particular SMEs. For such companies the information shall be adapted to their size and, where appropriate, to their shorter track record;

(f) if applicable, the public nature of the issuer.

3. The implementing measures referred to in paragraph 1 shall be based on the standards in the field of financial and non-financial information set out by international securities commission organisations, and in particular by IOSCO and on the indicative Annexes to this Directive.

[9467]

Article 8

Omission of information

1. Member States shall ensure that where the final offer price and amount of securities which will be offered to the public cannot be included in the prospectus:

(a) the criteria, and/or the conditions in accordance with which the above elements will be determined or, in the case of price, the maximum price, are disclosed in the prospectus; or

(b) the acceptances of the purchase or subscription of securities may be withdrawn for not less than two working days after the final offer price and amount of securities which will be offered to the public have been filed.

The final offer price and amount of securities shall be filed with the competent authority of the home Member State and published in accordance with the arrangements provided for in Article 14(2).

2. The competent authority of the home Member State may authorise the omission from the prospectus of certain information provided for in this Directive or in the implementing measures referred to in Article 7(1), if it considers that:

(a) disclosure of such information would be contrary to the public interest; or

(b) disclosure of such information would be seriously detrimental to the issuer, provided that the omission would not be likely to mislead the public with regard to facts and circumstances essential for an informed assessment of the issuer, offeror or guarantor, if any, and of the rights attached to the securities to which the prospectus relates; or

(c) such information is of minor importance only for a specific offer or admission to trading on a regulated market and is not such as will influence the assessment of the financial position and prospects of the issuer, offeror or guarantor, if any.

3. Without prejudice to the adequate information of investors, where, exceptionally, certain information required by implementing measures referred to in Article 7(1) to be included in a prospectus is inappropriate to the issuer's sphere of activity or to the legal form of the issuer or to the securities to which the prospectus relates, the prospectus shall contain information equivalent to the required information. If there is no such information, this requirement shall not apply.

4. In order to take account of technical developments on financial markets and to ensure uniform application of this Directive, the Commission shall, in accordance with the procedure referred to in Article 24(2), adopt implementing measures concerning paragraph 2.

[9468]

Article 9

Validity of a prospectus, base prospectus and registration document

1. A prospectus shall be valid for 12 months after its publication for offers to the public or admissions to trading on a regulated market, provided that the prospectus is completed by any supplements required pursuant to Article 16.

2. In the case of an offering programme, the base prospectus, previously filed, shall be valid for a period of up to 12 months.

3. In the case of non-equity securities referred to in Article 5(4)(b), the prospectus shall be valid until no more of the securities concerned are issued in a continuous or repeated manner.

4. A registration document, as referred to in Article 5(3), previously filed, shall be valid for a period of up to 12 months provided that it has been updated in accordance with Article 10(1). The registration document accompanied by the securities note, updated if applicable in accordance with Article 12, and the summary note shall be considered to constitute a valid prospectus.

[9469]

Article 10

Information

1. Issuers whose securities are admitted to trading on a regulated market shall at least annually provide a document that contains or refers to all information that they have published or made available to the public over the preceding 12 months in one or more Member States and in third countries in compliance with their obligations under Community and national laws and rules dealing with the regulation of securities, issuers of securities and securities markets. Issuers shall refer at least to the information required pursuant to company law directives, Directive 2001/34/EC and Regulation (EC) No 1606/2002 of the European Parliament and of the Council of 19 July 2002 on the application of international accounting standards.[1]

2. The document shall be filed with the competent authority of the home Member State after the publication of the financial statement. Where the document refers to information, it shall be stated where the information can be obtained.

3. The obligation set out in paragraph 1 shall not apply to issuers of non-equity securities whose denomination per unit amounts to at least EUR 50,000.

4. In order to take account of technical developments on financial markets and to ensure uniform application of this Directive, the Commission may, in accordance with the procedure referred to in Article 24(2), adopt implementing measures concerning paragraph 1. These measures will relate only to the method of publication of the disclosure requirements mentioned in paragraph 1 and will not entail new disclosure requirements. The first set of implementing measures shall be adopted by 1 July 2004.

[9470]

NOTES

[1] OJ L243, 11.9.2002, p 1.

Article 11

Incorporation by reference

1. Member States shall allow information to be incorporated in the prospectus by reference to one or more previously or simultaneously published documents that have been

approved by the competent authority of the home Member State or filed with it in accordance with this Directive, in particular pursuant to Article 10, or with Titles IV and V of Directive 2001/34/EC. This information shall be the latest available to the issuer. The summary shall not incorporate information by reference.

2. When information is incorporated by reference, a cross-reference list must be provided in order to enable investors to identify easily specific items of information.

3. In order to take account of technical developments on financial markets and to ensure uniform application of this Directive, the Commission shall, in accordance with the procedure referred to in Article 24(2), adopt implementing measures concerning the information to be incorporated by reference. The first set of implementing measures shall be adopted by 1 July 2004.

[9471]

Article 12

Prospectuses consisting of separate documents

1. An issuer which already has a registration document approved by the competent authority shall be required to draw up only the securities note and the summary note when securities are offered to the public or admitted to trading on a regulated market.

2. In this case, the securities note shall provide information that would normally be provided in the registration document if there has been a material change or recent development which could affect investors' assessments since the latest updated registration document or any supplement as provided for in Article 16 was approved. The securities and summary notes shall be subject to a separate approval.

3. Where an issuer has only filed a registration document without approval, the entire documentation, including updated information, shall be subject to approval.

[9472]

CHAPTER III

ARRANGEMENTS FOR APPROVAL AND PUBLICATION OF THE PROSPECTUS

Article 13

Approval of the prospectus

1. No prospectus shall be published until it has been approved by the competent authority of the home Member State.

2. This competent authority shall notify the issuer, the offeror or the person asking for admission to trading on a regulated market, as the case may be, of its decision regarding the approval of the prospectus within 10 working days of the submission of the draft prospectus.

If the competent authority fails to give a decision on the prospectus within the time limits laid down in this paragraph and paragraph 3, this shall not be deemed to constitute approval of the application.

3. The time limit referred to in paragraph 2 shall be extended to 20 working days if the public offer involves securities issued by an issuer which does not have any securities admitted to trading on a regulated market and who has not previously offered securities to the public.

4. If the competent authority finds, on reasonable grounds, that the documents submitted to it are incomplete or that supplementary information is needed, the time limits referred to in paragraphs 2 and 3 shall apply only from the date on which such information is provided by the issuer, the offeror or the person asking for admission to trading on a regulated market.

In the case referred to in paragraph 2 the competent authority should notify the issuer if the documents are incomplete within 10 working days of the submission of the application.

5. The competent authority of the home Member State may transfer the approval of a prospectus to the competent authority of another Member State, subject to the agreement of that authority. Furthermore, this transfer shall be notified to the issuer, the offeror or the person asking for admission to trading on a regulated market within three working days from the date of the decision taken by the competent authority of the home Member State. The time limit referred to in paragraph 2 shall apply from that date.

6. This Directive shall not affect the competent authority's liability, which shall continue to be governed solely by national law.

Member States shall ensure that their national provisions on the liability of competent authorities apply only to approvals of prospectuses by their competent authority or authorities.

7. In order to take account of technical developments on financial markets and to ensure uniform application of this Directive, the Commission may, in accordance with the procedure referred to in Article 24(2), adopt implementing measures concerning the conditions in accordance with which time limits may be adjusted.

[9473]

Article 14

Publication of the prospectus

1. Once approved, the prospectus shall be filed with the competent authority of the home Member State and shall be made available to the public by the issuer, offeror or person asking for admission to trading on a regulated market as soon as practicable and in any case, at a reasonable time in advance of, and at the latest at the beginning of, the offer to the public or the admission to trading of the securities involved. In addition, in the case of an initial public offer of a class of shares not already admitted to trading on a regulated market that is to be admitted to trading for the first time, the prospectus shall be available at least six working days before the end of the offer.

2. The prospectus shall be deemed available to the public when published either:

(a) by insertion in one or more newspapers circulated throughout, or widely circulated in, the Member States in which the offer to the public is made or the admission to trading is sought; or

(b) in a printed form to be made available, free of charge, to the public at the offices of the market on which the securities are being admitted to trading, or at the registered office of the issuer and at the offices of the financial intermediaries placing or selling the securities, including paying agents; or

(c) in an electronic form on the issuer's website and, if applicable, on the website of the financial intermediaries placing or selling the securities, including paying agents; or

(d) in an electronic form on the website of the regulated market where the admission to trading is sought; or

(e) in electronic form on the website of the competent authority of the home Member State if the said authority has decided to offer this service.

A home Member State may require issuers which publish their prospectus in accordance with (a) or (b) also to publish their prospectus in an electronic form in accordance with (c).

3. In addition, a home Member State may require publication of a notice stating how the prospectus has been made available and where it can be obtained by the public.

4. The competent authority of the home Member State shall publish on its website over a period of 12 months, at its choice, all the prospectuses approved, or at least the list of prospectuses approved in accordance with Article 13, including, if applicable, a hyperlink to the prospectus published on the website of the issuer, or on the website of the regulated market.

5. In the case of a prospectus comprising several documents and/or incorporating information by reference, the documents and information making up the prospectus may be published and circulated separately provided that the said documents are made available, free of charge, to the public, in accordance with the arrangements established in paragraph 2. Each document shall indicate where the other constituent documents of the full prospectus may be obtained.

6. The text and the format of the prospectus, and/or the supplements to the prospectus, published or made available to the public, shall at all times be identical to the original version approved by the competent authority of the home Member State.

7. Where the prospectus is made available by publication in electronic form, a paper copy must nevertheless be delivered to the investor, upon his request and free of charge, by the issuer, the offeror, the person asking for admission to trading or the financial intermediaries placing or selling the securities.

8. In order to take account of technical developments on financial markets and to ensure uniform application of the Directive, the Commission shall, in accordance with the procedure

referred to in Article 24(2), adopt implementing measures concerning paragraphs 1, 2, 3 and 4. The first set of implementing measures shall be adopted by 1 July 2004.

[9474]

Article 15

Advertisements

1. Any type of advertisements relating either to an offer to the public of securities or to an admission to trading on a regulated market shall observe the principles contained in paragraphs 2 to 5. Paragraphs 2 to 4 shall apply only to cases where the issuer, the offeror or the person applying for admission to trading is covered by the obligation to draw up a prospectus.

2. Advertisements shall state that a prospectus has been or will be published and indicate where investors are or will be able to obtain it.

3. Advertisements shall be clearly recognisable as such. The information contained in an advertisement shall not be inaccurate, or misleading. This information shall also be consistent with the information contained in the prospectus, if already published, or with the information required to be in the prospectus, if the prospectus is published afterwards.

4. In any case, all information concerning the offer to the public or the admission to trading on a regulated market disclosed in an oral or written form, even if not for advertising purposes, shall be consistent with that contained in the prospectus.

5. When according to this Directive no prospectus is required, material information provided by an issuer or an offeror and addressed to qualified investors or special categories of investors, including information disclosed in the context of meetings relating to offers of securities, shall be disclosed to all qualified investors or special categories of investors to whom the offer is exclusively addressed. Where a prospectus is required to be published, such information shall be included in the prospectus or in a supplement to the prospectus in accordance with Article 16(1).

6. The competent authority of the home Member State shall have the power to exercise control over the compliance of advertising activity, relating to a public offer of securities or an admission to trading on a regulated market, with the principles referred to in paragraphs 2 to 5.

7. In order to take account of technical developments on financial markets and to ensure uniform application of this Directive, the Commission shall, in accordance with the procedure referred to in Article 24(2), adopt implementing measures concerning the dissemination of advertisements announcing the intention to offer securities to the public or the admission to trading on a regulated market, in particular before the prospectus has been made available to the public or before the opening of the subscription, and concerning paragraph 4. The first set of implementing measures shall be adopted by the Commission by 1 July 2004.

[9475]

Article 16

Supplements to the prospectus

1. Every significant new factor, material mistake or inaccuracy relating to the information included in the prospectus which is capable of affecting the assessment of the securities and which arises or is noted between the time when the prospectus is approved and the final closing of the offer to the public or, as the case may be, the time when trading on a regulated market begins, shall be mentioned in a supplement to the prospectus. Such a supplement shall be approved in the same way in a maximum of seven working days and published in accordance with at least the same arrangements as were applied when the original prospectus was published. The summary, and any translations thereof, shall also be supplemented, if necessary to take into account the new information included in the supplement.

2. Investors who have already agreed to purchase or subscribe for the securities before the supplement is published shall have the right, exercisable within a time limit which shall not be shorter than two working days after the publication of the supplement, to withdraw their acceptances.

[9476]

CHAPTER IV
CROSS-BORDER OFFERS AND ADMISSION TO TRADING

Article 17

Community scope of approvals of prospectuses

1. Without prejudice to Article 23, where an offer to the public or admission to trading on a regulated market is provided for in one or more Member States, or in a Member State other than the home Member State, the prospectus approved by the home Member State and any supplements thereto shall be valid for the public offer or the admission to trading in any number of host Member States, provided that the competent authority of each host Member State is notified in accordance with Article 18. Competent authorities of host Member States shall not undertake any approval or administrative procedures relating to prospectuses.

2. If there are significant new factors, material mistakes or inaccuracies, as referred to in Article 16, arising since the approval of the prospectus, the competent authority of the home Member State shall require the publication of a supplement to be approved as provided for in Article 13(1). The competent authority of the host Member State may draw the attention of the competent authority of the home Member State to the need for any new information.

[9477]

Article 18

Notification

1. The competent authority of the home Member State shall, at the request of the issuer or the person responsible for drawing up the prospectus and within three working days following that request or, if the request is submitted together with the draft prospectus, within one working day after the approval of the prospectus provide the competent authority of the host Member State with a certificate of approval attesting that the prospectus has been drawn up in accordance with this Directive and with a copy of the said prospectus. If applicable, this notification shall be accompanied by a translation of the summary produced under the responsibility of the issuer or person responsible for drawing up the prospectus. The same procedure shall be followed for any supplement to the prospectus.

2. The application of the provisions of Article 8(2) and (3) shall be stated in the certificate, as well as its justification.

[9478]

CHAPTER V
USE OF LANGUAGES AND ISSUERS INCORPORATED IN THIRD COUNTRIES

Article 19

Use of languages

1. Where an offer to the public is made or admission to trading on a regulated market is sought only in the home Member State, the prospectus shall be drawn up in a language accepted by the competent authority of the home Member State.

2. Where an offer to the public is made or admission to trading on a regulated market is sought in one or more Member States excluding the home Member State, the prospectus shall be drawn up either in a language accepted by the competent authorities of those Member States or in a language customary in the sphere of international finance, at the choice of the issuer, offeror or person asking for admission, as the case may be. The competent authority of each host Member State may only require that the summary be translated into its official language(s).

For the purpose of the scrutiny by the competent authority of the home Member State, the prospectus shall be drawn up either in a language accepted by this authority or in a language customary in the sphere of international finance, at the choice of the issuer, offeror or person asking for admission to trading, as the case may be.

3. Where an offer to the public is made or admission to trading on a regulated market is sought in more than one Member State including the home Member State, the prospectus shall be drawn up in a language accepted by the competent authority of the home Member State and shall also be made available either in a language accepted by the competent

authorities of each host Member State or in a language customary in the sphere of international finance, at the choice of the issuer, offeror, or person asking for admission to trading, as the case may be. The competent authority of each host Member State may only require that the summary referred to in Article 5(2) be translated into its official language(s).

4. Where admission to trading on a regulated market of non-equity securities whose denomination per unit amounts to at least EUR 50,000 is sought in one or more Member States, the prospectus shall be drawn up either in a language accepted by the competent authorities of the home and host Member States or in a language customary in the sphere of international finance, at the choice of the issuer, offeror or person asking for admission to trading, as the case may be. Member States may choose to require in their national legislation that a summary be drawn up in their official language(s).

[9479]

Article 20

Issuers incorporated in third countries

1. The competent authority of the home Member State of issuers having their registered office in a third country may approve a prospectus for an offer to the public or for admission to trading on a regulated market, drawn up in accordance with the legislation of a third country, provided that:

(a) the prospectus has been drawn up in accordance with international standards set by international securities commission organisations, including the IOSCO disclosure standards;

(b) the information requirements, including information of a financial nature, are equivalent to the requirements under this Directive.

2. In the case of an offer to the public or admission to trading on a regulated market of securities, issued by an issuer incorporated in a third country, in a Member State other than the home Member State, the requirements set out in Articles 17, 18 and 19 shall apply.

3. In order to ensure uniform application of this Directive, the Commission may adopt implementing measures in accordance with the procedure referred to in Article 24(2), stating that a third country ensures the equivalence of prospectuses drawn up in that country with this Directive, by reason of its national law or of practices or procedures based on international standards set by international organisations, including the IOSCO disclosure standards.

[9480]

CHAPTER VI
COMPETENT AUTHORITIES

Article 21

Powers

1. Each Member State shall designate a central competent administrative authority responsible for carrying out the obligations provided for in this Directive and for ensuring that the provisions adopted pursuant to this Directive are applied.

However, a Member State may, if so required by national law, designate other administrative authorities to apply Chapter III.

These competent authorities shall be completely independent from all market participants.

If an offer of securities is made to the public or admission to trading on a regulated market is sought in a Member State other than the home Member State, only the central competent administrative authority designated by each Member State shall be entitled to approve the prospectus.

2. Member States may allow their competent authority or authorities to delegate tasks. Except for delegation of the publication on the Internet of approved prospectuses and the filing of prospectuses as mentioned in Article 14, any delegation of tasks relating to the obligations provided for in this Directive and in its implementing measures shall be reviewed, in accordance with Article 31 by 31 December 2008, and shall end on 31 December 2011. Any delegation of tasks to entities other than the authorities referred to in paragraph 1 shall be made in a specific manner stating the tasks to be undertaken and the conditions under which they are to be carried out.

These conditions shall include a clause obliging the entity in question to act and be organised in such a manner as to avoid conflict of interest and so that information obtained from carrying out the delegated tasks is not used unfairly or to prevent competition. In any case, the final responsibility for supervising compliance with this Directive and with its implementing measures and for approving the prospectus shall lie with the competent authority or authorities designated in accordance with paragraph 1.

Member States shall inform the Commission and the competent authorities of other Member States of any arrangements entered into with regard to delegation of tasks, including the precise conditions regulating such delegation.

3. Each competent authority shall have all the powers necessary for the performance of its functions. A competent authority that has received an application for approving a prospectus shall be empowered at least to:

(a) require issuers, offerors or persons asking for admission to trading on a regulated market to include in the prospectus supplementary information, if necessary for investor protection;

(b) require issuers, offerors or persons asking for admission to trading on a regulated market, and the persons that control them or are controlled by them, to provide information and documents;

(c) require auditors and managers of the issuer, offeror or person asking for admission to trading on a regulated market, as well as financial intermediaries commissioned to carry out the offer to the public or ask for admission to trading, to provide information;

(d) suspend a public offer or admission to trading for a maximum of 10 consecutive working days on any single occasion if it has reasonable grounds for suspecting that the provisions of this Directive have been infringed;

(e) prohibit or suspend advertisements for a maximum of 10 consecutive working days on any single occasion if it has reasonable grounds for believing that the provisions of this Directive have been infringed;

(f) prohibit a public offer if it finds that the provisions of this Directive have been infringed or if it has reasonable grounds for suspecting that they would be infringed;

(g) suspend or ask the relevant regulated markets to suspend trading on a regulated market for a maximum of 10 consecutive working days on any single occasion if it has reasonable grounds for believing that the provisions of this Directive have been infringed;

(h) prohibit trading on a regulated market if it finds that the provisions of this Directive have been infringed;

(i) make public the fact that an issuer is failing to comply with its obligations.

Where necessary under national law, the competent authority may ask the relevant judicial authority to decide on the use of the powers referred to in points (d) to (h) above.

4. Each competent authority shall also, once the securities have been admitted to trading on a regulated market, be empowered to:

(a) require the issuer to disclose all material information which may have an effect on the assessment of the securities admitted to trading on regulated markets in order to ensure investor protection or the smooth operation of the market;

(b) suspend or ask the relevant regulated market to suspend the securities from trading if, in its opinion, the issuer's situation is such that trading would be detrimental to investors' interests;

(c) ensure that issuers whose securities are traded on regulated markets comply with the obligations provided for in Articles 102 and 103 of Directive 2001/34/EC and that equivalent information is provided to investors and equivalent treatment is granted by the issuer to all securities holders who are in the same position, in all Member States where the offer to the public is made or the securities are admitted to trading;

(d) carry out on-site inspections in its territory in accordance with national law, in order to verify compliance with the provisions of this Directive and its implementing measures. Where necessary under national law, the competent authority or authorities may use this power by applying to the relevant judicial authority and/or in cooperation with other authorities.

5. Paragraphs 1 to 4 shall be without prejudice to the possibility for a Member State to make separate legal and administrative arrangements for overseas European territories for whose external relations that Member State is responsible.

[9481]

Article 22

Professional secrecy and cooperation between authorities

1. The obligation of professional secrecy shall apply to all persons who work or have worked for the competent authority and for entities to which competent authorities may have delegated certain tasks. Information covered by professional secrecy may not be disclosed to any other person or authority except in accordance with provisions laid down by law.

2. Competent authorities of Member States shall cooperate with each other whenever necessary for the purpose of carrying out their duties and making use of their powers. Competent authorities shall render assistance to competent authorities of other Member States. In particular, they shall exchange information and cooperate when an issuer has more than one home competent authority because of its various classes of securities, or where the approval of a prospectus has been transferred to the competent authority of another Member State pursuant to Article 13(5). They shall also closely cooperate when requiring suspension or prohibition of trading for securities traded in various Member States in order to ensure a level playing field between trading venues and protection of investors. Where appropriate, the competent authority of the host Member State may request the assistance of the competent authority of the home Member State from the stage at which the case is scrutinised, in particular as regards a new type or rare forms of securities. The competent authority of the home Member State may ask for information from the competent authority of the host Member State on any items specific to the relevant market.

Without prejudice to Article 21, the competent authorities of Member States may consult with operators of regulated markets as necessary and, in particular, when deciding to suspend, or to ask a regulated market to suspend or prohibit trading.

3. Paragraph 1 shall not prevent the competent authorities from exchanging confidential information. Information thus exchanged shall be covered by the obligation of professional secrecy, to which the persons employed or formerly employed by the competent authorities receiving the information are subject.

[9482]

Article 23

Precautionary measures

1. Where the competent authority of the host Member State finds that irregularities have been committed by the issuer or by the financial institutions in charge of the public offer or that breaches have been committed of the obligations attaching to the issuer by reason of the fact that the securities are admitted to trading on a regulated market, it shall refer these findings to the competent authority of the home Member State.

2. If, despite the measures taken by the competent authority of the home Member State or because such measures prove inadequate, the issuer or the financial institution in charge of the public offer persists in breaching the relevant legal or regulatory provisions, the competent authority of the host Member State, after informing the competent authority of the home Member State, shall take all the appropriate measures in order to protect investors. The Commission shall be informed of such measures at the earliest opportunity.

[9483]

CHAPTER VII
IMPLEMENTING MEASURES

Article 24

Committee procedure

1. The Commission shall be assisted by the European Securities Committee, instituted by Decision 2001/528/EC (hereinafter referred to as 'the Committee').

2. Where reference is made to this paragraph, Articles 5 and 7 of Decision 1999/468/EC shall apply, having regard to the provisions of Article 8 thereof and provided that the implementing measures adopted in accordance with this procedure do not modify the essential provisions of this Directive.

The period laid down in Article 5(6) of Decision 1999/468/EC shall be set at three months.

3. The Committee shall adopt its rules of procedure.

4. Without prejudice to the implementing measures already adopted, on the expiry of a four-year period following the entry into force of this Directive the application of its provisions providing for the adoption of technical rules and decisions in accordance with the procedure referred to in paragraph 2 shall be suspended. On a proposal from the Commission, the European Parliament and the Council may renew the provisions concerned in accordance with the procedure laid down in Article 251 of the Treaty and, to that end, shall review them prior to the expiry of the four-year period.

[9484]

Article 25

Sanctions

1. Without prejudice to the right of Member States to impose criminal sanctions and without prejudice to their civil liability regime, Member States shall ensure, in conformity with their national law, that the appropriate administrative measures can be taken or administrative sanctions be imposed against the persons responsible, where the provisions adopted in the implementation of this Directive have not been complied with. Member States shall ensure that these measures are effective, proportionate and dissuasive.

2. Member States shall provide that the competent authority may disclose to the public every measure or sanction that has been imposed for infringement of the provisions adopted pursuant to this Directive, unless the disclosure would seriously jeopardise the financial markets or cause disproportionate damage to the parties involved.

[9485]

Article 26

Right of appeal

Member States shall ensure that decisions taken pursuant to laws, regulations and administrative provisions adopted in accordance with this Directive are subject to the right to appeal to the courts.

[9486]

CHAPTER VIII
TRANSITIONAL AND FINAL PROVISIONS

Article 27

Amendments

With effect from the date set out in Article 29, Directive 2001/34/EC is hereby amended as follows:

1. Articles 3, 20 to 41, 98 to 101, 104 and 108(2)(c)(ii) shall be deleted;
2. in Article 107(3), the first subparagraph shall be deleted;
3. in Article 108(2)(a), the words 'the conditions of establishment, the control and circulation of listing particulars to be published for admission' shall be deleted;
4. Annex I shall be deleted.

[9487]

Article 28

Repeal

With effect from the date indicated in Article 29, Directive 89/298/EEC shall be repealed. References to the repealed Directive shall be construed as references to this Directive.

[9488]

Article 29

Transposition

Member States shall bring into force the laws, regulations and administrative provisions necessary to comply with this Directive not later than 1 July 2005. They shall forthwith inform the Commission thereof. When Member States adopt those measures they shall contain a reference to this Directive or shall be accompanied by such a reference on the occasion of their official publication. The methods for making such reference shall be laid down by Member States.

[9489]

Article 30

Transitional provision

1. Issuers which are incorporated in a third country and whose securities have already been admitted to trading on a regulated market shall choose their competent authority in accordance with Article 2(1)(m)(iii) and notify their decision to the competent authority of their chosen home Member State by 31 December 2005.

2. By way of derogation from Article 3, Member States which have used the exemption in Article 5(a) of Directive 89/298/EEC may continue to allow credit institutions or other financial institutions equivalent to credit institutions which are not covered by Article 1(2)(j) of this Directive to offer debt securities or other transferable securities equivalent to debt securities issued in a continuous or repeated manner within their territory for five years following the date of entry into force of this Directive.

3. By way of derogation from Article 29, the Federal Republic of Germany shall comply with Article 21(1) by 31 December 2008.

[9490]

Article 31

Review

Five years after the date of entry into force of this Directive, the Commission shall make an assessment of the application of this Directive and present a report to the European Parliament and the Council, accompanied where appropriate by proposals for its review.

[9491]

Article 32

Entry into force

This Directive shall enter into force on the day of its publication in the *Official Journal of the European Union*.

[9492]

Article 33

Addressees

This Directive is addressed to the Member States.

[9493]

Done at Brussels, 4 November 2003.

ANNEX I
PROSPECTUS

I. SUMMARY

The summary shall provide in a few pages the most important information included in the prospectus, covering at least the following items:

A. identity of directors, senior management, advisers and auditors
B. offer statistics and expected timetable
C. key information concerning selected financial data; capitalisation and indebtedness; reasons for the offer and use of proceeds; risk factors
D. information concerning the issuer
- — history and development of the issuer
- — business overview

E. operating and financial review and prospects
- — research and development, patents and licences, etc

— trends

F. directors, senior management and employees

G. major shareholders and related-party transactions

H. financial information
- — consolidated statement and other financial information
- — significant changes

I. details of the offer and admission to trading
- — offer and admission to trading
- — plan for distribution
- — markets
- — selling shareholders
- — dilution (equity securities only)
- — expenses of the issue

J. additional information
- — share capital
- — memorandum and articles of association
- — documents on display

II. IDENTITY OF DIRECTORS, SENIOR MANAGEMENT, ADVISERS AND AUDITORS

The purpose is to identify the company representatives and other individuals involved in the company's offer or admission to trading; these are the persons responsible for drawing up the prospectus as required by Article 5 of the Directive and those responsible for auditing the financial statements.

III. OFFER STATISTICS AND EXPECTED TIMETABLE

The purpose is to provide key information regarding the conduct of any offer and the identification of important dates relating to that offer.

A. Offer statistics

B. Method and expected timetable

IV. KEY INFORMATION

The purpose is to summarise key information about the company's financial condition, capitalisation and risk factors. If the financial statements included in the document are restated to reflect material changes in the company's group structure or accounting policies, the selected financial data must also be restated.

A. Selected financial data

B. Capitalisation and indebtedness

C. Reasons for the offer and use of proceeds

D. Risk factors

V. INFORMATION ON THE COMPANY

The purpose is to provide information about the company's business operations, the products it makes or the services it provides, and the factors which affect the business. It is also intended to provide information regarding the adequacy and suitability of the company's properties, plant and equipment, as well as its plans for future capacity increases or decreases.

A. History and development of the company

B. Business overview

C. Organisational structure

D. Property, plant and equipment

VI. OPERATING AND FINANCIAL REVIEW AND PROSPECTS

The purpose is to provide the management's explanation of factors that have affected the company's financial condition and results of operations for the historical periods covered by the financial statements, and management's assessment of factors and trends which are expected to have a material effect on the company's financial condition and results of operations in future periods.

A. Operating results

B. Liquidity and capital resources

C. Research and development, patents and licences, etc

D. Trends

VII. DIRECTORS, SENIOR MANAGEMENT AND EMPLOYEES

The purpose is to provide information concerning the company's directors and managers that will allow investors to assess their experience, qualifications and levels of remuneration, as well as their relationship with the company.

A. Directors and senior management
B. Remuneration
C. Board practices
D. Employees
E. Share ownership

VIII. MAJOR SHAREHOLDERS AND RELATED-PARTY TRANSACTIONS

The purpose is to provide information regarding the major shareholders and others that may control or have an influence on the company. It also provides information regarding transactions the company has entered into with persons affiliated with the company and whether the terms of such transactions are fair to the company.

A. Major shareholders
B. Related-party transactions
C. Interests of experts and advisers

IX. FINANCIAL INFORMATION

The purpose is to specify which financial statements must be included in the document, as well as the periods to be covered, the age of the financial statements and other information of a financial nature. The accounting and auditing principles that will be accepted for use in preparation and audit of the financial statements will be determined in accordance with international accounting and auditing standards.

A. Consolidated statements and other financial information
B. Significant changes

X. DETAILS OF THE OFFER AND ADMISSION TO TRADING DETAILS

The purpose is to provide information regarding the offer and the admission to trading of securities, the plan for distribution of the securities and related matters.

A. Offer and admission to trading
B. Plan for distribution
C. Markets
D. Holders of securities who are selling
E. Dilution (for equity securities only)
F. Expenses of the issue

XI. ADDITIONAL INFORMATION

The purpose is to provide information, most of which is of a statutory nature, that is not covered elsewhere in the prospectus.

A. Share capital
B. Memorandum and articles of association
C. Material contracts
D. Exchange controls
E. Taxation
F. Dividends and paying agents
G. Statement by experts
H. Documents on display
I. Subsidiary information

[9494]

ANNEX II
REGISTRATION DOCUMENT

I. IDENTITY OF DIRECTORS, SENIOR MANAGEMENT, ADVISERS AND AUDITORS

The purpose is to identify the company representatives and other individuals involved in the company's offer or admission to trading; these are the persons responsible for drawing up the prospectus and those responsible for auditing the financial statements.

II. KEY INFORMATION ABOUT THE ISSUER

The purpose is to summarise key information about the company's financial condition, capitalisation and risk factors. If the financial statements included in the document are restated to reflect material changes in the company's group structure or accounting policies, the selected financial data must also be restated.

A. Selected financial data
B. Capitalisation and indebtedness
C. Risk factors

III. INFORMATION ON THE COMPANY

The purpose is to provide information about the company's business operations, the products it makes or the services it provides and the factors which affect the business. It is also intended to provide information regarding the adequacy and suitability of the company's properties, plants and equipment, as well as its plans for future capacity increases or decreases.

A. History and development of the company
B. Business overview
C. Organisational structure
D. Property, plants and equipment

IV. OPERATING AND FINANCIAL REVIEW AND PROSPECTS

The purpose is to provide the management's explanation of factors that have affected the company's financial condition and results of operations for the historical periods covered by the financial statements, and management's assessment of factors and trends which are expected to have a material effect on the company's financial condition and results of operations in future periods.

A. Operating results
B. Liquidity and capital resources
C. Research and development, patents and licences, etc
D. Trends

V. DIRECTORS, SENIOR MANAGEMENT AND EMPLOYEES

The purpose is to provide information concerning the company's directors and managers that will allow investors to assess their experience, qualifications and levels of remuneration, as well as their relationship with the company.

A. Directors and senior management
B. Remuneration
C. Board practices
D. Employees
E. Share ownership

VI. MAJOR SHAREHOLDERS AND RELATED-PARTY TRANSACTIONS

The purpose is to provide information regarding the major shareholders and others that may control or have an influence on the company. It also provides information regarding transactions the company has entered into with persons affiliated with the company and whether the terms of such transactions are fair to the company.

A. Major shareholders
B. Related-party transactions
C. Interests of experts and advisers

VII. FINANCIAL INFORMATION

The purpose is to specify which financial statements must be included in the document, as well as the periods to be covered, the age of the financial statements and other information of a financial nature. The accounting and auditing principles that will be accepted for use in preparation and audit of the financial statements will be determined in accordance with international accounting and auditing standards.

A. Consolidated statements and other financial information
B. Significant changes

VIII. ADDITIONAL INFORMATION

The purpose is to provide information, most of which is of a statutory nature, that is not covered elsewhere in the prospectus.

A. Share capital
B. Memorandum and articles of association
C. Material contracts
D. Statement by experts
E. Documents on display
F. Subsidiary information

[9495]

ANNEX III
SECURITIES NOTE

I. IDENTITY OF DIRECTORS, SENIOR MANAGEMENT, ADVISERS AND AUDITORS

The purpose is to identify the company representatives and other individuals involved in the company's offer or admission to trading; these are the persons responsible for drawing up the prospectus and those responsible for auditing the financial statements.

II. OFFER STATISTICS AND EXPECTED TIMETABLE

The purpose is to provide key information regarding the conduct of any offer and the identification of important dates relating to that offer.
A. Offer statistics
B. Method and expected timetable

III. KEY INFORMATION ABOUT THE ISSUER

The purpose is to summarise key information about the company's financial condition, capitalisation and risk factors. If the financial statements included in the document are restated to reflect material changes in the company's group structure or accounting policies, the selected financial data must also be restated.
A. Capitalisation and indebtedness
B. Reasons for the offer and use of proceeds
C. Risk factors

IV. INTERESTS OF EXPERTS

The purpose is to provide information regarding transactions the company has entered into with experts or advisers employed on a contingent basis.

V. DETAILS OF THE OFFER AND ADMISSION TO TRADING

The purpose is to provide information regarding the offer and the admission to trading of securities, the plan for distribution of the securities and related matters.
A. Offer and admission to trading
B. Plan for distribution
C. Markets
D. Selling securities holders
E. Dilution (for equity securities only)
F. Expenses of the issue

VI. ADDITIONAL INFORMATION

The purpose is to provide information, most of which is of a statutory nature, that is not covered elsewhere in the prospectus.
A. Exchange controls
B. Taxation
C. Dividends and paying agents
D. Statement by experts
E. Documents on display

[9496]

ANNEX IV
SUMMARY NOTE

The summary note shall provide in a few pages the most important information included in the prospectus, covering at least the following items:
— identity of directors, senior management, advisers and auditors

- offer statistics and expected timetable
- key information concerning selected financial data; capitalisation and indebtedness; reasons for the offer and use of proceeds; risk factors
- information concerning the issuer
  - history and development of the issuer
  - business overview
- operating and financial review and prospects
  - research and development, patents and licences, etc
  - trends
- directors, senior management and employees
- major shareholders and related-party transactions
- financial information
  - consolidated statement and other financial information
  - significant changes
- details on the offer and admission to trading
  - offer and admission to trading
  - plan for distribution
  - markets
  - selling shareholders
  - dilution (for equity securities only)
  - expenses of the issue
- additional information
  - share capital
  - memorandum and articles of incorporation
  - documents available for inspection

[9497]

COMMISSION DIRECTIVE

of 22 December 2003

implementing Directive 2003/6/EC of the European Parliament and of the Council as regards the definition and public disclosure of inside information and the definition of market manipulation

(2003/124/EC)

(Text with EEA relevance)

NOTES

Date of publication in OJ: OJ L339, 24.12.2003, p 70. Notes are as in the original OJ version.

THE COMMISSION OF THE EUROPEAN COMMUNITIES,

Having regard to the Treaty establishing the European Community,

Having regard to Directive 2003/6/EC of the European Parliament and of the Council of 28 January 2003 on insider dealing and market manipulation (market abuse),[1] and in particular the second paragraph of Article 1 and the first, second and third indents of Article 6(10) thereof,

After consulting the Committee of European Securities Regulators (CESR)[2] for technical advice,

Whereas:

(1) Reasonable investors base their investment decisions on information already available to them, that is to say, on *ex ante* available information. Therefore, the question whether, in making an investment decision, a reasonable investor would be likely to take into account a particular piece of information should be appraised on the basis of the *ex ante* available information. Such an assessment has to take into consideration the anticipated impact of the information in light of the totality of the related issuer's activity, the reliability of the source of information and any other market variables likely to affect the related financial instrument or derivative financial instrument related thereto in the given circumstances.

(2) *Ex post* information may be used to check the presumption that the *ex ante* information was price sensitive, but should not be used to take action against someone who drew reasonable conclusions from *ex ante* information available to him.

(3) Legal certainty for market participants should be enhanced through a closer definition of two of the elements essential to the definition of inside information, namely the precise nature of that information and the significance of its potential effect on the prices of financial instruments or related derivative financial instruments.

(4) Not only does the protection of investors require timely public disclosure of inside information by issuers, it also requires such disclosure to be as fast and as synchronised as possible between all categories of investors in all Member States in which the issuer has requested or approved admission of its financial instruments to trading on a regulated market, in order to guarantee at Community level equal access of investors to such information and to prevent insider dealing. To this end Member States may officially appoint mechanisms to be used for such disclosure.

(5) In order to protect the legitimate interests of issuers, it should be permissible, in closely defined specific circumstances, to delay public disclosure of inside information. However, the protection of investors requires that in such cases the information be kept confidential in order to prevent insider dealing.

(6) In order to guide both market participants and competent authorities, signals have to be taken into account when examining possibly manipulative behaviours.

(7) The measures provided for in this Directive are in accordance with the opinion of the European Securities Committee,

[9498]

NOTES

1 OJ L96, 12.4.2003, p 16.
2 CESR was established by Commission Decision 2001/527/EC (OJ L191,13.7.2001, p 43).

HAS ADOPTED THIS DIRECTIVE:

Article 1

Inside information

1. For the purposes of applying point 1 of Article 1 of Directive 2003/6/EC, information shall be deemed to be of a precise nature if it indicates a set of circumstances which exists or may reasonably be expected to come into existence or an event which has occurred or may reasonably be expected to do so and if it is specific enough to enable a conclusion to be drawn as to the possible effect of that set of circumstances or event on the prices of financial instruments or related derivative financial instruments.

2. For the purposes of applying point 1 of Article 1 of Directive 2003/6/EC, 'information which, if it were made public, would be likely to have a significant effect on the prices of financial instruments or related derivative financial instruments' shall mean information a reasonable investor would be likely to use as part of the basis of his investment decisions.

[9499]

Article 2

Means and time-limits for public disclosure of inside information

1. For the purposes of applying Article 6(1) of Directive 2003/6/EC, Articles 102(1) and Article 103 of Directive 2001/34/EC of the European Parliament and of the Council[1] shall apply.

Furthermore, Member States shall ensure that the inside information is made public by the issuer in a manner which enables fast access and complete, correct and timely assessment of the information by the public.

In addition, Member States shall ensure that the issuer does not combine, in a manner likely to be misleading, the provision of inside information to the public with the marketing of its activities.

2. Member States shall ensure that issuers are deemed to have complied with the first subparagraph of Article 6(1) of Directive 2003/6/EC where, upon the coming into existence of a set of circumstances or the occurrence of an event, albeit not yet formalised, the issuers have promptly informed the public thereof.

3. Any significant changes concerning already publicly disclosed inside information shall be publicly disclosed promptly after these changes occur, through the same channel as the one used for public disclosure of the original information.

4. Member States shall require issuers to take reasonable care to ensure that the disclosure of inside information to the public is synchronised as closely as possible between all categories of investors in all Member States in which those issuers have requested or approved the admission to trading of their financial instruments on a regulated market.

[9500]

NOTES

[1] OJ L184, 6.7.2001, p 1.

Article 3

Legitimate interests for delaying public disclosure and confidentiality

1. For the purposes of applying Article 6(2) of Directive 2003/6/EC, legitimate interests may, in particular, relate to the following non-exhaustive circumstances:

(a) negotiations in course, or related elements, where the outcome or normal pattern of those negotiations would be likely to be affected by public disclosure. In particular, in the event that the financial viability of the issuer is in grave and imminent danger, although not within the scope of the applicable insolvency law, public disclosure of information may be delayed for a limited period where such a public disclosure would seriously jeopardise the interest of existing and potential shareholders by undermining the conclusion of specific negotiations designed to ensure the long-term financial recovery of the issuer;

(b) decisions taken or contracts made by the management body of an issuer which need the approval of another body of the issuer in order to become effective, where the organisation of such an issuer requires the separation between these bodies, provided that a public disclosure of the information before such approval together with the simultaneous announcement that this approval is still pending would jeopardise the correct assessment of the information by the public.

2. For the purposes of applying Article 6(2) of Directive 2003/6/EC, Member States shall require that, in order to be able to ensure the confidentiality of inside information, an issuer controls access to such information and, in particular, that:

(a) the issuer has established effective arrangements to deny access to such information to persons other than those who require it for the exercise of their functions within the issuer;

(b) the issuer has taken the necessary measures to ensure that any person with access to such information acknowledges the legal and regulatory duties entailed and is aware of the sanctions attaching to the misuse or improper circulation of such information;

(c) the issuer has in place measures which allow immediate public disclosure in case the issuer was not able to ensure the confidentiality of the relevant inside information, without prejudice to the second subparagraph of Article 6(3) of Directive 2003/6/EC.

[9501]

Article 4

Manipulative behaviour related to false or misleading signals and to price securing

For the purposes of applying point 2(a) of Article 1 of Directive 2003/6/EC, and without prejudice to the examples set out in the second paragraph of point 2 thereof, Member States shall ensure that the following non-exhaustive signals, which should not necessarily be deemed in themselves to constitute market manipulation, are taken into account when transactions or orders to trade are examined by market participants and competent authorities:

(a) the extent to which orders to trade given or transactions undertaken represent a significant proportion of the daily volume of transactions in the relevant financial instrument on the regulated market concerned, in particular when these activities lead to a significant change in the price of the financial instrument;

(b) the extent to which orders to trade given or transactions undertaken by persons with a significant buying or selling position in a financial instrument lead to significant changes in the price of the financial instrument or related derivative or underlying asset admitted to trading on a regulated market;

(c) whether transactions undertaken lead to no change in beneficial ownership of a financial instrument admitted to trading on a regulated market;

(d) the extent to which orders to trade given or transactions undertaken include position reversals in a short period and represent a significant proportion of the daily volume of transactions in the relevant financial instrument on the regulated market concerned, and might be associated with significant changes in the price of a financial instrument admitted to trading on a regulated market;

(e) the extent to which orders to trade given or transactions undertaken are concentrated within a short time span in the trading session and lead to a price change which is subsequently reversed;

(f) the extent to which orders to trade given change the representation of the best bid or offer prices in a financial instrument admitted to trading on a regulated market, or more generally the representation of the order book available to market participants, and are removed before they are executed;

(g) the extent to which orders to trade are given or transactions are undertaken at or around a specific time when reference prices, settlement prices and valuations are calculated and lead to price changes which have an effect on such prices and valuations.

[9502]

Article 5

Manipulative behaviours related to the employment of fictitious devices or any other form of deception or contrivance

For the purposes of applying point 2(b) of Article 1 of Directive 2003/6/EC, and without prejudice to the examples set out in the second paragraph of point 2 thereof, Member States shall ensure that the following non-exhaustive signals, which should not necessarily be deemed in themselves to constitute market manipulation, are taken into account when transactions or orders to trade are examined by market participants and competent authorities:

(a) whether orders to trade given or transactions undertaken by persons are preceded or followed by dissemination of false or misleading information by the same persons or persons linked to them;

(b) whether orders to trade are given or transactions are undertaken by persons before or after the same persons or persons linked to them produce or disseminate research or investment recommendations which are erroneous or biased or demonstrably influenced by material interest.

[9503]

Article 6

Transposition

1. Member States shall bring into force the laws, regulations and administrative provisions necessary to comply with this Directive by 12 October 2004 at the latest. They shall forthwith communicate to the Commission the text of the provisions and a correlation table between those provisions and this Directive.

When Member States adopt those provisions, they shall contain a reference to this Directive or be accompanied by such a reference on the occasion of their official publication. Member States shall determine how such reference is to be made.

2. Member States shall communicate to the Commission the text of the main provisions of national law which they adopt in the field covered by this Directive.

[9504]

Article 7

Entry into force

This Directive shall enter into force on the day of its publication in the *Official Journal of the European Union.*

[9505]

Article 8

Addressees

This Directive is addressed to the Member States.

[9506]

Done at Brussels, 22 December 2003.

COMMISSION DIRECTIVE

of 22 December 2003

implementing Directive 2003/6/EC of the European Parliament and of the Council as regards the fair presentation of investment recommendations and the disclosure of conflicts of interest

(2003/125/EC)

(Text with EEA relevance)

NOTES

Date of publication in OJ: OJ L339, 24.12.2003, p 73. Notes are as in the original OJ version.

THE COMMISSION OF THE EUROPEAN COMMUNITIES,

Having regard to the Treaty establishing the European Community,

Having regard to Directive 2003/6/EC of the European Parliament and of the Council of 28 January 2003 on insider dealing and market manipulation (market abuse),[1] and in particular the sixth indent of Article 6(10) thereof,

After consulting the Committee of European Securities Regulators (CESR)[2] for technical advice,

Whereas:

(1) Harmonised standards are necessary for the fair, clear and accurate presentation of information and disclosure of interests and conflicts of interest, to be complied with by persons producing or disseminating information recommending or suggesting an investment strategy, intended for distribution channels or for the public. In particular, market integrity requires high standards of fairness, probity and transparency when information recommending or suggesting an investment strategy is presented.

(2) Recommending or suggesting an investment strategy is either done explicitly (such as 'buy', 'hold' or 'sell' recommendations) or implicitly (by reference to a price target or otherwise).

(3) Investment advice, through the provision of a personal recommendation to a client in respect of one or more transactions relating to financial instruments (in particular informal short-term investment recommendations originating from inside the sales or trading departments of an investment firm or a credit institution expressed to their clients), which are not likely to become publicly available, should not be considered in themselves as recommendations within the meaning of this Directive.

(4) Investment recommendations that constitute a possible basis for investment decisions should be produced and disseminated in accordance with high standards of care in order to avoid misleading market participants.

(5) The identity of the producer of investment recommendations, his conduct of business rules and the identity of his competent authority should be disclosed, since it may be a valuable piece of information for investors to consider in relation to their investment decisions.

(6) Recommendations should be presented clearly and accurately.

(7) Own interests or conflicts of interest of persons recommending or suggesting investment strategy may influence the opinion that they express in investment recommendations. In order to ensure that the objectivity and reliability of the information can be evaluated, appropriate disclosure should be made of significant financial interests in any financial instrument which is the subject of the information recommending investment strategies, or of any conflicts of interest or control relationship with respect to the issuer to whom the information relates, directly or indirectly. However, this Directive should not require relevant persons producing investment recommendations to breach effective information barriers put in place in order to prevent and avoid conflicts of interest.

(8) Investment recommendations may be disseminated in unaltered, altered or summarised form by a person other than the producer. The way in which disseminators handle such recommendations may have an important impact on the evaluation of those recommendations by investors. In particular, the knowledge of the identity of the disseminator

of investment recommendations, his conduct of business rules or the extent of alteration of the original recommendation can be a valuable piece of information for investors when considering their investment decisions.

(9) Posting of investment recommendations on internet sites should be in accordance with the rules on transfer of personal data to third countries as laid down in Directive 95/46/EC of the European Parliament and of the Council of 24 October 1995 on the protection of individuals with regard to the processing of personal data and on the movement of such data.[3]

(10) Credit rating agencies issue opinions on the creditworthiness of a particular issuer or financial instrument as of a given date. As such, these opinions do not constitute a recommendation within the meaning of this Directive. However, credit rating agencies should consider adopting internal policies and procedures designed to ensure that credit ratings published by them are fairly presented and that they appropriately disclose any significant interests or conflicts of interest concerning the financial instruments or the issuers to which their credit ratings relate.

(11) This Directive respects the fundamental rights and observes the principles recognised in particular by the Charter of Fundamental Rights of the European Union and in particular by Article 11 thereof and Article 10 of the European Convention on Human Rights. In this regard, this Directive does not in any way prevent Member States from applying their constitutional rules relating to freedom of the press and freedom of expression in the media.

(12) The measures provided for in this Directive are in accordance with the opinion of the European Securities Committee,

[9507]

NOTES

1 OJ L96, 12.4.2003, p 16.
2 CESR was established by Commission Decision 2001/527/EC (OJ L191,13.7.2001, p 43).
3 OJ L281, 23.11.1995, p 31.

HAS ADOPTED THIS DIRECTIVE:

CHAPTER I
DEFINITIONS

Article 1

Definitions

For the purposes of this Directive, the following definitions shall apply in addition to those laid down in Directive 2003/6/EC:

1. 'investment firm' means any person as defined in Article 1(2) of Council Directive 93/22/EEC;[1]
2. 'credit institution' means any person as defined in Article 1(1) of Directive 2000/12/EC of the European Parliament and of the Council;[2]
3. 'recommendation' means research or other information recommending or suggesting an investment strategy, explicitly or implicitly, concerning one or several financial instruments or the issuers of financial instruments, including any opinion as to the present or future value or price of such instruments, intended for distribution channels or for the public;
4. 'research or other information recommending or suggesting investment strategy' means:
   (a) information produced by an independent analyst, an investment firm, a credit institution, any other person whose main business is to produce recommendations or a natural person working for them under a contract of employment or otherwise, that, directly or indirectly, expresses a particular investment recommendation in respect of a financial instrument or an issuer of financial instruments;
   (b) information produced by persons other than the persons referred to in (a) which directly recommends a particular investment decision in respect of a financial instrument;
5. 'relevant person' means a natural or legal person producing or disseminating recommendations in the exercise of his profession or the conduct of his business;
6. 'issuer' means the issuer of a financial instrument to which a recommendation relates, directly or indirectly;

7. 'distribution channels' shall mean a channel through which information is, or is likely to become, publicly available. 'Likely to become publicly available information' shall mean information to which a large number of persons have access;
8. 'appropriate regulation' shall mean any regulation, including self-regulation, in place in Member States as referred to by Directive 2003/6/EC.

[9508]

NOTES

[1] OJ L141, 11.6.1993, p 27.
[2] OJ L126, 26.5.2000, p 1.

CHAPTER II
PRODUCTION OF RECOMMENDATIONS

Article 2

Identity of producers of recommendations

1. Member States shall ensure that there is appropriate regulation in place to ensure that any recommendation discloses clearly and prominently the identity of the person responsible for its production, in particular, the name and job title of the individual who prepared the recommendation and the name of the legal person responsible for its production.

2. Where the relevant person is an investment firm or a credit institution, Member States shall require that the identity of the relevant competent authority be disclosed.

Where the relevant person is neither an investment firm nor a credit institution, but is subject to self-regulatory standards or codes of conduct, Member States shall ensure that a reference to those standards or codes is disclosed.

3. Member States shall ensure that there is appropriate regulation in place to ensure that the requirements laid down in paragraphs 1 and 2 are adapted in order not to be disproportionate in the case of non-written recommendations. Such adaptation may include a reference to the place where such disclosures can be directly and easily accessed by the public, such as an appropriate internet site of the relevant person.

4. Paragraphs 1 and 2 shall not apply to journalists subject to equivalent appropriate regulation, including equivalent appropriate self regulation, in the Member States, provided that such regulation achieves similar effects as those of paragraphs 1 and 2.

[9509]

Article 3

General standard for fair presentation of recommendations

1. Member States shall ensure that there is appropriate regulation in place to ensure that all relevant persons take reasonable care to ensure that:
   - (a) facts are clearly distinguished from interpretations, estimates, opinions and other types of non-factual information;
   - (b) all sources are reliable or, where there is any doubt as to whether a source is reliable, this is clearly indicated;
   - (c) all projections, forecasts and price targets are clearly labelled as such and that the material assumptions made in producing or using them are indicated.

2. Member States shall ensure that there is appropriate regulation in place to ensure that the requirements laid down in paragraph 1 are adapted in order not to be disproportionate in the case of non-written recommendations.

3. Member States shall require that all relevant persons take reasonable care to ensure that any recommendation can be substantiated as reasonable, upon request by the competent authorities.

4. Paragraphs 1 and 3 shall not apply to journalists subject to equivalent appropriate regulation in the Member States, including equivalent appropriate self regulation, provided that such regulation achieves similar effects as those of paragraphs 1 and 3.

[9510]

Article 4
Additional obligations in relation to fair presentation of recommendations

1. In addition to the obligations laid down in Article 3, where the relevant person is an independent analyst, an investment firm, a credit institution, any related legal person, any other relevant person whose main business is to produce recommendations, or a natural person working for them under a contract of employment or otherwise, Member States shall ensure that there is appropriate regulation in place to ensure that person to take reasonable care to ensure that at least:

(a) all substantially material sources are indicated, as appropriate, including the relevant issuer, together with the fact whether the recommendation has been disclosed to that issuer and amended following this disclosure before its dissemination;

(b) any basis of valuation or methodology used to evaluate a financial instrument or an issuer of a financial instrument, or to set a price target for a financial instrument, is adequately summarised;

(c) the meaning of any recommendation made, such as buy, sell or hold, which may include the time horizon of the investment to which the recommendation relates, is adequately explained and any appropriate risk warning, including a sensitivity analysis of the relevant assumptions, indicated;

(d) reference is made to the planned frequency, if any, of updates of the recommendation and to any major changes in the coverage policy previously announced;

(e) the date at which the recommendation was first released for distribution is indicated clearly and prominently, as well as the relevant date and time for any financial instrument price mentioned;

(f) where a recommendation differs from a recommendation concerning the same financial instrument or issuer, issued during the 12-month period immediately preceding its release, this change and the date of the earlier recommendation are indicated clearly and prominently.

2. Member States shall ensure that, where the requirements laid down in points (a), (b) or (c) of paragraph 1 would be disproportionate in relation to the length of the recommendation distributed, it shall suffice to make clear and prominent reference in the recommendation itself to the place where the required information can be directly and easily accessed by the public, such as a direct Internet link to that information on an appropriate internet site of the relevant person, provided that there has been no change in the methodology or basis of valuation used.

3. Member States shall ensure that there is appropriate regulation in place to ensure that, in the case of non-written recommendations, the requirements of paragraph 1 are adapted so that they are not disproportionate.

[9511]

Article 5
General standard for disclosure of interests and conflicts of interest

1. Member States shall ensure that there is appropriate regulation in place to ensure that relevant persons disclose all relationships and circumstances that may reasonably be expected to impair the objectivity of the recommendation, in particular where relevant persons have a significant financial interest in one or more of the financial instruments which are the subject of the recommendation, or a significant conflict of interest with respect to an issuer to which the recommendation relates.

Where the relevant person is a legal person, that requirement shall apply also to any legal or natural person working for it, under a contract of employment or otherwise, who was involved in preparing the recommendation.

2. Where the relevant person is a legal person, the information to be disclosed in accordance with paragraph 1 shall at least include the following:

(a) any interests or conflicts of interest of the relevant person or of related legal persons that are accessible or reasonably expected to be accessible to the persons involved in the preparation of the recommendation;

(b) any interests or conflicts of interest of the relevant person or of related legal persons known to persons who, although not involved in the preparation of the recommendation, had or could reasonably be expected to have access to the recommendation prior to its dissemination to customers or the public.

3. Member States shall ensure that there is appropriate regulation in place to ensure that the recommendation itself shall include the disclosures provided for in paragraphs 1 and 2. Where such disclosures would be disproportionate in relation to the length of the recommendation distributed, it shall suffice to make clear and prominent reference in the recommendation itself to the place where such disclosures can be directly and easily accessed by the public, such as a direct Internet link to the disclosure on an appropriate internet site of the relevant person.

4. Member States shall ensure that there is appropriate regulation in place to ensure that the requirements laid down in paragraph 1 are adapted in order not to be disproportionate in the case of non-written recommendations.

5. Paragraphs 1 to 3 shall not apply to journalists subject to equivalent appropriate regulation, including equivalent appropriate self regulation, in the Member States, provided that such regulation achieves similar effects as those of paragraphs 1 to 3.

[9512]

Article 6

Additional obligations in relation to disclosure of interests or conflicts of interest

1. In addition to the obligations laid down in Article 5, Member States shall require that any recommendation produced by an independent analyst, an investment firm, a credit institution, any related legal person, or any other relevant person whose main business is to produce recommendations, discloses clearly and prominently the following information on their interests and conflicts of interest:

(a) major shareholdings that exist between the relevant person or any related legal person on the one hand and the issuer on the other hand. These major shareholdings include at least the following instances:

— when shareholdings exceeding 5% of the total issued share capital in the issuer are held by the relevant person or any related legal person, or

— when shareholdings exceeding 5% of the total issued share capital of the relevant person or any related legal person are held by the issuer.

Member States may provide for lower thresholds than the 5% threshold as provided for in these two instances;

(b) other significant financial interests held by the relevant person or any related legal person in relation to the issuer;

(c) where applicable, a statement that the relevant person or any related legal person is a market maker or liquidity provider in the financial instruments of the issuer;

(d) where applicable, a statement that the relevant person or any related legal person has been lead manager or co-lead manager over the previous 12 months of any publicly disclosed offer of financial instruments of the issuer;

(e) where applicable, a statement that the relevant person or any related legal person is party to any other agreement with the issuer relating to the provision of investment banking services, provided that this would not entail the disclosure of any confidential commercial information and that the agreement has been in effect over the previous 12 months or has given rise during the same period to the payment of a compensation or to the promise to get a compensation paid;

(f) where applicable, a statement that the relevant person or any related legal person is party to an agreement with the issuer relating to the production of the recommendation.

2. Member States shall require disclosure, in general terms, of the effective organisational and administrative arrangements set up within the investment firm or the credit institution for the prevention and avoidance of conflicts of interest with respect to recommendations, including information barriers.

3. Member States shall require that for natural or legal persons working for an investment firm or a credit institution, under a contract of employment or otherwise, and who were involved in preparing the recommendation, the requirement under the second subparagraph of paragraph 1 of Article 5 shall include, in particular, disclosure of whether the remuneration of such persons is tied to investment banking transactions performed by the investment firm or credit institution or any related legal person.

Where those natural persons receive or purchase the shares of the issuers prior to a public offering of such shares, the price at which the shares were acquired and the date of acquisition shall also be disclosed.

4. Member States shall require that investment firms and credit institutions disclose, on a quarterly basis, the proportion of all recommendations that are 'buy', 'hold', 'sell' or equivalent terms, as well as the proportion of issuers corresponding to each of these categories to which the investment firm or the credit institution has supplied material investment banking services over the previous 12 months.

5. Member States shall ensure that the recommendation itself includes the disclosures required by paragraphs 1 to 4. Where the requirements under paragraphs 1 to 4 would be disproportionate in relation to the length of the recommendation distributed, it shall suffice to make clear and prominent reference in the recommendation itself to the place where such disclosure can be directly and easily accessed by the public, such as a direct Internet link to the disclosure on an appropriate internet site of the investment firm or credit institution.

6. Member States shall ensure that there is appropriate regulation in place to ensure that, in the case of non-written recommendations, the requirements of paragraph 1 are adapted so that they are not disproportionate.

[9513]

CHAPTER III
DISSEMINATION OF RECOMMENDATIONS PRODUCED BY THIRD PARTIES

Article 7

Identity of disseminators of recommendations

Member States shall ensure that there is appropriate regulation in place to ensure that, whenever a relevant person under his own responsibility disseminates a recommendation produced by a third party, the recommendation indicates clearly and prominently the identity of that relevant person.

[9514]

Article 8

General standard for dissemination of recommendations

Member States shall ensure that there is appropriate regulation in place to ensure that whenever a recommendation produced by a third party is substantially altered within disseminated information, that information clearly indicates the substantial alteration in detail. Member States shall ensure that whenever the substantial alteration consists of a change of the direction of the recommendation (such as changing a 'buy' recommendation into a 'hold' or 'sell' recommendation or vice versa), the requirements laid down in Articles 2 to 5 on producers are met by the disseminator, to the extent of the substantial alteration.

In addition, Member States shall ensure that there is appropriate regulation in place to ensure that relevant legal persons who themselves, or through natural persons, disseminate a substantially altered recommendation have a formal written policy so that the persons receiving the information may be directed to where they can have access to the identity of the producer of the recommendation, the recommendation itself and the disclosure of the producer's interests or conflicts of interest, provided that these elements are publicly available.

The first and second paragraphs do not apply to news reporting on recommendations produced by a third party where the substance of the recommendation is not altered.

In case of dissemination of a summary of a recommendation produced by a third party, the relevant persons disseminating such summary shall ensure that the summary is clear and not misleading, mentioning the source document and where the disclosures related to the source document can be directly and easily accessed by the public provided that they are publicly available.

[9515]

Article 9

Additional obligations for investment firms and credit institutions

In addition to the obligations laid down in Articles 7 and 8, whenever the relevant person is an investment firm, a credit institution or a natural person working for such persons under a contract of employment or otherwise, and disseminates recommendations produced by a third party, Member States shall require that:

(a) the name of the competent authority of the investment firm or credit institution is clearly and prominently indicated;

(b) if the producer of the recommendation has not already disseminated it through a distribution channel, the requirements laid down in Article 6 on producers are met by the disseminator;

(c) if the investment firm or credit institution has substantially altered the recommendation, the requirements laid down in Articles 2 to 6 on producers are met.

[9516]

CHAPTER IV
FINAL PROVISIONS

Article 10

Transposition

1. Member States shall bring into force the laws, regulations and administrative provisions necessary to comply with this Directive by 12 October 2004 at the latest. They shall forthwith communicate to the Commission the text of those provisions and a correlation table between these provisions and this Directive.

When Member States adopt those provisions, they shall contain a reference to this Directive or be accompanied by such a reference on the occasion of their official publication. Member States shall determine how such reference is to be made.

2. Member States shall communicate to the Commission the text of the main provisions of national law which they adopt in the field covered by this Directive.

[9517]

Article 11

Entry into force

This Directive shall enter into force on the day of its publication in the *Official Journal of the European Union*.

[9518]

Article 12

Addressees

This Directive is addressed to the Member States.

[9519]

Done at Brussels, 22 December 2003.

COMMISSION REGULATION

of 22 December 2003

implementing Directive 2003/6/EC of the European Parliament and of the Council as regards exemptions for buy-back programmes and stabilisation of financial instruments

(2273/2003/EC)

(Text with EEA relevance)

NOTES

Date of publication in OJ: OJ L336, 23.12.2003, p 33. Notes are as in the original OJ version.

THE COMMISSION OF THE EUROPEAN COMMUNITIES,

Having regard to the Treaty establishing the European Community,

Having regard to Directive 2003/6/EC of the European Parliament and the Council of 28 January 2003 on insider dealing and market manipulation (market abuse),[1] and in particular Article 8 thereof,

After consulting the Committee of European Securities Regulators (CESR)[2] for technical advice,

Whereas:

(1) Article 8 of Directive 2003/6/EC provides that the prohibitions provided therein shall not apply to trading in own shares in 'buy back' programmes or to the stabilisation of a financial instrument, provided such trading is carried out in accordance with implementing measures adopted to that effect.

(2) Activities of trading in own shares in 'buy-back' programmes and of stabilisation of a financial instrument which would not benefit from the exemption of the prohibitions of Directive 2003/6/EC as provided for by Article 8 thereof, should not in themselves be deemed to constitute market abuse.

(3) On the other hand, the exemptions created by this Regulation only cover behaviour directly related to the purpose of the buy-back and stabilisation activities. Behaviour which is not directly related to the purpose of the buy-back and stabilisation activities shall therefore be considered as any other action covered by Directive 2003/6/EC and may be the object of administrative measures or sanctions, if the competent authority establishes that the action in question constitutes market abuse.

(4) As regards trading in own shares in 'buy-back' programmes, the rules provided for by this Regulation are without prejudice to the application of Council Directive 77/91/EEC on coordination of safeguards which, for the protection of the interests of members and others, are required by Member States of companies within the meaning of the second paragraph of Article 58 of the Treaty, in respect of the formation of public limited liability companies and the maintenance and alteration of their capital, with a view to making such safeguards equivalent.[3]

(5) Allowable 'buy back' activities in order to benefit from the exemption of the prohibitions of Directive 2003/6/EC include issuers needing the possibility to reduce their capital, to meet obligations arising from debt financial instruments exchangeable into equity instruments, and to meet obligations arising from allocations of shares to employees.

(6) Transparency is a prerequisite for prevention of market abuse. To this end Member States may officially appoint mechanisms to be used for public disclosure of information required to be publicly disclosed under this Regulation.

(7) Issuers having adopted 'buy-back' programmes shall inform their competent authority and, wherever required, the public.

(8) Trading in own shares in 'buy-back' programmes may be carried out through derivative financial instruments.

(9) In order to prevent market abuse, the daily volume of trading in own shares in 'buy-back' programmes shall be limited. However, some flexibility is necessary in order to respond to given market conditions such as a low level of transactions.

(10) Particular attention has to be paid to the selling of own shares during the life of a 'buy-back' programme, to the possible existence of closed periods within issuers during which transactions are prohibited and to the fact that an issuer may have legitimate reasons to delay public disclosure of inside information.

(11) Stabilisation transactions mainly have the effect of providing support for the price of an offering of relevant securities during a limited time period if they come under selling pressure, thus alleviating sales pressure generated by short term investors and maintaining an orderly market in the relevant securities. This is in the interest of those investors having subscribed or purchased those relevant securities in the context of a significant distribution, and of issuers. In this way, stabilisation can contribute to greater confidence of investors and issuers in the financial markets.

(12) Stabilisation activity may be carried out either on or off a regulated market and may be carried out by use of financial instruments other than those admitted or to be admitted to the regulated market which may influence the price of the instrument admitted or to be admitted to trading on a regulated market.

(13) Relevant securities shall include financial instruments that become fungible after an initial period because they are substantially the same, although they have different initial dividend or interest payment rights.

(14) In relation to stabilisation, block trades shall not be considered as a significant distribution of relevant securities as they are strictly private transactions.

(15) When Member States permit, in the context of an initial public offer, trading prior to the beginning of the official trading on a regulated market, the permission covers 'when issued trading'.

(16) Market integrity requires the adequate public disclosure of stabilisation activity by issuers or by entities undertaking stabilisation, acting or not on behalf of these issuers. Methods used for adequate public disclosure of such information should be efficient and can take into account market practices accepted by competent authorities.

(17) There should be adequate coordination in place between all investment firms and credit institutions undertaking stabilisation. During stabilisation, one investment firm or credit institution shall act as a central point of inquiry for any regulatory intervention by the competent authority in each Member State concerned.

(18) In order to avoid confusion of market participants, stabilisation activity should be carried out by taking into account the market conditions and the offering price of the relevant security and transactions to liquidate positions established as a result of stabilisation activity should be undertaken to minimise market impact having due regard to prevailing market conditions.

(19) Overallotment facilities and 'greenshoe options' are closely related to stabilisation, by providing resources and hedging for stabilisation activity.

(20) Particular attention should be paid to the exercise of an overallotment facility by an investment firm or a credit institution for the purpose of stabilisation when it results in a position uncovered by the 'greenshoe option'.

(21) The measures provided for in this Regulation are in accordance with the opinion of the European Securities Committee,

[9520]

NOTES

1 OJ L96, 12.4.2003, p 16.
2 CESR was established by Commission Decision 2001/527/EC (OJ L191,13.7.2001, p 43).
3 OJ L26, 31.1.1977, p 1.

HAS ADOPTED THIS REGULATION:

CHAPTER I
DEFINITIONS

Article 1

Subject matter

This Regulation lays down the conditions to be met by buyback programmes and the stabilisation of financial instruments in order to benefit from the exemption provided for in Article 8 of Directive 2003/6/EC.

[9521]

Article 2

Definitions

For the purposes of this Regulation, the following definitions shall apply in addition to those laid down in Directive 2003/6/EC:

1. 'investment firm' means any legal person as defined in point (2) of Article 1 of Council Directive 93/22/EEC;[1]
2. 'credit institution' means a legal person as defined in Article 1(1) of Directive 2000/12/EC of the European Parliament and the Council;[2]
3. 'buy-back programmes' means trading in own shares in accordance with Articles 19 to 24 of Council Directive 77/91/EEC;
4. 'time-scheduled "buy-back" programme' means a 'buy-back' programme where the dates and quantities of securities to be traded during the time period of the programme are set out at the time of the public disclosure of the 'buy-back' programme;
5. 'adequate public disclosure' means disclosure made in accordance with the procedure laid down in Articles 102(1) and 103 of Directive 2001/34/EC of the European Parliament and of the Council;[3]
6. 'relevant securities' means transferable securities as defined in Directive 93/22/EEC, which are admitted to trading on a regulated market or for which a request for admission to trading on such a market has been made, and which are the subject of a significant distribution;

7. 'stabilisation' means any purchase or offer to purchase relevant securities, or any transaction in associated instruments equivalent thereto, by investment firms or credit institutions, which is undertaken in the context of a significant distribution of such relevant securities exclusively for supporting the market price of these relevant securities for a predetermined period of time, due to a selling pressure in such securities;
8. 'associated instruments' means the following financial instruments (including those which are not admitted to trading on a regulated market, or for which a request for admission to trading on such a market has not been made, provided that the relevant competent authorities have agreed to standards of transparency for transactions in such financial instruments):
   (a) contracts or rights to subscribe for, acquire or dispose of relevant securities;
   (b) financial derivatives on relevant securities;
   (c) where the relevant securities are convertible or exchangeable debt instruments, the securities into which such convertible or exchangeable debt instruments may be converted or exchanged;
   (d) instruments which are issued or guaranteed by the issuer or guarantor of the relevant securities and whose market price is likely to materially influence the price of the relevant securities, or vice versa;
   (e) where the relevant securities are securities equivalent to shares, the shares represented by those securities (and any other securities equivalent to those shares).
9. 'significant distribution' means an initial or secondary offer of relevant securities, publicly announced and distinct from ordinary trading both in terms of the amount in value of the securities offered and the selling methods employed;
10. 'offeror' means the prior holders of, or the entity issuing, the relevant securities;
11. 'allotment' means the process or processes by which the number of relevant securities to be received by investors who have previously subscribed or applied for them is determined;
12. 'ancillary stabilisation' means the exercise of an overallotment facility or of a greenshoe option by investment firms or credit institutions, in the context of a significant distribution of relevant securities, exclusively for facilitating stabilisation activity;
13. 'overallotment facility' means a clause in the underwriting agreement or lead management agreement which permits acceptance of subscriptions or offers to purchase a greater number of relevant securities than originally offered;
14. 'greenshoe option' means an option granted by the offeror in favour of the investment firm(s) or credit institution(s) involved in the offer for the purpose of covering overallotments, under the terms of which such firm(s) or institution(s) may purchase up to a certain amount of relevant securities at the offer price for a certain period of time after the offer of the relevant securities.

[9522]

NOTES

[1] OJ L141, 11.6.1993, p 27.
[2] OJ L126, 26.5.2000, p 1.
[3] OJ L184, 6.7.2001, p 1.

CHAPTER II
'BUY-BACK' PROGRAMMES

Article 3

Objectives of buy-back programmes

In order to benefit from the exemption provided for in Article 8 of Directive 2003/6/EC, a buy-back programme must comply with Articles 4, 5 and 6 of this Regulation and the sole purpose of that buy-back programme must be to reduce the capital of an issuer (in value or in number of shares) or to meet obligations arising from any of the following:

(a) debt financial instruments exchangeable into equity instruments;
(b) employee share option programmes or other allocations of shares to employees of the issuer or of an associate company.

[9523]

Article 4

Conditions for 'buy-back' programmes and disclosure

1. The 'buy-back' programme must comply with the conditions laid down by Article 19(1) of Directive 77/91/EEC.

2. Prior to the start of trading, full details of the programme approved in accordance with Article 19(1) of Directive 77/91/EEC must be adequately disclosed to the public in Member States in which an issuer has requested admission of its shares to trading on a regulated market.

Those details must include the objective of the programme as referred to in Article 3, the maximum consideration, the maximum number of shares to be acquired and the duration of the period for which authorisation for the programme has been given.

Subsequent changes to the programme must be subject to adequate public disclosure in Member States.

3. The issuer must have in place the mechanisms ensuring that it fulfils trade reporting obligations to the competent authority of the regulated market on which the shares have been admitted to trading. These mechanisms must record each transaction related to 'buy-back' programmes, including the information specified in Article 20(1) of Directive 93/22/EEC.

4. The issuer must publicly disclose details of all transactions as referred to in paragraph 3 no later than the end of the seventh daily market session following the date of execution of such transactions.

[9524]

Article 5

Conditions for trading

1. In so far as prices are concerned, the issuer must not, when executing trades under a 'buy-back' programme, purchase shares at a price higher than the higher of the price of the last independent trade and the highest current independent bid on the trading venues where the purchase is carried out.

If the trading venue is not a regulated market, the price of the last independent trade or the highest current independent bid taken in reference shall be the one of the regulated market of the Member State in which the purchase is carried out.

Where the issuer carries out the purchase of own shares through derivative financial instruments, the exercise price of those derivative financial instruments shall not be above the higher of the price of the last independent trade and the highest current independent bid.

2. In so far as volume is concerned, the issuer must not purchase more than 25% of the average daily volume of the shares in any one day on the regulated market on which the purchase is carried out.

The average daily volume figure must be based on the average daily volume traded in the month preceding the month of public disclosure of that programme and fixed on that basis for the authorised period of the programme.

Where the programme makes no reference to that volume, the average daily volume figure must be based on the average daily volume traded in the 20 trading days preceding the date of purchase.

3. For the purposes of paragraph 2, in cases of extreme low liquidity on the relevant market, the issuer may exceed the 25% limit, provided that the following conditions are met:

(a) the issuer informs the competent authority of the relevant market, in advance, of its intention to deviate from the 25% limit;

(b) the issuer discloses adequately to the public the fact that it may deviate from the 25% limit;

(c) the issuer does not exceed 50% of the average daily volume.

[9525]

Article 6

Restrictions

1. In order to benefit from the exemption provided by Article 8 of Directive 2003/6/EC, the issuer shall not, during its participation in a buy-back programme, engage in the following trading:

(a) selling of own shares during the life of the programme;
(b) trading during a period which, under the law of the Member State in which trading takes place, is a closed period;
(c) trading where the issuer has decided to delay the public disclosure of inside information in accordance with Article 6(2) of Directive 2003/6/EC.

2. Paragraph 1(a) shall not apply if the issuer is an investment firm or credit institution and has established effective information barriers (Chinese Walls) subject to supervision by the competent authority, between those responsible for the handling of inside information related directly or indirectly to the issuer and those responsible for any decision relating to the trading of own shares (including the trading of own shares on behalf of clients), when trading in own shares on the basis of such any decision.

Paragraphs 1(b) and (c) shall not apply if the issuer is an investment firm or credit institution and has established effective information barriers (Chinese Walls) subject to supervision by the competent authority, between those responsible for the handling of inside information related directly or indirectly to the issuer (including trading decisions under the 'buy-back' programme) and those responsible for the trading of own shares on behalf of clients, when trading in own shares on behalf of those clients.

3. Paragraph 1 shall not apply if:
(a) the issuer has in place a time-scheduled 'buy-back' programme; or
(b) the 'buy-back' programme is lead-managed by an investment firm or a credit institution which makes its trading decisions in relation to the issuer's shares independently of, and without influence by, the issuer with regard to the timing of the purchases.

[9526]

CHAPTER III
STABILISATION OF A FINANCIAL INSTRUMENT

Article 7

Conditions for stabilisation

In order to benefit from the exemption provided for in Article 8 of Directive 2003/6/EC, stabilisation of a financial instrument must be carried out in accordance with Articles 8, 9 and 10 of this Regulation.

[9527]

Article 8

Time-related conditions for stabilisation

1. Stabilisation shall be carried out only for a limited time period.

2. In respect of shares and other securities equivalent to shares, the time period referred to in paragraph 1 shall, in the case of an initial offer publicly announced, start on the date of commencement of trading of the relevant securities on the regulated market and end no later than 30 calendar days thereafter.

Where the initial offer publicly announced takes place in a Member State that permits trading prior to the commencement of trading on a regulated market, the time period referred to in paragraph 1 shall start on the date of adequate public disclosure of the final price of the relevant securities and end no later than 30 calendar days thereafter, provided that any such trading is carried out in compliance with the rules, if any, of the regulated market on which the relevant securities are to be admitted to trading, including any rules concerning public disclosure and trade reporting.

3. In respect of shares and other securities equivalent to shares, the time period referred to in paragraph 1 shall, in the case of a secondary offer, start on the date of adequate public disclosure of the final price of the relevant securities and end no later than 30 calendar days after the date of allotment.

4. In respect of bonds and other forms of securitised debt (which are not convertible or exchangeable into shares or into other securities equivalent to shares), the time period referred to in paragraph 1 shall start on the date of adequate public disclosure of the terms of the offer of the relevant securities(ie including the spread to the benchmark, if any, once it has been

fixed) and end, whatever is earlier, either no later than 30 calendar days after the date on which the issuer of the instruments received the proceeds of the issue, or no later than 60 calendar days after the date of allotment of the relevant securities.

5. In respect of securitised debt convertible or exchangeable into shares or into other securities equivalent to shares, the time period referred to in paragraph 1 shall start on the date of adequate public disclosure of the final terms of the offer of the relevant securities and end, whatever is earlier, either no later than 30 calendar days after the date on which the issuer of the instruments received the proceeds of the issue, or no later than 60 calendar days after the date of allotment of the relevant securities.

[9528]

Article 9

Disclosure and reporting conditions for stabilisation

1. The following information shall be adequately publicly disclosed by issuers, offerors, or entities undertaking the stabilisation acting, or not, on behalf of such persons, before the opening of the offer period of the relevant securities:

(a) the fact that stabilisation may be undertaken, that there is no assurance that it will be undertaken and that it may be stopped at any time;
(b) the fact that stabilisation transactions are aimed to support the market price of the relevant securities;
(c) the beginning and end of the period during which stabilisation may occur;
(d) the identity of the stabilisation manager, unless this is not known at the time of publication in which case it must be publicly disclosed before any stabilisation activity begins;
(e) the existence and maximum size of any overallotment facility or greenshoe option, the exercise period of the greenshoe option and any conditions for the use of the overallotment facility or exercise of the greenshoe option.

The application of the provisions of this paragraph shall be suspended for offers under the scope of application of the measures implementing Directive 2004/…/EC (prospectus Directive), from the date of application of these measures.

2. Without prejudice to Article 12(1)(c) of Directive 2003/6/EC, the details of all stabilisation transactions must be notified by issuers, offerors, or entities undertaking the stabilisation acting, or not, on behalf of such persons, to the competent authority of the relevant market no later than the end of the seventh daily market session following the date of execution of such transactions.

3. Within one week of the end of the stabilisation period, the following information must be adequately disclosed to the public by issuers, offerors, or entities undertaking the stabilisation acting, or not, on behalf of such persons:

(a) whether or not stabilisation was undertaken;
(b) the date at which stabilisation started;
(c) the date at which stabilisation last occurred;
(d) the price range within which stabilisation was carried out, for each of the dates during which stabilisation transactions were carried out.

4. Issuers, offerors, or entities undertaking the stabilisation, acting or not, on behalf of such persons, must record each stabilisation order or transaction with, as a minimum, the information specified in Article 20(1) of Directive 93/22/EEC extended to financial instruments other than those admitted or going to be admitted to the regulated market.

5. Where several investment firms or credit institutions undertake the stabilisation acting, or not, on behalf of the issuer or offeror, one of those persons shall act as central point of inquiry for any request from the competent authority of the regulated market on which the relevant securities have been admitted to trading.

[9529]

Article 10

Specific price conditions

1. In the case of an offer of shares or other securities equivalent to shares, stabilisation of the relevant securities shall not in any circumstances be executed above the offering price.

2. In the case of an offer of securitised debt convertible or exchangeable into instruments as referred to in paragraph 1, stabilisation of those instruments shall not in any circumstances be executed above the market price of those instruments at the time of the public disclosure of the final terms of the new offer.

[9530]

Article 11

Conditions for ancillary stabilisation

In order to benefit from the exemption provided for in Article 8 of Directive 2003/6/EC, ancillary stabilisation must be undertaken in accordance with Article 9 of this Regulation and with the following:

(a) relevant securities may be overallotted only during the subscription period and at the offer price;

(b) a position resulting from the exercise of an overallotment facility by an investment firm or credit institution which is not covered by the greenshoe option may not exceed 5% of the original offer;

(c) the greenshoe option may be exercised by the beneficiaries of such an option only where relevant securities have been overallotted;

(d) the greenshoe option may not amount to more than 15% of the original offer;

(e) the exercise period of the greenshoe option must be the same as the stabilisation period required under Article 8;

(f) the exercise of the greenshoe option must be disclosed to the public promptly, together with all appropriate details, including in particular the date of exercise and the number and nature of relevant securities involved.

[9531]

CHAPTER IV
FINAL PROVISION

Article 12

Entry into force

This Regulation shall enter into force in Member States on the day of its publication in the *Official Journal of the European Union*.

This Regulation shall be binding in its entirety and directly applicable in all Member States.

[9532]

Done at Brussels, 22 December 2003.

COUNCIL REGULATION

of 20 January 2004

on the control of concentrations between undertakings (the EC Merger Regulation)

(139/2004/EC)

NOTES

Date of publication in OJ: OJ L24, 29.1.2004, p 1. Notes are as in the original OJ version.

THE COUNCIL OF THE EUROPEAN UNION,

Having regard to the Treaty establishing the European Community, and in particular Articles 83 and 308 thereof,

Having regard to the proposal from the Commission,[1]

Having regard to the opinion of the European Parliament,[2]

Having regard to the opinion of the European Economic and Social Committee,[3]

Whereas:

(1) Council Regulation (EEC) No 4064/89 of 21 December 1989 on the control of concentrations between undertakings[4] has been substantially amended. Since further amendments are to be made, it should be recast in the interest of clarity.

(2) For the achievement of the aims of the Treaty, Article 3(1)(g) gives the Community the objective of instituting a system ensuring that competition in the internal market is not distorted. Article 4(1) of the Treaty provides that the activities of the Member States and the Community are to be conducted in accordance with the principle of an open market economy with free competition. These principles are essential for the further development of the internal market.

(3) The completion of the internal market and of economic and monetary union, the enlargement of the European Union and the lowering of international barriers to trade and investment will continue to result in major corporate reorganisations, particularly in the form of concentrations.

(4) Such reorganisations are to be welcomed to the extent that they are in line with the requirements of dynamic competition and capable of increasing the competitiveness of European industry, improving the conditions of growth and raising the standard of living in the Community.

(5) However, it should be ensured that the process of reorganisation does not result in lasting damage to competition; Community law must therefore include provisions governing those concentrations which may significantly impede effective competition in the common market or in a substantial part of it.

(6) A specific legal instrument is therefore necessary to permit effective control of all concentrations in terms of their effect on the structure of competition in the Community and to be the only instrument applicable to such concentrations. Regulation (EEC) No 4064/89 has allowed a Community policy to develop in this field. In the light of experience, however, that Regulation should now be recast into legislation designed to meet the challenges of a more integrated market and the future enlargement of the European Union. In accordance with the principles of subsidiarity and of proportionality as set out in Article 5 of the Treaty, this Regulation does not go beyond what is necessary in order to achieve the objective of ensuring that competition in the common market is not distorted, in accordance with the principle of an open market economy with free competition.

(7) Articles 81 and 82, while applicable, according to the case-law of the Court of Justice, to certain concentrations, are not sufficient to control all operations which may prove to be incompatible with the system of undistorted competition envisaged in the Treaty. This Regulation should therefore be based not only on Article 83 but, principally, on Article 308 of the Treaty, under which the Community may give itself the additional powers of action necessary for the attainment of its objectives, and also powers of action with regard to concentrations on the markets for agricultural products listed in Annex I to the Treaty.

(8) The provisions to be adopted in this Regulation should apply to significant structural changes, the impact of which on the market goes beyond the national borders of any one Member State. Such concentrations should, as a general rule, be reviewed exclusively at Community level, in application of a 'one-stop shop' system and in compliance with the principle of subsidiarity. Concentrations not covered by this Regulation come, in principle, within the jurisdiction of the Member States.

(9) The scope of application of this Regulation should be defined according to the geographical area of activity of the undertakings concerned and be limited by quantitative thresholds in order to cover those concentrations which have a Community dimension. The Commission should report to the Council on the implementation of the applicable thresholds and criteria so that the Council, acting in accordance with Article 202 of the Treaty, is in a position to review them regularly, as well as the rules regarding pre-notification referral, in the light of the experience gained; this requires statistical data to be provided by the Member States to the Commission to enable it to prepare such reports and possible proposals for amendments. The Commission's reports and proposals should be based on relevant information regularly provided by the Member States.

(10) A concentration with a Community dimension should be deemed to exist where the aggregate turnover of the undertakings concerned exceeds given thresholds; that is the case irrespective of whether or not the undertakings effecting the concentration have their seat or their principal fields of activity in the Community, provided they have substantial operations there.

(11) The rules governing the referral of concentrations from the Commission to Member States and from Member States to the Commission should operate as an effective corrective mechanism in the light of the principle of subsidiarity; these rules protect the competition interests of the Member States in an adequate manner and take due account of legal certainty and the 'one-stop shop' principle.

(12) Concentrations may qualify for examination under a number of national merger control systems if they fall below the turnover thresholds referred to in this Regulation. Multiple notification of the same transaction increases legal uncertainty, effort and cost for undertakings and may lead to conflicting assessments. The system whereby concentrations may be referred to the Commission by the Member States concerned should therefore be further developed.

(13) The Commission should act in close and constant liaison with the competent authorities of the Member States from which it obtains comments and information.

(14) The Commission and the competent authorities of the Member States should together form a network of public authorities, applying their respective competences in close cooperation, using efficient arrangements for information-sharing and consultation, with a view to ensuring that a case is dealt with by the most appropriate authority, in the light of the principle of subsidiarity and with a view to ensuring that multiple notifications of a given concentration are avoided to the greatest extent possible. Referrals of concentrations from the Commission to Member States and from Member States to the Commission should be made in an efficient manner avoiding, to the greatest extent possible, situations where a concentration is subject to a referral both before and after its notification.

(15) The Commission should be able to refer to a Member State notified concentrations with a Community dimension which threaten significantly to affect competition in a market within that Member State presenting all the characteristics of a distinct market. Where the concentration affects competition on such a market, which does not constitute a substantial part of the common market, the Commission should be obliged, upon request, to refer the whole or part of the case to the Member State concerned. A Member State should be able to refer to the Commission a concentration which does not have a Community dimension but which affects trade between Member States and threatens to significantly affect competition within its territory. Other Member States which are also competent to review the concentration should be able to join the request. In such a situation, in order to ensure the efficiency and predictability of the system, national time limits should be suspended until a decision has been reached as to the referral of the case. The Commission should have the power to examine and deal with a concentration on behalf of a requesting Member State or requesting Member States.

(16) The undertakings concerned should be granted the possibility of requesting referrals to or from the Commission before a concentration is notified so as to further improve the efficiency of the system for the control of concentrations within the Community. In such situations, the Commission and national competition authorities should decide within short, clearly defined time limits whether a referral to or from the Commission ought to be made, thereby ensuring the efficiency of the system. Upon request by the undertakings concerned, the Commission should be able to refer to a Member State a concentration with a Community dimension which may significantly affect competition in a market within that Member State presenting all the characteristics of a distinct market; the undertakings concerned should not, however, be required to demonstrate that the effects of the concentration would be detrimental to competition. A concentration should not be referred from the Commission to a Member State which has expressed its disagreement to such a referral. Before notification to national authorities, the undertakings concerned should also be able to request that a concentration without a Community dimension which is capable of being reviewed under the national competition laws of at least three Member States be referred to the Commission. Such requests for pre-notification referrals to the Commission would be particularly pertinent in situations where the concentration would affect competition beyond the territory of one Member State. Where a concentration capable of being reviewed under the competition laws of three or more Member States is referred to the Commission prior to any national notification, and no Member State competent to review the case expresses its disagreement, the Commission should acquire exclusive competence to review the concentration and such a concentration should be deemed to have a Community dimension. Such pre-notification referrals from Member States to the Commission should not, however, be made where at least one Member State competent to review the case has expressed its disagreement with such a referral.

(17) The Commission should be given exclusive competence to apply this Regulation, subject to review by the Court of Justice.

(18) The Member States should not be permitted to apply their national legislation on competition to concentrations with a Community dimension, unless this Regulation makes provision therefor. The relevant powers of national authorities should be limited to cases where, failing intervention by the Commission, effective competition is likely to be significantly impeded within the territory of a Member State and where the competition interests of that Member State cannot be sufficiently protected otherwise by this Regulation.

The Member States concerned must act promptly in such cases; this Regulation cannot, because of the diversity of national law, fix a single time limit for the adoption of final decisions under national law.

(19) Furthermore, the exclusive application of this Regulation to concentrations with a Community dimension is without prejudice to Article 296 of the Treaty, and does not prevent the Member States from taking appropriate measures to protect legitimate interests other than those pursued by this Regulation, provided that such measures are compatible with the general principles and other provisions of Community law.

(20) It is expedient to define the concept of concentration in such a manner as to cover operations bringing about a lasting change in the control of the undertakings concerned and therefore in the structure of the market. It is therefore appropriate to include, within the scope of this Regulation, all joint ventures performing on a lasting basis all the functions of an autonomous economic entity. It is moreover appropriate to treat as a single concentration transactions that are closely connected in that they are linked by condition or take the form of a series of transactions in securities taking place within a reasonably short period of time.

(21) This Regulation should also apply where the undertakings concerned accept restrictions directly related to, and necessary for, the implementation of the concentration. Commission decisions declaring concentrations compatible with the common market in application of this Regulation should automatically cover such restrictions, without the Commission having to assess such restrictions in individual cases. At the request of the undertakings concerned, however, the Commission should, in cases presenting novel or unresolved questions giving rise to genuine uncertainty, expressly assess whether or not any restriction is directly related to, and necessary for, the implementation of the concentration. A case presents a novel or unresolved question giving rise to genuine uncertainty if the question is not covered by the relevant Commission notice in force or a published Commission decision.

(22) The arrangements to be introduced for the control of concentrations should, without prejudice to Article 86(2) of the Treaty, respect the principle of non-discrimination between the public and the private sectors. In the public sector, calculation of the turnover of an undertaking concerned in a concentration needs, therefore, to take account of undertakings making up an economic unit with an independent power of decision, irrespective of the way in which their capital is held or of the rules of administrative supervision applicable to them.

(23) It is necessary to establish whether or not concentrations with a Community dimension are compatible with the common market in terms of the need to maintain and develop effective competition in the common market. In so doing, the Commission must place its appraisal within the general framework of the achievement of the fundamental objectives referred to in Article 2 of the Treaty establishing the European Community and Article 2 of the Treaty on European Union.

(24) In order to ensure a system of undistorted competition in the common market, in furtherance of a policy conducted in accordance with the principle of an open market economy with free competition, this Regulation must permit effective control of all concentrations from the point of view of their effect on competition in the Community. Accordingly, Regulation (EEC) No 4064/89 established the principle that a concentration with a Community dimension which creates or strengthens a dominant position as a result of which effective competition in the common market or in a substantial part of it would be significantly impeded should be declared incompatible with the common market.

(25) In view of the consequences that concentrations in oligopolistic market structures may have, it is all the more necessary to maintain effective competition in such markets. Many oligopolistic markets exhibit a healthy degree of competition. However, under certain circumstances, concentrations involving the elimination of important competitive constraints that the merging parties had exerted upon each other, as well as a reduction of competitive pressure on the remaining competitors, may, even in the absence of a likelihood of coordination between the members of the oligopoly, result in a significant impediment to effective competition. The Community courts have, however, not to date expressly interpreted Regulation (EEC) No 4064/89 as requiring concentrations giving rise to such non-coordinated effects to be declared incompatible with the common market. Therefore, in the interests of legal certainty, it should be made clear that this Regulation permits effective control of all such concentrations by providing that any concentration which would significantly impede effective competition, in the common market or in a substantial part of it, should be declared incompatible with the common market. The notion of significant impediment to effective competition in Article 2(2) and (3) should be interpreted as extending, beyond the concept of dominance, only to the anti-competitive effects of a concentration resulting from the non-coordinated behaviour of undertakings which would not have a dominant position on the market concerned.

(26) A significant impediment to effective competition generally results from the creation or strengthening of a dominant position. With a view to preserving the guidance that may be drawn from past judgments of the European courts and Commission decisions pursuant to Regulation (EEC) No 4064/89, while at the same time maintaining consistency with the standards of competitive harm which have been applied by the Commission and the Community courts regarding the compatibility of a concentration with the common market, this Regulation should accordingly establish the principle that a concentration with a Community dimension which would significantly impede effective competition, in the common market or in a substantial part thereof, in particular as a result of the creation or strengthening of a dominant position, is to be declared incompatible with the common market.

(27) In addition, the criteria of Article 81(1) and (3) of the Treaty should be applied to joint ventures performing, on a lasting basis, all the functions of autonomous economic entities, to the extent that their creation has as its consequence an appreciable restriction of competition between undertakings that remain independent.

(28) In order to clarify and explain the Commission's appraisal of concentrations under this Regulation, it is appropriate for the Commission to publish guidance which should provide a sound economic framework for the assessment of concentrations with a view to determining whether or not they may be declared compatible with the common market.

(29) In order to determine the impact of a concentration on competition in the common market, it is appropriate to take account of any substantiated and likely efficiencies put forward by the undertakings concerned. It is possible that the efficiencies brought about by the concentration counteract the effects on competition, and in particular the potential harm to consumers, that it might otherwise have and that, as a consequence, the concentration would not significantly impede effective competition, in the common market or in a substantial part of it, in particular as a result of the creation or strengthening of a dominant position. The Commission should publish guidance on the conditions under which it may take efficiencies into account in the assessment of a concentration.

(30) Where the undertakings concerned modify a notified concentration, in particular by offering commitments with a view to rendering the concentration compatible with the common market, the Commission should be able to declare the concentration, as modified, compatible with the common market. Such commitments should be proportionate to the competition problem and entirely eliminate it. It is also appropriate to accept commitments before the initiation of proceedings where the competition problem is readily identifiable and can easily be remedied. It should be expressly provided that the Commission may attach to its decision conditions and obligations in order to ensure that the undertakings concerned comply with their commitments in a timely and effective manner so as to render the concentration compatible with the common market. Transparency and effective consultation of Member States as well as of interested third parties should be ensured throughout the procedure.

(31) The Commission should have at its disposal appropriate instruments to ensure the enforcement of commitments and to deal with situations where they are not fulfilled. In cases of failure to fulfil a condition attached to the decision declaring a concentration compatible with the common market, the situation rendering the concentration compatible with the common market does not materialise and the concentration, as implemented, is therefore not authorised by the Commission. As a consequence, if the concentration is implemented, it should be treated in the same way as a non-notified concentration implemented without authorisation. Furthermore, where the Commission has already found that, in the absence of the condition, the concentration would be incompatible with the common market, it should have the power to directly order the dissolution of the concentration, so as to restore the situation prevailing prior to the implementation of the concentration. Where an obligation attached to a decision declaring the concentration compatible with the common market is not fulfilled, the Commission should be able to revoke its decision. Moreover, the Commission should be able to impose appropriate financial sanctions where conditions or obligations are not fulfilled.

(32) Concentrations which, by reason of the limited market share of the undertakings concerned, are not liable to impede effective competition may be presumed to be compatible with the common market. Without prejudice to Articles 81 and 82 of the Treaty, an indication to this effect exists, in particular, where the market share of the undertakings concerned does not exceed 25% either in the common market or in a substantial part of it.

(33) The Commission should have the task of taking all the decisions necessary to establish whether or not concentrations with a Community dimension are compatible with the common market, as well as decisions designed to restore the situation prevailing prior to the implementation of a concentration which has been declared incompatible with the common market.

(34) To ensure effective control, undertakings should be obliged to give prior notification of concentrations with a Community dimension following the conclusion of the agreement,

the announcement of the public bid or the acquisition of a controlling interest. Notification should also be possible where the undertakings concerned satisfy the Commission of their intention to enter into an agreement for a proposed concentration and demonstrate to the Commission that their plan for that proposed concentration is sufficiently concrete, for example on the basis of an agreement in principle, a memorandum of understanding, or a letter of intent signed by all undertakings concerned, or, in the case of a public bid, where they have publicly announced an intention to make such a bid, provided that the intended agreement or bid would result in a concentration with a Community dimension. The implementation of concentrations should be suspended until a final decision of the Commission has been taken. However, it should be possible to derogate from this suspension at the request of the undertakings concerned, where appropriate. In deciding whether or not to grant a derogation, the Commission should take account of all pertinent factors, such as the nature and gravity of damage to the undertakings concerned or to third parties, and the threat to competition posed by the concentration. In the interest of legal certainty, the validity of transactions must nevertheless be protected as much as necessary.

(35) A period within which the Commission must initiate proceedings in respect of a notified concentration and a period within which it must take a final decision on the compatibility or incompatibility with the common market of that concentration should be laid down. These periods should be extended whenever the undertakings concerned offer commitments with a view to rendering the concentration compatible with the common market, in order to allow for sufficient time for the analysis and market testing of such commitment offers and for the consultation of Member States as well as interested third parties. A limited extension of the period within which the Commission must take a final decision should also be possible in order to allow sufficient time for the investigation of the case and the verification of the facts and arguments submitted to the Commission.

(36) The Community respects the fundamental rights and observes the principles recognised in particular by the Charter of Fundamental Rights of the European Union.[5] Accordingly, this Regulation should be interpreted and applied with respect to those rights and principles.

(37) The undertakings concerned must be afforded the right to be heard by the Commission when proceedings have been initiated; the members of the management and supervisory bodies and the recognised representatives of the employees of the undertakings concerned, and interested third parties, must also be given the opportunity to be heard.

(38) In order properly to appraise concentrations, the Commission should have the right to request all necessary information and to conduct all necessary inspections throughout the Community. To that end, and with a view to protecting competition effectively, the Commission's powers of investigation need to be expanded. The Commission should, in particular, have the right to interview any persons who may be in possession of useful information and to record the statements made.

(39) In the course of an inspection, officials authorised by the Commission should have the right to ask for any information relevant to the subject matter and purpose of the inspection; they should also have the right to affix seals during inspections, particularly in circumstances where there are reasonable grounds to suspect that a concentration has been implemented without being notified; that incorrect, incomplete or misleading information has been supplied to the Commission; or that the undertakings or persons concerned have failed to comply with a condition or obligation imposed by decision of the Commission. In any event, seals should only be used in exceptional circumstances, for the period of time strictly necessary for the inspection, normally not for more than 48 hours.

(40) Without prejudice to the case-law of the Court of Justice, it is also useful to set out the scope of the control that the national judicial authority may exercise when it authorises, as provided by national law and as a precautionary measure, assistance from law enforcement authorities in order to overcome possible opposition on the part of the undertaking against an inspection, including the affixing of seals, ordered by Commission decision. It results from the case-law that the national judicial authority may in particular ask of the Commission further information which it needs to carry out its control and in the absence of which it could refuse the authorisation. The case-law also confirms the competence of the national courts to control the application of national rules governing the implementation of coercive measures. The competent authorities of the Member States should cooperate actively in the exercise of the Commission's investigative powers.

(41) When complying with decisions of the Commission, the undertakings and persons concerned cannot be forced to admit that they have committed infringements, but they are in any event obliged to answer factual questions and to provide documents, even if this information may be used to establish against themselves or against others the existence of such infringements.

(42) For the sake of transparency, all decisions of the Commission which are not of a merely procedural nature should be widely publicised. While ensuring preservation of the rights of defence of the undertakings concerned, in particular the right of access to the file, it is essential that business secrets be protected. The confidentiality of information exchanged in the network and with the competent authorities of third countries should likewise be safeguarded.

(43) Compliance with this Regulation should be enforceable, as appropriate, by means of fines and periodic penalty payments. The Court of Justice should be given unlimited jurisdiction in that regard pursuant to Article 229 of the Treaty.

(44) The conditions in which concentrations, involving undertakings having their seat or their principal fields of activity in the Community, are carried out in third countries should be observed, and provision should be made for the possibility of the Council giving the Commission an appropriate mandate for negotiation with a view to obtaining non-discriminatory treatment for such undertakings.

(45) This Regulation in no way detracts from the collective rights of employees, as recognised in the undertakings concerned, notably with regard to any obligation to inform or consult their recognised representatives under Community and national law.

(46) The Commission should be able to lay down detailed rules concerning the implementation of this Regulation in accordance with the procedures for the exercise of implementing powers conferred on the Commission. For the adoption of such implementing provisions, the Commission should be assisted by an Advisory Committee composed of the representatives of the Member States as specified in Article 23,

[9533]

NOTES

1 OJ C20, 28.1.2003, p. 4.
2 Opinion delivered on 9.10.2003 (not yet published in the Official Journal).
3 Opinion delivered on 24.10.2003 (not yet published in the Official Journal).
4 OJ L395, 30.12.1989, p 1. Corrected version in OJ L257, 21.9.1990, p 13. Regulation as last amended by Regulation (EC) No 1310/97 (OJ L180, 9.7.1997, p 1). Corrigendum in OJ L40,13.2.1998, p 17.
5 OJ C364, 18.12.2000, p 1.

HAS ADOPTED THIS REGULATION—

Article 1

Scope

1. Without prejudice to Article 4(5) and Article 22, this Regulation shall apply to all concentrations with a Community dimension as defined in this Article.

2. A concentration has a Community dimension where:

(a) the combined aggregate worldwide turnover of all the undertakings concerned is more than EUR 5,000 million; and

(b) the aggregate Community-wide turnover of each of at least two of the undertakings concerned is more than EUR 250 million,

unless each of the undertakings concerned achieves more than two-thirds of its aggregate Community-wide turnover within one and the same Member State.

3. A concentration that does not meet the thresholds laid down in paragraph 2 has a Community dimension where:

(a) the combined aggregate worldwide turnover of all the undertakings concerned is more than EUR 2,500 million;

(b) in each of at least three Member States, the combined aggregate turnover of all the undertakings concerned is more than EUR 100 million;

(c) in each of at least three Member States included for the purpose of point (b), the aggregate turnover of each of at least two of the undertakings concerned is more than EUR 25 million; and

(d) the aggregate Community-wide turnover of each of at least two of the undertakings concerned is more than EUR 100 million,

unless each of the undertakings concerned achieves more than two-thirds of its aggregate Community-wide turnover within one and the same Member State.

4. On the basis of statistical data that may be regularly provided by the Member States, the Commission shall report to the Council on the operation of the thresholds and criteria set out in paragraphs 2 and 3 by 1 July 2009 and may present proposals pursuant to paragraph 5.

5. Following the report referred to in paragraph 4 and on a proposal from the Commission, the Council, acting by a qualified majority, may revise the thresholds and criteria mentioned in paragraph 3.

[9534]

Article 2

Appraisal of concentrations

1. Concentrations within the scope of this Regulation shall be appraised in accordance with the objectives of this Regulation and the following provisions with a view to establishing whether or not they are compatible with the common market.

In making this appraisal, the Commission shall take into account:

(a) the need to maintain and develop effective competition within the common market in view of, among other things, the structure of all the markets concerned and the actual or potential competition from undertakings located either within or outwith the Community;

(b) the market position of the undertakings concerned and their economic and financial power, the alternatives available to suppliers and users, their access to supplies or markets, any legal or other barriers to entry, supply and demand trends for the relevant goods and services, the interests of the intermediate and ultimate consumers, and the development of technical and economic progress provided that it is to consumers' advantage and does not form an obstacle to competition.

2. A concentration which would not significantly impede effective competition in the common market or in a substantial part of it, in particular as a result of the creation or strengthening of a dominant position, shall be declared compatible with the common market.

3. A concentration which would significantly impede effective competition, in the common market or in a substantial part of it, in particular as a result of the creation or strengthening of a dominant position, shall be declared incompatible with the common market.

4. To the extent that the creation of a joint venture constituting a concentration pursuant to Article 3 has as its object or effect the coordination of the competitive behaviour of undertakings that remain independent, such coordination shall be appraised in accordance with the criteria of Article 81(1) and (3) of the Treaty, with a view to establishing whether or not the operation is compatible with the common market.

5. In making this appraisal, the Commission shall take into account in particular:

— whether two or more parent companies retain, to a significant extent, activities in the same market as the joint venture or in a market which is downstream or upstream from that of the joint venture or in a neighbouring market closely related to this market,

— whether the coordination which is the direct consequence of the creation of the joint venture affords the undertakings concerned the possibility of eliminating competition in respect of a substantial part of the products or services in question.

[9535]

Article 3

Definition of concentration

1. A concentration shall be deemed to arise where a change of control on a lasting basis results from:

(a) the merger of two or more previously independent undertakings or parts of undertakings, or

(b) the acquisition, by one or more persons already controlling at least one undertaking, or by one or more undertakings, whether by purchase of securities or assets, by contract or by any other means, of direct or indirect control of the whole or parts of one or more other undertakings.

2. Control shall be constituted by rights, contracts or any other means which, either separately or in combination and having regard to the considerations of fact or law involved, confer the possibility of exercising decisive influence on an undertaking, in particular by:

(a) ownership or the right to use all or part of the assets of an undertaking;

(b) rights or contracts which confer decisive influence on the composition, voting or decisions of the organs of an undertaking.

3. Control is acquired by persons or undertakings which:
   (a) are holders of the rights or entitled to rights under the contracts concerned; or
   (b) while not being holders of such rights or entitled to rights under such contracts, have the power to exercise the rights deriving therefrom.

4. The creation of a joint venture performing on a lasting basis all the functions of an autonomous economic entity shall constitute a concentration within the meaning of paragraph 1(b).

5. A concentration shall not be deemed to arise where:
   (a) credit institutions or other financial institutions or insurance companies, the normal activities of which include transactions and dealing in securities for their own account or for the account of others, hold on a temporary basis securities which they have acquired in an undertaking with a view to reselling them, provided that they do not exercise voting rights in respect of those securities with a view to determining the competitive behaviour of that undertaking or provided that they exercise such voting rights only with a view to preparing the disposal of all or part of that undertaking or of its assets or the disposal of those securities and that any such disposal takes place within one year of the date of acquisition; that period may be extended by the Commission on request where such institutions or companies can show that the disposal was not reasonably possible within the period set;
   (b) control is acquired by an office-holder according to the law of a Member State relating to liquidation, winding up, insolvency, cessation of payments, compositions or analogous proceedings;
   (c) the operations referred to in paragraph 1(b) are carried out by the financial holding companies referred to in Article 5(3) of Fourth Council Directive 78/660/EEC of 25 July 1978 based on Article 54(3)(g) of the Treaty on the annual accounts of certain types of companies[1] provided however that the voting rights in respect of the holding are exercised, in particular in relation to the appointment of members of the management and supervisory bodies of the undertakings in which they have holdings, only to maintain the full value of those investments and not to determine directly or indirectly the competitive conduct of those undertakings.

[9536]

NOTES

[1] OJ L222, 14.8.1978, p 11. Directive as last amended by Directive 2003/51/EC of the European Parliament and of the Council (OJ L178, 17.7.2003, p 16).

Article 4

Prior notification of concentrations and pre-notification referral at the request of the notifying parties

1. Concentrations with a Community dimension defined in this Regulation shall be notified to the Commission prior to their implementation and following the conclusion of the agreement, the announcement of the public bid, or the acquisition of a controlling interest.

Notification may also be made where the undertakings concerned demonstrate to the Commission a good faith intention to conclude an agreement or, in the case of a public bid, where they have publicly announced an intention to make such a bid, provided that the intended agreement or bid would result in a concentration with a Community dimension.

For the purposes of this Regulation, the term 'notified concentration' shall also cover intended concentrations notified pursuant to the second subparagraph. For the purposes of paragraphs 4 and 5 of this Article, the term 'concentration' includes intended concentrations within the meaning of the second sub-paragraph.

2. A concentration which consists of a merger within the meaning of Article 3(1)(a) or in the acquisition of joint control within the meaning of Article 3(1)(b) shall be notified jointly by the parties to the merger or by those acquiring joint control as the case may be. In all other cases, the notification shall be effected by the person or undertaking acquiring control of the whole or parts of one or more undertakings.

3. Where the Commission finds that a notified concentration falls within the scope of this Regulation, it shall publish the fact of the notification, at the same time indicating the names of the undertakings concerned, their country of origin, the nature of the concentration and the

economic sectors involved. The Commission shall take account of the legitimate interest of undertakings in the protection of their business secrets.

4. Prior to the notification of a concentration within the meaning of paragraph 1, the persons or undertakings referred to in paragraph 2 may inform the Commission, by means of a reasoned submission, that the concentration may significantly affect competition in a market within a Member State which presents all the characteristics of a distinct market and should therefore be examined, in whole or in part, by that Member State.

The Commission shall transmit this submission to all Member States without delay. The Member State referred to in the reasoned submission shall, within 15 working days of receiving the submission, express its agreement or disagreement as regards the request to refer the case. Where that Member State takes no such decision within this period, it shall be deemed to have agreed.

Unless that Member State disagrees, the Commission, where it considers that such a distinct market exists, and that competition in that market may be significantly affected by the concentration, may decide to refer the whole or part of the case to the competent authorities of that Member State with a view to the application of that State's national competition law.

The decision whether or not to refer the case in accordance with the third subparagraph shall be taken within 25 working days starting from the receipt of the reasoned submission by the Commission. The Commission shall inform the other Member States and the persons or undertakings concerned of its decision. If the Commission does not take a decision within this period, it shall be deemed to have adopted a decision to refer the case in accordance with the submission made by the persons or undertakings concerned.

If the Commission decides, or is deemed to have decided, pursuant to the third and fourth subparagraphs, to refer the whole of the case, no notification shall be made pursuant to paragraph 1 and national competition law shall apply. Article 9(6) to (9) shall apply *mutatis mutandis*.

5. With regard to a concentration as defined in Article 3 which does not have a Community dimension within the meaning of Article 1 and which is capable of being reviewed under the national competition laws of at least three Member States, the persons or undertakings referred to in paragraph 2 may, before any notification to the competent authorities, inform the Commission by means of a reasoned submission that the concentration should be examined by the Commission.

The Commission shall transmit this submission to all Member States without delay.

Any Member State competent to examine the concentration under its national competition law may, within 15 working days of receiving the reasoned submission, express its disagreement as regards the request to refer the case.

Where at least one such Member State has expressed its disagreement in accordance with the third subparagraph within the period of 15 working days, the case shall not be referred. The Commission shall, without delay, inform all Member States and the persons or undertakings concerned of any such expression of disagreement.

Where no Member State has expressed its disagreement in accordance with the third subparagraph within the period of 15 working days, the concentration shall be deemed to have a Community dimension and shall be notified to the Commission in accordance with paragraphs 1 and 2. In such situations, no Member State shall apply its national competition law to the concentration.

6. The Commission shall report to the Council on the operation of paragraphs 4 and 5 by 1 July 2009. Following this report and on a proposal from the Commission, the Council, acting by a qualified majority, may revise paragraphs 4 and 5.

[9537]

Article 5

Calculation of turnover

1. Aggregate turnover within the meaning of this Regulation shall comprise the amounts derived by the undertakings concerned in the preceding financial year from the sale of products and the provision of services falling within the undertakings' ordinary activities after deduction of sales rebates and of value added tax and other taxes directly related to turnover. The aggregate turnover of an undertaking concerned shall not include the sale of products or the provision of services between any of the undertakings referred to in paragraph 4.

Turnover, in the Community or in a Member State, shall comprise products sold and services provided to undertakings or consumers, in the Community or in that Member State as the case may be.

2. By way of derogation from paragraph 1, where the concentration consists of the acquisition of parts, whether or not constituted as legal entities, of one or more undertakings, only the turnover relating to the parts which are the subject of the concentration shall be taken into account with regard to the seller or sellers.

However, two or more transactions within the meaning of the first subparagraph which take place within a two-year period between the same persons or undertakings shall be treated as one and the same concentration arising on the date of the last transaction.

3. In place of turnover the following shall be used:

(a) for credit institutions and other financial institutions, the sum of the following income items as defined in Council Directive 86/635/EEC,[1] after deduction of value added tax and other taxes directly related to those items, where appropriate:

(i) interest income and similar income;

(ii) income from securities:

— income from shares and other variable yield securities,

— income from participating interests,

— income from shares in affiliated undertakings;

(iii) commissions receivable;

(iv) net profit on financial operations;

(v) other operating income.

The turnover of a credit or financial institution in the Community or in a Member State shall comprise the income items, as defined above, which are received by the branch or division of that institution established in the Community or in the Member State in question, as the case may be;

(b) for insurance undertakings, the value of gross premiums written which shall comprise all amounts received and receivable in respect of insurance contracts issued by or on behalf of the insurance undertakings, including also outgoing reinsurance premiums, and after deduction of taxes and parafiscal contributions or levies charged by reference to the amounts of individual premiums or the total volume of premiums; as regards Article 1(2)(b) and (3)(b), (c) and (d) and the final part of Article 1(2) and (3), gross premiums received from Community residents and from residents of one Member State respectively shall be taken into account.

4. Without prejudice to paragraph 2, the aggregate turnover of an undertaking concerned within the meaning of this Regulation shall be calculated by adding together the respective turnovers of the following:

(a) the undertaking concerned;

(b) those undertakings in which the undertaking concerned, directly or indirectly:

(i) owns more than half the capital or business assets, or

(ii) has the power to exercise more than half the voting rights, or

(iii) has the power to appoint more than half the members of the supervisory board, the administrative board or bodies legally representing the undertakings, or

(iv) has the right to manage the undertakings' affairs;

(c) those undertakings which have in the undertaking concerned the rights or powers listed in (b);

(d) those undertakings in which an undertaking as referred to in (c) has the rights or powers listed in (b);

(e) those undertakings in which two or more undertakings as referred to in (a) to (d) jointly have the rights or powers listed in (b).

5. Where undertakings concerned by the concentration jointly have the rights or powers listed in paragraph 4(b), in calculating the aggregate turnover of the undertakings concerned for the purposes of this Regulation:

(a) no account shall be taken of the turnover resulting from the sale of products or the provision of services between the joint undertaking and each of the undertakings concerned or any other undertaking connected with any one of them, as set out in paragraph 4(b) to (e);

(b) account shall be taken of the turnover resulting from the sale of products and the provision of services between the joint undertaking and any third undertakings. This turnover shall be apportioned equally amongst the undertakings concerned.

[9538]

NOTES

[1] OJ L372, 31.12.1986, p 1. Directive as last amended by Directive 2003/51/EC of the European Parliament and of the Council.

Article 6

Examination of the notification and initiation of proceedings

1. The Commission shall examine the notification as soon as it is received.

(a) Where it concludes that the concentration notified does not fall within the scope of this Regulation, it shall record that finding by means of a decision.

(b) Where it finds that the concentration notified, although falling within the scope of this Regulation, does not raise serious doubts as to its compatibility with the common market, it shall decide not to oppose it and shall declare that it is compatible with the common market.

A decision declaring a concentration compatible shall be deemed to cover restrictions directly related and necessary to the implementation of the concentration.

(c) Without prejudice to paragraph 2, where the Commission finds that the concentration notified falls within the scope of this Regulation and raises serious doubts as to its compatibility with the common market, it shall decide to initiate proceedings. Without prejudice to Article 9, such proceedings shall be closed by means of a decision as provided for in Article 8(1) to (4), unless the undertakings concerned have demonstrated to the satisfaction of the Commission that they have abandoned the concentration.

2. Where the Commission finds that, following modification by the undertakings concerned, a notified concentration no longer raises serious doubts within the meaning of paragraph 1(c), it shall declare the concentration compatible with the common market pursuant to paragraph 1(b).

The Commission may attach to its decision under paragraph 1(b) conditions and obligations intended to ensure that the undertakings concerned comply with the commitments they have entered into vis-à-vis the Commission with a view to rendering the concentration compatible with the common market.

3. The Commission may revoke the decision it took pursuant to paragraph 1(a) or (b) where:

(a) the decision is based on incorrect information for which one of the undertakings is responsible or where it has been obtained by deceit,

or

(b) the undertakings concerned commit a breach of an obligation attached to the decision.

4. In the cases referred to in paragraph 3, the Commission may take a decision under paragraph 1, without being bound by the time limits referred to in Article 10(1).

5. The Commission shall notify its decision to the undertakings concerned and the competent authorities of the Member States without delay.

[9539]

Article 7

Suspension of concentrations

1. A concentration with a Community dimension as defined in Article 1, or which is to be examined by the Commission pursuant to Article 4(5), shall not be implemented either before its notification or until it has been declared compatible with the common market pursuant to a decision under Articles 6(1)(b), 8(1) or 8(2), or on the basis of a presumption according to Article 10(6).

2. Paragraph 1 shall not prevent the implementation of a public bid or of a series of transactions in securities including those convertible into other securities admitted to trading on a market such as a stock exchange, by which control within the meaning of Article 3 is acquired from various sellers, provided that:

(a) the concentration is notified to the Commission pursuant to Article 4 without delay; and

(b) the acquirer does not exercise the voting rights attached to the securities in question or does so only to maintain the full value of its investments based on a derogation granted by the Commission under paragraph 3.

3. The Commission may, on request, grant a derogation from the obligations imposed in paragraphs 1 or 2. The request to grant a derogation must be reasoned. In deciding on the request, the Commission shall take into account *inter alia* the effects of the suspension on one or more undertakings concerned by the concentration or on a third party and the threat to competition posed by the concentration. Such a derogation may be made subject to conditions and obligations in order to ensure conditions of effective competition. A derogation may be applied for and granted at any time, be it before notification or after the transaction.

4. The validity of any transaction carried out in contravention of paragraph 1 shall be dependent on a decision pursuant to Article 6(1)(b) or Article 8(1), (2) or (3) or on a presumption pursuant to Article 10(6).

This Article shall, however, have no effect on the validity of transactions in securities including those convertible into other securities admitted to trading on a market such as a stock exchange, unless the buyer and seller knew or ought to have known that the transaction was carried out in contravention of paragraph 1.

[9540]

Article 8

Powers of decision of the Commission

1. Where the Commission finds that a notified concentration fulfils the criterion laid down in Article 2(2) and, in the cases referred to in Article 2(4), the criteria laid down in Article 81(3) of the Treaty, it shall issue a decision declaring the concentration compatible with the common market.

A decision declaring a concentration compatible shall be deemed to cover restrictions directly related and necessary to the implementation of the concentration.

2. Where the Commission finds that, following modification by the undertakings concerned, a notified concentration fulfils the criterion laid down in Article 2(2) and, in the cases referred to in Article 2(4), the criteria laid down in Article 81(3) of the Treaty, it shall issue a decision declaring the concentration compatible with the common market.

The Commission may attach to its decision conditions and obligations intended to ensure that the undertakings concerned comply with the commitments they have entered into vis-à-vis the Commission with a view to rendering the concentration compatible with the common market.

A decision declaring a concentration compatible shall be deemed to cover restrictions directly related and necessary to the implementation of the concentration.

3. Where the Commission finds that a concentration fulfils the criterion defined in Article 2(3) or, in the cases referred to in Article 2(4), does not fulfil the criteria laid down in Article 81(3) of the Treaty, it shall issue a decision declaring that the concentration is incompatible with the common market.

4. Where the Commission finds that a concentration:

(a) has already been implemented and that concentration has been declared incompatible with the common market, or

(b) has been implemented in contravention of a condition attached to a decision taken under paragraph 2, which has found that, in the absence of the condition, the concentration would fulfil the criterion laid down in Article 2(3) or, in the cases referred to in Article 2(4), would not fulfil the criteria laid down in Article 81(3) of the Treaty,

the Commission may:

— require the undertakings concerned to dissolve the concentration, in particular through the dissolution of the merger or the disposal of all the shares or assets acquired, so as to restore the situation prevailing prior to the implementation of the concentration; in circumstances where restoration of the situation prevailing before the implementation of the concentration is not possible through dissolution of the concentration, the Commission may take any other measure appropriate to achieve such restoration as far as possible,

— order any other appropriate measure to ensure that the undertakings concerned dissolve the concentration or take other restorative measures as required in its decision.

In cases falling within point (a) of the first subparagraph, the measures referred to in that subparagraph may be imposed either in a decision pursuant to paragraph 3 or by separate decision.

5. The Commission may take interim measures appropriate to restore or maintain conditions of effective competition where a concentration:

(a) has been implemented in contravention of Article 7, and a decision as to the compatibility of the concentration with the common market has not yet been taken;

(b) has been implemented in contravention of a condition attached to a decision under Article 6(1)(b) or paragraph 2 of this Article;

(c) has already been implemented and is declared incompatible with the common market.

6. The Commission may revoke the decision it has taken pursuant to paragraphs 1 or 2 where:

(a) the declaration of compatibility is based on incorrect information for which one of the undertakings is responsible or where it has been obtained by deceit; or

(b) the undertakings concerned commit a breach of an obligation attached to the decision.

7. The Commission may take a decision pursuant to paragraphs 1 to 3 without being bound by the time limits referred to in Article 10(3), in cases where:

(a) it finds that a concentration has been implemented

(i) in contravention of a condition attached to a decision under Article 6(1)(b), or

(ii) in contravention of a condition attached to a decision taken under paragraph 2 and in accordance with Article 10(2), which has found that, in the absence of the condition, the concentration would raise serious doubts as to its compatibility with the common market; or

(b) a decision has been revoked pursuant to paragraph 6.

8. The Commission shall notify its decision to the undertakings concerned and the competent authorities of the Member States without delay.

[9541]

Article 9

Referral to the competent authorities of the Member States

1. The Commission may, by means of a decision notified without delay to the undertakings concerned and the competent authorities of the other Member States, refer a notified concentration to the competent authorities of the Member State concerned in the following circumstances.

2. Within 15 working days of the date of receipt of the copy of the notification, a Member State, on its own initiative or upon the invitation of the Commission, may inform the Commission, which shall inform the undertakings concerned, that:

(a) a concentration threatens to affect significantly competition in a market within that Member State, which presents all the characteristics of a distinct market, or

(b) a concentration affects competition in a market within that Member State, which presents all the characteristics of a distinct market and which does not constitute a substantial part of the common market.

3. If the Commission considers that, having regard to the market for the products or services in question and the geographical reference market within the meaning of paragraph 7, there is such a distinct market and that such a threat exists, either:

(a) it shall itself deal with the case in accordance with this Regulation; or

(b) it shall refer the whole or part of the case to the competent authorities of the Member State concerned with a view to the application of that State's national competition law.

If, however, the Commission considers that such a distinct market or threat does not exist, it shall adopt a decision to that effect which it shall address to the Member State concerned, and shall itself deal with the case in accordance with this Regulation.

In cases where a Member State informs the Commission pursuant to paragraph 2(b) that a concentration affects competition in a distinct market within its territory that does not form a substantial part of the common market, the Commission shall refer the whole or part of the case relating to the distinct market concerned, if it considers that such a distinct market is affected.

4. A decision to refer or not to refer pursuant to paragraph 3 shall be taken:
   (a) as a general rule within the period provided for in Article 10(1), second subparagraph, where the Commission, pursuant to Article 6(1)(b), has not initiated proceedings; or
   (b) within 65 working days at most of the notification of the concentration concerned where the Commission has initiated proceedings under Article 6(1)(c), without taking the preparatory steps in order to adopt the necessary measures under Article 8(2), (3) or (4) to maintain or restore effective competition on the market concerned.

5. If within the 65 working days referred to in paragraph 4(b) the Commission, despite a reminder from the Member State concerned, has not taken a decision on referral in accordance with paragraph 3 nor has taken the preparatory steps referred to in paragraph 4(b), it shall be deemed to have taken a decision to refer the case to the Member State concerned in accordance with paragraph 3(b).

6. The competent authority of the Member State concerned shall decide upon the case without undue delay.

Within 45 working days after the Commission's referral, the competent authority of the Member State concerned shall inform the undertakings concerned of the result of the preliminary competition assessment and what further action, if any, it proposes to take. The Member State concerned may exceptionally suspend this time limit where necessary information has not been provided to it by the undertakings concerned as provided for by its national competition law.

Where a notification is requested under national law, the period of 45 working days shall begin on the working day following that of the receipt of a complete notification by the competent authority of that Member State.

7. The geographical reference market shall consist of the area in which the undertakings concerned are involved in the supply and demand of products or services, in which the conditions of competition are sufficiently homogeneous and which can be distinguished from neighbouring areas because, in particular, conditions of competition are appreciably different in those areas. This assessment should take account in particular of the nature and characteristics of the products or services concerned, of the existence of entry barriers or of consumer preferences, of appreciable differences of the undertakings' market shares between the area concerned and neighbouring areas or of substantial price differences.

8. In applying the provisions of this Article, the Member State concerned may take only the measures strictly necessary to safeguard or restore effective competition on the market concerned.

9. In accordance with the relevant provisions of the Treaty, any Member State may appeal to the Court of Justice, and in particular request the application of Article 243 of the Treaty, for the purpose of applying its national competition law.

[9542]

Article 10

Time limits for initiating proceedings and for decisions

1. Without prejudice to Article 6(4), the decisions referred to in Article 6(1) shall be taken within 25 working days at most. That period shall begin on the working day following that of the receipt of a notification or, if the information to be supplied with the notification is incomplete, on the working day following that of the receipt of the complete information.

That period shall be increased to 35 working days where the Commission receives a request from a Member State in accordance with Article 9(2)or where, the undertakings concerned offer commitments pursuant to Article 6(2) with a view to rendering the concentration compatible with the common market.

2. Decisions pursuant to Article 8(1) or (2) concerning notified concentrations shall be taken as soon as it appears that the serious doubts referred to in Article 6(1)(c) have been removed, particularly as a result of modifications made by the undertakings concerned, and at the latest by the time limit laid down in paragraph 3.

3. Without prejudice to Article 8(7), decisions pursuant to Article 8(1) to (3) concerning notified concentrations shall be taken within not more than 90 working days of the date on which the proceedings are initiated. That period shall be increased to 105 working days where the undertakings concerned offer commitments pursuant to Article 8(2), second subparagraph, with a view to rendering the concentration compatible with the common market, unless these commitments have been offered less than 55 working days after the initiation of proceedings.

The periods set by the first subparagraph shall likewise be extended if the notifying parties make a request to that effect not later than 15 working days after the initiation of proceedings pursuant to Article 6(1)(c). The notifying parties may make only one such request. Likewise, at any time following the initiation of proceedings, the periods set by the first sub-paragraph may be extended by the Commission with the agreement of the notifying parties. The total duration of any extension or extensions effected pursuant to this subparagraph shall not exceed 20 working days.

4. The periods set by paragraphs 1 and 3 shall exceptionally be suspended where, owing to circumstances for which one of the undertakings involved in the concentration is responsible, the Commission has had to request information by decision pursuant to Article 11 or to order an inspection by decision pursuant to Article 13.

The first subparagraph shall also apply to the period referred to in Article 9(4)(b).

5. Where the Court of Justice gives a judgment which annuls the whole or part of a Commission decision which is subject to a time limit set by this Article, the concentration shall be re-examined by the Commission with a view to adopting a decision pursuant to Article 6(1).

The concentration shall be re-examined in the light of current market conditions.

The notifying parties shall submit a new notification or supplement the original notification, without delay, where the original notification becomes incomplete by reason of intervening changes in market conditions or in the information provided. Where there are no such changes, the parties shall certify this fact without delay.

The periods laid down in paragraph 1 shall start on the working day following that of the receipt of complete information in a new notification, a supplemented notification, or a certification within the meaning of the third subparagraph.

The second and third subparagraphs shall also apply in the cases referred to in Article 6(4) and Article 8(7).

6. Where the Commission has not taken a decision in accordance with Article 6(1)(b), (c), 8(1), (2) or (3) within the time limits set in paragraphs 1 and 3 respectively, the concentration shall be deemed to have been declared compatible with the common market, without prejudice to Article 9.

[9543]

Article 11

Requests for information

1. In order to carry out the duties assigned to it by this Regulation, the Commission may, by simple request or by decision, require the persons referred to in Article 3(1)(b), as well as undertakings and associations of undertakings, to provide all necessary information.

2. When sending a simple request for information to a person, an undertaking or an association of undertakings, the Commission shall state the legal basis and the purpose of the request, specify what information is required and fix the time limit within which the information is to be provided, as well as the penalties provided for in Article 14 for supplying incorrect or misleading information.

3. Where the Commission requires a person, an undertaking or an association of undertakings to supply information by decision, it shall state the legal basis and the purpose of the request, specify what information is required and fix the time limit within which it is to be provided. It shall also indicate the penalties provided for in Article 14 and indicate or impose the penalties provided for in Article 15. It shall further indicate the right to have the decision reviewed by the Court of Justice.

4. The owners of the undertakings or their representatives and, in the case of legal persons, companies or firms, or associations having no legal personality, the persons authorised to represent them by law or by their constitution, shall supply the information

requested on behalf of the undertaking concerned. Persons duly authorised to act may supply the information on behalf of their clients. The latter shall remain fully responsible if the information supplied is incomplete, incorrect or misleading.

5. The Commission shall without delay forward a copy of any decision taken pursuant to paragraph 3 to the competent authorities of the Member State in whose territory the residence of the person or the seat of the undertaking or association of undertakings is situated, and to the competent authority of the Member State whose territory is affected. At the specific request of the competent authority of a Member State, the Commission shall also forward to that authority copies of simple requests for information relating to a notified concentration.

6. At the request of the Commission, the governments and competent authorities of the Member States shall provide the Commission with all necessary information to carry out the duties assigned to it by this Regulation.

7. In order to carry out the duties assigned to it by this Regulation, the Commission may interview any natural or legal person who consents to be interviewed for the purpose of collecting information relating to the subject matter of an investigation. At the beginning of the interview, which may be conducted by telephone or other electronic means, the Commission shall state the legal basis and the purpose of the interview.

Where an interview is not conducted on the premises of the Commission or by telephone or other electronic means, the Commission shall inform in advance the competent authority of the Member State in whose territory the interview takes place. If the competent authority of that Member State so requests, officials of that authority may assist the officials and other persons authorised by the Commission to conduct the interview.

[9544]

Article 12

Inspections by the authorities of the Member States

1. At the request of the Commission, the competent authorities of the Member States shall undertake the inspections which the Commission considers to be necessary under Article 13(1), or which it has ordered by decision pursuant to Article 13(4). The officials of the competent authorities of the Member States who are responsible for conducting these inspections as well as those authorised or appointed by them shall exercise their powers in accordance with their national law.

2. If so requested by the Commission or by the competent authority of the Member State within whose territory the inspection is to be conducted, officials and other accompanying persons authorised by the Commission may assist the officials of the authority concerned.

[9545]

Article 13

The Commission's powers of inspection

1. In order to carry out the duties assigned to it by this Regulation, the Commission may conduct all necessary inspections of undertakings and associations of undertakings.

2. The officials and other accompanying persons authorised by the Commission to conduct an inspection shall have the power:

(a) to enter any premises, land and means of transport of undertakings and associations of undertakings;
(b) to examine the books and other records related to the business, irrespective of the medium on which they are stored;
(c) to take or obtain in any form copies of or extracts from such books or records;
(d) to seal any business premises and books or records for the period and to the extent necessary for the inspection;
(e) to ask any representative or member of staff of the undertaking or association of undertakings for explanations on facts or documents relating to the subject matter and purpose of the inspection and to record the answers.

3. Officials and other accompanying persons authorised by the Commission to conduct an inspection shall exercise their powers upon production of a written authorisation specifying the subject matter and purpose of the inspection and the penalties provided for in Article 14, in the production of the required books or other records related to the business which is incomplete or where answers to questions asked under paragraph 2 of this Article are

incorrect or misleading. In good time before the inspection, the Commission shall give notice of the inspection to the competent authority of the Member State in whose territory the inspection is to be conducted.

4. Undertakings and associations of undertakings are required to submit to inspections ordered by decision of the Commission. The decision shall specify the subject matter and purpose of the inspection, appoint the date on which it is to begin and indicate the penalties provided for in Articles 14 and 15 and the right to have the decision reviewed by the Court of Justice. The Commission shall take such decisions after consulting the competent authority of the Member State in whose territory the inspection is to be conducted.

5. Officials of, and those authorised or appointed by, the competent authority of the Member State in whose territory the inspection is to be conducted shall, at the request of that authority or of the Commission, actively assist the officials and other accompanying persons authorised by the Commission. To this end, they shall enjoy the powers specified in paragraph 2.

6. Where the officials and other accompanying persons authorised by the Commission find that an undertaking opposes an inspection, including the sealing of business premises, books or records, ordered pursuant to this Article, the Member State concerned shall afford them the necessary assistance, requesting where appropriate the assistance of the police or of an equivalent enforcement authority, so as to enable them to conduct their inspection.

7. If the assistance provided for in paragraph 6 requires authorisation from a judicial authority according to national rules, such authorisation shall be applied for. Such authorisation may also be applied for as a precautionary measure.

8. Where authorisation as referred to in paragraph 7 is applied for, the national judicial authority shall ensure that the Commission decision is authentic and that the coercive measures envisaged are neither arbitrary nor excessive having regard to the subject matter of the inspection. In its control of proportionality of the coercive measures, the national judicial authority may ask the Commission, directly or through the competent authority of that Member State, for detailed explanations relating to the subject matter of the inspection. However, the national judicial authority may not call into question the necessity for the inspection nor demand that it be provided with the information in the Commission's file. The lawfulness of the Commission's decision shall be subject to review only by the Court of Justice.

[9546]

Article 14

Fines

1. The Commission may by decision impose on the persons referred to in Article 3(1)b, undertakings or associations of undertakings, fines not exceeding 1% of the aggregate turnover of the undertaking or association of undertakings concerned within the meaning of Article 5 where, intentionally or negligently:

(a) they supply incorrect or misleading information in a submission, certification, notification or supplement thereto, pursuant to Article 4, Article 10(5) or Article 22(3);

(b) they supply incorrect or misleading information in response to a request made pursuant to Article 11(2);

(c) in response to a request made by decision adopted pursuant to Article 11(3), they supply incorrect, incomplete or misleading information or do not supply information within the required time limit;

(d) they produce the required books or other records related to the business in incomplete form during inspections under Article 13, or refuse to submit to an inspection ordered by decision taken pursuant to Article 13(4);

(e) in response to a question asked in accordance with Article 13(2)(e),
- they give an incorrect or misleading answer,
- they fail to rectify within a time limit set by the Commission an incorrect, incomplete or misleading answer given by a member of staff, or
- they fail or refuse to provide a complete answer on facts relating to the subject matter and purpose of an inspection ordered by a decision adopted pursuant to Article 13(4);

(f) seals affixed by officials or other accompanying persons authorised by the Commission in accordance with Article 13(2)(d) have been broken.

2. The Commission may by decision impose fines not exceeding 10% of the aggregate turnover of the undertaking concerned within the meaning of Article 5 on the persons referred to in Article 3(1)b or the undertakings concerned where, either intentionally or negligently, they:

(a) fail to notify a concentration in accordance with Articles 4 or 22(3) prior to its implementation, unless they are expressly authorised to do so by Article 7(2) or by a decision taken pursuant to Article 7(3);

(b) implement a concentration in breach of Article 7;

(c) implement a concentration declared incompatible with the common market by decision pursuant to Article 8(3) or do not comply with any measure ordered by decision pursuant to Article 8(4) or (5);

(d) fail to comply with a condition or an obligation imposed by decision pursuant to Articles 6(1)(b), Article 7(3) or Article 8(2), second subparagraph.

3. In fixing the amount of the fine, regard shall be had to the nature, gravity and duration of the infringement.

4. Decisions taken pursuant to paragraphs 1, 2 and 3 shall not be of a criminal law nature.

[9547]

Article 15

Periodic penalty payments

1. The Commission may by decision impose on the persons referred to in Article 3(1)b, undertakings or associations of undertakings, periodic penalty payments not exceeding 5% of the average daily aggregate turnover of the undertaking or association of undertakings concerned within the meaning of Article 5 for each working day of delay, calculated from the date set in the decision, in order to compel them:

(a) to supply complete and correct information which it has requested by decision taken pursuant to Article 11(3);

(b) to submit to an inspection which it has ordered by decision taken pursuant to Article 13(4);

(c) to comply with an obligation imposed by decision pursuant to Article 6(1)(b), Article 7(3) or Article 8(2), second sub-paragraph; or;

(d) to comply with any measures ordered by decision pursuant to Article 8(4) or (5).

2. Where the persons referred to in Article 3(1)(b), undertakings or associations of undertakings have satisfied the obligation which the periodic penalty payment was intended to enforce, the Commission may fix the definitive amount of the periodic penalty payments at a figure lower than that which would arise under the original decision.

[9548]

Article 16

Review by the Court of Justice

The Court of Justice shall have unlimited jurisdiction within the meaning of Article 229 of the Treaty to review decisions whereby the Commission has fixed a fine or periodic penalty payments; it may cancel, reduce or increase the fine or periodic penalty payment imposed.

[9549]

Article 17

Professional secrecy

1. Information acquired as a result of the application of this Regulation shall be used only for the purposes of the relevant request, investigation or hearing.

2. Without prejudice to Article 4(3), Articles 18 and 20, the Commission and the competent authorities of the Member States, their officials and other servants and other persons working under the supervision of these authorities as well as officials and civil servants of other authorities of the Member States shall not disclose information they have acquired through the application of this Regulation of the kind covered by the obligation of professional secrecy.

3. Paragraphs 1 and 2 shall not prevent publication of general information or of surveys which do not contain information relating to particular undertakings or associations of undertakings.

[9550]

Article 18

Hearing of the parties and of third persons

1. Before taking any decision provided for in Article 6(3), Article 7(3), Article 8(2) to (6), and Articles 14 and 15, the Commission shall give the persons, undertakings and associations of undertakings concerned the opportunity, at every stage of the procedure up to the consultation of the Advisory Committee, of making known their views on the objections against them.

2. By way of derogation from paragraph 1, a decision pursuant to Articles 7(3) and 8(5) may be taken provisionally, without the persons, undertakings or associations of undertakings concerned being given the opportunity to make known their views beforehand, provided that the Commission gives them that opportunity as soon as possible after having taken its decision.

3. The Commission shall base its decision only on objections on which the parties have been able to submit their observations. The rights of the defence shall be fully respected in the proceedings. Access to the file shall be open at least to the parties directly involved, subject to the legitimate interest of undertakings in the protection of their business secrets.

4. In so far as the Commission or the competent authorities of the Member States deem it necessary, they may also hear other natural or legal persons. Natural or legal persons showing a sufficient interest and especially members of the administrative or management bodies of the undertakings concerned or the recognised representatives of their employees shall be entitled, upon application, to be heard.

[9551]

Article 19

Liaison with the authorities of the Member States

1. The Commission shall transmit to the competent authorities of the Member States copies of notifications within three working days and, as soon as possible, copies of the most important documents lodged with or issued by the Commission pursuant to this Regulation. Such documents shall include commitments offered by the undertakings concerned vis-à-vis the Commission with a view to rendering the concentration compatible with the common market pursuant to Article 6(2) or Article 8(2), second subparagraph.

2. The Commission shall carry out the procedures set out in this Regulation in close and constant liaison with the competent authorities of the Member States, which may express their views upon those procedures. For the purposes of Article 9 it shall obtain information from the competent authority of the Member State as referred to in paragraph 2 of that Article and give it the opportunity to make known its views at every stage of the procedure up to the adoption of a decision pursuant to paragraph 3 of that Article; to that end it shall give it access to the file.

3. An Advisory Committee on concentrations shall be consulted before any decision is taken pursuant to Article 8(1) to (6), Articles 14 or 15 with the exception of provisional decisions taken in accordance with Article 18(2).

4. The Advisory Committee shall consist of representatives of the competent authorities of the Member States. Each Member State shall appoint one or two representatives; if unable to attend, they may be replaced by other representatives. At least one of the representatives of a Member State shall be competent in matters of restrictive practices and dominant positions.

5. Consultation shall take place at a joint meeting convened at the invitation of and chaired by the Commission. A summary of the case, together with an indication of the most important documents and a preliminary draft of the decision to be taken for each case considered, shall be sent with the invitation. The meeting shall take place not less than 10 working days after the invitation has been sent. The Commission may in exceptional cases shorten that period as appropriate in order to avoid serious harm to one or more of the undertakings concerned by a concentration.

6. The Advisory Committee shall deliver an opinion on the Commission's draft decision, if necessary by taking a vote. The Advisory Committee may deliver an opinion even if some

members are absent and unrepresented. The opinion shall be delivered in writing and appended to the draft decision. The Commission shall take the utmost account of the opinion delivered by the Committee. It shall inform the Committee of the manner in which its opinion has been taken into account.

7. The Commission shall communicate the opinion of the Advisory Committee, together with the decision, to the addressees of the decision. It shall make the opinion public together with the decision, having regard to the legitimate interest of undertakings in the protection of their business secrets.

[9552]

Article 20

Publication of decisions

1. The Commission shall publish the decisions which it takes pursuant to Article 8(1) to (6), Articles 14 and 15 with the exception of provisional decisions taken in accordance with Article 18(2) together with the opinion of the Advisory Committee in the *Official Journal of the European Union*.

2. The publication shall state the names of the parties and the main content of the decision; it shall have regard to the legitimate interest of undertakings in the protection of their business secrets.

[9553]

Article 21

Application of the Regulation and jurisdiction

1. This Regulation alone shall apply to concentrations as defined in Article 3, and Council Regulations (EC) No 1/2003,[1] (EEC) No 1017/68,[2] (EEC) No 4056/86[3] and (EEC) No 3975/87[4] shall not apply, except in relation to joint ventures that do not have a Community dimension and which have as their object or effect the coordination of the competitive behaviour of undertakings that remain independent.

2. Subject to review by the Court of Justice, the Commission shall have sole jurisdiction to take the decisions provided for in this Regulation.

3. No Member State shall apply its national legislation on competition to any concentration that has a Community dimension.

The first subparagraph shall be without prejudice to any Member State's power to carry out any enquiries necessary for the application of Articles 4(4), 9(2) or after referral, pursuant to Article 9(3), first subparagraph, indent (b), or Article 9(5), to take the measures strictly necessary for the application of Article 9(8).

4. Notwithstanding paragraphs 2 and 3, Member States may take appropriate measures to protect legitimate interests other than those taken into consideration by this Regulation and compatible with the general principles and other provisions of Community law.

Public security, plurality of the media and prudential rules shall be regarded as legitimate interests within the meaning of the first subparagraph.

Any other public interest must be communicated to the Commission by the Member State concerned and shall be recognised by the Commission after an assessment of its compatibility with the general principles and other provisions of Community law before the measures referred to above may be taken. The Commission shall inform the Member State concerned of its decision within 25 working days of that communication.

[9554]

NOTES

[1] OJ L1, 4.1.2003, p 1.
[2] OJ L175, 23.7.1968, p 1. Regulation as last amended by Regulation (EC) No 1/2003 (OJ L1, 4.1.2003, p 1).
[3] OJ L378, 31.12.1986, p 4. Regulation as last amended by Regulation (EC) No 1/2003.
[4] OJ L374, 31.12.1987, p 1. Regulation as last amended by Regulation (EC) No 1/2003.

Article 22

Referral to the Commission

1. One or more Member States may request the Commission to examine any concentration as defined in Article 3 that does not have a Community dimension within the

meaning of Article 1 but affects trade between Member States and threatens to significantly affect competition within the territory of the Member State or States making the request.

Such a request shall be made at most within 15 working days of the date on which the concentration was notified, or if no notification is required, otherwise made known to the Member State concerned.

2. The Commission shall inform the competent authorities of the Member States and the undertakings concerned of any request received pursuant to paragraph 1 without delay.

Any other Member State shall have the right to join the initial request within a period of 15 working days of being informed by the Commission of the initial request.

All national time limits relating to the concentration shall be suspended until, in accordance with the procedure set out in this Article, it has been decided where the concentration shall be examined. As soon as a Member State has informed the Commission and the undertakings concerned that it does not wish to join the request, the suspension of its national time limits shall end.

3. The Commission may, at the latest 10 working days after the expiry of the period set in paragraph 2, decide to examine, the concentration where it considers that it affects trade between Member States and threatens to significantly affect competition within the territory of the Member State or States making the request. If the Commission does not take a decision within this period, it shall be deemed to have adopted a decision to examine the concentration in accordance with the request.

The Commission shall inform all Member States and the undertakings concerned of its decision. It may request the submission of a notification pursuant to Article 4.

The Member State or States having made the request shall no longer apply their national legislation on competition to the concentration.

4. Article 2, Article 4(2) to (3), Articles 5, 6, and 8 to 21 shall apply where the Commission examines a concentration pursuant to paragraph 3. Article 7 shall apply to the extent that the concentration has not been implemented on the date on which the Commission informs the undertakings concerned that a request has been made.

Where a notification pursuant to Article 4 is not required, the period set in Article 10(1) within which proceedings may be initiated shall begin on the working day following that on which the Commission informs the undertakings concerned that it has decided to examine the concentration pursuant to paragraph 3.

5. The Commission may inform one or several Member States that it considers a concentration fulfils the criteria in paragraph 1. In such cases, the Commission may invite that Member State or those Member States to make a request pursuant to paragraph 1.

[9555]

Article 23

Implementing provisions

1. The Commission shall have the power to lay down in accordance with the procedure referred to in paragraph 2:

(a) implementing provisions concerning the form, content and other details of notifications and submissions pursuant to Article 4;

(b) implementing provisions concerning time limits pursuant to Article 4(4), (5) Articles 7, 9, 10 and 22;

(c) the procedure and time limits for the submission and implementation of commitments pursuant to Article 6(2) and Article 8(2);

(d) implementing provisions concerning hearings pursuant to Article 18.

2. The Commission shall be assisted by an Advisory Committee, composed of representatives of the Member States.

(a) Before publishing draft implementing provisions and before adopting such provisions, the Commission shall consult the Advisory Committee.

(b) Consultation shall take place at a meeting convened at the invitation of and chaired by the Commission. A draft of the implementing provisions to be taken shall be sent with the invitation. The meeting shall take place not less than 10 working days after the invitation has been sent.

(c) The Advisory Committee shall deliver an opinion on the draft implementing provisions, if necessary by taking a vote. The Commission shall take the utmost account of the opinion delivered by the Committee.

[9556]

Article 24

Relations with third countries

1. The Member States shall inform the Commission of any general difficulties encountered by their undertakings with concentrations as defined in Article 3 in a third country.

2. Initially not more than one year after the entry into force of this Regulation and, thereafter periodically, the Commission shall draw up a report examining the treatment accorded to undertakings having their seat or their principal fields of activity in the Community, in the terms referred to in paragraphs 3 and 4, as regards concentrations in third countries. The Commission shall submit those reports to the Council, together with any recommendations.

3. Whenever it appears to the Commission, either on the basis of the reports referred to in paragraph 2 or on the basis of other information, that a third country does not grant undertakings having their seat or their principal fields of activity in the Community, treatment comparable to that granted by the Community to undertakings from that country, the Commission may submit proposals to the Council for an appropriate mandate for negotiation with a view to obtaining comparable treatment for undertakings having their seat or their principal fields of activity in the Community.

4. Measures taken under this Article shall comply with the obligations of the Community or of the Member States, without prejudice to Article 307 of the Treaty, under international agreements, whether bilateral or multilateral.

[9557]

Article 25

Repeal

1. Without prejudice to Article 26(2), Regulations (EEC) No 4064/89 and (EC) No 1310/97 shall be repealed with effect from 1 May 2004.

2. References to the repealed Regulations shall be construed as references to this Regulation and shall be read in accordance with the correlation table in the Annex.

[9558]

Article 26

Entry into force and transitional provisions

1. This Regulation shall enter into force on the 20th day following that of its publication in the *Official Journal of the European Union*.

It shall apply from 1 May 2004.

2. Regulation (EEC) No 4064/89 shall continue to apply to any concentration which was the subject of an agreement or announcement or where control was acquired within the meaning of Article 4(1) of that Regulation before the date of application of this Regulation, subject, in particular, to the provisions governing applicability set out in Article 25(2) and (3) of Regulation (EEC) No 4064/89 and Article 2 of Regulation (EEC) No 1310/97.

3. As regards concentrations to which this Regulation applies by virtue of accession, the date of accession shall be substituted for the date of application of this Regulation.

This Regulation shall be binding in its entirety and directly applicable in all Member States.

[9559]

Done at Brussels, 20 January 2004.

ANNEX
CORRELATION TABLE

Regulation (EEC) No 4064/89	*This Regulation*
Article 1(1), (2) and (3)	Article 1(1), (2) and (3)
Article 1(4)	Article 1(4)
Article 1(5)	Article 1(5)
Article 2(1)	Article 2(1)
—	Article 2(2)
Article 2(2)	Article 2(3)
Article 2(3)	Article 2(4)
Article 2(4)	Article 2(5)
Article 3(1)	Article 3(1)
Article 3(2)	Article 3(4)
Article 3(3)	Article 3(2)
Article 3(4)	Article 3(3)
—	Article 3(4)
Article 3(5)	Article 3(5)
Article 4(1) first sentence	Article 4(1) first subparagraph
Article 4(1) second sentence	—
—	Article 4(1) second and third subparagraphs
Article 4(2) and (3)	Article 4(2) and (3)
—	Article 4(4) to (6)
Article 5(1) to (3)	Article 5(1) to (3)
Article 5(4), introductory words	Article 5(4), introductory words
Article 5(4) point (a)	Article 5(4) point (a)
Article 5(4) point (b), introductory words	Article 5(4) point (b), introductory words
Article 5(4) point (b), first indent	Article 5(4) point (b)(i)
Article 5(4) point (b), second indent	Article 5(4) point (b)(ii)
Article 5(4) point (b), third indent	Article 5(4) point (b)(iii)
Article 5(4) point (b), fourth indent	Article 5(4) point (b)(iv)
Article 5(4) points (c), (d) and (e)	Article 5(4) points (c), (d) and (e)
Article 5(5)	Article 5(5)
Article 6(1), introductory words	Article 6(1), introductory words
Article 6(1) points (a) and (b)	Article 6(1) points (a) and (b)
Article 6(1) point (c)	Article 6(1) point (c), first sentence
Article 6(2) to (5)	Article 6(2) to (5)
Article 7(1)	Article 7(1)
Article 7(3)	Article 7(2)
Article 7(4)	Article 7(3)
Article 7(5)	Article 7(4)
Article 8(1)	Article 6(1) point (c), second sentence
Article 8(2)	Article 8(1) and (2)
Article 8(3)	Article 8(3)

Regulation (EEC) No 4064/89	*This Regulation*
Article 8(4)	Article 8(4)
—	Article 8(5)
Article 8(5)	Article 8(6)
Article 8(6)	Article 8(7)
—	Article 8(8)
Article 9(1) to (9)	Article 9(1) to (9)
Article 9(10)	—
Article 10(1) and (2)	Article 10(1) and (2)
Article 10(3)	Article 10(3) first subparagraph, first sentence
—	Article 10(3) first subparagraph, second sentence
—	Article 10(3) second subparagraph
Article 10(4)	Article 10(4) first subparagraph
—	Article 10(4), second subparagraph
Article 10(5)	Article 10(5), first and fourth subparagraphs
—	Article 10(5), second, third and fifth subparagraphs
Article 10(6)	Article 10(6)
Article 11(1)	Article 11(1)
Article 11(2)	—
Article 11(3)	Article 11(2)
Article 11(4)	Article 11(4) first sentence
—	Article 11(4) second and third sentences
Article 11(5) first sentence	—
Article 11(5) second sentence	Article 11(3)
Article 11(6)	Article 11(5)
—	Article 11(6) and (7)
Article 12	Article 12
Article 13(1) first subparagraph	Article 13(1)
Article 13(1) second subparagraph, introductory words	Article 13(2) introductory words
Article 13(1) second subparagraph, point (a)	Article 13(2) point (b)
Article 13(1) second subparagraph, point (b)	Article 13(2) point (c)
Article 13(1) second subparagraph, point (c)	Article 13(2) point (e)
Article 13(1) second subparagraph, point (d)	Article 13(2) point (a)
—	Article 13(2) point (d)
Article 13(2)	Article 13(3)
Article 13(3)	Article 13(4) first and second sentences
Article 13(4)	Article 13(4) third sentence
Article 13(5)	Article 13(5), first sentence

Regulation (EEC) No 4064/89	*This Regulation*
—	Article 13(5), second sentence
Article 13(6) first sentence	Article 13(6)
Article 13(6) second sentence	—
—	Article 13(7) and (8)
Article 14(1) introductory words	Article 14(1) introductory words
Article 14(1) point (a)	Article 14(2) point (a)
Article 14(1) point (b)	Article 14(1) point (a)
Article 14(1) point (c)	Article 14(1) points (b) and (c)
Article 14(1) point (d)	Article 14(1) point (d)
—	Article 14(1) points (e) and (f)
Article 14(2) introductory words	Article 14(2) introductory words
Article 14(2) point (a)	Article 14(2) point (d)
Article 14(2) points (b) and (c)	Article 14(2) points (b) and (c)
Article 14(3)	Article 14(3)
Article 14(4)	Article 14(4)
Article 15(1) introductory words	Article 15(1) introductory words
Article 15(1) points (a) and (b)	Article 15(1) points (a) and (b)
Article 15(2) introductory words	Article 15(1) introductory words
Article 15(2) point (a)	Article 15(1) point (c)
Article 15(2) point (b)	Article 15(1) point (d)
Article 15(3)	Article 15(2)
Articles 16 to 20	Articles 16 to 20
Article 21(1)	Article 21(2)
Article 21(2)	Article 21(3)
Article 21(3)	Article 21(4)
Article 22(1)	Article 21(1)
Article 22(3)	—
—	Article 22(1) to (3)
Article 22(4)	Article 22(4)
Article 22(5)	—
—	Article 22(5)
Article 23	Article 23(1)
—	Article 23(2)
Article 24	Article 24
—	Article 25
Article 25(1)	Article 26(1), first subparagraph
—	Article 26(1), second subparagraph
Article 25(2)	Article 26(2)
Article 25(3)	Article 26(3)
—	Annex

[9560]

COMMISSION NOTICE

Guidelines on the assessment of horizontal mergers under the Council Regulation on the control of concentrations between undertakings

(2004/C31/03)

NOTES

Date of publication in OJ: OJ C31, 5.2.2004, p 5. Notes are as in the original OJ version.

I. INTRODUCTION

1. Article 2 of Council Regulation (EC) No 139/2004 of 20 January 2004 on the control of concentrations between undertakings[1] (hereinafter: the 'Merger Regulation') provides that the Commission has to appraise concentrations within the scope of the Merger Regulation with a view to establishing whether or not they are compatible with the common market. For that purpose, the Commission must assess, pursuant to Article 2(2) and (3), whether or not a concentration would significantly impede effective competition, in particular as a result of the creation or strengthening of a dominant position, in the common market or a substantial part of it.

2. Accordingly, the Commission must take into account any significant impediment to effective competition likely to be caused by a concentration. The creation or the strengthening of a dominant position is a primary form of such competitive harm. The concept of dominance was defined in the context of Council Regulation (EEC) No 4064/89 of 21 December 1989 on the control of concentrations between undertakings (hereinafter 'Regulation No 4064/89') as:

> 'a situation where one or more undertakings wield economic power which would enable them to prevent effective competition from being maintained in the relevant market by giving them the opportunity to act to a considerable extent independently of their competitors, their customers and, ultimately, of consumers'.[2]

3. For the purpose of interpreting the concept of dominance in the context of Regulation No 4064/89, the Court of Justice referred to the fact that it 'is intended to apply to all concentrations with a Community dimension insofar as they are likely, because of their effect on the structure of competition within the Community, to prove incompatible with the system of undistorted competition envisaged by the Treaty'.[3]

4. The creation or strengthening of a dominant position held by a single firm as a result of a merger has been the most common basis for finding that a concentration would result in a significant impediment to effective competition. Furthermore, the concept of dominance has also been applied in an oligopolistic setting to cases of collective dominance. As a consequence, it is expected that most cases of incompatibility of a concentration with the common market will continue to be based upon a finding of dominance. That concept therefore provides an important indication as to the standard of competitive harm that is applicable when determining whether a concentration is likely to impede effective competition to a significant degree, and hence, as to the likelihood of intervention.[4] To that effect, the present notice is intended to preserve the guidance that can be drawn from past decisional practice and to take full account of past case-law of the Community Courts.

5. The purpose of this notice is to provide guidance as to how the Commission assesses concentrations[5] when the undertakings concerned are actual or potential competitors on the same relevant market.[6] In this notice such mergers will be denoted 'horizontal mergers'. While the notice presents the analytical approach used by the Commission in its appraisal of horizontal mergers it cannot provide details of all possible applications of this approach. The Commission applies the approach described in the notice to the particular facts and circumstances of each case.

6. The guidance set out in this notice draws and elaborates on the Commission's evolving experience with the appraisal of horizontal mergers under Regulation No 4064/89 since its entry into force on 21 September 1990 as well as on the case-law of the Court of Justice and the Court of First Instance of the European Communities. The principles contained here will be applied and further developed and refined by the Commission in individual cases. The Commission may revise this notice from time to time in the light of future developments.

7. The Commission's interpretation of the Merger Regulation as regards the appraisal of horizontal mergers is without prejudice to the interpretation which may be given by the Court of Justice or the Court of First Instance of the European Communities.

II. OVERVIEW

8. Effective competition brings benefits to consumers, such as low prices, high quality products, a wide selection of goods and services, and innovation. Through its control of mergers, the Commission prevents mergers that would be likely to deprive customers of these benefits by significantly increasing the market power of firms. By 'increased market power' is meant the ability of one or more firms to profitably increase prices, reduce output, choice or quality of goods and services, diminish innovation, or otherwise influence parameters of competition. In this notice, the expression 'increased prices' is often used as shorthand for these various ways in which a merger may result in competitive harm.[7] Both suppliers and buyers can have market power. However, for clarity, market power will usually refer here to a supplier's market power. Where a buyer's market power is the issue, the term 'buyer power' is employed.

9. In assessing the competitive effects of a merger, the Commission compares the competitive conditions that would result from the notified merger with the conditions that would have prevailed without the merger.[8] In most cases the competitive conditions existing at the time of the merger constitute the relevant comparison for evaluating the effects of a merger. However, in some circumstances, the Commission may take into account future changes to the market that can reasonably be predicted.[9] It may, in particular, take account of the likely entry or exit of firms if the merger did not take place when considering what constitutes the relevant comparison.[10]

10. The Commission's assessment of mergers normally entails:

(a) definition of the relevant product and geographic markets;

(b) competitive assessment of the merger.

The main purpose of market definition is to identify in a systematic way the immediate competitive constraints facing the merged entity. Guidance on this issue can be found in the Commission's Notice on the definition of the relevant market for the purposes of Community competition law.[11] Various considerations leading to the delineation of the relevant markets may also be of importance for the competitive assessment of the merger.

11. This notice is structured around the following elements:

(a) The approach of the Commission to market shares and concentration thresholds (Section III).

(b) The likelihood that a merger would have anti-competitive effects in the relevant markets, in the absence of countervailing factors (Section IV).

(c) The likelihood that buyer power would act as a countervailing factor to an increase in market power resulting from the merger (Section V).

(d) The likelihood that entry would maintain effective competition in the relevant markets (Section VI).

(e) The likelihood that efficiencies would act as a factor counteracting the harmful effects on competition which might otherwise result from the merger (Section VII).

(f) The conditions for a failing firm defence (Section VIII).

12. In order to assess the foreseeable impact[12] of a merger on the relevant markets, the Commission analyses its possible anti-competitive effects and the relevant countervailing factors such as buyer power, the extent of entry barriers and possible efficiencies put forward by the parties. In exceptional circumstances, the Commission considers whether the conditions for a failing firm defence are met.

13. In the light of these elements, the Commission determines, pursuant to Article 2 of the Merger Regulation, whether the merger would significantly impede effective competition, in particular through the creation or the strengthening of a dominant position, and should therefore be declared incompatible with the common market. It should be stressed that these factors are not a 'checklist' to be mechanically applied in each and every case. Rather, the competitive analysis in a particular case will be based on an overall assessment of the foreseeable impact of the merger in the light of the relevant factors and conditions. Not all the elements will always be relevant to each and every horizontal merger, and it may not be necessary to analyse all the elements of a case in the same detail.

III. MARKET SHARE AND CONCENTRATION LEVELS

14. Market shares and concentration levels provide useful first indications of the market structure and of the competitive importance of both the merging parties and their competitors.

15. Normally, the Commission uses current market shares in its competitive analysis.[13] However, current market shares may be adjusted to reflect reasonably certain future changes, for instance in the light of exit, entry or expansion.[14] Post-merger market shares are calculated on the assumption that the post-merger combined market share of the merging parties is the sum of their pre-merger market shares.[15] Historic data may be used if market shares have been volatile, for instance when the market is characterised by large, lumpy orders. Changes in historic market shares may provide useful information about the competitive process and the likely future importance of the various competitors, for instance, by indicating whether firms have been gaining or losing market shares. In any event, the Commission interprets market shares in the light of likely market conditions, for instance, if the market is highly dynamic in character and if the market structure is unstable due to innovation or growth.[16]

16. The overall concentration level in a market may also provide useful information about the competitive situation. In order to measure concentration levels, the Commission often applies the Herfindahl-Hirschman Index (HHI).[17] The HHI is calculated by summing the squares of the individual market shares of all the firms in the market.[18] The HHI gives proportionately greater weight to the market shares of the larger firms. Although it is best to include all firms in the calculation, lack of information about very small firms may not be important because such firms do not affect the HHI significantly. While the absolute level of the HHI can give an initial indication of the competitive pressure in the market post-merger, the change in the HHI (known as the 'delta') is a useful proxy for the change in concentration directly brought about by the merger.[19]

Market share levels

17. According to well-established case law, very large market shares—50% or more—may in themselves be evidence of the existence of a dominant market position.[20] However, smaller competitors may act as a sufficient constraining influence if, for example, they have the ability and incentive to increase their supplies. A merger involving a firm whose market share will remain below 50% after the merger may also raise competition concerns in view of other factors such as the strength and number of competitors, the presence of capacity constraints or the extent to which the products of the merging parties are close substitutes. The Commission has thus in several cases considered mergers resulting in firms holding market shares between 40% and 50%,[21] and in some cases below 40%,[22] to lead to the creation or the strengthening of a dominant position.

18. Concentrations which, by reason of the limited market share of the undertakings concerned, are not liable to impede effective competition may be presumed to be compatible with the common market. Without prejudice to Articles 81 and 82 of the Treaty, an indication to this effect exists, in particular, where the market share of the undertakings concerned does not exceed 25%[23] either in the common market or in a substantial part of it.[24]

HHI levels

19. The Commission is unlikely to identify horizontal competition concerns in a market with a post-merger HHI below 1,000. Such markets normally do not require extensive analysis.

20. The Commission is also unlikely to identify horizontal competition concerns in a merger with a post-merger HHI between 1,000 and 2,000 and a delta below 250, or a merger with a post-merger HHI above 2,000 and a delta below 150, except where special circumstances such as, for instance, one or more of the following factors are present:

(a) a merger involves a potential entrant or a recent entrant with a small market share;
(b) one or more merging parties are important innovators in ways not reflected in market shares;
(c) there are significant cross-shareholdings among the market participants;[25]
(d) one of the merging firms is a maverick firm with a high likelihood of disrupting coordinated conduct;
(e) indications of past or ongoing coordination, or facilitating practices, are present;
(f) one of the merging parties has a pre-merger market share of 50% of more.[26]

21. Each of these HHI levels, in combination with the relevant deltas, may be used as an initial indicator of the absence of competition concerns. However, they do not give rise to a presumption of either the existence or the absence of such concerns.

IV. POSSIBLE ANTI-COMPETITIVE EFFECTS OF HORIZONTAL MERGERS

22. There are two main ways in which horizontal mergers may significantly impede effective competition, in particular by creating or strengthening a dominant position:

(a) by eliminating important competitive constraints on one or more firms, which consequently would have increased market power, without resorting to coordinated behaviour (non-coordinated effects);

(b) by changing the nature of competition in such a way that firms that previously were not coordinating their behaviour, are now significantly more likely to coordinate and raise prices or otherwise harm effective competition. A merger may also make coordination easier, more stable or more effective for firms which were coordinating prior to the merger (coordinated effects).

23. The Commission assesses whether the changes brought about by the merger would result in any of these effects. Both instances mentioned above may be relevant when assessing a particular transaction.

Non-coordinated effects[27]

24. A merger may significantly impede effective competition in a market by removing important competitive constraints on one or more sellers, who consequently have increased market power. The most direct effect of the merger will be the loss of competition between the merging firms. For example, if prior to the merger one of the merging firms had raised its price, it would have lost some sales to the other merging firm. The merger removes this particular constraint. Non-merging firms in the same market can also benefit from the reduction of competitive pressure that results from the merger, since the merging firms' price increase may switch some demand to the rival firms, which, in turn, may find it profitable to increase their prices.[28] The reduction in these competitive constraints could lead to significant price increases in the relevant market.

25. Generally, a merger giving rise to such non-coordinated effects would significantly impede effective competition by creating or strengthening the dominant position of a single firm, one which, typically, would have an appreciably larger market share than the next competitor post-merger. Furthermore, mergers in oligopolistic markets[29] involving the elimination of important competitive constraints that the merging parties previously exerted upon each other together with a reduction of competitive pressure on the remaining competitors may, even where there is little likelihood of coordination between the members of the oligopoly, also result in a significant impediment to competition. The Merger Regulation clarifies that all mergers giving rise to such non-coordinated effects shall also be declared incompatible with the common market.[30]

26. A number of factors, which taken separately are not necessarily decisive, may influence whether significant non-coordinated effects are likely to result from a merger. Not all of these factors need to be present for such effects to be likely. Nor should this be considered an exhaustive list.

Merging firms have large market shares

27. The larger the market share, the more likely a firm is to possess market power. And the larger the addition of market share, the more likely it is that a merger will lead to a significant increase in market power. The larger the increase in the sales base on which to enjoy higher margins after a price increase, the more likely it is that the merging firms will find such a price increase profitable despite the accompanying reduction in output. Although market shares and additions of market shares only provide first indications of market power and increases in market power, they are normally important factors in the assessment.[31]

Merging firms are close competitors

28. Products may be differentiated[32] within a relevant market such that some products are closer substitutes than others.[33] The higher the degree of substitutability between the merging firms' products, the more likely it is that the merging firms will raise prices significantly.[34] For example, a merger between two producers offering products which a substantial number of customers regard as their first and second choices could generate a significant price increase. Thus, the fact that rivalry between the parties has been an important source of competition on the market may be a central factor in the analysis.[35] High pre-merger margins[36] may also make significant price increases more likely. The merging firms' incentive

to raise prices is more likely to be constrained when rival firms produce close substitutes to the products of the merging firms than when they offer less close substitutes.[37] It is therefore less likely that a merger will significantly impede effective competition, in particular through the creation or strengthening of a dominant position, when there is a high degree of substitutability between the products of the merging firms and those supplied by rival producers.

29. When data are available, the degree of substitutability may be evaluated through customer preference surveys, analysis of purchasing patterns, estimation of the cross-price elasticities of the products involved,[38] or diversion ratios.[39] In bidding markets it may be possible to measure whether historically the submitted bids by one of the merging parties have been constrained by the presence of the other merging party.[40]

30. In some markets it may be relatively easy and not too costly for the active firms to reposition their products or extend their product portfolio. In particular, the Commission examines whether the possibility of repositioning or product line extension by competitors or the merging parties may influence the incentive of the merged entity to raise prices. However, product repositioning or product line extension often entails risks and large sunk costs[41] and may be less profitable than the current line.

Customers have limited possibilities of switching supplier

31. Customers of the merging parties may have difficulties switching to other suppliers because there are few alternative suppliers[42] or because they face substantial switching costs.[43] Such customers are particularly vulnerable to price increases. The merger may affect these customers' ability to protect themselves against price increases. In particular, this may be the case for customers that have used dual sourcing from the two merging firms as a means of obtaining competitive prices. Evidence of past customer switching patterns and reactions to price changes may provide important information in this respect.

Competitors are unlikely to increase supply if prices increase

32. When market conditions are such that the competitors of the merging parties are unlikely to increase their supply substantially if prices increase, the merging firms may have an incentive to reduce output below the combined pre-merger levels, thereby raising market prices.[44] The merger increases the incentive to reduce output by giving the merged firm a larger base of sales on which to enjoy the higher margins resulting from an increase in prices induced by the output reduction.

33. Conversely, when market conditions are such that rival firms have enough capacity and find it profitable to expand output sufficiently, the Commission is unlikely to find that the merger will create or strengthen a dominant position or otherwise significantly impede effective competition.

34. Such output expansion is, in particular, unlikely when competitors face binding capacity constraints and the expansion of capacity is costly[45] or if existing excess capacity is significantly more costly to operate than capacity currently in use.

35. Although capacity constraints are more likely to be important when goods are relatively homogeneous, they may also be important where firms offer differentiated products.

Merged entity able to hinder expansion by competitors

36. Some proposed mergers would, if allowed to proceed, significantly impede effective competition by leaving the merged firm in a position where it would have the ability and incentive to make the expansion of smaller firms and potential competitors more difficult or otherwise restrict the ability of rival firms to compete. In such a case, competitors may not, either individually or in the aggregate, be in a position to constrain the merged entity to such a degree that it would not increase prices or take other actions detrimental to competition. For instance, the merged entity may have such a degree of control, or influence over, the supply of inputs[46] or distribution possibilities[47] that expansion or entry by rival firms may be more costly. Similarly, the merged entity's control over patents[48] or other types of intellectual property (e g brands[49] may make expansion or entry by rivals more difficult. In markets where interoperability between different infrastructures or platforms is important,[50] a merger may give the merged entity the ability and incentive to raise the costs or decrease the quality of

service of its rivals.[51] In making this assessment the Commission may take into account, *inter alia*, the financial strength of the merged entity relative to its rivals.[52]

Merger eliminates an important competitive force

37. Some firms have more of an influence on the competitive process than their market shares or similar measures would suggest. A merger involving such a firm may change the competitive dynamics in a significant, anti-competitive way, in particular when the market is already concentrated.[53] For instance, a firm may be a recent entrant that is expected to exert significant competitive pressure in the future on the other firms in the market.

38. In markets where innovation is an important competitive force, a merger may increase the firms' ability and incentive to bring new innovations to the market and, thereby, the competitive pressure on rivals to innovate in that market. Alternatively, effective competition may be significantly impeded by a merger between two important innovators, for instance between two companies with 'pipeline' products related to a specific product market. Similarly, a firm with a relatively small market share may nevertheless be an important competitive force if it has promising pipeline products.[54]

Coordinated effects

39. In some markets the structure may be such that firms would consider it possible, economically rational, and hence preferable, to adopt on a sustainable basis a course of action on the market aimed at selling at increased prices. A merger in a concentrated market may significantly impede effective competition, through the creation or the strengthening of a collective dominant position, because it increases the likelihood that firms are able to coordinate their behaviour in this way and raise prices, even without entering into an agreement or resorting to a concerted practice within the meaning of Article 81 of the Treaty.[55] A merger may also make coordination easier, more stable or more effective for firms, that were already coordinating before the merger, either by making the coordination more robust or by permitting firms to coordinate on even higher prices.

40. Coordination may take various forms. In some markets, the most likely coordination may involve keeping prices above the competitive level. In other markets, coordination may aim at limiting production or the amount of new capacity brought to the market. Firms may also coordinate by dividing the market, for instance by geographic area[56] or other customer characteristics, or by allocating contracts in bidding markets.

41. Coordination is more likely to emerge in markets where it is relatively simple to reach a common understanding on the terms of coordination. In addition, three conditions are necessary for coordination to be sustainable. First, the coordinating firms must be able to monitor to a sufficient degree whether the terms of coordination are being adhered to. Second, discipline requires that there is some form of credible deterrent mechanism that can be activated if deviation is detected. Third, the reactions of outsiders, such as current and future competitors not participating in the coordination, as well as customers, should not be able to jeopardise the results expected from the coordination.[57]

42. The Commission examines whether it would be possible to reach terms of coordination and whether the coordination is likely to be sustainable. In this respect, the Commission considers the changes that the merger brings about. The reduction in the number of firms in a market may, in itself, be a factor that facilitates coordination. However, a merger may also increase the likelihood or significance of coordinated effects in other ways. For instance, a merger may involve a 'maverick' firm that has a history of preventing or disrupting coordination, for example by failing to follow price increases by its competitors, or has characteristics that gives it an incentive to favour different strategic choices than its coordinating competitors would prefer. If the merged firm were to adopt strategies similar to those of other competitors, the remaining firms would find it easier to coordinate, and the merger would increase the likelihood, stability or effectiveness of coordination.

43. In assessing the likelihood of coordinated effects, the Commission takes into account all available relevant information on the characteristics of the markets concerned, including both structural features and the past behaviour of firms.[58] Evidence of past coordination is important if the relevant market characteristics have not changed appreciably or are not likely to do so in the near future.[59] Likewise, evidence of coordination in similar markets may be useful information.

Reaching terms of coordination

44. Coordination is more likely to emerge if competitors can easily arrive at a common perception as to how the coordination should work. Coordinating firms should have similar views regarding which actions would be considered to be in accordance with the aligned behaviour and which actions would not.

45. Generally, the less complex and the more stable the economic environment, the easier it is for the firms to reach a common understanding on the terms of coordination. For instance, it is easier to coordinate among a few players than among many. It is also easier to coordinate on a price for a single, homogeneous product, than on hundreds of prices in a market with many differentiated products. Similarly, it is easier to coordinate on a price when demand and supply conditions are relatively stable than when they are continuously changing.[60] In this context volatile demand, substantial internal growth by some firms in the market or frequent entry by new firms may indicate that the current situation is not sufficiently stable to make coordination likely.[61] In markets where innovation is important, coordination may be more difficult since innovations, particularly significant ones, may allow one firm to gain a major advantage over its rivals.

46. Coordination by way of market division will be easier if customers have simple characteristics that allow the coordinating firms to readily allocate them. Such characteristics may be based on geography; on customer type or simply on the existence of customers who typically buy from one specific firm. Coordination by way of market division may be relatively straightforward if it is easy to identify each customer's supplier and the coordination device is the allocation of existing customers to their incumbent supplier.

47. Coordinating firms may, however, find other ways to overcome problems stemming from complex economic environments short of market division. They may, for instance, establish simple pricing rules that reduce the complexity of coordinating on a large number of prices. One example of such a rule is establishing a small number of pricing points, thus reducing the coordination problem. Another example is having a fixed relationship between certain base prices and a number of other prices, such that prices basically move in parallel. Publicly available key information, exchange of information through trade associations, or information received through cross-shareholdings or participation in joint ventures may also help firms reach terms of coordination. The more complex the market situation is, the more transparency or communication is likely to be needed to reach a common under-standing on the terms of coordination.

48. Firms may find it easier to reach a common understanding on the terms of coordination if they are relatively symmetric,[62] especially in terms of cost structures, market shares, capacity levels and levels of vertical integration.[63] Structural links such as cross-shareholding or participation in joint ventures may also help in aligning incentives among the coordinating firms.[64]

Monitoring deviations

49. Coordinating firms are often tempted to increase their share of the market by deviating from the terms of coordination, for instance by lowering prices, offering secret discounts, increasing product quality or capacity or trying to win new customers. Only the credible threat of timely and sufficient retaliation keeps firms from deviating. Markets therefore need to be sufficiently transparent to allow the coordinating firms to monitor to a sufficient degree whether other firms are deviating, and thus know when to retaliate.[65]

50. Transparency in the market is often higher, the lower the number of active participants in the market. Further, the degree of transparency often depends on how market transactions take place in a particular market. For example, transparency is likely to be high in a market where transactions take place on a public exchange or in an open outcry auction.[66] Conversely, transparency may be low in a market where transactions are confidentially negotiated between buyers and sellers on a bilateral basis.[67] When evaluating the level of transparency in the market, the key element is to identify what firms can infer about the actions of other firms from the available information.[68] Coordinating firms should be able to interpret with some certainty whether unexpected behaviour is the result of deviation from the terms of coordination. For instance, in unstable environments it may be difficult for a firm to know whether its lost sales are due to an overall low level of demand or due to a competitor offering particularly low prices. Similarly, when overall demand or cost conditions fluctuate, it may be difficult to interpret whether a competitor is lowering its price because it expects the coordinated prices to fall or because it is deviating.

51. In some markets where the general conditions may seem to make monitoring of deviations difficult, firms may nevertheless engage in practices which have the effect of easing the monitoring task, even when these practices are not necessarily entered into for such purposes. These practices, such as meeting-competition or most-favoured-customer clauses, voluntary publication of information, announcements, or exchange of information through trade associations, may increase transparency or help competitors interpret the choices made. Cross-directorships, participation in joint ventures and similar arrangements may also make monitoring easier.

Deterrent mechanisms

52. Coordination is not sustainable unless the consequences of deviation are sufficiently severe to convince coordinating firms that it is in their best interest to adhere to the terms of coordination. It is thus the threat of future retaliation that keeps the coordination sustainable.[69] However the threat is only credible if, where deviation by one of the firms is detected, there is sufficient certainty that some deterrent mechanism will be activated.[70]

53. Retaliation that manifests itself after some significant time lag, or is not certain to be activated, is less likely to be sufficient to offset the benefits from deviating. For example, if a market is characterised by infrequent, large-volume orders, it may be difficult to establish a sufficiently severe deterrent mechanism, since the gain from deviating at the right time may be large, certain and immediate, whereas the losses from being punished may be small and uncertain and only materialise after some time. The speed with which deterrent mechanisms can be implemented is related to the issue of transparency. If firms are only able to observe their competitors' actions after a substantial delay, then retaliation will be similarly delayed and this may influence whether it is sufficient to deter deviation.

54. The credibility of the deterrence mechanism depends on whether the other coordinating firms have an incentive to retaliate. Some deterrent mechanisms, such as punishing the deviator by temporarily engaging in a price war or increasing output significantly, may entail a short-term economic loss for the firms carrying out the retaliation. This does not necessarily remove the incentive to retaliate since the short-term loss may be smaller than the long-term benefit of retaliating resulting from the return to the regime of coordination.

55. Retaliation need not necessarily take place in the same market as the deviation.[71] If the coordinating firms have commercial interaction in other markets, these may offer various methods of retaliation.[72] The retaliation could take many forms, including cancellation of joint ventures or other forms of cooperation or selling of shares in jointly owned companies.

Reactions of outsiders

56. For coordination to be successful, the actions of non-coordinating firms and potential competitors, as well as customers, should not be able to jeopardise the outcome expected from coordination. For example, if coordination aims at reducing overall capacity in the market, this will only hurt consumers if non-coordinating firms are unable or have no incentive to respond to this decrease by increasing their own capacity sufficiently to prevent a net decrease in capacity, or at least to render the coordinated capacity decrease unprofitable.[73]

57. The effects of entry and countervailing buyer power of customers are analysed in later sections. However, special consideration is given to the possible impact of these elements on the stability of coordination. For instance, by concentrating a large amount of its requirements with one supplier or by offering long-term contracts, a large buyer may make coordination unstable by successfully tempting one of the coordinating firms to deviate in order to gain substantial new business.

Merger with a potential competitor

58. Concentrations where an undertaking already active on a relevant market merges with a potential competitor in this market can have similar anti-competitive effects to mergers between two undertakings already active on the same relevant market and, thus, significantly impede effective competition, in particular through the creation or the strengthening of a dominant position.

59. A merger with a potential competitor can generate horizontal anti-competitive effects, whether coordinated or non-coordinated, if the potential competitor significantly

constrains the behaviour of the firms active in the market. This is the case if the potential competitor possesses assets that could easily be used to enter the market without incurring significant sunk costs. Anti-competitive effects may also occur where the merging partner is very likely to incur the necessary sunk costs to enter the market in a relatively short period of time after which this company would constrain the behaviour of the firms currently active in the market.[74]

60. For a merger with a potential competitor to have significant anti-competitive effects, two basic conditions must be fulfilled. First, the potential competitor must already exert a significant constraining influence or there must be a significant likelihood that it would grow into an effective competitive force. Evidence that a potential competitor has plans to enter a market in a significant way could help the Commission to reach such a conclusion.[75] Second, there must not be a sufficient number of other potential competitors, which could maintain sufficient competitive pressure after the merger.[76]

Mergers creating or strengthening buyer power in upstream markets

61. The Commission may also analyse to what extent a merged entity will increase its buyer power in upstream markets. On the one hand, a merger that creates or strengthens the market power of a buyer may significantly impede effective competition, in particular by creating or strengthening a dominant position. The merged firm may be in a position to obtain lower prices by reducing its purchase of inputs. This may, in turn, lead it also to lower its level of output in the final product market, and thus harm consumer welfare.[77] Such effects may in particular arise when upstream sellers are relatively fragmented. Competition in the downstream markets could also be adversely affected if, in particular, the merged entity were likely to use its buyer power vis-à-vis its suppliers to foreclose its rivals.[78]

62. On the other hand, increased buyer power may be beneficial for competition. If increased buyer power lowers input costs without restricting downstream competition or total output, then a proportion of these cost reductions are likely to be passed onto consumers in the form of lower prices.

63. In order to assess whether a merger would significantly impede effective competition by creating or strengthening buyer power, an analysis of the competitive conditions in upstream markets and an evaluation of the possible positive and negative effects described above are therefore required.

V. COUNTERVAILING BUYER POWER

64. The competitive pressure on a supplier is not only exercised by competitors but can also come from its customers. Even firms with very high market shares may not be in a position, post-merger, to significantly impede effective competition, in particular by acting to an appreciable extent independently of their customers, if the latter possess countervailing buyer power.[79] Countervailing buyer power in this context should be understood as the bargaining strength that the buyer has vis-à-vis the seller in commercial negotiations due to its size, its commercial significance to the seller and its ability to switch to alternative suppliers.

65. The Commission considers, when relevant, to what extent customers will be in a position to counter the increase in market power that a merger would otherwise be likely to create. One source of countervailing buyer power would be if a customer could credibly threaten to resort, within a reasonable timeframe, to alternative sources of supply should the supplier decide to increase prices[80] or to otherwise deteriorate quality or the conditions of delivery. This would be the case if the buyer could immediately switch to other suppliers,[81] credibly threaten to vertically integrate into the upstream market or to sponsor upstream expansion or entry[82] for instance by persuading a potential entrant to enter by committing to placing large orders with this company. It is more likely that large and sophisticated customers will possess this kind of countervailing buyer power than smaller firms in a fragmented industry.[83] A buyer may also exercise countervailing buying power by refusing to buy other products produced by the supplier or, particularly in the case of durable goods, delaying purchases.

66. In some cases, it may be important to pay particular attention to the incentives of buyers to utilise their buyer power.[84] For example, a downstream firm may not wish to make an investment in sponsoring new entry if the benefits of such entry in terms of lower input costs could also be reaped by its competitors.

67. Countervailing buyer power cannot be found to sufficiently off-set potential adverse effects of a merger if it only ensures that a particular segment of customers,[85] with particular

bargaining strength, is shielded from significantly higher prices or deteriorated conditions after the merger.[86] Furthermore, it is not sufficient that buyer power exists prior to the merger, it must also exist and remain effective following the merger. This is because a merger of two suppliers may reduce buyer power if it thereby removes a credible alternative.

VI. ENTRY

68. When entering a market is sufficiently easy, a merger is unlikely to pose any significant anti-competitive risk. Therefore, entry analysis constitutes an important element of the overall competitive assessment. For entry to be considered a sufficient competitive constraint on the merging parties, it must be shown to be likely, timely and sufficient to deter or defeat any potential anti-competitive effects of the merger.

Likelihood of entry

69. The Commission examines whether entry is likely or whether potential entry is likely to constrain the behaviour of incumbents post-merger. For entry to be likely, it must be sufficiently profitable taking into account the price effects of injecting additional output into the market and the potential responses of the incumbents. Entry is thus less likely if it would only be economically viable on a large scale, thereby resulting in significantly depressed price levels. And entry is likely to be more difficult if the incumbents are able to protect their market shares by offering long-term contracts or giving targeted pre-emptive price reductions to those customers that the entrant is trying to acquire. Furthermore, high risk and costs of failed entry may make entry less likely. The costs of failed entry will be higher, the higher is the level of sunk cost associated with entry.[87]

70. Potential entrants may encounter barriers to entry which determine entry risks and costs and thus have an impact on the profitability of entry. Barriers to entry are specific features of the market, which give incumbent firms advantages over potential competitors. When entry barriers are low, the merging parties are more likely to be constrained by entry. Conversely, when entry barriers are high, price increases by the merging firms would not be significantly constrained by entry. Historical examples of entry and exit in the industry may provide useful information about the size of entry barriers.

71. Barriers to entry can take various forms:

(a) Legal advantages encompass situations where regulatory barriers limit the number of market participants by, for example, restricting the number of licences.[88] They also cover tariff and non-tariff trade barriers.[89]

(b) The incumbents may also enjoy technical advantages, such as preferential access to essential facilities, natural resources,[90] innovation and R & D,[91] or intellectual property rights,[92] which make it difficult for any firm to compete successfully. For instance, in certain industries, it might be difficult to obtain essential input materials, or patents might protect products or processes. Other factors such as economies of scale and scope, distribution and sales networks,[93] access to important technologies, may also constitute barriers to entry.

(c) Furthermore, barriers to entry may also exist because of the established position of the incumbent firms on the market. In particular, it may be difficult to enter a particular industry because experience or reputation is necessary to compete effectively, both of which may be difficult to obtain as an entrant. Factors such as consumer loyalty to a particular brand,[94] the closeness of relationships between suppliers and customers, the importance of promotion or advertising, or other advantages relating to reputation[95] will be taken into account in this context. Barriers to entry also encompass situations where the incumbents have already committed to building large excess capacity,[96] or where the costs faced by customers in switching to a new supplier may inhibit entry.

72. The expected evolution of the market should be taken into account when assessing whether or not entry would be profitable. Entry is more likely to be profitable in a market that is expected to experience high growth in the future[97] than in a market that is mature or expected to decline.[98] Scale economies or network effects may make entry unprofitable unless the entrant can obtain a sufficiently large market share.[99]

73. Entry is particularly likely if suppliers in other markets already possess production facilities that could be used to enter the market in question, thus reducing the sunk costs of entry. The smaller the difference in profitability between entry and non-entry prior to the merger, the more likely such a reallocation of production facilities.

Timeliness

74. The Commission examines whether entry would be sufficiently swift and sustained to deter or defeat the exercise of market power. What constitutes an appropriate time period depends on the characteristics and dynamics of the market, as well as on the specific capabilities of potential entrants.[100] However, entry is normally only considered timely if it occurs within two years.

Sufficiency

75. Entry must be of sufficient scope and magnitude to deter or defeat the anti-competitive effects of the merger.[101] Small-scale entry, for instance into some market 'niche', may not be considered sufficient.

VII. EFFICIENCIES

76. Corporate reorganisations in the form of mergers may be in line with the requirements of dynamic competition and are capable of increasing the competitiveness of industry, thereby improving the conditions of growth and raising the standard of living in the Community.[102] It is possible that efficiencies brought about by a merger counteract the effects on competition and in particular the potential harm to consumers that it might otherwise have.[103] In order to assess whether a merger would significantly impede effective competition, in particular through the creation or the strengthening of a dominant position, within the meaning of Article 2(2) and (3) of the Merger Regulation, the Commission performs an overall competitive appraisal of the merger. In making this appraisal, the Commission takes into account the factors mentioned in Article 2(1), including the development of technical and economic progress provided that it is to the consumers' advantage and does not form an obstacle to competition.[104]

77. The Commission considers any substantiated efficiency claim in the overall assessment of the merger. It may decide that, as a consequence of the efficiencies that the merger brings about, there are no grounds for declaring the merger incompatible with the common market pursuant to Article 2(3) of the Merger Regulation. This will be the case when the Commission is in a position to conclude on the basis of sufficient evidence that the efficiencies generated by the merger are likely to enhance the ability and incentive of the merged entity to act pro-competitively for the benefit of consumers, thereby counteracting the adverse effects on competition which the merger might otherwise have.

78. For the Commission to take account of efficiency claims in its assessment of the merger and be in a position to reach the conclusion that as a consequence of efficiencies, there are no grounds for declaring the merger to be incompatible with the common market, the efficiencies have to benefit consumers, be merger-specific and be verifiable. These conditions are cumulative.

Benefit to consumers

79. The relevant benchmark in assessing efficiency claims is that consumers[105] will not be worse off as a result of the merger. For that purpose, efficiencies should be substantial and timely, and should, in principle, benefit consumers in those relevant markets where it is otherwise likely that competition concerns would occur.

80. Mergers may bring about various types of efficiency gains that can lead to lower prices or other benefits to consumers. For example, cost savings in production or distribution may give the merged entity the ability and incentive to charge lower prices following the merger. In line with the need to ascertain whether efficiencies will lead to a net benefit to consumers, cost efficiencies that lead to reductions in variable or marginal costs[106] are more likely to be relevant to the assessment of efficiencies than reductions in fixed costs; the former are, in principle, more likely to result in lower prices for consumers.[107] Cost reductions, which merely result from anti-competitive reductions in output, cannot be considered as efficiencies benefiting consumers.

81. Consumers may also benefit from new or improved products or services, for instance resulting from efficiency gains in the sphere of R & D and innovation. A joint venture company set up in order to develop a new product may bring about the type of efficiencies that the Commission can take into account.

82. In the context of coordinated effects, efficiencies may increase the merged entity's incentive to increase production and reduce prices, and thereby reduce its incentive to coordinate its market behaviour with other firms in the market. Efficiencies may therefore lead to a lower risk of coordinated effects in the relevant market.

83. In general, the later the efficiencies are expected to materialise in the future, the less weight the Commission can assign to them. This implies that, in order to be considered as a counteracting factor, the efficiencies must be timely.

84. The incentive on the part of the merged entity to pass efficiency gains on to consumers is often related to the existence of competitive pressure from the remaining firms in the market and from potential entry. The greater the possible negative effects on competition, the more the Commission has to be sure that the claimed efficiencies are substantial, likely to be realised, and to be passed on, to a sufficient degree, to the consumer. It is highly unlikely that a merger leading to a market position approaching that of a monopoly, or leading to a similar level of market power, can be declared compatible with the common market on the ground that efficiency gains would be sufficient to counteract its potential anti-competitive effects.

Merger specificity

85. Efficiencies are relevant to the competitive assessment when they are a direct consequence of the notified merger and cannot be achieved to a similar extent by less anticompetitive alternatives. In these circumstances, the efficiencies are deemed to be caused by the merger and thus, merger-specific.[108] It is for the merging parties to provide in due time all the relevant information necessary to demonstrate that there are no less anti-competitive, realistic and attainable alternatives of a non-concentrative nature (e g a licensing agreement, or a cooperative joint venture) or of a concentrative nature (e g a concentrative joint venture, or a differently structured merger) than the notified merger which preserve the claimed efficiencies. The Commission only considers alternatives that are reasonably practical in the business situation faced by the merging parties having regard to established business practices in the industry concerned.

Verifiability

86. Efficiencies have to be verifiable such that the Commission can be reasonably certain that the efficiencies are likely to materialise, and be substantial enough to counteract a merger's potential harm to consumers. The more precise and convincing the efficiency claims are, the better the Commission can evaluate the claims. Where reasonably possible, efficiencies and the resulting benefit to consumers should therefore be quantified. When the necessary data are not available to allow for a precise quantitative analysis, it must be possible to foresee a clearly identifiable positive impact on consumers, not a marginal one. In general, the longer the start of the efficiencies is projected into the future, the less probability the Commission may be able to assign to the efficiencies actually being brought about.

87. Most of the information, allowing the Commission to assess whether the merger will bring about the sort of efficiencies that would enable it to clear a merger, is solely in the possession of the merging parties. It is, therefore, incumbent upon the notifying parties to provide in due time all the relevant information necessary to demonstrate that the claimed efficiencies are merger-specific and likely to be realised. Similarly, it is for the notifying parties to show to what extent the efficiencies are likely to counteract any adverse effects on competition that might otherwise result from the merger, and therefore benefit consumers.

88. Evidence relevant to the assessment of efficiency claims includes, in particular, internal documents that were used by the management to decide on the merger, statements from the management to the owners and financial markets about the expected efficiencies, historical examples of efficiencies and consumer benefit, and pre-merger external experts' studies on the type and size of efficiency gains, and on the extent to which consumers are likely to benefit.

VIII. FAILING FIRM

89. The Commission may decide that an otherwise problematic merger is nevertheless compatible with the common market if one of the merging parties is a failing firm. The basic requirement is that the deterioration of the competitive structure that follows the merger

cannot be said to be caused by the merger.[109] This will arise where the competitive structure of the market would deteriorate to at least the same extent in the absence of the merger.[110]

90. The Commission considers the following three criteria to be especially relevant for the application of a 'failing firm defence'. First, the allegedly failing firm would in the near future be forced out of the market because of financial difficulties if not taken over by another undertaking. Second, there is no less anti-competitive alternative purchase than the notified merger. Third, in the absence of a merger, the assets of the failing firm would inevitably exit the market.[111]

91. It is for the notifying parties to provide in due time all the relevant information necessary to demonstrate that the deterioration of the competitive structure that follows the merger is not caused by the merger.

[9561]

NOTES

1 Council Regulation (EC) No 139/2004 of 20 January 2004 (OJ L24, 29.1.2004, p 1).

2 Case T-102/96, *Gencor v Commission*, [1999] ECR II-753, paragraph 200. See Joined Cases C-68/94 and C-30/95, *France and others v Commission* (hereinafter 'Kali and Salz'), [1998] ECR I-1375, paragraph 221. In exceptional circumstances, a merger may give rise to the creation or the strengthening of a dominant position on the part of an undertaking which is not a party to the notified transaction (see Case IV/M.1383—Exxon/Mobil, points 225–229; Case COMP/M.2434—Grupo Villar MIR/EnBW/Hidroelectrica del Cantabrico, points 67–71).

3 See also Joined Cases C-68/94 and C-30/95, Kali and Salz, paragraph 170.

4 See Recitals 25 and 26 of the Merger Regulation.

5 The term 'concentration' used in the Merger Regulation covers various types of transactions such as mergers, acquisitions, takeovers, and certain types of joint ventures. In the remainder of this notice, unless otherwise specified, the term 'merger' will be used as a synonym for concentration and therefore cover all the above types of transactions.

6 The notice does not cover the assessment of the effects of competition that a merger has in other markets, including vertical and conglomerate effects. Nor does it cover the assessment of the effects of a joint venture as referred to in Article 2(4) of the Merger Regulation.

7 The expression should be understood to also cover situations where, for instance, prices are decreased less, or are less likely to decrease, than they otherwise would have without the merger and where prices are increased more, or are more likely to increase, than they otherwise would have without the merger.

8 By analogy, in the case of a merger that has been implemented without having been notified, the Commission would assess the merger in the light of the competitive conditions that would have prevailed without the implemented merger.

9 See, e g Commission Decision 98/526/EC in Case IV/M.950—Hoffmann La Roche/Boehringer Mannheim, OJ L234, 21.8.1998, p 14, point 13; Case IV/M.1846—Glaxo Wellcome/SmithKline Beecham, points 70–72; Case COMP/M.2547—Bayer/Aventis Crop Science, points 324 et seq.

10 See, e g Case T-102/96, *Gencor v Commission*, [1999] ECR II-753, paragraphs 247–263.

11 OJ C372, 9.12.1997, p 5.

12 See Case T-102/96, *Gencor v Commission*, [1999] ECR II-753, paragraph 262, and Case T-342/99, *Airtours v Commission*, [2002] ECR II-2585, paragraph 280.

13 As to the calculation of market shares, see also Commission Notice on the definition of the relevant market for the purposes of Community competition law, OJ C372, 9.12.1997, p 3, paragraphs 54–55.

14 See, e g Case COMP/M.1806—Astra Zeneca/Novartis, points 150 and 415.

15 When relevant, market shares may be adjusted, in particular, to account for controlling interests in other firms (See, e g Case IV/M.1383—Exxon/Mobil, points 446–458; Case COMP/M.1879—Boeing/Hughes, points 60–79; Case COMP/JV 55—Hutchison/RCPM/ECT, points 66–75), or for other arrangements with third parties (See, for instance, as regards sub-contractors, Commission Decision 2001/769/EC in Case COMP/M.1940—Framatome/Siemens/Cogema, OJ L289, 6.11.2001, p 8, point 142).

16 See, e g Case COMP/M.2256—Philips/Agilent Health Care Technologies, points 31–32, and Case COMP/M.2609—HP/Compaq, point 39.

17 See, e g Case IV/M.1365—FCC/Vivendi, point 40; Case COMP/JV 55—Hutchison/RCPM/ECT, point 50. If appropriate, the Commission may also use other concentration measures such as, for instance, concentration ratios, which measure the aggregate market share of a small number (usually three or four) of the leading firms in a market.

18 For example, a market containing five firms with market shares of 40%, 20%, 15%, 15%, and 10%, respectively, has an HHI of 2,550 ($40^2 + 20^2 + 15^2 + 15^2 + 10^2 = 2{,}550$). The HHI ranges from close to zero (in an atomistic market) to 10,000 (in the case of a pure monopoly).

19 The increase in concentration as measured by the HHI can be calculated independently of the overall market concentration by doubling the product of the market shares of the merging firms. For example, a merger of two firms with market shares of 30% and 15% respectively would increase the HHI by 900 ($30 \times 15 \times 2 = 900$). The explanation for this technique is as follows: Before the merger, the market shares of the merging firms contribute to the HHI by their squares individually: $(a)^2 + (b)^2$. After the merger, the contribution is the square of their sum: $(a + b)^2$, which equals $(a)^2 + (b)^2 + 2ab$. The increase in the HHI is therefore represented by $2ab$.

20 Case T-221/95, *Endemol v Commission*, [1999] ECR II-1299, paragraph 134, and Case T-102/96,

Gencor v Commission, [1999] ECR II-753, paragraph 205. It is a distinct question whether a dominant position is created or strengthened as a result of the merger.

21 See, e g Case COMP/M.2337—Nestlé/Ralston Purina, points 48–50.

22 See, e g Commission Decision 1999/674/EC in Case IV/M.1221—Rewe/Meinl, OJ L274, 23.10.1999, p 1, points 98–114; Case COMP/M.2337—Nestlé/Ralston Purina, points 44–47.

23 The calculation of market shares depends critically on market definition. It must be emphasised that the Commission does not necessarily accept the parties' proposed market definition.

24 Recital 32 of the Merger Regulation. However, such an indication does not apply to cases where the proposed merger creates or strengthens a collective dominant position involving the 'undertakings concerned' and other third parties (see Joined Cases C-68/94 and C-30/95, Kali and Salz, [1998] ECR I-1375, paragraphs 171 et seq; and Case T-102/96, *Gencor v Commission*, [1999] ECR II-753, paragraphs 134 et seq).

25 In markets with cross-shareholdings or joint ventures the Commission may use a modified HHI, which takes into account such share-holdings (see, e g Case IV/M.1383—Exxon/Mobil, point 256).

26 See paragraph 17.

27 Also often called 'unilateral' effects.

28 Such expected reactions by competitors may be a relevant factor influencing the merged entity's incentives to increase prices.

29 An oligopolistic market refers to a market structure with a limited number of sizeable firms. Because the behaviour of one firm has an appreciable impact on the overall market conditions, and thus indirectly on the situation of each of the other firms, oligopolistic firms are interdependent.

30 Recital 25 of the Merger Regulation.

31 See, in particular, paragraphs 17 and 18.

32 Products may be differentiated in various ways. There may, for example, be differentiation in terms of geographic location, based on branch or stores location; location matters for retail distribution, banks, travel agencies, or petrol stations. Likewise, differentiation may be based on brand image, technical specifications, quality or level of service. The level of advertising in a market may be an indicator of the firms' effort to differentiate their products. For other products, buyers may have to incur switching costs to use a competitor's product.

33 For the definition of the relevant market, see the Commission's Notice on the definition of the relevant market for the purposes of Community competition law, cited above.

34 See for example Case COMP/M.2817—Barilla/BPS/Kamps, point 34; Commission Decision 2001/403/EC in Case COMP/M.1672—Volvo/Scania, OJ L143, 29.5.2001, p 74, points 107–148.

35 See, e g Commission Decision 94/893/EC in Case IV/M.430—Procter & Gamble/VP Schickedanz (II), OJ L354, 21.6.1994, p 32, Case T-290/94, *Kaysersberg v Commission*, [1997] II-2137, paragraph 153; Commission Decision 97/610/EC in Case IV/M.774—Saint-Gobain/Wacker-Chemie/NOM, OJ L247, 10.9.1997, p 1, point 179; Commission Decision 2002/156/EC in Case COMP/M.2097—SCA/Metsä Tissue, OJ L57, 27.2.2002, p 1, points 94–108; Case T-310/01, *Schneider v Commission*, [2002] II-4071, paragraph 418.

36 Typically, the relevant margin (m) is the difference between price (p) and the incremental cost (c) of supplying one more unit of output expressed as a percentage of price ($m = (p - c)p$)).

37 See, e g Case IV/M.1980—Volvo/Renault VI, point 34; Case COMP/M.2256—Philips Agilent/Health Care Solutions, points 33–35; Case COMP/M.2537—Philips/Marconi Medical Systems, points 31–34.

38 The cross-price elasticity of demand measures the extent to which the quantity of a product demanded changes in response to a change in the price of some other product, all other things remaining equal. The own-price elasticity measures the extent to which demand for a product changes in response to the change in the price of the product itself.

39 The diversion ratio from product A to product B measures the proportion of the sales of product A lost due to a price increase of A that are captured by product B.

40 Commission Decision 97/816/EC in Case IV/M.877—Boeing/McDonnell Douglas, OJ L336, 8.12.1997, p 16, points 58 et seq; Case COMP/M.3083—GE/Instrumentarium, points 125 et seq.

41 Sunk costs are costs which are unrecoverable upon exit from the market.

42 See e g Commission Decision 2002/156/EC in Case IV/M.877—Boeing/McDonnell Douglas, OJ L336, 8.12.1997, p 16, point 70.

43 See, e g Case IV/M. 986 Agfa Gevaert/DuPont, OJ L211, 29.7.1998, p 22, points 63–71.

44 See, e g Case COMP/M.2187—CVC/Lenzing, points 162–170.

45 When analysing the possible expansion of capacity by rivals, the Commission considers factors similar to those described in Section VI on entry. See, e g Case COMP/M.2187—CVC/Lenzing, points 162–173.

46 See, e g Case T-221/95, *Endemol v Commission*, [1999] ECR II-1299, paragraph 167.

47 See, e g Case T-22/97, *Kesko v Commission*, [1999], ECR II-3775, paragraphs 141 et seq.

48 See, eg Commission Decision 2001/684/EC in Case M.1671—Dow Chemical/Union Carbide OJ L245, 14.9.2001, p 1, points 107–114.

49 See, e g Commission Decision 96/435/EC in Case IV/M.623—Kimberly-Clark/Scott, OJ L183, 23.7.1996, p 1; Case T-114/02, *Babyliss SA v Commission* ('Seb/Moulinex'), [2003] ECR II-000, paragraphs 343 et seq.

50 This is, for example, the case in network industries such as energy, telecommunications and other communication industries.

51 Commission Decision 99/287/EC in Case IV/M.1069—Worldcom/MCI, OJ L116, 4.5.1999, p 1, points 117 et seq; Case IV/M.1741—MCI Worldcom/Sprint, points 145 et seq; Case IV/M.1795—Vodafone Airtouch/Mannesmann, points 44 et seq.

52 Case T-156/98 *RJB Mining v Commission* [2001] ECR II-337.

53 Commission Decision 2002/156/EC in Case IV/M.877—Boeing/McDonnell Douglas, OJ L336, 8.12.1997, p 16, point 58; Case COMP/M.2568—Haniel/Ytong, point 126.

54 For an example of pipeline products of one merging party likely to compete with the other party's pipeline or existing products, see, e g Case IV/M.1846—Glaxo Wellcome/SmithKline Beecham, point 188.

55 Case T-102/96, *Gencor v Commission*, [1999] ECR II-753, paragraph 277; Case T-342/99, *Airtours v Commission*, [2002] ECR II-2585, paragraph 61.

56 This may be the case if the oligopolists have tended to concentrate their sales in different areas for historic reasons.

57 Case T-342/99, *Airtours v Commission*, [2002] ECR II-2585, paragraph 62.

58 See Commission Decision 92/553/EC in Case IV/M.190—Nestlé/Perrier, OJ L356, 5.12.1992, p 1, points 117–118.

59 See, e g Case IV/M.580—ABB/Daimler-Benz, point 95.

60 See, e g Commission Decision 2002/156/EC in Case COMP/M.2097—SCA/Metsä Tissue, OJ L57, 27.2.2002, p 1, point 148.

61 See, e g Case IV/M.1298—Kodak/Imation, point 60.

62 Case T-102/96, *Gencor v Commission*, [1999] ECR II-753, paragraph 222; Commission Decision 92/553/EC in Case IV/M.190 Nestlé/Perrier, OJ L356, 5.12.1992, p 1, points 63–123.

63 In assessing whether or not a merger may increase the symmetry of the various firms present on the market, efficiency gains may provide important indications (see also paragraph 82 of the notice).

64 See, e g Commission Decision 2001/519/EC in Case COMP/M.1673—VEBA/VIAG, OJ L188, 10.7.2001, p 1, point 226; Case COMP/M.2567—Nordbanken/Postgirot, point 54.

65 See, e g Case COMP/M.2389—Shell/DEA, points 112 et seq; and Case COMP/M.2533—BP/E.ON, points 102 et seq.

66 See also Commission Decision 2000/42/EC in Case IV/M.1313—Danish Crown/Vestjyske Slagterier, OJ L20, 25.1.2000, p 1, points 176–179.

67 See, e g Case COMP/M.2640—Nestlé/Schöller, point 37; Commission Decision 1999/641/EC in Case COMP/M.1225—Enso/Stora, OJ L254, 29.9.1999, p 9, points 67–68.

68 See, e g Case IV/M.1939—Rexam (PLM)/American National Can, point 24.

69 See Case COMP/M.2389—Shell/DEA, point 121, and Case COMP/M.2533—BP/E.ON, point 111.

70 Although deterrent mechanisms are sometimes called 'punishment' mechanisms, this should not be understood in the strict sense that such a mechanism necessarily punishes individually a firm that has deviated. The expectation that coordination may break down for a certain period of time, if a deviation is identified as such, may in itself constitute a sufficient deterrent mechanism.

71 See, e g Commission Decision 2000/42/EC in Case IV/M.1313—Danish Crown/Vestjyske Slagterier, OJ L20, 25.1.2000, p 1, point 177.

72 See Case T-102/96, *Gencor v Commission*, [1999] ECR II-753, paragraph 281.

73 These elements are analysed in a similar way to non-coordinated effects.

74 See, e g Case IV/M.1630—Air Liquide/BOC, points 201 et seq. For an example of a case where entry by the other merging firm was not sufficiently likely in the short to medium term (Case T-158/00, *ARD v Commission*, [2003] ECR II-000, paragraphs 115–127).

75 Commission Decision 2001/98/EC in Case IV/M.1439—Telia/Telenor, OJ L40, 9.2.2001, p 1, points 330–331, and Case IV/M.1681—Akzo Nobel/Hoechst Roussel Vet, point 64.

76 Case IV/M.1630—Air Liquide/BOC, point 219; Commission Decision 2002/164/EC in Case COMP/M.1853—EDF/EnBW, OJ L59, 28.2.2002, p 1, points 54–64.

77 See Commission Decision 1999/674/EC in Case M.1221—Rewe/Meinl, OJ L274, 23.10.1999, p 1, points 71–74.

78 Case T-22/97, *Kesko v Commission*, [1999] ECR II-3775, paragraph 157; Commission Decision 2002/156/EC in Case M.877—Boeing/McDonnell Douglas, OJ L336, 8.12.1997, p 16, points 105–108.

79 See, e g Case IV/M.1882—Pirelli/BICC, points 73–80.

80 See, e g Case IV/M.1245—Valeo/ITT Industries, point 26.

81 Even a small number of customers may not have sufficient buyer power if they are to a large extent 'locked in' because of high switching costs (see Case COMP/M.2187—CVC/Lenzing, point 223).

82 Commission Decision 1999/641/EC in Case COMP/M.1225—Enso/Stora, OJ L254, 29.9.1999, p 9, points 89–91.

83 It may also be appropriate to compare the concentration existing on the customer side with the concentration on the supply side (Case COMP/JV 55—Hutchison/RCPM/ECT, point 119, and Commission Decision 1999/641/EC in Case COMP/M.1225—Enso/Stora, OJ L254, 29.9.1999, p 9, point 97).

84 Case COMP/JV 55—Hutchison/RCPM/ECT, points 129–130.

85 Commission Decision 2002/156/EC in Case COMP/M.2097—SCA/Metsä Tissue, OJ L57, 27.2.2002, point 88. Price discrimination between different categories of customers may be relevant in some cases in the context of market definition (See the Commission's notice on the definition of the relevant market, cited above, at paragraph 43).

86 Accordingly, the Commission may assess whether the various purchasers will hold countervailing buyer power, see, e g Commission Decision 1999/641/EC in Case COMP/M.1225—Enso/Stora, OJ L254, 29.9.1999, p 9, points 84–97.

87 Commission Decision 97/610/EC in Case IV/M.774—Saint-Gobain/Wacker-Chemie/NOM, OJ L247, 10.9.1997, p 1, point 184.

88 Case IV/M.1430—Vodafone/Airtouch, point 27; Case IV/M.2016—France Télécom/Orange, point 33.

89 Commission Decision 2002/174/EC in Case COMP/M.1693—Alcoa/Reynolds, OJ L58, 28.2.2002, point 87.

90 Commission Decision 95/335/EC in Case IV/M.754—Anglo American Corp./Lonrho, OJ L149, 20.5.1998, p 21, points 118–119.

91 Commission Decision 97/610/EC in Case IV/M.774—Saint-Gobain/Wacker-Chemie/NOM, OJ L247, 10.9.1997, p 1, points 184–187.

92 Commission Decision 94/811/EC in Case IV/M.269—Shell/Montecatini, OJ L332, 22.12.1994, p 48, point 32.

93 Commission Decision 98/327/EC in Case IV/M.833—The Coca-Cola Company/Carlsberg A/S, OJ L145, 15.5.1998, p 41, point 74.

94 Commission Decision 98/327/EC in Case IV/M.833—The Coca-Cola Company/Carlsberg A/S, OJ L145, 15.5.1998, p 41, points 72–73.

95 Commission Decision 2002/156/EC in Case COMP/M—2097 SCA/Metsä Tissue, OJ L57, 27.2.2002, p 1, points 83–84.

96 Commission Decision 2001/432/EC in Case IV/M.1813—Industri Kapital Nordkem/Dyno, OJ L154, 9.6.2001, p 41, point 100.

97 See, e g Commission Decision 98/475/EC in Case IV/M.986—Agfa-Gevaert/Dupont, OJ L211, 29.7.1998, p 22, points 84–85.

98 Case T-102/96, *Gencor v Commission*, [1999] ECR II-753, paragraph 237.

99 See, e g Commission Decision 2000/718/EC in Case IV/M.1578—Sanitec/Sphinx, OJ L294, 22.11.2000, p 1, point 114.

100 See, e g Commission Decision 2002/174/EC in Case COMP/M.1693—Alcoa/Reynolds, L58, 28.2.2002, points 31–32, 38.

101 Commission Decision 91/535/EEC in Case IV/M.68—Tetra Pak/Alfa Laval, OJ L290, 22.10.1991, p 35, point 3.4.

102 See Recital 4 of the Merger Regulation.

103 See Recital 29 of the Merger Regulation.

104 Cf Article 2(1)(b) of the Merger Regulation.

105 Pursuant to Article 2(1)(b), the concept of 'consumers' encompasses intermediate and ultimate consumers, i e users of the products covered by the merger. In other words, consumers within the meaning of this provision include the customers, potential and/or actual, of the parties to the merger.

106 Variable costs should be viewed as those costs that vary with the level of production or sales over the relevant time period. Marginal costs are those costs associated with expanding production or sales at the margin.

107 Generally, fixed cost savings are not given such weight as the relationship between fixed costs and consumer prices is normally less direct, at least in the short run.

108 In line with the general principle set out in paragraph 9 of this notice.

109 Joined Cases C-68/94 and C-30/95, Kali and Salz, paragraph 110.

110 Joined Cases C-68/94 and C-30/95, Kali and Salz, paragraph 114. See also Commission Decision 2002/365/EC in Case COMP/M.2314—BASF/Pantochim/Eurodiol, OJ L132, 17.5.2002, p 45, points 157–160. This requirement is linked to the general principle set out in paragraph 9 of this notice.

111 The inevitability of the assets of the failing firm leaving the market in question may, in particular in a case of merger to monopoly, underlie a finding that the market share of the failing firm would in any event accrue to the other merging party. See Joined Cases C-68/94 and C-30/95, Kali and Salz, paragraphs 115–116.

COMMISSION REGULATION

of 21 April 2004

implementing Council Regulation (EC) No 139/2004 on the control of concentrations between undertakings

(802/2004/EC)

NOTES

Date of publication in OJ: OJ L133, 30.4.2004, p 1. The text of this Regulation incorporates the corrigendum published in OJ L172, 6.5.2004, p 9. Notes are as in the original OJ version.

THE COMMISSION OF THE EUROPEAN COMMUNITIES,

Having regard to the Treaty establishing the European Community,

Having regard to the Agreement on the European Economic Area,

Having regard to Council Regulation (EC) No 139/2004 of 20 January 2004 on the control of concentrations between undertakings (EC Merger Regulation),[1] and in particular Article 23(1) thereof,

PART V EC LEGISLATION

Having regard to Council Regulation (EEC) No 4064/89 of 21 December 1989 on the control of concentrations between undertakings,[2] as last amended by Regulation (EC) No 1310/97,[3] and in particular Article 23 thereof,

Having consulted the Advisory Committee,

Whereas:

(1) Council Regulation (EEC) No 4064/89 of 21 December 1989 on the control of concentrations between undertakings has been recast, with substantial amendments to various provisions of that Regulation.

(2) Commission Regulation (EC) No 447/98[4] of 1 March 1998 on the notifications, time-limits and hearings provided for in Council Regulation (EEC) No 4064/89 must be modified in order to take account of those amendments. For the sake of clarity it should therefore be repealed and replaced by a new regulation.

(3) The Commission has adopted measures concerning the terms of reference of hearing officers in certain competition proceedings.

(4) Regulation (EC) No 139/2004 is based on the principle of compulsory notification of concentrations before they are put into effect. On the one hand, a notification has important legal consequences which are favourable to the parties to the proposed concentration, while, on the other hand, failure to comply with the obligation to notify renders the parties liable to fines and may also entail civil law disadvantages for them. It is therefore necessary in the interests of legal certainty to define precisely the subject matter and content of the information to be provided in the notification.

(5) It is for the notifying parties to make a full and honest disclosure to the Commission of the facts and circumstances which are relevant for taking a decision on the notified concentration.

(6) Regulation (EC) No 139/2004 also allows the undertakings concerned to request, in a reasoned submission, prior to notification, that a concentration fulfilling the requirements of that Regulation be referred to the Commission by one or more Member States, or referred by the Commission to one or more Member States, as the case may be. It is important to provide the Commission and the competent authorities of the Member States concerned with sufficient information, in order to enable them to assess, within a short period of time, whether or not a referral ought to be made. To that end, the reasoned submission requesting the referral should contain certain specific information.

(7) In order to simplify and expedite examination of notifications and of reasoned submissions, it is desirable to prescribe that forms be used.

(8) Since notification sets in motion legal time-limits pursuant to Regulation (EC) No 139/2004, the conditions governing such time-limits and the time when they become effective should also be determined.

(9) Rules must be laid down in the interests of legal certainty for calculating the time-limits provided for in Regulation (EC) No 139/2004. In particular, the beginning and end of time periods and the circumstances suspending the running of such periods must be determined, with due regard to the requirements resulting from the exceptionally tight legal timeframe available for the proceedings.

(10) The provisions relating to the Commission's procedure must be framed in such a way as to safeguard fully the right to be heard and the rights of defence. For these purposes, the Commission should distinguish between the parties who notify the concentration, other parties involved in the proposed concentration, third parties and parties regarding whom the Commission intends to take a decision imposing a fine or periodic penalty payments.

(11) The Commission should give the notifying parties and other parties involved in the proposed concentration, if they so request, an opportunity before notification to discuss the intended concentration informally and in strict confidence. In addition, the Commission should, after notification, maintain close contact with those parties, to the extent necessary to discuss with them any practical or legal problems which it discovers on a first examination of the case, with a view, if possible, to resolving such problems by mutual agreement.

(12) In accordance with the principle of respect for the rights of defence, the notifying parties must be given the opportunity to submit their comments on all the objections which the Commission proposes to take into account in its decisions. The other parties involved in the proposed concentration should also be informed of the Commission's objections and should be granted the opportunity to express their views.

(13) Third parties demonstrating a sufficient interest must also be given the opportunity of expressing their views, if they make a written application to that effect.

(14) The various persons entitled to submit comments should do so in writing, both in their own interests and in the interests of sound administration, without prejudice to their right to request a formal oral hearing, where appropriate, to supplement the written procedure. In urgent cases, however, the Commission must be enabled to proceed immediately to formal oral hearings of the notifying parties, of other parties involved or of third parties.

(15) It is necessary to define the rights of persons who are to be heard, to what extent they should be granted access to the Commission's file and on what conditions they may be represented or assisted.

(16) When granting access to the file, the Commission should ensure the protection of business secrets and other confidential information. The Commission should be able to ask undertakings that have submitted documents or statements to identify confidential information.

(17) In order to enable the Commission to carry out a proper assessment of commitments offered by the notifying parties with a view to rendering the concentration compatible with the common market, and to ensure due consultation with other parties involved, with third parties and with the authorities of the Member States as provided for in Regulation (EC) No 139/2004, in particular Article 18(1), 18(4), Article 19(1), 19(2), 19(3) and 19(5) thereof, the procedure and time-limits for submitting the commitments referred to in Article 6(2) and Article 8(2) of that Regulation should be laid down.

(18) It is also necessary to define the rules applicable to certain time limits set by the Commission.

(19) The Advisory Committee on Concentrations must deliver its opinion on the basis of a preliminary draft decision. It must therefore be consulted on a case after the inquiry in to that case has been completed. Such consultation does not, however, prevent the Commission from reopening an inquiry if need be.

[9562]

NOTES

1 OJ L24, 29.1.2004, p 1.
2 OJ L395, 30.12.1989, p 1.
3 OJ L180, 9.7.1997, p 1.
4 OJ L61, 2.3.1998, p 1. Regulation as amended by the 2003 Act of Accession.

HAS ADOPTED THIS REGULATION:

CHAPTER I
SCOPE

Article 1

Scope

This Regulation shall apply to the control of concentrations conducted pursuant to Regulation (EC) No 139/2004.

[9563]

CHAPTER II
NOTIFICATIONS AND OTHER SUBMISSIONS

Article 2

Persons entitled to submit notifications

1. Notifications shall be submitted by the persons or undertakings referred to in Article 4(2) of Regulation (EC) No 139/2004.

2. Where notifications are signed by representatives of persons or of undertakings, such representatives shall produce written proof that they are authorised to act.

3. Joint notifications shall be submitted by a joint representative who is authorised to transmit and to receive documents on behalf of all notifying parties.

[9564]

Article 3

Submission of notifications

1. Notifications shall be submitted in the manner prescribed by Form CO as set out in Annex I. Under the conditions set out in Annex II, notifications may be submitted in Short Form as defined therein. Joint notifications shall be submitted on a single form.

2. One original and [37] copies of the Form CO and the supporting documents shall be submitted to the Commission. The notification shall be delivered to the address referred to in Article 23(1) and in the format specified by the Commission.

3. The supporting documents shall be either originals or copies of the originals; in the latter case the notifying parties shall confirm that they are true and complete.

4. Notifications shall be in one of the official languages of the Community. For the notifying parties, this language shall also be the language of the proceeding, as well as that of any subsequent proceedings relating to the same concentration. Supporting documents shall be submitted in their original language. Where the original language is not one of the official languages of the Community, a translation into the language of the proceeding shall be attached.

5. Where notifications are made pursuant to Article 57 of the Agreement on the European Economic Area, they may also be submitted in one of the official languages of the EFTA States or the working language of the EFTA Surveillance Authority. If the language chosen for the notifications is not an official language of the Community, the notifying parties shall simultaneously supplement all documentation with a translation into an official language of the Community. The language which is chosen for the translation shall determine the language used by the Commission as the language of the proceeding for the notifying parties.

[9565]

NOTES

Para 2: figure in square brackets substituted by Commission Regulation 1792/2006/EC, Art 1, Annex, as from 1 January 2007.

Article 4

Information and documents to be provided

1. Notifications shall contain the information, including documents, requested in the applicable forms set out in the Annexes. The information shall be correct and complete.

2. The Commission may dispense with the obligation to provide any particular information in the notification, including documents, or with any other requirement specified in Annexes I and II where the Commission considers that compliance with those obligations or requirements is not necessary for the examination of the case.

3. The Commission shall without delay acknowledge in writing to the notifying parties or their representatives receipt of the notification and of any reply to a letter sent by the Commission pursuant to Article 5(2) and 5(3).

[9566]

Article 5

Effective date of notification

1. Subject to paragraphs 2, 3 and 4, notifications shall become effective on the date on which they are received by the Commission.

2. Where the information, including documents, contained in the notification is incomplete in any material respect, the Commission shall inform the notifying parties or their representatives in writing without delay. In such cases, the notification shall become effective on the date on which the complete information is received by the Commission.

3. Material changes in the facts contained in the notification coming to light subsequent to the notification which the notifying parties know or ought to know, or any new information coming to light subsequent to the notification which the parties know or ought to know and which would have had to be notified if known at the time of notification, shall be communicated to the Commission without delay. In such cases, when these material changes or new information could have a significant effect on the appraisal of the concentration, the notification may be considered by the Commission as becoming effective on the date on which the relevant information is received by the Commission; the Commission shall inform the notifying parties or their representatives of this in writing and without delay.

4. Incorrect or misleading information shall be considered to be incomplete information.

5. When the Commission publishes the fact of the notification pursuant to Article 4(3) of Regulation (EC) No 139/2004, it shall specify the date upon which the notification has been

received. Where, further to the application of paragraphs 2, 3 and 4 of this Article, the effective date of notification is later than the date specified in that publication, the Commission shall issue a further publication in which it shall state the later date.

[9567]

Article 6

Specific provisions relating to reasoned submissions, supplements and certifications

1. Reasoned submissions within the meaning of Article 4(4) and 4(5) of Regulation (EC) No 139/2004 shall contain the information, including documents, requested in accordance with Annex III to this Regulation.

2. Article 2, Article 3(1), third sentence, 3(2) to (5), Article 4, Article 5(1), 5 (2) first sentence, 5 (3), 5 (4), Article 21 and Article 23 of this Regulation shall apply *mutatis mutandis* to reasoned submissions within the meaning of Article 4(4) and 4(5) of Regulation (EC) No 139/2004.

Article 2, Article 3(1), third sentence, 3(2) to (5), Article 4, Article 5(1) to (4), Article 21 and Article 23 of this Regulation shall apply *mutatis mutandis* to supplements to notifications and certifications within the meaning of Article 10(5) of Regulation (EC) No 139/2004.

[9568]

CHAPTER III
TIME-LIMITS

Article 7

Beginning of time periods

Time periods shall begin on the working day, as defined in Article 24 of this Regulation, following the event to which the relevant provision of Regulation (EC) No 139/2004 refers.

[9569]

Article 8

Expiry of time periods

A time period calculated in working days shall expire at the end of its last working day.

A time period set by the Commission in terms of a calendar date shall expire at the end of that day.

[9570]

Article 9

Suspension of time limit

1. The time limits referred to in Articles 9(4), Article 10(1) and 10(3) of Regulation (EC) No 139/2004 shall be suspended where the Commission has to take a decision pursuant to Article 11(3) or Article 13(4) of that Regulation, on any of the following grounds:

(a) information which the Commission has requested pursuant to Article 11(2) of Regulation (EC) No 139/2004 from one of the notifying parties or another involved party, as defined in Article 11 of this Regulation, is not provided or not provided in full within the time limit fixed by the Commission;

(b) information which the Commission has requested pursuant to Article 11(2) of Regulation (EC) No 139/2004 from a third party, as defined in Article 11 of this Regulation, is not provided or not provided in full within the time limit fixed by the Commission owing to circumstances for which one of the notifying parties or another involved party, as defined in Article 11 of this Regulation, is responsible;

(c) one of the notifying parties or another involved party, as defined in Article 11 of this Regulation, has refused to submit to an inspection deemed necessary by the Commission on the basis of Article 13(1) of Regulation (EC) No 139/2004 or to cooperate in the carrying out of such an inspection in accordance with Article 13(2) of that Regulation;

(d) the notifying parties have failed to inform the Commission of material changes in the facts contained in the notification, or of any new information of the kind referred to in Article 5(3) of this Regulation.

2. The time limits referred to in Articles 9(4), Article 10(1) and 10(3) of Regulation (EC) No 139/2004 shall be suspended where the Commission has to take a decision pursuant to Article 11(3) of that Regulation, without proceeding first by way of simple request for information, owing to circumstances for which one of the undertakings involved in the concentration is responsible.

3. The time limits referred to in Articles 9(4), Article 10(1) and (3) of Regulation (EC) No 139/2004 shall be suspended:

(a) in the cases referred to in points (a) and (b) of paragraph 1, for the period between the expiry of the time limit set in the simple request for information, and the receipt of the complete and correct information required by decision;

(b) in the cases referred to in point (c) of paragraph 1, for the period between the unsuccessful attempt to carry out the inspection and the completion of the inspection ordered by decision;

(c) in the cases referred to in point (d) of paragraph 1, for the period between the occurrence of the change in the facts referred to therein and the receipt of the complete and correct information;

(d) in the cases referred to in paragraph 2 for the period between the expiry of the time limit set in the decision and the receipt of the complete and correct information required by decision.

4. The suspension of the time limit shall begin on the working day following the date on which the event causing the suspension occurred. It shall expire with the end of the day on which the reason for suspension is removed. Where such a day is not a working day, the suspension of the time-limit shall expire with the end of the following working day.

[9571]

Article 10

Compliance with the time-limits

1. The time limits referred to in Article 4(4), fourth subparagraph, Article 9(4), Article 10(1) and (3), and Article 22(3) of Regulation (EC) No 139/2004 shall be met where the Commission has taken the relevant decision before the end of the period.

2. The time limits referred to in Article 4(4), second subparagraph, Article 4(5), third subparagraph, Article 9(2), Article 22(1), second subparagraph, and 22(2), second subparagraph, of Regulation (EC) No 139/2004 shall be met by a Member State concerned where that Member State, before the end of the period, informs the Commission in writing or makes or joins the request in writing, as the case may be.

3. The time limit referred to in Article 9(6) of Regulation (EC) No 139/2004 shall be met where the competent authority of a Member State concerned informs the undertakings concerned in the manner set out in that provision before the end of the period.

[9572]

CHAPTER IV
EXERCISE OF THE RIGHT TO BE HEARD; HEARINGS

Article 11

Parties to be heard

For the purposes of the rights to be heard pursuant to Article 18 of Regulation (EC) No 139/2004, the following parties are distinguished:

(a) notifying parties, that is, persons or undertakings submitting a notification pursuant to Article 4(2) of Regulation (EC) No 139/2004;

(b) other involved parties, that is, parties to the proposed concentration other than the notifying parties, such as the seller and the undertaking which is the target of the concentration;

(c) third persons, that is natural or legal persons, including customers, suppliers and competitors, provided they demonstrate a sufficient interest within the meaning of Article 18(4), second sentence, of Regulation (EC) No 139/2004, which is the case in particular

— for members of the administrative or management bodies of the undertakings concerned or the recognised representatives of their employees;
— for consumer associations, where the proposed concentration concerns products or services used by final consumers.

(d) parties regarding whom the Commission intends to take a decision pursuant to Article 14 or Article 15 of Regulation (EC) No 139/2004.

[9573]

Article 12

Decisions on the suspension of concentrations

1. Where the Commission intends to take a decision pursuant to Article 7(3) of Regulation (EC) No 139/2004 which adversely affects one or more of the parties, it shall, pursuant to Article 18(1) of that Regulation, inform the notifying parties and other involved parties in writing of its objections and shall set a time limit within which they may make known their views in writing.

2. Where the Commission, pursuant to Article 18(2) of Regulation (EC) No 139/2004, has taken a decision referred to in paragraph 1 of this Article provisionally without having given the notifying parties and other involved parties the opportunity to make known their views, it shall without delay send them the text of the provisional decision and shall set a time limit within which they may make known their views in writing.

Once the notifying parties and other involved parties have made known their views, the Commission shall take a final decision annulling, amending or confirming the provisional decision. Where they have not made known their views in writing within the time limit set, the Commission's provisional decision shall become final with the expiry of that period.

[9574]

Article 13

Decisions on the substance of the case

1. Where the Commission intends to take a decision pursuant to Article 6(3) or Article 8(2) to (6) of Regulation (EC) No 139/2004, it shall, before consulting the Advisory Committee on Concentrations, hear the parties pursuant to Article 18(1) and (3) of that Regulation.

Article 12(2) of this Regulation shall apply *mutatis mutandis* where, in application of Article 18(2) of Regulation (EC) No 139/2004, the Commission has taken a decision pursuant to Article 8(5) of that Regulation provisionally.

2. The Commission shall address its objections in writing to the notifying parties.

The Commission shall, when giving notice of objections, set a time limit within which the notifying parties may inform the Commission of their comments in writing.

The Commission shall inform other involved parties in writing of these objections.

The Commission shall also set a time limit within which those other involved parties may inform the Commission of their comments in writing.

The Commission shall not be obliged to take into account comments received after the expiry of a time limit which it has set.

3. The parties to whom the Commission's objections have been addressed or who have been informed of those objections shall, within the time limit set, submit in writing their comments on the objections. In their written comments, they may set out all facts and matters known to them which are relevant to their defence, and shall attach any relevant documents as proof of the facts set out. They may also propose that the Commission hear persons who may corroborate those facts. They shall submit one original and 10 copies of their comments to the Commission to the address of the Commission's Directorate General for Competition. An electronic copy shall also be submitted at the same address and in the format specified by the Commission. The Commission shall forward copies of such written comments without delay to the competent authorities of the Member States.

4. Where the Commission intends to take a decision pursuant to Article 14 or Article 15 of Regulation (EC) No 139/2004, it shall, before consulting the Advisory Committee on

Concentrations, hear pursuant to Article 18(1) and (3) of that Regulation the parties regarding whom the Commission intends to take such a decision.

The procedure provided for in paragraph 2, first and second subparagraphs, and paragraph 3 shall apply, *mutatis mutandis*.

[9575]

Article 14

Oral hearings

1. Where the Commission intends to take a decision pursuant to Article 6(3) or Article 8(2) to (6) of Regulation (EC) No 139/2004, it shall afford the notifying parties who have so requested in their written comments the opportunity to develop their arguments in a formal oral hearing. It may also, at other stages in the proceedings, afford the notifying parties the opportunity of expressing their views orally.

2. Where the Commission intends to take a decision pursuant to Article 6(3) or Article 8(2) to (6) of Regulation (EC) No 139/2004, it shall also afford other involved parties who have so requested in their written comments the opportunity to develop their arguments in a formal oral hearing. It may also, at other stages in the proceedings, afford other involved parties the opportunity of expressing their views orally.

3. Where the Commission intends to take a decision pursuant to Article 14 or Article 15 of Regulation (EC) No 139/2004, it shall afford parties on whom it proposes to impose a fine or periodic penalty payment the opportunity to develop their arguments in a formal oral hearing, if so requested in their written comments. It may also, at other stages in the proceedings, afford such parties the opportunity of expressing their views orally.

[9576]

Article 15

Conduct of formal oral hearings

1. Formal oral hearings shall be conducted by the Hearing Officer in full independence.

2. The Commission shall invite the persons to be heard to attend the formal oral hearing on such date as it shall determine.

3. The Commission shall invite the competent authorities of the Member States to take part in any formal oral hearing.

4. Persons invited to attend shall either appear in person or be represented by legal representatives or by representatives authorised by their constitution as appropriate. Undertakings and associations of undertakings may also be represented by a duly authorised agent appointed from among their permanent staff.

5. Persons heard by the Commission may be assisted by their lawyers or other qualified and duly authorised persons admitted by the Hearing Officer.

6. Formal oral hearings shall not be public. Each person may be heard separately or in the presence of other persons invited to attend, having regard to the legitimate interest of the undertakings in the protection of their business secrets and other confidential information.

7. The Hearing Officer may allow all parties within the meaning of Article 11, the Commission services and the competent authorities of the Member States to ask questions during the formal oral hearing.

The Hearing Officer may hold a preparatory meeting with the parties and the Commission services, so as to facilitate the efficient organisation of the formal oral hearing.

8. The statements made by each person heard shall be recorded. Upon request, the recording of the formal oral hearing shall be made available to the persons who attended that hearing. Regard shall be had to the legitimate interest of the undertakings in the protection of their business secrets and other confidential information.

[9577]

Article 16

Hearing of third persons

1. If third persons apply in writing to be heard pursuant to Article 18(4), second sentence, of Regulation (EC) No 139/2004, the Commission shall inform them in writing of the nature and subject matter of the procedure and shall set a time limit within which they may make known their views.

2. The third persons referred to in paragraph 1 shall make known their views in writing within the time limit set. The Commission may, where appropriate, afford such third parties who have so requested in their written comments the opportunity to participate in a formal hearing. It may also in other cases afford such third parties the opportunity of expressing their views orally.

3. The Commission may likewise invite any other natural or legal person to express its views, in writing as well as orally, including at a formal oral hearing.

[9578]

CHAPTER V
ACCESS TO THE FILE AND TREATMENT OF CONFIDENTIAL INFORMATION

Article 17

Access to the file and use of documents

1. If so requested, the Commission shall grant access to the file to the parties to whom it has addressed a statement of objections, for the purpose of enabling them to exercise their rights of defence. Access shall be granted after the notification of the statement of objections.

2. The Commission shall, upon request, also give the other involved parties who have been informed of the objections access to the file in so far as this is necessary for the purposes of preparing their comments.

3. The right of access to the file shall not extend to confidential information, or to internal documents of the Commission or of the competent authorities of the Member States. The right of access to the file shall equally not extend to correspondence between the Commission and the competent authorities of the Member States or between the latter.

4. Documents obtained through access to the file pursuant to this Article may only be used for the purposes of the relevant proceeding pursuant to Regulation (EC) No 139/2004.

[9579]

Article 18

Confidential information

1. Information, including documents, shall not be communicated or made accessible by the Commission in so far as it contains business secrets or other confidential information the disclosure of which is not considered necessary by the Commission for the purpose of the procedure.

2. Any person which makes known its views or comments pursuant to Articles 12, Article 13 and Article 16 of this Regulation, or supplies information pursuant to Article 11 of Regulation (EC) No 139/2004, or subsequently submits further information to the Commission in the course of the same procedure, shall clearly identify any material which it considers to be confidential, giving reasons, and provide a separate non-confidential version by the date set by the Commission.

3. Without prejudice to paragraph 2, the Commission may require persons referred to in Article 3 of Regulation (EC) No 139/2004, undertakings and associations of undertakings in all cases where they produce or have produced documents or statements pursuant to Regulation (EC) No 139/2004 to identify the documents or parts of documents which they consider to contain business secrets or other confidential information belonging to them and to identify the undertakings with regard to which such documents are to be considered confidential.

The Commission may also require persons referred to in Article 3 of Regulation (EC) No 139/2004, undertakings or associations of undertakings to identify any part of a statement of objections, case summary or a decision adopted by the Commission which in their view contains business secrets.

Where business secrets or other confidential information are identified, the persons, undertakings and associations of undertakings shall give reasons and provide a separate non-confidential version by the date set by the Commission.

[9580]

CHAPTER VI
COMMITMENTS OFFERED BY THE UNDERTAKINGS CONCERNED

Article 19

Time limits for submission of commitments

1. Commitments offered by the undertakings concerned pursuant to Article 6(2) of Regulation (EC) No 139/2004 shall be submitted to the Commission within not more than 20 working days from the date of receipt of the notification.

2. Commitments offered by the undertakings concerned pursuant to Article 8(2) of Regulation (EC) No 139/2004 shall be submitted to the Commission within not more than 65 working days from the date on which proceedings were initiated.

Where pursuant to Article 10(3), second subparagraph, of Regulation (EC) No 139/2004 the period for the adoption of a decision pursuant to Article 8(1), (2) and (3) is extended, the period of 65 working days for the submission of commitments shall automatically be extended by the same number of working days.

In exceptional circumstances, the Commission may accept commitments offered after the expiry of the time limit for their submission within the meaning of this paragraph provided that the procedure provided for in Article 19(5) of Regulation (EC) No 139/2004 is complied with.

3. Articles 7, 8 and 9 shall apply *mutatis mutandis.*

[9581]

Article 20

Procedure for the submission of commitments

1. One original and 10 copies of commitments offered by the undertakings concerned pursuant to Article 6(2) or Article 8(2) of Regulation (EC) No 139/2004 shall be submitted to the Commission at the address of the Commission's Directorate General for Competition. An electronic copy shall also be submitted at the same address and in the format specified by the Commission. The Commission shall forward copies of such commitments without delay to the competent authorities of the Member States.

2. When offering commitments pursuant to Articles 6(2) or Article 8(2) of Regulation (EC) No 139/2004, the undertakings concerned shall at the same time clearly identify any information which they consider to be confidential, giving reasons, and shall provide a separate non-confidential version.

[9582]

CHAPTER VII
MISCELLANEOUS PROVISIONS

Article 21

Transmission of documents

1. Transmission of documents and invitations from the Commission to the addressees may be effected in any of the following ways:

(a) delivery by hand against receipt;

(b) registered letter with acknowledgement of receipt;

(c) fax with a request for acknowledgement of receipt;

(d) telex;

(e) electronic mail with a request for acknowledgement of receipt.

2. Unless otherwise provided in this Regulation, paragraph 1 also applies to the transmission of documents from the notifying parties, from other involved parties or from third parties to the Commission.

3. Where a document is sent by telex, by fax or by electronic mail, it shall be presumed that it has been received by the addressee on the day on which it was sent.

[9583]

Article 22

Setting of time limits

In setting the time limits provided for pursuant to Article 12(1) and (2), Article 13(2) and Article 16(1), the Commission shall have regard to the time required for the preparation of statements and to the urgency of the case. It shall also take account of working days as well as public holidays in the country of receipt of the Commission's communication.

Time limits shall be set in terms of a precise calendar date.

[9584]

Article 23

Receipt of documents by the Commission

1. In accordance with the provisions of Article 5(1) of this Regulation, notifications shall be delivered to the Commission at the address of the Commission's Directorate General for Competition as published by the Commission in the *Official Journal of the European Union*.

2. Additional information requested to complete notifications must reach the Commission at the address referred to in paragraph 1.

3. Written comments on Commission communications pursuant to Article 12(1) and (2), Article 13(2) and Article 16(1) of this Regulation must have reached the Commission at the address referred to in paragraph 1 before the expiry of the time limit set in each case.

[9585]

Article 24

Definition of working days

The expression working days in Regulation (EC) No 139/2004 and in this Regulation means all days other than Saturdays, Sundays, and Commission holidays as published in the *Official Journal of the European Union* before the beginning of each year.

[9586]

Article 25

Repeal and transitional provision

1. Without prejudice to paragraphs 2 and 3, Regulation (EC) No 447/98 is repealed with effect from 1 May 2004.

References to the repealed Regulation shall be construed as references to this Regulation.

2. Regulation (EC) No 447/98 shall continue to apply to any concentration falling within the scope of Regulation (EEC) No 4064/89.

3. For the purposes of paragraph 2, Sections 1 to 12 of the Annex to Regulation (EC) No 447/98 shall be replaced by Sections 1 to 11 of Annex I to this Regulation. In such cases references in those sections to the "EC Merger Regulation" and to the "Implementing Regulation" shall be read as referring to the corresponding provisions of Regulation (EEC) No 4064/89 and Regulation (EC) No 447/98, respectively.

[9587]

Article 26

Entry into force

This Regulation shall enter into force on 1 May 2004.

This Regulation shall be binding in its entirety and directly applicable in all Member States.

[9588]

Done at Brussels, 21 April 2004.

ANNEX I

FORM CO RELATING TO THE NOTIFICATION OF A CONCENTRATION PURSUANT TO REGULATION (EC) NO 139/2004

1. INTRODUCTION

1.1. The purpose of this Form

This Form specifies the information that must be provided by notifying parties when submitting a notification to the European Commission of a proposed merger, acquisition or other concentration. The merger control system of the European Union is laid down in Council Regulation (EC) No 139/2004 (hereinafter referred to as "the EC Merger Regulation"), and in Commission Regulation (EC) No xx/2004 (hereinafter referred to as "the Implementing Regulation"), to which this Form CO is annexed.[1] The text of these regulations, as well as other relevant documents, can be found on the Competition page of the Commission's Europa web site.

In order to limit the time and expense involved in complying with various merger control procedures in several individual countries, the European Union has put in place a system of merger control by which concentrations having a Community dimension (normally, where the parties to the concentration fulfil certain turnover thresholds)[2] are assessed by the European Commission in a single procedure (the "one stop shop" principle). Mergers which do not meet the turnover thresholds may fall within the competence of the Member States' authorities in charge of merger control.

The EC Merger Regulation requires the Commission to reach a decision within a legal deadline. In an initial phase the Commission normally has 25 working days to decide whether to clear the concentration or to "initiate proceedings", ie, to undertake an in-depth investigation[3]. If the Commission decides to initiate proceedings, it normally has to take a final decision on the operation within no more than 90 working days of the date when proceedings are initiated.[4]

In view of these deadlines, and for the "one stop shop" principle to work, it is essential that the Commission is provided, in a timely fashion, with the information required to carry out the necessary investigation and to assess the impact of the concentration on the markets concerned. This requires that a certain amount of information be provided at the time of notification.

It is recognised that the information requested in this Form is substantial. However, experience has shown that, depending on the specific characteristics of the case, not all information is always necessary for an adequate examination of the proposed concentration. Accordingly, if you consider that any particular information requested by this Form may not be necessary for the Commission's examination of the case, you are encouraged to ask the Commission to dispense with the obligation to provide certain information ("waiver"). See Section 1.3(g) for more details.

Pre-notification contacts are extremely valuable to both the notifying parties and the Commission in determining the precise amount of information required in a notification and, in the majority of cases, will result in a significant reduction of the information required. Notifying parties may refer to the Commission's Best Practices on the Conduct of EC Merger Control Proceedings, which provides guidance on pre-notification contacts and the preparation of notifications.

In addition, it should be noted that certain concentrations, which are unlikely to pose any competition concerns, can be notified using a Short Form, which is attached to the Implementing Regulation, as Annex II.

1.2. Who must notify

In the case of a merger within the meaning of Article 3(1)(a) of the EC Merger Regulation or the acquisition of joint control of an undertaking within the meaning of Article 3(1)(b) of the EC Merger Regulation, the notification shall be completed jointly by the parties to the merger or by those acquiring joint control, as the case may be.[5]

In case of the acquisition of a controlling interest in one undertaking by another, the acquirer must complete the notification.

In the case of a public bid to acquire an undertaking, the bidder must complete the notification.

Each party completing the notification is responsible for the accuracy of the information which it provides.

1.3. The requirement for a correct and complete notification

All information required by this Form must be correct and complete. The information required must be supplied in the appropriate Section of this Form.

In particular you should note that:

(a) In accordance with Article 10(1) of the EC Merger Regulation and Article 5(2) and (4) of the Implementing Regulation, the time-limits of the EC Merger Regulation linked to the notification will not begin to run until all the information that has to be supplied with the notification has been received by the Commission. This requirement is to ensure that the Commission is able to assess the notified concentration within the strict time-limits provided by the EC Merger Regulation.

(b) The notifying parties should verify, in the course of preparing their notification, that contact names and numbers, and in particular fax numbers and e-mail addresses, provided to the Commission are accurate, relevant and up-to-date.

(c) Incorrect or misleading information in the notification will be considered to be incomplete information (Article 5(4) of the Implementing Regulation).

(d) If a notification is incomplete, the Commission will inform the notifying parties or their representatives in writing and without delay. The notification will only become effective on the date on which the complete and accurate information is received by the Commission (Article 10(1) of the EC Merger Regulation, Articles 5(2) and (4) of the Implementing Regulation).

(e) Under Article 14(1)(a) of the EC Merger Regulation, notifying parties who, either intentionally or negligently, supply incorrect or misleading information, may be liable to fines of up to 1% of the aggregate turnover of the undertaking concerned. In addition, pursuant to Article 6(3)(a) and Article 8(6)(a) of the EC Merger Regulation the Commission may revoke its decision on the compatibility of a notified concentration where it is based on incorrect information for which one of the undertakings is responsible.

(f) You may request in writing that the Commission accept that the notification is complete notwithstanding the failure to provide information required by this Form, if such information is not reasonably available to you in part or in whole (for example, because of the unavailability of information on a target company during a contested bid).

The Commission will consider such a request, provided that you give reasons for the unavailability of that information, and provide your best estimates for missing data together with the sources for the estimates. Where possible, indications as to where any of the requested information that is unavailable to you could be obtained by the Commission should also be provided.

(g) You may request in writing that the Commission accept that the notification is complete notwithstanding the failure to provide information required by this Form, if you consider that any particular information required, in the full or short form version, may not be necessary for the Commission's examination of the case.

The Commission will consider such a request, provided that you give adequate reasons why that information is not relevant and necessary to its inquiry into the notified operation. You should explain this during your pre-notification contacts with the Commission and, submit a written request for a waiver, asking the Commission to dispense with the obligation to provide that information, pursuant to Article 4(2) of the Implementing Regulation.

1.4. How to notify

The notification must be completed in one of the official languages of the European Community. This language will thereafter be the language of the proceedings for all notifying parties. Where notifications are made in accordance with Article 12 of Protocol 24 to the EEA Agreement in an official language of an EFTA State which is not an official language of the Community, the notification must simultaneously be supplemented with a translation into an official language of the Community.

The information requested by this Form is to be set out using the sections and paragraph numbers of the Form, signing a declaration as provided in Section 11, and annexing supporting documentation. In completing Sections 7 to 9 of this Form, the notifying parties are invited to consider whether, for purposes of clarity, these sections are best presented in numerical order, or whether they can be grouped together for each individual affected market (or group of affected markets).

For the sake of clarity, certain information may be put in annexes. However, it is essential that all key substantive pieces of information, and in particular market share information for the parties and their largest competitors, are presented in the body of Form CO. Annexes to this Form shall only be used to supplement the information supplied in the Form itself.

Contact details must be provided in a format provided by the Commission's Directorate-General for Competition (DG Competition). For a proper investigatory process, it is essential that the contact details are accurate. Multiple instances of incorrect contact details may be a ground for declaring a notification incomplete.

Supporting documents are to be submitted in their original language; where this is not an official language of the Community, they must be translated into the language of the proceeding (Article 3(4) of the Implementing Regulation).

Supporting documents may be originals or copies of the originals. In the latter case, the notifying party must confirm that they are true and complete.

One original and [37] copies of the Form CO and the supporting documents shall be submitted to the Commission's Directorate-General for Competition.

The notification shall be delivered to the address referred to in Article 23 (1) of the Implementing Regulation and in the format specified by the Commission from time to time. This address is published in the *Official Journal of the European Union*. The notification must be delivered to the Commission on working days as defined by Article 24 of the Implementing Regulation. In order to enable it to be registered on the same day, it must be delivered before 17.00 hrs on Mondays to Thursdays and before 16.00 hrs on Fridays and workdays preceding public holidays and other holidays as determined by the Commission and published in the *Official Journal of the European Union*. The security instructions given on DG Competition's website must be adhered to.

1.5. Confidentiality

Article 287 of the Treaty and Article 17(2) of the EC Merger Regulation as well as the corresponding provisions of the EEA Agreement[6] require the Commission, the Member States, the EFTA Surveillance Authority and the EFTA States, their officials and other servants not to disclose information they have acquired through the application of the Regulation of the kind covered by the obligation of professional secrecy. The same principle must also apply to protect confidentiality between notifying parties.

If you believe that your interests would be harmed if any of the information you are asked to supply were to be published or otherwise divulged to other parties, submit this information separately with each page clearly marked "Business Secrets". You should also give reasons why this information should not be divulged or published.

In the case of mergers or joint acquisitions, or in other cases where the notification is completed by more than one of the parties, business secrets may be submitted under separate cover, and referred to in the notification as an annex. All such annexes must be included in the submission in order for a notification to be considered complete.

1.6. Definitions and instructions for purposes of this Form

Notifying party or parties: in cases where a notification is submitted by only one of the undertakings who is a party to an operation, "notifying parties" is used to refer only to the undertaking actually submitting the notification.

Party(ies) to the concentration or parties: these terms relate to both the acquiring and acquired parties, or to the merging parties, including all undertakings in which a controlling interest is being acquired or which is the subject of a public bid.

Except where otherwise specified, the terms notifying party(ies) and party(ies) to the concentration include all the undertakings which belong to the same groups as those parties.

Affected markets: Section 6 of this Form requires the notifying parties to define the relevant product markets, and further to identify which of those relevant markets are likely to be affected by the notified operation. This definition of affected market is used as the basis for requiring information for a number of other questions contained in this Form. The definitions thus submitted by the notifying parties are referred to in this Form as the affected market(s). This term can refer to a relevant market made up either of products or of services.

Year: all references to the word year in this Form should be read as meaning calendar year, unless otherwise stated. All information requested in this Form must, unless otherwise specified, relate to the year preceding that of the notification.

The financial data requested in Sections 3.3 to 3.5 must be provided in euros at the average exchange rates prevailing for the years or other periods in question.

All references contained in this Form are to the relevant articles and paragraphs of the EC Merger Regulation, unless otherwise stated.

1.7. Provision of information to Employees and their representatives

The Commission would like to draw attention to the obligations to which the parties to a concentration may be subject under Community and/or national rules on information and consultation regarding transactions of a concentrative nature vis-à-vis employees and/or their representatives.

SECTION 1

DESCRIPTION OF THE CONCENTRATION

1.1. Provide an executive summary of the concentration, specifying the parties to the concentration, the nature of the concentration (for example, merger, acquisition, or joint venture), the areas of activity of the notifying parties, the markets on which the concentration will have an impact (including the main affected markets[7]), and the strategic and economic rationale for the concentration.

1.2. Provide a summary (up to 500 words) of the information provided under Section 1.1. It is intended that this summary will be published on the Commission's website at the date of notification. The summary must be drafted so that it contains no confidential information or business secrets.

SECTION 2

INFORMATION ABOUT THE PARTIES

2.1. Information on notifying party (or parties)

Give details of:

2.1.1. name and address of undertaking;

2.1.2. nature of the undertaking's business;

2.1.3. name, address, telephone number, fax number and e-mail address of, and position held by, the appropriate contact person; and

2.1.4. an address for service of the notifying party (or each of the notifying parties) to which documents and, in particular, Commission decisions may be delivered. The name, telephone number and e-mail address of a person at this address who is authorised to accept service must be provided.

2.2. Information on other parties[8] to the concentration

For each party to the concentration (except the notifying party or parties) give details of:

2.2.1. name and address of undertaking;

2.2.2. nature of undertaking's business;

2.2.3. name, address, telephone number, fax number and e-mail address of, and position held by, the appropriate contact person; and

2.2.4. an address for service of the party (or each of the parties) to which documents and, in particular, Commission Decisions may be delivered. The name, e-mail address and telephone number of a person at this address who is authorised to accept service must be provided.

2.3. Appointment of representatives

Where notifications are signed by representatives of undertakings, such representatives must produce written proof that they are authorised to act. The written proof must contain the name and position of the persons granting such authority.

Provide the following contact details of any representatives who have been authorised to act for any of the parties to the concentration, indicating whom they represent:

2.3.1. name of representative;

2.3.2. address of representative;

2.3.3. name, address, telephone number, fax number and e-mail address of person to be contacted; and

2.3.4. an address of the representative (in Brussels if available) to which correspondence may be sent and documents delivered.

SECTION 3

DETAILS OF THE CONCENTRATION

3.1. Describe the nature of the concentration being notified. In doing so, state:

(a) whether the proposed concentration is a full legal merger, an acquisition of sole or joint control, a full-function joint venture within the meaning of Article 3(4) of the EC Merger Regulation or a contract or other means of conferring direct or indirect control within the meaning of Article 3(2) of the EC Merger Regulation;

(b) whether the whole or parts of parties are subject to the concentration;

(c) a brief explanation of the economic and financial structure of the concentration;

(d) whether any public offer for the securities of one party by another party has the support of the former's supervisory boards of management or other bodies legally representing that party;

(e) the proposed or expected date of any major events designed to bring about the completion of the concentration;

(f) the proposed structure of ownership and control after the completion of the concentration;

(g) any financial or other support received from whatever source (including public authorities) by any of the parties and the nature and amount of this support; and

(h) the economic sectors involved in the concentration.

3.2. State the value of the transaction (the purchase price or the value of all the assets involved, as the case may be).

3.3. For each of the undertakings concerned by the concentration[9] provide the following data[10] for the last financial year:

3.3.1. world-wide turnover;

3.3.2. Community-wide turnover;

3.3.3. EFTA-wide turnover;

3.3.4. turnover in each Member State;

3.3.5. turnover in each EFTA State;

3.3.6. the Member State, if any, in which more than two-thirds of Community-wide turnover is achieved; and

3.3.7. the EFTA State, if any, in which more than two-thirds of EFTA-wide turnover is achieved.

3.4. For the purposes of Article 1(3) of the EC Merger Regulation, if the operation does not meet the thresholds set out in Article 1(2), provide the following data for the last financial year:

3.4.1. the Member States, if any, in which the combined aggregate turnover of all the undertakings concerned is more than EUR 100 million; and

3.4.2. the Member States, if any, in which the aggregate turnover of each of at least two of the undertakings concerned is more than EUR 25 million.

3.5. For the purposes of determining whether the concentration qualifies as an EFTA cooperation case,[11] provide the following information with respect to the last financial year:

3.5.1. does the combined turnover of the undertakings concerned in the territory of the EFTA States equal 25% or more of their total turnover in the EEA territory?

3.5.2. does each of at least two undertakings concerned have a turnover exceeding EUR 250 million in the territory of the EFTA States?

3.6. Describe the economic rationale of the concentration.

SECTION 4

OWNERSHIP AND CONTROL[12]

4.1. For each of the parties to the concentration provide a list of all undertakings belonging to the same group.

This list must include:

4.1.1. all undertakings or persons controlling these parties, directly or indirectly;

4.1.2. all undertakings active on any affected market[13] that are controlled, directly or indirectly:

(a) by these parties;
(b) by any other undertaking identified in 4.1.1.

For each entry listed above, the nature and means of control should be specified.

The information sought in this section may be illustrated by the use of organization charts or diagrams to show the structure of ownership and control of the undertakings.

4.2. With respect to the parties to the concentration and each undertaking or person identified in response to Section 4.1, provide:

4.2.1. a list of all other undertakings which are active in affected markets (affected markets are defined in Section 6) in which the undertakings, or persons, of the group hold individually or collectively 10% or more of the voting rights, issued share capital or other securities;

in each case, identify the holder and state the percentage held;

4.2.2. a list for each undertaking of the members of their boards of management who are also members of the boards of management or of the supervisory boards of any other undertaking which is active in affected markets; and (where applicable) for each undertaking a list of the members of their supervisory boards who are also members of the boards of management of any other undertaking which is active in affected markets;

in each case, identify the name of the other undertaking and the positions held;

4.2.3. details of acquisitions made during the last three years by the groups identified above (Section 4.1) of undertakings active in affected markets as defined in Section 6.

Information provided here may be illustrated by the use of organization charts or diagrams to give a better understanding.

SECTION 5

SUPPORTING DOCUMENTATION

Notifying parties must provide the following:

5.1. copies of the final or most recent versions of all documents bringing about the concentration, whether by agreement between the parties to the concentration, acquisition of a controlling interest or a public bid;

5.2. in a public bid, a copy of the offer document; if it is unavailable at the time of notification, it should be submitted as soon as possible and not later than when it is posted to shareholders;

5.3. copies of the most recent annual reports and accounts of all the parties to the concentration; and

5.4. copies of all analyses, reports, studies, surveys, and any comparable documents prepared by or for any member(s) of the board of directors, or the supervisory board, or the other person(s) exercising similar functions (or to whom such functions have been delegated or entrusted), or the shareholders' meeting, for the purpose of assessing or analysing the concentration with respect to market shares, competitive conditions, competitors (actual and potential), the rationale of the concentration, potential for sales growth or expansion into other product or geographic markets, and/or general market conditions.[14]

For each of these documents, indicate (if not contained in the document itself) the date of preparation, the name and title of each individual who prepared each such document.

SECTION 6

MARKET DEFINITIONS

The relevant product and geographic markets determine the scope within which the market power of the new entity resulting from the concentration must be assessed.[15]

The notifying party or parties must provide the data requested having regard to the following definitions:

I. Relevant product markets:

A relevant product market comprises all those products and/or services which are regarded as interchangeable or substitutable by the consumer, by reason of the products' characteristics, their prices and their intended use. A relevant product market may in some cases be composed of a number of individual products and/or services which present largely identical physical or technical characteristics and are interchangeable.

Factors relevant to the assessment of the relevant product market include the analysis of why the products or services in these markets are included and why others are excluded by using the above definition, and having regard to, for example, substitutability, conditions of competition, prices, cross-price elasticity of demand or other factors relevant for the definition of the product markets (for example, supply-side substitutability in appropriate cases).

II. Relevant geographic markets:

The relevant geographic market comprises the area in which the undertakings concerned are involved in the supply and demand of relevant products or services, in which the conditions of competition are sufficiently homogeneous and which can be distinguished from neighbouring geographic areas because, in particular, conditions of competition are appreciably different in those areas.

Factors relevant to the assessment of the relevant geographic market include *inter alia* the nature and characteristics of the products or services concerned, the existence of entry barriers, consumer preferences, appreciable differences in the undertakings' market shares between neighbouring geographic areas or substantial price differences.

III. Affected markets:

For purposes of information required in this Form, affected markets consist of relevant product markets where, in the EEA territory, in the Community, in the territory of the EFTA States, in any Member State or in any EFTA State:

(a) two or more of the parties to the concentration are engaged in business activities in the same product market and where the concentration will lead to a combined market share of 15% or more. These are horizontal relationships;

(b) one or more of the parties to the concentration are engaged in business activities in a product market, which is upstream or downstream of a product market in which any other party to the concentration is engaged, and any of their individual or combined market shares at either level is 25% or more, regardless of whether there is or is not any existing supplier/customer relationship between the parties to the concentration.[16] These are vertical relationships.

On the basis of the above definitions and market share thresholds, provide the following information:[17]

— Identify each affected market within the meaning of Section III, at:
— the EEA, Community or EFTA level;
— the individual Member States or EFTA States level.

6.2. In addition, state and explain the parties' view regarding the scope of the relevant geographic market within the meaning of Section II that applies in relation to each affected market identified above.

IV. Other markets in which the notified operation may have a significant impact

6.3. On the basis of the above definitions, describe the product and geographic scope of markets other than affected markets identified in Section 6.1 in which the notified operation may have a significant impact, for example, where:

(a) any of the parties to the concentration has a market share larger than 25% and any other party to the concentration is a potential competitor into that market. A party may be considered a potential competitor, in particular, where it has plans to enter a market, or has developed or pursued such plans in the past two years;

(b) any of the parties to the concentration has a market share larger than 25% and any other party to the concentration holds important intellectual property rights for that market;

(c) any of the parties to the concentration is present in a product market, which is a neighbouring market closely related to a product market in which any other party to the concentration is engaged, and the individual or combined market shares of the parties in any one of these markets is 25% or more. Product markets are closely related neighbouring markets when the products are complementary to each other[18] or when they belong to a range of products that is generally purchased by the same set of customers for the same end use;[19]

where such markets include the whole or a part of the EEA.

In order to enable the Commission to consider, from the outset, the competitive impact of the proposed concentration in the markets identified under this Section 6.3, notifying parties are invited to submit the information under Sections 7 and 8 of this Form in relation to those markets.

SECTION 7

INFORMATION ON AFFECTED MARKETS

For each affected relevant product market, for each of the last three financial years:[20]

(a) for the EEA territory;

(b) for the Community as a whole;

(c) for the territory of the EFTA States as a whole;

(d) individually for each Member State and EFTA State where the parties to the concentration do business; and

(e) where in the opinion of the notifying parties, the relevant geographic market is different;

provide the following:

7.1. an estimate of the total size of the market in terms of sales value (in euros) and volume (units).[21] Indicate the basis and sources for the calculations and provide documents where available to confirm these calculations;

7.2. the sales in value and volume, as well as an estimate of the market shares, of each of the parties to the concentration;

7.3. an estimate of the market share in value (and where appropriate, volume) of all competitors (including importers) having at least 5% of the geographic market under consideration. On this basis, provide an estimate of the HHI index[22] pre- and post-merger, and the difference between the two (the delta).[23] Indicate the proportion of market shares used as a basis to calculate the HHI. Identify the sources used to calculate these market shares and provide documents where available to confirm the calculation;

7.4. the name, address, telephone number, fax number and e-mail address of the head of the legal department (or other person exercising similar functions; and in cases where there is no such person, then the chief executive) for the competitors identified under 7.3;

7.5. an estimate of the total value and volume and source of imports from outside the EEA territory and identify:

(a) the proportion of such imports that are derived from the groups to which the parties to the concentration belong;

(b) an estimate of the extent to which any quotas, tariffs or non-tariff barriers to trade, affect these imports; and

(c) an estimate of the extent to which transportation and other costs affect these imports;

7.6. the extent to which trade among States within the EEA territory is affected by:

(a) transportation and other costs; and

(b) other non-tariff barriers to trade;

7.7. the manner in which the parties to the concentration produce, price and sell the products and/or services; for example, whether they manufacture and price locally, or sell through local distribution facilities;

7.8. a comparison of price levels in each Member State and EFTA State by each party to the concentration and a similar comparison of price levels between the Community, the EFTA

States and other areas where these products are produced (eg Russia, the United States of America, Japan, China, or other relevant areas); and

7.9. the nature and extent of vertical integration of each of the parties to the concentration compared with their largest competitors.

SECTION 8

GENERAL CONDITIONS IN AFFECTED MARKETS

8.1. Identify the five largest independent[24] suppliers to the parties to the concentration and their individual shares of purchases from each of these suppliers (of raw materials or goods used for purposes of producing the relevant products). Provide the name, address, telephone number, fax number and e-mail address of the head of the legal department (or other person exercising similar functions; and in cases where there is no such person, then the chief executive) for each of these suppliers.

STRUCTURE OF SUPPLY IN AFFECTED MARKETS

8.2. Explain the distribution channels and service networks that exist in the affected markets. In so doing, take account of the following where appropriate:

(a) the distribution systems prevailing in the market and their importance. To what extent is distribution performed by third parties and/or undertakings belonging to the same group as the parties identified in Section 4?

(b) the service networks (for example, maintenance and repair) prevailing and their importance in these markets. To what extent are such services performed by third parties and/or undertakings belonging to the same group as the parties identified in Section 4?

8.3. Provide an estimate of the total Community-wide and EFTA-wide capacity for the last three years. Over this period what proportion of this capacity is accounted for by each of the parties to the concentration, and what have been their respective rates of capacity utilization. If applicable, identify the location and capacity of the manufacturing facilities of each of the parties to the concentration in affected markets.

8.4. Specify whether any of the parties to the concentration, or any of the competitors, have "pipeline products", products likely to be brought to market in the near term, or plans to expand (or contract) production or sales capacity. If so, provide an estimate of the projected sales and market shares of the parties to the concentration over the next three to five years.

8.5. If you consider any other supply-side considerations to be relevant, they should be specified.

STRUCTURE OF DEMAND IN AFFECTED MARKETS

8.6. Identify the five[25] largest independent customers of the parties in each affected market and their individual share of total sales for such products accounted for by each of those customers. Provide the name, address, telephone number, fax number and e-mail address of the head of the legal department (or other person exercising similar functions; and in cases where there is no such person, then the chief executive) for each of these customers.

8.7. Explain the structure of demand in terms of:

(a) the phases of the markets in terms of, for example, take-off, expansion, maturity and decline, and a forecast of the growth rate of demand;

(b) the importance of customer preferences, for example in terms of brand loyalty, the provision of pre- and after-sales services, the provision of a full range of products, or network effects;

(c) the role of product differentiation in terms of attributes or quality, and the extent to which the products of the parties to the concentration are close substitutes;

(d) the role of switching costs (in terms of time and expense) for customers when changing from one supplier to another;

(e) the degree of concentration or dispersion of customers;

(f) segmentation of customers into different groups with a description of the "typical customer" of each group;

(g) the importance of exclusive distribution contracts and other types of long-term contracts; and

(h) the extent to which public authorities, government agencies, State enterprises or similar bodies are important participants as a source of demand.

MARKET ENTRY

8.8. Over the last five years, has there been any significant entry into any affected markets? If so, identify such entrants and provide the name, address, telephone number, fax number and e-mail address of the head of the legal department (or other person exercising similar functions; and in cases where there is no such person, then the chief executive) and an estimate of the current market share of each such entrant. If any of the parties to the concentration entered an affected market in the past five years, provide an analysis of the barriers to entry encountered.

8.9. In the opinion of the notifying parties, are there undertakings (including those at present operating only outside the Community or the EEA) that are likely to enter the market? If so, identify such entrants and provide the name, address, telephone number, fax number and e-mail address of the head of the legal department (or other person exercising similar functions; and in cases where there is no such person, then the chief executive). Explain why such entry is likely and provide an estimate of the time within which such entry is likely to occur.

8.10. Describe the various factors influencing entry into affected markets, examining entry from both a geographical and product viewpoint. In so doing, take account of the following where appropriate:

(a) the total costs of entry (R& D, production, establishing distribution systems, promotion, advertising, servicing, and so forth) on a scale equivalent to a significant viable competitor, indicating the market share of such a competitor;

(b) any legal or regulatory barriers to entry, such as government authorization or standard setting in any form, as well as barriers resulting from product certification procedures, or the need to have a proven track record;

(c) any restrictions created by the existence of patents, know-how and other intellectual property rights in these markets and any restrictions created by licensing such rights;

(d) the extent to which each of the parties to the concentration are holders, licensees or licensors of patents, know-how and other rights in the relevant markets;

(e) the importance of economies of scale for the production or distribution of products in the affected markets; and

(f) access to sources of supply, such as availability of raw materials and necessary infrastructure.

RESEARCH AND DEVELOPMENT

8.11. Give an account of the importance of research and development in the ability of a firm operating the relevant market(s) to compete in the long term. Explain the nature of the research and development in affected markets carried out by the parties to the concentration.

In so doing, take account of the following, where appropriate:

(a) trends and intensities of research and development[26] in these markets and for the parties to the concentration;

(b) the course of technological development for these markets over an appropriate time period (including developments in products and/or services, production processes, distribution systems, and so on);

(c) the major innovations that have been made in these markets and the undertakings responsible for these innovations; and

(d) the cycle of innovation in these markets and where the parties are in this cycle of innovation.

COOPERATIVE AGREEMENTS

8.12. To what extent do cooperative agreements (horizontal, vertical, or other) exist in the affected markets?

8.13. Give details of the most important cooperative agreements engaged in by the parties to the concentration in the affected markets, such as research and development, licensing, joint production, specialization, distribution, long term supply and exchange of information agreements and, where deemed useful, provide a copy of these agreements.

TRADE ASSOCIATIONS

8.14. With respect to the trade associations in the affected markets:

(a) identify those of which the parties to the concentration are members; and

(b) identify the most important trade associations to which the customers and suppliers of the parties to the concentration belong.

Provide the name, address, telephone number, fax number and e-mail address of the appropriate contact person for all trade associations listed above.

SECTION 9

OVERALL MARKET CONTEXT AND EFFICIENCIES

9.1. Describe the world wide context of the proposed concentration, indicating the position of each of the parties to the concentration outside of the EEA territory in terms of size and competitive strength.

9.2. Describe how the proposed concentration is likely to affect the interests of intermediate and ultimate consumers and the development of technical and economic progress.

9.3. Should you wish the Commission specifically to consider from the outset[27] whether efficiency gains generated by the concentration are likely to enhance the ability and incentive of the new entity to act pro-competitively for the benefit of consumers, please provide a description of, and supporting documents relating to, each efficiency (including cost savings, new product introductions, and service or product improvements) that the parties anticipate will result from the proposed concentration relating to any relevant product.[28]

For each claimed efficiency, provide:

(i) a detailed explanation of how the proposed concentration would allow the new entity to achieve the efficiency. Specify the steps that the parties anticipate taking to achieve the efficiency, the risks involved in achieving the efficiency, and the time and costs required to achieve it;

(ii) where reasonably possible, a quantification of the efficiency and a detailed explanation of how the quantification was calculated. Where relevant, also provide an estimate of the significance of efficiencies related to new product introductions or quality improvements. For efficiencies that involve cost savings, state separately the one-time fixed cost savings, recurring fixed cost savings, and variable cost savings (in euros per unit and euros per year);

(iii) the extent to which customers are likely to benefit from the efficiency and a detailed explanation of how this conclusion is arrived at; and

(iv) the reason why the party or parties could not achieve the efficiency to a similar extent by means other than through the concentration proposed, and in a manner that is not likely to raise competition concerns.

SECTION 10

COOPERATIVE EFFECTS OF A JOINT VENTURE

10. For the purpose of Article 2(4) of the EC Merger Regulation, answer the following questions:

(a) Do two or more parents retain to a significant extent activities in the same market as the joint venture or in a market which is upstream or downstream from that of the joint venture or in a neighbouring market closely related to this market?[29]

If the answer is affirmative, please indicate for each of the markets referred to here:

— the turnover of each parent company in the preceding financial year;
— the economic significance of the activities of the joint venture in relation to this turnover;
— the market share of each parent.

If the answer is negative, please justify your answer.

(b) If the answer to (a) is affirmative and in your view the creation of the joint venture does not lead to coordination between independent undertakings that restricts competition within the meaning of Article 81(1) of the EC Treaty, give your reasons.

(c) Without prejudice to the answers to (a) and (b) and in order to ensure that a complete assessment of the case can be made by the Commission, please explain how the criteria of Article 81(3) apply. Under Article 81(3), the provisions of Article 81(1) may be declared inapplicable if the operation:

(i) contributes to improving the production or distribution of goods, or to promoting technical or economic progress;

(ii) allows consumers a fair share of the resulting benefit;
(iii) does not impose on the undertakings concerned restrictions which are not indispensable to the attainment of these objectives; and
(iv) does not afford such undertakings the possibility of eliminating competition in respect of a substantial part of the products in question.

SECTION 11

DECLARATION

Article 2(2) of the Implementing Regulation states that where notifications are signed by representatives of undertakings, such representatives must produce written proof that they are authorized to act. Such written authorization must accompany the notification.

The notification must conclude with the following declaration which is to be signed by or on behalf of all the notifying parties:

The notifying party or parties declare that, to the best of their knowledge and belief, the information given in this notification is true, correct, and complete, that true and complete copies of documents required by Form CO have been supplied, that all estimates are identified as such and are their best estimates of the underlying facts, and that all the opinions expressed are sincere.

They are aware of the provisions of Article 14(1)(a) of the EC Merger Regulation.

Place and date: ....

Signatures: ....

Name/s and positions: ....

On behalf of: ....

[9589]

NOTES

Para 1.4: figure in square brackets substituted by Commission Regulation 1792/2006/EC, Art 1, Annex, as from 1 January 2007.

1 Council Regulation (EC) No 139/2004 of 20 January 2004, OJ L24, 29.01.2004, p 1. Your attention is drawn to the corresponding provisions of the Agreement on the European Economic Area (hereinafter referred to as "the EEA Agreement"). See in particular Article 57 of the EEA Agreement, point 1 of Annex XIV to the EEA Agreement and Protocol 4 to the Agreement between the EFTA States on the establishment of a Surveillance Authority and a Court of Justice, as well as Protocols 21 and 24 to the EEA Agreement and Article 1 and the Agreed Minutes of the Protocol adjusting the EEA Agreement. Any reference to EFTA States shall be understood to mean those EFTA States which are Contracting Parties to the EEA Agreement. As of 1 May 2004, these States are Iceland, Liechtenstein and Norway.

2 The term "concentration" is defined in Article 3 of the EC Merger Regulation and the term "Community dimension" in Article 1 thereof. Furthermore, Article 4(5) provides that in certain circumstances where the Community turnover thresholds are not met, notifying parties may request that the Commission treat their proposed concentration as having a Community dimension.

3 See Article 10(1) of the EC Merger Regulation.

4 See Article 10(3) of the EC Merger Regulation.

5 See Article 4(2) of the EC Merger Regulation.

6 See, in particular, Article 122 of the EEA Agreement, Article 9 of Protocol 24 to the EEA Agreement and Article 17(2) of Chapter XIII of Protocol 4 to the Agreement between the EFTA States on the establishment of a Surveillance Authority and a Court of Justice (ESA Agreement).

7 See Section 6.III for the definition of affected markets.

8 This includes the target company in the case of a contested bid, in which case the details should be completed as far as is possible.

9 See Commission Notice on the concept of undertakings concerned.

10 See, generally, the Commission Notice on calculation of turnover. Turnover of the acquiring party or parties to the concentration should include the aggregated turnover of all undertakings within the meaning of Article 5(4) of the EC Merger Regulation. Turnover of the acquired party or parties should include the turnover relating to the parts subject to the transaction within the meaning of Article 5(2) of the EC Merger Regulation. Special provisions are contained in Articles 5(3), (4) and 5(5) of the EC Merger Regulation for credit, insurance, other financial institutions and joint undertakings.

11 See Article 57 of the EEA Agreement and, in particular, Article 2(1) of Protocol 24 to the EEA Agreement. A case qualifies as a cooperation case if the combined turnover of the undertakings concerned in the territory of the EFTA States equals 25% or more of their total turnover within the territory covered by the EEA Agreement; or each of at least two undertakings concerned has a turnover exceeding EUR 250 million in the territory of the EFTA States; or the concentration is

liable to create or strengthen a dominant position as a result of which effective competition would be significantly impeded in the territories of the EFTA States or a substantial part thereof.

12 See Articles 3(3), 3(4) and 3(5) and Article 5(4) of the EC Merger Regulation.

13 See Section 6 for the definition of affected markets.

14 As set out in introductory Parts 1.1 and 1.3(g), in the context of pre-notification, you may want to discuss with the Commission to what extent dispensation (waivers) to provide the requested documents would be appropriate. Where waivers are sought, the Commission may specify the documents to be provided in a particular case in a request for information under Article 11 of the EC Merger Regulation.

15 See Commission Notice on the definition of the relevant market for the purposes of Community competition law.

16 For example, if a party to the concentration holds a market share larger than 25% in a market that is upstream to a market in which the other party is active, then both the upstream and the downstream markets are affected markets. Similarly, if a vertically integrated company merges with another party which is active at the downstream level, and the merger leads to a combined market share downstream of 25% or more, then both the upstream and the downstream markets are affected markets.

17 As set out in introductory Parts 1.1 and 1.3(g), in the context of pre-notification, you may want to discuss with the Commission to what extent dispensation (waivers) to provide the requested information would be appropriate for certain affected markets, or for certain other markets (as described under IV).

18 Products (or services) are called complementary when, for example, the use (or consumption) of one product essentially implies the use (or consumption) of the other product, such as for staple machines and staples, and printers and printer cartridges.

19 Examples of products belonging to such a range would be whisky and gin sold to bars and restaurants, and different materials for packaging a certain category of goods sold to producers of such goods.

20 Without prejudice to Article 4(2) of the Implementing Regulation.

21 The value and volume of a market should reflect output less exports plus imports for the geographic areas under consideration. If readily available, please provide disaggregated information on imports and exports by country of origin and destination, respectively.

22 HHI stands for Herfindahl-Hirschman Index, a measure of market concentration. The HHI is calculated by summing the squares of the individual market shares of all the firms in the market. For example, a market containing five firms with market shares of 40%, 20%, 15%, 15%, and 10%, respectively, has an HHI of 2550 ($40^2 + 20^2 + 15^2 + 15^2 + 10^2 = 2550$). The HHI ranges from close to zero (in an atomistic market) to 10,000 (in the case of a pure monopoly). The post-merger HHI is calculated on the working assumption that the individual market shares of the companies do not change. Although it is best to include all firms in the calculation, lack of information about very small firms may not be important because such firms do not affect the HHI significantly.

23 The increase in concentration as measured by the HHI can be calculated independently of the overall market concentration by doubling the product of the market shares of the merging firms. For example, a merger of two firms with market shares of 30% and 15% respectively would increase the HHI by 900 ($30 \times 15 \times 2 = 900$). The explanation for this technique is as follows: Before the merger, the market shares of the merging firms contribute to the HHI by their squares individually: $(a)^2 + (b)^2$. After the merger, the contribution is the square of their sum: $(a + b)^2$, which equals $(a)^2 + (b)^2 + 2ab$. The increase in the HHI is therefore represented by 2ab.

24 That is, suppliers which are not subsidiaries, agents or undertakings forming part of the group of the party in question. In addition to those five independent suppliers the notifying parties can, if they consider it necessary for a proper assessment of the case, identify the intra-group suppliers. The same will apply in 8.6 in relation to customers.

25 Experience has shown that the examination of complex cases often requires more customer contact details. In the course of pre-notification contacts, the Commission's services may ask for more customer contact details for certain affected markets.

26 Research and development intensity is defined as research development expenditure as a proportion of turnover.

27 It should be noted that submitting information in response to Section 9.3 is voluntary. Parties are not required to offer any justification for not completing this section. Failure to provide information on efficiencies will not be taken to imply that the proposed concentration does not create efficiencies or that the rationale for the concentration is to increase market power. Not providing the requested information on efficiencies at the notification stage does not preclude providing the information at a later stage. However, the earlier the information is provided, the better the Commission can verify the efficiency claim.

28 For further guidance on the assessment of efficiencies, see the Commission Notice on the assessment of horizontal mergers.

29 For market definitions refer to Section 6.

ANNEX II
SHORT FORM FOR THE NOTIFICATION OF A CONCENTRATION PURSUANT TO REGULATION (EC) NO 139/2004

1. INTRODUCTION

1.1. The purpose of the Short Form

The Short Form specifies the information that must be provided by the notifying parties when submitting a notification to the European Commission of certain proposed mergers, acquisitions or other concentrations that are unlikely to raise competition concerns.

In completing this Form, your attention is drawn to Council Regulation (EC) No 139/2004 (hereinafter referred to as "the EC Merger Regulation"), and Commission Regulation (EC) No 802/2004 (hereinafter referred to as "the Implementing Regulation"), to which this Form is annexed.[1] The text of these regulations, as well as other relevant documents, can be found on the Competition page of the Commission's Europa web site.

As a general rule, the Short Form may be used for the purpose of notifying concentrations, where one of the following conditions is met:

1. in the case of a joint venture, the joint venture has no, or negligible, actual or foreseen activities within the territory of the European Economic Area (EEA). Such cases occur where:
   - (a) the turnover of the joint venture and/or the turnover of the contributed activities is less than EUR 100 million in the EEA territory; and
   - (b) the total value of the assets transferred to the joint venture is less than EUR 100 million in the EEA territory;
2. none of the parties to the concentration are engaged in business activities in the same relevant product and geographic market (no horizontal overlap), or in a market which is upstream or downstream of a market in which another party to the concentration is engaged (no vertical relationship);
3. two or more of the parties to the concentration are engaged in business activities in the same relevant product and geographic market (horizontal relationships), provided that their combined market share is less than 15%; and/or one or more of the parties to the concentration are engaged in business activities in a product market which is upstream or downstream of a product market in which any other party to the concentration is engaged (vertical relationships), and provided that none of their individual or combined market shares at either level is 25% or more; or
4. a party is to acquire sole control of an undertaking over which it already has joint control.

The Commission may require a full form notification where it appears either that the conditions for using the Short Form are not met, or, exceptionally, where they are met, the Commission determines, nonetheless, that a notification under Form CO is necessary for an adequate investigation of possible competition concerns.

Examples of cases where a notification under Form CO may be necessary are concentrations where it is difficult to define the relevant markets (for example, in emerging markets or where there is no established case practice); where a party is a new or potential entrant, or an important patent holder; where it is not possible to adequately determine the parties' market shares; in markets with high entry barriers, with a high degree of concentration or known competition problems; where at least two parties to the concentration are present in closely related neighbouring markets;[2] and in concentrations where an issue of coordination arises, as referred to in Article 2(4) of the EC Merger Regulation. Similarly, a Form CO notification may be required in the case of a party acquiring sole control of a joint venture in which it currently holds joint control, where the acquiring party and the joint venture, together, have a strong market position, or the joint venture and the acquiring party have strong positions in vertically related markets.

1.2. Reversion to the full Form CO notification

In assessing whether a concentration may be notified under the Short Form, the Commission will ensure that all relevant circumstances are established with sufficient clarity. In this respect, the responsibility to provide correct and complete information rests with the notifying parties.

If, after the concentration has been notified, the Commission considers that the case is not appropriate for notification under the Short Form, the Commission may require full, or where appropriate partial, notification under Form CO. This may be the case where:

- — it appears that the conditions for using the Short Form are not met
- — although the conditions for using the Short Form are met, a full or partial notification under Form CO appears to be necessary for an adequate investigation of possible competition concerns or to establish that the transaction is a concentration within the meaning of Article 3 of the EC Merger Regulation;
- — the Short Form contains incorrect or misleading information;
- — a Member State expresses substantiated competition concerns about the notified concentration within 15 working days of receipt of the copy of the notification; or
- — a third party expresses substantiated competition concerns within the time-limit laid down by the Commission for such comments.

In such cases, the notification may be treated as being incomplete in a material respect pursuant to Article 5(2) of the Implementing Regulation. The Commission will inform the notifying parties or their representatives of this in writing and without delay. The notification will only become effective on the date on which all information required is received.

1.3. Importance of pre-notification contacts

Experience has shown that pre-notification contacts are extremely valuable to both the notifying parties and the Commission in determining the precise amount of information required in a notification. Also, in cases where the parties wish to submit a Short Form notification, they are advised to engage in pre-notification contacts with the Commission in order to discuss whether the case is one for which it is appropriate to use a Short Form. Notifying parties may refer to the Commission's Best Practices on the Conduct of EC Merger Control Proceedings, which provides guidance on pre-notification contacts and the preparation of notifications.

1.4. Who must notify

In the case of a merger within the meaning of Article 3(1)(a) of the EC Merger Regulation or the acquisition of joint control of an undertaking within the meaning of Article 3(1)(b) of the EC Merger Regulation, the notification shall be completed jointly by the parties to the merger or by those acquiring joint control, as the case may be.[3]

In the case of the acquisition of a controlling interest in one undertaking by another, the acquirer must complete the notification.

In the case of a public bid to acquire an undertaking, the bidder must complete the notification.

Each party completing the notification is responsible for the accuracy of the information which it provides.

1.5. The requirement for a correct and complete notification

All information required by this Form must be correct and complete. The information required must be supplied in the appropriate Section of this Form.

In particular you should note that:

(a) In accordance with Article 10(1) of the EC Merger Regulation and Article 5(2) and (4) of the Implementing Regulation, the time-limits of the EC Merger Regulation linked to the notification will not begin to run until all the information that must be supplied with the notification has been received by the Commission. This requirement is to ensure that the Commission is able to assess the notified concentration within the strict time-limits provided by the EC Merger Regulation.

(b) The notifying parties should verify, in the course of preparing their notification, that contact names and numbers, and in particular fax numbers and e-mail addresses, provided to the Commission are accurate, relevant and up-to-date.

(c) Incorrect or misleading information in the notification will be considered to be incomplete information (Article 5(4) of the Implementing Regulation).

(d) If a notification is incomplete, the Commission will inform the notifying parties or their representatives in writing and without delay. The notification will only become effective on the date on which the complete and accurate information is received by the Commission (Article 10(1) of the EC Merger Regulation, Article 5(2) and (4) of the Implementing Regulation).

(e) Under Article 14(1)(a) of the EC Merger Regulation, notifying parties who, either intentionally or negligently, supply incorrect or misleading information, may be liable to fines of up to 1% of the aggregate turnover of the undertaking concerned. In addition, pursuant to Article 6(3)(a) and Article 8(6)(a) of the EC Merger Regulation the Commission may revoke its decision on the compatibility of a notified concentration where it is based on incorrect information for which one of the undertakings is responsible.

(f) You may request in writing that the Commission accept that the notification is complete notwithstanding the failure to provide information required by this Form, if such information is not reasonably available to you in part or in whole (for example, because of the unavailability of information on a target company during a contested bid).

The Commission will consider such a request, provided that you give reasons for the unavailability of that information, and provide your best estimates for missing data together with the sources for the estimates. Where possible, indications as to where any of the requested information that is unavailable to you could be obtained by the Commission should also be provided.

(g) You may request in writing that the Commission accept that the notification is complete notwithstanding the failure to provide information required by this Form, if you consider that any particular information required may not be necessary for the Commission's examination of the case.

The Commission will consider such a request, provided that you give adequate reasons why that information is not relevant and necessary to its inquiry into the notified operation. You should explain this during your pre-notification contacts with the Commission and submit a written request for a waiver, asking the Commission to dispense with the obligation to provide that information, pursuant to Article 4(2) of the Implementing Regulation.

1.6. How to notify

The notification must be completed in one of the official languages of the European Community. This language will thereafter be the language of the proceedings for all notifying parties. Where notifications are made in accordance with Article 12 of Protocol 24 to the EEA Agreement in an official language of an EFTA State which is not an official language of the Community, the notification must simultaneously be supplemented with a translation into an official language of the Community.

The information requested by this Form is to be set out using the sections and paragraph numbers of the Form, signing a declaration as provided in Section 9, and annexing supporting documentation. In completing Section 7 of this Form, the notifying parties are invited to consider whether, for purposes of clarity, this section is best presented in numerical order, or whether information can be grouped together for each individual reportable market (or group of reportable markets).

For the sake of clarity, certain information may be put in annexes. However, it is essential that all key substantive pieces of information, in particular, market share information for the parties and their largest competitors, are presented in the body of this Form. Annexes to this Form shall only be used to supplement the information supplied in the Form itself.

Contact details must be provided in a format provided by the Commission's Directorate-General for Competition (DG Competition). For a proper investigatory process, it is essential that the contact details are accurate. Multiple instances of incorrect contact details may be a ground for declaring a notification incomplete.

Supporting documents are to be submitted in their original language; where this is not an official language of the Community, they must be translated into the language of the proceeding (Article 3(4) of the Implementing Regulation).

Supporting documents may be originals or copies of the originals. In the latter case, the notifying party must confirm that they are true and complete.

One original and [37] copies of the Short Form and the supporting documents shall be submitted to the Commission's Directorate-General for Competition.

The notification shall be delivered to the address referred to in Article 23(1) of the Implementing Regulation and in the format specified by the Commission from time to time. This address is published in the *Official Journal of the European Union*. The notification must be delivered to the Commission on working days as defined by Article 24 of the Implementing Regulation. In order to enable it to be registered on the same day, it must be delivered before 17.00 hrs on Mondays to Thursdays and before 16.00 hrs on Fridays and workdays preceding public holidays and other holidays as determined by the Commission and published in the *Official Journal of the European Union*. The security instructions given on DG Competition's website must be adhered to.

1.7. Confidentiality

Article 287 of the Treaty and Article 17(2) of the EC Merger Regulation as well as the corresponding provisions of the EEA Agreement[4] require the Commission, the Member States, the EFTA Surveillance Authority and the EFTA States, their officials and other servants not to disclose information they have acquired through the application of the Regulation of the kind covered by the obligation of professional secrecy. The same principle must also apply to protect confidentiality between notifying parties.

If you believe that your interests would be harmed if any of the information you are asked to supply were to be published or otherwise divulged to other parties, submit this information separately with each page clearly marked "Business Secrets". You should also give reasons why this information should not be divulged or published.

In the case of mergers or joint acquisitions, or in other cases where the notification is completed by more than one of the parties, business secrets may be submitted under separate cover, and referred to in the notification as an annex. All such annexes must be included in the submission in order for a notification to be considered complete.

1.8. Definitions and instructions for purposes of this Form

Notifying party or parties: in cases where a notification is submitted by only one of the undertakings who is a party to an operation, "notifying parties" is used to refer only to the undertaking actually submitting the notification.

Party(ies) to the concentration or parties: these terms relate to both the acquiring and acquired parties, or to the merging parties, including all undertakings in which a controlling interest is being acquired or which is the subject of a public bid.

Except where otherwise specified, the terms notifying party(ies) and party(ies) to the concentration include all the undertakings which belong to the same groups as those parties.

Year: all references to the word year in this Form should be read as meaning calendar year, unless otherwise stated. All information requested in this Form must, unless otherwise specified, relate to the year preceding that of the notification.

The financial data requested in Sections 3.3 to 3.5 must be provided in euros at the average exchange rates prevailing for the years or other periods in question.

All references contained in this Form are to the relevant articles and paragraphs of the EC Merger Regulation, unless otherwise stated.

1.9. Provision of information to employees and their representatives

The Commission would like to draw attention to the obligations to which the parties to a concentration may be subject under Community and/or national rules on information and consultation regarding transactions of a concentrative nature vis-à-vis employees and/or their representatives.

SECTION 1

DESCRIPTION OF THE CONCENTRATION

1.1. Provide an executive summary of the concentration, specifying the parties to the concentration, the nature of the concentration (for example, merger, acquisition, joint venture), the areas of activity of the notifying parties, the markets on which the concentration will have an impact (including the main reportable markets),[5] and the strategic and economic rationale for the concentration.

1.2. Provide a summary (up to 500 words) of the information provided under Section 1.1. It is intended that this summary will be published on the Commission's website at the date of notification. The summary must be drafted so that it contains no confidential information or business secrets.

SECTION 2

INFORMATION ABOUT THE PARTIES

2.1. Information on notifying party (or parties)

Give details of:

2.1.1. name and address of undertaking;

2.1.2. nature of the undertaking's business;

2.1.3. name, address, telephone number, fax number and e-mail address of, and position held by, the appropriate contact person; and

2.1.4. an address for service of the notifying party (or each of the notifying parties) to which documents and, in particular, Commission Decisions may be delivered. The name, e-mail address and telephone number of a person at this address who is authorised to accept service must be provided.

2.2. Information on other parties[6] to the concentration

For each party to the concentration (except the notifying party or parties) give details of:

2.2.1. name and address of undertaking;

2.2.2. nature of undertaking's business;

2.2.3. name, address, telephone number, fax number and e-mail address of, and position held by, the appropriate contact person; and

2.2.4. an address for service of the party (or each of the parties) to which documents and, in particular, Commission Decisions may be delivered. The name, e-mail address and telephone number of a person at this address who is authorised to accept service must be provided.

2.3. Appointment of representatives

Where notifications are signed by representatives of undertakings, such representatives must produce written proof that they are authorised to act. The written proof must contain the name and position of the persons granting such authority.

Provide the following contact details of information of any representatives who have been authorised to act for any of the parties to the concentration, indicating whom they represent:

2.3.1. name of representative;

2.3.2. address of representative;

2.3.3. name, address, telephone number, fax number and e-mail address of person to be contacted; and

2.3.4. an address of the representative for service (in Brussels if available) to which correspondence may be sent and documents delivered.

SECTION 3

DETAILS OF THE CONCENTRATION

3.1. Describe the nature of the concentration being notified. In doing so state:

(a) whether the proposed concentration is a full legal merger, an acquisition of sole or joint control, a full-function joint venture within the meaning of Article 3(4) of the EC Merger Regulation or a contract or other means of conferring direct or indirect control within the meaning of Article 3(2) of the EC Merger Regulation;

(b) whether the whole or parts of parties are subject to the concentration;

(c) a brief explanation of the economic and financial structure of the concentration;

(d) whether any public offer for the securities of one party by another party has the support of the former's supervisory boards of management or other bodies legally representing that party;

(e) the proposed or expected date of any major events designed to bring about the completion of the concentration;

(f) the proposed structure of ownership and control after the completion of the concentration;

(g) any financial or other support received from whatever source (including public authorities) by any of the parties and the nature and amount of this support; and

(h) the economic sectors involved in the concentration.

3.2. State the value of the transaction (the purchase price or the value of all the assets involved, as the case may be);

3.3. For each of the undertakings concerned by the concentration[7] provide the following data[8] for the last financial year:

3.3.1. world-wide turnover;

3.3.2. Community-wide turnover;

3.3.3. EFTA-wide turnover;

3.3.4. turnover in each Member State;

3.3.5. turnover in each EFTA State;

3.3.6. the Member State, if any, in which more than two-thirds of Community-wide turnover is achieved; and

3.3.7. the EFTA State, if any, in which more than two-thirds of EFTA-wide turnover is achieved.

3.4. For the purposes of Article 1(3) of the EC Merger Regulation, if the operation does not meet the thresholds set out in Article 1(2), provide the following data for the last financial year:

3.4.1. the Member States, if any, in which the combined aggregate turnover of all the undertakings concerned is more than EUR 100 million; and

3.4.2. the Member States, if any, in which the aggregate turnover of each of at least two of the undertakings concerned is more than EUR 25 million.

3.5. For the purposes of determining whether the concentration qualifies as an EFTA cooperation case,[9] provide the following information with respect to the last financial year:

3.5.1. does the combined turnover of the undertakings concerned in the territory of the EFTA States equal 25% or more of their total turnover in the EEA territory?

3.5.2. does each of at least two undertakings concerned have a turnover exceeding EUR 250 million in the territory of the EFTA States?

3.6. In case the transaction concerns the acquisition of joint control of a joint venture, provide the following information:

3.6.1. the turnover of the joint venture and/or the turnover of the contributed activities to the joint venture; and/or

3.6.2. the total value of assets transferred to the joint venture.

3.7. Describe the economic rationale of the concentration.

SECTION 4

OWNERSHIP AND CONTROL[10]

For each of the parties to the concentration provide a list of all undertakings belonging to the same group.

This list must include:

4.1. all undertakings or persons controlling these parties, directly or indirectly;

4.2. all undertakings active in any reportable market[11] that are controlled, directly or indirectly:

(a) by these parties;
(b) by any other undertaking identified in 4.1.

For each entry listed above, the nature and means of control should be specified.

The information sought in this section may be illustrated by the use of organisation charts or diagrams to show the structure of ownership and control of the undertakings.

SECTION 5

SUPPORTING DOCUMENTATION

Notifying parties must provide the following:

5.1. copies of the final or most recent versions of all documents bringing about the concentration, whether by agreement between the parties to the concentration, acquisition of a controlling interest or a public bid; and

5.2. copies of the most recent annual reports and accounts of all the parties to the concentration.

SECTION 6

MARKET DEFINITIONS

The relevant product and geographic markets determine the scope within which the market power of the new entity resulting from the concentration must be assessed.[12]

The notifying party or parties must provide the data requested having regard to the following definitions:

I. Relevant product markets

A relevant product market comprises all those products and/or services which are regarded as interchangeable or substitutable by the consumer, by reason of the products' characteristics, their prices and their intended use. A relevant product market may in some cases be composed of a number of individual products and/or services which present largely identical physical or technical characteristics and are interchangeable.

Factors relevant to the assessment of the relevant product market include the analysis of why the products or services in these markets are included and why others are excluded by using the above definition, and having regard to, for example, substitutability, conditions of competition, prices, cross-price elasticity of demand or other factors relevant for the definition of the product markets (for example, supply-side substitutability in appropriate cases).

II. Relevant geographic markets

The relevant geographic market comprises the area in which the undertakings concerned are involved in the supply and demand of relevant products or services, in which the conditions of competition are sufficiently homogeneous and which can be distinguished from neighbouring geographic areas because, in particular, conditions of competition are appreciably different in those areas.

Factors relevant to the assessment of the relevant geographic market include *inter alia* the nature and characteristics of the products or services concerned, the existence of entry barriers, consumer preferences, appreciable differences in the undertakings' market shares between neighbouring geographic areas, or substantial price differences.

III. Reportable markets

For purposes of information required in this Form, reportable markets consist of all relevant product and geographic markets, as well as plausible alternative relevant product and geographic market definitions, on the basis of which:

(a) two or more of the parties to the concentration are engaged in business activities in the same relevant market (horizontal relationships);

(b) one or more of the parties to the concentration are engaged in business activities in a product market, which is upstream or downstream of a market in which any other party to the concentration is engaged, regardless of whether there is or is not any existing supplier/customer relationship between the parties to the concentration (vertical relationships).

6.1. On the basis of the above market definitions, identify all reportable markets.

SECTION 7

INFORMATION ON MARKETS

For each reportable market described in Section 6, for the year preceding the operation, provide the following:[13]

7.1. an estimate of the total size of the market in terms of sales value (in euros) and volume (units).[14] Indicate the basis and sources for the calculations and provide documents where available to confirm these calculations;

7.2. the sales in value and volume, as well as an estimate of the market shares, of each of the parties to the concentration. Indicate if there have been significant changes to the sales and market shares for the last three financial years; and

7.3. for horizontal and vertical relationships, an estimate of the market share in value (and where appropriate, volume) of the three largest competitors (indicating the basis for the estimates). Provide the name, address, telephone number, fax number and e-mail address of the head of the legal department (or other person exercising similar functions; and in cases where there is no such person, then the chief executive) for these competitors.

SECTION 8

COOPERATIVE EFFECTS OF A JOINT VENTURE

8. For the purpose of Article 2(4) of the EC Merger Regulation, please answer the following questions:

(a) Do two or more parents retain to a significant extent activities in the same market as the joint venture or in a market which is upstream or downstream from that of the joint venture or in a neighbouring market closely related to this market?[15]

If the answer is affirmative, please indicate for each of the markets referred to here:

— the turnover of each parent company in the preceding financial year;
— the economic significance of the activities of the joint venture in relation to this turnover;
— the market share of each parent.

If the answer is negative, please justify your answer.

(b) If the answer to (a) is affirmative and in your view the creation of the joint venture does not lead to coordination between independent undertakings that restricts competition within the meaning of Article 81(1) of the EC Treaty, give your reasons.

(c) Without prejudice to the answers to (a) and (b) and in order to ensure that a complete assessment of the case can be made by the Commission, please explain how the criteria of Article 81(3) apply. Under Article 81(3), the provisions of Article 81(1) may be declared inapplicable if the operation:

(i) contributes to improving the production or distribution of goods, or to promoting technical or economic progress;
(ii) allows consumers a fair share of the resulting benefit;
(iii) does not impose on the undertakings concerned restrictions which are not indispensable to the attainment of these objectives; and
(iv) does not afford such undertakings the possibility of eliminating competition in respect of a substantial part of the products in question.

SECTION 9

DECLARATION

Article 2(2) of the Implementing Regulation states that where notifications are signed by representatives of undertakings, such representatives must produce written proof that they are authorized to act. Such written authorization must accompany the notification.

The notification must conclude with the following declaration which is to be signed by or on behalf of all the notifying parties:

The notifying party or parties declare that, to the best of their knowledge and belief, the information given in this notification is true, correct, and complete, that true and complete copies of documents required by this Form have been supplied, that all estimates are identified as such and are their best estimates of the underlying facts, and that all the opinions expressed are sincere.

They are aware of the provisions of Article 14(1)(a) of the EC Merger Regulation.

Place and date: ....

Signatures: ....

Name/s and positions: ....

On behalf of: ....

[9590]

NOTES

Para 1.6: figure in square brackets substituted by Commission Regulation 1792/2006/EC, Art 1, Annex, as from 1 January 2007.

1 Council Regulation (EC) No 139/2004 of 20 January 2004, OJ L24, 29.01.2004, p 1. Your attention is drawn to the corresponding provisions of the Agreement on the European Economic Area (hereinafter referred to as "the EEA Agreement". See in particular Article 57 of the EEA Agreement, point 1 of Annex XIV to the EEA Agreement and Protocol 4 to the Agreement between the EFTA States on the establishment of a Surveillance Authority and a Court of Justice, as well as Protocols 21 and 24 to the EEA Agreement and Article 1, and the Agreed Minutes of the Protocol adjusting the EEA Agreement. Any reference to EFTA States shall be understood to mean those EFTA States which are Contracting Parties to the EEA Agreement. As of 1 May 2004, these States are Iceland, Liechtenstein and Norway.

2 Product markets are closely related neighbouring markets when the products are complementary to each other or when they belong to a range of products that is generally purchased by the same set of customers for the same end use.

3 See Article 4(2) of the EC Merger Regulation.

4 See, in particular, Article 122 of the EEA Agreement, Article 9 of Protocol 24 to the EEA Agreement and Article 17(2) of Chapter XIII of Protocol 4 to the Agreement between the EFTA States on the establishment of a Surveillance Authority and a Court of Justice (ESA Agreement).

5 See Section 6.III for the definition of reportable markets.

6 This includes the target company in the case of a contested bid, in which case the details should be completed as far as is possible.

7 See Commission Notice on the concept of undertakings concerned.

8 See, generally, the Commission Notice on calculation of turnover. Turnover of the acquiring party or parties to the concentration should include the aggregated turnover of all undertakings within the meaning of Article 5(4) of the EC Merger Regulation. Turnover of the acquired party or parties should include the turnover relating to the parts subject to the transaction within the meaning of Article 5(2) of the EC Merger Regulation. Special provisions are contained in Articles 5(3), (4) and 5(5) of the EC Merger Regulation for credit, insurance, other financial institutions and joint undertakings.

9 See Article 57 of the EEA Agreement and, in particular, Article 2(1) of Protocol 24 to the EEA Agreement. A case qualifies to be treated as a cooperation case if the combined turnover of the undertakings concerned in the territory of the EFTA States equals 25% or more of their total turnover within the territory covered by the EEA Agreement; or each of at least two undertakings concerned has a turnover exceeding EUR 250 million in the territory of the EFTA States; or the concentration is liable to create or strengthen a dominant position as a result of which effective competition would be significantly impeded in the territories of the EFTA States or a substantial part thereof.

10 See Articles 3(3), 3(4) and 3(5) and Article 5(4) of the EC Merger Regulation.

11 See Section 6.III for the definition of reportable markets.

12 See Commission Notice on the definition of the relevant market for the purposes of Community competition law.

13 In the context of pre-notification, you may want to discuss with the Commission to what extent dispensation (waivers) to provide the requested information would be appropriate for certain reportable markets.

14 The value and volume of a market should reflect output less exports plus imports for the geographic areas under consideration.

15 For market definitions refer to Section 6.

ANNEX III
FORM RS

(RS = REASONED SUBMISSION PURSUANT TO ARTICLE 4(4) AND (5) OF COUNCIL REGULATION (EC) NO 139/2004)
FORM RS RELATING TO REASONED SUBMISSIONS PURSUANT TO ARTICLES 4(4) AND 4(5) OF REGULATION (EC) NO 139/2004

INTRODUCTION

A. The purpose of this Form

This Form specifies the information that requesting parties should provide when making a reasoned submission for a pre-notification referral under Article 4(4) or (5) of Council Regulation (EC) No 139/2004 (hereinafter referred to as "the EC Merger Regulation").

Your attention is drawn to the EC Merger Regulation and to Commission Regulation (EC) No [802/2004] (hereinafter referred to as "the EC Merger Implementing Regulation"). The text of these regulations, as well as other relevant documents, can be found on the Competition page of the Commission's Europa web site.

Experience has shown that prior contacts are extremely valuable to both the parties and the relevant authorities in determining the precise amount and type of information required. Accordingly, parties are encouraged to consult the Commission and the relevant Member State/s regarding the adequacy of the scope and type of information on which they intend to base their reasoned submission.

B. The requirement for a reasoned submission to be correct and complete

All information required by this Form must be correct and complete. The information required must be supplied in the appropriate section of this Form.

Incorrect or misleading information in the reasoned submission will be considered to be incomplete information (Article 5(4) of the EC Merger Implementing Regulation).

If parties submit incorrect information, the Commission will have the power to revoke any Article 6 or 8 decision it adopts following an Article 4(5) referral, pursuant to Article 6(3)(a) or 8(6)(a) of the EC Merger Regulation. Following revocation, national competition laws would once again be applicable to the transaction. In the case of referrals under Article 4(4) made on the basis of incorrect information, the Commission may require a notification pursuant to Article 4(1). In addition, the Commission will have the power to impose fines for submission of incorrect or misleading information pursuant to Article 14(1)(a) of the EC Merger Regulation. (See point d below). Finally, parties should also be aware that, if a referral is made on the basis of incorrect, misleading or incomplete information included in Form RS, the Commission and/or the Member States may consider making a post-notification referral rectifying any referral made at pre-notification.

In particular you should note that:

(a) In accordance with Articles 4(4) and (5) of the EC Merger Regulation, the Commission is obliged to transmit reasoned submissions to Member States without delay. The time-limits for considering a reasoned submission will begin upon receipt of the submission by the relevant Member State or States. The decision whether or not to accede to a reasoned submission will normally be taken on the basis of the information contained therein, without further investigation efforts being undertaken by the authorities involved.

(b) The submitting parties should therefore verify, in the course of preparing their reasoned submission, that all information and arguments relied upon are sufficiently supported by independent sources.

(c) Under Article 14(1)(a) of the EC Merger Regulation, parties making a reasoned submission who, either intentionally or negligently, provide incorrect or misleading information, may be liable to fines of up to 1% of the aggregate turnover of the undertaking concerned.

(d) You may request in writing that the Commission accept that the reasoned submission is complete notwithstanding the failure to provide information required by this Form, if such information is not reasonably available to you in part or in whole (for example, because of the unavailability of information on a target company during a contested bid).

The Commission will consider such a request, provided that you give reasons for the non-availability of that information, and provide your best estimates for missing data together with the sources for the estimates. Where possible, indications as to where any of the requested information that is unavailable to you could be obtained by the Commission or the relevant Member State/s should also be provided.

(e) You may request that the Commission accept that the reasoned submission is complete notwithstanding the failure to provide information required by this Form, if you consider that any particular information requested by this Form may not be necessary for the Commission's or the relevant Member State/s' examination of the case.

The Commission will consider such a request, provided that you give adequate reasons why that information is not relevant and necessary to dealing with your request for a pre-notification referral. You should explain this during your prior contacts with the Commission and with the relevant Member State/s, and submit a written request for a waiver asking the Commission to dispense with the obligation to provide that information, pursuant to Article 4(2) of the EC Merger Implementing Regulation. The Commission may consult with the relevant Member State authority or authorities before deciding whether to accede to such a request.

C. Persons entitled to submit a reasoned submission

In the case of a merger within the meaning of Article 3(1)(a) of the EC Merger Regulation or the acquisition of joint control of an undertaking within the meaning of Article 3(1)(b) of the Merger Regulation, the reasoned submission must be completed jointly by the parties to the merger or by those acquiring joint control as the case may be.

In case of the acquisition of a controlling interest in one undertaking by another, the acquirer must complete the reasoned submission.

In the case of a public bid to acquire an undertaking, the bidder must complete the reasoned submission.

Each party completing a reasoned submission is responsible for the accuracy of the information which it provides.

D. How to make a reasoned submission

The reasoned submission must be completed in one of the official languages of the European Union. This language will thereafter be the language of the proceedings for all submitting parties.

In order to facilitate treatment of Form RS by Member State authorities, parties are strongly encouraged to provide the Commission with a translation of their reasoned submission in a language or languages which will be understood by all addressees of the information. As regards requests for referral to a Member State or States, the requesting parties are strongly encouraged to include a copy of the request in the language/s of the Member State/s to which referral is being requested.

The information requested by this Form is to be set out using the sections and paragraph numbers of the Form, signing the declaration at the end, and annexing supporting documentation. For the sake of clarity, certain information may be put in annexes. However, it is essential that all key substantive pieces of information are presented in the body of Form RS. Annexes to this Form shall only be used to supplement the information supplied in the Form itself.

Supporting documents are to be submitted in their original language; where this is not an official language of the Community, they must be translated into the language of the proceeding.

Supporting documents may be originals or copies of the originals. In the latter case, the submitting party must confirm that they are true and complete.

One original and 35 copies of the Form RS and of the supporting documents must be submitted to the Commission. The reasoned submission shall be delivered to the address referred to in Article 23(1) of the EC Merger Implementing Regulation and in the format specified by the Commission services.

The submission must be delivered to the address of the Commission's Directorate-General for Competition (DG Competition). This address is published in the *Official Journal of the European Union*. The submission must be delivered to the Commission on working days as defined by Article 24 of the EC Merger Implementing Regulation. In order to enable it to be registered on the same day, it must be delivered before 17.00 hrs on Mondays to Thursdays and before 16.00 hrs on Fridays and workdays preceding public holidays and other holidays as determined by the Commission and published in the *Official Journal of the European Union*. The security instructions given on DG Competition's website must be adhered to.

E. Confidentiality

Article 287 of the Treaty and Article 17(2) of the EC Merger Regulation require the Commission and the competent authorities of the Member States, their officials and other servants and other persons working under the supervision of these authorities as well as officials and civil servants of other authorities of the Member States, not to disclose information of the kind covered by the obligation of professional secrecy and which they have acquired through the application of the Regulation. The same principle must also apply to protect confidentiality between submitting parties.

If you believe that your interests would be harmed if any of the information supplied were to be published or otherwise divulged to other parties, submit this information separately with each page clearly marked "Business Secrets". You should also give reasons why this information should not be divulged or published.

In the case of mergers or joint acquisitions, or in other cases where the reasoned submission is completed by more than one of the parties, business secrets may be submitted in separate annexes, and referred to in the submission as an annex. All such annexes must be included in the reasoned submission.

F. Definitions and instructions for the purposes of this Form

Submitting party or parties: in cases where a reasoned submission is made by only one of the undertakings who is a party to an operation, "submitting parties" is used to refer only to the undertaking actually making the submission.

Party(ies) to the concentration or parties: these terms relate to both the acquiring and acquired parties, or to the merging parties, including all undertakings in which a controlling interest is being acquired or which is the subject of a public bid.

Except where otherwise specified, the terms "submitting party(ies)" and "party(ies) to the concentration" include all the undertakings which belong to the same groups as those "parties".

Affected markets: Section 4 of this Form requires the submitting parties to define the relevant product markets, and further to identify which of those relevant markets are likely to be affected by the operation. This definition of affected market is used as the basis for requiring information for a number of other questions contained in this Form. The definitions thus submitted by the submitting parties are referred to in this Form as the affected market(s). This term can refer to a relevant market made up either of products or of services.

Year: all references to the word "year" in this Form should be read as meaning calendar year, unless otherwise stated. All information requested in this Form relates, unless otherwise specified, to the year preceding that of the reasoned submission.

The financial data requested in this Form must be provided in Euros at the average exchange rates prevailing for the years or other periods in question.

All references contained in this Form are to the relevant Articles and paragraphs of the EC Merger Regulation, unless otherwise stated.

SECTION 1
BACKGROUND INFORMATION

1.0. Indicate whether the reasoned submission is made under Article 4(4) or (5).
— Article 4(4) referral
— Article 4(5) referral

1.1. Information on the submitting party (or parties)

Give details of:

1.1.1. the name and address of undertaking;

1.1.2. the nature of the undertaking's business;

1.1.3. the name, address, telephone number, fax number and electronic address of, and position held by, the appropriate contact person; and

1.1.4. an address for service of the submitting party (or each of the submitting parties) to which documents and, in particular, Commission decisions may be delivered. The name, telephone number and e-mail address of a person at this address who is authorised to accept service must be provided.

1.2. Information on the other parties[1] to the concentration

For each party to the concentration (except the submitting party or parties) give details of:

1.2.1. the name and address of undertaking;

1.2.2. the nature of undertaking's business;

1.2.3. the name, address, telephone number, fax number and electronic address of, and position held by the appropriate contact person;

1.2.4. an address for service of the party (or each of the parties) to which documents and, in particular, Commission Decisions may be delivered. The name, e-mail address and telephone number of a person at this address who is authorised to accept service must be provided.

1.3. Appointment of representatives

Where reasoned submissions are signed by representatives of undertakings, such representatives must produce written proof that they are authorized to act. The written proof must contain the name and position of the persons granting such authority.

Provide the following contact details of any representatives who have been authorized to act for any of the parties to the concentration, indicating whom they represent:

1.3.1. the name of the representative;

1.3.2. the address of the representative;

1.3.3. the name, address, telephone number, fax number and e-mail address of the person to be contacted; and

1.3.4. an address of the representative (in Brussels if available) to which correspondence may be sent and documents delivered.

SECTION 2
GENERAL BACKGROUND AND DETAILS OF THE CONCENTRATION

2.1. Describe the general background to the concentration. In particular, give an overview of the main reasons for the transaction, including its economic and strategic rationale.

Provide an executive summary of the concentration, specifying the parties to the concentration, the nature of the concentration (for example, merger, acquisition, or joint venture.), the areas of activity of the submitting parties, the markets on which the concentration will have an impact (including the main affected markets),[2] and the strategic and economic rationale for the concentration.

2.2. Describe the legal nature of the transaction which is the subject of the reasoned submission. In doing so, indicate:

(a) whether the whole or parts of the parties are subject to the concentration;

(b) the proposed or expected date of any major events designed to bring about the completion of the concentration;

(c) the proposed structure of ownership and control after the completion of the concentration; and

(d) whether the proposed transaction is a concentration within the meaning of Article 3 of the EC Merger Regulation.

2.3. List the economic sectors involved in the concentration.

2.3.1. State the value of the transaction (the purchase price or the value of all the assets involved, as the case may be).

2.4. Provide sufficient financial or other data to show that the concentration meets OR does not meet the jurisdictional thresholds under Article 1 of the EC Merger Regulation.

2.4.1. Provide a breakdown of the Community-wide turnover achieved by the undertakings concerned, indicating, where applicable, the Member State, if any, in which more than two-thirds of this turnover is achieved.

SECTION 3
OWNERSHIP AND CONTROL[3]

For each of the parties to the concentration provide a list of all undertakings belonging to the same group.

This list must include:

3.1. all undertakings or persons controlling these parties, directly or indirectly;

3.2. all undertakings active on any affected market[4] that are controlled, directly or indirectly:

(a) by these parties;

(b) by any other undertaking identified in 3.1.

For each entry listed above, the nature and means of control should be specified.

The information sought in this section may be illustrated by the use of organization charts or diagrams to show the structure of ownership and control of the undertakings.

SECTION 4
MARKET DEFINITIONS

The relevant product and geographic markets determine the scope within which the market power of the new entity resulting from the concentration must be assessed.[5]

The submitting party or parties must provide the data requested having regard to the following definitions:

I. Relevant product markets

A relevant product market comprises all those products and/or services which are regarded as interchangeable or substitutable by the consumer, by reason of the products' characteristics, their prices and their intended use. A relevant product market may in some cases be composed of a number of individual products and/or services which present largely identical physical or technical characteristics and are interchangeable.

Factors relevant to the assessment of the relevant product market include the analysis of why the products or services in these markets are included and why others are excluded by using the above definition, and having regard to, for example, substitutability, conditions of competition, prices, cross-price elasticity of demand or other factors relevant for the definition of the product markets (for example, supply-side substitutability in appropriate cases).

II. Relevant geographic markets

The relevant geographic market comprises the area in which the undertakings concerned are involved in the supply and demand of relevant products or services, in which the conditions of competition are sufficiently homogeneous and which can be distinguished from neighbouring geographic areas because, in particular, conditions of competition are appreciably different in those areas.

Factors relevant to the assessment of the relevant geographic market include *inter alia* the nature and characteristics of the products or services concerned, the existence of entry barriers, consumer preferences, appreciable differences in the undertakings' market shares between neighbouring geographic areas, or substantial price differences.

III. Affected markets

For the purposes of the information required in this Form, affected markets consist of relevant product markets where, in the Community, or in any Member State:

(a) two or more of the parties to the concentration are engaged in business activities in the same product market and where the concentration will lead to a combined market share of 15% or more. These are horizontal relationships;

(b) one or more of the parties to the concentration are engaged in business activities in a product market, which is upstream or downstream of a product market in which any other party to the concentration is engaged, and any of their individual or combined market shares at either level is 25% or more, regardless of whether there is or is not any existing supplier/customer relationship between the parties to the concentration.[6] These are vertical relationships.

On the basis of the above definitions and market share thresholds, provide the following information:

4.1. Identify each affected market within the meaning of Section III:

(a) at the Community level;

(b) in the case of a request for referral pursuant to Article 4(4), at the level of each individual Member State;

(c) in the case of a request for referral pursuant to Article 4(5), at the level of each Member State identified at Section 6.3.1 of this Form as capable of reviewing the concentration.

4.2. In addition, explain the submitting parties' view as to the scope of the relevant geographic market within the meaning of Section II in relation to each affected market identified at 4.1 above.

SECTION 5
INFORMATION ON AFFECTED MARKETS

For each affected relevant product market, for the last financial year,

(a) for the Community as a whole;

(b) in the case of a request for referral pursuant to Article 4(4), individually for each Member State where the parties to the concentration do business; and

(c) in the case of a request for referral pursuant to Article 4(5), individually for each Member State identified at Section 6.3.1 of this Form as capable of reviewing the concentration where the parties to the concentration do business; and

(d) where in the opinion of the submitting parties, the relevant geographic market is different;

provide the following information:

5.1. an estimate of the total size of the market in terms of sales value (in Euros) and volume (units).[7] Indicate the basis and sources for the calculations and provide documents where available to confirm these calculations;

5.2. the sales in value and volume, as well as an estimate of the market shares, of each of the parties to the concentration;

5.3. an estimate of the market share in value (and where appropriate volume) of all competitors (including importers) having at least 5% of the geographic market under consideration;

On this basis, provide an estimate of the HHI index[8] pre- and post-merger, and the difference between the two (the delta).[9] Indicate the proportion of market shares used as a basis to calculate the HHI; Identify the sources used to calculate these market shares and provide documents where available to confirm the calculation;

5.4. the five largest independent customers of the parties in each affected market and their individual share of total sales for such products accounted for by each of those customers;

5.5. the nature and extent of vertical integration of each of the parties to the concentration compared with their largest competitors;

5.6. identify the five largest independent[10] suppliers to the parties;

5.7. over the last five years, has there been any significant entry into any affected markets? In the opinion of the submitting parties are there undertakings (including those at present operating only in extra-Community markets) that are likely to enter the market? Please specify;

5.8. to what extent do cooperative agreements (horizontal or vertical) exist in the affected markets?

5.9. if the concentration is a joint venture, do two or more parents retain to a significant extent activities in the same market as the joint venture or in a market which is downstream or upstream from that of the joint venture or in a neighbouring market closely related to this market?[11]

5.10. describe the likely impact of the proposed concentration on competition in the affected markets and how the proposed concentration is likely to affect the interests of intermediate and ultimate consumers and the development of technical and economic progress.

SECTION 6
DETAILS OF THE REFERRAL REQUEST AND REASONS WHY THE CASE SHOULD BE REFERRED

6.1. Indicate whether the reasoned submission is made pursuant to Article 4(4) or 4(5) of the EC Merger Regulation, and fill in only the relevant sub-section:

— Article 4.4. referral
— Article 4.5 referral

Subsection 6.2
Article 4(4) Referral

6.2.1. Identify the Member State or Member States which, pursuant to Article 4(4), you submit should examine the concentration, indicating whether or not you have made informal contact with this Member State/s.

6.2.2. Specify whether you are requesting referral of the whole or part of the case.

If you are requesting referral of part of the case, specify clearly the part or parts of the case for which you request the referral.

If you are requesting referral of the whole of the case, you must confirm that there are no affected markets outside the territory of the Member State/s to which you request the referral to be made.

6.2.3. Explain in what way each of the affected markets in the Member State or States to which referral is requested presents all the characteristics of a distinct market within the meaning of Article 4(4).

6.2.4. Explain in what way competition may be significantly affected in each of the above-mentioned distinct markets within the meaning of Article 4(4).

6.2.5. In the event of a Member State/s becoming competent to review the whole or part of the case following a referral pursuant to Article 4(4), do you consent to the information contained in this Form being relied upon by the Member State/s in question for the purpose of its/their national proceedings relating to that case or part thereof? YES or NO

Subsection 6.3
article 4(5) referral

6.3.1. For each Member State, specify whether the concentration is or is not capable of being reviewed under its national competition law. You must tick one box for each and every Member State.

Is the concentration capable of being reviewed under the national competition law of each of the following Member States? You must reply for each Member State. Only indicate YES or NO for each Member State. Failure to indicate YES or NO for any Member State shall be deemed to constitute an indication of YES for that Member State.

Austria	YES	NO
Belgium	YES	NO
Cyprus	YES	NO
Czech Republic	YES	NO
Denmark	YES	NO
Estonia	YES	NO
Finland	YES	NO
France	YES	NO
Germany	YES	NO
Greece	YES	NO
Hungary	YES	NO
Ireland	YES	NO
Italy	YES	NO
Latvia	YES	NO
Lithuania	YES	NO
Luxembourg	YES	NO
Malta	YES	NO
Netherlands	YES	NO
Poland	YES	NO
Portugal	YES	NO
Slovakia	YES	NO
Slovenia	YES	NO
Spain	YES	NO
Sweden	YES	NO
United Kingdom	YES	NO

6.3.2. For each Member State, provide sufficient financial or other data to show that the concentration meets or does not meet the relevant jurisdictional criteria under the applicable national competition law.

6.3.4. Explain why the case should be examined by the Commission. Explain in particular whether the concentration might affect competition beyond the territory of one Member State.

SECTION 7
DECLARATION

It follows from Articles 2(2) and 6(2) of the EC Merger Implementing Regulation that where reasoned submissions are signed by representatives of undertakings, such representatives must produce written proof that they are authorized to act. Such written authorization must accompany the submission.

The reasoned submission must conclude with the following declaration which is to be signed by or on behalf of all the submitting parties:

The submitting party or parties declare that, following careful verification, the information given in this reasoned submission is to the best of their knowledge and belief true, correct, and complete, that true and complete copies of documents required by Form RS, have been supplied, and that all estimates are identified as such and are their best estimates of the underlying facts and that all the opinions expressed are sincere.

They are aware of the provisions of Article 14(1)(a) of the EC Merger Regulation.

Place and date: ....

Signatures: ....

Name/s and positions: ....

On behalf of: ....

[9591]

NOTES

Para D: figure in square brackets substituted by Commission Regulation 1792/2006/EC, Art 1, Annex, as from 1 January 2007.

1 This includes the target company in the case of a contested bid, in which case the details should be completed as far as is possible.

2 See Section 4 for the definition of affected markets.

3 See Article 3(3), 3(4) and 3(5) and Article 5(4).

4 See Section 4 for the definition of affected markets.

5 See Commission Notice on the definition of the relevant market for the purposes of Community competition law.

6 For example, if a party to the concentration holds a market share larger than 25% in a market that is upstream to a market in which the other party is active, then both the upstream and the downstream markets are affected markets. Similarly, if a vertically integrated company merges with another party which is active at the downstream level, and the merger leads to a combined market share downstream of 25% or more, then both the upstream and the downstream markets are affected markets.

7 The value and volume of a market should reflect output less exports plus imports for the geographic areas under consideration.

8 HHI stands for Herfindahl-Hirschman Index, a measure of market concentration. The HHI is calculated by summing the squares of the individual market shares of all the firms in the market. For example, a market containing five firms with market shares of 40%, 20%, 15%, 15%, and 10%, respectively, has an HHI of 2550 ($40^2 + 20^2 + 15^2 + 15^2 + 10^2 = 2550$). The HHI ranges from close to zero (in an atomistic market) to 10,000 (in the case of a pure monopoly). The post-merger HHI is calculated on the working assumption that the individual market shares of the companies do not change. Although it is best to include all firms in the calculation, lack of information about very small firms may not be important because such firms do not affect the HHI significantly.

9 The increase in concentration as measured by the HHI can be calculated independently of the overall market concentration by doubling the product of the market shares of the merging firms. For example, a merger of two firms with market shares of 30% and 15% respectively would increase the HHI by 900 ($30 \times 15 \times 2 = 900$). The explanation for this technique is as follows: Before the merger, the market shares of the merging firms contribute to the HHI by their squares individually: $(a)^2 + (b)^2$. After the merger, the contribution is the square of their sum: $(a + b)^2$, which equals $(a)^2 + (b)^2 + 2ab$. The increase in the HHI is therefore represented by 2ab.

10 That is suppliers which are not subsidiaries, agents or undertakings forming part of the group of the party in question. In addition to those five independent suppliers the notifying parties can, if they consider it necessary for a proper assessment of the case, identify the intra-group suppliers. The same applies in relation to customers.

11 For market definitions refer to Section 4.

Done at Brussels, 22 December 2003.

DIRECTIVE OF THE EUROPEAN PARLIAMENT AND OF THE COUNCIL

of 21 April 2004

on takeover bids

(2004/25/EC)

(Text with EEA relevance)

NOTES

Date of publication in OJ: OJ L142, 30.4.2004, p 12. Notes are as in the original OJ version.

THE EUROPEAN PARLIAMENT AND THE COUNCIL OF THE EUROPEAN UNION,

Having regard to the Treaty establishing the European Community, and in particular Article 44(1) thereof,

Having regard to the proposal from the Commission,[1]

Having regard to the opinion of the European Economic and Social Committee,[2]

Acting in accordance with the procedure laid down in Article 251 of the Treaty,[3]

Whereas:

(1) In accordance with Article 44(2)(g) of the Treaty, it is necessary to coordinate certain safeguards which, for the protection of the interests of members and others, Member States require of companies governed by the law of a Member State the securities of which are admitted to trading on a regulated market in a Member State, with a view to making such safeguards equivalent throughout the Community.

(2) It is necessary to protect the interests of holders of the securities of companies governed by the law of a Member State when those companies are the subject of takeover bids or of changes of control and at least some of their securities are admitted to trading on a regulated market in a Member State.

(3) It is necessary to create Community-wide clarity and transparency in respect of legal issues to be settled in the event of takeover bids and to prevent patterns of corporate restructuring within the Community from being distorted by arbitrary differences in governance and management cultures.

(4) In view of the public-interest purposes served by the central banks of the Member States, it seems inconceivable that they should be the targets of takeover bids. Since, for historical reasons, the securities of some of those central banks are listed on regulated markets in Member States, it is necessary to exclude them explicitly from the scope of this Directive.

(5) Each Member State should designate an authority or authorities to supervise those aspects of bids that are governed by this Directive and to ensure that parties to takeover bids comply with the rules made pursuant to this Directive. All those authorities should cooperate with one another.

(6) In order to be effective, takeover regulation should be flexible and capable of dealing with new circumstances as they arise and should accordingly provide for the possibility of exceptions and derogations. However, in applying any rules or exceptions laid down or in granting any derogations, supervisory authorities should respect certain general principles.

(7) Self-regulatory bodies should be able to exercise supervision.

(8) In accordance with general principles of Community law, and in particular the right to a fair hearing, decisions of a supervisory authority should in appropriate circumstances be susceptible to review by an independent court or tribunal. However, Member States should be left to determine whether rights are to be made available which may be asserted in administrative or judicial proceedings, either in proceedings against a supervisory authority or in proceedings between parties to a bid.

(9) Member States should take the necessary steps to protect the holders of securities, in particular those with minority holdings, when control of their companies has been acquired. The Member States should ensure such protection by obliging the person who has acquired control of a company to make an offer to all the holders of that company's securities for all of their holdings at an equitable price in accordance with a common definition. Member States should be free to establish further instruments for the protection of the interests of the holders of securities, such as the obligation to make a partial bid where the offeror does not acquire control of the company or the obligation to announce a bid at the same time as control of the company is acquired.

(10) The obligation to make a bid to all the holders of securities should not apply to those controlling holdings already in existence on the date on which the national legislation transposing this Directive enters into force.

(11) The obligation to launch a bid should not apply in the case of the acquisition of securities which do not carry the right to vote at ordinary general meetings of shareholders. Member States should, however, be able to provide that the obligation to make a bid to all the holders of securities relates not only to securities carrying voting rights but also to securities which carry voting rights only in specific circumstances or which do not carry voting rights.

(12) To reduce the scope for insider dealing, an offeror should be required to announce his/her decision to launch a bid as soon as possible and to inform the supervisory authority of the bid.

(13) The holders of securities should be properly informed of the terms of a bid by means of an offer document. Appropriate information should also be given to the representatives of the company's employees or, failing that, to the employees directly.

(14) The time allowed for the acceptance of a bid should be regulated.

(15) To be able to perform their functions satisfactorily, supervisory authorities should at all times be able to require the parties to a bid to provide information concerning themselves and should cooperate and supply information in an efficient and effective manner, without delay, to other authorities supervising capital markets.

(16) In order to prevent operations which could frustrate a bid, the powers of the board of an offeree company to engage in operations of an exceptional nature should be limited, without unduly hindering the offeree company in carrying on its normal business activities.

(17) The board of an offeree company should be required to make public a document setting out its opinion of the bid and the reasons on which that opinion is based, including its views on the effects of implementation on all the company's interests, and specifically on employment.

(18) In order to reinforce the effectiveness of existing provisions concerning the freedom to deal in the securities of companies covered by this Directive and the freedom to exercise voting rights, it is essential that the defensive structures and mechanisms envisaged by such companies be transparent and that they be regularly presented in reports to general meetings of shareholders.

(19) Member States should take the necessary measures to afford any offeror the possibility of acquiring majority interests in other companies and of fully exercising control of them. To that end, restrictions on the transfer of securities, restrictions on voting rights, extraordinary appointment rights and multiple voting rights should be removed or suspended during the time allowed for the acceptance of a bid and when the general meeting of shareholders decides on defensive measures, on amendments to the articles of association or on the removal or appointment of board members at the first general meeting of shareholders following closure of the bid. Where the holders of securities have suffered losses as a result of the removal of rights, equitable compensation should be provided for in accordance with the technical arrangements laid down by Member States.

(20) All special rights held by Member States in companies should be viewed in the framework of the free movement of capital and the relevant provisions of the Treaty. Special rights held by Member States in companies which are provided for in private or public national law should be exempted from the 'breakthrough' rule if they are compatible with the Treaty.

(21) Taking into account existing differences in Member States' company law mechanisms and structures, Member States should be allowed not to require companies established within their territories to apply the provisions of this Directive limiting the powers of the board of an offeree company during the time allowed for the acceptance of a bid and those rendering ineffective barriers, provided for in the articles of association or in specific agreements. In that event Member States should at least allow companies established within their territories to make the choice, which must be reversible, to apply those provisions. Without prejudice to international agreements to which the European Community is a party, Member States should be allowed not to require companies which apply those provisions in accordance with the optional arrangements to apply them when they become the subject of offers launched by companies which do not apply the same provisions, as a consequence of the use of those optional arrangements.

(22) Member States should lay down rules to cover the possibility of a bid's lapsing, the offeror's right to revise his/her bid, the possibility of competing bids for a company's securities, the disclosure of the result of a bid, the irrevocability of a bid and the conditions permitted.

(23) The disclosure of information to and the consultation of representatives of the employees of the offeror and the offeree company should be governed by the relevant national provisions, in particular those adopted pursuant to Council Directive 94/45/EC

of 22 September 1994 on the establishment of a European Works Council or a procedure in Community-scale undertakings and Community-scale groups of undertakings for the purposes of informing and consulting employees,[4] Council Directive 98/59/EC of 20 July 1998 on the approximation of the laws of the Member States relating to collective redundancies,[5] Council Directive 2001/86/EC of 8 October 2001 supplementing the statute for a European Company with regard to the involvement of employees[6] and Directive 2002/14/EC of the European Parliament and of the Council of 11 March 2002 establishing a general framework for informing and consulting employees in the European Community — Joint declaration of the European Parliament, the Council and the Commission on employee representation.[7] The employees of the companies concerned, or their representatives, should nevertheless be given an opportunity to state their views on the foreseeable effects of the bid on employment. Without prejudice to the rules of Directive 2003/6/EC of the European Parliament and of the Council of 28 January 2003 on insider dealing and market manipulation (market abuse),[8] Member States may always apply or introduce national provisions concerning the disclosure of information to and the consultation of representatives of the employees of the offeror before an offer is launched.

(24) Member States should take the necessary measures to enable an offeror who, following a takeover bid, has acquired a certain percentage of a company's capital carrying voting rights to require the holders of the remaining securities to sell him/her their securities. Likewise, where, following a takeover bid, an offeror has acquired a certain percentage of a company's capital carrying voting rights, the holders of the remaining securities should be able to require him/her to buy their securities. These squeeze-out and sell-out procedures should apply only under specific conditions linked to takeover bids. Member States may continue to apply national rules to squeeze-out and sell-out procedures in other circumstances.

(25) Since the objectives of the action envisaged, namely to establish minimum guidelines for the conduct of takeover bids and ensure an adequate level of protection for holders of securities throughout the Community, cannot be sufficiently achieved by the Member States because of the need for transparency and legal certainty in the case of cross-border takeovers and acquisitions of control, and can therefore, by reason of the scale and effects of the action, be better achieved at Community level, the Community may adopt measures, in accordance with the principle of subsidiarity as set out in Article 5 of the Treaty. In accordance with the principle of proportionality as set out in that Article, this Directive does not go beyond what is necessary to achieve those objectives.

(26) The adoption of a Directive is the appropriate procedure for the establishment of a framework consisting of certain common principles and a limited number of general requirements which Member States are to implement through more detailed rules in accordance with their national systems and their cultural contexts.

(27) Member States should, however, provide for sanctions for any infringement of the national measures transposing this Directive.

(28) Technical guidance and implementing measures for the rules laid down in this Directive may from time to time be necessary, to take account of new developments on financial markets. For certain provisions, the Commission should accordingly be empowered to adopt implementing measures, provided that these do not modify the essential elements of this Directive and the Commission acts in accordance with the principles set out in this Directive, after consulting the European Securities Commission established by Commission Directive 2001/528/EC.[9] The measures necessary for the implementation of this Directive should be adopted in accordance with the Council Decision 1999/468/EC of 28 June 1999 laying down the procedures for the exercise of implementing powers conferred on the Commission[10] and with due regard to the declaration made by the Commission in the European Parliament on 5 February 2002 concerning the implementation of financial services legislation. For the other provisions, it is important to entrust a contact committee with the task of assisting Member States and the supervisory authorities in the implementation of this Directive and of advising the Commission, if necessary, on additions or amendments to this Directive. In so doing, the contact committee may make use of the information which Member States are to provide on the basis of this Directive concerning takeover bids that have taken place on their regulated markets.

(29) The Commission should facilitate movement towards the fair and balanced harmonisation of rules on takeovers in the European Union. To that end, the Commission should be able to submit proposals for the timely revision of this Directive,

[9592]

NOTES

[1] OJ C45E, 25.2.2003, p 1.

2 OJ C208, 3.9.2003, p 55.
3 Opinion of the European Parliament of 16 December 2003 (not yet published in the Official Journal) and Council decision of 30 March 2004.
4 OJ L254, 30.9.1994, p 64. Directive as amended by Directive 97/74/EC (OJ L10, 16.1.1998, p 22).
5 OJ L225, 12.8.1998, p 16.
6 OJ L294, 10.11.2001, p 22.
7 OJ L80, 23.3.2002, p 29.
8 OJ L96, 12.4.2003, p 16.
9 OJ L191, 13.7.2001, p 45. Decision as amended by Decision 2004/8/EC (OJ L3, 7.1.2004, p 33).
10 OJ L184, 17.7.1999, p 23.

HAVE ADOPTED THIS DIRECTIVE:

Article 1

Scope

1. This Directive lays down measures coordinating the laws, regulations, administrative provisions, codes of practice and other arrangements of the Member States, including arrangements established by organisations officially authorised to regulate the markets (hereinafter referred to as 'rules'), relating to takeover bids for the securities of companies governed by the laws of Member States, where all or some of those securities are admitted to trading on a regulated market within the meaning of Directive 93/22/EEC[1] in one or more Member States (hereinafter referred to as a 'regulated market').

2. This Directive shall not apply to takeover bids for securities issued by companies, the object of which is the collective investment of capital provided by the public, which operate on the principle of risk-spreading and the units of which are, at the holders' request, repurchased or redeemed, directly or indirectly, out of the assets of those companies. Action taken by such companies to ensure that the stock exchange value of their units does not vary significantly from their net asset value shall be regarded as equivalent to such repurchase or redemption.

3. This Directive shall not apply to takeover bids for securities issued by the Member States' central banks.

[9593]

NOTES

1 Council Directive 93/22/EEC of 10 May 1993 on investment services in the securities field (OJ L141, 11.6.1993, p 27). Directive as last amended by Directive 2002/87/EC of the European Parliament and of the Council (OJ L35, 11.2.2003, p 1).

Article 2

Definitions

1. For the purposes of this Directive:
   (a) 'takeover bid' or 'bid' shall mean a public offer (other than by the offeree company itself) made to the holders of the securities of a company to acquire all or some of those securities, whether mandatory or voluntary, which follows or has as its objective the acquisition of control of the offeree company in accordance with national law;
   (b) 'offeree company' shall mean a company, the securities of which are the subject of a bid;
   (c) 'offeror' shall mean any natural or legal person governed by public or private law making a bid;
   (d) 'persons acting in concert' shall mean natural or legal persons who cooperate with the offeror or the offeree company on the basis of an agreement, either express or tacit, either oral or written, aimed either at acquiring control of the offeree company or at frustrating the successful outcome of a bid;
   (e) 'securities' shall mean transferable securities carrying voting rights in a company;
   (f) 'parties to the bid' shall mean the offeror, the members of the offeror's board if the offeror is a company, the offeree company, holders of securities of the offeree company and the members of the board of the offeree company, and persons acting in concert with such parties;

(g) 'multiple vote securities' shall mean securities included in a distinct and separate class and carrying more than one vote each.

2. For the purposes of paragraph 1(d), persons controlled by another person within the meaning of Article 87 of Directive 2001/34/EC[1] shall be deemed to be persons acting in concert with that other person and with each other.

[9594]

NOTES

1 Directive 2001/34/EC of the European Parliament and of the Council of 28 May 2001 on the admission of securities to official stock exchange listing and on information to be published on those securities (OJ L184, 6.7.2001, p 1). Directive as last amended by Directive 2003/71/EC (OJ L345, 31.12.2003, p 64).

Article 3

General Principles

1. For the purpose of implementing this Directive, Member States shall ensure that the following principles are complied with:

(a) all holders of the securities of an offeree company of the same class must be afforded equivalent treatment; moreover, if a person acquires control of a company, the other holders of securities must be protected;
(b) the holders of the securities of an offeree company must have sufficient time and information to enable them to reach a properly informed decision on the bid; where it advises the holders of securities, the board of the offeree company must give its views on the effects of implementation of the bid on employment, conditions of employment and the locations of the company's places of business;
(c) the board of an offeree company must act in the interests of the company as a whole and must not deny the holders of securities the opportunity to decide on the merits of the bid;
(d) false markets must not be created in the securities of the offeree company, of the offeror company or of any other company concerned by the bid in such a way that the rise or fall of the prices of the securities becomes artificial and the normal functioning of the markets is distorted;
(e) an offeror must announce a bid only after ensuring that he/she can fulfil in full any cash consideration, if such is offered, and after taking all reasonable measures to secure the implementation of any other type of consideration;
(f) an offeree company must not be hindered in the conduct of its affairs for longer than is reasonable by a bid for its securities.

2. With a view to ensuring compliance with the principles laid down in paragraph 1, Member States:

(a) shall ensure that the minimum requirements set out in this Directive are observed;
(b) may lay down additional conditions and provisions more stringent than those of this Directive for the regulation of bids.

[9595]

Article 4

Supervisory authority and applicable law

1. Member States shall designate the authority or authorities competent to supervise bids for the purposes of the rules which they make or introduce pursuant to this Directive. The authorities thus designated shall be either public authorities, associations or private bodies recognised by national law or by public authorities expressly empowered for that purpose by national law. Member States shall inform the Commission of those designations, specifying any divisions of functions that may be made. They shall ensure that those authorities exercise their functions impartially and independently of all parties to a bid.

2.

(a) The authority competent to supervise a bid shall be that of the Member State in which the offeree company has its registered office if that company's securities are admitted to trading on a regulated market in that Member State.
(b) If the offeree company's securities are not admitted to trading on a regulated market in the Member State in which the company has its registered office, the

authority competent to supervise the bid shall be that of the Member State on the regulated market of which the company's securities are admitted to trading.

If the offeree company's securities are admitted to trading on regulated markets in more than one Member State, the authority competent to supervise the bid shall be that of the Member State on the regulated market of which the securities were first admitted to trading.

(c) If the offeree company's securities were first admitted to trading on regulated markets in more than one Member State simultaneously, the offeree company shall determine which of the supervisory authorities of those Member States shall be the authority competent to supervise the bid by notifying those regulated markets and their supervisory authorities on the first day of trading.

If the offeree company's securities have already been admitted to trading on regulated markets in more than one Member State on the date laid down in Article 21(1) and were admitted simultaneously, the supervisory authorities of those Member States shall agree which one of them shall be the authority competent to supervise the bid within four weeks of the date laid down in Article 21(1). Otherwise, the offeree company shall determine which of those authorities shall be the competent authority on the first day of trading following that four-week period.

(d) Member States shall ensure that the decisions referred to in (c) are made public.

(e) In the cases referred to in (b) and (c), matters relating to the consideration offered in the case of a bid, in particular the price, and matters relating to the bid procedure, in particular the information on the offeror's decision to make a bid, the contents of the offer document and the disclosure of the bid, shall be dealt with in accordance with the rules of the Member State of the competent authority. In matters relating to the information to be provided to the employees of the offeree company and in matters relating to company law, in particular the percentage of voting rights which confers control and any derogation from the obligation to launch a bid, as well as the conditions under which the board of the offeree company may undertake any action which might result in the frustration of the bid, the applicable rules and the competent authority shall be those of the Member State in which the offeree company has its registered office.

3. Member States shall ensure that all persons employed or formerly employed by their supervisory authorities are bound by professional secrecy. No information covered by professional secrecy may be divulged to any person or authority except under provisions laid down by law.

4. The supervisory authorities of the Member States for the purposes of this Directive and other authorities supervising capital markets, in particular in accordance with Directive 93/22/EEC, Directive 2001/34/EC, Directive 2003/6/EC and Directive 2003/71/EC of the European Parliament and of the Council of 4 November 2003 on the prospectus to be published when securities are offered to the public or admitted to trading shall cooperate and supply each other with information wherever necessary for the application of the rules drawn up in accordance with this Directive and in particular in cases covered by paragraph 2(b), (c) and (e). Information thus exchanged shall be covered by the obligation of professional secrecy to which persons employed or formerly employed by the supervisory authorities receiving the information are subject. Cooperation shall include the ability to serve the legal documents necessary to enforce measures taken by the competent authorities in connection with bids, as well as such other assistance as may reasonably be requested by the supervisory authorities concerned for the purpose of investigating any actual or alleged breaches of the rules made or introduced pursuant to this Directive.

5. The supervisory authorities shall be vested with all the powers necessary for the purpose of carrying out their duties, including that of ensuring that the parties to a bid comply with the rules made or introduced pursuant to this Directive.

Provided that the general principles laid down in Article 3(1) are respected, Member States may provide in the rules that they make or introduce pursuant to this Directive for derogations from those rules:

(i) by including such derogations in their national rules, in order to take account of circumstances determined at national level

and/or

(ii) by granting their supervisory authorities, where they are competent, powers to waive such national rules, to take account of the circumstances referred to in (i) or in other specific circumstances, in which case a reasoned decision must be required.

6. This Directive shall not affect the power of the Member States to designate judicial or other authorities responsible for dealing with disputes and for deciding on irregularities committed in the course of bids or the power of Member States to regulate whether and under which circumstances parties to a bid are entitled to bring administrative or judicial proceedings. In particular, this Directive shall not affect the power which courts may have in a Member State to decline to hear legal proceedings and to decide whether or not such proceedings affect the outcome of a bid. This Directive shall not affect the power of the Member States to determine the legal position concerning the liability of supervisory authorities or concerning litigation between the parties to a bid.

[9596]

Article 5

Protection of minority shareholders, the mandatory bid and the equitable price

1. Where a natural or legal person, as a result of his/her own acquisition or the acquisition by persons acting in concert with him/her, holds securities of a company as referred to in Article 1(1) which, added to any existing holdings of those securities of his/hers and the holdings of those securities of persons acting in concert with him/her, directly or indirectly give him/her a specified percentage of voting rights in that company, giving him/her control of that company, Member States shall ensure that such a person is required to make a bid as a means of protecting the minority shareholders of that company. Such a bid shall be addressed at the earliest opportunity to all the holders of those securities for all their holdings at the equitable price as defined in paragraph 4.

2. Where control has been acquired following a voluntary bid made in accordance with this Directive to all the holders of securities for all their holdings, the obligation laid down in paragraph 1 to launch a bid shall no longer apply.

3. The percentage of voting rights which confers control for the purposes of paragraph 1 and the method of its calculation shall be determined by the rules of the Member State in which the company has its registered office.

4. The highest price paid for the same securities by the offeror, or by persons acting in concert with him/her, over a period, to be or determined by Member States, of not less than six months and not more than 12 before the bid referred to in paragraph 1 shall be regarded as the equitable price. If, after the bid has been made public and before the offer closes for acceptance, the offeror or any person acting in concert with him/her purchases securities at a price higher than the offer price, the offeror shall increase his/her offer so that it is not less than the highest price paid for the securities so acquired.

Provided that the general principles laid down in Article 3(1) are respected, Member States may authorise their supervisory authorities to adjust the price referred to in the first subparagraph in circumstances and in accordance with criteria that are clearly determined. To that end, they may draw up a list of circumstances in which the highest price may be adjusted either upwards or downwards, for example where the highest price was set by agreement between the purchaser and a seller, where the market prices of the securities in question have been manipulated, where market prices in general or certain market prices in particular have been affected by exceptional occurrences, or in order to enable a firm in difficulty to be rescued. They may also determine the criteria to be applied in such cases, for example the average market value over a particular period, the break-up value of the company or other objective valuation criteria generally used in financial analysis.

Any decision by a supervisory authority to adjust the equitable price shall be substantiated and made public.

5. By way of consideration the offeror may offer securities, cash or a combination of both.

However, where the consideration offered by the offeror does not consist of liquid securities admitted to trading on a regulated market, it shall include a cash alternative.

In any event, the offeror shall offer a cash consideration at least as an alternative where he/she or persons acting in concert with him/her, over a period beginning at the same time as the period determined by the Member State in accordance with paragraph 4 and ending when the offer closes for acceptance, has purchased for cash securities carrying 5% or more of the voting rights in the offeree company.

Member States may provide that a cash consideration must be offered, at least as an alternative, in all cases.

6. In addition to the protection provided for in paragraph 1, Member States may provide for further instruments intended to protect the interests of the holders of securities in so far as those instruments do not hinder the normal course of a bid.

[9597]

Article 6

Information concerning bids

1. Member States shall ensure that a decision to make a bid is made public without delay and that the supervisory authority is informed of the bid. They may require that the supervisory authority must be informed before such a decision is made public. As soon as the bid has been made public, the boards of the offeree company and of the offeror shall inform the representatives of their respective employees or, where there are no such representatives, the employees themselves.

2. Member States shall ensure that an offeror is required to draw up and make public in good time an offer document containing the information necessary to enable the holders of the offeree company's securities to reach a properly informed decision on the bid. Before the offer document is made public, the offeror shall communicate it to the supervisory authority. When it is made public, the boards of the offeree company and of the offeror shall communicate it to the representatives of their respective employees or, where there are no such representatives, to the employees themselves.

Where the offer document referred to in the first subparagraph is subject to the prior approval of the supervisory authority and has been approved, it shall be recognised, subject to any translation required, in any other Member State on the market of which the offeree company's securities are admitted to trading, without its being necessary to obtain the approval of the supervisory authorities of that Member State. Those authorities may require the inclusion of additional information in the offer document only if such information is specific to the market of a Member State or Member States on which the offeree company's securities are admitted to trading and relates to the formalities to be complied with to accept the bid and to receive the consideration due at the close of the bid as well as to the tax arrangements to which the consideration offered to the holders of the securities will be subject.

3. The offer document referred to in paragraph 2 shall state at least:

(a) the terms of the bid;
(b) the identity of the offeror and, where the offeror is a company, the type, name and registered office of that company;
(c) the securities or, where appropriate, the class or classes of securities for which the bid is made;
(d) the consideration offered for each security or class of securities and, in the case of a mandatory bid, the method employed in determining it, with particulars of the way in which that consideration is to be paid;
(e) the compensation offered for the rights which might be removed as a result of the breakthrough rule laid down in Article 11(4), with particulars of the way in which that compensation is to be paid and the method employed in determining it;
(f) the maximum and minimum percentages or quantities of securities which the offeror undertakes to acquire;
(g) details of any existing holdings of the offeror, and of persons acting in concert with him/her, in the offeree company;
(h) all the conditions to which the bid is subject;
(i) the offeror's intentions with regard to the future business of the offeree company and, in so far as it is affected by the bid, the offeror company and with regard to the safeguarding of the jobs of their employees and management, including any material change in the conditions of employment, and in particular the offeror's strategic plans for the two companies and the likely repercussions on employment and the locations of the companies' places of business;
(j) the time allowed for acceptance of the bid;
(k) where the consideration offered by the offeror includes securities of any kind, information concerning those securities;
(l) information concerning the financing for the bid;
(m) the identity of persons acting in concert with the offeror or with the offeree company and, in the case of companies, their types, names, registered offices and relationships with the offeror and, where possible, with the offeree company;

(n) the national law which will govern contracts concluded between the offeror and the holders of the offeree company's securities as a result of the bid and the competent courts.

4. The Commission shall adopt rules for the application of paragraph 3 in accordance with the procedure referred to in Article 18(2).

5. Member States shall ensure that the parties to a bid are required to provide the supervisory authorities of their Member State at any time on request with all the information in their possession concerning the bid that is necessary for the supervisory authority to discharge its functions.

[9598]

Article 7

Time allowed for acceptance

1. Member States shall provide that the time allowed for the acceptance of a bid may not be less than two weeks nor more than 10 weeks from the date of publication of the offer document. Provided that the general principle laid down in Article 3(1)(f) is respected, Member States may provide that the period of 10 weeks may be extended on condition that the offeror gives at least two weeks' notice of his/her intention of closing the bid.

2 Member States may provide for rules changing the period referred to in paragraph 1 in specific cases. A Member State may authorise a supervisory authority to grant a derogation from the period referred to in paragraph 1 in order to allow the offeree company to call a general meeting of shareholders to consider the bid.

[9599]

Article 8

Disclosure

1. Member States shall ensure that a bid is made public in such a way as to ensure market transparency and integrity for the securities of the offeree company, of the offeror or of any other company affected by the bid, in particular in order to prevent the publication or dissemination of false or misleading information.

2. Member States shall provide for the disclosure of all information and documents required by Article 6 in such a manner as to ensure that they are both readily and promptly available to the holders of securities at least in those Member States on the regulated markets of which the offeree company's securities are admitted to trading and to the representatives of the employees of the offeree company and the offeror or, where there are no such representatives, to the employees themselves.

[9600]

Article 9

Obligations of the board of the offeree company

1. Member States shall ensure that the rules laid down in paragraphs 2 to 5 are complied with.

2. During the period referred to in the second subparagraph, the board of the offeree company shall obtain the prior authorisation of the general meeting of shareholders given for this purpose before taking any action, other than seeking alternative bids, which may result in the frustration of the bid and in particular before issuing any shares which may result in a lasting impediment to the offeror's acquiring control of the offeree company.

Such authorisation shall be mandatory at least from the time the board of the offeree company receives the information referred to in the first sentence of Article 6(1) concerning the bid and until the result of the bid is made public or the bid lapses. Member States may require that such authorisation be obtained at an earlier stage, for example as soon as the board of the offeree company becomes aware that the bid is imminent.

3. As regards decisions taken before the beginning of the period referred to in the second subparagraph of paragraph 2 and not yet partly or fully implemented, the general meeting of shareholders shall approve or confirm any decision which does not form part of the normal course of the company's business and the implementation of which may result in the frustration of the bid.

4. For the purpose of obtaining the prior authorisation, approval or confirmation of the holders of securities referred to in paragraphs 2 and 3, Member States may adopt rules allowing a general meeting of shareholders to be called at short notice, provided that the meeting does not take place within two weeks of notification's being given.

5. The board of the offeree company shall draw up and make public a document setting out its opinion of the bid and the reasons on which it is based, including its views on the effects of implementation of the bid on all the company's interests and specifically employment, and on the offeror's strategic plans for the offeree company and their likely repercussions on employment and the locations of the company's places of business as set out in the offer document in accordance with Article 6(3)(i). The board of the offeree company shall at the same time communicate that opinion to the representatives of its employees or, where there are no such representatives, to the employees themselves. Where the board of the offeree company receives in good time a separate opinion from the representatives of its employees on the effects of the bid on employment, that opinion shall be appended to the document.

6. For the purposes of paragraph 2, where a company has a two-tier board structure 'board' shall mean both the management board and the supervisory board.

[9601]

Article 10

Information on companies as referred to in Article 1(1)

1. Member States shall ensure that companies as referred to in Article 1(1) publish detailed information on the following:

(a) the structure of their capital, including securities which are not admitted to trading on a regulated market in a Member State, where appropriate with an indication of the different classes of shares and, for each class of shares, the rights and obligations attaching to it and the percentage of total share capital that it represents;

(b) any restrictions on the transfer of securities, such as limitations on the holding of securities or the need to obtain the approval of the company or other holders of securities, without prejudice to Article 46 of Directive 2001/34/EC;

(c) significant direct and indirect shareholdings (including indirect shareholdings through pyramid structures and cross-shareholdings) within the meaning of Article 85 of Directive 2001/34/EC;

(d) the holders of any securities with special control rights and a description of those rights;

(e) the system of control of any employee share scheme where the control rights are not exercised directly by the employees;

(f) any restrictions on voting rights, such as limitations of the voting rights of holders of a given percentage or number of votes, deadlines for exercising voting rights, or systems whereby, with the company's cooperation, the financial rights attaching to securities are separated from the holding of securities;

(g) any agreements between shareholders which are known to the company and may result in restrictions on the transfer of securities and/or voting rights within the meaning of Directive 2001/34/EC;

(h) the rules governing the appointment and replacement of board members and the amendment of the articles of association;

(i) the powers of board members, and in particular the power to issue or buy back shares;

(j) any significant agreements to which the company is a party and which take effect, alter or terminate upon a change of control of the company following a takeover bid, and the effects thereof, except where their nature is such that their disclosure would be seriously prejudicial to the company; this exception shall not apply where the company is specifically obliged to disclose such information on the basis of other legal requirements;

(k) any agreements between the company and its board members or employees providing for compensation if they resign or are made redundant without valid reason or if their employment ceases because of a takeover bid.

2. The information referred to in paragraph 1 shall be published in the company's annual report as provided for in Article 46 of Directive 78/660/EEC[1] and Article 36 of Directive 83/349/EEC.[2]

3. Member States shall ensure, in the case of companies the securities of which are admitted to trading on a regulated market in a Member State, that the board presents an explanatory report to the annual general meeting of shareholders on the matters referred to in paragraph 1.

[9602]

NOTES

[1] Fourth Council Directive 78/660/EEC of 25 July 1978 on the annual accounts of certain types of companies (OJ L222, 14.8.1978, p 11). Directive as last amended by Directive 2003/51/EC of the European Parliament and of the Council (OJ L178, 17.7.2003, p 16).

[2] Seventh Council Directive 83/349/EEC of 13 June 1983 on consolidated accounts (OJ L193, 18.7.1983, p 1). Directive as last amended by Directive 2003/51/EC.

Article 11

Breakthrough

1. Without prejudice to other rights and obligations provided for in Community law for the companies referred to in Article 1(1), Member States shall ensure that the provisions laid down in paragraphs 2 to 7 apply when a bid has been made public.

2. Any restrictions on the transfer of securities provided for in the articles of association of the offeree company shall not apply vis-à-vis the offeror during the time allowed for acceptance of the bid laid down in Article 7(1).

Any restrictions on the transfer of securities provided for in contractual agreements between the offeree company and holders of its securities, or in contractual agreements between holders of the offeree company's securities entered into after the adoption of this Directive, shall not apply vis-à-vis the offeror during the time allowed for acceptance of the bid laid down in Article 7(1).

3. Restrictions on voting rights provided for in the articles of association of the offeree company shall not have effect at the general meeting of shareholders which decides on any defensive measures in accordance with Article 9.

Restrictions on voting rights provided for in contractual agreements between the offeree company and holders of its securities, or in contractual agreements between holders of the offeree company's securities entered into after the adoption of this Directive, shall not have effect at the general meeting of shareholders which decides on any defensive measures in accordance with Article 9.

Multiple-vote securities shall carry only one vote each at the general meeting of shareholders which decides on any defensive measures in accordance with Article 9.

4. Where, following a bid, the offeror holds 75% or more of the capital carrying voting rights, no restrictions on the transfer of securities or on voting rights referred to in paragraphs 2 and 3 nor any extraordinary rights of shareholders concerning the appointment or removal of board members provided for in the articles of association of the offeree company shall apply; multiple-vote securities shall carry only one vote each at the first general meeting of shareholders following closure of the bid, called by the offeror in order to amend the articles of association or to remove or appoint board members.

To that end, the offeror shall have the right to convene a general meeting of shareholders at short notice, provided that the meeting does not take place within two weeks of notification.

5. Where rights are removed on the basis of paragraphs 2, 3, or 4 and/or Article 12, equitable compensation shall be provided for any loss suffered by the holders of those rights. The terms for determining such compensation and the arrangements for its payment shall be set by Member States.

6. Paragraphs 3 and 4 shall not apply to securities where the restrictions on voting rights are compensated for by specific pecuniary advantages.

7. This Article shall not apply either where Member States hold securities in the offeree company which confer special rights on the Member States which are compatible with the Treaty, or to special rights provided for in national law which are compatible with the Treaty or to cooperatives.

[9603]

Article 12

Optional arrangements

1. Member States may reserve the right not to require companies as referred to in Article 1(1) which have their registered offices within their territories to apply Article 9(2) and (3) and/or Article 11.

2. Where Member States make use of the option provided for in paragraph 1, they shall nevertheless grant companies which have their registered offices within their territories the option, which shall be reversible, of applying Article 9(2) and (3) and/or Article 11, without prejudice to Article 11(7).

The decision of the company shall be taken by the general meeting of shareholders, in accordance with the law of the Member State in which the company has its registered office in accordance with the rules applicable to amendment of the articles of association. The decision shall be communicated to the supervisory authority of the Member State in which the company has its registered office and to all the supervisory authorities of Member States in which its securities are admitted to trading on regulated markets or where such admission has been requested.

3. Member States may, under the conditions determined by national law, exempt companies which apply Article 9(2) and (3) and/or Article 11 from applying Article 9(2) and (3) and/or Article 11 if they become the subject of an offer launched by a company which does not apply the same Articles as they do, or by a company controlled, directly or indirectly, by the latter, pursuant to Article 1 of Directive 83/349/EEC.

4. Member States shall ensure that the provisions applicable to the respective companies are disclosed without delay.

5. Any measure applied in accordance with paragraph 3 shall be subject to the authorisation of the general meeting of shareholders of the offeree company, which must be granted no earlier than 18 months before the bid was made public in accordance with Article 6(1).

[9604]

Article 13

Other rules applicable to the conduct of bids

Member States shall also lay down rules which govern the conduct of bids, at least as regards the following:

(a) the lapsing of bids;
(b) the revision of bids;
(c) competing bids;
(d) the disclosure of the results of bids;
(e) the irrevocability of bids and the conditions permitted.

[9605]

Article 14

Information for and consultation of employees' representatives

This Directive shall be without prejudice to the rules relating to information and to consultation of representatives of and, if Member States so provide, co-determination with the employees of the offeror and the offeree company governed by the relevant national provisions, and in particular those adopted pursuant to Directives 94/45/EC, 98/59/EC, 2001/86/EC and 2002/14/EC.

[9606]

Article 15

The right of squeeze-out

1. Member States shall ensure that, following a bid made to all the holders of the offeree company's securities for all of their securities, paragraphs 2 to 5 apply.

2. Member States shall ensure that an offeror is able to require all the holders of the remaining securities to sell him/her those securities at a fair price. Member States shall introduce that right in one of the following situations:

(a) where the offeror holds securities representing not less than 90% of the capital carrying voting rights and 90% of the voting rights in the offeree company,

or

(b) where, following acceptance of the bid, he/she has acquired or has firmly contracted to acquire securities representing not less than 90% of the offeree company's capital carrying voting rights and 90% of the voting rights comprised in the bid.

In the case referred to in (a), Member States may set a higher threshold that may not, however, be higher than 95% of the capital carrying voting rights and 95% of the voting rights.

3. Member States shall ensure that rules are in force that make it possible to calculate when the threshold is reached.

Where the offeree company has issued more than one class of securities, Member States may provide that the right of squeeze- out can be exercised only in the class in which the threshold laid down in paragraph 2 has been reached.

4. If the offeror wishes to exercise the right of squeeze-out he/she shall do so within three months of the end of the time allowed for acceptance of the bid referred to in Article 7.

5. Member States shall ensure that a fair price is guaranteed. That price shall take the same form as the consideration offered in the bid or shall be in cash. Member States may provide that cash shall be offered at least as an alternative.

Following a voluntary bid, in both of the cases referred to in paragraph 2(a) and (b), the consideration offered in the bid shall be presumed to be fair where, through acceptance of the bid, the offeror has acquired securities representing not less than 90% of the capital carrying voting rights comprised in the bid.

Following a mandatory bid, the consideration offered in the bid shall be presumed to be fair.

[9607]

Article 16

The right of sell-out

1. Member States shall ensure that, following a bid made to all the holders of the offeree company's securities for all of their securities, paragraphs 2 and 3 apply.

2. Member States shall ensure that a holder of remaining securities is able to require the offeror to buy his/her securities from him/her at a fair price under the same circumstances as provided for in Article 15(2).

3. Article 15(3) to (5) shall apply *mutatis mutandis*.

[9608]

Article 17

Sanctions

Member States shall determine the sanctions to be imposed for infringement of the national measures adopted pursuant to this Directive and shall take all necessary steps to ensure that they are put into effect. The sanctions thus provided for shall be effective, proportionate and dissuasive. Member States shall notify the Commission of those measures no later than the date laid down in Article 21(1) and of any subsequent change thereto at the earliest opportunity.

[9609]

Article 18

Committee procedure

1. The Commission shall be assisted by the European Securities Committee established by Decision 2001/528/EC (hereinafter referred to as 'the Committee').

2. Where reference is made to this paragraph, Articles 5 and 7 of Decision 1999/468/EC shall apply, having regard to Article 8 thereof, provided that the implementing measures adopted in accordance with this procedure do not modify the essential provisions of this Directive.

The period referred to in Article 5(6) of Decision 1999/468/EC shall be three months.

3. Without prejudice to the implementing measures already adopted, four years after the entry into force of this Directive, the application of those of its provisions that require the adoption of technical rules and decisions in accordance with paragraph 2 shall be suspended. On a proposal from the Commission, the European Parliament and the Council may renew the provisions concerned in accordance with the procedure laid down in Article 251 of the Treaty and, to that end, they shall review them before the end of the period referred to above.

[9610]

Article 19

Contact committee

1. A contact committee shall be set up which has as its functions:

(a) to facilitate, without prejudice to Articles 226 and 227 of the Treaty, the harmonised application of this Directive through regular meetings dealing with practical problems arising in connection with its application;

(b) to advise the Commission, if necessary, on additions or amendments to this Directive.

2. It shall not be the function of the contact committee to appraise the merits of decisions taken by the supervisory authorities in individual cases.

[9611]

Article 20

Revision

Five years after the date laid down in Article 21(1), the Commission shall examine this Directive in the light of the experience acquired in applying it and, if necessary, propose its revision. That examination shall include a survey of the control structures and barriers to takeover bids that are not covered by this Directive.

To that end, Member States shall provide the Commission annually with information on the takeover bids which have been launched against companies the securities of which are admitted to trading on their regulated markets. That information shall include the nationalities of the companies involved, the results of the offers and any other information relevant to the understanding of how takeover bids operate in practice.

[9612]

Article 21

Transposition

1. Member States shall bring into force the laws, regulations and administrative provisions necessary to comply with this Directive no later than 20 May 2006. They shall forthwith inform the Commission thereof.

When Member States adopt those provisions, they shall contain a reference to this Directive or shall be accompanied by such reference on the occasion of their official publication. The methods of making such reference shall be laid down by the Member States.

2. Member States shall communicate to the Commission the text of the main provisions of national law that they adopt in the fields covered by this Directive.

[9613]

Article 22

Entry into force

This Directive shall enter into force on the 20th day after that of its publication in the *Official Journal of the European Union*.

[9614]

Article 23

Addressees

This Directive is addressed to Member States.

[9615]

Done at Strasbourg, 21 April 2004.

DIRECTIVE OF THE EUROPEAN PARLIAMENT AND OF THE COUNCIL

of 21 April 2004

on markets in financial instruments amending Council Directives 85/611/EEC and 93/6/EEC and Directive 2000/12/EC of the European Parliament and of the Council and repealing Council Directive 93/22/EEC

(2004/39/EC)

NOTES

Date of Publication in OJ: OJ L145, 30.4.2004, p 1. The text of this Directive incorporates the corrigendum published in OJ L45, 16.2.2005, p 18. Notes are as in the original OJ version.

Note: the proposed transposition of Directive 2004/39/EC (originally 30 April 2006) has been subject to certain delays. See now the amendments made to this Directive by Directive 2006/31/EC and, in particular, Art 70 at **[9683]**. Note also that Directive 2006/31/EC itself has a transposition date of 31 January 2007 (see Art 2 of that Directive at **[9820]**).

Council Directive 1993/6/EEC: repealed and replaced by European Parliament and Council Directive 2006/49/EC.

European Parliament and Council Directive 2000/12/EC: repealed and replaced by European Parliament and Council Directive 2006/48/EC.

THE EUROPEAN PARLIAMENT AND THE COUNCIL OF THE EUROPEAN UNION,

Having regard to the Treaty establishing the European Community, and in particular Article 47(2) thereof,

Having regard to the proposal from the Commission,[1]

Having regard to the Opinion of the European Economic and Social Committee,[2]

Having regard to the opinion of the European Central Bank,[3]

Acting in accordance with the procedure laid down in Article 251 of the Treaty,[4]

Whereas:

(1) Council Directive 93/22/EEC of 10 May 1993 on investment services in the securities field[5] sought to establish the conditions under which authorised investment firms and banks could provide specified services or establish branches in other Member States on the basis of home country authorisation and supervision. To this end, that Directive aimed to harmonise the initial authorisation and operating requirements for investment firms including conduct of business rules. It also provided for the harmonisation of some conditions governing the operation of regulated markets.

(2) In recent years more investors have become active in the financial markets and are offered an even more complex wide-ranging set of services and instruments. In view of these developments the legal framework of the Community should encompass the full range of investor-oriented activities. To this end, it is necessary to provide for the degree of harmonisation needed to offer investors a high level of protection and to allow investment firms to provide services throughout the Community, being a Single Market, on the basis of home country supervision. In view of the preceding, Directive 93/22/EEC should be replaced by a new Directive.

(3) Due to the increasing dependence of investors on personal recommendations, it is appropriate to include the provision of investment advice as an investment service requiring authorisation.

(4) It is appropriate to include in the list of financial instruments certain commodity derivatives and others which are constituted and traded in such a manner as to give rise to regulatory issues comparable to traditional financial instruments.

(5) It is necessary to establish a comprehensive regulatory regime governing the execution of transactions in financial instruments irrespective of the trading methods used to

conclude those transactions so as to ensure a high quality of execution of investor transactions and to uphold the integrity and overall efficiency of the financial system. A coherent and risk sensitive framework for regulating the main types of order-execution arrangement currently active in the European financial marketplace should be provided for. It is necessary to recognise the emergence of a new generation of organised trading systems alongside regulated markets which should be subjected to obligations designed to preserve the efficient and orderly functioning of financial markets. With a view to establishing a proportionate regulatory new investment framework provision should be made for the inclusion of a service which relates to the operation of an MTF.

(6) Definitions of regulated market and MTF should be introduced and closely aligned with each other to reflect the fact that they represent the same organised trading functionality. The definitions should exclude bilateral systems where an investment firm enters into every trade on own account and not as a riskless counterparty interposed between the buyer and seller. The term 'system' encompasses all those markets that are composed of a set of rules and a trading platform as well as those that only function on the basis of a set of rules. Regulated markets and MTFs are not obliged to operate a 'technical' system for matching orders. A market which is only composed of a set of rules that governs aspects related to membership, admission of instruments to trading, trading between members, reporting and, where applicable, transparency obligations is a regulated market or an MTF within the meaning of this Directive and the transactions concluded under those rules are considered to be concluded under the systems of a regulated market or an MTF. The term 'buying and selling interests' is to be understood in a broad sense and includes orders, quotes and indications of interest. The requirement that the interests be brought together in the system by means of non-discretionary rules set by the system operator means that they are brought together under the system's rules or by means of the system's protocols or internal operating procedures (including procedures embodied in computer software). The term 'non-discretionary rules' means that these rules leave the investment firm operating an MTF with no discretion as to how interests may interact. The definitions require that interests be brought together in such a way as to result in a contract, meaning that execution takes place under the system's rules or by means of the system's protocols or internal operating procedures.

(7) The purpose of this Directive is to cover undertakings the regular occupation or business of which is to provide investment services and/or perform investment activities on a professional basis. Its scope should not therefore cover any person with a different professional activity.

(8) Persons administering their own assets and undertakings, who do not provide investment services and/or perform investment activities other than dealing on own account unless they are market makers or they deal on own account outside a regulated market or an MTF on an organised, frequent and systematic basis, by providing a system accessible to third parties in order to engage in dealings with them should not be covered by the scope of this Directive.

(9) References in the text to persons should be understood as including both natural and legal persons.

(10) Insurance or assurance undertakings the activities of which are subject to appropriate monitoring by the competent prudential-supervision authorities and which are subject to Council Directive 64/225/EEC of 25 February 1964 on the abolition of restrictions on freedom of establishment and freedom to provide services in respect of reinsurance and retrocession,[6] First Council Directive 73/239/EEC of 24 July 1973 on the coordination of laws, regulations and administrative provisions relating to the taking up and pursuit of direct insurance other than life assurance[7] and Council Directive 2002/83/EC of 5 November 2002 concerning life assurance[8] should be excluded.

(11) Persons who do not provide services for third parties but whose business consists in providing investment services solely for their parent undertakings, for their subsidiaries, or for other subsidiaries of their parent undertakings should not be covered by this Directive.

(12) Persons who provide investment services only on an incidental basis in the course of professional activity should also be excluded from the scope of this Directive, provided that activity is regulated and the relevant rules do not prohibit the provision, on an incidental basis, of investment services.

(13) Persons who provide investment services consisting exclusively in the administration of employee participation schemes and who therefore do not provide investment services for third parties should not be covered by this Directive.

(14) It is necessary to exclude from the scope of this Directive central banks and other bodies performing similar functions as well as public bodies charged with or intervening in the management of the public debt, which concept covers the investment thereof, with the exception of bodies that are partly or wholly State-owned the role of which is commercial or linked to the acquisition of holdings.

(15) It is necessary to exclude from the scope of this Directive collective investment undertakings and pension funds whether or not coordinated at Community level, and the depositaries or managers of such undertakings, since they are subject to specific rules directly adapted to their activities.

(16) In order to benefit from the exemptions from this Directive the person concerned should comply on a continuous basis with the conditions laid down for such exemptions. In particular, if a person provides investment services or performs investment activities and is exempted from this Directive because such services or activities are ancillary to his main business, when considered on a group basis, he should no longer be covered by the exemption related to ancillary services where the provision of those services or activities ceases to be ancillary to his main business.

(17) Persons who provide the investment services and/or perform investment activities covered by this Directive should be subject to authorisation by their home Member States in order to protect investors and the stability of the financial system.

(18) Credit institutions that are authorised under Directive 2000/12/EC of the European Parliament and of the Council of 20 March 2000 relating to the taking up and pursuit of the business of credit institutions[9] should not need another authorisation under this Directive in order to provide investment services or perform investment activities. When a credit institution decides to provide investment services or perform investment activities the competent authorities, before granting an authorisation, should verify that it complies with the relevant provisions of this Directive.

(19) In cases where an investment firm provides one or more investment services not covered by its authorisation, or performs one or more investment activities not covered by its authorisation, on a non-regular basis it should not need an additional authorisation under this Directive.

(20) For the purposes of this Directive, the business of the reception and transmission of orders should also include bringing together two or more investors thereby bringing about a transaction between those investors.

(21) In the context of the forthcoming revision of the Capital Adequacy framework in Basel II, Member States recognise the need to re-examine whether or not investment firms who execute client orders on a matched principal basis are to be regarded as acting as principals, and thereby be subject to additional regulatory capital requirements.

(22) The principles of mutual recognition and of home Member State supervision require that the Member States' competent authorities should not grant or should withdraw authorisation where factors such as the content of programmes of operations, the geographical distribution or the activities actually carried on indicate clearly that an investment firm has opted for the legal system of one Member State for the purpose of evading the stricter standards in force in another Member State within the territory of which it intends to carry on or does carry on the greater part of its activities. An investment firm which is a legal person should be authorised in the Member State in which it has its registered office. An investment firm which is not a legal person should be authorised in the Member State in which it has its head office. In addition, Member States should require that an investment firm's head office must always be situated in its home Member State and that it actually operates there.

(23) An investment firm authorised in its home Member State should be entitled to provide investment services or perform investment activities throughout the Community without the need to seek a separate authorisation from the competent authority in the Member State in which it wishes to provide such services or perform such activities.

(24) Since certain investment firms are exempted from certain obligations imposed by Council Directive 93/6/EEC of 15 March 1993 on the capital adequacy of investment firms and credit institutions,[10] they should be obliged to hold either a minimum amount of capital or professional indemnity insurance or a combination of both. The adjustments of the amounts of that insurance should take into account adjustments made in the framework of Directive 2002/92/EC of the European Parliament and of the Council of 9 December 2002 on insurance mediation.[11] This particular treatment for the purposes of capital adequacy should be without prejudice to any decisions regarding the appropriate treatment of these firms under future changes to Community legislation on capital adequacy.

(25) Since the scope of prudential regulation should be limited to those entities which, by virtue of running a trading book on a professional basis, represent a source of counterparty risk to other market participants, entities which deal on own account in financial instruments, including those commodity derivatives covered by this Directive, as well as those that provide investment services in commodity derivatives to the clients of their main business on an ancillary basis to their main business when considered on a group basis, provided that this main business is not the provision of investment services within the meaning of this Directive, should be excluded from the scope of this Directive.

(26) In order to protect an investor's ownership and other similar rights in respect of securities and his rights in respect of funds entrusted to a firm those rights should in particular be kept distinct from those of the firm. This principle should not, however, prevent a firm from doing business in its name but on behalf of the investor, where that is required by the very nature of the transaction and the investor is in agreement, for example stock lending.

(27) Where a client, in line with Community legislation and in particular Directive 2002/47/EC of the European Parliament and of the Council of 6 June 2002 on financial collateral arrangements,[12] transfers full ownership of financial instruments or funds to an investment firm for the purpose of securing or otherwise covering present or future, actual or contingent or prospective obligations, such financial instruments or funds should likewise no longer be regarded as belonging to the client.

(28) The procedures for the authorisation, within the Community, of branches of investment firms authorised in third countries should continue to apply to such firms. Those branches should not enjoy the freedom to provide services under the second paragraph of Article 49 of the Treaty or the right of establishment in Member States other than those in which they are established. In view of cases where the Community is not bound by any bilateral or multilateral obligations it is appropriate to provide for a procedure intended to ensure that Community investment firms receive reciprocal treatment in the third countries concerned.

(29) The expanding range of activities that many investment firms undertake simultaneously has increased potential for conflicts of interest between those different activities and the interests of their clients. It is therefore necessary to provide for rules to ensure that such conflicts do not adversely affect the interests of their clients.

(30) A service should be considered to be provided at the initiative of a client unless the client demands it in response to a personalised communication from or on behalf of the firm to that particular client, which contains an invitation or is intended to influence the client in respect of a specific financial instrument or specific transaction. A service can be considered to be provided at the initiative of the client notwithstanding that the client demands it on the basis of any communication containing a promotion or offer of financial instruments made by any means that by its very nature is general and addressed to the public or a larger group or category of clients or potential clients.

(31) One of the objectives of this Directive is to protect investors. Measures to protect investors should be adapted to the particularities of each category of investors (retail, professional and counterparties).

(32) By way of derogation from the principle of home country authorisation, supervision and enforcement of obligations in respect of the operation of branches, it is appropriate for the competent authority of the host Member State to assume responsibility for enforcing certain obligations specified in this Directive in relation to business conducted through a branch within the territory where the branch is located, since that authority is closest to the branch, and is better placed to detect and intervene in respect of infringements of rules governing the operations of the branch.

(33) It is necessary to impose an effective 'best execution' obligation to ensure that investment firms execute client orders on terms that are most favourable to the client. This obligation should apply to the firm which owes contractual or agency obligations to the client.

(34) Fair competition requires that market participants and investors be able to compare the prices that trading venues (i.e. regulated markets, MTFs and intermediaries) are required to publish. To this end, it is recommended that Member States remove any obstacles which may prevent the consolidation at European level of the relevant information and its publication.

(35) When establishing the business relationship with the client the investment firm might ask the client or potential client to consent at the same time to the execution policy as well as to the possibility that his orders may be executed outside a regulated market or an MTF.

(36) Persons who provide investment services on behalf of more than one investment firm should not be considered as tied agents but as investment firms when they fall under the definition provided in this Directive, with the exception of certain persons who may be exempted.

(37) This Directive should be without prejudice to the right of tied agents to undertake activities covered by other Directives and related activities in respect of financial services or products not covered by this Directive, including on behalf of parts of the same financial group.

(38) The conditions for conducting activities outside the premises of the investment firm (door-to-door selling) should not be covered by this Directive.

(39) Member States' competent authorities should not register or should withdraw the registration where the activities actually carried on indicate clearly that a tied agent has opted

for the legal system of one Member State for the purpose of evading the stricter standards in force in another Member State within the territory of which it intends to carry on or does carry on the greater part of its activities.

(40) For the purposes of this Directive eligible counterparties should be considered as acting as clients.

(41) For the purposes of ensuring that conduct of business rules (including rules on best execution and handling of client orders) are enforced in respect of those investors most in need of these protections, and to reflect well-established market practice throughout the Community, it is appropriate to clarify that conduct of business rules may be waived in the case of transactions entered into or brought about between eligible counterparties.

(42) In respect of transactions executed between eligible counterparties, the obligation to disclose client limit orders should only apply where the counter party is explicitly sending a limit order to an investment firm for its execution.

(43) Member States shall protect the right to privacy of natural persons with respect to the processing of personal data in accordance with Directive 95/46/EC of the European Parliament and of the Council of 24 October 1995 on the protection of individuals with regard to the processing of personal data and of the free movement of such data.[13]

(44) With the two fold aim of protecting investors and ensuring the smooth operation of securities markets, it is necessary to ensure that transparency of transactions is achieved and that the rules laid down for that purpose apply to investment firms when they operate on the markets. In order to enable investors or market participants to assess at any time the terms of a transaction in shares that they are considering and to verify afterwards the conditions in which it was carried out, common rules should be established for the publication of details of completed transactions in shares and for the disclosure of details of current opportunities to trade in shares. These rules are needed to ensure the effective integration of Member State equity markets, to promote the efficiency of the overall price formation process for equity instruments, and to assist the effective operation of 'best execution' obligations. These considerations require a comprehensive transparency regime applicable to all transactions in shares irrespective of their execution by an investment firm on a bilateral basis or through regulated markets or MTFs. The obligations for investment firms under this Directive to quote a bid and offer price and to execute an order at the quoted price do not relieve investment firms of the obligation to route an order to another execution venue when such internalisation could prevent the firm from complying with 'best execution' obligations.

(45) Member States should be able to apply transaction reporting obligations of the Directive to financial instruments that are not admitted to trading on a regulated market.

(46) A Member State may decide to apply the pre- and post-trade transparency requirements laid down in this Directive to financial instruments other than shares. In that case those requirements should apply to all investment firms for which that Member State is the home Member State for their operations within the territory of that Member State and those carried out cross border through the freedom to provide services. They should also apply to the operations carried out within the territory of that Member State by the branches established in its territory of investment firms authorised in another Member State.

(47) Investment firms should all have the same opportunities of joining or having access to regulated markets throughout the Community. Regardless of the manner in which transactions are at present organised in the Member States, it is important to abolish the technical and legal restrictions on access to regulated markets.

(48) In order to facilitate the finalisation of cross-border transactions, it is appropriate to provide for access to clearing and settlement systems throughout the Community by investment firms, irrespective of whether transactions have been concluded through regulated markets in the Member State concerned. Investment firms which wish to participate directly in other Member States' settlement systems should comply with the relevant operational and commercial requirements for membership and the prudential measures to uphold the smooth and orderly functioning of the financial markets.

(49) The authorisation to operate a regulated market should extend to all activities which are directly related to the display, processing, execution, confirmation and reporting of orders from the point at which such orders are received by the regulated market to the point at which they are transmitted for subsequent finalisation, and to activities related to the admission of financial instruments to trading. This should also include transactions concluded through the medium of designated market makers appointed by the regulated market which are undertaken under its systems and in accordance with the rules that govern those systems. Not all transactions concluded by members or participants of the regulated market or MTF are to be considered as concluded within the systems of a regulated market or MTF. Transactions which members or participants conclude on a bilateral basis and which do not comply with all the obligations established for a regulated market or an MTF under this Directive should be considered as transactions concluded outside a regulated market or an MTF for the purposes

of the definition of systematic internaliser. In such a case the obligation for investment firms to make public firm quotes should apply if the conditions established by this Directive are met.

(50) Systematic internalisers might decide to give access to their quotes only to retail clients, only to professional clients, or to both. They should not be allowed to discriminate within those categories of clients.

(51) Article 27 does not oblige systematic internalisers to publish firm quotes in relation to transactions above standard market size.

(52) Where an investment firm is a systematic internaliser both in shares and in other financial instruments, the obligation to quote should only apply in respect of shares without prejudice to Recital 46.

(53) It is not the intention of this Directive to require the application of pre-trade transparency rules to transactions carried out on an OTC basis, the characteristics of which include that they are ad-hoc and irregular and are carried out with wholesale counterparties and are part of a business relationship which is itself characterised by dealings above standard market size, and where the deals are carried out outside the systems usually used by the firm concerned for its business as a systematic internaliser.

(54) The standard market size for any class of share should not be significantly disproportionate to any share included in that class.

(55) Revision of Directive 93/6/EEC should fix the minimum capital requirements with which regulated markets should comply in order to be authorised, and in so doing should take into account the specific nature of the risks associated with such markets.

(56) Operators of a regulated market should also be able to operate an MTF in accordance with the relevant provisions of this Directive.

(57) The provisions of this Directive concerning the admission of instruments to trading under the rules enforced by the regulated market should be without prejudice to the application of Directive 2001/34/EC of the European Parliament and of the Council of 28 May 2001 on the admission of securities to official stock exchange listing and on information to be published on those securities.[14] A regulated market should not be prevented from applying more demanding requirements in respect of the issuers of securities or instruments which it is considering for admission to trading than are imposed pursuant to this Directive.

(58) Member States should be able to designate different competent authorities to enforce the wide-ranging obligations laid down in this Directive. Such authorities should be of a public nature guaranteeing their independence from economic actors and avoiding conflicts of interest. In accordance with national law, Member States should ensure appropriate financing of the competent authority. The designation of public authorities should not exclude delegation under the responsibility of the competent authority.

(59) Any confidential information received by the contact point of one Member State through the contact point of another Member State should not be regarded as purely domestic.

(60) It is necessary to enhance convergence of powers at the disposal of competent authorities so as to pave the way towards an equivalent intensity of enforcement across the integrated financial market. A common minimum set of powers coupled with adequate resources should guarantee supervisory effectiveness.

(61) With a view to protecting clients and without prejudice to the right of customers to bring their action before the courts, it is appropriate that Member States encourage public or private bodies established with a view to settling disputes out-of-court, to cooperate in resolving cross border disputes, taking into account Commission Recommendation 98/257/EC of 30 March 1998 on the principles applicable to the bodies responsible for out-of-court settlement of consumer disputes.[15] When implementing provisions on complaints and redress procedures for out of court settlements, Member States should be encouraged to use existing cross-border cooperation mechanisms, notably the Financial Services Complaints Network (FIN Net).

(62) Any exchange or transmission of information between competent authorities, other authorities, bodies or persons should be in accordance with the rules on transfer of personal data to third countries as laid down in Directive 95/46/EC.

(63) It is necessary to reinforce provisions on exchange of information between national competent authorities and to strengthen the duties of assistance and cooperation which they owe to each other. Due to increasing cross-border activity, competent authorities should provide each other with the relevant information for the exercise of their functions, so as to ensure the effective enforcement of this Directive, including in situations where infringements or suspected infringements may be of concern to authorities in two or more Member States. In the exchange of information, strict professional secrecy is needed to ensure the smooth transmission of that information and the protection of particular rights.

(64) At its meeting on 17 July 2000, the Council set up the Committee of Wise Men on the Regulation of European Securities Markets. In its final report, the Committee of Wise Men proposed the introduction of new legislative techniques based on a four-level approach, namely framework principles, implementing measures, cooperation and enforcement. Level 1, the Directive, should confine itself to broad general 'framework' principles while Level 2 should contain technical implementing measures to be adopted by the Commission with the assistance of a committee.

(65) The Resolution adopted by the Stockholm European Council of 23 March 2001 endorsed the final report of the Committee of Wise Men and the proposed four-level approach to make the regulatory process for Community securities legislation more efficient and transparent.

(66) According to the Stockholm European Council, Level 2 implementing measures should be used more frequently, to ensure that technical provisions can be kept up to date with market and supervisory developments, and deadlines should be set for all stages of Level 2 work.

(67) The Resolution of the European Parliament of 5 February 2002 on the implementation of financial services legislation also endorsed the Committee of Wise Men's report, on the basis of the solemn declaration made before Parliament the same day by the Commission and the letter of 2 October 2001 addressed by the Internal Market Commissioner to the chairman of Parliament's Committee on Economic and Monetary Affairs with regard to the safeguards for the European Parliament's role in this process.

(68) The measures necessary for the implementation of this Directive should be adopted in accordance with Council Decision 1999/468/EC of 28 June 1999 laying down the procedures for the exercise of implementing powers conferred on the Commission.[16]

[(69) The European Parliament should be given a period of three months from the first transmission of draft amendments and implementing measures to allow it to examine them and to give its opinion. However, in urgent and duly justified cases, it should be possible to shorten that period. If, within that period, a resolution is adopted by the European Parliament, the Commission should re-examine the draft amendments or measures.]

(70) With a view to taking into account further developments in the financial markets the Commission should submit reports to the European Parliament and the Council on the application of the provisions concerning professional indemnity insurance, the scope of the transparency rules and the possible authorisation of specialised dealers in commodity derivatives as investment firms.

(71) The objective of creating an integrated financial market, in which investors are effectively protected and the efficiency and integrity of the overall market are safeguarded, requires the establishment of common regulatory requirements relating to investment firms wherever they are authorised in the Community and governing the functioning of regulated markets and other trading systems so as to prevent opacity or disruption on one market from undermining the efficient operation of the European financial system as a whole. Since this objective may be better achieved at Community level, the Community may adopt measures in accordance with the principle of subsidiarity as set out in Article 5 of the Treaty. In accordance with the principle of proportionality, as set out in that Article, this Directive does not go beyond what is necessary in order to achieve this objective,

[9616]

NOTES

Recital 69 substituted by European Parliament and Council Directive 2006/31/EC, Art 1(1), as from 28 April 2006.

1 OJ C71E, 25.3.2003, p 62.
2 OJ C220, 16.9.2003, p 1.
3 OJ C144, 20.6.2003, p 6.
4 Opinion of the European Parliament of 25 September 2003 (not yet published in the Official Journal), Council Common Position of 8 December 2003 (OJ C60E, 9.3.2004, p 1), Position of the European Parliament of 30 March 2004 (not yet published in the Official Journal) and Decision of the Council of 7 April 2004.
5 OJ L141, 11.6.1993, p 27. Directive as last amended by Directive 2002/87/EC of the European Parliament and of the Council (OJ L35, 11.2.2003, p 1).
6 OJ L56, 4.4.1964, p 878/64. Directive as amended by the 1972 Act of Accession.
7 OJ L228, 16.8.1973, p 3. Directive as last amended by Directive 2002/87/EC.
8 OJ L345, 19.12.2002, p 1.
9 OJ L126, 26.5.2000, p 1. Directive as last amended by Directive 2002/87/EC.
10 OJ L141, 11.6.1993, p 1. Directive as last amended by Directive 2002/87/EC.
11 OJ L9, 15.1.2003, p 3.
12 OJ L168, 27.6.2002, p 43.
13 OJ L281, 23.11.1995, p 31.

[14] OJ L184, 6.7.2001, p 1. Directive as last amended by European Parliament and Council Directive 2003/71/EC (OJ L345, 31.12.2003, p 64.).
[15] OJ L115, 17.4.1998, p 31.
[16] OJ L184, 17.7.1999, p 23.

HAVE ADOPTED THIS DIRECTIVE:

TITLE I
DEFINITIONS AND SCOPE

Article 1

Scope

1. This Directive shall apply to investment firms and regulated markets.

2. The following provisions shall also apply to credit institutions authorised under Directive 2000/12/EC, when providing one or more investment services and/or performing investment activities:

— Articles 2(2), 11, 13 and 14,
— Chapter II of Title II excluding Article 23(2) second sub-paragraph,
— Chapter III of Title II excluding Articles 31(2) to 31(4) and 32(2) to 32(6), 32(8) and 32(9),
— Articles 48 to 53, 57, 61 and 62, and
— Article 71(1).

[9617]

Article 2

Exemptions

1. This Directive shall not apply to:

(a) insurance undertakings as defined in Article 1 of Directive 73/239/EEC or assurance undertakings as defined in Article 1 of Directive 2002/83/EC or undertakings carrying on the reinsurance and retrocession activities referred to in Directive 64/225/EEC;

(b) persons which provide investment services exclusively for their parent undertakings, for their subsidiaries or for other subsidiaries of their parent undertakings;

(c) persons providing an investment service where that service is provided in an incidental manner in the course of a professional activity and that activity is regulated by legal or regulatory provisions or a code of ethics governing the profession which do not exclude the provision of that service;

(d) persons who do not provide any investment services or activities other than dealing on own account unless they are market makers or deal on own account outside a regulated market or an MTF on an organised, frequent and systematic basis by providing a system accessible to third parties in order to engage in dealings with them;

(e) persons which provide investment services consisting exclusively in the administration of employee-participation schemes;

(f) persons which provide investment services which only involve both administration of employee-participation schemes and the provision of investment services exclusively for their parent undertakings, for their subsidiaries or for other subsidiaries of their parent undertakings;

(g) the members of the European System of Central Banks and other national bodies performing similar functions and other public bodies charged with or intervening in the management of the public debt;

(h) collective investment undertakings and pension funds whether coordinated at Community level or not and the depositaries and managers of such undertakings;

(i) persons dealing on own account in financial instruments, or providing investment services in commodity derivatives or derivative contracts included in Annex I, Section C 10 to the clients of their main business, provided this is an ancillary activity to their main business, when considered on a group basis, and that main business is not the provision of investment services within the meaning of this Directive or banking services under Directive 2000/12/EC;

(j) persons providing investment advice in the course of providing another professional activity not covered by this Directive provided that the provision of such advice is not specifically remunerated;

(k) persons whose main business consists of dealing on own account in commodities and/or commodity derivatives. This exception shall not apply where the persons that deal on own account in commodities and/or commodity derivatives are part of a group the main business of which is the provision of other investment services within the meaning of this Directive or banking services under Directive 2000/12/EC;

(l) firms which provide investment services and/or perform investment activities consisting exclusively in dealing on own account on markets in financial futures or options or other derivatives and on cash markets for the sole purpose of hedging positions on derivatives markets or which deal for the accounts of other members of those markets or make prices for them and which are guaranteed by clearing members of the same markets, where responsibility for ensuring the performance of contracts entered into by such firms is assumed by clearing members of the same markets;

(m) associations set up by Danish and Finnish pension funds with the sole aim of managing the assets of pension funds that are members of those associations;

(n) 'agenti di cambio' whose activities and functions are governed by Article 201 of Italian Legislative Decree No 58 of 24 February 1998.

2. The rights conferred by this Directive shall not extend to the provision of services as counterparty in transactions carried out by public bodies dealing with public debt or by members of the European System of Central Banks performing their tasks as provided for by the Treaty and the Statute of the European System of Central Banks and of the European Central Bank or performing equivalent functions under national provisions.

3. In order to take account of developments on financial markets, and to ensure the uniform application of this Directive, the Commission, acting in accordance with the procedure referred to in Article 64(2), may, in respect of exemptions (c)(i), and (k) define the criteria for determining when an activity is to be considered as ancillary to the main business on a group level as well as for determining when an activity is provided in an incidental manner.

[9618]

Article 3

Optional exemptions

1. Member States may choose not to apply this Directive to any persons for which they are the home Member State that:

— are not allowed to hold clients' funds or securities and which for that reason are not allowed at any time to place themselves in debit with their clients, and

— are not allowed to provide any investment service except the reception and transmission of orders in transferable securities and units in collective investment undertakings and the provision of investment advice in relation to such financial instruments, and

— in the course of providing that service, are allowed to transmit orders only to:

(i) investment firms authorised in accordance with this Directive;

(ii) credit institutions authorised in accordance with Directive 2000/12/EC;

(iii) branches of investment firms or of credit institutions which are authorised in a third country and which are subject to and comply with prudential rules considered by the competent authorities to be at least as stringent as those laid down in this Directive, in Directive 2000/12/EC or in Directive 93/6/EEC;

(iv) collective investment undertakings authorised under the law of a Member State to market units to the public and to the managers of such undertakings;

(v) investment companies with fixed capital, as defined in Article 15(4) of Second Council Directive 77/91/EEC of 13 December 1976 on coordination of safeguards which, for the protection of the interests of members and others, are required by Member States of companies within the meaning of the second paragraph of Article 58 of the Treaty, in respect of the formation of public limited liability companies and the maintenance and alteration of their capital, with a view to making such safeguards equivalent,[1] the securities of which are listed or dealt in on a regulated market in a Member State;

provided that the activities of those persons are regulated at national level.

2. Persons excluded from the scope of this Directive according to paragraph 1 cannot benefit from the freedom to provide services and/or activities or to establish branches as provided for in Articles 31 and 32 respectively.

[9619]

NOTES

1 OJ L26, 31.1.1977, p 1. Directive as last amended by the 1994 Act of Accession.

Article 4

Definitions

1. For the purposes of this Directive, the following definitions shall apply:

1) 'Investment firm' means any legal person whose regular occupation or business is the provision of one or more investment services to third parties and/or the performance of one or more investment activities on a professional basis;

Member States may include in the definition of investment firms undertakings which are not legal persons, provided that:

(a) their legal status ensures a level of protection for third parties' interests equivalent to that afforded by legal persons, and

(b) they are subject to equivalent prudential supervision appropriate to their legal form.

However, where a natural person provides services involving the holding of third parties' funds or transferable securities, he may be considered as an investment firm for the purposes of this Directive only if, without prejudice to the other requirements imposed in this Directive and in Directive 93/6/EEC, he complies with the following conditions:

(a) the ownership rights of third parties in instruments and funds must be safeguarded, especially in the event of the insolvency of the firm or of its proprietors, seizure, set-off or any other action by creditors of the firm or of its proprietors;

(b) the firm must be subject to rules designed to monitor the firm's solvency and that of its proprietors;

(c) the firm's annual accounts must be audited by one or more persons empowered, under national law, to audit accounts;

(d) where the firm has only one proprietor, he must make provision for the protection of investors in the event of the firm's cessation of business following his death, his incapacity or any other such event;

2) 'Investment services and activities' means any of the services and activities listed in Section A of Annex I relating to any of the instruments listed in Section C of Annex I;

The Commission shall determine, acting in accordance with the procedure referred to in Article 64(2):

— the derivative contracts mentioned in Section C 7 of Annex I that have the characteristics of other derivative financial instruments, having regard to whether, inter alia, they are cleared and settled through recognised clearing houses or are subject to regular margin calls

— the derivative contracts mentioned in Section C 10 of Annex I that have the characteristics of other derivative financial instruments, having regard to whether, inter alia, they are traded on a regulated market or an MTF, are cleared and settled through recognised clearing houses or are subject to regular margin calls;

3) 'Ancillary service' means any of the services listed in Section B of Annex I;

4) 'Investment advice' means the provision of personal recommendations to a client, either upon its request or at the initiative of the investment firm, in respect of one or more transactions relating to financial instruments;

5) 'Execution of orders on behalf of clients' means acting to conclude agreements to buy or sell one or more financial instruments on behalf of clients;

6) 'Dealing on own account' means trading against proprietary capital resulting in the conclusion of transactions in one or more financial instruments;
7) 'Systematic internaliser' means an investment firm which, on an organised, frequent and systematic basis, deals on own account by executing client orders outside a regulated market or an MTF;
8) 'Market maker' means a person who holds himself out on the financial markets on a continuous basis as being willing to deal on own account by buying and selling financial instruments against his proprietary capital at prices defined by him;
9) 'Portfolio management' means managing portfolios in accordance with mandates given by clients on a discretionary client-by-client basis where such portfolios include one or more financial instruments;
10) 'Client' means any natural or legal person to whom an investment firm provides investment and/or ancillary services;
11) 'Professional client' means a client meeting the criteria laid down in Annex II;
12) 'Retail client' means a client who is not a professional client;
13) 'Market operator' means a person or persons who manages and/or operates the business of a regulated market. The market operator may be the regulated market itself;
14) 'Regulated market' means a multilateral system operated and/or managed by a market operator, which brings together or facilitates the bringing together of multiple third party buying and selling interests in financial instruments—in the system and in accordance with its non-discretionary rules—in a way that results in a contract, in respect of the financial instruments admitted to trading under its rules and/or systems, and which is authorised and functions regularly and in accordance with the provisions of Title III;
15) 'Multilateral trading facility (MTF)' means a multilateral system, operated by an investment firm or a market operator, which brings together multiple third-party buying and selling interests in financial instruments—in the system and in accordance with non discretionary rules—in a way that results in a contract in accordance with the provisions of Title II;
16) 'Limit order' means an order to buy or sell a financial instrument at its specified price limit or better and for a specified size;
17) 'Financial instrument' means those instruments specified in Section C of Annex I;
18) 'Transferable securities' means those classes of securities which are negotiable on the capital market, with the exception of instruments of payment, such as:
    (a) shares in companies and other securities equivalent to shares in companies, partnerships or other entities, and depositary receipts in respect of shares;
    (b) bonds or other forms of securitised debt, including depositary receipts in respect of such securities;
    (c) any other securities giving the right to acquire or sell any such transferable securities or giving rise to a cash settlement determined by reference to transferable securities, currencies, interest rates or yields, commodities or other indices or measures;
19) 'Money-market instruments' means those classes of instruments which are normally dealt in on the money market, such as treasury bills, certificates of deposit and commercial papers and excluding instruments of payment;
20) 'Home Member State' means:
    (a) in the case of investment firms:
        (i) if the investment firm is a natural person, the Member State in which its head office is situated;
        (ii) if the investment firm is a legal person, the Member State in which its registered office is situated;
        (iii) if the investment firm has, under its national law, no registered office, the Member State in which its head office is situated;
    (b) in the case of a regulated market, the Member State in which the regulated market is registered or, if under the law of that Member State it has no registered office, the Member State in which the head office of the regulated market is situated;
21) 'Host Member State' means the Member State, other than the home Member State, in which an investment firm has a branch or performs services and/or activities or the Member State in which a regulated market provides appropriate arrangements so as to facilitate access to trading on its system by remote members or participants established in that same Member State;
22) 'Competent authority' means the authority, designated by each Member State in accordance with Article 48, unless otherwise specified in this Directive;

23) 'Credit institutions' means credit institutions as defined under Directive 2000/12/EC;

24) 'UCITS management company' means a management company as defined in Council Directive 85/611/EEC of 20 December 1985, on the coordination of laws, regulations and administrative provisions relating to undertakings for collective investment in transferable securities (UCITS);[1]

25) 'Tied agent' means a natural or legal person who, under the full and unconditional responsibility of only one investment firm on whose behalf it acts, promotes investment and/or ancillary services to clients or prospective clients, receives and transmits instructions or orders from the client in respect of investment services or financial instruments, places financial instruments and/or provides advice to clients or prospective clients in respect of those financial instruments or services;

26) 'Branch' means a place of business other than the head office which is a part of an investment firm, which has no legal personality and which provides investment services and/or activities and which may also perform ancillary services for which the investment firm has been authorised; all the places of business set up in the same Member State by an investment firm with headquarters in another Member State shall be regarded as a single branch;

27) 'Qualifying holding' means any direct or indirect holding in an investment firm which represents 10% or more of the capital or of the voting rights, as set out in Article 92 of Directive 2001/34/EC, or which makes it possible to exercise a significant influence over the management of the investment firm in which that holding subsists;

28) 'Parent undertaking' means a parent undertaking as defined in Articles 1 and 2 of Seventh Council Directive 83/349/EEC of 13 June 1983 on consolidated accounts;[2]

29) 'Subsidiary' means a subsidiary undertaking as defined in Articles 1 and 2 of Directive 83/349/EEC, including any subsidiary of a subsidiary undertaking of an ultimate parent undertaking;

30) 'Control' means control as defined in Article 1 of Directive 83/349/EEC;

31) 'Close links' means a situation in which two or more natural or legal persons are linked by:

(a) participation which means the ownership, direct or by way of control, of 20% or more of the voting rights or capital of an undertaking,

(b) control which means the relationship between a parent undertaking and a subsidiary, in all the cases referred to in Article 1(1) and (2) of Directive 83/349/EEC, or a similar relationship between any natural or legal person and an undertaking, any subsidiary undertaking of a subsidiary undertaking also being considered a subsidiary of the parent undertaking which is at the head of those undertakings.

A situation in which two or more natural or legal persons are permanently linked to one and the same person by a control relationship shall also be regarded as constituting a close link between such persons.

2. In order to take account of developments on financial markets, and to ensure the uniform application of this Directive, the Commission, acting in accordance with the procedure referred to in Article 64(2), may clarify the definitions laid down in paragraph 1 of this Article.

[9620]

NOTES

1 OJ L375, 31.12.1985, p 3. Directive as last amended by Directive 2001/108/EC of the European Parliament and of the Council (OJ L41, 13.2.2002, p 35).

2 OJ L193, 18.7.1983, p 1. Directive as last amended by Directive 2003/51/EC of the European Parliament and of the Council (OJ L178, 17.7.2003, p 16).

TITLE II
AUTHORISATION AND OPERATING CONDITIONS FOR INVESTMENT FIRMS

CHAPTER I
CONDITIONS AND PROCEDURES FOR AUTHORISATION

Article 5

Requirement for authorisation

1. Each Member State shall require that the performance of investment services or activities as a regular occupation or business on a professional basis be subject to prior authorisation in accordance with the provisions of this Chapter. Such authorisation shall be granted by the home Member State competent authority designated in accordance with Article 48.

2. By way of derogation from paragraph 1, Member States shall allow any market operator to operate an MTF, subject to the prior verification of their compliance with the provisions of this Chapter, excluding Articles 11 and 15.

3. Member States shall establish a register of all investment firms. This register shall be publicly accessible and shall contain information on the services and/or activities for which the investment firm is authorised. It shall be updated on a regular basis.

4. Each Member State shall require that:
- any investment firm which is a legal person have its head office in the same Member State as its registered office,
- any investment firm which is not a legal person or any investment firm which is a legal person but under its national law has no registered office have its head office in the Member State in which it actually carries on its business.

5. In the case of investment firms which provide only investment advice or the service of reception and transmission of orders under the conditions established in Article 3, Member States may allow the competent authority to delegate administrative, preparatory or ancillary tasks related to the granting of an authorisation, in accordance with the conditions laid down in Article 48(2).

[9621]

Article 6

Scope of authorisation

1. The home Member State shall ensure that the authorisation specifies the investment services or activities which the investment firm is authorised to provide. The authorisation may cover one or more of the ancillary services set out in Section B of Annex I. Authorisation shall in no case be granted solely for the provision of ancillary services.

2. An investment firm seeking authorisation to extend its business to additional investment services or activities or ancillary services not foreseen at the time of initial authorisation shall submit a request for extension of its authorisation.

3. The authorisation shall be valid for the entire Community and shall allow an investment firm to provide the services or perform the activities, for which it has been authorised, throughout the Community, either through the establishment of a branch or the free provision of services.

[9622]

Article 7

Procedures for granting and refusing requests for authorisation

1. The competent authority shall not grant authorisation unless and until such time as it is fully satisfied that the applicant complies with all requirements under the provisions adopted pursuant to this Directive.

2. The investment firm shall provide all information, including a programme of operations setting out inter alia the types of business envisaged and the organisational structure, necessary to enable the competent authority to satisfy itself that the investment firm has established, at the time of initial authorisation, all the necessary arrangements to meet its obligations under the provisions of this Chapter.

3. An applicant shall be informed, within six months of the submission of a complete application, whether or not authorisation has been granted.

[9623]

Article 8

Withdrawal of authorisations

The competent authority may withdraw the authorisation issued to an investment firm where such an investment firm:

(a) does not make use of the authorisation within 12 months, expressly renounces the authorisation or has provided no investment services or performed no investment activity for the preceding six months, unless the Member State concerned has provided for authorisation to lapse in such cases;

(b) has obtained the authorisation by making false statements or by any other irregular means;

(c) no longer meets the conditions under which authorisation was granted, such as compliance with the conditions set out in Directive 93/6/EEC;

(d) has seriously and systematically infringed the provisions adopted pursuant to this Directive governing the operating conditions for investment firms;

(e) falls within any of the cases where national law, in respect of matters outside the scope of this Directive, provides for withdrawal.

[9624]

Article 9

Persons who effectively direct the business

1. Member States shall require the persons who effectively direct the business of an investment firm to be of sufficiently good repute and sufficiently experienced as to ensure the sound and prudent management of the investment firm.

Where the market operator that seeks authorisation to operate an MTF and the persons that effectively direct the business of the MTF are the same as those that effectively direct the business of the regulated market, those persons are deemed to comply with the requirements laid down in the first subparagraph.

2. Member States shall require the investment firm to notify the competent authority of any changes to its management, along with all information needed to assess whether the new staff appointed to manage the firm are of sufficiently good repute and sufficiently experienced.

3. The competent authority shall refuse authorisation if it is not satisfied that the persons who will effectively direct the business of the investment firm are of sufficiently good repute or sufficiently experienced, or if there are objective and demonstrable grounds for believing that proposed changes to the management of the firm pose a threat to its sound and prudent management.

4. Member States shall require that the management of investment firms is undertaken by at least two persons meeting the requirements laid down in paragraph 1.

By way of derogation from the first subparagraph, Member States may grant authorisation to investment firms that are natural persons or to investment firms that are legal persons managed by a single natural person in accordance with their constitutive rules and national laws. Member States shall nevertheless require that alternative arrangements be in place which ensure the sound and prudent management of such investment firms.

[9625]

Article 10

Shareholders and members with qualifying holdings

1. The competent authorities shall not authorise the performance of investment services or activities by an investment firm until they have been informed of the identities of the shareholders or members, whether direct or indirect, natural or legal persons, that have qualifying holdings and the amounts of those holdings.

The competent authorities shall refuse authorisation if, taking into account the need to ensure the sound and prudent management of an investment firm, they are not satisfied as to the suitability of the shareholders or members that have qualifying holdings.

Where close links exist between the investment firm and other natural or legal persons, the competent authority shall grant authorisation only if those links do not prevent the effective exercise of the supervisory functions of the competent authority.

2. The competent authority shall refuse authorisation if the laws, regulations or administrative provisions of a third country governing one or more natural or legal persons with which the undertaking has close links, or difficulties involved in their enforcement, prevent the effective exercise of its supervisory functions.

3. Member States shall require any natural or legal person that proposes to acquire or sell, directly or indirectly, a qualifying holding in an investment firm, first to notify, in accordance with the second subparagraph, the competent authority of the size of the resulting holding. Such persons shall likewise be required to notify the competent authority if they propose to increase or reduce their qualifying holding, if in consequence the proportion of the voting rights or of the capital that they hold would reach or fall below or exceed 20%, 33% or 50% or the investment firm would become or cease to be their subsidiary.

Without prejudice to paragraph 4, the competent authority shall have up to three months from the date of the notification of a proposed acquisition provided for in the first subparagraph to oppose such a plan if, in view of the need to ensure sound and prudent management of the investment firm, it is not satisfied as to the suitability of the persons referred to in the first subparagraph. If the competent authority does not oppose the plan, it may fix a deadline for its implementation.

4. If the acquirer of any holding referred to in paragraph 3 is an investment firm, a credit institution, an insurance under-taking or a UCITS management company authorised in another Member State, or the parent undertaking of an investment firm, credit institution, insurance undertaking or a UCITS management company authorised in another Member State, or a person controlling an investment firm, credit institution, insurance undertaking or a UCITS management company authorised in another Member State, and if, as a result of that acquisition, the undertaking would become the acquirer's subsidiary or come under his control, the assessment of the acquisition shall be subject to the prior consultation provided for in Article 60.

5. Member States shall require that, if an investment firm becomes aware of any acquisitions or disposals of holdings in its capital that cause holdings to exceed or fall below any of the thresholds referred to in the first subparagraph of paragraph 3, that investment firm is to inform the competent authority without delay.

At least once a year, investment firms shall also inform the competent authority of the names of shareholders and members possessing qualifying holdings and the sizes of such holdings as shown, for example, by the information received at annual general meetings of shareholders and members or as a result of compliance with the regulations applicable to companies whose transferable securities are admitted to trading on a regulated market.

6. Member States shall require that, where the influence exercised by the persons referred to in the first subparagraph of paragraph 1 is likely to be prejudicial to the sound and prudent management of an investment firm, the competent authority take appropriate measures to put an end to that situation.

Such measures may consist in applications for judicial orders and/or the imposition of sanctions against directors and those responsible for management, or suspension of the exercise of the voting rights attaching to the shares held by the shareholders or members in question.

Similar measures shall be taken in respect of persons who fail to comply with the obligation to provide prior information in relation to the acquisition or increase of a qualifying holding. If a holding is acquired despite the opposition of the competent authorities, the Member States shall, regardless of any other sanctions to be adopted, provide either for exercise of the corresponding voting rights to be suspended, for the nullity of the votes cast or for the possibility of their annulment.

[9626]

Article 11

Membership of an authorised Investor Compensation Scheme

The competent authority shall verify that any entity seeking authorisation as an investment firm meets its obligations under Directive 97/9/EC of the European Parliament and of the Council of 3 March 1997 on investor-compensation schemes[1] at the time of authorisation.

[9627]

NOTES

[1] OJ L84, 26.3.1997, p 22.

Article 12

Initial capital endowment

Member States shall ensure that the competent authorities do not grant authorisation unless the investment firm has sufficient initial capital in accordance with the requirements of Directive 93/6/EEC having regard to the nature of the investment service or activity in question.

Pending the revision of Directive 93/6/EEC, the investment firms provided for in Article 67 shall be subject to the capital requirements laid down in that Article.

[9628]

Article 13

Organisational requirements

1. The home Member State shall require that investment firms comply with the organisational requirements set out in paragraphs 2 to 8.

2. An investment firm shall establish adequate policies and procedures sufficient to ensure compliance of the firm including its managers, employees and tied agents with its obligations under the provisions of this Directive as well as appropriate rules governing personal transactions by such persons.

3. An investment firm shall maintain and operate effective organisational and administrative arrangements with a view to taking all reasonable steps designed to prevent conflicts of interest as defined in Article 18 from adversely affecting the interests of its clients.

4. An investment firm shall take reasonable steps to ensure continuity and regularity in the performance of investment services and activities. To this end the investment firm shall employ appropriate and proportionate systems, resources and procedures.

5. An investment firm shall ensure, when relying on a third party for the performance of operational functions which are critical for the provision of continuous and satisfactory service to clients and the performance of investment activities on a continuous and satisfactory basis, that it takes reasonable steps to avoid undue additional operational risk. Outsourcing of important operational functions may not be undertaken in such a way as to impair materially the quality of its internal control and the ability of the supervisor to monitor the firm's compliance with all obligations.

An investment firm shall have sound administrative and accounting procedures, internal control mechanisms, effective procedures for risk assessment, and effective control and safeguard arrangements for information processing systems.

6. An investment firm shall arrange for records to be kept of all services and transactions undertaken by it which shall be sufficient to enable the competent authority to monitor compliance with the requirements under this Directive, and in particular to ascertain that the investment firm has complied with all obligations with respect to clients or potential clients.

7. An investment firm shall, when holding financial instruments belonging to clients, make adequate arrangements so as to safeguard clients' ownership rights, especially in the event of the investment firm's insolvency, and to prevent the use of a client's instruments on own account except with the client's express consent.

8. An investment firm shall, when holding funds belonging to clients, make adequate arrangements to safeguard the clients' rights and, except in the case of credit institutions, prevent the use of client funds for its own account.

9. In the case of branches of investment firms, the competent authority of the Member State in which the branch is located shall, without prejudice to the possibility of the competent authority of the home Member State of the investment firm to have direct access to those records, enforce the obligation laid down in paragraph 6 with regard to transactions undertaken by the branch.

10. In order to take account of technical developments on financial markets and to ensure the uniform application of paragraphs 2 to 9, the Commission shall adopt, in accordance with the procedure referred to in Article 64(2), implementing measures which specify the concrete organisational requirements to be imposed on investment firms performing different investment services and/or activities and ancillary services or combinations thereof.

[9629]

Article 14

Trading process and finalisation of transactions in an MTF

1. Member States shall require that investment firms or market operators operating an MTF, in addition to meeting the requirements laid down in Article 13, establish transparent and non-discretionary rules and procedures for fair and orderly trading and establish objective criteria for the efficient execution of orders.

2. Member States shall require that investment firms or market operators operating an MTF establish transparent rules regarding the criteria for determining the financial instruments that can be traded under its systems.

Member States shall require that, where applicable, investment firms or market operators operating an MTF provide, or are satisfied that there is access to, sufficient publicly available information to enable its users to form an investment judgement, taking into account both the nature of the users and the types of instruments traded.

3. Member States shall ensure that Articles 19, 21 and 22 are not applicable to the transactions concluded under the rules governing an MTF between its members or participants or between the MTF and its members or participants in relation to the use of the MTF. However, the members of or participants in the MTF shall comply with the obligations provided for in Articles 19, 21 and 22 with respect to their clients when, acting on behalf of their clients, they execute their orders through the systems of an MTF.

4. Member States shall require that investment firms or market operators operating an MTF establish and maintain transparent rules, based on objective criteria, governing access to its facility. These rules shall comply with the conditions established in Article 42(3).

5. Member States shall require that investment firms or market operators operating an MTF clearly inform its users of their respective responsibilities for the settlement of the transactions executed in that facility. Member States shall require that investment firms or market operators operating an MTF have put in place the necessary arrangements to facilitate the efficient settlement of the transactions concluded under the systems of the MTF.

6. Where a transferable security, which has been admitted to trading on a regulated market, is also traded on an MTF without the consent of the issuer, the issuer shall not be subject to any obligation relating to initial, ongoing or ad hoc financial disclosure with regard to that MTF.

7. Member States shall require that any investment firm or market operator operating an MTF comply immediately with any instruction from its competent authority pursuant to Article 50(1) to suspend or remove a financial instrument from trading.

[9630]

Article 15

Relations with third countries

1. Member States shall inform the Commission of any general difficulties which their investment firms encounter in establishing themselves or providing investment services and/or performing investment activities in any third country.

2. Whenever it appears to the Commission, on the basis of information submitted to it under paragraph 1, that a third country does not grant Community investment firms effective market access comparable to that granted by the Community to investment firms from that third country, the Commission may submit proposals to the Council for an appropriate mandate for negotiation with a view to obtaining comparable competitive opportunities for Community investment firms. The Council shall act by a qualified majority.

3. Whenever it appears to the Commission, on the basis of information submitted to it under paragraph 1, that Community investment firms in a third country are not granted national treatment affording the same competitive opportunities as are available to domestic

investment firms and that the conditions of effective market access are not fulfilled, the Commission may initiate negotiations in order to remedy the situation.

In the circumstances referred to in the first subparagraph, the Commission may decide, in accordance with the procedure referred to in Article 64(2), at any time and in addition to the initiation of negotiations, that the competent authorities of the Member States must limit or suspend their decisions regarding requests pending or future requests for authorisation and the acquisition of holdings by direct or indirect parent undertakings governed by the law of the third country in question. Such limitations or suspensions may not be applied to the setting-up of subsidiaries by investment firms duly authorised in the Community or by their subsidiaries, or to the acquisition of holdings in Community investment firms by such firms or subsidiaries. The duration of such measures may not exceed three months.

Before the end of the three-month period referred to in the second subparagraph and in the light of the results of the negotiations, the Commission may decide, in accordance with the procedure referred to in Article 64(2), to extend these measures.

4. Whenever it appears to the Commission that one of the situations referred to in paragraphs 2 and 3 obtains, the Member States shall inform it at its request:

- (a) of any application for the authorisation of any firm which is the direct or indirect subsidiary of a parent undertaking governed by the law of the third country in question;
- (b) whenever they are informed in accordance with Article 10(3) that such a parent undertaking proposes to acquire a holding in a Community investment firm, in consequence of which the latter would become its subsidiary.

That obligation to provide information shall lapse whenever agreement is reached with the third country concerned or when the measures referred to in the second and third subparagraphs of paragraph 3 cease to apply.

5. Measures taken under this Article shall comply with the Community's obligations under any international agreements, bilateral or multilateral, governing the taking-up or pursuit of the business of investment firms.

[9631]

CHAPTER II
OPERATING CONDITIONS FOR INVESTMENT FIRMS

SECTION 1
GENERAL PROVISIONS

Article 16

Regular review of conditions for initial authorisation

1. Member States shall require that an investment firm authorised in their territory comply at all times with the conditions for initial authorisation established in Chapter I of this Title.

2. Member States shall require competent authorities to establish the appropriate methods to monitor that investment firms comply with their obligation under paragraph 1. They shall require investment firms to notify the competent authorities of any material changes to the conditions for initial authorisation.

3. In the case of investment firms which provide only investment advice, Member States may allow the competent authority to delegate administrative, preparatory or ancillary tasks related to the review of the conditions for initial authorisation, in accordance with the conditions laid down in Article 48(2).

[9632]

Article 17

General obligation in respect of on-going supervision

1. Member States shall ensure that the competent authorities monitor the activities of investment firms so as to assess compliance with the operating conditions provided for in this Directive. Member States shall ensure that the appropriate measures are in place to enable the competent authorities to obtain the information needed to assess the compliance of investment firms with those obligations.

2. In the case of investment firms which provide only investment advice, Member States may allow the competent authority to delegate administrative, preparatory or ancillary tasks related to the regular monitoring of operational requirements, in accordance with the conditions laid down in Article 48(2).

[9633]

Article 18

Conflicts of interest

1. Member States shall require investment firms to take all reasonable steps to identify conflicts of interest between themselves, including their managers, employees and tied agents, or any person directly or indirectly linked to them by control and their clients or between one client and another that arise in the course of providing any investment and ancillary services, or combinations thereof.

2. Where organisational or administrative arrangements made by the investment firm in accordance with Article 13(3) to manage conflicts of interest are not sufficient to ensure, with reasonable confidence, that risks of damage to client interests will be prevented, the investment firm shall clearly disclose the general nature and/or sources of conflicts of interest to the client before undertaking business on its behalf.

3. In order to take account of technical developments on financial markets and to ensure uniform application of paragraphs 1 and 2, the Commission shall adopt, in accordance with the procedure referred to in Article 64(2), implementing measures to:

(a) define the steps that investment firms might reasonably be expected to take to identify, prevent, manage and/or disclose conflicts of interest when providing various investment and ancillary services and combinations thereof;

(b) establish appropriate criteria for determining the types of conflict of interest whose existence may damage the interests of the clients or potential clients of the investment firm.

[9634]

SECTION 2
PROVISIONS TO ENSURE INVESTOR PROTECTION

Article 19

Conduct of business obligations when providing investment services to clients

1. Member States shall require that, when providing investment services and/or, where appropriate, ancillary services to clients, an investment firm act honestly, fairly and professionally in accordance with the best interests of its clients and comply, in particular, with the principles set out in paragraphs 2 to 8.

2. All information, including marketing communications, addressed by the investment firm to clients or potential clients shall be fair, clear and not misleading. Marketing communications shall be clearly identifiable as such.

3. Appropriate information shall be provided in a comprehensible form to clients or potential clients about:

— the investment firm and its services,
— financial instruments and proposed investment strategies; this should include appropriate guidance on and warnings of the risks associated with investments in those instruments or in respect of particular investment strategies,
— execution venues, and
— costs and associated charges

so that they are reasonably able to understand the nature and risks of the investment service and of the specific type of financial instrument that is being offered and, consequently, to take investment decisions on an informed basis. This information may be provided in a standardised format.

4. When providing investment advice or portfolio management the investment firm shall obtain the necessary information regarding the client's or potential client's knowledge and experience in the investment field relevant to the specific type of product or service, his financial situation and his investment objectives so as to enable the firm to recommend to the client or potential client the investment services and financial instruments that are suitable for him.

5. Member States shall ensure that investment firms, when providing investment services other than those referred to in paragraph 4, ask the client or potential client to provide information regarding his knowledge and experience in the investment field relevant to the specific type of product or service offered or demanded so as to enable the investment firm to assess whether the investment service or product envisaged is appropriate for the client.

In case the investment firm considers, on the basis of the information received under the previous subparagraph, that the product or service is not appropriate to the client or potential client, the investment firm shall warn the client or potential client. This warning may be provided in a standardised format.

In cases where the client or potential client elects not to provide the information referred to under the first subparagraph, or where he provides insufficient information regarding his knowledge and experience, the investment firm shall warn the client or potential client that such a decision will not allow the firm to determine whether the service or product envisaged is appropriate for him. This warning may be provided in a standardised format.

6. Member States shall allow investment firms when providing investment services that only consist of execution and/or the reception and transmission of client orders with or without ancillary services to provide those investment services to their clients without the need to obtain the information or make the determination provided for in paragraph 5 where all the following conditions are met:

- the above services relate to shares admitted to trading on a regulated market or in an equivalent third country market, money market instruments, bonds or other forms of securitised debt (excluding those bonds or securitised debt that embed a derivative), UCITS and other non-complex financial instruments. A third country market shall be considered as equivalent to a regulated market if it complies with equivalent requirements to those established under Title III. The Commission shall publish a list of those markets that are to be considered as equivalent. This list shall be updated periodically,
- the service is provided at the initiative of the client or potential client,
- the client or potential client has been clearly informed that in the provision of this service the investment firm is not required to assess the suitability of the instrument or service provided or offered and that therefore he does not benefit from the corresponding protection of the relevant conduct of business rules; this warning may be provided in a standardised format,
- the investment firm complies with its obligations under Article 18.

7. The investment firm shall establish a record that includes the document or documents agreed between the firm and the client that set out the rights and obligations of the parties, and the other terms on which the firm will provide services to the client. The rights and duties of the parties to the contract may be incorporated by reference to other documents or legal texts.

8. The client must receive from the investment firm adequate reports on the service provided to its clients. These reports shall include, where applicable, the costs associated with the transactions and services undertaken on behalf of the client.

9. In cases where an investment service is offered as part of a financial product which is already subject to other provisions of Community legislation or common European standards related to credit institutions and consumer credits with respect to risk assessment of clients and/or information requirements, this service shall not be additionally subject to the obligations set out in this Article.

10. In order to ensure the necessary protection of investors and the uniform application of paragraphs 1 to 8, the Commission shall adopt, in accordance with the procedure referred to in Article 64(2), implementing measures to ensure that investment firms comply with the principles set out therein when providing investment or ancillary services to their clients. Those implementing measures shall take into account:

(a) the nature of the service(s) offered or provided to the client or potential client, taking into account the type, object, size and frequency of the transactions;
(b) the nature of the financial instruments being offered or considered;
(c) the retail or professional nature of the client or potential clients.

[9635]

Article 20

Provision of services through the medium of another investment firm

Member States shall allow an investment firm receiving an instruction to perform investment or ancillary services on behalf of a client through the medium of another investment firm to rely on client information transmitted by the latter firm. The investment firm which mediates the instructions will remain responsible for the completeness and accuracy of the information transmitted.

The investment firm which receives an instruction to undertake services on behalf of a client in this way shall also be able to rely on any recommendations in respect of the service or transaction that have been provided to the client by another investment firm. The investment firm which mediates the instructions will remain responsible for the appropriateness for the client of the recommendations or advice provided.

The investment firm which receives client instructions or orders through the medium of another investment firm shall remain responsible for concluding the service or transaction, based on any such information or recommendations, in accordance with the relevant provisions of this Title.

[9636]

Article 21

Obligation to execute orders on terms most favourable to the client

1. Member States shall require that investment firms take all reasonable steps to obtain, when executing orders, the best possible result for their clients taking into account price, costs, speed, likelihood of execution and settlement, size, nature or any other consideration relevant to the execution of the order. Nevertheless, whenever there is a specific instruction from the client the investment firm shall execute the order following the specific instruction.

2. Member States shall require investment firms to establish and implement effective arrangements for complying with paragraph 1. In particular Member States shall require investment firms to establish and implement an order execution policy to allow them to obtain, for their client orders, the best possible result in accordance with paragraph 1.

3. The order execution policy shall include, in respect of each class of instruments, information on the different venues where the investment firm executes its client orders and the factors affecting the choice of execution venue. It shall at least include those venues that enable the investment firm to obtain on a consistent basis the best possible result for the execution of client orders.

Member States shall require that investment firms provide appropriate information to their clients on their order execution policy. Member States shall require that investment firms obtain the prior consent of their clients to the execution policy.

Member States shall require that, where the order execution policy provides for the possibility that client orders may be executed outside a regulated market or an MTF, the investment firm shall, in particular, inform its clients about this possibility. Member States shall require that investment firms obtain the prior express consent of their clients before proceeding to execute their orders outside a regulated market or an MTF. Investment firms may obtain this consent either in the form of a general agreement or in respect of individual transactions.

4. Member States shall require investment firms to monitor the effectiveness of their order execution arrangements and execution policy in order to identify and, where appropriate, correct any deficiencies. In particular, they shall assess, on a regular basis, whether the execution venues included in the order execution policy provide for the best possible result for the client or whether they need to make changes to their execution arrangements. Member States shall require investment firms to notify clients of any material changes to their order execution arrangements or execution policy.

5. Member States shall require investment firms to be able to demonstrate to their clients, at their request, that they have executed their orders in accordance with the firm's execution policy.

6. In order to ensure the protection necessary for investors, the fair and orderly functioning of markets, and to ensure the uniform application of paragraphs 1, 3 and 4, the Commission shall, in accordance with the procedure referred to in Article 64(2), adopt implementing measures concerning:

(a) the criteria for determining the relative importance of the different factors that, pursuant to paragraph 1, may be taken into account for determining the best possible result taking into account the size and type of order and the retail or professional nature of the client;

(b) factors that may be taken into account by an investment firm when reviewing its execution arrangements and the circumstances under which changes to such arrangements may be appropriate. In particular, the factors for determining which venues enable investment firms to obtain on a consistent basis the best possible result for executing the client orders;

(c) the nature and extent of the information to be provided to clients on their execution policies, pursuant to paragraph 3.

[9637]

Article 22

Client order handling rules

1. Member States shall require that investment firms authorised to execute orders on behalf of clients implement procedures and arrangements which provide for the prompt, fair and expeditious execution of client orders, relative to other client orders or the trading interests of the investment firm.

These procedures or arrangements shall allow for the execution of otherwise comparable client orders in accordance with the time of their reception by the investment firm.

2. Member States shall require that, in the case of a client limit order in respect of shares admitted to trading on a regulated market which are not immediately executed under prevailing market conditions, investment firms are, unless the client expressly instructs otherwise, to take measures to facilitate the earliest possible execution of that order by making public immediately that client limit order in a manner which is easily accessible to other market participants. Member States may decide that investment firms comply with this obligation by transmitting the client limit order to a regulated market and/or MTF. Member States shall provide that the competent authorities may waive the obligation to make public a limit order that is large in scale compared with normal market size as determined under Article 44(2).

3. In order to ensure that measures for the protection of investors and fair and orderly functioning of markets take account of technical developments in financial markets, and to ensure the uniform application of paragraphs 1 and 2, the Commission shall adopt, in accordance with the procedure referred to in Article 64(2), implementing measures which define:

(a) the conditions and nature of the procedures and arrangements which result in the prompt, fair and expeditious execution of client orders and the situations in which or types of transaction for which investment firms may reasonably deviate from prompt execution so as to obtain more favourable terms for clients;

(b) the different methods through which an investment firm can be deemed to have met its obligation to disclose not immediately executable client limit orders to the market.

[9638]

Article 23

Obligations of investment firms when appointing tied agents

1. Member States may decide to allow an investment firm to appoint tied agents for the purposes of promoting the services of the investment firm, soliciting business or receiving orders from clients or potential clients and transmitting them, placing financial instruments and providing advice in respect of such financial instruments and services offered by that investment firm.

2. Member States shall require that where an investment firm decides to appoint a tied agent it remains fully and unconditionally responsible for any action or omission on the part of the tied agent when acting on behalf of the firm. Member States shall require the investment firm to ensure that a tied agent discloses the capacity in which he is acting and the firm which he is representing when contacting or before dealing with any client or potential client.

Member States may allow, in accordance with Article 13(6), (7) and (8), tied agents registered in their territory to handle clients' money and/or financial instruments on behalf and under the full responsibility of the investment firm for which they are acting within their territory or, in the case of a cross border operation, in the territory of a Member State which allows a tied agent to handle clients' money.

Member States shall require the investment firms to monitor the activities of their tied agents so as to ensure that they continue to comply with this Directive when acting through tied agents.

3. Member States that decide to allow investment firms to appoint tied agents shall establish a public register. Tied agents shall be registered in the public register in the Member State where they are established.

Where the Member State in which the tied agent is established has decided, in accordance with paragraph 1, not to allow the investment firms authorised by their competent authorities to appoint tied agents, those tied agents shall be registered with the competent authority of the home Member State of the investment firm on whose behalf it acts.

Member States shall ensure that tied agents are only admitted to the public register if it has been established that they are of sufficiently good repute and that they possess appropriate general, commercial and professional knowledge so as to be able to communicate accurately all relevant information regarding the proposed service to the client or potential client.

Member States may decide that investment firms can verify whether the tied agents which they have appointed are of sufficiently good repute and possess the knowledge as referred to in the third subparagraph.

The register shall be updated on a regular basis. It shall be publicly available for consultation.

4. Member States shall require that investment firms appointing tied agents take adequate measures in order to avoid any negative impact that the activities of the tied agent not covered by the scope of this Directive could have on the activities carried out by the tied agent on behalf of the investment firm.

Member States may allow competent authorities to collaborate with investment firms and credit institutions, their associations and other entities in registering tied agents and in monitoring compliance of tied agents with the requirements of paragraph 3. In particular, tied agents may be registered by an investment firm, credit institution or their associations and other entities under the supervision of the competent authority.

5. Member States shall require that investment firms appoint only tied agents entered in the public registers referred to in paragraph 3.

6. Member States may reinforce the requirements set out in this Article or add other requirements for tied agents registered within their jurisdiction.

[9639]

Article 24

Transactions executed with eligible counterparties

1. Member States shall ensure that investment firms authorised to execute orders on behalf of clients and/or to deal on own account and/or to receive and transmit orders, may bring about or enter into transactions with eligible counterparties without being obliged to comply with the obligations under Articles 19, 21 and 22(1) in respect of those transactions or in respect of any ancillary service directly related to those transactions.

2. Member States shall recognise as eligible counterparties for the purposes of this Article investment firms, credit institutions, insurance companies, UCITS and their management companies, pension funds and their management companies, other financial institutions authorised or regulated under Community legislation or the national law of a Member State, undertakings exempted from the application of this Directive under Article 2(1)(k) and (l), national governments and their corresponding offices including public bodies that deal with public debt, central banks and supranational organisations.

Classification as an eligible counterparty under the first subparagraph shall be without prejudice to the right of such entities to request, either on a general form or on a trade-by-trade basis, treatment as clients whose business with the investment firm is subject to Articles 19, 21 and 22.

3. Member States may also recognise as eligible counterparties other undertakings meeting pre-determined proportionate requirements, including quantitative thresholds. In the event of a transaction where the prospective counterparties are located in different jurisdictions, the investment firm shall defer to the status of the other undertaking as determined by the law or measures of the Member State in which that undertaking is established.

Member States shall ensure that the investment firm, when it enters into transactions in accordance with paragraph 1 with such undertakings, obtains the express confirmation from the prospective counterparty that it agrees to be treated as an eligible counterparty. Member States shall allow the investment firm to obtain this confirmation either in the form of a general agreement or in respect of each individual transaction.

4. Member States may recognise as eligible counterparties third country entities equivalent to those categories of entities mentioned in paragraph 2.

Member States may also recognise as eligible counterparties third country undertakings such as those mentioned in paragraph 3 on the same conditions and subject to the same requirements as those laid down at paragraph 3.

5. In order to ensure the uniform application of paragraphs 2, 3 and 4 in the light of changing market practice and to facilitate the effective operation of the single market, the Commission may adopt, in accordance with the procedure referred to in Article 64(2), implementing measures which define:

(a) the procedures for requesting treatment as clients under paragraph 2;

(b) the procedures for obtaining the express confirmation from prospective counterparties under paragraph 3;

(c) the predetermined proportionate requirements, including quantitative thresholds that would allow an undertaking to be considered as an eligible counterparty under paragraph 3.

[9640]

SECTION 3
MARKET TRANSPARENCY AND INTEGRITY

Article 25

Obligation to uphold integrity of markets, report transactions and maintain records

1. Without prejudice to the allocation of responsibilities for enforcing the provisions of Directive 2003/6/EC of the European Parliament and of the Council of 28 January 2003 on insider dealing and market manipulation (market abuse),[1] Member States shall ensure that appropriate measures are in place to enable the competent authority to monitor the activities of investment firms to ensure that they act honestly, fairly and professionally and in a manner which promotes the integrity of the market.

2. Member States shall require investment firms to keep at the disposal of the competent authority, for at least five years, the relevant data relating to all transactions in financial instruments which they have carried out, whether on own account or on behalf of a client. In the case of transactions carried out on behalf of clients, the records shall contain all the information and details of the identity of the client, and the information required under Council Directive 91/308/EEC of 10 June 1991 on prevention of the use of the financial system for the purpose of money laundering.[2]

3. Member States shall require investment firms which execute transactions in any financial instruments admitted to trading on a regulated market to report details of such transactions to the competent authority as quickly as possible, and no later than the close of the following working day. This obligation shall apply whether or not such transactions were carried out on a regulated market.

The competent authorities shall, in accordance with Article 58, establish the necessary arrangements in order to ensure that the competent authority of the most relevant market in terms of liquidity for those financial instruments also receives this information.

4. The reports shall, in particular, include details of the names and numbers of the instruments bought or sold, the quantity, the dates and times of execution and the transaction prices and means of identifying the investment firms concerned.

5. Member States shall provide for the reports to be made to the competent authority either by the investment firm itself, a third party acting on its behalf or by a trade-matching or reporting system approved by the competent authority or by the regulated market or MTF through whose systems the transaction was completed. In cases where transactions are reported directly to the competent authority by a regulated market, an MTF, or a trade-matching or reporting system approved by the competent authority, the obligation on the investment firm laid down in paragraph 3 may be waived.

6. When, in accordance with Article 32(7), reports provided for under this Article are transmitted to the competent authority of the host Member State, it shall transmit this

information to the competent authorities of the home Member State of the investment firm, unless they decide that they do not want to receive this information.

7. In order to ensure that measures for the protection of market integrity are modified to take account of technical developments in financial markets, and to ensure the uniform application of paragraphs 1 to 5, the Commission may adopt, in accordance with the procedure referred to in Article 64(2), implementing measures which define the methods and arrangements for reporting financial transactions, the form and content of these reports and the criteria for defining a relevant market in accordance with paragraph 3.

[9641]

NOTES

1 OJ L96, 12.4.2003, p 16.

2 OJ L166, 28.6.1991, p 77. Directive as last amended by Directive 2001/97/EC of the European Parliament and of the Council (OJ L344, 28.12.2001, p 76).

Article 26

Monitoring of compliance with the rules of the MTF and with other legal obligations

1. Member States shall require that investment firms and market operators operating an MTF establish and maintain effective arrangements and procedures, relevant to the MTF, for the regular monitoring of the compliance by its users with its rules. Investment firms and market operators operating an MTF shall monitor the transactions undertaken by their users under their systems in order to identify breaches of those rules, disorderly trading conditions or conduct that may involve market abuse.

2. Member States shall require investment firms and market operators operating an MTF to report significant breaches of its rules or disorderly trading conditions or conduct that may involve market abuse to the competent authority. Member States shall also require investment firms and market operators operating an MTF to supply the relevant information without delay to the authority competent for the investigation and prosecution of market abuse and to provide full assistance to the latter in investigating and prosecuting market abuse occurring on or through its systems.

[9642]

Article 27

Obligation for investment firms to make public firm quotes

1. Member States shall require systematic internalisers in shares to publish a firm quote in those shares admitted to trading on a regulated market for which they are systematic internalisers and for which there is a liquid market. In the case of shares for which there is not a liquid market, systematic internalisers shall disclose quotes to their clients on request.

The provisions of this Article shall be applicable to systematic internalisers when dealing for sizes up to standard market size. Systematic internalisers that only deal in sizes above standard market size shall not be subject to the provisions of this Article.

Systematic internalisers may decide the size or sizes at which they will quote. For a particular share each quote shall include a firm bid and/or offer price or prices for a size or sizes which could be up to standard market size for the class of shares to which the share belongs. The price or prices shall also reflect the prevailing market conditions for that share.

Shares shall be grouped in classes on the basis of the arithmetic average value of the orders executed in the market for that share. The standard market size for each class of shares shall be a size representative of the arithmetic average value of the orders executed in the market for the shares included in each class of shares.

The market for each share shall be comprised of all orders executed in the European Union in respect of that share excluding those large in scale compared to normal market size for that share.

2. The competent authority of the most relevant market in terms of liquidity as defined in Article 25 for each share shall determine at least annually, on the basis of the arithmetic average value of the orders executed in the market in respect of that share, the class of shares to which it belongs. This information shall be made public to all market participants.

3. Systematic internalisers shall make public their quotes on a regular and continuous basis during normal trading hours. They shall be entitled to update their quotes at any time. They shall also be allowed, under exceptional market conditions, to withdraw their quotes.

The quote shall be made public in a manner which is easily accessible to other market participants on a reasonable commercial basis.

Systematic internalisers shall, while complying with the provisions set down in Article 21, execute the orders they receive from their retail clients in relation to the shares for which they are systematic internalisers at the quoted prices at the time of reception of the order.

Systematic internalisers shall execute the orders they receive from their professional clients in relation to the shares for which they are systematic internalisers at the quoted price at the time of reception of the order. However, they may execute those orders at a better price in justified cases provided that this price falls within a public range close to market conditions and provided that the orders are of a size bigger than the size customarily undertaken by a retail investor.

Furthermore, systematic internalisers may execute orders they receive from their professional clients at prices different than their quoted ones without having to comply with the conditions established in the fourth subparagraph, in respect of transactions where execution in several securities is part of one transaction or in respect of orders that are subject to conditions other than the current market price.

Where a systematic internaliser who quotes only one quote or whose highest quote is lower than the standard market size receives an order from a client of a size bigger than its quotation size, but lower than the standard market size, it may decide to execute that part of the order which exceeds its quotation size, provided that it is executed at the quoted price, except where otherwise permitted under the conditions of the previous two subparagraphs. Where the systematic internaliser is quoting in different sizes and receives an order between those sizes, which it chooses to execute, it shall execute the order at one of the quoted prices in compliance with the provisions of Article 22, except where otherwise permitted under the conditions of the previous two subparagraphs.

4. The competent authorities shall check:

(a) that investment firms regularly update bid and/or offer prices published in accordance with paragraph 1 and maintain prices which reflect the prevailing market conditions;

(b) that investment firms comply with the conditions for price improvement laid down in the fourth subparagraph of paragraph 3.

5. Systematic internalisers shall be allowed to decide, on the basis of their commercial policy and in an objective non-discriminatory way, the investors to whom they give access to their quotes. To that end there shall be clear standards for governing access to their quotes. Systematic internalisers may refuse to enter into or discontinue business relationships with investors on the basis of commercial considerations such as the investor credit status, the counterparty risk and the final settlement of the transaction.

6. In order to limit the risk of being exposed to multiple transactions from the same client systematic internalisers shall be allowed to limit in a non-discriminatory way the number of transactions from the same client which they undertake to enter at the published conditions. They shall also be allowed, in a non-discriminatory way and in accordance with the provisions of Article 22, to limit the total number of transactions from different clients at the same time provided that this is allowable only where the number and/or volume of orders sought by clients considerably exceeds the norm.

7. In order to ensure the uniform application of paragraphs 1 to 6, in a manner which supports the efficient valuation of shares and maximises the possibility of investment firms of obtaining the best deal for their clients, the Commission shall, in accordance with the procedure referred to in Article 64(2), adopt implementing measures which:

(a) specify the criteria for application of paragraphs 1 and 2;

(b) specify the criteria determining when a quote is published on a regular and continuous basis and is easily accessible as well as the means by which investment firms may comply with their obligation to make public their quotes, which shall include the following possibilities:

(i) through the facilities of any regulated market which has admitted the instrument in question to trading;

(ii) through the offices of a third party;

(iii) through proprietary arrangements;

(c) specify the general criteria for determining those transactions where execution in several securities is part of one transaction or orders that are subject to conditions other than current market price;

(d) specify the general criteria for determining what can be considered as exceptional market circumstances that allow for the withdrawal of quotes as well as conditions for updating quotes;

(e) specify the criteria for determining what is a size customarily undertaken by a retail investor.

(f) specify the criteria for determining what constitutes considerably exceeding the norm as set down in paragraph 6;

(g) specify the criteria for determining when prices fall within a public range close to market conditions.

[9643]

Article 28

Post-trade disclosure by investment firms

1. Member States shall, at least, require investment firms which, either on own account or on behalf of clients, conclude transactions in shares admitted to trading on a regulated market outside a regulated market or MTF, to make public the volume and price of those transactions and the time at which they were concluded. This information shall be made public as close to real-time as possible, on a reasonable commercial basis, and in a manner which is easily accessible to other market participants.

2. Member States shall require that the information which is made public in accordance with paragraph 1 and the time-limits within which it is published comply with the requirements adopted pursuant to Article 45. Where the measures adopted pursuant to Article 45 provide for deferred reporting for certain categories of transaction in shares, this possibility shall apply *mutatis mutandis* to those transactions when undertaken outside regulated markets or MTFs.

3. In order to ensure the transparent and orderly functioning of markets and the uniform application of paragraph 1, the Commission shall adopt, in accordance with the procedure referred to in Article 64(2), implementing measures which:

(a) specify the means by which investment firms may comply with their obligations under paragraph 1 including the following possibilities:

(i) through the facilities of any regulated market which has admitted the instrument in question to trading or through the facilities of an MTF in which the share in question is traded;

(ii) through the offices of a third party;

(iii) through proprietary arrangements;

(b) clarify the application of the obligation under paragraph 1 to transactions involving the use of shares for collateral, lending or other purposes where the exchange of shares is determined by factors other than the current market valuation of the share.

[9644]

Article 29

Pre-trade transparency requirements for MTFs

1. Member States shall, at least, require that investment firms and market operators operating an MTF make public current bid and offer prices and the depth of trading interests at these prices which are advertised through their systems in respect of shares admitted to trading on a regulated market. Member States shall provide for this information to be made available to the public on reasonable commercial terms and on a continuous basis during normal trading hours.

2. Member States shall provide for the competent authorities to be able to waive the obligation for investment firms or market operators operating an MTF to make public the information referred to in paragraph 1 based on the market model or the type and size of orders in the cases defined in accordance with paragraph 3. In particular, the competent authorities shall be able to waive the obligation in respect of transactions that are large in scale compared with normal market size for the share or type of share in question.

3. In order to ensure the uniform application of paragraphs 1 and 2, the Commission shall, in accordance with the procedure referred to in Article 64(2) adopt implementing measures as regards:

(a) the range of bid and offers or designated market-maker quotes, and the depth of trading interest at those prices, to be made public;

(b) the size or type of orders for which pre-trade disclosure may be waived under paragraph 2;

(c) the market model for which pre-trade disclosure may be waived under paragraph 2 and in particular, the applicability of the obligation to trading methods operated by an MTF which conclude transactions under their rules by reference to prices established outside the systems of the MTF or by periodic auction.

Except where justified by the specific nature of the MTF, the content of these implementing measures shall be equal to that of the implementing measures provided for in Article 44 for regulated markets.

[9645]

Article 30

Post-trade transparency requirements for MTFs

1. Member States shall, at least, require that investment firms and market operators operating an MTF make public the price, volume and time of the transactions executed under its systems in respect of shares which are admitted to trading on a regulated market. Member States shall require that details of all such transactions be made public, on a reasonable commercial basis, as close to real-time as possible. This requirement shall not apply to details of trades executed on an MTF that are made public under the systems of a regulated market.

2. Member States shall provide that the competent authority may authorise investment firms or market operators operating an MTF to provide for deferred publication of the details of transactions based on their type or size. In particular, the competent authorities may authorise the deferred publication in respect of transactions that are large in scale compared with the normal market size for that share or that class of shares. Member States shall require MTFs to obtain the competent authority's prior approval to proposed arrangements for deferred trade-publication, and shall require that these arrangements be clearly disclosed to market participants and the investing public.

3. In order to provide for the efficient and orderly functioning of financial markets, and to ensure the uniform application of paragraphs 1 and 2, the Commission shall, in accordance with the procedure referred to in Article 64(2) adopt implementing measures in respect of:

(a) the scope and content of the information to be made available to the public;

(b) the conditions under which investment firms or market operators operating an MTF may provide for deferred publication of trades and the criteria to be applied when deciding the transactions for which, due to their size or the type of share involved, deferred publication is allowed.

Except where justified by the specific nature of the MTF, the content of these implementing measures shall be equal to that of the implementing measures provided for in Article 45 for regulated markets.

[9646]

CHAPTER III
RIGHTS OF INVESTMENT FIRMS

Article 31

Freedom to provide investment services and activities

1. Member States shall ensure that any investment firm authorised and supervised by the competent authorities of another Member State in accordance with this Directive, and in respect of credit institutions in accordance with Directive 2000/12/EC, may freely perform investment services and/or activities as well as ancillary services within their territories, provided that such services and activities are covered by its authorisation. Ancillary services may only be provided together with an investment service and/or activity.

Member States shall not impose any additional requirements on such an investment firm or credit institution in respect of the matters covered by this Directive.

2. Any investment firm wishing to provide services or activities within the territory of another Member State for the first time, or which wishes to change the range of services or activities so provided, shall communicate the following information to the competent authorities of its home Member State:

(a) the Member State in which it intends to operate;

(b) a programme of operations stating in particular the investment services and/or activities as well as ancillary services which it intends to perform and whether it intends to use tied agents in the territory of the Member States in which it intends to provide services.

In cases where the investment firm intends to use tied agents, the competent authority of the home Member State of the investment firm shall, at the request of the competent authority of the host Member State and within a reasonable time, communicate the identity of the tied agents that the investment firm intends to use in that Member State. The host Member State may make public such information.

3. The competent authority of the home Member State shall, within one month of receiving the information, forward it to the competent authority of the host Member State designated as contact point in accordance with Article 56(1). The investment firm may then start to provide the investment service or services concerned in the host Member State.

4. In the event of a change in any of the particulars communicated in accordance with paragraph 2, an investment firm shall give written notice of that change to the competent authority of the home Member State at least one month before implementing the change. The competent authority of the home Member State shall inform the competent authority of the host Member State of those changes.

5. Member States shall, without further legal or administrative requirement, allow investment firms and market operators operating MTFs from other Member States to provide appropriate arrangements on their territory so as to facilitate access to and use of their systems by remote users or participants established in their territory.

6. The investment firm or the market operator that operates an MTF shall communicate to the competent authority of its home Member State the Member State in which it intends to provide such arrangements. The competent authority of the home Member State of the MTF shall communicate, within one month, this information to the Member State in which the MTF intends to provide such arrangements.

The competent authority of the home Member State of the MTF shall, on the request of the competent authority of the host Member State of the MTF and within a reasonable delay, communicate the identity of the members or participants of the MTF established in that Member State.

[9647]

Article 32

Establishment of a branch

1. Member States shall ensure that investment services and/or activities as well as ancillary services may be provided within their territories in accordance with this Directive and Directive 2000/12/EC through the establishment of a branch provided that those services and activities are covered by the authorisation granted to the investment firm or the credit institution in the home Member State. Ancillary services may only be provided together with an investment service and/or activity.

Member States shall not impose any additional requirements save those allowed under paragraph 7, on the organisation and operation of the branch in respect of the matters covered by this Directive.

2. Member States shall require any investment firm wishing to establish a branch within the territory of another Member State first to notify the competent authority of its home Member State and to provide it with the following information:

(a) the Member States within the territory of which it plans to establish a branch;

(b) a programme of operations setting out inter alia the investment services and/or activities as well as the ancillary services to be offered and the organisational structure of the branch and indicating whether the branch intends to use tied agents;

(c) the address in the host Member State from which documents may be obtained;

(d) the names of those responsible for the management of the branch.

In cases where an investment firm uses a tied agent established in a Member State outside its home Member State, such tied agent shall be assimilated to the branch and shall be subject to the provisions of this Directive relating to branches.

3. Unless the competent authority of the home Member State has reason to doubt the adequacy of the administrative structure or the financial situation of an investment firm,

taking into account the activities envisaged, it shall, within three months of receiving all the information, communicate that information to the competent authority of the host Member State designated as contact point in accordance with Article 56(1) and inform the investment firm concerned accordingly.

4. In addition to the information referred to in paragraph 2, the competent authority of the home Member State shall communicate details of the accredited compensation scheme of which the investment firm is a member in accordance with Directive 97/9/EC to the competent authority of the host Member State. In the event of a change in the particulars, the competent authority of the home Member State shall inform the competent authority of the host Member State accordingly.

5. Where the competent authority of the home Member State refuses to communicate the information to the competent authority of the host Member State, it shall give reasons for its refusal to the investment firm concerned within three months of receiving all the information.

6. On receipt of a communication from the competent authority of the host Member State, or failing such communication from the latter at the latest after two months from the date of transmission of the communication by the competent authority of the home Member State, the branch may be established and commence business.

7. The competent authority of the Member State in which the branch is located shall assume responsibility for ensuring that the services provided by the branch within its territory comply with the obligations laid down in Articles 19, 21, 22, 25, 27 and 28 and in measures adopted pursuant thereto.

The competent authority of the Member State in which the branch is located shall have the right to examine branch arrangements and to request such changes as are strictly needed to enable the competent authority to enforce the obligations under Articles 19, 21, 22, 25, 27 and 28 and measures adopted pursuant thereto with respect to the services and/or activities provided by the branch within its territory.

8. Each Member State shall provide that, where an investment firm authorised in another Member State has established a branch within its territory, the competent authority of the home Member State of the investment firm, in the exercise of its responsibilities and after informing the competent authority of the host Member State, may carry out on-site inspections in that branch.

9. In the event of a change in any of the information communicated in accordance with paragraph 2, an investment firm shall give written notice of that change to the competent authority of the home Member State at least one month before implementing the change. The competent authority of the host Member State shall also be informed of that change by the competent authority of the home Member State.

[9648]

Article 33

Access to regulated markets

1. Member States shall require that investment firms from other Member States which are authorised to execute client orders or to deal on own account have the right of member-ship or have access to regulated markets established in their territory by means of any of the following arrangements:

(a) directly, by setting up branches in the host Member States;

(b) by becoming remote members of or having remote access to the regulated market without having to be established in the home Member State of the regulated market, where the trading procedures and systems of the market in question do not require a physical presence for conclusion of transactions on the market.

2. Member States shall not impose any additional regulatory or administrative requirements, in respect of matters covered by this Directive, on investment firms exercising the right conferred by paragraph 1.

[9649]

Article 34

Access to central counterparty, clearing and settlement facilities and right to designate settlement system

1. Member States shall require that investment firms from other Member States have the right of access to central counterparty, clearing and settlement systems in their territory for the purposes of finalising or arranging the finalisation of transactions in financial instruments.

Member States shall require that access of those investment firms to such facilities be subject to the same non-discriminatory, transparent and objective criteria as apply to local participants. Member States shall not restrict the use of those facilities to the clearing and settlement of transactions in financial instruments undertaken on a regulated market or MTF in their territory.

2. Member States shall require that regulated markets in their territory offer all their members or participants the right to designate the system for the settlement of transactions in financial instruments undertaken on that regulated market, subject to:

(a) such links and arrangements between the designated settlement system and any other system or facility as are necessary to ensure the efficient and economic settlement of the transaction in question; and

(b) agreement by the competent authority responsible for the supervision of the regulated market that technical conditions for settlement of transactions concluded on the regulated market through a settlement system other than that designated by the regulated market are such as to allow the smooth and orderly functioning of financial markets.

This assessment of the competent authority of the regulated market shall be without prejudice to the competencies of the national central banks as overseers of settlement systems or other supervisory authorities on such systems. The competent authority shall take into account the oversight/supervision already exercised by those institutions in order to avoid undue duplication of control.

3. The rights of investment firms under paragraphs 1 and 2 shall be without prejudice to the right of operators of central counterparty, clearing or securities settlement systems to refuse on legitimate commercial grounds to make the requested services available.

[9650]

Article 35

Provisions regarding central counterparty, clearing and settlement arrangements in respect of MTFs

1. Member States shall not prevent investment firms and market operators operating an MTF from entering into appropriate arrangements with a central counterparty or clearing house and a settlement system of another Member State with a view to providing for the clearing and/or settlement of some or all trades concluded by market participants under their systems.

2. The competent authority of investment firms and market operators operating an MTF may not oppose the use of central counterparty, clearing houses and/or settlement systems in another Member State except where this is demonstrably necessary in order to maintain the orderly functioning of that MTF and taking into account the conditions for settlement systems established in Article 34(2).

In order to avoid undue duplication of control, the competent authority shall take into account the oversight/supervision of the clearing and settlement system already exercised by the national central banks as overseers of clearing and settlement systems or by other supervisory authorities with a competence in such systems.

[9651]

TITLE III
REGULATED MARKETS

Article 36

Authorisation and applicable law

1. Member States shall reserve authorisation as a regulated market to those systems which comply with the provisions of this Title.

Authorisation as a regulated market shall be granted only where the competent authority is satisfied that both the market operator and the systems of the regulated market comply at least with the requirements laid down in this Title.

In the case of a regulated market that is a legal person and that is managed or operated by a market operator other than the regulated market itself, Member States shall establish how the different obligations imposed on the market operator under this Directive are to be allocated between the regulated market and the market operator.

The operator of the regulated market shall provide all information, including a programme of operations setting out inter alia the types of business envisaged and the organisational structure, necessary to enable the competent authority to satisfy itself that the regulated market has established, at the time of initial authorisation, all the necessary arrangements to meet its obligations under the provisions of this Title.

2. Member States shall require the operator of the regulated market to perform tasks relating to the organisation and operation of the regulated market under the supervision of the competent authority. Member States shall ensure that competent authorities keep under regular review the compliance of regulated markets with the provisions of this Title. They shall also ensure that competent authorities monitor that regulated markets comply at all times with the conditions for initial authorisation established under this Title.

3. Member States shall ensure that the market operator is responsible for ensuring that the regulated market that he manages complies with all requirements under this Title.

Member States shall also ensure that the market operator is entitled to exercise the rights that correspond to the regulated market that he manages by virtue of this Directive.

4. Without prejudice to any relevant provisions of Directive 2003/6/EC, the public law governing the trading conducted under the systems of the regulated market shall be that of the home Member State of the regulated market.

5. The competent authority may withdraw the authorisation issued to a regulated market where it:

(a) does not make use of the authorisation within 12 months, expressly renounces the authorisation or has not operated for the preceding six months, unless the Member State concerned has provided for authorisation to lapse in such cases;

(b) has obtained the authorisation by making false statements or by any other irregular means;

(c) no longer meets the conditions under which authorisation was granted;

(d) has seriously and systematically infringed the provisions adopted pursuant to this Directive;

(e) falls within any of the cases where national law provides for withdrawal.

[9652]

Article 37

Requirements for the management of the regulated market

1. Member States shall require the persons who effectively direct the business and the operations of the regulated market to be of sufficiently good repute and sufficiently experienced as to ensure the sound and prudent management and operation of the regulated market. Member States shall also require the operator of the regulated market to inform the competent authority of the identity and any other subsequent changes of the persons who effectively direct the business and the operations of the regulated market.

The competent authority shall refuse to approve proposed changes where there are objective and demonstrable grounds for believing that they pose a material threat to the sound and prudent management and operation of the regulated market.

2. Member States shall ensure that, in the process of authorisation of a regulated market, the person or persons who effectively direct the business and the operations of an already authorised regulated market in accordance with the conditions of this Directive are deemed to comply with the requirements laid down in paragraph 1.

[9653]

Article 38

Requirements relating to persons exercising significant influence over the management of the regulated market

1. Member States shall require the persons who are in a position to exercise, directly or indirectly, significant influence over the management of the regulated market to be suitable.

2. Member States shall require the operator of the regulated market:

(a) to provide the competent authority with, and to make public, information regarding the ownership of the regulated market and/or the market operator, and in particular, the identity and scale of interests of any parties in a position to exercise significant influence over the management;

(b) to inform the competent authority of and to make public any transfer of ownership which gives rise to a change in the identity of the persons exercising significant influence over the operation of the regulated market.

3. The competent authority shall refuse to approve proposed changes to the controlling interests of the regulated market and/or the market operator where there are objective and demonstrable grounds for believing that they would pose a threat to the sound and prudent management of the regulated market.

[9654]

Article 39

Organisational requirements

Member States shall require the regulated market:

(a) to have arrangements to identify clearly and manage the potential adverse consequences, for the operation of the regulated market or for its participants, of any conflict of interest between the interest of the regulated market, its owners or its operator and the sound functioning of the regulated market, and in particular where such conflicts of interest might prove prejudicial to the accomplishment of any functions delegated to the regulated market by the competent authority;

(b) to be adequately equipped to manage the risks to which it is exposed, to implement appropriate arrangements and systems to identify all significant risks to its operation, and to put in place effective measures to mitigate those risks;

(c) to have arrangements for the sound management of the technical operations of the system, including the establishment of effective contingency arrangements to cope with risks of systems disruptions;

(d) to have transparent and non-discretionary rules and procedures that provide for fair and orderly trading and establish objective criteria for the efficient execution of orders;

(e) to have effective arrangements to facilitate the efficient and timely finalisation of the transactions executed under its systems;

(f) to have available, at the time of authorisation and on an ongoing basis, sufficient financial resources to facilitate its orderly functioning, having regard to the nature and extent of the transactions concluded on the market and the range and degree of the risks to which it is exposed.

[9655]

Article 40

Admission of financial instruments to trading

1. Member States shall require that regulated markets have clear and transparent rules regarding the admission of financial instruments to trading.

Those rules shall ensure that any financial instruments admitted to trading in a regulated market are capable of being traded in a fair, orderly and efficient manner and, in the case of transferable securities, are freely negotiable.

2. In the case of derivatives, the rules shall ensure in particular that the design of the derivative contract allows for its orderly pricing as well as for the existence of effective settlement conditions.

3. In addition to the obligations set out in paragraphs 1 and 2, Member States shall require the regulated market to establish and maintain effective arrangements to verify that issuers of transferable securities that are admitted to trading on the regulated market comply with their obligations under Community law in respect of initial, ongoing or ad hoc disclosure obligations.

Member States shall ensure that the regulated market establishes arrangements which facilitate its members or participants in obtaining access to information which has been made public under Community law.

4. Member States shall ensure that regulated markets have established the necessary arrangements to review regularly the compliance with the admission requirements of the financial instruments which they admit to trading.

5. A transferable security that has been admitted to trading on a regulated market can subsequently be admitted to trading on other regulated markets, even without the consent of the issuer and in compliance with the relevant provisions of Directive 2003/71/EC of the European Parliament and of the Council of 4 November 2003 on the prospectus to be published when securities are offered to the public or admitted to trading and amending Directive 2001/34/EC.[1] The issuer shall be informed by the regulated market of the fact that its securities are traded on that regulated market. The issuer shall not be subject to any obligation to provide information required under paragraph 3 directly to any regulated market which has admitted the issuer's securities to trading without its consent.

6. In order to ensure the uniform application of paragraphs 1 to 5, the Commission shall, in accordance with the procedure referred to in Article 64(2) adopt implementing measures which:

(a) specify the characteristics of different classes of instruments to be taken into account by the regulated market when assessing whether an instrument is issued in a manner consistent with the conditions laid down in the second subparagraph of paragraph 1 for admission to trading on the different market segments which it operates;

(b) clarify the arrangements that the regulated market is to implement so as to be considered to have fulfilled its obligation to verify that the issuer of a transferable security complies with its obligations under Community law in respect of initial, ongoing or ad hoc disclosure obligations;

(c) clarify the arrangements that the regulated market has to establish pursuant to paragraph 3 in order to facilitate its members or participants in obtaining access to information which has been made public under the conditions established by Community law.

[9656]

NOTES

[1] OJ L345, 31.12.2003, p 64.

Article 41

Suspension and removal of instruments from trading

1. Without prejudice to the right of the competent authority under Article 50(2)(j) and (k) to demand suspension or removal of an instrument from trading, the operator of the regulated market may suspend or remove from trading a financial instrument which no longer complies with the rules of the regulated market unless such a step would be likely to cause significant damage to the investors' interests or the orderly functioning of the market.

Notwithstanding the possibility for the operators of regulated markets to inform directly the operators of other regulated markets, Member States shall require that an operator of a regulated market that suspends or removes from trading a financial instrument make public this decision and communicates relevant information to the competent authority. The competent authority shall inform the competent authorities of the other Member States.

2. A competent authority which demands the suspension or removal of a financial instrument from trading on one or more regulated markets shall immediately make public its decision and inform the competent authorities of the other Member States. Except where it could cause significant damage to the investors' interests or the orderly functioning of the market the competent authorities of the other Member States shall demand the suspension or removal of that financial instrument from trading on the regulated markets and MTFs that operate under their authority.

[9657]

Article 42

Access to the regulated market

1. Member States shall require the regulated market to establish and maintain transparent and non-discriminatory rules, based on objective criteria, governing access to or membership of the regulated market.

2. Those rules shall specify any obligations for the members or participants arising from:

(a) the constitution and administration of the regulated market;

(b) rules relating to transactions on the market;

(c) professional standards imposed on the staff of the investment firms or credit institutions that are operating on the market;
(d) the conditions established, for members or participants other than investment firms and credit institutions, under paragraph 3;
(e) the rules and procedures for the clearing and settlement of transactions concluded on the regulated market.

3. Regulated markets may admit as members or participants investment firms, credit institutions authorised under Directive 2000/12/EC and other persons who:
(a) are fit and proper;
(b) have a sufficient level of trading ability and competence;
(c) have, where applicable, adequate organisational arrangements;
(d) have sufficient resources for the role they are to perform, taking into account the different financial arrangements that the regulated market may have established in order to guarantee the adequate settlement of transactions.

4. Member States shall ensure that, for the transactions concluded on a regulated market, members and participants are not obliged to apply to each other the obligations laid down in Articles 19, 21 and 22. However, the members or participants of the regulated market shall apply the obligations provided for in Articles 19, 21 and 22 with respect to their clients when they, acting on behalf of their clients, execute their orders on a regulated market.

5. Member States shall ensure that the rules on access to or membership of the regulated market provide for the direct or remote participation of investment firms and credit institutions.

6. Member States shall, without further legal or administrative requirements, allow regulated markets from other Member States to provide appropriate arrangements on their territory so as to facilitate access to and trading on those markets by remote members or participants established in their territory.

The regulated market shall communicate to the competent authority of its home Member State the Member State in which it intends to provide such arrangements. The competent authority of the home Member State shall communicate, within one month, this information to the Member State in which the regulated market intends to provide such arrangements.

The competent authority of the home Member State of the regulated market shall, on the request of the competent authority of the host Member State and within a reasonable time, communicate the identity of the members or participants of the regulated market established in that Member State.

7. Member States shall require the operator of the regulated market to communicate, on a regular basis, the list of the members and participants of the regulated market to the competent authority of the regulated market.

[9658]

Article 43

Monitoring of compliance with the rules of the regulated market and with other legal obligations

1. Member States shall require that regulated markets establish and maintain effective arrangements and procedures for the regular monitoring of the compliance by their members or participants with their rules. Regulated markets shall monitor the transactions undertaken by their members or participants under their systems in order to identify breaches of those rules, disorderly trading conditions or conduct that may involve market abuse.

2. Member States shall require the operators of the regulated markets to report significant breaches of their rules or disorderly trading conditions or conduct that may involve market abuse to the competent authority of the regulated market. Member States shall also require the operator of the regulated market to supply the relevant information without delay to the authority competent for the investigation and prosecution of market abuse on the regulated market and to provide full assistance to the latter in investigating and prosecuting market abuse occurring on or through the systems of the regulated market.

[9659]

Article 44

Pre-trade transparency requirements for regulated markets

1. Member States shall, at least, require regulated markets to make public current bid and offer prices and the depth of trading interests at those prices which are advertised through

their systems for shares admitted to trading. Member States shall require this information to be made available to the public on reasonable commercial terms and on a continuous basis during normal trading hours.

Regulated markets may give access, on reasonable commercial terms and on a non-discriminatory basis, to the arrangements they employ for making public the information under the first subparagraph to investment firms which are obliged to publish their quotes in shares pursuant to Article 27.

2. Member States shall provide that the competent authorities are to be able to waive the obligation for regulated markets to make public the information referred to in paragraph 1 based on the market model or the type and size of orders in the cases defined in accordance with paragraph 3. In particular, the competent authorities shall be able to waive the obligation in respect of transactions that are large in scale compared with normal market size for the share or type of share in question.

3. In order to ensure the uniform application of paragraphs 1 and 2, the Commission shall, in accordance with the procedure referred to in Article 64(2) adopt implementing measures as regards:

(a) the range of bid and offers or designated market maker quotes, and the depth of trading interest at those prices, to be made public;

(b) the size or type of orders for which pre trade disclosure may be waived under paragraph 2;

(c) the market model for which pre-trade disclosure may be waived under paragraph 2, and in particular, the applicability of the obligation to trading methods operated by regulated markets which conclude transactions under their rules by reference to prices established outside the regulated market or by periodic auction.

[9660]

Article 45

Post-trade transparency requirements for regulated markets

1. Member States shall, at least, require regulated markets to make public the price, volume and time of the transactions executed in respect of shares admitted to trading. Member States shall require details of all such transactions to be made public, on a reasonable commercial basis and as close to real time as possible.

Regulated markets may give access, on reasonable commercial terms and on a non-discriminatory basis, to the arrangements they employ for making public the information under the first subparagraph to investment firms which are obliged to publish the details of their transactions in shares pursuant to Article 28.

2. Member States shall provide that the competent authority may authorise regulated markets to provide for deferred publication of the details of transactions based on their type or size. In particular, the competent authorities may authorise the deferred publication in respect of transactions that are large in scale compared with the normal market size for that share or that class of shares. Member States shall require regulated markets to obtain the competent authority's prior approval of proposed arrangements for deferred trade-publication, and shall require that these arrangements be clearly disclosed to market participants and the investing public.

3. In order to provide for the efficient and orderly functioning of financial markets, and to ensure the uniform application of paragraphs 1 and 2, the Commission shall, in accordance with the procedure referred to in Article 64(2) adopt implementing measures in respect of:

(a) the scope and content of the information to be made available to the public;

(b) the conditions under which a regulated market may provide for deferred publication of trades and the criteria to be applied when deciding the transactions for which, due to their size or the type of share involved, deferred publication is allowed.

[9661]

Article 46

Provisions regarding central counterparty and clearing and settlement arrangements

1. Member States shall not prevent regulated markets from entering into appropriate arrangements with a central counterparty or clearing house and a settlement system of another

Member State with a view to providing for the clearing and/or settlement of some or all trades concluded by market participants under their systems.

2. The competent authority of a regulated market may not oppose the use of central counterparty, clearing houses and/or settlement systems in another Member State except where this is demonstrably necessary in order to maintain the orderly functioning of that regulated market and taking into account the conditions for settlement systems established in Article 34(2).

In order to avoid undue duplication of control, the competent authority shall take into account the oversight/supervision of the clearing and settlement system already exercised by the national central banks as overseers of clearing and settlement systems or by other supervisory authorities with competence in relation to such systems.

[9662]

Article 47

List of regulated markets

Each Member State shall draw up a list of the regulated markets for which it is the home Member State and shall forward that list to the other Member States and the Commission. A similar communication shall be effected in respect of each change to that list. The Commission shall publish a list of all regulated markets in the *Official Journal of the European Union* and update it at least once a year. The Commission shall also publish and update the list at its website, each time the Member States communicate changes to their lists.

[9663]

TITLE IV
COMPETENT AUTHORITIES

CHAPTER I
DESIGNATION, POWERS AND REDRESS PROCEDURES

Article 48

Designation of competent authorities

1. Each Member State shall designate the competent authorities which are to carry out each of the duties provided for under the different provisions of this Directive. Member States shall inform the Commission and the competent authorities of other Member States of the identity of the competent authorities responsible for enforcement of each of those duties, and of any division of those duties.

2. The competent authorities referred to in paragraph 1 shall be public authorities, without prejudice to the possibility of delegating tasks to other entities where that is expressly provided for in Articles 5(5), 16(3), 17(2) and 23(4).

Any delegation of tasks to entities other than the authorities referred to in paragraph 1 may not involve either the exercise of public authority or the use of discretionary powers of judgement. Member States shall require that, prior to delegation, competent authorities take all reasonable steps to ensure that the entity to which tasks are to be delegated has the capacity and resources to effectively execute all tasks and that the delegation takes place only if a clearly defined and documented framework for the exercise of any delegated tasks has been established stating the tasks to be undertaken and the conditions under which they are to be carried out. These conditions shall include a clause obliging the entity in question to act and be organised in such a manner as to avoid conflict of interest and so that information obtained from carrying out the delegated tasks is not used unfairly or to prevent competition. In any case, the final responsibility for supervising compliance with this Directive and with its implementing measures shall lie with the competent authority or authorities designated in accordance with paragraph 1.

Member States shall inform the Commission and the competent authorities of other Member States of any arrangements entered into with regard to delegation of tasks, including the precise conditions regulating such delegation.

3. The Commission shall publish a list of the competent authorities referred to in paragraphs 1 and 2 in the *Official Journal of the European Union* at least once a year and update it continuously on its website.

[9664]

Article 49

Cooperation between authorities in the same Member State

If a Member State designates more than one competent authority to enforce a provision of this Directive, their respective roles shall be clearly defined and they shall cooperate closely.

Each Member State shall require that such cooperation also take place between the competent authorities for the purposes of this Directive and the competent authorities responsible in that Member State for the supervision of credit and other financial institutions, pension funds, UCITS, insurance and reinsurance intermediaries and insurance undertakings.

Member States shall require that competent authorities exchange any information which is essential or relevant to the exercise of their functions and duties.

[9665]

Article 50

Powers to be made available to competent authorities

1. Competent authorities shall be given all supervisory and investigatory powers that are necessary for the exercise of their functions. Within the limits provided for in their national legal frameworks they shall exercise such powers:

(a) directly; or

(b) in collaboration with other authorities; or

(c) under their responsibility by delegation to entities to which tasks have been delegated according to Article 48(2); or

(d) by application to the competent judicial authorities.

2. The powers referred to in paragraph 1 shall be exercised in conformity with national law and shall include, at least, the rights to:

(a) have access to any document in any form whatsoever and to receive a copy of it;

(b) demand information from any person and if necessary to summon and question a person with a view to obtaining information;

(c) carry out on-site inspections;

(d) require existing telephone and existing data traffic records;

(e) require the cessation of any practice that is contrary to the provisions adopted in the implementation of this Directive;

(f) request the freezing and/or the sequestration of assets;

(g) request temporary prohibition of professional activity;

(h) require authorised investment firms and regulated markets' auditors to provide information;

(i) adopt any type of measure to ensure that investment firms and regulated markets continue to comply with legal requirements;

(j) require the suspension of trading in a financial instrument;

(k) require the removal of a financial instrument from trading, whether on a regulated market or under other trading arrangements;

(l) refer matters for criminal prosecution;

(m) allow auditors or experts to carry out verifications or investigations.

[9666]

Article 51

Administrative sanctions

1. Without prejudice to the procedures for the withdrawal of authorisation or to the right of Member States to impose criminal sanctions, Member States shall ensure, in conformity with their national law, that the appropriate administrative measures can be taken or administrative sanctions be imposed against the persons responsible where the provisions adopted in the implementation of this Directive have not been complied with. Member States shall ensure that these measures are effective, proportionate and dissuasive.

2. Member States shall determine the sanctions to be applied for failure to cooperate in an investigation covered by Article 50.

3. Member States shall provide that the competent authority may disclose to the public any measure or sanction that will be imposed for infringement of the provisions adopted in

the implementation of this Directive, unless such disclosure would seriously jeopardise the financial markets or cause disproportionate damage to the parties involved.

[9667]

Article 52

Right of appeal

1. Member States shall ensure that any decision taken under laws, regulations or administrative provisions adopted in accordance with this Directive is properly reasoned and is subject to the right to apply to the courts. The right to apply to the courts shall also apply where, in respect of an application for authorisation which provides all the information required, no decision is taken within six months of its submission.

2. Member States shall provide that one or more of the following bodies, as determined by national law, may, in the interests of consumers and in accordance with national law, take action before the courts or competent administrative bodies to ensure that the national provisions for the implementation of this Directive are applied:

(a) public bodies or their representatives;
(b) consumer organisations having a legitimate interest in protecting consumers;
(c) professional organisations having a legitimate interest in acting to protect their members.

[9668]

Article 53

Extra-judicial mechanism for investors' complaints

1. Member States shall encourage the setting-up of efficient and effective complaints and redress procedures for the out-of-court settlement of consumer disputes concerning the provision of investment and ancillary services provided by investment firms, using existing bodies where appropriate.

2. Member States shall ensure that those bodies are not prevented by legal or regulatory provisions from cooperating effectively in the resolution of cross-border disputes.

[9669]

Article 54

Professional secrecy

1. Member States shall ensure that competent authorities, all persons who work or who have worked for the competent authorities or entities to whom tasks are delegated pursuant to Article 48(2), as well as auditors and experts instructed by the competent authorities, are bound by the obligation of professional secrecy. No confidential information which they may receive in the course of their duties may be divulged to any person or authority whatsoever, save in summary or aggregate form such that individual investment firms, market operators, regulated markets or any other person cannot be identified, without prejudice to cases covered by criminal law or the other provisions of this Directive.

2. Where an investment firm, market operator or regulated market has been declared bankrupt or is being compulsorily wound up, confidential information which does not concern third parties may be divulged in civil or commercial proceedings if necessary for carrying out the proceeding.

3. Without prejudice to cases covered by criminal law, the competent authorities, bodies or natural or legal persons other than competent authorities which receive confidential information pursuant to this Directive may use it only in the performance of their duties and for the exercise of their functions, in the case of the competent authorities, within the scope of this Directive or, in the case of other authorities, bodies or natural or legal persons, for the purpose for which such information was provided to them and/or in the context of administrative or judicial proceedings specifically related to the exercise of those functions. However, where the competent authority or other authority, body or person communicating information consents thereto, the authority receiving the information may use it for other purposes.

4. Any confidential information received, exchanged or transmitted pursuant to this Directive shall be subject to the conditions of professional secrecy laid down in this Article. Nevertheless, this Article shall not prevent the competent authorities from exchanging or

transmitting confidential information in accordance with this Directive and with other Directives applicable to investment firms, credit institutions, pension funds, UCITS, insurance and reinsurance intermediaries, insurance undertakings regulated markets or market operators or otherwise with the consent of the competent authority or other authority or body or natural or legal person that communicated the information.

5. This Article shall not prevent the competent authorities from exchanging or transmitting in accordance with national law, confidential information that has not been received from a competent authority of another Member State.

[9670]

Article 55

Relations with auditors

1. Member States shall provide, at least, that any person authorised within the meaning of Eighth Council Directive 84/253/EEC of 10 April 1984 on the approval of persons responsible for carrying out the statutory audits of accounting documents,[1] performing in an investment firm the task described in Article 51 of Fourth Council Directive 78/660/EEC of 25 July 1978 on the annual accounts of certain types of companies,[2] Article 37 of Directive 83/349/EEC or Article 31 of Directive 85/611/EEC or any other task prescribed by law, shall have a duty to report promptly to the competent authorities any fact or decision concerning that undertaking of which that person has become aware while carrying out that task and which is liable to:

(a) constitute a material breach of the laws, regulations or administrative provisions which lay down the conditions governing authorisation or which specifically govern pursuit of the activities of investment firms;
(b) affect the continuous functioning of the investment firm;
(c) lead to refusal to certify the accounts or to the expression of reservations.

That person shall also have a duty to report any facts and decisions of which the person becomes aware in the course of carrying out one of the tasks referred to in the first subparagraph in an undertaking having close links with the investment firm within which he is carrying out that task.

2. The disclosure in good faith to the competent authorities, by persons authorised within the meaning of Directive 84/253/EEC, of any fact or decision referred to in paragraph 1 shall not constitute a breach of any contractual or legal restriction on disclosure of information and shall not involve such persons in liability of any kind.

[9671]

NOTES

1 OJ L126, 12.5.1984, p 20.
2 OJ L222, 14.8.1978, p 11. Directive as last amended by Directive 2003/51/EC of the European Parliament and of the Council (OJ L178, 17.7.2003, p 16).

CHAPTER II
COOPERATION BETWEEN COMPETENT AUTHORITIES OF DIFFERENT MEMBER STATES

Article 56

Obligation to cooperate

1. Competent authorities of different Member States shall cooperate with each other whenever necessary for the purpose of carrying out their duties under this Directive, making use of their powers whether set out in this Directive or in national law.

Competent authorities shall render assistance to competent authorities of the other Member States. In particular, they shall exchange information and cooperate in any investigation or supervisory activities.

In order to facilitate and accelerate cooperation, and more particularly exchange of information, Member States shall designate one single competent authority as a contact point for the purposes of this Directive. Member States shall communicate to the Commission and to the other Member States the names of the authorities which are designated to receive requests for exchange of information or cooperation pursuant to this paragraph.

2. When, taking into account the situation of the securities markets in the host Member State, the operations of a regulated market that has established arrangements in a host Member State have become of substantial importance for the functioning of the securities markets and the protection of the investors in that host Member State, the home and host competent authorities of the regulated market shall establish proportionate cooperation arrangements.

3. Member States shall take the necessary administrative and organisational measures to facilitate the assistance provided for in paragraph 1.

Competent authorities may use their powers for the purpose of cooperation, even in cases where the conduct under investigation does not constitute an infringement of any regulation in force in that Member State.

4. Where a competent authority has good reasons to suspect that acts contrary to the provisions of this Directive, carried out by entities not subject to its supervision, are being or have been carried out on the territory of another Member State, it shall notify this in as specific a manner as possible to the competent authority of the other Member State. The latter authority shall take appropriate action. It shall inform the notifying competent authority of the outcome of the action and, to the extent possible, of significant interim developments. This paragraph shall be without prejudice to the competences of the competent authority that has forwarded the information.

5. In order to ensure the uniform application of paragraph 2 the Commission may adopt, in accordance with the procedure referred to in Article 64(2), implementing measures to establish the criteria under which the operations of a regulated market in a host Member State could be considered as of substantial importance for the functioning of the securities markets and the protection of the investors in that host Member State.

[9672]

Article 57

Cooperation in supervisory activities, on-the-spot verifications or in investigations

A competent authority of one Member State may request the cooperation of the competent authority of another Member State in a supervisory activity or for an on-the-spot verification or in an investigation. In the case of investment firms that are remote members of a regulated market the competent authority of the regulated market may choose to address them directly, in which case it shall inform the competent authority of the home Member State of the remote member accordingly.

Where a competent authority receives a request with respect to an on-the-spot verification or an investigation, it shall, within the framework of its powers:

(a) carry out the verifications or investigations itself; or
(b) allow the requesting authority to carry out the verification or investigation; or
(c) allow auditors or experts to carry out the verification or investigation.

[9673]

Article 58

Exchange of information

1. Competent authorities of Member States having been designated as contact points for the purposes of this Directive in accordance with Article 56(1) shall immediately supply one another with the information required for the purposes of carrying out the duties of the competent authorities, designated in accordance to Article 48(1), set out in the provisions adopted pursuant to this Directive.

Competent authorities exchanging information with other competent authorities under this Directive may indicate at the time of communication that such information must not be disclosed without their express agreement, in which case such information may be exchanged solely for the purposes for which those authorities gave their agreement.

2. The competent authority having been designated as the contact point may transmit the information received under paragraph 1 and Articles 55 and 63 to the authorities referred to in Article 49. They shall not transmit it to other bodies or natural or legal persons without the express agreement of the competent authorities which disclosed it and solely for the purposes for which those authorities gave their agreement, except in duly justified circumstances. In this last case, the contact point shall immediately inform the contact point that sent the information.

3. Authorities as referred to in Article 49 as well as other bodies or natural and legal persons receiving confidential information under paragraph 1 of this Article or under Articles 55 and 63 may use it only in the course of their duties, in particular:

(a) to check that the conditions governing the taking-up of the business of investment firms are met and to facilitate the monitoring, on a non-consolidated or consolidated basis, of the conduct of that business, especially with regard to the capital adequacy requirements imposed by Directive 93/6/EEC, administrative and accounting procedures and internal-control mechanisms;

(b) to monitor the proper functioning of trading venues;

(c) to impose sanctions;

(d) in administrative appeals against decisions by the competent authorities;

(e) in court proceedings initiated under Article 52; or

(f) in the extra-judicial mechanism for investors' complaints provided for in Article 53.

4. The Commission may adopt, in accordance with the procedure referred to in Article 64(2), implementing measures concerning procedures for the exchange of information between competent authorities.

5. Articles 54, 58 and 63 shall not prevent a competent authority from transmitting to central banks, the European System of Central Banks and the European Central Bank, in their capacity as monetary authorities, and, where appropriate, to other public authorities responsible for overseeing payment and settlement systems, confidential information intended for the performance of their tasks; likewise such authorities or bodies shall not be prevented from communicating to the competent authorities such information as they may need for the purpose of performing their functions provided for in this Directive.

[9674]

Article 59

Refusal to cooperate

A competent authority may refuse to act on a request for cooperation in carrying out an investigation, on-the-spot verification or supervisory activity as provided for in Article 57 or to exchange information as provided for in Article 58 only where:

(a) such an investigation, on-the-spot verification, supervisory activity or exchange of information might adversely affect the sovereignty, security or public policy of the State addressed;

(b) judicial proceedings have already been initiated in respect of the same actions and the same persons before the authorities of the Member State addressed;

(c) final judgment has already been delivered in the Member State addressed in respect of the same persons and the same actions.

In the case of such a refusal, the competent authority shall notify the requesting competent authority accordingly, providing as detailed information as possible.

[9675]

Article 60

Inter-authority consultation prior to authorisation

1. The competent authorities of the other Member State involved shall be consulted prior to granting authorisation to an investment firm which is:

(a) a subsidiary of an investment firm or credit institution authorised in another Member State; or

(b) a subsidiary of the parent undertaking of an investment firm or credit institution authorised in another Member State; or

(c) controlled by the same natural or legal persons as control an investment firm or credit institution authorised in another Member State.

2. The competent authority of the Member State responsible for the supervision of credit institutions or insurance undertakings shall be consulted prior to granting an authorisation to an investment firm which is:

(a) a subsidiary of a credit institution or insurance undertaking authorised in the Community; or

(b) a subsidiary of the parent undertaking of a credit institution or insurance undertaking authorised in the Community; or

(c) controlled by the same person, whether natural or legal, who controls a credit institution or insurance undertaking authorised in the Community.

3. The relevant competent authorities referred to in paragraphs 1 and 2 shall in particular consult each other when assessing the suitability of the shareholders or members and the reputation and experience of persons who effectively direct the business involved in the management of another entity of the same group. They shall exchange all information regarding the suitability of shareholders or members and the reputation and experience of persons who effectively direct the business that is of relevance to the other competent authorities involved, for the granting of an authorisation as well as for the ongoing assessment of compliance with operating conditions.

[9676]

Article 61

Powers for host Member States

1. Host Member States may, for statistical purposes, require all investment firms with branches within their territories to report to them periodically on the activities of those branches.

2. In discharging their responsibilities under this Directive, host Member States may require branches of investment firms to provide the information necessary for the monitoring of their compliance with the standards set by the host Member State that apply to them for the cases provided for in Article 32(7). Those requirements may not be more stringent than those which the same Member State imposes on established firms for the monitoring of their compliance with the same standards.

[9677]

Article 62

Precautionary measures to be taken by host Member States

1. Where the competent authority of the host Member State has clear and demonstrable grounds for believing that an investment firm acting within its territory under the freedom to provide services is in breach of the obligations arising from the provisions adopted pursuant to this Directive or that an investment firm that has a branch within its territory is in breach of the obligations arising from the provisions adopted pursuant to this Directive which do not confer powers on the competent authority of the host Member State, it shall refer those findings to the competent authority of the home Member State.

If, despite the measures taken by the competent authority of the home Member State or because such measures prove inadequate, the investment firm persists in acting in a manner that is clearly prejudicial to the interests of host Member State investors or the orderly functioning of markets, the competent authority of the host Member State, after informing the competent authority of the home Member State shall take all the appropriate measures needed in order to protect investors and the proper functioning of the markets. This shall include the possibility of preventing offending investment firms from initiating any further transactions within their territories. The Commission shall be informed of such measures without delay.

2. Where the competent authorities of a host Member State ascertain that an investment firm that has a branch within its territory is in breach of the legal or regulatory provisions adopted in that State pursuant to those provisions of this Directive which confer powers on the host Member State's competent authorities, those authorities shall require the investment firm concerned to put an end to its irregular situation.

If the investment firm concerned fails to take the necessary steps, the competent authorities of the host Member State shall take all appropriate measures to ensure that the investment firm concerned puts an end to its irregular situation. The nature of those measures shall be communicated to the competent authorities of the home Member State.

If, despite the measures taken by the host Member State, the investment firm persists in breaching the legal or regulatory provisions referred to in the first subparagraph in force in the host Member State, the latter may, after informing the competent authorities of the home Member State, take appropriate measures to prevent or to penalise further irregularities and, in so far as necessary, to prevent that investment firm from initiating any further transactions within its territory. The Commission shall be informed of such measures without delay.

3. Where the competent authority of the host Member State of a regulated market or an MTF has clear and demonstrable grounds for believing that such regulated market or MTF is

in breach of the obligations arising from the provisions adopted pursuant to this Directive, it shall refer those findings to the competent authority of the home Member State of the regulated market or the MTF.

If, despite the measures taken by the competent authority of the home Member State or because such measures prove inadequate, the said regulated market or the MTF persists in acting in a manner that is clearly prejudicial to the interests of host Member State investors or the orderly functioning of markets, the competent authority of the host Member State, after informing the competent authority of the home Member State, shall take all the appropriate measures needed in order to protect investors and the proper functioning of the markets. This shall include the possibility of preventing the said regulated market or the MTF from making their arrangements available to remote members or participants established in the host Member State. The Commission shall be informed of such measures without delay.

4. Any measure adopted pursuant to paragraphs 1, 2 or 3 involving sanctions or restrictions on the activities of an investment firm or of a regulated market shall be properly justified and communicated to the investment firm or to the regulated market concerned.

[9678]

CHAPTER III
COOPERATION WITH THIRD COUNTRIES

Article 63

Exchange of information with third countries

1. Member States may conclude cooperation agreements providing for the exchange of information with the competent authorities of third countries only if the information disclosed is subject to guarantees of professional secrecy at least equivalent to those required under Article 54. Such exchange of information must be intended for the performance of the tasks of those competent authorities.

Member States may transfer personal data to a third country in accordance to Chapter IV of Directive 95/46/EC.

Member States may also conclude cooperation agreements providing for the exchange of information with third country authorities, bodies and natural or legal persons responsible for:

(i) the supervision of credit institutions, other financial organisations, insurance undertakings and the supervision of financial markets;
(ii) the liquidation and bankruptcy of investment firms and other similar procedures;
(iii) carrying out statutory audits of the accounts of investment firms and other financial institutions, credit institutions and insurance undertakings, in the performance of their supervisory functions, or which administer compensation schemes, in the performance of their functions;
(iv) overseeing the bodies involved in the liquidation and bankruptcy of investment firms and other similar procedures;
(v) overseeing persons charged with carrying out statutory audits of the accounts of insurance undertakings, credit institutions, investment firms and other financial institutions,

only if the information disclosed is subject to guarantees of professional secrecy at least equivalent to those required under Article 54. Such exchange of information must be intended for the performance of the tasks of those authorities or bodies or natural or legal persons.

2. Where the information originates in another Member State, it may not be disclosed without the express agreement of the competent authorities which have transmitted it and, where appropriate, solely for the purposes for which those authorities gave their agreement. The same provision applies to information provided by third country competent authorities.

[9679]

TITLE V
FINAL PROVISIONS

Article 64

Committee procedure

1. The Commission shall be assisted by the European Securities Committee established by Commission Decision 2001/528/EC[1] (hereinafter referred to as the Committee).

2. Where reference is made to this paragraph, Articles 5 and 7 of Decision 1999/468/EC shall apply, having regard to the provisions of Article 8 thereof, provided that the implementing measures adopted in accordance with that procedure do not modify the essential provisions of this Directive.

The period laid down in Article 5(6) of Decision 1999/468/EC shall be set at three months.

[2a. None of the implementing measures enacted may change the essential provisions of this Directive.]

[3. Without prejudice to the implementing measures already adopted, on 1 April 2008 at the latest, the application of this Directive's provisions requiring the adoption of technical rules, amendments and decisions in accordance with paragraph 2 shall be suspended. Acting on a proposal from the Commission, the European Parliament and the Council may renew the provisions concerned in accordance with the procedure laid down in Article 251 of the Treaty and, to that end, they shall review them prior to the date referred to above.]

[9680]

NOTES

Para 2a inserted, and para 3 substituted, by European Parliament and Council Directive 2006/31/EC, Art 1(2), as from 28 April 2006.

[1] OJ L191, 13.7.2001, p 45.

[Article 65

Reports and review

1. By 31 October 2007, the Commission shall, on the basis of public consultation and in the light of discussions with competent authorities, report to the European Parliament and to the Council on the possible extension of the scope of the provisions of this Directive concerning pre and post-trade transparency obligations to transactions in classes of financial instruments other than shares.

2. By 31 October 2008, the Commission shall present the European Parliament and the Council with a report on the application of Article 27.

3. By 30 April 2008, the Commission shall, on the basis of public consultations and in the light of discussions with competent authorities, report to the European Parliament and to the Council on:

(a) the continued appropriateness of the exemption provided for in Article 2(1)(k) for undertakings whose main business is dealing on own account in commodity derivatives;

(b) the content and form of proportionate requirements for the authorisation and supervision of such undertakings as investment firms within the meaning of this Directive;

(c) the appropriateness of rules concerning the appointment of tied agents in performing investment services and/or activities, in particular with respect to the supervision of them;

(d) the continued appropriateness of the exemption provided for in Article 2(1)(i).

4. By 30 April 2008, the Commission shall present the European Parliament and the Council with a report on the state of the removal of the obstacles which may prevent the consolidation at European level of the information that trading venues are required to publish.

5. On the basis of the reports referred to in paragraphs 1 to 4, the Commission may submit proposals for related amendments to this Directive.

6. By 31 October 2006, the Commission shall, in the light of discussions with competent authorities, report to the European Parliament and to the Council on the continued appropriateness of the requirements for professional indemnity insurance imposed on intermediaries under Community law.]

[9681]

NOTES

Substituted by European Parliament and Council Directive 2006/31/EC, Art 1(3), as from 28 April 2006.

Articles 66–68

(Article 66 amends Council Directive 85/611/EEC, Art 5; Article 67 repealed by European Parliament and Council Directive 2006/49/EC, Art 52, Annex VIII, as from 20 July 2006; Article 68 repealed by European Parliament and Council Directive 2006/48/EC, Art 158, Annex XIII, as from 20 July 2006.)

[Article 69

Repeal of Directive 93/22/EEC

Directive 93/22/EEC shall be repealed with effect from 1 November 2007. References to Directive 93/22/EEC shall be construed as references to this Directive. References to terms defined in, or Articles of, Directive 93/22/EEC shall be construed as references to the equivalent term defined in, or Article of, this Directive.]

[9682]

NOTES

Substituted by European Parliament and Council Directive 2006/31/EC, Art 1(4), as from 28 April 2006.

Article 70

Transposition

[Member States shall adopt the laws, regulations and administrative provisions necessary to comply with this Directive by 31 January 2007. They shall forthwith inform the Commission thereof.

They shall apply these measures from 1 November 2007.]

When Member States adopt these measures, they shall contain a reference to this Directive or shall be accompanied by such reference on the occasion of their official publication. The methods of making such reference shall be laid down by the Member States.

[9683]

NOTES

Words in square brackets substituted by European Parliament and Council Directive 2006/31/EC, Art 1(5), as from 28 April 2006.

Article 71

Transitional provisions

[1. Investment firms already authorised in their home Member State to provide investment services before 1 November 2007 shall be deemed to be so authorised for the purposes of this Directive if the laws of that Member State provide that to take up such activities they must comply with conditions comparable to those provided for in Articles 9 to 14.

2. A regulated market or a market operator already authorised in its home Member State before 1 November 2007 shall be deemed to be so authorised for the purposes of this Directive if the laws of that Member State provide that the regulated market or market operator, as the case may be, must comply with conditions comparable to those provided for in Title III.

3. Tied agents already entered in a public register before 1 November 2007 shall be deemed to be so registered for the purposes of this Directive if the laws of Member States concerned provide that tied agents must comply with conditions comparable to those provided for in Article 23.

4. Information communicated before 1 November 2007 for the purposes of Articles 17, 18 or 30 of Directive 93/22/EEC shall be deemed to have been communicated for the purposes of Articles 31 and 32 of this Directive.

5. Any existing system falling under the definition of an MTF operated by a market operator of a regulated market shall, at the request of the market operator of the regulated market, be authorised as an MTF, provided that it complies with rules equivalent to those

required by this Directive for the authorisation and operation of MTFs and that the request concerned is made within eighteen months following 1 November 2007.]

6. Investment firms shall be authorised to continue considering existing professional clients as such provided that this categorisation has been granted by the investment firm on the basis of an adequate assessment of the expertise, experience and knowledge of the client which gives reasonable assurance, in light of the nature of the transactions or services envisaged, that the client is capable of making his own investment decisions and understands the risks involved. Those investment firms shall inform their clients about the conditions established in the Directive for the categorisation of clients.

[9684]

NOTES

Paras 1–5: substituted by European Parliament and Council Directive 2006/31/EC, Art 1(6), as from 28 April 2006.

Article 72

Entry into force

This Directive shall enter into force on the day of its publication in the *Official Journal of the European Union.*

[9685]

Article 73

Addressees

This Directive is addressed to the Member States.

[9686]

Done at Strasbourg, 21 April 2004.

ANNEX I
LIST OF SERVICES AND ACTIVITIES AND FINANCIAL INSTRUMENTS

SECTION A
INVESTMENT SERVICES AND ACTIVITIES

(1) Reception and transmission of orders in relation to one or more financial instruments.

(2) Execution of orders on behalf of clients.

(3) Dealing on own account.

(4) Portfolio management.

(5) Investment advice.

(6) Underwriting of financial instruments and/or placing of financial instruments on a firm commitment basis.

(7) Placing of financial instruments without a firm commitment basis

(8) Operation of Multilateral Trading Facilities.

[9687]

SECTION B
ANCILLARY SERVICES

(1) Safekeeping and administration of financial instruments for the account of clients, including custodianship and related services such as cash/collateral management;

(2) Granting credits or loans to an investor to allow him to carry out a transaction in one or more financial instruments, where the firm granting the credit or loan is involved in the transaction;

(3) Advice to undertakings on capital structure, industrial strategy and related matters and advice and services relating to mergers and the purchase of undertakings;

(4) Foreign exchange services where these are connected to the provision of investment services;

(5) Investment research and financial analysis or other forms of general recommendation relating to transactions in financial instruments;

(6) Services related to underwriting.

(7) Investment services and activities as well as ancillary services of the type included under Section A or B of Annex 1 related to the underlying of the derivatives included under Section C—5, 6, 7 and 10—where these are connected to the provision of investment or ancillary services.

[9688]

SECTION C
FINANCIAL INSTRUMENTS

(1) Transferable securities;

(2) Money-market instruments;

(3) Units in collective investment undertakings;

(4) Options, futures, swaps, forward rate agreements and any other derivative contracts relating to securities, currencies, interest rates or yields, or other derivatives instruments, financial indices or financial measures which may be settled physically or in cash;

(5) Options, futures, swaps, forward rate agreements and any other derivative contracts relating to commodities that must be settled in cash or may be settled in cash at the option of one of the parties (otherwise than by reason of a default or other termination event);

(6) Options, futures, swaps, and any other derivative contract relating to commodities that can be physically settled provided that they are traded on a regulated market and/or an MTF;

(7) Options, futures, swaps, forwards and any other derivative contracts relating to commodities, that can be physically settled not otherwise mentioned in C.6 and not being for commercial purposes, which have the characteristics of other derivative financial instruments, having regard to whether, inter alia, they are cleared and settled through recognised clearing houses or are subject to regular margin calls;

(8) Derivative instruments for the transfer of credit risk;

(9) Financial contracts for differences.

(10) Options, futures, swaps, forward rate agreements and any other derivative contracts relating to climatic variables, freight rates, emission allowances or inflation rates or other official economic statistics that must be settled in cash or may be settled in cash at the option of one of the parties (otherwise than by reason of a default or other termination event), as well as any other derivative contracts relating to assets, rights, obligations, indices and measures not otherwise mentioned in this Section, which have the characteristics of other derivative financial instruments, having regard to whether, inter alia, they are traded on a regulated market or an MTF, are cleared and settled through recognised clearing houses or are subject to regular margin calls.

[9689]

ANNEX II
PROFESSIONAL CLIENTS FOR THE PURPOSE OF THIS DIRECTIVE

Professional client is a client who possesses the experience, knowledge and expertise to make its own investment decisions and properly assess the risks that it incurs. In order to be considered a professional client, the client must comply with the following criteria:

I. Categories of client who are considered to be professionals

The following should all be regarded as professionals in all investment services and activities and financial instruments for the purposes of the Directive.

(1) Entities which are required to be authorised or regulated to operate in the financial markets. The list below should be understood as including all authorised entities carrying out the characteristic activities of the entities mentioned: entities authorised by a Member State under a Directive, entities authorised or regulated by a Member State without reference to a Directive, and entities authorised or regulated by a non-Member State:

(a) Credit institutions

(b) Investment firms
(c) Other authorised or regulated financial institutions
(d) Insurance companies
(e) Collective investment schemes and management companies of such schemes
(f) Pension funds and management companies of such funds
(g) Commodity and commodity derivatives dealers
(h) Locals
(i) Other institutional investors

(2) Large undertakings meeting two of the following size requirements on a company basis:
— balance sheet total: EUR 20,000,000,
— net turnover: EUR 40,000,000,
— own funds: EUR 2,000,000.

(3) National and regional governments, public bodies that manage public debt, Central Banks, international and supranational institutions such as the World Bank, the IMF, the ECB, the EIB and other similar international organisations.

(4) Other institutional investors whose main activity is to invest in financial instruments, including entities dedicated to the securitisation of assets or other financing transactions.

The entities mentioned above are considered to be professionals. They must however be allowed to request non-professional treatment and investment firms may agree to provide a higher level of protection. Where the client of an investment firm is an undertaking referred to above, the investment firm must inform it prior to any provision of services that, on the basis of the information available to the firm, the client is deemed to be a professional client, and will be treated as such unless the firm and the client agree otherwise. The firm must also inform the customer that he can request a variation of the terms of the agreement in order to secure a higher degree of protection.

It is the responsibility of the client, considered to be a professional client, to ask for a higher level of protection when it deems it is unable to properly assess or manage the risks involved.

This higher level of protection will be provided when a client who is considered to be a professional enters into a written agreement with the investment firm to the effect that it shall not be treated as a professional for the purposes of the applicable conduct of business regime. Such agreement should specify whether this applies to one or more particular services or transactions, or to one or more types of product or transaction.

II. Clients who may be treated as professionals on request

II.1. Identification criteria

Clients other than those mentioned in section I, including public sector bodies and private individual investors, may also be allowed to waive some of the protections afforded by the conduct of business rules.

Investment firms should therefore be allowed to treat any of the above clients as professionals provided the relevant criteria and procedure mentioned below are fulfilled. These clients should not, however, be presumed to possess market knowledge and experience comparable to that of the categories listed in section I.

Any such waiver of the protection afforded by the standard conduct of business regime shall be considered valid only if an adequate assessment of the expertise, experience and knowledge of the client, undertaken by the investment firm, gives reasonable assurance, in light of the nature of the transactions or services envisaged, that the client is capable of making his own investment decisions and understanding the risks involved.

The fitness test applied to managers and directors of entities licensed under Directives in the financial field could be regarded as an example of the assessment of expertise and knowledge. In the case of small entities, the person subject to the above assessment should be the person authorised to carry out transactions on behalf of the entity.

In the course of the above assessment, as a minimum, two of the following criteria should be satisfied:
— the client has carried out transactions, in significant size, on the relevant market at an average frequency of 10 per quarter over the previous four quarters,
— the size of the client's financial instrument portfolio, defined as including cash deposits and financial instruments exceeds EUR 500,000,

— the client works or has worked in the financial sector for at least one year in a professional position, which requires knowledge of the transactions or services envisaged.

II.2. Procedure

The clients defined above may waive the benefit of the detailed rules of conduct only where the following procedure is followed:

— they must state in writing to the investment firm that they wish to be treated as a professional client, either generally or in respect of a particular investment service or transaction, or type of transaction or product,

— the investment firm must give them a clear written warning of the protections and investor compensation rights they may lose,

— they must state in writing, in a separate document from the contract, that they are aware of the consequences of losing such protections.

Before deciding to accept any request for waiver, investment firms must be required to take all reasonable steps to ensure that the client requesting to be treated as a professional client meets the relevant requirements stated in Section II.1 above.

However, if clients have already been categorised as professionals under parameters and procedures similar to those above, it is not intended that their relationships with investment firms should be affected by any new rules adopted pursuant to this Annex.

Firms must implement appropriate written internal policies and procedures to categorise clients. Professional clients are responsible for keeping the firm informed about any change, which could affect their current categorisation. Should the investment firm become aware however that the client no longer fulfils the initial conditions, which made him eligible for a professional treatment, the investment firm must take appropriate action.

[9690]

COMMISSION DIRECTIVE

of 29 April 2004

implementing Directive 2003/6/EC of the European Parliament and of the Council as regards accepted market practices, the definition of inside information in relation to derivatives on commodities, the drawing up of lists of insiders, the notification of managers' transactions and the notification of suspicious transactions

(2004/72/EC)

(Text with EEA relevance)

NOTES

Date of publication in OJ: OJ L162, 30.4.2004, p 70. Notes are as in the original OJ version.

THE COMMISSION OF THE EUROPEAN COMMUNITIES,

Having regard to the Treaty establishing the European Community,

Having regard to Directive 2003/6/EC of the European Parliament and of the Council of 28 January 2003 on insider dealing and market manipulation (market abuse)[1], and in particular the second paragraph of point 1 and point 2(a) of Article 1 and the fourth, fifth and seventh indents of Article 6(10) thereof,

After consulting the Committee of European Securities Regulators (CESR)[2] for technical advice,

Whereas:

(1) Practising fairness and efficiency by market participants is required in order not to create prejudice to normal market activity and market integrity. In particular, market practices inhibiting the interaction of supply and demand by limiting the opportunities for other market participants to respond to transactions can create higher risks for market integrity and are, therefore, less likely to be accepted by competent authorities. On the other hand, market practices which enhance liquidity are more likely to be accepted than those practices reducing them. Market practices breaching rules and regulations designed to prevent market abuse, or

codes of conduct, are less likely to be accepted by competent authorities. Since market practices change rapidly in order to meet investors' needs, competent authorities need to be alert to new and emerging market practice.

(2) Transparency of market practices by market participants is crucial for considering whether a particular market practice can be accepted by competent authorities. The less transparent a practice is, the more likely it is not to be accepted. However, practices on non regulated markets might for structural reasons be less transparent than similar practices on regulated markets. Such practices should not be in themselves considered as unacceptable by competent authorities.

(3) Particular market practices in a given market should not put at risk market integrity of other, directly or indirectly, related markets throughout the Community, whether those markets be regulated or not. Therefore, the higher the risk for market integrity on such a related market within the Community, the less those practices are likely to be accepted by competent authorities.

(4) Competent authorities, while considering the acceptance of a particular market practice, should consult other competent authorities, particularly for cases where there exist comparable markets to the one under scrutiny. However, there might be circumstances in which a market practice can be deemed to be acceptable on one particular market and unacceptable on another comparable market within the Community. In case of discrepancies between market practices which are accepted in one Member State and not in another one, discussion could take place in the Committee of European Securities Regulators in order to find a solution. With regard to their decisions about such acceptance, competent authorities should ensure a high degree of consultation and transparency vis-à-vis market participants and end-users.

(5) It is essential for market participants on derivative markets the underlying of which is not a financial instrument, to get greater legal certainty on what constitutes inside information.

(6) The establishment, by issuers or persons acting on their behalf or for their account, of lists of persons working for them under a contract of employment or otherwise and having access to inside information relating, directly or indirectly, to the issuer, is a valuable measure for protecting market integrity. These lists may serve issuers or such persons to control the flow of such inside information and thereby manage their confidentiality duties. Moreover, these lists may also constitute a useful tool for competent authorities when monitoring the application of market abuse legislation. Identifying inside information to which any insider has access and the date on which it gained access thereto is necessary for issuers and competent authorities. Access to inside information relating, directly or indirectly, to the issuer by persons included on such a list is without prejudice to their duty to refrain from insider dealing on the basis of any inside information as defined in Directive 2003/6/EC.

(7) The notification of transactions conducted by persons discharging managerial responsibilities within an issuer on their own account, or by persons closely associated with them, is not only a valuable information for market participants, but also constitutes an additional means for competent authorities to supervise markets. The obligation by senior executives to notify transactions is without prejudice to their duty to refrain from insider dealing on the basis of any inside information as defined in Directive 2003/6/EC.

(8) Notification of transactions should be in accordance with the rules on transfer of personal data laid down in Directive 95/46/EC[3] of the European Parliament and of the Council of 24 October 1995 on the protection of individuals with regard to the processing of personal data and on the movement of such data.

(9) Notification of suspicious transactions by persons professionally arranging transactions in financial instruments to the competent authority requires sufficient indications that the transactions might constitute market abuse, ie transactions which give reasonable ground for suspecting that insider dealing or market manipulation is involved. Certain transactions by themselves may seem completely void of anything suspicious, but might deliver such indications of possible market abuse, when seen in perspective with other transactions, certain behaviour or other information.

(10) This Directive respects the fundamental rights and observes the principles recognised in particular by the Charta of Fundamental Rights of the European Union and in particular by Article 8 of the European Convention on Human Rights.

(11) The measures provided for in this Directive are in accordance with the opinion of the European Securities Committee,

[9691]

NOTES

[1] OJ L96, 12.4.2003, p 16.

[2] CESR was established by Commission Decision 2001/527/EC of 6 June 2001 (OJ L191, 13.7.2001, p 43).
[3] OJ L281, 23.11.1995, p 31.

HAVE ADOPTED THIS DIRECTIVE—

Article 1

Definitions

For the purpose of applying Article 6(10) of Directive 2003/6/EC:

1. 'Person discharging managerial responsibilities within an issuer' shall mean a person who is
   (a) a member of the administrative, management or supervisory bodies of the issuer;
   (b) a senior executive, who is not a member of the bodies as referred to in point (a), having regular access to inside information relating, directly or indirectly, to the issuer, and the power to make managerial decisions affecting the future developments and business prospects of this issuer.
2. 'Person closely associated with a person discharging managerial responsibilities within an issuer of financial instruments' shall mean:
   (a) the spouse of the person discharging managerial responsibilities, or any partner of that person considered by national law as equivalent to the spouse;
   (b) according to national law, dependent children of the person discharging managerial responsibilities;
   (c) other relatives of the person discharging managerial responsibilities, who have shared the same household as that person for at least one year on the date of the transaction concerned;
   (d) any legal person, trust or partnership, whose managerial responsibilities are discharged by a person referred to in point 1 of this Article or in letters (a), (b) and (c) of this point, or which is directly or indirectly controlled by such a person, or that is set up for the benefit of such a person, or whose economic interests are substantially equivalent to those of such person.
3. 'Person professionally arranging transactions' shall mean at least an investment firm or a credit institution.
4. 'Investment firm' shall mean any person as defined in Article 1(2) of Council Directive 93/22/EEC;[1]
5. 'Credit institution' shall mean any person as defined in Article 1(1) of Directive 2000/12/EC of the European Parliament and of the Council;[2]
6. 'Competent authority' shall mean the competent authority as defined in Article 1(7) of Directive 2003/6/EC.

[9692]

NOTES

[1] OJ L141, 11.6.1993, p 27.
[2] OJ L126, 26.5.2000, p 1.

Article 2

Factors to be taken into account when considering market practices

1. For the purposes of applying paragraph 2 of point 1 and point 2(a) of Article 1 of Directive 2003/6/EC, Member States shall ensure that the following non exhaustive factors are taken into account by competent authorities, without prejudice to collaboration with other authorities, when assessing whether they can accept a particular market practice:

(a) the level of transparency of the relevant market practice to the whole market;
(b) the need to safeguard the operation of market forces and the proper interplay of the forces of supply and demand;
(c) the degree to which the relevant market practice has an impact on market liquidity and efficiency;
(d) the degree to which the relevant practice takes into account the trading mechanism of the relevant market and enables market participants to react properly and in a timely manner to the new market situation created by that practice;

(e) the risk inherent in the relevant practice for the integrity of, directly or indirectly, related markets, whether regulated or not, in the relevant financial instrument within the whole Community;

(f) the outcome of any investigation of the relevant market practice by any competent authority or other authority mentioned in Article 12(1) of Directive 2003/6/EC, in particular whether the relevant market practice breached rules or regulations designed to prevent market abuse, or codes of conduct, be it on the market in question or on directly or indirectly related markets within the Community;

(g) the structural characteristics of the relevant market including whether it is regulated or not, the types of financial instruments traded and the type of market participants, including the extent of retail investors participation in the relevant market.

Member States shall ensure that competent authorities shall, when considering the need for safeguard referred to in point (b) of the first subparagraph, in particular analyse the impact of the relevant market practice against the main market parameters, such as the specific market conditions before carrying out the relevant market practice, the weighted average price of a single session or the daily closing price.

2. Member States shall ensure that practices, in particular new or emerging market practices are not assumed to be unacceptable by the competent authority simply because they have not been previously accepted by it.

3. Member States shall ensure that competent authorities review regularly the market practices they have accepted, in particular taking into account significant changes to the relevant market environment, such as changes to trading rules or to market infrastructure.

[9693]

Article 3

Consultation procedures and disclosure of decisions

1. For the purposes of applying paragraph 2 of point 1 and point 2(a) of Article 1 of Directive 2003/6/EC, Member States shall ensure that the procedures set out in paragraphs 2 and 3 of this Article are observed by competent authorities when considering whether to accept or continue to accept a particular market practice.

2. Without prejudice to Article 11(2) of Directive 2003/6/EC, Member States shall ensure that competent authorities, before accepting or not the market practice concerned, consult as appropriate relevant bodies such as representatives of issuers, financial services providers, consumers, other authorities and market operators.

The consultation procedure shall include consultation of other competent authorities, in particular where there exist comparable markets, ie in structures, volume, type of transactions.

3. Member States shall ensure that competent authorities publicly disclose their decisions regarding the acceptability of the market practice concerned, including appropriate descriptions of such practices. Member States shall further ensure that competent authorities transmit their decisions as soon as possible to the Committee of European Securities Regulators which shall make them immediately available on its website.

The disclosure shall include a description of the factors taken into account in determining whether the relevant practice is regarded as acceptable, in particular where different conclusions have been reached regarding the acceptability of the same practice on different Member States markets.

4. When investigatory actions on specific cases have already started, the consultation procedures set out in paragraphs 1 to 3 may be delayed until the end of such investigation and possible related sanctions.

5. A market practice which was accepted following the consultation procedures set out in paragraphs 1 to 3 shall not be changed without using the same consultation procedures.

[9694]

Article 4

Inside information in relation to derivatives on commodities

For the purposes of applying the second paragraph of point 1 of Article 1 of Directive 2003/6/EC, users of markets on which derivatives on commodities are traded, are deemed to expect to receive information relating, directly or indirectly, to one or more such derivatives which is:

(a) routinely made available to the users of those markets, or
(b) required to be disclosed in accordance with legal or regulatory provisions, market rules, contracts or customs on the relevant underlying commodity market or commodity derivatives market.

[9695]

Article 5

Lists of insiders

1. For the purposes of applying the third subparagraph of Article 6(3) of Directive 2003/6/EC, Member States shall ensure that lists of insiders include all persons covered by that Article who have access to inside information relating, directly or indirectly, to the issuer, whether on a regular or occasional basis.

2. Lists of insiders shall state at least:
(a) the identity of any person having access to inside information;
(b) the reason why any such person is on the list;
(c) the date at which the list of insiders was created and updated.

3. Lists of insiders shall be promptly updated:
(a) whenever there is a change in the reason why any person is already on the list;
(b) whenever any new person has to be added to the list;
(c) by mentioning whether and when any person already on the list has no longer access to inside information.

4. Member States shall ensure that lists of insiders will be kept for at least five years after being drawn up or updated.

5. Member States shall ensure that the persons required to draw up lists of insiders take the necessary measures to ensure that any person on such a list that has access to inside information acknowledges the legal and regulatory duties entailed and is aware of the sanctions attaching to the misuse or improper circulation of such information.

[9696]

Article 6

Managers' Transactions

1. For the purposes of applying Article 6(4) of Directive 2003/6/EC, and without prejudice to the right of Member States to provide for other notification obligations than those covered by that Article, Member States shall ensure that all transactions related to shares admitted to trading on a regulated market, or to derivatives or other financial instruments linked to them, conducted on the own account of persons referred to in Article 1 points 1 and 2 above, are notified to the competent authorities. The rules of notification to which those persons have to comply with shall be those of the Member State where the issuer is registered. The notification shall be made within five working days of the transaction date to the competent authority of that Member State. When the issuer is not registered in a Member State, this notification shall be made to the competent authority of the Member State in which it is required to file the annual information in relation to the shares in accordance with Article 10 of Directive 2003/71/EC.

2. Member States may decide that, until the total amount of transactions has reached five thousand Euros at the end of a calendar year, no notification is required or notification may be delayed until the 31 January of the following year. The total amount of transactions shall be computed by summing up the transactions conducted on the own account of persons referred to in Article 1 point 1 with the transactions conducted on the own account of persons referred to in Article 1 point 2.

3. The notification shall contain the following information:
(a) name of the person discharging managerial responsibilities within the issuer, or, where applicable, name of the person closely associated with such a person,
(b) reason for responsibility to notify,
(c) name of the relevant issuer,
(d) description of the financial instrument,
(e) nature of the transaction (e g acquisition or disposal),
(f) date and place of the transaction
(g) price and volume of the transaction.

[9697]

Article 7

Suspicious transactions to be notified

For the purposes of applying Article 6(9) of Directive 2003/6/EC, Member States shall ensure that persons referred to in Article 1 point 3 above shall decide on a case-by-case basis whether there are reasonable grounds for suspecting that a transaction involves insider dealing or market manipulation, taking into account the elements constituting insider dealing or market manipulation, referred to in Articles 1 to 5 of Directive 2003/6/EC, in Commission Directive 2003/124/EC[1] implementing Directive 2003/6/EC as regards the definition and public disclosure of inside information and the definition of market manipulation, and in Article 4 of this Directive. Without prejudice to Article 10 of Directive 2003/6/EC, persons professionally arranging transactions shall be subject to the rules of notification of the Member State in which they are registered or have their head office, or in the case of a branch, the Member State where the branch is situated. The notification shall be addressed to the competent authority of this Member State.

Member States shall ensure that competent authorities receiving the notification of suspicious transactions transmit such information immediately to the competent authorities of the regulated markets concerned.

[9698]

NOTES

[1] OJ L339, 24.12.2003, p 70.

Article 8

Timeframe for notification

Member States shall ensure that in the event that persons, as referred to in Article 1 point 3, become aware of a fact or information that gives reasonable ground for suspicion concerning the relevant transaction, make a notification without delay.

[9699]

Article 9

Content of notification

1. Member States shall ensure that persons subject to the notification obligation transmit to the competent authority the following information:

(a) description of the transactions, including the type of order (such as limit order, market order or other characteristics of the order) and the type of trading market (such as block trade);

(b) reasons for suspicion that the transactions might constitute market abuse;

(c) means for identification of the persons on behalf of whom the transactions have been carried out, and of other persons involved in the relevant transactions;

(d) capacity in which the person subject to the notification obligation operates (such as for own account or on behalf of third parties);

(e) any information which may have significance in reviewing the suspicious transactions.

2. Where that information is not available at the time of notification, the notification shall include at least the reasons why the notifying persons suspect that the transactions might constitute insider dealing or market manipulation. All remaining information shall be provided to the competent authority as soon as it becomes available.

[9700]

Article 10

Means of notification

Member States shall ensure that notification to the competent authority can be done by mail, electronic mail, telecopy or telephone, provided that in the latter case confirmation is notified by any written form upon request by the competent authority.

[9701]

Article 11

Liability and professional secrecy

1. Member States shall ensure that the person notifying to the competent authority as referred to in Articles 7 to 10 shall not inform any other person, in particular the persons on behalf of whom the transactions have been carried out or parties related to those persons, of this notification, except by virtue of provisions laid down by law. The fulfilment of this requirement shall not involve the notifying person in liability of any kind, providing the notifying person acts in good faith.

2. Member States shall ensure that competent authorities do not disclose to any person the identity of the person having notified these transactions, if disclosure would, or would be likely to harm the person having notified the transactions. This provision is without prejudice to the requirements of the enforcement and the sanctioning regimes under Directive 2003/6/EC and to the rules on transfer of personal data laid down in Directive 95/46/EC.

3. The notification in good faith to the competent authority as referred to in Articles 7 to 10 shall not constitute a breach of any restriction on disclosure of information imposed by contract or by any legislative, regulatory or administrative provision, and shall not involve the person notifying in liability of any kind related to such notification.

[9702]

Article 12

Transposition

1. Member States shall bring into force the laws, regulations and administrative provisions necessary to comply with this Directive by 12 October 2004 at the latest. They shall forthwith communicate to the Commission the text of the provisions and a correlation table between those provisions and this Directive.

When Member States adopt those provisions, they shall contain a reference to this Directive or be accompanied by such a reference on the occasion of their official publication. Member States shall determine how such reference is to be made.

2. Member States shall communicate to the Commission the text of the main provisions of national law which they adopt in the field covered by this Directive.

[9703]

Article 13

Entry into force

This Directive shall enter into force on the day of its publication in the *Official Journal of the European Union*.

[9704]

Article 14

Addressees

This Directive is addressed to the Member States.

[9705]

Done at Brussels, 29 April 2004.

COMMISSION REGULATION

of 29 April 2004

implementing Directive 2003/71/EC of the European Parliament and of the Council as regards information contained in prospectuses as well as the format, incorporation by reference and publication of such prospectuses and dissemination of advertisements

(809/2004/EC)

(Text with EEA relevance)

NOTES

Date of publication in OJ: this Regulation was originally published in OJ L149, 30.4.2004, p 1. Note that a corrigendum was published in OJ L215, 16.6.2004, p 3; that corrigendum set out the whole of this Regulation (with changes incorporated) and it is the version from that corrigendum that is reproduced here. Notes are as in the OJ version.

THE COMMISSION OF THE EUROPEAN COMMUNITIES,

Having regard to the Treaty establishing the European Community,

Having regard to Directive 2003/71/EC of the European Parliament and the Council of 4 November 2003 on the prospectus to be published when securities are offered to the public or admitted to trading and amending Directive 2001/34/EC,[1] and in particular Article 5(5), Article 7, Article 10(4), Article 11(3), Article 14(8) and Article 15(7) thereof,

After consulting the Committee of European Securities Regulators (CESR)[2] for technical advice,

Whereas:

(1) Directive 2003/71/EC lays down principles to be observed when drawing up prospectuses. These principles need to be supplemented as far as the information to be given therein, the format and aspects of publication, the information to be incorporated by reference in a prospectus and dissemination of advertisements are concerned.

(2) Depending on the type of issuer and securities involved, a typology of minimum information requirements should be established corresponding to those schedules that are in practice most frequently applied. The schedules should be based on the information items required in the IOSCO "Disclosure Standards for cross-border offering and initial listings" (part I) and on the existing schedules of Directive 2001/34/EC of the European Parliament and of the Council of 28 May on the admission of securities to official stock exchange listing and on information to be published on those securities.[3]

(3) Information given by the issuer, the offeror or the person asking for admission to trading on a regulated market, according to this Regulation, should be subject to European Union provisions relating to data protection.

(4) Care should be taken that, in those cases where a prospectus is composed of separate documents, duplication of information is avoided; to this end separate detailed schedules for the registration document and for the securities note, adapted to the particular type of issuer and the securities concerned, should be laid down in order to cover each type of security.

(5) The issuer, the offeror or the person asking for admission to trading on a regulated market are entitled to include in a prospectus or base prospectus additional information going beyond the information items provided for in the schedules and building blocks. Any additional information provided should be appropriate to the type of securities or the nature of the issuer involved.

(6) In most cases, given the variety of issuers, the types of securities, the involvement or not of a third party as a guarantor, whether or not there is a listing etc, one single schedule will not give the appropriate information for an investor to make his investment decision. Therefore the combination of various schedules should be possible. A non exhaustive table of combinations, providing for different possible combinations of schedules and "building blocks" for most of the different type of securities, should be set up in order to assist issuers when drafting their prospectus.

(7) The share registration document schedule should be applicable to shares and other transferable securities equivalent to shares but also to other securities giving access to the capital of the issuer by way of conversion or exchange. In the latter case this schedule should not be used where the underlying shares to be delivered have already been issued before the issuance of the securities giving access to the capital of the issuer; however this schedule should be used where the underlying shares to be delivered have already been issued but are not yet admitted to trading on a regulated market.

(8) Voluntary disclosure of profit forecasts in a share registration document should be presented in a consistent and comparable manner and accompanied by a statement prepared by independent accountants or auditors. This information should not be confused with the disclosure of known trends or other factual data with material impact on the issuers' prospects. Moreover, they should provide an explanation of any changes in disclosure policy relating to profit forecasts when supplementing a prospectus or drafting a new prospectus.

(9) Pro forma financial information is needed in case of significant gross change, i. e. a variation of more than 25% relative to one or more indicators of the size of the issuer's business, in the situation of an issuer due to a particular transaction, with the exception of those situations where merger accounting is required.

(10) The schedule for the share securities note should be applicable to any class of share since it considers information regarding a description of the rights attached to the securities and the procedure for the exercise of any rights attached to the securities.

(11) Some debt securities such as structured bonds incorporate certain elements of a derivative security, therefore additional disclosure requirements related to the derivative component in the interest payment should be included in the securities note schedule for debt securities.

(12) The additional "building block" related to guarantee should apply to any obligation in relation to any kind of security.

(13) The asset backed securities registration document should not apply to mortgage bonds as provided for in Article 5(4)(b) of Directive 2003/71/EC and other covered bonds. The same should apply for the asset backed securities additional "building block" that has to be combined with the securities note for debt securities.

(14) Wholesale investors should be able to make their investment decision on other elements than those taken into consideration by retail investors. Therefore a differentiated content of prospectus is necessary for debt and derivative securities aimed at those investors who purchase debt or derivative securities with a denomination per unit of at least EUR 50,000 or a denomination in another currency provided that the value of such minimum denomination when converted to EURO amounts to at least EURO 50,000.

(15) In the context of depository receipts, emphasis should be put on the issuer of the underlying shares and not on the issuer of the depository receipt. Where there is legal recourse to the depository over and above a breach of its fiduciary or agency duties, the risk factors section in the prospectus should contain full information on this fact and on the circumstances of such recourse. Where a prospectus is drafted as a tripartite document (i.e. registration document, securities note and summary), the registration document should be limited to the information on the depository.

(16) The banks registration document schedule should be applicable to banks from third countries which do not fall under the definition of credit institution provided for in Article 1(1)(a) of Directive 2000/12/EC of the European Parliament and of the Council of 20 March 2000 relating to the taking up and pursuit of the business of credit institutions[4] but have their registered office in a state which is a member of the OECD.

(17) If a special purpose vehicle issues debt and derivative securities guaranteed by a bank, it should not use the banks registration document schedule.

(18) The schedule "securities note for derivative securities" should be applicable to securities which are not covered by the other schedules and building blocks. The scope of this schedule is determined by reference to the other two generic categories of shares and debt securities. In order to provide a clear and comprehensive explanation to help investors understand how the value of their investment is affected by the value of the underlying, issuers should be able to use appropriate examples on a voluntary basis. For instance, for some complex derivatives securities, examples might be the most effective way to explain the nature of those securities.

(19) The additional information "building block" on the underlying share for certain equity securities should be added to the securities note for debt securities or substitute the item referring to "information required in respect of the underlying" of the schedule securities note for derivative securities, depending on the characteristics of the securities being issued.

(20) Member States and their regional or local authorities are outside the scope of Directive 2003/71/EC. However, they may choose to produce a prospectus in accordance with this Directive. Third country sovereign issuers and their regional or local authorities are not outside the scope of Directive 2003/71/EC and are obliged to produce a prospectus if they wish to make a public offer of securities in the Community or wish their securities to be admitted to trading on a regulated market. For those cases, particular schedules should be used for the securities issued by States, their regional and local authorities and by public international bodies.

(21) A base prospectus and its final terms should contain the same information as a prospectus. All the general principles applicable to a prospectus are applicable also to the final

terms. Nevertheless, where the final terms are not included in the base prospectus they do not have to be approved by the competent authority.

(22) For some categories of issuers the competent authority should be entitled to require adapted information going beyond the information items included in the schedules and building blocks because of the particular nature of the activities carried out by those issuers. A precise and restrictive list of issuers for which adapted information may be required is necessary. The adapted information requirements for each category of issuers included in this list should be appropriate and proportionate to the type of business involved. The Committee of European Securities Regulators could actively try to reach convergence on these information requirements within the Community. Inclusion of new categories in the list should be restricted to those cases where this can be duly justified.

(23) In the case of completely new types of securities which cannot be covered by the existing schedules or any of their combinations, the issuer should still have the possibility to apply for approval for a prospectus. In those cases he should be able to discuss the content of the information to be provided with the competent authority. The prospectus approved by the competent authority under those circumstances should benefit from the single passport established in Directive 2003/71/EC. The competent authority should always try to find similarities and make use as much as possible of existing schedules. Any additional information requirements should be proportionate and appropriate to the type of securities involved.

(24) Certain information items required in the schedules and building blocks or equivalent information items are not relevant to a particular security and thus may be inapplicable in some specific cases; in those cases the issuer should have the possibility to omit this information.

(25) The enhanced flexibility in the articulation of the base prospectus with its final terms compared to a single issue prospectus should not hamper the easy access to material information for investors.

(26) With respect to base prospectuses, it should be set out in an easily identifiable manner which kind of information will have to be included as final terms. This requirement should be able to be satisfied in a number of different ways, for example, if the base prospectus contains blanks for any information to be inserted in the final terms or if the base prospectus contains a list of the missing information.

(27) Where a single document includes more than one base prospectus and each base prospectus would require approval by a different home competent authority, the respective competent authorities should act in cooperation and, where appropriate, transfer the approval of the prospectus in accordance with Article 13(5) of Directive 2003/71/EC, so that the approval by only one competent authority is sufficient for the entire document.

(28) Historical financial information as required in the schedules should principally be presented in accordance with Regulation (EC) No 1606/2002 of the European Parliament and of the Council of 19 July 2002 on the application of international accounting standard[5] or Member States' accounting standards. Specific requirements should, however, be laid down for third country issuers.

(29) For the purposes of publication of the document referred to in Article 10 of Directive 2003/71/EC, issuers should be allowed to choose the method of publication they consider adequate among those referred to in Article 14 of that Directive. In selecting the method of publication they should consider the objective of the document and that it should permit investors a fast and cost-efficient access to that information.

(30) The aim of incorporation by reference, as provided for in Article 11 of Directive 2003/71/EC, is to simplify and reduce the costs of drafting a prospectus; however this aim should not be achieved to the detriment of other interests the prospectus is meant to protect. For instance, the fact that the natural location of the information required is the prospectus, and that the information should be presented in an easily and comprehensible form, should also be considered. Particular attention should be granted to the language used for information incorporated by reference and its consistency with the prospectus itself. Information incorporated by reference may refer to historical data, however if this information is no more relevant due to material change, this should be clearly stated in the prospectus and the updated information should also be provided.

(31) Where a prospectus is published in electronic form, additional safety measures compared to traditional means of publication, using best practices available, are necessary in order to maintain the integrity of the information, to avoid manipulation or modification from unauthorised persons, to avoid altering its comprehensibility and to escape from possible adverse consequences from different approaches on offer of securities to the public in third countries.

(32) The newspaper chosen for the publication of a prospectus should have a wide area of distribution and a high circulation.

(33) A home Member State should be able to require publication of a notice stating how the prospectus has been made available and where it can be obtained by the public. Where a home Member State requires publication of notices in its legislation, the content of such a notice should be kept to the necessary items information to avoid duplication with the summary. These home Member States may also require that an additional notice in relation to the final terms of a base prospectus is to be published.

(34) In order to facilitate centralising useful information for investors a mention should be included in the list of approved prospectuses posted in the web-site of the competent authority of the home Member State, indicating how a prospectus has been published and where it can be obtained.

(35) Member States should ensure effective compliance of advertising rules concerning public offers and admission to trading on a regulated market. Proper co-ordination between competent authorities should be achieved in cross-border offerings or cross-border admission to trading.

(36) In view of the interval between the entry into force of Regulation (EC) No 1606/2002 and the production of certain of its effects, a number of transitional arrangements for historical financial information to be included in a prospectus should be provided for, in order to prevent excessive burden on issuers and enable them to adapt the way they prepare and present historical financial information within a reasonable period of time after the entry into force of Directive 2003/71/EC.

(37) The obligation to restate in a prospectus historical financial information according to Regulation (EC) No 1606/2002 does not cover securities with a denomination per unit of at least EUR 50,000; consequently such transitional arrangements are not necessary for such securities.

(38) For reasons of coherence it is appropriate that this Regulation applies from the date of transposition of Directive 2003/71/EC.

(39) Whereas the measures provided for in this Regulation are in accordance with the opinion of the European Securities Committee,

[9706]

NOTES

1 OJ L345, 31.12.2003, p 64.

2 CESR was established by Commission Decision 2001/527/EC of 6 June 2001, OJ L191, 13 July 2001, p 43.

3 OJ L184, 6.7.2001, p 1. Directive as last amended by Directive 2003/71/EC.

4 OJ L126, 26.5.2000, p 1. Directive as last amended by the 2003 Act of Accession.

5 OJ L243, 11.9.2002, p 1.

HAS ADOPTED THIS REGULATION:

CHAPTER I
SUBJECT MATTER AND DEFINITIONS

Article 1

Subject matter

This Regulation lays down:

1. the format of prospectus referred to in Article 5 of Directive 2003/71/EC;

2. the minimum information requirements to be included in a prospectus provided for in Article 7 of Directive 2003/71/EC;

3. the method of publication referred to in Article 10 of Directive 2003/71/EC;

4. the modalities according to which information can be incorporated by reference in a prospectus provided for in Article 11 of Directive 2003/71/EC;

5. the publication methods of a prospectus in order to ensure that a prospectus is publicly available according to Article 14 of Directive 2003/71/EC;

6. the methods of dissemination of advertisements referred to in Article 15 of Directive 2003/71/EC.

[9707]

Article 2

Definitions

For the purposes of this Regulation, the following definitions shall apply in addition to those laid down in Directive 2003/71/EC:

1. "schedule" means a list of minimum information requirements adapted to the particular nature of the different types of issuers and/or the different securities involved;

2. "building block" means a list of additional information requirements, not included in one of the schedules, to be added to one or more schedules, as the case may be, depending on the type of instrument and/or transaction for which a prospectus or base prospectus is drawn up;

3. "risk factors" means a list of risks which are specific to the situation of the issuer and/or the securities and which are material for taking investment decisions;

4. "special purpose vehicle" means an issuer whose objects and purposes are primarily the issue of securities;

5. "asset backed securities" means securities which:

(a) represent an interest in assets, including any rights intended to assure servicing, or the receipt or timeliness of receipts by holders of assets of amounts payable there under; or

(b) are secured by assets and the terms of which provide for payments which relate to payments or reasonable projections of payments calculated by reference to identified or identifiable assets;

6. "umbrella collective investment undertaking" means a collective investment undertaking invested in one or more collective investment undertakings, the asset of which is composed of separate class(es) or designation(s) of securities;

7. "property collective investment undertaking" means a collective investment undertaking whose investment objective is the participation in the holding of property in the long term;

8. "public international body" means a legal entity of public nature established by an international treaty between sovereign States and of which one or more Member States are members;

9. "advertisement" means announcements:

(a) relating to an specific offer to the public of securities or to an admission to trading on a regulated market; and

(b) aiming to specifically promote the potential subscription or acquisition of securities.

10. "profit forecast" means a form of words which expressly states or by implication indicates a figure or a minimum or maximum figure for the likely level of profits or losses for the current financial period and/or financial periods subsequent to that period, or contains data from which a calculation of such a figure for future profits or losses may be made, even if no particular figure is mentioned and the word "profit" is not used.

11. "profit estimate" means a profit forecast for a financial period which has expired and for which results have not yet been published.

12. "regulated information" means all information which the issuer, or any person who has applied for the admission of securities to trading on a regulated market without the issuer's consent, is required to disclose under Directive 2001/34/EC or under Article 6 of Directive 2003/6/EC of the European Parliament and of the Council.[1]

[9708]

NOTES

[1] OJ L96, 12.4.2003, p 16.

CHAPTER II
MINIMUM INFORMATION

Article 3

Minimum information to be included in a prospectus

A prospectus shall be drawn up by using one or a combination of the following schedules and building blocks set out in Articles 4 to 20, according to the combinations for various types of securities provided for in Article 21.

A prospectus shall contain the information items required in Annexes I to XVII depending on the type of issuer and securities involved, provided for in the schedules and building blocks set out in Articles 4 to 20. [Subject to Article 4a(1), a competent authority shall not request that a prospectus contain information items which are not included in Annexes I to XVII.]

In order to ensure conformity with the obligation referred to in Article 5(1) of Directive 2003/71/EC, the competent authority of the home Member State, when approving a prospectus in accordance with Article 13 of that Directive, may require that the information provided by the issuer, the offeror or the person asking for admission to trading on a regulated market be completed, for each of the information items, on a case by case basis.

[9709]

NOTES

Words in square brackets substituted by Commission Regulation 211/2007/EC, Art 1(1), as from 1 March 2007.

Article 4

Share registration document schedule

1. For the share registration document information shall be given in accordance with the schedule set out in Annex I.

2. The schedule set out in paragraph 1 shall apply to the following:
   (1) shares and other transferable securities equivalent to shares;
   (2) other securities which comply with the following conditions:
      (a) they can be converted or exchanged into shares or other transferable securities equivalent to shares, at the issuer's or at the investor's discretion, or on the basis of the conditions established a the moment of the issue, or give, in any other way, the possibility to acquire shares or other transferable securities equivalent to shares; and
      (b) provided that these shares or other transferable securities equivalent to shares are or will be issued by the issuer of the security and are not yet traded on a regulated market or an equivalent market outside the Community at the time of the approval of the prospectus covering the securities, and that the underlying shares or other transferable securities equivalent to shares can be delivered with physical settlement.

[9710]

[Article 4a

Share registration document schedule in cases of complex financial history or significant financial commitment

1. Where the issuer of a security covered by Article 4(2) has a complex financial history, or has made a significant financial commitment, and in consequence the inclusion in the registration document of certain items of financial information relating to an entity other than the issuer is necessary in order to satisfy the obligation laid down in Article 5(1) of Directive 2003/71/EC, those items of financial information shall be deemed to relate to the issuer. The competent authority of the home Member State shall in such cases request that the issuer, the offeror or the person asking for admission to trading include those items of information in the registration document.

Those items of financial information may include pro forma information prepared in accordance with Annex II. In this context, where the issuer has made a significant financial commitment any such pro forma information shall illustrate the anticipated effects of the transaction that the issuer has agreed to undertake, and references in Annex II to "the transaction" shall be read accordingly.

2. The competent authority shall base any request pursuant to paragraph 1 on the requirements set out in item 20.1 of Annex I as regards the content of financial information and the applicable accounting and auditing principles, subject to any modification which is appropriate in view of any of the following factors:

(a) the nature of the securities;

(b) the nature and range of information already included in the prospectus, and the existence of financial information relating to an entity other than the issuer in a form that might be included in a prospectus without modification;

(c) the facts of the case, including the economic substance of the transactions by which the issuer has acquired or disposed of its business undertaking or any part of it, and the specific nature of that undertaking;

(d) the ability of the issuer to obtain financial information relating to another entity with reasonable effort.

Where, in the individual case, the obligation laid down in Article 5(1) of Directive 2003/71/EC may be satisfied in more than one way, preference shall be given to the way that is the least costly or onerous.

3. Paragraph 1 is without prejudice to the responsibility under national law of any other person, including the persons referred to in Article 6(1) of Directive 2003/71/EC, for the information contained in the prospectus. In particular, those persons shall be responsible for the inclusion in the registration document of any items of information requested by the competent authority pursuant to paragraph 1.

4. For the purposes of paragraph 1, an issuer shall be treated as having a complex financial history if all of the following conditions apply:

(a) its entire business undertaking at the time that the prospectus is drawn up is not accurately represented in the historical financial information which it is required to provide under item 20.1 of Annex I;

(b) that inaccuracy will affect the ability of an investor to make an informed assessment as mentioned in Article 5(1) of Directive 2003/71/EC; and

(c) information relating to its business undertaking that is necessary for an investor to make such an assessment is included in financial information relating to another entity.

5. For the purposes of paragraph 1, an issuer shall be treated as having made a significant financial commitment if it has entered into a binding agreement to undertake a transaction which, on completion, is likely to give rise to a significant gross change.

In this context, the fact that an agreement makes completion of the transaction subject to conditions, including approval by a regulatory authority, shall not prevent that agreement from being treated as binding if it is reasonably certain that those conditions will be fulfilled.

In particular, an agreement shall be treated as binding where it makes the completion of the transaction conditional on the outcome of the offer of the securities that are the subject matter of the prospectus or, in the case of a proposed takeover, if the offer of securities that are the subject matter of the prospectus has the objective of funding that takeover.

6. For the purposes of paragraph 5 of this Article, and of item 20.2 of Annex I, a significant gross change means a variation of more than 25%, relative to one or more indicators of the size of the issuer's business, in the situation of an issuer.]

[9710A]

NOTES

Inserted by Commission Regulation 211/2007/EC, Art 1(2), as from 1 March 2007.

Article 5

Pro-forma financial information building block

For pro forma financial information, information shall be given in accordance with the building block set out in Annex II.

Pro forma financial information should be preceded by an introductory explanatory paragraph that states in clear terms the purpose of including this information in the prospectus.

[9711]

Article 6

Share securities note schedule

1. For the share securities note information is necessary to be given in accordance with the schedule set out in Annex III.

2. The schedule shall apply to shares and other transferable securities equivalent to shares.

[9712]

Article 7

Debt and derivative securities registration document schedule for securities with a denomination per unit of less than EUR 50,000

For the debt and derivative securities registration document concerning securities which are not covered in Article 4 with a denomination per unit of less than EUR 50,000 or, where there is no individual denomination, securities that can only be acquired on issue for less than EUR 50,000 per security, information shall be given in accordance with the schedule set out in Annex IV.

[9713]

Article 8

Securities note schedule for debt securities with a denomination per unit of less than EUR 50,000

1. For the securities note for debt securities with a denomination per unit of less than EUR 50,000 information shall be given in accordance with the schedule set out in Annex V.

2. The schedule shall apply to debt where the issuer has an obligation arising on issue to pay the investor 100% of the nominal value in addition to which there may be also an interest payment.

[9714]

Article 9

Guarantees building block

For guarantees information shall be given in accordance with the building block set out in Annex VI.

[9715]

Article 10

Asset backed securities registration document schedule

For the asset backed securities registration document information shall be given in accordance with the schedule set out in Annex VII.

[9716]

Article 11

Asset backed securities building block

For the additional information building block to the securities note for asset backed securities information shall be given in accordance with the building block set out in Annex VIII.

[9717]

Article 12

Debt and derivative securities registration document schedule for securities with a denomination per unit of at least EUR 50,000

For the debt and derivative securities registration document concerning securities which are not covered in Article 4 with a denomination per unit of at least EUR 50,000 or, where there is no individual denomination, securities that can only be acquired on issue for at least EUR 50,000 per security, information shall be given in accordance with the schedule set out in Annex IX.

[9718]

Article 13

Depository receipts schedule

For depository receipts issued over shares information shall be given in accordance with the schedule set out in Annex X.

[9719]

Article 14

Banks registration document schedule

1. For the banks registration document for debt and derivative securities and those securities which are not covered by Article 4 information shall be given in accordance with the schedule set out in Annex XI.

2. The schedule set out in paragraph 1 shall apply to credit institutions as defined in point (a) of Article 1(1) of Directive 2000/12/EC as well as to third country credit institutions which do not fall under that definition but have their registered office in a state which is a member of the OECD.

These entities may also use alternatively the registration document schedules provided for under in Articles 7 and 12.

[9720]

Article 15

Securities note schedule for derivative securities

1. For the securities note for derivative securities information shall be given in accordance with the schedule set out in Annex XII.

2. The schedule shall apply to securities which are not in the scope of application of the other securities note schedules referred to in Articles 6, 8 and 16, including certain securities where the payment and/or delivery obligations are linked to an underlying.

[9721]

Article 16

Securities note schedule for debt securities with a denomination per unit of at least EUR 50,000

1. For the securities note for debt securities with a denomination per unit of at least EUR 50,000 information shall be given in accordance with the schedule set out in Annex XIII.

2. The schedule shall apply to debt where the issuer has an obligation arising on issue to pay the investor 100% of the nominal value in addition to which there may be also an interest payment.

[9722]

Article 17

Additional information building block on the underlying share

1. For the additional information on the underlying share, the description of the underlying share shall be given in accordance with the building block set out in Annex XIV.

In addition, if the issuer of the underlying share is an entity belonging to the same group, the information required by the schedule referred to in Article 4 shall be given in respect of that issuer.

2. The additional information referred to in the first subparagraph of paragraph 1 shall only apply to those securities which comply with both of the following conditions:

(1) they can be converted or exchanged into shares or other transferable securities equivalent to shares, at the issuer's or at the investor's discretion, or on the basis of the conditions established a the moment of the issue or give, in any other way, the possibility to acquire shares or other transferable securities equivalent to shares; and

(2) provided that these shares or other transferable securities equivalent to shares are or will be issued by the issuer of the security or by an entity belonging to the

group of that issuer and are not yet traded on a regulated market or an equivalent market outside the Community at the time of the approval of the prospectus covering the securities, and that the underlying shares or other transferable securities equivalent to shares can be delivered with physical settlement.

[9723]

Article 18

Registration document schedule for collective investment undertakings of the closed-end type

1. In addition to the information required pursuant to items 1, 2, 3, 4, 5.1, 7, 9.1, 9.2.1, 9.2.3, 10.4, 13, 14, 15, 16, 17.2, 18, 19, 20, 21, 22, 23, 24, 25 of Annex I, for the registration document for securities issued by collective investment undertakings of the closed-end type information shall be given in accordance with the schedule set out in Annex XV.

2. The schedule shall apply to collective investment undertakings of the closed-end type holding a portfolio of assets on behalf of investors that:

(1) are recognised by national law in the Member State in which it is incorporated as a collective investment undertaking of the closed end type; or

(2) do not take or seek to take legal or management control of any of the issuers of its underlying investments. In such a case, legal control and/or participation in the administrative, management or supervisory bodies of the underlying issuer(s) may be taken where such action is incidental to the primary investment objective, necessary for the protection of shareholders and only in circumstances where the collective investment undertaking will not exercise significant management control over the operations of that underlying issuer(s).

[9724]

Article 19

Registration document schedule for Member States, third countries and their regional and local authorities

1. For the registration document for securities issued by Member States, third countries and their regional and local authorities information shall be given in accordance with the schedule set out in Annex XVI.

2. The schedule shall apply to all types of securities issued by Member States, third countries and their regional and local authorities.

[9725]

Article 20

Registration document schedule for public international bodies and for issuers of debt securities guaranteed by a member state of the OECD

1. For the registration document for securities issued by public international bodies and for securities unconditionally and irrevocably guaranteed, on the basis of national legislation, by a state which is member of the OECD information shall be given in accordance with the schedule set out in Annex XVII.

2. The schedule shall apply to:

— all types of securities issued by public international bodies,

— to debt securities unconditionally and irrevocably guaranteed, on the basis of national legislation, by a state which is member of the OECD.

[9726]

Article 21

Combination of schedules and building blocks

1. The use of the combinations provided for in the table set out in Annex XVIII shall be mandatory when drawing up prospectuses for the types of securities to which those combinations correspond according to this table.

However, for securities not covered by those combinations further combinations may be used.

2. The most comprehensive and stringent registration document schedule, ie the most demanding schedule in term of number of information items and the extent of the information included in them, may always be used to issue securities for which a less comprehensive and stringent registration document schedule is provided for, according to the following ranking of schedules:

(1) share registration document schedule;

(2) debt and derivative securities registration document schedule for securities with a denomination per unit of less than EUR 50,000 ;

(3) debt and derivative securities registration document schedule for securities with a denomination per unit at least EUR 50,000.

[9727]

Article 22

Minimum information to be included in a base prospectus and its related final terms

1. A base prospectus shall be drawn up by using one or a combination of schedules and building blocks provided for in Articles 4 to 20 according to the combinations for various types of securities set out in Annex XVIII.

A base prospectus shall contain the information items required in Annexes I to XVII depending on the type of issuer and securities involved, provided for in the schedules and building blocks set out in Articles 4 to 20. A competent authority shall not request that a base prospectus contains information items which are not included in Annexes I to XVII.

In order to ensure conformity with the obligation referred to in Article 5(1) of Directive 2003/71/EC, the competent authority of the home Member State, when approving a base prospectus in accordance with Article 13 of that Directive, may require that the information provided by the issuer, the offeror or the person asking for admission to trading on a regulated market be completed, for each of the information items, on a case by case basis.

2. The issuer, the offeror or the person asking for admission to trading on a regulated market may omit information items which are not known when the base prospectus is approved and which can only be determined at the time of the individual issue.

3. The use of the combinations provided for in the table in Annex XVIII shall be mandatory when drawing up base prospectuses for the types of securities to which those combinations correspond according to this table.

However, for securities not covered by those combinations further combinations may be used.

4. The final terms attached to a base prospectus shall only contain the information items from the various securities note schedules according to which the base prospectus is drawn up.

5. In addition to the information items set out in the schedules and building blocks referred to in Articles 4 to 20 the following information shall be included in a base prospectus:

(1) indication on the information that will be included in the final terms;

(2) the method of publication of the final terms; if the issuer is not in a position to determine, at the time of the approval of the prospectus, the method of publication of the final terms, an indication of how the public will be informed about which method will be used for the publication of the final terms;

(3) in the case of issues of non equity securities according to point (a) of Article 5(4) of Directive 2003/71/EC, a general description of the programme.

6. Only the following categories of securities may be contained in a base prospectus and its related final terms covering issues of various types of securities:

(1) asset backed securities;

(2) warrants falling under Article 17;

(3) non-equity securities provided for under point (b) of Article 5(4) of Directive 2003/71/EC;

(4) all other non-equity securities including warrants with the exception of those mentioned in (2).

In drawing up a base prospectus the issuer, the offeror or the person asking for admission to trading on a regulated market shall clearly segregate the specific information on each of the different securities included in these categories.

7. Where an event envisaged under Article 16(1) of Directive 2003/71/EC occurs between the time that the base prospectus has been approved and the final closing of the offer of each issue of securities under the base prospectus or, as the case may be, the time that trading on a regulated market of those securities begins, the issuer, the offeror or the person asking for admission to trading on a regulated market shall publish a supplement prior to the final closing of the offer or the admission of those securities to trading.

[9728]

Article 23

Adaptations to the minimum information given in prospectuses and base prospectuses

1. Notwithstanding Articles 3 second paragraph and 22(1) second subparagraph, where the issuer's activities fall under one of the categories included in Annex XIX, the competent authority of the home Member State, taking into consideration the specific nature of the activities involved, may ask for adapted information, in addition to the information items included in the schedules and building blocks set out in Articles 4 to 20, including, where appropriate, a valuation or other expert's report on the assets of the issuer, in order to comply with the obligation referred to in Article 5(1) of Directive 2003/71/EC. The competent authority shall forthwith inform the Commission thereof.

In order to obtain the inclusion of a new category in Annex XIX a Member State shall notify its request to the Commission. The Commission shall update this list following the Committee procedure provided for in Article 24 of Directive 2003/71/EC.

2. By way of derogation of Articles 3 to 22, where an issuer, an offeror or a person asking for admission to trading on a regulated market applies for approval of a prospectus or a base prospectus for a security which is not the same but comparable to the various types of securities mentioned in the table of combinations set out in Annex XVIII, the issuer, the offeror or the person asking for admission to trading on a regulated market shall add the relevant information items from another securities note schedule provided for in Articles 4 to 20 to the main securities note schedule chosen. This addition shall be done in accordance with the main characteristics of the securities being offered to the public or admitted to trading on a regulated market.

3. By way of derogation of Articles 3 to 22, where an issuer, an offeror or a person asking for admission to trading on a regulated market applies for approval of a prospectus or a base prospectus for a new type of security, the issuer, the offeror or the person asking for admission to trading on a regulated market shall notify a draft prospectus or base prospectus to the competent authority of the home Member State.

The competent authority shall decide, in consultation with the issuer, the offeror or the person asking for admission to trading on a regulated market, what information shall be included in the prospectus or base prospectus in order to comply with the obligation referred to in Article 5(1) of Directive 2003/71/EC. The competent authority shall forthwith inform the Commission thereof.

The derogation referred to in the first subparagraph shall only apply in case of a new type of security which has features completely different from the various types of securities mentioned in Annex XVIII, if the characteristics of this new security are such that a combination of the different information items referred to in the schedules and building blocks provided for in Articles 4 to 20 is not pertinent.

4. By way of derogation of Articles 3 to 22, in the cases where one of the information items required in one of the schedules or building blocks referred to in 4 to 20 or equivalent information is not pertinent to the issuer, to the offer or to the securities to which the prospectus relates, that information may be omitted.

[9729]

Article 24

Content of the summary of prospectus and base prospectus

The issuer, the offeror or the person asking for admission to trading on a regulated market shall determine on its own the detailed content of the summary to the prospectus or base prospectus referred to in Article 5(2) of Directive 2003/71/EC.

[9730]

CHAPTER III
FORMAT OF THE PROSPECTUS, BASE PROSPECTUS AND SUPPLEMENTS

Article 25

Format of the prospectus

1. Where an issuer, an offeror or a person asking for the admission to trading on a regulated market chooses, according to Article 5(3) of Directive 2003/71/EC to draw up a prospectus as a single document, the prospectus shall be composed of the following parts in the following order:

(1) a clear and detailed table of contents;
(2) the summary provided for in Article 5 (2) of Directive 2003/71/EC;
(3) the risk factors linked to the issuer and the type of security covered by the issue;
(4) the other information items included in the schedules and building blocks according to which the prospectus is drawn up.

2. Where an issuer, an offeror or a person asking for the admission to trading on a regulated market chooses, according to in Article 5(3) of Directive 2003/71/EC, to draw up a prospectus composed of separate documents, the securities note and the registration document shall be each composed of the following parts in the following order:

(1) a clear and detailed table of content;
(2) as the case may be, the risk factors linked to the issuer and the type of security covered by the issue;
(3) the other information items included in the schedules and building blocks according to which the prospectus is drawn up.

3. In the cases mentioned in paragraphs 1 and 2, the issuer, the offeror or the person asking for admission to trading on a regulated market shall be free in defining the order in the presentation of the required information items included in the schedules and building blocks according to which the prospectus is drawn up.

4. Where the order of the items does not coincide with the order of the information provided for in the schedules and building blocks according to which the prospectus is drawn up, the competent authority of the home Member State may ask the issuer, the offeror or the person asking for the admission to trading on a regulated market to provide a cross reference list for the purpose of checking the prospectus before its approval. Such list shall identify the pages where each item can be found in the prospectus.

5. Where the summary of a prospectus must be supplemented according to Article 16(1) of Directive 2003/71/EC, the issuer, the offeror or the person asking for admission to trading on a regulated market shall decide on a case-by-case basis whether to integrate the new information in the original summary by producing a new summary, or to produce a supplement to the summary.

If the new information is integrated in the original summary, the issuer, the offeror or the person asking for admission to trading on a regulated market shall ensure that investors can easily identify the changes, in particular by way of footnotes.

[9731]

Article 26

Format of the base prospectus and its related final terms

1. Where an issuer, an offeror or a person asking for the admission to trading on a regulated market chooses, according to Article 5 (4) of Directive 2003/71/EC to draw up a base prospectus, the base prospectus shall be composed of the following parts in the following order:

(1) a clear and detailed table of contents;
(2) the summary provided for in Article 5 (2) of Directive 2003/71/EC;
(3) the risk factors linked to the issuer and the type of security or securities covered by the issue(s);
(4) the other information items included in the schedules and building blocks according to which the prospectus is drawn up.

2. Notwithstanding paragraph 1, the issuer, the offeror or the person asking for admission to trading on a regulated market shall be free in defining the order in the presentation of the

required information items included in the schedules and building blocks according to which the prospectus is drawn up. The information on the different securities contained in the base prospectus shall be clearly segregated.

3. Where the order of the items does not coincide with the order of the information provided for by the schedules and building blocks according to which the prospectus is drawn up, the home competent authority may ask the issuer, the offeror or the person asking for admission to trading on a regulated market to provide a cross reference list for the purpose of checking the prospectus before its approval. Such list should identify the pages where each item can be found in the prospectus.

4. In case the issuer, the offeror or the person asking for admission to trading on a regulated market has previously filed a registration document for a particular type of security and, at a later stage, chooses to draw up base prospectus in conformity with the conditions provided for in points (a) and (b) of Article 5(4) of Directive 2003/71/EC, the base prospectus shall contain:

(1) the information contained in the previously or simultaneously filed and approved registration document which shall be incorporated by reference, following the conditions provided for in Article 28 of this Regulation;

(2) the information which would otherwise be contained in the relevant securities note less the final terms where the final terms are not included in the base prospectus.

5. The final terms attached to a base prospectus shall be presented in the form of a separate document containing only the final terms or by inclusion of the final terms into the base prospectus.

In the case that the final terms are included in a separate document containing only the final terms, they may replicate some information which has been included in the approved base prospectus according to the relevant securities note schedule that has been used for drawing up the base prospectus. In this case the final terms have to be presented in such a way that they can be easily identified as such.

A clear and prominent statement shall be inserted in the final terms indicating that the full information on the issuer and on the offer is only available on the basis of the combination of base prospectus and final terms and where the base prospectus is available.

6. Where a base prospectus relates to different securities, the issuer, the offeror or the person asking for admission to trading on a regulated market shall include a single summary in the base prospectus for all securities. The information on the different securities contained in the summary, however, shall be clearly segregated.

7. Where the summary of a base prospectus must be supplemented according to Article 16(1) of Directive 2003/71/EC, the issuer, the offeror or the person asking for admission to trading on a regulated market shall decide on a case-by-case basis whether to integrate the new information in the original summary by producing a new summary, or by producing a supplement to the summary.

If the new information is integrated in the original summary of the base prospectus by producing a new summary, the issuer, the offeror or the person asking for admission to trading on a regulated market shall ensure that investors can easily identify the changes, in particular by way of footnotes.

8. Issuers, offerors or persons asking for admission to trading on a regulated market may compile in one single document two or more different base prospectuses.

[9732]

CHAPTER IV
INFORMATION AND INCORPORATION BY REFERENCE

Article 27

Publication of the document referred to in Article 10(1) of Directive 2003/71/EC

1. The document referred to in Article 10(1) of Directive 2003/71/EC shall be made available to the public, at the choice of the issuer, the offeror or the person asking for admission to trading on a regulated market, through one of the means permitted under Article 14 of that Directive in the home Member State of the issuer.

2. The document shall be filed with the competent authority of the home Member State and made available to the public at the latest 20 working days after the publication of the annual financial statements in the home Member State.

3. The document shall include a statement indicating that some information may be out-of-date, if such is the case.

[9733]

Article 28

Arrangements for incorporation by reference

1. Information may be incorporated by reference in a prospectus or base prospectus, notably if it is contained in one the following documents:

(1) annual and interim financial information;
(2) documents prepared on the occasion of a specific transaction such as a merger or de-merger;
(3) audit reports and financial statements;
(4) memorandum and articles of association;
(5) earlier approved and published prospectuses and/or base prospectuses;
(6) regulated information;
(7) circulars to security holders.

2. The documents containing information that may be incorporated by reference in a prospectus or base prospectus or in the documents composing it shall be drawn up following the provisions of Article 19 of Directive 2003/71/EC.

3. If a document which may be incorporated by reference contains information which has undergone material changes, the prospectus or base prospectus shall clearly state such a circumstance and shall give the updated information.

4. The issuer, the offeror or the person asking for admission to trading on a regulated market may incorporate information in a prospectus or base prospectus by making reference only to certain parts of a document, provided that it states that the non-incorporated parts are either not relevant for the investor or covered elsewhere in the prospectus.

5. When incorporating information by reference, issuers, offerors or persons asking for admission to trading on a regulated market shall endeavour not to endanger investor protection in terms of comprehensibility and accessibility of the information.

[9734]

CHAPTER V
PUBLICATION AND DISSEMINATION OF ADVERTISEMENTS

Article 29

Publication in electronic form

1. The publication of the prospectus or base prospectus in electronic form, either pursuant to points (c) (d) and (e) of Article 14(2) of Directive 2003/71/EC, or as an additional means of availability, shall be subject to the following requirements:

(1) the prospectus or base prospectus shall be easily accessible when entering the web-site;
(2) the file format shall be such that the prospectus or base prospectus cannot be modified;
(3) the prospectus or base prospectus shall not contain hyper-links, with exception of links to the electronic addresses where information incorporated by reference is available;
(4) the investors shall have the possibility of downloading and printing the prospectus or base prospectus.

The exception referred to in point 3 of the first subparagraph shall only be valid for documents incorporated by reference; those documents shall be available with easy and immediate technical arrangements.

2. If a prospectus or base prospectus for offer of securities to the public is made available on the web-sites of issuers and financial intermediaries or of regulated markets, these shall take measures, to avoid targeting residents in Members States or third countries where the offer of securities to the public does not take place, such as the insertion of a disclaimer as to who are the addressees of the offer.

[9735]

Article 30

Publication in newspapers

1. In order to comply with point (a) of Article 14(2) of Directive 2003/71/EC the publication of a prospectus or a base prospectus shall be made in a general or financial information newspaper having national or supra-regional scope;

2. If the competent authority is of the opinion that the newspaper chosen for publication does not comply with the requirements set out in paragraph 1, it shall determine a newspaper whose circulation is deemed appropriate for this purpose taking into account, in particular, the geographic area, number of inhabitants and reading habits in each Member State.

[9736]

Article 31

Publication of the notice

1. If a Member State makes use of the option, referred to in Article 14(3) of Directive 2003/71/EC, to require the publication of a notice stating how the prospectus or base prospectus has been made available and where it can be obtained by the public, that notice shall be published in a newspaper that fulfils the requirements for publication of prospectuses according to Article 30 of this Regulation.

If the notice relates to a prospectus or base prospectus published for the only purpose of admission of securities to trading on a regulated market where securities of the same class are already admitted, it may alternatively be inserted in the gazette of that regulated market, irrespective of whether that gazette is in paper copy or electronic form.

2. The notice shall be published no later than the next working day following the date of publication of the prospectus or base prospectus pursuant to Article 14(1) of Directive 2003/71/EC.

3. The notice shall contain the following information:
   (1) the identification of the issuer;
   (2) the type, class and amount of the securities to be offered and/or in respect of which admission to trading is sought, provided that these elements are known at the time of the publication of the notice;
   (3) the intended time schedule of the offer/admission to trading;
   (4) a statement that a prospectus or base prospectus has been published and where it can be obtained;
   (5) if the prospectus or base prospectus has been published in a printed form, the addresses where and the period of time during which such printed forms are available to the public;
   (6) if the prospectus or base prospectus has been published in electronic form, the addresses to which investors shall refer to ask for a paper copy;
   (7) the date of the notice.

[9737]

Article 32

List of approved prospectuses

The list of the approved prospectuses and base prospectuses published on the web-site of the competent authority, in accordance with Article 14(4) of Directive 2003/71/EC, shall mention how such prospectuses have been made available and where they can be obtained.

[9738]

Article 33

Publication of the final terms of base prospectuses

The publication method for final terms related to a base prospectus does not have to be the same as the one used for the base prospectus as long as the publication method used is one of the publication methods indicated in Article 14 of the Directive 2003/71/EC.

[9739]

Article 34

Dissemination of advertisements

Advertisements related to an offer to the public of securities or to an admission to trading on a regulated market may be disseminated to the public by interested parties, such as issuer, offeror or person asking for admission, the financial intermediaries that participate in the placing and/or underwriting of securities, notably by one of the following means of communication:

(1) addressed or unaddressed printed matter;
(2) electronic message or advertisement received via a mobile telephone or pager;
(3) standard letter;
(4) Press advertising with or without order form;
(5) catalogue;
(6) telephone with or without human intervention;
(7) seminars and presentations;
(8) radio;
(9) videophone;
(10) videotext;
(11) electronic mail;
(12) facsimile machine (fax);
(13) television;
(14) notice;
(15) bill;
(16) poster;
(17) brochure;
(18) web posting including internet banners.

[9740]

CHAPTER VI
TRANSITIONAL AND FINAL PROVISIONS

Article 35

Historical financial information

1. The obligation for Community issuers to restate in a prospectus historical financial information according to Regulation (EC) No 1606/2002, set out in Annex I item 20.1, Annex IV item 13.1, Annex VII items 8.2, Annex X items 20.1 and Annex XI item 11.1 shall not apply to any period earlier than 1 January 2004 or, where an issuer has securities admitted to trading on a regulated market on 1 July 2005 , until the issuer has published its first consolidated annual accounts with accordance with Regulation (EC) No 1606/2002.

2. Where a Community issuer is subject to transitional national provisions adopted pursuant Article 9 of Regulation (EC) No 1606/2002, the obligation to restate in a prospectus historical financial information does not apply to any period earlier than 1 January 2006 or, where an issuer has securities admitted to trading on a regulated market on 1 July 2005 , until the issuer has published its first consolidated annual accounts with accordance with Regulation (EC) No 1606/2002.

3. Until 1 January 2007 the obligation to restate in a prospectus historical financial information according to Regulation (EC) No 1606/2002, set out in Annex I item 20.1, Annex IV item 13.1, Annex VII items 8.2, Annex X items 20.1 and Annex XI item 11.1 shall not apply to issuers from third countries:

(1) who have their securities admitted to trading on a regulated market on 1 January 2007; and
(2) who have presented and prepared historical financial information according to the national accounting standards of a third country.

In this case, historical financial information shall be accompanied with more detailed and/or additional information if the financial statements included in the prospectus do not give a true and fair view of the issuer's assets and liabilities, financial position and profit and loss.

4. Third country issuers having prepared historical financial information according to internationally accepted standards as referred to in Article 9 of Regulation (EC) No 1606/2002 may use that information in any prospectus filed before 1 January 2007 , without being subject to restatement obligations.

[5. Subject to paragraph 5A, from 1 January 2007, third country issuers referred to in paragraphs 3 and 4 shall present their historical financial information in accordance with international accounting standards adopted under Regulation (EC) No 1606/2002 or a third country's national accounting standards equivalent to those standards. If such historical financial information is not in accordance with any such standards, it must be presented in the form of restated financial statements.]

[5A. Third country issuers are not subject to a requirement, under Annex I, item 20.1; Annex IV, item 13.1; Annex VII, item 8.2; Annex X, item 20.1 or Annex XI, item 11.1, to restate historical financial information or to a requirement under Annex VII, item 8.2.bis; Annex IX, item 11.1; or Annex X, item 20.1.bis, to provide a narrative description of the differences between international accounting standards adopted under Regulation (EC) No 1606/2002 and the accounting principles in accordance with which such information is drawn up, included in a prospectus filed with a competent authority before 1 January 2009, where one of the following conditions is met:

(a) the notes to the financial statements that form part of the historical financial information contain an explicit and unreserved statement that they comply with International Financial Reporting Standards in accordance with IAS 1 Presentation of Financial Statements;

(b) the historical financial information is prepared in accordance with the Generally Accepted Accounting Principles of either Canada, Japan or the United States of America;

(c) the historical financial information is prepared in accordance with the Generally Accepted Accounting Principles of a third country other than Canada, Japan or the United States of America, and the following conditions are satisfied:

 (i) the third country authority responsible for the national accounting standards in question has made a public commitment, before the start of the financial year in which the prospectus is filed, to converge those standards with International Financial Reporting Standards;

 (ii) that authority has established a work programme which demonstrates the intention to progress towards convergence before 31 December 2008; and

 (iii) the issuer provides evidence that satisfies the competent authority that the conditions in (i) and (ii) are met.

5B. By 1 April 2007, the Commission shall present to the European Securities Committee and the European Parliament a first report on the work timetable of the authorities responsible for national accounting standards in the US, Japan and Canada for the convergence between IFRS and the Generally Accepted Accounting Principles of those countries.

The Commission shall closely monitor, and regularly inform the European Securities Committee and the European Parliament about the amount of progress in the convergence between International Financial Reporting Standards and the Generally Accepted Accounting Principles of Canada, Japan and the United States of America and of progress on the elimination of reconciliation requirements that apply to Community issuers in those countries. In particular, it shall inform the European Securities Committee and the European Parliament immediately if the process is not proceeding satisfactorily.

5C. The Commission shall also regularly inform the European Securities Committee and the European Parliament about the development of regulatory discussions and the amount of progress in the convergence between International Financial Reporting Standards and the Generally Accepted Accounting Principles of third countries mentioned in paragraph 5A(c) and progress towards the elimination of any reconciliation requirements. In particular, the Commission shall inform the European Securities Committee and the European Parliament immediately if the process is not proceeding satisfactorily.

5D. In addition to the obligations under paragraphs 5B and 5C, the Commission shall engage in and maintain a regular dialogue with third country authorities and, before 1 April 2008 at the latest, the Commission shall present a report to the European Securities Committee and to the European Parliament on the progress in convergence and progress towards the elimination of any reconciliation requirements that apply to Community issuers under the rules of a third country covered by paragraph 5A (b) or (c). The Commission may request or require another person to prepare the report.

5E. At least six months before 1 January 2009, the Commission shall ensure a determination of the equivalence of the Generally Accepted Accounting Principles of third countries, pursuant to a definition of equivalence and an equivalence mechanism that it will have established before 1 January 2008 in accordance with the procedure referred to in Article 24 of Directive 2003/71/EC. When complying with this paragraph, the Commission shall first consult the Committee of European Securities Regulators on the appropriateness of the definition of equivalence, the equivalence mechanism and the determination of the equivalence that is made.]

6. The provisions of this Article shall also apply to Annex VI, item 3.

[9741]

NOTES

Para 5 substituted, and paras 5A–5E inserted, by Commission Regulation 1787/2006/EC, Art 1, as from 8 December 2006.

Article 36

Entry into force

This Regulation shall enter into force in Member States on the twentieth day after its publication in the *Official Journal of the European Union*.

It shall apply from 1 July 2005.

This Regulation shall be binding in its entirety and directly applicable in all Member States.

[9742]

Done at Brussels, 29 April 2004

ANNEXES

Annexes I to XVII: Schedules and building blocks

Annex XVIII: Table of combinations of schedules and building blocks

Annex XIX: List of specialist issuers

ANNEX I

MINIMUM DISCLOSURE REQUIREMENTS FOR THE SHARE REGISTRATION DOCUMENT (SCHEDULE)

1. PERSONS RESPONSIBLE

1.1. All persons responsible for the information given in the Registration Document and, as the case may be, for certain parts of it, with, in the latter case, an indication of such parts. In the case of natural persons including members of the issuer's administrative, management or supervisory bodies indicate the name and function of the person; in case of legal persons indicate the name and registered office.

1.2. A declaration by those responsible for the registration document that, having taken all reasonable care to ensure that such is the case, the information contained in the registration document is, to the best of their knowledge, in accordance with the facts and contains no omission likely to affect its import. As the case may be, a declaration by those responsible for certain parts of the registration document that, having taken all reasonable care to ensure that such is the case, the information contained in the part of the registration document for which they are responsible is, to the best of their knowledge, in accordance with the facts and contains no omission likely to affect its import.

2. STATUTORY AUDITORS

2.1. Names and addresses of the issuer's auditors for the period covered by the historical financial information (together with their membership in a professional body).

2.2. If auditors have resigned, been removed or not been re-appointed during the period covered by the historical financial information, indicate details if material.

3. SELECTED FINANCIAL INFORMATION

3.1. Selected historical financial information regarding the issuer, presented for each financial year for the period covered by the historical financial information, and any subsequent interim financial period, in the same currency as the financial information.

The selected historical financial information must provide the key figures that summarise the financial condition of the issuer.

3.2. If selected financial information for interim periods is provided, comparative data from the same period in the prior financial year must also be provided, except that the requirement for comparative balance sheet information is satisfied by presenting the year end balance sheet information.

4. RISK FACTORS

Prominent disclosure of risk factors that are specific to the issuer or its industry in a section headed "Risk Factors".

5. INFORMATION ABOUT THE ISSUER

5.1. *History and development of the issuer*

5.1.1. The legal and commercial name of the issuer

5.1.2. The place of registration of the issuer and its registration number

5.1.3. The date of incorporation and the length of life of the issuer, except where indefinite

5.1.4. The domicile and legal form of the issuer, the legislation under which the issuer operates, its country of incorporation, and the address and telephone number of its registered office (or principal place of business if different from its registered office)

5.1.5. The important events in the development of the issuer's business.

5.2. *Investments*

5.2.1. A description, (including the amount) of the issuer's principal investments for each financial year for the period covered by the historical financial information up to the date of the registration document

5.2.2. A description of the issuer's principal investments that are in progress, including the geographic distribution of these investments (home and abroad) and the method of financing (internal or external)

5.2.3. Information concerning the issuer's principal future investments on which its management bodies have already made firm commitments.

6. BUSINESS OVERVIEW

6.1. *Principal Activities*

6.1.1. A description of, and key factors relating to, the nature of the issuer's operations and its principal activities, stating the main categories of products sold and/or services performed for each financial year for the period covered by the historical financial information; and

6.1.2. An indication of any significant new products and/or services that have been introduced and, to the extent the development of new products or services has been publicly disclosed, give the status of development.

6.2. *Principal Markets*

A description of the principal markets in which the issuer competes, including a breakdown of total revenues by category of activity and geographic market for each financial year for the period covered by the historical financial information.

6.3. Where the information given pursuant to items 6.1 and 6.2 has been influenced by exceptional factors, mention that fact.

6.4. If material to the issuer's business or profitability, a summary information regarding the extent to which the issuer is dependent, on patents or licences, industrial, commercial or financial contracts or new manufacturing processes.

6.5. The basis for any statements made by the issuer regarding its competitive position.

7. ORGANISATIONAL STRUCTURE

7.1. If the issuer is part of a group, a brief description of the group and the issuer's position within the group.

7.2. A list of the issuer's significant subsidiaries, including name, country of incorporation or residence, proportion of ownership interest and, if different, proportion of voting power held.

8. PROPERTY, PLANTS AND EQUIPMENT

8.1. Information regarding any existing or planned material tangible fixed assets, including leased properties, and any major encumbrances thereon.

8.2. A description of any environmental issues that may affect the issuer's utilisation of the tangible fixed assets.

9. OPERATING AND FINANCIAL REVIEW

9.1. *Financial condition*

To the extent not covered elsewhere in the registration document, provide a description of the issuer's financial condition, changes in financial condition and results of operations for each year and interim period, for which historical financial information is required, including the causes of material changes from year to year in the financial information to the extent necessary for an understanding of the issuer's business as a whole.

9.2. *Operating results*

9.2.1. Information regarding significant factors, including unusual or infrequent events or new developments, materially affecting the issuer's income from operations, indicating the extent to which income was so affected.

9.2.2. Where the financial statements disclose material changes in net sales or revenues, provide a narrative discussion of the reasons for such changes.

9.2.3. Information regarding any governmental, economic, fiscal, monetary or political policies or factors that have materially affected, or could materially affect, directly or indirectly, the issuer's operations.

10. CAPITAL RESOURCES

10.1. Information concerning the issuer's capital resources (both short and long term);

10.2. An explanation of the sources and amounts of and a narrative description of the issuer's cash flows;

10.3. Information on the borrowing requirements and funding structure of the issuer;

10.4. Information regarding any restrictions on the use of capital resources that have materially affected, or could materially affect, directly or indirectly, the issuer's operations.

10.5. Information regarding the anticipated sources of funds needed to fulfil commitments referred to in items 5.2.3 and 8.1.

11. RESEARCH AND DEVELOPMENT, PATENTS AND LICENCES

Where material, provide a description of the issuer's research and development policies for each financial year for the period covered by the historical financial information, including the amount spent on issuer-sponsored research and development activities.

12. TREND INFORMATION

12.1. The most significant recent trends in production, sales and inventory, and costs and selling prices since the end of the last financial year to the date of the registration document.

12.2. Information on any known trends, uncertainties, demands, commitments or events that are reasonably likely to have a material effect on the issuer's prospects for at least the current financial year.

13. PROFIT FORECASTS OR ESTIMATES

If an issuer chooses to include a profit forecast or a profit estimate the registration document must contain the information set out in items 13.1 and 13.2:

13.1. A statement setting out the principal assumptions upon which the issuer has based its forecast, or estimate.

There must be a clear distinction between assumptions about factors which the members of the administrative, management or supervisory bodies can influence and assumptions about factors which are exclusively outside the influence of the members of the administrative, management or supervisory bodies; the assumptions must be readily understandable by investors, be specific and precise and not relate to the general accuracy of the estimates underlying the forecast.

13.2. A report prepared by independent accountants or auditors stating that in the opinion of the independent accountants or auditors the forecast or estimate has been properly compiled on the basis stated and that the basis of accounting used for the profit forecast or estimate is consistent with the accounting policies of the issuer.

13.3. The profit forecast or estimate must be prepared on a basis comparable with the historical financial information.

13.4. If a profit forecast in a prospectus has been published which is still outstanding, then provide a statement setting out whether or not that forecast is still correct as at the time of the registration document, and an explanation of why such forecast is no longer valid if that is the case.

14. ADMINISTRATIVE, MANAGEMENT, AND SUPERVISORY BODIES AND SENIOR MANAGEMENT

14.1. Names, business addresses and functions in the issuer of the following persons and an indication of the principal activities performed by them outside that issuer where these are significant with respect to that issuer:

(a) members of the administrative, management or supervisory bodies;
(b) partners with unlimited liability, in the case of a limited partnership with a share capital;
(c) founders, if the issuer has been established for fewer than five years; and
(d) any senior manager who is relevant to establishing that the issuer has the appropriate expertise and experience for the management of the issuer's business.

The nature of any family relationship between any of those persons.

In the case of each member of the administrative, management or supervisory bodies of the issuer and of each person mentioned in points (b) and (d) of the first subparagraph, details of that person's relevant management expertise and experience and the following information:

(a) the names of all companies and partnerships of which such person has been a member of the administrative, management or supervisory bodies or partner at any time in the previous five years, indicating whether or not the individual is still a member of the administrative, management or supervisory bodies or partner. It is not necessary to list all the subsidiaries of an issuer of which the person is also a member of the administrative, management or supervisory bodies;
(b) any convictions in relation to fraudulent offences for at least the previous five years;
(c) details of any bankruptcies, receiverships or liquidations with which a person described in (a) and (d) of the first subparagraph who was acting in the capacity of any of the positions set out in (a) and (d) of the first subparagraph was associated for at least the previous five years;
(d) details of any official public incrimination and/or sanctions of such person by statutory or regulatory authorities (including designated professional bodies) and whether such person has ever been disqualified by a court from acting as a member of the administrative, management or supervisory bodies of an issuer or from acting in the management or conduct of the affairs of any issuer for at least the previous five years.

If there is no such information to be disclosed, a statement to that effect is to be made.

14.2. Administrative, management, and supervisory bodies' and senior management conflicts of interests

Potential conflicts of interests between any duties to the issuer, of the persons referred to in item 14.1 and their private interests and or other duties must be clearly stated. In the event that there are no such conflicts, a statement to that effect must be made.

Any arrangement or understanding with major shareholders, customers, suppliers or others, pursuant to which any person referred to in item 14.1 was selected as a member of the administrative, management or supervisory bodies or member of senior management.

Details of any restrictions agreed by the persons referred to in item 14.1 on the disposal within a certain period of time of their holdings in the issuer's securities.

15. REMUNERATION AND BENEFITS

In relation to the last full financial year for those persons referred to in points (a) and (d) of the first subparagraph of item 14.1:

15.1. The amount of remuneration paid (including any contingent or deferred compensation), and benefits in kind granted to such persons by the issuer and its subsidiaries for services in all capacities to the issuer and its subsidiaries by any person.

That information must be provided on an individual basis unless individual disclosure is not required in the issuer's home country and is not otherwise publicly disclosed by the issuer.

15.2. The total amounts set aside or accrued by the issuer or its subsidiaries to provide pension, retirement or similar benefits.

16. BOARD PRACTICES

In relation to the issuer's last completed financial year, and unless otherwise specified, with respect to those persons referred to in point (a) of the first subparagraph of 14.1:

16.1. Date of expiration of the current term of office, if applicable, and the period during which the person has served in that office.

16.2. Information about members of the administrative, management or supervisory bodies' service contracts with the issuer or any of its subsidiaries providing for benefits upon termination of employment, or an appropriate negative statement.

16.3. Information about the issuer's audit committee and remuneration committee, including the names of committee members and a summary of the terms of reference under which the committee operates.

16.4. A statement as to whether or not the issuer complies with its country's of incorporation corporate governance regime(s). In the event that the issuer does not comply with such a regime, a statement to that effect must be included together with an explanation regarding why the issuer does not comply with such regime.

17. EMPLOYEES

17.1. Either the number of employees at the end of the period or the average for each financial year for the period covered by the historical financial information up to the date of the registration document (and changes in such numbers, if material) and, if possible and material, a breakdown of persons employed by main category of activity and geographic location. If the issuer employs a significant number of temporary employees, include disclosure of the number of temporary employees on average during the most recent financial year.

17.2. Shareholdings and stock options

With respect to each person referred to in points (a) and (d) of the first subparagraph of item 14.1. provide information as to their share ownership and any options over such shares in the issuer as of the most recent practicable date.

17.3. Description of any arrangements for involving the employees in the capital of the issuer.

18. MAJOR SHAREHOLDERS

18.1. In so far as is known to the issuer, the name of any person other than a member of the administrative, management or supervisory bodies who, directly or indirectly, has an interest in the issuer's capital or voting rights which is notifiable under the issuer's national law, together with the amount of each such person's interest or, if there are no such persons, an appropriate negative statement.

18.2. Whether the issuer's major shareholders have different voting rights, or an appropriate negative statement.

18.3. To the extent known to the issuer, state whether the issuer is directly or indirectly owned or controlled and by whom and describe the nature of such control and describe the measures in place to ensure that such control is not abused.

18.4. A description of any arrangements, known to the issuer, the operation of which may at a subsequent date result in a change in control of the issuer.

19. RELATED PARTY TRANSACTIONS

Details of related party transactions (which for these purposes are those set out in the Standards adopted according to the Regulation (EC) No 1606/2002), that the issuer has entered into during the period covered by the historical financial information and up to the date of the registration document, must be disclosed in accordance with the respective standard adopted according to Regulation (EC) No 1606/2002 if applicable.

If such standards do not apply to the issuer the following information must be disclosed:

(a) the nature and extent of any transactions which are – as a single transaction or in their entirety – material to the issuer. Where such related party transactions are not concluded at arm's length provide an explanation of why these transactions were not concluded at arms length. In the case of outstanding loans including guarantees of any kind indicate the amount outstanding;

(b) the amount or the percentage to which related party transactions form part of the turnover of the issuer.

20. FINANCIAL INFORMATION CONCERNING THE ISSUER'S ASSETS AND LIABILITIES, FINANCIAL POSITION AND PROFITS AND LOSSES

20.1. *Historical financial information*

Audited historical financial information covering the latest three financial years (or such shorter period that the issuer has been in operation), and the audit report in respect of each year. [If the issuer has changed its accounting reference date during the period for which historical financial information is required, the audited historical information shall cover at least 36 months, or the entire period for which the issuer has been in operation, whichever is the shorter.] Such financial information must be prepared according to Regulation (EC) No 1606/2002, or if not applicable to a Member State national accounting standards for issuers from the Community. For third country issuers, such financial information must be prepared according to the international accounting standards adopted pursuant to the procedure of Article 3 of Regulation (EC) No 1606/2002 or to a third country's national accounting standards equivalent to these standards. If such financial information is not equivalent to these standards, it must be presented in the form of restated financial statements.

The last two years audited historical financial information must be presented and prepared in a form consistent with that which will be adopted in the issuer's next published annual financial statements having regard to accounting standards and policies and legislation applicable to such annual financial statements.

If the issuer has been operating in its current sphere of economic activity for less than one year, the audited historical financial information covering that period must be prepared in accordance with the standards applicable to annual financial statements under the Regulation (EC) No 1606/2002, or if not applicable to a Member State national accounting standards where the issuer is an issuer from the Community. For third country issuers, the historical financial information must be prepared according to the international accounting standards adopted pursuant to the procedure of Article 3 of Regulation (EC) No 1606/2002 or to a third country's national accounting standards equivalent to these standards. This historical financial information must be audited.

If the audited financial information is prepared according to national accounting standards, the financial information required under this heading must include at least:

(a) balance sheet;

(b) income statement;

(c) a statement showing either all changes in equity or changes in equity other than those arising from capital transactions with owners and distributions to owners;

(d) cash flow statement;

(e) accounting policies and explanatory notes.

The historical annual financial information must be independently audited or reported on as to whether or not, for the purposes of the registration document, it gives a true and fair view, in accordance with auditing standards applicable in a Member State or an equivalent standard.

20.2. *Pro forma financial information*

In the case of a significant gross change, a description of how the transaction might have affected the assets and liabilities and earnings of the issuer, had the transaction been undertaken at the commencement of the period being reported on or at the date reported.

This requirement will normally be satisfied by the inclusion of pro forma financial information.

This pro forma financial information is to be presented as set out in Annex II and must include the information indicated therein.

Pro forma financial information must be accompanied by a report prepared by independent accountants or auditors.

20.3. *Financial statements*

If the issuer prepares both own and consolidated annual financial statements, include at least the consolidated annual financial statements in the registration document.

20.4. *Auditing of historical annual financial information*

20.4.1. A statement that the historical financial information has been audited. If audit reports on the historical financial information have been refused by the statutory auditors or if they contain qualifications or disclaimers, such refusal or such qualifications or disclaimers must be reproduced in full and the reasons given.

20.4.2. Indication of other information in the registration document which has been audited by the auditors.

20.4.3. Where financial data in the registration document is not extracted from the issuer's audited financial statements state the source of the data and state that the data is unaudited.

20.5. *Age of latest financial information*

20.5.1. The last year of audited financial information may not be older than one of the following:

(a) 18 months from the date of the registration document if the issuer includes audited interim financial statements in the registration document;

(b) 15 months from the date of the registration document if the issuer includes unaudited interim financial statements in the registration document.

20.6. *Interim and other financial information*

20.6.1. If the issuer has published quarterly or half yearly financial information since the date of its last audited financial statements, these must be included in the registration document. If the quarterly or half yearly financial information has been reviewed or audited, the audit or review report must also be included. If the quarterly or half yearly financial information is unaudited or has not been reviewed state that fact.

20.6.2. If the registration document is dated more than nine months after the end of the last audited financial year, it must contain interim financial information, which may be unaudited (in which case that fact must be stated) covering at least the first six months of the financial year.

The interim financial information must include comparative statements for the same period in the prior financial year, except that the requirement for comparative balance sheet information may be satisfied by presenting the years end balance sheet.

20.7. *Dividend policy*

A description of the issuer's policy on dividend distributions and any restrictions thereon.

20.7.1. The amount of the dividend per share for each financial year for the period covered by the historical financial information adjusted, where the number of shares in the issuer has changed, to make it comparable.

20.8. *Legal and arbitration proceedings*

Information on any governmental, legal or arbitration proceedings (including any such proceedings which are pending or threatened of which the issuer is aware), during a period covering at least the previous 12 months which may have, or have had in the recent past significant effects on the issuer and/or group's financial position or profitability, or provide an appropriate negative statement.

20.9. *Significant change in the issuer's financial or trading position*

A description of any significant change in the financial or trading position of the group which has occurred since the end of the last financial period for which either audited financial information or interim financial information have been published, or provide an appropriate negative statement.

21. ADDITIONAL INFORMATION

21.1. *Share capital*

The following information as of the date of the most recent balance sheet included in the historical financial information:

21.1.1. The amount of issued capital, and for each class of share capital:

(a) the number of shares authorised;

(b) the number of shares issued and fully paid and issued but not fully paid;
(c) the par value per share, or that the shares have no par value; and
(d) a reconciliation of the number of shares outstanding at the beginning and end of the year. If more than 10% of capital has been paid for with assets other than cash within the period covered by the historical financial information, state that fact.

21.1.2. If there are shares not representing capital, state the number and main characteristics of such shares.

21.1.3. The number, book value and face value of shares in the issuer held by or on behalf of the issuer itself or by subsidiaries of the issuer.

21.1.4. The amount of any convertible securities, exchangeable securities or securities with warrants, with an indication of the conditions governing and the procedures for conversion, exchange or subscription.

21.1.5. Information about and terms of any acquisition rights and or obligations over authorised but unissued capital or an undertaking to increase the capital.

21.1.6. Information about any capital of any member of the group which is under option or agreed conditionally or unconditionally to be put under option and details of such options including those persons to whom such options relate.

21.1.7. A history of share capital, highlighting information about any changes, for the period covered by the historical financial information.

21.2. *Memorandum and Articles of Association*

21.2.1. A description of the issuer's objects and purposes and where they can be found in the memorandum and articles of association.

21.2.2. A summary of any provisions of the issuer's articles of association, statutes, charter or bylaws with respect to the members of the administrative, management and supervisory bodies.

21.2.3. A description of the rights, preferences and restrictions attaching to each class of the existing shares.

21.2.4. A description of what action is necessary to change the rights of holders of the shares, indicating where the conditions are more significant than is required by law.

21.2.5. A description of the conditions governing the manner in which annual general meetings and extraordinary general meetings of shareholders are called including the conditions of admission.

21.2.6. A brief description of any provision of the issuer's articles of association, statutes, charter or bylaws that would have an effect of delaying, deferring or preventing a change in control of the issuer.

21.2.7. An indication of the articles of association, statutes, charter or bylaw provisions, if any, governing the ownership threshold above which shareholder ownership must be disclosed.

21.2.8. A description of the conditions imposed by the memorandum and articles of association statutes, charter or bylaw governing changes in the capital, where such conditions are more stringent than is required by law.

22. MATERIAL CONTRACTS

A summary of each material contract, other than contracts entered into in the ordinary course of business, to which the issuer or any member of the group is a party, for the two years immediately preceding publication of the registration document.

A summary of any other contract (not being a contract entered into in the ordinary course of business) entered into by any member of the group which contains any provision under which any member of the group has any obligation or entitlement which is material to the group as at the date of the registration document.

23. THIRD PARTY INFORMATION AND STATEMENT BY EXPERTS AND DECLARATIONS OF ANY INTEREST

23.1. Where a statement or report attributed to a person as an expert is included in the registration document, provide such person's name, business address, qualifications and material interest if any in the issuer. If the report has been produced at the issuer's request a statement to the effect that such statement or report is included, in the form and context in which it is included, with the consent of the person who has authorised the contents of that part of the registration document.

23.2. Where information has been sourced from a third party, provide a confirmation that this information has been accurately reproduced and that as far as the issuer is aware and is able to ascertain from information published by that third party, no facts have been omitted which would render the reproduced information inaccurate or misleading. In addition, identify the source(s) of the information.

24. DOCUMENTS ON DISPLAY

A statement that for the life of the registration document the following documents (or copies thereof), where applicable, may be inspected:

(a) the memorandum and articles of association of the issuer;

(b) all reports, letters, and other documents, historical financial information, valuations and statements prepared by any expert at the issuer's request any part of which is included or referred to in the registration document;

(c) the historical financial information of the issuer or, in the case of a group, the historical financial information for the issuer and its subsidiary undertakings for each of the two financial years preceding the publication of the registration document.

An indication of where the documents on display may be inspected, by physical or electronic means.

25. INFORMATION ON HOLDINGS

Information relating to the undertakings in which the issuer holds a proportion of the capital likely to have a significant effect on the assessment of its own assets and liabilities, financial position or profits and losses.

[9743]

NOTES

Words in square brackets in item 20.1 inserted by Commission Regulation 211/2007/EC, Art 1(3), as from 1 March 2007.

ANNEX II
PRO FORMA FINANCIAL INFORMATION BUILDING BLOCK

1. The pro forma information must include a description of the transaction, the businesses or entities involved and the period to which it refers, and must clearly state the following:

(a) the purpose to which it has been prepared;

(b) the fact that it has been prepared for illustrative purposes only;

(c) the fact that because of its nature, the pro forma financial information addresses a hypothetical situation and, therefore, does not represent the company's actual financial position or results.

2. In order to present pro forma financial information, a balance sheet and profit and loss account, and accompanying explanatory notes, depending on the circumstances may be included.

3. Pro forma financial information must normally be presented in columnar format, composed of:

(a) the historical unadjusted information;

(b) the pro forma adjustments; and

(c) the resulting pro forma financial information in the final column.

The sources of the pro forma financial information have to be stated and, if applicable, the financial statements of the acquired businesses or entities must be included in the prospectus

4. The pro forma information must be prepared in a manner consistent with the accounting policies adopted by the issuer in its last or next financial statements and shall identify the following:

(a) the basis upon which it is prepared;

(b) the source of each item of information and adjustment.

5. Pro forma information may only be published in respect of:
(a) the current financial period;
(b) the most recently completed financial period;
and/or
(c) the most recent interim period for which relevant unadjusted information has been or will be published or is being published in the same document.

6. Pro forma adjustments related to the pro forma financial information must be:
(a) clearly shown and explained;
(b) directly attributable to the transaction;
(c) factually supportable.

In addition, in respect of a pro forma profit and loss or cash flow statement, they must be clearly identified as to those expected to have a continuing impact on the issuer and those which are not.

7. The report prepared by the independent accountants or auditors must state that in their opinion:
(a) the pro forma financial information has been properly compiled on the basis stated;
(b) that basis is consistent with the accounting policies of the issuer.

[9744]

ANNEX III
MINIMUM DISCLOSURE REQUIREMENTS FOR THE SHARE SECURITIES NOTE (SCHEDULE)

1. PERSONS RESPONSIBLE

1.1. All persons responsible for the information given in the prospectus and, as the case may be, for certain parts of it, with, in the latter case, an indication of such parts. In the case of natural persons including members of the issuer's administrative, management or supervisory bodies indicate the name and function of the person; in case of legal persons indicate the name and registered office.

1.2. A declaration by those responsible for the prospectus that, having taken all reasonable care to ensure that such is the case the information contained in the prospectus is, to the best of their knowledge, in accordance with the facts and contains no omission likely to affect its import. As the case may be, declaration by those responsible for certain parts of the prospectus that, having taken all reasonable care to ensure that such is the case the information contained in the part of the prospectus for which they are responsible is, to the best of their knowledge, in accordance with the facts and contains no omission likely to affect its import.

2. RISK FACTORS

Prominent disclosure of risk factors that are material to the securities being offered and/or admitted to trading in order to assess the market risk associated with these securities in a section headed "Risk Factors".

3. KEY INFORMATION

3.1. *Working capital statement*

Statement by the issuer that, in its opinion, the working capital is sufficient for the issuer's present requirements or, if not, how it proposes to provide the additional working capital needed.

3.2. *Capitalisation and indebtedness*

A statement of capitalisation and indebtedness (distinguishing between guaranteed and unguaranteed, secured and unsecured indebtedness) as of a date no earlier than 90 days prior to the date of the document. Indebtedness also includes indirect and contingent indebtedness.

3.3. *Interest of natural and legal persons involved in the issue/offer*

A description of any interest, including conflicting ones that is material to the issue/offer, detailing the persons involved and the nature of the interest.

3.4. *Reasons for the offer and use of proceeds*

Reasons for the offer and, where applicable, the estimated net amount of the proceeds broken into each principal intended use and presented by order of priority of such uses. If the issuer is aware that the anticipated proceeds will not be sufficient to fund all the proposed uses, state the amount and sources of other funds needed. Details must be given with regard to the use of the proceeds, in particular when they are being used to acquire assets, other than in the ordinary course of business, to finance announced acquisitions of other business, or to discharge, reduce or retire indebtedness.

4. INFORMATION CONCERNING THE SECURITIES TO BE OFFERED/ ADMITTED TO TRADING

4.1. A description of the type and the class of the securities being offered and/or admitted to trading, including the ISIN (international security identification number) or other such security identification code.

4.2. Legislation under which the securities have been created.

4.3. An indication whether the securities are in registered form or bearer form and whether the securities are in certificated form or book-entry form. In the latter case, name and address of the entity in charge of keeping the records.

4.4. Currency of the securities issue.

4.5. A description of the rights attached to the securities, including any limitations of those rights, and procedure for the exercise of those rights.

Dividend rights:

— fixed date(s) on which the entitlement arises,
— time limit after which entitlement to dividend lapses and an indication of the person in whose favour the lapse operates,
— dividend restrictions and procedures for non-resident holders,
— rate of dividend or method of its calculation, periodicity and cumulative or non-cumulative nature of payments.

Voting rights.

Pre-emption rights in offers for subscription of securities of the same class.

Right to share in the issuer's profits.

Rights to share in any surplus in the event of liquidation.

— Redemption provisions.
— Conversion provisions.

4.6. In the case of new issues, a statement of the resolutions, authorisations and approvals by virtue of which the securities have been or will be created and/or issued.

4.7. In the case of new issues, the expected issue date of the securities.

4.8. A description of any restrictions on the free transferability of the securities.

4.9. An indication of the existence of any mandatory takeover bids and/or squeeze-out and sell-out rules in relation to the securities.

4.10. An indication of public takeover bids by third parties in respect of the issuer's equity, which have occurred during the last financial year and the current financial year. The price or exchange terms attaching to such offers and the outcome thereof must be stated.

4.11. In respect of the country of registered office of the issuer and the country(ies) where the offer is being made or admission to trading is being sought:

— information on taxes on the income from the securities withheld at source,
— indication as to whether the issuer assumes responsibility for the withholding of taxes at the source.

5. TERMS AND CONDITIONS OF THE OFFER

5.1. *Conditions, offer statistics, expected timetable and action required to apply for the offer*

5.1.1. Conditions to which the offer is subject.

5.1.2. Total amount of the issue/offer, distinguishing the securities offered for sale and those offered for subscription; if the amount is not fixed, description of the arrangements and time for announcing to the public the definitive amount of the offer.

5.1.3. The time period, including any possible amendments, during which the offer will be open and description of the application process.

5.1.4. An indication of when, and under which circumstances, the offer may be revoked or suspended and whether revocation can occur after dealing has begun.

5.1.5. A description of the possibility to reduce subscriptions and the manner for refunding excess amount paid by applicants.

5.1.6. Details of the minimum and/or maximum amount of application (whether in number of securities or aggregate amount to invest).

5.1.7. An indication of the period during which an application may be withdrawn, provided that investors are allowed to withdraw their subscription.

5.1.8. Method and time limits for paying up the securities and for delivery of the securities.

5.1.9. A full description of the manner and date in which results of the offer are to be made public.

5.1.10. The procedure for the exercise of any right of pre-emption, the negotiability of subscription rights and the treatment of subscription rights not exercised.

5.2. *Plan of distribution and allotment*

5.2.1. The various categories of potential investors to which the securities are offered. If the offer is being made simultaneously in the markets of two or more countries and if a tranche has been or is being reserved for certain of these, indicate any such tranche.

5.2.2. To the extent known to the issuer, an indication of whether major shareholders or members of the issuer's management, supervisory or administrative bodies intended to subscribe in the offer, or whether any person intends to subscribe for more than five per cent of the offer.

5.2.3. Pre-allotment disclosure:

(a) the division into tranches of the offer including the institutional, retail and issuer's employee tranches and any other tranches;

(b) the conditions under which the clawback may be used, the maximum size of such claw back and any applicable minimum percentages for individual tranches;

(c) the allotment method or methods to be used for the retail and issuer's employee tranche in the event of an over-subscription of these tranches;

(d) a description of any pre-determined preferential treatment to be accorded to certain classes of investors or certain affinity groups (including friends and family programmes) in the allotment, the percentage of the offer reserved for such preferential treatment and the criteria for inclusion in such classes or groups;

(e) whether the treatment of subscriptions or bids to subscribe in the allotment may be determined on the basis of which firm they are made through or by;

(f) a target minimum individual allotment if any within the retail tranche;

(g) the conditions for the closing of the offer as well as the date on which the offer may be closed at the earliest;

(h) whether or not multiple subscriptions are admitted, and where they are not, how any multiple subscriptions will be handled.

5.2.4. Process for notification to applicants of the amount allotted and indication whether dealing may begin before notification is made.

5.2.5. Over-allotment and "green shoe":

(a) the existence and size of any over-allotment facility and/or "green shoe".

(b) the existence period of the over-allotment facility and/or "green shoe".

(c) any conditions for the use of the over-allotment facility or exercise of the "green shoe".

5.3. *Pricing*

5.3.1. An indication of the price at which the securities will be offered. If the price is not known or if there is no established and/or liquid market for the securities, indicate the method for determining the offer price, including a statement as to who has set the criteria or is formally responsible for the determination. Indication of the amount of any expenses and taxes specifically charged to the subscriber or purchaser.

5.3.2. Process for the disclosure of the offer price.

5.3.3. If the issuer's equity holders have pre-emptive purchase rights and this right is restricted or withdrawn, indication of the basis for the issue price if the issue is for cash, together with the reasons for and beneficiaries of such restriction or withdrawal.

5.3.4. Where there is or could be a material disparity between the public offer price and the effective cash cost to members of the administrative, management or supervisory bodies or senior management, or affiliated persons, of securities acquired by them in transactions during the past year, or which they have the right to acquire, include a comparison of the public contribution in the proposed public offer and the effective cash contributions of such persons.

5.4. *Placing and underwriting*

5.4.1. Name and address of the coordinator(s) of the global offer and of single parts of the offer and, to the extend known to the issuer or to the offeror, of the placers in the various countries where the offer takes place.

5.4.2. Name and address of any paying agents and depository agents in each country.

5.4.3. Name and address of the entities agreeing to underwrite the issue on a firm commitment basis, and name and address of the entities agreeing to place the issue without a firm commitment or under "best efforts" arrangements. Indication of the material features of the agreements, including the quotas. Where not all of the issue is underwritten, a statement of the portion not covered. Indication of the overall amount of the underwriting commission and of the placing commission.

5.4.4. When the underwriting agreement has been or will be reached.

6. ADMISSION TO TRADING AND DEALING ARRANGEMENTS

6.1. An indication as to whether the securities offered are or will be the object of an application for admission to trading, with a view to their distribution in a regulated market or other equivalent markets with indication of the markets in question. This circumstance must be mentioned, without creating the impression that the admission to trading will necessarily be approved. If known, the earliest dates on which the securities will be admitted to trading.

6.2. All the regulated markets or equivalent markets on which, to the knowledge of the issuer, securities of the same class of the securities to be offered or admitted to trading are already admitted to trading.

6.3. If simultaneously or almost simultaneously with the creation of the securities for which admission to a regulated market is being sought securities of the same class are subscribed for or placed privately or if securities of other classes are created for public or private placing, give details of the nature of such operations and of the number and characteristics of the securities to which they relate.

6.4. Details of the entities which have a firm commitment to act as intermediaries in secondary trading, providing liquidity through bid and offer rates and description of the main terms of their commitment.

6.5. Stabilisation: where an issuer or a selling shareholder has granted an over-allotment option or it is otherwise proposed that price stabilising activities may be entered into in connection with an offer:

6.5.1. The fact that stabilisation may be undertaken, that there is no assurance that it will be undertaken and that it may be stopped at any time,

6.5.2. The beginning and the end of the period during which stabilisation may occur,

6.5.3. The identity of the stabilisation manager for each relevant jurisdiction unless this is not known at the time of publication,

6.5.4. The fact that stabilisation transactions may result in a market price that is higher than would otherwise prevail.

7. SELLING SECURITIES HOLDERS

7.1. Name and business address of the person or entity offering to sell the securities, the nature of any position office or other material relationship that the selling persons has had within the past three years with the issuer or any of its predecessors or affiliates.

7.2. The number and class of securities being offered by each of the selling security holders.

7.3. Lock-up agreements

The parties involved.

Content and exceptions of the agreement.
Indication of the period of the lock up.

8. EXPENSE OF THE ISSUE/OFFER

8.1. The total net proceeds and an estimate of the total expenses of the issue/offer.

9. DILUTION

9.1. The amount and percentage of immediate dilution resulting from the offer.

9.2. In the case of a subscription offer to existing equity holders, the amount and percentage of immediate dilution if they do not subscribe to the new offer.

10. ADDITIONAL INFORMATION

10.1. If advisors connected with an issue are mentioned in the Securities Note, a statement of the capacity in which the advisors have acted.

10.2. An indication of other information in the Securities Note which has been audited or reviewed by statutory auditors and where auditors have produced a report. Reproduction of the report or, with permission of the competent authority, a summary of the report.

10.3. Where a statement or report attributed to a person as an expert is included in the Securities Note, provide such persons' name, business address, qualifications and material interest if any in the issuer. If the report has been produced at the issuer's request a statement to the effect that such statement or report is included, in the form and context in which it is included, with the consent of the person who has authorised the contents of that part of the Securities Note.

10.4. Where information has been sourced from a third party, provide a confirmation that this information has been accurately reproduced and that as far as the issuer is aware and is able to ascertain from information published by that third party, no facts have been omitted which would render the reproduced information inaccurate or misleading. In addition, identify the source(s) of the information.

[9745]

ANNEX IV

MINIMUM DISCLOSURE REQUIREMENTS FOR THE DEBT AND DERIVATIVE SECURITIES REGISTRATION DOCUMENT (SCHEDULE)

(*Debt and derivative securities with a denomination per unit of less than EUR 50,000*)

1. PERSONS RESPONSIBLE

1.1. All persons responsible for the information given in the registration document and, as the case may be, for certain parts of it, with, in the latter case, an indication of such parts. In the case of natural persons including members of the issuer's administrative, management or supervisory bodies indicate the name and function of the person; in case of legal persons indicate the name and registered office.

1.2. A declaration by those responsible for the registration document that, having taken all reasonable care to ensure that such is the case the information contained in the registration document is, to the best of their knowledge, in accordance with the facts and contains no omission likely to affect its import. As the case may be, declaration by those responsible for certain parts of the registration document that, having taken all reasonable care to ensure that such is the case, the information contained in the part of the registration document for which they are responsible is, to the best of their knowledge, in accordance with the facts and contains no omission likely to affect its import.

2. STATUTORY AUDITORS

2.1. Names and addresses of the issuer's auditors for the period covered by the historical financial information (together with their membership in a professional body).

2.2. If auditors have resigned, been removed or not been re-appointed during the period covered by the historical financial information, details if material.

3. SELECTED FINANCIAL INFORMATION

3.1. Selected historical financial information regarding the issuer, presented, for each financial year for the period covered by the historical financial information, and any subsequent interim financial period, in the same currency as the financial information.

The selected historical financial information must provide key figures that summarise the financial condition of the issuer.

3.2. If selected financial information for interim periods is provided, comparative data from the same period in the prior financial year must also be provided, except that the requirement for comparative balance sheet data is satisfied by presenting the year end balance sheet information.

4. RISK FACTORS

Prominent disclosure of risk factors that may affect the issuer's ability to fulfil its obligations under the securities to investors in a section headed "Risk Factors".

5. INFORMATION ABOUT THE ISSUER

5.1. *History and development of the issuer*

5.1.1. the legal and commercial name of the issuer;

5.1.2. the place of registration of the issuer and its registration number;

5.1.3. the date of incorporation and the length of life of the issuer, except where indefinite;

5.1.4. the domicile and legal form of the issuer, the legislation under which the issuer operates, its country of incorporation, and the address and telephone number of its registered office (or principal place of business if different from its registered office);

5.1.5. any recent events particular to the issuer which are to a material extent relevant to the evaluation of the issuer's solvency.

5.2. *Investments*

5.2.1. A description of the principal investments made since the date of the last published financial statements.

5.2.2. Information concerning the issuer's principal future investments, on which its management bodies have already made firm commitments.

5.2.3. Information regarding the anticipated sources of funds needed to fulfil commitments referred to in item 5.2.2.

6. BUSINESS OVERVIEW

6.1. *Principal activities*

6.1.1. A description of the issuer's principal activities stating the main categories of products sold and/or services performed; and

6.1.2. an indication of any significant new products and/or activities.

6.2. *Principal markets*

A brief description of the principal markets in which the issuer competes.

6.3. The basis for any statements made by the issuer regarding its competitive position.

7. ORGANISATIONAL STRUCTURE

7.1. If the issuer is part of a group, a brief description of the group and of the issuer's position within it.

7.2. If the issuer is dependent upon other entities within the group, this must be clearly stated together with an explanation of this dependence.

8. TREND INFORMATION

8.1. Include a statement that there has been no material adverse change in the prospects of the issuer since the date of its last published audited financial statements.

In the event that the issuer is unable to make such a statement, provide details of this material adverse change.

8.2. Information on any known trends, uncertainties, demands, commitments or events that are reasonably likely to have a material effect on the issuer's prospects for at least the current financial year.

9. PROFIT FORECASTS OR ESTIMATES

If an issuer chooses to include a profit forecast or a profit estimate, the registration document must contain the information items 9.1 and 9.2:

9.1. A statement setting out the principal assumptions upon which the issuer has based its forecast, or estimate.

There must be a clear distinction between assumptions about factors which the members of the administrative, management or supervisory bodies can influence and assumptions about factors which are exclusively outside the influence of the members of the administrative, management or supervisory bodies; the assumptions must be readily understandable by investors, be specific and precise and not relate to the general accuracy of the estimates underlying the forecast.

9.2. A report prepared by independent accountants or auditors must be included stating that in the opinion of the independent accountants or auditors the forecast or estimate has been properly compiled on the basis stated and that the basis of accounting used for the profit forecast or estimate is consistent with the accounting policies of the issuer.

9.3. The profit forecast or estimate must be prepared on a basis comparable with the historical financial information.

10. ADMINISTRATIVE, MANAGEMENT, AND SUPERVISORY BODIES

10.1. Names, business addresses and functions in the issuer of the following persons, and an indication of the principal activities performed by them outside the issuer where these are significant with respect to that issuer:

(a) members of the administrative, management or supervisory bodies;

(b) partners with unlimited liability, in the case of a limited partnership with a share capital.

10.2. Administrative, management, and supervisory bodies' conflicts of interests

Potential conflicts of interests between any duties to the issuing entity of the persons referred to in item 10.1 and their private interests and or other duties must be clearly stated. In the event that there are no such conflicts, make a statement to that effect.

11. BOARD PRACTICES

11.1. Details relating to the issuer's audit committee, including the names of committee members and a summary of the terms of reference under which the committee operates.

11.2. A statement as to whether or not the issuer complies with its country's of incorporation corporate governance regime(s). In the event that the issuer does not comply with such a regime a statement to that effect must be included together with an explanation regarding why the issuer does not comply with such regime.

12. MAJOR SHAREHOLDERS

12.1. To the extent known to the issuer, state whether the issuer is directly or indirectly owned or controlled and by whom and describe the nature of such control, and describe the measures in place to ensure that such control is not abused.

12.2. A description of any arrangements, known to the issuer, the operation of which may at a subsequent date result in a change in control of the issuer.

13. FINANCIAL INFORMATION CONCERNING THE ISSUER'S ASSETS AND LIABILITIES, FINANCIAL POSITION AND PROFITS AND LOSSES

13.1. *Historical financial information*

Audited historical financial information covering the latest 2 financial years (or such shorter period that the issuer has been in operation), and the audit report in respect of each year. [If the issuer has changed its accounting reference date during the period for which historical financial information is required, the audited historical information shall cover at least 24 months, or the entire period for which the issuer has been in operation, whichever is the shorter.] Such financial information must be prepared according to Regulation (EC) No 1606/2002, or if not applicable to a Member States national accounting standards for issuers from the Community. For third country issuers, such financial information must be prepared according to the international accounting standards adopted pursuant to the procedure of Article 3 of Regulation (EC) No 1606/2002 or to a third country's national accounting standards equivalent to these standards. If such financial information is not equivalent to these standards, it must be presented in the form of restated financial statements.

The most recent year's historical financial information must be presented and prepared in a form consistent with that which will be adopted in the issuer's next published annual financial statements having regard to accounting standards and policies and legislation applicable to such annual financial statements.

If the issuer has been operating in its current sphere of economic activity for less than one year, the audited historical financial information covering that period must be prepared in accordance with the standards applicable to annual financial statements under the Regulation (EC) No 1606/2002, or if not applicable to a Member States national accounting standards where the issuer is an issuer from the Community. For third country issuers, the historical financial information must be prepared according to the international accounting standards adopted pursuant to the procedure of Article 3 of Regulation (EC) No 1606/2002 or to a third country's national accounting standards equivalent to these standards. This historical financial information must be audited.

If the audited financial information is prepared according to national accounting standards, the financial information required under this heading must include at least:

(a) balance sheet;
(b) income statement;
(c) cash flow statement; and
(d) accounting policies and explanatory notes

The historical annual financial information must have been independently audited or reported on as to whether or not, for the purposes of the registration document, it gives a true and fair view, in accordance with auditing standards applicable in a Member State or an equivalent standard.

13.2. *Financial statements*

If the issuer prepares both own and consolidated financial statements, include at least the consolidated financial statements in the registration document.

13.3. *Auditing of historical annual financial information*

13.3.1. A statement that the historical financial information has been audited. If audit reports on the historical financial information have been refused by the statutory auditors or if they contain qualifications or disclaimers, such refusal or such qualifications or disclaimers must be reproduced in full and the reasons given.

13.3.2. An indication of other information in the registration document which has been audited by the auditors.

13.3.3. Where financial data in the registration document is not extracted from the issuer's audited financial statements state the source of the data and state that the data is unaudited.

13.4. *Age of latest financial information*

13.4.1. The last year of audited financial information may not be older than 18 months from the date of the registration document.

13.5. *Interim and other financial information*

13.5.1. If the issuer has published quarterly or half yearly financial information since the date of its last audited financial statements, these must be included in the registration document. If the quarterly or half yearly financial information has been reviewed or audited the audit or review report must also be included. If the quarterly or half yearly financial information is unaudited or has not been reviewed state that fact.

13.5.2. If the registration document is dated more than nine months after the end of the last audited financial year, it must contain interim financial information, covering at least the first six months of the financial year. If the interim financial information is un-audited state that fact.

The interim financial information must include comparative statements for the same period in the prior financial year, except that the requirement for comparative balance sheet information may be satisfied by presenting the years end balance sheet.

13.6. *Legal and arbitration proceedings*

Information on any governmental, legal or arbitration proceedings (including any such proceedings which are pending or threatened of which the issuer is aware), during a period covering at least the previous 12 months which may have, or have had in the recent past, significant effects on the issuer and/or group's financial position or profitability, or provide an appropriate negative statement.

13.7. *Significant change in the issuer's financial or trading position*

A description of any significant change in the financial or trading position of the group which has occurred since the end of the last financial period for which either audited financial information or interim financial information have been published, or an appropriate negative statement.

14. ADDITIONAL INFORMATION

14.1. *Share capital*

14.1.1. The amount of the issued capital, the number and classes of the shares of which it is composed with details of their principal characteristics, the part of the issued capital still to be paid up, with an indication of the number, or total nominal value, and the type of the shares not yet fully paid up, broken down where applicable according to the extent to which they have been paid up.

14.2. *Memorandum and Articles of Association*

14.2.1. The register and the entry number therein, if applicable, and a description of the issuer's objects and purposes and where they can be found in the memorandum and articles of association.

15. MATERIAL CONTRACTS

A brief summary of all material contracts that are not entered into in the ordinary course of the issuer's business, which could result in any group member being under an obligation or entitlement that is material to the issuer's ability to meet its obligation to security holders in respect of the securities being issued.

16. THIRD PARTY INFORMATION AND STATEMENT BY EXPERTS AND DECLARATIONS OF ANY INTEREST

16.1. Where a statement or report attributed to a person as an expert is included in the registration document, provide such person's name, business address, qualifications and material interest if any in the issuer. If the report has been produced at the issuer's request a statement to that effect that such statement or report is included, in the form and context in which it is included, with the consent of that person who has authorised the contents of that part of the registration document.

16.2. Where information has been sourced from a third party, provide a confirmation that this information has been accurately reproduced and that as far as the issuer is aware and is able to ascertain from information published by that third party, no facts have been omitted which would render the reproduced information inaccurate or misleading. In addition, the issuer shall identify the source(s) of the information.

17. DOCUMENTS ON DISPLAY

A statement that for the life of the registration document the following documents (or copies thereof), where applicable, may be inspected:

(a) the memorandum and articles of association of the issuer;

(b) all reports, letters, and other documents, historical financial information, valuations and statements prepared by any expert at the issuer's request any part of which is included or referred to in the registration document;

(c) the historical financial information of the issuer or, in the case of a group, the historical financial information of the issuer and its subsidiary undertakings for each of the two financial years preceding the publication of the registration document.

An indication of where the documents on display may be inspected, by physical or electronic means.

[9746]

NOTES

Words in square brackets in item 13.1 inserted by Commission Regulation 211/2007/EC, Art 1(4), as from 1 March 2007.

ANNEX V
MINIMUM DISCLOSURE REQUIREMENTS FOR THE SECURITIES NOTE RELATED TO DEBT SECURITIES (SCHEDULE)

(*Debt securities with a denomination per unit of less than EUR 50,000*)

1. PERSONS RESPONSIBLE

1.1. All persons responsible for the information given in the prospectus and, as the case may be, for certain parts of it, with, in the latter case, an indication of such parts. In the case of natural persons including members of the issuer's administrative, management or supervisory bodies indicate the name and function of the person; in case of legal persons indicate the name and registered office.

1.2. A declaration by those responsible for the prospectus that, having taken all reasonable care to ensure that such is the case, the information contained in the prospectus is, to the best of their knowledge, in accordance with the facts and contains no omission likely to affect its import. As the case may be, declaration by those responsible for certain parts of the prospectus that the information contained in the part of the prospectus for which they are responsible is, to the best of their knowledge, in accordance with the facts and contains no omission likely to affect its import.

2. RISK FACTORS

2.1. Prominent disclosure of risk factors that are material to the securities being offered and/or admitted to trading in order to assess the market risk associated with these securities in a section headed "Risk Factors".

3. KEY INFORMATION

3.1. *Interest of natural and legal persons involved in the issue/offer*

A description of any interest, including conflicting ones, that is material to the issue/offer, detailing the persons involved and the nature of the interest.

3.2. *Reasons for the offer and use of proceeds*

Reasons for the offer if different from making profit and/or hedging certain risks. Where applicable, disclosure of the estimated total expenses of the issue/offer and the estimated net amount of the proceeds. These expenses and proceeds shall be broken into each principal intended use and presented by order of priority of such uses. If the issuer is aware that the anticipated proceeds will not be sufficient to fund all the proposed uses, state the amount and sources of other funds needed.

4. INFORMATION CONCERNING THE SECURITIES TO BE OFFERED/ ADMITTED TO TRADING

4.1. A description of the type and the class of the securities being offered and/or admitted to trading, including the ISIN (International Security Identification Number) or other such security identification code.

4.2. Legislation under which the securities have been created.

4.3. An indication of whether the securities are in registered form or bearer form and whether the securities are in certificated form or book-entry form. In the latter case, name and address of the entity in charge of keeping the records.

4.4. Currency of the securities issue.

4.5. Ranking of the securities being offered and/or admitted to trading, including summaries of any clauses that are intended to affect ranking or subordinate the security to any present or future liabilities of the issuer.

4.6. A description of the rights attached to the securities, including any limitations of those rights, and procedure for the exercise of those rights.

4.7. The nominal interest rate and provisions relating to interest payable.

— The date from which interest becomes payable and the due dates for interest

— The time limit on the validity of claims to interest and repayment of principal.

Where the rate is not fixed, description of the underlying on which it is based and of the method used to relate the two and an indication where information about the past and the further performance of the underlying and its volatility can be obtained.

— A description of any market disruption or settlement disruption events that affect the underlying

— Adjustment rules with relation to events concerning the underlying

— Name of the calculation agent.

If the security has a derivative component in the interest payment, provide a clear and comprehensive explanation to help investors understand how the value of their investment is affected by the value of the underlying instrument(s), especially under the circumstances when the risks are most evident.

4.8. Maturity date and arrangements for the amortisation of the loan, including the repayment procedures. Where advance amortisation is contemplated, on the initiative of the issuer or of the holder, it shall be described, stipulating amortisation terms and conditions.

4.9. An indication of yield. Describe the method whereby that yield is calculated in summary form.

4.10. Representation of debt security holders including an identification of the organisation representing the investors and provisions applying to such representation. Indication of where the public may have access to the contracts relating to these forms of representation.

4.11. In the case of new issues, a statement of the resolutions, authorisations and approvals by virtue of which the securities have been or will be created and/or issued.

4.12. In the case of new issues, the expected issue date of the securities.

4.13. A description of any restrictions on the free transferability of the securities.

4.14. In respect of the country of registered office of the issuer and the country(ies) where the offer being made or admission to trading is being sought:

— information on taxes on the income from the securities withheld at source;

— indication as to whether the issuer assumes responsibility for the withholding of taxes at the source.

5. TERMS AND CONDITIONS OF THE OFFER

5.1. *Conditions, offer statistics, expected timetable and action required to apply for the offer*

5.1.1. Conditions to which the offer is subject.

5.1.2. Total amount of the issue/offer; if the amount is not fixed, description of the arrangements and time for announcing to the public the definitive amount of the offer.

5.1.3. The time period, including any possible amendments, during which the offer will be open and description of the application process.

5.1.4. A description of the possibility to reduce subscriptions and the manner for refunding excess amount paid by applicants.

5.1.5. Details of the minimum and/or maximum amount of application, (whether in number of securities or aggregate amount to invest).

5.1.6. Method and time limits for paying up the securities and for delivery of the securities.

5.1.7. A full description of the manner and date in which results of the offer are to be made public.

5.1.8. The procedure for the exercise of any right of pre-emption, the negotiability of subscription rights and the treatment of subscription rights not exercised.

5.2. *Plan of distribution and allotment*

5.2.1. The various categories of potential investors to which the securities are offered. If the offer is being made simultaneously in the markets of two or more countries and if a tranche has been or is being reserved for certain of these, indicate any such tranche.

5.2.2. Process for notification to applicants of the amount allotted and indication whether dealing may begin before notification is made.

5.3. *Pricing*

5.3.1. An indication of the expected price at which the securities will be offered or the method of determining the price and the process for its disclosure. Indicate the amount of any expenses and taxes specifically charged to the subscriber or purchaser.

5.4. *Placing and underwriting*

5.4.1. Name and address of the co-ordinator(s) of the global offer and of single parts of the offer and, to the extend known to the issuer or to the offeror, of the placers in the various countries where the offer takes place.

5.4.2. Name and address of any paying agents and depository agents in each country.

5.4.3. Name and address of the entities agreeing to underwrite the issue on a firm commitment basis, and name and address of the entities agreeing to place the issue without a firm commitment or under "best efforts" arrangements. Indication of the material features of the agreements, including the quotas. Where not all of the issue is underwritten, a statement of the portion not covered. Indication of the overall amount of the underwriting commission and of the placing commission.

5.4.4. When the underwriting agreement has been or will be reached.

6. ADMISSION TO TRADING AND DEALING ARRANGEMENTS

6.1. An indication as to whether the securities offered are or will be the object of an application for admission to trading, with a view to their distribution in a regulated market or other equivalent markets with indication of the markets in question. This circumstance must be mentioned, without creating the impression that the admission to trading will necessarily be approved. If known, give the earliest dates on which the securities will be admitted to trading.

6.2. All the regulated markets or equivalent markets on which, to the knowledge of the issuer, securities of the same class of the securities to be offered or admitted to trading are already admitted to trading.

6.3. Name and address of the entities which have a firm commitment to act as intermediaries in secondary trading, providing liquidity through bid and offer rates and description of the main terms of their commitment.

7. ADDITIONAL INFORMATION

7.1. If advisors connected with an issue are mentioned in the Securities Note, a statement of the capacity in which the advisors have acted.

7.2. An indication of other information in the Securities Note which has been audited or reviewed by statutory auditors and where auditors have produced a report. Reproduction of the report or, with permission of the competent authority, a summary of the report.

7.3. Where a statement or report attributed to a person as an expert is included in the Securities Note, provide such persons' name, business address, qualifications and material interest if any in the issuer. If the report has been produced at the issuer's request a statement to that effect that such statement or report is included, in the form and context in which it is included, with the consent of that person who has authorised the contents of that part of the Securities Note.

7.4. Where information has been sourced from a third party, provide a confirmation that this information has been accurately reproduced and that as far as the issuer is aware and is able to ascertain from information published by that third party, no facts have been omitted which would render the reproduced information inaccurate or misleading. In addition, identify the source(s) of the information.

7.5. Credit ratings assigned to an issuer or its debt securities at the request or with the co-operation of the issuer in the rating process. A brief explanation of the meaning of the ratings if this has previously been published by the rating provider.

[9747]

ANNEX VI
MINIMUM DISCLOSURE REQUIREMENTS FOR GUARANTEES
(ADDITIONAL BUILDING BLOCK)

1. Nature of the guarantee

A description of any arrangement intended to ensure that any obligation material to the issue will be duly serviced, whether in the form of guarantee, surety, Keep well Agreement,

Mono-line Insurance policy or other equivalent commitment (hereafter referred to generically as "guarantees" and their provider as "guarantor" for convenience).

Without prejudice to the generality of the foregoing, such arrangements encompass commitments to ensure obligations to repay debt securities and/or the payment of interest and the description shall set out how the arrangement is intended to ensure that the guaranteed payments will be duly serviced.

2. Scope of the guarantee

Details shall be disclosed about the terms and conditions and scope of the guarantee. Without prejudice to the generality of the foregoing, these details should cover any conditionality on the application of the guarantee in the event of any default under the terms of the security and the material terms of any mono-line insurance or keep well agreement between the issuer and the guarantor. Details must also be disclosed of any guarantor's power of veto in relation to changes to the security holder's rights, such as is often found in Mono-line Insurance.

3. Information to be disclosed about the guarantor

The guarantor must disclose information about itself as if it were the issuer of that same type of security that is the subject of the guarantee.

4. Documents on display

Indication of the places where the public may have access to the material contracts and other documents relating to the guarantee.

[9748]

ANNEX VII
MINIMUM DISCLOSURE REQUIREMENTS FOR ASSET BACKED SECURITIES REGISTRATION DOCUMENT (SCHEDULE)

1. PERSONS RESPONSIBLE

1.1. All persons responsible for the information given in the registration document and, as the case may be, for certain parts of it, with, in the latter case, an indication of such parts. In the case of natural persons including members of the issuer's administrative, management or supervisory bodies indicate the name and function of the person; in case of legal persons indicate the name and registered office.

1.2. A declaration by those responsible for the registration document that, having taken all reasonable care to ensure that such is the case, the information given in the registration document is, to the best of their knowledge, in accordance with the facts and does not omit anything likely to affect its import. As the case may be, declaration by those responsible for certain parts of the registration document that having taken all reasonable care to ensure that such is the case, the information contained in that part of the registration document for which they are responsible is, to the best of their knowledge, in accordance with the facts and contains no omission likely to affect its import.

2. STATUTORY AUDITORS

2.1. Names and addresses of the issuer's auditors for the period covered by the historical financial information (together with any membership of any relevant professional body).

3. RISK FACTORS

3.1. The document must prominently disclose risk factors in a section headed "Risk Factors" that are specific to the issuer and its industry.

4. INFORMATION ABOUT THE ISSUER:

4.1. A statement whether the issuer has been established as a special purpose vehicle or entity for the purpose of issuing asset backed securities;

4.2. The legal and commercial name of the issuer;

4.3. The place of registration of the issuer and its registration number;

4.4. The date of incorporation and the length of life of the issuer, except where indefinite;

4.5. The domicile and legal form of the issuer, the legislation under which the issuer operates its country of incorporation and the address and telephone number of its registered office (or principal place of business if different from its registered office).

4.6. Description of the amount of the issuer's authorised and issued capital and the amount of any capital agreed to be issued, the number and classes of the securities of which it is composed.

5. BUSINESS OVERVIEW

5.1. A brief description of the issuer's principal activities.

5.2. A global overview of the parties to the securitisation program including information on the direct or indirect ownership or control between those parties.

6. ADMINISTRATIVE, MANAGEMENT AND SUPERVISORY BODIES

6.1. Names, business addresses and functions in the issuer of the following persons, and an indication of the principal activities performed by them outside the issuer where these are significant with respect to that issuer:

(a) members of the administrative, management or supervisory bodies;

(b) partners with unlimited liability, in the case of a limited partnership with a share capital.

7. MAJOR SHAREHOLDERS

7.1. To the extent known to the issuer, state whether the issuer is directly or indirectly owned or controlled and by whom, and describe the nature of such control and describe the measures in place to ensure that such control is not abused.

8. FINANCIAL INFORMATION CONCERNING THE ISSUER'S ASSETS AND LIABILITIES, FINANCIAL POSITION, AND PROFITS AND LOSSES

8.1. Where, since the date of incorporation or establishment, an issuer has not commenced operations and no financial statements have been made up as at the date of the registration document, a statement to that effect shall be provided in the registration document.

8.2. *Historical financial information*

Where, since the date of incorporation or establishment, an issuer has commenced operations and financial statements have been made up, the registration document must contain audited historical financial information covering the latest 2 financial years (or shorter period that the issuer has been in operation) and the audit report in respect of each year. [If the issuer has changed its accounting reference date during the period for which historical financial information is required, the audited historical information shall cover at least 24 months, or the entire period for which the issuer has been in operation, whichever is the shorter.] Such financial information must be prepared according to Regulation (EC) No 1606/2002, or if not applicable to a Member's State national accounting standards for issuers from the Community. For third country issuers, such financial information must be prepared according to the international accounting standards adopted pursuant to the procedure of Article 3 of Regulation (EC) No 1606/2002 or to a third country's national accounting standards equivalent to these standards. If such financial information is not equivalent to these standards, it must be presented in the form of restated financial statements.

The most recent year's historical financial information must be presented and prepared in a form consistent with that which will be adopted in the issuer's next annual published financial statements having regard to accounting standards and policies and legislation applicable to such annual financial statements.

If the issuer has been operating in its current sphere of economic activity for less than one year, the audited historical financial information covering that period must be prepared in accordance with the standards applicable to annual financial statements under Regulation (EC) No 1606/2002, or if not applicable to a Member States national accounting standards where the issuer is from the Community. For third country issuers, the historical financial information must be prepared according to the international accounting standards adopted pursuant to the procedure of Article 3 of Regulation (EC) No 1606/2002 or to a third country's national accounting standards equivalent to these standards. This historical financial information must be audited.

If the audited financial information is prepared according to national accounting standards, the financial information required under this heading must include at least the following:

(a) the balance sheet;
(b) the income statement;
(c) the accounting policies and explanatory notes.

The historical annual financial information must be independently audited or reported on as to whether or not, for the purposes of the registration document, it gives a true and fair view, in accordance with auditing standards applicable in a Member State or an equivalent standard.

8.2a. This paragraph may be used only for issues of asset backed securities having a denomination per unit of at least EUR 50,000.

Where, since the date of incorporation or establishment, an issuer has commenced operations and financial statements have been made up, the registration document must contain audited historical financial information covering the latest 2 financial years (or shorter period that the issuer has been in operation) and the audit report in respect of each year. [If the issuer has changed its accounting reference date during the period for which historical financial information is required, the audited historical information shall cover at least 24 months, or the entire period for which the issuer has been in operation, whichever is the shorter.] Such financial information must be prepared according to Regulation (EC) No 1606/2002 or, if not applicable, to a Member's State national accounting standards for issuers from the Community. For third country issuers, such financial information must be prepared according to the international accounting standards adopted pursuant to the procedure of Article 3 of Regulation (EC) No 1606/2002 or to a third country's national accounting standards equivalent to these standards. Otherwise, the following information must be included in the registration document:

(a) a prominent statement that the financial information included in the registration document has not been prepared in accordance with the international accounting standards adopted pursuant to the procedure of Article 3 of Regulation (EC) No 1606/2002 and that there may be material differences in the financial information had Regulation (EC) No 1606/2002 been applied to the historical financial information;
(b) immediately following the historical financial information a narrative description of the differences between the international accounting standards adopted pursuant to the procedure of Article 3 of Regulation (EC) No 1606/2002 and the accounting principles adopted by the issuer in preparing its annual financial statements.

The most recent year's historical financial information must be presented and prepared in a form consistent with that which will be adopted in the issuer's next annual financial statements having regard to accounting standards and policies and legislation applicable to such annual financial statements.

If the audited financial information is prepared according to national accounting standards, the financial information required under this heading must include at least the following:

(a) the balance sheet;
(b) the income statement;
(c) the accounting policies and explanatory notes.

The historical annual financial information must be independently audited or reported on as to whether or not, for the purposes of the registration document, it gives a true and fair view, in accordance with auditing standards applicable in a Member State or an equivalent standard. Otherwise, the following information must be included in the registration document:

(a) a prominent statement disclosing which auditing standards have been applied;
(b) an explanation of any significant departures from International Standards on Auditing.

8.3. *Legal and arbitration proceedings*

Information on any governmental, legal or arbitration proceedings (including any such proceedings which are pending or threatened of which the company is aware), during a period covering at least the previous 12 months, which may have, or have had in the recent past, significant effects on the issuer and/or group's financial position or profitability, or provide an appropriate negative statement.

8.4. *Material adverse change in the issuer's financial position*

Where an issuer has prepared financial statements, include a statement that there has been no material adverse change in the financial position or prospects of the issuer since the date of its last published audited financial statements. Where a material adverse change has occurred, this must be disclosed in the registration document.

9. THIRD PARTY INFORMATION AND STATEMENT BY EXPERTS AND DECLARATIONS OF ANY INTEREST

9.1. Where a statement or report attributed to a person as an expert is included in the registration document, provide such person's name, business address, qualifications and material interest if any in the issuer. If the report has been produced at the issuer's request a statement to that effect that such statement or report is included, in the form and context in which it is included, with the consent of that person who has authorised the contents of that part of the registration document.

9.2. Where information has been sourced from a third party, provide a confirmation that this information has been accurately reproduced and that as far as the issuer is aware and is able to ascertain from information published by that third party, no facts have been omitted which would render the reproduced information inaccurate or misleading In addition, the issuer shall identify the source(s) of the information.

10. DOCUMENTS ON DISPLAY

10.1. A statement that for the life of the registration document the following documents (or copies thereof), where applicable, may be inspected:

(a) the memorandum and articles of association of the issuer;

(b) all reports, letters, and other documents, historical financial information, valuations and statements prepared by any expert at the issuer's request any part of which is included or referred to in the registration document;

(c) the historical financial information of the issuer or, in the case of a group, the historical financial information of the issuer and its subsidiary undertakings for each of the two financial years preceding the publication of the registration document.

An indication of where the documents on display may be inspected, by physical or electronic means.

[9749]

NOTES

Words in square brackets in items 8.2, 8.2a inserted by Commission Regulation 211/2007/EC, Art 1(4), as from 1 March 2007.

ANNEX VIII
MINIMUM DISCLOSURE REQUIREMENTS FOR THE ASSET-BACKED SECURITIES ADDITIONAL BUILDING BLOCK

1. THE SECURITIES

1.1. The minimum denomination of an issue.

1.2. Where information is disclosed about an undertaking/obligor which is not involved in the issue, provide a confirmation that the information relating to the undertaking/obligor has been accurately reproduced from information published by the undertaking/obligor. So far as the issuer is aware and is able to ascertain from information published by the undertaking/obligor no facts have been omitted which would render the reproduced information misleading.

In addition, identify the source(s) of information in the Securities Note that has been reproduced from information published by an undertaking/obligor.

2. THE UNDERLYING ASSETS

2.1. Confirmation that the securitised assets backing the issue have characteristics that demonstrate capacity to produce funds to service any payments due and payable on the securities.

2.2. In respect of a pool of discrete assets backing the issue:

2.2.1. The legal jurisdiction by which the pool of assets is governed

2.2.2.

(a) In the case of a small number of easily identifiable obligors, a general description of each obligor.

(b) In all other cases, a description of: the general characteristics of the obligors; and the economic environment, as well as global statistical data referred to the securitised assets.

2.2.3. The legal nature of the assets;

2.2.4. the expiry or maturity date(s) of the assets;

2.2.5. the amount of the assets;

2.2.6. loan to value ratio or level of collateralisation;

2.2.7. the method of origination or creation of the assets, and for loans and credit agreements, the principal lending criteria and an indication of any loans which do not meet these criteria and any rights or obligations to make further advances;

2.2.8. an indication of significant representations and collaterals given to the issuer relating to the assets;

2.2.9. any rights to substitute the assets and a description of the manner in which and the type of assets which may be so substituted; if there is any capacity to substitute assets with a different class or quality of assets a statement to that effect together with a description of the impact of such substitution;

2.2.10. a description of any relevant insurance policies relating to the assets. Any concentration with one insurer must be disclosed if it is material to the transaction.

2.2.11. Where the assets comprise obligations of 5 or fewer obligors which are legal persons or where an obligor accounts for 20% or more of the assets, or where an obligor accounts for a material portion of the assets, so far as the issuer is aware and/or is able to ascertain from information published by the obligor(s) indicate either of the following:

(a) information relating to each obligor as if it were an issuer drafting a registration document for debt and derivative securities with an individual denomination of at least EUR 50,000 ;

(b) if an obligor or guarantor has securities already admitted to trading on a regulated or equivalent market or the obligations are guaranteed by an entity admitted to trading on a regulated or equivalent market, the name, address, country of incorporation, nature of business and name of the market in which its securities are admitted.

2.2.12. If a relationship exists that is material to the issue, between the issuer, guarantor and obligor, details of the principal terms of that relationship.

2.2.13. Where the assets comprise obligations that are not traded on a regulated or equivalent market, a description of the principal terms and conditions of the obligations.

2.2.14. Where the assets comprise equity securities that are admitted to trading on a regulated or equivalent market indicate the following:

(a) a description of the securities;

(b) a description of the market on which they are traded including its date of establishment, how price information is published, an indication of daily trading volumes, information as to the standing of the market in the country and the name of the market's regulatory authority;

(c) the frequency with which prices of the relevant securities, are published.

2.2.15. Where more than ten (10) per cent of the assets comprise equity securities that are not traded on a regulated or equivalent market, a description of those equity securities and equivalent information to that contained in the schedule for share registration document in respect of each issuer of those securities.

2.2.16. Where a material portion of the assets are secured on or backed by real property, a valuation report relating to the property setting out both the valuation of the property and cash flow/income streams.

Compliance with this disclosure is not required if the issue is of securities backed by mortgage loans with property as security, where there has been no revaluation of the properties for the purpose of the issue, and it is clearly stated that the valuations quoted are as at the date of the original initial mortgage loan origination.

2.3. In respect of an actively managed pool of assets backing the issue:

2.3.1. equivalent information to that contained in items 2.1 and 2.2 to allow an assessment of the type, quality, sufficiency and liquidity of the asset types in the portfolio which will secure the issue;

2.3.2. the parameters within which investments can be made, the name and description of the entity responsible for such management including a description of that entity's expertise and experience, a summary of the provisions relating to the termination of the appointment of such entity and the appointment of an alternative management entity, and a description of that entity's relationship with any other parties to the issue.

2.4. Where an issuer proposes to issue further securities backed by the same assets, a prominent statement to that effect and unless those further securities are fungible with or are subordinated to those classes of existing debt, a description of how the holders of that class will be informed.

3. STRUCTURE AND CASH FLOW

3.1. Description of the structure of the transaction, including, if necessary, a structure diagram.

3.2. Description of the entities participating in the issue and description of the functions to be performed by them.

3.3. Description of the method and date of the sale, transfer, novation or assignment of the assets or of any rights and/or obligations in the assets to the issuer or, where applicable, the manner and time period in which the proceeds from the issue will be fully invested by the issuer.

3.4. An explanation of the flow of funds including:

3.4.1. how the cash flow from the assets will meet the issuer's obligations to holders of the securities, including, if necessary, a financial service table and a description of the assumptions used in developing the table;

3.4.2. information on any credit enhancements, an indication of where material potential liquidity shortfalls may occur and the availability of any liquidity supports and indication of provisions designed to cover interest/principal shortfall risks;

3.4.3. without prejudice to item 3.4.2, details of any subordinated debt finance;

3.4.4. an indication of any investment parameters for the investment of temporary liquidity surpluses and description of the parties responsible for such investment;

3.4.5. how payments are collected in respect of the assets;

3.4.6. the order of priority of payments made by the issuer to the holders of the class of securities in question;

3.4.7. details of any other arrangements upon which payments of interest and principal to investors are dependent.

3.5. The name, address and significant business activities of the originators of the securitised assets.

3.6. Where the return on, and/or repayment of the security is linked to the performance or credit of other assets which are not assets of the issuer, items 2.2 and 2.3 are necessary.

3.7. The name, address and significant business activities of the administrator, calculation agent or equivalent, together with a summary of the administrator's/calculation agents responsibilities, their relationship with the originator or the creator of the assets and a summary of the provisions relating to the termination of the appointment of the administrator/calculation agent and the appointment of an alternative administrator/calculation agent.

3.8. The names and addresses and brief description of:

(a) any swap counterparties and any providers of other material forms of credit/liquidity enhancement;

(b) the banks with which the main accounts relating to the transaction are held.

4. POST ISSUANCE REPORTING

4.1. Indication in the prospectus whether or not it intends to provide post-issuance transaction information regarding securities to be admitted to trading and the performance of the underlying collateral. Where the issuer has indicated that it intends to report such

information, specify in the prospectus what information will be reported, where such information can be obtained, and the frequency with which such information will be reported.
[9750]

ANNEX IX
MINIMUM DISCLOSURE REQUIREMENTS FOR THE DEBT AND DERIVATIVE SECURITIES REGISTRATION DOCUMENT (SCHEDULE)

(*Debt and derivative securities with a denomination per unit of at least EUR 50,000*)

1. PERSONS RESPONSIBLE

1.1. All persons responsible for the information given in the registration document and, as the case may be, for certain parts of it, with, in the latter case, an indication of such parts. In the case of natural persons including members of the issuer's administrative, management or supervisory bodies indicate the name and function of the person; in case of legal persons indicate the name and registered office.

1.2. A declaration by those responsible for the registration document that, having taken all reasonable care to ensure that such is the case, the information contained in the registration document is, to the best of their knowledge, in accordance with the facts and contains no omission likely to affect its import. As the case may be, declaration by those responsible for certain parts of the registration document that, having taken all reasonable care to ensure that such is the case, the information contained in the part of the registration document for which they are responsible is, to the best of their knowledge, in accordance with the facts and contains no omission likely to affect its import.

2. STATUTORY AUDITORS

2.1. Names and addresses of the issuer's auditors for the period covered by the historical financial information (together with their membership in a professional body).

2.2. If auditors have resigned, been removed or not been re-appointed during the period covered by the historical financial information, details if material.

3. RISK FACTORS

3.1. Prominent disclosure of risk factors that may affect the issuer's ability to fulfil its obligations under the securities to investors in a section headed "Risk Factors".

4. INFORMATION ABOUT THE ISSUER

4.1. *History and development of the issuer*

4.1.1. the legal and commercial name of the issuer;

4.1.2. the place of registration of the issuer and its registration number;

4.1.3. the date of incorporation and the length of life of the issuer, except where indefinite;

4.1.4. the domicile and legal form of the issuer, the legislation under which the issuer operates, its country of incorporation, and the address and telephone number of its registered office (or principal place of business if different from its registered office;

4.1.5. any recent events particular to the issuer and which are to a material extent relevant to the evaluation of the issuer's solvency.

5. BUSINESS OVERVIEW

5.1. *Principal activities:*

5.1.1. A brief description of the issuer's principal activities stating the main categories of products sold and/or services performed;

5.1.2. The basis for any statements in the registration document made by the issuer regarding its competitive position.

6. ORGANISATIONAL STRUCTURE

6.1. If the issuer is part of a group, a brief description of the group and of the issuer's position within it.

6.2. If the issuer is dependent upon other entities within the group, this must be clearly stated together with an explanation of this dependence.

7. TREND INFORMATION

7.1. Include a statement that there has been no material adverse change in the prospects of the issuer since the date of its last published audited financial statements.

In the event that the issuer is unable to make such a statement, provide details of this material adverse change.

8. PROFIT FORECASTS OR ESTIMATES

If an issuer chooses to include a profit forecast or a profit estimate, the registration document must contain the information items 8.1 and 8.2 the following:

8.1. A statement setting out the principal assumptions upon which the issuer has based its forecast, or estimate.

There must be a clear distinction between assumptions about factors which the members of the administrative, management or supervisory bodies can influence and assumptions about factors which are exclusively outside the influence of the members of the administrative, management or supervisory bodies; be readily understandable by investors; be specific and precise; and not relate to the general accuracy of the estimates underlying the forecast.

8.2. Any profit forecast set out in the registration document must be accompanied by a statement confirming that the said forecast has been properly prepared on the basis stated and that the basis of accounting is consistent with the accounting policies of the issuer.

8.3. The profit forecast or estimate must be prepared on a basis comparable with the historical financial information.

9. ADMINISTRATIVE, MANAGEMENT, AND SUPERVISORY BODIES

9.1. Names, business addresses and functions in the issuer of the following persons, and an indication of the principal activities performed by them outside the issuer where these are significant with respect to that issuer:

(a) members of the administrative, management or supervisory bodies;

(b) partners with unlimited liability, in the case of a limited partnership with a share capital.

9.2. *Administrative, management, and supervisory bodies' conflicts of interests*

Potential conflicts of interests between any duties to the issuing entity of the persons referred to in item 9.1 and their private interests and or other duties must be clearly stated. In the event that there are no such conflicts, a statement to that effect.

10. MAJOR SHAREHOLDERS

10.1. To the extent known to the issuer, state whether the issuer is directly or indirectly owned or controlled and by whom, and describe the nature of such control, and describe the measures in place to ensure that such control is not abused.

10.2. A description of any arrangements, known to the issuer, the operation of which may at a subsequent date result in a change in control of the issuer.

11. FINANCIAL INFORMATION CONCERNING THE ISSUER'S ASSETS AND LIABILITIES, FINANCIAL POSITION AND PROFITS AND LOSSES

11.1. *Historical financial information*

Audited historical financial information covering the latest two financial years (or such shorter period that the issuer has been in operation), and the audit report in respect of each year. [If the issuer has changed its accounting reference date during the period for which historical financial information is required, the audited historical information shall cover at least 24 months, or the entire period for which the issuer has been in operation, whichever is the shorter.] Such financial information must be prepared according to Regulation (EC) No 1606/2002, or if not applicable to a Member's State national accounting standards for issuers from the Community. For third country issuers, such financial information must be prepared according to the international accounting standards adopted pursuant to the procedure of Article 3 of Regulation (EC) No 1606/2002 or to a third country's national accounting standards equivalent to these standards. Otherwise, the following information must be included in the registration document:

(a) a prominent statement that the financial information included in the registration document has not been prepared in accordance with the international accounting standards adopted pursuant to the procedure of Article 3 of Regulation (EC) No 1606/2002 and that there may be material differences in the financial information had Regulation (EC) No 1606/2002 been applied to the historical financial information;

(b) immediately following the historical financial information a narrative description of the differences between the international accounting standards adopted pursuant to the procedure of Article 3 of Regulation (EC) No 1606/2002 and the accounting principles adopted by the issuer in preparing its annual financial statements.

The most recent year's historical financial information must be presented and prepared in a form consistent with that which will be adopted in the issuer's next published annual financial statements having regard to accounting standards and policies and legislation applicable to such annual financial statements.

If the audited financial information is prepared according to national accounting standards, the financial information required under this heading must include at least the following:

(a) the balance sheet;

(b) the income statement;

(c) the accounting policies and explanatory notes.

The historical annual financial information must be independently audited or reported on as to whether or not, for the purposes of the registration document, it gives a true and fair view, in accordance with auditing standards applicable in a Member State or an equivalent standard. Otherwise, the following information must be included in the registration document:

(a) a prominent statement disclosing which auditing standards have been applied;

(b) an explanation of any significant departures from international standards on auditing.

11.2. *Financial statements*

If the issuer prepares both own and consolidated financial statements, include at least the consolidated financial statements in the registration document.

11.3. *Auditing of historical annual financial information*

11.3.1. A statement that the historical financial information has been audited. If audit reports on the historical financial information have been refused by the statutory auditors or if they contain qualifications or disclaimers, such refusal or such qualifications or disclaimers must be reproduced in full and the reasons given.

11.3.2. An indication of other information in the registration document which has been audited by the auditors.

11.3.3. Where financial data in the registration document is not extracted from the issuer's audited financial statements, state the source of the data and state that the data is unaudited.

11.4. *Age of latest financial information*

11.4.1. The last year of audited financial information may not be older than 18 months from the date of the registration document.

11.5. *Legal and arbitration proceedings*

Information on any governmental, legal or arbitration proceedings (including any such proceedings which are pending or threatened of which the issuer is aware), during a period covering at least the previous 12 months which may have, or have had in the recent past, significant effects on the issuer and/or group's financial position or profitability, or provide an appropriate negative statement.

11.6. *Significant change in the issuer's financial or trading position*

A description of any significant change in the financial or trading position of the group which has occurred since the end of the last financial period for which either audited financial information or interim financial information have been published, or an appropriate negative statement.

12. MATERIAL CONTRACTS

A brief summary of all material contracts that are not entered into in the ordinary course of the issuer's business, which could result in any group member being under an obligation or entitlement that is material to the issuer's ability to meet its obligation to security holders in respect of the securities being issued.

13. THIRD PARTY INFORMATION AND STATEMENT BY EXPERTS AND DECLARATIONS OF ANY INTEREST

13.1. Where a statement or report attributed to a person as an expert is included in the registration document, provide such person's name, business address, qualifications and material interest if any in the issuer. If the report has been produced at the issuer's request a statement to that effect that such statement or report is included, in the form and context in which it is included, with the consent of that person who has authorised the contents of that part of the registration document.

13.2. *Third party information*

Where information has been sourced from a third party, provide a confirmation that this information has been accurately reproduced and that as far as the issuer is aware and is able to ascertain from information published by that third party, no facts have been omitted which would render the reproduced information inaccurate or misleading; in addition, identify the source(s) of the information.

14. DOCUMENTS ON DISPLAY

A statement that for the life of the registration document the following documents (or copies thereof), where applicable, may be inspected:

(a) the memorandum and articles of association of the issuer;

(b) all reports, letters, and other documents, historical financial information, valuations and statements prepared by any expert at the issuer's request any part of which is included or referred to in the registration document;

(c) the historical financial information of the issuer or, in the case of a group, the historical financial information of the issuer and its subsidiary undertakings for each of the two financial years preceding the publication of the registration document.

An indication of where the documents on display may be inspected, by physical or electronic means.

[9751]

NOTES

Words in square brackets in item 11.1 inserted by Commission Regulation 211/2007/EC, Art 1(4), as from 1 March 2007.

ANNEX X

MINIMUM DISCLOSURE REQUIREMENTS FOR THE DEPOSITORY RECEIPTS ISSUED OVER SHARES (SCHEDULE)

Information about the Issuer of the Underlying Shares

1. PERSONS RESPONSIBLE

1.1. All persons responsible for the information given in the prospectus and, as the case may be, for certain parts of it, with, in the latter case, an indication of such parts. In the case of natural persons including members of the issuer's administrative, management or supervisory bodies indicate the name and function of the person; in case of legal persons indicate the name and registered office.

1.2. A declaration by those responsible for the prospectus that, having taken all reasonable care to ensure that such is the case, the information contained in the prospectus is, to the best of their knowledge, in accordance with the facts and contains no omission likely to affect its import. As the case may be, declaration by those responsible for certain parts of the prospectus that, having taken all reasonable care to ensure that such is the case, the information contained in the part of the prospectus for which they are responsible is, to the best of their knowledge, in accordance with the facts and contains no omission likely to affect its import.

2. STATUTORY AUDITORS

2.1. Names and addresses of the issuer's auditors for the period covered by the historical financial information (together with their membership in a professional body).

2.2. If auditors have resigned, been removed or not been re-appointed during the period covered by the historical financial information, indicate details if material.

3. SELECTED FINANCIAL INFORMATION

3.1. Selected historical financial information regarding the issuer, presented for each financial year for the period covered by the historical financial information, and any subsequent interim financial period, in the same currency as the financial information.

The selected historical financial information must provide the key figures that summarise the financial condition of the issuer.

3.2. If selected financial information for interim periods is provided, comparative data from the same period in the prior financial year shall also be provided, except that the requirement for comparative balance sheet information is satisfied by presenting the year end balance sheet information.

4. RISK FACTORS

Prominent disclosure of risk factors that are specific to the issuer or its industry in a section headed "Risk Factors".

5. INFORMATION ABOUT THE ISSUER

5.1. *History and development of the issuer*

5.1.1. the legal and commercial name of the issuer;

5.1.2. the place of registration of the issuer and its registration number;

5.1.3. the date of incorporation and the length of life of the issuer, except where indefinite;

5.1.4. the domicile and legal form of the issuer, the legislation under which the issuer operates, its country of incorporation, and the address and telephone number of its registered office (or principal place of business if different from its registered office);

5.1.5. the important events in the development of the issuer's business.

5.2. *Investments*

5.2.1. A description, (including the amount) of the issuer's principal investments for each financial year for the period covered by the historical financial information up to the date of the prospectus;

5.2.2. A description of the issuer's principal investments that are currently in progress, including the distribution of these investments geographically (home and abroad) and the method of financing (internal or external);

5.2.3. Information concerning the issuer's principal future investments on which its management bodies have already made firm commitments.

6. BUSINESS OVERVIEW

6.1. *Principal activities*

6.1.1. A description of, and key factors relating to, the nature of the issuer's operations and its principal activities, stating the main categories of products sold and/or services performed for each financial year for the period covered by the historical financial information.

6.1.2. An indication of any significant new products and/or services that have been introduced and, to the extent the development of new products or services has been publicly disclosed, give the status of development.

6.2. *Principal markets*

A description of the principal markets in which the issuer competes, including a breakdown of total revenues by category of activity and geographic market for each financial year for the period covered by the historical financial information.

6.3. Where the information given pursuant to items 6.1 and 6.2 has been influenced by exceptional factors, mention that fact.

6.4. If material to the issuer's business or profitability, disclose summary information regarding the extent to which the issuer is dependent, on patents or licences, industrial, commercial or financial contracts or new manufacturing processes.

6.5. The basis for any statements made by the issuer regarding its competitive position.

7. ORGANISATIONAL STRUCTURE

7.1. If the issuer is part of a group, a brief description of the group and the issuer's position within the group.

7.2. A list of the issuer's significant subsidiaries, including name, country of incorporation or residence, proportion of ownership interest and, if different, proportion of voting power held.

8. PROPERTY, PLANTS AND EQUIPMENT

8.1. Information regarding any existing or planned material tangible fixed assets, including leased properties, and any major encumbrances thereon.

8.2. A description of any environmental issues that may affect the issuer's utilisation of the tangible fixed assets.

9. OPERATING AND FINANCIAL REVIEW

9.1. *Financial condition*

To the extent not covered elsewhere in the prospectus, provide a description of the issuer's financial condition, changes in financial condition and results of operations for each year and interim period, for which historical financial information is required, including the causes of material changes from year to year in the financial information to the extent necessary for an understanding of the issuer's business as a whole.

9.2. *Operating results*

9.2.1. Information regarding significant factors, including unusual or infrequent events or new developments, materially affecting the issuer's income from operations, indicating the extent to which income was so affected.

9.2.2. Where the financial statements disclose material changes in net sales or revenues, provide a narrative discussion of the reasons for such changes.

9.2.3. Information regarding any governmental, economic, fiscal, monetary or political policies or factors that have materially affected, or could materially affect, directly or indirectly, the issuer's operations.

10. CAPITAL RESOURCES

10.1. Information concerning the issuer's capital resources (both short and long term).

10.2. An explanation of the sources and amounts of and a narrative description of the issuer's cash flows.

10.3. Information on the borrowing requirements and funding structure of the issuer.

10.4. Information regarding any restrictions on the use of capital resources that have materially affected, or could materially affect, directly or indirectly, the issuer's operations.

10.5. Information regarding the anticipated sources of funds needed to fulfil commitments referred to in items 5.2.3 and 8.1.

11. RESEARCH AND DEVELOPMENT, PATENTS AND LICENCES

Where material, provide a description of the issuer's research and development policies for each financial year for the period covered by the historical financial information, including the amount spent on issuer-sponsored research and development activities.

12. TREND INFORMATION

12.1. The most significant recent trends in production, sales and inventory, and costs and selling prices since the end of the last financial year to the date of the prospectus.

12.2. Information on any known trends, uncertainties, demands, commitments or events that are reasonably likely to have a material effect on the issuer's prospects for at least the current financial year.

13. PROFIT FORECASTS OR ESTIMATES

If an issuer chooses to include a profit forecast or a profit estimate the prospectus must contain the information items 13.1 and 13.2.

13.1. A statement setting out the principal assumptions upon which the issuer has based its forecast, or estimate.

There must be a clear distinction between assumptions about factors which the members of the administrative, management or supervisory bodies can influence and assumptions about factors which are exclusively outside the influence of the members of the administrative, management or supervisory bodies; the assumptions must be readily understandable by investors, be specific and precise and not relate to the general accuracy of the estimates underlying the forecast.

13.2. A report prepared by independent accountants or auditors stating that in the opinion of the independent accountants or auditors the forecast or estimate has been properly compiled on the basis stated and that the basis of accounting used for the profit forecast or estimate is consistent with the accounting policies of the issuer.

13.3. The profit forecast or estimate prepared on a basis comparable with the historical financial information.

13.4. If the issuer has published a profit forecast in a prospectus which is still outstanding, provide a statement setting out whether or not that forecast is still correct as at the time of the prospectus, and an explanation of why such forecast is no longer valid if that is the case.

14. ADMINISTRATIVE, MANAGEMENT, AND SUPERVISORY BODIES AND SENIOR MANAGEMENT

14.1. Names, business addresses and functions in the issuer of the following persons and an indication of the principal activities performed by them outside that issuer where these are significant with respect to that issuer:

(a) members of the administrative, management or supervisory bodies;

(b) partners with unlimited liability, in the case of a limited partnership with a share capital;

(c) founders, if the issuer has been established for fewer than five years;

(d) any senior manager who is relevant to establishing that the issuer has the appropriate expertise and experience for the management of the issuer's business.

The nature of any family relationship between any of those persons.

In the case of each member of the administrative, management or supervisory bodies of the issuer and person described in points (b) and (d) of the first subparagraph, details of that person's relevant management expertise and experience and the following information:

(a) the names of all companies and partnerships of which such person has been a member of the administrative, management or supervisory bodies or partner at any time in the previous five years, indicating whether or not the individual is still a member of the administrative, management or supervisory bodies or partner. It is not necessary to list all the subsidiaries of an issuer of which the person is also a member of the administrative, management or supervisory bodies;

(b) any convictions in relation to fraudulent offences for at least the previous five years;

(c) details of any bankruptcies, receiverships or liquidations with which a person described in points (a) and (d) of the first subparagraph who was acting in the capacity of any of the positions set out in points (a) and (d) of the first subparagraph member of the administrative, management or supervisory bodies was associated for at least the previous five years;

(d) details of any official public incrimination and/or sanctions of such person by statutory or regulatory authorities (including designated professional bodies) and whether such person has ever been disqualified by a court from acting as a member of the administrative, management or supervisory bodies of an issuer or from acting in the management or conduct of the affairs of any issuer for at least the previous five years.

If there is no such information to be disclosed, a statement to that effect must be made.

14.2. *Administrative, management, and supervisory bodies' and senior management conflicts of interests*

Potential conflicts of interests between any duties to the issuer of the persons referred to in the first subparagraph of item 14.1 and their private interests and or other duties must be clearly stated. In the event that there are no such conflicts, make a statement to that effect.

Any arrangement or understanding with major shareholders, customers, suppliers or others, pursuant to which any person referred to in the first subparagraph of item 14.1 was selected as a member of the administrative, management or supervisory bodies or member of senior management.

15. REMUNERATION AND BENEFITS

In relation to the last full financial year for those persons referred to in points (a) and (d) of the first subparagraph of item 14.1:

15.1. The amount of remuneration paid (including any contingent or deferred compensation), and benefits in kind granted, to such persons by the issuer and its subsidiaries for services in all capacities to the issuer and its subsidiaries by any person.

This information must be provided on an individual basis unless individual disclosure is not required in the issuer's home country and is not otherwise publicly disclosed by the issuer.

15.2. The total amounts set aside or accrued by the issuer or its subsidiaries to provide pension, retirement or similar benefits.

16. BOARD PRACTICES

In relation to the issuer's last completed financial year, and unless otherwise specified, with respect to those persons referred to in point (a) of the first subparagraph of item 14.1.

16.1. Date of expiration of the current term of office, if applicable, and the period during which the person has served in that office.

16.2. Information about members of the administrative, management or supervisory bodies' service contracts with the issuer or any of its subsidiaries providing for benefits upon termination of employment, or an appropriate negative statement.

16.3. Information about the issuer's audit committee and remuneration committee, including the names of committee members and a summary of the terms of reference under which the committee operates.

16.4. A statement as to whether or not the issuer complies with its country's of incorporation corporate governance regime(s). In the event that the issuer does not comply with such a regime, a statement to that effect together with an explanation regarding why the issuer does not comply with such regime.

17. EMPLOYEES

17.1. Either the number of employees at the end of the period or the average for each financial year for the period covered by the historical financial information up to the date of the prospectus (and changes in such numbers, if material) and, if possible and material, a breakdown of persons employed by main category of activity and geographic location. If the issuer employs a significant number of temporary employees, include disclosure of the number of temporary employees on average during the most recent financial year.

17.2. Shareholdings and stock options

With respect to each person referred to in points (a) and (b) of the first subparagraph of item 14.1, provide information as to their share ownership and any options over such shares in the issuer as of the most recent practicable date.

17.3. Description of any arrangements for involving the employees in the capital of the issuer.

18. MAJOR SHAREHOLDERS

18.1. In so far as is known to the issuer, the name of any person other than a member of the administrative, management or supervisory bodies who, directly or indirectly, has an interest notifiable under the issuer's national law in the issuer's capital or voting rights, together with the amount of each such person's interest or, if there are no such persons, an appropriate negative statement.

18.2. Whether the issuer's major shareholders have different voting rights, or an appropriate negative statement.

18.3. To the extent known to the issuer, state whether the issuer is directly or indirectly owned or controlled and by whom and describe the nature of such control and describe the measures in place to ensure that such control is not abused.

18.4. A description of any arrangements, known to the issuer, the operation of which may at a subsequent date result in a change in control of the issuer.

19. RELATED PARTY TRANSACTIONS

Details of related party transactions (which for these purposes are those set out in the Standards adopted according to Regulation (EC) No 1606/2002), that the issuer has entered into during the period covered by the historical financial information and up to the date of the prospectus must be disclosed in accordance with the respective standard adopted according to Regulation (EC) No 1606/2002 if applicable.

If such standards do not apply to the issuer the following information must be disclosed:

(a) the nature and extent of any transactions which are – as a single transaction or in their entirety – material to the issuer. Where such related party transactions are not concluded at arm's length provide an explanation of why these transactions were not concluded at arms length. In the case of outstanding loans including guarantees of any kind indicate the amount outstanding;

(b) the amount or the percentage to which related party transactions form part of the turnover of the issuer.

20. FINANCIAL INFORMATION CONCERNING THE ISSUER'S ASSETS AND LIABILITIES, FINANCIAL POSITION AND PROFITS AND LOSSES

20.1. *Historical financial information*

Audited historical financial information covering the latest 3 financial years (or such shorter period that the issuer has been in operation), and the audit report in respect of each year. [If the issuer has changed its accounting reference date during the period for which historical financial information is required, the audited historical information shall cover at least 36 months, or the entire period for which the issuer has been in operation, whichever is the shorter.] Such financial information must be prepared according to Regulation (EC) No 1606/2002, or if not applicable to a Member States national accounting standards for issuers from the Community. For third country issuers, such financial information must be prepared according to the international accounting standards adopted pursuant to the procedure of Article 3 of Regulation (EC) No 1606/2002 or to a third country's national accounting standards equivalent to these standards. If such financial information is not equivalent to these standards, it must be presented in the form of restated financial statements.

The last two years audited historical financial information must be presented and prepared in a form consistent with that which will be adopted in the issuer's next published annual financial statements having regard to accounting standards and policies and legislation applicable to such annual financial statements.

If the issuer has been operating in its current sphere of economic activity for less than one year, the audited historical financial information covering that period must be prepared in accordance with the standards applicable to annual financial statements under Regulation (EC) No 1606/2002, or if not applicable to a Member States national accounting standards where the issuer is an issuer from the Community. For third country issuers, the historical financial information must be prepared according to the international accounting standards adopted pursuant to the procedure of Article 3 of Regulation (EC) No 1606/2002 or to a third country's national accounting standards equivalent to these standards. This historical financial information must be audited.

If the audited financial information is prepared according to national accounting standards, the financial information required under this heading must include at least the following:

(a) the balance sheet;

(b) the income statement;

(c) a statement showing either all changes in equity or changes in equity other than those arising from capital transactions with owners and distributions to owners;

(d) the cash flow statement;
(e) the accounting policies and explanatory notes.

The historical annual financial information must be independently audited or reported on as to whether or not, for the purposes of the prospectus, it gives a true and fair view, in accordance with auditing standards applicable in a Member State or an equivalent standard.

20.1a. *This paragraph may be used only for issues of depository receipts having a denomination per unit of at least EUR 50,000.*

Audited historical financial information covering the latest three financial years (or such shorter period that the issuer has been in operation), and the audit report in respect of each year. [If the issuer has changed its accounting reference date during the period for which historical financial information is required, the audited historical information shall cover at least 36 months, or the entire period for which the issuer has been in operation, whichever is the shorter.] Such financial information must be prepared according to Regulation (EC) No 1606/2002, or if not applicable to a Member State's national accounting standards for issuers from the Community. For third country issuers, such financial information must be prepared according to the international accounting standards adopted pursuant to the procedure of Article 3 of Regulation (EC) No 1606/2002 or to a third country's national accounting standards equivalent to these standards. Otherwise, the following information must be included in the prospectus:

(a) a prominent statement that the financial information included in the registration document has not been prepared in accordance with the international accounting standards adopted pursuant to the procedure of Article 3 of Regulation (EC) No 1606/2002 and that there may be material differences in the financial information had Regulation (EC) No 1606/2002 been applied to the historical financial information;
(b) immediately following the historical financial information a narrative description of the differences between the international accounting standards adopted pursuant to the procedure of Article 3 of Regulation (EC) No 1606/2002 and the accounting principles adopted by the issuer in preparing its annual financial statements.

The last two years audited historical financial information must be presented and prepared in a form consistent with that which will be adopted in the issuer's next published annual financial statements having regard to accounting standards and policies and legislation applicable to such annual financial statements.

If the audited financial information is prepared according to national accounting standards, the financial information required under this heading must include at least the following:

(a) the balance sheet;
(b) the income statement;
(c) a statement showing either all changes in equity or changes in equity other than those arising from capital transactions with owners and distributions to owners;
(d) the cash flow statement;
(e) the accounting policies and explanatory notes.

The historical annual financial information must be independently audited or reported on as to whether or not, for the purposes of the prospectus, it gives a true and fair view, in accordance with auditing standards applicable in a Member State or an equivalent standard. Otherwise, the following information must be included in the prospectus:

(a) a prominent statement disclosing which auditing standards have been applied;
(b) an explanation of any significant departures from international standards on auditing.

20.2. *Financial statements*

If the issuer prepares both own and consolidated annual financial statements, include at least the consolidated annual financial statements in the prospectus.

20.3. *Auditing of historical annual financial information*

20.3.1. A statement that the historical financial information has been audited. If audit reports on the historical financial information have been refused by the statutory auditors or if they contain qualifications or disclaimers, such refusal or such qualifications or disclaimers must be reproduced in full and the reasons given.

20.3.2. Indication of other information in the prospectus which has been audited by the auditors.

20.3.3. Where financial data in the prospectus is not extracted from the issuer's audited financial statements state the source of the data and state that the data is unaudited.

20.4. *Age of latest financial information*

20.4.1. The last year of audited financial information may not be older than:

(a) 18 months from the date of the prospectus if the issuer includes audited interim financial statements in the prospectus;

(b) 15 months from the date of the prospectus if the issuer includes unaudited interim financial statements in the prospectus.

20.5. *Interim and other financial information*

20.5.1. If the issuer has published quarterly or half yearly financial information since the date of its last audited financial statements, these must be included in the prospectus. If the quarterly or half yearly financial information has been reviewed or audited the audit or review report must also be included. If the quarterly or half yearly financial information is unaudited or has not been reviewed, state that fact.

20.5.2. If the prospectus is dated more than nine months after the end of the last audited financial year, it must contain interim financial information, which may be unaudited (in which case that fact shall be stated) covering at least the first six months of the financial year.

The interim financial information must include comparative statements for the same period in the prior financial year, except that the requirement for comparative balance sheet information may be satisfied by presenting the years end balance sheet.

20.6. *Dividend policy*

A description of the issuer's policy on dividend distributions and any restrictions thereon.

20.6.1. The amount of the dividend per share for each financial year for the period covered by the historical financial information adjusted, where the number of shares in the issuer has changed, to make it comparable.

20.7. *Legal and arbitration proceedings*

Information on any governmental, legal or arbitration proceedings (including any such proceedings which are pending or threatened of which the issuer is aware), during a period covering at least the previous 12 months which may have, or have had in the recent past significant effects on the issuer and/or group's financial position or profitability, or provide an appropriate negative statement.

20.8. *Significant change in the issuer's financial or trading position*

A description of any significant change in the financial or trading position of the group which has occurred since the end of the last financial period for which either audited financial information or interim financial information have been published, or provide an appropriate negative statement.

21. ADDITIONAL INFORMATION

21.1. *Share capital*

The following information as of the date of the most recent balance sheet included in the historical financial information:

21.1.1. The amount of issued capital, and for each class of share capital:

(a) the number of shares authorised;

(b) the number of shares issued and fully paid and issued but not fully paid;

(c) the par value per share, or that the shares have no par value;

(d) a reconciliation of the number of shares outstanding at the beginning and end of the year. If more than 10% of capital has been paid for with assets other than cash within the period covered by the historical financial information, state that fact.

21.1.2. If there are shares not representing capital, state the number and main characteristics of such shares.

21.1.3. The number, book value and face value of shares in the issuer held by or on behalf of the issuer itself or by subsidiaries of the issuer.

21.1.4. The amount of any convertible securities, exchangeable securities or securities with warrants, with an indication of the conditions governing and the procedures for conversion, exchange or subscription.

21.1.5. Information about and terms of any acquisition rights and or obligations over authorised but unissued capital or an undertaking to increase the capital.

21.1.6. Information about any capital of any member of the group which is under option or agreed conditionally or unconditionally to be put under option and details of such options including those persons to whom such options relate.

21.1.7. A history of share capital, highlighting information about any changes, for the period covered by the historical financial information.

21.2. *Memorandum and Articles of Association*

21.2.1. A description of the issuer's objects and purposes and where they can be found in the memorandum and articles of association.

21.2.2. A summary of any provisions of the issuer's articles of association, statutes or charter and bylaws with respect to the members of the administrative, management and supervisory bodies.

21.2.3. A description of the rights, preferences and restrictions attaching to each class of the existing shares.

21.2.4. A description of what action is necessary to change the rights of holders of the shares, indicating where the conditions are more significant than is required by law.

21.2.5. A description of the conditions governing the manner in which annual general meetings and extraordinary general meetings of shareholders are called including the conditions of admission.

21.2.6. A brief description of any provision of the issuer's articles of association, statutes, charter or bylaws that would have an effect of delaying, deferring or preventing a change in control of the issuer.

21.2.7. An indication of the articles of association, statutes, charter or bylaws provisions, if any, governing the ownership threshold above which shareholder ownership must be disclosed.

21.2.8. A description of the conditions imposed by the memorandum and articles of association statutes, charter or bylaws governing changes in the capital, where such conditions are more stringent than is required by law.

22. MATERIAL CONTRACTS

A summary of each material contract, other than contracts entered into in the ordinary course of business, to which the issuer or any member of the group is a party, for the two years immediately preceding publication of the prospectus.

A summary of any other contract (not being a contract entered into in the ordinary course of business) entered into by any member of the group which contains any provision under which any member of the group has any obligation or entitlement which is material to the group as at the date of the prospectus.

23. THIRD PARTY INFORMATION, STATEMENT BY EXPERTS AND DECLARATIONS OF ANY INTEREST

23.1. Where a statement or report attributed to a person as an expert is included in the prospectus provide such person's name, business address, qualifications and material interest if any in the issuer. If the report has been produced at the issuer's request a statement to that effect that such statement or report is included, in the form and context in which it is included, with the consent of that person who has authorised the contents of that part of the prospectus.

23.2. Where information has been sourced from a third party, provide a confirmation that this information has been accurately reproduced and that as far as the issuer is aware and is able to ascertain from information published by that third party, no facts have been omitted which would render the reproduced information inaccurate or misleading. In addition, the issuer shall identify the source(s) of the information.

24. DOCUMENTS ON DISPLAY

A statement that for the life of the prospectus the following documents (or copies thereof), where applicable, may be inspected:

(a) the memorandum and articles of association of the issuer;

(b) all reports, letters, and other documents, historical financial information, valuations and statements prepared by any expert at the issuer's request any part of which is included or referred to in the prospectus;
(c) the historical financial information of the issuer or, in the case of a group, the historical financial information for the issuer and its subsidiary undertakings for each of the two financial years preceding the publication of the prospectus.

An indication of where the documents on display may be inspected, by physical or electronic means.

25. INFORMATION ON HOLDINGS

25.1. Information relating to the undertakings in which the issuer holds a proportion of the capital likely to have a significant effect on the assessment of its own assets and liabilities, financial position or profits and losses.

26. INFORMATION ABOUT THE ISSUER OF THE DEPOSITORY RECEIPTS

26.1. Name, registered office and principal administrative establishment if different from the registered office.

26.2. Date of incorporation and length of life of the issuer, except where indefinite.

26.3. Legislation under which the issuer operates and legal form which it has adopted under that legislation.

27. INFORMATION ABOUT THE UNDERLYING SHARES

27.1. A description of the type and the class of the underlying shares, including the ISIN (International Security Identification Number) or other such security identification code.

27.2. Legislation under which the underlying shares have been created.

27.3. An indication whether the underlying shares are in registered form or bearer form and whether the underlying shares are in certificated form or book-entry form. In the latter case, name and address of the entity in charge of keeping the records.

27.4. Currency of the underlying shares.

27.5. A description of the rights, including any limitations of these, attached to the underlying shares and procedure for the exercise of said rights.

27.6. Dividend rights:
(a) fixed date(s) on which the entitlement arises;
(b) time limit after which entitlement to dividend lapses and an indication of the person in whose favour the lapse operates;
(c) dividend restrictions and procedures for non-resident holders;
(d) rate of dividend or method of its calculation, periodicity and cumulative or non-cumulative nature of payments.

27.7. Voting rights
Pre-emption rights in offers for subscription of securities of the same class
Right to share in the issuer's profits
Rights to share in any surplus in the event of liquidation
Redemption provisions
Conversion provisions.

27.8. The issue date of the underlying shares if new underlying shares are being created for the issue of the depository receipts and they are not in existence at the time of issue of the depository receipts.

27.9. If new underlying shares are being created for the issue of the depository receipts, state the resolutions, authorisations and approvals by virtue of which the new underlying shares have been or will be created and/or issued.

27.10. A description of any restrictions on the free transferability of the underlying shares.

27.11. In respect of the country of registered office of the issuer and the country(ies) where the offer is being made or admission to trading is being sought:
(a) information on taxes on the income from the underlying shares withheld at source;
(b) indication as to whether the issuer assumes responsibility for the withholding of taxes at the source.

27.12. An indication of the existence of any mandatory takeover bids and/or squeeze-out and sell-out rules in relation to the underlying shares.

27.13. An indication of public takeover bids by third parties in respect of the issuer's equity, which have occurred during the last financial year and the current financial year. The price or exchange terms attaching to such offers and the outcome thereof must be stated.

27.14. Lock up agreements:
— the parties involved,
— content and exceptions of the agreement,
— indication of the period of the lock up.

27.15. *Information about selling share holders if any*

27.15.1. Name and business address of the person or entity offering to sell the underlying shares, the nature of any position office or other material relationship that the selling persons has had within the past three years with the issuer of the underlying shares or any of its predecessors or affiliates.

27.16. *Dilution*

27.16.1. Amount and percentage of immediate dilution resulting from the offer of the depository receipts.

27.16.2. In the case of a subscription offer of the depository receipts to existing shareholders, disclose the amount and percentage of immediate dilutions if they do not subscribe to the offer of depository receipts.

27.17. *Additional information where there is a simultaneous or almost simultaneous offer or admission to trading of the same class of underlying shares as those underlying shares over which the depository receipts are being issued.*

27.17.1. If simultaneously or almost simultaneously with the creation of the depository receipts for which admission to a regulated market is being sought underlying shares of the same class as those over which the depository receipts are being issued are subscribed for or placed privately, details are to be given of the nature of such operations and of the number and characteristics of the underlying shares to which they relate.

27.17.2. Disclose all regulated markets or equivalent markets on which, to the knowledge of the issuer of the depository receipts, underlying shares of the same class of those over which the depository receipts are being issued are offered or admitted to trading.

27.17.3. To the extent known to the issuer of the depository receipts, indicate whether major shareholders, members of the administrative, management or supervisory bodies intended to subscribe in the offer, or whether any person intends to subscribe for more than five per cent of the offer.

28. INFORMATION REGARDING THE DEPOSITORY RECEIPTS

28.1. A description of the type and class of depository receipts being offered and/or admitted to trading.

28.2. Legislation under which the depository receipts have been created.

28.3. An indication whether the depository receipts are in registered or bearer form and whether the depository receipts are in certificated or book-entry form. In the latter case, include the name and address of the entity in charge of keeping the records.

28.4. Currency of the depository receipts.

28.5. Describe the rights attaching to the depository receipts, including any limitations of these attached to the depository receipts and the procedure if any for the exercise of these rights.

28.6. If the dividend rights attaching to depository receipts are different from the dividend rights disclosed in relation to the underlying disclose the following about the dividend rights:
(a) fixed date(s) on which the entitlement arises;
(b) time limit after which entitlement to dividend lapses and an indication of the person in whose favour the lapse operates;
(c) dividend restrictions and procedures for non-resident holders;
(d) rate of dividend or method of its calculation, periodicity and cumulative or non-cumulative nature of payments.

28.7. If the voting rights attaching to the depository receipts are different from the voting rights disclosed in relation to the underlying shares disclose the following about those rights:
- voting rights.
- pre-emption rights in offers for subscription of securities of the same class.
- right to share in the issuer's profits.
- rights to share in any surplus in the event of liquidation.
- redemption provisions.
- conversion provisions.

28.8. Describe the exercise of and benefit from the rights attaching to the underlying shares, in particular voting rights, the conditions on which the issuer of the depository receipts may exercise such rights, and measures envisaged to obtain the instructions of the depository receipt holders – and the right to share in profits and any liquidation surplus which are not passed on to the holder of the depository receipt.

28.9. The expected issue date of the depository receipts.

28.10. A description of any restrictions on the free transferability of the depository receipts.

28.11. In respect of the country of registered office of the issuer and the country(ies) where the offer is being made or admission to trading is being sought:
(a) information on taxes on the income from the depository receipts withheld at source;
(b) indication as to whether the issuer assumes responsibility for the withholding of taxes at the source.

28.12. Bank or other guarantees attached to the depository receipts and intended to underwrite the issuer's obligations.

28.13. Possibility of obtaining the delivery of the depository receipts into original shares and procedure for such delivery.

29. INFORMATION ABOUT THE TERMS AND CONDITIONS OF THE OFFER OF THE DEPOSITORY RECEIPTS

29.1. *Conditions, offer statistics, expected timetable and action required to apply for the offer*

29.1.1. Total amount of the issue/offer, distinguishing the securities offered for sale and those offered for subscription; if the amount is not fixed, description of the arrangements and time for announcing to the public the definitive amount of the offer.

29.1.2. The time period, including any possible amendments, during which the offer will be open and description of the application process.

29.1.3. An indication of when, and under what circumstances, the offer may be revoked or suspended and whether revocation can occur after dealing has begun.

29.1.4. A description of the possibility to reduce subscriptions and the manner for refunding excess amount paid by applicants.

29.1.5. Details of the minimum and/or maximum amount of application (whether in number of securities or aggregate amount to invest).

29.1.6. An indication of the period during which an application may be withdrawn, provided that investors are allowed to withdraw their subscription.

29.1.7. Method and time limits for paying up the securities and for delivery of the securities.

29.1.8. A full description of the manner and date in which results of the offer are to be made public.

29.1.9. The procedure for the exercise of any right of pre-emption, the negotiability of subscription rights and the treatment of subscription rights not exercised.

29.2. *Plan of distribution and allotment*

29.2.1. The various categories of potential investors to which the securities are offered. If the offer is being made simultaneously in the markets of two or more countries and if a tranche has been or is being reserved for certain of these, indicate any such tranche.

29.2.2. To the extent known to the issuer, indicate whether major shareholders or members of the issuer's management, supervisory or administrative bodies intended to subscribe in the offer, or whether any person intends to subscribe for more than five per cent of the offer.

29.2.3. Pre-allotment disclosure:

29.2.3.1. The division into tranches of the offer including the institutional, retail and issuer's employee tranches and any other tranches.

29.2.3.2. The conditions under which the claw-back may be used, the maximum size of such claw back and any applicable minimum percentages for individual tranches.

29.2.3.3. The allotment method or methods to be used for the retail and issuer's employee tranche in the event of an over-subscription of these tranches.

29.2.3.4. A description of any pre-determined preferential treatment to be accorded to certain classes of investors or certain affinity groups (including friends and family programmes) in the allotment, the percentage of the offer reserved for such preferential treatment and the criteria for inclusion in such classes or groups.

29.2.3.5. Whether the treatment of subscriptions or bids to subscribe in the allotment may be determined on the basis of which firm they are made through or by.

29.2.3.6. A target minimum individual allotment if any within the retail tranche.

29.2.3.7. The conditions for the closing of the offer as well as the date on which the offer may be closed at the earliest;

29.2.3.8. Whether or not multiple subscriptions are admitted, and where they are not, how any multiple subscriptions will be handled.

29.2.3.9. Process for notification to applicants of the amount allotted and indication whether dealing may begin before notification is made.

29.2.4. Over-allotment and "green shoe" :

29.2.4.1. The existence and size of any over-allotment facility and/or "green shoe".

29.2.4.2. The existence period of the over-allotment facility and/or "green shoe".

29.2.4.3. Any conditions for the use of the over-allotment facility or exercise of the "green shoe".

29.3. *Pricing*

29.3.1. An indication of the price at which the securities will be offered. When the price is not known or when there is not an established and/or liquid market for the securities, indicate the method for determination of the offer price, including who has set the criteria or is formally responsible for its determination. Indication of the amount of any expenses and taxes specifically charged to the subscriber or purchaser.

29.3.2. Process for the disclosure of the offer price.

29.3.3. Where there is or could be a material disparity between the public offer price and the effective cash cost to members of the administrative, management or supervisory bodies or senior management, or affiliated persons, of securities acquired by them in transactions during the past year, or which they have the right to acquire, include a comparison of the public contribution in the proposed public offer and the effective cash contributions of such persons.

29.4. *Placing and underwriting*

29.4.1. Name and address of the co-coordinator(s) of the global offer and of single parts of the offer and, to the extend known to the issuer, of the placers in the various countries where the offer takes place.

29.4.2. Name and address of any paying agents and depository agents in each country.

29.4.3. Name and address of the entities agreeing to underwrite the issue on a firm commitment basis, and name and address of the entities agreeing to place the issue without a firm commitment or under "best efforts" arrangements. Indication of the material features of the agreements, including the quotas. Where not all of the issue is underwritten, a statement of the portion not covered. Indication of the overall amount of the underwriting commission and of the placing commission.

29.4.4. When the underwriting agreement has been or will be reached.

30. ADMISSION TO TRADING AND DEALING ARRANGEMENTS IN THE DEPOSITORY RECEIPTS

30.1. An indication as to whether the securities offered are or will be the object of an application for admission to trading, with a view to their distribution in a regulated market or other equivalent markets with indication of the markets in question. This circumstance must be mentioned, without creating the impression that the admission to trading necessarily will be approved. If known, the earliest dates on which the securities will be admitted to trading must be given.

30.2. All the regulated markets or equivalent markets on which, to the knowledge of the issuer, securities of the same class of the securities to be offered or admitted to trading are already admitted to trading.

30.3. If simultaneously or almost simultaneously with the creation of the securities for which admission to a regulated market is being sought securities of the same class are subscribed for or placed privately or if securities of other classes are created for public or private placing, details must be given of the nature of such operations and of the number and characteristics of the securities to which they relate.

30.4. Name and address of the entities which have a firm commitment to act as intermediaries in secondary trading, providing liquidity through bid and offer rates and description of the main terms of their commitment.

30.5. Stabilisation: where an issuer or a selling shareholder has granted an over-allotment option or it is otherwise proposed that price stabilising activities may be entered into in connection with an offer:

30.6. The fact that stabilisation may be undertaken, that there is no assurance that it will be undertaken and that it may be stopped at any time.

30.7. The beginning and the end of the period during which stabilisation may occur.

30.8. The identity of the stabilisation manager for each relevant jurisdiction unless this is not known at the time of publication.

30.9. The fact that stabilisation transactions may result in a market price that is higher than would otherwise prevail.

31. KEY INFORMATION ABOUT THE ISSUE OF THE DEPOSITORY RECEIPTS

31.1. *Reasons for the offer and use of proceeds*

31.1.1. Reasons for the offer and, where applicable, the estimated net amount of the proceeds broken into each principal intended use and presented by order of priority of such uses. If the issuer is aware that the anticipated proceeds will not be sufficient to fund all the proposed uses, state the amount and sources of other funds needed. Details must be given with regard to the use of the proceeds, in particular when they are being used to acquire assets, other than in the ordinary course of business, to finance announced acquisitions of other business, or to discharge, reduce or retire indebtedness.

31.2. *Interest of natural and legal persons involved in the issue/offer*

31.2.1. A description of any interest, including conflicting ones, that is material to the issue/offer, detailing the persons involved and the nature of the interest.

31.3. *Risk factors*

31.3.1. Prominent disclosure of risk factors that are material to the securities being offered and/or admitted to trading in order to assess the market risk associated with these securities in a section headed "Risk factors".

32. EXPENSE OF THE ISSUE/OFFER OF THE DEPOSITORY RECEIPTS

32.1. The total net proceeds and an estimate of the total expenses of the issue/offer.

[9752]

NOTES

Words in square brackets in items 20.1, 20.1a inserted by Commission Regulation 211/2007/EC, Art 1(3), as from 1 March 2007.

ANNEX XI
MINIMUM DISCLOSURE REQUIREMENTS FOR THE BANKS REGISTRATION DOCUMENT (SCHEDULE)

1. PERSONS RESPONSIBLE

1.1. All persons responsible for the information given in the registration document and, as the case may be, for certain parts of it, with, in the latter case, an indication of such parts. In the case of natural persons including members of the issuer's administrative, management or supervisory bodies indicate the name and function of the person; in case of legal persons indicate the name and registered office.

1.2. A declaration by those responsible for the registration document that, having taken all reasonable care to ensure that such is the case, the information contained in the registration document is, to the best of their knowledge, in accordance with the facts and contains no omission likely to affect its import. As the case may be, declaration by those responsible for certain parts of the registration document that, having taken all reasonable care to ensure that such is the case, the information contained in the part of the registration document for which they are responsible is, to the best of their knowledge, in accordance with the facts and contains no omission likely to affect its import.

2. STATUTORY AUDITORS

2.1. Names and addresses of the issuer's auditors for the period covered by the historical financial information (together with their membership in a professional body).

2.2. If auditors have resigned, been removed or not been reappointed during the period covered by the historical financial information, details if material.

3. RISK FACTORS

3.1. Prominent disclosure of risk factors that may affect the issuer's ability to fulfil its obligations under the securities to investors in a section headed "Risk factors".

4. INFORMATION ABOUT THE ISSUER

4.1. *History and development of the Issuer*

4.1.1. the legal and commercial name of the issuer;

4.1.2. the place of registration of the issuer and its registration number;

4.1.3. the date of incorporation and the length of life of the issuer, except where indefinite;

4.1.4. the domicile and legal form of the issuer, the legislation under which the issuer operates, its country of incorporation, and the address and telephone number of its registered office (or principal place of business if different from its registered office);

4.1.5. any recent events particular to the issuer which are to a material extent relevant to the evaluation of the issuer's solvency.

5. BUSINESS OVERVIEW

5.1. *Principal activities:*

5.1.1. A brief description of the issuer's principal activities stating the main categories of products sold and/or services performed;

5.1.2. An indication of any significant new products and/or activities.

5.1.3. Principal markets

A brief description of the principal markets in which the issuer competes.

5.1.4. The basis for any statements in the registration document made by the issuer regarding its competitive position.

6. ORGANISATIONAL STRUCTURE

6.1. If the issuer is part of a group, a brief description of the group and of the issuer's position within it.

6.2. If the issuer is dependent upon other entities within the group, this must be clearly stated together with an explanation of this dependence.

7. TREND INFORMATION

7.1. Include a statement that there has been no material adverse change in the prospects of the issuer since the date of its last published audited financial statements.

In the event that the issuer is unable to make such a statement, provide details of this material adverse change.

7.2. Information on any known trends, uncertainties, demands, commitments or events that are reasonably likely to have a material effect on the issuer's prospects for at least the current financial year.

8. PROFIT FORECASTS OR ESTIMATES

If an issuer chooses to include a profit forecast or a profit estimate the registration document must contain the information items 8.1 and 8.2.

8.1. A statement setting out the principal assumptions upon which the issuer has based its forecast, or estimate.

There must be a clear distinction between assumptions about factors which the members of the administrative, management or supervisory bodies can influence and assumptions about factors which are exclusively outside the influence of the members of the administrative, management or supervisory bodies; be readily understandable by investors; be specific and precise; and not relate to the general accuracy of the estimates underlying the forecast.

8.2. A report prepared by independent accountants or auditors stating that in the opinion of the independent accountants or auditors the forecast or estimate has been properly compiled on the basis stated and that the basis of accounting used for the profit forecast or estimate is consistent with the accounting policies of the issuer.

8.3. The profit forecast or estimate must be prepared on a basis comparable with the historical financial information.

9. ADMINISTRATIVE, MANAGEMENT, AND SUPERVISORY BODIES

9.1. Names, business addresses and functions in the issuer of the following persons, and an indication of the principal activities performed by them outside the issuer where these are significant with respect to that issuer:

(a) members of the administrative, management or supervisory bodies;

(b) partners with unlimited liability, in the case of a limited partnership with a share capital.

9.2. *Administrative, Management, and Supervisory bodies conflicts of interests*

Potential conflicts of interests between any duties to the issuing entity of the persons referred to in item 9.1 and their private interests and or other duties must be clearly stated. In the event that there are no such conflicts, make a statement to that effect.

10. MAJOR SHAREHOLDERS

10.1. To the extent known to the issuer, state whether the issuer is directly or indirectly owned or controlled and by whom, and describe the nature of such control, and describe the measures in place to ensure that such control is not abused.

10.2. A description of any arrangements, known to the issuer, the operation of which may at a subsequent date result in a change in control of the issuer.

11. FINANCIAL INFORMATION CONCERNING THE ISSUER'S ASSETS AND LIABILITIES, FINANCIAL POSITION AND PROFITS AND LOSSES

11.1. *Historical Financial Information*

Audited historical financial information covering the latest two financial years (or such shorter period that the issuer has been in operation), and the audit report in respect of each year. [If the issuer has changed its accounting reference date during the period for which historical financial information is required, the audited historical information shall cover at least 24 months, or the entire period for which the issuer has been in operation, whichever is the shorter.] Such financial information must be prepared according to Regulation (EC)

No 1606/2002, or if not applicable to a Member State national accounting standards for issuers from the Community. For third country issuers, such financial information must be prepared according to the international accounting standards adopted pursuant to the procedure of Article 3 of Regulation (EC) No 1606/2002 or to a third country's national accounting standards equivalent to these standards. If such financial information is not equivalent to these standards, it must be presented in the form of restated financial statements.

The most recent year's audited historical financial information must be presented and prepared in a form consistent with that which will be adopted in the issuer's next published annual financial statements having regard to accounting standards and policies and legislation applicable to such annual financial statements.

If the issuer has been operating in its current sphere of economic activity for less than one year, the audited historical financial information covering that period must be prepared in accordance with the standards applicable to annual financial statements under Regulation (EC) No 1606/2002, or if not applicable to a Member State national accounting standards where the issuer is an issuer from the Community. For third country issuers, the historical financial information must be prepared according to the international accounting standards adopted pursuant to the procedure of Article 3 of Regulation (EC) No 1606/2002 or to a third country's national accounting standards equivalent to these standards. This historical financial information must be audited.

If the audited financial information is prepared according to national accounting standards, the financial information required under this heading must include at least the following:

(a) the balance sheet;
(b) the income statement;
(c) in the case of an admission of securities to trading on a regulated market only, a cash flow statement;
(d) the accounting policies and explanatory notes.

The historical annual financial information must be independently audited or reported on as to whether or not, for the purposes of the registration document, it gives a true and fair view, in accordance with auditing standards applicable in a Member State or an equivalent standard.

11.2. *Financial statements*

If the issuer prepares both own and consolidated financial statements, include at least the consolidated financial statements in the registration document.

11.3. *Auditing of historical annual financial information*

11.3.1. A statement that the historical financial information has been audited. If audit reports on the historical financial information have been refused by the statutory auditors or if they contain qualifications or disclaimers, such refusal or such qualifications or disclaimers must be reproduced in full and the reasons given.

11.3.2. An indication of other information in the registration document which has been audited by the auditors.

11.3.3. Where financial data in the registration document is not extracted from the issuer's audited financial statements state the source of the data and state that the data is unaudited.

11.4. *Age of latest financial information*

11.4.1. The last year of audited financial information may not be older than 18 months from the date of the registration document.

11.5. *Interim and other financial information*

11.5.1. If the issuer has published quarterly or half yearly financial information since the date of its last audited financial statements, these must be included in the registration document. If the quarterly or half yearly financial information has been reviewed or audited the audit or review report must also be included. If the quarterly or half yearly financial information is unaudited or has not been reviewed state that fact.

11.5.2. If the registration document is dated more than nine months after the end of the last audited financial year, it must contain interim financial information, covering at least the first six months of the financial year. If the interim financial information is un-audited state that fact.

The interim financial information must include comparative statements for the same period in the prior financial year, except that the requirement for comparative balance sheet information may be satisfied by presenting the years-end balance sheet.

11.6. *Legal and arbitration proceedings*

Information on any governmental, legal or arbitration proceedings (including any such proceedings which are pending or threatened of which the issuer is aware), during a period covering at least the previous 12 months which may have, or have had in the recent past, significant effects on the issuer and/or group's financial position or profitability, or provide an appropriate negative statement.

11.7. *Significant change in the issuer's financial position*

A description of any significant change in the financial position of the group which has occurred since the end of the last financial period for which either audited financial information or interim financial information have been published, or an appropriate negative statement.

12. MATERIAL CONTRACTS

A brief summary of all material contracts that are not entered into in the ordinary course of the issuer's business, which could result in any group member being under an obligation or entitlement that is material to the issuer's ability to meet its obligation to security holders in respect of the securities being issued.

13. THIRD PARTY INFORMATION AND STATEMENT BY EXPERTS AND DECLARATIONS OF ANY INTEREST

13.1. Where a statement or report attributed to a person as an expert is included in the registration document, provide such person's name, business address, qualifications and material interest if any in the issuer. If the report has been produced at the issuer's request a statement to that effect that such statement or report is included, in the form and context in which it is included, with the consent of that person who has authorised the contents of that part of the registration document.

13.2. Where information has been sourced from a third party, provide a confirmation that this information has been accurately reproduced and that as far as the issuer is aware and is able to ascertain from information published by that third party, no facts have been omitted which would render the reproduced information inaccurate or misleading In addition, the issuer shall identify the source(s) of the information.

14. DOCUMENTS ON DISPLAY

A statement that for the life of the registration document the following documents (or copies thereof), where applicable, may be inspected:

(a) the memorandum and articles of association of the issuer;

(b) all reports, letters, and other documents, historical financial information, valuations and statements prepared by any expert at the issuer's request any part of which is included or referred to in the registration document;

(c) the historical financial information of the issuer or, in the case of a group, the historical financial information of the issuer and its subsidiary undertakings for each of the two financial years preceding the publication of the registration document.

An indication of where the documents on display may be inspected, by physical or electronic means.

[9753]

NOTES

Words in square brackets in item 11.1 inserted by Commission Regulation 211/2007/EC, Art 1(4), as from 1 March 2007.

ANNEX XII

MINIMUM DISCLOSURE REQUIREMENTS FOR THE SECURITIES NOTE FOR DERIVATIVE SECURITIES (SCHEDULE)

1. PERSONS RESPONSIBLE

1.1. All persons responsible for the information given in the prospectus and, as the case may be, for certain parts of it, with, in the latter case, an indication of such parts. In the case of natural persons including members of the issuer's administrative, management or supervisory bodies indicate the name and function of the person; in case of legal persons indicate the name and registered office.

1.2. A declaration by those responsible for the prospectus that, having taken all reasonable care to ensure that such is the case, the information contained in the prospectus is, to the best of their knowledge, in accordance with the facts and contains no omission likely to affect its import. As the case may be, declaration by those responsible for certain parts of the prospectus that, having taken all reasonable care to ensure that such is the case, the information contained in the part of the prospectus for which they are responsible is, to the best of their knowledge, in accordance with the facts and contains no omission likely to affect its import.

2. RISK FACTORS

Prominent disclosure of risk factors that are material to the securities being offered and/or admitted to trading in order to assess the market risk associated with these securities in a section headed "risk factors". This must include a risk warning to the effect that investors may lose the value of their entire investment or part of it, as the case may be, and/or, if the investor's liability is not limited to the value of his investment, a statement of that fact, together with a description of the circumstances in which such additional liability arises and the likely financial effect.

3. KEY INFORMATION

3.1. *Interest of natural and legal persons involved in the issue/offer*

A description of any interest, including conflicting ones that is material to the issue/offer, detailing the persons involved and the nature of the interest.

3.2. *Reasons for the offer and use of proceeds when different from making profit and/or hedging certain risks*

If reasons for the offer and use of proceeds are disclosed provide the total net proceeds and an estimate of the total expenses of the issue/offer.

4. INFORMATION CONCERNING THE SECURITIES TO BE OFFERED/ ADMITTED TO TRADING

4.1. *Information concerning the securities*

4.1.1. A description of the type and the class of the securities being offered and/or admitted to trading, including the ISIN (International security identification number) or other such security identification code.

4.1.2. A clear and comprehensive explanation to help investors understand how the value of their investment is affected by the value of the underlying instrument(s), especially under the circumstances when the risks are most evident unless the securities have a denomination per unit of at least EUR 50,000 or can only be acquired for at least EUR 50,000 per security.

4.1.3. Legislation under which the securities have been created.

4.1.4. An indication whether the securities are in registered form or bearer form and whether the securities are in certificated form or book-entry form. In the latter case, name and address of the entity in charge of keeping the records.

4.1.5. Currency of the securities issue.

4.1.6. Ranking of the securities being offered and/or admitted to trading, including summaries of any clauses that are intended to affect ranking or subordinate the security to any present or future liabilities of the issuer.

4.1.7. A description of the rights, including any limitations of these, attached to the securities and procedure for the exercise of said rights.

4.1.8. In the case of new issues, a statement of the resolutions, authorisations and approvals by virtue of which the securities have been or will be created and/or issued.

4.1.9. The issue date of the securities.

4.1.10. A description of any restrictions on the free transferability of the securities.

4.1.11.
— The expiration or maturity date of the derivative securities.
— The exercise date or final reference date.

4.1.12. A description of the settlement procedure of the derivative securities.

4.1.13. A description of how any return on derivative securities takes place, the payment or delivery date, and the way it is calculated.

4.1.14. In respect of the country of registered office of the issuer and the country(ies) where the offer is being made or admission to trading is being sought:
(a) information on taxes on the income from the securities withheld at source;
(b) indication as to whether the issuer assumes responsibility for the withholding of taxes at the source.

4.2. *Information concerning the underlying*

4.2.1. The exercise price or the final reference price of the underlying.

4.2.2. A statement setting out the type of the underlying and details of where information on the underlying can be obtained:
- an indication where information about the past and the further performance of the underlying and its volatility can be obtained,
- where the underlying is a security,
  - the name of the issuer of the security,
  - the ISIN (international security identification number) or other such security identification code,
- where the underlying is an index,
  - the name of the index and a description of the index if it is composed by the issuer. If the index is not composed by the issuer, where information about the index can be obtained,
- where the underlying is an interest rate,
  - a description of the interest rate,
- others:
  - Where the underlying does not fall within the categories specified above the securities note shall contain equivalent information.
- where the underlying is a basket of underlyings,
  - disclosure of the relevant weightings of each underlying in the basket.

4.2.3. A description of any market disruption or settlement disruption events that affect the underlying.

4.2.4. Adjustment rules with relation to events concerning the underlying.

5. TERMS AND CONDITIONS OF THE OFFER

5.1. *Conditions, offer statistics, expected timetable and action required to apply for the offer*

5.1.1. Conditions to which the offer is subject.

5.1.2. Total amount of the issue/offer; if the amount is not fixed, description of the arrangements and time for announcing to the public the amount of the offer.

5.1.3. The period of time , including any possible amendments, during which the offer will be open and description of the application process.

5.1.4. Details of the minimum and/or maximum amount of application, (whether in number of securities or aggregate amount to invest).

5.1.5. Method and time limits for paying up the securities and for delivery of the securities.

5.1.6. A full description of the manner and date in which results of the offer are to be made public.

5.2. *Plan of distribution and allotment*

5.2.1. The various categories of potential investors to which the securities are offered. If the offer is being made simultaneously in the markets of two or more countries and if a tranche has been or is being reserved for certain of these, indicate any such tranche.

5.2.2. Process for notification to applicants of the amount allotted and indication whether dealing may begin before notification is made.

5.3. *Pricing*

Indication of the expected price at which the securities will be offered or the method of determining the price and the process for its disclosure. Indicate the amount of any expenses and taxes specifically charged to the subscriber or purchaser.

5.4. *Placing and underwriting*

5.4.1. Name and address of the coordinator(s) of the global offer and of single parts of the offer and, to the extend known to the issuer or to the offeror, of the placers in the various countries where the offer takes place.

5.4.2. Name and address of any paying agents and depository agents in each country.

5.4.3. Entities agreeing to underwrite the issue on a firm commitment basis, and entities agreeing to place the issue without a firm commitment or under "best efforts" arrangements. Where not all of the issue is underwritten, a statement of the portion not covered.

5.4.4. When the underwriting agreement has been or will be reached.

5.4.5. Name and address of a calculation agent.

6. ADMISSION TO TRADING AND DEALING ARRANGEMENTS

6.1. An indication as to whether the securities offered are or will be the object of an application for admission to trading, with a view to their distribution in a regulated market or other equivalent markets with indication of the markets in question. This circumstance shall be mentioned, without creating the impression that the admission to trading necessarily will be approved. If known, the earliest dates on which the securities will be admitted to trading shall be given.

6.2. All the regulated markets or equivalent markets on which, to the knowledge of the issuer, securities of the same class of the securities to be offered or admitted to trading are already admitted to trading.

6.3. Name and address of the entities which have a firm commitment to act as intermediaries in secondary trading, providing liquidity through bid and offer rates and description of the main terms of their commitment.

7. ADDITIONAL INFORMATION

7.1. If advisors connected with an issue are mentioned in the Securities Note, a statement of the capacity in which the advisors have acted.

7.2. An indication of other information in the Securities Note which has been audited or reviewed by statutory auditors and where auditors have produced a report. Reproduction of the report or, with permission of the competent authority, a summary of the report.

7.3. Where a statement or report attributed to a person as an expert is included in the Securities Note, provide such person's name, business address, qualifications and material interest, if any, in the issuer. If the report has been produced at the issuer's request a statement to that effect that such statement or report is included, in the form and context in which it is included, with the consent of that person who has authorised the contents of that part of the Securities Note.

7.4. Where information has been sourced from a third party, provide a confirmation that this information has been accurately reproduced and that as far as the issuer is aware and is able to ascertain from information published by that third party, no facts have been omitted which would render the reproduced information inaccurate or misleading. In addition, the issuer shall identify the source(s) of the information.

7.5. An indication in the prospectus whether or not the issuer intends to provide post-issuance information. Where the issuer has indicated that it intends to report such information, the issuer shall specify in the prospectus what information will be reported and where such information can be obtained.

[9754]

ANNEX XIII
MINIMUM DISCLOSURE REQUIREMENTS FOR THE SECURITIES NOTE FOR DEBT SECURITIES WITH A DENOMINATION PER UNIT OF AT LEAST EUR 50,000 (SCHEDULE)

1. PERSONS RESPONSIBLE

1.1. All persons responsible for the information given in the prospectus and, as the case may be, for certain parts of it, with, in the latter case, an indication of such parts. In case of natural persons including members of the issuer's administrative, management or supervisory bodies indicate the name and function of the person; in case of legal persons indicate the name and registered office.

1.2. A declaration by those responsible for the prospectus that, having taken all reasonable care to ensure that such is the case, the information contained in the prospectus is, to the best of their knowledge, in accordance with the facts and contains no omission likely to affect its import. As the case may be, declaration by those responsible for certain parts of the prospectus that the information contained in the part of the prospectus for which they are responsible is, to the best of their knowledge, in accordance with the facts and contains no omission likely to affect its import.

2. RISK FACTORS

Prominent disclosure of risk factors that are material to the securities admitted to trading in order to assess the market risk associated with these securities in a section headed "Risk factors".

3. KEY INFORMATION

Interest of natural and legal persons involved in the issue

A description of any interest, including conflicting ones, that is material to the issue, detailing the persons involved and the nature of the interest.

4. INFORMATION CONCERNING THE SECURITIES TO BE ADMITTED TO TRADING

4.1. Total amount of securities being admitted to trading.

4.2. A description of the type and the class of the securities being admitted to trading, including the ISIN (international security identification number) or other such security identification code.

4.3. Legislation under which the securities have been created.

4.4. An indication of whether the securities are in registered or bearer form and whether the securities are in certificated or book-entry form. In the latter case, name and address of the entity in charge of keeping the records.

4.5. Currency of the securities issue.

4.6. Ranking of the securities being admitted to trading, including summaries of any clauses that are intended to affect ranking or subordinate the security to any present or future liabilities of the issuer.

4.7. A description of the rights, including any limitations of these, attached to the securities and procedure for the exercise of said rights.

4.8. The nominal interest rate and provisions relating to interest payable:

— The date from which interest becomes payable and the due dates for interest.
— The time limit on the validity of claims to interest and repayment of principal.

Where the rate is not fixed, description of the underlying on which it is based and of the method used to relate the two:

— A description of any market disruption or settlement disruption events that affect the underlying.
— Adjustment rules with relation to events concerning the underlying.
— Name of the calculation agent.

4.9. Maturity date and arrangements for the amortisation of the loan, including the repayment procedures. Where advance amortisation is contemplated, on the initiative of the issuer or of the holder, it must be described, stipulating amortisation terms and conditions.

4.10. An indication of yield.

4.11. Representation of debt security holders including an identification of the organisation representing the investors and provisions applying to such representation. Indication of where investors may have access to the contracts relating to these forms of representation.

4.12. A statement of the resolutions, authorisations and approvals by virtue of which the securities have been created and/or issued.

4.13. The issue date of the securities.

4.14. A description of any restrictions on the free transferability of the securities.

5. ADMISSION TO TRADING AND DEALING ARRANGEMENTS

5.1. Indication of the market where the securities will be traded and for which prospectus has been published. If known, give the earliest dates on which the securities will be admitted to trading.

5.2. Name and address of any paying agents and depository agents in each country.

6. EXPENSE OF THE ADMISSION TO TRADING

An estimate of the total expenses related to the admission to trading.

7. ADDITIONAL INFORMATION

7.1. If advisors are mentioned in the Securities Note, a statement of the capacity in which the advisors have acted.

7.2. An indication of other information in the Securities Note which has been audited or reviewed by auditors and where auditors have produced a report. Reproduction of the report or, with permission of the competent authority, a summary of the report.

7.3. Where a statement or report attributed to a person as an expert is included in the Securities Note, provide such person's name, business address, qualifications and material interest if any in the issuer. If the report has been produced at the issuer's request a statement to that effect that such statement or report is included, in the form and context in which it is included, with the consent of that person who has authorised the contents of that part of the Securities Note.

7.4. Where information has been sourced from a third party, provide a confirmation that this information has been accurately reproduced and that as far as the issuer is aware and is able to ascertain from information published by that third party, no facts have been omitted which would render the reproduced information inaccurate or misleading. In addition, identify the source(s) of the information.

7.5. Credit ratings assigned to an issuer or its debt securities at the request or with the cooperation of the issuer in the rating process.

[9755]

ANNEX XIV
ADDITIONAL INFORMATION BUILDING BLOCK ON UNDERLYING SHARE FOR SOME EQUITY SECURITIES

1. Description of the underlying share
   - 1.1. Describe the type and the class of the shares
   - 1.2. Legislation under which the shares have been or will be created
   - 1.3. Indication whether the securities are in registered form or bearer form and whether the securities are in certificated form or book-entry form. In the latter case, name and address of the entity in charge of keeping the records
   - 1.4. Indication of the currency of the shares issue
   - 1.5. A description of the rights, including any limitations of these, attached to the securities and procedure for the exercise of those rights:
     - — Dividend rights:
       - — fixed date(s) on which the entitlement arises,
       - — time limit after which entitlement to dividend lapses and an indication of the person in whose favour the lapse operates,
       - — dividend restrictions and procedures for non resident holders,

— rate of dividend or method of its calculation, periodicity and cumulative or non-cumulative nature of payments.
— Voting rights.
— pre-emption rights in offers for subscription of securities of the same class.
— right to share in the issuer's profits.
— rights to share in any surplus in the event of liquidation.
— redemption provisions.
— conversion provisions.

1.6. In the case of new issues, a statement of the resolutions, authorisations and approvals by virtue of which the shares have been or will be created and/or issued and indication of the issue date.

1.7. Where and when the shares will be or have been admitted to trading.

1.8. Description of any restrictions on the free transferability of the shares.

1.9. Indication of the existence of any mandatory takeover bids/or squeeze-out and sell-out rules in relation to the shares.

1.10. Indication of public takeover bids by third parties in respect of the issuer's equity, which have occurred during the last financial year and the current financial year. The price or exchange terms attaching to such offers and the outcome thereof must be stated.

1.11. Impact on the issuer of the underlying share of the exercise of the right and potential dilution effect for the shareholders.

2. When the issuer of the underlying is an entity belonging to the same group, the information to provide on this issuer is the one required by the share registration document schedule.

[9756]

ANNEX XV

MINIMUM DISCLOSURE REQUIREMENTS FOR THE REGISTRATION DOCUMENT FOR SECURITIES ISSUED BY COLLECTIVE INVESTMENT UNDERTAKINGS OF THE CLOSED-END TYPE (SCHEDULE)

In addition to the information required in this schedule, the collective investment undertaking must provide the following information as required under paragraphs and items 1, 2, 3, 4, 5.1, 7, 9.1, 9.2.1, 9.2.3, 10.4, 13, 14, 15, 16, 17.2, 18, 19, 20, 21, 22, 23, 24, 25 in Annex I (minimum disclosure requirements for the share registration document schedule).

1. **Investment objective and policy**

1.1. A detailed description of the investment objective and policy which the collective investment undertaking will pursue and a description of how that investment objectives and policy may be varied including any circumstances in which such variation requires the approval of investors. A description of any techniques and instruments that may be used in the management of the collective investment undertaking.

1.2. The borrowing and/or leverage limits of the collective investment undertaking. If there are no such limits, include a statement to that effect.

1.3. The regulatory status of the collective investment undertaking together with the name of any regulator in its country of incorporation.

1.4. The profile of a typical investor for whom the collective investment undertaking is designed.

2. **Investment restrictions**

2.1. A statement of the investment restrictions which apply to the collective investment undertaking, if any, and an indication of how the holders of securities will be informed of the actions that the investment manager will take in the event of a breach.

2.2. Where more than 20% of the gross assets of any collective investment undertaking (except where items 2.3 or 2.5 apply) may be:

(a) invested in, either directly or indirectly, or lent to any single underlying issuer (including the underlying issuer's subsidiaries or affiliates); or

(b) invested in one or more collective investment undertakings which may invest in excess of 20% of its gross assets in other collective investment undertakings (open-end and/or closed-end type); or

(c) exposed to the creditworthiness or solvency of any one counterparty (including its subsidiaries or affiliates);

the following information must be disclosed:

PART V
EC LEGISLATION

(i) information relating to each underlying issuer/collective investment undertaking/ counterparty as if it were an issuer for the purposes of the minimum disclosure requirements for the share registration document schedule (in the case of (a)) or minimum disclosure requirements for the registration document schedule for securities issued by collective investment undertaking of the closed-end type (in the case of (b)) or the minimum disclosure requirements for the debt and derivative securities with an individual denomination per unit of at least EUR 50,000 registration document schedule (in the case of (c)); or

(ii) if the securities issued by the underlying issuer/collective investment undertaking/ counterparty have already been admitted to trading on a regulated or equivalent market or the obligations are guaranteed by an entity admitted to trading on a regulated or equivalent market, the name, address, country of incorporation, nature of business and name of the market in which its securities are admitted.

This requirement shall not apply where the 20% is exceeded due to appreciations or depreciations, changes in exchange rates, or by reason of the receipt of rights, bonuses, benefits in the nature of capital or by reason of any other action affecting every holder of that investment, provided the investment manager has regard to the threshold when considering changes in the investment portfolio.

2.3. Where a collective investment undertaking may invest in excess of 20% of its gross assets in other collective investment undertakings (open ended and/or closed ended), a description of if and how risk is spread in relation to those investments. In addition, item 2.2 shall apply, in aggregate, to its underlying investments as if those investments had been made directly.

2.4. With reference to point (c) of item 2.2, if collateral is advanced to cover that portion of the exposure to any one counterparty in excess of 20% of the gross assets of the collective investment undertaking, details of such collateral arrangements.

2.5. Where a collective investment undertaking may invest in excess of 40% of its gross assets in another collective investment undertaking either of the following must be disclosed:

(a) information relating to each underlying collective investment undertaking as if it were an issuer under minimum disclosure requirements for the registration document schedule for securities issued by collective investment undertaking of the closed-end type;

(b) if securities issued by an underlying collective investment undertaking have already been admitted to trading on a regulated or equivalent market or the obligations are guaranteed by an entity admitted to trading on a regulated or equivalent market, the name, address, country of incorporation, nature of business and name of the market in which its securities are admitted.

2.6. *Physical commodities*

Where a collective investment undertaking invests directly in physical commodities a disclosure of that fact and the percentage that will be so invested.

2.7. *Property collective investment undertakings*

Where a collective investment undertaking is a property collective investment undertaking, disclosure of that fact, the percentage of the portfolio that is to be invested in the property, as well as a description of the property and any material costs relating to the acquisition and holding of such property. In addition, a valuation report relating to the properties must be included.

Disclosure of item 4.1. applies to:

(a) the valuation entity;

(b) any other entity responsible for the administration of the property.

2.8. *Derivatives financial instruments/money market instruments/currencies*

Where a collective investment undertaking invests in derivatives financial instruments, money market instruments or currencies other than for the purposes of efficient portfolio management (i.e. solely for the purpose of reducing, transferring or eliminating investment risk in the underlying investments of a collective investment undertaking, including any technique or instrument used to provide protection against exchange and credit risks), a statement whether those investments are used for hedging or for investment purposes, and a description of if and how risk is spread in relation to those investments.

2.9. Item 2.2 does not apply to investment in securities issued or guaranteed by a government, government agency or instrumentality of any Member State, its regional or local authorities, or OECD Member State.

2.10. Point (a) of item 2.2 does not apply to a collective investment undertaking whose investment objective is to track, without material modification, that of a broadly based and recognised published index. A description of the composition of the index must be provided.

3. **The applicant's service providers**

3.1. The actual or estimated maximum amount of all material fees payable directly or indirectly by the collective investment undertaking for any services under arrangements entered into on or prior to the date of the registration document and a description of how these fees are calculated.

3.2. A description of any fee payable directly or indirectly by the collective investment undertaking which cannot be quantified under item 3.1 and which is or may be material.

3.3. If any service provider to the collective investment undertaking is in receipt of any benefits from third parties (other than the collective investment undertaking) by virtue of providing any services to the collective investment undertaking, and those benefits may not accrue to the collective investment undertaking, a statement of that fact, the name of that third party, if available, and a description of the nature of the benefits.

3.4. The name of the service provider which is responsible for the determination and calculation of the net asset value of the collective investment undertaking.

3.5. A description of any material potential conflicts of interest which any of the service providers to the collective investment undertaking may have as between their duty to the collective investment undertaking and duties owed by them to third parties and their other interests. A description of any arrangements which are in place to address such potential conflicts.

4. **Investment manager/advisers**

4.1. In respect of any investment manager such information as is required to be disclosed under items 5.1.1 to 5.1.4 and, if material, under item 5.1.5 of Annex I together with a description of its regulatory status and experience.

4.2. In respect of any entity providing investment advice in relation to the assets of the collective investment undertaking, the name and a brief description of such entity.

5. **Custody**

5.1. A full description of how the assets of the collective investment undertaking will be held and by whom and any fiduciary or similar relationship between the collective investment undertaking and any third party in relation to custody:

Where a custodian, trustee, or other fiduciary is appointed:

(a) such information as is required to be disclosed under items 5.1.1 to 5.1.4 and, if material, under item 5.1.5 of Annex I;
(b) a description of the obligations of such party under the custody or similar agreement;
(c) any delegated custody arrangements;
(d) the regulatory status of such party and delegates.

5.2. Where any entity other than those entities mentioned in item 5.1, holds any assets of the collective investment undertaking, a description of how these assets are held together with a description of any additional risks.

6. **Valuation**

6.1. A description of how often, and the valuation principles and the method by which, the net asset value of the collective investment undertaking will be determined, distinguishing between categories of investments and a statement of how such net asset value will be communicated to investors.

6.2. Details of all circumstances in which valuations may be suspended and a statement of how such suspension will be communicated or made available to investors.

7. **Cross liabilities**

7.1. In the case of an umbrella collective investment undertaking, a statement of any cross liability that may occur between classes or investments in other collective investment undertakings and any action taken to limit such liability.

8. **Financial information**

8.1. Where, since the date of incorporation or establishment, a collective investment undertaking has not commenced operations and no financial statements have been made up as at the date of the registration document, a statement to that effect.

Where a collective investment undertaking has commenced operations, the provisions of item 20 of Annex I on the Minimum Disclosure Requirements for the share registration document apply.

8.2. A comprehensive and meaningful analysis of the collective investment undertaking's portfolio (if unaudited, clearly marked as such).

8.3. An indication of the most recent net asset value per security must be included in the securities note schedule (and, if un-audited, clearly marked as such).

[9757]

ANNEX XVI

MINIMUM DISCLOSURE REQUIREMENTS FOR THE REGISTRATION DOCUMENT FOR SECURITIES ISSUED BY MEMBER STATES, THIRD COUNTRIES AND THEIR REGIONAL AND LOCAL AUTHORITIES (SCHEDULE)

1. PERSONS RESPONSIBLE

1.1. All persons responsible for the information given in the registration document and, as the case may be, for certain parts of it, with, in the latter case, an indication of such parts. In the case of natural persons including members of the issuer's administrative, management or supervisory bodies indicate the name and function of the person; in case of legal persons indicate the name and registered office.

1.2. A declaration by those responsible for the registration document that, having taken all reasonable care to ensure that such is the case, the information contained in the registration document is, to the best of their knowledge in accordance with the facts and contains no omission likely to affect its import. As the case may be, declaration by those responsible for certain parts of the registration document that, having taken all reasonable care to ensure that such is the case the information contained in the part of the registration document for which they are responsible is, to the best of their knowledge, in accordance with the facts and contains no omission likely to affect its import.

2. RISK FACTORS

Prominent disclosure of risk factors that may affect the issuer's ability to fulfil its obligations under the securities to investors in a section headed "Risk factors".

3. INFORMATION ABOUT THE ISSUER

3.1. The legal name of the issuer and a brief description of the issuer's position within the national governmental framework.

3.2. The domicile or geographical location and legal form of the issuer and its contact address and telephone number.

3.3. Any recent events relevant to the evaluation of the issuer's solvency.

3.4. A description of the issuer's economy including:

(a) the structure of the economy with details of the main sectors of the economy;

(b) gross domestic product with a breakdown by the issuer's economic sectors over for the previous two fiscal years.

3.5. A general description of the issuer's political system and government including details of the governing body of the issuer.

4. PUBLIC FINANCE AND TRADE

Information on the following for the two fiscal years prior to the date of the registration document:

(a) the tax and budgetary systems;

(b) gross public debt including a summary of the debt, the maturity structure of outstanding debt (particularly noting debt with a residual maturity of less than one year) and debt payment record, and of the parts of debt denominated in the domestic currency of the issuer and in foreign currencies;

(c) foreign trade and balance of payment figures;

(d) foreign exchange reserves including any potential encumbrances to such foreign exchange reserves as forward contracts or derivatives;

(e) financial position and resources including liquid deposits available in domestic currency;

(f) income and expenditure figures.

Description of any auditing or independent review procedures on the accounts of the issuer.

5. SIGNIFICANT CHANGE

5.1. Details of any significant changes to the information provided pursuant to item 4 which have occurred since the end of the last fiscal year, or an appropriate negative statement.

6. LEGAL AND ARBITRATION PROCEEDINGS

6.1. Information on any governmental, legal or arbitration proceedings (including any such proceedings which are pending or threatened of which the issuer is aware), during a period covering at least the previous 12 months which may have, or have had in the recent past, significant effects on the issuer financial position, or provide an appropriate negative statement.

6.2. Information on any immunity the issuer may have from legal proceedings.

7. STATEMENT BY EXPERTS AND DECLARATIONS OF ANY INTEREST

Where a statement or report attributed to a person as an expert is included in the registration document, provide such person's name, business address and qualifications. If the report has been produced at the issuer's request a statement to that effect, that such statement or report is included, in the form and context in which it is included, with the consent of that person, who has authorised the contents of that part of the registration document.

To the extent known to the issuer, provide information in respect of any interest relating to such expert which may have an effect on the independence of the expert in the preparation of the report.

8. DOCUMENTS ON DISPLAY

A statement that for the life of the registration document the following documents (or copies thereof), where applicable, may be inspected:

(a) financial and audit reports for the issuer covering the last two fiscal years and the budget for the current fiscal year;

(b) all reports, letters, and other documents, valuations and statements prepared by any expert at the issuer's request any part of which is included or referred to in the registration document.

An indication of where the documents on display may be inspected, by physical or electronic means.

[9758]

ANNEX XVII

MINIMUM DISCLOSURE REQUIREMENTS FOR THE REGISTRATION DOCUMENT FOR SECURITIES ISSUED BY PUBLIC INTERNATIONAL BODIES AND FOR DEBT SECURITIES GUARANTEED BY A MEMBER STATE OF THE OECD (SCHEDULE)

1. PERSONS RESPONSIBLE

1.1. All persons responsible for the information given in the registration document and, as the case may be, for certain parts of it, with, in the latter case, an indication of such parts. In the case of natural persons including members of the issuer's administrative, management or supervisory bodies indicate the name and function of the person; in case of legal persons indicate the name and registered office.

1.2. A declaration by those responsible for the registration document, that, having taken all reasonable care to ensure that such is the case, the information contained in the registration document is, to the best of their knowledge, in accordance with the facts and contains no omission likely to materially affect its import. As the case may be, declaration by those responsible for certain parts of the registration document that, having taken all reasonable care to ensure that such is the case the information contained in the part of the registration document for which they are responsible is, to the best of their knowledge, in accordance with the facts and contains no omission likely to affect its import.

2. RISK FACTORS

Prominent disclosure of risk factors that may affect the issuer's ability to fulfil its obligations under the securities to investors in a section headed "Risk factors".

3. INFORMATION ABOUT THE ISSUER

3.1. The legal name of the issuer and a brief description of the issuer's legal status.

3.2. The location of the principal office and the legal form of the issuer and its contact address and telephone number.

3.3. Details of the governing body of the issuer and a description of its governance arrangements, if any.

3.4. A brief description of the issuer's purpose and functions.

3.5. The sources of funding, guarantees and other obligations owed to the issuer by its members.

3.6. Any recent events relevant to the evaluation of the issuer's solvency.

3.7. A list of the issuer's members.

4. FINANCIAL INFORMATION

4.1. The two most recently published audited annual financial statements prepared in accordance with the accounting and auditing principles adopted by the issuer, and a brief description of those accounting and auditing principles.

Details of any significant changes to the issuer's financial position which has occurred since the end of the latest published audited annual financial statement, or an appropriate negative statement.

5. LEGAL AND ARBITRATION PROCEEDINGS

5.1. Information on any governmental, legal or arbitration proceedings (including any such proceedings which are pending or threatened of which the issuer is aware), during a period covering at least the previous 12 months which are likely to have, or have had in the recent past, significant effects on the issuer's financial position, or provide an appropriate negative statement.

5.2. Information on any immunity the issuer may have from legal proceedings pursuant to its constituent document.

6. STATEMENT BY EXPERTS AND DECLARATION OF ANY INTERESTS

Where a statement or report attributed to a person as an expert is included in the registration document, provide such person's name, business address and qualifications. If the report has been produced at the issuer's request a statement to that effect, that such statement or report is included, in the form and context in which it is included, with the consent of that person.

To the extent known to the issuer, provide information in respect of any conflict of interests relating to such expert which may have an effect on the independence of the expert in the preparation of the report.

7. DOCUMENT ON DISPLAY

A statement that for the life of the registration document the following documents (or copies thereof), where applicable, will be made available on request:

(a) annual and audit reports of the issuer for each of the last two financial years prepared in accordance with the accounting and auditing principles adopted by the issuer;

(b) all reports, letters, and other documents, valuations and statements prepared by any expert at the issuer's request any part of which is included or referred to in the registration document;

(c) the issuer's constituent document.

An indication of where the documents on display may be inspected, by physical or electronic means.

[9759]

ANNEX XVIII
TABLE OF COMBINATIONS

ANNEX XVIII TYPES OF SECURITIES	REGISTRATION DOCUMENT					
	SCHEDULES					BUILDING BLOCK
	SHARE	DEBT and DERIVATIVE (<EUR 50000)	DEBT and DERIVATIVE (> or = EUR 50000)	ASSET BACKED SEC.	BANKS DEBT and DERIVATIVE	PRO FORMA INFORMATION
Shares (preference shares, redeemable shares, shares with preferential subscription rights; etc…)						
Bonds (vanilla bonds, income bonds, structured bonds, etc …) with a denomination of less than EUR 50 000		OR			OR	
Bonds (vanilla bonds, income bonds, structured bonds, etc …) with a denomination of at least EUR 50 000			OR		OR	
Debt securities guaranteed by a third party		OR	OR		OR	
Derivative sec. guaranteed by a third party		OR	OR		OR	
Asset backed securities						
Bonds exchangeable or convertible into third party shares or issuers' or group shares which are admitted on a regulated market		OR	OR		OR	
Bonds exchangeable or convertible into the issuer's shares not admitted on a regulated market						
Bonds exchangeable or convertible into group's shares not admitted on a regulated market		OR	OR		OR	
Bonds with warrants to acquire the issuer's shares not admitted to trading on a regulated market						
Shares with warrants to acquire the issuer's shares not admitted to trading on a regulated market						
Derivatives sec. giving the right to subscribe or to acquire the issuer's shares not admitted on a regulated market						
Derivatives sec, giving the right to acquire group's shares not admitted on a regulated market		OR	OR		OR	
Derivatives sec. giving the right to subscribe or to acquire issuer's or group shares which are admitted on a regulated market and derivatives sec. linked to any other underlying than issuer's or group shares which are not admitted on a regulated market (including any derivatives sec. entitling to cash settlement)		OR	OR		OR	

ANNEX XVIII	REGISTRATION DOCUMENT		
	SCHEDULES		
TYPES OF SECURITIES	COLLECTIVE INVESTMENT UNDERTAKING OF THE CLOSED-END TYPE	STATES AND THEIR REGIONAL AND LOCAL AUTHORITIES	PUBLIC INTERNATIONAL BODIES/Debt Securities guaranteed by a Member State of the OECD
Shares (preference shares, redeemable shares, shares with preferential subscription rights; etc…)			
Bonds (vanilla bonds, income bonds, structured bonds, etc …) with a denomination of less than EUR 50 000			
Bonds (vanilla bonds, income bonds, structured bonds, etc …) with a denomination of at least EUR 50 000			
Debt securities guaranteed by a third party			
Derivative sec. guaranteed by a third party			
Asset backed securities			
Bonds exchangeable or convertible into third party shares or issuers' or group shares which are admitted on a regulated market			
Bonds exchangeable or convertible into the issuer's shares not admitted on a regulated market			
Bonds exchangeable or convertible into group's shares not admitted on a regulated market			
Bonds with warrants to acquire the issuer's shares not admitted to trading on a regulated market			
Shares with warrants to acquire the issuer's shares not admitted to trading on a regulated market			
Derivatives sec. giving the right to subscribe or to acquire the issuer's shares not admitted on a regulated market			
Derivatives sec, giving the right to acquire group's shares not admitted on a regulated market			
Derivatives sec. giving the right to subscribe or to acquire issuer's or group shares which are admitted on a regulated market and derivatives sec. linked to any other underlying than issuer's or group shares which are not admitted on a regulated market (including any derivatives sec. entitling to cash settlement)			

ANNEX XVIII	SECURITIES NOTE						
	SCHEDULES				ADDITIONAL BUILDING BLOCKS		
TYPES OF SECURITIES	SHARE	DEBT (<EUR 50000)	DEBT (> or = EUR 50000)	DERIVATIVES SEC.	GUARANTEES	ASSET BACKED SEC.	UNDERLYING SHARE
Shares (preference shares, redeemable shares, shares with preferential subscription rights; etc…)							
Bonds (vanilla bonds, income bonds, structured bonds, etc …) with a denomination of less than EUR 50 000							
Bonds (vanilla bonds, income bonds, structured bonds, etc …) with a denomination of at least EUR 50 000							
Debt securities guaranteed by a third party		OR	OR				
Derivative sec. guaranteed by a third party							
Asset backed securities		OR	OR				
Bonds exchangeable or convertible into third party shares or issuers' or group shares which are admitted on a regulated market		OR	OR	only item 4.2.2			
Bonds exchangeable or convertible into the issuer's shares not admitted on a regulated market		OR	OR				
Bonds exchangeable or convertible into group's shares not admitted on a regulated market		OR	OR				
Bonds with warrants to acquire the issuer's shares not admitted to trading on a regulated market		OR	OR	AND except item 4.2.2			
Shares with warrants to acquire the issuer's shares not admitted to trading on a regulated market				AND except item 4.2.2			
Derivatives sec. giving the right to subscribe or to acquire the issuer's shares not admitted on a regulated market				except item 4.2.2			
Derivatives sec, giving the right to acquire group's shares not admitted on a regulated market				except item 4.2.2			
Derivatives sec. giving the right to subscribe or to acquire issuer's or group shares which are admitted on a regulated market and derivatives sec. linked to any other underlying than issuer's or group shares which are not admitted on a regulated market (including any derivatives sec. entitling to cash settlement)							

[9760]

ANNEX XIX
LIST OF SPECIALIST ISSUERS

— Property companies
— Mineral companies
— Investment companies
— Scientific research based companies
— Companies with less than three years of existence (start-up companies)
— Shipping companies.

[9761]

DIRECTIVE OF THE EUROPEAN PARLIAMENT AND OF THE COUNCIL

of 15 December 2004

on the harmonisation of transparency requirements in relation to information about issuers whose securities are admitted to trading on a regulated market and amending Directive 2001/34/EC

(2004/109/EC)

NOTES

Date of publication in OJ: OJ L390, 31.12.2004, p 38. Notes are as in the original OJ version.

THE EUROPEAN PARLIAMENT AND THE COUNCIL OF THE EUROPEAN UNION,

Having regard to the Treaty establishing the European Community, and in particular Articles 44 and 95 thereof,

Having regard to the proposal from the Commission,

Having regard to the opinion of the European Economic and Social Committee,[1]

Having regard to the opinion of the European Central Bank,[2]

Acting in accordance with the procedure laid down in Article 251 of the Treaty,[3]

Whereas:

(1) Efficient, transparent and integrated securities markets contribute to a genuine single market in the Community and foster growth and job creation by better allocation of capital and by reducing costs. The disclosure of accurate, comprehensive and timely information about security issuers builds sustained investor confidence and allows an informed assessment of their business performance and assets. This enhances both investor protection and market efficiency.

(2) To that end, security issuers should ensure appropriate transparency for investors through a regular flow of information. To the same end, shareholders, or natural persons or legal entities holding voting rights or financial instruments that result in an entitlement to acquire existing shares with voting rights, should also inform issuers of the acquisition of or other changes in major holdings in companies so that the latter are in a position to keep the public informed.

(3) The Commission Communication of 11 May 1999, entitled "Implementing the framework for financial markets: Action Plan", identifies a series of actions that are needed in order to complete the single market for financial services. The Lisbon European Council of March 2000 calls for the implementation of that Action Plan by 2005. The Action Plan stresses the need to draw up a Directive upgrading transparency requirements. That need was confirmed by the Barcelona European Council of March 2002.

(4) This Directive should be compatible with the tasks and duties conferred upon the European System of Central Banks (ESCB) and the Member States' central banks by the Treaty and the Statute of the European System of Central Banks and of the European Central Bank; particular attention in this regard needs to be given to the Member States' central banks whose shares are currently admitted to trading on a regulated market, in order to guarantee the pursuit of primary Community law objectives.

(5) Greater harmonisation of provisions of national law on periodic and ongoing information requirements for security issuers should lead to a high level of investor protection

throughout the Community. However, this Directive does not affect existing Community legislation on units issued by collective investment undertakings other than the closed-end type, or on units acquired or disposed of in such undertakings.

(6) Supervision of an issuer of shares, or of debt securities the denomination per unit of which is less than EUR 1000, for the purposes of this Directive, would be best effected by the Member State in which the issuer has its registered office. In that respect, it is vital to ensure consistency with Directive 2003/71/EC of the European Parliament and of the Council of 4 November 2003 on the prospectus to be published when securities are offered to the public or admitted to trading.[4] Along the same lines, some flexibility should be introduced allowing third country issuers and Community companies issuing only securities other than those mentioned above a choice of home Member State.

(7) A high level of investor protection throughout the Community would enable barriers to the admission of securities to regulated markets situated or operating within a Member State to be removed. Member States other than the home Member State should no longer be allowed to restrict admission of securities to their regulated markets by imposing more stringent requirements on periodic and ongoing information about issuers whose securities are admitted to trading on a regulated market.

(8) The removal of barriers on the basis of the home Member State principle under this Directive should not affect areas not covered by this Directive, such as rights of shareholders to intervene in the management of an issuer. Nor should it affect the home Member State's right to request the issuer to publish, in addition, parts of or all regulated information through newspapers.

(9) Regulation (EC) No 1606/2002 of the European Parliament and of the Council of 19 July 2002 on the application of international accounting standards[5] has already paved the way for a convergence of financial reporting standards throughout the Community for issuers whose securities are admitted to trading on a regulated market and who are required to prepare consolidated accounts. Thus, a specific regime for security issuers beyond the general system for all companies, as laid down in the Company Law Directives, is already established. This Directive builds on this approach with regard to annual and interim financial reporting, including the principle of providing a true and fair view of an issuer's assets, liabilities, financial position and profit or loss. A condensed set of financial statements, as part of a half-yearly financial report, also represents a sufficient basis for giving such a true and fair view of the first six months of an issuer's financial year.

(10) An annual financial report should ensure information over the years once the issuer's securities have been admitted to a regulated market. Making it easier to compare annual financial reports is only of use to investors in securities markets if they can be sure that this information will be published within a certain time after the end of the financial year. As regards debt securities admitted to trading on a regulated market prior to 1 January 2005 and issued by issuers incorporated in a third country, the home Member State may under certain conditions allow issuers not to prepare annual financial reports in accordance with the standards required under this Directive.

(11) This Directive introduces more comprehensive half-yearly financial reports for issuers of shares admitted to trading on a regulated market. This should allow investors to make a more informed assessment of the issuer's situation.

(12) A home Member State may provide for exemptions from half-yearly reporting by issuers of debt securities in the case of:

— credit institutions acting as small-size issuers of debt securities, or
— issuers already existing on the date of the entry into force of this Directive who exclusively issue debt securities unconditionally and irrevocably guaranteed by the home Member State or by one of its regional or local authorities, or
— during a transitional period of ten years, only in respect of those debt securities admitted to trading on a regulated market prior to 1 January 2005 which may be purchased by professional investors only. If such an exemption is given by the home Member State, it may not be extended in respect of any debt securities admitted to a regulated market thereafter.

(13) The European Parliament and the Council welcome the Commission's commitment rapidly to consider enhancing the transparency of the remuneration policies, total remuneration paid, including any contingent or deferred compensation, and benefits in kind granted to each member of administrative, management or supervisory bodies under its Action Plan for "Modernising Company Law and Enhancing Corporate Governance in the European Union" of 21 May 2003 and the Commission's intention to make a Recommendation on this topic in the near future.

(14) The home Member State should encourage issuers whose shares are admitted to trading on a regulated market and whose principal activities lie in the extractive industry to disclose payments to governments in their annual financial report. The home Member State

should also encourage an increase in the transparency of such payments within the framework established at various international financial fora.

(15) This Directive will also make half-yearly reporting mandatory for issuers of only debt securities on regulated markets. Exemptions should only be provided for wholesale markets on the basis of a denomination per unit starting at EUR 50,000, as under Directive 2003/71/EC. Where debt securities are issued in another currency, exemptions should only be possible where the denomination per unit in such a currency is, at the date of the issue, at least equivalent to EUR 50,000.

(16) More timely and more reliable information about the share issuer's performance over the financial year also requires a higher frequency of interim information. A requirement should therefore be introduced to publish an interim management statement during the first six months and a second interim management statement during the second six months of a financial year. Share issuers who already publish quarterly financial reports should not be required to publish interim management statements.

(17) Appropriate liability rules, as laid down by each Member State under its national law or regulations, should be applicable to the issuer, its administrative, management or supervisory bodies, or persons responsible within the issuer. Member States should remain free to determine the extent of the liability.

(18) The public should be informed of changes to major holdings in issuers whose shares are traded on a regulated market situated or operating within the Community. This information should enable investors to acquire or dispose of shares in full knowledge of changes in the voting structure; it should also enhance effective control of share issuers and overall market transparency of important capital movements. Information about shares or financial instruments as determined by Article 13, lodged as collateral, should be provided in certain circumstances.

(19) Articles 9 and 10(c) should not apply to shares provided to or by the members of the ESCB in carrying out their functions as monetary authorities provided that the voting rights attached to such shares are not exercised; the reference to a "short period" in Article 11 should be understood with reference to credit operations carried out in accordance with the Treaty and the European Central Bank (ECB) legal acts, in particular the ECB Guidelines on monetary policy instruments and procedures and TARGET, and to credit operations for the purpose of performing equivalent functions in accordance with national provisions.

(20) In order to avoid unnecessary burdens for certain market participants and to clarify who actually exercises influence over an issuer, there is no need to require notification of major holdings of shares, or other financial instruments as determined by Article 13 that result in an entitlement to acquire shares with regard to market makers or custodians, or of holdings of shares or such financial instruments acquired solely for clearing and settlement purposes, within limits and guarantees to be applied throughout the Community. The home Member State should be allowed to provide limited exemptions as regards holdings of shares in trading books of credit institutions and investment firms.

(21) In order to clarify who is actually a major holder of shares or other financial instruments in the same issuer throughout the Community, parent undertakings should not be required to aggregate their own holdings with those managed by undertakings for collective investment in transferable securities (UCITS) or investment firms, provided that such undertakings or firms exercise voting rights independently from their parent undertakings and fulfil certain further conditions.

(22) Ongoing information to holders of securities admitted to trading on a regulated market should continue to be based on the principle of equal treatment. Such equal treatment only relates to shareholders in the same position and does not therefore prejudice the issue of how many voting rights may be attached to a particular share. By the same token, holders of debt securities ranking pari passu should continue to benefit from equal treatment, even in the case of sovereign debt. Information to holders of shares and/or debt securities in general meetings should be facilitated. In particular, holders of shares and/or debt securities situated abroad should be more actively involved in that they should be able to mandate proxies to act on their behalf. For the same reasons, it should be decided in a general meeting of holders of shares and/or debt securities whether the use of modern information and communication technologies should become a reality. In that case, issuers should put in place arrangements in order effectively to inform holders of their shares and/or debt securities, insofar as it is possible for them to identify those holders.

(23) Removal of barriers and effective enforcement of new Community information requirements also require adequate control by the competent authority of the home Member State. This Directive should at least provide for a minimum guarantee for the timely availability of such information. For this reason, at least one filing and storage system should exist in each Member State.

(24) Any obligation for an issuer to translate all ongoing and periodic information into all the relevant languages in all the Member States where its securities are admitted to trading does not foster integration of securities markets, but has deterrent effects on cross-border admission of securities to trading on regulated markets. Therefore, the issuer should in certain cases be entitled to provide information drawn up in a language that is customary in the sphere of international finance. Since a particular effort is needed to attract investors from other Member States and third countries, Member States should no longer prevent shareholders, persons exercising voting rights, or holders of financial instruments, from making the required notifications to the issuer in a language that is customary in the sphere of international finance.

(25) Access for investors to information about issuers should be more organised at a Community level in order to actively promote integration of European capital markets. Investors who are not situated in the issuer's home Member State should be put on an equal footing with investors situated in the issuer's home Member State, when seeking access to such information. This could be achieved if the home Member State ensures compliance with minimum quality standards for disseminating information throughout the Community, in a fast manner on a non-discriminatory basis and depending on the type of regulated information in question. In addition, information which has been disseminated should be available in the home Member State in a centralised way allowing a European network to be built up, accessible at affordable prices for retail investors, while not leading to unnecessary duplication of filing requirements for issuers. Issuers should benefit from free competition when choosing the media or operators for disseminating information under this Directive.

(26) In order to further simplify investor access to corporate information across Member States, it should be left to the national supervisory authorities to formulate guidelines for setting up electronic networks, in close consultation with the other parties concerned, in particular security issuers, investors, market participants, operators of regulated markets and financial information providers.

(27) So as to ensure the effective protection of investors and the proper operation of regulated markets, the rules relating to information to be published by issuers whose securities are admitted to trading on a regulated market should also apply to issuers which do not have a registered office in a Member State and which do not fall within the scope of Article 48 of the Treaty. It should also be ensured that any additional relevant information about Community issuers or third country issuers, disclosure of which is required in a third country but not in a Member State, is made available to the public in the Community.

(28) A single competent authority should be designated in each Member State to assume final responsibility for supervising compliance with the provisions adopted pursuant to this Directive, as well as for international cooperation. Such an authority should be of an administrative nature, and its independence from economic players should be ensured in order to avoid conflicts of interest. Member States may however designate another competent authority for examining that information referred to in this Directive is drawn up in accordance with the relevant reporting framework and taking appropriate measures in case of discovered infringements; such an authority need not be of an administrative nature.

(29) Increasing cross-border activities require improved cooperation between national competent authorities, including a comprehensive set of provisions for the exchange of information and for precautionary measures. The organisation of the regulatory and supervisory tasks in each Member State should not hinder efficient cooperation between the competent national authorities.

(30) At its meeting on 17 July 2000, the Council set up the Committee of Wise Men on the Regulation of European securities markets. In its final report, that Committee proposed the introduction of new legislative techniques based on a four-level approach, namely essential principles, technical implementing measures, cooperation amongst national securities regulators, and enforcement of Community law. This Directive should confine itself to broad "framework" principles, while implementing measures to be adopted by the Commission with the assistance of the European Securities Committee established by Commission Decision 2001/528/EC[6] should lay down the technical details.

(31) The Resolution adopted by the Stockholm European Council of March 2001 endorsed the final report of the Committee of Wise Men and the proposed four-level approach to make the regulatory process for Community securities legislation more efficient and transparent.

(32) According to that Resolution, implementing measures should be used more frequently, to ensure that technical provisions can be kept up to date with market and supervisory developments, and deadlines should be set for all stages of implementing rules.

(33) The Resolution of the European Parliament of 5 February 2002 on the implementation of financial services legislation also endorsed the Committee of Wise Men's report, on the basis of the solemn declaration made before the European Parliament the same

day by the President of the Commission and the letter of 2 October 2001 addressed by the Internal Market Commissioner to the Chairman of the Parliament's Committee on Economic and Monetary Affairs with regard to safeguards for the European Parliament's role in this process.

(34) The European Parliament should be given a period of three months from the first transmission of draft implementing measures to allow it to examine them and to give its opinion. However, in urgent and duly justified cases, that period may be shortened. If, within that period, a Resolution is passed by the European Parliament, the Commission should re-examine the draft measures.

(35) Technical implementing measures for the rules laid down in this Directive may be necessary to take account of new developments on securities markets. The Commission should accordingly be empowered to adopt implementing measures, provided that they do not modify the essential elements of this Directive and provided that the Commission acts in accordance with the principles set out therein, after consulting the European Securities Committee.

(36) In exercising its implementing powers in accordance with this Directive, the Commission should respect the following principles:

— the need to ensure confidence in financial markets among investors by promoting high standards of transparency in financial markets;
— the need to provide investors with a wide range of competing investments and a level of disclosure and protection tailored to their circumstances;
— the need to ensure that independent regulatory authorities enforce the rules consistently, especially as regards the fight against economic crime;
— the need for high levels of transparency and consultation with all market participants and with the European Parliament and the Council;
— the need to encourage innovation in financial markets if they are to be dynamic and efficient;
— the need to ensure market integrity by close and reactive monitoring of financial innovation;
— the importance of reducing the cost of, and increasing access to, capital;
— the balance of costs and benefits to market participants on a long-term basis, including small and medium-sized businesses and small investors, in any implementing measures;
— the need to foster the international competitiveness of Community financial markets without prejudice to a much-needed extension of international cooperation;
— the need to achieve a level playing field for all market participants by establishing Community-wide regulations wherever appropriate;
— the need to respect differences in national markets where these do not unduly impinge on the coherence of the single market;
— the need to ensure coherence with other Community legislation in this area, as imbalances in information and a lack of transparency may jeopardise the operation of the markets and above all harm consumers and small investors.

(37) In order to ensure that the requirements set out in this Directive or the measures implementing this Directive are fulfilled, any infringement of those requirements or measures should be promptly detected and, if necessary, subject to penalties. To that end, measures and penalties should be sufficiently dissuasive, proportionate and consistently enforced. Member States should ensure that decisions taken by the competent national authorities are subject to the right of appeal to the courts.

(38) This Directive aims to upgrade the current transparency requirements for security issuers and investors acquiring or disposing of major holdings in issuers whose shares are admitted to trading on a regulated market. This Directive replaces some of the requirements set out in Directive 2001/34/EC of the European Parliament and of the Council of 28 May 2001 on the admission of securities to official stock exchange listing and on information to be published on those securities.[7] In order to gather transparency requirements in a single act it is necessary to amend it accordingly. Such an amendment however should not affect the ability of Member States to impose additional requirements under Articles 42 to 63 of Directive 2001/34/EC, which remain valid.

(39) This Directive is in line with Directive 95/46/EC of the European Parliament and of the Council of 24 October 1995 on the protection of individuals with regard to the processing of personal data and on the free movement of such data.[8]

(40) This Directive respects fundamental rights and observes the principles recognised in particular by the Charter of the Fundamental Rights of the European Union.

(41) Since the objectives of this Directive, namely to ensure investor confidence through equivalent transparency throughout the Community and thereby to complete the internal

market, cannot be sufficiently achieved by the Member States on the basis of the existing Community legislation and can therefore be better achieved at Community level, the Community may adopt measures, in accordance with the principle of subsidiarity as set out in Article 5 of the Treaty. In accordance with the principle of proportionality, as set out in that Article, this Directive does not go beyond what is necessary in order to achieve these objectives.

(42) The measures necessary for implementing this Directive should be adopted in accordance with Council Decision 1999/468/EC of 28 June 1999 laying down the procedures for the exercise of implementing powers conferred on the Commission,[9]

[9762]

NOTES

1 OJ C80, 30.3.2004, p 128.
2 OJ C242, 9.10.2003, p 6.
3 Opinion of the European Parliament of 30 March 2004 (not yet published in the Official Journal) and Council Decision of 2 December 2004.
4 OJ L345, 31.12.2003, p 64.
5 OJ L243, 11.9.2002, p 1.
6 OJ L191, 13.7.2001, p 45. Decision as amended by Decision 2004/8/EC (OJ L3, 7.1.2004, p 33).
7 OJ L184, 6.7.2001, p 1. Directive as last amended by Directive 2003/71/EC.
8 OJ L281, 23.11.1995, p 31. Directive as amended by Regulation (EC) No 1882/2003 (OJ L284, 31.10.2003, p 1).
9 OJ L184, 17.7.1999, p 23.

HAVE ADOPTED THIS DIRECTIVE:

CHAPTER I
GENERAL PROVISIONS

Article 1

Subject matter and scope

1. This Directive establishes requirements in relation to the disclosure of periodic and ongoing information about issuers whose securities are already admitted to trading on a regulated market situated or operating within a Member State.

2. This Directive shall not apply to units issued by collective investment undertakings other than the closed-end type, or to units acquired or disposed of in such collective investment undertakings.

3. Member States may decide not to apply the provisions mentioned in Article 16(3) and in paragraphs 2, 3 and 4 of Article 18 to securities which are admitted to trading on a regulated market issued by them or their regional or local authorities.

4. Member States may decide not to apply Article 17 to their national central banks in their capacity as issuers of shares admitted to trading on a regulated market if this admission took place before 20 January 2005.

[9763]

Article 2

Definitions

1. For the purposes of this Directive the following definitions shall apply:
   (a) "securities" means transferable securities as defined in Article 4(1), point 18, of Directive 2004/39/EC of the European Parliament and of the Council of 21 April 2004 on markets in financial instruments[1] with the exception of money-market instruments, as defined in Article 4(1), point 19, of that Directive having a maturity of less than 12 months, for which national legislation may be applicable;
   (b) "debt securities" means bonds or other forms of transferable securitised debts, with the exception of securities which are equivalent to shares in companies or which, if converted or if the rights conferred by them are exercised, give rise to a right to acquire shares or securities equivalent to shares;
   (c) "regulated market" means a market as defined in Article 4(1), point 14, of Directive 2004/39/EC;

(d) "issuer" means a legal entity governed by private or public law, including a State, whose securities are admitted to trading on a regulated market, the issuer being, in the case of depository receipts representing securities, the issuer of the securities represented;

(e) "shareholder" means any natural person or legal entity governed by private or public law, who holds, directly or indirectly:
   (i) shares of the issuer in its own name and on its own account;
   (ii) shares of the issuer in its own name, but on behalf of another natural person or legal entity;
   (iii) depository receipts, in which case the holder of the depository receipt shall be considered as the shareholder of the underlying shares represented by the depository receipts;

(f) "controlled undertaking" means any undertaking
   (i) in which a natural person or legal entity has a majority of the voting rights; or
   (ii) of which a natural person or legal entity has the right to appoint or remove a majority of the members of the administrative, management or supervisory body and is at the same time a shareholder in, or member of, the undertaking in question; or
   (iii) of which a natural person or legal entity is a shareholder or member and alone controls a majority of the shareholders' or members' voting rights, respectively, pursuant to an agreement entered into with other shareholders or members of the undertaking in question; or
   (iv) over which a natural person or legal entity has the power to exercise, or actually exercises, dominant influence or control;

(g) "collective investment undertaking other than the closed-end type" means unit trusts and investment companies:
   (i) the object of which is the collective investment of capital provided by the public, and which operate on the principle of risk spreading; and
   (ii) the units of which are, at the request of the holder of such units, repurchased or redeemed, directly or indirectly, out of the assets of those undertakings;

(h) "units of a collective investment undertaking" means securities issued by a collective investment undertaking and representing rights of the participants in such an undertaking over its assets;

(i) "home Member State" means
   (i) in the case of an issuer of debt securities the denomination per unit of which is less than EUR 1000 or an issuer of shares:
      — where the issuer is incorporated in the Community, the Member State in which it has its registered office;
      — where the issuer is incorporated in a third country, the Member State in which it is required to file the annual information with the competent authority in accordance with Article 10 of Directive 2003/71/EC.

   The definition of "home" Member State shall be applicable to debt securities in a currency other than Euro, provided that the value of such denomination per unit is, at the date of the issue, less than EUR 1000, unless it is nearly equivalent to EUR 1000;
   (ii) for any issuer not covered by (i), the Member State chosen by the issuer from among the Member State in which the issuer has its registered office and those Member States which have admitted its securities to trading on a regulated market on their territory. The issuer may choose only one Member State as its home Member State. Its choice shall remain valid for at least three years unless its securities are no longer admitted to trading on any regulated market in the Community;

(j) "host Member State" means a Member State in which securities are admitted to trading on a regulated market, if different from the home Member State;

(k) "regulated information" means all information which the issuer, or any other person who has applied for the admission of securities to trading on a regulated market without the issuer's consent, is required to disclose under this Directive, under Article 6 of Directive 2003/6/EC of the European Parliament and of the Council of 28 January 2003 on insider dealing and market manipulation (market abuse),[2] or under the laws, regulations or administrative provisions of a Member State adopted under Article 3(1) of this Directive;

(l) "electronic means" are means of electronic equipment for the processing (including digital compression), storage and transmission of data, employing wires, radio, optical technologies, or any other electromagnetic means;

(m) "management company" means a company as defined in Article 1a(2) of Council Directive 85/611/EEC of 20 December 1985 on the coordination of laws, regulations and administrative provisions relating to undertakings for collective investment in transferable securities (UCITS);[3]

(n) "market maker" means a person who holds himself out on the financial markets on a continuous basis as being willing to deal on own account by buying and selling financial instruments against his proprietary capital at prices defined by him;

(o) "credit institution" means an undertaking as defined in Article 1(1)(a) of Directive 2000/12/EC of the European Parliament and of the Council of 20 March 2000 relating to the taking up and pursuit of the business of credit institutions;[4]

(p) "securities issued in a continuous or repeated manner" means debt securities of the same issuer on tap or at least two separate issues of securities of a similar type and/or class.

2. For the purposes of the definition of "controlled undertaking" in paragraph 1(f)(ii), the holder's rights in relation to voting, appointment and removal shall include the rights of any other undertaking controlled by the shareholder and those of any natural person or legal entity acting, albeit in its own name, on behalf of the shareholder or of any other undertaking controlled by the shareholder.

3. In order to take account of technical developments on financial markets and to ensure the uniform application of paragraph 1, the Commission shall, in accordance with the procedure referred to in Article 27(2), adopt implementing measures concerning the definitions set out in paragraph 1.

The Commission shall, in particular:

(a) establish, for the purposes of paragraph 1(i)(ii), the procedural arrangements in accordance with which an issuer may make the choice of the home Member State;

(b) adjust, where appropriate for the purposes of the choice of the home Member State referred to in paragraph 1(i)(ii), the three-year period in relation to the issuer's track record in the light of any new requirement under Community law concerning admission to trading on a regulated market;

(c) establish, for the purposes of paragraph 1(l), an indicative list of means which are not to be considered as electronic means, thereby taking into account Annex V to Directive 98/34/EC of the European Parliament and of the Council of 22 June 1998 laying down a procedure for the provision of information in the field of technical standards and regulations.[5]

[9764]

NOTES

1 OJ L145, 30.4.2004, p 1.
2 OJ L96, 12.4.2003, p 16.
3 OJ L375, 31.12.1985, p 3. Directive as last amended by Directive 2004/39/EC.
4 OJ L126, 26.5.2000, p 1. Directive as last amended by Commission Directive 2004/69/EC (OJ L125, 28.4.2004, p 44).
5 OJ L204, 21.7.1998, p 37. Directive as last amended by the 2003 Act of Accession.

Article 3

Integration of securities markets

1. The home Member State may make an issuer subject to requirements more stringent than those laid down in this Directive.

The home Member State may also make a holder of shares, or a natural person or legal entity referred to in Articles 10 or 13, subject to requirements more stringent than those laid down in this Directive.

2. A host Member State may not:

(a) as regards the admission of securities to a regulated market in its territory, impose disclosure requirements more stringent than those laid down in this Directive or in Article 6 of Directive 2003/6/EC;

(b) as regards the notification of information, make a holder of shares, or a natural person or legal entity referred to in Articles 10 or 13, subject to requirements more stringent than those laid down in this Directive.

[9765]

CHAPTER II
PERIODIC INFORMATION

Article 4

Annual financial reports

1. The issuer shall make public its annual financial report at the latest four months after the end of each financial year and shall ensure that it remains publicly available for at least five years.

2. The annual financial report shall comprise:

(a) the audited financial statements;

(b) the management report; and

(c) statements made by the persons responsible within the issuer, whose names and functions shall be clearly indicated, to the effect that, to the best of their knowledge, the financial statements prepared in accordance with the applicable set of accounting standards give a true and fair view of the assets, liabilities, financial position and profit or loss of the issuer and the undertakings included in the consolidation taken as a whole and that the management report includes a fair review of the development and performance of the business and the position of the issuer and the undertakings included in the consolidation taken as a whole, together with a description of the principal risks and uncertainties that they face.

3. Where the issuer is required to prepare consolidated accounts according to the Seventh Council Directive 83/349/EEC of 13 June 1983 on consolidated accounts,[1] the audited financial statements shall comprise such consolidated accounts drawn up in accordance with Regulation (EC) No 1606/2002 and the annual accounts of the parent company drawn up in accordance with the national law of the Member State in which the parent company is incorporated.

Where the issuer is not required to prepare consolidated accounts, the audited financial statements shall comprise the accounts prepared in accordance with the national law of the Member State in which the company is incorporated.

4. The financial statements shall be audited in accordance with Articles 51 and 51a of the Fourth Council Directive 78/660/EEC of 25 July 1978 on the annual accounts of certain types of companies[2] and, if the issuer is required to prepare consolidated accounts, in accordance with Article 37 of Directive 83/349/EEC.

The audit report, signed by the person or persons responsible for auditing the financial statements, shall be disclosed in full to the public together with the annual financial report.

5. The management report shall be drawn up in accordance with Article 46 of Directive 78/660/EEC and, if the issuer is required to prepare consolidated accounts, in accordance with Article 36 of Directive 83/349/EEC.

6. The Commission shall, in accordance with the procedure referred to in Article 27(2), adopt implementing measures in order to take account of technical developments in financial markets and to ensure the uniform application of paragraph 1. The Commission shall in particular specify the technical conditions under which a published annual financial report, including the audit report, is to remain available to the public. Where appropriate, the Commission may also adapt the five-year period referred to in paragraph 1.

[9766]

NOTES

1 OJ L193, 18.7.1983, p 1. Directive as last amended by Directive 2003/51/EC of the European Parliament and of the Council (OJ L178, 17.7.2003, p 16).

2 OJ L222, 14.8.1978, p 11. Directive as last amended by Directive 2003/51/EC.

Article 5

Half-yearly financial reports

1. The issuer of shares or debt securities shall make public a half-yearly financial report covering the first six months of the financial year as soon as possible after the end of the

relevant period, but at the latest two months thereafter. The issuer shall ensure that the half-yearly financial report remains available to the public for at least five years.

2. The half-yearly financial report shall comprise:
(a) the condensed set of financial statements;
(b) an interim management report; and
(c) statements made by the persons responsible within the issuer, whose names and functions shall be clearly indicated, to the effect that, to the best of their knowledge, the condensed set of financial statements which has been prepared in accordance with the applicable set of accounting standards gives a true and fair view of the assets, liabilities, financial position and profit or loss of the issuer, or the undertakings included in the consolidation as a whole as required under paragraph 3, and that the interim management report includes a fair review of the information required under paragraph 4.

3. Where the issuer is required to prepare consolidated accounts, the condensed set of financial statements shall be prepared in accordance with the international accounting standard applicable to the interim financial reporting adopted pursuant to the procedure provided for under Article 6 of Regulation (EC) No 1606/2002.

Where the issuer is not required to prepare consolidated accounts, the condensed set of financial statements shall at least contain a condensed balance sheet, a condensed profit and loss account and explanatory notes on these accounts. In preparing the condensed balance sheet and the condensed profit and loss account, the issuer shall follow the same principles for recognising and measuring as when preparing annual financial reports.

4. The interim management report shall include at least an indication of important events that have occurred during the first six months of the financial year, and their impact on the condensed set of financial statements, together with a description of the principal risks and uncertainties for the remaining six months of the financial year. For issuers of shares, the interim management report shall also include major related parties transactions.

5. If the half-yearly financial report has been audited, the audit report shall be reproduced in full. The same shall apply in the case of an auditors' review. If the half-yearly financial report has not been audited or reviewed by auditors, the issuer shall make a statement to that effect in its report.

6. The Commission shall, in accordance with the procedure referred to in Article 27(2), adopt implementing measures in order to take account of technical developments on financial markets and to ensure the uniform application of paragraphs 1 to 5 of this Article.

The Commission shall, in particular:
(a) specify the technical conditions under which a published half-yearly financial report, including the auditors' review, is to remain available to the public;
(b) clarify the nature of the auditors' review;
(c) specify the minimum content of the condensed balance sheet and profit and loss accounts and explanatory notes on these accounts, where they are not prepared in accordance with the international accounting standards adopted pursuant to the procedure provided for under Article 6 of Regulation (EC) No 1606/2002.

Where appropriate, the Commission may also adapt the five-year period referred to in paragraph 1.

[9767]

Article 6

Interim management statements

1. Without prejudice to Article 6 of Directive 2003/6/EC, an issuer whose shares are admitted to trading on a regulated market shall make public a statement by its management during the first six-month period of the financial year and another statement by its management during the second six-month period of the financial year. Such statement shall be made in a period between ten weeks after the beginning and six weeks before the end of the relevant six-month period. It shall contain information covering the period between the beginning of the relevant six-month period and the date of publication of the statement. Such a statement shall provide:
— an explanation of material events and transactions that have taken place during the relevant period and their impact on the financial position of the issuer and its controlled undertakings, and

— a general description of the financial position and performance of the issuer and its controlled undertakings during the relevant period.

2. Issuers which, under either national legislation or the rules of the regulated market or of their own initiative, publish quarterly financial reports in accordance with such legislation or rules shall not be required to make public statements by the management provided for in paragraph 1.

3. The Commission shall provide a report to the European Parliament and the Council by 20 January 2010 on the transparency of quarterly financial reporting and statements by the management of issuers to examine whether the information provided meets the objective of allowing investors to make an informed assessment of the financial position of the issuer. Such a report shall include an impact assessment on areas where the Commission considers proposing amendments to this Article.

[9768]

Article 7

Responsibility and liability

Member States shall ensure that responsibility for the information to be drawn up and made public in accordance with Articles 4, 5, 6 and 16 lies at least with the issuer or its administrative, management or supervisory bodies and shall ensure that their laws, regulations and administrative provisions on liability apply to the issuers, the bodies referred to in this Article or the persons responsible within the issuers.

[9769]

Article 8

Exemptions

1. Articles 4, 5 and 6 shall not apply to the following issuers:

(a) a State, a regional or local authority of a State, a public international body of which at least one Member State is a member, the ECB, and Member States' national central banks whether or not they issue shares or other securities; and

(b) an issuer exclusively of debt securities admitted to trading on a regulated market, the denomination per unit of which is at least EUR 50,000 or, in the case of debt securities denominated in a currency other than Euro, the value of such denomination per unit is, at the date of the issue, equivalent to at least EUR 50,000.

2. The home Member State may choose not to apply Article 5 to credit institutions whose shares are not admitted to trading on a regulated market and which have, in a continuous or repeated manner, only issued debt securities provided that the total nominal amount of all such debt securities remains below EUR 100,000,000 and that they have not published a prospectus under Directive 2003/71/EC.

3. The home Member State may choose not to apply Article 5 to issuers already existing at the date of the entry into force of Directive 2003/71/EC which exclusively issue debt securities unconditionally and irrevocably guaranteed by the home Member State or by one of its regional or local authorities, on a regulated market.

[9770]

CHAPTER III
ONGOING INFORMATION

SECTION I
INFORMATION ABOUT MAJOR HOLDINGS

Article 9

Notification of the acquisition or disposal of major holdings

1. The home Member State shall ensure that, where a shareholder acquires or disposes of shares of an issuer whose shares are admitted to trading on a regulated market and to which voting rights are attached, such shareholder notifies the issuer of the proportion of voting

rights of the issuer held by the shareholder as a result of the acquisition or disposal where that proportion reaches, exceeds or falls below the thresholds of 5%, 10%, 15%, 20%, 25%, 30%, 50% and 75%.

The voting rights shall be calculated on the basis of all the shares to which voting rights are attached even if the exercise thereof is suspended. Moreover this information shall also be given in respect of all the shares which are in the same class and to which voting rights are attached.

2. The home Member States shall ensure that the shareholders notify the issuer of the proportion of voting rights, where that proportion reaches, exceeds or falls below the thresholds provided for in paragraph 1, as a result of events changing the breakdown of voting rights, and on the basis of the information disclosed pursuant to Article 15. Where the issuer is incorporated in a third country, the notification shall be made for equivalent events.

3. The home Member State need not apply:

(a) the 30% threshold, where it applies a threshold of one-third;

(b) the 75% threshold, where it applies a threshold of two-thirds.

4. This Article shall not apply to shares acquired for the sole purpose of clearing and settling within the usual short settlement cycle, or to custodians holding shares in their custodian capacity provided such custodians can only exercise the voting rights attached to such shares under instructions given in writing or by electronic means.

5. This Article shall not apply to the acquisition or disposal of a major holding reaching or crossing the 5% threshold by a market maker acting in its capacity of a market maker, provided that:

(a) it is authorised by its home Member State under Directive 2004/39/EC; and

(b) it neither intervenes in the management of the issuer concerned nor exerts any influence on the issuer to buy such shares or back the share price.

6. Home Member States under Article 2(1)(i) may provide that voting rights held in the trading book, as defined in Article 2(6) of Council Directive 93/6/EEC of 15 March 1993 on the capital adequacy of investment firms and credit institutions,[1] of a credit institution or investment firm shall not be counted for the purposes of this Article provided that:

(a) the voting rights held in the trading book do not exceed 5%, and

(b) the credit institution or investment firm ensures that the voting rights attaching to shares held in the trading book are not exercised nor otherwise used to intervene in the management of the issuer.

7. The Commission shall, in accordance with the procedure referred to in Article 27(2), adopt implementing measures in order to take account of technical developments on financial markets and to ensure the uniform application of paragraphs 2, 4 and 5 of this Article.

The Commission shall in particular specify the maximum length of the "short settlement cycle" referred to in paragraph 4, as well as the appropriate control mechanisms by the competent authority of the home Member State. In addition, the Commission may draw up a list of the events referred to in paragraph 2.

[9771]

NOTES

[1] OJ L141, 11.6.1993, p 1. Directive as last amended by Directive 2004/39/EC.

Article 10

Acquisition or disposal of major proportions of voting rights

The notification requirements defined in paragraphs 1 and 2 of Article 9 shall also apply to a natural person or legal entity to the extent it is entitled to acquire, to dispose of, or to exercise voting rights in any of the following cases or a combination of them:

(a) voting rights held by a third party with whom that person or entity has concluded an agreement, which obliges them to adopt, by concerted exercise of the voting rights they hold, a lasting common policy towards the management of the issuer in question;

(b) voting rights held by a third party under an agreement concluded with that person or entity providing for the temporary transfer for consideration of the voting rights in question;

(c) voting rights attaching to shares which are lodged as collateral with that person or entity, provided the person or entity controls the voting rights and declares its intention of exercising them;

(d) voting rights attaching to shares in which that person or entity has the life interest;

(e) voting rights which are held, or may be exercised within the meaning of points (a) to (d), by an undertaking controlled by that person or entity;

(f) voting rights attaching to shares deposited with that person or entity which the person or entity can exercise at its discretion in the absence of specific instructions from the shareholders;

(g) voting rights held by a third party in its own name on behalf of that person or entity;

(h) voting rights which that person or entity may exercise as a proxy where the person or entity can exercise the voting rights at its discretion in the absence of specific instructions from the shareholders.

[9772]

Article 11

1. Articles 9 and 10(c) shall not apply to shares provided to or by the members of the ESCB in carrying out their functions as monetary authorities, including shares provided to or by members of the ESCB under a pledge or repurchase or similar agreement for liquidity granted for monetary policy purposes or within a payment system.

2. The exemption shall apply to the above transactions lasting for a short period and provided that the voting rights attaching to such shares are not exercised.

[9773]

Article 12

Procedures on the notification and disclosure of major holdings

1. The notification required under Articles 9 and 10 shall include the following information:

(a) the resulting situation in terms of voting rights;

(b) the chain of controlled undertakings through which voting rights are effectively held, if applicable;

(c) the date on which the threshold was reached or crossed; and

(d) the identity of the shareholder, even if that shareholder is not entitled to exercise voting rights under the conditions laid down in Article 10, and of the natural person or legal entity entitled to exercise voting rights on behalf of that shareholder.

2. The notification to the issuer shall be effected as soon as possible, but not later than four trading days, the first of which shall be the day after the date on which the shareholder, or the natural person or legal entity referred to in Article 10,

(a) learns of the acquisition or disposal or of the possibility of exercising voting rights, or on which, having regard to the circumstances, should have learned of it, regardless of the date on which the acquisition, disposal or possibility of exercising voting rights takes effect; or

(b) is informed about the event mentioned in Article 9(2).

3. An undertaking shall be exempted from making the required notification in accordance with paragraph 1 if the notification is made by the parent undertaking or, where the parent undertaking is itself a controlled undertaking, by its own parent undertaking.

4. The parent undertaking of a management company shall not be required to aggregate its holdings under Articles 9 and 10 with the holdings managed by the management company under the conditions laid down in Directive 85/611/EEC, provided such management company exercises its voting rights independently from the parent undertaking.

However, Articles 9 and 10 shall apply where the parent undertaking, or another controlled undertaking of the parent undertaking, has invested in holdings managed by such management company and the management company has no discretion to exercise the voting rights attached to such holdings and may only exercise such voting rights under direct or indirect instructions from the parent or another controlled undertaking of the parent undertaking.

5. The parent undertaking of an investment firm authorised under Directive 2004/39/EC shall not be required to aggregate its holdings under Articles 9 and 10 with the holdings which such investment firm manages on a client-by-client basis within the meaning of Article 4(1), point 9, of Directive 2004/39/EC, provided that:

— the investment firm is authorised to provide such portfolio management under point 4 of Section A of Annex I to Directive 2004/39/EC;
— it may only exercise the voting rights attached to such shares under instructions given in writing or by electronic means or it ensures that individual portfolio management services are conducted independently of any other services under conditions equivalent to those provided for under Directive 85/611/EEC by putting into place appropriate mechanisms; and
— the investment firm exercises its voting rights independently from the parent undertaking.

However, Articles 9 and 10 shall apply where the parent undertaking, or another controlled undertaking of the parent undertaking, has invested in holdings managed by such investment firm and the investment firm has no discretion to exercise the voting rights attached to such holdings and may only exercise such voting rights under direct or indirect instructions from the parent or another controlled undertaking of the parent undertaking.

6. Upon receipt of the notification under paragraph 1, but no later than three trading days thereafter, the issuer shall make public all the information contained in the notification.

7. A home Member State may exempt issuers from the requirement in paragraph 6 if the information contained in the notification is made public by its competent authority, under the conditions laid down in Article 21, upon receipt of the notification, but no later than three trading days thereafter.

8. In order to take account of technical developments on financial markets and to ensure the uniform application of paragraphs 1, 2, 4, 5 and 6 of this Article, the Commission shall, in accordance with the procedure referred to in Article 27(2), adopt implementing measures:

(a) to establish a standard form to be used throughout the Community when notifying the required information to the issuer under paragraph 1 or when filing information under Article 19(3);
(b) to determine a calendar of "trading days" for all Member States;
(c) to establish in which cases the shareholder, or the natural person or legal entity referred to in Article 10, or both, shall effect the necessary notification to the issuer;
(d) to clarify the circumstances under which the shareholder, or the natural person or legal entity referred to in Article 10, should have learned of the acquisition or disposal;
(e) to clarify the conditions of independence to be complied with by management companies and their parent undertakings or by investment firms and their parent undertakings to benefit from the exemptions in paragraphs 4 and 5.

[9774]

Article 13

1. The notification requirements laid down in Article 9 shall also apply to a natural person or legal entity who holds, directly or indirectly, financial instruments that result in an entitlement to acquire, on such holder's own initiative alone, under a formal agreement, shares to which voting rights are attached, already issued, of an issuer whose shares are admitted to trading on a regulated market.

2. The Commission shall, in accordance with the procedure referred to in Article 27(2), adopt implementing measures in order to take account of technical developments in financial markets and to ensure the uniform application of paragraph 1. It shall in particular determine:

(a) the types of financial instruments referred to in paragraph 1 and their aggregation;
(b) the nature of the formal agreement referred to in paragraph 1;
(c) the contents of the notification to be made, establishing a standard form to be used throughout the Community for that purpose;
(d) the notification period;
(e) to whom the notification is to be made.

[9775]

Article 14

1. Where an issuer of shares admitted to trading on a regulated market acquires or disposes of its own shares, either itself or through a person acting in his own name but on the

issuer's behalf, the home Member State shall ensure that the issuer makes public the proportion of its own shares as soon as possible, but not later than four trading days following such acquisition or disposal where that proportion reaches, exceeds or falls below the thresholds of 5% or 10% of the voting rights. The proportion shall be calculated on the basis of the total number of shares to which voting rights are attached.

2. The Commission shall, in accordance with the procedure referred to in Article 27(2), adopt implementing measures in order to take account of technical developments in financial markets and to ensure the uniform application of paragraph 1.

[9776]

Article 15

For the purpose of calculating the thresholds provided for in Article 9, the home Member State shall at least require the disclosure to the public by the issuer of the total number of voting rights and capital at the end of each calendar month during which an increase or decrease of such total number has occurred.

[9777]

Article 16

Additional information

1. The issuer of shares admitted to trading on a regulated market shall make public without delay any change in the rights attaching to the various classes of shares, including changes in the rights attaching to derivative securities issued by the issuer itself and giving access to the shares of that issuer.

2. The issuer of securities, other than shares admitted to trading on a regulated market, shall make public without delay any changes in the rights of holders of securities other than shares, including changes in the terms and conditions of these securities which could indirectly affect those rights, resulting in particular from a change in loan terms or in interest rates.

3. The issuer of securities admitted to trading on a regulated market shall make public without delay of new loan issues and in particular of any guarantee or security in respect thereof. Without prejudice to Directive 2003/6/EC, this paragraph shall not apply to a public international body of which at least one Member State is member.

[9778]

SECTION II
INFORMATION FOR HOLDERS OF SECURITIES ADMITTED TO TRADING ON A REGULATED MARKET

Article 17

Information requirements for issuers whose shares are admitted to trading on a regulated market

1. The issuer of shares admitted to trading on a regulated market shall ensure equal treatment for all holders of shares who are in the same position.

2. The issuer shall ensure that all the facilities and information necessary to enable holders of shares to exercise their rights are available in the home Member State and that the integrity of data is preserved. Shareholders shall not be prevented from exercising their rights by proxy, subject to the law of the country in which the issuer is incorporated. In particular, the issuer shall:

(a) provide information on the place, time and agenda of meetings, the total number of shares and voting rights and the rights of holders to participate in meetings;
(b) make available a proxy form, on paper or, where applicable, by electronic means, to each person entitled to vote at a shareholders' meeting, together with the notice concerning the meeting or, on request, after an announcement of the meeting;
(c) designate as its agent a financial institution through which shareholders may exercise their financial rights; and
(d) publish notices or distribute circulars concerning the allocation and payment of dividends and the issue of new shares, including information on any arrangements for allotment, subscription, cancellation or conversion.

3. For the purposes of conveying information to shareholders, the home Member State shall allow issuers the use of electronic means, provided such a decision is taken in a general meeting and meets at least the following conditions:

(a) the use of electronic means shall in no way depend upon the location of the seat or residence of the shareholder or, in the cases referred to in Article 10(a) to (h), of the natural persons or legal entities;

(b) identification arrangements shall be put in place so that the shareholders, or the natural persons or legal entities entitled to exercise or to direct the exercise of voting rights, are effectively informed;

(c) shareholders, or in the cases referred to in Article 10(a) to (e) the natural persons or legal entities entitled to acquire, dispose of or exercise voting rights, shall be contacted in writing to request their consent for the use of electronic means for conveying information and, if they do not object within a reasonable period of time, their consent shall be deemed to be given. They shall be able to request, at any time in the future, that information be conveyed in writing, and

(d) any apportionment of the costs entailed in the conveyance of such information by electronic means shall be determined by the issuer in compliance with the principle of equal treatment laid down in paragraph 1.

4. The Commission shall, in accordance with the procedure provided for in Article 27(2), adopt implementing measures in order to take account of technical developments in financial markets, to take account of developments in information and communication technology and to ensure the uniform application of paragraphs 1, 2 and 3. It shall, in particular, specify the types of financial institution through which a shareholder may exercise the financial rights provided for in paragraph 2(c).

[9779]

Article 18

Information requirements for issuers whose debt securities are admitted to trading on a regulated market

1. The issuer of debt securities admitted to trading on a regulated market shall ensure that all holders of debt securities ranking pari passu are given equal treatment in respect of all the rights attaching to those debt securities.

2. The issuer shall ensure that all the facilities and information necessary to enable debt securities holders to exercise their rights are publicly available in the home Member State and that the integrity of data is preserved. Debt securities holders shall not be prevented from exercising their rights by proxy, subject to the law of country in which the issuer is incorporated. In particular, the issuer shall:

(a) publish notices, or distribute circulars, concerning the place, time and agenda of meetings of debt securities holders, the payment of interest, the exercise of any conversion, exchange, subscription or cancellation rights, and repayment, as well as the right of those holders to participate therein;

(b) make available a proxy form on paper or, where applicable, by electronic means, to each person entitled to vote at a meeting of debt securities holders, together with the notice concerning the meeting or, on request, after an announcement of the meeting; and

(c) designate as its agent a financial institution through which debt securities holders may exercise their financial rights.

3. If only holders of debt securities whose denomination per unit amounts to at least EUR 50,000 or, in the case of debt securities denominated in a currency other than Euro whose denomination per unit is, at the date of the issue, equivalent to at least EUR 50,000, are to be invited to a meeting, the issuer may choose as venue any Member State, provided that all the facilities and information necessary to enable such holders to exercise their rights are made available in that Member State.

4. For the purposes of conveying information to debt securities holders, the home Member State, or the Member State chosen by the issuer pursuant to paragraph 3, shall allow issuers the use of electronic means, provided such a decision is taken in a general meeting and meets at least the following conditions:

(a) the use of electronic means shall in no way depend upon the location of the seat or residence of the debt security holder or of a proxy representing that holder;

(b) identification arrangements shall be put in place so that debt securities holders are effectively informed;

(c) debt securities holders shall be contacted in writing to request their consent for the use of electronic means for conveying information and if they do not object within a reasonable period of time, their consent shall be deemed to be given. They shall be able to request, at any time in the future, that information be conveyed in writing; and

(d) any apportionment of the costs entailed in the conveyance of information by electronic means shall be determined by the issuer in compliance with the principle of equal treatment laid down in paragraph 1.

5. The Commission shall, in accordance with the procedure provided for in Article 27(2), adopt implementing measures in order to take account of technical developments in financial markets, to take account of developments in information and communication technology and to ensure the uniform application of paragraphs 1 to 4. It shall, in particular, specify the types of financial institution through which a debt security holder may exercise the financial rights provided for in paragraph 2(c).

[9780]

CHAPTER IV
GENERAL OBLIGATIONS

Article 19

Home Member State control

1. Whenever the issuer, or any person having requested, without the issuer's consent, the admission of its securities to trading on a regulated market, discloses regulated information, it shall at the same time file that information with the competent authority of its home Member State. That competent authority may decide to publish such filed information on its Internet site.

Where an issuer proposes to amend its instrument of incorporation or statutes, it shall communicate the draft amendment to the competent authority of the home Member State and to the regulated market to which its securities have been admitted to trading. Such communication shall be effected without delay, but at the latest on the date of calling the general meeting which is to vote on, or be informed of, the amendment.

2. The home Member State may exempt an issuer from the requirement under paragraph 1 in respect of information disclosed in accordance with Article 6 of Directive 2003/6/EC or Article 12(6) of this Directive.

3. Information to be notified to the issuer in accordance with Articles 9, 10, 12 and 13 shall at the same time be filed with the competent authority of the home Member State.

4. In order to ensure the uniform application of paragraphs 1, 2 and 3, the Commission shall, in accordance with the procedure referred to in Article 27(2), adopt implementing measures.

The Commission shall, in particular, specify the procedure in accordance with which an issuer, a holder of shares or other financial instruments, or a person or entity referred to in Article 10, is to file information with the competent authority of the home Member State under paragraphs 1 or 3, respectively, in order to:

(a) enable filing by electronic means in the home Member State;

(b) coordinate the filing of the annual financial report referred to in Article 4 of this Directive with the filing of the annual information referred to in Article 10 of Directive 2003/71/EC.

[9781]

Article 20

Languages

1. Where securities are admitted to trading on a regulated market only in the home Member State, regulated information shall be disclosed in a language accepted by the competent authority in the home Member State.

2. Where securities are admitted to trading on a regulated market both in the home Member State and in one or more host Member States, regulated information shall be disclosed:

(a) in a language accepted by the competent authority in the home Member State; and

(b) depending on the choice of the issuer, either in a language accepted by the competent authorities of those host Member States or in a language customary in the sphere of international finance.

3. Where securities are admitted to trading on a regulated market in one or more host Member States, but not in the home Member State, regulated information shall, depending on the choice of the issuer, be disclosed either in a language accepted by the competent authorities of those host Member States or in a language customary in the sphere of international finance.

In addition, the home Member State may lay down in its law, regulations or administrative provisions that the regulated information shall, depending on the choice of the issuer, be disclosed either in a language accepted by its competent authority or in a language customary in the sphere of international finance.

4. Where securities are admitted to trading on a regulated market without the issuer's consent, the obligations under paragraphs 1, 2 and 3 shall be incumbent not upon the issuer, but upon the person who, without the issuer's consent, has requested such admission.

5. Member States shall allow shareholders and the natural person or legal entity referred to in Articles 9, 10 and 13 to notify information to an issuer under this Directive only in a language customary in the sphere of international finance. If the issuer receives such a notification, Member States may not require the issuer to provide a translation into a language accepted by the competent authorities.

6. By way of derogation from paragraphs 1 to 4, where securities whose denomination per unit amounts to at least EUR 50,000 or, in the case of debt securities denominated in a currency other than Euro equivalent to at least EUR 50,000 at the date of the issue, are admitted to trading on a regulated market in one or more Member States, regulated information shall be disclosed to the public either in a language accepted by the competent authorities of the home and host Member States or in a language customary in the sphere of international finance, at the choice of the issuer or of the person who, without the issuer's consent, has requested such admission.

7. If an action concerning the content of regulated information is brought before a court or tribunal in a Member State, responsibility for the payment of costs incurred in the translation of that information for the purposes of the proceedings shall be decided in accordance with the law of that Member State.

[9782]

Article 21

Access to regulated information

1. The home Member State shall ensure that the issuer, or the person who has applied for admission to trading on a regulated market without the issuer's consent, discloses regulated information in a manner ensuring fast access to such information on a non-discriminatory basis and makes it available to the officially appointed mechanism referred to in paragraph 2. The issuer, or the person who has applied for admission to trading on a regulated market without the issuer's consent, may not charge investors any specific cost for providing the information. The home Member State shall require the issuer to use such media as may reasonably be relied upon for the effective dissemination of information to the public throughout the Community. The home Member State may not impose an obligation to use only media whose operators are established on its territory.

2. The home Member State shall ensure that there is at least one officially appointed mechanism for the central storage of regulated information. These mechanisms should comply with minimum quality standards of security, certainty as to the information source, time recording and easy access by end users and shall be aligned with the filing procedure under Article 19(1).

3. Where securities are admitted to trading on a regulated market in only one host Member State and not in the home Member State, the host Member State shall ensure disclosure of regulated information in accordance with the requirements referred to in paragraph 1.

4. In order to take account of technical developments in financial markets, to take account of developments in information and communication technology and to ensure the

uniform application of paragraphs 1, 2 and 3, the Commission shall adopt implementing measures in accordance with the procedure referred to in Article 27(2).

The Commission shall in particular specify:

(a) minimum standards for the dissemination of regulated information, as referred to in paragraph 1;

(b) minimum standards for the central storage mechanism as referred to in paragraph 2.

The Commission may also specify and update a list of media for the dissemination of information to the public.

[9783]

Article 22

Guidelines

1. The competent authorities of the Member States shall draw up appropriate guidelines with a view to further facilitating public access to information to be disclosed under Directive 2003/6/EC, Directive 2003/71/EC and this Directive.

The aim of those guidelines shall be the creation of:

(a) an electronic network to be set up at national level between national securities regulators, operators of regulated markets and national company registers covered by the First Council Directive 68/151/EEC of 9 March 1968 on coordination of safeguards which, for the protection of the interests of members and others, are required by Member States of companies within the meaning of the second paragraph of Article 48[1] of the Treaty, with a view to making such safeguards equivalent throughout the Community;[2] and

(b) a single electronic network, or a platform of electronic networks across Member States.

2. The Commission shall review the results achieved under paragraph 1 by 31 December 2006 and may, in accordance with the procedure referred to in Article 27(2), adopt implementing measures to facilitate compliance with Articles 19 and 21.

[9784]

NOTES

[1] The title has been adjusted to take account of the renumbering of the Articles of the Treaty establishing the European Community in accordance with Article 12 of the Treaty of Amsterdam; the original reference was to Article 58 of the Treaty.

[2] OJ L65, 14.3.1968, p 8. Directive as last amended by Directive 2003/58/EC of the European Parliament and of the Council (OJ L221, 4.9.2003, p 13).

Article 23

Third countries

1. Where the registered office of an issuer is in a third country, the competent authority of the home Member State may exempt that issuer from requirements under Articles 4 to 7 and Articles 12(6), 14, 15 and 16 to 18, provided that the law of the third country in question lays down equivalent requirements or such an issuer complies with requirements of the law of a third country that the competent authority of the home Member State considers as equivalent.

However, the information covered by the requirements laid down in the third country shall be filed in accordance with Article 19 and disclosed in accordance with Articles 20 and 21.

2. By way of derogation from paragraph 1, an issuer whose registered office is in a third country shall be exempted from preparing its financial statement in accordance with Article 4 or Article 5 prior to the financial year starting on or after 1 January 2007, provided such issuer prepares its financial statements in accordance with internationally accepted standards referred to in Article 9 of Regulation (EC) No 1606/2002.

3. The competent authority of the home Member State shall ensure that information disclosed in a third country which may be of importance for the public in the Community is disclosed in accordance with Articles 20 and 21, even if such information is not regulated information within the meaning of Article 2(1)(k).

4. In order to ensure the uniform application of paragraph 1, the Commission shall, in accordance with the procedure referred to in Article 27(2), adopt implementing measures

(i) setting up a mechanism ensuring the establishment of equivalence of information required under this Directive, including financial statements and information, including financial statements, required under the law, regulations or administrative provisions of a third country;

(ii) stating that, by reason of its domestic law, regulations, administrative provisions, or of the practices or procedures based on the international standards set by international organisations, the third country where the issuer is registered ensures the equivalence of the information requirements provided for in this Directive.

The Commission shall, in accordance with the procedure referred to in Article 27(2), take the necessary decisions on the equivalence of accounting standards which are used by third country issuers under the conditions set out in Article 30(3) at the latest five years following the date referred to in Article 31. If the Commission decides that the accounting standards of a third country are not equivalent, it may allow the issuers concerned to continue using such accounting standards during an appropriate transitional period.

5. In order to ensure uniform application of paragraph 2, the Commission may, in accordance with the procedure referred to in Article 27(2), adopt implementing measures defining the type of information disclosed in a third country that is of importance to the public in the Community.

6. Undertakings whose registered office is in a third country which would have required an authorisation in accordance with Article 5(1) of Directive 85/611/EEC or, with regard to portfolio management under point 4 of section A of Annex I to Directive 2004/39/EC if it had its registered office or, only in the case of an investment firm, its head office within the Community, shall also be exempted from aggregating holdings with the holdings of its parent undertaking under the requirements laid down in Article 12(4) and (5) provided that they comply with equivalent conditions of independence as management companies or investment firms.

7. In order to take account of technical developments in financial markets and to ensure the uniform application of paragraph 6, the Commission shall, in accordance with the procedure referred to in Article 27(2), adopt implementing measures stating that, by reason of its domestic law, regulations, or administrative provisions, a third country ensures the equivalence of the independence requirements provided for under this Directive and its implementing measures.

[9785]

CHAPTER V
COMPETENT AUTHORITIES

Article 24

Competent authorities and their powers

1. Each Member State shall designate the central authority referred to in Article 21(1) of Directive 2003/71/EC as central competent administrative authority responsible for carrying out the obligations provided for in this Directive and for ensuring that the provisions adopted pursuant to this Directive are applied. Member States shall inform the Commission accordingly.

However, for the purpose of paragraph 4(h) Member States may designate a competent authority other than the central competent authority referred to in the first subparagraph.

2. Member States may allow their central competent authority to delegate tasks. Except for the tasks referred to in paragraph 4(h), any delegation of tasks relating to the obligations provided for in this Directive and in its implementing measures shall be reviewed five years after the entry into force of this Directive and shall end eight years after the entry into force of this Directive. Any delegation of tasks shall be made in a specific manner stating the tasks to be undertaken and the conditions under which they are to be carried out.

Those conditions shall include a clause requiring the entity in question to be organised in a manner such that conflicts of interest are avoided and information obtained from carrying out the delegated tasks is not used unfairly or to prevent competition. In any case, the final responsibility for supervising compliance with the provisions of this Directive and implementing measures adopted pursuant thereto shall lie with the competent authority designated in accordance with paragraph 1.

3. Member States shall inform the Commission and competent authorities of other Member States of any arrangements entered into with regard to the delegation of tasks, including the precise conditions for regulating the delegations.

4. Each competent authority shall have all the powers necessary for the performance of its functions. It shall at least be empowered to:

(a) require auditors, issuers, holders of shares or other financial instruments, or persons or entities referred to in Articles 10 or 13, and the persons that control them or are controlled by them, to provide information and documents;

(b) require the issuer to disclose the information required under point (a) to the public by the means and within the time limits the authority considers necessary. It may publish such information on its own initiative in the event that the issuer, or the persons that control it or are controlled by it, fail to do so and after having heard the issuer;

(c) require managers of the issuers and of the holders of shares or other financial instruments, or of persons or entities referred to in Articles 10 or 13, to notify the information required under this Directive, or under national law adopted in accordance with this Directive, and, if necessary, to provide further information and documents;

(d) suspend, or request the relevant regulated market to suspend, trading in securities for a maximum of ten days at a time if it has reasonable grounds for suspecting that the provisions of this Directive, or of national law adopted in accordance with this Directive, have been infringed by the issuer;

(e) prohibit trading on a regulated market if it finds that the provisions of this Directive, or of national law adopted in accordance with this Directive, have been infringed, or if it has reasonable grounds for suspecting that the provisions of this Directive have been infringed;

(f) monitor that the issuer discloses timely information with the objective of ensuring effective and equal access to the public in all Member States where the securities are traded and take appropriate action if that is not the case;

(g) make public the fact that an issuer, or a holder of shares or other financial instruments, or a person or entity referred to in Articles 10 or 13, is failing to comply with its obligations;

(h) examine that information referred to in this Directive is drawn up in accordance with the relevant reporting framework and take appropriate measures in case of discovered infringements; and

(i) carry out on-site inspections in its territory in accordance with national law, in order to verify compliance with the provisions of this Directive and its implementing measures. Where necessary under national law, the competent authority or authorities may use this power by applying to the relevant judicial authority and/or in cooperation with other authorities.

5. Paragraphs 1 to 4 shall be without prejudice to the possibility for a Member State to make separate legal and administrative arrangements for overseas European territories for whose external relations that Member State is responsible.

6. The disclosure to competent authorities by the auditors of any fact or decision related to the requests made by the competent authority under paragraph (4)(a) shall not constitute a breach of any restriction on disclosure of information imposed by contract or by any law, regulation or administrative provision and shall not involve such auditors in liability of any kind.

[9786]

Article 25

Professional secrecy and cooperation between Member States

1. The obligation of professional secrecy shall apply to all persons who work or who have worked for the competent authority and for entities to which competent authorities may have delegated certain tasks. Information covered by professional secrecy may not be disclosed to any other person or authority except by virtue of the laws, regulations or administrative provisions of a Member State.

2. Competent authorities of the Member States shall cooperate with each other, whenever necessary, for the purpose of carrying out their duties and making use of their powers, whether set out in this Directive or in national law adopted pursuant to this Directive. Competent authorities shall render assistance to competent authorities of other Member States.

3. Paragraph 1 shall not prevent the competent authorities from exchanging confidential information. Information thus exchanged shall be covered by the obligation of professional secrecy to which the persons employed or formerly employed by the competent authorities receiving the information are subject.

4. Member States may conclude cooperation agreements providing for the exchange of information with the competent authorities or bodies of third countries enabled by their respective legislation to carry out any of the tasks assigned by this Directive to the competent authorities in accordance with Article 24. Such an exchange of information is subject to guarantees of professional secrecy at least equivalent to those referred to in this Article. Such exchange of information shall be intended for the performance of the supervisory task of the authorities or bodies mentioned. Where the information originates in another Member State, it may not be disclosed without the express agreement of the competent authorities which have disclosed it and, where appropriate, solely for the purposes for which those authorities gave their agreement.

[9787]

Article 26

Precautionary measures

1. Where the competent authority of a host Member State finds that the issuer or the holder of shares or other financial instruments, or the person or entity referred to in Article 10, has committed irregularities or infringed its obligations, it shall refer its findings to the competent authority of the home Member State.

2. If, despite the measures taken by the competent authority of the home Member State, or because such measures prove inadequate, the issuer or the security holder persists in infringing the relevant legal or regulatory provisions, the competent authority of the host Member State shall, after informing the competent authority of the home Member State, take, in accordance with Article 3(2), all the appropriate measures in order to protect investors. The Commission shall be informed of such measures at the earliest opportunity.

[9788]

CHAPTER VI
IMPLEMENTING MEASURES

Article 27

Committee procedure

1. The Commission shall be assisted by the European Securities Committee, instituted by Article 1 of Decision 2001/528/EC.

2. Where reference is made to this paragraph, Articles 5 and 7 of Decision 1999/468/EC shall apply, having regard to the provisions of Article 8 thereof, provided that the implementing measures adopted in accordance with that procedure do not modify the essential provisions of this Directive.

The period laid down in Article 5(6) of Decision 1999/468/EC shall be set at three months.

3. The Committee shall adopt its Rules of Procedure.

4. Without prejudice to the implementing measures already adopted by 20 January 2009 the application of the provisions of this Directive concerning the adoption of technical rules and decisions in accordance with the procedure referred to in paragraph 2 shall be suspended. On a proposal from the Commission, the European Parliament and the Council may renew the provisions concerned in accordance with the procedure laid down in Article 251 of the Treaty and, to that end, shall review them prior to the expiry of the four-year period.

[9789]

Article 28

Penalties

1. Without prejudice to the right of Member States to impose criminal penalties, Member States shall ensure, in conformity with their national law, that at least the appropriate administrative measures may be taken or civil and/or administrative penalties imposed in

respect of the persons responsible, where the provisions adopted in accordance with this Directive have not been complied with. Member States shall ensure that those measures are effective, proportionate and dissuasive.

2. Member States shall provide that the competent authority may disclose to the public every measure taken or penalty imposed for infringement of the provisions adopted in accordance with this Directive, save where such disclosure would seriously jeopardise the financial markets or cause disproportionate damage to the parties involved.

[9790]

Article 29

Right of appeal

Member States shall ensure that decisions taken under laws, regulations, and administrative provisions adopted in accordance with this Directive are subject to the right of appeal to the courts.

[9791]

CHAPTER VII
TRANSITIONAL AND FINAL PROVISIONS

Article 30

Transitional provisions

1. By way of derogation from Article 5(3) of this Directive, the home Member State may exempt from disclosing financial statements in accordance with Regulation (EC) No 1606/2002 issuers referred to in Article 9 of that Regulation for the financial year starting on or after 1 January 2006.

2. Notwithstanding Article 12(2), a shareholder shall notify the issuer at the latest two months after the date in Article 31(1) of the proportion of voting rights and capital it holds, in accordance with Articles 9, 10 and 13, with issuers at that date, unless it has already made a notification containing equivalent information before that date.

Notwithstanding Article 12(6), an issuer shall in turn disclose the information received in those notifications no later than three months after the date in Article 31(1).

3. Where an issuer is incorporated in a third country, the home Member State may exempt such issuer only in respect of those debt securities which have already been admitted to trading on a regulated market in the Community prior to 1 January 2005 from drawing up its financial statements in accordance with Article 4(3) and its management report in accordance with Article 4(5) as long as

(a) the competent authority of the home Member State acknowledges that annual financial statements prepared by issuers from such a third country give a true and fair view of the issuer's assets and liabilities, financial position and results;

(b) the third country where the issuer is incorporated has not made mandatory the application of international accounting standards referred to in Article 2 of Regulation (EC) No 1606/2002; and

(c) the Commission has not taken any decision in accordance with Article 23(4)(ii) as to whether there is an equivalence between the abovementioned accounting standards and
- the accounting standards laid down in the law, regulations or administrative provisions of the third country where the issuer is incorporated, or
- the accounting standards of a third country such an issuer has elected to comply with.

4. The home Member State may exempt issuers only in respect of those debt securities which have already been admitted to trading on a regulated market in the Community prior to 1 January 2005 from disclosing half-yearly financial report in accordance with Article 5 for 10 years following 1 January 2005, provided that the home Member State had decided to allow such issuers to benefit from the provisions of Article 27 of Directive 2001/34/EC at the point of admission of those debt securities.

[9792]

Article 31

Transposition

1. Member States shall take the necessary measures to comply with this Directive by 20 January 2007. They shall forthwith inform the Commission thereof.

When Member States adopt these measures, they shall contain a reference to this Directive or shall be accompanied by such reference on the occasion of their official publication. The methods of making such reference shall be laid down by Member States.

2. Where Member States adopt measures pursuant to Articles 3(1), 8(2), 8(3), 9(6) or 30, they shall immediately communicate those measures to the Commission and to the other Member States.

[9793]

Article 32

Amendments

With effect from the date specified in Article 31(1), Directive 2001/34/EC shall be amended as follows:

(1) In Article 1, points (g) and (h) shall be deleted;
(2) Article 4 shall be deleted;
(3) In Article 6, paragraph 2 shall be deleted;
(4) In Article 8, paragraph 2 shall be replaced by the following:

"2. Member States may make the issuers of securities admitted to official listing subject to additional obligations, provided that those additional obligations apply generally for all issuers or for individual classes of issuers.".

(5) Articles 65 to 97 shall be deleted;
(6) Articles 102 and 103 shall be deleted;
(7) In Article 107(3), the second subparagraph shall be deleted;
(8) In Article 108, paragraph 2 shall be amended as follows:
  (a) in point (a), the words "periodic information to be published by the companies of which shares are admitted" shall be deleted;
  (b) point (b) shall be deleted;
  (c) point (c)(iii) shall be deleted;
  (d) point (d) shall be deleted.

References made to the repealed provisions shall be construed as being made to the provisions of this Directive.

[9794]

Article 33

Review

The Commission shall by 30 June 2009 report on the operation of this Directive to the European Parliament and to the Council including the appropriateness of ending the exemption for existing debt securities after the 10-year period as provided for by Article 30(4) and its potential impact on the European financial markets.

[9795]

Article 34

Entry into force

This Directive shall enter into force on the twentieth day following that of its publication in the Official Journal of the European Union.

[9796]

Article 35

Addressees

This Directive is addressed to the Member States.

[9797]

Done at Strasbourg, 15 December 2004.

DIRECTIVE OF THE EUROPEAN PARLIAMENT AND OF THE COUNCIL

of 26 October 2005

on cross-border mergers of limited liability companies

(2005/56/EC)

(Text with EEA relevance)

NOTES

Date of publication in OJ: OJ L310, 25.11.2005, p 1. Notes are as in the original OJ version.

THE EUROPEAN PARLIAMENT AND THE COUNCIL OF THE EUROPEAN UNION,

Having regard to the Treaty establishing the European Community, and in particular Article 44 thereof,

Having regard to the proposal from the Commission,

Having regard to the opinion of the European Economic and Social Committee,[1]

Acting in accordance with the procedure laid down in Article 251 of the Treaty,[2]

Whereas:

(1) There is a need for cooperation and consolidation between limited liability companies from different Member States. However, as regards cross-border mergers of limited liability companies, they encounter many legislative and administrative difficulties in the Community. It is therefore necessary, with a view to the completion and functioning of the single market, to lay down Community provisions to facilitate the carrying-out of cross-border mergers between various types of limited liability company governed by the laws of different Member States.

(2) This Directive facilitates the cross-border merger of limited liability companies as defined herein. The laws of the Member States are to allow the cross-border merger of a national limited liability company with a limited liability company from another Member State if the national law of the relevant Member States permits mergers between such types of company.

(3) In order to facilitate cross-border merger operations, it should be laid down that, unless this Directive provides otherwise, each company taking part in a cross-border merger, and each third party concerned, remains subject to the provisions and formalities of the national law which would be applicable in the case of a national merger. None of the provisions and formalities of national law, to which reference is made in this Directive, should introduce restrictions on freedom of establishment or on the free movement of capital save where these can be justified in accordance with the case-law of the Court of Justice and in particular by requirements of the general interest and are both necessary for, and proportionate to, the attainment of such overriding requirements.

(4) The common draft terms of the cross-border merger are to be drawn up in the same terms for each of the companies concerned in the various Member States. The minimum content of such common draft terms should therefore be specified, while leaving the companies free to agree on other items.

(5) In order to protect the interests of members and others, both the common draft terms of cross-border mergers and the completion of the cross-border merger are to be publicised for each merging company via an entry in the appropriate public register.

(6) The laws of all the Member States should provide for the drawing-up at national level of a report on the common draft terms of the cross-border merger by one or more experts on behalf of each of the companies that are merging. In order to limit experts' costs connected with cross-border mergers, provision should be made for the possibility of drawing up a single report intended for all members of companies taking part in a cross-border merger operation. The common draft terms of the cross-border merger are to be approved by the general meeting of each of those companies.

(7) In order to facilitate cross-border merger operations, it should be provided that monitoring of the completion and legality of the decision-making process in each merging company should be carried out by the national authority having jurisdiction over each of those companies, whereas monitoring of the completion and legality of the cross-border merger should be carried out by the national authority having jurisdiction over the company resulting from the cross-border merger. The national authority in question may be a court, a notary or any other competent authority appointed by the Member State concerned. The national law

determining the date on which the cross-border merger takes effect, this being the law to which the company resulting from the cross-border merger is subject, should also be specified.

(8) In order to protect the interests of members and others, the legal effects of the cross-border merger, distinguishing as to whether the company resulting from the cross-border merger is an acquiring company or a new company, should be specified. In the interests of legal certainty, it should no longer be possible, after the date on which a cross-border merger takes effect, to declare the merger null and void.

(9) This Directive is without prejudice to the application of the legislation on the control of concentrations between undertakings, both at Community level, by Regulation (EC) No 139/2004,[3] and at the level of Member States.

(10) This Directive does not affect Community legislation regulating credit intermediaries and other financial undertakings and national rules made or introduced pursuant to such Community legislation.

(11) This Directive is without prejudice to a Member State's legislation demanding information on the place of central administration or the principal place of business proposed for the company resulting from the cross-border merger.

(12) Employees' rights other than rights of participation should remain subject to the national provisions referred to in Council Directive 98/59/EC of 20 July 1998 on collective redundancies,[4] Council Directive 2001/23/EC of 12 March 2001 on the safeguarding of employees' rights in the event of transfers of undertakings, businesses or parts of undertakings or businesses,[5] Directive 2002/14/EC of the European Parliament and of the Council of 11 March 2002 establishing a general framework for informing and consulting employees in the European Community[6] and Council Directive 94/45/EC of 22 September 1994 on the establishment of a European Works Council or a procedure in Community-scale undertakings and Community-scale groups of undertakings for the purposes of informing and consulting employees.[7]

(13) If employees have participation rights in one of the merging companies under the circumstances set out in this Directive and, if the national law of the Member State in which the company resulting from the cross-border merger has its registered office does not provide for the same level of participation as operated in the relevant merging companies, including in committees of the supervisory board that have decision-making powers, or does not provide for the same entitlement to exercise rights for employees of establishments resulting from the cross-border merger, the participation of employees in the company resulting from the cross-border merger and their involvement in the definition of such rights are to be regulated. To that end, the principles and procedures provided for in Council Regulation (EC) No 2157/2001 of 8 October 2001 on the Statute for a European company (SE)[8] and in Council Directive 2001/86/EC of 8 October 2001 supplementing the Statute for a European company with regard to the involvement of employees,[9] are to be taken as a basis, subject, however, to modifications that are deemed necessary because the resulting company will be subject to the national laws of the Member State where it has its registered office. A prompt start to negotiations under Article 16 of this Directive, with a view to not unnecessarily delaying mergers, may be ensured by Member States in accordance with Article 3(2)(b) of Directive 2001/86/EC.

(14) For the purpose of determining the level of employee participation operated in the relevant merging companies, account should also be taken of the proportion of employee representatives amongst the members of the management group, which covers the profit units of the companies, subject to employee participation.

(15) Since the objective of the proposed action, namely laying down rules with common features applicable at transnational level, cannot be sufficiently achieved by the Member States and can therefore, by reason of the scale and impact of the proposed action, be better achieved at Community level, the Community may adopt measures in accordance with the principle of subsidiarity as set out in Article 5 of the Treaty. In accordance with the principle of proportionality as set out in that Article, this Directive does not go beyond what is necessary to achieve that objective.

(16) In accordance with paragraph 34 of the Interinstitutional Agreement on better law-making,[10] Member States should be encouraged to draw up, for themselves and in the interest of the Community, their own tables which will, as far as possible, illustrate the correlation between this Directive and the transposition measures and to make them public,

[9798]

NOTES

[1] OJ C117, 30.4.2004, p 43.

2 Opinion of the European Parliament of 10 May 2005 (not yet published in the Official Journal) and Council Decision of 19 September 2005.

3 Council Regulation (EC) No 139/2004 of 20 January 2004 on the control of concentrations between undertakings (the EC Merger Regulation) (OJ L24, 29.1.2004, p 1).

4 OJ L225, 12.8.1998, p 16.

5 OJ L82, 22.3.2001, p 16.

6 OJ L80, 23.3.2002, p 29.

7 OJ L254, 30.9.1994, p 64. Directive as amended by Directive 97/74/EC (OJ L10, 16.1.1998, p 22).

8 OJ L294, 10.11.2001, p 1. Regulation as amended by Regulation (EC) No 885/2004 (OJ L168, 1.5.2004, p 1).

9 OJ L294, 10.11.2001, p 22.

10 OJ C321, 31.12.2003, p 1.

HAVE ADOPTED THIS DIRECTIVE:

Article 1

Scope

This Directive shall apply to mergers of limited liability companies formed in accordance with the law of a Member State and having their registered office, central administration or principal place of business within the Community, provided at least two of them are governed by the laws of different Member States (hereinafter referred to as cross-border mergers).

[9799]

Article 2

Definitions

For the purposes of this Directive:

1) "limited liability company", hereinafter referred to as "company", means:
   (a) a company as referred to in Article 1 of Directive 68/151/EEC,[1] or
   (b) a company with share capital and having legal personality, possessing separate assets which alone serve to cover its debts and subject under the national law governing it to conditions concerning guarantees such as are provided for by Directive 68/151/EEC for the protection of the interests of members and others;

2. "merger" means an operation whereby:
   (a) one or more companies, on being dissolved without going into liquidation, transfer all their assets and liabilities to another existing company, the acquiring company, in exchange for the issue to their members of securities or shares representing the capital of that other company and, if applicable, a cash payment not exceeding 10% of the nominal value, or, in the absence of a nominal value, of the accounting par value of those securities or shares; or
   (b) two or more companies, on being dissolved without going into liquidation, transfer all their assets and liabilities to a company that they form, the new company, in exchange for the issue to their members of securities or shares representing the capital of that new company and, if applicable, a cash payment not exceeding 10% of the nominal value, or in the absence of a nominal value, of the accounting par value of those securities or shares; or
   (c) a company, on being dissolved without going into liquidation, transfers all its assets and liabilities to the company holding all the securities or shares representing its capital.

[9800]

NOTES

1 First Council Directive 68/151/EEC of 9 March 1968 on coordination of safeguards which, for the protection of the interests of members and others, are required by Member States of companies within the meaning of the second paragraph of Article 58 of the Treaty, with a view to making such safeguards equivalent throughout the Community (OJ L65, 14.3.1968, p 8). Directive as last amended by the 2003 Act of Accession.

Article 3

Further provisions concerning the scope

1. Notwithstanding Article 2(2), this Directive shall also apply to cross-border mergers where the law of at least one of the Member States concerned allows the cash payment

referred to in points (a) and (b) of Article 2(2) to exceed 10% of the nominal value, or, in the absence of a nominal value, of the accounting par value of the securities or shares representing the capital of the company resulting from the cross-border merger.

2. Member States may decide not to apply this Directive to cross-border mergers involving a cooperative society even in the cases where the latter would fall within the definition of "limited liability company" as laid down in Article 2(1).

3. This Directive shall not apply to cross-border mergers involving a company the object of which is the collective investment of capital provided by the public, which operates on the principle of risk-spreading and the units of which are, at the holders' request, repurchased or redeemed, directly or indirectly, out of the assets of that company. Action taken by such a company to ensure that the stock exchange value of its units does not vary significantly from its net asset value shall be regarded as equivalent to such repurchase or redemption.

[9801]

Article 4

Conditions relating to cross-border mergers

1. Save as otherwise provided in this Directive,
   - (a) cross-border mergers shall only be possible between types of companies which may merge under the national law of the relevant Member States, and
   - (b) a company taking part in a cross-border merger shall comply with the provisions and formalities of the national law to which it is subject. The laws of a Member State enabling its national authorities to oppose a given internal merger on grounds of public interest shall also be applicable to a cross-border merger where at least one of the merging companies is subject to the law of that Member State. This provision shall not apply to the extent that Article 21 of Regulation (EC) No 139/2004 is applicable.

2. The provisions and formalities referred to in paragraph 1(b) shall, in particular, include those concerning the decision-making process relating to the merger and, taking into account the cross-border nature of the merger, the protection of creditors of the merging companies, debenture holders and the holders of securities or shares, as well as of employees as regards rights other than those governed by Article 16. A Member State may, in the case of companies participating in a cross-border merger and governed by its law, adopt provisions designed to ensure appropriate protection for minority members who have opposed the cross-border merger.

[9802]

Article 5

Common draft terms of cross-border mergers

The management or administrative organ of each of the merging companies shall draw up the common draft terms of cross-border merger. The common draft terms of cross-border merger shall include at least the following particulars:
- (a) the form, name and registered office of the merging companies and those proposed for the company resulting from the cross-border merger;
- (b) the ratio applicable to the exchange of securities or shares representing the company capital and the amount of any cash payment;
- (c) the terms for the allotment of securities or shares representing the capital of the company resulting from the cross-border merger;
- (d) the likely repercussions of the cross-border merger on employment;
- (e) the date from which the holding of such securities or shares representing the company capital will entitle the holders to share in profits and any special conditions affecting that entitlement;
- (f) the date from which the transactions of the merging companies will be treated for accounting purposes as being those of the company resulting from the cross-border merger;
- (g) the rights conferred by the company resulting from the cross-border merger on members enjoying special rights or on holders of securities other than shares representing the company capital, or the measures proposed concerning them;
- (h) any special advantages granted to the experts who examine the draft terms of the cross-border merger or to members of the administrative, management, supervisory or controlling organs of the merging companies;

(i) the statutes of the company resulting from the cross-border merger;
(j) where appropriate, information on the procedures by which arrangements for the involvement of employees in the definition of their rights to participation in the company resulting from the cross-border merger are determined pursuant to Article 16;
(k) information on the evaluation of the assets and liabilities which are transferred to the company resulting from the cross-border merger;
(l) dates of the merging companies' accounts used to establish the conditions of the cross-border merger.

[9803]

Article 6

Publication

1. The common draft terms of the cross-border merger shall be published in the manner prescribed by the laws of each Member State in accordance with Article 3 of Directive 68/151/EEC for each of the merging companies at least one month before the date of the general meeting which is to decide thereon.

2. For each of the merging companies and subject to the additional requirements imposed by the Member State to which the company concerned is subject, the following particulars shall be published in the national gazette of that Member State:
(a) the type, name and registered office of every merging company;
(b) the register in which the documents referred to in Article 3(2) of Directive 68/151/EEC are filed in respect of each merging company, and the number of the entry in that register;
(c) an indication, for each of the merging companies, of the arrangements made for the exercise of the rights of creditors and of any minority members of the merging companies and the address at which complete information on those arrangements may be obtained free of charge.

[9804]

Article 7

Report of the management or administrative organ

The management or administrative organ of each of the merging companies shall draw up a report intended for the members explaining and justifying the legal and economic aspects of the cross-border merger and explaining the implications of the cross-border merger for members, creditors and employees.

The report shall be made available to the members and to the representatives of the employees or, where there are no such representatives, to the employees themselves, not less than one month before the date of the general meeting referred to in Article 9.

Where the management or administrative organ of any of the merging companies receives, in good time, an opinion from the representatives of their employees, as provided for under national law, that opinion shall be appended to the report.

[9805]

Article 8

Independent expert report

1. An independent expert report intended for members and made available not less than one month before the date of the general meeting referred to in Article 9 shall be drawn up for each merging company. Depending on the law of each Member State, such experts may be natural persons or legal persons.

2. As an alternative to experts operating on behalf of each of the merging companies, one or more independent experts, appointed for that purpose at the joint request of the companies by a judicial or administrative authority in the Member State of one of the merging companies or of the company resulting from the cross-border merger or approved by such an authority, may examine the common draft terms of cross-border merger and draw up a single written report to all the members.

3. The expert report shall include at least the particulars provided for by Article 10(2) of Council Directive 78/855/EEC of 9 October 1978 concerning mergers of public limited

liability companies.[1] The experts shall be entitled to secure from each of the merging companies all information they consider necessary for the discharge of their duties.

4. Neither an examination of the common draft terms of cross-border merger by independent experts nor an expert report shall be required if all the members of each of the companies involved in the cross-border merger have so agreed.

[9806]

NOTES

[1] OJ L295, 20.10.1978, p 36. Directive as last amended by the 2003 Act of Accession.

Article 9

Approval by the general meeting

1. After taking note of the reports referred to in Articles 7 and 8, the general meeting of each of the merging companies shall decide on the approval of the common draft terms of cross-border merger.

2. The general meeting of each of the merging companies may reserve the right to make implementation of the cross-border merger conditional on express ratification by it of the arrangements decided on with respect to the participation of employees in the company resulting from the cross-border merger.

3. The laws of a Member State need not require approval of the merger by the general meeting of the acquiring company if the conditions laid down in Article 8 of Directive 78/855/EEC are fulfilled.

[9807]

Article 10

Pre-merger certificate

1. Each Member State shall designate the court, notary or other authority competent to scrutinise the legality of the cross-border merger as regards that part of the procedure which concerns each merging company subject to its national law.

2. In each Member State concerned the authority referred to in paragraph 1 shall issue, without delay to each merging company subject to that State's national law, a certificate conclusively attesting to the proper completion of the pre-merger acts and formalities.

3. If the law of a Member State to which a merging company is subject provides for a procedure to scrutinise and amend the ratio applicable to the exchange of securities or shares, or a procedure to compensate minority members, without preventing the registration of the cross-border merger, such procedure shall only apply if the other merging companies situated in Member States which do not provide for such procedure explicitly accept, when approving the draft terms of the cross-border merger in accordance with Article 9(1), the possibility for the members of that merging company to have recourse to such procedure, to be initiated before the court having jurisdiction over that merging company. In such cases, the authority referred to in paragraph 1 may issue the certificate referred to in paragraph 2 even if such procedure has commenced. The certificate must, however, indicate that the procedure is pending. The decision in the procedure shall be binding on the company resulting from the cross-border merger and all its members.

[9808]

Article 11

Scrutiny of the legality of the cross-border merger

1. Each Member State shall designate the court, notary or other authority competent to scrutinise the legality of the cross-border merger as regards that part of the procedure which concerns the completion of the cross-border merger and, where appropriate, the formation of a new company resulting from the cross-border merger where the company created by the cross-border merger is subject to its national law. The said authority shall in particular ensure that the merging companies have approved the common draft terms of cross-border merger in the same terms and, where appropriate, that arrangements for employee participation have been determined in accordance with Article 16.

2. To that end each merging company shall submit to the authority referred to in paragraph 1 the certificate referred to in Article 10(2) within six months of its issue together with the common draft terms of cross-border merger approved by the general meeting referred to in Article 9.

[9809]

Article 12

Entry into effect of the cross-border merger

The law of the Member State to whose jurisdiction the company resulting from the cross-border merger is subject shall determine the date on which the cross-border merger takes effect. That date must be after the scrutiny referred to in Article 11 has been carried out.

[9810]

Article 13

Registration

The law of each of the Member States to whose jurisdiction the merging companies were subject shall determine, with respect to the territory of that State, the arrangements, in accordance with Article 3 of Directive 68/151/EEC, for publicising completion of the cross-border merger in the public register in which each of the companies is required to file documents.

The registry for the registration of the company resulting from the cross-border merger shall notify, without delay, the registry in which each of the companies was required to file documents that the cross-border merger has taken effect. Deletion of the old registration, if applicable, shall be effected on receipt of that notification, but not before.

[9811]

Article 14

Consequences of the cross-border merger

1. A cross-border merger carried out as laid down in points (a) and (c) of Article 2(2) shall, from the date referred to in Article 12, have the following consequences:

(a) all the assets and liabilities of the company being acquired shall be transferred to the acquiring company;

(b) the members of the company being acquired shall become members of the acquiring company;

(c) the company being acquired shall cease to exist.

2. A cross-border merger carried out as laid down in point (b) of Article 2(2) shall, from the date referred to in Article 12, have the following consequences:

(a) all the assets and liabilities of the merging companies shall be transferred to the new company;

(b) the members of the merging companies shall become members of the new company;

(c) the merging companies shall cease to exist.

3. Where, in the case of a cross-border merger of companies covered by this Directive, the laws of the Member States require the completion of special formalities before the transfer of certain assets, rights and obligations by the merging companies becomes effective against third parties, those formalities shall be carried out by the company resulting from the cross-border merger.

4. The rights and obligations of the merging companies arising from contracts of employment or from employment relationships and existing at the date on which the cross-border merger takes effect shall, by reason of that cross-border merger taking effect, be transferred to the company resulting from the cross-border merger on the date on which the cross-border merger takes effect.

5. No shares in the acquiring company shall be exchanged for shares in the company being acquired held either:

(a) by the acquiring company itself or through a person acting in his or her own name but on its behalf;

PART V EC LEGISLATION

(b) by the company being acquired itself or through a person acting in his or her own name but on its behalf.

[9812]

Article 15

Simplified formalities

1. Where a cross-border merger by acquisition is carried out by a company which holds all the shares and other securities conferring the right to vote at general meetings of the company or companies being acquired:

— Articles 5, points (b), (c) and (e), 8 and 14(1), point (b) shall not apply,
— Article 9(1) shall not apply to the company or companies being acquired.

2. Where a cross-border merger by acquisition is carried out by a company which holds 90% or more but not all of the shares and other securities conferring the right to vote at general meetings of the company or companies being acquired, reports by an independent expert or experts and the documents necessary for scrutiny shall be required only to the extent that the national law governing either the acquiring company or the company being acquired so requires.

[9813]

Article 16

Employee participation

1. Without prejudice to paragraph 2, the company resulting from the cross-border merger shall be subject to the rules in force concerning employee participation, if any, in the Member State where it has its registered office.

2. However, the rules in force concerning employee participation, if any, in the Member State where the company resulting from the cross-border merger has its registered office shall not apply, where at least one of the merging companies has, in the six months before the publication of the draft terms of the cross-border merger as referred to in Article 6, an average number of employees that exceeds 500 and is operating under an employee participation system within the meaning of Article 2(k) of Directive 2001/86/EC, or where the national law applicable to the company resulting from the cross-border merger does not

(a) provide for at least the same level of employee participation as operated in the relevant merging companies, measured by reference to the proportion of employee representatives amongst the members of the administrative or supervisory organ or their committees or of the management group which covers the profit units of the company, subject to employee representation, or

(b) provide for employees of establishments of the company resulting from the cross-border merger that are situated in other Member States the same entitlement to exercise participation rights as is enjoyed by those employees employed in the Member State where the company resulting from the cross-border merger has its registered office.

3. In the cases referred to in paragraph 2, the participation of employees in the company resulting from the cross-border merger and their involvement in the definition of such rights shall be regulated by the Member States, *mutatis mutandis* and subject to paragraphs 4 to 7 below, in accordance with the principles and procedures laid down in Article 12(2), (3) and (4) of Regulation (EC) No 2157/2001 and the following provisions of Directive 2001/86/EC:

(a) Article 3(1), (2) and (3), (4) first subparagraph, first indent, and second subparagraph, (5) and (7);
(b) Article 4(1), (2), points (a), (g) and (h), and (3);
(c) Article 5;
(d) Article 6;
(e) Article 7(1), (2) first subparagraph, point (b), and second subparagraph, and (3). However, for the purposes of this Directive, the percentages required by Article 7(2), first subparagraph, point (b) of Directive 2001/86/EC for the application of the standard rules contained in part 3 of the Annex to that Directive shall be raised from 25 to 33⅓%;
(f) Articles 8, 10 and 12;
(g) Article 13(4);
(h) part 3 of the Annex, point (b).

4. When regulating the principles and procedures referred to in paragraph 3, Member States:

(a) shall confer on the relevant organs of the merging companies the right to choose without any prior negotiation to be directly subject to the standard rules for participation referred to in paragraph 3(h), as laid down by the legislation of the Member State in which the company resulting from the cross-border merger is to have its registered office, and to abide by those rules from the date of registration;

(b) shall confer on the special negotiating body the right to decide, by a majority of two thirds of its members representing at least two thirds of the employees, including the votes of members representing employees in at least two different Member States, not to open negotiations or to terminate negotiations already opened and to rely on the rules on participation in force in the Member State where the registered office of the company resulting from the cross-border merger will be situated;

(c) may, in the case where, following prior negotiations, standard rules for participation apply and notwithstanding these rules, determine to limit the proportion of employee representatives in the administrative organ of the company resulting from the cross-border merger. However, if in one of the merging companies employee representatives constituted at least one third of the administrative or supervisory board, the limitation may never result in a lower proportion of employee representatives in the administrative organ than one third.

5. The extension of participation rights to employees of the company resulting from the cross-border merger employed in other Member States, referred to in paragraph 2(b), shall not entail any obligation for Member States which choose to do so to take those employees into account when calculating the size of workforce thresholds giving rise to participation rights under national law.

6. When at least one of the merging companies is operating under an employee participation system and the company resulting from the cross-border merger is to be governed by such a system in accordance with the rules referred to in paragraph 2, that company shall be obliged to take a legal form allowing for the exercise of participation rights.

7. When the company resulting from the cross-border merger is operating under an employee participation system, that company shall be obliged to take measures to ensure that employees' participation rights are protected in the event of subsequent domestic mergers for a period of three years after the cross-border merger has taken effect, by applying *mutatis mutandis* the rules laid down in this Article.

[9814]

Article 17

Validity

A cross-border merger which has taken effect as provided for in Article 12 may not be declared null and void.

[9815]

Article 18

Review

Five years after the date laid down in the first paragraph of Article 19, the Commission shall review this Directive in the light of the experience acquired in applying it and, if necessary, propose its amendment.

[9816]

Article 19

Transposition

Member States shall bring into force the laws, regulations and administrative provisions necessary to comply with this Directive by 15 December 2007.

When Member States adopt these measures, they shall contain a reference to this Directive or shall be accompanied by such reference on the occasion of their official publication. The methods of making such reference shall be laid down by Member States.

[9817]

Article 20

Entry into force

This Directive shall enter into force on the 20th day following its publication in the *Official Journal of the European Union*.

[9818]

Article 21

Addressees

This Directive is addressed to the Member States.

[9819]

Done at Strasbourg, 26 October 2005.

DIRECTIVE OF THE EUROPEAN PARLIAMENT AND OF THE COUNCIL

of 5 April 2006

amending directive 2004/39/EC on markets in financial instruments, as regards certain deadlines

(2006/31/EC)

(Text with EEA relevance)

NOTES

Date of Publication in OJ: OJ L114, 27.4.2006, p 60. Notes are as in the original OJ version.

THE EUROPEAN PARLIAMENT AND THE COUNCIL OF THE EUROPEAN UNION,

Having regard to the Treaty establishing the European Community, and in particular Article 47(2) thereof,

Having regard to the proposal from the Commission,

After consulting the European Economic and Social Committee,

Having regard to the opinion of European Central Bank,[1]

Acting in accordance with the procedure laid down in Article 251 of the Treaty,[2]

Whereas:

(1) Directive 2004/39/EC of the European Parliament and of the Council of 21 April 2004 on markets in financial instruments[3] introduces a comprehensive regulatory regime to ensure a high quality of execution of investor transactions.

(2) Directive 2004/39/EC provides that Member States are to adopt the laws, regulations and administrative provisions necessary to comply with it by 30 April 2006. In order to ensure uniform application in the Member States, a significant number of complex provisions of that Directive need to be supplemented by implementing measures, to be adopted by the Commission during the period for transposition by Member States. Because Member States cannot fully prepare and finalise their national laws until the content of the implementing measures is clear, they may have difficulty in meeting the current transposition deadline.

(3) In order to comply with the requirements of Directive 2004/39/EC and national implementing legislation, investment firms and other regulated entities may have to introduce new information technology systems, new organisational structures, and reporting and recordkeeping procedures, or to make significant modifications to existing systems and practices. This can only be done once the contents of the implementing measures to be adopted by the Commission and of the national legislation transposing the Directive are settled.

(4) It is also necessary that Directive 2004/39/EC and its implementing measures be transposed into national law or apply directly in Member States simultaneously for the Directive to produce its full effect.

(5) It is therefore appropriate to extend the deadline for Member States to transpose Directive 2004/39/EC into national law. Similarly, the deadline for investment firms and

credit institutions to comply with the new requirements should be postponed for a period after the transposition into national law has been completed by the Member States.

(6) Given the interaction between the different provisions of Directive 2004/39/EC, it is appropriate that any extension of those deadlines apply to all the provisions of that Directive. Any extension of the transposition and application deadlines should be proportionate to, and not exceed, the needs of the Member States and regulated entities. In order to avoid fragmentation that could hamper the functioning of the internal market in securities, Member States should apply the provisions of Directive 2004/39/EC at the same time.

(7) In its Resolution of 5 February 2002 on the implementation of financial services legislation,[4] the European Parliament requested that it and the Council should have an equal role in supervising the way in which the Commission exercises its executive role in order to reflect the legislative powers of the European Parliament under Article 251 of the Treaty. In the solemn declaration made before the European Parliament the same day by its President, the Commission supported that request. On 11 December 2002, the Commission proposed amendments to Council Decision 1999/468/ EC of 28 June 1999 laying down the procedures for the exercise of implementing powers conferred on the Commission,[5] and then submitted an amended proposal on 22 April 2004. The European Parliament does not consider that this proposal preserves its legislative prerogatives. In the view of the European Parliament, it and the Council should have the opportunity of evaluating the conferral of implementing powers on the Commission within a determined period. It is therefore appropriate to limit the period during which the Commission may adopt implementing measures.

(8) The European Parliament should be given a period of three months from the first transmission of draft amendments and implementing measures to allow it to examine them and to give its opinion. However, in urgent and duly justified cases, it should be possible to shorten that period. If, within that period, a resolution is adopted by the European Parliament, the Commission should re-examine the draft amendments or measures.

(9) Further consequential amendments are necessary to postpone the dates for the repeal of Council Directive 93/22/EEC of 10 May 1993 on investment services in the securities field[6] and for the transitional provisions laid down in Directive 2004/39/EC, and to extend the timetable for the Commission's reporting obligations.

(10) Given the postponed deadline between the obligation for Member States to transpose Directive 2004/39/EC into national law and the deadline for investment firms and credit institutions to comply with the new requirements, the provisions of Directive 2004/39/EC will remain ineffective until 1 November 2007; it is therefore appropriate to repeal Directive 93/22/EEC with effect from 1 November 2007.

(11) Directive 2004/39/EC should therefore be amended accordingly,

[9820]

NOTES

1 OJ C323, 20.12.2005, p 31.
2 Opinion of the European Parliament of 13 December 2005 (not yet published in the Official Journal) and Council Decision of 10 March 2006.
3 OJ L145, 30.4.2004, p 1.
4 OJ C284E, 21.11.2002, p 115.
5 OJ L184, 17.7.1999, p 23.
6 OJ L141, 11.6.1993, p 27. Directive as last amended by Directive 2002/87/EC of the European Parliament and of the Council (OJ L35, 11.2.2003, p 1).

HAVE ADOPTED THIS DIRECTIVE:

Article 1

(*Amends Directive 2004/39/EC, Arts 64, 70, 71* (*and the recitals to that Directive*) *and substitutes Arts 65, 69* (*see* **[9616]** *at seq*).)

Article 2

1. Member States shall adopt the laws, regulations and administrative provisions necessary to comply with this Directive by 31 January 2007. They shall forthwith inform the Commission thereof. They shall apply these measures from 1 November 2007.

2. When Member States adopt these measures, they shall contain a reference to this Directive or shall be accompanied by such reference on the occasion of their official publication. The methods of making such reference shall be laid down by Member States.

[9820A]

Article 3

This Directive shall enter into force on the day following that of its publication in the Official Journal of the European Union.

[9821]

Article 4

This Directive is addressed to the Member States.

[9822]

Done at Strasbourg, 5 April 2006.

DIRECTIVE OF THE EUROPEAN PARLIAMENT AND OF THE COUNCIL

of 14 June 2006

relating to the taking up and pursuit of the business of credit institutions (recast)

(2006/48/EC)

(Text with EEA relevance)

NOTES

Date of publication in OJ: OJ L177, 30.6.2006, p 1. Notes are as in the original OJ version.

Only those provisions relevant to company law are reproduced; provisions not reproduced are not annotated.

THE EUROPEAN PARLIAMENT AND THE COUNCIL OF THE EUROPEAN UNION,

Having regard to the Treaty establishing the European Community, and in particular the first and third sentences of Article 47(2) thereof,

Having regard to the proposal from the Commission,

Having regard to the Opinion of the European Economic and Social Committee,[1]

Having regard to the Opinion of the European Central Bank,[2]

Acting in accordance with the procedure laid down in Article 251 of the Treaty,[3]

Whereas:

(1) Directive 2000/12/EC of the European Parliament and of the Council of 20 March 2000 relating to the taking up and pursuit of the business of credit institutions[4] has been significantly amended on several occasions. Now that new amendments are being made to the said Directive, it is desirable, in order to clarify matters, that it should be recast.

(2) In order to make it easier to take up and pursue the business of credit institutions, it is necessary to eliminate the most obstructive differences between the laws of the Member States as regards the rules to which these institutions are subject.

(3) This Directive constitutes the essential instrument for the achievement of the internal market from the point of view of both the freedom of establishment and the freedom to provide financial services, in the field of credit institutions.

(4) The Commission Communication of 11 May 1999 entitled "Implementing the framework for financial markets: Action plan", listed a number of goals that need to be achieved in order to complete the internal market in financial services. The Lisbon European Council of 23 and 24 March 2000 set the goal of implementing the action plan by 2005. Recasting of the provisions on own funds is a key element of the action plan.

(5) Measures to coordinate credit institutions should, both in order to protect savings and to create equal conditions of competition between these institutions, apply to all of them. Due regard should however be had to the objective differences in their statutes and their proper aims as laid down by national laws.

(6) The scope of those measures should therefore be as broad as possible, covering all institutions whose business is to receive repayable funds from the public, whether in the form of deposits or in other forms such as the continuing issue of bonds and other comparable securities and to grant credits for their own account. Exceptions should be provided for in the case of certain credit institutions to which this Directive cannot apply. The provisions of this

Directive should not prejudice the application of national laws which provide for special supplementary authorisations permitting credit institutions to carry on specific activities or undertake specific kinds of operations.

(7) It is appropriate to effect only the essential harmonisation necessary and sufficient to secure the mutual recognition of authorisation and of prudential supervision systems, making possible the granting of a single licence recognised throughout the Community and the application of the principle of home Member State prudential supervision. Therefore, the requirement that a programme of operations be produced should be seen merely as a factor enabling the competent authorities to decide on the basis of more precise information using objective criteria. A measure of flexibility should nonetheless be possible as regards the requirements on the legal form of credit institutions concerning the protection of banking names.

(8) Since the objectives of this Directive, namely the introduction of rules concerning the taking up and pursuit of the business of credit institutions, and their prudential supervision, cannot be sufficiently achieved by the Member States and can therefore, by reason of the scale and the effects of the proposed action, be better achieved at Community level, the Community may adopt measures, in accordance with the principle of subsidiarity as set out in Article 5 of the Treaty. In accordance with the principle of proportionality, as set out in that Article, this Directive does not go beyond what is necessary in order to achieve those objectives.

(9) Equivalent financial requirements for credit institutions are necessary to ensure similar safeguards for savers and fair conditions of competition between comparable groups of credit institutions. Pending further coordination, appropriate structural ratios should be formulated making it possible within the framework of cooperation between national authorities to observe, in accordance with standard methods, the position of comparable types of credit institutions. This procedure should help to bring about the gradual approximation of the systems of coefficients established and applied by the Member States. It is necessary, however to make a distinction between coefficients intended to ensure the sound management of credit institutions and those established for the purposes of economic and monetary policy.

(10) The principles of mutual recognition and home Member State supervision require that Member States' competent authorities should not grant or should withdraw an authorisation where factors such as the content of the activities programmes, the geographical distribution of activities or the activities actually carried on indicate clearly that a credit institution has opted for the legal system of one Member State for the purpose of evading the stricter standards in force in another Member State within whose territory it carries on or intends to carry on the greater Part of its activities. Where there is no such clear indication, but the majority of the total assets of the entities in a banking group are located in another Member State the competent authorities of which are responsible for exercising supervision on a consolidated basis, in the context of Articles 125 and 126 responsibility for exercising supervision on a consolidated basis should be changed only with the agreement of those competent authorities. A credit institution which is a legal person should be authorised in the Member State in which it has its registered office. A credit institution which is not a legal person should have its head office in the Member State in which it has been authorised. In addition, Member States should require that a credit institution's head office always be situated in its home Member State and that it actually operates there.

(11) The competent authorities should not authorise or continue the authorisation of a credit institution where they are liable to be prevented from effectively exercising their supervisory functions by the close links between that institution and other natural or legal persons. Credit institutions already authorised should also satisfy the competent authorities in that respect.

(12) The reference to the supervisory authorities' effective exercise of their supervisory functions covers supervision on a consolidated basis which should be exercised over a credit institution where the provisions of Community law so provide. In such cases, the authorities applied to for authorisation should be able to identify the authorities competent to exercise supervision on a consolidated basis over that credit institution.

(13) This Directive enables Member States and/or competent authorities to apply capital requirements on a solo and consolidated basis, and to disapply solo where they deem this appropriate. Solo, consolidated and cross-border consolidated supervision are useful tools in overseeing credit institutions. This Directive enables competent authorities to support cross border institutions by facilitating cooperation between them. In particular, the competent authorities should continue to make use of Articles 42, 131 and 141 to coordinate their activities and information requests.

(14) Credit institutions authorised in their home Member States should be allowed to carry on, throughout the Community, any or all of the activities listed in Annex I by establishing branches or by providing services.

(15) The Member States may also establish stricter rules than those laid down in Article 9(1), first subparagraph, Article 9(2) and Articles 12, 19 to 21, 44 to 52, 75 and 120 to 122 for credit institutions authorised by their competent authorities. The Member States may also require that Article 123 be complied with on an individual or other basis, and that the sub-consolidation described in Article 73(2) be applied to other levels within a group.

(16) It is appropriate to extend mutual recognition to the activities listed in Annex I when they are carried on by financial institutions which are subsidiaries of credit institutions, provided that such subsidiaries are covered by the consolidated supervision of their parent undertakings and meet certain strict conditions.

(17) The host Member State should be able, in connection with the exercise of the right of establishment and the freedom to provide services, to require compliance with specific provisions of its own national laws or regulations on the Part of institutions not authorised as credit institutions in their home Member States and with regard to activities not listed in Annex I provided that, on the one hand, such provisions are compatible with Community law and are intended to protect the general good and that, on the other hand, such institutions or such activities are not subject to equivalent rules under this legislation or regulations of their home Member States.

(18) The Member States should ensure that there are no obstacles to carrying on activities receiving mutual recognition in the same manner as in the home Member State, as long as the latter do not conflict with legal provisions protecting the general good in the host Member State.

(19) The rules governing branches of credit institutions having their head office outside the Community should be analogous in all Member States. It is important to provide that such rules may not be more favourable than those for branches of institutions from another Member State. The Community should be able to conclude agreements with third countries providing for the application of rules which accord such branches the same treatment throughout its territory. The branches of credit institutions authorised in third countries should not enjoy the freedom to provide services under the second paragraph of Article 49 of the Treaty or the freedom of establishment in Member States other than those in which they are established.

(20) Agreement should be reached, on the basis of reciprocity, between the Community and third countries with a view to allowing the practical exercise of consolidated supervision over the largest possible geographical area.

(21) Responsibility for supervising the financial soundness of a credit institution, and in particular its solvency, should lay with its home Member State. The host Member State's competent authorities should be responsible for the supervision of the liquidity of the branches and monetary policies. The supervision of market risk should be the subject of close cooperation between the competent authorities of the home and host Member States.

(22) The smooth operation of the internal banking market requires not only legal rules but also close and regular cooperation and significantly enhanced convergence of regulatory and supervisory practices between the competent authorities of the Member States. To this end, in particular, consideration of problems concerning individual credit institutions and the mutual exchange of information should take place in the Committee of European Banking Supervisors set up by Commission Decision 2004/5/EC.[5] That mutual information procedure should not in any case replace bilateral cooperation. Without prejudice to their own powers of control, the competent authorities of the host Member States should be able, in an emergency, on their own initiative or following the initiative of the competent authorities of home Member State, to verify that the activities of a credit institution established within their territories comply with the relevant laws and with the principles of sound administrative and accounting procedures and adequate internal control.

(23) It is appropriate to allow the exchange of information between the competent authorities and authorities or bodies which, by virtue of their function, help to strengthen the stability of the financial system. In order to preserve the confidential nature of the information forwarded, the list of addressees should remain within strict limits.

(24) Certain behaviour, such as fraud and insider offences, is liable to affect the stability, including the integrity, of the financial system, even when involving institutions other than credit institutions. It is necessary to specify the conditions under which exchange of information in such cases is authorised.

(25) Where it is stipulated that information may be disclosed only with the express agreement of the competent authorities, these should be able, where appropriate, to make their agreement subject to compliance with strict conditions.

(26) Exchanges of information between, on the one hand, the competent authorities and, on the other, central banks and other bodies with a similar function in their capacity as monetary authorities and, where appropriate, other public authorities responsible for supervising payment systems should also be authorised.

(27) For the purpose of strengthening the prudential supervision of credit institutions and the protection of clients of credit institutions, auditors should have a duty to report promptly to the competent authorities, wherever, during the performance of their tasks, they become aware of certain facts which are liable to have a serious effect on the financial situation or the administrative and accounting organisation of a credit institution. For the same reason Member States should also provide that such a duty applies in all circumstances where such facts are discovered by an auditor during the performance of his tasks in an undertaking which has close links with a credit institution. The duty of auditors to communicate, where appropriate, to the competent authorities certain facts and decisions concerning a credit institution which they discover during the performance of their tasks in a non-financial undertaking should not in itself change the nature of their tasks in that undertaking nor the manner in which they should perform those tasks in that undertaking.

(28) This Directive specifies that for certain own funds items qualifying criteria should be specified, without prejudice to the possibility of Member States to apply more stringent provisions.

(29) According to the nature of the items constituting own funds, this Directive distinguishes between on the one hand, items constituting original own funds and, on the other, those constituting additional own funds.

(30) To reflect the fact that items constituting additional own funds are not of the same nature as those constituting original own funds, the amount of the former included in own funds should not exceed the original own funds. Moreover, the amount of certain items of additional own funds included should not exceed one half of the original own funds.

(31) In order to avoid distortions of competition, public credit institutions should not include in their own funds guarantees granted them by the Member States or local authorities.

(32) Whenever in the course of supervision it is necessary to determine the amount of the consolidated own funds of a group of credit institutions, the calculation should be effected in accordance with this Directive.

(33) The precise accounting technique to be used for the calculation of own funds, their adequacy for the risk to which a credit institution is exposed, and for the assessment of the concentration of exposures should take account of the provisions of Council Directive 86/635/EEC of 8 December 1986 on the annual accounts and consolidated accounts of banks and other financial institutions,[6] which incorporates certain adaptations of the provisions of Seventh Council Directive 83/349/EEC of 13 June 1983 on consolidated accounts[7] or of Regulation (EC) No 1606/2002 of the European Parliament and of the Council of 19 July 2002 on the application of international accounting standards,[8] whichever governs the accounting of the credit institutions under national law.

(34) Minimum capital requirements play a central role in the supervision of credit institutions and in the mutual recognition of supervisory techniques. In that respect, the provisions on minimum capital requirements should be considered in conjunction with other specific instruments also harmonising the fundamental techniques for the supervision of credit institutions.

(35) In order to prevent distortions of competition and to strengthen the banking system in the internal market, it is appropriate to lay down common minimum capital requirements.

(36) For the purposes of ensuring adequate solvency it is important to lay down minimum capital requirements which weight assets and off-balance-sheet items according to the degree of risk.

(37) On this point, on 26 June 2004 the Basel Committee on Banking Supervision adopted a framework agreement on the international convergence of capital measurement and capital requirements. The provisions in this Directive on the minimum capital requirements of credit institutions, and the minimum capital provisions in Directive 2006/49/EC of the European Parliament and of the Council of 14 June 2006 on the capital adequacy of investment firms and credit institutions,[9] form an equivalent to the provisions of the Basel framework agreement.

(38) It is essential to take account of the diversity of credit institutions in the Community by providing alternative approaches to the calculation of minimum capital requirements for credit risk incorporating different levels of risk-sensitivity and requiring different degrees of sophistication. Use of external ratings and credit institutions' own estimates of individual credit risk parameters represents a significant enhancement in the risk-sensitivity and prudential soundness of the credit risk rules. There should be appropriate incentives for credit institutions to move towards the more risk-sensitive approaches. In producing the estimates needed to apply the approaches to credit risk of this Directive, credit institutions will have to adjust their data processing needs to their clients' legitimate data protection interests as governed by the existing Community legislation on data protection, while enhancing credit risk measurement and management processes of credit institutions to make methods for determining credit institutions' regulatory own funds requirements available that reflect the

sophistication of individual credit institutions' processes. The processing of data should be in accordance with the rules on transfer of personal data laid down in Directive 95/46/EC of the European Parliament and of the Council of 24 October 1995 on the protection of individuals with regard to the processing of personal data and on the free movement of such data.[10] In this regard, the processing of data in connection with the incurring and management of exposures to customers should be considered to include the development and validation of credit risk management and measurement systems. That serves not only to fulfil the legitimate interest of credit institutions but also the purpose of this Directive, to use better methods for risk measurement and management and also use them for regulatory own funds purposes.

(39) With regard to the use of both external and an institution's own estimates or internal ratings, account should be taken of the fact that, at present, only the latter are drawn up by an entity — the financial institution itself — which is subject to a Community authorisation process. In the case of external ratings use is made of the products of what are known as recognised rating agencies, which in the Community are not currently subject to an authorisation process. In view of the importance of external ratings in connection with the calculation of capital requirements under this Directive, appropriate future authorisation and supervisory process for rating agencies need to be kept under review.

(40) The minimum capital requirements should be proportionate to the risks addressed. In particular the reduction in risk levels deriving from having a large number of relatively small exposures should be reflected in the requirements.

(41) The provisions of this Directive respect the principle of proportionality, having regard in particular to the diversity in size and scale of operations and to the range of activities of credit institutions. Respect of the principle of proportionality also means that the simplest possible rating procedures, even in the Internal Ratings Based Approach ("IRB Approach"), are recognised for retail exposures.

(42) The "evolutionary" nature of this Directive enables credit institutions to choose amongst three approaches of varying complexity. In order to allow especially small credit institutions to opt for the more risk-sensitive IRB Approach, the competent authorities should implement the provisions of Article 89(1)(a) and (b) whenever appropriate. Those provisions should be read as such that exposure classes referred to in Article 86(1)(a) and (b) include all exposures that are, directly or indirectly, put on a par with them throughout this Directive. As a general rule, the competent authorities should not discriminate between the three approaches with regard to the Supervisory Review Process, ie credit institutions operating according to the provisions of the Standardised Approach should not for that reason alone be supervised on a stricter basis.

(43) Increased recognition should be given to techniques of credit risk mitigation within a framework of rules designed to ensure that solvency is not undermined by undue recognition. The relevant Member States' current customary banking collateral for mitigating credit risks should wherever possible be recognised in the Standardised Approach, but also in the other approaches.

(44) In order to ensure that the risks and risk reductions arising from credit institutions' securitisation activities and investments are appropriately reflected in the minimum capital requirements of credit institutions it is necessary to include rules providing for a risk-sensitive and prudentially sound treatment of such activities and investments.

(45) Operational risk is a significant risk faced by credit institutions requiring coverage by own funds. It is essential to take account of the diversity of credit institutions in the Community by providing alternative approaches to the calculation of operational risk requirements incorporating different levels of risk-sensitivity and requiring different degrees of sophistication. There should be appropriate incentives for credit institutions to move towards the more risk-sensitive approaches. In view of the emerging state of the art for the measurement and management of operational risk the rules should be kept under review and updated as appropriate including in relation to the charges for different business lines and the recognition of risk mitigation techniques. Particular attention should be paid in this regard to taking insurance into account in the simple approaches to calculating capital requirements for operational risk.

(46) In order to ensure adequate solvency of credit institutions within a group it is essential that the minimum capital requirements apply on the basis of the consolidated financial situation of the group. In order to ensure that own funds are appropriately distributed within the group and available to protect savings where needed, the minimum capital requirements should apply to individual credit institutions within a group, unless this objective can be effectively otherwise achieved.

(47) The essential rules for monitoring large exposures of credit institutions should be harmonised. Member States should still be able to adopt provisions more stringent than those provided for by this Directive.

(48) The monitoring and control of a credit institution's exposures should be an integral Part of its supervision. Therefore, excessive concentration of exposures to a single client or group of connected clients may result in an unacceptable risk of loss. Such a situation can be considered prejudicial to the solvency of a credit institution.

(49) Since credit institutions in the internal market are engaged in direct competition, monitoring requirements should be equivalent throughout the Community.

(50) While it is appropriate to base the definition of exposures for the purposes of limits to large exposures on that provided for the purposes of minimum own funds requirements for credit risk, it is not appropriate to refer on principle to the weightings or degrees of risk. Those weightings and degrees of risk were devised for the purpose of establishing a general solvency requirement to cover the credit risk of credit institutions. In order to limit the maximum loss that a credit institution may incur through any single client or group of connected clients it is appropriate to adopt rules for the determination of large exposures which take account of the nominal value of the exposure without applying weightings or degrees of risk.

(51) While it is desirable, pending further review of the large exposures provisions, to permit the recognition of the effects of credit risk mitigation in a manner similar to that permitted for minimum capital requirement purposes in order to limit the calculation requirements, the rules on credit risk mitigation were designed in the context of the general diversified credit risk arising from exposures to a large number of counterparties. Accordingly, recognition of the effects of such techniques for the purposes of limits to large exposures designed to limit the maximum loss that may be incurred through any single client or group of connected clients should be subject to prudential safeguards.

(52) When a credit institution incurs an exposure to its own parent undertaking or to other subsidiaries of its parent undertaking, particular prudence is necessary. The management of exposures incurred by credit institutions should be carried out in a fully autonomous manner, in accordance with the principles of sound banking management, without regard to any other considerations. Where the influence exercised by persons directly or indirectly holding a qualifying participation in a credit institution is likely to operate to the detriment of the sound and prudent management of that institution, the competent authorities should take appropriate measures to put an end to that situation. In the field of large exposures, specific standards, including more stringent restrictions, should be laid down for exposures incurred by a credit institution to its own group. Such standards need not, however be applied where the parent undertaking is a financial holding company or a credit institution or where the other subsidiaries are either credit or financial institutions or undertakings offering ancillary services, provided that all such undertakings are covered by the supervision of the credit institution on a consolidated basis.

(53) Credit institutions should ensure that they have internal capital that, having regard to the risks to which they are or may be exposed, is adequate in quantity, quality and distribution. Accordingly, credit institutions should have strategies and processes in place for assessing and maintaining the adequacy of their internal capital.

(54) Competent authorities have responsibility to be satisfied that credit institutions have good organisation and adequate own funds, having regard to the risks to which the credit institutions are or might be exposed.

(55) In order for the internal banking market to operate effectively the Committee of European Banking Supervisors should contribute to the consistent application of this Directive and to the convergence of supervisory practices throughout the Community, and should report on a yearly basis to the Community institutions on progress made.

(56) For the same reason, and to ensure that Community credit institutions which are active in several Member States are not disproportionately burdened as a result of the continued responsibilities of individual Member State competent authorities for authorisation and supervision, it is essential to significantly enhance the cooperation between competent authorities. In this context, the role of the consolidating supervisor should be strengthened. The Committee of European Banking Supervisors should support and enhance such cooperation.

(57) Supervision of credit institutions on a consolidated basis aims at, in particular, protecting the interests of the depositors of credit institutions and at ensuring the stability of the financial system.

(58) In order to be effective, supervision on a consolidated basis should therefore be applied to all banking groups, including those the parent undertakings of which are not credit institutions. The competent authorities should hold the necessary legal instruments to be able to exercise such supervision.

(59) In the case of groups with diversified activities where parent undertakings control at least one credit institution subsidiary, the competent authorities should be able to assess the financial situation of a credit institution in such a group. The competent authorities should at

least have the means of obtaining from all undertakings within a group the information necessary for the performance of their function. Cooperation between the authorities responsible for the supervision of different financial sectors should be established in the case of groups of undertakings carrying on a range of financial activities. Pending subsequent coordination, the Member States should be able to lay down appropriate methods of consolidation for the achievement of the objective of this Directive.

(60) The Member States should be able to refuse or withdraw banking authorisation in the case of certain group structures considered inappropriate for carrying on banking activities, in particular because such structures could not be supervised effectively. In this respect the competent authorities should have the necessary powers to ensure the sound and prudent management of credit institutions.

(61) In order for the internal banking market to operate with increasing effectiveness and for citizens of the Community to be afforded adequate levels of transparency, it is necessary that competent authorities disclose publicly and in a way which allows for meaningful comparison the manner in which this Directive is implemented.

(62) In order to strengthen market discipline and stimulate credit institutions to improve their market strategy, risk control and internal management organization, appropriate public disclosure by credit institutions should be provided for.

(63) The examination of problems connected with matters covered by this Directive, as well as by other Directives on the business of credit institutions, requires cooperation between the competent authorities and the Commission, particularly when conducted with a view to closer coordination.

(64) The measures necessary for the implementation of this Directive should be adopted in accordance with Council Decision 1999/468/EC of 28 June 1999 laying down the procedures for the exercise of implementing powers conferred on the Commission.[11]

(65) In its resolution of 5 February 2002 on the implementation of financial services legislation[12] the Parliament requested that it and the Council should have an equal role in supervising the way in which the Commission exercises its executive role in order to reflect the legislative powers of Parliament under Article 251 of the Treaty. In the solemn declaration made before the Parliament the same day by its President, the Commission supported this request. On 11 December 2002 the Commission proposed amendments to Decision 1999/468/EC, and then submitted an amended proposal on 22 April 2004. The Parliament does not consider that this proposal preserves its legislative prerogatives. In the view of the Parliament, it and the Council should have the opportunity of evaluating the conferral of implementing powers on the Commission within a determined period. It is therefore appropriate to limit the period during which the Commission may adopt implementing measures.

(66) The Parliament should be given a period of three months from the first transmission of draft amendments and implementing measures to allow it to examine them and to give its opinion. However, in urgent and duly justified cases, it should be possible to shorten this period. If, within that period, a resolution is adopted by the Parliament, the Commission should re-examine the draft amendments or measures.

(67) In order to avoid disruption to markets and to ensure continuity in overall levels of own funds it is appropriate to provide for specific transitional arrangements.

(68) In view of the risk-sensitivity of the rules relating to minimum capital requirements, it is desirable to keep under review whether these have significant effects on the economic cycle. The Commission, taking into account the contribution of the European Central Bank should report on these aspects to the European Parliament and to the Council.

(69) The arrangements necessary for the supervision of liquidity risks should also be harmonised.

(70) This Directive respects fundamental rights and observes the principles recognised in particular by the Charter of Fundamental Rights of the European Union as general principles of Community law.

(71) The obligation to transpose this Directive into national law should be confined to those provisions which represent a substantive change as compared with earlier directives. The obligation to transpose the provisions which are unchanged exists under the earlier directives.

(72) This Directive should be without prejudice to the obligations of the Member States relating to the time-limits for transposition into national law of the Directives set out in Annex XIII, Part B,

[9823]

NOTES

[1] OJ C234, 22.9.2005, p 8.

2 OJ C52, 2.3.2005, p 37.
3 Opinion of the European Parliament of 28 September 2005 (not yet published in the OJ) and Decision of the Council of 7 June 2006.
4 OJ L126, 26.5.2000, p 1. Directive as last amended by Directive 2006/29/EC (OJ L70, 9.3.2006, p 50).
5 OJ L3, 7.1.2004, p 28.
6 OJ L372, 31.12.1986, p 1. Directive as last amended by Directive 2003/51/EC of the European Parliament and of the Council (OJ L178, 17.7.2003, p 16).
7 OJ L193, 18.7.1983, p 1. Directive as last amended by Directive 2003/51/EC.
8 OJ L243, 11.9.2002, p 1.
9 See page 201 of this Official Journal.
10 OJ L281, 23.11.1995, p 31. Directive as amended by Regulation (EC) No 1882/2003 (OJ L284, 31.10.2003, p 1).
11 OJ L184, 17.7.1999, p 23.
12 OJ C284E, 21.11.2002, p 115.

HAVE ADOPTED THIS DIRECTIVE—

TITLE I
SUBJECT MATTER, SCOPE AND DEFINITIONS

Article 1

1. This Directive lays down rules concerning the taking up and pursuit of the business of credit institutions, and their prudential supervision.

2. Article 39 and Title V, Chapter 4, Section 1 shall apply to financial holding companies and mixed-activity holding companies which have their head offices in the Community.

3. The institutions permanently excluded pursuant to Article 2, with the exception, however, of the central banks of the Member States, shall be treated as financial institutions for the purposes of Article 39 and Title V, Chapter 4, Section 1.

[9824]

Article 2

This Directive shall not apply to the following:

— the central banks of Member States,

— post office giro institutions,

— in Belgium, the "Institut de Réescompte et de Garantie/Herdiscontering- en Waarborginstituut",

[— in Denmark, the "Dansk Eksportfinansieringsfond", the "Danmarks Skibskredit A/S" and the "KommuneKredit;"]

— in Denmark, the "Dansk Eksportfinansieringsfond", the "Danmarks Skibskreditfond", the "Dansk Landbrugs Realkreditfond", and the "KommuneKredit",

— in Germany, the "Kreditanstalt für Wiederaufbau", undertakings which are recognised under the "Wohnungsgemeinnützigkeitsgesetz" as bodies of State housing policy and are not mainly engaged in banking transactions, and undertakings recognised under that law as non-profit housing undertakings,

— in Greece, the "Ταμείο Παρακαταθηκών και Δανείων" (Tamio Parakatathikon kai Danion),

— in Spain, the "Instituto de Crédito Oficial",

— in France, the "Caisse des dépôts et consignations",

— in Ireland, credit unions and the friendly societies,

— in Italy, the "Cassa depositi e prestiti",

— in Latvia, the "krājaizdevu sabiedrības", undertakings that are recognised under the "krājaizdevu sabiedrību likums" as cooperative undertakings rendering financial services solely to their members,

— in Lithuania, the "kredito unijos" other than the "Centrinė kredito unija",

— in Hungary, the "Magyar Fejlesztési Bank Rt." and the "Magyar Export-Import Bank Rt.",

— in the Netherlands, the "Nederlandse Investeringsbank voor Ontwikkelingslanden NV", the "NV Noordelijke Ontwikkelingsmaatschappij", the "NV Industriebank Limburgs Instituut voor Ontwikkeling en Financiering" and the "Overijsselse Ontwikkelingsmaatschappij NV",

— in Austria, undertakings recognised as housing associations in the public interest and the "Österreichische Kontrollbank AG",
— in Poland, the "Spółdzielcze Kasy Oszczędnościowo — Kreditowe" and the "Bank Gospodarstwa Krajowego",
— in Portugal, "Caixas Económicas" existing on 1 January 1986 with the exception of those incorporated as limited companies and of the "Caixa Económica Montepio Geral",
— in Finland, the "Teollisen yhteistyön rahasto Oy/Fonden för industriellt samarbete AB", and the "Finnvera Oyj/Finnvera Abp",
— in Sweden, the "Svenska Skeppshypotekskassan",
— in the United Kingdom, the National Savings Bank, the Commonwealth Development Finance Company Ltd, the Agricultural Mortgage Corporation Ltd, the Scottish Agricultural Securities Corporation Ltd, the Crown Agents for overseas governments and administrations, credit unions and municipal banks.

[9825]

NOTES

Words in square brackets substituted by Commission Directive 2007/18/EC, Art 1(1), as from 17 April 2007. Note that Commission Directive 2007/18/EC has a transposition date of 1 October 2007 and that the substituted words previously read as follows—

"— in Denmark, the "Dansk Eksportfinansieringsfond", the "Danmarks Skibskreditfond", the "Dansk Landbrugs Realkreditfond", and the "KommuneKredit".".

Article 3

1. One or more credit institutions situated in the same Member State and which are permanently affiliated, on 15 December 1977, to a central body which supervises them and which is established in the same Member State, may be exempted from the requirements of Articles 7 and 11(1) if, no later than 15 December 1979, national law provides that:

(a) the commitments of the central body and affiliated institutions are joint and several liabilities or the commitments of its affiliated institutions are entirely guaranteed by the central body;
(b) the solvency and liquidity of the central body and of all the affiliated institutions are monitored as a whole on the basis of consolidated accounts; and
(c) the management of the central body is empowered to issue instructions to the management of the affiliated institutions.

Credit institutions operating locally which are permanently affiliated, subsequent to 15 December 1977, to a central body within the meaning of the first subparagraph, may benefit from the conditions laid down therein if they constitute normal additions to the network belonging to that central body.

In the case of credit institutions other than those which are set up in areas newly reclaimed from the sea or have resulted from scission or mergers of existing institutions dependent or answerable to the central body, the Commission, pursuant to the procedure referred to in Article 151(2) may lay down additional rules for the application of the second subparagraph including the repeal of exemptions provided for in the first subparagraph, where it is of the opinion that the affiliation of new institutions benefiting from the arrangements laid down in the second subparagraph might have an adverse effect on competition.

2. A credit institution referred to in the first subparagraph of paragraph 1, may also be exempted from the provisions of Articles 9 and 10, and also Title V, Chapter 2, Sections 2, 3, 4, 5 and 6 and Chapter 3 provided that, without prejudice to the application of those provisions to the central body, the whole as constituted by the central body together with its affiliated institutions is subject to those provisions on a consolidated basis.

In case of exemption, Articles 16, 23, 24, 25, 26(1) to (3) and 28 to 37 shall apply to the whole as constituted by the central body together with its affiliated institutions.

[9826]

Article 4

For the purposes of this Directive, the following definitions shall apply:

(1) "credit institution" means:

(a) an undertaking whose business is to receive deposits or other repayable funds from the public and to grant credits for its own account; or

(b) an electronic money institution within the meaning of Directive 2000/46/EC;[1]

(2) "authorisation" means an instrument issued in any form by the authorities by which the right to carry on the business of a credit institution is granted;

(3) "branch" means a place of business which forms a legally dependent Part of a credit institution and which carries out directly all or some of the transactions inherent in the business of credit institutions;

(4) "competent authorities" means the national authorities which are empowered by law or regulation to supervise credit institutions;

(5) "financial institution" means an undertaking other than a credit institution, the principal activity of which is to acquire holdings or to carry on one or more of the activities listed in points 2 to 12 of Annex I;

(6) "institutions", for the purposes of Sections 2 and 3 of Title V, Chapter 2, means institutions as defined in Article 3(1)(c) of Directive 2006/49/EC;

(7) "home Member State" means the Member State in which a credit institution has been authorised in accordance with Articles 6 to 9 and 11 to 14;

(8) "host Member State" means the Member State in which a credit institution has a branch or in which it provides services;

(9) "control" means the relationship between a parent undertaking and a subsidiary, as defined in Article 1 of Directive 83/349/EEC, or a similar relationship between any natural or legal person and an undertaking;

(10) "participation" for the purposes of points (o) and (p) of Article 57, Articles 71 to 73 and Title V, Chapter 4 means participation within the meaning of the first sentence of Article 17 of Fourth Council Directive 78/660/EEC of 25 July 1978 on the annual accounts of certain types of companies,[2] or the ownership, direct or indirect, of 20% or more of the voting rights or capital of an undertaking;

(11) "qualifying holding" means a direct or indirect holding in an undertaking which represents 10% or more of the capital or of the voting rights or which makes it possible to exercise a significant influence over the management of that undertaking;

(12) "parent undertaking" means:

(a) a parent undertaking as defined in Articles 1 and 2 of Directive 83/349/EEC; or

(b) for the purposes of Articles 71 to 73, Title V, Chapter 2, Section 5 and Chapter 4, a parent undertaking within the meaning of Article 1(1) of Directive 83/349/EEC and any undertaking which, in the opinion of the competent authorities, effectively exercises a dominant influence over another undertaking;

(13) "subsidiary" means:

(a) a subsidiary undertaking as defined in Articles 1 and 2 of Directive 83/349/EEC; or

(b) for the purposes of Articles 71 to 73, Title V, Chapter 2, Section 5, and Chapter 4 a subsidiary undertaking within the meaning of Article 1(1) of Directive 83/349/EEC and any undertaking over which, in the opinion of the competent authorities, a parent undertaking effectively exercises a dominant influence.

All subsidiaries of subsidiary undertakings shall also be considered subsidiaries of the undertaking that is their original parent;

(14) "parent credit institution in a Member State" means a credit institution which has a credit institution or a financial institution as a subsidiary or which holds a participation in such an institution, and which is not itself a subsidiary of another credit institution authorised in the same Member State, or of a financial holding company set up in the same Member State;

(15) "parent financial holding company in a Member State" means a financial holding company which is not itself a subsidiary of a credit institution authorised in the same Member State, or of a financial holding company set up in the same Member State;

(16) "EU parent credit institution" means a parent credit institution in a Member State which is not a subsidiary of another credit institution authorised in any Member State, or of a financial holding company set up in any Member State;

(17) "EU parent financial holding company" means a parent financial holding company in a Member State which is not a subsidiary of a credit institution authorised in any Member State or of another financial holding company set up in any Member State;

(18) "public sector entities" means non-commercial administrative bodies responsible to central governments, regional governments or local authorities, or authorities that in the view of the competent authorities exercise the same responsibilities as regional and local authorities, or non-commercial undertakings owned by central governments that have explicit guarantee arrangements, and may include self administered bodies governed by law that are under public supervision;

(19) "financial holding company" means a financial institution, the subsidiary undertakings of which are either exclusively or mainly credit institutions or financial institutions, at least one of such subsidiaries being a credit institution, and which is not a mixed financial holding company within the meaning of Article 2(15) of Directive 2002/87/EC;[3]

(20) "mixed-activity holding company" means a parent undertaking, other than a financial holding company or a credit institution or a mixed financial holding company within the meaning of Article 2(15) of Directive 2002/87/EC, the subsidiaries of which include at least one credit institution;

(21) "ancillary services undertaking" means an undertaking the principal activity of which consists in owning or managing property, managing data-processing services, or any other similar activity which is ancillary to the principal activity of one or more credit institutions;

(22) "operational risk" means the risk of loss resulting from inadequate or failed internal processes, people and systems or from external events, and includes legal risk;

(23) "central banks" include the European Central Bank unless otherwise indicated;

(24) "dilution risk" means the risk that an amount receivable is reduced through cash or non-cash credits to the obligor;

(25) "probability of default" means the probability of default of a counterparty over a one year period;

(26) "loss", for the purposes of Title V, Chapter 2, Section 3, means economic loss, including material discount effects, and material direct and indirect costs associated with collecting on the instrument;

(27) "loss given default (LGD)" means the ratio of the loss on an exposure due to the default of a counterparty to the amount outstanding at default;

(28) "conversion factor" means the ratio of the currently undrawn amount of a commitment that will be drawn and outstanding at default to the currently undrawn amount of the commitment, the extent of the commitment shall be determined by the advised limit, unless the unadvised limit is higher;

(29) "expected loss (EL)", for the purposes of Title V, Chapter 2, Section 3, shall mean the ratio of the amount expected to be lost on an exposure from a potential default of a counterparty or dilution over a one year period to the amount outstanding at default;

(30) "credit risk mitigation" means a technique used by a credit institution to reduce the credit risk associated with an exposure or exposures which the credit institution continues to hold;

(31) "funded credit protection" means a technique of credit risk mitigation where the reduction of the credit risk on the exposure of a credit institution derives from the right of the credit institution — in the event of the default of the counterparty or on the occurrence of other specified credit events relating to the counterparty — to liquidate, or to obtain transfer or appropriation of, or to retain certain assets or amounts, or to reduce the amount of the exposure to, or to replace it with, the amount of the difference between the amount of the exposure and the amount of a claim on the credit institution;

(32) "unfunded credit protection" means a technique of credit risk mitigation where the reduction of the credit risk on the exposure of a credit institution derives from the undertaking of a third party to pay an amount in the event of the default of the borrower or on the occurrence of other specified credit events;

(33) "repurchase transaction" means any transaction governed by an agreement falling within the definition of "repurchase agreement" or "reverse repurchase agreement" as defined in Article 3(1)(m) of Directive 2006/49/EC;

(34) "securities or commodities lending or borrowing transaction" means any transaction falling within the definition of "securities or commodities lending" or "securities or commodities borrowing" as defined in Article 3(1)(n) of Directive 2006/49/EC;

(35) "cash assimilated instrument" means a certificate of deposit or other similar instrument issued by the lending credit institution;

(36) "securitisation" means a transaction or scheme, whereby the credit risk associated with an exposure or pool of exposures is tranched, having the following characteristics:

(a) payments in the transaction or scheme are dependent upon the performance of the exposure or pool of exposures; and

(b) the subordination of tranches determines the distribution of losses during the ongoing life of the transaction or scheme;

(37) "traditional securitisation" means a securitisation involving the economic transfer of the exposures being securitised to a securitisation special purpose entity which issues securities. This shall be accomplished by the transfer of ownership of the securitised exposures from the originator credit institution or through sub-participation. The securities issued do not represent payment obligations of the originator credit institution;

(38) "synthetic securitisation" means a securitisation where the tranching is achieved by the use of credit derivatives or guarantees, and the pool of exposures is not removed from the balance sheet of the originator credit institution;

(39) "tranche" means a contractually established segment of the credit risk associated with an exposure or number of exposures, where a position in the segment entails a risk of credit loss greater than or less than a position of the same amount in each other such segment, without taking account of credit protection provided by third parties directly to the holders of positions in the segment or in other segments;

(40) "securitisation position" shall mean an exposure to a securitisation;

(41) "originator" means either of the following:

(a) an entity which, either itself or through related entities, directly or indirectly, was involved in the original agreement which created the obligations or potential obligations of the debtor or potential debtor giving rise to the exposure being securitised; or

(b) an entity which purchases a third party's exposures onto its balance sheet and then securitises them;

(42) "sponsor" means a credit institution other than an originator credit institution that establishes and manages an asset-backed commercial paper programme or other securitisation scheme that purchases exposures from third party entities;

(43) "credit enhancement" means a contractual arrangement whereby the credit quality of a position in a securitisation is improved in relation to what it would have been if the enhancement had not been provided, including the enhancement provided by more junior tranches in the securitisation and other types of credit protection;

(44) "securitisation special purpose entity (SSPE)" means a corporation trust or other entity, other than a credit institution, organised for carrying on a securitisation or securitisations, the activities of which are limited to those appropriate to accomplishing that objective, the structure of which is intended to isolate the obligations of the SSPE from those of the originator credit institution, and the holders of the beneficial interests in which have the right to pledge or exchange those interests without restriction;

(45) "group of connected clients" means:

(a) two or more natural or legal persons who, unless it is shown otherwise, constitute a single risk because one of them, directly or indirectly, has control over the other or others; or

(b) two or more natural or legal persons between whom there is no relationship of control as set out in point (a) but who are to be regarded as constituting a single risk because they are so interconnected that, if one of them were to experience financial problems, the other or all of the others would be likely to encounter repayment difficulties;

(46) "close links" means a situation in which two or more natural or legal persons are linked in any of the following ways:

(a) participation in the form of ownership, direct or by way of control, of 20% or more of the voting rights or capital of an undertaking;

(b) control; or

(c) the fact that both or all are permanently linked to one and the same third person by a control relationship;

(47) "recognised exchanges" means exchanges which are recognised as such by the competent authorities and which meet the following conditions:

(a) they function regularly;

(b) they have rules, issued or approved by the appropriate authorities of the home country of the exchange, defining the conditions for the operation of the exchange, the conditions of access to the exchange as well as the conditions that shall be satisfied by a contract before it can effectively be dealt on the exchange; and

(c) they have a clearing mechanism whereby contracts listed in Annex IV are subject to daily margin requirements which, in the opinion of the competent authorities, provide appropriate protection.

[9827]

NOTES

1 Directive 2000/46/EC of the European Parliament and of the Council of 18 September 2000 on the taking up, pursuit of and prudential supervision of the business of electronic money institutions (OJ L275, 27.10.2000, p 39).

2 OJ L222, 14.8.1978, p 11. Directive as last amended by Directive 2003/51/EC.

3 Directive 2002/87/EC of the European Parliament and of the Council of 16 December 2002 on the supplementary supervision of credit institutions, insurance undertakings and investment firms in a financial conglomerate (OJ L35, 11.2.2003, p 1). Directive as amended by Directive 2005/1/EC.

Article 5

Member States shall prohibit persons or undertakings that are not credit institutions from carrying on the business of taking deposits or other repayable funds from the public.

The first paragraph shall not apply to the taking of deposits or other funds repayable by a Member State or by a Member State's regional or local authorities or by public international bodies of which one or more Member States are members or to cases expressly covered by national or Community legislation, provided that those activities are subject to regulations and controls intended to protect depositors and investors and applicable to those cases.

[9828]

TITLE II
REQUIREMENTS FOR ACCESS TO THE TAKING UP AND PURSUIT OF THE BUSINESS OF CREDIT INSTITUTIONS

Article 6

Member States shall require credit institutions to obtain authorisation before commencing their activities. Without prejudice to Articles 7 to 12, they shall lay down the requirements for such authorisation and notify them to the Commission.

[9829]

Article 7

Member States shall require applications for authorisation to be accompanied by a programme of operations setting out, inter alia, the types of business envisaged and the structural organisation of the credit institution.

[9830]

Article 8

Member States may not require the application for authorisation to be examined in terms of the economic needs of the market.

[9831]

Article 9

1. Without prejudice to other general conditions laid down by national law, the competent authorities shall not grant authorisation when the credit institution does not possess separate own funds or in cases where initial capital is less than EUR 5 million.

"Initial capital" shall comprise capital and reserves as referred to in Article 57(a) and (b).

Member States may decide that credit institutions which do not fulfil the requirement of separate own funds and which were in existence on 15 December 1979 may continue to carry on their business. They may exempt such credit institutions from complying with the requirement contained in the first subparagraph of Article 11(1).

2. Member States may, subject to the following conditions, grant authorisation to particular categories of credit institutions the initial capital of which is less than that specified in paragraph 1:

(a) the initial capital shall be no less than EUR 1 million;
(b) the Member States concerned shall notify the Commission of their reasons for exercising this option; and
(c) the name of each credit institution that does not have the minimum capital specified in paragraph 1 shall be annotated to that effect in the list referred to in Article 14.

[9832]

Article 10

1. A credit institution's own funds may not fall below the amount of initial capital required under Article 9 at the time of its authorisation.

2. Member States may decide that credit institutions already in existence on 1 January 1993, the own funds of which do not attain the levels specified for initial capital in Article 9, may continue to carry on their activities. In that event, their own funds may not fall below the highest level reached with effect from 22 December 1989.

3. If control of a credit institution falling within the category referred to in paragraph 2 is taken by a natural or legal person other than the person who controlled the institution previously, the own funds of that credit institution shall attain at least the level specified for initial capital in Article 9.

4. In certain specific circumstances and with the consent of the competent authorities, where there is a merger of two or more credit institutions falling within the category referred to in paragraph 2, the own funds of the credit institution resulting from the merger may not fall below the total own funds of the merged credit institutions at the time of the merger, as long as the appropriate levels specified in Article 9 have not been attained.

5. If, in the cases referred to in paragraphs 1, 2 and 4, the own funds should be reduced, the competent authorities may, where the circumstances justify it, allow a credit institution a limited period in which to rectify its situation or cease its activities.

[9833]

Article 11

1. The competent authorities shall grant an authorisation to the credit institution only when there are at least two persons who effectively direct the business of the credit institution.

They shall not grant authorisation if these persons are not of sufficiently good repute or lack sufficient experience to perform such duties.

2. Each Member State shall require that:

(a) any credit institution which is a legal person and which, under its national law, has a registered office shall have its head office in the same Member State as its registered office; and
(b) any other credit institution shall have its head office in the Member State which granted its authorisation and in which it actually carries on its business.

[9834]

Article 12

1. The competent authorities shall not grant authorisation for the taking-up of the business of credit institutions unless they have been informed of the identities of the

shareholders or members, whether direct or indirect, natural or legal persons, that have qualifying holdings, and of the amounts of those holdings.

In determining a qualifying holding in the context of this Article, the voting rights referred to in Article 92 of Directive 2001/34/EC of the European Parliament and of the Council of 28 May 2001 on the admission of securities to official stock exchange listing and on information to be published on those securities[1] shall be taken into consideration.

2. The competent authorities shall not grant authorisation if, taking into account the need to ensure the sound and prudent management of a credit institution, they are not satisfied as to the suitability of the shareholders or members.

3. Where close links exist between the credit institution and other natural or legal persons, the competent authorities shall grant authorisation only if those links do not prevent the effective exercise of their supervisory functions.

The competent authorities shall also not grant authorisation if the laws, regulations or administrative provisions of a third country governing one or more natural or legal persons with which the credit institution has close links, or difficulties involved in the enforcement of those laws, regulations or administrative provisions, prevent the effective exercise of their supervisory functions.

The competent authorities shall require credit institutions to provide them with the information they require to monitor compliance with the conditions referred to in this paragraph on a continuous basis.

[9835]

NOTES

[1] OJ L184, 6.7.2001, p 1. Directive as last amended by Directive 2005/1/EC.

Article 13

Reasons shall be given whenever a decision not to grant an authorisation is taken and the applicant shall be notified thereof within six months of receipt of the application or, should the latter be incomplete, within six months of the applicant's sending the information required for the decision. A decision shall, in any case, be taken within 12 months of the receipt of the application.

[9836]

Article 14

Every authorisation shall be notified to the Commission.

The name of each credit institution to which authorisation has been granted shall be entered in a list. The Commission shall publish that list in the Official Journal of the European Union and shall keep it up to date.

[9837]

Article 15

1. The competent authority shall, before granting authorisation to a credit institution, consult the competent authorities of the other Member State involved in the following cases:
   - (a) the credit institution concerned is a subsidiary of a credit institution authorised in another Member State;
   - (b) the credit institution concerned is a subsidiary of the parent undertaking of a credit institution authorised in another Member State; or
   - (c) the credit institution concerned is controlled by the same persons, whether natural or legal, as control a credit institution authorised in another Member State.

2. The competent authority shall, before granting authorisation to a credit institution, consult the competent authority of a Member State involved, responsible for the supervision of insurance undertakings or investment firms in the following cases:
   - (a) the credit institution concerned is a subsidiary of an insurance undertaking or investment firm authorised in the Community;
   - (b) the credit institution concerned is a subsidiary of the parent undertaking of an insurance undertaking or investment firm authorised in the Community; or
   - (c) the credit institution concerned is controlled by the same person, whether natural or legal, as controls an insurance undertaking or investment firm authorised in the Community.

3. The relevant competent authorities referred to in paragraphs 1 and 2 shall in particular consult each other when assessing the suitability of the shareholders and the reputation and experience of directors involved in the management of another entity of the same group. They shall exchange any information regarding the suitability of shareholders and the reputation and experience of directors which is of relevance for the granting of an authorisation as well as for the ongoing assessment of compliance with operating conditions.

[9838]

Article 16

Host Member States may not require authorisation or endowment capital for branches of credit institutions authorised in other Member States. The establishment and supervision of such branches shall be effected in accordance with Articles 22, 25, 26(1) to (3), 29 to 37 and 40.

[9839]

Article 17

1. The competent authorities may withdraw the authorisation granted to a credit institution only where such an institution:

(a) does not make use of the authorisation within 12 months, expressly renounces the authorisation or has ceased to engage in business for more than six months, if the Member State concerned has made no provision for the authorisation to lapse in such cases;

(b) has obtained the authorisation through false statements or any other irregular means;

(c) no longer fulfils the conditions under which authorisation was granted;

(d) no longer possesses sufficient own funds or can no longer be relied on to fulfil its obligations towards its creditors, and in particular no longer provides security for the assets entrusted to it; or

(e) falls within one of the other cases where national law provides for withdrawal of authorisation.

2. Reasons shall be given for any withdrawal of authorisation and those concerned informed thereof. Such withdrawal shall be notified to the Commission.

[9840]

Article 18

For the purposes of exercising their activities, credit institutions may, notwithstanding any provisions in the host Member State concerning the use of the words "bank", "savings bank" or other banking names, use throughout the territory of the Community the same name as they use in the Member State in which their head office is situated. In the event of there being any danger of confusion, the host Member State may, for the purposes of clarification, require that the name be accompanied by certain explanatory particulars.

[9841]

Article 19

1. The Member States shall require any natural or legal person who proposes to hold, directly or indirectly, a qualifying holding in a credit institution first to inform the competent authorities, telling them of the size of the intended holding. Such a person shall likewise inform the competent authorities if he proposes to increase his qualifying holding so that the proportion of the voting rights or of the capital held by him would reach or exceed 20%, 33% or 50% or so that the credit institution would become his subsidiary.

Without prejudice to paragraph 2, the competent authorities shall have a maximum of three months from the date of the notification provided for in the first and second subparagraphs to oppose such a plan if, in view of the need to ensure sound and prudent management of the credit institution, they are not satisfied as to the suitability of the person concerned. If they do not oppose the plan, they may fix a maximum period for its implementation.

2. If the person proposing to acquire the holdings referred to in paragraph 1 is a credit institution, insurance undertaking or investment firm authorised in another Member State or the parent undertaking of a credit institution, insurance undertaking or investment firm authorised in another Member State or a natural or legal person controlling a credit institution, insurance undertaking or investment firm authorised in another Member State, and if, as a

result of that acquisition, the credit institution in which the acquirer proposes to hold a holding would become a subsidiary or subject to the control of the acquirer, the assessment of the acquisition shall be subject to the prior consultation provided for in Article 15.

[9842]

Article 20

The Member States shall require any natural or legal person who proposes to dispose, directly or indirectly, of a qualifying holding in a credit institution first to inform the competent authorities, telling them of the size of his intended holding. Such a person shall likewise inform the competent authorities if he proposes to reduce his qualifying holding so that the proportion of the voting rights or of the capital held by him would fall below 20%, 33% or 50% or so that the credit institution would cease to be his subsidiary.

[9843]

Article 21

1. Credit institutions shall, on becoming aware of any acquisitions or disposals of holdings in their capital that cause holdings to exceed or fall below one of the thresholds referred to in Article 19(1) and Article 20, inform the competent authorities of those acquisitions or disposals.

They shall also, at least once a year, inform the competent authorities of the names of shareholders and members possessing qualifying holdings and the sizes of such holdings as shown, for example, by the information received at the annual general meetings of shareholders and members or as a result of compliance with the regulations relating to companies listed on stock exchanges.

2. The Member States shall require that, where the influence exercised by the persons referred to in Article 19(1) is likely to operate to the detriment of the prudent and sound management of the institution, the competent authorities shall take appropriate measures to put an end to that situation. Such measures may consist in injunctions, sanctions against directors and managers, or the suspension of the exercise of the voting rights attaching to the shares held by the shareholders or members in question.

Similar measures shall apply to natural or legal persons who fail to comply with the obligation to provide prior information, as laid down in Article 19(1).

If a holding is acquired despite the opposition of the competent authorities, the Member States shall, regardless of any other sanctions to be adopted, provide either for exercise of the corresponding voting rights to be suspended, or for the nullity of votes cast or for the possibility of their annulment.

3. In determining a qualifying holding and other levels of holding referred to in this Article, the voting rights referred to in Article 92 of Directive 2001/34/EC shall be taken into consideration.

[9844]

Article 22

1. Home Member State competent authorities shall require that every credit institution have robust governance arrangements, which include a clear organisational structure with well defined, transparent and consistent lines of responsibility, effective processes to identify, manage, monitor and report the risks it is or might be exposed to, and adequate internal control mechanisms, including sound administrative and accounting procedures.

2. The arrangements, processes and mechanisms referred to in paragraph 1 shall be comprehensive and proportionate to the nature, scale and complexity of the credit institution's activities. The technical criteria laid down in Annex V shall be taken into account.

[9845]

TITLE III
PROVISIONS CONCERNING THE FREEDOM OF ESTABLISHMENT AND THE FREEDOM TO PROVIDE SERVICES

SECTION 1
CREDIT INSTITUTIONS

Article 23

The Member States shall provide that the activities listed in Annex I may be carried on within their territories, in accordance with Articles 25, 26(1) to (3), 28(1) and (2) and 29 to 37 either by the establishment of a branch or by way of the provision of services, by any credit institution authorised and supervised by the competent authorities of another Member State, provided that such activities are covered by the authorisation.

[9846]

SECTION 2
FINANCIAL INSTITUTIONS

Article 24

1. The Member States shall provide that the activities listed in Annex I may be carried on within their territories, in accordance with Articles 25, 26(1) to (3), 28(1) and (2) and 29 to 37 either by the establishment of a branch or by way of the provision of services, by any financial institution from another Member State, whether a subsidiary of a credit institution or the jointly-owned subsidiary of two or more credit institutions, the memorandum and Article of association of which permit the carrying on of those activities and which fulfils each of the following conditions:

(a) the parent undertaking or undertakings shall be authorised as credit institutions in the Member State by the law of which the financial institution is governed;

(b) the activities in question shall actually be carried on within the territory of the same Member State;

(c) the parent undertaking or undertakings shall hold 90% or more of the voting rights attaching to shares in the capital of the financial institution;

(d) the parent undertaking or undertakings shall satisfy the competent authorities regarding the prudent management of the financial institution and shall have declared, with the consent of the relevant home Member State competent authorities, that they jointly and severally guarantee the commitments entered into by the financial institution; and

(e) the financial institution shall be effectively included, for the activities in question in particular, in the consolidated supervision of the parent undertaking, or of each of the parent undertakings, in accordance with Title V, Chapter 4, Section 1, in particular for the purposes of the minimum own funds requirements set out in Article 75 for the control of large exposures and for purposes of the limitation of holdings provided for in Articles 120 to 122.

Compliance with these conditions shall be verified by the competent authorities of the home Member State and the latter shall supply the financial institution with a certificate of compliance which shall form Part of the notification referred to in Articles 25 and 28.

The competent authorities of the home Member State shall ensure the supervision of the financial institution in accordance with Articles 10(1), 19 to 22, 40, 42 to 52 and 54.

2. If a financial institution as referred to in the first subparagraph of paragraph 1 ceases to fulfil any of the conditions imposed, the home Member State shall notify the competent authorities of the host Member State and the activities carried on by that financial institution in the host Member State shall become subject to the legislation of the host Member State.

3. Paragraphs 1 and 2 shall apply mutatis mutandis to subsidiaries of a financial institution as referred to in the first subparagraph of paragraph 1.

[9847]

SECTION 3
EXERCISE OF THE RIGHT OF ESTABLISHMENT

Article 25

1. A credit institution wishing to establish a branch within the territory of another Member State shall notify the competent authorities of its home Member State.

2. Member States shall require every credit institution wishing to establish a branch in another Member State to provide the following information when effecting the notification referred to in paragraph 1:

(a) the Member State within the territory of which it plans to establish a branch;
(b) a programme of operations setting out, inter alia, the types of business envisaged and the structural organisation of the branch;
(c) the address in the host Member State from which documents may be obtained; and
(d) the names of those to be responsible for the management of the branch.

3. Unless the competent authorities of the home Member State have reason to doubt the adequacy of the administrative structure or the financial situation of the credit institution, taking into account the activities envisaged, they shall within three months of receipt of the information referred to in paragraph 2 communicate that information to the competent authorities of the host Member State and shall inform the credit institution accordingly.

The home Member State's competent authorities shall also communicate the amount of own funds and the sum of the capital requirements under Article 75 of the credit institution.

By way of derogation from the second subparagraph, in the case referred to in Article 24, the home Member State's competent authorities shall communicate the amount of own funds of the financial institution and the sum of the consolidated own funds and consolidated capital requirements under Article 75 of the credit institution which is its parent undertaking.

4. Where the competent authorities of the home Member State refuse to communicate the information referred to in paragraph 2 to the competent authorities of the host Member State, they shall give reasons for their refusal to the credit institution concerned within three months of receipt of all the information.

That refusal or a failure to reply, shall be subject to a right to apply to the courts in the home Member State.

[9848]

Article 26

1. Before the branch of a credit institution commences its activities the competent authorities of the host Member State shall, within two months of receiving the information referred to in Article 25, prepare for the supervision of the credit institution in accordance with Section 5 and if necessary indicate the conditions under which, in the interest of the general good, those activities shall be carried on in the host Member State.

2. On receipt of a communication from the competent authorities of the host Member State, or in the event of the expiry of the period provided for in paragraph 1 without receipt of any communication from the latter, the branch may be established and may commence its activities.

3. In the event of a change in any of the particulars communicated pursuant to points (b), (c) or (d) of Article 25(2), a credit institution shall give written notice of the change in question to the competent authorities of the home and host Member States at least one month before making the change so as to enable the competent authorities of the home Member State to take a decision pursuant to Article 25 and the competent authorities of the host Member State to take a decision on the change pursuant to paragraph 1 of this Article.

4. Branches which have commenced their activities, in accordance with the provisions in force in their host Member States, before 1 January 1993, shall be presumed to have been subject to the procedure laid down in Article 25 and in paragraphs 1 and 2 of this Article. They shall be governed, from 1 January 1993, by paragraph 3 of this Article and by Articles 23 and 43 as well as Sections 2 and 5.

[9849]

Article 27

Any number of places of business set up in the same Member State by a credit institution with headquarters in another Member State shall be regarded as a single branch.

[9850]

SECTION 4
EXERCISE OF THE FREEDOM TO PROVIDE SERVICES

Article 28

1. Any credit institution wishing to exercise the freedom to provide services by carrying on its activities within the territory of another Member State for the first time shall notify the competent authorities of the home Member State, of the activities on the list in Annex I which it intends to carry on.

2. The competent authorities of the home Member State shall, within one month of receipt of the notification provided for in paragraph 1, send that notification to the competent authorities of the host Member State.

3. This Article shall not affect rights acquired by credit institutions providing services before 1 January 1993.

[9851]

SECTION 5
POWERS OF THE COMPETENT AUTHORITIES OF THE HOST MEMBER STATE

Article 29

Host Member States may, for statistical purposes, require that all credit institutions having branches within their territories shall report periodically on their activities in those host Member States to the competent authorities of those host Member States.

In discharging the responsibilities imposed on them in Article 41, host Member States may require that branches of credit institutions from other Member States provide the same information as they require from national credit institutions for that purpose.

[9852]

Article 30

1. Where the competent authorities of a host Member State ascertain that a credit institution having a branch or providing services within its territory is not complying with the legal provisions adopted in that State pursuant to the provisions of this Directive involving powers of the host Member State's competent authorities, those authorities shall require the credit institution concerned to put an end to that irregular situation.

2. If the credit institution concerned fails to take the necessary steps, the competent authorities of the host Member State shall inform the competent authorities of the home Member State accordingly.

The competent authorities of the home Member State shall, at the earliest opportunity, take all appropriate measures to ensure that the credit institution concerned puts an end to that irregular situation. The nature of those measures shall be communicated to the competent authorities of the host Member State.

3. If, despite the measures taken by the home Member State or because such measures prove inadequate or are not available in the Member State in question, the credit institution persists in violating the legal rules referred to in paragraph 1 in force in the host Member State, the latter State may, after informing the competent authorities of the home Member State, take appropriate measures to prevent or to punish further irregularities and, in so far as is necessary, to prevent that credit institution from initiating further transactions within its territory. The Member States shall ensure that within their territories it is possible to serve the legal documents necessary for these measures on credit institutions.

[9853]

Article 31

Articles 29 and 30 shall not affect the power of host Member States to take appropriate measures to prevent or to punish irregularities committed within their territories which are contrary to the legal rules they have adopted in the interests of the general good. This shall include the possibility of preventing offending credit institutions from initiating further transactions within their territories.

[9854]

Article 32

Any measure taken pursuant to Article 30(2) and (3), or Article 31 involving penalties or restrictions on the exercise of the freedom to provide services shall be properly justified and communicated to the credit institution concerned. Every such measure shall be subject to a right of appeal to the courts in the Member State in which it was taken.

[9855]

Article 33

Before following the procedure provided for in Article 30, the competent authorities of the host Member State may, in emergencies, take any precautionary measures necessary to protect the interests of depositors, investors and others to whom services are provided. The Commission and the competent authorities of the other Member States concerned shall be informed of such measures at the earliest opportunity.

The Commission may, after consulting the competent authorities of the Member States concerned, decide that the Member State in question shall amend or abolish those measures.

[9856]

Article 34

Host Member States may exercise the powers conferred on them under this Directive by taking appropriate measures to prevent or to punish irregularities committed within their territories. This shall include the possibility of preventing offending credit institutions from initiating further transactions within their territories.

[9857]

Article 35

In the event of the withdrawal of authorisation, the competent authorities of the host Member State shall be informed and shall take appropriate measures to prevent the credit institution concerned from initiating further transactions within its territory and to safeguard the interests of depositors.

[9858]

Article 36

The Member States shall inform the Commission of the number and type of cases in which there has been a refusal pursuant to Articles 25 and 26(1) to (3) or in which measures have been taken in accordance with Article 30(3).

[9859]

Article 37

This Section shall not prevent credit institutions with head offices in other Member States from advertising their services through all available means of communication in the host Member State, subject to any rules governing the form and the content of such advertising adopted in the interests of the general good.

[9860]

TITLE IV
RELATIONS WITH THIRD COUNTRIES

SECTION 1
NOTIFICATION IN RELATION TO THIRD COUNTRIES' UNDERTAKINGS AND CONDITIONS OF ACCESS TO THE MARKETS OF THESE COUNTRIES

Article 38

1. Member States shall not apply to branches of credit institutions having their head office outside the Community, when commencing or carrying on their business, provisions which result in more favourable treatment than that accorded to branches of credit institutions having their head office in the Community.

2. The competent authorities shall notify the Commission and the European Banking Committee of all authorisations for branches granted to credit institutions having their head office outside the Community.

3. Without prejudice to paragraph 1, the Community may, through agreements concluded with one or more third countries, agree to apply provisions which accord to branches of a credit institution having its head office outside the Community identical treatment throughout the territory of the Community.

[9861]

SECTION 2
COOPERATION WITH THIRD COUNTRIES' COMPETENT AUTHORITIES REGARDING SUPERVISION ON A CONSOLIDATED BASIS

Article 39

1. The Commission may submit proposals to the Council, either at the request of a Member State or on its own initiative, for the negotiation of agreements with one or more third countries regarding the means of exercising supervision on a consolidated basis over the following:

(a) credit institutions the parent undertakings of which have their head offices in a third country; or

(b) credit institutions situated in third countries the parent undertakings of which, whether credit institutions or financial holding companies, have their head offices in the Community.

2. The agreements referred to in paragraph 1 shall, in particular, seek to ensure the following:

(a) that the competent authorities of the Member States are able to obtain the information necessary for the supervision, on the basis of their consolidated financial situations, of credit institutions or financial holding companies situated in the Community and which have as subsidiaries credit institutions or financial institutions situated outside the Community, or holding participation in such institutions; and

(b) that the competent authorities of third countries are able to obtain the information necessary for the supervision of parent undertakings the head offices of which are situated within their territories and which have as subsidiaries credit institutions or financial institutions situated in one or more Member States or holding participation in such institutions.

3. Without prejudice to Article 300(1) and (2) of the Treaty, the Commission shall, with the assistance of the European Banking Committee, examine the outcome of the negotiations referred to in paragraph 1 and the resulting situation.

[9862]

TITLE V
PRINCIPLES AND TECHNICAL INSTRUMENTS FOR PRUDENTIAL SUPERVISION AND DISCLOSURE

CHAPTER 1
PRINCIPLES OF PRUDENTIAL SUPERVISION

SECTION 1
COMPETENCE OF HOME AND HOST MEMBER STATE

Article 40

1. The prudential supervision of a credit institution, including that of the activities it carries on accordance with Articles 23 and 24, shall be the responsibility of the competent authorities of the home Member State, without prejudice to those provisions of this Directive which give responsibility to the competent authorities of the host Member State.

2. Paragraph 1 shall not prevent supervision on a consolidated basis pursuant to this Directive.

[9863]

Article 41

Host Member States shall, pending further coordination, retain responsibility in cooperation with the competent authorities of the home Member State for the supervision of the liquidity of the branches of credit institutions.

Without prejudice to the measures necessary for the reinforcement of the European Monetary System, host Member States shall retain complete responsibility for the measures resulting from the implementation of their monetary policies.

Such measures may not provide for discriminatory or restrictive treatment based on the fact that a credit institution is authorised in another Member State.

[9864]

Article 42

The competent authorities of the Member States concerned shall collaborate closely in order to supervise the activities of credit institutions operating, in particular through a branch, in one or more Member States other than that in which their head offices are situated. They shall supply one another with all information concerning the management and ownership of such credit institutions that is likely to facilitate their supervision and the examination of the conditions for their authorisation, and all information likely to facilitate the monitoring of such institutions, in particular with regard to liquidity, solvency, deposit guarantees, the limiting of large exposures, administrative and accounting procedures and internal control mechanisms.

[9865]

Article 43

1. Host Member States shall provide that, where a credit institution authorised in another Member State carries on its activities through a branch, the competent authorities of the home Member State may, after having first informed the competent authorities of the host Member State, carry out themselves or through the intermediary of persons they appoint for that purpose on-the-spot verification of the information referred to in Article 42.

2. The competent authorities of the home Member State may also, for purposes of the verification of branches, have recourse to one of the other procedures laid down in Article 141.

3. Paragraphs 1 and 2 shall not affect the right of the competent authorities of the host Member State to carry out, in the discharge of their responsibilities under this Directive, on-the-spot verifications of branches established within their territory.

[9866]

SECTION 2
EXCHANGE OF INFORMATION AND PROFESSIONAL SECRECY

Article 44

1. Member States shall provide that all persons working for or who have worked for the competent authorities, as well as auditors or experts acting on behalf of the competent authorities, shall be bound by the obligation of professional secrecy.

No confidential information which they may receive in the course of their duties may be divulged to any person or authority whatsoever, except in summary or collective form, such that individual credit institutions cannot be identified, without prejudice to cases covered by criminal law.

Nevertheless, where a credit institution has been declared bankrupt or is being compulsorily wound up, confidential information which does not concern third parties involved in attempts to rescue that credit institution may be divulged in civil or commercial proceedings.

2. Paragraph 1 shall not prevent the competent authorities of the various Member States from exchanging information in accordance with this Directive and with other Directives applicable to credit institutions. That information shall be subject to the conditions of professional secrecy indicated in paragraph 1.

[9867]

Article 45

Competent authorities receiving confidential information under Article 44 may use it only in the course of their duties and only for the following purposes:

(a) to check that the conditions governing the taking-up of the business of credit institutions are met and to facilitate monitoring, on a non-consolidated or consolidated basis, of the conduct of such business, especially with regard to the monitoring of liquidity, solvency, large exposures, and administrative and accounting procedures and internal control mechanisms;

(b) to impose penalties;
(c) in an administrative appeal against a decision of the competent authority; or
(d) in court proceedings initiated pursuant to Article 55 or to special provisions provided for in this in other Directives adopted in the field of credit institutions.

[9868]

Article 46

Member States may conclude cooperation agreements, providing for exchanges of information, with the competent authorities of third countries or with authorities or bodies of third countries as defined in Articles 47 and 48(1) only if the information disclosed is subject to guarantees of professional secrecy at least equivalent to those referred to in Article 44(1). Such exchange of information shall be for the purpose of performing the supervisory task of the authorities or bodies mentioned.

Where the information originates in another Member State, it may not be disclosed without the express agreement of the competent authorities which have disclosed it and, where appropriate, solely for the purposes for which those authorities gave their agreement.

[9869]

Article 47

Articles 44(1) and 45 shall not preclude the exchange of information within a Member State, where there are two or more competent authorities in the same Member State, or between Member States, between competent authorities and the following:
(a) authorities entrusted with the public duty of supervising other financial organisations and insurance companies and the authorities responsible for the supervision of financial markets;
(b) bodies involved in the liquidation and bankruptcy of credit institutions and in other similar procedures; and
(c) persons responsible for carrying out statutory audits of the accounts of credit institutions and other financial institutions;

in the discharge of their supervisory functions.

Articles 44(1) and 45 shall not preclude the disclosure to bodies which administer deposit-guarantee schemes of information necessary to the exercise of their functions.

In both cases, the information received shall be subject to the conditions of professional secrecy specified in Article 44(1).

[9870]

Article 48

1. Notwithstanding Articles 44 to 46, Member States may authorise exchange of information between the competent authorities and the following:
(a) the authorities responsible for overseeing the bodies involved in the liquidation and bankruptcy of credit institutions and in other similar procedures; and
(b) the authorities responsible for overseeing persons charged with carrying out statutory audits of the accounts of insurance undertakings, credit institutions, investment firms and other financial institutions.

In such cases, Member States shall require fulfilment of at least the following conditions:
(a) the information shall be for the purpose of performing the supervisory task referred to in the first subparagraph;
(b) information received in this context shall be subject to the conditions of professional secrecy specified in Article 44(1); and
(c) where the information originates in another Member State, it may not be disclosed without the express agreement of the competent authorities which have disclosed it and, where appropriate, solely for the purposes for which those authorities gave their agreement.

Member States shall communicate to the Commission and to the other Member States the names of the authorities which may receive information pursuant to this paragraph.

2. Notwithstanding Articles 44 to 46, Member States may, with the aim of strengthening the stability, including integrity, of the financial system, authorise the exchange of information between the competent authorities and the authorities or bodies responsible under law for the detection and investigation of breaches of company law.

In such cases Member States shall require fulfilment of at least the following conditions:

- (a) the information is for the purpose of performing the task referred to in the first subparagraph;
- (b) information received in this context is subject to the conditions of professional secrecy specified in Article 44(1); and
- (c) where the information originates in another Member State, it may not be disclosed without the express agreement of the competent authorities which have disclosed it and, where appropriate, solely for the purposes for which those authorities gave their agreement.

Where, in a Member State, the authorities or bodies referred to in the first subparagraph perform their task of detection or investigation with the aid, in view of their specific competence, of persons appointed for that purpose and not employed in the public sector, the possibility of exchanging information provided for in the first subparagraph may be extended to such persons under the conditions specified in the second subparagraph.

In order to implement the third subparagraph, the authorities or bodies referred to in the first subparagraph shall communicate to the competent authorities which have disclosed the information, the names and precise responsibilities of the persons to whom it is to be sent.

Member States shall communicate to the Commission and to the other Member States the names of the authorities or bodies which may receive information pursuant to this Article.

The Commission shall draw up a report on the application of the provisions of this Article.

[9871]

Article 49

This Section shall not prevent a competent authority from transmitting information to the following for the purposes of their tasks:

- (a) central banks and other bodies with a similar function in their capacity as monetary authorities; and
- (b) where appropriate, to other public authorities responsible for overseeing payment systems.

This Section shall not prevent such authorities or bodies from communicating to the competent authorities such information as they may need for the purposes of Article 45.

Information received in this context shall be subject to the conditions of professional secrecy specified in Article 44(1).

[9872]

Article 50

Notwithstanding Articles 44(1) and 45, the Member States may, by virtue of provisions laid down by law, authorise the disclosure of certain information to other departments of their central government administrations responsible for legislation on the supervision of credit institutions, financial institutions, investment services and insurance companies and to inspectors acting on behalf of those departments.

However, such disclosures may be made only where necessary for reasons of prudential control.

[9873]

Article 51

The Member States shall provide that information received under Articles 44(2) and 47 and information obtained by means of the on-the-spot verification referred to in Article 43(1) and (2) may never be disclosed in the cases referred to in Article 50 except with the express consent of the competent authorities which disclosed the information or of the competent authorities of the Member State in which on-the-spot verification was carried out.

[9874]

Article 52

This Section shall not prevent the competent authorities of a Member State from communicating the information referred to in Articles 44 to 46 to a clearing house or other similar body recognised under national law for the provision of clearing or settlement services for one of their national markets if they consider that it is necessary to communicate the information in order to ensure the proper functioning of those bodies in relation to defaults or potential defaults by market participants. The information received in this context shall be subject to the conditions of professional secrecy specified in Article 44(1).

The Member States shall, however, ensure that information received under Article 44(2) may not be disclosed in the circumstances referred to in this Article without the express consent of the competent authorities which disclosed it.

[9875]

SECTION 3
DUTY OF PERSONS RESPONSIBLE FOR THE LEGAL CONTROL OF ANNUAL AND CONSOLIDATED ACCOUNTS

Article 53

1. Member States shall provide at least that any person authorised within the meaning of Directive 84/253/EEC[1] performing in a credit institution the task described in Article 51 of Directive 78/660/EEC, Article 37 of Directive 83/349/EEC or Article 31 of Directive 85/611/EEC,[2] or any other statutory task, shall have a duty to report promptly to the competent authorities any fact or decision concerning that credit institution of which he has become aware while carrying out that task which is liable to:

(a) constitute a material breach of the laws, regulations or administrative provisions which lay down the conditions governing authorisation or which specifically govern pursuit of the activities of credit institutions;

(b) affect the continuous functioning of the credit institution; or

(c) lead to refusal to certify the accounts or to the expression of reservations.

Member States shall provide at least that that person shall likewise have a duty to report any fact or decision of which he becomes aware in the course of carrying out a task as described in the first sub-paragraph in an undertaking having close links resulting from a control relationship with the credit institution within which he is carrying out that task.

2. The disclosure in good faith to the competent authorities, by persons authorised within the meaning of Directive 84/253/EEC, of any fact or decision referred to in paragraph 1 shall not constitute a breach of any restriction on disclosure of information imposed by contract or by any legislative, regulatory or administrative provision and shall not involve such persons in liability of any kind.

[9876]

NOTES

1 Eighth Council Directive 84/253/EEC of 10 April 1984 on the approval of persons responsible for carrying out the statutory audits of accounting documents (OJ L126, 12.5.1984, p 20).

2 Council Directive 85/611/EEC of 20 December 1985 on the coordination of laws, regulations and administrative provisions relating to undertakings for collective investment in transferable securities (UCITS) (OJ L375, 31.12.1985, p 3). Directive as last amended by Directive 2005/1/EC.

SECTION 4
POWER OF SANCTION AND RIGHT TO APPLY TO THE COURTS

Article 54

Without prejudice to the procedures for the withdrawal of authorisations and the provisions of criminal law, the Member States shall provide that their respective competent authorities may, as against credit institutions, or those who effectively control the business of credit institutions, which breach laws, regulations or administrative provisions concerning the supervision or pursuit of their activities, adopt or impose penalties or measures aimed specifically at ending the observed breaches or the causes of such breaches.

[9877]

Article 55

Member States shall ensure that decisions taken in respect of a credit institution in pursuance of laws, regulations and administrative provisions adopted in accordance with this Directive may be subject to the right to apply to the courts. The same shall apply where no decision is taken, within six months of its submission, in respect of an application for authorisation which contains all the information required under the provisions in force.

[9878]

TITLE VII
TRANSITIONAL AND FINAL PROVISIONS

CHAPTER 1
TRANSITIONAL PROVISIONS

Article 152

1. Credit institutions calculating risk-weighted exposure amounts in accordance with Articles 84 to 89 shall during the first, second and third twelve-month periods after 31 December 2006 provide own funds which are at all times more than or equal to the amounts indicated in paragraphs 3, 4 and 5.

2. Credit institutions using the Advanced Measurement Approaches as specified in Article 105 for the calculation of their capital requirements for operational risk shall, during the second and third twelve-month periods after 31 December 2006, provide own funds which are at all times more than or equal to the amounts indicated in paragraphs 4 and 5.

3. For the first twelve-month period referred to in paragraph 1, the amount of own funds shall be 95% of the total minimum amount of own funds that would be required to be held during that period by the credit institution under Article 4 of Council Directive 93/6/EEC of 15 March 1993 on the capital adequacy of investment firms and credit institutions[1] as that Directive and Directive 2000/12/EC stood prior to 1 January 2007.

4. For the second twelve-month period referred to in paragraph 1, the amount of own funds shall be 90% of the total minimum amount of own funds that would be required to be held during that period by the credit institution under Article 4 of Directive 93/6/EEC as that Directive and Directive 2000/12/EC stood prior to 1 January 2007.

5. For the third twelve-month period referred to in paragraph 1, the amount of own funds shall be 80% of the total minimum amount of own funds that would be required to be held during that period by the credit institution under Article 4 of Directive 93/6/EEC as that Directive and Directive 2000/12/EC stood prior .to 1 January 2007.

6. Compliance with the requirements of paragraphs 1 to 5 shall be on the basis of amounts of own funds fully adjusted to reflect differences in the calculation of own funds under Directive 2000/12/EC and Directive 93/6/EEC as those Directives stood prior to 1 January 2007 and the calculation of own funds under this Directive deriving from the separate treatments of expected loss and unexpected loss under Articles 84 to 89 of this Directive.

7. For the purposes of paragraphs 1 to 6 of this Article, Articles 68 to 73 shall apply.

8. Until 1 January 2008 credit institutions may treat the Articles constituting the Standardised Approach set out in Title V, Chapter 2, Section 3, Subsection 1 as being replaced by Articles 42 to 46 of Directive 2000/12/EC as those Articles stood prior to 1 January 2007.

9. Where the discretion referred to in paragraph 8 is exercised, the following shall apply concerning the provisions of Directive 2000/12/EC:

- (a) the provisions of that Directive referred to in Articles 42 to 46 shall apply as they stood prior to 1 January 2007;
- (b) "risk-adjusted value" as referred to in Article 42(1) of that Directive shall mean "risk-weighted exposure amount";
- (c) the figures produced by Article 42(2) of that Directive shall be considered risk-weighted exposure amounts;
- (d) "credit derivatives" shall be included in the list of "Full risk" items in Annex II of that Directive; and
- (e) the treatment set out in Article 43(3) of that Directive shall apply to derivative instruments listed in Annex IV of that Directive whether on- or off-balance sheet and the figures produced by the treatment set out in Annex III shall be considered risk-weighted exposure amounts.

10. Where the discretion referred to in paragraph 8 is exercised, the following shall apply in relation to the treatment of exposures for which the Standardised Approach is used:

(a) Title V, Chapter 2, Section 3, Subsection 3 relating to the recognition of credit risk mitigation shall not apply;

(b) Title V, Chapter 2, Section 3, Subsection 4 concerning the treatment of securitisation may be disapplied by competent authorities.

11. Where the discretion referred to in paragraph 8 is exercised, the capital requirement for operational risk under Article 75(d) shall be reduced by the percentage representing the ratio of the value of the credit institution's exposures for which risk-weighted exposure amounts are calculated in accordance with the discretion referred to in paragraph 8 to the total value of its exposures.

12. Where a credit institution calculates risk-weighted exposure amounts for all of its exposures in accordance with the discretion referred to in paragraph 8, Articles 48 to 50 of Directive 2000/12/EC relating to large exposures may apply as they stood prior to 1 January 2007.

13. Where the discretion referred to in paragraph 8 is exercised, references to Articles 78 to 83 of this Directive shall be read as references to Articles 42 to 46 of Directive 2000/12/EC as those Articles stood prior to 1 January 2007.

14. If the discretion referred to in paragraph 8 is exercised, Articles 123, 124, 145 and 149 shall not apply before the date referred to therein.

[9878A]

NOTES

[1] OJ L141, 11.6.1993, p 1. Directive as last amended by 2005/1/EC.

Article 153

In the calculation of risk-weighted exposure amounts for exposures arising from property leasing transactions concerning offices or other commercial premises situated in their territory and meeting the criteria set out in Annex VI, Part 1, point 54, the competent authorities may, until 31 December 2012 allow a 50% risk weight to be assigned without the application of Annex VI, Part 1, points 55 and 56.

Until 31 December 2010, competent authorities may, for the purpose of defining the secured portion of a past due loan for the purposes of Annex VI, recognise collateral other than eligible collateral as set out under Articles 90 to 93.

In the calculation of risk weighted exposure amounts for the purposes of Annex VI, Part 1, point 4, until 31 December 2012 the same risk weight shall be assigned in relation to exposures to Member States' central governments or central banks denominated and funded in the domestic currency of any Member State as would be applied to such exposures denominated and funded in their domestic currency.

[9878B]

Article 154

1. Until 31 December 2011, the competent authorities of each Member State may, for the purposes of Annex VI, Part 1, point 61, set the number of days past due up to a figure of 180 for exposures indicated in Annex VI, Part 1, points 12 to 17 and 41 to 43, to counterparties situated in their territory, if local conditions make it appropriate. The specific number may differ across product lines.

Competent authorities which do not exercise the discretion provided for in the first subparagraph in relation to exposures to counterparties situated in their territory may set a higher number of days for exposures to counterparties situated in the territories of other Member States, the competent authorities of which have exercised that discretion. The specific number shall fall within 90 days and such figures as the other competent authorities have set for exposures to such counterparties within their territory.

2. For credit institutions applying for the use of the IRB Approach before 2010, subject to the approval of the competent authorities, the three-years' use requirement prescribed in Article 84(3) may be reduced to a period no shorter than one year until 31 December 2009.

3. For credit institutions applying for the use of own estimates of LGDs and/or conversion factors, the three year use requirement prescribed in Article 84(4) may be reduced to two years until 31 December 2008.

4. Until 31 December 2012, the competent authorities of each Member State may allow credit institutions to continue to apply to participations of the type set out in Article 57(o) acquired before 20 July 2006 the treatment set out in Article 38 of Directive 2000/12/EC as that article stood prior to 1 January 2007.

5. Until 31 December 2010 the exposure weighted average LGD for all retail exposures secured by residential properties and not benefiting from guarantees from central governments shall not be lower than 10%.

6. Until 31 December 2017, the competent authorities of the Member States may exempt from the IRB treatment certain equity exposures held by credit institutions and EU subsidiaries of credit institutions in that Member State at 31 December 2007.

The exempted position shall be measured as the number of shares as of 31 December 2007 and any additional share arising directly as a result of owning those holdings, as long as they do not increase the proportional share of ownership in a portfolio company.

If an acquisition increases the proportional share of ownership in a specific holding the exceeding Part of the holding shall not be subject to the exemption. Nor shall the exemption apply to holdings that were originally subject to the exemption, but have been sold and then bought back.

Equity exposures covered by this transitional provision shall be subject to the capital requirements calculated in accordance with Title V, Chapter 2, Section 3, Subsection 1.

7. Until 31 December 2011, for corporate exposures, the competent authorities of each Member State may set the number of days past due that all credit institutions in its jurisdiction shall abide by under the definition of "default" set out in Annex VII, Part 4, point 44 for exposures to such counterparts situated within this Member State. The specific number shall fall within 90 up to a figure of 180 days if local conditions make it appropriate. For exposures to such counterparts situated in the territories of other Member States, the competent authorities shall set a number of days past due which is not higher than the number set by the competent authority of the respective Member State.

[9878C]

Article 155

Until 31 December 2012, for credit institutions the relevant indicator for the trading and sales business line of which represents at least 50% of the total of the relevant indicators for all of its business lines accordance with Annex X, Part 2, points 1 to 4, Member States may apply a percentage of 15% to the business line "trading and sales".

[9878D]

CHAPTER 2
FINAL PROVISIONS

Article 156

The Commission, in cooperation with Member States, and taking into account the contribution of the European Central Bank, shall periodically monitor whether this Directive taken as a whole, together with Directive 2006/49/EC, has significant effects on the economic cycle and, in the light of that examination, shall consider whether any remedial measures are justified.

Based on that analysis and taking into account the contribution of the European Central Bank, the Commission shall draw up a biennial report and submit it to the European Parliament and to the Council, together with any appropriate proposals. Contributions from credit taking and credit lending parties shall be adequately acknowledged when the report is drawn up.

By 1 January 2012 the Commission shall, review and report on the application of this Directive with particular attention to all aspects of Articles 68 to 73, 80(7), 80(8) and 129, and shall submit this report to the Parliament and the Council together with any appropriate proposals.

[9879]

Article 157

1. By 31 December 2006 Member States shall adopt and publish the laws, regulations and administrative provisions necessary to comply with Articles 4, 22, 57, 61 to 64, 66, 68

to 106, 108, 110 to 115, 117 to 119, 123 to 127, 129 to 132, 133, 136, 144 to 149 and 152 to 155, and Annexes II, III and V to XII. They shall forthwith communicate to the Commission the text of those provisions and a correlation table between those provisions and this Directive.

Notwithstanding paragraph 3, Member States shall apply those provisions from 1 January 2007.

When Member States adopt those provisions, they shall contain a reference to this Directive or be accompanied by such a reference on the occasion of their official publication. They shall also include a statement that references in existing laws, regulations and administrative provisions to the directives repealed by this Directive shall be construed as references to this Directive. Member States shall determine how such reference is to be made and how that statement is to be formulated.

2. Member States shall communicate to the Commission the text of the main provisions of national law which they adopt in the field covered by this Directive.

3. Member States shall apply, from 1 January 2008, and no earlier, the laws regulations and administrative provisions necessary to comply with Articles 87(9) and 105.

[9880]

Article 158

1. Directive 2000/12/EC as amended by the Directives set out in Annex XIII, Part A, is hereby repealed without prejudice to the obligations of the Member States concerning the deadlines for transposition of the said Directives listed in Annex XIII, Part B.

2. References to the repealed Directives shall be construed as being made to this Directive and should be read in accordance with the correlation table in Annex XIV.

[9881]

Article 159

This Directive shall enter into force on the 20th day following its publication in the Official Journal of the European Union.

[9882]

Article 160

This Directive is addressed to the Member States.

[9883]

Done at Strasbourg, 14 June 2006.

ANNEX I

LIST OF ACTIVITIES SUBJECT TO MUTUAL RECOGNITION

1. Acceptance of deposits and other repayable funds

2. Lending including, inter alia: consumer credit, mortgage credit, factoring, with or without recourse, financing of commercial transactions (including forfeiting)

3. Financial leasing

4. Money transmission services

5. Issuing and administering means of payment (e g credit cards, travellers' cheques and bankers' drafts)

6. Guarantees and commitments

7. Trading for own account or for account of customers in:
   (a) money market instruments (cheques, bills, certificates of deposit, etc.);
   (b) foreign exchange;
   (c) financial futures and options;
   (d) exchange and interest-rate instruments; or
   (e) transferable securities.

8. Participation in securities issues and the provision of services related to such issues

9. Advice to undertakings on capital structure, industrial strategy and related questions and advice as well as services relating to mergers and the purchase of undertakings

10. Money broking
11. Portfolio management and advice
12. Safekeeping and administration of securities
13. Credit reference services
14. Safe custody services

The services and activities provided for in Sections A and B of Annex I to Directive 2004/39/EC of the European Parliament and of the Council of 21 April 2004 on markets in financial instruments,[1] when referring to the financial instruments provided for in Section C of Annex I of that Directive, are subject to mutual recognition according to this Directive.

[9884]

NOTES

[1] OJ L145, 30.4.2004, p 1. Directive as amended by Directive 2006/31/EC (OJ L114, 27.4.2006, p 60).

ANNEX XIII

PART A
REPEALED DIRECTIVES TOGETHER WITH THEIR SUCCESSIVE AMENDMENTS (REFERRED TO IN ARTICLE 158)

Directive 2000/12/EC of the European Parliament and of the Council of 20 March 2000 relating to the taking up and pursuit of the business of credit institutions

Directive 2000/28/EC of the European Parliament and of the Council of 18 September 2000 amending Directive 2000/12/EC relating to the taking up and pursuit of the business of credit institutions

Directive 2002/87/EC of the European Parliament and of the Council of 16 December 2002 on the supplementary supervision of credit institutions, insurance undertakings and investment firms in a financial conglomerate and amending Council Directives 73/239/EEC, 79/267/EEC, 92/49/EEC, 92/96/EEC, 93/6/EEC and 93/22/EEC, and Directives 98/78/EC and 2000/12/EC of the European Parliament and of the Council

Only Art 29.1(a)(b), Art 29.2, Art 29.4(a)(b), Art 29.5, Art 29.6, Art 29.7, Art 29.8, Art 29.9, Art 29.10, Art 29.11

Directive 2004/39/EC of the European Parliament and of the Council of 21 April 2004 on markets in financial instruments amending Council Directives 85/611/EEC and 93/6/EEC and Directive 2000/12/EC of the European Parliament and of the Council and repealing Council Directive 93/22/EEC

Only Art 68

Commission Directive 2004/69/EC of 27 April 2004 amending Directive 2000/12/EC of the European Parliament and of the Council as regards the definition of "multilateral development banks"

Directive 2005/1/EC of the European Parliament and of the Council of 9 March 2005 amending Council Directives 73/239/EEC, 85/611/EEC, 91/675/EEC, 92/49/EEC and 93/6/EEC and Directives 94/19/EC, 98/78/EC, 2000/12/EC, 2001/34/EC, 2002/83/EC and 2002/87/EC in order to establish a new organisational structure for financial services committees

Only Art 3

Non-Repealed Modifications

Act of Accession 2003

PART B
DEADLINES FOR TRANSPOSITION (REFERRED TO IN ARTICLE 158)

Directive	Deadline for transposition
Directive 2000/12/EC	—
Directive 2000/28/EC	27.4.2002
Directive 2002/87/EC	11.8.2004
Directive 2004/39/EC	30.04.2006 / 31.1.2007
Directive 2004/69/EC	30.6.2004
Directive 2005/1/EC	13.5.2005

[9885]

ANNEX XIV
CORRELATION TABLE

This Directive	**Directive 2000/12/EC**	**Directive 2000/28/EC**	**Directive 2002/87/EC**	**Directive 2004/39/EC**	**Directive 2005/1/EC**
Article 1	Art 2(1) and (2)				
Article 2	Art 2(3) Act of Accession				
Article 2	Art 2(4)				
Article 3	Art 2(5) and (6)				
Article 3(1), third subparagraph					Art 3(2)
Article 4(1)	Art 1(1)				
Article 4(2) to (5)		Art 1(2) to (5)			
Article 4(7) to (9)		Art 1(6) to (8)			
Article 4(10)			Art 29(1)(a)		
Article 4(11) to (14)	Art 1(10), (12) and (13)				
Article 4(21) and 22)			Art 29(1)(b)		
Article 4(23)	Art 1(23)				
Article 4(45) to (47)	Art 1(25) to (27)				
Article 5					
Article 6	Art 4				
Article 7	Art 8				
Article 8	Art 9				
Article 9(1)	Art 5(1) and 1(11)				
Article 9(2)	Art 5(2)				

This Directive	Directive 2000/12/EC	Directive 2000/28/EC	Directive 2002/87/EC	Directive 2004/39/EC	Directive 2005/1/EC
Article 10	Art 5(3) to (7)				
Article 11	Art 6				
Article 12	Art 7				
Article 13	Art 10				
Article 14	Art 11				
Article 15(1)	Art 12				
Article 15(2) and (3)			Art 29(2)		
Article 16	Art 13				
Article 17	Art 14				
Article 18	Art 15				
Article 19(1)	Art 16(1)				
Article 19(2)			Art 29(3)		
Article 20	Art 16(3)				
Article 21	Art 16(4) to (6)				
Article 22	Art 17				
Article 23	Art 18				
Article 24(1)	Art 19(1) to (3)				
Article 24(2)	Art 19(6)				
Article 24(3)	Art 19(4)				
Article 25(1) to (3)	Art 20(1) to (3), first and second subparagraphs				
Article 25(3)	Art 19(5)				
Article 25(4)	Art 20(3) third subparagraph				
Article 26	Art 20(4) to (7)				
Article 27	Art 1(3), second sentence				
Article 28	Art 21				
Article 29	Art 22				
Article 30	Art 22(2) to (4)				
Article 31	Art 22(5)				
Article 32	Art 22(6)				
Article 33	Art 22(7)				
Article 34	Art 22(8)				
Article 35	Art 22(9)				
Article 36	Art 22(10)				

PART V
EC LEGISLATION

This Directive	Directive 2000/12/EC	Directive 2000/28/EC	Directive 2002/87/EC	Directive 2004/39/EC	Directive 2005/1/EC
Article 37	Art 22(11)				
Article 38	Art 24				
Article 39(1) and (2)	Art 25				
Article 39(3)					Art 3(8)
Article 40	Art 26				
Article 41	Art 27				
Article 42	Art 28				
Article 43	Art 29				
Article 44	Art 30(1) to (3)				
Article 45	Art 30(4)				
Article 46	Art 30(3)				
Article 47	Art 30(5)				
Article 48	Art 30(6) and (7)				
Article 49	Art 30(8)				
Article 50	Art 30(9), first and second subparagraphs				
Article 51	Art 30(9), third subparagraph				
Article 52	Art 30(10)				
Article 53	Art 31				
Article 54	Art 32				
Article 55	Art 33				
Article 158	Art 67				
Article 159	Art 68				
Article 160	Art 69				
Annex I, points 1 to 14, excluding the final paragraph	Annex I				
Annex I, final paragraph				Art 68	

[9886]

NOTES

Note: parts of this table that relate to provisions not printed are omitted.

COMMISSION REGULATION

of 10 August 2006

implementing Directive 2004/39/EC of the European Parliament and of the Council as regards record-keeping obligations for investment firms, transaction reporting, market transparency, admission of financial instruments to trading, and defined terms for the purposes of that Directive

(1287/2006/EC)

(Text with EEA relevance)

NOTES

Date of publication in OJ: OJ L241, 2.9.2006, p 1. Notes are as in the original OJ version.

THE COMMISSION OF THE EUROPEAN COMMUNITIES,

Having regard to the Treaty establishing the European Community,

Having regard to Directive 2004/39/EC of the European Parliament and of the Council of 21 April 2004 on markets in financial instruments amending Council Directives 85/611/EEC and 93/6/EEC and Directive 2000/12/EC of the European Parliament and of the Council and repealing Council Directive 93/22/EEC,[1] and in particular Articles 4(1)(2), 4(1)(7) and 4(2), Article 13(10), Article 25(7), Article 27(7), Article 28(3), Article 29(3), Article 30(3), Article 40(6), Article 44(3), Article 45(3), Article 56(5), and Article 58(4) thereof,

Whereas:

(1) Directive 2004/39/EC establishes the general framework for a regulatory regime for financial markets in the Community, setting out, among other matters: operating conditions relating to the performance by investment firms of investment and ancillary services, and investment activities; organisational requirements (including record-keeping obligations) for investment firms performing such services and activities on a professional basis, and for regulated markets; transaction reporting requirements in respect of transactions in financial instruments, and transparency requirements in respect of transactions in shares.

(2) It is appropriate that the provisions of this Regulation take that legislative form in order to ensure a harmonised regime in all Member States, to promote market integration and the cross-border provision of investment and ancillary services, and to facilitate the further consolidation of the single market. Provisions relating to certain aspects of record-keeping, and to transaction reporting, transparency and commodity derivatives have few interfaces with national law and with detailed laws governing client relationships.

(3) Detailed and fully harmonised transparency requirements and rules regulating transaction reporting are appropriate so as to ensure equivalent market conditions and the smooth operation of securities markets throughout the Community, and to facilitate the effective integration of those markets. Certain aspects of record-keeping are closely allied as they make use of the same concepts as are defined for transaction reporting and transparency purposes.

(4) The regime established by Directive 2004/39/EC governing transaction reporting requirements in respect of transactions in financial instruments aims to ensure that relevant competent authorities are properly informed about transactions in which they have a supervisory interest. For those purposes it is necessary to ensure that a single data set is collected from all investment firms with a minimum of variation between Member States, so as to minimise the extent to which businesses operating across borders are subject to different reporting obligations, and so as to maximise the proportion of data held by a competent authority that can be shared with other competent authorities. The measures are also designed to ensure that competent authorities are in a position to carry out their obligations under that Directive as expeditiously and efficiently as possible.

(5) The regime established by Directive 2004/39/EC governing transparency requirements in respect of transactions in shares admitted to trading on a regulated market aims to ensure that investors are adequately informed as to the true level of actual and potential transactions in such shares, whether those transactions take place on regulated markets, multilateral trading facilities, hereinafter "MTFs", systematic internalisers, or outside those trading venues. Those requirements are part of a broader framework of rules designed to promote competition between trading venues for execution services so as to increase investor choice, encourage innovation, lower transaction costs, and increase the efficiency of the price formation process on a pan-Community basis. A high degree of transparency is an essential part of this framework, so as to ensure a level playing field

between trading venues so that the price discovery mechanism in respect of particular shares is not impaired by the fragmentation of liquidity, and investors are not thereby penalised. On the other hand, that Directive recognises that there may be circumstances where exemptions from pre-trade transparency obligations, or deferral of post-trade transparency obligations, may be necessary. This Regulation sets out details of those circumstances, bearing in mind the need both to ensure a high level of transparency, and to ensure that liquidity on trading venues and elsewhere is not impaired as an unintended consequence of obligations to disclose transactions and thereby to make public risk positions.

(6) For the purposes of the provisions on record-keeping, a reference to the type of the order should be understood as referring to its status as a limit order, market order, or other specific type of order. For the purposes of the provisions on record-keeping, a reference to the nature of the order or transaction should be understood as referring to orders to subscribe for securities or the subscription of securities, or to exercise an option or the exercise of an option, or similar client orders or transactions.

(7) It is not necessary at this stage to specify or prescribe in detail the type, nature and sophistication of the arrangements for the exchange of information between competent authorities.

(8) Where a notification made by a competent authority relating to the alternative determination of the most relevant market in terms of liquidity is not acted upon within a reasonable time, or where a competent authority does not agree with the calculation made by the other authority, the competent authorities concerned should seek to find a solution. It is open to the competent authorities, where appropriate, to discuss the matter in the Committee of European Securities Regulators.

(9) The competent authorities should coordinate the design and establishment of arrangements for the exchange of transaction information between themselves. Again it is open to the competent authorities to discuss those matters in the Committee of European Securities Regulators. Competent authorities should report to the Commission which should inform the European Securities Committee of those arrangements. In carrying out the coordination, competent authorities should consider the need to monitor the activities of investment firms effectively, so as to ensure that they act honestly, fairly and professionally and in a manner which promotes the integrity of the market in the Community, the need for decisions to be based on a thorough cost-benefit analysis, the need to ensure that transaction information is used only for the proper discharge of the functions of competent authorities and finally the need to have effective and accountable governance arrangements for any common system that might be considered necessary.

(10) It is appropriate to set the criteria for determining when the operations of a regulated market are of substantial importance in a host Member State and the consequences of that status in such a way as to avoid creating an obligation on a regulated market to deal with or be made subject to more than one competent authority where otherwise there would be no such obligation.

(11) ISO 10962 (Classification of financial instruments code) is an example of a uniform internationally accepted standard for financial instrument classification.

(12) If granting waivers in relation to pre-trade transparency requirements, or authorising the deferral of post-trade transparency obligations, competent authorities should treat all regulated markets and MTFs equally and in a non-discriminatory manner, so that a waiver or deferral is granted either to all regulated markets and MTFs that they authorise under Directive 2004/39/EC, or to none. Competent authorities which grant the waivers or deferrals should not impose additional requirements.

(13) It is appropriate to consider that a trading algorithm operated by a regulated market or MTF usually should seek to maximise the volume traded, but other trading algorithms should be possible.

(14) A waiver from pre-trade transparency obligations arising under Articles 29 or 44 of Directive 2004/39/EC conferred by a competent authority should not enable investment firms to avoid such obligations in respect of those transactions in liquid shares which they conclude on a bilateral basis under the rules of a regulated market or an MTF where, if carried out outside the rules of the regulated market or MTF, those transactions would be subject to the requirements to publish quotes set out in Article 27 of that Directive.

(15) An activity should be considered as having a material commercial role for an investment firm if the activity is a significant source of revenue, or a significant source of cost. An assessment of significance for these purposes should, in every case, take into account the extent to which the activity is conducted or organised separately, the monetary value of the activity, and its comparative significance by reference both to the overall business of the firm and to its overall activity in the market for the share concerned in which the firm operates. It should be possible to consider an activity to be a significant source of revenue for a firm even if only one or two of the factors mentioned is relevant in a particular case.

(16) Shares not traded daily should not be considered as having a liquid market for the purposes of Directive 2004/39/EC. However, if, for exceptional reasons, trading in a share is suspended for reasons related to the preservation of an orderly market or force majeure and therefore a share is not traded during some trading days, this should not mean that the share cannot be considered to have a liquid market.

(17) The requirement to make certain quotes, orders or transactions public pursuant to Articles 27, 28, 29, 30, 44 and 45 of Directive 2004/39/EC and this Regulation should not prevent regulated markets and MTFs from requiring their members or participants to make public other such information.

(18) Information which is required to be made available as close to real time as possible should be made available as close to instantaneously as technically possible, assuming a reasonable level of efficiency and of expenditure on systems on the part of the person concerned. The information should only be published close to the three minute maximum limit in exceptional cases where the systems available do not allow for a publication in a shorter period of time.

(19) For the purposes of the provisions of this Regulation as to the admission to trading on a regulated market of a transferable security as defined in Article 4(1)(18)(c) of Directive 2004/39/EC, in the case of a security within the meaning of Directive 2003/71/EC of the European Parliament and of the Council of 4 November 2003 on the prospectus to be published when securities are offered to the public or admitted to trading and amending Directive 2001/34/EC[2] there should be considered to be sufficient information publicly available of a kind needed to value that financial instrument.

(20) The admission to trading on a regulated market of units issued by undertakings for collective investment in transferable securities should not allow the avoidance of the relevant provisions of Council Directive 85/611/EEC of 20 December 1985 on the coordination of laws, regulations and administrative provisions relating to undertakings for collective investment in transferable securities (UCITS)[3] and in particular Articles 44 to 48 of that Directive.

(21) A derivative contract should only be considered to be a financial instrument under Section C(7) of Annex I to Directive 2004/39/EC if it relates to a commodity and meets the criteria in this Regulation for determining whether a contract should be considered as having the characteristics of other derivative financial instruments and as not being for commercial purposes. A derivative contract should only be considered to be a financial instrument under Section C(10) of that Annex if it relates to an underlying specified in Section C(10) or in this Regulation and meets the criteria in this Regulation for determining whether it should be considered as having the characteristics of other derivative financial instruments.

(22) The exemptions in Directive 2004/39/EC that relate to dealing on own account or to dealing or providing other investment services in relation to commodity derivatives covered by Sections C(5), C(6) and C(7) of Annex I to that Directive or derivatives covered by Section C(10) of that Annex I could be expected to exclude significant numbers of commercial producers and consumers of energy and other commodities, including energy suppliers, commodity merchants and their subsidiaries from the scope of that Directive, and therefore such participants will not be required to apply the tests in this Regulation to determine if the contracts they deal in are financial instruments.

(23) In accordance with Section B(7) of Annex I to Directive 2004/39/EC, investment firms may exercise the freedom to provide ancillary services in a Member State other than their home Member State, by performing investment services and activities and ancillary services of the type included under Section A or B of that Annex related to the underlying of the derivatives included under Sections C(5), (6), (7) and (10) of that Annex, where these are connected to the provision of investment or ancillary services. On this basis, a firm performing investment services or activities, and connected trading in spot contracts, should be capable to take advantage of the freedom to provide ancillary services in respect of that connected trading.

(24) The definition of a commodity should not affect any other definition of that term in national legislation and other community legislation. The tests for determining whether a contract should be considered as having the characteristics of other derivative financial instruments and not being for commercial purposes are only intended to be used for the purposes of determining whether contracts fall within Section C(7) or C(10) of Annex I to Directive 2004/39/EC.

(25) A derivative contract should be understood as relating to a commodity or to another factor where there is a direct link between that contract and the relevant underlying commodity or factor. A derivative contract on the price of a commodity should therefore be regarded as a derivative contract relating to the commodity, while a derivative contract on the transportation costs for the commodity should not be regarded as a derivative contract relating to the commodity. A derivative that relates to a commodity derivative, such as an option on a

commodity future (a derivative relating to a derivative) would constitute an indirect investment in commodities and should therefore still be regarded as a commodity derivative for the purposes of Directive 2004/39/EC.

(26) The concept of commodity should not include services or other items that are not goods, such as currencies or rights in real estate, or that are entirely intangible.

(27) The Committee of European Securities Regulators, established by Commission Decision 2001/527/EC[4] has been consulted for technical advice.

(28) The measures provided for in this Regulation are in accordance with the opinion of the European Securities Committee,

[9887]

NOTES

1 OJ L145, 30.4.2004, p 1. Directive as amended by Directive 2006/31/EC (OJ L114, 27.4.2006, p 60).

2 OJ L345, 31.12.2003, p 64.

3 OJ L375, 31.12.1985, p 3. Directive as last amended by Directive 2005/1/EC of the European Parliament and of the Council (OJ L79, 24.3.2005, p 9).

4 OJ L191, 13.7.2001, p 43.

HAS ADOPTED THIS REGULATION—

CHAPTER I
GENERAL

Article 1

Subject-matter and scope

1. This Regulation lays down the detailed rules for the implementation of Articles 4(1)(2), 4(1)(7), 13(6), 25, 27, 28, 29, 30, 40, 44, 45, 56 and 58 of Directive 2004/39/EC.

2. Articles 7 and 8 shall apply to management companies in accordance with Article 5(4) of Directive 85/611/EEC.

[9888]

Article 2

Definitions

For the purposes of this Regulation, the following definitions shall apply:

(1) "commodity" means any goods of a fungible nature that are capable of being delivered, including metals and their ores and alloys, agricultural products, and energy such as electricity;

(2) "issuer" means an entity which issues transferable securities and, where appropriate, other financial instruments;

(3) "Community issuer" means an issuer which has its registered office in the Community;

(4) "third country issuer" means an issuer which is not a Community issuer;

(5) "normal trading hours" for a trading venue or an investment firm means those hours which the trading venue or investment firm establishes in advance and makes public as its trading hours;

(6) "portfolio trade" means a transaction in more than one security where those securities are grouped and traded as a single lot against a specific reference price;

(7) "relevant competent authority" for a financial instrument means the competent authority of the most relevant market in terms of liquidity for that financial instrument;

(8) "trading venue" means a regulated market, MTF or systematic internaliser acting in its capacity as such, and, where appropriate, a system outside the Community with similar functions to a regulated market or MTF;

(9) "turnover", in relation to a financial instrument, means the sum of the results of multiplying the number of units of that instrument exchanged between buyers and sellers in a defined period of time, pursuant to transactions taking place on a trading venue or otherwise, by the unit price applicable to each such transaction;

(10) "securities financing transaction" means an instance of stock lending or stock

borrowing or the lending or borrowing of other financial instruments, a repurchase or reverse repurchase transaction, or a buy-sell back or sell-buy back transaction.

[9889]

Article 3

Transactions related to an individual share in a portfolio trade and volume weighted average price transactions

1. A transaction related to an individual share in a portfolio trade shall be considered, for the purposes of Article 18(1)(b)(ii), as a transaction subject to conditions other than the current market price.

It shall also be considered, for the purposes of Article 27(1)(b), as a transaction where the exchange of shares is determined by factors other than the current market valuation of the share.

2. A volume weighted average price transaction shall be considered, for the purposes of Article 18(1)(b)(ii), as a transaction subject to conditions other than the current market price and, for the purposes of Article 25, as an order subject to conditions other than the current market price.

It shall also be considered, for the purposes of Article 27(1)(b), as a transaction where the exchange of shares is determined by factors other than the current market valuation of the share.

[9890]

Article 4

References to trading day

1. A reference to a trading day in relation to a trading venue, or in relation to post-trade information to be made public under Article 30 or 45 of Directive 2004/39/EC in relation to a share, shall be a reference to any day during which the trading venue concerned is open for trading.

A reference to the opening of the trading day shall be a reference to the commencement of the normal trading hours of the trading venue.

A reference to noon on the trading day shall be a reference to noon in the time zone where the trading venue is established.

A reference to the end of the trading day shall be a reference to the end of its normal trading hours.

2. A reference to a trading day in relation to the most relevant market in terms of liquidity for a share, or in relation to post-trade information to be made public under Article 28 of Directive 2004/39/EC in relation to a share, shall be a reference to any day of normal trading on trading venues in that market.

A reference to the opening of the trading day shall be a reference to the earliest commencement of normal trading in that share on trading venues in that market.

A reference to noon on the trading day shall be a reference to noon in the time zone of that market.

A reference to the end of the trading day shall be a reference to the latest cessation of normal trading in that share on trading venues in that market.

3. A reference to a trading day in relation to a spot contract, within the meaning of Article 38(2), shall be a reference to any day of normal trading of that contract on trading venues.

[9891]

Article 5

References to transaction

For the purposes of this Regulation, a reference to a transaction is a reference only to the purchase and sale of a financial instrument. For the purposes of this Regulation, other than Chapter II, the purchase and sale of a financial instrument does not include any of the following:

PART V
EC LEGISLATION

(a) securities financing transactions;
(b) the exercise of options or of covered warrants;
(c) primary market transactions (such as issuance, allotment or subscription) in financial instruments falling within Article 4(1)(18)(a) and (b) of Directive 2004/39/EC.

[9892]

Article 6

First admission to trading of a share on a regulated market

For the purposes of this Regulation, the first admission to trading of a share on a regulated market referred to in Article 40 of Directive 2004/39/EC shall be considered to take place at a time when one of the following conditions applies:

(a) the share has not previously been admitted to trading on a regulated market;
(b) the share has previously been admitted to trading on a regulated market but the share is removed from trading on every regulated market which has so admitted it.

[9893]

CHAPTER II
RECORD-KEEPING: CLIENT ORDERS AND TRANSACTIONS

Article 7

Record-keeping of client orders and decisions to deal

(Article 13(6) of Directive 2004/39/EC)

An investment firm shall, in relation to every order received from a client, and in relation to every decision to deal taken in providing the service of portfolio management, immediately make a record of the following details, to the extent they are applicable to the order or decision to deal in question:

(a) the name or other designation of the client;
(b) the name or other designation of any relevant person acting on behalf of the client;
(c) the details specified in points 4, 6 and 16 to 19, of Table 1 of Annex I;
(d) the nature of the order if other than buy or sell;
(e) the type of the order;
(f) any other details, conditions and particular instructions from the client that specify how the order must be carried out;
(g) the date and exact time of the receipt of the order, or of the decision to deal, by the investment firm.

[9894]

Article 8

Record-keeping of transactions

(Article 13(6) of Directive 2004/39/EC)

1. Immediately after executing a client order, or, in the case of investment firms that transmit orders to another person for execution, immediately after receiving confirmation that an order has been executed, investment firms shall record the following details of the transaction in question:

(a) the name or other designation of the client;
(b) the details specified in points 2, 3, 4, 6 and 16 to 21, of Table 1 of Annex I;
(c) the total price, being the product of the unit price and the quantity;
(d) the nature of the transaction if other than buy or sell;
(e) the natural person who executed the transaction or who is responsible for the execution.

2. If an investment firm transmits an order to another person for execution, the investment firm shall immediately record the following details after making the transmission:

(a) the name or other designation of the client whose order has been transmitted;
(b) the name or other designation of the person to whom the order was transmitted;

(c) the terms of the order transmitted;
(d) the date and exact time of transmission.

[9895]

CHAPTER III
TRANSACTION REPORTING

Article 9

Determination of the most relevant market in terms of liquidity

(*Second subparagraph of Article 25(3) of Directive 2004/39/EC*)

1. The most relevant market in terms of liquidity for a financial instrument which is admitted to trading on a regulated market, hereinafter "the most relevant market", shall be determined in accordance with paragraphs 2 to 8.

2. In the case of a share or other transferable security covered by Article 4(1)(18)(a) of Directive 2004/39/EC or of a unit in a collective investment undertaking, the most relevant market shall be the Member State where the share or the unit was first admitted to trading on a regulated market.

3. In the case of a bond or other transferable security covered by Article 4(1)(18)(b) of Directive 2004/39/EC or of a money market instrument which, in either case, is issued by a subsidiary, within the meaning of Seventh Council Directive 83/349/EEC of 13 June 1983 on consolidated accounts,[1] of an entity which has its registered office in a Member State, the most relevant market shall be the Member State where the registered office of the parent entity is situated.

4. In the case of a bond or other transferable security covered by Article 4(1)(18)(b) of Directive 2004/39/EC or of a money market instrument which, in either case, is issued by a Community issuer and which is not covered by paragraph 3 of this Article, the most relevant market shall be the Member State where the registered office of the issuer is situated.

5. In the case of a bond or other transferable security covered by Article 4(1)(18)(b) of Directive 2004/39/EC or a money market instrument which, in either case, is issued by a third country issuer and which is not covered by paragraph 3 of this Article, the most relevant market shall be the Member State where that security was first admitted to trading on a regulated market.

6. In the case of a derivative contract or a financial contract for differences or a transferable security covered by Article 4(1)(18)(c) of Directive 2004/39/EC, the most relevant market shall be:

(a) where the underlying security is a share or other transferable security covered by Article 4(1)(18)(a) of Directive 2004/39/EC which is admitted to trading on a regulated market, the Member State deemed to be the most relevant market in terms of liquidity for the underlying security, in accordance with paragraph 2;

(b) where the underlying security is a bond or other transferable security covered by Article 4(1)(18)(b) of Directive 2004/39/EC or a money market instrument which is admitted to trading on a regulated market, the Member State deemed to be the most relevant market in terms of liquidity for that underlying security, in accordance with paragraphs 3, 4 or 5;

(c) where the underlying is an index composed of shares all of which are traded on a particular regulated market, the Member State where that regulated market is situated.

7. In any case not covered by paragraphs 2 to 6, the most relevant market shall be the Member State where the regulated market that first admitted the transferable security or derivative contract or financial contract for differences to trading is located.

8. Where a financial instrument covered by paragraphs 2, 5 or 7, or the underlying financial instrument of a financial instrument covered by paragraph 6 to which one of paragraphs 2, 5 or 7 is relevant, was first admitted to trading on more than one regulated market simultaneously, and all those regulated markets share the same home Member State, that Member State shall be the most relevant market.

Where the regulated markets concerned do not share the same home Member State, the most relevant market in terms of liquidity for that instrument shall be the market where the turnover of that instrument is highest.

For the purposes of determining the most relevant market where the turnover of the instrument is highest, each competent authority that has authorised one of the regulated markets concerned shall calculate the turnover for that instrument in its respective market for the previous calendar year, provided that the instrument was admitted to trading at the beginning of that year.

Where the turnover for the relevant financial instrument cannot be calculated by reason of insufficient or non-existent data and the issuer has its registered office in a Member State, the most relevant market shall be the market of the Member State where the registered office of the issuer is situated.

However, where issuer does not have its registered office in a Member State, the most relevant market for that instrument shall be the market where the turnover of the relevant instrument class is the highest. For the purposes of determining that market, each competent authority that has authorised one of the regulated markets concerned shall calculate the turnover for the instruments of the same class in its respective market for the preceding calendar year.

The relevant classes of financial instrument are the following:
(a) shares;
(b) bonds or other forms of securitised debt;
(c) any other financial instruments.

[9896]

NOTES

[1] OJ L193, 18. 7.1983, p 1.

Article 10

Alternative determination of most relevant market in terms of liquidity

(*Second subparagraph of Article 25(3) of Directive 2004/39/EC*)

1. A competent authority may, in January every year, notify the relevant competent authority for a particular financial instrument that it intends to contest the determination, made in accordance with Article 9, of the most relevant market for that instrument.

2. Within four weeks of the sending of the notification, both authorities shall calculate the turnover for that financial instrument in their respective markets over the period of the previous calendar year.

If the results of that calculation indicate that the turnover is higher in the market of the contesting competent authority, that market shall be the most relevant market for that financial instrument. Where that financial instrument is of a type specified in Article 9(6)(a) or (b), that market shall also be the most relevant market for any derivative contract or financial contract for differences or transferable security which is covered by Article 4(1)(18)(c) of Directive 2004/39/EC and in respect of which that financial instrument is the underlying.

[9897]

Article 11

List of financial instruments

(*Article 25(3) of Directive 2004/39/EC*)

The relevant competent authority for one or more financial instruments shall ensure that there is established and maintained an updated list of those financial instruments. That list shall be made available to the single competent authority designated as a contact point by each Member State in accordance with Article 56 of Directive 2004/39/EC. That list shall be made available for the first time on the first trading day in June 2007.

In order to assist competent authorities to comply with the first subparagraph, each regulated market shall submit identifying reference data on each financial instrument admitted to trading in an electronic and standardised format to its home competent authority. This information shall be submitted for each financial instrument before trading commences in that particular instrument. The home competent authority shall ensure the data is transmitted to the relevant competent authority for the financial instrument concerned. The reference data shall be updated whenever there are changes to the data with respect to an instrument. The requirements in this subparagraph may be waived if the relevant competent authority for that financial instrument obtains the relevant reference data by other means.

[9898]

Article 12

Reporting channels

(*Article 25(5) of Directive 2004/39/EC*)

1. The reports of transactions in financial instruments shall be made in an electronic form except under exceptional circumstances, when they may be made in a medium which allows for the storing of the information in a way accessible for future reference by the competent authorities other than an electronic form, and the methods by which those reports are made shall satisfy the following conditions:

   (a) they ensure the security and confidentiality of the data reported;

   (b) they incorporate mechanisms for identifying and correcting errors in a transaction report;

   (c) they incorporate mechanisms for authenticating the source of the transaction report;

   (d) they include appropriate precautionary measures to enable the timely resumption of reporting in the case of system failure;

   (e) they are capable of reporting the information required under Article 13 in the format required by the competent authority and in accordance with this paragraph, within the time limits set out in Article 25(3) of Directive 2004/39/EC.

2. A trade-matching or reporting system shall be approved by the competent authority for the purposes of Article 25(5) of Directive 2004/39/EC if the arrangements for reporting transactions established by that system comply with paragraph 1 of this Article and are subject to monitoring by a competent authority in respect of their continuing compliance.

[9899]

Article 13

Content of the transaction report

(*Article 25(3) and (5) of Directive 2004/39/EC*)

1. The reports of transactions referred to in Article 25(3) and (5) of Directive 2004/39/EC shall contain the information specified in Table 1 of Annex I to this Regulation which is relevant to the type of financial instrument in question and which the competent authority declares is not already in its possession or is not available to it by other means.

2. For the purposes of the identification of a counterparty to the transaction which is a regulated market, an MTF or other central counterparty, as specified in Table 1 of Annex I, each competent authority shall make publicly available a list of identification codes of the regulated markets and MTFs for which, in each case, it is the competent authority of the home Member State, and of any entities which act as central counterparties for such regulated markets and MTFs.

3. Member States may require reports made in accordance with Article 25(3) and (5) of Directive 2004/39/EC to contain information related to the transactions in question which is additional to that specified in Table 1 of Annex I where that information is necessary to enable the competent authority to monitor the activities of investment firms to ensure that they act honestly, fairly and professionally and in a manner that promotes the integrity of the market, and provided that one of the following criteria is met:

   (a) the financial instrument which is the subject of the report has characteristics which are specific to an instrument of that kind and which are not covered by the information items specified in that table;

   (b) trading methods which are specific to the trading venue where the transaction took place involve features which are not covered by the information items specified in that table.

4. Member States may also require a report of a transaction made in accordance with Article 25(3) and (5) of Directive 2004/39/EC to identify the clients on whose behalf the investment firm has executed that transaction.

[9900]

PART V EC LEGISLATION

Article 14

Exchange of information on transactions

(*Article 25(3) and (5) of Directive 2004/39/EC*)

1. The competent authorities shall establish arrangements designed to ensure that the information received in accordance with Article 25(3) and (5) of Directive 2004/39/EC is made available to the following:

   (a) the relevant competent authority for the financial instrument in question;
   (b) in the case of branches, the competent authority that has authorised the investment firm providing the information, without prejudice to its right not to receive this information in accordance with Article 25(6) of Directive 2004/39/EC;
   (c) any other competent authority that requests the information for the proper discharge of its supervisory duties under Article 25(1) of Directive 2004/39/EC.

2. The information to be made available in accordance with paragraph 1 shall contain the information items described in Tables 1 and 2 of Annex I.

3. The information referred to in paragraph 1 shall be made available as soon as possible.

With effect from 1 November 2008 that information shall be made available no later than the close of the next working day of the competent authority that received the information or the request following the day on which the competent authority has received the information or the request.

4. The competent authorities shall coordinate the following:

   (a) the design and establishment of arrangements for the exchange of transaction information between the competent authorities as required by Directive 2004/39/EC and this Regulation;
   (b) any future upgrading of the arrangements.

5. Before 1 February 2007, the competent authorities shall report to the Commission, which shall inform the European Securities Committee, on the design of the arrangements to be established in accordance with paragraph 1.

They shall also report to the Commission, which shall inform the European Securities Committee, whenever significant changes to those arrangements are proposed.

[9901]

Article 15

Request for cooperation and exchange of information

(*Article 58(1) of Directive 2004/39/EC*)

1. Where a competent authority wishes another competent authority to supply or exchange information in accordance with Article 58(1) of Directive 2004/39/EC, it shall submit a written request to that competent authority containing sufficient detail to enable it to provide the information requested.

However, in a case of urgency, the request may be transmitted orally provided that it is confirmed in writing.

The competent authority which receives a request shall acknowledge receipt as soon as practicable.

2. Where the information requested under paragraph 1 is internally available to the competent authority that receives the request, that authority shall transmit the requested information without delay to the competent authority which made the request.

However, if the competent authority that receives the request does not possess or control the information requested, it shall immediately take the necessary steps to obtain that information and to comply fully with the request. That competent authority shall also inform the competent authority that made the request of the reasons for not sending immediately the information requested.

[9902]

Article 16

Determination of the substantial importance of a regulated market's operations in a host Member State

(*Article 56(2) of Directive 2004/39/EC*)

The operations of a regulated market in a host Member State shall be considered to be of substantial importance for the functioning of the securities markets and the protection of investors in that host State where one of the following criteria is met:

(a) the host Member State has formerly been the home Member State of the regulated market in question;

(b) the regulated market in question has acquired through merger, takeover, or any other form of transfer the business of a regulated market which had its registered office or head office in the host Member State.

[9903]

CHAPTER IV
MARKET TRANSPARENCY

SECTION 1
PRE-TRADE TRANSPARENCY FOR REGULATED MARKETS AND MTFS

Article 17

Pre-trade transparency obligations

(*Articles 29 and 44 of Directive 2004/39/EC*)

1. An investment firm or market operator operating an MTF or a regulated market shall, in respect of each share admitted to trading on a regulated market that is traded within a system operated by it and specified in Table 1 of Annex II, make public the information set out in paragraphs 2 to 6.

2. Where one of the entities referred to in paragraph 1 operates a continuous auction order book trading system, it shall, for each share as specified in paragraph 1, make public continuously throughout its normal trading hours the aggregate number of orders and of the shares those orders represent at each price level, for the five best bid and offer price levels.

3. Where one of the entities referred to in paragraph 1 operates a quote-driven trading system, it shall, for each share as specified in paragraph 1, make public continuously throughout its normal trading hours the best bid and offer by price of each market maker in that share, together with the volumes attaching to those prices.

The quotes made public shall be those that represent binding commitments to buy and sell the shares and which indicate the price and volume of shares in which the registered market makers are prepared to buy or sell.

In exceptional market conditions, however, indicative or one-way prices may be allowed for a limited time.

4. Where one of the entities referred to in paragraph 1 operates a periodic auction trading system, it shall, for each share specified in paragraph 1, make public continuously throughout its normal trading hours the price that would best satisfy the system's trading algorithm and the volume that would potentially be executable at that price by participants in that system.

5. Where one of the entities referred to in paragraph 1 operates a trading system which is not wholly covered by paragraph 2 or 3 or 4, either because it is a hybrid system falling under more than one of those paragraphs or because the price determination process is of a different nature, it shall maintain a standard of pre-trade transparency that ensures that adequate information is made public as to the price level of orders or quotes for each share specified in paragraph 1, as well as the level of trading interest in that share.

In particular, the five best bid and offer price levels and/or two-way quotes of each market maker in that share shall be made public, if the characteristics of the price discovery mechanism permit it.

6. A summary of the information to be made public in accordance with paragraphs 2 to 5 is specified in Table 1 of Annex II.

[9904]

Article 18

Waivers based on market model and type of order or transaction

(*Articles 29(2) and 44(2) of Directive 2004/39/EC*)

1. Waivers in accordance with Article 29(2) and 44(2) of Directive 2004/39/EC may be granted by the competent authorities for systems operated by an MTF or a regulated market, if those systems satisfy one of the following criteria:

(a) they must be based on a trading methodology by which the price is determined in accordance with a reference price generated by another system, where that reference price is widely published and is regarded generally by market participants as a reliable reference price;

(b) they formalise negotiated transactions, each of which meets one of the following criteria:

(i) it is made at or within the current volume weighted spread reflected on the order book or the quotes of the market makers of the regulated market or MTF operating that system or, where the share is not traded continuously, within a percentage of a suitable reference price, being a percentage and a reference price set in advance by the system operator;

(ii) it is subject to conditions other than the current market price of the share.

For the purposes of point (b), the other conditions specified in the rules of the regulated market or MTF for a transaction of this kind must also have been fulfilled.

In the case of systems having functionality other than as described in points (a) or (b), the waiver shall not apply to that other functionality.

2. Waivers in accordance with Articles 29(2) and 44(2) of Directive 2004/39/EC based on the type of orders may be granted only in relation to orders held in an order management facility maintained by the regulated market or the MTF pending their being disclosed to the market.

[9905]

Article 19

References to negotiated transaction

(*Articles 29(2) and 44(2) of Directive 2004/39/EC*)

For the purpose of Article 18(1)(b) a negotiated transaction shall mean a transaction involving members or participants of a regulated market or an MTF which is negotiated privately but executed within the regulated market or MTF and where that member or participant in doing so undertakes one of the following tasks:

(a) dealing on own account with another member or participant who acts for the account of a client;

(b) dealing with another member or participant, where both are executing orders on own account;

(c) acting for the account of both the buyer and seller;

(d) acting for the account of the buyer, where another member or participant acts for the account of the seller;

(e) trading for own account against a client order.

[9906]

Article 20

Waivers in relation to transactions which are large in scale

(*Articles 29(2) and 44(2), and fifth subparagraph of Article 27(1) of Directive 2004/39/EC*)

An order shall be considered to be large in scale compared with normal market size if it is equal to or larger than the minimum size of order specified in Table 2 in Annex II. For the purposes of determining whether an order is large in scale compared to normal market size, all shares admitted to trading on a regulated market shall be classified in accordance with their average daily turnover, which shall be calculated in accordance with the procedure set out in Article 33.

[9907]

SECTION 2
PRE-TRADE TRANSPARENCY FOR SYSTEMATIC INTERNALISERS

Article 21

Criteria for determining whether an investment firm is a systematic internaliser

(*Article 4(1)(7) of Directive 2004/39/EC*)

1. Where an investment firm deals on own account by executing client orders outside a regulated market or an MTF, it shall be treated as a systematic internaliser if it meets the following criteria indicating that it performs that activity on an organised, frequent and systematic basis:

(a) the activity has a material commercial role for the firm, and is carried on in accordance with non-discretionary rules and procedures;

(b) the activity is carried on by personnel, or by means of an automated technical system, assigned to that purpose, irrespective of whether those personnel or that system are used exclusively for that purpose;

(c) the activity is available to clients on a regular or continuous basis.

2. An investment firm shall cease to be a systematic internaliser in one or more shares if it ceases to carry on the activity specified in paragraph 1 in respect of those shares, provided that it has announced in advance that it intends to cease that activity using the same publication channels for that announcement as it uses to publish its quotes or, where that is not possible, using a channel which is equally accessible to its clients and other market participants.

3. The activity of dealing on own account by executing client orders shall not be treated as performed on an organised, frequent and systematic basis where the following conditions apply:

(a) the activity is performed on an ad hoc and irregular bilateral basis with wholesale counterparties as part of business relationships which are themselves characterised by dealings above standard market size;

(b) the transactions are carried out outside the systems habitually used by the firm concerned for any business that it carries out in the capacity of a systematic internaliser.

4. Each competent authority shall ensure the maintenance and publication of a list of all systematic internalisers, in respect of shares admitted to trading on a regulated market, which it has authorised as investment firms.

It shall ensure that the list is current by reviewing it at least annually.

The list shall be made available to the Committee of European Securities Regulators. It shall be considered as published when it is published by the Committee of European Securities Regulators in accordance with Article 34(5).

[9908]

Article 22

Determination of liquid shares

(*Article 27 of Directive 2004/39/EC*)

1. A share admitted to trading on a regulated market shall be considered to have a liquid market if the share is traded daily, with a free float not less than EUR 500 million, and one of the following conditions is satisfied:

(a) the average daily number of transactions in the share is not less than 500;

(b) the average daily turnover for the share is not less than EUR 2 million.

However, a Member State may, in respect of shares for which it is the most relevant market, specify by notice that both of those conditions are to apply. That notice shall be made public.

2. A Member State may specify the minimum number of liquid shares for that Member State. The minimum number shall be no greater than five. The specification shall be made public.

3. Where, pursuant to paragraph 1, a Member State would be the most relevant market for fewer liquid shares than the minimum number specified in accordance with paragraph 2, the competent authority for that Member State may designate one or more additional liquid shares, provided that the total number of shares which are considered in consequence to be liquid shares for which that Member State is the most relevant market does not exceed the minimum number specified by that Member State.

The competent authority shall designate the additional liquid shares successively in decreasing order of average daily turnover from among the shares for which it is the relevant competent authority that are admitted to trading on a regulated market and are traded daily.

4. For the purposes of the first subparagraph of paragraph 1, the calculation of the free float of a share shall exclude holdings exceeding 5% of the total voting rights of the issuer, unless such a holding is held by a collective investment undertaking or a pension fund.

Voting rights shall be calculated on the basis of all the shares to which voting rights are attached, even if the exercise of such a right is suspended.

5. A share shall not be considered to have a liquid market for the purposes of Article 27 of Directive 2004/39/EC until six weeks after its first admission to trading on a regulated market, if the estimate of the total market capitalisation for that share at the start of the first day's trading after that admission, provided in accordance with Article 33(3), is less than EUR 500 million.

6. Each competent authority shall ensure the maintenance and publication of a list of all liquid shares for which it is the relevant competent authority.

It shall ensure that the list is current by reviewing it at least annually.

The list shall be made available to the Committee of European Securities Regulators. It shall be considered as published when it is published by the Committee of European Securities Regulators in accordance with Article 34(5).

[9909]

Article 23

Standard market size

(Fourth subparagraph of Article 27(1) of Directive 2004/39/EC)

In order to determine the standard market size for liquid shares, those shares shall be grouped into classes in terms of the average value of orders executed in accordance with Table 3 in Annex II.

[9910]

Article 24

Quotes reflecting prevailing market conditions

(Article 27(1) of Directive 2004/39/EC)

A systematic internaliser shall, for each liquid share for which it is a systematic internaliser, maintain the following:

(a) a quote or quotes which are close in price to comparable quotes for the same share in other trading venues;

(b) a record of its quoted prices, which it shall retain for a period of 12 months or such longer period as it considers appropriate.

The obligation laid down in point (b) is without prejudice to the obligation of the investment firm under Article 25(2) of Directive 2004/39/EC to keep at the disposal of the competent authority for at least five years the relevant data relating to all transactions it has carried out.

[9911]

Article 25

Execution of orders by systematic internalisers

(Fifth subparagraph of Article 27(3) and Article 27(6) of Directive 2004/39/EC)

1. For the purposes of the fifth subparagraph of Article 27(3) of Directive 2004/39/EC, execution in several securities shall be regarded as part of one transaction if that one transaction is a portfolio trade that involves 10 or more securities.

For the same purposes, an order subject to conditions other than the current market price means any order which is neither an order for the execution of a transaction in shares at the prevailing market price, nor a limit order.

2. For the purposes of Article 27(6) of Directive 2004/39/EC, the number or volume of orders shall be regarded as considerably exceeding the norm if a systematic internaliser cannot execute those orders without exposing itself to undue risk.

In order to identify the number and volume of orders that it can execute without exposing itself to undue risk, a systematic internaliser shall maintain and implement as part of its risk management policy under Article 7 of Commission Directive 2006/73/EC[1] a non-discriminatory policy which takes into account the volume of the transactions, the capital that the firm has available to cover the risk for that type of trade, and the prevailing conditions in the market in which the firm is operating.

3. Where, in accordance with Article 27(6) of Directive 2004/39/EC, an investment firm limits the number or volume of orders it undertakes to execute, it shall set out in writing, and make available to clients and potential clients, the arrangements designed to ensure that such a limitation does not result in the discriminatory treatment of clients.

[9912]

NOTES

[1] See page 26 of this Official Journal.

Article 26

Retail size

(*Fourth subparagraph Article 27(3) of Directive 2004/39/EC*)

For the purposes of the fourth subparagraph of Article 27(3) of Directive 2004/39/EC, an order shall be regarded as being of a size bigger than the size customarily undertaken by a retail investor if it exceeds EUR 7500.

[9913]

SECTION 3
POST-TRADE TRANSPARENCY FOR REGULATED MARKETS, MTFS AND INVESTMENT FIRMS

Article 27

Post-trade transparency obligation

(*Articles 28, 30 and 45 of Directive 2004/39/EC*)

1. Investment firms, regulated markets, and investment firms and market operators operating an MTF shall, with regard to transactions in respect of shares admitted to trading on regulated markets concluded by them or, in the case of regulated markets or MTFs, within their systems, make public the following details:

(a) the details specified in points 2, 3, 6, 16, 17, 18, and 21 of Table 1 in Annex I;
(b) an indication that the exchange of shares is determined by factors other than the current market valuation of the share, where applicable;
(c) an indication that the trade was a negotiated trade, where applicable;
(d) any amendments to previously disclosed information, where applicable.

Those details shall be made public either by reference to each transaction or in a form aggregating the volume and price of all transactions in the same share taking place at the same price at the same time.

2. By way of exception, a systematic internaliser shall be entitled to use the acronym "SI" instead of the venue identification referred to in paragraph 1(a) in respect of a transaction in a share that is executed in its capacity as a systematic internaliser in respect of that share.

The systematic internaliser may exercise that right only as long as it makes available to the public aggregate quarterly data as to the transactions executed in its capacity as a systematic internaliser in respect of that share relating to the most recent calendar quarter, or part of a calendar quarter, during which the firm acted as a systematic internaliser in respect of that share. That data shall be made available no later than one month after the end of each calendar quarter.

It may also exercise that right during the period between the date specified in Article 41(2), or the date on which the firm commences to be a systematic internaliser in relation to a share, whichever is the later, and the date that aggregate quarterly data in relation to a share is first due to be published.

3. The aggregated quarterly data referred to in the second subparagraph of paragraph 2 shall contain the following information for the share in respect of each trading day of the calendar quarter concerned:

(a) the highest price;
(b) the lowest price;
(c) the average price;
(d) the total number of shares traded;
(e) the total number of transactions;
(f) such other information as the systematic internaliser decides to make available.

4. Where the transaction is executed outside the rules of a regulated market or an MTF, one of the following investment firms shall, by agreement between the parties, arrange to make the information public:

(a) the investment firm that sells the share concerned;
(b) the investment firm that acts on behalf of or arranges the transaction for the seller;
(c) the investment firm that acts on behalf of or arranges the transaction for the buyer;
(d) the investment firm that buys the share concerned.

In the absence of such an agreement, the information shall be made public by the investment firm determined by proceeding sequentially from point (a) to point (d) until the first point that applies to the case in question.

The parties shall take all reasonable steps to ensure that the transaction is made public as a single transaction. For those purposes two matching trades entered at the same time and price with a single party interposed shall be considered to be a single transaction.

[9914]

Article 28

Deferred publication of large transactions

(*Articles 28, 30 and 45 of Directive 2004/39/EC*)

The deferred publication of information in respect of transactions may be authorised, for a period no longer than the period specified in Table 4 in Annex II for the class of share and transaction concerned, provided that the following criteria are satisfied:

(a) the transaction is between an investment firm dealing on own account and a client of that firm;
(b) the size of the transaction is equal to or exceeds the relevant minimum qualifying size, as specified in Table 4 in Annex II.

In order to determine the relevant minimum qualifying size for the purposes of point (b), all shares admitted to trading on a regulated market shall be classified in accordance with their average daily turnover to be calculated in accordance with Article 33.

[9915]

SECTION 4
PROVISIONS COMMON TO PRE- AND POST-TRADE TRANSPARENCY

Article 29

Publication and availability of pre- and post-trade transparency data

(*Articles 27(3), 28(1), 29(1), 44(1) and 45(1) of Directive 2004/39/EC*)

1. A regulated market, MTF or systematic internaliser shall be considered to publish pre-trade information on a continuous basis during normal trading hours if that information is published as soon as it becomes available during the normal trading hours of the regulated market, MTF or systematic internaliser concerned, and remains available until it is updated.

2. Pre-trade information, and post-trade information relating to transactions taking place on trading venues and within normal trading hours, shall be made available as close to real time as possible. Post-trade information relating to such transactions shall be made available in any case within three minutes of the relevant transaction.

3. Information relating to a portfolio trade shall be made available with respect to each constituent transaction as close to real time as possible, having regard to the need to allocate prices to particular shares. Each constituent transaction shall be assessed separately for the purposes of determining whether deferred publication in respect of that transaction is available under Article 28.

4. Post-trade information relating to transactions taking place on a trading venue but outside its normal trading hours shall be made public before the opening of the next trading day of the trading venue on which the transaction took place.

5. For transactions that take place outside a trading venue, post-trade information shall be made public:

(a) if the transaction takes place during a trading day of the most relevant market for the share concerned, or during the investment firm's normal trading hours, as close to real time as possible. Post-trade information relating to such transactions shall be made available in any case within three minutes of the relevant transaction;

(b) in a case not covered by point (a), immediately upon the commencement of the investment firm's normal trading hours or at the latest before the opening of the next trading day in the most relevant market for that share.

[9916]

Article 30

Public availability of pre- and post-trade information

(*Articles 27, 28, 29, 30, 44 and 45 of Directive 2004/39/EC*)

For the purposes of Articles 27, 28, 29, 30, 44 and 45 of Directive 2004/39/EC and of this Regulation, pre- and post-trade information shall be considered to be made public or available to the public if it is made available generally through one of the following to investors located in the Community:

(a) the facilities of a regulated market or an MTF;

(b) the facilities of a third party;

(c) proprietary arrangements.

[9917]

Article 31

Disclosure of client limit orders

(*Article 22(2) of Directive 2004/39/EC*)

An investment firm shall be considered to disclose client limit orders that are not immediately executable if it transmits the order to a regulated market or MTF that operates an order book trading system, or ensures that the order is made public and can be easily executed as soon as market conditions allow.

[9918]

Article 32

Arrangements for making information public

(*Article 22(2), 27, 28, 29, 30, 44 and 45 of Directive 2004/39/EC*)

Any arrangement to make information public, adopted for the purposes of Articles 30 and 31, shall satisfy the following conditions:

(a) it must include all reasonable steps necessary to ensure that the information to be published is reliable, monitored continuously for errors, and corrected as soon as errors are detected;

(b) it must facilitate the consolidation of the data with similar data from other sources;

(c) it must make the information available to the public on a non-discriminatory commercial basis at a reasonable cost.

[9919]

Article 33

Calculations and estimates for shares admitted to trading on a regulated market

(*Articles 27, 28, 29, 30, 44 and 45 of Directive 2004/39/EC*)

1. In respect of each share that is admitted to trading on a regulated market, the relevant competent authority for that share shall ensure that the following calculations are made in respect of that share promptly after the end of each calendar year:

(a) the average daily turnover;

(b) the average daily number of transactions;

(c) for those shares which satisfy the conditions laid down in Article 22(1)(a) or (b) (as applicable), the free float as at 31 December;

(d) if the share is a liquid share, the average value of the orders executed.

This paragraph and paragraph 2 shall not apply to a share which is first admitted to trading on a regulated market four weeks or less before the end of the calendar year.

2. The calculation of the average daily turnover, average value of the orders executed and average daily number of transactions shall take into account all the orders executed in the Community in respect of the share in question between 1 January and 31 December of the preceding year, or, where applicable, that part of the year during which the share was admitted to trading on a regulated market and was not suspended from trading on a regulated market.

In the calculations of the average daily turnover, average value of the orders executed and average daily number of transactions of a share, non-trading days in the Member State of the relevant competent authority for that share shall be excluded.

3. Before the first admission of a share to trading on a regulated market, the relevant competent authority for that share shall ensure that estimates are provided, in respect of that share, of the average daily turnover, the market capitalisation as it will stand at the start of the first day of trading and, where the estimate of the market capitalisation is EUR 500 million or more:

(a) the average daily number of transactions and, for those shares which satisfy the conditions laid down in Article 22(1)(a) or (b) (as applicable), the free float;

(b) in the case of a share that is estimated to be a liquid share, the average value of the orders executed.

The estimates shall relate to the six-week period following admission to trading, or the end of that period, as applicable, and shall take account of any previous trading history of the share, as well as that of shares that are considered to have similar characteristics.

4. After the first admission of a share to trading on a regulated market, the relevant competent authority for that share shall ensure that, in respect of that share, the figures referred to in points (a) to (d) of paragraph 1 are calculated, using data relating to the first four weeks' trading, as if a reference in point (c) of paragraph 1 to 31 December were a reference to the end of the first four weeks' trading, as soon as practicable after those data are available, and in any case before the end of the six-week period referred to in Article 22(5).

5. During the course of a calendar year, the relevant competent authorities shall ensure the review and where necessary the recalculation of the average daily turnover, average value of the orders executed, average daily number of transactions executed and the free float whenever there is a change in relation to the share or the issuer which significantly affects the previous calculations on an ongoing basis.

6. The calculations referred to in paragraphs 1 to 5 which are to be published on or before the first trading day in March 2009 shall be made on the basis of the data relating to the regulated market or markets of the Member State which is the most relevant market in terms of liquidity for the share in question. For those purposes, negotiated transactions within the meaning of Article 19 shall be excluded from the calculations.

[9920]

Article 34

Publication and effect of results of required calculations and estimates
(Articles 27, 28, 29, 30, 44 and 45 of Directive 2004/39/EC)

1. On the first trading day of March of each year, each competent authority shall, in relation to each share for which it is the relevant competent authority that was admitted to trading on a regulated market at the end of the preceding calendar year, ensure the publication of the following information:

(a) the average daily turnover and average daily number of transactions, as calculated in accordance with Article 33(1) and (2);

(b) the free float and average value of the orders executed, where calculated in accordance with Article 33(1) and (2).

This paragraph shall not apply to shares to which the second subparagraph of Article 33(1) applies.

2. The results of the estimates and calculations required under Article 33(3), (4) or (5) shall be published as soon as practicable after the calculation or estimate is completed.

3. The information referred to in paragraphs 1 or 2 shall be considered as published when it is published by the Committee of European Securities Regulators in accordance with paragraph 5.

4. For the purposes of this Regulation, the following shall apply:
  (a) the classification based on the publication referred to in paragraph 1 shall apply for the 12-month period starting on 1 April following publication and ending on the following 31 March;
  (b) the classification based on the estimates provided for in Article 33(3) shall apply from the relevant first admission to trading until the end of the six-week period referred to in Article 22(5);
  (c) the classification based on the calculations specified in Article 33(4) shall apply from the end of the six-week period referred to in Article 22(5), until:
    (i) where the end of that six-week period falls between 15 January and 31 March (both inclusive) in a given year, 31 March of the following year;
    (ii) otherwise, the following 31 March after the end of that period.

However, the classification based on the recalculations specified in Article 33(5) shall apply from the date of publication and, unless further recalculated under Article 33(5), until the following 31 March.

5. The Committee of European Securities Regulators shall, on the basis of data supplied to it by or on behalf of competent authorities, publish on its website consolidated and regularly updated lists of:
  (a) every systematic internaliser in respect of a share admitted to trading on a regulated market;
  (b) every share admitted to trading on a regulated market, specifying:
    (i) the average daily turnover, average daily number of transactions and, for those shares which satisfy the conditions laid down in Article 22(1)(a) or (b) (as applicable), the free float;
    (ii) in the case of a liquid share, the average value of the orders executed and the standard market size for that share;
    (iii) in the case of a liquid share which has been designated as an additional liquid share in accordance with Article 22(3), the name of the competent authority that so designated it; and
    (iv) the relevant competent authority.

6. Each competent authority shall ensure the first publication of the details referred to in points (a) and (b) of paragraph 1 on the first trading day in July 2007, based on the reference period 1 April 2006 to 31 March 2007. By way of derogation from paragraph 4, the classification based on that publication shall apply for the five-month period starting on 1 November 2007 and ending on 31 March 2008.

[9921]

CHAPTER V

ADMISSION OF FINANCIAL INSTRUMENTS TO TRADING

Article 35

Transferable securities

(*Article 40(1) of Directive 2004/39/EC*)

1. Transferable securities shall be considered freely negotiable for the purposes of Article 40(1) of Directive 2004/39/EC if they can be traded between the parties to a transaction, and subsequently transferred without restriction, and if all securities within the same class as the security in question are fungible.

2. Transferable securities which are subject to a restriction on transfer shall not be considered as freely negotiable unless that restriction is not likely to disturb the market.

3. Transferable securities that are not fully paid may be considered as freely negotiable if arrangements have been made to ensure that the negotiability of such securities is not restricted and that adequate information concerning the fact that the securities are not fully paid, and the implications of that fact for shareholders, is publicly available.

4. When exercising its discretion whether to admit a share to trading, a regulated market shall, in assessing whether the share is capable of being traded in a fair, orderly and efficient manner, take into account the following:

(a) the distribution of those shares to the public;

(b) such historical financial information, information about the issuer, and information providing a business overview as is required to be prepared under Directive 2003/71/EC, or is or will be otherwise publicly available.

5. A transferable security that is officially listed in accordance with Directive 2001/34/EC of the European Parliament and of the Council,[1] and the listing of which is not suspended, shall be deemed to be freely negotiable and capable of being traded in a fair, orderly and efficient manner.

6. For the purposes of Article 40(1) of Directive 2004/39/EC, when assessing whether a transferable security referred to in Article 4(1)(18)(c) of that Directive is capable of being traded in a fair, orderly and efficient manner, the regulated market shall take into account, depending on the nature of the security being admitted, whether the following criteria are satisfied:

(a) the terms of the security are clear and unambiguous and allow for a correlation between the price of the security and the price or other value measure of the underlying;

(b) the price or other value measure of the underlying is reliable and publicly available;

(c) there is sufficient information publicly available of a kind needed to value the security;

(d) the arrangements for determining the settlement price of the security ensure that this price properly reflects the price or other value measure of the underlying;

(e) where the settlement of the security requires or provides for the possibility of the delivery of an underlying security or asset rather than cash settlement, there are adequate settlement and delivery procedures for that underlying as well as adequate arrangements to obtain relevant information about that underlying.

[9922]

NOTES

[1] OJ L184, 6.7.2001, p 1. Directive as last amended by Directive 2005/1/EC.

Article 36

Units in collective investment undertakings

(*Article 40(1) of Directive 2004/39/EC*)

1. A regulated market shall, when admitting to trading units in a collective investment undertaking, whether or not that undertaking is constituted in accordance with Directive 85/611/EEC, satisfy itself that the collective investment undertaking complies or has complied with the registration, notification or other procedures which are a necessary precondition for the marketing of the collective investment undertaking in the jurisdiction of the regulated market.

2. Without prejudice to Directive 85/611/EEC or any other Community legislation or national law relating to collective investment undertakings, Member States may provide that compliance with the requirements referred to in paragraph 1 is not a necessary precondition for the admission of units in a collective investment undertaking to trading on a regulated market.

3. When assessing whether units in an open-ended collective investment undertaking are capable of being traded in a fair, orderly and efficient manner in accordance with Article 40(1) of Directive 2004/39/EC, the regulated market shall take the following aspects into account:

(a) the distribution of those units to the public;

(b) whether there are appropriate market-making arrangements, or whether the management company of the scheme provides appropriate alternative arrangements for investors to redeem the units;

(c) whether the value of the units is made sufficiently transparent to investors by means of the periodic publication of the net asset value.

4. When assessing whether units in a closed-end collective investment undertaking are capable of being traded in a fair, orderly and efficient manner in accordance with Article 40(1) of Directive 2004/39/EC, the regulated market shall take the following aspects into account:

(a) the distribution of those units to the public;

(b) whether the value of the units is made sufficiently transparent to investors, either by publication of information on the fund's investment strategy or by the periodic publication of net asset value.

[9923]

Article 37

Derivatives

(*Article 40(1) and (2) of Directive 2004/39/EC*)

1. When admitting to trading a financial instrument of a kind listed in points of Sections C(4) to (10) of Annex I to Directive 2004/39/EC, regulated markets shall verify that the following conditions are satisfied:

(a) the terms of the contract establishing the financial instrument must be clear and unambiguous, and enable a correlation between the price of the financial instrument and the price or other value measure of the underlying;

(b) the price or other value measure of the underlying must be reliable and publicly available;

(c) sufficient information of a kind needed to value the derivative must be publicly available;

(d) the arrangements for determining the settlement price of the contract must be such that the price properly reflects the price or other value measure of the underlying;

(e) where the settlement of the derivative requires or provides for the possibility of the delivery of an underlying security or asset rather than cash settlement, there must be adequate arrangements to enable market participants to obtain relevant information about that underlying as well as adequate settlement and delivery procedures for the underlying.

2. Where the financial instruments concerned are of a kind listed in Sections C (5), (6), (7) or (10) of Annex I to Directive 2004/39/EC, point (b) of paragraph 1 shall not apply if the following conditions are satisfied:

(a) the contract establishing that instrument must be likely to provide a means of disclosing to the market, or enabling the market to assess, the price or other value measure of the underlying, where the price or value measure is not otherwise publicly available;

(b) the regulated market must ensure that appropriate supervisory arrangements are in place to monitor trading and settlement in such financial instruments;

(c) the regulated market must ensure that settlement and delivery, whether physical delivery or by cash settlement, can be effected in accordance with the contract terms and conditions of those financial instruments.

[9924]

CHAPTER VI
DERIVATIVE FINANCIAL INSTRUMENTS

Article 38

Characteristics of other derivative financial instruments

(*Article 4(1)(2) of Directive 2004/39/EC*)

1. For the purposes of Section C(7) of Annex I to Directive 2004/39/EC, a contract which is not a spot contract within the meaning of paragraph 2 of this Article and which is not covered by paragraph 4 shall be considered as having the characteristics of other derivative financial instruments and not being for commercial purposes if it satisfies the following conditions:

(a) it meets one of the following sets of criteria:

(i) it is traded on a third country trading facility that performs a similar function to a regulated market or an MTF;

(ii) it is expressly stated to be traded on, or is subject to the rules of, a regulated market, an MTF or such a third country trading facility;

(iii) it is expressly stated to be equivalent to a contract traded on a regulated market, MTF or such a third country trading facility;

(b) it is cleared by a clearing house or other entity carrying out the same functions as a central counterparty, or there are arrangements for the payment or provision of margin in relation to the contract;

(c) it is standardised so that, in particular, the price, the lot, the delivery date or other terms are determined principally by reference to regularly published prices, standard lots or standard delivery dates.

2. A spot contract for the purposes of paragraph 1 means a contract for the sale of a commodity, asset or right, under the terms of which delivery is scheduled to be made within the longer of the following periods:

(a) two trading days;

(b) the period generally accepted in the market for that commodity, asset or right as the standard delivery period.

However, a contract is not a spot contract if, irrespective of its explicit terms, there is an understanding between the parties to the contract that delivery of the underlying is to be postponed and not to be performed within the period mentioned in the first subparagraph.

3. For the purposes of Section C(10) of Annex I to Directive 2004/39/EC, a derivative contract relating to an underlying referred to in that Section or in Article 39 shall be considered to have the characteristics of other derivative financial instruments if one of the following conditions is satisfied:

(a) that contract is settled in cash or may be settled in cash at the option of one or more of the parties, otherwise than by reason of a default or other termination event;

(b) that contract is traded on a regulated market or an MTF;

(c) the conditions laid down in paragraph 1 are satisfied in relation to that contract.

4. A contract shall be considered to be for commercial purposes for the purposes of Section C(7) of Annex I to Directive 2004/39/EC, and as not having the characteristics of other derivative financial instruments for the purposes of Sections C(7) and (10) of that Annex, if it is entered into with or by an operator or administrator of an energy transmission grid, energy balancing mechanism or pipeline network, and it is necessary to keep in balance the supplies and uses of energy at a given time.

[9925]

Article 39

Derivatives within Section C(10) of Annex I to Directive 2004/39/EC

(*Article 4(1)(2) of Directive 2004/39/EC*)

In addition to derivative contracts of a kind referred to in Section C(10) of Annex I to Directive 2004/39/EC, a derivative contract relating to any of the following shall fall within that Section if it meets the criteria set out in that Section and in Article 38(3):

(a) telecommunications bandwidth;

(b) commodity storage capacity;

(c) transmission or transportation capacity relating to commodities, whether cable, pipeline or other means;

(d) an allowance, credit, permit, right or similar asset which is directly linked to the supply, distribution or consumption of energy derived from renewable resources;

(e) a geological, environmental or other physical variable;

(f) any other asset or right of a fungible nature, other than a right to receive a service, that is capable of being transferred;

(g) an index or measure related to the price or value of, or volume of transactions in any asset, right, service or obligation.

[9926]

CHAPTER VII
FINAL PROVISIONS

Article 40

Re-examinations

1. At least once every two years, and after consulting the Committee of European Securities Regulators, the Commission shall re-examine the definition of "transaction" for the

purposes of this Regulation, the Tables included in Annex II, as well as the criteria for determination of liquid shares contained in Article 22.

2. The Commission shall, after consulting the Committee of European Securities Regulators, re-examine the provisions of Articles 38 and 39 relating to criteria for determining which instruments are to be treated as having the characteristics of other derivative financial instruments, or as being for commercial purposes, or which fall within Section C(10) of Annex I to Directive 2004/39/EC if the other criteria set out in that Section are satisfied in relation to them.

The Commission shall report to the European Parliament and to the Council at the same time that it makes its reports under Article 65(3)(a) and (d) of Directive 2004/39/EC.

3. The Commission shall, no later than two years after the date of application of this Regulation, after consulting the Committee of European Securities Regulators, re-examine Table 4 of Annex II and report on the results of this re-examination to the European Parliament and the Council.

[9927]

Article 41

Entry into force

This Regulation shall enter into force on the 20th day following its publication in the Official Journal of the European Union.

This Regulation shall apply from 1 November 2007, except Article 11 and Article 34(5) and (6), which shall apply from 1 June 2007.

[9928]

This Regulation shall be binding in its entirety and directly applicable in all Member States.

Done at Brussels, 10 August 2006.

ANNEX I

TABLE 1

LIST OF FIELDS FOR REPORTING PURPOSES

Field Identifier	Description
1. Reporting firm identification	A unique code to identify the firm which executed the transaction.
2. Trading day	The trading day on which the transaction was executed.
3. Trading time	The time at which the transaction was executed, reported in the local time of the competent authority to which the transaction will be reported, and the basis in which the transaction is reported expressed as Coordinated Universal Time (UTC) +/- hours.
4. Buy/sell indicator	Identifies whether the transaction was a buy or sell from the perspective of the reporting investment firm or, in the case of a report to a client, of the client.
5. Trading capacity	Identifies whether the firm executed the transaction: — on its own account (either on its own behalf or on behalf of a client), — for the account, and on behalf, of a client.

Field Identifier	Description
6. Instrument identification	This shall consist of: — a unique code, to be decided by the competent authority (if any) to which the report is made identifying the financial instrument which is the subject of the transaction, — if the financial instrument in question does not have a unique identification code, the report must include the name of the instrument or, in the case of a derivative contract, the characteristics of the contract.
7. Instrument code type	The code type used to report the instrument.
8. Underlying instrument identification	The instrument identification applicable to the security that is the underlying asset in a derivative contract as well as the transferable security falling within Article 4(1)(18)(c) of Directive 2004/39/EC.
9. Underlying instrument identification code type	The code type used to report the underlying instrument.
10. Instrument type	The harmonised classification of the financial instrument that is the subject of the transaction. The description must at least indicate whether the instrument belongs to one of the top level categories as provided by a uniform internationally accepted standard for financial instrument classification.
11. Maturity date	The maturity date of a bond or other form of securitised debt, or the exercise date/maturity date of a derivative contract.
12. Derivative type	The harmonised description of the derivative type should be done according to one of the top level categories as provided by a uniform internationally accepted standard for financial instrument classification.
13. Put/call	Specification whether an option or any other financial instrument is a put or a call.
14. Strike price	The strike price of an option or other financial instrument.
15. Price multiplier	The number of units of the financial instrument in question which are contained in a trading lot; for example, the number of derivatives or securities represented by one contract.
16. Unit price	The price per security or derivative contract excluding commission and (where relevant) accrued interest. In the case of a debt instrument, the price may be expressed either in terms of currency or as a percentage.
17. Price notation	The currency in which the price is expressed. If, in the case of a bond or other form of securitised debt, the price is expressed as a percentage, that percentage shall be included.
18. Quantity	The number of units of the financial instruments, the nominal value of bonds, or the number of derivative contracts included in the transaction.
19. Quantity notation	An indication as to whether the quantity is the number of units of financial instruments, the nominal value of bonds or the number of derivative contracts.

Field Identifier	Description
20. Counterparty	Identification of the counterparty to the transaction. That identification shall consist of: — where the counterparty is an investment firm, a unique code for that firm, to be determined by the competent authority (if any) to which the report is made, — where the counterparty is a regulated market or MTF or an entity acting as its central counterparty, the unique harmonised identification code for that market, MTF or entity acting as central counterparty, as specified in the list published by the competent authority of the home Member State of that entity in accordance with Article 13(2), — where the counterparty is not an investment firm, a regulated market, an MTF or an entity acting as central counterparty, it should be identified as "customer/client" of the investment firm which executed the transaction.
21. Venue identification	Identification of the venue where the transaction was executed. That identification shall consist in: — where the venue is a trading venue: its unique harmonised identification code, — otherwise: the code "OTC".
22. Transaction reference number	A unique identification number for the transaction provided by the investment firm or a third party reporting on its behalf.
23. Cancellation flag	An indication as to whether the transaction was cancelled.

TABLE 2
FURTHER DETAILS FOR USE OF COMPETENT AUTHORITIES

Field Identifier	Description
1. Reporting firm identification	If a unique code as referred to in Table 1 of Annex I is not sufficient to identify the counterparty, competent authorities should develop adequate measures that ensure the identification of the counterparty.
6. Instrument identification	The unique code, agreed between all the competent authorities, applicable to the financial instrument in question shall be used.
20. Counterparty	If a unique code, or unique harmonised identification code as referred to in Table 1 of Annex 1 is not sufficient to identify the counterparty, competent authorities should develop adequate measures that ensure the identification of the counterparty.

[9929]

ANNEX II

TABLE 1
INFORMATION TO BE MADE PUBLIC IN ACCORDANCE WITH ARTICLE 17

Type of system	Description of system	Summary of information to be made public, in accordance with Article 17
Continuous auction order book trading system	A system that by means of an order book and a trading algorithm operated without human intervention matches sell orders with matching buy orders on the basis of the best available price on a continuous basis.	The aggregate number of orders and the shares they represent at each price level, for at least the five best bid and offer price levels.
Quote-driven trading system	A system where transactions are concluded on the basis of firm quotes that are continuously made available to participants, which requires the market makers to maintain quotes in a size that balances the needs of members and participants to deal in a commercial size and the risk to which the market maker exposes itself.	The best bid and offer by price of each market maker in that share, together with the volumes attaching to those prices.
Periodic auction trading system	A system that matches orders on the basis of a periodic auction and a trading algorithm operated without human intervention.	The price at which the auction trading system would best satisfy its trading algorithm and the volume that would potentially be executable at that price.
Trading system not covered by first three rows	A hybrid system falling into two or more of the first three rows or a system where the price determination process is of a different nature than that applicable to the types of system covered by first three rows.	Adequate information as to the level of orders or quotes and of trading interest; in particular, the five best bid and offer price levels and/or two-way quotes of each market maker in the share, if the characteristics of the price discovery mechanism so permit.

TABLE 2
ORDERS LARGE IN SCALE COMPARED WITH NORMAL MARKET SIZE

(*in EUR*)

Class in terms of average daily turnover (ADT)	ADT < 500,000	500,000 ≤ADT < 1,000,000	1,000,000 ≤ADT < 25,000,000	25,000,000 ≤ ADT < 50,000,000	ADT ≥50,000,000
Minimum size of order qualifying as large in scale compared with normal market size	50,000	100,000	250,000	400,000	500,000

TABLE 3
STANDARD MARKET SIZES

(*in EUR*)

Class in terms of average value of transactions (AVT)	AVT < 10,000	10,000 ≤AVT < 20,000	20,000 ≤AVT < 30,000	30,000 ≤AVT < 40,000	40,000 ≤AVT < 50,000	50,000 ≤AVT < 70,000	70,000 ≤AVT < 90,000	Etc.
Standard market size	7,500	15,000	25,000	35,000	45,000	60,000	80,000	Etc.

TABLE 4
DEFERRED PUBLICATION THRESHOLDS AND DELAYS

The table below shows, for each permitted delay for publication and each class of shares in terms of average daily turnover (ADT), the minimum qualifying size of transaction that will qualify for that delay in respect of a share of that type.

		Class of shares in terms of average daily turnover (ADT)			
		ADT < EUR 100,000	EUR 100,000 ≤ADT < EUR 1,000,000	EUR 1,000,000 ≤ADT < EUR 50,000,000	ADT ≥EUR 50,000,000
		Minimum qualifying size of transaction for permitted delay			
Per mitted delay for publication	60 minutes	EUR 10,000	Greater of 5% of ADT and EUR 25,000	Lower of 10% of ADT and EUR 3,500,000	Lower of 10% of ADT and EUR 7,500,000
	180 minutes	EUR 25,000	Greater of 15% of ADT and EUR 75,000	Lower of 15% of ADT and EUR 5,000,000	Lower of 20% of ADT and EUR 15,000,000
	Until end of trading day (or roll-over to noon of next trading day if trade undertaken in final two hours of trading day)	EUR 45,000	Greater of 25% of ADT and EUR 100,000	Lower of 25% of ADT and EUR 10,000,000	Lower of 30% of ADT and EUR 30,000,000
	Until end of trading day next after trade	EUR 60,000	Greater of 50% of ADT and EUR 100,000	Greater of 50% of ADT and EUR 1,000,000	100% of ADT
	Until end of second trading day next after trade	EUR 80,000	100% of ADT	100% of ADT	250% of ADT
	Until end of third trading day next after trade		250% of ADT	250% of ADT	

[9930]

DIRECTIVE OF THE EUROPEAN PARLIAMENT AND OF THE COUNCIL

of 6 September 2006

amending Council Directive 77/91/EEC as regards the formation of public limited liability companies and the maintenance and alteration of their capital

2006/68/EC

(Text with EEA relevance)

NOTES

Date of publication in OJ: OJ L264, 25.9.2006, p 32. Notes are as in the original OJ version.

Note: Council Directive 77/91/EEC (the Second Council Directive on Company Law) is not reproduced in this Handbook as transposition of the main provisions was effected by CA1985 (see, in particular, Pts IV, V (except Chapter VIII), and VIII) and its principles are well established in UK law. For further implementation measures (including ones implementing the amending Council Directive 92/101/EEC), see the Companies (Membership of Holding Company) (Dealers in Securities) Regulations 1997, SI 1997/2306, the Companies (Investment Companies) (Distribution of Profits) Regulations 1999, SI 1999/2770, the Companies (Acquisition of Own Shares) (Treasury Shares) Regulations 2003, SI 2003/1116, the Companies (Acquisition of Own Shares) (Treasury Shares) No 2 Regulations 2003, SI 2003/3031, and the Companies Act 1985 (Investment Companies and Accounting and Audit Amendments) Regulations 2005, SI 2005/2280 (all of which amend CA 1985).

THE EUROPEAN PARLIAMENT AND THE COUNCIL OF THE EUROPEAN UNION,

Having regard to the Treaty establishing the European Community, and in particular Article 44(1) thereof,

Having regard to the proposal from the Commission,

Having regard to the opinion of the European Economic and Social Committee,[1]

Acting in accordance with the procedure laid down in Article 251 of the Treaty,[2]

Whereas:

(1) The second Council Directive 77/91/EEC of 13 December 1976 on coordination of safeguards which, for the protection of the interests of members and others, are required by Member States of companies within the meaning of the second paragraph of Article 58 of the Treaty, in respect of the formation of public limited liability companies and the maintenance and alteration of their capital, with a view to making such safeguards equivalent,[3] sets out the requirements for several capital-related measures taken by such companies.

(2) In its Communication of 21 May 2003 to the Council and the European Parliament entitled "Modernising Company Law and Enhancing Corporate Governance in the European Union – A Plan to Move Forward" the Commission draws the conclusion that a simplification and modernisation of Directive 77/91/EEC would significantly contribute to the promotion of business efficiency and competitiveness without reducing the protection offered to shareholders and creditors. Those objectives have the first priority but do not affect the need to proceed without delay to a general examination of the feasibility of alternatives to the capital maintenance regime which would adequately protect the interests of creditors and shareholders of a public limited liability company.

(3) Member States should be able to permit public limited liability companies to allot shares for consideration other than in cash without requiring them to obtain a special expert valuation in cases in which there is a clear point of reference for the valuation of such consideration. Nonetheless, the right of minority shareholders to require such valuation should be guaranteed.

(4) Public limited liability companies should be allowed to acquire their own shares up to the limit of the company's distributable reserves and the period for which such an acquisition may be authorised by the general meeting should be increased so as to enhance flexibility and reduce the administrative burden for companies which have to react promptly to market developments affecting the price of their shares.

(5) Member States should be able to permit public limited liability companies to grant financial assistance with a view to the acquisition of their shares by a third party up to the limit of the company's distributable reserves so as to increase flexibility with regard to changes in the ownership structure of the share capital of companies. This possibility should be subject to safeguards, having regard to this Directive's objective of protecting both shareholders and third parties.

(6) In order to enhance standardised creditor protection in all Member States, creditors should be able to resort, under certain conditions, to judicial or administrative proceedings where their claims are at stake as a consequence of a reduction in the capital of a public limited liability company.

(7) In order to ensure that market abuse is prevented, Member States should take into account, for the purpose of implementation of this Directive, the provisions of Directive 2003/6/EC of the European Parliament and of the Council of 28 January 2003 on insider dealing and market manipulation (market abuse),[4] Commission Regulation (EC) No 2273/2003 of 22 December 2003 implementing Directive 2003/6/EC of the European Parliament and of the Council as regards exemptions for buy-back programmes and stabilisation of financial instruments[5] and Commission Directive 2004/72/EC of 29 April 2004 implementing Directive 2003/6/EC of the European Parliament and of the Council as regards accepted market practices, the definition of inside information in relation to derivatives on commodities, the drawing up of lists of insiders, the notification of managers' transactions and the notification of suspicious transactions.[6]

(8) Directive 77/91/EEC should therefore be amended accordingly.

(9) In accordance with point 34 of the Interinstitutional Agreement on better law-making,[7] Member States are encouraged to draw up, for themselves and in the interest of the Community, their own tables illustrating, as far as possible, the correlation between this Directive and the transposition measures, and to make them public,

[9930A]

NOTES

1 OJ C294, 25.11.2005, p 1.
2 Opinion of the European Parliament of 14 March 2006 (not yet published in the Official Journal) and Council Decision of 24 July 2006.
3 OJ L26, 31.1.1977, p 1. Directive as last amended by the 2003 Act of Accession.
4 OJ L96, 12.4.2003, p 16.
5 OJ L336, 23.12.2003, p 33.
6 OJ L162, 30.4.2004, p 70.
7 OJ C321, 31.12.2003, p 1.

HAVE ADOPTED THIS DIRECTIVE:

Article 1

Directive 77/91/EEC is hereby amended as follows:

1. in Article 1(1), the 21st indent shall be replaced by the following:
   "— in Hungary:
   nyilvánosan működő részvénytársaság;";
2. the following Articles shall be inserted:

"Article 10a

1. Member States may decide not to apply Article 10(1), (2) and (3) where, upon a decision of the administrative or management body, transferable securities as defined in point 18 of Article 4(1) of Directive 2004/39/EC of the European Parliament and of the Council of 21 April 2004 on markets in financial instruments* or money-market instruments as defined in point 19 of Article 4(1) of that Directive are contributed as consideration other than in cash, and those securities or money-market instruments are valued at the weighted average price at which they have been traded on one or more regulated market(s) as defined in point 14 of Article 4(1) of that Directive during a sufficient period, to be determined by national law, preceding the effective date of the contribution of the respective consideration other than in cash.

However, where that price has been affected by exceptional circumstances that would significantly change the value of the asset at the effective date of its contribution, including situations where the market for such transferable securities or money-market instruments has become illiquid, a revaluation shall be carried out on the initiative and under the responsibility of the administrative or management body. For the purposes of the aforementioned revaluation, Article 10(1), (2) and (3) shall apply.

2. Member States may decide not to apply Article 10(1), (2) and (3) where, upon a decision of the administrative or management body, assets, other than the transferable securities and money-market instruments referred to in paragraph 1, are contributed as consideration other than in cash which have already been subject to a fair value opinion by a recognised independent expert and where the following conditions are fulfilled:

(a) the fair value is determined for a date not more than six months before the effective date of the asset contribution;

(b) the valuation has been performed in accordance with generally accepted valuation standards and principles in the Member State, which are applicable to the kind of assets to be contributed.

In the case of new qualifying circumstances that would significantly change the fair value of the asset at the effective date of its contribution, a revaluation shall be carried out on the initiative and under the responsibility of the administrative or management body. For the purposes of the aforementioned revaluation, Article 10(1), (2) and (3) shall apply.

In the absence of such a revaluation, one or more shareholders holding an aggregate percentage of at least 5% of the company's subscribed capital on the day the decision on the increase in the capital is taken may demand a valuation by an independent expert, in which case Article 10(1), (2) and (3) shall apply. Such shareholder(s) may submit a demand up until the effective date of the asset contribution, provided that, at the date of the demand, the shareholder(s) in question still hold(s) an aggregate percentage of at least 5% of the company's subscribed capital, as it was on the day the decision on the increase in the capital was taken.

3. Member States may decide not to apply Article 10(1), (2) and (3) where, upon a decision of the administrative or management body, assets, other than the transferable securities and money-market instruments referred to in paragraph 1, are contributed as consideration other than in cash whose fair value is derived by individual asset from the statutory accounts of the previous financial year provided that the statutory accounts have been subject to an audit in accordance with Directive 2006/43/EC of the European Parliament and of the Council of 17 May 2006 on statutory audits of annual accounts and consolidated accounts.**

The second and third subparagraphs of paragraph 2 shall apply *mutatis mutandis*.

Article 10b

1. Where consideration other than in cash as referred to in Article 10a occurs without an expert's report as referred to in Article 10(1), (2) and (3), in addition to the requirements set out in point (h) of Article 3 and within one month after the effective date of the asset contribution, a declaration containing the following shall be published:

(a) a description of the consideration other than in cash at issue;

(b) its value, the source of this valuation and, where appropriate, the method of valuation;

(c) a statement whether the value arrived at corresponds at least to the number, to the nominal value or, where there is no nominal value, the accountable par and, where appropriate, to the premium on the shares to be issued for such consideration;

(d) a statement that no new qualifying circumstances with regard to the original valuation have occurred.

That publication shall be effected in the manner laid down by the laws of each Member State in accordance with Article 3 of Directive 68/151/EEC.

2. Where consideration other than in cash is proposed to be made without an expert's report as referred to in Article 10(1), (2) and (3) in relation to an increase in the capital proposed to be made under Article 25(2), an announcement containing the date when the decision on the increase was taken and the information listed in paragraph 1 shall be published, in the manner laid down by the laws of each Member State in accordance with Article 3 of Directive 68/151/EEC, before the contribution of the asset as consideration other than in cash is to become effective. In that event, the declaration pursuant to paragraph 1 shall be limited to the statement that no new qualifying circumstances have occurred since the aforementioned announcement was published.

3. Each Member State shall provide for adequate safeguards ensuring compliance with the procedure set out in Article 10a and in this Article where a contribution for a consideration other than in cash is made without an expert's report as referred to in Article 10(1), (2) and (3).".

3. in Article 11(1), the first subparagraph shall be amended as follows:

(a) "Article 10" shall be replaced by "Article 10(1), (2) and (3)";

(b) the following sentence shall be added:

"Articles 10a and 10b shall apply mutatis mutandis.".

4. in Article 19, paragraph 1 shall be replaced by the following:

"1. Without prejudice to the principle of equal treatment of all shareholders who are in the same position, and to Directive 2003/6/EC of the European Parliament and of the Council of 28 January 2003 on insider dealing and market manipulation (market abuse),*** Member States may permit a company to acquire its own shares, either itself or through a person acting in his own name but on the company's behalf. To the extent that the acquisitions are permitted, Member States shall make such acquisitions subject to the following conditions:

(a) authorisation shall be given by the general meeting, which shall determine the terms and conditions of such acquisitions, and, in particular, the maximum number of shares to be acquired, the duration of the period for which the authorisation is given, the maximum length of which shall be determined by national law without, however, exceeding five years, and, in the case of acquisition for value, the maximum and minimum consideration. Members of the administrative or management body shall satisfy themselves that, at the time when each authorised acquisition is effected, the conditions referred to in points (b) and (c) are respected;

(b) the acquisitions, including shares previously acquired by the company and held by it, and shares acquired by a person acting in his own name but on the company's behalf, may not have the effect of reducing the net assets below the amount mentioned in points (a) and (b) of Article 15(1);

(c) only fully paid-up shares may be included in the transaction.

Furthermore, Member States may subject acquisitions within the meaning of the first subparagraph to any of the following conditions:

(i) that the nominal value or, in the absence thereof, the accountable par of the acquired shares, including shares previously acquired by the company and held by it, and shares acquired by a person acting in his own name but on the company's behalf, may not exceed a limit to be determined by Member States. This limit may not be lower than 10% of the subscribed capital;

(ii) that the power of the company to acquire its own shares within the meaning of the first subparagraph, the maximum number of shares to be acquired, the duration of the period for which the power is given and the maximum or minimum consideration are laid down in the statutes or in the instrument of incorporation of the company;

(iii) that the company complies with appropriate reporting and notification requirements;

(iv) that certain companies, as determined by Member States, may be required to cancel the acquired shares provided that an amount equal to the nominal value of the shares cancelled must be included in a reserve which cannot be distributed to the shareholders, except in the event of a reduction in the subscribed capital. This reserve may be used only for the purposes of increasing the subscribed capital by the capitalisation of reserves;

(v) that the acquisition shall not prejudice the satisfaction of creditors' claims.".

5. in Article 20(3), the words "Article 15(1)(a)" shall be replaced by the words "points (a) and (b) of Article 15(1)";

6. Article 23(1) shall be replaced by the following:

"1. Where Member States permit a company to, either directly or indirectly, advance funds or make loans or provide security, with a view to the acquisition of its shares by a third party, they shall make such transactions subject to the conditions set out in the second, third, fourth and fifth subparagraphs.

The transactions shall take place under the responsibility of the administrative or management body at fair market conditions, especially with regard to interest received by the company and with regard to security provided to the company for the loans and advances referred to in the first subparagraph. The credit standing of the third party or, in the case of multiparty transactions, of each counterparty thereto shall have been duly investigated.

The transactions shall be submitted by the administrative or management body to the general meeting for prior approval, whereby the general meeting shall act in accordance with the rules for a quorum and a majority laid down in Article 40. The administrative or management body shall present a written report to the general meeting, indicating the reasons for the transaction, the interest of the company in entering into such a transaction, the conditions on which the transaction is entered into, the risks involved in the transaction for the liquidity and solvency of the company and the price at which the third party is to acquire the shares. This report shall be submitted to the register for publication in accordance with Article 3 of Directive 68/151/EEC.

The aggregate financial assistance granted to third parties shall at no time result in the reduction of the net assets below the amount specified in points (a) and (b) of Article 15(1), taking into account also any reduction of the net assets that may have occurred through the acquisition, by the company or on behalf of the company, of its own shares in accordance with Article 19(1). The company shall include, among the liabilities in the balance sheet, a reserve, unavailable for distribution, of the amount of the aggregate financial assistance.

Where a third party by means of financial assistance from a company acquires that company's own shares within the meaning of Article 19(1) or subscribes for shares issued in the course of an increase in the subscribed capital, such acquisition or subscription shall be made at a fair price.".

7. the following Article shall be inserted:

"Article 23a

In cases where individual members of the administrative or management body of the company being party to a transaction referred to in Article 23(1), or of the administrative or management body of a parent undertaking within the meaning of Article 1 of Council Directive 83/349/EEC of 13 June 1983 on consolidated accounts**** or such parent undertaking itself, or individuals acting in their own name, but on behalf of the members of such bodies or on behalf of such undertaking, are counterparties to such a transaction, Member States shall ensure through adequate safeguards that such transaction does not conflict with the company's best interests.".

8. in Article 27(2), the second subparagraph shall be replaced by the following:

"Article 10(2) and (3) and Articles 10a and 10b shall apply.".

9. Article 32(1) shall be replaced by the following:

"1. In the event of a reduction in the subscribed capital, at least the creditors whose claims antedate the publication of the decision on the reduction shall at least have the right to obtain security for claims which have not fallen due by the date of that publication. Member States may not set aside such a right unless the creditor has adequate safeguards, or unless such safeguards are not necessary having regard to the assets of the company.

Member States shall lay down the conditions for the exercise of the right provided for in the first subparagraph. In any event, Member States shall ensure that the creditors are authorised to apply to the appropriate administrative or judicial authority for adequate safeguards provided that they can credibly demonstrate that due to the reduction in the subscribed capital the satisfaction of their claims is at stake, and that no adequate safeguards have been obtained from the company.".

10. Article 41(1) shall be replaced by the following:

"1. Member States may derogate from Article 9(1), the first sentence of point (a) of Article 19(1), and Articles 25, 26 and 29 to the extent that such derogations are necessary for the adoption or application of provisions designed to encourage the participation of employees, or other groups of persons defined by national law, in the capital of undertakings.".

[9930B]

NOTES

* OJ L145, 30.4.2004, p 1. Directive as last amended by Directive 2006/31/EC (OJ L114, 27.4.2006, p 60).

** OJ L157, 9.6.2006, p 87.

*** OJ L96, 12.4.2003, p 16.

****OJ L 193, 18.7.1983, p 1. Directive as last amended by Directive 2006/43/EC.

Article 2

1. Member States shall bring into force the laws, regulations and administrative provisions necessary to comply with this Directive by 15 April 2008.

When Member States adopt these measures, they shall contain a reference to this Directive or shall be accompanied by such reference on the occasion of their official publication. The methods of making such reference shall be laid down by Member States.

2. Member States shall communicate to the Commission the texts of the main provisions of national law which they adopt in the field covered by this Directive.

[9930C]

Article 3

This Directive shall enter into force on the 20th day following that of its publication in the *Official Journal of the European Union*.

[9930D]

Article 4

This Directive is addressed to the Member States.

[9930E]

Done at Strasbourg, 6 September 2006.

COMMISSION DIRECTIVE

of 10 August 2006

implementing Directive 2004/39/EC of the European Parliament and of the Council as regards organisational requirements and operating conditions for investment firms and defined terms for the purposes of that Directive

(2006/73/EC)

(Text with EEA relevance)

NOTES

Date of publication in OJ: OJ L241, 2.9.2006, p 26. Notes are as in the original OJ version.

THE COMMISSION OF THE EUROPEAN COMMUNITIES,

Having regard to the Treaty establishing the European Community,

Having regard to Directive 2004/39/EC of the European Parliament and of the Council of 21 April 2004 on markets in financial instruments amending Council Directives 85/611/EEC and 93/6/EEC and Directive 2000/12/EC of the European Parliament and of the Council and repealing Council Directive 93/22/EEC,[1] and in particular Article 4(2), Article 13(10), Article 18(3), Article 19(10), Article 21(6), Article 22(3) and Article 24(5) thereof,

Whereas:

(1) Directive 2004/39/EC establishes the framework for a regulatory regime for financial markets in the Community, governing, among other matters, operating conditions relating to the performance by investment firms of investment services and, where appropriate, ancillary services and investment activities; organisational requirements for investment firms performing such services and activities, and for regulated markets; reporting requirements in respect of transactions in financial instruments; and transparency requirements in respect of transactions in shares admitted to trading on a regulated market.

(2) The rules for the implementation of the regime governing organisational requirements for investment firms performing investment services and, where appropriate, ancillary services and investment activities on a professional basis, and for regulated markets, should be consistent with the aim of Directive 2004/39/EC. They should be designed to ensure a high level of integrity, competence and soundness among investment firms and entities that operate regulated markets or MTFs, and to be applied in a uniform manner.

(3) It is necessary to specify concrete organisational requirements and procedures for investment firms performing such services or activities. In particular, rigorous procedures should be provided for with regard to matters such as compliance, risk management, complaints handling, personal transactions, outsourcing and the identification, management and disclosure of conflicts of interest.

(4) The organisational requirements and conditions for authorisation for investment firms should be set out in the form of a set of rules that ensures the uniform application of the

relevant provisions of Directive 2004/39/EC. This is necessary in order to ensure that investment firms have equal access on equivalent terms to all markets in the Community and to eliminate obstacles, linked to authorisation procedures, to cross-border activities in the field of investment services.

(5) The rules for the implementation of the regime governing operating conditions for the performance of investment and ancillary services and investment activities should reflect the aim underlying that regime. That is to say, they should be designed to ensure a high level of investor protection to be applied in a uniform manner through the introduction of clear standards and requirements governing the relationship between an investment firm and its client. On the other hand, as regards investor protection, and in particular the provision of investors with information or the seeking of information from investors, the retail or professional nature of the client or potential client concerned should be taken into account.

(6) The form of a Directive is necessary in order to enable the implementing provisions to be adjusted to the specificities of the particular market and legal system in each Member State.

(7) In order to ensure the uniform application of the various provisions of Directive 2004/39/EC, it is necessary to establish a harmonised set of organisational requirements and operating conditions for investment firms. Consequently, Member States and competent authorities should not add supplementary binding rules when transposing and applying the rules specified in this Directive, save where this Directive makes express provision to this effect.

(8) However, in exceptional circumstances, it should be possible for Member States to impose requirements on investment firms additional to those laid down in the implementing rules. However, such intervention should be restricted to those cases where specific risks to investor protection or to market integrity including those related to the stability of the financial system have not been adequately addressed by the Community legislation, and it should be strictly proportionate.

(9) Any additional requirements retained or imposed by Member States in conformity with this Directive must not restrict or otherwise affect the rights of investment firms under Articles 31 and 32 of Directive 2004/39/EC.

(10) The specific risks addressed by any additional requirements retained by Member States at the date of application of this Directive should be of particular importance to the market structure of the State in question, including the behaviour of firms and consumers in that market. The assessment of those specific risks should be made in the context of the regulatory regime put in place by Directive 2004/39/EC and its detailed implementing rules. Any decision to retain additional requirements should be made with proper regard to the objectives of that Directive to remove barriers to the cross-border provision of investment service by harmonising the initial authorisation and operating requirements for investment firms.

(11) Investment firms vary widely in their size, their structure and the nature of their business. A regulatory regime should be adapted to that diversity while imposing certain fundamental regulatory requirements which are appropriate for all firms. Regulated entities should comply with their high level obligations and design and adopt measures that are best suited to their particular nature and circumstances.

(12) However, a regulatory regime which entails too much uncertainty for investment firms may reduce efficiency. Competent authorities are expected to issue interpretative guidance on provisions on this Directive, with a view in particular to clarifying the practical application of the requirements of this Directive to particular kinds of firms and circumstances. Non-binding guidance of this kind might, among other things, clarify how the provisions of this Directive and Directive 2004/39/EC apply in the light of market developments. To ensure a uniform application of this Directive and Directive 2004/39/EC, the Commission may issue guidance by way of interpretative communications or other means. Furthermore, the Committee of European Securities Regulators may issue guidance in order to secure convergent application of this Directive and Directive 2004/39/EC by competent authorities.

(13) The organisational requirements established under Directive 2004/39/EC are without prejudice to systems established by national law for the registration of individuals working within investment firms.

(14) For the purposes of the provisions of this Directive requiring an investment firm to establish, implement and maintain an adequate risk management policy, the risks relating to the firm's activities, processes and systems should include the risks associated with the outsourcing of critical or important functions or of investment services or activities. Such risks should include those associated with the firm's relationship with the service provider, and the potential risks posed where the outsourced activities of multiple investment firms or other regulated entities are concentrated within a limited number of service providers.

(15) The fact that risk management and compliance functions are performed by the same person does not necessarily jeopardise the independent functioning of each function. The conditions that persons involved in the compliance function should not also be involved in the performance of the functions that they monitor, and that the method of determining the remuneration of such persons should not be likely to compromise their objectivity, may not be proportionate in the case of small investment firms. However, they would only be disproportionate for larger firms in exceptional circumstances.

(16) A number of the provisions of Directive 2004/39/EC require investment firms to collect and maintain information relating to clients and services provided to clients. Where those requirements involve the collection and processing of personal data, firms should ensure that they comply with national measures implementing Directive 95/46/EC of the European Parliament and of the Council of 24 October 1995[2] on the protection of individuals with regard to the processing of personal data and on the free movement of such data.

(17) Where successive personal transactions are carried out on behalf of a person in accordance with prior instructions given by that person, the obligations under the provisions of this Directive relating to personal transactions should not apply separately to each such successive transaction if those instructions remain in force and unchanged. Similarly, those obligations should not apply to the termination or withdrawal of such instructions, provided that any financial instruments which had previously been acquired pursuant to the instructions are not disposed of at the same time as the instructions terminate or are withdrawn. However, those obligations should apply in relation to a personal transaction, or the commencement of successive personal transactions, carried out on behalf of the same person if those instructions are changed or if new instructions are issued.

(18) Competent authorities should not make the authorisation to provide investment services or activities subject to a general prohibition on the outsourcing of one or more critical or important functions or investment services or activities. Investment firms should be allowed to outsource such activities if the outsourcing arrangements established by the firm comply with certain conditions.

(19) For the purposes of the provisions of this Directive setting out conditions for outsourcing critical or important operational functions or investment services or activities, an outsourcing that would involve the delegation of functions to the extent that the firm becomes a letter box entity should be considered to undermine the conditions with which the investment firm must comply in order to be and remain authorised in accordance with Article 5 of Directive 2004/39/EC.

(20) The outsourcing of investment services or activities or critical and important functions is capable of constituting a material change of the conditions for the authorisation of the investment firm, as referred to in Article 16(2) of Directive 2004/39/EC. If such outsourcing arrangements are to be put in place after the investment firm has obtained an authorisation according to the provisions included in Chapter I of Title II of Directive 2004/39/EC, those arrangements should be notified to the competent authority where required by Article 16(2) of Directive 2004/39/EC.

(21) Investment firms are required by this Directive to give the responsible competent authority prior notification of any arrangement for the outsourcing of the management of retail client portfolios that it proposes to enter into with a service provider located in a third country, where certain specified conditions are not met. However, competent authorities are not expected to authorise or otherwise approve any such arrangement or its terms. The purpose of the notification, rather, is to ensure that the competent authority has the opportunity to intervene in appropriate cases. It is the responsibility of the investment firm to negotiate the terms of any outsourcing arrangement, and to ensure that those terms are consistent with the obligations of the firm under this Directive and Directive 2004/39/EC, without the formal intervention of the competent authority.

(22) For the purposes of regulatory transparency, and in order to ensure an appropriate level of certainty for investment firms, this Directive requires each competent authority to publish a statement of its policy in relation to the outsourcing of retail portfolio management to service providers located in third countries. That statement must set out examples of cases where the competent authority is unlikely to object to such outsourcing, and must include an explanation of why outsourcing in such cases is unlikely to impair the ability of the firm to comply with the general conditions for outsourcing under this Directive. In providing that explanation, a competent authority should always indicate the reasons why outsourcing in the cases in question would not impede the effectiveness of its access to all the information relating to the outsourced service that is necessary for the authority to carry out its regulatory functions in respect of the investment firm.

(23) Where an investment firm deposits funds it holds on behalf of a client with a qualifying money market fund, the units in that money market fund should be held in accordance with the requirements for holding financial instruments belonging to clients.

(24) The circumstances which should be treated as giving rise to a conflict of interest should cover cases where there is a conflict between the interests of the firm or certain persons connected to the firm or the firm's group and the duty the firm owes to a client; or between the differing interests of two or more of its clients, to whom the firm owes in each case a duty. It is not enough that the firm may gain a benefit if there is not also a possible disadvantage to a client, or that one client to whom the firm owes a duty may make a gain or avoid a loss without there being a concomitant possible loss to another such client.

(25) Conflicts of interest should be regulated only where an investment service or ancillary service is provided by an investment firm. The status of the client to whom the service is provided — as either retail, professional or eligible counterparty — is irrelevant for this purpose.

(26) In complying with its obligation to draw up a conflict of interest policy under Directive 2004/39/EC which identifies circumstances which constitute or may give rise to a conflict of interest, the investment firm should pay special attention to the activities of investment research and advice, proprietary trading, portfolio management and corporate finance business, including underwriting or selling in an offering of securities and advising on mergers and acquisitions. In particular, such special attention is appropriate where the firm or a person directly or indirectly linked by control to the firm performs a combination of two or more of those activities.

(27) Investment firms should aim to identify and manage the conflicts of interest arising in relation to their various business lines and their group's activities under a comprehensive conflicts of interest policy. In particular, the disclosure of conflicts of interest by an investment firm should not exempt it from the obligation to maintain and operate the effective organisational and administrative arrangements required under Article 13(3) of Directive 2004/39/EC. While disclosure of specific conflicts of interest is required by Article 18(2) of Directive 2004/39/EC, an over-reliance on disclosure without adequate consideration as to how conflicts may appropriately be managed is not permitted.

(28) Investment research should be a sub-category of the type of information defined as a recommendation in Commission Directive 2003/125/EC of 22 December 2003 implementing Directive 2003/6/EC of the European Parliament and of the Council as regards the fair presentation of investment recommendations and the disclosure of conflicts of interest,[3] but it applies to financial instruments as defined in Directive 2004/39/EC. Recommendations, of the type so defined, which do not constitute investment research as defined in this Directive are nevertheless subject to the provisions of Directive 2003/125/EC as to the fair presentation of investment recommendations and the disclosure of conflicts of interest.

(29) The measures and arrangements adopted by an investment firm to manage the conflicts of interests that might arise from the production and dissemination of material that is presented as investment research should be appropriate to protect the objectivity and independence of financial analysts and of the investment research they produce. Those measures and arrangements should ensure that financial analysts enjoy an adequate degree of independence from the interests of persons whose responsibilities or business interests may reasonably be considered to conflict with the interests of the persons to whom the investment research is disseminated.

(30) Persons whose responsibilities or business interests may reasonably be considered to conflict with the interests of the persons to whom investment research is disseminated should include corporate finance personnel and persons involved in sales and trading on behalf of clients or the firm.

(31) Exceptional circumstances in which financial analysts and other persons connected with the investment firm who are involved in the production of investment research may, with prior written approval, undertake personal transactions in instruments to which the research relates should include those circumstances where, for personal reasons relating to financial hardship, the financial analyst or other person is required to liquidate a position.

(32) Small gifts or minor hospitality below a level specified in the firm's conflicts of interest policy and mentioned in the summary description of that policy that is made available to clients should not be considered as inducements for the purposes of the provisions relating to investment research.

(33) The concept of dissemination of investment research to clients or the public should not include dissemination exclusively to persons within the group of the investment firm.

(34) Current recommendations should be considered to be those recommendations contained in investment research which have not been withdrawn and which have not lapsed.

(35) The same requirements should apply to the substantial alteration of investment research produced by a third party as apply to the production of research.

(36) Financial analysts should not become involved in activities other than the preparation of investment research where such involvement is inconsistent with the maintenance of that person's objectivity. The following involvements should ordinarily be

considered as inconsistent with the maintenance of that person's objectivity: participating in investment banking activities such as corporate finance business and underwriting, participating in "pitches" for new business or "road shows" for new issues of financial instruments; or being otherwise involved in the preparation of issuer marketing.

(37) Without prejudice to the provisions of this Directive relating to the production or dissemination of investment research, it is recommended that producers of investment research that are not investment firms should consider adopting internal policies and procedures designed to ensure that they also comply with the principles set out in this Directive as to the protection of the independence and objectivity of that research.

(38) Requirements imposed by this Directive, including those relating to personal transactions, to dealing with knowledge of investment research and to the production or dissemination of investment research, apply without prejudice to other requirements of Directive 2004/39/EC and Directive 2003/6/EC of the European parliament and of the Council of 28 January 2003 on insider dealing and market manipulation (market abuse)[4] and their respective implementing measures.

(39) For the purposes of the provisions of this Directive concerning inducements, the receipt by an investment firm of a commission in connection with investment advice or general recommendations, in circumstances where the advice or recommendations are not biased as a result of the receipt of commission, should be considered as designed to enhance the quality of the investment advice to the client.

(40) This Directive permits investment firms to give or receive certain inducements only subject to specific conditions, and provided they are disclosed to the client, or are given to or by the client or a person on behalf of the client.

(41) This Directive requires investment firms that provide investment services other than investment advice to new retail clients to enter into a written basic agreement with the client, setting out the essential rights and obligations of the firm and the client. However, it imposes no other obligations as to the form, content and performance of contracts for the provisions of investment or ancillary services.

(42) This Directive sets out requirements for marketing communications only with respect to the obligation in Article 19(2) of Directive 2004/39/EC that information addressed to clients, including marketing communications, should be fair, clear and not misleading.

(43) Nothing in this Directive requires competent authorities to approve the content and form of marketing communications. However, neither does it prevent them from doing so, insofar as any such pre-approval is based only on compliance with the obligation in Directive 2004/39/EC that information to clients, including marketing communications, should be fair, clear and not misleading.

(44) Appropriate and proportionate information requirements should be established which take account of the status of a client as either retail or professional. An objective of Directive 2004/39/EC is to ensure a proportionate balance between investor protection and the disclosure obligations which apply to investment firms. To this end, it is appropriate that less stringent specific information requirements be included in this Directive with respect to professional clients than apply to retail clients. Professional clients should, subject to limited exceptions, be able to identify for themselves the information that is necessary for them to make an informed decision, and to ask the investment firm to provide that information. Where such information requests are reasonable and proportionate investment firms should provide additional information.

(45) Investment firms should provide clients or potential clients with adequate information on the nature of financial instruments and the risks associated with investing in them so that their clients can take each investment decision on a properly informed basis. The level of detail of this information may vary according to the client's categorisation as either a retail client or a professional client and the nature and risk profile of the financial instruments that are being offered, but should never be so general as to omit any essential elements. It is possible that for some financial instruments only the information referring to the type of an instrument will be sufficient whereas for some others the information will need to be product-specific.

(46) The conditions with which information addressed by investment firms to clients and potential clients must comply in order to be fair, clear and not misleading should apply to communications intended for retail clients in a way that is appropriate and proportionate, taking into account, for example, the means of communication, and the information that the communication is intended to convey to the clients or potential clients. In particular, it would not be appropriate to apply such conditions to marketing communications which consist only of one or more of the following: the name of the firm, a logo or other image associated with the firm, a contact point, a reference to the types of investment services provided by the firm, or to its fees or commissions.

(47) For the purposes of Directive 2004/39/EC and of this Directive, information should be considered to be misleading if it has a tendency to mislead the person or persons to whom it is addressed or by whom it is likely to be received, whether or not the person who provides the information considers or intends it to be misleading.

(48) In determining what constitutes the provision of information in good time before a time specified in this Directive, an investment firm should take into account, having regard to the urgency of the situation and the time necessary for the client to absorb and react to the specific information provided, the client's need for sufficient time to read and understand it before taking an investment decision. A client is likely to require less time to review information about a simple or standardised product or service, or a product or service of a kind he has purchased previously, than he would require for a more complex or unfamiliar product or service.

(49) Nothing in this Directive obliges investment firms to provide all required information about the investment firm, financial instruments, costs and associated charges, or concerning the safeguarding of client financial instruments or client funds immediately and at the same time, provided that they comply with the general obligation to provide the relevant information in good time before the time specified in this Directive. Provided that the information is communicated to the client in good time before the provision of the service, nothing in this Directive obliges firms to provide it either separately, as part of a marketing communication, or by incorporating the information in a client agreement.

(50) In cases where an investment firm is required to provide information to a client before the provision of a service, each transaction in respect of the same type of financial instrument should not be considered as the provision of a new or different service.

(51) In cases where an investment firm providing portfolio management services is required to provide to retail clients or potential retail clients information on the types of financial instruments that may be included in the client portfolio and the types of transactions that may be carried out in such instruments, such information should state separately whether the investment firm will be mandated to invest in financial instruments not admitted to trading on a regulated market, in derivatives, or in illiquid or highly volatile instruments; or to undertake short sales, purchases with borrowed funds, securities financing transactions, or any transactions involving margin payments, deposit of collateral or foreign exchange risk.

(52) The provision by an investment firm to a client of a copy of a prospectus that has been drawn up and published in accordance with Directive 2003/71/EC of the European Parliament and of the Council of 4 November 2003 on the prospectus to be published when securities are offered to the public or admitted to trading[5] should not be treated as the provision by the firm of information to a client for the purposes of the operating conditions under Directive 2004/39/EC which relate to the quality and contents of such information, if the firm is not responsible under that directive for the information given in the prospectus.

(53) The information which an investment firm is required to give to a retail client concerning costs and associated charges includes information about the arrangements for payment or performance of the agreement for the provision of investment services and any other agreement relating to a financial instrument that is being offered. For this purpose, arrangements for payment will generally be relevant where a financial instrument contract is terminated by cash settlement. Arrangements for performance will generally be relevant where, upon termination, a financial instrument requires the delivery of shares, bonds, a warrant, bullion or another instrument or commodity.

(54) As regards collective investment undertakings covered by Council Directive 85/611/EEC of 20 December 1985 on the coordination of laws, regulations and administrative provisions relating to undertakings for collective investment in transferable securities (UCITS),[6] it is not the purpose of this Directive to regulate the content of the simplified prospectus as defined by Article 28 of Directive 85/611/EEC. No information should be added to the simplified prospectus as a result of the implementation of this Directive.

(55) The simplified prospectus provides, notably, sufficient information in relation to the costs and associated charges in respect to the UCITS itself. However, investment firms distributing units in UCITS should additionally inform their clients about all the other costs and associated charges related to their provision of investment services in relation to units in UCITS.

(56) It is necessary to make different provision for the application of the suitability test in Article 19(4) of Directive 2004/39/EC and the appropriateness test in Article 19(5) of that Directive. These tests have different scope with regards to the investment services to which they relate, and have different functions and characteristics.

(57) For the purposes of Article 19(4) of Directive 2004/39/EC, a transaction may be unsuitable for the client or potential client because of the risks of the financial instruments involved, the type of transaction, the characteristics of the order or the frequency of the trading. A series of transactions that are each suitable when viewed in isolation may be

unsuitable if the recommendation or the decisions to trade are made with a frequency that is not in the best interests of the client. In the case of portfolio management, a transaction might also be unsuitable if it would result in an unsuitable portfolio.

(58) In accordance with Article 19(4) of Directive 2004/39/EC, a firm is required to assess the suitability of investment services and financial instruments to a client only when it is providing investment advice or portfolio management to that client. In the case of other investment services, the firm is required by Article 19(5) of that Directive to assess the appropriateness of an investment service or product for a client, and then only if the product is not offered on an execution-only basis under Article 19(6) of that Directive (which applies to non-complex products).

(59) For the purposes of the provisions of this Directive requiring investment firms to assess the appropriateness of investment services or products offered or demanded, a client who has engaged in a course of dealings involving a specific type of product or service beginning before the date of application of Directive 2004/39/EC should be presumed to have the necessary experience and knowledge in order to understand the risks involved in relation to that product or investment service. Where a client engages in a course of dealings of that kind through the services of an investment firm, beginning after the date of application of that Directive, the firm is not required to make a new assessment on the occasion of each separate transaction. It complies with its duty under Article 19(5) of that Directive provided that it makes the necessary assessment of appropriateness before beginning that service.

(60) A recommendation or request made, or advice given, by a portfolio manager to a client to the effect that the client should give or alter a mandate to the portfolio manager that defines the limits of the portfolio manager's discretion should be considered a recommendation within the meaning of Article 19(4) of Directive 2004/39/EC.

(61) For the purposes of determining whether a unit in a collective investment undertaking which does not comply with the requirements of Directive 85/611/EC, that has been authorised for marketing to the public, should be considered as non-complex, the circumstances in which valuation systems will be independent of the issuer should include where they are overseen by a depositary that is regulated as a provider of depositary services in a Member State.

(62) Nothing in this Directive requires competent authorities to approve the content of the basic agreement between an investment firm and its retail clients. However, neither does it prevent them from doing so, insofar as any such approval is based only on the firm's compliance with its obligations under Directive 2004/39/EC to act honestly, fairly and professionally in accordance with the best interests of its clients, and to establish a record that sets out the rights and obligations of investment firms and their clients, and the other terms on which firms will provide services to their clients.

(63) The records an investment firm is required to keep should be adapted to the type of business and the range of investment services and activities performed, provided that the record-keeping obligations set out in Directive 2004/39/EC and this Directive are fulfilled. For the purposes of the reporting obligations in respect of portfolio management, a contingent liability transaction is one that involves any actual or potential liability for the client that exceeds the cost of acquiring the instrument.

(64) For the purposes of the provisions on reporting to clients, a reference to the type of the order should be understood as referring to its status as a limit order, market order, or other specific type of order.

(65) For the purposes of the provisions on reporting to clients, a reference to the nature of the order should be understood as referring to orders to subscribe for securities, or to exercise an option, or similar client order.

(66) When establishing its execution policy in accordance with Article 21(2) of Directive 2004/39/EC, an investment firm should determine the relative importance of the factors mentioned in Article 21(1) of that Directive, or at least establish the process by which it determines the relative importance of these factors, so that it can deliver the best possible result to its clients. In order to give effect to that policy, an investment firm should select the execution venues that enable it to obtain on a consistent basis the best possible result for the execution of client orders. An investment firm should apply its execution policy to each client order that it executes with a view to obtaining the best possible result for the client in accordance with that policy. The obligation under Directive 2004/39/EC to take all reasonable steps to obtain the best possible result for the client should not be treated as requiring an investment firm to include in its execution policy all available execution venues.

(67) For the purposes of ensuring that an investment firm obtains the best possible result for the client when executing a retail client order in the absence of specific client instructions, the firm should take into consideration all factors that will allow it to deliver the best possible result in terms of the total consideration, representing the price of the financial instrument and the costs related to execution. Speed, likelihood of execution and settlement, the size and

nature of the order, market impact and any other implicit transaction costs may be given precedence over the immediate price and cost consideration only insofar as they are instrumental in delivering the best possible result in terms of the total consideration to the retail client.

(68) When an investment firm executes an order following specific instructions from the client, it should be treated as having satisfied its best execution obligations only in respect of the part or aspect of the order to which the client instructions relate. The fact that the client has given specific instructions which cover one part or aspect of the order should not be treated as releasing the investment firm from its best execution obligations in respect of any other parts or aspects of the client order that are not covered by such instructions. An investment firm should not induce a client to instruct it to execute an order in a particular way, by expressly indicating or implicitly suggesting the content of the instruction to the client, when the firm ought reasonably to know that an instruction to that effect is likely to prevent it from obtaining the best possible result for that client. However, this should not prevent a firm inviting a client to choose between two or more specified trading venues, provided that those venues are consistent with the execution policy of the firm.

(69) Dealing on own account with clients by an investment firm should be considered as the execution of client orders, and therefore subject to the requirements under Directive 2004/39/EC and this Directive and, in particular, those obligations in relation to best execution. However, if an investment firm provides a quote to a client and that quote would meet the investment firm's obligations under Article 21(1) of Directive 2004/39/EC if the firm executed that quote at the time the quote was provided, then the firm will meet those same obligations if it executes its quote after the client accepts it, provided that, taking into account the changing market conditions and the time elapsed between the offer and acceptance of the quote, the quote is not manifestly out of date.

(70) The obligation to deliver the best possible result when executing client orders applies in relation to all types of financial instruments. However, given the differences in market structures or the structure of financial instruments, it may be difficult to identify and apply a uniform standard of and procedure for best execution that would be valid and effective for all classes of instrument. Best execution obligations should therefore be applied in a manner that takes into account the different circumstances associated with the execution of orders related to particular types of financial instruments. For example, transactions involving a customised OTC financial instrument that involve a unique contractual relationship tailored to the circumstances of the client and the investment firm may not be comparable for best execution purposes with transactions involving shares traded on centralised execution venues.

(71) For the purposes of determining best execution when executing retail client orders, the costs related to execution should include an investment firm's own commissions or fees charged to the client for limited purposes, in cases where more than one venue listed in the firm's execution policy is capable of executing a particular order. In such cases, the firm's own commissions and costs for executing the order on each of the eligible execution venues should be taken into account in order to assess and compare the results for the client that would be achieved by executing the order on each such venue. However, it is not intended to require a firm to compare the results that would be achieved for its client on the basis of its own execution policy and its own commissions and fees, with results that might be achieved for the same client by any other investment firm on the basis of a different execution policy or a different structure of commissions or fees. Nor is it intended to require a firm to compare the differences in its own commissions which are attributable to differences in the nature of the services that the firm provides to clients.

(72) The provisions of this Directive that provide that costs of execution should include an investment firm's own commissions or fees charged to the client for the provision of an investment service should not apply for the purpose of determining what execution venues must be included in the firm's execution policy for the purposes of Article 21(3) of Directive 2004/39/EC.

(73) It should be considered that an investment firm structures or charges its commissions in a way which discriminates unfairly between execution venues if it charges a different commission or spread to clients for execution on different execution venues and that difference does not reflect actual differences in the cost to the firm of executing on those venues.

(74) The provisions of this Directive as to execution policy are without prejudice to the general obligation of an investment firm under Article 21(4) of Directive 2004/39/EC to monitor the effectiveness of its order execution arrangements and policy and assess the venues in its execution policy on a regular basis.

(75) This Directive is not intended to require a duplication of effort as to best execution between an investment firm which provides the service of reception and transmission of order or portfolio management and any investment firm to which that investment firm transmits its orders for execution.

(76) The best execution obligation under Directive 2004/39/EC requires investment firms to take all reasonable steps to obtain the best possible result for their clients. The quality of execution, which includes aspects such as the speed and likelihood of execution (fill rate) and the availability and incidence of price improvement, is an important factor in the delivery of best execution. Availability, comparability and consolidation of data related to execution quality provided by the various execution venues is crucial in enabling investment firms and investors to identify those execution venues that deliver the highest quality of execution for their clients. This Directive does not mandate the publication by execution venues of their execution quality data, as execution venues and data providers should be permitted to develop solutions concerning the provision of execution quality data. The Commission should submit a report by 1 November 2008 on the market-led developments in this area with a view to assessing availability, comparability and consolidation at a European level of information concerning execution quality.

(77) For the purposes of the provisions of this Directive concerning client order handling, the reallocation of transactions should be considered as detrimental to a client if, as an effect of that reallocation, unfair precedence is given to the investment firm or to any particular client.

(78) Without prejudice to Directive 2003/6/EC, for the purposes of the provisions of this Directive concerning client order handling, client orders should not be treated as otherwise comparable if they are received by different media and it would not be practicable for them to be treated sequentially. For the further purposes of those provisions, any use by an investment firm of information relating to a pending client order in order to deal on own account in the financial instruments to which the client order relates, or in related financial instruments, should be considered a misuse of that information. However, the mere fact that market makers or bodies authorised to act as counterparties confine themselves to pursuing their legitimate business of buying and selling financial instruments, or that persons authorised to execute orders on behalf of third parties confine themselves to carrying out an order dutifully, should not in itself be deemed to constitute a misuse of information.

(79) Advice about financial instruments given in a newspaper, journal, magazine or any other publication addressed to the general public (including by means of the internet), or in any television or radio broadcast, should not be considered as a personal recommendation for the purposes of the definition of "investment advice" in Directive 2004/39/EC.

(80) This Directive respects the fundamental rights and observes the principles recognised in particular by the Charter of Fundamental Rights of the European Union and in particular by Article 11 thereof and Article 10 of the European Convention on Human Rights. In this regard, this Directive does not in any way prevent Member States from applying their constitutional rules relating to freedom of the press and freedom of expression in the media.

(81) Generic advice about a type of financial instrument is not investment advice for the purposes of Directive 2004/39/EC, because this Directive specifies that, for the purposes of Directive 2004/39/EC, investment advice is restricted to advice on particular financial instruments. However, if an investment firm provides generic advice to a client about a type of financial instrument which it presents as suitable for, or based on a consideration of the circumstances of, that client, and that advice is not in fact suitable for the client, or is not based on a consideration of his circumstances, depending on the circumstances of the particular case, the firm is likely to be acting in contravention of Article 19(1) or (2) of Directive 2004/39/EC. In particular, a firm which gives a client such advice would be likely to contravene the requirement of Article 19(1) to act honestly, fairly and professionally in accordance with the best interests of its clients. Similarly or alternatively, such advice would be likely to contravene the requirement of Article 19(2) that information addressed by a firm to a client should be fair, clear and not misleading.

(82) Acts carried out by an investment firm that are preparatory to the provision of an investment service or carrying out an investment activity should be considered as an integral part of that service or activity. This would include, for example, the provision of generic advice by an investment firm to clients or potential clients prior to or in the course of the provision of investment advice or any other investment service or activity.

(83) The provision of a general recommendation (that is, one which is intended for distribution channels or the public) about a transaction in a financial instrument or a type of financial instrument constitutes the provision of an ancillary service within Section B(5) of Annex I of Directive 2004/39/EC, and consequently Directive 2004/39/EC and its protections apply to the provision of that recommendation.

(84) The Committee of European Securities Regulators, established by Commission Decision 2001/527/EC[7] has been consulted for technical advice.

(85) The measures provided for in this Directive are in accordance with the opinion of the European Securities Committee,

[9931]

NOTES

1 OJ L145, 30.4.2004, p 1. Directive as amended by Directive 2006/31/EC (OJ L114, 27.4.2006, p 60).

2 OJ L281, 23.11.1995, p 31. Directive as amended by Regulation (EC) No 1882/2003 (OJ L284, 31.10.2003, p 1).

3 OJ L339, 24.12.2003, p 73.

4 OJ L96, 12.4.2003, p 16.

5 OJ L345, 31.12.2003, p 64.

6 OJ L375, 31.12.1985, p 3. Directive as last amended by Directive 2005/1/EC of the European Parliament and of the Council (OJ L79, 24.3.2005, p 9).

7 OJ L191, 13.7.2001, p 43.

HAS ADOPTED THIS DIRECTIVE:

CHAPTER I
SCOPE AND DEFINITIONS

Article 1

Subject-matter and scope

1. This Directive lays down the detailed rules for the implementation of Article 4(1)(4) and 4(2), Article 13(2) to (8), Article 18, Article 19(1) to (6), Article 19(8), and Articles 21, 22 and 24 of Directive 2004/39/EC.

2. Chapter II and Sections 1 to 4, Article 45 and Sections 6 and 8 of Chapter III and, to the extent they relate to those provisions, Chapter I and Section 9 of Chapter III and Chapter IV of this Directive shall apply to management companies in accordance with Article 5(4) of Directive 85/611/EEC.

[9932]

Article 2

Definitions

For the purposes of this Directive, the following definitions shall apply:

(1) "distribution channels" means distribution channels within the meaning of Article 1(7) of Commission Directive 2003/125/EC;

(2) "durable medium" means any instrument which enables a client to store information addressed personally to that client in a way accessible for future reference for a period of time adequate for the purposes of the information and which allows the unchanged reproduction of the information stored;

(3) "relevant person" in relation to an investment firm, means any of the following:

  (a) a director, partner or equivalent, manager or tied agent of the firm;

  (b) a director, partner or equivalent, or manager of any tied agent of the firm;

  (c) an employee of the firm or of a tied agent of the firm, as well as any other natural person whose services are placed at the disposal and under the control of the firm or a tied agent of the firm and who is involved in the provision by the firm of investment services and activities;

  (d) a natural person who is directly involved in the provision of services to the investment firm or to its tied agent under an outsourcing arrangement for the purpose of the provision by the firm of investment services and activities;

(4) "financial analyst" means a relevant person who produces the substance of investment research;

(5) "group", in relation to an investment firm, means the group of which that firm forms a part, consisting of a parent undertaking, its subsidiaries and the entities in which the parent undertaking or its subsidiaries hold a participation, as well as undertakings linked to each other by a relationship within the meaning of Article 12(1) of Council Directive 83/349/EEC on consolidated accounts;[1]

(6) "outsourcing" means an arrangement of any form between an investment firm and a service provider by which that service provider performs a process, a service or an activity which would otherwise be undertaken by the investment firm itself;

(7) "person with whom a relevant person has a family relationship" means any of the following:
  - (a) the spouse of the relevant person or any partner of that person considered by national law as equivalent to a spouse;
  - (b) a dependent child or stepchild of the relevant person;
  - (c) any other relative of the relevant person who has shared the same household as that person for at least one year on the date of the personal transaction concerned;

(8) "securities financing transaction" has the meaning given in Commission Regulation (EC) No 1287/2006;[2]

(9) "senior management" means the person or persons who effectively direct the business of the investment firm as referred to in Article 9(1) of Directive 2004/39/EC.

[9933]

NOTES

[1] OJ No L193, 18.7.1983, p 1.
[2] See page 1 of this Official Journal.

Article 3

Conditions applying to the provision of information

1. Where, for the purposes of this Directive, information is required to be provided in a durable medium, Member States shall permit investment firms to provide that information in a durable medium other than on paper only if:
  - (a) the provision of that information in that medium is appropriate to the context in which the business between the firm and the client is, or is to be, carried on; and
  - (b) the person to whom the information is to be provided, when offered the choice between information on paper or in that other durable medium, specifically chooses the provision of the information in that other medium.

2. Where, pursuant to Article 29, 30, 31, 32, 33 or 46(2) of this Directive, an investment firm provides information to a client by means of a website and that information is not addressed personally to the client, Member States shall ensure that the following conditions are satisfied:
  - (a) the provision of that information in that medium is appropriate to the context in which the business between the firm and the client is, or is to be, carried on;
  - (b) the client must specifically consent to the provision of that information in that form;
  - (c) the client must be notified electronically of the address of the website, and the place on the website where the information may be accessed;
  - (d) the information must be up to date;
  - (e) the information must be accessible continuously by means of that website for such period of time as the client may reasonably need to inspect it.

3. For the purposes of this Article, the provision of information by means of electronic communications shall be treated as appropriate to the context in which the business between the firm and the client is, or is to be, carried on if there is evidence that the client has regular access to the internet. The provision by the client of an e-mail address for the purposes of the carrying on of that business shall be treated as such evidence.

[9934]

Article 4

Additional requirements on investment firms in certain cases

1. Member States may retain or impose requirements additional to those in this Directive only in those exceptional cases where such requirements are objectively justified and proportionate so as to address specific risks to investor protection or to market integrity that are not adequately addressed by this Directive, and provided that one of the following conditions is met:

(a) the specific risks addressed by the requirements are of particular importance in the circumstances of the market structure of that Member State;
(b) the requirement addresses risks or issues that emerge or become evident after the date of application of this Directive and that are not otherwise regulated by or under Community measures.

2. Any requirements imposed under paragraph 1 shall not restrict or otherwise affect the rights of investment firms under Articles 31 and 32 of Directive 2004/39/EC.

3. Member States shall notify to the Commission:
(a) any requirement which it intends to retain in accordance with paragraph 1 before the date of transposition of this Directive; and
(b) any requirement which it intends to impose in accordance with paragraph 1 at least one month before the date appointed for that requirement to come into force.

In each case, the notification shall include a justification for that requirement.

The Commission shall communicate to Member States and make public on its website the notifications it receives in accordance with this paragraph.

4. By 31 December 2009 the Commission shall report to the European Parliament and the Council on the application of this Article.

[9935]

CHAPTER II
ORGANISATIONAL REQUIREMENTS

SECTION 1
ORGANISATION

Article 5

General organisational requirements

(Article 13(2) to (8) of Directive 2004/39/EC)

1. Member States shall require investment firms to comply with the following requirements:
(a) to establish, implement and maintain decision-making procedures and an organisational structure which clearly and in documented manner specifies reporting lines and allocates functions and responsibilities;
(b) to ensure that their relevant persons are aware of the procedures which must be followed for the proper discharge of their responsibilities;
(c) to establish, implement and maintain adequate internal control mechanisms designed to secure compliance with decisions and procedures at all levels of the investment firm;
(d) to employ personnel with the skills, knowledge and expertise necessary for the discharge of the responsibilities allocated to them;
(e) to establish, implement and maintain effective internal reporting and communication of information at all relevant levels of the investment firm;
(f) to maintain adequate and orderly records of their business and internal organisation;
(g) to ensure that the performance of multiple functions by their relevant persons does not and is not likely to prevent those persons from discharging any particular function soundly, honestly, and professionally.

Member States shall ensure that, for those purposes, investment firms take into account the nature, scale and complexity of the business of the firm, and the nature and range of investment services and activities undertaken in the course of that business.

2. Member States shall require investment firms to establish, implement and maintain systems and procedures that are adequate to safeguard the security, integrity and confidentiality of information, taking into account the nature of the information in question.

3. Member States shall require investment firms to establish, implement and maintain an adequate business continuity policy aimed at ensuring, in the case of an interruption to their systems and procedures, the preservation of essential data and functions, and the maintenance

of investment services and activities, or, where that is not possible, the timely recovery of such data and functions and the timely resumption of their investment services and activities.

4. Member States shall require investment firms to establish, implement and maintain accounting policies and procedures that enable them, at the request of the competent authority, to deliver in a timely manner to the competent authority financial reports which reflect a true and fair view of their financial position and which comply with all applicable accounting standards and rules.

5. Member States shall require investment firms to monitor and, on a regular basis, to evaluate the adequacy and effectiveness of their systems, internal control mechanisms and arrangements established in accordance with paragraphs 1 to 4, and to take appropriate measures to address any deficiencies.

[9936]

Article 6

Compliance

(Article 13(2) of Directive 2004/39/EC)

1. Member States shall ensure that investment firms establish, implement and maintain adequate policies and procedures designed to detect any risk of failure by the firm to comply with its obligations under Directive 2004/39/EC, as well as the associated risks, and put in place adequate measures and procedures designed to minimise such risk and to enable the competent authorities to exercise their powers effectively under that Directive.

Member States shall ensure that, for those purposes, investment firms take into account the nature, scale and complexity of the business of the firm, and the nature and range of investment services and activities undertaken in the course of that business.

2. Member States shall require investment firms to establish and maintain a permanent and effective compliance function which operates independently and which has the following responsibilities:

(a) to monitor and, on a regular basis, to assess the adequacy and effectiveness of the measures and procedures put in place in accordance with the first subparagraph of paragraph 1, and the actions taken to address any deficiencies in the firm's compliance with its obligations;

(b) to advise and assist the relevant persons responsible for carrying out investment services and activities to comply with the firm's obligations under Directive 2004/39/EC.

3. In order to enable the compliance function to discharge its responsibilities properly and independently, Member States shall require investment firms to ensure that the following conditions are satisfied:

(a) the compliance function must have the necessary authority, resources, expertise and access to all relevant information;

(b) a compliance officer must be appointed and must be responsible for the compliance function and for any reporting as to compliance required by Article 9(2);

(c) the relevant persons involved in the compliance function must not be involved in the performance of services or activities they monitor;

(d) the method of determining the remuneration of the relevant persons involved in the compliance function must not compromise their objectivity and must not be likely to do so.

However, an investment firm shall not be required to comply with point (c) or point (d) if it is able to demonstrate that in view of the nature, scale and complexity of its business, and the nature and range of investment services and activities, the requirement under that point is not proportionate and that its compliance function continues to be effective.

[9937]

Article 7

Risk management

(second subparagraph of Article 13(5) of Directive 2004/39/EC)

1. Member States shall require investment firms to take the following actions:

(a) to establish, implement and maintain adequate risk management policies and procedures which identify the risks relating to the firm's activities, processes and systems, and where appropriate, set the level of risk tolerated by the firm;

(b) to adopt effective arrangements, processes and mechanisms to manage the risks relating to the firm's activities, processes and systems, in light of that level of risk tolerance;

(c) to monitor the following:

(i) the adequacy and effectiveness of the investment firm's risk management policies and procedures;

(ii) the level of compliance by the investment firm and its relevant persons with the arrangements, processes and mechanisms adopted in accordance with point (b);

(iii) the adequacy and effectiveness of measures taken to address any deficiencies in those policies, procedures, arrangements, processes and mechanisms, including failures by the relevant persons to comply with such arrangements, processes and mechanisms or follow such policies and procedures.

2. Member States shall require investment firms, where appropriate and proportionate in view of the nature, scale and complexity of their business and the nature and range of the investment services and activities undertaken in the course of that business, to establish and maintain a risk management function that operates independently and carries out the following tasks:

(a) implementation of the policy and procedures referred to in paragraph 1;

(b) provision of reports and advice to senior management in accordance with Article 9(2).

Where an investment firm is not required under the first sub-paragraph to establish and maintain a risk management function that functions independently, it must nevertheless be able to demonstrate that the policies and procedures which it is has adopted in accordance with paragraph 1 satisfy the requirements of that paragraph and are consistently effective.

[9938]

Article 8

Internal audit

(second subparagraph of Article 13(5) of Directive 2004/39/EC)

Member States shall require investment firms, where appropriate and proportionate in view of the nature, scale and complexity of their business and the nature and range of investment services and activities undertaken in the course of that business, to establish and maintain an internal audit function which is separate and independent from the other functions and activities of the investment firm and which has the following responsibilities:

(a) to establish, implement and maintain an audit plan to examine and evaluate the adequacy and effectiveness of the investment firm's systems, internal control mechanisms and arrangements;

(b) to issue recommendations based on the result of work carried out in accordance with point (a);

(c) to verify compliance with those recommendations;

(d) to report in relation to internal audit matters in accordance with Article 9(2).

[9939]

Article 9

Responsibility of senior management

(Article 13(2) of Directive 2004/39/EC)

1. Member States shall require investment firms, when allocating functions internally, to ensure that senior management, and, where appropriate, the supervisory function, are responsible for ensuring that the firm complies with its obligations under Directive 2004/39/EC.

In particular, senior management and, where appropriate, the supervisory function shall be required to assess and periodically to review the effectiveness of the policies, arrangements and procedures put in place to comply with the obligations under Directive 2004/39/EC and to take appropriate measures to address any deficiencies.

2. Member States shall require investment firms to ensure that their senior management receive on a frequent basis, and at least annually, written reports on the matters covered by Articles 6, 7 and 8 indicating in particular whether the appropriate remedial measures have been taken in the event of any deficiencies.

3. Member States shall require investment firms to ensure that the supervisory function, if any, receives on a regular basis written reports on the same matters.

4. For the purposes of this Article, "supervisory function" means the function within an investment firm responsible for the supervision of its senior management.

[9940]

Article 10

Complaints handling

(Article 13(2) of Directive 2004/39/EC)

Member States shall require investment firms to establish, implement and maintain effective and transparent procedures for the reasonable and prompt handling of complaints received from retail clients or potential retail clients, and to keep a record of each complaint and the measures taken for its resolution.

[9941]

Article 11

Meaning of personal transaction

(Article 13(2) of Directive 2004/39/EC)

For the purposes of Article 12 and Article 25, personal transaction means a trade in a financial instrument effected by or on behalf of a relevant person, where at least one of the following criteria are met:

(a) that relevant person is acting outside the scope of the activities he carries out in that capacity;

(b) the trade is carried out for the account of any of the following persons:

(i) the relevant person;

(ii) any person with whom he has a family relationship, or with whom he has close links;

(iii) a person whose relationship with the relevant person is such that the relevant person has a direct or indirect material interest in the outcome of the trade, other than a fee or commission for the execution of the trade.

[9942]

Article 12

Personal transactions

(Article 13(2) of Directive 2004/39/EC)

1. Member States shall require investment firms to establish, implement and maintain adequate arrangements aimed at preventing the following activities in the case of any relevant person who is involved in activities that may give rise to a conflict of interest, or who has access to inside information within the meaning of Article 1(1) of Directive 2003/6/EC or to other confidential information relating to clients or transactions with or for clients by virtue of an activity carried out by him on behalf of the firm:

(a) entering into a personal transaction which meets at least one of the following criteria:

(i) that person is prohibited from entering into it under Directive 2003/6/EC;

(ii) it involves the misuse or improper disclosure of that confidential information;

(iii) it conflicts or is likely to conflict with an obligation of the investment firm under Directive 2004/39/EC;

(b) advising or procuring, other than in the proper course of his employment or contract for services, any other person to enter into a transaction in financial instruments which, if a personal transaction of the relevant person, would be covered by point (a) or Article 25(2)(a) or (b) or Article 47(3);

(c) without prejudice to Article 3(a) of Directive 2003/6/EC, disclosing, other than in the normal course of his employment or contract for services, any information or opinion to any other person if the relevant person knows, or reasonably ought to know, that as a result of that disclosure that other person will or would be likely to take either of the following steps:

(i) to enter into a transaction in financial instruments which, if a personal transaction of the relevant person, would be covered by point (a) or Article 25(2)(a) or (b) or Article 47(3);

(ii) to advise or procure another person to enter into such a transaction.

2. The arrangements required under paragraph 1 must in particular be designed to ensure that:

(a) each relevant person covered by paragraph 1 is aware of the restrictions on personal transactions, and of the measures established by the investment firm in connection with personal transactions and disclosure, in accordance with paragraph 1;

(b) the firm is informed promptly of any personal transaction entered into by a relevant person, either by notification of that transaction or by other procedures enabling the firm to identify such transactions;

In the case of outsourcing arrangements the investment firm must ensure that the firm to which the activity is outsourced maintains a record of personal transactions entered into by any relevant person and provides that information to the investment firm promptly on request.

(c) a record is kept of the personal transaction notified to the firm or identified by it, including any authorisation or prohibition in connection with such a transaction.

3. Paragraphs 1 and 2 shall not apply to the following kinds of personal transaction:

(a) personal transactions effected under a discretionary portfolio management service where there is no prior communication in connection with the transaction between the portfolio manager and the relevant person or other person for whose account the transaction is executed;

(b) personal transactions in units in collective undertakings that comply with the conditions necessary to enjoy the rights conferred by Directive 85/611/EEC or are subject to supervision under the law of a Member State which requires an equivalent level of risk spreading in their assets, where the relevant person and any other person for whose account the transactions are effected are not involved in the management of that undertaking.

[9943]

SECTION 2
OUTSOURCING

Article 13

Meaning of critical and important operational functions

(Article 13(2) and first subparagraph of Article 13(5) of Directive 2004/39/EC)

1. For the purposes of the first subparagraph of Article 13(5) of Directive 2004/39/EC, an operational function shall be regarded as critical or important if a defect or failure in its performance would materially impair the continuing compliance of an investment firm with the conditions and obligations of its authorisation or its other obligations under Directive 2004/39/EC, or its financial performance, or the soundness or the continuity of its investment services and activities.

2. Without prejudice to the status of any other function, the following functions shall not be considered as critical or important for the purposes of paragraph 1:

(a) the provision to the firm of advisory services, and other services which do not form part of the investment business of the firm, including the provision of legal advice to the firm, the training of personnel of the firm, billing services and the security of the firm's premises and personnel;

(b) the purchase of standardised services, including market information services and the provision of price feeds.

[9944]

Article 14

Conditions for outsourcing critical or important operational functions or investment services or activities

(Article 13(2) and first subparagraph of Article 13(5) of Directive 2004/39/EC)

1. Member States shall ensure that, when investment firms outsource critical or important operational functions or any investment services or activities, the firms remain fully responsible for discharging all of their obligations under Directive 2004/39/EC and comply, in particular, with the following conditions:

(a) the outsourcing must not result in the delegation by senior management of its responsibility;

(b) the relationship and obligations of the investment firm towards its clients under the terms of Directive 2004/39/EC must not be altered;

(c) the conditions with which the investment firm must comply in order to be authorised in accordance with Article 5 of Directive 2004/39/EC, and to remain so, must not be undermined;

(d) none of the other conditions subject to which the firm's authorisation was granted must be removed or modified.

2. Member States shall require investment firms to exercise due skill, care and diligence when entering into, managing or terminating any arrangement for the outsourcing to a service provider of critical or important operational functions or of any investment services or activities.

Investment firms shall in particular take the necessary steps to ensure that the following conditions are satisfied:

(a) the service provider must have the ability, capacity, and any authorisation required by law to perform the outsourced functions, services or activities reliably and professionally;

(b) the service provider must carry out the outsourced services effectively, and to this end the firm must establish methods for assessing the standard of performance of the service provider;

(c) the service provider must properly supervise the carrying out of the outsourced functions, and adequately manage the risks associated with the outsourcing;

(d) appropriate action must be taken if it appears that the service provider may not be carrying out the functions effectively and in compliance with applicable laws and regulatory requirements;

(e) the investment firm must retain the necessary expertise to supervise the outsourced functions effectively and manage the risks associated with the outsourcing and must supervise those functions and manage those risks;

(f) the service provider must disclose to the investment firm any development that may have a material impact on its ability to carry out the outsourced functions effectively and in compliance with applicable laws and regulatory requirements;

(g) the investment firm must be able to terminate the arrangement for outsourcing where necessary without detriment to the continuity and quality of its provision of services to clients;

(h) the service provider must cooperate with the competent authorities of the investment firm in connection with the outsourced activities;

(i) the investment firm, its auditors and the relevant competent authorities must have effective access to data related to the outsourced activities, as well as to the business premises of the service provider; and the competent authorities must be able to exercise those rights of access;

(j) the service provider must protect any confidential information relating to the investment firm and its clients;

(k) the investment firm and the service provider must establish, implement and maintain a contingency plan for disaster recovery and periodic testing of backup facilities, where that is necessary having regard to the function, service or activity that has been outsourced.

3. Member States shall require the respective rights and obligations of the investment firms and of the service provider to be clearly allocated and set out in a written agreement.

4. Member States shall provide that, where the investment firm and the service provider are members of the same group, the investment firm may, for the purposes of complying with this Article and Article 15, take into account the extent to which the firm controls the service provider or has the ability to influence its actions.

5. Member States shall require investment firms to make available on request to the competent authority all information necessary to enable the authority to supervise the compliance of the performance of the outsourced activities with the requirements of this Directive.

[9945]

Article 15

Service providers located in third countries

(Article 13(2) and first subparagraph of Article 13(5) of Directive 2004/39/EC)

1. In addition to the requirements set out in Article 14, Member States shall require that, where an investment firm outsources the investment service of portfolio management provided to retail clients to a service provider located in a third country, that investment firm ensures that the following conditions are satisfied:

(a) the service provider must be authorised or registered in its home country to provide that service and must be subject to prudential supervision;

(b) there must be an appropriate cooperation agreement between the competent authority of the investment firm and the supervisory authority of the service provider.

2. Where one or both of those conditions mentioned in paragraph 1 are not satisfied, an investment firm may outsource investment services to a service provider located in a third country only if the firm gives prior notification to its competent authority about the outsourcing arrangement and the competent authority does not object to that arrangement within a reasonable time following receipt of that notification.

3. Without prejudice to paragraph 2, Member States shall publish or require competent authorities to publish a statement of policy in relation to outsourcing covered by paragraph 2. That statement shall set out examples of cases where the competent authority would not, or would be likely not to, object to an outsourcing under paragraph 2 where one or both of the conditions in points (a) and (b) of paragraph 1 are not met. It shall include a clear explanation as to why the competent authority considers that in such cases outsourcing would not impair the ability of investment firms to fulfil their obligations under Article 14.

4. Nothing in this article limits the obligations on investment firms to comply with the requirements in Article 14.

5. Competent authorities shall publish a list of the supervisory authorities in third countries with which they have cooperation agreements that are appropriate for the purposes of point (b) of paragraph 1.

[9946]

SECTION 3
SAFEGUARDING OF CLIENT ASSETS

Article 16

Safeguarding of client financial instruments and funds

(Article 13(7) and (8) of Directive 2004/39/EC)

1. Member States shall require that, for the purposes of safeguarding clients' rights in relation to financial instruments and funds belonging to them, investment firms comply with the following requirements:

(a) they must keep such records and accounts as are necessary to enable them at any time and without delay to distinguish assets held for one client from assets held for any other client, and from their own assets;

(b) they must maintain their records and accounts in a way that ensures their accuracy, and in particular their correspondence to the financial instruments and funds held for clients;

(c) they must conduct, on a regular basis, reconciliations between their internal accounts and records and those of any third parties by whom those assets are held;

(d) they must take the necessary steps to ensure that any client financial instruments deposited with a third party, in accordance with Article 17, are identifiable separately from the financial instruments belonging to the investment firm and from financial instruments belonging to that third party, by means of differently titled accounts on the books of the third party or other equivalent measures that achieve the same level of protection;

(e) they must take the necessary steps to ensure that client funds deposited, in accordance with Article 18, in a central bank, a credit institution or a bank authorised in a third country or a qualifying money market fund are held in an account or accounts identified separately from any accounts used to hold funds belonging to the investment firm;

(f) they must introduce adequate organisational arrangements to minimise the risk of the loss or diminution of client assets, or of rights in connection with those assets, as a result of misuse of the assets, fraud, poor administration, inadequate record-keeping or negligence.

2. If, for reasons of the applicable law, including in particular the law relating to property or insolvency, the arrangements made by investment firms in compliance with paragraph 1 to safeguard clients' rights are not sufficient to satisfy the requirements of Article 13(7) and (8) of Directive 2004/39/EC, Member States shall prescribe the measures that investment firms must take in order to comply with those obligations.

3. If the applicable law of the jurisdiction in which the client funds or financial instruments are held prevents investment firms from complying with points (d) or (e) of paragraph 1, Member States shall prescribe requirements which have an equivalent effect in terms of safeguarding clients' rights.

[9947]

Article 17

Depositing client financial instruments

(Article 13(7) of Directive 2004/39/EC)

1. Member States shall permit investment firms to deposit financial instruments held by them on behalf of their clients into an account or accounts opened with a third party provided that the firms exercise all due skill, care and diligence in the selection, appointment and periodic review of the third party and of the arrangements for the holding and safekeeping of those financial instruments.

In particular, Member States shall require investment firms to take into account the expertise and market reputation of the third party as well as any legal requirements or market practices related to the holding of those financial instruments that could adversely affect clients' rights.

2. Member States shall ensure that, if the safekeeping of financial instruments for the account of another person is subject to specific regulation and supervision in a jurisdiction where an investment firm proposes to deposit client financial instruments with a third party, the investment firm does not deposit those financial instruments in that jurisdiction with a third party which is not subject to such regulation and supervision.

3. Member States shall ensure that investment firms do not deposit financial instruments held on behalf of clients with a third party in a third country that does not regulate the holding and safekeeping of financial instruments for the account of another person unless one of the following conditions is met:

(a) the nature of the financial instruments or of the investment services connected with those instruments requires them to be deposited with a third party in that third country;

(b) where the financial instruments are held on behalf of a professional client, that client requests the firm in writing to deposit them with a third party in that third country.

[9948]

Article 18

Depositing client funds

(Article 13(8) of Directive 2004/39/EC)

1. Member States shall require investment firms, on receiving any client funds, promptly to place those funds into one or more accounts opened with any of the following:

(a) a central bank;

(b) a credit institution authorised in accordance with Directive 2000/12/EC;

(c) a bank authorised in a third country;

(d) a qualifying money market fund.

The first subparagraph shall not apply to a credit institution authorised under Directive 2006/48/EC of the European Parliament and of the Council of 14 June 2006 relating to the taking up and pursuit of the business of credit institutions (recast)[1] in relation to deposits within the meaning of that Directive held by that institution.

2. For the purposes of point (d) of paragraph 1, and of Article 16(1)(e), a "qualifying money market fund" means a collective investment undertaking authorised under Directive 85/611/EEC, or which is subject to supervision and, if applicable, authorised by an authority under the national law of a Member State, and which satisfies the following conditions:

(a) its primary investment objective must be to maintain the net asset value of the undertaking either constant at par (net of earnings), or at the value of the investors' initial capital plus earnings;

(b) it must, with a view to achieving that primary investment objective, invest exclusively in high quality money market instruments with a maturity or residual maturity of no more than 397 days, or regular yield adjustments consistent with such a maturity, and with a weighted average maturity of 60 days. It may also achieve this objective by investing on an ancillary basis in deposits with credit institutions;

(c) it must provide liquidity through same day or next day settlement.

For the purposes of point (b), a money market instrument shall be considered to be of high quality if it has been awarded the highest available credit rating by each competent rating agency which has rated that instrument. An instrument that is not rated by any competent rating agency shall not be considered to be of high quality.

For the purposes of the second subparagraph, a rating agency shall be considered to be competent if it issues credit ratings in respect of money market funds regularly and on a professional basis and is an eligible ECAI within the meaning of Article 81(1) of Directive 2006/48/EC.

3. Member States shall require that, where investment firms do not deposit client funds with a central bank, they exercise all due skill, care and diligence in the selection, appointment and periodic review of the credit institution, bank or money market fund where the funds are placed and the arrangements for the holding of those funds.

Member States shall ensure, in particular, that investment firms take into account the expertise and market reputation of such institutions or money market funds with a view to ensuring the protection of clients' rights, as well as any legal or regulatory requirements or market practices related to the holding of client funds that could adversely affect clients' rights.

Member States shall ensure that clients have the right to oppose the placement of their funds in a qualifying money market fund.

[9949]

NOTES

[1] OJ L177, 30.6.2006, p 1.

Article 19

Use of client financial instruments

(Article 13(7) of Directive 2004/39/EC)

1. Member States shall not allow investment firms to enter into arrangements for securities financing transactions in respect of financial instruments held by them on behalf of a client, or otherwise use such financial instruments for their own account or the account of another client of the firm, unless the following conditions are met:

(a) the client must have given his prior express consent to the use of the instruments on specified terms, as evidenced, in the case of a retail client, by his signature or equivalent alternative mechanism;

(b) the use of that client's financial instruments must be restricted to the specified terms to which the client consents.

2. Member States may not allow investment firms to enter into arrangements for securities financing transactions in respect of financial instruments which are held on behalf of a client in an omnibus account maintained by a third party, or otherwise use financial instruments held in such an account for their own account or for the account of another client unless, in addition to the conditions set out in paragraph 1, at least one of the following conditions is met:

(a) each client whose financial instruments are held together in an omnibus account must have given prior express consent in accordance with point (a) of paragraph 1;

(b) the investment firm must have in place systems and controls which ensure that only financial instruments belonging to clients who have given prior express consent in accordance with point (a) of paragraph 1 are so used.

The records of the investment firm shall include details of the client on whose instructions the use of the financial instruments has been effected, as well as the number of financial instruments used belonging to each client who has given his consent, so as to enable the correct allocation of any loss.

[9950]

Article 20

Reports by external auditors

(Article 13(7) and (8) of Directive 2004/39/EC)

Member States shall require investment firms to ensure that their external auditors report at least annually to the competent authority of the home Member State of the firm on the adequacy of the firm's arrangements under Articles 13(7) and (8) of Directive 2004/39/EC and this Section.

[9951]

SECTION 4
CONFLICTS OF INTEREST

Article 21

Conflicts of interest potentially detrimental to a client

(Articles 13(3) and 18 of Directive 2004/39/EC)

Member States shall ensure that, for the purposes of identifying the types of conflict of interest that arise in the course of providing investment and ancillary services or a combination thereof and whose existence may damage the interests of a client, investment firms take into account, by way of minimum criteria, the question of whether the investment firm or a relevant person, or a person directly or indirectly linked by control to the firm, is in any of the following situations, whether as a result of providing investment or ancillary services or investment activities or otherwise:

(a) the firm or that person is likely to make a financial gain, or avoid a financial loss, at the expense of the client;

(b) the firm or that person has an interest in the outcome of a service provided to the client or of a transaction carried out on behalf of the client, which is distinct from the client's interest in that outcome;

(c) the firm or that person has a financial or other incentive to favour the interest of another client or group of clients over the interests of the client;

(d) the firm or that person carries on the same business as the client;

(e) the firm or that person receives or will receive from a person other than the client an inducement in relation to a service provided to the client, in the form of monies, goods or services, other than the standard commission or fee for that service.

[9952]

Article 22

Conflicts of interest policy

(Articles 13(3) and 18(1) of Directive 2004/39/EC)

1. Member States shall require investment firms to establish, implement and maintain an effective conflicts of interest policy set out in writing and appropriate to the size and organisation of the firm and the nature, scale and complexity of its business.

Where the firm is a member of a group, the policy must also take into account any circumstances, of which the firm is or should be aware, which may give rise to a conflict of interest arising as a result of the structure and business activities of other members of the group.

2. The conflicts of interest policy established in accordance with paragraph 1 shall include the following content:

(a) it must identify, with reference to the specific investment services and activities and ancillary services carried out by or on behalf of the investment firm, the circumstances which constitute or may give rise to a conflict of interest entailing a material risk of damage to the interests of one or more clients;

(b) it must specify procedures to be followed and measures to be adopted in order to manage such conflicts.

3. Member States shall ensure that the procedures and measures provided for in paragraph 2(b) are designed to ensure that relevant persons engaged in different business activities involving a conflict of interest of the kind specified in paragraph 2(a) carry on those activities at a level of independence appropriate to the size and activities of the investment firm and of the group to which it belongs, and to the materiality of the risk of damage to the interests of clients.

For the purposes of paragraph 2(b), the procedures to be followed and measures to be adopted shall include such of the following as are necessary and appropriate for the firm to ensure the requisite degree of independence:

(a) effective procedures to prevent or control the exchange of information between relevant persons engaged in activities involving a risk of a conflict of interest where the exchange of that information may harm the interests of one or more clients;

(b) the separate supervision of relevant persons whose principal functions involve carrying out activities on behalf of, or providing services to, clients whose interests may conflict, or who otherwise represent different interests that may conflict, including those of the firm;

(c) the removal of any direct link between the remuneration of relevant persons principally engaged in one activity and the remuneration of, or revenues generated by, different relevant persons principally engaged in another activity, where a conflict of interest may arise in relation to those activities;

(d) measures to prevent or limit any person from exercising inappropriate influence over the way in which a relevant person carries out investment or ancillary services or activities;

(e) measures to prevent or control the simultaneous or sequential involvement of a relevant person in separate investment or ancillary services or activities where such involvement may impair the proper management of conflicts of interest.

If the adoption or the practice of one or more of those measures and procedures does not ensure the requisite degree of independence, Member States shall require investment firms to adopt such alternative or additional measures and procedures as are necessary and appropriate for those purposes.

4. Member States shall ensure that disclosure to clients, pursuant to Article 18(2) of Directive 2004/39/EC, is made in a durable medium and includes sufficient detail, taking into account the nature of the client, to enable that client to take an informed decision with respect to the investment or ancillary service in the context of which the conflict of interest arises.

[9953]

Article 23

Record of services or activities giving rise to detrimental conflict of interest

(Article 13(6) of Directive 2004/39/EC)

Member States shall require investment firms to keep and regularly to update a record of the kinds of investment or ancillary service or investment activity carried out by or on behalf of the firm in which a conflict of interest entailing a material risk of damage to the interests of one or more clients has arisen or, in the case of an ongoing service or activity, may arise.

[9954]

Article 24

Investment research

(Article 19(2) of Directive 2004/39/EC)

1. For the purposes of Article 25, "investment research" means research or other information recommending or suggesting an investment strategy, explicitly or implicitly, concerning one or several financial instruments or the issuers of financial instruments,

including any opinion as to the present or future value or price of such instruments, intended for distribution channels or for the public, and in relation to which the following conditions are met:

(a) it is labelled or described as investment research or in similar terms, or is otherwise presented as an objective or independent explanation of the matters contained in the recommendation;

(b) if the recommendation in question were made by an investment firm to a client, it would not constitute the provision of investment advice for the purposes of Directive 2004/39/EC.

2. A recommendation of the type covered by Article 1(3) of Directive 2003/125/EC but relating to financial instruments as defined in Directive 2004/39/EC that does not meet the conditions set out in paragraph 1 shall be treated as a marketing communication for the purposes of Directive 2004/39/EC and Member States shall require any investment firm that produces or disseminates the recommendation to ensure that it is clearly identified as such.

Additionally, Member States shall require those firms to ensure that any such recommendation contains a clear and prominent statement that (or, in the case of an oral recommendation, to the effect that) it has not been prepared in accordance with legal requirements designed to promote the independence of investment research, and that it is not subject to any prohibition on dealing ahead of the dissemination of investment research.

[9955]

Article 25

Additional organisational requirements where a firm produces and disseminates investment research

(Article 13(3) of Directive 2004/39/EC)

1. Member States shall require investment firms which produce, or arrange for the production of, investment research that is intended or likely to be subsequently disseminated to clients of the firm or to the public, under their own responsibility or that of a member of their group, to ensure the implementation of all the measures set out in Article 22(3) in relation to the financial analysts involved in the production of the investment research and other relevant persons whose responsibilities or business interests may conflict with the interests of the persons to whom the investment research is disseminated.

2. Member States shall require investment firms covered by paragraph 1 to have in place arrangements designed to ensure that the following conditions are satisfied:

(a) financial analysts and other relevant persons must not undertake personal transactions or trade, other than as market makers acting in good faith and in the ordinary course of market making or in the execution of an unsolicited client order, on behalf of any other person, including the investment firm, in financial instruments to which investment research relates, or in any related financial instruments, with knowledge of the likely timing or content of that investment research which is not publicly available or available to clients and cannot readily be inferred from information that is so available, until the recipients of the investment research have had a reasonable opportunity to act on it;

(b) in circumstances not covered by point (a), financial analysts and any other relevant persons involved in the production of investment research must not undertake personal transactions in financial instruments to which the investment research relates, or in any related financial instruments, contrary to current recommendations, except in exceptional circumstances and with the prior approval of a member of the firm's legal or compliance function;

(c) the investment firms themselves, financial analysts, and other relevant persons involved in the production of the investment research must not accept inducements from those with a material interest in the subject-matter of the investment research;

(d) the investment firms themselves, financial analysts, and other relevant persons involved in the production of the investment research must not promise issuers favourable research coverage;

(e) issuers, relevant persons other than financial analysts, and any other persons must not before the dissemination of investment research be permitted to review a draft of the investment research for the purpose of verifying the accuracy of factual statements made in that research, or for any other purpose other than verifying compliance with the firm's legal obligations, if the draft includes a recommendation or a target price.

For the purposes of this paragraph, "related financial instrument" means a financial instrument the price of which is closely affected by price movements in another financial instrument which is the subject of investment research, and includes a derivative on that other financial instrument.

3. Member States shall exempt investment firms which disseminate investment research produced by another person to the public or to clients from complying with paragraph 1 if the following criteria are met:

(a) the person that produces the investment research is not a member of the group to which the investment firm belongs;

(b) the investment firm does not substantially alter the recommendations within the investment research;

(c) the investment firm does not present the investment research as having been produced by it;

(d) the investment firm verifies that the producer of the research is subject to requirements equivalent to the requirements under this Directive in relation to the production of that research, or has established a policy setting such requirements.

[9956]

CHAPTER III
OPERATING CONDITIONS FOR INVESTMENT FIRMS

SECTION 1
INDUCEMENTS

Article 26

Inducements

(Article 19(1) of Directive 2004/39/EC)

Member States shall ensure that investment firms are not regarded as acting honestly, fairly and professionally in accordance with the best interests of a client if, in relation to the provision of an investment or ancillary service to the client, they pay or are paid any fee or commission, or provide or are provided with any non-monetary benefit, other than the following:

(a) a fee, commission or non-monetary benefit paid or provided to or by the client or a person on behalf of the client;

(b) a fee, commission or non-monetary benefit paid or provided to or by a third party or a person acting on behalf of a third party, where the following conditions are satisfied:

(i) the existence, nature and amount of the fee, commission or benefit, or, where the amount cannot be ascertained, the method of calculating that amount, must be clearly disclosed to the client, in a manner that is comprehensive, accurate and understandable, prior to the provision of the relevant investment or ancillary service;

(ii) the payment of the fee or commission, or the provision of the non-monetary benefit must be designed to enhance the quality of the relevant service to the client and not impair compliance with the firm's duty to act in the best interests of the client;

(c) proper fees which enable or are necessary for the provision of investment services, such as custody costs, settlement and exchange fees, regulatory levies or legal fees, and which, by their nature, cannot give rise to conflicts with the firm's duties to act honestly, fairly and professionally in accordance with the best interests of its clients.

Member States shall permit an investment firm, for the purposes of point (b)(i), to disclose the essential terms of the arrangements relating to the fee, commission or non-monetary benefit in summary form, provided that it undertakes to disclose further details at the request of the client and provided that it honours that undertaking.

[9957]

SECTION 2
INFORMATION TO CLIENTS AND POTENTIAL CLIENTS

Article 27

Conditions with which information must comply in order to be fair, clear and not misleading

(Article 19(2) of Directive 2004/39/EC)

1. Member States shall require investment firms to ensure that all information they address to, or disseminate in such a way that it is likely to be received by, retail clients or potential retail clients, including marketing communications, satisfies the conditions laid down in paragraphs 2 to 8.

2. The information referred to in paragraph 1 shall include the name of the investment firm.

It shall be accurate and in particular shall not emphasise any potential benefits of an investment service or financial instrument without also giving a fair and prominent indication of any relevant risks.

It shall be sufficient for, and presented in a way that is likely to be understood by, the average member of the group to whom it is directed, or by whom it is likely to be received.

It shall not disguise, diminish or obscure important items, statements or warnings.

3. Where the information compares investment or ancillary services, financial instruments, or persons providing investment or ancillary services, the following conditions shall be satisfied:

(a) the comparison must be meaningful and presented in a fair and balanced way;
(b) the sources of the information used for the comparison must be specified;
(c) the key facts and assumptions used to make the comparison must be included.

4. Where the information contains an indication of past performance of a financial instrument, a financial index or an investment service, the following conditions shall be satisfied:

(a) that indication must not be the most prominent feature of the communication;
(b) the information must include appropriate performance information which covers the immediately preceding 5 years, or the whole period for which the financial instrument has been offered, the financial index has been established, or the investment service has been provided if less than five years, or such longer period as the firm may decide, and in every case that performance information must be based on complete 12-month periods;
(c) the reference period and the source of information must be clearly stated;
(d) the information must contain a prominent warning that the figures refer to the past and that past performance is not a reliable indicator of future results;
(e) where the indication relies on figures denominated in a currency other than that of the Member State in which the retail client or potential retail client is resident, the currency must be clearly stated, together with a warning that the return may increase or decrease as a result of currency fluctuations;
(f) where the indication is based on gross performance, the effect of commissions, fees or other charges must be disclosed.

5. Where the information includes or refers to simulated past performance, it must relate to a financial instrument or a financial index, and the following conditions shall be satisfied:

(a) the simulated past performance must be based on the actual past performance of one or more financial instruments or financial indices which are the same as, or underlie, the financial instrument concerned;
(b) in respect of the actual past performance referred to in point (a), the conditions set out in points (a) to (c), (e) and (f) of paragraph 4 must be complied with;
(c) the information must contain a prominent warning that the figures refer to simulated past performance and that past performance is not a reliable indicator of future performance.

6. Where the information contains information on future performance, the following conditions shall be satisfied:

(a) the information must not be based on or refer to simulated past performance;
(b) it must be based on reasonable assumptions supported by objective data;

(c) where the information is based on gross performance, the effect of commissions, fees or other charges must be disclosed;

(d) it must contain a prominent warning that such forecasts are not a reliable indicator of future performance.

7. Where the information refers to a particular tax treatment, it shall prominently state that the tax treatment depends on the individual circumstances of each client and may be subject to change in the future.

8. The information shall not use the name of any competent authority in such a way that would indicate or suggest endorsement or approval by that authority of the products or services of the investment firm.

[9958]

Article 28

Information concerning client categorisation

(Article 19(3) of Directive 2004/39/EC)

1. Member States shall ensure that investment firms notify new clients, and existing clients that the investment firm has newly categorised as required by Directive 2004/39/EC, of their categorisation as a retail client, a professional client or an eligible counterparty in accordance with that Directive.

2. Member States shall ensure that investment firms inform clients in a durable medium about any right that client has to request a different categorisation and about any limitations to the level of client protection that it would entail.

3. Member States shall permit investment firms, either on their own initiative or at the request of the client concerned:

(a) to treat as a professional or retail client a client that might otherwise be classified as an eligible counterparty pursuant to Article 24(2) of Directive 2004/39/EC;

(b) to treat as a retail client a client that is considered as a professional client pursuant to Section I of Annex II to Directive 2004/39/EC.

[9959]

Article 29

General requirements for information to clients

(Article 19(3) of Directive 2004/39/EC)

1. Member States shall require investment firms, in good time before a retail client or potential retail client is bound by any agreement for the provision of investment services or ancillary services or before the provision of those services, whichever is the earlier, to provide that client or potential client with the following information:

(a) the terms of any such agreement;

(b) the information required by Article 30 relating to that agreement or to those investment or ancillary services.

2. Member States shall require investment firms, in good time before the provision of investment services or ancillary services to retail clients or potential retail clients, to provide the information required under Articles 30 to 33.

3. Member States shall require investment firms to provide professional clients with the information referred to in Article 32(5) and (6) in good time before the provision of the service concerned.

4. The information referred to in paragraphs 1 to 3 shall be provided in a durable medium or by means of a website (where that does not constitute a durable medium) provided that the conditions specified in Article 3(2) are satisfied.

5. By way of exception to paragraphs 1 and 2, Member States shall permit investment firms, in the following circumstances, to provide the information required under paragraph 1 to a retail client immediately after that client is bound by any agreement for the provision of investment services or ancillary services, and the information required under paragraph 2 immediately after starting to provide the service:

(a) the firm was unable to comply with the time limits specified in paragraphs 1 and 2 because, at the request of the client, the agreement was concluded using a means of distance communication which prevents the firm from providing the information in accordance with paragraph 1 or 2;

(b) in any case where Article 3(3) of Directive 2002/65/EC of the European Parliament and of the Council of 23 September 2002 concerning the distance marketing of consumer financial services and amending Council Directive 90/619/EEC and Directives 97/7/EC and 98/27/EC[1] does not otherwise apply, the investment firm complies with the requirements of that Article in relation to the retail client or potential retail client, as if that client or potential client were a "consumer" and the investment firm were a "supplier" within the meaning of that Directive.

6. Member State shall ensure that investment firms notify a client in good time about any material change to the information provided under Articles 30 to 33 which is relevant to a service that the firm is providing to that client. That notification shall be given in a durable medium if the information to which it relates is given in a durable medium.

7. Member States shall require investment firms to ensure that information contained in a marketing communication is consistent with any information the firm provides to clients in the course of carrying on investment and ancillary services.

8. Member States shall ensure that, where a marketing communication contains an offer or invitation of the following nature and specifies the manner of response or includes a form by which any response may be made, it includes such of the information referred to in Articles 30 to 33 as is relevant to that offer or invitation:

(a) an offer to enter into an agreement in relation to a financial instrument or investment service or ancillary service with any person who responds to the communication;

(b) an invitation to any person who responds to the communication to make an offer to enter into an agreement in relation to a financial instrument or investment service or ancillary service.

However, the first subparagraph shall not apply if, in order to respond to an offer or invitation contained in the marketing communication, the potential retail client must refer to another document or documents, which, alone or in combination, contain that information.

[9960]

NOTES

[1] OJ L271, 9.10.2002, p 16.

Article 30

Information about the investment firm and its services for retail clients and potential retail clients

(first indent of Article 19(3) of Directive 2004/39/EC)

1. Member States shall require investment firms to provide retail clients or potential retail clients with the following general information, where relevant:

(a) the name and address of the investment firm, and the contact details necessary to enable clients to communicate effectively with the firm;

(b) the languages in which the client may communicate with the investment firm, and receive documents and other information from the firm;

(c) the methods of communication to be used between the investment firm and the client including, where relevant, those for the sending and reception of orders;

(d) a statement of the fact that the investment firm is authorised and the name and contact address of the competent authority that has authorised it;

(e) where the investment firm is acting through a tied agent, a statement of this fact specifying the Member State in which that agent is registered;

(f) the nature, frequency and timing of the reports on the performance of the service to be provided by the investment firm to the client in accordance with Article 19(8) of Directive 2004/39/EC;

(g) if the investment firm holds client financial instruments or client funds, a summary description of the steps which it takes to ensure their protection, including summary details of any relevant investor compensation or deposit guarantee scheme which applies to the firm by virtue of its activities in a Member State;

(h) a description, which may be provided in summary form, of the conflicts of interest policy maintained by the firm in accordance with Article 22;

(i) at any time that the client requests it, further details of that conflicts of interest policy in a durable medium or by means of a website (where that does not constitute a durable medium) provided that the conditions specified in Article 3(2) are satisfied.

2. Member States shall ensure that, when providing the service of portfolio management, investment firms establish an appropriate method of evaluation and comparison such as a meaningful benchmark, based on the investment objectives of the client and the types of financial instruments included in the client portfolio, so as to enable the client for whom the service is provided to assess the firm's performance.

3. Member States shall require that where investment firms propose to provide portfolio management services to a retail client or potential retail client, they provide the client, in addition to the information required under paragraph 1, with such of the following information as is applicable:

(a) information on the method and frequency of valuation of the financial instruments in the client portfolio;

(b) details of any delegation of the discretionary management of all or part of the financial instruments or funds in the client portfolio;

(c) a specification of any benchmark against which the performance of the client portfolio will be compared;

(d) the types of financial instrument that may be included in the client portfolio and types of transaction that may be carried out in such instruments, including any limits;

(e) the management objectives, the level of risk to be reflected in the manager's exercise of discretion, and any specific constraints on that discretion.

[9961]

Article 31

Information about financial instruments

(second indent of Article 19(3) of Directive 2004/39/EC)

1. Member States shall require investment firms to provide clients or potential clients with a general description of the nature and risks of financial instruments, taking into account, in particular, the client's categorisation as either a retail client or a professional client. That description must explain the nature of the specific type of instrument concerned, as well as the risks particular to that specific type of instrument in sufficient detail to enable the client to take investment decisions on an informed basis.

2. The description of risks shall include, where relevant to the specific type of instrument concerned and the status and level of knowledge of the client, the following elements:

(a) the risks associated with that type of financial instrument including an explanation of leverage and its effects and the risk of losing the entire investment;

(b) the volatility of the price of such instruments and any limitations on the available market for such instruments;

(c) the fact that an investor might assume, as a result of transactions in such instruments, financial commitments and other additional obligations, including contingent liabilities, additional to the cost of acquiring the instruments;

(d) any margin requirements or similar obligations, applicable to instruments of that type.

Member States may specify the precise terms, or the contents, of the description of risks required under this paragraph.

3. If an investment firm provides a retail client or potential retail client with information about a financial instrument that is the subject of a current offer to the public and a prospectus has been published in connection with that offer in accordance with Directive 2003/71/EC, that firm shall inform the client or potential client where that prospectus is made available to the public.

4. Where the risks associated with a financial instrument composed of two or more different financial instruments or services are likely to be greater than the risks associated with any of the components, the investment firm shall provide an adequate description of the components of that instrument and the way in which its interaction increases the risks.

5. In the case of financial instruments that incorporate a guarantee by a third party, the information about the guarantee shall include sufficient detail about the guarantor and the guarantee to enable the retail client or potential retail client to make a fair assessment of the guarantee.

[9962]

Article 32

Information requirements concerning safeguarding of client financial instruments or client funds

(first indent of Article 19(3) of Directive 2004/39/EC)

1. Member States shall ensure that, where investment firms hold financial instruments or funds belonging to retail clients, they provide those retail clients or potential retail clients with such of the information specified in paragraphs 2 to 7 as is relevant.

2. The investment firm shall inform the retail client or potential retail client where the financial instruments or funds of that client may be held by a third party on behalf of the investment firm and of the responsibility of the investment firm under the applicable national law for any acts or omissions of the third party and the consequences for the client of the insolvency of the third party.

3. Where financial instruments of the retail client or potential retail client may, if permitted by national law, be held in an omnibus account by a third party, the investment firm shall inform the client of this fact and shall provide a prominent warning of the resulting risks.

4. The investment firm shall inform the retail client or potential retail client where it is not possible under national law for client financial instruments held with a third party to be separately identifiable from the proprietary financial instruments of that third party or of the investment firm and shall provide a prominent warning of the resulting risks.

5. The investment firm shall inform the client or potential client where accounts that contain financial instruments or funds belonging to that client or potential client are or will be subject to the law of a jurisdiction other than that of a Member State and shall indicate that the rights of the client or potential client relating to those financial instruments or funds may differ accordingly.

6. An investment firm shall inform the client about the existence and the terms of any security interest or lien which the firm has or may have over the client's financial instruments or funds, or any right of set-off it holds in relation to those instruments or funds. Where applicable, it shall also inform the client of the fact that a depository may have a security interest or lien over, or right of set-off in relation to those instruments or funds.

7. An investment firm, before entering into securities financing transactions in relation to financial instruments held by it on behalf of a retail client, or before otherwise using such financial instruments for its own account or the account of another client, shall in good time before the use of those instruments provide the retail client, in a durable medium, with clear, full and accurate information on the obligations and responsibilities of the investment firm with respect to the use of those financial instruments, including the terms for their restitution, and on the risks involved.

[9963]

Article 33

Information about costs and associated charges

(fourth indent of Article 19(3) of Directive 2004/39/EC)

Member States shall require investment firms to provide their retail clients and potential retail clients with information on costs and associated charges that includes such of the following elements as are relevant:

(a) the total price to be paid by the client in connection with the financial instrument or the investment service or ancillary service, including all related fees, commissions, charges and expenses, and all taxes payable via the investment firm or, if an exact price cannot be indicated, the basis for the calculation of the total price so that the client can verify it;

(b) where any part of the total price referred to in point (a) is to be paid in or represents an amount of foreign currency, an indication of the currency involved and the applicable currency conversion rates and costs;

(c) notice of the possibility that other costs, including taxes, related to transactions in connection with the financial instrument or the investment service may arise for the client that are not paid via the investment firm or imposed by it;

(d) the arrangements for payment or other performance.

For the purposes of point (a), the commissions charged by the firm shall be itemised separately in every case.

[9964]

Article 34

Information drawn up in accordance with Directive 85/611/EEC

(second and fourth indent of Article 19(3) of Directive 2004/39/EC)

1. Member States shall ensure that in respect of units in a collective investment undertaking covered by Directive 85/611/EEC, a simplified prospectus complying with Article 28 of that Directive is regarded as appropriate information for the purposes of the second indent of Article 19(3) of Directive 2004/39/EC.

2. Member States shall ensure that in respect of units in a collective investment undertaking covered by Directive 85/611/EEC, a simplified prospectus complying with Article 28 of that Directive is regarded as appropriate information for the purposes of the fourth indent of Article 19(3) of Directive 2004/39/EC with respect to the costs and associated charges related to the UCITS itself, including the exit and entry commissions.

[9965]

SECTION 3
ASSESSMENT OF SUITABILITY AND APPROPRIATENESS

Article 35

Assessment of suitability

(Article 19(4) of Directive 2004/39/EC)

1. Member States shall ensure that investment firms obtain from clients or potential clients such information as is necessary for the firm to understand the essential facts about the client and to have a reasonable basis for believing, giving due consideration to the nature and extent of the service provided, that the specific transaction to be recommended, or entered into in the course of providing a portfolio management service, satisfies the following criteria:

(a) it meets the investment objectives of the client in question;

(b) it is such that the client is able financially to bear any related investment risks consistent with his investment objectives;

(c) it is such that the client has the necessary experience and knowledge in order to understand the risks involved in the transaction or in the management of his portfolio.

2. Where an investment firm provides an investment service to a professional client it shall be entitled to assume that, in relation to the products, transactions and services for which it is so classified, the client has the necessary level of experience and knowledge for the purposes of paragraph 1(c).

Where that investment service consists in the provision of investment advice to a professional client covered by Section 1 of Annex II to Directive 2004/39/EC, the investment firm shall be entitled to assume for the purposes of paragraph 1(b) that the client is able financially to bear any related investment risks consistent with the investment objectives of that client.

3. The information regarding the financial situation of the client or potential client shall include, where relevant, information on the source and extent of his regular income, his assets, including liquid assets, investments and real property, and his regular financial commitments.

4. The information regarding the investment objectives of the client or potential client shall include, where relevant, information on the length of time for which the client wishes to hold the investment, his preferences regarding risk taking, his risk profile, and the purposes of the investment.

5. Where, when providing the investment service of investment advice or portfolio management, an investment firm does not obtain the information required under Article 19(4) of Directive 2004/39/EC, the firm shall not recommend investment services or financial instruments to the client or potential client.

[9966]

Article 36

Assessment of appropriateness

(Article 19(5) of Directive 2004/39/EC)

Member States shall require investment firms, when assessing whether an investment service as referred to in Article 19(5) of Directive 2004/39/EC is appropriate for a client, to determine whether that client has the necessary experience and knowledge in order to understand the risks involved in relation to the product or investment service offered or demanded.

For those purposes, an investment firm shall be entitled to assume that a professional client has the necessary experience and knowledge in order to understand the risks involved in relation to those particular investment services or transactions, or types of transaction or product, for which the client is classified as a professional client.

[9967]

Article 37

Provisions common to the assessment of suitability or appropriateness

(Article 19(4) and (5) of Directive 2004/39/EC)

1. Member States shall ensure that the information regarding a client's or potential client's knowledge and experience in the investment field includes the following, to the extent appropriate to the nature of the client, the nature and extent of the service to be provided and the type of product or transaction envisaged, including their complexity and the risks involved:

(a) the types of service, transaction and financial instrument with which the client is familiar;

(b) the nature, volume, and frequency of the client's transactions in financial instruments and the period over which they have been carried out;

(c) the level of education, and profession or relevant former profession of the client or potential client.

2. An investment firm shall not encourage a client or potential client not to provide information required for the purposes of Article 19(4) and (5) of Directive 2004/39/EC.

3. An investment firm shall be entitled to rely on the information provided by its clients or potential clients unless it is aware or ought to be aware that the information is manifestly out of date, inaccurate or incomplete.

[9968]

Article 38

Provision of services in non-complex instruments

(first indent of Article 19(6) of Directive 2004/39/EC)

A financial instrument which is not specified in the first indent of Article 19(6) of Directive 2004/39/EC shall be considered as non-complex if it satisfies the following criteria:

(a) it does not fall within Article 4(1)(18)(c) of, or points (4) to (10) of Section C of Annex I to, Directive 2004/39/EC;

(b) there are frequent opportunities to dispose of, redeem, or otherwise realise that instrument at prices that are publicly available to market participants and that are either market prices or prices made available, or validated, by valuation systems independent of the issuer;

(c) it does not involve any actual or potential liability for the client that exceeds the cost of acquiring the instrument;

(d) adequately comprehensive information on its characteristics is publicly available and is likely to be readily understood so as to enable the average retail client to make an informed judgment as to whether to enter into a transaction in that instrument.

[9969]

Article 39

Retail client agreement

(Article 19(1) and 19(7) of Directive 2004/39/EC)

Member States shall require an investment firm that provides an investment service other than investment advice to a new retail client for the first time after the date of application of this

Directive to enter into a written basic agreement, in paper or another durable medium, with the client setting out the essential rights and obligations of the firm and the client.

The rights and duties of the parties to the agreement may be incorporated by reference to other documents or legal texts.

[9970]

SECTION 4
REPORTING TO CLIENTS

Article 40

Reporting obligations in respect of execution of orders other than for portfolio management

(Article 19(8) of Directive 2004/39/EC)

1. Member States shall ensure that where investment firms have carried out an order, other than for portfolio management, on behalf of a client, they take the following action in respect of that order:

(a) the investment firm must promptly provide the client, in a durable medium, with the essential information concerning the execution of that order;
(b) in the case of a retail client, the investment firm must send the client a notice in a durable medium confirming execution of the order as soon as possible and no later than the first business day following execution or, if the confirmation is received by the investment firm from a third party, no later than the first business day following receipt of the confirmation from the third party.

Point (b) shall not apply where the confirmation would contain the same information as a confirmation that is to be promptly dispatched to the retail client by another person.

Points (a) and (b) shall not apply where orders executed on behalf of clients relate to bonds funding mortgage loan agreements with the said clients, in which case the report on the transaction shall be made at the same time as the terms of the mortgage loan are communicated, but no later than one month after the execution of the order.

2. In addition to the requirements under paragraph 1, Member States shall require investment firms to supply the client, on request, with information about the status of his order.

3. Member States shall ensure that, in the case of orders for a retail clients relating to units or shares in a collective investment undertaking which are executed periodically, investment firms either take the action specified in point (b) of paragraph 1 or provide the retail client, at least once every six months, with the information listed in paragraph 4 in respect of those transactions.

4. The notice referred to in point (b) of paragraph 1 shall include such of the following information as is applicable and, where relevant, in accordance with Table 1 of Annex I to Regulation (EC) No 1287/2006:

(a) the reporting firm identification;
(b) the name or other designation of the client;
(c) the trading day;
(d) the trading time;
(e) the type of the order;
(f) the venue identification;
(g) the instrument identification;
(h) the buy/sell indicator;
(i) the nature of the order if other than buy/sell;
(j) the quantity;
(k) the unit price;
(l) the total consideration;
(m) a total sum of the commissions and expenses charged and, where the retail client so requests, an itemised breakdown;
(n) the client's responsibilities in relation to the settlement of the transaction,

including the time limit for payment or delivery as well as the appropriate account details where these details and responsibilities have not previously been notified to the client;

(o) if the client's counterparty was the investment firm itself or any person in the investment firm's group or another client of the investment firm, the fact that this was the case unless the order was executed through a trading system that facilitates anonymous trading.

For the purposes of point (k), where the order is executed in tranches, the investment firm may supply the client with information about the price of each tranche or the average price. Where the average price is provided, the investment firm shall supply the retail client with information about the price of each tranche upon request.

5. The investment firm may provide the client with the information referred to in paragraph 4 using standard codes if it also provides an explanation of the codes used.

[9971]

Article 41

Reporting obligations in respect of portfolio management

(Article 19(8) of Directive 2004/39/EC)

1. Member States shall require investments firms which provide the service of portfolio management to clients to provide each such client with a periodic statement in a durable medium of the portfolio management activities carried out on behalf of that client unless such a statement is provided by another person.

2. In the case of retail clients, the periodic statement required under paragraph 1 shall include, where relevant, the following information:

(a) the name of the investment firm;

(b) the name or other designation of the retail client's account;

(c) a statement of the contents and the valuation of the portfolio, including details of each financial instrument held, its market value, or fair value if market value is unavailable and the cash balance at the beginning and at the end of the reporting period, and the performance of the portfolio during the reporting period;

(d) the total amount of fees and charges incurred during the reporting period, itemising at least total management fees and total costs associated with execution, and including, where relevant, a statement that a more detailed breakdown will be provided on request;

(e) a comparison of performance during the period covered by the statement with the investment performance benchmark (if any) agreed between the investment firm and the client;

(f) the total amount of dividends, interest and other payments received during the reporting period in relation to the client's portfolio;

(g) information about other corporate actions giving rights in relation to financial instruments held in the portfolio;

(h) for each transaction executed during the period, the information referred to in Article 40(4)(c) to (l) where relevant, unless the client elects to receive information about executed transactions on a transaction-by-transaction basis, in which case paragraph 4 of this Article shall apply.

3. In the case of retail clients, the periodic statement referred to in paragraph 1 shall be provided once every six months, except in the following cases:

(a) where the client so requests, the periodic statement must be provided every three months;

(b) in cases where paragraph 4 applies, the periodic statement must be provided at least once every 12 months;

(c) where the agreement between an investment firm and a retail client for a portfolio management service authorises a leveraged portfolio, the periodic statement must be provided at least once a month.

Investment firms shall inform retail clients that they have the right to make requests for the purposes of point (a).

However, the exception provided for in point (b) shall not apply in the case of transactions in financial instruments covered by Article 4(1)(18)(c) of, or any of points 4 to 10 of Section C in Annex I to, Directive 2004/39/EC.

4. Member States shall require investment firms, in cases where the client elects to receive information about executed transactions on a transaction-by-transaction basis, to provide promptly to the client, on the execution of a transaction by the portfolio manager, the essential information concerning that transaction in a durable medium.

Where the client concerned is a retail client, the investment firm must send him a notice confirming the transaction and containing the information referred to in Article 40(4) no later than the first business day following that execution or, if the confirmation is received by the investment firm from a third party, no later than the first business day following receipt of the confirmation from the third party.

The second subparagraph shall not apply where the confirmation would contain the same information as a confirmation that is to be promptly dispatched to the retail client by another person.

[9972]

Article 42

Additional reporting obligations for portfolio management or contingent liability transactions

(Article 19(8) of Directive 2004/39/EC)

Member States shall ensure that where investment firms provide portfolio management transactions for retail clients or operate retail client accounts that include an uncovered open position in a contingent liability transaction, they also report to the retail client any losses exceeding any predetermined threshold, agreed between the firm and the client, no later than the end of the business day in which the threshold is exceeded or, in a case where the threshold is exceeded on a non-business day, the close of the next business day.

[9973]

Article 43

Statements of client financial instruments or client funds

(Article 19(8) of Directive 2004/39/EC)

1. Member States shall require investment firms that hold client financial instruments or client funds to send at least once a year, to each client for whom they hold financial instruments or funds, a statement in a durable medium of those financial instruments or funds unless such a statement has been provided in any other periodic statement.

The first subparagraph shall not apply to a credit institution authorised under Directive 2000/12/EC in respect of deposits within the meaning of that Directive held by that institution.

2. The statement of client assets referred to in paragraph 1 shall include the following information:

(a) details of all the financial instruments or funds held by the investment firm for the client at the end of the period covered by the statement;

(b) the extent to which any client financial instruments or client funds have been the subject of securities financing transactions;

(c) the extent of any benefit that has accrued to the client by virtue of participation in any securities financing transactions, and the basis on which that benefit has accrued.

In cases where the portfolio of a client includes the proceeds of one or more unsettled transactions, the information referred to in point (a) may be based either on the trade date or the settlement date, provided that the same basis is applied consistently to all such information in the statement.

3. Member States shall permit investment firms which hold financial instruments or funds and which carry out the service of portfolio management for a client to include the statement of client assets referred to in paragraph 1 in the periodic statement it provides to that client pursuant to Article 41(1).

[9974]

SECTION 5
BEST EXECUTION

Article 44

Best execution criteria

(Articles 21(1) and 19(1) of Directive 2004/39/EC)

1. Member States shall ensure that, when executing client orders, investment firms take into account the following criteria for determining the relative importance of the factors referred to in Article 21(1) of Directive 2004/39/EC:

(a) the characteristics of the client including the categorisation of the client as retail or professional;
(b) the characteristics of the client order;
(c) the characteristics of financial instruments that are the subject of that order;
(d) the characteristics of the execution venues to which that order can be directed.

For the purposes of this Article and Article 46, "execution venue" means a regulated market, an MTF, a systematic internaliser, or a market maker or other liquidity provider or an entity that performs a similar function in a third country to the functions performed by any of the foregoing.

2. An investment firm satisfies its obligation under Article 21(1) of Directive 2004/39/EC to take all reasonable steps to obtain the best possible result for a client to the extent that it executes an order or a specific aspect of an order following specific instructions from the client relating to the order or the specific aspect of the order.

3. Where an investment firm executes an order on behalf of a retail client, the best possible result shall be determined in terms of the total consideration, representing the price of the financial instrument and the costs related to execution, which shall include all expenses incurred by the client which are directly related to the execution of the order, including execution venue fees, clearing and settlement fees and any other fees paid to third parties involved in the execution of the order.

For the purposes of delivering best execution where there is more than one competing venue to execute an order for a financial instrument, in order to assess and compare the results for the client that would be achieved by executing the order on each of the execution venues listed in the firm's order execution policy that is capable of executing that order, the firm's own commissions and costs for executing the order on each of the eligible execution venues shall be taken into account in that assessment.

4. Member States shall require that investment firms do not structure or charge their commissions in such a way as to discriminate unfairly between execution venues.

5. Before 1 November 2008 the Commission shall present a report to the European Parliament and to the Council on the availability, comparability and consolidation of information concerning the quality of execution of various execution venues.

[9975]

Article 45

Duty of investment firms carrying out portfolio management and reception and transmission of orders to act in the best interests of the client

(Article 19(1) of Directive 2004/39/EC)

1. Member States shall require investment firms, when providing the service of portfolio management, to comply with the obligation under Article 19(1) of Directive 2004/39/EC to act in accordance with the best interests of their clients when placing orders with other entities for execution that result from decisions by the investment firm to deal in financial instruments on behalf of its client.

2. Member States shall require investment firms, when providing the service of reception and transmission of orders, to comply with the obligation under Article 19(1) of Directive 2004/39/EC to act in accordance with the best interests of their clients when transmitting client orders to other entities for execution.

3. Member States shall ensure that, in order to comply with paragraphs 1 or 2, investment firms take the actions mentioned in paragraphs 4 to 6.

4. Investment firms shall take all reasonable steps to obtain the best possible result for their clients taking into account the factors referred to in Article 21(1) of Directive 2004/39/EC. The relative importance of these factors shall be determined by reference to the criteria set out in Article 44(1)and, for retail clients, to the requirement under Article 44(3).

An investment firm satisfies its obligations under paragraph 1 or 2, and is not required to take the steps mentioned in this paragraph, to the extent that it follows specific instructions from its client when placing an order with, or transmitting an order to, another entity for execution.

5. Investment firms shall establish and implement a policy to enable them to comply with the obligation in paragraph 4. The policy shall identify, in respect of each class of instruments, the entities with which the orders are placed or to which the investment firm transmits orders for execution. The entities identified must have execution arrangements that enable the investment firm to comply with its obligations under this Article when it places or transmits orders to that entity for execution.

Investment firms shall provide appropriate information to their clients on the policy established in accordance with this paragraph.

6. Investment firms shall monitor on a regular basis the effectiveness of the policy established in accordance with paragraph 5 and, in particular, the execution quality of the entities identified in that policy and, where appropriate, correct any deficiencies.

In addition, investment firms shall review the policy annually. Such a review shall also be carried out whenever a material change occurs that affects the firm's ability to continue to obtain the best possible result for their clients.

7. This Article shall not apply when the investment firm that provides the service of portfolio management and/or reception and transmission of orders also executes the orders received or the decisions to deal on behalf of its client's portfolio. In those cases Article 21 of Directive 2004/39/EC applies.

[9976]

Article 46

Execution policy

(Article 21(3) and (4) of Directive 2004/39/EC)

1. Member States shall ensure that investment firms review annually the execution policy established pursuant to Article 21(2) of Directive 2004/39/EC, as well as their order execution arrangements.

Such a review shall also be carried out whenever a material change occurs that affects the firm's ability to continue to obtain the best possible result for the execution of its client orders on a consistent basis using the venues included in its execution policy.

2. Investment firms shall provide retail clients with the following details on their execution policy in good time prior to the provision of the service:

(a) an account of the relative importance the investment firm assigns, in accordance with the criteria specified in Article 44(1), to the factors referred to in Article 21(1) of Directive 2004/39/EC, or the process by which the firm determines the relative importance of those factors;

(b) a list of the execution venues on which the firm places significant reliance in meeting its obligation to take all reasonable steps to obtain on a consistent basis the best possible result for the execution of client orders;

(c) a clear and prominent warning that any specific instructions from a client may prevent the firm from taking the steps that it has designed and implemented in its execution policy to obtain the best possible result for the execution of those orders in respect of the elements covered by those instructions.

That information shall be provided in a durable medium, or by means of a website (where that does not constitute a durable medium) provided that the conditions specified in Article 3(2) are satisfied.

[9977]

SECTION 6
CLIENT ORDER HANDLING

Article 47

General principles

(Articles 22(1) and 19(1) of Directive 2004/39/EC)

1. Member States shall require investment firms to satisfy the following conditions when carrying out client orders:

(a) they must ensure that orders executed on behalf of clients are promptly and accurately recorded and allocated;

(b) they must carry out otherwise comparable client orders sequentially and promptly unless the characteristics of the order or prevailing market conditions make this impracticable, or the interests of the client require otherwise;

(c) they must inform a retail client about any material difficulty relevant to the proper carrying out of orders promptly upon becoming aware of the difficulty.

2. Where an investment firm is responsible for overseeing or arranging the settlement of an executed order, it shall take all reasonable steps to ensure that any client financial instruments or client funds received in settlement of that executed order are promptly and correctly delivered to the account of the appropriate client.

3. An investment firm shall not misuse information relating to pending client orders, and shall take all reasonable steps to prevent the misuse of such information by any of its relevant persons.

[9978]

Article 48

Aggregation and allocation of orders

(Articles 22(1) and 19(1) of Directive 2004/39/EC)

1. Member States shall not permit investment firms to carry out a client order or a transaction for own account in aggregation with another client order unless the following conditions are met:

(a) it must be unlikely that the aggregation of orders and transactions will work overall to the disadvantage of any client whose order is to be aggregated;

(b) it must be disclosed to each client whose order is to be aggregated that the effect of aggregation may work to its disadvantage in relation to a particular order;

(c) an order allocation policy must be established and effectively implemented, providing in sufficiently precise terms for the fair allocation of aggregated orders and transactions, including how the volume and price of orders determines allocations and the treatment of partial executions.

2. Member States shall ensure that where an investment firm aggregates an order with one or more other client orders and the aggregated order is partially executed, it allocates the related trades in accordance with its order allocation policy.

[9979]

Article 49

Aggregation and allocation of transactions for own account

(Articles 22(1) and 19(1) of Directive 2004/39/EC)

1. Member States shall ensure that investment firms which have aggregated transactions for own account with one or more client orders do not allocate the related trades in a way that is detrimental to a client.

2. Member States shall require that, where an investment firm aggregates a client order with a transaction for own account and the aggregated order is partially executed, it allocates the related trades to the client in priority to the firm.

However, if the firm is able to demonstrate on reasonable grounds that without the combination it would not have been able to carry out the order on such advantageous terms, or at all, it may allocate the transaction for own account proportionally, in accordance with its order allocation policy referred to in Article 48(1)(c).

3. Member States shall require investment firms, as part of the order allocation policy referred to in Article 48(1)(c), to put in place procedures designed to prevent the reallocation, in a way that is detrimental to the client, of transactions for own account which are executed in combination with client orders.

[9980]

SECTION 7
ELIGIBLE COUNTERPARTIES

Article 50

Eligible counterparties

(Article 24(3) of Directive 2004/39/EC)

1. Member States may recognise an undertaking as an eligible counterparty if that undertaking falls within a category of clients who are to be considered professional clients in

accordance with paragraphs 1, 2 and 3 of Section I of Annex II to Directive 2004/39/EC, excluding any category which is explicitly mentioned in Article 24(2) of that Directive.

On request, Member States may also recognise as eligible counterparties undertakings which fall within a category of clients who are to be considered professional clients in accordance with Section II of Annex II to Directive 2004/39/EC. In such cases, however, the undertaking concerned shall be recognised as an eligible counterparty only in respect of the services or transactions for which it could be treated as a professional client.

2. Where, pursuant to the second subparagraph of Article 24(2) of Directive 2004/39/EC, an eligible counterparty requests treatment as a client whose business with an investment firm is subject to Articles 19, 21 and 22 of that Directive, but does not expressly request treatment as a retail client, and the investment firm agrees to that request, the firm shall treat that eligible counterparty as a professional client.

However, where that eligible counterparty expressly requests treatment as a retail client, the provisions in respect of requests of non-professional treatment specified in the second, third and fourth sub-paragraphs of Section I of Annex II to Directive 2004/39/EC shall apply.

[9981]

SECTION 8
RECORD-KEEPING

Article 51

Retention of records

(Article 13(6) of Directive 2004/39(EC)

1. Member States shall require investment firms to retain all the records required under Directive 2004/39/EC and its implementing measures for a period of at least five years.

Additionally, records which set out the respective rights and obligations of the investment firm and the client under an agreement to provide services, or the terms on which the firm provides services to the client, shall be retained for at least the duration of the relationship with the client.

However, competent authorities may, in exceptional circumstances, require investment firms to retain any or all of those records for such longer period as is justified by the nature of the instrument or transaction, if that is necessary to enable the authority to exercise its supervisory functions under Directive 2004/39/EC.

Following the termination of the authorisation of an investment firm, Member States or competent authorities may require the firm to retain records for the outstanding term of the five year period required under the first subparagraph.

2. The records shall be retained in a medium that allows the storage of information in a way accessible for future reference by the competent authority, and in such a form and manner that the following conditions are met:

(a) the competent authority must be able to access them readily and to reconstitute each key stage of the processing of each transaction;

(b) it must be possible for any corrections or other amendments, and the contents of the records prior to such corrections or amendments, to be easily ascertained;

(c) it must not be possible for the records otherwise to be manipulated or altered.

3. The competent authority of each Member State shall draw up and maintain a list of the minimum records investment firms are required to keep under Directive 2004/39/EC and its implementing measures.

4. Record-keeping obligations under Directive 2004/39/EC and in this Directive are without prejudice to the right of Member States to impose obligations on investment firms relating to the recording of telephone conversations or electronic communications involving client orders.

5. Before 31 December 2009 the Commission shall, in the light of discussions with the Committee of European Securities Regulators, report to the European Parliament and the Council on the continued appropriateness of the provisions of paragraph 4.

[9982]

SECTION 9
DEFINED TERMS FOR THE PURPOSES OF DIRECTIVE 2004/39/EC

Article 52

Investment advice

(Article 4(1)(4) of Directive 2004/39/EC)

For the purposes of the definition of "investment advice" in Article 4(1)(4) of Directive 2004/39/EC, a personal recommendation is a recommendation that is made to a person in his capacity as an investor or potential investor, or in his capacity as an agent for an investor or potential investor.

That recommendation must be presented as suitable for that person, or must be based on a consideration of the circumstances of that person, and must constitute a recommendation to take one of the following sets of steps:

(a) to buy, sell, subscribe for, exchange, redeem, hold or underwrite a particular financial instrument;

(b) to exercise or not to exercise any right conferred by a particular financial instrument to buy, sell, subscribe for, exchange, or redeem a financial instrument.

A recommendation is not a personal recommendation if it is issued exclusively through distribution channels or to the public.

[9983]

CHAPTER IV
FINAL PROVISIONS

Article 53

Transposition

1. Member States shall adopt and publish, by 31 January 2007 at the latest, the laws, regulations and administrative provisions necessary to comply with this Directive. They shall forthwith communicate to the Commission the text of those provisions and a correlation table between those provisions and this Directive.

2. Member States shall apply those provisions from 1 November 2007.

3. When Member States adopt those provisions, they shall contain a reference to this Directive or be accompanied by such a reference on the occasion of their official publication. Member States shall determine how such reference is to be made.

4. Member States shall communicate to the Commission the text of the main provisions of national law which they adopt in the field covered by this Directive.

[9984]

Article 54

Entry into force

This Directive shall enter into force on the 20th day following its publication in the Official Journal of the European Union.

[9985]

Article 55

Addressees

This Directive is addressed to the Member States.

[9986]

Done at Brussels, 10 August 2006.

COMMISSION DIRECTIVE

of 8 March 2007

laying down detailed rules for the implementation of certain provisions of Directive 2004/109/EC on the harmonisation of transparency requirements in relation to information about issuers whose securities are admitted to trading on a regulated market

(2007/14/EC)

NOTES

Date of publication in OJ: OJ L69, 9.3.2007, p 27. Notes are as in the original OJ version.

THE COMMISSION OF THE EUROPEAN COMMUNITIES,

Having regard to the Treaty establishing the European Community,

Having regard to Directive 2004/109/EC of the European Parliament and of the Council of 15 December 2004 on the harmonisation of transparency requirements in relation to information about issuers whose securities are admitted to trading on a regulated market and amending Directive 2001/34/EC,[1] and in particular Articles 2(3)(a), 5(6), first subparagraph, and 5(6)(c), 9(7), 12(8)(b) to (e), 13(2), 14(2), 21(4)(a), 23(4)(ii) and 23(7) thereof,

After consulting the Committee of European Securities Regulators (CESR)[2] for technical advice,

Whereas:

(1) Directive 2004/109/EC establishes the general principles for the harmonisation of transparency requirements in respect of the holding of voting rights or financial instruments that result in an entitlement to acquire existing shares with voting rights. It seeks to ensure that, through the disclosure of accurate, comprehensive and timely information about security issuers, investor confidence is built up and sustained. By the same token, by requiring issuers to be informed of movements affecting major holdings in companies, it seeks to ensure that the latter are in a position to keep the public informed.

(2) The rules for the implementation of the rules governing transparency requirements should likewise be designed to ensure a high level of investor protection, to enhance market efficiency, and to be applied in a uniform manner.

(3) As regards the procedural arrangements in accordance with which investors are to be informed of the issuer's choice of home Member State, it is appropriate that such choices be disclosed in accordance with the same procedure as regulated information under Directive 2004/109/EC.

(4) As regards the minimum content of the condensed set of half-yearly financial statements, where that set is not prepared in accordance with international accounting standards, this should be such as to avoid giving a misleading view of the assets, liabilities, financial position and profit or loss of the issuer. The content of half-yearly reports should be such as to ensure appropriate transparency for investors through a regular flow of information about the performance of the issuer, and that information should be presented in such a way that it is easy to compare it with the information provided in the annual report of the preceding year.

(5) Issuers of shares who prepare consolidated accounts in accordance with International Accounting Standards (IAS) and International Financial Reporting Standards (IFRS) should apply the same definition of related party transactions in annual and half-yearly reports under Directive 2004/109/EC. Issuers of shares who do not prepare consolidated accounts and are not required to apply IAS and IFRS should, in their half-yearly reports under Directive 2004/109/EC, apply the definition of related party transactions set out in Council Directive 78/660/EEC of 25 July 1978 based on Article 54(3)(g) of the Treaty on the annual accounts of certain types of companies.[3]

(6) For the purposes of benefiting from the exemption from the notification of major holdings under Directive 2004/109/EC in the case of shares acquired for the sole purpose of clearing and settling, the maximum length of the "short settlement cycle" should be as short as possible.

(7) In order for the relevant competent authority to be able to monitor compliance as regards the derogation for market makers with respect to the notification of information about major holdings, the market maker seeking to benefit from that derogation should make known that it is acting or intends to act as market maker and for which shares or financial instruments.

(8) Conducting market making activities in full transparency is particularly important. Thus, the market maker should be capable upon request from the relevant competent authority of identifying the activities conducted in relation to the issuer in question, and in particular the shares or financial instruments held for market making activities purposes.

(9) As regards the calendar of trading days, it is appropriate, for the sake of ease of operation, that time limits be calculated by reference to the trading days in the Member State of the issuer. However, in order to enhance transparency, provision should be made for each competent authority to inform investors and market participants of the calendar of trading days applicable for the various regulated markets situated or operating on its territory.

(10) As regards the circumstances in which notification of major holdings is to be made, it is appropriate to determine when that obligation is triggered either individually or collectively, and how that obligation is to be complied with in the case of proxies.

(11) It is reasonable to assume that natural persons or legal entities exercise a high duty of care when acquiring or disposing of major holdings. It follows that such persons or entities will very quickly become aware of such acquisitions or disposals, or of the possibility to exercise voting rights, and it is therefore appropriate to specify only a very short period following the relevant transaction as the period after which they are deemed to have knowledge.

(12) The exemption from the obligation to aggregate major holdings should be available only to parent undertakings that can demonstrate that their subsidiary management companies or investment firms fulfil adequate conditions of independence. To ensure full transparency, a statement to that effect should be notified ex ante to the relevant competent authority. In this regard, it is important that the notification mentions the competent authority supervising the management companies' activities under the conditions laid down pursuant to Council Directive 85/611/EEC of 20 December 1985 on the coordination of laws, regulations and administrative provisions relating to undertakings for collective investment in transferable securities (UCITS),[4] irrespective of whether or not they are authorised under that Directive, provided in the latter case that they are supervised under national legislation.

(13) For the purposes of Directive 2004/109/EC, financial instruments should be taken into account in the context of notifying major holdings, to the extent that such instruments give the holder an unconditional right to acquire the underlying shares or discretion as to whether to acquire the underlying shares or cash on maturity. Consequently, financial instruments should not be considered to include instruments entitling the holder to receive shares depending on the price of the underlying share reaching a certain level at a certain moment in time. Nor should they be considered to cover those instruments that allow the instrument issuer or a third party to give shares or cash to the instrument holder on maturity.

(14) The financial instruments in Section C of Annex I of Directive 2004/39/EC of the European Parliament and of the Council[5] which are not mentioned in Article 11(1) of this Commission directive do not qualify as financial instruments within the meaning of Article 13(1) of Directive 2004/109/EC.

(15) Directive 2004/109/EC sets high-level requirements in the area of dissemination of regulated information. The mere availability of information, which means that investors must actively seek it out, is therefore not sufficient for the purposes of that Directive. Accordingly, dissemination should involve the active distribution of information from the issuers to the media, with a view to reaching investors.

(16) Minimum quality standards for the dissemination of regulated information are necessary to ensure that investors, even if situated in a Member State other than that of the issuer, have equal access to regulated information. Issuers should ensure that those minimum standards are met, whether by disseminating the regulated information themselves or by entrusting a third party to do so on their behalf. In the latter case, the third party should be capable of dissemination in adequate conditions and have adequate mechanisms in place to ensure that the regulated information it receives emanates from the relevant issuer and that there is no significant risk of data corruption or of unauthorised access to unpublished inside information. Where the third party provides other services or performs other functions, such as media, competent authorities, stock exchanges or the entity in charge of the officially appointed storage mechanism, such services or functions should be kept clearly separated from the services and functions relating to the dissemination of regulated information. When communicating information to the media, issuers or third parties should give priority to the use of electronic means and industry standard formats so as to facilitate and accelerate the processing of the information.

(17) Additionally, by way of minimum standards, regulated information should be disseminated in a way that ensures the widest possible public access, and where possible reaching the public simultaneously inside and outside the issuer's home Member State. That is without prejudice to the right of Member States to request issuers to publish parts or all

regulated information through newspapers, and to the possibility for issuers to make regulated information available on their own or other websites accessible to investors.

(18) Equivalence should be able to be declared when general disclosure rules of third countries provide users with understandable and broadly equivalent assessment of issuers' position that enable them to make similar decisions as if they were provided with the information according to requirements under Directive 2004/109/EC, even if the requirements are not identical. However, equivalence should be limited to the substance of the relevant information and no exception as regards the time limits set by Directive 2004/109/EC should be accepted.

(19) In order to establish whether or not a third country issuer is meeting equivalent requirements to those laid down in Article 4(3) of Directive 2004/109/EC, it is important to ensure that there is consistency with Commission Regulation (EC) No 809/2004 of 29 April 2004 implementing Directive 2003/71/EC of the European Parliament and of the Council as regards information contained in prospectuses as well as the format, incorporation by reference and publication of such prospectuses and dissemination of advertisements,[6] in particular the items dealing with Historical Financial Information to be included in a prospectus.

(20) As regards the equivalence of independence requirements, a parent undertaking of a management company or investment firm registered in a third country should be able to benefit from the exemption under Article 12(4) or (5) of Directive 2004/109/EC, independently of whether the authorisation is required by the law of the third country for the controlled management company or investment firm to conduct management activities or portfolio management activities, provided that certain conditions of independence are respected.

(21) The measures provided for in this Directive are in accordance with the opinion of the European Securities Committee,

[9987]

NOTES

1 OJ L390, 31.12.2004, p 38.

2 CESR was established by Commission Decision 2001/527/EC of 6 June 2001 (OJ L191, 13.7.2001, p 43).

3 OJ L222, 14.8.1978, p 11. Directive as last amended by Directive 2006/46/EC of the European Parliament and of the Council (OJ L224, 16.8.2006, p 1).

4 OJ L375, 31.12.1985, p 3, Directive as last amended by Directive 2005/1/EC of the European Parliament and of the Council (OJ L79, 24.3.2005, p 9).

5 OJ L145, 30.4.2004, p 1. Directive as amended by Directive 2006/31/EC (OJ L114, 27.4.2006, p 60).

6 OJ L149, 30.4.2004, p 1, as corrected by OJ L215, 16.6.2004, p 3. Regulation as amended by Regulation (EC) No 1787/2006 (OJ L337, 5.12.2006, p 17).

HAS ADOPTED THIS DIRECTIVE:

Article 1

Subject matter

This Directive lays down detailed rules for the implementation of Article 2(1)(i)(ii), the second subparagraph of Article 5(3), the second sentence of Article 5(4), Article 9(1), (2) and (4), Article 10, Article 12(1), (2), (4), (5) and (6), Article 12(2)(a), Article 13(1), Article 21(1), Article 23(1) and (6) of Directive 2004/109/EC.

[9988]

Article 2

Procedural arrangements for the choice of the home Member State

(Article 2(1)(i)(ii) of Directive 2004/109/EC)

Where the issuer makes a choice of home Member State, that choice shall be disclosed in accordance with the same procedure as regulated information.

[9989]

Article 3

Minimum content of half-yearly non-consolidated financial statements

(Article 5(3), second subparagraph, of Directive 2004/109/EC)

1. The minimum content of the condensed set of half-yearly financial statements, where that set is not prepared in accordance with international accounting standards adopted

pursuant to the procedure provided for under Article 6 of Regulation (EC) No 1606/2002, shall be in accordance with paragraphs 2 and 3 of this Article.

2. The condensed balance sheet and the condensed profit and loss account shall show each of the headings and subtotals included in the most recent annual financial statements of the issuer. Additional line items shall be included if, as a result of their omission, the half-yearly financial statements would give a misleading view of the assets, liabilities, financial position and profit or loss of the issuer.

In addition, the following comparative information shall be included:

(a) balance sheet as at the end of the first six months of the current financial year and comparative balance sheet as at the end of the immediate preceding financial year;

(b) profit and loss account for the first six months of the current financial year with, from two years after the date of entry into force of this Directive, comparative information for the comparable period for the preceding financial year.

3. The explanatory notes shall include the following:

(a) sufficient information to ensure the comparability of the condensed half-yearly financial statements with the annual financial statements;

(b) sufficient information and explanations to ensure a user's proper understanding of any material changes in amounts and of any developments in the half-year period concerned, which are reflected in the balance sheet and the profit and loss account.

[9990]

Article 4

Major related parties' transactions

(Article 5(4), second sentence, of Directive 2004/109/EC)

1. In the interim management reports, issuers of shares shall disclose as major related parties' transactions, as a minimum, the following:

(a) related parties' transactions that have taken place in the first six months of the current financial year and that have materially affected the financial position or the performance of the enterprise during that period;

(b) any changes in the related parties' transactions described in the last annual report that could have a material effect on the financial position or performance of the enterprise in the first six months of the current financial year.

2. Where the issuer of shares is not required to prepare consolidated accounts, it shall disclose, as a minimum, the related parties' transactions referred to in Article 43(1)(7b) of Directive 78/660/EEC.

[9991]

Article 5

Maximum length of the usual "short settlement cycle"

(Article 9(4) of Directive 2004/109/EC)

The maximum length of the usual "short settlement cycle" shall be three trading days following the transaction.

[9992]

Article 6

Control mechanisms by competent authorities as regards market makers

(Article 9(5) of Directive 2004/109/EC)

1. The market maker seeking to benefit from the exemption provided for in Article 9(5) of Directive 2004/109/EC shall notify to the competent authority of the Home Member State of the issuer, at the latest within the time limit laid down in Article 12(2) of Directive 2004/109/EC, that it conducts or intends to conduct market making activities on a particular issuer.

Where the market maker ceases to conduct market making activities on the issuer concerned, it shall notify that competent authority accordingly.

2. Without prejudice to the application of Article 24 of Directive 2004/109/EC, where in case the market maker seeking to benefit from the exemption provided for in Article 9(5) of that Directive is requested by the competent authority of the issuer to identify the shares or financial instruments held for market making activity purposes, that market maker shall be allowed to make such identification by any verifiable means. Only if the market maker is not able to identify the shares or financial instruments concerned, he may be required to hold them in a separate account for the purposes of that identification.

3. Without prejudice to the application of Article 24(4)(a) of Directive 2004/109/EC, if a market-making agreement between the market maker and the stock exchange and/or the issuer is required under national law, the market maker shall upon request of the relevant competent authority provide the agreement to such authority.

[9993]

Article 7

Calendar of trading days

(Article 12(2) and (6), and Article 14(1), of Directive 2004/109/EC)

1. For the purposes of Article 12(2) and (6), and Article 14(1), of Directive 2004/109/EC, the calendar of trading days of the home Member State of the issuer shall apply.

2. Each competent authority shall publish in its Internet site the calendar of trading days of the different regulated markets situated or operating on the territory within its jurisdiction.

[9994]

Article 8

Shareholders and natural persons or legal entities referred to in Article 10 of the Transparency Directive required to make the notification of major holdings

(Article 12(2) of Directive 2004/109/EC)

1. For the purposes of Article 12(2) of Directive 2004/109/EC, the notification obligation which arises as soon as the proportion of voting rights held reaches, exceeds or falls below the applicable thresholds following transactions of the type referred to in Article 10 of Directive 2004/109/EC shall be an individual obligation incumbent upon each shareholder, or each natural person or legal entity as referred to in Article 10 of that Directive, or both in case the proportion of voting rights held by each party reaches, exceeds or falls below the applicable threshold.

In the circumstances referred to in point (a) of Article 10 of the Directive 2004/109/EC, the notification obligation shall be a collective obligation shared by all parties to the agreement.

2. In the circumstances referred to in point (h) of Article 10 of Directive 2004/109/EC, if a shareholder gives the proxy in relation to one shareholder meeting, notification may be made by means of a single notification at the moment of giving the proxy provided that it is made clear in the notification what the resulting situation in terms of voting rights will be when the proxy may no longer exercise the voting rights at its discretion.

If, in the circumstances referred to in point (h) of Article 10, the proxy holder receives one or several proxies in relation to one shareholder meeting, notification may be made by means of a single notification at the moment of receiving the proxies provided that it is made clear in the notification what the resulting situation in terms of voting rights will be when the proxy may no longer exercise the voting rights at its discretion.

3. Where the duty to make a notification lies with more than one natural person or legal entity, notification may be made by means of a single common notification.

However, use of a single common notification may not be deemed to release any of the natural persons or legal entities concerned from their responsibility in relation to notification.

[9995]

Article 9

Circumstances under which the notifying person should have learned of acquisition or disposal or of possibility to exercise voting rights

(Article 12(2) of Directive 2004/109/EC)

For the purposes of point (a) of Article 12(2) of Directive 2004/109/EC, the shareholder, or the natural person or legal entity referred to in Article 10 of that Directive, shall be deemed to have knowledge of the acquisition, disposal or possibility to exercise voting rights no later than two trading days following the transaction.

[9996]

Article 10

Conditions of independence to be complied with by management companies and investment firms involved in individual portfolio management

(Article 12(4), first subparagraph, and Article 12(5), first subparagraph, of Directive 2004/109/EC)

1. For the purposes of the exemption to the aggregation of holdings provided for in the first subparagraphs of Article 12(4) and (5) of Directive 2004/109/EC, a parent undertaking of a management company or of an investment firm shall comply with the following conditions:

(a) it must not interfere by giving direct or indirect instructions or in any other way in the exercise of the voting rights held by that management company or investment firm;

(b) that management company or investment firm must be free to exercise, independently of the parent undertaking, the voting rights attached to the assets it manages.

2. A parent undertaking which wishes to make use of the exemption shall, without delay, notify the following to the competent authority of the home Member State of issuers whose voting rights are attached to holdings managed by the management companies or investment firms:

(a) a list of the names of those management companies and investment firms, indicating the competent authorities that supervise them or that no competent authority supervises them, but with no reference to the issuers concerned;

(b) a statement that, in the case of each such management company or investment firm, the parent undertaking complies with the conditions laid down in paragraph 1.

The parent undertaking shall update the list referred to in point (a) on an ongoing basis.

3. Where the parent undertaking intends to benefit from the exemptions only in relation to the financial instruments referred to in Article 13 of Directive 2004/109/EC, it shall notify to the competent authority of the home Member State of the issuer only the list referred to in point (a) of paragraph 2.

4. Without prejudice to the application of Article 24 of Directive 2004/109/EC, a parent undertaking of a management company or of an investment firm shall be able to demonstrate to the competent authority of the home Member State of the issuer on request that:

(a) the organisational structures of the parent undertaking and the management company or investment firm are such that the voting rights are exercised independently of the parent undertaking;

(b) the persons who decide how the voting rights are to be exercised act independently;

(c) if the parent undertaking is a client of its management company or investment firm or has holding in the assets managed by the management company or investment firm, there is a clear written mandate for an arms-length customer relationship between the parent undertaking and the management company or investment firm.

The requirement in point (a) shall imply as a minimum that the parent undertaking and the management company or investment firm must established written policies and procedures reasonably designed to prevent the distribution of information between the parent undertaking and the management company or investment firm in relation to the exercise of voting rights.

5. For the purposes of point (a) of paragraph 1, "direct instruction" means any instruction given by the parent undertaking, or another controlled undertaking of the parent undertaking, specifying how the voting rights are to be exercised by the management company or investment firm in particular cases.

"Indirect instruction" means any general or particular instruction, regardless of the form, given by the parent undertaking, or another controlled undertaking of the parent undertaking, that limits the discretion of the management company or investment firm in relation to the exercise of the voting rights in order to serve specific business interests of the parent undertaking or another controlled undertaking of the parent undertaking.

[9997]

Article 11

Types of financial instruments that result in an entitlement to acquire, on the holder's own initiative alone, shares to which voting rights are attached

(Article 13(1) of Directive 2004/109/EC)

1. For the purposes of Article 13(1) of Directive 2004/109/EC, transferable securities; and options, futures, swaps, forward rate agreements and any other derivative contracts, as referred to in Section C of Annex I of Directive 2004/39/EC, shall be considered to be financial instruments, provided that they result in an entitlement to acquire, on the holder's own initiative alone, under a formal agreement, shares to which voting rights are attached, already issued, of an issuer whose shares are admitted to trading on a regulated market.

The instrument holder must enjoy, on maturity, either the unconditional right to acquire the underlying shares or the discretion as to his right to acquire such shares or not.

A formal agreement means an agreement which is binding under the applicable law.

2. For the purposes of Article 13(1) of Directive 2004/109/EC, the holder shall aggregate and notify all financial instruments within the meaning of paragraph 1 relating to the same underlying issuer.

3. The notification required under Article 13(1) of Directive 2004/109/EC shall include the following information:

(a) the resulting situation in terms of voting rights;
(b) if applicable, the chain of controlled undertakings through which financial instruments are effectively held;
(c) the date on which the threshold was reached or crossed;
(d) for instruments with an exercise period, an indication of the date or time period where shares will or can be acquired, if applicable;
(e) date of maturity or expiration of the instrument;
(f) identity of the holder;
(g) name of the underlying issuer.

For the purposes of point (a), the percentage of voting rights shall be calculated by reference to the total number of voting rights and capital as last disclosed by the issuer under Article 15 of Directive 2004/109/EC.

4. The notification period shall be the same as laid down in Article 12(2) of Directive 2004/109/EC and the related implementing provisions.

5. The notification shall be made to the issuer of the underlying share and to the competent authority of the home Member States of such issuer.

If a financial instrument relates to more than one underlying share, a separate notification shall be made to each issuer of the underlying shares.

[9998]

Article 12

Minimum Standards

(Article 21(1) of Directive 2004/109/EC)

1. The dissemination of regulated information for the purposes of Article 21(1) of Directive 2004/109/EC shall be carried out in compliance with the minimum standards set out in paragraphs 2 to 5.

2. Regulated information shall be disseminated in a manner ensuring that it is capable of being disseminated to as wide a public as possible, and as close to simultaneously as possible in the home Member State, or the Member State referred to in Article 21(3) of Directive 2004/109/EC, and in the other Member States.

3. Regulated information shall be communicated to the media in unedited full text.

However, in the case of the reports and statements referred to in Articles 4, 5 and 6 of Directive 2004/109/EC, this requirement shall be deemed fulfilled if the announcement relating to the regulated information is communicated to the media and indicates on which website, in addition to the officially appointed mechanism for the central storage of regulated information referred to in Article 21 of that Directive, the relevant documents are available.

4. Regulated information shall be communicated to the media in a manner which ensures the security of the communication, minimises the risk of data corruption and unauthorised access, and provides certainty as to the source of the regulated information.

Security of receipt shall be ensured by remedying as soon as possible any failure or disruption in the communication of regulated information.

The issuer or the person who has applied for admission to trading on a regulated market without the issuer's consent shall not be responsible for systemic errors or shortcomings in the media to which the regulated information has been communicated.

5. Regulated information shall be communicated to the media in a way which makes clear that the information is regulated information, identifies clearly the issuer concerned, the subject matter of the regulated information and the time and date of the communication of the information by the issuer or the person who has applied for admission to trading on a regulated market without the issuer's consent.

Upon request, the issuer or the person who has applied for admission to trading on a regulated market without the issuer's consent shall be able to communicate to the competent authority, in relation to any disclosure of regulated information, the following:

(a) the name of the person who communicated the information to the media;
(b) the security validation details;
(c) the time and date on which the information was communicated to the media;
(d) the medium in which the information was communicated;
(e) if applicable, details of any embargo placed by the issuer on the regulated information.

[9999]

Article 13

Requirements equivalent to Article 4(2)(b) of Directive 2004/109/EC

(Article 23(1) of Directive 2004/109/EC)

A third country shall be deemed to set requirements equivalent to those set out in Article 4(2)(b) of Directive 2004/109/EC where, under the law of that country, the annual management report is required to include at least the following information:

(a) a fair review of the development and performance of the issuer's business and of its position, together with a description of the principal risks and uncertainties that it faces, such that the review presents a balanced and comprehensive analysis of the development and performance of the issuer's business and of its position, consistent with the size and complexity of the business;
(b) an indication of any important events that have occurred since the end of the financial year;
(c) indications of the issuer's likely future development.

The analysis referred to in point (a) shall, to the extent necessary for an understanding of the issuer's development, performance or position, include both financial and, where appropriate, non-financial key performance indicators relevant to the particular business.

[10000]

Article 14

Requirements equivalent to Article 5(4) of Directive 2004/109/EC

(Article 23(1) of Directive 2004/109/EC)

A third country shall be deemed to set requirements equivalent to those set out in Article 5(4) of Directive 2004/109/EC where, under the law of that country, a condensed set of financial statements is required in addition to the interim management report, and the interim management report is required to include at least the following information:

(a) review of the period covered;
(b) indications of the issuer's likely future development for the remaining six months of the financial year;

(c) for issuers of shares and if already not disclosed on an ongoing basis, major related parties transactions.

[10001]

Article 15

Requirements equivalent to Articles 4(2) and 5(2)(c) of Directive 2004/109/EC

(Article 23(1) of Directive 2004/109/EC)

A third country shall be deemed to set requirements equivalent to those set out in Articles 4(2)(c) and 5(2)(c) of Directive 2004/109/EC where, under the law of that country, a person or persons within the issuer are responsible for the annual and half-yearly financial information, and in particular for the following:

(a) the compliance of the financial statements with the applicable reporting framework or set of accounting standards;

(b) the fairness of the management review included in the management report.

[10002]

Article 16

Requirements equivalent to Article 6 of Directive 2004/109/EC

(Article 23(1) of Directive 2004/109/EC)

A third country shall be deemed to set requirements equivalent to those set out in Article 6 of Directive 2004/109/EC where, under the law of that country, an issuer is required to publish quarterly financial reports.

[10003]

Article 17

Requirements equivalent to Article 4(3) of Directive 2004/109/EC

(Article 23(1) of Directive 2004/109/EC)

A third country shall be deemed to set requirements equivalent to those set out in the first subparagraph of Article 4(3) of Directive 2004/109/EC where, under the law of that country, the provision of individual accounts by the parent company is not required but the issuer whose registered office is in that third country is required, in preparing consolidated accounts, to include the following information:

(a) for issuers of shares, dividends computation and ability to pay dividends;

(b) for all issuers, where applicable, minimum capital and equity requirements and liquidity issues.

For the purposes of equivalence, the issuer must also be able to provide the competent authority of the home Member State with additional audited disclosures giving information on the individual accounts of the issuer as a standalone, relevant to the elements of information referred to under points (a) and (b). Those disclosures may be prepared under the accounting standards of the third country.

[10004]

Article 18

Requirements equivalent to Article 4(3), second subparagraph, of Directive 2004/109/EC

(Article 23(1) of Directive 2004/109/EC)

A third country shall be deemed to set requirements equivalent to those set out in the second subparagraph of Article 4(3) of Directive 2004/109/EC in relation to individual accounts where, under the law of a third country, an issuer whose registered office is in that third country is not required to prepare consolidated accounts but is required to prepare its individual accounts in accordance with international accounting standards recognised pursuant to Article 3 of Regulation (EC) No 1606/2002 of the European Parliament and of the Council[1] as applicable within the Community or with third country national accounting standards equivalent to those standards.

For the purposes of equivalence, if such financial information is not in line with those standards, it must be presented in the form of restated financial statements.

In addition, the individual accounts must be audited independently.

[10005]

NOTES

[1] OJ L243, 11.9.2002, p 1.

Article 19

Requirements equivalent to Article 12(6) of Directive 2004/109/EC

(Article 23(1) of Directive 2004/109/EC)

A third country shall be deemed to set requirements equivalent to those set out in Article 12(6) of Directive 2004/109/EC where, under the law of that country, the time period within which an issuer whose registered office is in that third country must be notified of major holdings and within which it must disclose to the public those major holdings is in total equal to or shorter than seven trading days.

The time frames for the notification to the issuer and for the subsequent disclosure to the public by the issuer may be different from those set out in Articles 12(2) and 12(6) of Directive 2004/109/EC.

[10006]

Article 20

Requirements equivalent to Article 14 of Directive 2004/109/EC

(Article 23(1) of Directive 2004/109/EC)

A third country shall be deemed to set requirements equivalent to those set out in Article 14 of Directive 2004/109/EC where, under the law of that country, an issuer whose registered office is in that third country is required to comply with the following conditions:

- (a) in the case of an issuer allowed to hold up to a maximum of 5 % of its own shares to which voting rights are attached, it must make a notification whenever that threshold is reached or crossed;
- (b) in the case of an issuer allowed to hold up to a maximum of between 5 % and 10 % of its own shares to which voting rights are attached, it must make a notification whenever a 5 % threshold or that maximum threshold is reached or crossed;
- (c) in the case of an issuer allowed to hold more than 10 % of its own shares to which voting rights are attached, it must make a notification whenever the 5 % threshold or the 10 % threshold is reached or crossed.

For the purposes of equivalence, notification above the 10 % threshold need not be required.

[10007]

Article 21

Requirements equivalent to Article 15 of Directive 2004/109/EC

(Article 23(1) of Directive 2004/109/EC)

A third country shall be deemed to set requirements equivalent to those set out in Article 15 of Directive 2004/109/EC where, under the law of that country, an issuer whose registered office is in that third country is required to disclose to the public the total number of voting rights and capital within 30 calendar days after an increase or decrease of such total number has occurred.

[10008]

Article 22

Requirements equivalent to Articles 17(2)(a) and 18(2)(a) of Directive 2004/109/EC

(Article 23(1) of Directive 2004/109/EC)

A third country shall be deemed to set requirements equivalent to those set out in Article 17(2)(a) and 18(2)(a) of Directive 2004/109/EC, as far as the content of the information about meetings is concerned, where, under the law of that country, an issuer whose registered office is in that third country is required to provide at least information on the place, time and agenda of meetings.

[10009]

Article 23

Equivalence in relation to the test of independence for parent undertakings of management companies and investment firms

(Article 23(6) of Directive 2004/109/EC)

1. A third country shall be deemed to set conditions of independence equivalent to those set out in Article 12(4) and (5) of that Directive where, under the law of that country, a management company or investment firm as referred to in Article 23(6) of Directive 2004/109/EC is required to meet the following conditions:

   (a) the management company or investment firm must be free in all situations to exercise, independently of its parent undertaking, the voting rights attached to the assets it manages;

   (b) the management company or investment firm must disregard the interests of the parent undertaking or of any other controlled undertaking of the parent undertaking whenever conflicts of interest arise.

2. The parent undertaking shall comply with the notification requirements laid down in Article 10(2)(a) and (3) of this Directive.

In addition, it shall make a statement that, in the case of each management company or investment firm concerned, the parent undertaking complies with the conditions laid down in paragraph 1 of this Article.

3. Without prejudice to the application of Article 24 of Directive 2004/109/EC, the parent undertaking shall be able to demonstrate to the competent authority of the home Member State of the issuer on request that the requirements laid down in Article 10(4) of this Directive are respected.

[10010]

Article 24

Transposition

1. Member States shall bring into force the laws, regulations and administrative provisions necessary to comply with this Directive by 12 months after date of adoption at the latest. They shall forthwith communicate to the Commission the text of those provisions and a correlation table between those provisions and this Directive.

When Member States adopt those provisions, they shall contain a reference to this Directive or be accompanied by such a reference on the occasion of their official publication. Member States shall determine how such reference is to be made.

2. Member States shall communicate to the Commission the text of the main provisions of national law which they adopt in the field covered by this Directive.

[10011]

Article 25

This Directive shall enter into force on the 20th day following its publication in the Official Journal of the European Union.

[10012]

Article 26

This Directive is addressed to the Member States.

[10013]

Done at Brussels, 8 March 2007.

APPENDICES

Appendix 1: Companies Act 1948, Table A

FIRST SCHEDULE

TABLE A

PART I
REGULATIONS FOR MANAGEMENT OF A COMPANY LIMITED BY SHARES, NOT BEING A PRIVATE COMPANY

NOTES

The Table A which applies to any company is the Table A in force at the date of the company's registration, and if Table A is altered, the alteration does not affect a company registered before the alteration takes effect; see CA 1985, s 8(2), (3). Accordingly, Table A to the 1948 Act, which is specifically preserved by the Companies Consolidation (Consequential Provisions) Act 1985, s 31(8), is set out below both in its original form and in its form as amended at different dates.

Part I of Table A applies (subject to the savings set out in CA 1980, s 88(4)) in relation to private companies limited by shares as it applies in relation to public companies so limited (CA 1980, Sch 3, para 36(1)).

APPENDICES

INTERPRETATION

1. In these regulations:—

"the Act" means the Companies Act, 1948.

"the seal" means the common seal of the company.

"secretary" means any person appointed to perform the duties of the secretary of the company.

"the United Kingdom" means Great Britain and Northern Ireland.

Expressions referring to writing shall, unless the contrary intention appears, be construed as including references to printing, lithography, photography, and other modes of representing or reproducing words in a visible form.

Unless the context otherwise requires, words or expressions contained in these regulations shall bear the same meaning as in the Act or any statutory modification thereof in force at the date at which these regulations become binding on the company.

SHARE CAPITAL AND VARIATION OF RIGHTS

2. Without prejudice to any special rights previously conferred on the holders of any existing shares or class of shares, any share in the company may be issued with such preferred, deferred or other special rights or such restrictions, whether in regard to dividend, voting, return of capital or otherwise as the company may from time to time by ordinary resolution determine.

3. Subject to the provisions of *section 58 of the Act, any preference shares* may, with the sanction of an ordinary resolution, be issued on the terms that they are, or at the option of the company are liable, to be redeemed on such terms and in such manner as the company before the issue of the shares may by special resolution determine.

NOTES

Reg 3: for the words in italics there are substituted the words "Part III of CA 1981, any shares" by CA 1981, Sch 3, in relation to any company registered on or after 3 December 1981.

4. If at any time the share capital is divided into different classes of shares, the rights attached to any class (*unless otherwise provided by the terms of issue of the shares of that class*) may, whether or not the company is being wound up, be varied with the consent in writing of the holders of three-fourths of the issued shares of that class, or with the sanction of an extraordinary resolution passed at a separate general meeting of the holders of the shares of the class. *To every such separate general meeting the provisions of these regulations relating to general meetings shall apply, but so that the necessary quorum shall be two persons at least holding or representing by proxy one-third of the issued shares of the class and that any holder of shares of the class present in person or by proxy may demand a poll.*

NOTES

Words in italics repealed by CA 1980, Sch 4, in relation to any company registered on or after 22 December 1980.

5. The rights conferred upon the holders of the shares of any class issued with preferred or other rights shall not, unless otherwise expressly provided by the terms of issue of the shares of that class, be deemed to be varied by the creation or issue of further shares ranking pari passu therewith.

6. The company may exercise the powers of paying commissions conferred by section 53 of the Act, provided that the rate per cent or amount of the commission paid or agreed to be paid shall be disclosed in the manner required by the said section and the rate of the commission shall not exceed the rate of 10 per cent of the price at which the shares in respect whereof the same is paid are issued or an amount equal to 10 per cent of such price (as the case may be). Such commission may be satisfied by the payment of cash or the allotment of fully or partly paid shares or partly in one way and partly in the other. The company may also on any issue of shares pay such brokerage as may be lawful.

7. Except as required by law, no person shall be recognised by the company as holding any share upon any trust, and the company shall not be bound by or be compelled in any way to recognise (even when having notice thereof) any equitable, contingent, future or partial interest in any share or any interest in any fractional part of a share or (except only as by these regulations or by law otherwise provided) any other rights in respect of any share except an absolute right to the entirety thereof in the registered holder.

8. Every person whose name is entered as a member in the register of members shall be entitled without payment to receive within two months after allotment or lodgment of transfer (or within such other period as the conditions of issue shall provide) one certificate for all his shares or several certificates each for one or more of his shares upon payment of 2s 6d for every certificate after the first or such less sum as the directors shall from time to time determine. Every certificate shall be under the seal [or under the official seal kept by the company by virtue of section 2 of the Stock Exchange (Completion of Bargains) Act 1976] and shall specify the shares to which it relates and the amount paid up thereon. Provided that in respect of a share or shares held jointly by several persons the company shall not be bound to issue more than one certificate, and delivery of a certificate for a share to one of several joint holders shall be sufficient delivery to all such holders.

NOTES

Reg 8: words in square brackets inserted by the Stock Exchange (Completion of Bargains) Act 1976, s 2(3), in relation to any company registered on or after 2 February 1979.

9. If a share certificate be defaced, lost or destroyed, it may be renewed on payment of a fee of 2s 6d or such less sum and on such terms (if any) as to evidence and indemnity and the payment of out-of-pocket expenses of the company of investigating evidence as the directors think fit.

10. The company shall not give, whether directly or indirectly, and whether by means of a loan, guarantee, the provision of security or otherwise, any financial assistance for the purpose of or in connection with a purchase or subscription made or to be made by any person of or for any shares in the company or in its holding company nor shall the company make a loan for any purpose whatsoever on the security of its shares or those of its holding company, but nothing in this regulation shall prohibit transactions mentioned in the proviso to section 54(1) of the Act.

NOTES

Reg 10: repealed by CA 1981, Sch 4, in relation to any company registered on or after 3 December 1981.

LIEN

11. The company shall have a first and paramount lien on every share (not being a fully paid share) for all moneys (whether presently payable or not) called or payable at a fixed time in respect of that share, *and the company shall also have a first and paramount lien on all shares (other than fully paid shares) standing registered in the name of a single person for all moneys presently payable by him or his estate to the company*; but the directors may at any time declare any share to be wholly or in part exempt from the provisions of this regulation. The company's lien, if any, on a share shall extend to all dividends payable thereon.

NOTES

Words in italics repealed by CA 1980, Sch 4, in relation to any company registered on or after 22 December 1980.

12. The company may sell, in such manner as the directors think fit, any shares on which the company has a lien, but no sale shall be made unless a sum in respect of which the lien exists is presently payable, nor until the expiration of fourteen days after a notice in writing, stating and demanding payment of such part of the amount in respect of which the lien exists as is presently payable, has been given to the registered holder for the time being of the share, or the person entitled thereto by reason of his death or bankruptcy.

13. To give effect to any such sale the directors may authorise some person to transfer the shares sold to the purchaser thereof. The purchaser shall be registered as the holder of the shares comprised in any such transfer, and he shall not be bound to see to the application of the purchase money, nor shall his title to the shares be affected by any irregularity or invalidity in the proceedings in reference to the sale.

14. The proceeds of the sale shall be received by the company and applied in payment of such part of the amount in respect of which the lien exists as is presently payable, and the residue, if any, shall (subject to a like lien for sums not presently payable as existed upon the shares before the sale) be paid to the person entitled to the shares at the date of the sale.

CALLS ON SHARES

15. The directors may from time to time make calls upon the members in respect of any moneys unpaid on their shares (whether on account of the nominal value of the shares or by way of premium) and not by the conditions of allotment thereof made payable at fixed times, provided that no call shall exceed one-fourth of the nominal value of the share or be payable at less than one month from the date fixed for the payment of the last preceding call, and each member shall (subject to receiving at least fourteen days' notice specifying the time or times and place of payment) pay to the company at the time or times and place so specified the amount called on his shares. A call may be revoked or postponed as the directors may determine.

16. A call shall be deemed to have been made at the time when the resolution of the directors authorising the call was passed and may be required to be paid by instalments.

17. The joint holders of a share shall be jointly and severally liable to pay all calls in respect thereof.

18. If a sum called in respect of a share is not paid before or on the day appointed for payment thereof, the person from whom the sum is due shall pay interest on the sum from the day appointed for payment thereof to the time of actual payment at such rate not exceeding 5 per cent per annum as the directors may determine, but the directors shall be at liberty to waive payment of such interest wholly or in part.

19. Any sum which by the terms of issue of a share becomes payable on allotment or at any fixed date, whether on account of the nominal value of the share or by way of premium, shall for the purposes of these regulations be deemed to be a call duly made and payable on the date on which by the terms of issue the same becomes payable, and in case of non-payment all the relevant provisions of these regulations as to payment of interest and expenses, forfeiture or otherwise shall apply as if such sum had become payable by virtue of a call duly made and notified.

20. The directors may, on the issue of shares, differentiate between the holders as to the amount of calls to be paid and the times of payment.

21. The directors may, if they think fit, receive from any member willing to advance the same, all or any part of the moneys uncalled and unpaid upon any shares held by him, and upon all or any of the moneys so advanced may (until the same would, but for such advance, become payable) pay interest at such rate not exceeding (unless the company in general meeting shall otherwise direct) 5 per cent per annum, as may be agreed upon between the directors and the member paying such sum in advance.

TRANSFER OF SHARES

22. The instrument of transfer of any share shall be executed by or on behalf of the transferor and transferee, and, *except as provided by sub-paragraph (a) of paragraph 2 of the Seventh Schedule to the Act*, the transferor shall be deemed to remain a holder of the share until the name of the transferee is entered in the register of members in respect thereof.

NOTES

Words in italics repealed by CA 1967, Sch 8, Pt III, in relation to any company registered on or after 27 January 1968.

23. Subject to such of the restrictions of these regulations as may be applicable, any member may transfer all or any of his shares by instrument in writing in any usual or common form or any other form which the directors may approve.

24. The directors may decline to register the transfer of a share (not being a fully paid share) to a person of whom they shall not approve, and they may also decline to register the transfer of a share on which the company has a lien.

25. The directors may also decline to recognise any instrument of transfer unless:—

(a) a fee of 2s 6d or such lesser sum as the directors may from time to time require is paid to the company in respect thereof;

(b) the instrument of transfer is accompanied by the certificate of the shares to which it relates, and such other evidence as the directors may reasonably require to show the right of the transferor to make the transfer; and

(c) the instrument of transfer is in respect of only one class of share.

26. If the directors refuse to register a transfer they shall within two months after the date on which the transfer was lodged with the company send to the transferee notice of the refusal.

27. The registration of transfers may be suspended at such times and for such periods as the directors may from time to time determine, provided always that such registration shall not be suspended for more than thirty days in any year.

28. The company shall be entitled to charge a fee not exceeding 2s 6d on the registration of every probate, letters of administration, certificate of death or marriage, power of attorney, notice in lieu of distringas, or other instrument.

TRANSMISSION OF SHARES

29. In case of the death of a member the survivor or survivors where the deceased was a joint holder, and the legal personal representatives of the deceased where he was a sole holder, shall be the only persons recognised by the company as having any title to his interest in the shares; but nothing herein contained shall release the estate of a deceased joint holder from any liability in respect of any share which had been jointly held by him with other persons.

30. Any person becoming entitled to a share in consequence of the death or bankruptcy of a member may, upon such evidence being produced as may from time to time properly be required by the directors and subject as hereinafter provided, elect either to be registered himself as holder of the share or to have some person nominated by him registered as the transferee thereof, but the directors shall, in either case, have the same right to decline or suspend registration as they would have had in the case of a transfer of the share by that member before his death or bankruptcy, as the case may be.

31. If the person so becoming entitled shall elect to be registered himself, he shall deliver or send to the company a notice in writing signed by him stating that he so elects. If he shall elect to have another person registered he shall testify his election by executing to that person a transfer of the share. All the limitations, restrictions and provisions of these regulations relating to the right to transfer and the registration of transfers of shares shall be applicable to any such notice or transfer as aforesaid as if the death or bankruptcy of the member had not occurred and the notice or transfer were a transfer signed by that member.

32. A person becoming entitled to a share by reason of the death or bankruptcy of the holder shall be entitled to the same dividends and other advantages to which he would be entitled if he were the registered holder of the share, except that he shall not, before being registered as a member in respect of the share, be entitled in respect of it to exercise any right conferred by membership in relation to meetings of the company:

Provided always that the directors may at any time give notice requiring any such person to elect either to be registered himself or to transfer the share, and if the notice is not complied with within ninety days the directors may thereafter withhold payment of all dividends, bonuses or other moneys payable in respect of the share until the requirements of the notice have been complied with.

FORFEITURE OF SHARES

33. If a member fails to pay any call or instalment of a call on the day appointed for payment thereof, the directors may, at any time thereafter during such time as any part of the call or instalment remains unpaid, serve a notice on him requiring payment of so much of the call or instalment as is unpaid, together with any interest which may have accrued.

34. The notice shall name a further day (not earlier than the expiration of fourteen days from the date of service of the notice) on or before which the payment required by the notice is to be made, and shall state that in the event of non-payment at or before the time appointed the shares in respect of which the call was made will be liable to be forfeited.

35. If the requirements of any such notice as aforesaid are not complied with, any share in respect of which the notice has been given may at any time thereafter, before the payment required by the notice has been made, be forfeited by a resolution of the directors to that effect.

36. A forfeited share may be sold or otherwise disposed of on such terms and in such manner as the directors think fit, and at any time before a sale or disposition the forfeiture may be cancelled on such terms as the directors think fit.

37. A person whose shares have been forfeited shall cease to be a member in respect of the forfeited shares, but shall, notwithstanding, remain liable to pay to the company all moneys which, at the date of forfeiture, were payable by him to the company in respect of the shares, but his liability shall cease if and when the company shall have received payment in full of all such moneys in respect of the shares.

38. A statutory declaration in writing that the declarant is a director or the secretary of the company, and that a share in the company has been duly forfeited on a date stated in the declaration, shall be conclusive evidence of the facts therein stated as against all persons claiming to be entitled to the share. The company may receive the consideration, if any, given for the share on any sale or disposition thereof and may execute a transfer of the share in favour of the person to whom the share is sold or disposed of and he shall thereupon be registered as the holder of the share, and shall not be bound to see to the application of the purchase money, if any, nor shall his title to the share be affected by any irregularity or invalidity in the proceedings in reference to the forfeiture, sale or disposal of the share.

39. The provisions of these regulations as to forfeiture shall apply in the case of non-payment of any sum which, by the terms of issue of a share, becomes payable at a fixed time, whether on account of the nominal value of the share or by way of premium, as if the same had been payable by virtue of a call duly made and notified.

CONVERSION OF SHARES INTO STOCK

40. The company may by ordinary resolution convert any paid-up shares into stock, and reconvert any stock into paid-up shares of any denomination.

41. The holders of stock may transfer the same, or any part thereof, in the same manner, and subject to the same regulations, as and subject to which the shares from which the stock arose might previously to conversion have been transferred, or as near thereto as circumstances admit; and the directors may from time to time fix the minimum amount of stock transferable but so that such minimum shall not exceed the nominal amount of the shares from which the stock arose.

42. The holders of stock shall, according to the amount of stock held by them, have the same rights, privileges and advantages as regards dividends, voting at meetings of the company and other matters as if they held the shares from which the stock arose, but no such privilege or advantage (except participation in the dividends and profits of the company and in the assets on winding up) shall be conferred by an amount of stock which would not, if existing in shares, have conferred that privilege or advantage.

43. Such of the regulations of the company as are applicable to paid-up shares shall apply to stock, and words "share" and "shareholder" therein shall include "stock" and "stockholder".

ALTERATION OF CAPITAL

44. The company may from time to time by ordinary resolution increase the share capital by such sum, to be divided into shares of such amount, as the resolution shall prescribe.

45. The company may by ordinary resolution—

(a) consolidate and divide all or any of its share capital to shares of larger amount than its existing shares;

(b) sub-divide its existing shares, or any of them, into shares of smaller amount than is fixed by the memorandum of association subject, nevertheless, to the provisions of section 61(1)(d) of the Act;

(c) cancel any shares which, at the date of the passing of the resolution, have not been taken or agreed to be taken by any person.

46. The company may by special resolution reduce its share capital, any capital redemption reserve fund or any share premium account in any manner and with, and subject to, any incident authorised, and consent required, by law.

GENERAL MEETINGS

47. The company shall in each year hold a general meeting as its annual general meeting in addition to any other meetings in that year, and shall specify the meeting as such in the notices calling it; and not more than fifteen months shall elapse between the date of one annual general meeting of the company and that of the next. Provided that so long as the company holds its first annual general meeting within eighteen months of its incorporation, it need not hold it in the year of its incorporation or in the following year. The annual general meeting shall be held at such time and place as the directors shall appoint.

48. All general meetings other than annual general meetings shall be called extraordinary general meetings.

49. The directors may, whenever they think fit, convene an extraordinary general meeting, and extraordinary general meetings shall also be convened on such requisition, or, in default, may be convened by such requisitionists, as provided by section 132 of the Act. If at any time there are not within the United Kingdom sufficient directors capable of acting to form a quorum, any director or any two members of the company may convene an extraordinary general meeting in the same manner as nearly as possible as that in which meetings may be convened by the directors.

NOTICE OF GENERAL MEETINGS

50. An annual general meeting and a meeting called for the passing of a special resolution shall be called by twenty-one days' notice in writing at the least, and a meeting of the company other than an annual general meeting or a meeting for the passing of a special resolution shall be called by fourteen days' notice in writing at the least. The notice shall be exclusive of the day on which it is served or deemed to be served and of the day for which it is given, and shall specify the place, the day and the hour of meeting and, in case of special

business, the general nature of that business, and shall be given, in manner hereinafter mentioned or in such other manner, if any, as may be prescribed by the company in general meeting, to such persons as are, under the regulations of the company, entitled to receive such notices from the company:

Provided that a meeting of the company shall, notwithstanding that it is called by shorter notice than that specified in this regulation, be deemed to have been duly called if it is so agreed—

(a) in the case of a meeting called as the annual general meeting, by all the members entitled to attend and vote thereat; and

(b) in the case of any other meeting, by a majority in number of the members having a right to attend and vote at the meeting, being a majority together holding not less than 95 per cent in nominal value of the shares giving that right.

51. The accidental omission to give notice of a meeting to, or the non-receipt of notice of a meeting by, any person entitled to receive notice shall not invalidate the proceedings at that meeting.

PROCEEDINGS AT GENERAL MEETINGS

52. All business shall be deemed special that is transacted at an extraordinary general meeting, and also all that is transacted at an annual general meeting, with the exception of declaring a dividend, the consideration of the accounts, balance sheets, and the reports of the directors and auditors, the election of directors in the place of those retiring and the appointment of, and the fixing of the remuneration of, the auditors.

53. No business shall be transacted at any general meeting unless a quorum of members is present at the time when the meeting proceeds to business; save as herein otherwise provided *three members present in person shall be a quorum.*

NOTES

For the words in italics there are substituted the words "two members present in person or by proxy shall be a quorum" by CA 1980, Sch 3, in relation to any company registered on or after 22 December 1980.

54. If within half an hour from the time appointed for the meeting a quorum is not present, the meeting, if convened upon the requisition of members, shall be dissolved; in any other case it shall stand adjourned to the same day in the next week, at the same time and place or to such other day and at such other time and place as the directors may determine, *and if at the adjourned meeting a quorum is not present within half an hour from the time appointed for the meeting, the members present shall be a quorum.*

NOTES

Words in italics repealed by CA 1980, Sch 4, in relation to any company registered on or after 22 December 1980.

55. The chairman, if any, of the board of directors shall preside as chairman at every general meeting of the company, or if there is no such chairman, or if he shall not be present within fifteen minutes after the time appointed for the holding of the meeting or is unwilling to act the directors present shall elect one of their number to be chairman of the meeting.

56. If at any meeting no director is willing to act as chairman or if no director is present within fifteen minutes after the time appointed for holding the meeting, the members present shall choose one of their number to be chairman of the meeting.

57. The chairman may, with the consent of any meeting at which a quorum is present (and shall if so directed by the meeting), adjourn the meeting from time to time and from place to place, but no business shall be transacted at any adjourned meeting other than the business left unfinished at the meeting from which the adjournment took place. When a meeting is adjourned for thirty days or more, notice of the adjourned meeting shall be given as in the case of an original meeting. Save as aforesaid it shall not be necessary to give any notice of an adjournment or of the business to be transacted at an adjourned meeting.

58. At any general meeting a resolution put to the vote of the meeting shall be decided on a show of hands unless a poll is (before or on the declaration of the result of the show of hands) demanded—

(a) by the chairman; or
(b) by at least *three* members present in person or by proxy; or
(c) by any member or members present in person or by proxy and representing not less than one-tenth of the total voting rights of all the members having the right to vote at the meeting; or
(d) by a member or members holding shares in the company conferring a right to vote at the meeting being shares on which an aggregate sum has been paid up equal to not less than one-tenth of the total sum paid up on all the shares conferring that right.

Unless a poll be so demanded a declaration by the chairman that a resolution has on a show of hands been carried or carried unanimously, or by a particular majority, or lost and an entry to that effect in the book containing the minutes of the proceedings of the company shall be conclusive evidence of the fact without proof of the number or proportion of the votes recorded in favour of or against such resolution.

The demand for a poll may be withdrawn.

NOTES

For the word in italics there is substituted the word "two" by CA 1980, Sch 3, in relation to any company registered on or after 22 December 1980.

59. Except as provided in regulation 61, if a poll is duly demanded it shall be taken in such manner as the chairman directs, and the result of the poll shall be deemed to be the resolution of the meeting at which the poll was demanded.

60. In the case of an equality of votes, whether on a show of hands or on a poll, the chairman of the meeting at which the show of hands takes place or at which the poll is demanded, shall be entitled to a second or casting vote.

61. A poll demanded on the election of a chairman or on a question of adjournment shall be taken forthwith. A poll demanded on any other question shall be taken at such time as the chairman of the meeting directs, and any business other than that upon which a poll has been demanded may be proceeded with pending the taking of the poll.

VOTES OF MEMBERS

62. Subject to any rights or restrictions for the time being attached to any class or classes of shares, on a show of hands every member present in person shall have one vote, and on a poll every member shall have one vote for each share of which he is the holder.

63. In the case of joint holders the vote of the senior who tenders a vote, whether in person or by proxy, shall be accepted to the exclusion of the votes of the other joint holders; and for this purpose seniority shall be determined by the order in which the names stand in the register of members.

64. A member of unsound mind, or in respect of whom an order has been made by any court having jurisdiction in lunacy, may vote, whether on a show of hands or on a poll, by his committee, receiver, curator bonis, or other person in the nature of a committee, receiver or curator bonis appointed by that court, and any such committee, receiver, curator bonis or other person may, on a poll, vote by proxy.

65. No member shall be entitled to vote at any general meeting unless all calls or other sums presently payable by him in respect of shares in the company have been paid.

66. No objection shall be raised to the qualification of any voter except at the meeting or adjourned meeting at which the vote objected to is given or tendered, and every vote not disallowed at such meeting shall be valid for all purposes. Any such objection made in due time shall be referred to the chairman of the meeting whose decision shall be final and conclusive.

67. On a poll votes may be given either personally or by proxy.

68. The instrument appointing a proxy shall be in writing under the hand of the appointer or of his attorney duly authorised in writing, or, if the appointer is a corporation, either under seal, or under the hand of an officer or attorney duly authorised. A proxy need not be a member of the company.

69. The instrument appointing a proxy and the power of attorney or other authority if any, under which it is signed or a notarially certified copy of that power or authority shall be deposited at the registered office of the company or at such other place within the United Kingdom as is specified for that purpose in the notice convening the meeting, not less than 48 hours before the time for holding the meeting or adjourned meeting, at which the person named in the instrument proposes to vote, or, in the case of a poll, not less than 24 hours before the time appointed for the taking of the poll, and in default the instrument of proxy shall not be treated as valid.

70. An instrument appointing a proxy shall be in the following form or a form as near thereto as circumstances admit—

"..Limited

I/We, ... of ....

in the county of ....,

being a member/members of the above-named company,

hereby appoint .... of ....,

or failing him, ... of ....,

as my/our proxy to vote for me/us on my/our behalf at the [annual or extraordinary, as the case may be] general meeting of the company, to be held on

the .... day of .... 19...... , and at any adjournment thereof.

Signed this .... day of .... 19...... "

71. Where it is desired to afford members an opportunity of voting for or against a resolution the instrument appointing a proxy shall be in the following form or a form as near thereto as circumstances admit—

"..Limited

I/We, ... of ....

in the county of ....,

being a member/members of the above-named company,

hereby appoint .... of ....,

or failing him, ... of ....,

as my/our proxy to vote for me/us on my/our behalf at the [annual or extraordinary, as the case may be] general meeting of the company, to be held on

the .... day of .... 19...... , and at any adjournment thereof.

Signed this .... day of .... 19...... "

This form is to be used *in favour of/against the resolution. Unless otherwise instructed, the proxy will vote as he thinks fit.

* Strike out whichever is not desired."

72. The instrument appointing a proxy shall be deemed to confer authority to demand or join in demanding a poll.

73. A vote given in accordance with the terms of an instrument of proxy shall be valid notwithstanding the previous death or insanity of the principal or revocation of the proxy or of the authority under which the proxy was executed, on the transfer of the share in respect of which the proxy is given, provided that no intimation in writing of such death, insanity, revocation or transfer as aforesaid shall have been received by the company at the office before the commencement of the meeting or adjourned meeting at which the proxy is used.

APPENDICES

[73A. Subject to the provisions of CAs 1948 to *1980* a resolution in writing signed by all the members for the time being entitled to receive notice of and to attend and vote at general meetings (or being corporations by their duly authorised representatives) shall be as valid and effective as if the same had been passed at a general meeting of the company duly convened and held.]

NOTES

Added by CA 1980, Sch 3, in relation to any company registered on or after 22 December 1980; for the year in italics there is substituted the year "1981" by CA 1981, Sch 3, in relation to any company registered on or after 3 December 1981.

CORPORATIONS ACTING BY REPRESENTATIVES AT MEETINGS

74. Any corporation which is a member of the company may by resolution of its directors or other governing body authorise such person as it thinks fit to act as its representative at any meeting of the company or of any class of members of the company, and the person so authorised shall be entitled to exercise the same powers on behalf of the corporation which he represents as that corporation could exercise if it were an individual member of the company.

DIRECTORS

75. The number of the directors and the names of the first directors shall be determined in writing by the subscribers of the memorandum of association or a majority of them.

76. The remuneration of the directors shall from time to time be determined by the company in general meeting. Such remuneration shall be deemed to accrue from day to day. The directors may also be paid all travelling, hotel and other expenses properly incurred by them in attending and returning from meetings of the directors or any committee of the directors or general meetings of the company or in connection with the business of the company.

77. The shareholding qualification for directors may be fixed by the company in general meeting, and unless and until so fixed no qualification shall be required.

78. A director of the company may be or become a director or other officer of, or otherwise interested in, any company promoted by the company or in which the company may be interested as shareholder or otherwise, and no such director shall be accountable to the company for any remuneration or other benefits received by him as a director or officer of, or from his interest in, such other company unless the company otherwise direct.

BORROWING POWERS

79. The directors may exercise all the powers of the company to borrow money, and to mortgage or charge its undertaking, property and uncalled capital or any part thereof, and[, subject to section 14 of CA 1980] to issue debentures, debenture stock, and other securities whether outright or as security for any debt, liability or obligation of the company or of any third party:

Provided that the amount for the time being remaining undischarged of moneys borrowed or secured by the directors as aforesaid (apart from temporary loans obtained from the company's bankers in the ordinary course of business) shall not at any time, without the previous sanction of the company in general meeting, exceed the nominal amount of the share capital of the company for the time being issued, but nevertheless no lender or other person dealing with the company shall be concerned to see or inquire whether this limit is observed. No debt incurred or security given in excess of such limit shall be invalid or ineffectual except in the case of express notice to the lender or the recipient of the security at the time when the debt was incurred or security given that the limit hereby imposed had been or was thereby exceeded.

NOTES

Words in square brackets inserted by CA 1980, Sch 3, in relation to any company registered on or after 22 December 1980.

POWERS AND DUTIES OF DIRECTORS

80. The business of the company shall be managed by the directors, who may pay all expenses incurred in promoting and registering the company, and may exercise all such powers of the company as are not, by the *Act* or by these regulations, required to be exercised by the company in general meeting, subject, nevertheless, to any of these regulations, to the provisions of the *Act* and to such regulations being not inconsistent with the aforesaid regulations or provisions, as may be prescribed by the company in general meeting; but no regulation made by the company in general meeting shall invalidate any prior act of the directors which would have been valid if that regulation had not been made.

NOTES

For the words in italics there are substituted the words "Companies Acts 1948 to 1980" in both places by CA 1980, Sch 3, in relation to companies registered on or after 22 December 1980; in the text as substituted the year "1980" is substituted by the year "1981" by CA 1981, Sch 3, in relation to companies registered on or after 3 December 1981.

81. The directors may from time to time and at any time by power of attorney appoint any company, firm or person or body of persons, whether nominated directly or indirectly by the directors, to be the attorney or attorneys of the company for such purposes and with such powers, authorities and discretions (not exceeding those vested in or exercisable by the directors under these regulations) and for such period and subject to such conditions as they may think fit, and any such powers of attorney may contain such provisions for the protection and convenience of persons dealing with any such attorney as the directors may think fit and may also authorise any such attorney to delegate all or any of the powers, authorities and discretions vested in him.

82. The company may exercise the powers conferred by section 35 of the Act with regard to having an official seal for use abroad, and such powers shall be vested in the directors.

83. The company may exercise the powers conferred upon the company by sections 119 to 123 (both inclusive) of the Act with regard to the keeping of a dominion register, and the directors may (subject to the provisions of those sections) make and vary such regulations as they may think fit respecting the keeping of any such register.

84.—(1) A director who is in any way, whether directly or indirectly, interested in a contract or proposed contract with the company shall declare the nature of his interest at a meeting of the directors in accordance with section 199 of the Act.

(2) A director shall not vote in respect of any contract or arrangement in which he is interested, and if he shall do so his vote shall not be counted, nor shall he be counted in the quorum present at the meeting, but neither of these prohibitions shall apply to—

- (a) any arrangement for giving any director any security or indemnity in respect of money lent by him to or obligations undertaken by him for the benefit of the company; or
- (b) to any arrangement for the giving by the company of any security to a third party in respect of a debt or obligation of the company for which the director himself has assumed responsibility in whole or in part under a guarantee or indemnity or by the deposit of a security; or
- (c) any contract by a director to subscribe for or underwrite shares or debentures of the company; or
- (d) any contract or arrangement with any other company in which he is interested only as an officer of the company or as holder of shares or other securities;

and these prohibitions may at any time be suspended or relaxed to any extent, and either generally or in respect of any particular contract, arrangement or transaction, by the company in general meeting.

(3) A director may hold any other office or place of profit under the company (other than the office of auditor) in conjunction with his office of director for such period and on such terms (as to remuneration and otherwise) as the directors may determine and no director or intending director shall be disqualified by his office from contracting with the company either with regard to his tenure of any such other office or place of profit or as vendor, purchaser or otherwise, nor shall any such contract, or any contract or arrangement entered into by or on behalf of the company in which any director is in any way interested, be liable to be avoided, nor shall any director so contracting or being so interested be liable to account to the company

for any profit realised by any such contract or arrangement by reason of such director holding that office or of the fiduciary relation thereby established.

(4) A director, notwithstanding his interest, may be counted in the quorum present at any meeting whereat he or any other director is appointed to hold any such office or place of profit under the company or whereat the terms of any such appointment are arranged, and he may vote on any such appointment or arrangement other than his own appointment or the arrangement of the terms thereof.

(5) Any director may act by himself or his firm in a professional capacity for the company, and he or his firm shall be entitled to remuneration for professional services as if he were not a director; provided that nothing herein contained shall authorise a director or his firm to act as auditor to the company.

85. All cheques, promissory notes, drafts, bills of exchange and other negotiable instruments, and all receipts for moneys paid to the company, shall be signed, drawn, accepted, endorsed, or otherwise executed, as the case may be, in such manner as the directors shall from time to time by resolution determine.

86. The directors shall cause minutes to be made in books provided for the purpose—

(a) of all appointments of officers made by the directors;

(b) of the names of the directors present at each meeting of the directors and of any committee of the directors;

(c) of all resolutions and proceedings at all meetings of the company, and of the directors, and of committees of directors;

and every director present at any meeting of directors or committee of directors shall sign his name in a book to be kept for that purpose.

87. The directors on behalf of the company may pay a gratuity or pension or allowance on retirement to any director who has held any other salaried office or place of profit with the company or to his widow or dependants and may make contributions to any fund and pay premiums for the purchase or provision of any such gratuity, pension or allowance.

DISQUALIFICATION OF DIRECTORS

88. The office of director shall be vacated if the director—

(a) ceases to be a director by virtue of section 182 or 185 of the Act; or

(b) becomes bankrupt or makes any arrangement or composition with his creditors generally; or

(c) becomes prohibited from being a director by reason of any order made under section 188 of the Act [*or under section 28 of CA 1976*]; or

(d) becomes of unsound mind; or

(e) resigns his office by notice in writing to the company; or

(f) shall for more than six months have been absent without permission of the directors from meetings of the directors held during that period.

NOTES

Words in square brackets inserted by CA 1976, in relation to any company registered on or after 1 June 1977, and repealed by CA 1981, Sch 4, in relation to any company registered on or after 3 December 1981.

ROTATION OF DIRECTORS

89. At the first annual general meeting of the company all the directors shall retire from office, and at the annual general meeting in every subsequent year one-third of the directors for the time being, or, if their number is not three or a multiple of three, then the number nearest one-third, shall retire from office.

90. The directors to retire in every year shall be those who have been longest in office since their last election, but as between persons who became directors on the same day those to retire shall (unless they otherwise agree among themselves) be determined by lot.

91. A retiring director shall be eligible for re-election.

92. The company at the meeting at which a director retires in manner aforesaid may fill the vacated office by electing a person thereto, and in default the retiring director shall if offering himself for re-election be deemed to have been re-elected, unless at such meeting it is expressly resolved not to fill such vacated office or unless a resolution for the re-election of such director shall have been put to the meeting and lost.

93. No person other than a director retiring at the meeting shall unless recommended by the directors be eligible for election to the office of director at any general meeting unless not less than three nor more than twenty-one days before the date appointed for the meeting there shall have been left at the registered office of the company notice in writing, signed by a member duly qualified to attend and vote at the meeting for which such notice is given, of his intention to propose such person for election, and also notice in writing signed by that person of his willingness to be elected.

94. The company may from time to time by ordinary resolution increase or reduce the number of directors, and may also determine in what rotation the increased or reduced number is to go out of office.

95. The directors shall have power at any time, and from time to time, to appoint any person to be a director, either to fill a casual vacancy or as an addition to the existing directors, but so that the total number of directors shall not at any time exceed the number fixed in accordance with these regulations. Any director so appointed shall hold office only until the next following annual general meeting, and shall then be eligible for re-election but shall not be taken into account in determining the directors who are to retire by rotation at such meeting.

96. The company may by ordinary resolution, of which special notice has been given in accordance with section 142 of the Act, remove any director before the expiration of his period of office notwithstanding anything in these regulations or in any agreement between the company and such director. Such removal shall be without prejudice to any claim such director may have for damages for breach of any contract of service between him and the company.

97. The company may by ordinary resolution appoint another person in place of a director removed from office under the immediately preceding regulation, and without prejudice to the powers of the directors under regulation 95 the company in general meeting may appoint any person to be a director either to fill a casual vacancy or as an additional director. A person appointed in place of a director so removed or to fill such a vacancy shall be subject to retirement at the same time as if he had become a director on the day on which the director in whose place he is appointed was last elected a director.

PROCEEDINGS OF DIRECTORS

98. The directors may meet together for the despatch of business, adjourn, and otherwise regulate their meetings, as they think fit. Questions arising at any meeting shall be decided by a majority of votes. In case of an equality of votes, the chairman shall have a second or casting vote. A director may, and the secretary on the requisition of a director shall, at any time summon a meeting of the directors. It shall not be necessary to give notice of a meeting of directors to any director for the time being absent from the United Kingdom.

99. The quorum necessary for the transaction of the business of the directors may be fixed by the directors, and unless so fixed shall be two.

100. The continuing directors may act notwithstanding any vacancy in their body, but, if and so long as their number is reduced below the number fixed by or pursuant to the regulations of the company as the necessary quorum of directors, the continuing directors or director may act for the purpose of increasing the number of directors to that number, or of summoning a general meeting of the company, but for no other purpose.

101. The directors may elect a chairman of their meetings and determine the period for which he is to hold office; but if no such chairman is elected, or if at any meeting the chairman is not present within five minutes after the time appointed for holding the same, the directors present may choose one of their number to be chairman of the meeting.

102. The directors may delegate any of their powers to committees consisting of such member or members of their body as they think fit; any committee so formed shall in the exercise of the powers so delegated conform to any regulations that may be imposed on it by the directors.

103. A committee may elect a chairman of its meetings; if no such chairman is elected, or if at any meeting the chairman is not present within five minutes after the time appointed for holding the same, the members present may choose one of their number to be chairman of the meeting.

104. A committee may meet and adjourn as it thinks proper. Questions arising at any meeting shall be determined by a majority of votes of the members present, and in the case of an equality of votes the chairman shall have a second or casting vote.

105. All acts done by any meeting of the directors or of a committee of directors or by any person acting as a director shall, notwithstanding that it be afterwards discovered that there was some defect in the appointment of any such director or person acting as aforesaid, or that they or any of them were disqualified, be as valid as if every such person had been duly appointed and was qualified to be a director.

106. A resolution in writing, signed by all the directors for the time being entitled to receive notice of a meeting of the directors, shall be as valid and effectual as if it had been passed at a meeting of the directors duly convened and held.

MANAGING DIRECTOR

107. The directors may from time to time appoint one of more of their body to the office of managing director for such period and on such terms as they think fit, and, subject to the terms of any agreement entered into in any particular case, may revoke such appointment. A director so appointed shall not, whilst holding that office, be subject to retirement by rotation or be taken into account in determining the rotation of retirement of directors, but his appointment shall be automatically determined if he cease from any cause to be a director.

108. A managing director shall receive such remuneration (whether by way of salary, commission or participation in profits, or partly in one way and partly in another) as the directors may determine.

109. The directors may entrust to and confer upon a managing director any of the powers exercisable by them upon such terms and conditions and with such restrictions as they may think fit, and either collaterally with or to the exclusion of their own powers and may from time to time revoke, withdraw, alter or vary all or any of such powers.

SECRETARY

110. [Subject to Section 21(5) of CA 1976] the secretary shall be appointed by the directors for such term, at such remuneration and upon such conditions as they may think fit; and any secretary so appointed may be removed by them.

NOTES

Words in square brackets inserted by CA 1976, Sch 2, in relation to any company registered on or after 18 April 1977.

111. No person shall be appointed or hold office as secretary who is—

(a) the sole director of the company; or

(b) a corporation the sole director of which is the sole director of the company; or

(c) the sole director of a corporation which is the sole director of the company.

112. A provision of the Act or these regulations requiring or authorising a thing to be done by or to a director and the secretary shall not be satisfied by its being done by or to the same person acting both as director and as, or in place of, the secretary.

THE SEAL

113. The directors shall provide for the safe custody of the seal, which shall only be used by the authority of the directors or of a committee of the directors authorised by the directors in that behalf, and every instrument to which the seal shall be affixed shall be signed by a director and shall be countersigned by the secretary or by a second director or by some other person appointed by the directors for the purpose.

DIVIDENDS AND RESERVE

114. The company in general meeting may declare dividends, but no dividend shall exceed the amount recommended by the directors.

115. The directors may from time to time pay to the members such interim dividends as appear to the directors to be justified by the profits of the company.

116. *No dividend shall be paid otherwise than out of profits.*

NOTES

Substituted by CA 1980, Sch 3, in relation to any company registered on or after 22 December 1980, as follows—

"No dividend or interim dividend shall be paid otherwise than in accordance with the provisions of Part III of CA 1980 which apply to the company.".

117. The directors may, before recommending any dividend, set aside out of the profits of the company such sums as they think proper as a reserve or reserves which shall, at the discretion of the directors, be applicable for any purpose to which the profits of the company may be properly applied, and pending such application may, at the like discretion, either be employed in the business of the company or be invested in such investments (other than shares of the company) as the directors may from time to time think fit. The directors may also without placing the same to reserve carry forward any profits which they may think prudent not to divide.

118. Subject to the rights of persons, if any, entitled to shares with special rights as to dividend, all dividends shall be declared and paid according to the amounts paid or credited as paid on the shares in respect whereof the dividend is paid, but no amount paid or credited as paid on a share in advance of calls shall be treated for the purposes of this regulation as paid on the share. All dividends shall be apportioned and paid proportionately to the amounts paid or credited as paid on the shares during any portion or portions of the period in respect of which the dividend is paid; but if any share is issued on terms providing that it shall rank for dividend as from a particular date such share shall rank for dividend accordingly.

119. The directors may deduct from any dividend payable to any member all sums of money (if any) presently payable by him to the company on account of calls or otherwise in relation to the shares of the company.

120. Any general meeting declaring a dividend or bonus may direct payment of such dividend or bonus wholly or partly by the distribution of specific assets and in particular of paid up shares, debentures or debenture stock of any other company or in any one or more of such ways, and the directors shall give effect to such resolution, and where any difficulty arises in regard to such distribution, the directors may settle the same as they think expedient, and in particular may issue fractional certificates and fix the value for distribution of such specific assets or any part thereof and may determine that cash payments shall be made to any members upon the footing of the value so fixed in order to adjust the rights of all parties, and may vest any such specific assets in trustees as may seem expedient to the directors.

121. Any dividend, interest or other moneys payable in cash in respect of shares may be paid by cheque or warrant sent through the post directed to the registered address of the holder or, in the case of joint holders, to the registered address of that one of the joint holders who is first named on the register of members or to such person and to such address as the holder or joint holders may in writing direct. Every such cheque or warrant shall be made payable to the order of the person to whom it is sent. Any one of two or more joint holders may give effectual receipts for any dividends, bonuses or other moneys payable in respect of the shares held by them as joint holders.

122. No dividend shall bear interest against the company.

ACCOUNTS

123. The directors *shall cause proper books of account to be kept with respect to—*

(*a*) *all sums of money received and expended by the company and the matters in respect of which the receipt and expenditure takes place;*

(*b*) *all sales and purchases of goods by the company; and*

(*c*) *the assets and liabilities of the company.*

Proper books shall not be deemed to be kept if there are not kept such books of account as are necessary to give a true and fair view of the state of the company's affairs and to explain its transactions.

NOTES

For the words in italics there are substituted the words "shall cause accounting records to be kept in accordance with section 12 of CA 1976" by CA 1976, Sch 2, in relation to any company registered on or after 1 October 1977.

124. *The books of account shall be kept at the registered office of the Company, or, subject to section 147(3) of the Act, at such other place or places as the directors think fit, and shall always be open to the inspection of the directors.*

NOTES

Substituted by CA 1976, Sch 2, in relation to any company registered on or after 1 October 1977, as follows—

"The accounting records shall be kept at the registered office of the company or, subject to section 12(6) and (7) of CA 1976, at such other place or places as the directors think fit, and shall always be open to the inspection of the officers of the company.".

125. The directors shall from time to time determine whether and to what extent and at what times and places and under what conditions or regulations the accounts and books of the company or any of them shall be open to the inspection of members not being directors, and no member (not being a director) shall have any right of inspecting any account or book or document of the company except as conferred by statute or authorised by the directors or by the company in general meeting.

126. The directors shall from time to time, in accordance with *sections 148, 150 and 157 of the Act*, cause to be prepared and to be laid before the company in general meeting such profit and loss accounts, balance sheets, group accounts (if any) and reports as are referred to in those sections.

NOTES

For the words in italics there are substituted the words "sections 150 and 157 of the Act and sections 1, 6 and 7 of CA 1976" by CA 1976, Sch 2, in relation to any company registered on or after 1 October 1977.

127. A copy of every balance sheet (including every document required by law to be annexed thereto) which is to be laid before the company in general meeting, together with a copy of the auditors' report [and directors' report], shall not less than twenty-one days before the date of the meeting be sent to every member of, and every holder of debentures of, the company and to every person registered under regulation 31. Provided that this regulation shall not require a copy of those documents to be sent to any person of whose address the company is not aware or to more than one of the joint holders of any shares or debentures.

NOTES

Words in square brackets inserted by CA 1976, Sch 2, in relation to any company registered on or after 1 October 1977.

CAPITALISATION OF PROFITS

128. The company in general meeting may upon the recommendation of the directors resolve that it is desirable to capitalise any part of the amount for the time being standing to

the credit of any of the company's reserve accounts or to the credit of the profit and loss account or otherwise available for distribution, and accordingly that such sum be set free for distribution amongst the members who would have been entitled thereto if distributed by way of dividend and in the same proportions on condition that the same be not paid in cash but be applied either in or towards paying up any amounts for the time being unpaid on any shares held by such members respectively or paying up in full unissued shares or debentures of the company to be allotted and distributed credited as fully paid up to and amongst such members in the proportion aforesaid, or partly in the one way and partly in the other, and the directors shall give effect to such resolution:

Provided that a share premium account and a capital redemption reserve fund may, for the purposes of this regulation, only be applied in the paying up of unissued shares to be *issued* to members of the company as fully paid bonus shares.

NOTES

For the word in italics there is substituted the word "allotted" by CA 1980, Sch 3, in relation to any company registered on or after 22 December 1980.

[128A. The company in general meeting may on the recommendation of the directors resolve that it is desirable to capitalise any part of the amount for the time being standing to the credit of any of the company's reserve accounts or to the credit of the profit and loss account which is not available for distribution by applying such sum in paying up in full unissued shares to be allotted as fully paid bonus shares to those members of the company who would have been entitled to that sum if it were distributed by way of dividend (and in the same proportions), and the directors shall give effect to such resolution.]

NOTES

Added by CA 1980, Sch 3, in relation to any company registered on or after 22 December 1980.

129. *Whenever such a resolution as aforesaid shall have been passed* the directors shall make all appropriations and applications of the undivided profits resolved to be capitalised thereby, and all allotments and issues of fully-paid shares or debentures, if any, and generally shall do all acts and things required to give effect thereto, with full power to the directors to make such provision by the issue of fractional certificates or by payment in cash or otherwise as they think fit for the case of shares or debentures becoming distributable in fractions, and also to authorise any person to enter on behalf of all members entitled thereto into an agreement with the company providing for the allotment to them respectively, credited as fully paid up, of any further shares or debentures to which they may be entitled upon such capitalisation, or (as the case may require) for the payment up by the company on their behalf, by the application thereto of their respective proportions of the profits resolved to be capitalised, of the amounts or any part of the amounts remaining unpaid on their existing shares, and any agreement made under such authority shall be effective and binding on all such members.

NOTES

For the words in italics there are substituted the words "Whenever a resolution is passed in pursuance of regulation 128 or 128A above" by CA 1980, Sch 3, in relation to any company registered on or after 22 December 1980.

AUDIT

130. Auditors shall be appointed and their duties regulated in accordance with *sections 159 to 162 of the Act.*

NOTES

The regulation set out above applies to any company registered before 27 January 1968.

For the words in italics there are substituted the words "sections 159 to 161 of the Act and section 14 of the Companies Act 1967" by CA 1967, in relation to any company registered between 27 January 1968 and 17 April 1977; for the words in italics there are substituted the words "section 161 of the Act, section 14 of CA 1967 and sections 13 to 18 of CA 1976" by CA 1976, in relation to any company registered between 18 April 1977 and 2 December 1981, and for the words in italics there are substituted the words "section 161 of the Act, sections 14 and 23A of CA 1967, sections 13 to 18 of CA 1976 and sections 7 and 12 of CA 1981" by CA 1981, in relation to any company registered between 3 December 1981 and 30 June 1985.

NOTICES

131. A notice may be given by the company to any member either personally or by sending it by post to him or to his registered address, or (if he has no registered address within the United Kingdom) to the address, if any, within the United Kingdom supplied by him to the company for the giving of notice to him. Where a notice is sent by post, service of the notice shall be deemed to be effected by properly addressing, prepaying, and posting a letter containing the notice, and to have been effected in the case of a notice of a meeting at the expiration of 24 hours after the letter containing the same is posted, and in any other case at the time at which the letter would be delivered in the ordinary course of post.

132. A notice may be given by the company to the joint holders of a share by giving the notice to the joint holder first named in the register of members in respect of the share.

133. A notice may be given by the company to the persons entitled to a share in consequence of the death or bankruptcy of a member by sending it through the post in a prepaid letter addressed to them by name, or by the title of representatives of the deceased, or trustee of the bankrupt, or any like description, at the address, if any, within the United Kingdom supplied for the purpose by the persons claiming to be so entitled, or (until such an address has been so supplied) by giving the notice in any manner in which the same might have been given if the death or bankruptcy had not occurred.

134. Notice of every general meeting shall be given in any manner hereinbefore authorised to—

(a) every member except those members who (having no registered address within the United Kingdom) have not supplied to the company an address within the United Kingdom for the giving of notices to them;

(b) every person upon whom the ownership of a share devolves by reason of his being a legal personal representative or a trustee in bankruptcy of a member where the member but for his death or bankruptcy would be entitled to receive notice of the meeting; and

(c) the auditor for the time being of the company.

No other person shall be entitled to receive notices of general meetings.

WINDING UP

135. If the company shall be wound up the liquidator may, with the sanction of an extraordinary resolution of the company and any other sanction required by the Act, divide amongst the members in specie or kind the whole or any part of the assets of the company (whether they shall consist of property of the same kind or not) and may, for such purpose set such value as he deems fair upon any property to be divided as aforesaid and may determine how such division shall be carried out as between the members or different classes of members. The liquidator may, with the like sanction, vest the whole or any part of such assets in trustees upon such trusts for the benefit of the contributories as the liquidator, with the like sanction, shall think fit, but so that no member shall be compelled to accept any shares or other securities whereon there is any liability.

INDEMNITY

136. Every director, managing director, agent, auditor, secretary and other officer for the time being of the company shall be indemnified out of the assets of the company against any liability incurred by him in defending any proceedings, whether civil or criminal, in which judgment is given in his favour or in which he is acquitted or in connection with any application under section 448 of the Act in which relief is granted to him by the court.

PART II
REGULATIONS FOR THE MANAGEMENT OF A PRIVATE COMPANY LIMITED BY SHARES

1. The regulations contained in Part I of Table A (with the exception of regulations 24 and 53) shall apply.

2. The company is a private company and accordingly—

(*a*) *the right to transfer shares is restricted in manner hereinafter prescribed;*
(*b*) *the number of members of the company (exclusive of persons who are in the employment of the company and of persons who having been formerly in the employment of the company were while in such employment and have continued after the determination of such employment to be members of the company) is limited to fifty. Provided that where two or more persons hold one or more shares in the company jointly they shall for the purpose of this regulation be treated as a single member;*
(*c*) *any invitation to the public to subscribe for any shares or debentures of the company is prohibited;*
(*d*) *the company shall not have power to issue share warrants to bearer.*

3. The directors may, in their absolute discretion and without assigning any reason therefor, decline to register any transfer of any share, whether or not it is a fully paid share.

4. No business shall be transacted at any general meeting unless a quorum of members is present at the time when the meeting proceeds to business; save as herein otherwise provided two members present in person or by proxy shall be a quorum.

5. Subject to the provisions of the Act, a resolution in writing signed by all the members for the time being entitled to receive notice of and to attend and vote at general meetings (or being corporations by their duly authorised representatives) shall be as valid and effective as if the same had been passed at a general meeting of the company duly convened and held.

6. The directors may at any time require any person whose name is entered in the register of members of the company to furnish them with any information, supported (if the directors so require) by a statutory declaration, which they may consider necessary for the purpose of determining whether or not the company is an exempt private company within the meaning of subsection (4) of section 129 of the Act.

Note. Regulations 3 and 4 of this Part are alternative to regulations 24 and 53 respectively of Part I.

[A1]

NOTES

Pt II repealed by CA 1980, Sch 3, in relation to any company registered on or after 22 December 1980.

Reg 6 repealed by CA 1967, Sch 8, Pt III, in relation to any company registered on or after 27 January 1968.

Appendix 2: Companies Act 1985, Table A

(SI 1985/805, SCHEDULE)

TABLE A
REGULATIONS FOR MANAGEMENT OF A COMPANY LIMITED BY SHARES

NOTES

The Table A which applies to any company is the Table A in force at the date of the company's registration, and if Table A is altered, the alteration does not affect a company registered before the alteration takes effect; see CA 1985, s 8(2), (3). Accordingly, this table is set out below both in its original form and in its form as amended at different dates.

INTERPRETATION

1. In these regulations—

"the Act" means the Companies Act 1985 including any statutory modification or re-enactment thereof for the time being in force.

"the articles" means the articles of the company.

"clear days" in relation to the period of a notice means that period excluding the day when the notice is given or deemed to be given and the day for which it is given or on which it is to take effect.

["communication" means the same as in the Electronic Communications Act 2000.]

["electronic communication" means the same as in the Electronic Communications Act 2000.]

"executed" includes any mode of execution.

"office" means the registered office of the company.

"the holder" in relation to shares means the member whose name is entered in the register of members as the holder of the shares.

"the seal" means the common seal of the company.

"secretary" means the secretary of the company or any other person appointed to perform the duties of the secretary of the company, including a joint, assistant or deputy secretary.

"the United Kingdom" means Great Britain and Northern Ireland.

Unless the context otherwise requires, words or expressions contained in these regulations bear the same meaning as in the Act but excluding any statutory modification thereof not in force when these regulations become binding on the company.

NOTES

Definitions in square brackets inserted by the Companies Act 1985 (Electronic Communications) Order 2000, SI 2000/3373, art 32(1), Sch 1, para 1, as from 22 December 2000.

SHARE CAPITAL

2. Subject to the provisions of the Act and without prejudice to any rights attached to any existing shares, any share may be issued with such rights or restrictions as the company may by ordinary resolution determine.

3. Subject to the provisions of the Act, shares may be issued which are to be redeemed or are to be liable to be redeemed at the option of the company or the holder on such terms and in such manner as may be provided by the articles.

4. The company may exercise the powers of paying commissions conferred by the Act. Subject to the [provisions] of the Act, any such commission may be satisfied by the payment of cash or by the allotment of fully or partly paid shares or partly in one way and partly in the other.

NOTES

Word in square brackets substituted for original word "provision" by the Companies (Tables A to F) (Amendment) Regulations 1985, SI 1985/1052, reg 2, as from 1 August 1985.

5. Except as required by law, no person shall be recognised by the company as holding any share upon any trust and (except as otherwise provided by the articles or by law) the company shall not be bound by or recognise any interest in any share except an absolute right to the entirety thereof in the holder.

SHARE CERTIFICATES

6. Every member, upon becoming the holder of any shares, shall be entitled without payment to one certificate for all the shares of each class held by him (and, upon transferring a part of his holding of shares of any class, to a certificate for the balance of such holding) or several certificates each for one or more of his shares upon payment for every certificate after the first of such reasonable sum as the directors may determine. Every certificate shall be sealed with the seal and shall specify the number, class and distinguishing numbers (if any) of the shares to which it relates and the amount or respective amounts paid up thereon. The company shall not be bound to issue more than one certificate for shares held jointly by several persons and delivery of a certificate to one joint holder shall be a sufficient delivery to all of them.

7. If a share certificate is defaced, worn-out, lost or destroyed, it may be renewed on such terms (if any) as to evidence and indemnity and payment of the expenses reasonably incurred by the company in investigating evidence as the directors may determine but otherwise free of charge, and (in the case of defacement or wearing-out) on delivery up of the old certificate.

LIEN

8. The company shall have a first and paramount lien on every share (not being a fully paid share) for all moneys (whether presently payable or not) payable at a fixed time or called in respect of that share. The directors may at any time declare any share to be wholly or in part exempt from the provisions of this regulation. The company's lien on a share shall extend to any amount payable in respect of it.

9. The company may sell in such manner as the directors determine any shares on which the company has a lien if a sum in respect of which the lien exists is presently payable and is not paid within fourteen clear days after notice has been given to the holder of the share or to the person entitled to it in consequence of the death or bankruptcy of the holder, demanding payment and stating that if the notice is not complied with the shares may be sold.

10. To give effect to a sale the directors may authorise some person to execute an instrument of transfer of the shares sold to, or in accordance with the directions of, the purchaser. The title of the transferee to the shares shall not be affected by any irregularity in or invalidity of the proceedings in reference to the sale.

11. The net proceeds of the sale, after payment of the costs, shall be applied in payment of so much of the sum for which the lien exists as is presently payable, and any residue shall (upon surrender to the company for cancellation of the certificate for the shares sold and subject to a like lien for any moneys not presently payable as existed upon the shares before the sale) be paid to the person entitled to the shares at the date of the sale.

CALLS ON SHARES AND FORFEITURE

12. Subject to the terms of allotment, the directors may make calls upon the members in respect of any moneys unpaid on their shares (whether in respect of nominal value or premium) and each member shall (subject to receiving at least fourteen clear days' notice specifying when and where payment is to be made) pay to the company as required by the notice the amount called on his shares. A call may be required to be paid by instalments. A call may, before receipt by the company of any sum due thereunder, be revoked in whole or part and payment of a call may be postponed in whole or part. A person upon whom a call is made shall remain liable for calls made upon him notwithstanding the subsequent transfer of the shares in respect whereof the call was made.

13. A call shall be deemed to have been made at the time when the resolution of the directors authorising the call was passed.

14. The joint holders of a share shall be jointly and severally liable to pay all calls in respect thereof.

APPENDICES

15. If a call remains unpaid after it has become due and payable the person from whom it is due and payable shall pay interest on the amount unpaid from the day it became due and payable until it is paid at the rate fixed by the terms of allotment of the share or in the notice of the call or, if no rate is fixed, at the appropriate rate (as defined by the Act) but the directors may waive payment of the interest wholly or in part.

16. An amount payable in respect of a share on allotment or at any fixed date, whether in respect of nominal value or premium or as an instalment of a call, shall be deemed to be a call and if it is not paid the provisions of the articles shall apply as if that amount had become due and payable by virtue of a call.

17. Subject to the terms of allotment, the directors may make arrangements on the issue of shares for a difference between the holders in the amounts and times of payment of calls on their shares.

18. If a call remains unpaid after it has become due and payable the directors may give to the person from whom it is due not less than fourteen clear days' notice requiring payment of the amount unpaid together with any interest which may have accrued. The notice shall name the place where payment is to be made and shall state that if the notice is not complied with the shares in respect of which the call was made will be liable to be forfeited.

19. If the notice is not complied with any share in respect of which it was given may, before the payment required by the notice has been made, be forfeited by a resolution of the directors and the forfeiture shall include all dividends or other moneys payable in respect of the forfeited shares and not paid before the forfeiture.

20. Subject to the provisions of the Act, a forfeited share may be sold, re-allotted or otherwise disposed of on such terms and in such manner as the directors determine either to the person who was before the forfeiture the holder or to any other person and at any time before sale, re-allotment or other disposition, the forfeiture may be cancelled on such terms as the directors think fit. Where for the purposes of its disposal a forfeited share is to be transferred to any person the directors may authorise some person to execute an instrument of transfer of the share to that person.

21. A person any of whose shares have been forfeited shall cease to be a member in respect of them and shall surrender to the company for cancellation the certificate for the shares forfeited but shall remain liable to the company for all moneys which at the date of forfeiture were presently payable by him to the company in respect of those shares with interest at the rate at which interest was payable on those moneys before the forfeiture or, if no interest was so payable, at the appropriate rate (as defined in the Act) from the date of forfeiture until payment but the directors may waive payment wholly or in part or enforce payment without any allowance for the value of the shares at the time of forfeiture or for any consideration received on their disposal.

22. A statutory declaration by a director or the secretary that a share has been forfeited on a specified date shall be conclusive evidence of the facts stated in it as against all persons claiming to be entitled to the share and the declaration shall (subject to the execution of an instrument of transfer if necessary) constitute a good title to the share and the person to whom the share is disposed of shall not be bound to see to the application of the consideration, if any, nor shall his title to the share be affected by any irregularity in or invalidity of the proceedings in reference to the forfeiture or disposal of the share.

TRANSFER OF SHARES

23. The instrument of transfer of a share may be in any usual form or in any other form which the directors may approve and shall be executed by or on behalf of the transferor and, unless the share is fully paid, by or on behalf of the transferee.

24. The directors may refuse to register the transfer of a share which is not fully paid to a person of whom they do not approve and they may refuse to register the transfer of a share on which the company has a lien. They may also refuse to register a transfer unless—

(a) it is lodged at the office or at such other place as the directors may appoint and is accompanied by the certificate for the shares to which it relates and such other evidence as the directors may reasonably require to show the right of the transferor to make the transfer;

(b) it is in respect of only one class of shares; and

(c) it is in favour of not more than four transferees.

25. If the directors refuse to register a transfer of a share, they shall within two months after the date on which the transfer was lodged with the company send to the transferee notice of the refusal.

26. The registration of transfers of shares or of transfers of any class of shares may be suspended at such times and for such periods (not exceeding thirty days in any year) as the directors may determine.

27. No fee shall be charged for the registration of any instrument of transfer or other document relating to or affecting the title to any share.

28. The company shall be entitled to retain any instrument of transfer which is registered, but any instrument of transfer which the directors refuse to register shall be returned to the person lodging it when notice of the refusal is given.

TRANSMISSION OF SHARES

29. If a member dies the survivor or survivors where he was a joint holder, and his personal representatives where he was a sole holder or the only survivor of joint holders, shall be the only persons recognised by the company as having any title to his interest; but nothing herein contained shall release the estate of a deceased member from any liability in respect of any share which had been jointly held by him.

30. A person becoming entitled to a share in consequence of the death or bankruptcy of a member may, upon such evidence being produced as the directors may properly require, elect either to become the holder of the share or to have some person nominated by him registered as the transferee. If he elects to become the holder he shall give notice to the company to that effect. If he elects to have another person registered he shall execute an instrument of transfer of the share to that person. All the articles relating to the transfer of shares shall apply to the notice or instrument of transfer as if it were an instrument of transfer executed by the member and the death or bankruptcy of the member had not occurred.

31. A person becoming entitled to a share in consequence of the death or bankruptcy of a member shall have the rights to which he would be entitled if he were the holder of the share, except that he shall not, before being registered as the holder of the share, be entitled in respect of it to attend or vote at any meeting of the company or at any separate meeting of the holders of any class of shares in the company.

ALTERATION OF SHARE CAPITAL

32. The company may by ordinary resolution—

(a) increase its share capital by new shares of such amount as the resolution prescribes;

(b) consolidate and divide all or any of its share capital into shares of larger amount than its existing shares;

(c) subject to the provisions of the Act, sub-divide its shares, or any of them, into shares of smaller amount and the resolution may determine that, as between the shares resulting from the sub-division, any of them may have any preference or advantage as compared with the others; and

(d) cancel shares which, at the date of the passing of the resolution, have not been taken or agreed to be taken by any person and diminish the amount of its share capital by the amount of the shares so cancelled.

33. Whenever as a result of a consolidation of shares any members would become entitled to fractions of a share, the directors may, on behalf of those members, sell the shares representing the fractions for the best price reasonably obtainable to any person (including, subject to the provisions of the Act, the company) and distribute the net proceeds of sale in due proportion among those members, and the directors may authorise some person to

execute an instrument of transfer of the shares to, or in accordance with the directions of, the purchaser. The transferee shall not be bound to see to the application of the purchase money nor shall his title to the shares be affected by any irregularity in or invalidity of the proceedings in reference to the sale.

34. Subject to the provisions of the Act, the company may by special resolution reduce its share capital, any capital redemption reserve and any share premium account in any way.

PURCHASE OF OWN SHARES

35. Subject to the provisions of the Act, the company may purchase its own shares (including any redeemable shares) and, if it is a private company, make a payment in respect of the redemption or purchase of its own shares otherwise than out of distributable profits of the company or the proceeds of a fresh issue of shares.

GENERAL MEETINGS

36. All general meetings other than annual general meetings shall be called extraordinary general meetings.

37. The directors may call general meetings and, on the requisition of members pursuant to the provisions of the Act, shall forthwith proceed to convene an extraordinary general meeting for a date not later than eight weeks after receipt of the requisition. If there are not within the United Kingdom sufficient directors to call a general meeting, any director or any member of the company may call a general meeting.

NOTICE OF GENERAL MEETINGS

38. An annual general meeting and an extraordinary general meeting called for the passing of a special resolution or a resolution appointing a person as a director shall be called by at least twenty-one clear days' notice. All other extraordinary general meetings shall be called by at least fourteen clear days' notice but a general meeting may be called by shorter notice if it is so agreed—

(a) in the case of an annual general meeting, by all the members entitled to attend and vote thereat; and

(b) in the case of any other meeting by a majority in number of the members having a right to attend and vote being a majority together holding not less than ninety-five per cent in nominal value of the shares giving that right.

The notice shall specify the time and place of the meeting and the general nature of the business to be transacted and, in the case of an annual general meeting, shall specify the meeting as such.

Subject to the provisions of the articles and to any restrictions imposed on any shares, the notice shall be given to all the members, to all persons entitled to a share in consequence of the death or bankruptcy of a member and to the directors and auditors.

39. The accidental omission to give notice of a meeting to, or the non-receipt of notice of a meeting by, any person entitled to receive notice shall not invalidate the proceedings at that meeting.

PROCEEDINGS AT GENERAL MEETINGS

40. No business shall be transacted at any meeting unless a quorum is present. Two persons entitled to vote upon the business to be transacted, each being a member or a proxy for a member or a duly authorised representative of a corporation, shall be a quorum.

41. If such a quorum is not present within half an hour from the time appointed for the meeting, or if during a meeting such a quorum ceases to be present, the meeting shall stand adjourned to the same day in the next week at the same time and place or [to] such time and place as the directors may determine.

NOTES

Word in square brackets inserted by the Companies (Tables A to F) (Amendment) Regulations 1985, SI 1985/1052, reg 2, as from 1 August 1985.

42. The chairman, if any, of the board of directors or in his absence some other director nominated by the directors shall preside as chairman of the meeting, but if neither the chairman nor such other director (if any) be present within fifteen minutes after the time appointed for holding the meeting and willing to act, the directors present shall elect one of their number to be chairman and, if there is only one director present and willing to act, he shall be chairman.

43. If no director is willing to act as chairman, or if no director is present within fifteen minutes after the time appointed for holding the meeting, the members present and entitled to vote shall choose one of their number to be chairman.

44. A director shall, notwithstanding that he is not a member, be entitled to attend and speak at any general meeting and at any separate meeting of the holders of any class of shares in the company.

45. The chairman may, with the consent of a meeting at which a quorum is present (and shall if so directed by the meeting), adjourn the meeting from time to time and from place to place, but no business shall be transacted at an adjourned meeting other than business which might properly have been transacted at the meeting had the adjournment not taken place. When a meeting is adjourned for fourteen days or more, at least seven clear days' notice shall be given specifying the time and place of the adjourned meeting and the general nature of the business to be transacted. Otherwise it shall not be necessary to give any such notice.

46. A resolution put to the vote of a meeting shall be decided on a show of hands unless before, or on the declaration of the result of, the show of hands a poll is duly demanded. Subject to the provisions of the Act, a poll may be demanded—

(a) by the chairman; or

(b) by at least two members having the right to vote at the meeting; or

(c) by a member or members representing not less than one-tenth of the total voting rights of all the members having the right to vote at the meeting; or

(d) by a member or members holding shares conferring a right to vote at the meeting being shares on which an aggregate sum has been paid up equal to not less than one-tenth of the total sum paid up on all the shares conferring that right;

and a demand by a person as proxy for a member shall be the same as a demand by the member.

47. Unless a poll is duly demanded a declaration by the chairman that a resolution has been carried or carried unanimously, or by a particular majority, or lost, or not carried by a particular majority and an entry to that effect in the minutes of the meeting shall be conclusive evidence of the fact without proof of the number or proportion of the votes recorded in favour of or against the resolution.

48. The demand for a poll may, before the poll is taken, be withdrawn but only with the consent of the chairman and a demand so withdrawn shall not be taken to have invalidated the result of a show of hands declared before the demand was made.

49. A poll shall be taken as the chairman directs and he may appoint scrutineers (who need not be members) and fix a time and place for declaring the result of the poll. The result of the poll shall be deemed to be the resolution of the meeting at which the poll was demanded.

50. In the case of an equality of votes, whether on a show of hands or on a poll, the chairman shall be entitled to a casting vote in addition to any other vote he may have.

51. A poll demanded on the election of a chairman or on a question of adjournment shall be taken forthwith. A poll demanded on any other question shall be taken either forthwith or at such time and place as the chairman directs not being more than thirty days after the poll is demanded. The demand for a poll shall not prevent the continuance of a meeting for the transaction of any business other than the question on which the poll was demanded. If a poll is demanded before the declaration of the result of a show of hands and the demand is duly withdrawn, the meeting shall continue as if the demand had not been made.

52. No notice need be given of a poll not taken forthwith if the time and place at which it is to be taken are announced at the meeting at which it is demanded. In any other case at least seven clear days' notice shall be given specifying the time and place at which the poll is to be taken.

53. A resolution in writing executed by or on behalf of each member who would have been entitled to vote upon it if it had been proposed at a general meeting at which he was present shall be as effectual as if it had been passed at a general meeting duly convened and held and may consist of several instruments in the like form each executed by or on behalf of one or more members.

VOTES OF MEMBERS

54. Subject to any rights or restrictions attached to any shares, on a show of hands every member who (being an individual) is present in person or (being a corporation) is present by a duly authorised representative, not being himself a member entitled to vote, shall have one vote and on a poll every member shall have one vote for every share of which he is the holder.

55. In the case of joint holders the vote of the senior who tenders a vote, whether in person or by proxy, shall be accepted to the exclusion of the votes of the other joint holders; and seniority shall be determined by the order in which the names of the holders stand in the register of members.

56. A member in respect of whom an order has been made by any court having jurisdiction (whether in the United Kingdom or elsewhere) in matters concerning mental disorder may vote, whether on a show of hands or on a poll, by his receiver, curator bonis or other person authorised in that behalf appointed by that court, and any such receiver, curator bonis or other person may, on a poll, vote by proxy. Evidence to the satisfaction of the directors of the authority of the person claiming to exercise the right to vote shall be deposited at the office, or at such other place as is specified in accordance with the articles for the deposit of instruments of proxy, not less than 48 hours before the time appointed for holding the meeting or adjourned meeting at which the right to vote is to be exercised and in default the right to vote shall not be exercisable.

57. No member shall vote at any general meeting or at any separate meeting of the holders of any class of shares in the company, either in person or by proxy, in respect of any share held by him unless all moneys presently payable by him in respect of that share have been paid.

58. No objection shall be raised to the qualification of any voter except at the meeting or adjourned meeting at which the vote objected to is tendered, and every vote not disallowed at the meeting shall be valid. Any objection made in due time shall be referred to the chairman whose decision shall be final and conclusive.

59. On a poll votes may be given either personally or by proxy. A member may appoint more than one proxy to attend on the same occasion.

60. [The appointment of] a proxy shall be *in writing* executed by or on behalf of the appointor and shall be in the following form (or in a form as near thereto as circumstances allow or in any other form which is usual or which the directors may approve)—

"... PLC/Limited

I/We, ... of ....

being a member/members of the above-named company,

hereby appoint .... of ....,

or failing him, ... of ....,

as my/our proxy to vote in my/our name[s] and on my/our behalf at the annual/extraordinary general meeting of the company, to be held on

.... 19...... , and at any adjournment thereof.

Signed on .... 19...... "

NOTES

Words in square brackets substituted for original words "An instrument appointing", and words in italics revoked, by the Companies Act 1985 (Electronic Communications) Order 2000, SI 2000/3373, art 32(1), Sch 1, para 2, as from 22 December 2000.

61. Where it is desired to afford members an opportunity of instructing the proxy how he shall act the [appointment of] a proxy shall be in the following form (or in a form as near thereto as circumstances allow or in any other form which is usual or which the directors may approve)—

".. PLC/Limited

I/We, ... of ....

being a member/members of the above-named company,

hereby appoint .... of ....,

or failing him, ... of ....,

as my/our proxy to vote in my/our name[s] and on my/our behalf at the annual/extraordinary general meeting of the company, to be held on

.... 19...... , and at any adjournment thereof.

This form is to be used in respect of the resolutions mentioned below as follows:

Resolution No 1 *for *against

Resolution No 2 *for *against.

* Strike out whichever is not desired.

Unless otherwise instructed, the proxy may vote as he thinks fit or abstain from voting.

Signed this .... day of .... 19...... "

NOTES

Words in square brackets substituted for original words "instrument appointing" by the Companies Act 1985 (Electronic Communications) Order 2000, SI 2000/3373, art 32(1), Sch 1, para 3, as from 22 December 2000.

62. [The appointment of] a proxy and any authority under which it is executed or a copy of such authority certified notarially or in some other way approved by the directors may—

(a) [in the case of an instrument in writing] be deposited at the office or at such other place within the United Kingdom as is specified in the notice convening the meeting or in any instrument of proxy sent out by the company in relation to the meeting not less than 48 hours before the time for holding the meeting or adjourned meeting at which the person named in the instrument proposes to vote; or

[(aa) in the case of an appointment contained in an electronic communication, where an address has been specified for the purpose of receiving electronic communications—

(i) in the notice convening the meeting, or

(ii) in any instrument of proxy sent out by the company in relation to the meeting, or

(iii) in any invitation contained in an electronic communication to appoint a proxy issued by the company in relation to the meeting,

be received at such address not less than 48 hours before the time for holding the meeting or adjourned meeting at which the person named in the appointment proposes to vote;]

(b) in the case of a poll taken more than 48 hours after it is demanded, be deposited [or received] as aforesaid after the poll has been demanded and not less than 24 hours before the time appointed for the taking of the poll; or

(c) where the poll is not taken forthwith but is taken not more than 48 hours after it was demanded, be delivered at the meeting at which the poll was demanded to the chairman or to the secretary or to any director;

[and an appointment of proxy which is not deposited, delivered or received] in a manner so permitted shall be invalid.

[In this regulation and the next, "address", in relation to electronic communications, includes any number or address used for the purposes of such communications.]

NOTES

Words in first pair of square brackets substituted for original words "The instrument appointing", words in fifth pair of square brackets substituted for original words "and an instrument of proxy which is not deposited or delivered", and other words in square brackets inserted, by the Companies Act 1985 (Electronic Communications) Order 2000, SI 2000/3373, art 32(1), Sch 1, para 4, as from 22 December 2000.

63. A vote given or poll demanded by proxy or by the duly authorised representative of a corporation shall be valid notwithstanding the previous determination of the authority of the person voting or demanding a poll unless notice of the determination was received by the company at the office or at such other place at which the instrument of proxy was duly deposited [or, where the appointment of the proxy was contained in an electronic communication, at the address at which such appointment was duly received] before the commencement of the meeting or adjourned meeting at which the vote is given or the poll demanded or (in the case of a poll taken otherwise than on the same day as the meeting or adjourned meeting) the time appointed for taking the poll.

NOTES

Words in square brackets inserted by the Companies Act 1985 (Electronic Communications) Order 2000, SI 2000/3373, art 32(1), Sch 1, para 5, as from 22 December 2000.

NUMBER OF DIRECTORS

64. Unless otherwise determined by ordinary resolution, the number of directors (other than alternate directors) shall not be subject to any maximum but shall be not less than two.

ALTERNATE DIRECTORS

65. Any director (other than an alternate director) may appoint any other director, or any other person approved by resolution of the directors and willing to act, to be an alternate director and may remove from office an alternate director so appointed by him.

66. An alternate director shall be entitled to receive notice of all meetings of directors and of all meetings of committees of directors of which his appointor is a member, to attend and vote at any such meeting at which the director appointing him is not personally present, and generally to perform all the functions of his appointor as a director in his absence but shall not be entitled to receive any remuneration from the company for his services as an alternate director. But it shall not be necessary to give notice of such a meeting to an alternate director who is absent from the United Kingdom.

67. An alternate director shall cease to be an alternate director if his appointor ceases to be a director; but, if a director retires by rotation or otherwise but is reappointed or deemed to have been reappointed at the meeting at which he retires, any appointment of an alternate director made by him which was in force immediately prior to his retirement shall continue after his reappointment.

68. Any appointment or removal of an alternate director shall be by notice to the company signed by the director making or revoking the appointment or in any other manner approved by the directors.

69. Save as otherwise provided in the articles, an alternate director shall be deemed for all purposes to be a director and shall alone be responsible for his own acts and defaults and he shall not be deemed to be the agent of the director appointing him.

POWERS OF DIRECTORS

70. Subject to the provisions of the Act, the memorandum and the articles and to any directions given by special resolution, the business of the company shall be managed by the directors who may exercise all the powers of the company. No alteration of the memorandum or articles and no such direction shall invalidate any prior act of the directors which would

have been valid if that alteration had not been made or that direction had not been given. The powers given by this regulation shall not be limited by any special power given to the directors by the articles and a meeting of directors at which a quorum is present may exercise all powers exercisable by the directors.

71. The directors may, by power of attorney or otherwise, appoint any person to be the agent of the company for such purposes and on such conditions as they determine, including authority for the agent to delegate all or any of his powers.

DELEGATION OF DIRECTORS' POWERS

72. The directors may delegate any of their powers to any committee consisting of one or more directors. They may also delegate to any managing director or any director holding any other executive office such of their powers as they consider desirable to be exercised by him. Any such delegation may be made subject to any conditions the directors may impose, and either collaterally with or to the exclusion of their own powers and may be revoked or altered. Subject to any such conditions, the proceedings of a committee with two or more members shall be governed by the articles regulating the proceedings of directors so far as they are capable of applying.

APPOINTMENT AND RETIREMENT OF DIRECTORS

73. At the first annual general meeting all the directors shall retire from office, and at every subsequent annual general meeting one-third of the directors who are subject to retirement by rotation or, if their number is not three or a multiple of three, the number nearest to one-third shall retire from office; but, if there is only one director who is subject to retirement by rotation, he shall retire.

74. Subject to the provisions of the Act, the directors to retire by rotation shall be those who have been longest in office since their last appointment or reappointment, but as between persons who became or were last reappointed directors on the same day those to retire shall (unless they otherwise agree among themselves) be determined by lot.

75. If the company, at the meeting at which a director retires by rotation, does not fill the vacancy the retiring director shall, if willing to act, be deemed to have been reappointed unless at the meeting it is resolved not to fill the vacancy or unless a resolution for the reappointment of the director is put to the meeting and lost.

76. No person other than a director retiring by rotation shall be appointed or reappointed a director at any general meeting unless—

(a) he is recommended by the directors; or

(b) not less than fourteen nor more than thirty-five clear days before the date appointed for the meeting, notice executed by a member qualified to vote at the meeting has been given to the company of the intention to propose that person for appointment or reappointment stating the particulars which would, if he were so appointed or reappointed, be required to be included in the company's register of directors together with notice executed by that person of his willingness to be appointed or reappointed.

77. Not less than seven nor more than twenty-eight clear days before the date appointed for holding a general meeting notice shall be given to all who are entitled to receive notice of the meeting of any person (other than a director retiring by rotation at the meeting) who is recommended by the directors for appointment or reappointment as a director at the meeting or in respect of whom notice has been duly given to the company of the intention to propose him at the meeting for appointment or reappointment as a director. The notice shall give the particulars of that person which would, if he were so appointed or reappointed, be required to be included in the company's register of directors.

78. Subject as aforesaid, the company may by ordinary resolution appoint a person who is willing to act to be a director either to fill a vacancy or as an additional director and may also determine the rotation in which any additional directors are to retire.

79. The directors may appoint a person who is willing to act to be a director, either to fill a vacancy or as an additional director, provided that the appointment does not cause the number

of directors to exceed any number fixed by or in accordance with the articles as the maximum number of directors. A director so appointed shall hold office only until the next following annual general meeting and shall not be taken into account in determining the directors who are to retire by rotation at the meeting. If not reappointed at such annual general meeting, he shall vacate office at the conclusion thereof.

80. Subject as aforesaid, a director who retires at an annual general meeting may, if willing to act, be reappointed. If he is not reappointed, he shall retain office until the meeting appoints someone in his place, or if it does not do so, until the end of the meeting.

DISQUALIFICATION AND REMOVAL OF DIRECTORS

81. The office of a director shall be vacated if—
- (a) he ceases to be a director by virtue of any provision of the Act or he becomes prohibited by law from being a director; or
- (b) he becomes bankrupt or makes any arrangement or composition with his creditors generally; or
- (c) he is, or may be, suffering from mental disorder and either—
  - (i) he is admitted to hospital in pursuance of an application for admission for treatment under the Mental Health Act 1983 or, in Scotland, an application for admission under the Mental Health (Scotland) Act 1960, or
  - (ii) an order is made by a court having jurisdiction (whether in the United Kingdom or elsewhere) in matters concerning mental disorder for his detention or for the appointment of a receiver, curator bonis or other person to exercise powers with respect to his property or affairs; or
- (d) he resigns his office by notice to the company; or
- (e) he shall for more than six consecutive months have been absent without permission of the directors from meetings of directors held during that period and the directors resolve that his office be vacated.

REMUNERATION OF DIRECTORS

82. The directors shall be entitled to such remuneration as the company may by ordinary resolution determine and, unless the resolution provides otherwise, the remuneration shall be deemed to accrue from day to day.

DIRECTORS' EXPENSES

83. The directors may be paid all travelling, hotel, and other expenses properly incurred by them in connection with their attendance at meetings of directors or committees of directors or general meetings or separate meetings of the holders of any class of shares or of debentures of the company or otherwise in connection with the discharge of their duties.

DIRECTORS' APPOINTMENTS AND INTERESTS

84. Subject to the provisions of the Act, the directors may appoint one or more of their number to the office of managing director or to any other executive office under the company and may enter into an agreement or arrangement with any director for his employment by the company or for the provision by him of any services outside the scope of the ordinary duties of a director. Any such appointment, agreement or arrangement may be made upon such terms as the directors determine and they may remunerate any such director for his services as they think fit. Any appointment of a director to an executive office shall terminate if he ceases to be a director but without prejudice to any claim to damages for breach of the contract of service between the director and the company. A managing director and a director holding any other executive office shall not be subject to retirement by rotation.

85. Subject to the provisions of the Act, and provided that he has disclosed to the directors the nature and extent of any material interest of his, a director notwithstanding his office—
- (a) may be a party to, or otherwise interested in, any transaction or arrangement with the company or in which the company is otherwise interested;
- (b) may be a director or other officer of, or employed by, or a party to any transaction or arrangement with, or otherwise interested in, any body corporate promoted by the company or in which the company is otherwise interested; and
- (c) shall not, by reason of his office, be accountable to the company for any benefit

which he derives from any such office or employment or from any such transaction or arrangement or from any interest in any such body corporate and no such transaction or arrangement shall be liable to be avoided on the ground of any such interest or benefit.

86. For the purposes of regulation 85—
(a) a general notice given to the directors that a director is to be regarded as having an interest of the nature and extent specified in the notice in any transaction or arrangement in which a specified person or class of persons is interested shall be deemed to be a disclosure that the director has an interest in any such transaction of the nature and extent so specified; and
(b) an interest of which a director has no knowledge and of which it is unreasonable to expect him to have knowledge shall not be treated as an interest of his.

DIRECTORS' GRATUITIES AND PENSIONS

87. The directors may provide benefits, whether by the payment of gratuities or pensions or by insurance or otherwise, for any director who has held but no longer holds any executive office or employment with the company or with any body corporate which is or has been a subsidiary of the company or a predecessor in business of the company or of any such subsidiary, and for any member of his family (including a spouse and a former spouse) or any person who is or was dependent on him, and may (as well before as after he ceases to hold such office or employment) contribute to any fund and pay premiums for the purchase or provision of any such benefit.

PROCEEDINGS OF DIRECTORS

88. Subject to the provisions of the articles, the directors may regulate their proceedings as they think fit. A director may, and the secretary at the request of a director shall, call a meeting of the directors. It shall not be necessary to give notice of a meeting to a director who is absent from the United Kingdom. Questions arising at a meeting shall be decided by a majority of votes. In the case of an equality of votes, the chairman shall have a second or casting vote. A director who is also an alternate director shall be entitled in the absence of his appointor to a separate vote on behalf of his appointor in addition to his own vote.

89. The quorum for the transaction of the business of the directors may be fixed by the directors and unless so fixed at any other number shall be two. A person who holds office only as an alternate director shall, if his appointor is not present, be counted in the quorum.

90. The continuing directors or a sole continuing director may act notwithstanding any vacancies in their number, but, if the number of directors is less than the number fixed as the quorum, the continuing directors or director may act only for the purpose of filling vacancies or of calling a general meeting.

91. The directors may appoint one of their number to be the chairman of the board of directors and may at any time remove him from that office. Unless he is unwilling to do so, the director so appointed shall preside at every meeting of directors at which he is present. But if there is no director holding that office, or if the director holding it is unwilling to preside or is not present within five minutes after the time appointed for the meeting, the directors present may appoint one of their number to be chairman of the meeting.

92. All acts done by a meeting of directors, or of a committee of directors, or by a person acting as a director shall, notwithstanding that it be afterwards discovered that there was a defect in the appointment of any director or that any of them were disqualified from holding office, or had vacated office, or were not entitled to vote, be as valid as if every such person had been duly appointed and was qualified and had continued to be a director and had been entitled to vote.

93. A resolution in writing signed by all the directors entitled to receive notice of a meeting of directors or of a committee of directors shall be as valid and effectual as if it had been passed at a meeting of directors or (as the case may be) a committee of directors duly convened and held and may consist of several documents in the like form each signed by one or more directors; but a resolution signed by an alternate director need not also be signed by his appointor and, if it is signed by a director who has appointed an alternate director, it need not be signed by the alternate director in that capacity.

94. Save as otherwise provided by the articles, a director shall not vote at a meeting of directors or of a committee of directors on any resolution concerning a matter in which he has, directly or indirectly, an interest or duty which is material and which conflicts or may conflict with the interests of the company unless his interest or duty arises only because the case falls within one or more of the following paragraphs—

(a) the resolution relates to the giving to him of a guarantee, security, or indemnity in respect of money lent to, or an obligation incurred by him for the benefit of, the company or any of its subsidiaries;

(b) the resolution relates to the giving to a third party of a guarantee, security, or indemnity in respect of an obligation of the company or any of its subsidiaries for which the director has assumed responsibility in whole or part and whether alone or jointly with others under a guarantee or indemnity or by the giving of security;

(c) his interest arises by virtue of his subscribing or agreeing to subscribe for any shares, debentures or other securities of the company or any of its subsidiaries, or by virtue of his being, or intending to become, a participant in the underwriting or sub-underwriting of an offer of any such shares, debentures, or other securities by the company or any of its subsidiaries for subscription, purchase or exchange;

(d) the resolution relates in any way to a retirement benefits scheme which has been approved, or is conditional upon approval, by the Board of Inland Revenue for taxation purposes.

For the purposes of this regulation, an interest of a person who is, for any purpose of the Act (excluding any statutory modification thereof not in force when this regulation becomes binding on the company), connected with a director shall be treated as an interest of the director and, in relation to an alternate director, an interest of his appointor shall be treated as an interest of the alternate director without prejudice to any interest which the alternate director has otherwise.

95. A director shall not be counted in the quorum present at a meeting in relation to a resolution on which he is not entitled to vote.

96. The company may by ordinary resolution suspend or relax to any extent, either generally or in respect of any particular matter, any provision of the articles prohibiting a director from voting at a meeting of directors or of a committee of directors.

97. Where proposals are under consideration concerning the appointment of two or more directors to offices or employments with the company or any body corporate in which the company is interested the proposals may be divided and considered in relation to each director separately and (provided he is not for another reason precluded from voting) each of the directors concerned shall be entitled to vote and be counted in the quorum in respect of each resolution except that concerning his own appointment.

98. If a question arises at a meeting of directors or of a committee of directors as to the right of a director to vote, the question may, before the conclusion of the meeting, be referred to the chairman of the meeting and his ruling in relation to any director other than himself shall be final and conclusive.

SECRETARY

99. Subject to the provisions of the Act, the secretary shall be appointed by the directors for such term, at such remuneration and upon such conditions as they may think fit; and any secretary so appointed may be removed by them.

MINUTES

100. The directors shall cause minutes to be made in books kept for the purpose—

(a) of all appointments of officers made by the directors; and

(b) of all proceedings at meetings of the company, of the holders of any class of shares in the company, and of the directors, and of committees of directors, including the names of the directors present at each such meeting.

THE SEAL

101. The seal shall only be used by the authority of the directors or of a committee of directors authorised by the directors. The directors may determine who shall sign any

instrument to which the seal is affixed and unless otherwise so determined it shall be signed by a director and by the secretary or by a second director.

DIVIDENDS

102. Subject to the provisions of the Act, the company may by ordinary resolution declare dividends in accordance with the respective rights of the members, but no dividend shall exceed the amount recommended by the directors.

103. Subject to the provisions of the Act, the directors may pay interim dividends if it appears to them that they are justified by the profits of the company available for distribution. If the share capital is divided into different classes, the directors may pay interim dividends on shares which confer deferred or non-preferred rights with regard to dividend as well as on shares which confer preferential rights with regard to dividend, but no interim dividend shall be paid on shares carrying deferred or non-preferred rights if, at the time of payment, any preferential dividend is in arrear. The directors may also pay at intervals settled by them any dividend payable at a fixed rate if it appears to them that the profits available for distribution justify the payment. Provided the directors act in good faith they shall not incur any liability to the holders of shares conferring preferred rights for any loss they may suffer by the lawful payment of an interim dividend on any shares having deferred or non-preferred rights.

104. Except as otherwise provided by the rights attached to shares, all dividends shall be declared and paid according to the amounts paid up on the shares on which the dividend is paid. All dividends shall be apportioned and paid proportionately to the amounts paid up on the shares during any portion or portions of the period in respect of which the dividend is paid; but, if any share is issued on terms providing that it shall rank for dividend as from a particular date, that share shall rank for dividend accordingly.

105. A general meeting declaring a dividend may, upon the recommendation of the directors, direct that it shall be satisfied wholly or partly by the distribution of assets and, where any difficulty arises in regard to the distribution, the directors may settle the same and in particular may issue fractional certificates and fix the value for distribution of any assets and may determine that cash shall be paid to any member upon the footing of the value so fixed in order to adjust the rights of members and may vest any assets in trustees.

106. Any dividend or other moneys payable in respect of a share may be paid by cheque sent by post to the registered address of the person entitled or, if two or more persons are the holders of the share or are jointly entitled to it by reason of the death or bankruptcy of the holder, to the registered address of that one of those persons who is first named in the register of members or to such person and to such address as the person or persons entitled may in writing direct. Every cheque shall be made payable to the order of the person or persons entitled or to such other person as the person or persons entitled may in writing direct and payment of the cheque shall be a good discharge to the company. Any joint holder or other person jointly entitled to a share as aforesaid may give receipts for any dividend or other moneys payable in respect of the share.

107. No dividend or other moneys payable in respect of a share shall bear interest against the company unless otherwise provided by the rights attached to the share.

108. Any dividend which has remained unclaimed for twelve years from the date when it became due for payment shall, if the directors so resolve, be forfeited and cease to remain owing by the company.

ACCOUNTS

109. No member shall (as such) have any right of inspecting any accounting records or other book or document of the company except as conferred by statute or authorised by the directors or by ordinary resolution of the company.

CAPITALISATION OF PROFITS

110. The directors may with the authority of an ordinary resolution of the company—

(a) subject as hereinafter provided, resolve to capitalise any undivided profits of the company not required for paying any preferential dividend (whether or not they

APPENDICES

are available for distribution) or any sum standing to the credit of the company's share premium account or capital redemption reserve;

(b) appropriate the sum resolved to be capitalised to the members who would have been entitled to it if it were distributed by way of dividend and in the same proportions and apply such sum on their behalf either in or towards paying up the amounts, if any, for the time being unpaid on any shares held by them respectively, or in paying up in full unissued shares or debentures of the company of a nominal amount equal to that sum, and allot the shares or debentures credited as fully paid to those members, or as they may direct, in those proportions, or partly in one way and partly in the other: but the share premium account, the capital redemption reserve, and any profits which are not available for distribution may, for the purposes of this regulation, only be applied in paying up unissued shares to be allotted to members credited as fully paid;

(c) make such provision by the issue of fractional certificates or by payment in cash or otherwise as they determine in the case of shares or debentures becoming distributable under this regulation in fractions; and

(d) authorise any person to enter on behalf of all the members concerned into an agreement with the company providing for the allotment to them respectively, credited as fully paid, of any shares or debentures to which they are entitled upon such capitalisation, any agreement made under such authority being binding on all such members.

NOTICES

[111. Any notice to be given to or by any person pursuant to the articles (other than a notice calling a meeting of the directors) shall be in writing or shall be given using electronic communications to an address for the time being notified for that purpose to the person giving the notice.

In this regulation, "address", in relation to electronic communications, includes any number or address used for the purposes of such communications.]

NOTES

Substituted by the Companies Act 1985 (Electronic Communications) Order 2000, SI 2000/3373, art 32(1), Sch 1, para 6, as from 22 December 2000. The original reg 111 read as follows—

"111. Any notice to be given to or by any person pursuant to the articles shall be in writing except that a notice calling a meeting of the directors need not be in writing.".

112. The company may give any notice to a member either personally or by sending it by post in a prepaid envelope addressed to the member at his registered address or by leaving it at that address [or by giving it using electronic communications to an address for the time being notified to the company by the member]. In the case of joint holders of a share, all notices shall be given to the joint holder whose name stands first in the register of members in respect of the joint holding and notice so given shall be sufficient notice to all the joint holders. A member whose registered address is not within the United Kingdom and who gives to the company an address within the United Kingdom at which notices may be given to him[, or an address to which notices may be sent using electronic communications,] shall be entitled to have notices given to him at that address, but otherwise no such member shall be entitled to receive any notice from the company.

[In this regulation and the next, "address", in relation to electronic communications, includes any number or address used for the purposes of such communications.]

NOTES

Words in square brackets inserted by the Companies Act 1985 (Electronic Communications) Order 2000, SI 2000/3373, art 32(1), Sch 1, para 7, as from 22 December 2000.

113. A member present, either in person or by proxy, at any meeting of the company or of the holders of any class of shares in the company shall be deemed to have received notice of the meeting and, where requisite, of the purposes for which it was called.

114. Every person who becomes entitled to a share shall be bound by any notice in respect of that share which, before his name is entered in the register of members, has been duly given to a person from whom he derives his title.

115. Proof that an envelope containing a notice was properly addressed, prepaid and posted shall be conclusive evidence that the notice was given. [Proof that a notice contained in an electronic communication was sent in accordance with guidance issued by the Institute of Chartered Secretaries and Administrators shall be conclusive evidence that the notice was given.] A notice shall, *unless the contrary is proved,* be deemed to be given at the expiration of 48 hours after the envelope containing it was posted [or, in the case of a notice contained in an electronic communication, at the expiration of 48 hours after the time it was sent].

NOTES

Words in square brackets inserted by the Companies Act 1985 (Electronic Communications) Order 2000, SI 2000/3373, art 32(1), Sch 1, para 8, as from 22 December 2000; words in italics revoked by the Companies (Tables A to F) (Amendment) Regulations 1985, SI 1985/1052, reg 2, as from 1 August 1985.

116. A notice may be given by the company to the persons entitled to a share in consequence of the death or bankruptcy of a member by sending or delivering it, in any manner authorised by the articles for the giving of notice to a member, addressed to them by name, or by the title of representatives of the deceased, or trustee of the bankrupt or by any like description at the address, if any, within the United Kingdom supplied for that purpose by the persons claiming to be so entitled. Until such an address has been supplied, a notice may be given in any manner in which it might have been given if the death or bankruptcy had not occurred.

WINDING UP

117. If the company is wound up, the liquidator may, with the sanction of an extraordinary resolution of the company and any other sanction required by the Act, divide among the members in specie the whole or any part of the assets of the company and may, for that purpose, value any assets and determine how the division shall be carried out as between the members or different classes of members. The liquidator may, with the like sanction, vest the whole or any part of the assets in trustees upon such trusts for the benefit of the members as he with the like sanction determines, but no member shall be compelled to accept any assets upon which there is a liability.

INDEMNITY

118. Subject to the provisions of the Act but without prejudice to any indemnity to which a director may otherwise be entitled, every director or other officer or auditor of the company shall be indemnified out of the assets of the company against any liability incurred by him in defending any proceedings, whether civil or criminal, in which judgment is given in his favour or in which he is acquitted or in connection with any application in which relief is granted to him by the court from liability for negligence, default, breach of duty or breach of trust in relation to the affairs of the company.

[A2]

Appendix 3: Fees Instruments

CONTENTS OF APPENDIX 3

COMPANIES (INSPECTORS' REPORTS) (FEES) REGULATIONS 1981, SI 1981/1686

NOTES

Made: 24 November 1981.

Authority: Originally made under CA 1948, ss 168(2), 455(1) (repealed); now have effect under CA 1985, s 437(3)(b).

Commencement: 22 December 1981.

As of 1 July 2007, these Regulations had not been amended.

1. These Regulations may be cited as the Companies (Inspectors' Reports) (Fees) Regulations 1981 and shall come into operation on 22nd December 1981.

2. The fee prescribed for the furnishing of a copy of a report under section 168(2) of the Companies Act 1948 or for furnishing a copy of a report or part of a report under that section as it applies for the purposes of section 172 of that Act shall be 10 pence for each page copied.

NOTES

CA 1948, ss 168(2), 172 (repealed): see now CA 1985, ss 437(3)(b), 443, respectively.

INSOLVENCY FEES ORDER 1986, SI 1986/2030 (NOTE)

NOTES

This Order was revoked by the Insolvency Proceedings (Fees) Order 2004, SI 2004/593, art 3, Sch 1, as from 1 April 2004, except in relation to any case where a winding-up or bankruptcy order is made under the Insolvency Act 1986 before that date. It was also revoked by the Insolvency Proceedings (Fees) (Amendment) Order 2007, SI 2007/521, art 3(1), Schedule, as from 1 April 2007, in relation to any case where a winding-up or bankruptcy order was made under the Insolvency Act 1986 before 1 April 2004. See now the Insolvency Proceedings (Fees) Order 2004, SI 2004/593, *post*.

COMPANY AUDITORS (RECOGNITION ORDERS) (APPLICATION FEES) REGULATIONS 1990, SI 1990/1206 (NOTE)

NOTES

These Regulations were revoked by the Company Auditors (Recognition Orders) (Application Fees) and the Companies Act 1989 (Recognised Supervisory Bodies) (Periodical Fees) (Revocation) Regulations 2005, SI 2005/2243, reg 2, as from 5 September 2005. These Regulations prescribed the fees payable by bodies applying for recognition under CA 1989, Pt II (eligibility for appointment as company auditor). The majority of the functions of the Secretary of State under CA 1989, Pt II, including those in relation to the making of recognition orders, were transferred to the Professional Oversight Board for Accountancy by the Companies Act 1989 (Delegation) Order 2005, SI 2005/2337 (at **[7444]**). That Board will, accordingly, have the function of determining whether to prescribe any fees to replace the fees prescribed in these Regulations. Note also that on 5 May 2006 the Professional Oversight Board for Accountancy changed its name to the Professional Oversight Board. For more information, see www.frc.org.uk/poba/index.cfm.

MERGER (FEES) REGULATIONS 1990, SI 1990/1660 (NOTE)

NOTES

CA 1989, s 152 (under which these Regulations were made) was repealed by the Enterprise Act 2002, s 278(2), Sch 26, as from 29 December 2004. For transitional provisions in relation to anticipated and completed water mergers, see SI 2004/3233. For new fees made under the Enterprise Act 2002, see the Enterprise Act 2002 (Merger Fees and Determination of Turnover) Order 2003, SI 2003/1370, *post*.

COMPANIES (FEES) REGULATIONS 1991, SI 1991/1206 (NOTE)

NOTES

These Regulations were revoked by the Companies (Fees) Regulations 2004, SI 2004/2621, reg 3, as from 1 February 2005. For fees payable after 1 February 2005, and for transitional provisions, see the 2004 Regulations, *post*.

COMPANIES ACT 1989 (RECOGNISED SUPERVISORY BODIES) (PERIODICAL FEES) REGULATIONS 1993, SI 1993/1881 (NOTE)

NOTES

These Regulations were revoked by the Company Auditors (Recognition Orders) (Application Fees) and the Companies Act 1989 (Recognised Supervisory Bodies) (Periodical Fees) (Revocation) Regulations 2005, SI 2005/2243, reg 2, as from 5 September 2005. These Regulations prescribed the periodical fees payable by recognised supervisory bodies. The majority of the functions of the Secretary of State under CA 1989, Pt II, including those in relation to recognised supervisory bodies, were transferred to the Professional Oversight Board for Accountancy by the Companies Act 1989 (Delegation) Order 2005, SI 2005/2337 (at **[7444]**). That Board will, accordingly, have the function of determining whether to prescribe any fees to replace the fees prescribed in these Regulations. Note also that on 5 May 2006 the Professional Oversight Board for Accountancy changed its name to the Professional Oversight Board. For more information, see www.frc.org.uk/poba/index.cfm.

OPEN-ENDED INVESTMENT COMPANIES (INVESTMENT COMPANIES WITH VARIABLE CAPITAL) (FEES) REGULATIONS 1998, SI 1998/3087 (NOTE)

NOTES

These Regulations have been omitted from this Edition of the *Company Law Handbook* in order to create space for other legislation (ie, the Companies Act 2006 and the associated destination and derivation tables). They were printed in full in the 20th Edition of this work (at p 3299 et seq) and, as of 1 July 2007, they had not been amended since the publication of that Edition. These Regulations are, however, included in the CD version of this work (which may be ordered from the LexisNexis Butterworths Customer Services Department) and can be accessed in the online version of the *Company Law Handbook* which is updated fortnightly (at www.lexisnexis.com/uk/legal).

LIMITED LIABILITY PARTNERSHIPS (FEES) (NO 2) REGULATIONS 2001, SI 2001/969 (NOTE)

NOTES

These Regulations were revoked by the Limited Liability Partnerships (Fees) Regulations 2004, SI 2004/2620, reg 3, as from 1 February 2005. For fees payable after 1 February 2005, and for transitional provisions, see the 2004 Regulations, *post*.

APPENDICES

COMPANIES (COMPETENT AUTHORITY) (FEES) REGULATIONS 2002, SI 2002/502

NOTES

Made: 7 March 2002.
Authority: CA 1985, s 708(1), (2).
Commencement: 2 April 2002.
As of 1 July 2007, these Regulations had not been amended.

1. These Regulations may be cited as the Companies (Competent Authority) (Fees) Regulations 2002 and shall come into force on 2nd April 2002.

2. In these Regulations:
"the 2002 Regulations" means the Companies (Particulars of Usual Residential Address) (Confidentiality Orders) Regulations 2002;
"competent authority" shall have the meaning set out in the 2002 Regulations;
"the LLP Regulations" means the Limited Liability Partnerships (Particulars of Usual Residential Address) (Confidentiality Orders) Regulations 2002; and
"the LLP Fees Regulations" means the Limited Liability Partnerships (Competent Authority) (Fees) Regulations 2002.

3.—(1) For the making by the registrar of companies of each determination or variation of such determination under regulation 13 of the 2002 Regulations in respect of a competent authority as to the manner in which that competent authority and its officers, servants and representatives may inspect and take copies of the confidential record, the fee payable by that competent authority in respect of the determination or variation shall be calculated as follows:

(a) where a point of contact with a competent authority is to be through one or more addresses nominated by such competent authority, the fee shall be £50 in respect of each such new address nominated and included in a determination or variation;

(b) where a point of contact with a competent authority is to be through one or more nominated officers, servants and representatives, the fee shall be £50 in respect of each such new officer, servant or representative of that authority nominated and included in a determination or variation;

save that in either case no such fee shall be payable where a fee has already been paid in accordance with the LLP Fees Regulations in respect of such a determination or variation.

(2) Where a variation of a determination removes a previous point of contact with a given competent authority, no fee shall be incurred by such removal.

(3) In relation to the fee payable by a competent authority on each occasion such competent authority inspects or takes copies of the confidential record in relation to an individual beneficiary of a confidentiality order:

(a) the amount of the fee shall be £4 in respect of each named individual in respect of whom an inspection or copy of the confidential record is requested;

(b) such fee shall entitle the competent authority in question to an inspection or copy of both:

(i) the confidential record as maintained in relation to company directors, company secretaries or permanent representatives under the 2002 Regulations; and

(ii) the confidential record as maintained in relation to members of limited liability partnerships under the LLP Regulations;

in respect of such named individual;

(c) the search fee in respect of a named individual shall be payable even if information or a copy supplied by the registrar in response to a request to inspect or take a copy of the confidential record is taken, in the absence of the relevant information on the confidential record, from the information made publicly available by the registrar.

LIMITED LIABILITY PARTNERSHIPS (COMPETENT AUTHORITY) (FEES) REGULATIONS 2002, SI 2002/503

NOTES

Made: 7 March 2002.
Authority: CA 1985, s 708(1), (2).

Commencement: 2 April 2002.
As of 1 July 2007, these Regulations had not been amended.

1. These Regulations may be cited as the Limited Liability Partnerships (Competent Authority) (Fees) Regulations 2002 and shall come into force on 2nd April 2002.

2. In these Regulations:
"the 2002 Regulations" means the Limited Liability Partnerships (Particulars of Usual Residential Address) (Confidentiality Order) Regulations 2002;
"competent authority" shall have the meaning set out in the 2002 Regulations;
"the Companies (Particulars of Usual Residential Address) Regulations" means the Companies (Particulars of Usual Residential Address) (Confidentiality Orders) Regulations 2002; and
"the Companies Fees Regulations" means the Companies (Competent Authority) (Fees) Regulations 2002.

3.—(1) For the making by the registrar of companies of each determination or variation of such determination under regulation 13 of the 2002 Regulations in respect of a competent authority as to the manner in which that competent authority and its officers, servants and representatives may inspect and take copies of the confidential record, the fee payable by that competent authority in respect of the determination or variation shall be calculated as follows:
- (a) where a point of contact with a competent authority is to be through one or more addresses nominated by such competent authority, the fee shall be £50 in respect of each such new address nominated and included in a determination or variation;
- (b) where a point of contact with a competent authority is to be through one or more nominated officers, servants and representatives, the fee shall be £50 in respect of each such new officer, servant or representative of that authority nominated and included in a determination or variation;

save that in either case no such fee shall be payable where a fee has already been paid in accordance with the Companies Fees Regulations in respect of such determination or variation.

(2) Where a variation of a determination removes a previous point of contact with a given competent authority, no fee shall be incurred by such removal.

(3) In relation to the fee payable by a competent authority on each occasion such competent authority inspects or takes copies of the confidential record in relation to an individual beneficiary of a confidentiality order:
- (a) the amount of the fee shall be £4 in respect of each named individual in respect of whom an inspection or copy of the confidential record is requested;
- (b) such fee shall entitle the competent authority in question to an inspection or copy of both:
  - (i) the confidential record as maintained in relation to members of limited liability partnerships under the 2002 Regulations; and
  - (ii) the confidential record as maintained in relation to company directors, company secretaries or permanent representatives under the Companies (Particulars of Usual Residential Address) Regulations;

in respect of such named individual;
- (c) the search fee in respect of a named individual shall be payable even if information or a copy supplied by the registrar in response to a request to inspect or take a copy of the confidential record is taken, in the absence of the relevant information on the confidential record, from the information made publicly available by the registrar.

ENTERPRISE ACT 2002 (MERGER FEES AND DETERMINATION OF TURNOVER) ORDER 2003, SI 2003/1370

NOTES

Made: 23 May 2003.
Authority: Enterprise Act 2002, ss 28, 121, 124(2).
Commencement: 20 June 2003.
Only Pt 2 of this Order is reproduced here. For Pt 1 (General), and Pt 3 (Determination of Turnover), see this Order at **[7162]**. Pt 2 is reproduced as amended by the EC Merger Control (Consequential Amendments) Regulations 2004, SI 2004/1079, the Enterprise Act 2002 (Merger Fees and Determination of Turnover) (Amendment) Order 2004, SI 2004/3204, and the Enterprise Act 2002 (Merger Fees) (Amendment) Order 2005, SI 2005/3558.

PART 2
MERGER FEES

3 Matters in respect of which fees are payable

A fee of the amount specified in Article 5 shall be payable in respect of—

(a) the giving of a merger notice under section 96 of the Act;

(b) subject to article 4(1) and (2), the decision by the OFT in relation to a possible reference under section 22 or 33 of the Act that it is or may be the case that a relevant merger situation has been created or (as the case may be) that arrangements are in progress or in contemplation which, if carried into effect, will result in the creation of a relevant merger situation;

(c) subject to article 4(1), the decision by the Secretary of State in relation to a possible reference under section 45 of the Act that it is or may be the case that a relevant merger situation has been created or (as the case may be) that arrangements are in progress or in contemplation which, if carried into effect, will result in the creation of a relevant merger situation;

[(d) the making by the OFT of a merger reference to the Commission under section 32 of the Water Industry Act 1991.]

NOTES

Para (d) added by the Enterprise Act 2002 (Merger Fees and Determination of Turnover) (Amendment) Order 2004, SI 2004/3204, art 2(1), (3), as from 29 December 2004.

4 Circumstances in which certain fees are not payable

(1) A fee shall not be payable under article 3(b) or (c)—

(a) where a fee has been paid under article 3(a) in respect of a merger notice given in relation to proposed arrangements and either—

(i) the merger reference or, as the case may be, the OFT's or Secretary of State's decision not to make a merger reference is made in relation to those arrangements; or

(ii) if the fee under article 3(a) became due within the previous six months, the result of carrying those arrangements into effect is the creation or possible creation of a relevant merger situation which is the subject of the merger reference or, as the case may be, the OFT's or the Secretary of State's decision not to make a merger reference;

(b) where the creation or possible creation of the relevant merger situation depends or would depend on the operation of section 26(3) or (4)(b) of the Act.

(2) A fee shall not be payable under article 3(b) in relation to arrangements that are in progress or in contemplation which, if carried into effect, will result in the creation of a relevant merger situation, where the OFT decides that the arrangements concerned are not sufficiently far advanced, or are not sufficiently likely to proceed, to justify the making of a reference to the Commission pursuant to section 33(2)(b) of the Act.

5 Amount of fees

(1) The amount of the fee payable under [article 3(a) to (c)] shall be—

(a) where the value of the turnover in the United Kingdom of the enterprise which has been taken over or (as the case may be) which it is proposed or contemplated should be taken over, does not exceed £20 million, [£15,000];

(b) where the value of such turnover exceeds £20 million but does not exceed £70 million, [£30,000];

(c) where the value of such turnover exceeds £70 million, [£45,000].

(2) For the purposes of [paragraph (1)] the value of the turnover in the United Kingdom of the enterprise which has been taken over or (as the case may be) which it is proposed or contemplated should be taken over, shall be determined by taking the total value of the turnover in the United Kingdom of the enterprises which cease to be distinct enterprises and deducting—

(a) the turnover in the United Kingdom of any enterprise which continues to be carried on under the same ownership and control; or

(b) if no enterprise continues to be carried on under the same ownership and control, the turnover in the United Kingdom which, of all the turnovers concerned, is the turnover of the highest value.

(3) For the purposes of [paragraph (2)] the turnover in the United Kingdom of an enterprise shall be determined in accordance with article 11(2) to (4).

[(4) The amount of the fee payable under article 3(d) shall be—

(a) where the value of the turnover in England and Wales of the water enterprise which has been taken over or (as the case may be) which it is proposed should be taken over, does not exceed £20 million, [£15,000];

(b) where the value of such turnover exceeds £20 million but does not exceed £70 million, [£30,000];

(c) where the value of such turnover exceeds £70 million, [£45,000].

(5) For the purposes of paragraph (4) the value of the turnover in England and Wales of the water enterprise which has been taken over or (as the case may be) which it is proposed should be taken over, shall be determined by taking the total value of the turnover of the water enterprises ceasing to be distinct enterprises and deducting—

(a) the turnover of any water enterprise continuing to be carried on under the same ownership and control; or

(b) if there is no water enterprise continuing to be carried on under the same ownership and control, the turnover which, of all the turnovers concerned, is the turnover of the highest value.

(6) For the purposes of paragraph (5) the turnover in England and Wales of a water enterprise shall be determined in accordance with the Regulations made pursuant to section 33(4) of the Water Industry Act 1991.]

NOTES

Para (1): words in first pair of square brackets substituted by the Enterprise Act 2002 (Merger Fees and Determination of Turnover) (Amendment) Order 2004, SI 2004/3204, art 2(1), (4)(a), as from 29 December 2004; sums in square brackets in sub-paras (a)–(c) substituted by the Enterprise Act 2002 (Merger Fees) (Amendment) Order 2005, SI 2005/3558, art 2(1)–(4), as from 6 April 2006 (subject to transitional provisions as noted below).

Paras (2), (3): words in square brackets substituted by SI 2004/3204, art 2(1), (4)(b), (c), as from 29 December 2004.

Para (4): added, together with para (5), (6), by SI 2004/3204, art 2(1), (4)(d), as from 29 December 2004; sums in square brackets in sub-paras (a)–(c) substituted by SI 2005/3558, art 2(1), (5)–(7), as from 6 April 2006 (subject to transitional provisions as noted below).

Paras (5), (6): added as noted above.

Transitional provisions: the substitution of the sums in paras (1)(a)–(c) and (4)(a)–(c) above (and the revocation of art 6(5) below) do not apply in relation to: (i) a decision by the OFT or the Secretary of State in relation to a possible reference under ss 22 or 45(2) or (3) of the Enterprise Act 2002 that it is or may be the case that a relevant merger situation has been created; or (ii) the making by the OFT of a merger reference to the Commission under section 32(b) of the Water Industry Act 1991, where the decision or reference relates to two or more enterprises ceasing to be distinct enterprises before 6 April 2006 (see SI 2005/3558, art 1(2)). Note that the sums in both paras (1)(a)–(c) and (4)(a)–(c) were previously as follows: (a) £5,000; (b) £10,000; (c) £15,000.

6 Person by whom fees are payable

(1) In a case falling within article 3(a), the fee shall be payable by the person who gives the merger notice.

(2) Subject to article 7, in a case falling within article 3(b)[, (c) or (d)], the fee shall be payable by the acquirer.

(3) For the purposes of this article and article 7 "the acquirer" means the person, or group of persons, who has or have acquired or will, if those arrangements are carried into effect, acquire either—

(a) a controlling interest in one of the enterprises which was or is involved in the creation or possible creation of a relevant merger situation [or the merger or prospective merger of two or more water enterprises] which is the subject of the merger reference or, as the case may be, the OFT's or the Secretary of State's decision not to make such a merger reference, and in which he or they did not previously have such an interest; or

(b) in the case of such an enterprise carried on by a body corporate in which he or they did not previously have a controlling interest, a controlling interest in that body corporate.

(4) In a case where paragraph (3) applies to more than one person, whether by virtue of them being treated as associated persons, as defined in section 127 of the Act, or otherwise, the persons to whom it applies shall be jointly and severally liable for the fee in that case.

(5) …

NOTES

Para (2): words in square brackets substituted by the Enterprise Act 2002 (Merger Fees and Determination of Turnover) (Amendment) Order 2004, SI 2004/3204, art 2(1), (5)(a), as from 29 December 2004.

Para (3): words in square brackets inserted by SI 2004/3204, art 2(1), (5)(b), as from 29 December 2004.

Para (5): revoked by the Enterprise Act 2002 (Merger Fees) (Amendment) Order 2005, SI 2005/3558, art 2, as from 6 April 2006 (for transitional provisions see the note to art 5 above). This paragraph (as amended by SI 2004/3204) previously read as follows—

"(5) Where a fee is payable under article 3(b)[, (c) or (d)] but the acquirer is not—

(a) a United Kingdom national; or

(b) a body corporate incorporated under the law of the United Kingdom or of a part of the United Kingdom; or

(c) a person carrying on business in the United Kingdom, either alone or in partnership with one or more persons,

he shall not be liable to pay the fee unless the creation or possible creation of a relevant merger situation [or the merger or prospective merger of two or more water enterprises] which is the subject of the merger reference or, as the case may be, the OFT's or the Secretary of State's decision not to make such a merger reference, results wholly or partially from anything done by him within the United Kingdom.".

7 Exemption for acquisitions by small and medium sized enterprises

(1) In a case falling within article 3(a) no fee shall be payable by the person who gives the merger notice where—

(a) that person is the acquirer;

(b) the notified arrangements relate to the enterprise that will be taken over by the acquirer; and

(c) the acquirer qualifies as small or medium sized.

(2) In a case falling within article 3(b)[,(c) or (d)] no fee shall be payable by the acquirer where the acquirer qualifies as small or medium sized.

(3) For the purpose of paragraphs (1) and (2) an enterprise qualifies as small or medium sized if, immediately before the time at which the fee would otherwise become payable—

(a) it satisfies the requirements to be small or medium sized set out in subsections (3) to (6) of section 247 of the Companies Act 1985 ("the 1985 Act") in its most recent financial year, whether or not the enterprise is a company; and

(b) where it is a member of a group as defined in section 262 of the 1985 Act (whether or not the enterprise is a company), that group qualifies as small or medium sized within the meaning of subsection (3) to (5) of section 249 of the 1985 Act in its most recent financial year.

NOTES

Para (2): words in square brackets substituted by the Enterprise Act 2002 (Merger Fees and Determination of Turnover) (Amendment) Order 2004, SI 2004/3204, art 2(1), (6), as from 29 December 2004.

8 Person to whom fees are payable

In a case falling within article 3 the fee shall be payable to the OFT.

9 Time when fees are payable

(1) In a case falling within article 3(a), the fee shall be payable at the time when the merger notice is given.

(2) In a case falling within article 3(b) [or (d)], the fee shall be payable when the OFT publishes the merger reference or, as the case may be, publishes its decision not to make such a merger reference.

(3) In a case falling with article 3(c), the fee shall be payable when the Secretary of State publishes the merger reference or, as the case may be, publishes her decision not to make such a merger reference.

NOTES

Para (2): words in square brackets inserted by the Enterprise Act 2002 (Merger Fees and Determination of Turnover) (Amendment) Order 2004, SI 2004/3204, art 2(1), (7), as from 29 December 2004.

10 Repayment of fees

In a case falling within article 3(a)—

(a) the OFT shall repay the whole of the fee where the notified arrangements would not, if they were carried into effect, result in the creation of a relevant merger situation;

(b) the OFT shall repay the whole of the fee where it rejects the merger notice under section 99(5)(d) of the Act (rejection of merger notice where the notified arrangements are or would result in a concentration with a Community dimension);

(c) the OFT may repay the whole of the fee in any case to which section 22(3)(e) or section 33(3)(e) of the Act applies (request to European Commission pursuant to article [22(1) of the EC Merger Regulation]).

NOTES

Words in square brackets substituted by the EC Merger Control (Consequential Amendments) Regulations 2004, SI 2004/1079, reg 2, Schedule, para 5, as from 1 May 2004.

INSOLVENCY PRACTITIONERS AND INSOLVENCY SERVICES ACCOUNT (FEES) ORDER 2003, SI 2003/3363

NOTES

Made: 30 December 2003.
Authority: Insolvency Act 1986, s 415A.
Commencement: 30 January 2004 (art 2(3)); 1 April 2004 (otherwise).
Amended by: the Insolvency Practitioners and Insolvency Services Account (Fees) (Amendment) Order 2004, SI 2004/476 the Insolvency Practitioners and Insolvency Services Account (Fees) (Amendment) Order 2005, SI 2005/523; the Insolvency Practitioners and Insolvency Services Account (Fees) (Amendment) (No 2) Order 2005, SI 2005/3524; the Insolvency Practitioners and Insolvency Services Account (Fees) (Amendment) Order 2007, SI 2007/133.

1 Citation, Commencement, Interpretation and Extent

(1) This Order may be cited as the Insolvency Practitioners and Insolvency Services Account (Fees) Order 2003 and shall come into force on 1st April 2004 ("the principal commencement date") except for Article 2(3) which shall come into force on 30th January 2004.

(2) In this Order any reference to a numbered section is to the section so numbered in the Insolvency Act 1986.

(3) All the provisions of this Order except Article 5 and the Schedule to this Order extend to England and Wales and Scotland and Article 5 and the Schedule to this Order extend only to England and Wales.

2 Fees payable in connection with the recognition of professional bodies pursuant to section 391

(1) Every application by a body for recognition pursuant to section 391 shall be accompanied by a fee of £4,500.

[(2) On or before 1st April each year, there shall be paid to the Secretary of State by each body recognised pursuant to section 391 in respect of the maintenance of that body's recognition pursuant to section 391, a fee calculated as set out in paragraphs (2A) and (2B) below.

(2A) In respect of the fee due on or before 1st April 2006, the fee shall be calculated by multiplying £150 by the number of persons who as at the preceding 1st January in that year were authorised to act as insolvency practitioners by virtue of membership of that body.

(2B) In respect of the fee due on or before 1st April in each subsequent year, the fee shall be calculated by multiplying £200 by the number of persons who as at the preceding 1st January in that year were authorised to act as insolvency practitioners by virtue of membership of that body.]

(3) Each body recognised pursuant to section 391 shall on or before 31st January in each year submit to the Secretary of State a list of its members who as at 1st January in that year were authorised to act as insolvency practitioners by virtue of membership of that body.

NOTES

Paras (2)–(2B): substituted, for original para (2), by the Insolvency Practitioners and Insolvency Services Account (Fees) (Amendment) (No 2) Order 2005, SI 2005/3524, art 3(1), as from 30 January 2006, subject to transitional provisions in art 4 of that Order as follows—

"(1) This article applies to a body recognised pursuant to section 391 of the Insolvency Act 1986 that—

(a) pursuant to article 2(2) of the principal Order (as it stood before the coming into force of this Order) makes a payment by reference to the number of persons who as at 1st January 2006 were authorised to act as insolvency practitioners by virtue of membership of that body; and

(b) makes that payment in the period commencing on 1st January 2006 and ending with the day before the day on which this article comes into force.

(2) The insertion of article 2(2A) into the principal Order by article 3 of this Order shall not require a body to which this article applies to make any further payment by reference to the number of persons who as at 1st January 2006 were authorised to act as insolvency practitioners by virtue of membership of that body.".

3 Fees payable in connection with authorisations by the Secretary of State under section 393

(1) [Subject to paragraph (1A), every person] who on the principal commencement date is the holder of an authorisation to act as an insolvency practitioner granted by the Secretary of State pursuant to section 393 shall within 7 days of that date pay to the Secretary of State a fee in respect of the maintenance of that authorisation calculated in accordance with paragraph (2).

[(1A) Paragraph (1) does not apply to—

(a) any authorisation granted on the principal commencement date; or

(b) any authorisation granted on the 1st April in any year prior to the year 2004.]

(2) The fee payable by virtue of paragraph (1) shall be calculated by multiplying [£2,100] by the number of days in the period starting with the principal commencement date and ending with the date immediately before the next anniversary of the granting of the authorisation or the date of expiry of the authorisation (whichever occurs first) and dividing the result by 365.

(3) Every application made to the Secretary of State pursuant to section 392 for authorisation to act as an insolvency practitioner shall be accompanied by a fee of [£2,500].

(4) Subject to paragraph (5), every person who holds an authorisation granted by the Secretary of State pursuant to section 393 to act as an insolvency practitioner shall, on each anniversary of the granting of that authorisation when it is in force, pay to the Secretary of State in connection with the maintenance of that authorisation a fee of [£2,500].

(5) Where on the relevant anniversary the authorisation mentioned in paragraph (4) has less than a year to run, the fee shall be calculated by multiplying [£2,500] by the number of days that the authorisation has to run (starting with the day of the anniversary) and dividing the result by 365.

NOTES

Para (1): words in square brackets substituted by the Insolvency Practitioners and Insolvency Services Account (Fees) (Amendment) Order 2004, SI 2004/476, art 2(1), (2), as from 31 March 2004.

Para (1A): inserted by SI 2004/476, art 2(1), (3), as from 31 March 2004.

Para (2): sum in square brackets substituted by the Insolvency Practitioners and Insolvency Services Account (Fees) (Amendment) (No 2) Order 2005, SI 2005/3524, art 3(2), as from 1 April 2006.

Paras (3)–(5): sums in square brackets substituted by the Insolvency Practitioners and Insolvency Services Account (Fees) (Amendment) Order 2007, SI 2007/133, arts 2, 3, as from 1 April 2007.

4 Transitional cases—early applications for authorisation

(1) This article applies to an application made to the Secretary of State pursuant to section 392 for the granting of an authorisation to act as an insolvency practitioner—

(a) where the applicant was as at the date of its making the holder of an authorisation granted pursuant to section 393;

(b) where the application was made—

(i) after the date of the making of this Order but before the principal commencement date; and

(ii) more than three months before the expiry of the authorisation mentioned in sub-paragraph (a); and

(c) in respect of which as at the principal commencement date no decision as to whether to grant or refuse it has been taken.

(2) In respect of an application to which this article applies, there shall be paid to the Secretary of State by the applicant within 7 days of the principal commencement date a fee of £1,500.

5 Fees payable in connection with the operation of the Insolvency Services Account

There shall be payable in connection with the operation of the Insolvency Services Account fees as provided for in the Schedule to this Order.

6 Value Added Tax

Where Value Added Tax is chargeable in respect of the provision of a service for which a fee is prescribed by any provision of this Order, there shall be payable in addition to that fee the amount of the Value Added Tax.

SCHEDULE
FEES PAYABLE IN CONNECTION WITH THE OPERATION OF THE INSOLVENCY SERVICES ACCOUNT

Article 5

1 Interpretation for the purposes of the Schedule

(1) In this Schedule a reference to a numbered regulation is to the regulation so numbered in the Insolvency Regulations 1994

(2) In this Schedule "payment date" means any of the following dates in any year—

(a) 1st January;

(b) 1st April;

(c) 1st July; and

(d) 1st October.

[(2A) In this Schedule "working day" means any day other than a Saturday, a Sunday, Good Friday, Christmas Day or a Bank Holiday in England and Wales in accordance with the Banking and Financial Dealings Act 1971.]

(3) Subject to paragraphs (4) and (5), for the purposes of this Schedule an account is "maintained with the Secretary of State in respect of monies which may from time to time be paid into the Insolvency Services Account" where—

(a) in a winding up by the court or a bankruptcy the Secretary of State creates a record in relation to the winding up or, as the case may be, the bankruptcy for the purpose of recording payments into and out of the Insolvency Services Account relating to the winding up or, as the case may be, the bankruptcy; and

(b) in a voluntary winding up on the request of the liquidator the Secretary of State creates a record in relation to the winding up for the purposes of recording payments into and out of the Insolvency Services Account relating to the winding up.

[(4) An account ceases to be maintained with the Secretary of State in the case of a winding up by the court or a bankruptcy where—

(a) the liquidator or the trustee has filed a receipts and payments account with the Secretary of State pursuant to regulation 14 or regulation 28;

(b) the account contains, or is accompanied by, a statement that it is a final receipts and payments account; and

(c) four working days have elapsed since the requirements of paragraphs (a) and (b) have been met,

but an account is revived in the circumstances mentioned in paragraph (5).

(4A) An account ceases to be maintained with the Secretary of State in the case of a voluntary winding up where—

(a) no monies to which that account relates are held in the Insolvency Services Account (other than any unclaimed dividends or any amount that it is impracticable to distribute to creditors or is required for the payment of fees that are or will become payable while the account is maintained); and

(b) notice in writing has been given to the Secretary of State that the account is no longer required and four working days have elapsed since the receipt of that notice by the Secretary of State,

but an account is revived in the circumstances mentioned in paragraph (5).]

(5) The circumstances referred to in [paragraphs (4) and (4A)] are—

(a) the receipt by the Secretary of State of notice in writing given by the trustee or liquidator for the revival of the account; or

(b) the payment into the Insolvency Services Account of any sums to the credit of the company or, as the case may be, the estate of the bankrupt,

and on the occurrence of either of the circumstances mentioned above, an account is "maintained with the Secretary of State in respect of monies which may from time to time be paid into the Insolvency Services Account".

(6) References to a bankruptcy include a bankruptcy under the Bankruptcy Act 1914 and references to a winding up include a winding up under the provisions of the Companies Act 1985.

2 Fees payable in connection with the operation of the Insolvency Services Account

Fees shall be payable in relation to the operation of the Insolvency Services Account (including payments into and out of that account) in the circumstances set out in the table below—

Fee	*Description of fee and circumstances in which it is payable*	*Amount*
1.	**Banking fee; winding up by the court and bankruptcy** Where in any bankruptcy or winding up by the court an account is maintained with the Secretary of State in respect of monies which may from time to time be paid into the Insolvency Services Account, there shall be payable out of the estate of the bankrupt or, as the case may be, the assets of the company on each payment date where the liquidator or the trustee is not the official receiver, a fee of—	£15
2.	**Banking fee; voluntary winding up** Where in a voluntary winding up an account is maintained with the Secretary of State in respect of monies which may from time to time be paid into the Insolvency Services Account there shall be payable out of the assets of the company on each payment date a fee of—	£20
3.	**Cheque etc issue fee** Where a cheque, money order or payable order in respect of monies in the Insolvency Services Account is issued or reissued on the application of— (a) a liquidator pursuant to regulations 7 or 8; (b) a trustee pursuant to regulations 22 or 23; or (c) any person claiming any monies in that account pursuant to regulation 32, there shall be payable out of the assets of the company, the estate of the bankrupt or, as the case may be, by the claimant— —(i) where the application is made before principal commencement date, a fee in respect of that cheque, money order or payable order of—	£0.65
	—(ii) where the application is made on or after the principal commencement date, a fee in respect of that cheque, money order or payable order of—	£0.80

Fee	Description of fee and circumstances in which it is payable	Amount
[4.	**Electronic funds systems (CHAPs and BACs etc) fees** On the making or remaking of a transfer in respect of funds held in the Insolvency Services Account on an application made by— (a) a liquidator pursuant to regulations 7 or 8; (b) a trustee pursuant to regulations 22 or 23; or (c) any person claiming pursuant to regulation 32, any monies held in the Insolvency Services Account, there shall be payable out of the assets of the company, the estate of the bankrupt or, as the case may be, by the claimant, a fee in respect of that transfer as follows:	
	(i) where it is made through the Clearing House Automated Payments System (CHAPs), a fee of—	£10
	(ii) where it is made through the Bankers' Clearing System (BACs) or any electronic funds transfer system other than CHAPs, a fee of—	£0.15]

NOTES

Para 1: sub-para (2A) inserted, sub-paras (4), (4A) substituted for original sub-para (4), and words in square brackets in sub-para (5) substituted, by the Insolvency Practitioners and Insolvency Services Account (Fees) (Amendment) Order 2005, SI 2005/523, art 2, as from 1 April 2005.

Para 2: fee number 4 substituted by the Insolvency Practitioners and Insolvency Services Account (Fees) (Amendment) Order 2007, SI 2007/133, arts 2, 4, as from 1 April 2007.

INSOLVENCY PROCEEDINGS (FEES) ORDER 2004, SI 2004/593

NOTES

Made: 4 March 2004.

Authority: Insolvency Act 1986, ss 414, 415; Bankruptcy Act 1914, s 133; CA 1985, s 663(4).

Commencement: 1 April 2004.

Amended by: the Insolvency Proceedings (Fees) (Amendment) Order 2005, SI 2005/544; the Insolvency Proceedings (Fees) (Amendment) Order 2006, SI 2006/561; the Insolvency Proceedings (Fees) (Amendment) Order 2007, SI 2007/521.

Limited liability partnerships: this Order applies, with modifications, to limited liability partnerships; see the Limited Liability Partnerships Regulations 2001, SI 2001/1090, reg 10, Sch 6, Pt II (at **[6999]**), and the Interpretation Act 1978, ss 17(2)(a), 23(1), (2).

1 Citation and commencement

This Order may be cited as the Insolvency Proceedings (Fees) Order 2004 and shall come into force on 1st April 2004.

2 Interpretation

(1) In this Order—

"the Act" means the Insolvency Act 1986 (any reference to a numbered section being to the section so numbered in that Act);

"the commencement date" is the date referred to in Article 1;

"individual voluntary arrangement" means a voluntary arrangement pursuant to Part VIII of the Act; and

"the Rules" means the Insolvency Rules 1986 (any reference to a numbered Rule being to the Rule so numbered in the Rules).

(2) A reference to a fee by a means of letters and a number is a reference to the fee so designated in the table in Schedule 2.

3 Revocations and Transitional Provisions

The instruments listed in the Schedule 1 to this Order are revoked to the extent set out in that Schedule.

4 Fees payable in connection with bankruptcies, individual voluntary arrangements and winding up

(1) Subject to paragraphs (2) and (3) and article 8, the fees payable to the Secretary of State in respect of proceedings under Parts I to XI of the Act and the performance by the official receiver or Secretary of State of functions under those Parts shall be determined in accordance with the provisions of Schedule 2 to this Order.

(2) Paragraph (1) and the provisions of Schedule 2 shall not apply to a bankruptcy where the bankruptcy order was made before the commencement date except insofar as is necessary to enable the charging of—

(a) fee INV1; or

(b) as regards an individual voluntary arrangement proposed by, or entered into by, the bankrupt, fees IVA1, IVA2 or IVA3.

(3) Paragraph (1) and the provisions of Schedule 2 shall not apply to a winding up by the court where the winding-up order was made before the commencement date except insofar as is necessary to enable the charging of fee INV1.

(4) Each request for the purchase of any government securities made by a trustee in bankruptcy under the Bankruptcy Act 1914 or a liquidator in a winding up under the provisions of the Companies Act 1985 shall be accompanied by a fee of £50.

5 Fees payable to an insolvency practitioner appointed under section 273

Where a court appoints an insolvency practitioner under section 273(2) to prepare and submit a report under section 274 the court shall, on submission of the report, pay to the practitioner a fee of [£335] (that sum being inclusive of Value Added Tax).

NOTES

Sum in square brackets substituted by the Insolvency Proceedings (Fees) (Amendment) Order 2007, SI 2007/521, arts 2(1), (2), 4(1), (2), as from 1 April 2007 (note that this amendment shall only apply to reports submitted to the court in respect of debtors' petitions presented on or after that date; the previous sum was £310).

6 Deposits—winding up by the court and bankruptcy

(1) In this Article—

"appropriate deposit" means—

(a) in relation to a winding-up petition to be presented under the Act the sum of [£670];

(b) in relation to a bankruptcy petition to be presented under section 264(1)(b) the sum of [£335]; or

(c) in relation to a bankruptcy petition to be presented under sections 264(1)(a), [(ba), (bb),] (c) or (d) the sum of [£400];

"order" means a winding-up, or as the case may be, bankruptcy order;

"petition" means a winding-up, or as the case may be, bankruptcy petition;

"relevant assets" means the assets of the company or, as the case may be the assets comprised in the estate of the bankrupt; and

"relevant fees" means in relation to winding-up proceedings fee W1 and in relation to bankruptcy proceedings fee B1 together with any fees payable under section 273.

(2) [Where a bankruptcy or winding-up petition is presented the appropriate deposit is payable by the petitioner and the deposit] shall be security for the payment of the relevant fees and shall be used to discharge those fees to the extent that the relevant assets are insufficient for that purpose.

(3) Where a deposit is paid to the court, the court shall (except to the extent that a fee is payable by virtue of Article 5) transmit the deposit paid to the official receiver attached to the court.

(4) A deposit shall be repaid to the person who made it in a case where a petition is dismissed or withdrawn except in the case of a bankruptcy petition where it is required to pay any fees arising under Article 5.

(5) In any case where an order is made (including any case where the order is subsequently annulled, rescinded or recalled), any deposit made shall be returned to the person who made it save to the extent that the relevant assets are insufficient to discharge the fees for which the deposit is security.

NOTES

Para (1): sums in square brackets in paras (a), (b), (c) of the definition "appropriate deposit" substituted by the Insolvency Proceedings (Fees) (Amendment) Order 2007, SI 2007/521, arts 2(1), (3), 4(1), (3), as from 1 April 2007, in relation to petitions presented on or after that date (the sums applying before 1 April 2007 were £655, £325, and £390 respectively); words "(ba), (bb)," in square brackets in para (c) of that definition inserted by the Insolvency Proceedings (Fees) (Amendment) Order 2005, SI 2005/544, arts 4, 5(a), as from 1 April 2005.

Para (2): words in square brackets substituted by SI 2005/544, arts 4, 5(b), as from 1 April 2005.

7 Deposits—official receiver acting as nominee in individual voluntary arrangement

(1) Where a proposal for an individual voluntary arrangement with the official receiver acting as nominee is notified to the official receiver, the notification shall be accompanied by a deposit of [£310] as security for fee IVA1 and fee IVA2.

(2) The deposit shall be used to discharge fee IVA1 and fee IVA2.

(3) Where the official receiver declines to act in relation to a proposal of the kind mentioned in paragraph (1) the deposit mentioned in that paragraph shall be refunded to the person entitled to it

(4) Where the official receiver agrees to act as nominee in relation to a proposal of the kind mentioned in paragraph (1) but the proposal is rejected by the bankrupt's creditors, any balance of the deposit after deducting fee IVA2 shall be returned to the person who is entitled to it.

NOTES

Para (1): sum in square brackets substituted by the Insolvency Proceedings (Fees) (Amendment) Order 2007, SI 2007/521, art 2(1), (4), 4(1), (4), as from 1 April 2007, in relation to notifications sent to the official receiver on or after that date (the sum applying before 1 April 2007 was £315).

8 Reduction and refund of fees—individual voluntary arrangement following bankruptcy

Where proposals made by a bankrupt for an individual voluntary arrangement with the official receiver acting as supervisor are approved by the bankrupt's creditors, fee B1 shall be reduced to [£857.50] and any payments made in respect of fee B1 which exceed that amount shall be refunded to the credit of the estate of the bankrupt.

NOTES

Sum in square brackets substituted by the Insolvency Proceedings (Fees) (Amendment) Order 2007, SI 2007/521, art 2(1), (5), 4(1), (5), as from 1 April 2007, in relation to cases in which the bankruptcy order relating to the bankrupt was made on or after that date (the sum applying before 1 April 2007 was £812.50).

9 Value Added Tax

Where Valued Added Tax is chargeable in respect of the provision of a service for which a fee is prescribed by virtue of any provision of this Order (other than Article 5), there shall be payable in addition to that fee the amount of the Value Added Tax.

SCHEDULES

(Sch 1 (Revocations) omitted.)

SCHEDULE 2
FEES PAYABLE IN INSOLVENCY PROCEEDINGS

Article 4

1.—(1) In this Schedule—

"the bankruptcy ceiling" means in relation to a bankruptcy, the sum which is arrived at by adding together—

(a) the bankruptcy debts required to be paid under the Rules

[(b) any interest payable by virtue of sections 328(4) and 329(2)(b); and]

(c) the expenses of the bankruptcy as set out in Rule 6.224 other than—

APPENDICES

(i) any sums spent out of money received in carrying on the business of the bankrupt; and

(ii) fee B2 in the Table set out in paragraph 2;

"chargeable receipts" means those sums which are paid into the Insolvency Services Account after first deducting any amounts paid into the Insolvency Services Account which are subsequently paid out to secured creditors in respect of their securities or in carrying on the business of the company or the bankrupt; and

"the insolvency legislation" means the Insolvency Act 1986, the Insolvency Rules 1986 and the Insolvency Regulations 1994.

(2) In this Schedule, references to the performance of the "general duties" of the official receiver on the making of a winding-up or bankruptcy order—

(a) include the payment by the official receiver of any fees, costs or disbursements except for those associated with the realisation of assets or the distribution of funds to creditors; but

[(b) does not include anything done by the official receiver in connection with or for the purposes of—

(i) the appointment of agents for the purposes of, or in connection with, the realisation of assets;

(ii) the making of a distribution to creditors (including preferential or secured creditors or both such classes of creditor);

(iii) the realisation of assets on behalf of the holder of a fixed or floating charge or both types of those charges; or

(iv) the supervision of a special manager].

2. Fees payable to the Secretary of State in respect of proceedings under Parts I to XI of the Act and the performance by the official receiver and the Secretary of State of functions under those Parts shall be determined in accordance with the provisions of the Table of Fees set out below—

TABLE OF FEES

Fees payable in relation to winding up by the court only		
Designation of Fee	*Description of fee and circumstances in which it is charged*	*Amount of fee or applicable %*
W1	Winding up by the court—official receiver's administration fee For the performance by the official receiver of his general duties as official receiver on the making of a winding-up order[, including his duty to investigate and report upon the affairs of bodies in liquidation,] there shall be payable a fee of—	[£2,090]
W2	Winding up by the court—Secretary of State's administration fee For the performance by the Secretary of State of her general duties under the insolvency legislation in relation to the administration of the affairs of each company which is being wound up by the court, there shall be payable a fee (up to a maximum of £100,000) calculated as a percentage of total chargeable receipts relating to the company (but ignoring the first £2000) at the rate of—	17%

Fees payable in bankruptcies and both types of winding up		
Designation of Fee	*Description of fee and circumstances in which it is charged*	*Amount of fee or applicable %*
INV1	Investment fee—all cases Each request made by a trustee in bankruptcy or a liquidator in a compulsory or a voluntary winding up for the purchase of any government securities shall be accompanied by a fee of—	£50

NOTES

Para 1: para (b) of definition "the bankruptcy ceiling" substituted by the Insolvency Proceedings (Fees) (Amendment) Order 2007, SI 2007/521, art 2(1), (6), 4(1), (6), as from 1 April 2007, in relation to bankruptcy orders made on or after that date (prior to 1 April 2007, the paragraph read as follows "(b) any interest payable by virtue of section 328(4); and"); sub-para (2)(b) substituted by the Insolvency Proceedings (Fees) (Amendment) Order 2005, SI 2005/544, arts 4, 6, as from 1 April 2005 (in relation to any case where a winding-up is made on or after that date).

Fee W1: words in square brackets in column 2 inserted, and sum in square brackets in column 3 substituted, by SI 2007/521, art 2(1), (7)(c), 4(1), (9), as from 1 April 2007, in respect of winding-up orders made on or after that date (the sum applying before 1 April 2007 was £1,950).

Note: fees payable in respect of individual voluntary arrangements and fees payable in bankruptcies are omitted (outside the scope of this work).

EUROPEAN PUBLIC LIMITED-LIABILITY COMPANY (FEES) REGULATIONS 2004, SI 2004/2407

NOTES

Made: 13 September 2004.
Authority: Finance Act 1973, s 56(1), (2).
Commencement: 8 October 2004.
As of 1 July 2007, these Regulations had not been amended.

1. These Regulations may be cited as the European Public Limited-Liability Company (Fees) Regulations 2004 and shall come into force on 8th October 2004.

2. In these Regulations, unless the context otherwise requires—

"the 1985 Act" means the Companies Act 1985;

"the EC Regulation" means Council Regulation 2157/2001/EC of 8th October 2001 on the Statute for a European company;

"the principal Regulations" means the European Public Limited-Liability Company Regulations 2004;

"public company" means a public company as defined in section 744 of the 1985 Act;

"the registrar" means the registrar of companies as defined in section 744 of the 1985 Act;

"the relevant Community obligations" means the Community obligations of the United Kingdom set out in Articles 2, 3, 8 and 66 of the EC Regulation;

"SE" means a European public limited-liability company formed in pursuance of Article 1 of the EC Regulation.

3. The fees payable in connection with the services and facilities provided by the Department of Trade and Industry in pursuance of the relevant Community obligations relating to the matters set out in the first column of the Schedule to these Regulations, implemented in part by the principal Regulations, are the fees payable to the registrar set out in the second column of the Schedule.

SCHEDULE
FEES TO BE PAID TO THE REGISTRAR

Regulation 3

Matter in respect of which fee is payable	*Amount of fee*
1. For registration of an SE whose registered office is in Great Britain on its formation—	
(a) by merger in accordance with Article 2(1) of the EC Regulation	£20.00
(b) by the formation of a holding SE in accordance with Article 2(2) of the EC Regulation	£20.00
(c) by the formation of a subsidiary SE in accordance with Article 2(3) of the EC Regulation	£20.00
(d) by the transformation of a public company in accordance with Article 2(4) of the EC Regulation	£20.00
(e) by the formation of a subsidiary SE in accordance with Article 3(2) of the EC Regulation	£20.00
2. For registration of a public company by the conversion of an SE in accordance with Article 66 of the EC Regulation	£20.00
3. For registration of an SE on the transfer of its registered office to Great Britain in accordance with Article 8 of the EC Regulation	£20.00
4. For an application for a certificate under Article 8(8) of the EC Regulation attesting to the completion of the acts and formalities to be accomplished before the transfer of the registered office of an SE from Great Britain	£20.00

LIMITED LIABILITY PARTNERSHIPS (FEES) REGULATIONS 2004, SI 2004/2620

NOTES

Made: 6 October 2004.
Authority: CA 1985, s 708(1).
Commencement: 1 February 2005.
As of 1 July 2007, these Regulations had not been amended.

1 Citation and commencement

These Regulations may be cited as the Limited Liability Partnerships (Fees) Regulations 2004 and shall come into force on 1st February 2005.

2 Interpretation

In these Regulations—

"the 1985 Act" means the Companies Act 1985;

"the 2000 Act" means the Limited Liability Partnerships Act 2000;

"document package" means one of the sets of copies of documents relating to a limited liability partnership (in so far as such documents are delivered to the registrar of companies by the limited liability partnership) as described in one of the paragraphs in Schedule 2 and with the maximum number of documents in each package being as specified in Schedule 3, with the documents in the package being primarily determinable in reverse order of the dates of delivery to the registrar of companies;

"electronic information service" means a service by which information is accessed by the applicant in Hyper Text Markup Language using a website of the registrar of companies with no requirement for the applicant to deliver an access code;

"electronic subscription service" means a service by which information is accessed by the applicant in Hyper Text Markup Language using a website of the registrar of companies by delivering a non-encrypted access code;

"index" means one of the following indexes kept by the registrar of companies—
(a) the index of company and corporate names and numbers;
(b) the index of charges;

"limited liability partnership report" means a report containing the information relating to a limited liability partnership set out in Schedule 1 in so far as recorded by the registrar of companies in records kept by her for the purposes of the 1985 Act, as applied to limited liability partnerships;

"relevant document" means in relation to entry 2 in Schedule 3 a document which a limited liability partnership is required to deliver to the registrar of companies under any provisions of the 2000 Act or the 1985 Act, as applied to limited liability partnerships, other than a document in relation to the delivery of which a fee is specified in any other entry in Schedule 3;

"relevant period" means one of the following periods—
(a) the period beginning with the incorporation of a limited liability partnership and ending immediately after the delivery to the registrar of companies of its first annual return; or
(b) a period beginning immediately after delivery to the registrar of companies of an annual return and ending immediately after delivery to her of the next annual return;

"same day" means, in relation to a registration or provision of a certificate or certified copy, any such matter in relation to which—
(a) a request for same day registration, provision of a certificate or certified copy (as the case may be) and all documents required to be delivered to the registrar of companies in connection therewith, are received by the registrar of companies—
(i) in the case of a request for provision of a certificate or a certified copy, before 2.00 pm on the day in question, or
(ii) in other cases, before 3.00 pm on that day, and
(b) the registration (where requisite) is completed and the appropriate certificate or certified copy is issued to the applicant on that day;

"searchroom terminal" means a computer terminal operated by the applicant at an office of the registrar of companies.

APPENDICES

3 Revocations

(1) Subject to paragraph (2), these Regulations revoke the Limited Liability Partnerships (Fees) (No 2) Regulations 2001 and the Limited Liability Partnerships (Fees) (Amendment) Regulations 2002.

(2) The fee prescribed in relation to entry 2 in the Schedule to the Limited Liability Partnerships (Fees) (No 2) Regulations 2001 applies to the delivery of an annual return—
(a) in relation to which the return date is earlier than 1st February 2005; or
(b) which is delivered before 1st February 2005.

4 Fees payable to the registrar of companies

(1) Subject to paragraph (2), the fees set out in the second column of Schedule 3 shall be the fees payable in respect of the performance by the registrar of companies of her functions in relation to the matters specified in the first column of that Schedule and shall be payable—
(a) in relation to entries 2 and 15 in Schedule 3, as stated in those entries;
(b) in relation to all other matters, on the performance by the registrar of companies of the relevant function.

(2) The fee prescribed in relation to entry 15 in Schedule 3 is not payable in respect of any month for which the applicant pays a fee to the registrar of companies for an electronic subscription service under Regulations providing for fees in respect of functions of the registrar of companies in relation to companies or of the Department of Trade and Industry in relation to European Economic Interest Groupings.

5 Application of fees

The fees prescribed in regulation 4 apply—
(a) in relation to entries 1, 3, 4 and 5 in Schedule 3, to any matter in respect of which every document necessary for the registrar of companies to carry out her functions in respect of that matter is delivered to her on or after 1st February 2005;
(b) in relation to entry 2 in that Schedule, to the delivery of any annual return—
(i) in relation to which the return date is on or after 1st February 2005, and
(ii) which is delivered on or after 1st February 2005;

(c) in relation to entries 6 to 14 (inclusive) and 16 and 17 in that Schedule, to any matter in respect of which a request is received by the registrar of companies on or after 1st February 2005;

(d) in relation to entry 15 in that Schedule, in respect of February 2005 and any subsequent months.

SCHEDULES

SCHEDULE 1
CONTENTS OF LIMITED LIABILITY PARTNERSHIP REPORT

Regulation 2

Limited liability partnership register information

1. Information relating to the limited liability partnership including its registered number, its date of incorporation, its name and the number of registered charges.

2. Any previous names.

3. A list of dates including those relating to latest annual accounts and annual returns and dates for the next such documents to be delivered to the registrar of companies.

Appointments and charges

4. At the option of the applicant, either or both of the following sets of particulars—
   (a) particulars of members of the limited liability partnership;
   (b) particulars of charges registered in respect of the limited liability partnership

except that an applicant using electronic information service can not elect to have only the particulars under (b).

Recent filing history

5. List of documents delivered to the registrar of companies during the previous 18 months up to a maximum of 100 documents listed in the reverse order of the dates of delivery.

SCHEDULE 2
DOCUMENT PACKAGES

Regulation 2

Listed below are the document packages and the documents included in each package

1 General Package

Incorporation documents and name changes documents

Any documents relating to strike-off

Latest annual accounts and notices specifying accounting reference date or extending the period allowed for delivering the accounts and the auditors' report

Latest annual return

Notification of change among members and changes in registered office in each case since the date to which the latest annual return was made up

2 Current Package

Latest annual accounts and notices specifying accounting reference date or extending the period allowed for delivering the accounts and the auditors' report

Latest annual return

Notification of change among members and changes in registered office in each case since the date to which the latest annual return was made up

Any documents relating to strike-off

3 Charges Package

Charge related documents since incorporation

The limited liability partnership report containing the particulars in paragraph 4(b) of Schedule 1 but not the particulars in paragraph 4(a) of that Schedule

4 Insolvency Package

Company Voluntary Arrangements, Administration, Receivership, Winding Up, Dissolution and strike-off related documents delivered to the registrar of companies since April 1995

5 Accounts Package

Annual accounts and notices specifying accounting reference date or extending the period allowed for delivering the accounts and the auditors' report

The limited liability partnership report

6 Package of documents delivered in a calendar year selected by the applicant

Documents delivered to the registrar of companies by the limited liability partnership in a calendar year selected by the applicant (not available for years prior to 2003)

SCHEDULE 3

FEES PAYABLE TO THE REGISTRAR OF COMPANIES

Regulation 4

Matter in relation to which fee is payable	Amount of fee
1. Registration of a limited liability partnership on its incorporation under the 2000 Act—	
(a) other than same day registration	£20.00
(b) same day registration	£50.00
2. Delivery by a limited liability partnership of all relevant documents during a relevant period, payable at the end of that period on delivery by the limited liability partnership of its annual return under section 363 of the 1985 Act, as applied to limited liability partnerships by the Limited Liability Partnerships Regulations 2001	£30.00
3. Registration of a change of name of a limited liability partnership under paragraph 4 of the Schedule to the 2000 Act (other than a change made in response to a direction of the Secretary of State under paragraph 4(2) of that Schedule)—	
(a) other than same day registration	£10.00
(b) same day registration	£50.00
4. Registration of a charge under Part XII of the 1985 Act, as applied to limited liability partnerships	£13.00
5. Application by a limited liability partnership under section 652A of the 1985 Act, as applied to limited liability partnerships, for the limited liability partnership's name to be struck off the register	£10.00
6. Provision of a copy of an index page delivered by email or fax or on paper delivered by post or at an office of the registrar of companies	£2.00
7. Provision of particulars of the members of a limited liability partnership, particulars of charges registered in respect of a limited liability partnership, or particulars of memberships of limited liability partnerships held by a named person—	
(a) inspection of information using electronic subscription service or searchroom terminal	£1.00

APPENDICES

Matter in relation to which fee is payable	Amount of fee
(b) copy of information delivered by email or fax or on paper delivered by post or at an office of the registrar of companies	£3.00
8. Provision of a limited liability partnership report— (a) using electronic information service, electronic subscription service or searchroom terminal	£1.00
(b) delivered by email or fax or on paper delivered by post or at an office of the registrar of companies	£3.00
9. Provision of a copy of the register of charges with respect to a limited liability partnership	£3.00
10. Inspection or provision of a copy of a document—	
(a) inspection using electronic subscription service	£4.00
(b) inspection using searchroom terminal	£2.00
(c) provision of a copy without prior inspection using electronic information service, electronic subscription service or searchroom terminal	£1.00
(d) copy delivered by email or on paper delivered by post or at an office of the registrar of companies	£3.00
(e) copy requested by	£3.00
11. Printing a screen of information using searchroom terminal by the applicant at an office of the registrar of companies where no fee is chargeable for inspecting that information	£0.10
12. Provision of a document package of up to 25 documents requested at an office of the registrar of companies or using a searchroom terminal and delivered on paper at that office of the registrar of companies	£7.00
13. Provision of a document package of up to 50 documents requested using electronic subscription service—	
(a) delivered using the electronic subscription service	£4.00
(b) delivered by post on paper	£20.00
14. Inspection and provision of a copy of an original document delivered to the registrar of companies in legible form, when the record of the contents kept by the registrar of companies is illegible or unavailable—	
(a) inspection only	£6.00
(b) inspection and copy	£9.00
15. Fee for electronic subscription service, for each calendar month payable in arrears at the end of that month	£5.00
16. Provisions of a certified copy of a document or extract from a document provided pursuant to section 709(1)(b) of the 1985 Act, as applied to limited liability partnerships	
(a) up to 10 pages (including the tenth page)	£15.00
(b) each page thereafter	£1.00
(c) same day delivery	£50.00
(d) additional fee for same day delivery by fax	£3.00
17. Certificate of incorporation provided pursuant to section 710 of the 1985 Act, as applied to limited liability partnerships—	
(a) for the first certificate relating to a limited liability partnership provided on any one occasion	£15.00

Matter in relation to which fee is payable	Amount of fee
(b) each additional certificate relating to the same limited liability partnership provided on the same occasion	£10.00
(c) same day delivery	£50.00
(d) additional fee for same day delivery by fax	£3.00

COMPANIES (FEES) REGULATIONS 2004, SI 2004/2621

NOTES

Made: 6 October 2004.
Authority: Companies Act 1985, s 708(1).
Commencement: 1 February 2005.
As of 1 July 2007, these Regulations had not been amended.

1 Citation and commencement

These Regulations may be cited as the Companies (Fees) Regulations 2004 and shall come into force on 1st February 2005.

2 Interpretation

In these Regulations—

"the 1985 Act" means the Companies Act 1985 and in Schedule 4 any reference to a Part, Chapter, numbered section or Schedule is a reference to a Part, Chapter, or section of or Schedule to that Act;

"company" includes an oversea company except in relation to entries 1,2,3,5,10 and 24 in Schedule 4;

"company report" means a report containing the information relating to a company set out in Schedule 1 in so far as recorded by the registrar in records kept by her for the purposes of the 1985 Act;

"delivery of accounts" means in relation to an oversea company—

(a) delivery to the registrar by the company of copy accounts and reports under section 702 of the 1985 Act; or

(b) delivery to the registrar by the company of accounting documents under Schedule 21C or 21D to the 1985 Act;

"document package" means one of the sets of copies of documents relating to a company (in so far as such documents are delivered to the registrar by the company) as described in one of the paragraphs in Schedule 2 and with the maximum number of documents in each package being as specified in Schedule 4, with the documents in the package being primarily determinable in reverse order of the dates of delivery to the registrar;

"electronic information service" means a service by which information is accessed by the applicant in Hyper Text Markup Language using a website of the registrar with no requirement for the applicant to deliver an access code;

"electronic subscription service" means a service by which information is accessed by the applicant in Hyper Text Markup Language using a website of the registrar by delivering a non-encrypted access code;

"index" means one of the following indexes kept by the registrar—

(a) the index of company and corporate names and numbers;

(b) the index of company charges;

"long list of members" means a list of members delivered to the registrar under section 363 of the 1985 Act which—

(a) is delivered to the registrar by means of microfiche or magnetic tape; or

(b) exceeds 49 pages;

"oversea company" includes in relation to entry 6 in Schedule 4 any institution to which section 699A of the 1985 Act applies;

"relevant document" means in relation to entries 5 and 6 in Schedule 4, a document which a company is required to deliver to the registrar under any provisions of the 1985 Act, other than a document in relation to the delivery of which a fee is specified in any other entry in Schedule 4;

"relevant period" means one of the following periods—

(a) in relation to a company which is not an oversea company—
(i) the period beginning with its incorporation and ending immediately after the delivery to the registrar of its first annual return; or
(ii) a period beginning immediately after delivery to the registrar of an annual return and ending immediately after delivery to the registrar of the next annual return;
(b) in relation to an oversea company—
(i) the period beginning with the registration of the documents required to be delivered to the registrar by section 691 of the 1985 Act or of particulars required to be delivered to the registrar by paragraph 1 of Schedule 21A to the 1985 Act and ending immediately after the first delivery to the registrar of its accounts; or
(ii) a period beginning immediately after a delivery of accounts to the registrar and ending immediately after delivery to the registrar of the next accounts;

"same day" means, in relation to a registration, re-registration or provision of a certificate or certified copy, any such matter in relation to which—
(a) a request for same day registration, re-registration or provision of a certificate or certified copy (as the case may be) and all documents required to be delivered to the registrar in connection therewith, are received by the registrar—
(i) in the case of a request for provision of a certificate or a certified copy, before 2.00 pm on the day in question, or
(ii) in other cases, before 3.00pm on that day, and
(b) the registration or re-registration (where requisite) is completed and the appropriate certificate or certified copy is issued to the applicant on that day;

"searchroom terminal" means a computer terminal operated by the applicant at an office of the registrar.

3 Revocations

(1) The Regulations listed in Schedule 3 are revoked, subject to paragraph (2).

(2) The fee prescribed in relation to entry 2 in the Schedule to the Companies (Fees) Regulations 1991 applies to the delivery of an annual return—
(a) in relation to which the return date is earlier than 1st February 2005; or
(b) which is delivered before 1st February 2005.

4 Fees payable to the registrar

(1) Subject to paragraph (2), the fees set out in the second column of Schedule 4 shall be the fees payable in respect of the performance by the registrar of her functions in relation to the matters specified in the first column of that Schedule and shall be payable—
(a) in relation to entries 5, 6 and 22 in Schedule 4, as stated in those entries;
(b) in relation to all other matters, on the performance by the registrar of the relevant function.

(2) The fee prescribed in relation to entry 22 in Schedule 4 is not payable in respect of any month for which the applicant pays a fee to the registrar for an electronic subscription service under Regulations providing for fees in respect of functions of the registrar in relation to limited liability partnerships or of the Department of Trade and Industry in relation to European Economic Interest Groupings.

5 Application of fees

The fees prescribed by regulation 4 apply—
(a) in relation to entries 1 to 4 (inclusive) and 6 to 10 (inclusive) in Schedule 4, to any matter in respect of which every document necessary for the registrar to carry out her functions in respect of that matter is delivered to her on or after 1st February 2005;
(b) in relation to entry 5 in that Schedule, to the delivery of any annual return—
(i) in relation to which the return date is on or after 1st February 2005, and
(ii) which is delivered on or after 1st February 2005;
(c) in relation to entries 11 to 21 (inclusive) and 23 and 24 in that Schedule, to any matter in respect of which a request is received by the registrar on or after 1st February 2005;
(d) in relation to entry 22 in that Schedule, in respect of February 2005 and any subsequent months.

SCHEDULES

SCHEDULE 1
CONTENTS OF COMPANY REPORT

Regulation 2

Companies register information

1. Information relating to the company including its registered number, its date of incorporation, its name and the number of registered charges.

2. Any previous names.

3. A list of dates including those relating to latest annual accounts and annual returns and dates for the next such documents to be delivered to the registrar.

Appointments and charges

4. At the option of the applicant, either or both of the following sets of particulars—
   (a) particulars of the directors and secretary of the company;
   (b) particulars of charges registered in respect of the company;

except that an applicant using electronic information service can not elect to have only the particulars under (b).

Recent filing history

5. List of documents delivered to the registrar during the previous 18 months up to a maximum of 100 documents listed in the reverse order of the dates of delivery excluding returns of allotments unless requested by the applicant.

SCHEDULE 2
DOCUMENT PACKAGES

Regulation 2

Listed below are the document packages and the documents included in each package.

1 General Package

Incorporation documents and name changes documents

Resolutions and memorandum and articles of association

Any documents relating to strike-off

Latest annual accounts and notices specifying accounting reference date or extending the period allowed for laying and delivering accounts and reports

Latest annual return

Notification of change among directors or in secretary or their particulars and changes in registered office in each case since the date to which the latest annual return was made up

(at the option of the applicant) Returns of allotments of shares delivered to the registrar since the date to which the latest annual return giving full particulars of the members is made up

(long list of members not available)

2 Current Package

Latest annual accounts and notices specifying accounting reference date or extending the period allowed for laying and delivering accounts and reports

Latest annual return

Notification of change among directors or in secretary or their particulars and changes in registered office in each case since the date to which the latest annual return was made up

Any documents relating to strike-off

(at the option of the applicant) Returns of allotments of shares delivered to the registrar since the date to which the latest annual return giving full particulars of the members is made up

(long list of members not available)

3 Charges Package

Charge related documents since incorporation

The company report containing the particulars in paragraph 4(b) of Schedule 1 but not the particulars in paragraph 4(a) of that Schedule

4 Insolvency Package

Company Voluntary Arrangements, Administration, Receivership, Winding Up, Dissolution and strike-off related documents delivered to the registrar since April 1995

5 Accounts Package

Annual accounts and notices specifying accounting reference date or extending the period allowed for laying and delivering accounts and reports delivered to the registrar over the previous 5 years

The company report

6 Package of documents delivered in a calendar year selected by the applicant

Documents delivered to the registrar by the company in a calendar year selected by the applicant (not available for years prior to 2003)

(*Sch 3 revokes the Companies* (*Fees*) *Regulations 1991, SI 1991/1206 and the amending SI 1992/2876, SI 1994/2217, SI 1995/1423, SI 1996/1444, SI 1998/3088, SI 2000/3325, SI 2002/317, SI 2002/2894.*)

SCHEDULE 4
FEES PAYABLE TO THE REGISTRAR

Regulation 4

Matter in relation to which fee is payable	Amount of fee
1. Registration of a company on formation under Chapter I of Part I—	
(a) where all the requisite documents are sent to the registrar using electronic communications—	
(i) other than same day registration	£15.00
(ii) same day registration	£30.00
(b) where all the requisite documents are not sent to the registrar using electronic communications—	
(i) other than same day registration	£20.00
(ii) same day registration	£50.00
2. Registration of a company under Chapter II of Part XXII	£20.00
3. Re-registration of a company under Part II—	
(a) other than same day re-registration	£20.00
(b) same day re-registration	£50.00
4. Registration of documents required to be delivered to the registrar by section 691 in respect of the establishment of a place of business in Great Britain, or of particulars required to be delivered to the registrar by paragraph 1 of Schedule 21A in respect of an oversea company having opened a branch in a part of Great Britain	£20.00

Matter in relation to which fee is payable	Amount of fee
5. Delivery by a company of all relevant documents during a relevant period, payable on delivery by the company of its annual return under section 363 at the end of that period—	
(a) where the annual return is delivered using electronic communications	£15.00
(b) where the annual return is delivered not using electronic communications	£30.00
6. Delivery by an oversea company of all relevant documents during a relevant period, payable on delivery of accounts by the company at the end of that period	£30.00
7. Registration of a change of name under section 28 (other than a change made in response to a direction of the Secretary of State under section 28(2))—	
(a) other than same day registration	£10.00
(b) same day registration	£50.00
8. Registration of particulars of—	
(a) a change of corporate name of an oversea company delivered under section 692(2)	£10.00
(b) alteration of—	
(i) the corporate name of a company to which section 690A applies	£10.00
(ii) the name in which its business is carried on, delivered under paragraph 7 of Schedule 21A	£10.00
9. Registration of a charge under Part XII	£13.00
10. Application by a private company under section 652A to strike the company's name off the register	£10.00
11. Provision of a copy of an index page delivered by email or fax or on paper delivered by post or at an office of the registrar	£2.00
12. Provision of particulars of the directors and secretary of a company, particulars of charges registered in respect of a company, or particulars of directorships held by a named person—	
(a) inspection of information using electronic subscription service or searchroom terminal	£1.00
(b) copy of information delivered by email or fax or on paper delivered by post or at an office of the registrar	£3.00
13. Provision of a company report—	
(a) using electronic information service, electronic subscription service or searchroom terminal	£1.00
(b) delivered by email or fax or on paper delivered by post or at an office of the registrar	£3.00
14. Provision of a copy of the register of charges with respect to a company	£3.00
15. Inspection or provision of a copy of a document (other than a long list of members)—	
(a) inspection using electronic subscription service	£4.00
(b) inspection using searchroom terminal	£2.00

APPENDICES

Matter in relation to which fee is payable	Amount of fee
(c) provision of a copy without prior inspection using electronic information service, electronic subscription service or searchroom terminal	£1.00
(d) copy delivered by email or on paper delivered by post or at an office of the registrar	£3.00
(e) copy requested by telephone or using electronic subscription service and delivered by fax	£3.00
16. Printing a screen of information using searchroom terminal or a page printed from microfiche by the applicant at an office of the registrar where in either case no fee is chargeable for inspecting that information	£0.10
17. Provision of a document package of up to 25 documents requested at an office of the registrar or using a searchroom terminal and delivered on paper at that office of the registrar	£7.00
18. Provision of a document package of up to 50 documents requested using electronic subscription service—	
(a) delivered using the electronic subscription service	£4.00
(b) delivered by post on paper	£20.00
19. Provision of a copy of a long list of members—	
(a) microfiche copy	£12.50
(b) paper copy—	
(i) first 20 pages	£12.50
(ii) each additional page	£0.20
20. Inspection and provision of a copy of an original document delivered to the registrar in legible form, when the record of the contents kept by the registrar is illegible or unavailable—	
(a) inspection only	£6.00
(b) inspection and copy	£9.00
21. Provision of a microfiche copy of documents relating to a company (other than long list of members) received by the registrar up to and including 31st December 2002	£9.00
22. Fee for electronic subscription service, for each calendar month payable in arrears at the end of that month	£5.00
23. Provision of a certified copy of a document or extract from a document provided pursuant to section 709(1)(b)—	
(a) up to 10 pages (including the tenth page)	£15.00
(b) each page thereafter	£1.00
(c) same day delivery	£50.00
(d) additional fee for same day delivery by fax	£3.00
24. Certificate of incorporation provided pursuant to section 710—	
(a) for the first certificate relating to a company provided on any one occasion	£15.00
(b) each additional certificate relating to the same company provided on the same occasion	£10.00
(c) same day delivery	£50.00
(d) additional fee for same day delivery by fax	£3.00

EUROPEAN ECONOMIC INTEREST GROUPING (FEES) REGULATIONS 2004, SI 2004/2643

NOTES

Made: 11 October 2004.
Authority: Finance Act 1973, s 568(1), (2).
Commencement: 1 February 2005.
As of 1 July 2007, these Regulations had not been amended.

1 Citation and commencement

These Regulations may be cited as the European Economic Interest Grouping (Fees) Regulations 2004 and shall come into force on 1st February 2005.

2 Interpretation

In these Regulations—

"the Act" means the Companies Act 1985;

"the EC Regulation" means Council Regulation (EEC) No 2137/85 of 25th July 1985 on the European Economic Interest Grouping;

"EEIG" means a European Economic Interest Grouping formed in pursuance of article 1 of the EC Regulation;

"electronic information service" means a service by which information is accessed by the applicant in Hyper Text Markup Language using a website of the registrar of companies with no requirement for the applicant to deliver an access code;

"electronic subscription service" means a service by which information is accessed by the applicant in Hyper Text Markup Language using a website of the registrar of companies by delivering a non-encrypted access code;

"index" means one of the following indexes kept by the registrar of companies—

(a) the index of company and corporate names and numbers;

(b) the index of charges;

"the principal Regulations" means the European Economic Interest Grouping Regulations 1989;

"the registrar of companies" has the meaning specified in section 744 of the Act;

"the relevant Community obligations" means the Community obligations of the United Kingdom under article 39 of the EC Regulation;

"same day" means any provision of a certified copy, in relation to which a request for same day provision of that certified copy is received by the registrar of companies before 2.00 pm on the day in question and the certified copy is issued to the applicant on that day; and

"searchroom terminal" means a computer terminal operated by the applicant at an office of the registrar of companies.

3 Revocations

The Regulations listed in Schedule 1 are revoked.

4 Fees payable to the registrar of companies

(1) Subject to paragraph 2, the fees payable in connection with the services and facilities provided by the Department of Trade and Industry in pursuance of the relevant Community obligations relating to the matters set out in the first column of Schedule 2, implemented in part by the principal Regulations, are the fees payable to the registrar of companies set out in the second column of that Schedule.

(2) The fees prescribed in relation to entry 8 in Schedule 2 is not payable in respect of any month for which the applicant pays a fee to the registrar of companies for an electronic subscription service under Regulations providing for fees in respect of functions of the registrar of companies in relation to companies or limited liability partnerships.

5 Application of fees

The fees prescribed by regulation 4 apply—

(a) in relation to entries 1 to 3 (inclusive) in Schedule 2, to any matter in respect of which every document necessary for the Department of Trade and Industry to provide the services and facilities in respect of that matter is delivered to the registrar of companies on or after 1st February 2005;

(b) in relation to entries 4 to 7 (inclusive) and entry 9 in that Schedule, to any matter in respect of which a request is received by the registrar of companies on or before 1st February 2005;

(c) in relation to entry 8 in that Schedule, in respect of February 2005 and any subsequent months.

SCHEDULES

(Sch 1 revokes the European Economic Interest Grouping (Fees) Regulations 1999, SI 1999/268 and the amending SI 2000/3412, SI 2002/401 and SI 2002/2928.)

SCHEDULE 2

FEES PAYABLE TO THE REGISTRAR OF COMPANIES

Regulation 4

Matter in respect of which fee is payable	Amount of fee
1. (a) Registration under regulation 9 of the principal Regulations of an EEIG whose official address is in Great Britain	£20.00
(b) Registration under regulation 12 of the principal Regulations of an EEIG that is situating an establishment in Great Britain but whose official address is outside Great Britain	£20.00
2. Registration of a change of name of an EEIG under Regulation 11(2) of the principal Regulations	£10.00
3. Registration of a charge under paragraph 4 of Schedule 4 to the principal Regulations	£13.00
4. Provision of a copy of an index page delivered by email or fax or on paper delivered by post or at an office of the registrar of companies	£2.00
5. Inspection or provision of a copy of a document—	
(a) inspection using electronic subscription service	£4.00
(b) inspection using searchroom terminal	£2.00
(c) provision of a copy without prior inspection using electronic information service, electronic subscription service or searchroom terminal	£1.00
(d) copy delivered by email or on paper delivered by post or at an office of the registrar of companies	£3.00
(e) copy requested by telephone or using electronic subscription service and delivered by fax	£3.00
6. Printing a screen of information using searchroom terminal or a page printed from microfiche by the applicant at an office of the registrar of companies where in either case no fee is chargeable for inspecting that information	£0.10
7. Provision of a microfiche copy of documents relating to an EEIG received by the registrar of companies up to and including 31st December 2002	£9.00
8. Fee for electronic subscription service, for each calendar month payable in arrears at the end of that month	£5.00
9. Provision of a certified copy of a document or extract from a document—	
(a) up to 10 pages (including the tenth page)	£15.00
(b) each page thereafter	£1.00
(c) same day delivery	£50.00

Matter in respect of which fee is payable	Amount of fee
(d) additional fee for same day delivery by fax	£3.00

COMMUNITY INTEREST COMPANY REGULATIONS 2005, SI 2005/1788

NOTES

Made: 30 June 2005.

Authority: Companies (Audit, Investigations and Community Enterprise) Act 2004, ss 30(1)–(4), (7), 31, 32(3), (4), (6), 34(3), 35(4)–(6), 36(2), 37(7), 47(12), (13), 57(1), (2), 58, 59(1), 62(2), (3), Sch 4, para 4.

Commencement: 1 July 2005.

Only Pt 10 (reg 36) and Sch 5 are reproduced here. The remainder of the Regulations are set out at **[7399]** et seq.

The provisions below are reproduced as amended by: the Companies Act 2006 (Commencement No 2, Consequential Amendments, Transitional Provisions and Savings) Order 2007, SI 2007/1093.

PART 10
FEES

36 Fees payable by a community interest company

The fees set out in the second column of Schedule 5—

(a) shall be the fees payable in connection with the Regulator's functions in relation to the matters set out in the first column of that Schedule;

(b) shall be payable as stated in the third column of that Schedule; and

(c) shall be paid to the registrar of companies.

SCHEDULE 5
FEES PAYABLE TO THE REGISTRAR OF COMPANIES

Regulation 36

Matter in relation to which fee is payable	Amount of fee	When payable
Decision under section 36(4) of the 2004 Act as to whether a company is eligible to be formed as a community interest company	£15.00	On delivery to the registrar under section 10 of the 1985 Act [or Article 21 of the 1986 Order], section 36 of the 2004 Act and regulation 11 of the documents constituting an application to form a community interest company
Decision under section 38(3) of the 2004 Act as to whether a company is eligible to become a community interest company	£15.00	On delivery to the registrar under section 380 of the 1985 Act [or Article 388 of the 1986 Order], section 37 of the 2004 Act and regulation 12 of the documents constituting an application to the registrar to become a community interest company
Consideration of a community interest company report forwarded by the registrar under section 34(4) of the 2004 Act	£15.00	On delivery of the report to the registrar

APPENDICES

NOTES

Words in square brackets inserted by the Companies Act 2006 (Commencement No 2, Consequential Amendments, Transitional Provisions and Savings) Order 2007, SI 2007/1093, art 6(2), Sch 4, Pt 2, para 45, as from 6 April 2007.

[A3]

Appendix 4: Forms Table

CONTENTS OF APPENDIX 4

COMPANIES (REGISTERS AND OTHER RECORDS) REGULATIONS 1985, SI 1985/724

NOTES

Made: 8 May 1985.
Authority: CA 1985, s 723(4).
Commencement: 1 July 1985.
Regulations 1–6 of, and Sch 1 to, these Regulations are set out at **[6028]** et seq. Sch 2 to these Regulations prescribes the forms of notice to be given for the purposes of regs 3(1) and 5(1). The forms are not reproduced here but details are given in the table below.

Companies (Registers and Other Records) Regulations 1985

Form No	*Description*	*Status*
325a	Notice of place for inspection of register of directors' interests in shares etc which is kept in non-legible form, or of any change in that place	Prescribed by SI 1985/724, Sch 2, Pt I
353a	Notice of place for inspection of register of members which is kept in non-legible form, or of any change in that place	Prescribed by SI 1985/724, Sch 2, Pt I
362a	Notice of place for inspection of overseas branch register which is kept in non-legible form, or of any change in that place	Prescribed by SI 1985/724, Sch 2, Pt I
190a	Notice of place for inspection of register of holders of debentures which is kept in non-legible form, or of any change in that place	Prescribed by SI 1985/724, Sch 2, Pt II

COMPANIES (FORMS) REGULATIONS 1985, SI 1985/854

NOTES

Made: 4 June 1985.
Authority: originally made under CA 1985, ss 6(1)(b)(i), 10(2), 12(3), 21(5), 30(5), 43(3), 49(4), (8)(a), 51(4), 53(1)(b), 54(4), 65(3)(b), 72(2)(c), 77(5)(a), 88(2)(a), (3), 97(3)(a), 117(2), (3), 122(1), 123(2), 128(1), (3), (4), 129(1), (2), (3), 139(4), 147(3), 155(6), 156(1), 157(3), 169(1), 173(5), 176(3)(a), 190(5), 224(2), 225(1), (2), 241(3)(b), 242(3), 266(1), (3), 272(5), 273(7), 287(2), 288(2), 318(4), 325(5), 353(2), 362(3), 363(2), 364(1), 386(2), 395(1), 397(1), 398(1), (4), 400(2), 401(1), 403(1), 405(3), 409(1), 410(2), 413(2), 416(1), 417(1), 419(1), (5), 424(1), 428(2), 429(2), (3), 466(4), (5), 469(1), 470(3), 481(1)(b), (2), 482(1), 485(1), 486, 495(2)(a), (b), 496(1)(e), 497(2), 498(3), 600(1), 680(1), 681(6), 684(1)(a), (b), (2), 685(4), (4)(e), 686(1)(a), (2), 690(2), 691(1)(a), (b), 692(1), (2), 694(4)(a), (b), 698, 700(2), 701(2), (6), 744, Sch 13, para 27, Sch 14, para 1(1); the Companies Consolidation (Consequential Provisions) Act 1985, ss 2(1)(b), (4)(b), 4(1), (4).
Commencement: 1 July 1985.
Regulation 4 of these Regulations provides as follows—

APPENDICES

"(1) The forms set out in Schedule 3, other than those listed in Part I of Schedule 4, with such variations as circumstances require, are the forms prescribed for the purposes of the provisions of the new Acts which are referred to in those forms.

(2) The particulars contained in the forms listed in Parts I and II of Schedule 4 are the particulars prescribed for the purposes of the provisions of the Act which are referred to in those forms.".

The forms are not reproduced here but details are given in the table below. Unless otherwise indicated, the form number corresponds to the section of CA 1985 pursuant to which that form was made (or CA 2006 as appropriate). The forms are amended as noted below, and forms which have been replaced may continue to be used for a transitional period. See also, the note to CA 1985, s 272 at **[277]**.

Companies (Forms) Regulations 1985

Form No	*Presently prescribed by*	*Description*
6	1995/736	Cancellation of alteration to the objects of a company
10[4]	2002/691[3]	First directors and secretary and intended situation of registered office
12[5]	1995/736	Declaration on application for registration
30(5)(a)[6]	1995/736	Declaration on application for registration of a company exempt from the requirement to use the word "limited" or "cyfyngedig"
30(5)(b)[7]	1995/736	Declaration on application for registration under s 680 of the Companies Act 1985 of a company exempt from the requirement to use the word "limited" or "cyfyngedig"
30(5)(c)[8]	1995/736	Change of name omitting "limited" or "cyfyngedig"
43(3)	1995/736	Application by a private company for re-registration as a public company
43(3)(e)	1995/736	Declaration on application by a private company for re-registration as a public company
49(1)	1995/736	Application by a limited company to be reregistered as unlimited
49(8)(a)	1995/736	Members' assent to company being reregistered as unlimited
51	1995/736	Application by an unlimited company to be re-registered as limited
53	1995/736	Application by a public company for re-registration as a private company
54	1995/736	Application to the Court for cancellation of resolution for re-registration
88(2) (Revised 2005)[9]	2005/2747[22]	Return of allotment of shares
88(3) (Revised 2005)	2005/2747[22]	Particulars of a contract relating to shares allotted as fully or partly paid up allotments otherwise than in cash
97	1985/854	Statement of the amount or rate per cent of any commission payable in connection with the subscription of shares
117	1995/736	Application by a public company for a certificate to commence business

Companies (Forms) Regulations 1985

Form No	*Presently prescribed by*	*Description*
122[1]	1985/854; amended by 1987/752	Notice of consolidation, division, sub-division, redemption or cancellation of shares, or conversion, re-conversion of stock into shares
123	1985/854; amended by 1987/752	Notice of increase in nominal capital
128(1)[1]	1985/854; amended by 1987/752	Statement of rights attached to allotted shares
128(3)[1]	1985/854; amended by 1987/752	Statement of particulars of variation of rights attached to shares
128(4)[1]	1985/854; amended by 1987/752	Notice of assignment of name or new name to any class of shares
129(1)[1]	1985/854; amended by 1987/752	Statement by a company without share capital of rights attached to newly created class of members
129(2)[1]	1985/854; amended by 1987/752	Statement by a company without share capital of particulars of a variation of members' class rights
129(3)[1]	1985/854; amended by 1987/752	Notice by a company without share capital of assignment of a name or other designation to a class of members
139	1985/854; amended by 2006/3429	Application by a public company for re-registration as a private company following a Court Order reducing capital.
147	1985/854	Application by a public company for re-registration as a private company following cancellation of shares and reduction of nominal value of issued capital
155(6)a	1985/854	Declaration in relation to assistance for the acquisition of shares
155(6)b	1985/854	Declaration by the directors of a holding company in relation to assistance for the acquisition of shares
157[1]	1985/854; amended by 1987/752	Notice of application made to the Court for the cancellation of a special resolution regarding financial assistance for the acquisition of shares
169[21]	1987/752	Return by a company purchasing its own shares
169(1B)[21]	2003/2982	Return by a public company purchasing its own shares for holding in treasury
169A(2)[21]	2003/2982	Return by a public company cancelling or selling or transferring shares from treasury
173	1985/854	Declaration in relation to the redemption or purchase of shares out of capital
176[1]	1985/854; amended by 1987/752	Notice of application to the Court for the cancellation of a resolution for the redemption or purchase of shares out of capital
190	1995/736	Location of register of debenture holders

APPENDICES

Companies (Forms) Regulations 1985

Form No	*Presently prescribed by*	*Description*
224		*Revoked by 1996/594*
225[10]	1996/594[2]	Change of accounting reference date
225(1)		*Revoked by 1996/594*
225(2)		*Revoked by 1996/594*
242		*Revoked by 1990/572*
244	1990/572	Notice of claim to extension of period allowed for laying and delivering of accounts oversea business or interests
266(1)	1995/736	Notice of intention to carry on business as an investment company
266(3)	1995/736	Notice that company no longer wishes to be an investment company
287[11]	1995/736	Change in situation or address of Registered Office
287(I)	1998/1702	Change in situation or address of Registered office
288		*Revoked by 1995/736*
288a[12]	2002/691[3]	Appointment of director or secretary (pursuant to CA 1985, s 288(2))
288ab(I)	1998/1702	Resignation/appointment of director or secretary (pursuant to CA 1985, s 288(2))
288b[13]	1999/2356	Terminating appointment as director or secretary
288c[14]	2002/691[3]	Change of particulars for director or secretary (pursuant to CA 1985, s 288(2))
288c(I)	1998/1702	Change in the details of a director or secretary (pursuant to CA 1985, s 288(2))
318	1995/736	Location of directors' service contracts
325	1995/736	Location of register of directors' interests in shares etc (pursuant to CA 1985, s 325, Sch 13, para 27)
353	1995/736	Register of members
362[1]	1985/854; amended by 1987/752	Notice of place where an overseas branch register is kept, of any change in that place, or of discontinuance of any such register (pursuant to CA 1985, s 362, Sch 14, para 1)
363[15]		*Revoked by 1990/1766*
363a	2002/691[3]	Annual return
363b		*Revoked by 1999/2356*
363s[16]	2002/691[3]	Annual return declaration
386		*Replaced by Form 391*
391	1995/736	Notice of passing of resolution removing an auditor (replacing Form 386)
395	1985/854	Particulars of mortgage or charge
397	1985/854	Particulars for the registration of a charge to secure a series of debentures (pursuant to CA 1985, s 397)

Companies (Forms) Regulations 1985

Form No	*Presently prescribed by*	*Description*
397a	1985/854	Particulars of an issue of secured debentures in a series
398	1985/854	Certificate of registration in Scotland or Northern Ireland of a charge comprising property situate there
400[1]	1985/854; amended by 1987/752	Particulars of a mortgage or charge subject to which property has been acquired
401	1985/854	Register of charges, memoranda of satisfaction and appointments and cessation of receivers
403a[1]	1985/854; amended by 1987/752	Declaration of satisfaction in full or in part of mortgage or charge (pursuant to CA 1985, s 403(1))
403b[1]	1985/854; amended by 1987/752	Declaration that part of the property or undertaking charged (a) has been released from the charge; (b) no longer forms part of the company's property or undertaking (pursuant to CA 1985, s 403(1)(b))
405(1)	1985/854	Notice of appointment of receiver or manager
405(2)	1985/854	Notice of ceasing to act as receiver or manager
410 Scot	1985/854	Particulars of a charge created by a company registered in Scotland
413 Scot	1985/854	Particulars for the registration of a charge to secure a series of debentures (note 1)
413a Scot	1985/854	Particulars of an issue of Debentures out of a series of secured Debentures (note 1)
416 Scot[1]	1985/854; amended by 1987/752	Particulars of a charge subject to which property has been acquired by a company registered in Scotland
417 Scot	1985/854	Register of charges etc
419a Scot[1]	1985/854; amended by 1987/752	Application for registration of a memorandum of satisfaction in full or in part of a registered charge
419b Scot[1]	1985/854; amended by 1987/752	Application for registration of a memorandum of fact that part of the property charged (a) has been released from the charge; (b) no longer forms part of the company's property
428		*Revoked by 1987/752*[24]
429(2)		*Revoked by 1987/752*[24]
429(3)		*Revoked by 1987/752*[24]
429(4)		*See 980(1) below*
429dec		*See 980dec below*
430A		*See 984 below*
466 Scot	1985/854	Particulars of an instrument of alteration to a floating charge created by a company registered in Scotland
469 Scot		*Revoked by 1986/2097*

APPENDICES

Companies (Forms) Regulations 1985

Form No	*Presently prescribed by*	*Description*
470 Scot		*Revoked by 1986/2097*
478 Scot		*Revoked by 1986/2097*
481 Scot		*Revoked by 1986/2097*
482 Scot		*Revoked by 1986/2097*
495(2)(a)		*Revoked by 1986/2097*
495(3)a		*Revoked by 1986/2097*
495(3)b		*Revoked by 1986/2097*
497		*Revoked by 1986/2097*
600	1987/752	Notice of appointment of liquidator; voluntary winding up (Members or Creditors) (pursuant to IA 1986, s 109)
600a	1987/752	Notice of appointment of liquidator; voluntary winding up (Members or Creditors) (pursuant to IA 1986, s 109)
652a[17]	1995/1479	Application for striking off
652c[18]	1995/1479	Withdrawal of application for striking off (for the purposes of Companies Act 1985, s 652D)
680a	1985/854	Application by joint stock company for registration under Part XXII of the Companies Act 1985, and Declaration and related statements (pursuant to CA 1985, ss 680, 681, 684, 685, 686(2))
680b	1985/854	Application by a company which is not a joint stock company for registration under Part XXII of the Companies Act 1985, and Declaration and related statements (pursuant to CA 1985, ss 680, 681, 686)
684	1985/854	Registration under Part XXII of the Companies Act 1985: List of members—existing joint stock company (pursuant to CA 1985, s 684(1)(b))
685	1985/854	Declaration on application by a joint stock company for registration as a public company (pursuant to CA 1985, s 685(4)(e))
686	1985/854	Registration under Part XXII of the Companies Act 1985: Statutory Declaration verifying list of members (pursuant to CA 1985, s 686(2))
691	2002/691[3]	Return and declaration delivered for registration of a place of business of an oversea company
692(1)(a)	1985/854	Return of alteration in the charter, statutes, etc of an oversea company
692(1)(b)	2002/691[3]	Return of alteration in the directors or secretary of an oversea company or in their particulars

Companies (Forms) Regulations 1985

Form No	Presently prescribed by	Description
692(1)(c)	1985/854	Return of alteration in the names or addresses of persons resident in Great Britain authorised to accept service on behalf of an oversea company
692(2)	1985/854	Return of change in the corporate name of an oversea company
694(a)		*Replaced by Form 694(4)(a)*
694(b)		*Replaced by Form 694(4)(b)*
694(4)(a)	1992/3006	Statement of name, other than corporate name, under which an oversea company proposes to carry on business in Great Britain
694(4)(b)	1992/3006	Statement of name, other than corporate name, under which an oversea company proposes to carry on business in Great Britain in substitution for a name previously registered
701(2)		*Revoked by 1990/572*
701(6)a		*Revoked by 1990/572*
701(6)b		*Revoked by 1990/572*
701a		*Revoked by 1996/594*
701b		*Revoked by 1996/594*
701c		*Revoked by 1996/594*
703P(1)	1992/3006	Return by an oversea company that the company is being wound up
703P(3)	1992/3006	Notice of appointment of a liquidator of an oversea company
703P(5)	1992/3006	Notice by the liquidator of an oversea company concerning the termination of liquidation of the company
703Q(1)	1992/3006	Return by an oversea company which becomes subject to insolvency proceedings, etc
703Q(2)	1992/3006	Return by an oversea company on cessation of insolvency proceedings, etc
723SR[19]	2002/691	Notification of particulars of usual residential address by director who has obtained a confidentiality order
723 (change)[20]	2002/691	Notification of change in usual residential address by director who has obtained a confidentiality order
980(1)[23]	1987/752; amended by 2007/1093	Notice to non-assenting shareholders
980dec[23]	1987/752; amended by 2007/1093	Statutory Declaration relating to a notice to non-assenting shareholders
984[23]	1987/752; amended by 2007/1093	Notice to non-assenting shareholders
BR 1	2002/691[3]	Return delivered for registration of a branch of an oversea company (pursuant to CA 1985, Sch 21A, para 1)

APPENDICES

Companies (Forms) Regulations 1985

Form No	*Presently prescribed by*	*Description*
BR 2	1992/3006	Return by an oversea company subject to branch registration of an alteration to constitutional documents (pursuant to CA 1985, Sch 21A, para 7(1))
BR 3	1992/3006	Return by an oversea company subject to branch registration, for alteration of company particulars (pursuant to CA 1985, Sch 21A, para 7(1))
BR 4	2002/691[3]	Return by an oversea company subject to branch registration of change of directors or secretary or of their particulars (pursuant to CA 1985, Sch 21A, para 7(1))
BR 5	1992/3006	Return by an oversea company subject to branch registration of change of address or other branch particulars (pursuant to CA 1985, Sch 21A, para 7(1))
BR 6	2002/691[3]	Return of change of person authorised to accept service or to represent the branch of an oversea company or of any change in their particulars (pursuant to CA 1985, Sch 21A, para 7(1))
BR 7	1992/3006	Return by an oversea company of the branch at which the constitutional documents of the company have been registered in substitution for a previous branch (pursuant to CA 1985, Sch 21A, para 8(2))
R 7	1985/854	Application by an old public company for re-registration as a public company (pursuant to Companies Consolidation (Consequential Provisions) Act 1985, s 2(1))
R 7a[1]	1985/854; amended by 1987/752	Notice of application made to the Court for the cancellation of a special resolution by an old public company not to be re-registered as a public company (pursuant to Companies Consolidation (Consequential Provisions) Act 1985, s 4(1))
R 8	1985/854	Declaration by director or secretary on application by an old public company for re-registration as a public company (pursuant to Companies Consolidation (Consequential Provisions) Act 1985, s 2(4)(b))
R 9	1985/854	Declaration by old public company that it does not meet the requirements for a public company (pursuant to Companies Consolidation (Consequential Provisions) Act 1985, s 4)

NOTES

[1] Forms amended by SI 1987/752 may continue to be used in their unamended form if they are signed, or in the case of a statutory declaration made, by a person holding the office stated in the description of the signatory, or person making the declaration, given on those Forms.

2 Form 225 is prescribed for the purposes of s 225 including that section as applied by s 701.

3 Notwithstanding the prescription of new forms by SI 2002/691, the forms in use prior to the enactment of SI 2002/691 shall remain in use as alternatives to the forms prescribed by those Regulations, save that, the forms prescribed by the 2002 Regulations must be used where the director of a company in question is the beneficiary of a confidentiality order made under CA 1985, s 723B.

4 Welsh equivalent Form 10CYM prescribed by SI 2003/62. The 2003 Regulations also provide that the original form prescribed by SI 1995/734 may be used as an alternative in all circumstances except where the director of a company in question is the beneficiary of a confidentiality order made under CA 1985, s 723B.

5 Welsh equivalent Form 12CYM prescribed by SI 1995/1508.

6 Welsh equivalent Form 30(5)(a)CYM prescribed by SI 1995/1508.

7 Welsh equivalent Form 30(5)(b)CYM prescribed by SI 1995/1508.

8 Welsh equivalent Form 30(5)(c)CYM prescribed by SI 1995/1508.

9 Welsh equivalent Form 88(2)CYM (Rev 2005) prescribed by SI 2005/2746 to be used in relation to allotments of shares made on or after 1 December 2003. Form 88(2) CYM prescribed by SI 1999/2679 continues to be prescribed in relation to allotments made before 1 December 2003. It may also be used for returns made before 31 October 2006 in relation to allotments made on or after 1 December 2003.

10 Welsh equivalent Form 225CYM prescribed by SI 1996/595 (prescribed also for the purposes of CA 1985, s 225 as applied by s 701 thereof).

11 Welsh equivalent Form 287CYM prescribed by SI 1995/734.

12 Welsh equivalent Form 288aCYM prescribed by SI 2003/62. Alternative Welsh Form 288aCYM prescribed by SI 1995/734 may still be used except in the circumstances detailed in footnote 4 above.

13 Welsh equivalent Form 288bCYM prescribed by SI 1999/2357.

14 Welsh equivalent Form 288cCYM prescribed by SI 2003/62. Alternative Welsh Form 288cCYM prescribed by SI 1995/734 may still be used except in the circumstances detailed in footnote 4 above.

15 Welsh equivalent Form 363CYM prescribed by SI 2003/62. Alternative Welsh Form 363CYM prescribed by SI 1999/2357 may still be used except in the circumstances detailed in footnote 4 above.

16 Welsh equivalent Form 363sCYM prescribed by SI 2003/62. Alternative Welsh Form 363sCYM prescribed by SI 2000/2413 may still be used except in the circumstances detailed in footnote 4 above.

17 Welsh equivalent Form 652aCYM prescribed by SI 1995/1480.

18 Welsh equivalent Form 652cCYM prescribed by SI 1995/1480 (prescribed also for the purposes of CA 1985, s 652D(6)).

19 Welsh equivalent Form 723SRCYM prescribed by SI 2003/62.

20 Welsh equivalent Form 723(change)CYM prescribed by SI 2003/62.

21 SI 2003/2982 provides that form 169, prescribed by SI 1987/752 will apply only for the purposes of returns under CA 1985, s 169(1) and prescribes new forms for the purposes of returns under s 169(1B) and 169A(2).

22 Forms to be used in relation to allotments of shares made on or after 1 December 2003. The previous forms (Form 88(2) prescribed by SI 1999/2678 and Form 88(3) prescribed by SI 1985/854) continue to be prescribed in relation to allotments made before 1 December 2003. They may also be used for returns made before 31 October 2006 in relation to allotments made on or after 1 December 2003.

23 Forms 980(1), 980dec, 984 were originally forms 429(4), 429dec and 430(A) respectively. They were originally prescribed by SI 1987/752 and were renumbered (and amended) by SI 2007/1093 following the repeal of Part XIIIA of CA1985 (Takeovers) and its replacement by Part 28 (ss 942–992) of CA 2006.

24 The saving in SI 1987/752, reg 7 that the revoked forms 428, 429(2), 429(3) shall continue to be used in relation to an offer in respect of the scheme or contract mentioned in s 428(1) of this Act made before 30 April 1987, was itself revoked by SI 2007/1093, art 7, Sch 5, as from 6 April 2007.

INSOLVENCY RULES 1986, SI 1986/1925

NOTES

Made: 10 November 1986.

Authority: Insolvency Act 1986, ss 411, 412.

Commencement: 29 December 1986.

These Rules (in so far as relevant to this work) are reproduced at **[6060]** et seq. Sch 4 to the Rules sets out the forms to be used in insolvency proceedings (see r 12.7 at **[6541]**). The forms are not reproduced here but details are given in the table below. The forms have been amended as noted below.

APPENDICES

Insolvency Rules 1986		
Form No	*Description*	*Status*
	Part 1: Company Voluntary Arrangements	
1.1	Notice to registrar of companies of voluntary arrangement taking effect	Forms 1.1–1.19 substituted for Forms 1.1–1.4 by SI 2002/2712 (subject to transitional provisions)
1.2	Notice to registrar of companies of order of revocation or suspension of voluntary arrangement	Substituted as noted to Form 1.1
1.3	Notice to registrar of companies of supervisor's abstract of receipts and payments	Substituted as noted to Form 1.1
1.4	Notice to registrar of companies of completion or termination of voluntary arrangement	Substituted as noted to Form 1.1
1.5	Nominee's statement of opinion	Substituted as noted to Form 1.1
1.6	Statement of affairs	Substituted as noted to Form 1.1
1.7	Statement of eligibility for a moratorium	Substituted as noted to Form 1.1
1.8	Statement of consent to act by nominee	Substituted as noted to Form 1.1
1.9	Documents to be submitted to court to obtain moratorium	Substituted as noted to Form 1.1
1.10	Advertisement of coming into force or ending of moratorium	Substituted as noted to Form 1.1
1.11	Notice to registrar of companies of commencement of moratorium	Substituted as noted to Form 1.1
1.12	Notice to registrar of companies of extension or further extension or renewal or continuation of moratorium	Substituted as noted to Form 1.1
1.13	Notice to court of extension or further extension of moratorium	Substituted as noted to Form 1.1
1.14	Notice to the registrar of companies of ending of moratorium	Substituted as noted to Form 1.1
1.15	Nominee's notice to court of end of moratorium	Substituted as noted to Form 1.1
1.16	Notice to the registrar of companies of the withdrawal of nominee's consent to act	Substituted as noted to Form 1.1
1.17	Notice to court by nominee of withdrawal of consent to act	Substituted as noted to Form 1.1
1.18	Notice to the registrar of companies of the appointment of a replacement nominee	Substituted as noted to Form 1.1
1.19	Notice to court of appointment of replacement nominee	Substituted as noted to Form 1.1
	Part 2: Administration Procedure	
2.1B	Administration application	Forms 2.1B–2.40B substituted for Forms 2.1–2.23 by SI 2003/1730 (subject to transitional provisions as noted below). Amended by SI 2005/617

Insolvency Rules 1986

Form No	*Description*	*Status*
2.2B	Statement of proposed administrator	Substituted as noted to Form 2.1B
2.3B	Affidavit of service of administration application	Substituted as noted to Form 2.1B
2.4B	Administration order	Substituted as noted to Form 2.1B
2.5B	Notice of intention to appoint an administrator by holder of qualifying floating charge	Substituted as noted to Form 2.1B
2.6B	Notice of appointment of an administrator by holder of qualifying floating charge	Substituted as noted to Form 2.1B
2.7B	Notice of appointment of an administrator by holder of qualifying floating charge (For use in pursuance of Rule 2.19 of the Insolvency Rules 1986)	Substituted as noted to Form 2.1B
2.8B	Notice of Intention to Appoint an Administrator by Company or Director(s)	Substituted as noted to Form 2.1B; further substituted by SI 2004/584; further substituted by SI 2005/527
2.9B	Notice of Appointment of an Administrator by Company or Director(s)	Substituted as noted to Form 2.1B; further substituted by SI 2004/584
2.10B	Notice of appointment of an administrator by company or director(s) (where a notice of intention to appoint has not been issued)	Substituted as noted to Form 2.1B
2.11B	Notification of Appointment of Administrator (for Newspaper and London Gazette)	Substituted as noted to Form 2.1B; further substituted by SI 2004/584; further substituted by SI 2005/527
2.12B	Notice of administrator's appointment	Substituted as noted to Form 2.1B
2.13B	Notice requiring submission of a statement of affairs	Substituted as noted to Form 2.1B; further substituted by SI 2005/527
2.14B	Statement of affairs	Substituted as noted to Form 2.1B; further substituted by SI 2005/527
2.15B	Statement of concurrence	Substituted as noted to Form 2.1B
2.16B	Notice of statement of affairs	Substituted as noted to Form 2.1B
2.17B	Statement of administrator's proposals	Substituted as noted to Form 2.1B
2.18B	Notice of extension of time period	Substituted as noted to Form 2.1B
2.19B	Notice to attend meeting of creditors	Substituted as noted to Form 2.1B
2.20B	Notice of a meeting of creditors	Substituted as noted to Form 2.1B
2.21B	Creditor's request for a meeting	Substituted as noted to Form 2.1B
2.22B	Statement of administrator's revised proposals	Substituted as noted to Form 2.1B
2.23B	Notice of result of meeting of creditors	Substituted as noted to Form 2.1B
2.24B	Administrator's progress report	Substituted as noted to Form 2.1B

APPENDICES

Insolvency Rules 1986

Form No	*Description*	*Status*
2.25B	Notification of Conduct of Business by Correspondence	Substituted as noted to Form 2.1B; further substituted by SI 2004/584
2.26B	[Amended] Certificate of constitution of creditors' committee	Substituted as noted to Form 2.1B
2.27B	Notice by administrator of a change in committee membership	Substituted as noted to Form 2.1B
2.28B	Notice of order to deal with charged property	Substituted as noted to Form 2.1B
2.29B	Affidavit of debt	Substituted as noted to Form 2.1B
2.30B	Notice of automatic end of administration	Substituted as noted to Form 2.1B
2.31B	Notice of extension of period of administration	Substituted as noted to Form 2.1B
2.32B	Notice of end of administration	Substituted as noted to Form 2.1B
2.33B	Notice of court order ending administration	Substituted as noted to Form 2.1B
2.34B	Notice of move from administration to creditors' voluntary liquidation	Substituted as noted to Form 2.1B
2.35B	Notice of move from administration to dissolution	Substituted as noted to Form 2.1B
2.36B	Notice to registrar of companies in respect of date of dissolution	Substituted as noted to Form 2.1B
2.37B	Notice of intention to resign as administrator	Substituted as noted to Form 2.1B
2.38B	Notice of resignation by administrator	Substituted as noted to Form 2.1B
2.39B	Notice of vacation of office by administrator	Substituted as noted to Form 2.1B
2.40B	Notice of appointment of replacement/ additional administrator	Substituted as noted to Form 2.1B
	Part 3: Administrative Receivership	
3.1	Written acceptance of appointment by receiver	Inserted by SI 1987/1919
3.1A	Notice of appointment of administrative receiver (for newspaper or London Gazette)	Inserted by SI 1987/1919; substituted by SI 2005/527
3.1B	Notice requiring preparation and submission of administrative receivership statement of affairs	Substituted by SI 1987/1919 (for original Form 3.1)
3.2	Statement of affairs	Substituted by SI 2003/1730 (subject to transitional provisions as noted below); further substituted by SI 2005/527
3.3	Statement of affairs in administrative receivership following report to creditors	
3.4	Certificate of constitution [amended certificate] of creditors' committee	

Insolvency Rules 1986

Form No	*Description*	*Status*
3.5	Administrative receiver's report as to change in membership of creditors' committee	
3.6	Receiver or manager or administrative receiver's abstract of receipts and payments	
3.7	Notice of administrative receiver's death	
3.8	Notice of order to dispose of charged property	
3.9	Notice of resignation of administrative receiver pursuant to the Insolvency Act 1986, s 45(1)	
3.10	Administrative receiver's report	
	Part 4: Companies Winding Up	
4.1	Statutory demand under the Insolvency Act 1986, s 123(1)(a) or 222(1)(a)	Substituted by SI 1987/1919
4.2	Winding-up petition	Substituted by SI 2002/1307
4.3	—	Revoked by SI 2005/527
4.4	Affidavit of service of winding-up petition at registered office	
4.5	Affidavit of service of winding-up petition other than at registered office or on an oversea company	
4.6	Advertisement of winding-up petition	Substituted by SI 2005/527
4.7	Certificate that relevant provisions of Rules have been complied with	
4.8	Order for leave to withdraw winding-up petition	
4.9	Notice of intention to appear on petition	
4.10	List of persons intending to appear on the hearing of the petition	
4.11	Order for winding up by the court	Substituted by SI 2002/1307; further substituted by SI 2005/527
4.12	Order for Winding Up by the Court Following Upon the Cessation of the Appointment of an Administrator	Substituted by SI 2003/1730 (subject to transitional provisions as noted below); further substituted by SI 2005/527
4.13	Notice to Official Receiver of Winding-up Order	Substituted by SI 1987/1919; further substituted by SI 2005/527
4.14	Petition by contributory	Substituted by SI 2002/1307; further substituted by SI 2005/527
4.14A	Notice to official receiver of appointment of provisional liquidator	Inserted by SI 1987/1919
4.15	Order of appointment of provisional liquidator	Substituted by SI 2002/1307
4.15A	Notice of appointment of provisional liquidator in winding up by the court	Inserted by SI 2005/527

APPENDICES

Insolvency Rules 1986

Form No	*Description*	*Status*
4.16	Notice requiring preparation and submission of statement of company's affairs	Substituted by SI 1987/1919
4.17	Statement of Affairs	Substituted by SI 2003/1730 (subject to transitional provisions as noted below); further substituted by SI 2005/527
4.18	Statement of Affairs	Substituted by SI 2003/1730 (subject to transitional provisions as noted below); further substituted by SI 2005/527
4.19	Statement of Affairs	Substituted by SI 2003/1730 (subject to transitional provisions as noted below); further substituted by SI 2005/527
4.20	Statement of affairs under s 95/s 99 to registrar of companies	
4.21	Request by creditors for a meeting of the company's creditors [and contributories]	
4.22	Notice to creditors of meeting of creditors	
4.23	Notice to contributories of meeting of contributories	
4.24	Request by contributory/contributories for a meeting of the company's contributories	
4.25	Proof of debt—general form	Substituted by SI 2004/584
4.26	Affidavit of debt	
4.27	Certificate of appointment of liquidator by meeting	
4.28	Certificate of appointment of two or more liquidators by meeting	
4.29	Order of court appointing liquidator	
4.30	Order of court appointing two or more liquidators	
4.31	Notice of appointment of liquidator in winding up by the court (for registrar of companies)	
4.32	Notice to court of resignation of liquidator following meeting of creditors	Substituted by SI 1987/1919
4.33	Notice of resignation as voluntary liquidator under the Insolvency Act 1986, s 171(5)	
4.34	Order of court giving liquidator leave to resign	
4.35	Order of court granting voluntary liquidator leave to resign	
4.36	Notice to court of resignation of liquidator following leave of the court	

Insolvency Rules 1986

Form No	*Description*	*Status*
4.37	Certificate of removal of liquidator	
4.38	Certificate of removal of voluntary liquidator	
4.39	Order of court removing liquidator or directing liquidator to summon a meeting of creditors for purpose of his removal	
4.40	Notice of ceasing to act as voluntary liquidator	
4.41	Liquidator's application to the Secretary of State for his release	
4.42	Notice to court of final meeting of creditors	
4.43	Notice to registrar of companies of final meeting of creditors	
4.44	Notice of death of liquidator	
4.45	Notice to official receiver or Secretary of State by liquidator on loss of qualification as insolvency practitioner	
4.46	Notice of vacation of office by voluntary liquidator	
4.47	Certificate of constitution [amended certificate] of liquidation committee	
4.48	Notice of constitution of liquidation committee	
4.49	Report by liquidator of any change in membership of liquidation committee	
4.50	Liquidator's certificate that creditors paid in full	
4.51	Certificate that creditors have been paid in full	
4.52	Liquidator's certificate of continuance of liquidation committee	Substituted by SI 2003/1730 (subject to transitional provisions as noted below)
4.53	Notice of disclaimer under the Insolvency Act 1986, s 178	Substituted by SI 1987/1919
4.54	Notice to elect	
4.55	Notice of intended disclaimer to interested party	
4.56	Affidavit of liquidator in support of application for call	
4.57	Order giving leave to make a call	
4.58	Notice of call sanctioned by the court or the liquidation committee to be sent to contributory	
4.59	Order for payment of call due from contributory	
4.60	Order of appointment of special manager	

APPENDICES

Insolvency Rules 1986

Form No	*Description*	*Status*
4.61	Order of public examination	Substituted by SI 1987/1919
4.62	Notice to official receiver by creditor requesting him to make application for the holding of a public examination	
4.63	Notice to official receiver by contributory requesting him to make application for the holding of a public examination	
4.64	Order as to examination of person who lacks capacity to manage and administer his property and affairs or is suffering from mental disorder or physical affliction or disability	Substituted by SI 2007/1898
4.65	Affidavit of verification of record of the public examination	
4.66	Order of adjournment of public examination	Substituted by SI 1987/1919
4.67	Order appointing time for proceeding with public examination adjourned generally	Substituted by SI 1987/1919
4.68	Liquidator's Statement of Receipts and Payments	Substituted by SI 1987/1919; further substituted by SI 2005/527
4.69	Order of court on appeal against Secretary of State's decision under the Insolvency Act 1986, s 203(4) or 205(4)	
4.70	Members' voluntary winding up declaration of solvency embodying a statement of assets and liabilities	Substituted by SI 1987/1919
4.71	Return of final meeting in a members' voluntary winding up	Amended by SI 1991/495
4.72	Return of final meeting in creditors' voluntary winding up	Amended by SI 1991/495
	Part 7: Court Procedure and Practice	
7.1	Originating application	
7.2	Ordinary application	
7.3	Declaration by official shorthand writer	
7.4	Appointment of shorthand writer to take examination under the Insolvency Act 1986	
7.5	Declaration by shorthand writer	
7.6	Warrant for failure to attend examination under the Insolvency Act 1986, s 133	
7.7	Warrant of arrest etc under the Insolvency Act 1986, s 364	
7.8	Warrant of arrest etc under the Insolvency Act 1986, s 236 or 366	

Insolvency Rules 1986

Form No	*Description*	*Status*
7.9	Order for production of person arrested under warrant issued under the Insolvency Act 1986, s 134, 236, 364 or 366	Substituted by SI 1987/1919
7.10	Warrant to registrar of court in whose district a person against whom a warrant of arrest has been issued is believed to be	
7.11	Endorsement of warrant of arrest issued by a court to which the same has been sent for execution by the court which originally issued it	
7.12	Warrant of seizure of property under the Insolvency Act 1986, s 365	
7.13	Search warrant under the Insolvency Act 1986, s 365	
7.14	Order of discharge from custody under the Insolvency Act 1986 [General]	
7.15	Affidavit in support of application for committal for contempt of court	Substituted by SI 1987/1919
7.16	—	Revoked by SI 1987/1919
7.17	Warrant of committal for contempt	Amended by SI 1993/602
7.18	Order of discharge from custody for contempt	
7.19	Order appointing person to act for incapacitated person	
7.20	Application, affidavit and order confirming creditors' voluntary winding up	Inserted by SI 2002/1307
	Part 8: Proxies and Company Representation	
8.1	Proxy—company or individual voluntary arrangements	
8.2	Proxy—administration	
8.3	Proxy—administrative receivership	
8.4	Proxy—winding up by the court or bankruptcy	
8.5	Proxy—members' or creditors' voluntary winding up	
	Part 9: Examination of Persons Concerned in Company and Individual Insolvency	
9.1	Order under the Insolvency Act 1986, s 236 or 366	
	Part 12: Miscellaneous and General	
12.1	Notice to the Registrar of Companies in respect of order under section 176A	Inserted by SI 2003/1730 (subject to transitional provisions as noted below)

APPENDICES

NOTES

The substitution of Forms 2.1B–2.40B (for original Forms 2.1–2.23), the substitution of Forms 3.2, 4.12, 4.17, 4.18, 4.19, 4.52, and the insertion of Form 12.1, by SI 2003/1730, are subject to transitional provisions and savings (see the note preceding r 2.1 of these Rules at **[6097]**).

EUROPEAN ECONOMIC INTEREST GROUPINGS REGULATIONS 1989, SI 1989/638

NOTES

Made: 10 April 1989.
Authority: European Communities Act 1972, s 2(2).
Commencement: 1 July 1989.

These Regulations are reproduced at **[6602]** et seq. Sch 2 to the Regulations sets out the forms to be used in connection with the Regulations. The forms are not reproduced here but details are given in the table below.

As of 1 July 2007, the Forms in Sch 2 had not been amended.

By SI 1989/638, reg 2, "EEIG" means a European Economic Interest Grouping being a grouping formed in pursuance of Council Regulation (EEC) No 2137/85 (at **[9001]** et seq).

European Economic Interest Groupings Regulations 1989

Form No	*Description*
EEIG 1	Statement of name, official address, members, objects and duration for EEIG whose official address is in Great Britain
EEIG 2	Statement of name, establishment address in Great Britain and members of an EEIG whose official address is outside the UK
EEIG 3	Notice of manager's particulars, and of termination of appointment where the official address of the EEIG is in Great Britain
EEIG 4	Notice of documents and particulars required to be filed
EEIG 5	Notice of setting up or closure of an establishment of an EEIG
EEIG 6	Statement of name, other than registered name, under which an EEIG whose official address is outside Great Britain proposes to carry on business in Great Britain
EEIG 7	Statement of name, other than registered name, under which an EEIG whose official address is outside Great Britain proposes to carry on business in substitution for name previously approved

INSOLVENT COMPANIES (REPORTS ON CONDUCT OF DIRECTORS) RULES 1996, SI 1996/1909

NOTES

Made: 22 July 1996.
Authority: Insolvency Act 1986, s 411; Company Directors Disqualification Act 1986, s 21(2).
Commencement: 30 September 1996.

These Rules are reproduced at **[6916]** et seq. The Schedule to the Rules sets out the forms referred to in rr 3(2) and 4(3) (see r 5 at **[6919]**). The forms are not reproduced here but details are given in the table below. The forms have been amended as noted below.

By SI 1996/1909, r 1, the "1986 Act" means the Company Directors Disqualification Act 1986, and the "Rules" means the Insolvent Companies (Reports on Conduct of Directors) Rules 1996, SI 1996/1909.

Insolvent Companies (Reports on Conduct of Directors) Rules 1996

Form No	*Description*	*Status*
D1	Report under s 7(3) of the 1986 Act	Substituted by SI 2001/764
D2	Return by Office-holder under r 4 of the Rules	Substituted by SI 2001/764

LIMITED LIABILITY PARTNERSHIPS (FORMS) REGULATIONS 2001, SI 2001/927

NOTES

Made: 9 March 2001.

Authority: CA 1985, ss 190, 225, 244, 363, 391, 395, 397, 398, 400, 401, 403, 405, 410, 413, 416, 417, 419, 466, 652A, 652D.

Commencement: 6 April 2001.

These Regulations set out the forms (listed in the first table below) to be used for the purposes of the specified provisions of CA 1985 by limited liability partnerships, with such variations as the circumstances require. The Regulations also provide that the particulars or information contained in the forms listed in the second table below are the particulars or information prescribed for the purposes of the specified provisions of the 1985 Act.

As of 1 July 2007, these Regulations had not been amended.

In these Regulations, references to a section or to a numbered section are to a section of CA 1985 as applied to limited liability partnerships by the Limited Liability Partnerships Regulations 2001, SI 2001/1090, regs 3, 4.

Limited Liability Partnerships (Forms) Regulations 2001

Form No	*Section*	*Description*
LLP190	190	Location of register of debenture holders of a Limited Liability Partnership
LLP225	225	Change of accounting reference date of a Limited Liability Partnership
LLP244	244	Notice of extension of accounts delivery period of a Limited Liability Partnership
LLP363[1]	363	Annual return of a Limited Liability Partnership
LLP391	391	Notice of removal of auditor from a Limited Liability Partnership
LLP395	395	Particulars of a charge in respect of a Limited Liability Partnership
LLP397	397	Particulars for the registration of a charge to secure a series of debentures in respect of a Limited Liability Partnership
LLP397a	397	Particulars of an issue of secured debentures in a series in respect of a Limited Liability Partnership
LLP398	398	Limited Liability Partnership: Certificate of registration in Scotland or Northern Ireland of a charge comprising property situated there
LLP400	400	Particulars of a mortgage or charge on a property that has been acquired by a Limited Liability Partnership
LLP401	401	Register of charges, memoranda of satisfaction and appointments and cessations of receivers
LLP403a	403	Limited Liability Partnership: Declaration of satisfaction in full or part of mortgage or charge
LLP403b	403	Declaration that part of the property or undertaking charged (a) has been released from the charge; (b) no longer forms part of the limited liability partnership's property or undertaking
LLP405(1)	405	Notice of appointment of receiver or manager in respect of a Limited Liability Partnership
LLP405(2)	405	Notice of ceasing to act as receiver or manager in respect of a Limited Liability Partnership
LLP410(Scot)	410	Particulars of a charge created by a Limited Liability Partnership registered in Scotland

APPENDICES

Limited Liability Partnerships (Forms) Regulations 2001

Form No	*Section*	*Description*
LLP413(Scot)	413	Particulars for the registration of a charge to secure a series of debentures in respect of a Limited Liability Partnership
LLP413a(Scot)	413	Particulars of an issue of debentures out of a series of secured debentures in respect of a Limited Liability Partnership
LLP416(Scot)	416	Particulars of a charge subject to which property has been acquired by a Limited Liability Partnership registered in Scotland
LLP417(Scot)	417	Register of charges, memoranda of satisfaction and appointments and cessations of receivers
LLP419a(Scot)	419	Limited Liability Partnership: Memorandum of satisfaction in full or part of a registered charge
LLP419b(Scot)	419	Limited Liability Partnership: Memorandum of fact that a part of a property charged (a) has been released from the charge; (b) no longer forms part of the LLP's property
LLP466(Scot)	466	Particulars of an instrument of alteration to a floating charge created by a Limited Liability Partnership registered in Scotland
LLP652a	652A	Application for striking off a Limited Liability Partnership
LLP652c	652D	Withdrawal of application for voluntary strike off a Limited Liability Partnership

Prescribed particulars or information

Form	*Section*
LLP395	395
LLP397	397
LLP397a	397
LLP400	400
LLP401	401
LLP410 (Scot)	410
LLP413	413
LLP413a	413
LLP416	416
LLP417	417
LLP466	466
LLP625a	625A

NOTES

[1] The Limited Liability Partnerships (Forms) Regulations 2002, SI 2002/690 which come into force on 2 April 2002 prescribe a new Form LLP363. The new form is prescribed as an alternative which may be used in any circumstances but which must be used where a member of a limited liability partnership is the beneficiary of a confidentiality order made under CA 1985, s 723B, as applied to limited liability partnerships (see SI 2002/690, *post*).

Wales: the Limited Liability Partnerships (Welsh Language Forms) Regulations 2001, SI 2001/2917 (made under CA 1985, ss 225, 363, 652A, 652D, and in force on 17 September 2001) prescribe forms that correspond to those prescribed by SI 2001/927 and are in Welsh as well as English. See also the Limited Liability Partnerships (Welsh Language Forms) Regulations 2003, SI 2003/61 (details of which are given in the note to SI 2002/690, *post*).

COMPANIES (DISQUALIFICATION ORDERS) REGULATIONS 2001, SI 2001/967

NOTES

Made: 13 March 2001.

Authority: Company Directors Disqualification Act 1986, s 18.

Commencement: 6 April 2001.

These Regulations revoke and replace the Companies (Disqualification Orders) Regulations 1986 (SI 1986/2067) and are set out at **[6981A]**. Details of the forms are given in the table below. Note that the Companies (Disqualification Orders) (Amendment No 2) Regulations 2002, SI 2002/1834 (which came into force on 17 July 2002 and apply in relation to a disqualification order made after that date) prescribe a new Form DO1 to be added to these Regulations. The new form is added as an alternative which may be used in any circumstances but which must be used where the director of a company or member of a limited liability partnership in question is the beneficiary of a confidentiality order made under CA 1985, s 723B. Other than mentioned above, these Forms have not been amended.

Companies (Disqualification Orders) Regulations 2001

Form No	*Description*
DO1	Disqualification order against an individual
DO2	Disqualification order against a body corporate
DO3	Grant of leave in relation to a disqualification order
DO4	Variation or cessation of a disqualification order

LIMITED LIABILITY PARTNERSHIPS (FORMS) REGULATIONS 2002, SI 2002/690

NOTES

Made: 7 March 2002.

Authority: CA 1985, ss 363, 288A, 706.

Commencement: 2 April 2002.

These Regulations prescribe the forms (listed in the table below) to be used for the purposes of the specified provisions of CA 1985 by a member of a limited liability partnership who is the beneficiary of a confidentiality order made under the CA 1985, s 723B (as applied to limited liability partnerships and with such variations as the circumstances require).

As of 1 July 2007, these Regulations had not been amended.

Limited Liability Partnerships (Forms) Regulations 2002

Form No	*Description*
723SR	For the purpose of the notification to the registrar of a usual residential address as required by CA 1985, s 288A in respect of a member of a limited liability partnership who is a beneficiary of a confidentiality order made under s 723B of the 1985 Act.
723(change)	For the purpose of the notification to the registrar of a change in a usual residential address.
LLP 363[1]	For the purpose of the annual return of a limited liability partnership required by the Companies Act 1985, s 363.

NOTES

[1] Form LLP363 which was prescribed by the Limited Liability Partnerships (Forms) Regulations 2001, SI 2001/927, *ante*, shall remain in use as an alternative to the Form LLP363 prescribed by these Regulations, save that the new Form LLP363 must be used where a member

APPENDICES

of a limited liability partnership is the beneficiary of a confidentiality order made under the CA 1985, s 723B, as applied to limited liability partnerships.

Wales: the Limited Liability Partnerships (Welsh Language Forms) Regulations 2003, SI 2003/61 (made under CA 1985, ss 288A, 363(2), and in force on 27 January 2003) prescribe Welsh language alternatives of the forms prescribed by these Regulations.

EUROPEAN PUBLIC LIMITED-LIABILITY COMPANY REGULATIONS 2004, SI 2004/2326

NOTES

Made: 6 September 2004.
Authority: European Communities Act 1972, s 2(2).
Commencement: 8 October 2004.

These Regulations are reproduced at **[7249]** et seq. Sch 1 to the Regulations sets out the forms prescribed for use in connection with the formation, etc of Societas Europaea. The forms are not reproduced here but their numbers and titles are given in the table below.

As of 1 July 2007, the Forms in Sch 1 had not been amended.

European Public Limited-Liability Company Regulations 2004

Form No	*Title*
SE5	Formation by merger of Societas Europaea (SE) to be registered in GB
SE6	Formation of holding Societas Europaea (SE)
SE7	Formation of subsidiary Societas Europaea (SE) under Article 2(3) of Council Regulation (EC) No 2157/2001
SE8	Transformation of PLC to Societas Europaea (SE)
SE9(1)	Formation of subsidiary Societas Europaea (SE) under Article 3(2) of Council Regulation (EC) No 2157/2001
SE10	Transfer to GB of Societas Europaea (SE)
SE11	Transfer from GB of Societas Europaea (SE)
SE68(1)(a)	Proposed transfer from GB of Societas Europaea (SE)
SE68(2)(a)	Draft terms of formation of holding Societas Europaea (SE) involving a GB Registered Company or SE
SE68(3)(a)	Draft terms of conversion of PLC to Societas Europaea (SE)
SE70(1)	Notice of satisfaction of conditions for the formation of holding Societas Europaea (SE) by a GB Registered Company or SE
SE72(6)	Statement of solvency by members of Societas Europaea (SE) which is proposing to transfer from GB
SE79A	Appointment of a member of a supervisory organ of Societas Europaea (SE)
SE79B	Terminating appointment of a member of a supervisory organ of Societas Europaea (SE)
SE79C	Change of particulars of a member of a supervisory organ of Societas Europaea (SE)
SE82(1)(a)	Amendment of Statutes of Societas Europaea (SE)
SE82(1)(b)	Notice of initiation or termination of winding-up, liquidation, insolvency or cessation of payment procedures and decision to continue operating of Societas Europaea (SE)
SE85	Conversion of Societas Europaea (SE) to PLC
SE86	Notification of draft terms of conversion of Societas Europaea (SE) to PLC
SE(SR)	Usual Residential Addresses: Notification of details of usual residential address following grant of confidentiality order

European Public Limited-Liability Company Regulations 2004

Form No	*Title*
SE(SR)change	Usual Residential Addresses: Notification of change of usual residential address

CROSS-BORDER INSOLVENCY REGULATIONS 2006, SI 2006/1030

NOTES

These Regulations have been omitted from this Edition of the *Company Law Handbook* in order to create space for other legislation (ie, the Companies Act 2006 and the associated destination and derivation tables). They were printed in full in the 20th Edition of this work and, as of 1 July 2007, they had not been amended since the publication of that Edition. These Regulations are, however, included in the CD version of this work (which may be ordered from the LexisNexis Butterworths Customer Services Department) and can be accessed in the online version of the *Company Law Handbook* which is updated fortnightly (at www.lexisnexis.com/uk/legal).

[A4]

Appendix 5: Statutory Instruments made under FSMA 2000

NOTES

This table lists all statutory instruments made under the Financial Services and Markets Act 2000 that are of general UK application. Statutory instruments applying to Northern Ireland only are not listed. Statutory instruments that are no longer in force are printed in italics.

2007 Statutory Instruments
SI 2007/1821: Financial Services and Markets Act 2000 (Exemption) (Amendment No 2) Order 2007 Authority: FSMA 2000, ss 38, 428(3). This Order amends the Financial Services and Markets Act 2000 (Exemption) Order 2001, SI 2001/1201 (at **[4149]**). The Order provides certain exemptions for 'Invest Northern Ireland', freight forwarder and storage firms, and policyholder advocates
SI 2007/1339: Financial Services and Markets Act 2000 (Regulated Activities) (Amendment) Order 2007 Authority: FSMA 2000, ss 22(1), (5), 428(3), Sch 2, para 25. This Order amends the definition of "qualifying contracts of insurance" in art 2 of the RAO (at **[4003]**)
SI 2007/1083: Financial Services and Markets Act 2000 (Financial Promotion) (Amendment) Order 2007 Authority: FSMA 2000, s 21(5), (6). This Order substitutes the Financial Services and Markets Act 2000 (Financial Promotion) Order 2005, SI 2005/1529, Sch 3, Pt II at **[4804]** (list of certain investment exchanges operating relevant EEA markets)
SI 2007/800: Financial Services and Markets Act 2000 (Collective Investment Schemes) (Amendment) Order 2007 Authority: FSMA 2000, s 235(5). This Order amends the Schedule to the Financial Services Markets Act 2000 (Collective Investment Schemes) Order 2001, SI 2001/1062 (at **[4144]**) which sets out arrangements which are not to be regarded as collective investment schemes for the purposes of FSMA 2000. Paragraph 7 of that Schedule excludes certain funds relating to leasehold property. The amendment made by this Order extends this exclusion to arrangements where the participants have rights or interests in money held under a tenancy deposit scheme as provided for by Chapter 4 of Part 6 of the Housing Act 2004
SI 2007/763: Financial Services and Markets Act 2000 (Markets in Financial Instruments) (Amendment) Regulations 2007 Authority: FSMA 2000, ss 39(1), 349(1)–(3), 417(1), 428(3), Sch 3, para 22; European Communities Act 1972, s 2(2). These Regulations amend the Financial Services and Markets Act 2000 (Markets in Financial Instruments) Regulations 2007, SI 2007/126 (at **[7596]** et seq), the Financial Services and Markets Act 2000 (EEA Passport Rights) Regulations 2001, SI 2001/2511, reg 1 (at **[4448]**), and add the Financial Services and Markets Act 2000 (Appointed Representatives) Regulations 2001, SI 2001/1217, reg 4 (at **[4161A]**). They also make a consequential amendment to the Financial Services and Markets Act 2000 (Disclosure of Confidential Information) (Amendment) Regulations 2006, SI 2006/3413 (relating to the commencement of those Regulations). The Regulations implement, in part, Directive 2004/39/EC of the European Parliament and of the Council of 21 April 2004 on markets in financial instruments (MiFID)
SI 2007/383: Financial Services and Markets Act 2000 (Ombudsman Scheme) (Consumer Credit Jurisdiction) Order 2007 Authority: FSMA 2000, s 226A(2)(e). At **[4827]**. Section 226A of the 2000 Act was inserted by the Consumer Credit Act 2006. It provides that a complaint, relating to an act or omission of a licensee under a standard licence or a person authorised to carry on an activity by virtue of s 34A of the Consumer Credit Act 1974, qualifies to be dealt with under the financial ombudsman scheme if certain conditions are satisfied. One of the conditions is that at the time the act or omission occurs it has to have occurred in the course of a business of a type specified in an order made by the Secretary of State. This Order specifies the types of business for the purposes of section 226A(2)(e)
SI 2007/125: Financial Services and Markets Act 2000 (Exemption) (Amendment) Order 2007 Authority: FSMA 2000, ss 38, 428(3). This Order, which amends the Financial Services and Markets Act 2000 (Exemption) Order 2001, SI 2001/1201 at **[4149]**, implements, in part, Directive 2004/39/EC of the European Parliament and of the Council of 21 April 2004 on markets in financial instruments (MiFID)

2006 Statutory Instruments
SI 2006/3414: Financial Services and Markets Act 2000 (Appointed Representatives) (Amendment) Regulations 2006 Authority: FSMA 2000, ss 39(1), 417(1), 428(3). These Regulations, which amend the Financial Services and Markets Act 2000 (Appointed Representatives) Regulations 2001, SI 2001/1217 at **[4159]**, implement, in part, Directive 2004/39/EC of the European Parliament and of the Council of 21 April 2004 on markets in financial instruments (MiFID)
SI 2006/3413: Financial Services and Markets Act 2000 (Disclosure of Confidential Information) (Amendment) Regulations 2006 Authority: FSMA 2000, ss 349(1), (2), (3), 417(1), 428(3). These Regulations, which amend the Financial Services and Markets Act 2000 (Disclosure of Confidential Information) Regulations 2001, SI 2001/2188 at **[4372]**, implement, in part, Directive 2004/39/EC of the European Parliament and of the Council of 21 April 2004 on markets in financial instruments (MiFID)
SI 2006/3386: Financial Services and Markets Act 2000 (Recognition Requirements for Investment Exchanges and Clearing Houses) (Amendment) Regulations 2006 Authority: FSMA 2000, ss 286(1), (4A), (4B), (4C), (4D), 292(3)(a), 428(3). These Regulations amend the Financial Services and Markets Act 2000 (Recognition Requirements for Investment Exchanges and Clearing Houses) Regulations 2001, SI 2001/995. These Regulations implement, in part, Directive 2004/39/EC of the European Parliament and of the Council of 21 April 2004 on markets in financial instruments (MiFID)
SI 2006/3385: Financial Services and Markets Act 2000 (EEA Passport Rights) (Amendment) Regulations 2006 Authority: FSMA 2000, ss 428(3), Sch 3, paras 13(1)(b)(iii), 14(1)(b), 17(b), 22. These Regulations implement, in part, Directive 2004/39/EC of the European Parliament and of the Council on markets in financial instruments (MiFID). They amend the Financial Services and Markets Act 2000 (EEA Passport Rights) Regulations 2001, SI 2001/2511 at **[4448]**
SI 2006/3384: Financial Services and Markets Act 2000 (Regulated Activities) (Amendment No 3) Order 2006 Authority: FSMA 2000, ss 22(1), (5), 428(3), Sch 2, para 25. At **[4826A]**. This Order implements, in part, Directive 2004/39/EC of the European Parliament and of the Council on markets in financial instruments (MiFID). Part 2 of the Order amends the Financial Services and Markets Act 2000 (Regulated Activities) Order 2001, SI 2001/544. Parts 3 and 4 contain consequential amendments to other Acts and statutory instruments (including the Companies Act 1989, the Terrorism Act 2000, the Financial Services and Markets Act 2000 (Collective Investment Schemes) Order 2001, SI 2001/1062, the Financial Services and Markets Act 2000 (Carrying on Regulated Activities by Way of Business) Order 2001, SI 2001/1177, the Financial Services and Markets Act 2000 (Consultation with Competent Authorities) Regulations 2001, SI 2001/2509, the Money Laundering Regulations 2003, SI 2003/3075, and the Financial Services and Markets Act 2000 (Financial Promotion) Order 2005, SI 2005/1529)
SI 2006/3273: Lloyd's Sourcebook (Finance Act 1993 and Finance Act 1994) (Amendment) Order 2006 Authority: FSMA 2000, ss 417(1), 426(1). This Order substitutes references in the Finance Act 1993 and the Finance Act 1994 to the Lloyd's Sourcebook with references to the Insurance Prudential Sourcebook in consequence of the application of the latter Sourcebook to the operation of the market at Lloyd's. It revokes the Lloyd's Sourcebook (Amendment of the Finance Act 1993 and the Finance Act 1994) Order 2005, SI 2005/1538.
SI 2006/2383: Financial Services and Markets Act 2000 (Regulated Activities) (Amendment) (No 2) Order 2006 Authority: FSMA 2000, ss 22(1), (5), 426, 427, 428(3), Sch 2, para 25. At **[4820]**. This Order amends the Regulated Activities Order at **[4001]**. The effect of the Order is that the activities of entering into, administering, arranging and advising on regulated home reversion plans and regulated home purchase plans become regulated activities for the purposes of FSMA 2000. It also makes consequential amendments to primary legislation including CA 1985 and FSMA 2000 and various SIs made under FSMA 2000 (see **[4820]** et seq)

APPENDICES

2006 Statutory Instruments
SI 2006/1969: the Financial Services and Markets Act 2000 (Regulated Activities) (Amendment) Order 2006 Authority: FSMA 2000, ss 22(1), (5), 426, 427, 428(3), Sch 2, para 25. At **[4813]**. This Order amends the Regulated Activities Order at **[4001]**. The effect of the Order is that establishing, operating or winding up a personal pension scheme becomes a regulated activity for the purposes of FSMA 2000. It also makes consequential amendments to other SIs made under FSMA 2000 (see **[4813]** et seq)
SI 2006/1805: the Financial Services and Markets Act 2000 (Gibraltar) (Amendment) Order 2006 Authority: FSMA 2000, s 409(1). Amends the Financial Services and Markets Act 2000 (Gibraltar) Order 2001, SI 2001/3084 at **[4504]**
SI 2006/58: the Financial Services and Markets Act 2000 (Designated Professional Bodies) (Amendment) Order 2006 Authority: FSMA 2000, s 326. Amends the Financial Services and Markets Act 2000 (Designated Professional Bodies) Order 2001, SI 2001/1226 at **[4162]**

2005 Statutory Instruments
SI 2005/3392: Financial Services and Markets Act 2000 (Financial Promotion) (Amendment) Order 2005 Authority: FSMA 2000, ss 21(5), (6), 428(3). Amends the Financial Services and Markets Act 2000 (Financial Promotion) Order 2005, SI 2005/1529 at **[4717]**
SI 2005/3071: Financial Services and Markets Act 2000 (Disclosure of Confidential Information) (Amendment) Regulations 2005 Authority: FSMA 2000, ss 349(1)(b), (2), (3), 417(1). Amend the Financial Services and Markets Act 2000 (Disclosure of Confidential Information) Regulations 2001, SI 2001/2188 at **[4372]**
SI 2005/2967: Financial Services and Markets Act 2000 (Consequential Amendments) Order 2005 Authority: FSMA 2000, ss 426, 428(3). Amends the Consumer Credit Act 1974
SI 2005/1538: Lloyd's Sourcebook (Amendment of the Finance Act 1993 and the Finance Act 1994) Order 2005 Authority: FSMA 2000, ss 417(1), 426(1). Revoked by the Lloyd's Sourcebook (Finance Act 1993 and Finance Act 1994) (Amendment) Order 2006, SI 2006/3273
SI 2005/1532: Financial Services and Markets Act 2000 (Promotion of Collective Investment Schemes) (Exemptions) (Amendment) Order 2005 Authority: FSMA 2000, ss 238(6), (7), 428(3). Amends the Financial Services and Markets Act 2000 (Promotion of Collective Investment Schemes) (Exemptions) Order 2001, SI 2001/1060 at **[4112]**
SI 2005/1529: Financial Services and Markets Act 2000 (Financial Promotion) Order 2005 Authority: FSMA 2000, ss 21(5), (6), (9), (10), 428(3), Sch 2, para 25. At **[4717]**
SI 2005/1518: Financial Services and Markets Act 2000 (Regulated Activities) (Amendment) (No 2) Order 2005 Authority: FSMA 2000, ss 22(1), (5), 428(3), Sch 2, para 25. Amends the Financial Services and Markets Act 2000 (Regulated Activities) Order 2001, SI 2001/544 at **[4001]**
SI 2005/923: Open-Ended Investment Companies (Amendment) Regulations 2005 Authority: FSMA 2000, s 262. Amend the Open-Ended Investment Companies Regulations 2001, SI 2001/1228
SI 2005/922: Financial Services and Markets Act 2000 (Carrying on Regulated Activities by Way of Business) (Amendment) Order 2005 Authority: FSMA 2000, ss 419, 428(3). Amends the Financial Services and Markets Act 2000 (Carrying on Regulated Activities by way of Business) Order 2001, SI 2001/1177 at **[4145]**

2005 Statutory Instruments
SI 2005/680: Financial Services and Markets Act 2000 (Variation of Threshold Conditions) (Amendment) Order 2005 Authority: FSMA 2000, s 428(3), Sch 6, paras 8, 9. Amends the Financial Services and Markets Act 2000 (Variation of Threshold Conditions) Order 2001, SI 2001/2507. It varies the threshold conditions set out in Sch 6 to FSMA 2000 in their application to Swiss general insurance companies
SI 2005/594: Financial Services and Markets Act 2000 (Stakeholder Products) (Amendment) Regulations 2005 Authority: FSMA 2000, s 428 and SI 2001/544, art 52B(3). Amend the Financial Services and Markets Act 2000 (Stakeholder Products) Regulations 2004, SI 2004/2738 at **[4701]**
SI 2005/593: Financial Services and Markets Act 2000 (Regulated Activities) (Amendment) Order 2005 Authority: FSMA 2000, s 22(1), (5), 428(3), Sch 2, para 25. Amends the Financial Services and Markets Act 2000 (Regulated Activities) Order 2001, SI 2001/544 at **[4001]**
SI 2005/592: Financial Services and Markets Act 2000 (Exemption) (Amendment) Order 2005 Authority: FSMA 2000, ss 38, 428(3). Amends the Financial Services and Markets Act 2000 (Exemption) Order 2001, SI 2001/1201 at **[4149]**
SI 2005/274: Financial Services and Markets Act 2000 (Service of Notices) (Amendment) Regulations 2005 Authority: FSMA 2000, s 414. Amend the Financial Services and Markets Act 2000 (Service of Notices) Regulations 2001, SI 2001/1420 at **[4351]**
SI 2005/272: Financial Services and Markets Act 2000 (Disclosure of Information by Prescribed Persons) (Amendment) Regulations 2005 Authority: FSMA 2000, ss 353(1), 417(1). Amend the Financial Services and Markets Act 2000 (Disclosure of Information by Prescribed Persons) Regulations 2001, SI 2001/1857 at **[4368]**
SI 2005/270: Financial Services and Markets Act 2000 (Financial Promotion and Promotion of Collective Investment Schemes) (Miscellaneous Amendments) Order 2005 Authority: FSMA 2000, ss 21(5), (6), 238(6), (7), 428(3). Amends the Financial Services and Markets Act 2000 (Promotion of Collective Investment Schemes) (Exemptions) Order 2001, SI 2001/1060 at **[4112]**, and the Financial Services and Markets Act 2000 (Financial Promotion) Order 2001, SI 2001/1335 (*revoked*)
SI 2005/57: Financial Services and Markets Act 2000 (Collective Investment Schemes) (Amendment) Order 2005 Authority: FSMA 2000, s 235(5). Amends the Financial Services and Markets Act 2000 (Collective Investment Schemes) Order 2001, SI 2001/1062 at **[4141]**
SI 2005/1: Financial Services and Markets Act 2000 (Gibraltar) (Amendment) Order 2005 Authority: FSMA 2000, s 409(1). Amends the Financial Services and Markets Act 2000 (Gibraltar) Order 2001, SI 2001/3084 at **[4504]**

2004 Statutory Instruments
SI 2004/3352: Financial Services and Markets Act 2000 (Designated Professional Bodies) (Amendment) Order 2004 Authority: FSMA 2000, s 326. Amends the Financial Services and Markets Act 2000 (Designated Professional Bodies) Order 2001, SI 2001/1226 at **[4162]**
SI 2004/3351: Financial Services and Markets Act 2000 (Transitional Provisions) (General Insurance Intermediaries) Order 2004 Authority: FSMA 2000, ss 426–428. Effectively spent, see the note at **[4710]**
SI 2004/2738: Financial Services and Markets Act 2000 (Stakeholder Products) Regulations 2004 Authority: FSMA 2000, s 428 and SI 2001/544, art 52B(3). At **[4701]**
SI 2004/2737: Financial Services and Markets Act 2000 (Regulated Activities) (Amendment) (No 2) Order 2004 Authority: FSMA 2000, ss 22(1), (5), 428(3), Sch 2, para 25. Amends the Financial Services and Markets Act 2000 (Regulated Activities) Order 2001, SI 2001/544 at **[4001]**

2004 Statutory Instruments

SI 2004/2615: Financial Services and Markets Act 2000 (Transitional Provisions) (Mortgages) Order 2004
Authority: FSMA 2000, ss 426–428. Effectively spent, see the note at **[4695]**

SI 2004/1862: Financial Conglomerates and Other Financial Groups Regulations 2004
Authority: European Communities Act 1972, s 2(2); FSMA 2000, ss 183(2), 188(2), 417(1), 428(3). At **[4683]** These Regulations implement, in part, European Parliament and Council Directive 2002/87/EC on the supplementary supervision of credit institutions, insurance undertakings and investment firms in a financial conglomerate and amending Council Directives 73/239/EEC, 79/267/EEC, 92/49/EEC, 92/96/EEC, 93/6/EEC, 93/22/EEC, and Directives 98/78/EC and 2000/12/EC of the European Parliament and of the Council ("the conglomerates directive")

SI 2004/1610: Financial Services and Markets Act 2000 (Regulated Activities) (Amendment) Order 2004
Authority: FSMA 2000, ss 22(1), (5), 428(3), Sch 2, para 25. Amends the Financial Services and Markets Act 2000 (Regulated Activities) Order 2001, SI 2001/544 at **[4001]**, and the Financial Services and Markets Act 2000 (Regulated Activities) (Amendment) (No 2) Order 2003, SI 2003/1476 at **[4663]**

SI 2004/1609: Financial Services and Markets Act 2000 (Transitional Provisions) (Complaints Relating to General Insurance and Mortgages) (Amendment) Order 2004
Authority: FSMA 2000, ss 426–428. Amends the Financial Services and Markets Act 2000 (Transitional Provisions) (Complaints Relating to General Insurance and Mortgages) Order 2004, SI 2004/454 at **[4671]**

SI 2004/952: Financial Services and Markets Act 2000 (Transitional Provisions, Repeals and Savings) (Financial Services Compensation Scheme) (Amendment) Order
Authority: FSMA 2000, ss 360, 426–428. Amends the Financial Services and Markets Act 2000 (Transitional Provisions, Repeals and Savings) (Financial Services Compensation Scheme) Order 2001, SI 2001/2967

SI 2004/454: Financial Services and Markets Act 2000 (Transitional Provisions) (Complaints Relating to General Insurance and Mortgages) Order 2004
Authority: FSMA 2000, ss 426–428. At **[4671]**

SI 2004/453: Financial Services and Markets Act 2000 (Appointed Representatives) (Amendment) Regulations 2004
Authority: FSMA 2000, ss 39(1), 417(1), 428(3). Amend the Financial Services and Markets Act 2000 (Appointed Representatives) Regulations 2001, SI 2001/1217 at **[4159]**

SI 2004/355: Financial Services and Markets Act 2000 (Consequential Amendments) Order 2004
Authority: FSMA 2000, s 426. Amends CA 1985 at **[1]**, the Building Societies Act 1986, the Finance Act 1994, the Pensions Act 1995, the Public Offers of Securities Regulations 1995, SI 1995/1537 (*revoked*), and the Financial Services and Markets Act 2000 (Consequential Amendments) Order 2002, SI 2002/1555. Also contains various amendments to Northern Ireland legislation

2003 Statutory Instruments

SI 2003/3075: Money Laundering Regulations 2003
Authority: European Communities Act 1972, s 2(2); FSMA 2000, ss 168(4)(b), 402(1)(b), 417(1), 428(3). These Regulations implement European Parliament and Council Directive 2001/97/EC amending Council Directive 91/308/EEC on prevention of the use of the financial system for the purpose of money laundering

SI 2003/2822: Financial Services and Markets Act 2000 (Regulated Activities) (Amendment) (No 3) Order 2003
Authority: FSMA 2000, ss 22(1), (5), 428(3), Sch 2, para 25. Amends the Financial Services and Markets Act 2000 (Regulated Activities) Order 2001, SI 2001/544 at **[4001]**

SI 2003/2817: Financial Services and Markets Act 2000 (Disclosure of Confidential Information) (Amendment) (No 3) Regulations 2003
Authority: FSMA 2000, ss 349(1)(b), (2), 417(1). Amend the Financial Services and Markets Act 2000 (Disclosure of Confidential Information) Regulations 2001, SI 2001/2188 at **[4372]**

2003 Statutory Instruments
SI 2003/2174: Financial Services and Markets Act 2000 (Disclosure of Confidential Information) (Amendment) (No 2) Regulations 2003 Authority: FSMA 2000, ss 349(1)(b), (2), 417(1). Amend the Financial Services and Markets Act 2000 (Disclosure of Confidential Information) Regulations 2001, SI 2001/2188 at **[4372]**
SI 2003/2134: Financial Services and Markets Act 2000 (Administration Orders Relating to Insurers) (Amendment) Order 2003 Authority: FSMA 2000, ss 360, 426–428. Amends the Financial Services and Markets Act 2000 (Administration Orders Relating to Insurers) Order 2002, SI 2002/1242, and the Financial Services and Markets Act 2000 (Transitional Provisions, Repeals and Savings) (Financial Services Compensation Scheme) Order 2001, SI 2001/2967
SI 2003/2067: Financial Services and Markets Act 2000 (Promotion of Collective Investment Schemes etc) (Exemptions) (Amendment) Order 2003 Authority: FSMA 2000, ss 21(5), 238(6), (7), 428(3). Amends the Financial Services and Markets Act 2000 (Promotion of Collective Investment Schemes) (Exemptions) Order 2001, SI 2001/1060 at **[4112]**, and the Financial Services and Markets Act 2000 (Financial Promotion) Order 2001, SI 2001/1335 (*revoked*). This Order implements, in part, (i) European Parliament and Council Directive 2001/107/EC amending Council Directive 85/611/EEC on the coordination of laws, regulations and administrative provisions relating to undertakings for collective investment in transferable securities (UCITS) with a view to regulating management companies and simplified prospectuses, and (ii) European Parliament and Council Directive 2001/108/EC amending Council Directive 85/611/EEC on the coordination of laws, regulations and administrative provisions relating to undertakings for collective investment in transferable securities (UCITS) with regard to investments of UCITS
SI 2003/2066: Collective Investment Schemes (Miscellaneous Amendments) Regulations 2003 Authority: European Communities Act 1972, s 2(2); FSMA 2000, ss 183(2), 188(2), 213(10), 214(5), 224(4), 264(3), 349(1)(b), (2), (3), 417(1), 428(3), Sch 3, paras 13(1)(b)(iii), 14(1)(b), 17(b), 22. These Regulations amend the Financial Services and Markets Act 2000 at **[2001]**, the Financial Services and Markets Act 2000 (EEA Passport Rights) Regulations 2001, SI 2001/2511 at **[4448]**, the Financial Services and Markets Act 2000 (Consultation with Competent Authorities) Regulations 2001, SI 2001/2509 at **[4440]**, the Financial Services and Markets Act 2000 (Compensation Scheme: Electing Participants) Regulations 2001, SI 2001/1783 at **[4362]**, the Financial Services and Markets Act 2000 (Collective Investment Schemes Constituted in Other EEA States) Regulations 2001, SI 2001/2383 at **[4405]**, the Financial Services and Markets Act 2000 (Disclosure of Confidential Information) Regulations 2001, SI 2001/2188 at **[4372]**, and the Open-Ended Investment Companies Regulations 2001, SI 2001/1228. The Regulations also contains minor and consequential amendments to CA 1985 and other statutory instruments that are outside the scope of this work. These Regulations implement Directives 2001/107/EC and 2001/108/EC (see SI 2003/2066 above)
SI 2003/1676: Financial Services and Markets Act 2000 (Financial Promotion) (Amendment) Order 2003 Authority: FSMA 2000, ss 21(5), (9), (10), 428(3). Revoked by the Financial Services and Markets Act 2000 (Financial Promotion) Order 2005, SI 2005/1529
SI 2003/1675: Financial Services and Markets Act 2000 (Exemption) (Amendment) (No 2) Order 2003 Authority: FSMA 2000, ss 38, 428(3). Amends the Financial Services and Markets Act 2000 (Exemption) Order 2001, SI 2001/1201 at **[4149]**
SI 2003/1476: Financial Services and Markets Act 2000 (Regulated Activities) (Amendment) (No 2) Order 2003 Authority: FSMA 2000, ss 22(1), (5), 192(a), 426, 427, 428(3). At **[4663]** This Order implements, in part, European Parliament and Council Directive 2002/92/EC on insurance mediation
SI 2003/1475: Financial Services and Markets Act 2000 (Regulated Activities) (Amendment) (No 1) Order 2003 Authority: FSMA 2000, ss 22(1), (5), 426, 427, 428(3). At **[4657]**
SI 2003/1474: Financial Services and Markets Act 2000 (Misleading Statements and Practices) (Amendment) Order 2003 Authority: FSMA 2000, s 397(9), (14). Amends the Financial Services and Markets Act 2000 (Misleading Statements and Practices) Order 2001, SI 2001/3645 at **[4620]**

APPENDICES

2003 Statutory Instruments
SI 2003/1473: Insurance Mediation Directive (Miscellaneous Amendments) Regulations 2003 Authority: European Communities Act 1972, s 2(2); FSMA 2000, ss 349(1)(b), (2), (3), 417(1), 428(3), Sch 3 paras 14(1)(b), 17(a). Amend the Financial Services and Markets Act 2000 at **[2001]**, the Financial Services and Markets Act 2000 (EEA Passport Rights) Regulations 2001, SI 2001/2511 at **[4448]**, and the Financial Services and Markets Act 2000 (Disclosure of Confidential Information) Regulations 2001, SI 2001/2188 at **[4372]** These Regulations implement, in part, European Parliament and Council Directive 2002/92/EC on insurance mediation
SI 2003/1294: Financial Services and Markets Act 2000 (Communications by Actuaries) Regulations 2003 Authority: FSMA 2000, ss 342(5), 343(5), 428(3). At **[4655]**
SI 2003/1181: Financial Services and Markets Act 2000 (Collective Investment Schemes) (Designated Countries and Territories) Order 2003 Authority: FSMA 2000, ss 270, 426, 428(3). See the note to FSMA 2000, s 270 at **[2268]**
SI 2003/1092: Financial Services and Markets Act 2000 (Disclosure of Confidential Information) (Amendment) Regulations 2003 Authority: FSMA 2000, ss 349(1)(b), (2), 417(1). Revoked by the Financial Services and Markets Act 2000 (Disclosure of Confidential Information) (Amendment) (No 2) Regulations 2003, SI 2003/2174
SI 2003/693: Financial Services and Markets Act 2000 (Disclosure of Confidential Information) (Amendment) Regulations 2003 Authority: FSMA 2000, ss 349(1)(b), (2), 417(1), 428(3). Amend the Financial Services and Markets Act 2000 (Disclosure of Confidential Information) Regulations 2001, SI 2001/2188 at **[4372]** These Regulations implement, in part, European Parliament and Council Directive 2000/64/EC amending Council Directives 85/611/EEC, 92/49/EEC, 92/96/EEC and 93/22/EEC as regards exchange of information with third countries
SI 2003/47: Financial Services and Markets Act 2000 (Exemption) (Amendment) Order 2003 Authority: FSMA 2000, ss 38, 428(3). Amends the Financial Services and Markets Act 2000 (Exemption) Order 2001, SI 2001/1201 at **[4149]**

2002 Statutory Instruments
SI 2002/2707: Financial Services and Markets Act 2000 (Variation of Threshold Conditions) Order 2002 Authority: FSMA 2000, s 428(3), Sch 6, para 9. Amends the Financial Services and Markets Act 2000 at **[2001]**. This Order implements, in part, European Parliament and Council Directive 2000/26/EC on the approximation of the laws of the Member States relating to insurance against civil liability in respect of the use of motor vehicles and amending Council Directives 73/239/EEC and 88/357/EEC (Fourth motor insurance Directive)
SI 2002/2706: Financial Services and Markets Act 2000 (Fourth Motor Insurance Directive) Regulations 2002 Authority: European Communities Act 1972, s 2(2); FSMA 2000, ss 150(3), 417(1). These Regulations implement, in part, Directive 2000/26/EC (see SI 2002/2707 above). They make it clear that rules made by the FSA under FSMA 2000, s 138 may require authorised insurers effecting or carrying out contracts of insurance covering certain types of motor vehicle liability (or Lloyd's managing agents who manage syndicates who do such business) to make interest payments in certain specified circumstances. They also amend the Financial Services and Markets Act 2000 (Rights of Action) Regulations 2001, SI 2001/2256 at **[4395]**
SI 2001/2157: Financial Services and Markets Act 2000 (Financial Promotion) (Amendment) (Electronic Commerce Directive) Order 2002 Authority: FSMA 2000, ss 21(5), (6), 238(6),(7), 428(3). Revoked by the Financial Services and Markets Act 2000 (Financial Promotion) Order 2005, SI 2005/1529

2002 Statutory Instruments
SI 2002/1777: Financial Services and Markets Act 2000 (Commencement of Mortgage Regulation) (Amendment) Order 2002 Authority: FSMA 2000, ss 21(5), (9), (10), 22(1), (5), 327(6), 397(9), (10), (14), 428(3), Sch 2, para 25. Amends the Financial Services and Markets Act 2000 (Regulated Activities) Order 2001, SI 2001/544 at **[4001]**, the Financial Services and Markets Act 2000 (Professions) (Non-exempt Activities) Order 2001, SI 2001/1227 at **[4164]**, the Financial Services and Markets Act 2000 (Financial Promotion) Order 2001, SI 2001/1335 (*revoked*), the Financial Services and Markets Act 2000 (Regulated Activities) (Amendment) Order 2001, SI 2001/3544, the Financial Services and Markets Act 2000 (Misleading Statements and Practices) Order 2001, SI 2001/3645 at **[4620]**, and the Financial Services and Markets Act 2000 (Miscellaneous Provisions) Order 2001, SI 2001/3650
SI 2002/1776: Financial Services and Markets Act 2000 (Regulated Activities) (Amendment) (No 2) Order 2002 Authority: FSMA 2000, ss 22(1), (5), 428(3). Amends the Financial Services and Markets Act 2000 (Regulated Activities) Order 2001, SI 2001/544 at **[4001]**. This Order implements, in part, European Parliament and Council Directive 2000/31/EC on certain legal aspects of information society services, in particular electronic commerce, in the internal market ("Directive on electronic commerce")
SI 2002/1775: Electronic Commerce Directive (Financial Services and Markets) Regulations 2002 Authority: European Communities Act 1972, s 2(2); FSMA 2000, ss 349(1), 414, 428(3). At **[4639]**. These Regulations implement, in part, European Parliament and Council Directive 2000/31/EC on certain legal aspects of information society services, in particular electronic commerce, in the internal market ("Directive on electronic commerce")
SI 2002/1555: Financial Services and Markets Act 2000 (Consequential Amendments) Order 2002 Authority: FSMA 2000, ss 416(4), 426, 427. This Order is supplementary to the Financial Services and Markets Act 2000 (Consequential Amendments and Repeals) Order 2001, SI 2001/3649. It corrects or adjusts amendments made by SI 2001/3649, and makes additional amendments that are consequential upon the repeal of the legislation which established the regulatory regimes which have been replaced by FSMA 2000. It amends a large amount of legislation, the majority of which is not reproduced in this Handbook
SI 2002/1501: Financial Services and Markets Act 2000 (Consequential Amendments and Transitional Provisions) (Credit Unions) Order 2002 Authority: FSMA 2000, ss 426–428. Amends the Credit Unions Act 1979, the Trustee Savings Banks Act 1985, the Financial Services and Markets Act 2000 (Permission and Applications) (Credit Unions etc) Order 2002, SI 2002/704, and revokes various statutory instruments made under the 1979 Act
SI 2002/1409: Financial Services and Markets Act 2000 (Consequential Amendments) (Taxes) Order 2002 Authority: FSMA 2000, s 426. Amends the Income and Corporation Taxes Act 1988, the Finance Act 1989, the Insurance Companies (Taxation of Reinsurance Business) Regulations 1995, SI 1995/1730, the Insurance Companies (Reserves) (Tax) Regulations 1996, SI 1996/2991, the Friendly Societies (Modification of the Corporation Tax Acts) Regulations 1997, SI 1997/473 (*revoked*), and the Individual Savings Account Regulations 1998, SI 1998/1870
SI 2002/1310: Financial Services and Markets Act 2000 (Financial Promotion and Miscellaneous Amendments) Order 2002 Authority: FSMA 2000, ss 21(5), (6), 22(1), (5), 38, 238(6), (7), 428(3), Sch 2, para 25. Amends the Financial Services and Markets Act 2000 (Financial Promotion) Order 2001, SI 2001/1335 (*revoked*), the Financial Services and Markets Act 2000 (Promotion of Collective Investment Schemes) (Exemptions) Order 2001, SI 2001/1060 at **[4112]**, and the Financial Services and Markets Act 2000 (Regulated Activities) Order 2001, SI 2001/544 at **[4001]**
SI 2002/1242: Financial Services and Markets Act 2000 (Administration Orders Relating to Insurers) Order 2002 Authority: FSMA 2000, ss 355(2), 360, 426, 428(3). See **[4638A]**

2002 Statutory Instruments

SI 2002/765: Electronic Money (Miscellaneous Amendments) Regulations 2002
Authority: European Communities Act 1972, s 2(2); FSMA 2000, ss 417, 428(3), Sch 3, para 13(1)(b)(iii). Amend CA 1985 at **[1]**, FSMA 2000 at **[2001]**, the Public Offers of Securities Regulations 1995, SI 1995/1537 (*revoked*), the Cross-Border Credit Transfers Regulations 1999, SI 1999/1876, the Financial Markets and Insolvency (Settlement Finality) Regulations 1999, SI 1999/2979, the Competition Act 1998 (Small Agreements and Conduct of Minor Significance) Regulations 2000, SI 2000/262, the Competition Act 1998 (Determination of Turnover for Penalties) Order 2000, SI 2000/309, the Financial Services and Markets Act 2000 (EEA Passport Rights) Regulations 2001, SI 2001/2511 at **[4448]**, and the Companies (Northern Ireland) Order 1986. These Regulations implement, in part, European Parliament and Council Directive 2000/46/EC on the taking up, pursuit of and prudential supervision of the business of electronic money institutions, and European Parliament and Council Directive 2000/28/EC amending Directive 2000/12/EC relating to the taking up and pursuit of the business of credit institutions

SI 2002/704: Financial Services and Markets Act 2000 (Permission and Applications) (Credit Unions etc) Order 2002
Authority: FSMA 2000, ss 426–428. This Order sets out the transitional provisions relating to the expiry (on 2 July 2002) of the transitional exemption of credit unions from the general prohibition imposed by FSMA 2000, s 19; see the Financial Services and Markets Act 2000 (Exemption) Order 2001, SI 2001/1201, art 6

SI 2002/682: Financial Services and Markets Act 2000 (Regulated Activities) (Amendment) Order 2002
Authority: FSMA 2000, ss 22(1), (5), 428(3), Sch 2, para 25. At **[4636]**. This Order implements, in part, European Parliament and Council Directive 2000/46/EC on the taking up, pursuit of and prudential supervision of the business of electronic money institutions, and European Parliament and Council Directive 2000/28/EC amending Directive 2000/12/EC relating to the taking up and pursuit of the business of credit institutions

2001 Statutory Instruments

SI 2001/4040: Insurers (Winding Up) (Scotland) Rules 2001
Authority: IA 1986, s 411; FSMA 2000, s 379. These Rules supplement the Insolvency (Scotland) Rules 1986, SI 1986/1915 in relation to the winding up of insurers in Scotland. They revoke and replace, with modifications, the Insurance Companies (Winding Up) (Scotland) Rules 1986, SI 1986/1918

SI 2001/3801: Financial Services and Markets Act 2000 (Consequential Amendments) (No 2) Order 2001
Authority: FSMA 2000, ss 426, 427. Amends the Terrorism (United Nations Measures) Order 2001, SI 2001/3365 and the Terrorism (United Nations Measures) (Overseas Territories) Order 2001, SI 2001/3366

SI 2001/3800: Financial Services and Markets Act 2000 (Financial Promotion) (Amendment No 2) Order 2001
Authority: FSMA 2000, s 21(5). Revoked by the Financial Services and Markets Act 2000 (Financial Promotion) Order 2005, SI 2005/1529

SI 2001/3771: Financial Services and Markets Act 2000 (Scope of Permission Notices) Order 2001
Authority: FSMA 2000, ss 426–428. At **[4632]**

SI 2001/3681: Financial Services and Markets Act 2000 (Prescribed Markets and Qualifying Investments) (Amendment) Order 2001
Authority: originally made under FSMA 2000, s 118(3). However, following the amendment of Pt VIII of that Act by the Financial Services and Markets Act 2000 (Market Abuse) Regulations 2005, SI 2005/381, it now has effect as if made under s 130A(1). Amends the Financial Services and Markets Act 2000 (Prescribed Markets and Qualifying Investments) Order 2001, SI 2001/996 at **[4106]**

2001 Statutory Instruments
SI 2001/3650: Financial Services and Markets Act 2000 (Miscellaneous Provisions) Order 2001 Authority: FSMA 2000, ss 21(5), (9), (10), 235(5), 327(6), 426–428, Sch 2, para 25. Pt I of this Order provides for commencement, etc. Pt II amends the Financial Services and Markets Act 2000 (Collective Investment Schemes) Order 2001, SI 2001/1062 at **[4141]**, the Financial Services and Markets Act 2000 (Professions) (Non-Exempt Activities) Order 2001, SI 2001/1227 at **[4164]**, the Financial Services and Markets Act 2000 (Financial Promotion) Order 2001, SI 2001/1335 (*revoked*), the Financial Services and Markets Act 2000 (Transitional Provisions) (Authorised Persons etc) Order 2001, SI 2001/2636, and the Financial Services and Markets Act 2000 (Transitional Provisions) (Controllers) Order 2001, SI 2001/2637. Pt III of the Order makes miscellaneous provisions other than amendments. Arts 14, 15 modify FSMA 2000, s 367 (winding up petitions). Art 16 makes transitional provision in relation to provisions in FSA 1986, the Banking Act 1987 and the Rehabilitation of Offenders Act 1974 (Exceptions) Order 1975, SI 1975/1023 that confer an exception from the Rehabilitation of Offenders Act 1974. Art 17 retains in effect provisions regarding the disqualification from political office of members of the Financial Services Tribunal. Art 18 makes transitional savings of certain enactments that oblige auditors to communicate certain matters to the regulator. Art 19 provides that the FSA must fulfil its reporting obligations under FSA 1986 and the Banking Act 1987 by including the relevant information in the first report it makes of its activities under FSMA 2000. Article 20 contains similar provision in relation to the Treasury's report under the Insurance Companies Act 1982. Arts 21 22 provide for the FSA to devise a scheme for the transfer of the property, rights and liabilities of the self-regulating organisations. All liabilities for pre-commencement acts and omissions by these bodies are transferred to the FSA by art 22 and the FSA is, by art 23, substituted for the organisation in any legal proceedings pending at commencement. Art 24 deals with immunity from liability in damages in relation to actions before commencement or under repealed enactments. Arts 25–27 relate to fees. Art 28 revokes the Contracting Out (Functions in Relation to Insurance) Order 1998, SI 1998/2842. Arts 29, 30 concern corrections to scope of permission notices sent out to persons before commencement under the Financial Services and Markets Act 2000 (Transitional Provisions) (Authorised Persons etc) Order 2001
SI 2001/3649: Financial Services and Markets Act 2000 (Consequential Amendments and Repeals) Order 2001 Authority: FSMA 2000, ss 426, 427. This Order (which is made up of 610 articles) sets out the amendments to primary and secondary legislation consequential on the coming into force of FSMA 2000. The large majority of the amendments are consequential on the principal repeals and revocations made by art 3 (ie, the Policyholders Protection Act 1975, the Insurance Companies Act 1982, FSA 1986, the Banking Act 1987, the Insurance Companies (Reserves) Act 1995, the Policyholders Protection Act 1997, the Banking Coordination (Second Council Directive) Regulations 1992, SI 1992/3218, the Insurance Companies (Third Insurance Directives) Regulations 1994, SI 1994/1696, and the Investment Services Regulations 1995, SI 1995/3275). References in other legislation to the enactments repealed and revoked, or to expressions used in those enactments, are amended so that they refer to the appropriate provision or expression in FSMA 2000
SI 2001/3648: Financial Services and Markets Act 2000 (Confidential Information) (Bank of England) (Consequential Provisions) Order 2001 Authority: FSMA 2000, ss 426, 427. At **[4624]**
SI 2001/3647: Financial Services and Markets Act 2000 (Consequential Amendments and Savings) (Industrial Assurance) Order 2001 Authority: FSMA 2000, ss 339(1)–(3), 416(4), 426, 427. This Order makes transitional savings and consequential amendments pursuant to the repeal, by FSMA 2000, s 416, of the Industrial Assurance Act 1923, the Industrial Assurance and Friendly Societies Act 1948, and the revocation of the Industrial Assurance (Northern Ireland) Order 1978. It amends a large amount of legislation that is outside the scope of this Handbook

APPENDICES

2001 Statutory Instruments
SI 2001/3646: Financial Services and Markets Act 2000 (Transitional Provisions and Savings) (Information Requirements and Investigations) Order 2001 Authority: FSMA 2000, ss 426, 427, 428(3). This Order makes transitional provisions for requirements to provide information under the Banking Act 1987, FSA 1986, and the Insurance Companies Act 1982 and requirements made by recognised self-regulating organisations that are outstanding on 1 December 2001 ("commencement"). The Order also makes transitional provisions for requirements to supply a report by a skilled person that are pending at commencement which were made under the Banking Act 1987 or Insurance Companies Act 1982. The Order also makes transitional provisions for investigators appointed under the Insurance Companies Act 1982, the Banking Act 1987 and FSA 1986 where the investigations are in progress at commencement
SI 2001/3645: Financial Services and Markets Act 2000 (Misleading Statements and Practices) Order 2001 Authority: FSMA 2000, s 397(9), (10), (14). At **[4620]**.
SI 2001/3640: Financial Services and Markets Act 2000 (Savings, Modifications and Consequential Provisions) (Rehabilitation of Offenders) (Scotland) Order 2001 Authority: FSMA 2000, ss 426, 427, 428(3). This Order makes amendments, savings and modifications (in relation to Scotland only) which relate to the Rehabilitation of Offenders Act 1974. These provisions are necessary following the repeal of the Insurance Companies Act 1982, FSA 1986, and the Banking Act 1987. It also makes consequential amendments to the Rehabilitation of Offenders Act 1974 (Exceptions) Order 1975, SI 1975/1023
SI 2001/3639: Financial Services and Markets Act 2000 (Transitional Provisions and Savings) (Business Transfers) Order 2001 Authority: FSMA 2000, ss 426–428. This Order makes savings and transitional provisions for applications under the Insurance Companies Act 1982, Sch 2C for approval of a transfer of the whole or part of the long term business carried on by an insurance company, or approval of the transfer of rights and obligations under contracts of general insurance (including transfers of business to or from members of Lloyd's). In relation to any application that has been made, but not determined, before 1 December 2001, the relevant provisions of Sch 2C are saved, subject to modifications
SI 2001/3635: Insurers (Winding Up) Rules 2001 Authority: IA 1986, s 411; FSMA 2000, s 379. See **[4585]**
SI 2001/3633: Financial Services and Markets Tribunal (Legal Assistance Scheme—Costs) Regulations 2001 Authority: FSMA 2000, ss 134, 135, 428(1), (3). At **[4560]**
SI 2001/3632: Financial Services and Markets Tribunal (Legal Assistance) Regulations 2001 Authority: FSMA 2000, ss 134, 135, 428(1), (3). At **[4517]**
SI 2001/3629: Financial Services and Markets Act 2000 (Consequential Amendments) (Taxes) Order 2001 Authority: FSMA 2000, ss 426–428. This Order makes consequential amendments to primary and secondary legislation relating to matters under the care and management of the Commissioners of Inland Revenue (now the Commissioners for Her Majesty's Revenue and Customs). The matters involved include income tax, corporation tax, capital gains tax, national insurance contributions, inheritance tax, stamp duty and stamp duty reserve tax. It amends a large amount of legislation that is outside the scope of this Handbook
SI 2001/3626: Financial Services and Markets Act 2000 (Control of Transfers of Business Done at Lloyd's) Order 2001 Authority: FSMA 2000, ss 323, 428(3). This Order applies various provisions of FSMA 2000, Pt VII relating to insurance business transfers, to transfers of business from members (and certain former members) of Lloyd's
SI 2001/3625: Financial Services and Markets Act 2000 (Control of Business Transfers) (Requirements on Applicants) Regulations 2001 Authority: FSMA 2000, ss 108, 417(1), 428(3), Sch 12, para 6(2). At **[4511]**
SI 2001/3624: Financial Services and Markets Act 2000 (Disclosure of Confidential Information) (Amendment) (No 2) Regulations 2001 Authority: FSMA 2000, ss 349(1)(b), (2), 417(1), 426, 427, 428(3). Amend the Financial Services and Markets Act 2000 (Disclosure of Confidential Information) Regulations 2001, SI 2001/2188 at **[4372]**. These Regulations implement, in part, European Parliament and Council Directive 2001/34/EC on the admission of securities to official stock exchange listing and on information to be published on those securities

2001 Statutory Instruments
SI 2001/3623: Financial Services and Markets Act 2000 (Exemption) (Amendment) Order 2001 Authority: FSMA 2000, ss 38, 428(3). Amends the Financial Services and Markets Act 2000 (Exemption) Order 2001, SI 2001/1201 at **[4149]**
SI 2001/3592: Financial Services and Markets Act 2000 (Transitional Provisions) (Partly Completed Procedures) Order 2001 Authority: FSMA 2000, ss 426–428. This Order makes transitional provision for procedures which are partly completed on the day on which the main provisions of FSMA 2000 come into force (1 December 2001). Pt I of the Order provides for commencement and interpretation. Pt II sets out how applications which have been made under the repealed legislation are to be treated after commencement, and deals with situations where the FSA has started proceedings on its own initiative to withdraw, suspend or restrict authorisation under that legislation. Pt III deals with similar matters relating to friendly societies and building societies. Pt IV concerns pending authorisations of unit trust schemes and recognition of collective investment schemes. Pt V provides for the transition of other partly completed procedures, namely those in relation to (i) applications by people who will need to be approved persons for the purposes of Pt V of FSMA 2000; (ii) the making of public statements of misconduct under FSA 1986, s 60; (iii) persons who are subject to proceedings for disqualification under FSA 1986. Pt VI provides for the partly completed procedures of the recognised self-regulating organisations established under FSA 1986. Pt VII contains supplemental provisions regarding the content of notices served before commencement which are to be carried forward as a notice under an equivalent provision in FSMA 2000. Pt VIII deals with the position where an EEA firm is part way through exercising its EEA right to establish a branch or provide services in the UK, and where a UK firm is part way through exercising its EEA right to "passport" into another member State. Pt IX of the Order contains transitional provisions relating to appeals which are pending at commencement
SI 2001/3591: Bankruptcy (Financial Services and Markets Act 2000) (Scotland) Rules 2001 Authority: FSMA 2000, ss 372(4)(c), (9)(b), 428(3). These Rules relate to demands by the FSA (under s 372(4)(a) of FSMA 2000) to an individual to establish to the Authority's satisfaction that that individual has a reasonable prospect of being able to pay a regulated activity debt when it falls due. Rule 3 makes provision for the form of a demand. Rule 4 relates to service of a demand. Rules 5 and 6 relate to the setting aside of a demand. The Rules apply to Scotland only
SI 2001/3582: Financial Services and Markets Act 2000 (Dissolution of the Board of Banking Supervision) (Transitional Provisions) Order 2001 Authority: FSMA 2000, ss 426, 427, 428(3). This Order makes transitional provisions in connection with the final report of the Board of Banking Supervision (which is dissolved by FSMA 2000, s 416(3)(d))
SI 2001/3544: Financial Services and Markets Act 2000 (Regulated Activities) (Amendment) Order 2001 Authority: FSMA 2000, ss 22(1), (5), 428(3), Sch 2, para 25. Amends the Financial Services and Markets Act 2000 (Regulated Activities) Order 2001, SI 2001/544 at **[4001]**
SI 2001/3542: Financial Services and Markets Act 2000 (Law Applicable to Contracts of Insurance) (Amendment) Regulations 2001 Authority: FSMA 2000, ss 424(3), 417(1), 428(3). Amend the Financial Services and Markets Act 2000 (Law Applicable to Contracts of Insurance) Regulations 2001, SI 2001/2635
SI 2001/3538: Financial Services and Markets Act 2000 (Commencement No 7) Order 2001 Authority: FSMA 2000, ss 431(2), 428(3). Brings into force various provisions of the 2000 Act
SI 2001/3439: Financial Services and Markets Act 2000 (Official Listing of Securities) (Amendment) Regulations 2001 Authority: FSMA 2000, ss 75(3), 417(1), 428(3). Amend the Financial Services and Markets Act 2000 (Official Listing of Securities) Regulations 2001, SI 2001/2956 at **[4478]**
SI 2001/3437: Financial Services and Markets Act 2000 (Disclosure of Confidential Information) (Amendment) Regulations 2001 Authority: FSMA 2000, ss 349(1)(b), (2), (3), 417(1). Amend the Financial Services and Markets Act 2000 (Disclosure of Confidential Information) Regulations 2001, SI 2001/2188 at **[4372]**
SI 2001/3436: Financial Services and Markets Act 2000 (Commencement No 6) Order 2001 Authority: FSMA 2000, s 431(2). Brings into force various provisions of the 2000 Act

APPENDICES

2001 Statutory Instruments
SI 2001/3374: Financial Services and Markets Act 2000 (Interim Permissions) Order 2001 Authority: FSMA 2000, ss 426–428. This Order conferred an interim permission on certain applicants who applied to the FSA for permission under Pt IV of FSMA 2000 and whose application was still pending on the date when the main provisions of the Act came into force (1 December 2001). The scope of the Order is limited to those applicants who were lawfully carrying on the activity which was regulated for the first time under the Act
SI 2001/3338: Financial Services and Markets Act 2000 (Controllers) (Exemption) (No 2) Order 2001 Authority: FSMA 2000, ss 192(a), 428(3). At **[4508]**
SI 2001/3084: Financial Services and Markets Act 2000 (Gibraltar) Order 2001 Authority: FSMA 2000, ss 409(1), 428(3). At **[4504]**. This Order implements, in part, European Parliament and Council Directive 2000/12/EC relating to the taking up and pursuit of the business of credit institutions, and "the insurance directives" (ie, 73/239/EEC, 88/357/EEC, 92/49/EEC, 79/267/EEC, 90/619/EEC, and 92/96/EEC)
SI 2001/3083: Financial Services and Markets Act 2000 (Transitional Provisions and Savings) (Civil Remedies, Discipline, Criminal Offences etc) (No 2) Order 2001 Authority: FSMA 2000, ss 426, 427, 428(3). This Order revokes and re-enacts with certain modifications the Financial Services and Markets Act 2000 (Transitional Provisions and Savings) (Civil Remedies, Discipline, Criminal Offences etc) Order 2001, SI 2001/2657. It relates to the civil, prosecutorial and disciplinary powers of the FSA in relation to conduct that took place before the commencement of FSMA 2000, s 19 (the general prohibition). It also makes consequential amendments to the Financial Services and Markets Act 2000 (Consequential and Transitional Provisions) (Miscellaneous) (No 2) Order 2001, SI 2001/2659
SI 2001/2968: Financial Services and Markets Act 2000 (Treatment of Assets of Insurers on Winding Up) Regulations 2001 Authority: FSMA 2000, ss 378, 428(3). Revoked by the Insurers (Reorganisation and Winding Up) Regulations 2003, SI 2003/1102
SI 2001/2967: Financial Services and Markets Act 2000 (Transitional Provisions, Repeals and Savings) (Financial Services Compensation Scheme) Order 2001 Authority: FSMA 2000, ss 339(3), 416(4), 426–428. This Order makes transitional provisions in connection with the Financial Services Compensation Scheme which supersedes eight former compensation schemes; ie, the Policyholders Protection Scheme, the Deposit Protection Scheme, the Building Societies Investor Protection Scheme, the Investor Compensation Scheme, the section 43 Compensation Scheme, the Friendly Societies Protection Scheme, the Personal Investment Authority indemnity scheme, and the arrangements described in the ABI/ICS agreement ("the ABI scheme"). It implements, in part, European Parliament and Council Directive 94/19/EC on deposit-guarantee schemes, and European Parliament and Council Directive 97/9/EC on investor-compensation schemes
SI 2001/2966: Financial Services and Markets Act 2000 (Consequential Amendments) (Pre-Commencement Modifications) Order 2001 Authority: FSMA 2000, ss 426, 427. The modifications made by this Order are consequential on a number of provisions of FSMA 2000 which were brought into force by the Financial Services and Markets Act 2000 (Commencement No 5) Order 2001, SI 2001/2632. These include provisions relating to the making of applications and the granting of permissions to come into force on the day on which s 19 of the Act comes into force (1 December 2001), the doing of other preparatory acts by the FSA in advance of that day, and certain provisions relating to the Financial Services and Markets Tribunal. The modifications made by this Order ceased to have effect when s 19 came into force
SI 2001/2958: Financial Services and Markets Act 2000 (Offers of Securities) Order 2001 Authority: FSMA 2000, s 87(4), Sch 11, paras 8(2), 15, 17, 21, 22, 23, 25. Revoked by the Prospectus Regulations 2005, SI 2005/1433

2001 Statutory Instruments

SI 2001/2957: Financial Services and Markets Act 2000 (Official Listing of Securities) (Transitional Provisions) Order 2001
Authority: FSMA 2000, ss 426, 427, 428(3). This Order makes transitional provisions in connection with the official listing of securities following the repeal of FSA 1986, Pt IV and its replacement with the new regime in Pt VI of FSMA 2000. It provides, inter alia, for the continued effect of listing rules after commencement, and deals with the contravention of those rules before commencement and appeals in relation to decisions taken before commencement. These Regulations implement, in part, Council Directive 79/279/EEC coordinating the conditions for the admission of securities to official stock exchange listing, Council Directive 80/390/EEC coordinating the requirements for the drawing up, scrutiny and distribution of the listing particulars to be published for the admission of securities to official stock exchange listing (and the amending Directives 82/148/EEC, 87/345/EEC, 90/211/EEC and 94/18/EC), and Council Directive 82/121/EEC on information to be published on a regular basis by companies the shares of which have been admitted to official stock-exchange listing

SI 2001/2956: Financial Services and Markets Act 2000 (Official Listing of Securities) Regulations 2001
Authority: FSMA 2000, ss 75(3), 79(3), 103(1), 417(1), 428(3), Sch 10, para 9, Sch 11, paras 16(3), 16(4), 20(2). At **[4478]**. This Order implements, in part, Directives 79/279/EEC, 80/390/EEC (and the amending Directives 82/148/EEC, 87/345/EEC, 90/211/EEC and 94/18/EC), and Directive 82/121/EEC (see SI 2001/2957 above)

SI 2001/2659: Financial Services and Markets Act 2000 (Consequential and Transitional Provisions) (Miscellaneous) (No 2) Order 2001
Authority: FSMA 2000, ss 426, 427, 428(3). This Order makes consequential and transitional provisions for the purposes of a number of provisions of FSMA 2000 which were brought into force by the Financial Services and Markets Act 2000 (Commencement No 5) Order 2001, SI 2001/2632. Those provisions include the making of applications under the Act for permission or authorisation coming into force on the day on which s 19 of the Act comes into force, and in connection with Pt XI of the Act (information gathering and investigations)

SI 2001/2657: Financial Services and Markets Act 2000 (Transitional Provisions and Savings) (Civil Remedies, Discipline, Criminal Offences etc) Order 2001
Authority: FSMA 2000, ss 426, 427, 428(3). Revoked by the Financial Services and Markets Act 2000 (Transitional Provisions and Savings) (Civil Remedies, Discipline, Criminal Offences etc) (No 2) Order 2001, SI 2001/3083

SI 2001/2639: Financial Services and Markets Act 2000 (Own-initiative Power) (Overseas Regulators) Regulations 2001
Authority: FSMA 2000, ss 47(1), (3), 417(1), 428(3). At **[4475]**. These Regulations implement, in part, Council Directive 92/49/EEC on the coordination of laws, regulations and administrative provisions relating to direct insurance other than life assurance and amending Directives 73/239/EEC and 88/357/EEC (third non-life insurance Directive), Council Directive 92/96/EEC on the coordination of laws, regulations and administrative provisions relating to direct life assurance and amending Directives 79/267/EEC and 90/619/EEC (third life assurance Directive), Council Directive 91/371/EEC on the implementation of the Agreement between the European Economic Community and the Swiss Confederation concerning direct insurance other than life assurance, Council Directive 93/22/EEC on investment services in the securities field, and European Parliament and Council Directive 2000/12/EC relating to the taking up and pursuit of the business of credit institutions

SI 2001/2638: Financial Services and Markets Act 2000 (Controllers) (Exemption) Order 2001
Authority: FSMA 2000, ss 192(a), 428(3). At **[4473]**

SI 2001/2637: Financial Services and Markets Act 2000 (Transitional Provisions) (Controllers) Order 2001
Authority: FSMA 2000, ss 426–428. This Order makes transitional provision for people who are subject to a regime requiring them to notify a significant shareholding in an authorised person and who will fall within Pt XII of FSMA 2000. It deals both with the status after commencement of people who have been approved as shareholder controllers under existing regimes and with partly completed procedures

2001 Statutory Instruments
SI 2001/2636: Financial Services and Markets Act 2000 (Transitional Provisions) (Authorised Persons etc) Order 2001 Authority: FSMA 2000, ss 426–428. This Order sets out the transitional arrangements for ensuring that people who have been authorised to carry on particular business under the various regulatory regimes replaced by FSMA 2000 are treated as authorised persons with the appropriate permission for the purposes of that Act. The regulatory regimes covered by this Order are FSA 1986, the Banking Act 1987, the Insurance Companies Act 1982, the Friendly Societies Act 1992, the Building Societies Act 1986, the Banking Coordination (Second Council Directive) Regulations 1992, SI 1992/3218, and the Investment Services Regulations 1995, SI 1995/3275
SI 2001/2635: Financial Services and Markets Act 2000 (Law Applicable to Contracts of Insurance) Regulations 2001 Authority: FSMA 2000, ss 424(3), 417(1), 428(3). These Regulations specify the law that applies to contracts of insurance, the effecting or carrying out of which constitutes a regulated activity within the meaning of FSMA 2000. These Regulations implement, in part, Council Directive 78/473/EEC on the coordination of laws, regulations and administrative provisions relating to Community co-insurance
SI 2001/2634: Financial Services and Markets Act 2000 (Insolvency) (Definition of "Insurer") Order 2001 Authority: FSMA 2000, ss 355(2), 428(3). See **[4471]**
SI 2001/2633: Financial Services and Markets Act 2000 (Financial Promotion) (Amendment) Order 2001 Authority: FSMA 2000, ss 21(5), 238(6). Revoked by the Financial Services and Markets Act 2000 (Financial Promotion) Order 2005, SI 2005/1529
SI 2001/2632: Financial Services and Markets Act 2000 (Commencement No 5) Order 2001 Authority: FSMA 2000, s 431(2). Brings into force various provisions of the 2000 Act
SI 2001/2617: Financial Services and Markets Act 2000 (Mutual Societies) Order 2001 Authority: FSMA 2000, ss 334(1), (2), 335(1)–(4), 336(1), (2), 337, 338(1), (2), 339(1), (2), 426, 427, 428(3). FSMA 2000, Pt XXI provides for the transfer, to the FSA or to the Treasury, of functions of the Friendly Societies Commission, the Building Societies Commission, and the Registry of Friendly Societies (specifically the Chief Registrar of Friendly Societies, the central office of the registry of friendly societies, the assistant registrar of friendly societies for Scotland, and the other assistant registrars). This Order effects the transfer of these functions, contains general consequential and transitional provisions in relation to transferred functions, and provides for the dissolution of the bodies and office-holders whose functions are transferred
SI 2001/2587: Financial Services and Markets Act 2000 (Communications by Auditors) Regulations 2001 Authority: FSMA 2000, ss 342(5), 343(5), 428(3). At **[4469]**. These Regulations implement, in part, European Parliament and Council Directive 95/26/EC amending Directives 77/780/EEC and 89/646/EEC in the field of credit institutions, Directives 73/239/EEC and 92/49/EEC in the field of non- life insurance, Directives 79/267/EEC and 92/96/EEC in the field of life assurance, Directive 93/22/EEC in the field of investment firms and Directive 85/611/EEC in the field of undertakings for collective investment in transferable securities (UCITS), with a view to reinforcing prudential supervision
SI 2001/2512: Financial Services and Markets Act 2000 (Transitional Provisions) (Reviews of Pensions Business) Order 2001 Authority: FSMA 2000, ss 426–428. This Order makes transitional provisions with respect to the reviews of pension selling being conducted under FSA . The reviews concern (a) the selling of personal pension schemes between 29 April 1988 and 30 June 1994, and (b) the selling of free standing additional voluntary contribution schemes between 29 April 1988 and 15 August 1999
SI 2001/2511: Financial Services and Markets Act 2000 (EEA Passport Rights) Regulations 2001 Authority: FSMA 2000, ss 417(1), 426–428, Sch 3, paras 13(1)(b)(iii), 14(1)(b), 17(a)–(c), 18. 22. At **[4448]**
SI 2001/2510: Financial Services and Markets Act 2000 (Gaming Contracts) Order 2001 Authority: FSMA 2000, s 412(2), (6). At **[4446]**

2001 Statutory Instruments

SI 2001/2509: Financial Services and Markets Act 2000 (Consultation with Competent Authorities) Regulations 2001
Authority: FSMA 2000, ss 183(2), 188(2), 417(1), 428(3). At **[4440]**. These Regulations implement, in part, Council Directive 93/22/EEC on investment services in the securities field, and European Parliament and Council Directive 2000/12/EC relating to the taking up and pursuit of the business of credit institutions

SI 2001/2508: Financial Services and Markets Act 2000 (Appointed Representatives) (Amendment) Regulations 2001
Authority: FSMA 2000, ss 39(1), 417(1). Amend the Financial Services and Markets Act 2000 (Appointed Representatives) Regulations 2001, SI 2001/1217 at **[4159]**

SI 2001/2507: Financial Services and Markets Act 2000 (Variation of Threshold Conditions) Order 2001
Authority: FSMA 2000, s 428(3), Sch 6, paras 8, 9. This Order varies the threshold conditions in FSMA 2000, Sch 6, which authorised persons, and applicants for authorisation, under the Act must satisfy. See the notes to Sch 6, Pt I to the Act at **[2443]**

SI 2001/2476: Financial Services and Markets Tribunal Rules 2001
Authority: FSMA 2000, ss 132(3), 137(6), Sch 13, para 9. At **[4409]**

SI 2001/2383: Financial Services and Markets Act 2000 (Collective Investment Schemes constituted in other EEA States) Regulations 2001
Authority: FSMA 2000, ss 264, 417(1). At **[4405]**. These Regulations implement, in part, Council Directive 85/611/EEC on the coordination of laws, regulations and administrative provisions relating to undertakings for collective investment in transferable securities (UCITS)

SI 2001/2364: Financial Services and Markets Act 2000 (Commencement No 4 and Transitional Provision) Order 2001
Authority: FSMA 2000, ss 431(2), 428(3). Brings into force various provisions of the 2000 Act

SI 2001/2361: Financial Services and Markets Act 2000 (Meaning of "Policy" and "Policyholder") Order 2001
Authority: FSMA 2000, ss 424(2), 428(3). At **[4402]**

SI 2001/2326: Financial Services and Markets Act 2000 (Transitional Provisions) (Ombudsman Scheme and Complaints Scheme) Order 2001
Authority: FSMA 2000, ss 426–428. Articles 2–17 of this Order make transitional provision in relation to Pt XVI of FSMA 2000, which provides for the establishment of an ombudsman scheme. The Order provides for certain complaints relating to acts or omissions occurring before the commencement of Pt XVI, which fell (or would have fallen) within the scope of one of the "former schemes" (listed in art 1(2)), to be dealt with under the new scheme. The remainder of the Order makes transitional provisions concerned with complaints relating to certain matters occurring before the coming into force of FSMA 2000, s 19

SI 2001/2256: Financial Services and Markets Act 2000 (Rights of Action) Regulations 2001
Authority: FSMA 2000, ss 20(3), 71(2), (3), 150(3), (5), 202(2), 417(1), 428(3). At **[4395]**

SI 2001/2255: Financial Services and Markets Act 2000 (Transitional Provisions) (Designated Date for The Securities and Futures Authority) Order 2001
Authority: FSMA 2000, s 428(3), Sch 21, para 1. Sch 21 to FSMA 2000 makes transitional provisions in relation to the provisions of the FSA 1986 which relate to the recognition and subsequent supervision of recognised self-regulating organisations, pending the repeal of the 1986 Act. Sch 21 came into force on the passing of FSMA 2000 but applies in part from a date designated by the Treasury. This Order designates 13 July 2001 as the designated date for the Securities and Futures Authority Limited

SI 2001/2188: Financial Services and Markets Act 2000 (Disclosure of Confidential Information) Regulations 2001
Authority: FSMA 2000, ss 349(1)(b), (2), (3), 417(1), 426, 427, 428(3). At **[4372]**

SI 2001/1858: Financial Services and Markets Act 2000 (Competition Information) (Specification of Enactment etc) Order 2001
Authority: FSMA 2000, s 428(3), Sch 19. Lapsed on the repeal of FSMA 2000, Sch 19 by the Enterprise Act 2002, ss 247(k), 278(2), Sch 26

SI 2001/1857: Financial Services and Markets Act 2000 (Disclosure of Information by Prescribed Persons) Regulations 2001
Authority: FSMA 2000, ss 353(1), 417(1). At **[4368]**

2001 Statutory Instruments
SI 2001/1821: Financial Services and Markets Act 2000 (Consequential and Transitional Provisions) (Miscellaneous) Order 2001 Authority: FSMA 2000, ss 426–428. This Order makes consequential and transitional provisions in consequence of the Financial Services and Markets Act 2000 (Commencement No 3) Order, SI 2001/1820 which brought into force the provisions of FSMA 2000 relating to the constitution and rule making powers of the FSA and the scheme operator of the Ombudsman scheme
SI 2001/1820: Financial Services and Markets Act 2000 (Commencement No 3) Order 2001 Authority: FSMA 2000, s 431(2). Brings into force various provisions of the 2000 Act
SI 2001/1819: Financial Services and Markets Act 2000 (Regulations Relating to Money Laundering) Regulations 2001 Authority: FSMA 2000, ss 168(4)(b), 402(1)(b), 417(1). Revoked by the Money Laundering Regulations 2003, SI 2003/3075
SI 2001/1783: Financial Services and Markets Act 2000 (Compensation Scheme: Electing Participants) Regulations 2001 Authority: FSMA 2000, ss 213(10), 214(5), 224(4), 417(1), 428(3). At **[4362]**. These Regulations implement, in part, European Parliament and Council Directive 94/19/EC on deposit-guarantee schemes, and European Parliament and Council Directive 97/9/EC on investor-compensation schemes
SI 2001/1534: Financial Services and Markets Act 2000 (Transitional Provisions and Savings) (Rules) Order 2001 Authority: FSMA 2000, ss 426–428. This Order makes transitional provision in relation to the rule making powers conferred on the FSA under FSMA 2000. Pt I contains the commencement and interpretation provisions. Pt II concerns the power of the FSA to designate existing rules and legislative provisions which will be repealed or will lapse at commencement so that they continue in effect after commencement as if they were rules made by the FSA. This is an alternative to the FSA making new rules under its FSMA 2000 powers. Pt III of the Order contains transitional provisions in relation to consultation which the FSA has carried out in anticipation of the powers to be conferred on it by FSMA 2000. Where such consultations about rules, codes, statements of policy, etc, to be made under the Act was carried out before FSMA 2000 received Royal Assent, the procedure adopted may not have been fully compliant with the requirements laid down in the Act
SI 2001/1420: Financial Services and Markets Act 2000 (Service of Notices) Regulations 2001 Authority: FSMA 2000, ss 414, 428(3). At **[4351]**
SI 2001/1335: Financial Services and Markets Act 2000 (Financial Promotion) Order 2001 Authority: FSMA 2000, ss 22(1), (5), 428(3), Sch 2, para 25. Revoked and replaced by the Financial Services and Markets Act 2000 (Financial Promotion) Order 2005, SI 2005/1529
SI 2001/1283: Financial Services and Markets Act 2000 (Dissolution of the Insurance Brokers Registration Council) (Consequential Provisions) Order 2001 Authority: FSMA 2000, ss 416(4), 428(3). This Order makes provision consequential on the provisions of the FSMA 2000, s 416 which repeals the Insurance Brokers (Registration) Act 1977 and dissolves the Insurance Brokers Registration Council. The Grants Fund, comprising funds raised by levying practising insurance brokers and enrolled bodies, is transferred to the manager of the Investor Compensation Scheme established under FSA 1986, s 54. All other property, liabilities and rights to which the Council was entitled or subject immediately before 30 April 2001 transfer to the Treasury on that date. This Order also makes provision in respect of liabilities which the Council would have incurred if the Council had not been dissolved, legal proceedings to which the Council was, before 30 April 2001, a party and contracts, agreements and other instruments which relate to the property, rights and liabilities which, by virtue of this Order, become property, rights and liabilities of the Treasury. This Order also makes consequential amendments to other legislation which relates to the Council or which refers to the Insurance Brokers (Registration) Act 1977. The Order also permits the Treasury to disclose information which they acquire by virtue of this Order where the disclosure could have been made by the Council, but for its dissolution and the provisions of the Order
SI 2001/1282: Financial Services and Markets Act 2000 (Commencement No 2) Order 2001 Authority: FSMA 2000, s 431(2). Brings into force various provisions of the 2000 Act
SI 2001/1228: Open-Ended Investment Companies Regulations 2001 Authority: FSMA 2000, ss 262, 428(3). See **[4173]**

2001 Statutory Instruments
SI 2001/1227: Financial Services and Markets Act 2000 (Professions) (Non-Exempt Activities) Order 2001 Authority: FSMA 2000, ss 327(6), 428(3). At **[4164]**
SI 2001/1226: Financial Services and Markets Act 2000 (Designated Professional Bodies) Order 2001 Authority: FSMA 2000, s 326. At **[4162]**
SI 2001/1217: Financial Services and Markets Act 2000 (Appointed Representatives) Regulations 2001 Authority: FSMA 2000, ss 39(1), 417(1). At **[4159]**
SI 2001/1201: Financial Services and Markets Act 2000 (Exemption) Order 2001 Authority: FSMA 2000, ss 38, 428(3). At **[4149]**
SI 2001/1177: Financial Services and Markets Act 2000 (Carrying on Regulated Activities by Way of Business) Order 2001 Authority: FSMA 2000, ss 419, 428(3). At **[4145]**
SI 2001/1062: Financial Services and Markets Act 2000 (Collective Investment Schemes) Order 2001 Authority: FSMA 2000, s 235(5). At **[4141]**
SI 2001/1060: Financial Services and Markets Act 2000 (Promotion of Collective Investment Schemes) (Exemptions) Order 2001 Authority: FSMA 2000, s 238(6), (7). At **[4112]**
SI 2001/996: Financial Services and Markets Act 2000 (Prescribed Markets and Qualifying Investments) Order 2001 Authority: originally made under FSMA 2000, s 118(3). However, following the amendment of Pt VIII of that Act by the Financial Services and Markets Act 2000 (Market Abuse) Regulations 2005, SI 2005/381, it now has effect as if made under s 130A(1). At **[4106]**
SI 2001/995: Financial Services and Markets Act 2000 (Recognition Requirements for Investment Exchanges and Clearing Houses) Regulations 2001 Authority: FSMA 2000, ss 286(1), 426, 427, 428(3). These Regulations set out the recognition requirements which investment exchanges and clearing houses must satisfy in order to be, or remain, recognised by the FSA under FSMA 2000, s 290
SI 2001/544: Financial Services and Markets Act 2000 (Regulated Activities) Order 2001 Authority: FSMA 2000, ss 22(1), (5), 426, 428(3), Sch 2, para 25. At **[4001]**. This Order implements, in part, Council Directive 93/22/EEC on investment services in the securities field
SI 2001/516: Financial Services and Markets Act 2000 (Commencement No 1) Order 2001 Authority: FSMA 2000, s 431(2). Brings into force various provisions of the 2000 Act

2000 Statutory Instruments
SI 2000/1734: Financial Services and Markets (Transitional Provisions) (Designated Date for Certain Self-Regulating Organisations) Order 2000 Authority: FSMA 2000, s 428, Sch 21, paras 1, 2. Schedule 21 to FSMA 2000 makes transitional provisions in relation to the provisions of the Financial Services Act 1986 which relate to the recognition and subsequent supervision of recognised self-regulating organisations, pending the repeal of the 1986 Act. Schedule 21 came into force on the passing of FSMA 2000 but applies in part from a date designated by the Treasury. This Order designates 25 July 2000 as the designated date for the Personal Investment Authority Limited and for the Investment Management Regulatory Organisation Limited

[A5]

APPENDICES

Appendix 6: Domestic Implementation of EC Directives

NOTES

This table lists the UK implementing measures of the Directives reproduced in Part V of this Handbook. Directives that are no longer in force are printed in italics.

Directive	Implemented in the UK by
***89/298/EEC** coordinating the requirements for the drawing-up, scrutiny and distribution of the prospectus to be published when transferable securities are offered to the public* (Repealed by European Parliament and Council Directive 2003/71/EC (see below))	**SI 1999/734** Public Offers of Securities (Amendment) Regulations 1999 (spent)[1] **SI 1999/1146** Public Offers of Securities (Amendment) (No 2) Regulations 1999 (spent)[1] **SI 2001/2955** Public Offers of Securities (Exemptions) Regulations 2001 (spent)[1] **SI 2001/2956** Financial Services and Markets Act 2000 (Official Listing of Securities) Regulations 2001 at **[4478]** **SI 2001/2957** Financial Services and Markets Act 2000 (Official Listing of Securities) (Transitional Provisions) Order 2001
93/22/EEC Council Directive on investment services in the securities field (Repealed by European Parliament and Council Directive 2004/39/EC, as from 1 November 2007 (see below))	**SI 2001/544** Financial Services and Markets Act 2000 (Regulated Activities) Order 2001 at **[4001]** **SI 2001/2509** Financial Services and Markets Act 2000 (Consultation with Competent Authorities) Regulations 2001 at **[4440]** **SI 2001/2639** Financial Services and Markets Act 2000 Own-initiative Power) (Overseas Regulators) Regulations 2001 at **[4475]** **SI 2003/693** Financial Services and Markets Act 2000 (Disclosure of Confidential Information) (Amendment) Regulations 2003 **SI 2004/1862** Financial Conglomerates and Other Financial Groups Regulations 2004 at **[4683]**
97/9/EC Directive of the European Parliament and of the Council on investor-compensation schemes	**SI 2001/1783** Financial Services and Markets Act 2000 (Compensation Scheme: Electing Participants) Regulations 2001 at **[4362]** **SI 2001/2967** Financial Services and Markets Act 2000 (Transitional Provisions, Repeals and Savings) (Financial Services Compensation Scheme) Order 2001

Directive	Implemented in the UK by
***2000/12/EC** Directive of the European Parliament and of the Council relating to the taking up and pursuit of the business of credit institutions* (Repealed by European Parliament and Council Directive 2006/48/EC, as from 20 July 2006 (see below))	**SI 2000/2952** Banking Consolidation Directive (Consequential Amendments) Regulations 2000 **SI 2001/2509** Financial Services and Markets Act 2000 (Consultation with Competent Authorities) Regulations 2001 at **[4440]** **SI 2001/2639** Financial Services and Markets Act 2000 (Own-initiative Power) (Overseas Regulators) Regulations at **[4475]** **SI 2001/3084** Financial Services and Markets Act 2000 (Gibraltar) Order 2001 at **[4504]** **SI 2002/682** Financial Services and Markets Act 2000 (Regulated Activities) (Amendment) Order 2002 at **[4636]** **SI 2002/765** Electronic Money (Miscellaneous Amendments) Regulations 2002 **SI 2004/1862** Financial Conglomerates and Other Financial Groups Regulations 2004 at **[4683]**
2001/34/EC Directive of the European Parliament and of the Council on the admission of securities to official stock exchange listing and on information to be published on those securities	**SI 2001/3624** Financial Services and Markets Act 2000 (Disclosure of Confidential Information) (Amendment) (No 2) Regulations 2001
2002/87/EC Directive of the European Parliament and of the Council on the supplementary supervision of credit institutions, insurance undertakings and investment firms in a financial conglomerate and amending Council Directives 73/239/EEC, 79/267/EEC, 92/49/EEC, 92/96/EEC, 93/6/EEC and 93/22/EEC, and Directives 98/78/EC and 2000/12/EC of the European Parliament and of the Council	**SI 2004/1862** Financial Conglomerates and Other Financial Groups Regulations 2004 at **[4683]**
2003/6/EC Directive of the European Parliament and of the Council on insider dealing and market manipulation (market abuse)	**SI 2005/381** Financial Services and Markets Act 2000 (Market Abuse) Regulations 2005 at **[7355D]** **SI 2005/382** Investment Recommendation (Media) Regulations 2005 at **[7356]**
2003/71/EC Directive of the European Parliament and of the Council on the prospectus to be published when securities are offered to the public or admitted to trading and amending 2001/34	**SI 2005/1433** Prospectus Regulations 2005 at **[7398]**
2003/124/EC Commission Directive implementing Directive 2003/6/EC of the European Parliament and of the Council as regards the definition and public disclosure of inside information and the definition of market manipulation	**SI 2005/381** Financial Services and Markets Act 2000 (Market Abuse) Regulations 2005 at **[7355D]** **SI 2005/382** Investment Recommendation (Media) Regulations 2005 at **[7356]**
2003/125/EC Commission Directive implementing Directive 2003/6/EC of the European Parliament and of the Council as regards the fair presentation of investment recommendations and the disclosure of conflicts of interest	**SI 2005/381** Financial Services and Markets Act 2000 (Market Abuse) Regulations 2005 at **[7355D]** **SI 2005/382** Investment Recommendation (Media) Regulations 2005 at **[7356]**

APPENDICES

Directive	Implemented in the UK by
2004/25/EC Directive of the European Parliament and of the Council on takeover bids	**SI 2006/1183** Takeovers Directive (Interim Implementation) Regulations 2006 at **[7509]** et seq[2] **Companies Act 2006** ie, Pt 28 at **[S942]** et seq[2] **SI 2007/318** Companies Acts (Unregistered Companies) Regulations 2007
2004/39/EC Directive of the European Parliament and of the Council on markets in financial instruments amending Council Directives 85/611/EEC and 93/6/EEC and Directive 2000/12/EC of the European Parliament and of the Council and repealing Council Directive 93/22/EEC **Note:** Art 70 (at **[9683]**) provides that Member States shall adopt the laws, regulations and administrative provisions necessary to comply with this Directive by 31 January 2007 and shall apply the measures from 1 November 2007. The original date for transposition was 30 April 2006 but implementation has been delayed following the substitution of Art 70 by Directive 2006/31/EC. Art 2 of the 2006 Directive (at **[9820]**) provides for the same transposition dates as in the amended 2004/39/EC	**SI 2006/2975** Financial Services and Markets Act 2000 (Markets in Financial Instruments) (Modification of Powers) Regulations 2006 at **[7607]** **SI 2006/3384:** Financial Services and Markets Act 2000 (Regulated Activities) (Amendment No 3) Order 2006 **SI 2006/3385:** Financial Services and Markets Act 2000 (EEA Passport Rights) (Amendment) Regulations 2006 **SI 2006/3386** Financial Services and Markets Act 2000 (Recognition Requirements for Investment Exchanges and Clearing Houses) (Amendment) Regulations 2006 **SI 2006/3413** Financial Services and Markets Act 2000 (Disclosure of Confidential Information) (Amendment) Regulations 2006 **SI 2006/3414** Financial Services and Markets Act 2000 (Appointed Representatives) (Amendment) Regulations 2006 **SI 2007/124** Uncertificated Securities (Amendment) Regulations 2007 **SI 2007/125** Financial Services and Markets Act 2000 (Exemption) (Amendment) Order 2007 **SI 2007/126** Financial Services and Markets Act 2000 (Markets in Financial Instruments) Regulations 2007 **SI 2007/763** Financial Services and Markets Act 2000 (Markets in Financial Instruments) (Amendment) Regulations 2007
2004/72/EC Commission Directive implementing Directive 2003/6/EC of the European Parliament and of the Council as regards accepted market practices, the definition of inside information in relation to derivatives on commodities, the drawing up of lists of insiders, the notification of managers' transactions and the notification of suspicious transactions	**SI 2005/381** Financial Services and Markets Act 2000 (Market Abuse) Regulations 2005 at **[7355D]**
2004/109/EC Directive of the European Parliament and of the Council on the harmonisation of transparency requirements in relation to information about issuers whose securities are admitted to trading on a regulated market and amending Directive 2001/34/EC	**Companies Act 2006** ie, ss 1265–1268, 1270–1272 of the 2006 Act in Part 43 at **[S1265]** et seq
2005/56/EC of the European Parliament and of the Council on cross-border mergers of limited liability companies	No implementation measures as of 1 July 2007. The deadline for transposition is 15 December 2007 (see Art 19 at **[9817]**)

Directive	Implemented in the UK by
2006/31/EC Directive of the European Parliament and of the Council amending Directive 2004/39/EC on markets in financial instruments, as regards certain deadlines	See 2004/39/EC above
2006/48/EC Directive of the European Parliament and of the Council relating to the taking up and pursuit of the business of credit institutions (recast)	**SI 2006/3221** Capital Requirements Regulations 2006 at **[7545]** **Note:** this Directive is a re-enactment of Directive 2000/12/EC with certain new provisions. As such, only the new provisions require transposition (as to which see Art 157 at **[9880]**). As to the transposition of Directive 2000/12/EC, see above
2006/68/EC Directive of the European Parliament and of the Council amending Council Directive 77/91/EEC as regards the formation of public limited liability companies and the maintenance and alteration of their capital	No implementation measures as of 1 July 2007. The deadline for transposition is 15 April 2008 (see Art 2 at **[9930C]**)
2006/73/EC Commission Directive implementing Directive 2004/39/EC of the European Parliament and of the Council as regards organisational requirements and operating conditions for investment firms and defined terms for the purposes of that Directive	**SI 2006/2975** Financial Services and Markets Act 2000 (Markets in Financial Instruments) (Modification of Powers) Regulations 2006
2007/14/EC Commission Directive laying down detailed rules for the implementation of certain provisions of Directive 2004/109/EC on the harmonisation of transparency requirements in relation to information about issuers whose securities are admitted to trading on a regulated market	See the FSA's Transparency Rules made under provisions contained in CA 2006, Pt 43 (effective from 20 January 2007)

NOTES

1 Amended the Public Offers of Securities Regulations 1995, SI 1995/1537 and became spent on the revocation of the 1995 Regulations by the Prospectus Regulations 2005, SI 2005/1433, as from 1 July 2005.

2 The implementation date for the Takeovers Directive was 20 May 2006. In light of the fact that the Companies Act 2006 was still going through Parliament at this stage, interim implementation provisions were introduced under the European Communities Act 1972, s 2(2), ie, the Takeovers Directive (Interim Implementation) Regulations 2006, SI 2006/1183. The 2006 Regulations were revoked (subject to transitional provisions) on 6 April 2007 (the same date as CA 2006, Part 28 was brought into force).

[A6]

Appendix 7: Companies Act 2006 – Duties of Company Directors

COMPANIES ACT 2006
DUTIES OF COMPANY DIRECTORS

Ministerial Statements
DTI
June 2007

INTRODUCTION

Rt Hon Margaret Hodge MP MBE (Minister of State for Industry and the Regions)

I know that the new statutory duties of directors set out in Part 10 of the Companies Act 2006 were keenly debated while the Bill was going through Parliament, and I am sure they will continue to be seen as one of the most significant parts of the Act.

During those debates, I and the other Ministers were questioned about the meaning of the provisions. Some of our responses and statements may be helpful to people interested in what the provisions mean, and I am pleased to be publishing this structured collection of what we believe are the most useful of them.

There are two ways of looking at the statutory statement of directors' duties: on the one the hand it simply codifies the existing common law obligations of company directors; on the other – especially in section 172: the duty to act in the interests of the company – it marks a radical departure in articulating the connection between what is good for a company and what is good for society at large.

Continuity

The statutory expression of the duties is essentially the same as the existing duties established by case law, the only major exception being the new procedures for dealing with conflicts of interest.

The simple high-level guidance for directors in the box on the following page illustrates the way in which the codification maintains continuity with the existing law: this advice on how a director has to live up to his position of trust is applicable to the pre-existing common law as well as to the new codification. For most directors, who are working hard and put the interests of their company before their own, there will be no need to change their behaviour.

Guidance for company directors—

1) Act in the company's best interests, taking everything you think relevant into account.

2) Obey the company's constitution and decisions taken under it.

3) Be honest, and remember that the company's property belongs to it and not to you or to its shareholders.

4) Be diligent, careful and well informed about the company's affairs. If you have any special skills or experience, use them.

5) Make sure the company keeps records of your decisions.

6) Remember that you remain responsible for the work you give to others.

7) Avoid situations where your interests conflict with those of the company. When in doubt disclose potential conflicts quickly.

8) Seek external advice where necessary, particularly if the company is in financial difficulty.

Change

But compared with most text-book definitions of the common law duties of directors, the new statutory statement captures a cultural change in the way in which companies conduct their business. There was a time when business success in the interests of shareholders was thought to be in conflict with society's aspirations for people who work in the company or in supply chain companies, for the long-term well-being of the community and for the protection of the environment. The law is now based on a new approach. Pursuing the interests of shareholders and embracing wider responsibilities are complementary purposes, not contradictory ones.

I strongly believe that businesses perform better, and are more sustainable in the long term, when they have regard to a wider group of issues in pursuing success. That is a common-sense approach that reflects a modern view of the way in which businesses operate in their community: they interact with customers and suppliers; they make sure that employees are motivated and properly rewarded; and they think about their impact on communities and the environment. They do so at least partly because it makes good business sense.

The new expression of the duties is part of the wider recognition and encouragement of change in the Act. The enhanced business review, which for quoted companies must now include information on environmental, employee, social and community issues, is another key example that builds on the growing consensus that it is good business sense for companies to embrace wider social responsibilities.

I am sure that directors' duties will continue to evolve as times change and as societal norms are transformed. Corporate social responsibility has developed and evolved over time. The relationship between business interests and the wider world is changing all the time. The best way of achieving lasting cultural change is to go with the tide and the broad consensus of opinion.

Margaret Hodge

Notes on the ministerial statements

The quotations should be read in conjunction with the Act itself (available in hard copy at *www.tshop.co.uk* or online at *www.opsi.gov.uk*) and should not be regarded as a substitute for reading that Act or seeking legal advice. Full explanatory notes on the provisions of the Act are also available at *www.tsoshop.co.uk* and at *www.opsi.gov.uk* together with tables of origins and destinations for the Act's provisions.

It should be noted that on occasion the Parliamentary quotes have been edited in order to make it easier to read them. References to Hansard have been given so the full discussion can be seen if so desired.

COMPANIES ACT 2006 – DUTIES OF DIRECTORS

Collated Hansard extracts from debates on Companies Bill (originally Company Law Reform Bill)

Background

"The law commissions and the Company Law Review concluded that a statutory statement of duties would be helpful ... it is important that ... flexibility and ability to note changing circumstances are not lost".

Lord Goldsmith, Lords Grand Committee, 6 February 2006, column 242

"First … .the origins of the general duties [is] … that they are based in certain common law rules and equitable principles … the statutory statement replaces the common rule equitable principle … once the Act is passed, one will go to the statutory statement of duties to identify the duties to identify the duty the director owed".

Lord Goldsmith, Lords Grand Committee, 6 February 2006, column 243

" … the main purpose in codifying the general duties of directors is to make what is expected of directors clearer and to make the law more accessible to them and to others".

Lord Goldsmith, Lords Grand Committee, 6 February 2006, column 254

"We should remind ourselves that being a company director is a wonderful thing for the person who is a company director. But it is a position of great responsibility which involves running the affairs of a company for the benefit of other people. It is a heavy responsibility we should not water down".

Lord Goldsmith, Lords Grand Committee, 6 February 2006, column 291

APPENDICES

Interpretation by the courts

"The courts should be left to interpret the words Parliament passes".

Lord Goldsmith, Lords Grand Committee, 6 February 2006, column 243

"Although the duties in relation to directors have developed in a distinctive way, they are often manifestations of more general principles … [it] is intended to enable the courts to continue to have regard to development in the common law rules and equitable principles applying to these other types of fiduciary relationships. The advantage of that is it will enable the statutory duties to develop in line with relevant developments in the law as it applies elsewhere."

Lord Goldsmith, Lords Grand Committee, 6 February 2006, column 244

Effect of codification

"One proposition [is] that the result of this codification will be increased litigation. That is not how we see it … as in existing law, the general duties are owed by the director to the company. It follows that, as now, only the company can enforce them. Directors are liable to the company for loss to the company, and not more widely. It is quite rare for companies to sue their directors for breach of duty. That may well continue to be the position."

Lord Goldsmith, Lords Grand Committee, 6 February 2006, column 242

Effect of the provision of new duties

"[On] the provision of new duties, we do not see why that should lead to increased litigation either. For example … the need to have regard to the interests of employees as part of the main duty to promote the success of the company … was part of case law before becoming statute. It is an important principle, and plays a crucial part in business decisions … however … there is not evidence of which we are aware that it has led to legalistic decision making by companies, or people turning away from bringing their talent to the world of enterprise. We have no reason to expect that there will be a greater degree of litigation on those duties than there is now".

Lord Goldsmith, Lords Grand Committee, 6 February 2006, column 243

Statement of general duties

"The statement of general duties … is not intended to be an exhaustive list of all the duties owed by a director to his company. The directors may owe a wide range of duties to their companies in addition to the general duties listed. Those are general, basic duties which it is seen as right and important to set out in this way. The statement that these are the general duties does not allow a director to escape any other obligation he has, including obligations under the Insolvency Act 1986."

Lord Goldsmith, Lords Grand Committee, 6 February 2006, column 249

Enlightened shareholder value

"The Company Law Review considered and consulted on two main options. The first was "enlightened shareholder value", under which a director must first act in the way that he or she considers, in good faith, would be most likely to promote the success of the company for its members … The Government agrees this is the right approach. It resolves any confusion in the mind of directors as to what that the interests of the company are, and prevents any inclination to identify those interests with their own. It also prevents confusion between the interests of those who depend on the company and those of the members".

Lord Goldsmith, Lords Grand Committee, 6 February 2006, column 255

"For the first time, the Bill includes a statutory statement of directors' general duties. It provides a code of conduct that sets out how directors are expected to behave. That enshrines in statue what the law review called "enlightened shareholder value". It recognises that directors will be more likely to achieve long term sustainable success for the benefit of their shareholders if their companies pay attention to a wider range of matters … Directors will be required to promote the success of the company in the collective best interest of the shareholders, but in doing so they will have to have regard to a wider range of factors, including the interests of employees and the environment".

Alistair Darling, Commons Second Reading, 6 June 2006, column 125

Duty to promote the success of the company

"What is success? The starting point is that it is essentially for the members of the company to define the objective they wish to achieve. Success means what the members collectively want the company to achieve. For a commercial company, success will usually mean long-term increase in value. For certain companies, such as charities and community interest companies, it will mean the attainment of the objectives for which the company has been established".

Lord Goldsmith, Lords Grand Committee, 6 February 2006, column 255

" … for a commercial company, success will normally mean long-term increase in value, but the company's constitution and decisions made under it may also lay down the appropriate success model for the company. … it is essentially for the members of a company to define the objectives they wish to achieve. The normal way for that to be done—the traditional way—is that the members do it at the time the company is established. In the old style, it would have been set down in the company's memorandum. That is changing … but the principle does not change that those who establish the company will start off by setting out what they hope to achieve. For most people who invest in companies, there is never any doubt about it—money. That is what they want. They want a long-term increase in the company. It is not a snap poll to be taken at any point in time."

Lord Goldsmith, Lords Grand Committee, 6 February 2006, column 258

" … it is for the directors, by reference to those things we are talking about – the objective of the company – to judge and form a good faith judgment about what is to be regarded as success for the members as a whole … .they will need to look at the company's constitution, shareholder decisions and anything else that they consider relevant in helping them to reach that judgement … the duty is to promote the success for the benefit of the members as a whole – that is, for the members as a collective body – not only to benefit the majority shareholders, or any particular shareholder or section of shareholders, still less the interests of directors who might happen to be shareholders themselves. That is an important statement of the way in which directors need to look at this judgement they have to make".

Lord Goldsmith, Lords Grand Committee, 6 February 2006, column 256

" … we have included the words "amongst other matters". We want to be clear that the list of factors [for a director to have regard to] is not exhaustive".

Lord Goldsmith, Lords Grand Committee, 9 May 2006, column 846

"The clause does not impose a requirement on directors to keep records, as some people have suggested, in any circumstances in which they would not have to do so now."

Margaret Hodge, Commons Committee, 11 July 2006, column 592

"The Government believe that our enlightened shareholder value approach will be mutually beneficial to business and society. We do not, however, claim that the interests of the company and of its employees will always be identical; regrettably, it will sometimes be necessary, for example, to lay off staff. The drafting … must therefore clearly point directors towards their overarching objective. We have made it clear that [the clause] will make a difference, and a very important difference. The words "have regard to" mean "think about"; they are absolutely not about just ticking boxes. If "thinking about" leads to the conclusion, as we believe it will in many cases, that the proper course is to act positively to achieve the objectives in the clause, that will be what the director's duty is. In other words "have regard to" means "give proper consideration to" … Consideration of the factors will be an integral part of the duty to promote the success of the company for the benefit of its members as a whole. The clause makes it clear that a director is to have regard to the factors in fulfilling that duty. The decisions taken by a director and the weight given to the factors will continue to be a matter for his good faith judgment.".

Margaret Hodge, Commons Report, 17 October 2006, column 789

Duty to exercise independent judgement

" … the clause does not mean that a director has to form his judgement totally independently from anyone or anything. It does not actually mean that the director has to be independent

APPENDICES

himself. He can have an interest in the matter … It is the exercise of the judgement of a director that must be independent in the sense of it being his own judgement … The duty does not prevent a director from relying on the advice or work of others, but the final judgement must be his responsibility. He clearly cannot be expected to do everything himself. Indeed, in certain circumstances directors may be in breach of duty if they fail to take appropriate advice – for example, legal advice. As with all advice, slavish reliance is not acceptable, and the obtaining of outside advice does not absolve directors from exercising their judgement on the basis of such advice".

Lord Goldsmith, Lords Grand Committee, 6 February 2006, column 282

Standard of care owed by a director

" … the standard of care which a director owes is enormously important … it is now accepted that the duty of care … is accurately stated in Section 214(4) of the Insolvency Act 1986 … .Under the clause you take account both of the general knowledge, skills and experience that may be reasonably expected of a person carrying out those functions and the general knowledge, skills and experience that that director has. It is a cumulative requirement … I want to emphasise the point that it is not making a change from what is already the common law".

Lord Goldsmith, Lords Grand Committee, 6 February 2006, column 284

Duty to avoid conflicts of interest

" … the law already recognises that potential conflicts in certain circumstances are to be avoided … there is currently no absolute rule prohibiting directors from holding multiple directorships or even from engaging in business that competes with the company of which they are a director, but obviously a tension results from that degree of tolerance and the fiduciary duties which the director owes. The solution to it is … there is no prohibition of a conflict or potential conflict as long as it is has been authorised by the directors in accordance with the requirements set out in [the Act]".

Lord Goldsmith, Lords Grand Committee, 6 February 2006, column 288

" … we do not say that this should happen just because in the mind of a director it is all right; there should be a process for the company, through its members or directors, to make that decision, and that is what these new regulations permit".

Lord Goldsmith, Lords Grand Committee, 6 February 2006, column 289

"Following consultation, the Government have already adjusted the provision … to use instead the expression "if the situation cannot reasonably be regarded as likely to give rise to a conflict of interest". This introduces the concept of reasonableness which makes the situation easier from the point of view of a director and avoids a very harsh test, although it is still a heavy duty and intended to be so."

Lord Goldsmith, Lords Grand Committee, 6 February 2006, column 293

"So far as private companies are concerned, the default position is that the directors may authorise the matter unless there is a provision in the company's constitution saying otherwise. In the case of a public company … [d]irectors may authorise the matter only if the company's constitution includes provisions saying they can do so. It must follow that if the constitution does not do so, steps will have to be taken to amend it to that effect and the members of the company will be able to take a view about whether they think that is a good move".

Lord Goldsmith, Lords Grand Committee, 6 February 2006, column 294

" … the authorisation has to be given without relying on the votes of directors seeking the authorisation or any other director with an interest in it … .Those directors cannot count towards the quorum either … .[and] any requirements under the common law for what is necessary for a valid authorisation remain in force … Finally, in general terms, the directors who are giving the authorisation will need to comply with the general duties imposed on them. Those will include, specifically, the general duty … to act in such a way that in good faith they consider that authorisation is the course of action most likely to promote the success of the company".

Lord Goldsmith, Lords Grand Committee, 9 February 2006, column 327

"… the duty does not apply if the situation cannot reasonably be regarded as being likely to give rise to a conflict of interest. If the matter falls outside the ambit of the company's business, a real conflict of interest is unlikely".

Lord Goldsmith, Lords Grand Committee, 9 May 2006, column 864

"… the company's articles may contain provisions for dealing with conflicts of interests, and directors will not be in breach of duty if they act in accordance with those provisions. Examples might include arrangements whereby the directors withdraw from any board meeting at which the matters relating to conflicts of interest are discussed … our amendments will allow all the normal, perfectly acceptable, lawful ways in which companies and their directors deal with conflicts of interest to continue."

Lord Sainsbury of Turville, Lords Report, 23 May 2006, column 722

Duty not to accept benefits from third parties

"… the purpose of the clause … is to impose on a director a duty not to accept benefits from third parties. It applies only to benefits conferred because the director is a director of the company or because of something that the director does or doesn't do as director. The word "benefit" … includes benefits of any description, including non-financial benefits. The clause codifies … [the] long-standing rule, prohibiting the exploitation of the position of director for personal benefit. It does not apply to benefits that the director receives from the company, or from any associated company, or from any person acting on behalf of any of those companies … .I … draw attention to the fact that benefits are prohibited by the duty only if their acceptance is likely to give rise to a conflict of interest".

Lord Goldsmith, Lords Grand Committee, 9 February 2006, column 330

Duty to declare interest in proposed transaction or arrangement

"[This] clause … is deliberately intended to apply only to proposed transactions … if a company is told that a director has an interest in a proposed transaction, it can decide whether to enter into the transaction, on what terms and with what safeguards. [As for] "a director is treated as being aware of matters he ought reasonably to be aware" … I believe that the test is objective – that is, one judges objectively whether this is a matter of which the director ought to be aware reasonably".

Lord Goldsmith, Lords Grand Committee, 9 February 2006, column 334

Civil consequences of breach of general duties

"… we take the view that the "duty to exercise reasonable care, skill and diligence" is not a fiduciary duty. It may be owed by someone who is a fiduciary. But that is not the same thing …It is important to keep to the principle that these are enforceable in the same way as any other fiduciary duty owed to the company by its directors."

Lord Goldsmith, Lords Grand Committee, 9 February 2006, column 336

Consent, approval or authorisation by members

"[The Bill] permitted director authorisation of what would otherwise be impermissible conflicts of interests [and] … required declarations of interest in proposed company transactions. In both those cases, the general duty no longer requires the consent of the members. The common law rules or principles that refer to the failure to have had a conflict of interest approved by the member of a company under certain circumstances need to be set aside … .However … the company's constitution can reverse the change and can insist on certain steps being taken requiring the consent of the members in certain circumstances".

Lord Goldsmith, Lords Grand Committee, 9 February 2006, column 337

Indemnifying directors

"… the starting point for our reform package was a principle … that companies should be prohibited from exempting directors from, or indemnifying them against, liability for negligence, default, breach of duty or breach of trust in relation to the company. However the reform package also recognised that companies should be permitted to indemnify directors in respect of third-party claims in most circumstances … There are four main possible exceptions to indemnification: criminal penalties; penalties imposed by regulatory bodies: costs incurred by the director in defending criminal proceedings in which he is convicted; and costs incurred by the director in defending civil proceedings brought by the company in which final judgement is given against him".

Lord Goldsmith, Lords Grand Committee, 9 February 2006, column 364

"[The Companies (Audit, Investigations and Community Enterprise) Act 2004] … closed an important loophole concerning the indemnification of directors by third parties. It used to be the practice in some groups that one group company would indemnify the director of another group company … in effect to circumvent the rule that the company could not indemnify its own directors. We take the view that … continu[ing] to make directors properly accountable for what they do in relation to the company … should stand".

Lord Goldsmith, Lords Grand Committee, 9 February 2006, column 366

"It is also important to remember that at the same time as the loophole was closed, important reforms were introduced that permit all companies to indemnify directors against third-party claims, subject to … [certain] requirements. Although we agree that indemnification by a parent company of the directors is less likely to result in attempts at circumvention of the prohibition than indemnification by a wholly owned subsidiary company of the director of a holding company, we still believe there is scope for mischief. We cannot … accept [any] amendment".

Lord Sainsbury of Turville, Lords Report, 23 May 2006, column 724

Shadow directors

"The law is still developing. It would not be right for the general duties not to apply at all to a shadow directors, but the law may develop in such a way that some do and some don't. It is right to leave those areas, as now, to the courts … "

Lord Goldsmith, Lords Grand Committee, 9 May 2006, column 828

[A7]

Appendix 8: Table of commencements for the Companies Act 2006

NOTES

The commencement of the Companies Act 2006 is provided for by s 1300 (at **[S1300]**). See also the Orders made under that section, ie: the Companies Act 2006 (Commencement No 1, Transitional Provisions and Savings) Order 2006, SI 2006/3428 (at **[7574]**), and the Companies Act 2006 (Commencement No 2, Consequential Amendments, Transitional Provisions and Savings) Order 2007, SI 2007/1093 (at **[7614]**). See also the draft Companies Act 2006 (Commencement No 3, Consequential Amendments, Transitional Provisions and Savings) Order 2007 in Appendix 12 at **[A12]**.

This table lists the commencement dates for the 2006 Act. Where a date has been appointed for a section or Schedule the number of the relevant commencement order is given in the same column – or the abbreviation 'RA' (Royal Assent) is used, as appropriate. Details of commencements for limited purposes, transitional provisions and savings, etc, are given in the footnotes to this table. Other abbreviations used in this table are as follows:

- CO No 1: the Companies Act 2006 (Commencement No 1, Transitional Provisions and Savings) Order 2006, SI 2006/3428.
- CO No 2: the Companies Act 2006 (Commencement No 2, Consequential Amendments, Transitional Provisions and Savings) Order 2007, SI 2007/1093.
- CO No 3: the draft Companies Act 2006 (Commencement No 3, Consequential Amendments, Transitional Provisions and Savings) Order 2007.
- GB: Great Britain.
- NI: Northern Ireland.

Provision of CA 2006	Commencement
Part 1: General Introductory Provisions	
1 Companies	*Not in force*
2 The Companies Acts	1 Jan 2007 (certain purposes) (CO No 1)[1] 20 Jan 2007 (certain purposes) (CO No 1)[1] 6 Apr 2007 (otherwise) (CO No 2)[2]
3 Limited and unlimited companies	*Not in force*
4 Private and public companies	*Not in force*
5 Companies limited by guarantee and having share capital	*Not in force*
6 Community interest companies	*Not in force*
Part 2: Company Formation	
7 Method of forming company	*Not in force*
8 Memorandum of association	20 Jan 2007 (certain purposes) (CO No 1)[3] *Not in force* (otherwise)
9 Registration documents	*Not in force*
10 Statement of capital and initial shareholdings	20 Jan 2007 (certain purposes) (CO No 1)[3] *Not in force* (otherwise)
11 Statement of guarantee	20 Jan 2007 (certain purposes) (CO No 1)[3] *Not in force* (otherwise)
12 Statement of proposed officers	*Not in force*
13 Statement of compliance	*Not in force*
14 Registration	*Not in force*
15 Issue of certificate of incorporation	*Not in force*
16 Effect of registration	*Not in force*
Part 3: A Company's Constitution	
Chapter 1: Introductory	
17 A company's constitution	1 Oct 2007 (certain purposes) (CO No 3)[4] *Not in force* (otherwise)
Chapter 2: Articles of Association	
18 Articles of association	*Not in force*

Provision of CA 2006	Commencement
Part 3: A Company's Constitution	
Chapter 2: Articles of Association	
19 Power of Secretary of State to prescribe model articles	20 Jan 2007 (certain purposes) (CO No 1)[3] *Not in force* (otherwise)
20 Default application of model articles	*Not in force*
21 Amendment of articles	*Not in force*
22 Entrenched provisions of the articles	*Not in force*
23 Notice to registrar of existence of restriction on amendment of articles	*Not in force*
24 Statement of compliance where amendment of articles restricted	*Not in force*
25 Effect of alteration of articles on company's members	*Not in force*
26 Registrar to be sent copy of amended articles	*Not in force*
27 Registrar's notice to comply in case of failure with respect to amended articles	*Not in force*
28 Existing companies: provisions of memorandum treated as provisions of articles	*Not in force*
Chapter 3: Resolutions and Agreements Affecting a Company's Constitution	
29 Resolutions and agreements affecting a company's constitution	1 Oct 2007 (CO No 3)[5]
30 Copies of resolutions or agreements to be forwarded to registrar	1 Oct 2007 (CO No 3)[5]
Chapter 4: Miscellaneous and Supplementary Provisions	
31 Statement of company's objects	*Not in force*
32 Constitutional documents to be provided to members	20 Jan 2007 (certain purposes) (CO No 1)[3] *Not in force* (otherwise)
33 Effect of company's constitution	*Not in force*
34 Notice to registrar where company's constitution altered by enactment	*Not in force*
35 Notice to registrar where company's constitution altered by order	*Not in force*
36 Documents to be incorporated in or accompany copies of articles issued by company	*Not in force*
37 Right to participate in profits otherwise than as member void	*Not in force*
38 Application to single member companies of enactments and rules of law	*Not in force*
Part 4: A Company's Capacity and Related Matters	
39 A company's capacity	*Not in force*
40 Power of directors to bind the company	*Not in force*
41 Constitutional limitations: transactions involving directors or their associates	*Not in force*
42 Constitutional limitations: companies that are charities	*Not in force*
43 Company contracts	*Not in force*
44 Execution of documents	*Not in force*
45 Common seal	*Not in force*
46 Execution of deeds	*Not in force*

Provision of CA 2006	Commencement
Part 4: A Company's Capacity and Related Matters	
47 Execution of deeds or other documents by attorney	*Not in force*
48 Execution of documents by companies	*Not in force*
49 Official seal for use abroad	*Not in force*
50 Official seal for share certificates etc	*Not in force*
51 Pre-incorporation contracts, deeds and obligations	*Not in force*
52 Bills of exchange and promissory notes	*Not in force*
Part 5: A Company's Name	
Chapter 1: General Requirements	
53 Prohibited names	*Not in force*
54 Names suggesting connection with government or public authority	20 Jan 2007 (certain purposes) (CO No 1)[3] *Not in force* (otherwise)
55 Other sensitive words or expressions	20 Jan 2007 (certain purposes) (CO No 1)[3] *Not in force* (otherwise)
56 Duty to seek comments of government department or other specified body	20 Jan 2007 (certain purposes) (CO No 1)[3] *Not in force* (otherwise)
57 Permitted characters etc	20 Jan 2007 (certain purposes) (CO No 1)[3] *Not in force* (otherwise)
Chapter 2: Indications of Company Type or Legal Form	
58 Public limited companies	*Not in force*
59 Private limited companies	*Not in force*
60 Exemption from requirement as to use of "limited"	20 Jan 2007 (certain purposes) (CO No 1)[3] *Not in force* (otherwise)
61 Continuation of existing exemption: companies limited by shares	*Not in force*
62 Continuation of existing exemption: companies limited by guarantee	*Not in force*
63 Exempt company: restriction on amendment of articles	*Not in force*
64 Power to direct change of name in case of company ceasing to be entitled to exemption	*Not in force*
65 Inappropriate use of indications of company type or legal form	20 Jan 2007 (certain purposes) (CO No 1)[3] *Not in force* (otherwise)
Chapter 3: Similarity to Other Names	
66 Name not to be the same as another in the index	20 Jan 2007 (certain purposes) (CO No 1)[3] *Not in force* (otherwise)
67 Power to direct change of name in case of similarity to existing name	20 Jan 2007 (certain purposes) (CO No 1)[3] *Not in force* (otherwise)
68 Direction to change name: supplementary provisions	*Not in force*
69 Objection to company's registered name	*Not in force*
70 Company names adjudicators	*Not in force*
71 Procedural rules	*Not in force*
72 Decision of adjudicator to be made available to public	*Not in force*
73 Order requiring name to be changed	*Not in force*
74 Appeal from adjudicator's decision	*Not in force*

APPENDICES

Provision of CA 2006	Commencement
Part 5: A Company's Name	
Chapter 4: Other Powers of the Secretary of State	
75 Provision of misleading information etc	*Not in force*
76 Misleading indication of activities	*Not in force*
Chapter 5: Change of Name	
77 Change of name	*Not in force*
78 Change of name by special resolution	*Not in force*
79 Change of name by means provided for in company's articles	*Not in force*
80 Change of name: registration and issue of new certificate of incorporation	*Not in force*
81 Change of name: effect	*Not in force*
Chapter 6: Trading Disclosures	
82 Requirement to disclose company name etc	20 Jan 2007 (certain purposes) (CO No 1)[3] *Not in force* (otherwise)
83 Civil consequences of failure to make required disclosure	*Not in force*
84 Criminal consequences of failure to make required disclosures	20 Jan 2007 (certain purposes) (CO No 1)[3] *Not in force* (otherwise)
85 Minor variations in form of name to be left out of account	*Not in force*
Part 6: A Company's Registered Office	
86 A company's registered office	*Not in force*
87 Change of address of registered office	*Not in force*
88 Welsh companies	*Not in force*
Part 7: Re-Registration as a Means of Altering a Company's Status	
89 Alteration of status by re-registration	*Not in force*
90 Re-registration of private company as public	*Not in force*
91 Requirements as to share capital	*Not in force*
92 Requirements as to net assets	*Not in force*
93 Recent allotment of shares for non-cash consideration	*Not in force*
94 Application and accompanying documents	*Not in force*
95 Statement of proposed secretary	*Not in force*
96 Issue of certificate of incorporation on re-registration	*Not in force*
97 Re-registration of public company as private limited company	*Not in force*
98 Application to court to cancel resolution	*Not in force*
99 Notice to registrar of court application or order	*Not in force*
100 Application and accompanying documents	*Not in force*
101 Issue of certificate of incorporation on re-registration	*Not in force*
102 Re-registration of private limited company as unlimited	*Not in force*
103 Application and accompanying documents	20 Jan 2007 (certain purposes) (CO No 1)[3] *Not in force* (otherwise)
104 Issue of certificate of incorporation on re-registration	*Not in force*

Provision of CA 2006	Commencement
Part 7: Re-Registration as a Means of Altering a Company's Status	
105 Re-registration of unlimited company as limited	*Not in force*
106 Application and accompanying documents	*Not in force*
107 Issue of certificate of incorporation on re-registration	*Not in force*
108 Statement of capital required where company already has share capital	20 Jan 2007 (certain purposes) (CO No 1)[3] *Not in force* (otherwise)
109 Re-registration of public company as private and unlimited	*Not in force*
110 Application and accompanying documents	20 Jan 2007 (certain purposes) (CO No 1)[3] *Not in force* (otherwise)
111 Issue of certificate of incorporation on re-registration	*Not in force*
Part 8: A Company's Members	
Chapter 1: The Members of a Company	
112 The members of a company	*Not in force*
Chapter 2: Register of Members	
113 Register of members	*Not in force*
114 Register to be kept available for inspection	*Not in force*
115 Index of members	*Not in force*
116 Rights to inspect and require copies	20 Jan 2007 (certain purposes) (CO No 1)[3] 1 Oct 2007 (otherwise) (CO No 3)[6]
117 Register of members: response to request for inspection or copy	1 Oct 2007 (CO No 3)[6]
118 Register of members: refusal of inspection or default in providing copy	1 Oct 2007 (CO No 3)[6]
119 Register of members: offences in connection with request for or disclosure of information	1 Oct 2007 (CO No 3)[6]
120 Information as to state of register and index	*Not in force*
121 Removal of entries relating to former members	*Not in force*
122 Share warrants	*Not in force*
123 Single member companies	*Not in force*
124 Company holding its own shares as treasury shares	*Not in force*
125 Power of court to rectify register	*Not in force*
126 Trusts not to be entered on register	*Not in force*
127 Register to be evidence	*Not in force*
128 Time limit for claims arising from entry in register	*Not in force*
Chapter 3: Overseas Branch Registers	
129 Overseas branch registers	20 Jan 2007 (certain purposes) (CO No 1)[3] *Not in force* (otherwise)
130 Notice of opening of overseas branch register	*Not in force*
131 Keeping of overseas branch register	20 Jan 2007 (certain purposes) (CO No 1)[3] *Not in force* (otherwise)
132 Register or duplicate to be kept available for inspection in UK	*Not in force*

APPENDICES

Provision of CA 2006	Commencement
Part 8: A Company's Members	
Chapter 3: Overseas Branch Registers	
133 Transactions in shares registered in overseas branch register	*Not in force*
134 Jurisdiction of local courts	*Not in force*
135 Discontinuance of overseas branch register	*Not in force*
Chapter 4: Prohibition on Subsidiary being Member of its Holding Company	
136 Prohibition on subsidiary being a member of its holding company	*Not in force*
137 Shares acquired before prohibition became applicable	*Not in force*
138 Subsidiary acting as personal representative or trustee	*Not in force*
139 Interests to be disregarded: residual interest under pension scheme or employees' share scheme	*Not in force*
140 Interests to be disregarded: employer's rights of recovery under pension scheme or employees' share scheme	*Not in force*
141 Subsidiary acting as authorised dealer in securities	*Not in force*
142 Protection of third parties in other cases where subsidiary acting as dealer in securities	*Not in force*
143 Application of provisions to companies not limited by shares	*Not in force*
144 Application of provisions to nominees	*Not in force*
Part 9: Exercise of Members' Rights	
145 Effect of provisions of articles as to enjoyment or exercise of members' rights	1 Oct 2007 (CO No 3)[7]
146 Traded companies: nomination of persons to enjoy information rights	1 Oct 2007 (CO No 3)[7]
147 Information rights: form in which copies to be provided	1 Oct 2007 (CO No 3)[7]
148 Termination or suspension of nomination	1 Oct 2007 (CO No 3)[7]
149 Information as to possible rights in relation to voting	1 Oct 2007 (CO No 3)[7]
150 Information rights: status of rights	1 Oct 2007 (CO No 3)[7]
151 Information rights: power to amend	20 Jan 2007 (certain purposes) (CO No 1)[3] 1 Oct 2007 (otherwise) (CO No 3)[7]
152 Exercise of rights where shares held on behalf of others: exercise in different ways	1 Oct 2007 (CO No 3)[7]
153 Exercise of rights where shares held on behalf of others: members' requests	1 Oct 2007 (CO No 3)[7]
Part 10: A Company's Directors	
Chapter 1: Appointment and Removal of Directors	
154 Companies required to have directors	1 Oct 2007 (CO No 3)
155 Companies required to have at least one director who is a natural person	*Not in force*
156 Direction requiring company to make appointment	*Not in force*
157 Minimum age for appointment as director	*Not in force*

Provision of CA 2006	Commencement
Part 10: A Company's Directors	
Chapter 1: Appointment and Removal of Directors	
158 Power to provide for exceptions from minimum age requirement	20 Jan 2007 (certain purposes) (CO No 1)[3] *Not in force* (otherwise)
159 Existing under-age directors	*Not in force*
160 Appointment of directors of public company to be voted on individually	1 Oct 2007 (CO No 3)
161 Validity of acts of directors	1 Oct 2007 (CO No 3)[8]
162 Register of directors	20 Jan 2007 (certain purposes) (CO No 1)[3] *Not in force* (otherwise)
163 Particulars of directors to be registered: individuals	*Not in force*
164 Particulars of directors to be registered: corporate directors and firms	*Not in force*
165 Register of directors' residential addresses	*Not in force*
166 Particulars of directors to be registered: power to make regulations	20 Jan 2007 (certain purposes) (CO No 1)[3] *Not in force* (otherwise)
167 Duty to notify registrar of changes	*Not in force*
168 Resolution to remove director	1 Oct 2007 (CO No 3)[9]
169 Director's right to protest against removal	1 Oct 2007 (CO No 3)[9]
Chapter 2: General Duties of Directors	
170 Scope and nature of general duties	1 Oct 2007 (CO No 3)[10]
171 Duty to act within powers	1 Oct 2007 (CO No 3)
172 Duty to promote the success of the company	1 Oct 2007 (CO No 3)
173 Duty to exercise independent judgment	1 Oct 2007 (CO No 3)
174 Duty to exercise reasonable care, skill and diligence	1 Oct 2007 (CO No 3)
175 Duty to avoid conflicts of interest	*Not in force*
176 Duty not to accept benefits from third parties	*Not in force*
177 Duty to declare interest in proposed transaction or arrangement	*Not in force*
178 Civil consequences of breach of general duties	1 Oct 2007 (CO No 3)[10]
179 Cases within more than one of the general duties	1 Oct 2007 (CO No 3)
180 Consent, approval or authorisation by members	1 Oct 2007 (CO No 3)[10]
181 Modification of provisions in relation to charitable companies	1 Oct 2007 (CO No 3)[10]
Chapter 3: Declaration of Interest in Existing Transaction or Arrangement	
182 Declaration of interest in existing transaction or arrangement	*Not in force*
183 Offence of failure to declare interest	*Not in force*
184 Declaration made by notice in writing	*Not in force*
185 General notice treated as sufficient declaration	*Not in force*
186 Declaration of interest in case of company with sole director	*Not in force*
187 Declaration of interest in existing transaction by shadow director	*Not in force*

APPENDICES

Provision of CA 2006	Commencement
Part 10: A Company's Directors	
Chapter 4: Transactions with Directors Requiring Approval of Members	
188 Directors' long-term service contracts: requirement of members' approval	1 Oct 2007 (CO No 3)[11]
189 Directors' long-term service contracts: civil consequences of contravention	1 Oct 2007 (CO No 3)[11]
190 Substantial property transactions: requirement of members' approval	1 Oct 2007 (CO No 3)[12]
191 Meaning of "substantial"	1 Oct 2007 (CO No 3)[12]
192 Exception for transactions with members or other group companies	1 Oct 2007 (CO No 3)[12]
193 Exception in case of company in winding up or administration	1 Oct 2007 (CO No 3)[12]
194 Exception for transactions on recognised investment exchange	1 Oct 2007 (CO No 3)[12]
195 Property transactions: civil consequences of contravention	1 Oct 2007 (CO No 3)[12]
196 Property transactions: effect of subsequent affirmation	1 Oct 2007 (CO No 3)[12]
197 Loans to directors: requirement of members' approval	1 Oct 2007 (CO No 3)[13]
198 Quasi-loans to directors: requirement of members' approval	1 Oct 2007 (CO No 3)[13]
199 Meaning of "quasi-loan" and related expressions	1 Oct 2007 (CO No 3)[13]
200 Loans or quasi-loans to persons connected with directors: requirement of members' approval	1 Oct 2007 (CO No 3)[13]
201 Credit transactions: requirement of members' approval	1 Oct 2007 (CO No 3)[13]
202 Meaning of "credit transaction"	1 Oct 2007 (CO No 3)[13]
203 Related arrangements: requirement of members' approval	1 Oct 2007 (CO No 3)[13]
204 Exception for expenditure on company business	1 Oct 2007 (CO No 3)[13]
205 Exception for expenditure on defending proceedings etc	1 Oct 2007 (CO No 3)[13]
206 Exception for expenditure in connection with regulatory action or investigation	1 Oct 2007 (CO No 3)[13]
207 Exceptions for minor and business transactions	1 Oct 2007 (CO No 3)[13]
208 Exceptions for intra-group transactions	1 Oct 2007 (CO No 3)[13]
209 Exceptions for money-lending companies	1 Oct 2007 (CO No 3)[13]
210 Other relevant transactions or arrangements	1 Oct 2007 (CO No 3)[13]
211 The value of transactions and arrangements	1 Oct 2007 (CO No 3)[13]
212 The person for whom a transaction or arrangement is entered into	1 Oct 2007 (CO No 3)[13]
213 Loans etc: civil consequences of contravention	1 Oct 2007 (CO No 3)[13]
214 Loans etc: effect of subsequent affirmation	1 Oct 2007 (CO No 3)[13]
215 Payments for loss of office	1 Oct 2007 (CO No 3)[14]

Provision of CA 2006	Commencement
Part 10: A Company's Directors	
Chapter 4: Transactions with Directors Requiring Approval of Members	
216 Amounts taken to be payments for loss of office	1 Oct 2007 (CO No 3)[14]
217 Payment by company: requirement of members' approval	1 Oct 2007 (CO No 3)[14]
218 Payment in connection with transfer of undertaking etc: requirement of members' approval	1 Oct 2007 (CO No 3)[14]
219 Payment in connection with share transfer: requirement of members' approval	1 Oct 2007 (CO No 3)[14]
220 Exception for payments in discharge of legal obligations etc	1 Oct 2007 (CO No 3)[14]
221 Exception for small payments	1 Oct 2007 (CO No 3)[14]
222 Payments made without approval: civil consequences	1 Oct 2007 (CO No 3)[14]
223 Transactions requiring members' approval: application of provisions to shadow directors	1 Oct 2007 (CO No 3)
224 Approval by written resolution: accidental failure to send memorandum	1 Oct 2007 (CO No 3)
225 Cases where approval is required under more than one provision	1 Oct 2007 (CO No 3)
226 Requirement of consent of Charity Commission: companies that are charities	1 Oct 2007 (CO No 3)
Chapter 5: Directors' Service Contracts	
227 Directors' service contracts	1 Oct 2007 (CO No 3)[15]
228 Copy of contract or memorandum of terms to be available for inspection	1 Oct 2007 (CO No 3)[15]
229 Right of member to inspect and request copy	20 Jan 2007 (certain purposes) (CO No 1)[3] 1 Oct 2007 (otherwise) (CO No 3)[15]
230 Directors' service contracts: application of provisions to shadow directors	1 Oct 2007 (CO No 3)[15]
Chapter 6: Contracts with Sole Members who are Directors	
231 Contract with sole member who is also a director	1 Oct 2007 (CO No 3)[16]
Chapter 7: Directors' Liabilities	
232 Provisions protecting directors from liability	1 Oct 2007 (CO No 3)[17]
233 Provision of insurance	1 Oct 2007 (CO No 3)[17]
234 Qualifying third party indemnity provision	1 Oct 2007 (CO No 3)[17]
235 Qualifying pension scheme indemnity provision	1 Oct 2007 (CO No 3)[17]
236 Qualifying indemnity provision to be disclosed in directors' report	1 Oct 2007 (CO No 3)[17]
237 Copy of qualifying indemnity provision to be available for inspection	1 Oct 2007 (CO No 3)[18]
238 Right of member to inspect and request copy	20 Jan 2007 (certain purposes) (CO No 1)[3] 1 Oct 2007 (otherwise) (CO No 3)[18]
239 Ratification of acts of directors	1 Oct 2007 (CO No 3)[19]
Chapter 8: Directors' Residential Addresses: Protection From Disclosure	
240 Protected information	*Not in force*

APPENDICES

Provision of CA 2006	Commencement
Part 10: A Company's Directors	
Chapter 8: Directors' Residential Addresses: Protection From Disclosure	
241 Protected information: restriction on use or disclosure by company	*Not in force*
242 Protected information: restriction on use or disclosure by registrar	*Not in force*
243 Permitted use or disclosure by the registrar	20 Jan 2007 (certain purposes) (CO No 1)[3] *Not in force* (otherwise)
244 Disclosure under court order	*Not in force*
245 Circumstances in which registrar may put address on the public record	*Not in force*
246 Putting the address on the public record	*Not in force*
Chapter 9: Supplementary Provisions	
247 Power to make provision for employees on cessation or transfer of business	1 Oct 2007 (CO No 3)[20]
248 Minutes of directors' meetings	1 Oct 2007 (CO No 3)[21]
249 Minutes as evidence	1 Oct 2007 (CO No 3)[21]
250 "Director"	1 Oct 2007 (CO No 3)
251 "Shadow director"	1 Oct 2007 (CO No 3)
252 Persons connected with a director	1 Oct 2007 (CO No 3)
253 Members of a director's family	1 Oct 2007 (CO No 3)
254 Director "connected with" a body corporate	1 Oct 2007 (CO No 3)
255 Director "controlling" a body corporate	1 Oct 2007 (CO No 3)
256 Associated bodies corporate	1 Oct 2007 (CO No 3)
257 References to company's constitution	1 Oct 2007 (CO No 3)
258 Power to increase financial limits	20 Jan 2007 (certain purposes) (CO No 1)[3] 1 Oct 2007 (otherwise) (CO No 3)
259 Transactions under foreign law	1 Oct 2007 (CO No 3)
Part 11: Derivative Claims and Proceedings by Members	
Chapter 1: Derivative Claims in England and Wales or Northern Ireland	
260 Derivative claims	1 Oct 2007 (CO No 3)[22]
261 Application for permission to continue derivative claim	1 Oct 2007 (CO No 3)[22]
262 Application for permission to continue claim as a derivative claim	1 Oct 2007 (CO No 3)[22]
263 Whether permission to be given	20 Jan 2007 (certain purposes) (CO No 1)[3] 1 Oct 2007(otherwise) (CO No 3)[22]
264 Application for permission to continue derivative claim brought by another member	1 Oct 2007 (CO No 3)[22]
Chapter 2: Derivative Proceedings in Scotland	
265 Derivative proceedings	1 Oct 2007 (CO No 3)[22]
266 Requirement for leave and notice	1 Oct 2007 (CO No 3)[22]
267 Application to continue proceedings as derivative proceedings	1 Oct 2007 (CO No 3)[22]
268 Granting of leave	20 Jan 2007 (certain purposes) (CO No 1)[3] 1 Oct 2007(otherwise) (CO No 3)[22]
269 Application by member to be substituted for member pursuing derivative proceedings	1 Oct 2007 (CO No 3)[22]

Provision of CA 2006	Commencement
Part 12: Company Secretaries	
270 Private company not required to have secretary	*Not in force*
271 Public company required to have secretary	*Not in force*
272 Direction requiring public company to appoint secretary	*Not in force*
273 Qualifications of secretaries of public companies	*Not in force*
274 Discharge of functions where office vacant or secretary unable to act	*Not in force*
275 Duty to keep register of secretaries	20 Jan 2007 (certain purposes) (CO No 1)[3] *Not in force* (otherwise)
276 Duty to notify registrar of changes	*Not in force*
277 Particulars of secretaries to be registered: individuals	*Not in force*
278 Particulars of secretaries to be registered: corporate secretaries and firms	*Not in force*
279 Particulars of secretaries to be registered: power to make regulations	20 Jan 2007 (certain purposes) (CO No 1)[3] *Not in force* (otherwise)
280 Acts done by person in dual capacity	*Not in force*
Part 13: Resolutions and Meetings	
Chapter 1: General Provisions About Resolutions	
281 Resolutions	1 Oct 2007 (CO No 3)[23]
282 Ordinary resolutions	1 Oct 2007 (CO No 3)[23]
283 Special resolutions	1 Oct 2007 (CO No 3)[23]
284 Votes: general rules	1 Oct 2007 (CO No 3)[23]
285 Votes: specific requirements	1 Oct 2007 (CO No 3)[23]
286 Votes of joint holders of shares	1 Oct 2007 (CO No 3)[23]
287 Saving for provisions of articles as to determination of entitlement to vote	1 Oct 2007 (CO No 3)[23]
Chapter 2: Written Resolutions	
288 Written resolutions of private companies	1 Oct 2007 (CO No 3)[24]
289 Eligible members	1 Oct 2007 (CO No 3)[24]
290 Circulation date	1 Oct 2007 (CO No 3)[24]
291 Circulation of written resolutions proposed by directors	1 Oct 2007 (CO No 3)[24]
292 Members' power to require circulation of written resolution	1 Oct 2007 (CO No 3)[24]
293 Circulation of written resolution proposed by members	1 Oct 2007 (CO No 3)[24]
294 Expenses of circulation	1 Oct 2007 (CO No 3)[24]
295 Application not to circulate members' statement	1 Oct 2007 (CO No 3)[24]
296 Procedure for signifying agreement to written resolution	1 Oct 2007 (CO No 3)[24]
297 Period for agreeing to written resolution	1 Oct 2007 (CO No 3)[24]
298 Sending documents relating to written resolutions by electronic means	1 Oct 2007 (CO No 3)[24]
299 Publication of written resolution on website	1 Oct 2007 (CO No 3)[24]

APPENDICES

Provision of CA 2006	Commencement
Part 13: Resolutions and Meetings	
Chapter 2: Written Resolutions	
300 Relationship between this Chapter and provisions of company's articles	1 Oct 2007 (CO No 3)[24]
Chapter 3: Resolutions at Meetings	
301 Resolutions at general meetings	1 Oct 2007 (CO No 3)
302 Directors' power to call general meetings	1 Oct 2007 (CO No 3)
303 Members' power to require directors to call general meeting	1 Oct 2007 (CO No 3)[25]
304 Directors' duty to call meetings required by members	1 Oct 2007 (CO No 3)[25]
305 Power of members to call meeting at company's expense	1 Oct 2007 (CO No 3)[25]
306 Power of court to order meeting	1 Oct 2007 (CO No 3)[26]
307 Notice required of general meeting	1 Oct 2007 (CO No 3)[27]
308 Manner in which notice to be given	20 Jan 2007 (CO No 1)
309 Publication of notice of meeting on website	20 Jan 2007 (CO No 1)
310 Persons entitled to receive notice of meetings	1 Oct 2007 (CO No 3)[27]
311 Contents of notices of meetings	1 Oct 2007 (CO No 3)[27]
312 Resolution requiring special notice	1 Oct 2007 (CO No 3)[28]
313 Accidental failure to give notice of resolution or meeting	1 Oct 2007 (CO No 3)[29]
314 Members' power to require circulation of statements	1 Oct 2007 (CO No 3)[30]
315 Company's duty to circulate members' statement	1 Oct 2007 (CO No 3)[30]
316 Expenses of circulating members' statement	1 Oct 2007 (CO No 3)[30]
317 Application not to circulate members' statement	1 Oct 2007 (CO No 3)[30]
318 Quorum at meetings	1 Oct 2007 (CO No 3)[31]
319 Chairman of meeting	1 Oct 2007 (CO No 3)[31]
320 Declaration by chairman on a show of hands	1 Oct 2007 (CO No 3)[31]
321 Right to demand a poll	1 Oct 2007 (CO No 3)[31]
322 Voting on a poll	1 Oct 2007 (CO No 3)[31]
323 Representation of corporations at meetings	1 Oct 2007 (CO No 3)[31]
324 Rights to appoint proxies	1 Oct 2007 (CO No 3)[31]
325 Notice of meeting to contain statement of rights	1 Oct 2007 (CO No 3)[31]
326 Company-sponsored invitations to appoint proxies	1 Oct 2007 (CO No 3)[31]
327 Notice required of appointment of proxy etc	1 Oct 2007 (except sub-s (2)(c)) (CO No 3)[31] *Not on force* (otherwise)
328 Chairing meetings	1 Oct 2007 (CO No 3)[31]
329 Right of proxy to demand a poll	1 Oct 2007 (CO No 3)[31]
330 Notice required of termination of proxy's authority	1 Oct 2007 (except sub-s (6)(c)) (CO No 3)[31] *Not on force* (otherwise)
331 Saving for more extensive rights conferred by articles	1 Oct 2007 (CO No 3)[31]
332 Resolution passed at adjourned meeting	1 Oct 2007 (CO No 3)

Provision of CA 2006	Commencement
Part 13: Resolutions and Meetings	
Chapter 3: Resolutions at Meetings	
333 Sending documents relating to meetings etc in electronic form	20 Jan 2007 (CO No 1)
334 Application to class meetings	1 Oct 2007 (CO No 3)[32]
335 Application to class meetings: companies without a share capital	1 Oct 2007 (CO No 3)[32]
Chapter 4: Public Companies: Additional Requirements for AGMs	
336 Public companies: annual general meeting	1 Oct 2007 (CO No 3)[33]
337 Public companies: notice of AGM	1 Oct 2007 (CO No 3)[33]
338 Public companies: members' power to require circulation of resolutions for AGMs	1 Oct 2007 (CO No 3)[33]
339 Public companies: company's duty to circulate members' resolutions for AGMs	1 Oct 2007 (CO No 3)[33]
340 Public companies: expenses of circulating members' resolutions for AGM	1 Oct 2007 (CO No 3)[33]
Chapter 5: Additional Requirements for Quoted Companies	
341 Results of poll to be made available on website	1 Oct 2007 (CO No 3)
342 Members' power to require independent report on poll	1 Oct 2007 (CO No 3)[34]
343 Appointment of independent assessor	1 Oct 2007 (CO No 3)[34]
344 Independence requirement	20 Jan 2007 (certain purposes) (CO No 1)[3] 1 Oct 2007 (otherwise) (CO No 3)[34]
345 Meaning of "associate"	1 Oct 2007 (CO No 3)[34]
346 Effect of appointment of a partnership	1 Oct 2007 (CO No 3)[34]
347 The independent assessor's report	1 Oct 2007 (CO No 3)[34]
348 Rights of independent assessor: right to attend meeting etc	1 Oct 2007 (CO No 3)[34]
349 Rights of independent assessor: right to information	1 Oct 2007 (CO No 3)[34]
350 Offences relating to provision of information	1 Oct 2007 (CO No 3)[34]
351 Information to be made available on website	1 Oct 2007 (CO No 3)[34]
352 Application of provisions to class meetings	1 Oct 2007 (CO No 3)[34]
353 Requirements as to website availability	1 Oct 2007 (CO No 3)[34]
354 Power to limit or extend the types of company to which provisions of this Chapter apply	20 Jan 2007 (certain purposes) (CO No 1)[3] 1 Oct 2007 (otherwise) (CO No 3)[34]
Chapter 6: Records of Resolutions and Meetings	
355 Records of resolutions and meetings etc	1 Oct 2007 (CO No 3)[35]
356 Records as evidence of resolutions etc	1 Oct 2007 (CO No 3)[35]
357 Records of decisions by sole member	1 Oct 2007 (CO No 3)[35]
358 Inspection of records of resolutions and meetings	20 Jan 2007 (certain purposes) (CO No 1)[3] 1 Oct 2007 (otherwise) (CO No 3)[35]
359 Records of resolutions and meetings of class of members	1 Oct 2007 (CO No 3)[35]
Chapter 7: Supplementary Provisions	
360 Computation of periods of notice etc: clear day rule	1 Oct 2007 (CO No 3)
361 Meaning of "quoted company"	1 Oct 2007 (CO No 3)

APPENDICES

Provision of CA 2006	Commencement
Part 14: Control of Political Donations and Expenditure	
362 Introductory	1 Oct 2007 (GB subject to an exception) (CO No 3) 1 Nov 2007 (NI subject to an exception) (CO No 3) 1 Oct 2008 (exception noted above) (CO No 3)[36]
363 Political parties, organisations etc to which this Part applies	1 Oct 2007 (GB subject to an exception) (CO No 3) 1 Nov 2007 (NI subject to an exception) (CO No 3) 1 Oct 2008 (exception noted above) (CO No 3)[36]
364 Meaning of "political donation"	1 Oct 2007 (GB subject to an exception) (CO No 3) 1 Nov 2007 (NI subject to an exception) (CO No 3) 1 Oct 2008 (exception noted above) (CO No 3)[36]
365 Meaning of "political expenditure"	1 Oct 2007 (GB subject to an exception) (CO No 3) 1 Nov 2007 (NI subject to an exception) (CO No 3) 1 Oct 2008 (exception noted above) (CO No 3)[36]
366 Authorisation required for donations or expenditure	1 Oct 2007 (GB subject to an exception) (CO No 3) 1 Nov 2007 (NI subject to an exception) (CO No 3) 1 Oct 2008 (exception noted above) (CO No 3)[36]
367 Form of authorising resolution	1 Oct 2007 (GB subject to an exception) (CO No 3) 1 Nov 2007 (NI subject to an exception) (CO No 3) 1 Oct 2008 (exception noted above) (CO No 3)[36]
368 Period for which resolution has effect	1 Oct 2007 (GB) (CO No 3) 1 Nov 2007 (NI) (CO No 3)[36]
369 Liability of directors in case of unauthorised donation or expenditure	20 Jan 2007 (certain purposes) (CO No 1)[3] 1 Oct 2007 (otherwise, GB) (CO No 3) 1 Nov 2007 (otherwise, NI) (CO No 3)[36]
370 Enforcement of directors' liabilities by shareholder action	1 Oct 2007 (GB) (CO No 3) 1 Nov 2007 (NI) (CO No 3)[36]
371 Enforcement of directors' liabilities by shareholder action: supplementary	1 Oct 2007 (GB) (CO No 3) 1 Nov 2007 (NI) (CO No 3)[36]
372 Costs of shareholder action	1 Oct 2007 (GB) (CO No 3) 1 Nov 2007 (NI) (CO No 3)[36]
373 Information for purposes of shareholder action	1 Oct 2007 (GB) (CO No 3) 1 Nov 2007 (NI) (CO No 3)[36]
374 Trade unions	1 Oct 2007 (GB) (CO No 3) 1 Nov 2007 (NI) (CO No 3)[36]
375 Subscription for membership of trade association	1 Oct 2007 (GB) (CO No 3) 1 Nov 2007 (NI) (CO No 3)[36]
376 All-party parliamentary groups	1 Oct 2007 (GB) (CO No 3) 1 Nov 2007 (NI) (CO No 3)[36]
377 Political expenditure exempted by order	20 Jan 2007 (certain purposes) (CO No 1)[3] 1 Oct 2007 (otherwise, GB) (CO No 3) 1 Nov 2007 (otherwise, NI) (CO No 3)[36]

Provision of CA 2006	Commencement
Part 14: Control of Political Donations and Expenditure	
378 Donations not amounting to more than £5,000 in any twelve month period	1 Oct 2007 (GB subject to an exception) (CO No 3) 1 Nov 2007 (NI subject to an exception) (CO No 3) 1 Oct 2008 (exception noted above) (CO No 3)[36]
379 Minor definitions	1 Oct 2007 (GB) (CO No 3) 1 Nov 2007 (NI) (CO No 3)[36]
Part 15: Accounts and Reports	
Chapter 1: Introduction	
380 Scheme of this Part	*Not in force*
381 Companies subject to the small companies regime	*Not in force*
382 Companies qualifying as small: general	*Not in force*
383 Companies qualifying as small: parent companies	*Not in force*
384 Companies excluded from the small companies regime	*Not in force*
385 Quoted and unquoted companies	20 Jan 2007 (certain purposes) (CO No 1)[3] 1 Oct 2007 (certain purposes) (CO No 3)[4] *Not in force* (otherwise)
Chapter 2: Accounting Records	
386 Duty to keep accounting records	*Not in force*
387 Duty to keep accounting records: offence	*Not in force*
388 Where and for how long records to be kept	*Not in force*
389 Where and for how long records to be kept: offences	*Not in force*
Chapter 3: A Company's Financial Year	
390 A company's financial year	*Not in force*
391 Accounting reference periods and accounting reference date	*Not in force*
392 Alteration of accounting reference date	*Not in force*
Chapter 4: Annual Accounts	
393 Accounts to give true and fair view	*Not in force*
394 Duty to prepare individual accounts	*Not in force*
395 Individual accounts: applicable accounting framework	*Not in force*
396 Companies Act individual accounts	20 Jan 2007 (certain purposes) (CO No 1)[3] *Not in force* (otherwise)
397 IAS individual accounts	*Not in force*
398 Option to prepare group accounts	*Not in force*
399 Duty to prepare group accounts	*Not in force*
400 Exemption for company included in EEA group accounts of larger group	*Not in force*
401 Exemption for company included in non-EEA group accounts of larger group	*Not in force*
402 Exemption if no subsidiary undertakings need be included in the consolidation	*Not in force*
403 Group accounts: applicable accounting framework	*Not in force*

APPENDICES

Provision of CA 2006	Commencement
Part 15: Accounts and Reports	
Chapter 4: Annual Accounts	
404 Companies Act group accounts	20 Jan 2007 (certain purposes) (CO No 1)[3] *Not in force* (otherwise)
405 Companies Act group accounts: subsidiary undertakings included in the consolidation	*Not in force*
406 IAS group accounts	*Not in force*
407 Consistency of financial reporting within group	*Not in force*
408 Individual profit and loss account where group accounts prepared	*Not in force*
409 Information about related undertakings	20 Jan 2007 (certain purposes) (CO No 1)[3] *Not in force* (otherwise)
410 Information about related undertakings: alternative compliance	*Not in force*
411 Information about employee numbers and costs	*Not in force*
412 Information about directors' benefits: remuneration	20 Jan 2007 (certain purposes) (CO No 1)[3] *Not in force* (otherwise)
413 Information about directors' benefits: advances, credit and guarantees	*Not in force*
414 Approval and signing of accounts	*Not in force*
Chapter 5: Directors' Report	
415 Duty to prepare directors' report	*Not in force*
416 Contents of directors' report: general	20 Jan 2007 (certain purposes) (CO No 1)[3] *Not in force* (otherwise)
417 Contents of directors' report: business review	1 Oct 2007 (CO No 3)[37]
418 Contents of directors' report: statement as to disclosure to auditors	*Not in force*
419 Approval and signing of directors' report	*Not in force*
Chapter 6: Quoted Companies: Directors' Remuneration Report	
420 Duty to prepare directors' remuneration report	*Not in force*
421 Contents of directors' remuneration report	20 Jan 2007 (certain purposes) (CO No 1)[3] *Not in force* (otherwise)
422 Approval and signing of directors' remuneration report	*Not in force*
Chapter 7: Publication of Accounts and Reports	
423 Duty to circulate copies of annual accounts and reports	*Not in force*
424 Time allowed for sending out copies of accounts and reports	*Not in force*
425 Default in sending out copies of accounts and reports: offences	*Not in force*
426 Option to provide summary financial statement	20 Jan 2007 (certain purposes) (CO No 1)[3] *Not in force* (otherwise)
427 Form and contents of summary financial statement: unquoted companies	20 Jan 2007 (certain purposes) (CO No 1)[3] *Not in force* (otherwise)
428 Form and contents of summary financial statement: quoted companies	20 Jan 2007 (certain purposes) (CO No 1)[3] *Not in force* (otherwise)
429 Summary financial statements: offences	*Not in force*

Provision of CA 2006	Commencement
Part 15: Accounts and Reports	
Chapter 7: Publication of Accounts and Reports	
430 Quoted companies: annual accounts and reports to be made available on website	*Not in force*
431 Right of member or debenture holder to copies of accounts and reports: unquoted companies	*Not in force*
432 Right of member or debenture holder to copies of accounts and reports: quoted companies	*Not in force*
433 Name of signatory to be stated in published copies of accounts and reports	*Not in force*
434 Requirements in connection with publication of statutory accounts	*Not in force*
435 Requirements in connection with publication of non-statutory accounts	*Not in force*
436 Meaning of "publication" in relation to accounts and reports	*Not in force*
Chapter 8: Public Companies: Laying of Accounts and Reports Before General Meeting	
437 Public companies: laying of accounts and reports before general meeting	*Not in force*
438 Public companies: offence of failure to lay accounts and reports	*Not in force*
Chapter 9: Quoted Companies: Members' Approval of Directors' Remuneration Report	
439 Quoted companies: members' approval of directors' remuneration report	*Not in force*
440 Quoted companies: offences in connection with procedure for approval	*Not in force*
Chapter 10: Filing of Accounts and Reports	
441 Duty to file accounts and reports with the registrar	*Not in force*
442 Period allowed for filing accounts	*Not in force*
443 Calculation of period allowed	*Not in force*
444 Filing obligations of companies subject to small companies regime	20 Jan 2007 (certain purposes) (CO No 1)[3] *Not in force* (otherwise)
445 Filing obligations of medium-sized companies	20 Jan 2007 (certain purposes) (CO No 1)[3] *Not in force* (otherwise)
446 Filing obligations of unquoted companies	*Not in force*
447 Filing obligations of quoted companies	*Not in force*
448 Unlimited companies exempt from obligation to file accounts	*Not in force*
449 Special auditor's report where abbreviated accounts delivered	*Not in force*
450 Approval and signing of abbreviated accounts	*Not in force*
451 Default in filing accounts and reports: offences	*Not in force*
452 Default in filing accounts and reports: court order	*Not in force*
453 Civil penalty for failure to file accounts and reports	20 Jan 2007 (certain purposes) (CO No 1)[3] *Not in force* (otherwise)

APPENDICES

Provision of CA 2006	Commencement
Part 15: Accounts and Reports	
Chapter 11: Revision of Defective Accounts and Reports	
454 Voluntary revision of accounts etc	20 Jan 2007 (certain purposes) (CO No 1)[3] *Not in force* (otherwise)
455 Secretary of State's notice in respect of accounts or reports	*Not in force*
456 Application to court in respect of defective accounts or reports	*Not in force*
457 Other persons authorised to apply to the court	20 Jan 2007 (certain purposes) (CO No 1)[3] *Not in force* (otherwise)
458 Disclosure of information by tax authorities	*Not in force*
459 Power of authorised person to require documents, information and explanations	*Not in force*
460 Restrictions on disclosure of information obtained under compulsory powers	*Not in force*
461 Permitted disclosure of information obtained under compulsory powers	*Not in force*
462 Power to amend categories of permitted disclosure	20 Jan 2007 (certain purposes) (CO No 1)[3] *Not in force* (otherwise)
Chapter 12: Supplementary Provisions	
463 Liability for false or misleading statements in reports	20 Jan 2007 (CO No 1)[38]
464 Accounting standards	20 Jan 2007 (certain purposes) (CO No 1)[3] *Not in force* (otherwise)
465 Companies qualifying as medium-sized: general	*Not in force*
466 Companies qualifying as medium-sized: parent companies	*Not in force*
467 Companies excluded from being treated as medium-sized	*Not in force*
468 General power to make further provision about accounts and reports	20 Jan 2007 (certain purposes) (CO No 1)[3] *Not in force* (otherwise)
469 Preparation and filing of accounts in euros	*Not in force*
470 Power to apply provisions to banking partnerships	20 Jan 2007 (certain purposes) (CO No 1)[3] *Not in force* (otherwise)
471 Meaning of "annual accounts" and related expressions	*Not in force*
472 Notes to the accounts	*Not in force*
473 Parliamentary procedure for certain regulations under this Part	20 Jan 2007 (certain purposes) (CO No 1)[3] *Not in force* (otherwise)
474 Minor definitions	*Not in force*
Part 16: Audit	
Chapter 1: Requirement for Audited Accounts	
475 Requirement for audited accounts	*Not in force*
476 Right of members to require audit	*Not in force*
477 Small companies: conditions for exemption from audit	*Not in force*
478 Companies excluded from small companies exemption	*Not in force*
479 Availability of small companies exemption in case of group company	*Not in force*

Provision of CA 2006	Commencement
Part 16: Audit	
Chapter 1: Requirement for Audited Accounts	
480 Dormant companies: conditions for exemption from audit	*Not in force*
481 Companies excluded from dormant companies exemption	*Not in force*
482 Non-profit-making companies subject to public sector audit	*Not in force*
483 Scottish public sector companies: audit by Auditor General for Scotland	20 Jan 2007 (certain purposes) (CO No 1)[3] *Not in force* (otherwise)
484 General power of amendment by regulations	20 Jan 2007 (certain purposes) (CO No 1)[3] *Not in force* (otherwise)
Chapter 2: Appointment of Auditors	
485 Appointment of auditors of private company: general	1 Oct 2007 (CO No 3)[39]
486 Appointment of auditors of private company: default power of Secretary of State	1 Oct 2007 (CO No 3)[39]
487 Term of office of auditors of private company	1 Oct 2007 (CO No 3)[39]
488 Prevention by members of deemed re-appointment of auditor	1 Oct 2007 (CO No 3)[39]
489 Appointment of auditors of public company: general	*Not in force*
490 Appointment of auditors of public company: default power of Secretary of State	*Not in force*
491 Term of office of auditors of public company	*Not in force*
492 Fixing of auditor's remuneration	*Not in force*
493 Disclosure of terms of audit appointment	20 Jan 2007 (certain purposes) (CO No 1)[3] *Not in force* (otherwise)
494 Disclosure of services provided by auditor or associates and related remuneration	20 Jan 2007 (certain purposes) (CO No 1)[3] *Not in force* (otherwise)
Chapter 3: Functions of Auditor	
495 Auditor's report on company's annual accounts	*Not in force*
496 Auditor's report on directors' report	*Not in force*
497 Auditor's report on auditable part of directors' remuneration report	*Not in force*
498 Duties of auditor	*Not in force*
499 Auditor's general right to information	*Not in force*
500 Auditor's right to information from overseas subsidiaries	*Not in force*
501 Auditor's rights to information: offences	*Not in force*
502 Auditor's rights in relation to resolutions and meetings	*Not in force*
503 Signature of auditor's report	*Not in force*
504 Senior statutory auditor	20 Jan 2007 (certain purposes) (CO No 1)[3] *Not in force* (otherwise)
505 Names to be stated in published copies of auditor's report	*Not in force*
506 Circumstances in which names may be omitted	*Not in force*
507 Offences in connection with auditor's report	*Not in force*

Provision of CA 2006	Commencement
Part 16: Audit	
Chapter 3: Functions of Auditor	
508 Guidance for regulatory and prosecuting authorities: England, Wales and Northern Ireland	*Not in force*
509 Guidance for regulatory authorities: Scotland	*Not in force*
Chapter 4: Removal, Resignation, etc of Auditors	
510 Resolution removing auditor from office	*Not in force*
511 Special notice required for resolution removing auditor from office	*Not in force*
512 Notice to registrar of resolution removing auditor from office	*Not in force*
513 Rights of auditor who has been removed from office	*Not in force*
514 Failure to re-appoint auditor: special procedure required for written resolution	*Not in force*
515 Failure to re-appoint auditor: special notice required for resolution at general meeting	*Not in force*
516 Resignation of auditor	*Not in force*
517 Notice to registrar of resignation of auditor	*Not in force*
518 Rights of resigning auditor	*Not in force*
519 Statement by auditor to be deposited with company	*Not in force*
520 Company's duties in relation to statement	*Not in force*
521 Copy of statement to be sent to registrar	*Not in force*
522 Duty of auditor to notify appropriate audit authority	*Not in force*
523 Duty of company to notify appropriate audit authority	*Not in force*
524 Information to be given to accounting authorities	*Not in force*
525 Meaning of "appropriate audit authority" and "major audit"	*Not in force*
526 Effect of casual vacancies	*Not in force*
Chapter 5: Quoted Companies: Right of Members to Raise Audit Concerns at Accounts Meeting	
527 Members' power to require website publication of audit concerns	*Not in force*
528 Requirements as to website availability	*Not in force*
529 Website publication: company's supplementary duties	*Not in force*
530 Website publication: offences	*Not in force*
531 Meaning of "quoted company"	*Not in force*
Chapter 6: Auditors' Liability	
532 Voidness of provisions protecting auditors from liability	*Not in force*
533 Indemnity for costs of successfully defending proceedings	*Not in force*
534 Liability limitation agreements	*Not in force*
535 Terms of liability limitation agreement	20 Jan 2007 (certain purposes) (CO No 1)[3] *Not in force* (otherwise)

Provision of CA 2006	Commencement
Part 16: Audit	
Chapter 6: Auditors' Liability	
536 Authorisation of agreement by members of the company	*Not in force*
537 Effect of liability limitation agreement	*Not in force*
538 Disclosure of agreement by company	20 Jan 2007 (certain purposes) (CO No 1)[3] *Not in force* (otherwise)
Chapter 7: Supplementary Provisions	
539 Minor definitions	*Not in force*
Part 17: A Company's Share Capital	
Chapter 1: Shares and Share Capital of a Company	
540 Shares	1 Oct 2007 (sub-ss (1), (4) certain purposes) (CO No 3)[40] *Not in force* (otherwise)
541 Nature of shares	*Not in force*
542 Nominal value of shares	*Not in force*
543 Numbering of shares	*Not in force*
544 Transferability of shares	*Not in force*
545 Companies having a share capital	1 Oct 2007 (certain purposes) (CO No 3)[4] *Not in force* (otherwise)
546 Issued and allotted share capital	6 Apr 2007 (certain purposes) (CO No 2)[41] 1 Oct 2007 (certain purposes) (CO No 3)[4] 1 Nov 2007 (certain purposes) (CO No 3)[42] *Not in force* (otherwise)
547 Called-up share capital	*Not in force*
548 Equity share capital	1 Oct 2007 (certain purposes) (CO No 3)[4] *Not in force* (otherwise)
Chapter 2: Allotment of Shares: General Provisions	
549 Exercise by directors of power to allot shares etc	*Not in force*
550 Power of directors to allot shares etc: private company with only one class of shares	*Not in force*
551 Power of directors to allot shares etc: authorisation by company	*Not in force*
552 General prohibition of commissions, discounts and allowances	*Not in force*
553 Permitted commission	*Not in force*
554 Registration of allotment	*Not in force*
555 Return of allotment by limited company	20 Jan 2007 (certain purposes) (CO No 1)[3] *Not in force* (otherwise)
556 Return of allotment by unlimited company allotting new class of shares	20 Jan 2007 (certain purposes) (CO No 1)[3] *Not in force* (otherwise)
557 Offence of failure to make return	*Not in force*
558 When shares are allotted	6 Apr 2007 (certain purposes) (CO No 2)[41] *Not in force* (otherwise)
559 Provisions about allotment not applicable to shares taken on formation	*Not in force*
Chapter 3: Allotment of Equity Securities: Existing Shareholders' : Right of Pre-emption	
560 Meaning of "equity securities" and related expressions	*Not in force*
561 Existing shareholders' right of pre-emption	*Not in force*

APPENDICES

Provision of CA 2006	Commencement
Part 17: A Company's Share Capital	
Chapter 3: Allotment of Equity Securities: Existing Shareholders' : Right of Pre-emption	
562 Communication of pre-emption offers to shareholders	20 Jan 2007 (certain purposes) (CO No 1)[3] *Not in force* (otherwise)
563 Liability of company and officers in case of contravention	*Not in force*
564 Exception to pre-emption right: bonus shares	*Not in force*
565 Exception to pre-emption right: issue for non-cash consideration	*Not in force*
566 Exception to pre-emption right: securities held under employees' share scheme	*Not in force*
567 Exclusion of requirements by private companies	*Not in force*
568 Exclusion of pre-emption right: articles conferring corresponding right	*Not in force*
569 Disapplication of pre-emption rights: private company with only one class of shares	*Not in force*
570 Disapplication of pre-emption rights: directors acting under general authorisation	*Not in force*
571 Disapplication of pre-emption rights by special resolution	*Not in force*
572 Liability for false statement in directors' statement	*Not in force*
573 Disapplication of pre-emption rights: sale of treasury shares	*Not in force*
574 References to holder of shares in relation to offer	*Not in force*
575 Saving for other restrictions on offer or allotment	*Not in force*
576 Saving for certain older pre-emption requirements	*Not in force*
577 Provisions about pre-emption not applicable to shares taken on formation	*Not in force*
Chapter 4: Public Companies: Allotment Where Issue Not Fully Subscribed	
578 Public companies: allotment where issue not fully subscribed	*Not in force*
579 Public companies: effect of irregular allotment where issue not fully subscribed	*Not in force*
Chapter 5: Payment for Shares	
580 Shares not to be allotted at a discount	*Not in force*
581 Provision for different amounts to be paid on shares	*Not in force*
582 General rule as to means of payment	*Not in force*
583 Meaning of payment in cash	20 Jan 2007 (certain purposes) (CO No 1)[3] *Not in force* (otherwise)
584 Public companies: shares taken by subscribers of memorandum	*Not in force*
585 Public companies: must not accept undertaking to do work or perform services	*Not in force*
586 Public companies: shares must be at least one-quarter paid up	*Not in force*

Provision of CA 2006	Commencement
Part 17: A Company's Share Capital	
Chapter 5: Payment for Shares	
587 Public companies: payment by long-term undertaking	*Not in force*
588 Liability of subsequent holders of shares	*Not in force*
589 Power of court to grant relief	*Not in force*
590 Penalty for contravention of this Chapter	*Not in force*
591 Enforceability of undertakings to do work etc	*Not in force*
592 The appropriate rate of interest	20 Jan 2007 (certain purposes) (CO No 1)[3] *Not in force* (otherwise)
Chapter 6: Public Companies: Independent Valuation of Non-Cash Consideration	
593 Public company: valuation of non-cash consideration for shares	*Not in force*
594 Exception to valuation requirement: arrangement with another company	*Not in force*
595 Exception to valuation requirement: merger	*Not in force*
596 Non-cash consideration for shares: requirements as to valuation and report	*Not in force*
597 Copy of report to be delivered to registrar	*Not in force*
598 Public company: agreement for transfer of non-cash asset in initial period	*Not in force*
599 Agreement for transfer of non-cash asset: requirement of independent valuation	*Not in force*
600 Agreement for transfer of non-cash asset: requirements as to valuation and report	*Not in force*
601 Agreement for transfer of non-cash asset: requirement of approval by members	*Not in force*
602 Copy of resolution to be delivered to registrar	*Not in force*
603 Adaptation of provisions in relation to company re-registering as public	*Not in force*
604 Agreement for transfer of non-cash asset: effect of contravention	*Not in force*
605 Liability of subsequent holders of shares	*Not in force*
606 Power of court to grant relief	*Not in force*
607 Penalty for contravention of this Chapter	*Not in force*
608 Enforceability of undertakings to do work etc	*Not in force*
609 The appropriate rate of interest	20 Jan 2007 (certain purposes) (CO No 1)[3] *Not in force* (otherwise)
Chapter 7: Share Premiums	
610 Application of share premiums	*Not in force*
611 Group reconstruction relief	*Not in force*
612 Merger relief	*Not in force*
613 Merger relief: meaning of 90% equity holding	*Not in force*
614 Power to make further provision by regulations	20 Jan 2007 (certain purposes) (CO No 1)[3] *Not in force* (otherwise)
615 Relief may be reflected in company's balance sheet	*Not in force*
616 Interpretation of this Chapter	*Not in force*

APPENDICES

Provision of CA 2006	Commencement
Part 17: A Company's Share Capital	
Chapter 8: Alteration of Share Capital	
617 Alteration of share capital of limited company	*Not in force*
618 Sub-division or consolidation of shares	*Not in force*
619 Notice to registrar of sub-division or consolidation	20 Jan 2007 (certain purposes) (CO No 1)[3] *Not in force* (otherwise)
620 Reconversion of stock into shares	*Not in force*
621 Notice to registrar of reconversion of stock into shares	20 Jan 2007 (certain purposes) (CO No 1)[3] *Not in force* (otherwise)
622 Redenomination of share capital	*Not in force*
623 Calculation of new nominal values	*Not in force*
624 Effect of redenomination	*Not in force*
625 Notice to registrar of redenomination	20 Jan 2007 (certain purposes) (CO No 1)[3] *Not in force* (otherwise)
626 Reduction of capital in connection with redenomination	*Not in force*
627 Notice to registrar of reduction of capital in connection with redenomination	20 Jan 2007 (certain purposes) (CO No 1)[3] *Not in force* (otherwise)
628 Redenomination reserve	*Not in force*
Chapter 9: Classes of Share and Class Rights	
629 Classes of shares	1 Oct 2007 (certain purposes) (CO No 3)[4] *Not in force* (otherwise)
630 Variation of class rights: companies having a share capital	*Not in force*
631 Variation of class rights: companies without a share capital	*Not in force*
632 Variation of class rights: saving for court's powers under other provisions	*Not in force*
633 Right to object to variation: companies having a share capital	*Not in force*
634 Right to object to variation: companies without a share capital	*Not in force*
635 Copy of court order to be forwarded to the registrar	*Not in force*
636 Notice of name or other designation of class of shares	*Not in force*
637 Notice of particulars of variation of rights attached to shares	*Not in force*
638 Notice of new class of members	*Not in force*
639 Notice of name or other designation of class of members	*Not in force*
640 Notice of particulars of variation of class rights	*Not in force*
Chapter 10: Reduction of Share Capital	
641 Circumstances in which a company may reduce its share capital	*Not in force*
642 Reduction of capital supported by solvency statement	*Not in force*
643 Solvency statement	20 Jan 2007 (certain purposes) (CO No 1)[3] *Not in force* (otherwise)

Provision of CA 2006	Commencement
Part 17: A Company's Share Capital	
Chapter 10: Reduction of Share Capital	
644 Registration of resolution and supporting documents	20 Jan 2007 (certain purposes) (CO No 1)[3] *Not in force* (otherwise)
645 Application to court for order of confirmation	*Not in force*
646 Creditors entitled to object to reduction	*Not in force*
647 Offences in connection with list of creditors	*Not in force*
648 Court order confirming reduction	*Not in force*
649 Registration of order and statement of capital	20 Jan 2007 (certain purposes) (CO No 1)[3] *Not in force* (otherwise)
650 Public company reducing capital below authorised minimum	*Not in force*
651 Expedited procedure for re-registration as a private company	*Not in force*
652 Liability of members following reduction of capital	*Not in force*
653 Liability to creditor in case of omission from list of creditors	*Not in force*
Chapter 11: Miscellaneous and Supplementary Provisions	
654 Treatment of reserve arising from reduction of capital	20 Jan 2007 (certain purposes) (CO No 1)[3] *Not in force* (otherwise)
655 Shares no bar to damages against company	*Not in force*
656 Public companies: duty of directors to call meeting on serious loss of capital	*Not in force*
657 General power to make further provision by regulations	20 Jan 2007 (certain purposes) (CO No 1)[3] *Not in force* (otherwise)
Part 18: Acquisition by Limited Company of its Own Shares	
Chapter 1: General Provisions	
658 General rule against limited company acquiring its own shares	*Not in force*
659 Exceptions to general rule	*Not in force*
660 Treatment of shares held by nominee	*Not in force*
661 Liability of others where nominee fails to make payment in respect of shares	*Not in force*
662 Duty to cancel shares in public company held by or for the company	*Not in force*
663 Notice of cancellation of shares	20 Jan 2007 (certain purposes) (CO No 1)[3] *Not in force* (otherwise)
664 Re-registration as private company in consequence of cancellation	*Not in force*
665 Issue of certificate of incorporation on re-registration	*Not in force*
666 Effect of failure to re-register	*Not in force*
667 Offence in case of failure to cancel shares or re-register	*Not in force*
668 Application of provisions to company re-registering as public company	*Not in force*
669 Transfer to reserve on acquisition of shares by public company or nominee	*Not in force*
670 Public companies: general rule against lien or charge on own shares	*Not in force*

APPENDICES

Provision of CA 2006	Commencement
Part 18: Acquisition by Limited Company of its Own Shares	
Chapter 1: General Provisions	
671 Interests to be disregarded in determining whether company has beneficial interest	*Not in force*
672 Residual interest under pension scheme or employees' share scheme	*Not in force*
673 Employer's charges and other rights of recovery	*Not in force*
674 Rights as personal representative or trustee	*Not in force*
675 Meaning of "pension scheme"	*Not in force*
676 Application of provisions to directors	*Not in force*
Chapter 2: Financial Assistance for Purchase of Own Shares	
677 Meaning of "financial assistance"	*Not in force*
678 Assistance for acquisition of shares in public company	*Not in force*
679 Assistance by public company for acquisition of shares in its private holding company	*Not in force*
680 Prohibited financial assistance an offence	*Not in force*
681 Unconditional exceptions	*Not in force*
682 Conditional exceptions	*Not in force*
683 Definitions for this Chapter	*Not in force*
Chapter 3: Redeemable Shares	
684 Power of limited company to issue redeemable shares	*Not in force*
685 Terms and manner of redemption	*Not in force*
686 Payment for redeemable shares	*Not in force*
687 Financing of redemption	*Not in force*
688 Redeemed shares treated as cancelled	*Not in force*
689 Notice to registrar of redemption	20 Jan 2007 (certain purposes) (CO No 1)[3] *Not in force* (otherwise)
Chapter 4: Purchase of Own Shares	
690 Power of limited company to purchase own shares	*Not in force*
691 Payment for purchase of own shares	*Not in force*
692 Financing of purchase of own shares	*Not in force*
693 Authority for purchase of own shares	*Not in force*
694 Authority for off-market purchase	*Not in force*
695 Resolution authorising off-market purchase: exercise of voting rights	*Not in force*
696 Resolution authorising off-market purchase: disclosure of details of contract	*Not in force*
697 Variation of contract for off-market purchase	*Not in force*
698 Resolution authorising variation: exercise of voting rights	*Not in force*
699 Resolution authorising variation: disclosure of details of variation	*Not in force*
700 Release of company's rights under contract for off-market purchase	*Not in force*
701 Authority for market purchase	*Not in force*

Provision of CA 2006	Commencement
Part 18: Acquisition by Limited Company of its Own Shares	
Chapter 4: Purchase of Own Shares	
702 Copy of contract or memorandum to be available for inspection	*Not in force*
703 Enforcement of right to inspect copy or memorandum	*Not in force*
704 No assignment of company's right to purchase own shares	*Not in force*
705 Payments apart from purchase price to be made out of distributable profits	*Not in force*
706 Treatment of shares purchased	*Not in force*
707 Return to registrar of purchase of own shares	*Not in force*
708 Notice to registrar of cancellation of shares	20 Jan 2007 (certain purposes) (CO No 1)[3] *Not in force* (otherwise)
Chapter 5: Redemption or Purchase by Private Company Out of Capital	
709 Power of private limited company to redeem or purchase own shares out of capital	*Not in force*
710 The permissible capital payment	*Not in force*
711 Available profits	*Not in force*
712 Determination of available profits	*Not in force*
713 Requirements for payment out of capital	*Not in force*
714 Directors' statement and auditor's report	20 Jan 2007 (certain purposes) (CO No 1)[3] *Not in force* (otherwise)
715 Directors' statement: offence if no reasonable grounds for opinion	*Not in force*
716 Payment to be approved by special resolution	*Not in force*
717 Resolution authorising payment: exercise of voting rights	*Not in force*
718 Resolution authorising payment: disclosure of directors' statement and auditor's report	*Not in force*
719 Public notice of proposed payment	*Not in force*
720 Directors' statement and auditor's report to be available for inspection	*Not in force*
721 Application to court to cancel resolution	*Not in force*
722 Notice to registrar of court application or order	*Not in force*
723 When payment out of capital to be made	*Not in force*
Chapter 6: Treasury Shares	
724 Treasury shares	*Not in force*
725 Treasury shares: maximum holdings	*Not in force*
726 Treasury shares: exercise of rights	*Not in force*
727 Treasury shares: disposal	20 Jan 2007 (certain purposes) (CO No 1)[3] *Not in force* (otherwise)
728 Treasury shares: notice of disposal	*Not in force*
729 Treasury shares: cancellation	*Not in force*
730 Treasury shares: notice of cancellation	20 Jan 2007 (certain purposes) (CO No 1)[3] *Not in force* (otherwise)
731 Treasury shares: treatment of proceeds of sale	*Not in force*
732 Treasury shares: offences	*Not in force*

APPENDICES

Provision of CA 2006	Commencement
Part 18: Acquisition by Limited Company of its Own Shares	
Chapter 7: Supplementary Provisions	
733 The capital redemption reserve	*Not in force*
734 Accounting consequences of payment out of capital	*Not in force*
735 Effect of company's failure to redeem or purchase	*Not in force*
736 Meaning of "distributable profits"	*Not in force*
737 General power to make further provision by regulations	20 Jan 2007 (certain purposes) (CO No 1)[3] *Not in force* (otherwise)
Part 19: Debentures	
738 Meaning of "debenture"	*Not in force*
739 Perpetual debentures	*Not in force*
740 Enforcement of contract to subscribe for debentures	*Not in force*
741 Registration of allotment of debentures	*Not in force*
742 Debentures to bearer (Scotland)	*Not in force*
743 Register of debenture holders	*Not in force*
744 Register of debenture holders: right to inspect and require copy	20 Jan 2007 (certain purposes) (CO No 1)[3] *Not in force* (otherwise)
745 Register of debenture holders: response to request for inspection or copy	*Not in force*
746 Register of debenture holders: refusal of inspection or default in providing copy	*Not in force*
747 Register of debenture holders: offences in connection with request for or disclosure of information	*Not in force*
748 Time limit for claims arising from entry in register	*Not in force*
749 Right of debenture holder to copy of deed	20 Jan 2007 (certain purposes) (CO No 1)[3] *Not in force* (otherwise)
750 Liability of trustees of debentures	*Not in force*
751 Liability of trustees of debentures: saving for certain older provisions	*Not in force*
752 Power to re-issue redeemed debentures	*Not in force*
753 Deposit of debentures to secure advances	*Not in force*
754 Priorities where debentures secured by floating charge	*Not in force*
Part 20: Private and Public Companies	
Chapter 1: Prohibition of Public Offers by Private Companies	
755 Prohibition of public offers by private company	*Not in force*
756 Meaning of "offer to the public"	*Not in force*
757 Enforcement of prohibition: order restraining proposed contravention	*Not in force*
758 Enforcement of prohibition: orders available to the court after contravention	*Not in force*
759 Enforcement of prohibition: remedial order	*Not in force*
760 Validity of allotment etc not affected	*Not in force*

Provision of CA 2006	Commencement
Part 20: Private and Public Companies	
Chapter 2: Minimum Share Capital Requirement for Public Companies	
761 Public company: requirement as to minimum share capital	*Not in force*
762 Procedure for obtaining certificate	*Not in force*
763 The authorised minimum	20 Jan 2007 (certain purposes) (CO No 1)[3] *Not in force* (otherwise)
764 Power to alter authorised minimum	20 Jan 2007 (certain purposes) (CO No 1)[3] *Not in force* (otherwise)
765 Authorised minimum: application of initial requirement	*Not in force*
766 Authorised minimum: application where shares denominated in different currencies etc	20 Jan 2007 (certain purposes) (CO No 1)[3] *Not in force* (otherwise)
767 Consequences of doing business etc without a trading certificate	*Not in force*
Part 21: Certification and Transfer of Securities	
Chapter 1: Certification and Transfer of Securities: General	
768 Share certificate to be evidence of title	*Not in force*
769 Duty of company as to issue of certificates etc on allotment	*Not in force*
770 Registration of transfer	*Not in force*
771 Procedure on transfer being lodged	*Not in force*
772 Transfer of shares on application of transferor	*Not in force*
773 Execution of share transfer by personal representative	*Not in force*
774 Evidence of grant of probate etc	*Not in force*
775 Certification of instrument of transfer	*Not in force*
776 Duty of company as to issue of certificates etc on transfer	*Not in force*
777 Issue of certificates etc: cases within the Stock Transfer Act 1982	*Not in force*
778 Issue of certificates etc: allotment or transfer to financial institution	*Not in force*
779 Issue and effect of share warrant to bearer	*Not in force*
780 Duty of company as to issue of certificates on surrender of share warrant	*Not in force*
781 Offences in connection with share warrants (Scotland)	*Not in force*
782 Issue of certificates etc: court order to make good default	*Not in force*
Chapter 2: Evidencing and Transfer of Title to Securities Without Written Instrument	
783 Scope of this Chapter	*Not in force*
784 Power to make regulations	20 Jan 2007 (certain purposes) (CO No 1)[3] *Not in force* (otherwise)
785 Provision enabling procedures for evidencing and transferring title	20 Jan 2007 (certain purposes) (CO No 1)[3] *Not in force* (otherwise)
786 Provision enabling or requiring arrangements to be adopted	20 Jan 2007 (certain purposes) (CO No 1)[3] *Not in force* (otherwise)
787 Provision enabling or requiring arrangements to be adopted: order-making powers	20 Jan 2007 (certain purposes) (CO No 1)[3] *Not in force* (otherwise)

Provision of CA 2006	Commencement
Part 21: Certification and Transfer of Securities	
Chapter 2: Evidencing and Transfer of Title to Securities Without Written Instrument	
788 Provision that may be included in regulations	20 Jan 2007 (certain purposes) (CO No 1)[3] *Not in force* (otherwise)
789 Duty to consult	20 Jan 2007 (certain purposes) (CO No 1)[3] *Not in force* (otherwise)
790 Resolutions to be forwarded to registrar	*Not in force*
Part 22: Information About Interests in a Company's Shares	
791 Companies to which this Part applies	20 Jan 2007 (CO No 1)
792 Shares to which this Part applies	20 Jan 2007 (CO No 1)
793 Notice by company requiring information about interests in its shares	20 Jan 2007 (CO No 1)
794 Notice requiring information: order imposing restrictions on shares	20 Jan 2007 (CO No 1)
795 Notice requiring information: offences	20 Jan 2007 (CO No 1)
796 Notice requiring information: persons exempted from obligation to comply	20 Jan 2007 (CO No 1)
797 Consequences of order imposing restrictions	20 Jan 2007 (CO No 1)
798 Penalty for attempted evasion of restrictions	20 Jan 2007 (CO No 1)
799 Relaxation of restrictions	20 Jan 2007 (CO No 1)
800 Removal of restrictions	20 Jan 2007 (CO No 1)
801 Order for sale of shares	20 Jan 2007 (CO No 1)
802 Application of proceeds of sale under court order	20 Jan 2007 (CO No 1)
803 Power of members to require company to act	20 Jan 2007 (CO No 1)
804 Duty of company to comply with requirement	20 Jan 2007 (CO No 1)
805 Report to members on outcome of investigation	20 Jan 2007 (CO No 1)
806 Report to members: offences	20 Jan 2007 (CO No 1)
807 Right to inspect and request copy of reports	20 Jan 2007 (CO No 1)
808 Register of interests disclosed	20 Jan 2007 (CO No 1)[70]
809 Register to be kept available for inspection	20 Jan 2007 (CO No 1)[70]
810 Associated index	20 Jan 2007 (CO No 1)
811 Rights to inspect and require copy of entries	20 Jan 2007 (sub-ss (1)–(3)) (CO No 1) *Not in force* (otherwise)
812 Court supervision of purpose for which rights may be exercised	*Not in force*
813 Register of interests disclosed: refusal of inspection or default in providing copy	20 Jan 2007 (CO No 1)[43]
814 Register of interests disclosed: offences in connection with request for or disclosure of information	*Not in force*
815 Entries not to be removed from register	20 Jan 2007 (CO No 1)
816 Removal of entries from register: old entries	20 Jan 2007 (CO No 1)
817 Removal of entries from register: incorrect entry relating to third party	20 Jan 2007 (CO No 1)
818 Adjustment of entry relating to share acquisition agreement	20 Jan 2007 (CO No 1)
819 Duty of company ceasing to be public company	20 Jan 2007 (CO No 1)

Provision of CA 2006	Commencement
Part 22: Information About Interests in a Company's Shares	
820 Interest in shares: general	20 Jan 2007 (CO No 1)
821 Interest in shares: right to subscribe for shares	20 Jan 2007 (CO No 1)
822 Interest in shares: family interests	20 Jan 2007 (CO No 1)
823 Interest in shares: corporate interests	20 Jan 2007 (CO No 1)
824 Interest in shares: agreement to acquire interests in a particular company	20 Jan 2007 (CO No 1)
825 Extent of obligation in case of share acquisition agreement	20 Jan 2007 (CO No 1)
826 Information protected from wider disclosure	20 Jan 2007 (CO No 1)[43]
827 Reckoning of periods for fulfilling obligations	20 Jan 2007 (CO No 1)
828 Power to make further provision by regulations	20 Jan 2007 (CO No 1)
Part 23: Distributions	
Chapter 1: Restrictions on When Distributions may be Made	
829 Meaning of "distribution"	*Not in force*
830 Distributions to be made only out of profits available for the purpose	*Not in force*
831 Net asset restriction on distributions by public companies	*Not in force*
832 Distributions by investment companies out of accumulated revenue profits	*Not in force*
833 Meaning of "investment company"	*Not in force*
834 Investment company: condition as to holdings in other companies	*Not in force*
835 Power to extend provisions relating to investment companies	20 Jan 2007 (certain purposes) (CO No 1)[3] *Not in force* (otherwise)
Chapter 2: Justification of Distribution by Reference to Accounts	
836 Justification of distribution by reference to relevant accounts	*Not in force*
837 Requirements where last annual accounts used	*Not in force*
838 Requirements where interim accounts used	*Not in force*
839 Requirements where initial accounts used	*Not in force*
840 Successive distributions etc by reference to the same accounts	*Not in force*
Chapter 3: Supplementary Provisions	
841 Realised losses and profits and revaluation of fixed assets	*Not in force*
842 Determination of profit or loss in respect of asset where records incomplete	*Not in force*
843 Realised profits and losses of long-term insurance business	*Not in force*
844 Treatment of development costs	*Not in force*
845 Distributions in kind: determination of amount	*Not in force*
846 Distributions in kind: treatment of unrealised profits	*Not in force*
847 Consequences of unlawful distribution	*Not in force*
848 Saving for certain older provisions in articles	*Not in force*

Provision of CA 2006	Commencement
Part 23: Distributions	
Chapter 3: Supplementary Provisions	
849 Restriction on application of unrealised profits	*Not in force*
850 Treatment of certain older profits or losses	*Not in force*
851 Application of rules of law restricting distributions	*Not in force*
852 Saving for other restrictions on distributions	*Not in force*
853 Minor definitions	*Not in force*
Part 24: A Company's Annual Return	
854 Duty to deliver annual returns	*Not in force*
855 Contents of annual return: general	20 Jan 2007 (certain purposes) (CO No 1)[3] *Not in force* (otherwise)
856 Contents of annual return: information about share capital and shareholders	20 Jan 2007 (certain purposes) (CO No 1)[3] *Not in force* (otherwise)
857 Contents of annual return: power to make further provision by regulations	20 Jan 2007 (certain purposes) (CO No 1)[3] *Not in force* (otherwise)
858 Failure to deliver annual return	*Not in force*
859 Application of provisions to shadow directors	*Not in force*
Part 25: Company Charges	
Chapter 1: Companies Registered in England and Wales or in Northern Ireland	
860 Charges created by a company	20 Jan 2007 (certain purposes) (CO No 1)[3] *Not in force* (otherwise)
861 Charges which have to be registered: supplementary	*Not in force*
862 Charges existing on property acquired	20 Jan 2007 (certain purposes) (CO No 1)[3] *Not in force* (otherwise)
863 Charge in series of debentures	*Not in force*
864 Additional registration requirement for commission etc in relation to debentures	*Not in force*
865 Endorsement of certificate on debentures	*Not in force*
866 Charges created in, or over property in, jurisdictions outside the United Kingdom	*Not in force*
867 Charges created in, or over property in, another United Kingdom jurisdiction	*Not in force*
868 Northern Ireland: registration of certain charges etc affecting land	*Not in force*
869 Register of charges to be kept by registrar	*Not in force*
870 The period allowed for registration	*Not in force*
871 Registration of enforcement of security	*Not in force*
872 Entries of satisfaction and release	*Not in force*
873 Rectification of register of charges	*Not in force*
874 Consequence of failure to register charges created by a company	*Not in force*
875 Companies to keep copies of instruments creating charges	*Not in force*
876 Company's register of charges	*Not in force*
877 Instruments creating charges and register of charges to be available for inspection	20 Jan 2007 (certain purposes) (CO No 1)[3] *Not in force* (otherwise)

Provision of CA 2006	Commencement
Part 25: Company Charges	
Chapter 2: Companies Registered in Scotland	
878 Charges created by a company	20 Jan 2007 (certain purposes) (CO No 1)[3] *Not in force* (otherwise)
879 Charges which have to be registered: supplementary	*Not in force*
880 Duty to register charges existing on property acquired	20 Jan 2007 (certain purposes) (CO No 1)[3] *Not in force* (otherwise)
881 Charge by way of ex facie absolute disposition, etc	*Not in force*
882 Charge in series of debentures	*Not in force*
883 Additional registration requirement for commission etc in relation to debentures	*Not in force*
884 Charges on property outside United Kingdom	*Not in force*
885 Register of charges to be kept by registrar	*Not in force*
886 The period allowed for registration	*Not in force*
887 Entries of satisfaction and relief	*Not in force*
888 Rectification of register of charges	*Not in force*
889 Charges void unless registered	*Not in force*
890 Copies of instruments creating charges to be kept by company	*Not in force*
891 Company's register of charges	*Not in force*
892 Instruments creating charges and register of charges to be available for inspection	20 Jan 2007 (certain purposes) (CO No 1)[3] *Not in force* (otherwise)
Chapter 3: Powers of the Secretary of State	
893 Power to make provision for effect of registration in special register	20 Jan 2007 (certain purposes) (CO No 1)[3] *Not in force* (otherwise)
894 General power to make amendments to this Part	20 Jan 2007 (certain purposes) (CO No 1)[3] *Not in force* (otherwise)
Part 26: Arrangements and Reconstructions	
895 Application of this Part	*Not in force*
896 Court order for holding of meeting	*Not in force*
897 Statement to be circulated or made available	*Not in force*
898 Duty of directors and trustees to provide information	*Not in force*
899 Court sanction for compromise or arrangement	*Not in force*
900 Powers of court to facilitate reconstruction or amalgamation	*Not in force*
901 Obligations of company with respect to articles etc	*Not in force*
Part 27: Mergers and Divisions of Public Companies	
Chapter 1: Introductory	
902 Application of this Part	*Not in force*
903 Relationship of this Part to Part 26	*Not in force*
Chapter 2: Merger	
904 Mergers and merging companies	*Not in force*
905 Draft terms of scheme (merger)	*Not in force*
906 Publication of draft terms (merger)	*Not in force*

APPENDICES

Provision of CA 2006	Commencement
Part 27: Mergers and Divisions of Public Companies	
Chapter 2: Merger	
907 Approval of members of merging companies	*Not in force*
908 Directors' explanatory report (merger)	*Not in force*
909 Expert's report (merger)	*Not in force*
910 Supplementary accounting statement (merger)	*Not in force*
911 Inspection of documents (merger)	*Not in force*
912 Approval of articles of new transferee company (merger)	*Not in force*
913 Protection of holders of securities to which special rights attached (merger)	*Not in force*
914 No allotment of shares to transferor company or its nominee (merger)	*Not in force*
915 Circumstances in which certain particulars and reports not required (merger)	*Not in force*
916 Circumstances in which meeting of members of transferee company not required (merger)	*Not in force*
917 Circumstances in which no meetings required (merger)	*Not in force*
918 Other circumstances in which meeting of members of transferee company not required (merger)	*Not in force*
Chapter 3: Division	
919 Divisions and companies involved in a division	*Not in force*
920 Draft terms of scheme (division)	*Not in force*
921 Publication of draft terms (division)	*Not in force*
922 Approval of members of companies involved in the division	*Not in force*
923 Directors' explanatory report (division)	*Not in force*
924 Expert's report (division)	*Not in force*
925 Supplementary accounting statement (division)	*Not in force*
926 Inspection of documents (division)	*Not in force*
927 Report on material changes of assets of transferor company (division)	*Not in force*
928 Approval of articles of new transferee company (division)	*Not in force*
929 Protection of holders of securities to which special rights attached (division)	*Not in force*
930 No allotment of shares to transferor company or its nominee (division)	*Not in force*
931 Circumstances in which meeting of members of transferor company not required (division)	*Not in force*
932 Circumstances in which meeting of members of transferee company not required (division)	*Not in force*
933 Agreement to dispense with reports etc (division)	*Not in force*
934 Power of court to exclude certain requirements (division)	*Not in force*

Provision of CA 2006	Commencement
Part 27: Mergers and Divisions of Public Companies	
Chapter 4: Supplementary Provisions	
935 Expert's report: valuation by another person	*Not in force*
936 Experts and valuers: independence requirement	20 Jan 2007 (certain purposes) (CO No 1)[3] *Not in force* (otherwise)
937 Experts and valuers: meaning of "associate"	*Not in force*
938 Power of court to summon meeting of members or creditors of existing transferee company	*Not in force*
939 Court to fix date for transfer of undertaking etc of transferor company	*Not in force*
940 Liability of transferee companies for each other's defaults	*Not in force*
941 Meaning of "liabilities" and "property"	*Not in force*
Part 28: Takeovers etc	
Chapter 1: The Takeover Panel	
942 The Panel	6 Apr 2007 (CO No 2)
943 Rules	6 Apr 2007 (CO No 2)[44]
944 Further provisions about rules	6 Apr 2007 (CO No 2)
945 Rulings	6 Apr 2007 (CO No 2)
946 Directions	6 Apr 2007 (CO No 2)
947 Power to require documents and information	6 Apr 2007 (CO No 2)
948 Restrictions on disclosure	20 Jan 2007 (certain purposes) (CO No 1)[3] 6 Apr 2007 (otherwise) (CO No 2)
949 Offence of disclosure in contravention of section 948	6 Apr 2007 (CO No 2)
950 Panel's duty of co-operation	6 Apr 2007 (CO No 2)
951 Hearings and appeals	6 Apr 2007 (CO No 2)
952 Sanctions	6 Apr 2007 (CO No 2)
953 Failure to comply with rules about bid documentation	6 Apr 2007 (CO No 2)[44]
954 Compensation	6 Apr 2007 (CO No 2)
955 Enforcement by the court	6 Apr 2007 (CO No 2)
956 No action for breach of statutory duty etc	6 Apr 2007 (CO No 2)
957 Fees and charges	6 Apr 2007 (CO No 2)
958 Levy	20 Jan 2007 (certain purposes) (CO No 1)[3] 6 Apr 2007 (otherwise) (CO No 2)
959 Recovery of fees, charges or levy	6 Apr 2007 (CO No 2)
960 Panel as party to proceedings	6 Apr 2007 (CO No 2)
961 Exemption from liability in damages	6 Apr 2007 (CO No 2)
962 Privilege against self-incrimination	6 Apr 2007 (CO No 2)
963 Annual reports	6 Apr 2007 (CO No 2)
964 Amendments to Financial Services and Markets Act 2000	6 Apr 2007 (CO No 2)
965 Power to extend to Isle of Man and Channel Islands	20 Jan 2007 (certain purposes) (CO No 1)[3] 6 Apr 2007 (otherwise) (CO No 2)
Chapter 2: Impediments to Takeovers	
966 Opting in and opting out	20 Jan 2007 (certain purposes) (CO No 1)[3] 6 Apr 2007 (otherwise) (CO No 2)

APPENDICES

Provision of CA 2006	Commencement
Part 28: Takeovers etc	
Chapter 2: Impediments to Takeovers	
967 Further provision about opting-in and opting-out resolutions	6 Apr 2007 (CO No 2)
968 Effect on contractual restrictions	6 Apr 2007 (CO No 2)[45]
969 Power of offeror to require general meeting to be called	6 Apr 2007 (CO No 2)
970 Communication of decisions	6 Apr 2007 (CO No 2)
971 Interpretation of this Chapter	6 Apr 2007 (CO No 2)
972 Transitory provision	6 Apr 2007 (CO No 2)
973 Power to extend to Isle of Man and Channel Islands	20 Jan 2007 (certain purposes) (CO No 1)[3] 6 Apr 2007 (otherwise) (CO No 2)
Chapter 3: "Squeeze-Out" and "Sell-Out"	
974 Meaning of "takeover offer"	6 Apr 2007 (CO No 2)
975 Shares already held by the offeror etc	6 Apr 2007 (CO No 2)
976 Cases where offer treated as being on same terms	6 Apr 2007 (CO No 2)
977 Shares to which an offer relates	6 Apr 2007 (CO No 2)
978 Effect of impossibility etc of communicating or accepting offer	6 Apr 2007 (CO No 2)
979 Right of offeror to buy out minority shareholder	6 Apr 2007 (CO No 2)
980 Further provision about notices given under section 979	20 Jan 2007 (certain purposes) (CO No 1)[3] 6 Apr 2007 (otherwise) (CO No 2)
981 Effect of notice under section 979	6 Apr 2007 (CO No 2)
982 Further provision about consideration held on trust under section 981(9)	6 Apr 2007 (CO No 2)
983 Right of minority shareholder to be bought out by offeror	6 Apr 2007 (CO No 2)
984 Further provision about rights conferred by section 983	20 Jan 2007 (certain purposes) (CO No 1)[3] 6 Apr 2007 (otherwise) (CO No 2)
985 Effect of requirement under section 983	6 Apr 2007 (CO No 2)
986 Applications to the court	6 Apr 2007 (CO No 2)
987 Joint offers	6 Apr 2007 (CO No 2)
988 Associates	6 Apr 2007 (CO No 2)
989 Convertible securities	6 Apr 2007 (CO No 2)
990 Debentures carrying voting rights	6 Apr 2007 (CO No 2)
991 Interpretation	6 Apr 2007 (CO No 2)
Chapter 4: Amendments to Part 7 of the Companies Act 1985	
992 Matters to be dealt with in directors' report	6 Apr 2007 (CO No 2)
Part 29: Fraudulent Trading	
993 Offence of fraudulent trading	1 Oct 2007 (CO No 3)[46]
Part 30: Protection of Members Against Unfair Prejudice	
994 Petition by company member	1 Oct 2007 (CO No 3)[47]
995 Petition by Secretary of State	1 Oct 2007 (CO No 3)
996 Powers of the court under this Part	1 Oct 2007 (CO No 3)
997 Application of general rule-making powers	1 Oct 2007 (CO No 3)
998 Copy of order affecting company's constitution to be delivered to registrar	1 Oct 2007 (CO No 3)

Provision of CA 2006	Commencement
Part 30: Protection of Members Against Unfair Prejudice	
999 Supplementary provisions where company's constitution altered	1 Oct 2007 (CO No 3)[48]
Part 31: Dissolution and Restoration to the Register	
Chapter 1: Striking Off	
1000 Power to strike off company not carrying on business or in operation	*Not in force*
1001 Duty to act in case of company being wound up	*Not in force*
1002 Supplementary provisions as to service of letter or notice	*Not in force*
1003 Striking off on application by company	20 Jan 2007 (certain purposes) (CO No 1)[3] *Not in force* (otherwise)
1004 Circumstances in which application not to be made: activities of company	20 Jan 2007 (certain purposes) (CO No 1)[3] *Not in force* (otherwise)
1005 Circumstances in which application not to be made: other proceedings not concluded	*Not in force*
1006 Copy of application to be given to members, employees, etc	20 Jan 2007 (certain purposes) (CO No 1)[3] *Not in force* (otherwise)
1007 Copy of application to be given to new members, employees, etc	20 Jan 2007 (certain purposes) (CO No 1)[3] *Not in force* (otherwise)
1008 Copy of application: provisions as to service of documents	*Not in force*
1009 Circumstances in which application to be withdrawn	20 Jan 2007 (certain purposes) (CO No 1)[3] *Not in force* (otherwise)
1010 Withdrawal of application	*Not in force*
1011 Meaning of "creditor"	*Not in force*
Chapter 2: Property of Dissolved Company	
1012 Property of dissolved company to be bona vacantia	*Not in force*
1013 Crown disclaimer of property vesting as bona vacantia	*Not in force*
1014 Effect of Crown disclaimer	*Not in force*
1015 General effect of disclaimer	*Not in force*
1016 Disclaimer of leaseholds	*Not in force*
1017 Power of court to make vesting order	*Not in force*
1018 Protection of persons holding under a lease	*Not in force*
1019 Land subject to rentcharge	*Not in force*
1020 General effect of disclaimer	*Not in force*
1021 Power of court to make vesting order	*Not in force*
1022 Protection of persons holding under a lease	*Not in force*
1023 Liability for rentcharge on company's land after dissolution	*Not in force*
Chapter 3: Restoration to the Register	
1024 Application for administrative restoration to the register	*Not in force*
1025 Requirements for administrative restoration	*Not in force*
1026 Application to be accompanied by statement of compliance	*Not in force*

Provision of CA 2006	Commencement
Part 31: Dissolution and Restoration to the Register	
Chapter 3: Restoration to the Register	
1027 Registrar's decision on application for administrative restoration	*Not in force*
1028 Effect of administrative restoration	*Not in force*
1029 Application to court for restoration to the register	*Not in force*
1030 When application to the court may be made	*Not in force*
1031 Decision on application for restoration by the court	*Not in force*
1032 Effect of court order for restoration to the register	*Not in force*
1033 Company's name on restoration	*Not in force*
1034 Effect of restoration to the register where property has vested as bona vacantia	*Not in force*
Part 32: Company Investigations: Amendments	
1035 Powers of Secretary of State to give directions to inspectors	1 Oct 2007 (CO No 3)[49]
1036 Resignation, removal and replacement of inspectors	1 Oct 2007 (CO No 3)[49]
1037 Power to obtain information from former inspectors etc	1 Oct 2007 (CO No 3)[49]
1038 Power to require production of documents	1 Oct 2007 (CO No 3)[49]
1039 Disqualification orders: consequential amendments	1 Oct 2007 (CO No 3)[49]
Part 33: UK Companies Not Formed Under Companies Legislation	
Chapter 1: Companies Not Formed Under Companies Legislation but Authorised to Register	
1040 Companies authorised to register under this Act	*Not in force*
1041 Definition of "joint stock company"	*Not in force*
1042 Power to make provision by regulations	20 Jan 2007 (certain purposes) (CO No 1)[3] *Not in force* (otherwise)
Chapter 2: Unregistered Companies	
1043 Unregistered companies	20 Jan 2007 (certain purposes) (CO No 1)[3] 6 Apr 2007 (otherwise) (CO No 2)
Part 34: Overseas Companies	
1044 Overseas companies	*Not in force*
1045 Company contracts and execution of documents by companies	20 Jan 2007 (certain purposes) (CO No 1)[3] *Not in force* (otherwise)
1046 Duty to register particulars	20 Jan 2007 (certain purposes) (CO No 1)[3] *Not in force* (otherwise)
1047 Registered name of overseas company	*Not in force*
1048 Registration under alternative name	*Not in force*
1049 Accounts and reports: general	20 Jan 2007 (certain purposes) (CO No 1)[3] *Not in force* (otherwise)
1050 Accounts and reports: credit or financial institutions	20 Jan 2007 (certain purposes) (CO No 1)[3] *Not in force* (otherwise)
1051 Trading disclosures	20 Jan 2007 (certain purposes) (CO No 1)[3] *Not in force* (otherwise)
1052 Company charges	20 Jan 2007 (certain purposes) (CO No 1)[3] *Not in force* (otherwise)

Provision of CA 2006	Commencement
Part 34: Overseas Companies	
1053 Other returns etc	20 Jan 2007 (certain purposes) (CO No 1)[3] *Not in force* (otherwise)
1054 Offences	20 Jan 2007 (certain purposes) (CO No 1)[3] *Not in force* (otherwise)
1055 Disclosure of individual's residential address: protection from disclosure	20 Jan 2007 (certain purposes) (CO No 1)[3] *Not in force* (otherwise)
1056 Requirement to identify persons authorised to accept service of documents	20 Jan 2007 (certain purposes) (CO No 1)[3] *Not in force* (otherwise)
1057 Registrar to whom returns, notices etc to be delivered	20 Jan 2007 (certain purposes) (CO No 1)[3] *Not in force* (otherwise)
1058 Duty to give notice of ceasing to have registrable presence	20 Jan 2007 (certain purposes) (CO No 1)[3] *Not in force* (otherwise)
1059 Application of provisions in case of relocation of branch	*Not in force*
Part 35: The Registrar of Companies	
1060 The registrar	6 Apr 2007 (certain purposes) (CO No 1)[50] *Not in force* (otherwise)
1061 The registrar's functions	6 Apr 2007 (certain purposes) (CO No 1)[50] *Not in force* (otherwise)
1062 The registrar's official seal	*Not in force*
1063 Fees payable to registrar	20 Jan 2007 (certain purposes) (CO No 1)[3] 6 Apr 2007 (GB otherwise) (CO No 1)[51] *Not in force* (NI otherwise)
1064 Public notice of issue of certificate of incorporation	*Not in force*
1065 Right to certificate of incorporation	*Not in force*
1066 Company's registered numbers	*Not in force*
1067 Registered numbers of branches of overseas company	*Not in force*
1068 Registrar's requirements as to form, authentication and manner of delivery	1 Jan 2007 (sub-s (5), and sub-ss (1)–(4), (6), (7) for certain purposes) (CO No 1)[52] 15 Dec 2007 (sub-ss (1)–(4), (6), (7) for certain purposes) (CO No 3)[53] *Not in force* (otherwise)
1069 Power to require delivery by electronic means	20 Jan 2007 (certain purposes) (CO No 1)[3] *Not in force* (otherwise)
1070 Agreement for delivery by electronic means	*Not in force*
1071 Document not delivered until received	*Not in force*
1072 Requirements for proper delivery	*Not in force*
1073 Power to accept documents not meeting requirements for proper delivery	*Not in force*
1074 Documents containing unnecessary material	*Not in force*
1075 Informal correction of document	*Not in force*
1076 Replacement of document not meeting requirements for proper delivery	*Not in force*
1077 Public notice of receipt of certain documents	1 Jan 2007 (CO No 1)[54]
1078 Documents subject to Directive disclosure requirements	1 Jan 2007 (CO No 1)[54]
1079 Effect of failure to give public notice	1 Jan 2007 (CO No 1)[54]
1080 The register	1 Jan 2007 (CO No 1)[54]

APPENDICES

Provision of CA 2006	Commencement
Part 35: The Registrar of Companies	
1081 Annotation of the register	20 Jan 2007 (certain purposes) (CO No 1)[3] *Not in force* (otherwise)
1082 Allocation of unique identifiers	20 Jan 2007 (certain purposes) (CO No 1)[3] *Not in force* (otherwise)
1083 Preservation of original documents	*Not in force*
1084 Records relating to companies that have been dissolved etc	*Not in force*
1085 Inspection of the register	1 Jan 2007 (CO No 1)[54]
1086 Right to copy of material on the register	1 Jan 2007 (CO No 1)
1087 Material not available for public inspection	1 Jan 2007 (CO No 1)[54]
1088 Application to registrar to make address unavailable for public inspection	1 Jan 2007 (CO No 1)
1089 Form of application for inspection or copy	1 Jan 2007 (CO No 1)
1090 Form and manner in which copies to be provided	1 Jan 2007 (CO No 1)
1091 Certification of copies as accurate	1 Jan 2007 (CO No 1)
1092 Issue of process for production of records kept by the registrar	1 Jan 2007 (CO No 1)
1093 Registrar's notice to resolve inconsistency on the register	*Not in force*
1094 Administrative removal of material from the register	*Not in force*
1095 Rectification of register on application to registrar	20 Jan 2007 (certain purposes) (CO No 1)[3] *Not in force* (otherwise)
1096 Rectification of the register under court order	*Not in force*
1097 Powers of court on ordering removal of material from the register	*Not in force*
1098 Public notice of removal of certain material from the register	*Not in force*
1099 The registrar's index of company names	20 Jan 2007 (certain purposes) (CO No 1)[3] *Not in force* (otherwise)
1100 Right to inspect index	*Not in force*
1101 Power to amend enactments relating to bodies other than companies	20 Jan 2007 (certain purposes) (CO No 1)[3] *Not in force* (otherwise)
1102 Application of language requirements	1 Jan 2007 (CO No 1)
1103 Documents to be drawn up and delivered in English	1 Jan 2007 (CO No 1)[54]
1104 Documents relating to Welsh companies	1 Jan 2007 (CO No 1)[54]
1105 Documents that may be drawn up and delivered in other languages	1 Jan 2007 (CO No 1)[55]
1106 Voluntary filing of translations	1 Jan 2007 (CO No 1)
1107 Certified translations	1 Jan 2007 (CO No 1)
1108 Transliteration of names and addresses: permitted characters	20 Jan 2007 (certain purposes) (CO No 1)[3] *Not in force* (otherwise)
1109 Transliteration of names and addresses: voluntary transliteration into Roman characters	*Not in force*
1110 Transliteration of names and addresses: certification	20 Jan 2007 (certain purposes) (CO No 1)[3] *Not in force* (otherwise)

Provision of CA 2006	Commencement
Part 35: The Registrar of Companies	
1111 Registrar's requirements as to certification or verification	1 Jan 2007 (CO No 1)
1112 General false statement offence	*Not in force*
1113 Enforcement of company's filing obligations	*Not in force*
1114 Application of provisions about documents and delivery	1 Jan 2007 (certain purposes) (CO No 1)[56] *Not in force* (otherwise)
1115 Supplementary provisions relating to electronic communications	*Not in force*
1116 Alternative to publication in the Gazette	20 Jan 2007 (certain purposes) (CO No 1)[3] *Not in force* (otherwise)
1117 Registrar's rules	1 Jan 2007 (certain purposes) (CO No 1)[56] *Not in force* (otherwise)
1118 Payments into the Consolidated Fund	*Not in force*
1119 Contracting out of registrar's functions	*Not in force*
1120 Application of this Part to overseas companies	1 Jan 2007 (certain purposes) (CO No 1)[56] *Not in force* (otherwise)
Part 36: Offences Under the Companies Acts	
1121 Liability of officer in default	20 Jan 2007 (certain purposes) (CO No 1)[57] 6 Apr 2007 (certain purposes) (CO No 2)[41] 1 Oct 2007 (certain purposes) (CO No 3)[58] *Not in force* (otherwise)
1122 Liability of company as officer in default	20 Jan 2007 (certain purposes) (CO No 1)[57] 6 Apr 2007 (certain purposes) (CO No 2)[41] 1 Oct 2007 (certain purposes) (CO No 3)[58] *Not in force* (otherwise)
1123 Application to bodies other than companies	6 Apr 2007 (certain purposes) (CO No 2)[41] 1 Oct 2007 (certain purposes) (CO No 3)[58] *Not in force* (otherwise)
1124 Amendments of the Companies Act 1985	1 Oct 2007 (CO No 3)
1125 Meaning of "daily default fine"	20 Jan 2007 (certain purposes) (CO No 1)[57] 6 Apr 2007 (certain purposes) (CO No 2)[41] 1 Oct 2007 (certain purposes) (CO No 3)[58] *Not in force* (otherwise)
1126 Consents required for certain prosecutions	20 Jan 2007 (certain purposes) (CO No 1)[57] 6 Apr 2007 (certain purposes) (CO No 2)[41] 1 Oct 2007 (certain purposes) (CO No 3)[58] *Not in force* (otherwise)
1127 Summary proceedings: venue	20 Jan 2007 (certain purposes) (CO No 1)[57] 6 Apr 2007 (certain purposes) (CO No 2)[41] 1 Oct 2007 (certain purposes) (CO No 3)[58] *Not in force* (otherwise)
1128 Summary proceedings: time limit for proceedings	20 Jan 2007 (certain purposes) (CO No 1)[57] 6 Apr 2007 (certain purposes) (CO No 2)[41] 1 Oct 2007 (certain purposes) (CO No 3)[58] *Not in force* (otherwise)
1129 Legal professional privilege	20 Jan 2007 (certain purposes) (CO No 1)[57] 6 Apr 2007 (certain purposes) (CO No 2)[41] 1 Oct 2007 (certain purposes) (CO No 3)[58] *Not in force* (otherwise)
1130 Proceedings against unincorporated bodies	20 Jan 2007 (certain purposes) (CO No 1)[57] 6 Apr 2007 (certain purposes) (CO No 2)[41] 1 Oct 2007 (certain purposes) (CO No 3)[58] *Not in force* (otherwise)

APPENDICES

Provision of CA 2006	Commencement
Part 36: Offences Under the Companies Acts	
1131 Imprisonment on summary conviction in England and Wales: transitory provision	20 Jan 2007 (certain purposes) (CO No 1)[57] 6 Apr 2007 (certain purposes) (CO No 2)[41] 1 Oct 2007 (certain purposes) (CO No 3)[58] *Not in force* (otherwise)
1132 Production and inspection of documents where offence suspected	6 Apr 2007 (certain purposes) (CO No 2)[41] 1 Oct 2007 (certain purposes) (CO No 3)[58] *Not in force* (otherwise)
1133 Transitional provision	20 Jan 2007 (certain purposes) (CO No 1)[57] 6 Apr 2007 (certain purposes) (CO No 2)[41] 1 Oct 2007 (certain purposes) (CO No 3)[58] *Not in force* (otherwise)
Part 37: Companies: Supplementary Provisions	
1134 Meaning of "company records"	6 Apr 2007 (certain purposes) (CO No 2)[41] *Not in force* (otherwise)
1135 Form of company records	6 Apr 2007 (certain purposes) (CO No 2)[41] *Not in force* (otherwise)
1136 Regulations about where certain company records to be kept available for inspection	20 Jan 2007 (certain purposes) (CO No 1)[3] *Not in force* (otherwise)
1137 Regulations about inspection of records and provision of copies	20 Jan 2007 (certain purposes) (CO No 1)[3] *Not in force* (otherwise)
1138 Duty to take precautions against falsification	6 Apr 2007 (certain purposes) (CO No 2)[41] *Not in force* (otherwise)
1139 Service of documents on company	6 Apr 2007 (certain purposes) (CO No 2)[41] *Not in force* (otherwise)
1140 Service of documents on directors, secretaries and others	6 Apr 2007 (certain purposes) (CO No 2)[41] *Not in force* (otherwise)
1141 Service addresses	20 Jan 2007 (certain purposes) (CO No 1)[3] *Not in force* (otherwise)
1142 Requirement to give service address	*Not in force*
1143 The company communications provisions	20 Jan 2007 (CO No 1)[43]
1144 Sending or supplying documents or information	20 Jan 2007 (CO No 1)
1145 Right to hard copy version	20 Jan 2007 (CO No 1)
1146 Requirement of authentication	20 Jan 2007 (CO No 1)
1147 Deemed delivery of documents and information	20 Jan 2007 (CO No 1)
1148 Interpretation of company communications provisions	20 Jan 2007 (CO No 1)
1149 Application of valuation requirements	*Not in force*
1150 Valuation by qualified independent person	*Not in force*
1151 The independence requirement	20 Jan 2007 (certain purposes) (CO No 1)[3] *Not in force* (otherwise)
1152 Meaning of "associate"	*Not in force*
1153 Valuer entitled to full disclosure	*Not in force*
1154 Duty to notify registrar of certain appointments etc	*Not in force*
1155 Offence of failure to give notice	*Not in force*
1156 Meaning of "the court"	20 Jan 2007 (certain purposes) (CO No 1)[3] *Not in force* (otherwise)
1157 Power of court to grant relief in certain cases	*Not in force*

Provision of CA 2006	Commencement
Part 38: Companies: Interpretation	
1158 Meaning of "UK-registered company"	1 Oct 2007 (certain purposes) (CO No 3)[4] 1 Nov 2007 (certain purposes) (CO No 3)[42] *Not in force* (otherwise)
1159 Meaning of "subsidiary" etc	*Not in force*
1160 Meaning of "subsidiary" etc: power to amend	20 Jan 2007 (certain purposes) (CO No 1)[3] *Not in force* (otherwise)
1161 Meaning of "undertaking" and related expressions	*Not in force*
1162 Parent and subsidiary undertakings	*Not in force*
1163 "Non-cash asset"	*Not in force*
1164 Meaning of "banking company" and "banking group"	*Not in force*
1165 Meaning of "insurance company" and related expressions	*Not in force*
1166 "Employees' share scheme"	*Not in force*
1167 Meaning of "prescribed"	20 Jan 2007 (certain purposes) (CO No 1)[3] *Not in force* (otherwise)
1168 Hard copy and electronic form and related expressions	1 Jan 2007 (certain purposes) (CO No 1)[59] 20 Jan 2007 (certain purposes) (CO No 1)[59] 6 Apr 2007 (certain purposes) (CO No 2)[41] 1 Oct 2007 (certain purposes) (CO No 3)[4] 15 Dec 2007 (certain purposes) (CO No 3)[60] *Not in force* (otherwise)
1169 Dormant companies	*Not in force*
1170 Meaning of "EEA State" and related expressions	6 Apr 2007 (CO No 2)
1171 The former Companies Acts	*Not in force*
1172 References to requirements of this Act	*Not in force*
1173 Minor definitions: general	1 Jan 2007 (certain purposes) (CO No 1)[61] 20 Jan 2007 (certain purposes) (CO No 1)[61] 6 Apr 2007 (certain purposes) (CO No 2)[62] 1 Oct 2007 (certain purposes) (CO No 3)[63] 1 Nov 2007 (certain purposes) (CO No 3)[64] *Not in force* (otherwise)
1174 Index of defined expressions	*Not in force*
Part 39: Companies: Minor Amendments	
1175 Removal of special provisions about accounts and audit of charitable companies	*Not in force*
1176 Power of Secretary of State to bring civil proceedings on company's behalf	6 Apr 2007 (CO No 1)
1177 Repeal of certain provisions about company directors	6 Apr 2007 (CO No 1)
1178 Repeal of requirement that certain companies publish periodical statement	6 Apr 2007 (CO No 1)
1179 Repeal of requirement that Secretary of State prepare annual report	6 Apr 2007 (CO No 1)
1180 Repeal of certain provisions about company charges	*Not in force*
1181 Access to constitutional documents of RTE and RTM companies	20 Jan 2007 (certain purposes) (CO No 1)[3] *Not in force* (otherwise)

Provision of CA 2006	Commencement
Part 40: Company Directors: Foreign Disqualification etc	
1182 Persons subject to foreign restrictions	*Not in force*
1183 Meaning of "the court" and "UK company"	*Not in force*
1184 Disqualification of persons subject to foreign restrictions	20 Jan 2007 (certain purposes) (CO No 1)[3] *Not in force* (otherwise)
1185 Disqualification regulations: supplementary	20 Jan 2007 (certain purposes) (CO No 1)[3] *Not in force* (otherwise)
1186 Offence of breach of disqualification	20 Jan 2007 (certain purposes) (CO No 1)[3] *Not in force* (otherwise)
1187 Personal liability for debts of company	20 Jan 2007 (certain purposes) (CO No 1)[3] *Not in force* (otherwise)
1188 Statements from persons subject to foreign restrictions	20 Jan 2007 (certain purposes) (CO No 1)[3] *Not in force* (otherwise)
1189 Statements from persons disqualified	20 Jan 2007 (certain purposes) (CO No 1)[3] *Not in force* (otherwise)
1190 Statements: whether to be made public	*Not in force*
1191 Offences	20 Jan 2007 (certain purposes) (CO No 1)[3] *Not in force* (otherwise)
Part 41: Business Names	
Chapter 1: Restricted or Prohibited Names	
1192 Application of this Chapter	*Not in force*
1193 Name suggesting connection with government or public authority	20 Jan 2007 (certain purposes) (CO No 1)[3] *Not in force* (otherwise)
1194 Other sensitive words or expressions	20 Jan 2007 (certain purposes) (CO No 1)[3] *Not in force* (otherwise)
1195 Requirement to seek comments of government department or other relevant body	20 Jan 2007 (certain purposes) (CO No 1)[3] *Not in force* (otherwise)
1196 Withdrawal of Secretary of State's approval	*Not in force*
1197 Name containing inappropriate indication of company type or legal form	20 Jan 2007 (certain purposes) (CO No 1)[3] *Not in force* (otherwise)
1198 Name giving misleading indication of activities	*Not in force*
1199 Savings for existing lawful business names	*Not in force*
Chapter 2: Disclosure Required in Case of Individual or Partnership	
1200 Application of this Chapter	*Not in force*
1201 Information required to be disclosed	*Not in force*
1202 Disclosure required: business documents etc	20 Jan 2007 (certain purposes) (CO No 1)[3] *Not in force* (otherwise)
1203 Exemption for large partnerships if certain conditions met	*Not in force*
1204 Disclosure required: business premises	20 Jan 2007 (certain purposes) (CO No 1)[3] *Not in force* (otherwise)
1205 Criminal consequences of failure to make required disclosure	*Not in force*
1206 Civil consequences of failure to make required disclosure	*Not in force*
Chapter 3: Supplementary	
1207 Application of general provisions about offences	*Not in force*
1208 Interpretation	*Not in force*

Provision of CA 2006	Commencement
Part 42: Statutory Auditors	
Chapter 1: Introductory	
1209 Main purposes of Part	*Not in force*
1210 Meaning of "statutory auditor" etc	20 Jan 2007 (certain purposes) (CO No 1)[3] *Not in force* (otherwise)
1211 Eligibility for appointment as a statutory auditor: overview	*Not in force*
Chapter 2: Individuals and Firms	
1212 Individuals and firms: eligibility for appointment as a statutory auditor	*Not in force*
1213 Effect of ineligibility	*Not in force*
1214 Independence requirement	20 Jan 2007 (certain purposes) (CO No 1)[3] *Not in force* (otherwise)
1215 Effect of lack of independence	*Not in force*
1216 Effect of appointment of a partnership	*Not in force*
1217 Supervisory bodies	*Not in force*
1218 Exemption from liability for damages	*Not in force*
1219 Appropriate qualifications	*Not in force*
1220 Qualifying bodies and recognised professional qualifications	*Not in force*
1221 Approval of overseas qualifications	*Not in force*
1222 Eligibility of individuals retaining only 1967 Act authorisation	*Not in force*
1223 Matters to be notified to the Secretary of State	*Not in force*
1224 The Secretary of State's power to call for information	*Not in force*
1225 Compliance orders	*Not in force*
Chapter 3: Auditors General	
1226 Auditors General: eligibility for appointment as a statutory auditor	*Not in force*
1227 Individuals responsible for audit work on behalf of Auditors General	*Not in force*
1228 Appointment of the Independent Supervisor	20 Jan 2007 (certain purposes) (CO No 1)[3] *Not in force* (otherwise)
1229 Supervision of Auditors General by the Independent Supervisor	*Not in force*
1230 Duties of Auditors General in relation to supervision arrangements	*Not in force*
1231 Reports by the Independent Supervisor	20 Jan 2007 (certain purposes) (CO No 1)[3] *Not in force* (otherwise)
1232 Matters to be notified to the Independent Supervisor	*Not in force*
1233 The Independent Supervisor's power to call for information	*Not in force*
1234 Suspension notices	*Not in force*
1235 Effect of suspension notices	*Not in force*
1236 Compliance orders	*Not in force*
1237 Proceedings involving the Independent Supervisor	20 Jan 2007 (certain purposes) (CO No 1)[3] *Not in force* (otherwise)

APPENDICES

Provision of CA 2006	Commencement
Part 42: Statutory Auditors	
Chapter 3: Auditors General	
1238 Grants to the Independent Supervisor	*Not in force*
Chapter 4: The Register of Auditors etc	
1239 The register of auditors	20 Jan 2007 (certain purposes) (CO No 1)[3] *Not in force* (otherwise)
1240 Information to be made available to public	20 Jan 2007 (certain purposes) (CO No 1)[3] *Not in force* (otherwise)
Chapter 5: Registered Third Country Auditors	
1241 Meaning of "third country auditor", "registered third country auditor" etc	20 Jan 2007 (certain purposes) (CO No 1)[3] *Not in force* (otherwise)
1242 Duties of registered third country auditors	*Not in force*
1243 Matters to be notified to the Secretary of State	*Not in force*
1244 The Secretary of State's power to call for information	*Not in force*
1245 Compliance orders	*Not in force*
1246 Removal of third country auditors from the register of auditors	20 Jan 2007 (certain purposes) (CO No 1)[3] *Not in force* (otherwise)
1247 Grants to bodies concerned with arrangements under Schedule 12	*Not in force*
Chapter 6: Supplementary and General	
1249 Supplementary provision about second audits	*Not in force*
1250 Misleading, false and deceptive statements	*Not in force*
1251 Fees	20 Jan 2007 (certain purposes) (CO No 1)[3] *Not in force* (otherwise)
1252 Delegation of the Secretary of State's functions	20 Jan 2007 (certain purposes) (CO No 1)[3] *Not in force* (otherwise)
1253 Delegation of functions to an existing body	20 Jan 2007 (certain purposes) (CO No 1)[3] *Not in force* (otherwise)
1254 Directions to comply with international obligations	*Not in force*
1255 Offences by bodies corporate, partnerships and unincorporated associations	*Not in force*
1256 Time limits for prosecution of offences	*Not in force*
1257 Jurisdiction and procedure in respect of offences	*Not in force*
1258 Service of notices	*Not in force*
1259 Documents in electronic form	*Not in force*
1260 Meaning of "associate"	*Not in force*
1261 Minor definitions	20 Jan 2007 (certain purposes) (CO No 1)[3] *Not in force* (otherwise)
1262 Index of defined expressions	*Not in force*
1263 Power to make provision in consequence of changes affecting accountancy bodies	20 Jan 2007 (certain purposes) (CO No 1)[3] *Not in force* (otherwise)
1264 Consequential amendments	*Not in force*
Part 43: Transparency Obligations and Related Matters	
1265 The transparency obligations directive	8 Nov 2006 (RA)
1266 Transparency rules	8 Nov 2006 (RA)

Provision of CA 2006	Commencement
Part 43: Transparency Obligations and Related Matters	
1267 Competent authority's power to call for information	8 Nov 2006 (RA)
1268 Powers exercisable in case of infringement of transparency obligation	8 Nov 2006 (RA)
1269 Corporate governance rules	8 Nov 2006 (RA)
1270 Liability for false or misleading statements in certain publications	8 Nov 2006 (RA)
1271 Exercise of powers where UK is host member State	8 Nov 2006 (RA)
1272 Transparency obligations and related matters: minor and consequential amendments	8 Nov 2006 (certain purposes) (RA) *Not in force* (otherwise)[65]
1273 Corporate governance regulations	8 Nov 2006 (RA)
Part 44: Miscellaneous Provisions	
1274 Grants to bodies concerned with actuarial standards etc	8 Nov 2006 (RA)
1275 Levy to pay expenses of bodies concerned with actuarial standards etc	*Not in force*
1276 Application of provisions to Scotland and Northern Ireland	8 Nov 2006 (RA)
1277 Power to require information about exercise of voting rights	20 Jan 2007 (certain purposes) (CO No 1)[3] *Not in force* (otherwise)
1278 Institutions to which information provisions apply	20 Jan 2007 (certain purposes) (CO No 1)[3] *Not in force* (otherwise)
1279 Shares to which information provisions apply	20 Jan 2007 (certain purposes) (CO No 1)[3] *Not in force* (otherwise)
1280 Obligations with respect to provision of information	20 Jan 2007 (certain purposes) (CO No 1)[3] *Not in force* (otherwise)
1281 Disclosure of information under the Enterprise Act 2002	6 Apr 2007 (CO No 1)
1282 Payment of expenses of winding up	*Not in force*
1283 Amendment of memorandum or articles of commonhold association	*Not in force*
Part 45: Northern Ireland	
1284 Extension of Companies Acts to Northern Ireland	1 Jan 2007 (certain purposes) (CO No 1) 20 Jan 2007 (certain purposes) (CO No 1) 6 Apr 2007 (certain purposes) (CO No 1 & CO No 2) 1 Oct 2007 (certain purposes) (CO No 3) 1 Nov 2007 (certain purposes) (CO No 3) 15 Dec 2007 (certain purposes) (CO No 3) 1 Oct 2008 (certain purposes) (CO No 3) *Not in force* (otherwise)[66]
1285 Extension of GB enactments relating to SEs	*Not in force*
1286 Extension of GB enactments relating to certain other forms of business organisation	*Not in force*
1287 Extension of enactments relating to business names	*Not in force*
Part 46: General Supplementary Provisions	
1288 Regulations and orders: statutory instrument	8 Nov 2006 (RA)
1289 Regulations and orders: negative resolution procedure	8 Nov 2006 (RA)

Provision of CA 2006	Commencement
Part 46: General Supplementary Provisions	
1290 Regulations and orders: affirmative resolution procedure	8 Nov 2006 (RA)
1291 Regulations and orders: approval after being made	8 Nov 2006 (RA)
1292 Regulations and orders: supplementary	8 Nov 2006 (RA)
1293 Meaning of "enactment"	8 Nov 2006 (RA)
1294 Power to make consequential amendments etc	8 Nov 2006 (RA)
1295 Repeals	See Sch 16 below
1296 Power to make transitional provision and savings	8 Nov 2006 (RA)
1297 Continuity of the law	8 Nov 2006 (RA)
Part 47: Final Provisions	
1298 Short title	8 Nov 2006 (RA)
1299 Extent	8 Nov 2006 (RA)
1300 Commencement	8 Nov 2006 (RA)
Schedules	
Schedule 1—Connected Persons: References to an Interest in Shares or Debentures	1 Oct 2007 (CO No 3)
Schedule 2—Specified Persons, Descriptions of Disclosures etc for the Purposes of Section 948	
Part 1—Specified Persons	6 Apr 2007 (CO No 2)
Part 2—Specified Descriptions of Disclosures	20 Jan 2007 (certain purposes) (CO No 1)[3] 6 Apr 2007 (otherwise) (CO No 2)
Part 3—Overseas Regulatory Bodies	6 Apr 2007 (CO No 2)
Schedule 3—Amendments of Remaining Provisions of the Companies Act 1985 Relating to Offences	1 Oct 2007 (CO No 3)[67]
Schedule 4—Documents and Information Sent or Supplied to a Company	
Part 1—Introduction	20 Jan 2007 (CO No 1)
Part 2—Communications in Hard Copy Form	20 Jan 2007 (CO No 1)
Part 3—Communications in Electronic Form	20 Jan 2007 (CO No 1)
Part 4—Other Agreed Forms of Communication	20 Jan 2007 (CO No 1)
Schedule 5—Communications by a Company	
Part 1—Introduction	20 Jan 2007 (CO No 1)
Part 2—Communications in Hard Copy Form	20 Jan 2007 (CO No 1)
Part 3—Communications in Electronic Form	20 Jan 2007 (CO No 1)[68]
Part 4—Communications by Means of a Website	20 Jan 2007 (CO No 1)[68]
Part 5—Other Agreed Forms of Communication	20 Jan 2007 (CO No 1)
Part 6—Supplementary Provisions	20 Jan 2007 (CO No 1)
Schedule 6—Meaning of "Subsidiary" etc: Supplementary Provisions	*Not in force*

Provision of CA 2006	Commencement
Schedules	
Schedule 7—Parent and Subsidiary Undertakings: Supplementary Provisions	*Not in force*
Schedule 8—Index of Defined Expressions	*Not in force*
Schedule 9—Removal of Special Provisions About Accounts and Audit of Charitable Companies	
Part 1—The Companies Act 1985 (c 6)	*Not in force*
Part 2—The Companies (Northern Ireland) Order 1986 (SI 1986/1032 (NI 6))	*Not in force*
Schedule 10—Recognised Supervisory Bodies	
Part 1—Grant and Revocation of Recognition of a Supervisory Body	*Not in force*
Part 2—Requirements for Recognition of a Supervisory Body	*Not in force*
Part 3—Arrangements in which Recognised Supervisory Bodies are Required to Participate	*Not in force*
Schedule 11—Recognised Professional Qualifications	
Part 1—Grant and Revocation of Recognition of a Professional Qualification	*Not in force*
Part 2—Requirements for Recognition of a Professional Qualification	20 Jan 2007 (certain purposes) (CO No 1)[3] *Not in force* (otherwise)
Schedule 12—Arrangements in which Registered Third Country Auditors are Required to Participate	20 Jan 2007 (certain purposes) (CO No 1)[3] *Not in force* (otherwise)
Schedule 13—Supplementary Provisions with Respect to Delegation Order	20 Jan 2007 (certain purposes) (CO No 1)[3] *Not in force* (otherwise)
Schedule 14—Statutory Auditors: Consequential Amendments	*Not in force*
Schedule 15—Transparency Obligations and Related Matters: Minor and Consequential Amendments	
Part 1—Amendments of the Financial Services and Markets Act 2000	8 Nov 2006 (certain purposes) (RA) *Not in force* (otherwise)[65]
Part 2—Amendments of the Companies (Audit, Investigations and Community Enterprise) Act 2004	8 Nov 2006 (RA)
Schedule 16—Repeals	1 Jan 2007 (in part) (CO No 1) 20 Jan 2007 (in part) (CO No 1) 6 Apr 2007 (in part) (CO No 1 and CO No 2) 1 Oct 2007 (in part) (CO No 3) *Not in force* (otherwise)[69]

NOTES

[1] CO No 1, arts 2(2), 3(2) provide that this section shall come into force on 1 Jan 2007 and 20 Jan 2007 respectively so far as is necessary for the purposes of the provisions of this Act brought into force on those dates by that Order (see **[7575]**, **[7576]**). For transitional adaptations of s 2, see CO No 1, Sch 1, para 1 (at **[7582]**).

[2] For transitional adaptations of s 2, see CO No 2, Sch 1, para 1 (at **[7625]**).

[3] CO No 1, art 3(3) provides that the provisions CA 2006, in so far as not brought into force by s 1300(1) of that Act, or arts 2, 3(1), (2) of that Order, come into force on 20 Jan 2007 for the purpose of enabling the exercise of powers to make Orders or Regulations by statutory instrument.

[4] CO No 3, art 2(3) provides that this section shall come into force on 1 Oct 2007 so far as is necessary for the purposes of the provisions of this Act brought into force on that date by art 2(1), (2) of that Order (see **[A12]**). For transitional adaptations of ss 17, 1158, see CO No 3, Sch 1, paras 1, 21.
[5] For transitional provisions see CO No 3, Sch 3, para 1 (at **[A12]**).
[6] For transitional provisions see CO No 3, Sch 3, para 2 (at **[A12]**). For transitional adaptations of s 116, see CO No 3, Sch 1, para 2.
[7] For transitional provisions see CO No 3, Sch 3, para 3 (at **[A12]**). For transitional adaptations of ss 145, 146, 153, see CO No 3, Sch 1, paras 3–5.
[8] For transitional provisions see CO No 3, Sch 3, para 4 (at **[A12]**).
[9] For transitional provisions see CO No 3, Sch 3, para 5 (at **[A12]**).
[10] For transitional adaptations of ss 170, 178, 180, 181, see CO No 3, Sch 1, paras 6–9 (at **[A12]**).
[11] For transitional provisions see CO No 3, Sch 3, para 6 (at **[A12]**).
[12] For transitional provisions see CO No 3, Sch 3, para 7 (at **[A12]**). For transitional adaptations of s 191, see CO No 3, Sch 1, para 10.
[13] For transitional provisions see CO No 3, Sch 3, paras 8–11 (at **[A12]**). For transitional adaptations of s 205, see CO No 3, Sch 1, para 11.
[14] For transitional provisions see CO No 3, Sch 3, para 12 (at **[A12]**).
[15] For transitional provisions see CO No 3, Sch 3, para 13 (at **[A12]**).
[16] For transitional provisions see CO No 3, Sch 3, para 14 (at **[A12]**).
[17] For transitional provisions see CO No 3, Sch 3, para 15 (at **[A12]**). For transitional adaptations of s 234, see CO No 3, Sch 1, para 12.
[18] For transitional provisions see CO No 3, Sch 3, para 16 (at **[A12]**).
[19] For transitional provisions see CO No 3, Sch 3, para 17 (at **[A12]**).
[20] For transitional provisions see CO No 3, Sch 3, para 18 (at **[A12]**).
[21] For transitional provisions see CO No 3, Sch 3, para 19 (at **[A12]**).
[22] For transitional provisions see CO No 3, Sch 3, paras 20, 21 (at **[A12]**).
[23] For transitional provisions see CO No 3, Sch 3, paras 22, 23 (at **[A12]**).
[24] For transitional provisions see CO No 3, Sch 3, para 24 (at **[A12]**). For transitional adaptations of s 288 and the transitional insertion of ss 300A–300D, see CO No 3, Sch 1, para 13.
[25] For transitional provisions see CO No 3, Sch 3, para 25 (at **[A12]**).
[26] For transitional adaptations of s 306, see CO No 3, Sch 1, para 14 (at **[A12]**).
[27] For transitional provisions see CO No 3, Sch 3, para 26 (at **[A12]**).
[28] For transitional provisions see CO No 3, Sch 3, para 27 (at **[A12]**).
[29] For transitional provisions see CO No 3, Sch 3, para 28 (at **[A12]**).
[30] For transitional provisions see CO No 3, Sch 3, para 29 (at **[A12]**).
[31] For transitional provisions see CO No 3, Sch 3, para 30 (at **[A12]**).
[32] For transitional provisions see CO No 3, Sch 3, para 31 (at **[A12]**).
[33] For transitional provisions see CO No 3, Sch 3, paras 32–38 (at **[A12]**). For transitional adaptations of s 336, see CO No 3, Sch 1, para 15.
[34] For transitional provisions see CO No 3, Sch 3, para 39 (at **[A12]**).
[35] For transitional provisions see CO No 3, Sch 3, para 40 (at **[A12]**).
[36] CO No 3, arts 2(2), 3(1) (at **[A12]**) provide that Part 14 shall come into force on 1 Oct 2007 (in relation to Great Britain) and 1 Nov 2007 (in relation to Northern Ireland) except in so far as it relates to independent election candidates. Article 5 of that Order specifies certain words in ss 362–367, 378 which, accordingly, do not come into force until 1 Oct 2008. For transitional provisions in connection with the commencement of all of Part 14, see CO No 3, Sch 3, paras 41, 42.
[37] For transitional provisions see CO No 3, Sch 3, para 43 (at **[A12]**). For transitional adaptations of s 417, see CO No 3, Sch 1, para 16.
[38] For transitional provisions see CO No 1, Sch 5, Pt 2, para 3 (at **[7590]**).
[39] For transitional provisions see CO No 3, Sch 3, paras 44, 45 (at **[A12]**). For transitional adaptations of ss 485, 487, see CO No 3, Sch 1, paras 17, 18.
[40] CO No 3, art 2(3) provides that sub-ss (1), (4) shall come into force on 1 Oct 2007 so far as is necessary for the purposes of the provisions of this Act brought into force on that date by art 2(1), (2) of that Order (see **[A12]**).
[41] CO No 2, art 2(2) provides that this section shall come into force on 6 Apr 2007 so far as is necessary for the purposes of the provisions of this Act brought into force on that date by that Order (see **[7615]**). For transitional adaptations of s 1139, see CO No 2, Sch 1, para 5 (at **[7625]**).
[42] CO No 3, art 3(2) provides that this section shall come into force on 1 Nov 2007 so far as is necessary for the purposes of the provisions of this Act brought into force on that date by art 3(1) of that Order (see **[A12]**). For transitional adaptations of s 1158, see CO No 3, Sch 1, para 21.
[43] For transitional adaptations of ss 813, 826, 1143, see CO No 1, Sch 1, paras 2, 3 14, (at **[7582]**).
[44] For transitional adaptations of ss 943, 953, see CO No 2, Sch 1, paras 2, 3 (at **[7625]**).
[45] For transitional adaptations of s 968, see CO No 2, Sch 1, para 4 (at **[7625]**). Note also the prospective revocation of CO No 2, Sch 1, para 4 by CO No 3, art 11(b) (as from 1 Oct 2007).
[46] For transitional provisions see CO No 3, Sch 3, para 46 (at **[A12]**).
[47] For transitional adaptations of s 994, see CO No 3, Sch 1, para 19 (at **[A12]**).
[48] For transitional provisions see CO No 3, Sch 3, para 47 (at **[A12]**).
[49] For transitional provisions see CO No 3, Sch 3, para 48 (at **[A12]**).
[50] CO No 1, art 4(3) provides that this section shall come into force on 6 Apr 2007 so far as is necessary for the purposes of the provisions of this Act brought into force on that date by that Order (see **[7577]**).
[51] For transitional provisions see CO No 1, Sch 5, Pt 3, para 6 (at **[7591]**). Note also that the commencement of this section on 6 Apr 2007 by CO No 1 does not extend to Northern Ireland (see art 4(4) of that Order at **[7577]**).

52 CO No 1, art 2(2) provides that sub-ss (1)–(4), (6), (7) shall come into force on 1 Jan 2007 so far as is necessary for the purposes of the provisions of this Act brought into force on that date by that Order (see **[7575]**).

53 CO No 3, art 4(1) provides that sub-ss (1)–(4), (6), (7) shall come into force on 15 Dec 2007 so far as necessary for the purposes of any Regulations made before that date in implementation of Directive 2005/56/EC of the European Parliament and of the Council on cross-border mergers of limited liability companies (see **[A12]**).

54 For transitional adaptations of ss 1077–1080, 1085, 1087, 1103, 1104, see CO No 1, Sch 1, paras 4–11 (at **[7582]**). For savings in relation to the Companies (Welsh Language Forms and Documents) Regulations 1994 see CO No 1, Sch 5, Pt 1, para 1 (at **[7589]**).

55 For transitional adaptations of s 1105, see CO No 1, Sch 1, para 12 (at **[7582]**). Note also the prospective revocation of CO No 1, Sch 1, para 12(2) by CO No 3, art 11(a) (as from 1 Oct 2007).

56 CO No 1, art 2(2) provides that this section shall come into force on 1 Jan 2007 so far as is necessary for the purposes of the provisions of this Act brought into force on that date by that Order (see **[7575]**). For transitional adaptations of s 1120, see CO No 1, Sch 1, para 13 (at **[7582]**).

57 CO No 1, art 3(2) provides that this section shall come into force on 20 Jan 2007 so far as is necessary for the purposes of the provisions of this Act brought into force on that date by that Order (see **[7576]**).

58 CO No 3, art 2(1)(l) provides that ss 1121–1123, 1125–1133 shall come into force on 1 Oct 2007 in so far as applying to offences under CA 1985, Pts XIV, XV. Article 2(3)(h) of that Order further provides that ss 1121, 1122, 1125, 1127–1133 shall come into force on the same date so far as is necessary for the purposes of the provisions of this Act brought into force on that date by art 2(1), (2) of that Order (see **[A12]**).

59 CO No 1, arts 2(2), 3(2) provide that this section shall come into force on 1 Jan 2007 and 20 Jan 2007 respectively so far as is necessary for the purposes of the provisions of this Act brought into force on those dates by that Order (see **[7575]**, **[7576]**).

60 CO No 3, art 4(2) provides that this section shall come into force on 15 Dec 2007 so far as is necessary for the purposes of the provisions of this Act brought into force on that date by art 4(1) of that Order (see **[A12]**).

61 CO No 1, arts 2(2), 3(2) provide that specified definitions in this section shall come into force on 1 Jan 2007 and 20 Jan 2007 respectively so far as is necessary for the purposes of the provisions of this Act brought into force on those dates by that Order (see **[7575]**, **[7576]**).

62 CO No 2, art 2(2) provides that specified definitions in this section shall come into force on 6 Apr 2007 so far as is necessary for the purposes of the provisions of this Act brought into force on that date by that Order (see **[7615]**).

63 CO No 3, art 2(3) provides that specified definitions in this section shall come into force on 1 Oct 2007 so far as is necessary for the purposes of the provisions of this Act brought into force on that date by art 2(1), (2) of that Order (see **[A12]**).

64 CO No 3, art 3(2) provides that specified definitions in this section shall come into force on 1 Nov 2007 so far as is necessary for the purposes of the provisions of this Act brought into force on that date by art 3(1) of that Order (see **[A12]**).

65 Part 43 (ss 1265–1273, Sch 15) came into force on Royal Assent except in so far as relating to the amendment in Sch 15, Pt 1, para 11(2) to this Act to the definition of "regulated market" in FSMA 2000, s 103; see s 1300 of this Act (at **[S1300]**).

66 CO No 1, arts 2(2), 3(2), 4(3) provide that this section shall come into force on 1 Jan 2007, 20 Jan 2007 and 6 Apr 2007 respectively so far as is necessary for the purposes of the provisions of this Act brought into force on those dates by that Order (see **[7575]**–**[7577]**). For transitional adaptations of s 1284, see CO No 1, Sch 1, para 15 (at **[7582]**). CO No 2, art 2(1)(e) also provides that s 1284(1) comes into force on 6 Apr 2007 so far as relating to the provisions commenced by art 2(1)(a)–(c) of that Order and in so far as it relates to Part 2 of the Companies (Audit, Investigations and Community Enterprise) Act 2004. CO No 2, art 5 (at **[7618]**) further provides that s 1284(2) comes into force on 6 Apr 2007 in so far as relating to the repeals specified in Sch 2 to that Order (at **[7626]** et seq). CO No 3, arts 2(4), 3(2), 4(2) and 5(2) provide that this section shall come into force on 1 Oct 2007, 1 Nov 2007, 15 Dec 2007 and 1 Oct 2008 so far as is necessary for the purposes of the provisions of this Act brought into force on those dates by arts 2(1)(a)–(j), 3(1), 4(1) and 5(1) of that Order respectively (see **[A12]**). CO No 3, art 8 further provides that s 1284(2) comes into force on 1 Oct 2007 in so far as relating to the repeals specified in Sch 2 to that Order.

67 For transitional adaptations of Sch 3, see CO No 3, Sch 1, para 20 (at **[A12]**).

68 For transitional provisions see CO No 1, Sch 5, Pt 2, paras 4, 5 (at **[7590]**). For transitional adaptations of Sch 5, Pt 4, see CO No 1, Sch 1, para 16 (at **[7582]**). Note also the prospective revocation of CO No 1, Sch 1, para 16 by CO No 3, art 11(a) (as from 1 Oct 2007).

69 For details of the commencement of Sch 16 (Repeals) see that Schedule (at **[S1331]**).

70 For transitional provisions see CO No 1, Sch 5, Pt 2, para 2(3), (4) (at **[7590]**).

[A8]

Appendix 9: Draft Companies (Fees for Inspection etc) Regulations 2007

[DRAFT] COMPANIES (FEES FOR INSPECTION AND COPYING OF COMPANY RECORDS) REGULATIONS 2007

(2007 Draft)

NOTES

Made: ** 2007.
Authority: Companies Act 2006, ss 116(1)(b), (2), 229(2), 238(2), 358(4), 807(2), 811(2), 1167.
Commencement: 1 October 2007.

1 Citation, commencement and interpretation

(1) These Regulations may be cited as the Companies (Fees for Inspection and Copying of Company Records) Regulations 2007 and shall come into force on 1st October 2007.

(2) In these Regulations "the Act" means the Companies Act 2006.

2 Fee for inspection of registers

For the purposes of section 116(1)(b) (inspection of register and index of members' names) the fee prescribed is £3.50 for each hour or part thereof during which the right of inspection is exercised.

3 Fee for copy of registers

For the purposes of—

(a) section 116(2) of the Act (copy of company's register of members); and
(b) section 811(2) of the Act (copy of register of interests in shares disclosed),

the fee prescribed is—

(i) £3.50 for the first 50 entries or part thereof;
(ii) £31.50 for the next 950 entries or part thereof;
(iii) £20 for the next 4,000 entries or part thereof; and
(iv) £25 for every subsequent 5,000 entries or part thereof.

4 Fee for copy of company records

For the purposes of the following sections of the Act—

(a) section 229(2) (copy of director's service contract or memorandum setting out the terms of that contract);
(b) section 238(2) (copy of director's qualifying indemnity provision);
(c) section 358(4) (copy of records of resolutions and meetings); and
(d) section 807(2) (copy of report under section 805 of the Act),

the fee prescribed is 20 pence per thousand words or part thereof copied.

5 Revocation

In the Companies (Inspection and Copying of Registers, Indices and Documents) Regulations 1991 the following paragraphs in Schedule 2 are revoked—

(a) paragraph 1(d);
(b) paragraph 2(b);
(c) paragraph 2(d); and
(d) paragraph 3(b).

[A9]

Appendix 10: Draft LLP (Amendment) Regulations 2007

[DRAFT] LIMITED LIABILITY PARTNERSHIPS (AMENDMENT) REGULATIONS 2007

(2007 Draft)

NOTES

Made: ** 2007.
Authority: Limited Liability Partnerships Act 2000, s 15.
Commencement: 1 October 2007.

1 Citation, commencement and interpretation

(1) These regulations may be cited as the Limited Liability Partnerships (Amendment) Regulations 2007 and come into force on the 1st October 2007.

(2) In these Regulations "the principal regulations" means the Limited Liability Partnerships Regulations 2001.

2 Amendments of Schedule 2 to the principal regulations

(1) The first column of Part I of Schedule 2 to the principal regulations (provisions of the 1985 Act applied to limited liability partnerships) is amended as follows.

(2) After the entry relating to section 447 insert—

"447A (information provided: evidence)".

(3) After the entry relating to section 448 insert—

"448A (protection in relation to certain disclosures: information provided to Secretary of State)".

(4) After the entry relating to section 452 insert—

"453A (power to enter and remain on premises),

453B (power to enter and remain on premises: procedural),

453C (failure to comply with certain requirements)".

(5) After the entry relating to section 744A insert—

"Schedule 15C (security of information obtained: specified persons),

Schedule 15D (security of information obtained: specified disclosures)".

3 In the second column of Part 1 of Schedule 2 to the principal regulations (modifications of provisions applied), opposite the entry for section 453A (inserted by regulation 2(4) above) insert—

"In subsection (7), for the words "section 431, 432 or 442" substitute "section 431 or 432."".

4 Amendment of Schedule 6 to the principal regulations

In Part I of Schedule 6 to the principal regulations (application of subordinate legislation) after paragraph 6 insert—

"7. The Companies Act 1985 (Power to Enter and Remain on Premises: Procedural) Regulations 2005.".

[A10]

Appendix 11: Companies (Political Expenditure Exemption) Order 2007

COMPANIES (POLITICAL EXPENDITURE EXEMPTION) ORDER 2007

(SI 2007/2081)

NOTES

Made: 18 July 2007. Note this Order was published on 26 July 2007.
Authority: Companies Act 2006, ss 377, 1292(1)(c).
Commencement: in accordance with article 1(2) and (3).

1 Citation, commencement and interpretation

(1) This Order may be cited as the Companies (Political Expenditure Exemption) Order 2007 and shall come into force—

(a) for the purposes of its application to Great Britain, on 1st October 2007;
(b) for the purposes of its application to Northern Ireland, on 1st November 2007.

(2) In this Order, "news material" means material relating to—

(a) news,
(b) public and political affairs,
(c) public and political events, or
(d) views, opinion or comment on such news, affairs or events.

2 Exemption from authorisation

Political expenditure is exempt from the need for authorisation under Part 14 of the Companies Act 2006 if it is—

(a) political expenditure to which article 3 applies, and
(b) incurred by a company to which article 4 applies.

3 Description of political expenditure

(1) This article applies to political expenditure incurred in respect of the preparation, publication or dissemination of news material, where that material contains matter which would render that preparation, publication or dissemination on the part of the company an activity on the part of the company that is capable of being reasonably regarded as intended—

(a) to affect public support for a political party or other political organisation, or an independent election candidate, or
(b) to influence voters in relation to any national or regional referendum held under the law of a member State.

(2) Until 1st October 2008, paragraph (1)(a) has effect as if the words "or an independent election candidate" were omitted.

4 Description of company

(1) This article applies to any company whose ordinary course of business includes, or is proposed to include, the publication or dissemination to the public, or any part of the public, of news material, or the preparation of such material for publication or dissemination to the public, or any part of the public.

(2) For the purposes of paragraph (1), it is to be irrelevant—

(a) by which means or modes the news material is to be prepared, published or disseminated;
(b) where the public, or any part of the public, to which such material is published or disseminated is located or the identity or description of the public or any part of it.

[A11]

Appendix 12: Draft Third Commencement Order

[DRAFT] COMPANIES ACT 2006 (COMMENCEMENT NO 3, CONSEQUENTIAL AMENDMENTS, TRANSITIONAL PROVISIONS AND SAVINGS) ORDER 2007

(SI 2007 Draft)

NOTES

Made: This Order was made on 26 July 2007 (SI 2007/2194); see p vii of the Introduction *ante*.
Authority: Companies Act 2006, ss 1292, 1294, 1296, 1300(2).
Coming into force: in accordance with article 1(3).
Note: this is the second draft of this commencement order and it supersedes the draft published on 25 June 2007.

1 Citation, interpretation and coming into force

(1) This Order may be cited as the Companies Act 2006 (Commencement No 3, Consequential Amendments, Transitional Provisions and Savings) Order 2007.

(2) In this Order—
"the 1985 Act" means the Companies Act 1985; and
"the 1986 Order" means the Companies (Northern Ireland) Order 1986.

(3) The provisions of this Order come into force as follows—
(a) articles 1, 2, 8, 10 and 11 and Schedules 2, 4 and 5 come into force on 1st October 2007;
(b) article 3 comes into force on 1st November 2007;
(c) article 4 comes into force on 15th December 2007;
(d) article 5 comes into force on 1st October 2008;
(e) other provisions of this Order come into force on the same date as the provisions (or repeals) in relation to which they apply.

2 Provisions of the Companies Act 2006 coming into force on 1st October 2007

(1) The following provisions of the Companies Act 2006 come into force on 1st October 2007—
(a) sections 29 and 30 (resolutions and agreements affecting a company's constitution);
(b) sections 116 to 119 (inspection of register of members);
(c) sections 145 to 153 (exercise of members' rights);
(d) in Part 10 (a company's directors)—
section 154 (companies required to have directors);
section 160 (appointment of directors of public company to be voted on individually);
section 161 (validity of acts of directors);
sections 168 and 169 (removal of directors);
sections 170 to 181 (general duties of directors), except sections 175 to 177 (duty to avoid conflicts of interest, duty not to accept benefits from third parties and duty to declare interest in proposed transaction or arrangement);
sections 188 to 226 (transactions with directors requiring approval of members);
sections 227 to 230 (directors' service contracts);
section 231 (contract with sole member who is also a director);
sections 232 to 239 (directors' liabilities);
sections 247 to 259 (supplementary provisions);
(e) sections 260 to 269 (derivative claims and proceedings by members);
(f) in Part 13 (resolutions and meetings)—
sections 281 to 287 (general provisions about resolutions);
sections 288 to 300 (written resolutions);
sections 301 to 307, 310 to 326, 327(1), (2)(a) and (b) and (3), 328, 329, 330(1) to (5), (6)(a) and (b) and (7), 331, 332, 334 and 335 (resolutions at meetings);
sections 336 to 340 (public companies: additional requirements for AGMs);
sections 341 to 354 (additional requirements for quoted companies);

APPENDICES

sections 355 to 359 (records of resolutions and meetings);
sections 360 and 361 (supplementary provisions);

(g) section 417 (contents of directors' report: business review);
(h) sections 485 to 488 (appointment of auditors of private companies);
(i) section 993 (fraudulent trading);
(j) sections 994 to 999 (protection of members against unfair prejudice);
(k) sections 1035 to 1039 and 1124 and Schedule 3 (company investigations: amendments);
(l) sections 1121 to 1123 and 1125 to 1133 (general supplementary provisions relating to offences), as they apply to offences under Part 14 or 15 of the 1985 Act.

(2) Sections 362 to 379 of the Companies Act 2006 (control of political donations and expenditure), with the exception of the provisions specified in article 5 of this Order (which relate to independent election candidates), come into force in Great Britain on 1st October 2007.

(3) The following provisions of the Companies Act 2006 come into force on 1st October 2007 so far as necessary for the purposes of the provisions mentioned in paragraphs (1) and (2)—

(a) section 17 (a company's constitution);
(b) section 385 (quoted and unquoted companies);
(c) section 540(1) and (4) (shares);
(d) section 545 (companies having a share capital);
(e) section 546 (issued and allotted share capital);
(f) section 548 (equity share capital);
(g) section 629 (classes of shares);
(h) sections 1121, 1122, 1125 and 1127 to 1133 (provisions relating to offences);
(i) section 1158 (meaning of "UK-registered company");
(j) section 1168 (hard copy and electronic form and related expressions); and
(k) in section 1173 (minor definitions: general), the definitions of "body corporate" (and "corporation"), "firm" and "working day".

(4) Section 1284 of the Companies Act 2006 (extension of Companies Acts to Northern Ireland) comes into force on 1st October 2007 so far as necessary for the purposes of the provisions mentioned in paragraph (1)(a) to (j).

3 Provisions of the Companies Act 2006 coming into force on 1st November 2007

(1) Sections 362 to 379 of the Companies Act 2006 (control of political donations and expenditure), with the exception of the provisions specified in article 5 of this Order (which relate to independent election candidates), come into force in Northern Ireland on 1st November 2007.

(2) The following provisions of the Companies Act 2006 come into force on 1st November 2007 so far as necessary for the purposes of the provisions mentioned in paragraph (1)—

(a) section 546 (issued and allotted share capital);
(b) section 1158 (meaning of "UK-registered company");
(c) in section 1173 (minor definitions: general), the definition of "body corporate"; and
(d) section 1284 (extension of Companies Acts to Northern Ireland).

4 Provisions of the Companies Act 2006 coming into force on 15th December 2007

(1) Section 1068 of the Companies Act 2006 (registrar's requirements as to form, authentication and manner of delivery), other than subsection (5) (which is already wholly in force), comes into force on 15th December 2007 so far as necessary for the purposes of any regulations made before that date in implementation of Directive 2005/56/EC of the European Parliament and of the Council of 26th October 2005 on cross-border mergers of limited liability companies.

(2) The following provisions of the Companies Act 2006 come into force on 15th December 2007 so far as necessary for the purposes of the provisions mentioned in paragraph (1)—

(a) section 1168 (hard copy and electronic form and related expressions); and
(b) section 1284 (extension of Companies Acts to Northern Ireland).

5 Provisions of the Companies Act 2006 coming into force on 1st October 2008

(1) The following provisions of the Companies Act 2006 (which have the effect of applying the provisions about control of political donations and expenditure to independent election candidates) come into force on 1st October 2008—

(a) in section 362(a), the words "and to independent election candidates";
(b) in section 363(2)(a), the words "or an independent election candidate to whom";
(c) section 363(3);
(d) in section 363(4), the words "or independent election candidate" and "independent candidate";
(e) section 364(3);
(f) in section 365(1)(a) and (b)(i), the words "or an independent election candidate";
(g) in section 366(1)(a), the words "or to an independent election candidate";
(h) in section 367(3)(a), the words "or independent election candidates";
(i) in section 378(2), the words "or to an independent election candidate".

(2) Section 1284 of the Companies Act 2006 (extension of Companies Acts to Northern Ireland) comes into force on 1st October 2008 so far as necessary for the purposes of the provisions mentioned in paragraph (1).

6 Transitional adaptations of provisions brought into force

The provisions brought into force by this Order have effect subject to any transitional adaptations specified in Schedule 1 to this Order.

7 Interpretation of provisions brought into force

Where an expression in a provision brought into force by this Order (or in an adaptation made by this Order of such a provision)—

(a) is defined in the 1985 Act or the 1986 Order ("the old definition"); and
(b) is defined in the Companies Act 2006 by another provision that is not yet in force for the purposes of the provision brought into force ("the new definition"),

the expression has, for the purposes of the provision brought into force (or the adaptation), the meaning given by the old definition until the new definition is brought into force for the purposes of that provision.

8 Repeals

Sections 1284(2) and 1295 of, and Schedule 16 to, the Companies Act 2006 (repeals) come into force on 1st October 2007 so far as relating to the repeal of the provisions specified in Schedule 2 to this Order.

9 Transitional provisions and savings

Schedule 3 to this Order contains transitional provisions and savings relating to the provisions (and repeals) brought into force by this Order.

10 Consequential amendments and repeals

(1) The consequential amendments in Schedule 4 to this Order have effect.

(2) In that Schedule—

Part 1 contains amendments of provisions of the 1985 Act,
Part 2 contains amendments of the 1986 Order, and
Part 3 contains amendments of other enactments and instruments.

(3) The consequential repeals in Schedule 5 to this Order have effect.

11 Revocation of spent transitional adaptations

The following provisions (which make transitional adaptations that are no longer needed as a result of this Order) are revoked—

(a) in Schedule 1 to the Companies Act 2006 (Commencement No 1, Transitional Provisions and Savings) Order 2006, paragraphs 12(2) and 16;
(b) in Schedule 1 to the Companies Act 2006 (Commencement No 2, Consequential Amendments, Transitional Provisions and Savings) Order 2007, paragraph 4.

APPENDICES

12 General savings

(1) The amendments and repeals made by this Order do not affect the operation of section 1297 of the Companies Act 2006 (continuity of the law).

(2) Nothing in this Order affects any provision of the 1985 Act or the 1986 Order as applied by the Limited Liability Partnerships Regulations 2001 or the Limited Liability Partnerships Regulations (Northern Ireland) 2004 to limited liability partnerships.

SCHEDULES

SCHEDULE 1
TRANSITIONAL ADAPTATIONS OF PROVISIONS BROUGHT INTO FORCE

Article 6

A company's constitution (s 17)

1.—(1) Section 17 (a company's constitution) has effect with the following adaptation.

(2) Make the existing provision subsection (1).

(3) After that subsection insert—

"(2) Unless the context otherwise requires, references in this Act to a company's articles (including the reference in subsection (1) above) include the company's memorandum.".

Inspection of register of members (s 116)

2.—(1) Section 116 (rights to inspect and require copies of register and index of members' names) has effect with the following adaptation.

(2) After subsection (1) (right of inspection) insert—

"(1A) The right conferred by subsection (1) is not exercisable when the register is closed under section 358 of the Companies Act 1985 or Article 366 of the Companies (Northern Ireland) Order 1986.".

Exercise of members' rights (ss 145 to 153)

3.—(1) Section 145 (effect of provision of articles as to enjoyment or exercise of members' rights) has effect with the following adaptation.

(2) In subsection (3)(h), for "section 423 (right to be sent a copy of annual accounts and reports)" substitute "section 238 of the Companies Act 1985 or Article 246 of the Companies (Northern Ireland) Order 1986 (persons entitled to receive copies of accounts and reports).".

4.—(1) Section 146 (traded companies: nomination of persons to enjoy information rights) has effect with the following adaptations.

(2) In subsection (3)(b)(i), for "section 431 or 432 (right to require copies of accounts and reports)," substitute "section 239 of the Companies Act 1985 or Article 247 of the Companies (Northern Ireland) Order 1986 (right to demand copies of accounts and annual reports),".

(3) For the second sentence of subsection (4) substitute "Section 251 of the Companies Act 1985 or Article 259 of the Companies (Northern Ireland) Order 1986 (summary financial statements) applies to copies of accounts and reports required to be sent out by virtue of this section to a person nominated to enjoy information rights as it applies to copies of accounts and reports required to be sent out to a member of the company in accordance with section 238 of that Act or Article 246 of that Order.".

5.—(1) Section 153(1) (exercise of rights held on behalf of others: members' requests) has effect with the following adaptation.

(2) Omit paragraph (d).

General duties of directors (ss 170 to 181)

6.—(1) Section 170 (scope and nature of general duties) has effect with the following adaptations.

(2) In subsection (1), for "177" substitute "174".

(3) Omit subsection (2).

(4) In subsection (3) after "The general duties" insert "in sections 171 to 174".

7.—(1) Section 178 (civil consequences of breach of general duties) has effect with the following adaptation.

(2) In subsection (1), for "177" substitute "174".

8.—(1) Section 180 (consent, approval or authorisation by members) has effect with the following adaptations.

(2) Omit subsection (1).

(3) In subsection (2), omit the words from ", except that" to the end.

(4) In subsection (4), omit paragraph (b).

9.—(1) Section 181 (modification of provisions in relation to charitable companies) has effect with the following modifications.

(2) Omit subsections (2) and (3).

Transactions with directors requiring approval of members (ss 188 to 226)

10.—(1) Section 191 (meaning of "substantial" non-cash asset) has effect with the following adaptations.

(2) In subsection (4)—

(a) for "Part 15" substitute "Part 7 of the Companies Act 1985 or Part 8 of the Companies (Northern Ireland) Order 1986", and

(b) for "section 424" substitute "section 238A of that Act or Article 246A of that Order".

11.—(1) Section 205 (exception for expenditure on defending proceedings etc) has effect with the following adaptation.

(2) In subsection (5), for the words from "section 661(3)" to the end substitute—

"section 144(3) or (4) of the Companies Act 1985 or Article 154(3) or (4) of the Companies (Northern Ireland) Order 1986 (acquisition of shares by innocent nominee), or

section 727 of the Companies Act 1985 or Article 675 of the Companies (Northern Ireland) Order 1986 (general power to grant relief in case of honest and reasonable conduct).".

Directors' liabilities (ss 232 to 239)

12.—(1) Section 234 (qualifying third party indemnity provision) has effect with the following adaptation.

(2) In subsection (6), for the words from "section 661(3)" to the end substitute—

"section 144(3) or (4) of the Companies Act 1985 or Article 154(3) or (4) of the Companies (Northern Ireland) Order 1986 (acquisition of shares by innocent nominee), or

section 727 of the Companies Act 1985 or Article 675 of the Companies (Northern Ireland) Order 1986 (general power to grant relief in case of honest and reasonable conduct).".

Written resolutions (ss 288 to 300)

13.—(1) Section 288 (written resolutions of private companies) has effect with the following adaptations.

(2) In subsection (2) (resolutions that may not be passed as a written resolution)—

(a) in paragraph (b), for "a resolution under section 510" substitute "a resolution under section 391 of the Companies Act 1985 or Article 399 of the Companies (Northern Ireland) Order 1986";

(b) after that paragraph add—

"(c) a resolution under section 80A of the Companies Act 1985 or Article 90A of the Companies (Northern Ireland) Order 1986 revoking, varying or renewing the authority of the directors to allot securities.".

(3) After subsection (5) add—

"(6) A written resolution under any of the provisions of the Companies Act 1985 or the Companies (Northern Ireland) Order 1986 mentioned in sections 300A to 300D is not effective unless the procedural requirements specified in those sections are complied with.".

(4) After section 300 insert—

"Transitional application of procedural requirements

300A Disapplication of pre-emption rights

(1) This section applies to a written resolution—

(a) under section 95(2) of the Companies Act 1985 or Article 105(2) of the Companies (Northern Ireland) Order 1986 (disapplication of pre-emption rights), or

(b) renewing a resolution under that provision.

(2) The statement required by section 95(5) of that Act or Article 105(5) of that Order (statement by directors to be circulated with notice of meeting) must be sent or submitted to every eligible member at or before the time at which the resolution is sent or submitted to him.

(3) Section 95(6) of that Act or Article 105(6) of that Order (offences) applies in relation to the inclusion in any such statement of matter that is misleading, false or deceptive in a material particular.

300B Financial assistance for purchase of company's own shares or those of holding company

(1) This section applies to a written resolution under section 155(4) or (5) of the Companies Act 1985 or Article 165(4) or (5) of the Companies (Northern Ireland) Order 1986 (financial assistance for purchase of company's own shares or those of holding company).

(2) The documents referred to in section 157(4)(a) of that Act or Article 167(4)(a) of that Order (documents to be available at meeting) must be sent or submitted to every eligible member at or before the time at which the resolution is sent or submitted to him.

300C Authority for off-market purchase or contingent purchase contract of company's own shares

(1) This section applies to a written resolution—

(a) conferring authority to make an off-market purchase of the company's own shares under section 164(2) of the Companies Act 1985 or Article 174(2) of the Companies (Northern Ireland) Order 1986,

(b) conferring authority to vary a contract for an off-market purchase of the company's own shares under section 164(7) of that Act or Article 174(7) of that Order, or

(c) varying, revoking or renewing any such authority under section 164(3) of that Act or Article 174(3) of that Order.

(2) Section 164(5) of that Act or Article 174(5) of that Order (resolution ineffective if passed by exercise of voting rights by member holding shares to which the resolution relates) does not apply.

But for the purposes of section 289 of this Act (eligible members) a member holding shares to which the resolution relates shall not be regarded as a member who would be entitled to vote on the resolution.

(3) The documents referred to in section 164(6) of that Act or Article 174(6) of that Order (documents to be available at company's registered office and at meeting), and,

where that provision applies by virtue of section 164(7) of that Act or Article 174(7) of that Order, the further documents referred to in that provision, must be sent or submitted to every eligible member at or before the time at which the resolution is sent or submitted to him.

(4) Subsections (2) and (3) above also have effect in relation to a written resolution in relation to which the provisions of section 164(3) to (7) of the Companies Act 1985 or Article 174(3) to (7) of the Companies (Northern Ireland) Order 1986 apply by virtue of—

(a) section 165(2) of that Act or Article 175(2) of that Order (authority for contingent purchase contract), or

(b) section 167(2) of that Act or Article 177(2) of that Order (approval for release of rights under contracts approved under section 164 or 165 or Article 174 or 175).

300D Approval for payment out of capital

(1) This section applies to a written resolution giving approval under section 173(2) of the Companies Act 1985 or Article 183(2) of the Companies (Northern Ireland) Order 1986 (redemption or purchase of company's own shares out of capital).

(2) Section 174(2) of that Act or Article 184(2) of that Order (resolution ineffective if passed by exercise of voting rights by member holding shares to which the resolution relates) does not apply.

But for the purposes of section 289 of this Act (eligible members) a member holding shares to which the resolution relates shall not be regarded as a member who would be entitled to vote on the resolution.

(3) The documents referred to in section 174(4) of that Act or Article 184(4) of that Order (documents to be available at meeting) must be sent or submitted to every eligible member at or before the time at which the resolution is sent or submitted to him.".

Resolutions at meetings (ss 301 to 335)

14.—(1) Section 306 (power of court to order meeting) has effect with the following adaptation.

(2) In subsection (1)(b) for "or this Act" substitute "this Act, the Companies Act 1985 or the Companies (Northern Ireland) Order 1986".

Public companies: additional requirements for AGMs (ss 336 to 340)

15.—(1) Section 336 (public companies: annual general meeting) has effect with the following adaptations.

(2) In subsection (1), for "6 months" substitute "7 months".

(3) In subsection (2), for "notice under section 392 (alteration of accounting reference date)" substitute "notice under section 225 of the Companies Act 1985 or Article 233 of the Companies (Northern Ireland) Order 1986 (alteration of accounting reference date)".

Contents of directors' report: business review (s 417)

16.—(1) Section 417 (contents of directors' report: business review) has effect with the following adaptations.

(2) For subsection (1) substitute—

"(1) Unless the company is entitled to small companies exemption in relation to the directors' report, the report must contain a business review.

(1A) A company is entitled to small companies exemption in relation to the directors' report for a financial year if it—

(a) qualifies as small in relation to that year under Part 7 of the Companies Act 1985 or Part 8 of the Companies (Northern Ireland) Order 1986, and

(b) is not, and was not at any time within that year, an ineligible company as defined in section 247A(1B) of that Act or Article 255A(1B) of that Order.".

(3) For subsection (7) substitute—

APPENDICES

"(7) Where a company—

(a) qualifies as medium-sized in relation to a financial year under Part 7 of the Companies Act 1985 or Part 8 of the Companies (Northern Ireland) Order 1986, and

(b) is not, and was not at any time within that year, an ineligible company as defined in section 247A(1B) of that Act or Article 255A(1B) of that Order,

the directors' report for the year need not comply with the requirements of subsection (6) so far as they relate to non-financial information.".

Appointment of auditors of private company (ss 485 to 488)

17.—(1) Section 485 (appointment of auditors of private companies: general) has effect with the following adaptations.

(2) For paragraph (a) of subsection (2) substitute—

"(a) the end of the period allowed for delivering accounts and reports under section 244 of the Companies Act 1985 or Article 252 of the Companies (Northern Ireland) Order 1986, or".

(3) In paragraph (b) of subsection (2), for "section 423" substitute "section 238 of the Companies Act 1985 or Article 246 of the Companies (Northern Ireland) Order 1986".

18.—(1) Section 487 (term of office of auditors of private company) has effect with the following adaptation.

(2) In subsection (3) for "the provisions of this Part" substitute "the provisions of Chapter 5 of Part 11 of the Companies Act 1985 or Chapter 5 of Part 12 of the Companies (Northern Ireland) Order 1986".

Protection of members against unfair prejudice (ss 994 to 999)

19.—(1) Section 994(3) (meaning of "company") has effect with the following adaptation.

(2) For paragraph (a) substitute—

"(a) a company within the meaning of the Companies Act 1985 or the Companies (Northern Ireland) Order 1986;".

Company investigations: amendments relating to offences (s 1124 and Sch 3)

20.—(1) Schedule 3 (amendments of remaining provisions of the 1985 Act relating to offences) has effect with the following adaptations.

(2) Omit the words "or Northern Ireland" in the following provisions inserted in the 1985 Act—

(a) in the provision inserted by paragraph 1(2) as section 444(4)(b)(ii);
(b) in the provision inserted by paragraph 3(3) as section 449(6A)(b)(ii);
(c) in the provision inserted by paragraph 4(1) as section 450(3)(b)(ii);
(d) in the provision inserted by paragraph 5(1) as section 451(2)(b)(ii).

Meaning of "UK-registered company" (s 1158)

21.—(1) Section 1158 (meaning of "UK-registered company") has effect with the following adaptations.

(2) For "a company registered under this Act" substitute "a company within the meaning of the Companies Act 1985 or the Companies (Northern Ireland) Order 1986 or a company registered under section 680 of that Act or Article 629 of that Order.".

(3) For "an overseas company that has registered particulars under section 1046" substitute "an oversea company within the meaning of that Act or a Part 23 company within the meaning of that Order".

SCHEDULE 2
REPEALS

Article 8

NOTES

Only relevant entries of this Schedule are reproduced here; the entries omitted contain repeals to provisions in the following enactments: the Water Act 1989, the Political Parties, Elections and Referendums Act 2000, and the Civil Partnership Act 2004.

PART 1
GREAT BRITAIN

Short title and chapter	*Extent of repeal brought into force*
Companies Act 1985 (c 6)	Section 125(6). Section 234(1)(a). Section 234ZZB. Section 241, as it applies to private companies. In section 246(4)(a), the words "and 234ZZB (directors' report: business review)". Section 246A(2A). Sections 252 and 253. Section 282. Section 285. Section 292. Sections 303 and 304. Sections 309 to 309C. Sections 312 to 316. Sections 318 to 322. Section 322B. Sections 330 to 347. Sections 347A to 347K. Section 356. In section 357— (a) the words "section 356 (inspection)"; and (b) the words from "and the power of the court" to the end. Sections 366 to 379. Section 379A(1)(b) to (e). Section 380(1) and (4) to (5). Sections 381 to 383. Sections 384 and 385, as they apply to private companies. Sections 385A and 386. Sections 387 to 388A, as they apply to private companies. Section 393. In section 437— (a) in subsection (1), the second sentence; and (b) subsections (1B) and (1C). Section 442(2). Section 446. In section 448(7), the words from "and liable to a fine." to the end. Section 449(7). Section 450(4).

APPENDICES

Short title and chapter	Extent of repeal brought into force
	Section 451(3).
	Section 453(1A)(d) and the word "and" preceding it.
	Section 453A(6).
	Sections 458 to 461.
	Section 719.
	Section 730(5).
	Section 734(1).
	Section 741.
	Part 1 of Schedule 13.
	Schedule 15A.
	In Schedule 24, the entries relating to—
	(a) sections 210(3), 211(10), 214(5), 215(8), 216(3), 217(7), 218(3) and 219(3),
	(b) section 241(2), as it applies to private companies,
	(c) sections 314(3), 318(8), 322B(4), 323(2), 324(7), 326(2), (3), (4) and (5), 328(6), 329(3), 342(1), (2) and (3), 343(8), 356(5), 366(4), 367(3) and (5), 372(4) and (6), 376(7), 380(5), 381B(2), 382(5), 382B(2) and 383(4),
	(d) section 387(2), as it applies to private companies, and
	(e) sections 429(6), 430A(6), 444(3), 448(7), 449(6), 450, 451, 453A(5), 455(1) and (2), 458, 461(5) and 720(4).
Insolvency Act 1986 (c 45)	In Schedule 13, in Part 1, the entries relating to the following provisions of the Companies Act 1985—
	(a) section 380(4), and
	(b) section 461(6).
Companies Act 1989 (c 40)	Section 16.
	Section 113.
	Section 114(1).
	Section 115(2) and (3).
	Section 138.
	Section 143(8) and (9).
	In Schedule 10, paragraph 10.
	In Schedule 18, paragraphs 34 to 36.
	In Schedule 19, paragraphs 8, 9, and 17.
Companies (Audit, Investigations and Community Enterprise) Act 2004 (c 27)	Section 19(1).
	Section 20.
	In Schedule 2, paragraphs 7 to 9, 22 and 23.

(Sch 2, Pt 2 (Northern Ireland) contains various repeals to provisions in the Companies (Northern Ireland) Order 1986, the Companies (Northern Ireland) Order 1990, the

Companies (No 2) (Northern Ireland) Order 1990, and the Companies (Audit, Investigations and Community Enterprises) (Northern Ireland) Order 2005 (outside the scope of this work).)

SCHEDULE 3
TRANSITIONAL PROVISIONS AND SAVINGS
Article 9

Resolutions and agreements affecting a company's constitution (ss 29 and 30)

1.—(1) Sections 29 and 30 of the Companies Act 2006 (resolutions and agreements affecting a company's constitution) apply to resolutions passed and agreements made on or after 1st October 2007.

(2) The provisions of section 380(1) and (5) of the 1985 Act or Article 388(1) and (5) of the 1986 Order continue to apply in relation to resolutions passed and agreements made, but not forwarded to the registrar, before that date.

This does not affect the operation of section 1297 of the Companies Act 2006 (continuity of the law) in relation to things done under those provisions.

Inspection of register of members (ss 116 to 119)

2.—(1) Sections 116 to 119 of the Companies Act 2006 (inspection of register of members) apply where—

(a) the request is made on or after 1st October 2007, and
(b) the company is not obliged to deliver an annual return under section 363 of the 1985 Act or Article 371 of the 1986 Order made up to a date before 1st October 2008.

(2) Sections 356 and 357 of the 1985 Act or Articles 364 and 365 of the 1986 Order continue to apply to requests made before 1st October 2007 or after that date to a company that is so obliged.

Exercise of members' rights (ss 145 to 153)

3.—(1) Section 145 of the Companies Act 2006 (effect of provisions of articles as to enjoyment or exercise of members' rights) applies in relation to things required or authorised to be done as mentioned in subsection (2) of that section on or after 1st October 2007.

(2) Nominations under section 146 of that Act (traded companies: nomination of persons to enjoy information rights) may be made at any time on or after 1st October 2007.

A company is not required to act on a nomination before 1st January 2008; but if it does so, sections 147 to 150 apply.

(3) Section 152 of that Act (exercise of rights where shares held on behalf of others: exercise in different ways) applies in relation to the exercise of rights on or after 1st October 2007.

(4) A request may be made under section 153 of that Act (exercise of rights where shares held on behalf of others: members' requests) at any time on or after 1st October 2007.

Validity of acts of directors (s 161)

4.—(1) Section 161 of the Companies Act 2006 (validity of acts of directors) applies to acts done on or after 1st October 2007.

(2) Section 285 of the 1985 Act (validity of acts of director or manager) or Article 293 of the 1986 Order (validity of acts of director) continues to apply to acts done before that date.

Removal of directors (ss 168 and 169)

5.—(1) Section 169(5) of the Companies Act 2006 (circumstances in which representations need not be sent out or read out at the meeting) applies where the representations are received by the company on or after 1st October 2007.

(2) Section 304(4) of the 1985 Act or Article 312(4) of the 1986 Order continues to apply where the representations are received by the company before that date.

Transactions requiring members' approval: directors' long-term service contracts (ss 188 and 189)

6.—(1) Sections 188 and 189 of the Companies Act 2006 (directors' long-term service contracts: requirement of members' approval) apply to agreements made on or after 1st October 2007.

(2) A resolution passed before that date approving the provision made by such an agreement is effective for the purposes of those sections if it complies with the requirements of those sections.

(3) Section 188(4) (addition of unexpired period of earlier contract in determining guaranteed period under new contract) applies whether the original contract (within the meaning of that provision) was entered into before or after that date.

(4) Section 319 of the 1985 Act or Article 327 of the 1986 Order continues to apply to agreements made before that date.

Transactions requiring members' approval: substantial property transactions (ss 190 to 196)

7.—(1) Sections 190 to 196 of the Companies Act 2006 (substantial property transactions: requirement of members' approval) apply to arrangements or transactions entered into on or after 1st October 2007.

(2) A resolution passed before that date approving an arrangement or transaction is effective for the purposes of those sections if it complies with the requirements of those sections.

(3) Sections 320 to 322 of the 1985 Act or Articles 328 to 330 of the 1986 Order continue to apply in relation to arrangements or transactions entered into before that date.

Transactions requiring members' approval: loans, quasi-loans and credit transactions (ss 197 to 214)

8.—(1) Sections 197 to 214 of the Companies Act 2006 (loans, quasi-loans and credit transactions: requirement of members' approval) apply to transactions or arrangements entered into on or after 1st October 2007.

(2) A resolution passed before that date approving a transaction or arrangement is effective for the purposes of those sections if it complies with the requirements of those sections.

(3) Sections 330 to 342 of the 1985 Act or Articles 338 to 350 of the 1986 Order continue to apply in relation to a contravention occurring before that date.

9. Approval is not required under section 197, 198, 200 or 201 of the Companies Act 2006 (requirement of members' approval for loans etc) for anything done by a company in pursuance of an agreement entered into before 1st October 2007 that, by virtue of section 337A of the 1985 Act or Article 345A of the 1986 Order (funding of director's expenditure on defending proceedings), would not have required approval if done before that date.

10.—(1) This paragraph applies where before 1st October 2007 a company has done anything—

(a) pursuant to section 337(1) or (2) of the 1985 Act or Article 345(1) or (2) of the 1986 Order (funding of director's expenditure on duty to company), and

(b) on the condition mentioned in section 337(3)(b) of that Act or Article 345(3)(b) of that Order (condition requiring repayment of loan etc if approval of company in general meeting not given within six months).

(2) If that condition has not been satisfied before that date, it continues to apply notwithstanding the repeal of that section or that Article, but subject as follows.

(3) In the case of a private company that by reason of the repeal of section 366 of the 1985 Act or Article 374 of the 1986 Order with effect from that date ceases to be required to hold an annual general meeting, the condition shall be read as if it provided—

(a) that the approval of the company is required on or before the last date on which the company would have been required to hold an annual general meeting but for the repeal, and

(b) that the loan is to be repaid within six months from that date if such approval is not forthcoming.

11.—(1) This paragraph applies where before 1st October 2007 a company has done anything—

(a) pursuant to section 337A(1) or (3) of the 1985 Act or Article 345A(1) or (3) of the 1986 Order (funding of director's expenditure on defending proceedings), and

(b) on the terms mentioned in section 337A(4) of that Act or Article 345A(4) of that Order (terms requiring repayment of loan etc if defendant convicted, has judgment given against him or refused relief).

(2) If immediately before that date—

(a) it is not yet known whether repayment will be required, or

(b) repayment is required but had not been made,

those terms continue to apply notwithstanding the repeal of that section or that Article.

Transactions requiring members' approval: payments for loss of office (ss 215 to 222)

12.—(1) Sections 215 to 222 of the Companies Act 2006 (payments for loss of office: requirement of members' approval) apply in relation to any such loss of office or employment as is mentioned in section 215(1)(a) or (b), or any such retirement as is mentioned in section 215(1)(c) or (d), occurring on or after 1st October 2007.

(2) A resolution passed before that date approving a payment is effective for the purposes of those sections if it complies with the requirements of those sections.

(3) Sections 312 to 316 of the 1985 Act or Articles 320 to 324 of the 1986 Order continue to apply in relation to loss of office or retirement within the meaning of those provisions occurring before that date.

(4) For the purposes of this paragraph loss of office or retirement is regarded as occurring—

(a) in the case of a directorship, when the person ceases to be a director;

(b) in the case of any other office, when the person ceases to hold that office;

(c) in the case of employment, when the employment comes to an end.

Directors' service contracts (ss 227 to 230)

13.—(1) Sections 228 to 230 of the Companies Act 2006 (directors' service contracts) apply to—

(a) contracts within section 227(1) of that Act entered into on or after 1st October 2007,

(b) appointments within section 227(2) of that Act made on or after that date, and

(c) contracts to which section 318(1) of the 1985 Act or Article 326(1) of the 1986 Order applied immediately before that date.

(2) Until regulations under section 1136 of the Companies Act 2006 are made specifying a place for the purposes of section 228(2)(b), the copies and memoranda referred to in section 228 may be kept by a company—

(a) at any place where its register of members is kept, or

(b) at its principal place of business,

provided that place is situated in the part of the United Kingdom in which the company is registered.

(3) Until section 1068(1) of the Companies Act 2006 comes into force the notice referred to in section 228(4) must be given on the form prescribed for the purposes of section 318(4) of the 1985 Act or Article 326(4) of the 1986 Order.

(4) The provisions of section 318 of the 1985 Act or Article 326 of the 1986 Order continue to apply in relation to—

(a) any default before 1st October 2007 in complying with section 318(1) or (5) or Article 326(1) or (5);

(b) any request for inspection under section 318(7) or Article 326(7) made before that date;

(c) any duty to give notice under section 318(4) or Article 326(4) arising before that date.

Contracts with sole member who is a director (s 231)

14.—(1) Section 231 of the Companies Act 2006 (contracts with sole member who is a director) applies to contracts entered into on or after 1st October 2007.

(2) Section 322B of the 1985 Act or Article 330B of the 1986 Order continues to apply to contracts entered into before that date.

Directors' liabilities (ss 232 to 239)

15.—(1) Sections 232 to 236 of the Companies Act 2006 (restrictions on provision protecting directors from liability) apply to any provision made on or after 1st October 2007.

(2) Sections 309A, 309B and 309C(1) to (3) and (6) of the 1985 Act or Article 318 of the 1986 Order (so far as it relates to directors) continue to apply in relation to any provision to which they applied immediately before that date.

16.—(1) Sections 237 and 238 of the Companies Act 2006 (copies of qualifying indemnity provision to be available for inspection etc) apply to—

(a) qualifying indemnity provision within the meaning of section 237 made on or after 1st October 2007, and

(b) qualifying third party indemnity provision within the meaning of section 309B(1) of the 1985 Act to which section 309C(4) and (5) of that Act applied immediately before that date.

(2) Until regulations under section 1136 of the Companies Act 2006 are made specifying a place for the purposes of section 237(3)(b), the copies and memoranda referred to in section 237 may be kept by a company—

(a) at any place where its register of members is kept, or

(b) at its principal place of business,

provided that place is situated in the part of the United Kingdom in which the company is registered.

(3) Until section 1068(1) of the Companies Act 2006 comes into force the notice referred to in section 237(5) must be given on the form prescribed for the purposes of section 318(4) of the 1985 Act or Article 326(4) of the 1986 Order.

(4) The provisions of section 318 of the 1985 Act, as applied by section 309C(4) and (5), continue to apply in relation to—

(a) any default before 1st October 2007 in complying with section 318(1) or (5), as so applied;

(b) any request for inspection under section 318(7), as so applied, made before that date;

(c) any duty to give notice under section 318(4), as so applied, arising before that date.

17.—(1) Section 239 of the Companies Act 2006 (ratification of acts of directors giving rise to liability) applies to conduct by a director on or after 1st October 2007.

(2) Conduct by a director before that date is subject to the law relating to ratification that applied immediately before that date.

Power to make provision for employees on cessation or transfer of business (s 247)

18.—(1) Section 247 of the Companies Act 2006 (power to make provision for employees on cessation or transfer of business) applies to provision made on or after 1st October 2007 (subject to sub-paragraph (2)(b)).

(2) Section 719 of the 1985 Act or Article 668 of the 1986 Order continues to apply—

(a) to provision made before that date, and

(b) to anything sanctioned in accordance with subsection (3) of that section or paragraph (3) of that Article before that date.

Records of meetings of directors (ss 248 and 249)

19.—(1) Sections 248 and 249 of the Companies Act 2006 (records of meetings of directors) apply to meetings held on or after 1st October 2007.

(2) Section 382 of the 1985 Act or Article 390 of the 1986 Order continues to apply to meetings of directors held before that date.

Derivative claims and proceedings by members (ss 260 to 269)

20.—(1) On and after 1st October 2007 sections 260 to 264 of the Companies Act 2006 (derivative claims in England and Wales or Northern Ireland) apply to all derivative claims, subject to the following provisions.

(2) Those sections do not apply, and the law in force immediately before 1st October 2007 continues to apply, where the claimant (in Northern Ireland, the plaintiff) has applied for permission (in Northern Ireland, leave) to continue the claim before that date.

(3) If, or to the extent that, the claim arises from acts or omissions that occurred before 1st October 2007, the court must exercise its powers under those sections so as to secure that the claim is allowed to proceed as a derivative claim only if, or to the extent that, it would have been allowed to proceed as a derivative claim under the law in force immediately before that date.

21.—(1) This paragraph applies where an application is made under section 266 or 267 (derivative proceedings in Scotland).

(2) If the cause of action arises, wholly or to any extent, from an act or omission that occurred before 1st October 2007, the court shall exercise its powers under those sections so as to secure that the proceedings in respect of that act or omission are allowed to proceed as derivative proceedings only to the extent that they could have been pursued by the applicant under the law in force immediately before that date.

General provisions about resolutions (ss 281 to 287)

22.—(1) Sections 281 to 287 of the Companies Act 2006 (general provisions about resolutions), apply—

- (a) to written resolutions to which sections 288 to 300 of that Act apply (see paragraph 24);
- (b) to resolutions (other than written resolutions)—
  - (i) of which notice is given on or after 1st October 2007, or
  - (ii) that are proposed at a meeting of which notice is given on or after 1st October 2007, other than a meeting convened in pursuance of a requisition made under section 368 or 376 of the 1985 Act or Article 376 or 384 of the 1986 Order made before that date.

(2) The provisions of the 1985 Act or 1986 Order continue to apply to resolutions (other than written resolutions)—

- (a) of which notice is given before 1st October 2007, or
- (b) that are proposed at a meeting—
  - (i) of which notice was given before 1st October 2007, or
  - (ii) that is convened in pursuance of a requisition under section 368 or 376 of the 1985 Act or Article 376 or 384 of the 1986 Order made before that date.

(3) The provisions referred to in sub-paragraph (2) include—

section 370(6) of the 1985 Act or Article 378(6) of the 1986 Order (voting entitlement of members); and

section 378 of the 1985 Act or Article 386 of the 1986 Order (extraordinary and special resolutions).

(4) Where notice of a meeting is given over more than one day, it is treated for the purposes of this paragraph as given on the first of those days.

(5) Where copies of a requisition are deposited on more than one day, the references in this paragraph to the day on which the requisition is made shall be read as references to the first day on which the copies deposited are sufficient to require the company to act.

23. Any reference to an extraordinary resolution in a provision—

(a) of a company's memorandum or articles, or
(b) of a contract,

continues to have effect and shall continue to be construed in accordance with section 378 of the 1985 Act or Article 386 of the 1986 Order as if that section or Article had not been repealed.

Written resolutions (ss 288 to 300)

24.—(1) Sections 288 to 300 of the Companies Act 2006 (written resolutions) apply to resolutions for which the circulation date (see section 290) is on or after 1st October 2007.

(2) Section 381A to 381C of, and Schedule 15A to, the 1985 Act or Article 389A to 389C of, and Schedule 15A to, the 1986 Order continue to apply to resolutions sent or circulated to any relevant member before that date.

A "relevant member" means one whose signature is required by section 381A(1) or Article 389A(1).

Members' power to require directors to call meeting (ss 303 to 305)

25.—(1) Sections 303 to 305 of the Companies Act 2006 (meetings required by members) apply to requests made on or after 1st October 2007.

(2) Section 368 of the 1985 Act or Article 376 of the 1986 Order continues to apply to requisitions made before that date.

(3) Where requests are made or copies of a requisition are deposited on more than one day, the references in this paragraph to the day on which the request or requisition is made shall be read as references to the first day on which the requests made or copies deposited are sufficient to require the company to act.

Notice of meetings (ss 307, 310 and 311)

26.—(1) Sections 307, 310 and 311 of the Companies Act 2006 (notice of meetings) apply in relation to meetings of which notice is given on or after 1st October 2007.

(2) The provisions of the 1985 Act or the 1986 Order continue to apply in relation to a meeting of which notice was given before that date.

(3) The provisions referred to in sub-paragraph (2) include sections 369 and 370(2) of the 1985 Act or Articles 377 and 378(2) of the 1986 Order.

(4) Where notice of a meeting is given over more than one day, it is treated for the purposes of this paragraph as given on the first of those days.

Special notice (s 312)

27.—(1) Section 312 of the Companies Act 2006 (special notice) applies in relation to resolutions for which special notice is required where notice of the intention to move the resolution is given to the company on or after 1st October 2007.

(2) Section 379 of the 1985 Act or Article 387 of the 1986 Order continues to apply to resolutions for which special notice is required where notice of the intention to move the resolution is given to the company before that date.

Accidental failure to give notice of resolution or meeting (s 313)

28.—(1) Section 313 of the Companies Act 2006 (accidental failure to give notice of resolution or meeting) applies to resolutions or meetings of which notice is given on or after 1st October 2007.

(2) The reference in sub-paragraph (1) to cases in which notice is given on or after 1st October 2007 includes cases in which notice would be regarded as so given if section 313 applied.

Circulation of members' statements (ss 314 to 317)

29.—(1) Sections 314 to 317 of the Companies Act 2006 (circulation of members' statements) apply to requests made on or after 1st October 2007.

(2) Sections 376 and 377 of the 1985 Act or Articles 384 and 385 of the 1986 Order continue to apply in relation to requisitions made before that date.

(3) So long as such a requisition made to a private company under section 376(1)(b) or Article 384(1)(b) is not complied with, section 366 of the 1985 Act or Article 374 of the 1986 Order (duty to hold annual general meeting) continues to apply in relation to the company.

This does not apply if the company is not required to comply with the requisition (see section 377 of the 1985 Act or Article 385 of the 1986 Order).

(4) Where requests are made or copies of a requisition are deposited on more than one day, the references in this paragraph to the day on which the request or requisition is made shall be read as references to the first day on which the requests made or copies deposited are sufficient to require the company to act.

Procedure at meetings and proxies (ss 318 to 331)

30.—(1) Sections 318 to 323 of the Companies Act 2006 (procedure at meetings) and sections 324 to 331 (proxies) apply to meetings of which notice is given on or after 1st October 2007.

(2) The provisions of the 1985 Act or the 1986 Order continue to apply to meetings of which notice was given before that date.

(3) The provisions referred to in sub-paragraph (2) include sections 370, 370A, 372 to 375 and 378(4) of the 1985 Act or Articles 378, 378A, 380 to 383 and 386(4) of the 1986 Order.

(4) Where notice of a meeting is given over more than one day, it is treated for the purposes of this paragraph as given on the first of those days.

Application of provisions to class meetings (ss 334 and 335)

31.—(1) Sections 334 and 335 of the Companies Act 2006 (application of provisions of Chapter 3 to class meetings) apply to requests and meetings in relation to which the provisions applied by those sections have effect.

(2) Section 125(6) of the 1985 Act or Article 135(6) of the 1986 Order continues to apply to meetings of which notice is given before 1st October 2007.

(3) Where notice of a meeting is given over more than one day, it is treated for the purposes of sub-paragraph (2) as given on the first of those days.

Annual general meetings (ss 336 to 340)

32.—(1) The repeal of section 366 of the 1985 Act or Article 374 of the 1986 Order (duty to hold annual general meeting) does not affect any provision of a private company's memorandum or articles that expressly requires the company to hold an annual general meeting.

(2) Any such provision continues to have such effect as it had immediately before 1st October 2007.

(3) Provision specifying that one or more directors are to retire at an annual general meeting of the company is not provision expressly requiring the company to hold an annual general meeting.

33. The repeal of section 367 of the 1985 Act (default power of Secretary of State to call AGM) has effect in relation to a private company as from 1st October 2007, even if an application under that section has been made, or the Secretary of State has called or directed the calling of a meeting under that section, before that date.

34.—(1) The repeal of sections 376 and 377 of the 1985 Act or Articles 384 and 385 of the 1986 Order does not affect their application in relation to a requisition under section 376(1)(a) or Article 384(1)(a) made to a private company before 1st October 2007.

(2) So long as such a requisition has not been complied with, section 366 of the 1985 Act or Article 374 of the 1986 Order (duty to hold annual general meeting) continues to apply in relation to the company.

APPENDICES

This does not apply if the company is not required to comply with the requisition (see section 377 of the 1985 Act or Article 385 of the 1986 Order).

(3) Where copies of the requisition are deposited on more than one day, the reference in sub-paragraph (1) to the day on which the request or requisition is made shall be read as a reference to the first day on which the copies deposited are sufficient to require the company to act.

35.—(1) In the case of an existing public company—

(a) section 366 of the 1985 Act or section 374 of the 1986 Order (duty to hold annual general meeting) continues to apply to determine the date by which the company must hold its first annual general meeting after 30th September 2007, and

(b) section 336 of the Companies Act 2006 (public companies: annual general meeting) applies in relation to subsequent annual general meetings.

(2) An "existing public company" means a company formed and registered before 1st October 2007 that is a public company immediately before that date.

36. The repeal of section 367 of the 1985 Act (default power of Secretary of State to call AGM) does not affect the operation of that section in relation to a public company where an application under that section was made before 1st October 2007.

37.—(1) Section 337 of the Companies Act 2006 (public companies: notice of AGM) applies to meetings of which notice is given on or after 1st October 2007.

(2) Section 369 of the 1985 Act or Article 377 of the 1986 Order continues to apply in relation to meetings of which notice is given before that date.

(3) Where notice of a meeting is given over more than one day, it is treated for the purposes of this paragraph as given on the first of those days.

38.—(1) Sections 338 to 340 of the Companies Act 2006 (public companies: members' power to require circulation of resolutions for AGMs) apply to requests made on or after 1st October 2007.

(2) Sections 376 and 377 of the 1985 Act or Articles 384 and 385 of the 1986 Order continue to apply to requisitions made to a public company before that date.

(3) Where requests are made or copies of a requisition are deposited on more than one day, the references in this paragraph to the day on which the request or requisition is made shall be read as references to the first day on which the requests made or copies deposited are sufficient to require the company to act.

Additional requirements for quoted companies (ss 342 to 354)

39.—(1) Sections 342 to 354 of the Companies Act 2006 apply to polls taken at meetings of which notice was given on or after 1st October 2007.

(2) Where notice of a meeting is given over more than one day, it is treated for the purposes of this paragraph as given on the first of those days.

Records of resolutions and meetings (ss 355 to 359)

40.—(1) Sections 355 to 359 of the Companies Act 2006 (records of resolutions and meetings) apply to resolutions passed, meetings held or decisions taken on or after 1st October 2007.

(2) Sections 382, 382A, 382B and 383 of the 1985 Act or Articles 390, 390A, 390B and 391 of the 1986 Order continue to apply to resolutions passed, meetings held or decisions taken before that date.

Political donations and expenditure (ss 362 to 379)

41.—(1) Sections 362 to 379 of the Companies Act 2006 (political donations and expenditure) apply to donations made or expenditure incurred on or after 1st October 2007.

Section 379(2) of that Act applies as to the time when a donation is regarded as made or expenditure as incurred, including where it is made or incurred in pursuance of a contract entered into before that date.

(2) Part 10A of the 1985 Act continues to apply to donations or expenditure in relation to which the relevant time, as defined in section 347A(10) of that Act, is before that date.

(3) The repeal of that Part does not affect paragraph 3(4) of Schedule 7 to the 1985 Act (matters to be dealt with in directors' report: expressions to have same meaning as in Part 10A).

42. An approval resolution passed in accordance with section 347C of the 1985 Act before 1st October 2007 is treated as complying with the requirements of section 367 of the Companies Act 2006 (form of authorising resolution) although it does not comply with the requirements of that section as to the heads under which donations and expenditure are to be stated.

Contents of directors' report: business review (s 417)

43.—(1) Section 417 of the Companies Act 2006 (contents of directors' report: business review) applies to directors' reports for financial years beginning on or after 1st October 2007.

(2) Sections 234(1)(a), 234ZZB, 246(4)(a) and 246A(2A) of the 1985 Act or Articles 242(1), 242ZZB, 254(4)(a) and 254A(2A) of the 1986 Order continue to apply to directors' reports for financial years beginning before that date.

Appointment of auditors of private companies (ss 485 to 488)

44.—(1) Sections 485 to 488 of the Companies Act 2006 (appointment of auditors of private companies) apply in relation to appointments for financial years beginning on or after 1st October 2007.

(2) Sections 384 to 388A of the 1985 Act or Articles 392 to 396A of the 1986 Order continue to apply in relation to appointments for financial years beginning before that date.

(3) Where—

(a) a private company has elected under section 386 of the 1985 Act or Article 394 of the 1986 Order to dispense with the annual appointment of auditors, and

(b) the election is in force immediately before 1st October 2007,

section 487(2)(a) of the Companies Act 2006 (no deemed reappointment of auditors appointed by directors) does not prevent the deemed reappointment under that subsection of auditors first appointed before 1st October 2007.

45.—(1) This paragraph applies where immediately before 1st October 2007 a resolution of a private company under section 390A of the 1985 Act or Article 398A of the 1986 Order (remuneration of auditors) was in force and was expressed (in whatever terms) to continue to have effect so long as a resolution under section 386 of that Act or Article 394 of that Order (election to dispense with annual appointment of auditors) continued in force.

(2) The repeal of section 386 of the 1985 Act or Article 394 of the 1986 Order does not affect the continued operation of the resolution, which shall continue to have effect until—

(a) it is revoked or superseded by a further resolution,

(b) the auditors to which it applies cease to hold office, or

(c) it otherwise ceases to have effect in accordance with its terms.

Fraudulent trading (s 993)

46.—(1) Section 458 of the 1985 Act or Article 451 of the 1986 Order (offences of fraudulent trading) continues to apply to offences completed before 1st October 2007.

(2) Where, in the case of an offence—

(a) a relevant event occurs before 1st October 2007, and

(b) another relevant event occurs on or after 1st October 2007,

the offence must be charged under section 993 of the Companies Act 2006 (and not under section 458 of the 1985 Act or Article 451 of the 1986 Order).

(3) If in the case of any such offence a relevant event occurred before 15th January 2007 section 993(3)(a) applies with the substitution of "seven years" for "ten years".

(4) "Relevant event" means an act, omission or other event (including any result of one or more acts or omissions) proof of which is required for conviction of the offence.

Protection of members against unfair prejudice (ss 994 to 999)

47. Section 999 of the Companies Act 2006 (provisions applying where court order alters a company's constitution) does not apply (by virtue of section 1297 of that Act) to an order of the court made before 1st October 2007.

Company investigations (ss 1035 to 1039)

48. Sections 1035 to 1039 of the Companies Act 2006 (company investigations: amendments) apply where an inspector is appointed under a provision of Part 14 of the 1985 Act on or after 1st October 2007.

Repeal of requirement for private companies to lay accounts and reports before general meeting

49.—(1) The repeals of—
(a) section 241 of the 1985 Act or Article 264 of the 1986 Order (accounts and reports to be laid before company in general meeting) as it applies to private companies, and
(b) sections 252 and 253 of the 1985 Act or Articles 260 and 261 of the 1986 Order (election by private company to dispense with laying of accounts and report before general meeting),

have effect in relation to annual accounts and reports for financial years ending on or after 1st October 2007.

(2) Those provisions continue to have effect in relation to annual accounts for reports for financial years ending before that date.

Repeal of definition of "connected person"

50. The repeal of section 346 of and Schedule 13 to the 1985 Act or Article 354 of and Schedule 13 to the 1986 Order (meaning of "connected person") does not affect—
(a) section 317(3)(b) of the 1985 Act or Article 325(3)(b) of the 1986 Order (directors to disclose interest in contracts);
(b) section 7E and 7F(3) of the Industrial and Provident Societies Act 1965 or section 7D and 7E(3) of the Industrial and Provident Societies Act (Northern Ireland) 1969 (transactions with committee members: whether person "connected with" committee member or "associated with" society);
(c) section 96B(2)(a) of the Financial Services and Markets Act 2000 (disclosure rules: responsibility for compliance: meaning of person connected with person having managerial responsibilities within an issuer).

Provisions relating to trial and punishment of offences

51. Any saving in this Schedule for the effect of a provision of the 1985 Act or 1986 Order that creates an offence extends to the entry relating to that provision in Schedule 24 to that Act or Schedule 23 to that Order (punishment of offences).

SCHEDULE 4
CONSEQUENTIAL AMENDMENTS

Article 10(1)

PART 1
AMENDMENTS OF THE 1985 ACT

Resolutions and agreements affecting a company's constitution

1.—(1) In section 31(2) (resolution of directors changing of name of company to comply with direction of Secretary of State), omit the second sentence and after that subsection insert—

"(2A) Where such a resolution is passed by the directors, the company must give notice to the registrar of companies of the change.

(2B) Where a company changes its name under this section, the registrar of companies shall (subject to section 26) enter the new name on the register in place of the former name, and shall issue a certificate of incorporation altered to meet the circumstances of the case; and the change of name has effect from the date on which the altered certificate is issued.

(2C) A change of name by a company under this section does not affect any right or obligations of the company or render defective any legal proceedings by or against it; and any legal proceedings that might have been continued or commenced against it by its former name may be continued or commenced against it by its new name.".

(2) In section 51(4) (re-registration of unlimited company as limited: procedural requirements)—
- (a) omit the words from "The special resolution" to "15 days); and"; and
- (b) for "under section 380" substitute "under section 30 of the Companies Act 2006".

(3) In section 80(8) (resolution of company giving, varying, revoking or renewing authority of directors to allot shares), omit the words from "but it is in any case subject to section 380" to the end and substitute "but in any case Chapter 3 of Part 3 of the Companies Act 2006 (resolutions affecting a company's constitution) applies to it.".

(4) In section 128(1) (registration of particulars of special rights) for "section 380" substitute "section 30 of the Companies Act 2006".

(5) In section 129(1) (registration of newly created class rights) for "section 380" substitute "section 30 of the Companies Act 2006".

(6) In section 147(2) (resolution of directors altering memorandum on company ceasing to be public company following acquisition of its own shares), for the second sentence substitute "Chapter 3 of Part 3 of the Companies Act 2006 (resolutions affecting a company's constitution) applies to such a resolution.".

(7) In section 156(5)(a) (financial assistance by private company for acquisition of its own shares: statutory declaration to be delivered to registrar along with copy of special resolution), for "section 380" substitute "section 30 of the Companies Act 2006".

(8) In section 166 (authority for market purchase of own shares), for subsection (7) substitute—

"(7) Chapter 3 of Part 3 of the Companies Act 2006 (resolutions affecting a company's constitution) applies to a resolution of a company conferring, varying, revoking or renewing authority under this section.".

(9) In section 380(2) (resolutions or agreements to be embodied in copies of articles issued by the company), for "every such resolution or agreement" substitute "every resolution or agreement to which Chapter 3 of Part 3 of the Companies Act 2006 applies (resolutions and agreements affecting a company's constitution) and which is".

(10) In section 699 (oversea companies: provisions applying to Channel Islands and Isle of Man companies)—
- (a) in subsection (1) after "of this Act" insert "and the Companies Act 2006"; and
- (b) in subsection (3) for the words from "section 380" to "15 days)" substitute "Chapter 3 of Part 3 of the Companies Act 2006 (resolutions and agreements affecting a company's constitution)".

Reference to extraordinary resolution

2.—(1) In section 125(2) (variation of class rights) for "an extraordinary resolution" substitute "a special resolution".

(2) This amendment applies—
- (a) to written resolutions for which the circulation date (see section 290 of the Companies Act 2006) is on or after 1st October 2007;
- (b) to resolutions passed at a meeting of which notice is given on or after that date.

Provisions referring to general meetings of private companies

3.—(1) In section 235(1) (auditors' report on company's annual accounts), for the words from "are to be laid before the company" to the end substitute—

"are, during their tenure of office—

APPENDICES

(a) in the case of a private company, to be sent out to members under section 238(1);
(b) in the case of a public company, to be laid before the company in general meeting under section 241.".

(2) In section 238 (persons entitled to receive copies of accounts and reports)—
(a) in subsection (1) omit the words from "not less than 21 days" to the end;
(b) omit subsection (4); and
(c) in subsection (5) after "this section" insert "or section 238A".

(3) After that section insert—

"238A Time allowed for sending out copies of accounts and reports

(1) The time allowed for sending out copies of the company's annual accounts and reports is as follows.

(2) A private company must comply with section 238(1) not later than—
(a) the end of the period for delivering accounts and reports (see section 244), or
(b) if earlier, the date on which it actually delivers its accounts and reports under section 242.

(3) A public company must comply with section 238(1) not less than 21 days before the date of the meeting at which copies of the documents are to be laid in accordance with section 241.

(4) If in the case of a public company copies are sent out later than is required by subsection (3), they shall, despite that, be deemed to have been duly sent if it is so agreed by all the members entitled to attend and vote at the meeting.".

(4) References in any enactment or instrument to the period for laying and delivering accounts, and reports including those in section 244 (which defines that period), shall be read in relation to a private company as references to the period for delivering accounts and reports.

(5) In section 241 (accounts and reports to be laid before company in general meeting), in subsection (1) for "a company" substitute "a public company".

(6) In section 270(3) (distributions: justification by reference to company's last annual accounts) for the words from "that is to say" to the end substitute—

"that is to say—
(a) in the case of a private company, those prepared under Part 7 that were last sent to members in accordance with section 238(1);
(b) in the case of a public company, those prepared under Part 7 which were laid in respect of the last preceding accounting reference period in respect of which accounts so prepared were laid (and for this purpose accounts are laid if section 241(1) has been complied with in relation to them).".

(7) In section 271 (distributions: auditors' report on accounts), in subsection (4) omit the words from "and a copy" to the end and after that subsection insert—

"(4A) A copy of the auditors' statement under subsection (4) must—
(a) in the case of a private company, have been circulated to members along with the copies of the accounts sent to them under section 238(1);
(b) in the case of a public company, have been laid before the company in general meeting.".

(8) These amendments have effect for financial years ending on or after 1st October 2007.

Provisions referring to written resolutions of private companies

4.—(1) Section 390 (right of auditors to attend company meetings etc) is amended as follows.

(2) Omit subsection (1A).

(3) In subsection (2)—
(a) in the opening words, omit "in accordance with section 381A", and
(b) in paragraph (a), for "Schedule 15A" substitute "Chapter 2 of Part 13 of the Companies Act 2006".

References to loans, quasi-loans and other dealings in favour of directors etc

5. In section 317 (directors to disclose interest in contracts), in subsection (6) for "section 330" substitute "section 197, 198, 200, 201 or 203 of the Companies Act 2006".

6.—(1) Parts 2 and 3 of Schedule 6 (disclosure of information: loans, quasi-loans and other transactions in favour of directors etc) are amended as follows.

(2) In paragraphs 15(a) and 16(a) for "section 330" substitute "section 197, 198, 200, 201 or 203 of the Companies Act 2006".

(3) In paragraph 19(a) for "was prohibited by section 330" substitute "was one in respect of which approval was required under section 197, 198, 200, 201 or 203 of the Companies Act 2006".

(4) In paragraph 22(2)—
- (a) in paragraph (d) for "section 330(6) or (7) of this Act" substitute "section 203 of the Companies Act 2006"; and
- (b) in paragraph (e) for "section 330(6)" substitute "section 203(1)(b) of the Companies Act 2006".

(5) In paragraph 24(2)(c) for "subsection (6) or (7) of section 330" substitute "section 203 of the Companies Act 2006".

(6) In paragraph 26—
- (a) for "Section 345 of this Act" substitute "Section 258 of the Companies Act 2006", and
- (b) for "Part 10" substitute "Part 10 of that Act".

(7) In paragraph 27, for sub-paragraph (1) substitute—

"(1) The following provisions of the Companies Act 2006 apply for the purposes of this Part of this Schedule—
- (a) section 202 (meaning of "credit transaction");
- (b) section 211 (value of transactions and arrangements);
- (c) section 212 (person for whom a transaction or arrangement is entered into);
- (d) sections 252 to 255 and Schedule 1 (persons connected with a director).".

(8) In paragraph 28—
- (a) in paragraph (a) for "subsection (6) or (7) of section 330 of this Act" substitute "section 203 of the Companies Act 2006";
- (b) in paragraphs (b) and (c) for "either of those subsections" substitute "that section".

(9) In paragraph 29(3)—
- (a) for "Section 345 of this Act" substitute "Section 258 of the Companies Act 2006", and
- (b) for "Part 10" substitute "Part 10 of that Act".

(10) In paragraph 30 for the words from "of this Act" to the end of paragraph (b) substitute—

"of the Companies Act 2006 apply for the purposes of this Part of this Schedule—
- (a) section 199 (meaning of "quasi-loan"),
- (b) section 202 (meaning of "credit transaction"), and
- (c) section 212 (person for whom a transaction or arrangement is entered into);".

(11) These amendments apply in relation to arrangements and transactions entered into on or after 1st October 2007.

7.—(1) In Part 4 of Schedule 9 (special provisions for banking companies and groups: additional disclosure: emoluments of directors and others)—
- (a) in paragraph 2 (loans, quasi-loans and other dealings), for "section 330" substitute "section 197, 198, 200, 201 or 203 of the Companies Act 2006";
- (b) in paragraph 3(5) (other transactions, arrangements and agreements: meaning of "connected person"), for "Section 346 of this Act applies" substitute "Sections 252 to 255 of, and Schedule 1 to, the Companies Act 2006 apply".

(2) These amendments apply in relation to arrangements and transactions entered into on or after 1st October 2007.

APPENDICES

Provisions relating to the appointment of auditors

8.—(1) In section 384 (duty to appoint auditors)—
- (a) in subsection (1) for "Every company" substitute "Every public company";
- (b) in subsection (2) omit the words from "except in the case of a private company" to the end;
- (c) in subsection (3) omit the words from "or 385A(2)" to the end; and
- (d) omit subsection (4).

(2) In section 385 (appointment at general meeting at which accounts laid), in subsection (1) omit the words from "and to a private company" to the end.

(3) In section 387 (appointment by Secretary of State in default of appointment by company), in subsection (1) for "If in any case" substitute "If in the case of a public company".

(4) In section 388 (filling of casual vacancies)—
- (a) in subsection (1) after "The directors" insert "of a public company";
- (b) in subsection (3) for "a company" substitute "a public company".

(5) In section 388A (certain companies exempt from obligation to appoint auditors)—
- (a) in subsection (1) for "A company" substitute "A public company";
- (b) in subsection (2) for "a company" substitute "a public company";
- (c) omit subsection (4); and
- (d) in subsection (5), omit "or (4)".

(6) These amendments have effect in relation to appointments for financial years beginning on or after 1st October 2007.

References to provisions about protection of members from unfair prejudice

9. In section 126 (saving for court's powers under other provisions), for "sections 459 to 461 (protection of minorities)" substitute "Part 30 of the Companies Act 2006 (protection of members against unfair prejudice)".

10. In paragraph 9 of Schedule 21 (effect of registration under section 680: saving for powers of company to alter its constitution etc), for "None of the provisions of this Act (except section 461(3)" substitute "None of the provisions of this Act, and none of the provisions of the Companies Act 2006 (except section 996(2)),".

Removal of references to repealed enactments

11.—(1) Part 15 (orders imposing restrictions on shares) is amended as follows.

(2) In the Part heading for "SECTIONS 210, 216, 445" substitute "SECTION 445".

(3) In section 454(1), in the opening words, for the words from "pursuant to sections 210(5A)" to "of that order)" substitute "pursuant to section 445(1A) or 456(1A)".

(4) In section 454(2) for the words from "sections 210(5A)" to "section 216(1A)" substitute "section 445(1A) or 456(1A)".

(5) In section 454(3) for the words from "sections 210(5A)" to "section 216(1A)" substitute "section 445(1A) or 456(1A)".

(6) In section 455(1), in the opening words, for the words from "sections 210(5A)" to "section 216(1A)" substitute "section 445(1A) or 456".

(7) In section 455(2) for the words from "sections 210(5A)" to "section 216(1A)" substitute "section 445(1A) or 456".

(8) In section 456(2) omit the words from "and if the order" to the end.

(9) In section 456(3)(b) omit "210 or".

(10) In section 456(4), in the second sentence, omit the words from "(unless" to "section 216)".

(11) In section 456(5)(a) omit the words from "(unless" to "section 216)".

Supplementary provisions relating to offences

12. In section 730(1) (punishment of offences) after "offences under this Act" substitute "(other than an offence under Part 14 or 15)".

13. Omit section 730(5) (meaning of "officer in default") and after that section insert—

"730A Meaning of "officer in default"

(1) This section applies to—
(a) offences under this Act (other than an offence under Part 14 or 15),
(b) offences under the insider dealing legislation, and
(c) offences under the Companies Consolidation (Consequential Provisions) Act 1985.

(2) For the purposes of an offence to which this section applies "officer who is in default" means any officer who knowingly and wilfully authorises or permits the default, refusal or contravention in question.".

14.—(1) Section 731 (summary proceedings) is amended as follows.

(2) Before subsection (1) insert—

"(A1) This section applies to—
(a) offences under this Act (other than an offence under Part 14 or 15),
(b) offences under the insider dealing legislation, and
(c) offences under the Companies Consolidation (Consequential Provisions) Act 1985.".

(3) In subsection (1) for "any offence under the Companies Acts" substitute "an offence to which this section applies".

(4) In subsections (2) and (3) for "an offence under the Companies Acts" substitute "an offence to which this section applies".

15. In section 732 (prosecution by public authorities), for subsections (1) and (2) substitute—

"(1) Proceedings in England and Wales for an offence under section 245E or 245G may only be brought by or with the consent of the Secretary of State or the Director of Public Prosecutions.".

16.—(1) In section 733 (offences by bodies corporate)—
(a) in subsection (1) for the words from "any of sections 210" to "453A" substitute "section 245E(3), 245G(7) or 394A(1)"; and
(b) omit subsection (4).

(2) In section 734(1) (criminal proceedings against unincorporated bodies) for the words from "section 245E(3)" to "453A" substitute "section 245E(3), 245G(7) or 394A(1)".
(*Sch 4, Pt 2 (Amendments of the 1986 Order) contains various amendments to the Companies (Northern Ireland) Order 1986 (outside the scope of this work).*)

PART 3
AMENDMENTS OF OTHER ENACTMENTS AND INSTRUMENTS

NOTES

Only relevant paragraphs of this Part are reproduced here; the paragraphs omitted amend the following enactments: the Harbours Act 1964, the Industrial and Provident Societies Act 1965, the Industrial and Provident Societies Act (Northern Ireland) 1969, the Atomic Energy Authority Act 1971, the Local Government Act 1972, the Judicature (Northern Ireland) Act 1978, the Aircraft and Shipbuilding Industries (Northern Ireland) Order 1979, the Industry Act 1980, the Food Act 1984, the Industrial Development (Northern Ireland) Order 1982, the Building Societies Act 1986, the Local Government and Housing Act 1989, the Insolvency (Northern Ireland) Order 1989, the Companies (Northern Ireland) Order 1990, the Statutory Water Companies Act 1991, the Social Security Administration Act 1992, the Social Security Administration (Northern Ireland) Act 1992, the Taxation of Chargeable Gains Act 1992, the Friendly Societies Act 1992, the Trade Union and Labour Relations (Consolidation) Act 1992, the Electricity (Northern Ireland) Order 1992, the Industrial Relations (Northern Ireland) Order 1992, the Housing (Northern Ireland) Order 1992, the Charities Act 1993, the Leasehold Reform, Housing and Urban Development Act 1993, the Coal Industry Act 1994, the Value Added Tax Act 1994, the Airports (Northern Ireland) Order 1994, the Environment Act 1995, the Housing Act 1996, the Deregulation and

Contracting Out (Northern Ireland) Order 1996, the Commonwealth Development Corporation Act 1999, the Greater London Authority Act 1999, the Postal Services Act 2000, the Transport Act 2000, the Private Security Industry Act 2001, the Enterprise Act 2002, the Company Directors Disqualification (Northern Ireland) Order 2002, the Income Tax (Earnings and Pensions) Act 2003, the RTM Companies (Memorandum and Articles of Association) Regulations 2003, the Horserace Betting and Olympic Lottery Act 2004, the RTM Companies (Memorandum and Articles of Association) (Wales) Regulations 2004, the Gambling Act 2005, the Charities and Trustee Investment (Scotland) Act 2005, and the Water and Sewerage Services (Northern Ireland) Order 2006.

Companies Consolidation (Consequential Provisions) Act 1985 (c 9)

38. In section 2 of the Companies Consolidation (Consequential Provisions) Act 1985 (re-registration of old public company as public company), for subsection (3) substitute—

"(3) Chapter 3 of Part 3 of the Companies Act 2006 (resolutions affecting a company's constitution) applies to a resolution of the directors under this section.".

Insolvency Act 1986 (c 45)

39.—(1) Section 84 of the Insolvency Act 1986 (resolutions for voluntary winding up) is amended as follows.

(2) In subsection (1), omit paragraph (c).

(3) In subsection (2) for "any of the paragraphs" substitute "either of the paragraphs".

(4) For subsection (3) substitute—

"(3) Chapter 3 of Part 3 of the Companies Act 2006 (resolutions affecting a company's constitution) applies to a resolution under paragraph (a) of subsection (1) as well as a special resolution under paragraph (b).".

(5) These amendments apply—

(a) to written resolutions for which the circulation date (see section 290 of the Companies Act 2006) is on or after 1st October 2007;

(b) to resolutions passed at a meeting of which notice is given on or after that date.

40. In section 159 of that Act (powers of court to be cumulative) for "the Companies Act" substitute "the Companies Acts".

41.—(1) In section 165 of that Act (voluntary winding up: powers of liquidator)—

(a) in subsection (2)(a) for "extraordinary resolution" substitute "special resolution"; and

(b) in subsection (4)(c) for "special or extraordinary resolution" substitute "special resolution".

(2) These amendments apply—

(a) to written resolutions for which the circulation date (see section 290 of the Companies Act 2006) is on or after 1st October 2007;

(b) to resolutions passed at a meeting of which notice is given on or after that date.

42.—(1) Section 187 of that Act (power of liquidator to make payments to provide for employees or former employees on cessation or transfer of business) is amended as follows.

(2) In subsection (1) (power to act on decision of company made before commencement of winding up) for "section 719 of the Companies Act" substitute "section 247 of the Companies Act 2006".

(3) For subsection (2) (power of liquidator to make provision after winding up has commenced) substitute—

"(2) The liquidator may, after the winding up has commenced, make any such provision as is mentioned in section 247(1) if—

(a) the company's liabilities have been fully satisfied and provision has been made for the expenses of the winding up,

(b) the exercise of the power has been sanctioned by a resolution of the company, and

(c) any requirements of the company's memorandum or articles as to the exercise of the power conferred by section 247(1) are complied with.".

43. In section 251 of that Act (expressions used generally in First Group of Parts), for the closing words substitute—

"Any expression (other than one defined above in this section)—

(a) for whose interpretation provision is made by Part 26 of the Companies Act, or

(b) that is defined for the purposes of the Companies Acts,

has the same meaning in this Group of Parts.".

44. In sections 411(3) and 414(8) of, and paragraph 2(1) of Schedule 8 to, that Act (purposes for which company insolvency rules or fees orders may be made), for "the Companies Act" substitute "the Companies Acts".

45. In section 436 of that Act (expressions used generally in the Act), at the appropriate place insert—

""the Companies Acts" means the Companies Acts (as defined in section 2 of the Companies Act 2006) as they have effect in Great Britain;".

Company Directors Disqualification Act 1986 (c 46)

46. In section 4(1)(a) of the Company Directors Disqualification Act 1986 (disqualification for fraudulent trading), for "section 458 of the Companies Act" substitute "section 993 of the Companies Act 2006".

Companies Act 1989 (c 40)

52. In section 24(2) of the Companies Act 1989 (eligibility for appointment as company auditor: meaning of "company auditor"), after "Chapter 5 of Part 11 of the Companies Act 1985" insert "or Chapter 2 of Part 16 of the Companies Act 2006".

53. In section 53(1) of that Act (eligibility for appointment as auditor: definitions), in the definition of "company" after "section 384 of the Companies Act 1985" insert "or section 485 of the Companies Act 2006".

Financial Services and Markets Act 2000 (c 8)

92. In section 195(4)(c) of the Financial Services and Markets Act 2000 (exercise of power in support of overseas regulator: relevant functions) for "the Companies Act 1985" substitute "the Companies Acts (as defined in section 2 of the Companies Act 2006)".

93.—(1) Section 366 of that Act (insurers carrying out contracts of long-term insurance) is amended as follows.

(2) For subsection (4) substitute—

"(4) A winding up resolution may not be passed—

(a) as a written resolution (in accordance with Chapter 2 of Part 13 of the Companies Act 2006), or

(b) at a meeting called in accordance with section 307(4) to (6) or 337(2) of that Act (agreement of members to calling of meeting at short notice).".

(3) In subsection (5) for "section 380 of the 1985 Act (or Article 388 of the 1986 Order)" substitute "section 30 of the Companies Act 2006".

Uncertificated Securities Regulations 2001 (SI 2001/3755)

97.—(1) Regulation 16 of the Uncertificated Securities Regulations 2001 (resolution authorising transfer of securities by paperless means) is amended as follows.

(2) For paragraph (7) substitute—

"(7) In the event of default in complying with paragraph (4), an offence is committed by every officer of the issuer who is in default.

(7A) A person guilty of such an offence is liable—

(a) on conviction on indictment, to a fine;

(b) on summary conviction, to a fine not exceeding the statutory maximum.".

(3) After paragraph (8) insert—

"(8A) Chapter 3 of Part 3 of the Companies Act 2006 (resolutions affecting a company's constitution) applies to—

(a) a directors' resolution passed by virtue of paragraph (2), or

(b) a resolution of a company passed by virtue of paragraph (6) preventing or reversing such a resolution.".

Companies (Audit, Investigations and Community Enterprise) Act 2004 (c 27)

104. In section 34(3)(c) of the Companies (Audit, Investigations and Community Enterprise) Act 2004 (power to apply provisions of 1985 Act or 1986 Order relating to directors' reports), for "the 1985 Act or the 1986 Order" substitute "the 1985 Act, the 1986 Order or the Companies Act 2006".

105.—(1) Section 37 of that Act (requirements for company to become a community interest company) is amended as follows.

(2) In subsection (1)(b) for "the 1985 Act or the 1986 Order" substitute "the Companies Act 2006".

(3) For subsection (2) substitute—

"(2) Section 30 of the Companies Act 2006 (copies of resolutions to be forwarded to the registrar of companies) must be complied with in relation to each of the special resolutions at the same time.".

(4) In subsection (3)(b) for "section 380(1) of the 1985 Act or Article 388(1) of the 1986 Order" substitute "section 30(1) of the Companies Act 2006".

106. In section 43(3) of that Act (auditor's rights to information) omit the words from "as in relation" to the end.

107.—(1) Section 54 of that Act (requirements for company to cease being a community interest company and become a charity or a Scottish charity) is amended as follows.

(2) In subsection (1)(b) for "the 1985 Act of the 1986 Order" substitute "the Companies Act 2006".

(3) For subsection (2) substitute—

"(2) Section 30 of the Companies Act 2006 (copies of resolutions to be forwarded to the registrar of companies) must be complied with in relation to each of the special resolutions at the same time.".

(4) In subsection (3)(b) for "section 380(1) of the 1985 Act or Article 388(1) of the 1986 Order" substitute "section 30(1) of the Companies Act 2006".

Fraud Act 2006 (c 35)

111.—(1) Section 9 of the Fraud Act 2006 (participating in fraudulent business carried on by sole trader etc) is amended as follows.

(2) In subsection (2)(a) for "section 458 of the Companies Act 1985 or Article 451 of the Companies (Northern Ireland) Order 1986" substitute "section 993 of the Companies Act 2006".

(3) In subsection (3)—

(a) in the opening words for "section 458 of the 1985 Act" substitute "that section", and

(b) in paragraph (a) for "that Act" substitute "the Companies Act 1985 or the Companies (Northern Ireland) Order 1986".

(4) Omit subsection (4).

(5) In subsection (5) for "section 458 of the 1985 Act or Article 451 of the 1986 Order" substitute "that section".

(6) These amendments apply to an offence if any act, omission or other event (including any result of one or more acts or omissions) proof of which is required for conviction of the offence occurs on or after 1st October 2007.

SCHEDULE 5
CONSEQUENTIAL REPEALS

Article 10(3)

NOTES

Only relevant entries of this Schedule are reproduced here; the entries omitted contain repeals to provisions in the following enactments: the Companies Consolidation (Consequential Provisions) (Northern Ireland) Order 1986, the Companies (Northern Ireland) Order 1989, the Insolvency (Northern Ireland) Order 1989, the Statutory Water Companies Act 1991, the Friendly Societies Act 1992, the Housing (Northern Ireland) Order 1992, the Coal Industry Act 1994, the Deregulation and Contracting Out (Northern Ireland) Order 1996, the Deregulation (Northern Ireland) Order 1997, the Postal Services Act 2000, the Enterprise Act 2002, and the Civil Partnership Act 2004.

Short title and chapter	*Extent of repeal*
Companies Act 1985 (c 5)	Section 455(3). In section 456— (a) in subsection (2), the words from "and if the order" to the end; (b) in subsection (3)(b), the words "210 or"; (c) in subsection (4), in the second sentence, the words from "(unless" to "section 216)"; (d) in subsection (5)(a), the words from "(unless" to "section 216)".
Companies Consolidation (Consequential Provisions) Act 1985 (c 9)	Sections 14 and 15. In Schedule 2, the entries relating to— (a) section 53(1) of the Industrial and Provident Societies Act 1965; (b) the Atomic Energy Authority Act 1971; (c) section 3 of the Industry Act 1980; (d) the Food Act 1984.
Insolvency Act 1986 (c 45)	Section 84(1)(c).
Companies (Audit, Investigations and Community Enterprise) Act 2004	In section 43(3), the words from "as in relation" to the end.
Fraud Act 2006 (c 35)	Section 9(4).

[A12]

APPENDICES

Index

GLOSSARY OF WORDS AND PHRASES

accounting standards, **[260]**, **[S464]**
act as insolvency practitioner, **[3411]**
address, **[802]**
administrative receiver, **[3408]**
advertisement, **[9708]**
advocate, **[4518]**, **[4561]**
agent, **[629]**
allotment, **[619]**
ancillary document, **[501]**
annual accounts, **[266]**, **[S471]**
annual report, **[266]**
annuities on human life, **[4003]**
applicable turnover, **[7163]**
applicant, **[2311]**
application, **[2311]**
appropriate audit authority, **[S525]**
appropriate deposit, **[7206]**
appropriate qualification, **[780]**
appropriate rate, **[91]**
approved exchange, **[4482]**, **[6849]**
Article 21 relief application, **[7492]**, **[7504]**
articles, **[629]**
assessment methodology, **[7562]**
asset backed securities, **[9708]**
assets requirement, **[2048]**
assisted person, **[4518]**, **[4561]**
associate, **[464]**, **[801]**, **[S345]**, **[S1260]** , **[3453]**, **[7455]**
associated index, **[206]**
authorised agent, **[4448]**
authorised deposit-taker, **[6569]**
authorised incoming provider, **[4640]**
authorised insurance company, **[626]**
authorised insurance undertaking, **[206]**
authorised unit trust scheme, **[206]**
authority worker, **[4373]**
balance sheet date, **[266]**
bank, **[6796]**
bank holiday, **[629]**
banking company, **[625]**, **[S1164]**, **[6883]**
banking consolidation directive, **[7545]**
banking group, **[S1164]**
banking partnership, **[259]**
beneficiary of an order, **[7058]**, **[7080]**
body corporate, **[621]**, **[2414]**
books and papers, **[629]**
branch, **[4362]**, **[4479]**, **[9145]**, **[9181]**, **[9620]**, **[9827]**
broadcasting, **[3540]**
building, **[3228DA]**
building block, **[9708]**
building operations, **[3228DA]**
business, **[698]**, **[3044]**, **[6629]**
business day, **[3408]**, **[6570]**, **[6909]**
business year, **[7163]**
called-up share capital, **[618]**, **[S547]**
capital adequacy directive, **[7545]**
capitalisation, **[266]**, **[285]**
central bank, **[6948]**
central counterparty, **[6948]**
certified sophisticated investor, **[4135]**, **[4315]**
certified translation, **[6603]**
CGO, **[6693]**
CGO service, **[6693]**
CGO service charge, **[6693]**
CGO service member, **[6693]**
charge, **[6948]**
chattel leasing agreement, **[3408]**
chief executive, **[2414]**
claims representative, **[4448]**
clearing house, **[6948]**
client, **[9620]**
close links, **[9620]**
close relative, **[4003]**, **[4113]**, **[4265]**
collateral security, **[6948]**
collateral security charge, **[6948]**
collective investment scheme, **[2234]**
commercial communication, **[4640]**
commitment, **[4512]**
common interest group, **[4317]**
communications, **[629]**, **[4114]**
community law, **[3624]**
Companies Acts, **[629]**, **[S2]**
company, **[612]**, **[S1]**, **[7058]**
company (auditors), **[802]**
company (disqualification of directors), **[760]**
company (insider dealing), **[885]**
company auditor, **[773]**
company contributions, **[653D]**
company limited by guarantee, **[1]**, **[S3]**
company limited by shares, **[1]**, **[S3]**
company records, **[S1134]**
concentration, **[9536]**
confidential records, **[599]**
confidentiality order, **[599]**
connected with company, **[3406]**
consumers, **[2014]**, **[3624]**, **[4640]**
contract of insurance, **[4003]**
contract of long-term care insurance, **[4663]**
contractually-based investment, **[4003]**
contributory, **[3235]**
controller, **[2419]**
conversion rates, **[9199]**, **[9232]**
convertible securities, **[6849]**
core investment service, **[4004]**
corporation, **[621]**
country of origin, **[4640]**
court, **[629]**, **[S1156]**, **[S1183]**, **[3044]**
credit institution, **[266]**, **[547]**, **[683]**, **[684]**, **[S1173]**, **[6948]**, **[9145]**, **[9462]**, **[9827]**
credit transaction, **[331]**
creditor's voluntary winding-up resolution, **[6948]**
criminal conduct, **[4640]**
criminal investigation, **[4373]**
daily default fine, **[S1125]**
date of original annual accounts, **[6672]**
date of original directors' report, **[6672]**
date of revision, **[6672]**
date of the original directors' remuneration report, **[6672]**
dealing in securities, **[880]**
dealing on own account, **[9620]**
dealt with on a consolidated basis, **[6749]**
debenture, **[629]**, **[S738]**
debt, **[6568]**

decision notice, **[4518]**
decree, **[3660]**
deed of settlement, **[532]**
default arrangements, **[6948]**
default rules, **[858]**
dematerialised instructions, **[7003]**
dematerialised loan instrument, **[7003]**
depositary, **[2236]**
depositary receipt, **[206]**
derivatives, **[206]**
designated disadvantaged area, **[3228DA]**
designated professional body, **[4101A]**
designated system, **[6948]**
directive restrictions, **[4373]**
director, **[348]**, **[622]**, **[760]**, **[802]**, **[S250]**, **[2414]**, **[3408]**
director's service contract, **[S228]**
disciplinary proceedings authority, **[4373]**
disposable capital, **[4518]**
disposable income, **[4518]**
distributable profits, **[138]**, **[167]**, **[S683]**
distributions, **[268]**, **[S829]**
document, **[587]**, **[629]**, **[2414]**
document of debt, **[3660]**
donation, **[348]**
dormant, **[247]**, **[S1169]**
EEA activities, **[4448]**
EEA company, **[S1170]**
EEA competent authority, **[4373]**
EEA consolidation supervisor, **[7545]**
EEA market operator, **[2310D]**
EEA parent credit institution, **[7545]**
EEA parent investment firm, **[7545]**
EEA parent financial holding company, **[7545]**
EEA regulator, **[4640]**
EEA regulatory authority, **[4373]**, **[4625]**
EEA state, **[629]**, **[S1170]**, **[4640]**
EEA undertaking, **[S1170]**
EEIG, **[6603]**
elective resolution, **[395]**
electronic commerce communication, **[4114]**, **[4269]**
electronic commerce directive, **[4640]**
electronic communications, **[629]**
eligible debt security, **[7003]**
eligible Northern Ireland Treasury Bill, **[7003]**
eligible Treasury Bill, **[7003]**
emoluments, **[653D]**
e-money issuer, **[S474]**, **[S539]**
employees' share scheme, **[627]**, **[S1166]**
enactment, **[802]**
engineering operations, **[3228DA]**
equity security, **[79]**, **[S560]**, **[9462]**
equity share capital, **[629]**
equity shares, **[117]**, **[S616]**
established in the United Kingdom, **[802]**
EU political expenditure, **[348]**
EU political organisation, **[348]**
EU trade association, **[349]**
Euro unit, **[9199]**, **[9232]**
Euro-securities, **[6849]**
execution of orders on behalf of clients, **[9620]**
exempt person (regulated activities), **[2414]**
existing company, **[612]**
expert, **[63]**
exposure risk-weighting purposes, **[7562]**
feeder fund, **[4142]**
fellow subsidiary undertaking, **[S1161]**
financial assistance, **[138]**, **[S677]**
financial fixed assets, **[660]**
financial institution, **[547]**, **[683]**, **[684]**, **[S1173]**
financial instrument, **[9438]**, **[9620]**
financial system, **[2003]**
firm, **[802]**, **[S1173]**, **[3004]**
fixed assets, **[266]**
fixed security, **[501]**, **[3226]**, **[3659]**
floating charge, **[3408]**
former authorised deposit-take, **[6569]**
former CGO service member, **[6693]**
former Companies Acts, **[612]**
former regulated activities, **[4373]**
former regulated person, **[4373]**
former underwriting member, **[2322]**
franchise arrangements, **[4142]**
full accounts and reports, **[6883]**
funeral plan contract, **[4070]**
fungible assets, **[660]**, **[664]**
Gazette, **[629]**, **[S1173]**
general business, **[664]**
general insurance mediation activity, **[4665]**
general local authority security, **[7003]**
general partner, **[3056]**
general public sector security, **[7003]**
general UK Government security, **[7003]**
GISC Facility, **[4671]**
go into liquidation, **[3404]**
government, **[4396]**
group, **[266]**, **[802]**, **[S474]**, **[2418]**
group undertaking, **[S1161]**
guarantee, **[331]**
health insurance risks, **[4448]**
hire-purchase agreement, **[629]**
holding company, **[615]**, **[617]**
home member state, **[9145]**, **[9462]**, **[9620]**
home state deposit-guarantee scheme, **[4362]**
home state investor-compensation scheme, **[4362]**
host member state, **[9145]**, **[9462]**, **[9620]**
IAS Regulation, **[S474]**
incoming electronic commerce activity, **[4640]**
incoming electronic commerce communication, **[4114]**, **[4269]**
incoming firm, **[2193]**
incoming provider, **[4640]**
information made public, **[883]**
information society service, **[4640]**
inside information, **[881]**, **[9438]**
insiders, **[882]**
insolvency, **[3404]**
insolvency law, **[3446]**
insolvency legislation, **[6629]**
insolvency proceedings, **[6563]**, **[6629]**, **[9290B]**
insolvency work experience, **[6629]**
insolvent estate, **[6564]**
insolvent winding up, **[6356]**
insurance company, **[626]**, **[S1165]**, **[6883]**
insurance mediation activity, **[4101A]**
interconnected bodies corporate, **[3624]**
interest in a security, **[7003]**
interim relief application, **[7492]**

international accounting standards, **[S474]**
international organisation, **[4265]**, **[4396]**
investigator, **[4351]**
investment advice, **[9620]**
investment business, **[9181]**
investment company, **[271]**, **[S833]**
investment firm, **[2421A]**, **[4004]**, **[9145]**, **[9181]**, **[9620]**
investment service, **[9145]**
investment services and activities, **[9620]**
investor, **[9181]**
ISD investment firm, **[S474]**
issuer, **[4481]**, **[9462]**
issuer-instruction, **[7003]**
issuer register of securities, **[7003]**
joint enterprise, **[4003]**
joint investment business, **[9181]**
Joint Stock Companies Acts, **[612]**
joint stock company, **[525]**, **[S1041]**
lawful business name, **[698]**
lease, **[660]**, **[664]**
legal assistance, **[4518]**, **[4561]**
legal assistance order, **[4561]**
legal instruments, **[9199]**, **[9232]**
legible, **[587]**
liabilities, **[140]**
liability limitation agreement, **[S534]**
limit order, **[9620]**
limited company, **[S3]**, **[6749]**
limited liability partnership agreement, **[6983]**
limited partnership, **[6749]**
liquidation committee, **[6796]**
liquidator, **[9290B]**
listed company, **[206]**
limited liability company, **[9800]**
listed investment, **[664]**
listed public company, **[6883]**
listed security, **[660]**
local authority, **[27]**, **[698]**, **[S54]**, **[4003]**, **[4150]**, **[7003]**
local authority security, **[7003]**
local bank, **[6796]**
local bank account, **[6796]**
long lease, **[660]**, **[664]**
long term business, **[664]**
long-term care insurance mediation activity, **[4665]**
long term fund, **[664]**
main proceedings, **[6570]**
major audit **[S525]**
manager, **[2420]**
managing agent, **[4003]**
market abuse, **[2118]**
market charges, **[843]**, **[6693]**
market contracts, **[828]**
market maker, **[9620]**
market manipulation, **[9438]**
market operator, **[9620]**
market purchase, **[149]**
MCAS Scheme, **[4671]**
media public interest consideration, **[3540]**
member, **[23]**
member of company, **[3407]**
memorandum, **[629]**
merger, **[9800]**
merger notice, **[3591]**
merger reference, **[7163]**
modification or termination order, **[7492]**, **[7504]**
money-lending company, **[338]**
money market instruments, **[9145]**–**[9620]**
mortgage mediation activity, **[4659]**
multilateral trading facility, **[9620]**
national bureau, **[4448]**
national consolidation supervisor, **[7545]**
national currency units, **[9199]**, **[9232]**
national guarantee fund, **[4448]**
net assets, **[138]**, **[140]**
netting, **[6948]**
nominee, **[4351]**
non-business day, **[48]**
non-cash asset, **[620]**, **[S1163]**
non-EEA regulatory authority, **[4373]**, **[4625]**
non-equity securities, **[9462]**
non-equity shares, **[117]**
non-statutory accounts, **[227]**
occupational pension scheme, **[4003]**
offer to the public, **[623]**, **[9462]**
offering programme, **[9462]**
office copy, **[628]**
officer, **[629]**, **[S1173]**
officer in default, **[607]**
official list, **[2103]**
official notification, **[48]**
official seal, **[629]**
officially notified, **[48]**
off-market, **[149]**
old public company, **[702]**
open-ended investment company, **[2235]**
operator (collective investment scheme), **[206]**
operator-instruction, **[7003]**
operator register of securities, **[7003]**
operator-system, **[7003]**
operator (uncertificated securities), **[7003]**
ordinary application, **[6440]**
ordinary shares, **[S560]**
organisation, **[348]**
original, **[6672]**
originating application, **[6440]**
outgoing electronic commerce communication, **[4114]**, **[4269]**
oversea company, **[629]**
overseas applicant, **[2311]**
overseas company, **[S1044]**
overseas clearing house, **[2311]**
overseas investment exchange, **[2311]**
overseas person, **[4003]**
overseas regulatory authority, **[4373]**
paid-up, **[619]**
parent company, **[S1173]**
parent credit institution in an EEA State, **[7545]**
parent financial holding company in an EEA State, **[7545]**
parent investment firm in an EEA State, **[7545]**
parent undertaking, **[262]**, **[666]**, **[S1162]**, **[2417]**
Part IV financial resources requirement, **[4396]**
Part XIII financial resources requirement, **[4396]**
participating interests in, **[264]**
participating member states (single currency), **[9199]**, **[9232]**

participating security, **[7003]**
participation in Lloyd's syndicates, **[2322]**
partner, **[4518]**
partnership, **[3001]**
partnership property, **[3020]**
payment for loss of office, **[S215]**
pension fund management contract, **[4003]**
personal pension unit trust, **[4142]**
petitioner, **[6566]**
place for inspection (register), **[6028]**
place of business, **[629]**
police force, **[7058]**, **[7080]**
policy, **[4403]**
policyholder, **[4404]**
political donation, **[S364]**
political expenditure, **[S365]**
portfolio management, **[9620]**
power of intervention, **[2193]**
pre-existing transferee company, **[456]**
pre-1982 pre-emption requirement, **[81]**
preferential debts, **[182]**
prescribed, **[629]m [S1167]**
private company, **[1]**, **[S4]**
private person, **[4397]**
professional client, **[9620]**
professional intermediary, **[884]**
profit and loss account, **[S474]**
profit estimate, **[9708]**
profit forecast, **[9708]**
property, **[3454]**, **[3455]**
property collective investment undertaking, **[9708]**
prospectus, **[629]**
prove (debts), **[6276]**
provision for unexpired risks, **[664]**
proxy, **[6503]**
public authority, **[S54]**
public company, **[1]**, **[S4]**
public international body, **[9708]**
public sector body, **[885]**
public servant, **[482]**
publication, **[4113]**, **[4265]**
purchase price, **[266]**
qualified investors, **[9462]**
qualifying body, **[781]**
qualifying contract of insurance, **[4003]**
qualifying shares, **[148]**
quasi-loan, **[331]**, **[S199]**
quoted company, **[266]**, **[S385]**, **[S531]**
real time communications, **[4115]**
realised profit and losses, **[266]**
receiver, **[3226]**, **[3408]**
recognised clearing house, **[2283]**
recognised investment exchange, **[2283]**
recognition application, **[7492]**, **[7504]**
recognition order, **[7492]**, **[7504]**
recorded insurance intermediary, **[4101B]**
register, **[6028]**
register of directors' interests, **[6028]**
register of interests in shares, **[206]**
registered oversea company, **[554]**
registered party, **[348]**
registered third country auditor, **[S1241]**
registrar, **[6558]**
registrar of companies, **[629]**, **[6849]**
register of securities, **[6909]**
regulated activity, **[S474]**
regulated home purchase plan, **[4074F]**
regulated home reversion plan, **[4074B]**
regulated information, **[9708]**
regulated market, **[885]**, **[6779]**, **[9145]**–**[9620]**
regulated profession, **[4640]**
regulatory functions, **[804]**
relevant amounts, **[339]**
relevant balance sheet, **[49]**
relevant EEA regulator, **[4640]**
relevant employee shares, **[79]**
relevant investment exchange, **[206]**
relevant office-holder, **[859]**
relevant shares, **[79]**
relevant stock exchange, **[206]**
remuneration, **[414]**
repayable on demand, **[660]**
representative, **[4518]**, **[4561]**
responsible insolvency practitioner, **[6565]**
retail client, **[9620]**
retention of title agreement, **[3408]**
revised accounts, **[6672]**
revised report, **[6672]**
revision by replacement, **[6672]**
revision by supplementary note, **[6672]**
risk factors, **[9708]**
sale and option to resell transaction, **[660]**
sale and repurchase transaction, **[660]**
secondary proceedings, **[6570]**, **[7492]**
secretary of state worker, **[4373]**
secured creditor, **[3405]**
secured debenture, **[3226]**
securities, **[S783]**, **[7003]**, **[9462]**
securitisation risk-weighting purposes, **[7562]**
security, **[6779]**
series of secured debentures, **[3226]**
service address, **[7058]**, **[7080]**
settlement, **[7003]**
settlement account, **[6948]**
settlement agent, **[6948]**
settlement bank, **[6909]**, **[6693]**, **[7003]**
shadow director, **[622]**, **[760]**, **[S251]**
share, **[629]**, **[S540] [4499]**
share premium account, **[116]**
short lease, **[664]**
single market directive information, **[4373]**
small and medium-sized enterprises, **[9462]**
solicited and unsolicited real time communications, **[4116]**
solvent winding up, **[6356]**
special purpose vehicle, **[9708]**
special resolution, **[393]**
state within the European Economic Area, **[6768]**
statutory auditor, **[S1210]**
subsidiary, **[615]**, **[617]**, **[S1159]**, **[S1160]**
subsidiary undertaking, **[262]**, **[666]**, **[S1162]**, **[2417]**
substantial non-cash asset, **[S191]**
supervisory body, **[779]**, **[S1217]**
supply of goods, **[3624]**
system-beneficiary, **[6909]**
system-charge, **[6909]**
system-member, **[7003]**, **[6909]**
system-member instruction, **[7003]**
system-participant, **[7003]**